Nations of the World

2006
Sixth Edition

Nations of the World

A Political, Economic & Business Handbook

Grey House Publishing

Grey House Publishing

PUBLISHER: Leslie Mackenzie
EDITOR: Richard Gottlieb
EDITORIAL DIRECTOR: Laura Mars-Proietti
MARKETING DIRECTOR: Jessica Moody

Grey House Publishing, Inc.
185 Millerton Road
Millerton, NY 12546
518.789.8700
FAX 518.789.0545
www.greyhouse.com
e-mail: books @greyhouse.com

Central European Business Ltd

MANAGING DIRECTOR: Anthony Axon
PRODUCTION MANAGER: Elaine McCarthy
EDITORIAL: Ruth Davis, Roger Deakin, Anthony Griffin, Sue Hewitt, Patrick Ivory, Trevor Jones, Marianne Keating, Elaine McCarthy, Anthony Miller, Mick Sizer, Lena von Heimandahl, Sohpie von Heimandahl

World of Information
2 Market Street
Saffron Waldon
Essex CB10 1HZ, UK
Tel: +44 (0)1799 521150
Fax: +44 (0)1799 524805
e-mail: now@worldinformation.com

Every possible effort has been made to ensure that the information contained in this book is accurate at press time and the publishers cannot accept responsibility for any errors or omissions, however caused.

Except by express prior written permission of the Copyright Proprietor no part of this work may be copied by any means of publication or communication now known or developed hereafter including, but not limited to, use in any directory or compilation or other print publication, in any information storage and retrieval system, in any other electronic device, or in any visual or audio-visual device or product.

This publication is an original and creative work, and is fully protected by all applicable copyright laws, as well as by laws covering misappropriation, trade secrets and unfair competition.

Central European Business Ltd. and Grey House Publishing, Inc. will defend its rights in this publication.

Text Copyright © 2006 Central European Business Ltd. UK
Cover, Introduction and Format Copyright © 2006 Grey House Publishing, Inc. USA
All rights reserved
First edition published 2000
Sixth edition published 2006
Printed in the USA

Nations of the world: a political, economic & business handbook. – 6th ed. (2006) – 1741 p.
Annual

1. Almanacs, American. 2. Business travel – Handbooks, manuals, etc. 3. International trade – Handbooks, manuals, etc.

HF1010.N37
658-dc21
ISBN 10: 1-59237-079-9
ISBN 13: 978-1-597237-079-5

2001238305
softcover

Contents

Country Profiles

Afghanistan	1
Albania	8
Algeria	16
American Samoa	25
Andorra	29
Angola	33
Anguilla	42
Antigua and Barbuda	46
Argentina	50
Armenia	61
Aruba	68
Ascension Island	72
Australia	74
Austria	86
Azerbaijan	94
Bahamas	104
Bahrain	111
Bangladesh	119
Barbados	130
Barbuda see Antigua and Barbuda	
Belarus	135
Belgium	143
Belize	151
Benin	158
Bermuda	164
Bhutan	168
Bolivia	174
Bosnia and Hercegovina	184
Botswana	193
Brazil	200
British Virgin Islands	212
Brunei	216
Bulgaria	225
Burkina Faso	234
Burma see Myanmar	
Burundi	240
Caicos Islands see Turks and Caicos Islands	
Cambodia	246
Cameroon	254
Canada	262
Cape Verde	273
Cayman Islands	279
Central African Republic	283
Chad	289
Chile	295
China	304
Colombia	319
Comoros	329
Congo	335
Congo, Democratic Republic of	342
Cook Islands	351
Costa Rica	355
Côte d'Ivoire	364
Croatia	373
Cuba	382
Cyprus	391
Czech Republic	399
Denmark	408
Djibouti	416
Dominica	422
Dominican Republic	426
Easter Island	432
Ecuador	434
East Timor see Timor-Leste	
Egypt	442
El Salvador	452
Equatorial Guinea	459
Eritrea	465
Estonia	471
Ethiopia	479
Falkland Islands/Islas Malvinas	486
Faroe Islands	490
Fiji	493
Finland	499
France	508
French Guiana	519
French Polynesia	523
Futuna see Wallis and Futuna	
Gabon	527
The Gambia	535
Georgia	541
Germany	548
Ghana	560
Gibraltar	569
Greece	574

Greenland	583	Luxembourg	881
Grenada	587	Macao	888
Grenadines see St Vincent and the Grenadines		Macedonia	893
Guadeloupe	592	Madagascar	902
Guam	596	Malawi	909
Guatemala	600	Malaysia	917
Guinea	608	Maldives	928
Guinea-Bissau	614	Mali	933
Guyana	619	Malta	939
Haiti	627	Marshall Islands	945
Hercegovina see Bosnia & Hercegovina		Martinique	949
The Holy See see Vatican City		Mauritania	953
Honduras	633	Mauritius	959
Hong Kong	641	Mexico	966
Hungary	650	Federated States of Micronesia	977
Iceland	660	Moldova	981
India	666	Monaco	989
Indonesia	679	Mongolia	993
Iran	690	*Montenegro see Serbia and Montenegro*	
Iraq	699	Montserrat	999
Ireland	707	Morocco	1003
Islas Malvinas see Falkland Islands		Mozambique	1013
Israel	715	Myanmar	1021
Italy	726	Namibia	1029
Ivory Coast see Cote d'Ivoire		Nauru	1036
Jamaica	738	Nepal	1040
Japan	746	The Netherlands	1048
Jordan	758	The Netherlands Antilles	1058
Kazakhstan	767	*Nevis see St Kitts and Nevis*	
Kenya	776	New Caledonia	1062
Kiribati	785	New Zealand	1067
Korea, DPR (North)	790	Nicaragua	1077
Korea, Republic of Korea (South)	797	Niger	1086
Kuwait	808	Nigeria	1092
Kyrgyzstan	815	Niue	1103
Laos	823	Norfolk Island	1107
Latvia	830	Northern Marianas	1110
Lebanon	839	Norway	1113
Lesotho	848	Oman	1121
Liberia	855	Pakistan	1129
Libya	861	Palau	1140
Liechtenstein	868	Palestine	1144
Lithuania	872	Panama	1153

Papua New Guinea	1161	Sweden	1431
Paraguay	1169	Switzerland	1441
Peru	1178	Syria	1449
Philippines	1188	Taiwan	1458
Pitcairn Island	1198	Tajikistan	1467
Poland	1201	Tanzania	1477
Portugal	1211	Terres Australes	1487
Príncipe see São Tomé and Príncipe		Thailand	1489
Puerto Rico	1220	Timor-Leste	1500
Qatar	1226	*Tobago see Trinidad and Tobago*	
La Réunion	1233	Togo	1506
Romania	1237	Tokelau	1512
Russia	1248	Tonga	1515
Rwanda	1261	Trinidad and Tobago	1519
St Helena	1267	Tristan da Cunha	1527
St Kitts and Nevis	1270	Tunisia	1530
St Lucia	1274	Turkey	1539
St Vincent and the Grenadines	1279	Turkmenistan	1549
Samoa	1283	Turks and Caicos Islands	1558
San Marino	1287	Tuvalu	1562
São Tomé and Príncipe	1290	Uganda	1566
Saudi Arabia	1295	Ukraine	1574
Senegal	1305	United Arab Emirates	1584
Serbia and Montenegro	1313	United Kingdom	1593
Seychelles	1324	United States of America	1606
Sierra Leone	1329	United States' Virgin Islands	1619
Singapore	1336	Uruguay	1622
Slovakia	1346	Uzbekistan	1630
Slovenia	1355	Vanuatu	1640
Solomon Islands	1363	Vatican City	1645
Somalia	1369	Venezuela	1648
South Africa	1376	Vietnam	1658
South Georgia	1388	Wallis and Futuna	1669
Spain	1390	Yemen	1672
Sri Lanka	1401	*Yugoslavia see Serbia and Montenegro*	
Sudan	1410	Zambia	1679
Suriname	1419	Zimbabwe	1688
Swaziland	1424		

The World today	1697

Africa
Map	1698
Overview	1699
Currencies	1701
Key Indicators	1702

Americas
Maps	1703
Overviews	1706
Currencies	1708
Key Indicators	1709

Asia
Maps	1710
Overview	1712
Currencies	1713
Key Indicators	1714

Europe
Overview	1715
Map	1716
Currencies	1718
Key Indicators	1719

Middle East
Overview	1720
Map	1722
Currencies	1724
Key Indicators	1725

US Embassy addresses	1726

Contributors

Guy Arnold is a freelance writer who specialises in north-south relations and African affairs. His most recent publications include *A Third World Handbook*, *Wars in the Third World Since 1945* and *The End of the Third World*.

Barry Baxter has spent most his working life in Africa. He has worked as a journalist for 45 years, reporting from Botswana, South Africa, Zambia (and northern Rhodesia), Zimbabwe (and Southern Rhodesia), Angola, Kenya, Tanzania and Uganda. Since 1994, he has operated NewsWorld, an Africa news agency serving Reuters, the South African Press Association, Agencia EFE and several magazines.

Gopal Chandra Bose is a freelance journalist based in India and contributes articles on a political and economic themes for Asia. His work has been commissioned by the BBC.

Daniel Brett is a freelance journalist contributing articles on agricultural economics, protest movements and trade-related issues in Africa and Latin America as well as the politics and economics of other developing countries.

Ruth Davis has lived, worked and studied in south India and Japan. She has worked for the Department for International Development and is an analyst specialising in Asian countries.

Michael Fishpool is an analyst who specialises in international politics and security with a particular focus on Western Europe and the Balkans.

Shanjukta Ghosh is a graduate of Delhi University and writes on socioeconomic themes of the Indian subcontinent, with emphasis on high-technology.

John Gorvett is based in Istanbul, and has written extensively on the politics and economies of Turkey and Greece.

Anthony Griffin is a UK-based journalist specialising in emerging markets, with an emphasis on Spanish speaking countries. He regularly contributes articles British and international publications, on Europe and South America.

Aileen Herlihy, based in Australia, writes on health and welfare issues, with an emphasis on developing countries as well as Australia.

Fred J Hill is a development journalist specialising in the Caucasus, Central Asia and Latin America.

David Ivory has worked in various UK ministries and writes on governments and governance worldwide. His work includes analysis of elections and political leaderships results.

Niki Johnson is a research fellow at the Political Science Institute, Universidad de la República, Montevideo, Uruguay.

Trevor Jones is a freelance researcher and journalist, specialising in politico-economic developments in the Americas. He holds degrees from the University of Southampton, the London School of Economics and Darwin College, Cambridge.

Marianne Keating is a freelance writer contributing articles on various topics, in particular economic and political profiles, of Africa and Asia.

Ali Khalil is a business journalist at the UK-based *Asharq Al-Awsat* Arabic newspaper and writes on the Middle East.

Asbed Kotchikian is a doctoral student and lecturer at Boston University, US, specialising in the Middle East and the Caucasus. He has lectured at universities in Armenia, Georgia and Latvia.

Juma Kwayera is a sub-editor and writer for *The EastAfrican* newspaper and writes for *The Daily Nation* newspaper's KiSwahili edition in Kenya. He writes on east and central Africa

Marcela López Levy works as a researcher and editor at the UK-based Latin America Bureau, and writes on Latin America and the Caribbean.

Elaine McCarthy writes on agricultural and political trends within the European Union.

Ali Rafel al Mansour is a analyst based in the Middle East, who reports on the petroleum industry and OPEC.

Ben Marlow is a research student at the Institute of Latin American Studies, University of London.

Bhekie Matsebula is a Swaziland-based journalist and has written for the Pan-African News Agency and the BBC.

Meldun Mawson is a Swedish writer who specialises in travel and tourism issues, and the social and cultural implications of political change in Latin America, as well as northern Europe.

Dr **Anthony Miller** is a freelance journalist working in the NGO and thinktank sector, specialising in the Balkans, the Caucasus and the Middle East.

Neamat Nojumi is a former Afghani mujahideen soldier. Since 1991, he has been living in the US and works as a commentator on Central Asian affairs. He is author of *The Rise of the Taliban in Afghanistan*.

Gergana Noutcheva is a researcher specialising in Eastern Europe at the Centre for European Studies, based in Belgium.

Anita Parameswaran is a business analyst for a leading insurance company working on corporate strategy. She writes on North Africa and the Mediterranean.

Ibrahim Seaga Shaw is publisher and editor of www.expotimes.net which specialises in news and analysis of events in Africa and the African diaspora. He contributes to *New African* magazine and *The Guardian* newspaper.

Craig Stenhouse is a researcher specialising in Africa and the Middle East.

Bernadeta Tendyra specialises in Eastern Europe and has worked as a BBC World Service journalist.

Marian White is a freelance writer specialising in the politics and economics of the Pacific Rim with a particular interest in emerging economies.

William R Thomson is a former director and vice president in charge of the Asia Development Bank's lending programmes in over 25 Asian and Pacific countries. He advises both international investment houses and governments on regional economic developments and investment opportunities.

Damian Tobin is based in Ireland and the UK, lectures in economics and specialises in Europe and the Far East.

José Luis Velasco lectures in Mexican politics and holds a doctorate in political science from Boston University. He is the author of *El Debate Actual Sobre el Federalismo Mexicano*, published by Instituto Mora.

Main sources

It should be noted that the methodology used by the International Monetary Fund (IMF), World Bank, Organisation for Economic Co-operation and Development (OECD) and other main gatherers of international data can vary not only from each other but also from individual central banks and government departments. In order to ensure consistency and to allow like to be compared with like, *World of Information* uses the same single source for the Key Indicator data. Readers should be aware, however, that occasionally a more up to date figure is used in the body of the text that might not have been calculated in the same way. The principal sources used are: the IMF, World Bank, Asian Development Bank (ADB), African Development Bank (AfDB), Eastern Caribbean Central Bank (ECCB), Economic Commission for Latin America and the Caribbean (ECLAC), individual central bank reports and national statistics. Statistics have also been gathered from UN agencies including FAO, UNHCR and Unicef.

INTRODUCTION

This is the sixth edition of *Nations of the World: A Political, Economic & Business Handbook*. It profiles every nation and self-governing territory around the world in an easy-to-access, single-volume format. Political, economic and business information, supplemented by maps, charts and tables fill 1,800 pages.

This past year has witnessed once again what is being called the new post-9/11 world – one increasingly defined by a rise in volatility and violence. Warring nations and ethnic groups, warring political parties, and terrorist threats find world leaders and civilians alike immensely concerned at the state of the world. As a result, travel and tourism, although improving, is still far below pre-9/11 levels. The security industry continues to grow worldwide, although there is much discussion as to what's working and what's not. And devastation and hardship in unstable regions create growth and success in others.

But worldwide volatility and violence were not the only cause of devastation and hardship in 2005. Natural disasters, including tsunami, earthquakes, wildfires and hurricanes, all contributed to many nations of the world struggling for survival in 2005.

The 2006 edition of *Nations of the World* offers tremendous insight into the conditions, and social and economic climates of 230 nations, from those constantly in the headlines to those that seldom make the news. You will read about a world that, in the past year, held 77 political elections, resulting in 31 new heads of state, 64 new heads of government, and 18 changes of ruling party.

Every country profile in *Nations of the World* has been revised and updated. Contributors of the thoughtful and comprehensive country essays are experts in their fields, international correspondents who have contributed to some of the most influential books and periodicals in the world; see Contributor list following this Introduction..

Because *Nations of the World* is a reliable, careful compilation of essential information that is presented in a useful, organized format, this reference is critical for anyone doing business or traveling overseas. It has also proved to be an important reference tool for students from secondary school through college, as well as for professionals in the political arena.

ARRANGEMENT

Nations of the World is arranged in alphabetical order by nation or territory. Part one of each country chapter is a concise, independently written **Country Overview**. These overviews do not reflect the worldview of any particular government or intelligence agency. You will find current political and economic events, as well as an informed outlook toward the future. Most chapters include a **Map** with key places; some of the world's more obscure places are shown in relation to surrounding countries. All chapters include **Key Facts** -- official country name(s), ruling parties, language, basic area, population, unemployment, inflation figures, **Key Indicators** -- charted over five years and include population, GNP, imports/exports, foreign debt, exchange rate, and **Risk Assessment** – rates politics, economy and general stability of the region.

Part two of each chapter is a **Country Profile.** This section includes detailed historical information in easy-to-follow chronological order, political structure and parties, and a detailed look at the country's population, labor market, media, trade, industry, agriculture and energy. Business travelers will learn about that country's time zones, banking practices, entry requirements, dress codes, climate, health issues, hotels, working hours and the best way to travel to and from. *Noted are countries in political crises, with advice to visitors.*

The **Business Directory** is part three, with contact numbers and web sites for hotels, travel information and chambers of commerce, plus dozens of other useful numbers and addresses.

Following the country profiles is a **World Overview:** Africa; Americas; Asia and the Pacific; Europe; and the Middle East. Like the individual country chapters, these overviews offer an expertly written narrative on the political and economic climate. They include **Key Indicators, Currencies**, and a **Map** of the region. Nations of the World end with a **Global Overview** is also included.

Again this year, Grey House Publishing is offering an all-inclusive, searchable CD-ROM companion to the print book. With this new option, searching through this vast amount of text and finding a specific person or place has never been easier. To add the CD-ROM to your order, simply fill out and return the coupon in the back of the book. It will be shipped immediately.

With nearly 1,800 pages of critical political, economic and business information including narrative overviews, charts and maps, this newest edition of *Nations of the World: A Political, Economic & Business Handbook* – in both print and CD-ROM -- is a timely and immensely valuable reference acquisition to all public, academic and special library collections.

Afghanistan

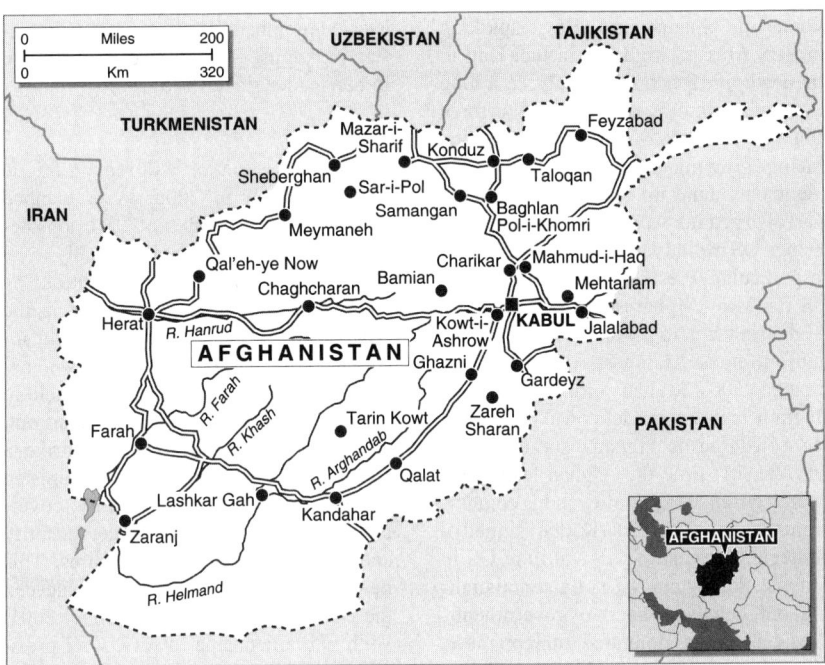

KEY FACTS

Official name: The Islamic Republic of Afghanistan

Head of State: President Hamid Karzai (since Jun 2002; democratically elected 9 Oct 2004)

Head of government: President Hamid Karzai

Ruling party: Members of the national assembly are elected as independent candidates.

Area: 647,497 square km

Population: 25.79 million (2004)

Capital: Kabul

Official language: Pashtu and Dari (named as official languages in the constitution ratified 4 Jan 2004)

Currency: Afghani (Af) = 100 puls

Exchange rate: Af43.00 per US$ (Oct 2005) (the afghani was re-valued on 3 Jan 2003)

GDP per capita: US$194 (2004)

GDP real growth: 7.50% (2004); *8.00% (2005)

Labour force: 8.47 million (2004)

Inflation: 13.00% (2004)

Balance of trade: -US$3.31 billion (2004)

Foreign debt: US$8.50 billion (2004)

Annual FDI: US$100.00 million (2004)

* estimated figure

It was a landmark year for the Islamic Republic of Afghanistan, with parliamentary and provincial elections being held for the first time in more than thirty years. A two-year disarmament programme, conducted by the UN, bore fruit in 2005, with tens of thousands of small arms being surrendered by militia groups. It was also one of the most violent 12-month periods since the toppling of the Taliban regime in 2001. The rise in the number and intensity of attacks by Taliban rebels was in part a bid to disrupt elections. The Afghan economy continued to expand rapidly and managed to reduce its dependence upon opium exports.

A reconstruction economy

With around US$3 billion in aid received by Afghanistan in 2005, the economy continued to experience a reconstruction boom-based shot in the arm. The IMF, which made an evaluation visit to the country in August, forecast an impressive 8 per cent GDP growth for Afghanistan in 2005. However, it also warned that major effort was needed in order to raise the level of domestic revenues and to diversify the export base. A UN report, also published in August, noted that opium export earnings still amounted to over 50 per cent of Afghanistan's total GDP, down from 61 per cent in 2004, and that Afghanistan was still home to around 90 per cent of the world's opium production. On the bright side the UN recorded a 21 per cent drop in the amount of land set aside for opium poppy cultivation.

Landmark elections

On 18 September, Afghans went to the polls to elect national and provincial parliaments for the first time since the early 1970s. The poll should have been held in May 2005 but on the recommendation of the UN, was delayed in order to address logistical and security concerns. Prior to the poll, dozens of former warlords and militia commanders were disqualified from standing, although controversially many more remained on ballot papers. Turnout was around 50 per cent, a drop of about 20 points when compared to the presidential election in October 2004. The substantial fall in the participation rate was undoubtedly influenced by an upsurge in fighting between US and government forces on the one hand and Taliban rebels on the other. Election results revealed a heterogeneous parliament featuring former warlords, ex-communists, human rights activists and Islamic clerics. Twenty-five per cent of seats were reserved for women and among those elected was Malalai Joya, famous for her condemnation of warlords at the 2003 national constitutional convention. Most MPs were elected as independents and local analysts estimate that 50–60 per cent of the parliament was broadly supportive of Afghan president, Hamid Karzai. The parliament held its inaugural session in December.

A surge in violence

It was one of the bloodiest years in Afghanistan since the fall of the Taliban regime in 2001. Around 80 US personnel and hundreds of Taliban rebels were killed in fighting that raged across most of Afghanistan's southern and eastern provinces. Zabul, Uruzgan and Kandahar provinces in the south and Kunar, Khost and Paktika provinces in the east were the source of most the violence. Some of the fighting can be explained as a bid to sabotage the September election. As well as battling US and Afghan government troops, the Taliban claimed responsibility for the killing of scores of pro-government clerics, police chiefs, aid workers, election officials, election candidates and government representatives. A number of foreign aid workers and tourists were also kidnapped, and in some cases executed, by groups claiming loyalty to the Taliban. The Taliban also managed to return to the airwaves in April, by establishing their own rebel radio station.

Afghanistan and the US

Relations between the two allies in the 'war on terror' entered a new phase in 2005, in large part due to external pressures beyond either government's control. A *New York Times* report published in May alleged that the US was operating a secret prison in the Bagram airbase in Afghanistan, where it held and tortured Afghan prisoners. Also in May, the US-based *Newsweek* magazine published allegations that US personnel desecrated a Koran at Guantánamo Bay, sparking anti-US riots in Afghanistan that lead to the death of 15 people. In July, in a long series of similar tragedies, the US airforce killed 17 civilians in a wayward airstrike. Facing growing calls from inside the country to stand up to the US, President Karzai urged his American counterpart to change US military tactics in Afghanistan. In particular, President Karzai called for US forces in Afghanistan to come under Afghan control, to put a stop to aggressive house-to-house searches, to release the estimated 500 Afghan citizens held in Bagram, and to focus less on al Qaeda and more on domestic Afghan insurgents. This was the first time the Afghan leader had openly criticised US policy in his country. Nonetheless, President Karzai signed a strategic partnership pact with the US in May, scotching any talk of a serious falling out between the two governments. President Karzai reiterated, in September, his call on the US to rethink its Afghan strategy.

A difficult border

In June, US president George W Bush was forced to intervene in a row between his two key South Asian allies, Afghanistan and Pakistan. What began as a brawl between border guards on the Afghanistan-Pakistan frontier threatened to turn into a major incident. The Afghan press, Afghan demonstrators and some inside the Afghan government accused Pakistan of being behind much of the violence in Afghanistan's eastern and southern provinces, by way of tolerating border crossings by insurgents. President Bush spoke to his Afghan and Pakistani counterparts by phone in a bid to defuse the crisis. In a bid to increase India's influence in the region, particularly at the expense of its long-time foe Pakistan, Indian prime minister Manmohan Singh visited Afghanistan in August – the first such visit by an Indian leader since 1976.

Outlook

The security situation will remain fragile in Afghanistan in 2006. With planned cut-backs in the number of US troops deployed in the country only partially to be met by an expanded contribution by NATO, there will be a reduction in the Afghan government's ability to fight insurgents. Much will depend on how a major international conference, to be held in London 31 January–1 February, pans out. The conference is designed to strike a five-year compact between Afghanistan and the international community, covering development, governance, security and the anti-drugs trade measures. This new 'Afghanistan Compact' will succeed the Bonn Agreement of December 2001. With parliament due to review all presidential decrees since 2002, both president and parliament will have to tread carefully if conflict is to be avoided or at least minimised. The IMF expects the economy to continue to grow, possibly in double-digit figures.

Risk assessment

Politics	Improving
Economy	Improving
Regional stability	Problematic

COUNTRY PROFILE

Historical profile

For centuries, Afghanistan's strategic location close to the heart of Central Asia made it the target of foreign powers. With its mixture of ethnic clans and feudal society ruled by powerful warlords, no foreign invader successfully managed to control Afghanistan for very long. In the nineteenth century, Afghanistan became the scene of the 'Great Game' as Britain tried to counter Russia's increasing influence in Central Asia.

In 1996, the Taliban, originally a group of Islamic scholars drawn from the Pashtun majority, seized Kabul after nearly two decades of conflict. Although its extreme version of Islam attracted widespread criticism, the Taliban remained in control of most of Afghanistan until its

KEY INDICATORS — Afghanistan

	Unit	2000	2001	2002	2003	2004
Population	m	22.70	23.00	24.70	25.25	25.79
Gross domestic product (GDP)	US$bn	18.00	4.60	2.84	4.60	*5.76
GDP per capita	US$	800	200	115	186	194
GDP real growth	%	–	–	28.6	15.7	7.5
Inflation	%	–	-43.4	52.3	10.3	13.0
Balance of trade	US$m	–	–	–	–	-3,313.0
Current account	US$m	–	-2,310.0	-6,260.0	3,400.0	4,400.0
Exchange rate	per US$	4,714.50	4,750.00	4,750.00	^43.00	43.00

* estimated figure
^ the afghani was re-valued on 3 Jan 2003

Afghanistan

refusal to hand over Osama bin Laden led to air strikes by the US and Britain in 2001. By the end of the year, the Taliban had been defeated and Hamid Kazai became interim head of a power-sharing government. Although some visible progress has been made since the fall of the Taliban government, many problems remain unsolved: militants continue to fight; there has been a boom in the drugs trade and Afghanistan has become the world's leading producer of opium.
1838–42 First Afghan War. Britain invaded Afghanistan to counter the threat to British India from expanding Russian influence in Afghanistan and was defeated by fierce resistance from Afghanistan's many ethnic tribes.
1878–80 Second Afghan War. After Britain invaded Afghanistan for the second time, parts of the country were absorbed into British India. Russia also seized parts of Afghani territory.
1907 Russia signed an agreement with Britain, promising no further interference in Afghanistan.
1919 Third Afghan War, after which Britain recognised Afghanistan's independence.
1926 Amanullah proclaimed himself King.
1929 Amanullah fled after civil unrest over his reforms; Mohammed Nadir Shah was proclaimed King. He reunited a fragmented Afghanistan and took steps to modernise the country, though less obtrusively than Amanullah.
1933 Nadir Shah was assassinated and his son, Zahir Shah, became King; his reign lasted 40 years.
1956 Afghanistan built a close relationship with the Soviet Union, gaining arms supplies and undertaking trade.
1964 A constitutional monarchy was introduced, which led to political polarisation and power struggles.
1965 The Communist People's Democratic Party of Afghanistan (PDPA) was formed.
1973 General Mohammed Daud deposed King Zahir Shah, who moved into exile in Italy, and Afghanistan was declared a republic.
1978 General Daud was assassinated in the Saur (April) Revolution, a coup by the pro-Communists, led by the PDPA's leader, Noor Taraki, who was declared president.
1979 The Soviet Union invaded Afghanistan after the nationalist foreign minister, Hafizullah Amin, deposed Taraki. Amin was executed and replaced by the pro-Soviet Babrak Karmal. Numerous Afghan factions formed the Mujahidin and began a guerrilla war against the Soviet occupation forces. Backed by the US, Pakistan, China, Iran and Saudi Arabia, the Mujahidin inflicted heavy losses on Soviet troops.
1985 The Mujahidin gathered in Pakistan, forming an alliance against Soviet forces. Half of the Afghan population was displaced by the war.
1986 Babrak Karmal was replaced by Najibullah Ahmadzai, the head of the Afghani secret police, as head of the Soviet-backed regime.
1988 Afghanistan, USSR, the US and Pakistan signed peace accords.
1989 The Soviet Union withdrew its last troops from Afghanistan. Civil war continued as the Mujahidin refused to co-operate with the Najibullah regime.
1991 The US and Russia agreed to end military aid to both sides.
1992 Afghanistan was declared an Islamic republic after the capture of Kabul by Mujahidin factions and Najibullah was forced to seek the UN's protection in Kabul. Rival militias vied for power.
1993 Burhanuddin Rabbani, an ethnic Tajik, was proclaimed president, and Gulbuddin Hekmatyar, who was strongly backed by the US during the Soviet occupation, was appointed prime minister.
1994 The Pashtun-dominated Islamic fundamentalist Taliban, formed in Kandahar, south Afghanistan, emerged as the major challenge to the Rabbani government.
1995 The Taliban swept through southern Afghanistan.
1996 The Taliban captured Kabul and quickly imposed a strict version of *sharia* (Islamic law). President Rabbani fled to join the anti-Taliban alliance in the north.
1997 Only Pakistan and Saudi Arabia recognised the Taliban as legitimate rulers of Afghanistan. Hostilities increased in the north between the Taliban and the militias of the United National Islamic Front for the Salvation of Afghanistan (UNIFSA) (also known as the Northern Alliance).
1998 The Taliban captured Mazar-i-Sharif, the last major city outside Taliban control; around 6,000 civilians were massacred following the city's capture. The US launched cruise missiles at suspected bases of Osama bin Laden, accused of bombing US embassies in Africa.
1999 The UN introduced economic sanctions against Afghanistan for harbouring Bin Laden.
2001 The Afghan resistance leader, Commander Massoud, was assassinated. The giant statues of Buddha in Bamian were destroyed by the Taliban. The US and Britain launched air strikes against the Taliban and al Qaeda, following the Taliban's refusal to hand over Bin Laden, also blamed for masterminding the 11 September 2001 terrorist attacks in the US. Opposition forces seized Mazar-i-Sharif, then Kabul and other key cities. Afghan groups agreed an interim government in UN-sponsored talks in Bonn, Germany. The Taliban gave up Kandahar, its last stronghold, at the end of the year and Pashtun royalist, Hamid Karzai was sworn in as head of a 30-member interim power-sharing government.
2002 The first contingent of foreign peacekeepers arrived. Hamid Karzai was elected interim president by the Loya Jirga. Former monarch, Zahir Shah, returned to Kabul, but made no claim to the throne. The Interim President narrowly escaped an assassination attempt in his home town of Kandahar. After 23 years, the Asian Development Bank resumed lending to Afghanistan.
2003 The afghani was re-valued. Afghanistan introduced a law banning armed factions from politics. NATO forces took control of security in Kabul.
2004 On 4 January, Afghanistan ratified a new constitution including a presidential system. In the October presidential elections Hamid Karzai, won 55 per cent of the vote, Yunus Qanuni 16 per cent, Mohammad Mohaqeq 12 per cent and Abdul Rashid Dostum 12 per cent. President Karzai was sworn in as Afghanistan's first democratically elected leader. Afghanistan was guaranteed US$8.2bn in aid until 2007.
2005 Parliamentary elections were held on 18 September. There was a turnout of 36 per cent in Kabul and 53 per cent across the country.

Political structure
Constitution
On 4 January 2004, Afghanistan ratified a new constitution, which establishes an Islamic republic, in which the president rules with a national assembly; women are recognised as equal citizens and have one-fifth of the lower house seats.
Form of state
Islamic republic
The executive
The president is the Head of State, leading a cabinet, with two vice presidents and 29 ministers.
National legislature
The bicameral parliament consists of the Wolesi Jirga (House of the People) (lower) and Meshrano Jirga (House of Elders) (senate). The lower house has 249 members, elected for five-year terms; members of the senate are elected for four years. The Kuchi (nomad) community is allocated 10 seats in the lower house; women also have guaranteed seats.
Legal system
The new constitution guarantees an independent judiciary, consisting of a Stera Mahkama (supreme court), high courts and appeal courts.

The president appoints the members of the supreme court, with the approval of the Wolesi Jirga.

Last elections
9 October 2004 (presidential); 18 September 2005 (parliamentary).

Results: Presidential: incumbent Hamid Karzai won 55 per cent of the vote, Yunus Qanuni 16 per cent, Mohammad Mohaqeq 12 per cent and Abdul Rashid Dostum 12 per cent.

Parliamentary: Turnout was 36 per cent in Kabul and 53 per cent across the country. There is no party breakdown as candidates ran as independents.

Next elections
2009 (presidential); 2010 (parliamentary)

Political parties
Ruling party
Members of the national assembly are elected as independent candidates.

Main opposition party
Jami'at e Islami (Islamic Society of Afghanistan) leads a loose alliance.

Population
25.79 million (2004)

Ethnic make-up
Pashtun (Pathan) (38 per cent), Tajik (25 per cent), Hazara (19 per cent), Uzbek (6 per cent), minority groups including Aimaks, Turkmen, Baluch and others (12 per cent).

The Pashtuns largely reside in south-eastern Afghanistan. Tajiks, Hazaras and Uzbeks are the main communities in northern and central Afghanistan.

Religions
Almost the entire population is Muslim (84 per cent Sunni Muslim, 15 per cent Shi'ite); Hindu, Sikh and Jewish minorities.

Education
The UN Educational, Scientific and Cultural Organisation (Unesco) assists the Afghan government in the education sector reconstruction by promoting universal primary education, especially for girls and the expansion of primary schooling with access to secondary education.

Unesco has extended its support for a computer centre at Kabul University, including Internet access for the young. It also funds the printing of text-books for all levels of education.

Literacy rate: 51.9 per cent and 21.9 per cent respectively for men and women; adult rates (Unesco 2000).

Enrolment rate: 15 per cent gross primary enrolment of relevant age group (including repeaters), rates for 2000–01 (Unesco 2002).

Health
The World Health Organisation (Who) reported that since September 2000, an estimated 180,000 internally displaced people (IDPs), mostly from Ghor and Badghis provinces had been living in the Maslakh camp outside the city of Herat, which has been the site of dire health conditions during the crisis. The mortality rate declined as international support enabled the establishment of more clinics inside the camp.

WHO continues to support the IDPs by providing essential medical supplies to clinics within the camps. There is provision for night health services and nutrition centres for malnourished children. Harsh winters in the region cause acute respiratory infections, while hot dry summers lead to diarrhoeal diseases.

Despite on-going security problems, UN relief agencies and the WHO provide emergency medical supplies and assistance to local hospitals.

Afghanistan has one of the highest numbers of polio victims in the world; the disease is endemic. In March 2002, the UN Children's Fund (Unicef) and the Afghan ministry of public health started a polio vaccination campaign in the southern and eastern regions of Afghanistan. The campaign had an initial target to vaccinate 1,950,000 children.

Life expectancy: 43.2 years (World Bank 2002).

Fertility rate/Maternal mortality rate: 6.8 births per woman (World Bank 2002).

Infant mortality rate: 165 per 1,000 live births (2002), 49 per cent of children aged under five were malnourished (World Bank).

Welfare
Many Afghans fled the country due to war, drought and earthquakes. The UNHCR estimated that, at its peak, more than 3.7 million Afghans survive outside their homeland; between 1.1–1.5 million were internally displaced. Over 520,000 refugees returned in 2005, the largest group, of 453,000, came from camps in Pakistan. International agencies and the government have been working hard for their rehabilitation, as well as for the thousands who returned in previous years.

The WFP has been working with the Afghan government to rehabilitate irrigation systems and expand its activities to cover the reconstruction of schools, hospitals, roads and bridges.

In March 2005, Japan donated US$29 million to *New Beginnings Programme* that offers ex-militia soldiers the opportunity of joining the official army or retraining in peacetime occupations such as farming or tailoring. Japan had already donated US$90 million to the project that required US$140 million to fund.

Main cities
Kabul (capital, estimated population 2.3 million in 2004), Kandahar (349,300), Mazar-i-Sharif (246,900), Herat (171,500), Jalalabad (163,600).

Languages spoken
The languages spoken by Afghanistan's two largest ethnic groups are Dari (Afghan Persian) (50 per cent) and Pashtu (35 per cent). Turkic languages (primarily Uzbek and Turkmen) (11 per cent), 30 minor languages (primarily Baluchi and Pashai) (4 per cent). Farsi (Persian) is spoken by the Tajiks. Some speak a second language, including English, Russian, French or German.

Official language/s
Pashtu and Dari (named as official languages in the constitution ratified 4 Jan 2004)

Media
Under the Taliban, the media was tightly controlled and used for propaganda purposes. The population were not alllowed access to western media while television and music was banned under *sharia*. This resulted in most media covering Afghanistan operating from other countries, although some publishing was undertaken in Taliban-free areas of northern Afghanistan.

After the fall of the Taliban in October 2001, the interim government promulgated the Media Law in Afghanistan, which came into effect in April 2002; it allows independent publications that can criticise government policy and express views on issues concerning Afghanistan.

Press
There are a number of Afghan publications with international circulations. Publications from the US include *Andiwal* and *Sobh-e Kabul*. Publications from Europe include *Aazarakhsh* (Switzerland) and *Dawat* (Norway). The UK's Institute for War and Peace Reporting (IWPR) has established an online news publication *Afghanweb* (http://www.afghanweb.org), which is run and produced by Afghani journalists living in Afghanistan.

Dailies: Government-sponsored publications include *Anis*, and *Hewad*. *Erada* (Pashto and Dari) is a independent newspaper.

Weeklies: *Payam-e-Mujahid* (www.payamemujahid.com) is an online publication. It is in Pushtu and Dari languages. In January 2002, *Kabul Weekly* was re-launched in Afghanistan; this independent newspaper is being funded by the UN. Government-sponsored publications include *Eslah* (bi-weekly), and *Kabul Times* (English, three times weekly). Non-governmental publications include *Afghanistan* (launched in 2003, in English, Pashto and Dari), *Cheragh* (launched in January 2004, in Pashto, Dari and English).

Omaid Weekly published in the US is one of the most widely read Afghani publications in the world.

Periodicals: International periodicals include *The Afghan Post* and *Zarnegaar*. *Sabawoon* is a cultural, social and political journal in Pashtu language (US) and *Voice of Peace* is a Afghanistan Peace Association publication (US).

Broadcasting

Radio: Radio Afghanistan is financed and controlled by the government.

There are several foreign radio broadcasting services received in Afghanistan. Radio Voice of Freedom, established in August 2002, is sponsored and run by the International Security Assistance Force (Isaf). The station broadcasts in Dari and Pashto 24 hours a day; it can be heard on 88.5 FM in Kabul.

Funded by USAID, Arman FM is Kabul's first commercial radio station. It began its transmissions in April 2003 on 98.1 MHz. Radio Arman broadcasts 18 hours daily, from 0600 until 2400.

Television: Television Afghanistan is financed and controlled by the government of Afghanistan. It was closed and banned by the Taliban, but its musical record archives were not destroyed. After the collapse of the Taliban, Television Afghanistan reopened with the support of Iran. The US embassy in Kabul delivered a new one-KW transmitter in early 2003 and the Japanese government has committed itself to rebuilding or replacing the company's old equipment by the end of 2004.

The first private television station, Aina Television, was launched on 18 January 2004 by the minister of information and culture.

Economy

The state of the country after the fall of the Taliban has left the government with political, economic and social burdens. However, Afghanistan has been experiencing significant economic improvements and stability, allowing improvements to be implemented. Extreme poverty is still estimated to affect 20 per cent of the population with a further 60 per cent being vulnerable. Long-term improvement will require substantial external financing, as well as government commitment to reform and to tackling the problems of an opium economy and domestic security issues.

The government's focus is on reviving the economy, particularly agriculture, energy, housing, education and export-related industries. Domestic revenues have increased, mainly due to tax reforms in 2004. For these revenues to meet the ambitious targets set, further improvement of revenue collection will be required. But the development of infrastructure remains heavily dependent on external backing. An estimated 80 per cent of the population are employed in the agricultural sector, most of which is subsistence farming. Illicit opium production forms an increasing percentage of the country's GDP, accounting for just over half with an estimated value of US$2.8 billion. The government and foreign donors are keen to tackle the opium trade, but this is likely to be extremely challenging due to the scale of production and its economic importance. Some success has been achieved, as there have been reports of fewer farmers sowing opium in 2005 in response to a government ban.

External trade

The low customs duties in Afghanistan, and the country's location have made the nation an important distribution point for re-exports in the past.

There is duty-free transit of goods from Pakistani ports into Afghanistan and a proposed preferential trade pact with Pakistan is likely to improve trade relations between the two countries. Suggested oil pipelines through Afghanistan to Pakistan would create an oil trade linking Central Asia with Pakistan.

The Trade and Investment Framework Agreement signed between the US and Afghanistan on 21 September 2004 is a step towards closer trading relations between the two countries.

Imports

Afghanistan mainly imports capital goods, foodstuffs, textiles and petroleum products. Imports totalled an estimates US$3.75 billion in 2003–04.

Main sources: Pakistan (25.2 per cent of total imports, 2004), US (8.7 per cent), South Korea (7.7 per cent), India (7.6 per cent), Germany (6.5 per cent), Turkmenistan (4.5 per cent), Turkey (4.1 per cent)

Exports

Opium, Afghanistan's largest export is primarily exported north through the Central Asian republics and on to Europe. However due to alarm over escalating opium production it is being heavily clamped down on by foreign governments. As opium represents a large proportion of the country's exports this could lead to revenues falling dramatically if this campaign is successful.

Principal non-opium exports are fruits and nuts, wool, cotton, hides, semi-precious and precious stones. Afghanistan was the world's largest exporter of raisins and a major producer of grapes, melons and other fruit.

Main destinations: India (23.1 per cent of total export, 2004), Pakistan (20.5 per cent), US (12.9 per cent), Germany (6 per cent)

Agriculture

Farming

The population is returning to the countryside and some rural areas have been transformed by the return of Afghan refugees from Pakistan and Iran. Development is impeded by the lack of finance for infrastructure repairs.

Twelve per cent of the total area is cultivated, another 10 per cent is pasture land and a further 5–6 per cent considered by some sources to have agricultural potential.

Most cultivated land is situated in river valleys or plains, which are often fertile; an estimated two-thirds of cultivated land is irrigated. Food output is frequently below what is required to feed the population. In total more than 12,000 out of 22,000 farming villages were abandoned or destroyed during the fighting of the 1990s. Drought was responsible for large-scale agricultural destruction in 2001.

Apart from the opium poppy, the main crops are wheat, fruit and vegetables, maize, rice, barley, cotton, sugar beet, sugar cane, oil seeds.

The livestock herd needs rebuilding. Livestock includes sheep, cattle, goats and poultry, with donkeys, horses, camels, mules and buffaloes kept as draught animals. Sheep provide a major source of protein and animal fat. Some 70 per cent of wool production, along with hides from karakul sheep, is exported.

After the fall of the Taliban, the farmers started to sow poppies again. In January 2002, Hamid Karzai banned opium poppy cultivation and trafficking, and offered farmers US$350 for each 0.2 hectare (ha) to be replanted with an alternative crop. This was only a fraction of what the farmers could earn from the poppy crop. Afghanistan recorded one of its highest opium harvests in 2002, regaining its position as the world's leading producer.

The area under poppy cultivation in 2004 increased by 64 per cent and only crop disease prevented it from being the largest opium harvest ever recorded. Until economic and social alternatives are developed, the local population remains dependent on the opium economy.

Forestry

Wooded land is limited to the eastern Hindu Kush region and along the Pakistani border. Many forests in these areas have been severely reduced due to trees being cut down and the wood smuggled out to surrounding countries.

Legitimate production in 2002 included 400,000 cubic metres (cum) sawnwood,

856,000cum sawlogs and veneers, 904,000cum industrial roundwood, 1.43 million cum woodfuel, 93,211 tonnes charcoal.

Tourism

Instability is an impediment to the development of a tourist sector in Afghanistan, although given the right conditions there is considerable potential. Some visitors are arriving and trekking trips have been arranged. Much work needs to be done to restore the necessary infrastructure. Accommodation in Kabul is limited to a few hotels and houses converted into guesthouses.

Mining

Natural resources include copper, chromite, lead, zinc, iron, salt, lapis lazuli, emeralds, talc and barium sulphate.
Long-term mineral development projects include copper mining and smelting at Ainak and high-grade iron ore mining at Hajigak in northern Afghanistan.

Hydrocarbons

Prior to the 1979 Soviet invasion, Afghanistan's total oil and condensate reserves were estimated at around 95 million barrels. Oil production was almost entirely halted during the 1980s and 1990s. The sector will require foreign investment to return to its pre-1979 status. Petroleum products are imported mainly from Pakistan and Turkmenistan.
Afghanistan has natural gas reserves of around 125 billion cubic metres. Political and military problems have hindered further development of the sector. Proposals for a pipeline connecting Pakistan, Afghanistan and Turkmenistan have made little progress.
There are small deposits of coal. An estimated 73 million tonnes of coal are located mainly in northern Afghanistan in the region between Herat and Badashkah.

Energy

The energy sector was badly damaged during the years of upheaval. Afghanistan has installed capacity of 450MW, generated by hydropower, of which only 271MW are available. Some border areas receive supplies from neighbouring countries. Electricity supply is only available to around 6 per cent of the population. Interruptions and blackouts are frequent.

Banking and insurance

Afghanistan has six banks (four of which have almost no assets) and two commercial banks – Pashtani and Milli – with assets. In September 2003, two banking laws were passed: the Central Banking Law and the Commercial Banking Law. The first laid the groundwork for the Central Bank to focus on monetary policy, pricing stability and oversight of the commercial markets; the second allowed for private ownership of commercial banks. By 2004 there were three commercial banks – Standard Chartered (UK), Microfinance Bank of Afghanistan and National Bank of Pakistan, with others being set up.

Central bank
Da Afghanistan Bank (re-opened January 2002).

Main financial centre
Kabul

Time

GMT plus 4.5 hours

Geography

Afghanistan is a landlocked country in south-western Asia. Its neighbours are Turkmenistan, Uzbekistan and Tajikistan to the north, Iran to the west, the People's Republic of China to the north-east and Pakistan to the east and south. The Hindu Kush mountains are in the north-east of the country.

Climate

The climate is generally dry and varies according to altitude. In Kabul (altitude 1,800 metres), winter temperatures can fall below -20 degrees Celsius (C), with average temperatures of 32 degrees C in July–August. Lower regions are warmer; summer temperatures can reach 40 degrees C plus. Most rainfall is from March–May (Kabul average 335mm).

Entry requirements

Passports
Required by all.

Visa
Required by all; application forms can be obtained via:
www.embassyofafghanistan.org/main/consulate/visa.cfm or local embassies. Business visas require a letter of introduction stating the purpose of visit and sponsorship information. A visa financial guarantee must be included with the application fee. For a multiply entry visa, a letter of introduction signed by the president of the organisation, must accompany the documentation.

Currency advice/regulations
Import of local and foreign currency is unlimited provided it is declared on arrival. Export of local currency is unlimited. Foreign currency up to the amount imported and declared can be exported.
US dollars, Pakistan rupees and afghani are widely used as cash currency.

Prohibited imports
Alcoholic beverages

Health (for visitors)

Mandatory precautions
Vaccination certificate for yellow fever if travelling from an infected zone.

Advisable precautions
Hepatitis 'A', anti-malarial precautions, polio, tetanus, typhoid. Diphtheria, hepatitis 'B', TB immunisations are recommended in some circumstances – seek further advice. Water precautions are advisable. There is a risk of rabies. Western-style medical care is not available except in Kabul where a well-equipped German hospital will accept foreign patients. Travellers should bring with them all necessary medications.

Hotels

There are only a few hotels and the accommodation tends to be spartan. The only international hotel in Kabul is the Intercontinental Hotel, Bagh-I-Balla, Kabul.

Public holidays

Fixed dates
21 Mar (Naw Roz/Persian New Year), 28 Apr (Islamic Revolution Day), 19 Aug (National Day).
Afghanistan uses the Persian calendar, which differs from the Gregorian calendar: there are 31 days in each of the first six months of the Persian calendar, 30 days in each of the next five months and 29 days in the last month, except in leap year when it has 30 days.
Persian year 1384: from 21 March 2005 to 20 March 2006.

Variable dates
Eid al Adha (three days), Ashura, Birth of the Prophet, First day of Ramadan, Eid al Fitr (three days).
Muslim holidays that occur on a Friday may be observed on the following Saturday.
The Islamic year contains 354 or 355 days, with the result that Muslim feasts advance by 10–12 days against the Gregorian calendar. Dates of feasts vary according to the sighting of the new moon, so cannot be forecast exactly.
Islamic year 1426: 10 February 2005 to 30 January 2006.

Working hours

The weekend is Friday.
Banking
Sat–Wed: 0800–1200, 1300–1630; Thu: 0800–1330.
Business
Sat–Wed: 0800–1200, 1300–1630; Thu: 0800–1330.
Government
Sat–Thu: 0800–1600.
Shops
Commercial shops keep long but varying hours, usually Sat–Thu: 0700–2300.

Telecommunications

Mobile phones
GSM 900/1800 services available in main cities only.

Afghanistan

Electricity supply
220 volts AC, 60 cycle electrical system, using European round, two-prong plugs. Supplies may be seriously affected and power cuts frequent.

Weights and measures
Metric system (local units are also in use).

Social customs/useful tips
It is customary to shake hands on meeting and taking leave. Among men, embracing is a traditional form of greeting. Islamic conventions apply. However, it is no longer necessary for women to wear a *burqa* (long veil), which was enforced under the Taliban. When sitting cross-legged on sofas or cushions, soles of feet must not be shown. Business meetings are usually conducted in English or Dari. Green or black tea, nuts and raisins are served. The form of greeting is *Salaam Aleykum* (peace be with you), followed by a firm handshake and placing the right hand over the heart. Several minutes are spent engaging in pleasantries about each other's countries. It is essential to build trust and to be patient.

Security
Foreign nationals are being advised not to travel to Afghanistan due to continuing instability in the country. Armed criminal and terrorist activity is high and there is also a high risk from fighting between rival tribal armies.
If travel is necessary, a visitor is advised to register with their embassy when leaving and only stay in parts of Afghanistan where international troops are assisting with security arrangements. The UK Foreign & Commonwealth Office (FCO) is suggesting that visitors who travel outside secure areas of Kabul should make arrangements to have armed protection.
In June 2002, a third of Afghanistan was put off-limits to UN workers, because of lack of security

Getting there
Air
National airline: Ariana Afghan Airlines (state-owned); UN Security Council financial sanctions were lifted in January 2002.
International airport/s: Kabul airport (KBL), 16km from Kabul; banking, buffet-bar, car park, post office and restaurant.
Surface
Road: There are links to Iran and Pakistan via the Asia Highway, with a bus service, and to the CIS via road and rail. Hostilities have periodically closed the Pakistan route; check before travelling.
Rail: Links exist between Kabul and the CIS.

Getting about
National transport
Air: The national airline, Ariana Afghan Airlines, flies domestic routes and to Germany, India, Iran, Pakistan, Turkey and the UAE.
Road: Main centres are linked by paved roads but secondary roads vary in condition and by season. There are approximately 22,000km of roads.
Buses: Bus service is available, but unreliable and dangerous for internal travel.
Water: There are 1,200km of navigable inland waterways, including the Amu Darya River.
City transport
Taxis: Taxis are available from Kabul airport to the city centre. Tipping is not usual. Fares are negotiable and can be high for foreigners.
Buses, trams & metro: A limited number of buses are operating.
Car hire
International driving licences are required if cars are available.

BUSINESS DIRECTORY

Telephone area codes
The international dialling code (IDD) for Afghanistan is +93, followed by the subscriber's number.

Chambers of Commerce
Afghan Chamber of Commerce and Industry, Mohammed Jan Khan Wattt, Kabul (tel/fax: 290-196).

Banking
Agricultural Development Bank, Jaddeh-Maiwand, Kabul.

Export Promotion Bank, Jaddah-Temorshahi, Kabul.

Industrial Promotion Bank, Shar-i-naw, Kabul.

Mortgage and Construction Bank, Shari-i-naw, Kabul.

Pashtany Tejaraty Bank, Mohmmad-Jankhan Watt, Kabul.
Central bank
Da Afghanistan Bank, Ibni Sina Watt, Kabul (tel: 240-7579).

Travel information
Ariana Afghan Airlines, PO Box 76, Ansari Watt, Kabul (tel: 873-762-523-844; fax: 873-762-523-846; e-mail: afghanairlines@yahoo.com).

Kabul Airport, PO Box 76, Anseri Watt, Kabul (tel: 25-541).

Ministries
Ministry of Communications (internet site: http://www.af-com-ministry.org).

Ministry of Finance (internet site: http://www.af/mof).

Ministry of Rural Rehabilitation and development (internet site: http://www.af/mrrd).

Ministry of Irrigation, Water Resources & Environment, Darulman, Kabul, Afghanistan

Other useful addresses
Afghan Islamic Press, House 208, Qafila Road, Tahkal Payan, Peshawar, Pakistan (tel: (92)91-570-1100; fax: (92)91-570-3355; e-mail: aip@pes.comsats.net.pk).

Afghanistan Assistance Co-ordination Authority (AACA), Flower House, Prime Minister Compound, Kabul (tel: 7028-2622; e-mail: info@afghanaca.com; internet site: http://www.af/aaca, http://www.af/aaca/procurement).

Afghanistan Embassy (USA), 2341 Wyoming Avenue, NW, Washington DC 20008 (tel: (1)202-234-3770; fax: (1)202-328-3516; internet site: http://afghanistanembassy.org).

Afghanistan Wireless Communication Corporation, Ministry of Communications Building, Mohammad Jan Khan Watt, Kabul (tel: 2020-0000; fax: 2020-0200; e-mail: info@afghan-wireless.com).

Arman FM, House #3, St 12, Wazir Akbar Khan, Kabul (tel: 7029-2690; 7028-9383; e-mail: saad.mohseni@mobycapital.com).

Fedex (Afghan Express), Karte 3, Khai Street, House 326, Kabul (tel: 2025-00525; fax: 2025-00524).

DHL Express, Street 10, Wazir Akbar Khan, House 310, Kabul (tel: 7027-6362; e-mail: kbl_hdesk@af.dhl.com).

TNT Express, Turabaz Khan Crossroads, Kabul (tel: 7027-6503; fax: 2029-0218).

Internet sites
Afghanistan Embassy (Australia): http://www.afghanembassy.net

Afghanistan Online: http://www.afghan-web.com

DariPashto Edition; http://www.af/daripashto

Donor Assistance Database: http://www.af/aaca/dad.html

Guide to Travellers to Kabul: http://www.afghanembassy.net/n_travel.html

LOTFA; http://www.undp.org.af/projects/lofta_july.html

UN Agencies: http://www.af/un

UN Development Business on-line subscription service: http://www.devbusiness.com
World Bank: http://www.worldbank.org/afghanistan

Albania

KEY FACTS

Official name: Republika ë Shqipërisë (Republic of Albania)

Head of State: President Alfred Moisiu (elected by the People's Assembly; sworn in 24 Jul 2002)

Head of government: Prime Minister Sali Berish (elected in 3 Jul 2005)

Ruling party: Coalition government, led by the Partia Demokratike ë Shqipërisë (PDS) (The Democratic Party of Albania) (DP), with the Partia Agrare Ambientaliste (AAP) Agrarian Environmentalist Party (AAP), the Partia Republikane e Shqipërisë (RP) Republican Party, the Partia Demokrate e Re (PDR) the New Democratic Party and the Partia Bashkimi për të Drejtat e Njeriut (UHRP) Union for Human Rights Party

Area: 28,748 square km

Population: 3.16 million (2004)

Capital: Tirana

Official language: Since 1945, the official language has been based on Tosk Albanian. The Albanian language is divided into two dialects – Gheg, north of the river Shkumbinit, and Tosk in the south.

Currency: Lek (L) = 100 qindarka

Exchange rate: L102.35 per US$ (Oct 2005)

GDP per capita: US$2,131 (2004)

GDP real growth: 5.90% (2004); *5.5 (2005)

Labour force: 1.62 million (2004)

Unemployment: 16.00% (2004)

Inflation: 2.90% (2004); 2.2 (first two quarters 2005)

Balance of trade: -US$1.52 billion (2004)

* estimated figure

It was a watershed year in Albanian politics, with an election in July bringing about a change in government for the first time in eight years. The elections also threw into relief Albania's relations with its neighbours, particularly on the status of Albanian communities in Macedonia, Greece and Serbia and Montenegro. The economy continued its steady run of GDP growth of around 6 per cent since 2000, with the IMF projecting 5.5 per cent growth for 2005.

Steady growth

Although representing a slowdown on 2004 figures (5.9 per cent), the IMF's projection for GDP growth in Albania for 2005 was proof that the Albanian economy had definitively left behind many of the problems of the 1990s. The country was virtually bankrupted in 1997 after the collapse of widely subscribed pyramid schemes. Inflation ran at 2.2 per cent in the first two quarters of 2005 – down from 2004's average of 2.9 per cent. A World Bank report, published in March, praised Albania's economic progress, particularly in the realm of banking reform and privatisation. However, it warned that declining levels of international aid and reliance on overseas remittances (estimated to be worth US$1 billion) posed a threat to Albania's economic prospects. In 2005, organic food produce emerged as a potentially lucrative new growth industry for Albania, based on the country's abundance of unpolluted land.

The return of Sali Berisha

At elections on 3 July 2005, four-times prime minister Fatos Nano and his Partia Socialiste ë Shqipërisë (PSS) (Socialist Party of Albania) was defeated. This was the first defeat for the PSS since it swept to power in 1997. Opposition leader Sali Berisha, himself a former president of Albania (1992–97), emerged as the new prime minister at the head of a seven-party coalition. The election was seen as an important test by the EU, as to whether or not Albania could be judged ready for further integration with the EU. Albania signed a Stabilisation and Association Agreement (SAA) with the EU in 2003 but was still in the process of implementing the required political and economic reforms. The campaign began with the usual trading of insults between long-time rivals Nano and Berisha, including allegations of drug trafficking and mafia connections. Although more peaceful than previous Albanian elections, Organisation for Security and Co-operation in Europe (OSCE) observers reported that the July election 'only partially' complied with democratic norms. The count was marred by irregularities and some ballots had to be re-run in August. However, despite Socialist claims of massive electoral fraud (rejected by the OSCE), it emerged that the opposition alliance had won a comfortable majority and Nano finally resigned on 1 September. Two days later, President Alfred Moisiu nominated Berisha as the country's next prime minister. In November, EU negotiators praised Albania's economic and political progress and stated that the SAA might be finalised in the coming months.

Making waves

Despite being hailed by President Moisiu as the most peaceful transition of power in Albania's post-communist era, there were signs that the new government was in the mood for aggressive policy and institutional changes. From September to December, the Berisha government clashed with the president over its reform agenda, specifically relating to the way in which the country's intelligence agency was structured, and the justice system. In October, the government overturned the previous government's decision to sell the state's telecom company, Albtelecom, to two Turkish buyers, citing legal irregularities. Widespread power cuts of up to 18 hours a day in November were blamed by Berisha on earlier PSS incompetence and prompted the government to announce the mass privatisation of the country's hydroelectric power stations.

As for the PSS itself, the durable Nano vacated the party chairmanship in October but was unable to install his preferred successor, instead losing out to Tirana mayor, Edi Rama. Mr Rama aggressively forged a post-Nano identity for the PSS, apologising to the nation for the mistakes of the previous PSS government.

Regional ethnic politics

Albania is exceptional among Balkan states in that there are nearly as many Albanians living within Albania's neighbours (approximately 2.3 million) as there are in Albania itself (3.4 million). Elections in Albania and developments in the region brought the issue of ethnic minorities to the fore in 2005. With a long-expected decision by the UN Security Council, in October, to open talks on the future status of Serbia's Albanian-populated Kosovo province, it was inevitable that the issue arose in the Albanian election. Both major parties in Albania pledged themselves to support the case for Kosovo's independence, complicating relations with Serbia. Calls from some ethnic Albanian politicians in Macedonia for the creation of a 'Greater Albania', uniting Albanian-population territories in Kosovo and Macedonia with Albania, prompted a string of reassurances from the Berisha government to its neighbours that Albania had no such designs.

Relations with Greece were strained in November, when a planned meeting between President Moisiu and his Greek counterpart, Karolos Papoulias, was disrupted by protestors from Albania's Cam (also known as Cham) community. The Cams were forcibly expelled from Greece in 1944, after being accused of collaborating with the Nazis. The Cams have since been campaigning for the restitution of their property rights in Greece but face widespread confiscations after the implementation, in November, of a new property law in Greece. The temperature of disagreements over national minorities had already been raised, in March, by the outgoing Greek president, Kostis Stephanopoulos. President Stephanopoulos had suggested that Greece revive old territorial claims to southern Albania on the grounds of a resident Greek minority.

Albania and the World

In November, Prime Minister Berisha reiterated Albania's long-standing desire to join NATO and the EU. Albania received backing for its NATO ambitions from Turkey in February. In September, the Adriatic Charter group, founded in 2003 and consisting of Albania, Croatia and Macedonia, agreed to accelerate and integrate efforts to meet NATO membership requirements.

Albania remained closely aligned with the US in 2005. In October, Albania sent another contingent of troops to Iraq; and in December, Albania's foreign minister, Besnik Mustafaj, explicitly identified the US as Albania's main strategic partner.

Outlook

The IMF expects economic growth in Albania to slow in 2006, to around 5.0 per cent. This will undoubtedly put pressure on the government, already grappling with an unemployment rate of around 15 per cent. Much will depend on the outcome of Albania's negotiations with the World Bank for a new Country Assistance Strategy (CAS) loan, aimed at promoting economic growth, development and improved service delivery.

With the Berisha government determined to implement political and institutional changes after eight years of socialist rule, the political climate will inevitably periodically heat up. Moreover, with the government committed to backing a new candidate for the presidency in 2007, further clashes with President Moisiu can be expected. On the other hand, the election of Mr Rama as PSS leader in October may signal a departure from the hyper-antagonism of previous parliamentary terms. Albania's post-communist politics has been dominated by the personal enmity between Mr Berisha and Mr Nano and the rise of Mr Rama in the PSS offers a chance of a new beginning.

With a final decision on the status of Kosovo looming, Albania will have to tread carefully. Appeals from Kosovo's Albanian politicians for firm backing from Tirana on the issue of Kosovan independence is growing. Albania must balance a sentimental desire to see Kosovo emerge as an independent state with the legitimate concerns of its neighbours, particularly Serbia and Macedonia. Also complicating Albania's regional relations in 2006 is the upcoming referendum on independence in Montenegro. Albania's relations with Montenegro will be under scrutiny from Montenegro's sister republic, Serbia. Moreover, with Montenegro's majority Slav population evenly split on the issue of independence, Montenegro's Albanian minority may end up casting the deciding vote. Albania will yet again have to tread carefully to avoid influencing outcomes beyond its borders.

KEY INDICATORS — Albania

	Unit	2000	2001	2002	2003	2004
Population	m	3.13	3.13	3.16	3.16	3.16
Gross domestic product (GDP)	US$bn	3.80	4.10	4.80	6.18	*7.59
GDP per capita	US$	1,214	1,302	1,516	1,958	2,131
GDP real growth	%	7.8	6.5	4.7	6.0	5.9
Inflation	%	4.2	3.1	5.3	3.3	2.9
Unemployment	%	16.8	14.5	14.3	15.0	–
Exports (fob) (goods)	US$m	255.7	304.6	330.0	426.0	552.4
Imports (fob) (goods)	US$m	1,070.0	1,331.6	1,400.0	1,800.0	2,076.0
Balance of trade	US$m	-814.3	-1,027.0	-1,096.0	-1,374.0	-1,523.6
Current account	US$m	-156.3	-217.7	-438.0	-500.0	-380.0
Foreign debt	US$bn	0.8	0.8	1.3	1.2	–
Total reserves minus gold	US$m	352.2	362.5	403.3	1,009.4	0.1
Foreign exchange	US$m	271.9	276.8	318.2	913.8	1,251.7
Exchange rate	per US$	143.71	143.48	137.26	120.17	98.50

* estimated figure

Nations of the World: A Political, Economic and Business Handbook

Risk assessment

Politics	stable
Economy	stable
Regional stability	stable

COUNTRY PROFILE

Historical profile
Albania was part of the Ottoman empire from 1385–1878, after which, regions of Albanian territory were occupied by neighbouring countries, notably Austria, Bulgaria, Montenegro, Serbia, Greece and for a longer period, Italy.

Albania is one of Europe's poorest countries, nevertheless, it possesses a rich blend of religions, cultures and landscapes. The country was effectively sealed off from the rest of the world by Enver Hoxha (pronounced Hodga). He was First Secretary of the Albanian Communist Party (ACP)'s politburo (the policy-making body) from 1944 until his death in 1985. Hoxha ruled Albania with an iron fist and stifled any dissension. Control over society and public institutions, which was near-absolute, was reinforced by the Sigurimi, the secret police. After Hoxha's death, Albania began to emerge from its isolation, although its political history since the fall of communism in 1992 has been, at best, chequered. Virtually every election has been an occasion for virulent controversy, with allegations of in-fighting.

1920s Italy withdrew from Albania and agreed to recognise its independence. Tirana was declared the capital city. Political instability ensued. Prime Minister Ahmet Beg Zogu took the crown, proclaiming himself King Zog I.
1939 Italian troops under Benito Mussolini invaded Albania and King Zog fled.
1940 The Italians used Albania as their platform for the invasion of Greece.
1941 The Albanian Communist Party (ACP) was formed, with Enver Hoxha as its leader.
1943 German forces invaded and occupied Albania following surrender by the Italians.
1944 The Germans were forced out by Communist resistance fighters led by Enver Hoxha, who proclaimed the constitution of the Democratic Government of Albania as a provisional government and became first secretary of the politburo.
1945–46 Tribunals were held which condemned thousands of 'war criminals' and 'enemies of the people' to death or to prison. Non-communists were purged from government positions.
1948 Albania broke its ties with Yugoslavia. The USSR began economic aid to Albania. The ACP was renamed the Party of Labour of Albania (PLA).
1955 Albania became a founding member of the Warsaw Pact.
1961 Relations with the USSR soured when Albania supported China in the Sino-Soviet ideology dispute. Albania withdrew from the Council for Mutual Economic Assistance (Comecon).
1967 The Communist government outlawed religion, making Albania the world's only atheist state.
1968 Albania withdrew from the Warsaw Pact over the Soviet-led invasion of Czechoslovakia.
1976 A new constitution was adopted. Albania declared itself the independent Peoples' Socialist Republic of Albania and reaffirmed its policy of self-reliance.
1985 Hoxha died and was replaced by Ramiz Alia as first secretary of the politburo.
1989 Communist rule in Eastern Europe collapsed. Freedom of religion was restored.
1990 The PLA was renamed the Partia Socialiste ë Shqipërisë (PSS) (Socialist Party of Albania) and pursued a more liberal democratic ideology. Albania legalised opposition parties. Albanians were granted the right to travel abroad; thousands of people tried to flee through Western embassies, and seized ships to sail illegally to Italy.
1991 After an interim constitution was approved, multiparty elections were won by the PSS. Ramiz Alia was elected by the People's Assembly to the new post of executive president. Fatos Nano was appointed head of government, but was forced to resign due to a deteriorating political and economic situation in the country. A caretaker government took power.
1992 The opposition Partia Demokratike ë Shqipërisë (PDS) (Democratic Party of Albania) won an overwhelming victory in parliamentary elections, ending five decades of communist rule. PDS leader, Sali Berisha, was elected president. Aleksander Meksi was appointed prime minister. Ramiz Alia, Fatos Nano and several others from the old Communist regime were arrested and charged with corruption.
1994 A national referendum rejected a new constitution which opponents said allowed the president too much power. Albania joined the NATO Partnership for Peace plan.
1995 Albania was admitted to the Council of Europe.
1996 The PDS won a landslide victory in parliamentary elections, which were tainted by accusations of fraud.
1997 After pyramid investment schemes collapsed, there were weeks of rioting. The government failed to convince the country that it had no part in the investment schemes. Rebels gained control of large sections of southern Albania and threatened the capital. Berisha dismissed the prime minister and the head of the army, closed down opposition newspapers and declared a state of emergency. Thousands of Albanians fled to Italy. An international force from eight European nations arrived to help restore order. Berisha was re-elected unopposed for a further five-year term by parliament which, boycotted by the opposition, was dominated by the PDS. As a proposed solution to the profound political crisis, fresh parliamentary elections were held; these were won by the Socialists and President Berisha resigned. He was succeeded by Socialist Rexhep Kemal. The convictions of communist-era leaders were overturned; Fatos Nano was elected prime minister. King Zog I returned from South Africa.
1998 Refugees from unrest in Kosovo (Serbia) entered Albania. Nano resigned due to protests over the economy, and was succeeded by Pandeli Majko. Voters approved Albania's first post-Communist constitution, which declared the country a parliamentary republic.
1999 There was a mass refugee exodus into Albania as thousands of Kosovans fled attacks by Serbian forces. Prime Minister Majko was succeeded by the Socialist, Ilir Meta.
2000 Albania joined the World Trade Organisation (WTO).
2001 Ilir Meta and the PSS won another term in office in the elections.
2002 Prime Minister Ilir Meta resigned after failing to resolve a party feud. Sali Berisha's opposition coalition announced that it would end its six-month boycott of Albania's parliament. The President asked Pandeli Majko to form a new cabinet. Alfred Moisiu was elected president by the People's Assembly. Pandeli Majko resigned and parliament approved a new government led by Prime Minister Fatos Nano. The royal family returned from exile.
2003 Albania and the EU began Stabilisation and Association Agreement (SAA) talks.
2004 In February, the opposition led a demonstration in Tirana protesting against the government's failure to improve living standards and demanding Prime Minister Nano's resignation.
2005 On 29 March, Albania signed a US$15 million deal with the US Occidental Petroleum Corporation for oil and natural gas drilling. The opposition, PDS, won the 10 July parliamentary elections, although the results were disputed by the ruling PSS. In September the PDS took office with Sali Berisha as prime minister.

Political structure
Constitution

The constitution adopted on 28 December 1976 was declared invalid in April

Albania

1991, when the Socialist Republic of Albania was renamed the Republic of Albania under an interim constitution.
A new constitution was agreed by referendum and came into effect on 28 November 1998. It provides for multi-party elections and guarantees freedom of speech, religion, press, assembly, and organisation.

Form of state
Unicameral parliamentary democratic republic

The executive
The president is head of state and shares control of the armed forces with the prime minister. The president is elected by parliament to a five-year term and is limited to two terms. The president appoints the prime minister nominated by the party or coalition of parties that has a majority of seats in the Assembly. If the Assembly fails to approve the president's appointee three times, the president dissolves parliament. The prime minister and Council of Ministers are in charge of the country's economic, social and cultural affairs. The president and prime minister are jointly responsible for foreign relations and security affairs.

National legislature
The Kuvendi Popullor (People's Assembly) has 140 members, who serve a four-year term – 100 directly elected and 40 elected by proportional representation. The Assembly meets twice a year. In addition to passing legislation, the Assembly approves the president's appointment of the prime minister and the prime minister's choices for the Council of Ministers.

Legal system
The court system is headed by the Supreme Court. Its members are appointed by the president to nine-year terms with the consent of the Assembly. Judges in appeals and district courts are appointed by the president upon the recommendations of the Higher Judicial Council, which is headed by the president and includes the chair of the Supreme Court and the minister of justice. A separate constitutional court rules on constitutional matters and consists of nine members appointed by the president with the Assembly's consent.

Last elections
10 July 2005 (parliamentary); 24 June 2002 (presidential).
Results: Paliamentary: the opposition, Partia Demokratike ë Shqipërisë (PDS) (Democratic Party of Albania), won the elections. Fatos Nano refused to concede defeat, citing violations in 30 constituencies and his party (PSS) filed complaints with the Central Electoral Commission, delaying the official certification of the election results.
Presidential: Alfred Moisiu won more than three-fifths of the presidential vote in parliament.

Next elections
2007 (presidential); 2009 (parliamentary).

Political parties
Ruling party
Coalition government, led by the Partia Demokratike ë Shqipërisë (PDS) (The Democratic Party of Albania) (DP), with the Partia Agrare Ambientaliste (AAP) Agrarian Environmentalist Party (AAP), the Partia Republikane e Shqipërisë (RP) Republican Party, the Partia Demokrate e Re (PDR) the New Democratic Party and the Partia Bashkimi për të Drejtat e Njeriut (UHRP) Union for Human Rights Party

Main opposition party
Partia Socialiste ë Shqipërisë (PSS) (Socialist Party of Albania)

Population
3.16 million (2004)

Ethnic make-up
Albanians make up 97 per cent of the population. The largest ethnic minority group is the Greeks, who account for around 2 per cent of the total. Other groups include Macedonian, Montenegrin, Vlach and Gypsy (Romany) groups.

Religions
Muslim (70 per cent), Christian Orthodox (20 per cent) and Roman Catholic (10 per cent).

Education
Despite its many failings, the communist regime virtually eliminated illiteracy. However, since 1991 the situation has deteriorated markedly, with equipment and buildings in a parlous state. Although high attendance rates in primary schools have been maintained, enrolment in pre-primary schooling and at the secondary or tertiary level has declined. In Albania, the government has closed down a third of public kindergartens and pre-school attendance has dropped dramatically. Unqualified teachers in elementary schools account for 10 per cent of teaching staff, and in the secondary schools, 8 per cent. The government has an ongoing programme to replace equipment and reconstruct buildings in urban areas and is also focussing on teacher training and enrolment rates. The current structure of the sector has resulted in a misalignment between the supply and demand of education. Consequently, the government is also engaged in a school construction programme to provide facilities for those areas where there are currently no school facilities.
The total expenditure on education is around 3 per cent of GDP.

Literacy rate: 98.5 per cent, adult rate (World Bank)
Enrolment rate: 100 per cent (primary); 71.5 per cent (secondary) (World Bank).
Pupils per teacher: 18 in primary schools.

Health
Although Albania's modest healthcare sector functioned adequately during the communist era, it suffered from substantial underfunding. The government recognises the problem and plans to strengthen managerial capacities and to decentralise health planning. It will take many years to create a system capable of providing even basic healthcare.

HIV/Aids
Albania had been screened from the initial impact of the Aids epidemic by the isolation imposed by the former communist state. However, the country opened its borders following the advent of democratic government in 1991 and the first HIV case of HIV was detected in 1993. By 2003, 177 cases had been reported of which 37 had died of Aids. Between 2001–03 the percentage of HIV positive females increased and their numbers now match male infection rates.

Life expectancy: 74.3 years (World Bank)
Fertility rate/Maternal mortality rate: 2.2 births per woman (World Bank)
Birth rate/Death rate: 18.2 per 1,000 crude birth rate; 6.5 per 1,000 crude death rate (USAID 2003).
Infant mortality rate: 18 per 1,000 live births in 2003; 14 per cent of children aged under five are malnourished (World Bank).
Head of population per physician/bed: 1.3 doctors per 1,000 people (USAID 2003).

Welfare
Albania's social infrastructure is in a poor state. Never well developed, social disintegration in 1997 led to further deterioration of virtually all services as funds dried up.
The collapse of central government authority in 1997 has led to already poor tax collection rates falling further. Neither the funds nor the infrastructure exist to provide adequate welfare coverage. It has been estimated that more than one million people are living below the poverty line. The Albanian Institute of Statistics reported in late-1999 that over one-third of families have only one income source averaging US$64 per month.
The government is attempting to remedy this by introducing community-based social services for vulnerable groups and is in the process of reorganising the state pension system based on the actuarial

model. The aim is to increase coverage in rural areas in order to reduce poverty.

Main cities
Tirana (capital, estimated population 353,400 in 2003), Durrës (Durrazzo) (113,900), Elbasan (97,000), Shkoder (Scutari) (85,900), Vlore (85,000), Korca (58,900), Fier (55,100), Berat (45,500).

Languages spoken
Greek, Romanian, Bulgarian, Serbian, Tosk and Gheg are also spoken. English, Italian, German and French are also spoken in business circles.

Official language/s
Since 1945, the official language has been based on Tosk Albanian. The Albanian language is divided into two dialects – Gheg, north of the river Shkumbinit, and Tosk in the south.

Media
The state news agency is the Albanian Telegraphic Agency (ATA) and it officially controls all newspapers. Although a vast improvement on the communist era, freedom of the press remains relative, with the printing of 'false information' an offence likely to attract a hefty fine. Due to the country's poor infrastructure, mountainous terrain and low economic development, access to media is poor.

Press
There are an estimated 35 daily newspapers per 1,000 people.
Dailies: Dailies include *Shekulli* (Albania's largest daily), *Zeri i Popullit* and *Bashkimi*. Others include *Balli I Kombit*, *Rilindja Demokratike*, *Ekonomia*, and *Gazeta Shqiptare*.
Weeklies: *Albanian Daily News* is published weekly.
Business: A bi-monthly foreign trade magazine is published by the Albanian Chamber of Commerce *Tregtia e Jashtme Popullore*.
Periodicals: Periodicals include *Klan*, *Spekter* and *XXL*.

Broadcasting
Radio: A wire relay service covers the whole country. Radio Tirana broadcasts in several European languages.
Television: There are stations at Tirana, Kukes, Berat and Pogradec. Greek and Austrian programmes are broadcast in Albania. Italian TV is relayed in censored form.

Economy
Albania ranks as the third poorest country in Europe and around a quarter of the population live below the poverty line. A socio-economic crisis in 1997, the Kosovo crisis in 1999 and political instability have hindered Albania's development. Low levels of productivity and capital investment combined with shortages of skilled labour have been major constraints on growth. GDP growth remains stable at around 6 per cent, but GDP per capita remains low.

Agriculture is the largest sector of the economy, contributing around 35 per cent of GDP. It has been an impetus of growth by attracting private-sector investment. The EU Common Agricultural Policy (Cap) subsidies on agricultural products has been an hindrance to the development of Albanian farming.

There is a heavy reliance on remittances from Albanians working mainly in Greece and Italy. These contribute around 21 per cent of GDP.

The rebuilding of the technical and physical infrastructure, from telecommunications to roads and railways, is a major priority. While the government encourages foreign investment in agriculture, agri-processing, manufacturing and export-oriented activities, poor basic services, such as electricity, discourage investor interest. Efforts to develop a larger tourist industry are also hindered by poor infrastructure and underinvestment. Corruption and organised crime, which may account for up to 50 per cent of GDP, are a further deterrent to foreign investment confidence.

EU membership is still a distant prospect, but the EU continues to fund infrastructure improvement in anticipation of eventual membership. International financial institutions, such as the World Bank and IMF, are also helping Albania's economic development.

External trade
Albania has been a member of the World Trade Organsiation (WTO) since 2000. There are free trade agreements with Macedonia, Croatia, the UN Mission in Kosovo (Unmik) and Bulgaria; negotiations with Romania, Bosnia and Hercegovina and Moldova are ongoing. Around 75 per cent of Albania's trade is with Greece, Italy and Turkey.

A Balkan oil pipeline that is due to be constructed from the Bulgarian port of Burgas to the Albanian port of Viore will allow transportation of Russian and Caspian oil.

Imports
Principal imports include chemicals, foodstuffs, machinery, textiles, vehicles, lubricants, and various consumer goods.
Main sources: Italy (36 per cent of 2004 total), Greece (20 per cent), Turkey (8.1 per cent), Germany (5.5 per cent)

Exports
Principal exports include chrome along with chrome products, copper wire, ferro-nickel ore, bitumen, crude oil, textiles and footwear, vegetables, fruits, tobacco and hydroelectricity.

Main destinations: Italy (71.9 per cent of 2004 total), Greece (6.3 per cent), Canada (4.4 per cent)

Agriculture
Farming
Agriculture, formerly the largest sector in the economy, has declined to less than 25 per cent of GDP, but remains an important social as well as economic factor in Albanian life. The sector is dominated by small-scale subsistence farming, which is underdeveloped and poorly financed. There is minimal mechanisation and little use of fertilisers and pesticides. Despite government attempts to privatise farmland, outside financial assistance has been needed to develop farming.

Crop production in 2004 included: 300,000 tonnes (t) wheat, 200,000t maize, 175,000t potatoes, 15,000t oats, 175,000t roots and tubers, 4,000t barley, 27,450t pulses, 2,200t citrus fruit, 80,000t grapes, 169,000t tomatoes, 40,000t sugar beet, 15,000t figs, 152,000t fruit in total, 679,100t vegetables in total. Livestock production included: 72,600t meat in total, 39,000t beef, 8,500t pig meat, 19,000t lamb and goat meat, 6,000t poultry, 25,800t eggs, 1,035,007t milk, 1,000t honey.

Fishing
Albania's fish catch declined sharply following the collapse of Communism and has not recovered. The sector is in generally poor shape. The fishing fleet comprises ageing and poorly equipped vessels and there is a shortage of fishermen. Development of the marine fisheries, including rehabilitation and construction of ports and other infrastructure, is a government priority.

There is some freshwater fishing in rivers, lakes and reservoirs. Fish farming of marine and freshwater species is increasingly important. Internal consumption of fish has increased in recent years, leaving about half of the approximately 4,000 tonnes of production for export, mainly to Greece and Italy.

Forestry
Forests cover less than two-fifths of the land area, the equivalent of 991,000 hectares (ha).

The forest industry is small-scale and is based mainly on imported raw materials to meet domestic production needs. Forestry is of little importance to GDP, with most timber production being used for domestic fuel. Timber processing and associated activities have been transferred to the private sector, but forest management remains in state hands.

Timber imports in 2004 amounted to US$24.7 million while exports amounted to US$7.4 million.

Production in 2004 included: 296,200 cubic metres (cum) roundwood, 75,200cum industrial roundwood, 97,000cum sawnwood, 62,100cum sawlogs and veneers, 37,000cum wood-based panels, 221,000cum wood fuel, 55,000t charcoal.

Industry and manufacturing
The industrialisation policy of the Communist era was aimed at making Albania completely self-sufficient. Although this meant that Albania was one of the few countries in the world without any foreign debt, it also meant that the industrial sector relied on outdated and inefficient machinery which produced poor quality goods unable to compete in international markets.

A side-effect of the search for higher productivity was a complete absence of environmental concerns, with industrial wastelands, oil slicks and abandoned equipment littering the country. Combined with thousands of broken concrete bunkers and derelict factories, Albania faces major, long-term environmental problems.

The industrial sector has experienced a disastrous decline in output since 1990. The sector is focussed mainly on engineering, chemicals, metals, construction materials, food processing and other agro-allied industries. The sector employs around 10 per cent of the workforce and accounts for around 19 per cent of GDP. There is virtually no light industry.

Foreign investment is the key to reviving industrial output, and consequently the government has been attempting to portray Albania as a low-wage manufacturing base with extensive natural resources on Western Europe's doorstep. Foreign companies have become involved in rehabilitating and modernising Albania's chrome industry by taking over a number of steel plants and mines.

Tourism
Albania's post-communist efforts to create a tourism sector virtually from scratch have been tardy and haphazard. Infrastructure is inadequate and the country needs cleaning-up. There were around 41,000 arrivals in 2004, There is considerable potential for attracting the wider and more lucrative international market, especially to its unspoilt beaches. Tourism is expected to contribute 4.7 per cent to GDP in 2005.

Environment
Macedonia and Albania participate in the Lake Ohrid Conservation Project (LOCP) which is a bilateral project supported by the World Bank.

Mining
The mining sector contributes as much as 20 per cent to GDP and employs some 15 per cent of the workforce.

Albania used to be the world's third-largest producer and second-largest exporter of chromium. The industry is undergoing rehabilitation. As with all areas of the Albanian economy, the mining sector suffers from obsolete technology and techniques, the disruption of supply lines and lack of management skills.

There are extensive reserves of copper, iron, zinc and nickel. In addition, there are smaller reserves of uranium, titanium-magnetite, gold and silver. Most of these reserves are in remote and mountainous areas of northern Albania, which increases production costs.

Hydrocarbons
Albania has recoverable oil reserves of 165 million barrels. Oil is produced onshore and is the primary source of energy. Two small oil fields at Patos and Morinza account for the majority of the oil production. Around 6,000 barrels per day (bpd) are produced, but with consumption of 24,000bpd there is a reliance on imports. Albania has natural gas reserves of 3.3 billion cubic metres. Production is around one billion cubic feet annually, which is sufficient to meet domestic requirements. Albania has coal reserves estimated at around 700 billion tonnes. Sufficient coal (of generally low quality) is produced for domestic consumption. Production is carried out at 21 mines in four basins run by various state-owned stock companies.

Oil production, natural gas and coal output have all fallen since the collapse of communism, as outdated equipment and a lack of investment, technology and management skills have taken their toll.

Energy
Nearly all of Albania's electricity is generated by hydroelectric power stations. The infrastructure is in poor condition; about a quarter of electricity generated is lost during distribution because of damaged network. Theft of electricity and non-payment of bills are common. Power cuts are frequent, sometimes occasioned by drought hitting the hydroelectric sources. To meet growing demand, Albania imports up to five million kilowatts of power a year, mainly from Greece and Macedonia.

Financial markets
Stock exchange
The Tirana Stock Exchange opened in mid-1996. Since the collapse of the pyramid schemes in 1997, it has been faced with the daunting task of rebuilding the confidence of potential investors.

Banking and insurance
The European Bank of Reconstruction and Development (EBRD) is involved in the development and privatisation of the banking system. An attempt to privatise the Savings Bank of Albania, the last state-owned bank, failed in June 2002 when two Italian banks pulled out of the tender.

Albania's central bank is the Banka e Shqipërisë (Bank of Albania). It has the power to authorise the creation of and supervise new banks, including those with foreign capital.
Central bank
Banka e Shqipërisë (Bank of Albania)

Time
GMT plus 1 hour (GMT plus two hours in summer months).

Geography
Albania's 28,748 square km are split into three main areas: a coastal plain, mountains and an inland plain. It shares a border with Montenegro and Kosovo (Serbia and Montenegro) to the north, the Former Yugoslav Republic of Macedonia (FYROM) to the north-west and Greece to the south. The Adriatic and Ionian Seas are to the west. The local name for Albania, 'eagles country', reflects its remote and mountainous nature (mountains cover about 75 per cent of the land area). The highest mountain entirely within Albania is Mt Jezerce at 2,694 metres in the north, although Mt Korab on the FYROM border reaches 2,751 metres.

The longest river, the Drini (285km), drains into Ohrid Lake on the border with FYROM. To the north the Drini joins the River Buna, the only navigable waterway in Albania. There are three natural freshwater lakes in Albania, all of which share borders with either Greece, Montenegro or the FYROM. Numerous artificial lakes have been created by hydroelectric power stations damming rivers, the largest of which are in the north around Kukes and Skhodra.

Climate
Albania has a Mediterranean climate, with long, hot and dry summers and cool, cloudy winters. Autumn has humid weather brought by the warm Sirocco wind. The high inland mountains can become cold during the winter months. July is the hottest month, and November, December and April the wettest months. It is warmest in the south-west and coldest in the north-east.

Dress codes
During the summer, light clothing is recommended, with warmer clothes essential during the winter months, particularly in mountainous regions.

Nations of the World: A Political, Economic and Business Handbook

Entry requirements
Passports
Required by all.
Visa
Not required by most citizens of Western Europe, North America, Australasia and a few Asian countries, however a US$10 entry tax is levied. For a full list of exemptions visit www.mfa.gov.al/english/info2.asp. An entry-exit form is issued at the border, the entry portion is handed in at passport control, and the exit portion should be kept until departure.
Currency advice/regulations
The import and export of local currency is not permitted.
The import of foreign currencies is allowed without limitations, although all amounts must be declared on arrival. Export of foreign currency is allowed within the limits of the declaration given, less the amounts exchanged or spent. Keep exchange receipts.
Traveller's cheques are accepted by banks and large tourist hotels.
Customs
All new or old personal items may be taken into Albania without incurring duty.

Health (for visitors)
Medical facilities are limited, and medicine is in short supply. Doctors and hospitals generally expect immediate cash payment for health services. Health care is free for citizens of countries with reciprocal health agreements.
Mandatory precautions
A vaccination certificate for yellow fever is required if travelling from an infected area.
Advisable precautions
It is advisable to have immunisations against hepatitis 'A', polio and tetanus. There is a risk of rabies. Access to clean water in the country is variable, and it is not usual to drink tap water.

Hotels
Bookings are handled by Albturist, except for business visitors who should make arrangements through business contacts. Increasing numbers of hotels can be contacted directly by telephone.

Credit cards
Major international hotels in Tirana accept American Express, Mastercard and Diners Club (but not Visa). Cases of credit card fraud have been reported.

Public holidays
Fixed dates
1 Jan (New Year's Day), 28 Nov (Independence and Liberation Day), 25 Dec (Christmas Day).
Variable dates
Orthodox Easter Monday, Labour Day (first Mon in May), Eid al Adha, Islamic New Year, Birth of the Prophet, Eid al Fitr. The Islamic year contains 354 or 355 days, with the result that Muslim feasts advance by 10–12 days against the Gregorian calendar. Dates of feasts vary according to the sighting of the new moon, so cannot be forecast exactly. Islamic year 1426: 10 February 2005 to 30 January 2006.

Working hours
Banking
Mon–Fri: 0700–1500.
Business
Mon–Fri: 0730–1530.
Government
Mon–Fri: 0700–1500.
Shops
Mon–Sat: 0800–1200, 1500–1900.l

Social customs/useful tips
It is customary to shake hands on meeting and taking leave. Business cards are exchanged. Albanian business meetings are reasonably relaxed. Delays to negotiations can be expected as bureaucratic tendencies still exist.
Some executives speak a second language – English, French, Italian or German.
Albanians are a naturally friendly and curious people with a good sense of humour, and are keen to talk to and meet foreigners.
Small gifts are appreciated. Round up the bill slightly when in restaurants.
Local body language customs: nodding the head up and down indicates no, and side to side indicates yes.

Security
It is advisable to be extremely cautious in Albania. Crime has increased significantly since 1990 and there are a large number of semi-automatic weapons in private hands since the collapse of social order in 1997. Armed criminal gangs also operate in the south, including near Lazarat.
Travel to the north-eastern border areas between Albania and Kosovo is not recommended.
Avoid giving anything to women and children asking you for money, as they target foreigners and will follow the compassionate whenever they see them again. Visitors should dress down and not display watches, cameras or other expensive items.

Getting there
Air
Albania is accessible by air from numerous European centres, including Athens, Bucharest, Budapest, Ioannina, Paris, Rome and Zurich.
National airline: Albanian Airlines.
International airport/s: Tirana-Rinas (TIA), 29km from Tirana.
Airport tax: US$10

Surface
Road: There are road links from all bordering countries, including Greece at Kakavia and Kristalopigi, and Kosovo (in Serbia and Montenegro) at Han-i-Hotit and Vrbnica, and Macedonia at Cafasan.
Rail: There are no passenger rail links between Albania and the rest of Europe and travel in some of the border regions is inadvisable.
Water: There are ferry services connecting Durrës and Vlora with Trieste, Ancona, Brindisi, Bari in Italy and Rijeka and Pula in Croatia. Others connect Durres to Kopa in Slovenia and Sarandra to Corfu.
Main port/s: Durrës, Vlora and Sarandra.

Getting about
National transport
Air: Ales Airlines (a private joint Italian-Albanian company licensed by the Albanian government) serves eight small airports across the country.
Road: Out of approximately 21,000km of roads, only 3,000km are paved. Road conditions can be unpredictable – narrow, unsurfaced or potholed, with the added risk of straying cattle or pedestrians. Mountain roads are often impassable. The roads are considered to be the worst in Europe.
Buses: Buses run frequently between Tirana and Durrës and other towns to the north and south. Tickets are sold on the bus.
Rail: The rail network is approximately 720km, single-track and unelectrified. Trains are diesel.
City transport
Taxis: The only city with a taxi service is Tirana. There are taxi transfers from Rinas airport to the city centre.
Buses, trams & metro: A flat-fare bus service operates in the main cities, including Tirana. Airport buses operate from the airport to the city centre every three hours. Journey duration is 30 minutes.
Car hire
Driving in Albania is only recommended for those with no other choice. An international driving permit or a national driving licence is required. It is advisable to hire a local car and driver through travel agencies. Traffic drives on the right.

BUSINESS DIRECTORY
The addresses listed below are a selection only. While World of Information makes every endeavour to check these addresses, we cannot guarantee that changes have not been made, especially to telephone numbers and area codes. We would welcome any corrections.

Telephone area codes
The international direct dialling code (IDD) for Albania is +355, followed by area code and subscriber's number:
Berat 623   Korca 824

Albania

Durrës	52	Shkoder	224
Elbasan	545	Tirana	4
Fier	642	Vlore	63

Useful telephone numbers
Police: 19
Fire: 17
Ambulance: 22235

Chambers of Commerce
Albanian British Chamber of Commerce and Industry, PO Box 1547, Tirana (tel: 227-000; fax: 230-636; e-mail: info:abcci.com).

American Chamber of Commerce in Albania, Rruga Deshmoret e 4 Shkurtit, Tirana (tel: 259-779; fax: 235-350; e-mail: info@amcham.com.al).

Korça Chamber of Commerce and Industry, Bulevard Republika, Korça (tel/fax: 824-457; e-mail: albchamber1@albchamber.com).

Tirana Chamber of Commerce and Industry, Rruga e Kavajes 6, Tirana (tel: 230-284; fax: 227-997; e-mail: ccitr@abissnet.com.al).

Union of Chambers of Commerce and Industry of Albania, Rruga e Kavajes 6, Tirana (tel: 230-283; fax: 227-997; e-mail: root@ccitr.tirana.al).

Banking
Albanian State Agricultural Bank, Tirana (tel: 27-738).

Albanian State Bank for Foreign Relations, Tirana.

Alpha Credit Bank, Deshmoret e Kombit Blvd 47, Tirana (Internet site: http://www.alpha.gr).

Arab Albanian Islamic Bank, Deshmoret e Kombit, Tirana (tel: 23-873).

Bank of Albania, Tirana (Internet site: http://www.bankofalbania.org).

Bankandertregtare (Intercommercial Bank), Tirana Tower, Rruga e Kavajes 59, Tirana (tel: 58-755/60; fax: 58-752; e-mail: icbs1@albaniaonline.net).

Banko Italo Albanese (Banka Italo Shqiptare) (Italian-Albanian Bank), Rruga e Barrikadave, Tirana (tel: 33-966; fax: 35-701).

Fefad Bank, Tirana (tel: 3-496, 37-958; fax: 33-481).

National Bank of Greece, Blvd. Deshmoret e Kombit, VEVE Business Centre, Tirana (tel: 33-621, 35-542).

National Commercial Bank of Albania, Tirana (tel: 50-955; fax: 50-960; e-mail: bkt@albmail.com).

Savings Bank of Albania, Rr Deshmoret e 4 Shkurti, 6 Tirana (tel: 24-540/051; fax: 23-587/695).

Tirana Bank, Blvd. Deshmoret e Kombit, NR55/1, Tirana (tel: 33-441).

Central bank
Banka e Shqiperise (Bank of Albania), Sheshi Skënderbej 1, Tirana (tel: 222-152; fax: 223-558; e-mail: public@bankofalbania.org).

Travel information
Lufthansa Tirana Rinas Airport Office (tel: 42-350/54/58; fax: 42-350/60).

Ministry of tourism
Ministry of Tourism, Blvd Deshmoret e Kombit, Tirana (tel: 28-123); fax: 27-922).

Ministries
Albanian Assembly, Kurvendi, Blvd Dëdhmotët e Kombit, nr 4, Tirana (tel: 42-37-418, 42-47-354,43-62-003; fax: 42-27-949; email: head-directory@parlament.al; internet: www.parlament.al).

Committee of Environmental Protection, Ministry of Health and Environmental Protection, Bulevari Bajran Curri, Tirana (tel: 42-682; 35-229; fax: 35-229).

Department of Economic Development and Foreign Aid Co-ordination, Tirana (tel: 28-467; fax: 28-363).

Industrialeksport – 4 Shkurti Street 6, Tirana (tel: 4550).

Institute of Statistics, Tirana (tel: 22-411; fax: 28-300).

Makinaimport (State Trade Organisation for the Import of Machinery), 4 Shkurti Street 6, Tirana (tel: 25-220, 25-221).

Mineralimpex (State Organisation for Export of Minerals), 4 Shkurti Street 6, Tirana (tel: 25-832, 23-848).

Ministry of Agriculture and Food, Blvd Dëdhmotët e Kombit Tirana (tel: 28-318, 32-675; fax: 23-806, 27-924).

Ministry of Energy and Mineral Resources (tel: 32-833; fax: 34-052).

Ministry of Finance and Economy, Dëdhmotët e Kombit, Tirana (tel: 28-405; fax: 28-494).

Ministry of Health and Environment, Ministria e Shendetesise, Tirana (tel and fax: 34-615).

Ministry of Industry, Transport and Trade, Sheshi Skenderbey, Tirana (tel: 25-353, 32-289; fax: 27-773, 616-835).

Ministry of Transport and Telecommunications, Sheshi Skenderbey, Tirana (tel: 25-353; tel/fax: 27-773/616/835).

National Agency for Privatisation (tel/fax: 27-937).

National Committee of Energy, Dëdhmotët e Kombit, Tirana (tel/fax: 28-475).

President's Office, Tirana (tel: 28-491; fax: 33-761).

Prime Minister's Office, Tirana (tel: 34-816; fax: 34-818).

Small and Medium-Sized Enterprises (SME) Foundation, c/o Ministry of Industry and Trade, 3 Rruga Andon Zako Cajupi, Tirana (fax: 34-892); EU Expert (fax: 42-413, 34-609).

Transshqip (State Organisation for the Transport of Goods in Foreign Trade), 4 Shkurti Street 6, Tirana (tel: 23-076, 24-659).

Other useful addresses
Agroeksport – State Trade Organisation for the Export of Agricultural and Food Products, 4 Shkurti Street 6, Tirana (tel: 25-227, 25-229, 23-128).

Albanian Embassy (USA), 2100 S Street, NW, Washington DC (tel: 202-223-4942; fax: 202-628-7342).

Albanian Telecom, Myslim Shyri 42, Tirina (tel: 32-047; fax: 33-323).

Albkontrol (Organisation for Inspection of Exported and Imported Goods), Rruga Skënderbeu 15, Durrës (tel: 22-354; fax: 22-791).

Artimpex (State Organisation for Export), 4 Shkurti Street 6, Tirana.

British Embassy, Ruga Vaso Pasha 7/1, Tirana (tel: 34-973; fax: 34-975).

Bureau for the Registration of Patents & Trade Marks, Konferenca e Pezes Street 6, Tirana.

Business Economic Development Department, c/o Ministry of Industry and Trade, 3 Rruga Andon Zamo Cajupi, Tirana (tel: 34-673; fax: 34-658).

Foreign Investment Promotion Centre, Ekspozita Shqiperia Sot (Protokolli), Blvd Jeanne d'Arc, Tirana (tel: 27-626; fax: 28-439, 42-133).

Insig, Insurance Institute, Rruga e Dibres 91, Tirana (tel: 341-84, 341-69, 341-70; fax: 341-80, 238-38).

US Embassy, 103 Rruga Elbasanit, Tirana (tel: 424-7285; fax: 423-2222; e-mail: wm_tirana@pd.state.gov).

Internet sites
Albanian Daily News: http://www.albaniannews.com

Albanian parliament: http://parlament.al

Albanian Economic Development Agency: http://aeda.gov.al

Albania Home Page: http://www.albanian.com

Albanian Ministry of Foreign Affairs: http://www.mfa.gov.al

Albanian Telegraphic Agency: http://www.ata-al.net

Land of the Eagles: http://www.albania.co.uk/

Algeria

KEY FACTS

Official name: Al Jumhuriya al Jazairiya ad Dimucratiya ash Shabiya (Democratic and Popular Republic of Algeria)

Head of State: President Abdelaziz Bouteflika (since 1999; re-elected 8 Apr 2004)

Head of government: Prime Minister Ahmed Ouyahia (since 5 May 2003; re-appointed by the President Apr 2004)

Ruling party: Coalition government (elected May 2002) led by the Front de Libération Nationale (FLN) (National Liberation Front), Rassemblement National pour la Démocratie (RND) (National Rally for Democracy), El Islah (Mouvement de la Société pour la Paix) (MSP) (Movement of the Society for Peace) and the Mouvement de la Renaissance Islamique (MRI) (Islamic Renaissance Movement)

Area: 2,381,741 square km

Population: 32.16 million (2004)

Capital: Algiers

Official language: Arabic

Currency: Algerian dinar (AD) = 100 centimes

Exchange rate: AD72.74 per US$ (Oct 2005)

GDP per capita: US$2,521 (2004)

GDP real growth: 5.30% (2004)

Labour force: 12.19 million (2004)

Unemployment: 25.40% (2004)

Inflation: 3.60% (2004)

Oil production: 1.93 million bpd (2004)

Balance of trade: US$16.91 billion (2004)

Foreign debt: US$21.90 billion (2004)

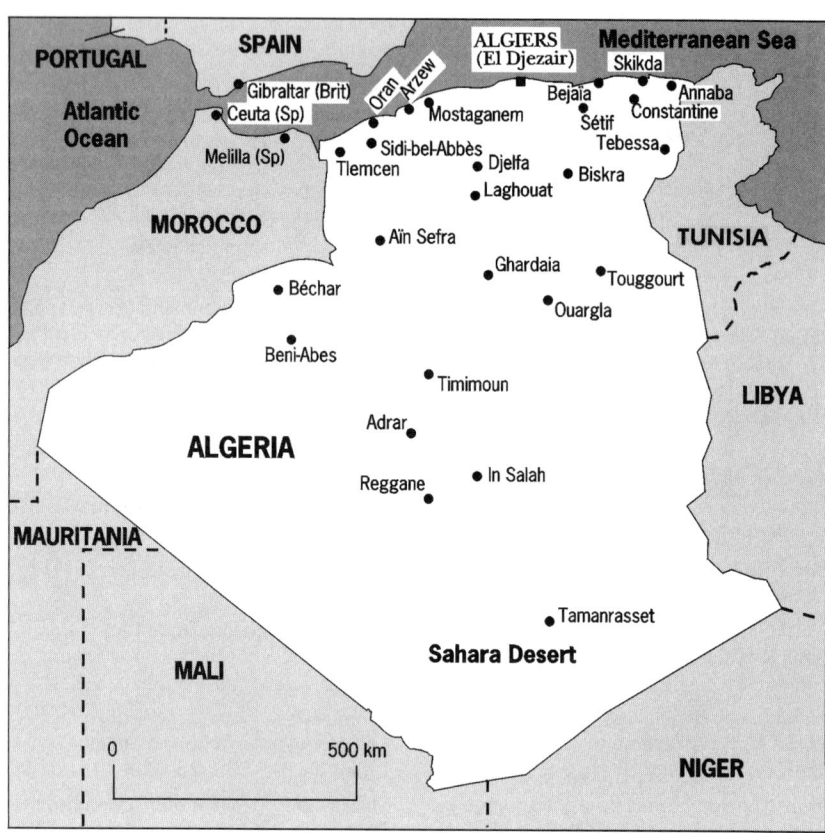

Despite a difficult socio-political environment, Algeria has adopted policies encouraging democratic principles which have led to the emergence of a vibrant civil society. Algeria has three key development challenges: how to use its oil and gas reserves for the long-run benefit of its people; how to create growth and employment in the non-oil economy to avoid social tensions caused by increased unemployment; and, how to provide better public services. Priority areas are to build a basis for sustained growth by better management of the hydrocarbon revenues so they benefit future as well as present generations. Perceived constraints to the growth of the private sector must be removed, particularly to allow private investment in infrastructure and support for the government's privatisation efforts.

Economy

Faced with low growth and high unemployment, Algeria four years ago adopted an IMF-endorsed plan to stimulate its economy. Real growth in gross domestic product has strongly recovered from its slowdown in 2000 – up from 2.4 per cent to 5.3 per cent in 2004. Although rising sharply in 2004 over 2003 to 3.6 per cent per annum inflation remains, in international terms, subdued.

The fiscal policy is expected to have led to an increase in the primary non-hydrocarbon budget deficit from 29.5 per cent of non-hydrocarbon GDP in 2003 to almost 32 per cent in 2004. Nevertheless, higher oil prices are expected to allow for an overall stronger fiscal position. With the control of public expenditure outlined in the 2005 budget, the non-hydrocarbon primary deficit as a percentage of non-hydrocarbon GDP is projected to be reduced gradually over the medium term. Algeria's economic outlook for 2005 and beyond remains favourable.

The hydrocarbons sector – petroleum and natural gas – accounts for roughly 60 per cent of budget revenues, 30 per cent of gross domestic product, and more than 95 per cent of export earnings. Algeria has the seventh-largest reserves of natural gas in the world and is the second-largest gas exporter; it ranks 14th in oil reserves.

Thanks to oil and gas, Algeria has impressive financial and macroeconomic indicators. It is running substantial trade surpluses and building up record foreign exchange reserves. The country's external position has strengthened significantly, with reserves at 42.3 billion dollars or 24 months of import cover in 2004 against external debt down to 24.7 per cent of GDP from 46.4 per cent four years ago. The budget has remained in surplus over the last five years.

Despite strong import growth, the external current account surplus is projected to increase further, reflecting higher world hydrocarbon export prices. Real GDP has risen due to higher oil output and increased government spending. The government's continued efforts to diversify the economy by attracting foreign and domestic investment outside the energy sector, however, have had little success in reducing high unemployment and improving living standards. Structural reform within the economy moves ahead slowly. Meeting current socio-economic challenges will require wide-ranging reforms – almost a change in national mindset.

Banking

Suggesting that a well-functioning banking sector can play an important role in channeling resources to the best firms and investment projects, the International Monetary Fund (IMF) has said economies served by better-developed financial systems tend to grow faster. In Algeria, public banks continue to account for 90 per cent of financial system assets and are burdened by sizeable non-performing loans to public enterprises. The Treasury has repurchased some of the non-performing loans, but these bail-outs have distorted risk pricing and stunted the development of an appropriate credit culture.

Many of these public banks should, says the IMF, be privatised.

Structural reforms

The Algerian authorities will need to accelerate the implementation of structural reforms. Achieving the appropriate balance between using large hydrocarbon revenues to accelerate the transition to a more diversified market economy and saving them for future generations represents a key challenge for a natural resource-rich economy. The government is to set fiscal policy within a long-term framework that delinks public spending from fluctuations in hydrocarbon revenue and the IMF has suggested transforming the current hydrocarbon stabilisation fund into a savings/financing account that is fully integrated into the budget.

While priority capital and social spending must be protected, including programmes for human capital development, long-term fiscal consolidation must put the public finances on a path that is compatible with the sustainable spending of hydrocarbon resources. This containment of spending in 2005 was seen as a first step towards reducing fiscal vulnerability. A decision to focus monetary policy on maintaining low inflation, will require curbs on excess liquidity and spending to maintain macroeconomic stability and the soundness of the financial system.

Politics

In the 1990s Algerian politics was dominated by a struggle involving the military and Islamist militants. In 1992 a general election won by an Islamist party was annulled, marking the beginning of a bloody campaign which saw the slaughter of more than 150,000 people. An amnesty in 1999 led many rebels to lay down their arms. Violence has largely abated, although a state of emergency remains in place.

Algeria under President Abdelaziz Bouteflika has won praise from the West for backing the US-led 'war on terror'. At home, many credit him with the return of security. But some campaigners say abuses by the security forces go on and rights group Amnesty International says allegations about the torture of detainees continue to be reported.

Since taking office in 1999, Bouteflika has focussed on national reconciliation and promised to restore national harmony and end years of bloodshed. He immediately released thousands of Muslim militants and won backing for a civil concord in 1999 which offered an amnesty to armed militants. Many accepted and the violence declined. He now supports a second amnesty for those remaining militants. The country backed his proposed 'charter for peace and reconciliation' in a 2005 referendum, one year after he was re-elected to a second term in a landslide victory. The military – traditionally a key player in Algerian politics – pledged neutrality during the poll.

Western Sahara

Algeria supports the exiled Sahrawi Polisario Front and rejects Moroccan

KEY INDICATORS — Algeria

	Unit	2000	2001	2002	2003	2004
Population	m	30.29	30.70	31.22	31.69	32.16
Gross domestic product (GDP)	US$bn	39.67	55.00	58.90	60.13	*84.65
GDP per capita	US$	1,725	1,789	1,918	1,830	2,521
GDP real growth	%	2.4	1.7	3.1	6.7	5.3
Inflation	%	0.3	3.4	1.4	2.6	3.6
Unemployment	%	28.0	28.5	27.8	28.4	25.4
Oil output	'000 bpd	1,579.0	1,563.0	1,659.0	1,520.0	1,933.0
Natural gas output	bn cum	89.3	78.2	80.4	82.8	82.0
Exports (fob) (goods)	US$m	21,700.0	19,100.0	18,700.0	19,500.0	32,160.0
Imports (fob) (goods)	US$m	9,200.0	9,800.0	11,300.0	10,600.0	15,250.0
Balance of trade	US$m	12,300.0	9,330.0	7,300.0	8,900.0	16,910.0
Current account	US$m	9,140.0	7,060.0	4,360.0	8,840.0	10,800.0
Foreign debt	US$bn	25.0	22.5	22.8	21.6	21.9
Total reserves minus gold	US$m	12,024.0	18,081.0	23,238.0	33,125.0	43,246.0
Foreign exchange	US$m	11,910.0	17,963.0	23,108.0	126.0	132.0
Exchange rate	per US$	75.26	77.22	78.09	75.73	71.80

* estimated figure

administration of Western Sahara; Algeria's border with Morocco remains an irritant to bilateral relations, each nation has accused the other of harbouring militants and arms smuggling; in an attempt to improve relations after unilaterally imposing a visa requirement on Algerians in the early 1990s, Morocco lifted the requirement in mid-2004 – a gesture not reciprocated by Algeria; Algeria remains concerned about armed bandits operating throughout the Sahel who sometimes destabilise southern Algerian towns; dormant disputes include Libyan claims of about 32,000 sq km still reflected on its maps of southeastern Algeria and the Algerian ruling coalition member National Liberation Front's assertions of a claim to Chirac Pastures in south eastern Morocco.

Risk assessment

Economic	Good
Political	Improving
Regional stability	Good

COUNTRY PROFILE

Historical profile

Algeria, a gateway between Africa and Europe, has been battered by violence over the past half-century. More than a million Algerians were killed in the fight for independence from France in 1962, and the country has recently emerged from a brutal internal conflict that followed the scrapped elections in 1992. A large country, more than four-fifths of Algeria's territory is covered by the Sahara desert. Part of the Turkish Ottoman empire from the sixteenth century, Algeria was conquered by the French in 1830. The country was given the status of a departement in its own right. The struggle for independence began in 1954 headed by the National Liberation Front, which came to power on independence in 1962. Algeria was originally inhabited by Berbers until the Arabs conquered North Africa in the seventh century. Staying mainly in the mountainous regions, the Berbers resisted the spreading Arab influence, managing to preserve much of their language and culture until the present day. The Berbers are Muslim but identify with their Berber rather than Arab cultural heritage. They have long agitated for autonomy, which the government is unlikely to grant but in 2001 it did agree to officially recognise the Berber language, after months of unrest involving Berber youths pressing for greater cultural and political recognition. It has now offered to teach the language in schools. Seventy per cent of the population over 15 years of age can read and write.

1830 Algeria was conquered by the French.
1848 It was made a *département* of France.
1954 The Front de Libération Nationale (FLN) (National Liberation Front) led the struggle for independence.
1962 Algeria gained independence and Ahmed ben Bella of the FLN was designated Algeria's first president.
1965 Ahmed ben Bella was ousted by Colonel Houari Boumédienne.
1976 Boumédienne won the presidential elections. He introduced a new constitution, which confirmed commitment to socialism, the FLN as the sole political party and Islam as the state religion. A programme of industrialisation was introduced.
1973–76 The Frente Popular para la Liberación de Saguia el Hamra y Río de Oro (Polisario) (Popular Front for the Liberation of Saguia el Hamra y Río de Oro) was formed with Algerian support, wanting self-determination for Spanish Sahara (later known as Western Sahara). Spain handed the territory over to Morocco and Mauritania, Polisario announced the formation of the Saharawi Arab Democratic Republic (SADR) and formed a government-in-exile.
1977–85 Fighting continued between Moroccan military and Polisario forces. Morocco left the African Unity in protest at the SADR's admission to the body.
1988 Full diplomatic relations with Morocco were resumed.
1978 President Boumédienne died and the FLN candidate, Colonel Chadli Benjedid, was elected president; he was re-elected in 1984 and 1989.
1986–91 Rising inflation and unemployment, exacerbated by the collapse of oil and gas prices, led to strikes and violent demonstrations. A UN-monitored cease-fire began in Western Sahara.
1989 The National People's Assembly revoked the ban on new political parties and the Front Islamique du Salut (FIS) (Islamic Salvation Front) was founded.
1991 The FIS won the first round of the parliamentary elections and the second round was cancelled when it seemed certain the FIS would gain an absolute majority in the next round.
1992 Outbreaks of violence followed the cancellation of the elections. The National People's Assembly was dissolved by presidential decree and President Chadli, apparently under pressure from the military leadership, resigned. A five-member Haut Conseil d'Etat (HCE) (High Council of State) was instituted. Violent clashes broke out between FIS supporters and security forces; after a state of emergency was declared, the FIS was banned. Mohammed Boudiaf, chairman of the HCE, was assassinated, allegedly by Islamists. The Armée Islamique du Salut (AIS) (Islamic Salvation Army), the military arm of the FIS, launched a campaign of guerrilla warfare, which killed an estimated 150,000 people.
1994 Liamine Zeroual became chairman of the HCE.
1995 Zeroual was elected president in the first multi-party democratic elections.
1997–98 The newly created Rassemblement Nationale Démocratique (RND) (National Democratic Rally) won the parliamentary elections.
1999 President Zeroual stood down (one year early) and Abdelaziz Bouteflika was elected president. A referendum approved Bouteflika's law on civil concord and thousands of members of the AIS and other armed groups were pardoned.
2000 Attacks continued by small groups of dissidents opposed to the civil accord.
2001 The Berber community were granted greater cultural and political recognition following months of unrest involving Berber youths in the Kabylie region.
2002 The Berber language, Tamazight, was officially recognised as a national language. Berber activists in Kabylie and several opposition parties elsewhere boycotted the parliamentary elections, which were won by the FLN.
2003 A major earthquake hit northern Algeria, the worst since 1980. The leader of the banned FIS and his deputy were freed from prison after serving 12-year sentences. Prime Minister Ali Benflis was dismissed by the President and Ahmed Ouyahia became prime minister.
2004 President Bouteflika was re-elected on 8 April and re-appointed Prime Minister Ouyahia.
2005 In January, Nourredine Boudiafi, the head of the AIS was arrested and his deputy killed. The government promised Berber leaders more investment in the Kabylie region and greater recognition for the Tamazight language. In March an official inquiry concluded that security forces abducted and killed over 6,000 citizens during the 1990s civil unrest. In September there was overwhelming agreement in a referendum, granting amnesty to many who were involved in the post-1992 killings.

Political structure
Constitution
The 1976 constitution has been amended three times.
In 1997, the government banned religion-based parties and imposed a law restricting the formation of political parties. All political parties must hold a founding conference attended by 400–500 delegates elected by 25,000 supporters from 25 of the country's 48 provinces. This

Algeria

policy is intended to limit the number of political parties and place at severe disadvantage all parties that lack funding – particularly those, such as the FIS (Islamic Salvation Front), without access to state funds.

Form of state
Republic

The executive
The head of state is the president, elected by universal suffrage for five years. He appoints a prime minister, who in turn appoints a government.

The president has the power to dissolve the government and request elections.

National legislature
The parliament is composed of the 380-member Al Majlis al Sha'abi al Watani (Assemblée Populaire Nationale) (National People's Assembly) and the 144-member Al Majlis al Umma (Conseil de la Nation) (National Council). Members of the National People's Assembly, which holds legislative power, are elected for five years by universal suffrage. Members of the National Council (the lower house) are elected by communal councils and the president.

Legal system
The legal system is based on French and Islamic law.

The judicial system consists of 183 courts and 31 appeal courts organised on a regional basis.

There are three special criminal courts in Oran, Constantine and Algiers, which deal with economic crimes against the state (against which there is no appeal) – the Court of State Security which is composed of judges and army officers, the court of audit and the Supreme Court in Algiers, which is the ultimate judicial authority.

Algeria has not accepted International Court of Justice (ICJ) jurisdiction.

Last elections
8 April 2004 (presidential); 30 May 2002 (parliamentary).

Results: Presidential: the incumbent president, Abdelaziz Bouteflika, won 85 per cent of the vote, former prime minister Ali Benflis 6.4 per cent and Abdallah Djaballah 5 per cent; turnout was 58.1 per cent.

Parliamentary: FLN won 199 seats out of 389; RND 48, El Islah (MSP) 38 and Parti du Travail (PT) (Workers' Party) 21; turnout was 46.1 per cent.

Next elections
2007 (parliamentary); 2009 (presidential)

Political parties
A law was passed in 1997 imposing restrictions on forming political parties.

Ruling party
Coalition government (elected May 2002) led by the Front de Libération Nationale (FLN) (National Liberation Front), Rassemblement National pour la Démocratie (RND) (National Rally for Democracy), El Islah (Mouvement de la Société pour la Paix) (MSP) (Movement of the Society for Peace) and the Mouvement de la Renaissance Islamique (MRI) (Islamic Renaissance Movement)

Main opposition party
The Mouvement pour la Démocratie en Algérie (Movement for Democracy in Algeria) and two parties representing the Berber minority, the Front des Forces Socialistes (FFS) (Front of Socialist Forces) and the Rassemblement pour la Culture et la Démocratie (RCD) (Rally for Culture and Democracy), boycotted the May 2002 elections.

Population
32.16 million (2004)

Ethnic make-up
The majority of Algerians are of Berber descent. The other significant ethnic group is Arab, although as a result of centuries of integration the two ethnic groups have become increasingly indistinguishable. The distinct Berber culture and language is best preserved in the north and eastern regions of Algeria.

The European population, most of whom are French, has declined from over one million before independence in 1962 to less than 50,000 in 2001.

Religions
Islam is the official religion. Approximately 99 per cent of the population is Sunni Muslim, while Christians make up about one per cent.

Education
Primary education lasts for six years. Secondary education, which begins at age 11, is divided into two courses of four years and three years. Approximately 13 per cent of students remain at tertiary level. Teaching is carried out in Arabic, although at higher levels French is widely used.

The government has encouraged girls to attend school to reduce the difference in literacy rates. A total of 86 per cent of girls are now educated to primary level, and 53 per cent to secondary level.

Total expenditure on education is 4–5 per cent of GDP.

Compulsory years: 6 to 15.

Enrolment rate: 98 per cent gross primary enrolment of relevant age group (including repeaters); 63 per cent gross secondary enrolment (World Bank).

Pupils per teacher: 27 in primary schools.

Health
Total expenditure on health is 3–6 of GDP, of which government spending is over 80 per cent.

All Algerians are entitled to free medical care. Medicines are sold through the state monopoly at subsidised prices, and are provided free to children and the elderly, though there have been some cutbacks. Health indicators point to a deterioration in public health, with infant mortality ratios and infectious diseases increasing. Health care infrastructure and personnel show considerable urban-rural disparities.

Life expectancy: 70.9 years (World Bank)

Infant mortality rate: 35 per 1,000 live births; 6 per cent of children aged under five are malnourished (World Bank).

Head of population per physician/bed: Eight physicians and 21 hospital beds per 10,000 people (World Bank 2004).

Welfare
During the 1990s, unemployment rates increased dramatically, poverty doubled and the purchasing power of the middle class experienced a huge drop. Government expenditure on social protection is relatively high, but the welfare system is criticised as unsustainable and inefficient. The most serious challenge to the government is tackling unemployment. The government continues to play a major role in providing housing and basic health services, particularly to urban populations. Substantial housing shortages have proven persistent, despite the deregulation efforts the government undertook to promote private sector construction.

Main cities
Algiers (capital, estimated population 1.8 million in 2004), Oran (794,200), Constantine (688,100), Annaba (246,700).

Languages spoken
Arabic (modern standard), known as *Fus'ha*, is used in the courts, mosques, most of the media and in education. About 80 per cent of Algerians speak the North African dialectal Arabic, *Darja*. French is widely spoken, especially as a language of commerce.

In 2003, Tamazight (the Berber language) was categorised as a national language, but the Berbers want it to have equal status alongside Arabic as an official language. Tamazight belongs to the Afro-Asiatic family and is related to ancient Egyptian and Ethiopian. Berber groups and their dialects include: Kabyles (Taqbaylit), Kabylie region, Kabyle dialect; Chaouia (Ishawiyan), Eastern Algeria, Tashawit dialect; Mozabites (Imzabiyan), northern edge of Sahara, Tamzabit dialect; Tuaregs (Tamachaq), extreme south, Tuareg dialect.

Official language/s
Arabic

Media

The 1990 media law bans visual or written media that contravene Islamic moral principles or national values or that encourage racism, fanaticism or treason. Journalists and editors are obliged to reveal sources to the authorities for articles regarding economic or defence 'secrets'. The law allows the formation of privately owned newspapers, radio and television stations, all of which have been state-owned in the past. Any new non-Arabic publication must first be approved by the independent Information Council.

The law guarantees freedom of access to information and freedom of expression in accordance with the constitution. However, it also makes it a criminal offence to publish or broadcast 'wrong or tendentious information harmful to state security or national unity'. Penalties for this range from five to 10 years in jail.

Media regulation and monitoring is delegated to a 12-member council, composed of three members appointed by the president, three appointed by the national assembly and six elected by journalists.

Press
Algeria has some 35 daily newspapers, most of which are in private ownership. The official press agency is the *Algérie Presse Service*.

Dailies: The main national papers include *El Khabar*, *Le Matin* and *El Watan*. Other leading national dailies in Arabic, French and English include *El Alam Essyassi* (Arabic), *El Moudjahid* (French and Arabic), *El Massa* (Arabic and French), *L'Authentique* (French), *Liberté*, *Latribune* (both in French), *Horizons* (English section) and *Ech-Chaab* (Arabic). The main provincial dailies include *An Nasr* (Arabic) and *Al Joumhourial* (Arabic).

Weeklies: Weeklies include *Azul de Kabylie* on tourism and employment news and *Echibek* covers sports.

Business: The monthly business periodical *L'Actuel Revue Economique* is useful for investors and financers.

Periodicals: *Le jeune indépendant* has 300 issues yearly. *Le Matin* covers current affairs.

Broadcasting
Broadcasting is controlled by the government through Radiodiffusion Télévision Algérienne (RTA).

Radio: Radio services are in Arabic, French and Tamazight.

Television: Television services are in Arabic and French. The network is operated by the state-run RTA.

Advertising
Although advertising is allowed and adverting agencies operate in Algeria, the impact of advertising is limited to basic consumer products. The market is underdeveloped and the foremost form of advertising is through print media and the RTA.

Economy

Algeria has to contend with the geopolitical reality of a north suffering from high population density and high unemployment and a south being richly endowed with hydrocarbon reserves; the benefits of the latter have only marginally enhanced the prospects of the former. Oil and gas accounts for almost 30 per cent of GDP, 60 per cent budget revenues and 95 per cent of export earnings.

In 2004 Algeria had over US$10 billion in its current account. The IMF has warned that the revenue from oil production could suppress dynamism in the economy and must be diversified and reinvested in the economy. The government embarked on a five-year US$55 billion spending programme in 2004 and the results have shown improvement in infrastructure and employment prospects.

GDP growth was good in 2004 at 5.3 per cent, however high unemployment at 28.4 per cent (and as much as 50 per cent in the youth group) in 2003 fell only slightly to 25.4 per cent in 2004. Social unrest could undermine the growth so far. Despite this, the nation has huge potential, mainly due to the rich natural resources it contains but also a strategic position close to the fast growing EU free-market.

The government's policy of turning Algeria's command economy into a market economy is an unpopular one. Industrial action in protest of the sale of public enterprises have continued and the IMF is cautious about the balance between deregulating the market and the sharp rise in job losses this would cause, against the long term good of the market. Nevertheless, privatisation will only be relatively successful if there is continued lack of investor interest in buying the state companies.

The state-owned Sonatrach company dominates hydrocarbon production and has been the foremost generator of government revenue for decades.

There is a policy of improving the investment climate in the tourist sector and the production of non-oil related goods. In reality obstacles remain for non-oil trade, primarily due to the repatriation of revenues in foreign currencies. A climate of unrest and violence has resulted in a reluctance on the part of private investors to put money into Algeria. This may improve with the pending WTO membership and the EU trade association agreements although the current ban on alcohol imports is undermining these trade agreements.

The civil war may have burned itself out, but it remains to be seen if Algeria can break the stranglehold oil and gas has on its economy and whether it can build a diverse market economy that offers a good standard of living to all citizens.

External trade

The strict control of imports combined with a broadening of hydrocarbons exports has traditionally produced a balance of trade surplus. Even so exports are heavily dependent on oil and gas. The government has introduced a series of measures designed to boost non-hydrocarbon exports, while cutting imports of consumer goods. However in 2004 non-hydrocarbon exports were in decline against 2003 activities with Europe and Sub-Sahara Africa being the only recipients of these goods.

Algeria belongs to the Union du Maghreb Arabe (UMA) (Arab Maghreb Union), together with Libya, Morocco, Mauritania and Tunisia. A desired membership of the WTO means Algeria is extensively assessing foreign trade policy in a bid to become a member. Nevertheless, a law passed in 2003 banning the importation of alcohol is against WTO rules and until it can be struck down it will impede membership.

An association agreement with the EU signed in 2001, provides for the gradual removal of import duties on industrial products over a period of 12 years and the liberalisation of Algeria's agricultural export market. A co-operation agreement was signed with the European Free Trade Association (EFTA) in 2002.

Imports
Principal imports are capital goods (typically around 24–26 per cent of total), semi-finished goods (24–26 per cent), food and tobacco (25 per cent), consumer goods (15–17 per cent), transport equipment (14–16 per cent), raw materials (5–8 per cent).

Imports totalled US$15.25 billion in 2004.

Main sources: France (31.6 per cent of total 2004), Italy (8.5 per cent), Germany (6.3 per cent), Spain (5.6 per cent), China (5.3 per cent), US (4.9 per cent), Turkey (4.5 per cent)

Exports
Principal exports are hydrocarbons (around 97 per cent) (of which natural gas 25 per cent, condensates 25 per cent, crude petroleum 24 per cent, petroleum products 21 per cent); wine, tobacco, foodstuffs. Exports totalled US$32.16 billion in 2004.

Algeria is one of the main natural gas suppliers to Europe.

Main destinations: US (22.5 per cent of total 2004), Italy (17.8 per cent), France (11.8 per cent), Spain (10.2 per cent),

Algeria

Canada (7.8 per cent), Belgium (4.8 per cent)

Agriculture

Farming

The sector employs about 25 per cent of the labour force and contributes around 10.5 per cent of GDP. Just over 40,000,000 hectares (ha) are given over to agriculture, or around 16 per cent of total land available, of which over 8,250,000ha are under arable and permanent crops.

Climatic conditions and the availability of water for irrigation directly affect crop yields. Despite extensive irrigation programmes and the dividing of state holdings into smaller units, agricultural output has failed to keep pace with the rate of population growth. Imports typically represent around 25 per cent of import costs. Government policy had been to reduce reliance on imported food, now, however, an open market is developing as state owned agricultural land is returned to private hands.

Underlying constraints to growth include soil erosion, desert encroachment, inefficient management in the state sector, poor marketing, recurrent droughts and the inability of farmers to secure loan finance due to problems with land security. Government plans to reduce dependence on imports by a series of measures, included investing in new technology, financial incentives for state and private sector farms to buy equipment, encouraging foreign investment, less interference in the private sector and tree planting to arrest desertification.

There has been a large increase in the number of vineyards now operating in Algeria, providing a boost in export revenue. Although wine consumption is banned under Islamic law, production has been increasing; since the end of the 1990s it has doubled to around 500,000 hectolitres by 2005. It has provided a healthy income for farmers, in semi-arid regions, when other food crops have failed.

Main cash crops are grapes, oranges, olives, dates, tobacco, sugar beet and tomatoes. Hard and soft wheat and barley are grown for the home market, as are vegetables, and pulses.

Crop production in 2004 included: 3,900,000 tonnes (t) cereals in total, 2,600,000t wheat, 1,314,000t barley, 1,800,000t potatoes, 514,890t citrus fruit, 170,000t olives, 815,000t tomatoes, 165,000t chillies & peppers, 32,000t almonds, 36,000t garlic, 120,000t apples, 275,000t grapes, 60,000t figs, 450,000t dates 5,7000t tobacco, 1,765,890t fruit in total, 49,267t oilcrops, 40,437t pulses, 2,919,200t vegetables in total. Livestock production included: 555,907t meat in total, 125,000t beef, 3,400t camel meat, 177,350t lamb and goat meat, 246,250t poultry, 165,000t eggs, 1,668,100t milk, 2,000t honey, 20,000t greasy wool, 12,900t cattle hides.

Fishing

The fisheries sector largely consists of small-scale private sector operators, virtually all of whom do their fishing in the Mediterranean. Main catches include sardines, anchovies, sprats, tuna and shellfish.

The government plans to boost fisheries by modernising the Mediterranean ports, where most of the catch is landed. It has also set up a partnership with West African states for fishing in the Atlantic Ocean.

Forestry

Less than 2 per cent of Algeria's total land area is covered with forest or wooded land and the country is one of the largest importers of wood in Africa.

Algeria's forest resources cover some 3.5 million hectares (ha), with the state monopoly processing some 272,000 cubic metres of wood annually. All of the forest and arable land is in a broad coastal strip, around 400km wide. As part of plans aimed at reducing desertification the government has established an extensive tract of plantation forests.

Algeria is among the world's largest producers of cork. Other forestry products include sawn timber, wood-based panels and paper based on non-wood fibres. Most domestic demand for forest products is met through imports.

Production in 2004 included 7,645,303 cubic metres (cum) roundwood, 100,300cum industrial roundwood, 12,800cum sawnwood, 7,545,003mcum woodfuel, 604,059t charcoal.

Industry and manufacturing

Industry represents 50 per cent of GDP and employs 23 per cent of the labour force. Algeria's industrial sector is dominated by large, inefficient state-owned companies that have largely survived only due to the credit extended them by the country's state-owned banks. Government attempts to privatise these industries have been frustrated by a lack of investor interest and the fear that the possible mass redundancies which may result will cause further social instability.

The largest company in Algeria is the state-owned hydrocarbons concern, Société Nationale pour la Recherche, la Production, le Transport, la Transformation et la Commercialisation des Hydrocarbures (Sonatrach).

Production is dominated by heavy industries such as steel, petrochemicals, fertilisers and cement, but the focus of development is changing to light industry. In November 2005 the first laptop computers produced in Algeria went on sale. The manufacturers, EEPAD, an Algerian Internet service provider, aim at producing one million units a year, enough to supply every home in Algeria, by 2010.

Traditional agri-allied industries are also important, particularly textiles, food processing and tobacco and cigarette production. However past lack of investment and inefficiencies in these industries resulted in generally low productivity. In an effort to modernise the government has allowed some entities to be expanded, charge competitive prices and invest profits. Industry is opening up to more foreign involvement, particularly in large-scale projects such as motor vehicle assembly. Main constraints to development are shortages of vital inputs and skilled labour, high production and transport costs and maintenance problems. Industrial development is centralised in the northern coastal strip, but plans exist to extend industry to the high plateaux in the south.

Tourism

Algeria's tourism, which always lagged behind that of neighbouring Morocco and Tunisia, was wrecked by the civil war in the 1990s, from which it has not yet recovered. Now that the violence and insecurity is likely to be rare, the government is trying to revive the sector, with the focus on up-market rather than mass tourism. Capital investment in the sector is estimated at 5.9 per cent of the total. New hotels are being built along the Mediterranean coast and adventure holidays are planned for tourists to the south.

French tourists are the largest group visiting, followed by Tunisian and other Arab citizens. The tourist sector only contributes around 1 per cent of GDP, and less than 6 per cent of total employment, however the potential for growth is great. There are a good supply of airports and docks that could be utilised quickly, although the countrywide infrastructure still has to be redeveloped to cater for the 5.1 per cent per annum growth rate (2005–15) expected in travel and tourism.

Mining

The mining and hydrocarbons sector employs 4 per cent of the labour force and contributes 40 per cent to GDP.

Algeria is rich in minerals, including iron ore, uranium, zinc, phosphates, gold, antimony, bituminous coal, tungsten, manganese, lead, mercury and salt. The mining of iron ore and phosphate for feedstocks (for local steel and fertiliser production, respectively) and for export are the most important.

Also located near the Moroccan border are iron-ore reserves estimated at two billion tonnes. The remote location and the Western Sahara/Morocco conflict have so far prevented exploitation.

Hydrocarbons

In 2004, oil reserves stood at 11.8 billion barrels, although new oil discoveries, improved data on existing fields and a recent increase in exploration are likely to mean that Algeria's reserves will be revised upwards.

Natural gas reserves stood at 4.55 trillion cubic metres in 2004 with production of 82 billion cubic metres in 2004, a decrease of 1 per cent on 2003.

Coal represents approximately 1 per cent of total energy consumption. Algeria's total recoverable coal reserves are estimated at 40 million tonnes.

The state-run Sonatrach announced, in 2005, that the responsibility for the oil and gas sectors will be divided between exploration, Agence Nationale pour la Valorisation des Resources en Hydrocarbures (Alnaft) and control and regulation of activities, Autorité de Régulation des Hydrocarbures (ARH). Alnaft will deal with technical regulations and the ARH with investment and development.

Approximately 90 per cent of Algeria's crude oil exports go to Western Europe, with Italy as the main market followed by Germany and France. The Netherlands, Spain and Britain are other important European markets. Algeria's Saharan blend oil, 45 degrees API with negligible (0.05 per cent) sulphur content, is considered among the highest quality in the world.

Energy

Algerian energy demand has been increasing by 5 per cent per annum and is expected to continue to grow at this rate as the government housing programme unfolds.

The existing 6,600MW of generating capacity is produced by oil and natural gas. Three new generating stations are under construction to add an extra 2,525MW to the network. In September 2005 Sonelgaz subsidiary electricity supply company announced a US$7 billion investment in a new power grid, incorporating high voltage power lines.

Financial markets
Stock exchange
The Algiers stock exchange (Bourse d'Alger) was formally opened in 1999.

Banking and insurance
The Algerian banking sector is dominated by six state-owned banks. There is a total of 17 commercial banks and 10 financial institutions. The banking sector remains inefficient, with the large state banks acting mainly as depository institutions and financing loss-making public sector companies.

Central bank
Banque d'Algérie.

Time
GMT plus one hour.

Geography
Algeria is the second largest country in Africa. With a total land area of 2.38 million square km, the country comprises three distinct regions: a narrow coastal plain, which has the most fertile soils and houses the majority of the country's population, agriculture and industry; the uplands of the Atlas mountain chain, which tend to be semi-arid steppe in the valleys; and the vast sandy desert to the south. Algeria has borders with Morocco to the west, Tunisia and Libya to the east and Niger, Mali and Mauritania to the south.

Climate
The coastal region has a temperate Mediterranean climate, averaging 13 degrees Celsius (C) to 24 degrees C throughout the year and rising to a daytime high of 32 degrees C during the summer (June to September). The rainy season is October to May, with rains especially heavy from November to February. The desert is constantly inhospitable, with temperatures rising to 45 degrees C during the day, falling to 10 degrees C at night, and with very little rainfall.

Dress codes
Western-style dress is acceptable, although lightweight or safari suits are recommended in summer. Women should not wear revealing clothes.

Entry requirements
Passports
Required by all
Visa
Visas are required by most nationals: visit http://algeria.embassyhomepage.com/ for details and application form or contact your local Algerian embassy. Visas are usually valid for 90 days.
Business visas must be accompanied by an invitation from an Algerian company (in duplicate).
Prohibited entry
Nationals of Israel
Currency advice/regulations
Visitors entering the country must change a fixed sum (AD1,000) of foreign exchange into Algerian dinars at the point of entry. Unlimited amounts of foreign currency may be imported but must be declared. Foreign exchange receipts must be repatriated within 120 days.
To enable re-export of any unchanged foreign currency, declaration forms issued on arrival should be kept, used at each successive currency change and surrendered on departure. Failure to comply with these regulations may mean visitors are liable to forfeit the currency. Export of local currency is prohibited. It can sometimes be difficult to reconvert dinars to foreign currency.

Health (for visitors)
Mandatory precautions
A yellow fever and/or cholera vaccination certificate is required if arriving from infected or endemic areas.
Advisable precautions
Hepatitis 'A', typhoid, tetanus and polio vaccinations are advisable. There is risk of malaria in some areas, therefore prophylaxis is recommended. There is also a rabies risk. Water precautions should be taken throughout the country. Bottled water is often hard to find, particularly in southern parts of the country.

Hotels
Hotels are classified from one- to five-star. Major hotels in the business centres tend to be expensive, but are generally of a reasonable standard. It is advisable to book well in advance as accommodation in Algiers is difficult to obtain. The service charge is usually 15 per cent.

Credit cards
The use of credit cards is restricted.

Public holidays
Fixed dates
1 Jan (New Year's Day), 1 May (Labour Day), 19 Jun (Revolutionary Readjustment), 5 Jul (Independence Day), 1 Nov (Anniversary of the Revolution).
Variable dates
Eid al Adha (two days), Eid al Fitr (two days), Islamic New Year, Ashura, Prophet's Birthday.
The Islamic year contains 354 or 355 days, with the result that Muslim feasts advance by 10–12 days against the Gregorian calendar. Dates of feasts vary according to the sighting of the new moon, so cannot be forecast exactly. Islamic year 1426: 10 February 2005 to 30 January 2006.

Working hours
The Muslim weekend is Thursday afternoon and Friday, but many industries close all day Thursday.
Banking
Sun–Thur: 0900–1530.
Business
Sat–Tue: 0800–1200 and 1300–1700; Wed 0800–1200 and 1300–1600.
Government
Sat–Wed: 0800–1200 and 1400–1730; Thur 0800–1200.
Shops
Sat–Wed 0800–1230 and 1430–1800; Thu: 0800–1300.

Algeria

Electricity supply
Electricity supply varies from 127–220V; a compensator for use with electronic/computer equipement is advisable. All types of plug fittings are used.

Social customs/useful tips
Business appointments should be made in advance. Business cards are exchanged after introductions. French-style courtesy should be adopted by visitors. Hospitality is regarded as very important, as it is throughout the Arab world.
Wives seldom accompany their husbands to social engagements outside the home.

Security
Violence has been endemic since 1991 however optimism following the end of the civil conflict may not bring instant peace and visitors should take precautions by avoiding travelling alone. Incidents of assaults on foreigners have been increasing. Economic hardship and unemployment have led to discontent and a rise in Islamic extremism, who have specifically targetted tourists.
Some 15,000 troops are stationed in and around Algiers. Many expatriates have left the country, and strict security measures have been put in place for those who remain.

Getting there
Air
National airline: Air Algérie (Compagnie Générale de Transports Aériens) (state-owned).
International airport/s: Algiers-Houari Boumédienne (ALG), 20km from city. Facilities include duty-free shop, restaurant, buffet, bank, post office, shops, car hire.
Other airport/s: Annaba-Les Salines (AAE), 12km from city; Constantine-Ain El-Bey (CZL), 9km from city; Oran-Es Senia (ORN), 10km from city.
Airport tax: None
Surface
Road: The National Travel and Transport Company (SNTV) operates bus services linking Libya, Niger, Morocco and Tunisia with Algeria. Road access is also possible from Mali by one of the trans-Saharan highways.
Rail: A daily train service (the Trans-Maghreb) links Tunis with Algiers and Oran.
Water: Regular ferry services connect Algiers with Marseilles and other Mediteranean ports.
Main port/s: Algiers, Annaba, Arzew, Bejaia, Oran.

Getting about
National transport
Air: There are frequent services from Algiers to Annaba, Constantine and Oran provided by Air Algérie. Regular flights also link these towns with other principal centres. Fares are generally low for domestic flights but overbooking can occur, especially in summer.
Road: Main roads are in good condition generally, but desert routes are rarely maintained.
Buses: Long-distance coach services are operated by SNTV and Altour. Bookings for long trips should be made well in advance.
Rail: The service is operated by SNTF. There are two classes; some services are air-conditioned and some have couchettes.
City transport
Taxis: Taxis are widely available in main centres; they are radio-controlled in Algiers. Taxis are identified by a local colour code. They are supposed to be metered, but owing to demand, usually operate without a meter and use a minimum fare system instead. A surcharge is imposed after dark. Tips are usually 10 per cent of fare.
Buses, trams & metro: State-owned service operates in Algiers. Can be overcrowded during rush hours. Daily and longer duration tickets are available.
Car hire
Car hire is available in most main towns and at airports. An international driving licence and third-party insurance are required. The maximum speed limit is 50kph in towns and 100kph on main roads.

BUSINESS DIRECTORY

The addresses listed below are a selection only. While World of Information makes every endeavour to check these addresses, we cannot guarantee that changes have not been made, especially to telephone numbers and area codes. We would welcome any corrections.

Telephone area codes
The international dialling code (IDD) for Algeria is + 213 followed by the area code and subscriber's number:

Algiers	21	Ghardaia	29
Annaba	38	Oran	41
Béchar	49	Sétif	36
Boumerdes	24	Tiemcen	43
Constantine	31	Tindouf	49

Useful telephone numbers
Directory enquiries: 19
Telegrams: 13
Police: 17

Chambers of Commerce
Algerian Chambre de Commerce et d'Industrie, Palais Consulaire, 6 Boulevard Amilcar Cabral, Place des Martyrs, PO Box 100, 16003 Algiers (tel: 715-160; fax: 710-174; e-mail: caci@wissal.dz).

Constantine Chambre de Commerce et d'Industrie, 6 Rue de 24 Novembre 1954, PO Box 394, 25000 Constantine (tel: 935-923; fax: 937-807).

Dhara Chambre de Commerce et d'Industrie, 1 Avenue Benyahia Belcacem, PO Box 99, Mostaganem (tel: 216-709; fax: 216-578).

French Chambre de Commerce et Industrie en Algerie, Villa Clarac, 3 Rue des Cèdres, El Mouradia, Alger (tel: 606-496; fax: 609-509; e-mail: cfcia@cfcia.org).

Oran Chambre de Commerce et d'Industrie, 8 Boulevard de la Soummam, Oran (tel: 391-299; fax: 396-312).

Banking
Banque Al Baraka, Haï Bouteldja Houidif, Villa No 1 Rocade Sud, Ben Aknoun, Algiers (tel: 916-450; fax: 916-457; e-mail: info@albaraka-bank.com).

Banque de l'Agrulture et du Developpement Rural, 17 Boulevard Colonel Amirouche, Algiers (tel: 634-922; fax: 635-146).

Banque de Developpement Local, 5 Rue Gaci Amar, Staoueli, Algiers (tel: 393-755; fax: 393-757).

Banque Extérieure d'Algérie, 3 Rue du Docteur Lucien Reynaud, Algiers (tel: 239-330; fax: 239-099; e-mail: dircom@bea.dz).

Banque Nationale d'Algérie, 8 Boulevard Ernesto Che Guevara, Algiers (tel: 714-719; fax: 712-424; e-mail: nb@bna.com.dz).

Caisse d'Epargne et de Prevoyance, 42 Rue Khelifa Boukhalfa, Algiers (tel: 713-395; fax: 714-131).

Crédit Populaire d'Algérie, 2 Boulevard Colonel Amirouche, Algiers (tel: 740-528; fax: 642-383).

Central bank
Banque d'Algérie, Villa Jolie, 38 Avenue Franklin Roosevelt, 16000 Algiers (tel: 230-023; fax: 260-856; e-mail: ba@bank-of-algeria.dz).

Travel information
Air Algérie, 1 Place Maurice Audin, PO 483, 1600 Algiers (tel: 653-340; fax: 509-389; e-mail: contact@)airalgerie.dz).

Algiers-Houari Boumediene Airport, BP130 Dar El-Baida, 16100 Algiers (tel: 506-000; fax: 509-219; e-mail: hlamyl@hotmail.com).

Ministry of tourism
Ministry of Tourism and Handicraft, Rue des Frères Ziata, 16070 Algiers (tel: 792-301; fax: 792-632).

National tourist organisation offices
ONAT (Entreprise Nationale Algérienne du Tourisme), 126 bis Rue Didouche Mourad, Algiers (tel: 744-448; fax: 743-214; e-mail: onat@onat.dz.com).

Nations of the World: A Political, Economic and Business Handbook

Ministries

Prime Minister's Office, Rue Docteur Saadane, 16001 Algiers (tel: 732-300; fax: 717-927).

Ministry of Agriculture and Rural Development, 12 Boulevard Colonel Amirouche, 16001 Algiers (tel: 711-712; fax: 745-986).

Ministry of Commerce, Rue Docteur Saadane, 16001 Algiers (tel: 732-340; fax: 735-478).

Ministry of Communications and Culture, Palais de la Culture, El-Anassers, 16502 Algiers (tel: 679-420; fax: 684-459).

Ministry of Defence, Avenue Ali Khodja, Les Tagarins, 16030 Algiers (tel: 711-515).

Ministry of Education, 8 Avenue de Pékin, 16070 Algiers (tel: 605-560; fax: 606-757).

Ministry of Energy and Mines, 80 Avenue Ahmed Ghermoul, 16014 Algiers (tel: 673-300; fax: 650-997).

Ministry of Finance, Immeuble Mauretania, Place du Pérou, 16001 Algiers (tel: 711-366; fax: 736-450).

Ministry of Fisheries and Marine Resources, 4 Rue des Quatre Canons, 16001 Algiers (tel: 433-947; fax: 433-168).

Ministry of Foreign Affairs, Place Med Seddik Benyahia, 16070, Algiers (tel: 504-545; fax: 504-242).

Ministry of Health, Population and Hospital Reform, 125 Rue Abderrahmane Laala, 16075Algiers (tel: 279-900; fax: 279-641).

Ministry of Higher Education and Scientific Research, 11 Rue Doudou Mokhtar, 16033 Algiers (tel: 912-323; fax: 912-113).

Ministry of Housing and Urbanism, 135 Rue Didouche Mourad, 16001 Algiers (tel: 740-722; fax: 747-664).

Ministry of Industry and Restructuring, Immeuble le Colisée, 4 Rue Ahmed Bey, 16030 Algiers (tel: 693-156; fax: 693-235; e-mail: info@mir-algeria.org).

Ministry of the Interior and Local Communities, Rue Docteur Saadane, 16001 Algiers (tel: 732-340; fax: 605-210).

Ministry of Justice, 8 Place Bir Hakem, 16030 Algiers (tel: 921-608; fax: 921-243).

Ministry of Labour and Social Protection, 44 Rue Med Belouizded, Belcourt, Algiers (tel: 683-366; fax: 745-306).

Ministry of Participation and Reforms Co-ordination (MPCR), Chemin Ibn Badis el Mouiz, 16030 Algiers (tel: 929-885; fax: 929-884).

Ministry of Post and Telecommunications, 4 Boulevard Krim Belkacem, 16027 Algiers (tel: 711-220; fax: 730-047).

Ministry of Public Works, 3 Rue du Caire, 16050 Algiers (tel: 689-500).

Ministry of Religious Affairs and Endowments, 4 Rue de Timgad, Algiers (tel: 608-555; fax: 600-936).

Ministry of Small and Medium Enterprises, Immeuble le Colisée, 4 Rue Ahmed Bey, 16030 Algiers (tel: 601-144; fax: 592-658).

Ministry of Transport, 119 rue Didouche Mourad, 16001 Algiers (tel: 740-699; fax: 646-637).

Ministry of Vocational Training and Professional Education, Route de Dély Ibrahim, 16033 Algiers (tel: 911-528; fax: 912-779).

Ministry of War Veterans, 9 Avenue Benarfa Mohamed, 16030 Algiers (tel: 922-355; fax: 922-739).

Ministry of Water Resources, 8 Place de Bir Hakem, 16030 Algiers (tel: 283-837; fax: 747-543).

Ministry of Youth and Sports, 3 Rue Mohamed Belouizdad, 16600 Algiers (tel: 683-350; fax: 657-778; e-mail: mjs@wissal.dz).

Other useful addresses

Algerian Embassy (USA), 2137 Wyoming Avenue, NW, Washington DC 20008 (tel: 202-265-2800; fax: 202-667-2174; e-mail: embalg.us@verizon.net).

APSI (investment promotion agency), Boulevard du 11 Décembre 1960, BP 336 El-Biar, 16030 Algiers (tel: 914-225; fax: 914-303; e-mail: apsi@wissal.dz).

British Embassy, 6 Avenue Souidani Boudiemaa, BP08 Alger-Gare, 16000, Algiers (tel: 230-068; fax: 230-067).

FINALEP (Algero-European Financial Participation Company), 11 Route Nationale, Staouéli, Algiers (tel: 393-494; fax: 392-020; e-mail: finalep@wissal.dz).

National Office of Statistics, 8/10 Rue des Moussebilines, BP 202 Ferhat Boussad, 16000 Algiers (tel: 744-100; fax: 743-839; e-mail: ons@onssiege.ons.dz).

SAFEX (Algerian fairs and exports company), Palais des Expositions, Pins Maritimes, BP 366 Alger Gare, Algiers (tel: 210-123; fax: 210-630; e-mail: safex@wissal.dz).

SNTF (national rail company), 21-23 Boulevard Mohamed V, Algiers (tel: 711-510; fax: 748-190).

Sonatrach (national oil and gas company), 10 Rue Djenane El-Malik, Hydra, 16035 Algiers (tel: 548-011; fax: 547-700; e-mail: sonatrach@sonatrach.dz).

US Embassy, 4 Chemin Cheikh Bachir El-Ibrahimi, BP 408 Alger-Gare, 16000, Algiers (tel: 691-255; fax: 693-979).

Internet sites

Africa Business Network: http://www.ifc.org/abn

AllAfrica.com: http://allafrica.com

African Development Bank: http://www.afdb.org

Algeria Interface: http://www.algeria-interface.com

Algeria News Agency: http://www.aps.dz

Algeria On-Line: http://www.djazaironline.net

Mbendi AfroPaedia: http://www.mbendi.co.za

American Samoa

COUNTRY PROFILE

Historical profile
The first Polynesians settled in what is now American Samoa around 600BC. American Samoa has been a territory of the United States of America since the signing of the 17 April 1900 *Deed of Cession*; the country was administered by the US Department of the Navy from 1900 until 1951. As Japan began to emerge as an international power, the US Naval Station began to acquire strategic importance, and by 1940, the port of Pago Pago had become a training and staging area for the US Marine Corps. The US built roads, airstrips, docks and medical facilities, while American Samoans continued to enlist and serve with distinction in the US Marine Corps. American Samoa has been administered by the US Department of the Interior since 1951.
1722 The Dutch navigator, Jacob Roggeveen, was the first European to sight the islands.
1831 The London Missionary Society arrived to convert native Samoans and established a British presence.
1872 The US gained exclusive use of the deep-water whaling port of Pago Pago.
1889 The Treaty of Berlin between Britain, the US and Germany promised an independent Samoan government.
1899 The Berlin Treaty was annulled by the Tripartite Treaty, which granted the US the right to all eastern islands of the Samoan group, giving Germany the remainder. In exchange, Britain gained control of Germany's rights in Tonga, Niue and the Solomon Islands (excluding Bougainville).
1900 American Samoa officially became a US territory. Traditional rights were protected in return for a military base and coaling station. Islanders became US nationals, but not citizens; they cannot vote in US elections.
1941 The US entered the Second World War and American Samoa became a strategic location, for the US Pacific Fleet.
1945 The US Marine Corps withdrew.
1951 The territory was transferred to the US Department of the Interior.
1956 The US appointed Peter Tali Coleman as the first Samoan governor; he went on to become the first popularly elected governor.
1960 A constitution was promulgated.
1967 A revised constitution was introduced, which guaranteed the rights of inhabitants in issues such as land ownership and civil rights.
2002 Following fears of overfishing in American Samoa's exclusive economic zone (EEZ) fishery, the Western Pacific Regional Fishery Management Council approved a decision to limit access of fleets to EEZ waters.
2003 Governor Tause Sunia died and his deputy Togiola (Tala) Tulafono was appointed acting governor.
2004 Cyclone Heta caused devastation in January, and President Bush declared the islands a federal disaster area. In November, incumbent Tulafono, won the gubernatorial elections.
2005 Cyclone Heta's damage to the Manu'a islands was estimated at US$2 million. On 19 April, the government owned KVZK-TV re-launched Channel 5, which had been off-air since 1991. From 1 May, travellers from American Samoa were required to obtain entry permits to enter Samoa.

Political structure
Constitution
The 1960 constitution was revised in 1967.
American Samoa is represented in the US by a senator and a non-voting representative.
American Samoans are not US citizens; they are classified as US nationals and have freedom of entry into the continental US, but no voting rights.
Form of state
American Samoa is an unincorporated and unorganized territory of the US, administered by the Office of Insular Affairs, US Department of the Interior.
The executive
Local executive power rests with a popularly elected governor and lieutenant governor, who serve four-year terms.
National legislature
The Fono (Legislative Assembly) has two chambers. It consists of an 18-member Senate, elected according to Samoan custom by *Matai* (local chiefs), for a four-year term, and a 21-seat House of Representatives (20 of which are elected by popular vote, and one who is an appointed, non-voting delegate from Swains Island) elected for two years.
Legal system
High Court – the chief justice and associate justices are appointed by the US Secretary of the Interior.
Last elections
2/16 November 2004 (gubernatorial)
Results: Gubernatorial (first round): incumbent Togiola (Tala) Tulafono won

KEY FACTS

Official name: Territory of American Samoa

Head of State: President George W Bush

Head of government: Governor Togiola (Tala) Tulafono (sworn in 7 Apr 2003; re-elected 16 Nov 2004)

Area: 196 square km (five islands); Tutuila: 135 square km

Population: 59,902 (2004)

Capital: Fagatogo (on Tutuila), usually known as Pago Pago

Official language: English and Samoan

Currency: US dollar (US$) = 100 cents

GDP per capita: US$4,300 (2003)

Unemployment: 6.00% (2003)

Inflation: 4.00% (2003)*

Balance of trade: -US$107.00 million (2003)

* estimated figure

48.4 per cent of the vote, Afoa Moega Lutu 39.4 per cent and Teo Fuavai 12.2 per cent.
Gubernatorial (second round): Togiola (Tala) Tulafono defeated Afoa Moega Lutu 56 per cent to 44 per cent.

Next elections
2008 (gubernatorial)

Population
59,902 (2004)

Ethnic make-up
Samoan (Polynesian) (89 per cent), Tongan (4 per cent), Caucasian (2 per cent), others (5 per cent).

Religions
Approximately half the population are Christian Congregational, but Roman Catholics, Latter Day Saints and Protestants are also represented.

Education
Extra federal funds will be provided in 2006 for schools with students from deprived backgrounds and aimed at those at risk of dropping out of education. There will also be schemes for early reading and English learning, and support for children with disabilities. Specific funding for American Samoa of US$29.5 million will be added to improve the island's education system.

Compulsory years: Six to 18

Health
Life expectancy: 75.8 years (2005): male 72.27 years; female 79.62 years (2005 estimate).
Fertility rate/Maternal mortality rate: 3.25 births per woman (2005 estimate).
Birth rate/Death rate: 25.9 births and three deaths per 1,000 population (2005 estimate)
Infant mortality rate: 9.3 deaths per 1,000 live births (2005 estimate)

Main cities
Fagatogo, the capital, on Tutuila, is usually known as Pago Pago (estimated population 4,100 in 2003), Tafuna (9,600), Nu'uuli (5,000).

Languages spoken
English is used for business and commerce but Samoan, (closely related to Hawaiian), is in common use among the local population.

Official language/s
English and Samoan

Media
Press
There are bi-lingual publications in English and Samoan including *Samoa News* (Monday to Friday), the semi-weekly *Samoa Journal* and the weekly *Advertiser*. Major international newspapers available on the island include *The International Herald Tribune*, *New York Times*, *The Washington Post* and *USA Today*. The *News Bulletin* is the island's own English newspaper and is published Monday to Friday.

Broadcasting
Radio: Radio Samoa broadcasts in English and Samoan and transmits 24 hours per day. KSBS FM broadcasts in English and Samoan 0600–2400.
Television: In 1991 Hurricane Val damaged the transmitter used by the state television, limiting broadcasts to Channel 2 only. KVZK-TV Channel 5 was re-launched on 19 April 2005.

Economy
The economy is reliant on agriculture, fishing, fish processing and aid from the US. The dependence on primary sectors means the economy is particularly vulnerable to adverse weather conditions and disease. Around half of the government's revenue is from US aid, making international support essential to the island's development.

Government efforts to attract investment to the territory have had limited success. Due to the islands natural beauty, tourism is a fast growing sector of the economy. The island is becoming an increasingly popular destination for the growing popularity in ecotourism. There are 10-year tax incentives for new businesses in the area, attempting to attract light manufacturing and service based industries.

The private sector continues to be dominated by the fish processing industry. However the canneries rely almost entirely on imported materials for production. Changing global environments have made it clear the territory can no longer depend on fish production for its survival, meaning diversification is essential for future development. Tuna processing is an important source of government revenue as it contributes 93 per cent of the island's exports. A decline in production would severely damage the local economy and lead to mass unemployment.

In April 2004, the government was awarded over US$1.4 million in federal grants, and over US$7.5 million for improvements at Pago Pago, Fitiuta and Ofu Airports. In February 2004 the Australian government pledged US$7 million to develop security forces in American Samoa. The Homeland Security Appropriations Act included US$5.03 million for American Samoa to use as funding for law enforcement training, terrorism prevention and port security. The 2005 appropriations bill includes US$23.1 million for American Samoa's government operations and US$10 million for capital improvement projects.

US Army recruitment, which is a considerable source of income and employment has dropped in recent years. It is believed that the decrease is due to the war in Iraq, which has had negative publicity, arising from the death of a number of American Samoan servicemen. According to Governor Togiola, on a per capita basis, they have 'the highest death rate in the US military at present'.

External trade
American Samoa benefits from duty free entry into the customs territory of the US. Canned fish is considered a domestic product in US statistics and is not reflected in export figures, nevertheless over 60 per cent of output from canneries goes to US markets.

Imports
Materials for the canneries (typically 56 per cent of total), food (8 per cent), petroleum products (7 per cent), machinery and parts (6 per cent). Imports totalled US$452 million in 2003.
Main sources: Japan (32.2 per cent of total 2004), New Zealand (30.4 per cent), Germany (14.6 per cent), Australia (9.2 per cent)

Exports
Canned tuna (typically 93 per cent of total). Exports totalled US$345 million in 2003.
Main destinations: Samoa (41.6 per cent of total 2004), Australia (21.8 per cent), Japan (16.6 per cent), New Zealand (7.7 per cent), Canada (4.2 per cent).
Canned fish to the US is not counted as an export.

Agriculture
Farming
The soil is volcanic. About 10 per cent of the land area is cultivable, half of which is under permanent cultivation.
Smallholding crop production in 2004 included: 4,700 tonnes (t) coconuts, 1,500t taro, 1,620t roots & tubers, 100t yams, 1,195t fruit in total, 750t bananas, 470t vegetables in total and 611t oilcrops.
Meat production was 344t in total, including: 3t beef, 315t pig meat and 26t poultry meat; 30t eggs, and 16t milk.

Fishing
Tuna and deep-sea fishing is important to the economy. American Samoa is the main processing site for the US tuna fishing fleet in the Pacific. Typical fish catches up to 2000 had been less than 600t but in 2001 the catch jumped to 3,600t and concerns about overfishing prompted a decision in 2002 to limit fleet access to American Samoa's waters.

Industry and manufacturing
The private sector is dominated by the fish processing industry, which employs one-third of the workforce. StarKist has the world's largest tuna cannery in American Samoa and has a 44 per cent US

market share. The two other producers are BumbleBee and Chicken of the Sea (a Thai owned company). Between them they produce 80–90 per cent of American Samoa's principal export, the majority of which is directed to the US market. The tuna canneries export around US$470 million processed tuna annually. StarKist and Chicken of the Sea employ more than 5,150 people or 74 per cent of the private sector workforce. Sales from StarKist canneries are reported to have increased sharply in recent years. American Samoa is fighting to exclude tuna from the US/Thailand Free Trade Agreement in order to save around 3,000 jobs.

Ecuador and Columbia are a threat to the tuna canneries as they have the production capacity to supply the entire US market and wipe out the economy of American Samoa.

Other industries include textiles, meat canning, dairy produce, jewellery, handicrafts and tourism. There are also factories processing soap, liquor and perfume. The US government is trying to encourage joint ventures and other foreign investment for any product with a 30 per cent local content.

Tourism
Tourism plays an increasing role in the islands' economy. It is still relatively underdeveloped, but has potential and development is a government priority. Tourist arrival figures are small and have tended to fluctuate. The cruise ship business is being encouraged. Ecotourism is an attraction following the creation of the National Park in 1993.

Mining
The only natural resources are pumice and pumicite.

Hydrocarbons
American Samoa does not produce gas, coal or oil. It relies entirely on imports of refined oil including gasoline, kerosene, distillate and jet fuel.

Energy
The monthly average generated is 8.4 million kW.

Banking and insurance
The Bank of Hawaii and the Amerika Samoa Bank provide 24-hour full banking services and correspond with banks in the US and the Pacific.

Time
GMT minus eleven hours

Geography
American Samoa comprises the seven islands of Tutuila, Tau, Olosega, Ofu, Aunuu, Rose and Swain's, lying in the southern central Pacific Ocean, about 3,700km (2,300 miles) south-west of Hawaii. Pago Pago has one of the best natural deepwater harbours in the South Pacific Ocean.

Climate
Wet and tropical, annual rainfall up to 750cm in mountainous areas. There are two main seasons; wet (Dec–Mar) and dry (Apr–Nov). Temperatures range from 20–32 degrees Celsius.

Entry requirements
Passports
Required by all except US citizens with proof of citizenship. Passports must be valid for at least 60 days beyond the intended length of stay.
Visa
US entry requirements apply. Visas required by all, except US citizens with proof of identity, and foreign nationals from countries that have visa free entry to the US and are in possession of machine readable passports under 'Visa Waiver Program' (VWP) due to be introduced in October 2005. All other visitors and passport holders must apply for a visa. Visits, (for both tourism and business) and visas are valid for up to 90 days. A return/onward ticket is also required.

Further information can be found at http://travel.state.gov/ including information on temporary business visas. More detailed information can be found at http://uscis.gov/graphics/services/visa_info.htm.

All visitors must have proof of adequate funds for up to 30 days and onward/return tickets. Entry to American Samoa does not give automatic entry to the US and visitors must apply separately to a US consulate.

Health (for visitors)
Mandatory precautions
Vaccination certificates required for yellow fever if travelling from infected area.
Advisable precautions
Vaccination for diphtheria, tuberculosis, hepatitis A and B, polio, tetanus and typhoid are advisable. There is a risk of rabies and dengue fever.

Public holidays
Fixed dates
1 Jan (New Year's Day), 17 Apr (Territorial Flag Day), 4 Jul (Independence Day), 11 Nov (Veterans' Day), 25 Dec (Christmas Day).
Variable dates
Martin Luther King's Birthday (third Mon in Jan), Washington's Birthday (third Mon in Feb), Memorial Day (last Mon in May), Labour Day (first Mon in Sep), Columbus Day (second Mon in Oct), Thanksgiving Day (fourth Thu in Nov).

Working hours
Banking
Mon–Fri: 0900–1500; Sat: 0800–1200.
Business
Mon–Fri: 0730/0830–1730/1800; Sat: 0830–1200.
Government
Mon–Fri: 0730/0830–1730/1800; Sat: 0830–1200.
Shops
Mon–Fri: 0800–1700; Sat: 0800–1300.

Weights and measures
Imperial

Social customs/useful tips
Visitors should be sensitive to local conventions and respect local customs and practices. Care should be taken when dressed casually; bikinis and shorts are acceptable in hotels, but they are not considered appropriate when visiting urban and rural areas.

Getting there
Air
National airline: Samoa Aviaton (TS).
International airport/s: Pago Pago International (PPG), 11km from town; duty-free shop, restaurant, shops and car hire.
Airport tax: None
Surface
Main port/s: Pago Pago is an international port. It is served by a number of passenger cruise and cargo lines including Farell Lines and Pacific Islands Transport Line.

Getting about
National transport
Air: In April 2004, over US$7.5 million was allocated to the American Samoa government for improvements at Pago Pago, Fitiuta and Ofu Airports.
Road: There are approximately 150km of paved roads and 200km of unpaved or secondary roads, the majority of which are on Tutuila. A new road and two bridges are being built in Pago Pago.
Buses: There is a local service operating between the airport and Pago Pago town centre. The Aiga bus service provides an inexpensive but non-timetabled service between Pago Pago and outlying villages.
Water: A weekly service operates between Pago Pago and the Manu'a islands.
Car hire
An international driving licence or valid national driving licence is required. Minimum age of 21. Traffic drives on the right.

BUSINESS DIRECTORY
The addresses listed below are a selection only. While World of Information makes every endeavour to check these addresses, we cannot guarantee that changes have not been made, especially

to telephone numbers and area codes. We would welcome any corrections.

Telephone area codes
The international direct dialling (IDD) code for American Samoa is +684, followed by subscriber's number.

Useful telephone numbers
International operator	0
Information	411
Police, fire and ambulance	911

Chambers of Commerce
American Samoa Chamber of Commerce, PO Box 2446, Pago Pago 96799 (tel: 699-6214; fax: 699-2219; e-mail: chamber@samoatelco.com).

Banking
Amerika Samoa Bank, PO Box 3790, Pago Pago 96799 (tel: 633-5053; fax: 633-5057).

Bank of Hawaii, PO Box 69, Pago Pago 96799 (tel: 633-4226; fax: 633-2918).

Travel information
Flight information: (tel: 699-9101, 0800-2200).

Pago Pago International Airport, PO Box 1539, Pago Pago 96799 (tel: 699-9101/2/3; fax: 633-5281).

National tourist organisation offices
Office of Tourism, Convention Centre, Pago Pago, 96799 (tel: 633-1091/92/93; fax: 633-1094).

Other useful addresses
Office of Economic Development and Planning, Territorial Planning Commission, Pago Pago, 96799 (tel: 633-5156).

Office of the Governor, American Samoa Government, Pago Pago (tel: 633-4828; fax: 633-2269).

Internet sites
Department of Commerce: http://www.amsamoa.com

Government: http://www.government.as

Newspaper on-line: http://www.samoanews.com

Office of the Governor: http//www.asg-gov.net

US Office of Insular affairs: http://www.doi.gov/oia

Andorra

COUNTRY PROFILE

Historical profile
One of the world's smallest countries, Andorra is also one of the oldest nations in Europe, established by Charlemagne in 803 as a buffer state against Spanish Muslims.
803 Charlemagne captured the area from Spanish Muslims and his son, Louis the Pious, presented the area's inhabitants with a charter of liberties.
843 The Valls d'Andorra (Valleys of Andorra) were granted to Sunifred, Count of Urgell.
1278 Co-principality established between France (originally represented by a nominee of the king, then the emperor and latterly the president himself) and Spain (in the person of the Bishop of Seu d'Urgel).
1419 A parliament, the Consell de la Terra (Council of the Land), was established to represent the Andorran people.
1866 The Consell General de las Valls (Council of the Valleys) replaced the Council of the Land, during the year of the New Reform, which introduced democratisation to Andorra.
1933–34 The Council of the Valleys was temporarily dissolved by the courts. Elections were held and all men over 25 years were granted the right to vote.
1981 Constitutional reforms are enacted to move power away from the feudal co-princes and towards the parliament.
1983 Introduction of income tax following storm damage and general recession.
1985 Universal suffrage was introduced.
1991 Andorra joined a customs union with the EU.
1993 Andorra introduced a new constitution, establishing the country as a sovereign parliamentary democracy, and a new 28-member parliament, the Consell General (General Council). The first elections were held; they were won by Agrupament Nacional Democratic (AND) (National Democratic Grouping).
1994 A coalition government was formed, led by Unió Liberal (UL), Marc Forné Molné of the Partit Liberal Andorra's (PLA) (Liberal Party of Andorra) was elected head of government by the General Council.
2001 The PLA was elected.
2002 The Organisation for Economic Co-operation and Development (OECD) blacklisted Andorra as a tax haven with 'prejudicial' tax practices. The principality refused to agree to lift the secrecy surrounding the banking sector, which is a source of international condemnation.
2003 Endesa of Spain will supply 50 per cent of Andorra's electricity requirements until 2008. On 12 May, Joan Enric Vives Sicília succeeded Joan Martí Alanís as Bishop of Seu d'Urgel and ex officio co-prince of Andorra.
2004 An agreement, on a Savings Tax Directive concerning tax withholding and savings, between the EU and Andorra was reached in June.
2005 The ruling PLA was re-elected on 24 April with 41.2 per cent of the vote (14 seats out of 28). Turnout was 80.4 per cent. Albert Pintat Santolària was elected head of government on 27 May by 15 votes against 12 for Jaume Bartumeu Cassany.

Political structure
Constitution
The first written constitution was adopted 14 March 1993 after a referendum. The constitution allows Andorra to hold full sovereignty, to be able to form trade unions and political parties, and to have an independent judiciary. It can also decide its own foreign policy and join international organisations.
Form of state
Andorra is a co-principality under the joint sovereignty of the President of France and the Spanish Bishop of Seu d'Urgel, who are represented locally by officials called *verguers*.
The executive
Nominally, the co-princes, the Bishop of Seu d'Urgel and President of France, are the heads of state. In reality, the country is governed by an administration formed by the party or coalition with the largest number of seats in the legislature.
National legislature
Day-to-day government is by an elected head of government and the 28-member Consell General (14 elected by a single national constituency and 14 to represent each of the seven *parroquies*, or parishes). Members serve for four years. The Cap de Govern (head of government) is elected by the Consell General.
Legal system
Independent judiciary
Last elections
24 April 2005 (parliamentary)
Results: Parliamentary: the ruling Partit Liberal Andorra (PLA) (Liberal Party of Andorra) won 41.2 per cent of the vote (14 seats out of 28), the Partit Socialdemòcrata (PSD) (Social-Democratic Party) 38.1 per

KEY FACTS

Official name: Principat d'Andorra (Principality of Andorra)

Head of State: Co-Princes: Bishop of Seu d'Urgel Joan Enric Vives Sicília (from 12 May 2003) and President Jacques Chirac of France

Head of government: Cap de Govern Albert Pintat Santolària (elected 27 May 2005)

Ruling party: Partit Liberal Andorra (PLA) (Liberal Party of Andorra) (elected 4 Mar 2001; re-elected 24 Apr 2005)

Area: 468 square km

Population: 73,100 (2004)

Capital: Andorra la Vella

Official language: Catalan

Currency: Euro (eur) = 100 cents

Exchange rate: eur0.83 per US$ (Oct 2005)

GDP per capita: US$19,000 (2003)

GDP real growth: 3.80% (2003)

Labour force: 33,000 (2003)

Inflation: 4.30% (2003)

Balance of trade: -US$1.02 billion (2003)

cent (12 seats), the Partit Demòcrata (PD) (Democratuc Party) 11 per cent (two seats), the Democratic Renovation 6.2 per cent (no seats) and the Greens 3.5 per cent (no seats); turnout was 80.4 per cent.

Next elections
2009 (parliamentary)

Political parties
Ruling party
Partit Liberal Andorra (PLA) (Liberal Party of Andorra) (elected 4 Mar 2001; re-elected 24 Apr 2005)
Main opposition party
Partit Socialdemòcrata (PSD) (Social-Democratic Party)

Population
73,100 (2004)
Ethnic make-up
Of Andorra's total population, only about 33 per cent are natives with the right to vote. The rest include Spaniards (43 per cent), Portuguese (11 per cent), French (7 per cent), English, Australians, Moroccans and others (6 per cent).
Religions
Roman Catholicism is predominant.

Education
A range of universal, free public French, Spanish and Andorran lay schools provide education up to the secondary level. Although schools are built and maintained by Andorran authorities, teachers are paid for the most part by France or Spain. The government provides free nursery schools, although supply falls short of demand. About 50 per cent of Andorran children attend the French primary schools, and the rest attend Spanish or Andorran schools. In July 1997, the University of Andorra was established, which serves principally as a centre for virtual studies, connected to Spanish and French universities. The only two graduate schools in Andorra are the Nursing School and the School of Computer Science.
Compulsory years: Four to 16

Health
Life expectancy: 79.6 years (WHO).
Fertility rate/Maternal mortality rate: 1.3 births per woman (WHO)
Birth rate/Death rate: 5.4 deaths to 10.29 births per 1,000 population (World Bank).
Infant mortality rate: 6 per 1,000 live births (World Bank)

Welfare
Social security in Andorra is based on a points system with two distinct programmes covering health and old-age insurance.
Health insurance covers illness, pregnancy, accidents at work, disability and death. Social security payments cover nearly 75 per cent and 90 per cent of expenditure relating to illness and hospitalisation respectively. There is no discrimination against disabled persons in employment, education, or in the provision of other state services.
Unemployment benefit includes 50 per cent of the average salary calculated in the first month and 66 per cent calculated from the second month onwards.

Pensions
People pay contributions towards their old-age pension and on retirement receive a pension proportional to the number of points collected. All salaried workers pay contributions to the Andorran Social Security Fund (CASS). Old-age pension is paid to those covered from the age of 65.

Family support
Maternity care and childbirth are fully covered by social security, while disability benefits are calculated in each individual case.

Main cities
Andorra la Vella (capital, estimated population 23,000 in 2003).

Languages spoken
French and Castilian
Official language/s
Catalan

Media
Press
Daily newspapers and local weeklies include *Diari d'Andorra*, *El Periodic d' Andorra*, *Poble Andorra*, *Correu Andorra*, *Informacions* and *Diari Informacions*.
Broadcasting
Around six TV stations and several radio stations can be received from France and Spain.
Radio: There are two radio stations. One state-owned (Radio Andorra) and one privately-owned (Radio Valira).

Economy
Economic activity in Andorra is dominated by commerce and tourism. With an estimated 10 million visitors every year, accounting for around 80 per cent of GDP, the country is heavily reliant on the tourist sector. The banking industry is characterised by security and contributes substantially to the economy. The principality is a tax haven although there are indirect taxes which contribute to 13 per cent of GDP. Andorra is a member of the EU customs union and is treated as an EU member with no tariffs on manufactured goods when trading with EU members.
There is a very small-scale agriculture industry with only around 2 per cent of the land being used for farming purposes; consequently there is a heavy reliance on food imports. Light industry in Andorra consists almost entirely of tobacco products and furniture, which are the nation's primary exports.
The most important activities of the country's service sector are commerce and the hotel trade, which employ almost 40 per cent of the workforce. There are insufficient modern and dynamic services, such as specialised services for businesses, and a reliance on traditional sectors which is limiting the economy's potential.
In 2003, the OECD named five countries as unco-operative tax havens, including Andorra. In June 2004, Andorra agreed to operate equivalent measures to those applied by EU's member states regarding taxation of income from savings in 2005.

External trade
Andorra is a member of the European Union Customs Union, and is a major entrepôt for numerous European goods owing to favourable excise duties. With agricultural products however, Andora is treated as a non-EU member and is subject to tariffs accordingly. Spain and France are Andorra's main export partners.
The Envalira tunnel, under the highest mountain pass in Europe, nearly 3km long and one of the longest road tunnels in the world, facilitates communications and transport between Andorra and France.
Imports
Three-quarters of Andorra's revenue is from import tariffs.
Main imports are foodstuffs, electricity, raw materials, manufactures and consumer goods. The relative volume of imports, equivalent to almost 90 per cent of GDP, is much higher than any other OECD country.
Main sources: Spain (typically 48 per cent of total), France (35 per cent), US (2 per cent)
Exports
Andorra's volume of exports are typically under 5 per cent of its GDP, a figure far below that of most OECD countries, indicating the unusual nature of the economy, based on retail sales to tourists. Main exports include tobacco products and furniture.
Main destinations: EU members take 99.5 per cent of exports, including France (typically 34 per cent of total) and Spain (58 per cent).

Agriculture
Farming
The agricultural sector is a small part of the economy and typically employs less than 1 per cent of the working population. Agricultural production is limited by a scarcity of arable land, and most food has to be imported. Milk is sourced domestically. Principal crops are tobacco and

Andorra

potatoes, rye, wheat, barley, oats. Some other vegetables are also grown.
The principal livestock activity is sheep husbandry.
Land use: 2 per cent permanent crops, 56 per cent forest and woodland, 20 per cent irrigated land.

Fishing
Andorra imports fish from Spain for domestic needs. Trout are plentiul in streams.

Forestry
One fifth of the land is forested. Exports of forest materials in 2004 amounted to US$800,000, while imports amounted to US$6.3 million. Logs are transported to Spain. Most reforestation is in pines.

Industry and manufacturing
The industrial sector has fallen to around 20 per cent of economic activity. The small manufacturing sector primarily services tourism, but also includes cigarettes, cigars and furniture.

Tourism
Andorra depends heavily on its tourist industry, which accounts for as much as 80 per cent of GDP. There are typically 10 million tourist visits per annum, three-quarters of which are day-trips. Tourists and day-trippers, the majority of whom are Spanish and French, are drawn by the principality's duty-free status and its skiing resorts. There are 270 hotels and 400 restaurants.

Environment
Current issues are deforestation and overgrazing of mountain meadows contributing to soil erosion. Natural hazards include snowslides and avalanches.

Mining
Forges in Andorra were once famed. There are small amounts of iron ore and lead but access is a problem.

Hydrocarbons
Even though Andorra has good hydroelectric facilities, around three-quarters of energy consumed is by imported oil from France and Spain. There are four gas companies. It does not import coal or natural gas.

Energy
From 2003 until 2008, Endesa of Spain will supply 50 per cent of Andorra's electricity requirements. Electricity demand for Andorra in 2003 was estimated at 500GWh, of which around 290GWh was supplied by Endesa, 90GWh by the country's only hydroelectric plant and the remaining 120GWh by Electricité de France (EDF).

Banking and insurance
The banking sector with its tax haven status contributes substantially to the economy. Seven commercial banks operate some 34 branches. Strict secrecy laws are maintained.
Andorra's financial service sector is benefiting from the eurozone which provides greater stability and enhanced opportunities. After being denounced as an unco-operative tax haven by the OECD in 2003, Andorra conceded to EU standards regarding taxation of income from savings. From 2005 the country has agreed to impose a withholding tax, up to 35 per cent, to be passed to the tax department of an EU citizen's country, instead of informing the relevant EU country about the amount of money in savings accounts. The anonymity of the saver will be preserved. Andorra refuses to back down from its commitment to banking secrecy, which is enshrined in the 1993 constitution.
Andorra has also agreed to supply information on tax fraud, for criminal or civil trials, and notify EU member states about additional malpractices.
There are 36 insurance companies in operation.

Central bank
European Central Bank (ECB)

Time
GMT plus one hour (GMT plus two hours from late Mar to late Sep).

Geography
Andorra is landlocked, lying in the eastern Pyrenees mountains, bounded by France and Spain. It is situated about midway between Barcelona and Toulouse.

Climate
Warm summers and moderately cold winters; temperatures range from 0–30 degrees Celsius (C).

Entry requirements
Passports
Required by all except for nationals of France and Spain, who only require an identity card.
Visa
Required by all; except nationals of EU and Schengen Accord signatory countries. Tourists from North America and Australasia may visit, visa-free, for up to 90 days. All other nationals, visiting for business purposes, should contact the nearest French embassy for a visa application form. Tourists travelling to further Schengen agreement countries may download a visa application (offered in several languages) from www.eurovisa.info/ApplicationForm.htm and submit it to the nearest French embassy.
Currency advice/regulations
No currency restrictions.

Health (for visitors)
Mandatory precautions
None

Advisable precautions
Up-to-date tetanus and polio immunisations are recommended.

Hotels
Around 250 hotels, most with modern facilities.

Public holidays
Fixed dates
1 Jan (New Year's Day), 6 Jan (Epiphany), 14 Mar (Constitution Day), 1 May (Labour Day), 24 Jun (St John's Day), 15 Aug (Assumption Day), 8 Sep (Mare de Deu de Meritxell, National Day), 1 Nov (All Saints' Day), 4 Nov (St Charles' Day), 8 Dec (Immaculate Conception), 24 Dec (Christmas Eve), 25–26 Dec (Christmas Holiday).
Variable dates
Good Friday, Easter Monday, Ascension Day, Whit Monday.

Working hours
Banking
Mon–Fri: 0900–1300, 1500–1700; Sat: 0900–1200.
Business
Considerable variation in times.
Shops
Mon–Sat: 0900–2000; Sun: 0900–1900.

Getting there
Air
International airport/s: The closest international airports are located in France and Spain, connecting to inter- and intracontinental destinations. Barcelona (Spain), 200km, and Toulouse-Blagnac (France), 180km from Andorra (approximately three hours drive).
Surface
Road: From Spain: Barcelona-Andorra via Puigcerda and La Seu d'Urgel; Barcelona-Andorra via Igualada, Calaf, Ponts and La Seu d'Urgel. Buses run regularly from Barcelona.
Mountainous roads exist over the Envalira pass to Perpignan, Tarbes and Toulouse. From France: from L'Hospitalet or La Tour de Carol to Pas de la Casa (approximately 2hrs 20 minutes), on the Andorran frontier, then Port d'Envalira.
A road runs from the Spanish to the French frontiers through Saint Julia, Andorra la Vella, Escaldes-Engordonay, Encamp, Camnillo and Soldeu.
A seasonal service runs from Aix-les-Thermes and services may be available from Seo de Urgel in Spain.
Rail: From Spain: Barcelona to Puigcerda, then by bus to La Seu d'Urgel and Andorra. Madrid to Lleida (Lérida), then bus to La Seu d'Urgel and Andorra. Routes from Perpignan, Villefranche and Toulouse go to La Tour de Carol 20km from Anodrra.
From France: trains to Aix-les-Thermes, L'Hospitalet or La Tour de Carol

(Toulouse-Perpignan lines), then bus to Andorra.

Getting about
National transport
Road: There are 186km of roads of which 162km are paved. Roads in poor condition, blocked by snow in winter and traffic jams in summer.
Buses: Constant minibus services link all the villages.

BUSINESS DIRECTORY

The addresses listed below are a selection only. While World of Information makes every endeavour to check these addresses, we cannot guarantee that changes have not been made, especially to telephone numbers and area codes. We would welcome any corrections.

Telephone area codes
The international direct dialling (IDD) code for Andorra is +376, followed by customer's number (no area code required).

Chambers of Commerce
Andorra Chamber of Commerce, Industry and Services, C/Prat de la Creu 8, Edifice le Mans 204, Andorra La Vella (tel: 863-232; fax:863-233; e-mail: ccis@andorra.ad).

Banking
Banc Agricol i Comercial d'Andorra, Mossen Cinto 6, Andorra la Vella (tel: 821-333).

Banca Cassany SA, Avinguda Meritxell 39-41, Andorra la Vella.

Banc Internacional, Avinguda Meritxell 32, Andorra la Vella (tel: 820-037).

Banca Mora SA, Placa Coprinceps 2, Les Escaldes (tel: 820-607).

Banca Reig, Avinguda Meritxell, Andorra la Vella (tel: 822-618).

Credit Andorra, Avinguda Princep Benlloch 19, Andorra la Vella (tel: 820-326).

La Caixa, Pl Rebés, Andorra la Vella (tel: 820-015).

Central bank
European Central Bank (ECB), Kaiserstrasse 29, D-60311 Frankfurt am Main, Germany (tel: +49(69) 13-440; fax: +49(69) 1344-6000).

Travel information
Caseta d'Informació i Turisme (tourism kiosk opposite Restaurant Martí), Andorra la Vella (tel: 827-117).

Sindicat d'Iniciativa Oficina de Turisme (national tourist office at the top of Carrer Doctor Vilanova between Plaça del Poble and Plaça Rebés), Andorra la Vella (tel: 820-214).

Ministries
Government of Andorra, C/ Prat de la Creu 62, Andorra La Vella (tel: 829-345; internet: www.govern.ad).

Ministry of Finance, Andorra la Vella (tel: 829-245).

Ministry of Commerce, Industry and Agriculture, Andorra la Vella.

Ministry of Tourism and Sport, Andorra la Vella.

Other useful addresses
French Embassy, C/ Les Canals 38-40, Andorra La Vella (tel: 820-809).

French Post Office, C/Bonaventura Armengol, Andorra la Vella (tel: 820-408).

General Syndic's Office (tel: 821-234).

Pas de la Casa Customs Post (Andorran frontier with France) (tel: 855-120).

Police, Andorra la Vella (tel: 821-222).

Sant Julia de Loria Customs Post (Andorran frontier with Spain) (tel: 841-090).

Servei de Telecomunicacions d'Andorra STA, Avinguda Meritxell 110, Andorra la Vella (tel: 821-021).

Sindicat d'Iniciativa de les Valls d'Andorra, c/Dr Vilanova, Andorra la Vella (tel: 820-214).

Spanish Embassy, C/ Prat de la Creu 34, Andorra La Vella (tel: 820-013).

Spanish Post Office, c/o Joan Maragall, Andorra la Vella (tel: 820-257).

Internet sites
Only Andorra yellow pages: http:// www.onlyandorra.com

Andorra information: http://www.andorra.ad/

Angola

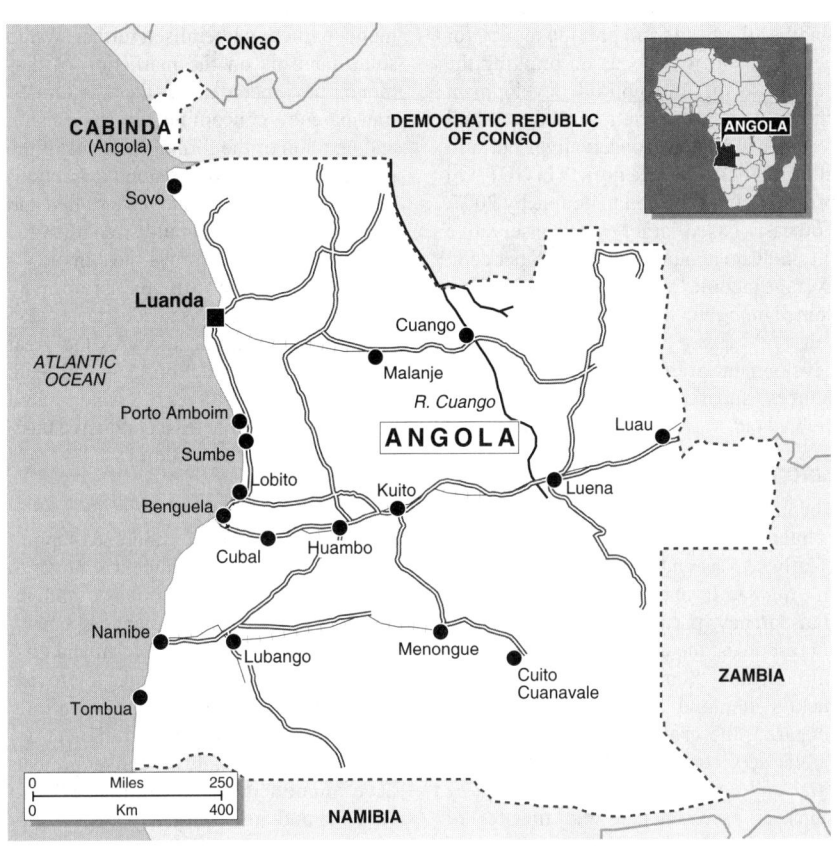

KEY FACTS

Official name: Republica de Angola (Republic of Angola)

Head of State: President José Eduardo dos Santos (since 1979)

Head of government: Prime Minister Fernando da Piedade Dias dos Santos (from 5 Dec 2002)

Ruling party: Government of Unity and National Reconciliation (GURN); dominated by Movimento Popular de Libertação de Angola (MPLA) (Popular Movement for the Liberation of Angola)

Area: 1,246,700 square km

Population: 15.94 million (2004)

Capital: Luanda

Official language: Portuguese

Currency: Kwanza (Kz) = 100 Lwei

Exchange rate: Kz89.21 per US$ (Oct 2005)

GDP per capita: US$1,305 (2004) (IMF)

GDP real growth: 11.20% (2004); *18.0% (2005)

Labour force: 6.25 million (2004)

Inflation: 43.60% (2004) (IMF)

Oil production: 991,000 bpd (2004)

Balance of trade: US$7.86 billion (2004)

Foreign debt: US$10.45 billion (2004)

* estimated figure

The post-war process of demobilisation and reintegration of former combatants in the Angolan civil war has been proceeding successfully, and the government has turned its attention to the challenges of post-conflict reconstruction. With much of both national and local infrastructure destroyed during more than 30 years of war, the challenge is enormous. Landmines and impassable roads have cut off large parts of the country. Many Angolans are dependent on food aid.

Future prosperity

Angola is a potentially wealthy country, with significant resources of oil, gas and diamonds, as well as considerable hydroelectric potential, varied agricultural land, and adequate rainfall. Despite this, the lack of any immediate substantial economic activity outside of the oil and diamond sectors has left most Angolans without sustainable incomes. A wild card that could come out of the pack at any time and would not contribute at all positively to their lot, is that much of Angola's oil wealth lies in the province of Cabinda, where a decades-long separatist conflict is simmering. The situation is contained by mainland troops and the undoubted, unpublicised, influence of international oil companies and their home governments.

Although since the end of the war, in which up to 1.5 million lives may have been lost and four million people displaced, growing revenues from oil and diamonds have boosted per capita income to over US$1,300, human development indicators remain poor. Infant mortality is 154 per 1,000, the prevalence of HIV/Aids 5.74 per cent, primary school enrolment only 74 per cent. On a macroeconomic level the outlook is far more favourable, a non-war economy has resulted in growth in gross domestic product of 11.2 per cent over 2004 and a forecast of 18 per cent for 2005. Apart from oil and diamonds, the economy is estimated to have grown at an annual rate of 9 per cent in 2004 as agricultural production has begun to recover with the return of displaced persons to their smallholdings. Foreign reserves have doubled to 1.8 months of import cover.

Annual inflation was 43.6 per cent over 2004, high, but down significantly from the 100 per cent of the early 2000s. The fiscal situation has also improved with the current account at US$6.8 million at the end of 2004, positive for the first time in four years. However, the financial framework remains fragile given the country's extreme dependence on the oil sector for half of its gross domestic product (GDP). To fully take advantage of all its rich natural resources – gold, diamonds, extensive forests, Atlantic fisheries, as well as the large oil deposits – Angola will need to continue reforming government policies and to reduce widespread corruption. A supplier of crude oil to the US and China, Angola has denied allegations that revenues have been squandered through corruption and mismanagement. Independent sources say over the years up to 50 per cent of the oil money has found its way into private bank accounts. At a September 2005 Washington meeting, the International Monetary Fund (IMF) said it was waiting for Angola to react to proposals for longer-term programmes, including some to curb corruption. Observers believe little will happen until the end of 2006, when President José Eduardo dos Santos has pledged to hold national elections. A new draft constitution is being prepared.

The IMF has recommended strengthening non-oil revenues while spending should be redirected toward social services and infrastructure. Oil 'boom revenues' – receipts derived from sales at, say, above the present price, should be used to stabilise the fiscus and provide money for development, with focus on bringing the private sector into non-oil development and on poverty alleviation. Budgetted oil receipts would be conservative, but still allow for considerable growth in GDP. Oil production is expected to double by 2007. Forecasts based largely on 'conservative oil' indicate annual growth of 18 per cent; average income levels in Angola could become among the highest in Africa as a result of rising oil production, the development of its extensive diamond resources, and the plentiful availability of arable land.

Reforming Sonangol

The fund has pulled no punches in its condemnation of the level of corruption it clearly sees as endemic to doing business in Angola. It underscores the need for transparency, particularly with respect to oil resources, the activities of the national oil company, Sonangol, and the government's diamond arm, Endiama; and to preparing the ground for a restoration of public services and a favorable agricultural and commercial environment. Key steps, it says, include the transfer of Sonangol's functions as regulator and government concessionaire to other agencies; the establishment of a government oil revenue management unit; and more rigorous reconciliation and analysis of tax payments and profitable oil allocations by international oil companies and Sonangol. In a similar vein, Endiama's regulatory and licensing functions could be separated from its commercial operations and diamond marketing liberalised further. While some controls on the marketing of diamonds have been eased, there is limited transparency concerning the supervision and taxation of the formal sector or of the granting of rights for diamond extraction.

Privatisation appears to have stalled and more fiscal stability would strengthen the private sector and improve the climate for private investment. Structural reform to improve competition is needed to develop the sector, which encompasses the great majority of the population. A World Bank report *The Cost of Doing Business* rated Angola as one of the least conducive business climates in the world.

World Bank

The World Bank already endorsed support for the dos Santos government's moves to enhance transparent governance and intensify capacity development, especially support for public sector reform and civil society empowerment. It looks to provide broad-based equitable growth, especially through improving the environment for the private sector. Five active projects have committed US$281 million: a Social Action Fund, an Emergency Demobilisation and Reintegration Programme, Technical Assistance, HIV/Aids, Malaria and Tuberculosis Control and an Emergency Multisector Recovery Programme. The NovoBanco Enterprise Bank of Angola has started disbursing loans to small businesses – US$5.5 million so far.

José Eduardo dos Santos, of the ruling Movimento Popular da Libertação de Angola (MPLA) (Movement for the Liberation of Angola), became president in 1979 after the death of Angola's first president and founder of the MPLA, Agostinho Neto. Born in 1942, he enlisted in the MPLA's guerrilla army at age 19. In the former Soviet Union he gained qualifications in petroleum engineering and radar telecommunications. He held ministerial posts before becoming president.

The MPLA and the rebel group União Nacional para a Independência Total de Angola (Unita) (Union for the Total Liberation of Angola) were bitter rivals even before the country gained independence from Portugal in 1975. The Soviet Union

KEY INDICATORS — Angola

	Unit	2000	2001	2002	2003	2004
Population	m	12.39	12.77	13.90	13.64	15.94
Gross domestic product (GDP)	US$bn	8.90	9.50	11.20	12.10	*20.11
GDP per capita	US$	715	743	858	901	1,305
GDP real growth	%	3.0	3.3	9.9	4.5	11.2
Inflation	%	325.0	152.6	108.9	115.0	43.6
Unemployment	%	–	–	50.0	*50.0	–
Oil output	'000 bpd	736.0	742.0	902.0	885.0	991.0
Exports (fob) (goods)	US$m	7,802.0	6,754.0	8,600.0	9,515.0	12,760.0
Imports (fob) (goods)	US$m	3,430.0	3,316.0	5,250.0	5,480.0	4,896.0
Balance of trade	US$m	4,372.0	3,438.0	3,350.0	4,035.0	7,864.0
Current account	US$m	79.0	-132.0	-31.0	-720.0	1,260.0
Total reserves minus gold	US$m	1,198.2	731.9	375.6	634.2	1,364.7
Foreign exchange	US$m	1,198.0	731.7	375.4	634.0	1,364.5
Exchange rate	per US$	10.04	22.06	45.19	68.85	82.38

* estimated figure

and Cuba supported the then-Marxist MPLA, while the US and white-ruled South Africa backed Unita as a bulwark against Soviet interests in Africa.

After 16 years of fighting during which 300,000 people were killed, a peace deal made it possible for elections to be held. But Unita rejected the outcome and resumed the war and hundreds of thousands more were killed. Another peace accord was signed in 1994, after which the UN sent in peacekeepers.

But the fighting steadily worsened and in 1999 the peacekeepers withdrew, leaving behind a country rich in natural resources but littered with landmines and the ruins of war. The connection between the civil war and the unregulated diamond trade – or 'blood diamonds' – was a source of international concern. The UN imposed a freeze on bank accounts holding funds from the trade which were being used to fund the war.

The death of Unita leader Jonas Savimbi in a gunfight with government forces in February 2002 raised the prospect of peace and the army and rebels signed a cease-fire two months later.

Elections are not due until 2007, 15 years after the first, and last, multi-party elections held in 1992.

Risk assessment

Economic	Improving
Political	Improving
Regional stability	Improving

COUNTRY PROFILE

Historical profile
Bantu speaking peoples, migrated to the area from west Africa in the thirteenth century, displacing the inhabitants the Khiosan people, and built several powerful kingdoms. The name Angola is thought to be derived from the Bantu word, of the Ndongo kingdom, for king, *ngola*.

Angola is a rich country; it is one of the world's largest producers of diamonds and has huge reserves of generally high quality crude oil. These riches will be the key to its development but has cause it immense suffering in the recent past. Angola's civil war was, for long a 'hot' front in the 'cold' war, with Cuban troops deployed against those of South Africa, each supporting opposing factions. When the cold war finally ceased, communism verses capitalism transformed into diamonds verses oil as the combatants of Angola had to turn to other sources to supply their war machine. Unita became the controller of up to 70 per cent of Angola's diamond production, with an illegal smuggling organisation that rivalled any legitimate operation. The MPLA led government turned to oil to fund its position with over US$900 million spent on the military hardware in the late 1990s.

The peace agreement of April 2002, signed following the death of rebel leader Jonas Savimbi in February, gave Angola a chance for economic recovery. After more than a quarter of a century of civil war, it will take a long time for a peace culture to replace the once prevailing war culture.

1482 The Portuguese arrived in Angola, which became a staging post for trade with India and south-east Asia.
1575 The Portuguese founded Luanda. The country became a major source of slaves, who were transported to Brazil.
1836 The slave trade was abolished.
1885 The borders of Angola were set following the Berlin Conference of imperial powers who, with an eye on exploitable assets in Africa, agreed to formal boundaries. Angola provided Portugal with minerals and agricultural products.
1951 Angola's status changed from a colony to an overseas territory.
1956 The Movimento Popular de Libertação de Angola (MPLA) (Popular Movement for the Liberation of Angola) was founded as a guerrilla force fighting against Portuguese rule.
1961 An uprising in which 50,000 Angolans were massacred led to increased repression by colonial security forces.
1962 The Frente Nacional para a Libertacao de Angola (FNLA) (National Front for the Liberation of Angola) was formed by refugees of the uprising, living mainly in what is now the Democratic Republic of Congo.
1966 The União Nacional de Independencia Total de Angola (Unita) (National Union for the Total Independence of Angola) was formed.
1972 The FNLA and MPLA assumed joint leadership of the liberation struggle.
1975 Angola gained independence from Portugal. Scheduled elections failed to take place when the MPLA took power. Unita and the FNLA formed an alliance aimed at defeating the MPLA government.
1979 José dos Santos (MPLA) became president, backed the Soviet Union and Cuba. A civil war ensued, with Unita, supported by the US and South Africa.
1988 An agreement between South Africa, Angola and Cuba was signed, all foreign troops to be withdrawn by mid-1991.
1990 A UN mission, to verify Cuban troop withdrawals, was initiated.
1991 The MPLA introduced multi-party democracy and officially dropped its commitment to Marxism in favour of social democracy. Talks with Unita began and Cuban troops withdrew.
1992 The first multi-party elections resulted in a coalition government formed by the MPLA, and minor parties. The newly-legalised Unita lost the ballot and rejected the election results, ending the UN-brokered cease-fire.
1994 A cease-fire peace agreement, the *Lusaka Protocol*, was signed between the government and Unita.
1997 Unita joined the ruling MPLA in a power-sharing government of national unity, however, it did not disarm.
1998 Renewed hostilities between MPLA and Unita broke out.
2002 Jonas Savimbi, the leader of Unita, was killed by government forces. The Angolan government offered an amnesty for all Unita rebels who surrendered. A cease-fire was signed, ending the civil war. Fernando da Piedade Dias dos Santos became prime minister.
2003 The World Bank approved a US$125 million assistance programme.
2004 More than 3,000 people were arrested in a crackdown on illegal diamond mining and trafficking (around 11,000 were deported in four months).
2005 An outbreak of the deadly Marburg disease infected 360 people, mainly in the northern province of Rige, and killed 325 people before finally burning itself out.

Political structure
Constitution
The Bicesse peace accords, signed in May 1991, led to the 1992 constitution. It recognises fundamental rights and duties, based on the principles of the major international treaties on human rights to which Angola is a signatory. It also established multi-party politics, enabling the first elections to be held in September 1992.
Form of state
Unitary republic
The executive
The president is the Head of State, elected by direct universal suffrage every five years.
Presidential elections have not been held since 1992.
National legislature
Unicameral legislature elected for a four-year term.
Legal system
The constitution defines the judiciary as an independent body that is nominated by the National Assembly on the decision of two-thirds of those casting their votes. The Judicial Proctorate is appointed for a four-year term of office and may be re-appointed for another four-year term.
Last elections
29/30 September 1992 (parliamentary and presidential).

Results: Parliamentary: the MPLA won 54 per cent of the votes.
Presidential: José Dos Santos received 49.6 per cent of the votes, making a run-off election necessary between him and second-place Jonas Savimbi; the run-off was not held and Savimbi's Unita disputed the results of the first election and led to a resumption of the civil war. Savimbi's death in 2002 resulted in a cease-fire and the end of the war.
Next elections
No date set

Political parties
Ruling party
Government of Unity and National Reconciliation (GURN); dominated by Movimento Popular de Libertação de Angola (MPLA) (Popular Movement for the Liberation of Angola)
Main opposition party
União Nacional de Independencia Total de Angola (Unita) (National Union for the Total Independence of Angola)

Population
15.94 million (2004)
Ethnic make-up
37 per cent Ovimbundu, 25 per cent Mbundu, 13 per cent Bakongo, 2 per cent Mestico (mixed European and indigenous descent), 1 per cent European.
Religions
Traditional beliefs (47 per cent), Christianity (38 per cent), mainly Roman Catholic.

Education
Primary school enrolment has increased slowly, although the increase in male enrolment has been higher than for females. Education expenditure amounts to round 6 per cent of the national budget.
The government allocated US$40 million to hire the graduates of a Unesco scheme, which is set to train around 29,000 school teachers as part of a development programme.
Total expenditure on education is around 3 per cent of GDP.
Literacy rate: 66.8 per cent total; 53.8 per cent female; adult rates.
Compulsory years: 6 to 9
Enrolment rate: 74 per cent gross primary enrolment of relevant age group (including repeater) (World Bank)
Pupils per teacher: 29 in primary schools

Health
Total spending on health, is around 2 per cent of GDP. Fifty per cent of the population has access to clean water and 40 per cent are undernourished, according to World Bank statistics.
Public health has become a priority as Angola's human development indicators are poor, it is recognised to having a high rate of infant mortality and has to repair the damage done by 27 years of civil war. One in four children under aged five are likely to die of malaria, the single largest cause of child mortality.
Until the country can exploit its vast natural resources and raise the living standards of the population as a whole, it has to contend with inadequate numbers of doctors and antiquated medical equipment. Preventative care has been described as almost non-existent and primary care, outside former provincial capitals, limited to infrequent and inadequate drug supplies.
Most doctors, who work within the private sector, live in the capital, Luanda. The government has prepared a large package of incentives to encourage health workers to work in the provinces, however most measures are awaiting the financial resources to implement them.

HIV/Aids
While the civil war wrought great destruction on the population, paradoxically it provided a buffer that stopped the disease from gaining a significant hold, as people were prevented from travelling. Now the citizens of Angola are free to travel and with a youthful population the government has taken measures to educate young people concerning the risks of HIV infection. A Unicef study presented in 2003 showed that almost 60 per cent of youths are sexually experienced by aged 15 years, and almost all by aged 18. A third of women had never heard of HIV/Aids and over half did not know that transmission could happen from mother to child.
In October 2005 there had been 17,620 cases of HIV/Aids reported. While prevalence rates for countries in the region range between 25–40 per cent and the rate in Angola is only 3.9 per cent, UN agencies are still concerned the following years could determine whether Angola is engulfed by the pandemic, particularly if education and basic health provisions remain lacking.
HIV prevalence: 3.9 per cent aged 15-49 in 2003 (World Bank)
Life expectancy: 46.7 years (World Bank)
Fertility rate/Maternal mortality rate: 6.8 births per woman; 1,700 maternal deaths per 100,000 live births (World Bank).
Infant mortality rate: 154 per 1,000 live births (2004); 42 per cent of all children are underweight for their age (World Bank).

Welfare
In 2005 plans to return 22,000 refugees living in Zambia got underway, however by November only 35,000 were able to make the return and the programme was extended into early 2006. The numbers of internally displaced persons (IDPs) total over 100,000 and are unable to return home due to poor access and mine infestation and lack of administrative capacity with basic services virtually non-existent. Mine clearance is ongoing as one in every 415 Angolans has been disabled by landmines, but it is estimated in 2005 that six million more remain to be destroyed.

Main cities
Luanda (capital, estimated population 2.4 million in 2004), Huambo (171,000), Lobito (136,000), Benguela (132,900), Lubango (75,000), Malanje (70,400).

Languages spoken
Local languages: principally Ovimbundu, Kimbundu (the language of the Mbundu), Bakongo and Chokwe.
Official language/s
Portuguese

Media
Press
Angola's only national daily newspaper is *O Jornal de Angola (JA)*. *Diário da República* (government news sheet) is published daily. Regional newspapers are published in several towns. *El Moujahid* is also circulated here. A few periodicals are also available. *Correio da Semana* is the Sunday newspaper.
Broadcasting
Radio: National radio service with broadcasts in Portuguese, English, French, Spanish and vernacular languages, operated by the state-owned Radio Nacional de Angola.
Television: Limited TV service operated by Televisão Popular de Angola (TPA). There are only 0.6 television sets per 100 inhabitants.

Economy
Angola remains one of the poorest countries in the world with one of the lowest GDP per capita rates. Although the nation has vast natural resources, around three-quarters of the population live on less than US$1 per day. GDP growth was strong in 2004 at 11.2 per cent, with inflation high at over 43.6 which, nevertheless, was a fall from the 115 per cent in 2003. These positive growth rates are attributable to a regional oil boom, although this has not yet filtered through to improve social indicators.
The Angolan economy is highly dependent on its offshore oil sector. Much of the population relies on farming, despite the poor level of productivity and high insecurity in the agricultural sector. The daily production of oil in 2004 was 991 million barrels per day. World oil prices are at a premium and Angola is currently receiving an unexpected windfall and should have the necessary funds to repay or service much of its foreign debt. In 2003/04

Angola

gross external borrowing of US$3.4 billion in oil-backed loans was incurred by the public sector and by June 2004 Angola's external debt was estimated at US$9.5 billion (or 49 per cent of GDP).

While Angola has the resources to sustain its debts the IMF has warned the government that governance and fiscal transparency is vital. Structural reforms in the economy are underway but the IMF maintains that the state still has to reduce the level of its influence in non-oil sectors and sustain macroeconomic management. Almost 30 years of civil war has left a legacy of damage and destruction in both human and infrastructure terms. Widespread poverty and low human development indicators, coupled with the rebuilding of the country and state institutions will take many years, Angola has the potential to provide a good level of income for its entire population. To do this though it must master an economy, open to corrupt practices, marshal its wealth and natural resources, invest wisely and develop an economy that is not wholly dependent on primary industries.

External trade

Angola has been a member of the WTO since November 1996. Main export partners are the US, China, Taiwan and France with exports consisting of oil, oil related products, natural gas and diamonds. Exports were US$12.76 billion in 2004; there is a significant surplus in the balance of trade. This is mainly used to finance government spending.

Imports

Principal imports are oil and electrical equipment, vehicles and spare parts, machinery, foodstuffs, medicines, textiles, consumer goods and military goods. Total imports in 2004 were US$4.86 billion.

Main sources: Portugal (1.8 per cent total 2004), US (13.1), South Africa (10.7 per cent), Japan (6.9 per cent), France (6.3 per cent), Brazil (5.6 per cent), UK (4.9 per cent), China (4.5 per cent)

Exports

Principal exports are crude oil, gas and derivatives (typically 92 per cent of total), diamonds (8 per cent), marble, coffee, sisal, fish and fish products, timber and cotton. Total iexports in 2004 were US$12.76 billion.

Main destinations: US (39.8 per cent total 2004 total), China (30.3 per cent), Taiwan (8.1 per cent), France (7.1 per cent)

Agriculture

Farming

Agriculture's share of GDP has slowly begun to rise as production has increased, as more displaced persons and ex-combatants have returned to their farms. Production was still severely hampered by a list of problems in 2005, including lack of seed and animals, as well as fertilisers, equipment and vehicles, landmines, lack of infrastructure, reduced capabilities of institutions and little access to investment. International donors and financial institutions have provided relief funds and personnel to improve the situation.

Even so, food insecurity is widespread and around 50 per cent of the population is undernourished.

Of the major crops, only coffee is produced in exportable volumes, while the cultivation of sisal and cotton has virtually ceased. Several overseas companies are reportedly interested in rehabilitating sugar cane, cotton and sisal estates. Livestock farming has been disrupted by insecurity, the neglect of veterinary services and recurrent droughts have affected much of the south and centre of Angola. Crop production in 2004 included: 5,600,000 tonnes (t) cassava, , 626,000t cereals in total, 510,000t maize, 430,000t sweet potatoes, 360,000t sugar cane, 300,000t bananas, 280,000t oil palm fruit, 96,000t millet, 78,000t citrus fruit, 40,000t pineapples, 16,000t rice, 66,000t pulses, 30,000t groundnuts, 82,127t oilcrops, 27,000t potatoes, 1,250t green coffee, 1,300t tobacco leaves, 450,000t fruit in total, 271,000t vegetables in total. Livestock production included: 138,610t meat in total, 85,000t beef, 27,885t pig meat, 10,485t lamb and goat meat, 7,740t poultry, 4,300t eggs, 195,000t milk, 23,000t honey, 10,956t cattle hides.

Fishing

The fishing sector represents less than 5 per cent of GDP. Government policy is aimed at increasing the amount of foreign fishing operations in territorial waters in order to increase foreign investment in the sector and increase licence revenue. Angola's 1,600km coastline offers some of the richest fishing grounds in Africa, with the annual catch averaging 450,000 tonnes per year before independence. Production has shown a turnaround with an estimate of over 200,000 tonnes, largely due to increased government support for the sector.

Forestry

Angola has around 18 per cent forest cover with an additional 43 per cent of other wooded land. Most forests are semi-deciduous and located in the north of the country. There are a large number of mangrove forests around Luanda, and in the south and west the forests give way to savannah forest. Around 6.6 per cent of the country's forests are protected, although Angola is the only African country which has not produced a forest law to bring forestry regulation up-to-date.

Angola has considerable timber resources. Valuable tree species, including rosewood, ebony, African sandalwood and mahogany, most of which can be found in the northern tropical forests that have not been commercially exploited since independence. Angola lost around 128,000 hectare of forest cover per year between 1990–2000, which is a modest 0.18 per cent per annum compared to the world average of 0.24 per cent and the African average of 0.78 per cent. In terms of wood products, Angola produces relatively small amounts of sawnwood, pulp and plywood panels. Most industrial roundwood is used for posts, poles and agricultural purposes. Averages annual charcoal production is under 240,000 tonnes and woodfuel just under 3.5 million cubic metres.

Timber imports in 2004 amounted to US$8.1 million while exports amounted to US$1 million.

Production in 2004 included: 4,582,673 cubic metres (cum) roundwood, 1,095,900cum industrial roundwood, 5,000cum sawnwood, 45,900cum sawlogs and veneers, 11,000cum wood-based panels, 3,486,773cum wood fuel, 237,678t charcoal.

Industry and manufacturing

Industrial production is centred on food processing, brewing, sugar, textiles and tobacco products. Also important are light manufactures, such as electrical goods (eg radio production), construction materials, steel production, motor vehicles, detergents, bicycles and chemicals. Manufacturing accounts for just 4 per cent of GDP.

Activity is concentrated in Luanda, Lobito and Huambo. Output is often sluggish due to shortages of foreign exchange, poor management and a low-paid labour force.

About 60 per cent of total production is accounted for by nationalised industries. The government has embarked upon a privatisation programme involving some 200 state-owned enterprises in a variety of industrial sectors. In early 2003, it passed laws to liberalise the sector and open it up to foreign investment.

The diamond industry has received a vital boom to the industry after De Beers agreed to a joint mining venture with Endiama. Angola is seeking to become one of the top three diamond producers in the world, increasing production to six million carrats between 2003–06.

Tourism

Much work still needs to be done to repair the war-damaged infrastructure, but visitor numbers continue to increase. The Ministry of Hotels and Tourism is attempting to attract foreign capital investment to rebuild the tourism sector. Hotels are in short supply and those that exist have a 99 per cent occupancy rate. The ministry estimates that 50 per cent of the hospitality sector's infrastructure needs renovating and coupled with the poor roads and internal air transport the sector has much to do but also much to gain. Travel and tourism demands are expected to grow by 13.5 per cent in 2005 and a steady 6.9 per cent between 2006–15. The sector contributes around 3 per cent of GDP but has the potential to rise sharply as more facilities become available.

Angola is in partnership with five of its southern African neighbours to establish a huge cross-border eco-tourism, game reserve and tourist resort. Angola has 13 national parks and reserves and has been underdeveloped since the 1960s so that once areas are designated free from landmines, tourism can expand into virtually untamed territories.

Mining

Before independence, Angola was a major producer of iron ore, gold and copper. However, the major disruptions to the country's infrastructure and economy throughout the war have meant that the country's considerable base metal and gold resources have been barely exploited.

Diamonds (mostly of gemstone quality) were the country's second-largest foreign exchange earner in 2004. Endiama is the state-owned diamond mining company dealing with all aspects of diamond exploitation.

Before the ban on Angolan 'conflict' diamonds in 2000, Angola was the fourth-largest diamond producer in the world, producing some US$600 million of rough diamonds per year. By 2003 US$1 billion rough diamonds were sold through the official trading company Sodiam, however the true figure can only be estimated as illegal mining and smuggling from the former Unita-held territories is still a major problem. Without punitive measures to deter this lucrative trade, the revenue from diamonds cannot be fully measured or used.

The government is introducing a register and to licence the many artisan prospectors and control the wholesale price of diamonds, and to establish an export certification scheme to identify legitimate production and sales.

Angola also has deposits of phosphates (Cabinda site, estimated 100 million tonnes; Kindonakasi, estimated 50 million tonnes), gold (at Cassinga and Lombige), copper, lead and zinc (in Tetelo and Alto Zambeze). There are deposits of marble and black granite in southern Angola. The production of ornamental stones was predominantly of black granite which was exported mainly to Spain and Portugal. Angostone Construction and Ornamental Rocks Ltd mines red granite from mines in Cunene province. With an initial investment of US$1.5 million, Angostone is producing 150 cubic metres of red granite per month.

Hydrocarbons

Angola's economic performance is largely determined by the level of oil production which accounts for 51.7 per cent of GNP and 92 per cent of exports and provides 90 per cent of government revenues. Production in 2004 was 991,000 barrels per day (bpd), with proven oil reserves of 8.8 million barrels.

In late 2005 both BP and ChevronTexaco, and the state-owned oil company, Sonangol, announced further oil discoveries in Angola's offshore fields. Added to the new discoveries of the Girassol oil field the level of reserves have substantially increased. Production is expected to peak at 1.8 million bpd by 2008. The planned construction of a new refinery in Benguela will open new opportunities to increase production. International interest in Angolan oil and investment in offshore exploration will further raise potential production.

Proven gas reserves stood at 79.57 billion cubic metres (cum) in 2004, but undiscovered reserves could exceed 700 billion cum. In 2005, Sonangol with Chevron and other partners, began the construction of a liquefied natural gas (LNG) plant, at Soyo, with an initial production capacity of five million tonnes of LNG. Until this plant is in production around 85 per cent of all natural gas production is flared.

Angola does not produce or import coal.

Energy

The state-owned Empresa Nacional de Electricidade (ENE) is responsible for the generation and supply of electricity in Angola. The country's total electricity generating capacity is estimated at 596MW. Half of this is provided by thermal generation and half through hydroelectric dams. Only 15 per cent of the population has access to electricity. Much of the country's electricity generation and transmission infrastructure was damaged during the civil war. The government estimates it will need US$500 million to recover electricity capacity. Around US$200 million has already been allocated to Angola's six dams, only three of which are working. Rehabilitation of the Matala and Cambambe dams was completed in 2002. Electricity production was also scheduled to begin at the Capanda dam on the Kwanza river in October 2005. The project's second phase, to install two new turbines will be completed in 2007. The first phase will produce 130MW and the second phase 520MW.

Angola has the potential to become a net exporter hydroelectricity.

Banking and insurance

The central bank is the Banco Nacional de Angola (BNA) (National Bank of Angola). It issues, and is responsible for, all foreign exchange transactions in conjunction with the ministries of planning, commerce and finance. The banking sector has long been undercapitalised and economically inept. However, the sector has seen some foreign interest, with Portuguese banks such as Banco Fomento Exterior and Banco Totta e Azores opening branches in Luanda.

In 2005 the Banco de Poupança e Crédito (Bank for Savings and Credit) and World Vision International, began a programme of micro-credit, by offering 1,900 families at least US$200 and 79 small farmers associations up to US$10,000 for agricultural purposes.

Central bank
Banco Nacional de Angola (BNA) started functioning in late-1996 as the central bank, ceasing its commercial activities, as part of the government's financial reforms.

Main financial centre
Luanda

Time
GMT plus one hour

Geography
Angola lies on the west coast of Africa, bordered by the Democratic Republic of Congo (DRC) to the north, Zambia to the east and Namibia to the south. The Cabinda district is separated from the rest of the country by the estuary of the River Congo and DRC, with the Republic of Congo lying to its north.

Climate
In Luanda and northern regions, October–April is hot and humid with usual temperature ranging from 28–32 degrees Celsius (C) with a maximum of 34 degrees C. April–September is hot but less humid with daytime temperatures ranging from 25–30 degrees C and cool evenings. Southern regions are more temperate and rainfall can be frequent and heavy, particularly in April.

Dress codes
Informal dress is suitable for most occasions. Lightweight suits are recommended for business meetings. Visitors to the central and southern plateaux will need warm clothes at night, as will visitors to the coastal region during May to September.

Angola

Entry requirements
Passports
Required by all. Passport must be valid for three months.
Visa
Required by all (except transit passengers remaining within the airport).
A business visitor requires sponsorship from a local Angolan company or state entity. Visas can be obtained in Luanda via the inviting company or government agency. An exit permit, provided by the same office that issued the visa, is also required.
Currency advice/regulations
There are no restrictions on the amount of money that can be taken in and out of the country. However, visitors are required to declare all their foreign currency to the Banco Nacional de Angola (BNA) within 24 hours of entering the country. All foreign exchange transactions must be arranged through the BNA.
Customs
No goods can be imported without the prior permission of the government. This permission is subject to various conditions.

Health (for visitors)
Mandatory precautions
Yellow fever vaccination certificate is required if travelling from an infected area.
Advisable precautions
Yellow fever, hepatitis A, typhoid, tetanus and polio vaccinations are recommended. Malaria prophylaxis is essential. There is a rabies risk.
Water precautions must be taken.
Travel insurance, including emergency medical evacuation, is strongly recommended. All medication, with prescriptions, should be carried by travellers.

Hotels
Accommodation shortages in the capital have intensified in the post-war atmosphere but a programme of hotel privatisation may help relieve the problem. Bookings must be made one month in advance and on official requisition to Anghotel. Bookings cannot be made by airline companies or at airport.

Credit cards
American Express accepted at Presidente and Tivoli hotels. Generally, credit cards are not accepted.

Public holidays
Fixed dates
1 Jan (New Year's Day), 4 Jan (Martyrs of the Colonial Repression Day), 4 Feb (Anniversary of Start of Independence War), 8 Mar (Women's Day), 4 Apr (Peace and Reconciliation Day), 1 May (May Day), 25 May (Africa Day), 1 Jun (International Children's Day), 1 Aug (Armed Forces Day), 17 Sep (National Heroes' Day), 2 Nov (All Souls' Day), 11 Nov (Independence Day), 25 Dec (Christmas Day).
Variable dates
Mardi Gras, Good Friday.

Working hours
Banking
Mon–Fri: 0800–1100, 1400–1500.
Business
0830–1230, 1430–1800. (Exceptions: Sat 0830–1230, Sun closed.)
Government
Mon–Fri: 0730–1230, 1430–1830.

Telecommunications
Telephone/fax
There are satellite links with Lisbon. International calls should be booked through the operator at least six hours in advance. Operator services: 155.

Electricity supply
220V AC, 50 cycles.

Social customs/useful tips
Travel permits may be required for travel outside Luanda province. Visitors are advised to carry spare passport photographs. Visitors should not attempt to photograph any public building, infrastructure or security forces.

Security
Travellers are advised against airport arrivals after dark. Use only the regulated taxi service at the airport and in Luanda. Travel by car in many parts of Luanda is relatively safe by day, but doors should be locked, windows closed and packages stored out of sight.
Although the civil war has ended, there is the possibility of banditry and danger from the extensive use of landmines during the war. Frequent checkpoints and poor infrastructure contribute to unsafe travel on roads outside the city. Police and military personnel are heavily armed and can be unpredictable; their authority should not be challenged. No travel should be undertaken on roads outside the city after nightfall.
Visitors should carry identity documents at all times.
Throughout Angola, taking photographs of anything that could be perceived as being of military or security interest, including government buildings, may result in problems with authorities and should therefore be avoided.

Getting there
Air
National airline: TAAG (Linhas Aéreas de Angola).
International airport/s: Luanda-4 de Fevereiro (Code: LAD), 4km from city, restaurant. No taxis, public telephones or banking services.
Airport tax: None

Surface
Road: Road travel is not generally practicable though access is now possible across the Namibian frontier to the south. Some 3,000 bridges were damaged during the war though a reconstruction programme has commenced.
Rail: Rail travel to Angola is difficult due to regional conflict and war damage which has destroyed railways and bridges.
Water: Angola has several ports along its Atlantic seaboard with the possibility of passenger traffic from other coastal African countries.
Main port/s: Cabinda, Lobito, Luanda, Namibe. Lobito and Luanda are being repaired.

Getting about
National transport
Air: Most of the country is only accessible by air. TAAG operates domestic flights connecting to main centres but these can be unreliable. There are separate helicopter services to the Cabinda enclave and some commercial companies, connected to the oil and diamond industries, who operate jet aircraft, may carry passengers. All passengers must carry authorisation to travel (guia de marcha), and business travellers should alert their embassy or representative of their travel plans.
Road: The 7,500km network of well made, major roads is still in relatively good condition and traffic is now free to travel at will along the main roads between provincial capitals. Identity papers should be carried.
Buses: There are buses throughout the country but the service is poor and the buses are generally very crowded.
Taxis: Are difficult to find and are expensive. If you arrive at the airport you will need to arrange to have someone meet you or use a transport service provided by one of the hotels.
Rail: The railway system is under repair, following the damage caused during the civil war. There are irregular passenger services on three routes from Luanda-Malanje, and Lobito-Dilolo, and Namibe-Menongue. Refreshments are available but no sleeping accommodation or air-conditioning is provided.
City transport
Taxis: Restricted service operated by state company. No service operated from airport to Luanda.
Buses, trams & metro: Local buses run

BUSINESS DIRECTORY

The addresses listed below are a selection only. While World of Information makes every endeavour to check these addresses, we cannot guarantee that changes have not been made, especially

to telephone numbers and area codes. We would welcome any corrections.

Telephone area codes
Telephone direct dialling code for Angola is +244 followed by area code (in the case of Luanda only) and subscriber's number.
Luanda   2

Chambers of Commerce
Angolan Chamber of Commerce and Industry, 14 Largo do Kinaxixi, PO Box 92, Luanda (tel: 344-506; fax: 344-629; e-mail: ccira@ebonet.net).

Banking
Banco de Comercio e Industria, 86 Avenida 4 de Fevereiro, Luanda (tel: 333-684; fax: 333-823; e-mail: secretariado@bci.ebonet.net).

Banco Comercial Angolano, 83A Avenida Comandante Valódia, PO Box 6900, Luanda (tel: 449-517; fax: 449-516; e-mail: bca@snet.co.ao).

Banco Africano de Investimentos, 34 Rua Major Kanhangulo, Luanda (tel: 337-369; fax: 335-486).

Banco de Poupança e Crédito, PO Box 1343, Luanda (tel: 233-9158).

Central bank
Banco Nacional de Angola, 151 Avenida 4 de Fevereiro, PO Box 1243, Luanda (tel: 332-633; fax: 390-579; e-mail: sec.gvb@bna.ao).

Travel information
Direcção de Emigração e Fronteiras de Angola (visa queries), Defa, Luanda (tel: 330-314, 330-019).

TAAG-Angola Airlines (Linhas Aéreas de Angola), Rua da Missão 123, CP 179, Luanda (tel: 332-485; fax: 393-548).

Ministry of tourism
Ministerio do Comercio e Turismo (Ministry of Commerce and Tourism), Largo 4 de Fevereiro 3, Luanda (tel: 338-741).

Ministries
Ministry of Agriculture and Rural Development, 2 Avenida Comandante Gika, CP 527 Luanda (tel: 322-694; fax: 323-217).

Ministry of Defence, Rua 17 de Setembro, Luanda (tel: 337-530; fax: 392-635).

Ministry of Education and Culture, Avenida Comandante Gika, CP 1281 Luanda (tel: 322-797; fax: 321-592).

Ministry of Energy and Water, 105 Avenida 4 de Fevereiro, CP 2229 Luanda (tel: 393-681; fax: 393-687).

Ministry of Ex-Servicemen and War Veterans, 2 Avenida Comandante Gika, CP 5466 Luanda (tel: 321-117; fax: 323-561).

Ministry of Family and Women's Advancement, Edifício Palácio de Vidro, Largo 4 de Fevereiro, 1242 Luanda (tel: 338-745; fax: 330-028).

Ministry of Finance, 127 Avenida 4 de Fevereiro, CP 592 Luanda (tel: 332-122; fax: 332-069).

Ministry of Fisheries and Environment, Edifício Atlantico, Avenida 4 de Fevereiro, CP 83 Luanda (tel: 390-690; fax: 333-814).

Ministry of Foreign Affairs, 8 Avenida Comandante Gika, CP 1500 Luanda (tel: 323-250; fax: 393-246).

Ministry of Geology and Mines, Avenida Comandante Gika, CP 1260 Luanda (tel: 326-724; fax: 321-655).

Ministry of Health, Rua 17 de Setembro, CP 1201 Luanda (tel: 322-797; fax: 321-592).

Ministry of Hotels and Tourism, Edifício Palácio de Vidro, Largo 4 de Fevereiro, CP 1242 Luanda (tel: 331-323; fax: 338-211).

Ministry of Industry, 25 Rua Cerqueira Lukoki, CP 594 Luanda (tel: 397-070; fax: 334-700).

Ministry of Information, 1 Avenida Comandante Valódia, CP 2608 Luanda (tel: 342-818; fax: 343-495).

Ministry of the Interior, 204 Avenida 4 de Fevereiro, CP 2723 Luanda (tel: 391-049; fax: 395-133).

Ministry of Justice, Rua 17 de Setembro, CP 2250 Luanda (tel: 330-327).

Ministry of Petroleum, Avenida 4 de Fevereiro, CP 1279 Luanda (tel: 337-440; fax: 372-373).

Ministry of Planning, Largo 17 de Setembro, Luanda (tel: 390-722; fax: 339-586).

Ministry of Posts and Telecommunications, 42 Avenida 4 de Fevereiro, CP 1459 Luanda (tel: 337-799; fax: 330-776).

Ministry of Public Administration, Employment and Social Security, 32 Rua 17 de Setembro, CP 1986 Luanda (tel: 338-654).

Ministry of Public Works and Town Planning, Rua Ed Mutamba, CP 1061 Luanda (tel: 336-717; fax: 333-814).

Ministry of Science and Technology, 25 Rua Cerqueira Lukoki, CP 1288 Luanda (tel: 338-987).

Ministry of Social Assistance and Reintegration, 117 Avenida dos Massacres, CP 102 Luanda (tel: 340-370; fax: 342-988).

Ministry of Territorial Administration, 8 Avenida Comandante Gika, Luanda (tel: 320-638; fax: 323-238).

Ministry of Trade, Edifício Palácio de Vidro, Largo 4 de Fevereiro, CP 1242 Luanda (tel: 338-737; fax: 370-804).

Ministry of Transport, 42 Avenida 4 de Fevereiro, Luanda (tel: 337-744; fax: 337-687).

Ministry of Youth and Sports, Avenida Comandante Gika, CP 5466 Luanda (tel: 321-117; fax: 323-561).

Other useful addresses
Angolan Embassy (USA), 2100 16th Street, NW, Washington DC 20009 (202-785-1156; fax: 202-785-1258; e-mail: angola@angola.org).

ANGOP (news agency), CP 2181, Luanda (tel: 334-945).

Associação Comercial de Luanda, CP 1275, Edificio Palácio de Comércio, 1e Andar, Luanda (tel: 322-453).

DHL International Ltd, Avenida Che Guevara 52–52a, CP 1545 (tel: 390-326, 390-376, 392-082).

Direcção dos Serviços de Comércio, CP 1337, Largo Diogo Cão, Luanda.

Direcção dos Serviços de Estatistica (statistical agency), CP 1215, Luanda.

Direcção da Aviacao Civil (National Civil Aviation Directorate), Rua Frederich Engels, 92-6 andar, CP 569, Luanda (tel: 339-412, 338-196, 338-596).

Direcção dos Caminhos de Ferro (National Railways Directorate), Rua Major Kanhangulo, CP 1250, Luanda (tel: 370-061).

Direcção Nacional de Correios e Telecomunicacoes (National Posts and Telecommunications Directorate), Rua Frederick Engels, CP 1459, Luanda (tel: 339-750).

Direcção Nacional da Marinha Mercante e Portos (National Merchant Navy and Ports Directorate), Rua Rainha Ginga, 74-4 andar, Luanda (tel: 332-032, 339-847, 339-848).

Direcção Nacional dos Transportes Rodoviarios (National Road Transport Directorate), Rua Rainha Ginga, 74-1 andar, Luanda (tel: 339-390).

Empresa Nacional de Construcão de Obrtas Industrials (National construction Company for Industrial Projects), Bairro do Cazenga, 5 Avenida Zona Industrial, CP 18612, Luanda (tel: 390-087, 391-478).

Empresa Nacional de Diamantes de Angola (Endiama-Angolan Diamond Company), Avenida Rainha Ginga, 73-3 andar, CP 1247, Luanda (tel: 393-336).

Empresa Nacional de Electricidada (ENE - National Electricity Company), Edeficio de Geologia e Minas 7, CP 772, Luanda

Angola

(tel: 323-382, 337-498, 323-568, 321-498, 321-499).

Importang (state import agency), Calçada do Município 10, CP 1003, Luanda (tel: 392-787).

Institute Foreign Investment, Rue Serqueira Lukoki 25 (tel: 334-700).

Instituto Nacional do Cafe de Angola (INCA – National Coffee Institute of Angola), Rua Dr Alves Maciel 17-1D, Luanda (tel: 370-386).

Instituto Nacional de Estradas de Angola (National Roads Institute), Rua Amilcar Cabral 35-4, Caixa Postal 5667, Luanda (tel: 332-828, 391-536; fax: 335-754).

Radio Nacional de Angola, CP 1389, Luanda.

Sociedade Nacional de Combustiveis (SONANGOL-Angola National Fuels Company), Rua I Congresso do MPLA, Caixa Postal 1316, Luanda (tel: 334-143/9; fax: 333-542/6, 391-782).

Televisão Popular de Angola (TPA), CP 2002, Luanda.

US Embassy, 32 Rua Houari Boumedienne, Luanda (tel: 445-481; fax: 446-924).

Internet sites

Africa Business Network: http://www.ifc.org/abn

AllAfrica.com: http://www.allafrica.com

African Development Bank: http://www.afdb.org

Africa Online: http://www.africaonline.com

Angola News: http://www.ourworld.compuserve.com/homepages/anginfolon/

Information on Angola including government, business and economics: http://www.angola.org/

Jornal de Angola (JA): http://www.ebonet.net/jornaldeangola

Anguilla

KEY FACTS

Official name: Anguilla

Head of State: Queen Elizabeth II; represented by Governor Alan E Huckle (from 28 May 2004)

Head of government: Chief Minister Osbourne Fleming (ANA) (since Mar 2000)

Ruling party: Anguilla United Front (AUF) alliance, comprising the Anguilla National Alliance (ANA) and the Anguilla Democratic Party (ADP) (since 2000; re-elected 21 Feb 2005)

Area: 96 square km (Anguilla 91 square km, Sombrero 5 square km)

Population: 12,600 (2004)

Capital: The Valley

Official language: English

Currency: East Caribbean dollar (EC$) = 100 cents

Exchange rate: EC$2.70 per US$ (fixed rate)

GDP per capita: US$8,600 (2003)

GDP real growth: 4.50% (2003)

Unemployment: 6.70% (2003)

Inflation: 7.00% (2003)

Balance of trade: -US$78.30 million (2003)

Foreign debt: US$11.00 million (2004)

Visitor numbers: 53,987 (2004)

COUNTRY PROFILE

Historical profile
Anguilla was originally settled about 1,500BC by Arawak Indians, who called it Malliouhana, and later by Carib Indians.
1650 The British established a colony on Anguilla.
1745 and 1796 Anguilla repelled attacks by France.
1882 Anguilla became part of a larger colony governed from St Kitts.
1967 St Kitts-Nevis-Anguilla became a state, in association with the UK. (The status of an associated state allowed St Kitts-Nevis-Anguilla to become independent internally while the British government retained responsibility for external affairs and defence).
1969 The Anguillians rebelled and British security forces were sent to Anguilla to install a British commissioner.
1971 The Anguilla Act was passed by the British parliament. A major provision of the Anguilla Act stated that, should St Kitts-Nevis-Anguilla initiate legislative steps to terminate the status of association, Anguilla could be separated formally from the other islands.
1980 Anguilla separated from St Kitts-Nevis and became a British Dependent Territory in December.
1982 A new constitution gave Anguilla greater control over its internal affairs.
1994 The Anguilla United Party (AUP) was elected and its leader, Hubert Hughes, became chief minister.
1999 Hubert Hughes was re-elected, but lost his majority when Victor Banks, leader of his coalition partner, the Anguilla Democratic Party (ADP), resigned.
2000 Hughes called a general election – four years early – in order to break the constitutional deadlock. Hughes and the ANP lost the election, which was won by the Anguilla United Front (AUF), comprising the Anguilla National Alliance (ANA) and the Anguilla Democratic Party (ADP); Osbourne Fleming (ANA) was appointed chief minister.
2005 The AUF was re-elected in the 21 February parliamentary elections.

Political structure
Constitution
The 1982 constitution gave Anguilla greater control over its internal affairs.
Form of state
British Caribbean dependency
The executive
Executive power rests with an appointed British governor, assisted by an executive council (chief minister, two ex-officio members and not more than three other ministers).
The governor, appointed by the British monarch, is responsible for defence and external affairs, but is required to consult the chief minister on matters relating to internal security, the police and civil service.
National legislature
The House of Assembly has seven elected members, for five-year terms, two nominated members and two ex-officio members.
Legal system
The legal system is based on English common law. Anguilla is a member of the Eastern Caribbean Supreme Court, which is responsible for the high court and court of appeals. Final appeal rests with the Privy Council in the UK.
Last elections
21 February 2005 (parliamentary)
Results: Parliamentary: the governing Anguilla United Front (AUF), comprising the ANA and the ADP, won 39 per cent of the vote (four seats out of seven), the ANSA 20 per cent (two) and the AUM 20 per cent (one). Turnout was 74.6 per cent.
Next elections
2010 (parliamentary)

Political parties
Ruling party
Anguilla United Front (AUF) alliance, comprising the Anguilla National Alliance (ANA) and the Anguilla Democratic Party (ADP) (since 2000; re-elected 21 Feb 2005)
Political situation
The general election on 21 February 2005 did not result in any major upset on the day. Six of the seven incumbent elected representatives were returned, the exception being the replacement for a retired member. The Anguilla United Front, headed by Osbourne Fleming, chief minister since 2000, won a majority of four seats and formed the new government on 22 February. Of the other three seats, two went to the Anguilla National Strategic Alliance (ANSA) and one to the Anguilla United Movement. Interest was added to the proceedings when Albert Hughes, one of the ANSA winners, placing country above party, as he claimed, defected from ANSA and joined the government, where he was found a position as parliamentary secretary. ANSA was left with a single representative.

Population
12,600 (2004)

Anguilla

Ethnic make-up
Mainly of African descent; some of Irish descent.

Religions
Anglican (40 per cent), Methodist (33 per cent), Seventh-Day Adventist (7 per cent), Baptist (5 per cent), Roman Catholic (3 per cent).

Health
Life expectancy: 77 years: male 74 years; female 80 years (2003).
Fertility rate/Maternal mortality rate: Two births per woman (2003).
Birth rate/Death rate: 15 births per 1,000 population; five deaths per 1,000 population (2003).
Infant mortality rate: 23 per 1,000 live births (2003)

Main cities
The Valley (capital, estimated population 830 in 2003), Sandy Ground (1,500).

Languages spoken
Official language/s
English

Media
Press
Dailies: *Chronicle* and *The Daily Herald* are published in St Martin cover Anguillan news.
Weeklies: The island has a weekly newspaper *The Anguillian*.
Business: *CEG Anguilla Newsletter* highlights developments in the international financial services sector and in Anguilla.
Periodicals: *What We Do in Anguilla* is a local monthly tourism paper. *Anguilla Life* is a quarterly magazine. *The Anguilla Guide* also carries news of the tourism industry.
Broadcasting
Radio: There are four radio stations. The government-owned Radio Anguilla transmits over 14hrs/day and the private Caribbean Beacon Radio transmits for 24hrs.
Television: ABC Channel 2 (Anguilla Broadcasting Corporation). A private cable 12-channel/24-hrs TV service is also in operation, using US satellite programming.

Economy
There are very few natural resources in Anguilla, which has come to rely on financial services, tourism, export of lobsters, emigrants' remittances, grants-in-aid from the UK and EU, customs duties, bank licence fees and the sale of stamps. The UK, Canada, EU and the Caribbean Development Bank (CDB) are the leading sources of development aid. Anguilla is entirely reliant on imports of fuel and food.
In 2002 the banking sector was removed from an international list of countries obstructing the fight against money laundering. A zero-tax jurisdiction with no income, corporate or inheritance taxes attracts domestic and offshore business. The Anguilla Commercial Online Registration Network (ACORN), the world's first online instant company registration system, has been very successful.
In March 2004, the European Commission (EC) provided US$10 million under the Ninth European Development Fund (EDF) for the development of Anguilla's air transport sector. The balance of previous unspent EDF funds of US$350,000 will also go towards this project.
There was a marked improvement in the economy in 2004, attributable to tourism, high private sector investment and major construction works, resulting in higher employment, output growth and improved public finances.

External trade
Anguilla's main export partners are the UK, US, Puerto Rico and Saint-Martin. Anguilla exports lobsters, fish, livestock and rum to these countries.
Imports
Principal imports include fuels, food products, chemicals, manufactures and textiles, vehicles.
Main sources: Typically US, Puerto Rico, UK
Exports
Principal exports include lobsters, fish and other seafood, livestock, salt, rum and concrete blocks.
Main destinations: Typically UK, US, Puerto Rico and other Caribbean islands.

Agriculture
The agriculture sector accounts for around 4 per cent of GDP. There is mainly small-scale farming of peas, corn, sweet potatoes, okra and tropical fruits. The average cultivated plot is less than 0.25ha. Traditional livestock raising (goats, sheep, poultry) is important, with some animals raised for export.

Fishing
Lobster fishing is a major employer and principal earner of foreign exchange; 70t are caught each year. The typical annual fish catch is 250t.

Industry and manufacturing
The manufacturing sector is based primarily on boatbuilding, construction and fish processing and contributes less than 1 per cent to GDP.

Tourism
Tourism is a major source of income for Anguilla, accounting for some 30 per cent of GDP and 28.6 per cent of the labour force. The island caters to both stay-over visitors and excursionists. Like other Caribbean destinations, Anguilla experienced a decline in visitors in 2002, due to a variety of factors; recovery was under way by late 2003 and completed by 2004. The number of stay-over visitors increased substantially in 2004. The most important market for visitors to Anguilla continues to be the US. Tourists from the UK and Germany have also increased in numbers. A new luxury resort, Temenos Anguilla, with a world-class hotel and an 18-hole golf course, is scheduled to open in 2006.

Banking and insurance
The island's banking sector is well-regulated and internationally competitive. With a neutral tax jurisdiction and no foreign exchange restrictions, Anguilla's financial services sector has attracted a lot of foreign interest over the years. Around 5,000 companies are registered in Anguilla, with most of them classified as International Business Companies (IBCs). The government began upgrading its regulatory framework in 2003, targetting captive insurance and mutual funds. This was in response to the international blacklisting by the OECD of a number of countries in the region as part of a drive against money laundering.
The seven members of the Organisation of Eastern Caribbean States (OECS), Antigua and Barbuda, Dominica,

KEY INDICATORS — Anguilla

	Unit	2000	2001	2002	2003	2004
Population	m	0.01	0.01	0.01	0.01	0.01
Gross domestic product (GDP)	US$bn	0.11	0.10	0.10	0.10	–
GDP per capita	US$	7,739	7,739	7,574	7,736	–
GDP real growth	%	0.2	2.7	0.9	4.5	–
Inflation	%	2.8	2.3	3.0	7.0	–
Total reserves minus gold	US$m	–	–	–	33.3	34.3
Foreign exchange	US$m	–	–	–	33.3	34.3
Exchange rate	per US$	2.70	2.70	2.70	2.70	2.70

Nations of the World: A Political, Economic and Business Handbook

Grenada, Montserrat, St Kitts and Nevis, St Lucia and St Vincent and the Grenadines, share a common currency and central bank. The British Virgin Islands and Anguilla are associate members.

As from July 2005 Anguilla has chosen to adhere to an EU tax directive and inform EU citizens' tax departments about the amount of money in savings accounts and allow tax to be levied from the home country, rather than imposing a withholding tax while retaining a saver's anonimity. Anguilla has also agreed to supply information on tax fraud, for criminal or civil trials, and notify EU member states about additional malpractices.

Central bank
Eastern Caribbean Central Bank, St Kitts and Nevis.

Offshore facilities
The offshore financial services sector in Anguilla is the responsibility of the governor, with day-to-day regulation carried out by the government's financial services department. There are strict laws to combat money laundering and only banks with a previous good track record can be licensed as offshore banks. Companies can be incorporated through the Anguilla Commercial Online Registration Network (ACORN).

Time
GMT minus four hours

Geography
Anguilla, a coralline island of 91 square km, is the most northerly of the Leeward Islands. It lies to the north-west of St Kitts and Nevis and 8km (5 miles) to the north of St Maarten, Netherlands Antilles. The island of Sombrero (48km north of Anguilla) is also included in the territory, as are several other uninhabited small islands.

Climate
Subtropical with a mean annual temperature of 27 degrees Celsius. It is hottest from July–October, coolest from December–February. Cooling trade winds blow throughout the year. Rain mainly falls September–December. Mean annual rainfall is 914mm.

Entry requirements
Passports
Valid passport required by all except US nationals, who can enter Anguilla on either a birth certificate with a photograph, an identification or registration card, or driver's licence with a photograph.
Visa
Required by all, in the form of an entry permit (see www.gov.ai/immigration/forms/Immigration_app_entry_clearance.pdf to download a copy of the entry form or contact the local embassy). Transit passengers do not usually require visas. All visitors require onward or return tickets and sufficient funds for their stay. Business travellers must give details of government or business contacts.
Currency advice/regulations
The import of local and foreign currency is unlimited. The export of local and foreign currency is limited to the amount imported and declared. Travellers are advised to take travellers cheques in US dollars to avoid additional exchange rate charges.

Health (for visitors)
Mandatory precautions
Vaccination certificate for yellow fever required if arriving from an infected area.
Advisable precautions
Water precautions advisable.

Hotels
Several high-quality hotels and a wide selection of villas and apartments.
A 10–15 per cent service charge is usually included in bill.
10 per cent government room tax.

Public holidays
Fixed dates
1 Jan (New Year's Day), 1 May (Labour Day), 25 Dec (Christmas Day), 26 Dec (Boxing Day).
Variable dates
Good Friday, Easter Monday, Anguilla Day (May), Whit Monday, Queen's Official Birthday (Jun), August Monday (first Mon in Aug), August Thursday (first Thu in Aug), Separation Day (third Mon in Dec).

Working hours
Banking
Mon–Thu: 0800–1500; Fri: 0800–1700.
Business
Mon–Fri: 0800–1200, 1300–1600.
Government
Mon–Fri: 1200–1600, 1700–2000.

Telecommunications
Mobile phones
GSM 850/1900 services are available.

Electricity supply
120/240V AC, 60 cycles

Getting there
Air
National airline: Air Anguilla.
International airport/s: Wallblake (AXA), 3km from The Valley. Daily air service with St Maarten (Netherlands Antilles) and St Thomas (US Virgin Islands) and regular air services from Antigua, St Kitts and San Juan (Puerto Rico). Air taxi and charter services are available from Air Anguilla and Tyden Air.
Airport tax: Departure tax US$15.

Surface
Water: Daily ferry services operate between Marigot Bay, St Martin (French Antilles) and Blowing Point.
Main port/s: Road Bay, Sandy Ground; Blowing Point is a smaller port.

Getting about
National transport
Road: Anguilla has about 150km of roads, of which 65km are surfaced. Public roads cover all parts of the island.
City transport
Taxis: Most generally used form of transport; readily available and inexpensive.
Car hire
Readily available. National licence needed to obtain temporary local licence. Drive on left.

BUSINESS DIRECTORY
The addresses listed below are a selection only. While World of Information makes every endeavour to check these addresses, we cannot guarantee that changes have not been made, especially to telephone numbers and area codes. We would welcome any corrections.

Telephone area codes
The international direct dialling code (IDD) for Anguilla is +1 264, followed by subscriber's number.

Useful telephone numbers
Airport: 497-2514
Cable & Wireless: 497-3100
Emergency: 911/999
Ferryboat port: 497-6665
Hospital: 497-25511
Offshore banking: 497-5881
Police: 497-2333
Post office: 497-2528

Chambers of Commerce
Anguilla Chamber of Commerce and Industry, PO Box 321, The Valley (tel/fax: 479-2839; e-mail: acoci@anguillanet.com).

Banking
Bank of Nova Scotia, PO Box 250, George Hill, The Valley (tel: 497-3333; fax: 497-3344).

Barclays Bank Plc (UK), PO Box 140, The Valley (tel: 497-2301/2304; fax: 497-2980).

Caribbean Commercial Bank (Anguilla) Ltd, PO Box 23, The Valley (tel: 497-2571/3; fax: 497-3570; e-mail: ccbaxa@anguillanet.com).

Caribbean Development Bank, PO Box 408, Wildey, st Michael, Barbados (1246) 431-1600; fax: (1246) 426-7269).

National Bank of Anguilla, PO Box 44, The Valley (tel: 497-2101/2104; fax: 497-3310).

Anguilla

Central bank
Eastern Caribbean Central Bank, Agency Office, PO Box 1385, Fairplay Commercial Complex, The Valley (tel: 497-5050; fax: 497-5150).

Travel information
Air Anguilla, PO Box 110, The Valley (tel: 497-2643; fax: 497-2982).

National tourist organisation offices
Anguilla Tourist Board, PO Box 1388, The Valley (tel: 497-2759; fax: 497-2710; e-mail: atbtour@anguillanet.com).

Ministries
Ministries: all located at The Secretariat, The Valley (tel: 497-2451).

Ministry of Finance, PO Box 60, The Secretariat, The Valley (tel: 497-5881/3881; fax: 497-5872; e-mail: anguillafsd@anguillanet.com).

Office of the Governor, Government House, PO Box 60, The Valley (tel: 497-2621/2, 497-3312/3; fax: 497-3314/3151; e-mail: govthouse@anguillanet.com).

Office of the Chief Minister, The Secretariat, The Valley (tel: 497-2518; fax: 497-3389).

Office of the Minister of Finance, Planning and Economic Development, The Secretariat, The Valley (tel: 497-2545/2451; fax: 497-3761).

Other useful addresses
Agriculture Department (tel: 497-2615).

All Island Cable TV, George Hill, PO Box 336 (tel: 497-3600; fax: 497-3602).

Anguilla Electricity Co Ltd, PO Box 400, The Valley (tel: 497-5200; fax: 497-5440).

Cable & Wireless (WI) Ltd, Telecoms House, PO Box 77, The Valley (tel: 497-3100; fax: 497-2501; internet site: http://www.anguillanet.com).

Caribbean Beacon Radio, PO Box 690, The Valley (tel: 497-4340).

Government of Anguilla Financial Services Department, The Secretariat, The Valley (tel: 497-5881; fax: 497-5872; e-mail: anguillafsd@anguillafsd.com; internet site: http://www.anguillaoffshore.com).

Immigration Office (tel: 497-2451, Ext 129).

Radio Anguilla, The Secretariat, The Valley (tel: 497-2218; fax: 497-2751).

Internet sites
ACORN:
http://www.anguillaoffshore.com

Anguilla Guide:
http://www.net.ai/main.html

Bob Green's Anguilla News:
http://www.news.ai

CEG Anguilla Newsletter:
http://www.ceg.ai/newsletters.htm

Local newspaper:
http://www.anguillian.com

Antigua and Barbuda

KEY FACTS

Official name: Antigua and Barbuda

Head of State: Queen Elizabeth II; Governor General Sir James B Carlisle (since 1993)

Head of government: Prime Minister Winston Baldwin Spencer (UPP) (sworn in 24 Mar 2004)

Ruling party: United Progressive Party (UPP) (elected 23 Mar 2004)

Area: 280 square km (Antigua), 160 square km (Barbuda)

Population: 70,700 (2004)

Capital: St John's (Antigua); Codrington (Barbuda)

Official language: English

Currency: Eastern Caribbean dollar (EC$) = 100 cents

Exchange rate: EC$2.70 per US$ (fixed)

GDP per capita: US$11,270 (2004)

GDP real growth: 4.10% (2004)

Labour force: 30,000 (2003)

Unemployment: 5.00% (2003)

Inflation: -1.30% (2004)

Balance of trade: -US$317.00 million (2003)

Foreign debt: US$231.00 million (2003)

COUNTRY PROFILE

Historical profile
1493 Columbus sighted Antigua.
1632 Antigua and Barbuda was settled by the British.
1667 Control was passed to Great Britain after a brief period of French control.
1674 First sugar colony was set up in Antigua by Christopher Codrington.
1685 Codrington leased the island of Barbuda from the British crown and imported African slaves to help grow tobacco and sugar.
1834 The slaves of Antigua were freed.
1860 Barbuda reverted to the British crown.
1871–1956 Antigua and Barbuda were administered together as part of the Leeward Islands federation.
1946 Vere Bird formed the Antigua Labour Party (ALP).
1958–62 A member of the Federation of the West Indies.
1967 The island of Antigua and its two dependencies, Barbuda and the uninhabited islet of Redonda, entered into a free association with other British dependencies in the Windward and Leeward Islands.
1969 A Barbuda separatist movement was formed.
1972 The sugar industry was closed down.
1981 Antigua and Barbuda achieved full independence, remaining a monarchy. The ALP won the first post-independence elections with Bird becoming prime minister.
1990 Vere Bird Jr, son of the prime minister, was declared unfit for office by a judicial enquiry which uncovered links with money laundering.
1993 Vere Bird Snr resigned as prime minister and was replaced by his son, Lester.
1994 Lester Bird and the ALP won the general elections.
1995 Riots erupted over the imposition of new taxes. Prime Minister Bird's brother, Ivor, was convicted of smuggling cocaine into Antigua and Barbuda. Hurricane Luis hit the islands, destroying 75 per cent of homes.
1998 The government closed down six Russian banks accused of money laundering.
1999 The ALP won the elections. The US State Department warned that the country's democratic institutions were being undermined by money laundering and corruption. Hurricane José caused severe damage to the country's infrastructure.
2001 After an investigation by the UK and US into the islands' banking sector and the government's subsequent adoption of a series of recommendations, the country was declared to be co-operative in fighting money laundering.
2002 The US$22 million Nevis Street pier was officially opened.
2004 The 23 March parliamentary elections were won by the United Progressive Party (UPP), ousting the Antigua Labour Party (ALP), which had dominated Antigua and Barbuda since the 1950s. Winston Baldwin Spencer was sworn in on 24 March.
2005 The development of a major tourist facility was initiated in December, with a land transfer to the US Federal Development LLC and Owens Development Group, in Hatton Bay, Antiqua. The multi-million dollar development will include a resort hotel, convention centre, casino and entertainment venue.
2006 The Twentieth meeting of the Council for Trade and Economic Development (COTED) was chaired by the Antigua and Barbuda finance minister. The meeting discussed the implementation of the Caricom single market economy, with regard to common external tariffs, rules of origin and standards.

Political structure
Form of state
Independent state; it is a member of the Commonwealth.
The executive
The British monarch is the head of state, represented by a governor general who acts on the advice of the prime minister and the cabinet.
National legislature
Legislative power rests with the bicameral parliament which consists of a 17-member House of Representatives (16 Antiguan seats and one representing Barbuda) elected every five years by universal suffrage, and a 17-member Senate, appointed by the governor general, mainly on the advice of the prime minister.
The prime minister and the cabinet are responsible to the parliament.
Legal system
The legal system embodies the principles of English statutory and common law. Antigua is responsible for its own magistrate's courts. The regional Eastern Caribbean Supreme Court is responsible for the

Antigua and Barbuda

high court and the court of appeals. The final court of appeal is to the Privy Council in the UK.

Last elections
23 March 2004 (parliamentary)
Results: Parliamentary: the United Progressive Party (UPP) won 55.3 per cent of the vote (12 seats out of 17); the Antigua Labour Party (ALP) 41.8 per cent of the vote (four seats); and the Barbuda People's Movement (BPM) one per cent (one seat).

Next elections
2009 (parliamentary)

Political parties
Ruling party
United Progressive Party (UPP) (elected 23 Mar 2004)

Main opposition party
Antigua Labour Party (ALP)

Political situation
After a landslide victory in the general election in March 2004, Winston Baldwin Spencer and the UPP ended the Bird family's 50-year reign. The election was bitterly fought, with accusations of sleaze and corruption. Spencer promised to stamp out corruption, prosecute those responsible and introduce electoral reform to stop the fraud that had marred previous elections.

Population
70,700 (2004)

Ethnic make-up
The majority of the population is of African descent; the remainder is of British, Portuguese, Lebanese and Syrian origin.

Religions
Anglican (90 per cent), Methodist, Moravian, Roman Catholic, Pentecostal, Baptist and Seventh Day Adventists.

Education
Literacy rate: 90 per cent (2003)
Enrolment rate: Primary education 6–11 years: 50 per cent; secondary education 33 per cent; tertiary education 20–24 years 6 per cent (2003).

Health
Life expectancy: 71.3 years: male 69 years; female 74 years (2003).
Fertility rate/Maternal mortality rate: 1.7 births per woman (2003)
Birth rate/Death rate: 18 births per 1,000 population; six deaths per 1,000 population (2003).
Infant mortality rate: 11 per 1,000 live births, 2003 (World Bank)
Head of population per physician/bed: 1,100 per physician (2003)

Main cities
St John's (capital of Antigua, estimated population 23,500 in 2003); Codrington (capital of Barbuda, 21,514).

Languages spoken
English patois is widely spoken. French also spoken by a small number of people.
Official language/s
English

Media
Press
Dailies: Main newspapers include *Antigua Sun*, *The Daily Observer* and *Antigua and Barbuda Today*.
Weeklies: *The Source* is an English language weekly published from St John's.
Business: *The Antigua Newsletter* (http://www.antiguatoday.com/newsletter/index.html) provides e-mail news on business and travel.

Broadcasting
There is one government radio and television service (The Antigua and Barbuda Broadcasting Service) plus one private radio service (ZDK). A private cable TV service (CTV) offers 17 channels of US television 24hrs/day.

Economy
Tourism dominates the economy of Antigua and Barbuda, accounting for over half of GDP. The size of the tourist sector means the islands are vulnerable to international economic downturn, especially if this occurs in the nearby US. The necessary diversification in the economy is a difficult challange as labour is attracted to the higher wages of the service sectors and away from agriculture and manufacturing industries.

One area into which the islands have successfully diversified is the growing industry of internet gambling sites. This resulted in a trade dispute with the US over restrictions on US citizens placing bets on these websites. A World Trade Organisation ruling in April 2005 will allow the websites to operate in the US.

External trade
There is heavy dependence on imported food and energy. The large trading deficit is only partially offset by re-exports (mostly manufactured goods) and earnings from tourism and capital inflows.

Imports
Principal imports include mineral fuel lubricants and related materials, food and live animals, machinery and transport equipment, other manufactures.
Main sources: US (21.8 per cent total 2004), Singapore (18.8 per cent), China (10.7 per cent), Poland (6.7 per cent) Trinidad and Tobago (10.3 per cent), UK (4.4 per cent)

Exports
Principal exports include petroleum products, chemicals, manufactured goods and materials, including transport equipment, food and live animals.
Main destinations: Germany (49.5 per cent total 2004), UK (29.7 per cent), France (3.5 per cent)

Agriculture
Agriculture typically accounts for around 4 per cent of GDP. Farming is faced with several problems that could weaken its contribution to GDP still further. Limit water supply, soil depletion and drought cause hardship and workers are turning to more lucrative employment in tourism and construction.

The majority of food grown is consumed locally. Fruit and sea-island cotton are grown for export.

Government policy is to encourage self-sufficiency in food. To expand agricultural production capacity, the government, with assistance from the European Development Fund, is promoting livestock development.

KEY INDICATORS — Antigua and Barbuda

	Unit	2000	2001	2002	2003	2004
Population	m	0.07	0.07	0.07	0.07	0.07
Gross domestic product (GDP)	US$bn	0.69	0.64	0.70	0.75	*0.80
GDP per capita	US$	10,615	9,714	10,597	11,000	11,270
GDP real growth	%	3.3	1.5	2.1	2.5	4.1
Inflation	%	0.7	1.5	1.0	2.5	-1.3
Exports (fob) (goods)	US$m	42.3	42.0	41.3	40.0	–
Imports (fob) (goods)	US$m	341.3	422.0	343.6	357.0	–
Balance of trade	US$m	-299.1	-380.0	-302.3	-317.0	–
Current account	US$m	-60.1	-60.0	-110.0	-100.0	-110.0
Total reserves minus gold	US$m	63.6	79.7	87.7	113.8	120.0
Foreign exchange	US$m	63.5	79.7	87.6	113.8	120.1
Exchange rate	per US$	2.70	2.70	2.70	2.70	2.70

* estimated figure

Nations of the World: A Political, Economic and Business Handbook

An agreement with Cuba has seen Antigua and Barbuda provided with technical assistance in a range of agricultural sectors, including tobacco, fertilisers, pesticides and irrigation.

Crop production in 2004 included: 70 tonnes (t) yams, 60t maize, 285t citrus, 200t sweet potatoes, 350t tomatoes, 220t bananas, 1,430t mangoes, 3,145t vegetables in total, 10,045t fruit in total, 95t seed cotton. Livestock production includes: 1,085t meat in total, 520t beef, 194t pig meat, 161t goat & lamb meat, 210t poultry, 250t eggs, 5,350t milk.

Fishing
Fishing is a growth area. There are shrimp and lobster farms in operation and the catch each year is over 300t. The typical annual fish catch is over 1,500t.

Industry and manufacturing
Activity is centred on food processing, galvanised sheet, paints and light industries (mainly assembly of household appliances, vehicles, garments, paper products). Industry contributes 19 per cent to GDP, of which the construction sector contributes about 13 per cent. Construction activity has been dominated by housing and infrastructure repair as a result of hurricanes.

Tourism
Tourism is the principal economic activity of Antigua and Barbuda, accounting for around 25 per cent of GDP, three-quarters of foreign exchange earnings and 35 per cent of the labour force.. The sector was hurt by the depredations of several hurricanes in the 1990s, the global economic downturn and, to a lesser extent, the 11 September 2001 terrorist attacks in the US. The lucrative stay-over market is recovering, with most visitors coming from the US and the UK. Cruise tourism has been targetted for expansion by the government, including development of the St John's waterfront, which, in its first year of operation, resulted in an increase of 45 per cent of cruise-ship arrivals in 2004 over the previous year. Proposals to improve the tourism product were announced in April 2004, with the formation of a National Tourism Task Force as a first step.

Mining
There are known deposits of high quality barytes, limestone and clay. Redonda island was once an important source of phosphates and guano.

Hydrocarbons
Anguilla does not produce any hydrocarbonsrelying on imported refined oil, primarily gasoline, jet fuel and distillate.

Energy
The government-owned Antigua Public Utilities Authority (APUA) provides all electricity services to the islands.

Banking and insurance
The seven members of the Organisation of Eastern Caribbean States (OECS), Antigua and Barbuda, Dominica, Grenada, Montserrat, St Kitts and Nevis, St Lucia and St Vincent and the Grenadines, share a common currency and central bank. The British Virgin Islands and Anguilla are associate members.

Central bank
Eastern Caribbean Central Bank, St Kitts and Nevis.

Main financial centre
St John's

Offshore facilities
There is an offshore financial sector offering full tax haven facilities to international business companies, trusts, banks and insurance companies. A corporate income tax was introduced in 1999. The International Financial Sector Regulatory Authority has full oversight of the offshore sector. Service providers are required to report suspicious transactions to the authority under the money laundering legislation.

Time
GMT minus four hours

Geography
The country comprises three islands – Antigua, Barbuda and the uninhabited rocky islet of Redonda. They are situated along the outer edge of the Leeward Islands chain in the West Indies. Barbuda is the most northerly, 40km north of Antigua; Redonda is 40km south-west of Antigua. Guadeloupe lies to the south of the country, Montserrat to the south-west and St Kitts Nevis to the west.

Climate
Tropical with temperature range from 21–32 degrees Celsius. Little variation throughout year, although driest from January–March.

Entry requirements
Passports
Required by all.

Visa
A full list of those who may visit for business or tourism without a visa can be found at www.antigua-barbuda.com or the local embassy can supply information. Visits must not exceed six months and visitors must have onward/return tickets.

Currency advice/regulations
No restrictions on import or export of local or foreign currency, as long as amount is declared on arrival.

Health (for visitors)
Mandatory precautions
Yellow fever vaccination certificate if arriving from an infected area.

Public holidays
Fixed dates
1 Jan (New Year's Day), 7 Oct (Merchant Holiday), 1 Nov (Independence Day), 25 Dec (Christmas Day), 26 Dec (Boxing Day).

Variable dates
Good Friday, Easter Monday, Labour Day (first Mon in May), Whit Monday, Queen's Official Birthday (Jun), Caricom Day (first Mon in Jul), Summer Carnival (first Mon and Tue in Aug).

Working hours
Banking
Mon–Fri: 0800–1300; (also Fri only) 1500–1700.

Government
Mon–Fri: 0800–1200, 1300–1630. Offices close at 1500 on Fridays.

Shops
Mon–Fri: 0830–1600. Some stores close between 1200 and 1300 daily. Most stores in St Johns close at noon on Thursdays. Sat: 0800–1200.

Electricity supply
220/110V AC, 60Hz. American-style two-pin plugs. Some hotels also have outlets for 240V AC; in this case European-style two-pin plugs are used.

Getting there
Air
National airline: Antigua is a shareholder in LIAT.
International airport/s: V.C. Bird International (ANU), 6km north-east of St John's; duty-free shop, restaurant, bank, post office, car hire.
Airport tax: Departure tax: US$20.

Surface
Main port/s: St John's Deepwater Harbour, Nelson's Dockyard, Crabbs Slipway.

Getting about
National transport
Air: Scheduled daily services between Antigua and Barbuda operated by LIAT.
Road: A network connects all main centres. Over 1,000km of roads, at least 40 per cent of which are all-weather.
Buses: Restricted service.
Rail: In 2003, there were 77km of track.

City transport
Taxis: Fixed rate system. Taxis are not metered and it is advisable to negotiate fares in advance.

Car hire
National or international licence required to obtain visitor's driving permit. Driving on the left. Maximum speed 64kph.

Antigua and Barbuda

BUSINESS DIRECTORY

The addresses listed below are a selection only. While World of Information makes every endeavour to check these addresses, we cannot guarantee that changes have not been made, especially to telephone numbers and area codes. We would welcome any corrections.

Telephone area codes

The international direct dialling code (IDD) for Antigua and Barbuda is +1 268, followed by subscriber's number.

Chambers of Commerce

Antigua and Barbuda Chamber of Commerce and Industry, North and Popeshead Street, PO Box 774, St John's (tel: 462-0743; fax: 462-4575; email: chamcom@candw.org).

Banking

Antigua and Barbuda Development Bank, 27 St Mary's St, Box 1279, St John's (tel: 462-0838; fax: 462-0839).

Antigua and Barbuda Investment Bank Ltd, High St, Box 1679, St John's (tel: 462-0067/1653; fax: 462-0804).

Antigua Commercial Bank, St Mary's and Thames Sts, PO Box 95, St John's (tel: 462-1217/9/2085/1860/4; fax: 462-1220).

Bank of Antigua, 1000 Airport Blvd, Box 315, St John's (tel: 462-4283; fax: 462-0040).

Bank of Nova Scotia, High St, Box 342, St John's (tel: 480-1500; fax: 480-1554).

Barclays Bank plc, High Street, Box 225, St John's (tel: 485-5000; fax: 462-4910).

Caribbean Banking Corporation Ltd, High Street, Box 1324, St John's (tel: 462-4217; fax: 462-5040).

CIBC Caribbean Ltd, High St and Corn Alley, Box 28, St John's (tel: 462-0836/7/0998/1278).

Royal Bank of Canada, High & Market Sts, Box 252, St John's (tel: 462-0325/6; fax: 462-1304).

Swiss American National Bank of Antigua, High St, Box 1302, St John's (tel: 462-4460; fax: 462-0274).

Central bank

Eastern Caribbean Central Bank, Agency Office, PO Box 741, Factory Road, St John's (tel: 462–2489; fax: 462-2490).

Travel information

Antigua Hotels and Tourist Association (AHTA), Lower Redcliffe St, PO Box 454, St John's (tel: 462-0374/3703; fax: 462-3702; e-mail: ahta@candw.ag).

LIAT (1974) Ltd, PO Box 819, VC Bird International Airport (tel: 462-0700; fax: 462-4765).

Ministry of tourism

Ministry of Tourism, Culture and the Environment, New Administration Building, Queen Elizabeth Highway, St John's (tel: 462-0787; fax: 462-2836).

National tourist organisation offices

Antigua and Barbuda Department of Tourism, PO Box 363, Long and Thames Streets, St John's (tel: 462-0480, 462-0029; fax: 462-2483).

Ministries

Minister of State in the Prime Minister's Office and Leader of Government Business in the Senate, Queen Elizabeth Highway, St John's (tel: 462-5933; fax: 462-3225).

Ministry of Agriculture, Lands, Fisheries, Planning and Co-operatives, Nevis & Temple Sts, St John's (tel: 462-1543/5571; fax: 462-6104).

Ministry of Education, Youth, Sports and Community Development, Church St, St John's (tel: 462-4959; fax: 462-4970).

Ministry of Finance and Social Security, High St, St John's (tel: 462-4301; fax: 462-1622/5093).

Ministry of Foreign Affairs, Queen Elizabeth Highway, St John's (tel: 462-4956; fax: 462-3225/9377).

Ministry of Health and Civil Service Affairs, Cross St, St John's (tel: 462-8783; fax: 462-9308/5003).

Ministry of Justice and Legal Affairs, Nevis St, St John's (tel: 462-8867; fax: 462-2465).

Ministry of Labour and Home Affairs, c/o State Insurance Building, Redcliffe St, St John's (tel: 462-0567; 462-1595).

Ministry of Public Utilities, Public Works and Energy, St John's St, St John's (tel: 462-3851/4772; fax: 462-4622).

Ministry of Trade, Industry and Commerce Affairs, Redcliffe Street, St John's (tel: 462-4951; fax: 462-5003).

Other useful addresses

Antigua and Barbuda Embassy (USA), 3216 New Mexico Avenue, NW, Washington DC 20016 (tel: 202-362-5122; fax: 202-362-5225).

Antigua Public Utility Authority (APUA), PO Box 416, St Mary's Street, St John's (tel: 462-4990; fax: 462-2516).

British High Commission, PO Box 483, 11 Old Parham Road, St John's (tel: 462-0008/9, 463-0010).

Cable and Wireless Telex Bureau, St Mary's Street, St John's (tel: 462-0840/2).

Directorate of Offshore Gaming, 2nd Floor, Mutual Finance Centre, 9 Factory Rd, Room 216, PO Box 588, St John's (tel: 481-3300; fax: 481-3305; e-mail: director@antiguagaming.com; internet site: http://antiguagaming.d2g.com).

Free Trade & Processing Zone, PO Box 817, St John's (tel: 460-5552; fax: 460-5553; e-mail: ftpzone@candw.ag; internet site: http://www.antiguafreezone.com).

Industrial Development Board, 34 Newgate Street, St John's (tel: 462-1038; fax: 462-2836).

Internet sites

Daily Observer:
http://www.antiguaobserver.com

East Caribbean Central Bank:
http://www.eccb-centralbank.org

Investment and general information:
http://www.antigua-barbuda.com

Official travel guide:
http://www.geographia.com/antigua-barbuda/

Argentina

KEY FACTS

Official name: República Argentina (Argentine Republic)

Head of State: President Néstor Kirchner (PJ) (inaugurated May 2003)

Head of government: President Néstor Kirchner

Ruling party: Partido Justicialista (PJ) (Justicialist Party, commonly referred to as the Perónist Party)

Area: 2,766,889 square km

Population: 38.47 million (2004)

Capital: Buenos Aires

Official language: Spanish

Currency: Peso (P) = 100 centavos

Exchange rate: P2.91 per US$ (Oct 2005) (peso floated Feb 2002)

GDP per capita: US$3,912 (2004)

GDP real growth: 9.00% (2004); *7.5% (2005)

Labour force: 15.40 million (2004)

Unemployment: 13.80% (2004)

Inflation: 4.40% (2004)

Oil production: 756,000 bpd (2004)

Balance of trade: US$13.27 billion (2004)

Foreign debt: US$168.00 billion (2004)

Annual FDI: US$1.80 billion (2004)

* estimated figure

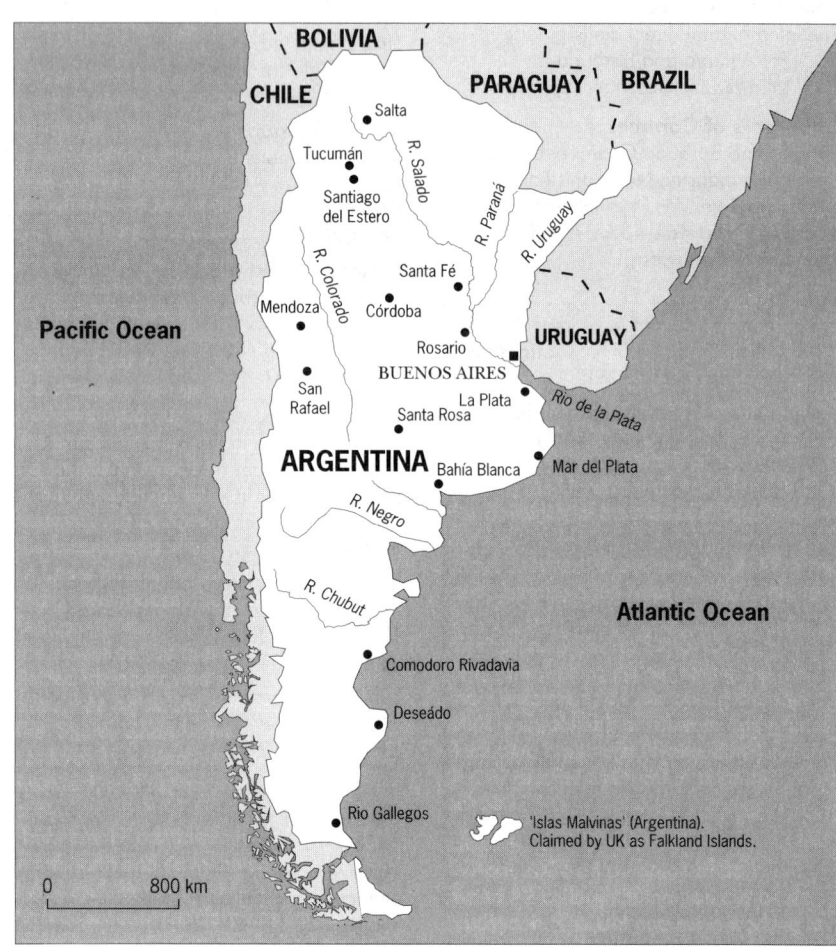

Two thousand and five was an eventful year for Argentina. It began with an audacious but ultimately successful debt restructuring offer made by the government to Argentine bondholders. Toward the end of the year the country hosted the Summit of the Americas. Once football icon and now television host Diego Maradona led trainloads of anti-American protestors to the gathering of political leaders. Maradona's rehabilitation from disgraced sports star and cocaine addict to pseudo-political leader has been nothing short of spectacular.

The Argentine economy, having imploded during the crisis of 2001–02 was in need of a similar scale recovery to that of the former soccer captain. Though progress has undoubtedly been made, especially in terms of macroeconomic restructuring, Argentina's economic recovery is by no means complete.

Along the road to recovery

The economy continued to grow strongly in 2005, but the country still remains a long way off its economic health prior to the spectacular debt default of 2001–02. The latest IMF growth estimate for 2005 is 7.5 per cent and though it represents a deceleration following the 9 per cent rate recorded in 2004, this figure remains positive. In a sign of the country's improving economic situation, Argentina's long-term debt rating was upgraded by the credit-rating agency Standard & Poors'

Argentina

(S&P) on 1 June 2005, from SD (collective default) to B- (stable outlook). Also in June, the government took the important step of tightening controls on capital inflows, thereby discouraging speculative investment funds and guarding against the possibility of the peso strengthening uncontrollably against the US dollar.

Generally, up until this point the government has done a solid job of knocking the economy into shape. Austere macroeconomic engineering has ensured this, but Argentines remain much worse off than they were prior to the catastrophe of the early 2000s. GDP per capita was US$3,912 in 2004, when as recently as 2000 the figure had been US$7,696. Argentina's total GDP, despite having risen year-on-year since 2002 still remains at almost half the figure for 2000.

Real prices were subject to deflationary pressures in 2000 (-0.9 per cent) and 2001 (-1.1 per cent) before suffering from very high upward pressure of 25.9 per cent in 2002. Until recently, Argentina's inflationary woes had been kept in check. The stabilisation of inflation was achieved when a 4.4 per cent annual rate was recorded in 2004, but it surged again in 2005, particularly toward the end of the year, when a rate as high as 12 per cent was forecast.

Bullying the bondholders

In early January the government of President Néstor Carlos Kirchner broke with almost a century of precedent when it refused to negotiate with Argentina's bondholders, who had suffered so greatly when the country defaulted its sovereign debt in 2001. Speaking to the *Financial Times* of London (*FT*) in January, Hans Humes, co-chairman of the Global Committee of Argentine Boldholders claimed that the government was 'just trying to bully people into an unacceptable offer'. This view was echoed by many as Argentina was repeatedly accused of treating the international financial system with disdain. The aggressive offer involved creditors writing off 75 per cent of their claims, inclusive of past due interest. This equated to some 50 per cent more than any country had ever achieved in the history of international debt swaps (the exchange of defunct, defaulted bonds for brand new paper).

The offer was even more audacious when it is factored in that Argentina's central bank reserves consisted of US$20 billion at the time of the offer – a substantial increase on US$8.8 billion in August 2002 – and the fiscal surplus was twice the limit agreed with the IMF. However, the government refused to budge and went head to head with the IMF over the acceptance rate required for the restructuring to proceed. While the fund demanded at least 80 per cent bondholder acceptance Argentina claimed that compliance by as few as 50 per cent of its creditors would be sufficient. On 3 March 2005 the government announced that private creditors holding 76 per cent of the defaulted bonds had agreed to the deal worth US$100 billion. Following a hold-out by the remaining 24 per cent of investors, Argentina continued with it bullish approach, refusing to re-negotiate. Despite appeals for further re-negotiation by developed and developing nations alike at the annual meetings of the World Bank and IMF in April, Argentina officially concluded its debt swap on 2 June 2005.

Kirchner and Lavagna

Roberto Lavagna's reign as Argentina's minister of finance ended on 28 November 2005. Lavagna, a giant on the country's political stage, was summoned to see the President to discuss export taxes on leather, but was probably little surprised to be sacked by Kirchner following recent policy disagreements on a whole range of topics. Lavagna was appointed by Kirchner's predecessor, Eduardo Duhalde, with whom the current president has since fallen out. Never afraid to voice disagreements with his boss, Lavagna effectively sealed his own fate. Eight days before his sacking he accused Julio de Vido, head of the ministry for planning and a key ally of the president, of allowing private contractors to swindle the government by overpricing several road construction projects.

Lavagna's political obituary will read well. He assumed his post at the depths of Argentina's crisis and helped drag his country to economic respectability. Staring the grim prospect of hyperinflation in the face, Lavagna imposed tight fiscal and monetary policies. In time, he addressed the country's inflationary misery and stabilised the exchange rate. Lavagna fiercely defended his country's interests when he took the fight to the IMF in early 2005, displaying real ruthlessness in dealings with Argentina's disgruntled bondholders. Serious disagreements with Kirchner persisted though, the latest variance revolving around the best strategy with which to fight rising inflation.

Outside observers have noted that Kirchner is now in a much stronger position having seen off rival contenders during the congressional elections in October and thus chose to remove his finance minister from the political equation. Many believe that Kirchner wanted rid of Lavagna for personal reasons, citing the fact that the two men were no longer on speaking terms. The relationship between a head of government and his/her finance minister is often the most fraught off all in political life, as observers of the British political arena will no doubt attest. In the Argentine

KEY INDICATORS — Argentina

	Unit	2000	2001	2002	2003	2004
Population	m	36.95	37.50	37.97	37.99	38.47
Gross domestic product (GDP)	US$bn	285.00	268.60	80.10	129.60	*151.50
GDP per capita	US$	7,696	7,169	2,109	3,222	3,912
GDP real growth	%	-0.8	-4.5	-11.0	8.7	9.0
Inflation	%	-0.9	-1.1	25.9	13.9	4.4
Unemployment	%	14.5	–	23.0	16.2	13.8
Oil output	'000 bpd	811.0	822.0	800.0	828.6	756.0
Natural gas output	bn cum	37.3	37.1	36.1	41.0	44.9
Exports (fob) (goods)	US$m	26,409.0	26,655.0	25,710.0	29,376.0	34,453.0
Imports (fob) (goods)	US$m	23,851.0	19,148.0	8,990.0	13,813.0	21,185.0
Balance of trade	US$m	2,558.0	6,370.0	16,400.0	15,563.0	13,267.0
Current account	US$m	-8,970.0	-4,550.0	9,590.0	7,390.0	3,060.0
Foreign debt	US$bn	146.4	170.0	134.2	155.0	168.0
Total reserves minus gold	US$m	25,147.0	14,533.0	10,490.0	14,153.0	18,884.0
Foreign exchange	US$m	24,414.0	14,542.0	10,400.0	13,145.0	18,007.0
Exchange rate	per US$	1.00	1.00	2.67	3.14	2.94

* estimated figure

case both men had apparently fallen out spectacularly during an official visit abroad in early 2005. However, the political persuasion of those promoted by Kirchner in his October reshuffle suggest a fundamental change in the strategic direction of his government, not simply a personal fall out with a high profile figure.

A shift to the left?

Lavagna's dismissal was the most widely publicised story of Kirchner's big re-shuffle, but his promotion of several maverick political figures has also raised eyebrows. *The Economist* of London recently quoted one government 'insider' as confirming a leftward change in direction for Argentina: 'This is the real Kirchner... he was always going to wait for the debt restructuring and the elections but now he's going to implement his ideals'. A brief run down of Kirchner's recent appointees appears to confirm this view. Mr Lavagna's successor Felisa Miceli, a former state bank chief, has denounced the IMF for its 'frighteningly simplistic theories'. She has also claimed, somewhat fantastically, that concerns about rising inflation are simply one of many arguments designed to 'maintain low wages'.

Rumours abound that Miceli will advocate the introduction of increased price controls, measures that the private investment community has not taken kindly to. Indeed, the Buenos Aires stock-exchange index shed 5.9 per cent in 48 hours following Miceli's appointment. Promotions elsewhere in the government have also increased the supposed leftward momentum of Kirchner's administration. Jorge Taiana, a card-carrying member of the Peronista left during the 1970s, was made foreign minister. Significantly, the defence brief was handed to Nilda Garré, former ambassador to Venezuela. Garré's appointment is particularly interesting given her alleged closeness to the Montonero guerrillas during the 1970s.

Foreign relations

Both Taiana and Garré, along with De Vido, have expressed their desire to build closer bilateral relations with the Chávez government in Venezuela. The promotions of Taiana and Garré is particularly significant in this respect and there are now genuine indications that Buenos Aires will gradually shift its foreign policy matrix toward Caracas and thus away from Washington. A closer alliance with Chávez would also presumably involve a loosening of ties with the IMF and this appears to have taken place in the latter half of 2005. The government paid off some of its substantial debt to the fund in late 2005.

Of considerable significance was Kirchner's decision to side with Venezuela against the recommencement of talks on the Washington-backed proposal for a Free-Trade Area of the Americas. Then, in December 2005 Kirchner paid a visit to Caracas to discuss strategy and regional integration with the Venezuelan president. Chávez agreed to increase the portion of Venezuela's reserves invested in Argentine bonds – the figure currently stands at US$1 billion. In return, Kirchner, who was accompanied on the trip by a select group of nuclear engineers, indicated that Argentina would be willing to be party to Venezuela's nuclear ambitions. Press reports in late 2005 suggested that Argentina was at one point willing to sell a nuclear reactor to Venezuela, which has been building links with another state eager to develop its own nuclear capacity: Iran.

Outlook

Kirchner's comprehensive victory in the 2005 parliamentary elections has strengthened his hand significantly. Many observers now contend that the president will steer his government on a leftward path and his recent cabinet appointments would appear to confirm this theory. The extent to which the government will shift away from its hitherto austere macroeconomic policies remains to be seen, but it is certainly the case that Kirchner now has more political clout than at any time since his election in 2003.

On the international front, Argentina looks set to pursue closer regional relations with Venezuela. Such a move would lead to much fist-banging in Washington and may endanger Argentina's strong relationship (among Latin American nations) with the United States that has been built up over recent years. However, with a re-election contest on the horizon a shift to the left and a populist foreign policy may be just what's required by Kirchner in a country growing increasingly anti-American with each passing month.

Risk assessment

Politics	Stable
Economy	Improving
Regional stability	Stable
Stock market	Improving

COUNTRY PROFILE

Historical profile

1916–22 and 1928–30 President Hipolito Yrigoyen was Argentina's first popularly elected president. He was ousted in his second term by the armed forces.

1939–1945 Argentina was neutral during the Second World War and initially refused to break diplomatic relations with Japan and Germany.

1943 A military government, with pro-fascist sympathies, assumed power.

1944 Argentina broke diplomatic relations with Japan and Germany and declared war on them.

1946 General Juan Domingo Perón, a leading figure in the military government, won a free presidential election. He and his wife, Evita, became increasingly popular as social services spending grew. However, foreign exchange reserves built up during the Second World War were squandered by nationalising the railways and other public utilities. President Perón became increasingly repressive towards his critics and the Catholic Church.

1949 A new constitution strengthened the power of the president and criticising the government became a criminal offence, leading to the jailing of Perón's opponents.

1951 Perón was re-elected with a large majority.

1952 Perón's popular wife, 'Evita', died of cancer and his support began to wane.

1955 An attempted coup by the navy in June was crushed by the army. However, in September the armed forces seized power, sending Perón into exile. A series of unstable military and civilian governments in subsequent years saw the Perónists win the few elections held.

1973 Following a Perónist electoral victory, Hector Campora became president. He resigned, following widespread civil disturbances and was succeeded by Perón who had been allowed to return from exile.

1974 Perón died and was succeeded by his wife, María. The country sank into political and economic chaos.

1976 The armed forces overthrew the government and installed General Jorge Videla as president. The military junta suppressed left-wing opposition groups – between 6–15,000 people 'disappeared' in the 'dirty war' that followed the coup.

1981 General Roberto Viola succeeded Videla as president. After Viola, General Leopoldo Galtieri became president.

1982 The military government invaded the Falkland Islands/Islas Malvinas. Argentina's defeat by the UK, on top of a collapsing economy, was a major factor in the end of military government and a return to democracy.

1983 Raul Alfonsín of the Unión Cívica Radical (UCR) (Radical Civic Union) won the presidential elections.

Argentina

1989 Perónist Carlos Ménem became president and began a programme of economic austerity in an effort to stabilise and restructure the ailing economy.
1990 Full diplomatic relations with the UK were restored, although Argentina continued to claim the Falklands.
1992 The peso was introduced as a new currency and was pegged to the US dollar at a one-to-one rate.
1995 Ménem was re-elected president.
1997 International pressure was applied when a judge in Spain called for the arrest of senior military officers involved in human rights violations during the 'dirty war'. However an amnesty protected them.
1998 Argentine judges ordered arrests in connection with the abduction of hundreds of children of women arrested during the 'dirty war'. A protracted recession began.
1999 Fernando de la Rúa won the presidential election, but his centre-left Alianza failed to secure an absolute majority in the lower house of Congress.
2001 The amnesty laws allowing members of the armed forces to escape prosecution for human rights abuses was overturned. The economy, devastated by years of recession, was near to collapse, leading to public protests. The Perónists won the mid-term parliamentary elections and both houses of Congress came under opposition control. President Fernando de la Rúa resigned, Ramon Puerta took over briefly before Adolfo Rodríguez Saa became president. Saa's presidency only lasted until mass demonstrations against his austerity measures resulted in his resignation. Eduardo Camaño assumed the presidency for a 48-hour period.
2002 Presidential elections resulted in Perónist, Eduardo Duhalde, becoming the fifth president in two weeks. The peso was devalued breaking the link with the US dollar. The president was given the power to pass some laws, without congressional approval, for the following two years. The peso was floated.
2003 Carlos Saúl Menem withdrew from the presidential election leaving Néstor Kirchner to win by default. Nearly twice the annual average rainfall fell in two days in Santa Fe province in May, causing major flooding.
2004 In April, an international arrest warrant was issued for the former president, Carlos Menem, over allegations of fraud. Menem returned from exile in Chile in December, following the cancellation of two international warrants for his arrest. In July, the IMF accepted that its handling of Argentina's financial crisis in 2001 had aggravated the deepening recession and that it had continued to lend Argentina money when its debt burden had become unsustainable.
2005 In March, Argentina's US$100 billion debt restructuring offer was accepted. The country hosted a thirty-four nation Summit of the Americas in November; violent protests accompanied proceedings.

Political structure
Constitution
Under the 1853 constitution which was reinstated by the military government in 1955, power is separated into executive, legislative and judicial branches at federal and state level. Each of the 22 states has its own subordinated constitution, elects its own executive and legislature and establishes its own judiciary.
Form of state
Federal presidential democratic republic
The executive
Executive power is vested in the president, who is elected by an electoral college for six years. Since 1994, presidents can run for a second term which is limited to four years. In January 2002, Congress suspended normal procedures for electing presidents and elected Eduardo Duhalde as president.
National legislature
Legislative power is held by the bicameral Congress, consisting of the Chamber of Deputies (257 members elected by universal suffrage for four years, with half the Chamber standing for re-election every two years) and the Senate (72 members). Senators were directly elected for the first time in 2001. The cabinet and chief of cabinet can be removed only by a majority vote in each congressional house.
Legal system
The judiciary is independent of the government and forms the third 'pillar' of the constitution. Since 1998, federal judges have been elected and dismissed by a body comprising lawyers and academics. The election of judges was intended to reduce the endemic political influence that had previously affected the Argentine legal system, especially at the local level, for many years. There is a Supreme Court system at national and provincial levels.
Last elections
27 April/18 May 2003 (presidential); 14 October 2001 (parliamentary).
Results: Presidential: Carlos Saúl Menem won 24.3 per cent of the vote, Néstor Kirchner 22 per cent, Ricardo López Murphy 16.4 per cent, Adolfo Rodríguez Saá 14.4 per cent and Elisa Carrio 14.2 per cent.
A run-off between Menem and Kirchner was to be held on 18 May, but Menem pulled out, leaving Néstor Kirchner to win by default.
Next elections
2007 (parliamentary and presidential)

Political parties
Ruling party
Partido Justicialista (PJ) (Justicialist Party, commonly referred to as the Perónist Party)
Main opposition party
Unión Cívica Radical (UCR) (Radical Civic Union)

Population
38.47 million (2004)
Ethnic make-up
White (97 per cent), principally descendants of Italian and Spanish immigrants. Minority groups include the Buenos Aires Jewish community and Anglo-Argentines throughout the country. The major indigenous nations are the Quechua of the north-west, the Mapuche of northern Patagonia and the Matacos, Tobas and others who inhabit the Chaco and north-eastern cities like Resistencia and Santa Fé.
Religions
Roman Catholic (92 per cent), Protestant (2 per cent), Jewish (2 per cent), others (4 per cent).

Education
Education is compulsory and free, so that Argentina has one of the highest literacy rates in Latin America. Secondary education consists of basic general education and polymodal education (multipurpose schools catering to ages between 15 and 18). In parallel to the polymodal cycle, there is a technical-,professional course, which leads after a further year's study to the title of *Técnico*. Higher education is provided by national and private universities, which are autonomous. There are 25 national universities. Technical institutes (Institutos de Formación Técnica) offer higher technical education, leading to the award of the *Título menor*. Professional courses are also available in a wide range of subjects.
Literacy rate: 97per cent, adult rate (World Bank 2004)
Compulsory years: 6 to 15
Enrolment rate: 120 per cent gross primary enrolment of relevant age group (including repeaters); 100 per cent gross secondary enrolment; 57 per cent in tertiary education (World Bank).
Pupils per teacher: 17 in primary schools

Health
The healthcare sector was deregulated in 2001. In effect, this gives Argentinians the right to choose between the union-administered healthcare system, known as *obras sociales*, and private healthcare providers. The reorganisation meant that those who paid into, or were already members of, a private health scheme, would no longer

have to pay 3 per cent of their salaries to the union-administered system.
Total health expenditure typically amounts to 10.3 per cent of GDP, of which public expenditure is equivalent to 4.9 per cent and private expenditure amounts to 5.4 per cent of GDP. Most children receive immunisations against childhood diseases.
HIV prevalence: 0.7 per cent aged 15–49 in 2003 (World Bank)
Life expectancy: 74.5 years (World Bank 2004)
Fertility rate/Maternal mortality rate: 2.4 births per woman; maternal deaths 38 per 100,000 live births (World Bank).
Infant mortality rate: 17 per 1,000 live births (2003); 5 per cent of children aged under five are malnourished (World Bank).
Head of population per physician/bed: 2.7 physicians and 3.3 hospital beds per 1,000 people.

Welfare
The main portion of the Argentine social security system is borne by a pay-as-you-go system where employers' and employees' contributions fund payments. Workers must contribute 11 per cent of their pay regardless of whether workers participate in a private, or the public, social security system; employers must contribute the equivalent of 16 per cent of each workers' salary to the public system. Non-salaried workers must pay the full amount of 27 per cent of their income.
The whole social security system is adversely affected when employers fail to pay or withhold their social security contributions. However, the percentage of non-registered employees in Argentina is very high. According to non-official records of the Argentine Ministry of Labour, 20 out of 100 employees are non-registered employees, thus depriving them of pensions. Measures have been taken by the Argentine Social Security Authority (SSA) to force employers to register employees and contribute to the social security fund.

Pensions
Argentina reformed its pension system in 1994 to a mixture of the old government-administered system and an individual retirement account programme administered by the Retirement and Pension Fund Administrators (AFJPs).
Argentina has retained the pay-as-you-go system. This system provides basic, universal old-age coverage (known as PBU) for all workers who reach retirement age and who have contributed for at least 30 years including a portion of the wealthiest Argentines' pensions. Payment of retirement benefits begin at age 65 for men and age 60 for women.

Main cities
Buenos Aires (capital, estimated population 11.9 million in 2004), Córdoba (1.5 million), Rosario (1.3 million), Mendoza (1.0 million), La Plata (838,600), Tucumán (814,500), Mar del Plata (683,700), Salta (516,600), Santa Fé (513,000).

Languages spoken
Italian, German and French are still maintained within their respective communities. English is generally spoken in business circles. There are 17 native Indian languages, the most widely spoken of which is Quechua.

Official language/s
Spanish

Media
Press
Dailies: The main dailies in Spanish and English languages include *Buenos Aires Herald* (English), *La Crónica* (national popular tabloid), *La Nación* (national daily independent broadsheet paper), *El Cronista*, *Página 12*, *La Prensa*, *Argentinisches Tageblatt* (German language national newspaper), *La Razón* (national popular broadsheet) and *Clarín*. Regional newspapers include *El Sol*, *El Atlántico* and the tabloid *Diario Popular*.
Weeklies: *Noticias* is published on every Saturday featuring business and curent affairs. Other weeklies include *El Fundador* and *Tiempos del Mundo*.
Business: Major daily business publications are *Buenos Aires Económicó* and *Ambito Financiero*. *El Tribuno* covers regional business. *Negocios* (monthly) and *Factor* features issues on industrial management. *La Prensa* also has sections on economy.
Periodicals: Periodicals of general interest are *168 Horas*, *Claudia Cosa* (Spanish) for domestic interest and *Super Campo* on farming and agriculture.

Broadcasting
Radio: The most popular radio station in Argentina is the nationwide Radio Rivadavia although in Buenos Aires alone at least a dozen FM stations operate. There are in the region of 21 million radios in Argentina, serving 90 per cent of the population.
Television: Legalisation of non-state television and the cable revolution have brought a wider variety of programming to the small screen. There are numerous (commercial) privately and state-owned stations.

Advertising
Press advertising accounts for approximately 45 per cent of total advertising expenditure, with commercial television taking between 25 and 30 per cent. Press, cinema, commercial TV and radio and direct mail opportunities are available. Outdoor sites such as wallposters and street stands are usually controlled by a few major or local companies or local authorities.

Economy
Argentina's economy continued to expand in 2005, with GDP growth of 7.2 per cent, though at a lower rate than the 2004 rate of 9 per cent. The IMF forecasts that real GDP growth will decrease further in 2006, to 4.2 per cent. Despite good economic growth the country is still suffering repercussions from its default on sovereign debt during the economic crisis of 2001–02. This crisis resulted in sharp increases in poverty and unemployment, and this problem has yet to be solved. Approximately 40 per cent of the population live below the poverty line compared to around half this figure between 1992–95. Even though Argentina has defaulted on a record US$140 billion, both the IMF and the World Bank have started policies of debt relief to encourage the continuation of growth. The nation's debt restructuring programme was accepted by 76 per cent of its original creditors. This involves an exchange of old bonds for new bonds, though at a lower market rate of 35 per cent of the original bond value. This provisional success attracted the attentions of the IMF and conversations over a US$13 billion loan agreement restarted in March 2005. In June 2005, the credit-rating agency Standard & Poor's, upgraded its long-term debt rating for Argentina from Selective Default (SD), to B- with a stable outlook.
Argentina's economy is underpinned by its vast natural resources and an export-oriented agricultural sector. The country is a major world producer of soya beans, beef and wheat. Financial services and tourism emerged as important sectors in Argentina's economic growth in the 1990s. Industry and manufacturing are also important and Argentina produces refined oil for export.
Recent economic growth is largely attributable to the increased soya bean demand from China. With China receiving around a third of Argentine soya exports and the industry growing by around 20 per cent every year, soya production is becoming a flourishing sector of the economy. China is also pursuing a policy of heavy investment in Latin America, with a planned US$20 billion being spent on Argentine infrastructure over the next 10 years.
Steady growth and political stability under President Kirchner is leading the country into recovery. The devaluation of the peso

has increased demand for Argentine exports and boosted the level of both investment and tourism. After consecutive year-on-year decreases in inflation from 2002–04 the level of inflation has increased to 7.7 per cent in 2005 but is expected to decrease again in 2006 to 6.0 per cent.

The 2004–05 World Bank Country Assistance Strategy (CAS) for Argentina has facilitated the injection of US$2 billion of World Bank financing to be spent on financial support for the country. The aim of CAS is to develop long-term strategies to sustain Argentinean growth and assist the country's recovery. Emphasis is being placed on equity, social inclusion and improved governance. An additional 35 projects constituting a total of US$5.5 billion are currently in operation from the bank.

External trade

The Mercosur trade group of Brazil, Argentina, Paraguay and Uruguay became a customs union in 1995. Trade disagreements with Brazil, following the devaluation of the Brazilian real in 1999, have slowed attempts to deepen Mercosur integration. However, Argentina's long-term commitment to Mercosur as a free trade area remains strong. The EU and Mercosur plan to negotiate a mutual free trade zone. Since May 2004 negotiations between the EU and Mercusor have been carried out on the basis of informal technical meetings between the two institutions. Ministers from both sides met in September 2005 to discuss ongoing negotiations on the formation of a mutual free trade bloc; a 'roadmap' for further technical summits in November 2005 and February 2006 was agreed on. The November meeting was concerned mainly with the political dimension of trade between the EU and Mercusor, focusing particularly on 'political dialogue' between both regions.

In December 2004, twelve South American countries signed an agreement to launch the South American Community of Nations (CSN), modelled on the European Union, to unite both politically and economically. The CSN seeks to integrate the Andean Union and Mercusor by 2007, with tariffs on non-sensitive products being abolished by 2014. Allan Wagner, Secretary of the Andean Union, has stated his belief that a complete union similar to that of the EU will be in effect by 2019.

Argentine plans to form a closer trading relationship with China have been in existence for some time due to the increasing soya trade between the two countries; coupled with Chinese investment in Argentina. Trade relations between the two countries have strengthened considerably with a memorandum on bilateral trade and investment co-operation being signed on 16 November 2004.

Imports

Principal imports include metal manufactures, machinery and equipment, vehicles, chemicals and plastics.

Main sources: Brazil (27.0 per cent total 2004), US (20.0 per cent), Germany (6.6 per cent), China (4.6 per cent) France (4.2 per cent) Italy (4.1 per cent)

Exports

Mineral products (typically 20 per cent of total), vegetable products (18 per cent), vehicles and parts (17.6 per cent), electrical machinery (7 per cent), live animals and related products (6 per cent), chemicals (6 per cent). These earnt an estimated US$33.78 billion f.o.b in 2004.

Main destinations: Brazil (16.5 per cent total 2004), Chile (10.9 per cent), US (10.2 per cent), China (8.5 per cent), Spain (4.5 per cent)

Agriculture
Farming

The agricultural sector as a whole contributes around 7 per cent to GDP and employs 11 per cent of the workforce, with the sector being composed predominantly of individual farmers and small companies. Arable land covers 12 per cent of Argentina's total land area. The country is an important producer of food, particularly soya beans, meat and wheat. Together, vegetable products and livestock account for nearly a quarter of total exports. Overall, the country is the fifth largest agricultural exporter in the world, with the sector accounting for 60 per cent of all Argentina's exports. It is the largest exporter of soy oil, soy flour oil and sunflower, the second largest exporter of corn after the United States, the third largest exporter of meat and the fifth largest flour producer.

Argentina's meat consumption is the highest in Latin America, at over 50kg per person per annum. Argentina is the world's third-largest organic meat producer, with 90 per cent of organic produce destined for export markets, particularly the EU. In previous years agricultural profitability has been hit by low international commodity prices, rising production costs, subsidiation of international competitors and an over-valued exchange rate which has diminished competitiveness. The weakness of the peso against the euro and the US dollar since the government ceased to peg the peso to the US dollar has provided a boost to sales volumes since 2002.

Crop production in 2004 included 34,212,000 tonnes (t) cereals in total, 14,560,000t wheat, 15,000,000t maize, 1,060,000t rice, 2,021,025t potatoes, 2,160,000t sorghum, 31,500,000t soya beans, 19,300,000t sugar cane, 1,262,444t apples, 2,690,000t citrus fruit, 2,365,000t grapes, 7,149,282t oilcrops, 180,000t bananas, 64,000t tea, 142,000 garlic, 118,000t tobacco, 676,000t tomatoes, 125,000t chillies & peppers, 7,067t peppermint, 7,169t various spices, 7.484,742t fruit in total, 3,184,982t vegetables in total. Livestock production included 4.16t meat in total, 2,700,000t beef, 150,200t pig meat, 61,270t lamb & goat meat, 55,600t horsemeat, 928,153t poultry, 300,000t eggs, 8,100,000t milk, 80,000t honey, 60,000t greasy wool, 378,000t cattle hides.

Fishing

Argentina has recently increased its fishing production and exports of surplus stock are becoming a valuable export earner, especially when processed into oil and fish meal. Because of the Argentines' preference for beef, the domestic demand for fish is relatively weak. Principal fishing ports are Mar del Plata and Bahía Blanca. The typical annual fish catch is around 925,000 tonnes, including 550,000 tonnes marine fish and 350,000 tonnes shellfish.

Forestry

About 12 per cent of Argentina's total land is covered by forest, equivalent to 34.6 million hectares, and a further 6 per cent of other wooded land.

Argentina is not self-sufficient in forestry goods, with most of the domestic harvest going towards lumber. Pine and cedar used for pulp are harvested in the north-west of the country. Significant quantities of sawn goods, wood-based panels and chemical pulps are produced from domestic hardwoods and softwoods. A large quantity of paper is imported, although Argentina's pulp and paper industry relies mainly on domestic pulp production.

Exports of timber products in 2004 amounted to US$280.7 and imports amounted to US$258.6 million. Timber production in 2004 included 9,307,000 cubic metres (cum) roundwood, 5,335,000cum industrial roundwood, 2,130,000cum sawnwood, 2,962,000cum pulpwood, 2,274,000cum sawlogs & veneer logs, 692,000cum wood-based panels, 185,000t newsprint, 304,000t printing and writing paper, 927,000t recovered paper, 3,972,000cum wood fuel.

Industry and manufacturing

Argentina's main industrial centres are Cordoba and to a lesser extent Buenos Aires. Industry as a whole contributes approximately 29 per cent to GDP and employs 24 per cent of the workforce. Major sectors of production include food, textiles, machinery and transport equipment, consumer durables, industrial chemicals, metal working, engineering, paper, iron and steel and electrical equipment. The beef industry has given rise to a number of associated industries, including hides, leather, meat extracts and processed meats. Sectors that have gained in prominence in recent years include software and petrochemicals.

The automobile sector represents an important growth sector for the economy. In recent years the sector has suffered from poor consumer demand and an uncompetitive exchange rate. Many car assembly plants have been closed and operations have been transferred to Brazil, where labour costs are lower and there is a more lucrative domestic market. With the exception of the automobile industry however, the manufacturing sector has been boosted by the acceleration of economic integration within Mercusor.

Tourism

Travel and tourism is a significant contributor to the economy. However, Argentina's tourism sector, which thrived during the 1990s (4,285,000 visitors in 1996), was badly affected by the country's political and economic problems, compounded by external events, such as the 11 September 2001 terrorist attacks in the US.

The World Travel and Tourism Council forecasts that the travel and tourism sector of Argentina will grow by more than 7 per cent in 2005, contributing some 2.6 per cent to GDP. The sector will generate over 1.3 million jobs (9.1 per cent of the total work force).

This recovery is on the back of Argentina's improving economic and political situation. Visitor numbers rose by 12 per cent in 2004, from 2.99 million to 3.35 million, with a rise in receipts of 28 per cent to US$2.56 billion.

Environment

Argentina's diverse environments have created a number of different ecological challenges from heavy pollution in Buenos Aires, deforestation in subtropical provinces to overgrazing in Patagonia.

Mining

The mining code was altered to create a more attractive investment environment in 1993, since when growth in the sector has picked up; mining exports in 2000 were estimated at US$1 billion and and had risen to US$2.3 billion by 2004. Altogether, there are over 70 companies with established projects in Argentina and some 40 companies actively seeking mining opportunities in the country.

Iron ore is the principal mineral extracted, mostly in Río Negro province, but output is only sufficient to supply about half of the requirements of the country's largest blast furnace complex, the remainder being made up from imports. Other minerals extracted include lead, zinc, tin, and uranium.

Argentina's largest mining project is the Alumbrera copper and gold mine in Catamarca province, thought to be the ninth largest copper mine in the world. Annual production of some 15 tonnes of gold is also expected until the end of its 20-year life in 2019. In addition, the Cerro Vanguardia silver and gold mine produces approximately five tonnes of gold per year. Now a significant gold producer Argentina – which occupies a top twenty world position – has recently seen considerable production activity in the north-west of the country, where the Veladero mine is situated. The Argentina-Chile border zone is particularly promising and output is predicted to rise in 2005 because of increased production in the area.

Hydrocarbons

Argentina has 2.7 billion barrels of proven oil reserves (as at year end 2004). It is the third-largest oil producer in Latin America, producing 756,000 barrels per day (bpd) and is the region's third-largest exporter. The oil sector is fully privatised.

Argentina is a net exporter of oil, consuming 393,000 bpd and exporting the remainder of its production.

At year end 2004, Argentina had 610 billion cubic metres (21.4 trillion cubic feet) of proven gas reserves, the third-largest in Latin America. It is the second-largest gas producer in Latin America after Mexico producing 44.9 billion cubic metres in 2004.

The gas sector is fully privatised and there are no restrictions on imports and exports. Chile is the largest consumer of Argentine gas exports and is supplied solely by the Neuquén gas fields . There are also pipelines to Argentina's second most important customer, Brazil.

Argentina has total coal reserves of 130 million tonnes. It produces 340,000 tonnes per year and consumes around 1.54 million tonnes per year.

Energy

The third largest power market in Latin America, Argentina relies predominantly on hydropower and natural gas to fuel its electricity generation. Argentina had 27 million KW of installed generation (as at end 2002), 49 per cent of which was fossil fuel based while 42 per cent was derived from hydroelectricity.

The Argentine electricity market for generation is highly competitive and is one of the most deregulated markets of its kind in the region. The liberated nature of the market combined with steadily rising demand through the 1990s ensured that the sector grew robustly. However, the economic crisis of 2001–02 led to a marked decrease in both production and consumption, though Argentina's relative stability in the last two years has allowed the sector to rebound.

Greater regulation in the distribution sector coupled with the domination of the market by three major organisations – Edenor, Edesur and Edelap – has resulted in a less competitive environment. Compania Nacional de Transporte Energetica en Alta Tension, or Transener, controls the market in electricity transmission, having secured a 95 year licence with the Argentine government in 1993. Hydroelectricity is of great importance to the energy sector, particular the Yacyreta hydroelectric dam, which helps power Argentina and neighbouring Paraguay. The Salto Grande dam is also co-owned by a bordering country, Uruguay, and as is the case with the Yacyreta, power generated from the project is shared equally between both nations.

Argentina relies on the Atucha I and Embalse nuclear power projects, both of which are operated by Nucleoelctrica Argentina SA. Construction of a further nuclear power station, Atucha II, was halted in 1994, though the national government formally announced in 2003 that it would invest US$300 million to complete construction by 2008.

Financial markets
Stock exchange

The growth of the pension fund market in Argentina has added considerable liquidity to the Argentine stock market since the late 1990s and increased the market capitalisation of the Buenos Aires stock exchange. However, the protracted recession has hit the stock exchange hard.

Banking and insurance

The country's economic crisis of 2001 severely undermined Argentina's banking system, when the freezing of deposit accounts and the conversion of deposits into pesos undermined liquidity in the financial system. The value of assets deteriorated throughout 2002 as the peso lost value and government bonds fell to a fraction of their purchase price. Banks were unable to meet claims on deposits, while savers filed law suits against institutions for failing to honour their deposits. As such, the entire banking system teetered on the edge of collapse in 2003. This led to the closure of many local subsidiaries of foreign banks. However, Argentina's recent

Argentina

economic recovery has enabled the sector to rehabilitate itself somewhat, with an increase in money supply demand and a significant recovery on bank deposits and loans. The acceptance of the national government's debt restructuring plan in early 2005 has led to a much needed increase in foreign capital inflow and greater stability in the sector. Despite this gradual upturn the banking sector remains very sensitive to macroeconomic conditions and though the level of credit is growing, it remains at a slow rate.

Central bank
Banco Central de la República Argentina

Main financial centre
Buenos Aires

Time
GMT minus three hours

Geography
Argentina lies east of Chile and west of the Atlantic Ocean. There are four main geographic provinces: the Andes, the lowland north, the Pampas and Patagonia. The Andes Mountains line Argentina's western edge, forming the boundary with Chile. The highest peak, Aconcagua, stands 6,960 metres (22,834 feet). Gently rolling plains extend eastward from the base of the Andes and descend gradually to sea level. Open savannas alternate with almost impenetrable thorn forests in the western part of the region. Vast, generally treeless plains of central Argentina gradually rise from the Atlantic coast to the Andes Mountains. These fertile plains are Argentina's breadbasket. They consist of the Humid Pampas along the coast and the Dry Pampas in the west and south.

Patagonia, south of the Pampas, is dry and desolate. The Patagonian steppes support flocks of sheep, the wool of which is exported to Europe.

The southernmost inhabited territory, Tierra del Fuego (Land of Fire), consists of various islands with the northern areas used for sheep farming, while the southern islands are mountainous and covered in glaciers and forests.

Climate
Argentina's climate ranges from sub-tropical in the north to sub-antarctic in the south. The densely populated central zone (including Buenos Aires) is temperate. Summer from December–March, is hot and humid with temperatures ranging from 26–35 degrees Celsius (C); autumn is in April–May, with temperatures in the range 10–25 degrees C; winter is from June–August, with temperatures of 0–20 degrees C, when nights can be cold with temperatures below freezing; spring is from September–November, with temperatures of 12–25 degrees C.

Dress codes
Dress codes are fairly formal in Buenos Aires. Suits are worn for business appointments and, for men, jackets and ties are required for dining out and other social occasions. Casual clothing is often worn on the coast, but shorts and beachwear should be worn only at the beach or pool.

Entry requirements
Passports
Passports are required by all visitors except nationals of neighbouring countries with identity cards.

Visa
All business travellers are advised to contact an Argentine embassy for requirements, before departure.
Tourist visas are not required by most nationals of the Americas, Europe, Australasia and some Asian countries. Citizens of neighbouring countries of Argentina need only national identification cards. For further exemptions and details check with the appropriate embassy or consulate before departure.

Currency advice/regulations
There are no restrictions on the import and export of local or foreign currency.

Health (for visitors)
Mandatory precautions
None

Advisable precautions
Cholera, typhoid and polio and hepatitis 'A' vaccinations are recommended. Yellow fever vaccinations are advised for visitors to the north-eastern forest area. Malaria prophylaxis is advisable for visits to some lowland tropical areas. Water precautions should be taken outside main towns.
There is some risk of dengue fever and anthrax outside urban areas.
Medical insurance is necessary and doctors often expect immediate cash payment before treatment.

Hotels
Wide range available, graded from one to five stars.
Service charge and sales tax of 21 per cent are usually included in bills. It is customary to tip 10 per cent on top of this.

Public holidays
Fixed dates
1 Jan (New Year's Day), 1 May (Labour Day), 25 May (Anniversary of the 1810 Revolution), 20 Jun (Flag Day), 10 Jul (Independence Day), 8 Dec (Immaculate Conception), 25 Dec (Christmas Day), 31 Dec (New Year's Eve).

Variable dates
Maundy Thursday, Good Friday, Malvinas Day (first Mon in Apr), Death of General José San Martin (third Mon in Aug), Columbus Day (second Mon in Oct).

Working hours
Banking
Mon–Fri: 0800–1700 (with regional variations).

Business
Most businesses work Mon–Fri: 0900–1900. Most offices break for lunch 1200–1400.

Government
Mon–Fri: 0800–1700.
Post offices: Mon–Fri: 0800–2000; Sat: 0800–1400.

Shops
Shopping centres Mon–Sun: 1000–2200. Supermarkets Mon–Sat: 0830–2030; Sun: 1000–2000.

Telecommunications
Mobile phones
GSM 850/1900 services are available in highly populated areas only.

Electricity supply
220V AC, 50 cycles

Social customs/useful tips
The normal form of greeting is a handshake. In general, European practices are followed. Standards on punctuality differ though and you may be kept waiting. Commercial quotations should be made in US dollars.
In their public behaviour, Argentines are very conscious of civilities. It is considered polite to first extend a greeting like *buenos dias* (good day) or *buenas tardes* (good afternoon) if you are approaching a stranger to ask for information.

Security
Although street crime is increasing in Argentina, personal security is a minor problem compared to other Latin American countries. Violent crime is rare in Buenos Aires. Travellers should take precautions against petty theft such as bag snatching, especially on trains.

Getting there
Air
National airline: Aerolíneas Argentinas.
International airport/s: Ezeiza Ministro Pistarini (EZE), 51km south-west of city: duty-free shop, restaurant, bank, car hire. A bus service operates to the city, every 30 minutes between 0500–2300, taking 45 minutes. Taxis are also available. A coach service also connects to Jorge Newbery airport (known locally as *Aeroparque*) for domestic flight connections.
Other airport/s: Jorge Newbery (commonly known as 'Aeroparque') (AEP), 8km north-east of Buenos Aires, domestic terminal also caters for certain international flights to neighbouring countries (Brazil, Chile, Paraguay, and Uruguay); duty-free shop, restaurant, bank, car hire.
Córdoba-Pajas Blancas (COR), 16km

from city; Jujuy-El Cadillal (JUJ), 40km from city; Rosario-Fisherton (ROS), 18km from city.

Airport tax: International departures US$18; regional and to Uruguay US$8. International arrivals US$10. These levies are subject to inflation.

Surface
Road: There are well-maintained roads between all the neighbouring countries. Four branches of the Pan-American Highway run from Buenos Aires to the borders of Bolivia, Brazil, Chile and Paraguay. Entry from Uruguay is possible via bridges over the Uruguay River at Puerto Colón, Puerto Unzué and the Salto Grande Dam. The long distances involved can make car journeys time-consuming: for example, the distance from Santiago in Chile to Buenos Aires is over 1,400 km.
Rail: The major direct route is north from Buenos Aires to Asunción in Paraguay. There are also direct rail links with Bolivia, Brazil and Chile. Services are often disrupted and delays can be expected.
Water: Ferry and hydrofoil services on the Río de la Plata link Colonia and Montevideo (Uruguay) with Buenos Aires. Ferries also operate from Paraguay on the Paraná River.
Main port/s: Buenos Aires, Ensenada (La Plata), Rosario and Bahía Blanca. There are numerous smaller ports and some specialised terminals (for oil, cereals, raw materials, etc).

Getting about
National transport
Air: Given the great distances involved, air travel is the logical method for reaching domestic destinations. Internal flights for Buenos Aires land at the Jorge Newbery airport (known as *Aeroparque*), 10 minutes from city centre by taxi.
An extensive domestic service is offered to regional airports and demand for services is high, so it is advisable to book flights in advance. Monthly unlimited travel tickets are available.
Road: The network has been improved over the last few years and links major centres. Tolls are collected on major roads. *Automóvil Club Argentino* is useful for information and advice on driving conditions.
Buses: Long-distance bus services are operated by a number of companies, mostly centred on Buenos Aires, and are extensive (e.g. routes to Mar del Plata, Córdoba, San Martín de Los Andes, Mendoza). Extended journey times leave these services only suitable for tourists. The Buenos Aires bus terminal is next to *Retiro*, the central rail station.
Rail: A comprehensive rail system links main towns. Long-distance Pullman services, with air-conditioning, sleeping facilities and restaurants, are recommended. It is advisable to book well in advance. Generally services have improved in the last few years. Unlimited travel tickets are available. Travelling by train is generally cheaper, but slower, than travelling by bus.
Water: There are regular sailings to Rosario and Corrientes via the Paraná River. River transport company Flota Fluvial operates services on the Plate, Paraná, Paraguay and Uruguay Rivers. Patagonian ports are also served, but sailings are irregular – check locally.

City transport
Taxis: Taxis, of which there are some 32,000 in Buenos Aires, generally have yellow roofs. They can be hailed or found on ranks and are metered within cities. For trips in the Buenos Aires centre which are less than six blocks, it is usually faster to walk than to take a taxi. Tips are not necessary, though generally expected from tourists.
Journey time from Ezeiza airport to city centre is 40 minutes and 10 minutes from the domestic airport, *Aeroparque Jorge Newbery*.
There is also a widely available and much-used system of chauffeured car hire. These cars, called *remises*, are slightly more expensive than normal taxis but offer a safer and more comfortable service. Remises are generally ordered by phone. Remises are also available for travel to and from the airports, where they can be booked at separate counters.
Buses, trams & metro: Within Buenos Aires there is a comprehensive public transport system with 'pay as you board' bus services, operating 24 hours. The metro (known as Subte) has five lines A–E, operating from early morning to late at night. Tokens can be purchased at booking offices.
All major towns have good local services.
Ferry: The principal ferry connection in Buenos Aires is to Colonia in Uruguay, and is frequented by tourists heading for the Uruguayan resort town of Punta del Este. River buses in the suburb of Tigre serve communities in the river delta and are a popular tourist attraction on weekends.

Car hire
Car hire is available in Buenos Aires and most main urban centres. An international driving licence is required, and must be validated by the *Automóvil Club Argentino* (www.aca.org.ar). Driving permits can be obtained from the *Dirección General de Tránsito* (Crnel. Roca 5252, Buenos Aires, from 0700 to 1300).

BUSINESS DIRECTORY

Telephone area codes
The international direct dialling code (IDD) for Argentina is +54, followed by area code and subscriber's number:

Bahía Blanca	291	Resistencia	3722
Balcarce	2266	Rio Cuarto	358
Buenos Aires	11	Rio Grande	2964
Catamarca	3833	Rosario	341
Córdoba	351	Salta	387
Formosa	3717	San Juan	264
Las Calera	351	San Lorenzo	3476
La Plata	221	San Miguel de Tucumen	381
Mar Del Plata	223	San Pedro	3329
Mendoza	261	San Rafael	2627
Neuquén	299	Santa Fé	342
Paraná	343	Santa Rosa	2954

Useful telephone numbers
Buenos Aires
Fire: 100
Police: 101
Emergency: 107

Chambers of Commerce
American Chamber of Commerce in Argentina, 1133 Viamonte, 1053 Buenos Aires (tel: 4371-4500; fax: 4371-8400; e-mail: amcham@amcham.com.ar).

Argentine Chamber of Commerce, 36 Avenida Leandro N Alem, 1003 Buenos Aires (tel: 5300-5000; fax: 5300-9058; e-mail: centroservices@cac.com.ar).

British-Argentine Chamber of Commerce, 457 Avenida Corrientes, 1043 Buenos Aires, CF (tel: 4394-2762; fax: 4394-3860; e-mail: info@ccab.com.ar).

Rosario Chamber of Commerce, 1868 Córdoba, 2000 Rosario (tel: 425-7147; fax: 425-7486; e-mail: ccer@commerce.com.ar).

Banking
Asociación de Bancos Argentinos (ADEBA), San Martín 1229, Piso 10, 1004 Buenos Aires, CF (tel: 4394-1430; fax: 4394-6340).

Banco Crédito-Op Cooperativo Ltdo, Reconquista 484, Zona postal 1003, Buenos Aires, CF (tel: 4394-0105/0122; fax: 4325-9104).

Banco de Crédito Argentino, Reconquista 2, Zona postal 1092, Buenos Aires, CF (tel: 4334-1181/89; fax: 4334-5618).

Banco de Galicia y Buenos Aires, Tte Gral Juan D Perón 407, Zona postal 1038, Buenos Aires, CF (tel: 4329-6000; fax: 4329-6100).

Banco de la Ciudad de Buenos Aires, Florida 302, Zona postal 1313, Buenos Aires, CF (tel: 4325-5881/89).

Banco de la Nación Argentina (BNA), Bartolomé Mitre 326, Zona postal 1036, Buenos Aires, CF (tel: 4347-6000; fax:

Argentina

4347-8078); international banking division (tel: 4347-8092; fax: 4347-8078); foreign trade promotion (tel: 4347-8763; fax: 4347-8764).

Banco de la Pampa, Reconquista 319, Zona postal 1003, Buenos Aires, CF (tel: 4325-3410; fax: 4325-8750).

Banco de la Provincia de Buenos Aires, San Martín 137, Zona postal 1004, Buenos Aires, CF (tel: 4331-2561/3584; fax: 4331-5154).

Banco del Buen Ayre, Cerrito 740, Zona postal 1309, Buenos Aires, CF (tel: 4350-020/054; fax: 4837-890).

Banco del Sud, Maipú 277, Zona postal 1084, Buenos Aires, CF (tel: 4326-3313, 4326-2965; fax: 4325-3177).

Banco Francés del Rio de la Plata, Reconquista 165, Zona postal 1003, Buenos Aires, CF (tel: 4331-7071; fax: 4954-8009).

Banco General de Negocios, Esmeralda 120, Zona postal 1035, Buenos Aires, CF (tel: 4394-3003, 4394-2879; fax: 4394-2698).

Banco Hipotecario Nacional, Balcarce 167, Zona postal 1064, Buenos Aires, CF (tel: 4342-9732; fax: 4331-0620).

Banco Holandés Unido, Florida 361, Zona postal 1005, Buenos Aires, CF (tel: 4394-4553; fax: 4322-0839).

Banco Medefín UNB, 25 de Mayo 489, Zona postal 1339, Buenos Aires, CF (tel: 4313-4125; fax: 4312-9450).

Banco Quilmes, Tte Gral Juan D Perón 564, Zona postal 1038, Buenos Aires, CF (tel: 4331-8111/9; fax: 4334-5235).

Banco República, Sarmiento 336, Zona postal 1041, Buenos Aires, CF (tel: 4331-8385/87; fax: 4331-2130).

Banco Río de la Plata, Bartolomé Mitre 480, Zona postal 1036, Buenos Aires, CF (tel: 4331-7551, 4331-8361; fax: 4331-7551; internet site: http://www.bancorio.com.ar).

Banco Roberts, 25 de Mayo 258, Zona postal 1002, Buenos Aires, CF (tel: 4334-1723, 4334-6682; fax: 4334-6679).

Banco Sudameris, Tte Gral Juan D Perón 500, Zona postal 1038, Buenos Aires, F (tel: 4331-4061/9; fax: 4331-2793).

Banco Supervielle Société Générale, Reconquista 330, Zona postal 1003, Buenos Aires, CF (tel: 4394-4051/9).

Banco Tornquist, Bartolomé Mitre 531, Zona postal 1036, Buenos Aires, CF (tel: 4343-784/49; fax: 4342-6090).

Banco Velox, San Martín 298, Zona postal 1004, Buenos Aires, CF (tel: 394-0115/0665; fax: 4394-8255).

Banesto Banco Shaw, Sarmiento 355, Zona postal 1041, Buenos Aires, CF (tel: 4325-6500; fax: 4312-4743).

Caja Nacional de Ahorro y Seguro, Hipólito Yrigoyen 1750, Zona postal 1308, Buenos Aires, CF (tel: 4476-4216; fax: 4111-568).

Deutsche Bank, Bartolomé Mitre 401, Zona postal 1036, Buenos Aires, CF (tel: 4343-2511/9; fax: 4343-3536).

The First National Bank of Boston, Florida 99, Zona postal 1005, Buenos Aires, CF (tel: 4342-3051/61; fax: 4343-7303).

Lloyds Bank, Reconquista 101, Zona postal 1003, Buenos Aires, CF (tel: 4331-3551/9; fax: 4342-7487).

Central bank
Banco Central de la República Argentina, Reconquista 266, 1003 Buenos Aires (tel: 4348-3500; fax: 4334-6489).

Travel information
Aerolíneas Argentinas, Paseo Colón 185, Zona postal 1063, Buenos Aires, CF (tel: 4320-2000; fax: 44317-3585; internet: www.austral.com.ar).

Austral Líneas Aéreas (ALA), Avda Corrientes 485, Piso 9, Zona postal 1398, Buenos Aires, CF (tel: 4340-7800, 4317-3605; fax: 4317-3992).

Ministry of tourism
Secretaría del Turismo, Presidencia de la Nación, Suípacha 1111, Piso 21, Zona potal 1360, Buenos Aires, CF (tel: 4312-5624, 4311-2089; fax: 4313-6834; internet site: http://www.sectur.gov.ar/eng/menu.htm).

National tourist organisation offices
Asociación Argentina de Agencias de Viaje y Turismo (Travel Agents' Association), Viamonte 640, Piso 10, Zona postal 1053, Buenos Aires, CF (tel: 4322-2804).

Ministries
Ministry of Culture and Education, Pizzurno 935, Zona postal 1020, Buenos Aires, CF (tel: 424-1551/9, 445-666, 448-110).

Ministry of Defence, Av. Paseo Colón 255, Zona postal 1063, Buenos Aires, CF (tel: 343-1561).

Ministry of Economy, Public Works and Services, Hipólito Yrigoyen 250, Zona posal 1310, Buenos Aires, CF (tel: 342-6411, 342-6421/9, 349-8814, 349-8810/2; fax: 331-0292, 331-2619, 331-2090; internet site: http://www.mecon.ar/default.htm).

Ministry of Foreign Affairs and International Trade, Reconquista 1088, Zona postal 1003, Buenos Aires, CF (tel: 331-0071, 312-1775, 312-3434; fax: 312-3593, 312-3423).

Ministry of the Interior, Balcarce 50, Zona postal 1064, Buenos Aires, CF (tel: 342-6081, 343-0880).

Ministry of Justice, Av Gral Gelly y Obes 2289, Piso 7, Zona postal 1425, Buenos Aires, CF (tel: 803-1051/3, 803-5453; fax: 803-3955).

Ministry of Labour and Social Security, Av L N Alem 650, Zona postal 1001, Buenos Aires, CF (tel: 311-3303, 311-2945).

Ministry of Public Health and Social Action, Av 9 de Julio 1925, Zona postal 1332, Buenos Aires, CF (tel: 381-8911, 381-8919).

Office of the President, Balcarce 50, Zona postal 1064, Buenos Aires, CF (tel: 331-5041, 303-608, 331-3183).

Other useful addresses
Administration of Agriculture and Agroindustrial Markets, Paseo Colón 922, Piso 1, Of 131, 1063 Buenos Aires (tel: 4349-2272/4; fax: 4349-2272).

Administration of Fish and Marine Resources, San Martín 459, Piso 2, 1004 Buenos Aires (tel: 4394-1869, 4394-5961).

Administration of Forestry Production, Av Paseo Colón 982, Piso 1, 1063 Buenos Aires (tel: 4349-2101, 4349-2103; fax: 4349-2108).

Administration of Geological and Mining Resources, Julio A Roca 651, Piso 8, 1322 Buenos Aires (tel: 4349-3131).

Administration of Livestock Markets, Paseo Colón 922, 1063 Buenos Aires (tel: 4349-2287, 4349-2294; fax: 4362-5144).

Administration of Markets of Non-Traditional Products, Paseo Colón 922, Buenos Aires (tel: 4362-1738, 4349-2280/2; fax: 4349-2280).

Administration of Mining Development, Av Julio A Roca 561, Piso 8, 1322 Buenos Aires (tel: 4349-3133).

Administration of Native Forestry Resources, San Martin 459, Piso 2, 1004 Buenos Aires (tel: 4394-1869).

Argentine Embassy (USA), 1600 New Hampshire Avenue, NW, Washington DC 20009 (te: 202-238-6400; fax: 202-332-3171; e-mail: info@embajadaargentinaeeuu.org).

Argentine Industry Association, Av L N 1067, Piso 10, 1001 Buenos Aires (tel: 4313-2012, 4313-2512, 4313-2561; fax: 4313-2413).

Argentine Institute of Plant Sanitation and Quality, Av Paseo Colón 982, 1063 Buenos Aires (tel: 4313-8311).

Argentine Petrochemical Institute, Av Santa Fe 1480, Piso 5, Buenos Aires (tel: 4813-3436; fax: 4813-3436).

Nations of the World: A Political, Economic and Business Handbook

Argentine Petroleum Institute, Maipú 645, Piso 3, Primer Cuerpo, Buenos Aires (tel: 4322-3233, 4322-3652, 4322-3244; fax: 4322-3233).

Association of Importers and Exporters, Av Belgrano 124, Piso 1, 1092 Buenos Aires (tel: 4342-0010/9; fax: 4342-1312).

British Embassy, Dr Luis Agote 2412/52, Casilla de Correo 2050, 1425 Buenos Aires (tel: 4803-7070/1; fax: 4803-1731).

Bolsa de Comercio de Buenos Aires (Stock Exchange), Sarmiento 299, 1st Floor, AR 1353 Buenos Aires (tel: 4311-1174, 4311-5231, 4311-5235; fax: 4312-9332, 4312-6636).

Bureau of Export Promotion, Av Julio A Roca 651, Piso 6, 1322 Buenos Aires (tel: 4334-2975; fax: 4331-2266).

Centre for Business Promotion, Buenos Aires Stock Exchange, Sarmlento 299, Piso 1, 1353 Buenos Aires (tel: 4311-5231/4, 4313-4812, 4313-4544; fax: 4312-9332).

Customs Authority, Hipólito Yrigoyen 250 Of 606, 1310 Buenos Aires (tel: 4331-7330; fax: 4331-9839).

Department of Public Works and Transport, 250 Hipólito Yrigoyen Street, 11th Floor, Office 1141, PC 1310, Buenos Aires (tel/fax: 4349-7728; e-mail: arco@meyosp.mecon.ar).

Federal Board of Investment, San Martín 871, 1004 Buenos Aires (tel: 4313-5557; fax: 4313-1486).

Junta Nacional de Carnes (National Meat Board), San Martin 459, 104 Buenos Aires (tel: 4394-5161; fax: 4322-9357).

National Administration of Customs, Azopardo 350, 1328 Buenos Aires (tel: 4343-0661/9, 4343-0101/9).

National Administration of Fishing and Aquaculture, Av Paseo Colón 982, Anexo Jardin, Piso 1, 1063 Buenos Aires (tel: 4349-2330/1; fax: 4349-2332).

National Administration of Fuels, Av Paseo Colón 171, Piso 6, Of. 620, 1063 Buenos Aires (tel: 4319-8030/1).

National Commission of Telecommunications, Sarmiento 151, Piso 4, Of 435, 1041 Buenos Aires (tel: 4331-1203).

National Institute of Industrial Technology, Av L N Alem 1067, Piso 7, 1001 Buenos Aires (tel: 4313-3013).

National Institute of Mining Technology, Parque Tecnológico Migueletes, Casilla de Correo 327, 1650 San Martín (tel: 4754-5151, 4754-4141; fax: 4754-4070, 4754-8307).

National Institute of Statistics and Census, Dirección de Difusión Estadistics, Centro de Servicios Estadísticos, Av Julio A Roca 615, 1067 Buenos Aires (tel: 4349-9651).

National Viticulture Institute, Av Julio A Roca 651, Piso 5, Of 22, 1067 Buenos Aires (tel/fax: 4343-3816).

Public Works and Transport Department, 250 Hipólito Yrigoyen Street, 11th Floor, Office 1141, PC 1310, Buenos Aires (tel/fax: 4349-7728; e-mail: arco@meyosp.mecon.ar).

Secretariat of Agriculture, Livestock and Fisheries, Av Paseo Colón 982, 1063 Buenos Aires (tel: 4362-2365, 4362-5091, 4362-5946; fax: 4349-2504).

Secretariat of Energy, Av Paseo Colón 171, Piso 8 Of 803, 1063 Buenos Aires (tel: 4349-8003/5; fax: 4343-6404).

Secretariat of Finance, Hipólito Yrigoyen 250, 1310 Buenos Aires (tel: 4331-0731, 4342-2937, 4341-8900; fax: 4331-0292).

Secretariat of Industry, Av Junio A Roca 651, 1322 Buenos Aires (tel: 4334-5065, 4342-7822; fax: 4331-3218).

Secretariat of International Economic Relations, Reconquista 1088, 1003 Buenos Aires (tel: 4331-7281, 4331-1073; fax: 4312-0965).

Secretariat of Mining, Av Junio A Roca 561, Sector 9, 1322 Buenos Aires (tel: 4349-3212, 4349-3232; fax: 4343-3525).

Secretariat of Public Works and Communications, Sarmiento 151, 1041 Buenos Aires (tel: 4499-481; fax: 4312-1283).

Secretariat of Transportation, Av. 9 de Julio 1925, 1332 Buenos Aires (tel: 4381-1435, 4381-4007).

Secretariat of Trade and Investment, Hipólito Yrigoyen 250, 1310 Buenos Aires (tel: 4331-2208).

Sociedad Rural Argentina (one of the main associations of big landowners), Florida 460, 1005 Buenos Aires (tel: 4392-2030, 4322-2111).

Subsecretariat of Economic Planning, Hipólito Yrigoyen 250, Of 843, 1310 Buenos Aires (tel: 4349-5079; fax: 4349-5730).

Superintendencia de Seguros de la Nación (Insurance Superintendency), Av Julio A Roca 721, 1067 Buenos Aires (tel: 4306-653).

Telecom Argentina Stet-France Telecom SA, Maipú 1210, 9th Floor, Buenos Aires (tel: 4968-3604, 4968-3606).

Trade Information and Opportunities, Reconquista 1098, 1003 Buenos Aires (tel: 4315-1125; fax: 4311-1331).

Undersecretariat of Air, River and Maritime Transport, Hipólito Yrigoyen 250, 1310 Buenos Aires (tel: 4349-7205; fax: 4342-6365).

Undersecretariat of Interior Security, Balearce 50 Post box 1064, Buenos Aires (tel: 4342-9440 Ext 579; fax: 4331-7051).

Undersecretariat of Investments, Hipólito Yrigoyen 250, Piso 10 Of 1010, 1310 Buenos Aires (tel: 4349-8515/6, 4349-5037; fax: 4349-8522).

Undersecretariat of Medical and Sanitary Inspection, 9 de Julio 1925, Piso 10, Of 1003, 1332 Buenos Aires (tel: 4383-1811; fax: 4381-8912).

Unión Industrial Argentina (main private sector industrial association), Avenida Leandro N Alem 1067, 11 Piso, 1001 Buenos Aires (tel: 4313-2762).

US Embassy, Avenida Colombia 4300, 1425 Buenos Aires (tel: 5777-4533; fax: 5777-4240).

World Trade Centre Buenos Aires, Moreno 584, Piso 6, 1091 Buenos Aires (tel: 4331-3432, 4331-2604; fax: 4343-4270).

Internet sites

Agricultural and economic information (in Spanish): http://www.inta.gov.ar

Argentina Business: http://www.invertir.com/index.html

Argentina wine business: http://www.winesofargentina.com/index.php

Business etiquette: http://www.businessculture.com/argentina/index.html

Information on Mercosur: http://www.ar/SECEC/index.htm

Inter-American Development Bank: http://www.iadb.org

Latin Trade Online: http://www.latintrade.com

Latin World (directory of Internet resources): http://wwwlatinworld.com

List of government department web sites: http://www.gksoft.com/govt/en/ar.html

Newspapers (in Spanish):
   http://www.clarin.com.ar
   http://www.pagina12.com.ar

Official Buenos Aires web site: http://www.buenosaires.com

Organisation of American States: http://www.oas.org

Web site of southern Argentina: http://www.surdelsur.com/

Armenia

Armenia made significant economic progress in 2005 and came close to making breakthroughs on a number of issues clouding its regional position. Armenia's domestic politics, however, remained volatile, with opposition forces again unable to make any significant impact on government policy, despite considerable popular support.

An exceptional economy

In the first eight months of 2005, Armenia's GDP grew by 11.7 per cent. This included significant production increases in the industrial and agricultural sectors. In September, at a launch in Yerevan, the United Nations Human Development Report for 2005 ranked Armenia 83rd in the world. This placed Armenia well ahead of its Caucasus neighbours, despite the fact that Armenia is resource poor in comparison. In October, the IMF praised Armenia, particularly its economic growth and poverty reduction programmes.

Domestic politics still fraught

After massive anti-government demonstrations in March 2003 and April 2004, Armenia's domestic scene was relatively quiet by comparison for much of 2005. However, a referendum on 27 November again polarised the country. The referendum was the culmination of years of work on the part of the Armenian government, in co-operation with the Council of Europe and the EU. It proposed several constitutional amendments, which would, among other things, reduce the powers of the presidency, strengthen the parliament and the judiciary and enshrine human rights provisions within the constitution.

KEY FACTS

Official name: Haikakan Hanrapetoutioun (Republic of Armenia)

Head of State: President Robert Kocharian (since 1998; re-elected Apr 2003)

Head of government: Prime Minister Andranik Margarian (HHK) (since May 2000)

Ruling party: Coalition government: Hayastani Hanrapetakan Kusaktsutyun (HHK) (Republican Party of Armenia), Hai Heghapokhakan Dashnaktsutiun (Dashnaktsutiun) (Armenian Revolutionary Federation), Orinants Erkir (OE) (Rule of Law Country) (elected 25 May 2003)

Area: 29,800 square km

Population: 3.00 million (2004)

Capital: Yerevan

Official language: Armenian

Currency: Dram (D) = Luma 100

Exchange rate: D444.10 per US$ (Oct 2005)

GDP per capita: US$1,093 (2004)

GDP real growth: 10.10% (2004); 11.7% (Jan–Aug 2005)

Labour force: 1.64 million (2004)

Unemployment: 20.00% (2004)*

Inflation: 7.00% (2004)

Balance of trade: -US$464.99 million (2004)

Foreign debt: US$1.11 billion (2004)

* estimated figure

While agreeing to many of the proposed changes in principle, Armenia's opposition parties preferred to use the referendum as a vote of no confidence in the government and thus urged a boycott combined with anti-government demonstrations. The opposition cried foul when Armenia's election commission declared a 64 per cent turnout and 93 per cent support for the amendments. The Council of Europe and the US State Department also questioned the validity of these figures but in the same breath backed the result.

Nagorno-Karabakh and Azerbaijan

In 2005, Armenia's President Robert Kocharian met twice with his Azeri counterpart, Ilham Aliyev, in an unprecedented effort to resolve a seventeen-year-old dispute over the territory of Nagorno-Karabakh (Artsakh in Armenian). Armenian forces and their Karabakh allies control approximately 20 per cent of Azerbaijan's territory, the spoils of an armed conflict that ended in 1994. In July, officials from both countries expressed optimism that a peace deal may be in sight but a summit in August between the two presidents did not deliver the anticipated breakthrough. Many analysts blamed the failure on the proximity of parliamentary elections in Azerbaijan, scheduled for November, in which the Azeri government did not wish to appear soft on Nagorno-Karabakh.

Complicating Armenia's relations with Azerbaijan was a Russo-Georgian agreement in May to evacuate Russian military bases from Georgian territory. Although initially tight-lipped about its role, it became evident in June that Armenia would host some of the relocated Russian military hardware. Azerbaijan immediately protested that this effectively bolstered Armenia's military capacity, and the Azeri president announced his intention to substantially boost military spending. In an effort to counter Azerbaijan's defence spending increase, the Armenian government announced plans of its own, in September, to increase the defence budget by 21 per cent (to US$166 million).

Easing out of the Russian bear-hug?

Since the military victory of the Armenian-backed separatists in Nagorno-Karabakh in 1994, Armenia has been able to maintain the status quo in part due to economic, military and diplomatic assistance from Russia. The price for this aid includes the stationing of Russian military bases on Armenian soil and, increasingly, Russian domination of Armenia's energy industry. In September, a Russian company took control of Armenia's electricity network and in December, Russia's gas giant and Armenia's main supplier Gazprom, moved to push up the price of gas.

Armenia has been seeking ways of easing the comprehensive nature of this Russian bear-hug. Since at least 2004, Armenia has been searching for alternative energy supplies and in December 2005 announced an agreement with Iran. This agreement enabled Armenia to import Iranian gas in exchange for Armenian electricity. In April, the Armenian government announced that it was investigating the possibility of building a second nuclear power plant in order to increase the country's indigenous energy supplies.

The government also opened talks with NATO in October, flagging the possibility of joining the organisation's Individual Partnership Action Plan (IPAP), and in the same month stepped up negotiations with the EU, specifically over Armenia's plans to bring its economic and political system in line with EU norms.

Lonely in a tough neighbourhood

Energy deals with Iran aside, Armenia still found it tough-going in the region in 2005. Because of Armenia's dispute with Azerbaijan over Nagorno-Karabakh, Armenia's long and potentially profitable border with Turkey has been closed since 1993. Turkey has backed Azerbaijan over this issue, in large part due to linguistic and cultural affinities, and has also refused to open diplomatic relations with Armenia. In September 2005, Azerbaijan, Georgia and Turkey announced an agreement to build a Baku-Tbilisi-Kars rail link, which by-passed Armenia, despite the fact that transit through Armenia provided the most direct (and cheapest) route. The opening, in May, of the equally circuitous Baku-Tbilisi-Ceyhan (BTC) oil pipeline, linking the same three countries, and the on-going construction of a parallel gas pipeline underscored Armenia's regional isolation.

One possible avenue for improvement in Armenia's regional relations emerged in April. Turkey suggested the establishment a joint commission to examine the deaths of hundreds or thousands of Armenians between 1915 and 1917 in the then Ottoman Empire. However, this idea met a cool reception in Armenia, which accuses Turkey of being in denial.

Outlook

Armenia is likely to experience further high levels of economic growth in 2006 and make further inroads into poverty. Armenia's improving relationship with Iran has the potential to ease dependence upon Russian hydrocarbon supplies and, by extension, influence. However, if the UN Security Council decides to impose economic sanctions on Tehran in light of its apparently illegal nuclear energy activities, this may complicate Armenia's efforts to diversify its energy sector.

Armenia's continuing ostracism from regional communications and energy supply networks will ensure that Armenia will remain reliant upon Russian

KEY INDICATORS — Armenia

	Unit	2000	2001	2002	2003	2004
Population	m	3.80	3.80	3.83	3.33	3.00
Gross domestic product (GDP)	US$bn	1.90	2.03	2.40	2.33	3.55
GDP per capita	US$	533	534	631	700	1,093
GDP real growth	%	6.0	9.6	12.9	7.0	10.1
Inflation	%	-0.8	2.9	1.1	2.2	7.0
Unemployment	%	10.9	9.8	9.7	20.0	*20.0
Exports (fob) (goods)	US$m	307.0	342.0	507.0	525.0	730.4
Imports (fob) (goods)	US$m	774.0	877.0	991.0	991.0	1,195.4
Balance of trade	US$m	-467.0	-535.0	-484.0	-466.0	-465.0
Current account	US$m	-278.0	-201.0	-160.0	–	-200.0
Foreign debt	US$bn	1.0	1.0	1.1	0.9	1.1
Total reserves minus gold	US$m	318.3	320.5	425.0	510.2	575.9
Foreign exchange	US$m	296.8	310.3	394.9	491.4	563.9
Exchange rate	per US$	539.53	555.08	574.36	558.14	521.07

* estimated figure

Armenia

friendship and patronage for the foreseeable future.

Opposition efforts to oust the government over the November referendum have failed to generate any momentum, in no small part due to Western approval of the referendum result, and it appears likely that there will be little change on the political scene until national elections scheduled for early 2007.

Risk assessment

Politics	stable
Economy	stable
Regional stability	stable

COUNTRY PROFILE

Historical profile
At its height, the Armenian empire stretched from the Caspian Sea to the Mediterranean, before being incorporated into the Roman empire in AD301. In the eleventh century, Armenia was incorporated into the Turkish Seljuk empire.
1915 The Ottoman empire killed around 1.5 million Armenians in response to the independence movement.
1916 Armenia was conquered by Russia. It joined an alliance with Georgia and Azerbaijan.
1918–20 Armenia was an independent republic for two years.
1920 Turkey and Russia invaded Armenia. An agreement with Russia led to Armenia proclaiming itself a socialist republic.
1922 Armenia was incorporated into the Union of Soviet Socialist Republics (USSR).
1923 Stalin drew the current recognised borders that placed the mainly ethnic Armenian Nagorno-Karabakh in Azerbaijan.
1930s The country suffered under Stalin's purges, but Armenia also underwent industrial development.
1988–93 An earthquake in northern Armenia in 1988 killed 25,000. Nagorno-Karabakh demanded unification with Armenia, and conflict between Azerbaijan and Armenia began. It lasted intermittently for five years.
1990 The Pan-Armenian National Movement (PNM) won the parliamentary elections. A declaration of independence was made, but ignored by Moscow.
1991 The republic boycotted the Soviet referendum on the preservation of the USSR. In a referendum held shortly after the failed anti-Gorbachev coup in Moscow, 94 per cent voted for secession from the USSR. Levon Ter-Petrossian was elected president. Independence was formally proclaimed by the President. Armenia joined the Commonwealth of Independent States (CIS). The US recognised Armenia's independence.
1992 Armenia joined the UN. Conflict over Nagorno-Karabakh turned into full-scale war between Armenia and Azerbaijan.
1994 The war with Azerbaijan over Nagorno-Karabakh settled into an uneasy stalemate, with local Armenians backed by Armenian forces in control of the disputed enclave. A Russian-brokered ceasefire between Azerbaijan and Armenia has generally been honoured.
1995 The first post-independence parliamentary elections resulted in victory for the ruling party, PNM. A constitution was approved by referendum which gave the president substantial powers, including the right to pass decrees.
1996 Levon Ter-Petrosian was re-elected president. There were protests over alleged electoral fraud.
1998 President Levon Ter-Petrosian was forced out of office after stating his wish to open negotiations with Azerbaijan. Robert Kocharian was elected president. The domestic political scene experienced growing instability and politically motivated violence. Deputy minister of defence, Colonel Vagram Khorkhoruni, was murdered. Arkady Gukasian was elected president of Nagorno-Karabakh.
1999 Deputy minister of the interior, Artsun Markarian, was murdered. Prime Minister Vazgen Sargissian and other politicians were assassinated in the National Assembly. Aram Sargissian, the former prime minister's younger brother, was appointed to succeed him. The gunmen accused the government of leading Armenia into political and economic ruin.
2000 Prime Minister Andranik Markarian admitted that those affected by the 1988 earthquake were still living in a disaster zone.
President Arkady Gukasian of Nagorno-Karabakh was seriously wounded in an assassination attempt.
2001 Armenia became a full member of the Council of Europe.
There was no result in the US-brokered talks on Nagorno-Karabakh between the presidents of Azerbaijan and Armenia.
2002 The first meeting between the foreign ministers of Armenia, Azerbaijan and Turkey was held in Iceland to try to find a settlement for the Nagorno-Karabakh conflict.
2003 Incumbent Robert Kocharian won the second round of the presidential elections and the ruling Hayastani Hanrapetakan Kusaktsutyun (HHK) (Republican Party of Armenia), loyal to President Kocharian, won the parliamentary elections. There were criticisms of both elections. A referendum rejected constitutional amendments giving more power to the National Assembly. The death penalty was abolished.
2004 In April, thousands of opposition supporters demonstrated against President Kocharian.
2005 A referendum, which endorsed constitutional change to strengthen parliament and limit presidential power, was held on 27 November.

Political structure
Constitution
Although the country has had a directly elected president since 1991, a constitution was only approved by referendum in July 1995. It gave the president substantial powers, including the right to pass decrees.
An attempt to amend the constitution to give the National Assembly more power was rejected by the electorate during a referendum on 25 May 2003.
In 2005 a referendum endorsed a number of constitutionals amendments, including reducing the power of the presidency, strengthening parliament and the judiciary, and enshrining in the constitution human rights provisions.
Form of state
Multi-party republic: divided into various *marz* (provincial divisions).
It is a member of the Commonwealth of Independent States (CIS).
The executive
The president has broad powers. He is elected by direct universal suffrage for a period of five years and has the right to pass decrees.
Although, under the 1995 constitution, the president is not the head of the executive power, in fact, he directs that power, as he forms the government, appoints the prime minister and upon the proposal of the latter – the cabinet ministers. He can dismiss the prime minister at any time. The president is not a member of the government, but he chairs the sittings and ratifies all the government decisions. He also defines the structure and the order of the functioning of the government. Having consulted with the prime minister, the president has the power to dissolve the National Assembly. The president is commander of the armed forces, represents the country in international negotiations, signs agreements and treaties and appoints the chief prosecutor.
National legislature
The Azgayin Zhoghov (National Assembly) is the supreme legislative body and comprises 131 directly elected deputies.
Legal system
The highest appellate court is the Court of Appeal, which ensures uniformity in how the country's laws are applied through its final review of cases. The Court of Appeal's members are nominated by the Council of Justice, an administrative body created to ensure independence of the

courts, and then appointed by the president. Armenia also has a Constitutional Court, which is charged with ensuring that legislative decisions and presidential decrees are consistent with the constitution. Of the Constitutional Court's nine members, five are appointed by the president and four by the National Assembly. The president of Armenia heads the Council of Justice. The minister of justice and the prosecutor general serve as deputy heads of the council.

In January 1999, a new civil code came into effect which creates the legal framework for property rights and contract enforcement, as well as the legal and institutional framework necessary for commercial banking activities. Despite this, the enforcement of laws and contracts remains weak.

Last elections
25 May 2003 (parliamentary); 19 February/5 March 2003 (presidential).
Results: Parliamentary: the ruling HHK, loyal to President Kocharyan, won 23.5 per cent of the vote and 35 seats in the National Assembly, the Justice bloc 13.6 per cent and 17 seats, OE 12.3 per cent and 18 seats, the Armenian Revolutionary Federation 11.4 per cent and 11 seats, National Unity (NU) 8.8 per cent and nine seats, and the United Labour Party (ULP) 5.7 per cent and six seats.
Presidential: incumbent Robert Kocharyan won 48.3 per cent of the vote, Stepan Demirchyan 27.4 per cent and Artashes Geghamyan 16.9 per cent; turnout was 61.2 per cent; Kocharian won a second term with 67.5 per cent of the vote in the run-off election on 5 March.

Next elections
2007 (presidential and parliamentary)

Political parties
Ruling party
Coalition government: Hayastani Hanrapetakan Kusaktsutyun (HHK) (Republican Party of Armenia), Hai Heghapokhakan Dashnaktsutiun (Dashnaktsutiun) (Armenian Revolutionary Federation), Orinants Erkir (OE) (Rule of Law Country) (elected 25 May 2003)
Main opposition party
Ardartyun (Justice) alliance; National Unity Party (AMK).

Population
3.00 million (2004)
Ethnic make-up
Armenians (93 per cent), Azerbaijanis (3 per cent), Russians (2 per cent); Kurdish and Yezidi minorities.
Religions
Armenian Apostolic Church (90 per cent), Armenian Catholic and Protestant (9 per cent), Russian and Greek Orthodox and Jewish.

Education
Primary education is followed by seven years of secondary school which is divided into a four-year first cycle (ages 12 to 16) and a three-year second cycle (ages 16 to 19). In the second cycle, students can opt between general or technical education. Higher education is provided by the Université Marien-Ngouabi, which is largely state subsidised. It has a yearly enrolment of about 12,000 students.
Literacy rate: 87.5 and 74.5 per cent respectively for males and females; adult rates (Unesco 2000).
Compulsory years: 6 to 11
Enrolment rate: 96 per cent gross primary enrolment, 87 per cent gross secondary enrolment, of relevant age groups, (including repeaters) World Bank.
Pupils per teacher: 19 in primary schools.

Health
The total expenditure on health is around 7.5 per cent of GDP, of which government spending is 42–43 per cent.
HIV prevalence: 0.1 per cent aged 15–49 in 2003 (World Bank)
Life expectancy: 75 years (World Bank)
Fertility rate/Maternal mortality rate: 1.2 births per woman (2003); maternal deaths 35 per 100,000 live births (World Bank).
Birth rate/Death rate: 6 deaths to 12 births per 1,000 people (World Bank).
Infant mortality rate: 31 per 1,000 live births; 3 per cent of children aged under five are malnourished (World Bank).
Head of population per physician/bed: 3 physicians and 0.7 hospital beds typically available per 1,000 people.

Welfare
The poverty family allowance system is based on the principle of voluntary involvement and aims to target the most needy. Welfare issues concerning the elderly are crucial as almost 97 per cent of them need constant medication and 41 per cent need home care.
Pensions
In order to improve the state pension system, the government has increased the level of contributions for certain income groups. Under the state system, pensioners receive a uniform payment. There are no private pension funds.

Main cities
Yerevan (capital, estimated population 1.2 million in 2004), Vanadzor (147,400), Gyumri (125,300).

Languages spoken
Russian and Kurdish.
Official language/s
Armenian

Media
Press
The National Press Club (NPC) of Armenia formed on May 1997 is a self-governing, apolitical, non-profit, independent public organisation that aims to support free and democratic press in Armenia.
Dailies: The most popular newspapers published in Armenia in Armenian and Russian languages include *Azg*, *Yerkir*, *Hayots Ashkharh*, *Hayastani Hanrapetutyun*, *Respublica Armenia* and *Golos Armenii*.
Weeklies: *Haykakan Zhamanak* is a popular weekly newspaper.
Broadcasting
Radio: State TV and Radio, Yerevan, is the national broadcaster.
Television: Ashtarak is a popular cable television station. State TV and Radio, Yerevan, is the national broadcaster.
In April 2002, the government removed the licences of two independent television companies, A-One Plus and Noyan Tapan, effectively leaving Armenia with no major independent news broadcast service.

Economy
Armenia's government has made structural reform a priority and efforts to make the economy a free market have resulted in steady growth since 1994. Agriculture, construction and services are the main drivers of growth. Current policy centres on reforming the tax and legal systems and the liberalisation of trade.
Privatisation policies have been successful with over two-thirds of small companies and three-quarters of large companies and agricultural land now being owned privately.
Nevertheless, privatisation has failed to reduce unemployment, which remains high at 20 per cent, while 43 per cent of the population live below the poverty line. The shortage of specialist skills and political instability have worsened the investor climate, which in turn has prevented poverty alleviation and has slowed the pace of job creation.
Projects supported by the World Bank have focussed on the development of the private sector and improving public services, in particular the health and education services.

External trade
Armenia is a net energy exporter, supplying Georgia and the Nagorno-Karabakh region in Azerbaijan. In 2003 Armenia joined the World Trade Organisation.
Imports
Imports of essential goods, including natural gas and petroleum, foodstuffs, tobacco products, equipment and diamonds.

Armenia

Main sources: Belgium (10.3 per cent total, 2004), Iran (10.2 per cent), Russia (9.8 per cent), Israel 8.6 per cent), US (7.7 per cent), UAE (6.2 per cent), Italy (5.4 per cent), Germany (5.0 per cent), France (4.6 per cent), Ukraine (4.5 per cent)

Exports
Principal exports are precious stones, including diamonds, semi-precious stones, precious metals, base metals, mineral products (together constituting over 50 per cent of total exports), transport equipment, electrical equipment. Armenia also exports energy.

Main destinations: Belgium (16.8 per cent total 2004), Israel (14.3 per cent), Russia (14.2 per cent), Germany (11.4 per cent), Iran (9.9 per cent), US (7.8 per cent), The Netherlands (5.8 per cent)

Agriculture
Farming
Armenia is a major producer of grapes, vegetables, dairy products and some cotton and sheep breeding. Agriculture contributes around 25 per cent to GDP and employs over 45 per cent of the work force. Armenia was the first former Soviet republic to privatise agricultural land. There are around 335,000 family farms, which account for the bulk of agricultural output. Development has been inhibited by lack of private investment, an inadequate agricultural financing system and poor infrastructure.

Crop production in 2004 included: 296,000 tonnes (t) wheat, 575,942t potatoes, 5,426t pulses, 575,942t roots and tubers, 148,892t grapes, 7,288t garlic, 222,047 tomatoes, 3,000t tobacco, 262,570t fruit in total, 714,431t vegetables in total. Livestock production included: 54,027t meat in total, 33,406t beef, 8,505t pig meat, 7,241t lamb, 4,275t poultry, 31,532t eggs, 555,240t milk, 1,000t honey, 5,320t cattle hides, 1,200t greasy wool.

Industry and manufacturing
The economy relies heavily on the industrial sector. Industry accounts for around 40 per cent of GDP and employs around 20 per cent of the workforce.

Industry is mainly based on the extraction and processing of natural resources, particularly ores and chemicals.

Other industries are mechanical engineering, electronic generators, textiles, synthetic rubber, wine and cognac, mineral water and food processing.

Tourism
Tourism is an increasingly important sector of the economy. Since 1997, much has had to be done to modernise and extend the infrastructure. Visitor numbers have increased by substantial annual percentages. Compared with 123,000 in 2001, there were 268,000 in 2004, with the trend continuing into 2005. A significant proportion of visitors are diaspora Armenians, but the numbers from other regions, including the EU and Asia, are growing. Tourism accounts for around five per cent of GDP.

Mining
Mining accounts for around 13 per cent of GDP and employs 3 per cent of the workforce.

There are large deposits of copper, zinc, aluminium and other metals, including gold. Copper accounts for 38 per cent of the reserve, iron and molybdenum 25 per cent each; gold 7.3 per cent, silver 1.6 per cent and lead and zinc 3.1 per cent. Armenia is rich in varieties of building stone, such as marble, granite, tuffa, limestone and gypsum, and in semi-precious and ornamental stones, such as agates, jasper, amethyst and turquoise.

The major markets for Armenia's mining products are Belgium, Georgia, Iran, Liechtenstein, Switzerland and Germany.

Hydrocarbons
Armenia has no oil reserves and is completely dependent on imports of petroleum products, all of which are transported by rail or truck since there are no oil pipelines into Armenia.

Armenia has no natural gas reserves and is totally reliant on imports, mainly from Turkmenistan through the Georgian and Russian gas pipelines in the north. It imported 49.4 billion cubic feet in 2003. When the Nagorno-Karabakh conflict erupted, Azerbaijan ceased shipments of natural gas to the country. A 140km pipeline to deliver natural gas from Iran to Armenia began construction in July 2004. The natural gas pipeline, which will commence delivery of one billion cubic metres a year in 2007, should enable Armenia to diversify its supplies.

Energy
Installed electricity capacity is 3.2GW, generated by thermal, hydro and nuclear power. 40 per cent of the total is supplied by the Metsamor nuclear station, which was reopened in 1995 after being closed after the 1988 earthquake. Armenia has been under international pressure to close the plant. There are 32 hydroelectric plants, which account for 34 per cent of production. Thermal power plants supply the remaining 26 per cent. Armenia is linked to Iran's grid, permitting two-way exchange of electricity.

Armenia and Iran are co-operating on development of renewable energy sources. A wind power plant with a capacity of 10.4MW, supported by Iranian money, was inaugurated in December 2005 and will supply the electricity grid.

Financial markets
Non-banking financial institutions (such as leasing organisations, insurance companies and investment funds) are either non-existent or at an early stage of development.

A Securities and Exchange Commission was established in November 1998.

Stock exchange
The Yerevan Stock Exchange (YSE) was liquidated in early 2001. The only stock exchange operating in Armenia is the Armenian Stock Exchange Self-Regulatory Organisation (Armex), which was established in February 2001.

Banking and insurance
The banking system in Armenia is growing but still experiences difficulties in attracting deposits (representing less than 10 per cent of GDP). Most lending is available at short maturities only and at high interest rates. The range of facilities and services on offer to customers is increasing. HSBC Armenia was one of the most active banks.

There are over 30 commercial banks in the country.

Central bank
Central Bank of the Republic of Armenia

Time
GMT plus three hours

Geography
Armenia is a landlocked country of high mountains and fertile valleys situated in south-west Transcaucasia. Georgia lies to the north of Armenia, to the west is the border with Turkey. Azerbaijan is to the east of the country – the ethnic Armenian enclave, Nagorno-Karabakh, is wholly within Azerbaijan – and to the south Armenia has a short frontier with Iran. The autonomous republic of Nankhchivan, an Azerbaijani territory, is an enclave within southern Armenia. Lake Sevan is at an altitude of 1,924 metres and is surrounded by mountain ranges reaching 4,090 metres at Mount Aragats. Numerous rivers and streams flow from the mountains into the River Araks which marks the south-western border of the country, its basin forming a fertile lowland to the south of Yerevan – the Ararat Plain.

Climate
Cool winters and hot summers characterise Armenia with the average January temperature in Yerevan at around 1 degree Celsius (C), while July averages 26 degrees C. Snow falls in early winter (November and December) and rain (April to June).

Annual rainfall in Yerevan averages 33cm but is much higher in mountain regions.

Entry requirements
Passports
Required by all. Must be valid six months after date of departure.
Visa
Required by all except nationals of all CIS countries. Tourist visas can be obtained online: www.armeniaforeignministry.am/eVisa/ for visits of up to 21days. An official invitation is only required for visits over 21 days and business travel.
Currency advice/regulations
Exchange booths are not common and ATMs are rare. US dollar notes or cheques can be changed at the Arm-econobank in Yerevan (see Business Directory, Banking).
Customs
Only a small amount of personal goods are duty-free. On arrival all foreign currency must be declared as well as valuable items such as jewellery, cameras, computers and musical instruments.

Health (for visitors)
Although a reciprocal health agreement for urgent medical treatment exists with the UK, payment by cash for medical assistance will be required, so obtain receipts. Proof of UK residence is required.
Mandatory precautions
Vaccination certificate is required for yellow fever if travelling from an infected area.
Advisable precautions
It is advisable to be 'in date' for the following immunisations: polio (within 10 years), tetanus (within 10 years), typhoid fever, hepatitis 'A' (moderate risk only); hepatitis 'B' (if you need to spend more than six to eight working weeks in the region); tuberculosis; malaria precautions for eastern border areas only; rabies (if travelling to rural areas).
Any medicines required should be taken by the visitor. It could be wise to have precautionary antibiotics if going outside major urban centres. Water precautions are recommended (water purification tablets may be useful).
A travel kit including a disposable syringe is a reasonable precaution.

Credit cards
Major credit cards and travellers cheques are accepted at the banks in Yerevan.

Public holidays
Fixed dates
1–2 Jan (New Year), 6 Jan (Orthodox Christmas), 8 Mar (Women's Day), 7 Apr (Motherhood and Beauty Day), 24 Apr (Genocide Memorial Day), 9 May (Victory and Peace Day), 28 May (First Republic Day), 5 Jul (Constitution Day), 21 Sep (Independence Day), 7 Dec (Earthquake Memorial Day), 31 Dec (New Year's Eve).

Variable dates
Good Friday

Working hours
Business
Mon–Fri: 0900–1800.
Shops
Mon: 0800–1900, Tue–Sat: 0800–2100.

Electricity supply
220V AC 50Hz

Weights and measures
Metric system

Social customs/useful tips
An interpreter is necessary in order to conduct business.
The Armenians are very hospitable, and will invite strangers into their homes for food. Being unable to speak their language will not be a problem.

Security
Visitors should not travel to the western region of Nagorno-Karabakh and the military occupied area surrounding it.

Getting there
Air
National airline: Armenian Airlines.
International airport/s: Zvartnots (EVN), 10km southwest of Yerevan; facilities include business and VIP halls plus duty-free shops. Flights arrive from Europe, Russia and Middle East.
Airport tax: An exit duty is levied of US$20, exclusive of transit passengers.
Surface
Road: A 192-metre road bridge over the Araks river, linking Armenia with Iran, was opened in January 1996 and is the most important international road link. It is possible to travel by road to the enclave of Nagorno-Karabakh.
The road linking Yerevan to Tblisi (capital of Georgia) has a high rate of highway robberies.
Rail: There is a line running from Batumi on the Black Sea, via Tbilisi and the Georgian border, to Yerevan. The *Gnatsk* is a through train, running on alternate days throughout the month. Of the four classes of carriage the *coupé* (with compartments and sleeping berths for 4), and *Luxe* (for two, with shared bathrooms between two compartments) are recommended. Refreshments must be carried onboard for the journey. Pre-booking is advised.
There are services running from Moscow, via Gyumri, to Yerevan.

Getting about
National transport
Internal travel, particularly by air, can be disrupted by fuel shortages and other problems.
Air: There is a small domestic airport at Yerevan, offering flights to major Armenian destinations.
Road: There are 7705km (4788 miles) of road network, although many of these can be very poor. It is possible to travel by road to the enclave of Nagorno-Karabakh.
Buses: Coaches also operate between major town and city centres.
City transport
Taxis: Taxis in Yerevan are unmetered. Expect to negotiate a fare from airport to city centre; journey time 20 minutes. Vans (route taxis) are available in Yerevan and a few major cities.
Buses, trams & metro: There is a metro in Yerevan. The journey time from the airport to the city centre is about 30 minutes.
Car hire
There are no car rental services available. It is usual to hire a car and driver. Traffic drives on the right.

BUSINESS DIRECTORY
The addresses listed below are a selection only. While World of Information makes every endeavour to check these addresses, we cannot guarantee that changes have not been made, especially to telephone numbers and area codes. We would welcome any corrections.

Telephone area codes
The international direct dialling (IDD) code for Armenia is +374, followed by area code and subscriber's number:
Abovyan 22 Yerevan 1

Chambers of Commerce
American Chamber of Commerce in Armenia, Hotel Armenia, 1 Amiryan Street, Yerevan 375010 (tel: 599-187; fax: 599-151; e-mail: amcham@arminco.com).

European Union Chamber of Commerce in Armenia, 8/1 Khorenatsi Street, Yerevan 375010 (tel: 547-760; fax: 547-780; e-mail: info@eucca.am).

Chamber of Commerce and Industry of the Republic of Armenia, 11 Khanjyan Street, Yerevan 375010 (tel: 560-184; fax: 587-871; e-mail: armcci@arminco.com).

Kotayk Marz Chamber of Commerce and Industry, 11 Sevani Street, Abovyan 378510 (tel: 26-035; fax: 233-97; e-mail: ccikotayk@ccikotayk.am).

Yerevan Chamber of Commerce and Industry, 11 Khanjyan Street, Yerevan 375010 (tel: 560-184; fax: 587-871; e-mail: yercci@arminco.com).

Banking
Ardshinbank of the Republic of Armenia, 3 Deghatan Street, Yerevan (tel: 560-611; fax: 151-155, 584-761).

Arminpex Bank, 2 Nalbandian Street, 375010 Yerevan (tel: 589-927, 567-183, 565-873; fax: 151-786).

Armenia

HSBC Armenia Bank, 1 Vramshapouh Arka Street, Yerevan (tel: 151-717; fax: 151-886).

Armeconombank, 32 G.Nzdehi Street, Yerevan 375026 (tel: 562-705, 531-115; fax: 151-149).

Armagrobank, 7a Movses Khorenacu Street, Yerevan 375015 (tel: 534-342; fax: 390-712-6).

Mellat, 1 P.Byusandy, Yerevan (tel: 581-354; fax: 151-811).

Prometeus, 19 Kochari Street, Yerevan 375012 (tel: 273-000; fax: 274-818).

Haykap, 22 Sarian Street, Yerevan 375002 (tel: 532-080; fax: 390-703-3).

Erebuni, 13 Khagakh- Don Street, Yerevan 375087 (tel: 577-256).

Credit - Yerevan, 2/8 Vramshapouh Arkay Street, Yerevan 375010 (tel: 589-065; fax: 580-083).

Central bank
Central Bank of Armenia, Vazgen Sargsyan Street 6, 375010 Yerevan (tel: 583-841; fax: 523-852); e-mail: mcba@cba.am).

Travel information
Armenian Airlines, Zvarnots Airport, 375042 Yerevan-42 (tel: 773-313).

Flight information (24 hours): CIS flights (tel: 533-311, 533-411); international flights (tel: 779-704).

Levon Travel Bureau, 10 Sayat Nova Avenue, 375001 Yerevan (tel: 525-210, 525-284, 583-193; fax: 151-133; e-mail: tourism@levontravel.am; internet site: http://www.levontravel.com).

Zvartnots International Airport, 375042 Yerevan (tel/fax: 151-392).

Ministries
Ministry of Agriculture and Food Supplies, 1 Government House, Republican Square, 375010 Yerevan (tel: 524-641; fax: 151-086, 151-583).

Ministry of Communications, 22 Sarian Street, 375002 Yerevan (tel: 526-632; fax: 151-446; 151-151); Union Bldg, Republic Square, Yerevan 375010.

Ministry of Culture, Youth and Sports, 5 Toumanian Street, 375010 Yerevan (tel: 528-869, 561-920; fax: 523-930).

Ministry of Defence, Proshian Settlement, 60 G. Shaush Road, Yerevan (tel: 357-822; fax: 526-560).

Ministry of Ecology and Natural Resources, 35 Moskovian Street, 375012 Yerevan (tel: 530-741; fax: 534-902).

Ministry of Economical Structural Reform, 1 Government House, Republic Square, Yerevan 375010 (tel: 151-069).

Ministry of Education and Science, 13 Movses Khorenatsi Street, 375010 Yerevan (tel: 526-602; fax: 151-150).

Ministry of Energy, 1 Government House, Republican Square, 375010 Yerevan (tel: 521-964; fax: 151-036).

Ministry of Finance and Economy, 1 Melik-Adamian Street, 375010 Yerevan (tel: 527-082; fax: 151-154).

Ministry of Foreign Affairs, 2 Government House, Republican Square, 375010 Yerevan (tel: 523-531; fax: 151-042).

Ministry of Health, 8 Tumanian Street, 375001 Yerevan (tel: 582-413; fax: 151-097).

Ministry of Industry and Trade, Division of Tourism, 5 Hanrapetutjan Street, 375010 Yerevan (tel: 560-274, 560-780, 589-472, 587-706; fax: 526-577).

Ministry of Internal Affairs and National Security, 2 Nalbandian, 375025 Yerevan (tel: 529-733).

Ministry of Justice, 8 Parliament Street, 375010 Yerevan (tel: 582-157; fax: 565-640).

Ministry of Local Government Affairs, 2 Government House, Yerevan (tel: 525-274).

Ministry of Operational Affairs, 1 Government House, Republican Square, Yerevan 375010 (tel: 151-036; fax: 520-321).

Ministry of Privatisation and Foreign Investment, 1 Government House, Republic Square, Yerevan 375010 (tel: 520-351; fax: 151-036).

Ministry of Social Security, 18 Issahakian Street, 375025 Yerevan (tel: 526-831; fax: 151-920).

Ministry of Statistics and Data, State Registrar, Republican Square, 375010 Yerevan (tel: 524-213).

Ministry of Transport, 10 Zakiyan Street, 375015 Yerevan (tel: 563-391; fax: 525-268).

Ministry of Urban Planning and Construction, 1 Government House, Republican Square, Yerevan (tel: 589-080; fax: 151-036).

Prime Minister's Office, 1 Government House, Republican Square, 375101 Yerevan (tel: 520-360; fax: 151-035).

Other useful addresses
Armenian Embassy (USA), 2225 R Street, NW, Washington DC 20008 (tel:202-319-1976; fax: 202-319-2982).

Armenian Foreign Trade Organisation, V/O Armentorg, Dom Pravitelstva, Ploschad Lenina, 375010 Yerevan.

Armenian Foundation for SMEs, 19 Khandjian Street, 375010 Yerevan (tel: 578-231; fax: 151-690; e-mail: smeda@arminco.com).

Armenian State Foreign Economic and Trade Association, Str 25 Hr Kochar, 375012 Yerevan (tel: 224-310; fax: 220-034).

Azat Mamoul (Dashnak News Agency), Yerevan (tel: 563-493; fax: 565-728).

British Embassy, 28 Charents Street, Yerevan (tel: 151-842; fax: 151-807).

Business Communication Centres, 6 Baghramian Avenue 2, 375009 Yerevan (tel: 222-145; fax: 151-934; e-mail: ggv@bcc.arminco.com).

Committee of Privatisation and Management of State Property, Ul Budakhian 1, 375014 Yerevan (tel: 280-120).

Department of Emergency Situations, Government House, Republican Square, Yerevan 375010 (tel: 531-612; fax: 151-036).

EC Energy Centre, Institute of Energy, Amaranotsayeen 127, Yerevan (tel/fax: 151-730).

Enterprise Development and Foreign Investment Promotion Armenian Agency (EDIPA), 23/1 Vramshapuh Arkah, Yerevan 375002 (tel: 538-929; fax: 151-149).

Secretariat of the Council of Ministers (tel: 520-360, 522-482; fax: 151-035, 141-036).

State Commission for Tax Inspection, Movses Khorenatsi, Yerevan 375010 (tel: 538-101, 538-073).

State Department for Statistics, State Register and Analysis of the Republic of Armenia, 3 Government House, Republic Square, Yerevan (tel: 524-213; fax: 521-921).

State TV and Radio, 5 Alex Manoogian, 375025 Yerevan (tel: 555-033).

TACIS (Technical Assistance to Commonwealth of Independent States), Ministry of Economy, 1 Government Building, Republic Square, Yerevan 10 (tel: 528-803; fax: 151-164).

US Embassy, 18 Baghramyan Avenue, Yerevan 375019 (tel: 520-791; fax: 520-800; e-mail: usinfo@arminco.com).

Internet sites
Armenian information: www.armgate.com

Armenia Business to Business Directory: www.armenian.com/business.html

Armenia Yellow Pages: www.armenian.com

Armenian Stock Exchange: www.armex.am

Aruba

KEY FACTS

Official name: Aruba

Head of State: Queen Beatrix of the Netherlands; Governor Fredis Refunjol (from 7 May 2004)

Head of government: Prime Minister Nelson Oduber (MEP) (since 2001, re-elected Sept 2005)

Ruling party: Movimiento Electoral di Pueblo (MEP) (People's Electoral Movement) (since 2001; re-elected Sept 2005)

Area: 193 square km

Population: 91,506 (2004)

Capital: Oranjestad

Official language: Dutch

Currency: Aruban guilder (Af) = 100 cents

Exchange rate: Af1.79 per US$ (Nov 2004)

GDP per capita: US$22,000 (2003)

GDP real growth: 3.50% (2004)

Unemployment: 0.60% (2003)

Inflation: 2.50% (2004)

Balance of trade: -US$330.00 million (2003)

Visitor numbers: 1.23 million (2003)

COUNTRY PROFILE

Historical profile
1499 First European sighting of the islands of the Netherlands Antilles by Spanish mariners.
1636 Dutch took over; Spanish and Portuguese Jews escaping from persecution in Europe settled in the islands.
1800–02 British Protectorate.
1825 Gold discovered and mined until 1916.
1863 Slavery completely abolished.
1954 Internal autonomy for Netherlands Antilles.
1986 Aruba seceded from Netherlands Antilles; both entities elected to remain part of the Kingdom of the Netherlands. Aruba has complete autonomy over its internal affairs, while the Netherlands is constitutionally responsible for defence and external affairs.
2001 Movimiento Electoral di Pueblo (MEP) (People's Electoral Movement) won the parliamentary elections and Nelson Oduber (MEP) became prime minister.
2003 A law was introduced in order to help fight money laundering more efficiently.
2004 Fredis Refunjol was sworn in as governor on 7 May.
2005 Negative publicity about the official investigation into the disappearance of a US teenager resulted in a drop in US visitor arrivals. In 24 September parliamentary elections, Prime Minister Nelson Oduber's People's Electoral Movement won 43 per cent of the vote (11 of 21 seats), the Aruban People's Party 33 per cent (8) and the Patriotic Movement of Aruba and the Real Democratic Party won 1 seat each. Turnout is 85 per cent.

Political structure
Form of state
Parliamentary democracy
The executive
The Head of State is the monarch of The Netherlands, who is represented by a governor. The governor is appointed by the monarch, upon the recommendation of the Aruban Council of Ministers. The seven-member Council of Ministers is vested with the executive power and headed by a prime minister. The Council is accountable to the Staten (parliament).
National legislature
The Staten has 21 members, elected for a four-year term by proportional representation.

Legal system
Aruba's judicial system, which has mainly been derived from the Dutch system, operates independently of the legislature and the executive. Jurisdiction, including appeal, lies with the Common Court of Justice of Aruba and the Supreme Court of Justice in The Netherlands.
Last elections
23 September 2005 (parliamentary)
Results: MEP won 43 per cent of the votes (11 seats), the AVP 33 per cent, (eight seats). The PPA and OLA won one seat each. Turnout was 85 per cent.

Political parties
Ruling party
Movimiento Electoral di Pueblo (MEP) (People's Electoral Movement) (since 2001; re-elected Sept 2005)
Main opposition party
Arubaanse Volks Partij (AVP) (Aruban People's Party)

Population
91,506 (2004)
Ethnic make-up
Carib and Arawak Indian, European and African heritage.
Religions
Roman Catholic (82 per cent), Protestant (8 per cent), Hindu, Muslim, Confucian, Jewish.

Education
Literacy rate: 97 per cent

Health
Life expectancy: 78.8 years: male 75.5 years; female 82.3 years (2003).
Fertility rate/Maternal mortality rate: Two births per woman (2003)
Birth rate/Death rate: 12 births per 1,000 population; six deaths per 1,000 population (2003).
Infant mortality rate: Six per 1,000 live births (2003)

Main cities
Oranjestad (capital, estimated population 20,700 in 2003), St Nicolas (17,400).

Languages spoken
Papiamento is the local language. Dutch, English and Spanish are widely spoken.
Official language/s
Dutch

Media
Press
Dailies are mainly in Dutch and in the native Papiamento language. These are *Extra Bondia Aruba*, *Diario Aruba*, *Corant*,

Aruba

Amigoe di Aruba (Dutch language Antillean newspaper), *Beurs* (Dutch). English language newspapers are the *News* and *Aruba Today*.

Broadcasting
Radio Victoria broadcasts in English. Television is operated by Tele-Aruba.

Advertising
All newspapers accept advertising in English. Advertising is also available on commercial radio and television.

Economy
Tourism, oil refining, and financial services are Aruba's economic mainstays. Tourism contributes some 38 per cent of GDP and employs 35 per cent of the workforce. Future economic growth depends on increased capacity utilisation, moves to further upgrade the quality of tourism, and the diversification of the economy. To encourage financial services and manufacturing investment, the government has developed the offshore financial sector and free trade zones.

The effects of the 11 September 2001 terrorist attacks on the US and the global economic downturn resulted in a weakening of the tourism industry. Consequently, there was a recession in 2001–02. In 2003, consumer spending and investments increased, marking the end of the recession, and GDP growth of 1.4 per cent was registered. With business confidence rising, the Aruban economy continued to improve and GDP grew by 3.5 per cent in 2004.

There have been recent warnings about Aruba's rapidly escalating government spending with public debt reaching 45.9 per cent of GDP at the end of 2004. The IMF warns that the island's vulnerability to downturns in the tourist industry means that debt accumulation should be managed with more prudence.

External trade
Main trading partners: US, The Netherlands, Japan, Taiwan, Colombia and Venezuela. Free zones are situated near the harbour of Oranjestad and Barcadera.

Imports
Main imports are crude oil, chemicals, machinery and electrical equipment, food and consumer goods. Imports totalled US$2.21 billion in 2003.

Main sources: US (55 per cent total, 2004), Netherlands (13.8 per cent), Venezuela (3.5 per cent)

Exports
Main exports include refined petroleum products, live animals, animal products, art and collectables, machinery and electronic equiptment and vehicles. Exports totalled US$1.88 billion in 2003.

Main destinations: US (79.9 per cent total, 2004), Netherlands (4.3 per cent), Canada (3.7 per cent)

Industry and manufacturing
Oil processing is the dominant industry in Aruba, despite the expansion of the tourism sector.

The Lago refinery, originally owned by a subsidiary of Exxon, was closed in 1985, depriving the island of one-third of its revenue, and later sold to the Aruban government for a nominal amount. It was rehabilitated by Coastal Oil and Gas Corporation of Houston and reopened in 1990. The refinery, by now owned by US-based El Paso, produced 169,000 barrels per day (bpd) of oil in the first quarter of 2003, around 50 per cent of capacity. El Paso announced in early 2003 that it intended to sell the refinery to pay off its debts, although it did not expect to receive the refinery's full US$1.3 billion book value.

In February 2004, El Paso agreed to sell the refinery and related marine, bunkering and marketing affiliates to Valero Energy Corporation, US, for US$465 million. The refinery has a throughput capacity of 315,000bpd.

Tourism
Tourism is the island's largest economic activity, accounting for 35 per cent of GDP. There has been considerable expansion in the sector in recent years with visitor figures exceeding one million by the year 2000. Further growth was stalled by events in 2001, especially the 11 September terrorist attacks in the US. Total visitor numbers have nevertheless remained relatively stable on average over subsequent years, but the more lucrative stay-over market, which was particularly affected, has not recovered; cruise visits on the other hand have experienced strong growth.

Three-quarters of visitors to the island come from the US. South American countries and The Netherlands make up most of the rest. The government is seeking to attract more visitors from Europe. A national short-haul airline, connecting with the Netherlands Antilles, has been set up. The Reina Beatrix airport can handle 2.6 million travellers.

Hydrocarbons
Aruba does not import either coal or gas. Crude oil makes up 97.4 percent of all oil imported with 235.1 thousand barrels daily being imported with some consumed domestically but most is refined and exported.

Energy
The government-owned power plant has a capacity of 114MW and distributes electricity through Elmar NV.

Financial markets
There is an offshore financial sector. There were growing international concerns about the island's use as a money laundering centre, although Aruba has been active in international efforts to quell the practice. Aruba is not on the OECD list of non-co-operative tax-havens.

Banking and insurance
The banking sector consists of six commercial banks, two of which are branches of banks established in The Netherlands and Curaçao, one is a subsidiary of a bank established in Curaçao and three have their head offices in Aruba.

KEY INDICATORS — Aruba

	Unit	2000	2001	2002	2003	2004
Population	m	0.09	0.09	0.09	0.09	0.09
Gross domestic product (GDP)	US$bn	1.86	1.88	1.88	1.88	1.88
GDP per capita	US$	20,530	20,755	20,495	22,000	–
GDP real growth	%	3.6	-0.7	-2.6	1.4	3.5
Inflation	%	4.0	2.9	3.2	3.2	2.5
Consumer prices	1995=100	115.0	118.6	122.5	*125.8	*128.3
Exports (fob) (goods)	US$m	2,521.0	2,418.0	1,483.2	2,045.1	–
Imports (fob) (goods)	US$m	2,579.3	2,364.0	2,013.4	2,378.8	–
Balance of trade	US$m	-57.8	-54.6	-530.1	-333.7	–
Current account	US$m	232.4	332.2	-329.4	-155.4	-113.6
Total reserves minus gold	US$m	208.0	293.7	339.7	295.2	295.4
Foreign exchange	US$m	208.0	293.7	339.7	295.2	295.4
Exchange rate	per US$	1.79	1.79	1.79	1.79	1.79

* estimated figure

Aruba is a signatory of a new EU tax agreement that was introduced in July 2005. It has agreed to pass on, to the tax department of an EU citizen's country, information concerning the amount of money in savings accounts, to allow tax to be levied from the account holder's home country.

Aruba has also agreed to supply information on tax fraud, for criminal or civil trials, and notify EU member states about additional malpractices.

Central bank
Centrale Bank van Aruba

Offshore facilities
The offshore banking sector has great potential. The Central Bank has been better equipped to regulate the banking sector since the enactment of the State Ordinance on the Supervision of the Credit System, 1998. The minimum issued capital of an offshore bank is Af5 million (US$2.8 million). Aruba has pledged to phase out all 'harmful tax practices' identified by the OECD by 2006.

Time
GMT minus four hours

Geography
Located in the Caribbean Sea north of Venezuela, Aruba is a flat island with large white sandy beaches and sparse vegetation. The highest point is Mount Jamanota which is 188 metres above sea level.

Climate
Aruba lies outside the Caribbean's hurricane zone. It has an almost constant temperature of 27 degrees Celsius with cooling trade winds and an absence of tropical storms and hurricanes. Low levels of humidity and rainfall.

Entry requirements
Passports
Required by all, except US and Canadian citizens, who only need proof of citizenship. A return or onward ticket and adequate subsistence are required.

Visa
Required by all, except nationals exempt from passport control, plus many European and South American countries, Australia, Japan (visiting for up to three months) and transit passengers. To clarify, and for further exceptions, visit http://www.visitaruba.com/travel/toaruba/customs.html or contact the nearest embassy.

Currency advice/regulations
From 2003, passengers with cash exceeding Af20,000 (US$11,173) must declare the full amount on arrival. The law was introduced in order to help fight illegal money laundering.

Customs
Besides articles for personal use, persons aged over 18 are allowed a 2 litres of liquor and 200 cigarettes, 50 cigars and 250 grammes of tobacco.

Health (for visitors)
Mandatory precautions
Yellow fever vaccination certificate required if arriving from an infected area.
Advisable precautions
Typhoid vaccination.

Hotels
It is advisable to book in advance. There are numerous tourist hotels. There is a 6 per cent government room tax and 11 per cent service charge added to the bill.

Public holidays
Fixed dates
1 Jan (New Year's Day), 18 Mar (National Anthem and Flag Day), 25 Mar (G F Croe's Day), 30 Apr (Queen's Day), 1 May (Labour Day), 25 Dec (Christmas Day), 26 Dec (Boxing Day).
Variable dates
Good Friday, Easter Monday, Ascension Day.

Working hours
Banking
Mon–Fri: 0800–1200, 1300–1600.
Business
Mon–Fri: 0800–1200, 1300–1700. Sat: 0800–1200.
Government
Mon–Fri: 0800–1200, 1300–1700. Sat: 0800–1200.
Shops
Mon–Sat: 0800–1800. Some stores close Tuesday afternoon; some close 1200–1400 every working day.

Telecommunications
Mobile phones
GSM 900/1800 services are available, with coverage throughout the island.

Electricity supply
110/120V 60 cycles

Getting there
Air
International airport/s: Reina Beatrix (AUA), 2.5km from Oranjestad, duty-free shop, bar, restaurant, post office, car hire.
Airport tax: Except for transit passengers, US destinations US$36.75, all other international destinations US$33.50.
Surface
Main port/s: Oranjestad, San Nicolas and Barcadera are deep-water harbours.

Getting about
National transport
Air: ALM operates services between Aruba and Netherlands Antilles.
Road: A well-developed road system connects all major towns.

Buses: Regular services in and around main centres. Also cars/ *jitney* services and sightseeing tours.
City transport
Taxis: Usually identified by 'TX' before the licence number. It is advisable to negotiate fares for tours in advance. Tipping is discretionary.
Car hire
Prices are reasonable. An international licence is required.

BUSINESS DIRECTORY

The addresses listed below are a selection only. While World of Information makes every endeavour to check these addresses, we cannot guarantee that changes have not been made, especially to telephone numbers and area codes. We would welcome any corrections.

Telephone area codes
The international dialling code (IDD) for Aruba is +297, followed by subscriber's number.

Chambers of Commerce
Aruba Chamber of Commerce and Industry, 10 JE Irausquin Boulevard, PO Box 140, Oranjestad (tel: 582-1566; fax: 583-3962; businessinfo@arubachamber.com).

Banking
ABN-AMRO Bank NV, Caya GF Betico Croes 89, Oranjestad (tel: 821-515; fax: 821-856).

Aruba Bank NV, Caya GF Betico Croes 41, PO Box 192, Oranjestad (tel: 821-550; fax: 829-152).

Aruban Investment Bank NV, Middenweg 20, PO Box 1011, Oranjestad (tel: 827-327; fax: 827-461).

Banco di Caribe, Caya GF Croes 90, Oranjestad (tel: 832-168; fax: 832-422).

Caribbean Mercantile Bank NV, Caya GF Betico Croes 53, PO Box 28, Oranjestad (tel: 823-118; fax: 824-373).

First National Bank of Aruba NV, Caya GF Betico Croes 67, Oranjestad (tel: 833-221; fax: 821-756).

Interbank Aruba, Caya GF Betico Croes 38, Oranjestad (tel: 831-080; fax: 824-058).

Central bank
Centrale Bank van Aruba, JE Irausquin Boulevard 8, Oranjestad (tel: 525-2100; fax: 525-2101).

Travel information
National tourist organisation offices
Aruba Tourism Authority, L G Smith Boulevard 172, Eagle (tel: 821-019; fax: 834-702).

Aruba Tourism Authority P R, A Schutte Str 2, Oranjestad (tel: 823-778, 823-779,

Aruba

837-254; fax: 830-075; internet site: http://www.arubatourism.com).

Ministries

Ministry of Economic Affairs and Tourism, Government of Aruba, L G Smith Boulevard 76, Oranjestad (tel: 826-977; fax: 835-084).

Ministry of Finance, Oranjestad (tel: 823-237; fax: 827-116).

Ministry of Public Works and Public Health, L G Smith Boulevard, Oranjestad (tel: 824-900; fax: 826-826).

Ministry of Traffic, Communications and Utilities, Oranjestad (tel: 824-900; fax: 835-985).

Cabinet of the Minister Plenipotentiary of Aruba, R J Schimmelpennincklaan 1, 2517 JN The Hague, The Netherlands (tel: (+3170) 356-6200; fax: (+3170) 356-6210).

Other useful addresses

Aruba Foreign Investment Agency, 85 Caya G F Betico Croes, Oranjestad (tel: 826-070; fax: 822-745).

Aruba Trade & Industry Association, Pedro Gallegostraat 6, PO Box 562, Oranjestad (tel: 827-593).

Department of Economic Affairs, Commerce and Industry, L G Smith Boulevard 160, Sun Plaza Building, Oranjestad (tel: 821-181, 821-482; fax: 834-494).

Elmar NV (electricity), Oranjestad (tel: 824-600, 837-681).

Internet sites

Bon Dia – on-line edition (local language): http://www.bondia.com

Ascension Island

KEY FACTS

Official name: Ascension Island

Head of State: Queen Elizabeth II, represented by Governor Michael Clancy (since 2004) (resides in St Helena)

Head of government: Administrator of Ascension Island Michael Thomas Hill (from Sep 2005) (the first Ascension Island government was established in Apr 2001)

Area: 88 square km

Population: 1,100 (2004)

Capital: Georgetown

Official language: English

Currency: Pound sterling (£) = 100 pence

Exchange rate: £0.57 per US$ (Oct 2005)

COUNTRY PROFILE

Historical profile
1501 Ascension Island was sighted by the Portuguese mariner Juan da Nova.
1815 The UK took possession (on Napoleon's exile to St Helena) and established a garrison.
1823 Responsibility for the island was taken over by the Admiralty Board until 1922, when it became a dependency of St Helena.
1922–64 The island was managed by the Eastern Telegraph Company (renamed Cable and Wireless in 1934).
1942 The US constructed a military airstrip and the island became an important transit point on the South African route between 1943–45.
1957 A US presence was re-established with the extension of the Eastern Test Range, and in 1967, a Nasa tracking station was built (since closed).
1964 In view of plans to establish BBC and Composite Signals Organisation (CSO) stations, an administrator was appointed.
1982 The island was re-garrisoned during the Falklands War and Ascension Island remains the intermediate stop for Royal Air Force (RAF) flights from the UK to the Falkland Islands.
1999 Geoffrey Fairhurst became the administrator of Ascension Island.
2001 The first Ascension Island government was established.
2002 Andrew Michael Kettlewell was appointed administrator.
2004 Michael Clancy became governor, resident in St Helena. Ascension Island is hoping to increase its population by building new homes. From April, the Ascension Island Base is the new name for the RAF base: command of RAF Ascension Island has been transferred from Headquarters Strike Command, based at RAF High Wycombe, to the Permanent Joint Headquarters (PJHQ), Northwood, London.
2005 In September, Michael Thomas Hill replaced Andrew Kettlewell as Administrator of Ascencion Island. Elections to the second AscensionIsland Council were held in November.

Political structure
Constitution
Ascension Island is governed by a Foreign and Commonwealth Office (FCO) administrator, responsible to the governor of St Helena and to the FCO.
Up to April 2001, the island infrastructure was paid for by user organisations. The Ascension Island government (AIG) was established in April 2001.
In conjunction with the St Helena government, the AIG is working out a new constitution. Income tax and customs duties will replace the former tax-free status. Local services are to be managed by the AIG and national matters by St Helena. By 2005 the Islanders had hoped they would have been granted right of abode and the right to purchase property. However the British government has said that Island Status is not feasible.
Last elections
16 November 2005
Results: The seven elected Councillors are independent members. Turn out was low at 39 per cent.

Population
1,100 (2004)
Ethnic make-up
St Helenians, UK and US citizens.
Religions
Anglican and Roman Catholic

Main cities
There are no cities. Georgetown is the administrative capital and port (estimated population 560 in 2003). Two Boats village is a residential area; Traveller's Hill is the RAF garrison; Cat Hill is the US base.

Languages spoken
Official language/s
English

Media
Press
The Islander is published and updated weekly.

Economy
Ascension Island's main importance is as a military base and communications centre. Public services, public works, healthcare facilities and the pier head are funded by the military and commercial organisations on the island. They each contribute an agreed sum annually.
Tax and customs duties were introduced in 2002.
The pier head facility is being developed and improved for both public and commercial use.
Cable and Wireless plc operates an international satellite telecommunications service and the Ariane Earth Station on behalf of the European Space Agency (ESA). The BBC operates its Atlantic relay station broadcasting to Africa and South America.

Ascension Island

Agriculture
Fishing
There is a species of marteralia or flying squid that inhabit the waters around Ascension.

Tourism
The island is renowned for its wildlife. From 2004, the RMS St Helena is based in Cape Town, South Africa, from September 2004, calling at the Namibian ports of Luderitz and Walvis Bay, St Helena and Ascension Island.

Environment
In 2002, the British government gave £500,000 to the Royal Society for the Protection of Birds (RSPB) to clear the Island of rats and feral cats that were destroying the seabird population. Ascension Island is also an important breeding colony for the green turtle.

Hydrocarbons
Ascension Island relies entirely on imports of hydrocarbons. It imports as much as its consumer requirement, which is around 200 barrels per day.

Banking and insurance
There are no international banking facilities on the island; the local bank is the St Helena Government Savings Bank.

Time
GMT

Geography
Ascension Island lies in the South Atlantic, north-west of St Helena. It is a rocky peak of volcanic origin with 44 craters. The last eruption took place about 600 years ago. The highest point is Green Mountain.

Climate
The climate is sub-tropical. Showers occur throughout the year with slightly heavier rain in January–April.

Entry requirements
Visa
All visitors must have the Administrator's written permission to land, before travelling. An 'Ascension Island Entry Permit' form, to be completed, can be downloaded from www.ascension-island.gov.ac/visitors.htm. Entry is only granted with evidence of visitors full medical insurance policy, covering medical evacuation by air, when necessary.

Customs
There is an £11 entry permit fee.
In April 2002, customs duties were introduced on alcohol, tobacco and petrol/diesel. Small amounts of personal goods are duty-free (see website above).

Hotels
A new consortium is operating all of Ascension Island's accommodation from March 2002, which includes the Georgetown Obsidian Hotel (www.obsidian.co.ac, tel/fax: 6246, e-mail: accommodation@atlantis.co.ac).

Working hours
Government
Mon–Fri: 0830–1230, 1330–1630.

Telecommunications
Telephone/fax
Direct satellite telephone

Getting there
Air
Wideawake Airfield is run by the US Space Command under the 1956 Bahamas Long Range Proving Ground Agreement. Negotiations with the US authorities concluded in October 2003 with the signing of an agreement, allowing air-charter access to the airfield.
Twice-weekly RAF Tristar flights (Mondays and Thursdays) to Ascension Island depart from RAF Brize Norton, Oxfordshire. Bookings can be made through Passenger Services Department, Andrew Weir Shipping Ltd, Dexter House, 2 Royal Mint Court, London EC N4XX, UK (tel: +44 (0)207-816-4800; fax: +44 (0)207-816-4802; e-mail: reservations@aws.co.uk).
There is a weekly USAF flight between Ascension, Antigua and Patrick Airforce Base for military personnel.

Surface
Water: There are irregular but timetabled calls by the RMS *St Helena*. From September 2004, the vessel will operate year-round in the South Atlantic, providing more frequent trips from Cape Town to Walvis Bay, St Helena and Ascension Island. The ship is operated under contract by Andrew Weir Shipping Ltd, on behalf of the owners, St Helena Line Ltd.
Bookings can be made through Passenger Services Department, Andrew Weir Shipping Ltd, Dexter House, 2 Royal Mint Court, London EC N4XX, UK (tel: +44 (0)207-575-6480; fax: +44 (0)207-575-6200; e-mail: reservations@aws.co.uk).
Main port/s: Georgetown

Getting about
Car hire
Cars can be hired for £20 per day.

BUSINESS DIRECTORY

Telephone area codes
The international dialling code (IDD) for Ascension Island is +247 followed by subscriber's number.

Travel information
Travel information (for air travel and bookings on the RMS St Helena): Passenger Services Department, Andrew Weir Shipping Ltd, Dexter House, 2 Royal Mint Court, London EC N4XX, UK (tel: +44 (0)207-575-6480; fax: +44 (0)207-575-6200; e-mail: reservations@aws.co.uk).

St Helena Line, Andrew Weir Shipping (SA) Pty Ltd, 3rd Floor, BP Centre, Thibault Square, Cape Town, South Africa (tel: +27-21-425-1165; fax: +27-21-421-7485; e-mail: sthelenaline@mweb.co.za).

Miss Kerry Yon, Solomon and Co plc, Jamestown, St Helena, South Atlantic (tel: +290-2523; fax: +290-2423; e-mail: solco.shipping@helanta.sh).

Ministries
Administrator's Office, Islander Building, Georgetown (tel: 6311; fax: 6152; e-mail: andrew.kettlewell@ascension.gov.ac; internet site: http://www.ascension-island.gov.ac).

Other useful addresses
From 3 February 2003, the AIG telephone number is 7000, which will take the caller to a pre-recorded menu, from which the caller can identify and dial the extension of the contact required.

Chief Executive Officer, Ascension Island Works and Services Agency (AIWSA), Jamestown, St Helena (tel: 6346; fax: 6139; e-mail: chiefexecutive.aiwsa@atlantis.co.ac).

St Helena Government Representative, Suite 5, 30b Wimpole St, London W1G 8YB, UK (tel: +44 (0)207-224-5025; fax: +44 (0)207-224-5035).

St Helena Desk Officer, Foreign and Commonwealth Office, Room, King Charles Street, London SW1A 2AH, UK (tel: +44 (0)207-270-2695).

Miles Apart (books, maps, videos on South Atlantic Islands), 5 Harraton House, Exning, Newmarket, Suffolk CB8 7HF, UK (tel: +44 (0)1638-577-627: fax: +44 (0)1638-577-874); 5929 Avon Drive, Bethesda, Maryland 20814, USA (tel/fax: +1301-571-8942; e-mail: familycarter@msn.com).

The Islander, Fort Hayes, Georgetown (tel/fax: 6327; e-mail: the-islander@org.ac; internet site: http://www.the-islander.org.ac).

Internet sites
Andrew Weir Shipping:
http://www.aws.co.uk

Ascension Island government:
http://www.ascension-island.gov.ac

St Helena web portal:
http://www.sthelenaonline.com

Australia

KEY FACTS

Official name: Commonwealth of Australia

Head of State: Queen Elizabeth II (since 1952), represented by Governor General Major General Michael Jeffery (from 11 Aug 2003)

Head of government: Prime Minister John Howard (leader of LP) (since Mar 1996; re-elected for a fourth term 9 Oct 2004)

Ruling party: Liberal Party (LP)-National Party (NP) coalition (since 1996; last re-elected 9 Oct 2004)

Area: 7,682,300 square km

Population: 20.23 million (2004); 19.88 million (OECD, 2003)

Capital: Canberra

Official language: English

Currency: Australian dollar (A$) = 100 cents

Exchange rate: A$1.31 per US$ (Oct 2005)

GDP per capita: US$30,445 (2004)

GDP real growth: 3.20% (2004)

Labour force: 10.35 million (2004)

Unemployment: 5.50% (OECD, 2004)

Inflation: 2.30% (2004)

Oil production: 541,000 bpd (2004)

Balance of trade: -US$18.22 billion (2004)

Foreign debt: US$495.60 billion (2004)

Annual FDI: US$118.20 billion (cumulative, 1995–2004, OECD); US$42.20 billion (OECD, 2004)*

* estimated figure

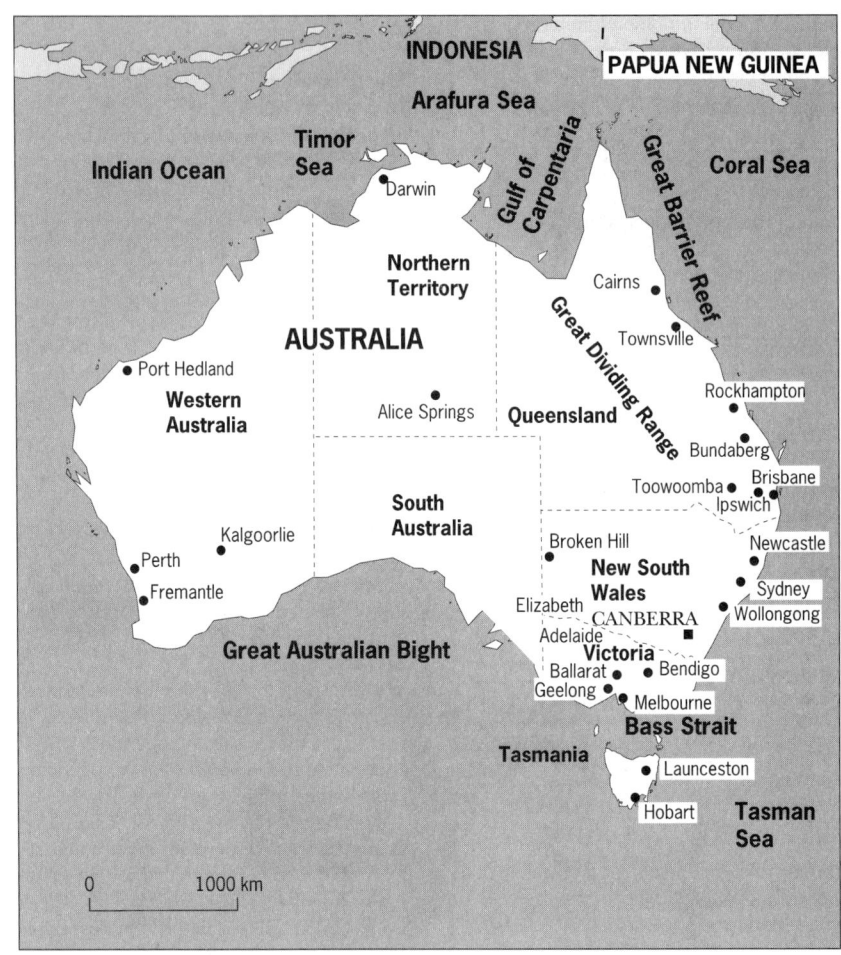

In winning his fourth term as prime minister in Australia's October 2004 general elections, John Howard of the Liberal-National coalition secured a place in the record books as one of Australia's longest serving leaders. His victory over his Labor party rival, Mark Latham, was despite vociferous opposition to Australia's strong support for the US-lead coalition of forces in Iraq. Mr Howard's victory came despite his less than charismatic personality and patrician manner, which contrasted sharply with the more down to earth, 'good bloke' image of his opponent, very much in the tradition of former Labor prime minister Bob Hawke who was famous for holding a beer drinking entry in *Guinness World Records*. As is the way of elections, though, in December 2005 Mr Howard made the record books as longest serving prime minister and Mr Latham was unceremoniously dumped by his party. For many Australians, for whom voting is compulsory, the political events of late 2004 paled into insignificance when compared to the sporting disaster that overtook the nation in 2005. For the first time in 14 years, Australia lost a nail-biting cricket series to England. The loss of the legendary Ashes caused national heart searching; losing at any sport comes hard to the Australian psyche. Losing to England is ten times harder.

Election changes

Cricket apart, the opinion polls had originally predicted a close-run race in an election contest in which the Iraq involvement had featured prominently. The first Bali bombings in October 2002 had claimed 89 Australian lives, the September 2005 bombing a further four, bringing in to sharp relief Australia's involvement in the Middle East. Iraq apart, the economy was prominent in both party campaigns. His election victory left Mr Howard with an increased majority in the lower house, but, of greater importance, it also gave his Liberal National coalition control of the Senate, the upper house. This will enable the coalition to contemplate introducing the privatisation legislation that it has long hankered after, but which in recent years had been blocked by the non-coalition majority in the upper house. The newly elected government took power, for its fourth term, in July 2005. Mr Howard also now has the opportunity to introduce long overdue reforms to Australia's creaky labour market, in which practices reminiscent of 1950s Britain still governed hours worked, allowed Australia's legendary 'sickies' (the practice of taking holiday leave disguised as sick leave) and in which so called 'allowable areas' have long prevailed. However, on the back of a leaked Treasury report, some analysts say this labour reform programme is linked to ideology not productivity.

Much of Australia's legislation and industrial practice relating to labour markets dates back to the creation of the Australian Industrial Relations Commission (AIRC) which requires employers to navigate their way through a labyrinth of industrial rules and regulations that, in most countries, would seem to be as absurd as they are childish,. However absurd they may seem, however, these rules and regulations affect the working day of some 20 per cent of the country's work force in some detail. Of those in the work force not covered by the AIRC regulations and provisions, many others come under what are known as 'enterprise bargaining schemes' introduced by the Labor government of Australia's iconic prime minister Bob Hawke in the 1980s. Much of Australia's labour legislation and provisions certainly goes towards creating what is, by international standards, a feather-bedded work force. 'Gods Own' is probably not a misnomer in a country where the minimum wage in 2005 was A$467 (US$365) a week, one of the highest in the world. Unsurprisingly, Australia's employers have long sought a relaxation of what is seen by most as a highly restrictive labour market.

Economy

2005 saw Australia move four places higher in the World Economic Forum's 'Global Competitiveness Report' for 2005–06, placing it in the top 10, ahead of Japan, the UK, Canada, Germany, Hong Kong and France. Australia was also designated 'the world's most resilient economy' for the fourth year in succession in the IMD *World Competitiveness Yearbook* for 2005. Showering accolades on the Australian economy, the same organisation rated Australia as having the highest overall productivity per person employed in the Asia Pacific region.

Australia had seen strong economic growth throughout 2004, in which GDP grew by 3.5 per cent. This level of growth – almost unique in the western developed economies – faltered slightly in 2005 due in some measure to record oil prices, but also to increased inflation and higher interest rates, which critically caused a drop in housing construction and related developments. Exports also registered a levelling off in 2005. None the less, 2005 was Australia's 15th consecutive year of growth, something very few developed economies could boast of. The economy's weaker performance in 2005 was the almost inevitable sequel to the pre-election boom created by the 2004/05 budget, which bore all the characteristics of a pre-election budget: these included extensive tax cuts, a A$13.3bn (US$10.4bn) increase in family allowances over a five year period and tax cuts of A$10bn (US$7.8bn) billion over the same period. In many respects, this was the Liberal-National coalition stealing the Labor party's clothes, but doing so on the back of a strong economy.

The pre-election boom, combined with exceptionally low unemployment, created extraordinary consumer confidence, which in turn inspired greater business confidence, particularly in the manufacturing sector. Perhaps predictably, much of this growth turned out to be short term as economic growth slumped to a near standstill at the end of the year. However, the economy had reverted to its longer term growth pattern by the end of the first quarter of 2005, with growth back up to 2.8 per cent. This figure concealed some potentially worrying developments. Capital investment dropped by an annual rate of 6.4 per cent. Household consumption registered growth at an annual rate of 3.1 per cent for the same period, but this was well down on the levels seen in 2003 and 2004. High household debt lead to expectations of a continued downturn in consumption.

By mid-2005 Australia's unemployment rate had fallen to almost 5.0 per cent, causing the central bank to highlight labour shortages in a number of industries, notably the construction, engineering and IT sectors. Australia's labour productivity has outgrown that of its competitors, at a rate of over 2.0 per cent. But Australia is something of an economic, as well as a geographic, anachronism. Despite the colourful images of its agricultural and

KEY INDICATORS — Australia

	Unit	2000	2001	2002	2003	2004
Population	m	19.20	19.40	19.56	19.89	20.23
Gross domestic product (GDP)	US$bn	445.44	357.40	400.00	518.40	*631.26
GDP per capita	US$	23,200	18,384	20,440	25,100	30,445
GDP real growth	%	3.3	2.7	3.6	3.3	*3.2
Inflation	%	4.3	4.4	3.0	2.8	2.3
Unemployment	%	6.3	6.7	6.3	6.0	5.5
Oil output	'000 bpd	812.0	733.0	730.0	731.0	541.0
Natural gas output	bn cum	31.1	32.7	34.5	33.2	35.2
Coal output	mtoe	155.6	168.1	183.6	188.7	199.4
Exports (fob) (goods)	US$m	64,041.0	63,667.0	64,990.0	70,358.0	*87,063.0
Imports (fob) (goods)	US$m	68,752.0	61,644.0	72,740.0	88,618.0	*105,278.0
Balance of trade	US$m	-4,711.0	2,023.0	-5,300.0	-18,260.0	*-18,215.0
Current account	US$m	-15,316.0	-9,194.0	-17,760.0	-30,675.0	-39,390.0
Total reserves minus gold	US$m	18,118.0	17,955.0	20,689.0	32,189.0	35,803.0
Foreign exchange	US$m	16,782.0	16,434.0	18,618.0	29,966.0	33,901.0
Exchange rate	per US$	1.66	1.82	1.86	1.55	1.36

* estimated figure

mining activities, Australia is very much an urban – more accurately a suburban – country. Around 90 per cent of the population live in or around the five major conurbations, four of which – Adelaide, Brisbane, Melbourne and Sydney – are on the East and South East coast. In the west, Perth is almost as close to Singapore as it is to Sydney. The services sector generates 80 per cent of Australia's economic output. Tourism currently generates around 5 per cent of GDP, roughly on a par with the mining sector. However, each of these sectors generates a disproportionately high foreign currency revenue.

Costello's budget

Peter Costello, Australia's treasurer (finance minister) benefited from the increased coal and iron-ore exports (mostly to China) to the extent that he was able to predict a fiscal surplus of A$7.4bn (US$5.78bn) in his 2005/06 budget. His tenth consecutive budget featured tax cuts of A$22bn (US$17.19bn). These cuts followed the pre-election cuts of over AS$15bn (US$11.72bn). In many respects Mr Costello's budget again possessed the characteristics of a pre-election budget, provoking comment that he was positioning himself for the leadership of the Liberal Party. The government maintains that all taxpayers benefit; the starting point for the top rate of income tax was raised from A$70,000 (US$54,700) to A$125,000 (US$70,650). In his budget speech, Mr Costello claimed that over 80 per cent of taxpayers would end up paying less than 30 per cent income tax. The 2005/06 budget did little to address the need for reforms to business tax incentives. Some economists raised fears about the budget's possible effect on inflation and, by extension, interest rates.

Inflation

Inflation had reached an annual rate of 2.4 per cent by the end of the first quarter of 2005, and was expected to continue upwards in the face of continued low unemployment. The central bank's upper limit for inflation is 3 per cent. Of concern to many economists is Australia's continued dependence on foreign borrowing to fund much of its growth in consumption. Net foreign liabilities represent an estimated 62 per cent of GDP, a figure which compares unfavourably with the 22 per cent registered in the USA. As long as the Asia Pacific region – notably China – continues to record high levels of demand for Australia's minerals and raw energy products, this dependence need not be a problem. But any significant downturn in Asian demand, or a slump in commodity prices, could spell trouble for the Australian economy.

Immigration

Any visitor to a major Australian city cannot fail to notice the growing presence of the country's Asian community. The enterprise and industry of Australia's Asian immigrants contrasts somewhat with the '£10 Aussies' of the 1950s. These were mostly British emigrants who decided that a boat trip to Australia, followed by a life in the sun with safe employment and housing was a better bet than life in the cold and rationing of post-war Europe. During the 1950s and 1960s the Department of Immigration undertook various campaigns to promote Australian citizenship to new migrants and the public more generally. The creation, in 1945, of a federal Immigration policy meant that by 1947, a post-war immigration boom was underway, with a large and growing number of arrivals of both government-assisted and other immigrants.

Agreements were reached with Britain, some European countries and with the International Refugee Organisation to encourage migrants, including displaced persons from war-torn Europe. By 1950, almost 200,000 people had arrived.

A million more migrants arrived in each of the following four decades. Today, nearly one in four of Australia's 20.3 million people was born overseas. Traditionally, Britain was the largest single source country of migrants, but other regions – notably Asia – have become more significant.

Currently more than 100,000 migrants each year are granted visas under the Skill and Family Streams of Australia's Migration Programme. More than 150,000 people now receive temporary entry visas to Australia each year, to undertake specific work or business, or to entertain, play sport or have a working holiday. In addition to these numbers, around 13,000 humanitarian entrants will also arrive in Australia each year to rebuild their lives, having fled persecution or suffering. According to the Australian government, immigration's contribution to population growth is likely to increase during the next 30 years as the ageing of Australia's population leads to a decline in growth. By the 2030s, immigration is likely to be the only source of growth in population.

Energy

In the thirty year period to 2004, total energy consumption in Australia had more than doubled. Coal is Australia's largest source of energy, with natural gas and various forms of of renewable energy gradually replacing oil as the country's second source of energy. Until the 1990s, energy consumption grew at a rate that closely tracked growth in GDP. Since the 1990s, energy consumption has grown more slowly than GDP, indicating a greater awareness of energy conservation in Australia's business and domestic consumers.

Australia's energy production grew by an estimated 1.5 per cent in the 2003–04 period. Coal production accounts for just over 50 per cent of total energy production. The predominance of coal is also seen in Australia's energy export statistics; Australia is a substantial energy exporter, its energy exports dominated by coal, which accounts for 40 per cent of total energy production, followed by uranium (29 per cent).

Australia is a net importer of crude oil and LPG. National production of crude oil and refined petroleum products are in decline, as are exports. Since 2000, refinery output is estimated to have fallen by 10 per cent. Electricity production is estimated to have risen by a similar amount over the same period.

Outlook

For some time, Australia's politics have been characterised by a 'steady as she goes' philosophy that an increasingly prosperous electorate have responded to positively. Some speculation surrounds the likelihood of Mr Howard stepping down from leadership of the Liberal Party. But Peter Costello, in December 2005, ruled out any challenge, and Howard's tenth anniversary will come in March 2006. Mr Howard himself has alluded to the need for an 'orderly transition', and remarks he made in April 2005 that he 'was not going anywhere' and boasting that he could beat Kim Beazly, Mr Latham's successor at the head of the Labor Party, suggest that – as is often the case with successful political leaders – Mr Howard may be around for longer than expected.

Risk assessment

Economic	Good
Political	Good
Regional stability	Good

COUNTRY PROFILE

Historical profile

The first Aborigines arrived from south-east Asia around 60,000BC and by 20,000BC had spread throughout the mainland and Tasmania. The Aborigines numbered a few hundred thousand when the British founded a penal settlement at Sydney in 1788, bringing over around 800 convicts. Free settlers arrived in increasing numbers, particularly after the discovery of gold in the mid-nineteenth century. Two centuries of discrimination and expropriation followed, and at one point the number of Aborigines fell as low as 60,000. Around 98.5 per cent of the present Australian population are of European or Asian descent, but calls for a formal apology for past injustices towards the Aborigines are still made. Indigenous Australians suffer high rates of unemployment, imprisonment and drug abuse. Migration continues to shape Australia, although it remains a sensitive issue and the country has taken a tough stance on unauthorised arrivals.

Although the country has considered cutting its ties with the British monarchy, in 1999 Australians voted against plans for the country to become a republic.

1778 Captain James Cook reached Australia and sailed the entire length of the East Coast. He claimed the land for Britain.

1788 British Naval captain, Arthur Phillip, founded a penal colony at Sydney. He had arrived with a fleet of 11 vessels and nearly 800 convicts.

1829 The Colony of Western Australia was established at Perth by Captain James Stirling.

1837 South Australia was established with Adelaide as its capital city.

1851 The discovery of gold in New South Wales sparked a wave of migration to Australia, known as the 'gold rush'. Within 10 years of the gold find, the population was estimated to have grown from 500,000 to 1.5 million. The Aborigines were treated badly.

1856 Australia became the first country to introduce the secret ballot for elections (known as the 'Australian ballot').

1877 The first Test cricket match between Australia and England was played in Melbourne.

1901 The Commonwealth of Australia was created. The former British colonies became the six states of Australia: New South Wales, Victoria, Queensland, Western Australia, South Australia and Tasmania. There are two self-governing states – the Northern Territory and the Australian Capital Territory.

1911 Canberra was founded as the capital city.

1914–1918 Australia fought alongside Britain during the First World War. Australian troops bore the brunt of the fighting and casualties during the ill-fated beach landing at Gallipoli in Turkey in 1915.

1929–31 Following the Wall Street Crash came the Great Depression, which hit the Australian economy badly. Recovery was slow and uneven. The Labor government was defeated in the elections.

1939–45 Australia fought alongside Britain and the US during the Second World War. In 1942, Japanese aircraft bombed Darwin (Northern Territory), the only direct foreign attack on Australia since its creation.

1948 Australia began to promote immigration from Europe and over the next three decades, more than a million people arrived, a third of whom came from Britain.

1950 Australia participated in the Korean War.

1951 Australia, New Zealand and the US signed the Anzus Pact, a security pact for the South Pacific.

1956 Australia hosted the Olympic games in Melbourne.

1963 The 'White Australia' policy of immigration restrictions was ended.

1965 Australia fought alongside the US in Vietnam. At the height of Australia's involvement, the task force numbered 8,500 troops.

1967 A national referendum approved changes to the constitution: the section which excluded Aboriginal people from the official census was removed and another change enabled the federal government to pass laws on Aboriginal issues.

1975 Australia restricted the immigration of non-skilled workers. The governor general, Sir John Kerr, dismissed Gough Whitlam's government following its repeated failure to pass the budget in the upper house of parliament. A caretaker government under Malcolm Fraser was installed.

1985 The issue of Aboriginal land rights was first addressed.

1986 Australia's legislative links with the UK were severed by the Australia Act, which abolished the UK parliament's residual legislative, executive and judicial controls over Australian state law.

1990 Bob Hawke and his Australian Labor Party (ALP) government narrowly won the federal election – the first ALP administration to win three consecutive elections.

1991 Paul Keating (ALP) succeeded Bob Hawke as prime minister.

1992 The Citizenship Act was amended to remove the obligation to swear an allegiance to the British Crown. Keating's government pledged to make Australia a republic and develop links with the rest of Asia.

1993 The ALP won the general election with an increased majority. The Native Title Act granted the Aborigines compensation for the loss of land rights.

1996 The Liberal Party (LP)-National Party (NP) coalition won a landslide victory in elections and John Howard, leader of the LP, took over as prime minister.

1998 The LP-NP coalition was re-elected at the general elections, but with a reduced majority. Delegates to a constitutional convention voted to replace the Queen with a president elected by parliament.

1999 Fifty-five per cent of votes cast in a national referendum opposed Australia becoming a republic. After East Timor voted for independence from Indonesia, Australia led an intervention force to counter pro-Indonesia militia violence. Australia's relationship with Indonesia worsened.

2000 Australia hosted the Olympic Games in Sydney; they became known as the 'friendly games'.

2001 Peter Hollingworth was sworn in as governor general. Prime Minister John Howard refused to apologise to 'stolen generations' of Aborigines who, as children, were forcibly removed from their parents to live with white families. Howard won a third term in the federal elections after gaining support for his 'Pacific Solution' – the policy of refusing entry to asylum seekers and directing them to other countries in Asia-Pacific.

2002 There were riots in the Woomera desert detention camp for asylum seekers. Eighty-eight Australian citizens were killed in a night club bombing in Bali, Indonesia.

2003 Australia sent 2,000 troops to the Iraq War. Governor General Peter Hollingworth stood down and Major General Michael Jeffery was appointed in his place. Bush fires raged across the country. The Senate passed a no-confidence motion against Prime Minister John Howard over his handling of the Iraq crisis. Australia headed a peacekeeping force in the Solomon Islands.

2004 On 1 February, the first passenger train to cross Australia from south to north (the Ghan) made its journey from Adelaide to Darwin. In February, the inhabitants of a predominantly Aborigine Sydney suburb rioted in protest at the death of a young Aborigine as the result of a police car chase. In the same month, a parliamentary committee cleared the government of lying about the threat posed by weapons of mass destruction in Iraq. In September, there was a bomb attack outside the Australian embassy in Jakarta, Indonesia. The LP-NP coalition government led by John Howard won a fourth term in October federal legislative elections. In November, the death of an Aboriginal man in police custody sparked more riots on Palm Island, off the north-east coast.

2005 In January, the worst bush fires for more than two decades killed nine people in South Australia. John Howard won a fourth term as prime minister in the 9 October election. Mr Howard's Liberal-National coalition won with an increased majority. In December there were riots in the Cronulla suburb of Sydney. Whether fuelled by racism, revenge or simply alcohol-induced aggression, the ferocity of the violence shocked Australia.

Political structure
Constitution
The Commonwealth of Australia is a constitutional monarchy with a parliamentary democracy. It consists of a federation of six states (New South Wales, Victoria, Queensland, South Australia, Western Australia and Tasmania) and two territories (Australian Capital Territory (ACT), Northern Territory). Each state has its own constitution, government, administration and judiciary. There are some 900 local government bodies at city, town, municipal and shire levels.

The federal government is located in Canberra, ACT. Federal responsibilities tend to be those with an international and national focus while state governments deal with regional issues. However, the overlap of power is considerable and companies must be prepared to deal with both levels of government.

Any amendment to the constitution must be passed by an absolute majority in each House of Parliament and must be approved in a referendum by the majority of electors in a majority of states and territories. In the past, three states (Tasmania, Queensland and Western Australia) have consistently blocked any changes to the constitution.

There is compulsory universal adult suffrage for Australian citizens, with a voting age of 18. An automatic fine of A$50 (US$35) is issued by post to those who fail to cast a vote, although this is rarely imposed through legal proceedings.

Form of state
Federal commonwealth, with the British monarch as Head of State.

The executive
The governor general represents and is appointed by the British sovereign. The role of governor general is largely ceremonial, but he has the power to dissolve parliament or the government and call new elections. He is also the commander-in-chief of the armed forces. If the governor general is ill, dies, resigns or is out of the country, an administrator is appointed to undertake the governor general's duties.

Day-to-day executive responsibility is held by the national government, which is composed of a cabinet of senior ministers formed by the party with a majority in the House of Representatives.

National legislature
Legislative powers are divided between the bicameral Australian Federal Parliament, with a 150-member House of Representatives and a 76-member Senate. The House of Representatives is directly elected by a preferential voting system for a three-year term.

The Senate is directly elected by proportional representation for a six-year term. One half of the Senate retires every three years, usually to coincide with elections for the House of Representatives. The Senate may not originate or amend money bills. In certain circumstances the governor general may dissolve the entire Senate.

The six state (or territory) parliaments also hold legislative powers. In five of the six states there is a bicameral legislature, in the other (Queensland) the legislature is unicameral.

Legal system
The legal system is based on the constitution of 1901. The governor general and state governors appoint judges on the advice of the cabinets of federal and state governments. Each state has state courts, federal courts, family courts and a supreme court. The High Court of Australia, which has seven judges, is the ultimate court of appeal. The High Court has jurisdiction to hear and determine appeals and judgments, decrees, orders and the sentences of most lower courts, but since 1984 cases have only been referred to it if there is a difference of opinion at lower levels. The High Court's main task is to interpret the Australian Constitution.

Last elections
9 October 2004 (federal legislative)
Results: Parliamentary: the coalition Liberal Party (LP)-National Party (NP) government led by John Howard won a third term.

Next elections
2007 (federal legislative)

Political parties
Ruling party
Liberal Party (LP)-National Party (NP) coalition (since 1996; last re-elected 9 Oct 2004)

Main opposition party
Australian Labor Party (ALP)

Population
20.23 million (2004); 19.88 million (OECD, 2003)

Ethnic make-up
The population is comprised mainly of immigrants and their descendants from over 120 countries, with Aboriginals and Torres Straits Islanders accounting for only 1.5 per cent of the population. The single largest immigrant group is from the British Isles, followed by Asians, New Zealanders, Italians, Croats, Serbs, Slovenes, Bosnians, Macedonians, Greeks, Germans, Vietnamese, Dutch, Poles and Lebanese. Over 20 per cent of the total population were born outside the country. More than half the Aboriginal population lives in urban areas.

Religions
Predominantly Christian (Anglican and Roman Catholic), although many are non-practising. There are significant Eastern Orthodox, Jewish, Muslim, Hindu and Buddhist communities in many cities.

Education
In most states, children start primary school at the age of five when they enrol in a preparatory or kindergarten year, after which primary education continues for either six or seven years followed by secondary education, available for either five or six years and may be completed by tertiary education of a student's level and choice.

State and Territory governments and the Federal government provide major financial support for primary and secondary education, delivered in public and fee-paying schools run by governments and non-government providers.

Links between the education and training sectors have been strengthened, through the introduction of the Australian National Training Authority (ANTA) national system of vocational education and training in co-operation with all levels of governments and industry. Two national communications campaigns began in late 2000 based on extensive market research into the vocational education and training needs of Australian individuals and enterprises.

Total expenditure on education is 5.3 per cent of GDP. In 2001, government expenditure on higher education totalled US$5.8 billion.

Compulsory years: 6 to 15; Tasmania: 6 to 16.
Pupils per teacher: 18 in primary schools.

Health
Total expenditure on health is around 9 per cent of GDP, of which government spending is 68 per cent; private expenditure is around 32 per cent, of which spending on pre-paid plans is 24 per cent.

While health care funds direct assistance to hospitals and rebates individuals under the Medicare national health insurance system, consideration of private medical insurance is central to federal health budget funding.

Primary healthcare is provided by independent and privately owned medical practices, offering general and specialist treatment including minor surgary.

Australia

Hospitals may be state, or privately run institutions.
HIV prevalence: 0.1 per cent aged 15–49 in 2003 (World Bank)
Life expectancy: 79.2 years (World Bank)
Fertility rate/Maternal mortality rate: 1.8 births per woman (World Bank)
Birth rate/Death rate: Seven deaths per 1,000 people (World Bank).
Infant mortality rate: 4.6 per 1,000 live births (World Bank).
Head of population per physician/bed: 2.5 physicians and 8.5 hospital beds per 1,000 people (World Bank 1995–2001).

Welfare
Social security payments are intended as a 'safety net' to help low income groups and anti-fraud measures are increasingly tough. In recent years, payments have been the subject of intense scrutiny to ensure that they are only distributed to those in genuine need, this has resulted in cuts in some benefits while other categories, especially disability and service pensions, have increased. Other priority groups have been defined as low-income: families with children; the long-term unemployed; and single parents.

Pensions
Australia has a forced savings 'superannuation' scheme for employees, the total value of which is approaching A$1 trillion (US$620 billion). The scheme involves compulsory contributions by employees of 9 per cent of their income. The scheme does not cover the self-employed or low-income workers. It is estimated that 94 per cent of pension schemes operate through trusts. Employees often have no choice in becoming a member and are ill-informed as to who heads the trust.

Main cities
Sydney, New South Wales (NSW) (state capital, estimated population 4.3 million in 2004); Melbourne, Victoria (Vic) (state capital, 3.7 million), Brisbane, Queensland (Qld) (state capital, 1.6 million); Perth, Western Australia (WA) (state capital, 1.4 million); Adelaide, South Australia (SA) (state capital, 1.1 million); Canberra, Australian Capital Territory (ACT) (national capital, 327,700); Newcastle, (NSW) (500,000); Gold Coast (Qld) (439,200); Hobart, Tasmania (Tas) (state capital, 189,400); Townsville (Qld) (137,900); Launceston (Tas) (98,400); Cairns (Qld) (129,200); Darwin, Northern Territory (NT) (territorial capital, 96,200); Alice Springs (NT) (20,000).

Languages spoken
Aboriginal dialects are becoming scarce. Italian is spoken by 2.6 per cent of the population and Greek by 1.8 per cent. A wide variety of other languages are spoken, particularly from Asia, reflecting the diverse origins of Australia's population.

Official language/s
English

Media
Press
Australia's media is free and operates only within legal and regulatory constraints. The Australian Press Council administers disputes about newspapers and magazines. Major newspapers are not associated with any political parties. Australia is said to have one of the highest per capita magazine and newspaper readerships in the world. There are 12 national or state/territory daily newspapers with Sunday newspapers reaching over 3.4 million. There are several additional major city newspapers, controlled by either Fairfax or Rupert Murdoch's News Corporation group. These groups also control extensive suburban newspaper networks. A variety of foreign language publications targetted at specific ethnic communities and trade publications are also available.
Dailies: The main national dailies include *The Sydney Morning Herald*, *The Sun-News Pictorial*, *The Age*, *Daily Mirror*, *The Telegraph* and *The Herald Sun*. *The Australian* is printed simultaneously in Sydney, Melbourne, Perth and Brisbane.
Weeklies: The main state weeklies are *Sunday Telegraph*, *The Sun-Herald*, *The Sunday Mail*, *The Sunday Times* and *The Sunday Sun*. Other regional weeklies are *The Weekend Independent*, *The Sunday Examiner* and *The Weekly Times*. *Beat Magazine* is a weekly street paper featuring arts and entertainment.
Business: There are numerous commercial and trade journals, including the reports of the Australian Bureau of Agricultural and Resources Economics (Abare) and the national daily *Australian Financial Review*. Other business newspapers are *Sydney Financial News*, *Business Sydney*, *Sydney Business Review*, *Daily Commercial News* and *Western Australian Business News*.
Periodicals: South Pacific editions of international publications, such as *Newsweek* and *Time*, and various international newspapers are widely available.

Broadcasting
The Australian Broadcasting Authority (ABA), an independent federal statutory authority, is the broadcast regulator for radio, TV and Internet content.
Radio: There are 144 stations broadcasting Australian Broadcasting Corporation (ABC) programmes, as well as 135 commercial radio networks.
Television: There are stringent broadcasting standards relating to issues such as violence on television. In addition there is concern to maintain the Australian content of programmes. The industry is dominated by Publishing and Broadcasting Limited (PBL) and the News Corporation.
The ABC operates a national public service channel, ABC TV. The other public service TV is the Special Broadcasting Service (SBS). It broadcasts in 68 languages. Commercial TV is provided by channels '7', Nine and Ten.
Digital services began in Canberra in 2001. The ABA has set a target for digital transmission in inland areas of New South Wales for 2004. An earlier transmission date of March 2003 was set for Southern New South Wales and Northern New South Wales.
There are more than 250 TV affiliates operating in Australia, some of which are private commercial stations, city-based or regional, while others transmit programmes of the ABC.

Advertising
Advertising is subject to the provisions of the Trade Practices Act. There are some restrictions on alcohol, tobacco, medical products and advertising to children. Cigarette advertising is not permitted on TV. The Advertising Standards Council interprets and applies the self-imposed codes created by advertisers, advertising agencies and media. In addition to commercial press and conventional TV and radio advertising, outdoor advertising is available in many forms, as well as direct mail facilities and house-to-house distribution of samples and literature.

Economy
Australia has evolved from an agrarian and mining economy pre-1980s when raw materials were exported, primarily sheep, wheat, coal and ore, without added value, to one based overwhelmingly on services which by early 2005 made up almost 80 per cent of output. Agricultural and mining products are still significant to Australia's export revenue but the country's location close to Asian markets, the diverse ethnic population (offering a large multilingual workforce with good IT skills), transparent legal system, good governance and financial services has made it a prime site as a regional hub for international companies. Tourism accounts for 5 per cent of GDP, roughly the same as all mining combined.
For over a decade Australia has enjoyed continued growth, low inflation and low unemployment. However the OECD considers the 5.1 per cent unemployment rate (a 30-year low) as too low for an advanced country. Australia suffers from labour shortages particularly in skilled and semi-skilled occupations, which prompted the government to establish 24 new technical colleges concentrating on trades,

mainly various engineering skills. Before trained workers are available this lack of skilled workers, coupled with infrastructure bottlenecks in rail links and port facilities, will continue to threaten Australia's exports with stagnation.

The economy has begun to slow with growth dropping to 0.3 per cent in the fourth quarter of 2004 from only 0.1 per cent increase in the previous quarter. However Australia appears to be avoiding the twin evils of recession and inflation with an independent central bank (released from government control in 1996) setting interest rates unfettered by political influence. Most analysts consider that Australia's economy is in good health with commercial profits, as a proportion of GDP, recording a 50-year high, business investment at 14.2 per cent of GDP and attracting, in 2004, a record US$42 billion foreign direct investment. To sustain the momentum however Australia has to overcome its labour shortage, infrastructure bottlenecks and lack of training.

External trade

Export marketing organisations established under government statutes supervise and promote the export of main income-earning commodities, and the Export Market Development Grants scheme provides taxable cash grants for developing overseas markets.

The tariff system is used to protect the car, textile and footwear manufacturing industries, with some use of import quotas.

In March 2004, the US signed a free-trade agreement with Australia, which excludes sugar and largely maintains US protection on dairy and beef produce. Australia and Thailand signed a free trade deal on 5 July 2004.

Imports
Principal imports are vehicles and equipment, industrial machinery, computers and office equipment, electrical goods, textiles and crude oil and petroleum products.
Main sources: US (14.8 per cent total, 2004), China (12.7 per cent), Japan (11.8 per cent), Germany (5.8 per cent), Singapore (4.4 per cent), UK (4.1 per cent)

Exports
Principal exports are minerals: coal, gold, alumina, iron ore; agricultural products: wheat, meat, wool; manufactures including: processed food, computers, telecommunications equipment, and vehicles.
Main destinations: Japan (18.6 per cent total, 2004), China (9.2 per cent), US (9.2 per cent), South Korea (7.7 per cent), New Zealand (7.4 per cent) India (4.6 per cent), UK (4.2 per cent)

Agriculture
Farming
Agricultural output has doubled since the early 1960s, but the sector now only contributes 4 per cent of GDP, a reduction from 14 per cent. Agricultural production still accounts for 22 per cent of exports. Larger, technologically-enhanced farms employing fewer workers are replacing many smaller operations; the number of farms has fallen by 25 per cent since the 1980s.

Weather, external pressures and commodity prices directly affect farming in Australia. A severe and prolonged drought which began in 2002 and affected much of the grain-producing and livestock grazing areas of northern New South Wales and southern Queensland, as well as central and western Australia, were relieved somewhat in 2003–04, but after some good rainfalls the threat of drought returned in 2004–05. By 2004 US$3.9 billion in rural exports were lost and the drought cut the economy by about 30 per cent. Australia was forced to import wheat and corn.

Government involvement tends to be focussed on improving infrastructure as a means of facilitating investment.

Australia is the world's fourth-largest wheat producer, after the EU, the US and Canada. Since the 1980s, Australia has successfully diversified its wheat production, increasing the number of varieties grown and improving marketing. China's membership of the WTO has benefited Australian wheat growers, who have seen a rise in exports to Asia. As living standards improve in Asia, consumption of higher value commodities such as rice and noodles will increase.

Crop production in 2004 included 31,340,500 tonnes (t) cereals in total, 20,376,000t wheat, 6,454,000t barley, 1,496,000t rapeseed (canola), 1,851,000t sorghum, 36,892,000t sugar cane, 1,057,000t oats, 1,200,000t potatoes, 1,668,000t pulses, 2,014,965t grapes, 392,000t maize, 391,000t rice, 546,000t citrus fruit, 400,000t tomatoes, 264,772t bananas, 7,149,282t oilcrops, 9,000t tobacco, 1,800t olives, 3,676,658t fruit in total, 1,356,200t vegetables in total. Livestock production included 3.8t meat in total, 2,033,000t beef, 406,000t pig meat, 561,000t lamb, 13,750t goat meat, 715,634t poultry, 155,000t eggs, 10,377,000t milk, 16,000t honey, 243,000t cattle hides, 121,421t sheepskins, 528,000t greasy wool.

Fishing
Australia typically produces 220,000 tonnes of seafood and 13,000 tonnes of freshwater fish per annum. Around 80 per cent of annual fishing production is exported. Rock lobsters from Western Australia account for 30 per cent of exports by value. Other species include prawns, molluscs, carp and eels. The main destinations for fish exports are Japan, Hong Kong and Taiwan, while exports to the US and Europe have benefited from the weakness of the Australian dollar.

South Australia has the world's first tuna fish farm industry. The tuna is caught at sea and transferred to holding pens for fattening before being sold on. The industry exports A$261 million (US$180 million) worth of fish to Japan, where the fresh tuna, delivered within 72 hours, fetches ¥2,800 (US$24.30) per kilo.

Forestry
There is a substantial forestry industry in tropical Queensland, producing approximately 22 million cubic metres of timber annually, worth over A$1 billion (US$694 million). Japan has traditionally been the sector's biggest customer, with New Zealand the second largest export market. The sector employs around 75,000 people. There are projects for new plantations to increase production by 300 per cent. In 2004, exports of forest products totalled US$1.3 billion and imports amounted to US$1.5 billion.

Production in 2003 included 29,826,000 cubic metres (cum) roundwood, 26,734,000cum industrial roundwood, 4,049,000cum sawnwood, 12,764,000cum sawlogs and veneers, 13,047,000cum pulpwood, round and split, 2,031,000cum wood-based panels, 3,092,000cum woodfuel, 23,350t charcoal.

Industry and manufacturing
Australia embarked on a basic reorientation of its economy in the 1980s, and has transformed itself from an inward-looking, import-substitution economy to an internationally competitive, export-oriented economy. In the early 1990s, the sector suffered from poor investment, despite boosts to exports provided by the low exchange rate. However, having shed labour, gained more effective investment and a sharper export focus, Australian industry has become more competitive internationally with manufacturers of wood and paper products, food, beverages and tobacco becoming dominant.

The Liberal Party (LP)-National Party (NP) coalition government, first elected in 1995, quickly made clear its aim of transforming a traditional commodity-based economy by value-added processing of domestic raw materials into high-value consumer products for the global market. At the heart of industrial policy is a package to support innovation and improve access to venture capital for the commercial application of research and

Australia

development. The government has also pledged to commit Australia to a free trade approach to the electronic market place – goods ordered and delivered electronically will remain duty free.

Tourism
Tourism is a major contributor to Australia's economy, accounting for around four per cent of GDP and employing 540,000 people. The country has become an increasingly popular destination for tourists from all around the world. While the largest market is New Zealand (exceeding a million visitors in 2004), significant numbers come from as far afield as the UK and other European countries, the US and east Asia. Arrivals increased annually for two decades until 2000, the year of the Sydney Olympics, encouraged by the relative weakness of the Australian currency. 4.9 million visitors were recorded in 2000 and the share of GDP was 4.6 per cent. Expectations of continuing growth to over five million visitors in 2001 were dashed, due to global conditions, including the 11 September terrorist attacks in the US, and a strengthening Australian dollar. As with many other countries, arrivals fell in 2001, but, against the general trend, the decline continued through 2002 and into 2003, when there were 4.75 million visitors. The sector recovered in 2004, when there were 5.2 million visitors, a trend which continued in 2005.

Environment
In June 2004 the government announced plans including A$1.5 billion (US$2.14 billion) on fuel tax breaks and A$700 million (US$1 billion) funds for investment in technology that could reduce greenhouse gas emissions. Critics have said this still favours oil and coal and pollution is unlikely to be reduced significantly.

Australia is the second-largest producer of greenhouse gas emissions (after the US) among western nations. The government claims that the country only produces 1.6 per cent of the global total and cannot therefore make an individual difference overall.

Australia, Philippines, Indonesia, Papua New Guinea and Solomon Islands are the countries with the most coral reef fish species.

Mining
Mining contributed around 8.5 per cent of GDP in 2004 and employs 4 per cent of the workforce. Australia has major deposits of a variety of minerals, possessing the world's biggest economic reserves of lead, uranium, silver, zinc, tantalum, mineral sands and low-cost uranium. Australia is a significant producer of gold, iron ore, bauxite, nickel, diamonds, alumina, ilmenute, zircon and rutile. Australia is the largest exporter of gold and iron ore in the world. Total mining exploration expenditure had fallen dramatically by 2001, but the trend had reversed by 2005 to levels equalling those of 1997, when spending on exploration was US$676 million.

Hydrocarbons
Australia has proven oil reserves totalled 1.5 billion barrels and produces around 550,000 barrels per day (bpd). The main oil-fields are situated offshore in the Bass Strait and Carnarvon Basin. The rate of production has been in decline since 2000, partly due to depleting reserves. Domestic consumption is around 900,000bpd. Australia imports over a third of its crude oil requirements, a proportion which is forecast to rise to 50 per cent by 2010. At current levels of production, Australian reserves should last for another 15 years, but exploration is taking place.

Australia has proven natural gas reserves of 2.54 trillion cubic metres. At a production rate of 34.5 billion cubic metres per annum, reserves should last for 40 years. There are expected to be significant increases in gas consumption in the future. It is projected that natural gas will increase to 22 per cent of Australia's total energy consumption by 2005.

Proven coal reserves are 86.5 billion tonnes, representing 8.3 per cent of world reserves. Coal production is around 373 million tonnes and is growing by four per cent a year. Australia exports 60 per cent of production.

Energy
Australia has a total generating capacity of 47.1GW. Around 85 per cent is produced by coal-fired power stations, most of the rest by gas and hydropower. The sector represents 1.4 per cent of GDP. Each state has its own pattern of electric power development. The government plans to increase generating capacity to 50GW by 2010. Expansion costs are estimated at US$9 billion.

Financial markets
Stock exchange
The Australian Stock Exchange (ASX) is the eleventh largest in the world.

Banking and insurance
There are 15 national and regional domestic banks in Australia, with an annual turnover of approximately US$34 billion.
Central bank
Reserve Bank of Australia
Main financial centre
Sydney

Time
GMT plus eight hours in Western Australia; GMT plus 9.5 hours in the Northern Territory and South Australia; GMT plus 10 hours in New South Wales, Queensland, Tasmania and Victoria; add one hour for summer time in all but Queensland, Northern Territory and Western Australia from 30 October–18 March.

Geography
Australia is an island continent with the Indian Ocean to the west, the Coral Sea to the east and the Tasman Sea and Pacific Ocean to the south. Australia is the flattest of the continents, the average elevation being less than 300 metres. It has three major landform features: the western plateau, the interior lowlands and the eastern uplands. Much of the land is desert.

Climate
The climate ranges from tropical to temperate. About half of Queensland and Western Australia and 80 per cent of the Northern Territory are within the tropics. The remainder of the states and territories – New South Wales, Victoria, South Australia, Tasmania and the Australian Capital Territory – are in the temperate zone. Temperatures vary greatly from warm to very hot in summer (December–February) to cool and rainy in winter (June–August). In July, the temperature in Sydney averages 11.7 degrees Celsius (C) and in Melbourne 9.4 degrees C. Average annual temperatures vary from 27 degrees C in the far north to 13 degrees C in the far south. For most of Australia the hottest month is January. In Tasmania and southern Victoria, the hottest month is February and in the tropical north near the coast, November.

Much of the country receives low rainfall, but some parts of Queensland, Tasmania, Victoria and New South Wales have annual rainfall of up to 4,200mm. Tropical cyclones develop over the seas to the north-west and the north-east in summer. An average of about three cyclones hit the Queensland coast every year. The Snowy Mountains in New South Wales, a famous ski resort, receives heavy snowfalls most years.

Some 70 per cent of the continent is arid, with extremes of daytime and night-time temperatures in the interior.

Dress codes
For business a suit and tie for men; suit, dress or skirt and blouse for women.

Entry requirements
Passports
Required by all.
Visa
Required by all and must be obtained in advance and outside Australia.
Most citizens of EU and North America can apply for an Electronic Travel Authority (ETA) which can be issued by a travel agent or airline, or can be applied for online. Visit http://www.eta.immi.gov.au/

ETAus1En.html for details of those eligible, and follow links to the application site. ETA-eligible business visitors may stay for up to three months without additional documentation.

Those not eligible for an ETA must apply using form 456, through the nearest embassy or mission. Business visas will require: a letter of invitation from a local company or organisation, a business letter from an employer stating purpose of trip and details of employee's function, proof of sufficient funds, and a full itinerary. Further details and application form can be obtained at http://www.immi.gov.au/allforms/visiting_business.htm.

Currency advice/regulations
There are no foreign exchange controls, although prior authorisation is needed to take amounts larger than A$5,000 (US$2,645) out of the country.

Customs
Personal effects are exempt and there are duty-free allowances of one litre of alcohol, 250 cigarettes and dutiable goods of up to A$400 (US$211). Duty-free shops are open to international visitors upon arrival in Australia.

Prohibited imports
Strict quarantine regulations make it inadvisable to carry food, fruit, vegetables, seeds, animals or plants without prior approval. Travellers are not permitted to carry fruit, vegetables or plants into the State of Victoria. Aircraft cabins are sprayed with insecticide before disembarkation.

Importation of certain items is prohibited, including narcotic and dangerous drugs, firearms and birds. Both import and export of protected wildlife or goods derived therefrom (ie made from skins, feathers, shell, bone, etc) is strictly prohibited.

Health (for visitors)
Mandatory precautions
Vaccination certificates are required for yellow fever if travelling from an infected area. Health rules are strictly enforced and heavy penalties can be incurred for infringement.

Advisable precautions
UK nationals can obtain free hospital treatment through a reciprocal arrangement between the two governments, but they must pay for other medical treatment. Australia provides moderately expensive, good quality medical care.
Travellers should be wary of exposure to the sun and the use of sun screening creams is advised. Australia has a high incidence of skin cancer.

Hotels
Hotels should be booked well in advance. A 10 per cent tip is optional.

Credit cards
Major international credit cards are accepted by virtually everyone. Some taxis also accept credit card payments, check with the driver before the journey begins.

Public holidays
In addition to official public holidays observed throughout Australia, extra statutory holidays are observed in individual states and the Australian Capital Territory (ACT).

Fixed dates
1 Jan (New Year's Day), 26 Jan (Australia Day), 25 Apr (Anzac Day), 27 Sep (Queen's Official Birthday, WA only), 25 Dec (Christmas Day), 26 Dec (Boxing Day).
If Christmas Day or New Year's Day falls on a Saturday, the next Monday is given as a holiday.

Variable dates
Good Friday, Easter Monday, Queen's Official Birthday (second Mon in Jun).

Working hours
Banking
Mon–Thu: 0930–1600; Fri: 0930–1700.
Business
Mon–Fri: 0900–1700.
Government
Mon–Fri: 0900–1700.
Shops
Mon–Fri: 0900–1700; Sat: 0900–1200. Late night shopping (to 2100) in Sydney, Perth and Darwin on Thursday, and in Melbourne, Brisbane, Hobart and Canberra on Friday.

Telecommunications
Mobile phones
GSM 3G service is available in major cities only, 900/1800 services are available in the most populated areas.

Electricity supply
220–250V AC, with 3-pin plug fittings (not UK style) and bayonet-type light sockets. Leading hotels also supply 110V outlets for razors and small appliances.

Weights and measures
Metric system.

Social customs/useful tips
Australians tend to be informal, first names are quickly adopted. A handshake is normal for greetings. Business, with traditional blunt, straight-to-the-point talk, is often conducted over lunch or dinner accompanied by local wines and beers. Australians love outdoor life and business tends to come to a standstill on weekends and public holidays, when there is a steady exodus to country areas, particularly beaches or ski-slopes depending on the season.
Visitors often complain about bureaucracy and patience is required in dealing with government departments and large corporations. There are no short-cuts and although sometimes an approach to the top official of a department might help speed up matters, this must be done with extreme caution as Australians do not tolerate queue-jumping.
Australia has strict drink and driving laws. Police conduct random roadside breath tests and penalties can be severe.

Security
Australian cities are relatively safe though care should be taken, particularly at night. Each capital city has separate emergency numbers on the inside cover of phone books. Otherwise dial 000 and the operator will direct you to the appropriate service.

Getting there
Air
National airline: Qantas Airways.
International airport/s: All states have international airports (with the exceptions of the capital territory, (which is served by NSW), and Tasmania) with connecting inter- and intra-state flights.
NSW: Kingsford Smith (SYD), 8km south of Sydney; Victoria: Tullamarine (MEL), 21km from Melbourne; Western Australia: Perth (PER), 10km from Perth, all of which have duty-free shop, bar, restaurant, bank, post office, shops; Queensland: Brisbane International (BNE), 11km north-east of city, with duty-free shop, bar, restaurant; South Australia: West Beach (ADL), 8km from Adelaide, with bar, restaurant, post office, shops; Northern Terrritory: Darwin (DRW), 8km from city with bar, money exchange and duty-free shops.
Other airport/s: Tasmania: Hobart (HBA), 17km north of city, with restaurant and bar. Queensland: Cairns (CNS), 4km north-west of Cairns, with duty-free shop, hotel reservations; Townsville (TSV), 5km from city. (More information on local airports is provided on: www.airportsaustralia.com/).
Airport tax: None
Surface
Water: There are ferries to main ports on the east coast of Australia from New Zealand, but these are not heavily used.
Main port/s: There are more than 30 ports. The main ports are at Sydney, Brisbane, Melbourne, Adelaide and Fremantle. Sea transport is extensively used for internal and international freight shipment. Containerised cargo facilities are available.

Getting about
National transport
Air: Air transport is widely used and well developed. Regular services linking main centres and nearly 440 airfields are operated by Australian Airlines, East-West

Australia

Airlines, Air Queensland and over 25 other operators. Charter aircraft are also available. Travellers holding international air tickets can obtain concessionary air, rail and bus fares within Australia.

Road: All cities have good arterial roads. Despite the vast distances, there are good highways and bus services between all major centres, but conditions in the interior are rugged, with road transport more limited. Seek advice from the appropriate local automobile association before travelling in remote areas, as roads may be affected by weather conditions.

Buses: Air-conditioned express coach services link main centres, including Tasmania via ferries. Buses provide good services on main town routes, but convenient cross-town transport is not always available.

Rail: Railways, mainly government-owned and operated, provide express inter-urban passenger services, electrified suburban services and long-distance freight services, using a 38,563km network of tracks. Long-distance passenger trains are air-conditioned, with dining and sleeping facilities, they are generally a slower option of transport than road or air. Advance booking is recommended.

The Ghan passenger train runs from the capital cities of Melbourne, Sydney and Adelaide direct to the 'Red Centre' of Australia. Alice Springs is the ideal base from which to explore the Red Centre, including Uluru/Ayers Rock and Kings Canyon. The 47-hour, 2,979km transcontinental journey began its regular services to and from Darwin in February 2004.

Water: There is a regular passenger/vehicle ferry link between Melbourne and Hobart, Tasmania.

City transport

Taxis: Metered taxis operate in all main cities and towns from major hotels, shopping areas and signposted taxi ranks. Radio-controlled taxis are listed in local telephone directories. Tipping is not expected, but a tip of the balance of the fare rounded up to the nearest dollar is sometimes given.

Buses, trams & metro: Sydney (NSW): the rail service AirportLink connects Sydney international airport with the city centre; trains depart at 10 minute intervals, journey time 13 minutes. State Transit run extensive services of buses, trains and ferries around the city.

Melbourne (Vic): VicTrip operate trams, buses and trains around the city. See http://www.victrip.com.au/ for journey planner. Skybus links the airport to city centre; services runs 24 hours, everyday with daytime departures every 15 minutes, journey time 20 minutes.

Brisbane (Qld): Buses and trains link the airport to the city centre, journey time 20 minutes, as well as to all other parts of the city.

Ferry: In Sydney, ferries are an easy, regular and enjoyable mode of transport to the city centre and harbour suburbs. The main ferry terminal is at Circular Quay. In Brisbane there are over a dozen passenger stops along the city's river.

Car hire

Hire cars are widely available. Current overseas licences are recognised, but International Drivers Permits are recommended. The required third-party insurance is normally included in car hire charge. Use of seat belts is compulsory and speed limit in towns is generally 60km per hour. Driving is on the left. Trams have the right of way. Drink driving rules are vigorously enforced, with sizeable fines.

BUSINESS DIRECTORY

The addresses listed below are a selection only. While World of Information makes every endeavour to check these addresses, we cannot guarantee that changes have not been made, especially to telephone numbers and area codes. We would welcome any corrections.

Telephone area codes

The international direct dialling (IDD) code for Australia is +61, followed by area code and subscriber's number:

Adelaide	8	Hobart	3
Brisbane	7	Launceston	3
Cairns	7	Melbourne	3
Canberra	2	Newcastle	2
Darwin	8	Perth	8
Gold Coast	7	Sydney	2
Wollongong	2	Townsville	7

Useful telephone numbers

Emergency Services: 000.

Chambers of Commerce

ACT and Region Chamber of Commerce and Industry, 12a Thesiger Court, PO Box 192, 2600 Deakin West (tel: 6283-5200; fax: 6260-3369; e-mail: chamber@actchamber.com.au).

Australian Business Chamber, 140 Arthur Street, Locked Bag 938, North Sydney, NSW 2059 (tel: 9458-7500; fax: 9923-1166; e-mail: moreld@abol.net).

Australian Chamber of Commerce and Industry, 50 Burwood Road, PO Box E14, Kingston, ACT 2604 (tel: 6273-2311; fax: 6273-3196; e-mail: acci@acci.asn.au).

Commerce Queensland, 375 Wickham Terrace, Brisbane, QLD 4000 (tel: 3842-2244; 3832-3195; fax: 3832-3195; e-mail: qcci@qcci.com.au).

New South Wales State Chamber of Commerce, Level 12, 83 Clarence Street, GPO Box 4280, Sydney NSW 2000 (tel: 9350-8100; fax: 9350-8199; e-mail: worldtradecentre@thechamber.com.au).

Northern Territory Chamber of Commerce and Industry, 5/2 Shepherd Street, GPO Box 1825, Darwin, NT 0800 (tel: 8936-3100; fax: 8981-1405; e-mail: darwin@ntcci.com.au).

South Australian Employers Chamber of Commerce, 136 Greenhill Road, Unley, SA 5061 (tel: 8300-0000; fax: 8300-0001; e-mail: enquiries@business-sa.com).

Tasmanian Chamber of Commerce and Industry, 30 Burnett Street, PO Box 793, 7001 Hobart (tel: 6234-5933; fax: 6231-1278; e-mail: admin@tcci.org.au).

Victoria Employers Chamber of Commerce asnd Industry, 196 Flinders Street, Melbourne, VIC 3000/ PO Box 4352QQ, Melbourne, VIC 3001 (tel: 8662-5333; fax: 8662-5462; e-mail: webmaster@vecci.org.au).

Western Australia Chamber of Commerce and Industry, 180 Hay Street, East Perth, WA 6004/ PO Box, East Perth, WA 6892 (tel: 9365-7555; fax: 9365-7550; e-mail: info@cciwa.com).

Banking

Australia and New Zealand Banking Group, 100 Queen Street, Melbourne, Vic 3000 (tel: 9273-5555).

Australia & New Zealand Savings Bank Ltd, Collins Place, 55 Collins Street, Melbourne, Vic 3000 (tel: 9275-5555).

Barclays Bank Australia Ltd, Barclays House, PO Box 3357, 25 Bligh Street, Sydney, NSW 2001 (tel: 9233-6622; fax: 9221-3060).

Colonial State Bank of New South Wales, PO Box 41, Sydney, NSW 2001 (tel: 9226-8000).

Commonwealth Bank of Australia, Pitt Street and Martin Place, Sydney, NSW 2000 (tel: 9378-2000; fax: 9312-9905).

Commonwealth Savings Bank of Australia, GPO Box 2719, Pitt Street & Martin Place, Sydney, NSW 2001 (9227-7111; fax: 9232-6573, 9235-1653).

National Australia Bank, 500 Bourke Street, PO Box 84A, Melbourne, Vic 3001 (tel: 9605-3500).

Natwest Australia Bank Ltd, 41st Level, Qantas International Centre, International Square, George Street, Sydney, NSW 2000 (tel: 9250-8500; fax: 9251-2763).

Rural & Industries Bank of Western Australia, PO Box E237, 54-58 Barrack Street, Perth, WA 6001 (tel: 9320-6206; fax: 9320-6444).

State Bank of Victoria, PO Box 267D, 385 Bourke Street, Melbourne, Vic 3001 (tel: 9604-7000; fax: 9602-2150).

State Bank of New South Wales, PO Box 41, Sydney, NSW 2001 (tel: 9226-8000).

State Bank of South Australia, 97 King William Street, PO Box 399, Adelaide, SA 5001 (tel: 9210-4411; fax: 9210-4758, 9212-3056).

Westpac Banking Corporation, 60 Martin Place, PO Box 1, Sydney, NSW 2001 (tel: 9226-3311).

Australian branches
Bank of New Zealand, 333 George Street, PO Box 507, Sydney, NSW 2001 (tel: 9290-6666).

Banque Nationale de Paris, 12 Castlereagh Street, PO Box 269, Sydney, NSW 2001 (tel: 9232-8733).

Central bank
Reserve Bank of Australia, 65 Martin Place, PO Box 3947, Sydney, NSW 2001 (tel: 9551-8111; fax: 9551-8000; e-mail: rbainfo@rba.gov.au).

Travel information
Australian Capital Territory Tourist Bureau, Canberra Centre, Northbourne Avenue, Canberra City, ACT 2601 (tel: 6233-3666).

Automobile Association of the Northern Territory (AANT), 79-81 Smith Street, Darwin, NT 0800 (tel: 8981-3837).

Holiday WA Centre, 772 Hay Street, Perth, WA 6000 (tel: 9322-2999).

National Roads and Motorists Association (NRMA), 151 Clarence Street, Sydney, NSW 2000 (tel: 9260-9222).

NSW Government Travel Centre, 16 Spring Street, Sydney, NSW 2000 (tel: 9231-444).

Northern Territory Government Tourist Bureau, 31 Smith Street, Darwin NT 5750 (tel: 8981-6611/3).

Qantas Airways, Qantas Centre, QCA9, 203 Coward Street, Sydney, NSW 2020 (tel: 9691-3472; fax: 9691-4547; internet site: http://www.anzac.com/qantas/qantas.com).

Queensland Government Tourist Bureau, Corner Adelaide and Edward Streets, Brisbane, QLD 4001 (tel: 3312-211; internet: www.tq.com.au).

Royal Automobile Club of Queensland (RACQ), 300 St Paul's Tce, Brisbane, QLD 4006 (tel: 3253-4444).

Royal Automobile Association of South Australia, 41 Hindmarsh Square, Adelaide, SA 5000 (tel: 8223-4555).

Royal Automobile Club of Tasmania (RACT), Corner Patrick & Murray Streets, Hobart, Tas 7001 (tel: 6382-200).

Royal Automobile Club of Victoria (RACV), 123 Queen Street, Melbourne, Vic 3174 (tel: 9790-2211).

Royal Automobile Club of Western Australia Inc (RACWA), 228 Adelaide Terrace, Perth, WA 6000 (tel: 9421-4444).

South Australian Government Travel Centre, 18 King William Street, Adelaide, SA 5000 (tel: 8212-1644).

Tasmanian Government Tourist Bureau, 80 Elizabeth Street, Hobart, Tas 7000 (tel: 6300-211).

Victoria Tourism Commission, 230 Collins Street, Melbourne, Vic 3000 (tel: 9619-9444).

VicRail Information: 619-1111 (Melbourne).

Ministry of tourism
Department of Tourism, Burns Memorial Building, 28 National Circuit, Forrest, ACT 2603 (tel: 6279-7111; fax: 6248-0734).

National tourist organisation offices
Australian Tourist Commission, 80 William Street, PO Box 2721, Sydney 2011 (tel: 9360-1111; fax: 9331-6469).

Ministries
Department of Administrative Services, GPO Box 1920, Canberra, ACT 2601 (tel: 6275-3000; fax: 6275-3819).

Department of Communications and the Arts, GPO Box 2154, Canberra, ACT 2601 (tel: 6279-1000; fax: 6279-1901; internet site: http//www.dcita.gov.au).

Department of Defence, Treasury Building, Newland Street, Parkes, ACT 2600 (tel: 6265-9111; fax: 6273-3021; internet site: http://www.defence.gov.au).

Department of Employment, Education and Training, GPO Box 9880, Canberra, ACT 2601 (tel: 6240-8111).

Department of Finance, Treasury Building, Newlands Street, Parkes, ACT 2600 (tel: 6263-2222; fax: 6273-3021; internet site: http://www.dofa.gov.au).

Department of Foreign Affairs and Trade, Administrative Building, Parkes Place, Parkes, ACT 2600 (tel: 6261-9111; fax: 6261-3111; internet site: http://www://dfat/gov.au).

Department of Housing and Regional Development, GPO Box 9834, Canberra, ACT 2601 (tel: 6289-2222).

Department of Human Services and Health, GPO Box 9848, Canberra, ACT 2601.

Department of Immigration and Ethnic Affairs, PO Box 25, Belconnen, ACT 2616 (tel: 6264-1111; internet site: http://www.immi.gov.au).

Department of Industrial Relations, GPO Box 9879, Canberra, ACT 2601 (tel: 6243-7333).

Department of Industry, Science and Technology, GPO Box 9839, Canberra, ACT 2601 (tel: 6276-1000; fax: 6276-1111; internet site: http://www.industry.gov.au).

Department of National Development and Industry, Tasman House, Hobart Place, PO Box 5, Canberra, ACT 2600.

Department of Primary Industries and Energy, GPO Box 858, Canberra, ACT 2601 (tel: 6272-3933; fax: 6272-5161).

Department of the Prime Minister and Cabinet, Locked Bag 14, Queen Victoria Terrace, Parkes, ACT 2600 (tel: 6271-5111; fax: 6271-5414; internet site: http://www.dpmc.gov.au).

Department of Social Security, Box 7788, Canberra Mail Centre, ACT 2610 (tel: 6244-7788).

Department of Transport, GPO Box 594, Canberra, ACT 2601 (tel: 6274-7111; fax: 6257-2505; internet site: http://www.dot.gov.au).

Department of the Treasury, The Treasury, Parkes Place, Parkes, ACT 2600 (tel: 6263-2111; fax: 6273-2614; internet site: http://www.treasury.gov.au).

Department of Veterans' Affairs, PO Box 21, Woden, ACT 2606 (tel: 6289-1111; fax: 6281-3822; internet site: http://www.dva.gov.au).

Foreign Investment Review Board, Department of the Treasury, Parkes Place, Parkes, ACT 2600 (tel: 6263-3795; fax: 6263-2940).

Other useful addresses
ACT Department of Business, Arts, Sport and Tourism, Level 8, FAI House, 197 London Circuit, Canberra, ACT 2601 (tel: 6207-5111; fax: 6205-0577).

Attorney-General, Suite MF 21, Parliament House, Canberra, ACT 2600 (tel: 6277-7300; fax: 6273-4102; internet site: http://www.law.gov.au).

Australian Bureau of Agriculture and Resource Economics, MacArthur House, Lyneham, ACT 2601 (tel: 6246-9111).

Australian Bureau of Statistics, Cameron Office, Chandler Street, Belconan, ACT 2617 (tel: 6252-7911).

Australian Dairy Corporation, Dairy Industry House, St Kilda Road, Melbourne, VIC 3004 (tel: 9819-4000).

Australian Embassy (USA), 1601 Massachusetts Avenue, NW, Washington DC 20036-2273 (tel: 202-797-3000; fax 202-797-3331; e-mail: library.washington@dfat.gov.au).

Australia

Australian Industrial Development Corporation, 212 Northbourne Avenue, Canberra, ACT 2600 (tel: 6479-411).

Australian Manufacturers' Export Council, MMI Building, PO Box 2, Civic Square, Canberra, ACT 2608 (tel: 6486-477; fax: 6486-993).

Australian Mining Industry Council, 216 Northbourne Avenue, Braddon, ACT 2601 (tel: 6249-8955).

Australian Securities Commission, Corporate Affairs Commission, National Mutual Centre, 15 London Court, Canberra City, ACT 2601 (tel: 6247-5011; internet site: http://www.asc.gov.au).

Australian Stock Exchange Ltd, Stock Exchange Center, 530 Collins Street, PO Box 1784 Q, AU Melbourne, VIC 3001 (tel: 9617-8611; fax: 9614-0303; internet site: http://www.asx.com.au).

Australia Trade Commission, AUSTRADE Centre Cnr Bary Drive and Northbourne Ave, Canberra City, ACT 2601 (tel: 6276-5111; fax: 6276-5105).

Australian Trade Development Council, Department of Trade and Resources, Canberra, ACT 2600.

Australian Wheat Board, Ceres House, Lonsdale Street, Melbourne, Victoria (tel: 9605-1555).

Australian Wool Corporation, Wool House, Royal Parade, Parkville, Victoria (tel: 9341-9111).

British High Commission, Commonwealth Avenue, Yarralumia, Canberra City, ACT 2600 (tel: 6270-6666; fax: 6273-3236).

Business Council of Australia, Ethos House, 28 Ainslie Avenue, Canberra City, ACT 2601 (tel: 6247-8208).

Business Victoria, Level 13, 55 Collins Street, melbourne, VIC 3000 (tel: 9651-9999; fax: 9651-9962).

BZW, Level 22, 255 George Street, Sydney 2000 (tel: 9259-5913; fax: 9259-5477); Airports Team, GPO Box 4675, Sydney 1042 (fax: 9259-5477).

Confederation of Australian Industry, 12a The Siger Court, Deakin, ACT 2600 (tel: 282-2199); PO Box E14, Queen Victoria Terrace, Canberra, ACT 2600 (tel: 6732-311; fax: 6733-196).

International Trade Department Centre, Edgecliff Centre, 203 New South Head Road, Edgecliff, NSW 2027 (tel: 9329-297).

Major Projects Tasmania, 10/fl, 22 Elizabeth Street, Hobart, TAS 7000 (tel: 6233-5869; fax: 6233-5755).

New South Wales Department of State, Level 44, Grosvenor Place, 225 George Street, Sydney, NSW 2000 (tel: 9242-6963; fax: 9242-6970).

New South Wales Government Department of Industrial Development and Decentralisation, GPO Box 4169, Sydney, NSW 2001 (tel: 9927-2741).

Northern Department of Asian Relations, Trade and Industry, 1/fl Development House, 76 The Esplande, Darwin, NT 0800 (tel: 8999-5210; fax: 8999-5106).

Northern Territory Development Corporation, GPO Box 2245, Darwin, NT 5794 (tel: 8989-4211).

Queensland Department of Economic Development & Trade, Executive Building, 100 George Street, Brisbane QLD 4000 (tel: 3224-5970; fax: 3225-8914).

South Australia Department of Trade and Industry, Terrace towers, 178 North Towers, Adelaide SA 5000 (tel: 8303-2400; fax: 9303-2410).

Telecom Australia, 199 William Street, Melbourne, VIC 3000 (tel: 9606-5511).

US Embassy, Moonah Place, Yarralumla, ACT 2600 (tel: 6214-5600; fax: 6214-5970).

Western Australia Department of Industry and Trade, 170 St Georges Terrace, Perth, WA 6000 (tel: 9327-5666; fax: 9322-3361).

Western Australian Development Corporation, 28th Floor, City Mutual Tower, 197 St George's Terrace, Perth, WA 6000 (tel: 9322-7933).

World Trade Promotions (trade fairs and exhibitions), 291 Sussex Street, Sydney, NSW 2000 (tel: 9267-5122).

Internet sites

Austrade (information for overseas business people):
http://www.austrade.gov.au/index.asp

British Chamber of Commerce:
http://www.whoswhere.com.au/abcc

Australian Capital Territory government:
http://www.act.gov.au

Customs service:
http://www.customs.gov.au

Federal Government:
http://www.fed.gov.au

General Information:
http://www.about-australia.com

Tourism: http://www.australia.com

ABC- Australian Broadcasting Corporation: http://www.abc.net.au

Stock Exchange: http://www.asx.com.au

Statistics: http://www.abs.gov.au

Reserve bank: http://www.rba.gov.au

Immigration Department:
http://www immi.gov.au

Qantas: http://www.qantas.com.au

Federal Parliament (Canberra):
http://www.aph.gov.au/

Taxation office: http://www.ato.gov.au

Tourism:
http://www.tourism.australia.com

White pages:
http://www.whitepages.com.au

Yellow pages:
http://www.Yellowpages.com.au

Department of Agriculture, Fisheries and Forestry: http://www.daff.gov.au

Department of the Environment and Heritage: http://www.environment.gov.au

Department of Health and Aged Care:
http://www.health.gov.au

Foreign Affairs & Trade Dept:
http://www.dfat.gov.au

Farmwide information on weather reports, commodity prices, etc:
http://www.farmwide.com.au

Invest Australia:
http://www.investaustralia.gov.au

New South Wales state government:
http://www.nsw.gov.au

Northern Territory state government:
http://www.nt.gov.au/

Queensland state government:
http://www.qld.gov.au/

South Australia: http://www.sa.gov.au

Tasmania state government:
http://www.tas.gov.au

Victoria state government:
http://www.vic.gov.au

Western Australia state government:
http://www.wa.gov.au/

Austria

KEY FACTS

Official name: Republik Österreich (Republic of Austria)

Head of State: Federal President Heinz Fischer (SPÖ) (sworn in 8 Jul 2004)

Head of government: Federal Chancellor Wolfgang Schüssel (leader of ÖVP) (since Feb 2000)

Ruling party: Coalition government sworn in 28 Feb 2003: the Österreichische Volkspartei (ÖVP) (Austrian People's Party) and the Bündis Zukunft Österreich (BZÖ) (Alliance for Austria's Future)

Area: 83,855 square km

Population: 8.08 million (2004); 8.07 million (OECD, 2003)

Capital: Vienna

Official language: German

Currency: Euro (eur) = 100 cents (from 1 Jan 2002; previous currency schilling, locked at S13.76 per euro)

Exchange rate: eur0.83 per US$ (Oct 2005)

GDP per capita: US$35,809 (2004)

GDP real growth: 2.00% (2004); *2.0% (2005)

Labour force: 3.45 million (2004)

Unemployment: 4.50% (OECD, 2004)

Inflation: 2.00% (2004)

Balance of trade: US$4.21 billion (2004)

Foreign debt: US$492.70 billion (2004)

Annual FDI: US$43.80 billion (cumulative, 1995–2004, OECD); US$4.90 billion (OECD, 2004)*

* estimated figure

Austria, one of the EU's smaller member states, frequently grabbed headlines and the limelight in Brussels in 2005 over its opposition to Turkish membership of the EU. With the EU committed to making a decision on accession talks for Turkey and Croatia by the end of 2005, Austria found itself isolated by the other 24 EU member states. Also producing headlines in Austria and abroad was the return to national politics of Austria's most prominent far-right politician, Jörg Haider.

A steady economy

The IMF forecast 2.0 per cent growth in GDP for Austria in 2005 and, in July 2005, praised Austria as one of the best-performing economies in the euro zone. Specifically, Austria was congratulated for achieving low budget deficits, low unemployment and tax reform. The IMF also remarked that Austrian businesses had done more than most pre-2004 EU members to seek out new opportunities in Eastern Europe's transitional economies, and was reaping the benefits in 2005.

EU and local politics merge

The 2005 domestic political scene in Austria was deeply affected by EU policy on enlargement, and in particular the question of opening membership accession talks with Turkey. A Eurobaromer poll conducted on behalf of the European Commission over May and June revealed Austria to be the most sceptical EU member state regarding both of these issues. It was found that only 10 per cent of Austrians favoured Turkish membership of the EU, that 78 per cent disliked the idea of new immigrants entering the country and that 73 per cent considered Turkish membership to be incompatible with European values and culture. On a continent charged with anti-enlargement, and in particular anti-Turkish membership, feeling, Austria took the first prize.

The Austrian government repeatedly insisted to its EU colleagues that Turkey be offered something less than full membership of the EU, full membership being the standard prize on offer in any accession treaty. This demand effectively sought to single out Turkey as different from all other accession candidates, of whom there were three others in 2005 – Bulgaria, Croatia and Romania. With Bulgaria and Romania signing accession treaties in April, Austria appeared to take issue with the EU's perceived favouring of Turkey over Croatia – a country with which Austria shares a long history. Analysts suggested that the EU decision to grant Turkey accession status in October was only possible after Austria's EU fellow member states agreed to give a similar green light to Croatia. In other words, the threat of an Austrian veto on enlargement, despite its isolation within the EU on the matter, appears to have worked.

Austria

Fear of EU enlargement, particularly eastwards to include Turkey, and perceived threats to European and Christian culture were very much reflected in Austria's national politics. In March, Jörg Haider, governor of Karinthia province and senior member of the far-right Freiheitliche Partei Österreichs (FPÖ) (Freedom Party of Austria), announced his intent to re-enter national politics. Haider attempted to retake the leadership of the FPÖ, a role he had relinquished in 2000, and, failing in this, launched, in April, a break-away party, the Bündnis Zukunft Österreich (BZÖ) (Alliance for Austria's Future). The BZÖ promptly netted the defection of all FPÖ ministers in the national coalition government and most FPÖ MPs.

In May 2005, Austria marked the 50th anniversary of the end of the Allied occupation of the country. This precipitated calls from some Austrian commentators and historians for Austria to undertake a comprehensive examination of the country's Nazi past. Others, including Jörg Haider, who is on record as having praised some of Adolf Hitler's policies, argued that Austria had done enough soul-searching and that it was time to move on. 'Moving on', or rather, the minimum requirement for doing so, was on the agenda again in November and December. In November, disgraced British historian David Irving was arrested in Austria on a charge of denying the Holocaust, a criminal offence under Austrian law. In December, the Austrian government decided to begin processing thousands of compensation claims from victims of the Holocaust and their relatives. The government made US$200 million available for such claims but insisted that 'legal closure' regarding Austria's role in the Holocaust be granted at the end of the process.

International relations

In a year more notable for Austria's actions within the EU, two events brought Austria international attention, both at the hands of Die Grünen/Die Grüne Alternative (Die Grünen) (The Greens/the Green Alternative) parliamentarian, Peter Pilz. In July, Austrian prosecutors, acting on information provided by Pilz, launched an investigation into the alleged role of newly elected Iranian president, Mahmoud Ahmadinejad, in the 1989 assassination of an exiled Iranian Kurd activist in Vienna. In December, Pilz also finally succeeded in a long-running campaign to have Austrian-born California governor Arnold Schwarzenegger's name removed from the Graz city sports stadium – Schwarzenegger was born near Graz and the city council had honoured the naturalised US citizen, in 1999, with the stadium dedication. Pilz argued that Governor Schwarzenegger had disgraced Austria by refusing to grant clemency to prisoners on death row. Governor Schwarzenegger intervened in December by insisting that his name be withdrawn from the stadium and renounced his ties to Graz in protest.

Outlook

The IMF forecasts continued healthy growth for Austria, especially in comparison with its euro-zone neighbours. The IMF also predicts that the Austrian budget deficit will continue to fall and that, due to pension reform in recent years, it is well placed to deal with the growing economic and social consequences of an ageing population.

Austria has already managed to place itself again in the centre of EU politics. After assuming the rotating EU presidency on 1 January 2006, the Austrian chancellor, Wolfgang Schüssel has since announced that he will use Austria's term as president to advocate a new EU constitution and the establishment of an EU tax. Both issues immediately divided EU member states and, regarding the constitution, stirred up opposition within his own cabinet.

Risk assessment

Politics	Fair
Economy	Good
Regional stability	Good

COUNTRY PROFILE

Historical profile

For centuries the Austrian (later Austro-Hungarian) Empire covered most of central Europe.
1918 After the Austro-Hungarian Empire was defeated in the First World War, the first Austrian Republic was declared; three-quarters of the Empire's territory was ceded to neighbouring states.
1933 Pro-fascist Engelbert Dollfuss (elected federal chancellor in 1932) gained dictatorial powers and banned all political opposition to his Vaterländische Front (VF) (Fatherland Front). Dollfuss forged a strong relationship with fascist Italy in an attempt to preserve Austria's independence.
1934 The government put down an uprising by Socialists in February. Dollfuss was assassinated in July by Austrian Nazis, who had been conspiring to oust the government and integrate Austria with Nazi Germany.
1938 The new chancellor, Kurt Von Schuschnigg, met with Adolf Hitler in an attempt to preserve Austria's independence. After refusing to meet Hitler's demands for concessions for the banned Austrian Nazi Party, Von Schuschnigg resigned as chancellor and was replaced by Arthur Seyss-Inquart (leader of the Austrian Nazi Party). In March, Austria was integrated with Nazi Germany. Austria was renamed Ostmark.
1945 After Nazi Germany was defeated in the Second World War; Austria re-emerged as an independent state but was divided into four zones of occupation by the US, UK, France and USSR. The conservative Österreichische Volkspartei (ÖVP) (Austrian People's Party) and the Sozialdemokratische Partei Österreichs

KEY INDICATORS — Austria

	Unit	2000	2001	2002	2003	2004
Population	m	8.11	8.13	8.15	8.07	8.08
Gross domestic product (GDP)	US$bn	189.80	188.70	204.70	251.50	290.11
GDP per capita	US$	23,300	23,100	24,990	30,250	35,809
GDP real growth	%	3.4	0.7	1.2	0.8	2.0
Inflation	%	2.4	2.7	1.8	1.3	2.0
Unemployment	%	3.7	3.6	4.2	4.3	4.5
Exports (fob) (goods)	US$m	64,684.0	66,899.0	73,700.0	70,000.0	111,134.0
Imports (fob) (goods)	US$m	67,415.0	68,227.0	70,100.0	74,000.0	106,929.0
Balance of trade	US$m	-2,732.0	-1,328.0	3,600.0	-4,000.0	4,205.0
Current account	US$m	-5,205.0	-4,103.0	800.0	-2,392.0	-1,980.0
Total reserves minus gold	US$m	14,318.0	12,509.0	13,189.0	8,470.0	7,858.0
Foreign exchange	US$m	13,492.0	11,444.0	12,020.0	7,144.0	6,763.0
Exchange rate	per US$	14.90	14.68	1.04	0.88	0.80

(SPÖ) (Social Democratic Party of Austria) formed a coalition government.
1955 The 1955 State Treaty confirmed Austria's independence and banned re-integration with Germany. Austria joined the UN, declared its neutrality and the occupation forces withdrew.
1960 Austria joined the European Free Trade Area (EFTA).
1966 The ÖVP came to power after 20 years of a coalition.
1970–87 The SPÖ was in power until 1983, when it formed a coalition government with the Freiheitliche Partei Österreichs (FPÖ) (Freedom Party of Austria).
1986 The presidential election was won by Kurt Waldheim (independent but with ÖVP's backing). Controversy surrounded allegations of his implication in Nazi atrocities in the Balkans (1942–45), culminating in his listing as an undesirable alien by the US Department of Justice.
1987 Following an inconclusive election, the SPÖ and the ÖVP formed a coalition.
1992 Waldheim stepped down and was replaced by Thomas Klestil.
1995 Austria joined the EU. The one-year-old governing coalition collapsed over the 1996 budget.
1997 Franz Vranitsky led the government as chancellor from 1995 until his resignation in 1997, when he was replaced by Viktor Klima.
1998 Federal President Klestil was re-elected for a second term of office.
1999 After indecisive election results, the ÖVP-SPÖ coalition collapsed, leading to a coalition between the ÖVP and the FPÖ.
2000 The ÖVP's Wolfgang Schüssel became chancellor. The inclusion of the FPÖ in the government led to EU diplomatic sanctions against Austria, which were formally lifted in September.
2002 Euro currency replaced the Austrian shilling. After three FPÖ ministers resigned, Schüssel announced that ÖVP was withdrawing from the coalition government. The ÖVP won the snap election.
2003 Chancellor Schüssel's coalition government was sworn in: the ÖVP and the right-wing populist FPÖ, with more power to the ÖVP than in the previous coalition.
2004 Heinz Fischer (SPÖ) won the 25 April presidential elections. On 6 July, President Klestil died after being critically ill for some time; Heinz Fischer was sworn in as president on 8 July.
2005 The Schüssel government survived a no-confidence vote on 5 April. The EU constitution was endorsed by parliament. The FPÖ split in April and a breakaway faction, the Bündis Zukunft Österreich (BZÖ) (Alliance for Austria's Future), joined the government coalition. In December, Austria began making payouts to those whose property was looted during the Holocaust. Most of the victims are elderly, and most are resident in the US.
2006 Austria assumed the presidency of the EU for the first six months of the year.

Political structure
Constitution
The 1920 constitution was amended in 1929.
The state is a federal republic consisting of nine Länder (states), each with its own state Ländtag (legislature) and government. The nine states are Burgenland, Carinthia, Lower Austria, Upper Austria, Salzburg, Styria, Tyrol, Vorarlberg and Vienna. A considerable amount of political power is devolved to the state assemblies, although all matters of national interest are decided in Vienna. Each state parliament appoints its own state governor.
For some functions (for example, appointing the new president) the Nationalrat (National Council) and the Bundesrat (Federal Council) of the federal Bundesversammlung (parliament) meet in joint session, as the Nationalversammlung (National Assembly). Certain issues may be put to the popular vote in a national referendum and the people may also force a direct vote in the Nationalrat if any petition gathers more than 200,000 signatures.
Traditionally, the government has been required to work according to the principles of the *sozialpartner* (social contract). This informal organisation, comprising the Chamber of Economy, Chamber of Agriculture, Chamber of Labour and trade unions, is at the heart of the policy-making process. Such a system has served Austria well in the past as it both guarantees and feeds on national consensus and unity. However, it is becoming unworkable in a fully globalised world economy.

Form of state
Federal parliamentary democratic republic

The executive
Executive power rests with the head of the federal government, who is the chancellor appointed by the president, and usually the leader of the largest party in the Nationalrat.
The president is elected by popular vote every six years for a maximum of two terms. He has no executive powers in peace time. He has special emergency powers, as well as overseeing elections and swearing in new chancellors and governments, but in practice, he acts in accordance with the decisions of the government.

National legislature
The bicameral parliament consists of the lower house, the Nationalrat, and the upper house, the Bundesrat.
The 183 constituent members of the Nationalrat are elected every four years by proportional representation. The seats are distributed first among 43 constituencies then among the nine states, and the remainder at federal level.
The 64 members of the Bundesrat are elected for various terms by the nine state legislatures and are chosen to reflect the party political strengths in their respective state parliaments. The chairmanship of the Bundesrat rotates on a six-monthly basis between the states.

Legal system
The legal system is divided between legislative, administrative and judicial power. There are three supreme courts Verfassungsgerichtshof (Constitutional Court), Verwaltungsgerichtshof (Administrative Court) and Oberster Gerichtshof (Judicial Court). There are around 200 local judicial courts (Bezirksgerichte), 17 provincial and district courts (Landes-und Kreisgerichte) and four higher provincial courts (Oberlandesgerichte) in Vienna, Graz, Innsbruck and Linz.

Last elections
13 June 2004 (European Parliament); 25 April 2004 (presidential); 24 November 2002 (parliamentary).
Results: European Parliament: SPÖ won 33.4 per cent of the vote (seven seats out of 18), ÖVP 32.7 per cent (six), List Hans-Peter Martin 14 per cent (two), Greens 12.8 per cent (two) and FPÖ 6.3 per cent (one); turnout 41.8 per cent. Presidential: Heinz Fischer (Sozialdemokratische Partei Österreichs (SPÖ) (Social Democratic Party)) won 52.4 per cent of the vote and Foreign Minister Benita Ferrero-Waldner (Österreichische Volkspartei (ÖVP) (Austrian People's Party)) 47.6 per cent; turnout was 70.8 per cent.
Parliamentary: the ÖVP won 42.3 per cent of the vote (79 seats out of 183), SPÖ 36.5 per cent (69), Freiheitliche Partei Österreichs (FPÖ) (Freedom Party of Austria) 10.0 per cent (18) and Die Grünen (Grüne) (Greens) 9.5 per cent (17); turnout was 80.5 per cent.

Next elections
2006 (parliamentary); 2010 (presidential).

Political parties
Ruling party
Coalition government sworn in 28 Feb 2003: the Österreichische Volkspartei (ÖVP) (Austrian People's Party) and the Bündis Zukunft Österreich (BZÖ) (Alliance for Austria's Future)

Main opposition party
Sozialdemokratische Partei Österreichs (SPÖ) (Social Democratic Party)

Population
8.08 million (2004); 8.07 million (OECD, 2003)

Austria

Ethnic make-up
Around 93 per cent are of German-Austrian origin. Minorities include Slovenes, Croats, Hungarians and Czechs and are mostly concentrated in the south-east. There are ethnic communities from Africa, the Middle East and Asia.

Religions
Roman Catholic (89 per cent); Protestant (6 per cent).

Education
Primary schooling lasts for four years. There are two main forms of secondary education; one academic and one geared more to technical and vocational education. The former, *Allgemeinbildende*, school may be attended for eight years or the latter, *Hauptschule*, attended for four years followed by a school offering specialised training of a technical or vocational nature. Tertiary education takes place in universities or specialist colleges including technology, music and art higher education institutions.
Compulsory years: 6 to 15
Enrolment rate: 103 per cent total primary enrolment, 99 per cent total secondary enrolment, 57 per cent tertiary enrolment; of relevant age groups (including repetition rates) World Bank.
Pupils per teacher: 12 in primary schools

Health
All Austrians have access to healthcare.
HIV prevalence: 0.3 per cent aged 15–49 in 2003 (World Bank)
Life expectancy: 79 years (World Bank)
Fertility rate/Maternal mortality rate: 1.4 births per woman (World Bank)
Infant mortality rate: 4.5 per 1,000 live births (World Bank)
Head of population per physician/bed: 3 physicians and 8.9 hospital beds per 1,000 people. The provision of hospital beds has declined from the level of the previous decade, when 11.2 were available per 1,000 people.

Welfare
Austrian social insurance is compulsory and covers health insurance, pension insurance, accident insurance and unemployment insurance. Contributions are shared by employers and employees.

Pensions
Reforms adopted in 2003, extend the years required for employee contributions from 40 to 45, before a worker can retire on a full pension with all benefits; the statutory retirement age was set at 65 for all; 10 disparate pension systems for various categories of workers were harmonised. This is expected to reverse the trend for early retirement. In 2003 the average age of retirement was 57.5, with less than 30 per cent of workers being in the 55–64 age range. With an ageing population the pension scheme will become progressively more expensive; it is expected that the new reforms wll limit spending by between 1.5–1.75 per cent of GDP a year. The government is proposing to stagger the rise in the official retirement age, while reducing state pensions by up to 30 per cent, in some cases.

Main cities
Vienna (capital, estimated population 1.5 million in 2004), Graz (219,500), Linz (185,300), Salzburg (145,500), Innsbruck (115,600), Klagenfurt (89,900), Villach (57,800), Wels (56,600), St Poelten (49,500), Dornbirn (42,800).

Languages spoken
About 94 per cent of Austrian nationals speak German, although a heavy dialect is in daily use. There are linguistic minorities of Slovenes, Croats, Hungarians, Slovaks and Czechs.

Official language/s
German

Media

Press
Dailies: *Der Standard* is a national daily with a liberal political outlook. Important dailies include *Die Presse*, *Neue Kronenzeitung*, *Wiener Zeitung* and *Kurier*. Other important regional dailies include *Kleine Zeitung*, *Tiroler Tageszeitung*, *Salzburger Nachrichten* and *Vorarlberger Nachrichten*.
Weeklies: Weekend editions of newspapers tend to be bigger than dailies and contain a large amount of advertising. Several weekly illustrated magazines, technical and trade magazines are published. *News* is a popular weekly news magazine. *Zur Zeit* covers weekly political issues and international affairs. *Samstag* is a family and general interest magazine.
Business: Major weekly and monthly business/political magazines include *Profil*, *Gewinn*, *Trend*, *Wirtschaft Nachrichten Sud* and *eurobusiness*.
Periodicals: Popular family and women's magazines include *Ehe und Familie*, *Okay* and *Woman*. *Rennbahn Express* is a monthly youth magazine. *Arbeit & Wirtschaft* covers labour issues.

Broadcasting
Österreichischer Rundfunk (ÖRF) (Austrian Broadcasting Corporation) is the national TV and radio broadcasting station.
Radio: Private radio stations began operating in 1990. ÖRF broadcasts three national radio stations, Radio Österreich 1 (ÖE1), Radio Österreich 3 (ÖE3) and FM4. Private domestic stations include Antenne and Orange.
Television: With satellite broadcasting and the trend for deregulation, state-run control of television is likely to diminish. There are two terrestrial TV stations, ÖRF1 and ÖRF2. Austria Television (ATV) was launched in January 2000, broadcasting via cable and digital satellite.

Advertising
Television advertising is popular but restricted facilities and high demand means space must be booked several months in advance. Newspapers (especially weekend editions) and magazines are also popular. Poster sites are available under the auspices of the municipal authorities. Advertising in cinemas and by direct mail is also widely used.

Economy
There has been a gradual shift away from agriculture towards heavy industry and services since the 1950s, leading to higher living standards and lower unemployment. The industrial sector has been largely restructured, but the process of divesting state holding company shares in large enterprises, which began in 1987, has not been entirely consistent.

Austria joined the EU in January 1995. It easily met the Maastricht convergence criteria and joined the Economic and Monetary Union (EMU) in January 1999. Austria became a member of the euro-zone in January 2002 as euro notes and coins replaced the schilling as Austria's national currency. It is well-placed to benefit from the euro as its trade is well integrated with its EU partners.

There is broad consensus among trades unions, business and government on commitment towards full employment and sustained economic growth. Austria has the third highest labour costs in the EU, but also one of the lowest levels of strikes. To ease the burden of an ageing population and to improve the economy, older citizens are being encouraged to enter the labour force by eliminating the pension system's incentives for early retirement. Strong exports pushed GDP growth to 2 per cent in 2004. The government needs to improve public-sector efficiency – public sector debt is high at 65 per cent of GDP – in order to balance the budget by 2008. The OECD said in its 2005 survey that Austria would also do well to improve its economic competitiveness. While a great deal is spent on higher education, graduation rates are among the lowest in the OECD, and better investment in education would spur growth.

External trade
Foreign trade is important to the Austrian economy. The EU is Austria's major trading area, accounting for more than 70 per cent of both imports and exports. By far the biggest individual partner is Germany, accounting for 40 per cent of trading exchange. Exports to the US and Eastern Europe have increased.

Heightened investment and trade with EU newcomers, initiated by Austria's banking and industrial sectors, has fuelled much of the country's recent economic success.

Imports
Major imports are oil and oil products, chemicals, vehicles, machinery, foodstuffs and consumer durables.

Main sources: Germany (45.9 per cent total, 2004), Italy (6.7 per cent), Switzerland (4.3 per cent)

Exports
Major exports include machinery, vehicles and parts, paper and paperboard, chemicals (chiefly plastics and pharmaceuticals) and manufactured goods, metal goods in iron and steel, textiles, foodstuffs.

Main destinations: Germany (31.4 per cent total, 2004), Italy (9.0 per cent), Switzerland (4.8 per cent), US (6.0 per cent), UK 4.4 per cent), France (4.2 per cent)

Agriculture
Farming
The agricultural sector contributes 2.2 per cent to GDP and employs 6.9 per cent of the labour force. The sector is dominated by small scale farming (50 per cent of farms cover less than 10 hectares), although the trend is towards larger, more mechanised units leading to increased productivity. Labour input is falling while workers' earnings are rising: by 2.5 per cent in real terms during 2004.

About 18.2 per cent of land is crop land, 24.1 per cent permanent pasture land and 39 per cent forests and woodland. Farming is concentrated in Upper Austria, the northern part of Lower Austria, Burgenland and Styria.

Principal products are milk, beef, veal, pork, sugar beet, maize, barley, wheat and wine, but government is encouraging diversification to oilseeds, herbs, spices, hops and fast-growing timber. Quality wine, improved since a 1985 wine scandal, has become a major export product. Although output fluctuates, the country remains almost 90 per cent self-sufficient. Fundamental reform to the Common Agricultural Policy (CAP) was introduced on 1 January 2005 in Austria. The subsidies paid on farm output, which tended to benefit large farms and encourage overproduction, were replaced by single farm payments not conditional on production. This is expected to reward farms that provide and maintain a healthy environment, food safety and animal welfare standards. The changes are also intended to encourage market conscious production and cut the cost of CAP to the EU taxpayer.

The growing of ornamental flowers and plants takes up much of Austria's horticultural land.

Crop production in 2004 included: 5,009,329 tonnes (t) cereals in total, 1,718,820t wheat, 1,653,750t maize, 1,006,740t barley, 2,934,744t sugar beets, 693,054t potatoes, 120,815t rapeseed (canola), 111,764t pulses, 351,000t grapes, 97,805t oilcrops, 484,096t apples, 1,131,613t fruit in total, 569,507t vegetables in total. Livestock production included: 995,545t meat in total, 215,000t beef, 654,000t pig meat, 7,600t lamb and goat meat, 112,365t poultry, 88,700t eggs, 3,582,500t milk, 9,000t honey, 23,000t cattle hides.

Fishing
The fisheries industry in Austria is based on professional lake fishing, which entails traditional breeding of trout, carp and other freshwater species. Austria promotes the EU's Common Fisheries Policy (CFP) as it benefits from the EU's structural funds for the development of aquaculture and the processing and marketing of products. Typically Austria's fishing haul is about 350 tonnes, amounting to 0.01 per cent of the EU total. Family firms run most businesses in both aquaculture and lake fishing. Despite its tradition of fish farming the sector suffers a lack of technical support.

Forestry
Forest and other wooded land occupy nearly a half of the total land area, with forest cover estimated at 3.8 million hectares (ha) in 2000. Forest cover increased an annual average of 0.20 per cent, the equivalent of 8,000ha between 1990–2000, as a result of afforestation in protected areas and natural extension onto agricultural land. Most of the forest is available for wood supply.

Forestry remains a major source of income within agriculture. Austria produces large quantities of paper and sawn wood, and is the fifth-largest exporter of sawnwood in the world with Germany, Italy and France the main export markets. The wood processing industry places an emphasis on value-added production including skis and solid wood panel manufacturing. A large proportion of raw materials including roundwood, pulp and recovered paper are imported.

Imports of forest materials amounted to US$3.0 billion, while exports totalled US$6.2 billion, in 2004. In 2002 forests were significantly harmed by windthrow, which had financial repercussions for forestry revenue in 2003–04.

Production in 2004 included: 16,482,000 cubic metres (cum) roundwood, 12,943,000cum industrial roundwood, 11,133,000cum sawnwood, 10,021,000cum sawlogs and veneer logs, 2,922,000cum pulpwood (round and split), 3,419,420cum wood-based panels, 3,539,000cum woodfuel; 1,344,663 tonnes (t) recovered paper, 421,697t newsprint, 2,506,196t printing and writing paper.

Industry and manufacturing
The industrial sector contributes 31 per cent to GDP and employs 34 per cent of the labour force.

Since 1985, the industrial workforce has fallen by more than 150,000 to just over 500,000, which can be partly explained by falling productivity growth and company restructuring during the late 1990s. Since then, the industrial sector has recovered. The steel industry in particular is flourishing. The sector's largest company, Voestalpine, has experienced record demand. Recent privatisation and deregulation of markets, along with tax and structural reform, have ensured that financially Austria is among the most successful of euro-zone nations.

Tourism
With the relaxation of border restrictions to Eastern Europe, overnight stays by visitors from neighbouring eastern countries are increasing. Overall arrivals in 2004 numbered 19 210 800, up on the previous year.

The tourism industry in Austria comprised an estimated 6.1 per cent of GDP in 2005 and accounted for 6.9% of total employment. Tourism was forecast to stimulate eur59.0 billion (US$78.7 billion) in 2005, with an increase in demand of 4.4 per cent.

Mining
The mining sector accounts for approximately 11 per cent of annual GDP and employs 1 per cent of the workforce. There are deposits of various minerals, notably magnesite (of which Austria is the world's largest producer), iron, lead and zinc ores, salt, graphite, coal and gypsum. Commercial exploitation is restricted by the very small number of viable deposits and geological difficulties.

Hydrocarbons
With extraction relatively expensive, estimated reserves of 86 million barrels (2003) are under-exploited and will last for little more than a decade. The main oil and gas company is Österreichische Mineralölverwaltung (ÖMV), the country's largest industrial concern. The government is the largest shareholder in ÖMV, with a 35 per cent stake.

Some 80 per cent of natural gas is imported, in particular from countries of the former Soviet bloc. Austrian gas reserves are projected to last until around 2015. Compliance with the first stage of the EU directive for liberalisation of the gas market in 2000 freed up half the market, which was largely controlled by ÖMV.

Austria

Austria produces over a million tonnes of coal per year, supplying approximately 20 per cent of domestic demand. Much of this production is low quality brown coal. The remainder of Austria's coal supplies are imported, particularly from Germany and the Czech Republic. At current production levels, Austrian coal reserves will last several decades.

Energy
Despite a successful energy conservation programme and an increase in local oil and gas production, there is still a heavy dependence on energy imports, especially gas from the former Soviet Union.

The country is more than self-sufficient in electricity, with hydroelectric power accounting for 70 per cent of total production. The Freudenau hydroelectric power plant on the Danube, which cost US$1.2 billion to build, has been operating since 1997 and is one of the world's most advanced hydroelectric power generating facilities.

Austria is one of the leading European nations in terms of solar energy utilisation.

Financial markets
Stock exchange
The Wiener Börse (Vienna Stock Exchange) is one of the smallest in Europe.

Banking and insurance
Consolidation of the Austrian banking sector began in 1997 when Bank Austria, the largest bank, took over Creditanstalt and Erste Bank took over Giro Credit. In 1998, Bank Austria merged with Germany's HypoVereinsbank. Bank Austria officially merged with Creditanstalt in May 2002. During the first half of 2005 Bank Austria Creditanstalt's (BA-CA) profits rose 59 per cent, up to eur453 million.

There are around 1,000 national and local banks in Austria. Many are active in Central and Eastern Europe. Austria remains overbanked. In order to remain competitive in the new European market, significant consolidation is required.

Central bank
Österreichische Nationalbank (OeNB) (Austrian National Bank); European Central Bank (ECB).

Time
GMT plus one hour (GMT plus two hours from late March to late September)

Geography
Austria's land surface area is 83,855 square km. Austria is famous for its Alpine terrain, but the bulk of the country's economic activity and all of its major population centres are based on the low-lying areas around Vienna and Linz, in the north and east, and around Salzburg, on the German border.

Climate
Climatic conditions vary widely across the country, with deep winter snows in the north and west, which are an essential element in the country's very important tourist economy. Seasonal variations are particularly marked: in Vienna, temperatures range from an average -1 degree Celsius (C) in January to 21 degrees C in July and August. Summers are often wet, with July and August recording averages of 84mm and 71mm of rainfall respectively.

Dress codes
Business dress is formal. Warm clothing is essential for the winter months.

Entry requirements
Passports
Required by all. Nationals of countries which are signatories of the Schengen Accords, which includes most EU member states may visit on national IDs.
Visa
Required by all except nationals of EU and Schengen Accord signatory countries; North America, Australasia, and Japan. For further exceptions contact the nearest embassy. A Schengen visa application (offered in several languages) can be downloaded on www.eurovisa.info/ApplicationForm.htm.
Currency advice/regulations
Exchange controls have been abolished and most currencies can be readily exchanged at a variety of facilities.
Customs
Personal items are not taxed. Standard EU customs controls are in place.
Prohibited imports
Narcotics and tickets relating to foreign lotteries are prohibited.

Health (for visitors)
Mandatory precautions
Vaccination certificates for cholera and yellow fever are required if travelling from infected areas.
Advisable precautions
Rabies is present in Austria although few incidents have been reported in recent years.

Hotels
Generally of a high standard with a large selection available in most cities. Classified from five stars to one star. Rates vary according to category but are generally cheaper outside the capital.

Credit cards
Eurocard, Mastercard, Visa and, less widely, American Express and Diners Club are accepted.

Public holidays
Fixed dates
1 Jan (New Year's Day), 6 Jan (Epiphany), 1 May (Labour Day), 15 Aug (Assumption Day), 26 Oct (National Day), 1 Nov (All Saints' Day), 8 Dec (Immaculate Conception), 25 Dec (Christmas Day), 26 Dec (St Stephen's Day).
Variable dates
Good Friday, Easter Monday, Ascension Day, Whit Monday, Corpus Christi (May/Jun).

Working hours
Banking
Mon–Wed and Fri: 0800–1230 and 1330–1500; Thu: 0800–1230 and 1330–1730. Banks are closed on Saturdays and Sundays. The exchange counters at airports and main railway stations are usually open from the first to the last plane or train, ie from 0800–2200 seven days a week.
Business
Mon–Fri: 0800–1230, 1300–1730. Many offices do not work Friday afternoon.
Government
Mon–Fri: 0800–1230, 1300–1730. Many offices do not work Friday afternoon.
Shops
Mon–Fri: 0800–1930; many shops close for two hours at midday. Sat: 0800–1700.

Telecommunications
Mobile phones
GSM G3 service operates in major cities only; 900 and 1800 services are available throughout the country

Electricity supply
220V AC

Social customs/useful tips
Appointments must be made in advance and punctuality is important; the usual form of address is *Herr* or *Frau*, followed by family or surname. People with an academic of professional title, eg *Doktor*, are addressed as *Herr* or *Frau Doktor*. Handshaking is universal in business and private meetings, both when arriving and leaving. Business is usually conducted in German. For restaurant meetings, dress formally, as for business meetings. Exchange pleasantries for a few minutes before getting down to business. When visiting private homes, it is usual to take flowers or confectionery for the host or hostess.

Security
There are no special problems and normal precautions apply. Vienna is possibly one of the safest cities in Europe.

Getting there
Air
National airline: Austrian Airlines
International airport/s: Vienna International (VIE), 18km south-east of city; facilities include duty-free, banks, bureaux de

change, post office, restaurants, left luggage, conference facilities, medical facilities, tourist information, car hire.
Other airport/s: Graz (GRZ), 12km from city; Salzburg (SZG), 4km from city; Innsbruck (INN), 5km from city; Klagenfurt (KLU), 4km from city; Linz (LNZ), 15km from city.
Airport tax: None
Surface
Road: There are good road links with all surrounding countries. Motorists should check advisability of routes, especially in winter, with ÖAMTC or ARBÖ (Austrian automobile clubs).
Rail: Austria participates in European rail pass schemes.
Water: Ships provide regular passenger services and cruises on the Danube, starting at Passau or Regensburg in Germany, to Vienna. There are also links with the Rhine and Main rivers and the Black Sea.

Getting about
National transport
Air: Austrian Air Services, Tyrolean Airways and Rheintalflug operate regular flights between Vienna and Graz, Linz, Klagenfurt, Innsbruck and Salzburg. Also between Innsbruck and Graz and Linz and between Linz and Salzburg.
Road: There is a good internal road network. Cars and trucks are charged an annual fee to use motorways and A-roads; a weekly fee can be paid by visitors.
Buses: Services are provided by federal and local authorities, in addition to private companies. There are more than 1,800 services in operation. For details of destinations consult the Austrian bus guide.
Rail: State-owned network of almost 6,000km, most of which is electrified. Also about 20 private railways covering a total 660km. There are frequent intercity services from Vienna to Salzburg, Innsbruck, Graz and Klagenfurt.
Water: There is a passenger ferry service between Vienna and the Black Sea and on upper Danube in mid-May to mid-September. Austrian Federal Railways operate passenger services on all the larger lakes.
City transport
Taxis: Widely available from stands or via radio/telephone services. The taxi journey time to the city centre from the airport is 25–30 minutes. Fares are metered but expensive, and in some areas zone charges or set charges for standard trips apply; a 10 per cent tip is usual.
Buses, trams & metro: Vienna has a very efficient, integrated system which avoids the crowded city traffic. Public transport operates between 0500 and 2400 and tickets, for all services, can be bought for 24 hour/3 day and set periods. An airport bus operates 24 hours every 20 minutes, and takes approximately 30 minutes to get to the city centre.
Trains: The OBB train service S7 operates between 0511–2216 every hour, and takes 25 minutes from the airport to the city centre.
Car hire
Self-drive and chauffeur-driven services available at railway stations, airports and in major cities. Rates per day vary with size of car, plus additional charge per kilometre, and fuel is extra, although weekly hire attracts cheaper initial rates. VAT at 20 per cent (32 per cent if rental over 21 days) must be paid but a 'green card' (third party motor insurance) is compulsory. The speed limit is 100kph on most roads and 130kph on motorways, in built-up areas it is 50kph, unless otherwise stipulated.
EU issued driving licenses are required, permitting the holders to drive in Austria for one year. Minimum driving age is 18.

BUSINESS DIRECTORY
The addresses listed below are a selection only. While World of Information makes every endeavour to check these addresses, we cannot guarantee that changes have not been made, especially to telephone numbers and area codes. We would welcome any corrections.

Telephone area codes
The international direct dialling code (IDD) for Austria is +43, followed by area code and subscriber's number:

Gmunden	7612	St Pölten	2742
Graz	316	Salzburg	662
Innsbruck	512	Steyr	7252
Kitzbühel	5356	Vienna	1
Klagenfurt	463	Villach	4242
Krems an der Donau	2732	Wels	7242
Leoben	3842	Wiener Neustadt	2622
Linz	70		

Chambers of Commerce
American Chamber of Commerce in Austria, 35 Porzellangasse, A-1090 Vienna (tel: 319-5751; fax: 319-5151; e-mail: office@amcham.or.at).

Austrian Economic Chamber, 63 Wiedner Hauptstrasse, A-1045 Vienna (tel/fax: 059-0900; e-mail: wkoe@wko.at).

Burgenland Economic Chamber, 1 Robert-Graf-Platz, A-7000 Eisenstadt (tel/fax: 059-0907; e-mail: wkgbld@wkbgld.at).

Kärnten Economic Chamber, 1 Europaplatz, A-9021 Klagenfurt (tel/fax: 059-0904; e-mail: wirtschaftskammer@wkk.or.at).

Lower Austria Economic Chamber, 10 Herrengasse, A-1014 Vienna (tel/fax: 015-3466; e-mail: wknoe@wknoe.at).

Salzburg Economic Chamber, 1 Julius-Raab-Platz, A-5027 (tel/fax: 0662-8888; e-mail: wirtschaftskammer@sbg.wk.or.at).

Steiermark Economic Chamber, 111 Körblergasse, A-8021 Graz (tel/fax: 031-6601; e-mail: office@wkstmk.at).

Tirol Economic Chamber, 14 Meinhardstrasse, A-6020 Innsbruck (te/fax: 059-0905; e-mail: office@wktirol.at).

Upper Austria Economic Chamber, 3 Hessenplatz, A-4010 Linz (tel/fax: 059-0909; e-mail: wirtschaftskammer@wkooe.at).

Vienna Economic Chamber, 8 Stubenring, A-1010 Vienna (tel/fax: 514-50; e-mail: postbox@wkw.at).

Vorarlberg Economic Chamber, 9 Wichnergasse, A-6800 Feldkirch (te/fax: 0552-2305; e-mail: praesidium@wkv.at).

Banking
Bank Austria Creditanstalt AG, Am Hof 2, A-1010 Vienna (tel: 531-240; fax: 5312-4155).

Bank für Arbeit und Wirtshaft AG (BAWAG), Seitzergasse 2 - 4, A-1010 Vienna (tel: 534-530; fax: 5345-32930).

Erste Bank, Graben 21, A1010 Vienna (tel: 531-000; fax: 5310-0625); also at Schubertring 5-7, A-1010 Vienna (tel: 711-940; fax: 713-7032).

Österreichische Postsparkasse, Georg Coch-Platz 2, A1020 Vienna (tel: 514-000; fax: 5140-01700).

Österreichische Volksbanken AG, Peregringasse 3, A-1090 Vienna (tel: 313-400; fax: 3134-03683).

Raiffeisen Zentralbank Österreich AG, Am Stadtpark 9, A-1030 Vienna (tel: 717-070).

Central bank
Österreichische Nationalbank, Otto Wagner-Platz 3, PO Box 61, A-1011 Vienna (tel: 404-20-2398; fax: 404-20-666; e-mail: oenb.info@oenb.co.at).

European Central Bank (ECB), Kaiserstrasse 29, D-60311 Frankfurt am Main, Germany (tel: +49(69)13-440; fax: +49(69)1344-6000; e-mail: info@ecb.int).

Travel information
Austrian Airlines (Österreichische Luftverkehrs), PO Box 50, Fontanastrasse 1, Vienna A-1010 (tel: 683-5110; fax: 685-505; internet site: http://www.aua.com).

Auto-, Motor- und Radfahrerbund Österreichs (ARBÖ), A-1150 Vienna, Mariahilfer Strasse 180 (tel: 891-217; fax: 891-236).

Austria

Lauda Air Luftfahrt, World Trade Centre, PO Box 56, Vienna-Schwechat A-1300 (tel: 7007-2081; fax: 7007-2091; internet site: http://www.laudaair.com/engl/indexe.htm).

ÖAMTC (Österreichischer Automobil-Motorrad und Touring Club), A-1010 Vienna, Schubertring 1-3 (tel: 711-990).

Tyrolean Airways (Tiroler Luftfahrt), Postfach 58, Innsbruck A-6026 (tel: 2222; fax: 293-490).

National tourist organisation offices

Österreich Werbung (Austrian National Tourist Office), A-1040 Vienna, Margarethenstr. 1 (tel: 587-2000; fax: 588-6620; email: info@anto.co.uk).

Ministries

Federal Chancellor's Office, Ballhausplatz 2, 1014 Vienna (tel: 531-150; fax: 535-0338).

Federal Ministry of Agriculture & Forestry, Environment and Water Resources, Stubenring 1, 1010 Vienna (tel: 711-000; fax: 715-9651).

Federal Ministry of Defence, Dampfschiffstr. 2, 1033 Vienna (tel: 515-950; fax: 515-9521).

Federal Ministry of Economic Affairs and Labour, Stubenring 1, 1010 Vienna (tel: 711-000; fax: 713-7995).

Federal Ministry of Education, Science and Culture, Minoritenplatz 5, 1014 Vienna (tel: 531-200; fax: 533-7797).

Federal Ministry of Finance, Himmelpfortgasse 8, 1015 Vienna (tel: 514-330; fax: 512-7869).

Federal Ministry of Foreign Affairs, Ballhausplatz 2, 1014 Vienna (tel: 531-150; fax: 533-2547).

Federal Ministry of the Interior, Herrengasse 7, 1010 Vienna (tel: 531-260; 531-263910).

Federal Ministry of Justice, Museumstrasse 7, 1070 Vienna (tel: 521-520; fax: 521-52727).

Federal Ministry of Public Affairs and Sport, Minoritenplatz 3, 1014 Vienna (tel: 531-150).

Federal Ministry of Social Security and Generations, Stubenring 1, 1010 Vienna (tel: 711-000; fax: 713-9311).

Federal Ministry of Transport, Innovation and Technology, Radetskystrasse 2, 1030 Vienna (tel: 711-620).

Other useful addresses

Austrian Business Agency, Opernring 3, A-1010 Vienna (tel: 202-588-5820; fax: 202-586-8659; e-mail: austrian.business@telecom.at; internet site: http://www.aba.qv.at).

Austria Presse-Agentur (APA) (Co-operative Agency of the Austrian Newspapers and Broadcasting Co), A-1199 Vienna, Gunoldstrasse 14 (tel: 36-050).

Austrian Telecommunications Regulatory Authority, Ministry of Science and Transport, Sektion IV, Kelsenstrasse 7, Vienna A-1030 (tel: 79731-4100; fax: 79731-4109; e-mail: Christian.Singer@bmv.gv.at).

Interpreters' Institute of Vienna University (tel: 347-649 ext. 298).

Österreichisches Statistisches Zentralamt (Central Statistical Office), Hintere Zollamtstrasse 2b, A-1030 Vienna (tel: 711-280; fax: 7112-87728).

Post und Telekom Austria AG, Postgasse 8, 1010 Vienna (tel: 515-510; fax: 512-8414).

US Embassy, Boltzmangasse 16, A-1090 Vienna (tel: 313-390; fax: 310-0682; e-mail: embassy@usembassy.at).

Vereinigung Österreichischer Industrieller (Association of Austrian Industrialists), A-1030 Vienna, Schwarzenbergplatz 4 (tel: 711-350).

Wiener Börse (Vienna Stock Exchange), A-1011 Vienna, Wipplingerstrasse 34 (tel: 53-499).

Internet sites

Austrian Business Agency: http://www.aba.gv.at

Austrian National Tourist Office: http://www.austria-tourism.at

Austrian Embassy, UK, consular information: http://www.austria.org.uk/visa.html

Government of Austria webpage: http://www.austria.gv.at/e/

Local government web site index (launches German language webpages): http://oultwood.com/localgov/austria.htm

Statistics Austria (in German): http://www.statistik.at/index.shtml

Azerbaijan

KEY FACTS

Official name: Azarbaijchan Respublikasy (Republic of Azerbaijan)

Head of State: President Kurmanbek Bakiyev (YAP) (sworn in 6 Aug 2005)

Head of government: Prime Minister Feliks Kulov (proposed by the President, endorsed by parliament Aug 2005)

Ruling party: Yeni Azerbaycan Partiyasi (YAP) (New Azerbaijan Party) (re-elected Nov 2005)

Area: 86,600 square km

Population: 8.32 million (2004)

Capital: Baku

Official language: Azeri (Turkic)

Currency: Manat (M) = 100 gopik

Exchange rate: M4,608.50 per US$ (Oct 2005)

GDP per capita: US$1,024 (2004)

GDP real growth: 10.10% (2004)

Labour force: 3.98 million (2004)

Unemployment: 14.00% (unofficial, 2004); 1.20% (official, 2004)

Inflation: 8.10% (2004)

Oil production: 318,000 bpd (2004)

Balance of trade: US$161.30 million (2004)

Foreign debt: US$1.60 billion (2004)

Annual FDI: US$4.40 billion (2004)

Azerbaijan featured prominently in international press headlines in 2005. Key developments were the impact of a continuing oil boom on the country's economy, and parliamentary elections, the first national poll since Ilham Aliyev won a deeply flawed presidential election in October 2003.

Hydrocarbon boom

With GDP growth of more than 10 per cent in 2004 and an estimated 14 per cent jump in growth in 2005, Azerbaijan is easily one of the fastest growing economies in the world. This growth is almost entirely dependent upon oil and gas sales, which make up 90 per cent of all Azeri exports to the rest of the world. Azeri oil and gas exports have been responsible for year-on-year GDP growth of around 10 per cent since 2000 but in 2005 Azerbaijan's hydrocarbon production capacity reached new heights. In May, the Baku-Tbilisi-Ceyhan (BTC) pipeline was officially opened, enabling Azerbaijan to transport oil from its vast Caspian Sea fields to the Mediterranean.

The project, which involved Georgia and Turkey (as transit countries) and an international consortium of oil companies, headed by British Petroleum (BP), cost an estimated US$3.6 billion. The development of the Azeri-Chirag-Gunashli (ACG) oil fields on the Caspian in the first quarter of 2005 also underwrote Azerbaijan's reputation as a major new producer. Record international prices for oil in 2005 also underpinned Azerbaijan's economic boom - in August, Azeri oil was selling at an unprecedented US$66 per barrel.

Azerbaijan took a large step towards becoming a major national gas exporter in 2005. Development of the Shah Deniz gas field in the Caspian, one of the world's largest gas discoveries in the last 20 years, gathered pace in 2005, with pipelines being laid in September. Parallel development of the South Caucasus Pipeline (SCP) or Baku-Tbilisi-Erzurum (BTE) pipeline also accelerated in 2005. This pipeline is designed to transport gas from the ACG and is expected to be operational by the end of 2006.

Azerbaijan

Fears of 'Dutch disease'

Aside from runaway economic growth, Azerbaijan's hydrocarbon boom has raised fears, both inside and outside the country, of 'Dutch disease'. In 2005, Azerbaijan showed symptoms of 'Dutch disease', namely an appreciation of the local currency, the manat (it recorded a 20 per cent jump in value against the US dollar in September), high inflation (around 15 per cent for the year), and persistent underdevelopment of non-hydrocarbon sectors of the economy. All of these factors threaten the long-term stability of Azerbaijan's economy, particularly as most energy experts predict that the Azeri hydrocarbon bonanza will fade after 2010.

Wary of the pitfalls of 'Dutch disease', the government continued its efforts to diversify the economy in 2005. President Aliyev issued a decree entitled *Long-term strategy on the Management of Oil and Gas Revenues*. This set out a series of programmes aimed at developing non-oil sectors of the economy and reducing poverty over 2005–25. Key to these programmes' success will be the State Oil Fund of Azerbaijan (SOFAZ), established in 1999 and funded by contributions from Azerbaijan's oil and gas revenues. In 2005, the SOFAZ was estimated to be worth US$1 billion. Encouragingly, the non-oil sector grew by 8 per cent in 2005, fuelled mainly by the construction industry. Both the IMF and the World Bank were active in 2005 in supporting Azerbaijan's efforts to reduce poverty levels, with around 40 per cent of the population currently living below the poverty line.

The big test

Azerbaijan's democratic credentials were seen by many to be put to the test in 2005. The Parliamentary Assembly of the Council of Europe (PACE) and the European Commission explicitly stated this to be the case. It was a test that Azerbaijan ultimately failed, at least for 2005. Although not actually taking place until 6 November, Azerbaijan's elections to its parliament, the Milli Mejlis (National Assembly), dominated the entire calendar year. There were essentially three major reasons for this:

- High expectations for free and fair elections. This election was the first nation-wide poll to take place in Azerbaijan since the election of Aliyev to the presidency in October 2003. These 2003 elections were widely condemned as fraudulent by Azeri opposition leaders and international bodies such as the Organisation for Security and Co-operation in Europe (OSCE). They were also tarnished by a post-poll crackdown on opposition party members, including mass arrests and sackings of public servants suspected of favouring non-governing parties. The Aliyev government was under pressure in 2005 from its domestic and international critics to clean up its act or at least improve upon the shambles of the 2003 election. In 2005, the US added its voice to those calling for a clean poll, with the US embassy in Baku being particularly vocal.
- Velvet, Orange and Tulip: Azerbaijan as the next 'colour' revolution? Since 2003, three former Soviet republics have experienced political upheavals and protest-led changes of government (Georgia, Ukraine, Kyrgyzstan). Outside observers and many within Azerbaijan, including the government, were keeping a close eye on the prospects for revolutionary change.
- Because of oil, Azerbaijan matters. The final major factor contributing to 2005 being a momentous year in Azeri politics was the fact that with Azerbaijan now exporting vast quantities of hydrocarbons, what happened in Azerbaijan now mattered to the rest of the world. In May, the presidents of Azerbaijan, Georgia, Turkey and Kazakhstan were in Baku for the BTC opening ceremony. Also in attendance was the US Energy Secretary. Opposition parties saw their chance and called for anti-government demonstrations – because of oil, the world was watching.

All three of these factors helped to galvanise opposition parties in Azerbaijan. In July, Azadliq (Freedom), a new electoral alliance consisting of three leading opposition parties was formed. Although the police did break up some rallies, large opposition rallies, never previously allowed in Azerbaijan, were held in May, June, September and October. President Aliyev issued two decrees calling for electoral reform, including allowing for Non-Governmental Organisation (NGO) monitoring of the election. Counting against real change was the fact that not all opposition parties were able, or willing, to unite before the election. More disturbingly, a prominent journalist and opposition figure, Elmar Huseynov, was murdered in March. This was the most extreme example in a series of kidnappings and beatings of opposition party figures in 2005. A leading Azadliq figure, Rusal Guliyev, was not allowed to return from exile and dozens of public figures, including two cabinet ministers, were sacked and arrested for allegedly favouring the opposition.

KEY INDICATORS — Azerbaijan

	Unit	2000	2001	2002	2003	2004
Population	m	8.05	8.10	8.17	8.25	8.32
Gross domestic product (GDP)	US$bn	5.30	4.50	6.10	6.18	*8.52
GDP per capita	US$	646	555	744	750	1,024
GDP real growth	%	11.1	9.9	10.6	9.5	10.1
Inflation	%	1.8	1.5	2.8	3.0	8.1
Unemployment	%	18.0	16.0	14.0	10.0	14.0
Oil output	'000 bpd	281.0	300.0	308.0	313.0	318.0
Natural gas output	bn cum	5.3	5.2	4.8	4.8	4.6
Exports (fob) (goods)	US$m	1,858.3	2,078.9	2,000.0	2,625.0	3,743.0
Imports (fob) (goods)	US$m	1,539.0	1,465.1	2,100.0	2,723.0	3,581.7
Balance of trade	US$m	319.3	613.9	-165.0	-98.0	161.3
Current account	US$m	-167.8	-51.8	-768.0	-2,021.0	-2,330.0
Foreign debt	US$bn	1.2	1.3	1.4	1.4	1.6
Total reserves minus gold	US$m	679.6	896.7	721.5	820.9	1,089.6
Foreign exchange	US$m	673.0	894.2	720.8	802.8	1,075.0
Foreign direct investment (FDI)	US$bn	–	–	–	–	1.1
Exchange rate	per US$	4,474.15	4,656.58	4,785.50	4,912.00	4,920.10

* estimated figure

Democracy bust

The election was in the end depressingly familiar for opposition supporters. The OSCE and the Council of Europe declared that the elections 'did not meet international standards despite some improvements' and opposition parties rejected the results out of hand. Although the ruling Yeni Azerbaycan Partiyasi (YAP) (New Azerbaijan Party) lost its legislative majority, the result revealed that the main opposition parties had won only ten seats. The election of scores of pro-government independent MPs ensured that YAP would not be denied a majority on most issues. Moreover, President Aliyev's wife and uncle won seats in parliament. Having dominated Azeri politics since 1969, these victories did nothing to dispel the notion that the Aliyev clan were, for all intents and purposes, a royal family.

Post-election demonstrations in Baku, the largest being 20,000-strong, took place in November and December. Riot police took a less forgiving view than they had prior to the election, which elicited a formal protest from the US State Department. After weeks of delay, Azerbaijan's Central Elections Commission announced in December that results in ten constituencies were to be overturned and elections re-run in May 2006. This did little to appease the opposition parties and those few who had managed to win seats launched a boycott of the Milli Mejlis. The NGO International Crisis Group (ICG) declared the elections to be a 'lost opportunity' and called upon the Council of Europe to suspend Azerbaijan's membership and for the international community to impose a diplomatic embargo on the regime in Baku.

Azerbaijan and the region

Due to high-profile domestic developments, 2005 was one of the few years in Azerbaijan's post-independence history not dominated by its dispute with Armenia over the separatist Nagorno-Karabakh enclave in the country's south-west. However, there were significant developments on this front, at least in terms of restarting dialogue. President Aliyev met with his Armenian counterpart, Robert Kocharian, twice in 2005 (in May and August), and their respective foreign ministers held several meetings. The OSCE Minsk Group, formed in 1992 to settle the dispute also insisted that momentum was gathering for a breakthrough, the last such occasion being in 2001.

Against these positive developments must be weighed other, less encouraging events. Dozens of Azeri and Armenian servicemen continued to be killed along the cease-fire line in small-scale clashes. More worryingly, in June, President Aliyev announced that he was nearly doubling defence spending for 2005 (to US$300 million) and would double it again in 2006. The Armenians duly promised to try and match these rises. Also in June, Nagorno-Karabakh's hard-line separatist administration was re-elected in a landslide.

Regarding its other neighbours, Azerbaijan's relations improved markedly with Iran. Azerbaijan-Iran relations have long been complicated by the presence of a 15–20 million-strong Azeri minority in north-western Iran – greater than the population of Azerbaijan-proper (eight million). However, President Aliyev visited Tehran in January and Iran agreed to provide its Nakhichevan enclave with natural gas. Azerbaijan also worked hard in 2005 to cultivate relations with Kazakhstan. At stake is control of the export route to Europe for Kazakh natural gas. Azerbaijan and its backers, including the US, favour south Caucasus routes such as the SCP, while Russia has lobbied for transit across its own territory. In December, the presidents of Azerbaijan and Kazakhstan signed agreements deepening trade relations between the two countries.

Outlook

With the SCP and BTC pipelines expected to become fully operational in 2006, thereby increasing Azerbaijan's capacity to exploit its oil and gas reserves on the Caspian, rapid economic growth is assured. However, this growth will almost certainly be dominated by the hydrocarbon sector. Although President Aliyev has promised to work towards diversifying the economy from 2005–25, the 'Long-term strategy' (op cit) is in its infancy. For now, the danger of 'Dutch disease' will continue to cloud Azerbaijan's medium and long-term future until structural changes are implemented.

The 'lost opportunity' of the 6 November election will, in 2006, likely remain just that – lost. Key opposition parties are insisting on a boycott of the Milli Mejlis and have not even indicated whether or not they will bother putting up candidates in the ten constituencies that will be re-contested in May 2006. US criticism of the regime became more muted in December 2005 and it appears unlikely that the kinds of embargoes recommended by the ICG will be implemented. Indeed, Russia has criticised the OSCE and Council of Europe's negative report card on Azerbaijan's elections, no doubt reminding Baku that it can always rely on support closer to home. An Azadliq leader, Jalal Sardaroglu, declared in December that the West had betrayed Azerbaijan's democrats. Given Azerbaijan's vast oil and gas reserves and the high price of energy resources, it seems unlikely that many governments will move to seriously jeopardise their relations with Baku. Rumours in the Azeri press of a US interest in establishing radar bases in Azerbaijan further reinforce the view that the Aliyev government has little to fear in the way of sanctions.

Risk assessment

Economic	Good
Political	Stable
Regional stability	Stable

COUNTRY PROFILE

Historical profile

Azerbaijan has at various times been part of the Persian, Muslim Arab, Turkish Seljuk, Mongol, Ottoman and Russian empires. The modern Republic was formed from territory ceded to Russia by Iran following the second of the two Russian-Persian wars.
1916 Azerbaijan joined an alliance with Armenia and Georgia.
1918–20 Azerbaijan existed as an independent republic until April 1920, when it became part of the Soviet Union.
1936 Assumed the status of a full Soviet member as the Azerbaijan Soviet Socialist Republic.
1988–94 War broke out with Nagorno-Karabakh, an ethnic Armenian enclave that lies wholly inside Azerbaijan territory, when Armenians in Nagorno-Karabakh voted to break away from Azerbaijan and join neighbouring Armenia. With the assistance of Armenian troops, separatists in Nagorno-Karabakh managed to expel Azeri forces by 1994 and have since maintained de facto independence from Azerbaijan. The self-proclaimed breakaway Nagorno-Karabakh Republic (Artsakh in Armenian) occupies approximately 4,400 square kilomtres, to which the separatists have added through military conquest some 7,700 square kilometres of Azerbaijan proper. The six-year war threw Azerbaijan into political turmoil.
1989 Azerbaijan became the first Soviet Republic outside the Baltics to declare its national sovereignty.
1991 Formal independence was declared.
1992 Violent demonstrations over repeated failures in the Nagorno-Karabakh war forced the Communist regime, under

Azerbaijan

the leadership of Ayaz Mutalibov, to flee. After presidential elections the Popular Front came to power, under the leadership of Abulfaz Elchibey.

1993 Suret Huseinov, a military commander, took advantage of Elchibey's military failures to organise a military insurrection, forcing Elchibey to abandon the presidency. Heidar Aliyev, a veteran politician, came out of retirement and won 70 per cent of the vote in the presidential referendum.

1994 A cease-fire agreement came into force. The conflict between Azerbaijan and Armenia over the predominantly Armenian region in western Azerbaijan resulted in an estimated 35,000 deaths and created 850,000 internally displaced persons, mainly Azeris, between 1988–94.

1995 A new constitution was adopted.

1996 The National Assembly election produced large majorities for the Aliyev-backed Yeni Azerbaycan Partiyasi (YAP) (New Azerbaijan Party). Artur Rasizade became prime minister.

1998 Aliyev returned to power.

2000 The ruling YAP won the general election, which was denounced as unfair by foreign observers, and leaders of five major opposition parties initiated a mass protest, calling for new elections.

2001 The government ordered that the local Azeri language should be written with a Latin, rather than Cyrillic, alphabet. Azerbaijan became a full member of the Council of Europe. There was no result in the US-brokered talks on Nagorno-Karabakh between the the presidents of Azerbaijan and Armenia.

2002 US sanctions, imposed in 1992 following the outbreak of war with Armenia over the Nagorno-Karabakh enclave, were lifted after Azerbaijan agreed to participate in the US-led war on terrorism. President Aliyev announced he would run for a third five-year term. Arkady Gukasyan was re-elected president of Nagorno-Karabakh. A referendum on amendments to the constitution was said to have received strong support from voters, but critics cited voting irregularities. In Baku, thousands of people held a protest against poor living conditions; they also demanded the resignation of Aliyev and the annulment of the referendum on constitutional change.

2003 France's TotalFinaElf revealed plans to invest about US$150 million in oil projects in Azerbaijan. Aliyev collapsed during a televised speech and was taken to Turkey for hospital treatment. The President's son, Ilham Aliyev, was elected prime minister by parliament so that he could stand in the presidential elections, in which he won a landslide victory. After President Ilham Aliyev's resignation as prime minister, Artur Rasizade's candidacy for the post was endorsed by parliament. On 12 December, former president (1993–2003) Heidar Aliyev died.

2004 In June, the government said that US$3.4 billion would be invested by 2006 in the first phase of development of the Azeri-Chirag-Guneshli oil field.

2005 The Baku-Tbilisi-Ceyhan (BTC) oil pipeline, which will carry one million barrels per day of Caspian oil to Western markets, opened on 25 May. In parliamentary elections in Nagorno-Karabakh, on 19 June, the Artsakhi Demokratakan Kusaktsutyun (ADK) (Democratic Party of Artsakh) won 31.1 per cent of the vote (12 seats), the Azat Hayrenik (Free Motherland) 26.7 per cent (10 seats), an alliance of Hai Heghapokhakan Dashnaktsutyun) (ARF) (Pan-Armenian social democratic party) and Movement 88 won 24.4 per cent (3 seats), independent candidates won 8 seats. Turnout was 73.6 per cent. In parliamentary elections in Azerbaijan, on November 6, the ruling YAP and its allies won more than half the available 125 seats. Turnout was around 47 per cent. OSCE and Council of Europe observers declared that the election fell short of democratic norms. On November 9, 15,000 people responded to opposition calls for election results to be anulled by marching in Baku. A new natural gas pipeline between Iran and Azerbaijan was inaugurated on 20 December.

Political structure

Constitution

A constitution was adopted by national referendum in November 1995, and was amended following a referendum in August 2002, which made changes to the parliamentary system. The changes included replacing proportional representation in the National Assembly with the majority system (first-past-the-post), and changing the election of the president from a two-thirds to a 50 per cent majority of the votes cast.

The Republic of Azerbaijan is officially a democratic, secular and unitary state, with power separated among three branches: executive, legislative and judicial. Administratively, the country is divided into 65 districts, the autonomous republic of Nakhichevan (which is separated from the main part of the country by southern Armenia), and the region of Nagorno-Karabakh (which has been occupied by Armenian forces since 1992).

Under the constitution, the autonomous republic of Nakhichevan is an autonomous state within the Republic of Azerbaijan. Executive power in Nakhichevan is implemented by the Cabinet of Ministers of Nakhichevan, which is appointed by the Nakhichevan prime minister on approval of the Milli Mejlis (National Assembly). However, presidential decrees have authority in Nakhichevan.

Form of state

Presidential republic, where despite democratic structures, there is no fair chance for the opposition.

The executive

The president is head of state. The president must be over 35-years-old and have been living permanently in the territory of Azerbaijan for over 10 years, having no previous convictions.

The president appoints a prime minister and Council of Ministers.

The president is also the supreme commander-in-chief of the armed forces and has powers to declare martial law and states of emergency.

Presidential elections are held every five years. The president is elected by a majority of half of all votes cast. If the presidential candidates fail to win a majority, a second round of elections is held between the two leading contestants. The candidate who wins the most votes in the second round is elected president.

According to the constitution, the president can only be removed from the post in cases of 'grave crimes'. In these cases the Supreme Court submits an application for removal to the Milli Mejlis (National Assembly), who must pass the application by a majority of 95 votes (over two-thirds majority).

National legislature

There is a one-chamber, 125-member Milli Mejlis (National Assembly). Its members are elected by majority vote (first-past-the-post). The National Assembly's term of authority is five years, with elections to take place every fifth year on the first Sunday in November.

Legislative power in the autonomous republic of Nakhichevan is held by a 45-member Ali Mejlis (Assembly) of Nakhichevan. The Ali Mejlis independently settles questions which according to the constitution fall under its competence: taxes, budget, economic development, social policy, environmental protection, tourism, health, science and culture. It also has powers to appoint and dismiss the prime minister and Cabinet of Ministers of Nakhichevan. However, the Ali Mejlis lacks power to 'contradict' the constitution and laws of the Republic of Azerbaijan.

Legal system

The highest judicial body is the Supreme Court, which is divided into criminal and civil sections. There is also a Constitutional Court, Economic Court, ordinary and specialised courts.

Judges of the Supreme Court are appointed by the Milli Mejlis on the recommendation of the president. It is the highest judicial body in civil, criminal, administrative and other cases directed to general and specialised courts.

The Constitutional Court consists of nine judges appointed in the same way as in the Supreme Court. It is constitutionally bound to inquire into the activities of the president, Milli Mejlis, Cabinet of Ministers, Supreme Court and Milli Mejlis of the autonomous republic of Nakhichevan. In 2002, the constitutional changes included the remit of the Constitutional Court to hear cases brought by individuals. The Economic Court is the highest court on matters of economic dispute (as envisaged by legislation) and oversees activities in the relevant specialised courts.

Judicial power in the autonomous republic of Nakhichevan is exercised by the courts of Nakhichevan, although the Republic of Azerbaijan's laws apply in most cases.

Last elections
15 October 2003 (presidential); 6 November 2005 (parliamentary).

Results: Presidential: fomer president Heidar Aliyev's son, Prime Minister Ilham Aliyev (YAP), won a landslide victory with 79.5 per cent of the vote; his nearest rival, Musavat Party leader, Isa Gambar, had 12.1 per cent; turnout was 71.6 per cent. Opposition leaders alleged electoral fraud.

Parliamentary: the ruling YAP, headed by Aliyev, wons comfortably. Turnout was 47 per cent. Opposition leaders alleged electoral fraud.

Next elections
2008 (presidential); 2010 (parliamentary).

Political parties
Ruling party
Yeni Azerbaycan Partiyasi (YAP) (New Azerbaijan Party) (re-elected Nov 2005)
Main opposition party
Azadliq (Freedom), an electoral alliance formed for the November 6, 2005 election and consisting of Müsavat Partiyasi (Equality Party), Azerbaycan Khalq Cabhasi Partiyasi (AXCP) (Popular Front of Azerbaijan), and the Azerbaycan Demokrat Partiyasi (ADP) (Azerbaijan Democratic Party) won 8 seats.

Population
8.32 million (2004)
Ethnic make-up
The majority are Azeri (90 per cent). Minority groups include Dagestani (3.2 per cent), Russians (2.5 per cent) and Armenian (2.3 per cent). Almost all Armenians live in the separatist Nagorno-Karabakh region.
Religions
The main religious affiliation is Shi'ite Muslim (93.4 per cent). Others include Russian Orthodox (2.5 per cent) and Armenian Orthodox (2.3 per cent).

Education
Compulsory schooling lasts for eight years, the last two of which can be undertaken in either general secondary schools, technical schools or vocational schools. Education is free, except for higher education for which there are student grants. There are approximately 4,500 schools, including 960 primary eight-year schools, more than 2,300 secondary schools, 20 higher schools, 74 colleges and 162 technical-vocational schools. In urban areas educational services are better than in rural areas.

Literacy rate: 97 per cent of the adult population
Compulsory years: Eight to 16
Pupils per teacher: 20 in primary schools

Health
Total expenditure on health is around 2 per cent of GDP, of which government spending is 44 per cent.

In conjunction with the IMF, a new health policy has been developed. The focus of government expenditure will be shifted away from input-based allocations (for example, based on the number of beds) to capital transfers based on the number and structure of local populations. Local autonomy will be increased in healthcare and the elements of a basic package are being developed, which the government will provide free of charge in all public health facilities.

Healthcare is universal and virtually free of charge but there is a chronic shortage of basic medicines and despite pay increases doctors' morale remains low. Over 60 per cent of health expenses goes to hospitals with acute care facilities and staffed by specialised doctors rather than to preventive and basic health care. Fifty per cent of the population are severely iodine deficient.

HIV prevalence: 0.1 per cent aged 15–49 in 2003 (World Bank)
Life expectancy: 65.2 years (World Bank)
Fertility rate/Maternal mortality rate: 2.1 births per woman; maternal deaths 43 deaths per 100,000 live births (World Bank).
Infant mortality rate: 75 per 1,000 live births; 10 per cent of children aged under five were malnourished (World Bank).
Head of population per physician/bed: 3.8 physicians and 9.7 hospital beds available for 1,000 people.

Welfare
Although it has an abundance of natural resources, Azerbaijan is classified as the poorest country in Europe with 60 per cent of the population living in poverty. The former Soviet Union developed an extensive welfare system but price liberalisation and soaring inflation have rendered pensions, unemployment benefit and money paid to single parent families virtually worthless. The government intends to initiate a participatory poverty reduction strategy, as existing social safety nets are not enough to keep the unemployed out of poverty.

Main cities
Baku (capital, estimated population 1.2 million in 2004), Gyandzha (303,000), Sumgayit (280,500), Mingechaur (100,100), Ali Bayramli (72,300), Sheki (64,200), Stepanakert, Lakataly, Geokchay, Kuba, Lenktran, Binkechevin, Tazlab, Haftalan and Shusha.

Languages spoken
Azeri is spoken by 95 per cent of the population. Russian (3 per cent as first language) and Armenian (2 per cent) are also spoken. English language lessons are being introduced in schools and colleges. Some Azeris speak Russian as a second language although the use of Russian is being phased out.
Official language/s
Azeri (Turkic)

Media
State control and censorship over the Azeri media have been widespread since independence, with newspapers often forced to appear with large white spaces, or not issued at all.

In response to international pressure, censorship of the media was abolished in 1998 prior to the presidential elections. Despite this, the government has not hesitated to launch prosecutions for 'libel' on newspapers that 'insult' the president or members of the government.
Press
There are 151 newspapers, of which 141 are in Azeri, 64 periodicals, of which 55 are in Azeri. The handful of newspapers that are aligned with and in some cases funded by opposition parties are virtually unobtainable outside Baku. The circulation of all newspapers is very small. Commencing August 2001, the government ordered a change from the Cyrillic script to the Latin one for newspapers and public documents.
Dailies: Daily tabloids include *Bakinskiy Rabochiy* and *Adalat* (Justice). Other important dailies include *Azadlyg* (Liberty) and *Azerbaijan* in Azeri and Russian.
Weeklies: *Ayna-Zerkalo* (Azeri language) is a tabloid with 156 issues yearly. Other important weeklies are *Cumhuriyyat* (Republic) and the English language *Baku Sun*.

Azerbaijan

Business: *Economics* is a weekly tabloid concentrating on finance and economics.
Periodicals: Magazines include *Azerbaijan International*.

Broadcasting
Radio: Radio Baku broadcasts in Azeri, Russian, Arabic, Persian and Turkish.
Television: Baku television broadcasts programmes in Azeri, Russian and English and is subservient to the government. There are also several privately owned television companies operating in Azerbaijan and a cable television provider.

Advertising
The Office of Advertising and Design (OAD) in Baku exercises supervisory oversight of the industry. Many newspapers in Baku carry advertising and their rates vary between US$70–350 depending on circulation and size of advertisement. TV advertising on state television is controlled by Miraj-Media.

The city of Baku is divided into six zones within which advertising is allowed. Advertising space in the city centre is more expensive than the outskirts, and foreign companies are charged more than Azeri ones.

Economy
Azerbaijan is one of the seven poorest countries in Europe and Central Asia, despite vast resources of oil and natural gas. Just under half the population live below the poverty line and access to services such as healthcare and education remains limited, particularly in rural areas.

Economic growth has been strong in recent years with GDP growth since 2000 averaging at 10 per cent. Growth reached 10.1 per cent in 2004 and is set to rise still further until 2007, largely due to rising world oil prices. This however has triggered inflation, which although high at 8.1 per cent in 2004, is set to decrease through the next two years. The economy is stable with the nation's debt under control.

The conflict with Armenia over the Nagorno-Karabakh region has the potential to destabilise the country's economic progress. Although a cease-fire was signed in 1994, no final agreement has been reached and the countries are in a stalemate situation.

Oil companies represent most foreign direct investment (FDI); foreign interest has not extended to other areas of the Azeri economy. FDI inflows into the oil sector rose from US$821 million in 2001 to US$1.7 billion in 2003. If diversification does not take place, the country faces the prospect of once more becoming a supplier of raw materials, but this time to the West rather than Russia. Consequently, it is essential that the government concentrates on the privatisation programme in conjunction with investment incentives.

The opening of the Baku-Tbilisi-Ceyhan (BTC) pipeline in May 2005 gave the oil industry a large boost. The pipeline is designed to transport Azerbaijan oil from the Caspian Sea to the Mediterranean and is expected to make its first complete sea-to-sea shipment by March 2006. A parallel project, the South Caucasus Pipeline (SCP), designed to transport Azerbaijan gas from the Caspian into Turkey, will be completed in September 2006. International companies that produce from the Caspian Sea resources contribute around US$200 million to government finances annually. It is estimated that revenues from these oil and natural gas resources may reach US$7 billion in the near future. The government has a policy of using oil wealth in a prudent fashion by meeting deficit targets of less than 2 per cent of GDP.

The government's 2004 budget provides for revenue of US$1.48 billion, an increase of 14.2 per cent, compared with the previous year, and expenditure of US$1.42 billion, an increase of 13.2 per cent. The government intentions are to follow a prudent policy, making government deficit a minimum at a predicted US$64.3 million. Allowing for the assets of state-owned enterprises and state funds, the national budget accounts for 37.6 per cent of total government revenue and 39 per cent of total government expenditure.

External trade
US sanctions, imposed in 1992 following the outbreak of war with Armenia over the Nagorno-Karabakh enclave, were lifted in January 2002 after Azerbaijan agreed to participate in the US-led war on terrorism. There are bilateral trade agreements with China, Germany, Kazakhstan, Norway and UK. Azerbaijan and the EU have a partnership agreement which was signed in June 1999. Azerbaijan is also part of a regional association for economic co-operation with Iran and Turkey.

Imports
Imports include machinery equipment, oil products, foodstuffs, metals and chemicals.
Main sources: UK (13.9 per cent total, 2004), Russia (13.1 per cent), Turkey (11.5 per cent), Germany (8.0 per cent), The Netherlands (5.3 per cent), China (5.0 per cent), US (4.7 per cent), Italy (4.5 per cent), Ukraine (4.3 per cent)

Exports
Exports and re-exports include: oil and gas (90 per cent of total exports), cotton fibre, machinery and foodstuffs.
Main destinations: Italy (31.1 per cent total, 2004), Czech Republic (14.5 per cent), Germany (9.4 per cent), Turkey (6.1 per cent), Russia (6.0 per cent), Georgia (5.3 per cent), France (4.9 per cent).

Agriculture
Farming
Agriculture has declined by more than 50 per cent since independence, but it continues to employ 30 per cent of the labour force and contributes about 17 per cent to GDP. It is the second-largest export sector with large potential markets in the Middle East, Europe and the former Soviet Union.

Around 2 million hectares (ha) out of a total land area of 8.7 million ha is classified as arable. Some 70 per cent of the 77 per cent of land used for agricultural purposes is irrigated through an extensive canal system. Most farming takes place in the fertile lowlands surrounding the Kura and Araz rivers, in central Azerbaijan.

The whole country is well endowed with fertile land, although adversely affected by periodic drought. A wide range of crops is grown, notably cotton, tobacco, nuts, grapes, grain, tea, vegetables and citrus fruits. Cattle, sheep, pigs and poultry are reared.

Grain is the leading agricultural product, followed by raw cotton (the country's largest cash crop).

Livestock, dairy products and alcoholic beverages are also important products. There is potential for agricultural development, greatly enhanced by the country's rich soils, wide agricultural plains and varied climatic conditions. There is scope for the cultivation of vegetables, fruits, cotton, tobacco, subtropical cultures, silkworm and sheep breeding.

However, agriculture comprises mainly smallholder farming, and is generally subsistence oriented. Despite the fact that 45 per cent of the country's population depend largely on agricultural income, the sector remains largely underdeveloped. Crop production in 2004 included 2,090,650 tonnes (t) cereals in total, 1,600,000t wheat, 150,000t maize, 930,000t potatoes, 320,000t barley, 20,000t rice, 39,000t citrus fruit, 55,000t grapes, 420,000t tomatoes, 19,534t oilcrops, 6,518t tobacco leaves, 60,000 sugar beets, 1,048t tea, 220,000t apples, 40,000 cotton lint, 33,200t treenuts, 475,387t fruit in total, 1,356,200t vegetables in total. Livestock production included: 145,500t meat in total, 73,100t beef, 1,400t pig meat, 43,900t lamb & goat meat, 27,100t poultry, 46,505t eggs, 1,214,000t milk, 500t honey, 100t cocoons, silk, 12,350t cattle hides, 5,220t sheepskins, 12,100t greasy wool.

Fishing
Salyan on the Kura River is the main centre for processing and canning fish. Azerbaijan once produced 10 per cent of the world's supply of caviar. The dividing of the Caspian Sea, which accounts for 90 per cent of world caviar production, has led to disputes between Azerbaijan and Russia. There is little effective policing of the Caspian, with smuggling and illegal fishing widespread. The Caspian is also being overfished, and combined with the threat of pollution, production levels are set to fall. International regulation of the trade in caviar was tightened in January 2006 and is expected to further restrict, for the forseeable future, Azerbaijan's caviar industry.

Forestry
Forest and other wooded land, mostly concentrated in the mountainous north, account for little more than one-tenth of its total land area. Estimates in 2000 showed that forest cover was slightly over one million hectares, with an annual average increase of 13,000 hectares, the equivalent of 1.27 per cent, between 1990–2000.

Forests in the flood plain areas remain in poor condition and are prone to overgrazing and pollution. There is no large-scale forest industry, with most wood products imported from the Russian Federation. Commercial exploitation is limited, and production is used mostly for domestic purposes. Most forest is classified as either 'protected' or 'preserved' and is public owned.

Industry and manufacturing
The oil industry dominates the Azeri economy, providing the driving force for all other sectors.

The emphasis on heavy industry, combined with substantial primary resources, enabled the development of a major oil equipment manufacturing sector in the Soviet era. However, the disintegration of the Soviet Union meant that supplies and markets dried up, leading to the virtual collapse of most industries.

It is hoped that the development of Azerbaijan's oil and gas industry will benefit all sectors of the economy, with widespread infrastructure improvements and developments essential. The construction industry has expanded particularly rapidly on the back of Azerbaijan's oil and gas boom (by 42 per cent in 2004).

In order to stimulate growth the government has developed a medium- and long-term strategy to restructure the economy in consultation with the IMF.

Industrial production increased by 12 per cent in 2004.

Tourism
During Soviet rule, there was considerable investment in tourist infrastructure such as hotels and Azerbaijan has inherited these assets. Little has been done to develop Azerbaijan's tourist potential since independence, despite the existence of many historical sites and sites of natural beauty. Tourist arrivals increased by 12.94 per cent in 2003, compared to 2002.

Environment
Pollution comes from four main sources – agriculture, industrial plants, oil exploitation and domestic waste. It will take time and investment to clean up Azerbaijan's environment.

Mining
The mining sector accounts for 1 per cent of GDP and since independence has suffered from a lack of infrastructure investment.

The republic has abundant mineral resources, including iron, lead, zinc and copper ores, cobalt, bauxite, matrium sulphate, marl, limestone, marble, lake and rock salts, and some small amounts of gold and silver. The largest iron ore field in the Caucasus region lies within Azerbaijan.

Copper reserves are attracting foreign investors. Azerbaijan has several deposits of pure copper, the largest of which is the Karadag, in western Azerbaijan, with reserves of about 320,000 tonnes.

Hydrocarbons
Oil from the Caspian basin has dominated the economic history of Azerbaijan since the late 19th Century. In 1891, half of the world's crude oil was extracted from Azerbaijan.

The Caspian is still the centre of oil exploration for Azerbaijan. Production averaged 319,000 bpd in 2004. Azerbaijan has two refineries, Azneftyag and Azneftyanajag, with a total refining capacity of 399,000bpd (2005 estimate).

The situation in the Caspian is complicated by a dispute between Iran, Russia and Azerbaijan over the division of the oil rich area. The government is placing huge store by the development of an oil-driven economic boom. While this may have negative implications for other industries, the estimated oil wealth that exists in the country could generate huge earnings and inward investment for years. As the Azeris lack the necessary financial resources and expertise to develop the fields on their own, foreign petrochemical corporations have been encouraged to invest. In order to keep control of the industry, however, the resulting exploration and production projects have usually been joint ventures between Socar and foreign companies.

Azerbaijan's main project is the Baku-Tbilisi-Ceyhan (BTC) oil pipeline, which will transport 50 million tonnes of oil per annum from the Sangachai Terminal in central Azerbaijan to Ceyhan in Turkey via Georgia. Construction of the 1,768km pipeline began in mid-2002 and it opened on 25 May 2005.

In June 2004, the government said that US$3.4 billion would be invested by 2006 in the first phase of development of the Azeri-Chirag-Guneshli (ACG) oil field. Several exploratory wells for oil have yielded natural gas instead, but this is economically less viable to produce given the current state of Azerbaijan's transportation infrastructure.

Azerbaijan's proven gas reserves total 850 billion cubic metres, although actual reserves are likely to be far higher. Natural gas production stood at 4.8 billion cubic metres in 2003.

The Bakhar gas field is the country's most important source of natural gas production, accounting for over 40 per cent of total production. However, future development is likely to concentrate on the Nakhichevan, Gunashli and Shah Deniz fields. The South Caucasus Pipeline (SPC), financed in large part by the consortium behind the BTC, is being built to transport Azerbaijani gas from the Shah Deniz field to Erzurum in Turkey through Georgia. In late 2005 the pipeline was 95 per cent complete and was projected to be fully operational by September 2006.

Energy
Azerbaijan is one of the region's largest power generators, with installed capacity of 5,200MW. Actual production is, however, limited to around 4,300MW due to ageing facilities. Thermal power plants produce 80 per cent of total electricity, the balance coming from hydroelectric sources. Azerbaijan also imports electricity from Iran for the autonomous Nakhichevan area.

Financial markets
Stock exchange
The Baku Stock Exchange, set up in August 1999, is regulated by the State Securities Committee.

Banking and insurance
Azerbaijan's banking sector is underdeveloped and dominated by four Soviet-era state-owned banks. The majority of Azerbaijani banks are undercapitalised and illiquid and during the course of 2005 several had their commercial licences revoked. In May 2005 there were 46 banks operating in Azerbaijan. Banking law states that foreign ownership of any bank in Azerbaijan cannot exceed 30 per cent.

Azerbaijan

Central bank
National Bank of Azerbaijan (NBA)

Main financial centre
Baku

Time
GMT plus three hours

Geography
Azerbaijan is situated in eastern Trans-Caucasia bordering Armenia, Georgia, the Russian Federation (Daghestan Autonomous Republic), Iran and the Caspian Sea. It is the largest of the three Trans-Caucasian republics, covering 87,000 square km. Azerbaijan is split in two, with the Nakhichevan Autonomous Republic separated from Azerbaijan proper by southern Armenia. Approximately 20 per cent of Azeri territory is occupied by Armenia. The ethnic Armenian enclave of Nagorno-Karabakh is an area of 4,000 square km situated in the south-west of the country.

The level of the largest salt water lake in the world, the Caspian Sea, is subject to continuous change. In 1929 its surface area was larger than the Black Sea at 422,000 square km, before it started to decline reaching a record low point in 1951. Since then it has risen to about 378,000 square km. Higher water levels are causing problems along the Azeri coast.

The greater part of the republic includes the lowlands of the River Kura and the lower reaches of its tributary, the Araks. The oil-rich Apsheron Peninsula, on which the country's capital city Baku is located, juts out into the Caspian Sea.

Climate
Azerbaijan is considered to contain nine of the world's 13 climatic zones, from Alpine meadows to the subtropics. In Baku the climate is dry and Mediterranean. Due to its diversity, there are extremes of temperature in many areas – harsh winters and hot summers. Baku and other places on the Caspian Sea have mild winters. Temperatures in Baku are 0–5 degrees Celsius (C) in winter and 25–35 degrees C in summer.

Dress codes
Business dress should include a jacket and tie for men, and smart 'business-like' clothes for women.

Entry requirements
Passports
Required by all.

Visa
Required by all with the exception of citizens from Bulgaria, Commonwealth of Independent States, Hungary, Romania and Vietnam.

For an online business visa application visit: www.azembassy.com/visa/application.pdf. Application and fee must be accompanied by an invitation from an Azerbaijan company submitted through the Consular Department of the Ministry of Foreign Affairs of Azerbaijan in Baku, and authorisation by employer, all to be submitted to the consular section of the local embassy. If time is limited, all documents should be faxed (including a letter from the employer of the traveller, and the invitation of the business partner in Azerbaijan) to the ministry in Baku, (contact the local embassy for further explanation). (For online information see www.azembassy.com).

Currency advice/regulations
Import/export of local currency by non-residents is prohibited.

There are no restrictions on the import of foreign currency by non-residents, although declaration on arrival is required. There are no limitations on the export of foreign currency, up to the amount declared on arrival.

US dollars, pounds sterling and euros are the preferred currencies and can be exchanged at the airport, bureaux de change, hotels, some restaurants and major banks. Hotels, exchange bureaux and restaurants will not accept US dollar bills dated before 1992 or those which are torn or in any way disfigured. Travellers are advised to take banknotes in small denominations and change small amounts of money as required. Rates offered by banks and bureaux de change are unlikely to vary significantly. Travellers cheques are accepted only by the International Bank of Azerbaijan.

Customs
On arrival declare all foreign currency and valuable items such as jewellery, cameras, computers etc.

Prohibited imports
Radioactive waste, narcotics and psychotropic drugs are prohibited.

Health (for visitors)
Only emergency medical treatment is available free to visitors, with small payments for medicines or hospital treatment. The level of care is limited. Private chemists in Baku stock a range of the more basic medicines. Travellers are advised to take out an insurance policy which includes emergency repatriation in case of serious illness or accident.

Mandatory precautions
None

Advisable precautions
It is advisable to be 'in date' for the following immunisations: polio (within 10 years), tetanus (within 10 years), hepatitis 'A' and 'B', tuberculosis. Anti-malarial precautions are advisable. There are cholera and diphtheria outbreaks and there may be some risk of meningitis, tick-borne encephalitis and leishmaniasis (cutaneous and visceral). Rabies is present.

It is advisable to take a supply of those medicines that are likely to be required (but check first that they may be legally imported). A travel kit including a disposable syringe is a reasonable precaution. Water precautions are recommended.

Hotels
Hotel space in Baku is very limited. Payment for the full stay is required in advance upon arrival at the hotel in cash (in US dollar bills which should be in good condition). VAT and service charges are included in all bills; tipping the waiters is appreciated but not compulsory.

Credit cards
Accepted in the major hotels, some restaurants and all banks in Baku. Credit cards can be used to purchase tickets at the airport.

Public holidays
Fixed dates
1 Jan (New Year), 20 Jan (Day of the Martyrs), 8 Mar (Women's Day), 20–21 Mar (Spring Holiday/Persian New Year), 9 May (Victory Day), 28 May (Republic Day), 15 Jun (Day of National Salvation), 18 Oct (Independence Day), 12 Nov (Constitution Day), 17 Nov (National Revival Day), 31 Dec (Solidarity Day).

Variable dates
Eid al Adha, Eid al Fitr.

The Islamic year contains 354 or 355 days, with the result that Muslim feasts advance by 10–12 days against the Gregorian calendar. Dates of feasts vary according to the sighting of the new moon, so cannot be forecast exactly. Islamic year 1426: 10 February 2005 to 30 January 2006.

Working hours
Banking
Mon–Fri: 0930–1730.

Business
Mon–Fri: 0900–1800.

Government
Mon–Fri: 0900–1300; 1400–1800.

Shops
Mon–Fri: 0900–1900.

Telecommunications
Telephone/fax
The domestic telephone system is sometimes unreliable.

International telephone and facsimile services exist at all major hotels. Calls placed outside regular business hours must be booked. Public telephones require tokens which can be purchased at subway stations.

Mobile phones
There are two GSM mobile phone companies, Azercell and Bakcell.

Electricity supply
Voltage is usually 220V, 50 Hz. There are occasionally electricity cuts in winter and high summer in Baku.

Weights and measures
Metric system

Social customs/useful tips
Azeri culture blends Soviet-style courtesy with Middle Eastern informality.
The approach to business is not very well developed by Western standards, although technical knowledge and education standards are high, so it is important not to patronise potential partners.
Although Azeris are Muslim, they are probably the most secular of all the Muslim people of the former Soviet Union, with many considering themselves Eastern European rather than Asian. Consequently, Azerbaijan bears little relation to the Middle East with the exception of its oil and gas reserves. Business and negotiation habits are more akin to those in the rest of the former Soviet Union than with Middle Eastern practices.
The business environment has been reported to suffer from a number of ills, including very low wages for civil servants which act as an encouragement to corruption, a lack of transparency in the legal system and the inability to make decisions at lower governmental levels.
Bribery and 'gifts' were part and parcel of everyday business life in the former Soviet Union, and little has changed since 1991. However, moderate gifts and souvenirs discreetly given are usually more suitable than offers of foreign trips and shopping sprees.
Office space – and quality – is limited in Baku, with many Western firms forced to work from the old Intourist Hotel or run-down buildings in the city.
Photocopying and word-processing facilities are scarce. Interpreters are available in Baku.

Security
Public transport in Baku should be avoided at night. Travellers should carry their passports with them at all times and ensure they travel with photocopies of their passports in case of theft.
Avoid all travel to the western region of Nagorno-Karabakh.

Getting there
Air
National airline: Azerbaijan Hava Yollari (Azal) (Azerbaijan Airlines)
International airport/s: Baku Bina International (BAK), is located 15km east of the city. Facilities include car hire, bank/bureau de change and VIP lounge.
Airport tax: None

Surface
Road: Inter-city bus routes link Baku with Makhachkala, Mineralnie Vody, Rostov-on-Don and other southern Russian cities.
Rail: There are rail connections to Tehran (Iran), Tbilisi (Georgia) and various cities in the Russian Federation, including Moscow.
Water: Passenger ferries on the Caspian Sea link Azerbaijan with the Russian Federation, Central Asia and Iran. Ferries sail regularly to Baku from Turkmenbashy in Turkmenistan and from Bandar Anzali and Bandar Nowshar in Iran. Winter storms may disrupt services.
Main port/s: Sumgayit, 35km north of Baku.

Getting about
Travel within some regions of the country is restricted and visitors must obtain special permission from the Ministry of Interior.

National transport
Road: Azerbaijan has more than 57,770km of roads, of which over 31,000km are paved. Roads are generally in bad repair and have deteriorated due to extensive military use during the six-year war with Armenia. Four-wheel drive vehicles are recommended, particularly for mountainous journeys. The main motorway runs from Baku to Russia via the Caspian Coast.
Rail: Azerbaijan has a rail network of approximately 2,100km (1,300km electrified). The rail network is the most important form of transport, handling an estimated 75 per cent of total traffic.

City transport
Taxis: Taxis can be distinguished by a sign on top. Agree a price beforehand. Taxis are cheap, but drivers are unlikely to speak English. As the cost of a trip can vary widely, it is better to use hotel taxis or pre-arrange a car with driver.
Buses, trams & metro: There is a metro in Baku with a total length of 28km.
Car hire
Care hire is available in Baku. An international driving licence is needed. Traffic drives on the right.

BUSINESS DIRECTORY

Telephone area codes
The international direct dialling code (IDD) for Azerbaijan is +994, followed by area code and subscriber's number:

Baku	12	Neftechala	153
Dashkasan	216	Sumgayit	164
Nakhichevan	136		

Useful telephone numbers
Fire	01
Police	02
Ambulance	03
Gas	04
Enquiries	001
General information	009
	933-544
Taxi services	621-256

Chambers of Commerce
American Chamber of Commerce in Azerbaijan, ISR Plaza, 340 Nizami Street, Baku 370000 tel: 971-333; fax: 971-091; e-mail: info@amchamaz.org).

Azerbaijan Chamber of Commerce and Industry, 31/33 Istiglaliyyat Street, Baku 370001 (tel: 928-912; fax: 971-997; e-mail: expo@chamber.baku.az).

Banking
Azakbank (private), 25 Xagani Street, 370070 Baku (tel: 983-109, 932-491; fax: 932-085).

Azcombank, 1 Inshaatchilar Avenue, 370073 Baku (tel: 388-323, 387-206).

AzEkoBank (joint stock bank), 11/39 Mustafa Subhi Street, Baku 370001 (tel: 929-433; fax: 980-406; e-mail: ecob@ecob.crack.azerbaijan.su; internet site: http://www.azekobank.com).

Azerbaijan Agricultural Industrial Bank, 125 Qadirli Street, Baku 370006 (tel: 389-293; fax: 389-115).

Azerbaijan Commercial Savings Bank, 71 Fizuli Street, Baku 370010 (tel: 930-561; fax: 939-489).

Azerbaijan Industrial Investment Bank, 71 Fizuli Street, 370010 Baku (tel: 931-701; fax: 931-266).

Azerbaijan National Bank, 19 Bulbul Ave, Baku 370070 (tel: 935-058; fax: 937-374).

Azerdemiryolbank, 31 Qarabagh Street, Baku 370008 (tel: 972-380, 675-321; fax: 987-936).

Azerigazbank, 37 Tbilisi Avenue, 370065 Baku (tel: 385-021; fax: 390-243).

Azerturkbank, 5 Islam Safarli Street, 370005 Baku (tel: 948-090; fax: 983-702).

Bakobank (private), 35 Yusif Safarov Street, 370025 Baku (tel: 666-549; fax: 981-927).

British Bank of the Middle East, 1 Bakihanov Street, Baku (tel: 981-234; fax: 980-817).

International Bank of Azerbaijan (IBA), 67 Nizami Street, Baku 370005 (tel: 930-091; fax: 934-091; e-mail: ibar@bar.az; internet site: http://www.ibar.az).

Most-Bank, 70 Nizami Street, Baku (tel: 971-070; fax: 972-094).

Promtekhbank (joint stock commercial bank), 69 Fizuli Street, Baku 370014 (tel: 957-874; fax: 958-360; e-mail: bank@devi.baku.az).

Azerbaijan

Rabitabank, 1 Buniat Sardarov Street, Baku 370001 (tel: 926-099; fax: 926-157).

Tajbank (commercial investment bank), 185 Azadlyg Ave, Baku 370087 (tel: 691-464; fax: 691-474).

Central bank

National Bank of Azerbaijan, 32 R. Behbudov Street, Baku (tel: 931-122; fax: 935-541; e-mail: mail@nba.az).

Travel information

Airlines information office (tel: 937-121).

Azal (Azerbaijan Hava Yollari) (Azerbaijan Airlines), Prospect Azadlig 11, Baku 370000 (tel: 934-434; fax: 985-237, 651-120).

Azerbaijani Railways, Dilara Aliyeva Str 230, 370010 Baku (tel: 984-467; fax: 984-280).

Azertur Travel Agency of the State Council for Foreign Tourism (tours, hotel reservations, translation and interpreting services), 1 Azadlyg Ave, Baku 370000 (tel: 933-481; fax: 933-481).

Baku Metro, 33 Azerbaijan Avenue, Baku 370002 (tel: 961-013).

Bina airport general enquiries (tel: 257-900, 242-018).

Central bus station (tel: 388-58.

Eur Tourism, 82 Topchubashev Str, Baku (tel: 973-444; fax: 986-810; e-mail: eurotourbaku@azeri.com).

Improtex (travel tours and conferences), 115 Azi Aslanov Str, Baku 370000 (tel: 930-896, 933-941; fax: 651-238; e-mail: toor@impro.Azerbaijan.su).

Marine passenger terminal (tel: 930-868).

Railway station (tel: 982-039, 995-480).

Train tickets (tel: 931-698, 931-702, 931-807, 931-946).

Ministries

Ministry of Agriculture and Food, 4 Shihali Kurbanov Street, Baku 370079 (tel: 935-355; fax: 943-952).

Ministry of Communications, 33 Azerbaijan Ave, Baku 370139 (tel: 930-004; fax: 984-285).

Ministry of Culture, Government House, Azadlyg Square, Baku 370016 (tel: 934-398; fax: 935-605).

Ministry of Defence, 3 Azerbaijan Ave, Azizbekov Baku 370601 (tel: 394-362; fax: 382-296).

Ministry of Economics, Government House, Azadlyg Square, Baku 370016 (tel: 936-920; fax: 932-025).

Ministry of Education, Government House, 1 Azadlyg Square, Baku 370016 (tel: 937-266; fax: 984-207).

Ministry of Finance, Sameda Vurguna Ul 6, Baku 370000 (tel: 933-012; fax: 987-969).

Ministry of Foreign Affairs, Gandjlar Meydani 3, Baku 370004 (tel: 923-401; fax: 629-756).

Ministry of Foreign Economic Relations, Lermontov Street 69, Baku 370601 (tel: 929-492; fax: 980-011).

Ministry of Grain Products, 13 Yusifzade Street, Baku 370033 (tel: 667-451; fax: 939-023).

Ministry of Health, Malaya Morskaya Street 4, Baku 370014 (tel: 932-977; fax: 988-559).

Ministry of Information and Press, 12 Ahmad Javad Street, Baku 370001 (tel: 926-357; fax: 926-747).

Ministry of Internal Affairs, 7 Gusi Hajiyev Street, Baku 370005 (tel: 986-396; fax: 923-471).

Ministry of Justice, 13 Kirov Avenue, Baku 370601 (tel: 939-785; fax: 938-367).

Ministry of Labour and Social Protection, Azadlyg Square, Baku 370016 (tel: 930-542; fax: 939-472).

Ministry of Material Resources, 83-23 Alaskar Alakbarov Street, Baku 370141 (tel: 394-296; fax: 399-176).

Ministry of National Security, 1 Azadlyg Square 1, Baku 370016 (tel: 931-000; fax: 936-296).

Ministry of Trade, Government House, Azadlyg Square 1, Baku 370016 (tel: 985-074; fax: 987-431).

Ministry of Youth and Sports, 98a Fatali Han Khoyski Avenue, Baku 370072 (tel: 981-426; fax: 643-650).

Office of the President of the Azerbaijan Republic, 19 Istiglaliyyat Street, Baku 370066 (tel: 983-113).

Other useful addresses

Azerbaijan News Service, Block 504, 1128 Street, Baku 370073 (building of the Institute of Zoology) (tel: 929-221/3; fax: 989-498).

Azerbintorg Foreign Trade Association, 14 Boyuk Gala Str, 370004 Baku (tel: 920-481, 926-492, 924-545; fax: 983-292).

Azerigaz, 23 Yusif Safarov Street, Baku 370025 (tel: 677-447; fax: 674-255).

Azerkimia, 86 Samed Vurgun Street, Baku 373200 (tel: 937-620).

Azertaj State Information Agency, Bulbul Avenue 18, 370000 Baku (tel: 935-445; fax: 938-138).

Baku General Customs Board, 62 Neftchilar Ave, Baku 370601 (tel: 939-588).

Baku Statistics Office, 10 Tabriz Street, Baku 370008 (tel: 669-327, 672-265).

Baku Telegraph Office, 41 Azerbaijan Avenue, Baku 370000 (tel: 936-142).

Baku Television, M. Husein St 1, Baku.

Board of Azerbaijan Railways, 230 Dilara Aliyeva Street, Baku 370010 (tel: 984-467).

British Embassy, 2 Izmir Street, 370065 Baku (tel: 924-813; fax: 985-558).

Caspian Shipping Company, 5 Rasulzade Street, Baku 370005 (tel: 922-058; fax: 935-339).

Central Post Office, 36 Uzeyir Hajibeyov Street, Baku 370000 (tel: 985-251).

EU Co-ordinating Unit in Azerbaijan, Government House, 8th Floor, Room 851, Baku 370016 (tel: 936-018; fax: 937-638).

Radio Baku, M Husein St 1, 370011 Baku.

Scientific Research and Test Constructive Institute of Oil Machinery of Azerbaijan Republic (Azinmash), Aras Street 4, Baku 370029 (tel: 670-888; fax: 672-888).

SME Development Agency 83, Mr Vagif G. Alikperov, S Vurguna, Azneftiechimprom Bld. 5th Floor, PO Box 114, 37000 Baku (tel: 957832; fax: 957832; e-mail: quirin@smeda.baku.az).

State Committee for Statistics, 24 Inshaatchylar Ave, Baku-136 370136 (tel: 381-171; fax: 380-577).

State Customs Committee, 2 Inshaatchilar Ave, Baku 370073 (tel: 927-545).

State Oil Company of the Azerbaijan Republic (SOCAR), 73 Neftchilar Ave, Baku 370004 (tel: 924-480, 920-745, 920-685; fax: 936-492, 923-204).

Statoil Caspian Region, 96 Nizami Street, 370010 Baku (tel: 977-340; fax: 977-944).

US Embassy, 83 Azadliq Avenue, Baku 370007 (tel: 980-335; fax: 983-755; e-mail: webbaku@pd.state.gov).

Internet sites

Department of co-ordination of foreign investment:
http://www.azinvestpromotion.com

Hyatt hotels: http://www.hyatt.com

President of Azerbaijan:
http://www.president.az/

State Property Committee of Azerbaijan Investment Information, Optimarket Inc, USA: http://www.optimarket.com

Virtual Azerbaijan: http://scf.usc.edu/~baguirov/azerbaijan.html

Bahamas

KEY FACTS

Official name: Commonwealth of The Bahamas

Head of State: Queen Elizabeth II, represented by Acting Governor General Paul Adderley (from 29 December 2005)

Head of government: Prime Minister Perry Christie (sworn in 3 May 2002)

Ruling party: Progressive Liberal Party (PLP) (elected May 2002)

Area: 13,935 square km

Population: 325,500 (2004)

Capital: Nassau

Official language: English

Currency: Bahamian dollar (B$) = 100 cents

Exchange rate: B$1.00 per US$ (fixed)

GDP per capita: US$17,486 (2004)

GDP real growth: 3.30% (2004)

Labour force: 167,000 (2004)

Unemployment: 10.20% (2004)

Inflation: 1.50% (2004)

Balance of trade: -US$1.21 billion (2004)

Visitor numbers: 5.00 million (2004)

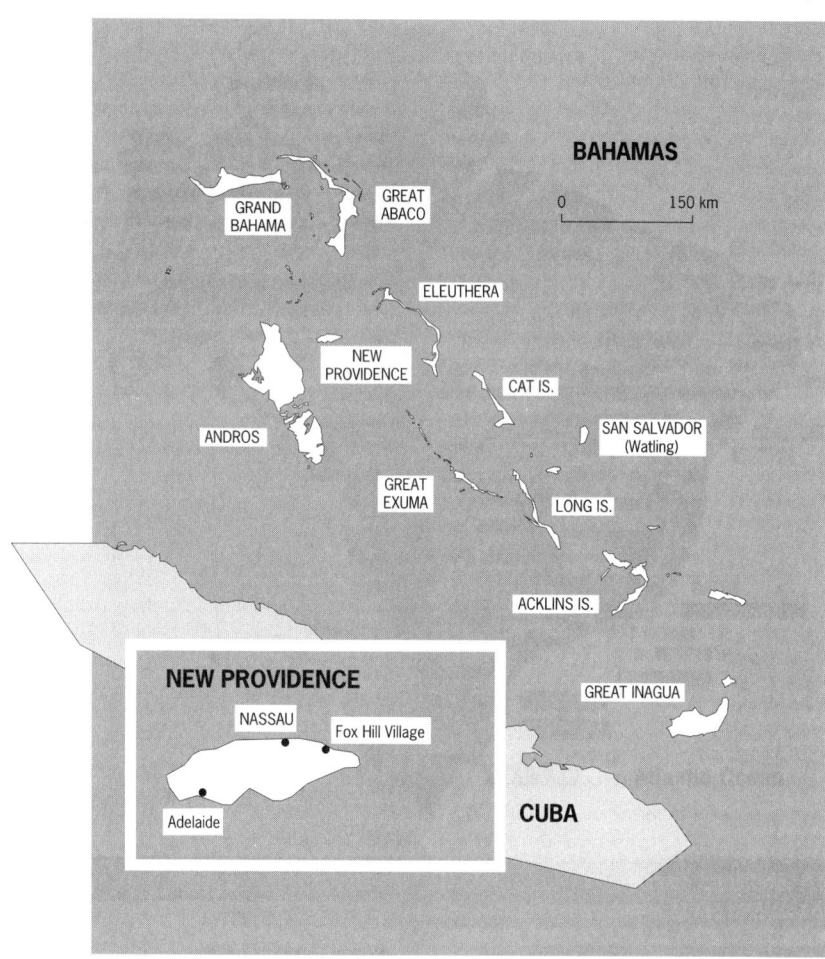

COUNTRY PROFILE

Historical profile
The islands of the Bahamas were formerly a British Dependency. For many years, the Bahamas were controlled by a white elite based on Bay Street, the main commercial thoroughfare of Nassau, known as the 'Bay Street Boys'.
1729 A parliamentary system of government was introduced.
1964 Internal self-government was granted.
1967 The first elections with universal adult suffrage were won by the Progressive Liberal Party (PLP), led by Lynden (later Sir Lynden) Pindling, with the support of the United Bahamian Party (UBP).
1973 The Bahamas gained full independence as a member of the Commonwealth.
1992 After 25 years in power, Sir Lynden Pindling and his PLP were unseated in the general election by the Free National Movement (FNM).
1997 The FNM won the parliamentary elections.
2000 The financial system was blacklisted by the Group of 7 (G7) countries.
2001 The US awarded the Bahamas certification as being one of 20 countries fully co-operating with anti-drug efforts. Dame Ivy Dumont, aged 71, became the first female governor general.
2002 The PLP won the parliamentary elections. Perry Christie was sworn in as prime minister.

2004 The Financial Action Task Force (FATF) of the OECD reported in July that it remains concerned about the ability of the Bahamian authorities to respond to foreign judicial and regulatory requests and it will therefore continue to monitor the situation.

2005 Dame Ivy Dumont announced her retirement; Deputy Governor, Paul Adderley, became Acting Governor General on 29 December.

Political structure
Constitution
The Bahamas gained independence from the UK in 1973 and a new constitution was enacted in the same year. Voting eligibility is for citizens of the Bahamas who are 18 years or older.

Form of state
Constitutional multi-party parliamentary democracy; it is a member of the Commonwealth.

The executive
The British monarch is the nominal head of state, represented on the islands by a governor general. The governor general is advised by a cabinet made up of the prime minister, who is the leader of the main party in the House of Assembly, the minister of finance and at least seven other ministers chosen on the prime minister's advice.

National legislature
The bicameral legislature consists of a 16-member Senate, appointed by the governor general, and a House of Assembly with 40 members. The parliamentary term runs for five years.

Legal system
The Bahamian legal system is based on British common law with elements of former colonial legislation. Much of the business legislation enacted since independence is based on the US system. The Privy Council in London is the highest court of appeal.

Last elections
2 May 2002 (parliamentary)

Results: Parliamentary: the Progressive Liberal Party (PLP) won with 50.8 per cent of the vote (29 of 40 seats) against 41.1 per cent (seven seats) for the former ruling party, Free National Movement (FNM), and 5.2 per cent (four seats) for independents.

Next elections
2007 (parliamentary)

Political parties
Ruling party
Progressive Liberal Party (PLP) (elected May 2002)

Main opposition party
Free National Movement (FNM)

Political situation
The Progressive Liberal Party (PLP) led by Perry Christie won a landslide election victory in 2003. Christie's large parliamentary majority enabled him to focus on reactivating the economy, which is heavily reliant on tourism. Over 1 million tourists visit the Bahamas each year. Tourism and related construction accounts for around 60 per cent of GDP and directly or indirectly employs 40 per cent of the archipelago's workforce.

Prime Minister Christie's position looks secure until the next elections in 2007, inspite of the mild stroke he suffered in May 2005. The PLP's large majority enables Mr Christie to overrule opponents within his own party. However, his decision to appoint some of the PLP's old guard to positions of power in government raised concerns of a possible return of corruption to political life. The previous PLP government of Sir Lynden Pindling (1967–92) was thrown out of power due to corruption in organised crime, particularly drug trafficking and money laundering. Christie's appointment of people closely associated with Pindling raised fears that the PLP had not learnt the lessons that led to a decade in opposition. He was also accused of disregarding the Code of Ethics passed by parliament in mid-2002.

The appointment of the old guard also risked tarnishing the government's image abroad. The country's location as a *de facto* offshore US island, with easy, largely unmonitored sea access to the northern coasts of Latin America, makes it a natural haven for international criminal gangs. The failure of the Bahamian judiciary to extradite alleged drug cartel members has often created friction between the Bahamas and the US. Under the Pindling administration, the Bahamas offshore banking regulations – or the lack of them – created widespread suspicions of money laundering. The Bahamas was removed from the OECD's money laundering blacklist in 2001.

The losing party, the FNM, is attempting to reform in a way that will attract lost voters. Tommy Turnquest is not seen as a charismatic leader and not only lost the election but lost his own parliamentary seat. Although a number of hopefuls are willing, it is also acknowledged that, the party has no obvious leader ready to replace Turnquest. The only candidate with the necessary allure, Hubert Ingraham, comes from the PLL party where he challenged his own leader to step down in the face of a poor report from a Commission of Inquiry. As a parliamentarian in isolation, former prime minister Ingraham has a reputation for integrity and an anti-corruption stance and could bring the electorate back to the FNM, however he could also spark a spilt in the party if nominated in the December 2005 party conference.

Population
325,500 (2004)

Ethnic make-up
African (85 per cent), European and mixed race (12 per cent), other (3 per cent).

Religions
Baptist (32 per cent), Anglican (20 per cent), Roman Catholic (19 per cent), Evangelical Protestant (12 per cent), Methodist (6 per cent), Church of God (6 per cent).

Education
There is an extensive primary and secondary school system, and education is free. There are numerous options for tertiary

KEY INDICATORS — Bahamas

	Unit	2000	2001	2002	2003	2004
Population	m	0.30	0.31	0.31	0.32	0.33
Gross domestic product (GDP)	US$bn	4.86	4.62	5.00	*5.26	5.60
GDP per capita	US$	16,050	15,000	16,156	17,000	17,486
GDP real growth	%	5.0	-1.0	-1.8	0.9	3.3
Inflation	%	1.6	2.0	1.9	1.7	1.5
Unemployment	%	7.0	6.9	9.0	6.9	10.2
Exports (fob) (goods)	US$m	549.8	931.0	921.0	636.0	424.7
Imports (fob) (goods)	US$m	1,905.0	1,765.0	1,530.0	1,630.0	1,630.2
Balance of trade	US$m	-1,355.2	-1,242.0	-606.0	-994.0	-1,205.6
Current account	US$m	-437.5	-348.0	-348.0	-420.0	-480.0
Total reserves minus gold	US$m	349.6	319.3	380.6	491.1	674.4
Foreign exchange	US$m	341.4	311.3	372.1	481.8	664.7
Exchange rate	per US$	1.00	1.00	1.00	1.00	1.00

* estimated figure

education, including the College of the Bahamas, which is affiliated with the University of the West Indies (UWI). Local post-secondary vocational and technical training is available in mechanical, electrical and automotive engineering, television and radio, technology, computer science, electronics, construction, carpentry, secretarial services, bookkeeping, printing, photography, straw craft and dressmaking. A scholarship programme provides university training abroad in medicine, agriculture, engineering, science, education and other subjects considered necessary for national development but not available locally.

Literacy rate: 96 per cent of adults (2003)
Compulsory years: Five to 16
Enrolment rate: 98 per cent, gross primary enrolment (World Bank).

Health

Total expenditure on health is around 8 per cent of GDP, of which government spending is 55 per cent.

There are three main hospitals in the Bahamas: Princess Margaret in Nassau and Rand Memorial in Freeport, both government owned, and the privately owned Doctors Hospital in Nassau. Lyford Cay Hospital is a smaller private establishment offering specialised treatment.

HIV/Aids

Deaths by Aids, once a leading cause, had by 2005 been halved due to the use of anti-retroviral (ARV) drugs – 1,600 patients received the treatment, up from 470 in 2002. Deaths from Aids dropped from 250 to 140 per annum between 2002–04.

Over 2,000 HIV positive patients are cared for by a speciality clinic in Nassau and it was reported that no new cases of infants born to HIV positive mothers were infected while patients. HIV-positive pregnant women's rate dropped from 2.7 per cent in 2001 to 1.6 per cent in 2004, nevertheless, child mortality was 25.21 per 1,000 live births in 2004.

HIV prevalence: 3.0 per cent aged 15–49 in 2003 (World Bank)
Life expectancy: 69.8 years (World Bank)
Fertility rate/Maternal mortality rate: 2.1 births per woman (World Bank)
Infant mortality rate: 11 per 1,000 live births (World Bank)

Welfare

Welfare conditions in the Bahamas are among the best in the Caribbean and the government is working towards ensuring that economic growth is accompanied by improvements in the social sector.

The National Insurance Act of 1972 set out the law governing social security. It provides for contributions from employers and employees to be paid to the National Insurance Fund. Anyone who is employed or self-employed is insured under the act, including non-Bahamians with work permits. Benefits include sickness and maternity payments, retirement and widows' pensions and social assistance payments.

Main cities

Nassau (capital and seat of government, on New Providence Island, estimated population 222,200 in 2003) and Freeport (on Grand Bahama Island, 49,500).

Languages spoken

English, Creole (among Haitian immigrants).

Official language/s

English

Media

Press

Dailies: The main dailies are the *Nassau Guardian*, *Tribune (Bahamas)* and *Freeport News* (daily newspaper for Grand Bahama).

Weeklies: *Punch* is published on Monday and Thursday. Other weeklies include *The Grand Bahama Sun* and the *Bahama Journal*.

Business: *The Bahamas Financial Digest* covers business.

Periodicals: Periodicals including *Bahamian Review* and *Bahamas Tourist News* feature business, finance and tourism. *Bahamas Magazine* (a tourist-oriented publication five times a year) and the *Bahamas Handbook* are other popular periodicals.

Broadcasting

The government-owned Bahamas Broadcasting Service operates three commercial radio and three television stations. Freeport is covered by cable television. American television can also be received.

Economy

Tourism and offshore financial banking are the mainstays of the Bahamian economy. This small open plan economy is becoming less dependent on the tourist sector, although tourism still contributes 18–19 per cent GDP. The Bahamas consequently ranks number seven in the world for the largest amount of tourism-GDP produced.

Cruise ship visitors typically account for over 50 per cent of all visitors to the Bahamas and growth in this sector has averaged 9 per cent over the past decade. However visitor numbers dropped by just over 50 per cent, due to hurricane damage. Nevertheless, visitor spending was US$2 billion or 11.4 per cent of overall economic growth in 2004, attributed in part by increased numbers of European tourists visiting due to a strong euro. Tourism in the Bahamas has benefited from oil price rises, against expectations, as US visitors are less willing to travel long distances. The heavy reliance on the US economy weakens the economy in the Bahamas. With America accounting for around 80 per cent of tourists to the Bahamas, downturns in the US economy feed through to the islands. The government is combating this problem by attempting to broaden the base of tourism and increasing investment in the financial centre. New financial service laws passed in July 2004 are set to increase the Bahaman's competitiveness in this sector. However, doubts on whether the Free Trade Area of the Americas will go ahead in 2005 were cast by the Bahamian Ministry of Trade and Industry.

The tax neutral environment, with no direct taxation makes the Bahamas banks attractive to international businesses. The financial centre accounts for around 20 per cent of the country's GDP and annual expenditures in the banking sector amount to US$400 million. Government policy is to improve the integrity of the banks, and after tightening controls the Bahamas has now been removed from an international list of countries with dubious banking sectors.

The high incidence of hurricanes in the Bahamas affects the economy, although due to the islands' general preparedness, the economic impact is kept to a minimum. In 2004 hurricanes affected 9 per cent of the population and it is estimated that they lowered GDP by around 1 per cent, principally due to the adverse impact on tourism.

Debt servicing is a budgetary priority. Total debt levels are estimated at over 35 per cent of GDP.

External trade

The Bahamas is a member of the Caribbean Community (CARICOM), however has not yet joined the open market. The large trade deficit is traditionally offset by invisible earnings from tourism, offshore financial business and shipping.

Imports

Principal imports include oil, machinery and transport equipment, manufactured goods, livestock and foodstuffs, and chemicals. Imports totalled US$1.82 billion in 2004.

Main sources: US (22.3 per cent total, 2004), South Korea (19 per cent), Japan (8.2 per cent), Brazil (8.2 per cent), Italy (8.1 per cent), Venezuela (6.8 per cent)

Exports

Exports include chemicals, pharmaceuticals, rum, crawfish, agricultural products, salt, ragonite, sponges, cosmetics and perfume. Exports totalled US$469.3 million in 2004.

Main destinations: US (42.1 per cent total, 2004), Spain (10.3 per cent), Poland (6.1 per cent), Germany (6.1 per cent),

Switzerland (4.9 per cent), Paraguay (4.8 per cent), France (4.5 per cent), Mexico (4.5 per cent)

Re-exports
Petroleum products

Agriculture
Farming
The agricultural and fisheries sector contributes approximately 3 per cent to annual GDP and employs about 5 per cent of the labour force.

Although only about 1 per cent of land area is cultivated, near self-sufficiency has been achieved in poultry, pork, eggs, fruit and vegetables. The expansion of export crops such as limes, pineapples, papayas, avocados, cucumbers and mangoes is being promoted.

The government has provided marketing facilities through the Product Exchange in Nassau for small-scale producers, and also supplies seed and fertilisers. There are special incentives to foreign investors in food production and processing.

The chicken industry accounts for 40 per cent of agricultural production.

Crop production in 2004 included: 355 tonnes (t) maize, 55,500t sugar cane, 700t potatoes, 880t sweet potatoes, 240t taro, 3,500t bananas, 21,700t citrus fruit, 5,000t tomatoes, 155t cassava, 125t pulses, 29,000t fruit in total, 25,709t vegetables in total. Livestock production included: 8,379t meat in total, 28t beef, 205t pig meat, 96t lamb and goat meat, 8,050t poultry, 900t eggs, 1,750t milk.

Fishing
The commercial fishing sector was originally reserved for Bahamians until 2002, when the authorities began opening up the sector to foreign participation. The sector employs around 9,000 Bahamians. The commercial harvesting of pearls and shells has seen a dramatic rise from the typical 8,400 units in 1997 to the high of 40,000 units in 2000; the annual harvest is now typically 13,000 units. The harvest of sponges averages 70,000 per annum.

Forestry
Total forest cover is estimated at 842,000 hectares, equivalent of 15 per cent of the total land area. Most forests are concentrated on the four islands of the north-western Bahamas including Ahaco, Andros, Grand Bahamas and New Providence.

Industry and manufacturing
The industrial sector is small-scale, contributing around 10 per cent to annual GDP and employing 10 per cent of the labour force.

The largest contributor to the industrial sector is the crude oil transshipment terminal operated by Burmah Oil. Re-exports of crude and refined oil (mainly to the US) are estimated to account for around 16 per cent of GDP.

Other activity is centred on the production of rum, chemicals and pharmaceuticals for export. The companies manufacturing these products are largely foreign-owned and located in the Freeport trade area on Grand Bahama.

Other light industries include rum production, food processing, confectionery, garments, small boat building and furniture making.

The Bahamas Agricultural and Industrial Corporation (BAIC) is encouraging light manufacturing, furniture, toiletries, cosmetics, jewellery, linens, beachwear and the assembly of air conditioners and refrigerators.

The construction industry is also important, fuelled by the tourist trade and financial institutions requiring offices.

Tourism
Tourism is one of the Bahamas' primary economic activities and accounts for around 19 per cent of GDP, with another 20 per cent in tourist related construction. Tourism, and visitor numbers in 2004 were damaged by hurricanes, which closed a major resort on Grand Bahama causing a drop in the number of cruise ships visiting. Overall, only 2,369,000 visitors arrived in 2004 compared to the 4,594,000 visitors who arrived in 2003. In mid-2005 the sector was showing a 5.32 per cent decline. Gross receipts for tourism in 2004 were US$2.06 billion. Employment in the tourist industry is forecast to be some 43,000, or 25.7 per cent of the total labour force, in 2005.

Mining
Mining contributes approximately 1 per cent to annual GDP and employs around 1 per cent of the labour force.

Crude salt is produced by solar evaporation in Great Inagua and Long Island and aragonite deposits are found near Bimini Island.

Hydrocarbons
The Bahamas does not have any significant oil reserves, but the country is an important re-exporter of oil and transshipment earns the islands a significant amount of foreign exchange. The state-owned Bahamas Oil Refining Company (Borco) is the principal domestic player on the petroleum market and has been involved in several joint ventures with larger international oil companies. The Bahamas is poised to increase its hydrocarbons re-export sector with the construction of new liquidified natural gas (LNG) re-gasification terminals in Ocean Cay connected by pipeline to nearby Florida in the US. Two companies – AES Ocean LNG, and Tractebel – have invested over US$1 billion for the new gas terminals in their bid to corner the Florida gas market. However, the Bahamian government had not, by mid-2005, approved the deal. The US Federal Energy Regulatory Commission and the Bahamas Environmental Impact Assessment have given approval to the bids despite local environmental concerns. The proposed US$144 million Calypso pipeline would convey about 23.5 million cubic metres of natural gas per day to Broward County, Florida, from a LNG terminal in Freeport.

Energy
The Bahamas imports all of its energy needs, mainly oil. It imports around 25,000 barrels per day (bpd).
Installed electrical capacity is estimated at 410MW.

Financial markets
Stock exchange
The Bahamas International Stock Exchange (BISX) began trading in 2000 as a virtual stock exchange – all transactions by brokers are carried out online – which acts as a listing of convenience for mutual funds administered from all over the world. The BISX was set up with technical and financial support from the Inter-American Development Bank (IADB).

Banking and insurance
Central bank
Central Bank of the Bahamas
Main financial centre
Nassau
Offshore facilities
The Bahamas is one of the largest offshore financial centres in the world. It was taken off the OECD's blacklist of countries that did not meet international requirements on taxation and transparency after it enacted new legislation which eliminated banking operations that did not have a physical presence in the Bahamas, and allowed for the exchange of tax information and the establishment of a comprehensive anti-money laundering regime. It resulted in the number of banks and trust companies licenced in the offshore sector declining.

Time
GMT minus five hours (GMT minus four hours from April to October)

Geography
The Bahamas archipelago, which consists of 700 islands and nearly 2,500 small islets or cays sprawled across roughly 259,000 square km, stretches south-east from the southern coast of Florida (US). Virtually all the islands are surrounded by coral reefs and sandbanks, and nearly all are low lying.

Climate

The Bahamas is said to have one of the finest climates in the world. There are two seasons, winter (November–April) which is cool and dry, and summer (May–October) which is warm and wet. The climate is semi-tropical with temperatures ranging from 20 degrees Celsius (C) in winter to 30 degrees C in summer. Hurricanes can occur between June–November.

Dress codes

Business dress is more formal in the Bahamas than elsewhere in the Caribbean or in Florida; a business suit and tie is recommended for men and conservative business dress for women. Visitors should bring lightweight or tropical clothing and rainwear during the wet season.

If invited to a Bahamian's home for dinner, dress should be business attire for men and conservative evening wear for women. Formal attire is worn when attending church.

Entry requirements

Passports

Passports valid for at least six months from the date of entry are required by all visitors, except nationals of Canada on a visit not exceeding three weeks and US *bona fide* visitors for a period not exceeding eight months. All visitors require evidence of citizenship, a return/onward ticket and sufficient funds to provide for maintenance during the stay in the Bahamas.

Visa

Required by most, for the full list of exceptions visit www.bahamas.com/. For visits up to three weeks visas are not required by citizens of UK, US and Canada. Business visits and sales tours that include order-taking require work permits, obtained from the Director of Immigration (Form 1), plus various extra documentation, see 'legal' section at www.bahamas.com/travel_tips/index.html. All other business trips are subject to tourist visa requirements.

Currency advice/regulations

Permission is required from the Central Bank of the Bahamas to import local currency, which may be exported up to a maximum of B$70. The import and export of foreign currency is unlimited.

US dollars are accepted as legal tender. To avoid additional exchange rate charges, travellers are advised to take travellers cheques in US dollars.

Prohibited imports

Narcotics, firearms and flick knives.

Health (for visitors)

Medical facilities are on a par with the US, but can be costly and therefore medical insurance is recommended.

Mandatory precautions

A yellow fever vaccination certificate is required if arriving from an infected area.

Advisable precautions

Recommended immunisations are typhoid, diphtheria, hepatitis 'A' and 'B', tuberculosis, polio and tetanus. Tap water is safe to drink, although it can often be salty in taste. Milk is pasteurised and dairy products are safe for consumption. Local meat, poultry, seafood, fruit and vegetables are generally considered safe to eat.

Hotels

Wide variety available. Bills usually include 15 per cent service charge, as well as a 10 per cent hotel room tax.

Public holidays

Fixed dates

1 Jan (New Year's Day), 10 Jul (Independence Day), 25 Dec (Christmas Day), 26 Dec (Boxing Day).

Holidays which fall on a Saturday or Sunday are observed on the following Monday.

Variable dates

Good Friday, Easter Monday, Whit Monday, Labour Day (first Mon in Jun), Emancipation Day (first Mon in Aug), discovery (second Mon in Oct).

Working hours

Banking

Mon–Thu: 0930–1500; Friday: 0930–1700.

Business

Mon–Fri: 0900–1700.

Government

Mon–Fri: 0900–1730.

Shops

Mon–Sat: 0900–1700. Sunday closing laws are generally strictly observed, except for some grocers open for a few hours, as well as the tourist shops on Bay Street in Nassau if cruise ships are docked.

Telecommunications

Mobile phones

A GSM 1900 service is available.

Electricity supply

110V AC, 60 cycles

Social customs/useful tips

Bahamians shake hands upon meeting and business cards may be exchanged. Address first-time business acquaintances by their last names – conversations generally move to a first-name basis more slowly than in most Western countries. Appointments for business meetings should be made in advance.

Business lunches are often held. If invited to dinner at home, it is customary to take a small gift for the hostess and send a thank-you card afterwards.

Security

Most visits to the Bahamas are trouble-free. Crime exists in the main cities of Nassau and Freeport, including incidents of murder and armed robbery. Much of this is within the local community, but tourists are often perceived as wealthy and have been the victims of robbery, particularly when alone or in isolated locations.

Visitors should take sensible precautions and be vigilant at all times. It is advisable not to carry large amounts of cash or jewellery. Do not offer resistance in the event of an attempted robbery as the assailant may be armed.

The outlying islands, known as the Family Islands, are attracting an increasing number of visitors. These islands are relatively free of crime, but sensible precautions should still be taken.

Penalties for possession or trafficking of drugs are severe. Pack all luggage yourself and do not carry anything through customs for anyone else unless you are aware of the contents.

Getting there

Air

National airline: Bahamasair

International airport/s: Grand Bahama International (FPO), 5km north of city, shop, bar, restaurant, buffet, shops, car hire; Nassau International (NAS), 16km west of city, shop, restaurant, bank, post office, car hire;

Other airport/s: Paradise Island (PID), 5km from Nassau; George Town (GGT), 6km from city.

Airport tax: Departure tax: US$15, except immediate transit passengers.

Surface

Water: All the major cruise lines operating out of Florida make calls in the Bahamas, either in Nassau or Freeport. There is a two-hour daily ferry service, the 'Cat', to the Bahamas from Port Everglades in Florida, US. It leaves Port Everglades at 1600 and returns each morning at 0930.

Main port/s: Freeport Container Port on Grand Bahama (is on one of the world's most important shipping lanes), Nassau on New Providence and Matthew Town on Inagua.

There are modern berthing facilities for cruise ships at Potters Cay on New Providence, Governor's Harbour on Eleuthera, Morgan's Bluff on North Andros and George Town on Exuma.

Getting about

National transport

Air: An extensive air charter network covers the islands, serving over 50 landing sites. Local enquiries should be made for particular requirements.

Road: The main centres are well served by 3,218km of surfaced roads.
Buses: There are few conventional buses but *jitneys* (mini-buses) serve New Providence Island.
Rail: There is no passenger rail service.
Water: Ferry and mail-boat services are operated between the various islands in the archipelago, but for business travellers the length and frequency of journeys may prove a major drawback.

City transport
Taxis: Taxis are often metered and use a fixed-rate system. A 15 per cent tip is usual.

Car hire
A national or international licence valid for three months is required. Rates vary according to the season. Traffic drives on the left.

BUSINESS DIRECTORY

The addresses listed below are a selection only. While World of Information makes every endeavour to check these addresses, we cannot guarantee that changes have not been made, especially to telephone numbers and area codes. We would welcome any corrections.

Telephone area codes
The international direct dialling code (IDD) for Bahamas is +1 242, followed by subscriber's number

Chambers of Commerce
Bahamas Chamber of Commerce, Shirley Street and Collins Avenue, PO Box N-665, Nassau (tel: 322-2145; fax: 322-4649; e-mail: bahamaschamber@coralwave.com).

Grand Bahama Chamber of Commerce, The Mall and Pioneer Way, PO Box F-40808, Freeport (tel: 352-8329; fax: 352-3280; e-mail: info@ thegrandbahamachamberofcommerce. com).

Banking
Bahamas Development Bank, West Bay Street, PO Box N-3034, Nassau (tel: 327-5780; fax: 322-6457).

Bank of the Bahamas Ltd, PO Box N-7118, Nassau (tel: 326-2560).

Bank of Nova Scotia, PO Box N-7518, Nassau (tel: 356-1400).

Banque Privée Edmond de Rothschild Ltd, 51 Frederick Street, PO Box N-1136, Nassau (tel: 328-8121; fax: 328-8115).

Barclays Bank, PO Box N-8350, Nassau (tel: 322-4921).

British-American Bank, PO Box N-7502, Nassau (tel: 327-5170).

Canadian Imperiam Bank of Commerce (CIBC), PO Box N-7125, Nassau (tel: 322-8455).

Citibank, PO Box N-8158, Nassau (tel: 322-4240).

Commonwealth Bank, PO Box SS-6263, Nassau (tel: 328-1854).

Finance Corporation of Bahamas Ltd, PO Box N-3038, Nassau (tel: 322-4822).

Handelsfinanz-CCF Bank International ltd, Maritime House, Frederick Street, PO Box N-10441, Nassau (tel: 328-8644, 328-1737; fax: 328-8600).

Inter-American Development Bank, PO Box N-3743, Nassau (tel: 393-7159).

Lloyds Bank International (Americas), PO Box N-1262, Bolam House, King and George Streets, Nassau (tel: 322-8711; fax: 322-8719).

Royal Bank of Canada, PO Box N-7537, Nassau (tel: 322-8700).

Central bank
Central Bank of the Bahamas, Frederick Street, PO Box N-4868, Nassau (tel: 322-2193; fax: 322-4321; e-mail: cbb@centralbankbahamas.com).

Travel information
Bahamasair, Windsor Field, PO Box N-4881, Nassau (tel: 327-8451; fax: 327-7409).

Bahamas Hotel Association, Dele West Bay Street, sub Dean's Lane, PO Box N-7799, Nassau (tel: 322-8381; fax: 326-5346).

Nassau/Cable Beach/Paradise Island Promotion Board, Dean's Lane, Fort Charlotte, PO Box N-7799, Nassau (tel: 322-8381; fax: 326-5346).

National tourist organisation offices
National Tourism Board, c/o Ministry of Tourism, PO Box N-3701, Nassau (tel: 322-7501/4, 322-8634/7; fax: 328-0945).

Ministries
Ministry of Agriculture and Industry, Levy Building, East Bay Street, Nassau (tel: 325-7502; fax: 322-1767).

Ministry of Economic Development, Manx Building, West Bay Street, Nassau.

Ministry of Education, Youth and Sports, Shirley Street, Nassau (tel: 322-5495; fax: 322-3267).

Ministry of Finance, Sir Cecil V Wallace Whitfield Centre, Cable Beach, PO Bx N-3017, Nassau (tel: 327-1530; fax: 327-1618).

Ministry of Foreign Affairs, Post Office Building, East Hill Street, Nassau (tel: 322-7624; fax: 328-8212).

Ministry of Health, Ministry of Health Building, Royal Victoria Gardens, Nassau (tel: 322-7425; fax: 322-7788).

Ministry of Housing and Social Development, Frederick House, Frederick Street, Nassau (tel: 356-0765; fax: 323-3883).

Ministry of Justice, Post Office Building, East Hill Street, Nassau.

Ministry of Labour and Immigration, Post Office Building, East Hill Street, Nassau (tel: 323-7240; fax: 326-7344).

Ministry of Public Works, John F Kennedy Drive, Nassau (tel: 323-7814; fax: 325-2016).

Ministry of Tourism, Market Plaza, Bay Street, Nassau (tel: 322-7500; fax: 322-4014).

Ministry of Transport, Aviation and Local Government, Pilot House Complex, Nassau (tel: 394-0451; fax: 394-5023).

Office of the Deputy Prime Minister, Churchill Building, Bay Street, Nassau (tel: 356-6792; fax: 356-6087).

Office of the Prime Minister, Cecil V Wallace Whitfield Centre, West Bay Street, Nassau (tel: 322-2805; fax: 328-8294).

Other useful addresses
Bahamas Agricultural and Industrial Corp, PO Box N-4940, Nassau (tel: 322-3740/3; fax: 322-2123).

Bahamas Economic Development Corporation, Bahamas Development Bank, Adderley Building, Bay Street/Rawson Square, PO Box N-3034, Nassau (tel: 327-5780; fax: 327-5907).

Bahamas Electricity Corporation, Big Pond and Tucker Road, PO Box N-7509, Nassau (tel: 328-7700).

Bahamas Employers' Confederation, PO Box N-166, Nassau (tel: 328-1757, 326-6644; fax: 328-1346).

Bahamas Financial Services Board (tel: 326-7001; e-mail: wwarren@bfsb-bahamas.com; internet site: http://www.bfsb-bahamas.com).

Bahamas Information Services, Nassau Court, PO Box N-8172 (tel: 325-6028).

Bahamas Investment Authority, Cecil Wallace Whitfield Centre, PO Box CB-10980, Nassau (tel: 327-5970/4; fax: 327-5907; e-mail: investbahama@batelnet.bs; internet site: http://www.opm.gov.bs).

Bahamas Telecommunications Corporations, J F Kennedy Drive, PO Box N-3048, Nassau (tel: 323-4911).

Bahamas Water and Sewerage Corporation, J F Kennedy Drive, PO Box N-3905, Nassau (tel: 323-3944).

British High Commission, Bitco Building, 3rd Floor, East Street, PO Box N-7516, Nassau (tel: 325-7471/2/3; fax: 323-3871).

Broadcasting Corporation of The Bahamas, PO Box N-1347, Nassau (tel: 32-4623, 322-4480).

Cabinet Office, Churchill Bldg, Rawson Square, PO Box N-7147, Nassau (tel: 322-2805; fax: 328-8294).

Central Post Office, Post Office Building, PO Box N-8302, Nassau (tel: 322-3344).

The Comptroller of Customs, Seaban Building, Oakes Field, PO Box N-155, Nassau (tel: 326-4401).

Department of Agriculture, East Bay Street, PO Box N-3028, Nassau (tel: 325-7502).

Department of Civil Aviation, Nassau International Airport, PO Box N-975, Nassau (tel: 327-7281).

Department of Fisheries, East Bay Street, PO Box N-3028, Nassau (tel: 393-1777).

Department of Housing, PO Box N 275, Nassau (tel: 356-0765; fax: 323-3883).

Department of Local Government, PO Box N 3040, Nassau (tel: 325-4560; fax: 326-5561).

Department of Statistics, c/o Ministry of Finance, Clarence Bain Building, PO Box N-3904, Nassau (tel: 325-6520).

Gaming Board of the Bahamas, West Bay Street, PO Box N-4565, Nassau (tel: 327-7478).

Government Publications Office (import regulations), East Bay Street, PO Box N-7147, Nassau (tel: 322-2410).

Hotel Corporation of the Bahamas, PO Box N-9520, Nassau (tel: 327-8395; fax: 327-6978).

Port Department, East Hill Street, PO Box N-8173 Nassau (tel: 326-7354).

Privatisation Office, c/o Office of the Deputy Prime Minister, PO Box N-3217, Nassau (tel: 356-6792; fax: 356-6087).

Securities Commission of the Bahamas, PO Box N-8347, Nassau (tel: 356-6271/2; fax: 356-7530; e-mail: secbd@batelnet.bs).

US Embassy, Mosmar Building, Queen Street, PO Box N-8197, Nassau (tel: 322-1181; fax: 328-3495; e-mail: embnas@state.gov).

Internet sites

Bahamas International Securities Exchange: http://www.bisxbahamas.com

Investment incentives: http://www.interknowledge.com/bahamas/investment

The Bahamian Web Community: http://www.tropitec.net

What's on Guide to Everything Bahamian: http://www.whatsonbahamas.com

Bahrain

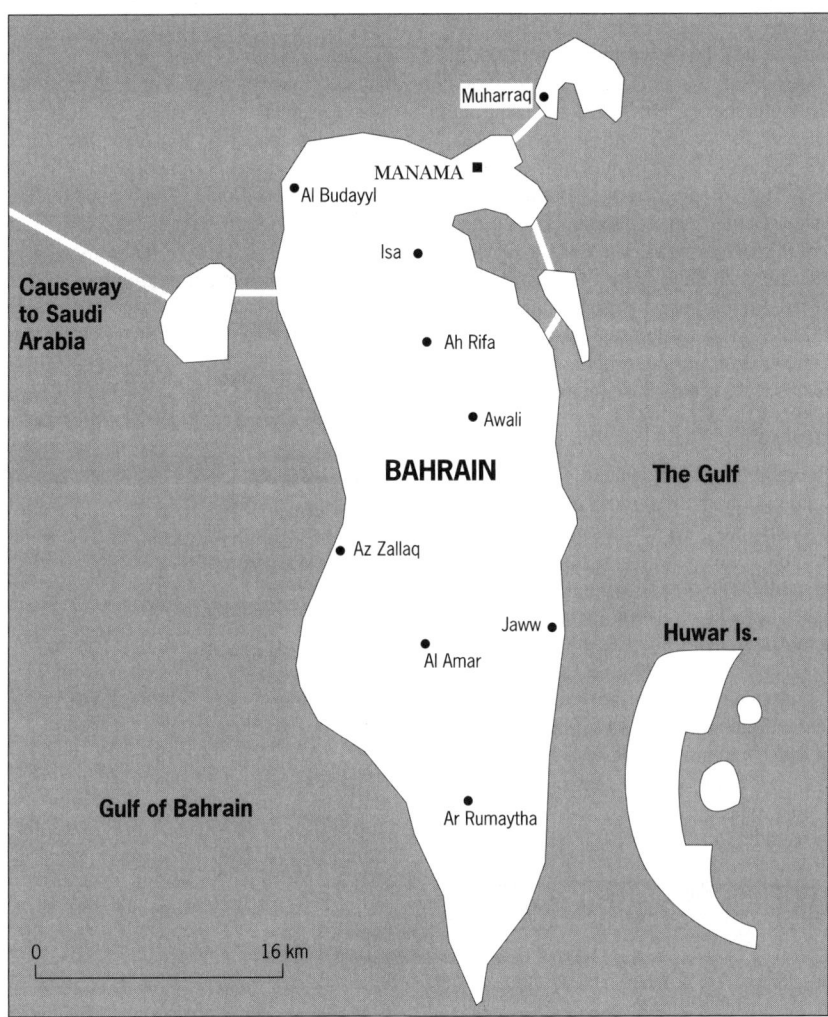

KEY FACTS

Official name: Al Mamlakah al Bahrayn (Kingdom of Bahrain)

Head of State: King Hamad bin Isa al Khalifa (ruler since Mar 1999; King since 14 Feb 2002)

Head of government: Prime Minister Sheikh Khalifa bin Sulman al Khalifa

Area: 676 square km (35 islands)

Population: 699,400 (2004)

Capital: Manama

Official language: Arabic

Currency: Bahraini dinar (BD) = 1,000 fils

Exchange rate: BD0.38 per US$ (fixed)

GDP per capita: US$13,848 (2004)

GDP real growth: 5.50% (2004);*6.0% (2005)

Labour force: 349,000 (2004)

Inflation: 4.90% (2004)

Balance of trade: US$1.49 billion (2004)

Foreign debt: US$6.21 billion (2004)

* estimated figure

In 2005, the Kingdom of Bahrain worked hard to emphasise its strengths and minimise its weaknesses. Faced with declining oil and gas reserves, the government invested heavily in the aluminium production and financial services sectors. Prior to the Iraqi elections in December 2005, when several women and ethnic minorities were elected to parliament, the government also continued to set the pace in the realm of Arab democracy.

The need to diversify

With no new significant oil or gas finds in recent years, Bahrain has had to maximise production efficiency in its existing fields, at Awali and Abu Sa'afa. To meet the challenges of declining hydrocarbon production and revenues, the government has invested heavily in aluminium production. In September, King Hamad bin Isa al Khalifa opened the world's longest aluminium smelter line. Production increased by 30 per cent in 2005, to around 820,000 tonnes. The state-owned Aluminium Bahrain (Alba) already contributes 8 per cent of Bahrain's GDP and this share is expected to increase to around 12 per cent once the new smelter line becomes fully operational.

Nations of the World: A Political, Economic and Business Handbook

The kingdom has also stepped up promotion of its status as the key financial centre in the Gulf region. From 1995–2005, the number of banks, insurance companies, investment houses and other financial organisations establishing themselves in Bahrain more than tripled, to 300. In December 2005, Bahrain was named the winner of the internationally prestigious Financial Centre of the Future award, in the Middle East and Africa category. This was welcome news in Bahrain, as it now faces competition for its status as the region's financial centre from Dubai's recently opened Dubai International Financial Centre (DIFC). Also in December, Bahrain further boosted its regional centre credentials by hosting the World Islamic Banking Conference.

A democracy, relatively speaking

Although political power is overwhelmingly dominated by the al Khalifa family – its members include the King, crown prince, prime minister, deputy prime minister, defenCe minister, foreign minister and finance minister – Bahrain has made much of its democratic credentials in recent years, 2005 being no exception. Bahrain caused a stir in the pan-Arab and local media when, in April, Alees Samaan became the first woman and non-Muslim anywhere in the Arab world to chair a house of parliament. Ms Samaan, a Christian, stood in as speaker of Bahrain's upper house, the Majlis al Shura (Consultative Assembly), by default, as she was the most senior parliamentarian available in the absence of the elected speaker and his deputies. However, that the event was permitted to occur at all was unprecedented in a region dominated by patriarchal societies. In November, Bahrain hosted the Forum for the Future, which brought together leaders from the Middle East and the Group of 8 (G8) countries to discuss political and economic reform in the region.

Abuse of guest workers

Bahrain generated news in 2005 over its treatment of guest workers, who make up about one third of Bahrain's population. In September, Alem Teklu, an Ethiopian citizen, went public with her story of having fallen victim to people traffickers and enduring virtual slavery in Bahrain. With the assistance of the International Organisation of Migration (IMO), Ms Alem drew attention to the plight of thousands of young Ethiopians who are trafficked to the Middle East, often suffering corporeal punishment, imprisonment, forced marriages and sexual abuse on arrival.

Outlook

Bahrain has taken constructive steps to minimise the fallout of declining hydrocarbon exports, which currently generate around 70 per cent of Bahrain's total foreign trade earnings. The high price of oil in 2005, and the likelihood that prices will remain high, especially if sanctions are imposed on Iran in 2006, has also delivered extra income for further diversification. Bahrain's reputation as the region's financial hub remains intact, although Bahrain will have to monitor developments in Dubai, where efforts are being stepped up to establish a rival financial centre.

Elections scheduled for September 2006 promise to be a more inclusive affair than those in 2002. The majority Shia community largely boycotted the latter and not a single woman candidate won a seat. King Hamad subsequently appointed six women to the Majlis al Shura. A poll conducted in January 2006 revealed that the electorate was much more favourable to voting for female candidates and some Shia community leaders indicated a greater willingness to participate. Bahrain will continue to attract some international attention over its record on the treatment of women in 2006. In December 2005, women's rights campaigner, Ghada Jamsheer, was cleared in court of defaming Family Court judges but still faces other charges related to her campaign to reform family law in the kingdom.

Risk assessment

Politics	Improving
Economy	Improving
Regional stability	Stable

COUNTRY PROFILE

Historical profile

Around 3000BC, the archipelago was the seat of the Dilmun trading empire linking Mesopotamia (southern Iraq) with the Indus Valley (India and Pakistan). Because of Dilmun's lush greenery in the midst of regions rapidly becoming arid, some scholars have suggested that it may have been the site of the biblical Garden of Eden. As well as a trading centre, it was also famous for pearl fishing. After being occupied by several other countries, the land subsequently became part of the Ottoman Empire. Later, it was administered by Britain until full independence. Since his accession to the throne in 1999, King Hamad bin Isa al Khalifa has instituted a process of political liberalisation. However, the process has been tightly controlled to ensure that the ruling Khalifa family and its close associates maintain control of both political and economic power.

1816 Bahrain's first treaty with Britain was signed
1861 The second treaty made it a British protectorate.
1869 Sheikh Isa bin Ali al Khalifa was named ruler.
1913 A treaty between Britain and Turkey recognised Bahrain as an independent state, but the country remained under British administration.
1923 After more than half a century of peace and stability, Sheikh Isa bin Ali al Khalifa abdicated in favour of his son, Sheikh Hamad.

KEY INDICATORS — Bahrain

	Unit	2000	2001	2002	2003	2004
Population	m	0.63	0.65	0.66	0.68	0.70
Gross domestic product (GDP)	US$bn	7.80	7.90	8.40	9.61	*10.00
GDP per capita	US$	10,600	11,141	12,700	10,096	13,848
GDP real growth	%	5.3	5.0	4.1	4.0	5.5
Inflation	%	-0.7	0.5	-1.0	0.4	4.9
Natural gas output	bn cum	8.6	8.9	9.2	9.6	9.8
Exports (fob) (goods)	US$m	5,700.5	5,386.0	5,790.0	6,592.0	7,620.7
Imports (fob) (goods)	US$m	4,373.4	4,418.0	4,990.0	5,357.0	6,135.4
Balance of trade	US$m	1,327.1	968.0	800.0	1,055.0	1,485.3
Current account	US$m	830.0	220.0	-520.0	-50.0	870.0
Total reserves minus gold	US$m	1,564.1	1,684.0	1,726.0	1,778.4	1,940.5
Foreign exchange	US$m	1,478.3	1,598.5	1,631.0	1,673.8	1,829.6
Exchange rate	per US$	0.38	0.38	0.38	0.38	0.38

* estimated figure

Bahrain

1928 Iran claimed ownership of Bahrain; the dispute was not resolved until 1970 when Iran accepted a UN report stating that the vast majority of Bahrainis wanted their complete independence.

1932 Bahrain became the first country in the Gulf to strike oil.

1942–61 Sheikh Hamad died in 1942 and his son, Sheikh Sulman bin Hamad al Khalifa ruled Bahrain until his death in 1961, when he was succeeded by Sheikh Isa bin Sulman al Khalifa.

1968 Britain announced its intention to withdraw from the Gulf by 1971. The British plan was to form a single state consisting of Bahrain, Qatar and the Trucial States, but this idea did not find favour with the states concerned.

1971 Bahrain and Qatar became independent states.

1973–74 Bahrain's constitution was promulgated; it limited the Sheikh's powers and established an elected 30-member National Assembly.

1975 The National Assembly refused to ratify a bill to arrest and detain people for up to three years without trial, and was dissolved by the ruler, Sheikh Isa. The government subsequently ruled by decree.

1981 Bahrain was one of the six founder members of the Gulf Co-operation Council (GCC).

1986 The opening of the King Fahd Causeway between Bahrain and Saudi Arabia gave a boost to business and tourism.

1991 Bahrain actively supported the allied forces against Iraq in the Gulf military conflict.

1994 The majority Shi'ites staged demonstrations demanding better living conditions and the return of an elected parliament. The Sunnis, although in a minority, are dominant in both politics and business.

1999 Sheikh Isa bin Sulman al Khalifa, who had ruled since 1961, died and was succeeded by his son, Sheikh Hamad bin Isa al Khalifa.

2000 For the first time, non-Muslims and women were appointed to the Consultative Council.

2001 A referendum on political reform was approved, under which Bahrain would become a constitutional monarchy with an elected lower chamber of parliament and an independent judiciary.

2002 Hamad bin Isa al Khalifa was declared king on 14 February, and the state became a constitutional monarchy. As part of the reform process, legislation was approved to allow women to vote in elections and run for national office. In legislative elections (the first since 1973), parliament became a mix of secular and Islamic candidates. The Shi'ite opposition boycotted the election resulting in a Sunni dominated parliament.

2004 In April, the first woman to be appointed head of a government ministry, Nada Haffadh, was made health minister. In September a free trade agreement was signed with the US.

2005 In March, King Hamad called for increasing global co-operation to combat international terrorism. Between March and June thousands protested in favour of a fully elected parliament.

Political structure

Constitution
The 1973 constitution was suspended in 1975 and reinstated by royal decree, with significant amendments, in February 2002.

By a charter, agreed through a referendum, Bahrain was declared a constitutional monarchy with a bicameral parliament and independent judiciary. The King is the symbol of the country and is inviolate.

Form of state
Constitutional monarchy

The executive
Executive power rests with the King, who is Head of State, he appoints a prime minister and members of the Consultative Council, which is an advisory body that, since 2002, is empowered to make laws. The King may dissolve or extend the term of the Consultative Council. The King has the right to initiate, ratify and promulgate laws.

The King is the head of the armed forces and head of the Judiciary.

National legislature
A bicameral national assembly; the Chamber of Deputies is a 40-member, popularly elected lower house legislature. The upper Consultative Council is a 40-member appointed chamber. Membership of both houses is four years. The King may renew membership of the Council and dissolve the Chamber of Deputies by decree. Terms of both houses may be extended by the King for up to two extra years.

The King and prime minister presents bills to the Chamber for consideration, before they are passed to the Consultative Council.

Legal system
The judiciary is a constitutionally independent body, whose function and organisation is regulated by law. It is a mixture, based on English common law and Sunni and Shi'a Sharia (Islamic law) traditions, where Sharia is the principal source of law.

The Supreme court is the final court of appeal for all civil, commercial and criminal matters.

Last elections
24 /31 October 2002 (parliamentary) (the first since 7 December 1973, after which, in 1975, the National Assembly was dissolved).
Results: Parliamentary: the 40-seat parliament was split between Islamists and secular and independent representatives; turnout was 51.3 per cent

Next elections
October 2006 (parliamentary)

Political parties
Political parties are not permitted, however, independently sitting MPs may be members of political societies.

Population
699,400 (2004)

Ethnic make-up
Bahrain's inhabitants are mostly Arab, with a sizeable minority of Iranian descent.

Approximately 38 per cent of the population are foreign residents, mostly from South Asia and other Arab countries.

Religions
According to the constitution, Islam is the state religion. Approximately 98 per cent of the indigenous population are Muslim – two-thirds Shi'as and the remainder belonging to the Sunni branch of Islam. The remaining 2 per cent are Jewish and Christian.

About half of the foreign population are non-Muslim, including Christians, Jews, Hindus, Baha'is, Buddhists and Sikhs.

Education
Primary schooling lasts for six years between the ages of six and 12. Secondary education lasts for three years and offers students a choice of three main branches: the general, the technical or the commercial.

The government is seeking to establish Bahrain as a regional centre for human resource development. In addition to several universities, there are a number of training centres, such as the Bahrain Training Institute (BTI) and the Bahrain Institute of Training and Finance (BITF) that are designed to prepare local graduates for the modern, technology driven workforce.

There are 188 government-owned and 42 private schools.
Literacy rate: 91 per cent and 82.6 per cent for males and females respectively (World Bank).
Compulsory years: 6 to 15
Enrolment rate: 105 per cent boys, 106 per cent girls total primary school enrolment of the relevant age group (including repetition rates) (World Bank).

Health
Health services in Bahrain are of a high quality and all Bahrainis receive free

health care from the state. There are a mixture of government and private hospitals, with additional government health centres and maternity hospitals.
HIV prevalence: 0.2 per cent aged 15–49 in 2003 (World Bank)
Life expectancy: 73.4 years (World Bank)
Fertility rate/Maternal mortality rate: 2.3 births per woman (World Bank)
Infant mortality rate: 12 per 1,000 live births (World Bank)
Head of population per physician/bed: 1 physician and 2.9 beds per 1,000 people

Welfare
The government provides direct financial assistance to those considered needy in addition to assistance provided by religious organisations and local charitable societies. There are seven social centres operated by the ministry of labour and social affairs (MoLSA) that provide training and assistance, especially to needy women. Public and private facilities for the elderly, handicapped and orphaned provide first class care, using the latest professional methods, approaches, and equipment. The number of needy families on government assistance lists has been growing for the past decade at double the rate of the population growth.
Family support
The social assistance programme provides approximately BD30 (US$80) per month to every family being assisted.

Main cities
Manama (capital, estimated population 149,900 in 2003), Rifa (91,800) Muharraq (84,500) Isa Town (69,100), Sitrah (62,500), Jid Hafs (53,000).

Languages spoken
English is widely spoken. Persian (Farsi), Hindi and Urdu are also frequently used.
Official language/s
Arabic

Media
The government is the most liberal of any in the Gulf towards broadcasting and the press, although its control over radio and television would be considered strict by Western standards.
Press
Dailies: The principal daily newspapers in Arabic are *Akhbar al Khaleej* and *al Ayam*. English-language dailies include *Bahrain Tribune*, *Gulf Daily News*, *Bahrain Voice* and *Middle Xpress*.
Business: Falcon Publishing Group and Al Hilal Publishing and Marketing Group, each produce several magazines and directories on business, industry, finance, banking and travel.

Broadcasting
Radio: The state-owned Bahrain Broadcasting Station transmits two services, one in Arabic and the other in English. Otherwise, it is possible to receive Capital Radio, the Voice of America, BBC World Service and services from Oman, Qatar, Abu Dhabi and the popular, music-oriented Aramco service from Dhahran.
Television: Bahrain Channel 4 in Arabic; Bahrain Channel 55 in English broadcast nightly. Other TV stations received in Bahrain include RAK (Ras al Khaimah), Dubai 10, Dubai 33, Dubai 41, Kuwait 8, Kuwait 10, Qatar 9, Qatar 11, Qatar 37, Oman 8, Abu Dhabi 5, Abu Dhabi 31, Saudi 6, Saudi 29 and Aramco 3 (English), depending on conditions.

Economy
Bahrain saw good GDP growth of 5.5 per cent in 2004 which is set to rise even further to around 6 per cent in 2005. However the country remains the least wealthy of the six Gulf states. Unemployment remains a problem in the country with 15 per cent of the labour force out of work. This is an even greater problem among the youth population. The Iraqi war has had no serious impact on Bahrain's economic growth, however investor confidence has declined after the conflict. This is mainly due to the threat of further conflict and terrorism.
The nation has only small hydrocarbon reserves and with the decline of crude oil production many jobs could be lost in the near future. By 2010 oil reserves are expected to be completely exhausted. Production of hydrocarbons accounts for 30 per cent of GDP and 60 per cent of government receipts. This means the government has a policy of increasing the rate of the diversification process in the country. Oil refining is a growing sector of the economy, even when oil reserves are exhausted the re-export industry may become a backbone of the economy.
The financial sector is another area of the economy that is in a state of intense development. In 2002 an international Islamic financial centre, dealing with products specifically complying with Sharia, was introduced. This International Islamic Financial Market (IIFM) is likely to grow and will assist Bahrain's need for diversification. The construction plans of a new airport and sea port in 2005 will further help the development of Bahrain as a regional hub.
Bahrain hopes to develop into a Free Trade and Service Hub in the region and has set up an Economic Development Board (EDB) to help realise its economic aims. Attracting foreign investment is a key objective. Bahrain is a member of the WTO and is well prepared to meet the demands of international competition. Bahrain is one of six members of the Gulf Co-operation council (GCC). This council's aims are to improve relations between the countries both economically and politically. The Unified Economic Agreement encourages the establishment of joint projects in agriculture, services and industry. There are plans in the near future to establish a customs union which will result in free trade between the six Gulf states. The GCC have also committed to issuing a common currency by 2010, this will have the effect of possibly changing the medium of oil transactions from the dollar to the new currency.

External trade
In September 2004 a Free Trade Agreement was signed with the US. This agreement will provide immediate access to 100 per cent of both countries non-textile industrial goods, 100 per cent of Bahrain's agricultural goods and 98 per cent of US agricultural goods. This trade agreement, however, violates the Unified Economic Agrement signed in 2001.
Imports
Main imports are crude oil, machinery, chemicals and foodstuffs.
Main sources: Saudi Arabia (33.1 per cent total, 2004), Japan (7.6 per cent), Germany (6.1 per cent), US (5.7 per cent), UK (5.6 per cent), France (4.9 per cent)
Exports
Main exports are petroleum and related goods, aluminim and textiles.
Main destinations: US (3.1 per cent total, 2004), South Korea (2.3 per cent), Japan (2.0 per cent)

Agriculture
Farming
The agricultural sector typically accounts for less than 1 per cent of GDP and employs 5 per cent of the workforce.
Apart from being a small island, development of agriculture is limited by labour shortages, lack of water and salinity of the soil. The major crop is alfalfa for animal fodder, although farmers produce modest amounts of crops including dates, watermelons, pomegranates, bananas, potatoes, eggplants and tomatoes for the local market.
Government agricultural plans emphasise drainage to reduce salinity, improvement of the soil and new irrigation and cultivation techniques; experiments with hydroponics are also under way.
The land tenure system, under which over 60 per cent of cultivable land is held on three-year leases, discourages the stability needed for development.
The lack of grazing inhibits livestock production. One large dairy has annual milk

Bahrain

production of 500,000 litres. Small dairy farmers, responsible for 15 per cent of production, have established a co-operative and constructed a milk pasteurising plant.

The estimated crop production for 2004 included: 11 metric tonnes (t) potatoes, 16,508mt dates, 730t bananas, 12t pulses, 950t citrus fruit, 130t grapes, 17,000t dates, 2,100t tomatoes, 345t treenuts, 22,010t fruit in total, 262t chillies & peppers, 1,300t onions 8,394t vegetables in total. The estimated livestock production included: 16,718t meat in total, 1,440t beef and veal, 83mt camel meat, 8,100t lamb, 1,455t goat meat, 5,640t poultry, 2,000t eggs, 18,487t milk, 240t cattle hides, 1,260t sheepskins, 8,000t greasy wool.

Fishing

The waters surrounding Bahrain have traditionally been rich, with more than 200 varieties of fish, many of which constitute a staple of the local diet. The discovery of oil in 1935 led to a steady decline in the fishing industry, which has been unable to meet domestic demand, noticeably since the 1970s. Moreover, pollution in the Gulf, since the 1980s, has increasingly threatened fish production and the shrimp industry.

Fish catches have dropped amid claims of illigal fishing, habitat destruction from land reclamation and environmental pollution that threatens overall fish stocks.

Industry and manufacturing

The industrial sector contributed 39.6 per cent of GDP in 2004, of which manufacturing was 10.8 per cent. The sector typically employs 34 per cent of the labour force.

Bahrain's most prominent non-oil industry is the Aluminium Bahrain (Alba) plant, which supplies various downstream manufacturing plants as well as the Gulf Aluminium Rolling Mill Company (Garmco). Aluminium exports are one of Bahrain's biggest earners as a result of increased world prices. Alba dominates the manufacturing sector with a production capacity of 500,000 tonnes per year. Alba commissioned its 450,000 tonnes per annum coke calcining plant and 41,000 cubic metres per day seawater desalination plant. This was the first plant of its kind in the Middle East. More than 50 per cent of the aluminium produced at Alba is sold on the local and regional market, while the remainder goes mainly to the Far East. Export-oriented small- and medium-sized industries have been attracted to free industrial zones established at Mina Sulman, Ma'amir, Abu Gazal and North Sitra, which enjoy tax and duty incentives. Industries located in these areas include plastics, paper, steel-wool and wire-mesh producers, marine service industries, aluminium, asphalt, cable manufacturing, prefabricated building and furniture. Iron and steel production is increasing. The Bahrain Ispat Company, under the control of the Indian Ispat Group (based in London), operates a plant with a capacity of 1.2 million tpy of iron briquettes produced from iron pellets.

Growth in industrial production fell to -0.2 per cent in 2004; whereas growth in 2003 was 2.9 per cent.

Tourism

Tourism is a major element of Bahrain's economic strategy of diversification to replace its depleted oil reserves. Bahrain is second only to Egypt in the number of arrivals, receiving over four million visitors each year. Around three-quarters of these come from neighbouring states, mainly Saudi Arabia and Kuwait, on short-term visits. The aim is to attract more visitors from the region, as well as from other markets. In addition to the existing causeway link with Saudi Arabia, a causeway to Qatar is scheduled to open in 2006. Bahrain is well-served with accommodation, leisure and conference facilities and continues to pursue an expansive infrastructure programme, involving private investment.

The sector is estimated to have accounted for 7.6 per cent of GDP in 2005 and provided 23.4 per cent of total employment. The revenues were estimated at US$2.1 billion or 19.5 per cent of export revenue in 2005, so its share of total capital investments at 4.2 per cent or US$54.2 million appears to be less than the government had planned.

Hydrocarbons

Oil accounts for more than 60 per cent of exports and around 65 per cent of government revenue; the government is attempting to diversify but the economy is heavily dependent on oil.

The Bahrain Petroleum Company has responsibility for all aspects of the oil industry including exploration, production, refining and distribution in both domestic and international markets.

Bahrain has 90 billion cubic metres (cum) of natural gas and produced 9.8 billion cum in 2004 – an increase of 1.4 per cent on 2003. With the imminent loss of all hydrocarbon reserves, Qatar has signed an agreement to supply Bahrain with natural gas in the future.

Bahrain does not produce or import coal.

Energy

Peak domestic demand for electricity has risen from 1,400MW in 2003 to 1,600MW by 2005. The government has restricted the price, to users, at a rate set in 1992. Responding to the rise in demand, capacity was increased by 675MW from a combined cycle gas turbine generating station at al Hidd, which went on-line in 2004. There are three other power stations at Rifa, with a capacity of 700MW, Manama with 167MW and Sitra with 125MW.

Financial markets

In December 2005 Bahrain won the Financial Centre of the Future Award, in the Middle East and Africa Category. It has a solid reputation as an international financial hub. Bahrain remains attractive as a result of a combination of factors, including its relative political stability, open and tax-free business climate, central geographical position, low costs, excellent communications and an accommodating government. The financial sector is one of the most diverse in the region and has the largest volume of transactions in the Middle East. The International Islamic Financial Market (IIFM) has attracted a number of major financial institutions to deal specifically in Sharia compliant deals.

Banking and insurance

There are more than 200 financial institutions in Bahrain. The Bahrain Monetary Agency (BMA) has full regulations for its Islamic banking community.

Central bank

Bahrain Monetary Agency (BMA) is an independent judicial organisation and the central monetary institution.

Main financial centre

Manama

Time

GMT plus three hours

Geography

Bahrain is an archipelago of 33 islands. Only three of the islands are inhabited. The main island of Bahrain contains most of the population and is linked by a causeway to the island of Muharraq. Another causeway links Bahrain to Saudi Arabia.

Climate

Summer temperatures are hot and humid, reaching 49 degrees Celsius (C) in the shade, while January, the coldest winter month, has temperatures ranging from 2.8 degrees C to 28.3 degrees C. Humidity, particularly on the coast, can be extreme. Between December and the end of March the climate is temperate, with temperatures ranging between 19 and 25 degrees C.

Dress codes

A lightweight suit or lightweight jacket and trousers are advised. A long-sleeved shirt with a tie should be worn at business and official meetings but a jacket need not be worn. Women should dress modestly. However, they can wear bikinis on certain beaches and the dress code for women is less severe than in Saudi Arabia or some other Islamic countries.

Entry requirements
Passports
Passports are required by all.
Visa
Visas are required by all except nationals of Kuwait, Oman, Qatar, Saudi Arabia and the United Arab Emirates (UAE).
For details of requirements for business and tourist visas visit: www.bahrainedb.com/lifestyle/visa.stm. Tourist visas can be obtained on arrival at Bahrain airport, business visas must be applied for in advance. Journalists must make prior arrangements with the Ministry of Information.
Women arriving in Bahrain alone and without a visa could be refused entry. Lone female travellers are advised to obtain a visa before departure.
Prohibited entry
Israeli nationals or anyone holding a passport with an Israeli visa/stamp may be denied entry.
Currency advice/regulations
Any currency may be freely imported and exported.
Customs
Personal effects duty free. The duty free allowance is 400 cigarettes or 50 cigars and two bottles of alcoholic beverages, for non-Muslim passengers only, and 227ml of perfume for personal use. Jewellery, drugs, firearms and ammunition are subject to import permits.
Prohibited imports
Pornographic and obscene literature and pictures, cultured or undrilled pearls, and goods of Israeli origin are prohibited.

Health (for visitors)
Medical services in Bahrain are of high quality with a good general hospital in Manama and modern health centres in smaller communities. Medical insurance is advised. Consultations are offered at the American Mission Hospital, 133 Isa Al-Kabeer Avenue, Manama (tel: 253-447).
Mandatory precautions
Yellow fever certificate, for visitors arriving from infected areas.
Advisable precautions
Recommended immunisations are hepatitis 'A' and 'B', polio, tetanus and typhoid. There is a risk of rabies.
Water should be boiled or sterilised, or use bottled water. Milk is unpasteurised and should therefore be boiled or avoided. Dairy products made from local milk should be avoided. Fruit should be peeled and vegetables cooked. Meat and fish should be well cooked and eaten hot.

Hotels
First-class hotel capacity for 175,000 average-stay visitors. A 12 per cent service charge is usual. Major hotels and most restaurants are licensed.

Credit cards
All major credit cards are accepted.

Public holidays
Fixed dates
1 Jan (New Year's Day), 16–17 Dec (National Day).
Variable dates
Eid al Adha (three days), Eid al Fitr (three days), Islamic New Year, Ashura, Prophet's Birthday.
The Islamic year has 354 or 355 days, with the result that Muslim feasts advance by 10–12 days against the Gregorian calendar each year. Dates of the Muslim feasts vary according to sightings of the new moon, so cannot be forecast exactly. Islamic year 1426: 10 February 2005 to 30 January 2006.

Working hours
Thursday and Friday are weekly holidays. Regular hours are subject to change during the month of Ramadan. Some banks and businesses close on Saturday.
Banking
Sat–Wed: 0730–1200; Thu: 0730–1100; some branches are open three days weekly in the afternoon; some offshore banking units close on Sunday; 1000–1330 during Ramadan.
Business
Sat–Thu: 0800–1530 or 0800–1300, 1500–1730.
Government
Sat–Tue: 0700–1415; Wed: 0700–1400. During Ramadan government offices open 0930–1430.
Shops
Sat–Thu: 0830–1230, 1530–1830; large superstores are open Sat–Thu: 0800–1900; late opening Wed and Thu: 0800–1200, 1530–2130; some are open for a few hours on Fri in the Souk.

Telecommunications
Mobile phones
GSM 900/1800 services are available throughout the country.

Electricity supply
230V 50 cycles AC everywhere except Awali, which has 120V 60 cycles; various types of plug fitting, normally three-pin flat.

Weights and measures
Metric system (local measures are also used).

Social customs/useful tips
Punctuality is not always a Bahraini virtue although this is changing. Traditionally much time is spent in exchanging small talk at business meetings; embarking on business matters before the atmosphere is favourable may cause offence. Decisions are often taken by consensus, according to the Arabian tradition, rather than exclusively on the advantages and disadvantages of the case submitted. In business, it is essential to create a mood of trust and to be persistent even when the case is apparently lost. Always shake hands on meeting and leaving. You may find the handshake lasts longer than in the West, but this is a sign of friendship. If you have made a good impression, the handshake on departure will be longer than that on arrival.
Muslims pray five times a day although shops and offices do not close during prayer. Although alcohol is not forbidden by law, like pork, it is forbidden by Islam and should be consumed with discretion. It is polite to avoid eating, drinking or smoking in the presence of Muslims during daylight hours in the month of Ramadan (it is illegal to do so in public). Unless addressing members of the royal family normal Western forms of address and greeting are usual.
Everyone, including the visitor, is subject to sharia (Islamic law) although it is less rigorously applied than in some other Islamic countries.

Security
Visitors to Bahrain should keep in touch with developments in the Middle East as any increase in regional tension might affect travel advice.
It is advisable to avoid village areas, especially after dark, and areas which have been the scene of demonstrations and incidents in the past. Local security precautions, religious and social sensitivities should be observed and respected.

Getting there
Air
National airline: Gulf Air (owned jointly with Qatar, Oman and Abu Dhabi).
International airport/s: Bahrain International, Muharraq (BAH), 6.5km north-east of city, with bar, restaurant, buffet, bank, shops, hotel reservations.
Airport tax: International departures BD3; not applicable for transit passengers.
Surface
Road: The Saudi-Bahrain Causeway links Bahrain, Saudi Arabia and Qatar.
Water: There are passenger ferries running between Iran and Bahrain; the trip takes about 16 hours each way. The route is served once every second week. There is a port tax of BD3.
Main port/s: Mina Sulman, Mina Manama and Mina Muharraq.

Bahrain

Getting about
National transport
Road: Bahrain's road network is fairly good. There are good tarmac roads between centres, and six-lane highways form a ring road by-pass system for Manama and Muharraq.
Buses: A national bus company provides public transport throughout the populated areas of the country.
Rail: There are no railways in Bahrain.
Water: Dhow trips are arranged most weekends to sand bars and nearby islands from the old wharf (Mina Manama) on King Faisal Road. Boat trips to neighbouring islands are frequently arranged on Friday and publicised in the local press.

City transport
It is easy to cover Manama and Muharraq on foot, though renting a car will make it easier to get to farther-flung locations.
Taxis: Taxis (with orange side wings and black-on-yellow number plates) are plentiful and fares are regulated. Agree a fare with the driver before booking. Fares are by meter and only vary when coming from the airport or when travelling by night. Taxis are readily available for the 6.5km journey from Bahrain International airport to Manama, for which there is a charge in addition to the meter reading. Recommended fares from the airport are displayed outside the arrivals terminal. Shared taxis or 'pick-ups' can be hailed from any bus stop. They do not use meters. Fares vary depending on the destination, but are lower than standard taxi fares. However, they can be very cramped and uncomfortable. The 'pick-ups' have white and orange number plates, and a yellow circle with the licence number in black painted on the driver's door.

Car hire
Insurance is compulsory and international driving licences must be validated at the Ministry of Interior Traffic Headquarters (near Isa Town) before use in Bahrain. Car hire firms are listed in the local telephone directory, and it is generally recommended to compare prices. Driving is on the right. Seatbelts are compulsory for both the driver and front seat passenger, and young children must be seated in the back. Road signs are in English and Arabic. The maximum speed limit on highways is 100kph, and on inner city roads it is generally between 50–80kph. If an accident occurs, the vehicle must not be moved until traffic police get to the scene.

BUSINESS DIRECTORY

The addresses listed below are a selection only. While World of Information makes every endeavour to check these addresses, we cannot guarantee that changes have not been made, especially to telephone numbers and area codes. We would welcome any corrections.

Telephone area codes
The international direct dialling code (IDD) for Bahrain is +973 followed by subscriber's number.

Useful telephone numbers
Emergency services 999
Directory enquiries 181
International enquiries 191
International bookings 151
Operator 100
Time in Arabic 141
Time in English 140
Telephone faults 121

Banking
Ahli United Bank Bahrain, 126 Government Avenue, PO Box 5941, Manama (tel: 221-700; fax: 224-322; e-mail: info@ahliunited.com).

Al Baraka Islamic Bank, PO Box 1882, Manama (tel: 535-300; fax: 533-993; e-mail: baraka@batelco.com.bh).

Arab Banking Corporation, ABC Tower, Diplomatic Area, PO Box 5698, Manama (tel: 543-000; fax: 533-163; e-mail: webmaster@arabbanking.com).

Bahrain Development Bank, PO Box 20501, Manama (tel: 537-007; fax: 534-005).

Bahrain Islamic Bank, Al Salam Tower, Diplomatic Area, PO Box 5240, Manama (tel: 535-888; fax: 535-707; e-mail: bahisi@batelco.com.bh).

Bahraini Saudi Bank, PO Box 1159, Manama (tel: 211-010; fax: 210-989; e-mail: helpdesk@bahrainisaudibank.com).

Bank of Bahrain & Kuwait, 43 Government Avenue, PO Box 597, Manama (tel: 223-388; fax: 229-822; e-mail: bbkonline@batelco.com.bh).

First Islamic Investment Bank EC, PO Box 1406, Manama (tel: 218-333; fax: 217-555).

Gulf International Bank, PO Box 1017, Al-Dowali Building, 3 Palace Avenue, Manama (tel: 534-000; fax: 522-633; e-mail: info@gibbah.com; internet site: http://www.gibonline.com).

National Bank of Bahrain, PO Box 106, Manama (tel: 228-800; fax: 228-998; e-mail: nbb@nbbonline.com).

TAIB Bank, Sehl Centre, Diplomatic Area, PO Box 20485, Manama (tel: 533-334; fax: 533-174; e-mail: taib@taib.com).

Central bank
Bahrain Monetary Agency, PO Box 27, Manama (tel: 535-535; fax: 533-342; e-mail: bmalbr@batelco.com.bh).

Travel information
Bahrain International Airport, PO Box 586, Manama (tel: 321-151; fax: 324-096).

Bahrain Tourism Company, PO Box 5831, Manama (tel: 534-321; fax: 531-353; e-mail: btc@alseyaha.com).

Gulf Air, PO Box 138, Manama (tel: 228-820; fax: 224-452).

Ministry of tourism
Tourism Affairs, Ministry of Information, PO Box 26613, Manama (tel: 201-203; fax: 211-717; e-mail: btour@bahraintourism.com).

Ministries
Ministry of Cabinet Affairs, PO Box 26141, Manama (tel: 731-544; fax: 731-863).

Ministry of Defence, PO Box 245, Manama (tel: 653-333; fax: 663-923).

Ministry of Education, PO Box 43, Manama (tel: 680-105; fax: 687-866).

Ministry of Electricity and Water, PO Box 2, Manama (tel: 546-666; fax: 533-035).

Ministry of Foreign Affairs, PO Box 547, Manama (tel: 227-555; fax: 212-603).

Ministry of Health, PO Box 12, Manama (tel: 255-555; fax: 252-569).

Ministry of Housing and Public Works, PO Box 5802, Manama (tel: 533-000; fax: 536-431).

Ministry of Information, PO Box 253, Manama (tel: 781-888; fax: 682-777).

Ministry of the Interior, PO Box 13, Manama (tel: 272-111; fax: 262-169).

Ministry of Justice and Islamic Affairs, PO Box 450, Manama (tel: 531-333; fax: 531-284).

Ministry of Labour and Social Affairs, PO Box 32333. Manama (tel: 687-800; fax: 686-954).

Ministry of Municipalities and Agriculture, PO Box 53, Manama (tel: 226-060; fax: 229-666).

Ministry of Oil, PO Box 1435, Manama (tel: 291-511; fax: 293-007).

Ministry of Transport, PO Box 10325, Manama (tel: 534-534; fax: 534-041).

Prime Minister's Office, PO Box 1000, Manama (tel: 200-000; fax: 532-839).

Other useful addresses
Aluminium Bahrain (Alba), PO Box 570, Manama (tel: 830-000; fax: 830-083; e-mail: alba@alba.com.bh).

Arabian Exhibition Management, PO Box 20200, Manama (tel: 550-033; fax: 553-288; aeminfo@batelco.com.bh).

Bahrain International Exhibition Centre, PO Box 11644, Manama (tel: 550-111;

fax: 553-447; e-mail: biec@batelco.com.bh).

Bahrain National Gas Company (Banagas), PO Box 29099, Manama (tel: 756-222; fax: 756-991; e-mail: bng@banagas.com.bh).

Bahrain Petroleum Company (Bapco), PO Box 25555, Awali (tel: 704-040; fax: 704-070; e-mail: info@bapco.net).

Bahrain Stock Exchange, PO Box 3203, Manama (tel: 261-260; fax: 256-362; e-mail: info@bahrainstock.com).

Central Municipal Council, PO Box 53, Manama (tel: 276-060; fax: 263-666).

Consultative Council (Majlis al-Shura), PO Box 2991 Manama (tel: 714-422; fax: 715-715).

Customs Directorate, PO Box 15, Manama (tel: 725-333; fax: 725-534).

Ports Directorate, PO Box 453, Manama (tel: 725-555; fax: 725-534).

Internet sites

Arab Banking Corporation BSC: http://www.arabbanking.com

Arab Net: http://www.arab.net

Arabia OnLine: http://www.arabia.com

Bahrain Promotions and Marketing Board: http://www.bpmb.com

Gulf business explorer: http://www.igulf.com/main.htm

Bangladesh

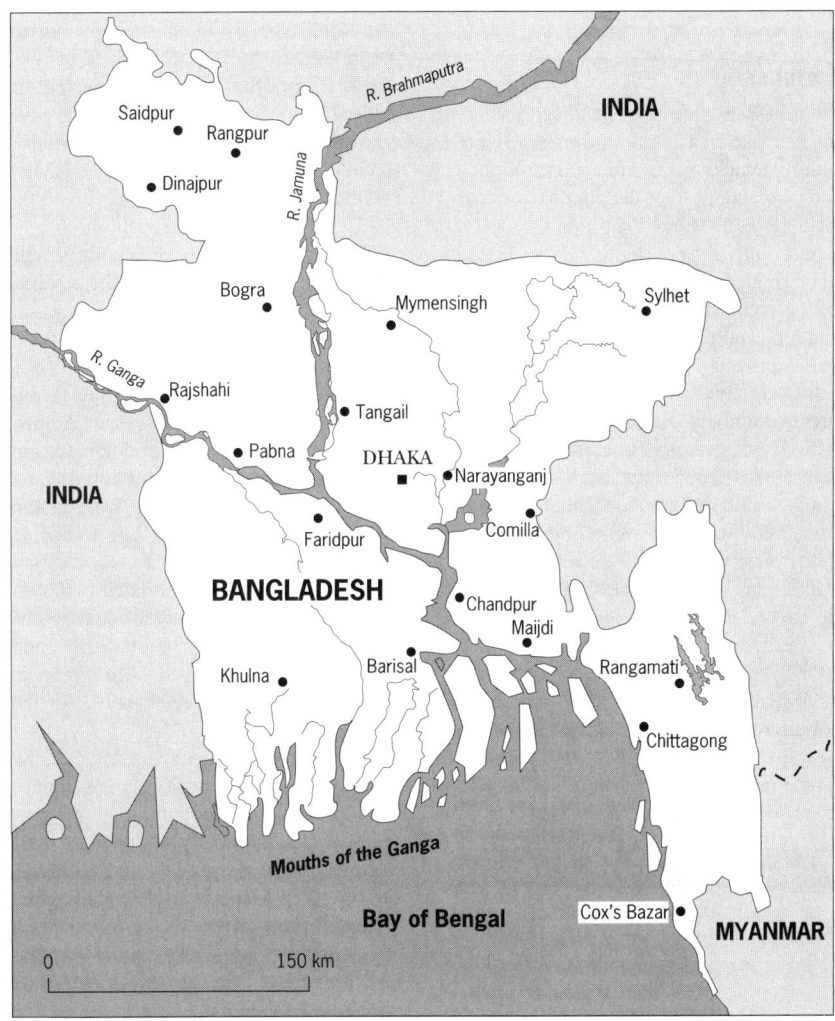

KEY FACTS

Official name: Gana Prajatantri Bangladesh (People's Republic of Bangladesh)

Head of State: President Iajuddin Ahmed (sworn in 6 Sep 2002)

Head of government: Prime Minister Begum Khaleda Zia (BNP) (elected 1 Oct 2001)

Ruling party: Four-party alliance led by Bangladesh Jatiyatabadi Dal (Bangladesh Nationalist Party) (BNP) (elected Oct 2001)

Area: 143,998 square km

Population: 146.39 million (2004)

Capital: Dhaka

Official language: Bengali (Bangla)

Currency: Taka (Tk) = 100 poisha

Exchange rate: Tk65.73 per US$ (Oct 2005)

GDP per capita: US$376 (2004)

GDP real growth: 5.40% (2004); *5.25% (2005)

Labour force: 72.39 million (2004)

Unemployment: 40.00% (2004) (includes underemployment)

Inflation: 6.10% (2004) *6.5% (2005)

Balance of trade: -US$2.55 billion (2004)

Foreign debt: US$19.97 billion (2004)

* Estimated figure

The year 2005 was a turbulent one in Bangladesh with severe floods and storms, the rise of domestic terrorist attacks and the country's first ever suicide bombing. The government has been forced to admit the unstable security situation and introduce new counter-terrorism laws, although before this year it claimed the country had no problem with extremists. The biggest triumph of the year was on the sports field: in June 2005 the country celebrated beating the world champions, Australia, at cricket in a one-day match. Bangladesh is considered one of the weakest sides in the international cricket league and their success defied bookmakers the world over.

Disaster

This year has been characteristically bad in terms of natural and manmade disasters. Ferry accidents are endemic in a country with many rivers prone to storms and flooding. Bad weather conditions are exacerbated by chronic overcrowding on public transport and a refusal to implement passenger number limits. The number of dead is often uncertain as there is no record of who travels on the ferries. In February 2005 120 people died when a ferry sunk in the Buriganga river near Dhaka during heavy storms. In May 60 people died on a ferry in storms in the south of the country. The ferry's capacity was limited legally to 80 people but was probably holding 200 when it capsized. Two days later a fishing boat tipped over near the capital Dhaka, killing nearly fifty. In the same week a third vessel sank, this time in the Meghna river. The combined death toll of this single fatal week reached 150. Another 25 people were feared to have died on a ferry heading towards Chittagong in November 2005 as a result of strong currents.

Severe weather which struck northern villages in March 2005 was to blame for a further 80 deaths. With winds of 100 kph, tornadoes damaged and blew away homes, crops and electricity supplies. 3,000 poorly constructed homes were destroyed. Heavy flooding in September caused a 3-metre rise in the waters of the Bay of Bengal and dozens of deaths.

In April 2005 a nine-storey factory collapsed in Savar in the country's central region, killing over 70 people. The building was illegally constructed on marshland and was demolished when the boiler blew up. This kind of incident is common due to unenforced legislation but there is international pressure on Bangladesh to ensure that its factories meet international safety and workplace standards. There is growing domestic agitation for greater safety measures too – in 2004 20 workplace protests were carried out. In March 2005 the UN appealed to Bangladeshi workers to enter into negotiations rather than engage in mass strikes to express labour grievances, because strikes and lost working days exert significant damage on the country's economy. There is doubt over the prospects for improved safety in Bangladeshi workplaces, however, because compliance with international labour standards could drive prices up and sales down.

Terrorism

2005 in Bangladesh was characterised by an increase in Islamic extremism. Unrelenting attacks were launched throughout the year and all over the country, but particularly targeting the judicial sector. Courtrooms and court workers are thought to be singled out because they are symbols of the secularism which militants wish to see replaced by Islamic rule. In a related development, madrasas, (Koranic schools), have been springing up in ever greater numbers. There are now thought to be 8,000 madrasas in operation.

In January 2005 three members of an Islamic militant group, Jagrata Muslim Janata (JMJ), were lynched by local residents near the country's western border with India. This led to clashes between the police and suspected extremists. Soon afterwards, an ex-finance minister belonging to the Bangladeshi opposition party, Shah AMS Kibria, was assassinated with a grenade thrown during a political rally. Five people died in total while many others sustained injuries. Three days of anti-government demonstrations, organised by the opposition Awami League, followed the deaths.

Eight development workers were injured in a series of attacked suspected of being carried out by Islamic extremists in February 2005. Homemade bombs were launched at the offices of the Bangladesh Rural Advancement Committee (Brac) and the Grameen Bank, both of which work for women's advancement.

A professor of Arabic, Muhammad Asadullah al Ghalib, was arrested in connection with the attacks, suspected of leading a fundamentalist faction. The government then banned two Islamic groups, Jamatul Mujahideen Bangladesh (JMB) and the JMJ and arrested 15 individuals on charges of incitement to rebellion.

The banning of these two Islamic groups was one of the first signs that the government was taking the threat seriously – it had been denying any problem until now. However, the ban did not stop the JMB implementing a co-ordinated attack involving 400 small explosives in August 2005. The devices were detonated in crowded spots throughout the country and killed two people. Leaflets were found calling for American and UK troops to leave Muslim territories.

In October 2005 co-ordinated bomb attacks were carried out in courtrooms around Lakshmipur, Chittagong and Chandpur. The outlawed JMB group is thought to have been responsible for the violence.

In November another attack targeted the legal system, this time killing two judges in the south of the country. The government reacted by swiftly outlawing a third Islamic group, Harkat-ul-Jihad al-Islami, or Huji. This group is also illegal in Britain and is thought to seek the introduction of a strict Islamic government in Bangladesh to replace the current secular rule. Huji is thought to have been implicated in the series of bombings in October and in the attempted murder of one-time prime minister, Sheikh Hasina.

In November 2005 the politician Abu Hena was expelled from the Bangladesh National Party, accused of sympathising with terrorists and for making allegations that the ruling coalition are complicit with terrorist factions. In the same month Bangladesh suffered its first ever suicide-bombing attack, carried out near a Gazipur courthouse and synchronised with an explosion in Chittagong. Nine people were killed. The prohibited organisations, JMB and JMJ, were the suspected culprits. Police and security forces fear that Jamaat-ul-Mujahideen has recruited

KEY INDICATORS — Bangladesh

	Unit	2000	2001	2002	2003	2004
Population	m	137.44	140.37	142.34	144.36	146.39
Gross domestic product (GDP)	US$bn	37.50	46.90	47.60	51.90	*56.84
GDP per capita	US$	291	334	333	358	376
GDP real growth	%	5.9	5.2	4.4	5.3	5.4
Inflation	%	3.4	1.4	5.0	6.0	6.1
Natural gas output	bn cum	10.3	10.8	11.2	12.2	13.2
Exports (fob) (goods)	US$m	6,399.2	6,467.0	5,930.0	6,549.0	7,478.0
Imports (fob) (goods)	US$m	8,052.9	9,363.0	7,700.0	8,707.0	10,030.0
Balance of trade	US$m	-1,653.7	-2,896.0	-1,768.0	-2,158.0	-2,552.0
Current account	US$m	-305.8	-806.0	240.0	–	-670.0
Foreign debt	US$bn	16.6	15.3	17.0	16.5	20.0
Total reserves minus gold	US$m	1,486.0	1,275.0	1,683.2	2,577.9	3,172.4
Foreign exchange	US$m	1,485.3	1,273.6	1,680.7	2,574.4	3,170.9
Exchange rate	per US$	52.14	55.81	57.58	58.39	59.28

* estimated figure

up to 2,000 potential suicide bombers. In December 2005 the government reacted to widespread security concerns by announcing that it would start monitoring telephone calls. Bangladeshi terrorists are known to plan their operations using mobile phones, of which there are eight million in use in the country. Following this announcement, the chief of the banned Jamaat-ul-Mujahideen group, Ataur Rahman Sunny, was arrested in Dhaka and found with explosives and weapons. This was a significant arrest and brings the total of arrested suspected extremists to 800.

In December the government declared the introduction of new counter-terrorism laws, allowing the imposition of the death penalty for convicted terrorists. Terrorist trials will also be accelerated. These measures bring some reassurance to the international community who suspect Bangladesh has been turning a blind eye to the intensification of anti-West and extremist sentiment, and to the development of terrorist capabilities.

Most, but not all, attacks were thought to be the work of Islamic fundamentalists. However, in October 2005, Mizanur Rahman, of the opposition group, the Bangladesh National Party, was assassinated in the town of Khulna and an illegal Maoist group is suspected to be behind the attack. The local Maoist presence has been found guilty of similar assaults on politicians and journalists in the past.

Foreign relations

There was sustained low-level tension between the normally amicable neighbours, India and Bangladesh, in 2005, which peaked in three hours of gunfire across their mutual border in March. The dispute was over an Indian fence which Bangladesh claims violates a no-build zone agreed in 1974. Then, in April, Indian border guards were accused of killing two Bangladeshi farmers – and Indian officials condemned Bangladesh for allowing military helicopters to stray into Indian territory. In August 2005 three people were killed in further border skirmishes provoked by mutual accusations of illegal construction on the banks of the Mahananda river. Villagers were evacuated on the Indian side for fear of violent fallout.

In September 2005 representatives from both Bangladesh and India met in Dhaka to resolve disagreements about water use in the Teesta river. They have both decided to reduce claims for water and share the river resources. India has also agreed not to link up the Ganges and the Brahmaputra rivers, in a large-scale project which was predicted would bring significant environmental damage to Bangladesh. Border skirmishes died down after this agreement.

Khaleda Zia, the Bangladeshi prime minister, made a speech in March 2005 condemning foreign interference in domestic affairs. NGOs and foreign governments have criticised the country's human rights reputation and insufficient counter-terrorism measures. The high profile US Assistant Secretary of State, Christina Rocca, visited Bangladesh in May 2005. She used this opportunity to condemn the Bangladeshi record on political violence in the wake of a spate of deaths – estimated to be 100 in the course of 2004–05. The UN criticised Bangladesh in July 2005 for accommodating 6,000 fleeing Burmese nationals on an unsafe tidal island. In response Bangladesh claimed the refugees, who left Burma during the 1990s junta, are illegal immigrants and they should leave the country. This group, the majority of whom have not been granted refugee status, have been largely forgotten and ignored by the international community, and live in fear of repatriation. In August 2005 Amnesty International accused Bangladesh of not doing enough to promote human rights, and letting known abusers walk free.

In November 2005 Bangladeshi corruption was to blame for a significant cancellation of aid by the World Bank. The Bank had planned to invest US$1 million in developing health services in the country but on the discovery of collusive bidding for the contract, it withdrew. However in November 2005 the government did successfully agree a four-year aid plan in conjunction with the UN Development Programme (UNDP). US$50 million will be poured into the troubled region of the Chittagong Hill Tracts in the hope of implementing a now faltering 1997 peace agreement. Rebels from the Jana Shangati Samity (JSS) group fighting for independence for the area have been involved in internal skirmishes and collisions with security forces for 20 years. It is hoped that a new injection of cash will raise living standards, combat poverty and so contribute to political stability in the region.

Economy

Bangladesh is ranked 158, officially joint bottom, in the Transparency International corruption survey, and has occupied this ignoble position for five years. Its degree of corruption was calculated at 1.7 out of 10 by the business community (10 being very clean). Tax evasion is rife and taxation revenue very low, which in 2005 contributed to the increase of the fiscal deficit. Tax reforms are under way but have not achieved any rise in revenue to date.

Overall fiscal management in 2005 was good. The economy continued its general upward trend with GDP growth estimated at 5.25 per cent. Macroeconomic stability was commended by the IMF Executive Board, especially as it was achieved in spite of political unrest.

Bangladesh's reputation for corruption did not stop a huge foreign investment deal going ahead in May 2005. The American company Global Vulcan Energy agreed to invest US$1.6 billion in fertiliser and power companies in Bangladesh. It is one of the biggest ever investments in the country's history. This was followed in November 2005 by an announcement by the Indian conglomerate, Tata, that it will invest even more money – US$3 billion – in the same areas. Tata will build a steel plant and a coal-fired power plant in the poor west of Bangladesh, which would expand the country's energy sector. These two large investments combined should give a significant boost to Bangladeshi infrastructure and, in turn, improve the exports market.

The factory-produced textiles sector, which makes up 75 per cent of the Bangladeshi exports market, experienced real change in 2005. In January the Multifibre Arrangement (MFA) production quotas, which had in effect guaranteed Bangladesh a role in the global market, were removed. This legislation had been introduced in the 1970s and its removal is one of the most significant recent events in the global economy. Retailers are now free to find the cheapest markets without restrictions. This deregulation means potentially much greater demand for Bangladeshi-made garments in the future, although it also puts great pressure on prices. Initially textile exports to the US and knitwear sales to the EU encountered good growth in sales: knitwear sales expanded by one third. However, EU demand for woven goods dropped. Overall, exports grew 14 per cent in 2004/05.

In June 2005 a populist budget was released to the public, including a US$100 million increase in agricultural subsidies. Bangladeshi finance minister, Saifur Rahman, earmarked US$10 billion for civil service administration costs, but also proposed increased welfare handouts. The once-cancelled export subsidy levied on the textile industry was re-introduced. The opposition Awami League, condemned the budget proposals as unfeasible.

Indeed the new budget measures did not manage to stabilise the economy before August 2005, when officials announced the creation of a two day weekend. From August government offices have been closing on Saturdays as well as Fridays and in a cost-cutting measure. The economy is in a fragile state due to lower than expected crop yields, which have been poor as a result of the summer's heavy storms and flooding. The annual harvest produced 4 per cent less food than in 2004. Rising global oil prices have also impacted negatively on the economy – savings of up to US$12 million are expected to be made on fuel costs as a result of an extra day's holiday per week. The working day will be one hour longer instead, although private practices are not affected by these measures and will continue with a six-day week.

Higher food prices as a result of shortages, along with flood relief efforts, contributed to the year's inflationary rise, up to 6.5 per cent. Imports grew more than exports in 2005, which contributed to the instability of the exchange rate. Foreign exchange reserves fell by US$200 million. GDP growth is projected at 5.5 per cent for 2006, driven by a stronger performance in the agriculture sector and growth in industry.

Social Developments

In March 2005 the Bangladeshi government outlawed smoking in public, including schools, workplaces and public transport. This, it is hoped, will go some way to curbing the high rates of smoking, and the huge cost of medical treatment for smoking-related diseases. Bangladesh had previously, in an uncharacteristically environmentally friendly move, banned all polythene bags in 2002. Amid fears of famine in September 2005 the government started a free food distribution scheme for the poorest. A bad harvest had sent the price of rice rocketing and led to a shortage in supply.

In August 2005 Bangladesh's two year old village governments, Gram Sarkars, were ruled illegal by the country's high court. They had been intended to localise government and administration, but were condemned for being undemocratic and unconstitutional.

Outlook

The government needs to implement, not just announce, counter-terrorism measures if the country is to stabilise and reduce the high numbers of bombs attacks. A primary barrier to economic growth is the corruption record: the government has made little effort to tackle this inveterate culture, but if this was to change, FDI could rocket. Similarly, a corruption crackdown would bring in much greater taxation revenues.

Agriculture and harvests are set to recover in 2006 and inflation is expected to fall to 6 per cent. Rising global oil prices are a concern but the government has so far managed to absorb a lot of the increases – consumers have not yet felt the full effects.

Elections will be held in January 2007: these could be preceded by further instability.

Risk assessment

Economic	Stable
Political	Poor
Regional Stability	Poor
Stock Market	Stable

COUNTRY PROFILE

Historical profile
1200 The start of five-and-a-half centuries of Muslim rule over the region began with the Sultanate era.
1757 The region gradually came under the influence of British rule after the battle of Plassey.
1947 Named East Pakistan, Bangladesh became a province of Pakistan following the partition of India.
1949 The Awami League (AL) was established to campaign for East Pakistan's autonomy from West Pakistan.
1970 The AL, under Sheikh Mujibur Rahman, won the elections in East Pakistan, but West Pakistan refused to accept the result, resulting in civil unrest.
1971 The People's Republic of Bangladesh was unilaterally declared; a de facto secession from Pakistan followed the nine-month Indo-Pakistan war. Around 10 million Bangladeshis fled to India during the conflict.
1972 Sheikh Mujibur became prime minister and, in an attempt to improve living standards, began a programme of industrial nationalisation.
1974 Severe flooding destroyed much of the grain harvest. A state of a emergency was declared as political unrest grew. A famine killed 100,000 people as wealthy farmers hoarded food that the poor could not afford to buy.
1975 Sheikh Mujibur became president, but was assassinated in a military coup. Martial law was imposed following the coup.
1976 Elections were postponed indefinitely. General Zia ur Rahman took over the post of Chief Martial Law Administrator from President Sayem.
1977 General Zia assumed the presidency, amending the constitution, making Islam, instead of secularism, its first basic principle.
1978 General Zia won the first direct presidential election.
1979 Parliamentary elections were won by Zia's Bangladesh Jatiyatabadi Dal (Bangladesh Nationalist Party) (BNP). Martial law was repealed and the state of emergency revoked.
1981 General Zia was assassinated.
1982 General Ershad seized power in a bloodless coup. The country was placed under martial law as the constitution and political parties were suspended.
1983–86 The country remained unstable, with opposition groups demanding the resignation of Ershad and his government. Ershad imposed Islam on the education system and forced teachers to teach in Arabic. This led to social unrest, particularly among the non-Muslim minority.
1986 Martial law ended and constitutional government was revived. Ershad was elected to a five-year term.
1987 A state of emergency was imposed during a wave of strikes and opposition demonstrations.
1988 Islam became the state religion. Floods covered around 75 per cent of the land and millions of people were made homeless.
1990 Ershad resigned following mass protests which made the country ungovernable.
1991 Elections resulted in a victory for the BNP, led by Begum Khaleda Zia, the widow of General Zia; she became prime minister. Ershad was jailed for corruption and the illegal possession of weapons. The position of president was made ceremonial and executive power was given to the office of prime minister.
1996 After two decades of military and authoritarian rule, the AL, led by Sheikh Hasina (Sheikh Mujibur's daughter), won the election .
1998 Floods covered two-thirds of the country, causing many deaths. Fifteen former army officers were sentenced to death for their involvement in the assassination of President Mujibur.
2000 Sheikh Hasina spoke out against military regimes and the government expelled a Pakistani diplomat for denying that three million Bangladeshis were murdered by Pakistani forces in 1971. Diplomatic relations broke down between Bangladesh and Pakistan.
2001 There were violent clashes, strikes and a growth in Islamic fundamentalism in the build-up to parliamentary elections. The alliance led by Zia's BNP won a

Bangladesh

landslide victory. AQM Badruddoza Chowdhury was sworn in as president.
2002 Chowdhury resigned and Iajuddin Ahmed was sworn in as president.
2004 The AL called 21 general strikes in a campaign to force early elections, accusing the government of being corrupt. The constitution was amended to reserve 45 parliamentary seats for women. Floods in July covered two-thirds of the country, killing over 800 people. Sheikh Hasina survived a grenade attack that killed 22 people at a party rally.
2005 In January a senior AL politician, Shah AMS Kibria, was killed in a grenade attack. In February a ferry capsized near Dhaka and killed over 140 people. Bangladesh signed the South Asia Free Trade Agreement (Safta), due to come into effect on 1 January 2006. Bombings aound the country in August and November blamed on Islamic militants.

Political structure
Constitution
The constitution was enacted in 1972. It was suspended following the coup of 1982, restored in 1986, and has been amended several times.
In 1977, the constitution was amended making Islam, instead of secularism, its first basic principle.
The country has six political divisions: Dhaka, Chittagong, Rajshahi, Barisal, Sylhet and Khulna. These are further subdivided into districts, thanas (parish-level government) and villages.

Form of state
Parliamentary republic

The executive
The president, who is elected by the legislature for a five-year term, performs ceremonial functions. The president is also commander-in-chief of the armed forces. The cabinet is led by the prime minister, who is usually the leader of the ruling party. The elections are preceded by a 'caretaker' government which is supposed to have no political affiliation, in order to allow elections to be fought on an equal and fair basis.

National legislature
Legislative authority is vested in the Jatiya Sangsad (parliament), a unicameral legislature; 300 members are elected by popular vote from single territorial constituencies every five years.
Over and above the 300 directly elected members, the May 2004 constitutional amendment includes reservation of 45 seats for women (formerly 30 seats were reserved), on a proportional representation basis for the next 10 years.

Legal system
The judiciary is a civil court system based on the British model. The highest court of appeal is the appellate division of the Supreme Court.

Last elections
October 2001 (parliamentary and presidential)
Results: Parliamentary: the four-party alliance led by Begum Khaleda Zia's Bangladesh Jatiyatabadi Dal (Bangladesh Nationalist Party) (BNP) won a landslide victory.
Presidential: A Q M Badruddoza Chowdhury was elected by parliament.

Next elections
October 2006 (parliamentary and presidential)

Political parties
Ruling party
Four-party alliance led by Bangladesh Jatiyatabadi Dal (Bangladesh Nationalist Party) (BNP) (elected Oct 2001)
Main opposition party
Awami League (AL) (People's League)

Population
146.39 million (2004)
Ethnic make-up
Bengalis (98 per cent) and Biharis. There are about one million tribal people, the majority of whom live in the Chittagong Hill Tracts in the east of the country. The tribes have distinct cultures of their own.
Religions
Islam (88 per cent), Hinduism (10 per cent), Buddhism and Christianity. Although Islam is the state religion, freedom of worship is guaranteed under the constitution.

Education
The investment in education amounts to 2.2 per cent of GDP.
In November 2003, the Asian Development Bank (ADB) announced it was leading the jointly financed Second Primary Education Development Program (PEDP-II), designed to reorganise primary education in Bangladesh, with a US$1.815 billion package, including US$654 million external financing, provided by, among others, 11 international donors. The programme will run over the six-year period 2004–09. The package includes a 32-year, US$100 million, loan. The objectives of PEDP-II are to raise standards in school governance, and teacher training, improve the quality of school buildings and enhance the accessibility of schooling for students, particularly those from poor families.
By 2004 nearly 18 million students were enrolled in over 78,000 primary level schools, in the world's largest primary education system. Bangladesh has gender parity and has strived to expand access to the very poor and disadvantaged, including those with special needs. Enrolment rates suggest that about four million primary school-aged children are absent from school and about one-third of children drop out before completing primary school; children in remote rural and tribal regions still have significantly less access to schooling. Despite Bangladesh's official policy of gender parity, gender differences in learning persist.
Government programmes include free education for girls up to class 10 and stipends for female students; food-for-education; and the total literacy movement.
Madrasas (schools offering an Islamic education to Muslim boys and girls) have increased in number from 1,500 in 1970 to 8,000 in 2004. Hindus and Buddhists also receive religious education at institutes called *Tol* and *Chatuspathi*.
Literacy rate: 41.1 per cent adult rate; 31.4 per cent female rate (World Bank).
Compulsory years: Six to 10
Enrolment rate: 98 per cent in primary education (2003) (ADB). Bangladesh aims to achieve universal primary school enrolment by 2015.
Pupils per teacher: 55 overall, and 67 in state schools (ADB 2003)

Health
In June 2003, the World Bank approved a US$300 million loan to implement the Poverty Reduction Strategy (PRS) and is taking a leading role in helping Bangladesh implement an integrated Health and Population Sector Programme. The focus is on nutrition, HIV/Aids and maternal and infant health.
In the past decade, the infant mortality rate has been reduced by half – a faster reduction than any other country. With the highest incidence of malnutrition in the world, Bangladesh has made great efforts to improve the nutritional status of women and children.
Primary health care facilities have been expanded throughout the country and are provided though government sponsored Union and Thana Health Complexes; secondary health care facilities are provided by District level hospitals, and tertiary healthcare facilities through Medical College Hospitals, Post-graduate Institutes and specialised hospitals at divisional and national levels.
It is estimated that at least 1.2 million people are exposed to poisoning by naturally occurring arsenic in groundwater, and about 40 million of Bangladesh's 144 million people are considered at risk. Since 1993, experts have found that tube wells in more than half of Bangladesh's 64 districts (mainly in the south-western, middle and north-eastern parts of the country) are likely to be contaminated with arsenic. The effects may take as long a 14 years to become visible but treatment can

be successful before levels of poison reaches a certain level.
A cheap filter, costing around US$4, was launched in 2002, which can process 25–30 litres of drinking water a day, enough for a family of five.

HIV/Aids
The HIV prevalence rate among adults between is relatively low; the rates among high-risk groups are greater – sex workers 0.5 per cent and unregistered injecting drug uses 1.7 per cent (World Bank).

HIV prevalence: 0.03 per cent ages of 15-49

Life expectancy: 62.4 years (World Bank)

Fertility rate/Maternal mortality rate: 2.9 births per woman (in 2003); maternal deaths 440 per 100,000 live births (World Bank).

Birth rate/Death rate: 28 births and 8 deaths per 1,000 (World Bank)

Infant mortality rate: 46 per 1,000 live births (World Bank)

Head of population per physician/bed: 0.2 physicians and 0.3 hospital beds per 1,000 people

Welfare
Over 67 million people live below the poverty line, and Bangladesh still has the highest incidence of poverty in South Asia; only India and China have higher numbers of poor. Added to which, Bangladesh has one of the highest density populations (roughly 800 people per square kilometre), however it has achieved near self sufficiency in food production and made good progress in improving natural disaster management and social safety nets. In the 2002/03 budget, an allowance of Tk125 each was given to 900,000 people, (up from a previous 600,000), deemed disadvantaged: orphans, retarded, very-old, widows, and deserted women.

The World Bank suggests that while economic development and lasting poverty reduction is being hampered by the absence of reliable power (an estimated 10 million rural households lack access to electricity), even poor households are eager to join community-based saving projects such as Safe Save, and the Social Investment Program Project designed to give the poor in remote areas access to decision-making processes through small-scale infrastructure and social assistance projects. Communities will be expected to provide participation by contributing at least 15 per cent of the expenditure needed and donors the remaining 85 per cent.

Main cities
Dhaka (capital, estimated population 9.4 million in 2004), Chittagong (2.6 million), Khulna (1.2 million), Rajshahi (712,400), Gazipur (520,800), Narayanganj (357,300), Comilla (318,600), Sylhet (307,500), Bogra (228,200).

Languages spoken
Bengali (Bangla) is spoken by 95 per cent of the population. The remaining 5 per cent speak various tribal dialects.
English is widely spoken and understood within the business community.

Official language/s
Bengali (Bangla)

Media
Press
Dailies: There are 83 national daily newspapers and 43 other daily periodicals, published in both Bengali and English.
Main English newspapers are *The Bangladesh Observer*, *The Bangladesh Times*, *The Daily Star*, *New Nation*, *The Independent* and *The Financial Express*.
Ittefaq is the most popular Bengali daily.
The Daily Inquilab is a bi-lingual daily newspaper.
Weeklies: *Muktakantha* and *JaiJaiDin* are weeklies published in Bengali. *Dhaka Courier* is an English language news weekly. *Holiday* is a weekly publication in English.
Periodicals: There are a number of fortnightly and monthly publications in both Bengali and English. *Nabajug* is a popular monthly covering articles, news and poetry.

Broadcasting
Radio: Radio Bangladesh has nine stations. Broadcasts are mainly in Bengali. However, there are daily programmes in English, Hindi, Arabic, Urdu and Nepalese. Radio Bangladesh also runs an external service beamed in seven languages towards Europe, the Middle East, Pakistan, India and Nepal.
Television: There are 10 relay stations at Chittagong, Sylhet, Khulna, Natore, Mymensing, Rangpur, Noakhali, Satkhira, Cox's Bazar and Rangamati.
Broadcasts are mainly in Bengali. There are also daily programmes in English, Hindi, Arabic, Urdu and Nepalese.

Advertising
Newspapers, radio and television accept advertising, as do some cinemas. Outdoor advertising sites in major towns, and some direct mail services are available.

Economy
Although there has been significant and continuous improvement of social indicators, Bangladesh has the highest incidence of poverty in Asia with around 45 per cent of people living below the poverty line. Vulnerability to typhoons, annual flooding and high population density obstruct development and place a huge strain on infrastructure. Floods in July 2004 alone affected a quarter of the population and damaged over 3 million homes. Poverty rates are in decline, with improvements in healthcare and education triggering social improvement.
The government is dedicated to reforms aimed at the liberalisation and stabilisation of the state-dominated economy. Annual GDP growth has averaged five per cent since 1995. Inflation remains in single figures, but is rising. The environment of reform has attracted some foreign direct investment (FDI) into the economy and created an entrepreneurial spirit. The main problem in attracting FDI is the crumbling physical infrastructure with little, if any, investment in ports, customs and trade-supporting utilities. This has helped foster the de-industrialisation of Bangladesh with a contraction in the manufacturing sector.
The government's target is to increase the growth rate to at least 8 per cent per annum in order to eliminate poverty by 2021. Despite its relatively high level of growth, Bangladesh remains one of the poorest and most vulnerable countries in the world. Government revenues rely on foreign aid, which contributes 40 per cent to total revenue figures. International financial institutions continue to urge the government to tackle obstacles to development by changing and introducing policies.

External trade
Bangladesh was one of the 32 developing nations designated in 1985 for exemption from US competitive trade requirements in accordance with the Generalised System of Preferences. A liberal trade policy was introduced.
There are export processing zones in Chittagong, Dhaka, and Gazipur. Wholly foreign-owned companies are permitted to operate in these zones, but both Indian and foreign companies have to export their entire output in order to qualify for exemption from customs duties.

Imports
Main imports are manufactured goods, machinery and transport equipment, petroleum and petroleum products, chemicals and pharmaceuticals, cement, raw cotton, food, vegetable oil, fats and foodgrains.
Main sources: India (14.6 per cent total, 2004), China (11.7 per cent), Singapore (7.8 per cent), Japan (5.8 per cent), Hong Kong (4.8 per cent)

Exports
Main exports typically include jute manufactures and raw jute (over 20 per cent of total), garments, frozen fish and seafood, leather, ceramics and tea.

Main destinations: US (22.7 per cent total, 2004), Germany (14.5 per cent), UK (10.8 per cent), France (6.7 per cent)

Agriculture
Farming
Agriculture dominates the economy and contributes around 20 per cent to GDP. It employs 66 per cent of the labour force and determines incomes and consumption for the vast majority of Bangladeshis. Bangladesh is largely self-sufficient in food grains, although a food deficit may occur when weather conditions are adverse.

Rice is the principal crop, accounting for about 70 per cent of cropped land. Improvements in rice production have been achieved through research, which has produced high-yielding rice varieties, improved farming methods, greater use of fertiliser and more widespread irrigation. Agricultural employment increased with the use of high-yield rice, which is between 20 and 50 per cent more labour-intensive than traditional varieties. Other crops are pulses, wheat, jute, oil seeds, sugar cane, tea, spices, vegetables and fruit. The livestock sector contributes about 3 per cent to GDP.

The amount of cultivable land under irrigation has increased to about 35 per cent. Much of the land is broken into tiny plots. Farms of less than one acre account for about 40 per cent, while about 5 per cent of farm households own and operate more than 25 per cent of agricultural land. The government leases farm machinery to groups of farmers forming co-operatives and increasing farm sizes. Bangladesh is the world's largest exporter of raw jute and jute goods, amounting to around half of the world shipments. The jute industry has been restructured and modernised with aid from the World Bank. About 2 per cent of the world's tea is grown in Bangladesh on some 150 plantations in the north-east region of Sylhet. After meeting domestic demand, a significant amount is exported to other Asian countries and Europe.

Crop production in 2004 included 37,910,000 tonnes rice, 4,000,000t cassava, 1,253,000t wheat, 3,908,000t potatoes, 6,484,000t sugar cane, 320,000t sweet potatoes, 800,000t jute, 700,000t bananas, 211,000t rapeseed (canola), 243,000t mangoes, 138,000t allspice, 10,000t maize, 57,000t millet, 89,000t coconuts, 48,000t ginger, 122,000t lentils, 352,000t pulses, 103,000t tomatoes, 65,627t tea, 40,000t tobacco, 48,000t citrus fruit, 146,170t oilcrops, 45,000t seed cotton, 1,605,000t fruit in total, 2,059,000t vegetables in total. Livestock production included 440,600t meat in total, 180,000t beef, 3,600t buffalo meat, 133,000t lamb & goat meat, 115,000t poultry, 115,000t eggs, 2,175,930t milk, 30,600t cattle hides,

Fishing
Fishing has been identified by the government as a rapidly growing sector with increased production, which could generate revenue and foreign earnings while improving local nutrition. The sector has grown by 8 per cent per year since 1996 and contributes 3.3 per cent to GDP and directly employs around 1.3 million people. The typical annual catch is over 1.7 million tonnes.

Development by government, NGOs and private initiatives include: new hatcheries, extensive marine fisheries in the Bay of Bengal, south of the country, supporting infrastructure and training programmes.

Forestry
Bangladesh's total forest cover is estimated at 1.3 million hectares. The forestry sector typically contributes about 2.5 per cent to GDP, providing raw materials for the construction industry.

Bangladesh is one of the world's most densely populated countries and, as a consequence, its forests are subject to heavy demand pressures, both in wood production and competing land uses. An estimated 80 per cent of wood production is used for fuel; most of the remainder is converted to sawnwood. Coastal forests comprise mangroves, which account for nearly half of total forest cover, and bamboo. Inland valley forests comprise *sal, gamari, chaplish, telsu, jarui, teak, garjan, chandon* and *sundari*.

The import of forest products in 2004 amounted to US$197 million, while exports amounted to US$421,000. Production in 2004 included: 27.9 million cubic metres (cum) roundwood, 282,000cum industrial roundwood, 388,000 cum sawnwood, 174,000 cum sawlogs and veneers, 27.7 million cum woodfuel, 304,016 tonnes charcoal.

Industry and manufacturing
The industrial sector accounts for around 26 per cent of GDP and employs 10 per cent of the workforce. Some 40 per cent of industrial capacity is publicly-owned, mostly in jute and textile milling, steel and chemical production. Around one-third of fixed assets in manufacturing enterprises are held by the public sector, but account for less than 10 per cent of output. The main activities are jute processing, contributing around 15 per cent to gross manufacturing output, and cotton spinning and weaving.

The garment industry, which is the principal exporter, grew rapidly during the 1990s, helped by economic liberalisation, fiscal incentives and a relatively disciplined workforce. It is the largest industrial employer, with about 1.5 million workers.

Other industries include leather goods, newsprint, cement, refined sugar, beverages, pharmaceuticals, electronic components and fertilisers. The US$510 million fertiliser plant in Chittagong exports 500 tonnes of ammonia and 1,725 tonnes of urea a day, mainly to India and China; earnings are estimated at US$100 million a year.

Bangladesh has established export processing zones in Chittagong, Dhaka, and Gazipur. Improving the efficiency and flexibility of labour and the financial markets and public enterprise reform will be critical for the performance of the industrial sector.

Long-term financing is virtually impossible to obtain and few companies have access to overseas financing, resulting in only modest growth in the industrial sector, the garments industry aside. Low wage rates, labour and an entrepreneurial society make the country an ideal manufacturing base, although poor infrastructure, high tariffs, corruption and bad governance still need to be addressed. Power constraints are also cited as a reason for low investment, although the government has opened the energy sector to private and foreign investment.

Tourism
Tourism is undeveloped in Bangladesh. The government recognised the potential of the sector in the early 1990s, but promotion has been minimal. Bangladesh's proneness to natural disasters, especially flooding, is a disadvantage. The 11 September 2001 terrorist attacks in the US, the ensuing Afghan war and the Sars scare in 2003 adversely affected the sector. Of around 200,000 visitors, only a fifth are holiday-makers.

Environment
In 2002, a ban was put on the production and use of polythene bags which had caused serious problems blocking the drainage system.

Mining
The 550km of coastline hold large resources of beachsands with rare mineral deposits spread over 17 areas containing monazite, ilmenite, zircon, rutile and magnetite. There are large limestone deposits, which are used to produce cement. The Jaipurhat Limestone Mining and Cement Works extracts one million tonnes per year of limestone to operate the plant. Other mineral resources include peat, white clay and mineral-bearing sands. The general trend of government incentives to foreign investors, including share holding and

private investment in exploration activities, is likely to develop the mining sector.

Hydrocarbons
Bangladesh has oil reserves of 57 million barrels and produces around 6,200 barrels per day (bpd) of oil. The breakdown of the monopoly of the state oil and gas company, Petrobangla, sparked foreign interest and has in recent years resulted in the arrival of several foreign oil companies.

Bangladesh has proven natural gas reserves of 374.7 billion cubic metres (cum)and produces around 11 billion cum per year.

The large gas reserves and Bangladesh's proximity to the potentially huge energy market in India has resulted in a wave of energy companies. Bangladesh could also become a major natural gas transit corridor, linking India's easternmost states with West Bengal.

An adequate regulatory framework is required. Bangladesh has been ill-equipped to cope with even the bidding round for the remaining gas and oil blocs. This deficiency would need to be addressed to ensure increased certainty in investments. Bangladesh's coal reserves remained unexploited until recently. The Barapukuria coal mine in north-west Bangladesh, the first major coal mine was opened in April 2003. The mine has a production capacity of one million tonnes per annum, which will be mainly used for electricity generation.

Energy
Bangladesh has an electricity generation capacity of 3.8GW, 87 per cent of which is generated by natural gas and the remainder by oil and hydro-power.

The electricity generation and distribution sectors have deteriorated while demand has grown. Plant efficiency is low, power supply is erratic and electricity theft is widespread. Blackouts are common, putting a severe strain on industry. The sector is faced with a severe shortage of funds and investment needed to maintain and improve the electricity sector's infrastructure. The government's Power System Master Plan (PSMP) projects a required doubling of electric generating capacity between 2000 and 2010 to keep up with demand. The government aims for universal electrification by 2020.

Financial markets
Stock exchange
There has been an equity market in Bangladesh since colonial times. There are small, long-established, stock exchanges in Dhaka and Chittagong. However, their size and lack of liquidity means that foreign interest is minimal. Total market capitalisation is less than 1 per cent of GDP. The market is also too small to appear in the Morgan Stanley indices and this further restricts interest from investors. Eleven private commercial banks and six leasing companies are due to go public in 2004. This should broaden the market's capital base and boost investor interest in equities.

Banking and insurance
The banking system dominates the financial sector, accounting for about 97 per cent of the market in terms of assets. There are four nationalised commercial banks, six development banks, 27 private banks and 19 non-bank financial institutions. The four nationalised commercial banks have consistently accounted for over 60 per cent of assets since the mid-1990s, while private domestic banks account for about 32 per cent, and foreign banks for the remaining 6–7 per cent.

Successive Bangladeshi governments have failed to address the inefficiencies and mis-allocation of funds by the state-owned banks. The government's emphasis on private sector led growth, if implemented, requires the development of a more efficient, transparent financial sector. Development of a properly regulated banking system is one priority in this regard, the equity market is another.

Central bank
Bangladesh Bank
Main financial centre
Dhaka

Time
GMT plus six hours

Geography
Bangladesh is bordered mostly by India except for a short border with Myanmar to the south-east. The Bay of Bengal washes the southern edge of the country. The Ganges (Padma) and Brahmaputra (Jamuna) rivers flow from the Himalayas into the Bay of Bengal and each river has a massive and ever-changing delta system where they meet the sea. The silt deposits from these rivers have created a vast alluvial plain where the soils are among the most agriculturally rich in the world. Apart from some hills around Aylhet in the north-east and the Chittagong Hills in the south-east, the country is flat and low-lying, and is criss-crossed by numerous waterways.

Climate
Bangladesh has a sub-tropical monsoon climate and is dominated by the seasonally-reversing monsoons. There are three main seasons: winter (November–February) with an average temperature of 19 degrees Celsius (C); summer (March–May) when the average temperature is 29 degrees C and the climate is remarkably equable; and monsoon (June–October) which is humid and warm and accounts for 80 per cent of the country's annual rainfall of 1,200–3,500mm. It is normal for monsoon floods to cover around one-third of the country each year.

Dress codes
Lightweight cottons and linens are suitable during all seasons except winter when warm clothing is required.

Most Bangladeshis still wear traditional dress: *lungi* (sarong) and *kurta* (loose shirt) for men and *sari* for women. However, urban and professional men prefer Western clothes: trousers, suits and ties; very few women wear skirts.There is no recognised national dress, but at official functions, Bengali men are expected to wear a closed collar jacket and trousers; for less formal occasions, safari suits are popular.

Visiting businessmen should wear a lightweight or tropical suit and tie, and women should dress modestly.

Entry requirements
Passports
Required for nationals of all countries. Passports must be valid three months beyond the intended length of stay. A return ticket is required.

Visa
Are required by most, for a list of the few exemptions visit www.erdbd.org/informationcenter/visa.jsp. For a breakdown of visa categories and the permits allowed visit www.bdesh.info/. Lengths of stay can vary from three months (tourist visa) to one year (business visa).

Prohibited entry
Nationals of Israel

Currency advice/regulations
The import and export of local currency is limited to Tk100. Reconversion of local currency is permitted up to Tk500 or 25 per cent of the amount exchanged on arrival. The import of foreign currency is allowed but amounts greater than US$150 must be declared on arrival. The export of foreign currency is limited to US$150 or the amount declared on arrival.

All foreign currency exchanged must be entered on a currency declaration form. Many shops in the cities will offer better rates of exchange than the banks. Travellers cheques can be exchanged on arrival at Dhaka Airport. To avoid additional exchange rate charges, it is advisable to take travellers cheques in US dollars or UK pounds sterling.

Customs
Personal effects duty-free provided they are declared on entry.

Prohibited imports
Firearms and some animals.

Bangladesh

Health (for visitors)
Mandatory precautions
A vaccination certificate is required for yellow fever if travelling from an infected area. Health regulations may change, and it is best to make detailed enquiries before travelling.

Advisable precautions
Immunisations are recommended for tetanus, typhoid, polio and hepatitis 'A'. In some circumstances, immunisations for tuberculosis, hepatitis 'B' and Japanese 'B' encephalitis are advisable – seek medical advice. Anti-malarial precautions should be taken. There is a rabies risk. Tap water is not safe to drink anywhere.

Hotels
Hotel bills must be paid in a major convertible currency or with travellers cheques.
Provincial towns have government rest-houses with fairly Spartan accommodation, for which booking well in advance is advisable.

Credit cards
Credit cards are accepted. There is limited acceptance of Mastercard, Diners Club and American Express outside Dhaka.

Public holidays
Fixed dates
1 Jan (New Year's Day), 21 Feb (Shaheed Day), 26 Mar (National Day), 14 Apr (Bengali New Year), 1 May (Labour Day), 7 Nov (National Revolution Day), 16 Dec (Victory Day), 25 Dec (Christmas Day), 31 Dec (New Year's Eve).

Variable dates
Eid al Adha, Islamic New Year, Birth of the Prophet, July Bank Holiday (first Mon in Jul), Ascent of the Prophet, Shab e-Qadr (Oct/Nov), Eid al Fitr (second and third day).
The Islamic year contains 354 or 355 days, with the result that Muslim feasts advance by 10–12 days against the Gregorian calendar. Dates of feasts vary according to the sighting of the new moon, so cannot be forecast exactly. Islamic year 1426: 10 February 2005 to 30 January 2006.

Working hours
Banking
Sun–Thu: 0900–1500.
Business
Sun–Thu: 0900–1700.
Government
Sun–Thu: 0900–1700.
Shops
Sat–Thu: 0900–2000; Fri 0900–1230; 1400–2000.

Telecommunications
Mobile phones
The use of mobile phones is extremely limited.

Electricity supply
220V AC, with British-type 2 or 3 round pin plug fittings.

Weights and measures
Metric system

Social customs/useful tips
Normal Muslim customs predominate. Food and drink should be proffered with the right hand only. It is offensive to drink, eat or smoke in public or in the presence of Muslims during the month of Ramadan. Pork is considered unclean. However, alcohol is not prohibited and is available. Muslim women should not be photographed unless it is certain that no objection will be made. Females are expected to dress soberly and act discreetly. If travelling without a man, women sit together at the front of the bus.
People are usually warm and informal and do not hesitate to invite foreigners to their homes. The attitude towards punctuality is lax but getting less so.
Gratuities in restaurants are around 10 per cent and 5 per cent for taxis.

Security
While thefts and burglary are not uncommon, street violence is rare, especially against foreigners. Ostentatious displays of wealth such as money, watches and cameras should be avoided.

Getting there
Air
National airline: Biman Bangladesh Airlines
International airport/s: Zia International (DAC), 2km north of Dhaka, with VIP lounge, duty-free shop, bank, post office, restaurant and car hire; Patenga (CGP), 22km from Chittagong.
Other airport/s: Sylhet (ZYL), in the north-east of the country catering for visitors to the highlands of Sylhet.
Airport tax: Tk300 for all passengers, excluding those under two-years-old and immediate transit passengers.
Surface
Road: It is possible to travel by road from a number of points in India, including West Bengal, Assam and Tripura. Travel may be difficult during monsoon seasons.
Main port/s: Chittagong, Chalna.

Getting about
National transport
Transport links in Bangladesh are often slow and prone to disruption by bad weather. Allow time for delays.
Air: There are regular daily flights between Dhaka, Chittagong, Sylhet and Khulna operated by Air Parabat. Biman Bangladesh serves main centres. There are regional airports at Barisal, Jessore, Saidpur, Sylhet, Cox's Bazar, Thakurgaon and Rajshahi. Local storms can disrupt schedules.
Road: Bangladesh has an extensive road system, but does not have the capacity to deal with the amount of traffic. An estimated 7 per cent of roads are paved, and around half are metalled. Travel on roads during monsoon season is difficult. The 4.8km long road/rail bridge across the Jamuna River links the eastern and western parts of the country. Numerous ferry crossings sometimes make journey times unpredictable.
Buses: There are express buses and local ones which stop en route. The latter charge around 25 per cent less, but are slow. In remote areas local buses are often the only means of transport.
Rail: About one-third of Bangladesh is serviced by railways. Inter City (IC) trains are frequent, clean and reasonably punctual, especially in the eastern zone, although they may be relatively slow. Six classes of rail travel are available: 'first' and 'express' are recommended for air-conditioned coaches that also provide more room.
Water: The river is the traditional means of transport. There are 8,000km of navigable waterways, although flooding in the monsoon season, silting in the dry season, and fogs may make routes inaccessible. The main routes are covered by the Bangladesh Inland Waterway Transport Corporation (BIWTC), but there are many private companies operating on shorter routes. Passage should be booked well in advance.
City transport
Taxis: Taxis, generally identifiable by their black body and yellow top, are few and far between in Dhaka; they are available at main hotels and airports. Negotiate fares before undertaking a journey. A 10 per cent service charge is usual.
It is probably best to organise a car from the hotel for the 20km trip from Dhaka Zia International Airport; journey time is 30 minutes.
Rickshaws and autorickshaws are available, but are not recommended for use at night. Autorickshaws should be metered, but often are not. Negotiate fares in advance.
Buses, trams & metro: There is a shuttle bus between Zia International Airport and Dhaka city centre; journey time is 35–45 minutes.
Car hire
There are a number of private car hire companies can be found in Dkaka and other cities. The Bangladesh Parjatan Corporation (BPC), a government organisation, has a fleet of air-conditioned and non air-conditioned cars, microbuses and jeeps for hire. The BPC also offers a

transfer service for tourists between Dhaka airport and the city centre and main hotels.
Driving is on the left. A national licence or international driving permit is required.

BUSINESS DIRECTORY

The addresses listed below are a selection only. While World of Information makes every endeavour to check these addresses, we cannot guarantee that changes have not been made, especially to telephone numbers and area codes. We would welcome any corrections.

Telephone area codes
The international direct dialling code (IDD) for Bangladesh is + 880, followed by area code and subscriber's number:

Bagerhat	401	Khulna	41
Barisal	431	Kushtia	71
Bogra	51	Moulvi Bazar	861
Chittagong	31	Mymensingh	91
Comilla	81	Narayanganj	671
Dhaka	2	Patvakhali	441
Dinajpur	531	Rajshashi	721
Jamalpur	981	Sylhet	821

Useful telephone numbers
Police: 866-551/3, 842-501/8.
Fire and ambulance: 955-5555, 955-6666.
Directory enquiries: 17 or 254-222.
Trunk booking (overseas): 501-777, 832-359, 419-313, 608-080.
Trunk booking (inland): 109.
Trunk enquiries: 103.
Time: 14.

Chambers of Commerce
American Chamber of Commerce in Bangladesh, Dhaka Sheraton Hotel, 1 Minto Road, Dhaka 1000 (tel: 861-3391; fax: 831-2915; e-mail: amcham@bangla.net).

Chittagong Chamber of Commerce and Industry, Agrabad Commercial Area, Chittagong (tel: 711-355; fax: 710-183; e-mail: ccci@globalctg.net).

Dhaka Chamber of Commerce and Industry, 65 Motijheel Commercial Area, Dhaka 1000 (tel: 955-2562; fax: 956-0830; e-mail: dcci@bangla.net).

Federation of Bangladesh Chambers of Commerce and Industry, 60 Motijheel Commercial Area, Dhaka 1000 (tel: 956-0102; fax: 861-3213; e-mail: fbcci@bol-online.com).

Foreign Investors Chamber of Commerce and Industry, 35-1 Purana Paltan Line, Inner Circular Road, Dhaka 1000 (tel: 831-9448; fax: 831-9449; e-mail: ficci@bangla.net).

Khulna Chamber of Commerce and Industry, 5 KDA Commercial Area, Khan-A-Sabur Road, Khulna (tel: 721-695; fax: 731-213).

Metropolitan Chamber of Commerce and Industry, 122 Motijheel Commercial Area, Dhaka 1000 (tel: 956-5208; fax: 956-5212; e-mail: sg@citechco.net).

Banking
Agrani Bank, Agrani Bank Building, 9D Motijheel C/A, Dhaka 1000 (tel: 956-6160; fax: 956-2346).

Arab Bangladesh Bank, BCIC Bhaban, 30-31 Dilkusha C/A (8th, 9th & 11th Floors), Dhaka 1000 (tel: 956-0312; fax 956-4122).

Bangladesh Krishi Bank (Agricultural Bank), 83-85 Motijheel C/A, Dhaka 100 (tel: 956-0021; fax: 867-102).

Bangladesh Shilpa Bank (Industrial Bank),PO Box 975, 8 Rajuk Avenue, Dhaka (tel: 955-8326; fax: 956-2061).

Banque Indosuez, 47 Motijheel C/A, Dhaka 1000 (tel: 956-6566; fax: 956-5707).

Citibank N A, Chamber Building, 122-124 Motijheel C/A, Dhaka 1000 (tel: 955-0061; fax: 956-2236).

Dutch-Bangla Bank Limited, 3rd & 4th Floor, Sena Kalyan Bhaban, 195 Motijheel Commercial Area, Dhaka 1000 (tel: 956-8537, 956-8542-44; fax: 956-1889; e-mail: dbbl@bdmail.net).

Grameen Bank, Grameen Bank Bhaban, Mirpur, Section-2, Dhaka-1216, Bangladesh (tel: 900-5256; e-mail: grameen.bank@grameen.net).

Hongkong & Shanghai Banking Corporation, Anchor Tower (5th Floor), 1.1-B Sonargaon Road, Dhaka 1205 (tel: 966-0536; fax: 966-0554).

International Finance Investment and Commercial Bank, BSB Building, 8 Rajuk Avenue, Dhaka 1000.

Islam Bank Bangladesh, PO Box 233, Islami Bank Tower, 40 Dilkusha Commercial Area, Dhaka 1000 (tel: 956-3182; fax: 956-4532).

Janata Bank, Janata Bhadan, 110 Motijheel C/A, PO Box 468, Dhaka 1000 (tel: 956-000; fax: 956-4644).

National Bank Limited, 18 Dilkusha C/A, Dhaka 1000 (tel: 956-3081/5; fax: 956-3953; e-mail: nblho@citechco.net).

Pubali Bank Ltd, 26 Dikusha C/A, Dhaka 1000 (tel: 956-9050; fax: 956-4009).

Rupali Bank Ltd, 34 Dilkusha C/A, Dhaka 1000 (tel: 955-1624; fax: 956-4148).

Sonali Bank, Motijheel C/A, PO Box 147, Dhaka 1000 (tel: 955-0426; fax: 956-1410).

Standard Chartered Bank, 18-20 Motijheel C/A, Dhaka 1000 (tel: 956-1465; fax: 956-1758).

United Commercial Bank, 60 Motijheel C/A, Dhaka 1000.

Uttara Bank, 90 Motijheel C/A, Dhakar 1000 (tel: 955-1162; fax: 863-539).

Central bank
Bangladesh Bank, Motijheel Commercial Area, PO Box 325, Dhaka 1000 (tel: 956-6203; fax: 956-6212; e-mail: banglabank@bangla.net).

Travel information
Automobile Association of Bangladesh, 3/B Outer Circular Road, Dhaka 17 (tel: 402-241).

Biman Bangladesh Airlines, Biman Bhaban, 100 Motijheel Commercial Area, Dhaka 1000 (tel: 240-151/90; fax: 863-005); airport (tel: 894-771/79); flight enquiries (tel: 894-350, 894-870).

Railway enquiries (tel: 409-686).

National tourist organisation offices
Bangladesh Parjatan Corporation, 233 Airport Road, Tejgaon, Dhaka 12 (tel: 817-855; fax: 817-235).

Ministries
Ministry of Agriculture, Bangladesh Secretariat, Dhaka 1000 (tel: 869-277; fax: 867-040).

Ministry of Civil Aviation and Tourism, Bangladesh Secretariat, Dhaka 1000 (tel: 867-244; fax: 869-206).

Ministry of Commerce, Bangladesh Secretariat, Dhaka 1000 (tel: 869-679; fax: 865-741).

Ministry of Communications, Bangladesh Secretariat, Dhaka 1000 (tel: 864-977; fax: 866-636).

Ministry of Cultural Affairs, Bangladesh Secretariat, Dhaka 1000 (tel: 868-977; fax: 860-290).

Ministry of Defence, Ganabhaban Complex, Shere-e-Banglanagar, Dhaka 1207 (tel: 816-955; fax: 817-945).

Ministry of Disaster Management & Relief, Bangladesh Secretariat, Dhaka 1000 (tel: 868-744; fax: 869-623).

Ministry of Education, Bangladesh Secretarieat, Dhaka 1000 (tel: 868-711; fax: 867-577).

Ministry of Energy and Mineral Resources, Bangladesh Secretariat, Dhaka 1000 (tel: 866-188; fax: 861-110).

Ministry of Environment & Forest, Bangladesh Secretariat, Dhaka 1000 (tel: 860-587; fax: 869-210).

Ministry of Finance, Finance Division, Bangladesh Secretariat, Dhaka 1000 (tel: 860-406; fax: 865-581).

Ministry of Fisheries and Livestock, Bangladesh Secretariat, Dhaka 1000 (tel: 864-700).

Bangladesh

Ministry of Food, Bangladesh Secretariat, Dhaka 1000 (tel: 862-240; fax: 860-762).

Ministry of Foreign Affairs, Foreign Affairs Building, Segunbagicha, Dhaka 1000 (tel: 955-6020; fax: 956-2557).

Ministry of Health & Family Welfare, Bangladesh Secretariat, Dhaka 1000 (tel: 866-975; fax: 869-077).

Ministry of Home Affairs, Bangladesh Secretariat, Dhaka 1000 (tel: 864-611; fax: 869-667).

Ministry of Industries, Shilpa Bhaban, 91 Motijheel C/A, Dhaka 1000 (tel: 956-3549; fax: 956-3553).

Ministry of Information, Bangladesh Secretariate, Dhaka 1000 (tel: 868-555; fax: 862-211).

Ministry of Jute, Bangladesh Secretariat, Dhaka 1000 (tel: 862-250; fax: 868-766).

Ministry of Labour and Manpower, Bangladesh Secretariat, Dhaka 1000 (tel: 862-141; fax: 868-660).

Ministry of Land, Bangladesh Secretariat, Dhaka 1000 (tel: 869-644; fax: 862-989).

Ministry of Law, Justice and Parliamentary Affairs, Bangladesh Secretariat, Dhaka 1000 (tel: 860-560; fax: 868-557).

Ministry of Local Government and Rural Development, Bangladesh Secretariat, Dhaka 1000 (tel: 869-176; fax: 864-374).

Ministry of Planning, Sher-e-Banglanagar, Dhaka 1207 (tel: 815-175; fax: 814-638).

Ministry of Post and Telecommunications, Bangladesh Secretariat, Dhaka 1000 (tel: 864-800; fax: 865-775).

Ministry of Primary and Mass Education, Bangladesh Secretariat, Dhaka 1000 (tel: 862-484; fax: 868-871).

Ministry of Religious Affairs, Bangladesh Secretariat, Dhaka 1000 (tel: 860-682; fax: 865-040).

Ministry of Science & Technology, Bangladesh Secretariat, Dhaka 1000 (tel: 866-144; fax: 869-606).

Ministry of Shipping, Bangladesh Secretariat, Dhaka 1000 (tel: 868-155; fax: 862-219).

Ministry of Social Welfare, Bangladesh Secretariat, Dhaka 1000 (tel: 860-452; fax: 868-969).

Ministry of Textiles, Bangladesh Secretariat, Dhaka 1000 (tel: 864-388; fax: 860-600).

Ministry of Water Resources, Bangladesh Secretariat, Dhaka 1000 (tel: 868-688; fax: 862-400).

Ministry of Women and Children Affairs, Bangladesh Secretariat, Dhaka 1000 (tel: 861-012; fax: 867-550).

Ministry of Youth and Sports, Bangladesh Secretariat, Dhaka 1000 (tel: 867-053; fax: 862-344).

President's Office, Bangabhaban, Dhaka 1000 (tel: 966-8041; fax: 946-6242).

Prime Minister's Office, Old Sangsad Bhaban, Tejgaon, Dhaka (tel: 888-160; fax: 813-244).

Other useful addresses

Asian Development Bank, Bangladesh Resident Mission, BSL Office Complex, Second Floor, Sheraton Hotel Annex, 1 Minto Road, Ramna, Dhaka 1000 (tel: 933-4017; fax: 933-4012; e-mail: abddrm@mail.asiandevbank.org; internet site: http://asiandevbank.org/).

Bangladesh Agricultural University, Mymensingh (tel: 4333, 4191/93).

Bangladesh Export Processing Zones Authority, 222 New Eskaton Road, Dhaka (tel: 832-553; fax: 834-963).

Bangladesh Jute Mills Corporation, Adanjee Court, Motijheel C/A, Dhaka (tel: 238-182/6, 238-192/6; fax: 883-329, 883-985).

Bangladesh Small and Cottage Industries Corporation, 137-138 Motijheel Comercial Area, Dhaka (tel: 865-161).

Bangladesh Telegraph and Telephone Board, 36/1 Mymensingh Road, Dhaka (tel: 831-500; fax: 832-477).

Board of Investment, Shilpa Bhaban, 91 Motijheel Commercial Area, Dhaka (tel: 955-9378; fax: 956-2312; internet site: http://www.boibd.org/).

Bangladesh University of Engineering & Technology, Ramna, Dhaka 2 (tel: 505-171-5).

British High Commission, United Nations Road, PO Box 6079, Baridhara, Dhaka 12 (tel: 882-705/9; fax: 883-437).

Chittagong Port Authority, Port Road, Chittagong (tel: 712-504; fax: 710-593).

Chittagong Stock Exchange, 1/F Kashfia Plaza, 923/A Sheikh Mujib Road, Chittagong (tel: 714-100; fax: 714-101).

Department of Environment, Poribesh Bhaban, Plot £16 Agargaon, Sher-e-Bangla Nagar, Dhaka (tel: 812-416).

Department of Fisheries, Matsa Bhaban Segunbagicha, Dhaka (tel: 956-9320).

Department of Immigration and Passports, 17 Segunbagicha, Dhaka (tel: 834-320; fax: 956-2787).

Department of Shipping, 8/F, 141-143, Motijheel Commercial Area, Dhaka (tel: 955-5128).

Department of Textiles, Bastra Bhaban, Kazi Nazrul Islam Avenue, Dhaka (911-6385).

Dhaka Electric Supply Authority, 1 Abdul gani Road, Dhaka (tel: 956-3520).

Dhaka Stock Exchange, 9F Motijheel Commercial Area, Dhaka 1000 (tel: 955-1935; fax: 867-552).

Export Promotion Bureau, Chamber Building, 122-124 Motijheel Commercial Area, Dhaka 1000 (tel: 955-2245/9; fax: 956-8000; e-mail: epb.tic@pradeshta.net).

Infrastructure Development Co Ltd, c/o Economic Relations Division, Block 16, Room 3, Sher-e-Bangla Nagar, Dhaka (tel: 811-971; fax: 811-660).

Mongla Port Authority, Mongla, Bagerhat (tel: 416-2331; fax: 403-1224).

National Board of Revenue, Segunbagicha, Dhaka (tel: 838-120; fax: 836-143).

Planning Commission, G.O. Hostel, Sher-e-Bangla Nagar, Dhaka.

Power Development Board, WAPDA Building, Motijheel Commercial Area, Dhaka (tel: 956-2154; fax: 956-4765).

Privatisation Board, 14/F Joban Bima Tower, 10 Dilkusha Commecial Area, Dhaka (tel: 956-3763; fax: 956-3723).

Registrar of Joint Stock Companies and Firms, 24-25 Dilkusha Commercial Area, Dhaka (tel: 956-4005).

Securities and Exchange Commission, Jiban bima Tower, 10 Dilkusha Commercial Area, Dhaka (tel: 956-8101; fax: 956-3721).

US Embassy, Madani Avenue, Baridhara, Dhaka 1212 (tel: 882-4700; fax: 882-3744; e-mail: dhaka@pd.state.gov).

Water Sewerage Authority, 98 Kazi Nazrul Islam Avenue, Dhaka (el: 816-792; fax: 812-109).

Internet sites

Asia Business Connection (gareway site): http://www.asiabiz.com

Asian Sources Online: http://www.asiansources.com

Bangladesh News: http://www.bangla.org/news/amitech/

Bangladesh search engine: http://www.dhaka-bd.com

Commonwealth Online: http://www.thecommonwealth.org

Export opportunites: http://www.bdexport.com/

Travel and Tourism: http://www.discoverybangladesh.com

Barbados

KEY FACTS

Official name: Barbados

Head of State: Queen Elizabeth II, represented by Governor General Sir Clifford Straughn Husbands (since 1996)

Head of government: Prime Minister Owen S Arthur (BLP) (since 1994)

Ruling party: Barbados Labour Party (BLP) (since 1994; last re-elected 21 May 2003)

Area: 430 square km

Population: 270,540 (2004)

Capital: Bridgetown

Official language: English

Currency: Barbados dollar (BD$) = 100 cents

Exchange rate: BD$2.00 per US$ (Oct 2005)

GDP per capita: US$10,334 (2004)

GDP real growth: 3.00% (2004)

Labour force: 152,000 (2004)

Unemployment: 9.80% (2004)

Inflation: 1.50% (2004)

Balance of trade: -US$945.50 million (2004)

Foreign debt: US$643.50 million (2004)

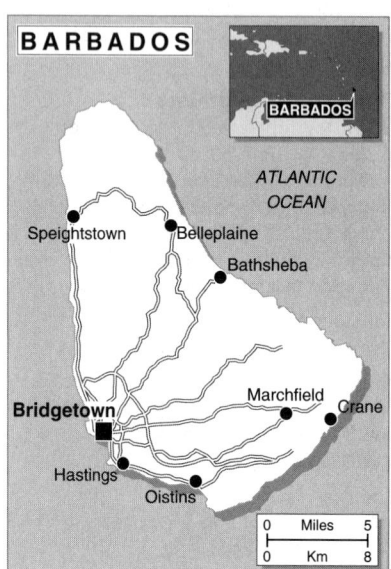

COUNTRY PROFILE

Historical profile
Barbados was formerly a British colony and is now an independent sovereign state.
1951 Universal adult suffrage was introduced. The Barbados Labour Party (BLP) won the general election, and held office until 1961.
1961 Barbados achieved full internal self-government. The Democratic Labour Party (DLP) won the elections.
1966 Barbados gained independence.
1994 The BLP won the election. Owen Arthur became prime minister.
2002 Barbados was removed from the Organisation for Economic Co-operation and Development (OECD's) blacklist of non-co-operative countries in OECD efforts to combat money laundering.
2003 The ruling BLP won the general elections.
2004 A new radio service – Radio Caricom, the Voice of the Caribbean Community – was officially launched at the Conference of the Heads of Government in Grenada on 4 July. Barbados is a 'pilot state' in the project.
2005 The prime minister announced he was relinquishing a number of ministerial responsibilities so that he could oversee and encourage the development of major foreign investment programmes.

Political structure
Constitution
This was promulgated on 30 November 1966.
Form of state
Parliamentary democracy; it is a member of the Commonwealth.
The executive
Executive power is vested in the British monarch, represented by a governor general, who is appointed by the monarch.
National legislature
Legislative power is exercised through the bicameral parliament, comprising a 21-member Senate (appointed) and a 30-member House of Assembly (elected by direct popular vote, at least every five years).
Following legislative elections, the leader of the majority party, or majority coalition, is appointed prime minister by the governor general. The cabinet is appointed by the governor general on the advice of the prime minister.
Legal system
The legal system is based on English common law. Judges are appointed by the service commissions for the judicial and legal service. There is no judicial review of legislative acts.
Last elections
21 May 2003 (legislative)
Results: Parliamentary: the Barbados Labour Party (BLP) won 23 seats out of 30 and the Democratic Labour Party (DLP) won seven seats.
Next elections
2008 (legislative)

Political parties
Ruling party
Barbados Labour Party (BLP) (since 1994; re-elected 21 May 2003)
Main opposition party
Democratic Labour Party (DLP)

Population
270,540 (2004)
Ethnic make-up
African (90 per cent), mixed race (6 per cent), European (4 per cent).
Religions
Mainly Christian, with an Anglican majority and dozens of smaller sects, plus small Jewish, Hindu and Muslim communities. Anglican (40 per cent), Pentecostal (8 per cent), Methodist (7 per cent), Roman Catholic (4 per cent).

Barbados

Education
Educational spending is around US$150 million per year. Expenditure on primary education typically fluctuates between 25–29 per cent of total public expenditure on education. The government provides assistance to all private secondary schools.

Public education at primary and secondary levels is free, although parents can opt to send their children to private schools. Primary education begins at aged five and lasts for six years.

The secondary school programme begins at aged 11 years and last until aged 16, when students choose between academic higher education or applied further education.

The Samuel Jackman Prescod Polytechnic (SJPP), the Barbados Community College (BCC), Erdiston College and the University of the West Indies cater for higher education. Eligible students also pursue their studies in North American colleges and universities.

Compulsory years: 5 to 16
Enrolment rate: 94.7 per cent to 100 per cent, primary school enrolment of the relevant age group.
Pupils per teacher: 18 in primary schools

Health
Total expenditure on health is 6–7 per cent of GDP, of which government spending is 65 per cent.

With 16 per cent of the population aged 60 years and over, Barbados has the highest percentage of elderly population in the English speaking Caribbean. Barbados provides high quality primary and secondary care with free treatment for young children. The Queen Elizabeth Hospital benefits from government aid. There is universal access to improved water and sanitation facilities.

HIV prevalence: 1.5 per cent aged 15–49 in 2003 (World Bank)
Life expectancy: 74.8 years World Bank
Fertility rate/Maternal mortality rate: 1.8 births per woman (World Bank)
Birth rate/Death rate: 13 births per 1,000 population; nine deaths per 1,000 population (2003).
Infant mortality rate: 13 per 1,000 live births (2003)

Welfare
The government provides an extensive welfare programme for the poor and the elderly. Assistance for the elderly comprises housing, transportation, home care and free utilities (water and utilities), assistance in kind, and food vouchers.

Financial assistance is provided to parents of underprivileged children as well as subsidies for school expenses.

Low rent housing is available to all residents; some housing is available to be purchased by low income earners.

Pensions
There is universal pension coverage from a non-contributory pension.

Main cities
Bridgetown (capital, estimated population 98,900 in 2003), Speightstown (3,600), Oistins, Holetown.

Languages spoken
A local Bajan dialect is spoken.
Official language/s
English

Media
Press
Dailies: Two are published *The Daily Nation* and *Barbados Advocate*.
Weeklies: Include *Caribbean Week, Eastern Caribbean News, Sunday Advocate, Sunday Sun, Weekend Investigator* and *WeekEnd Nation*.
Business: *The Broad Street Journal* is a weekly publication for Barbados and the Caribbean. Others include the *Barbados Business Update* and an English monthly on finance *CANA Business*.

Broadcasting
Radio: Four national services provide approximately 19 hrs/day. A cable radio (Rediffusion) exists.
Radio Caricom, the Voice of the Caribbean Community began broadcasting in 2005.
Television: Government-owned Caribbean Broadcasting Corporation operates CBC-TV colour/commercial station.

Economy
Traditionally economic activity has centred around sugarcane production, but has diversified into the tourist industry and offshore banking. GDP growth reached 3 per cent in 2004 after an economic contraction in 2002/03, which was a result of the US economic slowdown. Barbados has the most developed infrastructure in the Caribbean region, however its vulnerability to changes in the global economy and seasonal hurricane damage are challenges which the government has to face each year. Nevertheless the ongoing development of the financial service sector will ensure a stable economy in the long run.

The inflow of divestment proceeds along with weak demand for private loans led to a high level of excess liquidity in 2004. The financial sector also saw a 6.3 per cent increase in the number of international businesses and financial service firms being established in the country. Barbados relies heavily on imports of foodstuffs, fuel and consumer goods. As a result the government runs a high trade deficit which has to be financed by issuing securities. The budget deficit is narrowing due to cutbacks to capital expenditure and increasing revenues.

The 2004 budget included a planned US$100 million for preparation of the cricket World Cup in 2007. This sum was funded by the issuing of US$75 million of bonds in early 2005. The World Cup is likely to create an all time high in tourist numbers, especially as Barbados is hosting the final. The competition has triggered investment in home improvement, both government and privately funded. It is expected that thousands of visitors will opt for home-style accommodation.

In July 2005 a spending package of US$2.4 billion was put forward, funded by

KEY INDICATORS — Barbados

	Unit	2000	2001	2002	2003	2004
Population	m	0.27	0.27	0.27	0.27	0.27
Gross domestic product (GDP)	US$bn	2.60	2.54	2.54	*2.63	*2.80
GDP per capita	US$	9,702	9,444	9,462	10,000	10,334
GDP real growth	%	3.1	-2.8	-1.8	1.6	3.0
Inflation	%	2.5	2.6	1.5	1.5	1.5
Unemployment	%	9.4	9.9	10.3	10.0	9.8
Exports (fob) (goods)	US$m	286.4	252.0	241.5	227.0	312.4
Imports (fob) (goods)	US$m	1,030.3	1,144.0	1,070.8	987.0	1,277.9
Balance of trade	US$m	-743.9	-809.3	-829.3	-760.0	-945.5
Current account	US$m	-145.5	-90.0	-170.0	-210.0	-280.0
Total reserves minus gold	US$m	472.7	690.4	668.5	737.9	579.9
Foreign exchange	US$m	466.6	684.4	661.9	730.5	571.8
Exchange rate	per US$	1.99	1.99	2.00	2.00	2.01

* estimated figure

increased VAT, reforms in the tax system and the sale of various government assets.

External trade
Even though the government sees the high trade deficit as excessive Barbados is reliant on imports of basic goods such as foodstuffs.
On 1 January 2006, Barbados, which has been re-designated a 'high income' country, will lose its preferential trade status; such designation allows products of developing countries to pay lower customs duties when they enter the markets of developed countries, with no obligation of reciprocity.

Imports
Principal imports are machinery (typically 17 per cent of total), food and beverages (15 per cent), fuels (5 per cent), vehicles (3 per cent), and other include consumer goods, construction materials and electrical components.
Main sources: US (31.6 per cent total, 2004), Trinidad and Tobago (21.6 per cent), UK (7.9 per cent), Japan (5.3 per cent)

Exports
Principal exports are sugar and molasses (typically 30 per cent of total), electrical and electronic components (25 per cent), clothing (12 per cent), chemicals (11 per cent), others include rum, foods and beverages.
Main destinations: Trinidad and Tobago (14.2 per cent total, 2004), US (13.9 per cent), UK (13.0 per cent), Jamaica (7.7 per cent), Saint Lucia (5.8 per cent), Spain (5.8 per cent), Saint Vincent and the Grenadines (4.6 per cent)

Agriculture
Farming
The agricultural sector contributes around 7 per cent to GDP and employs around 5 per cent of the labour force.
Around 76 per cent of the total land area is under cultivation, mostly for sugar cane production.
The sugar sector contributes about 3 per cent to GDP.
Emphasis has been placed on diversifying production away from sugar and towards the farming of sea island cotton, green vegetables and market garden produce.
There are around 50 sugar plantations in Barbados, directly employing 3,000–4,000 workers. The cost of producing sugar is high, averaging around BD$1,400 (US$700) per tonne. The EU guarantees a price of BD$800 (US$400) per tonne under the EU sugar quota system and many producers are reliant on government handouts worth around US$8 million per year to remain in business. The EU quota of just under 50,000 tonnes per year and its guaranteed price mechanism will come to an end in 2007. The pressure is on Barbados to make the sugar sector profitable, although it seems unlikely that the island will be able to compete with low-cost producers and the heavily subsidised sugar beet farmers in North America and the EU. As well as trade liberalisation, the Barbados sugar sector will have to cope with environmental degradation and the rising price of land.
Crop production in 2004 included: 270 tonnes (t) maize, 2,700t sweet potatoes, 370,000t sugar cane, 1,800t coconuts, 1,375t yams, 240t taro, 1,550t okra, 1,250t tomatoes, 1,300t chillies & peppers, 1,025t pulses, 635t bananas, 261t oilcrops, 430t cassava, 3,415t fruit in total, 14,960t vegetables in total. Livestock production included: 14,191t meat in total, 416t beef, 2,185t pig meat, 120t lamb and goat meat, 11,470t poultry, 1,750t eggs, 7,200t milk.

Fishing
There are complaints that the small fishing industry has not been supported by the government. The government issued fish importing licences permitting processors to import fish, when the domestic catch could have provided for domestic processing needs.

Industry and manufacturing
Manufacturing employs around 9 per cent of the workforce and construction and quarrying, 11 per cent.
Production is centred on light manufacturing and assembly of electrical and electronic goods, food processing, clothing, sugar refining, petrochemicals and beverages.
Most new foreign-owned export-oriented industries are based on the island's nine purpose-built industrial estates, which are largely managed by the Barbados Industrial Development Corporation.
Emphasis is placed on expanding the number of value-added joint venture assembly industries. The sugar refining sector is in the process of consolidation, with the closure of a mill in 2002 and one of the remaining two mills closed in 2005.

Tourism
Tourism accounts for around 11 per cent of GDP, employing 21 per cent of the workforce, generating 70 per cent of foreign exchange earnings. Visitor numbers grew by 10 per cent and cruise ship passengers by 32 per cent, in 2004.

Hydrocarbons
Proven oil reserves were estimated at 2.5 million barrels in early 2003.
The Barbados National Oil Company (BNOC) is using horizontal drilling techniques to increase production. As Barbados has no refining capacity, its oil is refined in Trinidad and returned to Barbados for domestic consumption. Most oil produced is used domestically.
By 2003, Barbados had 142 million cubic metres of natural gas reserves. There are plans for a pipeline to be built that would link Trinidad and Tobago to other islands in the Caribbean including Barbados.

Energy
Barbados relies on imported oil for most of its energy requirements. Under the San José pact, Mexico and Venezuela supply crude oil and refined products on concessionary terms.
There are plans to expand solar and wind energy programmes.

Banking and insurance
The financial sector grew by 2 per cent in 2004.
Central bank
Central Bank of Barbados
Main financial centre
Bridgetown
Offshore facilities
Barbados is a major international business centre. It has several tax treaties in place with developed countries including Canada. Offshore banking institutions fell from 14 in 2003 to two in 2004.

Time
GMT minus four hours

Geography
Barbados is the most easterly of the Caribbean islands, lying about 320km (200 miles) north-east of Trinidad. It is relatively flat and is one of the few coral-capped islands in the region.

Climate
Generally warm but cooled by trade winds with temperature around 26–30 degrees Celsius (C) in the day and 15–18 degrees C at night. Rainy season: July–November. Humidity rises in the rainy season.

Dress codes
Business suits may be worn with jackets removed. Generally, smart casual wear is suitable in restaurants, although some restaurants may require suits and ties for men. Lightweight cottons are advised.

Entry requirements
Passports
Required by all.
Visa
Visas are not required by most European, American, Australasian and some Asian citizens. For a list of those that do, see http://www.barbados.org/docs.htm. All visitors must have return/onward passage.
Currency advice/regulations
No restrictions on import and export of local currency. Export of foreign currency limited to amounts declared on arrival.

Barbados

Health (for visitors)
Mandatory precautions
Yellow fever vaccination certificate if arriving from an infected area.
Advisable precautions
Typhoid/polio vaccination.

Hotels
There is wide range of first-class hotels available. A 5 per cent government tax and 10 per cent service charge are generally applied.

Public holidays
Fixed dates
1 Jan (New Year's Day), 21 Jan (Errol Barrow Day), 28 Apr (National Heroes' Day), 1 May (Labour Day), 30 Nov (Independence Day), 25 Dec (Christmas Day), 26 Dec (Boxing Day).
Variable dates
Good Friday, Easter Monday, Whit Monday, Emancipation/Kadooment Day (first Mon in Aug).

Working hours
Banking
Mon–Thu: 0800–1500; Fri: 0800–1700.
Business
Mon–Fri: 0800–1600/1630; Sat: 0800–1200.
Government
Mon–Fri: 0800–1600/1630.

Telecommunications
Mobile phones
GSM 900/1900, 900/1800 services are available throughout most of the island.

Electricity supply
110V AC, 50Hz. American-style two-pin plugs are in use.

Social customs/useful tips
Make and confirm appointments before travelling. Many hotels do not start check-in procedures until 1500 so advise the hotel if arriving earlier. Most hotels have a business centre, although facilities vary.

Getting there
Air
International airport/s: Grantley Adams International (BGI), 13km east of Bridgetown; duty-free shops, restaurant, bank, hotel reservations, car hire.
Airport tax: Departure tax BD$25; not applicable to transit passengers.
Surface
Main port/s: Bridgetown Harbour.

Getting about
National transport
Road: There are over 2,000km of surfaced road. Main roads radiate from Bridgetown.
Buses: Frequent and efficient standard fare services operate throughout the island.

City transport
Taxis: Taxis are easily available. They can be hailed, ordered by telephone or found on ranks. The Tourism Board publishes a list of standard fares.
Some hotels run pick-up services.
Car hire
A local driver's permit must be obtained; they are available at police stations and the licensing authority or through car rental agencies on presentation of a national driving licence. Traffic drives on the left and is often heavy in the morning and at night. Strict speed limits of 20mph in Bridgetown and Speightstown and 30mph elsewhere.

BUSINESS DIRECTORY
The addresses listed below are a selection only. While World of Information makes every endeavour to check these addresses, we cannot guarantee that changes have not been made, especially to telephone numbers and area codes. We would welcome any corrections.

Telephone area codes
The international direct dialling code (IDD) for Barbados is +1 246, followed by subscriber's number.

Chambers of Commerce
Barbados Chamber of Commerce and Industry, Nemwil House, Collymore Rock, St Michael (tel: 426-2056; fax: 429-2907; e-mail: bdscham@caribsurf.com).

Banking
Bank of Nova Scotia, PO Box 202, Broad St, Bridgetown (tel: 431-3000; fax: 426-0969).

Barbados Agency for Microenterprise Development Ltd (Fund Access), 30 Tudor Street, Bridgetown (tel: 228-1366; fax: 228-1343).

Barbados National Bank, PO Box 1002, Broad St, Bridgetown (tel: 431-5700; fax: 426-0969).

Barclays Bank PLC, PO Box 301, Broad St, Bridgetown (tel: 431-5151; fax: 436-7957).

Caldon Finance Merchant Bank Ltd, Hilton Hotel, 7 Shopping Arcade, St Michael (tel: 437-7550; fax: 436-4999).

Caribbean Commercial Bank, PO Box 1007C, Broad St, Bridgetown (tel: 431-2500; fax: 431-2530).

Caribbean Development Bank, PO Box 408 Wildey, St Michael, Barbados (tel: 431-1600; fax: 426-7269).

Intel Overseas Bank Inc, Suite No 7, Goding House, Spry St, Bridgetown (tel: 436-8826).

Mutual Bank of the Caribbean Inc, Triden House, Lower Broad St, Bridgetown (tel: 436-8335; fax: 429-5734).

Royal Bank of Canada, PO Box 68, Broad Street, Bridgetown (tel: 431-6700; fax: 427-8393).

Central bank
Central Bank of Barbados, Spry Street, PO Box 1016, Bridgetown (tel: 436-6870; fax: 427-3334; e-mail: cbb.libr@caribsurf.com).

Travel information
Caribbean Airways, Terminal 1, Grantley Adams International Airport, Christ Church (tel: 428-1950; fax: 428-1652; e-mail: info@caribairways.com; internet site: http://www.caribairways.com).

Ministry of tourism
Ministry of Foreign Affairs, Tourism and International Transport, Tourism Division, Sherbourne Conference Centre, Two Mile Hill, St Michael (tel: 436-4830; fax: 436-4828).

National tourist organisation offices
Barbados Tourism Authority, Harbour Road, PO Box 242, Bridgetown (tel: 427-2623/4; fax: 426-4080).

Ministries
Ministry of Agriculture and Rural Development, Graeme Hall, Christ Church (tel: 428-4061; fax: 420-8444).

Ministry of Education, Youth Affairs and Culture, Jemmotts Ln, St Michael (tel: 426-5416; fax: 436-2411).

Ministry of Finance and Economic Affairs, Civil Service, Government Headquarters, Bay St, St Michael (tel: 426-3179; fax: 436-9280).

Ministry of Health and the Environment, Jemmotts Ln, St Michael (tel: 426-4669; fax: 426-5570).

Ministry of Home Affairs, Sir Frank Walcott Bldg, Culloden Rd, St Michael (tel: 431-7750; fax: 437-3794).

Ministry of Industry, Commerce and Business Development, Reef Rd, Fontabelle, St Michael (tel: 426-4452; fax: 431-0056).

Ministry of International Trade and Business, 1 Culloden Rd, St Michael (tel: 427-0427; fax: 429-6652).

Ministry of Labour, Community Development and Sports, National Insurance Bldg, Fairchild St, Bridgetown, St Michael (tel: 427-2326; fax: 426-8959).

Ministry of Public Works, Transport and Housing, The Pine, St Michael (tel: 429-3495; fax: 437-8133).

Ministry of Trade, Industry and Commerce, Savannah Lodge, Garrison, St Michael (tel: 427-270).

Prime Minister's Office, Government Headquarters, Bay St, St Michael (tel: 426-3179; fax: 436-9280).

Nations of the World: A Political, Economic and Business Handbook

Other useful addresses

Barbados External Telecommunications, Wildey, St Michael (tel: 427-5200; fax: 427-5808).

Barbados Investment and Development Corporation, Pelican House, Princess Alice Highway, St Michael (tel: 427-5350; fax: 426-7802; internet site: http://www.bidc.com/index.htm).

Barbados Manufacturers' Association, Prescod Blvd, Harbour Road, Bridgetown (tel: 426-4474, 427-9898; fax: 436-5182).

Barbados National Trust, 10th Avenue Relleville, St Michael (tel: 436-9033); The Future Centre Trust, Edgehill Street, St Thomas (fax: 425-0075).

Barbados Tourism Investment Inc, 2nd Floor, Nemwil House, Collymore Rock, St. Michael (tel: 426-7085; fax: 426-7086; e-mail: btii@tourisminvest.com.bb; internet site: http://barbadostourisminvestment.com).

British High Commission, PO Box 676, Lower Collymore Rock, St Michael (tel: 436-6694; fax: 436-5398, 426-7916).

Caribbean Broadcasting Corporation, PO Box 900, Bridgetown (tel: 429-2041).

US Embassy, PO Box 302, Canadian Imperial Bank of Commerce Building, Broad Street, Bridgetown (tel: 436-4950; fax: 429-5246).

Internet sites

Government information service: http://www.bgis.gov.bb/

Barbados Nation (newspaper): http://nationnews.com

Travel and Tourism Encyclopedia: http://www.barbados.org

Belarus

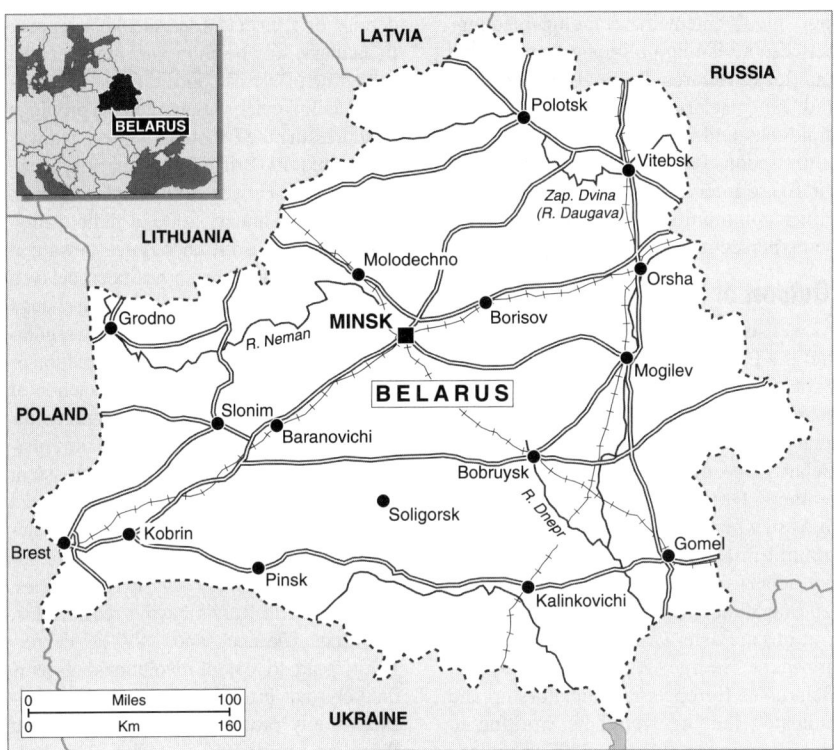

In 2005, there was a flurry of activity on the part of the government in Belarus, aimed at ensuring that the incumbent president, Alexander Lukashenko, would win presidential elections scheduled for March 2006. This included jailing opposition politicians, banning the flow of foreign funds to Belarus' political parties and NGOs, and clamping down on the country's ethnic Pole minority. There was also an air of self-congratulation on the matter of the Belarus economy.

Economic improvements

The IMF forecasts that the Belarus economy grew by 8.5–10.0 per cent in 2005. Inflation, running at 18.1 per cent in 2004, was reined to around 11 per cent in 2005; and the current account deficit, having surged in 2004, was also reversed in 2005. Andrei Kobyakov, Belarus' representative on the World Bank Board of Governors, heaped praise on Belarus' economic achievements since 1991 and in particular the country's achievements in 2005. However, the IMF also noted, in 2005, that such growth was unsustainable without major structural reforms and warned of difficult times ahead.

Gagging internal opposition

With President Lukashenko scheduled to face the electorate for only the second time in his long reign, in March 2006, the government assiduously prepared the ground for an incumbent victory. On the back of jailing prominent opposition figure, Mikhail Marinich, in December 2004, the government passed legislation, in August 2005, designed to block all foreign funding for Belarus' political parties and NGOs. Such funding was considered by both those in favour and against the bill as the last remaining financial lifeline for organisations expressing non-government views. Legislation was also passed in December making it illegal to circulate material that 'discredits' the state, and making it more difficult to hold anti-government demonstrations. The head of Belarus'

KEY FACTS

Official name: Respublika Belarus (Republic of Belarus)

Head of State: President Aleksandr Lukashenko (since 1994; re-elected 2001)

Head of government: Prime Minister Syarhey Sidorski (from 19 Dec 2003)

Ruling party: Coalition of Kommunisticheskaya Partuya Belarusi (KPB) (Communist Party of Belarus) and Agrarnaya Partiya Belarusi (APB) (Agrarian Party of Belarus) (since 1995)

Area: 208,000 square km

Population: 9.88 million (2004)

Capital: Minsk

Official language: Belarusian since 1990 and Russian since 1995 referendum.

Currency: Rouble (R)

Exchange rate: R2,152.50 per US$ (Oct 2005) (official) (currency was re-valued Jan 2000)

GDP per capita: US$2,641 (2004)

GDP real growth: 11.00% (2004)

Labour force: 5.37 million (2004)

Unemployment: 2.00% (official, 2004) (additional large number of underemployed)

Inflation: 18.10% (2004); *11.0% (2005)

Balance of trade: -US$2.06 billion (2004)

Foreign debt: US$600.00 million (2004)

KGB, Stepan Sukhorenko, stated that these laws were designed to resist an 'Orange Revolution'-style reaction to the presidential poll result in March 2006.

The main political opposition adopted two new tactics in 2005 in an effort to have their voice heard. On the 16th of every month, citizens were urged to place a candle in their windows. This was devised as a way of protesting against the regime that minimised the chance of being arrested or beaten by the police. In a reference to successful efforts to topple entrenched regimes elsewhere in the world, the opposition also adopted blue denim as their official colour, thus anticipating a 'denim revolution'. This came about in September after opposition supporter Mikita Sasim fashioned a flag out of his denim shirt just prior to being beaten unconscious by the police. Denim is also considered by many in the former USSR as a symbol of the West. In October, Belarus' main opposition parties united behind a single candidate to run in the March 2006 presidential election. Joint candidate Alexander Milinkevich, a former science professor, warned that he would take to the streets if the poll were rigged.

Belarus and the Poles

In June 2005, Belarus publicly clashed with its Polish neighbour. The diplomatic row was sparked by Poland's concern over the treatment by Belarus of its ethnic Polish minority. There are around 400,000 ethnic Poles living in Belarus, largely in the west of the country, which, between 1921–45, had been under Polish rule. President Lukashenko accused Poland and the Polish community in Belarus of seeking to overthrow him, and, in 2005, the Belarus authorities began to hound the main organisation representing Poles within Belarus. Two senior figures in the Zwiazek Polaków na Bialorusi (Union of Poles) were arrested in July, ostensibly for their involvement in arranging meetings between a visiting politician from Poland and local Belarus Poles. Between June and July, Belarus expelled three Polish diplomats and in July Poland recalled its ambassador. Poland subsequently urged the EU to intervene on behalf of Belarus' Polish community, arguing that they were being persecuted.

'Outpost of tyranny'

As well as drawing the attention of Poland and the EU in 2005, Belarus also elicited criticism from the US. In her confirmation hearing in January, the incoming US Secretary of State, Condoleezza Rice, called Belarus one of the world's 'outposts of tyranny'. Dr Rice reiterated her comments in April when, on the sidelines of a NATO summit in Lithuania, she met opposition politicians from Belarus. Just prior to attending Victory in Europe (VE) Day celebrations in Eastern Europe, May 2005, US president George W Bush singled out Belarus as Europe's last dictatorship and indicated that he would be working to make sure the March 2006 elections would be 'free and fair'. The US had already imposed a series of diplomatic sanctions on Belarus in the wake of widely criticised parliamentary elections in October 2004.

Outlook

Belarus will garner much foreign attention in 2006, primarily because of its presidential election in March. Given previous statements from the EU and the US on the matter, it is no surprise that the West favours the demise of President Lukashenko's regime. In January, this position was made crystal clear when Belarus opposition leader Alexander Milinkevich was granted the privilege of addressing the Polish parliament and was later fêted in Brussels by the European Commission. However, an EU plan to set up and fund, in January 2006, a radio station designed to transmit uncensored news and information into Belarus has been delayed until May. As for the prospect of real change in March, along the lines of a 'denim revolution', much will depend upon the reaction of Belarus' security forces and the reaction of Russia, Belarus' main economic and political sponsor over the past decade. Some analysts have noted that Russian president Vladimir Putin has in recent years distanced himself from President Lukashenko, particularly regarding the latter's desire for a political union between the two countries. However, with Russia having recently lost Georgia, Ukraine and, to a degree, Kyrgyzstan, to 'colour revolutions' it seems unlikely that President Putin would acquiesce in any protest-driven push to unseat President Lukashenko in March. The decision by Gazprom, Russia's state-owned gas monopoly company and main supplier of gas to Belarus, to cap Belarus' gas bill at 2005 levels while insisting in January 2006 that Ukraine pay more is indicative of this sentiment.

Risk assessment

Politics	Potentially explosive
Economy	Improving
Regional stability	Fragile

COUNTRY PROFILE

Historical profile
During the thirteenth and fourteenth centuries, Belarus was part of the Grand Duchy of Lithuania.
1500s The Grand Duchy was united with Poland.
1800s The dismemberment of Poland led to Belarus becoming a part of the Russian empire.
1918 Belarus became part of the Soviet Union, following the Russo-German treaty of Brest Litovsk.
1941–44 Belarus was occupied by Nazi Germany.

KEY INDICATORS — Belarus

	Unit	2000	2001	2002	2003	2004
Population	m	9.93	9.94	9.95	9.90	9.88
Gross domestic product (GDP)	US$bn	1.12	12.20	14.30	17.50	*22.85
GDP per capita	US$	1,104	1,220	1,403	1,430	2,641
GDP real growth	%	5.8	3.0	4.7	4.8	11.0
Inflation	%	168.9	61.1	42.6	29.0	18.1
Unemployment	%	2.1	2.3	2.6	2.1	2.0
Exports (fob) (goods)	US$m	6,932.3	7,240.1	7,530.0	10,092.0	13,916.8
Imports (fob) (goods)	US$m	7,840.0	8,018.8	8,460.0	11,326.0	15,982.5
Balance of trade	US$m	-907.7	-778.7	-935.0	-1,264.0	-2,065.7
Current account	US$m	-231.5	-270.3	-377.5	–	-680.0
Foreign debt	US$bn	0.9	0.9	0.9	0.9	0.6
Total reserves minus gold	US$m	350.5	390.7	618.8	594.8	749.4
Foreign exchange	US$m	350.3	390.3	618.5	594.8	749.3
Exchange rate	per US$	876.75	1,390.00	1,782.75	2,046.00	2,178.50

* estimated figure

Belarus

After the war, Belarus was returned to its status as a Soviet republic, although, uniquely, it was granted membership of the UN in its own right.

1988 The Narodni Front Belarusi (NFB) (Belarusian Popular Front) was formed.

1991 Independence was declared. Following the disintegration of the Soviet Union, the Kommunisticheskaya Partuya Belarusi (KPB) (Communist Party of Belarus) quickly established itself as the main political force. Stanislau Shushkevich (NFB), a moderate reformer, was chosen as head of the Supreme Soviet, a body dominated by old-guard communists.

1994 Shushkevich was dismissed after a vote of no-confidence. The constitution was settled. Belarus was influential in the creation of the Commonwealth of Independent States (CIS). The first free presidential elections were won by Aleksandr Lukashenko.

1996 A constitutional referendum changed the structure of government and gave the president sweeping powers. It also extended President Lukashenko's term of office until 2001.

1997 Belarus and Russia ratified the treaty establishing a Union of Russia and Belarus.

1998 Belarus and Russia agreed to begin steps to merge their currencies and taxation systems.

2000 The Belarus rouble exchange rate was re-denominated on 1 January. Prime Minister Sergei Ling was dismissed at the president's request; he had been prime minister since November 1996. The parliamentary elections were boycotted by the opposition. The presidents of Belarus, Kazakhstan, Kyrgyzstan, Russia and Tajikistan (formerly the Customs Five) established the Eurasion Economic Community (EEC).

2001 The Russian Federation Council approved the introduction of a single currency (the Russian rouble) for Russia and Belarus as of 1 January 2005. President Lukashenko was returned to power and began a second five-year term amid controversy over the fairness of the election. The president appointed Henadz Navitski as prime minister.

2002 The IMF refused financial assistance stating that Belarus had not made sufficient reforms.

2003 Nearly 73 per cent of voters took part in Belarus's local elections on 2 March. On 10 July, President Lukashenko dismissed Prime Minister Navitski; Syarhey Sidorski became prime minister. In September, Russia, Ukraine, Kazakhstan and Belarus signed an economic union treaty.

2004 Parliamentary election and a referendum were held on 17 October. Of the 110 seats in the House of Representatives, 107 were won by government supporters; an approval for a change to the constitution enabled Lukashenko to stand for a third term as president in 2006.

2005 The 2006 budget was passed by the Council of the Republic on 21 December.

Political structure
Constitution
The 1994 constitution vested legislative power in a 260-member Sejm (Supreme Council).

The first free presidential elections were held in 1994, after which differences emerged over the distribution of power between the president and the Supreme Council.

The constitutional referendum held in late 1996 and the subsequent introduction of a new constitution allowed an expansion of presidential powers and introduced a new two-chamber National Assembly, replacing the Sejm.

Form of state
Authoritarian presidential republic, where political life is dominated by the president and no real opposition is allowed.

The executive
The president is directly elected for a maximum of two five-year terms and also serves as commander-in-chief of the armed forces, appoints the cabinet and prime minister and has the power to declare a state of emergency, but not to dissolve parliament.

National legislature
The Natsionalnoye Sobranie (National Assembly has two chambers.

The Soviet Respubliki (Council of the Republic) is the upper house. Eight of the 64 members are appointed directly by the president and form the Council of Ministers, and the 56 are indirectly elected by members of the local soviets in the six Belarusian regions and Minsk (eight each). The list of candidates is subject to the final approval by President Lukashenko.

The 110-member Palata Predstavitely (House of Representatives) is the the lower house. Members are elected for four-year terms.

Legal system
Judicial power in the Republic of Belarus is vested in courts. The Constitutional Court adjudicates on whether law is constitutional. The prosecutor general is responsible for ensuring that all laws and presidential decrees are executed properly and uniformly across all state bodies and local Soviets.

Last elections
31 October 2004 (second round parliamentary); 9 September 2001 (presidential).

Results: Parliamentary: 107 of 110 deputies were elected, all supporters of the government, with 12 of them representing political parties. The remaining three seats are to be decided in a second round. Presidential: the official election commission said that President Lukashenko won with 75.6 per cent of the vote. There was controversy over the results.

Next elections
19 March 2006 (presidential); 2008 (parliamentary).

Political parties
Ruling party
Coalition of Kommunisticheskaya Partuya Belarusi (KPB) (Communist Party of Belarus) and Agrarnaya Partiya Belarusi (APB) (Agrarian Party of Belarus) (since 1995)

Main opposition party
Respublikanskaya Partiya Pratsy y Spravyadivasti (RPPS) (Republican Party of Labour and Justice)

Population
9.88 million (2004)
Ethnic make-up
Belorussian (78 per cent), Russian (13 per cent), Polish (4 per cent), Ukranian (3 per cent), other (2 per cent).
Religions
Eastern Orthodox (80 per cent), Roman Catholic, Protestant, Jewish and Islam (20 per cent).

Education
School education is divided into three stages: primary from aged four; basic from aged nine; then secondary schooling, from aged 11. Secondary schooling may be taught through gymnasiums, lyceums or colleges, as well as specialised or technical schools. Gymnasiums provide secondary education at a higher level, while lyceums provide vocational education. The certificate of lyceum education gives right of admission to any higher education institution.

Specialised secondary education lasts for two to four years. Colleges are a new type of institution in Belarus and provide advanced specialist training.

Public expenditure on education is estimated at some 6 per cent of annual gross national income.

Literacy rate: 99.7 per cent total adult literacy in 2002 (World Bank).

Compulsory years: 4 to 9.

Enrolment rate: 94.2 per cent net primary enrolment; 77.5 per cent net secondary enrolment, of the relevant age groups (including repetition rates), in 2002 (World Bank).

Pupils per teacher: 19 in primary schools.

Nations of the World: A Political, Economic and Business Handbook

Health
Expenditure on health is estimated at 5.7 of GDP, of which government spending is 82.8 per cent. The population declined by 0.5 per cent per annum between 1994–2000 and is projected to decline at the same rate between 1999–2015. The Ministry of Statistics and Analysis reported that the cause of the decrease is due to the number of deaths exceeding the number of births. The dramatic fall in life expectancy since the early 1990s is caused by environmental degradation, economic distress and the ever-present radiation from Chernobyl fall-out which continues to affect health, particularly among children.

Medical care in Belarus is limited. There is a severe shortage of basic medical supplies, including anaesthetics, vaccines and antibiotics.

Life expectancy: 68.2 years in 2003 (World Bank).

Fertility rate/Maternal mortality rate: 1.3 births per woman in 2003; maternal deaths 28 per 100,000 live births (World Bank).

Birth rate/Death rate: 14 deaths to 9 births per 1,000 people (World Bank).

Infant mortality rate: 13 per 1,000 live births in 2003 (World Bank).

Head of population per physician/bed: 4.3 physicians and 12.2 hospital beds per 1,000 people.

Welfare
For some years now both economic and political standards have deteriorated under President Lukashenko. As long ago as 1998, a poll by the Ministry of Economy reported that almost 80 per cent of families believed their material well-being had worsened since the collapse of the Soviet Union. Although the state exercises control and mobilises funds for social care and protection, Belarus, along with other Eastern European countries, is planning to privatise its social security systems. Foreign citizens and people permanently living in Belarus have equal rights to social services.

Since independence, the number of local non-governmental organisations (NGOs) has increased dramatically in Belarus. To strengthen the NGO sector, USAID has created the Counterpart Alliance Program (CAP), which provides seed grants to social service organisations in Belarus.

There is a two tiered system of social security coverage: general employed workers and special employees (such as aviators, civil servants and certain medical personnel). Contributions are acquired from three sources: workers, 1 per cent of earnings; employer, 4.7–35 per cent of the payroll, dependent on industry or enterprise; government revenue covers the cost of social pensions and subsidies as needed.

Social security payments are made to the unemployed and those without pension rights through a general social insurance.

Pensions
Pensions are provided for old age (beginning for men at age 60 and women at age 55, with 25 or 20 years contributions, respectively), disabilities and survivors, including payments for sickness and maternity benefits.

Main cities
Minsk (capital, estimated population 1.7 million in 2004), Homel (Gomel) (502,200), Brest (306,300), Hrodna (Grodno) (314,100), Mahileu (Mogilev) (374,000), Vitsebsk (Vitebsk) (355,800). Names in brackets are the Russian place-names.

Minsk is the headquarters for the Commonwealth of Independent States (CIS).

Languages spoken
Ukrainian, Polish and Yiddish.

Official language/s
Belarusian since 1990 and Russian since 1995 referendum.

Media
Press
Dailies: All the major widely circulated national newspapers (some of them heavily subsidised) are owned by the state. The most influential dailies include *Narodnaya Gazeta*, *Belaruska Niva* and *Sovetskaya Belorussia*. Independent newspapers include *Narodnaya Volya*, *Naviny* and *Nasha Niva*. *Belorusskaya Delovaya Gazeta* contains political and economic analysis and is the leading opposition newspaper. Russian newspapers have a strong hold on the Belarusian market. *Vecherny Minsk* is a national daily that is privately owned.

Weeklies: There are four national weekly newspapers, including *Argumenti i Facti*.

Business: *Minsk Economic News* provides recent economic and political information for businessmen, scientists, and analysts.

Broadcasting
The Belarusian National State Teleradio company operates domestic radio and TV channels and an external (international) radio service. Radio Baltic Waves (RBW) (Baltijos Bangos) was established in 1999 to deliver uncensored news and information to Belarus, incurring the complaints from the Belarusian government. RBW also relays Belarusian language broadcasts from Poland, Lithuania and the Czech Republic. In similar vein, Radio Ratsyya (Radio Reason) broadcasts in Belarusian from Bialystok in Poland.

Radio: Radio stations include Radio Minsk, Belarusian Radio 1 and 2, Radio VA and Radio Fox. Independent radio stations broadcast only entertainment shows.

Television: BTV is the state-run channel; there are also Russian, and occasionally Polish and Ukrainian, channels available.

Advertising
The advertising market has been developing very slowly. Advertisers use radio, television, newspapers (rarely used by foreign advertisers) and outdoor media.

Economy
During the Soviet era, the Belarus economy was geared towards industrial production of chemicals, metals and machinery, resulting in serious environmental problems. The break-up of the Soviet Union in 1991 had a strongly negative impact on the economy. Despite this, Belarus entered on a period of privatisation and preliminary reform supported by several international organisations. Continuing dependency on Russia for trade and aid undermined Belarus, particularly following the Asian financial crisis of 1997/98, which threw Russia and consequently Belarus into turmoil.

Since being swept to power in 1994 in the wake of public disillusionment with the negative effects of liberalisation, President Lukashenko has gradually reversed the economic reforms and returned to Soviet-style centralised planning. Price controls were reintroduced, exchange regulations reimposed, privatisation halted and the government has continued to prevent output collapse through subsidised credits to enterprises and farms. More than 95 per cent of the economy is in state control.

Industry and services are the mainstays of the economy, but rely on imports of raw materials and energy. There is a continuing and heavy reliance on Russia for trade, particularly for the import of gas and oil. The removal of gas subsidies from Russia in 2002 cost Belarus an estimated US$700 million per annum.

There was strong growth in the economy in 2004 with GDP increasing by 11 per cent, compared with 4.8 per cent in 2003. Potential in the economy is high as the country has a strategic location between Russian and central European markets. The policy of centralisation means there is a severe lack of foreign investment in the industry and infrastructure. The economy is diverse, with a high level of industrialisation, producing machinery, vehicles, construction materials and chemicals. The labour force is highly skilled with a large number of engineers and scientists.

External trade
For political reasons there have been US sanctions on Belarus since October 2004.

Belarus

Trading relations with Russia have strained over the last few years due to arguments over natural gas subsidies. By the end of 2005 arrangements had been made for gas supplies, and the pricing was capped at 2005 rates.

Imports
Principal imports include mineral products, machinery and equipment, metals, gas and energy, chemicals, foodstuffs.
Main sources: Russia (50 per cent total, 2004), Germany (13.3 per cent), Ukraine (4.3 per cent), Poland (4.2 per cent)

Exports
Principal exports include machinery and transport equipment, mineral products, chemicals, foodstuffs, metals and textiles.
Main destinations: Russia (38.7 per cent of total, 2004), Poland (6.5 per cent), Germany (5.1 per cent), Latvia (5.1 per cent), Ukraine (5.1 per cent)

Agriculture
Farming
About 60 per cent of arable land is used for livestock (cattle and pigs), the rest being used for cultivation of potatoes, grain, sugar beet and flax. Although agricultural lands occupy 9.4 million hectares (45.2 per cent of the total area), more than 30 per cent of the land is still contaminated as a consequence of the Chernobyl nuclear plant explosion in Ukraine in 1986. Particularly badly hit was the area around Gomel, where high levels of contamination are still recorded.

The sector receives heavy state support in the form of tax reductions, consumer goods, fertilisers and fuels and remains collectivised, although there are huge unpaid wage arrears on collective farms.

The climate in Belarus means that production is concentrated on hardier crops, including grains, flax, sugar beet and potatoes, of which Belarus is a leading producer.

Belarus meets its own food needs except for feed grains, sugar and vegetable oils, which the government has targetted for increased production. Agriculture is oriented towards meeting domestic market demands for food products with a trend towards animal production.

There has been a steady growth in the amount of agricultural land under private ownership, although the process is slow and obstructed by political and bureaucratic problems.

Crop production in 2004 included: 6,585,000 tonnes (t) cereals in total, 1,025,000t wheat, 2,070,000t barley, 1,480,000t rye, 3,088,200t sugar beets, 9,902,100t potatoes, 175,000t rapeseed (canola), 200,000t apples, 65,000t maize, 431,000t pulses, 150,000t tomatoes, 77,900t oilcrops, 1,400t tobacco, 357,900t fruit in total, 2,042,300t vegetables in total. Livestock production included: 440,600t meat in total, 180,000t beef, 318,000t pig meat, 2,000t lamb, 92,500t poultry, 160,500t eggs, 5,206,700t milk, 3,100t honey, 30,600t cattle hides, 80,000t sheepskins lamb, 1,400t wool, greasy.

Fishing
All fishing in Belarus is derived from rivers, lakes and reservoirs, mainly with drag nets by small teams moving from location to location. There is some fish farming, owned by the state or joint stock companies with government shareholdings. Belarus has the capacity to process up to 20,000 tonnes per year of mainly smoked and salted fish, with a total of around 300 organisations involved in the fishery industry. The main traditional products include cold smoked fish, salted, preserved and canned fish. Government programmes include increasing the level of catches, the volume and efficiency of fish processing activity by introducing new technologies. Belarus has had an agreement with Russia since 2002, under which Belarus receives fish quotas in the Russian exclusive economic zone for 10 years, Russian-Belarussian joint ventures base their fleets in Russian ports and both countries co-ordinate their fisheries policies.

Forestry
Forest and other wooded land accounts for over two-fifths of the land area, with forest cover of 9.4 million hectares. About three-quarters of the forest is available for wood supply. Timber includes spruce and birch, which are generally of high quality. The state owns all forest and other wooded land. The Belavezhskaja Pusha Nature Reserve (north of Brest on the Polish border) is Europe's largest remaining area of primeval forest, totalling 1,300 square km in size.

In the period 1990–2000, afforestation increased forest cover at an annual average rate of 3.23 per cent, the equivalent of 256,000 hectares.

The forest sector in Belarus makes an important contribution to the economy. The government has attempted to turn back the sector's deterioration in recent years by increasing exports of wood, wood processing and pulp products. It has also investigated environmentally sustainable forestry and has launched a programme of information collation, using satellite technology, to assess the best use of forestry resources.

There is abundant roundwood production, which is mainly used for sawnwood in both large state-owned and small private enterprises. A significant proportion of roundwood and nearly half of pulpwood production is exported. There is very little domestic consumption of production of sawnwood and panels, but pulp and paper production do not meet domestic demand.

In 2004, imports of forest materials amounted to US$211.3 million and exported stood at US$258.4 million. Production in 2004 included: 7,500,000 cubic metres (cum) roundwood, 2,300,000cum sawnwood, 2,300,000cum sawlogs and veneer logs, 1,600,000cum pulpwood (round and split), 814,600cum wood-based panels, 29,000cum veneer sheets, 1,100,000cum woodfuel, 279,300 tonnes (t) paper and paperboard, 8,300t printing and writing paper, 60,600t woodpulp.

Industry and manufacturing
The industrial sector accounts for 25.5 per cent of GDP and employs 40 per cent of the workforce. It has benefited from Soviet-era industrialisation, which transformed Belarus from an agricultural economy into the region's industrial hub. The sector is diverse and comprises heavy machine production, micro-electronics, computers, chemical and mineral processing, synthetic fibre production, textiles, consumer durables and food processing. Raw materials have to be imported and manufacturing is reliant on energy imports, mainly from Russia.

One of the prime industrial sub-sectors is the automative industry. Belarus is the world's third largest producer of tractors and also produces a large number of lorries, motorbikes and other vehicles, which are exported mainly to Europe. The Minsk Tractor Works (MTZ) produces up to 8 per cent of the world's tractors, which are exported to more than 100 countries.

Belarus' electronics sector is highly developed, due to its role in supplying the Soviet military machine. It manufactures radios, televisions and electronic devices used in engineering, as well as supplying consumer goods, including refrigerators and freezers, to countries inside and outside the former Soviet Union.

Production of chemicals is concentrated in Soligorsk, Gomel and Grodno. The chemical sector produces potassium and nitrate fertilisers, aminophosphate, medicines, polymers and plastics, chemical and synthetic fibres, pesticides, rubber goods and building materials.

Tourism
Despite government intentions to reinvigorate the tourist sector, it remains in the doldrums. 64,000 arrivals were recorded for 2004. Tourist facilities are inadequate with poor quality hotels and bureaucratic obstacles hindering visitors; visas cost more than those charged by neighbouring states, border crossings are tedious and costly, while levies on hotel rooms for tourists put them out of the reach of most

visitors. Investment in upgrading facilities and conserving historic tourist attractions is in short supply. Tourism is expected to contribute 1.9 per cent to GDP in 2005.

Environment
One-third of the nation's agricultural land has been unusable since it was contaminated by fall-out from the 1986 Chernobyl nuclear accident.

Mining
Belarus is not rich in natural resources, except for deposits of peat, used in power stations and for the manufacture of chemicals. There are significant deposits of potassium, which is a major export, and rock salt. Other resources include clay, sand, iron ore, cobalt, phosphate, silver and gold. Many known mineral deposits await development, while a full survey of the country's resources has yet to be carried out.

Hydrocarbons
Belarus has proven oil reserves of 198 million barrels. The country typically produces over 35,000 barrels per day (bpd), but imports 75 per cent of its oil needs, all of which come from Russia. Refining capacity is over 300,000bpd, higher than both domestic production and consumption. There are two refineries in the regions of Novopolotsk Vitebsk and Gomel. Natural gas reserves stand at 2.83 billion cubic metres (cum). Belarus produces around 210 million cum of natural gas, but with consumption amounting to 19.6 billion cum, the country is heavily reliant on Russian gas imports.

There are deposits of brown coal of little value. Coal is not produced, but is imported from Russia.

Energy
Belarus has a total electricity generating capacity of 7.5GW. Net electricity imports amount to 20 per cent of annual electricity demand. Gas accounts for approximately 71 per cent of electricity generation and oil for the rest. Fears of accelerating inflation have slowed the implementation of tariff reform and price rises have been consistently outstripped by inflation.

Banking and insurance
The National Bank of the Republic of Belarus (NBRB) (central bank) and the Commercial Bank for Foreign Economic Activity (CBFEA) were established in 1991. All enterprises were instructed to transfer hard currency funds from the Russian Vnesheconombank to the CBFEA. The banking system has seen an increase in state participation since President Lukashenko was first elected in 1994. Priorbank is the largest private bank and holds 8 per cent of the total assets of the banking system, making it the fifth largest in Belarus. Foreign capital participation is present in 19 banks, including two which are wholly foreign owned. Credit to the private sector amounts to 9 per cent of GDP. In January 2003, Austria's Raiffeisen Bank bought a 50 per cent stake in Priorbank for US$30.5 million, injecting competition into the sector.

Central bank
The National Bank of the Republic of Belarus

Time
GMT plus two hours (GMT plus three hours from late March to late September)

Geography
Belarus is situated in north-eastern Europe. It has a short frontier with Poland to the west. Lithuania lies to the north-east, Latvia to the north, Russia to the north, north-east and east, and Ukraine to the south-east and south. The land is a plain with numerous lakes, swamps and marshes. There is an area of low hill country north of Minsk. The highest point, Mount Dzyarzhynskaya, is only 346 metres above sea-level. The southern part of the country is a low flat marshland. Forests cover some 30 per cent of the territory. The main rivers are the Dnepr which flows south to the Black Sea, and the Pripyat which flows eastwards to the Dnepr through the Pripyat Marshes.

Climate
Temperature ranges from -6 degrees Celsius (C) in January, to a high of 18 degrees C in August. The average annual rainfall is 550mm to 700mm.

Dress codes
With grey, freezing winters and wet summers, fashion takes second place to practicality in Belarus. Smart dress is required for business.

Entry requirements
Passports
Valid passport required by all. Must be valid for six months after departure.
All foreign nationals must register their passports at the local police station within three days of their arrival. If staying at a hotel, reception will do this automatically.
Visa
Visas are required by almost all. Some exceptions include nationals of the CIS, travelling as tourists. For further details of those exempt and full requirements for visas visit www.mfa.gov.by/eng/consul/3. Business visas allow stays up to 90 days. Applications must include an invitation, (may be originally supplied as fax) on official letterhead and should have a signature of the head of a company as well as a corporate seal. It should also indicate the expected period of stay and a pledge by the host company to provide the invited person full support during their stay in Belarus including all possible medical expenses.
Exit permits are required by foreigners intending to leave the country with expired visas.
Currency advice/regulations
Import and export of the local currency up to R100 is permitted. Import of foreign currency is unlimited, while export is possible within the limits of the declaration given, less amounts exchanged or spent. The Belarus rouble is non-convertible outside Belarus.
US dollars and euros should be imported since many public services can only be paid for in hard currencies.
Customs
Small amounts of personal goods are duty-free. On arrival declare all foreign currency and valuable items such as jewellery, cameras, computers and musical instruments.

Health (for visitors)
Medical insurance is required by all foreign citizens visiting Belarus.
Mandatory precautions
None
Advisable precautions
Water precautions are recommended (water purification tablets may be useful) and the avoidance of dairy products, mushrooms and fruits of the forest (all of which may still be contaminated by radiation from the Chernobyl disaster). Some immunisations may be advantageous: polio, typhoid, diphtheria and tetanus, and hepatitis 'A' for longer term visitors.
It is wise to carry adequate supplies of prescribed medicines, and have precautionary antibiotics if going outside major urban centres. A travel kit including a disposable syringe is a reasonable precaution.
A reciprocal health agreement for urgent medical treatment exists with the UK. Proof of UK residency is essential.

Hotels
There are no Western-standard hotels in Belarus. Intourist operates a number of hotels that can be booked from the West, but visitors have reported bad conditions.

Credit cards
Only valid in a few locations such as major hotels.

Public holidays
Fixed dates
1 Jan (New Year), 7 Jan (Orthodox Christmas Day), 8 Mar (Women's Day), 15 Mar (Constitution Day), 1 May (Labour Day), 9 May (Victory Day), 3 Jul (Independence Day), 2 Nov (Dzyady/Remembrance Day), 7 Nov (Day of the October Revolution), 25 Dec (Christmas Day).

Belarus

Variable dates
Good Friday, Orthodox Good Friday, Easter Monday, Orthodox Easter Monday.

Working hours
Banking
Mon–Fri: 0930–1730. Priorbank, Minsk 2 airport, daily: 0900–1700.
Exchange outlets are open all day until late, and some open 24 hours.
Business
Mon–Fri: 0900–1800 (appointments best between 0900–1000).
Shops
Most food stores are now open Mon–Sat: 0900–1400 and 1500–2000. Sat: 0900–1800.
General stores open Mon to Fri: 1000–1400 and 1500–1900. Sat: 1000–1800.
There are some 24-hour food stores.

Electricity supply
220V AC 50Hz. European-style round two-pin plugs are in use.

Social customs/useful tips
A firm handshake is important as is negotiating an agenda at the beginning of the meeting. Smoking in meetings is very common. Ask permission before lighting a cigarette and offer cigarettes generously. Written communications are particularly important with large bureaucracies. Address the recipient formally and keep a copy of everything. It is customary to take a small gift on a business or social visit. Offering basic food is considered insulting. Offer little luxuries. It is impolite to take along people who are not invited to a social function.
Business is conducted formally and appointments are essential. Gratuities are not obligatory but are becoming more widespread. Vodka is drunk.

Security
Crime levels have risen since 1991 as the economic situation has deteriorated. However, crime is still negligible in this police state and visitors should be more fearful of the law enforcers and avoid political demonstrations.

Getting there
Air
National airline: Belavia Belorus (Belarusian Airlines)
International airport/s: Minsk 2 (MSQ), 43km east of the city, facilities include banks and bureaux de change, bars, car hire, duty-free shops, post office and restaurants.
Airport tax: None.
Surface
Road: Good road connections exist with Ukraine, the Baltic States, Poland and Russia. Visitors arriving by car are advised to insure their vehicle with a Belarusian insurer (eg Belingosstrakh); offices can be found at crossing sites. Note that petrol is limited and only 4-star and diesel are available. Most petrol stations only accept cash.
Rail: There are train connections with all neighbouring countries, with express trains from most European capitals.

Getting about
National transport
Road: Belarus has a road network of over 55,000km, the majority of which is hard surfaced. It is advisable to keep away from military establishments. Petrol is limited; only 4-star and diesel are available; and most petrol stations only accept cash. Motorways connect many of the major cities.
Rail: Total railtrack is about 5,523km broad gauge, of which approximately 875km is electrified. Train tickets and reservations can be purchased at Francyska Skaryny Prospekt No 18, Minsk.
Water: Belarus is landlocked, but there is an extensive network of inland waterways (3,800km) which mainly convey cargo goods. The Mukhavets and Pripyat rivers in south Belarus are connected by the strategic Dnepr-Buh Canal, which in turn gives access to the Baltic and Black Seas.
City transport
Taxis: Taxis are plentiful; they can be found waiting in front of hotels, at the airport, railway station and bus station. Journey time from the airport to city centre is about 40 minutes.
Buses, trams & metro: The city of Minsk has a metro that covers the central district (16 stations) and is in the process of being expanded. Trains run between 0600-0100; buses, trams and trolleybuses between 0535-0055. Tickets for buses, trams and trolleybuses can be purchased at news-stands or kiosks and are punched on board. Entry to the underground is by tokens which are obtainable from stations. There are buses from the international airport to city centre, journey time about 60 minutes.
Car hire
Cars can be rented, with or without a driver. An international driving licence with international permit is required. There are numerous restrictions that apply to driving. It is illegal to drive after consuming any amount of alcohol, no matter how little. Driving is on the right. International traffic signs and regulations are in use. Speed limits are 60kph (37mph) in towns and cities and 90kph (55mph) on country lanes.

BUSINESS DIRECTORY
The addresses listed below are a selection only. While World of Information makes every endeavour to check these addresses, we cannot guarantee that changes have not been made, especially to telephone numbers and area codes. We would welcome any corrections.

Telephone area codes
The international direct dialling (IDD) code for Belarus is +375, followed by area code and subscriber's number:

Brest	16	Minsk	17
Gomel	23	Mogilev	22
Grodno	15	Vitebsk	21

Chambers of Commerce
Belarussian Chamber of Commerce and Industry, 14 Masherova Avenue, 220035 Minsk (tel: 226-9127; fax: 226-9860; e-mail: mbox@cci.by).

Brest Chamber of Commerce and Industry, 14 Kubysheva Street, 224016 Brest (tel: 223-2400; fax: 223-4854; e-mail: bo@tppbrs.belpak.brest.by).

Grodno Chamber of Commerce and Indutry, Sovetskaya Street, 20023 Grodno (tel: 224-9070; e-mail: anat@grocci.belpark.grodno.by).

Minsk Chamber of Commerce and Industry, 65 Ya Kolas Street, 220113 Minsk (tel: 266-0473; fax: 266-2604; e-mail: secret@mdbcci.belpak.minsk.by).

Vitebsk Chamber of Commerce and Industry, Kosmonavtov Street, 210001 Vitebsk (tel: 236-3052; fax: 236-4674; e-mail: vitebsk@cci.by).

Banking
Belagroprom Bank, 44 Kropotkina Street, Minsk 220002 (tel: 503-958).

Bel Vnesh Econom Bank (Belarus Bank for Foreign Economic Affairs), 10 Zaslavskaya Street, Minsk 220004 (tel: 269-757, 267-022; fax: 269-759).

Commercial Bank for Reconstruction and Development (Belbusinessbank), 6a Partizansky Ave, 220033 Minsk (tel: 298-147, 768-942; fax: 298-147, 768-504).

Central bank
The National Bank of the Republic of Belarus, 20 F Skorina Avenue, 220008 Minsk (tel: 219-2303; fax: 227-4879; e-mail: email@nbrb.by).

Travel information
Belavia Belarussian Airlines, Minsk Aerodromnaya, Str 4, Minsk 220065 (tel: 255-902, 250-836; fax: 251-566, 250-629).

Belavia Belarusian Airlines, 14 Nemiga Street, Minsk 220004 (tel: 229-2290; fax: 229-2383).

National tourist organisation offices
Belintourist, 19 Masherov Avenue, 220004 Minsk (tel: 226-9840; fax: 223-1143; email: office@belintourist.by; internet: www.belintourist.by).

Nations of the World: A Political, Economic and Business Handbook

Ministries

Department of Foreign Economic Co-operation (tel: 269-169).

Department of International Relations (tel: 269-187; fax: 269-936).

Ministry of Agriculture, Dom Pravitelstva, Minsk (tel: 271-377, 271-352, 205-492).

Ministry of Finance, Dom Pravitelstva, 220010 Minsk (tel: 296-949).

Ministry of Foreign Affairs, ul. K. Mark 16, 220050 Minsk (tel: 272-011; fax: 293-383).

Ministry of Information, Prospekt Mashirova 11, Minsk (tel: 237-574).

Ministry of Statistics and Analysis of the Republic of Belarus, 12 Partizan Avenue, Minsk 220658 (tel: 491-261, 495-200; fax: 492-204).

Ministry of Trade, Kirov St. Building, Minsk 220084 (tel: 276-121).

State Committee for Foreign Economic Relations, House of Government, Minsk 220010 (tel: 296-345).

State Committee for Economic Planning, Dom Pravitelstva, Minsk (tel: 296-944).

Other useful addresses

Belarusintorg, Foreign Trade Organisation, Ulitsa Kollektornaya 10, 220048 Minsk (tel: 207-812, 209-756, 208-188; fax: 209-470, 204-763).

British Embassy, 37 Karl Marx Street, Minsk 220016 (tel: 292-303/4/5, 172105920; fax: 292-306, 172292306); Visa and Consulate Section (tel: 292-310; fax: 292-311).

Minsk Expo Exhibition Company, pr. Masherova 14, Minsk 220035 (tel: 226-9193/9890; fax: 226-9192/9936; e-mail: minskexpo@brm.minsk.by; internet site: http://www.minskexpo.com.by).

National Centre for Marketing and Price Study, 7-1117 Masherov Avenue, Minsk, PO 220004 (to reach the National Centre call for voice connection and/or fax: 266-758).

News Agency, Minsk (tel: 293-040).

Union of Enterpreneurs, 13 Internatsional'naya St, Minsk 220050 (tel: 172-587; fax: 271-596).

US Embassy, 46 Starovilenskaya Street, Minsk 220002 (tel: 210-1283; fax: 234-7853).

Internet sites

Belarus Railways: http://www.belrw.com

Belarusian web links: http://www.belarusian.com/links/

Belarusian web sites: http://www.ac.by/country/belwww.html

General information: http://www.belarus.net

Investment: http://www.ib.by

Chamber of Commerce: http://www.cci.by

Business information: http://www.delobelarus.com

General information: http://www.open.by

Belgium

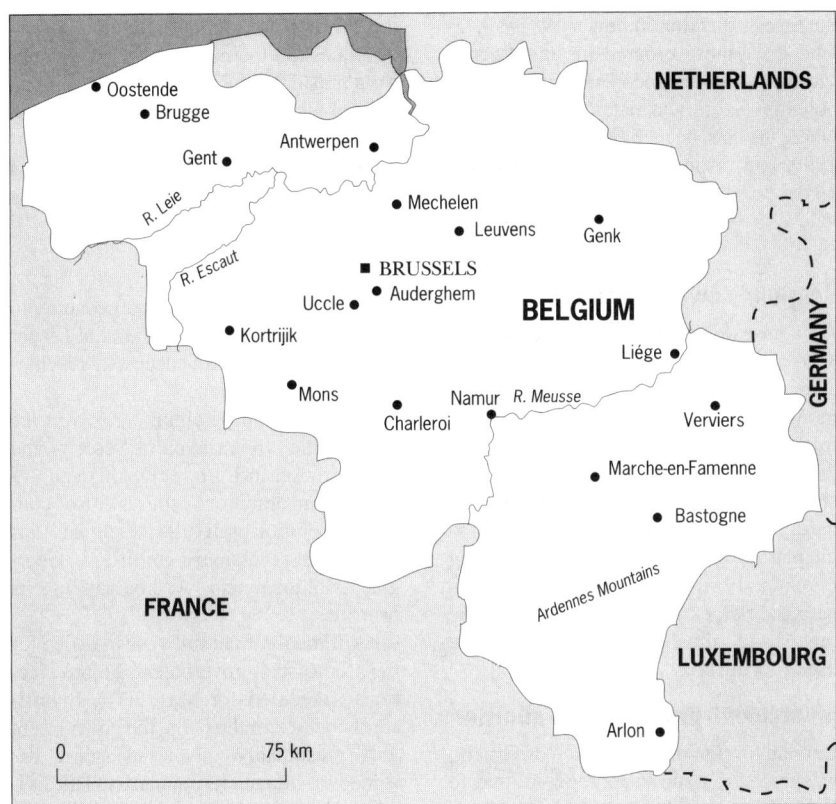

In 2005, Belgium spent much time reflecting on and dealing with the consequences of actions and events that took place both inside and outside Belgium. Belgium had to deal with a slowdown in the economy, inherited from the end of 2004. Atrocities committed in Africa, some of them more than a century ago, also had repercussions in Belgium.

Slow economic recovery

An economic downturn, apparent at the end of 2004, continued to dog Belgium in 2005. GDP growth slipped to 1.5 per cent in 2005, down from 2.7 per cent the previous year. A debt reduction programme also slowed, partly as a result of the downturn and partly as a result of the government taking on the debt of the national rail company, estimated to be around 2.5 per cent of GDP. Government efforts to reform the national pension scheme resulted in 24-hour strikes in October, drastically effecting schools, transport systems and other public services.

Linguistic politics

The coalition government of Prime Minister Guy Verhofstadt, first elected to office in 1999, was forced to a no-confidence motion in May 2005, due to a dispute over language rights in a constituency in suburban Brussels. Belgium is divided into three federal units, Flanders (Flemish-speaking), Wallonia (French-speaking) and Brussels (bi-lingual). Political parties also reflect this linguistic divide, meaning, for example, that a French-speaking party will have a sister party in the Flemish-speaking half of the country. Immigration, in recent years, of French-speakers into Brussels suburbs that are administratively part of Flanders has given rise to disputes over which political parties will represent the electorate – French-speaking ones, as reflected in

KEY FACTS

Official name: Royaume de Belgique (French), Koninkrijk België (Dutch), Königreich Belgien (German) (Kingdom of Belgium)

Head of State: King Albert II (since 1993)

Head of government: Federal Prime Minister Guy Verhofstadt (VLD) (since Jun 1999)

Ruling party: Coalition government: Vlaamse Liberalen en Demokraten (VLD) (Flemish Liberal and Democrats), Socialistische Partij Anders-Spirit (SPA-Spirit) (Socialist Party-Spirit), Parti Socialiste (PS) (Socialist Party) and Mouvement Réformateur (MR) (Reform Movement) (from Jul 2003; new government sworn in on 20 Jul 2004)

Area: 30,518 square km

Population: 10.41 million (2004); 10.37 million (OECD, 2003)

Capital: Brussels

Official language: Dutch (Flemish), French and German

Currency: Euro (eur) = 100 cents (from 1 Jan 2002; previous currency Belgian franc, locked at Bf40.34 per euro)

Exchange rate: eur0.83 per US$ (Oct 2005)

GDP per capita: US$34,244 (2004)

GDP real growth: 2.70% (2004); *1.5% (2005)

Labour force: 4.45 million (2003)

Unemployment: 7.80% (OECD, 2004)

Inflation: 1.90% (2004)

Balance of trade: US$8.99 billion (2004)

Foreign debt: US$949.47 billion (2004)

Annual FDI: US$34.40 billion (OECD, 2004)*

* estimated figure

Headscarf politics

In March, Naima Amzil, a Belgian originally from Morocco, quit her job after receiving a death threat that singled her out due to her religion and her use of a headscarf. The incident drew national attention, as both Ms Amzil and her employer had been receiving threats since November 2005 and had received public support from politicians, trade unions and even the King. Despite the shock expressed by many, in a country better known for its tolerance, the issue of wearing headscarves has polarised Belgium in recent years. In Antwerp, police are now able to reprimand or even imprison a woman for wearing a *burqa*.

Busy courts

In November, 13 men went on trial for supporting the recent bombings in Madrid and Casablanca. Regarded by many analysts as the most important terrorism trial in Europe to take place since 11 September 2001, the men are alleged to be members of the Moroccan Islamic Combat Group (MICG).

Belgium's judiciary was also busy dealing with individuals charged under the country's 'universal jurisdiction law', passed in 1993. Under this law, crimes committed anywhere in the world could be brought to trial in Belgium if local courts were unable or unwilling to do so. Following the first successful conviction under the law in 2001, a flood of cases has been brought before Belgian courts. Of these, two made significant progress in 2005. In June, two Rwandans were found guilty of assisting in the Hutu-led genocide against Rwanda's ethnic Tutsi community. In September, a warrant for the arrest of former Chadian dictator, Hissène Habré, was issued on the basis of charges brought before a Belgian court. Victims of the former dictator, in power 1982–90, allege that Habré ordered his intelligence services to torture and kill his political opponents. Habré was detained in Senegal, where he has been living in exile since 1990, and responsibility for the decision on his extradition was passed by the Senegalese government to the African Union (AU).

Belgium's own African past

A major exhibition opened in Brussels in March 2005, bringing together an unprecedented collection of photographs, testimony and analysis related to Belgium's role in its former colony of Congo (now the Democratic Republic of Congo, since changing its name from Zaire in 1997). In particular, the exhibition drew attention to the period 1878–1908, when Belgian king Leopold II brutally ran the Congo as his personal fief, extracting a fortune in ivory, rubber and mineral resources through the use of local slave labour.

An accident-prone foreign minister

Belgian foreign minister, Karel de Grucht, was forced to issue an apology, in June, to Netherlands prime minister Jan Peter Balkenende. De Grucht had called Dutch voters 'superficial' for their recent rejection of the EU constitution and had called Prime Minster Balkenende 'a mix between Harry Potter and a brave rigid bourgeois'. It was de Grucht's third public gaffe in recent months, having twice upset the authorities in the former Belgian colony of the Democratic Republic of Congo (DRC), in October 2004 and February 2005. De Grucht was accused of denigrating the DRC's political elite and calling into question the nationality of the country's president, Joseph Kabila. During an official visit to the DRC in October 2004, de Grucht was himself ironically caricatured by the DRC information minister as Tintin, a colonial-era Belgian cartoon character.

Outlook

The IMF expects the Belgian economy to grow at an improved rate of around 1.9 per cent during 2006 and a successful resumption of debt reduction.

In January 2006, Belgium took over the chair of the Organisation of Security and Co-operation in Europe (OSCE) and announced an ambitious programme of conflict resolution activities. Belgium has singled out secessionist conflicts in Georgia, Moldova and Azerbaijan as its priorities.

It will be the final full year in office for the Verhofstadt government, before elections scheduled for May 2007. Significantly behind in the polls, the government will presumably unveil measures designed to shore up its popularity. The divisive issue of language rights within the suburban constituencies of Brussels was delayed for two years back in May 2005, meaning that it will again return just in time for the 2007 election.

Risk assessment

Politics	Stable
Economy	Improving
Regional stability	Stable

COUNTRY PROFILE

Historical profile

In the eighth and ninth centuries, the area which is now Belgium was part of the Charlemagne empire. It achieved independence by the tenth century. Flemish towns, with their large textile industries, enjoyed great financial and political power.
1322 The area fell under French control again.
1419 The accession of Philip of Burgundy ended a period of instability.
1477 The Low Countries (Belgium and the Netherlands) passed to the Habsburgs

KEY INDICATORS — Belgium

	Unit	2000	2001	2002	2003	2004
Population	m	10.24	10.30	10.33	10.37	10.41
Gross domestic product (GDP)	US$bn	231.00	229.90	247.10	296.44	*349.83
GDP per capita	US$	23,100	22,400	24,100	28,700	34,244
GDP real growth	%	3.7	0.9	0.9	1.3	2.7
Inflation	%	2.5	2.5	1.6	1.5	1.9
Unemployment	%	10.9	6.6	7.3	8.2	7.8
Exports (fob) (goods)	US$m	166,982.0	161,428.0	223,520.0	255,300.0	244,552.0
Imports (fob) (goods)	US$m	164,197.0	158,113.0	208,870.0	235,500.0	-23,559.0
Balance of trade	US$m	2,785.0	3,315.0	17,500.0	19,900.0	8,993.0
Current account	US$m	11,844.0	13,037.0	11,600.0	14,600.0	14,910.0
Total reserves minus gold	US$m	9,994.0	11,266.0	11,855.0	10,989.0	10,361.0
Foreign exchange	US$m	7,988.0	8,743.0	8,909.0	7,651.0	7,715.0
Exchange rate	per US$	43.68	43.05	1.04	0.88	0.80

* estimated figure

of Spain on the death of Philip's son, Charles the Bold.
1500–55 Under the reign of Emperor Charles V, Antwerp was a leading commercial centre and financial centre.
1555–98 Reign of Philip II, King of Spain. The Belgians and the Dutch reacted against the tyranny of Philip II. There was trouble between the protestants and the catholics.
1580s The northern Netherlands managed to secede. King Philip reconquered the south, where catholicism was imposed. The leading traders and intellectuals migrated to the north.
1598–1621 Under Archduke Albert and Archduchess Isabella (daughter of Philip II), the southern Netherlands (Belgium excluding Liège) became semi-autonomous.
1648 The Peace of Westphalia confirmed this position.
1700–13 The War of the Spanish Succession resulted in the southern Netherlands passing to the Austrian Habsburgs. Liège remained independent within the Holy Roman Empire.
1790 The United States of Belgium was established after a local revolution inspired by the French revolution.
1792 French troops conquered the southern Netherlands and Liège.
1793 The Austrians reoccupied the territory.
1794 The southern Netherlands and Liège were invaded by the French and the newly integrated territories were annexed to France. When Napoleon came to power, Belgium became part of the French empire.
1814–15 After the defeat of Napoleon, the allies met at the Congress of Vienna and decided to unite the northern and southern Netherlands and the princedom of Liège under the rule of King William I. The catholic church refused to accept a protestant King. William tried to impose Dutch in Flanders. The young Walloon and Flemish upper classes, which spoke French, were afraid that their careers would be affected.
1828 The Catholics and young Liberals formed an association called Unionism and drew up a programme of demands.
1830 Revolution erupted in Brussels and the south broke away from the north and formed an independent Belgian state.
1831–65 Leopold I of Saxe-Coburg became the first King of Belgian.
1865–1909 His son Leopold II succeeded him. He backed expeditions to Africa. In 1908, Congo was transferred to the Belgian state.
1909–34 King Albert I reigned.
1914 Following the outbreak of the First World War, Germany invaded Belgium and the country became a battlefield until the end of the war in 1918.
1918–39 Inter-war years saw rapid industrialisation, developing colonial wealth in Africa and the forging of regional links, leading to the Belgium-Luxembourg Economic Union (BLEU).
1940–45 Belgium was invaded and occupied by Nazi Germany.
1947 Belgium formed a customs union with Luxembourg and the Netherlands, known as Benelux.
1951 King Leopold III, who had been on the throne since 1934, abdicated in favour of his son, Baudouin (Boudewijn) I.
1958 Belgium was a founder member of the forerunner of the EU, the European Economic Community (EEC), with Brussels becoming the favoured location for the organisation.
1960 Belgium withdrew rapidly from the Belgian Congo.
1970s There was a succession of unstable coalition governments.
1979–92 Christian Democrat Wilfried Martens was appointed prime minister twice during this period, with Mark Eyskens serving for some months in 1981.
1992 Jean-Luc Dehaene was appointed prime minister.
1993 King Baudouin I died and was succeeded by his brother, Albert II. Belgium became a federal state.
1999 Belgium was one of the first 11 countries to adopt the euro. Guy Verhofstadt was appointed prime minister.
2001 A government reform package was approved, which provided more money for schools in the French-speaking communities of the south and more political influence for the Dutch-speaking Flemish around Brussels even though they are a minority.
2002 Euro currency replaced the Belgian franc.
2003 The May parliamentary elections were won by the Vlaamse Liberalen en Demokraten (VLD) (Flemish Liberal and Democrats), led by Guy Verhofstadt, who formed a coalition government in July, which included the Socialistische Partij Anders-Spirit (SPA-Spirit) (Socialist Party-Spirit), Parti Socialiste (PS) (Socialist Party) and Mouvement Réformateur (MR) (Reform Movement).
2004 A new government was sworn in on 20 July.
2005 After failing to resolve a dispute between French and Dutch speakers over the re-drawing of the country's biggest electoral district, Prime Minister Guy Verhofstadt's liberal-socialist coalition government comfortably won a parliamentary vote of confidence on 13 May.

Political structure
Constitution
A new constitution was introduced in 1994, re-defining the federal structure and introducing devolution on both a regional and language-speaking level. In 2001, a constitutional amendment allowed greater autonomy in taxation, spending, agricultural and trade policy. The federal state is responsible for economic, domestic, foreign, defence, legal, welfare and health policy.
The are three Régions/Gewests (Regions) of Flemish, Wallonia and Brussels. Each has its own executive and assembly, responsible for regional policies (such as transport and housing).
Overlapping the Regions are three Communautés/Gemeenschaps (Communities), representing Belgium's Flemish, French and German-speakers. They are responsible for policy on language and cultural affairs. The French and German Communities operate separate parliaments. The Flemish Region and Community (which represent the same geographical area) operate a joint assembly. Language and cultural affairs in the Brussels Region are divided between the Flemish and French Communities.
In May 2003 electoral reforms allowed changes to electoral districts for the House of Representatives, which now match the borders of the provinces, a new system of distribution of seats, an electoral threshold and Belgians abroad allowed to vote.

Form of state
Federal parliamentary democratic monarchy

The executive
Executive responsibilities reside with the federal prime minister and Council of Ministers (cabinet) and with the regional prime ministers and cabinets. The monarch has a largely ceremonial role.
The Council of Ministers is appointed by the monarch and approved by parliament. Following legislative elections, the leader of the majority party or the leader of the majority coalition is usually appointed prime minister by the monarch and then approved by parliament.

National legislature
Legislative power is vested in a bicameral parliament, consisting of the Senate (71 seats; 40 members are directly elected by popular vote, 31 are indirectly elected; members serve four-year terms) and the Chamber of Representatives (150 seats; members are directly elected by popular vote on the basis of proportional representation to serve four-year terms). Both chambers can propose and veto legislation.

Legal system
The *Code Napoléon*, became the basis of civil law in Belgium.
The constitution guarantees the independence of the judiciary from the executive and legislative branches. Court hearings

are public and trials of a serious nature are heard before a jury of civilians.
The highest court is the Cour de Cassation (Supreme Court), composed of judges appointed by the Crown. A Cour d'Arbitration rules on conflicts of authority between the many layers of federal and national government and their legal instruments.

A Consultation Committee, made up of regional and national representatives including the prime minister, is the final recourse for conflicts of interest arising from devolution. Formed with equal numbers of French and Dutch/Flemish speakers, it makes its decisions by consensus.

Last elections
13 June 2004 (European Parliament); 18 May 2003 (parliamentary).

Results: European Parliament: CD&V won 16.4 per cent of the vote (four seats out of 24), VB 13.5 per cent (three), PS 13.4 per cent (four), VLD 12.8 per cent (three), SPA-Spirit 10.4 per cent (three), MR 10.4 per cent (three), CDH 5.7 per cent (one), Agalev 4.7 per cent (one), Ecolo 3.9 per cent (one), Christlich Soziale Partei-Europäische Volkspartei (one). Turnout 90.8 per cent.

Parliamentary: the Vlaamse Liberalen en Demokraten (VLD) (Flemish Liberals and Democrats), led by Guy Verhofstadt, won 15.4 per cent of the vote (25 seats out of 150), the Socialistische Partij Anders-Spirit (SPA-Spirit) (Socialist Party-Spirit) (Flemish Socialists) 14.9 per cent (23 seats), the Christen-Democratisch & Vlaams (CD&V) (Flemish Christian Democrats) 13.3 per cent (21), the Parti Socialiste (PS) (French Socialists) 13.0 per cent (25), the Vlaams Blok (VB) (Flemish Bloc) 11.6 per cent (18), the Mouvement Réformateur (MR) (French Liberals) 11.4 per cent (24), the Centre Démocrate Humaniste (CDH) (French Christian Democrats) 5.5 per cent (eight), the Ecologistes Confédérés (Ecolo) (French Greens) 3.1 per cent (four), the Nieuw-Vlaamse Alliantie (N-VA) (New Flemish Alliance) 3.1 per cent (one), the Anders Gaan Leven (Agalev) (Flemish Greens) 2.5 per cent (no seats) and the Front National (FN) (National Front) 2.0 per cent (one).

Next elections
2007 (parliamentary)

Political parties
Ruling party
Coalition government: Vlaamse Liberalen en Demokraten (VLD) (Flemish Liberal and Democrats), Socialistische Partij Anders-Spirit (SPA-Spirit) (Socialist Party-Spirit), Parti Socialiste (PS) (Socialist Party) and Mouvement Réformateur (MR) (Reform Movement) (from Jul 2003; new government sworn in on 20 Jul 2004)

Main opposition party
Christen-Democratische en Vlaamse (CD&V) (Christian Democratic and Flemish)

Population
10.41 million (2004); 10.37 million (OECD, 2003)

Ethnic make-up
Around 57 per cent of the population live in Dutch-speaking Flanders, 32 per cent in French-speaking Wallonia, 10 per cent in bilingual Brussels and 1 per cent in the German-speaking border region. There are also some 860,000 foreign expatriates and immigrants. The largest expatriate communities are Italian, French, Moroccan, Dutch, Turkish and Spanish. Foreigners comprise about 27 per cent of the population of Brussels.

Religions
Predominantly Roman Catholic (75 per cent). Also Protestant, Jewish and Muslim.

Education
Education budgets are set by the French, Dutch/Flemish and German language communities.

Most schools are state-run and free. Catholic and international schools are fee-paying. The Belgian education system is widely recognised as being of a very high standard. Government expenditure on education typically accounts for 3 per cent of GDP.

Primary schooling lasts from age six to 12 when students undertake exams to determine progression to one of four different schools and programmes: general, technical, artistic or vocational.

Universities and colleges offer a full range of subjects and qualifications.

Compulsory years: 6 to 18.
Enrolment rate: 103 per cent, gross primary enrolment; 146 per cent, gross secondary enrolment; of the relevant age group (including repeaters and training for the unemployed); 56 per cent teriary enrolment (World Bank).
Pupils per teacher: 12 in primary schools.

Health
Total expenditure on health is 8–9 per cent of GDP, of which 71–72 per cent is government spending.

Adequate healthcare is provided for all citizens. The patient pays for treatment, but the fee is reimbursed by his or her health insurance company. The reimbursement may cover almost all of the cost or very little, depending on the patient's choice of doctor. The *mutuelles* (health insurance companies) also have their own clinics where basic healthcare, optometry and dentistry can be obtained for a token fee.

HIV prevalence: 0.2 per cent aged 15–49 in 2003 (World Bank)
Life expectancy: 78.3 years (World Bank)
Fertility rate/Maternal mortality rate: 1.6 births per woman; maternal deaths 8 per 100,000 (World Bank)
Infant mortality rate: 4 per 1,000 live births (World Bank)

Welfare
A social insurance scheme covers welfare payments. Contributions are taken from all workers at 7.5 per cent of earnings and pensioners 0.5–2 per cent of pensions or pre-pensions; employers pay 8.86 per cent of the payroll and the government provides annual subsidies.

Old age pensions, disability, sickness, maternity benefits, survivors pensions are dependent on contributions to worker's insurance funds.

Workers' contributions cover around 70 per cent of social security costs. Unemployment benefits are administered by three regional offices, the Vlaamse Dienst Arbeidsbemiddeling Beroepsopleiding (VDBA) in Flanders, the Organisme de Formation et d'Emploi de la Wallonie (FOREM) in Wallonia and the Office Régional Bruxellois d'Emploi-Brusselse Gewestelijke Dienst voor Arbeidsbemiddeling (ORBEM-BGDA) in Brussels.

Pensions
The statutory age of retirement is 65 and 62 for men and women respectively; in 2009 it will be set at 65 for all.

Main cities
Brussels (Bruxelles, Brussel, Brüssel, Bruessel) (capital, estimated population 981,200 in 2003), Antwerp (Anvers, Antwerpen) (450,000), Gent (Ghent) (226,900), Charleroi (201,200), Liège (Luik, Lüttich, Liege, Luettich, Luttich) (185,700), Brugge (Bruges)(117,200), Namur (105,700), Mons (91,200).

Languages spoken
The northern part of Belgium, Flanders, is Dutch-speaking and the southern part, Wallonia, is French-speaking. Brussels is officially bilingual, but over 80 per cent of its population are French-speakers. There is also a small German-speaking area in eastern Wallonia, which became part of Belgium after the First World War. English, Luxembourgish, Italian, Spanish, Greek, Arabic and Turkish are also spoken.

Official language/s
Dutch (Flemish), French and German

Media
The press is free of government control and there is no formal censorship. However, press freedoms are not codified in any legislation and the media sometimes

Belgium

does not cover anti-government or anti-police events.

Press
There are over 530 newspapers and 700 magazines, reaching 58 per cent of the adult population.

Dailies: There are over 30 dailies in both French and Dutch languages. Important dailies include a broadsheet-sized newspaper *Libre Belgique Gazette de Liège*, *Nieuwsblad*, *Het Volk* (popular in Flemish part of Belgium), *Le Soir*, *Vers l'Avenir*, *De Morgen* (Flemish), *De Standaard*, *Het Laatste Nieuws* and *Gazet van Antwerpen*.

Weeklies: *Les Nouvelles du Dimanche Matin* is a Sunday newspaper. *Le 7e Soir* is a national weekly. Other weekly publications include *Knack* and *Le Vif/L'Express*.

Business: Principal business papers/magazines include dailies like *L'Echo*, *De Financieel Ekonomische Tijd*, weeklies like *Intermediair* and *Trends/Tendances*, *Belgian Economic Journal* and *Industrie Magazine* (monthly). *Le Courrier de la Bourse et de la Banque* is a national daily for private investors and stockbrokers.

Periodicals: Periodicals include bi-monthly publication *Banking Review* covering all aspects of finance and banking and *The Corporate Traveller*. *Het Bedrijf Industrial Digest* is a business journal in Dutch. *Conscience Européenne* covers European political and current affairs.

Broadcasting
Radio: There are around 300 radio stations, of which 200 are commercial.

Television: Belgium has 11 television stations, nine of which are commercial. In the north, VTM has a greater market share than the non-commercial TV1. In the south RTL/TV1 retains the lead. Radio-Télévision Belge de la Communauté Française (RTBF) broadcasts in French, and Vlaamse Radio en Televisie (VRT) in Dutch. Commercial stations include RTBF (French language) and VTM (Dutch). Through cable television, Belgian TV viewers can tune in to a great number of channels from their own country and from Germany, France, Luxembourg, The Netherlands, Spain, Italy and the UK.

Advertising
Nationwide advertising is complicated by language problems. However, information about regional advertising is available from the Ministry of Economic Affairs and Scientific Research, 23 Square de Meeûs, 1000 Brussels (tel: 506-5111; fax: 514-4683). Besides advertising carried by commercial television and radio channels (46 per cent of total advertising by expenditure), other popular forms of advertising include telemarketing, catalogues, direct mail, the Internet, department stores and shops.

Economy
Belgium has used its geographic situation at the heart of the EU to develop a sophisticated transport system of roads, rail, canals and ports. With this network in place, and although it has few natural resources and has to import almost all its raw materials, Belgium never-the-less has a diversified industrial sector, generally in the north (Flanders) and based on a highly skilled, productive and multi-lingual work force. Per capita exports from Belgium are five times as great as Japan's, and twice as great as Germany's. Industry accounts for some 24 per cent of GDP, the services sector 74 per cent and agriculture 2 per cent. It has one of the world's most open economies measured by the value of exports and imports relative to GDP, largely thanks to its highly integrated, economic interdependence with its three main neighbours – France, Germany and the Netherlands. Around 75 per cent of all trade is contracted with EU countries.

The government has run an economy that was close to balance in 2005 with only a slight risk of a deficit. Unemployment throughout was 7.8 per cent in 2004, although this figure masks considerable differences between the prosperous north and Wallonia in the south with double Flander's unemployment rate. GDP growth is expected to slow from 2.7 per cent in 2004 to 1.5 per cent in 2005, with interest rates remaining stable, although they are expected to edge up in 2006.

OECD recommendations for increasing productivity include:
- increasing competition in rail freight transport by abolishing laws and regulations governing competition in rail transport provision
- relaxing labour laws and allowing flexibility in employment contracts
- providing more support for entrepreneurship by reducing business licences and permits
- increasing quality of tertiary education by giving universities the ability to adapt their employment contracts as necessary and introducing tuition fees.

External trade
Belgium and Luxembourg operate a customs union known as the Belgo-Luxembourg Economic Union (BLEU). However, Belgium has been accumulating large current account surpluses in its own right, without being dependent on Luxembourg's substantial services income.

Imports
Imports consist of diamonds, machinery and equipment, metal products, pharmaceuticals, foodstuffs, vehicles and products, chemicals and oil products

Main sources: Germany (18.4 per cent total, 2004), The Netherlands (17.0 per cent), France (12.5 per cent), UK (6.8 per cent), Ireland (6.3 per cent), US (5.5 per cent)

Exports
Many companies export more than 80 per cent of their production. Principal exports include machinery and equipment, diamonds, metals and metal products, glass, chemicals, motor vehicles, foodstuffs and carpets.

Main destinations: Germany (19.9 per cent total, 2004), France (17.2 per cent), The Netherlands (11.8 per cent), UK (8.2 per cent), US (6.5 per cent), Italy (5.2 per cent)

Agriculture
Farming
The agriculture sector accounts for around 1.4 per cent of GDP and employs 2.5 per cent of the workforce. Although small-scale, cultivation is intensive, especially in Flanders, which has better soils for arable farming. Here one quarter of the organically managed land is used for arable crops. Belgium is self-sufficient in sugar, eggs, butter and meat, and is an exporter of vegetables and horticultural produce. The amount of land under cultivation (approximately 25 per cent of total land area) is falling.

Reform to the EU Common Agricultural Policy (CAP) was introduced on 1 January 2005 in Belgium, whereby subsidies paid on farm output, which tended to benefit large farms and encourage overproduction, were replaced by single farm payments not conditional on production. This is expected to reward farms that provide and maintain a healthy environment, food safety and animal welfare standards. The changes are also intended to encourage market conscious production and cut the cost of CAP to the EU taxpayer.

The crop production in 2004 included: 2,951,015 tonnes (t) cereals in total, 1,913,177t wheat, 637,807t maize, 3,299,622t potatoes, 304,777t barley, 31,273t oats, 395t hops, 100t vanilla, 250,000t tomatoes, 13,876t oilcrops, 1,221t tobacco, 6,215,850t sugar beets, 323,800t apples, 589,830t fruit in total, 1,819,000t vegetables in total. Livestock production included: 1,745,145t meat in total, 280,000t beef, 1,050,000t pig meat, 3,545t lamb & goat meat, 407,000t poultry, 179,250t eggs, 3,350,000t milk, 1,600t honey, 27,000t cattle hides, 1,050t sheepskins, 4,300t horsemeat.

Fishing
Fishing is a smaller and less important industry in Belgium than in neighbouring countries, largely because of its short coastline. The mussel- and oyster-bearing

waters of the Scheldt estuary are bordered on both sides by the Netherlands. Belgium has a flotilla of small offshore trawlers, but no major deep sea fleet.

Forestry
Forest and other wooded land cover around 22 per cent of the land area – one of the lowest ratios in Europe. The majority of timber materials imported come from Germany and France.
In 2004, imports of forest materials amounted US$4.7 billion, while exports were valued at US$3.9 billion.
Production in 2004 included: 4,765,000 cubic metres (cum) roundwood, 4,215,000cum industrial roundwood, 1,215,000cum sawnwood, 2,690,000cum sawlogs and veneer logs, 1,325,000cum pulpwood (round and split), 2,698,000cum wood-based panels, 48,000cum veneer sheets, 550,000cum wood fuel; 173,000 tonnes (t) newsprint, 1,062,000t printing and writing paper, 491,000t wood-pulp, 1,846,000t recovered paper.

Industry and manufacturing
The large-scale, export-based industrial sector accounts for 22 per cent of GDP and employs approximately 28 per cent of the labour force.
Belgium's industrial sector is strongly regional. Flanders, which accounts for some 60 per cent of GDP, has a modern industrial base. It is also more integrated into international markets than other regions, with around 85 per cent of its output going abroad and accounting for some 70 per cent of total Belgian exports. The region of Wallonia, on the other hand, accounts for 25 per cent of GDP and is burdened with declining heavy industry. The government has made considerable efforts to restructure the industrial base in Wallonia, with substantial investment incentives available.
The government's policy is aimed at facilitating the renewal and restructuring of industry so that it can adapt to new technologies and maintain its competitive position internationally. This includes encouraging domestic and foreign investment in industry with tax incentives, particularly in advanced technology fields.

Tourism
Tourism is expected to account for 3.6 per cent of GDP in 2005. Belgium's historic towns and rich cultural heritage are particularly attractive to short-stay visitors, mainly from neighbouring countries.
There were around seven million arrivals in 2004

Mining
The mining sector accounts for approximately 0.3 per cent of GDP and employs 0.4 per cent of the workforce. There is no longer a mining industry. Only clay and sand are mined on any scale.

Hydrocarbons
Belgium has no oil or gas reserves. Belgium imports 16 billion cubic metres of gas annually and one million barrels per day (bpd) of oil, of which 436,000bpd is re-exported. Belgian refineries have a total capacity of 805,000bpd. Belgium's coal-mining industry having been closed down, only a negligible quantity of coal is produced by tip-washing; coal has to be imported to meet domestic demand.

Energy
Belgium has the highest energy consumption per capita in the EU. Electricity capacity is 16GW. Nuclear power is the primary source of energy, accounting for around 60 per cent of electricity output; most of the rest comes from thermal sources, fired by gas, coal and oil. There are seven nuclear stations. Legislation adopted in 2002 provides for nuclear energy to be phased out by 2025, but Belgium's environmental obligations are leading to second thoughts.

Financial markets
Stock exchange
The Brussels Stock Exchange is part of Euronext, an integrated cross-border single currency stock, derivatives and commodities market composed of the Brussels, Paris and Amsterdam exchanges. This arrangement gives the relatively small Belgian stock exchange important external visibility.

Banking and insurance
The banking sector is divided into three main groups – commercial banks, public credit institutions and private savings banks.
Belgium's efforts to meet the conditions for European Economic and Monetary Union (Emu) involved major restructuring of the financial sector.
Central bank
Banque Nationale de Belgique; European Central Bank (ECB)

Time
GMT plus one hour

Geography
Belgium is a small European state bordered to the north by the North Sea and The Netherlands, to the east by The Netherlands, Germany and Luxembourg, and to the south and west by France. It is flat near the coast, but hillier in the Ardennes region in the south-east.

Climate
The country has a temperate climate; the proximity of the sea reduces the harshness of winter, but makes summers relatively cool.
Temperatures overall do not show great variations. The average for the hottest month, July, is 17 degrees Celsius (C) and for the coldest, January, 3 degrees C. Temperatures tend to be slightly higher along the coast and cooler in the Ardennes.
There is regular but moderate rainfall with average annual precipitation of 800mm.

Dress codes
Belgian dress codes are in general the same as those in other industrialised nations. Suit and tie for men are usual for business and formal occasions, but often a jacket and trousers are sufficient. For women, a suit, dress or skirt and blouse are suitable for most business and social occasions.

Entry requirements
Passports
Belgium is a member of the Schengen Visa Accord and citizens of other signatory states do not require passports. Passports are required for citizens of other countries.
Visa
Required by all except nationals of EU and Schengen Accord signatory countries, North America, Australasia, or Japan. For further exceptions contact the nearest embassy. A Schengen visa application (offered in several languages) can be downloaded on www.eurovisa.info/ApplicationForm.htm.
Currency advice/regulations
No restrictions on foreign or local currency movements.

Health (for visitors)
EU nationals visiting or temporarily resident in Belgium are entitled to emergency medical treatment for sickness or accident on the same basis as insured Belgians.
Mandatory precautions
There are no mandatory health precautions for entry into Belgium.
Advisable precautions
It is advisable to have up-to-date tetanus and polio immunisations. Tap water is safe to drink.

Hotels
It is advisable to book hotel or pension in advance either directly or through Belgium Tourist Reservations. By law, all tariffs must be displayed. Service charges are usually included. Tipping is roughly 10 per cent. Major credit cards are accepted.

Public holidays
Fixed dates
1 Jan (New Year's Day), 1 May (Labour Day), 21 Jul (Independence Day), 15 Aug (Assumption Day), 1 Nov (All Saints' Day), 2 Nov (All Souls' Day), 11 Nov (Armistice Day), 25 Dec (Christmas Day), 26 Dec (St Stephen's Day). Also community public

Belgium

holidays: 11 Jul (Flemish Community); 27 Sep (French-speaking community). Fixed-date holidays that fall on a Sunday are observed on the following Monday.

Variable dates
Easter Monday, Ascension Day, Whit Monday.

Working hours
Banking
Mon–Fri: 0900–1600. Banks are open most days, although a few small banks close at lunch-time.

Business
Mon–Fri: 0830–1730; Sat: 0900–1200. The mornings are the best time for phone contacts. Lunch is usually one or two hours, and in the latter case, the business day is likely to end at 1800.

Government
Mon–Fri: 0900–1700.

Shops
Mon–Sat: 0900/1000–1800/1900. In large cities, convenience stores (*magasins de nuit/avondwinkels*) stay open either all night or until around 2200 every day, including Sundays.

Electricity supply
220V AC

Social customs/useful tips
It can be considered impolite to use French in Dutch-speaking Flanders or Dutch in Wallonia due to historical friction between the two language groups. English is quite widely understood and has made headway as a *lingua franca*, in Brussels in particular.
In Flanders, the names of Walloon cities are generally in Flemish and vice versa in Wallonia. There are also different names for German place names in both Belgium and Germany.
Business relations require some degree of formality and the use of the formal pronoun in French and Dutch (vous/U). It is customary to shake hands at the beginning and end of a meeting. Punctuality is valued.
Belgium has one of the highest ratios of police to population of any western European country and officers are permitted to undertake random identity checks. It is compulsory to have a passport or identity card with you at all times.
Alcohol is sold freely at any time of day or night. Smoking is banned in public places (including stations and airports).
Traffic coming from the right has priority in most situations (if the driver who has priority slows down or hesitates, he/she still has priority; a driver who has priority only loses this after having stopped and started moving again). Therefore, foreign drivers should be aware that vehicles could suddenly emerge from side-streets to their right.

Security
There is very little street crime or violence in Belgium, though the inner cities have isolated problem areas.

Getting there
Air
National airline: SN Brussels Airlines is the successor to the failed national airline, Sabena.
International airport/s: Antwerp International (ANR), 3km from city; Brussels National (BRU), 13km north-east of city centre; Brussels-South Charleroi (CRL), 55km south-east of Brussels; Ostend International (OST), 6km from city.
Airport tax: None
Surface
There is good road and rail access from the main centres of The Netherlands, France, Germany and Luxembourg.
Water: There are daily crossings by ferry or jetfoil to Ostend or Zeebrugge from the UK and Norway.
Main port/s: Antwerp, Ghent, Zeebrugge, Ostend, Brussels, Liège.

Getting about
National transport
Road: There is an extensive road network. Toll-free motorways serve all main towns with the exception of those in the Ardennes. Comprehensive coach services, particularly to rural areas, are operated by Société Nationale des Chemins de Fer Belges (SNCB) and Société Nationale des Chemins de Fer Vicinaux (SNCV).
Rail: First- and second-class services run between all main towns. Combined tickets allowing for stop-overs in main towns offer best value. Express trains (TEE) ensure rapid connection with all French, Dutch and German cities. Over half the railway network is electrified.
Water: There are over 1,500km of inland waterways. Services are operated by Administration des Voies Hydrauliques. Inland canals connect with major French, Dutch and German ports.

City transport
Taxis: Readily available. Standardised fare system, which includes service charge. Chauffeur-driven cars are cheaper on long journeys.
Buses, trams & metro: Flat fares are charged on tram and bus service. There are metro services in Brussels and Antwerp.
Trains: Special airport shuttle service operates from Brussels Central Station and North Station, departing every hour.
Car hire
Available at aiports and in most main towns. Speed limit: urban roads 60kph, main roads 90kph. Maximum speed on motorways 120kph, minimum speed 70kph. Drive on the right. The wearing of seat belts is compulsory. It is prohibited for children under 12 to sit in front seats.

BUSINESS DIRECTORY
The addresses listed below are a selection only. While World of Information makes every endeavour to check these addresses, we cannot guarantee that changes have not been made, especially to telephone numbers and area codes. We would welcome any corrections.

Telephone area codes
The international direct dialling code (IDD) for Belgium is +32, followed by area code and subscriber's number:

Antwerp	3	Ypres	57
Arlon	63	Liège	41
Bastogne	61	La Louvière	64
Brugge	50	Libramont	61
Brussels	2	Mechelen	15
Charleroi	71	Mons	65
Chimay	60	Ostende	59
Dendermonde	52	Verviers	87
Ghent	9	Zeebrugge	50

Chambers of Commerce
American Chamber of Commerce, 50 Avenue des Arts, 1000 Brussels (tel: 513-6770; fax: 513-3590; e-mail: gch@postl.amcham.be).

Antwerp Chamber of Commerce, 12 Markgravestraat, 2000 Antwerp (tel: 232-2219; fax: 233-6442; e-mail: eic@kkna.be).

British Chamber of Commerce, Egmont House, 15 Rue d'Egmont, 1000 Brussels (tel: 540-9030; fax: 512-8363; e-mail: brit.cham@britcham.be).

Bruges Chamber of Commerce and Industry, 25 Ezelstraat, 8000 Bruges (tel: 333-696; fax: 342-297; e-mail: brugge@ccibkw.be).

Brussels Chamber of Commerce and Industry, 500 Avenue Louise, 1050 Brussels (tel: 648-5002; fax: 640-9328; e-mail: inscription@ccib.irisnet.be).

Charleroi Chamber of Commerce and Industry, 1a Avenue Général Michel, 6000 Charleroi (tel: 321-160; fax: 334-218; e-mail: info@ccic.be).

Federation of Chambers of Commerce and Industry of Belgium, 1-2 Avenue des Arts, 1210 Brussels (tel: 209-1550; fax: 209-0568; e-mail: fedcci@cci.be).

Ghent Chamber of Commerce and Industry, 41 Martelaarslaan, 9000 Ghent (tel: 266-1440; fax: 266-1441; e-mail: kkngent@cci.be).

Liège Chamber of Commerce and Industry, Palais des Congrès de Liège, 2 Esplanade de l'Europe, 4020 Liège (tel: 343-9292; fax: 343-9267; e-mail: info@ccilg.be).

Nations of the World: A Political, Economic and Business Handbook

Banking
AXA Bank Belgium, 214 Grotesteenweg, 2600 Antwerp (tel: 286-2211; fax: 286-2407; e-mail: contact@axa.be).

ING Belgium., 24 Avenue Marnix, 1000 Brussels (tel: 547-2111; fax: 547-3844; e-mail: info@ing.be).

KBC Bank and Insurance, Havenlaan 2, 1080 Brussels (tel: 429-1111; fax: 429-8123; e-mail: kbc.bank@kbc.be).

Central bank
Banque Nationale de Belgique, Boulevard de Berlaimont 14, 1000 Brussels (tel: 221-2111; fax: 221-3100; e-mail: secretariat@nbb.be).

European Central Bank (ECB), Kaiserstrasse 29, D-60311 Frankfurt am Main, Germany (tel: +49(69)13-440; fax: +49(69)1344-6000; e-mail: info@ecb.int).

Travel information
Brussels Airport, 1930 Zaventem (tel: 753-4200; fax: 753-4250; e-mail: info@biac.be).

Brussels International Tourism and Congress, Hôtel de Ville, Grand Place, 1000 Brussels (tel: 513-8940; fax: 513-8320; e-mail: info@brusselstourism.be).

National tourist organisation offices
Belgian Tourist Office (Brussels and Ardennes), 61 Rue du Marché aux Herbes, 1000 Brussels (tel: 504-0390; fax: 504-0270; e-mail: info@opt.be).

Belgian Tourist Office (Tourism Flanders), 63 Rue du Marché aux Herbes, 1000 Brussels (tel: 504-0390; fax: 504-0270; e-mail: info@toerismevlaanderen.be).

Ministries
Ministry of Agriculture and Small and Medium-Sized Enterprises, 1 Rue Marie-Thérèse, 1000 Brussels (tel: 211-0611; fax: 219-6130).

Ministry of the Budget, 180 Rue Royale, 1000 Brussels (tel: 219-1911; fax: 217-3328).

Ministry for the Civil Service, Résidence Palace, 51 Rue de la Loi, 1040 Brussels (tel: 790-5800; fax: 790-5790).

Ministry of Consumer Affairs, Public Health and Environment, 7 Avenue des Arts, 1210 Brussels (tel: 220-2011; fax: 220-2067; e-mail: environment@health.fgov.be).

Ministry of Defence, 8 Rue Lambermont, 1000 Brussels (tel: 550-2811; fax: 550-2919).

Ministry of Economic Affairs and Scientific Research, 23 Square de Meeûs, 1000 Brussels (tel: 506-5111; fax: 514-4683).

Ministry of Employment, 51 Rue Belliard, 1040 Brussels (tel: 233-5111; fax: 230-1067; e-mail: info@cabmeta.fgov.be).

Ministry of Finance, 12 Rue de la Loi, 1000 Brussels (tel: 238-8111; fax: 233-8003; e-mail: contact@ckfin.minfin.be).

Ministry of Foreign Affairs, 15 Rue des Petits Carmes, 1000 Brussels (tel: 501-8211; fax: 511-6385; internet site: http://www.diplobel.fgov.be/default_em.htm).

Ministry of Interior Affairs, 60 Rue Royale, 1000 Brussels (tel: 504-8511; fax: 504-8500; e-mail: info@mibz.fgov.be).

Ministry of Justice, 115 Boulevard de Waterloo, 1000 Brussels (tel: 542-7911; fax: 538-0767; info@just.fgov.be).

Ministry of Mobility and Transport, 65 Rue de la Loi, 1040 Brussels (tel: 237-6711; fax: 230-1824).

Ministry of Social Affairs and Pensions, 62 Rue de la Loi, 1040 Brussels (tel: 238-2811; fax: 230-3895).

Ministry of Telecommunications, Public Enterprises and Participations, 7 Queteletplein, 1030 Brussels (tel: 250-0303; fax: 219-0914; e-mail: info@telcobel.be).

Prime Minister's Office, 16 Rue de la Loi, 1000 Brussels (tel: 501-0211; fax: 512-6953).

Other useful addresses
Belgian Association of International Trading Houses (ABNEI), 7 Israëlietenstraat, 2000 Antwerp (tel: 226-0712; fax: 231-9969; e-mail: tradechem@cmc.be).

Belgian Embassy (USA), 3330 Garfield Street, NW, Washington DC 20008 (tel: 202-333-6900; fax: 202-333-3079).

Belgian Foreign Trade Board, World Trade Centre, Tower 1, 30/36 Boulevard du Roi Albert II, 1000 Brussels (tel: 206-3511; fax: 203-1812; e-mail: info@obcebdbh.be).

Belgian Institute of Standardisation, 29 Avenue de la Brabançonne, 1000 Brussels (tel: 738-0111; fax: 733-4264; e-mail: info@ibn.be).

British Embassy, 85 Rue d'Arlon, 1040 Brussels (tel: 287-6211; fax: 287-6360; e-mail: info@britain.be).

Brussels Regional Development Agency, 6 Rue Gabrielle Petit, 1080 Brussels (tel: 422-5111; fax: 422-5112; info@sdrb.irisnet.be).

Ducroire/Delcredere (export credit agency), 40 Square de Meêus, 1000 Brussels (tel: 509-4211; fax: 513-5059; e-mail: ducroire@ondd.be).

Euronext Brussels (stock exchange), Palais de la Bourse, Place de la Bourse, 1000 Brussels (tel: 509.1211; fax: 509-1212; e-mail: info@euronext.be).

Federation of Belgian Companies (VBO-FEB), 4 Rue Ravenstein, 1000 Brussels (tel: 515-0811; fax: 515-0999; e-mail: info@vbo-feb.be).

Flemish Economic Alliance (VEV), 5 Brouwersvliet, 2000 Antwerp (tel: 202-4400; fax: 233-7660; e-mail: vev@vev.be).

Flemish Foreign Trade Board, 40 Boulevard du Régent, 1000 Brussels (tel: 504-8711; fax: 504-8899; e-mail: info@export.vlaanderen.be).

Investment Company for Flanders (GIMV), 37 Karel Oomsstraat, 2018 Antwerp (tel:290-2100; fax: 290-2105; e-mail: receptie@gimv.be).

US Embassy, 27 Boulevard du Régent, 1000 Brussels (tel: 508-2111; fax: 511-2725; e-mail: ic@usinfo.be).

Walloon Business Union (UWE), 1-3 Chemin du Stockoy, 1300 Wavre (tel: 471-940; fax: 453-343; e-mail: info@uwe.be).

Walloon Export Agency (AWEX), 2 Place Sainctelette, 1080 Brussels (tel: 421-8211; fax: 421-8787; e-mail: mail@awex.wallonie.be).

Internet sites
Belgium companies: http://www.belgium.com/business/tradecontact.php

Belgium Federal Information Service: http://www.belgium.fgov.be/

Belgium Foreign Trade Board: http://www.obcebdbh.be

Belgium white pages: http://www.infobel.be

Europa (Gateway site): http://europa.eu.int

Export services: http://exportservices.be

Travel information: http://www.visitbelgium.com

Railway information: http://www.b-rail.be

Statistics: http://www.statbel.fgov.be

Le Soir (newspaper): http://www.lesoir.be

La Poste (newspaper) http://www.brusselspost.com

Government of Flanders: http://www.flanders.be

Government of Wallonia: http://www.wallonie.com

Flight information: http://www.brusselsairport.be

Hotels and restaurants: http://www.brussels-online.com

Belize

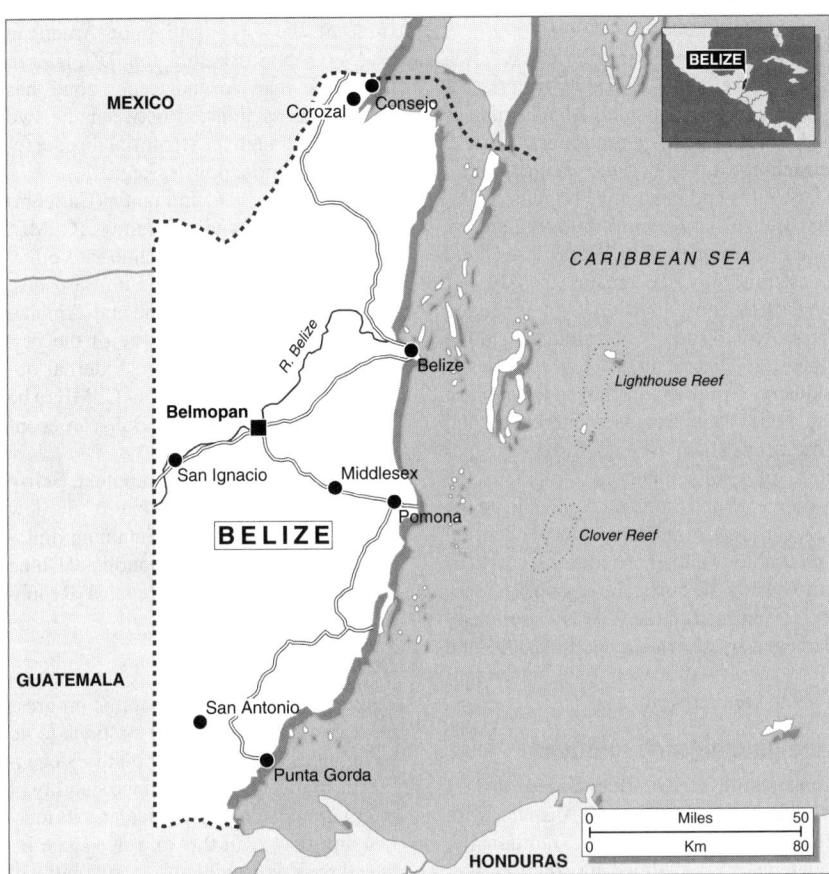

KEY FACTS

Official name: Belize

Head of State: Queen Elizabeth II (since 1952); Governor General Sir Colville Norbert Young (since 1993)

Head of government: Prime Minister Said Musa (leader of PUP) (since 1998)

Ruling party: People's United Party (PUP) (since 1998; re-elected 5 Mar 2003)

Area: 22,965 square km

Population: 269,000 (2004)

Capital: Belmopan

Official language: English

Currency: Belize dollar (Bz$) = 100 cents

Exchange rate: Bz$1.97 per US$ (Oct 2005)

GDP per capita: US$3,977 (2004)

GDP real growth: 3.00% (2004); *2.2% (2005)

Labour force: 101,000 (2004)

Inflation: 2.70% (2004); *2.2% (2005)

Balance of trade: -US$178.50 million (2004)

Foreign debt: US$950.90 million (2004)

* estimated figure

A parliamentary democracy on the British Westminster model, Belize's head of state is Queen Elizabeth II. The Monarch is represented in the country by the Governor General of Belize, Sir Colville Norbert Young, who acts on the advice provided to him by the prime minister and his/her cabinet. Owing to its historical status as a former British colony the country differs from its immediate neighbours in that English is the official language.

Aside from its British characteristics, Belize is blessed with many other diverse peoples and cultures that are representative of the Latin American continent as a whole. Spanish-speaking Mestizos (of mixed European and Maya Indian heritage), Creoles (of African and African-European descent) and Garifuna, whose lineage is Carib Indian and African, constitute a sizeable portion of the total population.

Spanish is now beginning to challenge English as the national language following the recent declaration of an amnesty for Guatemalan, Honduran and Nicaraguan immigrants. Still, with a population of just 269,000 the country's political and business elite continue to dominate proceedings in this Central American state.

The Musa effect

The domestic political arena has been dominated by Prime Minister Said Wilbert Musa since his election in 1998. The University of Manchester (UK) law graduate, of Palestinian descent, is the leader of the Peoples' United Party (PUP) and served as his own foreign minister (1998–2002) before resigning the post to concentrate on the premiership. Said to have attended his own swearing in ceremony in a pair of jeans and a t-shirt, Musa is also strongly alleged to be conducting an affair with a mistress.

A strong two-party system operates in Belize with the PUP and opposition United Democratic Party (UDP) operating something of an electoral duopoly in the country. In the 2003 elections the PUP claimed 22 seats out of a total of 29 in the House of Representatives on 53.2 per cent of the total vote, while the UDP, despite achieving a 45.6 per cent share, won just 7 seats. The PUP is a Christian democratic organisation, while the UDP presents itself as the party of the progressive left.

For a country not particularly known as a hotbed of political and social unrest, the outbreak of strikes and riots in 2005 was somewhat surprising. In January both public and private sector workers struck, citing their displeasure at new budget measures, including an increase in taxation. In April, the were violent protests in the streets of the capital Belmopan. Anti-government sentiment was right at the heart of the protesters' motives and this would suggest that Musa, after almost eight years in power, is starting to lose his midas touch.

Economic progress

Prior to the twenty first century the Belizean economy was almost entirely reliant on the forestry industry for export revenue. However, over recent years the tourism industry has expanded considerably and is now of importance to the country's economic wellbeing. Growth has remained consistent since the early 2000s and came in at 3 per cent in 2004. The latest IMF forecast for growth in 2005 stands at 2.2 per cent with an expansion of 2.7 per cent predicted for 2006. Inflation remains low by the standards of the region and indeed by developed countries' standards. In 2004 the inflation rate was 2.7 per cent per annum and the IMF predicts a continued low rate of inflation for Belize; 2.2 per cent for 2005, potentially falling to 1 per cent by 2006.

The longest barrier reef in the Western Hemisphere is in Belizean waters, together with several small islands and superb fishing opportunities. These attractions, together with the country's Maya ruins and raw jungle regions ensure that Belize's travel and tourism industry continues to grow. The World Travel and Tourism Council estimates that 20 per cent of Belize's total GDP is generated from tourism activity and almost the same figure (19.7 per cent) is employed in the industry. Crucially, capital investment in the sector has increased markedly and now stands at almost one quarter (24.5 per cent) of total capital investment in the economy. The continued wellbeing of the nascent tourism industry is dependent on favourable weather conditions, particularly during the hurricane season. The sector's infrastructure was seriously damaged by Hurricane Keith (2000) and Hurricane Iris (2001), but has since managed to recover well.

Foreign and trade relations

The festering sore on Belize's regional relations has long been its dispute with neighbouring Guatemala. Traditionally, Guatemala has claimed jurisdiction over Belizean territory and even after Belize's independence was confirmed in 1981 its western neighbour refused to recognise its existence. Some 10 years later, in 1991, Guatemala did finally recognise the state of Belize and diplomatic relations were established. A series of negotiations have taken place over the past decade including mediations in Miami, Florida (USA) in February 2000 and a separate meeting in front of the Organisation of American States (OAS) in Washington, DC, later in that same year. An 'adjacency zone' has since been established between the two countries, though the territorial dispute remains a potential powder keg.

The Caribbean Community (Caricom) Single Market and Economy (CSME) treaty (Caricom CSME) came into effect on 1 January 2006. Along with Barbados, Jamaica, Guyana, Suriname and Trinidad and Tobago, Belize was one of the first full members of the treaty. External observers consider the Caricom CSME to be a major stimulant for the Belizean economy and the wider region.

In a wider foreign policy context, Belize is interesting in that it is one of the few countries in the world maintaining diplomatic relations with the Republic of China (Taiwan), rather than the Peoples' Republic of China (China).

Outlook

Belize has made solid economic progress in recent years and should continue to do so in 2006. However, the country's economy is highly dependent on the stability of international markets, particularly its tourism industry. A further oil price spike induced by a worsening of the international geopolitical environment will probably lead to a deceleration in the economies of the major developed counties. Such a global economic downturn would be especially bad for the tourism sector, as would a series of severe hurricanes and tropical storms. The country's political situation is generally stable, but 2005 revealed the beginnings of social unrest and dissatisfaction with Prime Minister Musa.

Risk assessment

Economy	Stable
Politics	Deteriorating
Regional stability	Stable
Stock market	Stable

COUNTRY PROFILE

Historical profile
1802 Spain recognised British sovereignty of what became known as British Honduras, but after gaining their independence

KEY INDICATORS — Belize

	Unit	2000	2001	2002	2003	2004
Population	m	0.25	0.25	0.26	0.26	0.27
Gross domestic product (GDP)	US$bn	0.60	0.80	0.84	1.28	*1.90
GDP per capita	US$	2,400	3,160	3,230	4,900	3,977
GDP real growth	%	11.1	5.1	3.5	4.9	3.0
Inflation	%	0.6	1.2	1.2	1.5	2.7
Exports (fob) (goods)	US$m	212.3	198.0	310.4	290.0	401.4
Imports (fob) (goods)	US$m	403.7	434.0	500.3	430.0	579.9
Balance of trade	US$m	-191.4	-236.0	-189.9	-140.0	-178.5
Current account	US$m	-139.5	-176.0	-162.7	–	-150.0
Total reserves minus gold	US$m	122.9	112.0	114.5	84.7	48.3
Foreign exchange	US$m	115.8	105.0	106.7	76.1	39.1
Exchange rate	per US$	1.98	1.97	2.00	1.97	1.98

* estimated figure

Belize

from Spain, both Mexico and Guatemala laid claim to the territory.
1970 Belmopan became the captial after Belize City was devastated by a hurricane.
1973 The territory was renamed Belize.
1981 Belize attained independence from the UK.
1984 After 30 years in power, the People's United Party (PUP) was defeated by the United Democratic Party (UDP). Manuel Esquivel became prime minister.
1989 The PUP narrowly won the general election.
1993 The UDP won the general election; Esquivel became prime minister again.
1998 In elections, the PUP defeated the UDP.
2000 The government began reforming the offshore banking sector following international criticism of the country's reputation as a tax haven for the rich. Hurricane Keith caused extensive damage.
2001 Hurricane Iris devastated the southern part of Belize. The UK government suspended its plan to grant Belize US$14 million of debt relief due to the government's failure to reform the financial services sector and abolish tax breaks.
2002 The Supreme Court advised holding a public hearing of the environmental lawsuit against Fortis Inc, a Newfoundland-based power company, regarding the proposed Chalillo hydro project.
2003 The ruling PUP won the 5 March general elections.
2004 In January Britain's Privy Council dismissed an appeal by environmental protesters against the proposed construction of the Chalillo dam. On 16 August, the Prime Minister accepted the resignations of seven members of the cabinet.
2005 Workers in the private and public sectors struck in January citing tax increases and low salaries. In April anti-government riots broke out in the capital Belmopan.

Political structure
Constitution
The governor general is advised by the cabinet (led by the prime minister) which holds executive power.
Form of state
Independent state with the British monarch as head of state, represented by the governor general.
The executive
The cabinet, led by the prime minister, holds executive power.
National legislature
The legislature is the bicameral National Assembly consisting of the Senate (nine members, appointed for a five-year term), and the House of Representatives (29 members elected by universal adult suffrage for a five-year term in single-seat constituencies).
Last elections
5 March 2003 (parliamentary)
Results: Parliamentary: the ruling People's United Party (PUP) won 22 seats out of 29 in the National Assembly.
Next elections
2008 (parliamentary)

Political parties
Ruling party
People's United Party (PUP) (since 1998; re-elected 5 Mar 2003)
Main opposition party
United Democratic Party (UDP) (three seats)

Population
269,000 (2004)
Ethnic make-up
Mestizos (44 per cent), Creoles (30 per cent), Mayans (15 per cent), Garifunas (7 per cent), Mennonites (3 per cent). Other races: Spanish, British, Lebanese, Chinese and Eastern Indian.
Religions
Roman Catholic (62 per cent), Anglican (12 per cent), Methodist (6 per cent), Mennonite (4 per cent), Seventh-Day Adventist (3 per cent).

Education
About 22.35 per cent of the budget expenditure in 2002/03 was allocated to the education sector, of which a total of Bz$61 million (US$31 million) and Bz$16 million (US$8.1 million) were budgeted for salaries and education grants respectively. Since 1998, dozens of new school buildings have been constructed, with more than 700 new classrooms catering for additional 3,000 students. The government contributes some Bz$20 million (US$10.1 million) towards higher education student loans for the University of Belize.
Literacy rate: 92.7 per cent total, 92.4 per cent female; adult rates (World Bank).
Enrolment rate: 123 per cent for boys, 119 per cent for girls; total primary school enrolment of the relevant age group (including repetition rates) (World Bank).

Health
In its 2002/03 budget plans, the government proposed to reform health care at the primary level so that 60 to 70 per cent of the medical conditions can be attended effectively. Government expenditure on medical supplies increased to Bz$9 million (US$4.5 million).
The ministry of health plans to implement the National Health Insurance as part of its overall health sector reform programme, with Bz$4 million (US$2 million) from the Social Security Fund.
HIV prevalence: 2.5 per cent aged 15–49 in 2003 (World Bank)
Life expectancy: 71.2 years (World Bank 2003)
Fertility rate/Maternal mortality rate: 3.1 births per woman (World Bank 2003)
Infant mortality rate: 33 per 1,000 live births (World Bank)

Welfare
As part of its poverty alleviation strategy, the Social Investment Fund (SIF) has sought assistance from the World Bank to spend some Bz$10.5 million (US$5.2 million) in water supply, sanitation, health, education and social services projects. The government budget in 2002/03 allocated Bz$24 million (US$12 million) for public utilities.
Seven per cent of a worker's weekly earning is paid into the social security fund; a ratio is determined and divided between the employer and employee. Benefits include maternity, sickness, injury and dependant's grants.
Pensions
Old age pensions are paid to those aged between 60 and 65 who have made at least 130 contributions.

Main cities
Belmopan (capital, estimated population 8,700 in 2003), Belize City (52,600), Orange Walk (14,400), San Ignacio (14,200), Dangriga (9,400).

Languages spoken
Spanish, Creole, Garifuna and Mayan dialects are widely spoken throughout the country.
Official language/s
English

Media
Press
Weeklies: The most widely read weeklies include *Amandala*, *The Reporter*, *The Belize Times*, *The Beacon*, *The People's Pulse* and *The San Pedro Sun*.
Broadcasting
Radio: Belize Broadcasting Network transmits in Spanish and English; Radio KREM (a private station), in English.
A new radio service – Radio Caricom, the Voice of the Caribbean Community – was officially launched at the 25th Meeting of the Conference of the Heads of Government in Grenada on 4 July 2004. Barbados, Belize, Grenada and St Lucia are 'pilot states' in the project, which will eventually be available to all member states.
Television: Controlled satellite services are available on about 12 television stations.

Economy
The economy in Belize has more in common with the nearby Caribbean region as opposed to its South American neighbours. A small enterprise economy, in the

past it has been dominated by the agricultural sector, on which the country's well being was dependent. Although Belize is still dependent on agricultural exports, tourism is the fastest growing sector in the economy and now accounts for around 20 per cent of the nation's GDP and almost one fifth of total employment. The growth in tourism is predominantly attributable to the rapidly expanding cruise sector in the country which grew by 71.7 per cent in 2004. The services sector contributes approximately 60 per cent to GDP and is based around a number of privately owned monopoly utilities, such as Belize Telecommunications Limited (BTL). Economic policy has recently focussed on expansionary policies teaming low taxes with high government spending and investment. This has led to both an increased current account deficit and public debt. The problem of public debt is spiralling upwards 41 per cent of GDP in 1998 to 93 per cent in 2004. It is planned that the improvements in the nation's infrastructure will attract foreign and private investment and offset the growing debt problems. Belize remains in the top ten of the most heavily indebted emerging-economy governments.

The expansionary policy resulted in strong GDP growth in 2000 of 11.1 per cent from 1.5 per cent two years previously. The devastation caused by hurricane Iris, which struck Belize in October 2001, affected the economy in 2002. However, a quick rebound in 2003, with sugar cane and banana production recovering from the hurricane and tourism surging helped the economy recover with growth of 4.9 per cent in 2003. GDP growth in 2004 fell to 3.0 per cent and the International Monetary Fund (IMF) predicts growth for 2005 to slow to 2.2 per cent before improving slightly in 2006, at 2.7 per cent. Though growth has been steady since 1999 worries persist among international observers as to the large trade deficit and high level of foreign debt in the country.

External trade
Belize relies on imports to fuel economic activity. Imports have a value of over 65 per cent of total GDP while exports account for around 35 per cent.
Belize is a member of the Caribbean Community (Caricom), Caribbean Single Market and Economy (CSME), which came into effect January 2006. The country is also a non-resident member of the World Trade Organisation (WTO).

Imports
Main imports are machinery and transport equipment, food, beverages, tobacco, manufactured goods, fuels, chemicals and pharmaceuticals.

Main sources: US (32.7 per cent total, 2004), Mexico (14.4 per cent), Cuba (6.5 per cent), Japan (4.7 per cent)

Exports
Principal exports are sugar, bananas, citrus concentrate, garments, fish and cultured shrimp, molasses and timber.

Main destinations: US (36.8 per cent of total, 2004), UK (28.5 per cent), Thailand (3.6 per cent)

Agriculture
Farming
The agricultural sector forms the mainstay of the economy contributing approximately 20 per cent of total GDP and employing 25 per cent of the workforce. The sector accounts for about 65 per cent of foreign exchange earnings and the banana industry is the country's largest employer. Approximately 65 per cent of the country's land mass is considered to have arable potential but only 2 per cent is used for farming; 45 per cent of the total land mass is forest, much of which is commercially exploitable.

Sugar is the main cash crop though Belize has diversified into exporting other crops, particularly banana and citrus production (mainly oranges), and fisheries. Winter vegetables, papayas, mangoes and cocoa are also grown for export, while rice, maize, roots, beans and vegetables are produced for livestock consumption.

Crop production in 2004 included: 1.1 million tonnes (t) sugar cane, 58,000t cereals in total, 35,000t maize, 13,000t rice, 750t potatoes, 10,000t sorghum, 28,500t plantains, 70,000t bananas, 208,000t citrus fruit, 12,000t papayas, 1,250t mangoes, 1,500t cassava, 1,500t tomatoes, 1,100t coconuts, 1,820t soya beans, 200t sweet potatoes, 235t green coffee, 510t oilcrops, 7,000t pulses, 325,100t fruit in total, 11,263t vegetables in total. Livestock production included: 17,008t meat in total, 2,250t beef, 1,060t pig meat, 13t lamb, 13,684t poultry, 1,530t eggs, 3,850t milk, 50t honey.

Fishing
Fishing, mainly for lobsters, conch and shrimp, contributes significantly to the economy.

Forestry
Forestry has played an integral role in the economy of Belize but the rise of the tourism industry has reduced its importance. Over half of the country's land mass is covered by forests, though the majority of this area has now been logged. Of the lumber cut, the majority is sold in local markets including that of mahogany, soft pine, cedar, santa maria and yemeri. Recent years have also seen an increased interest in chicle harvesting throughout the country.

Industry and manufacturing
Centered on agricultural processing such as sugar-milling, citrus-processing and the processing of domestic foodstuffs, the industrial sector is small-scale. Garment manufacturing previously played a prominent role in the economy of Belize but has decreased in significance since the 1990s. In all, manufacturing contributes approximately one fifth of GDP (including a manufacturing contribution of 12.6 per cent). Manufacturing employs about 10 per cent of the workforce and construction employs 6 per cent.

Tourism
Tourism is Belize's principal economic activity, contributing up to 23 per cent of GDP and accounting for a quarter of jobs and foreign earnings. Diving, sailing and fishing on the coral reef and among the islands, archaeology and wildlife tours inland are the main attractions. The annual increase in the number of arrivals was stalled by the economic downturn in the United States and the effects of the 11 September 2001 terrorist attacks. Recovery came in 2003 when 207,930 holidaymakers were recorded and the surge in numbers continued into the first half of 2004. Americans account for over 50 per cent of visitors, increasing by 7.3 per cent in 2004. The number of Canadian tourists visiting the country also increased significantly in 2004, by 23 per cent. Some 357 cruise ships arrived at Belize's ports in 2004, bringing with them 747,746 passengers, an increase of 55.1 per cent on the 2003 figure. One in every five jobs in the country is in the tourism industry and travel and tourism constitute an estimated 20 per cent of total GDP in 2005.

Environment
Scientists have warned that the proposed Chalillo hydro project, which involves building a 50-metre high dam in the rainforest, would destroy rare habitat for jaguar, tapir and a sub-species of scarlet macaw. The Belize Supreme Court halted construction at the end of 2002. However, in January 2004, the Privy Council in London, ruled that work on the controversial Chalillo Dam could proceed.

Mining
Belize has insignificant mineral deposits. During the 1980s extensive drilling was undertaken in the country in a vain attempt to discover oil. Nowadays, mining mainly involves surface removal of gravel for use in the construction industry. Approximately 0.4 per cent of the workforce is employed in the mining and quarrying sector.

Belize

Hydrocarbons
Despite an extensive oil exploration programme, commercial quantities have not so far been found. Consequently Belize still relies on the import of refined oil for its energy needs. Imports come primarily from Venezuela and Mexico under the San Jose Pact, signed in 1988, which obliges both countries to offer concessions of up to 25 per cent on the market price of their oil. In 1991 the terms of the San Jose agreement were revised, increasingly the amount of oil available at a discounted price to each of the signatories.

Energy
With no reserves of its own, Belize imports oil from Mexico and Venezuela under the auspices of the San Jose Pact and the Caracas Energy Accord. Belize purchases around 50 per cent of electricity from Mexico, 30 per cent is generated from the Mollejon dam and the remaining 20 per cent is derived from thermal plants. The government has outlined plans to develop a 7MW Chalillo dam on the Macal river.

Banking and insurance
Belize's banking sector is small, but contains both an offshore and onshore sector. The offshore sector is undergoing continued expansion owing to generous tax schemes and there are now eight banks, one insurance house and more than 22,000 international business companies. The International Financial Services Commission acts as the regulator of the offshore sector.

The onshore sector is composed of five domestic commercial banks, seven international banks and three quasi-governmental institutions, with credit unions also being prominent. Belize Banking Ltd retains a dominant market position with 45 per cent of domestic banks' assets. The Central Bank of Belize supervises banking activity and the Register of Co-operatives is the Credit union regulator.

The country's insurance sector is also small with 17 firms competing in the market; six insurance houses, nine general companies and three composites. At present there are no reinsurance firms in Belize.

Central bank
Central Bank of Belize

Main financial centre
Belize City

Offshore facilities
Belize has an important offshore banking sector. In April 2002, Belize was taken off the Organisation for Economic Co-operation and Development's (OECD) blacklist of 'un-co-operative tax havens' after the government made a commitment to greater transparency of its tax and regulatory systems and agreed to exchange information on tax matters with OECD countries from end-2005.

Time
GMT minus six hours

Geography
Belize lies on the Caribbean coast of Central America, with Mexico to the north-east and Guatemala to the south-west.

Climate
Sub-tropical with temperatures ranging from 10–30 degrees Celsius. Hottest months between March–September and rainy season June–October.

Entry requirements
Passports
All visitors must travel on an unexpired passport, the validity must be for at least six months longer than the intended period of stay.

Visa
Required by all, except north American, most European and Australasian citizens. For further exemptions contact the local embassy.
For a copy of the visa application visit www.un.int/belize/visappli.pdf.
All visitors should show that they have sufficient funds for the purpose and period of their stay (US$50 per person per day), and must be in possession of a valid return or onward ticket. Evidence in support of both funds and travel arrangements must be presented with applications for visas. Visitors are permitted to stay in Belize for a period not exceeding 30 days.

Currency advice/regulations
A currency declaration form must be completed on arrival. Visitors are advised to keep a copy of the declaration form because travellers are not permitted to export more than this amount of currency.

Health (for visitors)
Mandatory precautions
Yellow fever vaccination certificate if travelling from infected area.

Advisable precautions
Typhoid, polio and rabies vaccinations. Malaria prophylaxis advisable. Water precautions should be taken.

Hotels
Approximately 270 hotels and guest houses. Five per cent government tax and usually 10 per cent service charge.

Public holidays
Fixed dates
1 Jan (New Year's Day), 9 Mar (Baron Bliss Day), 1 May (Labour Day), 24 May (Commonwealth Day), 10 Sep (St George's Caye Day), 21 Sep (Independence Day), 12 Oct (Columbus Day), 19 Nov (Garifuna Settlement Day), 25–26 Dec (Christmas Holiday).

Variable dates
Good Friday, Easter Monday.

Working hours
Banking
Mon–Thu: 0800–1300; Fri: 0800–1300 and 1500–1800.

Business
Mon–Fri: 0800–1200, 1300–1700. Some businesses are open on Fridays.

Government
Mon–Fri: 0800–1200, 1300–1700; closes 1630 on Fridays.

Electricity supply
110/220/V AC, 60 cycles. Most of the electricity is provided by diesel/generator sets.

Getting there
Air
International airport/s: PSW Goldson International (BZE), 16km west of Belize City; duty-free shops, bar, buffet, post office, bank.
Airport tax: International departures Bz$20.

Surface
Road: Main routes are from Melchor de Mencos (Guatemala) and Chetumal (Mexico).
Main port/s: Belize City.

Getting about
National transport
Air: Maya Airways and Tropic Air operate domestic services to main centres.
Road: Over 1,500km of surfaced road – but difficulties in rainy weather are often reported.
A new all-weather road to Caracol, the largest and most important archeological site in Belize, is expected to be completed by late-2004; the project will cost around US$2.5 million.
Buses: Service operates within Belize City; long-distance coach services to major centres.
Water: Regular ferry services and small boats ply to offshore cays.

City transport
Taxis: Taxis are available in towns and resort areas, and at the airport. They are easily recognised by their green licence plates.
Fixed rates apply within Belize City (higher at night). No meters. It is advisable to agree fare beforehand. Tipping is discretionary.

Car hire
Foreign or international licence acceptable for 30 days. Driver must be over 18 years old. Driving on the right.

BUSINESS DIRECTORY
The addresses listed below are a selection only. While World of Information makes every endeavour to check these addresses, we cannot guarantee that

changes have not been made, especially to telephone numbers and area codes. We would welcome any corrections.

Telephone area codes
The international dialling code (IDD) for Belize is +501 followed by the area code and subscriber's number:
Belize City 2   Dangriga 5
Belmopan 8   Independence 6
Corozal 4   San Ignacio 92

Useful telephone numbers
Directory enquiries: 113.
Local and regional operator-assisted calls: 114.
International operator-assisted calls: 115.
Fire and ambulance: 90.
Police: 911.

Chambers of Commerce
Belize Chamber of Commerce and Industry, 63 Regent Street, PO Box 291, Belize City (tel: 227-3148; fax: 227-4984; e-mail: bcci@btl.net).

Banking
Alliance Bank of Belize Ltd, PO Box 1988, 18 Cnr New Road & Hydes Lane, Belize City (tel: 236-783, 236-784; fax: 236-785).

Atlantic Bank Ltd, PO Box 481, Cor Cleghorn & Freetown Road, Belize City (tel: 234-123, 277-124; fax: 233-907, 234-150).

Atlantic International Bank Ltd, PO Box 481, Cnr Freetown Road & Cleghorn Streets, Belize City (tel: 230-681; fax: 230-677).

Banca Serfin of Mexico, PO Box 1636, Cor. Eyre & Hudson Streets, Belize City (tel: 027-8179, 027-8225; fax: 027-8970).

Bank of Nova Scotia, PO Box 708, Albert Street, Belize City (tel: 027-7027/030/415/416; fax: 027-7416).

Barclays Bank PLC, PO Box 363, Albert Street, Belize City (tel: 027-7211; fax: 027-8572).

Belize Bank Ltd, PO Box 364, 60 Market Square, Belize City (tel: 277-132, 272-390; fax: 272-712, 274-519).

Development Finance Corporation, PO Box 40, Bliss Parade, Belmopan, Cayo District (tel: 082-2360, 082-2350; fax: 082-3096).

National Development Foundation of Belize, PO Box 1210, 109 Cemetery Road, Belize City (tel: 027-2139, 027-2874; fax: 027-8437).

Provident Bank & Trust of Belize Limited, PO Box 1867, 1st Floor, 35 Barrack Road, Belize City (tel: 235-698; fax: 230-368).

Central bank
Central Bank of Belize, Gabourel Lane, PO Box 852, Belize City (tel: 223-6194; fax: 223-6226; e-mail: info@centralbank.org.bz).

Travel information
AeroBelize, P S W Goldson International Airport, Ladyville (tel: 252-535).

Belize Airport Authority, PSW Goldson International Airport, Ladyville (tel: 252-045; fax: 252-439).

Belize Hotel Association (tel: 230-065; fax: 231-857; e-mail: miller@btl.net).

Belize Port Authority, Caesar Ridge Road, Belize City (tel: 272-439; fax: 273-571).

Belize Tourism Board (tel: 231-913; fax: 231-943; e-mail: btbb@btl.net; internet sites: http://www.travelbelize.org; www.belizetourism.org).

Belize Tourism Industry Association (BTIA), 99 Albert Street, PO Box 62, Belize City (tel: 275-717; fax: 271-144; e-mail: btia@btl.net).

Maya Airways (administrative office), 6 Fort St, PO Box 458, Belize City (tel: 272-312; fax: 30-585); P S W Goldson International Airport, Ladyville (tel: 252-336).

Ministry of tourism
Ministry of Tourism and The Environment, Belmopan (tel: 223-394; fax: 222-862).

National tourist organisation offices
Belize Tourist Board, PO Box 325, 83 North Front Street, Belize City (tel: 277-213; fax: 277-490; e-mail: btbb@btl.net).

Ministries
Ministry of Agriculture and Fisheries, West Block, Belmopan (tel: 222-332, 222-241; fax: 222-409).

Ministry of Budget Management, Investment and Trade, Central Bank of Belize Building, Gaol Lane, Belize City (tel: 232-128, 236-194; fax: 235-097; e-mail: chalilio@bti.net).

Ministry of Economic Development, PO Box 42, Belmopan (tel: 222-526, 222-527, 222-023, 222-672; fax: 223-111, 223-673).

Ministry of Education and Public Service, West Block, Belmopan (tel: 222-329, 222-798, 222-067; fax: 223-389, 222-206).

Ministry of Energy, Science, Technology and Transportation, Belmopan (tel: 222-435; fax: 223-317).

Ministry of Finance, Belmopan (tel: 222-169; fax: 2222-886).

Ministry of Foreign Affairs, PO Box 174, Belmopan (tel: 222-322; fax: 222-854).

Ministry of Health and Sports, Belmopan (tel: 222-325; fax: 222-942).

Ministry of Home Affairs and Labour, Belmopan (tel: 222-281; fax: 222-016).

Ministry of Housing, Urban Development and Co-operatives, Belmopan (tel: 223-339; fax: 223-298).

Ministry of Human Resources, Community and Youth Development, Culture and Women's Affairs, Belmopan (tel: 222-161; fax: 223-175).

Ministry of National Security, Belmopan (tel: 222-225; fax: 222-615).

Ministry of Natural Resources, Belmopan (tel: 222-331, 222-249; fax: 222-333).

Ministry of Statistics, Central Statistical Office, Belmopan (tel: 222-207; fax: 223-206).

Ministry of Tourism and The Environment, Belmopan (tel: 223-394; fax: 222-862).

Ministry of Trade and Industry, Belmopan (tel: 222-199; fax: 222-329).

Ministry of Works, Belmopan (tel: 222-139; fax: 223-282).

Other useful addresses
Association of National Development Agencies (ANDA), Princess Margaret Drive, Belize City (tel: 35-115; fax: 32-362).

Attorney General's Ministry, Belmopan (tel: 222-504; fax: 223-390).

Belize Electricity Board, 115 Barrack Road, Belize City (tel: 277-141; fax: 231-905).

Belize Embassy (USA), 2535 Massachusetts Avenue, NW, Washington DC 20008 (tel: 202-332-9636; fax: 202-332-6888).

Belize Export and Investment Promotion Unit (BEIPU), PO Box 291, 63 Regent Street, Belize City (tel: 273-148, 274-394, 275-108/9; fax: 274-984).

Belize Information Service, P.O. Box 60, Belmopan (tel: 222-019; fax: 223-242).

Belize Marketing Board, 117 North Front Street, PO Box 479, Belize City (tel: 272-439; fax: 273-571).

Belize Port Authority (tel: 272-439; fax: 273-571; e-mail: portbze@btl.net).

Belize Offshore Centre (tel: 234-351; fax: 233-501; e-mail: cititrust@btl.net).

Belize Telecommunications Ltd. St Thomas Street, PO Box 603, Belize City (tel: 232-868; fax: 277-600; internet site: http://www.btl.net).

Belize Trade and Investment Development Services (BELTRAIDE) (tel: 223-737; fax: 220-595; e-mail: beltraide@belize.gov.bz).

British High Commission, PO Box 91, Belmopan (tel: 222-146; fax: 222-717).

Central Statistical Office (CSO), Ministry of Finance, Belmopan (tel: 222-207; fax: 222-206).

Citrus Control Board, 87 Commerce Bight, Melinder Road, Dangriga Town (tel: 222-145, 222-447; fax: 222-686).

Customs & Excise, PO Box 146, Fort Street, Belize City (tel: 277-405; fax: 277-091).

Export Processing Zone, Ministry of Trade and Industry, Belmopan (tel: 222-199, 222-153; fax: 222-923).

Fisheries Department, Princess Margaret Drive, Belize City (tel: 244-552, 232-623; fax: 232-983; e-mail: species@btl.net).

Forest Department, Forestry Drive, Belmopan (tel: 223-629; fax: 222-083).

Geology and Petroleum Office, Unity Boulevard, Belmopan (tel: 222-178, 222-651; fax: 223-538).

National Development Foundation of Belize, 2882 Coney Drive Coral Grove, Belize City (tel: 231-207, 231-132; fax: 231-195).

Society for the Promotion of Education & Research (SPEAR), Corner Pickstock and New Road, PO Box 1766, Belize City (tel: 231-668; fax: 232-367).

Water and Sewerage Authority, Central American Boulevard, Belize City (tel: 224-757; fax: 224-759).

Internet sites

Belize yellow pages: http://www.ipl.com.gt/cgi-bin/busca-beling

Latin American Network Information Center: http://www.lanic.utexas.edu

Benin

KEY FACTS

Official name: République du Bénin (Republic of Benin)

Head of State: President Mathieu Kérékou (since Mar 1996; re-elected Mar 2001)

Head of government: President Mathieu Kérékou (since May 1998)

Ruling party: The Mouvance Présidentielle (Presidential Movement) (a large coalition of parties backing President Mathieu Kérékou) (elected 30 Mar 2003)

Area: 112,622 square km

Population: 6.94 million (2004)

Capital: Porto-Novo (administrative); Cotonou (seat of government)

Official language: French

Currency: CFA franc (CFAf) = 100 centimes (Communauté Financière Africaine (African Financial Community) franc). New notes have been issued; old notes cease to be legal tender from Jan 2005.

Exchange rate: CFAf544.07 per US$ (Oct 2005); CFAf655.95 per euro (pegged from Jan 1999)

GDP per capita: US$565 (2004)

GDP real growth: 3.00% (2004)

Labour force: 3.14 million (2004)

Inflation: 2.60% (2004)

Balance of trade: -US$213.60 million (2004)

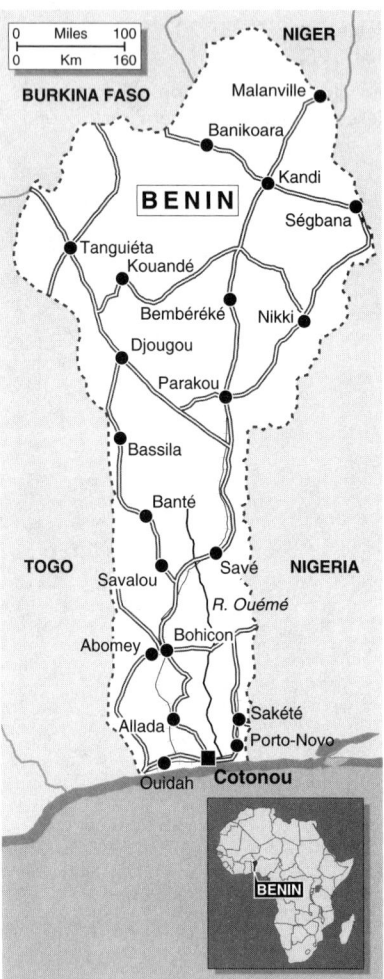

Benin's major challenge of ensuring sustainable, high economic growth by diversifying its economy and reviving the private sector obstinately persists. Recent economic and financial developments have been marked by negative external shocks in the form of a significant drop in the international prices for cotton, and Nigeria's intensification of restrictions on trade that ban imports of a growing list of products from Benin and elsewhere. As a result, smuggling and criminality along the Benin-Nigeria border has been on the rise.

Economy

In July 2005, the country applied to the International Monetary Fund (IMF) for assistance with the implementation of a three year programme to meet this challenge and to obtain more convincing results in its IMF-endorsed fight against poverty, not only through higher growth but also through more resolute implementation of economic and social policies.

Benin was seeking US$9.1 million. The IMF had only six months previously finally wiped off US$265 million of Benin's international debt. This new approach fell on favourable ears: Benin had qualified for the debt relief because of its 'overall satisfactory recent macroeconomic performance and progress in poverty reduction' and the IMF 'looked forward to working with Benin to help it develop a strong and stable economy'. The application was approved in August.

The numbers that took Benin to the IMF again were a drop in growth in GDP over 2004 to 3.0 per cent, against over 5.0 per cent in each of three previous years, and targets of 6.5 per cent. The fiscal deficit worsened by 0.8 per cent of GDP and would have been greater, had the government not reduced other expenditures; and money supply contracted by five per cent. Two banks liquidated, although two new ones replaced them, and the 43 per cent government owned Continental Bank was in difficulties.

The reasons for this fall in GDP were a drop in production of cotton fibre, and the virtual closure of the country to transit traffic because of the trade restrictions imposed by Nigeria and the loss of the port of Cotonou to transit traffic because of Nigerian initiated roadblocks and highway controls.

Benin has promised the IMF that the sought after aid will 'ensure Benin's economic recovery by improving its competitiveness through wide-ranging structural reforms', enable it to realise a real annual growth rate of 5.5 per cent by 2008 and keep annual inflation down to three per cent. Deficit-budgeting will be contained to a maximum 4.5 of GDP, the current account balanced to within 7.4 per cent.

To achieve these objectives, the government will intensify its efforts to mobilise revenues, in particular to collect taxes. The target is that tax revenues account for 17.8 per cent of GDP by 2008. That will allow overall expenditures to stay at 22.2 per cent of GDP by 2008 and primary expenditures at 17.7 per cent.

There are suggestions as to how, at least internally, the cotton industry will be revived, but no ideas on how big and powerful brother Nigeria will be brought into line.

In an ambitious privatisation programme, the 2005/06 cotton crop will be ginned by private enterprise, says the government – and bids for the three major ginneries have been awarded. Telecommunications and port administration will also soon be offered to the private sector.

Overall, the economy of Benin is underdeveloped although there are small oil deposits, as well as limestone, marble and timber. It remains dependent on subsistence agriculture, cotton production, and regional trade. There are allegations that the country is a transshipment point for illicit drugs associated with Nigerian trafficking organisations and most commonly destined for Western Europe and the US; and that it is vulnerable to money laundering due to a poorly regulated financial infrastructure.

Politics

President Mathieu Kerekou, a former military leader of Benin, seized power in 1972 as Major Kerekou. He began to restore civilian rule and during the 1980s resigned from the army to become a civilian head of state. He immediately set about liberalising the economy.

He was born in 1933 and educated in Senegal and Mali before joining the French army. He held senior posts in the Adwoman military before 1972. He first proclaimed Marxism-Leninism as the official ideology, earning for the country the label 'Africa's Cuba'. Following pressure from creditor nations and domestic unrest related to economic hardship, he dropped the ideology. He later lost the 1991 presidential elections but was returned in the 1996 elections. Kerekou was re-elected for a second term in 2002 but is barred by the constitution from running for a third term in the presidential polls planned for March 2006. Reclusive, he calls himself a born-again Christian, and seldom makes public appearances.

Border disputes

Only some 100 miles wide for half its length, Benin has border disputes with all four of its neighbours. It accuses Burkina Faso of moving boundary pillars; much of the Benin-Niger boundary, including the tri-point with Nigeria, remains undemarcated. A joint boundary commission continues to resurvey the boundary with Togo to verify Benin's claim that Togo moved the boundary stones. And the Nigerians, although not disputing the border, have virtually closed all crossing points, serverly curtailing the important cross-border trade.

COUNTRY PROFILE

Historical profile

With little known about the history of northern Benin, much of the area now comprising the country belonged to the ancient kingdom of Dahomey (located in the south of the country and the strongest of three kingdoms founded by three brothers). At its height, in the seventeenth century, the kingdom boasted a royal court complex as large as a European town, with palaces and buildings decorated with carvings and copper castings and housing bronze and ivory treasures. The wealth of the kingdoms was built on slave trading, a lucrative business that sold over 10,000 prisoners a year up to the nineteenth century. In 1879 the royal court of the Oba King was destroyed and its treasures looted; most pieces ended up in the British Museum. France, with a strategy of denying other European powers expansion into the region, overthrew King Behanzin and declared Dahomey a protectorate in 1893. In 1904 it was later absorbed into French West Africa, and gained autonomous status in 1946. Following independence from France in 1960 until 1972 the Republic of Dahomey endured a period of chronic instability enduring five coups, nine changes in government and five different constitutions.

1960 Gained independence from France as the Republic of Dahomey. Hubert Maga, was elected president.
1963 Maga was overthrown by General Christophe Soglo leading a military coup d'état.
1965 Soglo declared himself head of state.
1967 A military coup deposed Soglo.
1969 Lt Col Paul-Émile de Souza became president.
1970 Election were scheduled but failed to take place due to irreconcilable differences between politicians of the north and south. Instead, a three-man presidential council was formed; with a two-year rotating precedency for each.
1972 Maga, the first president, was replaced, without incident in May, by Justin Ahomadegbé. In October, the military staged another coup and installed an 11-man government headed by Major Mathieu Kérékou who declared Benin a Marxist-Leninist state.
1975 The Republic of Dahomey was renamed The People's Republic of Benin.
1990 With the country bankrupt and on the brink of social collapse, President Kérékou handed power to a national conference. The government abandoned Marxism-Leninism and committed itself to political reform.
1991 Nicéphore Soglo became president and introduced sweeping austerity measures.
1995 Parties opposed to the president won a majority in the National Assembly in the legislative elections.
1996 Kérékou became president and Adrien Houngbédji, leader of the Parti du Renouveau Démocratique (PRD) (Party of Democratic Renewal), assumed the role of prime minister.

KEY INDICATORS — Benin

	Unit	2000	2001	2002	2003	2004
Population	m	6.23	6.40	6.57	65.85	6.94
Gross domestic product (GDP)	US$bn	2.30	2.40	2.70	2.63	*4.08
GDP per capita	US$	373	375	450	400	565
GDP real growth	%	5.8	5.0	5.8	5.5	3.0
Inflation	%	3.0	4.0	2.4	1.5	2.6
Exports (fob) (goods)	US$m	246.0	210.0	375.0	207.0	720.9
Imports (fob) (goods)	US$m	453.0	661.0	647.7	479.0	934.5
Balance of trade	US$m	-207.0	-451.0	-272.7	-272.0	-213.6
Current account	US$m	-180.0	-159.0	-240.0	-300.0	-350.0
Total reserves minus gold	US$m	458.1	578.0	615.7	509.8	442.9
Foreign exchange	US$m	455.2	574.9	612.6	506.3	439.5
Exchange rate	per US$	711.98	733.04	696.99	574.89	496.63

* estimated figure

1998 Houngbédji resigned, a new government was formed without a post of prime minister.

1999 After National Assembly elections, the Parti de la Renaissance du Benin (PRB) (Benin Renaissance Party), led by former president Soglo's wife, Rosine, emerged as the largest single opposition party. Adrien Houngbédji (PRD) was elected president of the new Assembly.

2001 President Kérékou was re-elected for his last five-year term since, in 2006, he will be over the age limit of 70 years for presidential candidates.

2002 The European Commission adopted a programme of co-operation with Benin for the period 2002–07. The first municipal elections were held.

2003 A large coalition of parties backing President Mathieu Kérékou won the 30 March National Assembly elections.

2004 In July, an International Development Association (IDA) credit of US$45 million was approved to assist Benin in expanding electrification and restructuring its power sector. Benin and Nigeria agreed to a redefine their mutual border.

2005 The International Court of Justice awarded Benin most of the river islands that had been disputed along the Niger/Benin border.

Political structure
Constitution
The 1990 constitution provides for multi-party politics and a president to be directly elected by popular vote. Presidential candidates cannot be aged over 70. No provision is made for a prime minister; the president is head of government.
Form of state
Republic
The executive
The president is directly elected by popular vote for a five-year term and has ultimate power and control.
National legislature
Benin has a directly elected legislature, the 83-member Assemblée Nationale (National Assembly), with a maximum life of four years.
Legal system
The legal system is based on French civil law and customary law.
Last elections
30 March 2003 (parliamentary); March 2001 (presidential).
Results: Parliamentary: won by the Mouvance Présidentielle (President Movement) – a large coalition of parties backing President Mathieu Kérékou.
Next elections
March 2006 (presidential); 2007 (parliamentary).

Political parties
There are over 100 registered parties in Benin, but only a handful are represented in parliament.
Ruling party
The Mouvance Présidentielle (Presidential Movement) (a large coalition of parties backing President Mathieu Kérékou) (elected 30 Mar 2003)
Main opposition party
Parti de la Renaissance du Bénin (PRB) (Party for the Rebirth of Benin); Parti du Renouveau Démocratique (PRD) (Party of Democratic Renewal).

Population
6.94 million (2004)
Ethnic make-up
African (99 per cent) (42 ethnic groups, most important being Fon, Adja, Yoruba, Bariba), European (1 per cent).
Religions
Animists (70 per cent), Christians (15 per cent) and Muslims (15 per cent).

Education
Annual expenditure on education is 3–3.5 per cent of GDP of which over 55 per cent is spent on primare education.
Literacy rate: 33.6 per cent adult rate; 25 per cent female rate.
Enrolment rate: 99 per cent gross primary enrolment, of relevant age group (including repeaters); 20 per cent net secondary enrolment (UN HDR)
Pupils per teacher: 52 in primary schools.

Health
HIV/Aids
70,000 people, 3,000 of whom are aged under 15 (World Bank). Half of sex workers have tested positive, so a pandemic could cause future problems if issues of contraceptive use are not addressed.
HIV prevalence: 1.9 per cent aged 15–49 in 2003 (World Bank)
Life expectancy: 53 years (World Bank 2003).
Fertility rate/Maternal mortality rate: 5.2 births per woman (World Bank)
Infant mortality rate: 91 per 1,000 live births; 23 per cent of children aged under five were malnourished (World Bank).
Head of population per physician/bed: Six doctors per 100,000 people.

Welfare
The National Social Security fund provides for general workers and farmers who have made contributions. The fund is supervised by the Ministry of Labour although its assets are autonomous and administered by trustees. Every employer must provide a contribution for each worker to cover disability and family allowances. Old age pension benefits are accrued by workers contributions to the fund.

Main cities
Cotonou (seat of government, estimated population 734,600 in 2003), Porto-Novo (administrative capital, 231,600), Parakou (205,300), Abomey (120,700), Natitingou (111,600), Ouidah (89,600).

Languages spoken
African languages (Yoruba, Bariba and Fon) are widely used in everyday life.
Official language/s
French

Media
Press
Dailies: The government information bureau publishes the daily *Le Nation*. *Ehuzu* is the other widely read national daily. *Le Matinal En Ligne* is a French language daily.
Weeklies: The Chamber of Commerce publishes a weekly bulletin. *La Gazette du Golfe* is a weekly sport publication.
Periodicals: Periodicals include a fortnightly publication of the government information bureau *Journal Officiel de la République du Benin*.
Broadcasting
The state-owned Office des Radiodiffusion et Télévision du Bénin (ORTB) broadcasts radio services in French, English and 18 local languages and television transmissions for eight hours weekly.
Advertising
Advertising is available in the press, on radio, in Benin's seven cinemas and on hoardings and trains.

Economy
Benin was forced to restructure its economy in the early 1990s following the devaluation of the CFA franc. This, coupled with sound market-orientated economic policies that followed, gave the country sustained growth for over a decade.
In 2004 GDP growth fell to 3.0 per cent, from 5.5 in 2003. The IMF in a 2005 review commended the government for its 'prudent macroeconomic policies' that had resulted in growth and low inflation. The economy is reliant on primary industries with agriculture providing 36.9 per cent of GDP, of which cotton accounts for 80 per cent of exports. Benin is one of Africa's largest cotton producers. Just under 30 per cent of its labour force depend on cotton production for their livelihood. A decline in cotton production along with restrictions on exports to Nigeria and the continuation of cotton subsidies in developed countries resulted in a fall in exports in 2004/05. Most other agricultural products grown are sold on local markets or are subsistence crops.
Despite the progress made, poverty and social indicators have not improved significantly over the past decade. Benin

remains one of the poorest countries in the world, with 29 per cent of the population living below the national poverty line; it is rated at 162 out of 177, by UN Human Development Reports.

In 2004 the economy weakened under external pressures and budgetary slippage. The government finally implemented the delayed wage settlement with its civil service. However, the IMF warned that public expenditure management with enhanced transparency and governance of public finances was vital.

The government's policy is focussed on attempting to increase the level of foreign direct investment. This is hoped to be achieved by attracting investment into the growing tourist industry and communication sectors. Approval of a natural gas pipeline from Nigeria will help the nation's poor energy situation, this in turn should create jobs and an enhanced business climate.

The World Bank and IMF agreed in 2005 to approve a three-year arrangement of US$9.1 million, with a first tranche of US$1.3 million. This follows on from the 2003 final disbursement of US$460 million that successfully completed the debt relief under the enhanced Heavily Indebted Poor Countries (HIPC) initiative, after Benin fulfilled several conditions. These included implementing a poverty reduction strategy, maintenance a macroeconomic framework, and introducing structural and social reforms to improve poverty reduction, school enrolment and governance in other areas. Donors also pressed for further action to reduce the civil service and privatise state enterprises. However only limited success was achieved on the latter as state control of the cotton sector has yet to be relinquished, although the government has plans for reforms due after the 2006 national elections.

Corruption and the informal sector also dog government control of the economy. Smuggling, including of people, between Benin and Nigeria is rife and it has been estimate that the informal sector can account for over 45 per cent of gross national income.

External trade
Benin has lodged a complaint with the WTO, along with Burkina Faso, Mali and Chad, calling for the removal of cotton subsidies in developed countries, which have artificially lowered the trading price of cotton.

Nigeria's ban on a number of imports from Benin continues to damage trade. In 2002, the US approved Benin as being eligible for tariff preferences under the Africa Growth and Opportunities Act (AGOA).

Imports
Principal imports are foodstuffs, capital goods, fuel and energy.
Main sources: China (29.7 per cent total, 2004), France (13.8 per cent), Thailand (7.2 per cent), Côte d'Ivoire (4.6 per cent)

Exports
Principal exports are crude oil, palm products, cotton, coffee and cocoa.
Main destinations: China (30.2 of total, 2004), India (15.6 per cent), Thailand (6 per cent), Ghana (5.9 per cent), Niger (4.5 per cent)

Agriculture
Farming
The agricultural sector is the most important economic sector. It accounted for 36.9 per cent of GDP in 2004 and employs over 55 per cent of the workforce. Cotton is the principal cash crop and foreign exchange earner, farmed mainly on large industrial plantations. It is also important to the rural economy as it supports almost half of rural households. Other cash crops include palm oil, coffee, sugar, cocoa, karité nuts and tobacco. Subsistence farming (mainly collectivised) shows low productivity but the country is virtually self-sufficient in food. Livestock farming is particularly important in the north. The principal food crops are yams, cassava, sorghum, beans, millet, maize and rice.

Crop production in 2004 included: 1,102,100 tonnes (t) cereals in total, *4,000,000t cassava, *2,500,000t yams, *800,000t maize, 425,000t seed cotton, 150,000t cotton lint, *200,000t oil palm fruit, 190,000t sorghum, 130,000t groundnuts in shell, *170,000t tomatoes, *70,000t rice, *75,000t sweet potatoes, 40,000t millet, 115,170t oilcrops, *70,000t sugar cane, 106,000t pineapples, 41,100t treenuts in total, 128,000t pulses, *45,500t chillies & peppers, *1,000t tobacco leaves, *12,000t citrus fruit, 15,500t sesame seed, 249,000t fruit in total, 414,500t vegetables in total. Livestock production included: 53,501t meat in total, 21,109t beef, 3,892t pig meat, 7,300t lamb & goat meat, 15,200t poultry, 9,360t eggs, 34,323t milk, 3,454t cattle hides.
* estimate

Fishing
Fishing is confined mainly to inland waters and augments local food supplies.

Industry and manufacturing
The industrial sector is small-scale, contributing 8.4 per cent to GDP and employing 6 per cent of the workforce. Manufacturing activity is centred on processing primary products (palm oil, fats, sugar, beverages, cotton) for export, and the manufacture of consumer goods and construction materials for home consumption.

Cement production and oil refining are the main heavy industries.

The government has encouraged foreign investment in canning, paper processing, glass manufacturing, salt processing, agribusiness, pharmaceuticals, clothing, palm oil, building materials and chemicals.

In 2000, the cottonseed oil plant at Bohicon was extended and modernised, raising capacity to 12,000 tonnes of oil, and a sugar producing enterprise, which had been closed since 1990, was reopened.

Tourism
Tourism in Benin is at a formative stage of development. The government recognises its potential value to the economy and is encouraging promotion of the country's under-exploited attractions and the expansion of infrastructure. Tourist arrivals increased by 2.75 per cent in 2003, compared to 2002.

Mining
The mining sector accounts for 5.5 per cent of GDP and employs 3 per cent of the workforce.

Activity is confined to extraction of limestone for the local cement industry, and marble. There is a limestone quarry at Onigbolo. There are known reserves of phosphate, chromite, uranium, low grade iron ore, marble and gold. The government has awarded a number of gold exploration licences to foreign investors. Under Beninese law, all mineral resources belong to the state, which grants exclusive rights for exploration, development and mining activities.

Hydrocarbons
Proven reserves of oil have fallen from the eight million barrels in 2003 and ongoing exploration has been unsuccessful. Oil production is on a very small scale, with the downstream oil industry dependent on refined petroleum products imported from neighbouring Nigeria. An oil terminal with a capacity of 55,000 cubic metres (cum) of crude is based at Cotonou.

Proven gas reserves totalled 1.2 billion cubic metres. When it is complete, the US$260 million West African Gas Pipeline (WAGP) will supply natural gas from Nigeria's Escravos field to Benin, Togo and Ghana. The WAGP consortium will invest about US$500 million to pipe Nigerian natural gas across the region. The 1,000km pipeline is to be managed by Chevron Texaco and was expected to come into operation in 2005. However, protracted debate on the environmental impact of the pipeline has delayed construction. Nigeria has said it will use gas that at the moment is being flared off, but has so far (early 2006) refused to name the wells. Benin is expected to consume only 5 per cent of the piped gas until a market for it is fully established.

Energy
Benin produces about 25 million kilowatt-hours of electricity each year. Traditional fuels account for over 70 per cent of total energy consumption. The rest is mainly hydroelectric power.
Electricity is imported from the hydroelectric Akosombo Dam in Ghana. The Akosombo and Nkong hydroelectric dams generate about 1,072MW annually.
A joint hydroelectric power project with Togo on the river Mono has been in full operation since the building of the Nangbeto Dam.
In 2004, a US$45 million International Development Association (IDA) credit was approved to assist Benin in expanding electrification and restructuring the power sector, with private sector participation in the distribution of electricity.

Banking and insurance
Central bank
Banque Centrale des États de l'Afrique de l'Ouest
Main financial centre
Cotonou and Parakou

Time
GMT plus one hour

Geography
Benin is a narrow stretch of territory 700km long running north/south. The country has an Atlantic coastline of about 100km, flanked by Nigeria to the east and Togo to the west. In the north it is bordered by Burkina Faso and Niger.

Climate
Equatorial in the south with average daytime temperatures reaching 30–38 degrees Celsius (C). Main dry season from January–March. Rainy seasons from May–July and from September–December. Very humid in coastal areas. The north is tropical with more extreme temperatures, and single dry and rainy seasons. Length of rainy seasons varies with location but it is generally very wet from July–October.

Entry requirements
Passports
Required by all except nationals of certain African countries who have identification documents.
Visa
Required by all, except for nationals of Denmark, Germany, France and Sweden and those of Economic Community Of West African States. For the latest requirements and to apply, contact the local embassy or representative.

Currency advice/regulations
There are no restrictions on import of local or foreign currency, but amounts of foreign currency must be declared on arrival.
Foreign currency exports are allowed up to the equivalent of CFAf500.

Health (for visitors)
Mandatory precautions
A yellow fever vaccination certificate is required by all.
Advisable precautions
Hepatitis A, typhoid, tetanus and polio vaccinations. Malaria prophylaxis should be taken.
Water precautions are necessary, especially outside towns.
There is a rabies risk.

Hotels
Available in all main towns. Accommodation in Cotonou is limited. Advance booking essential. Service charge usually included in bill, otherwise 10 per cent tip.

Credit cards
Access, Mastercard, Visa accepted on limited basis. Some banks may advance cash on Visa cards, check with card company.

Public holidays
Fixed dates
1 Jan (New Year's Day), 10 Jan (Traditional Day), 1 May (Labour Day), 1 Aug (Independence Day), 15 Aug (Assumption Day), 26 Oct (Armed Forces Day), 1 Nov (All Saints' Day), 30 Nov (National Day), 25 Dec (Christmas Day).
Variable dates
Easter Monday, Ascension Day, Whit Monday, Eid al Adha, Eid al Fitr, Birth of the Prophet.
The Islamic year contains 354 or 355 days, with the result that Muslim feasts advance by 10–12 days against the Gregorian calendar. Dates of feasts vary according to the sighting of the new moon, so cannot be forecast exactly. Islamic year 1426: 10 February 2005 to 30 January 2006.

Working hours
Banking
Mon–Fri: 0800–1100, 1500–1700.
Business
Mon–Fri: 0800–1230, 1530–1900. (Sat) 0900–1300.
Government
Mon–Fri: 0800–1230, 1500–1830.
Shops
Mon–Sat: 0830–1300, 1600–1930; (Sun) 0800–1200. Shops that open Sun mainly close Mon am.

Electricity supply
Electricity supply 220V AC 50 cycles.

Getting there
Air
International airport/s: Cotonou-Cadjehoun (COO), 6km west of city; taxi and limousine service (15–20 minutes to city centre), restaurant, business centre, 24 hours medical facility.
Airport tax: None
Surface
Road: There are routes from Burkina Faso, Togo, Nigeria and Niger.
Rail: A line linking Niger to Benin is under construction.
Water: Shipping lines from Marseille (France) and Lagos (Nigeria).
Main port/s: Porta Nova

Getting about
National transport
Air: Regular services between Cotonou, Parakou, Natitingou, Kandi and Djougou.
Road: Good main roads in south connecting towns to Cotonou and Porto Novo.
Mainly laterite, but the main coast road, which connects Lagos with Accra, is surfaced, and the road north from Cotonou is surfaced to Savalou.
In northern areas some roads are only passable in dry season.
Buses: Bus services link towns on these main routes.
Rail: There is only one operation railway line going north from Cotonou to Bohicon, Savé and Parakou. Facilities are limited.
City transport
Taxis: Fixed charge within towns, but advisable to negotiate fares in advance. Tipping is optional.
Car hire
Available in Cotonou. Chauffeur-driven services are recommended. Insurance/liability position should be checked. International driving licence required.

BUSINESS DIRECTORY
The addresses listed below are a selection only. While World of Information makes every endeavour to check these addresses, we cannot guarantee that changes have not been made, especially to telephone numbers and area codes. We would welcome any corrections.

Telephone area codes
The international direct dialling code (IDD) for Benin is +229, followed by subscriber's number.

Chambers of Commerce
Benin Chamber of Commerce and Industry, Avenue Général de Gaulle, PO Box 31, Cotonou (tel: 312-081; fax: 313-299; e-mail: ccib@bow.intnet.bj).

Benin

Banking

Bank of Africa Bénin (BOA), BP 08-0879, Ave Pape Jean Paul II, Cotonou (tel: 313-228; fax: 313-117).

Banque Centrale des Etats de l'Afrique de l'Ouest, BP 325, Ave Jean Paul II, Cotonou (tel: 312-466/7; fax: 312-465).

Banque Internationale du Bénin (BIBE) BP 03-2098, Carrefour des 3 Banques, Cotonou (315-549, 315-621; fax:312-365, 312-707).

Continental Bank Bénin, 01 BP, Avenue Pope Jean-Paul II, 2020 Cotonou (tel: 312-424, 313-393; fax: 315177).

Ecobank Bénin, BP 1280, Rue du Gouverneur Bayol, 01 Cotonou (tel: 314-023, 313-069; fax: 313-385, 313-718).

Financial Bank Bénin (FBB), BP 2700, Rue du Commandant Decoeur, Cotonou (tel: 313-100, 313-103, 313-104; fax: 313-102).

Central bank

Banque Centrale des États de l'Afrique de l'Ouest, PO Box 325, Avenue Jean Paul I, Cotonou (tel: 312-466; fax: 312-465; e-mail: webmaster@bceao.int).

Travel information

Transports Aériens du Bénin (tel: 314-797).

National tourist organisation offices

Office National du Tourisme et de l'Hôtellerie (ONATHO), BP 89, Contonou (tel: 315-402).

Ministries

Ministry of Public Service, Labour and Administrative Reform (tel: 313-112).

Ministry of Public Works and Transport, PO Box 16, Cotonou, Benin (tel: 313-380).

State Ministry of Government Co-ordination, Planning, Development and Employment Promotion (tel: 301-553).

Other useful addresses

Agence Bénin-Presse, BP 120, Cotonou.

Benin Embassy (USA), 2737 Cathedral Avenue, NW, Washington DC 20008 (tel: 232-6656; fax: 265-1996).

Import/Export Alimentation de Bénin, BP 53, Cotonou.

Institut National de la Statistique et de L'Analyse Economique, BP 323, Cotonou (tel: 314-101/103).

Mission de Co-opération et d'Action Culturelle, BP 476, Cotonou (tel: 300-824).

Mission Permanente d'Aide et de Co-opération, BP 476, Cotonou (administers aid from France).

Organisation Commune Benin-Niger des Chemins de fer et des Transports (OCBN) (Benin Railways), PO Box 16, Cotonou, Benin (tel: 313-380).

Société Nationale d'Equipement, BP 2042, Cotonou (deals with capital goods).

Société Nationale de Commercialisation et d'Exportation du Bénin (Sonaceb), BP 933, Cotonou (tel: 312-822).

Société Nationale de Commercialisation des Produits Pétroliers (Sonacop), BP 245, Cotonou (tel: 312-290).

Société Nationale d'Importation du Bénin, BP 2042, Cotonou.

Syndicat National des Commerçants et Industriels Africains du Bénin, BP 367, Cotonou.

Internet sites

Africa Business Network: http://www.ifc.org/abn

AllAfrica.com: http://www.allafrica.com

African Development Bank: http://www.afdb.org

Africa Online: http://www.africaonline.com

Benin: http://www.guide-benin.

Embassy in Paris: http://www.ambassade-benin.org

General tourist information: http://www.africaguide.com/

Mbendi AfroPaedia (information on companies, countries, industries and stock exchanges in Africa): http://mbendi.co.za

Mission to the UN: http://www.un.int/benin

Bermuda

KEY FACTS

Official name: Bermuda

Head of State: Queen Elizabeth II; represented by Governor Sir John Vereker (sworn in 11 Apr 2002)

Head of government: Prime Minister Alex Scott (PLP) (sworn in 29 Jul 2003)

Ruling party: Progressive Labour Party (PLP) (since Nov 1998; re-elected 24 Jul 2003)

Area: 55 square km

Population: 65,000 (2004)

Capital: Hamilton

Official language: English

Currency: Bermudan dollar (BD$) = 100 cents

Exchange rate: BD$1.00 per US$ (fixed)

GDP per capita: US$36,000 (2004)

GDP real growth: 0.50% (2003)

Labour force: 37,472 (2003)

Unemployment: 4.50% (2003)

Inflation: 2.30% (2003)

Balance of trade: -US$668.00 million (2003)

Foreign debt: US$145.00 million (2003)

Visitor numbers: 477,757 (2004)

COUNTRY PROFILE

Historical profile
1503 A Spaniard, Juan de Bermudez, sighted the islands.
1609 Settled by the British.
1612 A charter was given by James I to the Virginia Company to include Bermuda in the dominion. The first permanent settlers arrived shortly afterwards.
1684 The islands were sold to the City of London and became the property of the Crown.
1620 Bermuda was granted limited self-government.
1700s Bermuda developed links with the American colonies.
1940 An agreement between the US and Britain granted about 10 per cent of Bermuda's land to the US for military use.
1968 Bermuda was granted internal self-government. The first elections were won by the United Bermuda Party (UBP).
1998 The UBP lost power for the first time since 1968 when the Progressive Labour Party (PLP) won the general election.
2001 Regulation of the insurance sector was moved from the ministry of finance to the Monetary Authority, in order to increase the transparency of the sector.
2002 The Bermuda Companies Amendment Act simplifying the procedure for forming companies was passed.
2003 The ruling PLP won the 24 July parliamentary elections. Following a revolt in the PLP, Prime Minister Jennifer Smith resigned and Alex Scott was sworn in as premier on 29 July. In September, Bermuda was struck by Hurricane Fabian, the most powerful storm to hit the island in 50 years.
2004 The PLP published plans for independence from the UK.
2005 Bermuda entered into a tax sharing agreement with Australia, only its second after the US; it will be able to request and pass information on a specific tax matter under investigation or audit. The OECD welcomed the agreement as a measure to 'counter abuse of the financial system'.

Political structure
Bermuda has had a broad measure of internal self-government since 1968. Queen Elizabeth II is represented by a UK-appointed governor who is responsible for defence, external affairs and internal security. The governor is guided on most internal matters by a cabinet appointed from the bicameral legislature.

Form of state
Representative democracy; crown colony of the UK.

The executive
The prime minister is chosen from the majority party and heads a cabinet of no more than 14 members of the legislature.

National legislature
The legislature is bicameral. The upper house, the Senate, consists of 11 members, five appointed by the governor on the advice of the prime minister, three on the advice of the leader of the opposition and three by the governor. The lower house, the 40-member House of Assembly, is directly elected for a maximum term of five years.

Legal system
The legal system and Bermudian law are based on the British model. The ultimate court of appeal is the Judicial Committee of the Privy Council in the UK.

Last elections
24 July 2003 (parliamentary)
Results: Parliamentary: the ruling Progressive Labour Party (PLP) won 22 seats (51.7 per cent of the vote) and the United Bermuda Party (UBP) 14 seats (48 per cent).

Next elections
2008 (parliamentary)

Political parties
Ruling party
Progressive Labour Party (PLP) (since Nov 1998; re-elected 24 Jul 2003)
Main opposition party
United Bermuda Party (UBP)

Political situation
In June 2004, Alex Scott, prime minister and leader of the PLP, published his plans for independence for Bermuda from the UK. The proposals expect that legal documents could be prepared by 2006–07, and public debate would be undertaken in the meantime. The PLP is proposing that Bermudans should vote on the change during the next general election. The opposition party, UBP, has argued that only a referendum could give unequivocal acceptance by the electorate, while the UK has expressed concern that, unless there was sufficient turnout, the legitimacy of independence could always be open to doubt.

Bermuda

Population
65,000 (2004)
Ethnic make-up
African (58 per cent), European (36 per cent). Approximately 73 per cent of the population is Bermuda-born.
Religions
Non-Anglican Protestant (39 per cent), Anglican (27 per cent), Roman Catholic (15 per cent), African Methodist Episcopal (10 per cent), Methodist (6 per cent), Seventh-Day Adventist (3 per cent).

Health
Life expectancy: 77 years: male 75 years; female 79 years (2003).
Fertility rate/Maternal mortality rate: Two births per woman (2003)
Birth rate/Death rate: 12 births per 1,000 population; eight deaths per 1,000 population (2003).
Infant mortality rate: Nine per 1,000 live births (2003)

Welfare
An insurance scheme takes contributions from the employer and employee to benefit workers during sickness, or disability, for maternity leave or survivors of deceased workers, funded by contributions of a set amount, paid by both the employer and employee, each paying 50 per cent of the sum per week.
Pensions
There is an old age pension scheme funded by contributions of a set amount, paid by both the employer and employee, each paying 50 per cent of the sum per week.

Main cities
Hamilton (capital city, estimated population 97,000 in 2003), St George's (St George's Island) (1,800).

Languages spoken
English and Portuguese.
Official language/s
English

Media
Press
Dailies: The only daily is *The Royal Gazette*.
Weeklies: There are several weekly publications, including *Mid-Ocean News* and *Bermuda Sun*.
Periodicals: Regular magazines include *Bermudian*, *Bottom Line* and *Bermudian Business*.
Broadcasting
Two television and three radio channels operated by the Bermuda Broadcasting Corporation, which are commercial and privately owned. Also one independent radio station, the St George's Broadcasting Company, which also operates a microwave pay-TV service. Bermuda Cablevision runs an island-wide cable television service.
Advertising
Available on all forms of media.

Economy
Despite its small size and negligible resource base, Bermuda has one of the highest per capita incomes in the world. The economy is based upon tourism and international business transactions, which take advantage of Bermuda's offshore banking status.
Inflation has been kept low through the policy of fixing the Bermudan dollar at parity with the US dollar. Bermuda has low levels of public debt and although borrowing has risen due to an increase in capital spending, debt remains well below the government's ceiling of 10 per cent of GDP.
In the last three months of 2003, 428 new companies, partnerships and permits were created, representing the second highest number since the Bermuda Monetary Authority (BMA) began reporting the data in 2001. The strong trend continued into the first quarter of 2004 which recorded a further 416 incorporations, substantially higher than the 296 seen in the first quarter of 2003.
In 2004, the Bermudan based consulting firm Accenture (formerly known as Anderson Consulting) won the US$10 billion contract to administer the US visitor and immigrant indicator technology (US VISIT) programme, as part of the US homeland security measures. The US senate voted that this contract would be the last one awarded to an offshore company. Homeland security measures came into force as a result of the 2001 terrorist attacks on the US.
Uninsured costs to government for damage caused by Hurricane Fabian reduced the projected current account surplus in 2003/04 by some BD$10 million.
Prices of houses rose by nearly 180 per cent between 2000 and 2004. Consequently, only 21 per cent of locals own their own homes with a mortgage, and 23 per cent of locals without a mortgage. The 2004/05 budget includes some moderate increases to Bermuda's tax structure. In addition, the introduction of new government fees, including an annual fee for cellular telephones, will generate additional revenue of BD$28 million. It also includes plans to provide affordable housing.

External trade
The large trade deficit is offset by net invisible earnings from tourism and international business, especially insurance and shipping registration. High import duties on all items are the government's main source of income.
Imports
Principal imports include foodstuffs, tobacco, clothing, fuels, chemicals, machinery, transport equipment, and live animals.
Main sources: Kazakhstan (typically 36.6 per cent total, 2004), France (19.1 per cent), Japan 15.1 (per cent), Italy (10.6 per cent), US (8.2 per cent)
Exports
Principal goods exported are rum, flowers.
Main destinations: France (73.8 per cent total, 2004), UK (6.2 per cent), Sweden (2.6 per cent)
Re-exports
Pharmaceuticals and petroleum

Agriculture
Agriculture contributes about 1 per cent to GDP annually. Less than 6 per cent of total area is cultivated arable land, most of which is used by tenant farmers for growing fruit, vegetables and flowers. Although self-sufficient in eggs and milk, around 80 per cent of food requirements need to be imported. There is a small fishing industry.

KEY INDICATORS — Bermuda

	Unit	2000	2001	2002	2003	2004
Population	m	0.06	0.06	0.06	0.06	0.07
Gross domestic product (GDP)	US$bn	2.08	2.10	2.11	2.25	*2.34
GDP per capita	US$	33,000	33,000	33,000	35,000	36,000
GDP real growth	%	1.9	1.2	1.0	0.5	–
Inflation	%	2.7	2.9	2.3	2.3	–
Exports (fob) (goods)	US$m	56.0	45.0	–	51.0	–
Imports (fob) (goods)	US$m	739.0	750.0	–	719.0	–
Balance of trade	US$m	-683.0	-705.0	–	-668.0	–
Tourist numbers	'000	534.0	–	–	482.7	477.8
Exchange rate	per US$	1.00	1.00	1.00	1.00	1.00

* estimated figure

Nations of the World: A Political, Economic and Business Handbook

Crop production in 2004 included: 700 tonnes (t) potatoes, 90t sweet potatoes, 115t tomatoes, 330t bananas, 330t fruit in total, 2,855t vegetables in total. Livestock production included: 177t meat in total, 25t beef, 2t goat meat, 50t pig meat, 101t poultry, 280t eggs 1,350t milk.

The typical annual fish catch is over 350t, plus 25t per annum other seafood.

Industry and manufacturing
Manufacturing and construction combined contribute around 10 per cent to GDP and employ less than 5 per cent of the workforce. Major activities include ship repair, small boat building and manufacture of paints, perfumes, pharmaceuticals, mineral water extracts and handicraft souvenirs. The emphasis is on encouraging light industry in the Freeport area on Ireland Island North. Bermuda has large marine engineering interests, and operates one of the world's largest flag of convenience shipping fleets.

Tourism
Tourism, formerly the mainstay of the economy, is now second to the financial sector as a source of income. Due in part to the high cost of visiting the island, a decline in visitor numbers had already set in even before the terrorist events of 11 September 2001, which affected the all-important US market. The US has accounted for as much as 80 per cent of Bermuda's arrivals. In 2001, the total number of visitors fell below the half-million mark for the first time since 1973. Signs of recovery in 2002 and 2003 were set back by Hurricane Fabian in September 2003, the most powerful storm to hit the island in 50 years. Arrivals in 2003 nevertheless totalled 482,673, only a little under the previous year's figures and an improvement on those for 2001. The overall decline has resulted in a fall in income, accommodation and hotel employment. In an attempt to reverse the downward trend, the government and the hoteliers joined forces in 2001 to form the Alliance for Tourism, which offers concessions to encourage the redevelopment of hotels and investment in new properties. US visitors were still accounting for some 80 per cent of tourists in 2005, although in the first three quarters of the year numbers fell to 66,664, 11.5 per cent down on the same period in 2004. Canadian visitors increased by 4.5 per cent. Total tourist arrivals for the first three quarters of the year were 215,005, 0.5 per cent down on 2004.

Hydrocarbons
Bermuda relies on imported refined oil products and does not produce oil, natural gas or coal. Only ExxonMobil and Shell Oil Company are allowed to sell petroleum products on the market. Refined oils are imported to run electricity generators.

Gas is used mainly for domestic appliances and some commercial machines. It is imported by Shell from Argentina and is supplied by three commercial gas companies. There is no national grid; gas is supplied in cylinders and pumped into appliances.

Financial markets
Stock exchange
The Bermuda Stock Exchange (BSX) is rapidly becoming one of the world's leading offshore electronic securities markets. The BSX launched a securities depository in 2001.

Banking and insurance
Central bank
Bermuda Monetary Authority
Main financial centre
Hamilton
Offshore facilities
In 2000, Bermuda signed a letter of commitment with the Organisation for Economic Co-operation and Development (OECD) agreeing to exchange information with overseas authorities in criminal tax matters by 31 December 2003 and in civil tax matters by 31 December 2005. Following the 11 September 2001 terrorist attacks on the US, a number of new reinsurance companies located on the island.

Time
GMT minus four hours (GMT minus three hours from April to October).

Geography
The Bermudas or Somers Islands are an isolated archipelago, comprising about 150 islands in the Atlantic Ocean about 917km (570 miles) off the coast of South Carolina, USA. Ten of the islands are linked by bridges and causeways to form the principal mainland.

Climate
Semi-tropical with temperatures usually ranging between 16–28 degrees Celsius, from winter (Nov–Mar) to summer (Apr–Oct), with no marked rainy season. Bermuda is located more than 1,600km north of the Caribbean and is subjected to occasional hurricane-force winds between June and September.

Dress codes
There is no occasion on the island when shorts cannot be worn. For the office, tailored shorts of one colour may be worn, with long socks to the knees with at least an inch to turn over.

Entry requirements
Passports
Required by all visitors except UK, US and Canadian nationals with other documentary proof of identification. A return ticket is required by all visitors.
Visa
Visas are not required by transit passengers and most citizens of the Americas, Europe, Australasia and some Asian countries, provided their stay does not exceed six months. For further details visit www.barbados.org/docs.htm, or contact the local diplomatic or consular mission. All visitors must have return/onward passage.
Currency advice/regulations
There is no limit to the import of local or foreign currency, provided it is declared on arrival. The export of local currency is limited to BD$250. The export of foreign currency is limited to the amount imported and declared.

Health (for visitors)
Mandatory precautions
Yellow fever vaccination certificate if travelling from an infected area.
Advisable precautions
Hepatitis, typhoid, tetanus and polio vaccinations.

Hotels
Generally expensive. Reduced rates are avaliable in the November–March period. 7.25 per cent government tax payable on check-out in addition to room rates. Ten per cent tip is expected except where 10–15 per cent service charge added to bill.

Credit cards
Credit cards are accepted at most hotels, restaurants and shops.

Public holidays
Fixed dates
1 Jan (New Year's Day), 24 May (Bermuda Day), 11 Nov (Remembrance Day), 25 Dec (Christmas Day), 26 Dec (Boxing Day).
Variable dates
Good Friday, Queen's Official Birthday (second Mon in Jun), Cup Match and Somers' Day (Thu and Fri before the first Mon in Aug), Labour Day (first Mon in Sep).

Working hours
Banking
Mon–Fri: 0900–1500; also 1630–1730 Fridays only.
Business
Mon–Fri: 0900–1700.
Government
Mon–Fri: (summer) 1145–1600, 1715–2000; (winter) 1245–1700, 1815–2100.

Bermuda

Shops
Mon–Sat: 0900–1700. During summer many stores stay open until 2100.

Telecommunications
Mobile phones
GSM 1900 coverage is available throughout the islands

Electricity supply
115–230V AC, 80 cycles

Getting there
Air
International airport/s: Bermuda International Airport (BDA), 16km from Hamilton; bar, restaurant, bank, shops, hotel reservations.
Airport tax: A departure tax of BD$25 is included in air tickets.
Surface
Main port/s: Hamilton, St George's. Weekly cruises link Bermuda with several east coast US ports during the summer months.

Getting about
National transport
Road: There are around 250km of well-surfaced roads.
Buses: Regularly scheduled buses operate at frequent intervals to most destinations throughout Bermuda. Passengers must have the exact fare, tokens or transport passes which provide unlimited travel by bus or ferry which can be purchased at the Central Terminal in Hamilton.
Water: Ferries to and from Hamilton, Paget, Warwick, Somerset and Dockyard.
City transport
Taxis: Metered taxis with 25 per cent surcharge between midnight and 0600; tariffs are fixed by law. Taxis displaying a small blue flag are approved by the Department of Tourism for sightseeing purposes.
Car hire
Visitors are not permitted to drive cars. Motor-assisted cycles (mopeds and scooters) for hire at liveries throughout the island and through hotel and guest-houses. Law requires all persons riding motorised cycles to wear safety helmets.

BUSINESS DIRECTORY

The addresses listed below are a selection only. While World of Information makes every endeavour to check these addresses, we cannot guarantee that changes have not been made, especially to telephone numbers and area codes. We would welcome any corrections.

Telephone area codes
The international direct dialling (IDD) code for +1441, followed by subscriber's number.

Chambers of Commerce
Bermuda Chamber of Commerce, 1 Point Pleasant Road, PO Box HM 655, Hamilton HM CX (tel: 295-4201; fax: 292-5779; e-mail: info@bermudacommerce.com).

Banking
Bank of Bermuda, 6 Front Street, Hamilton HM DX (tel: 295-4000, 299-5005; fax: 299-6501, 295-1386).

The Bank of N T Butterfield & Son Ltd, PO Box HM 195, 65 Front Street, Hamilton HM AX (tel: 295-1111; fax: 295-0658).

Bermuda Commercial Bank Ltd, 44 Church Street, Hamilton HM 12 (tel: 295-5678; fax: 295-8091).

Central bank
Bermuda Monetary Authority, Burnaby House, 26 Burnaby Street, Hamilton HM 11 (tel: 295-5278; fax: 292-7471; e-mail: Info@bma.bm).

Travel information
National tourist organisation offices
Department of Tourism, Global House, 43 Church Street, Hamilton HM 12 (tel: 292-0023; fax: 292-7537; internet site: http://www.bermudatourism.org).

Ministries
Ministry of Finance, Government Administration Building, 30 Parliament Street, Hamilton HM 12 (tel: 295-5151; fax: 295-5727).

Office of The Governor, Government House, 11 Langton Hill, Pembroke, Hamilton HM 13 (tel: 292-3600; fax: 292-6831; e-mail: governor@gov.bm).

Other useful addresses
Bermuda Broadcasting Company, PO Box HM 452, Hamilton HM BX (tel: 295-2828; fax: 295-4282).

Bermuda Hotel Association, 102 Reid Street, Hamilton HM 19 (tel: 295-2127; fax: 292-6671; internet site: http://www.bermudahotels.com).

Bermuda International Business Association (BIBA), Suite 203, 48 Par-la-Ville Road, Hamilton HM 11 (tel: 292-0632; fax: 292-1797).

Bermuda Insurance Management Association (BIMA), PO Box HM 1752, Hamilton HM GX (tel: 295-4864; fax: 292-7375).

Bermuda Small Business Development Corp, PO Box HM 637, Hamilton HM CX (tel: 292-5570; fax: 295-1600).

Bermuda Stock Exchange, PO Box HM 1369, 3 F Washington Mall, Church Street, Hamilton HM FX (tel: 292-7212; fax: 292-7619; e-mail: info@bsx.com; internet site: http://www.bsx.com).

Department of Civil Aviation, Bermuda International Air Terminal, 2 Kindley Field Rd, St George's GE CX (tel: 293-1640; fax: 293-2417).

Government Information Services, Global House, 43 Church Street, Hamilton HM 12 (tel: 292-6384; fax: 292-5267).

Government Statistical Department, 43 Church Street, Hamilton HM 12 (PO Box HM 3015, Hamilton HM MX) (tel: 297-7761; fax: 295-8390).

Insurance Information Office, PO Box HM 2911, Hamilton HM LX (tel: 292-9829; fax: 295-3532).

The Registrar of Companies, Government Administration Building, 30 Parliament Street, Hamilton HM 12 (tel: 295-5151; fax: 292-6640; internet site: http://www.roc.bdagov.bm).

Internet sites
Bermuda Sun:
http://www.bermudasun.bm/

Bermuda Yellow Pages:
http://www.bermudayp.com/

Bermuda online:
http://www.bermuda-online.org

Bhutan

KEY FACTS

Official name: Druk-yul (The Kingdom of Bhutan)

Head of State: Druk Gyalpo (Dragon King) Jigme Singye Wangchuk (since Jul 1972)

Head of government: Prime Minister (Chairman of the Council of Ministers) Lyonpo Sangey Ngedup (took office 5 Sept 2005); the post is rotated annually among the ministers.

Area: 47,000 square km

Population: 2.22 million (2004)

Capital: Thimphu

Official language: Dzongkha

Currency: Ngultrum (Nu) = 100 chetrums

Exchange rate: Nu43.97 per US$ (Oct 2005) (pegged to Indian rupee)

GDP per capita: US$817 (2004)

GDP real growth: 7.00% (2004)

Labour force: 433,000 (2004)

Unemployment: 2.90% (2004)

Inflation: 4.50% (2004)

Balance of trade: -US$42.00 million (2003)

Visitor numbers: 9,000 (2004)

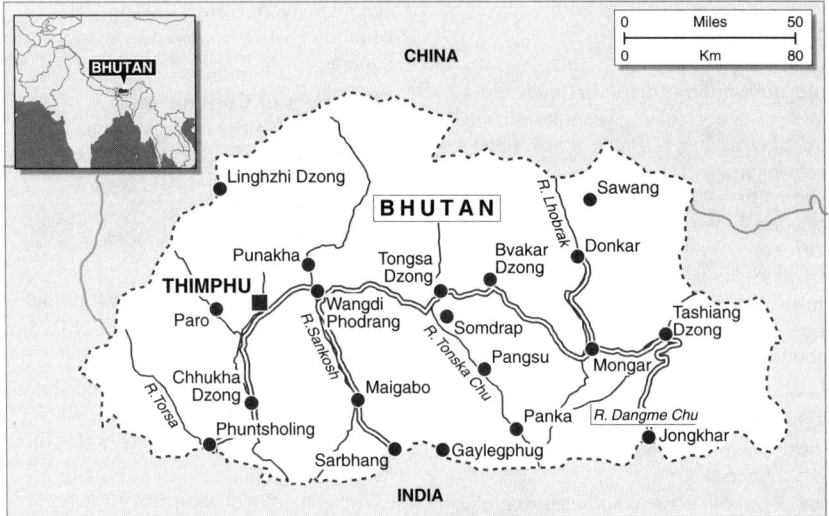

This landlocked Himalayan kingdom nestles between India and China and is ruled by the reformist King Jigme Singye Wangchuk. Bhutan existed in isolation for years and until 1998 the monarchy exerted absolute power. In December 2005, however, the 50-year old king declared that democratic national elections would be held in 2008, putting an end to four generations of the Wangchuk family dynasty. The crown will be passed down to King Wanchuck's son, but stripped of most of its power. The Bhutanese have the highest per capita income in South Asia, despite the king's policy of maximising 'gross national happiness' rather than gross domestic product.

Economy

GDP growth has been an average 8 per cent since 2000, and reached 7.0 per cent in 2004. Foreign observers have praised the country's good macroeconomic management. The hydropower sector is one of the main drivers of the economy, and thanks to new investment, looks set to generate lucrative profits from 2006 onwards. The private sector has been faring well and as a result non performing loans (NPL) have decreased.

Government spending increased in 2005 as a result of civil service wage increases, introduced in January. This is expected to cost more than 1.5 per cent of GDP annually. Domestic debt has been bumped up as a result of borrowing for the Tala hydropower project and for new aircraft for Druk Air.

The Bhutanese administration has generally not exploited the country's workers with low wages in order to gain a competitive edge, as many other Asian countries have done. Barriers to foreign investment and trade have been enforced, limiting the amount of cheap produce entering the country. Farmers have received the benefits of education, electricity and healthcare.

However, Bhutan cannot, it seems, resist the pressures of globalisation for ever. There is talk of entering the World Trade Organisation (WTO) and allowing a stream of FDI from global companies and banks. In November 2004, Bhutan held the first ever WTO working party meeting. The IMF has commended Bhutan for its recent structural reforms which align the country more with international practices.

Democracy

The King, who has ruled since the age of 16, enjoys huge popularity in Bhutan. Currently the king rules alongside a government and assembly. In the new democratic system, however, the king will assume more of a figurehead role and will be replaced by two houses of parliament: a National Assembly and a smaller National Council. The new 34-article constitution will be put to the people in a referendum at the end of 2006, in preparation for national elections in 2008. The democratic document will supersede the 1953 royal decree which conferred absolute power on the king. The international community has praised the king's free decision to introduce democracy and surrender his powers.

Refugees

Critics claim that King Wangchuk is merely putting on a show for foreign observers and that democracy will not be fully permitted. The organisation adds that the country's new constitutional developments are a smokescreen for the still messy refugee situation. The country's ethnic Nepalese were re-defined as illegal immigrants after a census in 1988: the king sought to protect the nation's Buddhist culture against alien influence. Hindu Nepalese have been marginalised and persecuted by the government and their language banned from schools. This antagonism led to violent disturbances and the expression of pro-democracy, anti-government sentiment in 1990.

The worsening situation led to 100,000 ethnic Nepalese leaving the country, most of whom arrived as refugees in Nepal. These refugees are housed in seven camps, prohibited from earning a salary and must depend on food aid. To date, Bhutan has not accepted the return of these former Bhutanese residents – instead it is claiming that the refugees were illegal immigrants with no right to return. Since then, Bhutan and Nepal have sat down at the negotiating table 15 times, but no deal has been signed. Bhutan has forbidden the UN High Commission for Refugees to enter the country.

In 2003, Bhutan recognised the theoretical right of many ethnic Nepalese in one particular camp to return, but imposed long delays in repatriation in which the refugees were to demonstrate their loyalty to Bhutan.

In August 2005 the UN announced progress on the fate of the 100,000 ethnic Nepalese refugees. There were new suggestions that these refugees could be sent on to Western countries, although Nepal did not support this proposal without some concessions from the Bhutan administration.

The plight of the exiles worsened with the rising global oil prices: the increases are sucking money out of the UN's fuel budget for cooking and lighting for the refugees. The problem is set to continue through 2000.

Foreign relations

In December 2005, 300 Chinese soldiers were alleged to have crossed the border into Bhutan on an unsolicited road and bridge building mission. India responded by condemning China for not adhering to a 1998 peace pact that it had agreed with Bhutan. There has been speculation that China is flexing its muscle in response to feeling threatened by the imminent introduction of democracy so close to its borders.

Social

On 1 March 2005 a nationwide smoking ban in public places came into force. This follows legislation passed two months previously, rendering the selling of cigarettes and tobacco illegal – probably the first such ruling anywhere in the world.

Outlook

The Tala hydropower plant will come on stream in 2006–07 and is expected to boost annual growth to 8–9 per cent. The IMF recommends that Bhutan accelerate liberalising reforms to facilitate greater private sector activity, trade and more non-power business. The IMF also seeks tax reforms to increase government revenue. The refugee stand-off looks likely to rumble on in 2006 while in Bhutan democratic institutions are gradually being established.

Risk assessment

Economic	Stable
Political	Stable
Regional Stability	Tension with Nepal
Stock Market	Small

COUNTRY PROFILE

Historical profile
1907 The first hereditary king was enthroned.
1910 The Anglo-Bhutanese Treaty was signed, granting the government of British India full control of Bhutan's foreign relations.
1949 India became independent and the 1910 treaty was re-negotiated. Bhutan became free to pursue its own foreign policy, although it agreed to seek India's advice.
1952 King Jigme Dorji Wangchuk was enthroned and established the Tsogdu (National Assembly) in 1953.
1958 The Lhotshampa population of the southern districts of Bhutan was granted Bhutanese citizenship and tenure of lands.
1965 The Lodoi Tsokde (Royal Advisory Council) was established.
1972 King Jigme Singye Wangchuk was enthroned.
1979 Bhutan supported China in preference to India at the UN, beginning a gradual reorientation of foreign policy away from India.
1987 Bhutan's Sixth Five Year Plan included a policy of 'one nation, one people'. A code of traditional Drukpa dress and etiquette (Driglam Namzhag) was introduced. This led to discontent in the 1990s.

KEY INDICATORS — Bhutan

	Unit	2000	2001	2002	2003	2004
Population	m	2.09	2.10	2.15	2.17	2.22
Gross domestic product (GDP)	US$bn	0.49	0.53	0.59	0.61	*0.67
GDP per capita	US$	234	252	274	287	817
GDP real growth	%	5.7	6.5	6.7	6.5	7.0
Inflation	%	4.8	3.6	5.0	2.0	4.5
Exports (fob) (goods)	US$m	114.0	104.0	98.0	154.0	–
Imports (fob) (goods)	US$m	185.0	212.0	188.0	196.0	–
Balance of trade	US$m	-71.0	-108.0	-90.0	-42.0	–
Current account	US$m	0.0	-108.0	56.0	-71.0	-53.0
Foreign debt	US$bn	0.2	0.3	0.3	0.2	–
Total reserves minus gold	US$m	295.4	284.6	354.9	366.6	398.6
Foreign exchange	US$m	293.8	283.1	353.2	364.7	396.6
Exchange rate	per US$	44.94	47.19	48.61	46.81	44.46

* estimated figure

1990 The teaching of Nepali in schools was halted. Mass public demonstrations in southern Bhutan were held.
1998 King Wangchuk handed over full executive power to a Lhengye Zhungtshog (Council of Ministers).
1999 The King granted the Tsogdu the right to dismiss a reigning monarch. The WTO Working Party on Accession for the Kingdom of Bhutan was established.
2001 A draft constitution included proposals for a democratic system of government.
2002 The Ninth Five Year Plan (July 2002–June 2007) was drawn up to continue Bhutan's decentralisation process and promote 'Gross National Happiness'.
2003 On 17 February, the representative of the Kingdom of Bhutan to the WTO delivered Memorandum on the Foreign Trade Regime, describing all aspects of Bhutan's economy and legal system and its compliance with WTO norms and requirements. A new government was installed on 10 July with Lyonpo Jigme Yozer Thinley as prime minister.
2004 After being chased away from Bhutan in December 2003, Indian insurgents entered Nepal and were reported to be working with Nepalese Maoists with a view to attacking Bhutan's royal palace.
2005 A draft constitution was unveiled in April that aims to transform the country's absolute monarchy into a two-party democracy. On 5 September, Lyonpo Sangey Ngedup took office as prime minister. In December, the king announced that elections would be held in 2008 and Bhutan would become a constitutional democracy.

Political structure
Constitution
There is no written constitution.
A draft constitution aiming to transform the country's absolute monarchy into a two-party democracy was drawn up in April 2005. It will be put to the people in a referendum during 2006.
Form of state
Hereditary monarchy
The executive
On 20 July 1998, King Jigme Singye Wangchuk handed over full executive power to the six-member Lhengye Zhungtshog (Council of Ministers).
The king is Head of State, assisted by the 10-member Lodoi Tsokde (Royal Advisory Council), the Tsogdu (National Assembly) and the monastic head of the kingdom's Buddhist priesthood.
National legislature
Elections for 105 seats in the 150-member Tsogdu (National Assembly) (established in 1953) are by universal adult suffrage; the remaining seats are reserved for representatives of religious bodies and industry, and for officials nominated by the government; not all elections are held simultaneously, so there are overlaps in tenure, which is for three years.
The Tsogdu meets bi-annually; it is required to pass a vote of confidence in the king by a two-thirds majority every three years.
The chairman of the Council of Ministers is head of government (prime minister), a position which is rotated on an annual basis among the elected ministers.

Political parties
There are no legal political parties. Illegal political organisations are: Bhutan People's Party (BPP); People's Forum for Human Rights (PFHR); United Liberation People's Front (ULPF).

Population
2.22 million (2004)
Ethnic make-up
There are many ethnic groups: the Sharchhop in the east (the largest group), the Ngalong in the west, the Lhotsampas, who speak Nepali, in the south and the Bumtaps, Khengpas, Layaps, Doyas and other nomadic groups.
Religions
Mahayana Buddhism is the state religion; Hinduism. Christianity is banned.

Education
The United Nations Children's Fund (Unicef) reported that in four decades, the government established 343 primary schools and a college that offers undergraduate degrees in arts and commerce. Since education remains a national priority in the country's development process, more than 150 community schools are available from which every school-age child may choose. However, classrooms are in short supply and most schools lack basic sanitation facilities. Each teacher may have an average of 37 students but in some schools, class sizes can reach 70 pupils.
Literacy rate: 61.1 per cent and 33.6 per cent for men and women respectively; adult rates (World Bank 2002).
Enrolment rate: 45 per cent enrolment for girls in primary schools.
Pupils per teacher: 37 in primary schools.

Health
The total expenditure on health is around 4.1 per cent of GDP, of which government spending is 90 per cent.
Although improvement in the primary healthcare system has reduced the maternal mortality rate the figure is still one of the highest in south and east Asia. The United Nations Children's Fund (Unicef) reports that about four out of five women still deliver at home, without professional help.
Bhutan conducts national and regional immunisation days annually to achieve 90 per cent coverage. Unicef estimates that 22.2 per cent of households do not have safe drinking water.
Out-reach clinics spread across rural Bhutan provide low cost health care. A network of 145 basic health units supports the clinics, with each unit serving communities of 2,000 to 5,000 people. There are 28 hospitals, which provide more advanced and referral treatment.
The Asian Development Bank (ADB) provided the government with a loan of about US$10 million covering the five years 2001–2005 to improvement of the health sector.
Unicef initiated model villages established in almost all the 202 sub-district blocks in the country have adopted a variety of health and education programmes. Its initial success has prompted Unicef to expand the model village experience into a more general community development programme.
Life expectancy: 63.5 years (World Bank).
Fertility rate/Maternal mortality rate: 5.1 births per woman 2003, (World Bank)
Infant mortality rate: 70 per 1,000 live births; around 19 per cent of children aged under five are malnourished (World Bank).

Welfare
In October 2001, the Bhutan government and the Asian Development Bank (ADB) signed a partnership agreement aimed at poverty reduction by 2012 through income and employment generation led by the private sector. Emphasis will be put on lifting monthly average rural incomes to about Nu3,000 (about US$65) per head.
In March 2002, the ADB agreed to provide a US$700,000 grant to prepare a rural electrification and network expansion project.
There is a national pension plan and provident fund plan that currently provides for government employees and members of the armed forces. Between 16 per cent and 24 per cent of monthly earnings are paid into the funds, to provide for workers and their dependents. The amounts paid are split evenly between the employer and employee. These schemes are expected to be offered to other salaried workers over the next few years.

Main cities
Thimphu (capital, estimated population 60,200 in 2003), Phuntsholing (58,300), Punakha (21,200), Somdrup Jongkhar (13,600), Gaylegphug (6,600), Paro (4,400).

Bhutan

Languages spoken
There are 19 dialects and languages in Bhutan. Dzongkha bears similarities to Tibetan. English (the working language), Bumthangkha, Sharchop, Nepali and other dialects also spoken.
Official language/s
Dzongkha

Media
Press
Dailies: There is one national newspaper *Kuensel*.
Broadcasting
Bhutan Broadcasting Service (BBS) is government-operated.
Radio: Bhutan had approximately 40,000 radios in 2002. There are several radio stations, including those broadcasting flood information. Radio broadcast stations include AM 0, FM 1, shortwave 1. The country's government-owned radio broadcasts in English, Dzonghka and Nepali. Bhutan Broadcasting Service (BBS) Radio broadcasts in Nepali and Scharchop.
Television: Bhutan, which had previously banned television, finally decided to have its own national TV channel in 1999. BBS TV started a pilot service covering mainly the capital, Thimphu, broadcasting in English (the working language) and Dzongkha (the national language).

Economy
This small landlocked country has achieved good economic growth and considerable improvement in its social indicators over the last decade. Around 36 per cent of the population live below the upper poverty line, with the majority of these living in remote rural areas of the country. India and international organisations support the government's development plans.
Government policy is directed towards conservative economic modernisation. Work has been carried out on tariff reform, liberalising foreign exchange and foreign direct investment (FDI) regulations, and deregulating interest rates. Policy is targeting poverty alleviation through improvement of infrastructures such as healthcare and education. These projects receive substantial international support. The wellbeing of the population relies on agriculture and forestry. Bhutan is almost entirely self-sufficient in the production of food. The agricultural sector employs around 90 per cent of the labour force and accounts for 26 per cent of total GDP.
Tourism has strong potential for growth, although travellers are restricted to pre-packaged holidays and arranged tours, while independent travellers are strongly discouraged.

The growing strength of the economy is due to the hydroelectric power sector. New power projects have led to significant growth in the construction and transport sectors. These projects include the Tala hydropower project, expected to produce 1 gigawatt of energy, which is now nearing completion (2006–05). Most of the electricity is exported to India. These exports provide 45 per cent of government revenue.
Growth of foreign investment continues to be restrained by problematic policies in finance, labour and trade. Difficulties in industrial licensing stem from the government's policy towards environmental protection. The current five-year plan intends to encourage growth in communication technology, energy and tourism with clearer legal and regulatory systems to enable this. Bhutan's application to join the WTO could spur foreign investment, if successful.

External trade
Bhutan is one of the 32 developing nations designated in 1985 to receive exemption from US competitive trade requirements in accordance with a law known as the Generalised System of Preferences (GSP).
Bhutan is in the middle of negotiations to join the World Trade Organisation.
Imports
Principal imports are fuel and lubricants, rice, machinery parts, vehicles and fabrics.
Main sources: India (71.3 per cent total, 2004), Japan (7.8 per cent), Austria (3.0 per cent)
Exports
Main exports include electricity, cardamom, gypsum, timber, handicrafts, cement, fruit, precious stones and spices
Main destinations: India (87.9 per cent total, 2004), Bangladesh (4.6 per cent), Philippines (2 per cent)

Agriculture
Farming
Agriculture annually contributes around 26 per cent to GDP and employs 90 per cent of the workforce.
Approximately 15 per cent of the land area is fertile lowland arable and 72.5 per cent is forested. No trees can be cut down without a special permit.
Main crops are rice, maize, potatoes, citrus fruits, wheat, buckwheat, barley, millet, vegetables, mustard, apples and cardamom. Vegetable production is hindered by the cold climate.
Cattle, yaks, sheep, goats and pigs are raised.
Crop production in 2004 included 97,350 tonnes (t) cereals, 4,800t wheat, 45,000t rice, 40,000t maize, 40,000t potatoes, 43,500t fruit in total, 36,000t citrus fruit, 5,800t nutmeg, 1,318t oilcrops, *1,600t pulses, 61,800t roots and tubers, 2,800t chillies & peppers, 350t jute, *4,600t vegetables in total. Livestock production included 6,901t meat in total, 5,100t beef, 1,285t pig meat, *225t lamb &goat meat, 259t poultry, 240t eggs, *41,440t milk, 1,080t cattle hides.
* estimate

Industry and manufacturing
The industrial sector contributes around 43 per cent to GDP annually. Manufacturing accounts for around 7.5 per cent of GDP, with cement as the principal product.
Small-scale local industries produce woodwork, fruit processing, weaving, textiles, soap, metals, handicrafts, carpets, matches and plywood manufacture. Most manufacturing industries are owned by the government.
Industrial growth has risen mainly because of increased value of electricity exports to India (from the Chukha hydroelectric plant). The Tala project will further enhance growth when it comes on stream in 2006–07. There has also been significant hydropower investment in industry.

Tourism
The annual number of visitors is kept deliberately low by the government. The object of this policy is to protect the country's environmental and cultural integrity from the adverse effects of mass tourism. Visitor numbers are regulated by measures such as a high tariff (US$200 each per day) and restriction of travel arrangements to authorised Bhutanese operators. In addition, visits may only be made to designated regions and holy sites. Government policy is to increase visitor numbers gradually to 20,000 by 2012. Arrivals peaked in 2000 at 7,559, but fell sharply in the following years due to external events. By 2004, the sector had recovered its momentum, registering 9,249 arrivals.

Mining
Mining contributes about 1 per cent to GDP and employs 1 per cent of the workforce.
Deposits of many minerals exist, but quarrying is restricted to limestone, dolomite, gypsum and slate due to difficulties of access. Talcum powder is the major mineral export.

Hydrocarbons
Bhutan has no known oil or gas reserves. Around 1,000 barrels per day of oil are imported.
Bhutan has coal reserves of 1.3 million tonnes and produces only 1,000 tonnes of coal per annum, which are used for domestic consumption. Some exploration is being carried out in the southern

borders and the New Policy is encouraging private sector investment into exploration and production.

Energy
Hydropower is Bhutan's most important economic asset and supplies 97 per cent of total installed generating capacity of 457MW. Domestic consumption is around 112MW. The surplus is exported to India and is the largest component of Bhutan's total exports, contributing around 45 per cent of total revenues. The main hydroelectric facility is the Chukha plant, which generates around 336MW of electricity and is connected to the Indian electricity grid. A hydroelectric plant with a capacity of 1.02 GW, due to be commissioned in 2006, is being built at Tala. It is expected eventually to increase total revenues to 60 per cent.

More than 90 per cent of Bhutan's domestic energy requirements are provided by biomass, such as firewood, due to low levels of rural electrification. Over 70 per cent of domestic energy consumption is accounted for by the household sector.

Financial markets
Stock exchange
In 1993, a Royal Securities Exchange was established, supervised by the Royal Monetary Authority (RMA) and capitalised by the four financial institutions – the Bank of Bhutan, the Royal Insurance Corporation of Bhutan, Unit Trust of Bhutan and the Bhutan Development Finance Corporation. In 1996, auctions of government securities were introduced and the Unit Trust of Bhutan was converted into the country's second commercial bank, the Bhutan National Bank.

Banking and insurance
Central bank
Royal Monetary Authority (RMA)
Main financial centre
Phuntsholing

Time
GMT plus six hours

Geography
Bhutan lies in the Himalayan range of mountains, with the People's Republic of China to the north and India to the south.

Climate
In Thimphu, the likely temperature range between June–September (monsoon season) is 10–20 degrees Celsius (C), for December–February, the likely maximum is 13 degrees C with temperatures frequently below freezing. In southern areas/Duars Plain, temperatures are generally higher. Annual rainfall of 7,500mm is sometimes recorded, although over 5,000mm is usual.

Entry requirements
Passports
Required by all, except Indian nationals.
Visa
All visitors require visas and these must be arranged prior to arrival.
Independent travel is not permitted, even for business purposes. Businessmen and tourists are admitted only in groups by pre-arrangement through registered tour operators in Bhutan. This can be done directly or through a travel agent abroad. A minimum daily tariff is regulated and fixed by the government. The rate includes all accommodation, meals, transport, and services.
Visa applications should be made at least three months in advance. Add an extra three weeks for business visas, when a letter of introduction from a Bhutan company and an employer's guarantee, plus an itinerary should accompany applications.
The only airline servicing Bhutan is Druk-Air, which will only board travellers with visa clearance from the tourism authority. Entry is via India, Bangladesh, Nepal, or Thailand.
The visa is also required for exit from Bhutan.
If travelling overland from India a transit pass from the Indian authorities is required to permit passage through prohibited areas of the India-Bhutan border. For this, apply to the Indian Ministry of External Affairs in Delhi some months before travelling.
Enquiries can be made to: Bhutan Tourism Corporation (state-run operator), PO Box 159, Thimphu (tel: 322-647; fax: 323-392; e-mail: btcl@druknet.net.bt). Although Bhutan has no formal diplomatic representation in Europe or the US, it has a Permanent Mission to the UN at 2 United Nations Plaza, 27th Floor, New York, NY 10017 (tel: (00-1) (212) 826-1919), which has consular jurisdiction in the US. Informal contact is maintained between the Bhutanese and US Embassy in New Delhi (India).

Health (for visitors)
Mandatory precautions
A vaccination certificate for yellow fever is required if arriving from an infected area.
Advisable precautions
Anti-malarial precautions are advisable. Bhutanese hospitals only provide basic care. Comprehensive medical insurance should therefore be obtained.

Hotels
All hotel bookings are made through the Bhutan Tourism Corporation. Private hotels are open only to Bhutan nationals, some Indian nationals and certain business contacts; state hotels are of adequate standard.

Public holidays
Fixed dates
2 May (Third King's Birthday), 2 Jun (Coronation Day), 8 Aug (Independence Day), 11 Nov (three days, Birthday of HM Jigme Singye Wangchuck), 17 Dec (National Day).
Variable dates
Winter Solstice (Jan), Offerings Day (Jan), Losay (Lunar New Year) (two days Feb), Shabdrung Kuchoe (Apr/May), Buddha Parinirvana (May/Jun), Buddha's First Sermon (Jul/Aug), Third King's Death (Jul), Guru Rinpoche's Birthday (Jul), Blessed Rainy Day (Sep), Dashaim (Oct), Buddha Descension Day (Oct/Nov).
Buddhist festivals are declared according to local astronomical observations.

Working hours
Banking
Bank of Bhutan: 0630–0930 and 1200–1600. Other banks, Mon–Fri: 0900–1700; 0900–1300 (cash transactions); Sat: 0900–1100.
Business
Mon–Fri: 0900–1700.
Shops
Mon–Sun: 0900–2000. Closed Tuesday.

Weights and measures
Metric system

Social customs/useful tips
Prior authority is required to visit some of the religious and administrative buildings (Dzongs) and special permits are required to visit certain areas.

Security
Most visits are trouble-free and the country is generally peaceful.

Getting there
Air
Air transport into Bhutan is by Druk-Air, which flies from India (New Delhi and Calcutta), Nepal (Kathmandu), Bangladesh and Thailand. Druk-Air bookings can only be arranged after a visa has been issued and must also be obtained from a Bhutanese tour operator.
National airline: Druk-Air (Royal Bhutan Airlines).
International airport/s: Paro (PBH), 8km south of Paro, 68km from Thimpu..
Airport tax: International departures Nu300.
Surface
Road: Overland access is via the road from the Indian frontier (Jaigaon) to Phuntsholing.

Getting about
National transport
Road: The road network comprises some 2,280km, largely surfaced. The mountain roads are hazardous and subject to landslides in the monsoon season.

Bhutan

Buses: Bus services are available between main centres. Local enquiries are recommended.

City transport
Taxis: Thimphu to airport journey time 90 minutes, between hours 0500–2000.
Buses, trams & metro: Druk-Air service from Thimphu to airport every two hours, journey time 90 minutes.
Car hire
Certain services are available, and local enquiries are recommended.

BUSINESS DIRECTORY

The addresses listed below are a selection only. While World of Information makes every endeavour to check these addresses, we cannot guarantee that changes have not been made, especially to telephone numbers and area codes. We would welcome any corrections.

Telephone area codes
The international dialling code (IDD) for Bhutan is +975, followed by area code and subscriber's number:
Jakar 3 Thimphu 2

Chambers of Commerce
Bhutan Chamber of Commerce and Industry, PO Box 147, Doybum Lam, Thimphu (tel: 322-742; fax: 323-936; e-mail: bsdbcci@druknet.net.bt).

Banking
Bank of Bhutan, (tel: 322-621, 322-266; fax: 323-433).

Bhutan National Bank, PO Box 439, Thimphu (tel: 322-767, 323-602; fax: 323-601; e-mail: mdbnb@druknet.net.bt).

Central bank
Royal Monetary Authority of Bhutan, PO Box 154, Thimphu (tel: 323-111; fax: 322-847; e-mail: rma@rma.org.bt).

Travel information
Bhutan Yod Sel Tours and Treks, PO Box 574, Thimphu (tel: 323-912; fax: 323-589; e-mail: dawa@druknet.net.bt).

Tourism Authority of Bhutan, P.O. Box 126, Thimphu, (tel: 223-251, 223-252; fax 223-695).

Ministry of tourism
Tourism Authority of Bhutan (supplies lists of operators and trekking agencies), PO Box 126, Thimphu (tel: 323-251/2, 325-121/2; fax: 323-695; e-mail: tab@druknet.net.bt).

National tourist organisation offices
Bhutan Tourism Corporation Ltd (BTCL) (state-run operator), PO Box 159, Thimphu (tel: 322-045, 322-854, 322-647, 324-045; fax: 323-392, 322-479; e-mail: btcl@druknet.net.bt; btcl1@druknet.net.bt; ynorbu@druknet.net.bt; internet site: http://www.kingdomofbhutan.com/).

Ministries
Ministry of Trade and Industries, PO Box 126 Thimphu (tel: 23-251; fax: 23-695).

Other useful addresses
Bhutanese Permanent Mission to the UN, 2 United Nations Plaza, 27th Floor, New York, NY 10017 (tel: (00-1) (212) 826-1919; fax: 212-826-2998).

State Trading Corp of Bhutan, 52 Trivoli Court, Ballygange Circular Road, Calcutta, 700019, India.

United Nations Development Programme, United Nations Building, Dremton Lam, GPO Box 162, Thimphu (tel: 322 424; fax: 322-657; e-mail: fo.btn@undp.org).

Internet sites
Bhutan Consular Information:
http://travel.state.gov/bhutan.html
Bhutan news:
http://www.bhutannewsonline.com
Online Magazine:
http://wwwbhutannewsonline.com/

Bolivia

KEY FACTS

Official name: República de Bolivia (Republic of Bolivia)

Head of State: President Eduardo Rodríguez (from 10 Jun 2005); Evo Morales won the Dec 2005 elections and will be inaugurated on 22 Jan 2006.

Head of government: President Eduardo Rodríguez (from 10 Jun 2005); Evo Morales won the Dec 2005 elections and will be inaugurated on 22 Jan 2006.

Ruling party: Movimiento al Socialismo (MAS) (Movement to Socialism) (from Dec 2005)

Area: 1,098,581 square km

Population: 8.88 million (2004)

Capital: La Paz (administrative); Sucre (legislative and judicial)

Official language: Spanish

Currency: Boliviano (B) = 100 centavos

Exchange rate: B8.04 per US$ (Oct 2005)

GDP per capita: US$1,125 (2004)

GDP real growth: 3.80% (2004); 3.9% (2005)*

Labour force: 3.75 million (2004)

Unemployment: 11.70% (2004) (additional widespread underemployment)

Inflation: 4.40% (2004)

Balance of trade: US$391.00 million (2004)

Foreign debt: US$5.44 billion (mid-2004)

* estimated figure

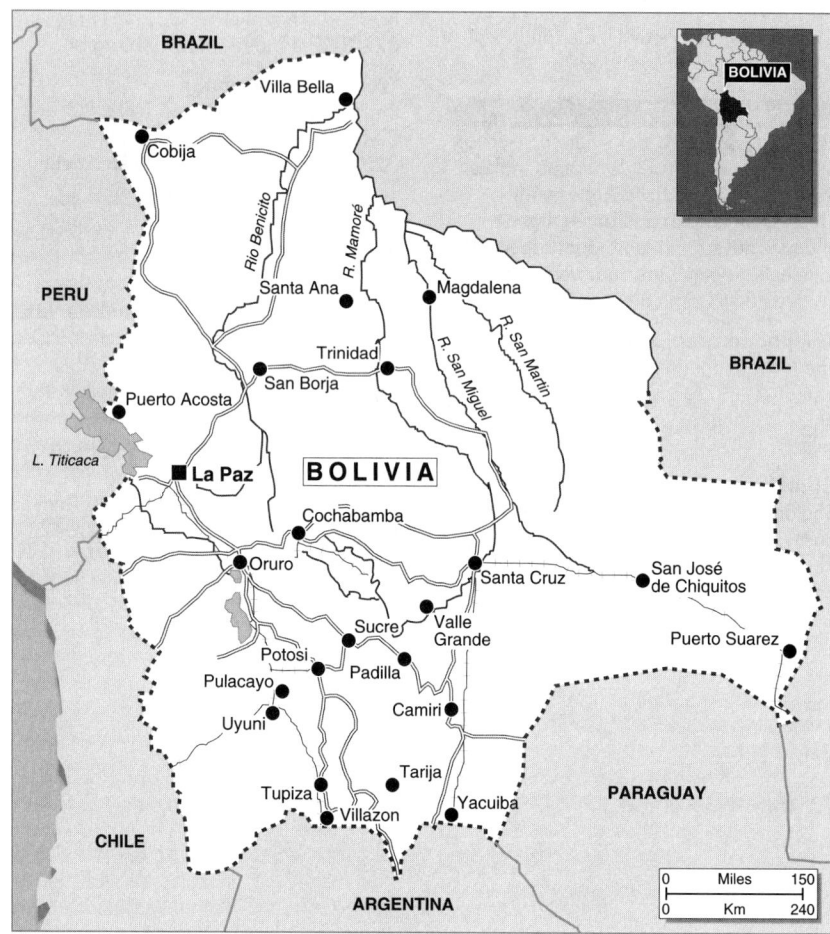

Bolivia is one of, if not *the* poorest nation in Latin America. Two-thousand and five has proved to be the dawning of a new era for all Bolivians, but particularly the indigenous population, which for many years has suffered a series of injustices at the hands of the ruling elite. During the year the president was ousted and replaced by an interim leader, who set an electoral contest in motion. As soon as the starting gun was fired in the presidential race, a flamboyant, charismatic and, most significantly, indigenous, candidate was hot favourite to win.

Ejection of a president

President Carlos Mesa was ejected from office on 6 June 2005 following an escalation of social unrest in the country. A well known historian, newspaper journalist and television pundit, Mesa had assumed the presidency in 2003. He came under extreme political pressure in early 2005 as the so-called 'Bolivian Gas War' came back to haunt the political establishment. The second largest proven natural gas reserves on the South American continent, Bolivia's 0.89 trillion cubic metres are of high stakes. A resumption of the protests seen in the early 2000s led Mesa to offer his resignation in March. This offer was rejected by congress.

Though under extreme political pressure, Mesa, an independent, remained popular among the population at large, with approval ratings as high as 70 per cent even in March. But the president's popular support began to crumble, as his authority ebbed away in the midst of increased protests over the ensuing months. Mesa's standing was further damaged by related street protests alleging that he had given in to US big business in conducting Bolivia's foreign and trade policy.

As tens of thousands marched into La Paz in early June the government became increasing unable to exercise civil order. Mesa again tendered his resignation on 6 June, and this time it was accepted by congress, four days later on 10 June. The head of the Supreme Court Eduardo Rodríguez Veltzé was sworn in as president by Bolivia's legislators in an emergency procedure designed to calm the increasing social unrest. Almost immediately, Rodríguez, in line with his constitutional duty, announced that elections would be held in due course.

Victory for Morales

Bolivia became the latest in an increasing long line of Latin American countries to elect a left-wing candidate as president when Juan Evo 'Morales' Aima (popularly known as Evo) recorded an absolute majority with 54 per cent of votes cast on 18 December 2005. Morales, an Aymara Indian and leader of the *cocalero* (coca growers) movement, is Bolivia's first ever indigenous president. His party, the Movimiento al Socialismo (MAS) (Movement for Socialism) was confirmed as having won 72 of 130 seats in the chamber of deputies and 12 of 27 in the senate.

The flamboyant Morales, noted for his trademark striped sweater, beat Jorge Quiroga of Poder Democratico Nacional (Podemos) into second place in the presidential race. However, MAS was not as successful in the respective regional gubernatorial races and this could well restrict Morales' power. The regional governor posts were contested electorally for the first time in 2005 and are expected to wield considerable power.

Charismatic and unorthodox, Morales has an interesting past. The *cocalero* leader shot to national and international prominence when he first ran for president, finishing runner-up, in 2002. Prior to his bid for the presidency Morales was dismissed from his congressional seat on charges of connections with terrorist activities during riots in Sacaba in January 2002. Brought up in tough conditions in a mining town in Bolivia's Altiplano region, Morales joined the military at the age of seventeen. He boasts of the superior education he received at the 'university of life', before entering the cut-throat world of Bolivian union politics.

There were three major tenets to Morales electoral programme: nationalisation of Bolivia's natural gas reserves, the formation of a constituent assembly in order to rewrite the constitution with a commitment to indigenous rights and third, the 'depenalisation' (Morales' own phrase) of the coca leaf, but not the drug itself.

Economy

Liquefied natural gas (LNG) is Bolivia's key natural resource and is crucial to the country's economic well-being, in terms of generating foreign exchange. Political stability and economic performance correlate closely in most economies, but in Bolivia this truism is especially sound. It was therefore imperative, as Mesa undoubtedly realised in offering his resignation on two separate occasions, that the growing social unrest was diffused. Despite several years of growth, Bolivia remains a very poor country and aid accounts for some 10 per cent of total GDP. GDP per-capita in 2004 was a miniscule US$1,125, though this figure has in fact risen from US$853 in 2003 as overall GDP has expanded.

The rate of inflation rose to 4.4 per cent by the end of 2004 and the IMF forecasts the rate to remain around this figure for 2005. Though inflationary pressure has risen year on year since 2001 the overall annual rate still remains respectable by developing economy standards. Bolivia's foreign debt reduced in 2005 as government coffers filled up with foreign exchange tax revenue courtesy of the LNG industry. However, the number of Bolivians that are officially unemployed has risen significantly in recent years, including a 3.7 per cent increase (to 11.3 per cent) from 2003 to 2004, and is largely responsible for the social upheaval witnessed in 2005.

An increase in the price of natural gas on the back of increased demand owing to supply shortages elsewhere in the world sustained the Bolivian economy in 2005. Given the revenues to be derived from this lucrative business, pressure grew among the population to nationalise the industry, which helped to energise Morales' electoral platform. A hydrocarbons law, that doubled the taxation rate on oil and gas firms, was passed in early 2005 by president Mesa in a bid to placate growing dissatisfaction, yet still Bolivians demanded a greater share of the proceeds of their national resource wealth. In light of Morales' nationalisation commitment, foreign companies such as Petrobras of Brazil and Repsol YPF (Spain) have not taken kindly to the potential revocation of their large contracts, having invested some US$3.5 billion in Bolivia.

Foreign policy: no time-wasted

Perhaps the most interesting facet of Morales' election as president is the effect it will have on Bolivian foreign policy. Already in the space of just a few months since becoming president-elect and then president Morales has embarked on an extraordinary world tour. First up was the

KEY INDICATORS — Bolivia

	Unit	2000	2001	2002	2003	2004
Population	m	8.33	8.52	8.70	8.79	8.88
Gross domestic product (GDP)	US$bn	8.30	8.00	7.60	8.00	*8.77
GDP per capita	US$	995	935	875	853	1,125
GDP real growth	%	2.4	1.2	2.5	2.6	3.8
Inflation	%	4.6	1.6	2.4	3.3	4.4
Unemployment	%	0.0	0.0	0.0	7.6	11.3
Natural gas output	bn cum	3.3	4.1	5.4	5.2	8.5
Exports (fob) (goods)	US$m	1,229.6	1,285.0	1,190.0	1,479.0	1,986.0
Imports (fob) (goods)	US$m	1,610.1	1,724.0	1,740.0	1,675.0	1,595.0
Balance of trade	US$m	-380.5	-440.0	-500.0	-196.0	391.0
Current account	US$m	-464.2	-292.0	-330.0	0.0	250.0
Foreign debt	US$bn	6.8	5.8	4.5	5.9	5.4
Total reserves minus gold	US$m	779.9	767.0	580.4	716.8	872.4
Foreign exchange	US$m	732.8	721.5	531.2	663.3	817.3
Exchange rate	per US$	6.18	6.61	7.19	7.65	7.95

* estimated figure

obligatory visit, a must for all revolutionary Latin American presidents, to Fidel Castro's Cuba. Having been feted by the communist dictator Morales then moved on to Caracas, the home of the man of the moment on the continent, President Hugo Chávez. The two presidents signed a new hydrocarbon exchange deal, whereby Bolivia will receive 150,000 barrels of diesel in exchange for export of Bolivian agricultural products to Venezuela.

From Caracas Morales flew to a meeting with Spanish prime minister José Luis Rodríguez 'Zapatero' and then King Juan Carlos at the royal palace. In a piece of smooth diplomacy Morales engineered the cancellation of Bolivia's eur120 million (US$162 million) debt to Spain. While in Spain Morales continued to make waves. Following an attack by the Spanish media on his choice of multicoloured garb, former Conservative prime minister José María Aznar announced his intention to combat the rise of leftist leaders in Latin America, using funds from his new political lobbying organisation.

Morales also visited France, where he secured a guarantee of economic support so long as French interests in Bolivia were protected. Next stop was the Netherlands, where Dutch foreign minister Ben Bot agreed a new aid package of eur15 million (US$20 million) per annum. A similar assurance to that given to the French president was provided to Javier Solana (High Representative for the Common Foreign and Security Policy of the EU) during a meeting in Brussels, regarding existing European investments in Bolivia. Following a quick stop in China where he met Hu Jintao and invited Chinese investment in Bolivia, Morales was on the move again, this time to South Africa. In Pretoria, underlining his manifesto commitment to indigenous rights, Morales compared the struggle of black Africans during the apartheid era to that of the indigenous peoples of Latin America.

Rounding off the tour, Morales called on President da Silva of Brazil, where he emphasised his dedication to regional solidarity in the Americas, referring to his Brazilian counterpart as a 'comrade and brother'. Morales' proposed nationalisation of the natural gas production industry had previously disturbed Brazil, the largest importer of Bolivian gas, but Morales' assurances would appear to have diffused any potential tension between the two countries.

Washington, which has been alarmed by the leftward momentum building in Latin America generally, made its opposition to Morales firmly known prior to his election victory. US trade preferences to Bolivia equate to US$150 million in export earnings and prop up about 100,000 manufacturing jobs. Crucially, they expire in 2006 and Washington is unlikely to renew them given recent developments. The US government has presented a US$593 million aid carrot as an alternative to extending its trade preferences, but is unlikely to formerly put the deal on the table until Morales changes his tune on the legality of coca.

Outlook

It will be challenging for Morales to keep his coalition tightly knit, while dampening some of the fervent optimistism among his supporters. In his honeymoon period as president he has trotted around the world striking deals with world leaders in exchange for the protection of their countries' interests in Bolivia. This ploy may come back to haunt Bolivia as Morales' domestic policy of complete nationalisation of the LNG industry is seemingly contradicted by such promises. The new president may find himself caught in an uncomfortable bind in 2006 as he sets about appeasing domestic demand for radicalism while ensuring that foreign aid, upon which the Bolivian economy is so dependent, continues to flow.

A warning sign appeared when a week prior to the elections, on 10 December 2005, a grouping of trade unions and social movements announced that Morales had 90 days to eliminate the neo-liberal economy. 'If Evo lets us down', one of the president's supporters is quoted as saying 'we'll throw him out too'! In his victory speech Morales insisted that 'governing will be the hard part'. Such words may prove prophetic.

Risk assessment

Politics	Stable
Economy	Stable/improving
Regional stability	Stable

COUNTRY PROFILE

Historical profile
Bolivia was inhabited by the ancient Aymará peoples, who were conquered by the Incas.
1538 The Incas were conquered by the Spanish.
1825 There were many revolts against Spanish rule; independence was finally gained under the leadership of Simón Bolívar.
1826 Bolivia's first constitution was established.
1879–83 War of the Pacific between Bolivia, Peru and Chile over disputed territory along the Pacific coast. Bolivia and Peru suffered a humiliating defeat against Chile's armed forces. A new elite, with mining interests, combined with the traditional ruling oligarchy, supported by external capitalist interests, gained power and polarised civil society into conservative and liberal factions.
1890s The successful exploitation of tin brought a degree of prosperity and peace after years of turbulent and unstable government. A new constitution established centralised political control and the separation of powers between the legislature, executive-style and judiciary. The indigenous population was excluded from political life when property and literacy were made a prerequisite.
1933–35 Defeat during the Chaco Wars with Paraguay led to a large part of the Chaco region, much of it arid and infertile, being annexed by Paraguay. The defeat discredited the ruling elite and formed the basis for a realignment of Bolivian politics with the middle-class joining the working-class and *campesinos* (peasant farmers) to form a broad revolutionary movement.
1941 Formation of the Movimiento Nacionalista Revolucionario (MNR) (Nationalist Revolutionary Movement), a broad multi-class coalition to resist the power of the traditional oligarchy and what was seen as US imperialism.
1951 A military *Junta* prevented the newly elected president, Victor Paz Estenssoro (MNR) from taking office. With the help of a militia, recruited from the national police, miners and peasants, a rebellion succeeded in installing a revolutionary council. It nationalised tin holdings and instigated land reform. Universal suffrage was extended to the indigenous population. A state-capitalist development programme was initiated, backed by the IMF and later by the US programme 'Alliance for Progress'.
1964 Vice President René Barrientos Ortuño led a *coup d'état*. The military continued to implement similar policies to the MNR's state-capitalist model.
1969 Barrientos died in a mysterious helicopter crash that many suspected was an assassination. A brief period of military populism was followed by the succession of the Bolivian left, the expulsion of the US Peace Corps and the creation of a Soviet-style People's Assembly.
1971 A violent coup led by Colonel Hugo Bánzer Suárez led to the repression of labour leaders and left-wing politicians in a period of a *Junta* known as the *Banzerato*.
1978 Strains within the ruling elite and pressure from US President Jimmy Carter forced Bánzer to call elections.

Bolivia

1978–1982 A period of political turbulence: seven military and two civilian governments held office for an average of six months each. Meanwhile, political parties split into different factions, resulting in 70 different parties – the MNR alone split into thirty parties – resulting in a weak civil society.

1979 The Acción Democrática Nacionalista (ADN) (Democratic Nationalist Action) was formed by Bánzer.

1982 Siles Zuazo was elected president, his rule was ineffective as he struggled to appease both the IMF and growing militant elements within the civilian population. Meanwhile, the Bolivian economy collapsed from hyperinflation and high levels of foreign debt.

1985 Elections followed Siles' resignation. President Paz Estenssoro (MNR) implemented austere fiscal policies and brought about economic liberalisation. He also signed a Pact for Democracy with the ADN to resolve the impasse between the executive and legislature.

1989 The new president, Paz Zamora (MIR), offered tax incentives for direct foreign investment in the mining industry.

1993 Gonzalo Sánchez de Lozada (MNR) won the presidential election.

1998 Hugo Bánzer was elected president following popular discontent with economic liberalisation measures initiated by the MNR. Bánzer's rule intensified efforts to restructure the economy prescribed by the IMF, while implementing a coca-eradication programme demanded by the US.

2001 Bánzer resigned due to ill health and was replaced by Vice President Jorge Quiroga.

2002 Hugo Bánzer died. Congress appointed Lozada (known universally by his nickname 'Goni') Gonzalo Sánchez de as president.

2003 Civil unrest throughout the year led to the resignation of President Lozada on 17 October. Vice President Carlos Mesa was sworn in as president.

2004 In April, President Mesa signed a natural gas export deal with Argentina. Opponents criticised the deal as a pre-emption of the referendum on gas exports due on 18 July.

2005 On 6 March, President Mesa offered his resignation to Congress after 17 months in office, as a new wave of anti-government protests spread throughout Bolivia; it was unanimously rejected. He resigned again on 6 June, in an effort to resolve the crisis over how to divide up the country's natural gas wealth, and on 10 June it was accepted. Eduardo Rodríguez was appointed president, after both presidents of the Congress and Chamber of Deputies declined the post. On Sunday 18 December, leftist candidate Evo Morales won the presidential election, beating former president, Jorge Quiroga. He has said that his government would call for a referendum on how to control coca production and would study whether to increase the amount of coca that can be legally grown. He will be inaugurated on 22 January.

Political structure
Constitution
The first constitution was promulgated in 1826. The 1947 constitution was revised in 1967, and again in 1994.
Bolivia is divided into nine departments, each of which elects three Senators. The prefect of each department is appointed by the president. There is obligatory universal adult suffrage.

Form of state
Presidential democratic republic

The executive
Executive power is vested in the president and his appointed cabinet.
The president is directly elected for a five-year term, but is chosen by Congress if no candidate gains a majority of the vote.
An incumbent president cannot seek immediate re-election and candidates for president and vice president must be at least 35 years old. In the event of the president's death or failure to assume office, the next in line would be the vice president followed by the president of the Senate.

National legislature
Legislative power is held by the bicameral Congress, comprising a Senate (27 members) and a Chamber of Deputies (130 members). Senators must be over the age of 35. The Deputies must be over 25 years. Both Senators and Deputies hold office for five years. Half the Deputies are elected under party lists; the rest – although identified with political parties – must run for the representation of a particular district.

Legal system
There are five levels of jurisdiction headed by the Supreme Court.
From 1 June 2001, a criminal code was introduced which allows for public jury trials and a prosecution service independent of the police.

Last elections
18 July 2004 (referendum on oil and gas industries); 18 December 2005 (presidential and parliamentary)
Results: Oil and gas referendum: approval of the five questions proposed by the government in order to define Bolivia's new energy policy; endorsement of an increased role for the state in the natural gas sector.
Presidential: Evo Morales (MAS) won about 54 per cent of the vote, former president Jorge Quiroga (Podemos) about 29 per cent, Samuel Doria Medina (FUN) about 8 per cent and Michiaki Nagatani (MNR) about 6 per cent. Turnout was around 85 per cent.
Parliamentary: (Chamber of Deputies) MAS won 72 out of 130 seats, Podemos won 43 seats, FUN won 8 seats and MNR won 7 seats. (Senate) Podemos won 13 out of 27 seats, MAS 12 seats, FUN and MNR 1 seat each.

Next elections
2010 (presidential and parliamentary)

Political parties
Ruling party
Movimiento al Socialismo (MAS) (Movement to Socialism) (from Dec 2005)
Main opposition party
Poder Democrático y Social (Podemos) (Democratic and Socialist Power)

Population
8.88 million (2004)
Ethnic make-up
Official figures estimate that approximately 4.2 million Bolivians (50.6 per cent of the population) are indigenous, comprising 37 different indigenous and aboriginal peoples. Of these, most live in the Andean highlands.
Religions
In 1961, the church was separated from the state and there is complete freedom of worship. The majority of the population is Roman Catholic, although Protestant denominations are expanding. Many indigenous groups mix Christian symbolism with pre-Columbian worship.

Education
Education is free of charge. Nevertheless, the average schooling completed is less than seven years.
The need to integrate education policy into broader anti-poverty strategies is exemplified by a high rate of primary school drop out among poor children. In Bolivia the wealth gap contributes to more than 90 per cent of the shortfall in primary-school completion. Education deprivation and poverty intersects with gender disparities, particularly in the case of Bolivia's indigenous population. More than half of indigenous males and two-thirds of indigenous females do not complete primary education.
Public expenditure on education is equivalent to approximately 5 per cent of annual GDP and includes subsidies to private education at the primary, secondary and tertiary levels. Bolivia has one of the lowest levels of provision in the developing world.
Literacy rate: 93 per cent and 81 per cent for men and women respectively; adult rates (World Bank).
Compulsory years: Six to 14

Enrolment rate: 114 per cent gross primary enrolment of relevant age group (including repeaters); 84 per cent gross secondary enrolment; 39 per cent gross tertiary enrolment (World Bank).

Health
The total expenditure on health is around 6.7 per cent of GDP, of which government spending is 72.4 per cent. Some companies provided private medical care for their employees.
International funding has been donated to provide increased family planning and community based healthcare.
Yellow fever continues to be an important public health problem in the Americas. In 2000, Bolivia introduced the yellow fever vaccine in their child vaccination schedule, as well as the vaccination of all age groups in enzootic areas.
HIV prevalence: 0.5 per cent aged 15–49 in 2003 (World Bank)
Life expectancy: 64.1 years (World Bank)
Fertility rate/Maternal mortality rate: 3.7 births per woman (World Bank)
Infant mortality rate: 53 per 1,000 live births (in 2003); 10 per cent of children aged under five tend to be malnourished (World Bank).
Head of population per physician/bed: 1.3 physicians and 1.7 hospital beds typically available per 1,000 people

Welfare
The social security scheme is a defined contribution system based on individual capitalisation accounts and managed by the private sector. To avoid high marketing costs, Bolivia has two private consortia to administer its private pension system: The Spanish BBVA, y AFP Futuro de Bolivia S.A. and Zurich Financial Services Group with roughly equal shares of the market.
Employers and employees contribute 13 per cent of employee salary to the AFPs, of which 10 per cent is put aside for a capitalisation fund, 2 per cent to a disability fund and 1 per cent for a workers compensation fund. Proceeds from the capitalisation programme (in 1997, when the previous pension scheme was reformed) were used to pay an annuity to all Bolivians 65 and older. The collection system is streamlined so that non-payment, one of the major difficulties with the previous pay-as-you-go system, can be more readily identified.

Main cities
La Paz (administrative capital, estimated population 830,500 in 2004), Sucre (legislative and judicial capital, 203,200), Santa Cruz (1.2 million), Cochabamba (815,800), El Alto (728,500), Oruro (211,700), Tarija (142,000), Potosi (139,700).

Languages spoken
Approximately half the population speak Spanish as their first language. The *campesinos* (peasant farmers) often speak only Aymará or Quechua, but these languages are seldom written and are of limited commercial importance. Aymará is mainly spoken in the departments of Oruro, La Paz and Potosí. Quechua (often mixed with Spanish) is spoken in the departments of Cochabamba, Potosí and Sucre.
Official language/s
Spanish

Media
Press
Dailies: The five principal dailies in La Paz are: *Diario, Hoy, Jornada*, and *Ultima Hora*. Two dailies in Santa Cruz: *La Crónica* and *El Mundo*; two in Cochabamba: *Prensa Libre* and *Los Tiempos*; one in Oruro *El Expreso* and one in Tarija: *La Verdad*. Other dailies are *El Deber, La Razón, El Día* and *Opinión*.
Weeklies: The English-language newspaper, *Bolivian Times*, also has an on-line edition (www.boliviantimes.com).
Broadcasting
Radio: The government-controlled broadcasting authority is the Dirección General de Telecomunicaciones. There are 130 mostly private owned radio stations ranging in size from 25 kW (Radio Illimani) to 0.5 kW in rural areas. La Paz has 40 radio stations. Most of the stations are privately owned and operated, although there are some in public ownership. Radio provides a particularly effective way of reaching the rural populations by broadcasting in Aymará and Quechua languages.
Television: The government television network, Empresa Nacional de Televisión, operates stations in La Paz, Oruro, Cochabamba, Sucre, Potosí, Beni, Pando, Tarija and Santa Cruz. There are five private television channels in La Paz; a sixth is available in Oruro, Cochabamda, Santa Cruz, Potosí and Sucre. There are also a few private channels operating in other areas. The university television service, Televisión Universitaria, provides educational programmes.

Economy
Political and social upheaval has hindered economic development in Bolivia over the years, though the economy has continued to record positive, albeit slow growth in recent times. The International Monetary Fund (IMF) expects growth of 3.9 per cent in 2005, though the rate of growth in real GDP is predicted to slow to 2.5 per cent in 2006.

Despite recent growth and a wealth of hydrocarbon resources Bolivia remains South America's poorest nation. An estimated 70 per cent of the population lives below the poverty line, the majority in rural areas. While recent economic reforms have stabilised the nation's economy and brought steady, if unspectacular, economic growth, they have also forced thousands of people into the informal economy and concentrated wealth among Bolivia's small upper class.
There have been efforts to develop manufacturing and improve public services. However this has been met with hostility as many in Bolivia believe liberalisation and diversification of the economy will lead to greater problems. The government, backed by international financial institutions, has cut fiscal expenditure in response to a rising budget deficit, has privatised some of the public sector and is attempting to eradicate coca production in the nation (although this particular aspect of government policy may be changed under the Morales regime). These measures, which will eventually strengthen the economy, are highly unpopular and contribute to the fast declining political stability.
The economy is largely dependent on hydrocarbons. Bolivia has US$120 billion worth of natural gas reserves and President Evo Morales has pledged to nationalise the industry. This is a popular argument as many wish to ensure profits from the industry will flow directly to ordinary Bolivians and help address income inequality throughout the country. Though this argument has its merits, nationalisation of the industry would undoubtedly have an adverse effect on foreign investment in other areas of the economy, as business confidence is rapidly plummeting.
Mining is an important industry, though Bolivian tin mines have in recent years faced growing competition from South East Asia. This has resulted in the closure of several mines throughout the country. Agriculture is also a key component of the economy, especially the growing of coffee, soybeans, wheat, rice and potatoes. Bolivia is the third largest coca cultivator in the world. The presence of such a large illegal trade in the country has harmed Bolivian development as a sizable proportion of the country's labour force is engaged in the coca production business. In a move that has angered international observers, particularly the United States, President Morales has pledged to resist efforts to eradicate coca.

External trade
Bolivia is a full member of the World Trade Organisation (WTO) and enjoys free trade with the nations of the Andean

Pact signatories. The country is also a beneficiary of the US's Andean Trade Preference Act. Free trade agreements have also been signed with Brazil and with Mercosur in addition to a preferential trade deal signed with Chile. Bolivia also has Generalised System of Preferences (GSP) status with the United States, the European Union and Japan.

Imports
Manufactured goods, petroleum products, plastics, paper, aircraft and aircraft parts, machinery and vehicles, chemical products and foodstuffs.

Main sources: Brazil (25.3 per cent total, 2004), Argentina (17.0 per cent), US (13.1 per cent), Chile (9.2 per cent), Peru (7.2 per cent)

Exports
Principal exports are natural gas, soya beans and soya products, crude oil, zinc, ore and tin.

Main destinations: Brazil (33.9 per cent of total, 2004), US (12.7 per cent), Colombia (11.8 per cent), Venezuela (11.6 per cent), Peru (5.1 per cent), Japan (4.2 per cent)

Agriculture
Farming
Although agricultural produce remains Bolivia's main export, agriculture's share of GDP has fallen from 30 per cent in the early 1960s to around 15 per cent by the end of the century. Yet it is still economically important, employing nearly half the country's labour force. Most agricultural activities in rural areas are performed in small family units with low levels of productivity and income.

The cultivation of commercial crops is central to the advancement of Bolivia's 'agricultural frontier' and an intrinsic element of Bolivia's export-oriented development programme. This development drive is backed by a major road-building programme and changes in land tenure laws.

Since the 1990s, the Bolivian government has fought a US-backed war against the production of coca leaves – the raw source of cocaine. By 2002, the government had eliminated a total of 40,000 hectares of the crop, representing the eradication of 95 per cent of the country's coca fields since the programme began. Before the initiation of the eradication programme, coca production represented nearly 10 per cent of the country's GDP, so efforts are being made to replace coca production with alternative economic activities, such as commercial crops and textile manufacturing.

Unlike the Colombian drug fiefdoms, coca production in Bolivia was largely associated with indigenous peasants who have grown the crops as a traditional medicine since pre-Colombian times and, latterly, as a cash crop to alleviate their enduring poverty. Unsurprisingly, the government's efforts to destroy coca crops damaged the rural economy and inflamed social and racial tensions. Protests by coca farmers, who rely on the crop for their income, have culminated in mass unrest.

Significantly, President Evo Morales has underlined his opposition to the previous government's crackdown on coca production. In a hugely populist move he has pledged to reverse the policy.

Crop production in 2004 included 1,102,100 tonnes (t) cereals in total, 1,670,000t soya beans, 4,800,000t sugar cane, 107,870t wheat, 686,110t maize, 304,530t rice, 827,690t potatoes, 151,080t sorghum, 62,100t barley, 646,310t bananas, 380,971t oilcrops, 186,500t plantains, 258,730t citrus fruit, 40,810t pulses, 130,110t tomatoes, 1,372,670t roots and tubers, 4,330t cocoa beans,
24,670t green coffee, 434,040t cassava, 72,840t treenuts, 29,850t grapes, 25,600t cotton lint, 3,640t tea, 11,670t natural rubber, 1,290,800t fruit in total, 571,940t vegetables in total. Livestock production included 445,6285t meat in total, 172,000t beef, 107,750t pig meat, 23,786t lamb and goat meat, 133,703t poultry, 38,680t eggs, 274,590t milk, 20,840t cattle hides, 5,643t sheep skins, 8,550t greasy wool.

Fishing
Bolivia produces approximately 6,000 tons of fresh water fish per year, almost entirely for the domestic market. Bolivia's lakes, among them Lake Titicaca the world's highest navigable lake, provide the basis for this yield. However, the fishing industry does suffer from limited access to external markets, which is exacerbated by poor road transport infrastructure owing to the extreme altitude of the lakes. In addition to the domestic catch, about 7,000 tons of marine fish are imported per year.

Forestry
With a total land mass of 1.1 million sq km (424,164 sq miles), 53 per cent of which is covered by forests and woodlands, Bolivia has the potential to be one of the world's most significant forestry nations.

Sawnwood accounts for more than 90 per cent of Bolivia's total export of forest products. Brazil nuts, palm hearts and rubber are also important sources of income and are mainly derived from the Amazon forests. The export of more value-added products, such as material for doors, window frames and furniture, has increased rapidly in recent years, surpassing the levels of sawn wood, Bolivia's traditional forest export. This diversification of forest products and improvement in production processes has increased the commercial viability of Bolivian forestry. There continue to be significant problems with the forestry sector however. Legal efforts to promote diversification and sustainability are limited and deforestation continues to out-pace forest regeneration. Forest cover decreased at an annual average rate of 0.30 per cent, the equivalent of 161,000 hectares in 1990–2000 and is still decreasing rapidly.

Though productivity has improved with the introduction of more sophisticated technology in the sawing and drying processes, there are still comparatively few sawmills for a country of Bolivia's forestry capacity and the industry suffers from poor transport infrastructure. The majority of the sawmills are located in the eastern region around Santa Cruz, where the standard of roads is particularly poor. Small- and medium-sized forestry companies that use old technology and outmoded production methods continue to operate with inefficient capacity and no method of producing value-added products. Valuable tree species such as mahogany, oak and cedar are dwindling in numbers. As well as contributing to the overall decline of biodiversity in the Amazon, these precious woods are now below commercial volumes. Efforts to control logging are limited as illegal colonisation of the forests and 'slash and burn' techniques continue.

Timber production in 2003 included: 2,855,626 cubic metres (cum) roundwood, 650,000cum industrial roundwood, 299,000cum sawnwood, 650,000cum sawlogs & veneer logs, 2,205,626cum wood fuel, 29,000t charcoal.

Industry and manufacturing
Although it constitutes approximately 18 per cent to the total GDP of Bolivia, the industrial sector is considerably underdeveloped. Manufacturing in Bolivia is also capital intensive, employing just 14 per cent of the total work force.

Production is centred on the processing of minerals (mainly tin, lead and zinc smelting) and agricultural products. Oil refining and cement production are also important activities. There is a large workshop and artisan sector of small-scale domestic industries producing textiles, clothing and food. Bolivia is a producer of natural textile fibres: cotton, alpaca wool, llama wool, merino lambswool and rabbit fur. There is no heavy industry or electronics industry.

Bolivian industry is under pressure to become more competitive. Traditionally, unprocessed or semi-processed materials have dominated Bolivian exports. The government has created new and more decentralised industries, to stimulate the development of competitive industries, particularly agro-based industries.

Tourism
The Bolivian tourism industry is undergoing expansion. The country's wealth of diversity and cultural and natural attractions has made it a destination for eco-tourists and backpackers. Most of the country's hotels are located in the capital La Paz, but there has been an expansion of hotel accommodation in other cultural centres. The travel and tourism industry generated 9.2 per cent of total GDP in 2005 and visitor levels continued to rise. The continued expansion of the Bolivian tourism industry will depend significantly on the relative level of civil unrest in future years.

Mining
Mining has long been a mainstay of the Bolivian economy and its importance to the country continues today. The mining sector contributes up to one fifth of GDP and employs 10 per cent of the labour force. Mining accounts for approximately 45 per cent of the country's total export earnings and the country's unexploited mineral potential is significant.

The industry has continued to show an improved performance especially, the mining of tin, silver and gold. Total tin reserves are estimated at 1.6 million tonnes and are mainly composed of low quality ore and accounts for approximately 17 per cent of total mining production. Bolivia is the world's fifth-largest tin producer and one of the world's leading producers of antimony and tungsten. Other minerals extracted include zinc, silver, gold, lead, copper and limestone, while large reserves of iron ore, lithium and potassium are as yet unexploited. Zinc accounts for 27 per cent of total mining production. Gold production is significant, totalling some 14 tonnes per year. Privately owned mining enterprises account for the majority of output. Most mining operations are small and inefficient, with many of the more promising deposits occupied by co-operatives, with little exploration being carried out.

Hydrocarbons
With 441 million barrels of proven oil (as at end 2003) reserves, Bolivia has considerable oil supplies. With a consumption rate of 53,000 barrels per day (bpd) and production of 40,700 bpd Bolivia is relatively self-sufficient in oil. Despite its significant proven reserves however, Bolivia does suffer from poor transport infrastructure and a challenging topography which render the transportation of oil extremely difficult, as many of the country's oil fields are located in remote areas.

Bolivia's natural gas reserves are second only to Venezuela in South America; the country's potential gas reserves are estimated at approximately 1.32 trillion cubic metres. Proven gas reserves are vast, recorded at 890 billion cubic metres (as at end 2004) with a total output of around 8.5 billion cubic metres (2004), an almost 50 per cent increase over the figure for 2003. Due to the extensive exploration in recent years, there have been several large discoveries of oil fields holding over 10 million cubic metres of natural gas. There is particular interest in exporting to the large markets of the US and Mexico and there are plans to link the gas reserves to Paraguay via a new pipeline. The domestic gas market is small but there are plans to install 230,000 residential gas connections by 2007 and so the market is set to grow.

In July 2004 Bolivians voted 66.4 per cent in favour of repealing the 1996 law that allowed foreign energy companies to exploit Bolivia's considerable natural gas reserves. Bolivia's reserves are greater in size than those of Canada – 52.3 trillion cubic feet. On 22 July 2004, then president Carlos Mesa signed a 10-year supply deal with Argentine President Nestor Kirchner. The deal includes completion of a US$1 billion pipeline to be operational by 2007, from which Bolivia will earn around US$500 million annually. Bolivia does not produce or import coal.

Energy
Bolivia's capacity to generate electricity has improved markedly over the decade to 2005. This increase is predominantly attributable to an increase in thermoelectric power plants, with around two thirds of the country's electricity output now being generated by such plants. Hydroelectric power and other sources of renewable energy have contributed to the growth in recent years of electricity generation. Bolivia's consumption of energy has also grown considerably, with an increase of 70 per cent throughout the 1990s. The annual growth rate in 2004 was approximately 5.5 per cent in terms of energy consumption.

The Bolivian electricity market is dominated by four electricity companies, all of which are controlled by foreign (mostly US) investors.

Financial markets
Stock exchange
The Bolsa Boliviana de Valores (Bolivian Stock Exchange) was granted official status in 1989. Trading in securities is thin.

Banking and insurance
Bolivia's banking system has been undergoing extensive reform since the mid-1990s. The last decade has seen the full-scale privatisation of formerly state-owned banks and significant regulatory upheaval. A high level of dollarisation has meant that approximately 90 per cent of Bolivian deposits are denominated in US dollars and the holding of deposits is highly concentrated in the country's wealthy elite. This means that the banking system is highly dependent on the financial fortunes of a select number of wealthy Bolivians. Concern has been expressed in various quarters that President Evo Morales will seek to redistribute income to the poor. Thus the banking system may feel the effects of diminished holdings by wealthy clients in future years.

Bolivia's banking system has remained largely immune from the contagious effects of financial sector turmoil that inflicted the region in the early part of the decade. This fact owes to Bolivia's comparatively low exposure to international capital markets; the majority of Bolivia's debt is with foreign states and multilateral institutions, which have worked to change the structure of the country's debt portfolio and maintain vital foreign currency reserves.

Central bank
Banco Central de Bolivia
Main financial centre
La Paz

Time
GMT minus four hours

Geography
Bolivia straddles the Andes and is made up of mountainous areas with cold desolate plateaux and semi-tropical and fertile lowlands. It is landlocked with Chile and Peru to the west, Brazil to the north and east and Argentina to the south. The Andean range is at its widest in Bolivia, some 650km.

The Western Cordillera separating Bolivia and Chile has peaks of between 6,000 metres and 6,500 metres above sea level and a number of volcanoes along its crest. Passes across the Cordillera are at 4,000 metres. To the east of the range lies the bleak treeless Altiplano also at around 4,000 metres. The Altiplano makes up about 10 per cent of the country and is divided into basins by spurs of mountains. Around 70 per cent of the population lives on the Altiplano, particularly the northern part where most of the larger cities are located. In the south, the parched desert landscape is mostly unpopulated.

Lake Titicaca, the highest navigable lake in the world, is situated at the northern end of the Altiplano. It is 171km in length,

Bolivia

64km in breadth and 280 metres at its deepest point. The immense depth of water keeps the lake at an even temperature of 10 degrees Celsius and modifies extremes of winter and night temperatures on the surrounding land, thereby making the basin favourable for farming.

The Eastern Cordillera rises sharply from the Altiplano in the east and four of its peaks rise to above 6,000 metres. These north-eastern slopes are heavily forested and are indented by fertile valleys in an area known as the Yungas.

In the north and east, the Oriente has dense tropical forest and in the centre there are plains covered with rough pasture, swamp and scrub.

Climate
The climate varies with the area. It is tropical in the lowlands (eastern region) with an average temperature of 25 degrees Celsius (C); temperate in the highland valley regions (middle of the country), average temperature 15 degrees C, and cooler in the Altiplano (highland) areas (western region), average temperature 10 degrees C.

La Paz is in the Altiplano where temperatures vary between 3.5 degrees C in June and 24.5 degrees C in November and December. In the highlands the rainy season begins in December and ends in late March.

Dress codes
For business meetings men should wear a suit and tie, women a two-piece suit, or equivalent, and hosiery. Warm clothing is required in the high plateau region. Lightweight clothing is needed during the day and warmer clothing for the evenings in the valleys, and very lightweight clothing for both day and night in the tropical valleys.

Entry requirements
Travellers who arrive without the correct documentation will be fined.

Passports
Passports are required by all (with at least one year of validity remaining) except holders of Cedula de Identidad issued to nationals of Argentina, Paraguay and Uruguay.

Visa
A visa is not required for tourist visits up to 90 days, by nationals of most of the Americas, Western Europe, Australasia and some Asian countries. For further details contact the local embassy or see www.embassyofbolivia.co.uk/visas.html#2.

The 'specific purpose visa', for business visits, require a letter of introduction, including an itinerary and letters of guarantee by employer and host company. See www.embassyofbolivia.co.uk/visaformfiles/specificvisaform.html for copy.

Currency advice/regulations
There are no restrictions on the import and export of local or foreign currency; currency must be declared.

US dollar travellers cheques are the best form of currency to take. UK sterling cheques can sometimes be exchanged, but only with difficulty.

Customs
Visitors are not required to declare valuable personal effects such as cameras and radios. Business samples are duty-free as long as they are re-exported within 90 days.

Health (for visitors)
Mandatory precautions
A yellow fever vaccination certificate is required for visitors arriving from infected areas, and for those travelling to high risk areas such as the Departments of Beni, Cochabamba, Santa Cruz and the sub-tropical area of La Paz Department.

Advisable precautions
Typhoid, paratyphoid, hepatitis 'A', tetanus and polio vaccinations. Malaria risk exists in rural areas – prophylaxis recommended. Owing to the altitude of La Paz and other places in the Altiplano region, sufferers from heart or lung complaints should seek medical advice before leaving for Bolivia. Water precautions should be taken.

Hotels
There is a wide range available. Service charge and local tax are added to the bill. Tipping 5–10 per cent.

Credit cards
Mastercard, Diners Club, Visa and American Express have limited acceptance.

Public holidays
Fixed dates
1 Jan (New Year's Day), 1 May (Labour Day), 6 Aug (Independence Day), 1 Nov (All Saints' Day), 25 Dec (Christmas Day). There are other additional holidays celebrated in individual provinces and towns.

Variable dates
Carnival (Feb, seven days), Good Friday, Corpus Christi (May/Jun).

Working hours
Banking
Mon–Fri: 0830–1200, 1430–1800; Sat: 0830–1200.
Business
Mon–Fri: 0830–1200, 1430–1830.
Government
Mon–Fri: 0800–1200, 1430–1830.
Shops
Mon–Fri: 0930–1230, 1500–1930; Sat: 1000–1500.

Telecommunications
Mobile phones
GSM 1900 service available.

Electricity supply
110V and 200V in La Paz and 220V in Cochabamba and most other towns; US-type flat-prong plugs.

Weights and measures
The metric system is standard, although the Imperial is sometimes used.

Social customs/useful tips
In business circles, local customs are similar to those in Europe or North America. While English is widely used in commercial and business circles, a knowledge of Spanish is a valuable asset to the visitor. Correspondence in Spanish is almost essential. On business visits, cards are presented and it is normal to shake hands when arriving or leaving. It is advisable to arrange appointments before visiting. Bolivians are informal about observing prescribed times and will often arrive 30–45 minutes late.

It is customary to address persons by their professional title, eg, doctor, engineer and *licenciado* for social science graduates. Holders of law degrees are addressed as doctor.

It is offensive to refer to rural Indians as *indios*; they are referred to as *campesinos* (peasants).

It is customary to give gratuities in a hotel or restaurant of around 5–10 per cent even if a service charge has been added to the bill. The minimum drinking age is 21 years.

Security
Since the civil disruption in February 2003, road blockades can happen on all main roads at any time. Visitors should not attempt to breach road blockades and should stay away from demonstrations.

Getting there
Air
National airline: Lloyd Aéreo Boliviano (LAB).
International airport/s: La Paz/El Alto (LPB), 14km from city, duty-free shop, bar, restaurant, bank, post office, hotel reservations.
Other airport/s: Santa Cruz/Viru-Viru (SRZ), 16km from city, duty-free shop, restaurant.
Airport tax: US$25 for all adults, excluding 12-hour transit passengers. An additional exit tax is levied for all passengers staying over 90 days.

Surface
Road: Road access is possible from Peru (Peruvian part of route may be difficult), Argentina (Bolivian roads may not be passable after rain) and Chile (road generally recommended).

Travellers who use overland routes are generally advised to check border post opening hours.
Rail: Rail services connect La Paz with Chile (Arica and Calama) and Argentina (Buenos Aires). The Expreso del Sur is a special train service from La Paz to Buenos Aires.
Water: It is possible to take the steamer on Lake Titicaca from Puno (Peru) to Guaqui.
Main port/s: Although Bolivia is landlocked, access to the sea (and in certain cases free port facilities) has been granted by Paraguay (via River Paraguay), Brazil (Belem, Santos, Corumbá, Port Velho) and Argentina (Buenos Aires, Rosario).

Getting about
National transport
Air: Lloyd Aéreo Boliviano (LAB), AeroSur, TAM (army airline) and Aero Xpress (AX) operate domestic services to main centres, offering the best method of travelling around the country.
Road: Around 40,000km of road exists, but only 5.5 per cent is paved and only 20 per cent can be classed as all-weather road. A toll permit system is in operation; garage and petrol services are sparse outside main centres.
Camión (truck) rides are available, although they can be rough, and it is advisable to book in advance and take warm clothing.
Buses: *Flotas* are long-distance buses, they mostly leave in the evening and travel overnight, except on the major routes where there are some daytime departures. It is advisable to book in advance and take warm clothing.
Rail: A north-south line runs from La Paz to Oruro and Uyuni, with spurs to Cochabamba, Uncia, Potosi, Sucre and Villazón at the Argentine border. The eastern system runs from Santa Cruz to Yacuiba and to Corumbá at the Brazilian border. Sleeper and first-class services are available; advance booking is essential.
Water: Half of Bolivia's territory lies in the Amazon Basin. Transport is by cargo boats, which carry passengers, vehicles and livestock. The tributaries of the Amazon are the Ichilo, Mamoré, Beni, Madre de Dios and Guaporé rivers.
City transport
Taxis: There are *remise* (yellow cabs) which have fixed rates applicable per passenger – the cabs are frequently shared. Within La Paz, *trufis* (cabs with green flags) ply along fixed routes. Tips are not expected.
Car hire
An international driving permit is required. This may be issued in Bolivia by the Federación Inter-Americana de Touring Automovil on presentation of a national licence. Drivers must also buy a *hoja de ruta*, a form which notes the driver's itinerary. Traffic drives on the right.

BUSINESS DIRECTORY
The addresses listed below are a selection only. While World of Information makes every endeavour to check these addresses, we cannot guarantee that changes have not been made, especially to telephone numbers and area codes. We would welcome any corrections.

Telephone area codes
The international direct dialling code (IDD) for Bolivia is + 591, followed by area code and subscriber's number:

Beni	3465	Potosi	262
Buena Vista	3932	Saavedra	3924
Cochabamba	441	Santa Cruz	33
La Belgica	3923	Sucre	4691
La Paz	22	Tarija	466
Montero	3922	Trinidad	346
Oruro	252	Villamontes	4672
Portachuelo	3924		

Useful telephone numbers
Police: 110
Fire: 119
Ambulance (La Paz): 118

Chambers of Commerce
American Chamber of Commerce of Bolivia, Avenida 6 de Agosto, Edificio Hilda, PO Box 8268, La Paz (tel: 244-3939; fax: 244-3972; e-mail: amgalin@caoba.entelnet.bo).

Cochabamba Chamber of Commerce, 336 Calle Sucre, Cochabamba (tel: 425-7715; fax: 425-7717; e-mail: sistema@cadeco.org).

Chuquisaca Chamber of Industry and Commerce, 64 Calle España, Sucre (tel: 645-1194; fax: 645-1850; e-mail: info@cicch.com).

National Chamber of Commerce, 1392 Avenida Mariscal Santa Cruz, La Paz (tel: 237-8606; fax: 239-1004; e-mail: cnc@boliviocomercio.org.bo).

Santa Cruz Chamber of Industry, Commerce and Services, 7 Avenida Las Américas esquina Saavedra, Santa Cruz (tel: 333-4555; fax: 334-2353; e-mail: cainco@cainco.org.bo).

Banking
Banco Bisa, Avenida 16 de Julio 1628, La Paz (tel: 359-471; fax: 316-597; e-mail: bancbisa@caoba.entelnet.bo).

Banco de Crédito de Bolivia, Calle Colón esquina Mercado 1308, La Paz (tel: 360-025; fax: 391-044).

Banco de la Nación Argentina, Avenida 16 de Julio 1486, La Paz (tel: 359-218; fax: 391-392; e-mail: bancnalp@caoba.entelnet.bo).

Banco Económico, Calle Ayacucho 166, Santa Cruz (tel: 361-177; fax: 361-184; e-mail: baneco@roble.scz.entelnet.bo).

Banco Ganadero, Calle 24 de Septiembre 110, Santa Cruz (tel: 361-616; fax: 361-617; e-mail: bangan@roble.scz.entelnet.bo).

Banco Mercantil, Calle Ayacucho esquina Mercado, La Paz (tel: 315-131; fax: 391-442; e-mail: bercant@caoba.entelnet.bo).

Banco Nacional de Bolivia, Avenida Camacho esquina Colón 1312, La Paz (tel: 318-732; fax: 359-146; e-mail: info@bnb.com.bo).

Banco Real, Avenida 16 de Julio 1642, La Paz (tel: 334-477; fax: 335-588; e-mail: real@caob.entelnet.bo).

Banco Santa Cruz, Calle Junín 154, Santa Cruz (tel: 369-911; fax: 350-114; e-mail: bancruz@mail.bsc.com.bo).

Banco Sollidario, Calle Nicolás Acosta 289, La Paz (tel: 484-242; fax: 486-468; e-mail: info@bancosol.com.bo).

Banco Unión, CalleLibertad 165, Santa Cruz (tel: 366-869; fax: 340-684; e-mail: info@bancounion.com.bo).

Interbanco, Calle Mercado No 1046, PO Box 14758, La Paz (tel: 317-707; fax: 316-787).

Central bank
Banco Central de Bolivia, PO Box 3118, Calle Mercado esquina Ayacucho, La Paz (tel: 409-090; fax: 406-598; e-mail: bancocentraldebolivia@bcb.gov.bo).

Travel information
AeroSur, Calle Colón esqina Avenida Irala, Santa Cruz (tel: 364-446; fax: 365-246; e-mail: mail@aerosur.com).

Lloyd Aéreo Boliviano, Aeropuerto Jorge Wilstermann, Cochabamba (tel: 25-903; fax: 50-744; email: gergen@labairlines.com).

Ministry of tourism
Viceministerio de Turismo, Avenida Mariscal Santa Cruz, Edificio Palacio de Comunicacióones, Piso 16, La Paz (tel: 236 7463/4; fax: 237 4630; e-mail: vturismo@mcei.gov.bo; internet: www.mcei.gov.bo).

National tourist organisation offices
Secretaría Nacional de Turismo, Calle Mercado 1328, Edificio Ballivián, La Paz (tel: 367-441; fax: 374-630).

Ministries
Ministry of Agriculture and Rural Development, Avenida Camacho 1471, La Paz (tel: 367-968; fax: 313-601).

Ministry of Defence, Avenida 20 de Octubre esquina Pedro Salazar, La Paz (tel: 431-364; fax: 433-159).

Bolivia

Ministry of Economic Development, Palacio de Comunicaciones, Avenida Mariscal Santa Cruz, La Paz (tel: 375-000, fax: 360-534; e-mail: contactos@desarrollo.gov.bo).

Ministry of Education, Culture and Sport, Avenida Arce 2147, La Paz (tel: 440-160; fax: 440-376).

Ministry of Finance, Palacio de Comunicaciones, Avenida Mariscal Santa Cruz, La Paz (tel: 392-220; fax: 359-955).

Ministry of Foreign Affairs, Calle Ingavi esquina Junín, La Paz (tel: 336-200; fax: 333-521; email: mreuno@rree.gov.bo).

Ministry of Foreign Trade and Investment, Palacio de Comunicaciones, Avenida Mariscal Santa Cruz, La Paz (tel: 343-519; fax: 377-451; internet site: http://www.mcei-bolivia.com).

Ministry of Government [Interior], Avenida Arce 2409 esquina Belisario Salinas, La Paz (tel: 440-114; fax: 442-589).

Ministry of Health and Social Security, Plaza del Estudiante, La Paz (tel: 371-373; fax: 391-590; e-mail: minsalud@ceibo.entelnet.bo).

Ministry of Housing, Avenida 20 de Octubre 2230, La Paz (tel: 372-241; fax: 371-335; e-mail: minviv@ceibo.entelnet.bo).

Ministry of Information, Edificio La Urbana, Avenida Camacho 1485, La Paz (339-027; fax: 391-607).

Ministry of Justice and Human Rights, Avenida 16 de Julio 1769, La Paz (tel: 361-083; fax: 392-982).

Ministry of Labour and Micro-enterprises, Yanacocha esquina Mercado, La Paz (tel: 407-740; fax: 406-867).

Ministry of Presidency, Palacio de Gobierno, Plaza Murillo, La Paz (tel: 371-082; fax: 371-388).

Ministry of Sustainable Development and Planning, Avenida Mariscal Santa Cruz 1092, La Paz (tel: 330-074; fax: 330-540).

Other useful addresses

Bolivian Embassy (USA), 3014 Massachusetts Avenue, NW, Washington DC 20008 (tel: 202-483-4410; fax: 202-3712; e-mail: embassy@bolivia-usa.org).

Bolsa Boliviana de Valores, Calle Montevideo 142, La Paz (tel: 443-232; fax: 442-308; e-mail: info@bolsa-valores-bolivia.com).

British Embassy, Avenida Arce 2732, La Paz (tel: 357-424; fax: 431-073).

Confederación de Empresarios Privados de Boliva, Avenida Mariscal Santa Cruz 1392, Edificio Camara Nacional de Comercio, La Paz (tel: 315-562: fax: 379-970; e-mail: cepbol@ceibo.entelnet.bo).

Empresa Nacional de Electricidad (ENDE), Calle Colombia 655, Cochabamba (tel: 59-500; fax: 59-509).

Eurocentro de Cooperación Empresarial de Bolivia, Calle Suárez de Figueroa 127, Santa Cruz (tel: 334-555; fax: 365-108; e-mail: eurocentro@cainco.org.bo).

US Embassy, Avenida Arce 2780 esquina Cordero, La Paz (tel: 430-120; fax: 432-051).

Internet sites

Bolsa Boliviana de Valores SA (Bolivian Chamber of Commerce): http://www.bolsa-valores-bolivia.com

Bolivia Business Online: http://www.boliviabiz.com

Bolivia Government website: http://boliviaweb.com/gov.htm

Bolivian Times: http://www.boliviantimes.com

Export services: http://exportservices.be/bolivia.htm

Bosnia and Hercegovina Republic

KEY FACTS

Official name: Republika Bosne i Hercegovine (BiH) (Republic of Bosnia and Hercegovina). BiH consists of two distinct entities: Federacija Bosne i Hercegovine (FBiH) (Federation of Bosnia and Hercegovina) and Republika Srpska (RS) (Serb Republic)

Head of State: Three-member rotating collective presidency: Borislav Paravac (Serb); Sulejman Tihic (Muslim); Ivo Miro Jovic (Croat).

Head of government: Prime Minister Adnan Terzic (appointed 20 Dec 2002)

Ruling party: Coalition government (approved 13 Jan 2003) led by the Stranka Demokratske Akcije (SDA) (Democratic Action Party), Hrvatska Demokratska Zajednica BiH (HDZ BiH) (Croatian Democratic Community) and Srpska Demokratska Stranka (SDS) (Serb Democratic Party)

Area: 51,129 square km

Population: 4.36 million (2004)

Capital: Sarajevo (BiH)

Official language: Bosanski (Bosnian)

Currency: Konvertibilna marka (KM) (Yugoslav dinar and Croatian kuna also circulate widely)

Exchange rate: KM1.62 per US$ (Oct 2005) (pegged at KM1.96 per euro)

GDP per capita: US$2,129 (2004)

GDP real growth: 5.20% (2004)

Labour force: 1.95 million (2004)

Unemployment: 44.00% (2004)

Inflation: 0.80% (2004)

Balance of trade: -US$4.57 billion (2004)

Foreign debt: US$3.00 billion (2004)

It was a turbulent year in Bosnia and Hercegovina (BiH), with several political and constitutional reform programmes coming before the republic's various parliaments. Only heavy pressure from the US, the EU and the Office of the High Representative (OHR), the civilian body appointed by the guarantors of the 1995 Dayton Peace Accord to oversee the implementation of the peace accord, brought about the necessary changes. The reward was the opening, in 2005, of accession talks for the EU's Stabilisation and Association Agreement (SAA). IMF reports in April and June noted some good economic progress in BiH but warned that substantial improvements were still needed if BiH was to survive an inevitable decline in international aid contributions.

The economic struggles go on ...

BiH's GDP has tripled since 1995, the year in which its civil war ended, although around 40 per cent of GDP is reckoned to be comprised of the grey economy. However, GDP is still only around 60 per cent of its pre-war size. The steady decline in international aid is also expected to raise pressure on BiH to increase its domestic savings. US financial assistance to BiH was US$51.0 million in 2005 while the EU contributed US$121.4 million. Worryingly, unemployment also increased, to 47.7 per cent in 2005. IMF reports in April and June noted progress in 2005, particularly regarding plans to introduce a value added tax (VAT) code. The IMF projects that GDP growth will be around 5.4 per cent for the year. In 2005, BiH's lucrative snail farming sector expanded to 300 farms and delivered its produce to tables Rome, London and even Paris.

... and so do the politics

Dividing BiH's already fractious political scene in 2005 was the prospect of securing an SAA, usually viewed as the first step on the long road to EU membership. A deadline of 15 September was set for meeting the SAA criteria and police reform was targetted as the main stumbling block by EU negotiators. Each entity within BiH, the Republika Srpska (Serb Republic) (RS) and the Federacija Bosne i Hercegovine (FBiH) (Federation of Bosnia and Hercegovina) operated separate police forces. It was required of BiH that if it desired further integration into Europe, it must unify its police services. At each stage of inter-entity negotiations, the RS fought hard to maintain the autonomy of its police force, so much so that the September deadline was missed. However, after being threatened with sanctions by the OHR, the Bosnian Serbs acceded to the police unification requirement and the SAA process was declared open on 21 October.

Running parallel to the police reform process was an effort by the OHR to dissolve the hitherto separate defence ministry operated by the RS. This was seen as a minimum requirement for BiH to join NATO's Partnership for Peace (PfP) programme. After months of pressure from BiH's central government and the international community, the RS, in August, formally disbanded its defence ministry and agreed to transfer its troops to state level control. In September, the FBiH followed suit.

While grudging progress was achieved on the RS front, the OHR had to deal with growing discontent among BiH's Croat community. Lord Paddy Ashdown, the OHR High Representative, sacked Dragan Čović, the Croat member on BiH's collective presidency. Čović was facing serious corruption charges and had refused to step down. One of Čović's predecessors, Ante Jelavic, was sentenced in absentia in September for embezzlement and attempting to set up a separate Croatian state within BiH. In November, the main Bosnian Croat political party, the Hrvatska Demokratska Zajednica Bosne i Hercegovine (HDZ-BiH) called for a third (ie Croat) level of governance in BiH.

In November, the leaders of BiH's three constituent communities agreed to key constitutional changes, including replacing the former tripartite presidency with a single, largely symbolic president, and the strengthening of the prime minister and cabinet. These changes were seen as crucial for BiH's case for EU and NATO membership.

Ghosts of the past

On 11 July, BiH marked the tenth anniversary of the Srebrenica massacre, in which Bosnian Serb forces killed around 8,000 mostly unarmed Bošniak men and boys. The anniversary prompted responses suggesting that years of denial were coming to an end in RS and Serbia-proper. In an unprecedented move, the Serbian parliament observed a minute's silence for those killed in and around Srebrenica. In October, the RS government submitted a list of names to BiH's state prosecutor's office of all Bosnian Serb personnel involved in the 1995 attack on Srebrenica. And in December, Serbia's president, Boris Tadić, made an apology to BiH for crimes committed in the name of the Serb people. The two men considered most responsible for the massacre, former RS president Radovan Karadic, and former Bosnian Serb army commander General Ratko Mladić remained on the run in 2005. In December, EU military officials in BiH admitted that neither was likely to be caught soon.

Other reminders of the Srebrenica massacre were unearthed in 2005, with the discovery of at least three mass graves in eastern Bosnia, thought to hold the remains of Srebrenica's Bošniak dead. Also, five suspected war criminals, all of them senior military figures at the time of the Bosnian War, were extradited to, or handed themselves into the International War Crimes Tribunal in The Hague.

Outlook

With stubbornly high unemployment, falling levels of international aid, corporate malaise and economic growth of around 5 per cent, Azra Hadžiahmetović, a former Bosnian foreign trade minister, says that BiH will probably struggle to reach its pre-war GDP level before 2015. However, tax reform, implemented in January 2006 is expected to improve revenue collection and strengthen the state. Further European assistance with economic reform is also anticipated under the SAA.

BiH faces a number of political challenges in 2006, all of which will be thrown into sharp relief by a national election due by the end of the year. The various political parties must still finalise how the new presidency will function. The current Serb representative on the BiH presidency, Borislav Paravac, is also expected to continue his campaign against his own country's efforts to bring Serbia-Montenegro before the International Court of Justice on charges of aggression and genocide. Sulejman Tihić, leader of the largest Bošniak political party will also probably continue his campaign for BiH to join the Organisation of the Islamic Conferences

KEY FACTS

Official name: Republika Srpska (RS) (Serb Republic)

Head of State: President Dragan Čović(SDS) (elected 5 Oct 2002)

Head of government: Prime Minister Pero Bukejlovic (elected by parliament 15 Feb 2005)

Ruling party: Coalition government: Sloga (Harmony), dominated by Stranka Nezavisnih Socijaldemokrata (SNSD) (Independent Social Democrat Party)

Capital: Banja Luka

Currency: Konvertibilna marka (KM) pegged to the euro at KM1 per eur0.51 (since 2001); the KM is the only legal tender

Exchange rate: KM1.51 per US$ (Nov 2004)

Labour force: 0

Unemployment: 40.10% (2001)*

Inflation: 11.00% (2001); 5.0% (2002)*

* estimated figure

Nations of the World: A Political, Economic and Business Handbook

KEY FACTS

Official name: Federacija Bosne i Hercegovine (FBiH) (Federation of Bosnia-Hercegovina)

Head of State: President Niko Lozancic (from 27 Jan 2003) (rotating presidency)

Head of government: Prime Minister Ahmet Hadzipasic (elected and sworn in 14 Feb 2003)

Ruling party: Coalition government led by Stranka Demokratski Akcije (SDA) (Party of Democratic Action) and the Hrvatska Demokratska Zajednica Bosne i Hercegovine (HDZ BiH) (Croatian Democratic Union Bosnia and Hercegovina)

Capital: Sarajevo

Currency: Konvertibilna marka (KM) Yugoslav dinar and Croatian kuna also circulate widely

Exchange rate: KM1.51 per US$ (Jul 2004) (pegged at KM1.96 per euro)

GDP per capita: US$2,129

GDP real growth: 5.20% (2001)*

Unemployment: 39.40% (2001)*

Inflation: 0.80% (2001); 2.0% (2002)*

* estimated figure

(OIC), a move guaranteed to alienate many non-Muslim Bosnians. Although the Bosnian Croats have been told by the OHR that they will not be granted separate governing status within BiH, agitation will almost certainly continue. The OHR itself will undergo a shake-up on 31 January 2006, when Lord Ashdown retires as High Representative. After Lord Ashdown earned the enmity of many local elites for his tough stance against transgressors of the Dayton Accord, there will be those eager to test how far they can push his successor, Christian Schwarz-Schilling.

Having been identified by both the US and Saudi Arabia as a safe haven for suspected al Qaeda members, BiH will also have to come to grips with the less savoury activities of some of its adopted citizens.

Risk assessment

Economy	Poor
Politics	Improving
Regional stability	Improving

COUNTRY PROFILE

Historical profile

1463 Bosnia and Hercegovina (BiH) became a province of the Ottoman empire. Many of BiH's Christian Slavic population (principally Serb and Croat) were converted to Islam.
1877–78 The Congress of Berlin assigned BiH to the Austro-Hungarian Empire following the end of the Russo-Turkish War.
1914 Gavrilo Princip, a Serbian nationalist, assassinated Austrian Archduke Ferdinand in Sarajevo (capital of BiH), precipitating the First World War.
1918 The defeat of the Austro-Hungarian empire during the First World War saw the creation of the Kingdom of the Serbs, Croats and Slovenes, encompassing BiH, Croatia, parts of Dalmatia and Macedonia, Montenegro, Serbia, Slavonia and Slovenia.
1929 The Kingdom was renamed Yugoslavia.
1941 Parts of Yugoslavia were occupied by the Germans, Italians, Hungarians and Bulgarians. Most of BiH was incorporated into Croatia, which was granted independence by the Axis powers and ruled by the country's fascist Ustasha movement. Two opposition movements, the communist Partisans led by Josip Broz Tito and the royalist Chetniks led by Draza Mihailovic and backed by the Allied powers, formed to resist Nazi rule.
1944–45 After hostilities broke out between the Chetniks and Partisans, the Allies withdrew support for the Chetniks and backed the Partisans. The Partisans then defeated the occupying forces, the Ustasha, and the Chetniks.
1945 BiH became a constituent republic of a new Yugoslav federation. Tito assumed power and a Soviet-style constitution was adopted. The rest of the Yugoslav federation comprised Croatia, Macedonia, Slovenia, Montenegro, Serbia and the two autonomous regions of Vojvodina and Kosovo. In an attempt to create a Yugoslav unity, Tito imposed restrictions on religious worship while socialism was encouraged as the country's national ideology.
1953 Constitutions adopted in 1953, 1963 and 1974 increased the autonomy of the constituent republics.
1989 Following the death of Tito in 1980 and the fall of communism elsewhere in Eastern Europe, friction between the wealthier republics, Slovenia and Croatia, and the different ethnic groupings intensified.
1990 Multi-party elections in BiH brought to power a government which supported outright independence.
1992 After independence from Yugoslavia, civil war engulfed the whole of BiH.
1995 Hostilities were brought to an end by the Dayton Peace Agreement in late 1995. BiH was divided almost equally into two distinctive entities, based along ethnic lines: the Federacija Bosne i Hercegovine (FBiH) (Federation of Bosnia and Hercegovine) (comprising the Croat and Muslim population, 51 per cent of BiH) and the RS (comprising the Serb population, 49 per cent of BiH).
The disputed region of Brcko in the north-west of the country became a self-governing district within BiH. A multi-national Nato military force was deployed in BiH to enforce the military aspects of Dayton.
1996 A democratic government was elected comprising the main nationalist parties of the three ethnic communities: the Muslim Stranka Demokratski Akije (SDA) (Party of Democratic Action), Hrvatska Demokratska Zajednica Bosne i Hercegovine (HDZ BiH) (Croatian Democratic Union Bosnia and Hercegovina) and the Srpska Demokratska Stranka (SDS) (Serb Democratic Party). Alija Izetbegovic, Ante Jelavic and Zivko Radisic were elected to the three-member collective presidency.
2000 Nationalists did well in the general election and international hopes of multi-ethnic political co-operation declined. The Organisation for Security and Co-operation in Europe (OSCE) reported that several political parties abused the regulations during the elections.
2001 Ante Jelavic was dismissed from the BiH presidency by the then UN High Representative, Wolfgang Petritsch, after he threatened to form his own government in

Bosnia and Hercegovina Republic

Croat-dominated parts of the FBiH. He was replaced by Jozo Krizanovic. The BiH parliament elected Zlatko Lagumdzija as prime minister to replace Bozidar Matic, who had resigned.

2002 Dragan Covic (Croat), Mirko Sarovic (Serb) and Sulejman Tihic (Muslim) were elected to the BiH presidency in the presidential elections. The SDA won the BiH parliamentary elections.

2003 Borislav Paravac replaced Mirko Sarovic who resigned from the BiH presidency in April after accusations of being involved with illegal arms sales to Iraq. In June, Dragan Covic became the chairman of the presidency.

2004 Sulejman Tihic became chairman of the presidency in February. On 29 June, the High Representative, Lord (Paddy) Ashdown, dismissed 60 top officials in the RS, including the interior minister, Zoran Djeric, for failing to implement measures to catch Radovan Karadzic, the Bosnian Serb leader, and his military commander, General Ratko Mladic, both of whom are indicted on war-crimes charges. In December, the EU force (EUFOR) took over NATO's peacekeeping mission in Bosnia. On 17 December, the prime minister of the RS, Dragan Mikerevic, resigned.

2005 On 15 February, the RS parliament elected Pero Bukejlovic as prime minister. Dragan Covic, was dismissed by the High Representative on 29 March. On 4 May, Ivo Miro Jovic was appointed as the Croat member of the presidency. In November the EU agreed to stabilisation and association agreement talks as pre-entry measures for BiH to join the EU.

2006 Christian Schwarz-Schilling will take office as UN High Representative on 31 January, following the retirement of Lord Ashdown.

Political structure
Constitution
The effective founding constitution of modern Republika Bosne i Hercegovine (BiH) (Republic of Bosnia and Hercegovina) is the 1995 Dayton Peace Agreement. This set out the federal state, divided between the Federacija Bosne i Hercegovine (FBiH) (Federation of Bosnia and Hercegovina) and the Republika Srpska (RS) (Serb Republic). The two republics are then subdivided into cantons based on the Swiss model.

The disputed region of Brcko in the northwest of the country was placed under international arbitration in 1995. In March 1998, the Brcko Tribunal declared the Brcko municipality a separate self-governing neutral district under the sovereignty of BiH. In March 2002, the FBiH and RS governments signed an agreement to make constitutional amendments designed to give equal status to all ethnic Muslims, Croats and Serbs in BiH.

Under the terms of the Dayton Agreement, the BiH is responsible for foreign affairs, foreign trade, monetary policy and law enforcement. The FBiH and RS are primarily responsible for fiscal policy, defence and law.

Constitutional government is not yet in full operation. The UN's Office of the High Representative (OHR) is responsible for overseeing and implementing the civilian aspects of the Dayton Agreement.

Universal suffrage at 18 years of age (16 years if employed).

The 2001 election law only allows voters to cast ballots for members of their own ethnic group in elections for the collective three-member presidency. Voters may only vote in constituencies where they lived prior to the 1992–95 civil war.

Form of state
Confederal parliamentary democratic republic, separated into two constituent states – Bosnia-Hercegovina Federation and Bosnia Serb Republic (RS).

The executive
BiH has a three-member collective presidency, one representative from each of the three main ethnic groups. Although this is nominally the executive for the whole country, in practice, the RS appointed its own president and has frequently disregarded the authority of the three-man presidency.

In 2002, the collective presidency was elected for a four-year mandate as opposed to a two-year mandate in previous elections.

In December 2005, the post of prime minister was enhanced, with the power to appoint and dismiss members of cabinet.

National legislature
BiH has three national legislatures, of which two are fully operational.

The bicameral Skupstina (parliament) represents the whole republic. The Zastupnicki dom (House of Representatives) (lower house) has 42 members elected for a two-year term by proportional representation, with 28 members elected from the FBiH and 14 from the RS; the Dom Naroda (House of the Nations) (upper house) has 15 members elected by the Zastupnicki dom, 10 representing the FBiH and five the RS.

The FBiH's parliament has two chambers: the Zastupicki dom Federacije (House of Representatives of the Federation) has 140 members elected for a two-year term by proportional representation; the Dom Naroda is divided equally between Croat and Muslim appointees.

The RS has its own parliament, the Narodna Skuptstina Republika Srpska (Serb Republic National Parliament), with 83 members elected for a two-year term by proportional representation.

National government: the Council of Ministers includes six ministers, one of whom is appointed chairman (prime minister) on a rotating basis for eight months at a time.

Legal system
Civil law system of former Yugoslavia. Legal infrastructure has been in disarray since the war.

Last elections
5 October 2002 (presidential and parliamentary)

Results: Presidential: the tri-presidency was won by the Muslim Party of Democratic Action's Sulejman Tihic with 37.2

KEY INDICATORS — Bosnia and Hercegovina Republic

	Unit	2000	2001	2002	2003	2004
Population	m	3.88	3.90	3.92	4.14	4.36
Gross domestic product (GDP)	US$bn	4.21	4.60	5.20	7.00	*8.12
GDP per capita	US$	972	1,196	1,327	1,544	2,129
GDP real growth	%	5.9	5.6	3.9	3.3	5.2
Inflation	%	5.4	3.3	0.3	1.1	0.8
Unemployment	%	39.8	40.0	40.0	40.0	44.0
Exports (fob) (goods)	US$m	1,066.2	1,166.4	1,000.0	1,272.0	2,086.7
Imports (fob) (goods)	US$m	2,896.0	3,917.9	2,700.0	3,890.0	6,656.2
Balance of trade	US$m	-1,829.8	-2,751.5	-1,600.0	-2,618.0	-4,569.5
Current account	US$m	-610.0	-850.0	-1,230.0	-1,250.0	-1,430.0
Foreign debt	US$bn	2.1	2.2	2.7	2.8	3.0
Total reserves minus gold	US$m	497.0	1,221.0	1,321.0	1,796.0	2,408.0
Foreign exchange	US$m	486.0	1,215.0	1,318.0	1,792.0	2,407.0
Exchange rate	per US$	2.12	2.19	2.04	1.72	1.49

* estimated figure

per cent of the vote, the Croatian Democratic Union's Dragan Covic with 61.5 per cent of the vote and the Serbian Democratic Party's Mirko Sarovic with 35.5 per cent of the vote; voter turnout was 55.5 per cent.

Parliamentary: the SDA won 10 seats out of 42, followed by the HDZ BiH and SDS with five seats each. The SDA, HDZ BiH and SDS also won the largest proportion of seats in the FBiH and RS parliamentary elections.

Next elections
2006 (parliamentary and presidential)

Political parties
Ruling party
Coalition government (approved 13 Jan 2003) led by the Stranka Demokratske Akcije (SDA) (Democratic Action Party), Hrvatska Demokratska Zajednica BiH (HDZ BiH) (Croatian Democratic Community) and Srpska Demokratska Stranka (SDS) (Serb Democratic Party)

Main opposition party
Socijaldemokratska Partija Bosne i Hercegovine-Socijaldemokrati (SPD) (Social Democratic Party BiH)

Population
4.36 million (2004)

Ethnic make-up
Muslims (44 per cent), Serbs (31 per cent) and Croats (17 per cent). The RS is a mostly Serb enclave, while Muslims (also known as 'Bosniaks') and Croats control and inhabit the FBiH.

Religions
Islam (Muslims), Serbian Eastern Orthodoxy (Serbs), Roman Catholicism (Croats).

Education
The education system in BiH was largely destroyed by the civil war and is now influenced by politics. International aid and tax revenues are being used by the entity governments to re-build and fund the education system. In the FBiH, each canton has responsibility for education. The RS has responsibility for its own education system. Despite the FBiH and RS signing the Declaration and Agreement on Education in BiH in 2000 to introduce much-needed reforms to the post-war education system, educational curriculums in each of the entities follow ethnic and religious lines. Segregation of students along ethnic lines is not uncommon.

BiH has universities at Banja Luka, Mostar, Sarajevo and Tuzla. Higher education is also poorly financed and most international aid has come from non-governmental organisations (NGOs).

Health
The health system in BiH is poor and receives little funding from the central government, having handed down the funding responsibilities to cantonal and local government. The health system is largely dependent on aid but is also financed through employee insurance schemes.

HIV prevalence: 0.5 per cent aged 15–49 in 2003 (World Bank)
Life expectancy: 74 years (World Bank)
Fertility rate/Maternal mortality rate: 1.3 births per woman (World Bank)
Infant mortality rate: 14 per 1,000 live births (World Bank)
Head of population per physician/bed: 1.4 physicians per 1,000 people

Welfare
Higher spending on specific areas of the welfare system compared to other areas of the economy has become a major impediment to achieving economic growth in BiH. The welfare system is highly geared to supporting military veterans, war widows and their families, thus only benefiting around 230,000 people – about six per cent of the population. According to the IMF, benefits and spending for military invalids and war widows in the FBiH and the RS account for 10–12 per cent of the country's government revenues. These payments also accounted for over 80 per cent of the annual pension fund.

The unemployment benefit system in BiH is of limited assistance to the claimant. Unemployment benefits – 30 per cent of the state average wage – in the FBiH are only available for six months – although these are available longer for those who had been in continuous employment for more than five years. Claimants need to have paid through an insurance scheme to gain unemployment benefits, while military invalids and war widows are funded by the state. As a result of the system, few register as unemployed, confusing official statistics of the unemployed in BiH (estimated at 40 per cent in 2003). About 5 per cent of those registered as unemployed actually receive state benefits.

Main cities
Sarajevo (capital, estimated population 581,500 in 2003), Banja Luka (capital of RS) (189,700), Zenica (134,900), Tuzla (119,200), Prijedor (112,000), Mostar (the main town in Hercegovina province) (75,600), Bihac (62,300).

Languages spoken
Bosanski (Bosnian) is one of the southern Slavonic languages and is most closely related to Serbian, Croatian and Slovene. Croatian and Serbian are also spoken. Bosnian is written in Latin script but can also be seen written in the Cyrillic alphabet.

German is a useful language for the business traveller. English is not widely spoken, but is becoming more common as a language for business.

Official language/s
Bosanski (Bosnian)

Media
Press
Alternativna Informativna Mreza (AIM) is a press agency that unites journalists from BiH, Croatia and Serbia and Montenegro who work for alternative and other independent media. AIM enables them to share information, work together on some issues, standardise their approach in different regions and communicate about the feedback they get.

Dailies: The main Sarajevo daily is *Dnevni Avaz*. *Oslobodjenje* is an independent Sarajevo daily, but was formerly state-run during the communist era. Other newspapers and magazines include *Nezavisne Novine*, *Dnevne Novostli*, *Hrvatska Rijec*, *Nik Avaz* and *Slobodna Bosna*.

Weeklies: *Reporter* an independent bi-weekly published in Banja Luka (RS).
Periodicals: *Vozdra* (What's up) is the magazine for teens. *Izbor iz Stampe* covers monthly news and tourist information. *Bosnia Report* is a quarterly publication. *Dani* is an independent magazine in BiH and is an important source of objective reporting from Sarajevo.

Broadcasting
Radio: There are about 168 radio stations in BiH, including Radio Free Europe/Radio Liberty and the Nato-run Radio Mir.
Television: There are over 50 television stations in BiH, which are mostly independent. The largest companies are Radio Televizija Bosne i Hercegovine (RTVBiH) (Radio Television Bosnia and Hercegovina) in the FBiH and Radio Televizija Republike Srpske (RTRS) in the RS.

Economy
Since the Dayton peace accord in 1995, the country has achieved substantial success in post-war reconstruction efforts and social stabilisation. This has been achieved through a high level of international support, with a total of US$1.9 billion being committed to the nation's development from 60 donors. As a result, GDP has more than tripled since 1995. Despite impressive growth, there are still significant challenges ahead for Bosnia and Hercegovina (BiH) as poverty affects a fifth of the population and 30 per cent of the population could easily descend below the poverty line.

In 2004 GDP growth was 5.2 per cent, an increase from the 3.3 per cent in 2003, and was due to strong growth in the regional export market. Inflation remained

Bosnia and Hercegovina Republic

low at 0.8 per cent, however unemployment is high. The IMF, in June 2005, reported a fall in rates to around 25 per cent; although unofficial rates, including underemployment, pushes this figure higher.

Measures to harmonise BiH and EU tax structures, customs levies and indirect taxation were pooled at state level; VAT will be introduced at the end of 2006, at 17 per cent, replacing dual-sales tax.

A court ruling on compensation for land and property seizure by the former Yugoslavia is expected to have a significant impact on BiH's economy over the medium-term. The IMF has warned that it could destabilise government fiscal plans unless restitution payments are postponed 'until the burden of domestic debts' is clarified. The government announced its commitment to increasing foreign direct investment through privatisation programmes. In August 2004 the sale of the Zenica steelworks to the LNM Group gave a boost of 12.4 per cent in industrial production and the resurgent metals sector. It was the largest sum of foreign investment since the 1980s, of US$215 million. LNM has increased production but is expected to raise it further when its high volume supply of electricity, from the state-owned energy company, can be assured.

Recently the status of BiH was changed from a post-conflict economy to a transition economy, showing the improvements made in GDP growth. Currently BiH is moving towards accession into the EU, with pre-entry talks agreed in November 2005. It is also undertaking NATO's Partnership for Peace programme and membership of the World Trade Organisation (WTO). For membership status in the EU, BiH will have to encourage the development of the private sector along with increasing competitiveness within the country.

Since the civil war ended in 1995 BiH has required international peace-keeping operations to improve its fragile stability. It still has deep divisions within its civil society although, politically, the three rival groups have come together and agreed to strengthen central government. This should enhance its chances of improving the economy for all the regions.

External trade

BiH has been working towards WTO membership and in October 2004 bilateral market access negotiations started. A Stabilisation and Association Agreement (SAA) with the EU was initiated in November 2005 and is expected to further enhance trading links.

Exports of goods and services recorded an annual average growth of 8.9 per cent in 2004 and is expected to grow by 12.8 per cent between 2004–08.

Imports

Imports consist of fuels, foodstuffs, chemicals, machinery and equipment.

Main sources: Croatia (26.4 per cent total, 2004), Germany (14.9 per cent), Slovenia (13.4 per cent), Italy (12.0 per cent), Austria (6.9 per cent), Hungary (6.4 per cent)

Exports

Exports consist of mainly metals, clothing and timber products.

Main destinations: Italy (22.9 per cent total, 2004), Croatia (22.1 per cent), Germany (20.3 per cent), Austria (7.5 per cent), Slovenia (6.9 per cent), Hungary (4.9 per cent)

Agriculture

Farming

The legacy of war in the region has implications for BiH's agricultural policy. There is considerable uncertainty over land rights, with fragmented and small-sized farm units hindering any large-scale investment opportunities.

The varying climatic conditions in BiH offer wide possibilities both in terms of crop choice and cultivation of land farming, fruit-growing, vine-growing, vegetable-growing, forage crops and livestock production.

Agricultural activities in the RS extend over different farming systems including mixed farming enterprises (crops and cattle) on lower flat lands that alternate with more extensive sheep grazing systems in mountainous areas.

Most of the FBiH is mountainous, with farms in the south and south-east growing vegetables, fruits and rearing livestock. The issue of land mines in rural areas complicates policies related to post-war agricultural development.

Agriculture provided 11.9 per cent of GDP in 2004, with an average annual growth of 15.8 per cent.

The estimated crop production in 2004 included 1,158,800 tonnes (t) cereals in total, 250,000t wheat, 800,000t maize, 12,000t rye, 350,000t potatoes, 31,800t barley, 30,000t pimento, 50,000t oats, 18,450t pulses, 350,000t roots and tubers, 19,700t grapes, 130,110t tomatoes, 2,999t oilcrops, 4,000t tobacco, 3,064t treenuts, 35,000t apples, 30,000t chillies and peppers, 8,000t soya beans, 157,719t fruit in total, 713,937t vegetables in total. Estimated livestock production included 32,300t meat in total, 13,000t beef, 8,200t pig meat, 2,700t lamb, 8,400t poultry, 15,100t eggs, 476,000t milk, 900t honey, 2,368t cattle hides.

Fishing

Fishing is of little importance to BiH's agricultural sector as a whole with the fish catch totalling some 2,500 tonnes per year.

Forestry

Over half of BiH's land area is forested, covering over 2.2 million hectares (ha). Three-fifths of woodland are used for wood supply, mostly for export. Most of the woodland is state-owned. The country has a small forest sector, which produces mainly sawnwood and wood-based panels from domestic resources.

Exports in 2004 amounted to US$65.3 million, while imports amounted to US$23.9 million.

Production in 2004 included: 3,993,000 cubic metres (cum) roundwood, 2,677,000cum industrial roundwood, 887,900cum sawnwood, 2,247,000cum sawlogs and veneers, 196,000cum pulpwood, 1,316,000cum woodfuel.

Industry and manufacturing

The industrial sector accounted for 27.5 per cent of GDP in 2004, of which manufacturing was 12.5 per cent. Average annual growth was 2.5 per cent and 2.9 per cent respectively.

Since the end of the civil war, the construction industry has been the main engine of industrial growth, and since the Zenica steelworks was sold to LNM Group in 2004 steel production has boosted state industrial production based on the resurgent metals sector, as well as the civil engineering projects and Balkan regeneration.

State-owned telecommunication entities are due to be one of the first organisations offered up for privatisation.

Tourism

Travel and tourism is expected to have contributed US$118.3 million or 1.3 per cent of GDP in 2005 and has a hard road to travel before tourist numbers match those of its neighbour, Croatia. There was little tourist infrastructure before 2004 and by 2006 its market is centred on adventure holidays to its unspoilt mountains and lakes. An estimated US$138 million or 7.8 per cent of total capital investment was spent on travel and tourism, in 2005. Direct flights from the UK to Sarajevo have helped to provide access, with the re-opening of the bridge at Mostar, the national symbol of reconciliation, being used as a tourist attraction.

Mining

BiH has deposits of iron ores and good reserves of bauxite, as it used to be a major source of minerals for former Yugoslavia.

Hydrocarbons
BiH imports all of its oil and gas supplies from Russia. Oil imports total over 20,000 barrels per day (bpd). Consumption of gas, at around 311 million cubic metres per year, is covered by imports from Russia via the Bratsvo gas pipeline through Hungary and Serbia and Montenegro.

BiH has deposits of coal and produces enough for its own consumption. The Visca mines, near Tuzla, in the north, produce 1,000 tonnes of coal a day. The coal industry is one of the big loss-makers in the state sector.

Energy
BiH's electricity network has been returned to about 80 per cent of its pre-war capacity with international loans to re-build and develop the energy sector.
Elektroprivreda RS, a state-owned power company, exports electricity to Serbia.

Financial markets
Stock exchange
The Sarajevo Stock Exchange (SASE) and Banja Luka Stock Exchange both have official markets (for blue chip companies only) and free markets.

Banking and insurance
BiH's banking system has undergone reform since 1995. Although heavily indebted and close to bankruptcy, a number of banks underwent privatisation in the late 1990s. Foreign companies that have already invested in BiH banking have streamlined and modernised major banks. Croatia's Zagrebacka Banka has taken a major share in the banking sector, acquiring stakes in four banks. Three RS banks were granted licences from the Federation Banking Agency (FBA) and opened branches in the FBiH, assisted by the introduction of a harmonised banking code between the entities.
The central bank has responsibility as the monetary authority and currency board.
Central bank
The Centralna Banka Bosne i Hercegovine (CBBH) (Central Bank of Bosnia and Hercegovina)

Time
GMT plus one hour (GMT plus two hours from late Mar to late Sep).

Geography
BiH is a mountainous territory with only about 20km (12 miles) of coastline. Croatia forms its western border (running from north-west to south-east, along the Dinaric Alps) and its northern border. Serbia and Montenegro lies to the north-east and to the south-east.
The ancient province of BiH lies between the Sava, Drina and Una rivers. There are fertile lowlands along the River Sava which forms the northern border.

Climate
The climate in BiH is continental with hot summers and cold winters. The temperature averages one degree Celsius (C) in January and 21 degrees C in July. As the country is dominated by mountainous and hilly terrain, with central and southern BiH dominated by the Dinaric Alps, the weather can be unpredictable and isolated in valley areas in the spring and winter months.

Dress codes
During the summer, light clothing is recommended, with warmer clothes essential during the winter months.

Entry requirements
Passports
Required by all except citizens of Croatia who only need an identity card.
Visa
Are not required for either business or tourist reasons, by citizens of Europe, North America and some Middle Eastern countries. See www.sarajevo-tourist.org/visas.htm for more details.
Visa fees vary according to nationality and the type of visa required.
Currency advice/regulations
BiH has a cash economy. The Konvertibilna marka (KM) and euro are the most commonly used currencies. The Croatian kuna can still be used in some parts of BiH. If a visitor uses euros, however, it is likely that change will be supplied in KM. Credit card facilities are limited, although many hotels, restaurants and shops in the major cities and towns are beginning to accept them. While traveller's cheques will be changed by a few banks in major cities, they are not recommended.
Customs
A single and uniform customs territory has been established in BiH. All new or old personal items may be taken into the country without incurring duty.

Health (for visitors)
Medical services are not comprehensive. Visitors should carry a sufficient supply of medicines or prescription drugs.
Ensure that personal accident and evacuation insurance covers all eventualities.

Credit cards
Credit cards can be used in some shops, hotels and travel agencies (Croatia Airlines, Air Bosna) in Sarajevo and is accepted by the Privredna Banka Sarajevo for cash withdrawals.

Public holidays
Fixed dates
1 Jan (New Year's Day), 7 Jan (Orthodox Christmas Day), 14 Jan (Orthodox New Year), 1 Mar (Independence Day), 1 May (Labour Day), 15 Aug (Assumption Day), 28 Aug (Orthodox Assumption Day), 8 Sep (Nativity of the Virgin Mary), 21 Sep (Orthodox Nativity of the Virgin Mary), 1 Nov (All Saints' Day), 2 Nov (All Souls' Day), 25 Nov (National Statehood Day), 25 Dec (Christmas Day).
Variable dates
Easter, Orthodox Easter, Eid al Adha, Birth of the Prophet, Eid al Fitr.
The Islamic year contains 354 or 355 days, with the result that Muslim feasts advance by 10–12 days against the Gregorian calendar. Dates of feasts vary according to the sighting of the new moon, so cannot be forecast exactly. Islamic year 1426: 10 February 2005 to 30 January 2006.

Working hours
Banking
Mon–Fri: 0730–1900.
Business
Mon–Fri: 0800–1530.
Government
Mon–Fri: 0730–1530, except Wed, 0730–1730.
Shops
Mon–Fri: 0800–1200 and 1700–2000, Sat: 0800–1500, but many shops open throughout day.

Telecommunications
Mobile phones
GSM 900 facilities are available throughout most of the country.

Electricity supply
220V AC

Social customs/useful tips
It is traditional for the chairman to welcome his guests formally with drinks before commencing a meeting. Punctuality depends on the region: it is important in some, more casual in others. As elsewhere, it is customary to shake hands on meeting and taking leave.

Security
Crime is reportedly low in BiH. However, visitors are advised to keep clear of demonstrations or crowds, particularly in rural areas where refugees are attempting to return to their homes.

Getting there
Air
National airline: Air Bosna
International airport/s: Sarajevo International Airport (SJJ), 12km south of the city centre. Flights connect from Europe and Turkey.
Other airport/s: Mostar, Banja Luka and Tuzla.
Airport tax: None
Surface
Road: From Zagreb (Croatia) the border can be crossed at Zupanja/Orasje, Stara

Bosnia and Hercegovina Republic

Gradiska/Bosanska Gradiska, Maljevac/Velika Kladusa and Licko Petrovo Selo/Izacic.
From Split (Croatia): Kamensko/Livno and Metkovic/Capljina.
Water: Bosnia has 20km of coastline on the Adriatic, but no ports.

Getting about
National transport
Air: The BiH national airline is Air Bosna. Additionally, Air Srpska operates from the RS.
Road: Night travel by road is not advised and travellers on back roads risk landmines left over from the war. Drivers should also be aware of the local population's disregard for the country's traffic laws. Speeding, particularly on dangerous valley roadways, is commonplace. Horse transport is used by substantial numbers of the local population to travel around the country's roads.
Buses: Buses run between Split and Zagreb to Sarajevo. Journey times from Split vary between five hours during the summer to six in the winter. Journey times from Zagrab take eight hours in the summer and 11 in the winter.
Rail: The country's two railway services are BiH's Zeljeznice Bosne i Hercegovina (ZBH) and RS's Zeljeznice Republike Srpska (ZRS).

City transport
Taxis: Inexpensive taxi services operate in all the main cities. All taxis are metered, but there is no basic charge. A 10 per cent tip is usual.
Buses, trams & metro: Most city centres are served by trams, while buses serve the suburbs. The service is generally cheap and regular. Bus transfers operate out of Sarajevo airport.

Car hire
Avis and Hertz and other international car hire companies operate in neighbouring Croatia. Although the majority of hire cars have Croatian licence plates and are normally insured for travelling within BiH, it is advisable to check before booking.
Car rental firms mainly operate from Sarajevo airport.
Because the international Green Card is not applicable in BiH, car insurance is restricted to Third Party only. Travellers are likely to be asked for either a large deposit or to leave an open credit card voucher with the hire company.
Should travellers have an accident in BiH which is reported to the police, the hire company will impose an automatic charge fine, over and above any other hire costs; check all agreements carefully.
Drivers should be 21 years with a minimum of two years' driving experience.

It is recommended that visitors who rent a car also hire a driver, especially if they intend to travel outside Sarajevo.

BUSINESS DIRECTORY
The addresses listed below are a selection only. While World of Information makes every endeavour to check these addresses, we cannot guarantee that changes have not been made, especially to telephone numbers and area codes. We would welcome any corrections.

Telephone area codes
The international direct dialling (IDD) code for Bosnia is +387 followed by area code and subscriber's number.

Banja Luka	51	Sarajevo	33
Mostar	36	Tuzla	35
Pale	57	Zenica	72

Useful telephone numbers
General emergencies: 112
Emergency hospital, Koldovorska Street, Sarajevo (English spoken): 611-111

Chambers of Commerce
American Chamber of Commerce in Bosnia and Hercegovina, 4 Zmaja Od Bosne, 71000 Sarajevo (tel: 269-230; fax: 269-232; e-mail: amcham@lsinter.net).

Bosnia-Hercegovina Chamber of Foreign Trade, 10 Branislava Durdeva, 71000 Sarajevo (tel: 663-631; fax: 663-632; e-mail: cis@komorabih.com).

Federation of Bosnia-Hercegovina Chamber of Economy, 10 Branislava Durdeva, 71000 Sarajevo (tel: 217-782; fax: 217-783; e-mail: info@kfbih.com).

Sarajevo Canton Chamber of Economy, 8 La Benevolencije, 71000 Sarajevo (tel: 250-100; fax: 250-137).

Banking
Aurobanka, Mostar (tel: 444-444, 444-445, 444-456; fax: 444-400; internet site: http://www.aurobanka.com; e-mail: aurobanka.com).

Gospodarska Banka, International Division, Ferhadija 11/III, 71000 Sarajevo (tel: 208-907, 667-688; fax: 444-605).

Hercegovacka banka, Kneza Domagoja Street, Sarajevo (tel: 320-555; fax: 324-771; internet site: http://www.hercegovacka-banka.com; e-mail: herbank@hercegovacka-banka.com).

Hrvatska Banka, Kardinala Stepinca bb, 88000 Mostar (tel: 312-112; fax: 312-121).

Hrvatska Postanska Banka, Kneza Domagoja, Mostar (tel/fax: 316-020; e-mail: hpb-hb@int.tel.hr).

Investment Bank of the Federation of Bosnia and Hercegovina, Igmanska 1, 71000 Sarajevo (tel: 277-900; fax: 668-952; e-mail: info@ibf-bih.com).

Komercijalna Banka, Dzafer mahala 65/67, 75000 Tuzla (tel/fax: 259-000, 252-630; internet site: http://www.kombanka.com.ba; e-mail: kombanka@kombanka.com.ba).

Privredna Banka Sarajevo, Obala Vojvode Stepe 19, 71000 Sarajevo (tel: 213-144).

Universal Banka, Branilaca sarajeva 20/V, 71000 Sarajevo (tel: 664-139; fax: 668-239; internet site: http://www.universalbanka.ba; e-mail: uniba@bih.net.ba).

Central bank
Central Bank of Bosnia and Hercegovina, Maršala Tita 25, 71000 Sarajevo (tel: 278-100; fax: 278-299; e-mail: contact@cbbh.ba).

Travel information
Air Bosna, Sarajevo office No 1 (tel: 610-000; fax: 667-954); Sarajevo office No 2 (tel: 203-330; fax: 209-350).

Air Commerce, Sarajevo (tel: 663-396; fax: 663-395).

Avio Express, Sarajevo (tel/fax: 653-179).

Air Srpska, Veselina Maslese 28, 78000 Banja Luka (tel: 212-806; fax: 211-348).

Ministries
Ministry of External Trade and International Communication, 9 Musala, 71000 Sarajevo (tel: 664-831; fax: 655-060).

Ministry of Foreign Affairs of BiH, Musala 2, Sarajevo (tel: 281-100; internet site: http://www.mvp.gov.ba/Index_eng.htm).

RS Ministry of Foreign Economic Affairs, Vuka Karadzica 4, 51000 Banja Luka (tel: 331-430; fax: 331-436).

RS Ministry of Trade and Tourism, Vuka Karadzica 4, 51000 Banja Luka (tel: 331-523; fax: (331-499).

Other useful addresses
Agency for Privatisation in Federation of Bosnia and Hercegovina, Alipasina 41, Sarajevo (tel: 218-550; fax: 218-552; e-mail: apftbiro@bih.net.ba).

US Embassy of Bosnia and Hercegovina, 2109 E Street, NW, Washington DC 20037 (tel: 337-1500; fax: 337-1502; e-mail: info@bosnianembassy.org).

British Embassy, BFPO 543, 8 Tina Ujevica, Sarajevo (tel: 444-429; fax: 666-131; e-mail: britemba@bih.net.ba).

British Embassy Commercial Department, Petrakijina 22, Sarajevo (tel: 204-781, 204-782, 679-635; fax: 204-780).

Communications and Regulatory agency (CRA), Vilsonovo Setaliste 10, 71000 Sarajevo.

Directorate for Reconstruction and Development, Saravejo (tel: 650-563).

RS Directorate for Privatisation, Mladena Stojanovica 4, Banja Luka (tel: 308-311; fax: 311-245; e-mail: dip@inecco.net).

Elektrodistribucija (Power Distribution Company), Sarajevo (tel: 472-462).

Elektroprivreda BiH, Vilsonovo setaliste 20, 71000 Sarajevo (tel: 651-722; fax: 653-004).

Gras (Public Transport Company), Sarajevo (tel: 664-624).

Institute for City Development Planning, Saravejo (tel: 664-638).

Institute for City Construction, Saravejo (tel: 663-901).

Institute for Information and Statistics, Saravejo (tel: 664-450).

Office of the High Representative, Emerika Bluma 1, 71 000 Sarajevo (tel: 283-500; fax: 283-501).

Public Information Office HQ SFOR, Butmir Camp, 71 000 Sarajevo (tel: 495-149).

PTT (Post/Telegraph/Telephone), Sarajevo (tel: 664-813).

Sarajevo City Council, Reisa Dz Causevica Street No 3, Sarajevo (tel: 664-773; fax: 648-016).

Sarajevogas (Gas Company), Sarajevo (tel: 467-713).

Sarajevostan (Housing Company), Saravejo (tel: 663-522).

Sarajevski Sajam (trade fairs), Terezije bb, 71 000 Sarajevo (tel: 664-163, 201-208, 445-156; fax: 201-178, 201-208).

Telekom Srpske (e-mail: tskabinet@telekom-rs.com).

World Bank Resident Mission, Bosnia and Hercegovina, Hidrogradnja Building, 5th Florr, Hamdije Kresevljakovica 19, 71000 Sarajevo (tel: 440-293; fax: 440-108).

Internet sites

RS Directorate for Privatisation: http://www.rsprivatizacija.com

Parliament of the FBiH: http://www.fbihvlada.gov.ba

Republika Srpska Government: http://www.vladars.net

United States BiH Embassy: http://www.bosnianembassy.org

World Bank Resident Mission: http://www.worldbank.org.ba

UN Office of the High Representative: http://www.ohr.int

Botswana

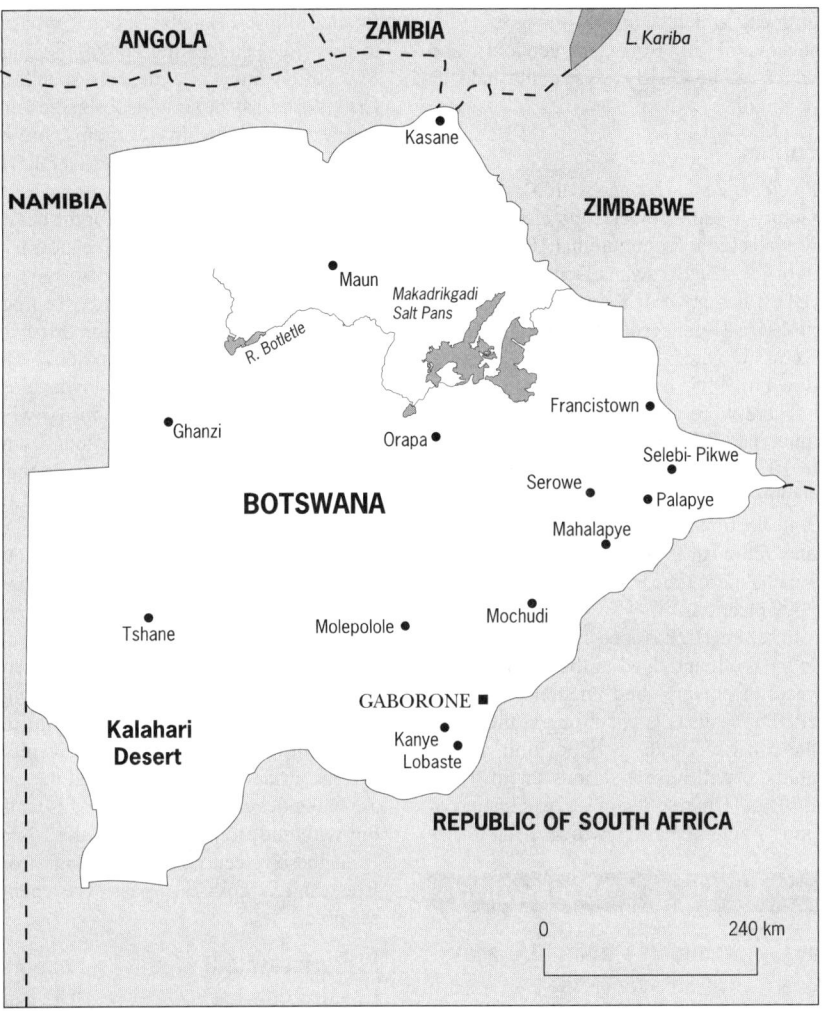

KEY FACTS

Official name: Republic of Botswana

Head of State: President Festus Mogae (since Apr 1998; re-elected for final term 30 Oct 2004)

Head of government: President Festus Mogae

Ruling party: Botswana Democratic Party (BDP) (since 1965; last re-elected 30 Oct 2004)

Area: 582,000 square km

Population: 1.80 million (2004)

Capital: Gaborone

Official language: English (official); Setswana (national).

Currency: Pula (P) = 100 thebe

Exchange rate: P5.41 per US$ (Oct 2005) (pula devalued by 7.5 per cent on 5 Feb 2004)

GDP per capita: US$5,740 (2004)

GDP real growth: 5.20% (2004)

Labour force: 759,000 (2004)

Unemployment: 23.80% (2004); *28.0% (2005)

Inflation: 6.30% (2004)

Balance of trade: US$685.00 million (2004)

Foreign debt: US$531.00 million (2004)

* estimated figure

Botswana's economic growth has averaged seven per cent over the past two decades; one of the highest in the developing world. The mining industry, essentially diamonds although there is extensive prospecting for other minerals, contributes 35 per cent of Botswana's gross domestic product (GDP), between upwards of 80 per cent of export revenues and a direct 50 per cent of government revenues. It has no foreign debt to speak of, and is not subject to any financial or structural reconstruction schemes. It is in fact a contributor to the World Bank International Development Association. It houses, and was a founder member of, the 14-member Southern African Development Community (SADC), in part a brainchild of Botswana's first president, Sir Seretse Khama.

A middle-income country

Per capita income of US$5,740 means Botswana is considered an upper middle-income country. The government has managed the country's resources prudently and has kept its recurrent expenditure within its revenue, allowing for investment in human and physical capital. The government's revenue from diamonds, as well as profits from the large foreign exchange reserves of the Bank of Botswana – equivalent to more than 24 months of import cover – has largely cushioned Botswana from the recessions that have buffeted most countries in the region.

But high unemployment

With such a record, can there be any cracks? Yes. Botswana is mining country and mining is never for ever. Now-a-days it is also capital intensive, which does not help Botswana's growing unemployment problem – 28 per cent official unemployment, discount a growing informal sector and there are 40 per cent of a 600,000 workforce looking for jobs. The solution was seen as diversification of the economy with more labour intensive manufacturing industries. The campaigns still continue, but competition from South Africa – just four driving hours down the road – inhibits their success.

The new approach is more money from the diamond mines through international marketing in co-operation with, instead of by, the De Beers Diamond Trading Company (DTC). De Beers is a 50 per cent shareholder in Botswana's diamond industry and is to co-operate in setting up a Botswana DTC. And because diamonds are not for ever, the government has encouraged an exploration and exploitation boom: copper, gold – a mine has opened; coal – a new power station is proposed, and methane – the energy hungry US is supporting a project. There will also be a new lease of life for the existing copper-nickel mines – new technology will eliminate the need for smelting.

But there are still few new job creating industries. There are tax packages, factory shells, well educated but unemployed workers up to graduate level. This is Oxford economist President Festus Mogae's biggest headache. He is also grappling with a 'culture of dependency on the government' which he openly attributes to the success of the Botswana economy and which, as he clearly says, could help its downfall.

Politics

President Festus Mogae scored a landslide victory in the October 2004 elections and was elected to complete his 10 year term in office. His Botswana Democratic Party (BDP) has governed since independence in 1966. He succeeded former president Ketumile Quett Masire when he stepped down in 1998.

There were rumblings of political disquiet in 2005. Limited by the constitution to 10 years in office, Mogae says he will step down in 2008, ahead of the next general elections. He has denied reports he may retire early to give vice president Ian Khama more time to organise ahead of the 2009 elections.

Seretse's BDP is seen as somewhat long in the tooth and dyed in the wool after 40 years of power – and unemployment fuelled opposition is champing at the bit. If the alliance of three opposition groups holds, it will pose a serious threat to the BDP and Khama. There is also a history of poor implementation which Khama has tried to solve, but without a great deal of success. But he, a former army commander, is tough and resilient. The hope is now an e-government serving an e-society within five years, but there are major infrastructure problems in this vast, mainly desert country.

Botswana will remain in business – good balanced business – for many years, finance minister Baledzi Gaolathe will see to that. He balances the books, there are few deficit budgets – he cuts spending. Critics often say he should loosen the reins and reflate a tightening economy, but he rejects out of hand any sign of red ink. He remains confident a surge in mining revenues will work and buy time for the development of more labour intensive industry.

Botswana's tourist hot spots shine as brightly as any of its diamonds. Tourism has been identified as a major driver of Botswana's efforts to create jobs. The government is funding primary development, but has thrown the industry wide open to investors to develop lodges and hotels and to diversify Botswana's tourism product. The effort, believes the government, will see tourism's share of Botswana's gross domestic product up from 7 per cent to 20 per cent over the next 10 years. 'Destination Gaborone' is an initiative of the city fathers and the private sector to divert some of the tourist dollars away from the hotspots of the Okavango Delta and Chobe National park into the tills of the shopping malls in the capital. Tourist attractions in and around the city are being developed – the newest is walking with and riding elephants just 15kms from the city centre, and buildings from Botswana's colonial past are being restored.

Risk assessment

Political	Good
Economic	Fair
Regional stability	Fair

COUNTRY PROFILE

Historical profile

The majority Tswana people settled in the area during the great Bantu migration. Under threat of incorporation into the Boer settlements of Inner Africa and faced by economic and social destruction through white adventurers, cattle raiders, profiteers and other forerunners of European civilisation, the Tswana chiefs called for Imperial British protection and rule in 1884. A crown colony was created in the southern parts in 1885, while a protectorate was established in the north. The colony was then integrated into existing

KEY INDICATORS — Botswana

	Unit	2000	2001	2002	2003	2004
Population	m	1.63	1.70	1.69	1.75	1.80
Gross domestic product (GDP)	US$bn	5.57	5.60	5.30	7.40	*8.66
GDP per capita	US$	3,420	3,315	3,202	4,554	5,740
GDP real growth	%	8.7	4.3	2.6	5.4	5.2
Inflation	%	7.9	6.6	5.5	10.1	6.3
Unemployment	%	15.8	21.0	21.0	40.0	23.8
Exports (fob) (goods)	US$m	2,690.0	2,817.0	2,280.0	3,038.0	2,940.0
Imports (fob) (goods)	US$m	2,040.0	2,409.0	1,600.0	2,039.0	2,255.0
Balance of trade	US$m	657.0	468.1	683.0	999.0	685.0
Current account	US$m	449.0	471.0	327.0	500.0	580.0
Foreign debt	US$bn	0.4	0.4	0.3	0.4	0.5
Total reserves minus gold	US$m	6,318.2	5,897.3	5,473.9	5,339.8	5,661.4
Foreign exchange	US$m	6,256.2	5,829.6	5,397.2	5,244.9	5,576.1
Exchange rate	per US$	5.10	5.84	6.09	4.92	4.40

* estimated figure

white-ruled colonies in South Africa which (in 1910) were combined in the Union of South Africa.
The protectorate, however, survived as the Bechuanaland Protectorate as a political entity separate from South Africa. Economically, the protectorate was very dependent on its larger neighbour, a fact recognised by the protectorate's inclusion in the Southern Africa Customs Union. The role assigned to the Bechuanaland Protectorate was that of supplier of migrant labour. During most of the British colonial period Bechuanaland was never given any positive social, cultural or political development. When, at a relatively late stage of de-colonisation in Africa, British rule ended, the newly created Republic of Botswana was generally regarded as an economic hostage to South Africa. Two things changed that perception: first the discovery of mineral wealth – diamonds now account for more than a third of GDP and 80 per cent of total exports – and post independence governments' determination to pursue a policy of independence from then white-ruled South Africa.
1885 Britain declared the country a protectorate and called it Bechuanaland, defining its modern borders.
1966 Independence for Botswana came a year after the territory's first election, which was won by Seretse Khama and his Botswana Democratic Party (BDP).
1980 On his death, Khama was succeeded by his vice president, Quett Ketumile Masire.
1984 and 1989 The ruling BDP easily won elections but was tainted by allegations of corruption.
1994 In the elections, the opposition party, Botswana National Front (BNF), took 13 seats and unseated three ministers.
1998 President Sir Quett Ketumile Masire retired from the presidency.
1999 The legislative elections were won by the BDP. The National Assembly chose Festus Mogae as president.
2001–02 The government's policy towards the San people (formerly called the Bushmen) in the Central Kalahari Game Reserve has been criticised internationally for its refusal to recognise the ownership rights of the Bushmen over the land they have lived on for at least 20,000 years. The Reserve was originally created in 1961 to constitute a refuge for the marginalised San people. However, the potential for tourism and diamonds increased the value of these marginal lands, leading the government to relocate the original inhabitants.
2003 A partnership between the government, a pharmaceutical giant and the Bill and Melinda Gates Foundation began providing free anti-retroviral drugs to the country's HIV-infected population.
2004 The pula was devalued by 7.5 per cent on 5 February. Festus Mogae won a landslide victory in October when he was elected for a second (and final), five-year term.

Political structure
Constitution
The constitution came into effect on 30 September 1966. It enshrines a code of human rights.
The approval of a 15-member House of Chiefs is needed for some measures, but it cannot veto legislation.
Form of state
Multi-party democratic republic
The executive
The National Assembly elects a president who has executive power for a maximumu of two five-year terms. He appoints a vice president and the cabinet, over which he presides. The president is an ex-officio member of the Assembly.
National legislature
The legislature is the National Assembly, which comprises 63 members, 57 of whom are elected for five years by universal adult suffrage and four are elected by the elected assembly members. The membership is expanded every 10 years following the census.
A 15-member House of Chiefs advises on tribal and customary matters.
Legal system
Roman-Dutch law. Rural areas have customary courts.
Last elections
30 October 2004 (presidential and parliamentary)
Results: Parliamentary: the ruling Botswana Democratic Party (BDP) won with 51.7 per cent of the vote (44 seats out of 57 contested), Botswana National Front (BNF) 26.1 per cent (12 seats) and Botswana Congress Party (BCP) 16.6 per cent (one seat).
Presidential: Festus Mogae was elected in a landslide victory for a second (and final) five-year term.
Next elections
2009 (presidential and parliamentary)

Political parties
Ruling party
Botswana Democratic Party (BDP) (since 1965; last re-elected 30 Oct 2004)
Main opposition party
Coalition of Botswana National Front (BNF), Botswana Congress Party (BCP) and Botswana Alliance Movement (BAM).

Population
1.80 million (2004)
Ethnic make-up
The Batswana, of which the largest group is the Bamangwato, comprise 79 per cent of the total population. The Kalanga 11 per cent, Basarwa (the Bushmen) 3 per cent, Kgalagadi and the rest 7 per cent.
Religions
Most of the population are Christians (about 49 per cent); other religions include various traditional beliefs, including animism, mostly in rural areas (50 per cent), and a small Muslim population.

Education
Primary education is free but with a high drop-out rate. In 2001, the gender gap in primary enrolment was 25 per cent, with net enrolment among girls remaining at only 50 per cent.
Secondary schooling starts from the age of 12 and lasts till the age of 18.
The National Policy on Education (1977) and the Revised National Policy on Education (1994) have provided the policy framework for the education system in Botswana.
The United Nations International Children's Emergency Fund's (Unicef) Girls' Education Programme has focussed on the prevention of HIV/Aids, particularly among children aged 6–15. Unicef in association with the government has been formulating primary school curricula and developing four 'model' community-based pre-schools.
Literacy rate: 74 per cent males, 79 per cent females; adult rates (World Bank 2002).
Compulsory years: 6 to 11 years.
Enrolment rate: 84 per cent, primary school enrolment; 10 per cent for girls and 24 per cent for boys gross enrolment for secondary schools.
Pupils per teacher: 28 in primary schools.

Health
The annual total expenditure on health is around 6 per cent of GDP, of which government spending is approximately 63 per cent.
HIV/Aids
Projections by UNAids show that the impact of HIV on firms could equal 4.9 per cent of their total wage bill between 1996–2004. It also reported that Botswana was the first country to begin providing antiretroviral drugs through its public health system, courtesy of a bigger health budget and drug price reductions negotiated with pharmaceutical companies.
UNAids said in September 2003 'rampant epidemics are under way in southern Africa' including Botswana, with a national adult HIV prevalence rising higher than thought possible.
Testing for HIV has been considered by most NGOs as best done voluntarily. In Botswana the testing has been changed to routine, any test that requires a blood

Nations of the World: A Political, Economic and Business Handbook

sample will be checked for HIV/Aids, unless the donor expressly forbids it. This change in policy was initiated in January 2004 to overcome the reluctance of people to know their status regarding the disease. The head of the Botswana Aids Treatment Programme, Dr Darkoh, points out that without knowing their status patients cannot be treated in time or effectively. He also changed the method of testing with patients attending open, rather than separate, clinics. Testing for HIV/Aids has increased from 20 per cent to 95 per cent.

The change from voluntary to regular testing has not been welcomed by all, some rights activists fear the discrimination of patients if their results become public.

HIV prevalence: 37.3 per cent aged 15–49 in 2003 (World Bank). One of the highest in the world.

Life expectancy: 38.0 years (World Bank).

Fertility rate/Maternal mortality rate: 3.7 births per woman (World Bank)

Infant mortality rate: 82 per 1,000 live births; 17 per cent of children under aged five are malnourished (World Bank).

Head of population per physician/bed: 1.6 hospital beds per 1,000 people.

Welfare

Botswana provides a non-contributory social pension for about 80,000 elderly citizens of 65 years and older, a flat-rate 151 Pula each month. This income has become an important source of revenue for families and communities and has had a significant impact on poverty reduction, as it alleviates the needs of more than just the elderly. Studies have shown that multi-generational households derive a 'safety-net' against economic hardship and these pensions support families where grandparents are fostering children of HIV/Aids parents. Pensioners are economically independent and valuable family members, this contradicts any perception that they may be a financial burden on their offspring.

Main cities

Gaborone (capital, estimated population 195,000 in 2003), Francistown (87,000), Molepolole (57,200), Selebi-Phikwe (52,300), Maun (45,900).

Languages spoken
Official language/s
English (official); Setswana (national).

Media
Press
Dailies: *Botswana Daily News* is owned by the government. *Daily News Online* (http://www.gov.bw/cgi-bin/news.cgi) is a news service provided by the Botswana Press Agency. *Mmegi* with on-line edition (http://www.mmegi.bw/) is an independent weekly.

Weeklies: Weekly publications are *Botswana Guardian*, *Gazette*, *Midweek Sun* and *Mmegi Monitor*.

Business: *Business Gazette* covers financial and business interests.

Periodicals: *Marung* is a monthly periodical and *The Voice* is an irregular publication from Francistown.

Broadcasting
Radio: National service in Setswana and English operated by Radio Botswana, based in Gaborone.

Television: South African and Bophuthatswana transmissions can be received.

Economy

Botswana continues to live off its large diamond reserves and remains one of the fastest growing economies in the world. Since independence in 1966, Botswana has achieved average annual GDP growth of around 7 per cent, transforming it from one of the world's poorest countries into a thriving middle-income country. In recent years, the government has initiated strategies to diversify export markets and has invested heavily in communications and water. Despite attempts to increase foreign involvement in the non-mining sectors through privatisation and other measures, diamonds are still a motor for the economy providing 80 per cent of export earnings and increasing the country's wealth. A further 10 per cent is provided by nickel and copper production.

Botswana is basically an open desert about the size of France. There is little room for agricultural diversification beyond livestock rearing and the country does not have a population or domestic market that is large enough to warrant a significantly large industrial sector. There is a small but growing tourist industry, consisting mainly of up-market hunters. The government is attempting to diversify and increase the tourist industry, but the main attraction, lions, are fast declining. Although Botswana's infrastructure is highly developed and therefore attractive to foreign investors, the possibility that it can compete with South Africa within the Southern African Development Community (SADC) in manufactured goods is remote, particularly given the cost of start-up and the generally higher wage rates.

2003 saw sustained growth in GDP at 5.4 per cent, followed by 5.2 per cent in 2004. High unemployment levels remain a large issue for the country.

Despite the economy's health, the IMF has warned of the Aids time-bomb that is likely to hit the country's workforce in coming years. The government has led a concerted and largely successful Aids campaign, increasing the availability of drugs and giving financial aid to orphans. The IMF is concerned about the wider costs of the disease which had, by 2003, infected around 40 per cent of the adult population.

The growing macroeconomic impact of Aids-related problems is likely to coincide with a decline in the value of diamond exports, which the IMF believes have reached a plateau.

External trade

In 2002, the US approved Botswana as being eligible for tariff preferences under the African Growth and Opportunities Act (AGOA).

Imports
Principal imports are foodstuffs, machinery and electrical goods, transport equipment, chemical and rubber products, wood and paper products, textiles, footwear, metals and metal products, tobacco.

Main sources: Southern African Customs Union (SACU) (over 70 per cent), EFTA (over 15 per cent), Zimbabwe (around 5 per cent)

Exports
Principal exports are diamonds and copper, nickel (typically 80 per cent of total), soda-ash, textiles, meat and meat products.

Main destinations: European Free Trade Association (EFTA) (typically over 80 per cent,), Southern African Customs Union (SACU) (around 10 per cent), Zimbabwe (around 5 per cent)

Agriculture
Farming
The agricultural sector contributes around 3.5 per cent to GDP and employs 60 per cent of the workforce.

Production is divided between small, traditional farms and around 360 large-scale commercial units (including Barolong Farms, Pandamantenga and Tuli Block). The climate and poor soil are suitable for extensive ranching, with the result that livestock produce accounts for about 80 per cent of marketed output. In the past, rearing of livestock has been hampered by frequent outbreaks of foot-and-mouth disease – now largely controlled – and more recently by drought. However, the livestock sector has predominated due to a lack of cultivatable land – only 5 per cent of the land is suitable for arable production – in a country which is mostly arid and contributes around 80 per cent of agriculture's share of GDP. Beef is one of the country's main exports and the Botswana Meat Commission (BMC) operates three abattoirs with a combined capacity of up to 2,000 head of cattle and smaller stock every day.

Government aims for self-sufficiency in basic foodstuffs, such as maize, millet, beans and sorghum, are far from being realised. There is potential for investment in adding value to primary products through increasing processing capacity. There is also a growing market in farm machinery, irrigation and water pumps. The crop production for 2004 included 45,250 tonnes (t) cereals in total, 32,000t sorghum, *10,000t maize, 550t wheat, *17,500t pulses, *93,000t roots and tubers, *1,100t millet, *600t citrus fruit, 3,306t oilcrops, *770t cotton lint, *10,600t fruit in total, *16,400t vegetables in total. Estimated livestock production included 54,095t meat in total, 28,000t beef, *375t pig meat, *8,160t lamb and goat meat, 11,000t game meat, 5,360t poultry, *3,000t eggs, *105,350t milk, *3,500t cattle hides, 330t sheepskins.

* estimate

Fishing

Botswana has a small freshwater fishing industry with annual average catches amounting to 2,000 tonnes.

Forestry

About 25 per cent of the total land area has forest cover. Another 20 per cent of its terrain is classified as wooded land. There are several large game reserves in the west, including the Central Kalahari Game Reserve, the largest protected area in Africa. In 1990–2000, deforestation accounted for an annual average decrease in forest cover of 0.91 per cent. There are no large-scale forest industries in the country. Some varieties of woods are used for fuel consumption and for the manufacture of wooden handicrafts.

Industry and manufacturing

The industrial sector as a whole contributes around 5 per cent to GDP and employs 10 per cent of the workforce.

The manufacturing sector is underdeveloped. There is a wide range of consumer products manufactured by a relatively small number of enterprises. There is also a large number of village industries, mainly producing handicrafts. The main industrial base depends on the livestock sector. Beverages, chemicals, paper, plastics and electrical goods are also produced.

The small domestic market has hampered attempts to stimulate production. Emphasis is on expansion of the export market for traditional products, such as textiles, leather goods, processed meat and import substitution.

The government is pushing for increased value-added on the country's primary goods production. The soda ash industry has helped develop the local manufacture of detergents, potash and fertilisers. The country also produces electrical components, which utilise copper and nickel production.

The government has set up the Botswana Development Corporation (BDC) in an effort to promote industrial development, particularly in sugar refining, furniture, clothing, milling, brewing, packaging and handicrafts.

Tourism

Botswana's tourism sector is being actively developed as part of a strategy to diversify the economy away from dependence on diamond mining. The sector accounts for around 5 per cent of GDP. The main attractions are the country's rich variety of wildlife and its wilderness areas. Around 40 per cent of the land is dedicated to national parks, game reserves and wildlife management areas. Long-term sustainability is a key element of development policy. Botswana has tended to cater to up-market tourists, but in order to expand the market and the variety of the attractions, eco-tourism, in which private investors collaborate with local communities, is being fostered.

Mining

Exploitation of rich mineral reserves, notably diamonds, provided the key to Botswana's rapid economic growth, with the mining sector accounting for up to 50 per cent of GDP and employing 7 per cent of the workforce. Botswana's diamond reserves are expected to last until 2030 at current production rates.

Diamonds, together with copper and nickel production, are the main focus of prospecting activities and account for most of the country's export revenue. Botswana is the largest producer of diamonds, and second-largest producer of gem diamonds, in the world, after Russia. All diamond mining is carried out by De Beers Botswana Mining Company (Debswana), a company jointly owned by the government and UK-based De Beers of South Africa. De Beers produces 60 per cent of the world's diamond output, a significant proportion of which comes from Botswana.

In November 2005 President Mogae proposed that diamonds mined in southern Africa should be sent to Botswana for processing. This would return more of the profits to the producers in the scheme, after value-added cutting and polishing had been included.

Hydrocarbons

Botswana has the largest known coal reserves in Africa: proven reserves are 17 billion tonnes, total reserves are estimated at about 50 billion tonnes, although of low quality. Coal output from the Morupule coal mine, which is mainly used in domestic power stations, has increased to around 900,000 tonnes.

There are no known domestic oil reserves; all refined petroleum products are sourced via South Africa.

Energy

Total installed electricity generating capacity (all thermal) is 220MW. Consumption per capita is estimated at 874kWh; only 22 per cent of the population have access to electricity. Electricity prices are the highest in Southern Africa and consequently demand is falling. There is potential for hydroelectric generation and solar power. Half of total primary energy requirements is met by fuelwood.

Financial markets

Stock exchange

Botswana Stock Exchange (BSE) was launched in 1989 and became a fully-fledged stock market in 1995. The Contributory Funded Pension Scheme was launched in 2000. The BSE is dominated by Barclays and Standard Chartered and is widely seen as a small but vibrant market.

Banking and insurance

Of the established commercial banks, the largest is Barclays Bank of Botswana, which was launched in 1950 and has approximately 42 branches and agencies. It has 19.6 per cent local equity with the rest held by the UK's Barclays Bank. Standard Chartered Bank of Botswana has been operating in the country since 1897 and has 14 branches and four agencies.

Central bank

Bank of Botswana

Main financial centre

Gaborone

Time

GMT plus two hours

Geography

Botswana is a landlocked country in southern Africa, with South Africa to the south and east, Zimbabwe to the north-east and Namibia to the west and north. A short section of the northern frontier adjoins Zambia.

Climate

Sub-tropical, with hot summers and dry winters. Temperatures range from about 5–23 degrees Celsius (C) in July to 18–31 degrees C in January.

Entry requirements

Passports

Required by all. Passports should be valid for at least 12 months.

Visa

Required by all except citizens of North America, Western Europe, Australasia and

Japan, plus transit passengers. All other visitors should confirm requirements from consular sections of local embassy before travelling.

Business visas should be accompanied by letters of invitation.

Currency advice/regulations

Import and export of foreign currency is unlimited, provided it is declared on arrival.

Import of local currency is unlimited but export is restricted to P50. Botswana is not part of the Rand area.

Customs

Member of Southern African Customs Union, therefore virtually no restrictions on movement of goods from South Africa, Namibia, Lesotho and Swaziland.

Health (for visitors)
Mandatory precautions

No compulsory vaccinations required.

Advisable precautions

Hepatitis 'A', 'B' and 'C', tuberculosis, tetanus and typhoid immunisations are advisable. Anti-malarial prophylaxis is necessary for visitors to northern regions. To avoid the risk of bilharzia, only use well maintained, chlorinated swimming pools.

An examination is advisable within 10 days if bitten by insects, while visiting game reserves, in case of sleeping sickness, insect repellent is a necessary precaution.

AIDS infection rates are high throughout the country but particularly in Francistown and Gaborone.

Medical insurance is essential.

Hotels
First-class hotels available in all main towns. Generally advisable to book in advance – essential at weekends and during public holidays.

Credit cards
American Express, Access/MasterCard, Barclaycard/Visa, Diners.

Public holidays
Fixed dates

1–3 Jan (New Year), 1 Jul (Sir Seretse Khama Day), 18–19 Jul (President's Day), 30 Sep–1 Oct (Botswana Day), 25–27 Dec (Christmas Holiday).

Variable dates

Good Friday, Easter Monday, Ascension Day, President's Day (third Tue and Wed in Jul).

Working hours
Banking

Mon–Fri: 0815–1245; Sat: 0815–1045.

Business

Mon–Fri, Apr–Oct: 0800–1300, 1400–1700; Mon–Fri, Oct–Apr: 0730–1630.

Government

Mon–Fri: 0730–1230, 1345–1630.

Shops

Mon–Fri: 0830–1300, 1400–1700; Sat: 0830–1300.

Telecommunications
Telephone/fax

Land lines connect the 12 main towns by microwave links. Botswana is directly connected to South Africa, Zimbabwe, Zambia and Namibia.

Mobile phones

Mascom and Vista Cellular provide CSM 900 network, though coverage is limited to main towns.

Social customs/useful tips
A lightweight or tropical suit should be worn for meetings, casual clothes are acceptable at other times.

Most people rise early in the morning and nightlife is limited.

The noun for the people of Botswana is: singular, Motswana; plural, Batswana.

Getting there
Air

National airline: Air Botswana

International airport/s: The Sir Seretse Khama international airport (GBE) is 15km from Gaborone. Facilities include left luggage, bank, bar, restaurant, post office, shops and car hire.

There are no regular bus services to and from the airport but several hotels run minibuses

Taxis are available to the city centre.

Other airport/s: Francistown (FRW), 6km from city; Maun (MUB), Kasane (BBK) and Selebi-Phikwe (PKW).

Airport tax: There is no airport tax.

Surface

Road: Bitumised roads link Botswana with South Africa in the south, and Zambia and Zimbabwe in the north.

The Trans-Kalahari highway provides a shorter all-tarred road link between Namibia and South Africa's Gauteng province, crossing south-west Botswana, via Kanye and Ghanzi.

Botswanan border posts are at Ngoma Bridge and Shakawe. The road from Namibia, via Shakawe border post, is paved all the way to Maun.

Rail: There are good connections between South Africa and Zimbabwe with Botswana. Passengers are advised to take their own refreshments as the alternatives are limited. There are three classes, and sleeping compartments are available. First-class cars have comfortable reclining seats.

Plans to extend the network include the extension of the line into Namibia, following the construction of the Limpopo line from Zimbabwe to Mozambique.

Water: A car ferry operates across the Zambezi River to Zambia.

Getting about
National transport

Air: Air travel is the best way to get around Botswana.

Regular flights operated by Air Botswana connect Gaborone, Francistown, Maun and Selebi-Pikwe. Air Botswana also provides direct charter flights to other airstrips throughout country.

Road: There are over 13,000km of well-developed roads, of which some 1,900km are tarred and a further 1,000km gravelled. They carry 92 per cent of vehicle traffic. The network of bitumised roads extends along the populated eastern side of the country.

Most major towns are connected by good roads. Travellers to Okavango should note that the road to Maun is tarred, but it is impossible to travel further without use of an overland vehicle.

Buses: Bus services remain underdeveloped. Services between Gaborone and Francistown, going on to Nata and Maun.

Rail: Botswana's railway system consists of 641km of main line plus three branch lines – between Morupule and Palapye, Selebi-Phikwe and Serule, and between Sua Pan and Francistown.

The main Cape Town (South Africa)-Bulawayo (Zimbabwe) railway runs for over 700km through Botswana, linking several towns. This section is operated by Botswana Railways, along with freight-only lines to Selebi-Phikwe and Sua Pan. Botswana Railways has lost a great deal of freight business to road transporters. It has established the Gaborone Container Terminal (Gabcon), a dry port facility acting as a container terminal, specifically for locally based importers and exporters.

City transport

Taxis: Taxis are available in the capital. Tips are not common; if offered, 10 per cent would be acceptable.

Car hire

Foreign or international driving licence is required. Speed limits: 120kph on main roads, 60kph in built-up areas. Seat-belts must be worn. Facilities are available to hire Avis car in South Africa and deposit it in Botswana, or vice versa. Hire cars are only available for driving from Botswana to Zimbabwe or Zambia by special prior arrangement.

BUSINESS DIRECTORY
The addresses listed below are a selection only. While World of Information makes every endeavour to check these addresses, we cannot guarantee that changes have not been made, especially to telephone numbers and area codes. We would welcome any corrections.

Botswana

Telephone area codes
The international direct dialling (IDD) code for Botswana is +267, followed by area code and subscriber's number:

Francistown	24	Jwaneng	588
Gaborone	39	Maun	68
Lobatse	533		

Chambers of Commerce

Botswana Chamber of Commerce and Industry, PO Box 00290, Gaborone (tel: 359-292; fax: 372-467).

Botswana Confederation of Commerce, Industry and Manpower, Boccim House, Old Lobatse Road, PO Box 432, Gaborone (tel: 353-459; fax: 373-142; e-mail: boccim@info.bw).

Francistown Chamber of Commerce and Industry, PO Box 196, Francistown (tel: 241-2149; fax: 241-2175; e-mail: boccim@info.bw).

Banking

Barclays Bank of Botswana, PO Box 478, Barclays House, Plot 8842 Khama Crescent, Gaborone (tel: 352-041; fax: 313-672).

National Development Bank, PO Box 225, Development House, Plot 1123, The Mall, Gaborone (tel: 352-801; fax: 374-446).

Standard Chartered Bank Botswana Ltd, PO Box 496, 5th Floor, Standard House, The Mall, Gaborone (tel: 360-1500, 353-111; fax: 372-933, 353-446).

Central bank
Bank of Botswana, Private Bag 154, 1863 Khama Crescent, Gaborone (tel: 360-6000; fax: 372-984).

Travel information

Air Botswana, Sir Seretse Khama Airport, PO Box 92, Gaborone (tel: 352-812; fax: 374-802).

Botswana National Parks Reservations, Maun (tel: 661-265; fax: 661-264).

Ministry of tourism
Department of Tourism, 2nd Floor, Standard House, Main Mall, Private Bag 0047, Gaborone (tel: 353-024, 313-314; fax: 308-675; e-mail: botswanatourism@gov.bw; internet site: http://www.botswanatourism.org).

Ministries

Ministry of Agriculture, Private Bag 003, Gaborone (tel: 350-500; fax: 356-027).

Ministry of Commerce and Industry, Private Bag 004, Gaborone (tel: 360-1200; fax: 371-539).

Ministry of External Affairs, Private Bag 00368, Gaborone (tel: 360-0700; fax: 313-366).

Ministry of Finance and Development Planning, Private Bag 008, Gaborone (tel: 350-100, 355-272; fax: 356-086).

Ministry of Mineral Resources and Water Affairs, Private Bag 0018, Gaborone (tel: 352-452; fax: 372-733).

Ministry of Works, Transport and Communications, Private Bag 007, Gaborone (tel: 358-500, 355-563, 355-303; fax: 358-500, 313-303).

Office of the President, Private Bag 001, Gaborone (tel: 350-800).

Other useful addresses

Botswana Development Corporation Ltd, Private Bag 160, Gaborone (tel: 351-790; fax: 305-375).

Botswana Diamond Company (Pty) Ltd, Debswana House, The Mall, Gaborone (tel: 351-131; fax; 356-110).

Botswana Enterprise Development Unit (promotes industrial & rural development), PO Box 0014, Gaborone.

Botswana Meat Commission, Private Bag 4, Lobatse (tel: 330-321; fax: 330-530).

Botswana Power Corporation, Motlakase House, Macheng Way, PO Box 48, Gaborone (tel: 360-300; fax: 373-563).

Botswana Telecommunications Corporation, PO Box 700, Gaborone (tel: 358-000).

Botswanan Embassy (USA), Suite 7M, 3400 International Drive, NW, Washington DC 20008 (tel: 202-244-4990; fax: 202-244-4164)

Debswana Diamond Company, Gaborone (tel: 351-131; fax: 356-110).

Department of Geological Survey, Private Bag 14, Lobatse (tel: 330-0327; fax: 332-013).

Department of Information and Broadcasting, Private Bag 0060, Gaborone (tel: 365-8000, 365-3081; fax: 357-138, 301-675; e-mail: ib.publicity@info.bw).

Department of Mines, Private Bag 0049, Gaborone (tel: 352-641; fax: 352-141).

Department of Trade and Investment Promotion (TIPA), Private Bag 004, Gaborone (tel: 351-790; fax: 305-375).

Stockbrokers Botswana Ltd, Ground Floor, Barclays House, Khama Crescent, Post Bag 00417, Gaborone (tel: 357-900; fax: 357-901).

Water Utilities Corporation, Private Bag 00276, Gaborone (tel: 352-521).

Internet sites

Africa Business Network: http://www.ifc.org/abn

AllAfrica.com: http://www.allafrica.com

African Development Bank: http://www.afdb.org

Africa Online: http://www.africaonline.com

Harambee Afrika (UK business club for traders with east, central and southern Africa; includes annotated web resource list): http://www.harambee.co.uk

Mbendi AfroPaedia (information on companies, countries, industries and stock exchanges in Africa): http://mbendi.co.za

Brazil

KEY FACTS

Official name: Republica Federativa do Brasil (Federative Republic of Brazil)

Head of State: President Luiz Inácio da Silva ('Lula') (PT) (sworn in 1 Jan 2003)

Head of government: President Luiz Inácio da Silva

Ruling party: Coalition government led by the Partido dos Trabalhadores (PT) (Workers' Party)

Area: 8,511,965 square km

Population: 181.20 million (2004)

Capital: Brasília

Official language: Portuguese

Currency: Real (R$) (plural reais)

Exchange rate: R$2.22 per US$ (Oct 2005)

GDP per capita: US$3,417 (2004)

GDP real growth: 5.20% (2004); 3.3% (2005)

Labour force: 83.34 million (2004)

Unemployment: 11.50% (2004)

Inflation: 6.60% (2004)

Oil production: 1.54 million bpd (2004)

Balance of trade: US$33.69 billion (2004)

Foreign debt: US$219.80 billion (2004)

Annual FDI: US$18.17 billion (2004)

Following the Brazilian economy's renaissance year of 2004, when the highest real GDP growth rate for ten years was recorded, the country's economy has consolidated in 2005. However, ever since allegations of malpractice were first connected to officials within the governing Partido dos Trabalhadores (PT) (Workers' Party) business and consumer confidence have declined and prospects for growth, have, in turn, fallen. Taking the year as a whole, the IMF has forecast growth of 3.3 per cent for 2005. Despite the degree of uncertainty created by allegations of corruption, a great deal of progress has been made in terms of fiscal consolidation. Monetary policy, by and large, continues to be implemented with the long-term in mind. Persistently strong export performance, courtesy of a boom in agricultural commodities sold on foreign markets, has resulted in a transformation of the country's level of external debt. The economy would now appear to be well on the road to an established recovery. Fulfillment of Brazil's considerable potential for economic growth will depend heavily on the maintenance of a continued prudent macroeconomic policy as well as the internal political situation in the economy.

Lula's third year

President Luiz Inácio 'Lula' da Silva's third year in power was most notable for his PT party's alleged involvement in the so-called *mensalão* scandal; *mensalão* denotes the 'big monthly' payoffs supposedly made using public funds to members of Congress voting with the government. The allegations led to three official inquiries, the dismissal of one of the cabinet's most prominent members, five resignations and two expulsions from Congress and the substitution of the higher echelon of PT with new members. The allegations of corruption first surfaced when a member of the postal service was filmed taking a bribe and the scandal is set to run into 2006, as two of the aforementioned parliamentary inquiries are ongoing and not due to report until March 2006.

Legislative logjam

Many months of allegations, claims and counter claims concerning *mensalão* have dominated the political cycle. But Lula and his allies have also struggled with opposition to their reform agenda from within the 'big tent' governing coalition. In February, PT suffered a humiliating defeat when it lost the leadership of the lower house. The new lower house president, Severino Cavalcanti, whose Partido Progessista (PP) (Progressive Party) is a coalition member, was outspoken in his criticism of the government's draft bills, referring to finance minister Antonio Palocci as an 'insensitive technocrat'.

Cavalcanti's jibes were quickly followed by demands from other coalition member parties. The Partido do Movimento Democrático Brasileiro (PMDB) (Democratic Movement Party), the Partido Trabalhista Brasileiro (PTB) (Brazilian Labour Party) and the Partido Liberal (PL) (Liberal Party) all attempted to hold PT to ransom, demanding that they be provided with ministerial posts in exchange for continued support. The concentration of cabinet posts in PT is a festering sore for other allied parties, who cite the fact that PT only holds 24 per cent of the seats in the lower house of Congress yet retains 70 per cent of cabinet posts. The government suffered a significant defeat when its tax reform bill, despite the granting of significant concessions to opponents, was rejected by Congress in April. The third defeat of the year for the government came when Congress rejected Lula's nominee to head the budget watchdog. Insult was added to injury when the government was defeated for a fourth time, over a flagship minimum salary bill.

News of the *mensalão* allegations broke early in the summer and exercised a further brake on the government's legislative agenda. The scandal is a reminder of the infestation of corruption in Brazilian public life which, according to the *Financial Times* of London, is a 'fact of daily life and the chances of being punished for it are close to zero'. The funding scandal plunged Brazil into its deepest political crisis since Lula was elected in 2002. The secretary general of PT was forced to resign in July and later in the same month opposition parties filed a lawsuit against PT. The party's president and treasurer were also eventually forced out.

The fightback

Broad coverage of the official hearings on television and in the print media increased the government's woes. But the president rejected an opposition proposal that he give up his right to re-election in 2006 – thereby making himself a lame duck – in order to diffuse the issue, confidently asserting that '…they (the opposition) will have to stomach me again because the Brazilian people want it'. Despite the negative publicity attracted to PT by the ongoing saga, the Brazilian president seems not to have lost his teflon touch, as Lula's approval rating actually rose 2.5 percentage points to 59.9 per cent at one point. Whether Brazilians' look quite so fondly on the man once popularly known as 'the saviour' when elections roll round in October 2006 is another matter however. Lula and PT ran on something of an ethically pure platform in 2002 and this strategy may come back to haunt the governing party in light of *mensalão* and other related issues.

After the damaging testimony of his former campaign manager during a Congressional hearing, Lula used a nationally televised address to rebut allegations of improper conduct on his part. 'I am not ashamed to say that we have to apologise', he said before continuing 'I want to tell you not to lose hope… I know you are angry. I certainly am as angry as any Brazilian or more'. Though he pointedly stated that he felt 'betrayed by unacceptable practices that I never knew about'. The president's fight back was genuinely launched though, when yet another scandal ended the career of Severino Cavalcanti, his staunch opponent as leader of the lower house of representatives. Cavalcanti's resignation allowed Lula to nominate his preferred candidate, who was promptly installed as lower house leader. Lula's favoured candidate was also selected by members of PT to be party president, constituting a further important victory.

Stalemate once more

Despite these two important victories, the government struggled to assert its authority. Eye-catching tax legislation, offering US$1.6 billion in tax breaks to boost exports and investment, was abandoned because the amendments made to it by legislators had increased the bill's cost by almost one hundred per cent. This humiliating climb down was quickly followed by an outbreak of foot and mouth disease, which Lula attempted to blame on the individual farmer responsible for the

KEY INDICATORS — Brazil

	Unit	2000	2001	2002	2003	2004
Population	m	170.12	172.40	174.50	177.82	181.20
Gross domestic product (GDP)	US$bn	624.20	502.40	463.90	492.30	*604.86
GDP per capita	US$	3,762	2,987	2,722	2,774	3,417
GDP real growth	%	4.4	1.5	1.5	0.5	5.2
Inflation	%	7.0	7.7	12.5	*11.0	6.6
Unemployment	%	7.1	6.9	7.4	11.4	11.5
Oil output	'000 bpd	1,268.0	1,337.0	1,500.0	1,552.0	1,542.0
Natural gas output	bn cum	7.7	7.7	9.1	10.1	11.1
Coal output	mtoe	3.2	2.1	2.2	1.9	1.6
Exports (fob) (goods)	US$m	55,087.0	58,224.0	58,000.0	73,084.0	96,475.0
Imports (fob) (goods)	US$m	55,783.0	55,579.0	46,000.0	48,260.0	62,782.0
Balance of trade	US$m	-696.0	2,645.0	13,100.0	24,824.0	33,693.0
Current account	US$m	-24,632.0	-23,208.0	-10,000.0	2,700.0	11,670.0
Foreign debt	US$bn	236.2	226.1	226.4	233.7	19.8
Total reserves minus gold	US$m	33,011.0	35,740.0	37,684.0	49,111.0	52,740.0
Foreign exchange	US$m	32,488.0	35,729.0	37,409.0	49,108.0	52,736.0
Exchange rate	per US$	1.83	2.36	2.38	3.18	2.92

* estimated figure

original outbreak. The government's most vocal critics were quick to highlight what they viewed as poor management on the part of the authorities, citing a sizeable reduction in public spending on animal sanitation since 2002.

Poor central management and a general lack of preparedness were also cited when flooding in the Amazon region left some 30,000 families without transport or food. Later in October, a referendum banning the sale of firearms and ammunition that had been promoted by the government as part of its war on gun crime, was comprehensively defeated. PT then became further impaled by the *mensalão* scandal as a Congressional hearing unearthed even greater wrongdoing at the very heart of the party. Lula's former chief of staff, José Dirceu, was expelled from Congress and high profile finance minister Antonio Palocci came under attack for his alleged involvement in the affair.

Domestic growth

Brazil recorded its highest real GDP growth for ten years in 2004 and the country has received glowing reviews from institutions such as the Organisation for Economic Cooperation and Development (OECD), commending its 'prudent policy stance'. Brazil's export performance has also been strong which in turn has strengthened the economy's resilience to external shocks. However, growth slowed in 2005, down to 3.3 per cent from 5.2 per cent in 2004. A general consolidation of economic activity after twelve months of robust growth in addition to a decline in business and consumer confidence following repeated allegations of corruption in Brazilian public life, resulted in an inevitable deceleration. Over recent months investors have taken flight and at one point in June the São Paulo Stock Exchange fell by over 4 per cent while the real fell more than 1 per cent against the US dollar.

Foreign trade: agriculture to the fore

Over recent years Brazil's exports, especially agricultural products, have performed strongly. According to the Food and Agriculture Organisation, Brazil is second only to the EU-15 and the United States in the international league of agri-business exporters, selling approximately US$6.2 billion on to world markets each year. Brazil has risen to become something of an 'agricultural superpower' and the national government has clearly stated its intention to improve transport infrastructure by investing US$408 million in a comprehensive revamp of the national railway, in order to increase accessibility for exports. In April 2005, Brazil registered its largest ever monthly trade surplus, which was largely attributable to the sale of agricultural exports on international markets, with exports constituting US$3.8 billion more in goods and services than imports during the month. In September this record was beaten once again, as April's figure was eclipsed.

Despite the overall success of Brazil's agricultural exports, the country's soya-farmers have been hit hard by a decline in demand in recent years and this trend continued in 2005. Exports of steel have also tailed off as global demand for the metal has decreased. Toward the end of 2005, Brazil's cattle farmers were dealt a considerable blow as the national government confirmed an outbreak of foot and mouth disease. Consequently, the country's cattle exports decreased significantly in the final weeks of 2005 as sizeable herds were culled in the cattle farming region bordering Paraguay. Brazil's successful citrus growers were also faced with negative news in the form of the US government's decision to impose import duties on citrus products. In November, at the Summit of the Americas, US President George W Bush and President da Silva presented a united front, but divisions remain over international trade issues and the Brazilian government has pledged to fight the US import policy.

Macroeconomic policy

The Brazilian Central Bank raised the standard rate of interest to 18.25 per cent during the year and a new annual inflation target of 4.5 per cent, to be met by 2007, was set. Brazil's macroeconomic framework remains in good shape, but the country's prudent economic path needs to be maintained into the future if stability and continued growth are to be achieved. The OECD has listed several requirements for the government to meet during the coming 12 months, such as the need to cut public expenditure, improve the investment climate in the country and revamp welfare spending. Public pronouncements to the contrary by members of the increasingly fragmented governing coalition have placed the continuation of Palocci's hitherto austere approach in doubt. Parties on the left of the 'big tent' centrist coalition have begun to berate the treasury for not increasing public spending in a bid to alleviate the plight of Brazil's poor. A shift to the left on macroeconomic policy cannot be ruled out for as long as the governing coalition remains in a fragile state, reliant as it is on leftist political parties to sustain its existence.

Outlook

The outlook for Brazil's economy remains stable, though the continuation of the country's prudent macroeconomic policy will be dependent on opposition or support from within the increasingly fragile coalition. Economic growth is forecast at somewhere between the 3–4 per cent range, but Brazil's vast potential for economic development is largely dependent on the stability of the political system. If investors are able to view Brazil as a stable country with a minimum of political unrest and corruption scandals then they will continue to place faith in this emerging economic power of the South. Should corruption allegations and Congressional hearings continue to overshadow public life in the country however, economic growth will undoubtedly suffer.

Risk assessment

Economy	Stable
Politics	Poor
Regional stability	Good
Stock market	Stable

COUNTRY PROFILE

Historical profile
1500 First sighted by Portuguese mariner, Pedro Alvares Cabral. The area was claimed by the Portuguese crown.
Sugar cane plantations were started by the Portuguese, with Indian slave labour. The Indians were decimated by disease and the survivors fled to the interior. The Portuguese turned to Africa as another source of slaves.
1807 Portuguese imperial court moved to Brazil after the invasion of Portugal by Napoleon's armies and Brazil became a kingdom within the Portuguese empire. Following Napoleon's retreat, Prince Pedro, the son of João VI, became regent of Brazil.
1822 Brazil gained independence from Portugal and Emperor Pedro became Brazil's first monarch. The immediate post-independence period was marked by minor civil wars, slave rebellions and attempts at secession, with many in the south favouring a republican form of government.
1831 Pedro I abdicated following a period of political turmoil. He was succeeded by his five-year-old son, Pedro II, under a regency.
1840 Emperor Pedro II was granted full powers as monarch at the age of 14,

Brazil

ending the regency period. Although his reign was characterised by stability and a move towards political liberalism, wealth was concentrated in the hands of a small feudal elite while the rest of the population remained illiterate and poor.
1850 Pedro II abolished the slave trade.
1864–70 Brazil, Argentina and Uruguay were at war with Paraguay, ending with Paraguay's defeat and ruination.
1888 Pedro II abolished slavery, leading to a revolt by the country's landed gentry.
1889 The monarchy was overthrown by a revolution led by Manuel Deodoro da Fonseca and the king was sent into exile. A federal republic was established, although ruled in the interest of coffee plantation owners.
1929 Turmoil caused by the Wall Street crash led to a military coup which installed a civilian politician, Gertulio Vargas, as president in 1930.
1937 Vargas assumed dictatorial powers and began a revolution in welfare provision and reformed laws governing industry.
1939–45 Brazil remained neutral in the Second World War, but received a large number of exiled Nazis after the defeat of Germany.
1945 Vargas was ousted in a military coup. Elections were held under a new caretaker government and a new constitution was promulgated.
1951 Vargas was narrowly elected president.
1954 Vargas commited suicide after the military gave him the option of resigning or being overthrown.
1956 Juscelino Kubitschek, a strong democrat, came to power after fresh elections. Construction of the new capital, Brasília, began.
1960 Brasília was declared the country's new capital city.
1964 João Goulart was elected president, but after months of hyperinflation leading to the country's virtual bankruptcy he was overthrown by the military. General Humberto Castello Branco was installed as president, overseeing a period of political repression and economic growth based on state-owned industries.
1974 General Ernesto Geisel became president and introduced reforms which allowed limited political activity and elections.
1982 Brazil defaulted on its foreign debt repayments, which were among the world's biggest.
1985 Tancredo Neves was elected president, but died before his inauguration. His vice-president, José Sarney, was declared president, taking over a country wracked by hyperinflation.
1986 Sarney introduced the Cruzado Plan which froze prices and wages in an effort to control inflation. However, growing public opposition led to the abandonment of the controls thereby maintaining hyperinflation.
1988 A new constitution was promulgated, reducing presidential powers.
1989 Fernando Collor de Mello was elected president. He introduced a radical economic reform, which involved trade liberalisation, privatisation and a controversial freeze on savings and bank accounts. However, this failed to meet expectations, inflation remained high and the country defaulted on its debt repayments.
1992 Earth Summit in Rio. Collor resigned after being accused of corruption, of which he was later cleared. He was replaced by Vice President Itamar Franco.
1994 Fernando Henrique Cardoso won the presidential election.
1997 The constitution was changed to allow presidents to run for a second term in office.
1998 President Cardoso was re-elected.
2000 Brazil's 500th anniversary celebrations were disrupted by protests by indigenous peoples on the issue of land reform and against the legacy of European colonialism, including genocide and the destruction of their cultures.
2001 Corruption scandals rocked the political establishment and a number of senior figures in government and Congress resigned.
2002 Luiz Inácio da Silva (known as Lula), leader of the Partido dos Trabalhadores (PT) (Workers' Party), was elected president.
2003 Lula was sworn in as president on 1 January, heading a broad coalition government, led by the PT. In May, the centrist Partido do Movimento Democratico Brasileiro (PMDB) (Democratic Movement Party) joined the coalition, ensuring a congressional majority to pass social security and tax reforms.
2004 In April, the Moviemento dos Trabalhadores Rurais Sem Terra (MST) (Landless Workers' Movement) launched its biggest wave of farm occupations to force speedier expropriation and redistribution of unused farmland. The campaign was known as Red April. Brazil applied for a permanent seat on the UN Security Council in September. In October, the country launched its first rocket into space.
2005 In March, a death squad carried out a massacre in Rio de Janeiro, killing thirty people. In June, allegations of corruption were made against the ruling Workers' party (PT). President Lula later made a televised apology to the nation, while denying any personal responsibility for illegal actions. In October a referendum was held on a proposal to ban the sale of firearms and a 'no' vote was returned.

Political structure
Constitution
The 1988 constitution is the country's seventh charter since independence from Portugal in 1822. The federal republic consists of 26 states and one federal district (Brasília). Congress passed a constitutional amendment in 1997 allowing Fernando Henrique Cardoso to become the first president to stand for re-election.
Form of state
Federal presidential democratic republic
The executive
Executive power is exercised by the president, aided by ministers of state who are appointed by the president. The president is elected for a four-year term.
The president is also assisted by the Council of the Republic, an advisory body consisting of the vice president of the republic, the presidents of the Chamber of Deputies and the Senate, the leaders of the majority and minority in each house, the minister of justice, and six other members (two appointed by the president of the republic, two elected by the Chamber of Deputies and two elected by the Senate). These six members have a three-year term of office. The national defence council is the president's advisory body on defence matters. It consists of the vice president of the republic, the presidents of the Chamber of Deputies and the Senate, the minister of justice, ministers of the army, navy and air force, and the ministers of foreign affairs and planning.
National legislature
The Congress consists of the Federal Senate (upper house) and the Chamber of Deputies (lower house). The Federal Senate has 81 members, of which two-thirds are directly elected and one-third indirectly elected. Members are elected in rotation for eight years. The Chamber of Deputies has 513 members directly elected on a constituency basis for a period of four years.
All decrees must be submitted to Congress. As well as fiscal and budgetary control, Congress must be consulted on matters concerning payments of external debt. Congressional committees have powers of oversight on nominations to important posts proposed by the executive. The Senate must approve issues of treasury bills. Constitutional amendments must be approved by a three-fifths majority of both the Chamber of Deputies and the Senate.
Legal system
An 11-member Supreme Federal Tribunal is Brazil's highest judicial body. Judges are appointed by the president of the republic and approved by the Senate. It gives

decisions in cases involving the president, vice president, ministers of state, members of Congress, its own members and judges of other courts. It interprets the constitution, judges disputes between the federal and state authorities, between different state authorities, between federal and state authorities and foreign governments, between different levels of the judicial system, and cases involving extradition, *habeas corpus* and *habeas data*.

The Higher Tribunal of Justice is composed of at least 33 members and gives decisions in cases involving state governors. Its members are appointed by the president and approved by the Senate. Regional federal tribunals have at least seven members, who are appointed by the president. The Higher Labour Tribunal is composed of 27 members appointed by the president and approved by the Senate. The Higher Electoral Tribunal includes at least seven judges, three from the Supreme Federal Tribunal, two elected by secret ballot from the Higher Tribunal of Justice and two appointed by the president. The labour and electoral tribunals each have regional counterparts. The Higher Military Tribunal is composed of 15 judges appointed by the president and approved by the Senate for life. Four of its judges are selected from the army, three from the navy and three from the air force. The remaining five are civilians. There is a federal court of appeal. The Federal Audit Court provides for the administrative review of national and state accounts.

Last elections
6 October 2002 (parliamentary); 6/27 October 2002 (presidential).
Results: Presidential: Luiz Inácio da Silva (known as Lula), leader of the Partido dos Trabalhadores (PT) (Workers' Party), was elected president.

Next elections
2006 (presidential and parliamentary)

Political parties
Ruling party
Coalition government led by the Partido dos Trabalhadores (PT) (Workers' Party)
Main opposition party
Partido da Social Democracia Brasileira (PSDB) (Party of Brazilian Social Democracy)

Population
181.20 million (2004)
Ethnic make-up
European (54 per cent), mixed race (39 per cent), black (6 per cent) and Japanese (1 per cent). The major cities in the centre-south area of the country contain substantial communities of Portuguese, Italian, Lebanese and German immigrants. There are an estimated 210 indigenous groups in Amazonia, making up only 0.2 per cent of the total population of Brazil.

Religions
Catholic (90 per cent); Protestant (5 per cent). Brazil is the largest Catholic country in the world. There is freedom of worship and many other religions are represented.

Education
The investment in education amounts to 4.2 per cent of GDP.
State education is free from pre-primary level. Primary education begins at the age of seven and lasts for eight years. Secondary education, which is not compulsory, begins at the age of 15 and lasts for four years.

Primary and secondary education suffer from scarce resources. Although the initial enrolment rate is similar between the rich and the poor, the inequality is evident at later stages. Only 15 per cent of poor children compared to 80 per cent of children from the richest households complete primary school. Inequalities in budget affect enrolment patterns between those prosperous regions and the north-east where over half of rural children receive less than four years of schooling, and one-quarter of the population has had no schooling at all.

Brazil has doubled the number of students reaching their final year in secondary school but has only places for 11 per cent of them. If the country is to compete internationally it will have to increase this amount to at least 40 per cent, to match even its neighbour Argentina.

To combat the problem of lack of opportunity for poorer students in higher education, the president introduced tax concessions, in July 2004, for private universities who reserve at least 20 per cent of their places to black or native Indian students. It is expected that these tax breaks will provided places for up to 100,000 underprivileged students.

Literacy rate: 85 per cent, adult rate (World Bank).
Compulsory years: 7 to 14.
Pupils per teacher: 24 in primary schools.

Health
Total expenditure on health is around 6 per cent of GDP, of which government spending is typically 60 per cent.
In theory, medical, pharmaceutical and dental treatment is free. However, in practice the social health system is underfunded and cannot meet the growing needs of the population. Private health insurance and healthcare facilities are widely available for those who can afford them. The National Social Security and Assistance Institute for Medical Care (INAMPS) is responsible for healthcare.

HIV/Aids
The UNAID/WHO reported that an estimated 105,000 Brazilians were receiving antiretroviral drugs, through the public health system.
HIV prevalence: 0.7 per cent aged 15–49 in 2003 (World Bank)
Life expectancy: 68.7 years (World Bank)
Fertility rate/Maternal mortality rate: 2.1 births per woman (2003); maternal mortality 160 per 100,000 live births (World Bank).
Birth rate/Death rate: 7 deaths to 20 births per 1,000 people respectively.
Infant mortality rate: 33.0 per 1,000 live births; 6 per cent of children aged under five are malnourished (World Bank).
Head of population per physician/bed: 1.3 physicians and 3.1 hospital beds typically available per 1,000 people.

Welfare
Employers pay 20 per cent of the payroll into the Social Insurance Scheme to cover payments for social benefits: pensions, invalidity pensions, sickness pay, family allowances, funeral grants, maternity grants, prisoners' family pensions, widows' pensions and special pensions for workers in dangerous jobs. The state sets aside taxes to cover the costs of collection and administration. Brazil shows a highly unequal distribution of income among households and individuals in both rural and urban economies. Pensions can vary from matching the minimum wage of R$130 to the maximum of R$1,200, dependant of contributions.

The Instituto Nacional de Providencia Social (INPS) (National Social Security Institute), administers the scheme for all workers except military personnel, civil servants and agricultural workers, who are covered by a separate system.

Pensions
The retirement ages for those in urban areas are 70 and 65 for men and women respectively, with 35 years contributions; in rural areas 60 and 55 for men and women respectively, with 30 years contributions.

Main cities
Brasília, (capital, estimated population 2.2 million in 2004), São Paulo (10.3 million), Rio de Janeiro (6.2 million), Salvador (2.6 million), Belo Horizonte (2.4 million), Fortaleza (2.3 million), Curitiba (1.7 million), Manaus (1.7 million), Recife (1.5 million), Belém (1.4 million), Porto Alegre (1.4 million), Goiânia (1.2 million), Guarulhos (1.2 million), Campinas (1.0 million), Nova Iguaçu (1.0 million).

Languages spoken
Many business people and officials speak English. Spanish, Italian, French and

German are also widely spoken, especially in tourist areas. There are nearly 200 indigenous languages.
Official language/s
Portuguese

Media
Press
Dailies: There are around 280 daily newspapers, although there are no national dailies due to the difficulty of distribution in such a large country. There are also hundreds of magazines. Main newspapers include *Notícias Populares, A Tarde, Correio Brazilense, O Dia, Jornal do Brasil, O Globo, Folha de São Paulo* and *Jornal da Tarde. Zero Hora* covers sports, weather and news from the south of Brazil in Portuguese. *O Estado de São Paulo* is one of the largest Brazilian newspapers in Portuguese. *Jornal de Santa Catarina* is a major South Brazilian daily. There are four domestic news agencies, all run by newspapers. They are *Agencia Globo, Agencia Jornal do Brasil, Agencia do Estado de São Paulo* and *Agencia Folha de São Paulo.*
Business: Business publications include *Jornal do Comercio, Valor Economico* and *Gazeta Mercantil.*
Periodicals: Popular magazines published in Portuguese include *Epoca, Isto E* and *Veja. Brazzil* is an English-language magazine covering the Brazilian economy, politics and culture.
Broadcasting
The Ministry of Communications is responsible for radio and television broadcasting, overseen by the state body Empresa Brasileira de Radiodifusão (Radiobras).
Radio: There are about 2,300 radio stations with an estimated 59 million radio receivers. Over 80 per cent of homes have access to radio.
Television: There are about 298 television stations broadcasting to an estimated 52 million television sets. Over 80 per cent of households have access to a television set.
Television is dominated by the powerful Rede Globo network, which claims an average 59 per cent of viewers with a technical standard comparable to the best United States or European stations. It is owned by the Marinho family, whose conservative influence has been notable.

Economy
The Brazilian economy recorded increased growth of 5.2 per cent in 2004. The IMF forecasts real GDP growth of around 3.3 per cent in 2005 and 3.5 per cent in 2006. Despite this steady growth the economy suffered considerably in 2005 from a lack of consumer and business confidence induced by the scandal currently engulfing the governing Workers' party (PT).
Brazil has a diverse economy which is rated the ninth-largest in the world. The industrial base is broad, including the production of aircraft, motor vehicles, armaments and oil refining, while the agricultural sector produces a significant amount of exports, notably coffee and soya. Poverty remains a large problem in Brazil with large income inequalities and almost a third of the country living below the poverty line. Social reform, although occurring, is taking a back seat to the priority of stabilising the macroeconomy and lowering the country's budget deficit.
Since the mid-1990s, Brazil has moved from a policy of import substituting industrialisation and protectionism to one of free markets and liberalisation in a programme known as the 'Plano Real'. This was in response to a number of structural problems in the economy, namely persistent hyperinflation, high levels of external debt, low growth and an inability to adapt to adverse external situations. The government was forced to shift policy again after the Asian financial crisis. The crisis saw the government unable to maintain the overvalued exchange rate, which had become a central part of its efforts to encourage capital inflows and reduce the current account deficit.
Since the financial crisis of 1998 the government has attempted to stabilise the economy and institute policies to initiate recovery, under the auspices of the IMF. In an effort to reduce the debt burden, the government has resorted to cuts in expenditure with a reduction in social spending, freezing of public sector wages and a dramatic decrease in infrastructural investment. Such austere measures have allowed the national government to reduce its debt burden. In December 2005 President da Silva announced the early repayment of the outstanding US$15.5 billion of an original US$33.7 billion IMF loan. The interest rate gap between Brazilian and US Treasury bonds fell to its lowest level in eight years on the back of news of the early repayment. Having controlled inflation relatively well in recent years the central bank cut its target interest rate in October 2005 by half a percentage point, to 19 per cent a year. Credit rating agencies Moody's and Fitch Ratings both upgraded Brazil's sovereign rating in 2005, from B1 to Ba3. Brazil was also voted the most investor friendly emerging market country in December 2005 by the Institute for International Finance (IIF). Most significantly, the country's current account deficit has been transformed in recent years on the back of an export boom, the result of China-led global growth. Net public debt now stands at 50.3 per cent, down from 55.5 per cent in 2002.
However, the electoral funding scandal surrounding the governing party has hindered potential growth. The alleged involvement of President Lula and minister of finance, Antonio Palocci, led to a decline in business confidence. Consequently the economy recorded a contraction of 1.2 per cent in the third quarter of the year, compared with quarter two. The scandal appears to have opened up fault lines within PT over economic policy as prominent cabinet ministers have signalled their displeasure at Palocci's hitherto austere reign, calling for an increase in public expenditure. Fulfillment of Brazil's significant potential for economic growth will depend heavily on the political climate in the country throughout 2006, leading up to presidential elections in October.

External trade
Brazil is a member of the Mercusor trade group, established as a customs union in 1995. Other members include Argentina, Paraguay and Uruguay. Trade spats between Brazil and neighbouring Argentina following the revaluation of the real initially halted efforts to strengthen Mercusor. The South American Continent of Nations (SACN) is now being promoted as a potential free trade bloc modelled on the European Union. The SACN seeks to merge Mercusor and the Andean Pact in future years.
Imports
Principal imports include mineral fuels and products (typically 49 per cent of total), machinery and electrical equipment, chemicals, vegetable products, vehicle products, chemical products.
Main sources: US (22.4 per cent 2002, total), Germany (9.2 per cent), Argentina (8.1 per cent), China (5.5 per cent)
Exports
Principal exports include agricultural products (typically 35 per cent of total), iron ore and steel products, transport equipment, soya, footwear and, coffee.
Main destinations: US (21.2 per cent 2002, total), China (7.8 per cent), Argentina (6.0 per cent), Germany (5.1 per cent), The Netherlands (4.8 per cent)

Agriculture
Farming
Brazil's agricultural sector accounts for 8.8 per cent of total GDP. This figure is no higher than that in comparable countries, but the significance of Brazil's agriculture sector lies in the fact that it has not declined as a percentage of GDP as development has gathered pace. Approximately 60 million hectares of the total land mass is used for agricultural purposes with another 90 million hectares

available for cultivation. Large-scale farming is concentrated in the south and south-east of Brazil.

Brazil has shown remarkable progress in agribusiness development, which includes not just farming production but also increased investment in the sale of farm machinery and processing activities. Brazil's agribusiness offers a diversified range of products from several regions and supplies cost-effective high quality food products. It accounts for over 40 per cent of the country's total exports.

Irrigated fruit growing in the São Francisco River and the Açu River Valleys, both located in north-eastern part of Brazil has contributed to its prosperous agribusiness sector.

Major agricultural exports include coffee (the world's largest producer and exporter), sugar cane (world's largest producer) and soya beans (world's second-largest producer after US). Orange juice (supplies 85 per cent of world market for orange juice concentrates), tobacco, cocoa, cotton, butter, maize and cattle (around 10 per cent of total world trade) are also significant.

Though agriculture has performed well in recent years, the sector's growth potential continues to be held back by poor transport infrastructure. Only 10 per cent of Brazil's roads are paved.

Crop production in 2004 included 20,591,000 tonnes (t) cereals in total, 41,863,756t maize, 13,251,200t rice, 24,038,888t cassava, 2,891,530t potatoes, 5,962,604t wheat, 2,138,754t sorghum, 10,039,641t oilcrops, 6,602,750t bananas, 410,983,008t sugar cane, 3,419,664t tomatoes, 2,973,700t coconuts, 1,650,000t papayas, 20,594,000t citrus fruit, 2,475,780t green coffee, 1,278,885t grapes, 27,660,418t roots and tubers, 49,205,384t soya beans, 1,435,190t pineapples, 928,338t tobacco, 169,416t cocoa beans, 3,017,560t pulses, 211,757t cashew nuts, 28,500t Brazil nuts, 64,540t pepper spice, 97,000 natural rubber, 3,621,860t seed cotton, 1,195,500t cotton lint, 192,395t sisal, 35,996,238t fruit in total, 7,682,018t vegetables in total. Livestock production included 19,919,135t meat in total, 7,774,000t beef, 3,110,000t pig meat, 116,500t lamb and goat meat, 8,895,410t poultry, 1,619,500t eggs, 23,455,000t milk, 24,500t honey, 11,000t cocoons, silk, 792,000t cattle hides.

Fishing
Brazil has a coastline of 8,500km, 12 per cent of the world's freshwater reserves and two million hectares of flooded land. The country is yet to fulfill its vast potential for marine and freshwater fishing despite efforts by the national government to promote fish as an export commodity. Brazil's annual catch is typically in the range of 980,000 metric tonnes (mt) including 505,957mt marine fish and 117,863mt shellfish.

Forestry
Brazil has vast forest areas; some 543.9 million hectares with the humid tropical areas of the Amazon forests in the north-west of the country accounting for 95 per cent of the total forested area. There are approximately five million hectares of forest plantations, the majority of which are pine and eucalyptus. However, vast areas of protected woodland land exist; 30 million hectares inclusive of state parks and national reserves.

Timber production in 2003 included 235,536,476 cubic metres (cum) roundwood, 102,994,000cum industrial roundwood, 21,200,000cum sawnwood, 45,861,000cum pulpwood, 49,290,000cum sawlogs & veneer logs, 6,283,000cum wood-based panels, 163,000t newsprint, 2,272,000t printing and writing paper, 13,542,476cum wood fuel, 873,000t recovered paper, 12,679,630t charcoal.

Industry and manufacturing
Brazil's industrial sector is one of the most well developed in Latin America. Manufacturing contributes over 23 per cent to annual GDP and industrial goods account for up to 60 per cent of exports. Industry as a whole accounts for approximately 29 per cent of GDP and employs 20 per cent of the labour force.

Industry has relied primarily on imports of capital and intermediary goods, which are either higher quality or cheaper than domestically produced goods. This has caused balance of payments problems and depressed some sectors of industry, such as machine tools. In a drive to replace imports with domestically produced goods, the government has encouraged multinational investment in key sectors of industry. Problems arose in the pharmaceutical, biotechnology and computer industries when the government's desire for self-sufficiency caused it to ignore foreign patent rights and the payment of royalties.

Tourism
The Brazilian travel and tourism industry has developed massively in recent years and is expected to contribute US$55.1 billion of economic activity in 2005. The tourism industry accounts for 7 per cent of total employment and 7.2 per cent of the country's total GDP.

The September 2001 terrorist attacks in the US and domestic uncertainties at the beginning of the decade had severe consequences on the industry, visitor arrivals falling from a record 5,313,463 in 2000 to 3,783,400 in 2002. The government began a shake-up of the sector's administration in 2003. The tourism authority, Embratur, was redefined as an agency to market Brazil abroad and the Ministry of Tourism was established.

Investment in infrastructure and services, particularly in the north-eastern coastal area, is being pursued through the government's Tourism Development Programme (PRODETUR). Cultural and eco-tourism are being developed. Brazil has long been a destination for the world's backpackers and continues to be immensely popular at the budget end of the market.

The Brazilian airline industry underwent upheaval in 2004, with the Department of Civil Aviation (DAC) introducing a new policy of fare control, whereby the government banned the sale of airfares it considered to be too low. Despite the new DAC regulations Brazil's first budget airline GOL, established in 2001, had a very profitable year.

Embratur, the Brazilian Institute of Tourism, has launched its largest ever promotional programme, which aims to make Brazil one of the top twenty most-visited destinations by 2007. Embratur has targeted the US, EU countries and China in a bid to attract greater numbers of visitors in the future.

Environment
Environmentalists have been concerned over the rate of destruction of the Brazilian rain forest. A major problem is illegal logging and many logging firms have falsified land titles with the help of corrupt officials to claim land.

In August 2002, the Global Environment Facility (GEF) provided US$30 million to fund the implementation of the Amazon Region Protected Areas Project. The total cost of the project, which is co-financed by the Brazilian government, the World Wildlife Fund (WWF) and the KfW development bank in Germany, is US$81.5 million.

Mining
Brazil is a major mining nation, ranking twelve in the world gold production league (second in Latin America) with an annual output of 55 million tonnes. Forty tonnes is accounted for by formal mines and the remainder is generated by alluvial operations which are worked by prospectors.

The mineral potential of Brazil has not been fully assessed. Less than one-third of the country has been thoroughly prospected. The authorities are keen to exploit the country's raw material wealth and a comprehensive aerial survey has been completed by the government's National Mineral Resources Company (CPRM).

The centre of the mining industry is the state of Minas Gerais, named after the large number of gold and precious stone mines discovered in colonial times. Minas Gerais is also Brazil's main producer of mica, beryl, talc, marble, dolomite, graphite, zirconium, bauxite and nickel. There are also large known reserves of minerals scattered throughout the country with concentrations in the state of Rio Grande do Sul (copper, lead, zinc and wolfram), Bahia (lead, barite, quartz crystal and magnesite), Amapa (manganese) and São Paulo (lead, wolfram and zinc). Brazil ranks as the world leader in production and reserves of niobium/colombium and as the world's top producer of tantalite (28 per cent of total world output). It is the second largest producer of iron ore, third largest producer of bauxite and fourth largest producer of tin. The Carajas mineral deposit contains most of these reserves.

Brazil has vast iron ore reserves, reportedly the world's sixth largest in volume, and is one of the world's leading iron ore exporters. Iron ore is produced from the Quadrilateral area of Minas Gerais in the south-east and the Carajas region in Southern Para. The privatised Companhia Vale do Rio Doce (CVRD), which operates the Carajas deposit with 67 per cent iron metal content, is one of the world's top iron ore exporters.

Brazil is also an important gold producer. Gold production has been decentralised and the market has become more accessible. Minas Gerais is Brazil's main gold producing area, accounting for 45 per cent of the sector's total exports.

Copper has been mined from two sources, the state-owned Caraiba Metals in Bahia and a small mine in Rio Grande do Sul. Production at these two sites is uneconomic. CVRD expects to initiate production from Salobo in the Carajas complex.

Hydrocarbons

Brazil is the third-largest oil producer in Latin America. Due to intensified oil exploration and development, particularly in the offshore Campos basin, and falling domestic consumption, the government is working to become self-sufficient in oil by 2006. Total proven oil reserves were 11.2 billion (as at end 2004), total oil reserves and production totalled 1.5 million barrels per day (bpd). However, with consumption estimated at 1.8 million bpd in the same year, Brazil is a net importer of oil. Much of this is crude, imported from Venezuela and Argentina. Brazil's oil refining capacity, with 13 refineries, was estimated at 1.94 million bpd in 2004. Natural gas reserves totalled 330 billion cubic metres (cum), (2004). The country's largest gas fields are located in the Campos and Santos basins with Petrobrás dominating the natural gas market. Gas production was 11.1cum (2004), which satisfies about 95 per cent of Brazil's annual consumption. However as demand for natural gas is growing there is an increasing need for new pipelines.

There are two international pipelines running into Brazil from Bolivia and Argentina. Other pipelines are planned, mainly from Argentina, including the extension of the Cruz del Sur, which runs from Argentina to Uruguay. There are strong possibilities that new pipelines will be built connecting newly discovered gas fields in Bolivia. There is also a likelihood of pipelines from Venezuelan gas fields as well as Liquefied Natural Gas (LNG) imports from Trinidad and Tobago.

At 10.1 billion tonnes (2004), Brazil has the largest coal reserves in Latin America. However production was 1.6 million tonnes of oil equivalent (toe) and consumption of coal is 11.4 million toe in 2004. This means Brazil relies on imports to meet domestic demand.

Energy

Brazil has installed electric capacity of 82.5GW. Approximately 90 per cent of electricity is generated by hydropower. Brazil and Paraguay jointly run the world's largest hydroelectric complex, Itaipu on the Paraná river, which has a capacity of 12.6GW. Other electricity generation comes from coal and natural gas. The majority of the electricity imported by Brazil comes from Argentina.

Rapid growth in the demand for electricity in the 1990s was not met by similar increases in generating capacity and the country's heavy reliance on hydroelectricity became a liability.

Many blame the government's privatisation programme for the problems of underdevelopment in the energy sector. The sale of plants and transmission lines piecemeal in smaller constituent parts has arguably undermined the ability of the electricity sector to attract sufficient investment. Efforts to reduce the country's debt through expenditure cuts under the auspices of the IMF have also discouraged public investment in the electricity infrastructure. Large profits from the state-owned electricity company, Eletrobrás, have not been ploughed back into capital investment, but instead have gone towards maintaining the government's fiscal accounts in order to satisfy IMF demands. The oil and gas corporation, Petrobrás, was also prevented from investing its profits in the electricity sector, which could have bolstered gas-fired generation and helped Brazil off dependency on hydroelectricity.

Conventional thermal plants generate only 7.4 per cent of Brazil's total electricity. President Lula has expressed his administration's desire to expand hydroelectric power plants and thus the future of conventional thermal generation is unclear

Brazil has two nuclear power plants, both of which are operated by a subsidiary of Electrobras, Electronuclear. The construction of the country's third nuclear facility, Angra-3 has been slowed by political disagreements and a shortfall of funds. A final decision on the completion of the plant is expected from the Brazilian government in early 2006.

Financial markets
Stock exchange
Brazil has major stock exchanges in São Paulo and Rio de Janeiro and smaller bourses in seven other cities. The Bolsa de Valores de São Paulo (Bovespa) has usually accounted for about 60 per cent of all transactions. Together, the two major exchanges account for 90 per cent of total transactions. They both have computerised operations.

Banking and insurance
The government of President Lula da Silva, signalled its more cautious approach to bank privatisation, with the cancellation of the sale of a 17.8 per cent stake in Banco do Brasil, Latin America's largest retail bank. Less than a quarter of the banking industry in Brazil is owed by foreign institutions. The major market operators are domestic finance houses.
Central bank
Banco Central do Brasil
Main financial centre
Rio de Janeiro and São Paulo

Time
São Paulo, Rio de Janeiro and Brasília are GMT -3hrs. Of the other major cities, Manaus, Campo Grande and Corumba are GMT -4hrs. Some parts of the extreme west of Brazil are GMT -5hrs. In recent years, the government has introduced daylight-saving time from late Oct to late Feb and, during this period, clocks run one hour ahead of normal Brazilian time, making the time difference in Rio de Janeiro, for instance, GMT -2hrs.

Geography
Brazil borders all South American countries except Chile and Ecuador. The distance from north to south is 5,320km, and from east to west 4,328km. Brazil has a land frontier of 15,719km and an Atlantic coastline of 7,408km.

Although Brazil's topography varies greatly, it can be divided roughly into five zones: the Amazon basin, the River Plate basin, the Guiana highlands, the Brazilian highlands and the coastal strip.

Nations of the World: A Political, Economic and Business Handbook

The densely forested Amazon basin covers some 40 per cent of Brazil's territory but has only one inhabitant per square km. It receives heavy rainfall and floods annually.

The River Plate basin in southern Brazil is less heavily forested. The land is higher and the climate cooler. The Guiana highlands, north of the Amazon, are part forest and part scrubland. The Brazilian highlands, lying between the Amazon and the River Plate basin, form a tableland from 300 metres to 900 metres high. There are a few mountain ranges, mostly in south-eastern Brazil.

Climate

The average annual temperature increases from south to north. On the equator in the Amazon basin, average temperatures are 27 degrees Celsius (C) with no seasonal variation. From the latitude of the port of Recife to the border with Uruguay, the average temperature range is 17–19 degrees C. The two winter months in the south are June and July. Humidity is relatively high in Brazil, particularly in the Amazon basin and on the coast. The rainy seasons are January–April in the north, April–July in the north-east and November–March in the southern coastal area.

Dress codes

Suits are normally worn to business meetings, particularly in Brasília. They are also worn for formal social events and in exclusive restaurants and clubs. For other occasions smart casual clothes are suitable. Lightweight clothing is advisable for all seasons in the north and for all but the two winter months in the south, when warmer clothing is necessary. Rainproof clothing or umbrellas are necessary during the rainy seasons.

Entry requirements

Passports
Required by all.
Visa
Required by all, except most citizens of Europe and South America (both tourist and business visits). The application for a temporary visa type II, for business purposes, can be found online, or supplied by local consular sections of Brazilian embassies, plus a list of those nationals who are exempt from visas. When submitting, the application should include a letter from the applicant's employer, stating visit, giving guarantees, the contacts to be maintained by the applicant, and signed by an authorised, senior staff member. A certificate of vaccination against yellow fever, (if arriving from an infected country), should also be included.

Currency advice/regulations
There is no restriction on the import and export of local currency. Foreign currency import is unlimited but amounts must be declared; export of foreign currency is allowed up to amount declared on arrival. Regulations may change at short notice. International credit cards are widely used, though cash advances are only paid in local currency.

Health (for visitors)

Mandatory precautions
A yellow fever certificate not more than 10 years old is compulsory for travellers who within the last three months before arrival in Brazil have been in any of the following countries: Angola, Bolivia, Cameroon, Colombia, Democratic Republic of Congo, Ecuador, Gambia, Guinea Republic, Mali, Nigeria, Peru and Sudan.

Advisable precautions
Yellow fever vaccinations are essential for visits to infected areas within Brazil; these include Mato Grosso, Rondônia and states surrounding the Amazon. Typhoid/paratyphoid, hepatitis, tetanus and polio vaccinations are also recommended. Malaria prophylaxis is advisable for visits to Amazon regions. The World Health Organisation warned of a high risk of catching dengue fever. Water precautions should be taken.

Hotels

Graded from one- to five-stars. Wide range available in main towns but sometimes heavily booked (especially during Carnival) and advance booking advisable. Listings available from local tourist offices. Only five-star hotels are not price controlled.
A service charge is usually included in bill; if not, a 10 per cent tip is usual.

Credit cards

Amex, Diners, Mastercard and Visa widely accepted for purchases other than fuel.

Public holidays

Fixed dates
1 Jan (New Year's Day), 21 Apr (Tiradentes Day), 1 May (Labour Day), 7 Sep (Independence Day), 12 Oct (Our Lady Aparecida, Patroness of Brazil), 2 Nov (All Souls' Day), 15 Nov (Proclamation of the Republic), 25 Dec (Christmas Day).
Variable dates
Carnival (five days, Feb), Good Friday, Corpus Christi (May/Jun).

Working hours

In Rio de Janeiro and São Paulo there is no siesta break; in Brasília there is a three-hour siesta from 1200–1500.
Banking
Mon–Fri: 1000–1630.
Business
Mon–Fri: 0900–1200; 1400–1800.
Government
Mon–Fri: 0930–1800.
Shops
Mon–Fri: 0900–1830/1900, Sat: 0900–1300. Shopping centres Mon–Sat: 0900–2200.

Telecommunications

Mobile phones
GSM 900 and 1800 services available in most regions of the country.

Electricity supply

127V AC (Bahia (Salvador) and Manaus); 220V AC, 60Hz (Brasília and Recife); 110/220V AC, 60Hz (Rio de Janeiro and São Paulo).
Most hotels provide 100V and 220V outlets, transformers and adaptors.

Social customs/useful tips

There is generally a relaxed attitude towards timekeeping in Rio de Janeiro and the north-east, but people are much more punctual in São Paulo and Brasília. It is the usual practice to shake hands in greeting and on departure. When invited to someone's home for a meal, a gift of flowers for the hostess is customary.

Security

The Brazilian authorities insist on extensive personal documentation. This should be carried at all times.
Brazil's big coastal cities, particularly Rio de Janeiro and those situated in the north-east, have serious crime problems. Street robberies are common and press estimates put the number of armed assaults on bus passengers in Rio alone at about 20 per day.
First-time visitors to Rio are advised to be extremely cautious in allowing strangers to engage them in conversation, especially in areas such as the Avenida Atlantica (the Copacabana sea-front) and the western suburbs. It is inadvisable to visit the Baixada Fluminense, where a murder rate of 20 deaths per day makes the district one of the most violent areas in the world.

Getting there

Air
National airline: VARIG (Viação Aérea Rio Grandense).
International airport/s: The capital city's airport is Brasilia-International (BSB), 11km from centre, with duty-free shop, bar, restaurant, buffet, bank, post office, shops, hotel reservations, car hire.
Other airport/s: Rio de Janeiro (RIO), 12km north of city, bar, hotel, taxi, duty-free shop, restaurant; International Galeão (GIG), and São Paulo-Cumbica (GRU) 25km north-east of the city, Recife, Fortaleza, Salvador-Dois de Julho (SSA),

Brazil

Belem-Val de Cans (BEL), 12km from city; Belo Horizonte-Pampulha (BHZ).
Airport tax: Adult international departures US$36; domestic amounts change on a daily basis; not applicable to transit passengers and infants under two years.

Surface
Road: It is possible to reach Brazil by road from Argentina, Bolivia, Paraguay and Uruguay.
Rail: There are rail connections to Argentina and Uruguay.
Water: There are boats sailing along the Rio Paraguay between Asunción in Paraguay and Corumba. There are also boat services to Peru along the Amazon.

Getting about
When travelling between cities on public transport, visitors must carry passports as proof of identity is required.

National transport
Air: Regular domestic and charter flights to all main cities. Main form of long-distance travel. Air taxis available at most domestic airports. Advance booking not necessary for shuttle flights between Rio de Janeiro and São Paulo (about one hour). Main internal airlines are VARIG, Cruzeiro, Transbrasil and VASP. Domestic flights are expensive, although safety and quality of service are good.
Road: All main centres are connected by surfaced highways, with particularly good roads in the north. Many of the local roads are in need of urgent repair. In total, around 1.6 million km of roads are supervised by the Departmento Nacional de Estradas de Rodagem (DNER).
Buses: Buses are the most popular means of transport with frequent inter-city bus services between main centres. Standards are variable although many routes are now served by modern high quality coaches. Sleeping berths (leito) are available on some routes.
Rail: State- and privately-owned railways operate limited services to most main centres throughout the country. Service is generally slower than bus and long distance travelling can be uncomfortable. Good sleeper services with restaurant cars operate between São Paulo, Rio de Janeiro and Belo Horizonte.
Water: Services on São Francisco River between Juazeiro and Pirapora and up the Amazon to Manaus. Hydrofoil service between Rio de Janeiro and Niteroi.

City transport
Taxis: Metered taxis, identified by their roof lights, are available almost everywhere in urban areas. They are inexpensive and often rudimentary. The fare is regularly adjusted according to a table posted on the inside of a rear window. In Rio de Janeiro, there are several types; these include so-called 'common' taxis (yellow with checkered stripe) and the more expensive radio taxi (white, with a red and yellow stripe). A 40 per cent surcharge operates between 2300–0600, on Sundays and public holidays. Tipping is optional.
Travellers arriving by plane are advised to use the main taxi companies which operate desks at major airports and run on a fixed-charge basis. Their cars are big and air-conditioned and although rates are more expensive than those officially charged by standard taxis, it is advisable to use them to avoid frequent exploitation of unwary travellers by individual operators.
Buses, trams & metro: Extensive services operate in all main centres. Efficient though crowded. Two types – regular and special (fresces).
Metro: Two-line service in Rio de Janeiro. Line one goes from Botafogo Station to Saenz Peña Station (Tijuca): Mon–Sat: 0600–2300. Line two cuts across the city's centre, from Estácio Station to the Maria de Graca Station: Mon–Sat: 0600–2000. There is also a two-line network in São Paulo.
Integrated bus/metro tickets available.

Car hire
Car hire is expensive and involves a frustratingly bureaucratic process.
An international driving licence is required, which must be validated by Automovil Club do Brasil. Traffic is often congested in main cities. Petrol is of poor quality and expensive.
Service stations are rare on some roads and often close on Sundays.

BUSINESS DIRECTORY
The addresses listed below are a selection only. While World of Information makes every endeavour to check these addresses, we cannot guarantee that changes have not been made, especially to telephone numbers and area codes. We would welcome any corrections.

Telephone area codes
The international dialling code (IDD) for Brazil is +55 followed by the area code:

Belem	91	Porto Alegre	51
Belo Horizonte	31	Recife	81
Brasilia	61	Rio de Janeiro	21
Campinas	19	Salvador	71
Curitiba	41	Santos	132
Fortaleza	81	São Paulo	11
Manaus	92		

Chambers of Commerce
American Chamber of Commerce in Brazil (Rio de Janeiro), Praça Pio X 15, 20040-020 Rio de Janeiro (tel: 2203-2477; fax: 2223-0438; e-mail: achambr@amchamrio.com.br).

American Chamber of Commerce in Brazil (São Paulo), Rua da Paz 1431, Chácara Santo Antônio, 04713-001 São Paulo (tel: 5180-3804; fax: 5180-3777; e-mail: amhost@amcham.com.br).

Brazilian International Chamber of Commerce, 1.200 Rua Timbiras, 30140-060 Belo Horizonte (tel/fax: 3273-7021; e-mail: camint@camint.com.br).

British Chamber of Commerce in Brazil (Rio de Janeiro), Avenida Graça Aranha 1, Centro, 20030-002, Rio de Janeiro (tel: 2262-5926; fax: 2240-1058; e-mail: rio@britcham.com.br).

British Chamber of Commerce in Brazil (São Paulo), Rua Ferreira de Araújo 741, Pinheiros, 05428-002 São Paulo (tel: 3819-0265; fax: 3819-7908; e-mail: britcham@britcham.com.br).

Rio de Janeiro Chamber of Commerce and Industry, Rua da Assembléia 93, Centro, 20011-001 Rio de Janeiro (tel: 2532-0089; fax: 2532-1918; e-mail: chamber@ccirj.com).

São Paulo Associação Comercial, 51 Rua Boa Vista, Centro, 01014-911 São Paulo (tel: 3244-3322; fax: 3244-3355; e-mail: infocem@acsp.com.br).

Banking
Banco America do Sul, Alameda Ribeirão Preto 87, 7 andar, Zona postal 01331, PO Box 8075, São Paulo (tel: 287-7955; fax: 287-2762).

Banco Bandeirantes, Rua Boa Vista 162, 7 andar, Zona postal 01014-902, São Paulo (tel: 823-1122; fax: 239-5959).

Banco Boavista, Familia Paula Machado, Zona postal 20091-040, PO Box 1560, Rio de Janeiro (tel: 211-1711; fax: 253-9036).

Banco Bozano Simonsen, Av Rio Branco 138, Zona postal 20057, PO Box 3074, Rio de Janeiro (tel: 271-8232; fax: 271-8160).

Banco Brasileiro Iraquiano, Praça Pio X 54 Centro, Zona postal 20091, Rio de Janeiro (tel: 253-2020/ 2255; fax: 253-3498).

Banco Chase Manhattan, Rua Alvares Penteado 131, Zona postal 01012, São Paulo (tel: 345-751; fax: 239-0594).

Banco de Credito Nacional, Rua Boa Vista 208, Zona postal 01014-030, PO Box 4222, São Paulo (tel: 235-1079, 235-1118; fax: 356-892).

Banco de la Nación Argentina, Av Paulista 2319, Sobreloja, Zona postal 01311, PO Box 22-25, São Paulo (tel: 280-2674; fax: 881-4630).

Banco de la Provincia de Buenos Aires, Rua L Badaró 425, 26 andar, Zona postal 01009, São Paulo (tel: 258-8798; fax: 257-4557).

Banco de la República Oriental del Uruguay, Av Paulista 1776, 9 andar, Zona postal 01310, São Paulo (tel: 251-2699/ 2454; fax: 289-8245).

Banco de Montreal, Trav do Ouvidor 4, Zona postal 20149, Rio de Janeiro (tel: 270-209/ 0210; fax: 221-2706).

Banco do Estado de São Paulo, Praça Antonio Prado 06, 6 andar, Zona postal 01062-900, PO Box 35565, São Paulo (tel: 259-6622, 259-7722; fax: 348-523).

Banco Exterior de España, Av Paulista 1963, 1 andar, Zona postal 01311, PO Box 51623, São Paulo (tel: 251-4344; fax: 288-8015).

Banco Francés e Brasileiro, Av Paulista 1294, 12 andar, zona postal 01310-915, PO Box 8017, São Paulo (tel: 252-7163/64; fax: 283-0794).

Banco Geral do Comercio, Rua Funchai 160, 5 andar, Zona postal 04551-060, São Paulo (tel: 828-7322; fax: 828-7208).

Banco Mercantil de São Paulo, Av Paulista 1450, 9 andar, Zona postal 01310-917, PO Box 4077, São Paulo (tel: 252-2121/2228; fax: 284-3312).

Banco Mitsubishi Brasileiro, Rua Libero Badaró 6633/641, Zona postal 01009-904, PO Box 8449, São Paulo (tel: 239-5244; fax: 362-128, 362-060).

Banco Noroeste, Rua Alvares Penteado 216, 3 andar, Zona postal 010102, PO Box 8119, São Paulo (tel: 239-0844, 378-401; fax: 354-858).

Banco Real, Av Paulista 1347, 3 andar, Zona postal 01310-916, PO Box 5766, São Paulo (tel: 285-5645, 251-9796; fax: 251-9222).

Banco Region de Desenv do Extremo Sul, Rua Uruguai, 155-4, andar, Porto Alegre (tel: 228-9200; fax: 228-8283).

Banco Safra, Av Paulista 2100, Bela Vista, Zona postal 01310, PO Box 9139, São Paulo (tel: 251-7575; fax: 251-7211).

Banco Sogeral, Av Paulista 1355, 12 andar, Zona postal 01311-924, São Paulo (tel: 251-5533; fax: 283-1449).

Banco Sudameris Brasil, Av Paulista 1000, 14 andar, Zona postal 01310-100, PO Box 3481, São Paulo (tel: 283-9251/9260; fax: 283-9269).

Unibanco-União de Bancos Brasileiros, Av Euzébio Matoso 891, 4 andar, Zona postal 05423-901, PO Box 8185, São Paulo (tel: 817-4322; fax: 815-5084).

Central bank
Banco Central do Brasil, Quadra 03, Bloco B, Edificio do Banco Central do Brasil, PO Box 08670, 70074-900 Brasília DF (tel: 414-2401; fax: 321-9453; e-mail: cap.secre@bcb.gov.br).

Travel information
American Express, Avenida Atlantica 2316, Copacabana, Rio de Janeiro.

EMBRATUR (Empresa Brasileira de Turismo), Rua Mariz e Barros 13, 7-28 andar, 20270 Rio de Janeiro (tel: 273-2212).

Tourist Information Centre, Brata Ribeiro 272, Copacabana, Rio de Janeiro.

VARIG SA, Edif Varig, Avenida Almirante Silvio Noronha 365, 20021 Rio de Janeiro (tel: 272-5000; fax: 272-5700).

Ministry of tourism
Conselho Nacional de Turismo (CNTUR), Ministry of Infrastructure, Rua Mariz e Barros 13, 5 andar, 20270 Rio de Janeiro (tel: 273-0691).

National tourist organisation offices
Centro Brasileiro de Informação Turística (CEBITUR) (Brazilian Tourist Office), Rua Mariz e Barros 13, 6 andar, Praça da Bandeira, 20270-000 Rio de Janeiro (tel: 293-1313; fax: 273-9290).

Ministries
Ministry of Administration, Esplanada dos Ministérios, Bloco C, CEP 70046-900 Brasília-DF (tel: 224-2682; fax: 225-8927).

Ministry of Agrarian Policy, SBN Ed Palácio do Desenvolvimento, CEP 70057-900 Brasilia-DF (tel: 223-8852; fax: 226-8727).

Ministry of Agriculture, Esplanada dos Ministerios, Bloco D, 8 andar, CEO 70043-900 Brasília DF (tel: 226-5161, 226-5380; fax: 225-9046).

Ministry of the Air Force, Esplanada dos Ministérios, Bloco M, CEP 70045-900 Brasília-DF (tel: 321-5303; fax: 223-2592).

Ministry of the Armed Forces, Esplanada dos Ministérios, Bloco Q, CEP 70049-900 Brasília-DF (tel: 223-5356; fax: 321-2477).

Ministry of the Army, QG/EX, Bloco A, SMU, CEP 70630-900 Brasília-DF (tel: 315-5200, 224-2844; fax: 223-1145).

Ministry of Communications, Esplanada dos Ministerios, Bloco R, 80 andar, CEP 70040-900 Brasília DF (tel: 225-9381, 224-9723; fax: 226-3980).

Ministry of Culture, Esplanada dos Ministérios, Bloco B, CEP 70068-900 Brasília-DF (tel: 224-6064; fax: 225-9162).

Ministry of Education, Esplanada dos Ministérios, Bloco L, CEP 70047-900 Brasília-DF (tel: 321-1076; fax: 224-3618).

Ministry of Environment, Water Resources and Amazonia, Esplanada dos Ministérios, Bloco B, CEP 70068-900 Brasília-DF (tel: 322-7819; fax: 226-7101).

Ministry of External Relations, Esplanada dos Ministérios, Palácio do Itamaraty, CEP 70170-900 Brasília-DF (tel: 211-6100; fax: 223-7362).

Ministry of Finance, Esplanada dos Ministérios, Bloco P, CEP 70048-900 Brasília-DF (tel: 314-4805; fax: 322-5009).

Ministry of Health, Esplanada dos Ministérios, Bloco G, CEP 70058-900 Brasília-DF (tel: 224-5269).

Ministry of Industry, Trade and Tourism, Esplanad dos Ministerios, Bloco J, CEP 70056-900 Brasília DF (tel: 325-2001; fax: 325-2209).

Ministry of Institutional Reform, Palácio do Planalto, Praca dos Tres Poderes, CEP 70150-900 Brasília-DF (tel: 322-9619; fax: 211-1192).

Ministry of Justice, Esplanada dos Ministérios, Bloco T, Ed Sede, CEP 70064-900 Brasília-DF (tel: 226-2296; fax: 322-6817).

Ministry of Labour, Esplanada dos Ministérios, Bloco F, CEP 70056-900 Brasília-DF (tel: 226-6137; fax: 226-3577).

Ministry of Mines and Energy, Esplanada dos Ministerios, Bloco U, 70 andar, CEP 70065-900 Brasília DF (tel: 218-5447, 223-9059; fax: 225-5407).

Ministry of the Navy, Esplanada dos Ministerios, Bloco N, 20 andar, CEP 70055-900 Brasília DF (tel: 223-6858, 312-1000; fax: 312-1202).

Ministry of Planning and Budget, Esplanada dos Ministérios, Bloco K, CEP 70048-900 Brasília-DF (tel: 224-0679; fax: 225-4032).

Ministry of Science and Technology, Esplanada dos Ministérios, Bloco E, CEP 70067-900 Brasília-DF (tel: 224-4364; fax: 225-1141).

Ministry of Social Security, Esplanada dos Ministérios, Bloco F, CEP 70059-900 Brasília DF (tel: 224-5914; fax: 223-2293).

Ministry of Sport, Esplanada dos Ministérios, Bloco A, CEP 70054-900 Brasília-DF (tel: 224-5285; fax: 224-3618).

Ministry of Transport, Esplanada dos Ministerios, Bloco R, CEP 70040-900

Brasília DF (tel: 224-0185, 224-0995; fax: 226-4864).

President's Office, Palácio do Planalto, 40 andar, CEP 70150-900 Brasília-DF (tel: 211-1303, 211-1034; fax: 226-2078, 321-5804).

Other useful addresses

Associação do Comercio Exterior do Brasil (Exporters' Association), Avenida General Justo 335, Rio de Janeiro (tel: 240-5048).

Bolsa de Valores de Rio de Janeiro (Rio de Janeiro Stock Exchange), Praça 15 de Novembro 20, 2010 Rio de Janeiro (tel: 271-1001; fax: 221-2151).

Bolsa de Valores de São Paulo (São Paulo Stock Exchange), Alvares Peuteado 151, São Paulo (tel: 233-2147; fax: 233-2226).

Brazilian Embassy (USA), 3006 Massachusetts Avenue, NW, Washington DC 20008 (tel: 202-238-2700; fax 202-238-2827; e-mail: webmaster@brasilemb.org).

British Consulate-General, Praia do Flamengo 284, 22210-030 Rio de Janeiro (tel: 553-3223; fax: 553-6850).

British Embassy, Setor de Embaixadas Sul, Quadra 801, Loto 8, Conjunto K, 70408-900 Brasília DF (tel: 225-2710, 223-5357; fax: 225-1777).

Central Post Office, Praça Correio, São Paulo.

Central Post Office, Setor Hoteleiro Sul, Brasília.

Central Post Office, Rua Primeiro do Marco 64, Rio de Janeiro.

Companhia Vale do Rio Doce (CVRD – State Mining Company), Avenida Graca Aranha 26, Bairro Castelo, 20005 Rio de Janeiro (tel: 272-4477).

Confederação Nacional de Agricultura (CNA – National Agriculture Federation), Brasília DF (tel: 225-3150).

Confederação Nacional da Industria (CNI – National Confederation of Industry, comprising the 21 state industry federations), Edificio Roberto Simonsen, 16 andar, 70040 Brasília DF (tel: 224-1328).

Council of the State's Reform Programme, Av Borges de Medeiros, No 1501, 7 Andar, CEP 90119-900, Porte Alegre, Rio Grande do Sul (tel: 228-2708, 334-5275; fax: 226-5893, 382-4607).

Departamento Nacional de Telecomunicaes (Dentel), Via N2, Anexo do Ministerio das Comunicações, Esplanada dos Ministerios, Bloco R, 70044 Brasília DC (tel: 223-3229).

Divisão de Feiras e Turismo-Departamento de Promocão Comercial (Organisers of Trade Fairs and Tourism), Ministerio das Relacões Exteriores, Esplanada dos Ministerios, 2 andar, 70170 Brasília (tel: 211-6644).

Fundacão Instituto Brasileiro de Geografia e Estatistica (IBGE – Brazil Institute of Geography and Statistics), Avenida Franklin Rossevelt 166, Castelo, 20021 Rio de Janeiro (tel: 220-6671).

National Department of Foreign Trade, Avenida Presidente Vargas 328, 11 andar, 20091 Rio de Janeiro (tel: 271-7504).

Petrolo Brasileiro–Petrobras Segen/Gasbol (State Oil Company), Rua General Canabarro 500-6 andar, CEP 20271-201, Maracana, Rio de Janeiro (tel: 566-3733; fax: 566-5723/5299).

Rede Ferroviaria Federal (SA – Federal Railway Corporation), Praça Procopio Ferreira 86, 2221 Rio de Janeiro (tel: 223-5795).

Secretaria Especial de Desenvolvimento Industrial (Industrial Development Council), Ministerio de Desenvolvimento da Industria e Comercio, Lotes 2/5-2/8, Bloco G, 8 andar, 70070 Brasília DF (tel: 225-7556).

Superintendencia da Zona Franca de Manaus (Manaus Free Zone Authority), Rua Ministro João Gonçalves de Souza, Cidade Universitaria, Distrito Industrial, 69000 Manaus (tel: 237-3288).

US Embassy, Avenida das Naçoes, Lote 3, 70403-900 Brasília DF (tel: 321-7272; fax: 225-9136).

World Trade Centre (WTC), Av das Naçoes Unidas, 12-551, Sao Paulo (tel: 893-7113; fax: 893-7101).

Internet sites

Banco do Brasil: http://www.bancobrasil.com.br

Banco Itaú: http://www.itau.com.br

Brazilian Embassy in London: http://www.brazil.org.uk

Brazilinfo: http://www.brazilinfo.net

Brazil American Chamber of Commerce: http://www.amcham.com.br/

Brazil Statistics: http://www.ibge.gov.br

Brazzil (English-language magazine): http://www.brazzil.com

National Industry Confederation (markets and industry information): http://www.cni.org.br

British Virgin Islands

KEY FACTS

Official name: British Virgin Islands

Head of State: Queen Elizabeth II; represented by Governor Thomas T Macan (sworn in 14 Oct 2002)

Head of government: Chief Minister Orlando Smith (sworn in 17 Jun 2003)

Ruling party: National Democratic Party (NDP) (elected 16 Jun 2003)

Area: 153 square km

Population: 22,700 (2004)

Capital: Road Town

Official language: English

Currency: US dollar (US$) = 100 cents

GDP per capita: US$16,000 (2004)

GDP real growth: 1.00% (2004)

Labour force: 12,770 (2004)

Inflation: 1.00% (2004)

COUNTRY PROFILE

Historical profile
1493 The islands were sighted by Columbus.
1595 Sir Francis Drake visited the channel which runs through the islands and which now bears his name.
1648 The islands were settled by the Dutch.
1666 English settlers arrived.
1672 Tortola was taken over by the English.
1872 The islands became part of the UK colony of the Leeward Islands. The islands continued to come under the authority of the governor of the Leeward Islands until 1960.
1960 An appointed administrator (renamed governor in 1971) assumed responsibility for the islands.
1967 Lavity Stoutt of the Virgin Islands Party (VIP) became the first chief minister as the islands were granted internal self-government.
1995 The VIP won the elections.
1997 The National Democratic Party (NDP) was formed.
1999 The VIP was re-elected.
2003 The NDP won the 16 June parliamentary elections and Orlando Smith became chief minister.
2005 From July the BVI began imposing a withholding tax on EU citizens' savings. The tax is passed to the relevant EU country, although the savers' names will be withheld. The BVI government purchased the Virgin Gorda Airport in August, for US$2.9 million. The airport will be upgraded and fully licenced to maintain the tourist interests of the territory's second most populated island.

Political structure
Constitution
The constitution of June 1977 gives the islands a large measure of internal self-government. The governor has direct responsibility for external affairs, defence and internal security (including the police), the public services and the administration of the courts. The constitution provides for a ministerial system of government headed by the governor, an Executive Council (ExCo) and Legislative Council (LegCo).
The governor is appointed by the British monarch.

Form of state
British Caribbean dependency

The executive
The Executive Council is made up of the governor, attorney general, chief minister and three other ministers and has responsibility for finance.

National legislature
The Legislative Council has 15 members, 13 members elected for a four-year term in single-seat constituencies, one ex-officio member and one speaker chosen from outside the Council.

Legal system
The legal system is based on the English common law system with local variations. Justice is administered by the Eastern Caribbean Supreme Court. A resident puisne judge presides over the High Court, Admiralty, and associated courts. There is a Court of Appeal. Final appeals go to the Privy Council in the UK.

Last elections
16 June 2003 (parliamentary)
Results: Parliamentary: the opposition party, the National Democratic Party (NDP), won eight seats out of 13, defeating the Virgin Islands Party (VIP); turnout was 72 per cent.

Next elections
2007 (parliamentary)

Political parties
Ruling party
National Democratic Party (NDP) (elected 16 Jun 2003)
Main opposition party
Virgin Islands Party (VIP)

Population
22,700 (2004)
Ethnic make-up
African (83 per cent), white, Indian, Asian and mixed race.
Religions
Methodist (45 per cent), Anglican (21 per cent), Church of God (7 per cent), Seventh-Day Adventist (5 per cent), Baptist (4 per cent).

Education
The education sector will receive US$46.7 million from the 2004 Budget.

Health
A national health insurance scheme is being planned. In the 2004 budget, US$37.3 million was allocated to the health and welfare sector.
Life expectancy: 76 years: male 75 years; female 77 years (2003).
Fertility rate/Maternal mortality rate: Two births per woman (2003)

British Virgin Islands

Birth rate/Death rate: 15 births per 1,000 population; five deaths per 1,000 population (2003).
Infant mortality rate: 19 per 1,000 live births (2003)

Welfare
A social security scheme exists for workers between the ages of 16 and 65. The scheme covers old age pensions, disability and a survivors fund. Contributions are shared between the employer and employee, each providing 3.25 per cent of salary. Self-employed workers pay the full 6.5 per cent.

Main cities
Road Town, on Tortola island (capital, estimated population 9,100 in 2003), East End-Long Look (5,200).

Languages spoken
Official language/s
English

Media
Press
Local newspapers are issued at regular intervals, mostly weeklies in circulation. The readership is somewhat less than 100 newspapers per 1,000 persons. The island has an abundant supply of international and regional newspapers, including radio, television and specialised publications. Newspapers operate freely without any government influence or pressure and openly criticise policies and actions.
Weeklies: There are three. *The Island Sun* with on-line version (www.islandsun.com) is the oldest newspaper and is published on Fridays. *The BVI Beacon* is the second oldest newspaper published on Thursdays (www.bvibeacon.com). The *BVI Penny Saver* is published on Tuesdays. On-line news service from the island includes *Islands On-line* (www.islandsonline.com) which provides information on tourism and finance.
In addition to local newspapers there are regional and international publications including the *Daily News* (St Thomas), *Avis* (St Croix), *San Juan Star* (Puerto Rico), *The Barbados Advocate*, *Wall Street Journal* (New York), and *New York Times*. There are also a number of newspapers from other Caribbean countries circulated on a delayed basis.
Broadcasting
Radio: Two radio stations: Radio ZBVI and ZRODFM. ZBVI operates a daily commercial station from Tortola.
Television: VITV (Virgin Islands Television) Network. Cable television.

Economy
The economy is dependent on tourism and the financial services sector, which is based on the large offshore sector; the services sector contributes approximately 75 per cent to annual GDP.

Economic growth has been restrained by the effects of the global economic slowdown and the decline in tourism following the 11 September 2001 terrorist attacks on the US. Nevertheless, tourist numbers and company registrations are rising. An increase in public investment has also stimulated the economy.
The 2004 budget prioritised education, health and welfare and youth development, involving an 18 per cent increase in government spending. The budget also included plans to purchase new land for a home ownership programme, to diversify the financial services sector and the rehabilitation of the capital, Road Town. Government revenues for 2004 increased by nearly 10 per cent to US$194.40 million, compared to US$180.60 million collected in 2003.
The government lifted the ceiling of tax-exempt income from US$3,000 to US$7,500 per annum in 2004.

External trade
The visible trade deficit is offset by tourist spending, capital inflows and by workers' remittances from overseas.
Imports
Principal imports are machinery and equipment, building materials, vehicles, foodstuffs and fuel.
Main sources: US Virgin Islands, Puerto Rico, US
Exports
Principal exports are fruit, vegetables, fish, rum and gravel and sand.
Main destinations: US Virgin Islands, Puerto Rico, US

Agriculture
Farming
The agricultural sector contributes approximately 15 per cent to annual GDP. About 60 per cent of the total land area is agricultural.
Production is centred on livestock farming, fishing (langoustine, prawns), food crops (mainly fruit and vegetables) and sugar cane for rum production.
Main areas of activity are Tortola, Virgin Gorda and Jost Van Dyke.
The expansion of the tourist industry has increased the dependence on imported foodstuffs, mainly from the US.

Crop production in 2004 included: 340 tonnes (t) bananas, 420t fruit in total, 25t coconuts, 3t oilcrops. Livestock production included: 266t meat in total, 139t beef, 36t goat meat, 71t lamb, 20t pig meat.
Fishing
The typical annual fish catch has declined since a 116mt high in 1998.

Industry and manufacturing
The industrial sector typically contributes around 10 per cent to annual GDP. Industries include construction, concrete and rum production.

Tourism
Tourism is the mainstay of the economy. The British Virgin Islands (BVI) are marketed as a quality tourist destination offering such activities as diving, yachting and boat chartering, with a stress on return visits, and eschewing mass-market attractions such as casinos. The infrastructure is proving inadequate to meet the demands of increasing cruise tourism. The BVI Tourist Board was allocated US$10 million in the 2004 budget to assist with resources for expanding the sector.

Hydrocarbons
The British Virgin Islands do not produce coal, oil or gas. They import refined oil products, but not coal or gas.

Banking and insurance
The business and financial services sector is the largest contributor to government income, accounting for around 60 per cent of the total. There are over 500,000 International Business Corporations (IBC) incorporated in the British Virgin Islands. In 2002, the government established the Financial Services Commission (FSC) to replace the Directorate of Financial Services (DFS). The FSC operates as an independent regulator and is responsible for domestic and offshore finance.
The seven members of the Organisation of Eastern Caribbean States (OECS), Antigua and Barbuda, Dominica, Grenada, Montserrat, St Kitts and Nevis, St Lucia and St Vincent and the Grenadines, share a common currency and central bank. The British Virgin Islands and Anguilla are associate members.

KEY INDICATORS — British Virgin Islands

	Unit	2000	2001	2002	2003	2004
Population	m	0.02	0.02	0.02	0.02	0.02
Gross domestic product (GDP)	US$bn	0.31	0.32	0.34	0.32	0.36
GDP per capita	US$	16,000	16,000	17,000	16,000	16,000
GDP real growth	%	6.0	8.7	5.1	1.0	1.0
Exchange rate	per US$	1.00	1.00	1.00	1.00	1.00

Under a new EU tax directive, introduced in July 2005 in a number of associate and dependent EU countries, the BVI imposed a withholding tax for EU citizens. The tax will be passed to the relevant EU tax department while retaining the anonymity of the saver. Withholding taxes began at 15 per cent and will rise to 35 per cent by 2011.

BVI has also agreed to supply information on tax fraud, for criminal or civil trials, and notify EU member states about additional malpractices.

Central bank
There is no central bank.

Main financial centre
Tortola

Offshore facilities
The British Virgin Islands Financial Services Commission licenses and regulates all service providers operating within the offshore sector.

Time
GMT minus four hours

Geography
At the northern end of the Leeward Islands, in the eastern Caribbean, the British Virgin Islands consist of more than 60 islands and cays, of which only 16 are inhabited. Most of the islands are mountainous and of volcanic origin; the coralline island of Anegada is the only exception of any size. They lie about 100km to the east of Puerto Rico and adjoin the US Virgin Islands.

Climate
The climate is sub-tropical, with no marked seasonal variation in temperature – generally 24–30 degrees Celsius (C) during the day and 10 degrees C cooler at night. Rainfall is generally low, although tropical storms may occur from July–November.

Entry requirements
Passports
Required by all.
Visa
Not required by tourists for visits up to one month, with return/onwards tickets, pre-arranged accommodation and sufficient funds for stay. Longer stays require premission from the immigration department.
Some visitors will, and business visitors may, require a visa; see www.bvitourism.com/immigration for more details.

Currency advice/regulations
No restriction on import of foreign currency but amounts should be declared. Exports limited to the amounts declared on arrival.

Health (for visitors)
Mandatory precautions
None.

Advisable precautions
Typhoid vaccinations. Dengue fever is a viral disease transmitted by mosquitoes, which are most likely to bite two hours after sunrise and two hours before sunset. Use an effective insect repellent on all exposed skin. Take water precautions.

Hotels
Expensive, but wide range available. Seven per cent hotel tax and 10 per cent service charge usually added to bill.

Public holidays
Fixed dates
1 Jan (New Year's Day), 1 Jul (Territory Day), 21 Oct (St Ursula's Day), 25–26 Dec (Christmas Holiday).
Variable dates
Commonwealth Day (second Mon in Mar), Good Friday, Easter Monday, Whit Monday, Queen's Official Birthday (Jun).

Working hours
Banking
Mon–Fri: 0900–1400; also Fri: 1600–1730.
Business
Mon–Fri: 0830/0900–1630/1700.
Government
Mon–Fri: 1230–2030.

Telecommunications
Mobile phones
GSM 900/1900 coverage throughout the islands.

Electricity supply
120/208V AC, 60 cycles

Getting there
Air
National airline: Virgin Islands Airways (Air BVI).
International airport/s: Terrance B Lettsome International Airport (EIS) on Beef Island, 15km from Road Town on Tortola. Only inter-island and intra-Carribbean flights arrive at this airport, including regular flights from Puerto Rico, US Virgin Islands and Antigua.
Airport tax: Departures tax US$20, not applicable to transit passengers.

Getting about
National transport
Air: Air BVI operates domestic flights linking Tortola, Virgin Gorda and Anegada. Charter services are also available.
Road: The main highway from Beef Island through Road Town to West End is surfaced. There is a bridge connecting Beef Island with Tortola. There is also a surfaced road on the northern ridge from east to west. Roads on Virgin Gorda are in variable condition.
Water: Various types of boats ply between islands. Regular ferry services operate between Road Town and West End (Tortola) and Charlotte Amalie (St Thomas, US Virgin Islands).

City transport
Taxis: Widely available. Taxi rank in Road Town is opposite central post office and Taxi Association on Wickhams Cay. Tipping is optional. Taxis can be hired on a time basis.

Car hire
Can be hired on Tortola and Virgin Gorda. Temporary licences can easily be obtained from rental agency on production of national driving licence. Traffic drives on the left.

BUSINESS DIRECTORY
The addresses listed below are a selection only. While World of Information makes every endeavour to check these addresses, we cannot guarantee that changes have not been made, especially to telephone numbers and area codes. We would welcome any corrections.

Telephone area codes
The international direct dialling (IDD) code for the British Virgin Islands is +284, followed by subscriber's number.

Chambers of Commerce
BVI Chamber of Commerce and Hotel Association, James Frett Building, PO Box 376, Road Town, Tortola (tel: 494-3514; fax 494-6179; e-mail: bviccha@surfbvi.com).

Banking
Banco Popular de Puerto Rico, PO Box 67, Road Town, Tortola (tel: 494-2117; fax: 494-5294).

Bank of Nova Scotia, PO Box 434, Road Town, Tortola (tel: 494-2526; fax: 494-4657).

Barclays Bank International, PO Box 70, Road Town, Tortola (tel: 494-2171; fax: 494-4315).

Chase Manhattan Bank, PO Box 435, Road Town, Tortola (tel: 494-2662; fax: 494-3863).

CITCO Ban (BVI) Ltd, PO Box 662, Road Town, Tortola (tel: 494-2217; fax: 494-3917).

Crorebridge Bank, PO Box 71, Road Town, Tortola (tel: 494-2233; fax: 494-3547).

Disa Bank BVI, PO Box 985, Road Town, Tortola (tel: 494-4977; fax: 494-4980).

Guyerzeller Bank, PO Box 3162, Road Town, Tortola (tel: 494-5414; fax: 494-5417).

London International Bank and Trust Company, PO Box 3151, Road Town, Tortola (tel: 494-3045; fax: 494-3050).

Rathbone Bank, PO Box 986, Road Town, Tortola (tel: 494-6544; fax: 494-6532).

British Virgin Islands

The Bank of East Asia, PO Box 901, Road Town, Tortola (tel: 495-5588; fax: 494-4513).

United Chinese Bank, PO Box 901, Road Town, Tortola (tel: 494-6775; fax: 494-8180).

VP Bank, PO Box 3463, Road Town, Tortola (tel: 494-1100; fax: 494-1199).

Travel information

Air BVI, PO Box 85, Road Town, Tortola (tel: 42-777/8; fax: 42-136); airport (tel: 52-346).

British Virgin Islands Tourist Board, Joshua Smith Building, PO Box 134, Road Town, Tortola (tel: 43-134; fax: 43-866).

Ministries

Governor's Office, Government House, PO Box 702, Road Town, Tortola (tel: 494-2345, 494-2370, 494-3520; fax: 468-4490).

Other useful addresses

BVI Hotel and Commerce Association, PO Box 376, Wickhams Cay, Road Town, Tortola (tel: 43-514, 42-947; fax: 46-179).

BVI Financial Services Commission, Pasea Estate, Road Town, Tortola (tel: 494-4190; fax: 494-9399; e-mail: commissioner@bvifsc.vg; internet site: http://www.bvi.org).

BVI Offshore Financial Centre, Financial Services Department, Ministry of Finance, Pasea Estate, Road Town, Tortola (tel: 494-6430; fax: 494-5016; internet site: http://www.bvi.org).

Cable and Wireless (West Indies), PO Box 440, Road Town, Tortola (tel: 44-444; fax: 42-506).

Immigration Department, Road Town, Tortola (tel: 494-3701, 494-3471; fax: 494-4399).

Trade and Investment Promotion, Trade Department, Central Administration Complex, Road Town, Tortola (tel: 494-3701; fax: 494-5676).

VITV (Virgin Islands Television) Network, Butu Mountain, PO Box 118, Road Town, Tortola (tel: 494-8488/2257; fax: 494-5323).

ZBVI Radio, PO Box 78, Road Town, Tortola (tel: 494-2250; fax: 494-1139).

ZRODFM (radio station), PO Box 992, Road Town, Tortola (tel: 494-1037/5832; fax: 494-4564).

Internet sites

British Virgin Islands homepage: http://www.britishvirginislands.com

Islands on-line: http://www.islandsonline.com

The Island Sun: http://www.islandsun.com

Brunei

KEY FACTS

Official name: Negara Brunei Darussalam (The Sultanate of Brunei)

Head of State: Sultan Haji Hassanal Bolkiah Mu'izzaddin Waddaulah, the Sultan and Yang Di-Pertuan of Brunei Darussalam (since 1997)

Head of government: Sultan Haji Hassanal Bolkiah Mu'izzaddin Waddaulah, the Sultan and Yang Di-Pertuan of Brunei Darussalam

Ruling party: There is no ruling party.

Area: 5,765 square km

Population: 371,100 (2004)

Capital: Bandar Seri Begawan

Official language: Behasa Melayu

Currency: Brunei dollar (B$) = 100 cents

Exchange rate: B$1.69 per US$ (Oct 2005) (the Brunei dollar is set at parity with the Singapore dollar.)

GDP per capita: US$15,612 (2004)

GDP real growth: 1.10% (2004)

Labour force: 169,000 (2004)

Unemployment: 4.80% (2004)

Inflation: 0.90% (2004)

Oil production: 211,000 bpd (2004)

Balance of trade: US$2.96 billion (2003)

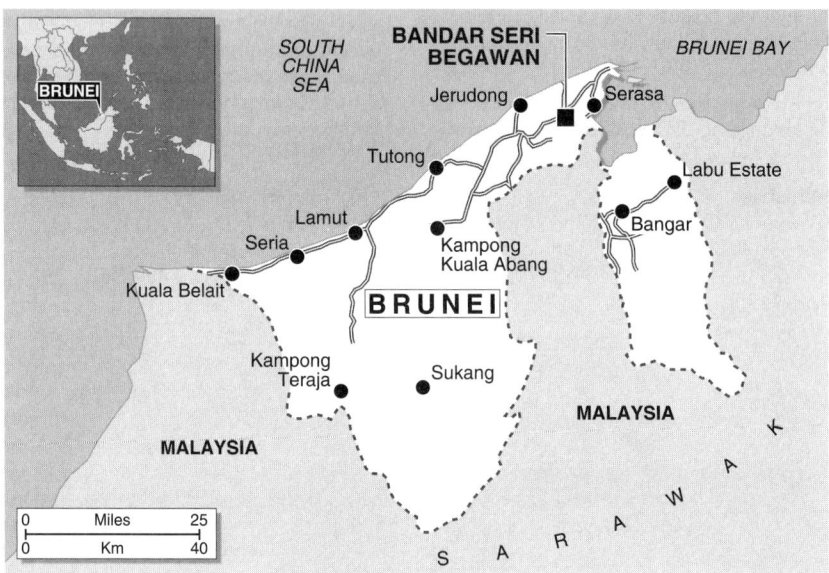

Brunei gained its independence in 1984 after a period of British rule. Now the very small, tax-free country has one of the highest average living standards in the world. Brunei's size and oil wealth have tended to make the tiny sultanate easy to govern. Yet, the ruling monarchy, led by Sultan Hassanal Bolkiah, one of the richest men in the world, is changing, aware that an abundance of oil cannot sustain economic development or the adulation of its subjects.

A rise in political and religious militancy in neighbouring Malaysia, Indonesia and Philippines, along with growing violent opposition to the monarchy in oil-rich Saudi Arabia, has prompted Sultan Hassanal Bolkiah to seek a more ethical approach involving a strictly controlled Islamicisation of Brunei's society. At the same time, the monarchy is attempting to diversify the economy to reduce dependency on foreign workers and encourage domestic employment. But the possibility that a surge in radical Islamic activity could spill over into Brunei puts the sultanate in a hazardous position with uncertainty over how the local population would respond. This threat has prompted Brunei to engage in regional security initiatives as well as joint military exercises with the UK.

Four cabinet ministers were dismissed by the Sultan in 2005. For the first time a minister with sole responsibility for energy was appointed, as were some younger figures and some with experience in private business. The education minister, of 20 years experience, is believed to have lost his job due to a controversial plan to overhaul the curriculum in favour of conservative Islamic teaching. Middle class Brunei parents sought science teaching rather than an emphasis on religion and Jawi, a lesser-known Malay dialect. Another political first was the elevation of a non-Muslim to the sultanate's government.

Monarchy plays safe

The embarrassing corruption scandals of the 1990s had led to a shift in government behaviour in an attempt to maintain popular support. In a Muslim country where humility is respected and ostentation is avoided, the monarchy has made efforts to portray itself as virtuous in order to overcome its tarnished reputation. Members of the royal family have distanced themselves from the greed and carnality associated with the disgraced Prince Jefri, who stole billions of US dollars from the government in the Amedeo scandal, in favour of displays of religious piety. The government has staged a number of religious ceremonies in an attempt to display its commitment to Islamic values.

While the Islamicisation of Brunei is an attempt to re-establish the Sultan's legitimacy and tighten his control of the population, the form it has taken cannot be compared to the Wahhabi fundamentalism exported from Saudi Arabia to countries such as Afghanistan and Pakistan. Brunei remains one of the closest regional allies of the UK and the US and is regarded as one of Asia's most pro-Western states in international relations. Yet the trend towards religious conservatism has promoted an insularity which borders on xenophobia and seems in conflict with the monarchy's professed desire to embrace globalisation.

Brunei depends on foreign workers, particularly from South Asia, who take on the menial jobs that the local population is unwilling to perform, such as maidservants and labourers. In an effort to purge Brunei of 'immoral' foreign influences, foreigners are put under extraordinary levels of surveillance – although most expatriate workers are Muslims. The police regularly raid night-spots and detain foreigners if they are seen associating with non-related members of the opposite sex.

Brunei's increasingly hard approach towards the immigrant community has brought it into conflict with foreign governments. India and Pakistan have lodged complaints over the introduction of flogging for visitors who breach the terms of their visas. They argue that many expatriate workers in Brunei are illiterate and hand their passports to their employers when they arrive, so they are often unaware of visa requirements or if they have overstayed.

Diversifying for future growth

Brunei is heavily reliant on its hydrocarbons sector, which accounts for around 40 per cent of GDP, 90 per cent of exports and 90 per cent of government revenue. The country's oil wealth has enabled the government to provide free healthcare to its citizens, while the civil service employs over half the workforce.

GDP growth in 2004 was 1.1 per cent, a reduction on the 3 per cent of the previous year. The figure for 2005 however was expected to climb back up to 3 per cent. Small improvements were seen in the agriculture, forestry, fishery, mining, manufacturing, construction and communication sectors.

The 2004 CPI figure was 101.1, up 0.9 per cent on 2003. Food and alcohol helped push up prices, especially meat – the price of this climbed 10.7 per cent, with beef rocketing up 20 per cent. Government finances were expected to show a large surplus – in 2004 the surplus was B$1,217.6 million (US$751.6 million). The current account balance increased by 6.5 per cent. Total trade expanded 9 per cent in 2004. Exports increased 11 per cent although garment exports fell, pushing down the value of non-oil and gas exports. While exports to India rose from 2 per cent (2003) to 6.8 per cent (2004), exports to China dropped by one third. There was a 41 per cent surge in the imports of drinks and tobacco and a 9 per cent rise in chemicals imports. Manufactured EU goods came into Brunei in greater volumes.

Brunei may have one of the most stable and wealthiest economies in the region, but it is also having to come to terms with the steady depletion of oil reserves. At production rates of 211,000 barrels per day (bpd) in 2004, Brunei's oil reserves are only expected to last for around 25 years, unless new finds are made. The oil and gas sector contracted 1.5 per cent in 2004 – a steep decline from the 3.6 per cent growth recorded in 2003. The price of crude oil was an average US$34.00 per barrel.

The government is looking towards economic diversification, including the development of the natural gas, manufacturing, tourism and financial services sectors. The main obstacles facing investors are the attitudes of the native workforce, high public sector wages and complex bureaucracy that make Brunei uncompetitive and unattractive. The government has stated its desire to introduce reforms and develop non-oil sectors.

In 2004 the non-oil and gas sectors grew 5.1 per cent, up on the previous year's 3.6 per cent. Agriculture had an impressive year with growth of 10.8 per cent in 2004; and the forestry and fishery sectors were even better with growth rates of 29 per cent each. The transport and communications sectors expanded 14 per cent, up two percentage points on 2003 figures.

The wholesale sector grew 9 per cent in 2004. The only sectors not participating in this growth were the restaurant and hotel industries, which shrank 0.2 per cent in 2004, banking and finance, which contracted 6.2 per cent, and real estate.

The government is Brunei's major employer. The entire labour force comprises 160,000 people with an unemployment rate of 4.8 per cent. Seventy per cent of private sector workers come from abroad.

The Brunei dollar is pegged to the Singapore dollar and has been stable in recent years.

Outlook

Growth in manufacturing and Brunei's entry into the Islamic financial market are unlikely to substantially broaden the non-oil sector. The main impetus for non-oil growth is likely to come from liquefied natural gas (LNG). Brunei is the world's fourth-largest LNG producer, with more than 90 per cent of its LNG exported to Japan. Long-term prospects for LNG are good, with the ongoing development of the Egret gas field fuelling growth in the sector and new long-term supply contracts with South Korea. Rising gas

KEY INDICATORS — Brunei

	Unit	2000	2001	2002	2003	2004
Population	m	0.34	0.35	0.36	0.37	0.37
Gross domestic product (GDP)	US$bn	4.70	4.20	4.40	4.50	5.20
GDP per capita	US$	14,094	12,295	12,911	12,335	15,612
GDP real growth	%	2.8	1.5	3.0	3.0	1.1
Inflation	%	1.5	1.2	-2.0	1.0	0.9
Unemployment	%	6.0	10.0	4.6	–	4.8
Oil output	'000 bpd	193.0	195.0	210.0	214.0	211.0
Natural gas output	bn cum	11.6	11.4	11.5	12.4	12.1
Exports (fob) (goods)	US$m	3,500.0	3,727.0	2,730.0	4,505.0	–
Imports (fob) (goods)	US$m	1,600.0	1,030.0	1,730.0	1,540.0	–
Balance of trade	US$m	1,870.0	2,697.0	998.0	2,965.0	–
Current account	US$m	3,530.0	3,500.0	3,120.0	3,810.0	4,240.0
Exchange rate	per US$	1.72	1.79	1.79	1.72	1.66

output is also likely to increase investor interest in petrochemicals and smelting production in Brunei.

The development of the non-oil sector will no doubt help the government achieve the goals of the Nineth National Development Plan 2006–10.

However, it may not provide sufficient work opportunities for the native labour force, which will mean that the government will remain the main employer for the majority of Brunei's citizens. The monarchy is reluctant to scale back its role in the economy. Concern about civil unrest will continue to motivate government policy in Brunei, a small area of stability in a turbulent region.

Risk assessment

Economic	Good
Political	Good
Regional stability	Good

COUNTRY PROFILE

Historical profile
1839 When an English explorer, James Brooke, arrived on the island of Borneo, he helped the Sultan to suppress an uprising against the rule of the Brunei Sultanate. As a reward for the role he played in quelling the rebellion, in 1841, the Pengiran Mahkota of Brunei made Brooke the Rajah of Sarawak on the north-west coast of Borneo (Sarawak is now the largest state in Malaysia). The British North Borneo Company was expanding its influence on the island.
1888 Brunei became a British protectorate, keeping the Sultanate out of the Malaysian confederacy. Brunei's monarch retained control over internal matters while the British took charge of external affairs.
1906 A treaty with Britain assured Brunei's status as a protectorate and the succession of the ruling dynasty. Executive power, including the right to advise the Sultan on all affairs except religion, was transferred to the British.
1929 Oil was discovered in the Seria field, ensuring the country's future prosperity.
1941–45 Brunei was occupied by the Japanese.
1959 An agreement was drawn up to allow Brunei internal self-government.
1962 In the run-up to Brunei's proposed amalgamation with Malaysia, the British pressured Sultan Omar Saifudd (the present Sultan's father) into holding elections. The opposition Partai Rakyat Brunei (PRB) (Brunei People's Party) won a convincing victory, campaigning against unification, for complete independence from the UK and the creation of a constitutional monarchy. The Sultan's rejection of the result and his plans to unite with Malaysia led to an armed uprising which was quickly crushed (with British backing). The Sultan decided against union with Malaysia.
1979 Brunei concluded a treaty of friendship with the UK.
1984 Brunei became independent from the UK, under Sultan Haji Hassanal Bolkiah Mu'izzaddin Waddaulah, who had ruled since the abdication of his father in 1967.
1991 The sale of alcohol was forbidden. Nationals were required to wear muslim garments.
1998 Prince al Muhtadee Billah, the Sultan's eldest son, was inaugurated as crown prince.
2000 Legal action was initiated against Prince Jefri Bolkiah, younger brother and former favourite of the Sultan, for misusing US$15 billion while head of the state investment agency.
2001 The Association of Southeast Asian Nations (Asean) summit was held in Brunei and agreed to step up co-operation to combat terrorism in the region.
2002 Licences were awarded to two foreign consortiums, Royal Dutch/Shell and TotalFinaElf, to explore for oil deposits in Brunei's 200-mile Exclusive Economic Zone (EEZ) in the South China Sea.
2003 A battalion of the British Brigade of Gurkhas is to continue to be stationed in Brunei for another five years from the end of September 2003.
2004 In September, Parliament was reconvened for first time since 1984.
2005 The Sultan sacked four members of his cabinet, replacing them with younger, more progressive candidates, and introduced reform measures.

Political structure
Constitution
The Sultanate of Brunei (Negara Brunei Darussalam) became a fully independent sovereign state on 1 January 1984, when a ministerial system of government was established. Previously it had been a protectorate of Britain.
The Sultan rules partly by decree, and a state of emergency has been in force since a large-scale revolt in December 1962 which resulted in the suspension of sections of the constitution.
In lieu of democracy and to act as conduits of two-way communication between government and populace, there is a system of village and rural-district consultative councils.
In addition to the cabinet or council of ministers, three other councils advise the Sultan on the running of the country. These are:

- the Religious Council, which advises on all Islamic matters. The council also gives advice on legal matters; the Islamic court falls under its jurisdiction.
- the Privy Council, which is concerned with constitutional matters such as the exercising of royal prerogative and the awarding of honorary titles.
- the Council of Succession, which is empowered to determine the succession to the throne should the need arise.

In September 2004 the Sultan signed a new constitution that will allow limited elections of up to 15 members to an expanded 45-seat legislative council; 30 council members will be appointed by the Sultan. No timetable for the elections has been announced although a new parliament building is planned.

Form of state
Autocratic sultanate

The executive
The Sultan and Yang Di-Pertuan (paramount ruler) is the sovereign head of state and prime minister, retaining supreme executive authority. He is also head of the Islamic faith in Brunei and minister for defence.

A ministerial system of government was introduced following independence in 1984. The cabinet, presided over by the Sultan in his position as prime minister, consists mostly of members of the Sultan's family. Ministers are appointed to hold office at the Sultan's pleasure.

National legislature
The Legislative Council of 20 appointees was abolished at independence in 1984, ending a purely consultative role.
A General Assembly of 1,000 village chiefs from 150 villages and 35 *mukim* (village groups) took place in 1996, described as an expression of a 'grassroots political system' by the government. Chiefs were chosen by secret ballot of villagers but government appointed the Assembly's advisers.

Legal system
Syariah (Islamic) courts were established in 1996 to handle family and criminal law. Their emphasis on publicly shaming offenders is designed to prevent anti-social and anti-Islamic activities.
Brunei has an independent legal system. It is a distinctive, separate branch of government, based on the English common law system. Apart from the *Syariah* courts, the legal system includes:

- the High Court, which hears appeals in criminal and civil matters from subordinate courts. It is presided over by the chief justice and various commissioners.
- the Court of Appeal, which hears appeals against High Court decisions. It consists of a president and two commissioners.

- subordinate courts, which have limited jurisdiction in civil and criminal cases, and are presided over by a chief magistrate.
- the Courts of Kathis, which deal with certain religious (Islamic) matters. These are marriage, divorce, inheritance and sexual crimes. The Courts of Kathis have jurisdiction over Muslims and supercede the civil law only in these matters.

In 1993, Brunei ended the arrangement with Hong Kong under which Hong Kong's judges took up appointments in the Brunei Supreme Court as Judicial Commissioners. By early 1997, the majority of senior positions in the judiciary were held by Bruneians, while from 1995 appeals in criminal cases to the Judicial Committee of the Privy Council in London were abolished, although they have been retained in civil matters.

Political parties
The sole political party of note – Partai Kebangsaan Demokratic Brunei (PKDB) (Brunei National Democratic Party) – has been banned since 1988. The Partai Perpaduan Kebangsaan Brunei (PPKB) (Brunei National Solidarity Party), which split from the PKDB in 1986, is the country's only legal party, although it plays a minimal role in public life, speaking out mainly on international affairs affecting Muslims. The Parti Rakyat Brunei (PRB) (Brunei People's Party) has been banned since 1962, when it attempted an armed rebellion, and operates in exile.

Ruling party
There is no ruling party.

Main opposition party
The absence of any recognisable opposition movement is explained by a number of factors, not least the state of emergency, press censorship and the growing influence of Melaya Islam Berjaya (MIB) (Malay Islam Monarchy) policy (which emphasises obedience and deters the questioning of authority).

Population
371,100 (2004)

Ethnic make-up
Indigenous (predominantly Malay) (69 per cent), Chinese (18 per cent), Indian (3 per cent), other (10 per cent). There are severe obstacles to further Chinese naturalisation and their emigration to China has been encouraged. The 50,000 Chinese living in Brunei play a negligible role in the country's political life, although they are vital to its economic success. Around a third of the Chinese population is naturalised. The same is true of the non-Malay indigenous population, which remains on the fringe of society but forms a crucial part of the workforce.

Religions
Sunni Islam (official faith and religion of all Malays). Members of the Chinese community are either Buddhist, Confucianist, Taoist or Christian. There are also ancient native religions.

Education
Primary schooling includes one year of compulsory pre-school education. Secondary education is divided into junior schools, lasting for three years between the ages of 12 and 15, and upper secondary schools, for another two years. Pre-university further education lasts for up to two years.

In 1985, the government established the University of Brunei Darussalam. In addition, there are two state-run teacher training colleges and six technical schools. If a university course is not available in Brunei, the government will pay for its students to study at a foreign university.

Education for expatriate children is provided by missionary schools, the International School and Chinese schools. All are fee paying and education at the International School follows a UK curriculum, but only caters for children up to the age of 12.

Literacy rate: 91 per cent, adult rates (World Bank)

Compulsory years: Five to 12

Health
The total expenditure on health is around 3 per cent of GDP, of which government spending is 80 per cent.

The government has used its revenues from oil to provide one of the best healthcare systems in Asia. Health services are free for Brunei citizens, although there is a nominal fee for hospital and dentist treatment.

The healthcare system is based on health clinics, which provide primary care and include mobile clinics to reach the most isolated regions, health centres and district hospitals. The central hospital in Bandar Seri Begawan (Raja Isteri Pengiran Anak Saleha) has 550 beds and provides diagnostic and therapeutic facilities for the whole country. There are also government-operated hospitals in Tutong, Temburong and Kuala Belait. A Flying Medical Service reaches areas inaccessible by road. British Shell Petroleum (BSP) has its own private facilities in Seria.

The government is committed to increase its expenditure towards health care and building more clinics. Brunei continues to rely on expatriate doctors to run its health system. Government health surveys have shown that local doctors have made up only 10 per cent, and local dentists 32 per cent, of the medical workforce in the country.

HIV prevalence: 0.1 per cent aged 15–49 in 2003 (World Bank)

Life expectancy: 76.8 years (World Bank)

Fertility rate/Maternal mortality rate: 2.5 births per woman (World Bank)

Infant mortality rate: 5.0 per 1,000 live births (World Bank)

Welfare
The Employees Trust Fund or Tabung Amanah Pekerja (Tap) provides membership to a providence fund that is open to all government workers and private sector employees. The scheme requires compulsory contributions from both the employer and the employee at a contribution rate of 5 per cent each. Universal old age pensions are granted those who have been residents for 30 years.

The ministry of culture, youth and sport oversees the distribution of pensions to citizens not holding contributory pensions and also provides welfare provisions for needy families and the handicapped. The government subsidises housing and food. Under the National Housing Scheme (NHS), the state grants housing to those who have lived under Temporary Occupation Licences (TOL). The Housing Scheme for Landless Citizens also gives land title deeds to those who have been occupying land under TOL.

Main cities
Bandar Seri Begawan (capital, estimated population 78,000 in 2003), Kuala Belait (27,800), Seria (oil field) (23,400).

Languages spoken
The national education system is formally bilingual for all, in Malay and English. Chinese is spoken; English is the principal commercial language.

Official language/s
Behasa Melayu

Media
The absence of any significant political opposition to the government has much to do with Brunei's mainly government-owned and controlled media. The few private publications produced in the Sultanate are forced to be circumspect in their reporting, stifling any criticism of the government and royal family, concentrating instead on pursuing the concept of Melaya Islam Berjaya (MIB) (Malay Islam Monarchy). MIB is an attempt to create a national ideology based on the idea that the best form of government for Brunei is for a Malay ruler to turn it into an Islamic state.

Press
The government stresses the role of the media to establish a harmonious relationship between the people and the government. The press is encouraged to print

'positive' news, mainly associated with the activities of the royal family.

Foreign newspapers available include the *Singapore Straits Times* and several Chinese publications produced in Sarawak and Singapore. These publications provide a variety of views and information beyond anything the straitjacketed Brunei press is able to achieve.

Dailies: The privately owned daily newspaper *Borneo Bulletin* (founded in 1990) is published in Kuala Belait.

Weeklies: *Pelita Brunei* is published in Malay, by the government and resembles a curious cross between court bulletin and religious tract. The *Brunei Darussalam Newsletter,* a fortnightly publication in English, is also produced by the government. *The Newsletter* is mainly concerned with reporting the Sultan's latest activities. Brunei Shell Petroleum (BSP) publishes *Salam* in English and Malay.

Broadcasting

The government operates all local television and radio broadcasts. Local broadcasting is entirely controlled by the Department of Broadcasting and Information through Radio Television Brunei.

Radio: There are two radio networks, one broadcasting in Malay and the other in English, Chinese and Nepali. Most homes can receive Malaysian radio broadcasts.

Television: The government-operated television station transmits one channel, with programming in Malay and English, in colour. Malaysian Channels RTM 1 and 2 are received. Malaysia's TV3 is increasingly accessible. A selection of channels from other satellite networks is available. Television runs on the PAL system.

Advertising

Press advertising is only accepted by *Borneo Bulletin*. Radio Television Brunei accepts advertising in Malay and English.

Economy

Brunei is the richest, in terms of GDP per capita, and the smallest, Asean member, with an economy based on the extraction of natural gas and oil, which account for over half of GDP and over 90 per cent of export earnings.

Brunei enjoys a high standard of living, with medical services, education and pensions provided free. Half of Brunei's income comes from its international investment portfolio, managed by the Brunei Investment Agency (BIA). The exact value of these assets is secret.

A central issue is economic diversification and an increase in foreign investment by US$4.5 billion by 2008. This is essential to maintain growth and long-term viability. Key to this is the country's transformation into an offshore financial centre and tourist destination. Between 2000–03, the government attempted to develop Brunei as a service hub for trade and tourism (SHuTT), to enable the country to take advantage of regional economic integration. The launch of the Brunei International Financial Centre (BIFC) helped to establish the first securities exchange, the International Brunei Exchange (IBX), and awarded its first offshore banking licence. Economic development has concentrated on infrastructure, roads, schools and numerous government buildings. The eighth national development plan (2001–2005) concentrated on promoting tourism, aiming to boost GDP growth to 5–6 per cent per year. Alongside this Brunei intends to increase the financial sector and energy-intensive industries, especially petrochemicals.

Major obstacles to growth include labour shortages, as many Bruneian unemployed workers are unwilling to do manual work. Complex bureaucracy and high wages are also cited as deterrents to foreign investment.

External trade

As Asean moves towards the creation of a free trade area, Brunei is likely to benefit from increased transit trade and the rapidly developing economies of its neighbours, particularly within the East Asean Growth Area (EAGA).

Imports

Brunei's limited industrial and agricultural base require a range of principal imports including machinery, transport equipment, manufactured goods, food and chemicals.

Most items can be imported under an open general licence. There are some restricted goods which require special licences, including used vehicles, certain listed drugs, livestock, some foodstuffs and gambling equipment (eg fruit machines). The banning of alcohol in 1999 created a lucrative trade in illegal alcohol smuggling from the neighbouring Sarawak region of Malaysia.

Main sources: Singapore (33.1 per cent total, 2004), Singapore (33.1 per cent), Malaysia (21.5 per cent), Japan (7.3 per cent), UK (6.8 per cent)

Exports

Crude petroleum (typically 50 per cent of the total exports) and natural gas (around 40 per cent) and refined products dominate the export schedule.

The government is encouraging exports from the non-hydrocarbons sector. Some items are heavily subsidised by the government and their export is consequently restricted. Such goods include rice, petrol, kerosene and diesel fuels. Exports of cigarettes are also restricted.

Main destinations: Japan (37.8 per cent total, 2004), South Korea (13.6 per cent), Australia (11.1 per cent), US (9.0 per cent), Thailand (7.9 per cent)

Agriculture

Farming

The agricultural sector plays only a minor role in Brunei's economy, typically accounting for less than 3 per cent of GDP and employing 2 per cent of the workforce. Brunei has to import 80 per cent of its food needs. Only around 15 per cent of the total land area is cultivated or under grazing.

Brunei's agricultural base consists mainly of small farms growing rice and vegetables. Farming is primarily a part-time occupation. The main crops are rice, vegetables, arable crops and fruits. A wide range of tropical fruit varieties are produced, but in low volumes. Vegetable production is intensive and concentrated in the fertile alluvial plain close to the urban centres. With smallholding rice production declining, the government has initiated a pilot large-scale rice mechanisation project aimed at increasing output; it is hoped that once fully mechanised, 30 per cent of Brunei's rice needs will be met by domestic production.

Government attempts to increase the importance of the sector and moves towards self-sufficiency are hampered by the population's lack of interest in outdoor, manual work. Another disincentive is that farming is perceived as less lucrative than other areas of the economy, so reducing further the likelihood of significant small-scale development. High wage costs mean that the expansion of larger-scale production depends very much on increased mechanisation rather than labour-intensive techniques, unless large scale immigrant labour can be guaranteed.

Crop production in 2004 included: 618 tonnes (t) rice, *1,800t cassava, 990 pineapples, 215t natural rubber, *220t sweet potatoes, 2,360t roots and tubers, *640t bananas, 28t pepper spice, 395t citrus fruit, 5,525t fruit in total, *10,000t vegetable in total. Livestock production included: 20,607t meat in total, *3,450t beef, *540t buffalo, 196t pig meat, 59t lamb and goat meat, 16,363t poultry, 5,853t eggs, 115t milk.
* estimate

Fishing

Since 1990, the government has attempted to expand the fishing industry. The ministry of industry and primary resources granted more fishing licences to match the extension of the country's fishing boundary to 200 miles offshore. Several other sites were located for aquaculture projects. The government also improved the distribution system to ensure that the local catch reaches more remote areas of the country. The trawling industry has also been developed. The important trawling areas are Pulau Tambisan and north of Sandakan (Marchesa and Labuk Bay).

Typical annual fish production is over 1,600 tonnes and other seafood over 400 tonnes.

Forestry

About 70 per cent of Brunei is covered by primary and secondary rain forest; 37 per cent of the country is designated as a national Forest Reserve. There is growing concern locally about the conservation of the forests and the environment, and exports of timber and logs are now strictly limited. Consequently timber production of logs and sawnwood is for domestic consumption only. Some natural rubber is produced. The government hopes to develop the forestry sector as part of its diversification strategy, but investment opportunities are limited by legal restrictions. Private companies wishing to become involved in the sector must have local business participation of 51 per cent.

Typical annual timber production is 230,000 cubic metres (cum) roundwood, 90,000cum sawnwood, 206,000cum sawlogs & veneer logs and over 11,500cum wood fuel.

Industry and manufacturing

The industrial sector, including hydrocarbons, accounts for approximately 44 per cent of GDP and employs almost a quarter of the workforce. The industrial structure, long dependent on export of oil and gas, consists mainly of small-scale enterprises. Apart from the energy and construction sectors, Brunei's industrial base is limited. The small domestic market, high wage costs, bureaucracy and poor co-ordination between government departments has deterred both local and foreign investment.

Despite the government's emphasis on diversification, the industrial sector remains underdeveloped. The manufacturing sector is small and consists mainly of the production of materials for the construction sector, petroleum refining, food-processing and garment manufacture. There are also factories producing canned food, mineral water and dairy products.

Areas the government wants to develop include the manufacture of furniture, pottery, tiles, cement, chemicals, plywood and glass. As part of the industrial development programme a number of industrial estates have been established. These include a 40 hectare site near Bandar Seri Begawan and the Beribi Light Industrial Complex, which consists of four blocks including textiles, food and electrical manufacturers.

The government is eager to promote the development of a financial centre and of export-oriented, value-added industries. Investment policy is open and flexible and welcomes investors, both local and foreign, in any productive industrial activity which furthers diversification.

Tourism

Tourism is relatively undeveloped, although the government is actively trying to promote the sector. Efforts have been made to attract visitors to such attractions as the 20ha Sungai Basong National Park at Bukit Bendera and the Jerudong Park Playground.

Brunei is marketing itself as a service hub for trade and tourism (ShuTT), using the country as a stop-off point for international travellers.

Despite areas of extensive natural beauty that could be visited by tourists, expansion of the sector is hampered by strict rules affecting clothing and alcohol and the difficulties associated with travelling caused by the relative scarcity of taxi drivers. Tourism is expected to contribute 3.3 per cent to GDP in 2005.

Environment

Brunei is prone to occasional typhoons, earthquakes and flooding. Environmental management is overseen by the ministry of development, ministry of health and the ministry of industry and primary resources. Brunei is party to major international environmental agreements that include endangered species, ozone layer protection, ship pollution and whaling.

Mining

Brunei possesses only limited raw materials. Its principal resources are clay and silica in the form of 20 million tonnes of high quality beach sands at Tutong.

Hydrocarbons

Brunei's international status depends upon its oil and gas. Revenues from hydrocarbons make up over 50 per cent of GDP and 90 per cent of Brunei's exports. Brunei has proven crude oil reserves of 1.3 billion barrels, with a production rate of 214,000 barrels per day (bpd). Brunei has plans to diversify the oil-based economy, which should lead to a greater emphasis on natural gas in the future. At a meeting in May 2004, member states of the Asia Co-operation Dialogue planned to ensure the security and reliability of the oil market by improving their regional co-operation.

Brunei has seven offshore fields of which the largest, Champion, contains about 40 per cent of total reserves and accounts for 50,000bpd in output. There are believed to be significant undeveloped oil reserves in the existing fields and these will be tapped by advanced technology and modern drilling methods.

Brunei has natural gas reserves of 350 billion cubic metres and produces around 12.2 billion cubic metres per year. Brunei is south-east Asia's third-largest gas producer (after Indonesia and Malaysia), and the world's fourth-largest producer of liquefied natural gas (LNG). Brunei LNG operates the LNG plant at Lumut, which ranks as one of the largest in the world, processing almost all of Brunei's LNG, the majority of which is exported to Japan. Brunei does not produce or import coal.

Energy

Electricity generation capacity is around 500MW. All Brunei's electricity is produced by gas-fired power plants. Electricity demand is expanding by 7–10 per cent annually, making long-term electricity development a priority. A programme of electricity expansion includes the construction of a 400MW power plant in Tutong, which will feature new, more efficient combine cycle turbines.

Banking and insurance

The regulatory system is based on the 1906 British Banking Act, although various modifications have been made to bring it up-to-date with modern banking requirements.

In 2001, the fourth pillar of the Brunei International Financial Centre (BIFC), the International Insurance and Takaful Order, was set up, designed to provide for foreign investors in the banking scene. This will enable Brunei to have a fully operational foreign offshore banking sector. In January 2002, the Royal Bank of Canada (RBC) became the first foreign bank to operate in the BIFC. RBC is focussing its activities on private bank services for the rich and assisting the management of Islamic funds.

Three local banks dominate the domestic banking sector – the Islamic Bank of Brunei (IBB), Baiduri Bank (BB) and the Development Bank of Brunei. IBB was established in 1993, replacing the International Bank of Brunei. It conducts its savings and loans operations in accordance with Islamic law. The Sultan and his family own 80 per cent of IBB's paid up capital, Japan's Daiichi Kangyo Bank holds the other 20 per cent.

The three largest foreign banks in Brunei are Citibank, the Hong Kong and Shanghai Banking Corporation (HSBC) and Standard Chartered Bank. Other foreign banks include the Overseas Union Bank, Malayan Banking and the United Malayan Banking Corporation.

Central bank

Brunei has no central bank; the main duties are carried out by the ministry of finance.

Main financial centre
Bandar Seri Begawan

Time
GMT plus eight hours

Geography
Brunei lies 442km north of the equator on the island of Borneo. It consists of two wedges of land, separated by the Malaysian province of Sarawak. To the south, both strips of land continue to be bordered by Sarawak, and to the north lies the South China sea.

The country is divided into separate administrative districts, Brunei/Muara, Tutong and Seria/Belait in the west, and Temburong, which makes up the entire eastern section of the country. Although there is a mountainous region in the eastern half of the country, Brunei mostly consists of a low-lying coastal plain. The highest peak is Bukit Pagon (1,841 metres). Brunei has four main rivers – the Belait, Tutong, Brunei and Temburong. Approximately 75 per cent of the total land area is covered by tropical rain forest.

Climate
The climate is typically equatorial. Humidity averages 82 per cent, and daily temperatures range between 24 and 31 degrees Celsius (C). The rainy season lasts from September to January, although rainfall can be expected throughout the year. It can reach up to 7,500mm in the interior, but on the coast it tends to average around 2,500mm. The driest months are from January to April.

Dress codes
Lightweight clothing is suitable. In deference to the Islamic culture, Western business women should dress modestly at all times.

Entry requirements
Passports
Required by all. Must be valid for six months.
Visa
Required by all. Exceptions are granted for short stays of up to 14 days and to certain nationals, see www.mfa.gov.bn/consular, for a full list. Business visas require a sponsorship letter from a local company or government entity, for full details see www.immigration.gov.bn/visiting.htm.
When filling out a transit visa application form, be sure to write the correct point of departure, otherwise you will not be allowed to leave Brunei.
Prohibited entry
Holders of Israeli passports, unless they have an invitation from a Brunei citizen. Visa applications for nationals of Israel must be submitted to the Brunei Immigration Authority for approval.
Currency advice/regulations
Unlimited import of both foreign and local currency, with the exception of Singapore currency, which is generally restricted to B$1,000 in bank notes. Indian and Indonesian bank notes are prohibited. Export of local currency is restricted to B$1,000, and export of foreign currency is limited to amount imported. Brunei dollar is at par with Singapore dollar and the currencies are interchangeable in both countries.
Customs
Personal effects are allowed duty-free. Tobacco, cigarettes and perfumes are liable for taxation.
Prohibited imports
Trafficking and illegal importation of controlled drugs are very serious offences carrying the death penalty.

Health (for visitors)
Health services are not free as for Brunei citizens but there is only a very nominal charge for permanent residents and expatriate government officials and their dependants. Malaria has been eradicated in Brunei. Certificates of vaccination for both cholera and yellow fever are advisable. Normal precautions should be taken for food and drink. The authorities are becoming concerned over the growing amount of drug abuse.
Mandatory precautions
Vaccination certificates for yellow fever are required for travellers over one year of age travelling from an infected area.
Advisable precautions
Chest X-ray and blood film examination for malaria are required for the issue and renewal of labour permits as Brunei is malaria-free. Immunisations are recommended for hepatitis 'A', polio, tetanus, typhoid, and also advice should be sought regarding diphtheria, hepatitis 'B', Japanese encephalitis and TB. There is a risk of rabies.

Hotels
Rooms in major hotels have air-conditioning, telephones, TV, bathrooms and showers. A 10 per cent service charge is usual.

Credit cards
Major credit cards are accepted at some hotels and at some shops.

Public holidays
Fixed dates
1 Jan (New Year's Day), 23 Feb (National Day), 31 May (Armed Forces Day), 15 Jul (Sultan's Birthday), 25 Dec (Christmas Day).
Variable dates
Chinese New Year (Jan–Feb), Eid al Adha, Eid al Fitr, Islamic New Year, Birth of the Prophet, Ascension of the Prophet, First day of Ramadan, Revelation of the Quran Anniversary.
Friday and Sunday are not working days. If a holiday falls on those days, then Saturday or Monday are substituted. Banks close on 30 June and 30 December.
The Islamic year contains 354 or 355 days, with the result that Muslim feasts advance by 10–12 days against the Gregorian calendar. Dates of feasts vary according to the sighting of the new moon, so cannot be forecast exactly. Islamic year 1426: 10 February 2005 to 30 January 2006.

Working hours
Banking
Mon–Fri: 0900–1500; Sat: 0900–1100. Many banks close during lunch hour.
Business
Mon–Thur: 0745–1215, 1330–1630; Sat: 0800–1200.
Government
Mon–Thu, Sat: 0745–1215, 1330–1630. Fasting month (Ramadan) 0800–1400.
Shops
Mon–Sat: 0800–1900/2100, 1000–2200 (most shopping centres). Post offices: Mon–Thu, Sat: 0730–1600; Fri: 0830–0930.

Electricity supply
230V AC, with 3-pin round or 3-pin square plug fittings.

Weights and measures
The metric system is now in full use.

Social customs/useful tips
The public sale and consumption of alcohol is prohibited by law. Muslims do not eat pork or drink alcohol. The right hand should be used for offering or receiving anything, from food to money. Refusal of offered refreshment is discourteous.
To point with the index finger is also considered discourteous; the thumb of the right hand should be used instead with the four fingers folded beneath it. To call a taxi or attract someone's attention, wave the whole hand with the palm facing downwards. Do not smack the fist of your right hand into your left palm; it has a different meaning in Brunei to that of Western countries. It is not customary to shake hands with members of the opposite sex. When visiting a mosque, you should always remove your shoes first and you should not pass in front of a person at prayer, or touch the Qur'an. Women should cover their heads, and not have their knees or arms exposed.

Security
There is no major problem with petty crime in Brunei.

Brunei

Getting there

Air
National airline: Royal Brunei Airlines (RBA)

International airport/s: Bandar Seri Begawan International (BWN), 5km north of city, with car hire and taxi service.

Airport tax: Departures to Singapore and Malaysia B$5. International departures to all other destinations B$12.

Surface
Road: Road connections between Brunei and Sarawak (Malaysia) are good. There is a bitumen road between Miri and Kuala Belait.

Water: Most sea traffic is handled by the deep-water port at Muara, while the smaller port at Kuala Belait handles shallow-draught vessels.

Main port/s: Muara (27km from Bandar Seri Begawan), Kuala Belait, Lumut.

Getting about

National transport
Road: The total road network is around 2,500km. Brunei has 1,500km of main roads, 500km of district roads and 500km of unpaved road surface. There is no road connecting the Temburong district but a water taxi service is available. A main highway links Bandar Seri Begawan with Kuala Belait and Seria, with a road linking Muara and Tutong providing access to western districts.

Buses: There are six bus lines in Bandar Seri Begawan. Services operate betwen Bandar Seri Begawan and Kuala Belait and Seria, and also serve rural areas. Buses run from 0630–1800, every 15–20 minutes.

Water: The Brunei, Belait and Tutong rivers are the main inland waterways and are principally used for passenger traffic. River-going vessels use the old port at Bandar Seri Begawan. Large river taxis operate to the Temburong district; service starts at 0745 and ends at 1600. River taxi and boat services are also available to Limbang in Sarawak and Labuan in Sabah.

City transport
The City Transport Service (CTS) is the easiest way to travel in the city. Fixed fare within the CTS zone.

Taxis: From the airport to the city centre, metered taxis are in operation 0700–0030. Metered taxis are also available from hotels and shopping centres near the capital to all parts of Brunei, but are otherwise scarce. Tipping is not usual.

Buses, trams & metro: From the airport to the city centre, buses operate 0630–1800, every 15–20 minutes.

Car hire
Self-drive and chauffeur-driven cars are available from major hotels and the airport. An international driving licence is required.

BUSINESS DIRECTORY

The addresses listed below are a selection only. While World of Information makes every endeavour to check these addresses, we cannot guarantee that changes have not been made, especially to telephone numbers and area codes. We would welcome any corrections.

Telephone area codes
The international direct dialling (IDD) code for Brunei is +673, followed by subscriber's number.

Useful telephone numbers
Police: 993
Fire: 995
Ambulance: 991
Flight information: 331-747
Directory enquiries: 0213
International calls: 000

Chambers of Commerce
Brunei Darussalam International Chamber of Commerce and Industry, PO Box 2246, Bandar Seri Bagawan 1922 (tel: 2 228382; fax: 2 228389).

Brunei Malay Chamber of Commerce, PO Box 1099, Bandar Seri Begawan 8672 (tel: 2 422752; fax: 2 422753).

Chinese Chamber of Commerce, 72 Jalan Roberts, PO Box 281, Bandar Seri Begawan 8670 (tel: 2 235494; fax: 2 235492).

National Chamber of Commerce and Industry, 144 2nd Floor Jalan Pemancha, Bandar Seri Begawan BS8711 (tel: 2 243321; fax: 2 228737).

Banking
Baiduri Bank Berhad (BB), 145 Jalan Pemancha, PO Box 2220, Bandar Seri Begawan 1922 (tel: 233-233; fax: 235-722).

Citibank, 12-15 Bangunan Darussalam, Bandar Seri Begawan (tel: 243-983; fax: 225-704).

Development Bank of Brunei Bhd, 1st Floor RBA Plaza, Jalan Sultan Bandar Seri Begawan 2085 (tel: 233-430; fax: 233-429).

Hongkong & Shanghai Banking Corporation, cnr Jalan Sultan and Jalan Pemancha, PO Box 59, Jalan Sultan, Bandar Seri Begawan (tel: 242-305/10, 242-204; fax: 241-316).

Islamic Bank of Brunei Berhad (IBB), lot 159, Jalan Pemancha, Bandar Seri Begawan (tel: 235-686/7; fax: 235-722).

Malayan Banking Berhad, 148 Jalan Pemancha, Bandar Seri Begawan 2085 (tel: 242-494).

Overseas Union Bank (OUB), Unit G5, RBA Plaza, Jalan Sultan, Bandar Seri Begawan 2089 (tel: 225-477; fax: 240-792).

Sime Bank Berhad, Unit G 02, Kompleks Yayasan Sultan Haji Hassanal Bolkiah, Bandar Seri Begawan (tel: 222-516).

Standard Chartered Bank, 51-55 Jalan Sultan, Bandar Seri Begawan (tel: 242-386; fax: 242-390).

Central bank
Brunei Currency and Monetray Board, Simpang 295, Jalan Kebangsaan, PO Box 660, Bandar Seri Begawan BS 8670 (tel: 238-3999; fax: 238-2232; e-mail: bcb@brunet.bn).

Travel information
Brunei Travel Service, Sdn Bhd, Bandar Seri Begawan (tel: 225-664).

Department of Civil Aviation, Ministry of Communications, Brunei International Airport, 2015 (tel: 330-483, 330-142/3; fax: 331-7066).

Royal Brunei Airlines, PO Box 737, Bandar Seri Begawan 1907 (tel: 240-500, 242-222; fax: 244-737).

Tourist information (on arrival level at airport) (tel: 331-747).

Ministries
Ministry of Communications, Old Airport, Berakas, Bandar Seri Begawan 1150 (tel: 383-838; fax: 380-127).

Ministry of Culture, Youth and Sports, Jalan Residency, Bandar Seri Begawan 1200 (tel: 240-585; fax: 241-620).

Ministry of Defence, Bolkiah Garrison, Bandar Seri Begawan 1110 (tel: 230-130; fax: 230-110).

Ministry of Development, Old Airport, Berakas, Bandar Seri Begawan 1190 (tel: 241-911; fax: 240-271).

Ministry of Education, Old Airport, Berakas, Bandar Seri Begawan 1170 (tel: 244-233; fax: 240-250).

Ministry of Finance, Bandar Seri Begawan 1130 (tel: 242-405; fax: 241-829).

Ministry of Foreign Affairs, Jalan Subok, Bandar Seri Begawan 1120 (tel: 241-177; fax: 224-709).

Ministry of Health, Old Airport, Berakas, Bandar Seri Begawan 1210 (tel: 226-640; fax: 240-980).

Ministry of Home Affairs, Bandar Seri Begawan 1140 (tel: 223-225).

Ministry of Industry and Primary Resources, Old Airport, Berakas, Bandar Seri Begawan 1220 (tel: 224-822; fax: 244-811).

Ministry of Law, Jalan Tutong, Bandar Seri Begawan 1160 (tel: 244-872; fax: 223-100).

Ministry of Religious Affairs, Bandar Seri Begawan 1180 (tel: 242-565).

Other useful addresses

Asean Investment Promotion Agency, Ministry of Industry and Primary Resources, Bandar Seri Begawan 1220 (tel: 238-119; fax: 238-811).

British High Commission, 2.01, 2nd Floor, Block D, Komplexs Bangunan Yayasan, Sultan Haji Ilassanal Boklkiah, Jalan Pretty, PO Box 2197, Bandar Seri Begawan 1921 (tel: 222-231; fax: 226-002).

Brunei Darussalam Embassy (USA), 3520 International Court, NW, Washington DC 20008 (tel: 202-237-1838; fax: 202-885-0560; e-mail: info@bruneiembassy.org).

Brunei Industrial Development Authority (BINA), Km 8, Jalan Gadong, BE 1118 (tel: 444100; fax: 423300; e-mail: bruneibina@brunet.bn).

Controller of Customs and Excise, Jabatan Customs and Excise Di-Raja, Bandar Seri Begawan (tel: 222-342).

Economic Development Board, Ministry of Finance, 2nd Floor, RBA Plaza, Jalan Sultan, Bandar Seri Begawan 2085 (postal address: Locked Bag 15, Bandar Seri Begawan 1999) (tel: 229-269; fax: 241-417).

University of Brunei Darussalam, Gadong, Bandar Seri Begawan (tel: 227-001).

US Embassy, 3rd Floor, Teck Guan Plaza, cnr Jalan Sultan and Jalan MacArthur, Bandar Seri Begawan (tel: 229-670; fax: 225-293).

Internet sites

Brunei Darussalam homepage: http://www.brunet.bn

Far Eastern Economic Review: http://www.feer.com

Government of Brunei: http://www.brunei.gov.bn

Bulgaria

KEY FACTS

Official name: Republika Bulgaria (Republic of Bulgaria)

Head of State: President Georgi Parvanov (inaugurated 22 Jan 2002)

Head of government: Prime Minister Sergey Stanishev (BSP) (took office 15 Aug 2005)

Ruling party: Koalicija za Bulgaria (KzB) (Coalition for Bulgaria) (since 15 Aug 2005): led by the Bulgarska Socialistièska Partija (BSP) (Bulgarian Socialist Party), with the Nacionale Dvisenie Simeon Tvori (NDST) (National Movement for Simeon II), Dvisenie za Pravata i Svobodie (DPS) (Movement for Rights and Freedoms)

Area: 110,994 square km

Population: 7.91 million (2004)

Capital: Sofia

Official language: Bulgarian

Currency: Lev (Lev) = 100 stotinki

Exchange rate: Lev1.62 per US$ (Oct 2005) (pegged at KM1.96 per euro)

GDP per capita: US$3,074 (2004)

GDP real growth: 5.70% (2004); *6.0% (2005)

Labour force: 4.05 million (2004)

Unemployment: 12.00% (2004); 10.73% (Dec 2005)

Inflation: 6.10% (2004); 6.5% (2005)

Balance of trade: -US$3.35 billion (2004)

Foreign debt: US$16.10 billion (2004)

* estimated figure

It was a tense year in 2005 for Bulgaria, politically and economically. After last minute warnings from EU officials of delays, Bulgaria was allowed to begin accession talks for EU membership on 25 April. High GDP growth in 2005 was tempered by repeated warnings from the IMF that Bulgaria's current account deficit was widening. Also, despite going to the polls on 25 June, Bulgarians had to wait until 16 August before a new government was sworn in. Weeks of haggling and abortive coalition-building were responsible for the delay, sparking fears that Bulgaria's EU accession progress could be adversely affected.

High growth and debt fears

The European Commission forecasts that Bulgarian GDP grew by 6.0 per cent in 2005. The tourism sector continued to expand, both in terms of visitor numbers and revenue generated, although industry analysts remain wary about the impact of unrestrained resort expansion on Bulgaria's popular Black Sea coast region. In October, the IMF expressed concerns about Bulgaria's growing current account deficit. Inflation also reached a 5-year high, of 6.5 per cent. The new Socialist-led government adopted a fiscally conservative outlook upon taking office in August and authorised ahead of schedule repayments to the IMF and the World Bank in December 2005 and January 2006.

One battle ends, others begin

The primary goal of Bulgaria's leadership in 2005 was ensuring that the country signed an accession treaty with the EU. Despite warnings from the EU that Bulgaria might struggle to make the deadline, Bulgaria duly signed the accession agreement on 25 April. Initially, it was announced that Bulgaria and fellow signatory Romania would be in line for full membership on 1 January 2007. However, the rejection in referenda by France and The Netherlands in May and June respectively, of the proposed EU Constitution caused many observers to reassess the issue of expansion. In September and October, EU officials, including European Commission president, Jose Manuel

Barroso, warned Bulgaria that significant progress was required if it expected to meet the 2007 deadline. Corruption and the lack of judicial reform were continually cited as key obstacles to full EU membership. An EU report on corruption and mafia activity in Bulgaria was leaked in December, underscoring fears among some EU members, particularly The Netherlands and Germany, that Bulgaria simply was not ready to join.

Politics: a divisive year

With parliamentary elections due in 2005, local politics was combative to say the least. The ruling coalition of then prime minister, Simeon Borisov Sakskoburggotski, suffered a partial break-up and the threat of a no-confidence motion in January. A reshuffle in February and the prospect of EU accession in April bought some time for the government but by May it was forced to call a general election. Although the results of the 25 June election saw an alliance led by the opposition Bulgarska Socialistièska Partija (BSP) (Bulgarian Socialist Party) emerge as the single biggest bloc in parliament, the government remained in limbo for another six weeks. Out-going prime minister Simeon attempted to cobble together a new centre-right government after it became clear that the BSP was experiencing difficulties attracting sufficient coalition partners. Eventually, in August, the BSP formed a coalition with Simeon's Nacionale Dvisenie Simeon Tvori (NDST) (National Movement for Simeon II) and the ethnic Turk-based Dvisenie za Pravata i Svobodie (DPS) (Movement for Rights and Freedoms). BSP leader, Sergey Stanishev became prime minister.

The new government was immediately faced with a number of challenges, some of which it met, others it struggled to come to grips with. Faced with rising debt and warnings from the IMF, the government acted to shore up the economy by paying back a large sum of its national debt owed to the IMF and the World Bank. The release, in September, of the UN's report into corruption relating to Iraq's 'oil for food' programme made life difficult for the government as a number of Bulgarian companies were named as suspect participants. Opposition pressure for an inquiry mounted in November but the collapse of the main opposition centre-right alliance in the same month took some of the sting out of the attacks. From November, the government was also forced to deny that it had allowed the CIA to operate secret prisons on Bulgarian soil and faced growing opposition from nationalist parties to negotiations with the US over setting up military bases in Bulgaria. Popular with the public was the full withdrawal of Bulgarian troops from Iraq by the end of December.

The election of a far-right nationalist party, Ataka (Attack), to parliament in June threatened to upset Bulgaria's ethnic balance. With the predominantly Turkish-based DPS in government, many DPS figures were well-placed in August to take over a number of oblast (regional) governorships. Led by Ataka, nationalists protested the appointments as encouraging Turkish separatism. In a separate development, the European Court of Human Rights (ECHR) ruled, in October, that Bulgaria was guilty of persecuting ethnic Macedonian-based political parties.

Outlook

The European Commission forecasts continued high GDP growth for Bulgaria, in the vicinity of 5.5 per cent. Moreover, the government has taken off some budgetary pressure by paying back ahead of time some of its international loans. Politically, the government is still in its infancy and it remains to be seen whether or not a coalition featuring socialists, a movement based on a former king and a minority Turkish party can survive for long. Thus far it has proved adept at meeting the political and economic challenges ahead of it. Of paramount importance will be the decision by the EU, expected sometime in 2006, on whether or not to allow Bulgaria to become a full EU member on 1 January 2007. Issues also bound to concern the government in 2006 are negotiations with the US over the use of Bulgarian military facilities, due to conclude in March 2006; and the continuing detention of five Bulgarian nurses in Libya, facing a retrial for their alleged role in the deliberate infection of Libyan children with HIV-positive blood. Planned oil pipelines linking the Black Sea with the Aegean and Adriatic Seas through Bulgarian territory look set to go ahead in 2006.

Risk assessment

Politics	Fragile
Economy	Improving
Regional stability	Good

COUNTRY PROFILE

Historical profile
The Bulgars were a Finno-Ugrian people, whose ancestors crossed the River Danube in the seventh century and merged with the Slavonic population. Bulgaria is the oldest surviving state in Europe to have retained its original name.
681 The state of Bulgaria was founded.
811–927 After defeating the Byzantine Empire, Bulgaria expanded into the Balkans.
1014–18 The Byzantines regained control of lost territory and took over much of Bulgaria.
1185–97 The Bulgarians revolted against Byzantine rule. Bulgaria re-emerged as a state and major Balkan empire.

KEY INDICATORS — Bulgaria

	Unit	2000	2001	2002	2003	2004
Population	m	8.10	8.03	7.96	7.94	7.91
Gross domestic product (GDP)	US$bn	12.05	13.60	16.20	19.90	*24.13
GDP per capita	US$	1,484	1,759	2,130	2,591	3,074
GDP real growth	%	5.8	4.0	4.0	4.5	5.7
Inflation	%	10.4	7.4	5.8	2.4	6.1
Unemployment	%	19.0	17.5	16.4	14.8	12.7
Coal output	mtoe	4.5	4.7	4.5	4.5	4.4
Exports (fob) (goods)	US$m	4,824.6	5,107.0	5,690.0	7,445.0	9,858.6
Imports (fob) (goods)	US$m	6,000.1	7,261.0	7,280.0	9,923.0	13,211.5
Balance of trade	US$m	-1,175.5	-1,700.5	-1,700.0	-1,778.0	-3,352.9
Current account	US$m	-701.2	-828.0	-677.0	–	-1,770.0
Foreign debt	US$bn	10.4	10.6	10.9	10.3	16.1
Total reserves minus gold	US$m	3,342.0	3,390.0	4,407.0	6,291.0	8,776.3
Foreign exchange	US$m	3,215.0	3,347.0	4,362.0	6,174.6	8,171.2
Exchange rate	per US$	2.12	2.18	2.04	1.71	1.57

* estimated figure

Bulgaria

1396 Bulgaria was conquered by Ottoman Turkey and became its European stronghold for the next 500 years.
1800s The Ottoman Empire began to fall apart as many Balkan states launched uprisings.
1878 Russia defeated Turkey and Bulgaria came into existence again as a sovereign state.
1908 German Ferdinand Saxe-Coburg-Gotha proclaimed himself Tsar of Bulgaria.
1912 The Balkan powers of Bulgaria, Greece and Montenegro defeated the remnants of the Ottoman Empire.
1913 In the Second Balkan War, Bulgaria tried to take Macedonia from Serbia, but was defeated. Balkan states ended the war by signing the Treaty of Bucharest, which also reduced the territorial size of Bulgaria.
1915 Bulgaria invaded Serbia and Macedonia, after joining on the side of the Central Powers (Germany and Austro-Hungary).
1918 The Entente powers (Great Britain, France and Russia) defeated Bulgaria and an armistice was signed in September. The Bulgarian defeat led to the abdication of Tsar Ferdinand I and his son, Boris, was crowned.
1923 As internal divisions intensified between the peasants, ethnic Macedonians and communists, the army overthrew the government, which was dominated by agrarian parties. Prime Minister Alexander Stambolisky was assassinated. Alexander Tsankov formed a new pro-democracy government.
1924–25 Violence from communist militants and Macedonian nationalists prevented the Tsankov government from bringing political stability to Bulgaria.
1926 An ethnic Macedonian, Andrei Liapchev, replaced Tsankov as prime minister.
1929–31 The Great Depression devastated the Bulgarian economy. Thousands of jobs were lost and a wave of strikes hit the country. In the 1931 parliamentary election, the Liapchev government was defeated by the centre-left Naroden Blok (NB) (People's Bloc), led by Alexander Malinov.
1934 A coalition of political parties, led by Zveno's Kimon Georgiev and Colonel Damyan Velchev of the Voenni Sayuz (VZ) (Military Union), overthrew Malinov's government. The new government introduced one-party rule and turned Bulgaria into an authoritarian state.
1935 Disillusioned by the government's authoritarianism, Tsar Boris III began a personal dictatorship of Bulgaria.
1939–1941 Having remained neutral at the start of the Second World War, Bulgaria joined the Axis powers (Germany, Italy and Japan) in 1941. Bulgaria ruled German-captured Macedonia and Western Thrace in Greece.
1943 Boris III died of a heart attack. The heir to the Bulgarian throne, Simeon II, was too young to rule. A three-man regency was established to rule on Tsar Simeon II's behalf and Prime Minister Bogdan Filov became the *de facto* head of state.
1944 The Soviet Union invaded Bulgaria. The Fatherland Front, a left-wing alliance dominated by the Soviet-backed Bulgarska Komunistieska Partija (BKP) (Bulgarian Communist Party), gained power.
1946 A referendum abolished the monarchy, which had ruled Bulgaria periodically since the ninth century.
1947 All opposition parties were abolished. Political trials and executions on the Stalinist model were carried out under Vulko Chervenkov until 1953 when Todor Zhivkov became the general secretary of the BKP.
1962–88 Zhivkov cemented his position as leader of Bulgaria and the country moved politically and economically closer to the Soviet Union.
1989 Petur Mladenov was appointed Zhivkov's successor.
1990 The BCK changed its name to the Bulgarska Socialistièska Partija (BSP) (Bulgarian Socialist Party). The BSP won the first multi-party elections in Bulgaria since the inter-war period. However, growing political infighting and nationwide strikes led to its fall. An interim government was confirmed, under the leadership of Dimitur Popov.
1991 The BSP lost power in the parliamentary elections. The Sajuz na Demokratienite Sili (SDS) (Union of Democratic Forces) formed a government.
1992 The SDS's Zhelyu Zhelev became Bulgaria's first directly-elected president.
1994 The BSP returned to government in the parliamentary elections.
1996 Amid a severe economic and political crisis, Petar Stoyanov won the presidential elections.
1997 An early general election was held, resulting in a win for the SDS-led centre-right coalition, the Obedineni Demokratièni Sili (ODS) (United Democratic Forces).
2001 The Nacionale Dvisenie Simeon Tvori (NDST) (National Movement for Simeon II) won the general election. The NDST's leader and former king, Simeon II, accepted the nomination to be prime minister and formed a coalition government. The BSP's Georgi Parvanov won the run-off presidential elections.
2002 NATO invited Bulgaria to join the alliance in 2004.
2003 In January, the IMF signalled its approval of Bulgaria's efforts to improve its macroeconomic situation with a loan tranche of US$36 million. On 29 May, a no-confidence motion against Prime Minister Simeon Borisov Sakskoburggotski's government was defeated.
2004 In April, Bulgaria was admitted to NATO.
2005 The Koalicija za Balgarija (KzB) (Coalition for Bulgaria) (led by the BSP) won the 25 June parliamentary elections, defeating the ruling NDST. On 27 July parliament approved Sergey Stanishev as prime minister.

Political structure
Constitution
A democratic constitution was passed in July 1991, defining Bulgaria as a republic with a parliamentary form of government.
Form of state
Parliamentary democratic republic
The executive
The Council of Ministers is the supreme executive body of the government and usually consists of elected members of the National Assembly. The right to initiate new legislation is vested in the deputies and the Council of Ministers.
The head of state is the president of the Republic, elected by a direct popular vote every five years, and assisted by a vice president. The president is not allowed to initiate or veto new laws, but can bring a law back to parliament for further consideration.
National legislature
Legislative functions are carried out by the Narodno Sabranie (National Assembly) consisting of 240 deputies elected for a four-year term by universal adult suffrage.
Legal system
The legal system is based on the 1991 constitution.
The judiciary is the third component within the political system. It is an autonomous power with an independent budget. The Supreme Legal Council has 45 members. The Constitutional Court is the supreme arbiter.
Last elections
25 June 2005 (parliamentary); 11–18 November 2001 (presidential).
Results: Parliamentary: the KzB coalition led by the BSP won 31.1 per cent of the vote (82 seats out of 240), the ruling NDST 19.9 per cent (53), the DPS 12.7 per cent (34), the Ataka 8.2 per cent (21), ODS 7.7 per cent (20), DSB 6.5 per cent (17) and the BNS 5.2 per cent (13). Presidential: the BSP's Georgi Parvanov won the run-off presidential elections.
Next elections
November 2006 (presidential); 2009 (parliamentary).

Nations of the World: A Political, Economic and Business Handbook

Political parties
Ruling party
Koalicija za Bulgaria (KzB) (Coalition for Bulgaria) (since 15 Aug 2005): led by the Bulgarska Socialistièska Partija (BSP) (Bulgarian Socialist Party), with the Nacionale Dvisenie Simeon Tvori (NDST) (National Movement for Simeon II), Dvisenie za Pravata i Svobodie (DPS) (Movement for Rights and Freedoms)

Population
7.91 million (2004)
Ethnic make-up
Turks, Gypsies (around one million in 2002), Russians, Armenians, Jews and Greeks.
Religions
Eastern Orthodoxy is the main religion, but Catholic, Protestant, Jewish and Muslim communities also exist.

Education
Primary education comprises basic education and pre-secondary education. Secondary school education lasts for four or five years and is provided in three types of schools – comprehensive (general secondary) schools, profile-oriented schools and vocational (technical and vocational-technical) schools. Universities, institutes and academies provide higher education. Some universities are private. Public expenditure on education is typically equivalent to 3.2 per cent of annual gross national income.
Literacy rate: 99 per cent and 97.9 per cent, men and women respectively; adult rates (World Bank).
Compulsory years: 7 to 18.
Enrolment rate: 100 per cent boys and 98 per cent girls, total primary school enrolment of the relevant age group, (World Bank).
Pupils per teacher: 17 in primary schools.

Health
Health care reform was initiated in 2000 with the introduction of outpatient care reform, with future plans for transforming the hospitals into commercial enterprises. The IMF and the World Bank agreed to extend a loan of over US$60 million towards the health fund reform.
The National Health Insurance Fund (NHIF) is responsible for the development of the compulsory health insurance scheme in Bulgaria. Health insurance financing by the NHIF will replace funding through taxes for nearly 90 per cent of hospitals.
HIV prevalence: 0.1 per cent aged 15–49 in 2003 (World Bank)
Life expectancy: 72.1 years (World Bank)
Fertility rate/Maternal mortality rate: 1.2 births per woman (2003); maternal mortality 1.5 per 1,000 live births (World Bank).
Infant mortality rate: 12.3 per 1,000 live births (World Bank)

Welfare
The Bulgarian social security system consists of a public pay-as-you-go system, a mandatory state-funded system of privately managed savings accounts and an additional voluntary private contribution. The National Social Security Institute (NSSI) administers mandatory insurance programmes for maternity, sickness, disability and old age benefits including those related to work injuries and occupational diseases. It is also responsible for the collection, control and information services for all obligatory contributions. The current system of funding benefits was instigated in 2002. A mandatory social insurance scheme provides universal coverage for all members; contributions by individuals to a private insurance fund provide for old age pensions. These schemes are open to all employees, farmers, and artists who pay 21.75 per cent of earning for the social insurance and 0.5 per cent for the private insurance. Employers pay 8.25 per cent of payroll as a whole into these funds. The self-employed pay 31 per cent in total to the funds. The retirement is at aged 61.5 years (men) and 56.5 years (women), however the age is being increased every year until 2009 when retirement will be at age 63 (men) and 60 (women).

Main cities
Sofia (capital, estimated population 1.1 million in 2004), Plovdiv (338,200), Varna (312,300), Burgas (192,000), Ruse (161,000), Stara Zagora (143,000).

Languages spoken
Turkish (permitted since 1992), Macedonian, Romani, Gagauz, Tartar and Albanian.
Official language/s
Bulgarian

Media
Press
There are around 170 newspapers and 133 magazines, which reach 58.7 per cent of adults.
Dailies: The only English-language daily is *Daily Chronicle*. *Monitor* is a daily newspaper covering local and international politics, business, and sports. Other dailies include *24 Chassa*, *Kontinent*, *Trud*, *Zhult Trud*, *Nie*, *Zhenite*, *Duma*, *Vestnik za Zhenata*, *Standart* and *Democratzia*.
Weeklies: The main Sunday newspapers are *Komunistichesko Delo* and *The Sofia Echo*. Other weeklies of general interest include *168 Chassa* and *Kapital Weekly*.
Business: Business publications in main European languages include *Bulgarian Foreign Trade* (bi-monthly), *Economic News of Bulgaria* (a monthly of the Bulgarian Chamber of Commerce and Industry), *Sofia News* and *Bulgaria Today*. *Bulgarian Economic Review* is a fortnightly English-language edition of *PARI*, a financial and business news daily. There is a monthly foreign trade magazine, *Vanshna Targoviya*. *The Insider* is a monthly political and economic digest published by Eltex.
Periodicals: Periodicals include a half-yearly publication *Information Technology in Bulgaria*.
Broadcasting
Radio: There are around 92 commercial radio stations. Four home service radio programmes and several local stations. Foreign service broadcasts several hours each week.
Television: The TV market is monopolised by state-owned Bulgarian National Television (BNT). Russian ORT, French TV5 and CNN as well as Turkish, Greek, Macedonian, Serbian and Romanian TV stations (in border regions) are all accessible without the need for additional equipment. Cable and satellite TV are received.

Economy
With the end of the Soviet Union in 1991, Bulgaria's economic decline reflected the general trend in central and eastern Europe, with falling GDP growth, rising inflation and unemployment. After near economic collapse in 1996, Bulgaria began to stabilise and reform its economy with support from the IMF and other donors. With EU accession in mind, trade switched from Russia to western European markets, which reduced the impact of the 1998 Russian rouble crisis.
The government achieved macroeconomic stabilisation over the period 1997–2001, based on the three-year economic 'Bulgaria 2001' programme, which was launched in 1998. Much of the improved economic performance was achieved through restrictive fiscal and monetary policy and economic reforms, such as privatisation. The government introduced a currency board, pegging the lev to the then Deutsche mark. International loans assisted the government in its economic programme, but contributed to a burgeoning current account deficit.
The government has made poverty reduction one of its major policy priorities and has received loans from the IMF under its Poverty Reduction and Growth Facility (PRGF).
Government has introduced measures to reduce taxes, curtail corruption and attract foreign investment. Other priorities included public sector reform, completion

Bulgaria

of the privatisation process, including the public utilities, promoting the development of a domestic capital market and, ultimately, reducing unemployment and improving the standard of living for the Bulgarian people.

Restructuring and increased investment contributed to a better performance by the manufacturing sector and an improvement in export performance. Economic growth and rising investment have generated new jobs and reduced the unemployment rate. The IMF approved the progress made by Bulgaria with structural reform, particularly restructuring of the energy and railway sectors, simplification of business regulations and judicial reform.

GDP grew by 5.7 per cent in 2004.

External trade
Bulgaria's trade with EU countries is increasing rapidly.

Imports
Principal imports include energy, mining, metallurgical and petroleum equipment, raw materials, perfumes and cosmetics, chemicals and plastics.

Main sources: Germany (15.7 per cent total, 2004), Italy (10.9 per cent), Russia (9.0 per cent), Greece (8.0 per cent), Turkey (7.5 per cent), France (4.7 per cent), Austria (4 per cent)

Exports
Significant exports include clothing, footwear, iron and steel, machinery and equipment and fuels.

Main destinations: Italy (13.2 per cent total, 2004), Germany (11.5 per cent), Turkey (9.7 per cent), Belgium (6.4 per cent), Greece (6.1 per cent), US (5.6 per cent), France (5.1 per cent), Russia (1.4 per cent)

Agriculture
Farming
Agriculture accounts for around 11 per cent of GDP. About 16 per cent of Bulgaria's workforce is employed in farming. Land for agricultural use covers 6.16 million hectares (ha). Principal crops are wheat, maize, barley, sugar beet; other crops include sunflowers, grapes and tobacco.

In February 2001, the Bulgarian government approved proposals to establish market-based institutions, including the revival of its land market, and make the farming sector more competitive. The government supported funding to promote economic diversification, particularly in the rural areas.

Official policy towards land reform has mainly focused on restoring property rights, which included over 99.58 per cent of agricultural land and 90 per cent for wooded areas.

With the exception of cereals, farm prices and trade have been liberalised. The outlook for wheat producers has brightened since the reduction of a 15 per cent tax on wheat export earnings to 10 per cent.

There is a sizeable wine industry, which accounts for around a third of agricultural exports. Bulgaria exports 80 per cent of its wine output, amounting to about 220,000 litres, of which 25 prer cent are exported to the UK, still the biggest market for Bulgarian wine.

Long-term development of agriculture is based on further concentration and specialisation, mechanisation, improved irrigation, increased grain production and expansion of the dairy sector. The government offers subsidised credits to farmers owning more than 10 cows.

Crop production in 2004 included: 7,462,821 million tonnes (t) cereals in total, 3,961,178t wheat, 2,123,022t maize, 573,579t potatoes, 101,486t oats, 1,180,830t barley, 28,116t rice, 1,078,832t sunflower seeds, 25,850t pulses, *6,300t treenuts, *400,000t grapes, *400,000t tomatoes, 457,802t oilcrops, *60,000t tobacco, 800t cotton lint, 160,000t chillies & peppers, 566,400t fruit in total, 1,377,852t vegetables in total. Livestock production included: 479,100t meat in total, 69,700t beef, 300t buffalo meat, *250,000t pig meat, 36,900t lamb, 7,100t goat meat, *110,000t poultry, *92,000t eggs, 1,598,042t milk, *5,000t honey, 10,560t cattle hides, *15,000t sheepskins, *6,600t greasy wool, *50t cocoons, silk.
* estimate

Fishing
Bulgaria's implementation of EU fisheries legislation is yet to be completed. Since progress in the compilation of standardised market data has been slow, privatisation of the processing and marketing sectors has been largely affected. Bulgaria is collaborating on a draft convention on fishing and conservation of resources in the Black Sea, which provides an abundance of fish for domestic and external markets, although it is under-utilised. The main species caught include sprats, mussels and turbot.

Forestry
Forest and other wooded land accounts for over a third of the total land area, with 3.6 million hectares of forest cover. The proportion of forest cover has been increasing as a result of afforestation intended chiefly for soil protection, rather than wood production. Plantations account for more than a quarter of the forest area.

Most of the forest and wooded land is available for wood supply with the main species being beech and oak. Coniferous species include Norwegian spruce and Austrian pine. Up until 1999, all of the forests were state-owned, but by 2002 some 33 per cent were state-owned, 50 per cent municipal and 17 per cent privately owned.

Local demand for sawn wood, panels, pulp and paper is generally met by using domestic wood. Large amounts of sawlogs are also exported.

Export of forest products in 2004 amounted to US$139.3 million, while imports were valued at US$154.3 million. The estimated production in 2004 included: 4,800,000 cubic metres (cum) roundwood, 332,000cum sawnwood, 1,600,000cum sawlogs and veneers, 971,223cum pulpwood, 532,970cum wood-based panels, 2,200,000cum woodfuel; 171,000 tonnes (t) paper and paperboard, 3,000t printing and writing paper, 92,000t woodpulp.

Industry and manufacturing
The industrial sector accounts for around 30 per cent of GDP and employs 38 per cent of the workforce.

Economic growth in the 1990s was led by the manufacturing sector, which contributes around 18 per cent to GDP. The industrial sector is well-developed, and the metal processing, machine building, chemicals, pharmaceuticals, electronics, textiles and food-processing sectors are particularly strong.

The machine building sector includes over 400 enterprises specialising in various areas including casting, machine tools, wood processing machines, machines for the mining industry, machines for the textile industry, machines for the food processing industry, agricultural machines, shipbuilding, vehicle manufacture, fine mechanics, metal constructions and household instruments.

The key markets are the EU (particularly Germany and the Netherlands), Russia and North America.

Since 2003, the manufacturing sector has picked up and there has been an improvement in export performance, with total industrial production increasing by over 5 per cent in 2004.

Tourism
Bulgaria has become a major tourist destination, despite limited infrastructure. The sector is expected to contribute around 4.6 per cent to GDP in 2005.

Winter ski-ing and Black Sea summer resorts are the main attractions for an increasing flow of tourists. Investment is urgently needed in the existing, increasingly inadequate infrastructure, which is in danger of being overwhelmed, and in new development. The sector is short of up-market facilities. The authorities are seeking to diversify away from package tourism and to spread the benefits of tourism throughout the country, by encouraging cultural, rural and eco-tourism. A Ministry of Culture and Tourism was created in 2005.

Arrivals grew from three million in 2002 to four million in 2004 and the upward trend continued into 2005. The majority of visitors come from south-eastern Europe, especially Greece, followed by Germany, the UK and Russia.

Mining

The mining sector accounts for 2 per cent of GDP and employs 2 per cent of the workforce.

Bulgaria has some deposits of iron, manganese and chromium, and large reserves of zinc, lead and copper.

Apart from zinc, lead and copper, the non-ferrous ores contain some gold, silver and other precious metals. The Chala gold deposit in the area of Haskovski Mineralni Bani is one of Bulgaria's richest. The average gold content is higher than that in Madjarovo where it exceeds three grammes per tonne.

Large deposits of copper ore have been discovered in the Sredna Gora mountains. There are deposits of marl, limestone, granite, sandstone and clay, and plenty of stone which can be used in the building industry.

Hydrocarbons

Known oil and natural gas deposits are of small amounts and at considerable depth. Exploration for oil and gas is concentrated in the north of the country and in the Black Sea.

Bulgaria has oil reserves of around 15 million barrels. Bulgaria is a net importer of oil, with most of the supply coming from Russia. In December 2004, Bulgaria, Macedonia and Albania agreed to construct a 900km oil pipeline linking the Bulgarian Black Sea port of Burgas with Vlore on the Adriatic coast of Albania. In April 2005, Russia, Bulgaria and Greece agreed to construct a 285km oil pipeline linking Burgas with Alexandropoulis on the Mediterranean coast of Greece. Natural gas reserves total 210 billion cubic feet. Production is negligible and Bulgaria is dependent on Russia for the 6.5 billion cubic metres of natural gas it consumes annually. In October 2003 Russia and Bulgaria agreed 10–15 year extension of an agreement guaranteeing gas supplies. Bulgaria also transits Russian gas to other countries in the Balkans and Eastern Europe that do not have access to the pipelines.

Deposits of coal are estimated at around three billion tonnes, mostly of a low calorific value. Around 25 million tonnes of coal is produced annually.

Energy

Bulgaria's installed electricity capacity is approximately 12.5GW, composed of 5.8GW of coal-powered thermal power, 3.8GW of nuclear power and 2.9MW of hydroelectric power.

The coal-fired Maritsa Iztok complex accounts for 60 per cent of the power generated by coal-fired plants. A new thermal plant, agreed in December 2005, is to be constructed at Maritsa Iztok to replace capacity lost by the closure of two nuclear reactors at the Kozloduy power plant after the EU had raised safety concerns. In early 2003, the supreme administrative court blocked Bulgaria's 2002 agreement with the EU to close another two Kuzloduy reactors by 2006. In June 2004, the government announced that it will build a new nuclear power plant on the river Danube, to take over when the remaining plants go off-line. The new plant is expected to keep Bulgaria the leading exporter of electricity in Europe's south-east.

Financial markets

Stock exchange

Trading volumes are low despite the number of large companies that are quoted. Most trading on the Bulgarian Stock Exchange (BSE) is concentrated in the free markets, where privatised stakes under the government's privatisation programme are placed.

Banking and insurance

There is a two-tier system in which an independent central bank supervises and regulates commercial banks and has exclusive rights over the issue of currency. There are approximately 33 commercial banks, with total bank credit to the private sector accounting for 14 per cent of GDP, one of the lowest rates of former Soviet countries.

Central bank

Bulgarska Narodna Banka (BNB) (Bulgarian National Bank)

Time

GMT plus two hours (GMT plus three hours from late March to late September)

Geography

Bulgaria lies in south-eastern Europe, on the east of the Balkan Peninsula. It is situated on the western shores of the Black Sea and shares borders with Romania to the north, Turkey to the south-east, Greece to the south, Serbia to the north-west and Macedonia (FYROM) to the south-west. The lower River Danube forms most of the border with Romania. The Balkan Mountains dominate central Bulgaria, running from west to east and separating the Danubian plains in the north from the Thracian plains of Eastern Rumelia in the south-east. The Rhodope Mountains occupy south-west Bulgaria and separate it from Greece and Macedonia.

The Sofia depression in the west of the country is hill country which separates the Balkan Mountains from the southern mountains. It is the main centre of population and communications.

The fertile Bulgarian plateau, between the Danubian border and the Balkan Mountains, averages some 100km in width and contains several tributaries of the Danube, the major one being the Iskur. The main rivers south of the Balkan watershed are the Struma and the Maritza which run into the Aegean Sea. The broad Maritza Valley, which leads on to the Thracian plains, is one of the principal agricultural areas.

Climate

Summer is hot and dry, April–September average temperature 23 degrees Celsius (C). Cold winters, average temperature -1 degree C, with heavy snow.

Dress codes

Dress for business is usually quite conservative but not overly formal.

Entry requirements

Passports

Passports are required by all visitors.

Visa

Not required by North American, European, Australasian and some Asian citizens (a full list is given at www.bulgaria-embassy.org/consular section), visiting for less than 30 days and includes business trips. For those businessmen who require visas, other documentation required includes a letter of invitation from a company registered in Bulgaria endorsed by the Bulgarian Chamber of Commerce.

All visitors, tourist and business, must have travel and medical insurance to cover emergency medical expenses, repatriation, transport of mortal remains, funeral and hospitalisation.

When applying for a visa, a copy of the policy, with legible policy number, company name, duration of validity and sum of coverage or a letter from the insurance company including such data, should be submitted with the application.

Currency advice/regulations

Travellers cheques can be changed at official bureaux. It is a serious offence under Bulgarian law to exchange money anywhere except at an officially authorised exchange office. An exchange receipt must always be obtained and kept for Customs inspection on departure. It is illegal to import and export lev. The import of foreign currency is unlimited, although amounts exceeding US$2,200 must be declared. Export is restricted to amounts imported and declared.

Customs
Small quantities of spirits, wines and beverages are allowed in duty-free. Valuable personal effects should be declared verbally to Customs on entry. There are no restrictions on goods bought for foreign exchange in duty free shops at ports of entry.

Health (for visitors)
Foreign travellers must present valid evidence of health insurance to the Bulgarian border authorities in order to be admitted into the country.
Mandatory precautions
None
Advisable precautions
Recommended immunisations: hepatitis 'A', polio, tetanus, tick-borne encephalitis, typhoid.

Hotels
Deluxe, first- and second-class ratings system. Hotels have been upgraded to attract business people. Radisson and Hilton opened hotels in Sofia in 2001.

Credit cards
Main international credit cards are accepted in larger hotels and stores, especially in Sofia and on the Black Sea coast, and in some restaurants in larger cities.

Public holidays
Fixed dates
1 Jan (New Year's Day), 3 Mar (National Day), 1 May (Labour Day), 6 May (St George's Day), 24 May (St Cyril and Methodius Day/Culture Day), 6 Sep (Unification Day), 22 Sep (Independence Day), 1 Nov (Leaders of the Bulgarian Revival Day), 24–26 Dec (Christmas Holiday).
Variable dates
Orthodox Good Friday, Orthodox Easter Monday.

Working hours
Banking
Mon–Fri: 0800–1230, 1330–1530; Sat: 0830–1130.
Business
Mon–Fri: 0800 (0900)–1730 (1800).
Government
Mon–Fri: 0800 (0900)–1730 (1800).
Shops
Mon–Fri: 1000–2000; Sat: 0800–1400.

Electricity supply
220–240V AC/50 HZ

Social customs/useful tips
A nod of the head means 'No', a shake of the head means 'Yes'. Shaking hands is the traditional form of greeting. It is usual to invite your host to a good restaurant.

Security
By Western standards, the streets of Sofia and other towns and cities are generally safe. Street crime is slowly rising and the usual precautions should be taken.

Getting there
Air
Main international airlines operate flights to Sofia. Flight frequencies from some western cities are low. Travellers from Scandinavia, UK and the Netherlands may find it more convenient to fly to Vienna or Zurich and take connecting flights.
National airline: Balkan Air Tour.
International airport/s: Sofia (SOF) Vrajdebna airport, 12km from city centre.
Other airport/s: Varna (VAR), 9km from city; Burgas (BOJ), 13km from city.
Airport tax: None
Surface
Road: Frontier exit/entry points in Yugoslavia: Kalotina, Zlatarevo, Gjueshevo and Vrashkachuka. Turkey: Svilengrad and Capitan Andreevo. Romania: Rousse, Kardam and Durankulak. Greece: Koulata.
Rail: There are no direct rail services between Bulgaria and Western Europe. Links exist to Yugoslavia, Turkey, Romania and Greece.
Water: Ships provide regular passenger service and cruises on the Danube, starting at Passau in Germany, to Vienna, passing through Slovakia, Hungary and Serbia. There are also links with the Rhine, Black Sea and Main.
Main port/s: Burgas, Varna.

Getting about
National transport
Air: Balkan Air Tour operate domestic lines connecting Sofia with all main towns. Shuttle service to Varna and Burgas. Fares are generally inexpensive.
Road: The overall quality of the 13,000km of roads linking the major cities is good but some roads are in poor repair and full of potholes. International road signs are used and traffic drives on the right.
Rail: Approximately 6,500km of track connect all main towns. First-class travel is recommended. It is necessary to make reservations.
City transport
Taxis: Taxis are plentiful and cheap. Official taxis have meters, although some privately operated ones may not. A 5–10 per cent tip in local currency is usual.
Taxis to Sofia airport have a journey time of 15 minutes. Fares should be agreed before departure.
Buses, trams & metro: Efficient and cheap tram and bus services operate in Sofia. Flat rate fares are charged. Trolleybus services are available in Plovdiv and Varna.
Buses to the city centre from the airport run every 10 minutes during the day and every 20 minutes between 2100–0030, and take 25 minutes.
Car hire
An international driving permit is required. A green card (international car insurance) is compulsory. Most car hire accounts are transacted in hard currency. Drivers are normally given special petrol coupons, which can be used throughout the country. Speed limits: out of town 90kph and 120kph on motorways, in town 50kph. Drinking and driving is strictly prohibited. Tolls on motorways and other major roads were introduced in 1997. Fees must be paid in US dollars or Deutsche marks.

BUSINESS DIRECTORY
The addresses listed below are a selection only. While World of Information makes every endeavour to check these addresses, we cannot guarantee that changes have not been made, especially to telephone numbers and area codes. We would welcome any corrections.

Telephone area codes
The international direct dialling (IDD) code for Bulgaria is +359, followed by area code and subscriber's number:

Blagoevgrad	73	Rousse	82
Burgas	56	Smoliyan	301
Dobritch	58	Sofia	2
Gabrovo	66	Stara Zagora	42
Lovech	68	Varna	52
Plovdiv	32	Veliko Tûrnovo	62

Useful telephone numbers
Ambulance: 150
Fire brigade: 160
Police: 166
Operator: (inland) 121
   (international) 123
Directory enquiries: (corporate lines)144
   (private lines)145
Traffic police: 165
Road service: 146
Taxi: 142

Chambers of Commerce
American Chamber of Commerce in Bulgaria, Building 2, Mladost 4 Area, Business Park Sofia, 1715 Sofia (tel: 976-9565; fax: 976-9569; e-mail: amcham@amcham.bg).

British Bulgarian Chamber of Commerce, 8 Charles Darwin Street, 1113 Sofia (tel: 971-4756; fax: 738-331; e-mail: info@bbcc.bg).

Bulgarian Chamber of Commerce and Industry, 42 Parchevich Street, 1058 Sofia (tel: 987-2631; fax: 987-3209; e-mail: bcci@bcci.bg).

Burgas Chamber of Commerce and Industry, 12B L Karavelov Street, PO Box 644, 8000 Sofia (tel: 812-007; fax: 810-130; e-mail: bscci@bcci.bg).

Dobritch Chamber of Commerce and Industry, 14 Nezavisimost Street, PO Box 182, 9300 Dobritch (tel: 601-433; fax:601-434; e-mail: dbcci@bcci.bg).

Gabrovo Chamber of Commerce and Industry, 1Vazrazhdane Square, PO Box 217, 5300 Gabrovo (tel: 288-39; fax: 341-83; e-mail: gbcci@mbox.eda.bg).

Plovdev Chamber of Commerce and Industry, 7 Samara Street, 4003 Plovdev (tel: 652-645; fax: 652-647; e-mail: pcci@plovdiv-chamber.org).

Sousse Chamber of Commerce and Industry, 3 A Ferdinand Boulevard, PO Box 484, 7000 Rousse (tel: 825-884; fax: 825-873; e-mail: info@chamber.rousse.bg).

Stara Zagora Chamber of Commerce and Industry, 66 GS Rakovski Street, 6000 Stara Zagora (tel: 461-94; fax: 260-33; e-mail: office@chambersz.com).

Varna Chamber of Commerce and Industry, 135 Primorsky Boulevard, 9000 Varna (tel: 615-140; fax: 612-146; e-mail: office@vcci.bg).

Banking
Biochim Bank, 1 Ivan Vazov Street, 1040 Sofia (tel: 926-9210; fax: 981-9151; e-mail: info@biochim.com).

BulBank Ltd, 7 Sveta Nedelya Square, 1000 Sofia (tel: 984-1111; fax: 988-4636, 988-5370; e-mail: infor@sof.bulbank.bg).

Bulgarian Post Bank, 1 Bulgaria Square, 1414 Sofia (tel: 963-2104/5; e-mail: iap@postbank.bg).

DSK Bank, 19 Moskovska Street, 1040 Sofia (tel: 939-1220; fax: 980-6477).

Central bank
Bulgarska Narodna Banka, 1 Alexander Battenberg Square, 1000 Sofia (tel: 85-51; fax: 980-2425).

Travel information
Balkantourist, 1 Vitosha Boulevard, 1040 Sofia (tel: 43-331; fax: 800-134).

Balkan-Bulgarian Airlines, Sofia Airport, 1540 Sofia (tel: 881-800).

Central Railway Station, Maria Luisa Boulevard, Sofia (tel: 231-111).

Committee for Tourism, 1 Sveta Nedelya Square, 1000 Sofia (tel: 879-664; fax: 882-066).

Lufthansa Airport Office, Sofia (tel and fax: 793-695); town office (tel: 882-310, 884-223; fax: 981-2911).

Rila International Travel Offices, 5 Gurko Street, Sofia (tel: 870-777).

Sofia Airport (tel: 661-616; fax: 709-217).

Tourist Publicity Centre, 4 Triaditsa Street, 1000 Sofia (tel: 835-906).

Vrajdebna Airport (723-696).

Ministries
Ministry of Agriculture and Forests, 55 Hristo Botev Boulevard, 1000 Sofia (tel: 981-1546; fax: 885-557).

Ministry of Culture, 17 Alexander Stamboliiski Boulevard., 1000 Sofia (tel: 980-5384; fax: 981-8145).

Ministry of Defence, 3 Vassil Levsky Street, 1000 Sofia (tel: 862-4135; fax: 873-626).

Ministry of Economy, 12 Kniaz Alexander Batenberg Street, 1000 Sofia (tel: 981-9965, 987-9778; fax: 981-2515, 981-5039).

Ministry of Education and Science, 2a Doundukov Boulevard, 1000 Sofia (tel: 84-81; fax: 987-1289).

Ministry of Environment and Waters, 67 Gladstone Street, 1000 Sofia (tel: 814-269; fax: 521-634).

Ministry of Finance, 102 Georgi Rakovski Street, 1000 Sofia (tel: 869-1870; fax: 980-6863); external department (tel: 869-223; fax: 876-008).

Ministry of Foreign Affairs, 2 Alexander Jendov Street, 1000 Sofia (tel: 714-3507; fax: 736-069).

Ministry of Health, 5 Sveta Nedelya Square, 1000 Sofia (tel: 86-31; fax: 875-040).

Ministry of the Interior, 23 Gurko Street, 1000 Sofia (tel: 877-511; fax: 824-047).

Ministry of Justice, 1 Slavianska Street, 1000 Sofia (tel: 86-01; fax: 876-3226).

Ministry of Labour and Social Policy, 2 Triaditza Street, 1000 Sofia (tel: 981-1717; fax: 800-609).

Ministry of Regional and Urban Development, 17 Kiril & Methodius Street, 1000 Sofia (tel: 83-841; fax: 872-517).

Ministry of Transport, 9 Levski Street, 1000 Sofia (tel: 872-862; fax: 885-094).

Other useful addresses
Agency for Economic Co-ordination and Development, 1 Vassil Levsky Street, 1000 Sofia (tel: 543-386; fax: 833-323).

Agency for Privatisation, 29 Aksakov St, 1000 Sofia (tel: 873-188; fax: 882-938, 885-395).

Amex Representative Office, BICD, Rila Hotel, 6 Kalojan Street, Sofia 1000 (tel: 871-516).

Board of Customs Houses at the Ministry of Finance, 1 Aksakov Street, Sofia 1000 (tel: 869-528; fax: 884-909).

British Embassy, 38 Boulevard Vassil, Levski, Sofia 1000 (tel: 980-1220; fax: 988-5367).

Bulgarian Academy of Sciences, 1 7-mi Noemvri Street, 1000 Sofia (tel: 841-41; fax: 803-023).

Bulgarian Embassy (USA), 1621 22nd Street, NW, Washington DC 20008 (tel: 202-387-0174; fax: 202-234-7973; e-mail: office@bulgaria-embassy.org).

Bulgarian Foreign Investment Agency, 3 Sveta Sofia Street, 1000 Sofia (tel: 980-0918; fax: 980-1320; e-mail: fia@geobiz.com; internet site: http://www.bfia.org).

Bulgarian Industrial Association (BISA), 14 Alabin Street, 1000 Sofia (tel: 879-611, 872-960; fax: 872-604).

Bulgarian National Television, 29 San Stefano Str, 1504 Sofia (tel: 446-329; fax: 662-388).

Bulgarian News Agency (BTA), 49 Tzarigradsko Chaussee Blvd, 1024 Sofia (tel: 877-363, 877-739; fax: 802-488).

Bulgarian Telecommunication Company (BTC), 8 Totleben Blvd (tel: 870-143; fax: 875-885).

Bulgarian Telegraph Agency, Trakija Boulevard 49, Sofia (tel: 8461).

Bulgarian Translators' Union, 16 Graf Ignatiev Street, 1000 Sofia (tel: 661-602, 662-564; fax: 510-845, 661-233).

Bulgarreklama (advertising agency), 42 Parchevich Street, Sofia 1040 (tel: 85-151).

Central Co-operative Union, 99 Rakovski Street, 1000 Sofia (tel: 84-41; fax: 878-157).

Central Post Office, 4 Gurko Street, Sofia.

Committee for Energy, 8 Triaditsa Street, 1000 Sofia (tel: 861-91; fax: 876-279).

Committee for Forests, 17 Antim I Street, 1000 Sofia (tel: 861-71; fax: 873-235).

Committee for Geology and Mineral Resources, 22 Maria Louisa Blvd, 1000 Sofia (tel: 832-767; fax: 833-976).

Committee for Posts and Telecommunications, 6 Gourko Street, 1000 Sofia (tel: 889-646, 871-837; fax: 814-512, 800-044).

Committee for Television, 29 San Stefano Street, 1504 Sofia (tel: 43-481).

Committee for Standardisation and Metrology, 21 6-ti Septemvri Street, 1000 Sofia (tel: 85-91; fax: 801-402).

Council of Ministers, 1 Dondoukov Blvd., 1000 Sofia (tel: 8501; fax: 884-252).

EU Energy Centre (Thermie), 51 James Boucher Blvd, 1407 Sofia (tel: 681-461, 683-542; fax: 681-461).

Euro Information Centre, Network/Correspondence Centre, 54 Dr GM Dimitrov Blv, 1125 Sofia (tel: 738-448; fax: 730-435).

Bulgaria

First Bulgarian Stock Exchange, 1 Macedonia Square, 1040 Sofia (tel: 815-711; fax: 875-566; internet site: http://www.bse-sofia.bg).

Foreign Aid Agency, 1 Vrabcha Street, 1000 Sofia (tel: 881-951; fax: 885-039).

Intercommerce (import, export, re-export and transit operations, compensation deals and foreign trade transactions), 21 Aksakov Str, 1000 Sofia (tel: 879-364; fax: 873-753).

International Fair – Plovdiv, G. Dimitrov Boulevard 37 (tel: 553-191, 553-146, 26-129, 26-139).

International Road Transport (SO MAT), Gorublyane, 1738 Sofia (tel: 712-121, 758-015; fax: 758-015).

Interpred World Trade Center (representation of foreign companies), 36 Dragan Tzankov Boulevard, 1040 Sofia (tel: 7146-4646; fax: 700-006, 706-401).

Law Offices for Foreign Legal Matters (tel: 877-782).

Medical Industry Association, Bademova Gora Street 20-a, Sofia 1404 (tel: 592-111).

Scientific Institute for International Co-operation and Foreign Economic Activities, 3A 165 Street, Zh K Izgreva, 1113 Sofia (tel: 708-336; fax: 705-154, 700-131).

Small and Medium-Sized Enterprises (SME) Development Programme, Agency for Privatisation, 29 Aksakov Str, 1046 Sofia (tel: 871-913; fax: 871-912).

Sofia Press Agency, 113 Tsarigradsko Shosse Blvd. (tel: 878-428; fax: 883-455).

Sofia Customs Office, 1 Aksakov Street, 1000 Sofia (tel: 800-402; fax: 884-909).

State Insurance Institute, 3 Benkovski Street, 1000 Sofia (tel: 879-341; fax: 871-429).

Union for Private Economic Enterprise, 2a Suborna Street, 1000 Sofia (tel: 659-371; fax: 659-411).

Internet sites

Background information on the government and useful links: http://www.vii.org/afgrbulg.htm

Bulgaria business catalogue and useful links: http://www.bulgaria.com

Bulgarian Economic Forum: http://www.biforum.org/

Bulgaria financial and business newspaper: http://www.pari.bg/

Bulgarian Internation Business Association: http://www.biba.bg/

Bulgarian News Agency: http://www.bta.bg/site/en/indexe.shtml

SG Expressbank AD: http://www.sgexpressbank.bg

Burkina Faso

KEY FACTS

Official name: République Démocratique Populaire de Burkina Faso (Popular Democratic Republic of Burkina Faso)

Head of State: President Captain Blaise Compaoré (since 1987, re-elected 13 November 2005)

Head of government: Prime Minister Paramanga Ernest Yonli (since Nov 2000)

Ruling party: Coalition led by Congrès pour la Démocratie et le Progrès (CDP) (Congress for Democracy and Progress)

Area: 274,000 square km

Population: 12.44 million (2004)

Capital: Ouagadougou

Official language: French

Currency: CFA franc (CFAf) = 100 centimes (Communauté Financière Africaine (African Financial Community) franc). New notes have been issued; old notes cease to be legal tender from Jan 2005.

Exchange rate: CFAf544.07 per US$ (Oct 2005); CFAf655.95 per euro (pegged from Jan 1999)

GDP per capita: US$412 (2004)

GDP real growth: 4.80% (2004)

Labour force: 5.77 million (2004)

Inflation: -0.40% (2004)

Balance of trade: -US$447.70 million (2004)

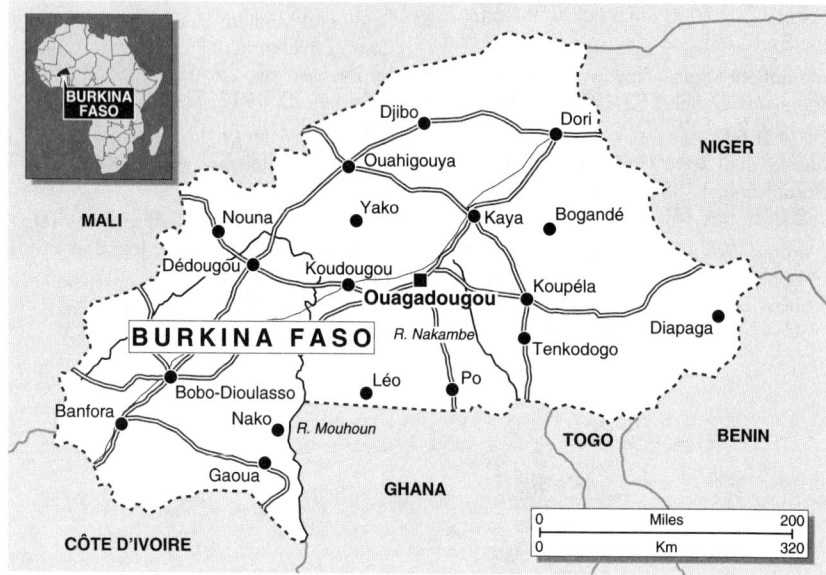

Finance minister Jean-Baptiste Compaoré – not to be confused with President Blaise Compaoré, head of the family and the country – outlines Burkina Faso's strategy for further development as primarily focussed on diversification of the cotton based economy.

Economy

Like many African countries, Burkina Faso relies economically on one commodity, over which it does not have absolute control. This means the economy remains very vulnerable to external shocks. Growth of 6.8 per cent in 2003 became 4.8 per cent in 2004 – not all due to world prices and markets: there was an invasion of locusts and poor rainfall. A major obstacle to growth remains farm subsidies by western governments which cut into demand for Burkinabe cotton. Like most African countries Burkina Faso is an outspoken critic of this perceived inequity. Burkinabe workers are attracted to the more economically viable plantations of neighbouring Côte d'Ivoire and Gabon – and many do not return home.

While the country, unlike many in Africa, spends substantially on social services and regularly improves its key indicators of education and health, to boost its social spending, it needs to rely on a significant increase in external aid flows over the medium-term. Longer-term, economic diversification and increased productivity will focus on rural development, the reform of public utilities and improvements in governance, with the aim of strengthening the business climate.

But the tax screw is tightening. The continued orientation of expenditures toward key social services, notably health and education, as well as growth and productivity-enhancing capital investments has been welcome, but it carries a price. Improvements in tax administration have already contributed to an increase in revenues by half a percentage point of GDP. Structural measures will broaden the tax base and improve tax compliance. After a taxpayer census, a joint tax-customs brigade will conduct comprehensive tax audits. There are moves towards automatic price adjustment mechanisms for domestic petroleum products and the phasing out of subsidies on utilities, but in line with diversification into agriculture subsidies on fertilisers, which will remain.

Clearly supportive of a leading role for the private sector in development and transparency in doing business, Compaoré, is supporting a number of programmes to help small- and medium-sized enterprises engaged in construction and other services. Through a General Organisational Framework for Budgetary Support, he has made the government more accountable for how it uses resources. The private sector will be invited to participate in the energy and telecommunications sectors. Tourism is set to become a new money earner and, as importantly, a source of new jobs. The World Travel and Tourism Council forecasts annual revenue will reach US$720 million by 2015 and 131,000 jobs will have been created.

But Compaoré wants a quid pro quo and has told donors that as his government strives for fiscal transparency, its donor partners should support it by introducing mechanisms suited to (his) national environment, so that exogenous shocks that so often beset an aid-recipient country may be better taken into account. This would be a partnership that allowed for real government ownership of its policies, essential for achieving sustainable development.

IMF funding

In September 2005, the International Monetary Fund (IMF) released a further US$5.1 million to Burkina Faso for poverty reduction and growth, bringing the total so far made available to US$25.5 million.

Full of praise, the IMF first deputy managing director commended Burkina Faso for sound macroeconomic policies. A sharp decline in world cotton prices and an increase in world oil prices had reduced economic growth prospects for 2005, but the country's programme struck an appropriate balance between the need for fiscal restraint in the face of economic shock and the need to push ahead with priority expenditures in support of poverty reduction strategy. Expenditures had remained oriented toward key social services, notably health and education, as well as growth and productivity-enhancing capital investments.

The government had encouraged cotton producers to find their own solution to the drop in prices without recourse to budget subsidies. The government would continue to support the sector through projects to improve infrastructure, enhance productivity, and conduct research.

Over the past decade, Burkina Faso has maintained an average annual real growth rate of more than six per cent, but the 5.7 per cent of 2001 and 6.8 per cent of 2003 were down to 3.5 per cent over 2005. Since 2001, the trade balance has remained reasonably constant at a negative 300 per cent. Preliminary figures for 2005 show little change. The headcount poverty index declined by eight percentage points between 1998 and 2003, but Burkina Faso continues to rank among the poorest countries in the world.

Politics

Burkina Faso has spent many of its post-independence years under military rule. The last but one coup was in 1983, led by Thomas Sankara who adopted a policy of nonalignment. His rule was cut short after only four years, when in the final coup to date he was overthrown by his minister of state Blaise Compaoré and subsequently executed.

In 1991 Burkina Faso adopted a constitution which provided for direct multi-party elections. Blaise Compaoré was returned as president in elections the following year and continued to dominate the politics of Burkina Faso. Compaoré, having successfully managed the multi-party coalition democracy he subsequently created is now in his nineteenth year of presidency. Not until the 2002 elections was the grip of his Congrès pour la Démocratie et le Progrès (CDP) (Congress for Democracy and Progress) party on the national assembly broken. The main opposition parties, which had boycotted previous elections in 1992 and 1998, succeeded in reducing the CDP's representation in the 111-seat assembly from 103 seats to 57. This democracy in action did not please Compaoré and tension between the two sides continues.

Compaoré won his third straight term in November 2005 by a landslide, beating 11 other contenders and taking 80 per cent of the vote. Born in 1950 and trained as a soldier, he has disarmed local militias and, despite his reputed left-wing leanings, embarked on a programme of privatisation and austerity measures urged upon him by the IMF.

The president of Burkina Faso exercises executive power and appoints the prime minister. Compaoré keeps a tight hold over the military and government and portrays himself as the guarantor of political stability and economic progress. His prime minister is Paramanga Ernest Yonli, foreign minister Youssouf Ouedraogo and finance minister Jean-Baptiste Marie Pascal Compaoré.

The country faces international censure over its record of human rights and, more recently, that it was involved in the smuggling of 'blood diamonds' from Sierra Leone to world markets. This was tacit support for rebels opposing the Sierra Leone government and using money from the sale of the gems to fund their campaign. Similarly, there is tension with Côte d'Ivoire, which accuses Burkina Faso of backing rebels who hold the north of that country.

Outlook

The anticipated low (cotton) and high (oil) prices are expected to, at least for a year or so, take the shine off Burkina Faso's IMF-lauded sound macroeconomic policies and structural reforms. Structural reforms will be necessary to establish the conditions for a resumption of robust economic growth.

A donor-backed aid package is funding an Education For All Fast Track Initiative (EFA-FTI) to provide every child with primary school education by 2015. It will

KEY INDICATORS — Burkina Faso

	Unit	2000	2001	2002	2003	2004
Population	m	11.90	11.90	12.19	12.31	12.44
Gross domestic product (GDP)	US$bn	2.20	2.30	2.80	2.68	*4.82
GDP per capita	US$	185	193	230	218	412
GDP real growth	%	2.2	5.7	5.2	6.5	4.8
Inflation	%	-0.2	4.9	2.7	1.7	-0.4
Exports (fob) (goods)	US$m	210.0	230.0	254.0	250.0	418.6
Imports (fob) (goods)	US$m	530.0	510.0	574.0	525.0	866.3
Balance of trade	US$m	-320.0	-280.0	-320.0	-275.0	-447.7
Current account	US$m	-320.0	-290.0	-300.0	-320.0	-440.0
Total reserves minus gold	US$m	243.6	260.5	313.4	434.8	430.6
Foreign exchange	US$m	233.8	250.9	303.1	423.6	419.1
Exchange rate	per US$	711.98	733.04	696.99	574.89	496.63

* estimated figure

include education about the HIV/Aids epidemic. With 6.5 per cent of its adult population suffering from the disease, Burkina Faso has the second highest infection rate in West Africa. The United Nations estimates life expectancy down to 47 years for men, 48 years for women.

Risk assessment

Economic	Poor
Political	Satisfactory
Regional stability	Poor

COUNTRY PROFILE

Historical profile
Formerly an ancient African kingdom, the area was taken over by France in the nineteenth century, who did little to develop it preferring to provide local workers for neighbouring Côte d'Ivoire.
Translated into English as the 'land of honest men', Burkina Faso (known as Upper Volta until 1938) was created as an administrative unit, by the French, as late as 1947. It became politically independent in 1960, ruled by a civilian government under Maurice Yameogo. He was ousted by the army in 1966 following mass opposition to austerity measures. To its credit, the army had been reluctant to assume power and set about organising the introduction of a new civilian government, drawing up the 1970 constitution which provided for semi-civilan rule for the next four years. Fractional struggles within the civilian political parties came to a head in 1974 and the army again formally took over government. Later all political parties were banned. A wave of strikes in 1976 finally forced the complete demilitarisation of politics. Instability – in the form of *coups d'état* and even assassinations – remained the determining feature of Burkinabe politics until the early 1990s.
1958 The country was given self-government.
1960 Granted full independence from France as Upper Volta. Maurice Yameogo became first president.
1966 Yameogo was ousted in a military coup by Colonel Sangoule Lamizama.
1970 A new constitution was agreed by a referendum, it detailed the introduction of an elected president and civilian administration by 1975.
1974 Lamizama suspended the constitution and assumed the presidency.
1978 Multiparty elections for president and National Assembly were held. Lamizama and his followers won and he retained the presidency.
1980 Yameogo, was overthrown in a coup by Colonel Saye Zerbo.
1982 Major Jean-Baptiste Ouédraogo overthrew Zerbo.
1983 Captain Thomas Sankara led a coup and took over as president.
1984 Upper Volta's name was changed.
1987 Sankara was assassinated. Captain Blaise Compaoré seized power backed by the Organisation pour la Démocratie Populaire-Mouvement du Travail (ODP-MT) (Organization for People's Democracy-Workers' Movement).
1991 Compaoré was elected president, following the withdrawal of opposition candidates.
1992 The ODP-MT won a convincing victory in the national legislature elections.
1996 The ODP-MT merged with the Parti pour la Démocratie et le Progrès (Party for Democracy and Progress) to become the Congrès pour la Démocratie et le Progrès (CDP) (Congress for Democracy and Progress).
1998 Compaoré won the presidential election, which was boycotted by opposition parties.
1999 Prime Minister Ouédraogo and his cabinet resigned, but he and his cabinet were reinstated by presidential decree.
2000 A UN report accused the president of not only allowing Burkina Faso to be involved in sanctions busting of UN embargoes to Angola but also of being in personal receipt of payments for diamond smuggling activities undertaken through his country by Unita rebels.
2001 International donors agreed to fund a US$85 million programme to combat the HIV/Aids epidemic.
2002 The CDP retained its majority in parliamentary election.
2004 Burkina Faso was included on the US African Growth and Opportunity Act (AGOA) list of countries allowed preferential trading with the US.
2005 Blaise Compaoré was re-elected president 13 November with 80.3 per cent of the votes, while Bénéwendé Stanislas Sankara won 4.9 per cent. Turnout was 57.5 per cent.

Political structure
Constitution
Constitutional changes were adopted in January 1997. These included the abolition of the limit of two seven-year terms for the president, and an increase in the number of seats in the legislature from 107 to 111.
Form of state
Unitary and secular state
The executive
Executive power is vested in the head of state (the president), who is elected by universal suffrage for a seven-year term. The president may serve unlimited terms. The Council of Ministers is appointed by the president on the recommendation of the prime minister who is also appointed by the president, with the consent of the legislature.
National legislature
The parliament comprises two chambers, the Assemblée des Députés Populaires (ADP) (National Assembly) and the Chambre Des Représentants (House of Representatives).
The multi-party ADP has 111 members, who are elected for a four-year term. The House of Representatives, which acts only as a consultative chamber, has 120 members, who are elected for a three-year term.
Last elections
5 May 2002 (parliamentary); 15 November 1998 (presidential).
Results: Parliamentary: the CDP retained its majority, although its number of seats in the 111-seat declined from 103 to 57; the ADF-RDA became the main opposition party with 17 seats.
Presidential: Blaise Compaore was re-elected with 87.5 per cent of the vote.
Next elections
2005 (presidential); 2006 (parliamentary).

Political parties
Ruling party
Coalition led by Congrès pour la Démocratie et le Progrès (CDP) (Congress for Democracy and Progress)
Main opposition party
Alliance pour la Démocratie et la Féderation- Rassemblement Démocratique Africain (ADF-RDA) (Alliance for Democracy and Federation-African Democratic Rally)

Population
12.44 million (2004)
Ethnic make-up
There are a number of ethnic groups, the most numerous of whom are the Mossi in the north (49 per cent), the Gourma in the east and the Bobo in the south-west. Other sizeable groups include the Fulani, the Hausa, the nomadic Tuareg with their Bella domestic serfs in the north-west and the Lobi in the south.
Religions
Animist (55 per cent), Muslim (40 per cent), Catholic (5 per cent).

Education
Only two in five children are able to attend school, due to the chronic lack of places.
Burkina Faso secured financial aid from the international donor community in 2002, in the form of a three-year package aimed at building capacity in education. The agreement encompassed the Education For All Fast Track Initiative (EFA-FTI) with the goal of providing every child with primary school education by 2015. The first phase of financing is aimed at the 1.2 million children currently unable to attend primary school. The initial financing will

also be used to train new teachers, pay teachers' salaries, build new schools, help education systems, respond to HIV/Aids, and put in place other steps to ensure a quality primary education for all children.
Literacy rate: 33 per cent men, 13 per cent women; adult rates (World Bank).
Pupils per teacher: 47 in primary schools.

Health
Total expenditure on health is some 4–5 per cent of GDP, of which government spending is 70 per cent.
HIV/Aids
Burkina Faso has the second highest infection rate in West Africa, next to Côte d'Ivoire. In February 2003, the UN Development Programme (UNDP) announced the provision of US$9.5 million in funding for the fight against HIV/Aids, poverty reduction and other activities in Burkina Faso. It is expected that half of the funding will be concentrated on the HIV/Aids programme, including prevention of HIV transmission, improved co-ordination and monitoring, and care for infected and affected persons.

A programme to provide anti-retroviral drugs was scaled down in December 2004, instead of the 27,000 patients WHO said should receive treatment, it is expected in 2005 that only 15,000 patients will be targetted. Lack of political commitment, poor infrastructure – with a lack of medical personnel – and a centralised distribution network are sited as major contributing factors in the programme's shortcomings.
HIV prevalence: 4.2 per cent aged 15–49 in 2003 (World Bank)
Life expectancy: 42.8 years (World Bank)
Fertility rate/Maternal mortality rate: 6.2 births per woman (World Bank)
Infant mortality rate: 107 per 1,000 live births; 34 per cent of children aged under five are malnourished (World Bank).
Head of population per physician/bed: 1 physician per 32,000 people

Welfare
The Social Insurance Scheme provides benefits for old age pensions, disability and a survivor's fund. The fund is open to workers who contribute 4.5 per cent of the wages and this is matched by their employer.

Main cities
Ouagadougou (capital, estimated population 962,100 in 2003), Bobo Dioulasso (319,500), Koudougou (72,600).

Languages spoken
African languages include More, Dioula, Gourmantche and Peul. French is the universal medium for documentation.
Official language/s
French

Media
Press
Dailies: The main national dailies are *Sidwaya* (government-controlled), *Le Pays*, *l'Observateur* (Burkinabe daily newspaper) and *24 Heures*.
Weeklies: Weeklies published from Ouagadougou include *Indépendent*, *Intrus Journal du Jeudi*, *Observateur* and *Le Journal du Soir*.
Periodicals: Several periodicals mainly economic and industrial are published.
Broadcasting
Radio: Radio Burkina broadcasts in French and 13 African languages. Also private FM stereo radio (Horizon FM).
Television: Télévision Nationale du Burkina provides transmissions seven days a week to Ouagadougou and Bobo Dioulasso, Koudougou and Ouahigouya, in French and African languages.

Economy
Burkina Faso is a mainly agrarian economy. The sector accounted for around 31 per cent of GDP in 2004. More than 80 per cent of the population is engaged in subsistence agriculture and nomadic livestock rearing. It is one of the poorest countries in Africa, with 45 per cent of the population, mainly in the countryside, living below the poverty line in 2004. Reforms since 1991, supported by the IMF and the World Bank, have contributed to growth in GDP, stabilisation of inflation and some reduction in the poverty rate, but Burkino Faso continues to be dependent on foreign aid. The economy, despite positive developments, remains fragile and vulnerable to weather conditions and world commodity prices. The growing strength of the economy is encouraging foreign support for poverty reduction and reform. Since 2003, instability in neighbouring Côte d'Ivoire has added to Burkino Faso's problems, with the need to divert resources to humanitarian assistance and security measures.

Cotton is the main source of foreign currency, accounting for around 65 per cent of export earnings. World prices fell in 2004, but not before Burkino Faso had sold most of its crop early in the year. Prices improved in 2005, but competition from subsidised cotton growers, especially in the US and other OECD countries, is a continuing threat to the market. The World Bank and the IMF are encouraging Burkino Faso to diversify as a means of strengthening the economy against external shocks.

External trade
Imports
Main imports are foodstuffs, fuel and energy, and capital goods.
Main sources: France (31.5 per cent total, 2004), Côte d'Ivoire (13.9 per cent), Togo (8.5 per cent)

Exports
Main exports include cotton, gold, live animals, hides and skins.
Main destinations: China (32.3 per cent total, 2004), Singapore (10.7 per cent), Bangladesh (4.5 per cent), Ghana 94.4 per cent), Colombia (4.4 per cent)

Agriculture
Farming
The agricultural sector accounts for around a third of GDP and employs three-quarters of the workforce. It accounts for around 65 per cent of export earnings. Over 80 per cent of the population is engaged in subsistence farming and nomadic stock raising.

Burkina Faso is prone to drought and has poor soil. Only 10 per cent of the total land area is cultivated. There are plans to mechanise farming and open up new areas for development.

Principal food crops are sorghum, millet, yams, maize, rice and beans.

Cotton is the main cash crop and is the country's principal foreign exchange earner; others are sheanuts, sesame and sugar cane.

Livestock production is concentrated in the north, mainly for export to Côte d'Ivoire (which has severely restricted its Burkinabè beef imports in recent years) and Ghana. Crop production in 2004 included: 3,062,501 tonnes (mt) cereals in total, 1,481,212t sorghum, 880,912t millet, 1.5mt sorghum, 594,580t maize, 95,168t rice, *37,000t sweet potatoes, *25,000t yams, 450,000t sugar cane, 301,000t groundnuts (in shells), 15,000t sesame seed, *391,000t pulses, *65,500t roots and tubers, 177,120t oilcrops, 575,000t seed cotton, 210,000t cotton lint, *78,110t fruit in total, *232,000t vegetables in total. Livestock production included: 146,026t meat in total, 58,080t beef, 9,708t pig meat, 14,040t lamb, 27,487t goat meat, *28,240t poultry, *18,200t eggs, 241,200t milk, 9,504t cattle hides, 3,432t sheepskins.
* estimate
Forestry
Production in 2004 included: 12.9 million cubic metres (cum) roundwood, 85,000cum sawlogs and veneers, 11.7 million cum woodfuel, 495,851t charcoal.

Industry and manufacturing
The industrial sector as a whole contributes around 20 per cent to GDP and employs 10 per cent of the workforce; manufacturing contributes 13.5 per cent. Production is centred on the processing of agricultural commodities (flour milling, sugar refining, manufacture of cotton yarn and textiles) and production of consumer goods, including moped/bicycle assembly, footwear and soap manufacture.

Nations of the World: A Political, Economic and Business Handbook

Foreign investment is minimal and development remains handicapped by the chronic shortages of raw materials and spares.

Tourism
Tourism is at an early stage of development. While hotel accommodation is expanding, most of it is confined to Ouagadougou and Bobo Diaoulasso, and access to some tourist sites is difficult. Burkina Faso received around 130,000 arrivals in 2004. The sector is expected to contribute 2.1 per cent to GDP in 2005. Europe is the main source of visitors, especially France, followed by Africa. The country comprises four tourist regions. Ouagadougou is an artistic and business centre, while the west specialises in indigenous culture, the Sahel in adventure holidays, and the east, which is home to two national parks, in safaris and hunting. The economic importance of the sector is recognised, with rural and eco-tourism being the focus of further development.

Mining
The sector contributes around 7 per cent to GDP and employs 2 per cent of the workforce.
Activity is confined to extraction of gold-bearing quartz at Poura (reserves estimated at 30 tonnes), marble and antimony.
There are viable deposits of zinc and silver at Perkoa, and some 15 million tonnes of manganese deposits at Tambao, as well as known reserves of limestone, bauxite, nickel, phosphates and lead.
Exploitation of resources is hindered by weak infrastructure.
Burkina Faso has a geological structure similar to that of the world's richest gold producing areas.

Hydrocarbons
There are no known reserves of oil or gas. Burina Faso relies entirely on imports of refined oil, mainly gasoline and distillate. Nigeria has made trade deals of oil with Burkina Faso as a way of improving relations.

Energy
The rural population relies on wood as a fuel for cooking, which is leading to deforestation and desertification in some areas.
Electricity supply is overseen by the Societé Nationale Burkinabe d'Electricité (Sonabel). Installed generation capacity is estimated at around 90MW. Only 14 per cent of the country, mainly the urban areas, has access to electricity and there is no national electricity grid. 85 per cent of electricity is supplied by thermal power. Some electricity is imported from Côte d'Ivoire.

Electricity is regarded as crucial to the country's development and the government is keen to extend transmission lines and improve supply to meet growing demand.

Financial markets
Burkina Faso has no stock exchange.

Banking and insurance
The banking sector has undergone liberalisation in recent years, with the government restricting its involvement to around a quarter of the sector.
Central bank
Banque Centrale des Etats de l'Afrique de l'Ouest (central banking authority for the members of the West African Monetary Union)
Main financial centre
Ouagadougou

Time
GMT

Geography
Burkina Faso is a landlocked country in West Africa, bordered by Mali to the west and north, by Niger to the east, and by Benin, Togo, Ghana and Côte d'Ivoire to the south.

Climate
The climate is tropical. The dry season runs from November–March, when the Harmattan wind blows, keeping the humidity low. Temperatures in Ouagadougou range from 14 degrees Celsius (C) at night to over 35 degrees C during the day. The main rainy season is from June–October. The highest rainfall is in the south, lowest in the far north where an arid desert climate prevails.

Entry requirements
Passports
Required by all except holders of national identity cards issued to nationals of Benin, Central African Republic, Côte d'Ivoire, Guinea, Mali, Mauritania, Niger, Senegal and Togo.
Passports must be valid for six months after departure.
Visa
Required by all, except citizens of Ecowas territories. Applications for tourist and business visas should include itineraries and vaccination certificates against yellow fever. Business visas require a company letter of introduction.
An onward or return ticket is also required.
Currency advice/regulations
There are no restrictions on the import/export of foreign currency or local currency.

Health (for visitors)
Mandatory precautions
Yellow fever vaccination certificate.

Advisable precautions
Typhoid, tetanus, hepatitis A and polio vaccinations are recommended. Malaria prophylaxis should be taken as risk exists throughout the country. Water precautions are also advisable. There is a risk of rabies. Visitors should seek advice with regard to vaccinations for diphtheria, heptaitis B, meningitis and tuberculosis.

Hotels
Hotels are available in Ouagadougou and Bobo Dioulasso with limited availability elsewhere. It is advisable to book in advance. Service is included in bills and gratuities are customary for taxis and porters.

Public holidays
Fixed dates
1 Jan (New Year's Day), 3 Jan (Anniversary of the 1966 Coup d'État), 8 Mar (Women's Day), 1 May (Labour Day), 4 Aug (Revolution Day), 5 Aug (Independence Day), 15 Aug (Assumption Day), 15 Oct (Anniversary of the 1987 Coup d'État), 1 Nov (All Saints' Day), 11 Dec (Proclamation of the Republic), 25 Dec (Christmas Day).
Variable dates
Easter Monday, Ascension Day, Eid al Adha, Eid al Fitr, Islamic New Year, Birth of the Prophet.
The Islamic year contains 354 or 355 days, with the result that Muslim feasts advance by 10–12 days against the Gregorian calendar. Dates of feasts vary according to the sighting of the new moon, so cannot be forecast exactly. Islamic year 1426: 10 February 2005 to 30 January 2006.

Working hours
Banking
Mon–Fri: 0830–1130 and 1530–1630.
Business
Mon–Fri: 0730–1230 and 1500–1730.
Government
Mon–Fri: 0730–1230 and 1500–1730.
Shops
(Mon–Sat) 0800–1300 and 1500–1900; (Sun) 0800–1200.

Electricity supply
220/380 V AC, 50 cycles.

Getting there
Air
National airline: Air Burkina
International airport/s: Ouagadougou (OUA), 8km from city, restaurant, car hire.
Other airport/s: Bobo Dioulasso (BOY), 1.9km from city.
Surface
Road: Most practical during dry seasons – from Mali (Bamako) and Niger (Niamey), when buses operate on these routes. The road from Ghana is being improved.

Land journeys are also possible from Côte d'Ivoire, Benin and Togo.
Rail: Daily express service from Abidjan (Côte d'Ivoire) to Bobo Dioulasso and Ouagadougou. Sleeping and dining cars.

Getting about
National transport
Air: Air Burkina serves Ouagadougou, Bobo Dioulasso and other main centres. Light aircraft can be chartered from Air Burkina. The airline also operates flights to surrounding countries, Mali, Togo, Benin, Côte d'Ivoire and Niger.
Road: Conditions vary; some roads are only passable in dry season, although international roads are all-weather.
Buses: Services from Ouagadougou to main towns.
Rail: Daily railcar service runs Ouagadougou-Bobo Dioulasso and on to Côte d'Ivoire; two classes; some restaurant cars, sleeping accommodation and air-conditioning. Service can become overloaded.
City transport
Taxis: Unmetered and available in main centres. A 10 per cent tip is usually given.
Buses, trams & metro: Frequent in Ouagadougou and Bobo Dioulasso.
Car hire
National licence plus permit or international driving licence required. Use of chauffeur-driven cars advised.

BUSINESS DIRECTORY

Telephone area codes
The international direct dialling code (IDD) for Burkina Faso is +226, followed by subscriber's number.

Useful telephone numbers
Police: 17
Fire: 18
Ambulance: 3066-43/44/45

Chamber of Commerce
Burkina Faso Chamber of Commerce, Industry and Handicrafts, 118/220 Rue 3.119, 01 PO Box 502, Ouagadougou (tel: 306-114; fax: 306-116; e-mail: ccia-bf@ccia.bf).

Banking
Banque Internationale du Burkina, BP 1336, Av Nelson Mandela 800, Ouagadougou 01 (tel: 307-888, 307-878; fax: 310628).

Banque Internationale du Burkina SA, BP 362, Rue de la Chance, Ouagadougou 01 (tel: 306 170, 306-171; fax: 300-171, 310-094).

Banque Internationale pour le Commerce, l'Industrie et l'Agriculture du Burkina SA, BP 8, Avenue Dr Kwamé N'Krumah 479, Ouagadougou 01 (tel: 306-226/8, 306-227; fax: 311-955).

Caisse Nationale de Crédit Agricole du Burkina (CNCAB), BP 1644, Avenue Gamal Abdel Naser 2, Ouagadougou 01 (tel: 333-333).

Ecobank-Burkina, BP 145, Rue Maurice Bishop 633, Espace Fadima, Ouagadougou 01 (tel: 318-975, 318-980; fax: 318-981, 318-982).

Société Générale de Banque au Burkina (SGBB), BP 585, Rue du Marché 4, Ouagadougou 01 (tel: 323-232; fax: 310-561).

Central bank
Banque Centrale des Etats de l'Afrique de l'Ouest, Avenue Gamal Abdel Nasser, PO Box 356, Ouagadougou (tel: 306-015; fax: 310-122).

Travel information
Air Burkina, Siège Sociale, avenue Loudun, BP 1459, Ouagadougou 307676 (tel: 306-144; fax: 310-268).

Division du Tourisme et de l'Hôtellerie, BP 624, Ouagadougou (tel: 332-448).

Ministry of tourism
Ministry of Transport and Tourism, 03 BP 7068, Ouagadougou 03 (tel: 306-211).

National tourist organisation offices
Faso Tours (national travel agency), BP 1318, Ouagadougou (tel: 335-350).

Ministries
Ministry of Agriculture, 03 BP 7005, Ouagadougou 03 (tel: 324-114).

Ministry of Administration, 03 BP 7034, Ouagadougou 03 (tel: 324-833).

Ministry of Commerce and Industry, 01 BP 365 Ouagadougou 01 (tel: 324-786).

Ministry of Communications, 03 BP 7045, Ouagadougou 03 (tel: 324-833).

Ministry of Defence, 01 BP 496, Ouagadougou 01 (tel: 307-214).

Ministry of Education, 03 BP 7032, Ouagadougou 03 (tel: 324-870).

Ministry of Employment and Social Security, 03 BP 7016, Ouga 03 (tel: 310-960).

Ministry of Energy and Mines, 01 BP 3922 Ouagadougou 01 (tel: 324-786).

Ministry of the Environment and Water, 03 BP 7044 Ouagadougou 01 (tel: 324-074).

Ministry of the Family, 01 BP 515, Ouagadougou 01 (tel: 310-960).

Ministry of Finance and Economy, 03 BP 7012, Ouagadougou 03 (tel: 306-995).

Ministry of Foreign Affairs, 03 BP 7038, Ouagadougou 03 (tel: 324-733; fax: 308-792; internet: www.mae.gov.bf/).

Ministry of Health, 03 P 7009 Ouagadougou (tel: 324-158).

Ministry of Higher Education and Scientific Research, 03 BP 7047, Ouagadougou 03 (tel: 324-567).

Ministry of Integration and African Affairs, 01 BP 6943, Ouagadougou 01 (tel: 324-833).

Ministry of the Interior, 03 BP 7011, Ouagadougou 03 (tel: 324-905).

Ministry of Justice, 01 BP 526, Ouagadougou 01 (tel: 324-833).

Ministry of Public Relations and Modernisation of Administration, 03 BP 7006, Ouagadougou 03 (tel: 306-995).

Ministry of Youth and Sports, 03 BP 7035, Ouagadougou 03 (tel: 324-786).

Other useful addresses
Burkina Faso Embassy (USA), 2340 Massachusetts Avenue, NW, Washington DC 20008 (tel: 202-332-5577; fax: 202-667-1882; e-mail: ambawdc@rcn.com).

Groupement des Petits Commerçants, BP 952, Ouagadougou.

Institut de la Statistique et de la Démographie, BP 374, Ouagadougou (tel: 335-537).

Office National de Commerce Extérieur, BP 389, Ouagadougou (tel: 336-225).

Société de Commercialisation, BP 531, Ouagadougou (tel: 333-007); BP 375, Bobo-Dioulasso (tel: 390-423).

Syndicat des Entrepreneurs et Industriels, BP 446, Ouagadougou.

Télévision Nationale du Burkina, BP 7029, Ouagadougou (tel: 336-801).

West African Economic Community, BP 643, Ouagadougou.

Internet sites
Africa Business Network: http://www.ifc.org/abn

AllAfrica.com: http://www.allafrica.com

African Development Bank: http://www.afdb.org

Africa Online: http://www.africaonline.com

Burkina Faso: http://www.fasobusiness.com

Mbendi AfroPaedia (information on companies, countries, industries and stock exchanges in Africa): http://mbendi.co.za

Burundi

KEY FACTS

Official name: Republika y'Uburundi (Republic of Burundi)

Head of State: President Pierre Nkurunziza (Hutu) (from 26 Aug 2005)

Head of government: President Pierre Nkurunziza (Hutu) (from 26 Aug 2005)

Ruling party: Conseil National pour la Défense de la Démocratie-Forces pour la Défense de la Démocratie (CNDD-FDD), (National Council for Defence of Democracy-Force for the Defence of Democracy)

Area: 27,834 square km

Population: 7.80 million (2004)

Capital: Bujumbura

Official language: Kirundi and French

Currency: Burundi franc (Buf) = 100 centimes

Exchange rate: Buf1,035.95 per US$ (Oct 2005)

GDP per capita: US$91 (2004)

GDP real growth: 5.50% (2004)

Labour force: 3.92 million (2004)

Inflation: 7.90% (2004); 12.6 (monthly figure May 2005)

Balance of trade: -US$106.36 million (2004)

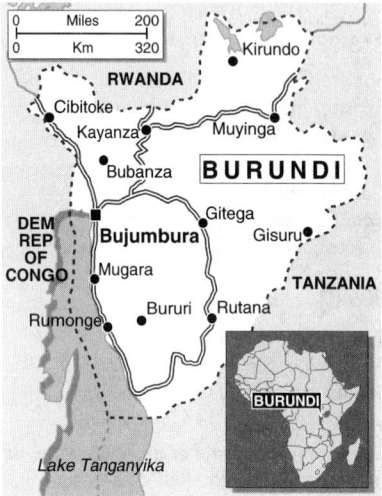

Burundi has made good progress with macroeconomic policy and structural reforms despite a complex political environment. The political transition process has advanced significantly and further progress has been made in securing peace. Hostilities in most of the country have ceased, but the adverse effects of the decade-long conflict will continue to be felt for at least another generation and sporadic fighting continues to disrupt access to health and education services.

2005: a year of voting

There was a successful referendum on a new constitution in February 2005, local elections were held in June, parliamentary elections in July, and the new president chosen by parliament in August. An ethnically balanced army and national police are being created and the integration and demobilisation of former combatants is proceeding. An army of 80,000 men is being reduced to one of 25,000.

Economic progress

Financial programmes over 2005 were aimed at strengthening public financial management and to support the revival of private sector investment seen as necessary to achieve sustainable growth. In particular, there was a focus on privatisation. It is the belief of the International Monetary Fund (IMF) that Burundi will require significant technical and financial support on very concessional terms from the international community for many years to come – its external debt is unsustainable even after the full use of traditional debt relief mechanisms.

Fiscal performance in the first quarter of 2005 was mixed. Macroeconomic objectives for the remainder of 2005 and for 2006 are to sustain economic recovery, secure financial stability and deepen structural reforms. Growth is projected at five per cent, supported by continued vigour in the service sectors but tempered by a lower coffee crop. A tighter monetary policy is to aim for budgetary discipline and to reverse the acceleration of year on year inflation to 10 per cent or lower. Gross international reserves are projected to increase to around six and a half months of import cover. The primary fiscal deficit target is 3.5 per cent of GDP. Revenues are conservatively projected to increase by at least 10 per cent largely via improved tax collections, while primary expenditure should remain constant.

Structural reform

The structural reform agenda is focused on promoting private sector-led growth and reducing poverty. A key component of the strategy is the reform of the coffee sector, with the 2006 crop to be produced by the private sector. It is recognised that liberalisation of the economy will not produce real economic growth without being accompanied by privatisation in a broad range of sectors. The government has committed to initiating this process. There are promises of further efforts to publicise government decisions, decrees, laws and financial and economic data. New anti-money laundering and bankruptcy laws are under consideration.

The medium-term macroeconomic outlook shows real growth averaging five per cent, led by initially buoyant export growth as the quality of coffee exports improve and with further development of non-traditional exports. Domestic revenue mobilisation should remain at the current level of 18–20 per cent of GDP and inflation stabilise at four per cent. The external current account deficit (excluding official grants) is expected to be high in the short term, reflecting an initial hump in reconstruction activity, but thereafter to follow a high but declining path to about 18.5 per cent of GDP by 2010.

The main risks are regional tensions and setbacks in the political and security situation. Overall, these appear contained given Burundi's track record so far and the international community's commitment to support the transition and peace process.

Politics

President Pierre Nkurunziza, a Hutu former rebel leader, is the first president to be chosen through democratic means since the start of Burundi's civil war. He was the sole candidate in the August 2005 vote in the National Assembly and the Senate after his Force for the Defence of Democracy (FDD) won parliamentary elections in June. The vote was one of the final steps in a peace process intended to end years of fighting between Hutu rebels and the Tutsi-controlled army. His chosen vic -presidents are drawn from Hutu and Tutsi ethnic groups – major protagonists in the war. Similarly, members of the national assembly, council of ministers and Senate are an ethnic mix.

Born in 1964 in Burundi's Ngozi province, Nkurunziza is one of Africa's youngest leaders. His father, a former MP, was killed in ethnic violence in 1972. He joined the Hutu rebellion in 1995 and rose through the ranks to become head of the FDD in 2001. The married father of two is a born-again Christian.

Outlook

In landlocked Burundi, where the economy is predominantly agricultural and the manufacturing sector underdeveloped, only one in two children go to school, half the population can neither read nor write, and approximately one in 10 adults has HIV/Aids. Food, medicine, and electricity remain in short supply. Tutsi, Hutu, other conflicting ethnic groups, associated political rebels, armed gangs, and various government forces continue fighting in the Great Lakes region which transcends the boundaries of Burundi, Democratic Republic of the Congo, Rwanda and Uganda in an effort to gain control over populated and natural resource areas. Government heads pledge to end the conflict, but localised violence continues despite the presence of about 6,000 peacekeepers from the UN Operation in Burundi (ONUB).

Risk assessment

Economic	Improving
Political	Slightly improving
Regional stability	Improving

COUNTRY PROFILE

Historical profile

Virtually unheard of until its first round of massacres in 1972–73, in which a quarter of a million people died, Burundi is a small, poor and overpopulated African republic. For years, Burundi's politics were unhappily preoccupied with the maintenance of Tutsi supremacy over the majority Hutu people.

Although the origins of Burundi's second major civil war, which broke out in 1993, were ethnic, the conflict degenerated into a bewildering free-for-all in which an estimated 300,000 people died. At issue was a struggle for control of one of Africa's poorest countries, with a GDP of less than US$1 billion.

1899 Burundi and its neighbour, Rwanda, were incorporated into German East Africa.
1916 Belgium occupied the area.
1923 Re-named Ruanda-Urundi, Belgium continued its administration.
1959 Many Tutsi refugees from Rwanda sought shelter from ethnic violence.
1962 On July 1, the Kingdom of Burundi became independent from Belgium under a Tutsi King, Mwambutsa IV.
1963 Many Hutus fled into Rwanda due to ethnic violence.
1965 Hutu candidates won a majority in parliamentary elections. However, Mwambutsa refused to appoint a Hutu prime minister. A Hutu coup led by Michel Micombero failed and the Hutu elite were massacred in retaliation.
1966 In July Mwambutsa was deposed by his son Ntare V. In November Micombero led a successful *coup d'état*.
1972 Ntare was killed, supposedly by Hutus, sparking violence that led to the killing of 150,000 Hutus.
1976–87 Micombero was deposed by Tutsi Colonel Jean-Baptiste Bagaza. Bagaza's dictatorship was notorious for its violations of human rights.
1987 Bagaza was overthrown by Tutsi Major Pierre Buyoya.
1988 Thousands of Hutu were killed and many more fled into Rwanda
1992 A new constitution endorsed multi-party elections.
1993 Melchior Ndadaye, who was committed to reforming the Tutsi-dominated army, won the elections and became the first Hutu president. Ndadaye was assassinated in October by pro-Bagazza paratroopers. More massacres followed.
1994 Cyprien Ntaryamira, a Hutu, was appointed president by the National Assembly. He and the Hutu president of Rwanda were killed in a plane crash. Sylvestre Ntibantuganya, a Hutu, became president.
1995 A coalition government was formed under Antoine Nduwayu, a Tutsi. Ethnic violence continued.
1996 Major Pierre Buyoya seized power and suspended the constitution.
1998 Buyoya came to an agreement with parliament under a transitional constitution and was formally sworn in as president.
1999 Tutsi and Hutu factions agreed to talks brokered by former Tanzanian president Julius Nyerere.
2000 President Buyoya and 13 political parties signed the Arusha peace accord but two important Hutu groups refused to sign.
2001 In talks chaired by former South Africa president Nelson Mandela, it was agreed that Buyoya, a Tutsi, should remain president for 18 months of a new three-year transitional government, when a Hutu vice president would become

KEY INDICATORS — Burundi

	Unit	2000	2001	2002	2003	2004
Population	m	6.36	6.50	6.63	7.22	7.80
Gross domestic product (GDP)	US$bn	0.83	0.66	0.62	0.69	*0.66
GDP per capita	US$	126	97	92	95	91
GDP real growth	%	-2.3	2.0	4.1	-0.5	5.5
Inflation	%	24.3	9.2	-1.4	11.0	7.9
Exports (fob) (goods)	US$m	49.1	48.0	57.0	26.0	31.8
Imports (fob) (goods)	US$m	107.9	157.0	183.0	135.0	138.2
Balance of trade	US$m	-58.8	-109.0	-126.0	-109.0	-106.4
Current account	US$m	-70.0	-50.0	-40.0	-40.0	-160.0
Total reserves minus gold	US$m	32.9	17.7	58.8	67.0	65.8
Foreign exchange	US$m	25.2	17.2	58.1	66.3	64.8
Exchange rate	per US$	720.67	830.35	967.28	1,065.00	1,060.00

* estimated figure

president. A three-year Transitional Government of National Unity was installed even though the main rebel group had refused to signed a cease-fire.
2002 The Burundi franc was devalued by 20 per cent to the US dollar. Violence between government forces and Hutu rebel groups continued.
2003 In April, Vice President Domitien Ndayizeye was sworn in as president in accordance with the power-sharing agreement. The president and Pierre Nkurunziza, the leader of the main rebel group the Conseil National de Défense de la Démocratie-Forces de Défense de la Démocratie (CNDD-FDD) Forces for Defence of Democracy, signed an agreement to end the civil war.
2004 A South African-style truth and reconciliation commission was set up. An electoral commission undertook to manage the 2005 elections. A new constitution was deferred until the transitional government was replaced with a fully elected Assembly.
2005 On 28 February, a referendum approved a new power-sharing constitution. The main former rebel Hutu group, CNDD-FDD, won the 4 July parliamentary elections. Pierre Nkurunziza was sworn in as president on 26 August. Martin Nduwimana (Tutsi) and Alice Nzomukunda (Hutu) were appointed vice presidents.

Political structure
Constitution
The constitution endorses multi-party elections by universal suffrage.
The February 2005 referendum approved a new power-sharing constitution, under which Burundi's president has a deputy from each of the ethnic groups while 60 per cent of the cabinet is Hutu and 40 per cent Tutsi.
Representation in the National Assembly is apportioned on a 60/40 basis between the Hutu and Tutsi with three seats reserved for the Twa ethnic group. In the Senate (upper house) two members are elected from each of Burundi's 17 provinces (one Hutu and one Tutsi), plus three from the Twa ethnic group. Women must account for at least 30 per cent. Four former presidents were also co-opted as senators in July 2005.
The army and the police service are staffed equally along ethnic lines.

Form of state
Republic

The executive
Executive power is vested directly in the elected president, with one each Hutu and Tutsi vice presidents.

National legislature
Legislative power is vested in the Assemblée Nationale (National Assembly) and Senate. The National Assembly is elected for a five-year term by universal suffrage. Senators are appointed by the President.

Legal system
Burundi law is based on Belgian and German law. The legal system is composed of a Supreme Court, Constitutional Court and a Courts of Appeal.

Last elections
4 July 2005 (parliamentary); 19 August 2005 (presidential)
Results: National Assembly: CNDD-FDD won 59 per cent of the vote (59 seats, out of 100), Frodebu 22 per cent (25) and Uprona 7 per cent (10), National Council for the Defence of Democracy (CNDD) 4 per cent (4), Movement for the Rehabilitation of Citizens-Rurenzangemero (MRC-Rurenzangemero) 2 per cent (2). In order to comply with the 60/40 Hutu/Tutsi split, and the 30 per cent quota for women, a further 18 members were co-opted after the elections. Of these, 5 each were allocated to the CNDD-FDD, Frodebu and Uprona, and three to the ethnic Twa, making a total in the National Assembly of 118.
Senate: CNDD-FDD won 30 seats, plus 2 co-opted members (out of 34 seats plus 15 co-opted and other members), Frodebu won 3 seats (plus 2 co-opted), CNDD 1 seat (plus 2 co-opted), Uprona (2 co-opted), ethnic Twa (3 co-opted), ex-presidents 4
Presidential: Pierre Nkurunziza (CNDD-FDD) was elected president by the National Assembly and Senate by 151 votes out of 160 votes.

Next elections
2010 (parliamentary).

Political parties
Ruling party
Conseil National pour la Défense de la Démocratie-Forces pour la Défense de la Démocratie (CNDD-FDD), (National Council for Defence of Democracy-Force for the Defence of Democracy)
Main opposition party
Front pour la Démocratie au Burundi (Frodebu) (Front for the Democracy in Burundi) (Hutu),

Population
7.80 million (2004)
Ethnic make-up
The Hutu people are believed to comprise 85 per cent of the population, the Tutsi 14 per cent and the Twa 1 per cent, but there have never been any census statistics on ethnic groups.
Religions
Christianity (over 60 per cent), 32 per cent traditional beliefs.

Education
Burundi typically spends around 3 per cent of its public expenditure on education, however this will increase following an announcement by the president that primary education will be free. Primary education will be boosted by a US$4 million Unicef grant aimed at doubling enrolment by March 2006. Classrooms are due to be refurbished and upgraded and 3,000 qualified teachers will be recruited, as well as training for less skilled teachers. Secondary education is divided into two: academic and technical. Academic secondary education is available for four years between ages 12 and 16, then a national test determines access to higher education. Technical secondary education lasts from ages 12–19.
Kirundi is the language of instruction in primary schools and French in secondary schools.
Higher education is mainly provided by the Université du Burundi, which is largely financed by the government.
Literacy rate: 50.4 per cent total; 43.6 per cent female; adult rates (World Bank).
Compulsory years: Six to 12.
Enrolment rate: 55 per cent boys and 46 per cent girls, total primary school enrolment for the relevant age groups (including repetition rates) (World Bank).
Pupils per teacher: 42 in primary schools.

Health
The annual total expenditure on health is around 3 per cent of GDP, of which government spending is approximately 59 per cent.
Burundi's infant mortality rate is relatively high compared to the other African countries. Although women have a higher life expectancy, it is still less than the other East African countries. Immunisation campaigns have resulted in high levels of vaccinations against measles, TB, polio and other childhood deseases.
HIV/Aids
There were 220,000 adults living with HIV/Aids, of which 130,000 were women, as well as another 27,000 children diagnosed as HIV positive in 2003. The number of HIV/Aids cases has risen dramatically, particularly in rural areas. It is estimated that 20 per cent of the urban population, and six per cent of the rural population, are HIV positive. Infection rates in girls aged 15–19 are four times greater than boys of the same age and there are over 200,000 children orphaned by Aids.
HIV prevalence: 6.0 per cent aged 15–49 in 2003 (World Bank)
Life expectancy: 41.6 years (World Bank)

Burundi

Fertility rate/Maternal mortality rate: 5.7 births per woman (World Bank)
Infant mortality rate: 114 per 1,000 live births (World Bank)
Head of population per physician/bed: 0.1 physicians and 0.7 hospital beds per 1,000 people.

Welfare
Burundi has 800,000 internally displaced people, while another 250,000 refugees fled to Tanzania.
The National Social Security Institute administers the old age, disability and survivor's pension insurance fund. It is a scheme funded by workers who contribute 2.6 per cent of their wages (3.8 per cent if working an arduous job), and employers contribute 3.9 per cent of the payroll (5.7 for arduous occupations). Old age pensions are paid at aged 60 (45 for arduous work).

Main cities
Bujumbura (capital, estimated population 330,500 in 2005), Muyinga (71,000).

Languages spoken
French is the administrative language; KiSwahili is used commercially. English is a compulsory subject in secondary academic education.
Official language/s
Kirundi and French

Media
Press
Dailies: The main government controlled daily newspaper in French is *Le Renouveau du Burundi*.
Weeklies: Weeklies include *Ubumwe* (Kirundi weekly) that is government-controlled and *l'Indépendant*.
Periodicals: Periodicals include *Carrefour des Idées*, *Le Citoyen* (twice monthly), *l'Aube de la Démocratie* (published twice monthly by the Frodebu party), *Intahe*, *Burakeyei* and *Kanura*.
Broadcasting
Radio: Radio service in Kirundi, KiSwahili, French and English, operated by the state broadcasting station Voix de la Révolution.
Television: State-owned La Radiodiffusion et Télévision Nationale de Burundi (RTNB) is the only TV service and was established in 1984.

Economy
The government in 2005 is attempting to manage a post-conflict economy and has called on the resources of the IMF and World Bank to bring about some order and direction. In analysis the IMF has outlined an agenda that defines the necessary structural reforms capable of providing long-term benefits.
The priorities highlighted include managing the strengthening public finances, supporting the revival of private sector investment and all activities that achieve sustainable growth. In turn the IMF acknowledges Burundi will require significant technical and financial support on highly preferential terms from the international community for many years to come and also substantial debt relief under the enhanced Heavily Indebted Poor Countries (HIPC) initiative. In August 2005 the IMF and World Bank agreed to forward US$826 million in debt relief under the HIPC programme. Burundi's debt service payments are expected to reduce by about US$1.5 billion over the period of the loans. Foreign donors pledged US$981 million for 2003–05 to support the peace effort and national reconstruction.
The country relies primarily on agricultural exports, with tea and coffee as the main cash crops. A bumper harvest of coffee in 2004 boosted real growth but a drought and grain crop disease in the north offset the benefits. As part of the restructuring, the government has undertaken to reform the coffee sector by privatising production facilities, commercialising the market and defining new roles for coffee sector institutions.
Higher food prices and the record prices for imported oil pushed up inflation which had dropped to 7.9 per cent in 2004, to 12.6 per cent by end-May 2005. Nevertheless GDP rose to 5.5 per cent in 2004, following the input of foreign aid, and the Burundi franc and bank interest rates remained relatively stable.
Social deprivation and measures in poverty alleviation have to be monitored so that any changes can generate a response. Burundi needs a social fund for the welfare of its citizens and needs an economy to sustain it. Measures that enhance government revenue such as taxes and investments not only have to be, and also seen to be, administered well.
Macroeconomic policies are beginning to be effective through the liberalisation of the economy while privatising most sectors including agriculture and finance and improving governance and transparency, are all on the government's agenda.

External trade
Imports
Principal imports are capital goods, machinery and equipment, petroleum products, foodstuffs.
Main sources: Kenya (11.7 per cent total, 2004), Tanzania (9.6 per cent), US (9.1 per cent), Belgium (9.0 per cent), France (8.8 per cent), Italy (5.4 per cent), Japan (4.8 per cent), Uganda (4.8 per cent), Zambia (4.2 per cent)

Exports
Principal exports are coffee (normally 75 per cent of total), manufactures, tea, sugar, cotton and hides.
Main destinations: Switzerland (25.8 per cent total, 2004), Germany (12.2 per cent), Belgium (7.9 per cent), US (5.5 per cent), Thailand (5.3 per cent), Rwanda (5.2 per cent)

Agriculture
Farming
The agriculture sector is the mainstay of the economy, although there was a sharp drop in agricultural output due to disruptions caused by the civil war. The sector has to contend with a damaged infrastructure, broken market networks and poor productivity. Internally displaced persons (IDP) caught up in the civil war were made to over-exploit land causing ecological damage. Although Burundi is potentially self-sufficient in food, large numbers of IDP rely on humanitarian assistance. Food products account for around 13 per cent of all imports.
The main cash crop is coffee, which accounts for up to three-quarters of the country's exports. More than 90 per cent of coffee production is arabica, which is being encouraged for its higher producer prices. The Burundian brand of coffee has won international best quality prizes. Burundi saw a bumper coffee harvest in 2004 and world prices remain strong. Other cash crops include tea, cotton, palm oil and tobacco.
Agriculture traditionally employs around 90 per cent of the population and contributes around 50 per cent of GDP. Most land under cultivation is devoted to subsistence crops – mainly cassava, bananas, sweet potatoes, pulses, maize and sorghum
Cattle rearing is also an important source of food, as is fishing on Lake Tanganyika.
Crop production in 2004 included: 280,095 tonnes (t) cereals in total, 64,532t rice, *7,493t wheat, 123,199t maize, 709,574t cassava, 834,394t sweet potatoes, 26,091t potatoes, 74,171t sorghum, *1,600,000t bananas, 255,518t pulses, 1,641,674t roots and tubers, 61,703t taro, 20,100t coffee, *180,000t sugar cane, 210,000t cotton lint, 6,600t tea, 1,685,000t fruit in total, *250,000t vegetables in total.
* estimate
Estimated livestock production included: 23,393t meat in total, 9,100t beef, 4,160t pig-meat, 1,020t lamb, 2,850t goat meat, 6,065t poultry, 3,002t eggs, 28,300t milk, 240t honey, 1,750 cattle hides.
Fishing
Lake Tanganyika is a rich source of fish.

Nations of the World: A Political, Economic and Business Handbook

Forestry
Almost 4 per cent of the land area, around 95,000 hectares, is forest. Around 8.7 million cubic metres of wood is felled each year, of which 8 million cubic metres is used for firewood.

Industry and manufacturing
The industrial sector, which is centred almost entirely in Bujumbura, is based on import substitution and typically accounts for around 20 per cent of GDP. Production includes beer, soft drinks, cigarettes, glass, textiles, insecticides, cement, oxygen and coffee processing.
The civil war discouraged foreign investment and high import costs hampered development of industrial capital, with strengthening peace these trends are reversing.

Tourism
The sector has only had two years since the civil conflict precluded tourists from visiting Burundi and therefore the US$22.6 million or 2.7 per cent of GDP expected in 2005 is remarkable. Capital investment in tourism is expected to reach 8.7 per cent of total investment in 2005, while one in every 26 jobs is in travel and tourism,.

Mining
Gold and tungsten are mined.
Substantial nickel reserves (up to 5 per cent of world total) have been found, but low world prices and an inadequate infrastructure mean extraction is not economically viable. Deposits of vanadium and uranium are being surveyed.
Phosphates and limestone are used for cement production.

Hydrocarbons
Burundi is reliant on imported petroleum. Petroleum reserves have been located under the Ruzizi Plain and under Lake Tanganyika.
Plans, put forward in 2000, for an extension to be added to a proposed oil pipeline between Kenya and Uganda, supplying Burundi, Rwanda, north-western Tanzania and eastern DRC have not progressed due to lack of investment.

Energy
Biomass, including wood, charcoal and peat, provides around 85 per cent of all energy consumption.
Burundi has three power stations and around 90 per cent of electricity services are consumed in the capital, by about 1.5–2 per cent of the country's population.
Burundi is hoping to secure finance for the development of the electricity sector, which has been fully liberalised, including the first phase of the Mpanda power station. This will involve the construction of a 10.4MW hydroelectric power station. Rwanda and Burundi are also looking at joint plans to construct a hydroelectric dam on the Ruzizi river.

Banking and insurance
Central bank
Banque de la République du Burundi
Main financial centre
Bujumbura

Time
GMT plus two hours

Geography
Burundi is a landlocked country lying on the eastern shore of Lake Tanganyika, in central Africa, just south of the Equator. It borders Rwanda to the north, Tanzania to the south and east, and the Democratic Republic of Congo to the west.

Climate
Around Lake Tanganyika (including Bujumbura), equatorial with hot, humid temperatures 23–33 degrees Celsius (C), and frequent winds. Elsewhere is temperate with average temperatures of 20 degrees C. The rainy season is from October–May (except brief dry period December–January); the long dry season is from June–September.

Entry requirements
Passports
Required by all.
Visa
Required by all. Applications for tourist and business visas should include itineraries and vaccination certificates against yellow fever and cholera. Business visas require a company letter of introduction from the employer and a local host company.
Currency advice/regulations
Foreign currency is unlimited subject to declaration on entry. Import and export of the Burundi Franc is limited; seek advice from the local diplomatic mission.

Health (for visitors)
Mandatory precautions
Cholera vaccination certificates are required by all visitors. Visitors arriving from countries where yellow fever is endemic are required to have meningitis and yellow fever vaccination certificates.
Advisable precautions
Yellow fever and cholera vaccinations are considered essential. Occasionally a certificate for meningococcal meningitis is required. Vaccinations for hepatitis A, polio, tetanus and typhoid are recommended. Malaria prophylaxis should be taken as risk exists throughout the country. Bilharzia risk is present in the lakes and rivers; visitors are advised to bathe only in well-maintained swimming pools.
Drinking water precautions are essential and all foods should be cooked. AIDS is widespread: 15 per cent seropositivity among adults in Bujumbura.
Visitors should seek advice on diphtheria, hepatitis B, dysentery and tuberculosis vaccinations. A travel kit including a disposable syringe is a reasonable precaution, for use during local treatment involving hypodermic needles or blood transfusions. Medical insurance, including repatriation, is essential and, as local supplies of medicines are in short supply, always take adequate personal provisions.
There is a rabies risk.

Hotels
Advisable to book in advance. Very little accommodation available outside Bujumbura. A 10 per cent tip is usual.

Public holidays
Variable dates
Ascension Day

Working hours
Banking
Mon–Fri: 0800–1130; 1500–1600.
Business
Mon–Fri: 0730–1200, 1400–1730.
Government
Mon–Fri: 0730–1200, 1400–1730.
Shops
Mon–Fri: 0830–1200, 1500–1800. Sat: 0830–1230.

Electricity supply
220V AC

Getting there
Air
There are no direct flights from either Europe or the US.
National airline: Air Burundi (state-owned).
International airport/s: Bujumbura (code: BJM), 11km north of city; café, currency exchange and post office.
Airport tax: Departure tax: US$20.
Surface
There are good roads from Bukavu (Democratic Republic of Congo) and Kigali (Rwanda) to Bujumbura. Roads from Tanzania are generally in poor condition.
Main port/s: Bujumbura (on Lake Tanganyika). Ferries operate from Kigoma (Tanzania), Kalenjie (DRC) and Mpulungu (Zambia). Dar es Salaam is the nearest sea port.

Getting about
National transport
Air: There are no scheduled internal flights operating at the moment. Aircraft may be chartered at Bujumbura.
Road: Most of the roads leading to provincial towns are surfaced. Unsurfaced roads elsewhere can be difficult in rainy season. Surfaced routes are being extended and local advice should be sought. Border areas are regarded as dangerous to travel through.

Buses: Very little public transport is available and is considered dangerous outside Bujumbura.
Water: Local boats may be available on Lake Tanganyika.
City transport
Taxis: Available in Bujumbura.
Car hire
Local firms only. International driving licence is required.

BUSINESS DIRECTORY

The addresses listed below are a selection only. While World of Information makes every endeavour to check these addresses, we cannot guarantee that changes have not been made, especially to telephone numbers and area codes. We would welcome any corrections.

Telephone area codes
The international direct dialling (IDD) code for Burundi is +257, followed by area code and subscriber's number:

Bubanza	42	Gitega	40
Bujumbura	2	Muramvya	43
Bururi	50	Ngozi	30
Cibitoke	41		

Useful telephone numbers
Police: 18, 19.

Chambers of Commerce
Burundi Chamber of Commerce, Industry, Agriculture and Handicrafts, Avenue du 18 Septembre, PO Box 313, Bujumbura (tel: 222-280; fax: 227-895; e-mail: ccib@cbinf.com).

Banking
Banque Commerciale du Burundi, PO Box 990, Libere Ndabakwaje, Bujumbura (tel: 222-317; fax: 221-018).

Banque de Crédit de Bujumbura, PO Box 300, Avenue Patrice Emery Lumumba, Bujumbura (tel: 222-091; fax: 223-007).

Central bank
Banque de la République du Burundi, PO Box 705, Avenue du Gouvernement, Bujumbura, Burundi (tel: 225-142 fax: 223-128).

Travel information
Air Burundi, BP 2460, Avenue du Commerce, Bujumbura (tel: 223-460; fax: 223-452).

Bujumbura International Airport, PO Box 694, Bujumbura (tel: 223-707; 223-797; fax: 223-428).

Tourist office (for accommodation) 7 place de L'Indépendance, Bujumbura, BP 1402, (tel: 222-321, 220-704; email: nitra@cbinf.com).

National tourist organisation offices
Office National du Tourisme, 2 Avenue des Euphorbes, BP 902, Bujumbura (tel: 222-202/023; fax: 222-390; email: ontbur@cbinf.com); internet (in French): www.burundi.gov.bi).

Ministries
Ministry of Agriculture, Bujumbura (tel: 210-342; fax: 222-873).

Ministry of Commerce, Industry and Tourism, Bujumbura (tel: 217-775; fax: 225-595).

Ministry of Communication with the Government, Bujumbura (tel: 212-601; fax: 216-318).

Ministry of Community Development, Bujumbura (tel: 213-098; fax: 224-678).

Ministry of Defence, Bujumbura (tel: 219-994; fax: 225-686).

Ministry of Education, Bujumbura (tel: 217-776; fax: 226-839).

Ministry of Energy and Mines, Bujumbura (tel: 218-586; fax: 223-337).

Ministry of the Environment, Bujumbura (tel: 221-649; fax: 228-902).

Ministry of Finance, Bujumbura (tel: 217-918; fax: 223-827).

Ministry of Foreign Affairs and Co-operation, Bujumbura (tel: 217-595; fax: 226-313).

Ministry of Health, Bujumbura (tel: 218-200; fax: 229-916).

Ministry of Human Rights, Law Reforms and Relations with the National Assembly, Bujumbura (tel: 217-365; fax: 213-847).

Ministry of the Interior, Bujumbura (tel: 212-480; fax: 223-904).

Ministry of Justice, Bujumbura (tel: 210-595; fax: 222-148).

Ministry of Labour, Public Office and Professional Education, Bujumbura (tel: 217-928; fax: 224-079).

Ministry of Peace Process, Bujumbura (tel: 219-457; fax: 219-459).

Ministry of Planning, Development and Reconstruction, Bujumbura (tel: 219-079; fax: 224-193).

Ministry of Public Works and Equipment, Bujumbura (tel: 219-646; fax: 226-840).

Ministry of Repatriation of Displaced Persons, Bujumbura (tel: 218-184; fax: 218-201).

Ministry of Social Action and Promotion of Women, Bujumbura (tel: 210-376; fax: 216-102).

Ministry of Transport, Post and Telecommunications, Bujumbura (tel: 210-462; fax: 226-900).

Ministry of Youth Sport and Culture, Bujumbura (tel: 216-729; fax: 226-231).

Office of the President, Bujumbura (tel: 217-806; fax: 226-424).

Other useful addresses
APEE (export promotion) BP 3535, Bujumbura (tel: 225-997; fax: 222-767).

BCC (Burundi Coffee Co) BP 780 Bujumbura.

Burundi Embassy (USA), Suite 212, 2233 Wisconsin Avenue, NW, Washington DC 20007 (tel: 202-342-2574; fax: 202-342-2578).

Burundi Mining Co. BP468 Bujumbura (tel: 223-229).

CIGERCO (Cotton growers), BP 2571 Bujumbura (tel: 222-208).

Internet sites
Africa Business Network: http://www.ifc.org/abn

AllAfrica.com: http://www.allafrica.com

African Development Bank: http://www.afdb.org

Africa Online: http://www.africaonline.com

Harambee Afrika (UK business club for traders with east, central and southern Africa; includes annotated web resource list): http://www.harambee.co.uk

Mbendi AfroPaedia (information on companies, countries, industries and stock exchanges in Africa): http://mbendi.co.za

Cambodia

KEY FACTS

Official name: Preah Réachéanachâkr Kâmpuchéa (The Kingdom of Cambodia)

Head of State: King Norodom Sihamoni (from 14 Oct 2004)

Head of government: Prime Minister Samdech Hun Sen (KPK) (since 1985); Speaker of the National Assembly: Prince Norodom Ranariddh (since Nov 1998)

Ruling party: Coalition government: Kanakpak Pracheachon Kâmpuchéa (KPK) (Cambodian People's Party) and United National Front for an Independent, Neutral, Peaceful and Co-operative Cambodia (Funcinpec) (sworn in 16 Jul 2004)

Area: 181,035 square km

Population: 13.81 million (2004)

Capital: Phnom Penh

Official language: Khmer

Currency: Riel (R) = 100 sen

Exchange rate: R4,120.00 per US$ (Oct 2005)

GDP per capita: US$314 (2004)

GDP real growth: 4.30% (2004); *6.3% (2005)

Labour force: 6.81 million (2004)

Unemployment: 3.10% (2004)

Inflation: 2.00% (2004); *5.0% (2005)

Balance of trade: -US$818.00 million (2004)

* estimated figure

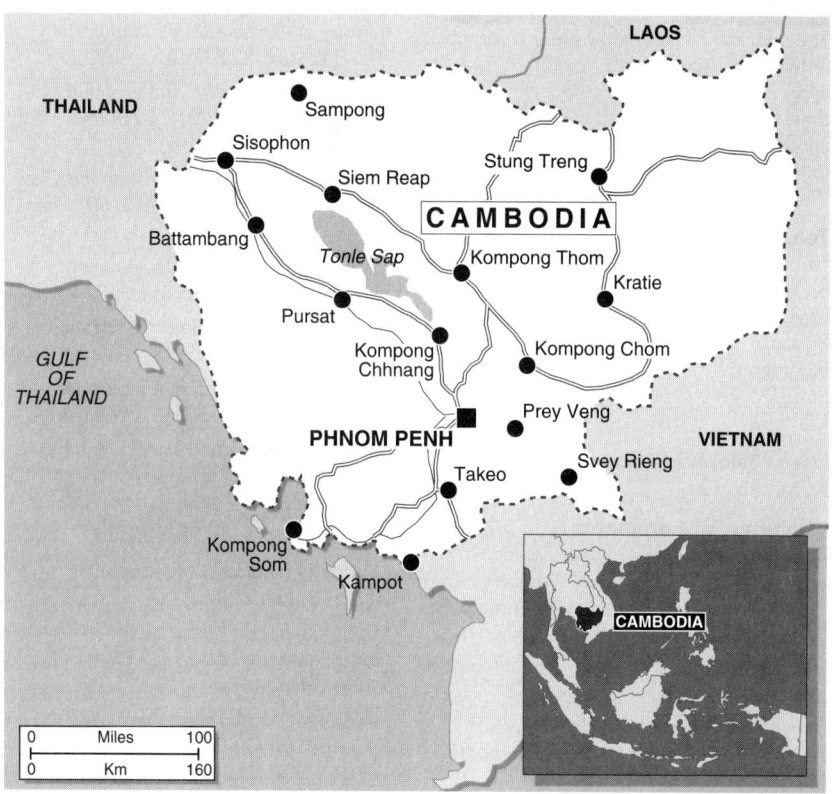

Cambodia took steps in 2005 to confront its past and redress some of the terrible wrongs of the Khmer Rouge regime which lasted from 1975–79. The funds for a tribunal to investigate the remaining accused commanders were finally raised, fuelling expectation that judicial proceedings will begin in 2006. Despite this progression, human rights groups have complained of ongoing abuses such as unlawful imprisonment of government critics. Also in 2005 there was a worrying spate of undemocratic sales of land to the country's richest and most powerful figures. Indigenous people appealed to the UN in October for help in lobbying the government for protectionist legislation. In March 2005 a man in southern Cambodia contracted and died of the avian 'flu virus, the country's second fatality.

Economy

In December 2005 the IMF announced that Cambodia qualified for 100 per cent debt relief amounting to the cancellation of US$82 million pounds. Repayments are now freed up and can be ploughed into much-needed investment. GDP growth averaged 7.75 per cent from 1999–2004 and reached 6.3 per cent in 2005. These figures were underpinned by robust textile export sales to the US and an expanding tourist sector. The IMF praised the country's sound macroeconomic management and trade liberalisation. Rising global oil prices prompted a rise in inflation, to 5–6 per cent but generally inflationary rates have been low. The government should take further measures to increase taxation revenue.

Textiles industry

The factory-produced textiles sector, which accounts for a huge 80 per cent of Cambodian exports, experienced real change in 2005. In January the Multifibre Arrangement (MFA) production quotas, which had in effect guaranteed Cambodia a role in the global market, were removed. This legislation had been introduced in the 1970s and its removal is one of the most significant recent events in the global economy. The resulting shake-up of the industry is particularly worrying for Cambodia – no other country is so dependent on a single sector. Retailers are now free to find the cheapest markets without restrictions. This deregulation puts great pressure on prices and China is expected to dominate the market at least initially.

Cambodia has sought to promote itself as an ethical source of textiles, allowing independent foreign inspections of their factories by the International Labour Organisation (ILO) and others. This has given the country an edge over China: global brands perceive Cambodia to have some of the highest health and safety standards in the region, although Chinese production is quicker and of higher quality. US global brand Gap buys 15 per cent of Cambodian exports, keen to please politically-aware consumers. The sting in the tail, however, is that the price of efficiently and ethically produced textiles is bumped up by corrupt civil servants. Layers of bureaucracy – nearly 50 papers have to be signed before a cargo can leave Cambodia – are cut through with offerings of unofficial fees.

The Cambodian export market was worth US$2.3 billion in 2004 but it will struggle to maintain this level in the wake of increased competition. The World Bank has predicted that Cambodia's GDP growth will fall several percentage points as a result of the deregulation. From January to May 2005 30,000 jobs were cut in the garment sector. In May 2005 labourers attacked factory owners for using the removal of quotas as an excuse to regress on progressive working conditions. Cambodia's garment manufacturing association, GMAC, announced that it was considering cost-cutting measures such as reducing holiday entitlement, cutting pay allowances for night workers, phasing out factory crèches and clamping down on trade union powers. The number of disputes rose in the first few months of 2005 and workers said that police were called in to dismantle strikes, on one occasion using tear gas.

Farming

Textiles and tourism are virtually the country's only industries. The threat to the textiles industry as a result of the removal of quotas prompted Cambodia to consider other sources of income. The Cambodian government is planning to expand the organic sector and ship produce to health-conscious Europe and the US. Profit margins could be potentially greater as organic prices are higher and do not require expensive fertilizers. A German aid agency has funded the organic certification process in the hope that Cambodia will develop a niche market.

Corruption

Cambodia is ranked 130 out of 158 countries in the Transparency International survey of perceived corruption, making it one of the most corrupt countries in the world. In February 2005 the then president of the World Bank, James Wolfensohn, advised Cambodia that its three biggest tasks were 'fighting corruption, fighting corruption, and fighting corruption'. Cambodia is not seen as a credible investment environment as a result of excessive bureaucracy and widespread fraud and bribery. This culture is ingrained and few official measures have been taken to tackle it. As a result investor confidence is low and FDI is now only one fifth of the 1998 level. Investment of US$250 million in 1998 has plummeted to its current level of US$50 million.

In February 2005, in response to World Bank criticism, the Cambodian prime minister, Hun Sen, pledged to increase civil servant wages to lessen the incentive for accepting bribes. He also vowed to cut red tape and delays in exporting goods. However, this kind of rhetoric has been aired before without any accompanying action. There is some skepticism about whether this time will be any different.

Banking

During Pol Pot's tyrannical regime in the 1970s the use of money was abolished and private property was prohibited. Even when banks were hastily established in the 1990s, they were often shambolic and unregulated operations which resulted in many people losing their savings when these banks went out of business. Banking is, as a result, an underdeveloped sector in Cambodia. Many rural-dwellers have never used banking facilities. Total bank deposits in Cambodia equate to only 19 per cent of GDP, as opposed to the Asian average of 90 per cent. Aceleda bank, supported by the UN, has been trying to instill consumer confidence in the banking for a decade. They provide credit for small businesses and in 2004 generated profits of US$2 million. Aceleda aims to be eventually self-sufficient rather than relying on foreign aid. The business seems to be winning over people's trust, as they have doubled their deposits over a twelve month period, to a total of US$60 million in November 2005.

In August 2005 ANZ Royal Bank opened in Cambodia. The company, jointly run by the Australian bank ANZ and the Cambodian company Royal Group, experienced quick success. Over a thousand people opened accounts in the company's first few weeks of operation and in September they announced the

KEY INDICATORS — Cambodia

	Unit	2000	2001	2002	2003	2004
Population	m	13.10	13.20	13.50	13.65	13.81
Gross domestic product (GDP)	US$bn	3.20	4.50	3.70	3.82	*4.60
GDP per capita	US$	289	260	274	280	314
GDP real growth	%	5.4	5.3	5.5	5.2	4.3
Inflation	%	-0.8	0.6	3.3	3.5	2.0
Exports (fob) (goods)	US$m	1,327.1	1,451.0	1,500.0	1,380.0	2,311.0
Imports (fob) (goods)	US$m	1,525.1	1,950.0	1,760.0	1,730.0	3,129.0
Balance of trade	US$m	-198.0	-240.0	-262.0	-350.0	-818.0
Current account	US$m	-110.0	-40.0	-40.0	-140.0	-100.0
Total reserves minus gold	US$m	501.7	586.8	776.1	815.5	943.2
Foreign exchange	US$m	501.5	586.3	775.6	815.3	943.1
Exchange rate	per US$	3,840.80	3,916.30	3,835.00	3,912.50	3,918.00

* estimated figure

installation of the first international ATM machines in the country.

Politics

Domestic political crisis started to unfold at the beginning of 2005. In February the ruling coalition stripped three opposition MPs of parliamentary immunity: the party's namesake, Sam Rainsy, Cheam Channy and Chea Poch. Rainsy responded by leaving the country in the knowledge that the government's action was the first step towards prosecuting the men for defamation. Channy was indeed arrested while Poch went into hiding. By removing these three main Sam Rainsy party figures, the government effectively dismantled the opposition. From Paris, Rainsy implored the international community to intervene. The opposition leader also asked the Cambodian king to override the government and restore opposition MPs' immunity from prosecution. The Sam Rainsy party boycotted parliament for six months after February.

In August 2005 Cheam Channy was condemned to seven years imprisonment, accused by a military court of working to overthrow the prime minister, Hun Sen. The Cambodian administration claimed that Channy's dissent could threaten national security. However human rights observers say the trial was staged to send a warning to opposition activity throughout the country.

In December 2005 Rainsy was sentenced in abstension to 18 months in prison. He was alleged to have made false accusations against the government, when he claimed it to be implicated in the launching of a hand grenade in the middle of an opposition protest eight years ago.

By January 2006 analysts were suggetsing that this, the harshest crackdown on the opposition in years, was Hun Sen's final move to consolidate absolute power.

Kem Sokha, leader of the Cambodian Center for Human Rights was also arrested in December 2005. He was accused of carrying a slanderous banner at International Human Rights Day on 10 December 2005. He is the fourth person to be awaiting trial on charges of anti-government activity.

In December 2005 a UN human rights envoy echoed domestic fears about infringements of human rights. The visitors expressed alarm at the crackdown on opposition members and freedom of speech. A climate of fear is growing as the government becomes increasingly tyrannical. UN officials visited opposition politicians in jail and the EU is also keen to send a delegation to the country.

Khmer Rouge justice

Cambodia still has not mounted a trial of the Khmer Rouge perpetrators of genocide. These atrocities were committed in the 1970s and led to the deaths of 1.7 million Cambodians. The leader, Pol Pot, died in 1998 but there are thought to be ten leaders still alive in Cambodia who have yet to be tried. Two high profile suspects, Kaing Khek Iev and Ta Mok, are in custody awaiting charges. A tribunal supported by the UN has been established to investigate the Khmer Rouge incidents and charge those responsible. However, proceedings were delayed by a shortage of funds. By April 2005 the full US$56 million had been raised, largely thanks to a sizeable Japanese contribution. This has led to speculation that the trials could begin in early 2006. UN offices were set up in December 2005. In March 2005, human rights groups asked for assurances that witnesses in the future trial would be protected from intimidation from former Khmer Rouge members. They called for the use of video evidence and other safety measures to ensure a fair trial.

Crime and punishment

In June 2005 four armed young men stormed an international school in Siem Reap, north-western Cambodia. The kindergarten classes were taken hostage while the men asked for money, rifles, shotguns and a getaway car in return for the children's release. Before the siege was ended by armed police, a two-year old Canadian child was shot dead by the captors, frustrated by the lack of success in their demands. The hostage-takers were arrested. In December 2005 one of the gang members was sentenced to life imprisonment for the murder of the Canadian boy. Four men were given 20-year prison sentences and two others received lighter punishments. When questioned, hostage-taker Chea Sokhom explained that his motive for the siege was humiliation earned at the hands of his South Korean employer. The boss, who had children at the school, smacked Sokhom in public when he arrived at work late.

In November 2005 the British government and the Cambodian authorities announced the beginning of greater co-operation between the two countries over the capture and prosecution of UK paedophiles and sex offenders. A new Child Exploitation and Online Protection Centre had been established and now courts in either country can prosecute offenders.

Outlook

The human rights outlook is depressing: a trend of unlawful imprisonment shows no sign of stopping, despite international criticism. The financial outlook is good, with 6 per cent GDP growth predicted for 2006. However, high global oil prices will continue to be a concern.

Risk assessment

Economic	Good
Political	Poor
Regional Stability	Stable

COUNTRY PROFILE

Historical profile
1863 Cambodia was made a French Protectorate.
1941 Prince Norodom Sihanouk became King. Cambodia was occupied by the Japanese during the Second World War.
1945 Japanese occupation ended.
1946 France re-imposed its protectorate. A new constitution permitted Cambodians to form political parties. Communist guerrillas began an insurgency against French rule.
1953 Cambodia became independent with King Sihanouk as head of state.
1955 Sihanouk abdicated to pursue a political career as prime minister. His father, Norodom Suramarit, became King.
1960 King Suramarit died and Sihanouk became head of state.
1965 Sihanouk cut off relations with the US and gave support to North Vietnamese guerrillas fighting the US-backed regime in South Vietnam.
1969 The US began bombing Cambodia.
1970 Sihanouk was overthrown in a US-backed coup. General Lon Nol became president, proclaimed the Khmer Republic and began fighting the North Vietnamese in Cambodia. Sihanouk formed a guerrilla movement, known as the Khmer Rouge, while in exile in China.
1970–75 Civil war and intensive American bombing caused widespread destruction.
1975 Lon Nol was overthrown by the Khmer Rouge, led by Pol Pot. Sihanouk briefly served as head of state.
1975–79 Under the Khmer Rouge regime, around 1.7 million people were killed and towns and industry destroyed. The cities were emptied and people were forced into the countryside to become agricultural workers.
1976 Sihanouk was replaced by Khieu Samphan as head of state and Pol Pot as prime minister.

Cambodia

1979 The Khmer Rouge was ejected by a Vietnamese invasion and the regime's policies were reversed.
1981 The pro-Vietnamese Kampuchean People's Revolutionary Party (KPRP) won the elections to the National Assembly, but the international community, led by the US, refused to recognise the new government. Instead, Cambodia was represented in the UN by the Khmer Rouge.
1985 Hun Sen became prime minister.
1989 Vietnam claimed to have withdrawn its remaining troops from the country. Hun Sen abandoned his socialist programme in an effort to appease the US and gain international recognition.
1991 The signing of a peace agreement brought to an end 13 years of civil war. A UN transitional authority was established to share power between the country's varius factions. Sihanouk became head of state.
1993 The UN organised elections. The Cambodian National Unity Party (Khmer Rouge) guerrilla group boycotted the poll. The two main parties, United National Front for an Independent, Neutral, Peaceful and Co-operative Cambodia (Funcinpec) and Kanakpak Pracheachon Kâmpuchéa (KPK) (Cambodian People's Party), agreed on a joint government under which they would share power. A constitutional monarchy was established and, in May, the country was renamed the Kingdom of Cambodia. The government-in-exile lost its seat in the UN.
1994 Thousands of Khmer Rouge fighters surrendered after the government called an amnesty.
1997 Second Prime Minister Hun Sen (KPK) seized power, removing First Prime Minister Prince Norodom Ranariddh (Funcinpec) from office, in a move condemned by the international community.
1998 The Khmer Rouge founder, Pol Pot, died. The KPK won the elections, but the opposition parties objected saying the election was fraudulent. A coalition government was formed with Funcinpec. Hun Sen became prime minister and Ranariddh became president of the National Assembly.
1999 Two Khmer Rouge leaders were arrested and charged with genocide.
2001 Parliament approved a law to create a special tribunal to bring genocide charges against Khmer Rouge leaders.
2002 The KPK scored an overwhelming victory in the country's first multi-party local elections, giving it control of over 98 per cent of the country's communes.
2003 Anti-Thai riots in January were set off by claims that Angkor Wat really belonged to Thailand and not to Cambodia. The KPK was re-elected in the 27 July parliamentary elections, but failed to secure the two-thirds majority required under the constitution to govern alone.
2004 In July, the two main political parties, KPK and Funcinpec, agreed to form a coalition government with Hun Sen remaining as prime minister, ending a government crisis that had crippled the kingdom for almost a year; the coalition government was sworn in on 16 July. Cambodia became a member of the WTO on 13 October. On 14 October, the Council of the Throne chose Prince Norodom Sihamoni as the new King.
2005 In October, Cambodia concluded a border agreement with Vietnam.
2006 The 22 January elections to the Senate were won by the ruling KPK.

Political structure
Constitution
The 1993 constitution provides for a pluralistic, liberal democratic political system and for a limited monarchy.
To govern alone, a political party is required to have a two-thirds majority.
Form of state
Multiparty liberal democracy under a constitutional monarchy established in 1993.
The executive
Executive power is vested in the Council of Ministers led by the prime minister. The King appoints the prime minister from the representatives of the largest party in parliament on the recommendation of the president of the National Assembly.
National legislature
Under the constitution, the National Assembly has at least 120 members who are all elected by universal suffrage. Only those who were Cambodian citizens at birth and who are aged over 25 years are entitled to stand for election. The National Assembly is elected every five years.
Legal system
The judiciary is granted independence under the constitution. The Supreme Council of the Magistracy, chaired by the King, has the right to discipline any judge who breaks the law, but judges cannot be dismissed. The King has sole authority to appoint judges on the advice of the Supreme Council of the Magistracy.
Last elections
27 July 2003 (parliamentary); 23 January 2005 (Senate).
Results: Parliamentary: The ruling coalition was re-elected – the Kanakpak Pracheachon Kâmpuchéa (KPK) (Cambodian People's Party) won 73 seats out of 123; the United National Front for an Independent, Neutral, Peaceful and Co-operative Cambodia (Funcinpec) party 26 seats and the Sam Rainsy Party (SRP) 24. Senate: The KPK increased their seats in the Senate winning 43 of the 57 seats. They had previously held 35.

Next elections
2008 (parliamentary)
Political parties
Ruling party
Coalition government: Kanakpak Pracheachon Kâmpuchéa (KPK) (Cambodian People's Party) and United National Front for an Independent, Neutral, Peaceful and Co-operative Cambodia (Funcinpec) (sworn in 16 Jul 2004)
Main opposition party
Sam Rainsy Party (SRP)

Population
13.81 million (2004)
Religions
Theravada Buddhism, Christianity (Roman Catholicism).

Education
Primary school lasts between the ages of six and 12.
Secondary education is divided into lower secondary and upper secondary lasting for three years each. All students follow the same curriculum through the six years.
Nearly 40 per cent of total expenditure in primary schools is paid through household contributions. Public expenditure on education typically amounts to around 3 per cent of annual gross national income.
Literacy rate: 59 per cent men, 21 per cent women; adult rates (World Bank).
Enrolment rate: 123 per cent and 104 per cent for boys and girls respectively, total primary school enrolment of the relevant age group (including repetition rates) (World Bank).
Pupils per teacher: 44 in primary schools.

Health
Total expenditure on health is 11–12 per cent of GDP, of which government spending is 15 per cent.
HIV prevalence: 2.6 per cent aged 15–49 in 2003 (World Bank)
Life expectancy: 54 years (World Bank)
Fertility rate/Maternal mortality rate: 3.9 births per woman; maternal mortality ratio 470 deaths per 100,000 live births (World Bank).
Infant mortality rate: 97 per 1,000 live births; 47 per cent of children under aged five are malnourished (World Bank).
Head of population per physician/bed: 0.3 physicians and 2.1 hospital beds per 1,000 people.

Welfare
Five Cambodian government ministries and their departments directly or indirectly offer social welfare support for the general population, including people with disabilities. There is provision for pensions of disabled veterans. There are no universal social security benefit entitlements in Cambodia.

Main cities
Phnom Penh (capital, estimated population 1.2 million in 2004), Bat Dâmbâng (207,000), Siem Reab (149,800), Preah Sihanouk (95,500).

Languages spoken
French is spoken. English is becoming the most commonly used business language, superseding French.
Official language/s
Khmer

Media
Press
Dailies: *Cambodia Daily* (www.camnet.com.kh/cambodia.daily/) is a non-profit daily newspaper, published in English and Khmer. *Koh Santepheap Daily* (www.kohsantepheapdaily.com.kh) and *Kampuchea.com* (www.kampuchea.com) are both regularly updated English language news portals.
Weeklies: Weeklies are *Moha Samakki Kraom Tong Ranakse* (Great Solidarity Under the Front Banner) and *Pracheachon* (The People) twice weekly. *Phnom Penh Post* (www.phnompenhpost.com) is an English-language independent newspaper published weekly. *Cambodia Journal* (www.cambodiajournal.com) is an on-line news service.
Business: Business and investment news is available from www.business-in-cambodia.com/cambodia.htm.
Broadcasting
Radio: Radio services include CARN Internet Edition (www.cambodianradio.net/carn/index.html) as the leading Khmer Language radio and the Voice of Cambodia Radio International (http://khmer.sanetech.com/).

Economy
Cambodia is for the most part a rural, developing country, but despite extensive reforms and massive donor support, its economic basis remains weak. Cambodia is one of the least developed countries in the world with 36 per cent of the population living below the poverty line, 90 per cent in rural areas. Sustainable development is not possible without greater private sector commitment coupled with social programmes.
Cambodia has a market economy which is subject to hardly any government restrictions. Economic growth has been driven by increases in garment production, tourism inflows, agriculture and construction activity. Donors have criticised the speed of reform with regard to good governance, forest management, law and especially anti-corruption measures.
Cambodia became a member of the World Trade Organisation (WTO) in 2004. Although Cambodia's economy is small, the decision to join the WTO could increase commerce and prosperity. Although Cambodia lacks many laws like bankruptcy and incorporation statutes, through entry to the WTO, guidance will be available to help it to create a modern legal framework for commerce.
The major economic challenge for Cambodia over the next decade will be to encourage a private sector that can create enough jobs for Cambodia's young population. About 60 per cent of the population is 20 years or younger and most of these people will seek to enter the workforce over the course of the next 10 years.

External trade
Imports
Main imports are petroleum products, vehicles and machinery, construction materials, pharmaceutical products, cigarettes, gold, artificial textiles, cotton yarns and cotton textiles.
Main sources: Thailand (23.9 per cent total, 2004), Hong Kong (15 per cent), China (13.5 per cent), Singapore (11.5 per cent), Vietnam (7.6 per cent), Taiwan (7.3 per cent)
Exports
Major exports are clothing timber, rubber rice, fish, tobacco and footwear.
Main destinations: US (56.2 per cent total, 2004), Germany (11.5 per cent), UK (7.0 per cent), Canada (4.3 per cent)

Agriculture
Farming
Agriculture accounts for 33 per cent of GDP and employs around 75 per cent of the workforce. Agriculture is hampered by poor soil fertility and irrigation and unclear land-ownership rights.
The principal crop is rice (both hill and lowland types), which is grown on 70 per cent of the cultivated land. Rice output accounts for around 17 per cent of GDP. Only 16 per cent of rice lands are irrigated and there have been no large-scale projects since the 1960s.
Other crops include rubber (a major export), maize, cassava and fruit and vegetables. The smuggling of rubber to neighbouring countries, to get a better price, is a problem. Cambodia also produces jute and sawn timber products. Cattle stocks are improving, but fish represents the only animal protein for most people.
Crop production in 2004 included: 4,170,000 million tonnes (t) cereals in total, 256,000t maize, 550,000t sorghum, 140,000t cassava, 135,000t potatoes, 34,00t sweet potatoes, 1,200,000t oil palm fruit, 148,000t bananas, 370,000t tomatoes, *24,000t pulses, *71,000t coconuts, *68,200t citrus fruit, 25,733t oilcrops, 310t green coffee, *35,000t mangoes, 46,000t natural rubber, *2,400t pepper spice, *220,000t sugar cane, 7,500t ginger, *650t jute, *39,000t soya beans, 7,361t tobacco leaves, 324,700t fruit in total, *475,000t vegetables in total. Livestock production included: 193,550t meat in total, *54,000t beef, *12,800t buffalo meat, 102,500t pig meat, 24,250t poultry, 17,050t eggs, *20,400t milk, 300t cocoons, silk, 13,500t cattle hides.
* estimate
Forestry
Exports of forest products in 2004 amounted to US$13.9 million and imports to 18.9 million.
The estimated production for 2004 included: 9.5 million cubic metres (mcum) roundwood, 4,000 cubic metres (cum) sawnwood, 100,000cum sawlogs and veneers, 5,000cum wood-based panels, 1,000cum veneer sheets, 9.3mcum woodfuel, 32,669 tonnes charcoal.

Industry and manufacturing
The industrial sector accounts for 29 per cent of GDP and employs around 20 per cent of the workforce.
Most of what little industry Cambodia possessed was wrecked during the 1970s under the Khmer Rouge, particularly by the virtual closure of the towns in the drive to force people back to the land. Development has been hampered by the absence of adequate transport and other infrastructure. The manufacturing sector is beset by shortages of power and raw materials and by poor quality products. A number of state factories have been leased to the private sector since 1990 and joint ventures established in enterprises such as hotels, rattan, mineral water, wood processing, a tannery, plywood, tyres and textiles.
Industrial expansion has been led by the growth in the garment-manufacturing sector, but the level of growth might be affected by the ending of garment quotas by the WTO in 2005. In order to offset this, the government will need to create a more investor-friendly environment.

Tourism
The government has a target of three million tourists per annum by 2010. Particular focus is geared towards the cultural attractions such as the ancient city of Angkor Wat. Tourism, which has had to overcome the effects of years of upheaval, has led growth in the services sector. After a disappointing year in 2003, occasioned by external events, the sector recovered in 2004, receiving just over a million visitors, rising to over 1.4 million in 2005. The main market is South Korea, followed by Japan, USA and the UK. Tourism is expected to contribute 7.3 per cent to GDP in 2005.

Cambodia

Mining
The mining sector typically contributes 9 per cent to GDP and employs 1 per cent of the workforce.
There are deposits of iron ore, copper, manganese, gold and bauxite, but exploitation is hindered by the absence of transport facilities. Phosphates are the only economically viable mineral and are mined for use in the local fertiliser industries. Gemstones are also mined.

Hydrocarbons
Cambodia has no oil or natural gas reserves. Cambodia is dependent on imports of refined oil, mainly from Thailand. Exploration is being undertaken particularly in offshore areas, where indications of oil and gas have been detected.
There are indications of small coal reserves.

Energy
Cambodia has an electricity generating capacity of around 150MW nationally, a level insufficient to sustain rapid economic growth. About 15 per cent of the population have access to electricity, but only in Phnom Penh and provincial towns. Generation is small-scale and inefficient, mostly oil-fired with some hydropower. There is no national power grid and rural consumers as well as industries frequently use costly generators to ensure an uninterrupted supply. The cost of electricity is the highest and consumption the lowest in the region.

Banking and insurance
The banking system is underdeveloped. The economy is highly dollarised, with foreign currency making up 70 per cent of the total money supply. This hinders the central bank's ability to implement an effective monetary policy.
Since 2000, Cambodia has been reforming the banking sector, introducing a minimum capitalisation requirement of US$11 million. This led to the closure of 11 banks by 2002.
Central bank
National Bank of Cambodia

Time
GMT plus seven hours

Geography
Cambodia occupies part of the Indochinese peninsula in South-East Asia. It is bordered by Thailand and Laos to the north, by Vietnam to the east and by the Gulf of Thailand to the south.

Climate
Generally hot and very humid, with a rainy season from June to October/November. Likely temperatures in Phnom Penh are 22–30 degrees Celsius (C) from November–December and 24–34 degrees C in April.

Entry requirements
Passports
Required by all. Must be valid for six months.
Visa
Visas are required by all. A one-month visa, for both tourist and business trips, can be issued on arrival at the Pochentong (Phnom Penh) and Siem Reap airports, as well as the Poi Pet international checkpoint, overland from Thailand. If planning to arrive by boat from Vietnam, or overland at checkpoints other than Poi Pet, a visa must be obtained prior to arrival; the place of entry must be specified.
Currency advice/regulations
Import and export of local currency is prohibited. Import of foreign currency must be declared on arrival; export of foreign currency up to amount declared.

Health (for visitors)
Mandatory precautions
Vaccination certificates for yellow fever if travelling from an infected area.
Advisable precautions
Vaccinations recommended for diphtheria, tuberculosis, hepatitis 'A' and 'B', Japanese B encephalitis. Anti-malarial precautions should be taken. There is risk of rabies.

Credit cards
Credit cards are only accepted in large hotels and shops.

Public holidays
Fixed dates
1 Jan (New Year's Day), 7 Jan (Victory Day), 8 Mar (Women's Day), 13–15 Apr (Traditional Cambodia New Year), 1 May (Labour Day), 1 Jun (International Children's Day), 18 Jun (Queen's Birthday), 24 Sep (Constitution and Coronation Day), 14 Oct (Pchum Ben Day), 23 Oct (Paris Peace Agreement), 9 Nov (Independence Day).
Variable dates
Birth of Buddha Day (Visaka Buja Day, May), Royal Ploughing Ceremony (May), Water Festival (three days, Nov).
The religious festivals are determined by the Buddhist lunar calendar.

Working hours
Banking
Mon–Fri: 0800–1500.
Business
Mon–Sat: 0700–1700 (siesta time is between 1130 and 1400). Some offices close on Saturday afternoons.
Government
Mon–Sat: 0700–1700 (siesta time is between 1130 and 1400). Some offices close on Saturday afternoons.
Shops
0700–1800.

Social customs/useful tips
Business cards are essential and are usually exchanged during introductions, when offering and receiving business cards with both hands is considered particularly polite. Punctuality is important and visitors should allow plenty of time for travelling. It is acceptable to shake hands with both men and women.
In conversation speak clearly using a moderate pace and complete sentences. Always give time for your host to answer and maintain courtesies.
Even during difficult negotiations remain calm as anger will give a poor impression. Criticism of the Royal Family and Buddhism should be avoided.
Learning some Cambodian greetings will both surprise and impress yours host. Photography is permitted although it is polite to ask permission before photographing Cambodian people, particularly monks.
Gratuities are welcome in restaurants and hotels.
The minimum drinking age is 18 years.

Security
The government has taken action to reduce crime but visitors are still advised not to walk alone at night in many areas of the city. Most hotels can arrange cars with drivers.
When visiting the temples at Angkor Wat, travel by air to Siem Reap airport, remain within the main temple complex and do not attempt to travel to Banteay Srei or to other outlying temples.

Getting there
Air
National airline: Royal Air Cambodge stopped all flying operations in October 2001 and went into bankruptcy.
International airport/s: Pochentong International (PNH), 8km from Phnom Penh.
Airport tax: International US$20; domestic US$10.
Surface
There is no overland or water crossing between Laos and Cambodia.
Road: Overland access is via Thailand or Vietnam.
Water: Access to Cambodia is possible by boat from Vietnam.
Main port/s: Mekong river port, Phnom Penh, Kompong Som (formerly Sihanoukville).

Getting about
National transport
Air: Domestic flights connect major cities. Siem Reap Airways flies one domestic route between Phnom Penh and Siem Reap. Royal Phnom Penh Airways flies to Siem Reap, Battambang, Stung Treng and Rattanakiri. President Airlines flies two

daily services between Phnom Penh and Siem Reap.

Road: There are 13,500km of roads. Only 12 per cent of national highways are paved, meaning that many communities are cut off during the rainy season. In November 1998, the Asian Development Bank (ADB) approved loans amounting to US$40 million and US$100 million to Cambodia and Viet Nam, respectively, from the ADB's Special Fund resources for rehabilitation of parts of the Phnom Penh-Ho Chi Minh City (HCMC) Highway Project over the 10-year period from 2002 to 2012.

Buses: Some bus or passenger truck services are available.

Rail: There are 612km of track. Rail services operate between Phnom Penh-Aranyaprathet, and Phnom Penh-Kompong Som. The government is aware of the critical need to improve infrastructure over the medium-term. It is aiming first to rehabilitate its railways to build links to Thailand through refurbishment of the Phnom Penh-Poipet line and construct a new line linking Phnom Penh and Ho Chi Minh City. These projects are part of the Asian Development Bank's (ADB) Greater Mekong sub-regional co-operation scheme. The Phnom Penh- Ho Chi Minh City link is part of the Trans-Asia railway aimed at linking Singapore to Kunming in the Yunnan province of China.

Water: Public boat travel is available.

City transport
The most convenient way to travel around the capital is by cyclo (tricycle) or motodops (motorcycles).

Taxis: There are ranks of cars with 'taxi' signs at the airport, but cruising taxis are not the norm.

Car hire
Most hotels can arrange cars with drivers.

BUSINESS DIRECTORY

The addresses listed below are a selection only. While World of Information makes every endeavour to check these addresses, we cannot guarantee that changes have not been made, especially to telephone numbers and area codes. We would welcome any corrections.

Telephone area codes
The international direct dialling (IDD) code for Cambodia is +855, followed by area code and subscriber's number.

Battambang	53	Pusat	52
Kampong Som	62	Stung Treng	74
Phnom Penh	23	Siem Riep	63

Useful telephone numbers
Police: 722-353
Fire: 723-555
Ambulance: 723-173

Chambers of Commerce
Phnom Penh Chamber of Commerce, 7B Street 81 corner Street 109, Sangkat Beung Raing, Daun Penh District, Phnom Penh (tel: 212-265; fax: 212-270; e-mail: ppcc@camnet.com.kh).

Banking
Cambodia Mekong Bank Public Ltd, 1 Kramuon Sar Street, Khan Daun Penh, Phnom Penh (tel: 217-112; fax: 217-122).

Cambodian Commercial Bank Limited, 26 Monivong Road, Sangkat Phsar Thmei 2, Khan Daun Penh, Phnom Penh (tel: 426-145, 426-639, 213-601, 213-602, 426-638; fax: 426-116).

Cambodian Public Bank Ltd, Villa No. 23, Street 114, Vithei Kramounsar, Phnom Penh (tel: 426-067; fax:426-068).

Canadia Bank Ltd, 265-269 Prash Ang Doung Street, Sangkath Wattphnom, Khan Daun Penh, Phnom Penh (tel:-266-046, 725-548).

Crédit Agricole Indosuez, 70 Blvd Norodom, Phnom Penh (tel: 427-233).

First Commercial Bank, 263 Ang Duong St, Phnom Penh (tel: 210-026; fax: 210-029).

Foreign Trade Bank of Cambodia, 24/26 Preah Morodom Boulevard, Phnom Penh (tel: 724-466, 723-866, 722-466, 723-466).

National Bank of Cambodia, PO Box 25, 22-24 Preah Norodom Blvd, Phnom Penh (tel: 428-105, 722-563; fax: 426-117).

Singapore Banking Corporation Ltd, 68 Samdech Pan Street (St. 214), Sangkat Beung Raing, Khan Daun Penh, Phnom Penh (tel: 217-771).

Singapore Commercial Bank Ltd, 316 Preah Monivong Boulevard, Sangkat Chak To Mok, Khan Daun Penh, Phnom Penh (tel: 427-471).

Union Commercial Bank Plc, UCB Bldg, No. 61, 130 Road, Psa Chas Quater, Khan Daun Penh, Phnom Penh (tel: 724-831, fax: 427-997).

Central bank
National Bank of Cambodia, 22-24 Preah Boulevard Norodom, Phnom Penh (tel/fax: 426-117).

Travel information
Ministry of tourism
Ministry of Tourism, Boulevard Monivong/Street 232, Phnom Penh (tel: 426-107, 724-807; fax: 426-877).

Ministries
Ministry of Agriculture, 200 Norodom Blvd, Phnom Penh (tel: 723-689, 722-127).

Ministry of Commerce, Boulevard Norodom, Phnom Penh (tel: 723-263; fax: 426-396).

Ministry of Culture, Monivong Blvd/Red Cross Street, Phnom Penh (tel: 724-769).

Ministry of Defence, Pochentong Blvd, Phnom Penh (tel: 725-697).

Ministry of Education, Youth and Sport, 80 Blvd Norodom, Phnom Penh (tel: 362-338; fax: 426-791).

Ministry of Finance, 60 St 92, Phnom Penh (tel: 426-841).

Ministry of Foreign Affairs and International Co-operation, Sisowath Quay/St 240, Phnom Penh (tel: 426-146, 724-441; fax: 26-144).

Ministry of Health, 153-153 Blvd Kampuchea Krom, Phnom Penh (tel: 725-833, 724-573).

Ministry of Industry, 45 Norodom Boulevard/St 45, Phnom Penh (tel: 723-477; fax: 427-840).

Ministry of Information, 62 Boulevard Monivong, Phnom Penh (tel: 23-369, 22-869).

Ministry of the Interior, 275 Norodom Blvd, Phnom Penh (tel: 426-494).

Ministry of Justice, Sothearos Blvd, Phnom Penh (tel: 724-543, 360-329).

Ministry of Planning, 386 Boulevard Monivong, Phnom Penh (tel: 725-143, 724-543).

Ministry of Posts and Telecommunications, Street 13/Street 102, Phnom Penh (tel: 723-911, 426-817; fax: 426-786).

Ministry of Public Works and Transport, Boulevard Norodom/Mahaksatriyani St, Phnom Penh (tel: 427-862; fax: 427-862).

Ministry of Religious Affairs, Sothearos Blvd/St 240, Phnom Penh (tel: 725-699).

Ministry of Rural Development, Blvd Pochentong, Phnom Penh (tel: 426-814).

Ministry of Social Welfare, 68 Blvd Norodom, Phnom Penh (tel: 725-191, 427-322).

Prime Minister's Office, 22 Street 214, Phnom Penh (tel: 26-053/4, 26-025).

Other useful addresses
ASEAN Investment Promotion Agency, Cambodian Investment Board, Government Palace, Sisowath Quay, Wat Phnom, Phnom Penh (tel: 50-428; fax: 61-616, 60-606).

ASEAN Secretariat, 70 A J1 Sisingamangaraja, Jakarta 12110, Indonesia (tel: 62(21)726-2991, 724-3372; fax: 724-3504, 739-8234).

Asian Development Bank, Cambodia Resident Mission, 93 Preah Norodom

Boulevard, Phnom Penh (tel: 725-805; fax: 725-807).

British Embassy, 27-29 Street 75, Phnom Penh (tel: 427-124; fax: 427-124/5).

Cambodian Development Council (CDC), Phnom Penh.

Cambodian Embassy (USA), 4530 16th Street, NW, Washington DC 20011 (tel:202- 726-7742; fax:202-726-8381; e-mail: cambodia@embassy.org).

Cambodia Mine Action Centre, 22 Street 122, Phnom Penh (tel: 913-506).

Chemins de Fer du Cambodge, Moha Vithei Pracheathippatay, Phnom Penh (tel: 25-156).

Department of Civil Aviation, 62 Boulevard Norodom, Phnom Penh (tel: 427-141; fax: 26-169).

Global, Business Centre, 378 EO Sivutha Street, Group 1, Sangkat Olympic, Khan Chamcarmon, Phnom Penh (tel: 27-124; fax: 27-125).

Phnom Penh Port Authority (tel: 23-369).

Prime Minister's Office, 22 Street 214, Phnom Penh (tel: 26-053/4, 26-025).

Internet sites

Asian Development Bank: http://www.adb.org/carm

Cambodia web sites: http://mekong.net/cambodia/links.htm

Cambodian web directory: http://www.kampuchea.com/

UN Food and Aid administration: http://www.fao.org/waicent/search/default.asp

Cameroon

KEY FACTS

Official name: République du Cameroun (Republic of Cameroon)

Head of State: President Paul Biya (since 1982; last re-elected 11 Oct 2004)

Head of government: Prime Minister Ephraïm Inoni (appointed by the President 8 Dec 2004)

Ruling party: Coalition: Rassemblement Démocratique du Peuple Camerounais (RDPC) (Cameroon People's Democratic Rally) and Union Nationale pour la Démocratie et le Progrès (UNDP) (National Union for Democracy and Progress)

Area: 475,442 square km

Population: 16.79 million (2004)

Capital: Yaoundé

Official language: French, English

Currency: CFA franc (CFAf) = 100 centimes (Communauté Financière Africaine (African Financial Community) franc)

Exchange rate: CFAf544.07 per US$ (Oct 2005); CFAf655.95 per euro (pegged from Jan 1999)

GDP per capita: US$831 (2004)

GDP real growth: 4.30% (2004)

Labour force: 6.83 million (2004)

Inflation: 0.30% (2004)

Oil production: 62,000 bpd (2004)

Balance of trade: US$466.00 million (2004)

Foreign debt: US$8.46 billion (2004)

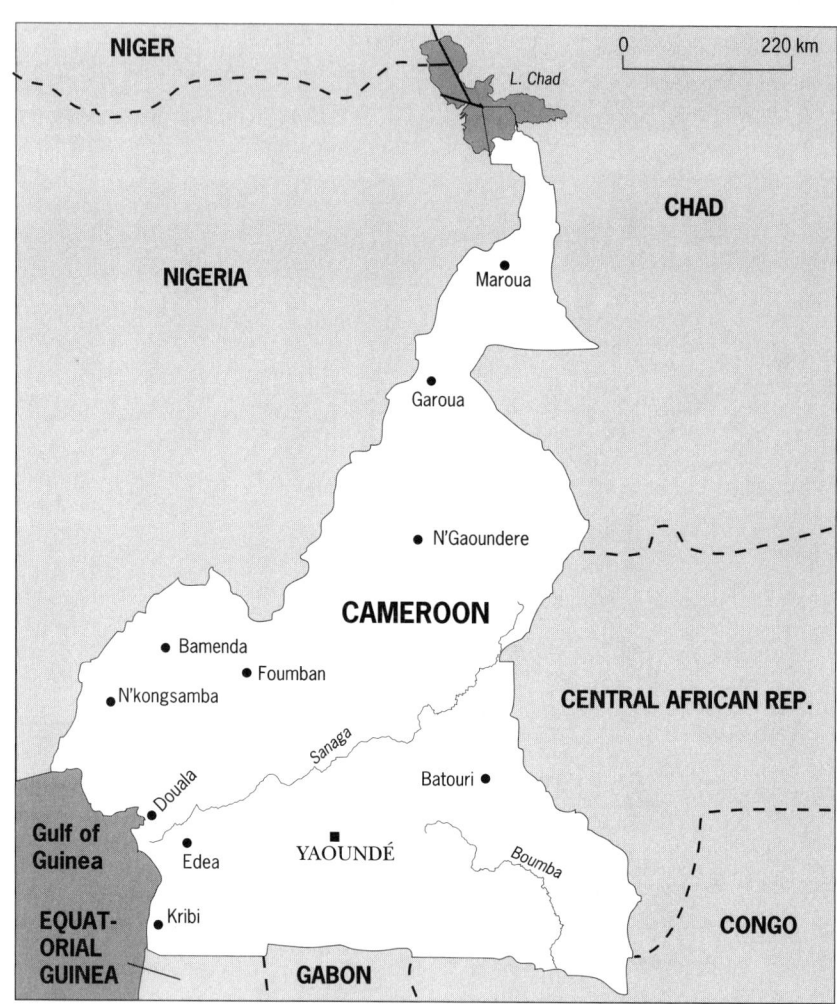

Cameroon has one of the best-endowed primary commodity economies in sub-Saharan Africa, with its oil resources and favourable agricultural conditions.

IMF funding

After a year of negotiations, Cameroon in October 2005 realised an ambitious International Monetary Fund (IMF)-backed arrangement to bring its economy into line. Over three years, the IMF will make available US$35 million to support the government's programme of economic reform and poverty reduction. Targets include annual real growth up to 4.5 per cent from 2.8 per cent, with non-oil growth of 5.1 per cent from 3.7 per cent. This will be in the face of declining oil output – down to 74,000 barrels per day (bpd) from 82,000bpd, and at three dollars a barrel less. Growth in exports of the non-oil sector will reach 5.4 per cent (negative 3.7 per cent in 2005) while growth in oil exports will have slowed to 3.2 per cent.

Total government revenue is set to remain reasonably constant at 17 per cent of GDP; while expenditure will jump to 17 per cent from 15 per cent. Debt servicing after debt relief will be cut to 4.2 per cent of GDP from 6.7 per cent. The current account balance will worsen from a negative 2.4 per cent to 4.8 per cent.

Monitoring of the programme so far (over 2005) has seen 'broadly satisfactory' performance. The policies have contributed to solid growth, low inflation and a narrowing of the current account deficit, but progress in structural reforms needs to be strengthened, particularly with respect to improving governance and the business climate, privatisation and fuel price adjustments. There is also considerable room for improvement in the transparency of government operations.

In recent years, the business climate has also been adversely affected by the government's failure to pay salaries and slow progress in restructuring loss-making public enterprises. The targets doggedly assume an end to this and although oil production is expected to decline over the medium term, growth in the non-oil economy is expected to strengthen as the business climate improves.

The economy is mainly agricultural. The principal commercial crops are cocoa, coffee, tobacco, cotton, and bananas. Petroleum products make up more than half of all exports. Timber is also a major export. Potential includes bauxite, iron ore, timber and hydropower. Underlying economic and policy weaknesses were exposed in 1985, when sharp declines in coffee, cocoa and oil prices had led to a 60 per cent degeneration in the external terms of trade. In late 1996, Cameroon changed course and committed itself to correcting the years of economic mismanagement. The success of government reforms (forestry, transportation, banking system, and privatisation of public utilities) supported by the IMF and the World Bank translated into better economic performance, but impetus flagged because of a top-heavy civil service and a generally unfavorable climate for business enterprise.

Politics

Cameroon has generally enjoyed stability, but despite movement toward democratic reform, political power remains firmly in the hands of an ethnic oligarchy. The anglophone community has felt for some time that it is discriminated against by a remote Yaoundé-based government and has long campaigned for greater autonomy, seeing itself as increasingly marginalised in the francophone-dominated country. Most in the anglophone community favour the reintroduction of a federal system.

Cameroon has the advantage of one of the best literacy rates in Africa. Almost all members of the indigenous population over 15 years of age can read and write.

However, the country's continued development is hampered by a level of corruption that is among the highest in the world. Ratings agency Standard and Poor's in January 2006 reaffirmed Cameroon's CCC long term and C short term ratings, saying they reflected the country's weak public finances.

Veteran Cameroon leader Paul Biya won his third term in presidential elections in October 2004, with more than 70 per cent of the vote. Commonwealth observers accepted the result, but said the poll lacked credibility in key areas. Opposition parties alleged widespread fraud. Biya has been in power since 1982. Born in 1933, he was educated in Cameroon and France, where he studied law at the Sorbonne. Before becoming president, he spent his entire political career in the service of previous president Ahmadou Ahidjo, becoming his prime minister in 1975. When Ahidjo resigned in 1982 he assumed the leadership and set about replacing his predecessor's northern allies with his own fellow southerners. In 1983 he accused Ahidjo of organising a coup against him, forcing the former president to flee the country.

Risk assessment

Economic	Fair
Political	Fair
Regional stability	Improving

COUNTRY PROFILE

Historical profile

At the end of the First World War, the German protectorate over Douala was divided between Britain and France. In 1958, the French granted their region self-government which led to independence as the Republic of Cameroon. In 1961 British Southern Cameroon was federated with the Republic of Cameroon, while British Northern Cameroon joined Nigeria.

Cameroon began its independence with a bloody insurrection which was suppressed only with the help of French forces. This was followed by 20 years of repressive government under Ahidjo. In 1994, and briefly in 1996, Cameroon fought a border war with Nigeria over the disputed oil-rich Bakassi Peninsula. An international court awarded sovereignty over Bakassi to Cameroon in 2002, although Nigeria has yet to withdraw its troops from the territory. Internally, there are tensions over the two mainly English-speaking southern provinces. A secessionist movement, the Southern Cameroon National Council (SCNC), emerged in the 1990s and has been declared as illegal.

1470s Portuguese mariners arrived and gave Cameroon its name. Having found what they thought to be shrimps (*camaroes*) in the main river, they named it *Rio dos Camaroes*.

1884 Germany established the protectorate of Kamerun.

1916 The German administration was ousted by Allied forces in the First World War.

The post-war League of Nations gave mandates for four-fifths of the territory to France, and the remainder to Britain.

1960 French East Cameroon gained its independence.

KEY INDICATORS — Cameroon

	Unit	2000	2001	2002	2003	2004
Population	m	14.88	15.20	15.50	16.14	16.79
Gross domestic product (GDP)	US$bn	8.90	8.50	9.40	12.40	*14.73
GDP per capita	US$	593	559	606	841	831
GDP real growth	%	4.2	5.3	6.5	4.2	4.3
Inflation	%	0.8	2.8	6.3	0.6	0.3
Oil output	'000 bpd	88.0	80.0	72.0	68.0	62.0
Exports (fob) (goods)	US$m	2,124.0	2,129.0	1,790.0	2,078.0	2,445.0
Imports (fob) (goods)	US$m	1,538.0	1,617.0	1,830.0	1,962.0	1,979.0
Balance of trade	US$m	586.0	512.0	-39.0	116.0	466.0
Current account	US$m	-153.0	-350.0	-690.0	-300.0	-240.0
Foreign debt	US$bn	9.9	6.6	8.5	8.5	8.5
Total reserves minus gold	US$m	212.0	331.8	629.7	639.6	829.3
Foreign exchange	US$m	203.6	331.1	627.7	637.2	827.6
Exchange rate	per US$	711.98	733.04	683.75	574.89	528.29

* estimated figure

1961 British West Cameroon gained its independence.
1972 A unified state was formed, with the Union Nationale Camerounaise (UNC) (Cameroonian National Union) dominating both the executive and legislative branches.
1982 Prime Minister Paul Biya became president after the resignation of President Ahidjo.
1985 Biya renamed the ruling party the Rassemblement Démocratique du Peuple Camerounais (RDPC) (Cameroon People's Democratic Rally), and introduced a number of political reforms which were largely viewed as cosmetic.
1990 A multi-party political system was legalised. Although this change marked the gradual opening of the Cameroonian political system, subsequent elections were marred by irregularities and accusations of electoral fraud.
1997 President Paul Biya was re-elected. The elections were boycotted by the three main opposition parties after their complaints about the handling of voter registration were ignored. Biya won 92 per cent of the vote.
1999 English-speaking secessionists, led by the Southern Cameroon National Council (SCNC), announced a breakaway Federal Republic of Southern Cameroon.
2001 Demonstrations calling for decentralisation of power were banned and several southern Cameroon separatists were killed.
2002 The ruling RDPC increased its number of seats in the legislative elections. The International Court of Justice gave Cameroon sovereignty of the potentially oil-rich Bakassi Peninsula, claimed by Cameroon and Nigeria.
2003 The communications minister ordered the closure of an English-speaking private radio station, Magic FM, for running programmes critical of the government.
2004 Biya was re-elected in the 11 October presidential elections. On 8 December, Ephraïm Inoni was appointed prime minister. In September Nigeria failed to withdraw troops from the Bakassi Peninsula.
2005 In May, Presidents Obasanjo and Biya and UN Secretary Annan failed to resolve the dispute concerning Bakassi Peninsula, thought to hold about 10 per cent of the world's oil and gas reserves.

Political structure
Constitution
The constitution was promulgated in 1972 and revised in 1975 and 1996. The main provisions of the 1996 revision were for a more decentralised government, the creation of a unicameral national assembly (Assemblée Nationale), and the extension of the president's term of office from five years to seven, at the same time allowing a fourth consecutive term.
Form of state
Unitary republic
The executive
Executive power is vested in the president, who appoints a cabinet. The president serves a seven-year term. A prime minister, who acts as head of government, is appointed by the president. The president names and dismisses cabinet members and judges, ratifies treaties, heads the armed forces, controls legislation and can rule by decree.
National legislature
Legislative power is held by the 180-member unicameral Assemblée Nationale (National Assembly), elected for a five-year term.
Legal system
Cameroon's legal system is based on French civil law with common law influences. The country has a Supreme Court, the judges of which are appointed by the president. Provisions in the 1996 constitution for judicial independence have not been put into force. Cameroon does not accept the compulsory jurisdiction of the International Court of Justice, but does belong to the International Court of Arbitration of the International Chamber of Commerce.
Last elections
11 October 2004 (presidential); 30 June 2002 (parliamentary).
Results: Presidential: Paul Biya was re-elected with 70.9 per cent of the vote against 17.4 per cent for John Fru Ndi, 4.5 per cent for Adamou Ndam Njoya and 3.7 per cent for Garga Haman Adji. Turnout was 82.8 per cent.
Parliamentary: The ruling RDPC increased its seats from 116 to 133 (149 after the Supreme Court ordered, on 15 September 2002, a re-run after allegations of electoral irregularities); SDF won 21 (22 after the re-run) seats, down from 43; the UDC retained its five seats; the Union des Populations du Cameroun (UPC) (Cameroon Peoples' Union) won three seats, up from one seat in 1997; the UNDP won only one seat, down from 68 in 1997.
Next elections
2007 (parliamentary); 2011 (presidential).
Political parties
Ruling party
Coalition: Rassemblement Démocratique du Peuple Camerounais (RDPC) (Cameroon People's Democratic Rally) and Union Nationale pour la Démocratie et le Progrès (UNDP) (National Union for Democracy and Progress)

Main opposition party
Social Democratic Front (SDF); Union Démocratique du Cameroun (UDC) (Democratic Union of Cameroon).

Population
16.79 million (2004)
Ethnic make-up
Cameroon has a highly diversified population comprising some 200 ethnic groups, including Cameroon Highlanders (31 per cent), Equatorial Bantu (19 per cent) and Kirdi (11 per cent). There are about 200,000 Europeans in the country, mainly French speakers.
Religions
Indigenous beliefs are practiced by 40 per cent of the population, another 40 per cent are Christian, and 20 per cent are Muslim.

Education
Literacy rate: 81per cent men, 69 per cent women; adult rates (World Bank).
Enrolment rate: 107 per cent gross primary enrolment, 33 per cent gross secondary enrolment; of relevant age groups (including repeaters) (World Bank).
Pupils per teacher: 44 in primary schools.

Health
The total expenditure on health is 3–4 per cent of GDP, of which government spending is about 37 per cent.
HIV prevalence: 5.5 per cent aged 15–49 in 2004 (World Bank)
Life expectancy: 48 years (World Bank)
Fertility rate/Maternal mortality rate: 4.5 births per woman
Birth rate/Death rate: 34.7 births and 15.4 deaths per 1,000 population (2005)
Infant mortality rate: 95 per 1,000 live births; 22 per cent of children aged under five are malnourished (World Bank).
Head of population per physician/bed: 26 hospital beds and one physician per 10,000 people.

Welfare
Cameroon's social insurance system provides cover for old-age pension, disability pension, sickness and maternity benefits, work injuries and family allowances.

Main cities
Douala (commercial centre, estimated population 1.3 million in 2004), Yaoundé (capital, 1.2 million), Garoua (387,000), Kousséri (313,800), Bamenda (290,300), Maroua (284,200), Bafoussam (250,500).

Languages spoken
24 major African language groups including Bamileke, Ewondo, Bassa and Bamoun are spoken. Around 80 per cent of the population speak French as a second language (francophone Cameroon) and 20 per cent speak English as a

Cameroon

second language (anglophone – formerly British West Cameroon).

Official language/s
French, English

Media
Press
Dailies: Privatisation of the media has steadily increased the size of the press over the years, as no authorisation is needed to start a newspaper. The official state-owned daily paper *Cameroon Tribune* (French) is also published in English twice weekly. Other English and French-language dailies include *Le Messager*, *Cameroun Today*, *Camnet Actualites* and *Wagne*.

Weeklies: Weeklies include *Socialist Chronicle*, *Star Headlines*, *Weekly Post*, *Temps*, *Perspectives hebdo*, *Le Phare*, *Politiks*, *Cameroon Post*, *Cigale*, *Héraut* and *Generation*.

Business: Business news is carried by a bi-weekly publication *La Dépeche économique*.

Periodicals: Monthly periodicals include *L'Aube des temps nouveaux*, *Contact magazine*, *La Démocrate*, *Dikalo*, *Effets du septennat*, *La Foi qui sauve*, *Le Météo*, *Le Devoir*, *Le Journal de Douala*, *Le Proces*, *Reforme*, *Revelation* and *Le Météo*.

Broadcasting
From Yaoundé, Cameroon Radio and Television Corporation (CRTV) operates a radio service in French, English and local languages (there are independent stations in all provincial centres), and the television network covers most of the country. Service is financed mainly by commercial advertising with some state input.

Advertising
There is a wide range of media for advertising in Cameroon. Radio and television airtime is available from state broadcasters, as well as on Gabon's 'Africa Number One' radio station. Cinema audiences in Yaoundé, Douala and Bafoussa can also be reached. Billboard space, once a state monopoly, has been liberalised. The Cameroonian chamber of commerce organises an annual trade fair, and the thriving independent press offers an alternative to advertising in the official newspapers.

Economy
Cameroon has, for a number of years, been working in close co-operation with the IMF to improve its economic policies. It has introduced structural reforms with adjustments to emphasise non-oil revenue, to improve public finance management and reporting. There was a marked improvement through 2004 with real growth at 4.3 per cent and inflation at just 0.3 per cent and a reduction in the external current account deficit. However, at the same time public finances deteriorated, poverty was still widespread and public investment remained low. Nevertheless the government has been advised that it should remain firm on improving governance, enterprise restructuring, privatisation and removing fuel price subsidies. The IMF has stated that reform priorities should include increasing public investment in infrastructure and removing obstacles to private sector activities.

In October 2005 the IMF announced that Cameroon had been awarded a three-year arrangement of US$26.8 million under the Poverty Reduction and Growth facility. This followed the additional amount of US$8.2 million offered under the Heavily Indebted Poor Countries Initiative, which will be released from late 2005 through to 2006.

Oil and cocoa prices have a great impact on the economy. Both commodities rose in price in 2004 bringing an unexpected surge in revenue, which the IMF advised should be used for poverty reduction programmes and debt reduction.

Cameroon has the possibility of becoming a major net exporter of oil and gas if it can reach agreement with Nigeria concerning Bakassi Peninsula, thought to hold about 10 per cent of the world's oil and gas reserves. An international ruling and top-level mediation has not solved this *impasse* as it seems Nigeria does not want to give up this potentially lucrative land to Cameroon.

External trade
Cameroon benefits from the tariff preferences under the U S African Growth and Opportunities Act (AGOA).

Imports
Imports consist mainly of semi-processed products and industrial outputs, machinery and food products. There is also some importing of light crude oil for the country's refineries. Imports consist principally of machines and electrical equipment, transport equipment, fuel and food. Import volume has been constrained because of the strong growth of domestic industries (especially in food processing) which are offering cheaper alternatives to expensive imported goods.

Main sources: France (28.2 cent total, 2004), Nigeria (9.4 per cent), Belgium (7.6 per cent), US (4.8 per cent), Germany (4.6 per cent), China (4.4 per cent), Italy (4 per cent)

Exports
Principal exports include crude oil and petroleum products, timber, cocoa beans, aluminium, coffee, cotton.

Main destinations: Spain (16.2 per cent total, 2004), Italy (14.1 per cent), France (10.2 per cent), UK (9.9 per cent), US (9.6 per cent), The Netherlands (5.1 per cent)

Agriculture
Farming
In order to broaden the country's economic base and increase the value added to domestic production, the government is encouraging development of its full agricultural potential. Agricultural production as a percentage of GDP has been steadily increasing since the early 1980s, reaching 43.9 per cent of national output in 2004. Some 70 per cent of Cameroon's labour force is employed in the agricultural sector, although only 2 per cent of Cameroon's land area is used for permanent crops. Principal crops include cocoa, coffee, bananas, cotton and oil palms. Virtually all food requirements are met by local production. Most agricultural production is in the hands of smallholders, with the exception of rubber and palm, which are run under the plantation system.

Mayuka, located in the northern region of Cameroon, is the centre of the cocoa industry, where business made sweeping profits as prices soared following the political crisis in Côte d'Ivoire. As demand for cocoa rises, so the government aims to double the amount of production.

Crop production in 2004 included: 1,412,400 million tonnes (t) cereals in total, 1,950,000t cassava, 1,200,000t taro, 265,000t yams, 1,450,000t sugar cane, 1,200,000t oil palm fruit, 750,000t maize, *1,200,000t plantains, 50,000t millet, 135,000t potatoes, 175,000t sweet potatoes, 550,000t sorghum, 240,000t seed cotton, 109,000t cotton lint, 62,000t rice, 200,000t groundnuts in shells, 630,000t bananas, 291,090t oilcrops, 266,600t pulses, *4,000t tea, 370,000t tomatoes, 45,000t pineapples, *4,500t tobacco, *130,000t cocoa beans, *60,000t green coffee, *45,892t natural rubber, 2,042,927t fruit in total, 1,290,870t vegetables in total. Livestock production included: 223,649t meat in total, 54,000t beef, *16,200t pig meat, *16,380t lamb, *15,700t goat meat, *50,000t game meat, *30,000t poultry, *13,400t eggs, *189,300t milk, *3,000t honey, 300t cocoons, silk, *13,000t cattle hides, *2,730t sheepskins.
* estimate

Fishing
As a consequence of its short coastline and the intrusion on its territorial waters of Bioko Island, which belongs to Equatorial Guinea, Cameroon's fishing industry is underdeveloped. Offshore waters are not well stocked, as the currents which provide richer fishing grounds off Nigeria and other parts of West Africa do not flow close to Cameroon's coastline. Nevertheless, catches of both freshwater and marine fish have been steadily increasing in recent years.

Fisheries legislation in Cameroon contains specific clauses dealing with the aquaculture sector, covering issues related to registration and licensing, and the export/import of fish species. It aims to improve artisanal fishing methods, preservation and processing of fishery products.

Forestry
While the country is well-forested, with more than 40 per cent forest cover and an additional 30 per cent of other wooded land, unsustainable deforestation led to the loss of 222,000 hectares between 1990–2000. Nevertheless Cameroon is the second-largest area of tropical rainforest in Africa after the Democratic Republic of Congo (DRC). It is one of Africa's leading producers and exporters of tropical logs and sawn timber; smaller quantities of veneer and plywood are also exported. Important non-wood forest products include medicinal plants, nuts, wild fruits, rattan and bushmeat.
Three-quarters of Cameroon's forestry exports consist of industrial roundwood, with sawnwood accounting for another 18 per cent. Forestry imports to Cameroon are composed almost exclusively of paper and paperboard, totalling 96.5 per cent of forestry imports. Exports in 2004 amounted to just over US$400 million, while imports were US$37 million.
Timber production in 2004 included 10,956,789 cubic metre (cum) roundwood, 1,550,000cum industrial roundwood, 658,100cum sawnwood, 1,400,000cum sawlogs and veneer logs, 9,406,789cum wood fuel, 371,712t charcoal.

Industry and manufacturing
The industrial sector has been contracting and accounted for only 15.6 per cent of GDP in 2004, while services accounted for 40.5 per cent. However, the agri-industrial sub-sector has been growing, gradually substituting imports with domestically produced goods. The sector employs around 10 per cent of the workforce. Industrial output accounts for 25 per cent of Cameroon's exports.
The government has been a major participant in the industrial sector, mainly through the Société Nationale d'Investissement (SNI) (National Investment Agency), however economic imperatives have required that public entities become market driven and private enterprise has yet to become competitive. The Technical Commission for the Rehabilitation of Public Enterprises oversees privatisation and restructuring of all state-owned companies.
Industrial production increased by 7.2 per cent in 2004.

Tourism
There is considerable potential for tourism in Cameroon although development has been slow due to expensive air fares, the high cost of tourist visas, limited tourist infrastructure and the relatively high prices of hotels. A Tourist Development Plan is being undertaken in co-operation with the World Tourism Organisation (WTO). The government has devised a special investment code to encourage private investors. The deregulation of air traffic should help reduce air fares.

Environment
Cameroon's tropical forest is the second largest in the world but it is being exploited at a faster rate than is sustainable. There is little monitoring of forest management. As the forests have become more accessible, poachers are shooting antelope, chimpanzees and gorillas, and selling them.
In October 2005 a UN inspection team warned that a natural dam in the north-west province was in imminent danger of collapsing and flooding the Nyos Valley. The cost to repair the dam is estimated at US$15 million.

Mining
The mining sector accounts for around 10 per cent of GDP and employs 2 per cent of the workforce. Bauxite deposits of some 1,100 million tonnes at Adamaoua Province have been identified but remain unexploited, although an upturn in world aluminium prices encouraged Société des Bauxitese de Cameroun (SBC) to begin mining operations. There are deposits of iron ore at Kribi (reserves estimated at 197 million tonnes), and potential reserves of gold, diamonds, uranium, rutile, industrial clays and low-grade nickel and cobalt. Tin is mined on a very small scale. Investment by large mining companies is needed to exploit underground riches.

Hydrocarbons
Cameroon used to be sub-Saharan Africa's fifth-largest oil producer but by 2005 had dropped to seventh place as Equatorial Guinea and Chad have developed their oil reserves. Crude oil production in 2004 was 62,000 barrels per day (bpd); proven oil reserves were 400 million barrels in 2003.
The country also had natural gas reserves of 110.7 billion cubic metres in 2004. The industry is still in early stages of development, but would take off dramatically if the territorial dispute with Nigeria over the Bakassi Peninsula were to be resolved in Cameroon's favour. The Bakassi Peninsula is reckoned by some to hold some 10 per cent of the world oil and gas reserves. The government also believes there is considerable potential in two largely unexplored areas – the Logone Birni and Douala basins – and is also hoping for the discovery of big offshore finds. However, the coastline is limited and the country's maritime area is small.

Energy
Total electricity generation capacity is estimated at 850MW, nearly 90 per cent of which is hydroelectric. Although Cameroon has the greatest hydroelectric power potential in Africa after the Democratic Republic of Congo (DRC), its plants are old, having been mainly built in the 1950s, and operate well below capacity. Therefore, gas will be especially important as an alternative source of power in the dry season. Cameroon expects its demand for power to double in the course of the next decade. Production from the Edéa Dam complex, Lagdo near Garoua and Song-Loulou generate enough to meet 85 per cent of needs. All electricity is produced by the Société Nationale d'Electricité du Cameroun (AES-Sonel), which is 51 per cent owned by the US's AES Sirocco. AES-Sonel increased tariff charges annually over 2001–04 to improve its commercial viability ahead of the sale of the government's remaining 49 per cent stake in the company.
The government decided in October 2004, to go ahead with plans for the Lom-Pangar hydroelectric project, which includes a 50 metre high barrage flooding an area of 610 square km and a hydroelectric plant of approximately 50MW. An environmental impact study is to be the initial step and construction of the project probably will not start before 2008.
It is estimated that only 2 per cent of the population has access to electricity supplies and only 9 per cent of the capitial's potential consumers use electricity; most of the country relies on wood fuel.
To comply with a World Bank loan to develop the electricity sector emphasis on sustainable energy has increased

Banking and insurance
Cameroon's banking sector has become significantly stronger as the result of IMF-led restructuring, but is still poorly developed. The last state-owned bank in Cameroon was bought by a French banking company in 1999. Cameroon's largest bank is the Société Générale de Banques au Cameroun (SGBC). The commercial banking sector is made up of nine commercial banks with 60 branches, but suffers from a lack of available capital, an unwillingness to take risks and outdated products.

Central bank
Banque des Etats de l'Afrique Centrale

Main financial centre
Douala

Cameroon

Time
GMT plus one hour

Geography
Cameroon lies at the elbow of Africa where West Africa meets Southern Africa. Nigeria is to the west, Chad and the Central African Republic to the north-east and east, and the Republic of Congo, Equatorial Guinea and Gabon to the south. The country can be divided into four main regions. The coastal plain is tropical but tempered by the effects of the sea. The tropical plateau in the south is heavily forested and cut through by a number of rivers flowing west into the Bight of Biafra or south-east to join the River Zaire. The Adamawa and Bamenda highlands rise to 2,500 metres and are drier and cooler than the forest areas. The highlands are volcanic in origin, and include Mount Cameroon (4,070 metres). The savannah grasslands to the north lie between Nigeria and Chad, and stretch northwards to Lake Chad.

Climate
In the north the single wet season is between April and September, and there is a dry season during the rest of the year. It is tropical in the south with fairly constant average temperatures throughout the year, ranging between 18 degrees Celsius (C) at night and 30–32 degrees C during the day. In the south rainfall is distributed throughout the year with two wet seasons and two dry seasons.

Dress codes
Tropical clothes are advised, with warmer clothes required for the higher altitudes. Lightweight raincoats are recommended for the rainy season.

Entry requirements
Passports
Passports are required by all and should be valid for at least six months upon arrival.
Visa
Required by all before arrival. Citizens of those countries without embassy representation may be issued with a visa at the border if notification of arrival is made beforehand. A visa application form for American visitors can be found at www.ambacam-usa.org/formstofill.html. A business visa requires a letter from applicant's company outlining purpose of visit, proof of sufficient funds and a letter from business partners in Cameroon (endorsed by the local police), plus a full itinerary. An onward/return ticket, is required by all.
Currency advice/regulations
Foreign currency import is unlimited, but amounts must be declared. Local currency import is also unlimited, but export is limited to CFAf20,000 (approximately US$30) without official authorisation. Traveller's cheques are accepted on a limited basis.
Prohibited imports
Pornographic materials, illegal drugs, weapons and ammunitions may not be brought into Cameroon. Alcohol and other spirits (maximum 30 bottles) should be sent separately.
An invoice must accompany all furniture and electrical appliances to prove that they are more than six months old. Newer items are subject to customs duties and taxes. Home computers do not qualify as personal effects, and are subject to customs duties and taxes.

Health (for visitors)
Mandatory precautions
An international certificate of vaccination against yellow fever.
Advisable precautions
The principal health hazards are cholera, malaria and HIV. Vaccination against tetanus, typhoid, polio, meningitis, and hepatitis 'A' and 'B' are all advisable. Rabies and bilharzia also occur, and necessary precautions should be taken. Avoid swimming in fresh water; well-chlorinated swimming pools should be safe. Bottled water is readily available. Milk is unpasteurised and should be boiled; meat and vegetables should be cooked and fruit peeled.
Medical care is adequate, but can be expensive.

Hotels
Good hotel accommodation is available in main centres. Advisable to book in advance, and confirmation should be obtained from the selected hotel in writing. Service charges usually added to bill.

Credit cards
There is limited acceptance of the major credit cards only.

Public holidays
Fixed dates
1 Jan (New Year's Day), 11 Feb (Youth Day), 1 May (Labour Day), 20 May (National Day), 21 May (Sheep Festival), 15 Aug (Assumption Day), 25 Dec (Christmas Day).
Variable dates
Good Friday, Easter Monday, Ascension Day, Eid al Adha, Eid al Fitr, Birth of the Prophet.
The Islamic year contains 354 or 355 days, with the result that Muslim feasts advance by 10–12 days against the Gregorian calendar. Dates of feasts vary according to the sighting of the new moon, so cannot be forecast exactly. Islamic year 1426: 10 February 2005 to 30 January 2006.

Working hours
Different hours are kept in the French-speaking (including Yaoundé and Douala) and English-speaking areas (south-west and north-west frontier areas) of Cameroon.
Banking
French-speaking areas: 0800–1200 and 1515–1630 (Mon–Fri).
English-speaking areas: 0800–1330 (Mon–Fri).
Business
French-speaking areas: 0730–1200 and 1430–1800 (Mon–Fri).
English-speaking areas: 0730–1500 (Mon–Fri); 0730–1200 (Sat).
Government
French-speaking areas: 0730–1200 and 1430–1800 (Mon–Fri).
English-speaking areas: 0730–1500 (Mon–Fri); 1730–1200 (Sat).
Shops
French-speaking areas: 0700/0800–1230 and 1430/1500–1830–1900 (Mon–Sat).
English-speaking areas: 0700/0800–1200 and 1430/1530–1830–1900 (Mon–Sat).
Post offices:
French-speaking areas: 0800–1200 and 1400–1700 (Mon–Fri); 0800–1200 (Sat)
English-speaking areas: 0800–1200 and 1430–1700 (Mon–Fri).

Telecommunications
Mobile phones
Cellular telephones services are available.

Electricity supply
220V AC, 50 cycles; plugs are of the two-pin round type.

Social customs/useful tips
Handshaking is the customary form of greeting. Business is conducted primarily in English and French.
Care should be taken to respect Islamic and other local religious practices and conventions, and visitors should be aware of restrictions on food and drink in Muslim areas, particularly during the Islamic fasting period of Ramadan.
Visitors should take care when photographing. It is considered polite to ask permission to photograph traditional dances, and it is advisable not to take pictures of official buildings or military installations.
If there is no service charge included in a bill, gratuities in hotels and restaurants are up to 10 per cent.

Security
Muggings and pickpocketing have increased in recent years, mainly in the large cities, and it is unwise to carry valuables or large amounts of cash in the street. Bandit attacks are known to occur along the N1 highway which runs through

Cameroon's Far North Province between Nigeria and Chad. At the international airports, to avoid luggage being stolen, care should be taken to employ only the official porters.

Getting there
Air
National airline: Cameroon Airlines (Camair)
International airport/s: Douala International (DLA), is 5km from the city and has a duty-free shop, bar, restaurant, buffet, bank, post office and shops.
Other airport/s: Yaoundé (YAO), 4km from the capital city, and Garoua International (GOU), 6km from the city, also accepts international flights.
Airport tax: None.
Surface
Road: Road access is possible from Nigeria, Chad, Gabon, Equatorial Guinea and the Central African Republic. However, these routes are considered rough and may become impassable during rainy seasons. Bush taxis and minibuses are available. There have been many bandit attacks along the N1 highway which runs through Cameroon Far North Province between Nigeria and Chad.
Rail: Rail access is available from N'Gaoundal and Belabo in the Central African Republic.
Water: There are two boats a day from Calabar (Nigeria) across the Cross River to Oron, and from Ikang (Nigeria) there are speedboats to Ekondo Titi.
Douala offers more freights links with Europe than other Central African ports. Cameroon Shipping Lines (Camshiplines) maintains an office in Paris.
Main port/s: Douala. Other ports are at Limbe, Kribi and Garoua (on the River Bénoué), which handle river trade during the dry season.

Getting about
National transport
Air: Cameroon airlines operates domestic services between the main cities, including several daily flights between Yaoundé and Douala. Early arrival at the airport terminal is advisable, as overbookings are common. However, air services are generally efficient and certainly the fastest means of travelling within Cameroon.
Road: Cameroon's road network totals 31,800km of roads. Surfaced roads run between main centres although there are no tarmac road links between Yaoundé and Ngaoundéré. Major routes are from Douala to Limbé, Buea, Bafoussam, Sangmelima, Bamenda and Yaoundé (all-weather road). Most other roads are unsurfaced and are often impassable during rainy season.

Buses: There are few fixed schedules and routes outside main centres are subject to suspension in the rainy season.
Rail: The track network extends 1,168km. Cameroon Railways (Camrail) links Kumba, Douala, Yaoundé and Ngaoundéré. An overnight service runs from Yaoundé to Ngaoundéré (12 hours). Second-class travel is cheap but uncomfortable. Sleeping facilities are available on some trains. There is an express three-hour service between Yaoundé and Douala with good facilities.
City transport
Taxis: Taxis are not metered but have a minimum fare and fixed prices. Long journeys and daily hire should be negotiated. A 10 per cent tip is optional. There are taxis from the airport to Douala city centre.
Car hire
Chauffeur- or self-driven cars are available in Yaoundé and Douala, but can be expensive. An international driving licence is required.

BUSINESS DIRECTORY
The addresses listed below are a selection only. While World of Information makes every endeavour to check these addresses, we cannot guarantee that changes have not been made, especially to telephone numbers and area codes. We would welcome any corrections.

Telephone area codes
The international direct dialling code (IDD) for Cameroon is +237 followed by the subscriber's number.

Useful telephone numbers
Police: 17
Fire: 18
Ambulance: 23-40-20

Chambers of Commerce
Cameroon Chamber of Commerce, Industry and Mines, Rue de Chambre de Commerce, PO Box 4011, Douala (tel: 342-6855; fax: 342-5596; e-mail: cride-g77@camnet.cm).

Banking
Amity Bank Cameroon, PO Box 2705, Douala (tel: 432-055; fax: 432-046).

Banque Internationale pour le Commerce et l'Industrie du Cameroun (BICIC), PO Box 1925, Avenue du Général-de-Gaulle, Douala (tel: 428-431, 420-001; fax: 424-184, 424-116).

Commercial Bank of Cameroon, PO Box 4004, Douala (tel: 420-202; fax: 433-802).

First Investment Bank; PO Box 13276, Douala (tel: 431-304; fax: 428-423).

International Bank of Africa-Cameroon, PO Box 3300, Douala (tel: 428-422; fax: 428-423).

Société Générale de Banques au Cameroun, PO Box 4042, 78 Rue Joss, Douala (tel: 427-010, 427-004; fax: 430-353).

Standard Chartered Bank Cameroon, PO Box 1784, Boulevard de la Liberté, Douala (tel: 424-191; fax: 422-789).

Central bank
Banque des États de l'Afrique Centrale, Direction Nationale, PO Box 83, Yaoundé (tel: 223-0511; fax: 223-3380; e-mail: beacyde@beac.int).

Travel information
Cameroon Airlines, Littoral BP 4092, 3 Avenue General de Gaulle, Douala (tel: 422-525, 424-949; fax: 422-487, 423-459).

Douala International Airport, BP 3131, Douala (tel: 423-630, 423-577; fax: 423-758).

Ministry of tourism
Ministry of Tourism, Yaoundé (tel: 223-353, 235-258; fax: 221-295).

National tourist organisation offices
Société Camerounaise de Tourisme (Socatour), BP 7138, Yaoundé (tel: 233-219).

Ministries
Ministry of Agriculture, Yaoundé (tel: 234-085, 225-166, 231-190).

Ministry of Communications, Yaoundé (tel: 234-075; 223-155, 233-974).

Ministry of External relations, Yaoundé (tel: 220-133).

Ministry of Economy and Finance, BP 18, Yaoundé (tel: 234-000, 232-299).

Ministry of Environment and Forestry, BP 14276, Yaoundé (tel: 229-483, 221-225).

Ministry of Industrial and Commercial Development, Yaoundé (tel: 234-040, 225-085).

Ministry of Culture, Yaoundé (tel: 223-155, 233-974).

Ministry of Livestock, Fisheries and Animal Industries, Yaoundé (tel: 223-311, 220-443).

Ministry of Mines, Water and Energy, Yaoundé (tel: 233-404).

Ministry of Post and Telecommunications, Yaoundé (tel: 234-016; fax: 223-497).

Ministry of Public Works and Transport, Yaoundé (tel: 232-236).

Other useful addresses
British Embassy, Avenue Winston Churchill, BP 547, Yaoundé (tel: 220-545, 220-796; fax: 220-148).

Cameroon Development Corporation (CDC), BP 28, Bota, Limbe (tel: 332-251).

Cameroon Embassy (USA), 2349 Massachusetts Avenue, NW, Washington DC 20008 (tel: 202-265-8790; fax: 202-387-3826; e-mail: info@ambacam-usa.org).

Cameroon Press and Publishing Co, BP 1218, Yaoundé (tel: 234-012).

Cameroon Telecommunications, BP 1571, Yaoundé (tel: 234-065; fax: 230-303).

Commission Technique de la Mission de Réhabilitation des Entreprises due Secteur Public et Parapublic, SNI Building, 9th Floor, Yaoundé (tel: 239-750; fax: 235-108).

Centre National d'Assistance aux Petites et Moyennes Entreprises, BP 1377, Douala (tel: 425-858).

Centre National du Commerce Exterieur (CNCE), BP 2461, Douala (tel: 421-685).

Department of Statistics, BP 25, Yaoundé (tel: 220-788).

EU Delegate, BP 847, Yaoundé (tel: 221-387, 222-149).

FEICOM (Special Equipment and Intercommunity Intervention Fund), BP 718 Yaoundé (tel/fax: 231-759).

National Tenders Board, Mballa II, 4th Floor, PO Box 6604, Yaoundé (tel: 201-803; fax: 206-042; e-mail: DGTC@GCNET.CM).

Office National du Café et du Cacao (ONCC), BP 378, Douala (tel: 426-776, 425-088) – sole marketing agency for cocoa, coffee, cotton, groundnuts, palm kernels.

Office de Radiodiffusion-Télévision Camerounaise (CRTV), BP 1634, Yaoundé (tel: 234-088).

Regifercam, BP 304, Douala (tel: 407-159; fax: 423-205).

Société Camerounaise des Depots Petroliers, Siège Social BP 2271, Douala (tel: 405-445; fax: 404-796).

Société de Développement du Cacao SODECAO), BP 1651, Yaoundé (tel: 220-991).

Société de Développement du Coton, Headquarters, BP 302, Garoua (tel: 271-556; fax: 272-068).

Société Nationale des Eaux du Cameroun, BP 157 Douala (tel: 433-066, 430-067; fax: 422-945).

Société Nationale de Raffinage, Cape Limboh, PO Box 365, Limbe (tel: 423-815, 423-817; fax: 423-444, 424-199).

Société Nationale d'Investissement, BP 423, Place de la Poste, Yaoundé (tel: 224-499, 224-422).

Société de Recouvrement des Créances du Cameroun, BP 11991, Yaoundé (tel: 223-739, 220-911, 230-067; fax: 233-833).

Sydicate of Wood Producers and Exporters (SPEBC), BP 2064, Douala (tel/fax: 428-617).

Syndicat des Commerçants, Importateurs et Exportateurs du Cameroun (SCIEC), BP 562, Douala (tel: 420-304).

Syndicat des Industriels du Cameroun, BP 1516, Yaoundé (tel: 222-468; BP 673, Douala (tel: 423-058).

Technical Committee for Privatisation and Liquidations, SNI Building, 9th Floro, Yaoundé (tel: 239-750; fax: 235-108).

US Embassy, rue Nachtigal, BP 817, Yaoundé (tel: 234-014).

Internet sites

Africa Business Network: http://www.ifc.org/abn

AllAfrica.com: http://allafrica.com

African Development Bank: http://www.afdb.org

Africa Online: http://www.africaonline.com

Harambee Afrika (UK business club for traders with east, central and southern Africa; includes annotated web resource list): http://www.harambee.co.uk

Mbendi AfroPaedia (information on companies, countries, industries and stock exchanges in Africa): http://mbendi.co.za

Federal Republic of Southern Cameroons: http://www.southerncameroons.org/

Canada

KEY FACTS

Official name: Canada

Head of State: Queen Elizabeth II (since 1952), represented by Governor General Michaëlle Jean (since 2005)

Head of government: Prime Minister Stephen Harper (from 6 Feb 2006)

Ruling party: Conservative Party of Canada (CPC) (elected 23 January 2006)

Area: 9,976,139 square km

Population: 31.75 million (2004); 31.63 million (OECD, 2003)

Capital: Ottawa

Official language: English, French

Currency: Canadian dollar (C$) = 100 cents

Exchange rate: C$1.16 per US$ (Oct 2005)

GDP per capita: US$31,209 (2004)

GDP real growth: 2.80% (2004); 2.8% (2005)*

Labour force: 17.18 million (2004)

Unemployment: 7.20% (OECD, 2004)

Inflation: 1.80% (2004); 2.1% (2005)*

Oil production: 3.09 million bpd (2004)

Balance of trade: US$51.73 billion (2004)

Foreign debt: US$608.11 billion (2004)

Annual FDI: US$206.60 billion (cumulative, 1995–2004, OECD); US$6.30 billion (OECD, 2004)*

* estimated figure

Two thousand and five was an important year for Canada. The country celebrated the confirmation of a new Governor General and discovered a huge amount of oil. The economy also continued to grow steadily. On the political front, the government became mired in scandal before gearing up for an electoral showdown in early 2006.

The investiture of Michaëlle Jean, a glamorous one-time television presenter and former Haitian refugee, as Governor General in September 2005 personified a country of ambition, social mobility and diversity that Canada is today. Ms Jean's acceptance speech pronouncement that Canada was no longer a divided land of Anglo- and Francophones received wide acclaim. The respected *Globe and Mail* newspaper of Toronto applauded the 'remarkable new governor general who personifies the free and open country Canada wants to be'.

A question of sovereignty

Despite the new *de facto* head of state's claim to harmony among English-speaking Canadians and their Quebecan kin, this is not nearly the full story. Quebecers voted 'no' to independence in 1980 and rejected the notion again in 1995, albeit by a most paper-thin of margins (50.6 to 49.4 per cent). But the prospect of eventual succession remains strong. Though the separatist Parti Québécois (PQ) is in opposition, a large portion of the local population remains committed to their independent ideals. PQ's cause was further enhanced by the province's intense anger at the then governing Liberal Party's 'sponsorship scandal', which exposed wide-scale sleaze in the federal programme to promote Canada in Quebec following the 1995 referendum.

Quebec is 'a lion in a cage' according to PQ leader Alain Boisclair and at some point, the earliest possible date being 2007/08, his party will return to power. Soon after this eventuality Quebeckers will be asked the sovereignty question again. At the end of 2005, everything remained to be played for however. A poll published in *Globe and Mail* revealed evidence from which both camps can take heart. When surveyed, 58 per cent of Quebeckers said that they considered themselves as either Quebeckers and Canadians in equal measure or as Canadians first and foremost, while 40 per cent thought of themselves as Quebeckers primarily.

Alberta's black gold

The to and fro knock about of Quebec's ongoing separatist debate usually ensures the territory a monopoly of international news coverage among Canada's ten provinces. But in 2005 Alberta stole at least some of the limelight. The province's economy is booming owing to a discovery of new bitumen-like oil sands and high oil prices induced by geopolitical uncertainty in many of the globe's oil producing regions and related concerns over US energy security. Alberta's economy grew by 4.5 per cent in 2004, by far the largest expansion of any of the country's provinces.

There are about a dozen planned oil sand projects and Chinese firms, among other nations, are keen to grab a slice of the action. The process of extraction is difficult however, and only the very best technology will succeed in mining the surface by injecting steam into wells before finally refining the substance into crude. Luckily for Alberta's three million or so residents, the big oil firms have just what is required to churn out the lucrative black gold. Recent estimates suggest that Alberta's oil sands output may treble to three million barrels per day (bpd) by 2012. This would ensure Canada a seat at the high table of oil producing states, making it the world's fourth largest oil producer after Saudi Arabia, Russia and the US.

Alberta's economy is truly burgeoning on the back of its new found energy sector royalties, which now constitute about a third of budget revenues. Total budget revenues for the province were expected to rise to the equivalent of US$7.7 billion by the end of fiscal year 2005/06, a one hundred per cent increase on the previous year's total. Debt repayment was a priority of Alberta's government in 2005. The governing Progressive Conservative Party is reported to have paid off approximately 90 per cent of the territory's total debt. Business and consumer confidence soared in Alberta in 2005 as the province's residents spent their new disposable income with abandon. In a market that is generally feeling the pinch in North America, BMW motorcar sales in Alberta rocketed, leading the company to open an extra sales outlet in order to match demand.

Economic performance in 2005

One of the richest nations in the world, Canada's economy has been historically well managed and its natural resources sensibly exploited. Macroeconomic indicators in Canada remained positive in 2005. The growth rate was maintained at around its 2004 level, with the IMF's latest forecast indicating steady growth of 2.8 per cent for 2005. Inflation has been low throughout the 2000s; the annual rate dropped in 2004 and the IMF has predicted a low rate of 2.1 per cent for 2005.

Canada's trade surplus rose by a slender margin in data recorded in October 2005, to US$6 billion equivalent. The figure was slightly higher than analysts' predictions and the unexpected swell is mainly attributable to export revenues derived from sales of natural gas abroad. The neighbouring US, which has experienced a particularly harsh winter and is beset by energy security worries, was a particularly keen purchaser of Canadian natural gas over the year.

Unemployment, which has hovered around the 7 per cent mark throughout most of the 2000s, fell to a three decade low in October 2005. Approximately 69,000 new jobs were created in the month of October, bringing the total for the 11 months to November to 204,000 new positions. Analysts cited Alberta's oil and gas bonanza as a partial explanation for the reduction in unemployment levels.

Gangs and guns

The related vices of gang warfare and gun crime are on the increase in Canada. For the very first time in December 2005, transport police in Vancouver were issued with individual hand guns. Shootings outside nightclubs are particularly rife and nightclub owners throughout the city have taken to introducing metal detectors at the entrance to their premises. Other cities suffer from the same problem, such as Toronto, where over 50 murders involving firearms were recorded in 2005. The Royal Canadian Mounted Police commissioned a study into gun crime in British Columbia (BC) in the latter part of the year; its findings made for alarming reading. According to the report the number of criminal gangs operating in BC had doubled over the past two years from 52 to 108. Police seizures of firearms jumped by over 50 per cent in the province over the last three years.

The alarming rise in gun-related crime left many Canadians aghast, not least of them the Mayor of Toronto. Mayor David Miller, a colourful character at the best of times, accused the United States during the autumn of 'exporting gun crime' north of the border. This created general uproar among the governing US Republican Party, who told the Canadians to concentrate on keeping their own house in order. And well they might. Canada's burgeoning cannabis trade has a lot to do with the problem, as arguably had the Liberal

KEY INDICATORS — Canada

	Unit	2000	2001	2002	2003	2004
Population	m	30.75	31.10	31.40	31.58	31.75
Gross domestic product (GDP)	US$bn	711.10	700.10	733.60	834.40	*979.76
GDP per capita	US$	23,100	22,500	23,440	27,199	31,209
GDP real growth	%	5.2	1.8	3.4	2.0	2.8
Inflation	%	2.7	2.5	2.0	2.8	1.8
Unemployment	%	6.8	7.2	7.6	7.8	7.2
Oil output	'000 bpd	2,721.0	2,763.0	2,880.0	2,800.0	3,085.0
Natural gas output	bn cum	167.8	172.0	183.5	180.5	182.8
Coal output	mtoe	37.2	37.6	35.5	33.3	34.9
Exports (fob) (goods)	US$m	284,445.0	267,915.0	287,170.0	272,054.0	*331,070.0
Imports (fob) (goods)	US$m	244,613.0	226,490.0	252,000.0	245,618.0	*279,337.0
Balance of trade	US$m	39,833.0	41,425.0	34,700.0	26,436.0	*51,734.0
Current account	US$m	18,014.0	19,479.0	11,030.0	18,630.0	26,040.0
Total reserves minus gold	US$m	31,924.0	33,962.0	36,984.0	36,222.0	34,430.0
Foreign exchange	US$m	28,841.0	30,484.0	32,685.0	31,537.0	30,167.0
Exchange rate	per US$	1.49	1.55	1.60	1.43	1.30

* estimated figure

government's policy approach to domestic matters. Despite then prime minister Paul Martin's reactionary decision to advocate a total ban on handguns, Conservative Party leader Stephen Harper made great play of issues surrounding gun and gang crime during the 2005–06 election campaign. The Conservative leader called for tougher sentences for dug trafficking, an abandonment of plans to decriminalise marijuana and the abolishment of a neutral injection zone for Vancouver heroin users.

Election 2006

Canada's Conservative Party returned to power for the first time in 11 years on 23 January 2006. They failed to win an outright majority in the House of Commons however and have already been forced to participate in political horse trading in order to govern effectively. The Conservatives won 124 out of a possible 308 seats while the Liberal Party, courtesy of some effective campaigning, polled a respectable 103, a reduction of 30 from their previous total. The limited mandate for Harper's tories reflected a tiredness of the incumbent scandal-stained Liberals among Canada's 32 million strong population, but a resistance to fundamental change. After thirteen years in power and tainted by allegations of corruption the incumbent Liberals were fighting an uphill battle and looked unlikely to stretch the democratic elastic for a fifth successive term in office. Moderate candidates of all political colours faired well, while the Quebec nationalists polled poorly, to the delight of the Ottawa political elite. The defeat of three fundamentalist Christian Conservatives in British Columbia also brought broad smiles to many faces.

For Harper however, any kind of victory was a success, having lost to Paul Martin of the Liberal Party in 2004. The election was fought in the mammoth shadow of corruption allegations and investigations into government practice. Martin's minority government lost a vote of confidence in November following evidence of government member's having profited from illegal kickbacks derived from public funds. As well as taking the fight to the government over the issue of cleaner government, Harper promoted policies of sales tax reduction, combating crime and improving the publicly funded health system. By contrast, Martin at first ran a campaign premised on a buoyant economy with eight years of budget and trade surpluses.

When he realised that a positive campaign based on the merits of his admirable economic record would not be sufficient to overcome dissatisfaction with alleged malpractice, Martin reverted to an increasingly negative approach. He portrayed Harper as 'extreme' and communicated his message to the Canadian voters that the Conservative leader would sell out the country's proud foreign policy to Washington if he ever became prime minister. The campaign, which was tetchy from the moment it began, turned particularly fierce in the lead up to polling day. In the second of three live televised debates Harper asked his opponent 'how many criminal investigations are going on in this government?' before accusing the government of 'stealing money from the taxpayer'. In reply, apparently dismissing widespread dissatisfaction and distrust of his government among the electorate at large, Martin accused the Conservative leader of promoting nothing but 'drive-by-smears'.

Following his defeat at the polls Martin announced his intention to stand down as Liberal Party leader. Martin's legacy will read better in the history books than it did on 11 January's newspaper front pages. After taking office as prime minister in December 2003, his government had pursued a successful economic policy and Martin made several principled foreign policy stands independent of Washington. One man that stands to benefit from Martin's departure as party leader is former Harvard University professor Michael Ignatieff.

The former Oxbridge academic won the seat of Etobicoke-Lakeshore and is tipped for great things, perhaps even the party leadership one day. A measure of the influence wielded by Ignatieff so early on in his political career was evident during the campaign when Harper urged voters to 'send that Ignatieff fellow back to Harvard'. Ignatieff has shown unique promise and an acute political brain so far in his nascent career but the Liberal Party leadership contest, expected toward the end of 2006, may come a little too soon. Ignatieff needs time to overcome elements of hostility toward him within his own party for supporting the US-led invasion of Iraq, and a reputation as a 'carpetbagger', having returned to Canada to fight the election after more three decades spent living abroad.

Missiles and Arctic islands

Following the decision by the government of the day not to support the US-led invasion of Iraq without a fresh UN mandate, relations between Canada and its southern neighbour have been increasingly strained. Though Canadian troops continued to serve alongside their American counterparts in Afghanistan during 2005, diplomatic procedure between the two countries has been far from straightforward. In February the Canadian government announced that it would pull out of the US's proposed ballistic missile defence system. Ottawa claimed that it would commit no further than the existing arrangements specified under the North American Aerospace Command (Norad).

Anti-American sentiment runs high in Canada owing to a general dislike of George W Bush's policies and Martin's decision was taken to be a direct snub of the US President. Future prospects for closer relations have been enhanced by two factors however. The first of these is an American willingness to gain a share of Canada's growing energy market. US treasury secretary John Snow recently pronounced his government's northern neighbour as 'our closet ally' and enthused that 'Canada, with these resources available… is a huge contributor to energy security for North America'. Until the devastation of Hurricane Katrina focussed his attention elsewhere US vice president Dick Cheney was expected to visit the oil-laden lands of Alberta. Second, and just as important, is the election of Harper's Conservatives, who are ideologically much closer to the governing US Republicans. A slender electoral mandate and adverse public opinion may hinder any ploy to snuggle up to Washington any time soon though.

No snuggling of any sort was done with the Danish government in 2005. Ottawa and Copenhagen fell out during a war of words centring on a section of Artic rock called Hans Island. Both countries traded diplomatic insults with one another at various junctures during the dispute over the ownership of the rock. A rapprochement was achieved in September, when the foreign ministers met in New York City. A protocol for managing future dealings was drafted and signed, but neither country chose to officially renounce its claim to sovereignty over the island.

Outlook

Politically, Canadians opted for a change in the 2006 election, but not much of one. Having grown tired of scandal and 13 years of Liberal government the electorate endorsed Harper's Conservatives. The margin of electoral victory for Harper however, revealed contentment within the Canadian psyche with the economic status

Canada

quo, which has been carefully managed by the Liberals over the years. The size of Harper's victory means that he will not veer off to the right any time soon, choosing to stay on the centre-right of the political spectrum while he and his party finds its feet. With increased energy exports owing to significant new oil finds in Alberta and an unquenched thirst for gas and oil south of the border, Canada's continued economic stability looks assured, for the time being at least.

Risk assessment

Politics	Stable
Economics	Good
Regional stability	Excellent
Stock market	Good

COUNTRY PROFILE

Historical profile

1497 John Cabot claimed Newfoundland for Henry VII of England.
1534 Jacques Cartier explored Newfoundland and charted the Gulf of St Lawrence as far as what is now Québec city and Montréal. He claimed this land for France.
1600 King Henry IV of France granted fur trading rights in the Gulf of St Lawrence to a group of French merchants.
1608 Founding of Québec as France's first colony by Samuel Champlain.
1629 Québec city was captured by the English fleet.
1632 Québec was returned to France by the treaty of St Germain-en-Laye.
1642 Founding of Ville Marie, which later became Montréal.
1660 The English Navigation Act prohibited foreigners from trading with English colonies.
1663 Louis XIV assumed personal control of the French settlements that included Québec, Montréal, Nova Scotia, New Brunswick and the area around the Gulf of St Lawrence and called this *Nouvelle France* (New France). Québec became a royal province.
1665 Jean Talon came from France to administer colonial affairs and brought about a significant expansion of the colony, encouraging agriculture, arts and business that stimulated immigration. By this time, the English, fighting for territorial dominance, controlled 10 colonies on the Atlantic coast and exceeded New France in terms of population and self-sufficiency.
1670 In competition with the French, the English established the Hudson Bay Company, giving themselves a monopoly on the fur trade in the Hudson Bay area.
1702 Queen Anne's War broke out between the English and the French. This led to the capture of Port Royal by the English.
1713 Peace was established under the Treaty of Utrecht. This required France to surrender the Hudson Bay Area, Newfoundland and Acadia to Britain. France was permitted to keep Cape Breton island and her inland colonies.
1754 The French and Indian War began in North America; it became the Seven Years War when fighting spread to Europe.
1755–56 The British attacked Québec, the nerve-centre of the French empire. Québec came under British rule.
1759 Montréal, cut off from reinforcements and supplies from France, fell to the British.
1774 Britain passed the Québec Act, that officially recognised French civil law and granted religious freedom to Roman Catholics. Britain assumed full control of the North Atlantic provinces: Canada, Nova Scotia, New Brunswick, Prince Edward Island and Newfoundland.
1858 British Columbia became a Crown Colony.
1862 The British withdrew troops from Canada.
1867 Ontario, Québec, Nova Scotia and New Brunswick joined together under the terms of the British North America Act to become the Dominion of Canada. These four territories became provinces with their own governments, law making bodies and lieutenant governors.
1870 Manitoba joined the Dominion, followed by British Columbia and Prince Edward Island. Hudson Bay became part of Canada and was renamed the Northwest Territories.
1898 The territory of Yukon was carved out of the Northwest Territories and entered the Dominion. The Territories, unlike the provinces that existed within their own right, were subject to federal legislative power. The federal government had the right to intrude in administrative and social affairs.
1905 Alberta and Saskatchewan became provinces of Canada.
1914–18 Canada joined the allies in the First World War.
1931 The Statute of Westminster was passed by the British parliament, granting dominion parliaments the right to reject the laws of British parliament and allowing British dominions, including Canada, complete autonomy. Canada became a free associate of the British Commonwealth of Nations, but had to swear allegiance to the British Crown.
1939–45 Canada joined the allies against Nazi Germany, Italy and Japan in the Second World War.
1949 Newfoundland became Canada's tenth province.
1969 Canada recognised English and French as its two official languages.
1977 Following an amendment to the Citizenship Act, Canadians ceased to be British subjects.
1980 A referendum to make Québec a separate country was rejected by the people of Québec.
1982 The Constitution Act stated that Canada no longer required British approval for new laws.
1995 The Canadian parliament passed a resolution recognising Québec as a distinct society within Canada. A referendum in Québec produced another 'no' vote for independence.
1999 Nunavut, created out of part of the Northwest Territories, became Canada's third territory.
2000 Jean Chrétien called snap elections, in which the Liberal Party of Canada (LPC) took 40.8 per cent of the vote, winning 172 seats.
2001 Québec's premier, Lucien Bouchard, resigned. Bernard Landry took over the post. Canada became the first country to legalise cannabis for people suffering from chronic medical conditions and terminal illnesses.
2002 Jean Chrétien announced that he would not seek a fourth term but would remain in office until 2004.
2003 Toronto was seriously hit by an outbreak of the flu-like Sars virus. A power blackout – the biggest in North American history – hit Toronto, Ottawa and other parts of Ontario, as well as cities in the north-eastern US. Paul Martin took over as prime minister after Jean Chrétien's retirement.
2004 The ruling LPC won the 28 June parliamentary elections, but lost its majority.
2005 On 19 May, Paul Martin's minority LPC won a vote-of-confidence in the House of Commons. Haitian-born Michaëlle Jean was appointed as Governor General in August. On 28 November the government lost a no-confidence vote.
2006 The 23 January elections were won by the Conservatives, but without an overall majority.

Political structure
Constitution
Although Canada is formally a constitutional monarchy with the British monarch as the nominal head of state, for all practical purposes the country is a sovereign state. The governor general is the Queen's representative in Canada.
The Canadian government has a federal structure, with 10 provincial governments plus the three northern territories of the Northwest Territories, Yukon and Nunavut on the lower tier and a national government on the upper tier.
The constitution is contained in the Constitution Act of 1982, although the

province of Québec did not agree to this legislation. The division of power between the national and provincial governments is set out in the constitution which also contains a Charter of Rights and Freedoms. The federal government has authority over areas of national interest, while provincial governments have specific authority over local matters, including education, hospitals and public lands (including natural resources). The provinces exercise considerable autonomy over their affairs. Each province has an elected legislature together with an executive led by a provincial premier.

All Canadian citizens aged 18 years and over have the right to vote.

Form of state
Constitutional monarchy

The executive
The executive comprises the prime minister, appointed by the governor general, and his cabinet. The prime minister is the leader of the majority party in the House of Commons; the cabinet is also drawn from the ruling party's ranks.

National legislature
The bicameral federal parliament, based in Ottawa, is styled on the British model. The House of Commons (lower house) has 301 seats, for which constituency elections must be held at least once every five years. The upper house, the Senate, has very little influence, although it may delay legislation. It has a total membership of 105 senators who are appointed on a regional basis, by the prime minister, and who may serve until their 75th birthday.

Legal system
Based on English common law, except in Québec, where a French civil law system prevails.

The prime minister, through the governor general, appoints all judges to the federal courts, but not those to the provincial courts. Apart from this, the judiciary is independent of the executive. The Supreme Court of Canada is the highest court of appeal in both civil and criminal cases. Each province has its own court structure, headed by a provincial Supreme Court.

Last elections
23 January 2006 (parliamentary)
Results: Parliamentary: the Conservative Party of Canada (CPC) won 36.25 per cent of the vote (124 seats out of 308), the Liberal Party of Canada (LPC) 30.2 per cent (1039), the New Democratic Party/Nouveau Parti Démocratique (NDP) 17.5 per cent (29), the Bloc Québécois (BQ) 10.5 per cent (51), and independents 0.1 per cent (1).

Next elections
2011 (parliamentary)

Political parties
Ruling party
Conservative Party of Canada (CPC) (elected 23 January 2006)
Main opposition party
The Liberal Party of Canada (LPC).

Population
31.75 million (2004); 31.63 million (OECD, 2003)
Ethnic make-up
British and Irish origin (28 per cent), French origin (23 per cent), other European origin (15 per cent), indigenous (2 per cent), other (including Asian, African, Arab) (6 per cent), mixed background (26 per cent).

In 2002, about 52 per cent of immigrants settled in Toronto, 15 per cent in Vancouver and 11 per cent in Montréal; the populations of many rural areas are declining.

Religions
Christianity is the prevailing religion in Canada. Approximately 45 per cent of the population belong to the Roman Catholic Church. The leading Protestant churches are the Anglican Church of Canada and the United Church of Canada. Orthodox Churches are also represented. Jews make up 1.2 per cent of the population and Muslims just under 1 per cent.

Education
Public investment in education amounts to 5.5 per cent of GDP. Universal primary education and gender parity, at this level and in secondary schools, have been achieved. Although methods of funding higher education vary from province to province, the federal and provincial governments fund approximately 85 per cent of the expenditure. Total government spending on education in 2002/03 amounted to C$25 billion (US$39 billion). Canada has strong initiatives to monitor and detect inequities in schooling across the provinces. There is stiff entrance exams for teaching courses and extensive in-service training for qualified teachers, which affords them high status in the community.

Each province is responsible for its own education system. In general, education is provided free of charge to the end of the secondary level. The number of private schools is small, except in the province of Québec. Levels of educational attainment continue to rise, with record numbers attending university. However, enrolments at elementary and secondary schools have steadily declined since the late 1960s, reflecting the decline in both the birth rate and the number of new immigrants.

The proportion of young people attending full-time university and college courses continues to expand, while part-time higher education courses for mature students are becoming increasingly popular.

Canada has over 80 universities and 160 community and technical colleges, as well as 35 colleges of religious study. Education services for indigenous students are an area of responsibility that is not clearly defined between provincial, territorial and federal government, who along with various local authorities have come up with different plans. There has been a rapid development of non-formal educational programmes, provided by non-governmental organisations. Citizenship education is a subject of renewed interest in the education curriculum.

Enrolment rate: 100 per cent total gross primary enrolment; 107 per cent boys, 106 per cent girls, gross secondary enrolment of relevant age groups (including repeaters) (Unesco).
Pupils per teacher: 16 in primary schools.

Health
Total health expenditure is typically 9.5 per cent of GDP, of which government spending is approximately 70 per cent. Private expenditure averages 29 per cent of GDP, 39 per cent of which is funded by prepaid health plans and 52 per cent in out-of-pockets expenses.

Nationwide state-sponsored health insurance is achieved through a series of interlocking provincial plans, with the federal government providing substantial financial support through national Hospital Insurance and Medical Care Programmes. The insurance programmes are designed to ensure that all residents have access to medical services as needed. Most hospitals are run by non-profit, non-governmental, corporations.

In the 2004 Budget it was announced that health spending in 2004 was to be C$36.8 billion (US$25.73 billion). A new Canada Public Health Agency – as a focal point for disease control and emergency response – is being set up with an immediate budget of C$665 million (US$465 million), plus added funds of approximately C$400 million (US$280 million) transfered from Health Canada to deal with public health emergencies.

HIV prevalence: 0.3 per cent aged 15–49 in 2003 (World Bank)
Life expectancy: 79.3 years (World Bank)
Fertility rate/Maternal mortality rate: 1.5 births per woman (World Bank)
Infant mortality rate: 5 per 1,000 live births (World Bank)
Head of population per physician/bed: 2.2 physicians per 1,000 people (WHO)

Welfare
Canada has a comprehensive welfare system, which is administered at both federal and provincial levels of government. The

system provides for social assistance, old age pensions, family allowances and unemployment insurance. Family allowances are credited for dependent children up to the age of 18.
Pensions
Old age pensions become payable at the age of 65 and are indexed to inflation. There are essentially two social security programmes aimed at providing income for the elderly in Canada.
The Old Age Security (OAS) pension is given to people aged 65 and over, who meet residence requirements. Those who have little or no other income are eligible for the Guaranteed Income Supplement (GIS). People who have lived in Canada for less than 40 years receive a reduced pension.

Main cities
Ottawa (capital, estimated population 852,100 in 2004), Toronto (4.6 million), Montréal (3.3 million), Vancouver (1.9 million), Calgary (921,600), Edmonton (810,000), Québec City (670,000), Winnipeg (630,500), Hamilton (636,900).

Languages spoken
English is spoken by 61 per cent of the population, French by 26 per cent and both languages by 13 per cent. French predominates in the province of Québec (Montréal is the second largest French-speaking city in the world). A wide variety of other languages are spoken, reflecting the diverse origins of Canada's population.
Official language/s
English, French

Media
Press
Dailies: Major national dailies include the *National Post* and *Globe & Mail* in major urban centres across Canada. The vastness of the country has prevented the development of a strong national press, so the majority of newspapers are essentially local in character. Most major metropolitan centres have their own daily publications. These include the *Toronto Star*, *The Toronto Sun*, *Le Journal de Montréal*, *The Chronicle Herald*, *The Edmonton Journal*, *The Vancouver Sun*, *Winnipeg Free Press* and *This Week*.
Weeklies: Weeklies including major Sunday papers are *This Week*, *Times Colonist*, *Now*, *Edmonton Sun*, *The Mail Star*, *Maclean's News Magazine*, *National Post*, *La Presse* and *The London Free Press*.
Business: The *Financial Post* (daily, Toronto) is the national business newspaper. Other publications include *All-Canadian Mutual Fund Guide*, *National Post Business* and *Report on Business Magazine*.
Periodicals: Popular Canadian magazines include *L'Actualité*, *Report News Magazine*, *The Wal-Mart Profile on Entertainment*, *The Readers Showcase*, *TV Guide*, *Time Toronto Life* and *Western Living*. *News Canada Chatelaine* and *Saturday Night* are published monthly.
Broadcasting
The Canadian Radio-Television and Telecommunications Commission (CRTC) is responsible for regulating broadcasting. The Canadian Broadcasting Corporation (CBC) operates radio and television networks in both English and French.
By March 2004 there were an annual 4,367 licences granted, issued to provide all broadcasting services, including radio, network television, pay-per-view television and digital broadcasting. In the same period 663 licences were issued to provide cable television.
Radio: There are numerous independent regional AM–FM radio stations. The CBC, which operates on both AM and FM, can be received in most areas of the country; there are also community-owned stations.
Television: Apart from CBC, there are several other major broadcasting companies in Canada. Canadian Television (CTV) broadcasts in both English and French. It is privately owned by the multi-media company, Bell Globemedia. Global TV, privately owned by the CanWest Global Communications Corporation, is a smaller network operating in densely populated areas of southern Ontario, and some parts of western Canada, Atlantic Canada, and Québec. Groupe TVA, an independent French network, consists of 10 stations and operates in Québec and parts of New Brunswick.
In addition to 15 independent stations, there are privately-owned and operated cable vision systems which transmit both US and Canadian transmissions.
Advertising
Advertisers use a variety of media to access the Canadian market. Television accounts for the greatest part of net revenue from advertising. It is followed by magazines and newspapers.
Although most Canadians speak English, the Francophone market (concentrated in Québec) is generally considered a separate market, as Québec is served extensively by its own French-language press, radio and television.

Economy
The Canadian economy has grown gradually since growth of over 5 per cent was recorded in 2000. Since 2003 real GDP growth of between 2 and 3 per cent has been recorded. The IMF has forecast growth for 2005 to come in at 2.9 per cent with a slight rise to 3.2 per cent in 2006. The rate of inflation remains low and is forecast to fall to around 1 per cent by 2006.

Canada's economy is reliant on that of its main trading partner the US. Approximately 80 per cent of Canada's exports and 70 per cent of imports are with the US. The economy has maintained growth in the face of global currency fluctuations and a strong Canadian dollar that caused increased prices for energy and non-energy commodity exports. This led to reduced exports in a marketplace of growing competition from emerging market economies. Net exports have had a negative impact on the economy, nevertheless the commodity producing sectors have expanded and domestic consumer confidence is high.
Unemployment was 7.2 per cent in 2004, a figure that has crept up slightly since the beginning of the decade.

External trade
Canada's largest trading partner by far is the US and the country is now the leading export market for 35 separate US states. In 1994 the North American Free Trade Agreement (Nafta) was established. Since Nafta's inception, bilateral US-Canada trade increased by approximately 40 per cent. The US is also Canada's primary agricultural market and a sizeable amount of energy trading is done between the two countries.
At the Ottawa summit of March 2004 Canada and the EU agreed a Partnership Agenda, encompassing bilateral trade as well as other issues.
Canada has a growing trading relationship with China. China is now Canada's third largest trading partner after the US and Japan.
The government department with responsibility for international trade and export/import policies is International Trade Canada (ITCan). The new department was created in November 2003, following the divison of the former Department of Foreign Affairs and International Trade into two separate departments.
Imports
Main imports are machinery and equipment, vehicles and parts, industrial materials, crude oil, consumer goods, foodstuffs, durable consumer goods and construction materials.
Main sources: US (58.9 per cent total, 2004), China (6.8 per cent), Mexico (3.8 per cent)
Exports
Canada, as a member of the North American Free Trade Association (Nafta), exports the majority of its goods and services to the US, in particular energy, crude oil and natural gas. Other exports include vehicles and parts, industrial machinery, aircraft, telecommunications equipment; chemicals, plastics, fertilisers;

wood pulp, timber, aluminium other manufactures and agricultural products.
Main destinations: US (85.2 per cent total, 2004), Japan (2.1 per cent), UK (1.6 per cent)

Agriculture
Farming
The agricultural industry is of considerable importance to the country's economy. Canada has somewhere in the region of 280,000 farms and is the world's second-largest wheat exporter, with its high-quality spring wheat commanding a premium price on world markets. The country is also a sizeable producer of other grains, notably barley, rapeseed (canola) and oats. Livestock rearing is as important a source of income as field crops.

Despite the relative importance of agriculture in the Canadian economy compared with other industrialised nations, the federal government tends to argue that it cannot afford to match the plentiful subsidies and other aid offered to farmers in the EU and US. However, delays in co-ordinated elimination of the world's farm subsidies through the WTO are focussing the government's attention on support programmes for Canadian farmers.

Cattle exports to US markets were due to resume in early 2005, following a ban placed on imports in May 2003, after one case of bovine spongiform encephalopathy (BSE) was detected. However another two cases were identified and prompted the US to reinstate its ban in 2005. About two million head of young cattle were due to be exported in 2005. The number of cattle on farms in January 2005 reached a record high of 15.1 million head (22.9 per cent increase on 2004 figure).

During the embargo of live cattle, plans were advanced to expand slaughtering facilities and increase the amount of Canadian processed beef, and open new export markets. The latest ban increased the enthusiasm for the plans, and has had added impetus since a US Senate decision in April 2005 not to designate Canada as an area of 'minimal risk' from BSE, and a US cattle association won a temporary injunction blocking any US government move to reopen the border to live cattle imports.

In March 2005 the government announced a US$820 billion support package for its farmers to offset the drop in sales due to the strong Canadian dollar and low prices for some produce on international markets. Beef producers are eligible for US$24.6 billion from the package with the rest distributed between grain and oilcrop growers.

Crop production in 2004 included: 52,680,400 tonnes (t) cereal in total, 25,860,400t wheat, 8,835,700t maize, 5,170,790t potatoes, 13,186,400t barley, 3,680,000t oats, 3,048,000t soya beans, 4,580,300t pulses, 7,728,100t rapeseed (canola), 3,799,427t oilcrops, 743,900t sugar beets, 3,338,200t dry peas, 370,338t apples, 78,120t grapes, 48,000 tobacco leaves, 689,598t fruit in total, 2,508,055t vegetables in total. Livestock production included: 4,547,920t meat in total, 1,460,000t beef, 1,930,000t pig meat, 16,100t lamb, 1,123,020t poultry, 376,560t eggs, 8,000,000t milk, 32,755t honey, 2,625t sheepskins, 107,500t cattle hides.

Fishing
Canada remains the largest exporter of fish in the world. Approximately half of the country's sizeable annual fish catch is processed for export. Aggressive fishing depleted Canada's stocks causing the closure of Canada's Atlantic fisheries in 1992, which led to a bitter salmon war with the US when wild salmon stocks dipped to perilously low levels. Such were the tensions, annually renewed during the salmon spawning season, that Canada encouraged the capture of fish bound for rivers in Washington and Oregon, in retaliation for rising US catches of Canadian-origin salmon. A deal agreed in 1999 will be effective for 10 years along the coast and for 12 years along the Fraser River run, which should enable flexible reductions in catches through a managed scheme, replacing the more rigid quota system formerly in effect. Despite past tension between the national governments on this issue the US remains the largest market for Canadian fish exports.

Criticism has been raised that Canada has not protected its wild salmon population of fish. Three of the world's largest salmon farming companies operate in British Columbia and overall there are 17 companies managing 105 salmon farms. The fear is that Canada is raising non-native species of salmon and feeding them fish protein that creates risks for other species of wild fish. The resulting intermingling of populations risks the spread of disease, a competition for habitat and the alteration of the wild salmon gene pool. A salmon enhancement programme has been set up to enable the annual catch to reach 150,000 tonnes instead of the current average 70,000 tonnes.

Canada has imposed a moratorium on commercial cod fishing and has a 320km exclusion zone off its eastern coast, patrolled by an increased number of coast guard vessels.

The minister of fisheries and oceans announced in May 2004 that limited cod fishing in the northern and southern Gulf of St Lawrence would be opened in the 2004–05 season, with maximum removals up to 3,500 tonnes in the northern, and 3,000 tonnes in the southern, gulf.

Forestry
Over 70 per cent of Canada's total landmass is covered with forests and woodland. The country accounts for approximately 10 per cent of the world's forests and the forestry industry accounts for more than US$24 billion annually. Canada is the largest exporter of newsprint, softwood timber and wood pulp worldwide. There is enormous variation in forest types across this vast country, including temperate softwood rainforests in coastal British Columbia, mixed boreal shield forests in central Canada, the maritime forests of New Brunswick and Nova Scotia on the Atlantic seaboard, and the sparse and slow-growing forests found at the Arctic tree line.

Québec, Ontario and British Columbia have the largest forest resources. Most forest and other wooded land is publicly owned, with 71 per cent under provincial jurisdiction and a further 23 per cent under the wing of the federal and territorial governments. Just 6 per cent is privately owned, and is generally located in the more productive regions. Large areas of forest land are under legislative protection, including the almost 8 per cent protected from harvesting.

A three-way agreement between environmentalists, indigenous tribes and logging company MacMillan Bloedel was concluded in 1999, regulating logging in Clayoquot Sound. The agreement binds Iisaak Forest Resources, which is 49 per cent-owned by Macmillan Bloedel, and 51 per cent owned by the Nuu-Chah-Nuluth Indians, not to log trees in Clayoquot Sound's remaining old-growth watersheds, part of the lush coastal rainforest of Vancouver Island. US forestry giant Weyerhauser took over MacMillan Bloedel in the same year. Canada is the world's largest exporter of market pulp (almost 30 per cent of world total) and newsprint (near 40 per cent), with most production located in British Columbia, Ontario and Québec. Exports of standard forestry products total some US$27 billion while imports amount to around US$4 billion.

Non-wood forest products in Canada include maple syrup, berries, mushrooms, medicinal plants and game.

In 2003 state authorities in British Columbia announced a radical overhaul of its forest industry. Unhappy with the loss of revenue from the lack of softwood sales, the authority decided to withdraw some timber rights from the biggest companies and transfer them to First Nation organisations.

In a typical year for the Canadian forestry industry, exports of forest materials amount to approximately US$24 billion while imports constitute US$4.2 billion.

Industry and manufacturing

In a typical year for the Canadian economy the industrial sector contributes approximately 27 per cent to total GDP. The sector also accounts for around 18 per cent of the country's workforce.

Canada's traditional manufacturing sectors include petroleum refining, pulp and paper mills, motor vehicles, steel, sawmills and planing mills, the dairy products industry, motor vehicle spare parts and accessories, metal stamping and pressing, smelting and refining, industrial chemicals, food processing, commercial printing, communications equipment, feed industries, plastics fabricating industries and aircraft and aircraft parts. Notable new sectors are in advanced telecommunications and network technology. Production of primary metals and transport equipment has grown in recent years, reflecting exceptional growth in the automotive industry. The vast majority of automobile production is exported to the US.

Tourism

Canada's travel and tourism industry has expanded in recent years and contributes 11.8 per cent of total GDP. Employment in the sector accounts for 12.8 per cent of the country's total workforce and capital investment in the industry has also increased, representing 8.1 per cent of total capital investment in the Canadian economy.

The majority of visits, usually about three-quarters of the total, are made by US residents. Visitor numbers flattened out in 2001 and 2002, following the 11 September 2001 terrorist attacks in the US. Prospects of recovery in 2003, which started well, were impeded by the Iraq war and the Sars outbreak in Toronto, and compounded by the weakening of the US dollar against the Canadian dollar so that 2003 was deemed to be the sector's worst year. The Sars outbreak, which was the subject of a World Health Organisation advisory, was particularly damaging to the Toronto area and 2004 started badly, but by April numbers had picked up. The country received 20,585,600 visitors in 2004, an increase of over 900,000 on the figure for 2000.

Mining

Canada remains a significant producer of gold and the country's reserves of the yellow metal more than trebled over the 1983–2003 period, to an estimated 1,500 tonnes. Other base metal and metal stocks have declined, but Canada remains a major producer of nickel, copper, zinc, lead, iron ore and diamonds. Most of Canada's exploration is focussed on diamonds, mainly in Northwest Territories, Alberta, Québec and Saskatchewan. The country's first diamond mine opened in 1998.

Hydrocarbons

Canada had proven reserves of 178.9 billion barrels of oil (including 174.4 billion barrels from Alberta's oilsands) in 2004, with oil production averaging 3.1 million barrels per day (bpd) and consumption at 2.2 million bpd. Most oil is extracted from the west of the country, particularly Alberta which typically produces 55 per cent of Canada's total oil production. While oil production is steadily declining in the west, it is rising in the east, where production costs are higher and reserves are smaller. The US is the largest supplier of refined oil products to Canada. Bitumen production from Canada's oilsands is due to expand over the next decade with several large investment projects being developed. Currently this form of production is reliant on natural gas, however due to the high prices of natural gas this industry is seeking alternative methods of production. Until it becomes economically viable the development of this industry could be slow.

There are two major pipeline networks. The Enbridge Pipelines cover 14,000km, delivering oil from Edmonton, Alberta, to Montréal, Québec, eastern Canada and refineries in the US Great Lakes region. The Trans-Mountain Pipeline (TMPL) delivers oil from Alberta to Vancouver and British Columbia as well as the US state of Washington.

Canada had 1.6 trillion cubic metres (cum) of natural gas reserves in 2004 and produced 183 billion cum per year, making it the world's third-largest gas producer after Russia and the US and the second-largest gas exporter after Russia. Canada's gas exports are exclusively destined for the US. Domestic gas consumption is rising due to an increase in demand from the electricity generating sector.

The 3,000km Alliance Pipeline, opened in 2000, carries 36.8 million cum of gas per day from western Canada to the Chicago area in the US. The Millennium Pipeline is planned to connect Canadian gas fields to New York and Pennsylvania in the US. The first phase is expected to be completed by 2006.

Canada's coal reserves amounted to around 6.6 billion tonnes in 2004. The estimated coal production was 34.9 million tonnes oil equivalent (Mtoe). Canadian coal consumption of around 20.5 mtoe is primarily used for electricity generation with the remainder used for steel production.

Energy

Canada currently has one of the world's most diversified electricity generation bases. The country retains hydroelectricity, natural gas, oil, coal and nuclear power sources, which are used to produce electricity.

By the end of the 1990s, Canada's electricity generating capacity was 109.8GW, of which 60 per cent was hydroelectric, 26 per cent was thermal, 12 per cent was nuclear and 1 per cent was produced from geothermal and other sources. The use of gas in electricity generation is on the rise, with a 300 per cent increase in gas-fired electricity capacity by 2010. There are 22 nuclear reactors, of which 5 are inoperative until refurbishments have been completed. Canada exports its reactor technology with projects in Argentina, China, Romania and South Korea with the most being built in India.

Under the Canadian constitution, electricity production is the responsibility of the provincial administrations. Most electricity generation, transmission and distribution facilities are owned by the provinces. Alberta had a fully deregulated market by the beginning of 2001, while Ontario commenced deregulation in mid-2002.

In 2003 a massive power failure left most of Ontario and the US Midwest and Northeast without power. Initial recriminations swung across the border as each authority, under heavy public criticism, sort to shift blame for the outage away from themselves. The final report concluded that the blackout was caused by procedural failures such as inadequate backup facilities; operations not kept within secure limits; ineffective training; poor judgement about the nature of the critical conditions, and poor communications within neighbouring systems; and the lack of a guiding overview. The power was cut when vegetation, that should have been cut-back, short-circuited powerlines and no one was available to stop the cascade of disruption this caused. Regulatory bodies have introduced mandatory systems to provide management and regulatory procedures, and compliance to standards, in both Canada and the US.

Financial markets

Stock exchange

The principal Canadian stock market is the Toronto Stock Exchange (TSE), which is the fourth most active stock exchange in North America after the NYSE, Nasdaq and Chicago.

Banking and insurance

Toronto Dominion Bank is Canada's largest banking and financial services institution, in terms of both its retail network and overall personal deposits and lending, having merged with Canada Trust in 2000.

In 2001, financial legislation, Bill C–8, was passed to ease mergers. This allows foreign and local banks to increase stakes in Canadian banks and to encourage global competitiveness and economic growth. The legislation allows a single shareholder to hold up to 20 per cent of the voting shares of a big Canadian bank, and opened the way to strategic alliances with foreign banks

Central bank
Bank of Canada

Main financial centre
Toronto

Time
Canada has six time zones:
Newfoundland: GMT minus three and a half hours;
Atlantic standard time (maritimes and Labrador): GMT minus four hours;
Eastern zone (Québec and most of Ontario): GMT minus five hours;
Central zone (Manitoba, north-west Ontario and eastern Saskatchewan): GMT minus six hours;
Mountain zone (west Saskatchewan, Alberta and north-east Columbia): GMT minus seven hours;
Pacific zone (Yukon and the bulk of British Columbia): GMT minus eight hours.
Daylight saving time operates from early April to late October.

Geography
Canada is the second-largest country in the world (Russia is the largest) and it stretches from the Atlantic Ocean to the Pacific. Apart from the border with Alaska in the north-west, Canada's frontier with the US follows the upper St Lawrence Seaway and the Great Lakes, extending westwards along latitude 49 degrees N.
There are six principal geographical regions. The south-east corner is the most densely populated part of the country and comprises the Atlantic Provinces and the lowland area to the north of the Great Lakes and the St Lawrence Seaway. To the north and west of this region lies the Canadian Shield, which is covered by forests, bare rock and lakes. Further to the west are the Interior Plains which are largely prairies, while the coastal area along the Pacific is dominated by the Rocky Mountains. The Northwest Territories extend into the Arctic with a barren landscape and sparse population density.

Climate
The climate is extreme, especially inland. Winter temperatures drop well below freezing, but summers are usually warm. There are often heavy snowfalls in winter, making travel difficult.

Dress codes
Canadians are generally casual about dress. It is best to ask about dress codes if you are unsure.

Entry requirements
Passports
Required by all except US citizens permanently resident in US.
Visa
Are required by all except citizens of EU, the Commonwealth and US. For further information on exceptions visit www.cic.gc.ca/english/visit/visas.html. Business visitors from exempted countries do not need to fulfil extra entry criteria, as long as their permanent employment is typically outside Canada, however work may not be undertaken beyond that allowed; to see such permission visit www.cic.gc.ca/english/work/exempt-1.html.

Currency advice/regulations
There are no restrictions on the import and export of currency.
Income tax clearance certificates are not required when leaving the country.

Customs
Personal effects are allowed duty-free. Certain items, such as plants, meat, cereals, dairy products and live animals are subject to import licensing.

Prohibited imports
Goods prohibited for import include firearms, weapons, used motor vehicles, films, reprints of work copyrighted in Canada and some game birds.

Health (for visitors)
Advisable precautions
No vaccinations or certificates are required. Comprehensive travel and medical insurance is essential though, as medical treatment can be very expensive.

Hotels
It is advisable to book rooms in advance. Goods and services tax of 7 per cent applies to all hotel bills, and provincial sales tax is applied to bills in some provinces. For visitors travelling by car, good quality motels are available around all major towns and cities where rates are considerably less than those charged by city-centre hotels. Most large hotels have facilities for small displays or exhibitions, and smaller rooms may be rented as sample rooms. Most hotels impose a substantial surcharge on telephone calls.

Credit cards
Credit cards are widely used.

Public holidays
Fixed dates
1 Jan (New Year's Day), 1 Jul (Canada Day), 11 Nov (Remembrance Day), 25 Dec (Christmas Day), 26 Dec (Boxing Day).
When Canada Day falls on a Sunday, the next day is considered a holiday.
When Christmas Day or Boxing Day fall at a weekend, an extra day is given in lieu.
In addition to statutory federal public holidays observed throughout the country, additional holidays are observed in certain provinces.
Variable dates
Good Friday, Easter Monday, Victoria Day (Mon preceding 25 May), Labour Day (first Mon in Sep), Thanksgiving Day (second Mon in Oct).

Working hours
Working hours vary throughout the country. Some small businesses close completely in July and August and government departments may work variable hours during the summer months.
Banking
Mon–Thu: 1000–1500/1630; Fri: 1000–1800. Some banks in large centres operate much longer hours, including Saturdays.
Business
Mon–Fri: 0830–1700.
Government
Mon–Fri: 0830–1700.
Shops
There is a five-day working week, but most retail stores in cities open on Saturday and a few on Sunday as well. Late shopping (to 2100) on Thursday or Friday is common in large cities; in suburban shopping centres, supermarkets often stay open until 2100 or 2200 Monday–Friday. Some convenience stores and supermarkets remain open 24 hours per day, especially in heavily populated areas.

Electricity supply
120–240V (mostly 120V) 60 cycles AC, with two-pin flat-prong plug fittings (or three-pin with one round and two flat prongs) and screw-type lamp sockets. Adapters and transformers are available for appliances using other voltages.

Weights and measures
Metric system (Imperial and US systems also still in use).

Social customs/useful tips
When making introductions, the hand shake is considered rather formal unless you are meeting someone for the first time. To Canadians, eye contact is very important in conversation as it shows that you are paying attention.
It is best to avoid touching people unless you know someone fairly well. Touching someone of the opposite sex may well be considered harassment but touching the arm of your conversation partner is acceptable.

Tipping is expected and tends to be more generous in Canada than in other countries. 10 or 12 per cent would be considered frugal.

Getting there
Air
National airline: Air Canada
International airport/s: Ottawa (YOW), 13km south of the capital city. All major airports have full banking and catering facilities, duty-free shops and car hire. Airport-to-city bus and taxi services and, in some cases, rail links, are available. Toronto Pearson International (YYZ), 27km north-west of Toronto, is Canada's busiest airport. It has three terminals catering for domestic and international flights and another terminal is under construction.
Other airport/s: Calgary (YYC), 8km north of city. Edmonton (YEG), 28km south of city. Montréal Dorval (YUL), 25km west of Montréal. Vancouver (YVR), 15km south-west of city. Winnipeg (YWG), 10km north-west of city.
Airport tax: There are two taxes that may or may not be included in the price of the ticket.
Both levies vary depending on destination, the Airport Improvement Fee (AIF) is C$5 for intrastate, C$10 interstate and US, and C$15 for all other international flights; the Air Travellers Security Charge is C$12 for intrastate and C$24 for interstate and all international flights. Travel agents and airport information can provided last minute details.
Surface
Road: Numerous border crossings from the US link directly with the Canadian highway system. Avoid crossings during peak times at weekends during the summer months when there are long delays.
Rail: Via Rail Canada Inc. provides links with the US. Routes include: Montréal-New York; Toronto-New York; Toronto-Chicago; Toronto-Cleveland/Detroit.
Water: Ferries connect the east coast of the US with Canada across the great lakes. Hudson Bay ports are subject to closure during winter months.
Main port/s: On the Atlantic Ocean: Halifax (Nova Scotia), St John (New Brunswick) and St John's (Newfoundland). Montréal and Québec have ports on the St Lawrence Seaway (linking the Atlantic with the Great Lakes). Toronto's port is on the north-western shore of Lake Ontario. Montréal is the only port for passenger liners from Europe.
On the Pacific Ocean: Vancouver (British Columbia).

Getting about
National transport
Air: There are frequent and extensive air services connecting all towns and cities of importance with 68 major airports and over 700 smaller ones lacking control tower facilities. Privatised Air Canada serves the main routes, and several regional carriers operate as well. Air travel is the most widely recommended form of travel between major cities, except between Toronto, Montréal and Ottawa, where train service is comfortable, reasonably priced and usually punctual.
Road: There are about 392,000km of roads, about 84 per cent surfaced. Motorways connect some large industrial centres and most large cities have a motorway network.
Buses: Long-distance coach services link all major centres. They are very well air-conditioned, and it is often recommended that travellers keep a sweater handy.
Rail: The rail network comprises around 100,000km of track. The Canadian National Railway (CN) and Canadian Pacific Rail are the two main railway services, but passenger services are operated by Via Rail, a government agency. Air-conditioning, refreshment facilities and sleeping accommodation are available on long-distance passenger services. The Transcontinental, which takes the northern route through Saskatoon, Edmonton and Jasper, runs three times a week; the Canadian, which took the southern route through Regina, Calgary and Banff, has been cut completely due to reduction in government subsidy. It is advisable to book seats/sleepers as early as possible. Canrail passes give unlimited travel for certain areas and routes.
Water: The St Lawrence Seaway provides deep-water passage from the Atlantic to the Great Lakes, and there are 3,017km of canals, mainly used for leisure.
City transport
Taxis: Good taxi services operate in all major cities; rates vary between cities.
Buses, trams & metro: Toronto, Montréal, Vancouver and Edmonton have efficient, safe and clean underground systems. Most cities have reliable and extensive bus services.
Car hire
Car hire is widely available. Overseas driving licences may be used for the first three months of a visitor's stay (six months in British Columbia). Driving is on the right-hand side of the road.

BUSINESS DIRECTORY
The addresses listed below are a selection only. While World of Information makes every endeavour to check these addresses, we cannot guarantee that changes have not been made, especially to telephone numbers and area codes. We would welcome any corrections.

Telephone area codes
The international direct dialling (IDD) code for Canada is +1, followed by area code and subscriber's number:

Calgary	403	Québec	514
Edmonton	780	Saskatoon	306
Fredericton	506	St John	506
Halifax	902	St John's	709
Kingston	613	Toronto	416
London	519	Vancouver	604
Montréal	514	Windsor	519
Niagara Falls	905	Winnipeg	204
Ottawa	613		

Chambers of Commerce
American Chamber of Commerce in Canada, 260 Adelaide Street, PO Box 160, Toronto, Ontario, M5A 1N1 (tel: 777-8512; fax: 738-7714; e-mail: info@amchamcanada.ca).

British Canadian Chamber of Trade and Commerce, PO Box 1358, Station 'K', Toronto, Ontario, M4P 3J4 (tel: 502-0847; fax: 502-9319; e-mail: central@bcctc.ca).

Canadian Chamber of Commerce, Delta Office Towers, 350 Sparks Street, Ottawa, Ontario, K1R 7S8 (tel: 238-4000; fax: 238-7643; e-mail: info@chamber.ca).

British Columbia Chamber of Commerce, 750 West Pender Street, Vancouver, British Columbia, V6C 2T8 (tel: 683-0700; fax: 683-0416; e-mail: bccc@bcchamber.org).

Halifax Chamber of Commerce, 7 Spectacle Lake Drive, Dartmouth, Nova Scotia (tel: 468-7111; fax: 468-7333;e-mail: info@halifaxchamber.com).

Kingston Chamber of Commerce, 67 Brock Street, Kingston, Ontario, K7K 1R7 (tel: 5448-4453; fax: 548-4743; e-mail: info@kingstonchamber.on.ca).

Manitoba Chambers of Commerce, 227 Portage Avenue, Winnipeg, Manitoba, R3B 2A6 (tel: 948-0100; fax: 948-0110; e-mail: mbchamber@mbchamber.mb.ca).

Montréal Board of Trade, 380 St Antoine Street West, Montréal, Québec, H2Y 3X7 (tel: 871-4000; fax: 871-1255; e-mail: info@ccmm.qc.ca).

North Vancouver Chamber of Commerce, 124 West 1st Street, North Vancouver, British Columbia, V7M 3N3 (tel: 987-4488; fax: 987-8272; e-mail: info@nvchamber.bc.ca).

Ontario Chamber of Commerce, 180 Dundas Street West, Toronto, Ontario M5G 1Z8 (tel: 482-5222; fax: 482-5879; e-mail: info@occ.on.ca).

Ottawa Chamber of Commerce, 1701 Woodward Drive, Ottawa, Ontario, K2C 0R4 (tel: 236-3630; fax: 236-7498; info@greaterottawachamber.com).

Québec Federation of Chambers of Commerce, 500 Place d'Armes, Montréal, Québec, H2Y 2W2 (tel: 844-9571; fax: 844-0226; e-mail: info@ccq.ca).

Toronto Board of Trade, 1 First Canadian Place, PO Box 60, Toronto, Ontario, M5X 1C1 (tel: 366-6811; fax: 366-8406; e-mail: info@bot.com).

Vancouver Board of Trade, World Trade Centre, 999 Canada Place, Vancouver, British Columbia, V6C 3E1 (tel: 681-2111; fax: 681-0437; e-mail: contactus@boardoftrade.com).

Winnipeg Chamber of Commerce, 259 Portage Avenue, Winnipeg, Manitoba, R3B 2A9 (tel: 944-8484; fax: 944-8492; e-mail: info@winnipeg-chamber.com).

Banking
Bank of Montréal, First Canadian Place, Concourse Level, PO Box 3, Toronto, Ontario M5X 1A1 (tel: 867-7662).

Bank of Nova Scotia, 44 King Street West, Toronto, Ontario M5H 1H1 (tel: 866-6161).

Business Development Bank of Canada, 3rd Floor, 5 Place Ville Marie, Montréal, Québec H4Z 1L4 (tel: 283-5904; fax: 496-8036).

Canadian Imperial Bank of Commerce (CIBC), Commerce Court, Toronto, Ontario M5L 1G9 (tel: 980-2211).

National Bank of Canada, 50 O'Connor Street, Suite 1224, Ottawa, Ontario K1P 6C2 (tel: 238-8383).

Royal Bank of Canada, 200 Bay Street, Royal Bank Plaza, Toronto, Ontario M5J 2J5 (tel: 974-5151; internet site: http://www.royalbank.com).

Toronto Dominion Bank, PO Box 1, Toronto Dominion Centre, 55 King Street, Toronto, Ontario M5K 1A2 (tel: 982-7730).

Central bank
Bank of Canada, 234 Wellington Street, Ottawa, Ontario, K1A 0G9 (tel: 782-8111; fax: 782-7713; e-mail: paffairs@bankofcanada.ca).

Travel information
Tourism Industry Association of Canada, 130 Albert Street, Suite 1016, Ottawa K1P 5G4 (tel: 238-3883).

Air Transport Association of Canada, 99 Bank St, Suite 747, Ottawa, ON, K1P 6B9 (tel: 233-7727; fax: 230-8648).

Ministry of tourism
Tourism Canada, Federal Department of Industry, Science and Technology, 235 Queen Street, 4th Floor East, Ottawa K1A 0H6 (tel: 954-3851).

Ministries
Ministry of Agriculture and Agri-Food, Sir John Carling Building, 930 Carling Avenue, Ottawa, Ontario, K1A 0C5 (tel: 995-8963).

Ministry of Foreign Affairs and International Trade, Lester B Pearson Building, 125 Sussex Drive, Ottawa, Ontario, K1A 0G2 (tel: 996-9134; fax: 952-3904).

Ministry of Industry, CD Howe Building, 235 Queen Street, Ottawa, Ontario, K1A 0H5 (tel: 952-4782).

Ministry of Natural Resources, 580 Booth Street, Ottawa, Ontario, K1A 0E4 (tel: 995-0947; fax: 992-6424/5230).

Ministry of Public Works and Government Services, Sir Charles Tupper Building, Confederation Heights, Ottawa, Ontario, K1A 0M2 (tel: 736-2027; fax: 736-23440).

Other useful addresses
Alberta Stock Exchange, 10th Floor, 300 Fifth Avenue SW, Calgary T2P 3C4 (tel: 974-7400; fax: 237-0450).

Bourse de Montréal (Stock Exchange), Tour de la Bourse, CP 61, 800 Square Victoria, Montréal H4Z 1A9 (tel: 871-2424; fax: 871-3553; e-mail: info@me.org).

British High Commission, 80 Elgin Street, Ottawa, Ontario, K1P 5K7 (tel: 237-1530; fax: 237-7980).

Canadian Broadcasting Corporation, 1500 Bronson Avenue, PO Box 8478, Ottawa, Ontario K1G 3J5 (tel: 724-1200; fax: 738-6843).

Canadian Embassy (USA), 501 Pennsylvania Avenue, NW, Washington DC 20001 (tel: 202-682-1740; fax: 202-682-7701; e-mail: webmaster@canadianembassy.org).

Canadian Importers' Association, 210 Dundas St West, Suite 700, Toronto, Ontario, M5G 2E8 (tel: 595-5333; fax: 595-8226).

Canadian Manufacturers' Association, One Yonge St, Toronto, Ontario, M5E 1J9 (tel: 363-7261; fax: 363-3779).

CTV Television Network, 42 Charles St East, Toronto, Ontario, M4Y 1T5 (tel: 928-6000; fax: 928-0907).

Department of Energy, Mines and Resources, 580 Booth St, Ottawa, Ontario, K1A 0E4 (tel: 995-3065; fax: 996-9094).

Department of Finance, 140 O'Connor St, Ottawa, Ontario, K1A 0G5 (tel: 992-1575; fax: 996-2690).

Department of Labour, Labour Canada, Ottawa, Ontario, K1A 0J2 (tel: 997-2617; fax: 953-0176).

Department of Regional Industrial Expansion, 235 Queen St, Ottawa, Ontario, K1A 0H5 (tel: 995-9001).

Economic Council of Canada, PO Box 527, Ottawa, Ontario, K1P 5V6 (tel: 993-1253; fax: 991-4904).

Investment Canada, PO Box 2800, Station 'D', Ottawa, Ontario, K1P 6A5 (tel: 996-2515; fax: 995-0465).

Ontario International Trade Corporation, 5th Floor, Hearst Block, 900 Bay Street, Toronto, Ontario, M7A 2E1 (tel: 325-6514; fax: 325-6509).

Retail Council of Canada, 210 Dundas St West, Suite 600, Toronto, Ontario, M5G 2E8 (tel: 598-4684; fax: 598-3707).

Statistics Canada, Statistical Reference Centre, Ottawa, Ontario, K1A 0T6 (tel: 951-8116; internet site: http://www.statcan.ca/start.html).

Toronto Stock Exchange, The Exchange Tower, 2 First Canadian Place, Toronto, Ontario, M5X 1J2 (tel: 947-4700, 947-9301; fax: 947-4662).

Vancouver Stock Exchange, Stock Exchange Tower, 609 Granville Street, PO Box 10333, Vancouver, BC V7Y 1H1 (tel: 689-3334; fax: 688-6051).

Winnipeg Stock Exchange, 620 One Lombard Place, Winnipeg, Manitoba R3B 0X3 (tel: 987-7070; fax: 987-7079).

Internet sites
Asia-Pacific Economic Co-operation (APEC): http://www.apecsec.org.sg

Air Canada: http://www.aircanada.ca/

Canada Online: http://strategis.ic.gc.ca/

Canada Yellow Pages: http://www.canadayellowpages.com/

Canadian Airlines: http://www.cdnair.ca

Canadian Energy: http://www.centreforenergy.com

Canadian International Development Agency (CIDA): http://www.acdi-cida.gc.ca/

Canadian Parliament: http://www.parl.gc.ca/

Canadian Statistics: http://www.statcan.ca

Government of Canada (all dept): http://www.canada.gc.ca

Inuit and Artic news: http://www.nunatsiaq.com

Strategis: http://strategis.ic.ca

Thomas Register: http://www2.thomasregister.com/

Cape Verde

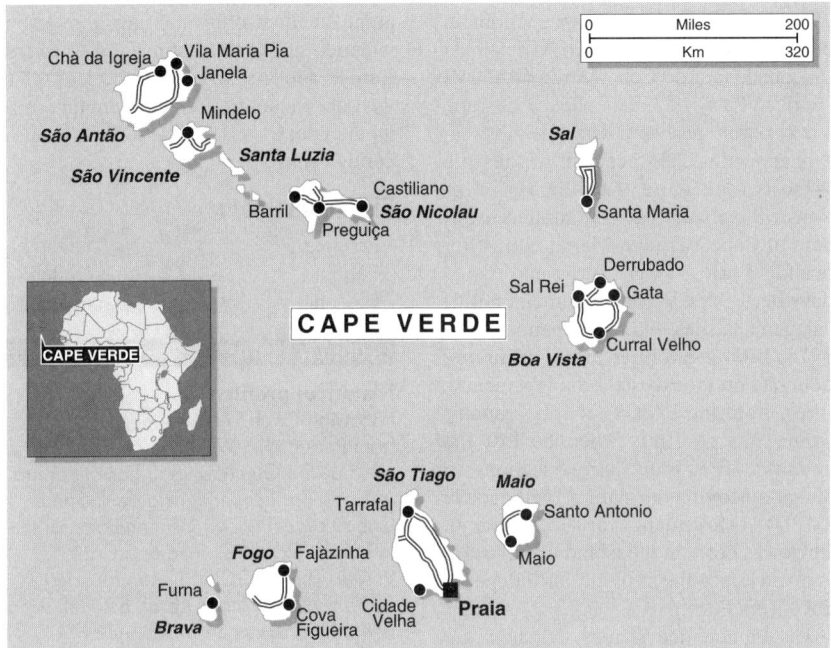

Macroeconomic policies in Cape Verde have strengthened significantly over recent years, enabling the country to correct the severe macroeconomic imbalances that emerged in 2000 in the run-up to parliamentary and presidential elections. External and domestic debt have declined, international reserves have been built up. There has been progress on structural reforms to support investment and improve the business climate. Real growth has averaged six per cent since 2000 and inflation has remained low.

Economic progress

The construction sector continues to provide key support to economic activity, notably through private investment in tourism facilities and public investment in infrastructure. These trends have been backed by increasing foreign direct investment and concessional assistance from Cape Verde's bilateral and multilateral partners. The fiscal deficit for 2005 is projected to be 2.8 per cent of gross domestic, up over 1.5 per cent in 2004, but fully financed through higher external assistance.

In view of continuing low inflation, a strong balance of payments and stable money and credit growth, the Bank of Cape Verde has been able to lower the required reserve ratio and standing lending facility rate. These moves have been followed by a reduction in commercial banks' lending rates.

The remaining enterprises on the government's privatisation agenda are being prepared for sale, tender under concession contracts, or liquidation. While progress in some areas is behind schedule, the programme is expected to be largely completed by the end of 2006. A rare remark at a recent IMF meeting with the Cape Verde authorities was that the country's socio-economic performance was paving the way for Cape Verde's graduation to middle-income status in the near future.

The meeting stressed that domestic resource mobilisation and export diversification should remain high priorities and noted the importance of a prudent fiscal policy, especially in the run-up to elections in early 2006. Taxes and spending were commented on: there was scope for further improvement in revenue

KEY FACTS

Official name: República de Cabo Verde (Republic of Cape Verde)

Head of State: President Pedro Verona Rodrigues Pires (PAICV) (elected 11/25 February 2001; inaugurated 22 March 2001)

Head of government: Prime Minister José María Neves (PAICV) (elected 14 January 2001; inaugurated 1 February 2001; re-elected January 2006)

Ruling party: Partido Africano da Independência de Cabo Verde (PAICV) (African Party of Independence of Cape Verde) (elected Jan 2001; re-elected January 2006)

Area: 4,033 square km (nine islands and 10 islets)

Population: 463,600 (2004)

Capital: Praia

Official language: Portuguese and Creole (national language)

Currency: Cape Verde escudo (CVEsc) = 100 centavos

Exchange rate: CVEsc92.10 per US$ (Oct 2005) (pegged CVEsc110.27 per euro)

GDP per capita: US$2,097 (2004)*

GDP real growth: 4.00% (2004)

Labour force: 204,000 (2004)

Inflation: -1.90% (2004)

Balance of trade: -US$326.19 million (2004)

* estimated figure

performance, including measures to strengthen tax administration and rationalise tax exemptions; it was important to continue to prioritise spending.

The economy is service-oriented, with commerce, transport, tourism, and public services accounting for 72 per cent of gross domestic product. Although almost 70 per cent of the population lives in rural areas, the share of agriculture in GDP in 2004 was just 12 per cent. The fishing potential, mostly lobster and tuna, is not fully exploited. Cape Verde annually runs a high trade deficit, financed by foreign aid and remittances from emigrants which supplement GDP by more than 20 per cent. During the twentieth century severe droughts caused the deaths of 200,000 people, prompting heavy emigration, with the result that more people with origins in Cape Verde live outside the country than inside it. The money that they send home brings in much-needed foreign currency. Nonetheless, the country enjoys a per capita income that is higher than that of many continental African nations (US$2,097 in 2004). Tourism is growing in importance, but there are concerns that it poses a threat to Cape Verde's rich marine life. It is an important nesting site for loggerhead turtles and humpback whales feed in the island waters.

World aid

The World Bank has approved 21 credits for Cape Verde for a total amount of US$197.93 million. The commitment value of seven ongoing International Development Agency-financed operations is US$58.1 million. The operations are in the sectors of: education; energy and mining; finance, industry and trade; health and social services; law and justice; transportation; and water, sanitation and flood protection.

Politics

Considered a veteran left winger, Pedro de Verona Rodrigues Pires is due to contest presidential elections in February 2006 when his sole opponent will again be Carlos Veiga. His Partido Africano da Independência de Cabo Verde (PAICV) (African Party of Independence of Cape Verde) won parliamentary elections in January with 52.34 per cent of the vote (41 seats, one more than the last elections). Pires was first inaugurated president of Cape Verde in March 2001 after beating Carlos Veiga. Pires and Veiga have been Cape Verde's dominant political personalities since independence in 1975. Both are former prime ministers, both had previously held the presidency. Pires, from the PAICV, led the country from 1975 to 1991, when he lost the country's first multi-party elections to Veiga's Movimento para a Democracia (MPD) (Movement for Democracy). Pires was born on the island of Fogo. He is a veteran of the struggle for independence from Portugal.

The uninhabited islands that now are Cape Verde were colonised by the Portuguese in the fifteenth century; Cape Verde subsequently became a trading center for African slaves and later an important coaling and resupply stop for whaling and transatlantic shipping. Following independence in 1975 a one-party system was established and maintained until multi-party elections were held in 1990.

Outlook

Cape Verde continues to exhibit one of Africa's most stable democratic governments. Cape Verde's expatriate population is greater than its domestic one and will continue to underpin the economy. One worrying development is the allegations that Cape Verde is a transshipment point for illicit drugs moving from Latin America and Asia destined for Western Europe and that it is only the lack of a well-developed financial system that limits the country's utility as a money-laundering centre.

Risk assessment

Economic	Good
Political	Excellent
Regional stability	Excellent

COUNTRY PROFILE

Historical profile
Following Cape Verde's independence from Portugal in 1975, the country was ruled by the Guinea-Bissau based Partido Africano da Independência da Guiné e Cabo Verde (PAIGC) (African Party for the Independence of Guinea and Cape Verde). The PAIGC had been founded in 1956 by Dr Amilcar Cabral, as a left-wing nationalist movement which led an 11-year guerrilla struggle in mainland Guinea-Bissau from 1963 to 1974 for independence from Portuguese rule. The PAIGC was prevented by Portuguese repression from establishing an effective organisation in the Cape Verde islands. In 1974, following the April coup in Lisbon, Portugal's new military leaders agreed to give the islands their independence, although there was more hesitation in the case of Cape Verde in view of the island republic's strategic mid-Atlantic importance. Cape Verde was actually granted independence 10 months later than Guinea-Bissau. The historical ties between the two countries are strong – the majority of Cape Verdians are descended from slaves transported from the African mainland – principally from what are now Guinea-Bissau and Senegal.
1462 The previously uninhabited islands were colonised by the Portuguese and became one of the most important slaving stations in West Africa.
1961 The movement for independence gathered strength, adopting guerrilla tactics against the Portuguese.
1975 Cape Verde gained independence after the fall of the dictatorship in Portugal.
1975–80 Moves to unite Cape Verde and Guinea-Bissau were made, but came to

KEY INDICATORS — Cape Verde

	Unit	2000	2001	2002	2003	2004
Population	m	0.43	0.45	0.46	0.46	0.48
Gross domestic product (GDP)	US$bn	0.56	0.59	0.62	0.65	*0.95
GDP per capita	US$	1,297	1,311	1,348	1,400	*2,097
GDP real growth	%	6.7	3.0	4.6	5.0	4.0
Inflation	%	-2.4	3.8	1.8	1.2	-1.9
Exports (fob) (goods)	US$m	24.0	24.0	42.0	30.0	61.1
Imports (fob) (goods)	US$m	260.0	260.0	245.0	220.0	387.3
Balance of trade	US$m	-236.0	-205.0	-200.0	-190.0	-326.2
Current account	US$m	-60.0	-60.0	-70.0	-80.0	-80.0
Total reserves minus gold	US$m	28.2	45.5	79.8	93.6	139.5
Foreign exchange	US$m	28.1	45.5	79.8	93.6	139.5
Exchange rate	per US$	115.88	123.21	114.38	108.95	95.05

* estimated figure

Cape Verde

nothing following the overthrow of President Luiz Cabral in Guinea-Bissau.
1980 The constitution was adopted.
1981 A revision to the constitution was passed.
1990 A multi-party system was introduced.
1991 Cape Verde's first free multi-party elections were won by the Movimento para a Democracia (MPD) (Movement for Democracy) and a government under Carlos Veiga was formed.
1992 A new constitution was adopted.
1995 The MPD secured an absolute majority in the elections to the National Assembly.
1996 President Antonio Mascarenhas Monteiro (MPD) was re-elected; no other parties put up candidates.
1999 Amendment to constitution.
2001 The MPD was ousted by Partido Africano da Independência de Cabo Verde (PAICV) (African Party of Independence of Cape Verde) in the elections. Pedro Pires was elected president and José María Neves was appointed prime minister.
2003 The IMF approved a three-year programme for US$11.5 million under the Poverty Reduction and Growth Facility (PRGF).
2004 Poor rainfall and locust damage resulted in reduced harvests and a larger than usual food deficit.
2006 The January elections to the national assembly were won by the PAICV with 52.34 per cent of the vote against the 43.93 per cent won by the MPD. PAICV have 41 seats, the MPD 29 seats.

Political structure
Cape Verde has a mixed presidential/parliamentary form of government.
Constitution
A new constitution was adopted in 1992 and amended in 1999. There are 17 municipios (administrative districts).
Form of state
Unitary republic
The executive
Executive power rests with the prime minister and the Council of Ministers, proposed by the prime minister and appointed by the president. The prime minister is appointed by the president, in consultation with the National Assembly. The president is elected by universal suffrage by electors registered in the electoral census in the national territory and abroad, for a five-year term. The presidential candidate must be a Capeverdean citizen by origin, thirty-five or more years of age on the date of his candidature, and, in the three years immediately preceding that date, have had permanent residence in the national territory.

National legislature
The legislative unicameral parliament, the Assembléia Nacional (National Assembly), serves a five-year term. It has 66 deputies elected in Cape Verde by universal suffrage, under a system of proportional representation, and six deputies elected by Cape Verdeans living abroad (two each for Africa, the Americas and the rest of the world).
Legal system
The legal system is derived from that of Portugal.
Last elections
22 January 2006 (parliamentary); 11/25 February 2001 (presidential).
Results: Presidential: Pedro Pires (PAICV) was elected president with 49.43 per cent of the votes; Carlos Veiga (MPD) 49.42 per cent.
Parliamentary: Partido Africano da Independência de Cabo Verde (PAICV) (African Party of Independence of Cape Verde) 41 seats (52.34 per cent), Movimento para a Democracia (MPD) (Movement for Democracy) 29 seats (43.93 per cent)
Next elections
12 February 2006 (presidential).

Political parties
There are six registered political parties.
Ruling party
Partido Africano da Independência de Cabo Verde (PAICV) (African Party of Independence of Cape Verde) (elected Jan 2001; re-elected January 2006)
Main opposition party
Movimento para a Democracia (MPD) (Movement for Democracy)

Population
463,600 (2004)
Ethnic make-up
Creole (mulatto) (71 per cent), African (28 per cent), European (1 per cent).
Religions
Constitutional separation of church and state allows for freedom of religion. Christian (97 per cent Roman Catholic).

Education
The National Development Plan of 2002–06 aims to increase vocational training and job creation and reduce illiteracy in an effort to generate foreign investment and therefore increase employment.
Literacy rate: 74 per cent adult population.
Enrolment rate: 100 per cent of children age six to 11 will enrol for school in 2015, Oxfam estimate.

Health
Annual total expenditure on health is around 4–5 per cent of GDP, of which government spending is approximately 84 per cent.

HIV/Aids
The government had a National Aids programme in place for the period 2001–04, financed by the World Bank.
Life expectancy: 69.2 years (World Bank)
Fertility rate/Maternal mortality rate: 3.5 births per woman (World Bank)
Infant mortality rate: 26 per 1,000 births (World Bank).

Welfare
Around a third of the population live under the poverty line with around 14 per cent living in absolute poverty. Unemployment is estimated at 25 per cent, while underemployment is far higher. Poverty is worse in rural areas where employment opportunities are poor and incomes are declining. As a result, there is a steady migration to urban areas, creating pockets of extreme poverty within cities and towns.

Main cities
Praia, on Santiago Island (capital, estimated population 99,400 in 2003); Mindelo, on São Vicente (commercial centre, 66,100).

Languages spoken
Official language/s
Portuguese and Creole (national language)

Media
Press
Dailies: *Horizonte*, which was established in 1998 as a weekly, went daily in November 2000. It is the country's sole daily newspaper and is owned by the government. *Expresso das Ilhas* (www.expressodasilhas.cv) is a privately-owned web-based news service.
Weeklies: *Novo Jornal Cabo Verde* and *A Semana*.
Periodicals: Periodicals include *Terra Nova* the Catholic Church monthly publication, *Opinião*, *Noticias* (independent publication) and *Agaviva*.
Broadcasting
Radio: The two main radio stations are Radio Nova and Radio Nacional de Cabo Verde (National Radio of Cape Verde).
Television: Televisao Nacional De Cabo Verde (TNCV) is the country's only television station.

Economy
Cape Verde has limited natural resources. Only 20 per cent of the total land area can be used for agriculture, because of the rugged volcanic nature of the landscape, erosion and persistent periods of severe drought. Most essentials, including food and fuel, have to be imported. Tourism is being developed as the main generator of economic growth. The number of visitors has steadily risen year-on-year, despite restricted facilities;

major expansion of infrastructure is underway. The sector is expected to contribute around 11 per cent to GDP in 2005.
The islands continue to remain heavily dependent upon external donor assistance and food aid. Around half of the country's development expenses are funded by foreign aid with basic products (cereals, cooking oil, milk) making up 20 per cent of public development aid. Much aid is now also aimed at transforming the country into a self-sustainable economy. Mass emigration following serious droughts in the twentieth century has benefited the economy by the inflow of remittances. There is a high rate of unskilled workers – 30–40 per cent of the population – and foreign investors are able take advantage of low wage rates.

External trade
The trade deficit is partly offset by income from ship servicing, workers' remittances from abroad and substantial aid flows. Cape Verde is eligible for tariff preferences under the US Africa Growth and Opportunities Act (AGOA). The legislation requires that countries are only eligible for greater access to US markets provided they have made continued progress toward a market-based economy, the rule of law, free trade, poverty reduction and the protection of workers' rights. This process is reviewed annually.
Imports
Principal imports are foodstuffs such as rice, wheat and maize, cooking oil and milk; industrial products, transport equipment, fuels, machinery and textiles.
Main sources: Portugal (43.2 per cent total, 2004), US (12.5 per cent), The Netherlands (8.7 per cent)
Exports
Principal exports are fuel, shoes, garments, fish, hides, salt and entrepôt trade.
Main destinations: Portugal (62.5 per cent total, 2004), US (15.8 per cent), UK (11.3 per cent)

Agriculture
Farming
The agricultural sector forms the backbone of the economy, even though only 20 per cent of total area is cultivable, with 48 per cent of the population engaged in subsistence farming. Agriculture accounts for around 13 per cent of GDP. Most arable land is on the island of São Tiago. Recurrent drought, interrupted by torrential rains and floods, soil erosion, disease and a weak infrastructure have reduced agricultural production considerably, but there are schemes for water conservation and irrigation.
Beans and maize are the staple foodstuffs. Maize covers 25–80 per cent of cultivated land according to rainfall. Only 10 per cent of food is produced locally.

Other crops include bananas, sweet potatoes, yams, manioc, pumpkins, sugar cane, coffee and groundnuts. About 90 per cent of food requirements are met by imports, largely in the form of food aid. The estimated crop production for 2004 included: 4,042 tonnes (t) maize, *3,000t cassava, *3,500t potatoes, 6,000t bananas, *4,000t sweet potatoes, *5,000t pulses, *10,500t roots and tubers, *6,000t coconuts, *4,500t tomatoes, 1,000t pimento, *792t oilcrops, *14,000t sugar cane, *15,000t fruit in total, *15,665t vegetables in total. Estimated livestock production included: 8,554t meat in total, *450t beef, 7,200t pig meat, 509t lamb and goat meat, 395t poultry, 1,476t eggs, 10,900t milk, 85t cattle hides.
* estimate

Fishing
Although fishing (lobster and tuna) has been of growing importance, supporting some 20,000 people and accounting for over 60 per cent of export revenues and 4 per cent of GDP, it is under-exploited. Construction of a fishing port in Mindelo on São Vicente was completed in 2001.

Industry and manufacturing
The industrial sector accounts for around 19 per cent of GDP and employs 15 per cent of the workforce.
Industries include ship repair and fuelling, construction, fish processing and canning, flour milling, soft drinks, cigar manufacture and garment making. Construction and civil engineering contribute about 10 per cent of GDP and are primarily related to the development of the tourism sector. Two zones have been set up with industrial parks: Lazareto on São Vicente and Achada Grande Tras in Praia.

Tourism
Tourism is a primary contributor to the economy and is being vigorously developed as an engine of economic growth. Visitor arrivals have increased steadily, from 13,000 in 1986 to around 70,000 in 2000, then accelerating to 178,000 by 2004. The increase in 2005 is expected to be around 2 per cent. Most tourist activity is centred on Sal, whose airport has been the only one catering to charter flights from Europe. Most visitors come from Portugal and Italy. In October 2005, a new international airport was inaugurated on Santiago near the capital, Praia, which will open up Santiago and other islands to tourism. Other infrastructure works are in progress, including the Santiago Golf Club, a huge resort near Praia, scheduled to open in 2006. Tourism is expected to contribute around 11 per cent to GDP in 2005.

Environment
Cape Verde faces serious environmental problems, particularly concerning water management. Serious drought caused by global warming and the country's geographical location has undermined agriculture as well as plant cover. The government has drawn upon the Global Environment Facility (GEF) to help protect biodiversity and is supported by the UN's Food and Agriculture Organisation (FAO) in a forestry action plan.

Mining
The mining sector employs about 1 per cent of the workforce.
Activity is largely confined to exploitation of pozzolana (volcanic derivative) at São Antão, gypsum at Maio and production of salt on Sal and in Mindelo by evaporation method.

Hydrocarbons
Cape Verde has no oil or gas reserves. Oil requirements are imported mainly from Portugal and West African countries. Imported refined oil products supply 96 per cent of the country's energy needs. Current consumption of oil products is around 20,000 tonnes per annum. The downstream industry is regulated by Direcão Geral da Energia and distribution is by Shell Capo Verde and Enacol.

Energy
Cape Verde is dependent on oil imports for electricity generation. Around 96 per cent of energy needs come from oil-derived products.

Banking and insurance
Central bank
Banco de Cabo Verde
Main financial centre
Praia

Time
GMT minus one hour

Geography
Cape Verde is an archipelago of 10 islands and five islets in the North Atlantic Ocean, about 500km (300 miles) west of Dakar, Senegal.

Climate
Hot with very little rainfall. Temperatures range from around 20 degrees Celsius (C) at night to 32 degrees C during the day. Hottest months are July, August and September and rain most likely from August–September.

Entry requirements
Passports
Required by all. Passport must be valid for duration of stay.
Visa
Required by all except citizens of West African States (ECOWAS). Business visas requirements include a business letter and

Cape Verde

an itinerary. For full details and application form, contact the nearest embassy or consulate.
Currency advice/regulations
Import and export of local currency prohibited.
No restriction on import of foreign currency, but amounts must be declared. Export of foreign currency is limited to equivalent of CVEsc20,000 unless a higher amount is declared on arrival.

Health (for visitors)
Mandatory precautions
Yellow fever certificates if arriving from countries having notified cases in the last six years.
Advisable precautions
Typhoid, tetanus, hepatitis A and polio vaccinations. Malaria limited risk exists September to November in São Tiago Island. Water precautions should be taken. There is a rabies risk. There is a slight risk of cholera. Milk is unpasteurised and should be boiled. Dairy products should be avoided.

Hotels
Accommodation is available in all islands but the best establishments are situated in Fogo, Sal, Santiago, São Vicente.

Credit cards
Credit cards are only accepted in the bigger hotels.

Public holidays
Fixed dates
1 Jan (New Year's Day), 20 Jan (Heroes' Day), 1 May (Labour Day), 5 Jul (Independence Day), 15 Aug (Assumption Day), 12 Sep (National Day), 1 Nov (All Saints' Day), 25 Dec (Christmas).
Variable dates
Carnival (Feb)

Working hours
Banking
Mon–Fri: 0800–1400.
Business
Mon–Fri: 0800–1230, 1430–1800.
Shops
Mon–Fri: 0800–1300, 1500–1900. Sat: 0900–1300. Closed all day Sunday.

Electricity supply
220V AC

Weights and measures
Metric system

Getting there
Air
A new airline service, by TAAG of Angola, flies weekly from São Tomé and Príncipe.
National airline: Transportes Aéreos de Cabo Verde (TACV) guarantees daily inter-island flights and weekly flights. South African Airlines, TAP Air Portugal and Tower Airlines also service Cape Verde.

International airport/s: Sal Amilcar Cabral International (Code: SID), 2km south of Espargos.
Airport tax: There is no airport tax.

Getting about
National transport
Air: Transportes Aéreos de Cabo Verde (TACV) flies daily to all islands except Brava and Santo Antâo. The Cape Verde Airpass from TACV offers discounts to frequent flyers.
Flights from West African coast use San Pedro regional airport, near Praia on Santiago.
Buses: Buses available on main islands.
Water: Boats ply between the islands.
City transport
Taxis: Available on main islands. Taxis are available from Sal Amilcar Cabral International Airport to city centre.

BUSINESS DIRECTORY
The addresses listed below are a selection only. While World of Information makes every endeavour to check these addresses, we cannot guarantee that changes have not been made, especially to telephone numbers and area codes. We would welcome any corrections.

Telephone area codes
The international dialling code (IDD) for Cape Verde is +238 followed by subscriber's number.
NB From 3 July 2004, standard and cellular numbers have seven digits: add '2' to the beginning of the existing standard number; add '9' to the beginning of the existing cellular number.

Useful telephone numbers
Praia, Santiago
Airport docks: 2615-821, 2615-646
Electricity Board: 2611-909
Fire brigade: 2612-727
Ambulance: 2612-462
Police: 2613-637

Chambers of Commerce
Barlavento Cámara de Comércio, Indústria, Agricultura e Serviços, Rua de Luz 31, PO Box 728, Mindelo, São Vicente (tel: 2328-495; fax: 2328-496; e-mail: camera.com @mail.cvtelecom.cv).

Sotavento Cámara de Comércio, Indústria e Serviços, Rua Andrade Corvo, PO Box 105, Praia, Santiago (tel: 2617-234; fax: 2617-235; e-mail: cciss@mail,cvtelecom.cv).

Banking
Banco Insular (IFI), PO Box 556, Conjunto Residencial Comunidades, Lote Oito- Bloco D Fracção Oitava, Achada Santo Antonio-Praia (e-mail: bancoinsular@mail.cvtelecom.cv).

Banco Comercial do Atlantico, PO Box 474, Avenida Amílcar Cabral, Praia (tel: 2614-953; fax: 2613-235).

Banco Interatlântico, Avenida Cidade de Lisboa 131-A, Praia (tel: 2614-008, 2613-829, 2614-425; fax: 2614-712, 2614-752).

Caixa Económica de Cabo Verde SARL, PO Box 199, Avenida Cidade de Lisboa, Praia (tel: 2615-561; fax: 2615-560).

Central bank
Banco de Cabo Verde, Avenida Amilcar Cabral, PO Box 101, Praia (tel: 2615-526; fax: 2611-914; e-mail: drs@bcv.cv).

Travel information
Agencia Cabetur, Viagens e Turismo, Rua Guerra Mendes 4, Praia (tel: 2615-551; fax: 2615-553).

Intertur SARL, Av Cidade de Lisboa, 2 Esq Fazenda, Praia (tel: 614-643; fax: 614-644); Rua 5 de Julho Espargos, Sal (tel: 2411-580/590).

Orbitur, Rua Roberto Duarte Silva, CP 161, Praia (tel: 2615-737; fax: 2613-888).

Praiatur, 100 Av Amilcar Cabral, CP 470, Praia (tel: 2615-746/7; fax: 2614-500).

Sal Amilcar Cabral International Airport, ASA-Empresa Nacional de Aeroportos E Seguranca Aerea-EP, PB 50, Ilha do Sal (tel: 2411-135, 2411-394, 2411-468; fax: 2411-570, 2411-323; e-mail: asacv@milton.cvtelecom.cv).

Transportes Aéreos de Cabo Verde (TACV), Av Amilcar Cabral, CP 1, Praia (tel: 2615-813; fax: 2615-905).

Ministries
Ministry of Agriculture, Alimentation and Environment, Praia (tel: 2615-716; fax: 2614-717).

Ministry of Defence, Praia (tel: 2610-372; fax: 2611-286).

Ministry of Economic Co-ordination, Avenue Amilcar Cabral, Praia (tel: 2613-210; fax: 2611-922).

Ministry of Education, Science and Culture, Praia (tel: 2610-507; fax: 2612-764).

Ministry of Foreign Affairs, Praia (tel: 2614-773; fax: 2611-960).

Ministry of Health and Social Promotion, Praia (tel: 2615-721; fax: 2613-991).

Ministry of Justice and Internal Administration, Praia (tel: 2615-687; fax: 2611-396).

Ministry of Sea, Praia (tel: 2616-662; fax: 2611-770).

Ministry of Transport and Infrastructure, Praia (tel: 2615-709; fax: 2614-822).

Prime Minister's Office, Palacio do Governo, Praia (tel: 2610-513; fax: 2612-288).

Other useful addresses

Associação Commercial e Agricola de Sotavento de Cabo Verde, CP 78, Praia (tel: 2612-991).

Associação Comercial Barlavento, CP 62, Mindelo, S Vicente (tel: 2313-281).

Cabo Verde Motors, CP 51-B, Praia (tel: 2612-345; fax: 2612-612).

Ceris, Sociedade Caboverdiana de Cerveja e Refrigerantes (beer and refrigeration), CP 320, Praia (tel: 2615-575; fax: 2614-488).

Direcção-Geral das Alfandegas (customs body), CP 98, Praia (tel: 2613-835, 2613-026).

Direcção-Geral do Comércio (trade body), CP 105, Praia (tel: 2614-159).

Direcção-Geral de Estatistica (Statistics Department of the Ministry of Economic Co-ordination), Avenida Amilcar Cabral, Praia (fax: 2611-922).

Direcção-Geral das Pescas (national fisheries authority), Praia (tel: 2612-976).

Direcção-Geral do Plano (Planning Department of the Ministry of Economic Co-ordination), Avenida Amilcar Cabral, Praia (fax: 2611-922).

Embassy of Portugal, Achada de S António, Praia (tel: 2615-602).

Empresa Nacional de Aeroportos e Segurança Aérea, Aeroporto Amilcar Cabral, Ilha do Sal (tel: 2411-394).

Empresa Nacional de Combustivels (national combustibles corporation), CP 1, Mindelo, S Vicente (tel: 2313-659).

Garantia (insurance company) (tel: 2615-661, 2615-662; fax: 2313-221, 2313-470).

Promex (Centro de Promoção Turística, do Investimento e das Exportações), CP89c, Praia (tel: 2622-736; fax: 2622-657; e-mail: promex@cvtelecom.cv).

Radio Nacional de Cabo Verde, CP 26, Praia (tel: 2613-729).

Shell Cabo Verde, CP 4, S Vicente (tel: 2314-470; fax: 2314-755).

US Embassy, R Abilio Macedo, Praia (tel: 2615-616).

Internet sites

Africa Business Network: http://www.ifc.org/abn

African Development Bank: http://www.afdb.org

Africa Online: http://www.africaonline.com

Allafrica.com: http://allafrica.com

Mbendi AfroPaedia (information on companies, countries, industries and stock exchanges in Africa): http://mbendi.co.za

Cayman Islands

COUNTRY PROFILE

Historical profile
1503 Little Cayman and Cayman Brac were sighted by Christopher Columbus during his fourth and final voyage to the New World. The islands were first named Las Tortugas (turtles); the name was later changed to Lagartos (alligator or large lizard).
1540 The name Caymanas was given to the islands, derived from the Carib word for marine crocodile.
1585–86 Sir Frances Drake visited the islands.
During the sixteenth, seventeenth and eighteenth centuries, Dutch, English, Spanish and French ships used the islands for watering and provisioning.
1655 The islands came under British control when Jamaica was captured from the Spanish.
1670 In the Treaty of Madrid, Spain recognised UK sovereignty over Jamaica and the Cayman Islands.
The early settlers were ex-soldiers from Oliver Cromwell's army, and other settlers transplanted from Jamaica, together with shipwrecked or marooned sailors.
1773 Grand Cayman's population reached 400.
1831 It was resolved that representatives should be appointed for the five different districts of Grand Cayman for the purpose of forming local laws for better government. After elections in the five districts, the legislative assembly met in George Town.
1833 Cayman Brac and Little Cayman were settled permanently.
1835 The proclamation was read declaring the emancipation of all slaves throughout the colonies.
1962 When Jamaica became independent, Caymanians retained direct links with the Crown and the Cayman islands became a separate British Crown Colony.
1971 The first governor was appointed.
1972 The constitution was adopted.
1994 Ministries were created.
2000 Only independents were elected in the parliamentary elections in November.
2001 The United Democratic Party (UDP) was formed in November. Its leader, W McKeeva Bush, became the leader of government business in December.
2002 The People's Progressive Movement (PPM) was formed in June.
2004 Hurricane Ivan struck the Cayman Islands in September, causing flooding and extensive structural damage and delayed the November general elections.
2005 The PPM won the 11 May parliamentary elections; Kurt Tibbetts became leader of government business.

Political structure
Constitution
The constitution of 1972, revised in 1994, created ministers and ministries and provided for a system of government headed by a governor, an Executive Council (ExCo) and Legislative Assembly. Unlike other Caribbean Overseas Territories, there is no chief minister, but a leader of government business. The appointed governor retains responsibility for the civil service, defence, external affairs and internal security.

Form of state
Self-governing British Crown Colony

The executive
The British monarch is Head of State, represented by the governor. Government is exercised by the Executive Council (ExCo) presided over by the governor, consisting of three official members appointed by the governor and five members drawn from the elected members of the Legislative Assembly. As ministers, the five elected members of the ExCo have direct responsibility for government portfolios.

National legislature
The Legislative Assembly has 18 members, 15 elected members (MLAs) for a four-year term in two-seat constituencies, and three members ex-officio.

Legal system
The legal system is based on English common law with local changes. Courts: Juvenile Court, Summary Court Grand Court and the Cayman Islands Court of Appeal. Final appeals go to the Privy Council in the UK.

Last elections
11 May 2005 (parliamentary)
Results: Parliamentary: the People's Progressive Movement (PPM) won nine seats out of 15; the United Democratic Party (UDP) won five seats; one independent candidate was returned.

Next elections
2009 (parliamentary)

Political parties
Ruling party
People's Progressive Movement (PPM) (elected 11 May 2005)
Main opposition party
United Democratic Party (UDP)

KEY FACTS

Official name: Cayman Islands

Head of State: Queen Elizabeth II; represented by Governor Stuart Jack (from Nov 2005)

Head of government: Leader of Government Business: Kurt Tibbetts (PPM)

Ruling party: People's Progressive Movement (PPM) (elected 11 May 2005)

Area: 259 square km

Population: 48,800 (2004)

Capital: George Town (Grand Cayman)

Official language: English

Currency: Cayman Islands dollar (CI$) = 100 cents

Exchange rate: CI$0.83 per US$ (Oct 2005)

GDP per capita: US$33,300 (2004)

GDP real growth: 2.00% (2004)

Inflation: 4.40% (2004)*

* estimated figure

Nations of the World: A Political, Economic and Business Handbook

Political situation

The two national parties included proposals to modernise the constitution in their manifestos for the general election, scheduled for November 2004, but postponed to May 2005 (following the devastation of Hurrican Ivan). Both took the view that a popular vote in the election would be a mandate to amend the constitution without a referendum. Critics argue that previous legislative assembly resolutions preclude such changes without a full plebiscite. The UK has said that it would wait on a Cayman Island timetable for amendments, bolstering the argument that any amendment to the constitution should not be rushed.

Population

48,800 (2004)

Ethnic make-up

Mixed race (40 per cent), white (20 per cent), black (20 per cent). Thirty-four per cent of the population are foreign residents, of whom 10 per cent are British or American.

Religions

Mainly Presbyterian with Anglican, Roman Catholic, Seventh-Day Adventists, Pilgrims, Pilgrim Holiness Church of God, Jehovah's Witnesses and Baha'i minorities on Grand Cayman. Baptists on Cayman Brac.

Health

The Cayman Islands has a variety of modern medical facilities. There are government-operated hospitals on Grand Cayman and Cayman Brac. The George Town Hospital on Grand Cayman is affiliated with the Baptist Hospital of Miami, USA, for patient referrals involving advanced care or treatment.

Life expectancy: 80 years: male 77 years; female 82 years (2003).

Fertility rate/Maternal mortality rate: Two births per woman (2003)

Birth rate/Death rate: 13 births per 1,000 population; five deaths per 1,000 population (2003).

Infant mortality rate: Nine per 1,000 live births (2003)

Main cities

George Town, on Grand Cayman (capital, estimated population 29,400 in 2003); other islands are Cayman Brac and Little Cayman.

Languages spoken

Spoken English has a distinctive 'brogue'. The Jamaican patois and a stronger accent is also common. Spanish, particularly regional dialects of Central America and Cuba, is also spoken.

Official language/s

English

Media

Press

Cayman Net News (http://www.caymannetnews.com) is an on-line publication covering local news and business.

Dailies: *The Caymanian Compass* published from Monday to Friday.

Weeklies: *New Caymanian* is a weekly newspaper.

Periodicals: Monthly magazines include *Financial and Business Journal* and *Newstar*.

Broadcasting

Radio: Consists of the government radio station, Radio Cayman, and education/cultural station ICCI-FM.

Television: There is no domestic television service.

Economy

The economy is dominated by the offshore financial services sector and tourism, which are virtually the sole sources of export earnings. The Cayman Islands is also dependent on imports for the bulk of its consumption and investment requirements. This level of openness renders the economy vulnerable in the face of such external events as recession in the US, the operations of the financial sector or natural catastrophes, such as Hurricane Ivan, which struck in 2004.

After an average 5 per cent growth rate through the 1990s, the Cayman Islands economy suffered a setback as a result of recession in the US. Growth fell to below 1 per cent in 2001, but started picking up again in 2002, a trend which continued into 2004. Tourism and construction, as well as financial services, expanded. Consumer demand continued to increase, leading to higher rate of inflation in 2004 of 4.4 per cent, compared to 2.8 per cent in the previous year. The unemployment rate declined to 4.1 per cent in 2003, but rose to 5.7 per cent in 2004. GDP was expected to increase by up to 4 per cent in 2004, but the arrival of Hurricane Ivan in September wreaked havoc on the Cayman Islands. The economic impact of the disaster was estimated at US$2.9 billion (189 per cent of GDP), with the prospect of negative growth in 2005.

External trade

The Cayman Islands depend on fuel, food and tourism-related imports. A substantial deficit is traditionally run on the merchandise trade account, which is usually covered by invisible earnings and capital inflows from tourism and financial services.

Imports

Principal imports are foodstuffs, petroleum and derivatives, machinery and transport equipment, tourist-related goods. In 2003, imports totalled US$457.40 million.

Main sources: US, Trinidad and Tobago, UK, The Netherlands Antilles, Japan

Exports

Principal exports are turtle products and manufactured consumer goods

Main destinations: US, Costa Rica, UK, Canada, Jamaica.

Agriculture

Farming

Poor soil conditions and scarcity of land make agriculture uneconomic. Only about 8 per cent of the total land area is farmed. The Cayman Islands do not produce enough food to meet local demand and are reliant on imports. A National Tree Crop Husbandry Programme has increased the output of mangoes, citrus fruit and bananas. Government policies focus on sustainable development and using new technologies.

Crop production in 2004 included: 32 tonnes (t) yams, 33t plantains, 36t mangoes, 206t bananas, 56t citrus, 27t tomatoes, 18t cassava, 10t coconuts, 344t fruit in total, 118t vegetables in total. Livestock production included: 5t eggs, 9t honey.

Fishing

The typical annual fish catch is 125t. All spawning areas for groupers were closed for fishing for a period of eight years from 2003, in a move aimed at preserving stocks for future generations. Groupers take eight years to mature.

KEY INDICATORS — Cayman Islands

	Unit	2000	2001	2002	2003	2004
Population	m	0.04	0.04	0.04	0.05	0.05
Gross domestic product (GDP)	US$bn	0.86	1.00	1.18	1.42	1.39
GDP per capita	US$	23,800	24,500	27,442	30,000	32,300
GDP real growth	%	1.0	0.6	1.7	*2.0	1.7
Inflation	%	2.3	1.2	2.4	2.8	*4.4
Unemployment	%	–	–	–	4.1	5.7
Exchange rate	per US$	0.82	0.80	0.82	0.82	0.82

* estimated figure

Cayman Islands

Industry and manufacturing
The industrial sector makes only a very small contribution to the economy; diversification is hampered by factors such as high labour costs and a shortage of labour. Activity is centred on building materials (concrete blocks and tiles) and tourist-related industries such as jewellery, printing and food processing.

Tourism
Tourism is the most important sector of the economy, accounting for a projected 9.4 per cent of GDP in 2005 and employing 13.2 per cent of the labour force. The majority of visitors come from the US. Most arrivals are by cruise ship. The growth in cruise ship arrivals was encouraged by government measures to relax the restriction on the number of passengers allowed to disembark and the number of ships allowed to dock. Arrivals by air, after falling off for several years, were on the rise again by 2004. The sector was badly hit in September 2004 when Hurricane Ivan devastated the islands.

Hydrocarbons
The Cayman Islands do not produce any hydrocarbons. To supply the only public electrical utility, refined oil products, primarily diesel, are imported. 2,410 barrels were imported daily in 2001 from refineries in the Carribean and the Gulf of Mexico. It does not import coal or gas.

Financial markets
Stock exchange
The Cayman Islands Stock Exchange (CSX) started operations in 1997 as an offshore investment market.

Banking and insurance
In 2000, the Cayman Islands made a commitment to the OECD, agreeing to exchange information with overseas authorities in criminal and civil tax matters by December 2005. The banking sector came under harsh criticism and was initially blacklisted by the OECD and US for money laundering activities, however it had implemented nearly all the OECD recommended regulations by 2002.
Under an EU tax directive introduced in July 2005 in dependent EU countries, the Cayman Islands now informs all EU citizens' tax departments about the amount of money in savings accounts to allow tax to be levied from the home country rather than impose a withholding tax while retaining a saver's anonyimity.
The Cayman Islands has also agreed to supply information on tax fraud, for criminal or civil trials, and notify EU member states about additional malpractices.

Central bank
The Cayman Islands Monetary Authority (CIMA) was established in January 1997.

Main financial centre
George Town, Grand Cayman

Time
GMT minus five hours

Geography
The Cayman Islands are located in the western Caribbean, south of Cuba and north-west of Jamaica.
The three islands of Grand Cayman, Cayman Brac and Little Cayman are limestone outcroppings, the tops of a submarine mountain range called the Cayman Ridge, which extends west-south-west from the Sierra Maestra range of the south-east part of Cuba to the Misteriosa Bank near Belize. There are no rivers or streams because of the porous nature of the limestone rock. All three islands are surrounded by healthy coral reefs.

Climate
Prevailing north-east trade winds; moderate, otherwise hot climate. Average temperatures 24–29 degrees Celsius. The rainy season is May–Oct, but annual rainfall is low.

Dress codes
Neat, casual, tropical attire is appropriate. Public nudity and topless bathing are strictly prohibited by law.

Entry requirements
Passports
Required by all except citizens of the UK, US and Canada with proof of citizenship (authenticated birth certificate and photographic identity document) and a return ticket.
The pink immigration slip given upon arrival should be kept with travel documents and presented when departing.

Visa
Not required by transit passengers or nationals of the EU, North America, Australasia or Japan, provided their stay does not exceed 30 days. For further exceptions see http://cayman.com.ky/visiting/reqs.htm.
Salespeople planning to solicit business and take orders require a temporary work permit, applications should be obtained in advance from the Department of Immigration.

Currency advice/regulations
There is no restriction on import of foreign or local currency, apart from import of Jamaican dollars, which are restricted to J$20.

Customs
Products made from farmed green sea turtles are offered only for local consumption and cannot be exported.

Prohibited imports
Illegal drugs, including marijuana (ganja), are strictly prohibited by law. Firearms of any kind, spearguns (or pole spears or Hawaiian slings), live plants and plant cuttings, raw fruits and vegetables are also restricted.

Health (for visitors)
Modern medical facilities are available, particularly on Grand Cayman and Cayman Brac. The George Town Hospital is well equipped for any diving accidents.
Mandatory precautions
None.
Advisable precautions
Immunisation against typhoid, and less so TB, diphtheria and hepatitis 'B' and 'C'. Outbreaks of dengue fever and dengue haemorrhagic fever can occur. Hepatitis 'A' has been reported in the northern Caribbean generally.

Hotels
There is a wide choice of hotels throughout the islands, mainly on the beach. There is a government room tax of 10 per cent and an automatic gratuity of 10 per cent of the room rate. Restaurants often add a 15 per cent gratuity to their bills.

Credit cards
Major credit cards are widely accepted.

Public holidays
Fixed dates
1 Jan (New Year's Day), 20 Jan (Heroes' Day), 1 May (Labour Day), 5 Jul (Independence Day), 15 Aug (Assumption Day), 12 Sep (National Day), 1 Nov (All Saints' Day), 25 Dec (Christmas Day).
Variable dates
Carnival (Feb)

Working hours
Banking
Mon–Thu: 0900–1600; Fri: 0900–1630.
Business
Mon–Fri: 0830–1700.
Government
Mon–Fri: 1330–1800, 1900–2200.
Shops
Mon–Sat: 0900–1700.

Electricity supply
110V AC, 60Hz. American-style (flat) two-pin plugs are standard.

Getting there
Air
National airline: Cayman Airways.
International airport/s: Owen Roberts International (GCM), 3km from the centre of George Town, duty-free shop, bar, restaurant, buffet, money exchange, shops.
Other airport/s: Gerrard Smith (CYB) on Cayman Brac. Little Cayman is served by inter-island flights arriving at the Edward Bodden Airstrip.
Airport tax: Departure tax US$25

Getting about
National transport
Air: Cayman Airways operates a service from Grand Cayman to Cayman Brac.

Island Air offers a four-times-a-day service between Grand Cayman and both Cayman Brac and Little Cayman.
Road: There are over 175km of road, mostly surfaced. Speed limits of 50, 40, 30, 25mph are strictly enforced. Most hotels have bicycles available for complimentary guest use.
Buses: Daily bus services start at 0600. There are regular bus services between West Bay and George Town, and between the latter and Bodden Town and East End. Mini-buses are operated by licensed operators.

City transport
Taxis: Taxis are readily available at hotels and airport. Fares are based on a fixed place-to-place tariff. Tipping optional.
Car hire
An international licence is recommended. A local permit is obtainable on production of a national licence. Traffic drives on the left. Wearing seat belts is mandatory.

BUSINESS DIRECTORY

The addresses listed below are a selection only. While World of Information makes every endeavour to check these addresses, we cannot guarantee that changes have not been made, especially to telephone numbers and area codes. We would welcome any corrections.

Telephone area codes
The international direct dialling code (IDD) for the Cayman Islands is + 1 345, followed by subscriber's number.

Useful telephone numbers
Emergency service (island-wide): 911.

Chambers of Commerce
Cayman Islands Chamber of Commerce, Harbour Centre, PO Box 1000, George Town, Grand Cayman (tel: 949-8090; fax: 949-0220; e-mail: info@caymanchamber.ky).

Banking
The Bank of Nova Scotia, PO Box 689, Grand Cayman (tel: 949-7666; fax: 949-0020).
Bank of Butterfield International (Cayman) Ltd, PO Box 705 G, Grand Cayman (tel: 949-7055; fax: 949-7761).
Barclays Bank International, PO Box 68 G, Grand Cayman (tel: 949-7300; fax: 949-7179).
Canadian Imperial Bank of Commerce and Trust Co (Cayman), PO Box 694 G, Grand Cayman (tel: 949-8666; fax: 949-7904).

The Cayman Islands Bankers' Association, PO Box 1321, Grand Cayman (tel: 949-0330).
Cayman National Bank and Trust Co, PO Box 1097, Grand Cayman (tel: 949-4655; fax: 949-7506); Galleria Branch, PO Box 1097, Grand Cayman (tel: 949-7137; fax: 949-7506).
First Home Banking, PO Box 914, Grand Cayman (tel: 949-7822; fax: 949-6064).
The Royal Bank of Canada, PO Box 245 G, Grand Cayman (tel: 949-4600; fax: 949-7396).
Swiss Bank and Trust Corporation Ltd, PO Box 852 G, Grand Cayman (tel: 949-7344; fax: 949-7308).

Central bank
Cayman Islands Monetary Authority, PO Box 10052 APO, Elizabethan Square, 80e Shedden Road, Grand Cayman (tel: 949-7089; fax: 949-2532; e-mail: cima@cimoney.com.ky).

Travel information
Cayman Airways, PO Box 1101, George Town, Grand Cayman (tel: 949-2311/8272; fax: 949-7607).

Ministry of tourism
Ministry of Tourism, Aviation and Commerce, Government Administration Building, Grand Cayman (tel: 949-7900; fax: 949-1746).

National tourist organisation offices
Cayman Islands Department of Tourism, PO Box 67, The Pavilion, Cricket Square, George Town, Grand Cayman (tel: 949-0623; fax: 949-4053; fax: 949-4053; internet sites: http://www.caymanislands.ky; http://www.divecayman.ky).

Ministries
Governor's Office, 4th Floor, Government Administration Building, Elgin Avenue, George Town, Grand Cayman (tel: 949-7900; fax: 945-4131).
Ministry of Agriculture, Environment, Communications and Works, Government Administration Building, Grand Cayman (tel: 949-7900; fax: 949-2922).
Ministry of Community Development, Sports, Women's and Youth Affairs, Government Administration Building, Grand Cayman (tel: 949-7900; fax: 949-0726).
Ministry of Education and Planning, Government Administration Building, Grand Cayman (tel: 949-7900; fax: 949-9343).
Ministry of Health, Drug Abuse, Prevention and Rehabilitation, Government Administration Building, Grand Cayman (tel: 949-7900; fax: 949-7544).
Ministry of Internal and External Affairs, Government Administration Building, Grand Cayman (tel: 949-7900; fax: 949-7544).
Ministry of Finance and Development, Government Administration Building, Grand Cayman (tel: 949-7900; fax: 949-9838).
Ministry of Legal Affairs, Government Administration Building, Grand Cayman (tel: 949-7900; fax: 949-1746).
Sports Office, Ministry of Community Development, Sports, Women's and Youth Affairs, Third Floor, Tower Building, Grand Cayman (tel: 914-3480; fax: 949-8487).

Other useful addresses
Cable and Wireless (West Indies) Ltd, PO Box 293, George Town (tel: 949-7800; fax: 949-5472).
Cayman Islands Port Authority, PO Box 1358, Georgetown, Grand Cayman (tel: 949-2055; fax: 949-5820; e-mail: info@caymanport.com).
Cayman Islands Stock Exchange, Fourth Floor, Elizabethan Square, P.O Box 2408GT, Grand Cayman (tel: 945-6060; fax: 945-6061; e-mail: csx@csx.com.ky; internet site: http://www.csx.com.ky).
Civil Aviation Authority, PO Box 278, George Town, Grand Cayman (tel: 949-7811).
Customs Department, PO Box 898GT, Grand Cayman (tel: 949-2473; fax: 945-1573).
Government Information Services, Broadcasting House, Grand Cayman (tel: 949-8092; fax: 949-5936).
Immigratioon Department (tel: 949-8344; fax: 949-8486).
Radio Cayman, PO Box 1110, George Town, Grand Cayman (tel: 949-7799).
Registrar of Companies, Ground Floor, Tower Building, Grand Cayman (tel: 949-7999; fax: 949-0969).

Internet sites
Cayman Islands information: http://www.cayman.com.ky/cayman.htm
Cayman Net News: http://www.caymannetnews.com

Central African Republic

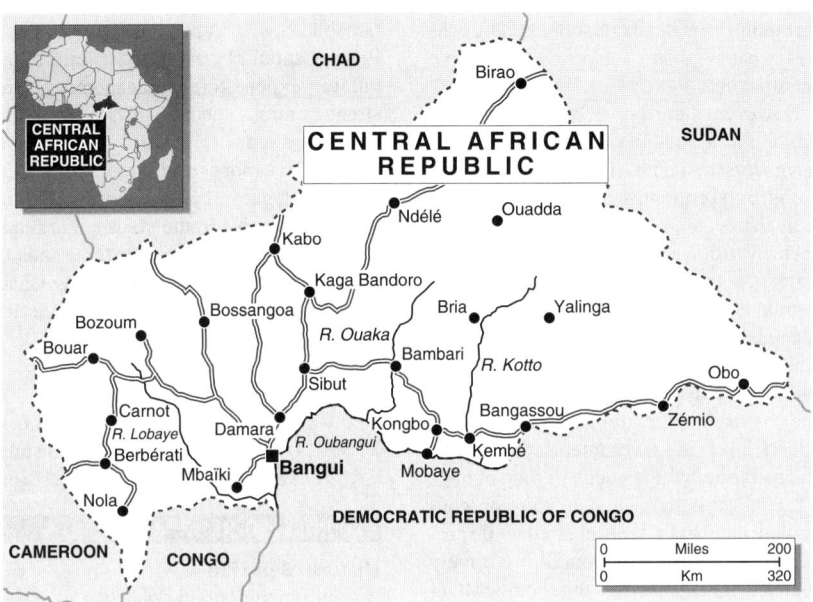

The Central African Republic (CAR) has been unstable since independence from France in 1960. During an internationally notorious period, self-declared emperor, Jean-Bedel Bokassa, presided over a brutal regime and pursued an extravagant lifestyle. The Bokassa era ended in 1979, when he was overthrown in a coup led by David Dacko, backed by French commandos based in the country. After just two years in office Dacko was toppled by André Kolingba, who eventually allowed multi-party presidential elections – and was duly rejected in the first round. Kolingba's successor, Ange-Félix Patassé, had to contend with serious unrest, which culminated in riots, and looting in 1997 by unpaid soldiers. In 1999, Patassé beat nine other candidates to become president again, although there were allegations of electoral fraud.

General Francois Bozizé took more than 64 per cent of the vote in the second round of the CAR's presidential elections in May 2005, ending two years of military rule. The newly elected president called for national unity. He had pledged in his campaign to bring security to the coup-prone country. He himself first took power in a 2003 coup, when he ousted the unpopular Ange-Félix Patassé – who was out of the country at the time. Bozizé promised to return the CAR to democratic rule and ran as an independent in the 2005 poll. He is no stranger to politics. He stood for president in the republic's first democratic elections in 1993, but lost to Patassé. Bozizé had previously led an unsuccessful coup in 1983 against military ruler Kolingba and was suspected of being involved in a coup attempt against Patassé in 2001, which was thwarted with the help of Libyan troops. Patassé was eventually overthrown, by Bozizé in 2003, and went into exile in Togo.

In 2005, Bozizé and his Convergence Nationale (Kwa Na Kwa) (KNK) (National Convergence) coalition won the May 2005 elections. He now has the support of civil society groups and the main political factions, and control of a country politically and economically destroyed by three tumultuous decades of misrule – mostly by military governments – which will take years to re-establish.

Economy

Subsistence agriculture and forestry are the traditional backbone of the economy of the CAR. Timber accounts for about 16 per cent of export earnings and the diamond industry for 54 per cent, yet the

KEY FACTS

Official name: République Centrafricaine (Central African Republic)

Head of State: President General François Bozizé (proclaimed himself president 15 Mar 2003; elected 8 May 2005)

Head of government: Prime Minister Elie Doté (from 13 Jun 2005)

Ruling party: A transitional government is in power, including members from all political parties and civic groups (the National Convergence coalition won the Mar 2005 elections).

Area: 622,984 square km

Population: 4.09 million (2004)

Capital: Bangui

Official language: French

Currency: CFA franc (CFAf) = 100 centimes (Communauté Financière Africaine (African Financial Community) franc)

Exchange rate: CFAf544.07 per US$ (Oct 2005); CFAf655.95 per euro (pegged from Jan 1999)

GDP per capita: US$331 (2004)

GDP real growth: 2.20% (2004)

Labour force: 1.85 million (2004)

Inflation: -2.20% (2004)

Balance of trade: US$32.00 million (2003)

agricultural sector as a whole generates half of the country's gross domestic product. There is understandable caution on the part of investors as they add to the mix the country's landlocked position, a poor transportation system, a largely unskilled work force, and a legacy of misdirected macroeconomic policies. Factional fighting between the government and its opponents remains a drag on economic revitalisation, with growth at 0.5 per cent in 2004. Distribution of income is extraordinarily unequal. Grants from France and the international community can only partially meet humanitarian needs.

In 2004, somewhat remarkably, the International Monetary Fund endorsed reports of economic growth of 2.2 per cent. A pick up in both private sector credit and net credit to government, although the increase in private sector credit, largely associated with petroleum imports and several large loans in the forestry sector late in the year, has partly receded.

But external debt payment arrears continue to accumulate to both bilateral and multilateral creditors – the most recent estimate is US$335 million or 25 per cent of gross domestic product. Serious weaknesses in public finances remain, and the large gap between expenditures and revenue continues to weigh heavily on the ability of the government to provide basic public services. While revenue increased in 2004, at around eight per cent of GDP, it is still very low even relative to other low-income African countries. Weaknesses in tax and customs administration, rooted partly in corruption, continue to hamper efforts to improve revenue performance.

There has been a serious loss of control on expenditure. Although salaries have been frozen since 1985, the public wage bill continues to increase because of the creation of high-level posts carrying salary premiums, and new recruitment paired with delays in retirements. Developments in the banking sector continue to be dominated by the government's heavy reliance on commercial banks' resources. The central bank has suspended reserve requirements.

However, it must be acknowledged that while social conditions in the country have worsened with life expectancy worsening by six months every year, significant achievements have been made on the security front and in ensuring a smooth transition to democratic rule. The presidential and legislative elections were conducted peacefully and were generally free. The security situation has improved with the support of several hundred troops from the country's international partners.

The level of government revenue remains far below the needs of the country. Taxes must be collected, corruption controlled, payment arrears cleared while current obligations are honoured in a timely manner. Longer-term, the competitiveness of the economy must be improved. This will require rebuilding the infrastructure, enhancing security, and advancing on structural reforms. Improved infrastructure – especially for land and river transport – and better security in rural areas will be instrumental in reducing costs faced by agricultural producers and exporters. Steps to strengthen the judiciary and improve property rights and contract enforcement should also contribute to reducing the cost of doing business in the CAR, and thereby enhancing competitiveness.

Outlook

Governance problems are at the heart of the weak management of public resources and the poor climate for private sector activity. The CAR's debt situation is unsustainable. Social indicators are very poor. Priority should be accorded to improving public expenditure management and strengthening tax and customs administration.

Illegal weapons proliferate across the CAR, the legacy of years of unrest. Armed groups are active in the volatile north and have prompted the flight of thousands of Central Africans into neighbouring Chad. Corruption is rife and mostly affects the timber and diamond industries.

Risk assessment

Economic	Poor
Political	Optimistic
Regional stability	Average

COUNTRY PROFILE

Historical profile

Among Africa's varied political and economic entities, since its independence in 1960 the Central African Republic (CAR) has had a more colourful history than most – for all the wrong reasons. In 1966, the notorious Jean-Bedel Bokassa seized power, declaring himself 'President for Life' in 1972, bestowing upon himself countless, and ever more absurd, military honours, a fixation that dated from his enthusiastic service in France's colonial army. In 1977, Bokassa went a stage further, crowning himself emperor in a ceremony that reportedly cost one quarter of the CAR annual income.

The CAR's strategic location in mid-Africa, bordering five other republics, meant that during the Cold War, France had little option but to pander to the erratic Bokassa's whims, providing budgetary and financial assistance to the ailing CAR. Bokassa brought the CAR to bankruptcy, but his own personal wealth, which he banked outside the country, was reported to be enormous. He also established an unwelcome precedent for the country's future governments, beset by corruption, instability and inefficiency at all levels.

1889 The French established themselves at Bangui.

1907 The colony of Oubangi-Shari (named after two main rivers) was founded.

1958 The country was proclaimed a republic.

KEY INDICATORS — Central African Republic

	Unit	2000	2001	2002	2003	2004
Population	m	3.72	3.80	3.86	3.97	4.09
Gross domestic product (GDP)	US$bn	0.97	0.98	1.10	1.17	*1.33
GDP per capita	US$	259	255	270	306	331
GDP real growth	%	2.6	1.5	2.0	-5.8	2.2
Inflation	%	3.2	3.8	2.3	4.2	-2.2
Exports (fob) (goods)	US$m	142.0	160.0	175.0	134.0	–
Imports (fob) (goods)	US$m	140.0	151.0	165.0	102.0	–
Balance of trade	US$m	2.0	9.0	10.0	32.0	–
Current account	US$m	-30.0	-20.0	-30.0	-60.0	-60.0
Total reserves minus gold	US$m	133.3	118.8	123.2	132.4	148.3
Foreign exchange	US$m	133.1	118.6	123.1	132.2	145.6
Exchange rate	per US$	711.98	733.04	683.75	574.89	496.63

* estimated figure

Central African Republic

1960 David Dacko became the president of the independent and newly named country
1966 Dacko's cousin, Jean-Bedel Bokassa, an army commander, seized power, declaring himself life-president in 1972.
1977 Bokassa crowned himself emperor – the coronation consumed about one quarter of the country's annual income.
1979 Bokassa's repressive regime was forced from office when French troops reinstated David Dacko.
1981 Dacko was ousted by the army chief of staff, General André Kolingba.
1986 Kolingba established a one-party state.
1990 Opposition groups united and forced the government to adopt a multi-party system.
1992 Elections were held but the results were nullified after several groups boycotted the poll.
1993 Ange-Félix Patassé became president in the first multi-party elections.
1995 A democratic constitution was adopted.
1996 Three episodes of army mutiny erupted, the last, in November, degenerated into ethnic violence and was suppressed by French troops in January 1997.
1997 Patassé appointed Michel Gbezera-Bira at the head of an 11-party coalition government.
1998 Parliamentary elections were indecisive.
1999 Some deputies defected to Patassé's Mouvement de Libération du Peuple Centrafricain (MLPC) (Movement for the Liberation of the Central African People) and it then had a slight majority. Presidential elections confirmed support for Patassé. France withdrew its troops.
2001 Libya sent troops to protect the Patassé from military overthrow.
2002 Rebels seized part of Bangui; they were fought off by the army, aided by Libyan warplanes.
2003 General François Bozizé led a military coup that captured Bangui while President Patassé was abroad. Bozizé proclaimed himself president, suspended the constitution and dissolved the National Assembly.
2004 The National Transitional Council created an independent commission to oversee elections. A new constitution was approved in December.
2005 The Convergence Nationale (Kwa Na Kwa) (KNK) (National Convergence) coalition won the May parliamentary elections and incumbent François Bozizé was elected president. Elie Doté was named as prime minister.

Political structure
Constitution
A new constitution was approved in December 2004.
Form of state
Republic
The executive
Under the new constitution, approved in December 2004, the presidential term has been reduced from six to five years. Presidents can only serve a maximum of two terms in office.
National legislature
The National Assembly has a five-year mandate.
Last elections
13 March 2005 (presidential and parliamentary)
Results: Presidential: incumbent François Bozizé won 64.7 per cent of the vote and Martin Ziguélé 35.3 per cent; turnout was 64.6 per cent.
Parliamentary: the Convergence Nationale 'Kwa Na Kwa') (KNK) (National Convergence 'Kwa Na Kwa') coalition won 42 seats out of 105 (including the Party for National Unity with three seats and the Movement for Democracy and Development with two), the Liberation Movement of the Central African People 11, the Central African Democratic Rally eight, the Social Democratic Party four, the Patriotic Front for Progress two, the Alliance for Democracy two, the Londo Association one and independents 34.
Next elections
2010 (presidential and parliamentary)

Political parties
Ruling party
A transitional government is in power, including members from all political parties and civic groups (the National Convergence coalition won the Mar 2005 elections).
Main opposition party
Mouvement de Libération du Peuple Centrafricain (MLPC) (Movement for the Liberation of the Central African People)

Population
4.09 million (2004)
Ethnic make-up
Bayas (34 per cent), Bandas (27 per cent), Manzas (21 per cent), Saras (10 per cent), Mbums (4 per cent), Mbakas (4 per cent)
Religions
About 24 per cent of the population hold traditional beliefs; 25 per cent Protestants; 25 per cent Catholics; 15 per cent Muslims.

Education
Only 60 per cent of eligible children receive education. Basic education lasts for 10 years divided into six years' basic first stage and four years' basic second stage. General secondary school lasts for three years, which gives access to higher education. Only 10 per cent of secondary school-aged children are enrolled due to limited resources. Technical education at the secondary level is offered at two levels. School instruction is primarily in French, but the government has sought to promote Sango literacy and encourages its use in schools.
Higher education is offered at the Université de Bangui, which also has a teacher training college.
Literacy rate: 59 per cent men, 33 per cent women; adult rates (World Bank).
Compulsory years: Six to 14

Health
Total expenditure on health is 4–5 per cent of GDP, of which government spending is 51 per cent.
Modern healthcare facilities exist only in Bangui (with one major hospital) and a few other towns.
In July 2004, CAR launched a 10-year programme to reduce maternal deaths and infant mortality rates.
HIV prevalence: 13.5 per cent aged 15–49 in 2003 (World Bank)
Life expectancy: 41.8 years (World Bank).
Fertility rate/Maternal mortality rate: 4.6 births woman; maternal mortality 1,100 per 100,000 live births (World Bank).
Infant mortality rate: 115 per 1,000 live births; 23 per cent of children under aged five are malnourished (World Bank).
Head of population per physician/bed: 0.1 physicians and 0.9 hospital beds available per 1,000 people (World Bank).

Welfare
Amnesty International reports that some 30,000 mostly Yakoma civilians and members of the armed forces had escaped to the neighbouring Democratic Republic of the Congo (DRC) and northern Republic of the Congo following the coup attempt in May 2001. Most refugees survived without basic humanitarian assistance and were prone to malnutrition for more than six months. The government started preparations to repatriate refugees from the DRC in December 2001, although efforts to stabilise the situation could falter without the support of international donors. The country is in deep poverty, with two out of three people earning less than US$1 a day. All social security programmes are administered by the Central African Social Security Office.
In the first half of 2002, the UN's World Food Programme (WFP) provided assistance to 6,000 internally displaced people mostly in Batangafo and Kabo for a period of three months. The WFP is expected to provide food rations until the end of the year despite drastic cuts in its food stock.

Main cities
Bangui (capital, estimated population 669,800 in 2003), Berbérati (65,000), Bouar (56,400).

Languages spoken
Sango, Banda, Baye and Zanda are widely spoken.
Official language/s
French

Media
Press
Dailies: The print media is relatively free from arbitrary government interference. There are some independent newspapers in circulation, although their influence remains limited. These include *Le Citoyen*, *L'Echo de Centrafrique*, *Le Novateur*, *L'Hirondelle* and *Le Démocrate*. The Sango-language *E Le Songo* is another daily published in Bangui.
Periodicals: A few periodicals are also published in Bangui, including *Journal Officiel de la République Centrafricaine*.
Broadcasting
Radio: The state-owned Radiodiffusion-Télévision Centrafrique broadcasts in Sango and French. The UN-sponsored Radio Ndeke Luka in Bangui rebroadcasts international news. Other radio services include *Radio Centrafrique*, *Radio Notre-Dame*, *Radio Nostalgie*, *Africa No 1* and *Radio France Internationale*.

Economy
The economy is dominated by subsistence agriculture and is vulnerable to the adverse effects of drought and of domestic and regional political strife. Diamonds are the principal export, accounting for over half all export earnings.

The Central African Republic's (CAR) landlocked position and relative isolation provide considerable problems in exploiting economic potential and foreign technical and financial assistance will remain necessary for some time. Poverty is hindering development. It is estimated that two-thirds of the population live on less than US$1 a day and CAR has one of the highest rates of urban poverty in Africa. The workforce is largely unskilled with only half of the population over 15 years of age being literate. The wealth of natural resources are largely unexploited with the exception of diamonds, which account for a large proportion of the country's exports.

Serious reform is necessary to attract foreign investment. The economy would be enhanced by improved transport facilities and domestic reforms by the government. Under pressure from the World Bank and the IMF, CAR has privatised state-owned enterprises and introduced other measures to encourage investment and combat corruption.

The Economic Community of Central African States (CEEAC), of which CAR is a member, is hoping to set up a free trade area by 2007, which should increase incentives to foreign investors as there will be immediate access to the 100 million consumers in the CEEAC trade agreement.

External trade
On 31 December 2002, the US approved the Central African Republic as being eligible for tariff preferences under the African Growth and Opportunities Act (AGOA). The legislation requires that countries are only eligible for greater access to US markets provided they have made continued progress toward a market-based economy, the rule of law, free trade, poverty reduction and the protection of workers' rights. This process is reviewed annually.
Imports
Principal imports are food, textiles, petroleum products, machinery, electrical equipment, motor vehicles, chemicals and pharmaceuticals.
Main sources: France (19.4 per cent total, 2004), US (16.3 per cent), Cameroon (8.3 per cent), Belgium (5.6 per cent)
Exports
Principal exports are diamonds, coffee, timber, cotton, tobacco, leather, natural rubber, gold, wax.
Main destinations: Belgium (41 per cent total, 2004), Italy (8.9 per cent), Spain (8.5 per cent), Indonesia (7.6 per cent), France (6.3 per cent), US (5.3 per cent)

Agriculture
Farming
Agriculture and forestry are the mainstays of the economy. Agriculture accounts for around 55 per cent of GDP and employs 66 per cent of the workforce. Around 12 per cent of the total land is arable; much of the rest is savannah.

The sector consists mainly of subsistence farming and animal husbandry. The main crops are maize, cassava, sorghum, groundnuts, sesame and rice. Cotton and tobacco are also cultivated. The main export crop is coffee.

Production is hampered by soil erosion, widespread drought and underdeveloped marketing and infrastructure, as well as poor internal security and mass migration. The estimated crop production for 2004 included: 201,800 tonnes (t) cereals in total, 119,000t maize, 350,000t yams, *100,000t taro, *563,000t cassava, 42,480t sorghum, 29,700t rice, *110,000t bananas, *80,000t plantains, 27,000t pulses, 1,014,000t roots and tubers, *26,100t citrus fruit, 73,462t oilcrops, 90,000t sugar cane, *243,800t fruit in total, 7,500t green coffee, 63,900t vegetables in total. Estimated livestock production included: 127,300t meat in total, 74,000t beef, 13,500t pig meat, 11,500t goat meat, 14,000t game meat, 4,000t poultry, *1,476t eggs, *65,000t milk, *13,000t honey, *9,460t cattle hides.
* estimate
Forestry
Forest covers 50 per cent of the country. There is significant forestry potential, including over 60 species of commercially viable trees, but it is under-exploited because of poor transport infrastructure. Exports of forest materials amounted to US$89.8 billion in 2004, while imports amounted to US$2.8 million
Production in 2004 included: 2,8 million cubic metres (cum) roundwood, 69,000cum sawnwood, 524,000cum sawlogs and veneers, 2.0 million cum woodfuel, 21,000t charcoal.

Industry and manufacturing
The industrial sector typically accounts for around 18 per cent of GDP and employs 9 per cent of the workforce. Manufacturing accounts for around 9 per cent of GDP.

Manufacturing is relatively small-scale and is concentrated in the brewing, tanning, food processing, soap manufacture and textile sectors. There are also import substitution industries such as motor cycle and bicycle assembly.

The main industrial centre is the Bangui district.

Tourism
The tourist sector is under-developed, although with a wealth of natural resources, the potential, especially for eco-tourism, is considerable. Tourism is expected to contribute 3.0 per cent to the economy in 2005 and provide employment to 2.4 per cent of the workforce.

Mining
The mining sector officially accounts for around 4 per cent of GDP, employs 3 per cent of the workforce and generates 40 per cent of the country's export earnings. Smuggling is endemic and production and trade is likely to be far higher than official estimates.

Around 80,000 autonomous artisanal miners are engaged in mining production, mostly of diamonds and gold. Diamond output is around 500,000 carats per year, over half of which are gem quality. Other mineral deposits include uranium, limestone, iron ore, copper and manganese. In mid-2003, the Bozizé government withdrew mining licences and seized mines belonging to foreigners and figures associated with the government of former president Patassé. The measures were

Central African Republic

taken as part of an anti-corruption campaign which targetted divested interests associated with vital revenue-generating sectors.

Hydrocarbons
There are no known oil or gas fields in the Central African Republic, but exploration is being undertaken in the expectation of locating deposits. The downstream oil industry relies on imports from neighbouring African countries. Petroleum products provide around 90 per cent of the country's energy demands and the revenue from taxes on refined oil products provides over 50 per cent of the total revenue from indirect taxes.

Energy
There is a strong dependence on imported fuels.
Around 80 per cent of electricity production is generated at the country's two hydro-stations: Boali and M'Bali, a joint project with the Democratic Republic of Congo.

Banking and insurance
Central bank
Banque des Etats de l'Afrique Centrale
Main financial centre
Bangui

Time
GMT plus one hour

Geography
The Central African Republic is a landlocked country in the heart of equatorial Africa. It is bounded by Chad to the north, and Sudan to the east, by the Republic of Congo and the Democratic Republic of Congo to the south and Cameroon to the west.

Climate
Hot all year with temperatures up to 36 degrees Celsius. The dry season runs from November–February with cooler nights. The rainy season runs from May–October.

Entry requirements
Passports
Required by all except certain African and French document holders.
Visa
Visas are required by all except citizens of France, Germany, Israel and Switzerland. Visas can be issued in neighbouring countries, generally within 24 hours but are expensive. Visas can be obtained in advance from the Central African Republic Embassy in Paris, 30 rue des Perchamps, 75116 Paris. A business letter and itinerary must accompany the application for a business visa.
Currency advice/regulations
No restrictions on import of foreign currency, but amount must be declared; export up to declared amount allowed.

Unlimited import of local currency; export limited to CFAf75,000.

Health (for visitors)
Mandatory precautions
Yellow fever vaccination certificate required by all.
Advisable precautions
Typhoid, tetanus, hepatitis A and polio vaccinations are recommended. Malaria prophylaxis should be taken as risk exists throughout country. There is a rabies risk. Water precautions are necessary – bilharzia risk in some areas. AIDS risk.

Hotels
Good standard hotels are available in Bangui – limited accommodation elsewhere. Where service charge is not included in bill a 10 per cent tip is usual.

Public holidays
Fixed dates
1 Jan (New Year's Day), 29 Mar (President Boganda's Remembrance Day), 13 Aug (Independence Day), 15 Aug (Assumption Day), 1 Nov (All Saints' Day), 1 Dec (National Day), 25 Dec (Christmas Day).
Variable dates
Easter Monday

Working hours
Banking
Mon–Fri: 0730–1130.
Business
Mon–Fri: 0730–1530.
Government
Mon–Fri: 0700–1200, 1430–1700; Sat: 0700–1200.
Shops
(Mon–Sat) 0800–1200; 1600–1900.

Electricity supply
220/380V AC, 50 cycles

Weights and measures
The metric system is used.

Getting there
Air
National airline: Air Afrique (Central African Republic is a shareholder). Air France and Sudan Airways serve CAR.
International airport/s: Bangui-M'Poko (Code: BGF), 4km from city, restaurant, post office, shops, car hire.

Getting about
National transport
Air: Small light aircraft can be chartered from Air Afrique.
Road: Eight main roads run from Bangui to the main towns and those that are surfaced are toll roads. The Trans-African Lagos-Mombasa highway passes through the Central African Republic. Most other roads can become impassable during rainy season. NB Spare parts and petrol stations tend to be sparse outside Bangui.

Buses: Limited coach service operates between Bangui and Bangassou.
Water: Large volume of freight carried on rivers. The principal trading route is on the Oubangui River south of the capital Bangui which runs into the River Congo, connecting Bangui to the former Zaïre and the Congo (including Brazzaville, from where railway runs to Pointe-Noire). Also services from Salo on the Sangha River.
City transport
Taxis: Available in Bangui; fares by negotiation.
Car hire
Self- or chauffeur-driven cars available. International driving licence required.

BUSINESS DIRECTORY

The addresses listed below are a selection only. While World of Information makes every endeavour to check these addresses, we cannot guarantee that changes have not been made, especially to telephone numbers and area codes. We would welcome any corrections.

Telephone area codes
Dialling code for Central African Republic: IDD access code +236 followed by subscriber's number.

Chambers of Commerce
Chambre de Commerce, d'Industrie, des Mines et d'Artisinat de Centrafrique, PO Box 252/ 813, Bangui (tel: 611.668; fax: 613-561; e-mail: ccima@intnet.cf).

Chambre de d'Agriculture, d'Elevage, des Eaux, Forêts, Chasses, Pêches et du Tourisme, PO Box 850, Bangui (tel:/fax: 619-052; e-mail: denissio@intnet.cf).

Banking
Banque de Crédit Agricole et de Développement, BP 801, Place de la République, Bangui (tel: 613-200).

Banque Internationale pour le Centrafrique, BP 910, Place de la République, Bangui (tel: 610-042; fax: 616-136, 613-438).

Banque Populaire Maroco-Centrafricaine, BP 844, Rue Guerlliot, Bangui (tel: 613-190, 611-290; fax: 616-230).

Caisse Nationale d'Epargne, BP 839, Siège social, Bangui (tel: 612-296).

Commercial Bank Centrafrique SA, BP 839, Rue de Brazza, Bangui (tel: 612-990; fax: 613-454).

Central bank
Banque des États de l'Afrique Centrale, Direction Nationale, PO Box 851, Bangui (tel: 612-405; fax: 611-995; e-mail: beacbgf@beac.int).

Travel information
Inter-RCA, BP 1413, Bangui.

Ministry of Water, Forests, Wildlife, Fisheries and Tourism, Bangui.

Office Centrafricain de Tourisme (OCATOUR), BP 655, Bangui (tel: 614-566).

Ministries

Ministry of Economy and Finance, Planning and International Co-operation, Bangui (tel: 610-811).

Ministry of Energy, Mines, Geology and Water Resources, Bangui.

Ministry of Posts and Telecommunications, Bangui (tel: 612-946).

Ministry of Rural Development, Bangui (tel: 612-800).

Ministry of Trade, Industry and Small- and Medium-scale Enterprises, Bangui (tel: 614-488).

Ministry of Transport and Civil Aviation, Bangui (tel: 612-307).

Other useful addresses

Central African Republic Embassy (USA), 1618 22nd Street, NW, Washington DC 20008 (tel: 202-483-7800; fax: 202-332-9893).

European Development Fund, BP 1298, Bangui (tel: 613-053, 610-113).

Office of the President, Palais de la Renaissance, Bangui (tel: 610-323).

Société Centrafricaine de Développement Agricole (SOCADA), ave David Dacko, BP 997, Bangui (tel: 613-033).

Internet sites

Africa Business Network: http://www.ifc.org/abn

AllAfrica.com: http://allafrica.com

African Development Bank: http://www.afdb.org

Africa Online: http://www.africaonline.com

Harambee Afrika (UK business club for traders with east, central and southern Africa; includes annotated web resource list): http://www.harambee.co.uk

Mbendi AfroPaedia (information on companies, countries, industries and stock exchanges in Africa): http://mbendi.co.za

Chad

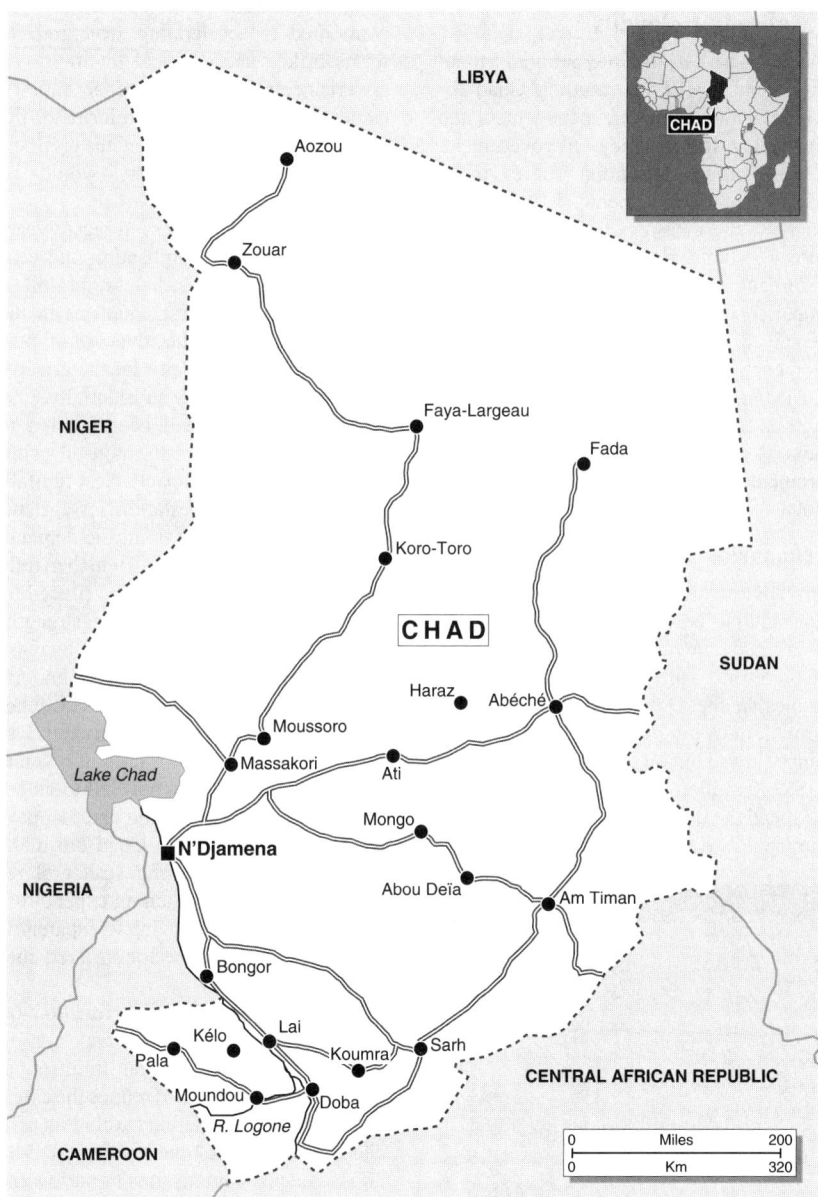

KEY FACTS

Official name: République du Tchad (Republic of Chad)

Head of State: President Colonel Idriss Déby (MPS) (since 1990; re-elected 21 May 2001)

Head of government: Prime Minister Pascal Yoadimnadji (from 3 Feb 2005)

Ruling party: Mouvement Patriotique du Salut (MPS) (Patriotic Movement for Salvation) (re-elected Apr 2002)

Area: 1,284,000 square km

Population: 8.21 million (2004)

Capital: N'Djamena

Official language: French and Arabic

Currency: CFA franc (CFAf) = 100 centimes (Communauté Financière Africaine (African Financial Community) franc)

Exchange rate: CFAf544.07 per US$ (Oct 2005); CFAf655.95 per euro (pegged from Jan 1999)

GDP per capita: US$523 (2004)

GDP real growth: 30.50% (2004)

Labour force: 4.02 million (2004)

Inflation: -4.80% (2004)

Oil production: 168,000 bpd (2004)

Balance of trade: -US$690.00 million (2004)

In an unexpected display of displeasure at a development agreement with Chad being virtually torn up by that country, the World Bank in January 2006 withheld new loans and grants and suspended the disbursement of US$124 million International Development Association funds. It froze Chad's account at Citibank, London, into which revenues from the transfer of oil through a pipeline to Cameroon are paid. Chad had amended its Petroleum Revenue Management Law, which, said the Bank, would substantially weaken programmes intended to improve the lives of Chad's poor which the World Bank had been supporting. The Bank's action will reverberate around the donor-world.

Nations of the World: A Political, Economic and Business Handbook

World Bank withdraws ...

Chad had fundamentally altered the Petroleum Revenue Management Law which was the basis for the agreement, the Bank alleged. It said oil revenues which under the agreement would have been used to alleviate poverty would be diverted to address pressing financial difficulties of the government. The Bank had previously offered to assist the government of Chad to address those difficulties by analysing the relevant financial issues and how public finances should be managed. It had also proposed a review of how the law would be implemented. In the run-up to the passage of the amendments, the Bank had expressed its concern and remained open to dialogue with the government on the best ways to address its current financial crisis while protecting poverty reduction programmes.

The law was, in the Bank's analysis, the deciding factor in its support for the Chad–Cameroon oil pipeline project, which represented a unique opportunity for Chad to use its oil revenues to finance desperately needed poverty reduction. As part of the loan agreement with the World Bank, the government of Chad specifically undertook not to amend or waive any provisions of the law in ways that would 'materially and adversely affect' the direction of revenue to agreed priority sectors such as health, education and rural development. A Future Generations Fund ensured there would be some benefits to the population once the oil reserves were exhausted.

The government added more priority sectors – essentially territorial administration and security – and eliminated the Future Generations Fund, allowing the transfer of more than US$36 million already accumulated there to the general budget. It also gave itself the power to add more priority sectors by decree and doubled the share of royalties and dividends that could be allocated to non-priority sectors.

... after IMF plaudits

One year earlier, the International Monetary Fund (IMF) was lauding Chad for strengthening economic management and improving transparency in government. Chad had made substantial progress in the transparent management of its oil resources, and measures to curtail expenditure in response to substantial shortfalls in external budget support and non-oil revenue. Economic growth was high, inflation remained subdued, and the external position continued to strengthen. At that time, the IMF also approved a three year US$40 million package for Chad to be spent on poverty reduction and to support the government's economic programme into 2008.

Economy

In 2004, earnings from Chad's primarily agricultural economy became insignificant beside the promise of US$2.5 billion in oil revenues after finds by two US companies in the Doba basin. Total export growth rates hit 200 per cent. They have since slowed but oil exports are on track at US$200 million a year. This issue of how to spend the oil simmers, but the oil keeps flowing.

The non-oil targets of Chad's development programmes are to create conditions for sustained private sector-led growth and poverty reduction. Within this overall framework, the programmes focus on consolidating the fiscal position through measures to enhance non-oil revenue collection, and strengthen the budgetary process and spending policy.

Chad had convinced the IMF it was committed to accelerating structural reforms in key areas critical for improved governance and increased economic efficiency. It had emphasised reforms of the cotton and energy sectors and the civil service. The cotton industry would be privatised.

Chad has made progress in recent years in macroeconomic stabilisation and economic reforms. Nevertheless, pre-oil it was one of the poorest countries in the world. The IMF saw the advent of oil production as an opportunity for the government to reduce poverty substantially.

In 2004, growth had been limited to about two per cent in the non-oil economy, because of the impact of low rainfall, the desert locust infestation on agricultural output, and weak domestic demand. Inflation remained subdued, which mainly reflected a bumper crop in the preceding year. Chad's external position strengthened further with the significant increase in oil exports and the decline in imports following the completion of the oil pipeline. Fiscal performance was mixed. Despite spending cuts, shortfalls in revenue and external budget support led to an accumulation of domestic and external payments arrears. Although Chad did make progress in implementing structural reforms aimed at strengthening expenditure management and improving transparency, reforms in the cotton sector suffered considerable delays.

Macroeconomic objectives for 2005–07 are to achieve an annual real non-oil growth of 5.5 per cent a year; limit annual inflation to 3 per cent and reduce the external current account deficit (excluding official transfers) to 4.4 per cent of GDP by 2007. The programme aims to narrow the non-oil primary base deficit to 4.1 per cent of non-oil GDP by 2007, through the implementation of measures to strengthen non-oil revenue performance and a prudent expenditure policy. Structural reforms to strengthen budgetary procedures, as well as expenditure and cash management will be critical.

KEY INDICATORS — Chad

	Unit	2000	2001	2002	2003	2004
Population	m	7.89	7.90	8.10	8.16	8.21
Gross domestic product (GDP)	US$bn	1.40	1.60	2.00	1.76	*4.29
GDP per capita	US$	182	202	247	216	523
GDP real growth	%	1.0	8.5	10.9	11.8	30.5
Inflation	%	3.7	12.4	4.5	2.8	-4.8
Oil output	'000 bpd	–	–	–	–	168.0
Exports (fob) (goods)	US$m	181.0	191.0	177.0	197.0	–
Imports (fob) (goods)	US$m	243.0	560.0	867.0	570.0	–
Balance of trade	US$m	-62.0	-369.0	-690.0	-373.0	-690.0
Current account	US$m	-250.0	-590.0	-1,115.0	-1,040.0	-760.0
Total reserves minus gold	US$m	110.7	122.4	218.7	187.1	221.7
Foreign exchange	US$m	110.3	122.0	218.3	186.7	221.2
Exchange rate	per US$	711.98	733.04	696.99	574.89	496.63

* estimated figure

Chad

Politics

Chad endured three decades of civil warfare as well as invasions by Libya before a semblance of peace was finally restored in 1990. The government eventually suppressed or came to terms with most political-military groups, settled a territorial dispute with Libya on terms favorable to Chad, drafted a democratic constitution, and held multi-party presidential elections in 1996 which were won by Idriss Déby. He was re-elected in 2001. Voters have backed a change to the constitution which will allow Déby to stand for a third term in 2006. The opposition cried foul.

Chad's post-independence history has been marked by instability and violence stemming mostly from tension between the mainly Arab-Muslim north and the predominantly Christian and animist south. In 1969 Muslim dissatisfaction with the first president, Ngarta Tombalbaye – a Christian southerner – had developed into a guerrilla war. This, combined with a severe drought, undermined his rule and in 1975 President Tombalbaye was killed in a coup led by another southerner, Felix Malloum. Malloum, too, failed to end the war, and in 1979 he was replaced by a Libyan-backed northerner, Goukouki Oueddei. But the fighting continued, this time with a former defence minister, Hissèné Habré, on the opposite side.

In 1982, with French help, Habré captured the capital, N'Djamena, and Oueddei escaped to the north, where he formed a rival government. The standoff ended in 1990, when Habré was toppled by the Libyan-backed Déby.

Outlook

Despite movement toward democratic reform, power in Chad remains in the hands of an ethnic minority. Rebellion sporadically flares in the north despite two peace agreements signed in 2002 and 2003 between the government and the rebels. 2006 is unlikely to see this change.

Risk assessment

Economic	Improving
Political	Poor/improving
Regional stability	Improving

COUNTRY PROFILE

Historical profile

Once described as a land of lost opportunities, this huge land-locked state with its reserves of gold, uranium and oil remains one of the world's poorest countries.
Chad's post-independence governments have failed to give the country the unified platform it requires for serious economic development. Instead, Chad has been plagued with innumerable variations on the themes of civil war, human rights violations, regional conflicts, economic mismanagement and rampant corruption.
1900s France defeated the local ruler, Rabeh Zubeit, at a battle in Kousseri in 1916, and the territory of Chad was formed.
1929 A northern, Saharan, segment was added.
1946 Chad was granted status as a French overseas territory and gained its own regional assembly.
1960 Chad was granted independence. A one-party regime was imposed under President Francois Tombalbaye. A series of rebellions against Tombalbaye's rule were repressed.
1975 Tombalbaye was killed in a coup and replaced by Colonel Félix Malloum. Malloum agreed to share power with a rebel leader, Hissène Habré.
1979 Habré forced Malloum out of N'Djamena after a violent power struggle.
1980 A new alliance was formed between Habré and Goukouni Oueddei, which lasted until 1980 when Libya sided with Goukouni and Habré fled. Libyan troops and Chadian factions defeated Habré, at which point France intervened and the invading force was driven back from N'Djamena, leaving Habré in nominal control of the country.
1987 After several years of stalemate, an effort was made to resolve the conflict by President Mitterand of France and Colonel al Qadafi of Libya, who both agreed to withdraw their forces from Chad. The French troops withdrew but those of Libya did not. The French returned and pushed Libya back across the Chad-Libya border.
1989–90 A rebellion was launched by Idriss Déby, an army commander. Habré fled to Senegal and Déby proclaimed himself president.
1996 In Chad's first multi-party presidential elections, Idriss Déby was elected to remain as Chad's president.
1997 Legislative elections were won by the Mouvement Patriotique du Salut (MPS) (Patriotic Movement for Salvation).
2001 President Déby was re-elected. A peace agreement was signed in Libya between the Chadian government and the northern rebel movement, Mouvement pour la Démocratie et la Justice au Tchad (MDJT) (Movement for Democracy and Justice in Chad).
2002 The ruling MPS won the parliamentary elections. Haroun Kabadi was appointed prime minister by the president after the resignation of Nagoum Yamassoum.
2003 In January, Chad and the Central African Republic began peace talks. Moussa Faki became prime minister on 24 June and formed his cabinet. Chad became an oil exporter, with the opening of a pipeline from its oil fields to Cameroon.
2004 Early in the year, thousands of Sudanese refugees arrived in Chad to escape unrest in the Darfur region of western Sudan; in April, the fighting spilled across the border and Chadian troops clashed with pro-Sudanese government militias.
2005 On 3 February, Prime Minister Moussa Faki resigned and was replaced by Pascal Yoadimnadji.

Political structure
Constitution
A referendum in March 1996 passed (with 61.46 per cent of votes) a constitution based on the French model, providing for a unitary state.
Form of state
Republic
The executive
The executive branch consists of the president who is head of state, and the prime minister and cabinet. The president is elected by popular vote to serve a five-year term; the prime minister is appointed by the president.
National legislature
The legislature consists of a National Assembly (155 seats; members elected by popular vote to serve four-year terms).
Legal system
Based on the French civil law system and customary law.
Last elections
21 April 2002 (parliamentary); 20 May 2001 (presidential).
Results: Parliamentary: the ruling Mouvement Patriotique du Salut (MPS) (Patriotic Movement for Salvation) won 112 seats out of 155, Rassemblement pour la Démocratie et le Progrès (RDP) (Rally for Democracy and Progress) 10 seats and Front des Forces d'Action pour la République (FAR) (Front of Action Forces for the Republic) nine seats.
Next elections
2006 (presidential and parliamentary)

Political parties
Ruling party
Mouvement Patriotique du Salut (MPS) (Patriotic Movement for Salvation) (re-elected Apr 2002)
Main opposition party
Rassemblement pour la Démocratie et le Progrès (RDP) (Rally for Democracy and Progress).

Population
8.21 million (2004)
Ethnic make-up
There are 200 distinct groups of Chadeans. In the north and centre: Arabs,

Gorane (Toubou, Daza, Kreda), Zaghawa, Kanembou, Ouaddai, Baguirmi, Hadjerai, Fulbe, Kotoko, Hausa, Boulala, and Maba, most of whom are Muslim; in the south: Sara (Ngambaye, Mbaye, Goulaye), Moundang, Moussei, Massa, most of whom are Christian or animist. About 1,000 French citizens live in Chad. Of the population, 48 per cent of over 15s can read and write.

Religions
Muslim (44 per cent), traditional beliefs, Christians (33 per cent).

Education
As reform in the education sector has been slow following from the period of disturbances, local communities continue to play a greater role in financing and operating their schools. To rebuild the education system, the government of Chad developed an Education-Training-Employment strategy for 1990–2000 with the help of the International Labour Organisation, and other UN development agencies.

French is the primary language of instruction in most higher education institutions. The University of N'Djamena is the country's main university, with three faculties.

Literacy rate: 45.8 per cent total, 37.5 per cent female; adult rates (World Bank).

Enrolment rate: 73 per cent gross primary enrolment, 12 per cent gross secondary enrolments; of relevant age groups, inlcuding repeaters (World Bank).

Pupils per teacher: 67 in primary schools.

Health
As one of the poorest countries in the world, Chad has the largest proportion of external resources committed to health at 62.9 per cent of all spending on healthcare.

Unicef and the Public Health Ministry have begun a campaign to inoculate nearly 90,000 children - half of them Sudanese refugees - against measles in the most remote areas, in 2004; their target is children aged between six months and 15 years. As well as the inoculations, staff will distribute Vitamin A to children to reinforce their immune systems and protect them from blindness.

Total expenditure on health, is 2–3 per cent of GDP, of which government spending is 80 per cent.

HIV prevalence: 4.8 per cent aged 15–49 in 2003 (World Bank)

Life expectancy: 48.3 years (World Bank)

Fertility rate/Maternal mortality rate: 6.2 births per woman (World Bank)

Infant mortality rate: 117 per 1,000 live births (World Bank)

Head of population per physician/bed: Less than 0.05 physicians and 0.7 hospital beds available per 1,000 people (World Bank)

Welfare
An old age pension is paid at age 55 to workers with full contributions who pay 2 per cent of their wages. An employer pays 10 per cent of a worker's wage overall, for old age, disability and survivors' pensions. The government does not pay social security benefits. Roughly half the workforce has no jobs.

While Chad remains a traditional society, the role of women is expected to remain unchanged. Female Genital Mutilation (FGM) is practiced on 60 per cent of females, prior to puberty; and girls as young as 11 may be forced into an arranged marriage. Wives are subservient to their husbands and domestic violence is not uncommon. In 2003 a law was passed prohibiting FGM.

Main cities
N'Djamena (capital, formerly Fort Lamy, estimated population 609,600 in 2003), Moundou (127,500), Sarh (86,700), Abéché (62,700).

Languages spoken
The language group in Chad is Afro-Asiatic; Arabic is spoken by most of the population and there are more than 50 African dialects.

Official language/s
French and Arabic

Media
Press
There are some independent newspapers that circulate freely in the capital, N'Djamena, but have little impact among the largely rural and illiterate population. Weeklies include *Le Progres*, *N'Djamena Hebdo* (independent), *Le Contact* (bi-weekly) and *Le Temps*. A few newspapers and periodicals are published, including *Info-Tchad* (a daily news bulletin) and *Journal Officiel de la République du Tchad*. *L'Observateur* is an independent bi-monthly publication.

Broadcasting
Radio: The state primarily controls the broadcast media. Radio is the main medium of mass communication. Government radio station, Radio Diffusion Nationale Tchadienne, broadcasts from N'Djamena, with stations at Moundou, Sarh and Abéché. Private commercial radio hardly exists due to high licensing fees. The Catholic Church owns one private radio station.

Television: The only television station, Télé-Chad, is state-owned and its coverage favours the government. Télé-Chad has transmitted since December 1987 in French and Arabic.

Economy
Chad is one of the poorest countries in the world, brought about by drought, civil war and permanent instability. It has been highly dependent on cotton exports, the value of which varies considerably as prices fluctuate on the world market and the climate changes. The completion of the Doba oil pipeline (allowing Chad to export its oil production via Cameroon) in July 2003, however, is set to double Chad's GDP, as well as the government's income. Despite production predicted to peak at 225,000 barrels per day (bpd), the country will remain dependent on imports of refined petroleum products as there are no refineries in Chad.

The agricultural sector, which until 2003 accounted for the bulk of GDP, employment and export earnings, was hit by adverse weather conditions in 2002 and 2003, leading to a down turn in cotton output. Then in 2004 a plague of locusts destroyed large areas of maize, millet and sorghum.

The economy has been undergoing a programme of liberalisation under the auspices of the IMF's Poverty Reduction and Growth Facility (PRGF). This has been coupled with debt service relief under an enhanced Heavily Indebted Poor Countries (HIPC) initiative.

Under the regime of liberalisation, the government has privatised public enterprises, aimed to secure macroeconomic stability and strengthen its fiscal position, as well as bring down inflation. In terms of broad indicators, the programme has brought mixed success. Between 1996–2000, inflation fell from 11.3 to 3.7 per cent. After a 12.4 per cent increase in 2001, it fell again until by 2004 it was a negative -4.8 per cent. Meanwhile GDP has risen sharply, to 30.5 per cent in 2004, on the back of oil production and exports. Chad in 2005 is one of the fastest growing economies in the world, even though in 2004 GDP per capita was a mere US$112, one of the lowest in the world.

External trade
On 31 December 2002, the US approved Chad as being eligible for tariff preferences under the African Growth and Opportunities Act (AGOA). The legislation requires that countries are only eligible for greater access to US markets provided they have made continued progress toward a market-based economy, the rule of law, free trade, poverty reduction and the protection of workers' rights. This process is reviewed annually.

Imports
Principal imports are machinery and transportation equipment, industrial goods, petroleum products, foodstuffs and textiles.

Main sources: France (22.9 per cent total, 2004), Cameroon (13.7 per cent), US (11.8 per cent), Portugal (10.9 per cent), Germany (7.7 per cent), Belgium (4.8 per cent)

Exports
Principal exports are oil, raw cotton (typically 48 per cent of total), textiles, fish, meat and cattle, hides, natron, gum arabic and resins.
Main destinations: US (74.2 per cent total, 2004), China (14.8 per cent), Portugal (5.2 per cent)

Agriculture
Farming
The agricultural sector forms the mainstay of the economy, accounting for around 40 per cent of GDP and 60 per cent of employment. Around 20 per cent of land is arable and most of this is the southern flood plains of the Logone and Chari rivers.
Rice is produced on the irrigated land along the banks of the Oubangi river north of Lake Chad. Subsistence farming and livestock predominate in the north.
The country's main food crops are sorghum, millet, dry beans, sesame, potatoes, rice and maize. Cash crops include oil seeds (groundnuts and sesame), sugar cane and tobacco. Cotton is the most important agricultural product.
Cattle farming involves nearly 40 per cent of the population. It contributes 39 per cent to total agricultural production and 20 per cent to Chad's GDP. About 90 per cent of beef production is exported to Nigeria.
In 2004 the worst locust plague for 15 years attacked crops across much of west Africa and the Sahel region of southern Sahara. The UN organised a nine-country response group with Morocco and Algeria sending aid of vehicles and pesticide but, a year after the warning was first given, it was estimated that only 3 per cent of the 4.3 million hectares that required spraying were treated. Mauritania is the hatching ground for the largest swarms, although the insects are breeding elsewhere in the region.
Crop production for 2004 included: 1,394,000 tonnes (t) cereals in total, 400,000t groundnuts in shell, *325,000t cassava, *430,000t millet, *120,000t maize, *230,000t yams, *560,000t sorghum, 109,000t rice, *121,000t pulses, 684,000t roots and tubers, 176,690t oilcrops, 366,000t sugar cane, 64,000T sweet potatoes, 233,000t seed cotton, 81,5000t cotton lint, *113,000t fruit in total, *95,000t vegetables in total. Estimated livestock production included: 125,123t meat in total, 80,160t beef, 481t pig meat, 13,282t lamb, 21,438t goat meat, 3,200t game meat, 1,386t camel meat, 4,900t poultry, 4,680t eggs, 238,783t milk, *960t honey, 14,696t cattle hides, 2,239t sheepskins.
* estimate

Industry and manufacturing
The industrial sector contributes around 15 per cent of GDP and employs 10 per cent of the workforce.
The sector is small-scale and underdeveloped. Activity is centred in N'Djamena, Moundou and Sarh and is based on agriculture, particularly food processing, textiles, brewing, tobacco processing, leather and construction materials.

Tourism
Tourist arrivals increased by 10.26 per cent in 2003, compared to 2002. The World Travel and Tourism Council forecast in 2004 that tourism will grow at an annualised rate of 7.70 per cent over the period 2005–14.

Mining
Mining contributes less than 3 per cent to GDP. The only minerals extracted in any quantities are soda and rock salt (which are exported mainly to Nigeria) and natron from Lake Chad (used in preservation of meat and in tanning).
Known deposits of chromium, tungsten, titanium, iron, wolfram, gold, uranium and tin remain unexploited.
Other mineral deposits are thought to lie in the disputed Aouzou Strip along the Libyan border.

Hydrocarbons
West Africa is one of the world's fastest growing oil regions. It is projected that 25 per cent of US oil imports will be from this region by 2010. The development of Chad's oil industry is the subject of intense debate, although it could hold the key to the country's development. Chad has proven oil reserves of one billion barrels, most of which is located in the Doba basin. In November 1996, a consortium (Exxon Mobil (40 per cent), Royal Dutch/Shell (40 per cent), Elf Aquitaine (20 per cent)) signed a memorandum of understanding (MOU) with the government to develop the Doba fields and construct a 1,070km pipeline to offshore facilities in Cameroon. In April 2000, Chevron and Petronas replaced TotalFinaElf and Royal Dutch/Shell in the consortium. Development of the project began in October 2000 and was completed ahead of schedule in July 2003. Both the development of the oil fields and the construction of the pipeline have been the subject of political wrangling. While politicians squabble over oil revenues, organisations involved in environmental protection and human rights have criticised the Chad-Cameroon pipeline. The World Bank (which provided US$200 million of financing for the US$3.70 billion project) initially hailed the project as a model of poverty alleviation in Africa, but, according to its critics, the Doba development will increase regional problems, particularly in relation to conflict and corruption. Oil production in 2003 was 40,000 barrels per day (bpd) and Chad started exporting oil with the opening of the pipeline connecting its oil fields with Cameroon.
Chad's upstream oil industry is entirely reliant on imports of refined oil products from Nigeria and Cameroon. All energy requirements are fuelled by petroleum, athough currently Chad has no refinery. There are plans to build a small refinery in N'Djamena to process the oil from Sedigi in the Lake Chad Basin. The upfield oil industry is regulated by the Ministry of Mines, Energy and Oil.
Chad is not known to have either natural gas or coal reserves.

Energy
Chad has an installed electricity generation capacity of 29MW with electricity generation of 90 million kWh. Only 2 per cent of the population have access to electricity. The electricity supply is provided by two power stations in N'Djamena and plants in Moundou, Sarh and Abéché. Imports from Nigeria and Cameroon provide most of Chad's power requirements.
The Société Tchadienne d'Eau et d'Électricité (STEE) is the company responsible for electricity generation and supply in Chad. STEE is scheduled for privatisation under the terms of the country's IMF structural adjustment programme.

Banking and insurance
The banking sector was fully privatised in 1999. The two main banks in Chad are the Banque Internationale de l'Afrique au Tchad (BIAT) and the Société Générale de Banque Tchadienne (SGBT).
Central bank
Banque des Etats de l'Afrique Centrale.
Main financial centre
N'Djamena

Time
GMT plus one hour

Geography
Chad is a landlocked country in north central Africa, bordered to the north by Libya, to the south by the Central African Republic, to the west by Niger and Cameroon and to the east by Sudan.

Climate
Hot and arid in northern desert regions, and wet and tropical in the south. Southern rainy season from May to October, central rainy season from June to September with temperatures ranging from 20 degrees Celsius (C) at night to as high as

40 degrees C during the day. Dry season throughout the rest of the year, lower evening temperatures.

Entry requirements
Passports
Required by all except nationals of certain African countries. Passports must be valid for three months.
Visa
Required by all, except a number of nationals of West and Central Africa. Business visa applications must be accompanied by a letter from an employer/company stating the purpose of the visit.
All visitors must register with authorities on arrival. Exit permits must also be obtained if leaving via Niger or Sudan.
Currency advice/regulations
No restriction on import of foreign currency, but amounts must be declared; export limited to declared amount.
Unlimited import of local currency which must also be declared.

Health (for visitors)
Mandatory precautions
Yellow fever vaccination certificate required if arriving from an infected area.
Advisable precautions
Hepatitis A, tetanus, typhoid and polio vaccinations. Malaria prophylaxis recommended as risk exists throughout the country. There is a rabies risk. Water precautions necessary outside the capital.

Hotels
Reservations should be made well in advance of visit. If service charge is not included in bill a 10 per cent tip is usual. Limited availability outside of N'Djamena.

Public holidays
Fixed dates
1 Jan (New Year's Day), 13 Apr (National Day), 1 May (Labour Day), 25 May (Africa Day), 11 Aug (Independence Day), 1 Nov (All Saints' Day), 28 Nov (Proclamation of the Republic), 1 Dec (Day of Liberty and Democracy), 25 Dec (Christmas Day).
Variable dates
Easter Monday, Eid al Adha, Eid al Fitr. The Islamic year contains 354 or 355 days, with the result that Muslim feasts advance by 10–12 days against the Gregorian calendar. Dates of feasts vary according to the sighting of the new moon, so cannot be forecast exactly. Islamic year 1426: 10 February 2005 to 30 January 2006.

Working hours
Banking
Mon–Thu and Sat: 0700–1100; Fri: 0700–1030.
Business
Mon–Sat: 0900–1230, 1600–1930.

Government
Mon–Thu and Sat: 0700–1400; Fri: 0700–1200. Specific times vary within this period.

Electricity supply
220V AC, 50 cycles

Getting there
Air
National airline: Air Tchad (98 per cent government-owned).
International airport/s: N'Djamena (NDJ), 4km from city. Post office, bank, refreshments, bar and duty-free.
Limited flights from surrounding countries and Paris, France.
Airport tax: CFAf5000 (tourist tax) and CFAf3000 (security tax), except students and transit passengers continuing their journey within 24 hours.
Surface
Road: Access is possible by road from Bangui (Central African Republic), from Maroua (Cameroon), Niger and Sudan. Road conditions are variable and access can be very difficult, especially in the rainy season.
Water: The main overland points of entry are by ferry across the Chari River to N'Djamena from Cameroon, or from Maiduguri (Nigeria), via Cameroon.

Getting about
National transport
Air: Restricted domestic service operated by Air Tchad. Scheduled services occasionally commandeered by armed forces.
Road: There are surfaced roads around N'Djamena; most other roads are not in good condition and are often impassable during rainy season (Jun–Oct). Permits and four-wheel drive vehicles required for all travel outside N'Djamena.
City transport
Taxis: Available in N'Djamena and the principal towns – Sarh and Moundou; set-fare system in operation; 10 per cent tip is usual; can be hired on a time basis or by the day.
Car hire
Limited availablity in N'Djaména. French or international driving licence is required.

BUSINESS DIRECTORY

Telephone area codes
The international dialling code (IDD) for Chad is + 235 followed by subscriber's number.

Chambers of Commerce
Chad Chamber of Commerce, Industry, Agriculture, Mines and Handicrafts, PO Box 458, N'Djamena (tel: 525-264; fax: 521-452; e-mail: cciamat@hotmail.com).

Banking
Banque Agricole du Soudan au Tchad, BP 1727, 1727 NDjamena (tel: 519-041, 519-042; fax: 519-040).

Banque Commerciale du Chari Tchad, BP 757, NDjamena (tel: 515-958, 515-231; fax: 516-249).

Banque de Développement du Tchad, BP 19, NDjamena (tel: 522-829, 523-284; fax: 523-318).

Banque Internationale pour l'Afrique au Tchad, BP 87, Ave Charles de Gaulle, NDjamena (tel: 525-684, 524-321; fax: 523-053, 522-345).

Banque Tchadienne de Crédit et de Dépôts, BP 461, NDjamena (tel: 524-203, 522-801, 524-195; fax: 523-713).

Financial Bank, BP 804, NDjamena (tel: 523-389, 522-660; fax: 522-905).

Central bank
Banque des États de l'Afrique Centrale, Direction Nationale, PO Box 50, N'Djamena (tel: 525-014; fax: 524-487; e-mail: beacndj@beac.int).

Travel information
Air Tchad, 27 Avenue du Président Tombalbaye, BP 168, N'Djaména (tel: 515-090, 513-581, 514-564).

Direction du Tourisme, BP 86, N'Djaména (tel: 515-032, 512-303, 512-305).

Ethiopian Airlines, BP 989, N'Djaména (tel: 513-027, 513-143).

Sudan Airways, BP 167, N'Djaména (tel: 515-148).

Other useful addresses
Chad Embassy (USA), 2002 R Street, NW, Washington DC 20009 (tel: 202-462-4009; fax: 202-265-1937; e-mail: info@chadembassy.org).

Chambre Consulaire du Tchad, BP 458, N'Djamena (tel: 515-264).

Commission for Trade and Industry, BP 453, N'Djamena (tel: 515-656).

European Development Fund, BP 532, N'Djamena (tel: 515-977, 512-276).

Office National des Céréales (ONC), BP 21, N'Djamena (tel: 513-731, 574-014).

Internet sites
Africa Business Network:
http://www.ifc.org/abn

AllAfrica.com: http://allafrica.com

African Development Bank:
http://www.afdb.org

Africa Online:
http://www.africaonline.com

Chad: http://www.tchadrepertoire.com

Chile

KEY FACTS

Official name: República de Chile (Republic of Chile)

Head of State: President Ricardo Lagos Escobar (CPD) (since Jan 2000)

Head of government: President Ricardo Lagos Escobar

Ruling party: Concertación de Partidos por la Democracia (CPD) (Coalition of Pro-Democracy Parties) (centre-left coalition, comprising the Partido Demócrata Christiano (PDC) (Christian Democratic Party), Partido Radical Social Demócrata (PRSD) (Social Democratic Radical Party), Partido Socialista (PS) (Socialist Party) and Partido por la Democracia (PPD) (Party for Democracy) (re-elected Dec 2001)

Area: 756,626 square km

Population: 15.48 million (2004)

Capital: Santiago

Official language: Spanish

Currency: Chilean peso (CH$) = 100 centavos

Exchange rate: CH$528.75 per US$ (Oct 2005)

GDP per capita: US$5,856 (2004)

GDP real growth: 6.00% (2004); *5.9% (2005)

Labour force: 6.76 million (2004)

Unemployment: 8.50% (2004)

Inflation: 1.10% (2004)

Balance of trade: US$9.02 billion (2004)

Foreign debt: US$44.60 billion (2004)

Annual FDI: US$7.60 billion (2004)

* estimated figure

Economically, Chile performed very well in 2005. Strong growth continued, the result of increased exports and a sound macroeconomic framework put in place by President Ricardo Froilán 'Lagos' Escobar of the Partido Socialista de Chile (SP) (Socialist Party of Chile) in the Concertación de Partidos por la Democracia (CPD) (Coalition of Parties for Democracy). Indeed, 2005 was Lagos' last full year at the wheel of the Chilean economy, as electoral politics dominated the country's popular press in the run up to elections. Having served all six years of his only term as president Lagos will hand over to the historic winner of Chile's 2006 presidential run off. But it was the plight of a former president that occupied the headlines early in 2005.

Pinochet

To the delight of millions of Chileans, former military dictator General Augusto Pinochet was placed under house arrest in January following a decision by Chile's Supreme Court, which facilitated his standing trial for alleged human rights atrocities. After later being released on bail the military strong man, facing accusations of complicity in the kidnapping of nine individuals and the murder of one during 1976–77, was ruled by a panel of judges to be too old and infirm to defend himself and was therefore unfit for trial. However, the dictator did lose his former status of immunity from prosecution when, two days before his ninetieth birthday, he was indicted and put under house arrest on charges of tax evasion and mass corruption. Bail of CH$12 million (US$22,000) was placed on Pinochet following the ruling.

Boom and boom

Chile is famous in the economic world for its embrace of the ideals of economic liberalism – as espoused by the Chicago School – in the early 1970s. Some three decades later the country's economy is booming. In 2005, in economic terms relative to the rest of the region, Chile was sitting pretty. Chileans are relatively rich in comparison to their immediate neighbours, with GDP per capita income of US$5,856 in 2004, a big increase on the US$4,408 recorded in 2003. Figures released in March 2005 suggested that Chileans were, in dollar terms, some 10 per cent better off than they were in March 2004, following good growth in 2004. Inflation is at its lowest level since the decade began, at 1.1 per (2004), and the balance of trade and current account are increasingly healthy. Unemployment, at 8.5 per cent (2004), is falling while growth in real GDP was a very healthy 6 per cent in 2004.

When Lagos took over the helm in 2000 Chile was suffering from the effects of the Asian crisis of the late 1990s, having build up a strong trading relationship with several of the 'tiger' economies in the region. Like a well-conditioned racehorse however, Chile with all of its neo-classical economic pedigree, has pulled away from the pack and is now performing better than most states in the region.

The decision taken by Chile's exporters to diversify their international markets has succeeded in annulling the problem of over-reliance on one specific trading region, the scourge of the Chilean economy following the Asian crisis. A new free trade deal with the United States, which was ratified in 2004, has undoubtedly assisted the Chilean economic revival, but it is important to note that the country's exporters have also been busy reconstructing once failed relationships with Asian countries, as well as forming new ones. China for example, is now one of Chile's largest trading partners.

As the far eastern powerhouse continues to expand, so too will Chile's export growth, as China's new nascent middle class looks set to raise its demand for Chilean specialities such as wine, copper and fruit. In an interview with the *Financial Times* of London (*FT*) outgoing president Lagos talked of Chile building a 'bridge between the Pacific and the Atlantic'. 'Geography is part of our opportunity' he said. Though Lagos, who's six-year term finishes in March 2006, is right when he talks of the need to continue Chile's export success, a continuation of his sagacious macroeconomic policies is also required.

Breaking the mould

Verónica Michelle Bachelet Jeria of SP became the first-ever Chilean female president when she won the electoral run-off on 15 January 2006, after various candidates split the vote in the initial poll on 11 December 2005. The contrast between both candidates could not have been more stark: Michelle Bachelet, a dyed in the wool socialist, verses Harvard PhD, billionaire businessman and former senator Sebastián Piñera, of Renovación Nacional (RN), a centre-right member party of the Alianza por Chile (Alliance for Chile) coalition. Bachelet was victorious with 53.5 per cent of the vote, having campaigned on a mixed platform of promoting Chile's free-market heritage and increasing social benefits to alleviate poverty. The telegenic 55-year old previously served as minister of defence and minister of health under President Lagos. A self confessed atheist – unusual in Catholic Chile – and single mother of three, Bachelet is competent in 5 different languages.

Bachelet has an unconventional background for a Chilean presidential candidate. Born into a middle class family in Santiago she went to medical school at the university in the city. Bachelet's father was detained and tortured by the Chilean authorities under instruction from Pinochet in 1973, having disobeyed orders and been charged with treason; he later died in prison. In January 1975 Bachelet along with her mother was detained and tortured, but both were later allowed to seek exile in Australia and later East Germany. Bachelet returned to Chile in 1979 and completed her medical degree, graduating in 1983. A shrewd networker and relationship builder Bachelet became involved in politics in the early 1990s following Chile's democratic transition. After becoming an advisor at the ministry of health she branched out into military strategy studies and transformed her area of expertise, taking up an official post in the Chilean defence department.

During her time as a student Bachelet became increasingly left-wing, firstly as a member of the Socialist Youth group and then SP. She still retains something of a reputation of a radical and is most certainly a mould breaker. Bachelet is the first woman who was not the spouse of a previous head of state or political leader to be directly elected to the Presidency in a Latin American country. The new president has also made a bold commitment to fill half her cabinet appointments with women.

Foreign relations

In May 2005 Chile's minister of the interior, José Miguel Insulza, was elected

KEY INDICATORS — Chile

	Unit	2000	2001	2002	2003	2004
Population	m	15.21	15.40	15.20	15.34	15.48
Gross domestic product (GDP)	US$bn	70.20	66.30	63.50	72.40	*94.11
GDP per capita	US$	4,617	4,316	4,176	4,408	5,856
GDP real growth	%	4.4	2.8	2.0	3.3	6.0
Inflation	%	3.8	3.6	2.5	3.4	1.1
Unemployment	%	9.2	9.2	9.2	8.5	8.5
Exports (fob) (goods)	US$m	18,159.0	18,050.0	19,130.0	19,898.0	32,025.0
Imports (fob) (goods)	US$m	16,721.0	16,334.0	17,150.0	18,009.0	23,006.0
Balance of trade	US$m	1,438.0	2,090.0	2,400.0	1,889.0	9,019.0
Current account	US$m	-991.0	-1,241.0	-320.0	-916.0	1,390.0
Foreign debt	US$bn	42.5	38.5	39.0	43.4	44.6
Total reserves minus gold	US$m	14,729.3	14,219.4	15,341.1	15,839.6	15,993.8
Foreign exchange	US$m	14,380.5	13,881.7	14,813.9	15,211.0	15,495.4
Exchange rate	per US$	535.47	634.94	696.60	652.95	609.36

* estimated figure

secretary general of the Organisation of American States (OAS). The decision marked a distinct setback for the United States in the region, after Washington had failed to garner enough support for its preferred candidates for the role. Though US Secretary of State Condoleezza Rice agreed to back Insulza at the very last minute, the Bush Administration had previously endorsed Mexico's foreign minister Luis Derbez. Insulza's victory was an important blow for Santiago to have struck in the region's geopolitical mix. The top job at the OAS is a plum diplomatic position in the Americas and its leader (and corresponding country) traditionally wields considerable influence.

Chile and Peru seem to be perennially at each other's throats and 2005, for a short while at least, was no different. On 7 November 2005 officials from the Peruvian state department travelled to Santiago on a mission to extradite former Peruvian president Alberto Fuijimori, after he turned up in the Chilean capital having left Japan, his home in exile. In a direct show of political muscle, Lima also sent its minister of the interior and anti-corruption prosecutor to Santiago. By January 2006, nothing concrete had come of the negotiations.

Outlook

For Chile, these are good times. Economic growth was strong in 2004 and 2005 and looks set to continue. Now that Chile's exporters have diversified their international markets, the economy is no longer solely leashed to tigers in the Far East. Continued Chinese economic growth is particularly beneficial to the Chilean economy but here the Chileans have little to worry about, for the Chinese economy looks set to keep on expanding at a healthy rate of knots. With Lagos soon to depart the political scene, dynamic new president Bachelet will need to ensure a smooth transition. Simultaneously, the new government will be required to act as macroeconomic guardian to Chile throughout 2006 and beyond, as Lagos did so successfully.

Risk assessment

Politics	Good
Economy	Good
Regional stability	Stable

COUNTRY PROFILE

Historical profile

Inca rule barely touched Chile, with Aymara and Atacameno farmers and herders pre-dating the Incas. Chango Indians fished along the coastal areas while Diaguitas farmed the interior of Coquimbo. Beyond the central valley, Araucanian or Mapuche Indians resisted Inca aggression.
1535 Indigenous Araucanian people successfully resisted the first Spanish invasion of Chile.
1540 Santiago was founded by Pedro de Valdivia, who began the Spanish conquest of Chile.
1553 Araucanians captured and executed Valdivia.
1553–58 Indigenous people staged an uprising against Spanish colonialism, however most of the country was eventually subdued, although the Mapuche managed to hold onto their remaining territory for almost three centuries.
1578 Sir Francis Drake, an English adventurer, led a raid on the port of Valparaíso, which was repulsed by the Spanish armies.
1700 For most of the eighteenth century it was ruled by a small oligarchy of landowners.
1759 Chile began reforms under the auspices of the Bourbon monarchs, who succeeded the Habsburg dynasty in Spain.
1788 Irish-born Ambrosio O'Higgins y Ballenary began his tenure as governor of Chile. He outlawed slavery and forced labour, strengthened production and administration and bolstered the power of the military. Chile was granted more autonomy than most other Latin American colonies.
1807 Napoleon Bonaparte's invasion of Spain fuelled the independence movement in Chile.
1810 Independence leader Bernardo O'Higgins Riquelme, son of Ambrosio O'Higgins, led a revolt against José Miguel Carrera Verdugo, the Chilean leader who had brought more autonomy to the country.
1814 Spanish troops reconquered Chile.
1818 Bernado O'Higgins joined forces with José de San Martín in Argentina and led successful battles against the Spanish that resulted in Chile's independence from Spain. Bernado O'Higgins became Chile's first post-independence leader.
1823 O'Higgins was forced to resign. Civil war between liberal federalists and conservative centralists ensued, lasting for seven years.
1830 The Conservatives won the civil war.
1851–61 President Manuel Montt liberalised the constitution, reducing the power of landowners and the Roman Catholic Church.
1879–84 Chile's victory in the War of the Pacific against Peru and Bolivia increased its territory by one-third.
1880s–90s The pacification of the Araucanians led to increased European immigration. Mining of nitrates and copper began.
1891 A civil war over a constitutional dispute between the president and congress led to a congressional victory, with the role of the president reduced to a figurehead.
1925 A new constitution saw the disestablishment of the church.
1927 General Carlos Ibañez del Campo seized power in a military coup and established a dictatorship.
1938–46 A Popular Front coalition was formed by communists, socialists and radicals.
1948–58 The Communist Party was banned.
1952 Carlos Ibañez was elected president, promising to strengthen law and order.
1964 Eduardo Frei Montalva was elected president, pledging to introduce limited social reform.
1970 Salvador Allende Gossens was elected president and imposed an extensive programme of nationalisation.
1973 The government failed to win a congressional majority in the elections as opposition to its policies mounted and the country faced ever increasing economic problems. Food shortages followed high inflation and fighting broke out between pro- and anti-government activists. Backed by the CIA, the armed forces intervened. President Allende died during the military takeover.
1974 General Augusto Pinochet Ugarte became president, remaining in power for 16 years.
1988 Chilean voters rejected Pinochet's bid to extend his power until 1997.
1989 Patricio Aylwin defeated both Pinochet's protégé and a right-wing independent candidate in the presidential election.
1993 Eduardo Frei Ruíz-Tagle won the presidential election. He began reducing the military's influence in government.
1998 Pinochet retired from the army and was made senator-for-life. He was arrested in the UK on a warrant issued by a Spanish magistrate on murder charges related to his 'caravan of death' in the 1970s.
2000 Ricardo Lagos Escobar won the elections and became Chile's first socialist president since 1973. The UK government declared Pinochet unfit for extradition to Spain and the former dictator was returned to Chile. A Chilean judge subsequently charged Pinochet with kidnap.
2001 Chile's appeal court ruled that General Augusto Pinochet was mentally unfit to stand trial on human rights violation charges. The ruling centre-left coalition held on to its majority in Congress in the legislative elections.

Nations of the World: A Political, Economic and Business Handbook

2002 All charges against Pinochet were dropped after the Supreme Court upheld a verdict finding him mentally unfit to stand trial for human rights crimes. Pinochet resigned from his post as a lifelong senator.

2003 There was a series of cases alleging corruption involving members of the government.

2004 In May, President Lagos signed a new law giving Chileans the right to divorce, despite continued opposition from the Roman Catholic Church. Chile's court lifted Pinochet's immunity from prosecution.

2005 The 11 December first round of the presidential elections was won by Michelle Bachelet with 46 per cent of the vote, the governing centre-left *Concertación* coalition candidate.

2006 Dr Bachelet won the run-off election and became Chile's first woman president. She will take office on 11 March.

Political structure
Constitution
The constitution dates from 1980, when it was accepted by two-thirds of voters in a plebiscite organised by the military government. Following a further plebiscite in 1989, 54 reforms passed into law. They included increasing the number of directly elected members in the Senate, abolishing Article 8 (which outlawed Marxist groups) and balancing the number of civilian and military representatives on the powerful Council of National Security. Further changes to the constitution require a two-thirds majority in both houses of the Congreso Nacional (National Congress).

Form of state
Presidential democratic republic

The executive
Executive power is held by the president and cabinet. The president is head of state and commander-in-chief of the armed forces. Elected for a fixed term of six years, the president cannot be re-elected for the following period.

The relationship between the executive and the armed forces is enshrined in the constitution. The president should take note of discussions within the Council of National Security. This consists of eight members, four military and four civilian. The four military members are the heads of the army, navy, air force and police. The four civilian members are the president of the republic, president of the Senate, president of the Supreme Court and the comptroller general of the republic. According to the constitution, the Council of National Security provides a forum within which it is possible to present, at the highest level, the military's opinion. The armed forces see the council as having the function of letting civilian governments know of potential conflicts between military and civilian interests, thereby acting to prevent future military intervention in government.

National legislature
The bicameral National Congress, together with the president of the republic, co-legislate within a multi-party system legislature. The 38 elected and 10 appointed senators of the Senado (Senate), the upper chamber, serve for eight years. Four of the latter are chosen by the Council of National Security, three by the Supreme Court and two by the president. Ex-presidents who served for six uninterrupted years are also given a seat. The 120 deputies of the lower chamber are elected for four-year terms. Laws can originate in either of the chambers or be proposed by the president of the republic.

Legal system
The main tribunals of the independent judiciary system are the Supreme Court, 16 regional courts of appeal and the lower courts. The Supreme Court consists of 16 members appointed for life by the president from a list of five names proposed by the Supreme Court as vacancies arise. Members of the courts of appeal are appointed in the same way as those of the Supreme Court. Judges in lower courts are appointed in a similar manner, but from lists submitted by the court of appeal of the district in which the vacancies arise.

Last elections
16 December 2001 (parliamentary); January 2006 (presidential)

Results: Presidential: The first round was won by Michelle Bachelet of the governing centre-left *Concertación* coalition with just under 46 per cent. In the second round on 15 January 2006 Ms Bachelet won 53.3 per cent of the vote, while Sebastián Piñera, a moderate conservative, won 46.5 per cent.

Parliamentary: (Chamber of Deputies) the *Concertación* won with 47.9 per cent of the vote. (Senate) Following partial elections, coupled with those elected in 2001, *Concertación* hold 20 seats and the Alliance 17 seats.

Political parties
Ruling party
Concertación de Partidos por la Democracia (CPD) (Coalition of Pro-Democracy Parties) (centre-left coalition, comprising the Partido Demócrata Christiano (PDC) (Christian Democratic Party), Partido Radical Social Demócrata (PRSD) (Social Democratic Radical Party), Partido Socialista (PS) (Socialist Party) and Partido por la Democracia (PPD) (Party for Democracy) (re-elected Dec 2001)

Main opposition party
Alianza por Chile (Alliance for Chile coalition), comprising the Unión Demócrata Independiente (UDI) (Independent Democratic Union) and the Renovación Nacional (RN) (National Renewal).

Population
15.48 million (2004)

Ethnic make-up
Mixed European and indigenous peoples (mestizos) account for approximately 75 per cent of the population, with a further 23 per cent of European descent and 2 per cent Indians, mainly Mapuches, in the south.

Religions
Approximately 85 per cent Roman Catholic, 10 per cent Protestant, with small minorities of Jews, Muslims and other religions.

Education
The investment in education amounts to 4.0 per cent of GDP. This figure has doubled since the early 1990s. Chile has achieved gender parity in both primary and secondary education and has extended the school year by around 15 per cent.

Education is free and compulsory for the first eight years, beginning at the age of five or six.

Over 80 per cent of children complete secondary education, which begins at the age of 13 or 14 years and is divided into a humanities/science programme or a technical/vocational programme. Higher education consists of universities, professional and technical institutes.

Literacy rate: 96 per cent and 95 per cent for men and women respectively; adult rates (World Bank).

Compulsory years: Five or six to 13 or 14 (eight years in total)

Enrolment rate: 103 per cent boys, 100 per cent girls, total primary school enrolment of the relevant age group (including repetition rates), (World Bank).

Pupils per teacher: 30 in primary schools

Health
Total expenditure on health is around 7 per cent of GDP, of which government spending is 44 per cent.

Care for pregnant women, children under six and members of indigent and low income families is free. More specialised medical consultation and care is given at hospitals and maternity units. For patients who voluntarily choose the state system, a contribution of 25 to 30 per cent of the cost is required (depending on income). People under any social security scheme are entitled to preventive medical services (periodical health examinations) and in the case of illness, are granted full-paid sick leave. Occupational accidents or disease are covered by a special fund.

Chile

Life expectancy: 76.4 years (World Bank)
Fertility rate/Maternal mortality rate: 2.2 births per woman (World Bank 2003)
Infant mortality rate: 8.0 deaths per 1,000 live births; 1 per cent of children aged under five are malnourished (World Bank).
Head of population per physician/bed: 1.1 physicians and 2.7 hospital beds per 1,000 people

Welfare
The statutory age of retirement is 65 years for men and 60 years for women. The system requires 13 per cent of a worker's wage to be deducted and accumulated in one of seven independently managed mutual-fund companies selected by the worker, with a small part of the contribution going towards disability insurance. Neither employers nor the government contribute to the individual accounts. The contributions remain under the workers' control, if they change jobs, and are deferred from any tax.

Main cities
Santiago (capital, estimated population 4.4 million in 2004), Puente Alto (508,200), Viña del Mar (303,100), Antofagasta (302,400), Valparaíso (274,100), Talcahuano (252,800), San Bernardo (247,800), Temuco (247,200), Iquique (218,300), Concepción (217,600).

Languages spoken
English is the main second language.
Official language/s
Spanish

Media
Press
Dailies: Santiago daily newspapers are *La Cuarta*, *Diario Oficial de la República de Chile*, *La Epoca*, *Fortón Diario*, *El Mercurio*, *La Nación*, *La Segunda*, *La Tercera de la Hora*, *Las Ultimas Noticias*. The *News Review* is in English.
In political terms, daily newspapers range from the conservative upmarket *El Mercurio* and the liberal upmarket *La Epoca*, to the populist conservative *La Tercera* and *Las Ultimas Noticias* and the radical *Fortín Mapocho* and radical populist *La Cuarta*.
The evening paper is *La Segunda*.
Business: *Prensa Al Día* carries summary news about finance, economy and information technology. *Santiago Times* provides business briefs as well. *Business News Americas* (www.bnamericas.com) is the English daily on-line digest of business news. Other publications are *Estrategia* and *Infoweek*.

Broadcasting
Radio: Over 300 radio stations broadcast on short and medium wave and FM. Most are commercial and in Spanish.
Television: Three main TV channels and numerous stations, mostly commercial. Televisión Nacional de Chile operates over 100 stations and reaches around 90 per cent of the country. Cable TV network is available in Santiago.
Of the three main television stations, state-run Channel 7, with 108 stations, is the only station which reaches more than 90 per cent of the country. Channel 11 is run by the Television Corporation of the University of Chile, while Channel 13 is owned by the Television Corporation of the Catholic University. Channels 11 and 13 reach around 60 per cent of the country.

Advertising
Advertising spending is dominated by TV (59 per cent), newspapers (13 per cent) and magazines (4 per cent).

Economy
Chile remains one of Latin America's most robust economies. Successful exploitation of the country's natural resource base and diversification into non-traditional sectors continue to fuel growth. The boom in international copper prices from 2004 has maintained the economy's key strength. Chile's export sector is relatively strong and diversified, with copper typically accounting for 35 per cent of export earnings, compared with 80 per cent in 1973. The IMF predicts growth in real GDP to reach 5.9 per cent in 2005 and 5.8 per cent in 2006.
Chile's reputation for sound economic management has created a level of international confidence without equal in Latin America. At the heart of these policies lies the government's concentration on sound monetary, fiscal and exchange rate policies. Interest rates have traditionally been high, but were progressively eased from 2002 as the authorities sought to counter the effects of falling consumer demand and rapidly rising unemployment. The economy has been liberalised through an extensive privatisation policy, tax revenue increases and allowing the peso to float freely, enabling the country to maintain its competitiveness. Key to the government's economic policy has been investment, with foreign direct investment (FDI) flowing into the mining, construction and telecommunications sectors in particular.
Points of major concern include high unemployment and the influence of copper prices on the exchange rate and their tendency to distort the wider economy.
Though interest rates are low domestic demand remains sluggish, the growth of Chile's export sector has barely impacted on domestic consumption and investment. Despite lacklustre domestic demand the rebound of the world's economy in recent years and the increased Chinese demand for copper has boosted prices and increased Chilean copper exports. A likely continuation of this trend should encourage robust growth throughout 2006 and the outlook for the Chilean economy remains positive.

External trade
Chile is an associate member of Mercusor, which was established as a customs union in 1995. Other members include Argentina, Brazil, Paraguay and Uruguay. Plans are afoot to create a free trade bloc modelled on the European Union, under the auspices of the South American Community of Nations (SACN). The SACN seeks to merge two existing free trade zones in the region, the Andean Community and Mercusor.

Imports
Main imports include petroleum and petroleum products, natural gas, chemicals, electrical and telecommunications equipment, industrial machinery and vehicles.
Main sources: Argentina (17 per cent total, 2004), US (14.1 per cent), Brazil (11.1 per cent), China (7.1 per cent)

Exports
Major exports include copper, fruit, fish products, paper and pulp, chemicals and wine.
Main destinations: US (14 per cent total, 2004), Japan (11.4 per cent), China (9.9 per cent), South Korea (5.5 per cent), The Netherlands (5.1 per cent), Brazil (4.3 per cent), Italy (4.1 per cent), Mexico (4.0 per cent)

Agriculture
Farming
The contribution of the agricultural sector to the Chilean economy is significant, employing 15 per cent of the total workforce and generating 6 per cent of GDP. Approximately 8 per cent of the total land mass is cultivated. The country's soil is fertile and well irrigated, particularly in the central area and main river valleys. Dependence on imported foodstuffs has been reduced by improved wheat, sugar and vegetable oil production. Other important crops are oats, barley, rice, beans, lentils, maize and chickpeas. Important cash/export crops are maize, beans, asparagus, onions and garlic.
The production and export of a variety of fruit have all recorded impressive figures, given Chile's favourable growing conditions and good soil, relatively cost-effective labour and protection from disease. Table grapes, citrus fruits, avocados, pears, nectarines, peaches, kiwis, plums and nuts have done well. Chilean wine is

growing in importance as a value-added agricultural product and a highly important export.

Livestock farming is concentrated in the south of the country.

Crop production in 2004 included: 3,956,406 million tonnes (t) cereals, 1,921,652t wheat, 1,320,606t maize, 1,144,170t potatoes, 2,370,483t sugar beets, 265,000t citrus fruit, 1,900,000t grapes, 1,350,000t tomatoes, 1,152,920t roots and tubers, 119,265t rice, 12,576t oilcrops, 538,600t oats, 16,000t olives, 130,000t kiwi fruit, 105,478t pulses, 63,000t chillies & peppers, 1,250,000t apples, 9,321t tobacco leaves, 22,565t treenuts, 4,580,350t fruit in total, 2,832,300t vegetables in total. Livestock production included: 1,126,039t meat in total, 208,258t beef, 363,605t pig meat, 9,539t lamb, 5,220t goat meat, 10,900t horsemeat, 528,517t poultry, 118,000t eggs, 2,309,750t milk, 16,000t honey, 29,564t cattle hides, 2,655t sheepskins, 15,100t greasy wool.

Fishing

The Fishing industry in Chile is one of the economy's most important export industries. Chile is second only to Norway as a producer of fresh, frozen and prepared salmon, with annual exports totalling more than US$800 million. The productivity of the fishing industry is largely attributable to the large number of salmon farms in the south of the country.

Fishing and fish processing have become a diversified industry. Pilchards have traditionally been the main species of fish landed (75 per cent), with jack mackerel second. Abalone is exported to Japan, algae to Taiwan, hake to Spain, fresh salmon to the US and canned pilchards to the UK. Such diversification has been fuelled by substantial and continued increases in investment.

The typical annual fish catch is 4.3million tonnes, including 3.6 million tonnes marine fish and 164,477 tonnes shellfish.

Forestry

Chile has a significant amount of forested land, approximately 15.5 million hectares (ha), equating to 23 per cent of the total land area. In the period 1990–2000, deforestation accounted for a decrease of forest cover by an average of 0.13 per cent per annum or 20,000ha. Forestry is an important sector suitable for commercial exploitation.

Chile has abundant softwood plantations used for the manufacture of forest products. The forestry industry is primarily located in the south, stretching from the Seventh to the Tenth region, with the main concentration in the Eighth Region around Concepción. The three ports of the area (San Vicente, Lirquén and Talcahuano) handle up to 95 per cent of all forestry exports.

The sawn wood sector is characterised by a wide variety of producers, ranging from small portable sawmills to large highly automated mills. The larger sawmills tend to specialise in *pinus radiata*. Sawnwood production is largely a seasonal industry, with the highest activity occurring between spring and autumn (September to April). In the global market, Chile is the third-largest exporter of woodchips while nearly 50 per cent of its sawn timber, panels and softwood pulp production are exported.

Japan is the single most important purchaser of Chilean wood cellulose. Paper production has a large domestic market. The government has promoted private sector investment in forestry with land tax exemptions, rebates and subsidies. Estimated timber production in 2004 included: 40,203,371 cubic metres (cum) roundwood, 27,491,000cum industrial roundwood, 7,004,000cum sawnwood, 15,087cum sawlogs & veneer logs, 12,221,000cum pulpwood, 1,739,000cum wood-based panels, 12,712,371cum wood fuel, 251,897t charcoal.

Industry and manufacturing

Chile's manufacturing sector employs approximately one quarter of the country's total workforce. The sector also contributes around a third of Chilean GDP. Financial conglomerates control a substantial section of denationalised industries, although small firms with less than 10 employees still dominate. Export-based industries include petrochemicals, pulp and paper, base metals, plastics, rubber and food processing (particularly fish and malted barley). Domestic market industries include textiles, footwear, cement, food processing, beverages and machinery.

Tourism

Chile's tourism industry continues to grow, with the country's variety of natural environments and climates attracting an increasing number of visitors. In line with the expansion of the industry Chile's infrastructure is being expanded to cater for the growth of the sector. In 2005 travel and tourism accounted for 6.5 per cent of total GDP and 6.8 per cent of total employment, a rise of 11.8 per cent on 2004 in the latter. The largest market is Argentina, but many tourists come from further afield, including a considerable number from the US and Europe. Capital investment in the industry rose by 9.4 per cent on the figure for 2004 and now represents 8.7 per cent of total capital investment in the country.

Environment

Santiago suffers from a serious smog problem, which is at its worst May–September and is aggravated when the winter weather is interrupted by spells of milder temperatures.

Mining

The mining sector is of great importance to the Chilean economy, contributing 9 per cent to GDP and providing employment for 6 per cent of the workforce. It is the main export earner and a major focus of foreign investment in the country. Activity is concentrated in copper, of which Chile is the world's leading producer and holds around 30 per cent of the world's proven reserves. The state-owned copper enterprise, Corporación Nacional del Cobre de Chile (Codelco), holds 70 per cent of national reserves and administers the four largest mines: Chuquicamata, El Teniente, Andina and El Salvador. Copper is also extracted from the Escondida mine, the biggest proven deposit in the world.

The sector was hit by falling copper prices until 2003 when demand for copper was fuelled by Chinese expansion in particular and prices rose. Copper continued to rise at a rapid rate in 2005, in line with increased demand in the international market.

Mining of silver, gold (the El Indio mine ranks among the highest grade mines in the world), iron ore, manganese and lead is also undertaken. Other mining sub-sectors include natural nitrates, mercury, marble, coal, sulphur and limestone Proven and probable reserves at the Fachinal mine in southern Chile (Coeur d'Alene Mines Corporation) are estimated at 317,915 ounces of gold and 14.6 million ounces of silver.

Hydrocarbons

The country is a net importer of energy and is heavily reliant on imports of crude oil. Chile's domestic oil production, which is extracted mainly from offshore fields at the Straits of Magellan and onshore at Tierra del Fuego and the southern mainland, provides only 6 per cent of domestic consumption. Chile's oil reserves totalled only 150 million barrels in 2005. Production was around 18,400 barrels per day (bpd), while consumption was around 225,000 bpd in 2004. There were plans to privatise Empresa Nacional de Petróleo (ENAP), the state oil company, but these were shelved by President Lagos in 2003. The country's oil sector is controlled by ENAP including the three primary refineries which between them produce 226,800bpd.

Investments by ENAP in exploration outside Chile have not been successful.

Chile

Chile had 100 billion cubic metres of proven natural gas reserves in 2005. Production is limited, and is geared to the urban markets of central Chile, particularly Santiago. However since 1997 gas consumption has risen by an average 21.7 per cent per year, and most of this growth is satisfied through increased imports of natural gas.

Liquid natural gas (LNG) production is being increased; ENAP called for international tenders, in July 2005, for the construction of a LNG terminal. The government held talks with various international LNG suppliers, while ENAP concluded agreements with domestic energy companies to supply the LNG. Chile's coal resources come mainly from Lota/Coronel and the extreme south of Tierra del Fuego. All domestic coal production goes to power generation. Chile has total recoverable coal reserves of 1.3 million tonnes and typically produces around 500,000 tonnes a year.

Energy

Generation, transmission and distribution are undertaken by private companies. The sector is jointly regulated by the Ministerio de Economía y Energía (MEE) (ministry of economy and energy) and Comisión Nacional de Energía (CNE) (national energy commission).

Chile generates a total capacity of 10.5GW electricity. Some 43 per cent of the country's electricity is generated by thermal power sources and 41 per cent by hydroelectricity. Renewable energy sources account for the remainder.

Around 90 per cent of the country is served by the Central Grid, while the rest is supplied by the Northern Grid and the Aisén and Magallanes systems which supply the south. Empresa Nacional de Electricidad (Endesa), part of the Enersis Group owned by Spain's Endesa, is the country's largest electricity producer with 50 per cent of output. US-owned Gener is the second largest producer, generating 20 per cent of national power.

Banking and insurance

Chile's banking and insurance sector was once an exclusive enclave of the economy where only the rich were able to access financial services. However, the 1990s saw an expansion of the banking sector throughout the country. Today Chile has one of Latin America's most developed and sophisticated banking sectors and Chilean banks have shown relative strength in a weak economic environment. The authorities do not allow new banks to enter the Chilean market, except via the purchase of an existing bank. Restrictions remain on the range of activities a bank can undertake, with pension fund management reserved for private pension fund companies.

Competitive pressures have increased with domestic banks facing increased competition from Spanish banks. Following Banco Santander Central Hispano's (BSCH) takeover of Banco Santiago and Santander Chile – two of Chile's largest banks – BSCH has a market share of just under 30 per cent.

Central bank
Banco Central de Chile

Main financial centre
Santiago

Time

GMT -4 hours (GMT -3 hours October to March).

Geography

Chile occupies a thin strip of land, rarely more than 200km wide, which stretches 4,640km down the west coast of Latin America from north of the tropic of Capricorn to Cape Horn. Geography and climate range from hot deserts in the north to icy Andean peaks at almost 7,000 metres high in the east and thousands of rainswept islets in the south.

Chile is bordered by the Pacific to the west, by Argentina to the east, by Bolivia in the north-east and Peru to the north. Several Pacific islands, including the Juan Fernandez archipelago and Easter Island, are Chilean. Of the mainland area, 2.2 per cent is suitable for crops, 17.1 per cent for livestock and 10.8 per cent for forestry. The remaining 69.9 per cent is considered unproductive and is mostly covered by deserts or mountains.

There are three main geographical belts running from north to south – the Andes, the central valley, and the narrow coastal range. The Andes are characterised not only by their great height but also by being a broad mass, generally over 80km wide, and making a superb natural border with Argentina. West of the Andes, the central valley has a varied form. In the north, it is a high desert basin, characterised by inward drainage and near complete aridity. Further south it disappears, until re-emerging near Santiago. From Santiago to Puerto Montt, it constitutes the agricultural heart of Chile, until it disappears under the sea at Puerto Montt. The coastal range, significantly lower than the Andes and generally under 3,000 metres, forms a barrier between the populated central valley and the coast, except for certain gaps made by powerful rivers, as at Concepción in the south.

Climate

Generally hot and dry in north, Mediterranean in central region (cool nights) and wet and cold in the south. Temperatures in Santiago range from 10–33 degrees Celsius (C) in summer (December–March) and 2–20 degrees C in winter (June–September). The rainy season in the Santiago area is from May to September.

Dress codes

Relatively formal. A suit or a jacket and tie for men and skirts for women are usual for business.

Entry requirements

Passports
Required by all, with the exception of tourists travelling direct to Chile from Argentina, Brazil, Colombia, Paraguay and Uruguay, for whom national identity cards are sufficient.

Visa
Visas are not required by citizens of neighbouring countries or most EU states. For further details contact the local embassy. Business visas are not required by those citizens who do not need a tourist visa, all others, including those who do not normally require them but who are visiting on short-term contracts or receive fees from a local company, do need a visa.
On arrival a 'tourist card' is issued and must be returned when leaving.

Currency advice/regulations
No restrictions on import and export of foreign or Chilean currency. International credit cards are widely accepted. Receipts for money changed on entry should be retained.

Health (for visitors)

Mandatory precautions
None

Advisable precautions
Typhoid, polio, hepatitis 'A' and tetanus vaccinations are useful.
Water precautions should be taken (avoid tap water) and eating unpeeled fruit or uncooked vegetables is not advised. Foreigners may get free primary health care from the state-run health service's hospitals, but for more serious cases they are required to pay the costs. Travel health insurance is advised if not already covered by one's own national health insurance.

Hotels

Numerous luxury and first-class hotels as well as good hotels in lower price range. The Stars Classification System in operation. Bookings may be made at the Sernatur information office at Pudahuel Airport. An 18 per cent hotel tax is added to bill. Service charge is usually included, but an extra 5–10 per cent tip is usual.

Public holidays

Fixed dates
1 Jan (New Year's Day), 1 May (Labour Day), 21 May (Navy Day), 28 Jun (St Peter and St Paul Day), 15 Aug (Assumption Day), 18 Sep (Independence Day), 19 Sep (Army Day), 12 Oct (Columbus Day), 1

Nations of the World: A Political, Economic and Business Handbook

Nov (All Saints' Day), 8 Dec (Immaculate Conception), 25 Dec (Christmas Day), 31 Dec (New Year's Eve).

Variable dates
Good Friday, Holy Saturday, Corpus Christi (May/Jun), Reconciliation Day (first Mon in Sep).

Working hours
Banking
Mon–Fri: 0900–1400.
Business
Mon–Fri: 0830–1230 and 1400–1800; Sat: 0900–1300.
Business visits are best made outside the summer month of February when the great majority of people are on holiday.
Government
Mon–Fri: 0830–1730.
Shops
Mon–Sat: 0900–2000. Supermarkets and many shopping centres are open continuously until 2100, including Sundays and public holidays.

Telecommunications
Telephone/fax
GSM 1900 service available in populated areas only.

Electricity supply
220V AC, with two-pin plugs.

Social customs/useful tips
People are expected to be punctual for business appointments. However, for social appointments, being 30 or 40 minutes late is quite usual. Chileans are very hospitable and do not necessarily expect reciprocity. Entertaining at home is common practice and a small gift of thanks is acceptable.
In Latin American Spanish it is acceptable to address others in a familiar form *tu*, or in a polite form *usted*. The latter is more appropriate for business although the familiar form is often rapidly adopted. Chileans are quite easy about smoking habits, but it is banned in cinemas, theatres, churches and public transport.
It is necessary to carry car documents when driving.

Security
Santiago is generally regarded as a safe city with low incidences of assault and mugging compared with other Latin American capitals. However, pickpocketing is common in the city centre and on buses.

Getting there
Air
National airline: LAN-Chile (Línea Aérea Nacional de Chile).
International airport/s: Santiago-Comodoro Arturo Merino Benítez (often known as 'Pudahuel') (SCL), 21km west of city; bar, restaurant, bank, post office, shops, hotel reservations, car hire. A bus service to the city runs 24 hours.
Other airport/s: Arica-Chacalluta (ARI), 18km from city; bar, restaurant, buffet, shops, car hire.
Airport tax: For flights over 500km, US$26.

Surface
Road: The road system is dominated by the 3,455km Pan-American Highway, which links the Peruvian frontier to Puerto Montt in the south. Between Santiago and Puerto Montt, the Pan-American follows the course of the central valley. A trans-Andean highway links Valparaíso with the Argentine city of Mendoza. This is frequently closed during winter due to snow, when more southerly and lower passes have to be used.
Rail: Five lines to neighbouring Argentina, Bolivia and Peru are operated by the government-owned Ferrocarriles del Estado.
Water: Empremar (Valparaíso) is the principal port with developed passenger routes mainly to Argentina. Chile has around 60 ports.

Getting about
National transport
Air: Línea Aérea del Cobre (Ladeco) provides most domestic services. Lanexpress also operate frequent flights to major centres only. Air taxi services also operate. The south of the country relies heavily on air links and seats must be booked well in advance.
Road: There are 80,000km of good roads including the Pan-American Highway running north-south and qualified as first-class. It is only possible to reach Punta Arenas by land from Rio Gallengos (Argentina).
Buses: Express coaches link main centres and are generally recommended (eg Santiago-Arica, typically one departure daily; Santiago-Valparaíso, approx hourly service).
Rail: A fast diesel-electric train service is available. The main line runs from Santiago to Puerto Montt (includes sleeper service, restaurant cars, air-conditioning, typical total journey time around 18 hours); Japanese-built train links between Santiago and Concepción (first-class service and a journey time around nine hours including bus service from Chillián to Concepción).

City transport
Taxis: From Santiago's Arturo Merino Benitez airport, there are metered taxis into town.
Taxis are cheap and widely available in main towns. An initial charge (*Bajada de Bandera*) is displayed on front windscreen. Large blue taxis do not have meters. Tipping is not customary. Radio taxis charge higher fares.
Within Santiago and Chile's main towns black and yellow taxis can be hailed but are scarce at rush hour. These taxis are mostly metered but for long journeys fares should be negotiated in advance. There are extra charges at night and on holidays. Taxis operating from the airport require a special permit, and it is advised that visitors check a taxi's authenticity before boarding. The journey to central Santiago takes about 30 minutes. However, any taxi can go to the airport and the fare is often cheaper than from the airport.
Buses, trams & metro: Frequent inner city bus service. Shuttle service – minibuses for several passengers – from airport to city centre.
Fast, frequent, clean and safe metro system in Santiago consisting of two main lines: line 1 San Pablo-Escuela Militar line; line 2 Lo Ovalle-Cal y Canto line which has 13 stations. Trains run 0700–2245.

Car hire
A national or international licence is accepted. Car hire can be arranged at the airport and in most major towns. A large deposit may be required. All car drivers require a 'Carnet de Passages et Douanes' issued by the Automobile Club. Traffic drives on the right.

BUSINESS DIRECTORY

Telephone area codes
The international dialling code (IDD) for Chile is +56, followed by area code and subscriber's number:

Antofagasta	55	Linares	73
Arica	58	Punta Arenas	61
Chillán	42	Santiago	2
Concepción	41	Temuco	45
Coquimbo	51	Valparaíso	32
Iquique	57	Vina del Mar	32
La Serena	51		

Chambers of Commerce
American Chamber of Commerce in Chile, Avenida Kennedy 5735, Las Condes, Santiago (tel: 290-9700; fax: 212-0515; e-mail: amcham@amchamchile.cl).

British-Chilean Chamber of Commerce, Avenida Suecia 155-C, Providencia, Santiago (tel: 231-4366; fax: 231-8211; e-mail: cambrit@entelchile.net).

Antofagasta Cámara de Comercio, Servicios y Turismo, Latorre 2580, Antofagasta (tel: 225-175; fax: 55-222-053; e-mail: info@comercioantofagusta.cl).

Arica Cámara de Comercio, Industria, Servicios y Turismo, Rafael Sotomayor 252, Arica (tel: 224-643; fax: 253-718; e-mail: comercio@camaracomercioarica.cl).

Iquique Cámara de Comercio, Industria, Servicios y Turismo, San Martín 225, Iquique (tel: 412-942; fax: 414-090; e-mail: info@iquiquenegocios.cl).

Talca Cámara de Comercio, Servicios y Turismo, 2 Sur 1061, Talca (tel/fax: 233-569; e-mail: contact@camaradecomerciotalca.cl).

Temuco Cámara de Comercio, Servicios y Turismo, Vicuña Mackenna 396, Temuco (tel: 210-556; fax: 237-047; e-mail: camcotem@entelchile.cl).

Valparaiso Cámara Regional del Comercio y la Produccion, Pasaje Ross 149, Valparaiso (tel: 253-065; fax: 212-770).

Banking
Banco de A. Edwards, Huérfanos 740, Santiago (tel: 388-3000; fax: 388-4100; e-mail: marketing@baenet.cl).

Banco de Chile, Ahumada 251, Santiago (tel: 637-1111; fax: 637-3434)

Banco de Crédito e Inversiones, Huérfanos 1134, Santiago (tel: 692-7000; fax: 699-0729; e-mail: consulta@bcl.cl).

Banco del Estado de Chile, Avenida Libertador Bernardo O'Higgins 1111, Santiago (tel: 670-7000; fax: 670-5478; e-mail: msoto9@bech.cl).

Central bank
Banco Central de Chile, Agustinas 1180, Santiago (Tel: 670-2000; fax: 670-2099; e-mail: bcch@bcentral.cl).

Travel information
LADECO (Línea Aérea del Cobre), Avenida Américo Vespucio 901, Santiago (tel: 661-3131; fax: 639-5757; e-mail: josecotd@cmbchile.cl).

LAN-Chile (Línea Aérea Nacional de Chile), Avenida Américo Vespucio 901, Santiago (tel: 687-2525; fax: 687-2483; e-mail:sdelpino@lanchile.cl).

National tourist organisation offices
Servicio Nacional de Turismo (SERNATUR), (National Tourist Service) Avenida Providencia 1550, Santiago (tel: 236-1416; fax: 251-8469; internet: www.visit-chile.org; e-mail: sernatur@ctc-mundo.net or info@sernatur.cl).

Ministries
Ministry of Agriculture, Teatinos 40, Santiago (tel: 393-5000; fax:672-5654; e-mail: xbarrera@minagri.gob.cl).

Ministry of Defence, Edificio Diego Portales, Villavicencio 364, Santiago (tel: 222-1202; fax: 634-5339; e-mail: dn@defensa.cl).

Ministry of Economy, Mining and Energy, Teatinos 120, Santiago (tel: 672-5522; fax: 672-6040; e-mail: conomia@minecon.cl).

Ministry of Education, Avenida Libertado Bernardo O'Higgins 1371, Santiago (tel: 390-4000; fax: 380-0317; e-mail: ineduc@chilnet.cl).

Ministry of the Government, Palacio de la Moneda, Santiago (tel: 671-4103; fax: 699-1657).

Ministry of Housing, Avenida Libertado Bernardo O'Higgins 924, Santiago (tel: 638-0801; fax: 633-3892; e-mail: martinez@minvu.cl).

Ministry of the Interior, Palacio de la Moneda, Santiago (tel: 690-4000; fax: 699-2165; e-mail: alopez@interior.gov.cl).

Ministry of Justice, Morandé 107, Santiago (tel: 696-8151; fax: 696-6952).

Ministry of Labour and Social Security, Huérfanos 1273, Santiago (tel: 695-5133; fax: 671-6539).

Ministry of Mining, Teatinos 120, Santiago (tel: 671-4373; fax: 698-9262; e-mail:chileminero@mixmail.com).

Ministry of National Properties, Pdte. Juan Antonio Rios 6, Santiago (tel: 633-9305; fax: 633-6521; e-mail: aleonp@mbienes).

Ministry of Planning and Co-operation, Ahumada 48, Santiago (tel: 675-1400; fax: 672-1879; e-mail: misoto@mideplan.cl).

Ministry of the Presidency, Palacio de la Moneda, Santiago (tel: 690-4000; fax: 698-4656).

Ministry of Public Health, Enrique Mac-Iver 541, Santiago (tel: 639-4001; fax: 633-5875; e-mail: info@minsal.cl).

Ministry of Public Works, Morandé 59, Santiago (tel/fax: 361-2700; e-mail: mop.doh@chilnet.cl).

Ministry of Transport and Telecommunications, Amunategui 139 Santiago (tel: 672-6503; fax: 699-5138).

Ministry of Women's Affairs, Teatinos 950, Santiago (tel: 549-6100; fax: 549-6247; e-mail:sernam@entelchile.net).

Other useful addresses
Asociación de Exportadores de Manufacturas (ASEXMA Chile), Nueva Tajamar, Santiago (tel: 203-6699; fax: 203-6730; e-mail: asexma@asexmachile.cl).

Bolsa de Comercio de Santiago, La Bolsa 64, Santiago (Tel: 698-2001; fax: 697-2236; e-mail: fledermann@comercio.bolsantiago.cl).

British Embassy, Avenida el Bosque Norte 125, Piso 3, Las Condes, Santiago (tel: 231-3737; fax: 231-9771; e-mail: embsan@portal.cl).

Chilean Embassy (USA), 1732 Massachusetts Avenue, NW, Washington DC 20036 (tel: 202-785-1746; fax: 202-887-557; e-mail: embassy@embassyofchile.org).

Comisión Chilena del Cobre (Cochilco), Agustinas 1161, Santiago (tel: 382-8100; fax: 382-8300; e-mail: cochilco@cochilco.cl).

Comisión Económica para America Latina y el Caribe (CEPAL) (Economic Commission for Latin America - ECLAC), United Nations Building, Avenida Dag Hammarskjold s/n, Santiago (tel: 210-2000; fax: 208-0252).

Comité de Inversiones Extranjeras, Teatinos 120, Santiago (tel: 698-4254; fax: 698-9476; e-mail: investment@cinver.cl).

Corporación de Fomento de la Producción (CORFO) (Development Corporation), Moneda 921, Santiago (tel: 631-8692; fax: 631-8686; e-mail: drmetro@corfo.cl).

Corporación Nacional de Cobre (CODELCO), Huérfanos 1270, Santiago (tel: 690-3000; fax: 690-3059; e-mail: comunica@stgo.codelco.cl).

Empresa Nacional de Minería (ENAMI), MacIver 459, Santiago (tel: 664-7244; fax: 637-5436;e-mail: ghormaza@enami.cl).

Empresa Nacional de Petróleo (ENAP), Vitacura 2736, Santiago (tel: 280-3000; fax: 280-3199).

Instituto de Promoción de Exportaciones (ProChile), Avenida Libertador Bernardo O'Higgins 1315, Santiago (tel: 565-9000; fax: 696-0639; e-mail: info@prochile.cl).

Instituto Nacional de Estadísticas (INE), Avenida Presidente Bulnes 418, Santiago (tel: 366-7777; fax: 671-2169; e-mail: inecedoc@terra.cl).

Sociedad de Formento Fabril (SOFOFA)(Chilean Federation of Industry), Avenida Andrés Bello 2777, Santiago (tel: 391-3100; fax: 391-3200; e-mail: sofofa@sofofa.cl).

US Embassy, Avenida Andrés Bello 2800, Santiago (tel: 232-2600; fax: 330-3710).

Internet sites
Chile Business Directory:
http://www.chilnet.cl/

Chile Trade Commission:
http://www.prochile.cl

Government of Chile:
http://www.gobiernodechile.cl

Latin Trade Online:
http://www.latintrade.com

Organisation of American States:
http://www.oas.org

China

KEY FACTS

Official name: Zhonghua Renmin Gongheguo (Zhongguo) (People's Republic of China)

Head of State: State President Hu Jintao (elected 15 Mar 2003)

Head of government: Premier of the State Council Wen Jiabao (appointed 16 Mar 2003)

Ruling party: Zhongguo Gongchangdang (Chinese Communist Party) (CCP)

Area: 9,596,961 square km

Population: 1.34 billion (2004)

Capital: Beijing (Peking)

Official language: Putonghua (Mandarin Chinese – Beijing dialect).

Currency: Renminbi yuan (Rmb) = 100 fen

Exchange rate: Rmb8.09 per US$ (Oct 2005) (In Jul 2005, the currency peg with the US$ ended and there was a 2.1 per cent revaluation of the renminbi)

GDP per capita: US$1,269 (2004)

GDP real growth: 10.10% (2004); 9.9% (2005)*

Labour force: 778.50 million (2004)

Unemployment: 9.80% (2004, urban areas); 20.00% (2004, urban and rural areas)

Inflation: 3.90% (2004)

Oil production: 3.49 million bpd (2004)

Balance of trade: US$30.70 billion (2004))*; US$44.6 billion (IMF, 2003)

Foreign debt: US$233.30 billion (2004)*

Annual FDI: US$53.50 billion (2004)*

* estimated figure

If there were any doubts left as to China's status as the 'next big thing' on the world stage, these were surely dispelled in 2005. New figures released in December 2005 indicated that China's GDP in 2004 was in fact 10.1 per cent (16.8 per cent larger than the earlier recorded figure of 9.5 per cent). This meant that China officially became the world's sixth largest economy, drawing ahead of Italy. Moreover, GDP growth of 9.9 per cent in 2005, China's third consecutive yearly growth figure of circa 10 per cent, had analysts suggesting that China was in reality the fourth biggest economy in the world, ahead of Britain and France.

In January 2005, China's population passed the 1.3 billion mark and in February, China overtook the US as the world's biggest consumer of basic agricultural and industrial goods. In October, China launched its second manned mission to space, confirming its status as only the third country, after Russia and the US, in the world to do so. Combined with an announcement in March of plans to increase annual defence spending by 12 per cent, China inevitably had to spend much time in 2005 assuring its neighbours that its rise was not synonymous with hegemony.

Global implications: hydrocarbons

The sheer size of China's economy, and the pace of its growth, were topics that exercised the minds of many, both inside China and internationally. China's growth, largely fuelled by hydrocarbon-based energy, contributed to soaring demand for oil in 2005. Since 2001, China has accounted for more than 40 per cent of the global demand for oil and is currently the world's biggest consumer of oil, after the US. Combined with supply problems, related to ongoing difficulties in Iraq and hurricane damage to Gulf of Mexico production facilities, global demand led to a 30 per cent increase in the price of oil in 2005. In August, oil prices reached an unprecedented US$70.85 per barrel. In an effort to secure its economic growth, China scoured the globe for energy resources. Two Chinese state-owned oil companies made multi-billion dollar bids for foreign oil firms in 2005. Most prominent among these was a bid, in June, by China National Offshore Oil Company (CNOOC) for US-based oil giant Unocal; and a bid, in

August, by China National Petroleum Company (CNPC) for the Canadian-listed PetroKazakhstan. In November, China signed a deal with neighbouring Mongolia that would enable China to develop Mongolia's coal fields. In December, an oil pipeline linking Kazakh oil fields with Chinese consumers was officially opened. Also in December, China held its first ever summit with the Organisation of the Petroleum Exporting Countries (OPEC), to discuss ways of supplying China's growing hydrocarbon demands. CNPC investment in Sudanese oil fields and refineries also continued apace in 2005, with China now importing around 7 per cent of its oil supplies from Sudan.

Global implications: trade surpluses

China's trade surplus with the rest of the world tripled in 2005, to US$102 billion. This imbalance caused many in the US and the EU to call for restrictions on Chinese exports, particularly manufactured goods such as textiles, the export of which had been regulated by a deal originally struck in the mid-1970s. Faced with tariff threats and import restrictions, China was forced to negotiate on how to deal with widening trade gaps with its major trading partners. In June and November, China signed agreements with the EU and the US respectively, stipulating temporary artificial slowdowns in the number of Chinese textile products exported to these countries.

Global implications: the yuan

Throughout 2005, several countries and NGOs warned China that its policy of keeping the value of its currency, the yuan, artificially low was a threat to the global economy and to China's own economic growth. The low value of the yuan against other major currencies meant Chinese products were cheaper to import than rival products. This in turn helped to fuel China's massive trade surplus with its trading partners. The IMF in particular, warned that as China's boom was largely dependent upon exports and production, at the expense of domestic consumption, this could leave the Chinese economy dangerously exposed to downturns in global demand. In July, China made an effort to address these concerns by revaluing the yuan 2.1 per cent higher, removing its peg to the US dollar and permitting a 0.3 per cent fluctuation in the yuan's value on currency markets. In September, China further freed up the yuan against a basket of international currencies, including the yen, pound sterling, euro, rouble and baht, but refused further liberalisation against the US dollar. By November, the Organisation for Economic Co-operation and Development (OECD) was urging yet another freeing up of the yuan.

The domestic scene

The upper echelons of China's ruling Zhongguo Gongchangdang (Communist Party) experienced no dramatic change in 2005. President Hu Jintao consolidated his position as China's supreme leader by formally taking over, in March, command of the army – the last of the three positions to be vacated (in Septemmber 2004) by his predecessor, Jiang Zemin. The government also confidently dealt with two potentially difficult events, the death of purged former party leader Zhao Ziyang in January, and the anniversary of the birthday, in November, of another purged party leader, the late Hu Yaobang, whose death in 1989 sparked the Tiananmen Square protests.

However, the government had to deal with several domestic crises that threatened, if left unchecked, to chip away at its grip on power. Government figures for 2005 indicate a 6 per cent rise in public disturbances. Unrest, including riots and assaults against police and government officials, in rural China caught many in the government off-guard. Protests in Zhejiang, Hebei and Guandong provinces in April, June and December respectively were caused by dissatisfaction on the part of locals over the appropriation of land by corrupt officials. An estimated 66 million people have lost their land since 1995. In the most dramatic of these land protests, in April 2005, around 20,000 peasants drove off 1,000 police sent to quell protesters. Rural unrest over pollution and the inability to oust corrupt officials also led, in April and July, to violent clashes in Zhejiang and Guandong provinces respectively.

The government also came under fire from a normally quiescent Chinese media for failing to respond adequately to, or cover up, a series of disasters, both human and environmental. With more than 400 killed in coal mine accidents in 2005, the government, in September, promised to close dangerous pits and provide full disclosure of death tolls. However, the government was again accused in the media of a cover-up when, in November, a massive toxic spill contaminated the Songhua River (in Heilong Jiang province), threatening the safety of millions. Information about outbreaks of avian bird 'flu (H5N1) in June, August and October was also tightly controlled, to the detriment of locals.

To counter growing social unrest, the government initiated or stepped up a series of reforms. Prominent among these

KEY INDICATORS — China

	Unit	2000	2001	2002	2003	2004
Population	m	1,270.00	1,271.90	1,280.90	1,308.37	1,335.84
Gross domestic product (GDP)	US$bn	1,076.90	1,179.70	1,275.90	1,378.00	*1,649.33
GDP per capita	US$	865	930	1,010	1,060	1,269
GDP real growth	%	8.0	7.3	8.0	8.5	9.5
Inflation	%	0.4	0.7	-0.8	0.6	3.9
Unemployment	%	7.0	3.5	4.0	10.2	20.0
Oil output	'000 bpd	3,252.0	3,308.0	3,387.0	3,396.0	3,490.0
Natural gas output	bn cum	27.7	30.3	32.6	34.1	40.8
Coal output	mtoe	498.0	548.5	703.0	842.6	989.8
Exports (fob) (goods)	US$m	249,131.0	266,155.0	325,570.0	413,600.0	583,100.0
Imports (fob) (goods)	US$m	214,657.0	243,610.0	295,200.0	384,900.0	552,400.0
Balance of trade	US$m	34,474.0	22,545.0	30,400.0	44,652.0	30,700.0
Current account	US$m	20,518.0	17,405.0	35,420.0	16,300.0	70,000.0
Foreign debt	US$bn	149.8	170.0	155.7	150.0	233.3
Total reserves minus gold	US$m	168,278.0	215,605.0	291,128.0	408,151.0	614,500.0
Foreign exchange	US$m	165,574.0	212,165.0	286,407.0	403,251.0	609,932.0
Exchange rate	per US$	8.28	8.28	8.28	8.28	8.28

* estimated figure

was an anti-corruption drive, which had netted some 50,000 individuals since 2004. However, it was only in December 2005 that a high-ranking official was actually convicted. The government also announced, in August, new income tax measures designed to narrow the widening gap between rich and poor, seen by many in the government as the primary cause of social unrest. Also in August, it was announced that 7,000 coal mines deemed to be unsafe were to be closed. In November, plans were announced to scrap the much despised *hukou* system, by which millions of rural people were effectively prevented from moving to urban centres. After warnings, in 2005, from officials that 70 per cent of China's lakes and rivers had been polluted as a by-product of its rapid economic growth, and that 360 million rural people did not have access to safe drinking water, the government began tightening its environmental impact laws.

Alongside these measures, the government also attempted to tighten its grip on the activities of its citizens. In August, the government curbed the number of foreign satellite TV stations allowed to operate in the country, and in September, new restrictions were placed on online news bulletins. A number of high profile political dissidents, including Peng Ming and Xu Wanping were also jailed.

Human rights

A UN Human Rights Commission *rapporteur* declared, visiting China in September, that he was 'guardedly optimistic' about China's human rights record. However, incidences of torture, forced abortions and sterilisation, and the execution of child prisoners were still reported in China in 2005. Two anniversaries marked by the government also underscored China's poor human rights record in relation to its ethnic and religious minorities. In 2005, the government celebrated fifty years of Communist rule in Xinjiang province and forty years since the establishment of an autonomous Communist administration in Tibet. Both regions were forcibly incorporated into the Peoples' Republic of China after the Second World War, having previously broken away from Chinese rule. US-based NGO Human Rights Watch (HRW) co-published, in April, a damning report documenting China's continuing abuse of its Uighur minority, an ethnic Turkic and predominantly Muslim people living in Xinjiang.

China also flexed its muscles in relation to Hong Kong, dispelling any misapprehension that the former British colony was anything other than under Beijing's control. In March, China eased the unpopular Chief Executive of Hong Kong, Tung Chee-hwa, from office and, in June, replaced him with its favoured candidate, Donald Tsang. This followed a request from the Hong Kong government in April, only the second such request since the territory returned to Chinese rule in 1997, to sort out the succession issue. This was, in effect, a plea to interpret the Basic Law, Hong Kong's mini-constitution guaranteeing it special administrative status within China. That the request occurred at all underscored the reality of the power China exercised over the territory.

China and its neighbourhood

China's continuing rise to global economic prominence in 2005 caused unease in many of its neighbours, particularly over how China would use its burgeoning economic clout. Two significant developments in favour of China making direct contributions to neighbourhood stability can be cited. In January 2005 and 2006, direct air links between China and Taiwan were again allowed for travel over Chinese New Year (the number of flights permitted rose from 48 in 2005 to 72 in 2006); and in April, China signed an agreement with old regional rival India, establishing a framework for the solving of a border dispute. However, fears were not allayed in March, when China's government announced a 12 per cent increase in defence spending. At April's 26-member Asia Co-operation Dialogue summit in Pakistan, China's prime minister Wen Jiabao assured his audience that China's rise was a peaceful one, without an agenda for hegemony. President Hu reiterated these sentiments before Vietnam's parliament in November.

Such assurances may have been deemed hollow by some, given developments in the months surrounding the summit. In March, China adopted a law specifically designed to allow military action in the event of Taiwan formally seceding from China. The so-called 'anti-secession' law sparked demonstrations in Taiwan's capital, Taipei, where hundreds of thousands protested against China's aggression. China's relationship with the Taiwan government was not helped by China's decision in May to host Taiwan's then opposition leader, Lien Chan.

The anti-secession law also stymied EU attempts to lift an arms embargo it had imposed upon China in the wake of 1989's Tiananmen Square massacre. Despite pressure from France, Germany and Britain to lift the embargo, against the wishes of the US and Japan, the EU decided that the anti-secession law warranted leaving the embargo in place.

Eyebrows were also raised in international circles when China became the first state to send a high-ranking official to Nepal after a royal coup in that country in February. Following the coup, most countries had imposed an arms embargo on Nepal and had pressured the royalist regime to restore democracy. China, on the other hand, in March and April, was reported to be supplying Nepal with arms and ammunition. With Nepal unable to rely upon its traditional ally and arms supplier India for arms, China's influence correspondingly rose.

China's often fraught relationship with Japan took several turns for the worse in 2005. Adding to the usual Sino-Japanese fracas over visits by Japanese prime minister Junichiro Koizumi to the Yasukuni Shrine, which honours Japanese war dead, including convicted war criminals, were a number of more physical confrontations. A spate of violent anti-Japanese protests rocked China in April, causing damage to Japanese property and consulates. There were two main catalysts for the protests. The first was Japan's decision to seek a permanent seat on the UN Security Council, and the second was a decision by the Japanese education ministry to approve school textbooks that contained material which, according to the Chinese government, downplayed Japanese atrocities committed during Japan's 1936–45 war with China. Analysts noted that the Chinese government gave tacit backing to some of the protests. Compounding these problems were two disputes over China's maritime boundary with Japan in the Yellow Sea. At stake were drilling rights to gas fields potentially worth billions of dollars. In April and July, Japan granted exploration licences to companies, and in September, China was accused by Japan of drilling in the disputed area. All of these disputes, from textbooks to gas fields, precipitated several pointed and high profile snubs, on the part of the Chinese government, of Japanese officials. A Chinese government official went so far as to say, in April, that Sino-Japanese relations were at a 30-year low. Accordingly, in December, the Japanese foreign minister, Taro Aso, called China a military threat to the region.

China and the US

It was a critical year for Sino-American relations, and one reconfirming the vital nature of this relationship, for both the Pacific region and the world. High on Washington's agenda was China's massive trade surplus. In 2005, China's trade surplus with the US was more than US$20 billion, part of which the US Trade Department blamed on China's regulation of the yuan in relation to other currencies. US pressure on China resulted in two revaluations of the yuan, in July and September, although Beijing made sure to maintain the key restriction of not allowing the yuan to fluctuate by more than 0.3 per cent in a single day's trading. This ensured that China's trade surplus with the US was not fundamentally altered in 2005. Also on the matter of trade surpluses, China fought hard to ensure that the US did not impose trade sanctions over the issue of China's textile exports to the US. China managed to strike a deal with the US in November, restricting the growth in its textile exports to US markets.

The attempt in June by China's CNOOC to purchase US-based oil company Unocal threatened to touch off a new dispute between China and the US within the economic sphere. Having offered over US$18 billion for the company, CNOOC found itself the target of sharp criticism within the US Congress. Politicians from both major parties in the US attacked the take-over bid as a strategic threat to their country and its hydrocarbon needs. An American company, Chevron, offered a smaller bid for Unocal, receiving in the process bipartisan support from US legislators. By August, CNOOC was forced to abandon its bid, as it had become clear that China was perceived as a competitor in the global demand for oil.

Relations were also strained by accusations from the Pentagon that China had deployed over 700 ballistic missiles in close proximity to US ally Taiwan. China's ambition, in 2005, to secure a lifting of an EU arms embargo, in place since 1989, was in part thwarted by US lobbying. Further tensions were raised when a Chinese general threatened, in July, nuclear strikes on America's west coast if the US intervened in any Chinese conflict with Taiwan. Secretary of Defense, Donald Rumsfeld, raised further concerns about Chinese missile deployments in October.

China worked hard to decrease US influence in the region in 2005, particularly through its neighbours to the north and west. In May, China was one of the few countries in the world to publicly back President Islam Karimov of Uzbekistan after his violent crackdown against dissidents in the town of Andijan. In July, the Shanghai Co-operation Organisation (SCO), comprised of China, Russia, Uzbekistan, Kyrgyzstan, Kazakhstan and Tajikistan, demanded that the US set a timetable for the evacuation of its bases in Central Asia. In August, China conducted joint military exercises, the first of its kind, with Russia.

In November, a much-anticipated visit to China by US president George W Bush was intended to smooth over nearly a year's worth of sometimes very public differences. However, China brushed off President Bush's appeal for greater freedom and democracy in China and there were no further agreements, either of an economic or military nature, signed during the visit.

Outlook

Data released in January 2006 confirmed China's place as the world's fourth largest economy, behind the US, Japan and Germany. It is predicted by most analysts that its will overtake Germany by 2010. In short, the economic growth of recent years is set to continue apace. However, of concern to China in 2006 will be fears of domestic oversupply, particularly in the steel sector. Moreover, some analysts predict a fall of around 20 per cent in export growth, stemming from a rise in the yuan and a decline in US demand for Chinese imports. Also in January 2006, China's economic growth featured heavily in World Economic Forum (WEF) talks in Davos, Switzerland. China's delegates were on hand to ensure that their country was treated as an 'equal member of the international community', and had to field numerous queries on the future of the yuan and Chinese trade surpluses in general.

China's relationship with the US will continue to be problematic in 2006, although both countries need each other now more than ever. China relies upon access to US markets to underpin much of its economic growth and the US relies on China to buy US bonds that underpin America's budget deficit. China is being relied upon by the US to 'deliver' North Korea in its ongoing talks about terminating North Korea's nuclear capabilities. Although there were signs in 2005 that China wants to see North Korea enter into constructive talks, China looks to be in opposition to the other pillar of America's nuclear disarmament strategy, Iran. In January 2006, China signalled its willingness to back Russia's bid to revive negotiations with Iran over its nuclear programme. Close to the heart of this decision lies China's energy needs and its desire to continue importing Iranian oil. This should underscore the fact that China, like the US and other countries, will relentlessly pursue its strategic objectives in 2006, particularly when it comes to the economy. In terms of China's regional policies, China will no doubt continue to lobby for the closure of US bases in Central Asia, primarily through the SCO forum, and continue to court Taiwan's main opposition party, the Kuomintang (KMT), in the hope of KMT electoral success in presidential elections scheduled for 2008.

Risk assessment

Politics	Stable
Economy	Improving
Regional stability	Stable

COUNTRY PROFILE

Historical profile

From the nineteenth century onwards, the ruling Qing Dynasty (1644–1911) came under increasing pressures from internal demographic and economic imbalances, and incursions from Western powers. Following defeat at the hands of the Japanese (1895) and escalating concessions to Western powers after the Boxer Uprising (1901), the centuries-old system of promotion to the civil service via examinations ended in 1905 and dynastic rule collapsed in 1911. Yuan Shikai failed to become emperor and a chaotic period of rule by 'warlords', regional power-brokers with military resources, ensued.
1920s The Zhongguo Gongchangdang (CCP) (Chinese Communist Party) was formed and declared the southern province of Jiangxi an autonomous 'soviet' in 1927. The Communists were brutally suppressed by the rival Kuomintang (Nationalist Party).
1935 Mao Zedong took control of the CCP during the 'Long March', begun in October 1934, in which thousands of Communist fighters fled Jiangxi for the northern Shanxi province.
1937–45 The Japanese occupied increasingly large areas of China. The government of Chiang Kai-shek and the Kuomintang retreated to Sichuan province in the west of China.
1949 The People's Republic of China was established in October following the victory of Communist guerrilla forces led by Mao Zedong over the Kuomintang government, which fled to the island province of Formosa (now Taiwan).
1950 Tibet (Xizang), an independent region of western China, was occupied by Chinese Communist forces.

Nations of the World: A Political, Economic and Business Handbook

1958–60 In Mao's Great Leap Forward to collectivise agriculture and bring about a socialist economic system, some 40 million people died from hunger.
1965 Tibet became an autonomous region of China, but has not enjoyed any real political or cultural autonomy.
1966 To prevent the establishment of a ruling class and to destroy his enemies within the CCP, Chairman Mao launched the Great Proletarian Cultural Revolution. Some 800,000 died in the cities, but the wider effects of enforced rural re-education were widespread psychological trauma and the breakdown of industry and educational institutions.
1980–97 During this period, the CCP with over 40 million members and political control, was dominated by China's elder statesman, Deng Xiaoping, who initiated gradualist economic reform designed to create a 'socialist market economy'.
1986 The CCP Central Committee adopted a resolution redefining the general ideology of the CCP to provide a theoretical basis for the programme of modernisation and the 'open door' policy of economic reform. An anti-corruption campaign was launched and there was significant liberalisation in the field of culture and the arts. However, student demonstrations in major cities were regarded by China's leaders as excessive 'bourgeois liberalisation'.
1987 In the ensuing clampdown, in January, Hu Yaobang unexpectedly resigned as CCP general secretary, accused of 'mistakes on major issues of political principles'. The thirteenth National Congress of the CCP opened in October. The 'reformist' faction within the Chinese leadership emphasised the need for further reform and the extension of the 'open door' policy. Li Peng became premier of the state council.
1989 The death of Hu Yaobang in Beijing served as a catalyst for the most serious student demonstrations ever seen in the People's Republic of China. The protests were against alleged corruption and nepotism within the government and sought a limited degree of Soviet-style *glasnost* in public life. A state of martial law was declared in Beijing. With the government fearing for its security, the army attacked protesters in and around Tiananmen Square. All over China, similar demonstrations were put down using force. The reformist Zhao Ziyang, CCP general secretary, was confined under house arrest. Deng brought in Jiang Zemin as general secretary to replace him. Jiang was also made chairman of the central military commission.
1990 Martial law was lifted.

1993 Deng retired from his civilian offices, but continued to exert influence over the 'third generation' of leaders, including Jiang, who was elected state president.
1997 China re-established sovereignty over Hong Kong, which had been under British control under a treaty signed during the Qing dynasty.
1998 The Quanguo Renmin Daibiao Dahui (National People's Congress) (NPC) re-elected Jiang as president and chairman of the government's central military commission. Li Peng stepped down as premier, but was named chairman of the NPC and retained his number two ranking in the party hierarchy, officially outranking the new premier Zhu Rongji. The NPC also approved major changes in the leadership, bringing in a new cabinet of younger technocrats.
2000 China signed bilateral trade deals with the EU and the US in preparation for its eventual accession to the World Trade Organisation (WTO) and consequent deeper integration within the global trading system.
2001 Tajikistan, China, Russia, Kazakhstan, Kyrgyzstan and Uzbekistan formed the Shanghai Co-operation Organisation (SCO) and agreed to fight ethnic and religious militancy, while promoting investment and trade. Beijing won its bid to host the 2008 Olympic Games. In October, President Jiang Zemin offered China's support to the US for military action aimed at terrorist activities following the 11 September attacks in the US. China was formally admitted to the WTO. Jiang launched his 'Three Represents' theory.
2002 China began the first round of trade talks with the Association of Southeast Asian Nations (Asean) for the establishment of a free trade zone no later than 2010. Vice President Hu Jintao was formally appointed General Secretary of the CCP.
2003 Due to the spread of the flu-like virus, Severe Acute Respiratory Syndrome (Sars), China threatened to execute or jail for life anyone who intentionally spread Sars. Hu was elected as state president and Zeng Qinghong replaced Hu as vice president. Wen Jiabao was appointed premier. Jiang retained the chairmanship of the Central Military Commission (head of the armed forces). China and Egypt joined a WTO agreement on removing all tariff barriers to information technology products, such as personal computers and telecommunications equipment. China became the third country to put a man in space.
2004 In April, legislators ruled out direct elections for a Hong Kong leader in 2007. Instead of waiting until 2007, Jiang Zemin resigned as chairman of the Central Military Commission on 18 September and President Hu Jintao assumed supreme authority as head of the armed forces, as well as the party and the state.
2005 In March, China's National People's Congress passed an anti-secession law, enshrining Beijing's claim of sovereignty and its threat of military force in the event of Taiwan's formal independence; more than one million people took to the streets in Taipei to express opposition to the law. There were anti-Japanese protests in April, opposing Japan's becoming a permanent member of the UN Security Council. In July, China scrapped its decade-old currency peg with the US dollar and sanctioned a 2.1 per cent revaluation of the renminbi against the dollar.
On 13 November a blast at a chemical factory in Jilin, north-east China, resulted in a spillage of highly toxic benzene and nitrobenzene into the Songhua river, which is the main water source for the city of Harbin and its surrounds (some nine million people in total). The Songhua is a tributary of the Amur river which runs through south-east Russia where cities which draw their water supplies from the Amur prepared for the slick. Yao Wenyuan, last of the 'Gang of Four' died at the end of December.

Political structure
Constitution
The current constitution came into effect in 1982 and mandates complete CCP rule of the country. China's constitution emphasises strict ideological homogeneity and forbids acts that endanger the state security. It states that the Chinese people must adhere to Marxism-Leninism and Mao Zedong Thought.
The People's Republic of China, a unitary state consisting of 22 provinces, four special municipalities under central government control and five autonomous regions, was established in October 1949. The provinces, special municipalities and autonomous regions elect local people's congresses and are administered by people's governments.
Form of state
People's republic
The executive
The executive is the 15-member State Council which is elected by the National People's Congress (NPC). State Council members, including the premier of the State Council, who is appointed by the president, may not serve more than two consecutive five-year terms. The NPC also elects the 155 members of the Standing Committee which convenes annually when the NPC is not in session.
Effective political control is in the hands of the CCP which has over 40 million members. All ministers are party members. The

party's central committee of 175 full members meets irregularly for plenary sessions. A National Congress is usually held every five years when a new central committee is elected.

The political bureau (politburo) of the CCP sets policy and controls all administrative, legal and executive appointments; the nine-man politburo standing committee is the focus of power.

CCP committees are the key decision-making bodies in the provinces, cities and regions into which China is divided.

The president, who plays no formal role in administration, and vice president, are elected for a maximum of two consecutive five-year terms by the NPC.

National legislature
Legislative authority is vested in the unicameral NPC, the 2,979 members of which are elected for five years by provinces, municipalities, autonomous regions and the armed forces.

Legal system
The Chinese legal system is an opaque mix of custom and statute. The judiciary and the government are closely connected. Much of the legal system remains at a partial stage of development.

The hierarchy of people's courts, ranging from Local People's Courts through Intermediate and then Higher People's Courts to the Supreme People's Court, is headed by the Ministry of Justice. The ministry was re-established in 1979 (it had been abolished in 1959 during Mao's 'Great Leap Forward'). Before 1979, arrests and sentences had to be approved by Communist Party committees. Although this practice was abolished in 1979, criminal law is still largely applied by the government as a form of public education, with periodic campaigns of mass arrests and executions used to frighten law-breakers.

People's courts, at all levels, deal with criminal, civic and economic matters in separate tribunals. Local people's mediation committees supplement the work of the courts by dealing with minor criminal offences and civil disputes, as well as helping implement government policy (such as the one-child per couple policy) at street level.

There is a similar hierarchy of people's procurates, re-established in 1978 after their abolition in the cultural revolution, extending from the localities to the Supreme People's Procurate. These monitor the work of state officials in the courts and the public security organs to ensure that they are observing the constitution and the law.

Supreme People's Court judges are appointed by the National People's Congress (NPC).

Last elections
October 2002/March 2003 (National People's Congress (NPC), presidential and State Council).

Results: Parliamentary: no parties other than the Zhongguo Gongchangdang CCP and the eight 'democratic' parties — all members of the China People's Political Consultative Conference — were allowed at the elections. The CCP forms the government.

Next elections
Due by March 2008 (National People's Congress (NPC)); March 2008 (presidential and State Council).

Political parties
Ruling party
Zhongguo Gongchangdang (Chinese Communist Party) (CCP)

Main opposition party
Opposition parties are strictly controlled and do not offer alternative policies. There are no multi-party democratic elections.

Population
1.34 billion (2004)

Ethnic make-up
The largest ethnic group is the Han, constituting 93.3 per cent of the population, which is largely concentrated around the basins of the main rivers (the Yellow River, the Yangtse and the Pearl River) and along the coast. Of the 55 other ethnic groups, 15 number over a million people each, including the Zhuang (Guangxi province), Hui (Muslims), Uygurs (in Xinjiang), Manchus, Tibetans, Mongolians and Koreans. The rest vary in size from several hundred thousand down to a few hundred.

Religions
China is officially atheist, but religion is tolerated to the extent that it does not challenge the state. Buddhism, Taoism, Islam, Catholicism and Protestantism all have followings. The formerly dominant belief system, Confucianism, continues to influence habits throughout society. Old temples, mosques and churches are being reopened and new ones built, but numbers are still far short of pre-revolutionary days. The Falun Gong religious movement is one of the religions considered to be subversive and its members have been arrested and imprisoned.

Education
The Ministry of Education in China estimates that 99 per cent of school-age children enter primary education, the length of which is six years. The retention rate in primary education for the whole country is 93 per cent.

Secondary education extends over six years, divided into general secondary education and vocational/technical secondary education. Both include two stages, junior secondary and senior secondary, of three years each. There are specialised schools and skilled workers' schools which cater for vocational training. The Ministry of Education estimated that 94 per cent of pupils finishing primary education enter secondary schools. It also says that half of pupils finishing junior secondary schools enter senior high education.

The Ministry of Education has encouraged the establishment of community colleges in major cities across China. Public expenditure on education was equivalent to less than 3 per cent of annual GDP in 2001 and included subsidies to private education at the primary, secondary and tertiary levels.

Literacy rate: 91 per cent men, 75 per cent women; adult rates (World Bank).
Compulsory years: 7 to 16.
Pupils per teacher: 24 in primary schools.

Health
Total expenditure on health is around 5.5 per cent of GDP, of which government spending is approximately 37 per cent. Employers pay for the medical care of most Chinese city-dwellers, while the rural population is in theory covered by local insurance schemes, village collectives or rural factories. The state and collective entities, such as factories or villages, run all large hospitals. There are a large number of private practitioners and privately run clinics.

It is estimated that more than one in five Chinese will be 60 years or older by 2030, which is likely to increase state expenses towards old age health care.

World Bank estimates show that 68 per cent and 24 per cent respectively in urban and rural areas have access to improved sanitation. Safe water facilities are available to 94 per cent of the urban population and 66 per cent of the rural population. Around 90 per cent of women use contraceptives, mainly due to the government's drive to keep down the birth rate.

Chinese consumption of tobacco products is popular and estimates say two-thirds of men smoke by the age of 25, with the vast majority maintaining the habit for many years. It is estimated that one third of Chinese men will die from smoking-related diseases, with the annual death toll reaching three million by 2050.

Hospitals rely on drug sales for 70 per cent of their budgets; in May 2004 the Chinese government ordered price cuts for antibiotics, which account for 35 per cent of the Rmb49.6 billion (US$6 billion) pharmaceutical market. This measure is expected to have repercussions as it decreases hospital sales. Analysts say antibiotics are prescribed unnecessarily and the government is concerned about incentives, legal and illegal, that have resulted in hospital doctors prescribing them to about 80 per cent of in-patients.

HIV/Aids
In 2003 there were over 840,000 people reported as living with Aids and there were 44,000 reported deaths due to Aids. The virus is now present in 31 regions and has exploited distinct risk groups. The prevalence of HIV infection among injecting drug users ranges from 35–80 per cent in Xinjiang, and 20 per cent of the population in Guangdong. Some rural communities in Anhui, Henan and Shandong have been hit by infection levels of 10–20 per cent, and as much as 60 per cent in the worst hit areas, where locals sold their blood plasma to supplement their poor incomes. Death rates in these areas are high, although not yet significant enough to affect national statistics.

HIV prevalence: 0.1 per cent aged 15–49 in 2003 (World Bank).
Life expectancy: 70.8 years (World Bank)
Fertility rate/Maternal mortality rate: 1.9 births per woman (2003); maternal mortality 55 per 100,000 live births (World Bank).
Birth rate/Death rate: 7 deaths and 16 births per 1,000 people
Infant mortality rate: 30 deaths per 1,000 live births (World Bank)
Head of population per physician/bed: 1.6 doctors and 2.9 hospital beds per 1,000 people.

Welfare
China's economic development is uneven, with a wide gap between cities and the countryside and between regions. China's social security expenses are typically equivalent to around 10 per cent of GDP. The social insurance system includes provision for old age pensions, unemployment, medical care and industrial injury. Social insurance is implemented in accordance with state laws. The current focus of reform is on old age pension and unemployment insurance systems for urban enterprises. Social security entitlements have been allocated on a geographical footing with the working population being divided into urban and rural residents with the latter receiving far less in terms of benefits. Moreover, the urban population has been further split up into various layers depending on the size and importance of the employing enterprise or work unit. Therefore, a key state-owned enterprise (SOE) would offer better pension rights, wages and medical benefits than a smaller SOE or a township collective enterprise (COE).

In 2003 the government announced that it was increasing the availability of the social security fund to more beneficiaries. The pension system will be available to 150 million people, up from 130 million; the unemployment insurance system will benefit approximately 110 million up from 100 million; and the medicare insurance system will treat 100 million, an increase of 10 million people. Nevertheless, the cost of providing a national farmers' social insurance system was one expense considered too much.

Another safety net beneath these systems is the minimum livelihood guarantee (MLG), which is administered by the Ministry of Civil Affairs (MCA). There are unemployment insurance schemes and some regions have started reforms of the basic medical insurance system.

In 2003, the government announced that it would phase out a jobs-for-life system for the country's 30 million civil servants.

Pensions
There is a partially funded pension scheme, which was launched in 1997, with two mandatory elements, a pay-as-you-go state pension administered by provinces, and individual pension accounts. There are also voluntary company pensions and for those most disadvantaged a social security fund. The pay-as-you-go system is based on contributions from employers and employees with the funds being pooled into a general account. In case of any shortfall, it is the responsibility of the local government to ensure funds are available to pay basic pension allowances. Government statistics indicate that SOEs contribute the majority of cash to pension funds.

In general, the contribution of the employer does not exceed 20 per cent of the overall wage bill of an enterprise. Employee contributions are between 4 and 8 per cent with employees in more developed areas paying the higher rate. The lower tier pension, known as the basic pension, is calculated at 20 per cent of the average wage of employees in the town or city.

As yet, China does not have a national policy for pension provision. Nevertheless the government is aware that with an ageing population and falling fertility rate China's dependency ratio – the numbers in work supporting the numbers in retirement – is projected to drop from 9:1 to 2.6:1 by 2045.

In August 2005 the government awarded operating licenses to 15 investment managers to operate China's new corporate pension scheme. Of the 15, four are foreign financial services ING, Fortis, Deutsche Bank and Bank of Montreal which are required to be in joint Chinese partnership. The new scheme will hold pension contributions in a legally distinct fund governed by trust law.

Main cities
Beijing (capital, estimated population 6.7 million in 2004), Shanghai (9.1 million), Tianjin (4.4 million), Wuhan (4.0 million), Shenyang (3.6 million), Guangzhou (Canton, 3.5 million), Harbin (2.9 million), Xian (2.7 million), Chongqing (2.4 million), Jiulong (2.1 million), Changchun (2.0 million), Chendu (2.0 million), Nanjing (1.9 million), Taiyuan (1.8 million), Jinan (1.8 million), Dalian (1.7 million), Qingdao (1.5 million), Fushun (1.5 million), Lanzhou (1.4 million), Xianggang (1.4 million), Zhengzhou (1.4 million), Datong (1.3 million), Hangzhou (1.3 million), Anshan (1.3 million), Changsha (1.3 million), Guiyang (1.2 million), Jilin (1.2 million), Shijiazhuang (1.2 million), Urumqi (1.1 million), Nanchang (1.1 million), Shenzhen (1.1 million), Fuzhou (1.0 million).

Languages spoken
There are seven main Chinese dialects, but the written language is the same for all dialects. Other languages include Tibetan, Uygur (a Turkic language) and Mongolian.

English is not widely spoken, especially outside the main cities, although there will usually be someone who can speak a little in hotels, restaurants and taxi stations.

Official language/s
Putonghua (Mandarin Chinese – Beijing dialect).

Media
All forms of media in China are directly controlled by the Chinese Communist Party (CCP) or its subordinate organisations. All television and radio stations are run by the state. There are national radio and television networks, and all provinces and some cities have their own stations. Central television stations are under the supervision of the CCP's propaganda department, but provincial stations tend to be less orthodox, buying programmes independently from abroad, which they finance by selling advertising space to foreign firms for hard currency.

The New China News Agency (Xinhua), the official government news agency, has a network of correspondents throughout China and in many posts abroad. A prime responsibility is to provide news reports on foreign and domestic affairs to other official Chinese publications. It has a regular wire called China Economic Information. The service is a daily digest of economic news with specialist and general information. The service carries items in English and Chinese about Chinese market and investment opportunities and data on economic co-operation and trade between

China and other countries. Another official agency is the China News Service which provides news of China to Chinese-language newspapers abroad.

Press

Dailies: Most major cities have both morning and evening newspapers. Major dailies include *People's Daily* (official Communist party newspaper), *Shanghai Wenhui Daily* (official newspaper), *China Youth Daily Yangtse Evening Post* and *Shanghai Liberation Daily*. Some other dailies in HongKong include *Apple Daily*, *HKiMail* and *Sing Tao Daily*. In Shanghai, *News Digest* provides daily local government news. Some of the Chinese language dailies are *JiNan Daily*, *JiNan Times* and *Qingdao News*. The English-language *China Daily* is published in Beijing. *Inside China Today* is a source of daily news, business, politics, and travel information for China.

Apart from the official publications publicly distributed, there is another set of newspapers and magazines, which are 'internal', meant for restricted circulation among different levels of officials. The largest of these internal publications, which are all produced by the New China News Agency, is *Reference News*, a digest of foreign news reports which has a daily circulation of more than three million copies. *Reference Information* is published twice daily for a senior restricted readership and there is an even more tightly restricted publication called *Internal Reference*.

Weeklies: *Guangzhou Morning Post* is published weekly in Chinese.

Business: *Hong Kong Commercial Daily* gives daily news for Hong Kong, Taiwan and specialises in financial news. *Shanghai Daily* focusses on business and the latest information about the city.

Periodicals: After liberalisation of the market in the 1980s there was a proliferation of new titles. Some 6,400 magazines, the bulk of them technical, are published. *Outlook* is a magazine published by the official New China News Agency. *Beijing Scene* is a bilingual lifestyle magazine.

Broadcasting

Various foreign companies have sought good relations with China in an effort to penetrate the presumably vast Chinese market.

In 2001, a landmark deal was established. China granted News Corporation and AOL Time Warner the right to broadcast into Chinese homes in the Pearl River Delta area of the southern province of Guangdong, in return for an agreement to deliver a government-owned Chinese channel (CCTV) in the US. For News Corporation's Chairman, Rupert Murdoch, the approval is a welcome reward after years of wooing Chinese leaders. In mid-2002, News Corp and AOL were negotiating an agreement with Guangdong Cable, which was hoping for a substantial slice of the profits. The agreement, while revolutionary in itself, does not signify a willingness by the Chinese authorities to give up their monopoly of the Chinese television market.

Radio: There are over 1,100 radio stations. Domestic radio services broadcast in the major languages and dialects, with external services in numerous languages.

Television: The China Central Television service is networked throughout the country by a variety of means, including satellite. There are thousands of registered ground receiving stations in China which, as well as providing access to broadcasts from Beijing, enable some users to watch foreign programmes and record them for sale. China has by far the world's largest television audience. There are over 750 cable television stations in China with an estimated 100 million customers.

Advertising

The Advertising Law of 1995 regulates advertising. The state controls the price of advertisements in the various media and foreign advertisers pay a premium. Advertisements must not offend the dignity of the state and should be written in Mandarin. Radio, television, billboards and printed publications are the main forms of advertising, although sponsorship of sports teams and events is also permitted.

Economy

When the Chinese Communist Party (CCP) gained power in 1949, China was a predominantly rural, economically under-developed country. The CCP embarked on a massive industrialisation programme -- the 'Great Leap Forward' - from 1958, which resulted in a marked increase in China's industrial capacity, but was also accompanied by widespread and serious social consequences. Centralisation, government planning and huge industrial combines have characterised the Chinese economy since then, although beginning in 1978, the characteristics of a market economy have been gradually introduced under the tight political leadership of the CCP. Decentralisation of economic decisions grew apace in the 1980s and although the commanding heights of industry remain in state hands, the previous policy of collectivisation in agriculture has been replaced by a system of household responsibility and power has devolved slowly downward to local officials and plant managers. The private sector, although still relatively small, is the fastest growing sector in the economy. With freer economic development has come a strain on natural resources, especially water, and the potential for severe damage to China's natural environment.

The 1980s and 1990s also saw greater emphasis placed on light industrial development, both for exports and to provide consumer goods for domestic consumption. As the government has switched production from labour-intensive to higher technology industries, officials and industrial managers are increasingly marked by their technocratic, rather than ideological background. Against these generally positive trends, corruption remains a problem and economic expansion has outstripped regulatory and financial reform, rendering an uncertain environment for investors who have not been deterred from entering the Chinese market in large numbers.

China is becoming the world's manufacturing centre, as well as its biggest growth market. Since 1996 China has contributed one quarter of the global growth in output and international trade; in the more difficult times since late 2000 it has effectively contributed the whole of growth worldwide.

China has overtaken the US as the world's largest destination of foreign direct investment (FDI) in absolute terms, inflows hitting a record US$57 billion in 2004. Booming investment and growing exports, which generated GDP growth of around ten per cent in 2005, took China from sixth to fourth place in the league of world's biggest economies, after the US, Japan and Germany. Investment accounted for around half of the growth.

In 2005, China revalued its currency by 2.1 per cent. The yuan, which had been pegged to the US$ for ten years, was widely regarded as a cheap currency, giving Chinese exports an unfair advantage in the world market. China had built up a huge trade surplus. Pressure to break the link with the US$ increased, especially after joining the WTO. In July, China complied and delinked the currency from the US dollar, revalued it by 2.1 per cent and allowed it to fluctuate by up to 0.3 per cent on the currency markets. While this measure might slow the rate of growth of China's exports, it was not expected that there would be any marked effect, at least in the near term.

External trade

In 2001, China finally entered the WTO, after 15 years of negotiation and hesitation on the part of the US. Following China's entry into the global trading community, a proposal came from Hong Kong's then chief executive Tung Chee-Hua to create a Free Trade Area (FTA) with the Special Administrative Region (SAR). Hong Kong SAR feared that with increased access to the Chinese market for other countries, it would lose its privileged access to the mainland and was keen to ensure that the Chinese government retained its privileges towards the territory.

Imports
Main categories are light industrial and metal products, machinery and equipment, oil and mineral fuels, plastics, optical and medical equipment, organic chemicals, iron and steel.
Main sources: Japan (16.1 per cent total, 2004), Taiwan (10.9 per cent), South Korea (10.4 per cent), US (7.7 per cent), Hong Kong (7.4 per cent), Germany (5.4 per cent)

Exports
Primary products (food and oil) have declined significantly since the late 1970s, while manufactured goods (especially clothing and textiles) are rising sharply since China joined the WTO. There has been a distinct softening of the official ban on trade with Taiwan. Principal exports include machinery and equipment, plastics, optical and medical equipment, iron and steel.
Main destinations: US (22.8 per cent total, 2004), Hong Kong (16.2 per cent), Japan (12.4 per cent), South Korea (4.4 per cent), Germany (4 per cent)

Agriculture
Farming
China's economy has traditionally been based on agriculture, but since collectivisation and the Mao-era requirement for self-sufficiency in food was replaced with co-operatives in 1976, farming has experienced the progressively hard realities of the market place with large unprofitable state farms closing down and workers made redundant. Agriculture remains an important sector, employing 50 per cent of the labour force, while contributing around 15 per cent of GDP. Since China joined the WTO in 2001 its domestic farmers have been in competition from foreign imports and in 2005, for the first time in decades, China was a net importer of food. There has also been a shift from land-intensive farming of grains to labour intensive crops such as fruit and vegetable to relieve the pressure on farmland and to soak up the abundance of workers.

With a burgeoning industrial base, China is experiencing rapid urbanisation and rural workers, looking for better wages and a share of China's increasing standard of living, have joined the factory line. A land reform law, which took effect in March 2003, enabled farm collectives and members to sell their land; the government's ultimate aim is land privatisation. About 5 per cent of farmland, or 6.7 million hectares (ha), have been lost to mainly industrial development since 1997 and pressure on resources, such as water, is, in some areas, becoming critical. Land use and erosion have resulted in pollution and flooding, which prompted the government to modify the new reforms, including delisting 70 per cent of development zones, thus saving over 24,000 square kilometres of farmland. Although all land is officially owned by the state, land ownership comes in the form of 'land use rights', which give the title-owner rights for between 30–70 years. Forty million farmers have lost the rights to their land since 1984 and rural communities are protesting at the manner of the purchase and sale of farmland.

Re-designated land use has also been initiated by the government with 5.4 million ha of arable land given over to forestry, while cotton growing has dropped by over 7 per cent. Both of these measures, and the reinforced embankment of the middle and lower reaches of the Yangtze and Yellow rivers, are measures designed to stem the disastrous flooding seen increasingly since the early 1990s.

Government policy, incorporating the changes that entry to the WTO has imposed, is mostly concerned with food security. The government's traditional agricultural policy has been to encourage farmers to increase production to meet the needs of the cities, while keeping prices low. This has involved guaranteeing farmers a price for a proportion of their crop and offering it at a subsidised price in the towns. Grain imports prompted government funding for rural regional development with rice procurement prices increased by 20 per cent in 2004.

The government is attempting to increase farm incomes – which are markedly below those in the cities – in the hope that the sector can provide the impetus for growth of consumer products. The government is considering changing agricultural policy to focus more on grain quality rather than quantity in order to cope with external competition. There is likely to be increased rural poverty and unemployment in the medium-term as cheaper imports bite. The conundrum remains of how to increase rural incomes and provide food for a huge population without significant state intervention and, by extension, state distortion of the market.

From 2005, a policy that limits foreign producers of genetically modified (GM) seed crops from accessing the Chinese market runs concurrently with the country's own research and development to produce its GM crops in cotton and rice (US$121 million in 2004). The government's problematic position is hampered by its appreciation of the sales potential for unmodified crops in overseas markets that are reluctant to take GM crops, against the need for higher domestic yields and the possibility for sales of Chinese patented GM seed crops abroad. According to the Centre for Chinese Agricultural Policy, China will need to produce more than 1.5 times the 1999 level of grain output to feed a population of 1.6 billion by 2030. The demand for livestock and aquatic products is forecast to double in the same period.

Crop production ('000) in 2004 included: 413,568 tonnes (t) cereal in total, 177,434t rice, 132,160t maize, 4,202t cassava, 1,646t taro, 91,330t wheat, 70,048t potatoes, 14,385t groundnuts in shell, 13,040t rapeseed (canola), 18,960t seed cotton, 6,320t cotton lint, 105,197t sweet potatoes, 5,800t sugar beets, 3,110t sorghum, 16,618t oilcrops, 14,655t citrus fruit, 3,582t mangoes, 2,410t tobacco, 90,635t sugar cane, 30,142t tomatoes, 12,028t chillies & peppers, 10,578t garlic, 6,420t bananas, 22,163t apples, 5,528t grapes, 1,327t treenuts, 4,929t pulses, 80,646t fruit in total, 423,369t vegetables in total, 861t tea, 260t ginger, 400t various spices, 6000t natural rubber. Livestock production included: 74,432t meat in total, 6,494t beef, 48,267t pig meat, 2,201t lamb, 1,753t goat meat, 14,170t poultry, 2,260t duck meat, 28,434t eggs, 22,914t milk, 306t honey, 1,652t cattle hides, 290t cocoons, silk.

Fishing
With its extensive river network and long coastline, China produces a substantial quantity of fish and exports much of it to its regional neighbours. The total marine fishing ground area is about 818,000 square nautical miles and China has a total of 150 commercially exploitable marine species in its waters. The main species are silver carp, bighead carp, grass carp and tilapia.

China's marine fishing production is made up of small-scale fisheries and the state-owned enterprises (SOEs). The small scale fisheries produce an estimated 90 per cent of the total seafood supply. The reform of SOEs has improved productivity in large-scale fishing operations. In common with other fishing grounds, stocks in the South and East China Seas are becoming depleted. Inland fishing is showing an increase, following a period of decline caused by the depletion of inland freshwater habitats due to dam-building, industrial pollution and land reclamation for agriculture.

Forestry
China has around 14 per cent forest cover, almost evenly divided between coniferous and broadleaved forests. Southern forests are mainly lowland rain forests and monsoon forests. In the north, the majority of forests are mixed coniferous.

The government has embarked on a policy of reforestation. Deforestation was partially blamed for the disastrous extent of the 1998–99 floods which killed thousands and swamped cities, agricultural land and industrial enterprises. Huge coniferous forests have been planted and it is hoped that slower-growing deciduous trees will augment them in the reforested areas.

The State Forestry Administration, has set ambitious targets for China to raise afforestation by 26 per cent by 2050.

China is one of the world's five largest wood-producing countries, although the majority of production is burned as fuel. It is a net exporter of wood products and also produces a large amount of non-wood forest products such as resins, tung oil, essential oils, bamboo poles and bamboo shoots, nuts, mushrooms, honey and medicinal plants.

Exports of forest materials in 2004 amounted to US$4.4 billion, while imports amounted to US$17 billion. Production in 2004 included: 286,104,808 cubic metres (cum) roundwood, 95,061,000cum industrial roundwood, 12,211,000cum sawnwood, 52,623,000cum sawlogs and veneers, 6,678,000cum pulpwood, 41,709,000cum wood-based panels, 191,043,808cum wood fuel, 119,991 tonnes charcoal.

Industry and manufacturing

China's industrial base is highly diversified and ranges from the production of metals and oil refining to light industry such as textiles and computer hardware. The manufacturing sector accounts for around 37 per cent of GDP. The major industries are mechanics, electronics, metallurgy, chemicals, building materials, furniture, woodwork, textiles, clothing, food, petroleum and coal processing. The government has been focussing on restructuring the industrial sector and introducing advanced technology. The government hopes to phase out small scale production and encourage foreign participation, particularly in the chemicals industry. The development of effective, low-cost chemicals for agricultural use is a top priority.

China has become a production centre for a multitude of labour-intensive assembly industries. China produces around 75 per cent of the global supply of textiles. There is considerable foreign investment coming from Hong Kong (which accounts for most of new funding in the Shenzhen Special Economic Zone), Japan and the US. China has the ability to exploit vertical economic linkages from its impressive natural resources to heavy industry and the manufacturing of white goods, which has shown impressive growth since the early 1990s.

China is a net exporter of aluminium and stands to become one of the world's largest aluminium producers. It is also a major exporter of magnesium, although competitors have complained that China has driven down global magnesium prices through price dumping on commodity markets. China is the world's largest steel producer. Steel exports more than doubled in 2004 and the growth continued into 2005, making China the third leading exporter of steel after Japan and Russia. At the same time, imports of steel have fallen.

Vehicle production is an important growth sector. On the basis of growth levels sustained since the late 1990s, China stands to become one of the world's largest car exporters by 2010.

China's attraction as a foreign investment destination has increased since it became a WTO member, since low production costs and cheap labour have encouraged many foreign businesses to transfer their operations to the mainland. The main concern is that increased competition will have a devastating effect on state-owned industries. More joint-venture companies are likely to evolve over time, leading to mixed-ownership control in the industrial sector.

Chinese industry is faced with an increasing domestic oversupply problem. At the same time, domestic demand has fallen as state-owned enterprises lay off workers as part of the government's restructuring programme. This has increased competition within Chinese industry, causing deflation and putting pressure on factory gate prices. The problems facing the industrial sector have led to concerns that Chinese companies, stimulated by the government's fiscal pump-priming of the economy, have been investing too much in increasing capacity.

Problems facing China's industrial sector are the lack of workable bankruptcy laws and the corruption of local officials, who are keeping failing industries afloat. State-owned banks are forced to carry the burden of the industrial sector's debt, a burden that is unsustainable. An eventual clamp-down on non-performing loans within the banking sector will affect the industrial sector. The government is encouraging investment in privately-owned industrial firms, with the possibility of opening up the sector to further foreign investment.

Tourism

China is one of the world's most visited destinations. In 2004, China displaced Italy as the world's fourth most popular desination. The tourism sector is being vigorously developed and promoted. Its contribution to the economy is growing and is expected to account for 2.4 per cent of GDP in 2005. Infrastructure is being continuously expanded and will receive extra impetus from the preparations for the 2008 Olympic Games in Beijing. The upward trend of tourist numbers was interrupted for the first time in 2003 as a result of the Sars outbreak, but recovery has been quick. Visitor numbers increased by 27 per cent in 2004 to 42 million.

Environment

While a project of land reclamation has been in operation since 2001, in the North Western Ningxia Hui autonomous region, where willows and grass are helping to beat back the desert, for many regions around China the prospects are not so good. Over 1,350 square miles of land is lost to desert each year which covers about 18 per cent of the land. Desertification is accelerating and threatens a further one-third of the country and 400 million people. The national policy of self-sufficiency in food in the past resulted in the cultivation of unsuitable grain crops in desert frontiers and, coupled with logging and over-exploitation exacerbated by a natural lack of water and rainfall has led to rapid soil erosion.

The beginnings of a forest have been planted in Yanchi in an effort to avert the spring sand storms that sweep through Beijing each spring.

Mining

China's mining industry ranks as one of the largest in the world, although production statistics are sketchy. Most of China's mineral production is consumed locally by state-owned enterprises (SOEs). There are around 80,000 SOEs and 200,000 collectively-owned mines. China is an important producer of copper, tungsten, antimony, lithium and molybdenum, and also produces significant quantities of zinc, lead, manganese, tin, mercury and rare earths. China ranks among the top five countries for its reserves of antimony, barite, graphite, magnesite, fluorite, molybdenum, tin and tungsten. China imports alumina, chromite, cobalt, copper, iron ore, manganese and other platinum-group metals. China is an extremely important market for the global minerals industry and is one of the largest mineral exporters, importers and producers in the world.

China is becoming increasingly important in the molybdenum market and has substantially more deposits of rare earth elements than the rest of the world, 97 per cent of them in the Bayan Obo iron ore mined in Inner Mongolia.

Hydrocarbons

China had proven oil reserves of 17.1 billion barrels in 2004 and produced around 3.5 million bpd. Ninety per cent of Chinese oil production is located onshore, with Daqing in north-eastern China accounting for nearly a third of total production. Offshore exploration is concentrated on the Bohai Sea, which is believed to have 1.5 billion barrels of reserves. The Pearl River Delta is also a major area of exploration. Oil production is currently dominated by several large state-owned firms and the government is in the process of restucturing state sector oil companies. China is one of the largest oil consumers in the world, overtaking Japan to be second to the US. Consumption in 2004 was 6.7 million barrels per day (bpd), increasing by 15.8 per cent from 2003. China, whose oil requirements are increasing year by year to feed the burgeoning economic expansion, is a net importer of oil and is active in securing supplies around the world.

China had natural gas reserves of 2.23 trillion cubic metres (cum) in 2004, mainly located in Xinjiang Uyghur Autonomous region and Inner Mongolia. Production was at 40.8 billion cum, increasing by 18.5 per cent on 2003. Consumption was just under this figure at 39.0 billion cum. Demand is increasing at a greater rate than production. With investment increasing by around 20 per cent annually, production is likely to continue increasing. A 4,000km pipeline, bringing gas to the urban coastal areas, opened in 2005. China plans to replace coal with gas as the main source of power generation in homes in the main urban areas and this pipeline could eventually be extended to tap the large gas reserves of Central Asia. China had coal reserves of 114.5 billion tonnes in 2004 and produced 989.8 million tonnes oil equivalent (mtoe). Consumption was 956.9 mtoe and is expected to increase. The main export destinations for Chinese coal are South Korea and Japan. China is becoming more open to foreign investment in its coal industry.

Energy

China's total installed generating capacity stood at 508GW in 2005 and continues to expand to meet the demands of the onward economic rush. Around 70 per cent is supplied by coal, reserves of which China has in abundance. Although more coal will be used for generation in the future and a large number of new coal-fired power stations are projected, the proportion of natural gas use is rising. Electric consumption by sector is: heavy industry – 60 per cent, light industry – 15 per cent, residential – 10 per cent, government – 7 per cent, agriculture – 6 per cent, transport and telecommunications – 2 per cent.

The use of hydropower for generation is being expanded with new stations being constructed. On completion in 2009, the giant Three Gorges dam will have a capacity of 18.2GW produced by 26 separate 700MW generators. Another large hydroelectric project will involve a series of dams on the Yellow River, with 25 generating stations with a combined installed capacity of 15.8GW.

The government is also expanding nuclear power generating capacity, with the construction of a number of plants in joint ventures with Russian, French and Canadian firms.

The government hopes eventually to unify electricity distribution into one national power grid with power generators selling their electricity at rates determined by a free market.

Financial markets

Stock exchange

In 1986, the stock market in Shanghai, the largest in East Asia before 1949, re-opened to trade shares and bonds. China has since opened securities exchanges in 44 cities, including the capital Beijing, but trading so far has been thin. Shanghai and the Shenzhen Stock Exchange (formally opened in 1991) remain the two major markets for both domestic and foreign investors. Both markets list 'A' shares (for domestic investors) and 'B' shares (for foreign investors) as well as bonds and warrants. As a result of further planned privatisation, Shanghai's total market capitalisation is expected to increase from US$600 billion in 2002 to US$2 trillion by 2010, although there are uncertainties surrounding the government's commitment to the privatisation programme. The market, driven by millions of retail investors, is thought to be overvalued and subject to illegal manipulations.

Banking and insurance

China's accession to the WTO in late 2001 means that reform in the country's banking sector became essential for China's domestic banks to compete with foreign-owned banks in the future. This meant eliminating corruption at the highest levels of management. Under the WTO agreement, foreign banks were allowed to offer renminbi banking services to Chinese corporations from 2004, and will be allowed to offer services to Chinese individuals from 2007.

In 2003, the country was dominated by four large banks, the Bank of China, the Agricultural Bank of China, China Construction Bank and Industrial and Commercial Bank of China, which between them controlled 80 per cent of banking services. WTO membership gives foreign banks the right to compete with domestic ones and all restrictions on the setting up, operation and licensing of foreign banks were eliminated by 2005. In addition, state-owned banks are to provide foreign currency services. In December 2001, HSBC became the first foreign bank to obtain equity in mainland China when it acquired 8 per cent in the Bank of Shanghai.

Central bank

People's Bank of China. The central bank became an autonomous financial institution in 1995.

Time

GMT plus eight hours (except north-west Xinjiang province: GMT plus six hours). From April to September (summertime) GMT plus nine hours (Xinjiang: GMT plus seven hours).

Geography

China is the third-largest country in the world after Russia and Canada. Its 28,000km land boundary touches North Korea, Russia, Mongolia, Afghanistan, Pakistan, India, Nepal, Bhutan, Myanmar, Laos and Vietnam.

China is bounded by the Yellow and East China Seas to the east and by the South China Sea to the south.

Deserts and semi-arid grasslands make up much of the western and northern parts of the country. Central and eastern China are the most heavily populated parts of the country. The plains of north and north-east China are flat and fertile, but frequently suffer from prolonged drought. Mountain ranges occupy 33 per cent of China's area. Most of China's main rivers run west to east. The longest is the Yangtze River, followed by the Yellow River. The Yangtze River is known as Chiangjiang ('long river') in China. Much of China was once covered by forest, but due to dense settlement and intensive agriculture, most forests have disappeared.

Climate

China has an extremely diverse climate, with tropical areas in the south contrasting with the subarctic north and mountainous Tibet. Most of China, especially coastal areas, has a relatively temperate climate. The average temperature there in summer is 20 degrees Celsius (C). However, in the interior a number of cities are known as 'freezing hells in winter, furnaces in summer'. In winter, the average temperature in southern and central China is about 4 degrees C. Most rain falls in summer, the season when typhoons often hit the south-east coast.

China is hit every summer by severe floods. The worst affected areas are the middle and upper reaches of the Yangtze River. This contrasts to an increasing water shortage in north China, with the Yellow River typically running dry before it reaches the sea because of farmers' use of the river as a source for irrigation.

Dress codes

Foreign businessmen generally wear suits and ties to negotiating sessions with Chinese counterparts, who have abandoned the Mao suit for Western dress. Less formal attire is acceptable outside the main cities.

Fashion-consciousness is growing among younger urban Chinese, but attire is not as important as it is in the West. However, foreigners need a supply of more formal clothes for business and social occasions with other members of the foreign community.

Entry requirements

Passports
All visitors need to hold a passport with validity of a minimum of six months. Passports should have at least a few blank pages for visas and entry and exit stamps.

Visa
Required by all, except transit passengers. Business visits can only be made with an invitation of a Chinese organisation such as a ministry or commercial institution. Foreign firms may request such invitations from a trading corporation. An invitation in the form of a fax is usually sufficient for the visa application which should also include a business letter and itinerary. For up-to-date information concerning visas contact the nearest consulate.

It is possible for individuals to organise their own itinerary and when this has been confirmed by the authorities, the visitor must finance the cost of accommodation and the tour by depositing the amount, through a home bank, with China International Travel Service.

If arriving from Mongolia: airlines in Ulaanbaatar require holders of foreign passports to have a Chinese visa in order to board the aircraft for flights to Beijing. This requirement applies regardless of the length of time in transit at Beijing, where there is no airside transit facility.

Currency advice/regulations
Unlimited import of foreign currency is allowed, provided it is declared on arrival. Export and import of local currency is limited to Rmb20,000; export of foreign currency up to the amount imported and declared is permitted. Local currency is available in exchange for traveller's cheques. US dollars and pounds sterling are available in China. There is a black market but the parallel rate does not diverge radically from the official rate.

Customs
Certain items produced in China before 1949, such as embroidery, silks, porcelain, scrolls and *objets d'art*, may be subject to export restrictions. When arriving, list tape recorders and camera gear on customs forms; if these items are not with the traveller on departure, the traveller is liable to pay duty on them. Receipts for any major purchases, especially paintings and antiques, should be kept.

Prohibited imports
It is illegal to import any printed material, films, tapes, etc. However, this only applies to material that is viewed to be adverse to China's politics, economy, culture and ethics.

Health (for visitors)

In April 2003, the World Health Organisation (WHO) temporarily advised travellers against visiting Beijing in a move to halt the global spread of Sars, a flu-type disease. Although the disease seems to have been contained there are still the occasional cases reported, especially in the south.

Mandatory precautions
Vaccination certificates are required for yellow fever if travelling from an infected area.

Advisable precautions
Take precautions against AIDS and malaria (generally confined to the southern part of China near the border with Myanmar and Vietnam, although in the summer months the Yangtze River basin is also affected). Rabies is endemic and bilharzia is present in southern and eastern parts of the country. Vaccinations should be taken against hepatitis 'A' and 'B', diphtheria, tuberculosis, Japanese 'B' encephalitis, polio, tetanus and typhoid. Drink only bottled water, avoid unpeeled fruit and salads and try to ensure all food has been thoroughly cooked. It is advisable to have emergency medical insurance; in Beijing two companies – Asia Emergency Assistance (AEA) and International SOS Assistance – offer evacuation services.

Hotels

There is no shortage of accommodation in peak seasons. The main hotels in major cities are of a reasonable standard, but many hotels are frugal, often with fixed-time, fixed-menu meals and even cold water only during certain hours in the evening and morning. There are new hotels built with foreign assistance (in Nanjing, Guangzhou, Beijing and Zhjanjiang) and international-standard joint-venture hotels (in Tianjin, Hainan, Xiamen, Fujian, Hangzhou and Shenzen). Charges for government guest houses, which are used to accommodate hotel overflows, are high.

Reservations for business visitors are made by their host organisations. Joint venture hotels are able to accept bookings from outside China. Hotel reservations for over 70 Chinese cities are being computerised. Tipping is officially forbidden in China, although small tips are occasionally 'expected' by porters and bell boys in larger hotels. The custom is uneven, and tips will often be refused.

Credit cards

Credit cards are accepted at tourist hotels and tourist shops in major cities. Use of cash or traveller's cheques is more usual. Cash withdrawals from banks are possible with major cards, but are not encouraged and frequently entail long delays.

Public holidays

Fixed dates
1–2 Jan (New Year's Holiday), 1–3 May (May Day), 1–3 Oct (National Day).

Variable dates
Chinese New Year (Jan/Feb)

Working hours

Banking
Mon–Fri: 0900–1200, 1400–1700.

Business
Mon–Fri: 0800–1130, 1300–1700.

Government
Mon–Fri: 0800–1200, 1300–1700.

Shops
Mon–Sun: 0900–1900.

Electricity supply

220/240V AC, 50Hz. Two-pin sockets and some three-pin sockets used. Mostly flat plug fittings, with two-pin round as well in some hotels, and generally, screw-type light bulb fittings.

Weights and measures

Metric system (with Chinese units in use).

Social customs/useful tips

Although tipping is officially discouraged, it is now more common in places such as the Special Economic Zones (SEZs), although even there it is still optional. However, it is courteous to thank hotel and restaurant staff for their services. It is customary to present a business card. The full title of the People's Republic of China should be used for formal communications.

Doing business needs patience; punctuality is vital, being especially valued on the part of the visitor. Contact with nationals has become easier recently, although local sensitivities still remain. Discussing politics or religion is strictly forbidden. Unofficial contact between foreigners and local Chinese was effectively banned until reforms gathered momentum in the 1980s and 1990s. The borderline of what is permissible remains unclear, and contact by Chinese with some categories of foreigners such as journalists may still attract adverse attention.

Taiwan (Formosa) is considered a province of China, and should not be referred to as a country. It is quite acceptable nowadays to discuss Taiwan, though the visitor may have to ask questions with considerable art as the Chinese do not volunteer much information.

Bureaucratic procedures are many and the frustrations of grappling with the Chinese bureaucracy are considerable. The visitor should assume that virtually all negotiations are going to take far longer than would be necessary in a Western country.

It is advisable to have a destination written in Chinese characters.

Eating can be a tricky business but there are a few important things to remember to save embarrassment on the part of the foreigner. When dining with the Chinese, and certainly with professionals, you should wait until your seat is 'allocated' by a nod or a subtle indication by the host. The Chinese have great respect for authority and title and this determines where a person will be seated at a table. One should not begin eating until indicated to do so. Take care not to 'upset' the presentation of the food as this is considered very offensive. When eating with chopsticks do not position them upright in your ricebowl. The gesture is symbolic of death and should be avoided.

When being served tea, it is customary to tap the table with your forefingers as a gesture of thanks.

The Chinese are highly 'face' conscious and try to avoid self-embarrassment at all costs. It is important that foreigners endeavour not to mock, satirise or embarrass their Chinese counterparts in any way as this will definitely ruin any developing relationship.

Security

China's cities probably rate among the world's safest after dark, although some, such as Shenzhen and Wuhan have a worse reputation. Only a tiny handful of the several million foreign visitors to enter China in recent years have been the victims of violent crime. Thefts are relatively rare, perhaps because the authorities investigate and punish crimes against foreigners with special vigour. The usual precautions should be taken with valuables.

Organised gangs, some of them Hong Kong-based, are reported to operate in the southern city of Guangzhou (formerly Canton). Their methods include drugging and robbing businessmen.

Chinese criminal law is much harsher than in most Western countries, and Chinese society is still very puritanical in sexual matters.

Getting there
Air
Air China dominates inbound travel, although foreign airlines do land in China. There are various air routes into the country, but landing in Hong Kong is significantly cheaper than mainland China.
National airline: Air China.
International airport/s: Capital (PEK), 26km north of Beijing, with duty-free shop.
Hongqiao (SHA), 12km from Shanghai, with restaurant, shops; Pudong International, 30km from Shanghai, 60 minutes by car. There are special buses; services to and from the city run from 06.00–19.00. Facilities include internet cafés, restaurants, bars, duty-free shops and short-stay hotel rooms for passengers. Baiyun International (CAN) – the new airport opened in August 2004 – 12km north of Guangzhou (capital of Guangdong Province).
Other airport/s: Include: Chengdu; Guilin; Haikou; Kunming and Tianjin.
Airport tax: Domestic Rmb15–50; international Rmb90–120, including 24-hour transit passengers.
Surface
Road: Motorways have been built between Guangzhou and Shenzhen and Guangzhou and Zhuhai. These roads link the cities of Dongguan, Zhongshan, Foshan, Jiangmen, Huizhou and Shunde to Hong Kong and Macau. Motorway links to major cities from neighbouring countries are few, partly reflecting the fact that most of China's neighbours, including Laos and North Korea, are poorer than China itself.
Rail: The Kowloon-Canton Railway Corporation (KCRC) has express trains serving Kowloon-Guangzhou and an indirect Kowloon-Lowu service.
The Trans-Siberian Express operates two weekly services, a train to Russia serving Moscow-Beijing via Harbin and a China train via Ulaanbaatar.
Nanning, in Guangxi province, is linked by rail to Hanoi, Vietnam. A second cross-border runs from Kunming, the capital of China's south-western province of Yunnan, via Lao Cai, to Hanoi.
Water: Daily hovercraft services operate between Hong Kong and Guangzhou, and also serve Shekou, Shenzhen and Zhuhai. There are also regular services between Weihai and Inchon in South Korea, and a weekly service between Shanghai and Osaka in Japan.

Getting about
National transport
Air: The Civil Aviation Administration of China (CAAC) controls internal air travel and operates several domestic airlines including China Eastern, China Northern, China Southern and Yunnan Airlines. These provide regular services between the major cities, with first-class service on some routes. Flights are always overbooked and seats should be confirmed as a matter of course. Independent regional airlines also operate. Tickets not booked through an official guide/travel service should be booked and collected well in advance. Allow plenty of time for inevitable and often prolonged delays in services. Airport announcements are not multilingual.
Road: There are 1.18 million km of internal roads, but most are narrow and poorly surfaced and only 241,300km are paved, making long-distance travel time-consuming. A superhighway links Beijing and Tianjin, and a 138km four-lane toll highway links Hangzhou and the port of Ningbo in Zhejiang Province. These are linked into a network of 12 major highways across the country.
Buses: Extensive, long distance services are available, it is advisable to book seats in advance.
Rail: The rail network has over 64,900km of track, with 10,400km electrified, although most locomotives are steam-powered. Rail services operate between main cities. Deluxe rail services, with opulent German-made sleeping cars and private dining coaches, are available. Generally, rail travel is comfortable but time-consuming because long distances are involved.
Water: Inland waterways and coastal shipping services are an important form of transport.
City transport
Taxis: Taxi service is available in all major cities. It can be difficult to find a taxi except at hotels. Metered taxis may be hailed in the street in Guangzhou and Shenzhen. Taxis hired by the day charge on the basis of distance travelled and waiting time. If possible, it is best to retain a taxi until returning to the hotel, paying the driver a small waiting fee during appointments or meals. Tipping is not practised.
Buses, trams & metro: Beijing has an underground railway; Shanghai is constructing one and Guangzhou is planning one. There are extensive local bus services in main cities, generally inexpensive but crowded.
Car hire
Foreigners are generally not allowed to drive in China so self-drive car hire is not available. Chauffeur-driven cars may be hired at a standard rate on a daily basis. Bicycle hire is available in some towns, but it is advisable to carry proof of identity when riding.

China

BUSINESS DIRECTORY

The addresses listed below are a selection only. While World of Information makes every endeavour to check these addresses, we cannot guarantee that changes have not been made, especially to telephone numbers and area codes. We would welcome any corrections.

Telephone area codes

The International direct dialling (IDD) code for China is +86, followed by the area code:

Beijing	10	Shanghai	21
Dalian	411	Shenyang	24
Fuzhou	591	Shenzen	755
Guangzhou	20	Tianjin	22
Jinan	531	Wenzhou	577
Nanjing	25	Wuhan	27
Qingdao	532	Xi'an	29

Useful telephone numbers

Beijing

Police	110
International calls, English-language	337-431
	553-536
Local, long-distance enquiries	116
Cable and telex information	664-900
Taxis	557-671
Airport-flight enquiries	552-515
	555-531, ext 382

Shanghai

Ambulance	120
Police	110
Fire	119

Chambers of Commerce

American Chamber of Commerce -PRC, 1903 China Resources Building, 8 Jianguomenbai Dajie, Beijing 100005 (tel: 8519-1920; fax: 8519-1910; e-mail: amcham@amcham-china.org.cn).

British Chamber of Commerce in China, China Life Tower, 16 Chaoyangmenwai Avenue, Beijing 100020 (tel: 8525-1111; fax: 8525-1100; email: director@pek.britcham.org).

Banking

Agricultural Bank of China, Jia 23 Fu Xing Road, Beijing 100036 (tel: 6847-5321; fax: 6829-7160).

Bank of China, 410 Fuchengmen Nei Dajie, Beijing 100818 (tel: 6601-6688; fax: 6601-6869).

Beijing City Commercial Bank Corp Ltd, 2nd Floor, Tower B Beijing International Financial Building, 156 Fuxingmennei Street, Beijing 100031 (tel: 6642-6928; fax: 6642-6691/9).

Bank of Communications, 18 Xianxia Lu, Shanghai 200335 (tel: 6275-1234; fax: 6275-6784).

China Construction Bank, No 25 Finance Street, Beijing 100032 (tel: 6759-8050; fax: 6759-7353).

China Minsheng Banking Corporation Ltd, 4 Zheng Yi Lu, Dong Cheng District, Beijing 100006 (tel: 6526-9578).

Hua Xia Bank, Xidan International Mansion, No. 111 Xidan North Avenue, Xicheng District, Beijing 100032 (tel: 6615-1199, 6612-9139; fax: 6618-8484).

Central bank

People's Bank of China, 32 Chengfang Street, Xicheng District, Beijing 100800 (tel: 6619-4114; fax: 6601-5346; e-mail: master@pbc.gov.cn).

Travel information

Air China, Beijing Capital Airport, Beijing 100621 (tel: 6456-3201; fax: 6456-3831; e-mail: webmaster@airchina.com.cn).

Beijing Capital Airport, Beijing 100621(tel: 6456-4247; fax: 6457-0487).

China Eastern Airlines, 2550 Hingqiaolu, Shanghai 200335 (tel: 6268-6268; fax: 6268-6116; e-mail: webmaster@ce-air.com).

China International Travel Service (CITS), 103 Fuxingmennei Dajie, Beijing 100800 (tel: 6601-1122; fax: 6601-2021; e-mail: webmaster@cits.net).

China Southern Airlines, Baiyun International Airport, Guangzhou 510405 (tel: 8612-4738; fax: 8665-9040; e-mail: webmaster@cs-air.com).

Shanghai Hongqiao Airport, Shanghai 200335 (tel: 6269-0029; fax: 6269-0027).

National tourist organisation offices

National Tourism Administration of the People's Republic of China (CNTA), 9A Jianguomennei Avenue, Beijing 100740 (tel: 6520-1114; fax: 6512-2096; internet site: http://www.cnta.gov.cn/lyen/index.asp).

Ministries

Ministry of Agriculture, 11 Nonzhanguan Nanli, Beijing 100026 (tel: 6419-1114; fax: 64192468).

Ministry of Civil Affairs, 147 Beiheyan Dajie, Beijing 100721 (tel: 6523-5511; fax: 6513-5332).

Ministry of Communications, 11 Jianguomennei Dajie, Beijing 100736 (tel: 6529-2114; fax: 6529-2345).

Ministry of Construction, Baiwanzhuang, Haidian District, Beijing 100835 (tel: 6839-3970; fax: 6839-3333).

Ministry of Culture, A83 Dong'anmen Beijie, Beijing 100722 (tel: 6401-2255; fax: 6403: 1266).

Ministry of Defence, 20 Jinshanquianjie, Beijing 100009 (tel: 6673-0000).

Ministry of Education, 37 Damucang Hutong, Xidian, Beijing 100820 (tel: 6609-6114; fax: 6601-1049).

Ministry of Foreign Affairs, 2 Chaonei Dajie, Dongcheng Districti, Beijing 100701 (tel: 8596-1114).

Ministry of Health, 44 Beiheyan, Xicheng District, Beijing 100725 (tel: 6403-4433; fax: 6401-2369).

Ministry of Information Industry, 13 Xichang'anjie, Beijing 10084 (tel: 6601-4249; fax: 6201-6362).

Ministry of Justice, 10 Chaoyangmen Nandajie, Beijing 100020 (tel: 6520-5254).

Ministry of Labour and Social Security, 12 Hepingli Zhongjie, Dongcheng District, Beijing 100716 (tel: 6421-3240).

Ministry of Land and Natural Resources, 64 Funeidajie, Xicheng District, Beijing 100812 (tel: 6616-5566; e-mail: master@mail.mlr.gov.cn).

Ministry of Personnel, 12 Hepingli Zongjie, Beijing 100716 (tel: 6421-3240).

Ministry of Public Security, 14 Dongchang'anjie, Beijing 100741 (tel: 6512-1967).

Ministry of Railways, 10 Fuxinglu, Haidian District, Beijing 100844 (tel: 6324-0114; fax: 6324-2150).

Ministry of Science and Technology, 15 Fuxinglu, Haidian District, Beijing 100038 (tel: 6851-5544; fax: 6851-5004).

Ministry of State Security, 14 Dongchang'anjie, Beijing 100741 (tel: 6524-4702).

Ministry of Supervision, 4 Zaojunmiao, Haidian District, Beijing 100081 (tel: 6225-4129).

Ministry of Water Resources, 2 Ertiao, Baiguanglu, Xuanwu District, Beijing 100053 (tel: 6320-2114; fax: 6320-2650).

Other useful addresses

China International Trust and Investment Corporation (CITIC), Capital Mansion, 6 Xinuan Nanlu, Beijing (tel: 6466-0088; fax: 6466-1186; e-mail: g-office@citic.com.cn).

China National Chemicals Import & Export Corporation (SINOCHEM), A2 Fuxingmenwai Dajie, Beijing 100046 (tel: 6856-8888; fax: 6856-8890).

China National Instruments Import & Export Corporation, Erligou, Xijiao, Beijing 100044 (tel: 6831-7393; fax: 6831-59251).

China National Light Industrial Products Import & Export Corporation (CHINALIGHT), 910 Jinsongjiu Qu,

Beijing 100747 (tel: 6776-6688; fax: 6774-7245).

China National Machinery Import & Export Corporation, PO Box 49, Erligou, Xijiao, Beijing (tel: 6849-4851; fax: 6831-4143).

China National Metals & Minerals Import & Export Corporation, Building 15, Block 4, Anhui Li, Chaoyang District, Beijing 100101 (tel: 6491-6666; fax: 6491-7031).

China National Offshore Oil Corporation, PO Box 4705, 6 Dongzhimenwai Xioajie, Beijing 100027 (tel: 8452-1010; fax: 8452-1044; e-mail: webmaster@cnooc.com.cn).

China National Petroleum Corporation, 6 Liupukang Jie, Xicheng District, Beijing 100724 (tel: 6422-2946; fax: 6426-6302; e-mail: webmaster@hq.cnpc.com.cn).

China National Technical Import and Export Corporation (CNTIC), Jiuling Building, 21 Xisanhuan Bei Lu, Beijing 100081 (tel: 6840-4106; fax: 6841-4877).

China Ocean Shipping Agency (PENAVICO), Tower Crest Plaza, 3 Maizidian Road West, Chaoyang District, Beijing (tel: 6461-1188; fax: 6467-3118; e-mail: general@penavico.com.cn).

Chinese Embassy (US), 2300 Connecticut Avenue, NW, Washington DC 20008 (tel: 202-238-5000; fax: 202-588-0032; e-mail: chinaembassy_us@fmprc.gov.cn).

Chinese Export Commodities Fair, 117 Liuhua Road, Guangzhou (tel: 8666-1664; fax: 8333-5880; e-mail: info@cecf-info.com).

General Administration of Customs, 6 Jiannei Dajie, Beijing 100730 (tel: 6519-4114; fax: 6519-4004).

Shanghai Advertising Corporation, 117 Xianggang Road, Shanghai 200002 (tel: 6321-7599; 6329-0068).

State Administration for Industry and Commerce, 8 Sanlihe Donglu, Xicheng District, Beijing 100820 (tel: 6803-2233; fax: 6857-0848).

State Administration of Entry-Exit Inspection and Quarantine, A10 Chaowai Dajie, Chaoyang District, Beijing 100020 (tel: 6599-4600; fax: 6599-4306).

Internet sites

Archive of Chinese news digest, also contains links to other Chinese sites: http://www.cnd.org.

Beijing Landmark Towers Hotel: http://www.chinatour.com.

China Business Pages: http://www.chinapages.com.

China Web (investment data, Shanghai city information, stock prices, travel arrangements and a searchable directory of key figures in commerce, industry and government): http://www.comnex.com

China Window information on country, government and business activities: http://china-window.com/

Shanghai business: http://www.sh.com

Colombia

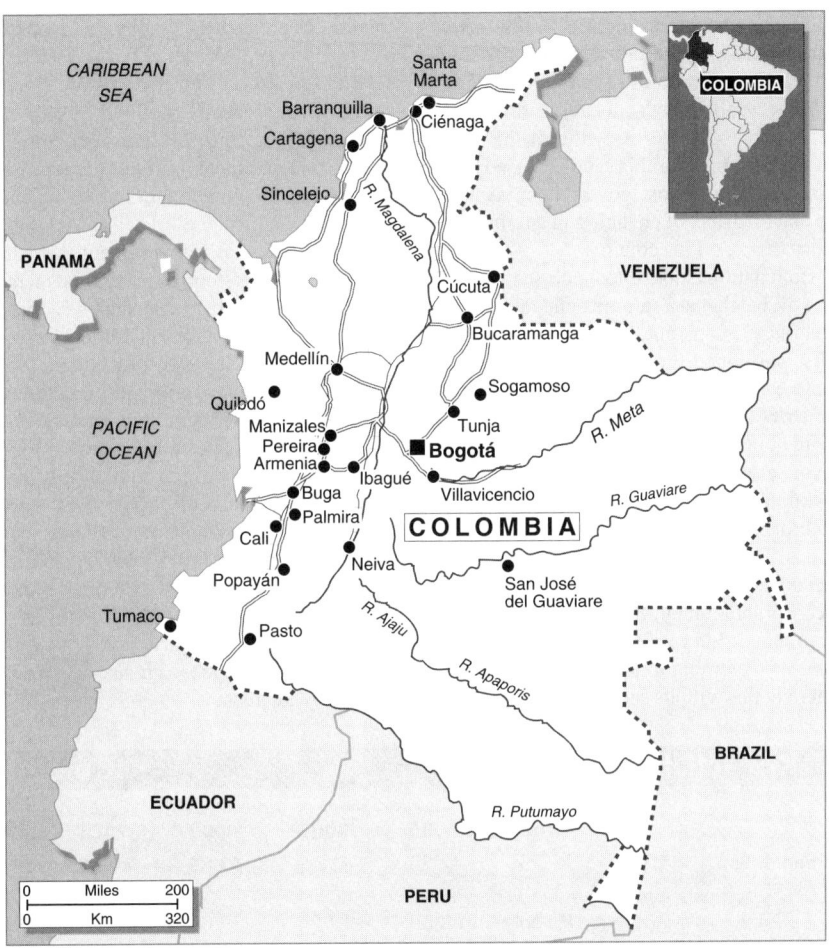

KEY FACTS

Official name: República de Colombia (Republic of Colombia)

Head of State: President Álvaro Uribe Vélez (sworn in 7 Aug 2002)

Head of government: President Álvaro Uribe Vélez

Ruling party: As President Uribe was elected on an independent platform (Primero Colombia (Colombia First)), there is no ruling party, although he enjoys the support of a majority of members of Congress.

Area: 1,138,914 square km

Population: 45.30 million (2004)

Capital: Santa Fé de Bogotá

Official language: Spanish

Currency: Colombian peso (Col$) = 100 centavos

Exchange rate: Col$2,289.70 per US$ (Oct 2005)

GDP per capita: US$2,099 (2004)

GDP real growth: 4.00% (2004)

Labour force: 20.22 million (2004)

Unemployment: 13.60% (2004)

Inflation: 5.90% (2004)

Oil production: 551,000 bpd (2004)

Balance of trade: US$1.13 billion (2004)

Foreign debt: US$38.70 billion (2004)

Annual FDI: US$2.35 billion (2004)

President Álvaro Uribe Vélez, who ran as an independent candidate in 2002, eventually secured the right to seek a second consecutive term in 2006 following the Colombian Constitutional Court's decision to amend the constitution. Despite this success and his continuing widespread popularity, Uribe's third year has been marred by the related problems of violence and drug-trafficking that has been traditionally endemic in the country. The level of violence and political instability must be set in context however, for the Uribe government's hard line approach has yielded significant results. The number of kidnappings fell by 49 per cent in 2004, to 746, and the land from which cocaine is cultivated has now been halved, to approximately 212,000 acres.

The ongoing battle with Farc

The beginning of 2005 was characterised by rising levels of violence, as more than 50 soldiers and 12 civilians were killed in attacks by the Fuerzas Armadas Revolucionarias de Colombia–Ejército del Pueblo (Farc) (Revolutionary Armed Forces of Colombia-People's Army). The outbreak of the insurgency marked the worst patch of sustained violence since Uribe was elected in 2002 and raised fears that the government was beginning to lose its hitherto tight grip on the insurgents' advances. Throughout the spring months though, the military forces appeared to regain the upper hand, driving Farc members into isolated strongholds. In May however, ten hostages seized by Farc rebels at a remote jungle camp were executed and the president's anti-insurgency tactics were once again thrown into the spotlight. The government's failure to successfully resolve the crisis prompted Uribe, during a visit to the United States, to seek to begin the renewal process for Plan Colombia, Washington's anti-insurgent military aid package.

Official talks with the right-wing Autodefensas Unidas de Colombia (AUC) (United Self-Defence Forces of Colombia) collapsed in April, as both parties failed to reach an agreement, but there was greater success in beginning peace negotiations with left-wing group Ejército de Liberación Nacional (ELN) (National Liberation Army). In early December 2005 the government dispatched a peace envoy to meet with an ELN delegation and later in the month both parties commenced peace talks in Havana, Cuba. The Farc offensive continued however, as the extreme left wing group launched a 300-rebel offensive on government troops near the Sierra Macarena national park, killing 29 soldiers in late December 2005. The attack was thought to be the opening salvo in a renewed insurgency in the run up to presidential elections in May 2006.

Constitutional success for Uribe

In an historic ruling, the Colombian constitutional court concluded by a margin of eight to one that incumbent Uribe would be able to seek re-election to the presidency in May 2006. Despite the fact that he had previously ruled out an amendment to the country's constitution during his campaign for the presidency in 2002 Uribe has since changed his attitude to the issue, firstly in private and then publicly, when he sought a congressional amendment. Prior to the constitutional court's decision, Colombia's armed forces were placed on high alert. The attack by Farc rebels in December, the largest since Uribe came to power, is thought to have been in response to the ruling and the widely held expectation that the incumbent will be comfortably returned to power.

Close to Bush but frosty with Chávez

Relations between Colombia and its Andean neighbour Venezuela sunk to their lowest level for fifteen years in early 2005. In mid-January Uribe accused Venezuela of 'harbouring terrorists' and 'violating its sovereignty', following the capture, under mysterious circumstances by operatives who were paid by Colombia, of Farc rebel Rodrigo Granda in December 2004 in Caracas and his subsequent handing over to Colombian officials. Venezuela demanded an apology for what it called the 'kidnapping' of Mr Granda and promptly halted all commercial trade with Colombia. In response, Uribe cited what he called 'proof' of Venezuela's protection of seven Farc leaders. This accusation led Venezuela's firebrand leader Hugo Chávez to withdraw his ambassador to Colombia and accused the United States, whose government is close to that of Uribe, of engaging in an 'imperialist' attack on his country.

Both nations looked to be close to burying the hatchet at a summit scheduled for 4 February 2005, but Colombian officials first postponed the meeting for 24 hours before cancelling it altogether, on account of Uribe suffering a somewhat mysterious bought of food poisoning. With the diplomatic elastic between the two countries at breaking point, both leaders met on 15 February 2005 in Caracas and resolved the crisis. The fact that Uribe visited the Venezuelan capital and not vice versa, may be seen as something of a diplomatic victory for Chávez but is perhaps more emblematic of Colombia's need to restore commercial ties with its second largest trading partner. A significant portion of Colombia's economic growth is attributable to increased exports to Venezuela and the permanent severing of commercial links with its neighbour would be economically unthinkable.

Colombia continues to enjoy a strong relationship with the United States. Washington's regard for its junior ally was expressed by its attitude to a perceived escalation in Venezuela's military capability. In February, Venezuela expressed its desire to procure military hardware from Brazil having recently acquired extensive weaponry from the Russian Federation. The US Department of State cautioned Moscow of the 'potential destabilising effect on the hemisphere' of selling arms to Chávez left-leaning government, which was widely understood as an endorsement of Colombia's concern that such weapons may end up in the hands of Farc rebels. Indeed, the United States is fully committed to the Colombian government's hard-line opposition to Farc and the country remains the third-largest recipient of US military aid. Following a meeting between Uribe and US President George W Bush in Crawford, Texas, Plan Colombia was extended for one year to September 2006. The US has also sought to replicate the techniques employed by Uribe's government to combat illegal drug trafficking in its military operations against the warlords of Afghanistan.

KEY INDICATORS — Colombia

	Unit	2000	2001	2002	2003	2004
Population	m	42.38	43.08	43.89	44.59	45.30
Gross domestic product (GDP)	US$bn	83.00	83.00	89.00	77.59	*97.38
GDP per capita	US$	1,960	1,940	2,030	1,740	2,099
GDP real growth	%	2.8	1.6	1.7	3.4	4.0
Inflation	%	9.2	8.7	6.3	6.1	5.9
Unemployment	%	19.7	16.4	15.7	14.4	13.6
Oil output	'000 bpd	711.0	627.0	601.0	564.0	551.0
Natural gas output	bn cum	5.9	6.1	6.2	6.1	6.4
Coal output	mtoe	27.5	27.6	25.7	32.1	35.8
Exports (fob) (goods)	US$m	13,620.0	12,759.0	11,900.0	12,900.0	17,011.0
Imports (fob) (goods)	US$m	11,090.0	12,267.0	13,030.0	12,500.0	15,878.0
Balance of trade	US$m	2,531.0	492.0	-1,000.0	400.0	1,134.0
Current account	US$m	740.0	-1,110.0	-1,370.0	-1,190.0	-1,010.0
Foreign debt	US$bn	36.0	37.1	40.0	38.4	38.7
Total reserves minus gold	US$m	8,916.0	10,154.0	10,732.0	10,784.0	13,394.0
Foreign exchange	US$m	8,409.0	9,659.0	10,190.0	10,188.0	12,769.0
Exchange rate	per US$	2,087.90	2,299.63	2,567.55	2,811.75	2,627.33

* estimated figure

Colombia

Consistent economic growth

Since coming to power the government has largely succeeded in stabilising the country's macroeconomic direction. Though real GDP growth was initially slow in the early stages of Uribe's first term, particularly in 2002, the economy has since rebounded, recording growth of 3.4 per cent in 2003 and 4 per cent in 2004. The current IMF forecast for growth in 2005 and 2006 also stands at a healthy 4 per cent. Colombia's economy has been assisted by a rise in private investment as the government has improved security in the country. Its export revenues have also increased owing to strong external demand. The rate of inflation has almost been halved since the level of 9.2 per cent was recorded in 2000 and now stands at 5.9 per cent.

In recent years fiscal matters have remained the fulcrum of economic debate with various solutions being floated to improve Colombia's high level of debt. The government has also put before congress new social security reform legislation that seeks to improve the system's financial feasibility. In May 2004 negotiations began on the conclusion of a new trade deal involving the United States, Peru and Ecuador. The country's external relations remain of importance to the domestic economy, as was evident in February 2005 when relations with Venezuela, Colombia's second largest trade partner, became increasingly strained. It is estimated that trade between the two countries constitutes US$5.2 billion per annum and many of Colombia's export products, which are vital to the country's economic growth, are sold to its Andean neighbour. Therefore, a stable bilateral relationship between the two countries is imperative.

The constitutional court's decision to permit an alteration to Colombia's electoral law (which will allow Uribe to stand again) is good news for business and consumer confidence. Following the court's ruling Luis Carlos Villegas, president of business confederation Andi, echoed the majority view of Colombia's business leaders when he said that 'the private sector receives the court's decision with enormous satisfaction'. International investors are also likely to view the ruling favourably, as Uribe is widely considered to have improved the climate for investment in the country.

Outlook

Colombia's economic development has been consistently strong over recent years and looks set to remain so. As is so often the case on the South American continent however, the country's economic prospects depend heavily on the social and political climate. Despite intermittent surges of violence in 2005, the Farc offensive seems to be, on the whole, under control. But government forces must remain vigilant if they are to stave off the challenge from the extreme-left wing group in the run up to elections in May 2006. Re-election for Uribe in 2006, which at present looks likely, would endow the president with renewed political capital and ensure that the government's hitherto successful campaign against the guerrilla fighters would continue.

Risk assessment

Economy	Good
Politics	Stable
Regional stability	Good
Stock market	Good

COUNTRY PROFILE

Historical profile
1820 Colombia became independent from Spain.
1800s Outbreaks of fighting erupted sporadically throughout the nineteenth century, often between anti-clerical Liberals and pro-church Conservatives.
1899–1903 The (Civil) War of 1,000 Days in which some 100,000 people were killed. Panama separated from Colombia during the war and became an independent state.
1930 A Liberal president was elected, leading to social reform.
1948–57 The two major parties, the Partido Social Conservador (PSC) (Social Conservative Party) and the Partido Liberal (PL) (Liberal Party) became more extreme – the Conservatives veering towards fascism and the Liberals towards left-wing populism. Civil war broke out, resulting in up to 300,000 deaths.
1957 The civil war ended and the PSC and PL agreed on a power-sharing pact with the presidency going alternately to a PL and PSC member, and seats in cabinet and Congress to be split equally.
1965 The Ejército de Liberación Nacional (ELN) (National Liberation Army) was formed by guerrillas.
1966 Another rebel group, the Fuerzas Armadas Revolucionarias de Colombia–Ejército del Peublo (Farc) (Revolutionary Armed Forces of Colombia– Peoples' Army), was formed.
1970 After disputed elections, elements of the defeated Alianza Nacional Popular (Anapo) formed an armed movement (M-19) to fight the PSC government. They were joined by dissident members of the Farc.
1970s Guerrilla violence increased.
1982 President Belisario Betancur granted guerrillas an amnesty and freed political prisoners.
1984 The assassination of the justice minister led to a step-up in the government war on drugs traffickers.
1985 M-19 guerrillas stormed the Palace of Justice, killing 11 judges and 90 other people.
1989 M-19 became a legal political party after reaching agreement with the government, but other guerrilla groups remained active.
1991 A new constitution was adopted which legalised divorce and gave indigenous people democratic rights, although it fell short of addressing their territorial claims.
1994 Ernesto Samper won the presidential election.
1998 Andrés Pastrana won the presidential election, bringing the Partido Conservador Colombiano (PCC) (Colombian Conservative Party) to power and ending 12 years of rule by the PL. Demilitarised areas were handed over to rebels.
1999 President Pastrana began formal peace talks with the Farc in an attempt to end the region's longest-running civil war. After only two weeks, the rebels ended the talks. The two rebel movements, the Farc and the ELN, were estimated to control 40 per cent of Colombia.
2000 President Pastrana issued 11 emergency decrees to increase the armed forces from 10,000 to 42,000 by the end of the year, with further increases to 52,000 by end-2001. The demilitarised areas were disbanded.
2001 The Farc and government agreed to begin the exchanges of sick prisoners.
2002 Peace talks collapsed. Attacks were carried out on the country's infrastructure. Threats from the Farc and the Autodefensas Unidas de Colombia (AUC) (United Self-Defence Forces of Colombia) made campaigning in the rural areas for the legislative elections very risky and, despite a security operation involving 150,000 troops and police, only 48 per cent of the population voted. The PCC and the PL remained the largest groups in the legislature. Álvaro Uribe Vélez won the presidential election. An assassination attempt on President Uribe was foiled.
2003 In May, the IDB said that lenders' confidence had grown since Uribe gained congressional approval of legislation raising tax revenues and boosting funding for the state pension system.
2004 May saw Farc guerrilla Ricardo Palmera sentenced to 35 years imprisonment. In July, the right wing AUC movement and the national government began

peace talks. Later in the same month AUC leaders addressed the Colombian Congress.
2005 In January relations with Venezuela deteriorated over the kidnapping of a Farc guerrilla on Venezuelan soil. In February the Presidents of both countries held a summit to resolve the matter. The national government passed new legislation in June, reducing jail terms for members of paramilitary groups who turn themselves in to authorities and submit their arms. In Cuba in December, tentative peace talks began with ELN. Also in December, President Uribe agreed to withdraw troops from a small area of mountainous terrain as a means to commencing talks on potential prisoner exchanges with Farc.

Political structure
Constitution
The current constitution dates from 6 July 1991. Colombia has a representative democracy composed of an executive, legislative and a judicial branch.
Administratively, the country is divided into 32 departments ruled by governors, representing the executive branch, and a Departmental Assembly representing the legislative branch. Cities are governed by a mayor and a municipal council. All are elected by democratic vote.
Colombian citizens aged 18 and over are eligible to vote.
Form of state
Presidential democratic republic
The executive
Executive power is vested in the president, elected by universal adult suffrage for four years but not for consecutive terms. The president appoints a cabinet.
National legislature
The legislature is the bicameral Congreso (Congress), which comprises the 167-member Cámara de Representantes (Chamber of Representatives) and the 102-member Senado de la República (Senate of the Republic). Members of Congress are elected for four-year terms by universal suffrage.
Legal system
The judicial system maintains formal independence but has experienced problems operating normally in circumstances that have extended to massed attacks using heavy firepower on major court institutions.
Last elections
26 May 2002 (presidential); 10 March 2002 (congressional).
Results: Presidential: Álvaro Uribe Vélez, an independent candidate backed by the PCC, won the presidential election with 53 per cent of the vote against Horacio Serpa of the PL, 32 per cent.
Parliamentary: although the traditional parties lost seats, they remained the two largest groups in the legislature: the PCC was left with 13 senators and 21 representatives in Congress and the PL, 28 senators and 54 representatives.
Next elections
2006 (presidential and congressional)
Political parties
Ruling party
As President Uribe was elected on an independent platform (Primero Colombia (Colombia First)), there is no ruling party, although he enjoys the support of a majority of members of Congress.
Main opposition party
Partido Liberal (PL) (Liberal Party) is the largest political group in Congress with 54 representatives and 28 senators (elected 10 Mar 2002). The Partido Conservador Colombiano (PCC) (Colombian Conservative Party) (21 representatives and 13 senators) is the second largest party in Congress and supported Uribe's candidacy in the 2002 presidential elections.

Population
45.30 million (2004)
Ethnic make-up
Mestizo 57 per cent, white 20 per cent, mulatto 14 per cent, Indian 1 per cent, and others 8 per cent.
Religions
Roman Catholicism is the official religion and the vast majority of Colombians consider themselves Catholic. There is freedom of worship.

Education
Financing for the education sector is decentralised and municipalities are required to use 30 per cent of the resources transferred to them from central government for education purposes.
Although the illiteracy rate averages 8 per cent among adults over 15 years of age, drop-out rates are increasing on an annual basis; Oxfam estimates that one in every four children drops out before completing primary education and girls' enrolment rates, estimated at 65 per cent, are at least 30 per cent lower than boys' enrolment rates. Primary education has also suffered due to cuts in government budget, while per capita spending is 12 times higher in the tertiary sector.
The New School Programme, known as the *Escuela Nueva*, was begun in the mid-1970s and governs the principles of the Colombian education system. It emphasises flexible school schedules and an appropriate curriculum catering to the needs of the poor rural areas.
Literacy rate: 91 per cent, adult rates, in urban areas; 68 per cent, adult rates, in rural areas.
Compulsory years: Nine years in urban areas; Five years in rural areas
Enrolment rate: 113 per cent in primary; 67 per cent in secondary, of relevant age groups (including repitition rates) (World Bank).
Pupils per teacher: 25 in primary schools

Health
HIV prevalence: 0.7 per cent aged 15–49 in 2003 (World Bank)
Life expectancy: 71.9 years (World Bank).
Fertility rate/Maternal mortality rate: 2.5 births per woman (2003); maternal mortality 80 per 100,000 live births (World Bank).
Infant mortality rate: 18 per 1,000 live births; 7 per cent of children aged under five were malnourished (World Bank).
Head of population per physician/bed: 1.1 physicians and 1.5 hospital beds typically available for 1,000 people.

Welfare
UN agency World Food Programme (WPF) stated that in 2003 there were two million internally displaced persons (IDP) who had fled their homes due to conflict and violence; 80 per cent of the two million lacked access to food production. Food aid is being provided for over 300,000 people, particularly in the northern states. International medical aid provides primary care, prenatal treatment and vaccinations for victims of the internal conflict, and the rural and urban disadvantaged.

Pensions
Colombia undertook major reforms in its pension system in the 1990s by shifting its priorities from government-run pay-as-you-go systems to multi-tier systems characterised by a privately run and fully-funded scheme. New workers have the choice of a pay-as-you-go defined-benefit as the primary system, if they prefer. An individual can only be a member of one scheme. In addition, there is a redistributive scheme for the elderly poor who are not entitled to a social insurance pension. Estimates show that only 30 per cent of individuals above the age of 60, or 2 per cent of the population, receive a pension. Consequently, compared to other industrial countries, the average pension remains very high and is estimated at about twice the GDP per capita.

Main cities
Bogotá (capital, estimated population 7.0 million in 2004, 2,640 metres above sea-level), Cali (2.3 million), Medellín (2.0 million), Barranquilla (1.4 million), Cartagena (853,900), Cucuta (657,100), Bucaramanga (542,400), Pereira (419,600), Ibagué (411,700), Santa

Colombia

Marta (404,800). More than 30 cities have populations of over 100,000.

Languages spoken
Some 200 Indian dialects are spoken. English is spoken in the business community.

Official language/s
Spanish

Media
Press
Publishing companies are predominantly owned by supporters of either the Liberal Party or the Conservative Party. Corporate advertisers and the Medellín drug cartel have also exerted pressure on newspapers.

Dailies: Daily newspapers published in Bogotá include *El Bogotano, El Espacio, El Espectador, El Nuevo Siglo, La Prensa, La República, El Tiempo,* and *El Vespertino*. Cali's daily newspapers are *El Occidente, El País,* and *El Pueblo. El Colombiano* and *El Mundo* are published daily in Medellín. Principal US and west European dailies are available at larger newsstands in main cities. Other popular Spanish language dailies include *El Heraldo, El Mundo, La Nación, La Patria, La Tarde, El Universal, Vanguardia Liberal* and *El Diario del Otún*.

Broadcasting
Broadcasting is closely controlled by the government although most programmes are produced by commercial companies.

Radio: Colombia has over 450 commercial radio stations. Every home has an average of 4.3 radios. Primera Cadena Radial Colombiana (Caracol) is the largest network, followed by Circuito Todelar de Colombia, the official Radio Cadena Nacional (RCN) and Super Radio.

Television: The state-owned Instituto Nacional de Radio y Televisión (Inravisión) runs the two national commercial television channels and one educational channel. There are three regional channels. Airtime is leased out on the commercial channels and is dominated by programming companies, which are selected by public tender.

Television dominates mass communications and absorbs around 60 per cent of all advertising, against about 20 per cent for newspapers, 15 per cent for radio and 5 per cent for magazines.

Advertising
Advertising expenditure is equivalent to 2.1 per cent of GDP.

Economy
The economy of Colombia is forecast by the IMF to grow by 4 per cent in 2005 and by 4 per cent again in 2006. The country's rate of growth is steady but not spectacular, as the Colombian economy is still struggling to recover from the economic crisis of 1998/99. With political unrest destabilising investor confidence and the two major export commodities—oil and coffee—facing a degree of uncertainty, the Colombian economy is in need of considerable reform.

President Álvaro Uribe took office in August 2002 emphasising fiscal and structural reform as a government priority. Since the change in presidency five economic reforms passed through Congress in January 2003 with emphasis placed on changing the tax, pension, labour, public administration and banking systems. These are hoped to spark growth and increase investor confidence. However there are still major economic problems of debts, high unemployment and oil production slowdown.

Economic recovery is gaining momentum with inflation decreasing to 5.9 per cent in 2004, from its previous level of 6 per cent in 2003. Unemployment is also falling: from the previous level of 14.2 per cent to 13.6 per cent. GDP has returned to 1999 levels of US$97 billion. Discussions on free trade agreements with the US and between the Andean Group have had a beneficial effect to confidence levels.

External trade
Colombia is a full member of the WTO having joined the organisation when it was established in 1994. The US is by far Colombia's largest trading partner, receiving 44 per cent of Colombian exports and providing 38 per cent of its imports. Bilateral trade with the US has doubled in the last decade; Colombia is now the US's four largest trading partner in the Western Hemisphere outside of NAFTA, trailing only Brazil and Venezuela. Colombia has a strategic location at the geographical crossroads of the Western Hemisphere and other important trading partners include the EU, Japan and Andean Pact countries.

Traditionally coffee has accounted for half or more of hard-currency income, but the relative importance of the commodity is declining as earnings from oil, coal, ferro-nickel and other non-traditional products are increasing. Coffee prices plunged to 30-year lows in 2002. Social unrest in Colombia's major coffee growing areas also dramatically affected production. Consequently, coffee earnings dropped.

The government fears that around 50,000 jobs could be lost after the US decided to give trade preferences to Central America and the Caribbean through the extension of the Caribbean Basin Initiative (CBI) in 2002. Under the new tariff regime, CBI countries can export clothing to the US free of tariffs and quotas as long as it is assembled from US-made fabric. Meanwhile, Colombian clothing producers will have to pay a 17 to 20 per cent tariff on cotton clothing exported to the US, forcing many US textile companies in Colombia to consider relocation to Central America. Colombians feel aggrieved that nothing is being done to enhance growth areas such as textiles to guarantee them legitimate employment while the US contributes millions of dollars into strengthening the military.

Plans are afoot to create a free trade bloc modelled on the European Union, under the auspices of the South American Community of Nations (SACN). The SACN seeks to merge two existing free trade zones in the region, the Andean Community and Mercusor.

Imports
Principal imports include industrial equipment, vehicles and equipment, consumer goods, chemicals, paper products, fuels and electricity, plastics and natural rubber products

Main sources: US (30.6 per cent total, 2004), Venezuela (5.8 per cent), Brazil (5.2 per cent), Japan (5.2 per cent), Germany (5.1 per cent), Mexico (5.0 per cent), China (4.2 per cent)

Exports
Principal exports are crude oil and derivatives, coffee, coal, clothing, bananas and cut flowers.

Main destinations: US (40.9 per cent total, 2004), Ecuador (5.8 per cent), Venezuela (4.8 per cent)

Agriculture
Farming
The agricultural sector has traditionally played a prominent role in the Colombian economy and it continues to contribute a sizable amount to total GDP. A wide variety of crops are grown throughout Colombia, depending on the altitude in a given region, but coffee is by far the most lucrative crop farmed.

Agricultural exports, primarily coffee, earn US$2 billion or more annually, and when prices have been high, have generated over half of the country's US dollar income. Colombia is the world's second largest producer of coffee after Brazil. Other important cash-export crops include bananas, exotic fruits, cut flowers, tobacco, cotton, sugar cane and cocoa.

The price of coffee on the international markets fell dramatically in 2001, partly caused by a surge in coffee production in Vietnam which led to high levels of oversupply. This damaged production prospects for Colombian coffee producers and there were fears after the 2002 season that coffee growers would shift to growing cocaine. However, coffee prices had recovered by the end of 2004.

Nations of the World: A Political, Economic and Business Handbook

The illegal export of cocaine, and to a lesser extent marijuana, has been estimated to earn the country between US$500 million and US$1 billion per year.

The government has been successful in promoting the diversification of agricultural export crops and lessening the economy's dependence on coffee revenues. Projects included drainage and irrigation schemes to bring more land under cultivation, cheaper credit for farmers, the improvement of road networks and taking electricity to isolated areas. Basic food subsidies in favour of urban consumers were revised to increase incentives for farmers.

Colombia's flower industry began in 1970 and the country is now the world's second-largest exporter of cut flowers after The Netherlands. The US is the main destination for this product. Climatic conditions are ideal, with no special heating or cooling conditions required. Colombia produces over 3.5 billion flowers a year, mostly on the plains near Bogotá. Shipments of fresh and processed tropical fruit are also increasing.

Meat production was hit by guerrilla violence in ranching zones. The government has launched emergency development programmes in low-income farming districts as part of its plans to boost agricultural output and to passify politically turbulent regions.

Crop production in 2004 included: 4,450,469 million tonnes (t) cereals in total, 2,663trice, 1,458t maize, 2,959t potatoes, 2,218t cassava, 37,100t sugar cane, 3,150t oil palm fruit, 2,950t plantains, 1,450t bananas, 325t yams, 305t citrus fruit, 169t pulses, 70t tomatoes, 30t chillies & peppers, 5,578t roots & tubers, 742t oilcrops, 49t cocoa beans, 664t green coffee, 18t grapes, 28t tobacco leaves, 6,866t fruit in total, 1,773t vegetables in total. Livestock production included: 1,511,714t meat in total, 90,000t beef buffalo meat, 119,000t pig meat, 6,670t lamb, 6,594t goat meat, 5,750t horsemeat, 680,000t poultry, 465,000t eggs, ,700,000t milk, 2,550t honey, 1,150t sheepskins, 2,795t greasy wool, 73,700t cattle hides.

Fishing

Despite a substantial coastline of 2,880km and recent modest successes in developing the shrimp and shellfish industries, the fishing industry as a whole remains underdeveloped. As a member state of the Andean Community Colombia has benefitted form special duty-free status and is increasing its shipments of canned tuna to the EU. Exports of artificially reared shrimps are rising as the sector gathers strength.

The typical annual catch is 190,000mt, inclusive of 91,420mt marine fish and 20,580mt shellfish.

Forestry

Approximately half of Colombia's total landmass is forested. There are 49.6 million hectares (ha) of forests in the country. Most of the forests are located in the south-east of the country and form part of the Amazon jungle. Around 20 per cent of forested land is protected, with 40 national parks and reserves. In the period 1990–2000, deforestation resulted in the decrease of forest cover by an average of 0.38 per cent per annum, the equivalent of 190,000ha.

Despite its extensive forest resources, Colombia has a very modest production of industrial round timber. Sawn timber and panels have a large domestic market. Import of paper meets nearly one-third of the country's demand.

Timber production in 2003 included 9,958,513 million cubic metres (cum) roundwood, 2,068,000cum industrial roundwood, 599,000 cubic metres (cum) sawnwood, 836,000cum pulpwood, 1,148,000cum sawlogs & veneer logs, 207,000cum wood-based panels, 7,890,513cum wood fuel, 722,000t charcoal.

Industry and manufacturing

Manufacturing accounts for 14.3 per cent of Colombia's total GDP. Products include textiles and garments, chemicals, metal products, cement, cardboard containers, plastic resins and manufactures, beverages, wood products, pharmaceuticals, machinery and electrical equipment.

The industrial sector typically contributes a quarter of GDP, including the manufacturing sector which contributes 13 per cent, and employs 46 per cent of the workforce.

Food processing, beverages and textiles are the largest industries, followed by chemicals, leather goods, shoes and clothing, capital goods industries and motor vehicles. Metals, tobacco, cement, electrical engineering and paper are also important.

Tourism

Colombia's tourism industry is concentrated on the coastal region and the cities, especially Cartagena. Over the years Colombia's travel and tourism industry has suffered greatly from the ongoing civil conflict in the country. The industry has been severely damaged since its heyday in the 1990s, suffering from an image problem which was exacerbated by a reputation as the 'kidnap capital' of the world. The travel and tourism industry is now beginning to make a moderate recovery. The industry now employs 5.9 per cent of the total workforce, a growth of 3.5 per cent year on year. The GDP contribution of the sector is 6.6 per cent of the country's total in 2005.

Mining

Mining in Colombia is concentrated on gold and other precious metals, iron ore, nickel and coal. In a typical year the mining industry contributes 4 per cent to the country's total GDP and employs 5 per cent of the total workforce. The industry is Colombia's main legal source of foreign exchange.

In recent years foreign investors have become fully aware of Colombia's potential for coal mining. With 20,000 tonnes of proven and inferred reserves the country's coal resource base is extensive and the quality of Colombian coal is high. Colombia is the second largest exporter of coal to Europe and the largest exporter to the US.

Colombia is one of the largest gold producers in the world, the fifth largest in Latin America after Peru, Brazil, Chile and Argentina. About 70 per cent of Colombian gold originates from the mines of Buritaca in Antioquia, using small-scale and primitive methods. Other precious minerals include silver and platinum (fourth largest producer of platinum), which are found in Choco Province along the Pacific coast.

Colombia is the world's top producer of high-grade emeralds, accounting for over 90 per cent of world output. The Muzo mine in the Eastern Andes near Bogotá is the world's largest emerald mine. Estimates put total emerald exports at US$250 million, of which a little more than 15 per cent is exported legally, for the most part (90 per cent) to Japan. Worker supervision in many of the emerald mines is minimal, fuelling the problems of smuggling.

Reserves of 100 million tonnes of iron ore assure Colombia of self-sufficiency until 2050. The known reserves are owned by Colombia's only steel company, Acerías Paz del Rio. The reserves are on the whole deep, expensive to extract and of low quality with a high sulphur content. A large part of the industry is located north-east of Bogotá, including the fully integrated steel works of Acerías Paz del Río.

Colombia has a high output of nickel supplying around 12 per cent of world demand. The country also mines copper, lime, sulphur, manganese, phosphates and salt.

Hydrocarbons

Colombia has the fifth largest proven crude oil reserves in South America, at 1.5 billion barrels. However, this figure marks a 13 per cent decline from that of

Colombia

2004. 530,000 barrels per day (bpd) were produced in 2004, 5 per cent less than the 2003 level. The country's oil production level has declined steadily since 1999. This fact together with the recent revised estimate of proven reserves and the toll taken on the industry by the country's long standing civil conflict, demonstrates how the oil industry has suffered. Colombian officials recently warned that unless considerable new oil supplies are discovered, the country will become a net importer of petroleum in the near future. Crude oil remains Colombia's largest export earner, a key source of foreign exchange earnings and is a major contributor to the fiscal revenues.

Natural gas production stands at 6.1 billion cubic metres, just exceeding consumption at 6 billion cubic metres. Reserves are estimated to stand at 110 billion cubic metres. However demand is set to increase due to the government's Plan de Masificacion de Gas Natural programme, which is aiming to increase natural gas use.

Colombia has high-quality proven coal reserves of around 7.3 billion tonnes (as at end 2004) and is the largest producer in Latin America. Much of the coal production goes to power plants both at home and abroad. Sixty per cent of Colombia's coal reserves lie in the interior around Bogotá, where the giant El Cerrejón Norte mine is located. New development is centred on this open-cast mine in Guajira. Coal is Colombia's third most important export after oil and coffee. With government investment in the promotion of the coal industry it is estimated that output will double between 2000 and 2010.

Although the privatisation of Carbocol (the state coal mining company and 50 per cent partner in El Cerrejón Norte) in 2001 added impetus to the improvement of the sector's infrastructure network and port facilities, many are worried about future security problems. Several incidents, including the destruction of railway lines by the guerrillas, have worried observers about the feasibility of the project to expand the sector.

Energy
With a generating capacity of 13.1GW Colombia has been self sufficient in energy since 1984. Approximately 44.9 billion kilowatthours (kwh) of electricity is generated each year and 41.1 kwh is consumed.

Seventy-seven per cent of total electricity generated is hydroelectric with conventional thermal and renewable sources constituting the remainder.

The electricity sector has been plagued by rebel attacks that damaged infrastructure. Grid connections have been blown up, leaving the country divided into small grids. A plan to connect Colombia's Atlantic coast and the capital city Bogotá was put on hold in 2002 due to increased guerrilla attacks.

The energy sector was deregulated in the 1990s and is now composed of a mixture of private and publicly owned operators. Colombia actively trades electricity with neighbouring countries, particularly Ecuador. Plans to increase electricity trade with Venezuela and other Andean Community nations have also been promoted.

Financial markets
Stock exchange
To improve stock market efficiency, the three stock markets: Bolsa de Valores de Bogotá, Bolsa de Valores de Medellín in Antioquia and Bolsa de Valores de Occidente in Cali merged in July 2001 to provide a combined capitalisation of Col$13 billion (US$5.8 million), with 42 member brokers.

Banking and insurance
Both Bancolombia and BBVA Colombia, two of the country's largest banking houses, have enjoyed significant profitability in recent years. Bancolombia, one of the oldest banks in Latin America, recorded pre tax profits of US$339 million in 2004, an increase of 53 per cent on the previous year's total. BBVA Colombia reported an earnings increase of 80 per cent in 2004. Both banks have indicated the likelihood of continued robust growth in 2005.

Following several years of a difficult economic and financial environment in the Colombia, the country's banking sector is now considered to be one of the leading markets in Latin America.

Central bank
Banco de la República
Main financial centre
Bogotá

Time
GMT minus five hours

Geography
Colombia, covering 1.14 million square km, is split between a coastal plain, high Andean peaks rising to more than 5,000 metres and a tropical Amazonian lowland. The only nation in South America with both Pacific and Caribbean coastlines, Colombia is bordered by Venezuela and Brazil to the east, Peru and Ecuador to the south and Panama to the north. Colombia owns several small Pacific and Caribbean islands. Its territorial waters border those of nations as distant as Honduras and Haiti. Around 80 per cent of the population is concentrated in the Andean region, which covers around a quarter of the country's area. The Andes fan out northwards from the Ecuadorian border into three high cordilleras (parallel ranges) separated by deep valleys. Many of the peaks are volcanic. Colombia's highest mountain, the Pico Cristobal Colón, reaches 5,800 metres; it is 50km from the Caribbean coast in the Sierra de Santa Marta, which is isolated from the three main cordilleras. Just over half of the country lies east of the Andes. Known as Los Llanos, most of this region is virtually unexplored and sparsely populated jungle. A low plain fringes most of the coast in the west and the north. About a fifth of the population lives in this area, which is also about a fifth of the total land area.

Climate
The equator runs across the south of Colombia. The low coastal plain and the jungle regions east of the Andes have a tropical climate, with frequent rains and temperatures between 24–28 degrees Celsius (C). Temperatures fall with the higher altitudes. In Bogotá, at 2,650 metres, temperatures average around 14 degrees C.

Dress codes
Dress codes in Colombia are partly determined by formality but mostly by climate. In the capital, Bogotá, at 2,650 metres, suits for men and skirts for women are usual for business. Residents recommend a light coat for the evenings. In low-lying cities such as Cali in the south or Cartagena on the Caribbean coast, informal lightweight clothing is common.

Entry requirements
Passports
Required by all with few exceptions (eg certain nationals of Ecuador and certain tourist visitors from Trinidad and Tobago).
Visa
Are required for all business visits and must be obtained before arrival. A letter, issued by the traveller's company, giving name and position of applicant, a detailed summary of intended purpose of trip, an itinerary, and the acceptance of full responsibility for any expenses incurred during the term of stay must be submitted with the application, (an original and copy, to be translated into Spanish), which will be notarised by the Colombian embassy.

Tourist visas are not required by citizens of North America, most EU and West European and most South American countries for stays up to 90 days. For further details and confirmation, contact the nearest embassy.
Currency advice/regulations
There are no limitations on the import of foreign and local currency. The export of foreign currency is limited to US$25,000.

Nations of the World: A Political, Economic and Business Handbook

Travellers' cheques are recommended. Banks are generally the only reliable location for changing travellers' cheques or cash.

Prohibited imports
Any chemicals which could be used in the extraction or refining of narcotics are likely to arouse suspicion. Toy weapons have been banned in an attempt to reduce the pervasiveness of violence in Colombian societies.

Health (for visitors)
Mandatory precautions
None, although vaccination against yellow fever is essential for visitors travelling to certain parts of the country, notably the central valley of the Magdalena River, the inland border areas (with Ecuador, Peru, Brazil and Venezuela), Uraba district, the south-eastern part of the Sierra Nevada de Santa Marta and the forest area along the Guaviare River.

Advisable precautions
Precautions should be taken against malaria and hepatitis. In 1998 the World Health Organisation warned of the high risk of catching dengue fever.
Tap water is not considered safe to drink. Milk is unpasteurised and should therefore be boiled or avoided. It is advised to avoid uncooked vegetables and dairy products made from local milk. Fruit should be peeled. Visitors to Bogotá should take it easy for a few days to get used to the altitude, which may induce drowsiness, dizziness or altitude sickness.

Hotels
Hotels are graded from one- to five-star by the National Tourist Corporation. There is a tourist tax of 5 per cent on rooms; most hotels charge a minimum fee per night for insurance against theft. It is advisable to book well in advance. Higher tariff operates from December to April. Service charge is normally added to bill, otherwise a 10 per cent tip is expected.

Credit cards
American Express, Diners, Visa and Master Card are widely used.

Public holidays
Fixed dates
1 Jan (New Year's Day), ^6 Jan (Epiphany), ^19 Mar (St Joseph's Day), 1 May (Labour Day), ^17 Jun (Sacred Heart of Jesus/Thanksgiving Day), ^29 Jun (St Peter and St Paul Day), 20 Jul (Independence Day), 7 Aug (Battle of Boyacá), ^15 Aug (Assumption Day), ^12 Oct (Columbus Day), ^1 Nov (All Saints' Day), ^11 Nov (Independence of Cartagena), 8 Dec (Immaculate Conception), 25 Dec (Christmas Day).

^ If it does not fall on a Monday, the holiday is observed on the following Monday.

Variable dates
Maundy Thursday, Good Friday, *Ascension Day, *Corpus Christi (May/Jun). (NB *If it does not fall on a Monday, the holiday is observed on the following Monday).

Working hours
Banking
In Bogotá: Mon–Thu: 0900–1500; Fri: 0900–1530.
Other cities: 0800–1230 and 1400–1630.
On the last working day of the month, service is available only up to 1200.
Business
Mon–Fri: 0800–1230, 1400–1800.
Shops
Mon–Fri: 0900–1900 or 2000.

Telecommunications
Mobile phones
Some GSM 850 and 1900 services available in limited areas.

Electricity supply
110V AC 60 cycles; two-pin flat blade plugs.

Social customs/useful tips
It is customary to tip porters but not maids or clerks in hotels.

Security
With a virtual war being fought between the government, drug barons and Farc insurgents, realistic security measures must be carried out as kidnapping, armed robbery and bomb explosions are frequent hazards. Visitors should exert due care and vigilance at all times. It is advisable that embassy officials be informed of their national's presence in Colombia and itinerary, particularly if travelling to the north of the country.
Colombia has the highest murder rate in the Americas and one of the worst reputations, in South America, for street crime, which is common during daylight hours in main cities. Visitors are advised not to display jewellery and to carry as little cash and documentation as possible; watches and briefcases are prime targets. It is advisable to keep a copy of all documents in an hotel safe in case of mishap. Much crime is drug-related and visitors should be wary of any unwarranted attention from strangers.

Getting there
Air
National airline: Avianca (Aerovías Nacionales de Colombia).
International airport/s: Bogotá-El Dorado (BOG), 12km from city, duty-free shop, bar, restaurant, buffet, bank, shops, hotel reservations, car hire.
Other airport/s: Barranquilla-Ernesto Cortissos (BAQ), 10km from city, car hire; Cali-Palmaseca (CLO), 19km from city, restaurant; Cartagena-Crespo (CTG), 2km north-east of city; Medellín-Rionegro (MDE), 15 minutes' flight by scheduled and frequent helicopter service to city, (36km south-east of Medellín).
Airport tax: International departures US$25–29, not applicable to transit passengers.
An exit tax of US$19 is charged to travellers whose stay exceeds two months.
Surface
Road: Access is possible from Ecuador and Venezuela by road.
Main port/s: Caribbean: Santa Marta, Barranquilla, and Cartagena. Pacific: Buenaventura and Tumaco.

Getting about
National transport
Air: Frequent and cheap air services between Bogotá and all main centres. Major air companies operating internal flights are Avianca, SAM, ACES, Aires Colombia, Intercontinental de Aviación and SATENA. Around 15 smaller companies also operate domestic services.
Road: Fifty per cent of the main roads wind through steep cordilleras, with bridges and tunnels in constant need of repair.
Only 4,600km of the country's 120,000km road network are considered to be in good condition and less than 13,000km are paved.
There are highway links for Bogotá-Cali; for other journeys local enquiries are advisable.
Buses: Buses can usually be flagged down – in most cases there are no scheduled stops. Within cities buses tend to be crowded; long-distance bus journeys are generally for more adventurous travellers and care is needed – Bogotá-Medellín inter-city service, however, is fairly reliable and comfortable.
Rail: The rail service has deteriorated, and taking a train is not recommended. The rail system, which carries about a million tons of cargo a year, has less than 1,700km of line in service.
Water: Cargo boats and some hire boats operate on the four major hydrographic systems. The Magdalena River carries the most traffic. There are 10,000km of navigable rivers between the three main Andean ranges.
City transport
Taxis: Within Bogotá, usually metered with minimum charge and extra at night, holidays, Sundays and for out of town journeys; can be hailed; tipping not usual. For unmetered taxis fares should be agreed in advance of journey. Shared taxis, colectivos, operate within cities and suburbs. Green and white taxis have English-speaking drivers and can be rented by the hour/day at major hotels.

Colombia

Car hire
National or international licences are acceptable for up to three months, but must be accompanied by an official translation. Traffic drives on the right and during the working day is heavily congested in main towns.

BUSINESS DIRECTORY
The addresses listed below are a selection only. While World of Information makes every endeavour to check these addresses, we cannot guarantee that changes have not been made, especially to telephone numbers and area codes. We would welcome any corrections.

Telephone area codes
The international dialling code (IDD) for Colombia is +57 followed by the area code:

Armenia	67	Cartagena	5
Baranquilla	5	Cucuta	70
Bogotá	1	Manizales	69
Bucaramanga	73	Medellín	4
Cali	2		

Chambers of Commerce
American-Colombian Chamber of Commerce, 22-64 Calle 98, Bogotá (tel: 623-7088; fax: 621-6838; e-mail: info@amchamcolombia.com.co).

Barranquilla Chamber of Commerce, 36-135 Via 40, Barranquilla (tel: 330-3701; fax: 330-3750;e-mail: info@camarabaq.org.co).

Bogotá Chamber of Commerce, 16-21 Carrera 9, Bogotá (tel: 2381-0270; fax: 284-7735; e-mail: ccbcentro@ccb.org.co).

British-Colombian Chamber of Commerce, 77A-52 Carrera 12A, Bogotá (tel: 321-7077; fax: 321-7964; e-mail: britanica@cable.net.co).

Bucaramanga Chamber of Commerce, 36-20 Carrera 19, Bucaramanga (tel: 652-7000; fax: 633-4062).

Cali Chamber of Commerce, 3-14 Calle 8, Cali (tel: 886-1300; fax: 886-1399; e-mail: contacto@ccc.org.co).

Cartagena Chamber of Commerce, 32-41 Calle Santa Teresa, Cartagena (tel: 660-0795; fax: 660-0802; e-mail: camaradecomercio@cccartagena.org.co).

Colombian Confederation of Chambers of Commerce, 27-47 Carrera 13, Oficina 502, Bogotá (tel: 346-7055; fax: 346-7026; e-mail: confecamaras@confecamaras.org.co).

Cucuta Chamber of Commerce, 4-38 Calle 10, Cucuta (tel: 571-5922; fax: 571-2502; e-mail: cccuc02@col1.telecom.com.co).

Manizales Chamber of Commerce, 26-60 Carrera 23, Manizales (tel: 884-1840; fax: 884-0919; e-mail: ccm@ccm.org.co).

Medellín Chamber of Commerce, 52-82 Avenida Oriental, Medellín (tel: 511-6111; fax: 513-7757; e-mail: subcontramed@camaramed.org.co).

Pereira Chamber of Commerce, 23-09 Carrera 8, Local 10, Risaralda, Pereira (tel: 252-587; fax: 250-957; e-mail: camarap@pereira.multi.net.co).

Banking
Banco Andino, Carrera 7a No 14-23, Piso 3, Apdo Postal 6826, Bogotá (tel: 284-8800; fax: 286-7919).

Banco Anglo Colombiano (associated to Lloyds Bank plc), Cra 8 No 15-46/60, Zonal postal 1, Bogotá (tel: 334-5088; fax: 286-1383).

Banco Cafetero, Calle 28 No 13 A-15, Apdo Postal 240332, Bogotá (tel: 282-7742; fax: 284-5430).

Banco Caldas, Calle 72 No 7-64, Apdo Postal 240332, Bogotá (tel: 282-7742; fax: 284-5430).

Banco Central Hipotecario, Carrera 6a No 15-32, Zona postal 1, Bogotá (tel: 283-7100; fax: 283-2802).

Banco Colombo Americano, Carrera 7a No 16-36, Piso 10, Apdo Postal 12327, Bogotá (tel: 334-5530; fax: 283-2939).

Banco Colpatria, Calle 13, No 7-90, Piso 2, Apdo Postal 30241, Bogotá (tel: 283-1567; fax: 286-3914).

Banco Co-operativo de Colombia (Bancoop), Calle 98 No 14-41, Apdo Postal 12242, Bogotá (tel: 257-7411; fax: 218-1601).

Banco de Antioquia (Bancoquia), Calle 12 No 746, Bogotá (tel: 334-9040).

Banco de Bogotá, PO Box 3436, Calle 36 No 7-47, Bogotá (tel: 3320032 fax: 3383302).

Banco de Colombia, Calle 30A No 6-38, zona postal 1, Apdo Postal 6836, Bogotá (tel: 285-6767; fax: 287-0595).

Banco de Cio Exterior de Colombia (Bancoldex) (Foreign Trade Bank of Colombia), Calle 28 No 13A-15, Apdo Postal 240-092, Bogotá (tel: 341-0677; fax: 282-5071).

Banco de Crédito, Calle 27 No 6-48, zona postal 1, Bogotá (tel: 286-8400; fax: 282-7256).

Banco del Occidente, Carrera 5a No 12-42, Apdo Postal 7607, Cali, Valle (tel: 824-081; fax: 822-705).

Banco del Estado, Carrera 10 No 18-15, Apdo Postal 8711, Bogotá (tel: 282-8471; fax: 284-9775).

Banco Extebandes de Colombia, Calle 74 No 6-65, Zona postal 2, Bogotá (tel: 217-7200; fax: 212-5786).

Banco Ganadero, Carrera 9A No 72-21, Apdo Postal 53851/9, Bogotá (tel: 217-0100; fax: 255-2457).

Banco Industrial Colombiano, Carrera 52 No 50-20, Apdo Postal 768, Medellín, Antioquia (tel: 251-5216; fax: 251-4716).

Banco Latino de Colombia, calle 72 No 10-07, Apdo Postal 056397, Bogotá (tel: 210-999; fax: 284-0056).

Banco Mercantil Colombia, Carrera 9A No 99-02, Zona postal 8, Bogotá (tel: 618-2249; fax: 618-2111).

Banco Popular, Calle 17 No 7-35, Zona postal 1, Bogotá (tel: 334-9640; fax: 282-4246).

Banco Real de Colombia, Carrera 7a No 33-80, Apdo Postal 034262, Bogotá (tel: 269-8523; fax: 287-0507).

Banco Sudameris Colombia, Carrera 8a No 15-42, Zona postal 1, Bogotá (tel: 283-8700; fax: 281-6191).

Banco Superior, Carrera 10a No 64-28, Bogotá (tel: 217-3888; fax: 235-4352).

Banco Tequendama, diagonal 27 No 6-70, Apdo Postal 29799, Bogotá (tel: 285-9900; fax: 287-7020).

Banco Uconal, Calle 72 No 8-56, Bogotá (tel: 310-5155; fax: 212-2094).

Banco Unión Colombiano, Piso 2, Carrera 7 N°71-52, Bogotá (tel: 3120411 fax: 3120843).

Caja de Crédito Agrario Industrial y Minero, Carrera 8a No 15-43, Zona postal 1, Bogotá (tel: 334-9066; fax: 286-5824).

Caja Social, Calle 72 No 10-71, Apdo Postal 58175, Bogotá (tel: 310-0099; fax: 211-6036).

Citibank, Carrera 9a No 99-02, Bogotá (tel: 618-4455; fax: 618-2515).

Central bank
Banco de la República, Carrera 7, No 14-78, Bogotá (tel: 342-1111; fax: 286-1686; e-mail: wbanco@banrep.gov.co).

Travel information
American Express, TMA, Cra.10 No 27-91, Offices 1-26, Bogotá (tel: 283-2955).

Avianca (Aerovías Nacionales de Colombia), Avenida, Eldorado 93-30, Piso 4, Bloque 1, Bogotá (tel: 413-9511; fax: 413-8325).

Fondo de Promoción Turistica de Colombia, Carrera 16A No 78-55 Of. 604, Bogotá (tel: 611-4330, 611-4185; fax: 236-3640; e-mail:

turismocolombia@andinet.com; internet site: http://www.turismocolombia.com).

National tourist organisation offices
National Tourist Office, Calle 28 No. 13A-15 P 17 Y 18, Bogotá (tel: 283-9466; fax: 283-8945).

Ministries
Ministry of Agriculture and Rural Development, Avenida Jiménez No. 7-65, Santafé de Bogotá (tel: 334-1199; fax: 284-1775).

Ministry of Communications, Edificio Murillo Toro, Carrera 7 y 8 Calle 12 y 13, Santafé de Bogotá (tel: 286-6911; fax: 286-1185).

Ministry of Culture, Calle 8 No 6-67, Santafé de Bogotá (tel: 282-0854; fax: 282-0666).

Ministry of Economic Development, Carrera 13 No. 28-01, Apartado Aéreo 99412, Santafé de Bogotá (tel: 320-0077; fax: 287-6025).

Ministry of the Environment, Calle 38 No 8-61, Santafé de Bogotá (tel:288-6010; fax: 243-3004).

Ministry of Finance and Public Credit, Carrera 7a No. 6-45, Santafé de Bogotá (tel: 284-5400; fax: 284-5396).

Ministry for Foreign Affairs, Palacio de San Carlos, Calle 10 No. 5-51, Santafé de Bogotá (tel: 282-7811, 287-6800; fax: 341-6777).

Ministry of Foreign Trade, Calle 28 No. 13A-15 P 5,6,7,9, Santafé de Bogotá (tel: 286-9111; fax: 284-9537, 334-9908).

Ministry of Health, Carrera 13 No. 32-76, Santafé de Bogotá (tel: 336-5066; fax: 336-0116, 336-0296).

Ministry of the Interior, Palacio Echeverry, Carrera 8a No. 8-09, Santafé de Bogotá (tel: 283-0676, 283-6853; fax: 281-5884, 286-8025).

Ministry of Justice and Law, Avenida Jiménez No. 8-89, Santafé de Bogotá (tel: 286-0211, 286-5888, 286-9711; fax: 281-6384, 283-2761).

Ministry of Labour and Social Security, Carrera 7a No. 34-50, Santafé de Bogotá (tel: 287-3434, 285-8362, 285-7092, 285-7361, 285-7098, 287-5045; fax: 285-7091, 287-3861, 285-8342).

Ministry of Mines and Energy CAN, Santafé de Bogotá (tel: 222-4555, 2068, 222-0179; fax: 222-3651).

Ministry of National Defence, Avenida El Dorado Cra 52 CAN, Santafé de Bogatá (tel: 220-4999; fax: 222-1874).

Ministry of National Education, CAN, Santafé de Bogotá (tel: 222-2800; fax: 222-0324).

Ministry of Transport, CAN, Santafé de Bogotá (tel: 222-4411, 222-7577, 7966; fax: 222-1647, 222-1121).

Other useful addresses
Asociación Nacional de Industriales (ANDI), Carrera 13 No 26-45, Bogotá (tel: 334-6673, 281-0600).

Bolsa de Bogotá (Stock Exchange), Carrera 8a, No 13-82, Apartado Aéreo 3584, Bogotá (tel: 243-6501, 243-8471; fax: 281-3170).

Bolsa de Medellín S.A. (Stock Exchange), Carrera 50 No 50-48 Piso 2, Medellín (tel: 260-3000; fax: 251-1981).

British Embassy, Apartado Aéreo 4508, Torre Propaganda Sancho, Calle 98, No 9-03, Piso 4, Bogotá (tel: 218-5111; fax: 218-2330, 218-2460).

Caja de Crédito Agrario Industrial y Minero, Carrera 8 No 15-43, Bogotá (tel: 284-4600).

Carbones de Colombia (CARBOCOL), Carrera 7, No 31-10, Pisos 5-18, Bogotá (tel: 287-3100).

Colombian Embassy (USA), 2118 Leroy Place, NW, Washington DC 20008 (tel: 202-387-8338; fax: 202-232-8643; e-mail: emwash@colombiaemb.org).

Colombian Government Trade Bureau (Proexport Colombia) Calle 28 No. 13 A - 15 Piso 35, Santafé de Bogotá, (tel: 341-2066; fax: 282-8130, 282-8230).

Departamento Administrativo de Aeronáutica Civil (DAAC), Aeropuerto Internacional El Dorado, Bogotá (tel: 266-2237).

Departamento Administrativo Nacional de Estadísticas (DANE), Oficina 222, CAN-Avenida Eldorado, Bogotá.

Departamento Nacional de Planeación, Calle 26 No 13-19, Bogotá (tel: 282-4055; fax: 281-3348).

Empresa Colombiana de Mina (ECOMINAS), Calle 32, No 13-07, Apartado Aéreo 17878, Bogotá (tel: 287-7136; fax: 287-4606).

Empresa Colombiana de Petróleos (ECOPETROL), Carrera 13 No 36-24, Bogotá (tel: 285-6400).

Empresa Nacional de Telecomunicaciones (TELECOM), Calle 23 No 13-49, Bogotá (tel: 286-0077, 282-8280).

Federación Nacional de Cafeteros de Colombia, Calle 73 No 8-13, Apartado Aéreo 57534, Bogotá DE (tel: 217-0600).

Instituto Colombiana de Comercio Exterior (INCOMEX), Edifico Centro Comercio Internacional, Calle 28 No 13A-15, Bogotá (tel: 281-2200).

Instituto de Fomento Industrial (IFI), Calle 16, No 6-66, Pisos 7-15, Bogotá (tel: 282-2055).

Instituto Nacional de Investigaciones Geológico-Mineras (INGEOMINAS), Diagonal 53, No 34-53, Apartado Aéreo 4865, Bogotá (tel: 222-1811; fax: 222-3597).

Instituto Nacional de Radio y Televisión, Via del Aeropuerto Eldorado, Bogotá (tel: 222-0700; fax: 222-0080).

Invertir Corporation of Colombia (COINVERTIR), Cra 7 no 71-52 Torre A, Oficina 702, Bogotá (tel: 312-0312; fax: 312-0318).

US Embassy, Calle 38, No 8-61, Bogotá (tel: 285-1300; fax: 288-5687).

Internet sites
Business News, Latin Trade online: http://www.latintrade.com

Organisation of American States: http://www.oas.org

President of the Republic (in Spanish): http://www.presidencia.gov.co/webpresi/

Colombia Trade: http://www.coltrade.org/

Comoros

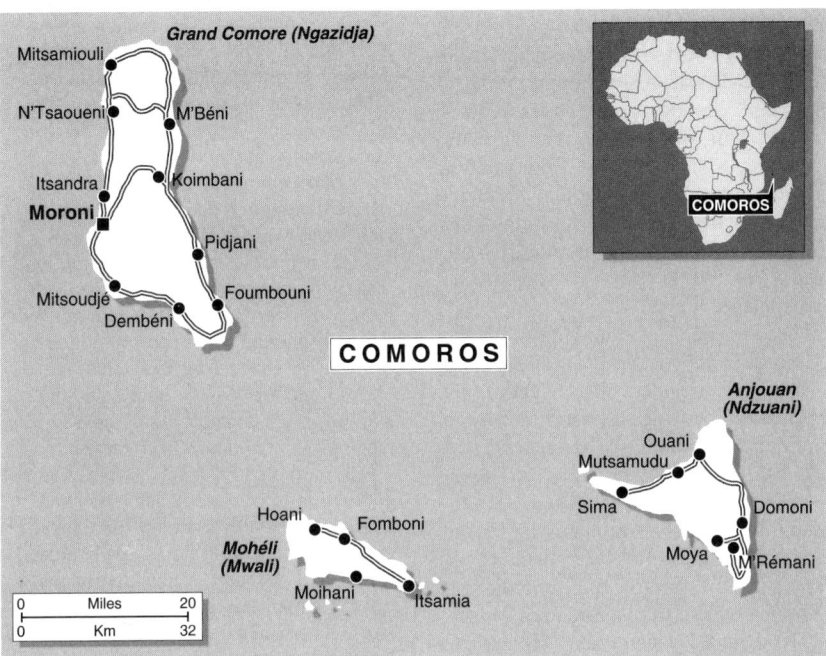

KEY FACTS

Official name: Udzima wa Komori (L'Union des Comores) (The Union of the Comoros) (from Jan 2002)

Head of State: Federal President Azali Assoumani (from 26 May 2002)

Head of government: Federal President Azali Assoumani

Ruling party: The first federal government was sworn in on 14 Jul 2004.

Area: 2,171 square km

Population: 766,000 (2004)

Capital: Moroni

Official language: Arabic and French

Currency: Comoros franc (Cf) = 100 centimes

Exchange rate: Cf408.05 per US$ (Oct 2005) (pegged Cf491.97 per euro)

GDP per capita: US$582 (2004)

GDP real growth: 1.90% (2004)

Labour force: 290,000 (2004)

Inflation: 4.30% (2004)

Balance of trade: -US$23.50 million (2003)

There has been significant political progress in the Comoros. On the three small islands inhabited by less than 800,000 people political infighting and coups have been regular occurrences since independence from France in 1975, but national reconciliation has advanced, helped by domestic leadership as well as by concerted international support. The African Union, the United Nations Development Programme (UNDP) and regional partners in the Southern African Development Community (SADC) have played critical roles. Progress on the political front has also benefited economic performance.

Economy

The delineation of fiscal competencies and revenue-sharing arrangements between the union and island governments led to improved inter-island co-operation and enhanced growth over 2005. On the other hand, the envisaged privatisation of Comores-Telecom and Société Comorienne des Hydrocarbures remains outstanding, reflecting in part a lack of external assistance but also a lack of domestic reform momentum. Preparations for customs reforms are also taking longer than originally envisaged.

The near term economic assessment is that on the basis of ongoing political progress, rising donor support, and fairly good prospects for the tourism sector, real growth could strengthen to above three per cent over 2006 and the large external current account deficit start to decline. The budget envisages a domestic primary surplus of around one per cent of GDP, with much-needed capital spending set to almost double to above seven per cent of GDP. The main risks to achieving the fiscal objectives relate to the domestic revenue and civil service wage bill targets. The civil service is excessively large, and its wages absorb 60 per cent of domestic revenue.

The International Monetary Fund (IMF) said at the end of 2005 that it was too early to negotiate assistance for Comoros, but this would be reviewed early in 2006. It was hoped that progress in policy reforms that could open the door for future debt relief would be sufficiently deep and rapid so that Comoros could enter into an agreement with the IMF before the end of 2006.

The people of the Comoros are among the poorest in Africa and are heavily dependent on foreign aid. Natural resources are in short supply and the islands' chief exports – vanilla, cloves and perfume essence – are prone to price fluctuations. Money sent home by Comorans living abroad is an important source of foreign exchange. The descendants of Arab traders, Malay immigrants and African peoples contribute to the islands' complex ethnic mix.

The islands have inadequate transportation links and a young and rapidly increasing population. The low educational level of the labour force contributes to a subsistence level of economic activity, high unemployment, and a heavy dependence on foreign grants and technical assistance. Agriculture, including fishing, hunting, and forestry, contributes 40 per cent to GDP, employs 80 per cent of the labour force, and provides most of the exports. The country is not self-sufficient in food production; rice, the main staple, accounts for the bulk of food imports. The government is struggling to upgrade education and technical training, privatise commercial and industrial enterprises, improve health services, diversify exports, promote tourism, and reduce the high population growth rate. Increased foreign support is essential if annual growth targets are to be met.

Politics

Potentially a holiday paradise, the Comoros islands are trying to consolidate political stability amid tensions between semi-autonomous islands and the central government. A history of political violence has left the islands desperately poor. At times, the country has teetered on the brink of disintegration.

The three Indian Ocean islands have experienced more than 20 coups or attempted coups, beginning just weeks after independence from France in 1975 when President Ahmed Abdallah was toppled in a coup assisted by French mercenary Colonel Bob Denard. To add to the country's troubles, the islands of Anjouan and Moheli declared unilateral independence in a violent conflict in 1997. In an effort to bring them back into the fold, Moheli, Anjouan and the largest island, Grande Comore, were in 2001 granted their own presidents and greater autonomy. The Union of Comoros retained control of security and financial matters. The Comoros lay claim to French-administered Mayotte Island, which has one of only two ports in the archipelago.

The President of the Union of the Comoros in 2006 is Azali Assoumani. He was named president after elections in April 2002. The title was confirmed by an international committee overseeing the islands' transition to the Union of Comoros. The presidents of the three semi-autonomous islands – Anjouan, Moheli and Grande Comore – are vice presidents of the Union of Comoros. A 33-member national assembly sits on Grande Comore. Under the 2001 constitution, Assoumani, a native of Grande Comore, is expected to step down at elections in 2006 to allow the presidency to be passed to another island.

Risk assessment

Economic	Poor
Political	Poor
Regional stability	Fair

COUNTRY PROFILE

Historical profile

Long ruled by Arab potentates, the Comoros first attracted French attention in the nineteenth century. The first French settlement began in Mayotte in 1841. But it was not until 1912, 71 years later, that the other large islands in the archipelago – Grand Comore, Anjouan and Mohéli – became French colonies. French settlement was motivated mainly by the desire to set up sugar plantations on the model of those in Réunion and Mauritius – although sugar was later replaced by cocoa, coffee, sisal, perfume plants – particularly yiang-yiang, (the base of 90 per cent of French perfumes) – timber, cloves and vanilla. The French settlers, French companies and wealthy Arab landlords, who owned the islands, effectively held sway over the impoverished, and 90 per cent illiterate, Comorian villagers. In Mayotte, three families, the Henry, the Giraud and the Novou, dominated the economic and political life of the island. Since its independence from France in 1975, Comoros has been rocked by a succession of coups and secessionist movements, led by a motley assortment of military officers, drug traffickers, mercenaries and chancers. Many Comorians, not to mention some foreigners, have learnt that to pursue their political interests within the island group, they simply have to land a boat and storm the local police station – preferably after lunch.

1843 The Comoros was ceded to France by Portugal.
1947 The Comoros became a separate French Overseas Territory, detached from administration by Madagascar.
1961 It achieved internal self government.
1972 Elections produced a large majority for parties advocating independence and Ahmed Abdallah Abderrahman became president of the government council.
1973 Abderrahman was restyled president of the government.
1975 The Federal Islamic Republic of the Comoros gained independence from France, Mayotte was the only island in the archipelago that voted to retain links with France.
1978 A constitution was approved by referendum.
1982 Constitutional amendments increased the president's power by reducing those of each island's governor.
1989 Abderrahman was assassinated.
1990 In Comoros' first democratic elections, Said Mohamed Djohar was elected president.
1992 A new constitution was approved that included the new post of prime minister.

KEY INDICATORS — Comoros

	Unit	2000	2001	2002	2003	2004
Population	m	0.71	0.73	0.75	0.76	0.77
Gross domestic product (GDP)	US$bn	0.17	0.20	0.26	0.32	*0.37
GDP per capita	US$	238	269	348	417	582
GDP real growth	%	-1.1	1.0	2.3	2.1	1.9
Inflation	%	4.5	3.5	3.0	4.5	4.3
Exports (fob) (goods)	US$m	20.0	10.0	17.0	16.3	–
Imports (fob) (goods)	US$m	78.0	45.0	49.0	39.8	–
Balance of trade	US$m	-58.0	-35.0	-32.0	-23.5	-24.0
Current account	US$m	-5.5	-0.8	-10.0	-20.0	-10.0
Total reserves minus gold	US$m	43.2	62.3	79.9	94.3	103.7
Foreign exchange	US$m	42.3	61.6	79.2	93.5	102.9
Exchange rate	per US$	533.98	549.78	522.74	462.34	408.14

* estimated figure

Comoros

1995 An abortive coup to toppled Djohar was foiled by French troops.
1996 Mohammed Taki Abdoul-Karim won the presidential election. Constitutional changes adopted *sharia* as law.
1997 The islands of Anjouan (Ndzuani) and Mohéli (Mwali) declared their independence from the Comoros. Economic depression was sited as the reason for their wish for reintegration with France. The central government led an unsuccessful invasion of the island.
1998 President Taki Abdoul-Karim died. Tajidine ben Said Massonde became president.
1999 Colonel Azali Assoumani seized power in a bloodless coup and became president. In legislative elections on Anjouan, hardline secessionists won every seat.
2001 A military, unionist force on Anjouan took control in August. Attempts to wrest control from it failed and in December the Comoran government, with amendment to the constitution, implemented a change to unify the country in a lose federation as a decentralised Comoran Union of three autonomous islands: Anjouan, Mohéli and Grand Comoros.
2002 The country's name was changed to L'Union des Comores (The Union of the Comoros). In May, Assoumani was declared president of The Union. Mohamed Bacar was elected president of Anjouan. Mohamed Said Fazul was elected president in Mohéli, and Abdou Soule Elbak was elected president of Grande Comore.
2003 Power-sharing agreements were signed to allow national elections to take place. The presidency rotates between the islands.
2004 In April, parliamentary elections were held in which the opposition parties won 27 seats against six seats for the President's party. The first federal government was sworn in on 14 July.
2005 Mount Karthala, a volcano on Gran Comore, erupted in April and again in November, causing population flights and public health concerns.

Political structure
Constitution
The constitution of 1992 was suspended after the 1999 military coup.
The new national constitution, ratified in 2002, created a federation – The Union of the Comoros – with greater autonomy for each of the three islands.
Each island has its own president, with a federal president assuming overall authority. The federal presidency rotates every four years between the three islands. Each island has its own legislature, constitution and budget. Foreign relations, defence and currency are the responsibility of the Union.

Form of state
Federal republic

The executive
Under the federal constitution, the president of The Union of the Comoros, the central government, is elected for a four-year term. The federal presidency rotates every four years between the three islands.

National legislature
The 33-member Assemblée de l'Union (parliament) has 15 members appointed by the three island legislatures (five each) and 18 elected through direct universal suffrage. Each island has its own assembly.

Legal system
French and Sharia (Islamic) law in a new consolidated code.

Last elections
18 and 25 April 2004 (parliamentary); 17 and 21 March 2004 (autonomous islands' assemblies); 14 April 2002 (presidential).
Results: Second round parliamentary: the islands' candidates won 12 seats, the supporters of The Union, six. Turnout in the election for those 18 seats was over 65 per cent. The remaining 15 seats in the 33-seat assembly will be nominated by the island parliaments.
Autonomous islands' assemblies:
Grande Comore: supporters of the island president won 13 seats out of 20 and supporters of the federal president, seven.
Anjouan: supporters of the island president won 23 seats out of 25 and supporters of the federal president, two.
Mohéli: supporters of the island president won nine seats out of 10 and supporters of the federal president, one.
Presidential: Colonel Azali Assoumani was elected president of The Union with about 75 per cent of the vote, but the electoral commission declared the poll invalid. The two opposition candidates and most voters of Anjouan, boycotted the vote. Nevertheless, on 26 May 2002, Azali Assoumani was declared president of The Union.

Next elections
2006 (presidential); 2009 (parliamentary).

Political parties
President Azali Assoumani's Convention pour le Renouveau des Comores (CRC) (Convention for the Renewal of the Comoros) is the only national political party.
The CRC was opposed in the 2004 parliamentary elections by a loose coalition of opposition groups, the Camp des Iles Autonomes (Camp of the Autonomous Islands), organised by the presidents of the three islands.

Ruling party
The first federal government was sworn in on 14 Jul 2004.

Population
766,000 (2004)

Ethnic make-up
Antalote, Cafre, Makao, Oimatsaha, Sakalava. The descendants of Arab traders, Malay immigrants and African peoples contribute to the islands' complex ethnic mix.

Religions
Sunni Muslim 86 per cent (official religion), Roman Catholic 14 per cent.

Education
Unicef concluded that school enrolment dropped due to insufficient classrooms and qualified teachers, among other infrastructural inadequacies. Education also suffers from poor performance and quality. A Unicef-sponsored humanitarian action plan in 2002 provided US$122,000 towards basic education.
Literacy rate: 59 per cent; adult rates (World Bank 2002).
Enrolment rate: 60 per cent (Unicef).

Health
The World Health Organisation (WHO), in 2003, funded health projects aimed at reducing mortality from common diseases and encouraging better use of existing health facilities, while improving the quality of healthcare overall. It also organised mosquito control activities to reduce the incidence of malaria.
Annual total expenditure on health is around 3 per cent of GDP, of which government spending is about 60 per cent (40 per cent coming from external sources).

HIV/Aids
Although prostitution is relatively rare, over 60 per cent of sex workers in Moroni tested HIV positive.
HIV prevalence: 0.12 per cent aged 15–49 in 2000
Life expectancy: 61.6 years (World Bank).
Fertility rate/Maternal mortality rate: 4.0 births per woman; maternal mortality five per 1,000 live births (World Bank).
Infant mortality rate: 54 per 1,000 live births; 26 per cent of children aged under five years are malnourished (World Bank).

Welfare
There is no minimum wage, there are no laws prohibiting bonded or forced labour and no protection for anti-union practices by employers. The labour code allows for one day off per week and one month of paid leave per year, although the government generally does not enforce the law due to a lack of provision.
The World Bank reported, in October 2003, that 47 per cent of households

were living in poverty and 42 per cent of the population were malnourished. It stated that the government were poor in implementing, even in partnership, basic social infrastructure, and health and educational services tended to be of low quality and poorly utilised. Local communities were found to be keen to undertake projects in partnership with a World Bank poverty reduction plan, the 'Social Fund Project,' to creat small, income-generating activities. In future, proposed projects will rely mainly on village committees, community groups, NGOs and private firms.

Main cities
Moroni (on Grand Comore (Ngazidja) (capital, estimated population 60,200 in 2003), Mutsamudu (on Anjouan (Ndzuani), (30,900), Mutsamudu (30,900), Mitsamiouli (21,400), Domoni (19,100), Fomboni (on Mohéli (Mwali) (13,300).

Languages spoken
Shikomor and numerous African languages are spoken. English is rarely spoken.
Official language/s
Arabic and French

Media
Press
The semi-official weekly *Al Watwan* and several private newspapers are published in the capital Moroni. The weekly *La Gazette de Comores* and the monthly *L'Archipel* are sharply critical of the government.
Broadcasting
Radio: Radio Comoros broadcasts in Comoran, French, Arabic and Swahili. A few private television and radio stations operate without overt government interference. Transmissions from French- controlled Mayotte are easily received and some people have access to satellite and other international broadcasting.
Television: There is no national television.

Economy
Comoros's economy is based on local services and agriculture. Exports consist mainly of agricultural products, including cloves, ylang-ylang and vanilla, of which Comoros is a major world producer. In recent years, the economy showed modest improvement in its macroeconomic indicators.
Part of the country's success was due to the pegging of the Comoran franc to the euro, which ensured exchange rate stability while depreciating the currency's parity with the US dollar, making its exports generally more attractive on world markets. The economy also benefited from the rising international prices of its main cash crops. In 2004, however, world prices for vanilla, which accounts for two-thirds of Comoros's agricultural exports, collapsed, contributing, along with crop and livestock diseases, to a slowdown in growth. At the same time, the cost of petroleum products rose, adding to the pressures on inflation, which was 4.5 per cent in 2003 and 4.3 per cent in 2004. The adverse effects of these developments was ameliorated to some extent by the increase in remittances from expatriates, especially those taking advantage of cheaper air flights to visit home in the summer.
The distribution of wealth between the islands is a problem, given the lack of constitutional clarity over revenue collection, but an agreement to transfer shared revenues to a special account at the Central Bank has been reached to secure fiscal policy in 2005. Harmonisation of custom tariffs is expected increase revenue by about 0.4 per cent of GDP. The government has embarked on a number of counter-measures to limit expenditure and reassure investors.

External trade
Comoros runs annual deficits on its trade account, largely because of a limited export base. The IMF has urged better customs control as customs revenue represents over half of state financial receipts.
Imports
Principal imports are rice and other foodstuffs, consumer goods; petroleum products, cement and transport equipment
Main sources: France (24.4 per cent total, 2004), South Africa (11.5 per cent), UAE (7.3 per cent), Kenya (6.1 per cent), Italy (5.1 per cent), Mauritius (4.8 per cent), Singapore (4.2 per cent)
Exports
Principal exports are vanilla, ylang-ylang, cloves, perfume oil, copra
Main destinations: US (42.2 per cent total, 2004), France (18 per cent), Singapore (16 per cent), Turkey (4.7 per cent)

Agriculture
Farming
The agriculture sector is the principal source of export earnings. It contributes around 40 per cent to GDP and employs 65 per cent of the workforce.
Although as much as 50 per cent of the total land area is cultivated, the agricultural sector remains underdeveloped (due to poor soil, adverse weather conditions and inadequate facilities) and over 50 per cent of the country's food requirements (notably rice) have to be imported.
Major food crops grown are cassava, sweet potatoes, rice and bananas; yams and coconuts are also produced, while main cash crops are cocoa, ylang-ylang (perfumes), vanilla and cloves.
Crop production in 2004 included: *21,000 tonnes (t) cereals in total, *17,000t rice, *4,000t maize, *58,000t cassava, 5,500t sweet potatoes, 9,200t taro, 4,000t yams, 65,000t bananas, 14,320t pulses, 77,200t roots and tubers, *77,000t coconuts, *10,271t oilcrops, *27t cocoa beans, *100t green coffee, 140t vanilla, 3,000t cloves, 68,600t fruit in total, 3,715t vegetables in total. Estimated livestock production included: 2,095t meat in total, 1,100t beef, 350t goat meat, 560t poultry, *776t eggs, *4,550t milk.
* estimate
Fishing
Fishing is underexploited, with tuna being the main catch. The fishing sector has received considerable aid from Japan and the EU.
Forestry
Deforestation, caused by clearing for the cultivation of the ylang-ylang crop, is an increasing ecological problem.

Industry and manufacturing
The industrial sector contributes around 13 per cent to GDP and employs 5 per cent of the workforce; manufacturing contributes 5.4 per cent. The sector is underdeveloped, with activity confined to distillation of essences and perfumes (particularly from ylang-ylang), vanilla processing, soft drinks, plastics and woodwork.

Tourism
The tourism sector has potential, but remains under-developed. Tourists have been deterred by political instability and social turmoil, although there are no reports of attacks on foreigners. Tourism contributes around 4 per cent to GDP.

Mining
There is no mining activity.

Hydrocarbons
There are no known oil or gas reserves and the country relies on imports of refined oil for its energy needs. However, consumption is low, around 670 barrels per day. There is only one oil company in Comoros, the Société Comorienne des Hydrocarbures (SCH), which owns two storage depots.

Energy
There is heavy dependence on imports for all fuel requirements. The electricity generating infrastructure is poor and there are frequent blackouts, partly due to generator breakdowns and partly due to a lack of fuel. Electricity is provided by the parastatal utility Electricite et Eaux des Comores (EEDC).

Banking and insurance
The Banking sector is composed of the Banque Centrale des Comores (BCC), the

Comoros

central bank, the Banque de Développement des Comores (BDC), which focusses on development lending, and the Banque pour l'Industrie et le Commerce des Comores (BIC). The BDC stopped lending in 1997 due to liquidity problems, but still exists and is scheduled for restructuring some time in the future. The BIC is linked to France's BNP-Paribas and provides full international trade finance as well as local personal and business banking services.

Central bank
Banque Centrale des Comores (BCC)
Main financial centre
Moroni

Time
GMT plus three hours

Geography
The Comoros is an archipelago in the Mozambique Channel, between the island of Madagascar and the east coast of the African mainland. The group comprises four main islands (Grand Comore, Anjouan, Mohéli and Mayotte) and numerous islets and coral reefs. Mayotte is a French overseas territory, politically separate from the Comoros.

Climate
Tropical. Dry season May to October with average temperature 24 degrees Celsius (C). Rainy season from November to April with temperature 27-35 degrees C. Very hot and humid on coasts, cooler on inner highlands.

Entry requirements
Passports
Required by all.
Visa
Required by all. They can be bought on arrival at the airport, the cost varies to the length of stay. Return/onward ticket and exit permit are also needed.
Currency advice/regulations
No restrictions.
Prohibited imports
Weapons, ammunition and radio transmission equipment, plants and soil.

Health (for visitors)
Mandatory precautions
Yellow fever vaccination certificates requested from visitors arriving from infected areas.
Advisable precautions
Typhoid, hepatitis A, tetanus and polio vaccinations recommended. Malaria prophylaxis advisable as risk exists throughout the country. Water precautions should be taken. There is a rabies risk. Seek further advice with regard to vaccinations for diphtheria, hepatitis B, meningitis and tuberculosis.

Hotels
Advisable to book in advance. Limited first-class accommodation available on Grande Comore, Anjouan and Mayotte (Maore), but several high-quality resort hotels have been built.

Public holidays
Fixed dates
18 Mar (Anniversary of the Death of President Said Mohamed Cheikh), 25 May (Africa Day), 29 May (Anniversary of the Death of President Ali Soilih), 6 Jul (Independence Day), 26 Nov (Anniversary of the Death of President Ahmed Abdallah), 25 Dec (Christmas Day).
Variable dates
Eid al Adha, Islamic New Year, Ashura, Eid al Fitr.
The Islamic year contains 354 or 355 days, with the result that Muslim feasts advance by 10–12 days against the Gregorian calendar. Dates of feasts vary according to the sighting of the new moon, so cannot be forecast exactly. Islamic year 1426: 10 February 2005 to 30 January 2006.

Working hours
Banking
Mon–Thu: 0800–1400; Fri: 0800–1100.
Business
Mon–Thu: 0730–1430; Fri: 0730–1100, Sat: 0730–1200.
Government
Mon–Thu: 0730–1200 and 1500–1730, Fri: 0730–1100, Sat: 0730–1200.
Shops
Closed daily between 1200–1500.

Electricity supply
220V AC

Getting there
Air
There is an international airport on Grande Comore. Air Mauritius, Air France and South African Airways are the principal airlines that fly to the island.
National airline: Air Comores (state-owned).
International airport/s: International Prince Said Ibrahim (Code: HAH), 25km north of Moroni, on Ngazidja.
Airport tax: None.
Surface
Main port/s: Moroni (Grand Comore) and Fomboni (Anjouan): both have offshore anchorage for larger vessels.

Getting about
National transport
Air: Each island is served by Air Comores. There are regular flights between the islands.
Road: Surfaced roads on Grande Comore and Anjouan; other islands' roads can be difficult in rainy season. Mohéli has only very basic tracks.

Water: Small boats, which can be hired, ply between islands.
City transport
Taxis: Service is provided by taxi-brousse (bush taxis) on each island. The journey from the International Airport to the city centre takes 30 minutes.
Car hire
International driving licence required.

BUSINESS DIRECTORY
The addresses listed below are a selection only. While World of Information makes every endeavour to check these addresses, we cannot guarantee that changes have not been made, especially to telephone numbers and area codes. We would welcome any corrections.

Telephone area codes
The international direct dialling code (IDD) for Comoros is +269, followed area code and subscriber's number:
Anjouan 71 Moroni 73
Mohali 72

Useful telephone numbers
Emergency services: 744-890

Chambers of Commerce
Chambre de Commerce, d'Industries et d'Agriculture, PO Box 763, Moroni (tel: 730-958;fax: 731-983; e-mail: pride@snpt.km).

Banking
Banque de Development des Comores, Place de France, BP-298 Moroni (tel: 730-154, 730-818; fax: 730-397, e-mail: bdc@snpt.km).

Banque pour l'Industrie et le Commerce - Comores, BP 175, Place de France, Moroni (tel: 730-243, 730-225, 730-289; fax: 731-229).

Central bank
Banque Centrale des Comores, PO Box 405, Place de France, Moroni (tel: 731-814; fax: 730-349).

Travel information
Comorian Association of Tourism (ACT) (tel: 732-847, 731-942; fax: 732-846).

Société Comorienne de Tourisme et d'Hotellerie (COMOTEL), Itsandra Hotel, Ngazidja (tel: 732-365).

International Prince Said Ibrahim Airport, BP 1003, Moroni (tel: 731-593, 732-452, 732-135; fax: 731-468).

Ministry of tourism
Ministry of Transport, Tourism, Post and Telecommunications, BP 97 Moroni (tel: 744-242; fax: 744-241).

Ministries
Ministry of Culture, Youth and Sports, Moroni (tel: 744-044).

Ministry of the Economy, Commerce, Handicrafts and Investment, BP 474 Moroni (tel: 744-232; fax: 730-144).

Ministry of Education, Professional Formation and Human Rights, BP 73 Moroni (tel: 744-185; 744-180).

Ministry of Equipment, Energy and Urbanism, Moroni (tel: 744-500).

Ministry of Finance, Budget and Privatisation, BP 324 Moroni (tel: 744-141; fax: 744-140).

Ministry of Foreign Affairs and Co-operation, BP 428 Moroni (tel: 744-100; fax: 744-111).

Ministry of Health, Population and Women's Affairs, Moroni (tel: 744-070).

Ministry of the Interior and Decentralisation, BP 686 Moroni (tel: 744-666; fax: 744-688).

Ministry of Justice and Islamic Affairs, Moroni (tel: 744-200).

Ministry of Production and the Environment, BP41 Moroni (tel: 744-630; fax: 744-632).

Ministry of Public Service, Employment and Labour, Moroni (tel: 744-540).

Other useful addresses

British Honorary Consulate, BP 986, Moroni (tel/fax: 733-182).

Comoros Embassy (USA), East 50th Street, New York, NY 10022 (tel: 202-972-8010; fax: 202- 983-4712; e-mail: comun@undp.org).

Société Internationale des Comores, BP 175, Moroni (tel: 730-243).

Internet sites

Africa Business Network: http://www.ifc.org/abn

AllAfrica.com: http://allafrica.com

African Development Bank: http://www.afdb.org

Africa Online: http://www.africaonline.com

Harambee Afrika (UK business club for traders with east, central and southern Africa; includes annotated web resource list): http://www.harambee.co.uk

Mbendi AfroPaedia (information on companies, countries, industries and stock exchanges in Africa): http://mbendi.co.za

Congo

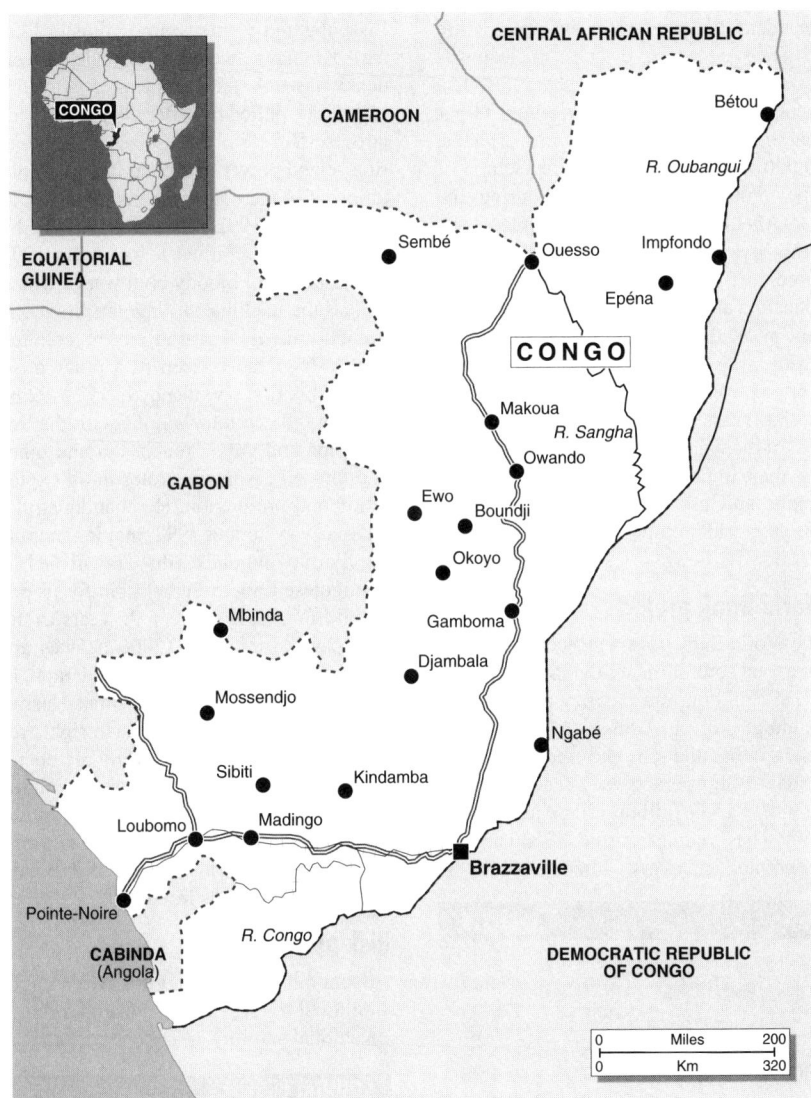

KEY FACTS

Official name: République du Congo (Republic of Congo)

Head of State: President Denis Sassou-Nguesso (PCT) (since 1997; elected 10 Mar 2002)

Head of government: Isidore Mvouba (appointed 7 Jan 2005. President Sassou-Nguesso made the appointment to a post that does not exist under the new constitution)

Ruling party: Coalition of Parti Congolais du Travail (PCT) (Congolese Labour Party), Forces Démocratiques Unies (FDU) (United Democratic Forces) and independents

Area: 342,000 square km

Population: 3.47 million (2004)

Capital: Brazzaville (political); Pointe-Noire (economic)

Official language: French

Currency: CFA franc (CFAf) = 100 centimes (Communauté Financière Africaine (African Financial Community) franc)

Exchange rate: CFAf544.07 per US$ (Oct 2005); CFAf655.95 per euro (pegged from Jan 1999)

GDP per capita: US$1,427 (2004)

GDP real growth: 4.00% (2004)

Labour force: 1.56 million (2004)

Inflation: 2.00% (2004)

Oil production: 240,000 bpd (2004)

Balance of trade: US$1.47 billion (2004)

The Republic of Congo continues to face major challenges. Its problems are those of many African one-commodity nations – economic diversification to provide jobs and a need to restructure politically and economically to reduce the numbers of people living below poverty levels. There's a lot of competition for development dollars, and increasingly Africa-wise monetary funds, international banks and donor nations will neither give nor lend unless the, to them, all important social restructure has reasonable priority. And this has to be followed by continued transparency – not a favourite of many African governments.

Economy

Congo is oil rich – its one of sub-Saharan Africa's main oil producers – but in terms of economic diversity, poor. It has been bedeviled by civil conflict. The non-oil sector – timber, potash, lead, zinc, uranium, copper, phosphates, gold, magnesium, natural gas, hydropower – increased by about 9.5 per cent on average during 2000–04,

335

propelled by improvements in agriculture, commerce, and transportation. There is more potential, but to unlock it the government needs to tackle structural weaknesses in key sectors of the economy, including banking and electricity.

Congo is ahead before going to the donors and agencies having planned to use oil revenues in excess of budget assumptions to fund poverty alleviation programmes, accelerate the clearance of arrears to external creditors, and normalise relations with domestic creditors. It will also strengthen the management of public finances and monitor public spending to improve the business climate and enhance the overall governance framework.

IMF aid

Congo's development aims are backed by a current US$85 million IMF-endorsed programme. This focuses on economic and social recovery within the framework of a *Nouvelle Espérance* (New Hope) programme. Macroeconomic performance is strengthening. Improved economic management, coupled with an exceptionally favourable international environment – a strong rise in oil prices – has resulted in increased growth and stronger fiscal and current account balances. There are steps to enhance transparency with regard to oil sector transactions – a full audit report of the national oil company is to be published and quarterly revenue reports certified.

But a long way to go

Once classified as a lower-middle-income economy, in donor terms Congo is now a Highly Indebted Poor Country (HIPC). It is likely to qualify for early debt relief provided its macroeconomic programme remains on track. A decade of conflicts has had devastating effects on the economy and the welfare of its people. Congo experienced a continuous decline in per capita income from the mid-1980s to the late 1990s. The infrastructure has suffered considerable damage; for example, entire provinces do not have access to clean water, and institutions are in shambles. The social crisis is acute and worsening: 11 per cent of children under 15 are orphans, 60,000 women and girls were victims of rape, 5,000 children fought during the war. About 70 per cent of Congolese currently live below the poverty line, compared to 30 per cent in 1993. Primary education attendance dropped from 90 per cent in 1990 to 40 per cent in 2000; and, during the same time life expectancy dropped from 52 years in the early 1990s to 48.6 years in 2002. More than 50 per cent of the workforce is unemployed, with less than 30 per cent of 15 to 25 year-olds in jobs, and less than two per cent of 15 to 25 year olds employed in the formal sector.

World Bank projects

The World Bank has six projects in Congo, for a total commitment of US$157 million: a US$7 million transparency and capacity building project, US$40 million emergency rehabilitation and reconstruction, US$41 million emergency recovery/community, US$19 million HIV/Aids, US$20 million basic education and US$30 million economic recovery credit (this is essentially to make recovery and development in Congo pro-poor. A new World Bank programme is planned by June 2006.

Politics

President Sassou-Nguesso began a seven-year term in March 2002 after winning presidential elections in which two of his main rivals – former president Pascal Lissouba and former prime minister Bernard Kolelas – were excluded by a residency law. A third contender – André Milongo – pulled out after alleging irregularities. Born in 1943, Sassou-Nguesso first seized power in a coup in 1979, only to lose it in the country's first multi-party elections in 1992 which were won by Lissouba. He returned to power in 1997 after a brief but bloody civil war in which he had the backing of Angolan troops. A French-trained paratroop colonel, Sassou-Nguesso is seen as a pragmatist. During his first presidency in 1979–92 he loosened the country's links with the Soviet bloc and gave French, US and other Western oil companies roles in oil exploration and production. He abandoned the one-party system in 1992, making the ruling Parti Congolaise du Travail (PTC) (Congolese Labour Party) fight for its political life after more than 20 years as the sole party. In January 2006 he was appointed chairman of the African Union, in place of Sudan's President Omar Hassan Ahmad al Bashir whose human rights record was questioned by several members.

Civil wars and militia conflicts have plagued the Republic of Congo throughout its recent past and the country is struggling to build on a peace accord signed with southern rebels in 2003.

Risk assessment

Economic	Poor/improving
Political	Poor/improving
Regional stability	Average

COUNTRY PROFILE

Historical profile

With its small population – 3.5 million in 2004 – and varied mineral wealth, Congo should be better placed than most African countries to realise its potential. In fact, on a GDP per capita basis, it is not even in the 10 wealthiest African countries. After three relatively peaceful but coup-ridden decades of independence, the former French colony experienced the first of two destructive bouts of fighting in 1993 when disputed parliamentary elections led to bloody, ethnically-based fighting between pro-government forces and the opposition. A ceasefire agreement

KEY INDICATORS — Congo

	Unit	2000	2001	2002	2003	2004
Population	m	3.02	3.10	3.19	3.23	3.47
Gross domestic product (GDP)	US$bn	2.80	2.80	3.00	2.91	*4.38
GDP per capita	US$	927	903	938	900	1,427
GDP real growth	%	7.9	2.9	3.5	1.2	4.0
Inflation	%	0.4	-0.1	3.3	2.0	2.0
Oil output	'000 bpd	275.0	271.0	258.0	243.0	240.0
Exports (fob) (goods)	US$m	2,559.0	2,181.0	1,880.0	2,400.0	2,224.0
Imports (fob) (goods)	US$m	966.0	1,153.0	1,230.0	730.0	749.3
Balance of trade	US$m	1,593.0	1,028.0	646.0	1,670.0	1,474.7
Current account	US$m	260.0	-90.0	66.0	–	330.0
Total reserves minus gold	US$m	222.0	68.9	31.6	34.8	119.6
Foreign exchange	US$m	221.3	68.0	27.7	–	111.5
Exchange rate	per US$	711.98	733.04	683.75	574.89	528.29

* estimated figure

Congo

followed by the inclusion of some opposition members in the government helped to restore peace, but in 1997 ethnic and political tensions exploded into a full-scale civil war, fuelled in part by the prize of the country's offshore oil wealth, which motivated many of the warlords. The army split along ethnic lines, with most northern officers joining President Denis Sassou-Nguesso who was also backed by Angola, and most southerners backing the rebels. These were supporters of the former president, Pascal Lissouba, who had been deposed by Sassou-Nguesso in 1997. There was a ceasefire in 1999, but rebel remnants, known as Ninjas, are still active in the southern region. Most of the rebels have yet to disarm and many have turned to banditry.

From the fifteenth century, the Bakongo, Bateke and Sanga began settling what is now the Republic of Congo.

1482 Portuguese explorer Diogo Cao mapped the coastline.
1880s The colonisation of what is now Congo began in the late nineteenth century after the French explorer Pierre Savorgnan de Brazza signed a treaty with the Chief of the Batekes to establish a French protectorate over the north bank of the Congo river.
1910 Middle Congo, as the country was then known, became a colony of French Equatorial Africa.
1928 Africans revolted over forced labour which was used to build the Congo railway. More than 17,000 Africans died in the revolt.
1946 Congo was granted a territorial assembly by the French and representation in the French parliament.
1960 Congo became independent with a catholic priest, Abbé Fulbert Youlou, as president.
1963 Alfonse Massamba-Debat became president and Pascal Lissouba became prime minister. The country became a one-party socialist state.
1969 Captain Marien Ngouabi led a coup against Massamba-Debat and became president. The Parti Congolais du Travail (PCT) (Congolese Workers' Party) was declared the only legal political party.
1970 Ngouabi proclaimed Congo a Marxist state.
1977 Ngouabi was assassinated by forces loyal to Massamba-Debat, who in turn was executed for treason. Joachim Yhombi-Opango of the Comité Militaire du Parti (CMP) (Party of the Military Committee) became president.
1979 Colonel Denis Sassou-Nguesso took over the PCT, and remained in power under one-party PCT rule until 1992.
1990 The PCT abandoned Marxism.
1992 A new constitution was approved by referendum. Multi-party legislative elections were won by the Union Panafricaine pour la Démocratie Sociale (UPADS) (Pan-African Union for Social Development), led by Pascal Lissouba. Lissouba was elected president, defeating Sassou-Nguesso.
1993 Political unrest forced new elections, which were won by UPADS. Civil war broke out over disputes over the elections.
1994 A peace agreement saw members of the opposition join the government. The currency was devalued.
1997 Civil war broke out after the government attempted to disarm rebels militia loyal to Sassou-Nguesso. Thousands of people were killed and tens of thousands forced to flee their homes. After several months of fighting Sassou-Nguesso succeeded in overthrowing the government of Pascal Lissouba. Sassou-Nguesso assumed the presidency at the head of the Conseil National de Transition (CNT) (National Transitional Council).
1999 The warring factions signed a peace accord with the government.
2001 A peace conference proposed a new constitution and 15,000 militia were demobilised through financial incentives. In December, Lissouba was convicted *in absentia* of treason and corruption and sentenced to 30 years' hard labour. Congo signed a treaty establishing the Gulf of Guinea Commisssion.
2002 The new constitution was endorsed by 80 per cent of the electorate, which strengthen the power of the president. Sassou-Nguesso was elected president. The legislative elections led to the creation of a pro-Sessou-Nguesso coalition consisting of the PCT, the Forces Démocratiques Unies (FDU) (United Democratic Forces) and a number of independents. Electoral disputes led to intense fighting, which reached Brazzaville, between government forces and the rebels in the south. An agreement on power-sharing was reached between the government and two main rebel groups, but fighting continued in the east.
2003 All parties signed a peace agreement ending the civil war. A new constitution was adopted paving the way for elections.
2004 The Congo, which was held responsible for large-scale diamond smuggling from the Democratic Republic of Congo, was expelled from the Kimberley Process Certification Scheme, severely limiting its exports of diamonds.
2005 On 7 January, Isidore Mvouba was named to the new post of prime minister (a post which does not exist under the constitution). Floods and mudslides, caused by heavy rains in December, left thousands of people without shelter in the capital, Brazzaville.

Political structure
Constitution
A new constitution was agreed in April 2001 and endorsed by referendum in 2002. As a result the power of the president was increased.
Form of state
Republic
The executive
Executive authority is vested in the directly elected president, who serves a seven-year term.
National legislature
Parliament consists of the National Assembly and the Senate. Parliament does not have the power to impeach the president.
Legal system
Based on the French civil, and traditional customary law
Last elections
10 March 2002 (presidential); 12 May/9 June 2002 (parliamentary).
Results: Presidential: Denis Sassou-Nguesso was elected with 89.4 per cent of the vote, Joseph Kignoumbi Kia Mboungou 2.7 per cent.
Parliamentary: PCT won 53 seats, FDU 30, URD six, UDAPS four, independents 60.
Next elections
May 2007 (parliamentary); 2009 (presidential).

Political parties
Ruling party
Coalition of Parti Congolais du Travail (PCT) (Congolese Labour Party), Forces Démocratiques Unies (FDU) (United Democratic Forces) and independents
Main opposition party
Union pour la Renouveau Démocratique/Mwinda (URD) (Union for Democratic Renewal); Union Panafricaine pour la Démocratie Sociale (UDAPS) (Pan-African Union for Social-Democracy).

Population
3.47 million (2004)
Ethnic make-up
Kongo (48 per cent), Sangha (17 per cent), Teke (17 per cent).
Religions
Traditional beliefs (over 50 per cent), Christianity (about 40 per cent, mainly Roman Catholic, some Protestant).

Education
Primary education is followed by seven years of secondary school which is divided into a four-year first cycle (ages 12 to 16) and a three-year second cycle (ages 16 to 19). In the second cycle, students can opt between general or technical education. Higher education is provided by the

Université Marien-Ngouabi, which is largely state subsidised. It has a yearly enrolment of about 12,000 students.
Public expenditure on education typically amounts to 6 per cent of annual gross national income.
Literacy rate: 83.8 per cent adult rate; 78.4 per cent female rate.
Compulsory years: Six to 12
Enrolment rate: 120 per cent for boys, 109 per cent for girls, total primary school enrolment of the relevant age group (including repetition rates) (World Bank)
Pupils per teacher: 70 in primary schools.

Health
In February 2004 a measles epidemics broke out in remote regions of northern Congo due to 'weak vaccination coverage' in earlier programmes and it was expected that, without a thorough immunisation campaign, measles would continue to return in two- to three-year cycles.
Pneumonic plague broke out in February 2005 in the north-east killing over 60 people and prompted control teams to be sent by international medical agencies to treat the victims. Many locals had fled the area and raised the fear of the infection spreading.
Annual total expenditure on health is around 2 per cent of GDP, of which government spending is approximately 64 per cent.
HIV prevalence: 4.9 per cent aged 15–49 in 2003 (World Bank)
Life expectancy: 48.6 years (World Bank).
Fertility rate/Maternal mortality rate: 6.3 births per woman (World Bank)
Infant mortality rate: 81 per 1,000 live births; 16 per cent of children aged under five were malnourished (World Bank).
Head of population per physician/bed: 0.3 physicians and 3.4 hospital beds available per 1,000 people (World Bank).

Welfare
The World Food Programme (WFP) in 2004 appealed for US$1.5 million, warning that without the necessary funding, food aid to vulnerable people would have to be reduced or entirely cut.
In moves to encourage full cessation following the peace agreement of 2003, international donors have contributed over US$900,000 to projects set up to reintegrate demobilised soldiers into society. These projects were a second phase, the first built on credit offered by the World Bank of US$5 million.

Main cities
Brazzaville (political capital, estimated population 1.2 million in 2004), Pointe-Noire (economic capital, 544,200), Loubomo (89,900), Nkayi (83,400).

Languages spoken
French is used for all business documentation. Numerous African languages are also spoken, including Lingala and Kikongo.
Official language/s
French

Media
Press
Main newspapers include *Semaine Africaine* (Catholic), the government-owned *Mweti* (four times a week), *Agence Congolaise d'Information* (official bulletin), *Soleil*, *La Madu Kutsekele*, *Le Pays*, *Choc* and *Aujourd'hui*. Several journals and periodicals, including *Etumba* and *Le Stade*.
Broadcasting
Radio and television are state-run. The fighting in the country has affected the communications, and radio and television can only be received in Brazzaville and environs (February 2000).
Radio: Radiodiffusion-Télévision Nationale Congolaise broadcasts programmes in French, Lingala and Kikongo.
Television: Broadcasts 80 hrs/week.

Economy
The war in Congo took its toll with deteriorating standards of living and widespread damage of essential infrastructure. The peace deal signed in 2001 gave the economy a much needed break from the devastation and encouraged international financial institutions, led by the IMF, to aid recovery through economic means.
In a post-conflict time the Congo is attempting to strengthen its medium-term macroeconomic and financial framework in an attempt to achieve steady growth and reduce its levels of poverty. The oil industry is the powerhouse of the economy generating around 60 per cent of GDP, and the IMF has targetted petroleum refining as one of the first structural challenges the government has to tackle, and in particular public resource management and fiscal discipline. Revenue from oil exports rose by 20 per cent in 2004 even though production was slightly down on 2003.
The Banking and electricity sectors are also deemed necessary for an overhaul. The agricultural sector, farming and forestry, is the country's largest employer. Subsistence farming does not produce enough food to feed the population; about half the area of forest is exploitable for commercial logging, while only 5 per cent remains protected from development Even though the country's economic performance has steadily increased since the end of the civil war it has been unable to alleviated problems of poverty and underdevelopment.
The government's main fiscal policy is to increase revenue to pay for the post-war reconstruction and meet IMF fiscal targets. On-going plans are to increase the amount of foreign investment in Congo. World Bank donors have pledged up to US$3.9 billion, with around three-quarters of this sum being invested in the transportation system. Improvements in the country's roads and mass transit could further encourage foreign investment.
With the unexpected rise in world prices of oil Congo is benefiting from a windfall, although the IMF has already suggested that any such bonuses should be spent on poverty-related expenditures (such as basic health and education) and debt repayment both domestic and international. Oil production has fallen in recent years and is not expected to increase until new oil fields come online at Libondo, Tchibeli, Litanzi and Yanga-Sud. Therefore, the government will have to broaden the tax base and improve revenue collection. Oil price rises in 2004 will also improve state revenues as will the resumption of the privatisation programme.
GDP growth was sluggish in 2003, but rebounded in 2004 and growth should escalate with President Sassou-Nguesso's economic programme dubbed the *Nouvelle Espérance* (New Hope) which is scheduled to run from 2003–10. The IMF and World Bank are satisfied with the government's policies and are entering negotiations on the cancellation of around US$13 billion of external debt.

External trade
There is a regular large trade surplus from oil export earnings, but invisibles and debt payments keep the current account in deficit.
Imports
Principal imports capital equipment, construction materials and foodstuffs.
Main sources: France (20.2 per cent total, 2004), China (6.6 per cent), Italy (6.5 per cent), India (4.8 per cent), Belgium (4.7 per cent), US (4.6 per cent)
Exports
Principal exports are petroleum, timber, plywood, sugar, cocoa, coffee and diamonds.
Main destinations: China (30.8 per cent total, 2004), US (18.2 per cent), Taiwan (16.8 per cent), South Korea (11.2 per cent), Trinidad and Tobago (5.6 per cent)

Agriculture
Farming
The agricultural sector contributes around 25 per cent of GDP and employs a third of the workforce. Agriculture has been

overshadowed by development of the petroleum industry.

Approximately a third of the total land area is given over to agriculture, of that almost all is pasture land. Only an estimated 2 per cent of the total land area is under cultivation (mainly in the alluvial Niari Valley). Farming is small-scale with output concentrated on subsistence crops such as plantains, cassava, yams, groundnuts, manioc, potatoes, wheat, maize, beans and paddy rice. Despite some growth in food production, Congo relies heavily on food imports.

The main cash crops are coffee, cocoa, tobacco and sugar. Attempts to expand production of other cash crops include the rehabilitation of oil palm estates and a major new cocoa project.

Crop production in 2004 included: 880,800 tonnes (t) cassava, 7,200t maize, 4,800t potatoes, 6,000t sweet potatoes, 12,000t yams, 90,000t oil palm fruit, 1,500t rice, 88,000t bananas, 73,000t plantains, 9,300t pulses, 940,800t roots and tubers, 90,000t oil palm fruit, 6,200t avocados, 10,700t citrus fruit, 25,000t mangoes, 3,200t tomatoes, 3,300t pineapples, 26,919t oilcrops, *100t tobacco, 1,260t cocoa beans, 1,700t green coffee, 4,000t coconuts, 460,000t sugar cane, 1,350t natural rubber, 229,200t fruit in total, 41,555t vegetables in total. Livestock production included: 30,423t meat in total, 20,000t game meat, 2,028t beef, *2,072t pig meat, 340t lamb, 783t goat meat, 5,200t poultry, *1,185t eggs, 1,100t milk.
* estimate

Fishing
Fishing is underdeveloped but is practised commercially on a small scale.

Forestry
The main agricultural export is timber, mostly Okoumé logs (of which Congo is a major world supplier). About half the total timber output is used for wood processing. Approximately 60 per cent of the country is covered by woodlands and forests, much of it unsuitable for commercial exploitation. There are large eucalyptus (fast growing) plantations near Pointe-Noire.

Exports of forest materials amount to US$214.2 million while imports amounted to US$4.8 million in 2003. Production in 2004 included 2,453,401 cubic metres (cum) roundwood, 1,251,000cum industrial roundwood, 314,500cum sawnwood, 520,000cum sawlogs and veneers, 361,000cum pulpwood, 29,600 cum wood-based panels, 21,000 cum veneer sheets, 1,202,401cum wood fuel, 4,701t charcoal.

Industry and manufacturing
The industrial sector contributes over 10 per cent to GDP and employs a fifth of the workforce. The manufacturing sector is largely underdeveloped, contributing less than 5 per cent to GDP. Construction contributes a further 5 per cent, although this figure could grow rapidly, particularly in the repair of the damaged infrastructure, if political stability remains calm and reconstruction efforts are sustained.

Most manufacturing enterprises operate in the Brazzaville and Pointe-Noire districts and in the Niari Valley. Activity is centred on agri-food and timber processing, textiles and oil refining.

There are also a few small-scale import substitution industries (footwear, soft drinks, metal working, chemicals) and a cement plant.

Structure and ownership of parastatals is being reformed and the privatisation programme is expected to be renewed after years of delay. Emphasis is on joint-venture enterprises, particularly in pulp/paper and light manufacturing.

Tourism
The tourist industry had great potential for eco-tourism, but until peace can by assured foreign governments continue to advise strongly that their citizens do not visit Congo unless absolutely necessary.

Mining
Congo has significant deposits of magnesium, gold, diamonds, cement, potash and salt. Commercial exploitation of these deposits was either damaged by the civil war or have yet to be developed.

In July 2004, Congo was expelled from the Kimberley Process, set up to curb the trade in 'conflict diamonds', when the Congo could not account for the discrepancy between reported production and its exports of rough diamonds. As these diamonds are mined mostly by artisans the government claimed it was unable to confirm production, or curb smuggling along its uncontrolled borders. The ban on Congo diamonds effectively suspended legal exports of diamonds.

Gold production from the Yangadou Mine experienced technical problems and production has only amounted to 4kg per month since it opened in 2003, instead of the 1,500kg as expected.

A major magnesium processing plant at Kouilou could have a significant role in the economy when it is up and running. The plan, by Canada's MagIndustries Corporation (MagMetals), is to construct a 72,000 tonnes per annum (tpa) smelter of the local magnesium salt deposits and produce 60,000tpa of magnesium alloy. However, by the beginning of 2005 the project was still awaiting financial backing.

As a by-product of the magnesium mining MagMetals also proposes to exploit the potash and salt deposits found in the locale, with a 300,000tpa potash fertiliser plant and 400,000tpa salt plant.

Hydrocarbons
Congo is sub-Saharan Africa's fifth largest oil producer with proven reserves of 1.5 billion barrels. Production fell slightly in 2004 to around 235,000 barrels per day (bpd) due to mature fields yielding less and new fields not ready to come online. Other new fields – Libondo, Tchibeli, Litanzi and Yanga-Sud – are expect to begin production by 2006, and offset the reduced output. Western Europe and North America are Congo's predominant markets although there is hope of future expansion into Asian Markets.

France's TotalFina has the dominant role in oil production in the Congo, although it has lost its monopoly status as other foreign companies, especially Italy's Agip have begun investing in the country's petroleum industry.

The Congo has as yet no refining capacity and limited port facilities, which will hamper future growth in the short- to medium-term.

In 2004, natural gas reserves stood at around 90.4 billion cubic metres, most of which is oil-associated. A lack of infrastructure and investment means that most gas is vented or flared. The new 25MW gas plant in Djeno utilises gas for electricity production for supply to the Pointe Noire area.

Congo does not produce or import coal.

Energy
Installed generating capacity is 89MW, although generating potential is estimated at 3,000MW. Most electricity is produced by the 74MW Bouenza and the 15MW Djoué hydroelectric plants. Around a quarter of the country's electricity requirements are imported from the Democratic Republic of Congo (DRC). The development of the postponed US$925 million Sounda Gorge hydroelectric project could increase capacity by 1,000MW and turn the country into a net electricity exporter. Consumption is low as most rural inhabitants rely on wood fuel as a primary source of power.

The power infrastructure is in need of repairs and upgrading. The Congo and two Chinese companies signed a US$220 million contract to build a 120MW hydroelectric power plant on the Congo River and when completed in 2006, it is expected to double Congo's power generating capacity.

Banking and insurance
In 2004 the banking system was considered fragile by the IMF, with credit growth

limited by the lack of viable projects and a reluctance by banks to make loans as loan recovery is problematic. Of the four domestic banks two have been classified as in good condition and two in either a fragile or critical condition and in need of restructuring.

Central bank
Banque des Etats de l'Afrique Centrale

Main financial centre
Brazzaville

Time
GMT plus one hour

Geography
The Republic of Congo is an equatorial country on the west coast of Africa. A flat, treeless plane stretches down from the highlands to the coast. The coastline stretches about 170km along the Atlantic Ocean. The rain-forested highlands extends northward to Cameroon and the Central African Republic. Congo is bordered by Gabon in the west, and with the Democratic Republic of Congo to the east. In the south there is a short frontier with the Cabinda enclave of Angola.

Climate
Equatorial or sub-equatorial. Main dry season from June–September with average temperatures ranging from 15 degrees Celsius (C) at night to 32 degrees C during the day. Rainy season from October–May with higher average temperatures and high humidity. Generally hotter and more humid in Congo Basin, drier and cooler in highlands.

Entry requirements
Passports
Required by all.

Visa
Required by all except tourists from Gabon. If on business, a letter, issued by the traveller's company, giving a detailed summary of intended purpose of trip, a full itinerary including intended contacts with host company, and the acceptance of full responsibility for any expenses incurred during the term of stay, and repatriation expenses in case of emergency, must be submitted with the application to the local embassy.

Currency advice/regulations
There is no limit to the amount of foreign currency or CFA francs which can be taken into the country but receipts must be provided. The amount of local currency that can be exported in notes is limited to CFAf25,000.

Health (for visitors)
Medical and dental facilities are inadequate.

Mandatory precautions
A yellow fever vaccination certificate is required by all.

Advisable precautions
Typhoid, polio, hepatitis 'A' and tetanus vaccinations are recommended. Malaria prophylaxis should be taken, as a risk exists throughout the country. Water precautions should be taken. Visitors should avoid uncooked fruit and vegetables. There is an Aids risk and a risk of rabies. In February 2003, there was an outbreak of ebola hemorrhagic fever in the Congo/Gabon border region.

Hotels
Good hotels are available in Brazzaville, Pointe-Noire and Loubomo; few elsewhere. It is advisable to book well in advance. A 10 per cent tip is usual.

Credit cards
Two hotels in Brazzaville and several in Pointe Noire accept major credit cards.

Public holidays
Fixed dates
1 Jan (New Year's Day), 5 Feb (President's Day), 8 Mar (Women's Day), 18 Mar (Marien Ngouabi Day), 1 May (Labour Day), 22 Jun (Army Day), 31 Jul (Revolution Day), 13–15 Aug (Independence celebrations), 25 Dec (Christmas – Christians only), 31 Dec (Republic Day).

Working hours
Banking
Mon–Fri: 0630–1300. Counters close at 1130.

Business
Mon–Fri: 0800–1200 and 1430–1730, Sat: 0800–1200.

Government
Mon–Fri: 0700–1400, Sat: 0700–1200.

Shops
Mon–Fri: 0800–1200 and 1530–1800. Sat: 0800–1200 and 1530–1800/1900. Some shops close on Mon afternoons; a few open Sun mornings.

Telecommunications
Mobile phones
There there are two GSM 900 networks operating.

Electricity supply
220V AC 50 cycles; the voltage varies erratically.

Weights and measures
The metric system is used.

Getting there
Air
International airport/s: Brazzaville-Maya Maya Airport (BZV), 4km from city; restaurant.
Other airport/s: Pointe-Noire Airport (PNR), 6km from city.
Airport tax: None.
Surface
Road: There is a road from Lambaréné, in Gabon, to Loubomo and Brazzaville; this is not surfaced all the way. Entry from Cameroon is only practicable in the dry season. There is a surfaced road from the Cabinda enclave of Angola.
Water: A ferry service across the River Congo is operational daily from 0800–1200 and 1400–1700 between Kinshasa (Democratic Republic of Congo) and Brazzaville. Cars can be carried. The ferry takes about half an hour. There is also a vedette service for passengers only, which takes 15 minutes. Both services are liable to short-notice cancellation or delay.

Main port/s: Pointe-Noire. Brazzaville is the inland river port.

Getting about
National transport
Air: Internal air service operated by Lina Congo to Pointe-Noire (two or three times daily) and the main provincial towns.
Road: There are 243km of tarred roads; other routes are mainly tracks which can be impassable when wet.
There are very few metalled roads outside Brazzaville and Pointe-Noire, while the roads within the towns are generally poor. The main route from Pointe-Noire, through Brazzaville to Ouesso, is not uniform in quality; the section from Loubomo to Pointe-Noire is liable to become impassable in the rainy season.
Rail: The principal railway line is the Chemin de Fer Congo-Océan from Pointe-Noire to Brazzaville – 520km, which is part of the parastatal organisation Agence Transcongolaise de Communications. The service has been improved, but the journey can take 10 hours or more.
About half-way between Brazzaville and Point-Noire, the Congo-Océan railway is joined by the Comilog railway from Mbinda on the Congo/Gabon border – 280km. This line is used mainly for the carriage of manganese ore produced by Comilog, but the company which runs the Congo-Océan line is responsible for passengers and general freight.
The railways are suffering from lack of maintenance and general upkeep.
Water: The ferries on the rivers Congo and Oubangui are a principal form of transport.
City transport
Taxis: Freely available in Brazzaville and Pointe-Noire; tipping is not usual. Can be hired by the hour or day. Fares should be negotiated in advance of journey.
Car hire
Available from main hotels in Brazzaville and Pointe-Noire. International or national driving licence accepted. Traffic drives on the right.

Congo

BUSINESS DIRECTORY

The addresses listed below are a selection only. While World of Information makes every endeavour to check these addresses, we cannot guarantee that changes have not been made, especially to telephone numbers and area codes. We would welcome any corrections.

Telephone area codes

The international direct dialling code (IDD) for Congo is + 242, followed by subscriber's number.

Useful telephone numbers

Fire: 18.
Police: 17.
Ambulance: 822-365/368.

Chambers of Commerce

Congo National Chamber of Commerce, Industry and Agriculture, PO Box 1119, Brazzaville (tel: 832-956).

Brazzaville Chamber of Commerce, Industr, Agriculture and Crafts, Avenue Amilcar Cabral, PO Box 92, Brazzaville (tel/fax: 811-608; e-mail: cciam_brazza@hotmail.com).

Dolisie Regional Chamber of Commerce, Industry and Agriculture, PO Box 78, Dolisie (Tel: 910.017).

La Sangha Regional Chamber of Commerce, Industrie and Agriculture, PO Box 122, Ouessa (tel: 983-200).

Pointe-Noire Chamber of Commerce, Agriculture, Industry and Crafts, PO Box 665, Pointe-Noire (tel: 941-280; fax: 943-467; e-mail: cciampnr@cg.celtelplus.com).

Banking

Banque de Développement des Etats de l'Afrique Centrale, PO Box 1177, Brazzaville (tel: 811-885, 811-761; fax: 811-880).

Banque des États de l'Afrique Centrale, PO Box 126, Brazzaville (tel: 832-814/5, 833-626, 833-362; fax: 836-342).

Banque Internationale du Congo, PO Box 33, Avenue Amilcar Cabral, Brazzaville (tel: 830-308, 831-411; fax: 815-092, 835-382).

Crédit pour l'Agriculture, l'Industrie et le Commerce (CAIC), PO Box 2889, Brazzaville (tel: 810-978, 814-050; fax: 810-977, 835-352).

Mutuelle Congolaise d'Epargne et de Crédit, PO Box 13237, Brazzaville (tel: 837-001; fax: 837-930).

Union Congolaise de Banques; PO Box 147, Avenue Amilcar Cabral, Brazzaville (tel: 833-000; fax: 836-845).

Central bank

Banque des États de l'Afrique Centrale, Direction Nationale, PO Box 126, Brazzaville (tel: 811-073; fax: 811-094; e-mail: beacbzv@beac.int).

Travel information

Afri-Congo, Brazzaville. Direction Générale du Tourisme, BP 456, Brazzaville (tel: 830-953).

Ministries

Ministry of Construction and Urban Development, BP 1218, Brazzaville.

Ministry of Decentralisation and Regional Development, BP 630, Brazzaville.

Ministry of Defence, BP 1219, Brazzaville.

Ministry of the Economy, BP 2120, Brazzaville.

Ministry of Finance and the Budget, BP 64, Brazzaville (tel: 411-266; fax: 814-145).

Ministry of Foreign Affairs, BP 2070, Brazzaville.

Ministry of Industry, Fisheries and Crafts, Palais du Peuple, Brazzaville (tel: 835-130).

Ministry of the Interior and of Security, BP 64, Brazzaville.

Ministry of Trade and Small- and Medium-sized Enterprises, Brazzaville (tel: 831-827).

Ministry of Transport and Civil Aviation, BP 2146, Brazzaville.

Other useful addresses

Agence Congolaise d'Information (ACI), BP 2144, Brazzaville

Bureau pour le Développement de la Production Agricole, BP 2222, Brazzaville.

Direction de la Statistique, BP 2031, Brazzaville (tel: 834-324).

Institut de Développement Economique de la République Populaire du Congo, c/o The Presidency, Brazzaville.

Office du Café et du Cacao (OCC), BP 2488, Brazzaville (tel: 831-902).

Office Congolais des Bois (OCB), BP 1229, Pointe-Noire (tel: 948-248).

Office Congolais de l'Entretien Routier (OCER), BP 2073, Brazzaville.

Office National du Commerce (ONC), BP 2305, Brazzaville (tel: 834-399).

Republic of Congo Embassy (USA), 4891 Colorado Avenue, NW, Washington DC 20011 (tel: 726-5500; fax: 726-1860; e-mail: info@embassyofcongo.org).

Société Nationale de Recherche et d'Exploitation Pétrolières (Hydro Congo), BP 2008, Brazzaville (tel: 833-560).

Syndicat des Commerçants, Importateurs et Exportateurs de l'Afrique Equatoriale (Sycomimpex), BP 84, Brazzaville.

Internet sites

Africa Business Network: http://www.ifc.org/abn

AllAfrica.com: http://allafrica.com

African Development Bank: http://www.afdb.org

Africa Online: http://www.africaonline.com

Congo-Brazzaville (French only, Actualité dossier): http://www.solcongolais.net/

Mbendi AfroPaedia (information on companies, countries, industries and stock exchanges in Africa): http://mbendi.co.za

Democratic Republic of Congo

KEY FACTS

Official name: République Démocratique du Congo (Democratic Republic of Congo) (DRC)

Head of State: Interim President Major General Joseph Kabila (appointed 25 Jan 2001) (in Dec 2002, the DRC government signed a peace deal with the two main rebel groups: Joseph Kabila is to remain president until elections)

Head of government: Interim President Major General Joseph Kabila

Ruling party: Transitional government (installed 30 Jun 2003; in Aug 2004, Tutsi-led RCD-Goma left the government.)

Area: 2,345,409 square km

Population: 58.78 million (2004)

Capital: Kinshasa

Official language: French

Currency: Congolese franc (Cf)

Exchange rate: Cf461.50 per US$ (Oct 2005); (currency floated 28 May 2001)

GDP per capita: US$112 (2004)

GDP real growth: 6.80% (2004)

Labour force: 22.08 million (2004)

Inflation: 3.90% (2004)

Balance of trade: -US$223.00 million (2003)

Foreign debt: US$12.90 billion (2003)

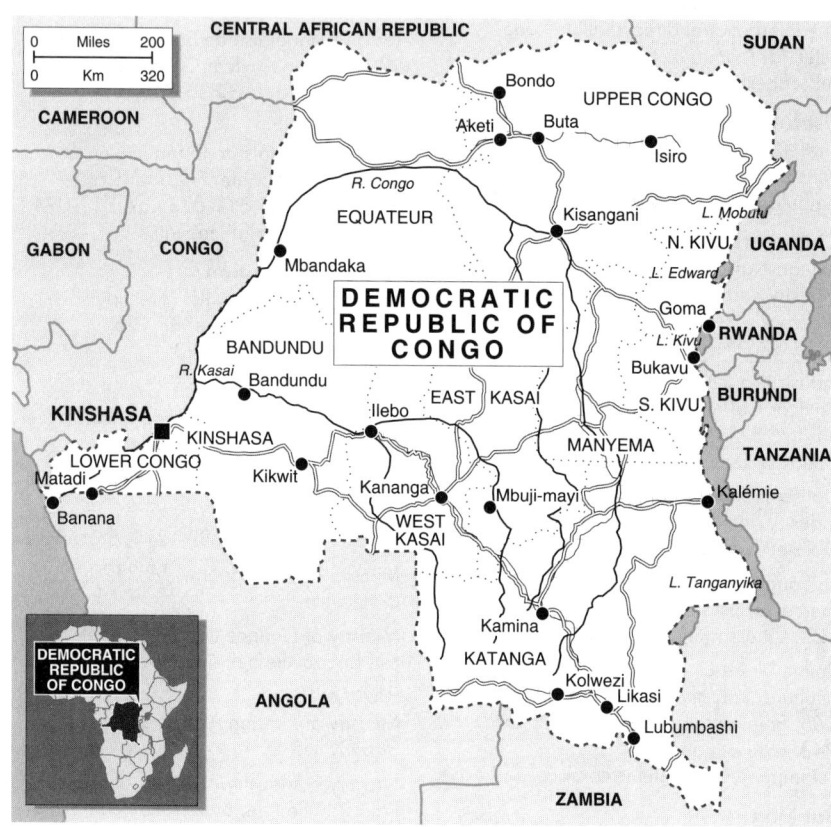

A vast country with immense economic resources, the Democratic Republic of Congo (DRC) is at centre of Africa's potentially most serious region of conflict. A five year civil war has pitted government forces, supported by Angola, Namibia and Zimbabwe, against rebels backed by Uganda and Rwanda. Despite a 2003 peace deal and the formation of a transition government, the threat of more conflict remains. The fighting was fuelled by the country's vast mineral wealth, with all sides taking advantage of the anarchy to plunder its natural resources.

The history of the DRC has been one of civil war and corruption. After independence in 1960, the country immediately faced an army mutiny and an attempt at secession by its mineral-rich province of Katanga. A year later, its prime minister, Patrice Lumumba, was seized and killed by troops loyal to army chief Joseph Mobutu. In 1965 Mobutu seized power, later renaming the country Zaïre and himself Mobutu Sese Seko. He turned Zaïre into a springboard for operations against Soviet-backed Angola and thereby ensured US backing. But he also made Zaïre synonymous with corruption.

After the Cold War, Zaïre ceased to be of interest to the US. In 1997 anti-Mobutu rebels quickly captured the capital, Kinshasa, installed Laurent Kabila as president and renamed the country. A rift between Kabila and his former allies backed by Rwanda and Uganda sparked a new rebellion. Angola, Namibia and Zimbabwe took Kabila's side and the country became a vast battleground. The United Nations has maintained more than 14,000 peacekeepers in the region since 1999.

Since 2001, the DRC has experienced a significant turnaround under difficult circumstances, but the figures do not tell the full story. In some instances, overall economic objectives have been met, but the composition of expenditure did not improve as envisaged. Low levels of spending on public investment and social sectors are offset by overspending by security and political institutions. Militias, rebel and other armed groups remain active in the illegal exploitation of minerals in the east. The Kinshasa government has no control over large parts of the country and tension remains high in the east. The Crisis Group, a Brussels-based think-tank, said in 2005 that 1,000 people were dying every day from war-related causes, including disease, hunger and violence. A transition government has difficulty reaching a broad consensus on essential reforms.

Insecurity and corruption

Corruption remains a major obstacle to any economic improvements, but the most important risks to progress are insecurity and social tensions. Although legislation has been adopted to intensify the fight against corruption, renewed impetus is needed to rebuild institutions, strengthen budget procedures and reporting, improve transparency in tax administration, and pursue the auditing and restructuring of public enterprises. Bringing the political transition process to a successful conclusion is key. There needs to be co-ordinated efforts to simultaneously tackle political, economic and security challenges. The more active involvement of UN peacekeepers in the east has succeeded in containing the activities of militias although widespread human rights violations continue.

There has been some progress. Since the declared end of the civil war in 2001, the country has experienced a significant turnaround. An extended transition government will, by the time it ends in the first quarter of 2006, have spent two and a half years reunifying the country and strengthening public institutions. An integrated army and a police force are being created and the combatants demobilised and disarmed, albeit with some delays. Economic activity has started to recover after 13 years of decline. There are new investment, forestry and mining codes on the table. Nevertheless, much remains to be done to enforce laws and procedures. The focus is on fiscal consolidation, monetary control, liberal exchange and trade regimes and improved governance, especially in the management of public resources, including the country's abundant natural resources. However, implementation is slowed by the difficulties of reaching a consensus within the transition government, especially on issues that could potentially affect the fragile balance of power among political parties.

Delays in completing the political transition process continue to lead to political and social tensions which undermine macroeconomic stability. The presidential, legislative and local elections have been postponed to early 2006 because of delays in adopting key laws, and the complexities of organisation in a country as vast as the DRC.

The long-term challenge for the DRC is to create an environment that is conducive to private sector-led growth and capitalises on the country's large resource endowment and potential. The macroeconomic framework for 2005–08 envisages average real growth of 7 per cent, implying an average increase in per capita gross domestic product of 4 per cent to US$117, a decline in inflation to 5 per cent (better than most economies in Africa), and a gradual build-up in gross international reserves to about nine weeks of non-aid-related imports.

Much needs to be done to strengthen budget execution, contain current expenditure, observe spending priorities, and improve capacity to implement poverty-reducing projects and fight corruption, but this, hopefully, is a pre-election period and little can be expected until after the poll, whenever that might be. And there will no attempts to digest bitter pills of enhanced tax collection before then. However, while the forthcoming elections may make reaching decisions difficult, progress in key areas is essential to attract private investment and maintain the momentum for growth. Particular effort should be made to address delays in reforming the mining sector and public enterprises and to ensure that the pace of reforms in the social sectors is sustained.

Politics

President Joseph Kabila heads a transition government, formed in June 2003, which includes members of former rebel groups, opposition politicians and Kabila loyalists. Planned general elections – the first since independence from Belgium in 1960 – have been delayed and are expected to be held in 2006.

Kabila was barely 30 and a political novice when in 2001 he inherited a nation decimated by civil war, following the murder of his father, Laurent. He surprised diplomats and observers by declaring that he wanted to seek a peaceful end to the war and introduce a multi-party democracy to the country.

He is the eldest of 10 children and spent much of his early life in East Africa, where his father lived in exile. He received military training in Rwanda and Uganda. Unlike his father, he was perceived to be shy, unassuming and quietly-spoken. He fought in his father's rebel army during the military campaign that brought him to power.

The DRC's largest former rebel groups are the Rassemblement Congolais pour la Démocratie-Goma (RCD-Goma) (Congolese Democratic Coalition) and the Mouvement de liberation du Congo (MLC) (Movement for the Liberation of Congo). The RCD received backing from Rwanda while Uganda supported the MLC. Under the terms of a peace deal signed in December 2002, both groups each received seven ministries in the transition government. Four vice presidents represent the former government, former rebel groups, and the political opposition.

KEY INDICATORS — Democratic Republic of Congo

	Unit	2000	2001	2002	2003	2004
Population	m	50.95	53.00	54.00	56.39	58.78
Gross domestic product (GDP)	US$bn	23.00	7.30	5.70	5.70	*6.57
GDP per capita	US$	452	138	106	90	112
GDP real growth	%	-7.0	-4.4	3.0	5.0	6.8
Inflation	%	553.7	357.0	25.7	12.8	3.9
Exports (fob) (goods)	US$m	760.0	940.0	1,010.0	1,128.0	–
Imports (fob) (goods)	US$m	1,035.0	702.0	955.0	1,351.0	–
Balance of trade	US$m	-275.0	238.0	58.0	-223.0	-223.0
Current account	US$m	-200.0	-250.0	-150.0	-80.0	-160.0
Foreign debt	US$bn	11.4	12.9	8.2	12.9	–
Exchange rate	per US$	21.82	164.00	344.13	369.00	409.25

* estimated figure

Nations of the World: A Political, Economic and Business Handbook

There are many other rebel groups, usually ethnically-linked and with fluid political allegiances. A government ruling in May 2001 allowed conventional political parties to operate, as long as they informed the government in writing that they intended to do so.

Risk assessment

Economic	Improving
Political	Poor
Regional stability	Poor

COUNTRY PROFILE

Historical profile
The Democratic Republic of Congo (DRC), formerly Zaïre, was once the colony, Belgian Congo, which won independence in 1960. It is the biggest, and should be the richest, country in Central Africa. Its area is more than twice that of Nigeria with half the population; the civil wars which have ravaged the country for a decade have done little to encourage population growth, quite the contrary. The DRC possesses legendary mineral wealth, much of which has been plundered during the civil war. Before the civil war it was the world's largest producer of industrial diamonds and a major exporter of copper, tin, manganese and cobalt. It also has exploitable resources of gold, uranium, tungsten, aluminium, nickel and lithium. In addition, the DRC has millions of acres of extremely fertile land, some of the richest in the world.

The thirteenth century saw the rise of the Kongo empire, which covered northern Angola and western Congo.

1482 Portuguese navigator Diogo Cao became the first European to visit the country and the Portuguese subsequently formed ties with the Kongo empire.

During the sixteenth and seventeenth centuries, the British, Dutch, Portuguese and French bought slaves from the Kongo empire.

1870 King Leopold II of Belgium decided to colonise the Kongo empire.
1879–87 British explorer, Henry Stanley, established Belgian authority over the Congo basin.
1884–85 European governments recognised Leopold's claim to the Congo basin.
1885 Leopold established the Congo Free State.
1891–92 Belgium conquered Katanga.
1892–94 Belgium conquered eastern Congo, which was controlled by Arab and east African merchants.
1908 The Belgian state annexed Congo.
1959 A nationalist uprising based in Leopoldville (now Kinshasa) began the disintegration of Belgian colonial authority.
1960 Congo gained independence. Joseph Kasavuba became president. The Belgian community fled and too few professionals were left to run the government. Chaos ensued as the diamond and copper mining province of Katanga attempted to secede under the leadership of Joseph Tshombe.
1961 Prime Minister Patrice Lumumba was deposed and murdered, allegedly by Katangan separatists. Marshal Joseph Mobutu was appointed prime minister. UN soldiers began disarming the Katangese soldiers on behalf of the Kasavuba government.
1963 Tshombe agreed to end the Katangan separatist war.
1964 President Kasavuba dismissed Mobutu and appointed Tshombe as prime minister.
1965 Mobutu seized power after a coup.
1971 Congo was renamed Zaïre. Mobutu renamed himself Mobutu Sese Seko.
1973–74 Mobutu nationalised foreign firms and forced foreign investors out of the country.
1977 French, Belgian and Moroccan troops fought an attack on Katanga by Angolan-based rebels.
1989 Zaïre defaulted on its debt servicing to Belgium; the economy began to deteriorate as development programmes were suspended.
1990 Mobutu appointed a transitional government and lifted the ban on mulit-party politics.
1991 A series of short-lived coalition governments were presided over by President Mobutu, who retained control of security and key ministries.
1993 Rival pro- and anti-Mobutu governments were formed
1996 Tutsi rebels, of eastern Zaire, captured much of the eastern border area
1997 Mobutu fled to Togo when the Alliance des Forces Démocratiques pour la Libération (AFDL) (Alliance of Democratic Forces for Liberation), led by Laurent-Désiré Kabila, seized Kinshasa, after a seven-month campaign. Kabila was backed by Tutsi rebels and the Rwandan government. Zaïre was renamed the Democratic Republic of Congo (DRC). Kabila became president. All government institutions were dissolved and a new constitution drafted. Mobutu Sese Seko died in Morocco.
1998 The Rassemblement Congolais pour la Démocratie-Goma (RCD-Goma) (Congolese Democratic Coalition) was formed, supported by Rwanda, Burundi and Uganda, and aimed at overthrowing Kabila, who was backed by Zimbabwe, Namibia and Angola. A full-scale civil war broke out. Peace talks began in Zambia but were ultimately unsuccessful.
1999 A split developed between the Mouvement pour la Libération Congolaise (MLC) (Movement for Congolese Liberation) backed by Uganda and the RCD-Goma supported by Rwanda. The six countries involved in the war signed a cease-fire, and the RCD-Goma and MLC signed later.
2000 A 5,500-strong UN force to monitor the supposed cease-fire: fighting continued between government and rebel forces and Rwandan and Ugandan forces.
2001 President Kabila was assassinated. His son, Major General Joseph Kabila became president. A peace agreement between DCR, Uganda and Rwanda allowed foreign troops to withdraw. An estimated 2.5 million people had died in the conflict and the UN declared the warring parties continued the fighting to mask plundering DCR's rich mineral assets.
2002 Goma was devastated by the eruption of Mount Nyiragongo. Rwanda and the DRC signed a peace deal whereby Rwanda withdrew troops and DRC disarmed and arrested Rwandan Hutu militia held responsible for the genocide in Rwanda in 1994. The DRC government signed a peace deal with the two main rebel groups. UN sponsored power-sharing talks were undertaken in South Africa.
2003 A transitional constitution sanctioned an interim government pending democratic elections to be held within two years. Leaders of the principal former rebel groups were sworn in as vice presidents.
2004 In August, the massacre of 160 mostly Tutsi DRC refugees in Burundi prompted renewed warnings of war, and the Tutsi-led RCD-Goma, the former main rebel group during the DRC's civil war, suspended its participation in the power-sharing government.
2005 In March nine UN peacekeepers were killed in the north-east; UN troops retaliated, killing over 50 militia members. In May, The National Assembly adopted a draft constitution, which had been agreed by former rebel groups. A referendum on the new constitution was held on 18/19 December. The result (released on 11 January 2006) was resounding approval for the changes with 84.31 per cent voting 'yes'. The result paves the way for presidential and parliamentary elections to be held in March 2006.
2006 In January Etienne Tshisekedi, leader of the opposition Union pour la Démocratie et le Progrès Social (UDPS) (Union for Democracy and Social Progress) withdrew his call for a boycott of the general elections due in March.

Political structure
Constitution
A draft of a new constitution was approved by the national assembly in May

Democratic Republic of Congo

2005, and by a majority (84.31 per cent) of the people in a referendum held in December. The new constitution allows greater autonomy for some of the mineral-rich regions and lowers the minimum age for presidents from 35 to 30, thereby allowing 33-year-old Joseph Kabila, who has been president since the death of Laurent Kabila (his father) in 2001

Form of state
Presidential republic

The executive
Under an accord signed in 2002 by the government, rebel groups and the civilian opposition, President Joseph Kabila was expected to remain in office until election in 2004, however elections have been postponed to 2006. The president is assisted by four vice presidents, each representing the government, two armed rebel groups and the civilian opposition.

National legislature
The legislature consists of a 500-member National Assembly and a 120-member Senate.

Legal system
The civil code is based on the Belgian system, including the structure of the Supreme Court. Legal issues at the local level are usually dealt with according to tribal law.

Last elections
There have been no democratic elections since independence in 1960. A referendum on a new constitution was held 18/19 December 2005.
Results: Referendum: 83 per cent 'yes', 17 per cent 'no'.

Next elections
29 April 2006 (presidential and parliamentary; postponed from June 2005); 2 June 2006 (presidential run-off if needed).

Political parties
President Joseph Kabila lifted restrictions on political parties on 17 May 2001.

Ruling party
Transitional government (installed 30 Jun 2003; in Aug 2004, Tutsi-led RCD-Goma left the government.)

Main opposition party
Mouvement Populaire de la Revolution (MPR) (Popular Movement of the Revolution)

Population
58.78 million (2004)

Ethnic make-up
There are over 200 ethnic groups in DRC. The largest is the Kongo, which predominates in Bandundu province. The Mongo are mainly found in the heavily forested north and north-west. The Luba predominate in the two Kasai provinces and the Shabans and Bemba live mainly in Katanga (formerly Shaba) province. Other large ethnic groups include the Zande, the Bwaka, the Lulua and the Songe. There are a large number of people of Nilotic origin, mainly concentrated in the eastern North Kivu province.

Religions
Some 50 per cent of the population adhere to animist beliefs. The remainder are mostly Christian, of which a majority are Roman Catholic. Muslims make up some 10 per cent of the population, residing mainly in North Kivu province.

Education
Estimates by major non-government organisations show that at least four out of every 10 children of primary school age are denied the basic right to education in the DRC. Several obstacles towards accessing basic education include the inability of parents to pay school fees, massive displacement of population and destruction of school buildings during the civil war. Between 1997 and 2003, millions of children had no access to schools, leading to an increase in the dropout rate from 49 per cent to 75 per cent during the period.
The UN Children's Fund (UNICEF) has helped in the rehabilitation of seven schools and four health centres in Kisangani (damaged in 2000), which cater for 20,000 children. Unicef will also provide financial assistance towards training teachers and for various educational materials.
Literacy rate: 72 per cent men and 49 per cent women, adult rates (World Bank).
Compulsory years: Six to 12.
Pupils per teacher: 45 in primary schools.

Health
Annual total expenditure on health is some 3.4 per cent of GDP, of which 44–45 per cent is government spending. The Mobutu government had placed a low priority on standards of health and welfare, and continuing civil war inhibited improvement. From this low base, expenditure has slowly risen from the 1.5 per cent in 2000.
Only one-third of the population, mostly those in the larger cities, have access to local healthcare. There are more than 900 hospitals with a total capacity of over 75,000 beds, but many of these are not operating due to a lack of resources and loss of unpaid staff. There are an estimated 1,900 physicians working in the DRC, for a population of 58 million. Tuberculosis incidence is about 260 per 100,000 population.
Unicef in association with the DRC government started a major measles immunisation campaign in October 2002, targetting some 15 million children initially.
Forty five per cent of the population have access to an improved water sources.

HIV/Aids
One million people were HIV positive in 2003, of which 570,000 were women, plus there were 110,000 children infected and 770,000 orphans (aged 0–17) created. Deaths from Aids amounted to 100,000 in 2003.
An HIV infection rate of 12 per cent has been characteristic for women who were caught up in civil war atrocities, or attacked by exiled Hutu Militia, and been raped. Such militia erroneously believe that raping a woman will be protection from HIV infection.
HIV prevalence: 4.2 per cent aged 15–49 in 2003 (World Bank)
Life expectancy: 45.2 years (World Bank 2003).
Fertility rate/Maternal mortality rate: 6.7 births per woman (2003); maternal mortality 9.4 per 1,000 (World Bank)
Birth rate/Death rate: 15 deaths to 45 births per 1,000 people (World Bank 2001).
Infant mortality rate: 129 per 1,000 live births; 34 per cent of children aged under five were malnourished (World Bank 2004).
Head of population per physician/bed: 0.006 doctors per 1,000 people.

Welfare
While several UN agencies and non-governmental organisations, through a diverse range of activities, manage the welfare situation in the DRC, there have been setbacks when humanitarian teams were withdrawn for safety reasons. The western provinces of the country have remained stable, but the eastern provinces, featuring unrivalled poverty and insecurity, are gripped by a humanitarian emergency. Over 3.3 million people are estimated to have been killed or died as a result of the war, to overthrow the DRC government, which started in 1998.
The UN estimates that there are 3.4 million internally displaced persons (IDPs), and the UN World Food Programme (WFP) estimates that 16 million people (including refugees from Angola), are in need of emergency food aid, or have been cut off from traditional means of subsistence. In early 2004, two million people benefited from WFP's programmes, at a total cost of US$196 million.

Main cities
Kinshasa (capital, estimated population 6.8 million in 2004), Lubumbashi (1.1 million), Mbuji-Mayi (938,000), Kolwezi (832,400), Kananga (557,800), Kinsangani (523,000).

Languages spoken
Among the many African languages spoken, Lingala, KiSwahili, Tshiluba and Kikongo are the most prominent in DRC.
Official language/s
French

Media
Press
The press is able to criticise government bodies and some publications serve as mouthpieces for opposition parties, despite the fact that these were suspended shortly after Laurent Kabila became president in 1997. Journalists are often harassed, prompting many to exercise self-censorship.

The main publications are: *La Tempête des Tropiques, Le Potential, Elima, Le Phare, Le Palmarés, L'Avenir, Umoja, Alerte-Plus, Le Grognon, L'Eveil* and *La Cloche*.

Broadcasting
Radio: There is a domestic radio service broadcast in French and four African languages (KiSwahili, Lingala, Kiluba and Kikongo). Educational programmes are broadcast by Radio Candip.

Television: There is a limited television service broadcast by the government-owned commercial station.

Economy
The Democratic Republic of Congo (DRC) with its huge mineral wealth of cobalt, copper, gold, diamonds and uranium, its rivers with abundant hydroelectric potential, its fertile land and its virgin forests should have become Africa's economic powerhouse. Unfortunately, political instability, conflict and corruption have hindered its economic growth. Throughout the civil war, Uganda and Rwanda (supporters of rebels in the east of the country) and Angola, Namibia and Zimbabwe (supporters of the government) looted mines and smuggled out commodities, such as diamonds and coffee which helped fund the supply of weaponry to the warring factions. After a decade or more of economic contraction, growth, which began in 2002, reached 6.8 per cent by 2004.

The slow implementation of the peace agreement has stabilised the economy, particularly in government-controlled areas. Improved relations with the IMF came about after the government cleared its arrears and in 2005 DRC received the fifth tranche of US$39.2 million from the IMF's Poverty Reduction and Growth Facility (PRGF) arrangement. In total, the DRC will have received US$813.2 million from the PRGF by March 2006 to implement wide-ranging macroeconomic and structural policies. The political situation still has an effect on the economic performance of DRC. However, the government has ended exchange controls and shored up the fiscal regime with greater budgetary control and is attempting to strengthened public expenditure management by modernising its tax administration and increasing the fight against smuggling, fraud and corruption.

Poverty is a major problem in the DRC and grew steadily worse during the civil war. Social indicators are poor with the DRC having the highest infant mortality rate in Africa, while around 70 per cent of the population have no access to healthcare.

Diplomatic tension and militia fighting in the border region with Burundi has isolated the area from total government control, nevertheless the DRC is making faltering steps as a country towards a viable economy that can provide the necessary development to sustain its citizens.

External trade
The narrow export base, concentrated mainly on minerals, with some agricultural cash crops, has made the DRC's balance of trade susceptible to the vagaries of world commodity markets. Under-investment and regular strikes have further weakened the mining industry.

In 2002, the US approved the DRC as being eligible for tariff preferences under the African Growth and Opportunities Act (AGOA), which requires that countries are only eligible for greater access to US markets provided they have made continued progress toward a market-based economy, the rule of law, free trade, poverty reduction and the protection of workers' rights. This process is reviewed annually.

Imports
Principal imports are foodstuffs, mining and other machinery, transport equipment and fuels.

Main sources: South Africa (18.5 per cent total, 2004), Belgium (15.6 per cent), France (10.9 per cent), US (6.2 per cent), Germany (5.9 per cent), Kenya (4.9 per cent)

Exports
Principal exports are copper, diamonds, cobalt, crude oil and coffee.

Main destinations: Belgium (42.5 per cent total, 2004), Finland (17.8 per cent), Zimbabwe (12.2 per cent), US (9.2 per cent), China (6.5 per cent)

Agriculture
Farming
Agriculture contributes around 50 per cent of GDP, around half of which is derived from subsistence farming, even though it provides the livelihood of 57 per cent of the population. There are almost 23 million hectares (ha) of agricultural land available, of which 7.8 million ha is given over to permanent arable and 15 million ha to pasture.

Despite enormous agricultural potential, the sector has been handicapped by transport problems, occasional drought, smuggling and inflexible pricing policies. Farmers in the eastern provinces have also had to contend with lethal Hutu militia, exiled from Rwanda, who target isolated farms and villages for supplies while often committing atrocities.

The government is developing the forestry sector with multilateral financial assistance.

Main food crops are cassava, maize, rice and plantain. Production is insufficient to meet demand, and poor transport restricts supplies to the urban areas. Main cash and export crops are plantation-grown coffee, cocoa, oil palm, rubber, tea, cotton, sugar and tobacco.

Crop production in 2004 included: 1,155,030 million tonnes (t) maize, 14,950,500t cassava, 1,150,000t oil palm fruit, 92,300t potatoes, 224,450t sweet potatoes, 84,000t yams, 315,130t rice, 65,690t taro, 54,000t sorghum, 36,690t millet, 1,199,000t plantains, 313,000t bananas, 184,641t pulses, 341,086t oilcrops, 15,486,940t roots and tubers, 211,000t papayas, 61,000t avocados, 196,800t citrus fruit, 200,000t mangoes, 193,000t pineapples, *3,700t tobacco, 5,800t cocoa beans, 33,000t green coffee, 1,400t tea, 363,850t groundnuts in shell, 1,787,300t sugar cane, *7,000t natural rubber, 33,000t allspice, 30,000t seed cotton, 8,000t cotton lint, 2,433,800t fruit in total, *449,550t vegetables in total. Livestock production included: 218,083t meat in total, 12,423t beef, 95,000t game meat, 23,810t pig meat, 2,775t lamb, 18,471t goat meat, 10,604t poultry, *6,000t eggs.
* estimate

Fishing
Although the DRC has only a narrow coastline, the fisheries sector is evenly based between inland and coastal resources. Around 150,000 artisanal fisherman operate in the DRC, providing 90 per cent of the total national catch. Excluding subsistence production, inland fishing in the many rivers and lakes produces around 150,000 tonnes, comparable with the 160,000 for seafood production. The country is a substantial net importer of seafood and freshwater fish.

Forestry
DRC has 135.2 million hectares (ha) of tropical forest, roughly half the timber resources of the African continent. The first industrial exploitation started in 1930 at Mayumbe. The sector is vastly under-exploited and holds out much potential, particularly in terms of export revenue. From 1970 onwards, the focus of activity

Democratic Republic of Congo

shifted from Mayumbe to the Cuvette region. Forest cover fell by 532,000 hectares or 0.4 per cent per annum in 1990–2000. The DRC produces large quantities of sawnwood, as well as plywood and veneer and tropical hardwood logs and sawnwood are the principal exports. However the principal use of timber is as domestic firewood.

In 2004, the export of forest products amounted to US$25,665 million while imports totalled US$4,772 million. Production in 2004 included 73,430,400 cubic metres (cum) roundwood, 3,653,000cum industrial roundwood, 40,000cum sawnwood, 170,000cum sawlogs and veneers, 69,777,400cum woodfuel, 1,645,773t charcoal.

Industry and manufacturing

The industrial sector contributes around 17 per cent to GDP and employs around 10 per cent of the workforce. Approximately three-quarters of production is centred around Kinshasa or in Katanga province, owing to the availability of electricity and adequate transport facilities in these areas.

In an environment of political instability, endemic corruption and poor regulation, few manufacturing industries have developed. The few that remain have also been hindered by a lack of technical and management expertise, the comparatively poor transport infrastructure and a chronic decline in domestic purchasing power eroded by inflation and lack of foreign exchange to purchase essential manufacturing inputs.

Output is geared towards the domestic market and is mainly concentrated on brewing, food processing, textiles, consumer goods, construction industry inputs and transport equipment.

Mismanagement and shortages of spare parts and materials have led to cut-backs in production with most firms operating at below half capacity. The government is attempting to increase production by encouraging foreign investment and offering substantial tax incentives.

Tourism

Tourism was never an important economic activity, but with its immense rainforests and rich bio-diversity, a peaceful DRC would provide a rich abundance of eco-tourist destinations for the adventurous traveller. The infrastructure deteriorated as a result of warfare and this will have to be improved if there is to be any major growth in the sector.

Capital investment in the tourist industry was a modest US$74.6 million in 2004, which accounted for 5.1 per cent of total capital investment; the government invested US$20.4 million, which was 2.5 per cent of total government spending, on tourism in 2004. The country earned US$58.7 million, or 1.2 per cent of GDP from the sector and it employed 8,300 people, or 1.1 per cent of total employment while achieving a 0.3 per cent growth in 2004.

With the necessary investment and a return to civilian government the projected annualised growth in travel and tourism is 5.5 per cent (2006–15).

Mining

The country is rich in mineral resources and is potentially one of Africa's richest countries. DRC's copper reserves are estimated at 75 million tonnes with iron at one billion tonnes, 240 million carats of diamonds and over 600 tonnes of gold. In the past, mining contributed around a third of GDP and employed 5 per cent of the workforce.

Moves towards peace should lead to a resumption of investment in the mining sector, backed by planned new mining and investment codes. Mining is likely to be the driving force of the economy over the medium-term.

Diamonds are mined on a commercial scale by the Société Minière de Bakwanga (Miba) at Bakwanga in Kasai Oriental, but artisanal diggers account for almost three-quarters of total output.

Gold production has been erratic and has fallen to record lows during the years of war. However, renewed investor interest will increase production.

There is tin mining and small-scale mining of cadmium, cassiterite and wolframite. Activity is concentrated in the copper-rich Katanga (formerly Shaba) province. Twangiza gold deposits are estimated at 4.1 million tonnes of ore. With the exception of diamonds, these minerals have been hit by weak world demand.

Katanga Province is part of the Central African Copperbelt, which extends from Angola through the DRC into Zambia. The state-run Gécamines has holdings containing the biggest concentrations of copper and cobalt in the world. Gécamines' troubles are rooted in long-term problems of corruption and mismanagement. Its misfortune is exacerbated by the civil war, which has led to foreign partners scaling down or pulling out of joint ventures.

In October 2002, Australia's Anvil Mining began production at the Dikulushi copper and silver mine.

Hydrocarbons

Proven oil reserves totalled 187 million barrels in 2005, most of which are located off the Atlantic coastline and in the River Congo estuary. Oil production totalled 21,100 barrels per day (bpd) in 2004, however all oil has to be exported as DRC does not have a refinery. Total natural gas reserves stood at 990 million cubic metres in 2005, most of which is located beneath Lake Kivu, however the cost of exploiting this reserve has made production non-viable.

In 2005 coal reserves stood at 88 million tonnes, with production running at 9.9 million tonnes per annum. Mines are located at Luena and Kalemie.

Energy

The DRC has the potential to produce 100,000MW of electricity, twice the power necessary to supply the entire southern African region, if it were able to harness the power of its rivers. The civil war has left the country without the infrastructure and investors needed to exploit the natural resources and in the meantime actual electricity production in 2005 was estimated at no more than 650–750MW. Hydroelectric power, produced by the Inga Dam near the port of Matadi at the mouth of the Congo River, supplies around 30 per cent of the electricity consumed in Brazzaville, the capital of the Republic of Congo. The dam also supplies the copper mines in Katanga, and produces two-thirds of the rest of DRC's consumption.

In September 2004 an agreement with the Republic of Congo to supply a further 620MW of electricity from the Inga Dam was signed. The energy is necessary for manganese and aluminium smelting plants in Congo's Kouilou region. The Inga power plant will be expanded and upgraded, by Germany's Siemens, to provided the extra energy.

Energy in rural areas is mainly derived from charcoal and wood.

The DRC imports most of its oil requirements, due to the inability to refine its own crude oil.

Banking and insurance

The banking system is virtually non-existent as persistent hyperinflation has led to the collapse of all the country's banks.

Central bank
Banque du Congo

Main financial centre
Kinshasa

Time

GMT plus one hour in Kinshasa and the western provinces; GMT plus two hours elsewhere.

Geography

The DRC is a large and diverse country, straddling the equator. Much of the interior is covered by dense forest, with a large number of rivers flowing into the Congo river (formerly known as the Zaïre river, and as the Congo river in the People's Republic of Congo), which provides a major transport system. The land is highest in the east, along the border with

Nations of the World: A Political, Economic and Business Handbook

Uganda, Rwanda and Burundi, and falls gradually to a very narrow Atlantic coastline. The southern part of the country is savannah grassland.

Most of the population is concentrated in areas with the best communications: near Kinshasa in the far west, along the Congo River and other main rivers, and in the southern and eastern border regions.

Climate
The climate varies widely owing to the size of the country. The lowlands in the western region are hot and humid, including Kinshasa, where rain is concentrated in the period from November to March and temperatures reach 32 degrees Celsius (C) in the hottest month, January, with 26 degrees C in the coolest month, June.

On the central plateau, the likely temperature range is 18–20 degrees C. In the south and the eastern province of Kivu the climate has a Mediterranean type climate and is slightly cooler, particularly in the winter months.

Dress codes
There are no particular restrictions on dress. Lightweight clothing is essential, especially if visiting during the rainy season.

Entry requirements
Visitors are advised to contact embassy representatives in advance to ascertain current entry requirements. Visitors are also advised to register their presence in DRC with their local embassy representative.

Passports
Required by all. All passports must be revalidated two months prior to expiry date and all documents must be issued in French.

Visa
Required by all except nationals of Zimbabwe.

Applications for a business visa require a letter from a tour company stating the trip has been paid in full, or from an employer accepting responsibility for any expenses incurred; proof of status and a letter of finance giving proof of sufficient funds and a full itinerary. An official letter of invitation endorsed by the DRC authorities must also accompany the application.

Travel regulations should be studied carefully beore a visit as restrictions apply.

Prohibited entry
Those with visas/entry/exit stamps for Rwanda, Burundi or Uganda are likely to be refused entry.

Currency advice/regulations
The import or export of local currency is prohibited. Foreign currency import is limited to declared amount. Currency declaration forms must be kept and all currency exchanges should be recorded.

Customs
Visitors are advised not to take in any equipment which may arouse suspicion, such as cameras, binoculars, maps or any kind of tools or military equipment.

Health (for visitors)
Mandatory precautions
Yellow fever vaccination certificate is required if arriving from an infected area.

Advisable precautions
Visitors should take precautions against all tropical diseases. Anti-malaria tablets are essential, and AIDS is widespread among both men and women. Dysentery, typhoid and typhus are also prevalent, especially outside Kinshasa. Bubonic plague exists in the Bunia region.

Tap water must be treated as unsafe unless boiled and filtered (bottled water is available in the main cities).

Outside Kinshasa and Lubumbashi, it is not advisable to eat raw vegetables or ice cubes.

There was an outbreak of ebola in December 2001.

Hotels
Several major hotels in main cities. Most tend to be expensive and are often heavily booked. A service charge is usually added to bill and further tipping is optional.

Public holidays
Fixed dates
1 Jan (New Year's Day), 4 Jan (Commemoration of the Martyrs of Independence), 17 Jan (National Heroes' Day), 1 May (Labour Day), 17 May (National Liberation Day), 30 Jun (Independence Day), 17 Nov (Army Day), 24 Nov (New Regime Anniversary), 25 Dec (Christmas Day).

Working hours
Banking
Mon–Fri: 0800–1130.
Business
Mon–Fri: 0730–1200, 1430–1700; Sat: 0730–12.00.
Government
Mon–Fri: 0730–1500; Sat: 0730–1200, although it is normal practice for ministers and senior officials to work from 0830–1300 and from 1600–2000.
Shops
Mon–Fri: 0800–1200, 1500–1700; Sat: 0800–1200.

Electricity supply
220V AC

Social customs/useful tips
With its vast range of ethnic groups and huge land area, there are many different traditions, according to the locality. The most recent, the campaign of Zaïreanisation introduced by President Mobutu in the 1970s, was officially abandoned in 1990 as part of sweeping political changes. As a result of this campaign, conventional 'Christian' names were changed to African names, public sector employees abandoned the wearing of jackets and ties in favour of a tailored jacket known as an abacost, women wearing Western clothing were frowned on, and local people addressed each other as Citoyen and Citoyenne (Citizen). Since 1990, however, Monsieur and Madame have been acceptable forms of address.

As in most French-speaking African countries, business etiquette when visiting government and (to a lesser degree) private commercial offices is more formal than in English-speaking Africa.

Do not openly criticise the government or attempt to photograph public buildings. Military installations are also best avoided if possible.

Security
The security situation in DRC since late 1998 has been volatile. Street crime is rife, especially in Kinshasa. Visitors are advised not to wear expensive jewellery or watches or to carry cameras conspicuously. To achieve anything expect to pay *katamulomo* tips, especially to soldiers (both genuine and fake), who are seldom paid and who man the roadblocks. Visitors should beware of unofficial 'porters' at N'djili airport. Those visiting for the first time should try to arrange for a local business associate or friend to meet them at the airport. Visitors are advised to stay in their hotels after dark. They should avoid public transport altogether and use hire cars rather than taxis whenever possible. The DRC is undergoing profound political change which means that any official efforts which may be made to protect foreign visitors are unlikely to be effective outside Kinshasa. The best advice is to contact embassy representatives in advance in order to check the safety of the region to which you wish to travel.

Getting there
Air
Several Arican carriers fly into DRC.
National airline: Congo Airlines.
International airport/s: Kinshasa-N'djili International airport (FIH) is 25km from central Kinshasa. As N'djili is located a long way from the city, it is advisable to pre-arrange transport either with a hotel or local car hire firm such as Hertz (office within the shopping gallery at the Inter-Continental Hotel) or to arrange for a business or social contact to meet first-time visitors to the country at the airport.
Other airport/s: Lubumbashi-Luano (Code: FBM), 6.5km from city; Gbadolite (BDT).
Airport tax: There is no airport tax.

Democratic Republic of Congo

Surface
Road: There are 2,400km of poorly maintained asphalted roads leading to neighbouring countries. However, most borders are closed and the roads leading to them are considered very dangerous.
Rail: The three main lines into DRC are the Voie Nationale running from Matadi port to Kinshasa (366km); the eastern route entering from Tanzania at Kalemie and the northern route entering from the Sudan at Mungbere. There are also links to southern African states via Zambia. An end to Angola's civil war would allow reconstruction of the Benguela line from Shaba to Lobito port in Angola, but this could take several years.
Water: From Kinshasa there is a regular ferry service to Brazzaville although it is subject to distruption.
Main port/s: The main port is Matadi, about 150km inland on the Congo River. Kinshasa is the main inland river port and the ferry crossing point from Brazzaville.

Getting about
National transport
Air: There are connections from Kinshasa-N'djili to over 40 local destinations. Charter facilities are available.
Road: There are indefinite restrictions on travel through the country. A permit from the interior ministry is required for travel outside Kinshasa.
The 240,000km road network is in poor condition outside main population centres and some parts have become impassable through lack of maintenance. Bridges should be checked before crossing and banditry is common.
Buses: Very irregular, crowded and infrequent service.
Rail: A network of over 5,000km is operated by Société Nationale des Chemins de Fer Zaïroise (SNCZ), but some parts are inoperable while others subject to disruption. Of the four classes – 'deluxe' and first-class are advisable.
Water: Inland navigation is important, particularly for freight on the Congo River between Kinshasa and Kisangani and the Kasai River from Ilebo to the Congo River north of Kinshasa. However, all routes around Kisangani have been disrupted by the civil war. When available, passenger services run on all major rivers and lakes. It is advisable to travel luxury or first class.

City transport
There is little or no public transport outside Kinshasa.
Taxis: Volatile inflation rates and political instability mean it is virtually impossible to keep track of taxi fares in local currency. If resorting to a local taxi, it is absolutely essential to negotiate a fixed fare before starting the journey.

Car hire
Self-drive cars available in Kinshasa and at airport. A deposit is required unless an acceptable credit card can be produced. International driving licence required. Traffic drives on the right.

BUSINESS DIRECTORY
The addresses listed below are a selection only. While World of Information makes every endeavour to check these addresses, we cannot guarantee that changes have not been made, especially to telephone numbers and area codes. We would welcome any corrections.

Telephone area codes
The international direct dialling (IDD) code for DRC is +243, followed by the area code and subscriber's number:
Kinshasa 12 Lubumbashi 2
Cellular network 88

Chambers of Commerce
Fédération des Entreprises du Congo, 10 Avenue des Aviateurs, PO Box 7247, Kinshasa (tel: 880-7297; fax: 780-0660; e-mail: feccongo@hotmail.com).

Franco-Congolaise Chambre de Commerce et d'Industrie, 407 Avenue Roi Baudouin, PO Box 8.211, Kinshasa 1 (tel: 780-5871; fax: 880-7158).

Banking
Banque Commerciale du Congo SARL, BP 2798, Boulevard du 30 Juin, Kinshasa/Gombe (tel: 217-73, 217-76; fax: 221-770).

Banque Continentale Africaine (Zaïre) SARL, 4 Avenue de la Justice, Kinshasa/Gombe (tel: 28-006, 28-537; fax: 25-243).

Banque Internationale de Credit SARL, 191 Ave de l'Equateur, Kinshasa/Gombe (tel: 882-0404, 884-1940, 884-5631, 884-3159, 884-3790, 880-1487; fax: 880-1125, 377-97900/34).

Citibank NA Congo, BP 9999, Citibank Building, Coin des Avenues Colonel Lukusa et Ngongo Lutete, Kinshasa/Gombe 1 (tel: 20555/57; fax: 40015).

Fransabank (Congo) SARL, BP 9497, Avenue du Port, 14/16 Immeuble Zaïre-Shell, Kin. 1, Kinshasa/Gombe (tel: 12-20119, 20121/2/3/4; fax: 12-20199).

Nouvelle Banque de Kinshasa, 1 Place du Marché, Kinshasa/Gombe 1 (tel: 12-20562-5, 12-0459-60, 12-3461-63; fax: 12-581-496180043).

Stanbic Bank Congo SARL, 12 Avenue de la Mongala, Kinshasa/Gombe (tel: 88-48445, 88-41984, 88-43453, 88-43419, 88- 04512; fax: 88-46216).

Union de Banques SARL, BP 197, Coin des Avenues de la Nation et des Aviateurs, Kinshasa/Gombe (tel: 88-4133, 88-43620, 88-44887; fax: 88-46628).

Central bank
Banque Centrale du Congo, 563 Boulevard Colonel Tshashi, PO Box 2697, Kinshasa-Gombe (tel: 20-704; fax: 880-5152; e-mail: cabgouv@bcc.cd).

Travel information
Air Zaïre, BP 10120, Airport de N'Djili, Kinshasa (tel: 20-939; fax: 20-940).

N'Djili International Airport, BP 10124, Kinshasa 24 (tel: 23-570).

SNCZ Railways, BP 597, Kinshasa.

Ministry of tourism
Ministry of Tourism, BP12.348, 15 Avenue Papa Ileo (ex des Cliniques), Kinshasa 1 (tel: 34-390, 88-02-394; fax: 88-44-987).

National tourist organisation offices
Office National du Tourisme de la République Démocratique du Congo, BP 9502, Kinshasa 1 (tel: 89-32-2238, 815-091-627, 99-31-939; fax: 33-781; e-mail: ont-rdc@raga.net).

Ministries
Civil Service Ministry, Avenue des Ambassadeurs, BP 3, Kinshasa-Gombe.

Ministry of Agriculture, Boulevard du 30 Juin, Building Sozacom, 3e Etage, BP 8722 KIN I, Kinshasa-Gombe.

Ministry of Economy, Industry and Commerce, Boulevard du 30 Juin, Building ONATRA, BP 8500 KIN I, Kinshasa-Gombe.

Ministry of Energy, 239 Avenue de la Justice, Building SNEL, BP 5137 KIN I, Kinshasa-Gombe.

Ministry of Environment and Tourism, 15 Avenue des Cliniques, BP 12348 KIN I, Kinshasa-Gombe.

Ministry of Finance, Boulevard du 30 Juin, BP 12998 KIN I, Kinshasa-Gombe.

Ministry of Foreign Affairs and International Co-operation, Place de l'Indépendance, BP 7100, Kinshasa-Gombe 14 (tel: 32-450, 30-248, 32-239, 30-996, 32-735, 33-325; fax: 88-02-368; internet site: http://www.minaffeci-rdcongo.net/).

Ministry of Health, Boulevard du 30 Juin, BP 3088 KIN I, Kinshasa-Gombe.

Ministry of Home Affairs, Kinshasa-Gombe.

Ministry of Information and Cultural Affairs, Avenue du 24 Novembre, BP 3171 KIN I, Kinshasa-Kabinda.

Ministry of International Co-Operation, Avenue de la Justice, Enceinte SNEL, Kinshasa-Gombe.

Ministry of Justice, 228 Avenue des 3 Z, Kinshasa-Gombe.

Ministry of Mines, 239 Avenue de la Justice, Building SNEL, BP 5137 KIN I, Kinshasa-Gombe.

Ministry of National Education, Enceinte de l'Institut de la Gombe, BP 3163, Kinshasa-Gombe.

Ministry of Planning and Development, 4155 Avenue des Coteaux, BP 9378 KIN I, Kinshasa-Gombe.

Ministry of Post and Telecommunications, 4484 Avenue des Huiles, Building KILOU, BP 800 KIN I, Kinshasa-Gombe.

Ministry of Public Works, Building TRAVAUX PUBLICS, Kinshasa-Gombe.

Ministry of Reconstruction, Boulevard Colonel Tshatshi, Building TRAVAUX PUBLICS, BP 26, Kinshasa-Gombe.

Ministry of Transport, Boulevard du 30 Juin, Building ONATRA, BP 3304, Kinshasa-Gombe.

Ministry of Youth and Sports, 77 Avenue de la Justice, BP 8541 KIN I, Kinshasa-Gombe.

Other useful addresses

Democratic Republic of Congo Embassy (USA), 1800 New Hampshire Avenue, NW, Washington DC 20009 (tel: 202-234-7690; fax: 202-237-0748).

Foire Internationale de Kinshasa, BP 1397, Kinshasa (annual international fair in July).

Internet sites

Africa Business Network: http://www.ifc.org/abn

AllAfrica.com: http://allafrica.com

African Development Bank: http://www.afdb.org

Africa Online: http://www.africaonline.com

Democratic Republic of Congo (French only): http://www.congonline.com

Harambee Afrika (UK business club for traders with east, central and southern Africa; includes annotated web resource list): http://www.harambee.co.uk

Mbendi AfroPaedia (information on companies, countries, industries and stock exchanges in Africa): http://mbendi.co.za

Cook Islands

COUNTRY PROFILE

Historical profile
1200 The islands were believed to have been settled by neighbouring Tahitians.
1596 The Spaniard, Alvaro de Mendana, was thought to be the first European to sight the islands.
1733 The islands were named in honour of Captain James Cook.
1789 Rarotonga, the main island, was sighted by the Bounty mutineers.
1888 The islands became a British protectorate.
1901 New Zealand became colonial administrators of the Cook Islands.
1965 The islands became self-governing, as a New Zealand dependency. Albert Henry of the Cook Islands Party (CIP) became prime minister.
1978 The Democratic Party (DP) won the election and Tom Davis became prime minister.
1994 The CIP won the general elections with 20 seats in the 25-seat parliament – the greatest margin of victory in 30 years and Geoffrey Henry became prime minister.
1999 The CIP lost the general election and Terepai Maoate of the Democratic Party (DP) formed a government with the New Alliance (NA).
2001 The Cook Islands was placed on the international money laundering blacklist.
2002 Maoate was ousted as prime minister in a vote of no-confidence. Robert Woonton (DP) formed an all-party coalition.
2003 The DP and the NA merged into the Democratic Alliance Party (DAP). Cook Islands Mäori became an official language.
2004 Prime Minister Woonton's DAP won the 7 September parliamentary elections. On 13 December, Queen's Representative Sir Fred Goodwin dissolved the government after a recount found that the votes in the prime minister's constituency had been split evenly between he and a rival candidate. On 14 December, Jim Marurai was elected prime minister of a CIP government.
2005 In February, the Cook Islands was removed from the OECD international money laundering blacklist.

Political structure
Constitution
Under the 1965 constitution, New Zealand has responsibility for defence and foreign affairs and the Cook Islands government has full responsibility for internal affairs. Local affairs are handled by island councils and village committees in the outer islands.
In 2003, a constitutional amendment allowed that a voter be either a Cook Islander, or a New Zealand citizen, or have permanent residence.
Form of state
Self-governing state in free association with New Zealand.
The executive
The British monarch delegates, to an appointed representative, executive power in constitutional affairs.
National legislature
The parliament comprises 25 members (10 representing the main island of Rarotonga, 14 representing constituencies on other islands, and one representing those Cook Islanders who have left for less than three years), elected by universal suffrage for a five-year term.
Parliament chooses a prime minister from among its members, who then appoints a cabinet.
The assembly of 15 hereditary chiefs, the House of Ariki (the upper house of the legislature), has advisory functions only.
Last elections
7 September 2004 (parliamentary)
Results: Parliamentary: Prime Minister Robert Woonton's Democratic Party (DP) won 14 seats, the Cook Islands Party (CIP) nine and independents one; turnout 74 per cent.
Next elections
2009 (parliamentary)

Political parties
Ruling party
Cook Islands Party (CIP)
Main opposition party
Democratic Party (DP)

Political situation
The general election held on 7 September 2004 was not a straightforward as it could have been. Just as Robert Woonton (DAP) and Sir Geoffry Henry (CIP) were set to make history by sharing the premiership, one following the other, each in a two-year stint, a challenge to Woonton's election result collapsed the deal. After it had been revealed that there was a tie in Woonton's constituency the courts forced him to stand down pending a by-election and rendered him ineligible to stand for the post of prime minister.
In due time the parliament elected Jim Marurai of the Demo Tumu Party as prime minister, with Henry as his deputy.

KEY FACTS

Official name: Cook Islands

Head of State: Queen Elizabeth II; represented by Frederik Goodwin (DP) (since 2001)

Head of government: Prime Minister Jim Marurai (elected 14 Dec 2004)

Ruling party: Cook Islands Party (CIP)

Area: 234 square km (15 islands); Rarotonga (67 square km)

Population: 13,999 (2004)

Capital: Avarua, on the island of Rarotonga

Official language: English and Cook Islands' Mäori

Currency: New Zealand dollar (NZ$) = 100 cents; Cook Islands' own currency is defunct

Exchange rate: NZ$1.46 per US$ (Jan 2006)

GDP per capita: US$9,621 (2004)

GDP real growth: 3.40% (2004)

Inflation: 0.30% (2004)

Visitor numbers: 83,028 (2004)

Population
13,999 (2004)

Ethnic make-up
Polynesian (81 per cent), Polynesian and European mixed (8 per cent), Polynesian and non-European mixed (8 per cent), European 2 per cent.

Religions
The majority are Cook Islands Christian Church (70 per cent), although Roman Catholics, Latter Day Saints, Seventh-Day Adventists and Assembly of God are also represented.

Labour market and unemployment
The government has been the main source of paid work even though 1,000 public sector employees were sacked in 1998, followed by the dismissal of two-thirds of the civil service in 1999. The Public Service Association has the largest membership of worker associations and is influential. Other unions are relatively small (Cook Islands Industrial Union of Waterside Workers and the Airport Workers' Union).

During 2004/05, poor job opportunities and the high cost of living continued to push young Cook Islanders out of the country. While foreign workers entered to take up promised employment, overall the local population declined in number, primarily due to lack of employment.

Health
The total expenditure on health is around 4.6 per cent of GDP, of which government spending is typically over 90 per cent.

Life expectancy: 71.0 years (WHO)
Fertility rate/Maternal mortality rate: 3.2 births per woman (WHO 2003)
Infant mortality rate: 21 per 1,000 live births

Main cities
Avarua, on the island of Rarotonga (capital, estimated population 10,500 in 2003).

Languages spoken
Rarotongan is spoken on Rarotonga; Pukapuka and Nassau both have their own quite different languages, while other islands have differing versions of Cook Islands Māori. Most of the islanders also speak English.

Official language/s
English and Cook Islands' Māori

Media
Press
Dailies: *Cook Islands News*, a privately owned newspaper, is published in English. Online, the Tuatua-tika, offers news briefs, (www.ck/tuatua.htm). The *New Zealand Herald* is also available.
Business: There is a business section in *Cook Islands News*.

Broadcasting
Radio: Cook Islands Broadcasting Corporation (CIBC) broadcasts 18hrs/day, seven days/week in English and Māori, including bulletins from Australian and New Zealand national stations. Radio Kia Orana Country FM103 operates an FM station broadcasting general programmes 18hrs/day, seven days/week in English and Māori. BBC World Service is on MHz15.36.

In September 2004, a state-owned radio station started operating from the grounds of the office of the prime minister.

Television: CIBC operates Television Cook Islands. The station broadcasts daily showing footage on local sports, news and cultural programmes, as well as New Zealand and World News from Television New Zealand. Broadcasting hours are from 1700–2300 daily.

Economy
The economy is based mainly on tourism although subsistence agriculture and fishing continue to be important activities. Remittances from migrant workers, aid from New Zealand, sales of postage stamps and export of agricultural produce also continue to have significant roles in the economy. The pearl industry based on the islands of Manihiki and Penrhyn is showing success. On the southern atolls, there has been a shift to paid labour and small businesses, although many still work their own plantations. A significant offshore banking business has developed and the sale of fishing licenses to foreign fleets is also a key revenue earner.

Major projects include expansion of the electricity system, solarisation in the Northern Group Islands, improvements in both telecommunications and in the harbour and shipping service.

The government has problems in maintaining basic health and education services on the outer islands, due to continued migration of skilled workers to New Zealand. Financial assistance received by the Cook Islands, as party to the Cotonou Agreement with the EU, is earmarked for these services.

Offshore banking regulations have been revised and the Financial Supervisory Commission established, allowing for further improvements to be implemented. Tourism is the country's main source of income, providing a third of the local jobs and accounting for almost 25 per cent of GDP. The tourism sector has not been helped by poor marketing and a general lack of resources and funds. In a recent industry study the beauty of Cook Islands beaches was perceived as generic to any South Pacific destination and the implication is that there has been little loyalty for the Cook Islands engendered in the tourist market.

In May 2004, the EU pledged a total of US$1.6 million towards the Outer Island Development Programme.

In September 2004, the governments of Cook Islands, New Zealand and Australia signed an agreement marking the first official joint New Zealand and Australian aid programme to the Cook Islands. New Zealand promised US$4 million and Australia US$1 million in programmed aid every year to help Cook Islands reduce administrative processes in the management of aid programmes.

External trade
The Cook Islands suffer from an adverse balance of trade. There is free trade with New Zealand.

Imports
Principal imports are manufactured goods, foodstuffs, textiles, fuels, timber, capital goods. Imports totalled US$50.7 million in 2003.
Main sources: New Zealand (61 per cent total, 2004), Fiji (19 per cent), US (9 per cent), Australia (6 per cent), Japan (2 per cent)

Exports
Principal exports are copra, papayas, fresh and canned citrus fruit, coffee, fish, pearls and pearl shells and clothing.
Main destinations: Australia (34 per cent total, 2004), Japan (27 per cent), New Zealand (25 per cent), US (8 per cent)

KEY INDICATORS — Cook Islands

	Unit	2000	2001	2002	2003	2004
Population	m	0.01	0.01	0.01	0.01	0.01
Gross domestic product GDP)	US$bn	0.05	0.07	0.05	0.11	0.14
GDP per capita	US$	3,499	5,000	3,882	5,000	9,621
GDP real growth	%	4.1	3.0	3.9	3.1	3.4
Inflation	%	3.2	8.7	3.9	2.4	0.3
Unemployment	%	0.0	0.0	0.0	13.0	0.0
Exchange rate	per US$	2.10	2.26	2.14	1.72	1.42

Cook Islands

Agriculture
Farming
The rich volcanic soil on the southern islands helps subsistence farming cater for local consumption.
Crop production in 2004 included: 1,250 tonnes (t) cassava, 900t papayas, 250t mangoes, 550t sweet potatoes, 3,800t roots & tubers, 234t oilcrops, 81t citrus fruit, 250t tomatoes 15t pineapples, 650t papayas, 1,800t coconuts, 1,461t fruit in total and 1,301t vegetables in total. Livestock production included: 569t meat in total, with 2t beef, 2t goat meat, 550t pig meat, 14t poultry meat and 25t eggs and 1t honey.

Fishing
Long-line fishing of tuna and billfish catches are most often exported to either American Samoa or Japan. The problems of the Cook Islands' huge fishery exclusive economic zone includes the continued attraction of illegal operators, too little data on migratory fish stock and the high cost of its operation. In order to develop the domestic fishing industry, the government introduced exemption on levies for fuel, bait and equipment, but labour shortages are a constant constraint. Since 2000 the number of licences issued for fishing has dropped from 60 to less than 20 boats and the Cook Islands marines minister began discussion with his counterpart in French Polynesia in July 2005 to address the problem. His proposals include issuing licences to Tahitian fishing operators with the expectation that any catch would be processed at the Cook Island processing factory. New Zealand would also be approached for assistance.

Pearl farming used to be the second-largest income earner, after tourism. In 2000 the black pearl fishing industry was hit hard by disease, due to overcrowding in the main producing lagoon, and the growth in good quality cultivated pearls for China. Foreign production took a large share of the Cook Islands' market so that production had fallen by a third by 2002. By 2004 an average annual rise of 20 per cent was forecast, nevertheless commercial fishing now generates three times as much export income as pearl production. The bases for pearl fishing are the northern group atolls Manihiki, Penrhyn and Rakahanga.

Industry and manufacturing
The Cook Islands economy earns around US$4.5 million per annum from its pearl industry. The other main secondary industries include agricultural exports, clothing manufacture, fruit canning/processing, electronic component assembly and handicrafts.

Tourism
Tourism continues to be the main element in economic growth, with the Islands receiving more visitors pre capita than any other South Pacific destination. However the government is interested in re-developing the industry away from 'sun and sand' holidays to value added geotourism, 'that sustains or enhances the geographical character of a place – its environment, culture, aesthetics, heritage, and well-being of its residents'.

The islands have quintessential tropical beaches with soft white-sand, fringed with coconut palms and beautifully clear waters.

Visitor numbers reached 83,333 in 2004, surpassing its previous record of 78,328 in 2003. The largest number of visitors came from New Zealand, with a 46.5 per cent share (38,755 people) followed by Europe with 24.5 per cent and Australia with 14.2 per cent. New Zealand's share has increased by 7.1 per cent whereas most other country's share has fallen. Virgin Blue, a subsidiary of UK based Virgin Airlines, allow passengers to join their low-cost flights en route to and from Christchurch, New Zealand. Routes from Australia to Rorotonga are also available.

Mining
The Japanese government's Metal Mining Agency has discovered significant reserves of manganese in nodules on the seabed in Cook Islands territorial waters. New techniques are being developed to exploit this resource.

Hydrocarbons
There are no oil, gas or coal reserves. The Islands rely entirely on the import of refined oil, importing 390 barrels per day of jet fuel, distillate and gasoline.

Banking and insurance
Legislation to enable Cook Islands' development as an offshore financial centre and tax haven was enacted in 1981/82. Since 2001, when the Cook Islands was among nine countries listed by the OECD as havens for money laundering, offshore banking regulations have been revised and the Financial Supervisory Commission established in 2003 to license and regulate all trustee companies both domestic and international.

In February 2005, the Cook Islands came off the list of non-co-operative countries and territories of the OECD Financial Action Task Force (FATF).

There have been limited attempts to consolidate the banking sector, with 16 licensed banks in operation.

Main financial centre
Avarua (on Rarotonga).

Offshore facilities
The offshore financial industry provides 8 per cent of GDP.

Time
GMT minus ten hours.

Geography
The Cook Islands comprise 13 inhabited and two uninhabited islands located in the southern Pacific Ocean, between American Samoa to the west and French Polynesia to the east. The islands are spread over about two million square km (more than 750,000 square miles) of ocean, and form two groups – the northern Cook Islands which are all atolls and include Pukapuka, Rakahanga and Manihiki, and the southern Cook Islands which include Aitutaki, Mangaia and Rarotonga, all volcanic islands.

Climate
Damp and tropical, mild from Apr–Nov but Dec–Mar hot and humid, with likelihood of hurricanes. The mean temperature is 23.9 degrees Celsius, with average yearly rainfall over 2,000mm; heaviest on the forested volcanic slopes of the southern islands.

Entry requirements
Passports
Required by all and valid for the intended length of stay.
Proof of onward passage, adequate funds and suitable booked accommodation are also required.

Visa
For tourist purposes, visas are not required for stays of up to 31 days. All business visitors require a visa, length of stay 21 days, this can be issued on arrival but any business must be completed within this period. Tourist visas for stays beyond a month must be made either in advance of arrival, or when staying, within 14 days of expiry.
For further details contact the local embassy or where they have no consular offices, contact a New Zealand embassy or High Commission.

Currency advice/regulations
Unlimited import of local and foreign currency. No restrictions on export.

Customs
Import licences are required for goods from countries other than New Zealand. Incoming passengers are permitted to bring in a maximum of 200 cigarettes, one litre of wine and spirits or 4.5 litres of beer.

Health (for visitors)
Mandatory precautions
None.

Nations of the World: A Political, Economic and Business Handbook

Advisable precautions
Vaccinations for diphtheria, tuberculosis, hepatitis A and B, polio, tetanus and typhoid are recommended.
The World Health Organisation has warned of a high risk of catching dengue fever.

Hotels
A 10 per cent Government Turnover Tax applies. Tipping is not customary.

Credit cards
Visa and Mastercard are accepted.

Public holidays
Fixed dates
1 Jan (New Year's Day), 25 Apr (Anzac Day), 25 Jul (Gospel Day, Rarotonga), 4 Aug (Constitution Day) 26 Oct (Gospel Day), 25 Dec (Christmas Day), 26 Dec (Boxing Day).
Variable dates
Good Friday, Easter Monday, Queen's Official Birthday (first Mon in Jun).

Working hours
Banking
Mon–Fri: 0900–1500.
Business
Mon–Fri: 0800–1600.
Government
Mon–Fri: 0800–1600.
Shops
Mon–Fri: 0800–1600; Sat: 0800–1200.

Telecommunications
Telephone/fax
There are automatic telephone exchanges in Rarotonga and Aitutaki. International telecommunications are via Cable and Wireless and Peacesat satellite links.

Electricity supply
240V DC/50 cycle.

Social customs/useful tips
Bargaining is discouraged. Gratuities are not customary, as tradition requires that something is given in return.
Dress: Brief attire (eg bikinis) should not be worn in towns or villages. Nude or topless sunbathing will cause offence.

Getting there
Air
There are limited services from Hawaii via American Samoa and Auckland, plus a new weekly flight from Christchurch, New Zealand.
International airport/s: Rarotonga (RAR), three kilometres west of Avarua. Hotel coaches meet each flight and taxis and buses are also available.
Airport tax: NZ$25 international departure tax, excluding transit passengers.
Surface
Water: Inter-island shipping services are provided by major passenger carrying cargo lines, operators include Express Cook Islands Line Shipping Ltd and Hawaii-Pacific Maritime Ltd.
Main port/s: Avatiu (on Rarotonga), and Aitutaki. Penrhyn Island (northern Cook Islands) is also a Port of Entry.

Getting about
National transport
Air: Air Rarotonga operates inter-island services. Airstrips for small planes on Aitutaki, Penryhn, Rakahanga, Mitiaro, Atiu, Mauke, Mangala and Manitiki. Services do not operate on Sunday.
Road: A surfaced road of about 33km runs around Rarotonga coast.
Buses: *The Island Bus* (yellow buses) – a round-the-island service (Mon–Fri 0700–1630; Sat 0800–1200). A night time service is available Mon–Thu 1800–2200; Fri 1800–0130; Sat 1800–2300.
Taxis: Taxi service is available on Rarotonga.
Water: There are harbours on Aitutaki, Atiu, Penrhyn and Suwarrow. Local advice should be sought transfers.
Car hire
Car, scooter and bicycle hire are available on Rarotonga and Aitutaki. Driving is on the left.
A local licence is required; they can be obtained from the police station on Avarua, on presentation of an international or Commonwealth national driving licence.

BUSINESS DIRECTORY

The addresses listed below are a selection only. While World of Information makes every endeavour to check these addresses, we cannot guarantee that changes have not been made, especially to telephone numbers and area codes. We would welcome any corrections.

Telephone area codes
The international direct dialling (IDD) for Cook Islands is +682 followed by subscriber's number.

Useful telephone numbers
Police: 999
Fire: 996
Ambulance: 998

Chambers of Commerce
Cook Islands Chamber of Commerce PO Box 242, Avarua, Rarotonga (tel: 209-25; fax: 209-69).

Banking
Bank of the Cook Islands, PO Box 113, Rarotonga (tel: 29-341; fax: 29-343).

Wall Street Banking Corporation Ltd, PO Box 3012, CITC House, Avarua (tel: 23-445; fax: 23-446; e-mail: info@wallbank.co.ck).

Westpac Banking Corporation, PO Box 42, Rarotonga (tel: 22-014; fax: 20-014).

Travel information
Air Rarotonga (tel: 22-888; e-mail: bookings@airraro.co.ck; internet site: http://www.airraro.com).

Flight information (24 hours) (tel: 25-890).

Government Information Office, PO Box 106 (tel: 29-304; fax: 20-856).

Principal Immigration Officer, Ministry of Foreign Affairs and Immigration, PO Box 105, Rarotonga (tel: 29-347; fax: 21-247).

Rarotonga International Airport, PO Box 90, Rarotonga (tel: 25-890; fax: 21-890; e-mail: aaci@airport.gov.ck).

National tourist organisation offices
Cook Islands Tourism Corporation, PO Box 14, Avarua, Rarotonga (tel: 29-435; fax: 21-435; e-mail: tourism@cookislands.gov.ck; internet: www.cook-islands.com).

Other useful addresses
Asian Development Bank (ADB), South Pacific Regional Mission, La Casa di Andrea, Fr. Dr. W. H. Lini Highway; PO Box 127, Port Vila (tel: +678 2 23-300; fax: +678 2 23-183; email: adbsprm@adb.org; internet: http://www.adb.org/SPRM).

Cook Islands Development Investment Board, Rarotonga (tel: 24-296; fax: 24-298; e-mail: cidib@oyster.net.ck; internet site: http://www.cookislands-invest.com).

Cook Islands Investment Corporation, Rarotonga (tel: 29-391; fax: 29-381; e-mail: ciic@oyster.net.ck).

Cook Islands News, PO Box 15, Rarotonga (tel: 22-999; fax: 25-303; e-mail: editor@cookislandsnews.com; internet site: http://www.cinews.co.ck).

Internet sites
Yellow pages: http://www.yellowpages.co.ck

Cook Islands government: http://www.cook-islands.gov.ck

Cook Islands News: http://www.cinews.co.ck

Cook Islands shipping movements: http://www.ck/shipping.htm

Cook Islands website: http://www.ck

Tourism Council of the South Pacific: http://www.tcsp.com

Costa Rica

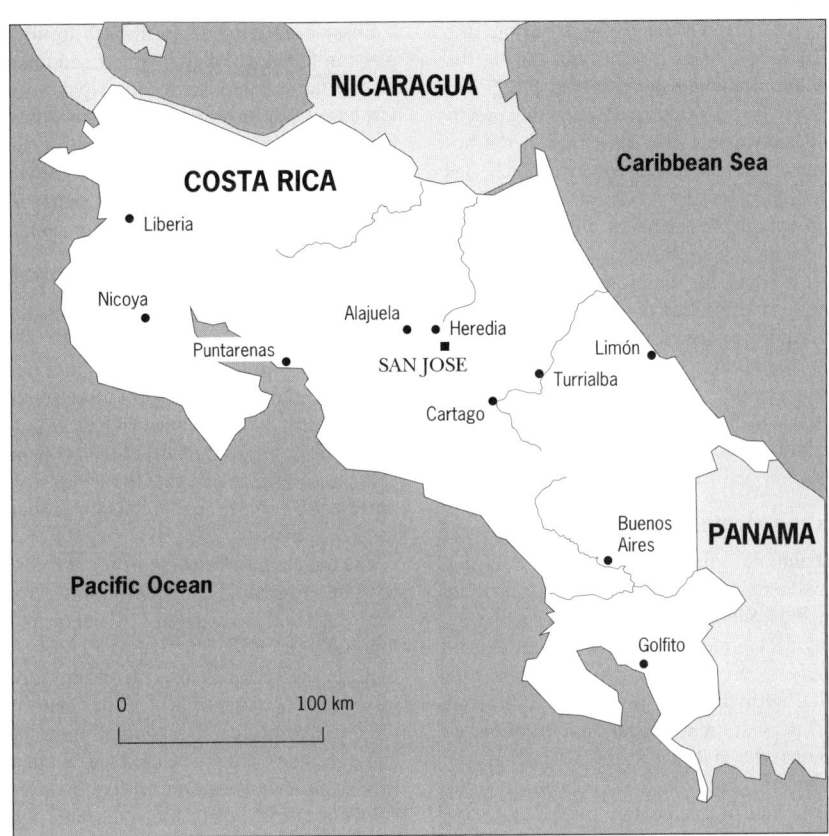

KEY FACTS

Official name: República de Costa Rica (Republic of Costa Rica)

Head of State: President Abel Pacheco de la Espriella (PUSC) (elected 8 May 2002)

Head of government: President Abel Pacheco de la Espriella

Ruling party: Partido Unidad Social Cristiana (PUSC) (Social Christian Unity Party) (re-elected Feb 2002)

Area: 51,060 square km

Population: 4.27 million (2004)

Capital: San José

Official language: Spanish

Currency: Colón (CC) = 100 céntimos

Exchange rate: CC487.45 per US$ (Oct 2005)

GDP per capita: US$4,361 (2004)

GDP real growth: 4.20% (2004); *3.2% (2005)

Labour force: 1.67 million (2004)

Unemployment: 6.60% (2004)

Inflation: 12.30% (2004)

Balance of trade: -US$1.66 billion (2004)

Foreign debt: US$5.96 billion (2004)

* estimated figure

Over recent decades Costa Rica has emerged as a fully developed democratic polity with a healthy respect for human rights. In sharp contrast to many of its Central American neighbours the country – which has no national army – has fostered strong democratic institutions and devised an orderly constitutional process for governmental succession. Historically, the political scene has been dominated by the governing Partido Unidad Social Cristiana (PUSC) (Social Christian Unity Party) and the Partido Liberación Nacional (PLN) (National Liberation Party), both broadly of the centre-right.

However, just fourteen months after its founding, a new party, the Partido Acción Ciudadana (PAC) (Citizen's Action Party) ruffled the feathers of the political establishment when its economist candidate Otton Solnis ran a strong campaign for president in 2002. Other parties include the Partido Movimiento Libertario (ML) (Libertarian Movement Party) and smaller political organisations such as the Partido Renovación Costarricense (PRC) and Fuerza Democrática (FD). The Partido Unión para el Cambio (PUC) (Union for Change Party) along with other minor parties, will contest the February 2006 presidential elections for the first time.

Owing to term limits specified in the country's constitution, President Abel Pacheco de la Espriella will be unable to stand for consecutive re-election. The popular former psychiatrist and television presenter has been elected on a platform of austere monetary policies and market reform. Despite his government's success in continuing Costa Rica's macroeconomic stability and prudent path to reform, Pacheco became something of a lame duck toward the end of 2005, as all eyes turned to the 2006 elections that will determine his successor as head of state.

2006 elections: the candidates

When Costa Ricans go to the polls on 6 February 2006 they will have a host of candidates to choose from, though former president Óscar Arías is currently the clear favourite to succeed Pacheco as president. PAC's Ottón Solís, who ran strongly as the third party candidate in 2002, will contest the presidency again. He is expected to garner some support for his anti-Central American Free Trade Agreement (Cafta) stance, having stated his belief that the proposed free trade agreement would be disadvantageous for Costa Rica: 'I never imagined Cafta was going to be so one sided... the law of the jungle benefits the big beast. We are a very small beast'.

Otto Guevara Guth of ML is a libertarian who advocates a slashing of government expenditure. Throughout 2005 he also emphasised his belief that Costa Rica should play a more active role in making the case for political liberty in the Central American and Caribbean region. He is a vehement critic of Castro's authoritarian rule in Cuba and has attacked other Latin American politicians for not vocally opposing authoritarianism throughout the region. Antonio Álvarez is the confirmed candidate of the UPC and has so far adopted a hard line on illegal Nicaraguan immigration. He has also advocated harsher penalties for employers of illegal immigrants, suggesting that many Nicaraguans are being unfairly exploited for cheap labour by Costa Rican landowners.

Ricardo Toledo, a close personal friend of President Pacheco, has been nominated by the PUSC. He is an experienced politician having held many prominent positions within his party. Nevertheless, Arías remains the man to beat. Recent polls have confirmed the former president and Nobel laureate as the frontrunner. Arías, who served as head of state from 1986–1990 is known for his role in securing the Esquipulas Peace Agreement during the 1980s, for which he received the Nobel Peace Prize. After receiving the prestigious award in 1987 he established a human rights advocacy group which has worked toward resolving conflicts throughout the Americas. In a recent interview for the *Al Día* newspaper Arías set out his stall for the presidency highlighting his twin policy objectives of reducing inflation and the cost of living in the country. He has also stated that the breaking of the previous political duopoly held by PLN and PUSC was a positive development in a bid to emphasise his credentials as a 'moderniser'.

Economic performance

Economic growth during the Pacheco presidency reached a high of 4.2 per cent in 2004. Since then however, the economy has decelerated, though not to an alarmingly slow rate. The IMF predicts real GDP growth of 3.2 per cent in 2005 and 2.7 per cent in 2006, but high inflation remains the country's biggest economic problem. Though the Pacheco government has implemented market reforms and pursued austere public finance policies it has only been able to contain, rather than substantially reduce the annual rate of inflation, which stood at 9 per cent in 2005. Former president Arías' emphasis on tackling the problem of high inflation is largely responsible for his position as presidential frontrunner, as Costa Ricans regard the rising cost of living to be their major everyday concern.

Costa Rica climbed from 54th to 46th place in the index of economic freedom, a league table compiled by the right-wing US-based Heritage Foundation in 2005, highlighting a slight liberalisation in the make-up of the economy. Positive growth was recorded in the agricultural sector in 2005, with an expansion of 4.1 per cent, a vast improvement on the 0.8 per cent growth rate recorded in the industry in 2004. Overall, the agricultural industry now accounts for approximately 30 per cent of total GDP, though this figure has declined greatly over the past 30 years as the economy has been successfully diversified. Still, approximately 261,000 people are employed in the industry, representing 15 per cent of the total labour force.

The travel and tourism industry of Costa Rica has continued its expansion over recent years and contributed 13.7 per cent to total GDP in 2005. The level of employment in the sector is also increasing rapidly and now represents 13.3 per cent of the total workforce. The tourism industry achieved good growth despite the fact that the Costa Rican Institute of Tourism recently confirmed that a room shortage had meant the country's hoteliers were, in certain cases, forced to turn away up to 50 per cent more visitors. Given this fact, it was perhaps just as well that the Queen Mary II cruise ship was forced to abandon docking on her inaugural visit to Costa Rica due to a heavy swell at Port of Moin. Costa Rica's tourism industry will need to continue attracting outside investment if it is to fulfill its immense potential for development.

Outlook

Costa Rica has one of the most stable democracies in Latin America with a fully competitive party system. The country's political elite continues to be a leading advocate for human rights throughout the Central American and Caribbean region. With the economy under-performing, the first task for the country's new president will be a reduction in the rate of inflation, followed by a continuing implementation of market reforms. If, as recent polls predict, former president Arías is elected in

KEY INDICATORS — Costa Rica

	Unit	2000	2001	2002	2003	2004
Population	m	3.64	3.90	4.00	4.13	4.27
Gross domestic product (GDP)	US$bn	15.80	16.20	16.30	16.54	*18.40
GDP per capita	US$	4,127	4,105	4,075	4,002	4,361
GDP real growth	%	1.7	0.9	2.8	3.0	4.2
Inflation	%	11.5	11.2	9.1	9.7	12.3
Unemployment	%	5.2	6.1	6.8	6.7	6.6
Exports (fob) (goods)	US$m	5,850.0	4,932.0	4,910.0	6,029.0	6,184.0
Imports (fob) (goods)	US$m	6,350.0	6,564.0	6,650.0	7,700.0	7,842.0
Balance of trade	US$m	-500.0	-1,540.0	-1,700.0	-1,671.0	-1,658.0
Current account	US$m	-758.0	-750.0	-850.0	–	-890.0
Foreign debt	US$bn	4.5	3.2	48.3	4.8	6.0
Total reserves minus gold	US$m	1,317.8	1,329.8	1,496.5	1,836.3	1,917.9
Foreign exchange	US$m	1,291.3	1,304.6	1,469.3	1,806.5	1,886.7
Exchange rate	per US$	308.90	328.87	360.67	398.67	439.08

* estimated figure

Costa Rica

February 2006, he will bring a wealth of administrative experience to the post, coupled with a much needed determination to rid the economy of chronic inflationary pressures.

Risk assessment

Politics	Good
Economy	Stable
Regional stability	Good
Stock market	Stable

COUNTRY PROFILE

Historical profile
1502 Christopher Columbus visited the region, naming it Costa Rica (Rich Coast).
1561 Colonisation of Costa Rica began. The country became a dependency of Nicaragua within the kingdom of Guatemala in the vice-royalty of Mexico, then known as Nuevo España (New Spain).
1808 Coffee was introduced into Costa Rica and became the country's main crop.
1821 The Central American provinces (Costa Rica, Guatemala, Honduras, Nicaragua and El Salvador) declared independence from Spain.
1822 Central American confederation annexed itself to the Mexican Empire, under General Agustín de Iturbde, later Emperor Agustín I.
1823 Agustín I was overthrown and Mexico became a republic. The Central American states formed the United Provinces of Central America.
1825 Costa Rica, Guatemala, Honduras, Nicaragua and El Salvador formed the Central American Federation (CAF).
1838 The CAF was dissolved and Costa Rica became a fully independent republic.
1849 Under the leadership of Juan Rafael Mora, Costa Rica helped organise Central American resistance against William Walker, the US bucaneer who took over Nicaragua.
1859 A coup d'état saw Mora lose power.
1870 Costa Rican leader, Tomás Guardía, began a process of development, encouraging foreign investment in the rail system.
1874 The United Fruit Company began operations in Costa Rica.
1889 The country embraced democracy and Bernardo Soto was elected as the country's first president.
1940 President Rafael Angel Calderón Guardía, founder of the Partido Unidad Social Christiana (PUSC) (Social Christian Unity Party), introduced social reforms, including labour rights and a minimum wage.
1948 The result of the presidential election was annulled after the government's candidate, Rafael Calderón, who came second, refused to accept defeat. An opposition leader, José Figueres Ferrer, led a revolt in favour of the winning candidate, Otilio Ulate. An interim regime was set up, the constitution was changed, the army was abolished and Otilio Ulate became president.
1953 José Figueres Ferrer, a democratic socialist and leader of the Partido Liberación Nacional (PLN) (National Liberation Party), won the election. He began to effect social reforms with the help of the reformist bishop of San José and a communist union leader, remaining president until 1958.
1982 Luis Alberto Monge (PLN) was elected president. He introduced a programme of austerity measures designed to stabilise the deteriorating economy.
1986 Oscar Arías Sánchez (PLN) was elected president and began brokering a peace plan with the leaders of Nicaragua, El Salvador, Guatemala and Honduras to end regional political turbulence and civil war.
1987 Arías won the Nobel Peace Prize for securing a regional peace deal.
1990 Rafael Angel Calderón Fournier of the PUSC was elected president and enacted a series of austerity measures.
1994 José María Figueres (PLN) won the presidential election.
1998 Miguel Angel Rodríguez of the PUSC was elected president.
2000 Costa Rica and Nicaragua reached an agreement to end a dispute over navigation along the San Juan river, which serves as the border between the two countries.
2001 Privatisation of Costa Rica's Pacific ports commenced.
2002 The PUSC defeated the PLN in the parliamentary elections. Abel Pacheco de la Espriella (PUSC) won the run-off election and became president.
2003 Strikes were held by energy and telecommunications workers over President Pacheco's privatisation plans for the sector and by primary and secondary school teachers over problems in paying their salaries. The strikes led to the resignations of three ministers.
2004 In July, three Chilean diplomats were murdered by a security guard at the Chilean embassy in San Jose. October saw three former presidents – Jose Maria Figueres, Miguel Angel Rodriguez and Rafael Angel Calderon – investigated over allegations of corruption.
2005 A national state of emergency was declared in January after days of heavy rainfall resulted in severe flooding.

Political structure
Constitution
Under the November 1949 constitution, government consists of three branches: legislative, executive and judicial.

In April 2003, the constitutional court annulled a constitutional reform enacted by the Legislative Assembly in 1969, barring presidents from running for re-election; the law reverts to the 1949 constitution, which states that presidents may run for re-election after being out of office for two presidential terms – eight years.
Voting: compulsory over 18 years.
Form of state
Presidential democratic republic
The executive
Executive power is held by the president, elected by popular vote for one four-year term – if a 40 per cent vote for any candidate is not obtained, a second ballot is held. The president is also head of government. The president appoints and is assisted by a 15-member cabinet.
National legislature
The unicameral 57-member Asamblea Legislativa (Legislative Assembly) is elected every four years.
Legal system
The legal system is based on the Spanish civil law system. There are judicial reviews of legislative acts in the Supreme Court. Justices are elected for renewable eight-year terms by the Legislative Assembly. Costa Rica has not accepted compulsory International Court of Justice (ICJ) jurisdiction.
Last elections
April 2002 (second round presidential); February 2002 (presidential and parliamentary)
Results: Presidential: in the first round of the elections, no candidate won the 40 per cent needed, but Abel Pacheco de la Espriella (PUSC) decisively won the run-off election with 58 per cent of the vote. Parliamentary: the Partido Unidad Social Cristiana (PUSC) won 29.8 per cent of the vote (19 seats), defeating the Partido Liberación Nacional (PLN) (National Liberation Party), 27.1 per cent (17 seats)..
Next elections
February 2006 (presidential and parliamentary)

Political parties
Ruling party
Partido Unidad Social Cristiana (PUSC) (Social Christian Unity Party) (re-elected Feb 2002)
Main opposition party
Partido Liberación Nacional (PLN) (National Liberation Party)

Population
4.27 million (2004)
Ethnic make-up
The majority of the population, 98 per cent, is white or racially mixed, except in Limón province on the Caribbean coast, where an estimated 70,000 blacks and 5,000 Indians live. The Northern

Guanacaste province also has a sizeable Indian population.

Religions
Roman Catholic (approximately 2.33 million followers); Methodist (estimated 6,000 followers); Baptist and Episcopalian.

Education
Education is compulsory at the elementary level, between the ages of six and 13, and is free at both elementary and secondary level. State-owned and private primary and secondary schools are of a high standard and the country has one of the highest literacy rates in Latin America. The adult illiteracy rate is estimated at 4.4 per cent and 4.3 per cent for men and women respectively. World Bank estimates show that the total primary school enrolment of the relevant age group typically stood at 104 per cent for boys and 103 per cent for girls (including repetition rates) between 1994 and 2000.

Costa Ricans are very proud of their education system, with about 12,000 university graduates joining the workforce each year. Costa Rica has 250,000 graduates from higher education per annum and 630,000 graduates from secondary academic schools and around 50,000 graduates of vocational schools.

Public expenditure on education typically amounts to 5–6 per cent of annual gross national income according to UN surveys.
Pupils per teacher: 29 in primary schools.

Health
Total expenditure on health is some 6–7 per cent of GDP, of which 68–69 per cent is government spending.

It is estimated that 10 per cent of all deaths are caused by prenatal or infectious diseases. Immunisation programmes against measles, diphtheria, polio and tetanus are very successful with between 85 and 95 per cent of all relevant ages being immunised.

Improved water sources and sanitation facilities are available to 98 per cent and 96 per cent of the population, respectively.

The Ministry of Health units operate a preventive health programme in all parts of the country. Most of Costa Rica's health services are supplied by the Caja Costarricense del Seguro Social (CCSS) (Costa Rican Social Security Agency), an independent state institution which operates a national insurance fund.
HIV prevalence: 0.6 per cent aged 15–49 in 2003 (World Bank)
Life expectancy: 78.6 years (World Bank)
Fertility rate/Maternal mortality rate: 2.3 births per woman (2003); maternal mortality 29 per 100,000 live births (World Bank).
Infant mortality rate: 8 per 1,000 live births; 5 per cent of children aged under five are malnourished (World Bank).
Head of population per physician/bed: 1.4 doctors per 1,000 people (WHO)

Welfare
The state-owned National Insurance Institute (INS) administers all social security insurance. Wage-earners and their dependants enjoy disability and retirement pensions, workers' compensation and family assistance. A pay-as-you-go system operates alongside voluntary individual accounts which provide second-tier benefits. The pay-as-you-go benefit, financed by employee, employer, and government contributions, is equal to a proportion of adjusted average monthly earnings.

Main cities
San José (capital, estimated population 1.5 million in 2004), Alajuela (791,900), Cartago (475,100), Puntarenas (397,700), Heredia (390,400), Limón (380,200).

Languages spoken
Business is conducted in Spanish, but many executives speak English. French, German and Italian are also spoken.
Official language/s
Spanish

Media
Press
Dailies: The major daily newspapers are *La Nación*, *La República*, *Al Día*, *La Prensa Libre* and *La Extra*.
Weeklies: The financial weekly *El Financiero* is published every Monday. The *Tico Times* is an independent English-language weekly, with on-line edition (http://www.ticotimes.net/) covering news, business, tourism, and cultural developments in Costa Rica and Central America. *Costa Rica Today* is a bi-lingual English/Spanish weekly covering tourism.
Broadcasting
Radio: There are over 100 commercial radio stations and several cultural and religious networks. It is estimated that 98 per cent of the population has a radio.
Television: There are eight commercial stations, covering 90 per cent of the country and a state-owned system. Three cable companies offer international programming. There are over 650,000 television sets.
Advertising
Even though the advertising market in Costa Rica is growing, it is still relatively small and fragmented.

Economy
The Costa Rican economy is predicted to grow by 3.2 per cent in 2005 and 2.7 per cent in 2006, according to the IMF. The economy is now growing slowly but steadily and sustained economic development has been coupled with an increase in social services available to most Costa Ricans. The last 15 years have seen a marked reduction in the level of poverty in the country. The Costa Rican economy relies predominantly on a combination of tourism, agriculture and electronics exports.

Until recently coffee, bananas, beef and sugar dominated exports. However Costa Rica managed to diversify its economy which is now reliant on tourism and exports of electrical goods along with agriculture. Tourism accounts for around 13 per cent of total GDP and is Costa Rica's largest sector.

A series of external shocks brought about the debt crisis of the 1980s. Stabilisation programmes were introduced in Costa Rica but unlike elsewhere in the region, the authorities were careful not to cut back too heavily on social spending. By the early 1990s growth had recovered and much needed export diversification gave rise to a new phase of industrial activity. The opening of an Intel Corporation plant was a major boost to the economy, and electrical components soon overtook both bananas and coffee as the country's greatest export product.

The rapid rise in the industrial sector and growth in tourism has not fully absorbed the impact of the decline in the agricultural sector, spurred on by falling international prices. The fall in coffee prices has caused problems for rural areas, although Costa Rica has avoided the kind of deterioration seen in other Central American states.

Growth of real GDP continued in 2003 and 2004 and extreme poverty has been halved since 1990. The government's economic policy emphasises human development and fulfilling basic social needs. Costa Rica has the best social indicators in Central America with strong education, health and high life expectancy. These indicators along with a relatively stable economy continue to attract foreign investment to Costa Rica. However the World Bank suggests that the pace of such improvements is slowing and that projections do not suggest consistent economic growth. Although poverty has been reduced distribution of income has remained highly unequal.

External trade
Costa Rica was one of the founding members of the WTO in 1995 and is also a member of the Cairns Group of 17

Costa Rica

agricultural exporting countries. The country is also a constituent of the Mercado Común Centroamericano (MCCA), the common market of Central America. Other members if MCCA include Guatemala, El Salvador, Honduras and Nicaragua. In 2004 Costa Rica signed a free trade agreement with the US (Cafta) and the agreement is currently being considered for ratification by the Costa Rican National Assembly.

The diversification of the Costa Rican economy into producing electronics for export has meant that the country has been dependent on the demand for high-tech products in the US. The collapse of the US high-tech sector at the end of 2000 hit exports. This has raised concerns that relying on high-tech exports, such as semi-conductors, will mean the country's export market will experience extreme volatility in the future.

Costa Rica remains the second largest banana supplier to the EU, behind Ecuador, but the majority of its trade is conducted with the US. The US currently receives 23.7 per cent of the country's exports and 35.5 per cent of Costa Rican imports come from the US.

Imports
Main imports are industrial raw materials (typically 40 per cent of total), raw materials, consumer goods, capital equipment and petroleum.
Main sources: US (35.5 per cent total, 2004), Japan (4.8 per cent), Mexico (3.7 per cent)
Exports
Main exports are coffee, bananas, sugar; pineapples; textiles, electronic components and., medical equipment.
Main destinations: US (23.7 per cent total, 2004), Netherlands (7.7 per cent), UK (6.6 per cent)

Agriculture
Farming
Costa Rica's agricultural sector is an important contributor to the country's GDP. The sector represents approximately17 per cent of total GDP and employs a fifth of the workforce.

The most important cash crops are coffee, bananas and sugar. A considerable amount of meat, mostly beef, is also exported. The share of traditional agricultural exports declined from 95 per cent of total exports in 1990 to less than 30 per cent by 2004. Bananas account for just over a fifth of Costa Rica's exports. Costa Rica is the world's second-largest banana exporter, representing 12 per cent of the world's banana trade.

Around 10 per cent of the total land is cultivated arable land and 25 per cent is pasture.

Production of cash crops has risen in recent years, but increased exports have tended to be offset by falling prices. Staple food crops including rice, maize and beans are grown, although Costa Rica is not self-sufficient in these. Non-traditional products include tropical fruits, ornamental plants and cut flowers. Crop production in 2004 included: 3,945,000 million tonnes (t) sugar cane, 2,230,000t bananas, 1,080,000t oil palm fruit, 12,200t maize, 222,142t rice, 80,000t potatoes, 725,224t pineapples, 20,000t yams, 400,920t citrus fruit, 50,000t tomatoes, 126,000t green coffee, 206,197t roots and tubers, 209,543t oilcrops, 10,500t pulses, 708t cocoa beans, 36,000t mangoes, 25,000t avocados, 1,070t chillies & peppers, 71,197t cassava, 3722,762t fruit in total, 431,939t vegetables in total. Livestock production included: 190,372t meat in total, 68,799t beef, 38,395t pig meat, 83,158t poultry, 50,412t eggs, 790,000t milk, 10,450t cattle hides.

Fishing
industry has the potential for positive growth. However, the industry has suffered from a lack of organisation and infrastructure over the years.

The majority of the fishing industry is concentrated on the Pacific coastline. Shrimp fishing has decreased due to overfishing, but the potential for tuna, shark and sardine fishing has remained largely untapped due to a lack of investment in modern canning factories.

In a typical year the annual fish catch is 35,003mt, including 19,838mt marine fish and 6,341mt shellfish.

Forestry
Approximately 25 per cent of Costa Rica's total landmass is forested. Significant variations in elevation and topography have led to the development of a wide array of vegetative zones ranging from coastal mangroves to sub-alpine paramó. The predominant forests of Costa Rica can be broadly classified according to elevation and precipitation. The most extensive are lowland humid tropical forests in the south-east of the country and on the Peninsula de Osa. Common species are guacimo colorado (Luehea seemanii) and laurel (Cordia alliodora). Dry tropical forests are characteristic of the Guanacaste province in the north-west. The most extensive montane forests occur in the Cordillera de Talamanca mountain range in the south. Quercus are the most common trees at higher elevations. Costa Rica has an extensive network of protected areas with more than 25 per cent of the country´s land area protected as forest reserves, national parks, and reservations for indigenous peoples.

Costa Rica produces a moderate amount of roundwood, three-quarters of which is used as fuel. The majority of industrial roundwood is used for sawn timber, but Costa Rica also has small wood-based panels and paper industries. Most pulp and paper is imported.

Industry and manufacturing
The Costa Rican industrial sector contributes approximately 23 per cent to the country's total GDP. The sector is also responsible for 24 per cent of Costa Rica's total level of employment.

The manufacturing sector alone contributes 18 per cent to GDP and is concentrated on export-oriented processing of agricultural products and electronic components. Costa Rica's manufacturing sector is divided into small- and medium-sized companies producing among other things shoes, packing materials, glass and leather goods, and larger companies involved in producing beer, cement, paper, textiles and palm oil. There is also a growing number of companies involved in the processing of fish, fruit and meat. Other important industries are petroleum refining and pulp/paper processing.

There are industrial free zones (Zonas Francas), where incentives apply, at Puerto Limón, Puntarenas and Cartago. The government's promotion of the manufacturing sector, with investment incentives and tax holidays, has largely been curtailed in the name of fiscal discipline. Costa Rica has one of the lowest unit costs among developing countries for the creation of new jobs.

Tourism
Travel and tourism is one of Costa Rica's most significant economic sectors and now accounts for 13.7 per cent of total GDP. Employment is predicted to rise by 8.3 per cent in 2005 and now constitutes 13.3 per cent of total employment in Costa Rica.

Eco-tourism and resorts, coupled with the country's stability, are the main attractions. The sector doubled in size during the nineties, passing the million visitors mark by 1999, and is projected to double again by 2012. In 2001, despite the 11 September terrorist attacks in the US, tourist arrivals numbered a record 1,132,000, but the effects were felt the following year when the number fell to 1,113,000. The downturn was temporary and 2003 saw a resurgence, with record arrivals by air and cruise vessels, a trend that has continued into 2004 and 2005. The US, together with Canada, is the main market, followed by Europe.

Nations of the World: A Political, Economic and Business Handbook

Environment
Since the 1960s and 1970s, the Costa Rican authorities have been increasingly anxious to protect the environment.
By 2001, over a quarter of the total land area was protected. There has also been a great deal of success in protecting valuable natural resources in a sustainable way, while at the same time promoting a growing eco-tourism sector.

Mining
The mining sector in Costa Rica is not a substantial contributor to total GDP. However, Costa Rica does have substantial deposits of various precious metals and the industry is notable for the activity of Canadian firms in the country. In October 2005 two of the largest Canadian corporations operating in Costa Rica announced positive news. Glencairn announced that the Bellavista mine, which it operates, was nearing completion, while Vannessa Ventures Ltd announced the go-ahead of its Las Crucitas Project.
Gold and silver are mined in the western part of Costa Rica. Deposits of manganese, nickel, mercury and sulphur are largely unused. Petroleum deposits are found in the south, but not exploited. Salt is produced from seawater. Large gold deposits in Costa Rica are found near the border with Nicaragua, although estimates vary wildly on the level of reserves. The government is reluctant to explore other reserves found in national parks in the Peninsula de Osa region, due to the environmental impact.
Deposits of manganese, bauxite, aluminium, zinc, copper and sulphur exist in Costa Rica, although their quantity and potential for commercial mining is unknown. Discovery of a valuable bauxite deposit in Boruca area prompted large-scale investment in an aluminium smelting plant. Commercial deposits of iron ore may also be present.

Hydrocarbons
Costa Rica is thought to possess considerable oil reserves. However, exploration and exploitation of these potential reserves has so far proved illusive as the process has proved too costly. Foreigners are permitted to undertake exploration exercises but have been met by environmental protesters on several occasions.
Costa Rica imports its oil from Venezuela and Mexico and the state-run oil monopoly Refinadora Costarricense de Petróleo (Recope) refines it at Moin on the Caribbean coast.
Costa Rica produces neither natural gas nor coal. The country imports approximately 54,000 tonnes of coal each year.

Energy
The majority of Costa Ricans, approximately 80 per cent, have access to electricity. Hydroelectricity is responsible for 90 per cent of total electricity generated and Costa Rica is considered to have huge potential for further hydroelectric generation. Other energy sources include geothermal power and wind generation. The government estimates that the electricity sector requires over US$10 billion in investment between 2001–2011 in order to satisfy demand, which is forecast to grow by 6 per cent annually up to 2020. The government hopes to build 29 hydroelectric power plants by 2020.
In 1998, the government initiated a plan to liberalise the country's electricity generating market and introduced full competition to the sector in 2003. Instituto Costarricense de Electricidad (ICE), the state power monopoly, is undergoing restructuring to make it profitable, although privatisation remains highly unpopular.

Financial markets
Stock exchange
The main stock exchange in Costa Rica, the Bolsa Nacional de Valores (BNV), was established in 1976. Most transactions are in finance ministry debt and central bank monetary stabilisation bonds. The stock market index is the ALDESA and all shares are traded electronically. There is another exchange, the Bolsa Electrónica de Valores de Costa Rica (BEVCR), which trades in the same amount of paper and shares. There is an agricultural commodities exchange, set up in 1990 and trading in coffee, maize, potatoes and timber.

Banking and insurance
Costa Rica's financial services sector is composed of the Central Bank, three state-owned commercial banking houses, nineteen private commercial banks (including one jointly owned state bank), one workers' bank, one state-owned mortgage bank and four mutual house-building companies. There are also 15 private finance companies, 27 savings and loans co-operatives and 30 investment and retirement funds/trusts.
Both local and international companies have looked to raise capital abroad because of the poor service and high costs offered by the state banks in Costa Rica. Some of the larger private banks have capitalised on this by offering a wide range of international services and financing in dollars through offshore banks affiliated to them. However, reforms introduced under the administration of Manuel Angel Rodríguez (1998–2002) introduced regulations for the interbank market and for offshore banking operations and made the banking sector more flexible.
By opening up the financial sector to both domestic and foreign investors, Costa Rica is going down the same path as other Latin American countries which have secured economic stability by having a foreign presence in the financial sector. The last few years have seen a number of joint ventures and takeovers by both domestic and foreign banking groups. The banks with the most presence in Costa Rica's banking system include Citibank, Banco de la Industria, Bancrecén, Banco de San José, Banco del Pacifíco, Banca Promérica and Scotiabank.
There is also a sizable offshore banking service with the financial services sector. In recent years the Costa Rican authorities have co-operated with international agencies in order to guard against money laundering.
Central bank
Banco Central de Costa Rica
Main financial centre
San José

Time
GMT minus six hours

Geography
Costa Rica is the second smallest country in Central America after El Salvador. The country lies between Nicaragua and Panama and has coastlines on the Caribbean Sea and the Pacific Ocean. A low, thin line of hills between Lake Nicaragua and the Pacific is prolonged into northern Costa Rica, broadening and rising into high and rugged mountains in the centre and south. The capital city, San José, lies in the Meseta central basin set in these highlands.
Both coasts have lowland areas. The sparsely inhabited east coast has a narrow swamp strip and tropical forests as the terrain slopes inland. The Pacific coast has two peninsulas: the mountainous Nicoya peninsula in the north and the lowland Osa peninsula in the south. A rich lowland savannah patched by deciduous forests stretches along the Pacific coast between the two peninsulas.

Climate
Costa Rica's weather is influenced by altitude. The Pacific coast is drier while the Caribbean coast has the most rainfall – about 300 days a year. It is hot and humid in lowland coastal areas; temperate and warm in central highlands. The dry season is December–May; the rainy season runs from June–November. The temperature in San José ranges from a high of 24–27 degrees Celsius (C) to a low of 14–16 degrees C. The hottest months are March and April.

Dress codes
Formal dress is required for business engagements. Shorts, especially for women,

Costa Rica

are for the beach or country club and should not be worn in restaurants or at parties. Women can wear trousers. Strapless dresses are only acceptable for evening events.

Entry requirements
Passports
Passports are required by all, and must be carried at all times. Passports must be valid for at least six months.
Visa
Required by all, except many citizens of the Americas, Europe and Australasia, visiting either as tourists or for business purposes, for up to 30 or 90 days. For confirmation and further details contact the nearest consulate or email: miginfor@racsa.co.cr. Business visitors should carry a company letter stating that they represent a foreign company on legitimate business.
Those staying up to 90 days must obtain an exit visa from the Immigration Department in San José at least three days before leaving. Those whose stay is less than 30 days need only their disembarkation card (issued on arrival).
Prohibited entry
Entry is refused to persons of unkempt appearance or without sufficient funds (minimum US$200), who will be deported immediately.
Currency advice/regulations
No restrictions on import of foreign or local currency. Foreign currency should be changed only at banks and authorised bureaux. Street-corner foreign exchange transactions are illegal. Visitors may change excess local currency back to US dollars, but only at main offices of state commercial banks and on production of an onward airline ticket and passport.
Customs
It is prohibited to import arms and drugs. Import tariffs range from 1 to 20 per cent except for vehicles, textiles, shoes, clothing (which are higher). Food products and medicines require registration.

Health (for visitors)
Mandatory precautions
There are no compulsory vaccinations.
Advisable precautions
Typhoid, tetanus, hepatitis 'A' and polio vaccinations are advised.
There is a malaria risk in some low-lying areas – prophylaxis is advisable if visiting the provinces of Limón, Guanacaste, Alajuela and Heredia. Dengue fever mosquitoes are present throughout the country.
Water precautions should be taken outside of San José. There is a risk of rabies.

Hotels
It is advisable to book well in advance. A 3 per cent tourism tax, 10 per cent sales tax and 10 per cent service charge will be added to the bill. Gratuities of around 5–10 per cent are also expected.

Public holidays
Fixed dates
1 Jan (New Year's Day), 19 Mar (Feast of San José (San José only)), 11 Apr (Anniversary of the Battle of Rivas), 1 May (Labour Day), 29 Jun (St Peter and St Paul Day), 25 Jul (Guanacaste Annexation), 2 Aug (Our Lady of the Angels), 15 Aug (Assumption/Mothers' Day), 15 Sep (Independence Day), 12 Oct (Columbus Day), 8 Dec (Immaculate Conception), 24 Dec (Christmas Eve), 25 Dec (Christmas Day), 31 Dec (New Year's Eve).
Most businesses close for Holy Week and between Christmas and New Year.
Variable dates
Maundy Thursday, Good Friday, Corpus Christi (Mon/Jun).

Working hours
Banking
Mon–Fri: 0900–1500.
Business
Mon–Fri: 0800–1200; 1400–1600.
Government
Mon–Fri: 0800–1600.
Shops
Mon–Sat: 0900–1800/1900.

Telecommunications
Mobile phones
GSM 1800 service available.

Electricity supply
110/220V AC, 60Hz. Two-pin plugs are standard.

Social customs/useful tips
Appointments must be made in advance. It is customary to shake hands on meeting and taking leave. The usual form of address is Don for a man, and Doña for a woman, followed by the first name. Business cards to indicate academic/professional titles are exchanged after introduction.
Costa Ricans are not very punctual for social activities, except for football matches, the cinema and weddings, but are more formal with their business appointments. Mothers are regarded as the leading family figures; grandparents and elders are highly respected.
The national pastimes are football and politics. The people have a strong sense of democracy.
Costa Ricans are called Ticos for short. Visitors from Colombia are subject to strict searches for drugs.
Although a service charge is added to restaurant and hotel bills, gratuities of 5–10 per cent are also expected.

Security
Petty crime is frequent. Thefts, especially in urban areas, and car break-ins are common. Thefts take place on the street and from cars. The loss or theft of a passport should be reported immediately to the local police and the relevant embassy. Some remote trails in national parks have been closed because of the low number of visitors and reported robberies of hikers in the area. Tourists should check with forest rangers for current park conditions. There are pickpockets in downtown San José. Beware of mugging in the national parks at night and of theft at beaches and ports.

Getting there
Air
National airline: LACSA (Líneas Aréas Costarricenses).
International airport/s: San José-Juan Santamaría International/El Coco (SJO), 22km from city; duty-free shop, bar, restaurant, buffet, bank, post office, shops, hotel reservations, car hire.
Airport tax: International departures: nationals US$37, resident aliens US$57, non-residents US$15.
Surface
Road: It is possible to travel overland from North or Central America. The nearest US town is Brownsville, Texas, on the Mexican border. From there it is about 4,000km by road to San José, crossing Mexico and going through Guatemala, Honduras, Nicaragua and into Costa Rica. There is one major crossing point between Nicaragua and Costa Rica at Peñas Blancas, which is not a town, so there is nowhere to stay. There are two border crossings between Panama and Costa Rica.
Rail: There is no rail link with neighbouring countries.
Water: Freighters may accept a small number of passengers, and private yachts cruise down the Pacific coast from North America.
Main port/s: Limón, Puntarenas

Getting about
National transport
Air: SANSA is the main domestic carrier and operates very cheap regular flights from San José to provincial towns (eg San José to Golfito near the south-west border, 55 minutes). Travelair also provides domestic services. There is a bus service from the airline office in San José to the airport. It is advisable to book in advance. A number of smaller airlines provide internal flights. There are over 200 small airfields throughout the country.
Road: Total network of some 30,000km of all-weather roads. Main routes are the Pan-American Highway; San José-Caldera; San José-Guapiles; and San José-Puerto Limón. Tolls are paid on all four-lane highways entering San José.

Taxis are a form of public transport outside urban areas and can be hired by the hour, half-day or the day. Arrange the fare beforehand.

Buses: There are bus services around the country, but both the quality of services and prices vary considerably. Major tourist areas are better provided with short-distance bus services.

Rail: There is a short commuter train which links San José with Heredia and one which links Puerto Limón with the Río Estrella area. There is also a 'banana train' which travels on a section of track in the banana plantations around Guápiles.

Water: There are passenger and car ferries in operation.

City transport

Taxis: Within San José taxis can be hailed or ordered by telephone (235-9966, 221-8466, 221-2552); they have white number plates; checking fixed-rate fare beforehand is generally advised. Tipping is unnecessary. All taxis are red except those serving the Juan Santamaría international airport which are orange. In San José make sure the electronic meter is used from 0600–2100.

Car hire

A temporary permit must be obtained from local traffic authorities on production of a national licence. Always carry a driving licence. There are tough drink-drive laws – the penalty includes having your driving licence impounded for a minimum of three years.

BUSINESS DIRECTORY

The addresses listed below are a selection only. While World of Information makes every endeavour to check these addresses, we cannot guarantee that changes have not been made, especially to telephone numbers and area codes. We would welcome any corrections.

Telephone area codes

The international direct dialling (IDD) code for Costa Rica is +506 followed by the subscriber's number.

Useful telephone numbers

Emergencies: 911
Ambulance: 128
Fire: 118
Police: 222-1365, 221-5337
Highway police: 222-9330, 222-8245

Chambers of Commerce

American-Costa Rican Chamber of Commerce, PO Box 4946-1000, San José (tel: 220-2200; fax: 220-2300; e-Mail: chamber@amcham.co.cr).

Costa Rican Cámara de Comercio, PO Box 1114-1000, San José (tel: 221-0005; fax: 233-7091; e-mail: servicos@camara-comercio.com).

Costa Rica Cámara de Industrias, PO Box 10003-1000, San José (tel: 281-0006; fax: 234-6163; e-mail: cicr@cicr.com).

Franco-Costa Rican Chambre de Commerce et d'Industrie, PO Box 912-1007 Centro Colon, San José (tel: 257-1138; fax: 257-1345; e-mail: cfcci@camarafranco-cr.org).

German-Costa Rican Cámara de Comercio, PO Box 2139-1000, San José (tel: 222-4789; fax: 221-1219; e-mail: cacoral@racsa.co.cr).

Unión Costarricense de Cámaras y Asociaciones de la Empresa Privada, PO Box 539-1002 Paseo de los Estudiantes, San José (tel: 290-5594; fax: 290-5596; e-mail: uccaep@uccaep.or.cr).

Banking

Banco Banex, Apdo 7983, 1000 San José (tel: 233-4855; fax: 223-7192).

Banco BCT, Apdo 7698, 1000 San José (tel: 233-6611; fax: 233-6833).

Banco Continental, Apdo 7969, 1000 San José (tel: 257-1155; fax: 255-3983).

Banco Co-operativo Costarricense, Apdo 8593, 1000 San José (tel: 233-5044; fax: 233-9661).

Banco Crédito Agrícola de Cartago, Apdo 5572, 1000 San José (tel: 251-3011; fax: 252-0364).

Banco de Costa Rica, Apdo 10035, 1000 San José (tel: 255-1100; fax: 255-0911).

Banco del Comercio SA, Apdo 1106, 1000 San José (tel: 233-6011; fax: 222-3706).

Banco de Fomento Agrícola, Apdo 6531, 1000 San José (tel: 231-4444; fax: 232-7476).

Banco de la Construcción, Apdo 5099, 1000 San José (tel: 221-5811; fax: 222-6567).

Banco de la Industria, Apdo 4254, 1000 San José (tel: 221-3355; fax: 233-8383).

Banco de San José, Apdo 5445, 1000 San José (tel: 221-9911; fax: 222-8208).

Banco Federado de Co-operativas de Ahorro y Crédito, Apdo 4748, 1000 San José (tel: 222-3323; fax: 257-1724).

Banco Fincomer, Apdo 57, Cartago (tel: 251-1351, 233-7822; fax: 222-0405).

Banco Germano Centroamericano, Apartado 2559, 1000 San José (tel: 233-8022; fax: 222-2648).

Banco Interfín, Apdo 6899, 1000 San José (tel: 221-8022; fax: 233-4823).

Banco Internacional de Costa Rica, Apdo 6116, 1000 San José (tel: 223-6522; fax: 233-6572).

Banco Lyon, Apdo 10184, 1000 San José (tel: 221-2611; fax: 221-6795).

Banco Mercantil de Costa Rica, Apdo 32101, 1000 San José (tel: 231-0724, 255-3636; fax: 255-3076).

Banco Metropolitano, Apdo 3932, 1000 San José (tel: 233-8111; fax: 222-8840).

Banco Nacional de Costa Rica, Apdo 10015, 1000 San José (tel: 223-2166; fax: 255-2436).

Corporación Costarricense de Financiamiento Industrial, Apdo 10507, 1000 San José (tel & fax: 221-2212).

Central bank

Banco Central de Costa Rica, Avenida Central y Primera, Calles 2 y 4, Apdo 10058, San José (tel: 243-3333; fax: 243-3011).

Travel information

American Airlines, Calle 26 & 28, Paseo Colón, San José (tel: 257-1266; fax: 222-5213).

British Airways, Calle 32, paseo Colón and Avenida 2, San José (tel: 223-5648; fax: 223-4863).

SANSA (Servicios Aéreos Nacionales), Apdo 999-1007, Centro Colón, San José (tel: 233-2714, 233-1673; fax: 255-2176).

Tourist Information Office, Plaza de la Cultura, Calle 5, Avenida 0-2, San José (tel: 223-1733 Ext 277; fax: 222-1090).

Ministry of tourism

Ministry of Tourism, Apdo 777-1000, San José (tel: 233-9605; fax: 255-4997).

National tourist organisation offices

Instituto Costarricense de Turismo (ICT) (Tourism Institute main office), Edificio Genaro Valverde, Calles 5 y 7, Avenida 4, PO Box 777, 1000 San José (tel: 223-8423; fax: 255-4997, 223-5452).

Ministries

Ministry of Agriculture and Livestock, Science and Technology, Apdo 10094, 1000 San José (tel: 232-4496; fax: 232-2103).

Ministry of Culture, Apdo 10227, 1000 San José (tel: 223-1658; fax: 233-7066).

Ministry of Economy, Industry and Commerce, Foreign Commerce, Apdo 10216-1000, San José (tel: 222-1016; fax: 222-2305).

Ministry of Environment and Energy, Apdo 10104 1000 San José (tel: 257-1417; fax: 257-0697).

Ministry of Finance, Apdo 5016, San José (tel: 222-2481; fax: 255-4874).

Ministry of Foreign Affairs, Apdo 10027-1000, San José (tel: 223-7555; fax: 223-9328).

Ministry of Foreign Trade, Apdo 96-2050 Mtes de Oca, San José (tel: 222-5910; fax: 233-5090).

Costa Rica

Ministry of Health, Apdo 10123, 1000 San José (tel: 233-0683; fax: 255-4997).

Ministry of Housing, Apdo 222-1002 Paseo de Los Estudiantes, San José (tel: 233-3665; fax: 255-1976).

Ministry of Information, PO Box 520-2010, Zapote (tel: 225-9936/9797; fax: 253-6984).

Ministry of the Interior, Police and Public Security, Apdo 10006, 1000 San José (tel: 223-8354; fax: 222-7726).

Ministry of Justice, Apdo 5685, 1000 San José (tel: 223-9739; fax: 223-3879).

Ministry of Labour and Social Security, Apdo 10133, 1000 San José (tel: 221-0238; fax: 222-8085).

Ministry of the Presidency and Planning, Apdo 520 Zapote, San José (tel: 224-4092; fax: 253-6984).

Ministry of Public Education, Apdo 10087, 1000 San José (tel: 222-0229; fax: 255-2868).

Ministry of Public Security, Apdo 55-4874, San José (tel: 226-0093; fax: 226-6581).

Ministry of Public Works and Transport, Apdo 10176, 1000 San José (tel: 226-7311; fax: 227-1434).

Ministry of Science And Technology, Apdo 5589-1000, San José (tel: 253-7446; fax: 224-8295).

Other useful addresses

Bolsa Nacional De Valores S.A. (Stock Exchange), Central Street, 1st Avenue, PO Box 1736-1000, San José (tel: 221-8011; fax: 255-0131).

British Embassy, Apdo 815, 11th Floor, Edificio Centro Colón, 1007 San José (tel: 221-5566, 255-2937; fax: 233-9938).

Centro de Promoción de Exportaciones e Inversiones (CENPRO) (Costa Rican Export & Investment Promotion Centre), Apdo 5.418, San José (tel: 221-7166; fax: 223-5722).

Costa Rican Electricity Institute (ICE), Apdo 10032, 10 San José (tel: 220-7720; fax: 220-1555).

Costa Rican Embassy (USA), 2114 S Street, NW, Washington DC 20008 (tel: 202-234-2945; fax: 202-265-4795; e-mail: embassy@costarica-embassy.com).

Costa Rican Institute of Pacific Ports (INCOP), Calle 36, Avenida 3, San José (tel: 223-7111).

Costa Rican Investment and Development Corporation (CINDE), P.O. Box 7170-100 San José (tel: 220-0366, 220-4755; fax: 220-4750, 220-4754).

Costa Rican Investment Promotion Programme (CINDE-EUROPE), Eisenhowerlaan 128, 22517 KM Den Haag, The Netherlands (tel: (31-70)512-1212, 515-010).

Costa Rican Oil Refinery (RECOPE), Apdo 43351, 1000 San José (tel: 223-9611; fax: 255-2049).

Costa Rican Stock Exchange (BNVSA), Apartado 1736-1000, San José (tel: 222-8011; fax: 255-0131).

Ferias Internacionales SA (FERCORI), Apartado 1843, 1000 San Jose (tel: 233-6990; fax: 233-5791).

Free Zones Export Corporation, Apdo 96, 2020 Montes de Oca (tel: 222-5855).

Grupo Centro, PO Box 6133, 1000 San José (tel: 235-4509; fax: 240-7591).

National Association for Economic Development (ANFE), Apartado 3577-1000, San José (tel: 253-4497).

Red Nacional de Televisión, PO Box 7-1980, 1000 San José (tel: 231-333; fax: 231-6604).

Sistema Nacional de Radio y Televisión Cultural (SINART), PO Box 27941, Administración Central, 1000 San Jose (tel: 231-6474; fax: 231-6604).

Televisora de Costa Rica, PO Box 3786, 1000 San Jose (tel: 232-2222; fax: 231-7545).

TNT Correos de Costa Rica, Calle 34-36, Avenida 1RA, San Jose (tel: 233-4993; fax: 221-5046).

Union Pack de Costa Rica (UPS), Aveida 3, Calle 30 & 32, San Jose (tel: 257-7447; fax: 257-5343).

US Embassy, Pavas Frente Centre Comercial, Apdo 920-1200, San José (tel: 220-3939; fax: 220-2305).

Internet sites

Information about the country, investment and the Stock Exchange: http://incostarica.net/

Bolsa Nacional de Valores (stock market): http://www.bnv.co.cr/

Central Bank: http://www.bccr.fi.cr/

Côte d'Ivoire

KEY FACTS

Official name: République de Côte d'Ivoire (Republic of Côte d'Ivoire)

Head of State: President Laurent Gbagbo (FPI) (since Oct 2000)

Head of government: Interim Prime Minister Charles Konan Banny (from 4 Dec 2005). The transition period is due to end in Oct 2006.

Ruling party: Government of National Unity formed Mar 2003: Front Populaire Ivorienne (FPI)(Ivorian Popular Front); Parti Democratique de la Côte d'Ivoire (PDCI)(Democratic Party of Côte d'Ivoire) ^ ; Rassemblement des Républicains (RDR)(Rally of Republicans); Parti Ivoirien des Travailleurs (PIT)(Ivorian Workers' Party); Union des Démocrates de Côte d'Ivoire (UDCI)(Union of Democrats of Côte d'Ivoire); Mouvement des Forces d'Avenir (MFA)(Movement of the Forces of the Future); and independents. (^ On 4 Mar 2004, the PDCI pulled out of the coalition government.)

Area: 322,630 square km

Population: 18.95 million (2004)

Capital: Yamoussoukro (administrative capital); Abidjan (economic centre)

Official language: French

Currency: CFA franc (CFAf) = 100 centimes (Communauté Financière Africaine (African Financial Community) franc). New notes have been issued; old notes cease to be legal tender from Jan 2005.

Exchange rate: CFAf544.07 per US$ (Oct 2005); CFAf655.96 per euro (pegged Jan 1999)

GDP per capita: US$852 (2004)

GDP real growth: -0.90% (2004)

Labour force: 7.08 million (2004)

Inflation: 1.50% (2004)

Balance of trade: US$1.76 billion (2004)

Foreign debt: US$11.81 billion (2004)

* estimated figure

An armed rebellion in 2002 split Côte d'Ivoire in two, and the main players in the conflict have so far failed to find a political solution, or to implement the terms of a peace accord.

For more than three decades after independence, under the leadership of its first president, Felix Houphouet-Boigny, Côte d'Ivoire was conspicuous for its religious and ethnic harmony. Its economy was among the most developed on the continent. All this ended when the late Robert Guei led a coup which toppled Felix Houphouet-Boigny's successor, Henri Bédié, in 1999.

Bédié fled, but not before planting the seeds of ethnic discord by trying to stir up xenophobia against Muslim northerners, including his main rival, Alassane Ouattara. A subsequent civil war in 2002 left the country divided between the rebel-held north and army-controlled south.

Terms of a 2003 peace deal have yet to be fully implemented. UN peacekeepers have joined French troops on the ground. Elections planned for October 2005 were postponed.

The central government has yet to exert control over the northern regions and tensions remain high between President Laurent Gbagbo and rebel leaders. Thousands were killed in the conflict and although the fighting has stopped, Côte d'Ivoire remains divided. Ten thousand French and West African troops remain in Côte d'Ivoire. They patrol a buffer zone which separates the rebel-held north and the government-controlled south. Political efforts to reunite the nation have so far failed. Although the fighting has stopped, Côte d'Ivoire remains a nation divided.

In January 2006, UN peacekeepers clashed with supporters of President Gbagbo protesting at a UN suggestion the country's interim parliament be dissolved as it had outrun its mandate. They accused the UN of interfering in domestic affairs. The protesters called upon the Bangladeshi and French peacekeepers to leave and surrounded the UN building and the French embassy, whose occupants were under siege.

Gbagbo's ruling party pulled out of the transitional government, but a few days later returned to parliament. He then renewed the mandate of the transitional government until October 2006 when elections are expected.

Economy

Côte d'Ivoire is rich in petroleum, natural gas, diamonds, manganese, iron ore, cobalt, bauxite, copper, gold, nickel, tantalum, silica sand, clay, cocoa beans, coffee, palm oil and hydropower. It should be economically sound but for the civil conflict.

The country is among the world's largest producers and exporters of coffee, cocoa beans, and palm oil. Consequently, the economy is highly sensitive to fluctuations in international prices for these products and weather conditions. Despite government attempts to diversify the economy, it is still heavily dependent on agriculture and related activities, which engage 68 per cent of the population.

After several years of poor performance, the economy began a comeback in 1994, due to the 50 per cent devaluation of the CFA franc and improved prices for cocoa and coffee, growth in non-traditional primary exports such as pineapples and rubber, limited trade and banking liberalisation, offshore oil and gas discoveries and generous external financing and debt rescheduling by multilateral lenders and France. Moreover, government adherence to donor-mandated reforms led to a jump to five per cent annual growth during 1996–99. Growth was negative over most of 2000–03 because of the difficulty of meeting the conditions of international donors, continued low prices of key exports, and severe civil war. In November 2004 the situation deteriorated when Gbagbo's troops attacked and killed nine French members of the peacekeeping forces and the UN imposed an arms embargo. Foreign investment has shriveled, businessmen have fled, travel within the country has fallen and criminal elements that traffic in weapons and diamonds have gained ground.

The country is an illicit producer of cannabis, mostly for local consumption; and a transshipment point for Southwest and Southeast Asian heroin to Europe and the US, and for Latin American cocaine destined for Europe and South Africa. Rampant corruption and inadequate supervision leave the banking system vulnerable to money laundering, but ironically, the lack of a developed financial system limits the country's utility as a major money-laundering centre.

Rebel and ethnic fighting against the central government has spilled over into neighbouring states and harmed regional economies by driving out foreign cocoa workers from nearby countries.

Politics

Amid an uprising against his predecessor, Laurent Gbagbo proclaimed himself president in October 2000, at the age of 55. He had spent 30 years in opposition and derives much of his support from the mostly-Christian south and west of the country.

Under the terms of a peace deal brokered in 2003 his government is required to disarm militias and to pass political and legal reforms. In return, rebels in the north are to lay down their weapons.

But nationwide elections – scheduled for October 2005 when Gbagbo's five-year term was set to end – were postponed after the president invoked a law which he said allowed him to stay in office. The African Union recommended that he should stay in power for a further 12 months, but urged him to appoint a prime minister – acceptable to all parties – with executive powers.

A historian by profession, Gbagbo is a former trade union activist who, since the 1980s, has taken a strongly nationalist stance, espousing the concept of pure Ivorian parentage.

He spent two years in prison in the early 1970s for 'subversive' teaching and eight years in exile in France in the 1980s, before returning in 1988 – to campaign for the multi-party democracy he no longer found favour with in 2005.

In December 2005 Charles Konan Banny was chosen by Nigerian President Olusegun Obasanjo and South African President Thabo Mbeki – asked by the UN to resolve the crisis in Ivory Coast – as prime minister of Côte d'Ivoire after talks with Ivorian political parties.

Banny has now been tasked with organising elections – scheduled for October 2006 – and with disarming rebels in the north and militias loyal to the president. The UN says he will be given the necessary powers to do this.

An economist by profession, Banny is a one-time governor of the Central Bank of West African States.

Risk assessment

Economic	Poor
Political	Poor
Regional stability	Poor

COUNTRY PROFILE

Historical profile

When Côte d'Ivoire became independent from France in 1960, it had only just acquired a secondary school, the colonial

KEY INDICATORS — Côte d'Ivoire

	Unit	2000	2001	2002	2003	2004
Population	m	16.40	16.70	16.98	17.97	18.95
Gross domestic product (GDP)	US$bn	9.40	10.40	11.00	12.76	*15.29
GDP per capita	US$	573	634	646	710	852
GDP real growth	%	-2.3	-0.9	0.5	-2.2	-0.9
Inflation	%	2.5	4.3	3.5	3.4	1.5
Exports (fob) (goods)	US$m	3,972.9	3,745.0	5,020.0	4,400.0	5,124.0
Imports (fob) (goods)	US$m	2,175.5	1,277.0	2,790.0	2,500.0	3,360.0
Balance of trade	US$m	1,797.4	1,023.0	2,230.0	1,900.0	1,764.0
Current account	US$m	-290.0	-120.0	720.0	550.0	500.0
Foreign debt	US$bn	14.0	9.7	16.4	10.3	10.3
Total reserves minus gold	US$m	667.8	1,018.9	1,863.3	2,230.5	2,422.1
Foreign exchange	US$m	666.2	1,017.8	1,861.5	2,229.3	2,420.9
Exchange rate	per US$	711.98	733.04	683.75	574.89	528.29

* estimated figure

practice of forced labour had only been abolished a couple of years earlier and industrial development was virtually nil, whether in the dense tropical forests of the coast and west, or the central savannah and dry north. A few thousand French settlers eked out a desultory trading or farming existence and a few thousand more Ivorian followed them into cocoa and coffee farming. Economically Côte d'Ivoire ranked among the world's poorest, with little prospect of hauling itself up the development ladder. No mineral wealth seemed readily exploitable, the internal market of five millions (today the population numbers around 19 million) was not tempting for large-scale industrial foreign investment, the commodities on which the country depended for foreign exchange were fluctuating wildly on world markets: cocoa, coffee and timber seemed a highly unstable base.

However, by the late twentieth century Côte d'Ivoire become an example of a certain style of African enterprise and capitalism. Airlines linked Abidjan with dozens of capitals and it was an established port of call for the world's businessmen. For Paris, it was the most thriving of its former West African colonies.

1960 Côte d'Ivoire gained independence from France. Felix Houphouet-Boigny, selected by French colonial rulers as the most promising successor to their rule, established a benevolent authoritarian regime which tended towards paternalism. Politics were based around oligarchs who gained power through government position, ran state-owned companies or gained positions in the ruling party, the Parti Démocratique de la Côte d'Ivoire (PDCI) (Democratic Party of Côte d'Ivoire.

1970s–1980s Economic decline increased the pressure for political reform. Laurent Gbagbo, a lecturer and long-term dissident, emerged as the main opposition leader. He went into exile in 1982.

1988 Gbagbo returned from exile and founded the Front Populaire d'Ivoirie (FPI) (Ivorian Popular Front) to campaign for multi-party democracy.

1990 Houphouet-Boigny was forced to call elections, which were won by the PDCI. Houphouet-Boigny was elected president.

1993 President Felix Houphouet-Boigny died after 30 years in power. Henri Konan-Bédié became president.

1995 Legislative and presidential elections were convincingly won by Konan-Bédié and the PDCI party.

1999 President Bédié was toppled in a military coup and General Robert Gueï seized the presidency. Gueï continued the incitement instigated by Bédié to heighten inter-communal tension, between the Muslim north and Christian south, by banning Alassane Ouattara the northern Arab leader from standing in the forthcoming presidential election.

2000 Laurent Gbagbo declared himself president following controversial elections as supporters of Ouattara were killed in protest at the election results.

2002 An uprising split the country, with rebels taking control of the north. Alassane Ouattara, the main opposition leader, was granted citizenship. A cease-fire was negotiated and a French-manned buffer zone imposed between north and south.

2003 10,000 UN and French troops separated the warring sides.

2004 Rebels appointed ministers to join a coalition government. On 4 March, PDCI pulled out of the power-sharing cabinet amid ongoing violence. Abidjan came under bombardment from rebel forces. When the Côte d'Ivoire airforce targetted the rebel held town of Bouake it killed nine French soldiers in the air raid. The French airforce retaliated by wiping out the Côte d'Ivoire airforce. Pro-government demonstrators erupted onto the capital's streets, looting and threatening foreign, particulary French, targets.

2005 A UN report accused both rebel and government forces of atrocities including torture, systematic rape and mass execution. In April, the government, rebel and opposition leaders signed a deal to end the civil war which had started in 2002; the deal was brokered by South Africa's President Thabo Mbeki. A previous Government of National Reconciliation was revived to take over until elections were held. However, the October presidential elections were cancelled. On 4 October Presidents Obasanjo and Mbeki of Nigeria and South Africa respectively named Charles Konan Banny as interim prime minister. Prime Minister Banny will have powers to run an interim government (which is planned to end in Oct 2006) and organise presidential elections. He announced his cabinet on 29 December.

2006 Banny faced his first test in January when international mediators called for the dissolution of parliament, which backs President Gbagbo. As a result the ruling Front Populaire Ivorienne (FPI) (Ivorian Popular Front) briefly withdrew from the transitional government, accusing the mediators of a 'constitutional coup d'etat'. The FPI leader, Pascal Affi N'Guessan, threatened to set up a 'government of liberation' to remove the New Forces from the north. Former prime minister Alassane Ouattara returned from three years in exile in late January.

Political structure
Constitution
A multi-party system is enshrined in the constitution, but in practice no party other than Parti Démocratique de la Côte d'Ivoire (PDCI) (Democratic Party of Côte d'Ivoire) was allowed to operate until May 1990 when the government legalised party political activity.

A 1990 constitutional amendment allowed for the appointment of a prime minister, with the speaker of the National Assembly empowered to assume the office of president of the republic prior to a presidential election in the event of a sudden presidential vacancy.

The constitution was suspended following a military takeover in December 1999. In 2000, the constitution was revised, stipulating that presidential candidates must be of Ivorian origin, born of parents who are not naturalised Ivorians, should not have dual nationality and must have lived in Côte d'Ivoire for a minimum and uninterrupted period of five years. Those with at least 21 years of Ivorian citizenship are eligible to vote.

Form of state
Republic

The executive
Executive power rests with the president (elected by universal suffrage for a five-year term) who appoints the cabinet. The president can veto legislation, but his veto can in theory be overridden by a two-thirds vote of the National Assembly.

National legislature
The 175-member National Assembly was dissolved in December 1999 and replaced by an appointed National Council for Public Salvation formed by the military junta. This was dissolved following elections to a new 225-seat assembly in December 2000 and January 2001. From time to time, the president also summons an informal grass-roots body known as the National Council for Consultations on Controversial Issues.

Legal system
All civil, criminal, commercial and administrative cases come under the jurisdiction of the tribunaux de première instance (magistrates' courts), the assize courts and the court of appeal.

Last elections
22 October 2000 (presidential); 10 December 2000 (parliamentary).

Results: Parliamentary: Front Populaire Ivorienne (FPI) (Ivorian Popular Front) won 96 seats, Parti Democratique de la Côte d'Ivoire (PDCI) (Democratic Party of Côte d'Ivoire) 94.

Presidential: Laurent Gbagbo won 59.4 per cent of the vote, Robert Guei 32.7 per cent, Francis Wodie 5.7 per cent.

Next elections
Parliamentary and presidential elections scheduled for 30 October 2005 were postponed after a political stalemate between northern rebels and the government prevented the electoral rolls being drawn

Côte d'Ivoire

up. A UN resolution, based on African Union recommendations, to extend President Gbagbo's term as president by one year was rejected by the rebels.

Political parties
Ruling party
Government of National Unity formed Mar 2003: Front Populaire Ivoirienne (FPI)(Ivorian Popular Front); Parti Democratique de la Côte d'Ivoire (PDCI)(Democratic Party of Côte d'Ivoire)*; Rassemblement des Républicains (RDR)(Rally of Republicans); Parti Ivoirien des Travailleurs (PIT)(Ivorian Workers' Party); Union des Démocrates de Côte d'Ivoire (UDCI)(Union of Democrats of Côte d'Ivoire); Mouvement des Forces d'Avenir (MFA)(Movement of the Forces of the Future); and independents. (*On 4 Mar 2004, the PDCI pulled out of the coalition government.)

Main opposition party
Parti Democratique de la Côte d'Ivoire (PDCI)(Democratic Party of Côte d'Ivoire).

Population
18.95 million (2004)

Ethnic make-up
Akan (the Baoule subgroup accounts for 23 per cent of the population), Kru (the Bete subgroup accounts for 18 per cent), Senoufo 15 per cent, Malinke 11 per cent, Agni, Mande. There are nearly 3 million foreign Africans (mainly from Burkina Faso and Mali) and an estimated 130,000–330,000 non-Africans (French 30,000 and Lebanese 100,000–300,000).

Religions
Islam (60 per cent), Christianity (mainly Roman Catholic) (22 per cent), traditional animist beliefs (18 per cent) (some of these are also numbered among the Christians and Muslims).

Education
Education is provided free of charge. Primary education lasts for six years from the age of six. Secondary education lasts for up to seven years from the age of 13. There are universities at Abidjan and Yamoussoukro, but many students attend French universities.
Only 50 per cent of girls attend primary school.
Pupils per teacher: 41 in primary schools.

Health
The annual total expenditure on health is around 2.7 per cent of GDP, of which government spending is 37 per cent.
HIV/Aids
Aids-related costs typically absorb 11 per cent of the total public health budget.
HIV prevalence: 7.0 per cent aged 15–49 in 2003 (World Bank)
Life expectancy: 45.1 years (World Bank)

Fertility rate/Maternal mortality rate: 4.5 births per woman; maternal mortality six per 1,000 live births (World Bank).
Infant mortality rate: 117 per 1,000 live births; 24 per cent of children under aged five are malnourished (World Bank).
Head of population per physician/bed: 0.01 physicians and 0.8 hospital beds typically available for 1,000 people.

Welfare
An employer must declare each worker employed to the Caisse National de Prevoyance Sociale (CNPS), the national social security fund, and is responsible for deducting social security contributions paid by the worker. Large firms are also expected to provide in-house medical care.
Social security is divided into three areas: family allowances, retirement pensions, medical care and compensation payments in case of accident at work. There are no payments for illness unconnected to work. Contributions are paid every quarter by firms employing fewer than 20, and each month for those employing over 20, people. The CNPS funds are ring-fenced from the government's main budget.
The social security system does not cover unemployment, which is paid monthly through labour exchanges and financed by a national solidarity contribution of 1 per cent of salary, which is levied on each employee's wages.
Child labour is used in domestic service, farming, mining and factory work as well as casual labour in street markets. Law restricting the age of employment is enforced in large enterprises but is more lax in small industries and the informal sector. Local opinion concerning child labour is equivocal; while rural children are needed for subsistence farming, and urban street children can avoid destitution through work, the need for change would seem to be moot.

Main cities
Abidjan (economic centre and site of embassies, estimated population 3.6 million in 2004), Yamoussoukro (political capital since 1983, 185,600), Bouaké (549,800), Daloa (206,200), Korhogo (169,200).

Languages spoken
Approximately 60 local African languages are spoken, including Dioula, Baoule, Akan, Kru and Bete.
Official language/s
French

Media
Press
At independence in August 1960, Côte d'Ivoire had only two publications, *Fraternité* and *Abidjan-Matin*, and one radio station, Radio-Abidjan. The two official newspapers were merged in 1964 into the daily *Fraternité Matin*. Other official newspapers include *Ivoire Soir* (Mon–Fri) *Fraternité-Hebdo* and the PDCI party weekly. Other publications include *Abidjan 7 Jours*, *Le Griot* and *Le Guido*, a guide to movies, television and restaurants.
Broadcasting
The government gradually created its own information network after independence in 1960, founding the Ivorian news agency, Agence Ivoirienne de Presse, in 1961, taking full control of the radio station in 1962 and setting up a television station in 1963. On two channels, Télévision Ivoirienne broadcasts in French from stations in many parts of the country, several hours a day. Colour television was introduced in 1973.
Radio: Radiodiffusion Ivoirienne, the government radio station, broadcasts in French, English and 13 African languages. It has 13 transmitters which cover 85 per cent of the country. The commercial service is known as Radio Abidjan-Inter.
Television: A ground station at Akakro, near Abidjan, allows Côte d'Ivoire to receive television pictures by satellite from around the world. Transmissions (including colour) last for several hours a day with stations in many parts of the country.

Economy
Although classified by the World Bank as a low income economy, Côte d'Ivoire in good times has been sub-Saharan Africa's second most developed economy, after South Africa. Despite Côte d'Ivoire's dependence on a limited range of traditional exports, when not suffering from a civil war, it is one of Africa's most diversified economies. Its location geographically and economically at the hub of francophone West Africa leaves it ideally placed to capitalise on the economic development of the region.
Apart from coffee and cocoa, which are the mainstays of the economy, other agricultural exports include sugar, rubber, bananas and cotton. Industry is dominated by processing agricultural produce and the import substitution of consumer goods. A growing financial services sector and tourism have also been important to the economy in recent years.
The civil war adversely affected the economy, which stagnated in 2003 as a result of a contraction in the agricultural sector. With the country split between rebel and government-held areas and rail and road links between the two halves of the country closed down, the movement of goods ground to a halt. People fled the economically important cocoa-growing areas, leaving crops to rot and starving the

economy of its most important source of foreign exchange. Food prices rose sharply, as agricultural output, particularly meat supply from the north, fell. The decline in food output and problems with supply led to hunger in the north of the country. Continuing instability during 2004 and 2005 impeded any prospects of a return to growth. The country's debt arrears led to the cessation of World Bank and IMF projects. Although the tax base has been eroded by the poor economic conditions, the proceeds from cocoa exports and oil exploration concessions have been healthy enough to keep the government afloat.

External trade
The trade balance consistently registered a surplus throughout the 1990s, with the devaluation of the CFA franc in 1994 initially aiding a recovery in exports. The deterioration of commodity prices and the rapid decline in cocoa exports has caused a large fall in the surplus since the 1999 coup. Côte d'Ivoire's current account has shown a rising deficit in recent years, largely due to large financial outflows in the form of debt service obligations.
On 31 December 2002, the US approved Côte d'Ivoire as being eligible for tariff preferences under the Africa Growth and Opportunities Act (AGOA). The legislation requires that countries are only eligible for greater access to US markets provided they have made continued progress toward a market-based economy, the rule of law, free trade, poverty reduction and the protection of workers' rights. This process is reviewed annually. On 1 January 2005, Côte d'Ivoire's eligibility status was cancelled, because of its poor law enforcement record.

Imports
Principal imports include fuel, capital equipment and foodstuffs.
Main sources: France (24.7 per cent total, 2004), Nigeria (18.5 per cent), Italy (4.0 per cent)

Exports
Principal exports include cocoa (typically 36 per cent of total), coffee, timber, petroleum, cotton, bananas, pineapples, palm oil and fish.
Main destinations: US (11.3 per cent total, 2004), Netherlands (10.1 per cent), France (9.4 per cent), Italy (5.3 per cent), Belgium (4.7 per cent), Germany (4.3 per cent)

Agriculture
Farming
The agricultural sector is the mainstay of the economy. It accounts for around 30 per cent of GDP, earns over 60 per cent of export revenues and employs some 54 per cent of the workforce. The climate in some parts of the north is suitable for the production of wheat to support an estimated local consumption of about 200,000 tonnes a year.
The principal cash crops are cocoa and coffee. Côte d'Ivoire could account for 39 per cent of total world cocoa production. The cocoa and coffee sectors have undergone liberalisation and institutional reform since 1995. This has included transferring some responsibility for price stabilisation to the private sector, making operations more transparent, and reducing customs duties on cocoa and abolishing them for coffee. Price liberalisation was achieved for coffee in 1998 and cocoa in 1999, with the price stabilisation fund, Caistab, disbanded and replaced by a private-sector operation. Privatisation of the coffee and cocoa sectors was highly controversial among farmers.
In 2002, the government set up a new cocoa and coffee marketing institution, the Fonds de Regulation et de Controle (FRC), which took over the financial aspects of marketing from the Bourse du Café et Cacao (BCC). The BCC were been set up in July 2001 and was two-thirds owned by farmers and one-third by exporters. The FRC is owned by the farmers (45 per cent), banks (20 per cent), insurance companies (20 per cent) and the government (15 per cent). It determines minimum guaranteed farm-gate prices and bears the cost of implementing the price stabilisation mechanism, which cushions farmers' exposure to volatile international markets. Coffee and cocoa production is regulated by the Autorité de Regulation du Café et Cacao (ARCC), which determines export quotas.
Since the fighting began in 2002 these developments have become more or less irrelevant and exports have fallen.
Crop production for 2004 included: 2,205,000 million tonnes (t) cereals in total, 1,500,000t cassava, 370,000t taro, 3,050,000t yams, 930,000t sugar cane, 1,400,000t oil palm fruit, 1,331,494t cocoa beans, 1,150,000t rice, 910,000t maize, *43,000t sweet potatoes, 70,000t sorghum, 252,423t bananas, 1,350,000t plantains, 4,968,000t roots and tubers, *240,000t coconuts, *61,250t citrus fruit, *170,000t tomatoes, 300,000t seed cotton, 152,000t cotton lint, 150,000t groundnuts in shell, 176,917t pineapples, 430,732t oilcrops, *10,200t tobacco, 159,769t green coffee, 99,630t treenuts, 136,872t natural rubber, 14,000t pimento allspices, *22,500t chillies & peppers, 1,881,790t fruit in total, 633,910t vegetables in total. Livestock production included: 170,689t meat in total, 52,200t beef, 13,000t game meat, 11,760t pig meat, 9,429t lamb and goat meat, *69,300t poultry, *31,214t eggs, *25,912t milk, 6,804t cattle hides, 1,245t sheepskins.
* estimate

Fishing
Côte d'Ivoire is the second largest exporter of canned tuna in the world. The port of Abidjan handles more than 400,000 tonnes of fish a year. The government has launched a series of initiatives to modernise local fishing and assist local fishermen to benefit from the country's 150,000 hectares of lagoon and 350,000 hectares of lakes and rivers. The EU and Côte d'Ivoire run a fisheries agreement which provides EU fishermen with fishing rights in Côte d'Ivoire waters in return for the funding of research and training programmes.

Forestry
Côte d'Ivoire has 17 per cent forest cover and an additional 25 per cent of other wooded land. Ten per cent of forests are inside protected reserves, including the Parc National de Tai which has the largest tract of primary rainforest in West Africa. The southern half of the country, which was once covered by tropical forest, has suffered extensive deforestation for logging and agriculture. The northern half contains savannah woodland. Between 1990–2000, Côte d'Ivoire lost on average 3.12 per cent of forest cover per year. Forestry is important and Côte d'Ivoire has been Africa's leading exporter of sawn timber. Wood is also an important source of domestic fuel.
Exports of forest materials in 2004 amounted to US$183 million, while imports were valued at US$38 million. Production in 2002 included 11,000,000 cubic metres (cum) roundwood, 620,000cum sawnwood, 2,000,000cum sawlogs and veneers, 323,000cum wood-based panels, 247,000cum veneer sheets, 8,600,000cum woodfuel, 49,000t charcoal.

Industry and manufacturing
The industrial sector contributes around 20 per cent to GDP, but output has fallen due to instability since 2002.
The industrial and manufacturing sectors expanded rapidly following independence in 1960, but suffered some setbacks in the late 1980s as a result of increased foreign competition and a decline in consumer purchasing power. In addition, the industrial plant is ageing and has often not been renewed on account of the low level of private investment.
During the 1990s, privatisation reduced the state's role in industry and manufacturing. Policy has focussed upon encouraging private sector involvement in the hydrocarbons sector which it is hoped will encourage the expansion of the industrial and manufacturing sectors.

Côte d'Ivoire

Mining
The mining sector holds considerable potential and could become the second mainstay of the economy. It contributes around 3.7 per cent to GDP annually and employs 1 per cent of the workforce. A state company, Société pour le Développement Minier Ivorien (Sodemi) carries out exploration and production, in some cases in joint ventures with foreign companies. Gold is found in three main reserves: Issia, Lobo and Ity.

Diamonds have traditionally been mined by small independent prospectors, but the incidence of diamond smuggling and consequent loss of revenue prompted the Ministry of Mines to introduce licences for prospectors and diamond purchasing offices in 2000. Diamonds are produced at Séguéla and Tortiya. Reserves at Séguéla are estimated at 150,000 carats, and at Tortiya 450,000 carats.

Grand-Lehou produces 90,000 to 100,000 tonnes of manganese per year. A deposit, estimated at 1.2 million tonnes (47 per cent manganese), was discovered at Ziemougoula, near Odienne.

A large iron ore deposit at Monogaga-Victory has estimated reserves of 140 million tonnes. Further reserves, estimated at three billion tonnes, are located on the border with Guinea at Mount Nyumba and Mount Kalayo.

Hydrocarbons
Côte d'Ivoire is self-sufficient in oil and natural gas. Proven oil reserves in 2005 were 100 million barrels (bpd) and natural gas reserves 1 trillion cubic feet. Most of the oil and gas wells are located offshore in the shallow waters Espoir field and, since August 2005, the deep-water Baobab field. Oil production is around 33,000 barrels per day, but set to increase as new fields come on-stream. Côte d'Ivoire's oil refinery has a capacity of 65,200bpd, sufficient to supply domestic requirements as well as some export volumes for neighbouring countries. The refinery is connected to the Lion and Panther fields and receives crude oil from Nigeria for processing.

Consumption of natural gas is expected to increase by 50 per cent. Côte d'Ivoire is in line to become a regional exporter of natural gas. In 1999 Côte d'Ivoire signed agreements with Ghana for a feasability study in building a pipeline running from Abidjan to Takoradi in Ghana. There is also a possibility that this gas pipeline would be eventualy linked to the West Africa Gas Pipeline.

Côte d'Ivoire does not produce or import coal.

Energy
Installed electricity generating capacity is 911 megawatts. More than 50 per cent of annual production is generated by gas-powered plants, with a declining contribution from hydroelectric sources. Côte d'Ivoire is an exporter of electricity, supplying Ghana, Benin, Togo, Mali and Burkina Faso.

Access to electricity is concentrated mainly in the cities and towns. Electricity reaches less than 15 per cent of the rural population, a shortcoming which the government is seeking to remedy by progressive connection of rural communities to the distribution system.

Financial markets
Stock exchange
The Abidjan bourse is a regional stock exchange serving eight West African Economic and Monetary Union countries – Côte d'Ivoire, Benin, Burkina Faso, Mali, Niger, Senegal, Togo and Guinea-Bissau.

Banking and insurance
Abidjan is traditionally a major regional banking centre. There is no clear distinction between commercial, merchant and development banks since they may all accept deposits and engage in long- and short-term financing. Local banks generally handle retail banking and export-crop financing as well as funding small- and medium-sized businesses and housing. Some specialise in development of industry, agriculture and small businesses. Côte d'Ivoire has a liberal policy towards foreign banks, but entry has become more difficult in recent years because of the large number of banks already present. A minimum capital is required for a new bank to start operating, but Ivorian particiipation is not obligatory.

Political instability has undermined the Ivorian banking sector, with the African Development Bank (AfDB) tranferring its head-quarters from Côte d'Ivoire to Tunisia in early 2003.

Central bank
Banque Centrale des Etats de l'Afrique de l'Ouest

Main financial centre
Abidjan

Time
GMT

Geography
Côte d'Ivoire is in West Africa on the Atlantic coast, bordered by Liberia and Guinea to the west, Mali and Burkina Faso to the north, and Ghana to the east. To the south is a 470 kilometre coastline on the Gulf of Guinea, the eastern part of which is inset with lagoons.

The terrain rises from the coastal plains to a plateau, 300 metres high for most of its length, rising to 1,200 metres near the country's western border.

The three main geographical areas are the equatorial zone along the coast, the tropical rain forests of the south and the drier savannah belt in the north.

There are four main rivers, the Bandama, Comoe, Sassandra and Cavally, but they are not navigable for long distances due to rapids.

Climate
There are four seasons in the south. The long dry season runs from December–April and the long rains from May–July. Then comes the short dry season in August and September and the short rains during October–November. Average temperatures on the coastal plains are 21–34 degrees Celsius (C). Humidity is 80–90 per cent. Annual rainfall can be as heavy as 2.5 metres spread over about 140 days.

In the tropical zone, temperature ranges are 14–39 degrees C. Annual rainfall varies from 1–2.5 metres.

In the northern savannah the climate is more extreme, but less humid with temperatures between 21–40 degrees C. Rainfall averages 1.4 metres a year. There are two seasons, rains from July–November and the dry season from December–June.

Dress codes
When calling on government ministers, senior civil servants, bankers, diplomats and heads of large organisations and international bodies, businessmen should wear suits, even though this may be uncomfortable in Abidjan's hot and humid climate. Otherwise loose-fitting, lightweight clothing is advisable.

European women generally wear sleeveless cotton dresses or lightweight skirts and blouses, and this mode of dress is adequate for business calls.

Entry requirements
Passports
Required by all except particular document holders of certain African countries.

Visa
Required by all except citizens of other ECOWAS countries, and nationals of Andorra, Chad, Monaco, Morocco, Seychelles, Tunisia and Vatican City, for stays of up to three months. Applications for business visas require a letter from the visitor's company accepting responsibility for any expenses incurred, and a letter of invitation (can be faxed copy) from host company in Côte d'Ivoire.

Currency advice/regulations
There is no limit to the amount of foreign currency which can be taken in, although it must be declared (excepting euros). A limited amount of CFA francs per person may be taken out.

Health (for visitors)
Mandatory precautions
Yellow fever vaccination certificate.

Advisable precautions
Cholera, hepatitis 'A' and 'E' and typhoid vaccinations are strongly recommended and polio immunisation is a benefit. Malaria prophylaxis should be taken as risk exists throughout the country all year. Avoid tap water and drink only bottled beverages (including water) or beverages made with boiled water; cooked food is advisable and all fruit should be peeled. Bilharzia is present, only use well chlorinated swimming pools. Rabies and sleeping sickness are a risk. It is advisable to pack a sterilised syringe kit.

Hotels
Abidjan has several high-class hotels. Wide range in the other main centres. Tipping usually 10–15 per cent.

Credit cards
American Express and Mastercard are widely accepted.

Public holidays
Fixed dates
1 Jan (New Year's Day), 1 May (Labour Day), 7 Aug (Independence Day), 15 Aug (Assumption Day), 1 Nov (All Saints' Day), 9 Nov (Day of Mourning), 15 Nov (Peace Day), 7 Dec (Félix Houphouët-Boigny Remembrance Day), 25 Dec (Christmas Day).
Variable dates
Easter Monday, Ascension Day, Whit Monday, Eid al Adha, Eid al Fitr, Birth of the Prophet, Ascent of the Prophet.
The Islamic year contains 354 or 355 days, with the result that Muslim feasts advance by 10–12 days against the Gregorian calendar. Dates of feasts vary according to the sighting of the new moon, so cannot be forecast exactly. Islamic year 1426: 10 February 2005 to 30 January 2006..

Working hours
Banking
Mon–Fri: 0800–1130 and 1430–1630.
Business
Mon–Fri: 0800–1200 and 1430–1700.
Government
Mon–Fri: 0730/0800–1200 and 1430–1730.
Shops
Mon–Fri: 0800–1200 and 1530–1830/1900, Sat: 0800–1200 and 1430–1730.

Electricity supply
220V AC, 50 cycles

Social customs/useful tips
Ivorians like to shake hands and exchange greetings and other pleasantries before getting down to business. Small tokens of appreciation such as business gifts with company logos or souvenirs from home will be welcome. It is considered polite to arrive punctually to social occasions when kissing on the cheek and hugging are reserved only for old friends.

Security
The government is concerned about the level of street crime in the cities and it is advisable not to walk around the city streets after dark.

Getting there
Air
National airline: Air Ivoire (Société Ivoirienne de Transport Aériens) (government-owned) operates internally and to Mali and Burkina Faso.
International airport/s: Abidjan-Félix Houphouet-Boigny (ABJ), 16km from city; duty-free shop, restaurant, bank, post office, shops, car hire. Yamoussoukro (ASK) has been upgraded to international standards.
Airport tax: Departure tax to African countries: CFAf3,000; all other international destinations: CFAf5,000.
Surface
Road: There are good links from Ghana, Burkina Faso, Guinea and Liberia.
Rail: There are good, regular daily services from Burkina Faso, connecting Ouagadougou with Abidjan. Sleeping and restaurant facilities are available for these long journeys.

Getting about
National transport
Air: Air Ivoire operates regular flights from Abidjan to major locations around the country. Departure tax: CFAf800.
Road: Extensive network of good roads stretching from south to north with transverse roads interconnecting.
Buses: Extensive service, with air-conditioned vehicles, operated countrywide by private companies, including daily between Abidjan and major cities.
Taxis: Bush taxis run to all parts of the country.
Rail: A 1,145km network from Abidjan to Ouagadougou passes through Agboville, Dimbokra, Bouaké, Katiola and Ferkessedougou including express trains (with first and second class, sleeping and dining cars).
City transport
Taxis: Red taxis with meters can be hailed or ordered by telephone in main centres. Two tariffs operate: one from 0600–2400, the other 2400–0600. The early morning tariff is double that for the day and evening. Do not hesitate to haggle over the fare, especially if the meter is not running, or if arriving at the airport.
Buses, trams & metro: Buses usually run from 0600–2100 or 2200, operated in Abidjan by state-run Sotra. Most hotels have their own free airport buses. Check at hotel booths near the terminal exit.
Car hire
Self-drive and chauffeur-driven cars can be hired in Abidjan, Bouaké, Daloa, Gagnoa, Man and Sassandra.
An international driving licence is required (not less than 12 months old). Drivers must be at least 21-years-old. Seat-belts must be worn in front seats. Traffic drives on the right.

BUSINESS DIRECTORY
The addresses listed below are a selection only. While World of Information makes every endeavour to check these addresses, we cannot guarantee that changes have not been made, especially to telephone numbers and area codes. We would welcome any corrections.

Telephone area codes
The international direct dialling (IDD) code for Côte d'Ivoire is +225, followed by subscriber's number.

Useful telephone numbers
Ambulance (SAMU): 185, 443-445, 445-353.
Police (emergency): 111, 170.
International telephone enquiries: 160.
National telephone enquiries: 120.

Chambers of Commerce
American Chamber of Commerce, 01 PO Box 3394, Abidjan 01 (tel: 214-616; fax: 222-437; e-mail: amcham@AfricaOnline.co.ci).

Côte d'Ivoire Chambre de Commerce et Industrie, 6 Avenue Joseph Anoma, PO Box 1399, Abidjan 01 (tel: 331-600; fax 323-942; e-mail: mail@ccici.org).

French Chambre de Commerce et d'Industrie, 141 Boulevard de Marseille, Immeuble Jean Lefebvre, 01 PO Box 189, Abidjan 18 (tel: 258-206; fax: 241-000; e-mail: ccifci@ccif.ci).

Banking
Bank of Africa Côte d'Ivoire, BP 4132, 11 Ave Joseph Anoma, Abidjan 01 (tel: 2033-1536; fax: 2033-2398, 2032-8993).

Banque Atlantique - Côte d'Ivoire SA); BP 04, Immeuble Atlantique, Avenue Nogues, 1036 Abidjan 04 (tel: 2031-5950; fax: 2021-6852).

Banque de l'Habitat de Côte d'Ivoire, BP 2325, 22 Ave Joseph Anoma, Abidjan 01 (tel: 2022-6000; fax: 2022-5818).

Banque Internationale pour le Commerce et l'Industrie de la Côte d'Ivoire SA; Avenue Franchet d'Espérey, 01 BP 1298 Abidjan 01 (tel: 2020-1600, 2020-1700; fax: 2020-1700) .

Côte d'Ivoire

Banque Paribas Côte d'Ivoire; BP 09, 17 Avenue Terrasson de Fougères, Abidjan 17 (tel: 2021-8686, 2021-3032; fax: 2021-8823).

BIAO-Côte d'Ivoire; BP 1274, 8/10 Avenue Joseph Anoma, Abidjan 01 (tel: 2020-0720, 2020-0722; fax: 2020-0700).

Caisse Autonome d'Amortissement Société d'Etat, BP 670, Immeuble SCIAM, Ave Marchant, Abidjan 01 (tel: 2021-0611, 2032-8575; fax: 2021-3578).

Cofipa Investment Bank Côte d'Ivoire, BP 411, Rue Botreau Roussel/ Ave Delafosse, Abidjan 04 (tel: 2021-8452; fax: 2021-8599).

Compagnie Bancaire de l'Atlantique en Côte d'Ivoire,01 BP, Immeuble Atlantique, Avenue Nogues, 522 Abidjan 01 (tel: 2021-2804, 2030-1520; fax: 2021-0798).

Compagnie Financière de la Côte d'Ivoire; BP 1566, Tour BICICI 01, Rue Gourgas 15e étage, Abidjan 01 (tel: 2021-2732; fax: 2021-2643, 2020-1700).

Ecobank Côte d'Ivoire SA, BP 4107, Immeuble Alliance, 1 Av Terrasson de Fougères, Abidjan 01 (tel: 2031-9200, 2021-1041; fax: 2021-8816).

Société Générale de Banques en Côte d'Ivoire SA; BP 1355, 5 & 7 Avenue Joseph Anoma, Abidjan 01 (tel: 2020-1234, 2020-1111; fax: 2020-1482, 2020-1486).

Société Générale de Financement et de Participation en Côte d'Ivoire (SOGEFINANCE); BP 3904, 5-7 Avenue Joseph Anoma, Abidjan 01 (tel: 2022-5530, 2022-1234; fax: 2032-6760, 2020-1492).

Société Ivoirienne de Banque, BP 1300, Immeuble Alpha 2000, 34 Boulevard de la Republique, Abidjan 01 (tel: 2020-0000; fax: 2021-9741).

Central bank
Banque Centrale des Etats de l'Afrique de l'Ouest, Direction National, Angle Boulevard Botreau-Roussel et Avenue Delafosse, PO Box 1769, Abidjan (tel: 208-500; fax: 222-852).

Travel information
Air Ivoire, 2 Avenue du Général de Gaulle, PO Box 1027, Abidjan 01 (tel: 213-429).

Félix Houphouet-Boigny International Airport (tel: 277-322, 234-000).

Wagonlits (Railway Information), Boulevard de Marseille, Abidjan (tel: 212-066, 213-910).

Ministry of tourism
Ministry of Tourism, BP V184, Abidjan (tel: 445-500, 445-129, 446-474, 446-953; fax: 445-580).

National tourist organisation offices
Office Ivoirien du Tourisme et de l'Hôtellerie (OITH), Place de la République, BP 8538, Abidjan 01 (tel: 206-528; fax: 225-624; email: oith@africaonline.co.ci; internet: www.tourisme.ci/tourisme).

Ministries
Ministry of Agriculture and Animal Resources, Immeuble de la Caisse de Stabilisation, BP V84, Abidjan (tel: 2021-3858; fax: 2021-4618; e-mail: minagra@cimail.net).

Ministry of Communication and Information Technology, Tour C, Tours Administratives, BP V138, Abidjan (tel: 2021-1116; fax: 2021-8495).

Ministry of Construction and Urbanism, Tour D, Tours Administratives, 20 BP 650, Abidjan (tel: 2021-8235; fax: 2021-3568).

Ministry of Defence and Civil Protection, Immeuble EECI, BP V 241, Abidjan (tel: 2021-2682; fax: 2022-4175).

Ministry of Economic Infrastructures, Immeuble Postel 2001, 18 BP 2203, Abidjan (tel: 2034-4273; fax: 2034-7322).

Ministry of Economy and Finance, Immeuble SCIAM, BP V163, Abidjan (tel: 2020-0842; fax: 2021-3208).

Ministry of Education, Tour D, Tours Administratives, BP V 120, Abidjan (tel: 2022-7406; fax: 2022-9322).

Ministry of Family, Women and Children, Tour E, Tours Administratives, BP 200, Abidjan (tel: 2021-7626; fax: 2021-4461).

Ministry of Foreign Affairs, Bloc Ministériel, Boulevard Angoulvand, BP V109, Abidjan (tel: 2022-7150; fax: 2033-2308).

Ministry of Health, Tour C, Tours Administratives, 01 BP V 04, Abidjan (tel: 2021-0871; fax: 2021-5240).

Ministry of Higher Education and Scientific Research, Tour C, Tours Administratives, BP V 151, Abidjan (tel: 2021-3316; fax: 2021-2225).

Ministry of the Interior and Decentralisation, Bloc Ministériel, Boulevard Angoulvand, BP V 121, Abidjan (tel: 2022-3816; fax: 2022-3648).

Ministry of Justice and Public Freedom, Bloc Ministériel, Boulevard Angoulvand, BP V 107, Abidjan (tel: 2021-1727; fax: 2033-1259).

Ministry of Labour, Civil Service and Administrative Reform, Immeuble Fonction Publique, Boulevard Angoulvand, BP V 93, Abidjan (tel: 2021-4290; fax: 2021-1286).

Ministry of Mines and Energy, Immeuble Postel 2001, BP V 40, Abidjan (tel: 2034-4851; fax: 2021-3730).

Ministry of Trade, Immeuble CCIA, Rue Jean-Paul II, BP V65, Abidjan (tel: 2021-6473; fax: 2021-6474).

Ministry of Transport, Immeuble Postel 2001, BP V 06, Abidjan (tel: 2034-7315; fax: 2021-3730).

Other useful addresses
Agence des Télécommunications de Côte d'Ivoire (ATCI), BP 2203, Immeuble Postel 2001, Rue le Coeur, Abidjan 18 (tel: 344-255; fax: 344-254).

Association of Businessmen and Industry of Côte d'Ivoire, Imm Lefébre, Bd de Marseille, 01 BP 464, Abidjan 01.

Association of Exporters of Coffee-Cocoa, Imm CCIA, 01 BP 1399, Abidjan 01 (tel: 225-446/5).

Association of Fishing Industry, Port de Pêche, 01 BP 14, Abidjan 01 (tel: 257-998; fax: 252-065).

Association of Import and Export Traders, Imm Résidence du Front Lagunaire 2 étage, 01 BP 3792, Abidjan 01 (tel: 325-427; fax: 325-652).

Association of West African Home Grown Product Dealers, Imm CCIA 7 étage, O & BP 5407, Abidjan 01 (tel: 225-795).

Bourse des Valeurs Abidjan, Ave Marchand 10, BP 1878, 01 Abidjan (tel: 215-783, 215-742; fax: 221-657).

British Embassy, 3rd Floor, Immeuble Les Harmonies, Angle Boulevard Carde et Avenue Dr Jamot, BP 2581, Plateau, 01 Abidjan (tel: 226-850/2, 328-209; fax: 223-221).

Bureau National d'Etudes Techniques et de Développement (BNETD) (National Office for Technical and Development Studies), BP 945, 04 Abidjan (tel: 442-805, 445-877; fax: 445-666; e-mail: nzoro@bnetd.sita.net; internet site: http://www.bnetd.sita.net.).

Caisse de Stabilisation (CAISTAB), BP V132, Abidjan (tel: 202-700; fax: 218-994).

Centre de Commerce Internationale d'Abidjan (conference bookings), Abidjan (tel: 224-070).

Centre de Promotion des Investissements en Côte d'Ivoire (CEPICI), CCIA-WTR 5th Floor, BP V152, Abidjan 01 (tel: 214-070; fax: 214-071).

Committee of Insurers, Imm Les Arcades, 01 BP 3873, Abidjan 01 (tel: 225-437; fax: 211-835).

Committee of Privatisation, 6 Boulevard de l'Indénié, Abidjan-Plateau, BP 1141, Abidjan 01 (tel: 222-231/232/236; fax: 222-235).

Compagnie Ivoirienne pour le Développement des Textiles, BP 622, Bouaké (tel: 633-113, 633-013; fax: 634-167).

Conseil Economique et Social, 04 BP 301, Abidjan (tel: 212-060).

Cote d'Ivoire Embassy (USA), 3421 Massachusetts Avenue, NW, Washington DC 20007 (tel: 202-797-0300; fax: 202-265-2454).

The Customs Department, Boulevard de la République, BP V 25, Abidjan (tel: 215-223).

Direction et Controle des Grands Travaux, Département Industrie et Energie, Boulevard de la Corniche, Cocody, 04 BP 945, Abidjan 04 (tel: 442-118; fax: 445-866).

Energie Electrique de la Côte d'Ivoire, BP 1345, 1 place de la REpublique, Abidjan (tel: 206-000; fax: 327-477).

French Embassy (tel: 210-404).

General Surveillance Co (Responsible for Import Controls), PO Box 795, Abidjan (tel: 211-290).

Ivorian Investment Promotion in Côte d'Ivoire (CEPECI), PO Box V 152, Abidjan 01 (tel: 214-070; fax: 214-071; internet site: http://www.cepici.go.ci).

Ivory Coast Embassy, 2424 Massachusetts Avenue, NW, Washington DC 20008 (tel: 797-0300).

National Enterprise Assistance and Promotion Centre (CAPEN), Immeuble La Pyramide, 9th floor, 08 BP 868, Abidjan 08 (tel: 320-145).

Organisation Centrale pour la Commercialisation de l'Ananas et la Banane (OCAB), Imm Corniche, 16 BP 1908, Abidjan 16 (tel: 325-882; fax: 321-060).

Port Autonome d'Abidjan, BP V85, Abidjan (tel: 240-866, 242-640; fax: 242-328).

Professional Association of the Oil Industry, 13 Impasse Paris Village, 01 BP 1777, Abidjan 01 (tel: 217-320; fax: 222-858).

Société des Mines d'Ity, BP 872, Abidjan 08 (tel: 446-363; fax: 444-100).

Société Ivoirienne de la Poste et de L'Epargne, BP 105, Abidjan 17 (tel: 347-004; fax: 347-107).

Société Ivoirienne de Raffinage (SIR), Boulevard de Petit-Bassam, BP 1269, Abidjan 01 (tel: 270-427, 270-160; fax: 271-798, 273-217).

Société Nationale d'Opérations Petroliéres de la Côte d'Ivoire, BP V194, Abidjan (tel: 214-058).

Société pour le Développement Minier de la Côte d'Ivoire, BP 2816, Abidjan (tel: 212-994).

SODEMI (State Company for Mineral Development), BP 2816, 31 Boulevard Latrille, Abidjan Cocody-Nord, Abidjan 01 (tel: 4420994; fax: 440-821).

US Embassy, 5 rue Jesse Owens, 01 BP 171, Abidjan 01 (tel: 210-979).

World Trade Centre, PO Box V 68, Abidjan (tel: 216-189, 224-072/3; fax: 227-112).

Internet sites

Africa Business Network: http://www.ifc.org/abn

AllAfrica.com: http://allafrica.com

African Development Bank: http://www.afdb.org

Africa Online: http://www.africaonline.com

Mbendi AfroPaedia (information on companies, countries, industries and stock exchanges in Africa): http://mbendi.co.za

Croatia

KEY FACTS

Official name: Republika Hrvatska (Republic of Croatia)

Head of State: President Stjepan (Stipe) Mesić (HNS) (from 2000; re-elected 16 Jan 2005))

Head of government: Prime Minister Ivo Sanader (HDZ) (appointed by the President 9 Dec 2003)

Ruling party: Coalition government from Dec 2003: Hrvatska Demokratska Zajednica (HDZ) (Croatian Democratic Community) and Hrvatska Socialna Liberalna Stranka-Demokratski Centar (HSLS-DC) (Croatian Social Liberal Party-Democratic Centre)

Area: 56,538 square km

Population: 4.38 million (2004)

Capital: Zagreb

Official language: Croatian

Currency: Kuna (K) = 100 lipas

Exchange rate: K6.16 per US$ (Oct 2005)

GDP per capita: US$7,378 (2004)

GDP real growth: 3.80% (2004); 3.5% (2005)

Labour force: 2.12 million (2004)

Unemployment: 13.80% (2004)

Inflation: 2.10% (2004); *2.9% (2005)

Balance of trade: -US$8.35 billion (2004)

Foreign debt: US$26.40 billion (2004)

* estimated figure

It was a year of high drama for Croatia in 2005. Faced with the prospect of a start date for European Union (EU) membership accession talks, Croatia was repeatedly warned by EU officials that progress was dependent upon its ability to extradite a key war crimes suspect, General Ante Gotovina. Croatia therefore found itself in the unenviable position of having the fate of its key strategic goal since 1991, European integration, resting in the hands of a fugitive.

Robust economy

The Croatian economy continued to stand apart from all of its fellow former Yugoslav republics, bar Slovenia, in terms of growth and stability. The European Bank for Reconstruction and Development (EBRD) forecasts GDP growth of 3.5 per cent for Croatia in 2005, and an inflation rate of 2.9 per cent. The IMF praised Croatia in September for having reduced its budget deficit but also noted a rise in its overall external debt. During the year, Croatia finalised three loan agreements with the World Bank, aimed at revitalising its underdeveloped regions. Part of this process was to assist Croatia in meeting requirements for EU accession talks.

Exorcising the past ...

Despite Croatia's efforts to separate the two, the question of Croatian membership of the EU and the alleged war crimes of General Gotovina have travelled hand in hand since 2001. In that year, Croatia paved the way for future EU membership by signing a Stabilisation and Association Agreement (SAA) with the EU. However, the International Criminal Tribunal for the former Yugoslavia (ICTY), also in 2001, indicted Gotovina for war crimes committed in 1995 against Croatia's Serb minority. Ever since, Croatia's EU ambitions have been bedevilled by its inability, and at times unwillingness, to address Gotovina's alleged crimes.

... for a European future

In February 2005, Croatia's SAA with the EU finally came into force. However, although Croatia had been told that accession talks for full membership could begin on 17 March, it suffered an embarrassing suspension due to its perceived failure to co-operate in the capture of General Gotovina. The Croatian government lobbied hard during the rest of the year to prove to the EU that Gotovina had long since fled the country and was beyond Croatia's remit. A number of EU countries urged the European Commission to de-link the issues of Croatia's membership with Gotovina's arrest, but to no avail. ICTY's chief prosecutor, Carla Del Ponte, remained resolute that co-operation with The Hague was a minimum European standard and clearly had the ear of officials in charge of EU enlargement. This state of limbo remained in place until 4 October, when both Del Ponte and the EU gave Croatia the green light for accession talks to begin, despite Gotovina's fugitive status. The Croatian government claimed vindication for its position that Gotovina was no longer in Croatia when, on 8 December, Gotovina was finally arrested inside Spanish territory.

Another troubling event from Croatia's 1991–95 conflict with its Serb minority continued to dog Croatia in 2005. Croatia was criticised by NGOs in December for failing to facilitate adequately the return of Croatian Serb refugees, most of whom had fled during Operation Storm – the Croatian army operation that in August 1995 crushed the then separatist Serb Krajina republic. By the end of 2005, only one third of the more than 300,000 Serbs who had fled had returned to their homes. However, in an unprecedented move, Croatian president Stjepan Mesić publicly apologised, at a ceremony marking the tenth anniversary of Operation Storm, to all those who had been harmed by the campaign.

Border dispute

Croatia's long-running dispute with neighbouring Slovenia over terrestrial and maritime borders came to a head in 2005. Despite a joint pledge in June to prevent the border disagreement from generating incidents on the ground, Croatia and Slovenia were at loggerheads from August over a Slovene decision to declare an exclusive maritime zone in the Adriatic. Although some within the Slovene governing coalition threatened to make life difficult for Croatia in its accession talks with the EU, the European Commission assured Croatia in December that the dispute would not influence negotiations.

Local politics

In office since December 2003, the governing coalition of Prime Minister Ivo Sanader came under considerable pressure for early elections in 2005. The defeat of Sanader's preferred presidential candidate to incumbent, Stjepan Mesić, in January kicked off a difficult year for the government. Although generally co-operative with the government, President Mesić was often out of step on issues such as Croatia's relationship with its former Yugoslav neighbours, the EU and Croatia's wartime legacy. As in his first term in office (2000–05), Mesić urged his fellow Croats to undertake a more honest assessment of what precisely had been done in Croatia's name during its war of independence. Continuing embarrassment over the failure to secure EU accession talks, a split in the coalition's senior party, the Hrvatska Demokratska Zajednica (HDZ) (Croatian Democratic Union), and a poor showing in local elections in May also had Sanader on the defensive. However, with accession talks affirmed in October and Gotovina's arrest in December, the pressure eased.

Outlook

After the stress of Croatia's drawn out negotiations over EU accession talks in 2005, the New Year looks quiet in comparison. With the start of talks, Croatia can expect access to extra EU funding and greater economic stability. The Croatian government has made it clear that it expects serious progress in the accession talks by June 2006 and full membership in 2009 and so far there is little to fundamentally contradict this expectation. The European Commission has already signalled to Croatia that it will not hold the border dispute with Slovenia against it. However, it remains to be seen how a long-running dispute with Italy over claims to compensation for the expulsion of ethnic Italians from Dalmatia after the Second World War will play out. The Italian government threatened, in October 2005, to hold this over Croatia during the accession process. The Croatian government also stands a realistic chance of being invited to join NATO in 2006.

Risk assessment

Politics	Stable
Economy	Stable
Regional stability	Improving

COUNTRY PROFILE

Historical profile

The Croats formed an independent kingdom during the tenth century.

KEY INDICATORS — Croatia

	Unit	2000	2001	2002	2003	2004
Population	m	4.39	4.40	4.39	4.38	4.38
Gross domestic product (GDP)	US$bn	19.00	20.30	22.40	27.34	*34.20
GDP per capita	US$	4,183	4,626	5,325	6,240	7,378
GDP real growth	%	3.7	4.1	5.0	3.7	3.8
Inflation	%	6.2	6.2	2.2	2.0	2.1
Unemployment	%	22.0	23.1	23.8	21.9	13.8
Exports (fob) (goods)	US$m	4,567.0	4,752.1	4,800.0	6,300.0	8,208.2
Imports (fob) (goods)	US$m	7,770.7	8,763.8	9,000.0	14,200.0	16,554.5
Balance of trade	US$m	-3,203.7	-4,011.7	-4,300.0	-7,900.0	-8,346.3
Current account	US$m	-399.2	-623.3	-661.0	-2,000.0	-1,790.0
Foreign debt	US$bn	10.4	10.6	11.8	16.5	26.4
Total reserves minus gold	US$m	3,524.4	4,703.2	5,884.9	8,190.5	8,758.2
Foreign exchange	US$m	3,376.9	4,595.6	5,883.2	8,190.2	8,757.9
Foreign direct investment (FDI)	US$bn	0.9	1.3	–	2.0	–
Exchange rate	per US$	8.28	8.34	7.85	6.64	5.82

* estimated figure

Croatia

1089 Inner Croatia came under the control of Hungary and then the Habsburg empire, remaining that way for eight centuries.
1529 After Hungary's defeat by the Ottoman Turks, a militarised border was formed between Croatia and Bosnia-Hercegovina.
1918 The defeat of the Austro-Hungarian empire during the First World War saw the creation of the Kingdom of the Serbs, Croats and Slovenes, encompassing Bosnia-Hercegovina, Croatia, parts of Dalmatia and Macedonia, Montenegro, Serbia, Slavonia and Slovenia.
1921 Prince Alexander, Regent of Serbia, became King.
1929 Following disputes between Serbs and Croats, King Alexander assumed dictatorial powers and the country was renamed Yugoslavia.
1934 King Alexander of Yugoslavia was assassinated in France by Croatian extremists. Power passed to Prince Paul, acting as Regent to 11-year-old King Peter II. He ruled with the support of the armed forces.
1939 Croatia was granted internal autonomy.
1941 A coup by air force officers replaced Prince Paul and the pro-Nazi Germany government with the 17-year-old King Peter II and established a pro-Allied government. In response, German and Italian forces invaded Yugoslavia, forcing the royal family and government into exile. The fascist Ustasha movement, led by Ante Pavelic, created the Nezavisna Drzava Hrvatska (NDH) (Independent State of Croatia).
1943 Civil war ensued between two rival groups, the communist partisans, led by General Tito, and the Royalist Chetniks. The partisans proclaimed their own government in liberated areas.
1944 King Peter II was deposed.
1945 The Federal People's Republic of Yugoslavia was proclaimed, with Josip Broz Tito as prime minister – a Croat opposed to expressions of Croat (or any other) nationalism. Croatia became a constituent republic of the federation. The other republics were: Bosnia-Hercegovina, Macedonia, Slovenia, Montenegro, Serbia and the two autonomous regions of Vojvodina and Kosovo.
1953 Constitutions were adopted and Tito became president of Yugoslavia. Increased autonomy for the constituent republics was extended in 1963 and 1974.
1971 A mass movement in favour of Croatian nationalist revival was crushed by Tito.
1989 Following the death of Tito in 1980 and the fall of communism elsewhere in Eastern Europe, friction between the wealthier republics, Slovenia and Croatia, and the different ethnic groupings intensified.
1990 Following Slovenia's secession from Yugoslavia, Croatia held its own free elections which were won by the nationalist Hrvatska Demokratska Zajednica (HDZ) (Croatian Democratic Community). Franjo Tudjman became the first president of the Republic of Croatia. In August, Croatian Serbs held their own referendum, which favoured maintaining their cultural autonomy. Rebel Serbs took control of the Krajina and two other regions in Croatia – Eastern and Western Slavonia.
1991 Independence from Yugoslavia was unilaterally declared.
1992–94 Croatia was recognised as an independent state by the then European Community (EC) on 15 January and became a member of the UN. Franjo Tudjman was re-elected president. The declaration of independence was followed by several months of war, first against the Yugoslav National Army and then against local rebel ethnic Serbs. The Croatian government began to finance and support Bosnian Croat attempts to separate from Bosnia-Hercegovina. This exacerbated the civil war in Bosnia between the Muslim and Bosnian Croats, until a cease-fire was achieved and the Muslim-Croat Federation of Bosnia-Hercegovina was established in 1994.
1995 After nearly four years of Serb control, western Slavonia and Krajina were recaptured by the Croatian army. Tudjman's ruling nationalist HDZ won the parliamentary elections and Zlatko Matesa became prime minister. President Tudjman of Croatia, along with President Slobodan Milosevic of Yugoslavia and President Alija Izetbegovic of Bosnia-Hercegovina, agreed to end the Bosnian civil war.
1996 Yugoslavia (consisting of Serbia and Montenegro and the two autonomous regions of Kosovo and Vojvodina) and Croatia signed an agreement on mutual recognition, formally ending five years of hostility.
1997 The HDZ won a majority in the upper house of the Sabor and President Franjo Tudjman was re-elected.
1998 Eastern Slavonia (some 5 per cent of Croatia's total territory) was handed back to Croatia by the UN Transition Authority for Eastern Slavonia (UNTAES).
1999 Due to Tudjman's deteriorating health, the president of the House of Representatives, Vlatko Pavletic, took over as acting Croatian president in November. Franjo Tudjman died on 10 December.
2000 The Socialdemokratska Partija (SDP) (Social Democratic Party) won the general election. A centre-left coalition government was formed, led by the SDP, with Ivica Racan (SDP) as prime minister. Stipe Mesic of the Hrvatska Narodna Stranka (HNS) (Croatian People's Party) and regarded as an ally of the SDP, was sworn in as president.
2001 A constitutional amendment abolished of the upper house of parliament, the Zupanijski dom (House of Counties). Croatia agreed to extradite several suspected war criminals to the International Criminal Tribunal for former Yugoslavia (ICTY) at The Hague in The Netherlands. War veteran groups protested strongly at the government's co-operation.
2002 Ivica Racan resigned as prime minister, but was reappointed and formed a new centre-left coalition government, comprising the SDP, HNS, Hrvatska Seljacka Stranka (HSS) (Croatian Peasant Party), Liberalna Stranka (LS) (Liberal Party) and Libra.
2003 Croatia submitted its formal application for EU membership. The HDZ – Croatian nationalists – defeated the pro-Western parties in parliamentary elections. President Mesić appointed Ivo Sanader (HDZ) as prime minister and a coalition government was formed by the HDZ and the Hrvatska Socialna Liberalna Stranka, Demokratski Centar (HSLS, DC) (Croatian Social Liberal Party, Democratic Centre).
2004 Milan Babić, a Croatian Serb, was jailed for 13 years by the ICTY Tribunal in The Hague for war crimes during his leadership, in the early 1990s, of the self-proclaimed Krajina Serb republic.
2005 In the run-off presidential elections on 16 January, incumbent Stjepan Mesić won 66 per cent of the vote, defeating Jadranka Kosor with 34 per cent. In October EU began accession talks with Croatia; they had been stalled because Croatia was deemed unco-operative in handing over suspected war criminals. In December, the fugitive, General Ante Gotovina was arrested in the Canary Islands and sent to the war crimes tribunal in The Hague.

Political structure
Constitution

The written constitution was first adopted in December 1990, with amendments in November 2000 and March 2001 that cut back presidential powers and abolish the upper house of parliament.
Under the constitution there is a principle of the separation of power into legislative, executive and judicial branches, which are limited by the right to local and regional self-government.
The laws of Croatia must conform to the constitution
The electoral law gives the vote to all Croatians over the age of 18, including those living abroad. Ethnic minorities are equal with ethnic Croats according to the

constitution. However, in recent years the international community has raised strong objections to laws that *de facto* discriminate against other groups – specifically returning Serb refugees. Until these problems are solved, Croatia is unlikely to be recognised as a fully democratic state. The administration of Croatia is divided into 21 *zupanije* (counties). There are also two *kotari*, or special districts, at Glina and Knin, which are under direct Serb control.

Form of state
Unitary, democratic republic

The executive
Executive power is vested in the president who is Head of State and supreme commander of the armed forces and is directly elected for five years and a maximum of two terms.

The president appoints the prime minister and, by recommendation of the prime minister, other members of the government. These appointments are subject to confirmation by the House of Representatives.

National legislature
In March 2001, a constitutional amendment abolished Croatia's bicameral legislature and the upper house, the Zupanijski dom (House of Counties). The remaining chamber, Zastupnici dom (House of Representatives), is composed of 152 members, each elected for a four-year term in multi-member constituencies.

Following the 2001 amendment, the House of Representatives has been referred to more commonly as the Sabor (parliament).

Legal system
All civil and criminal cases are dealt with by basic and higher courts. The Supreme Court is the highest authority for civil and criminal law, charged with ensuring uniform application of laws and equality of citizens. All judges and other judicial officials are appointed by the Judicial Council, an elected body that is answerable to the parliament. The Judicial Council also acts as the Constitutional Court to determine the conformity of national legislation with the Constitution.

All prosecutions are the responsibility of the Office of the Public Prosecutor. There is also a Public Attorney. The Justice Ministry is the administrative authority of the Croatian judiciary. Its major instrument is the Croatian police, which falls under the jurisdiction of the interior minister.

Last elections
16 January 2005 (run-off presidential); 2 January 2005 (first round presidential); 23 November 2003 (parliamentary).

Results: Presidential second round: Stipe Mesic won 66 per cent of the vote, defeating Jadranka Kosor with 34 per cent.

Parliamentary: the HDZ won 66 seats, the SDP, won 34 seats and the Hrvatska Narodna Stranka (HNS) (Croatian People's Party) 10 seats, Hrvatska Socialna Liberalna Stranka, Demokratski Centar (HSLS, DC) (Croatian Social Liberal Party, Democratic Centre) won two and one seats respectively.

Next elections
2007 (parliamentary); 2009 (presidential).

Political parties
Ruling party
Coalition government from Dec 2003: Hrvatska Demokratska Zajednica (HDZ) (Croatian Democratic Community) and Hrvatska Socialna Liberalna Stranka-Demokratski Centar (HSLS-DC) (Croatian Social Liberal Party-Democratic Centre)

Main opposition party
Socijaldemokratska Partija Hrvatske (SPH) (Social Democratic Party of Croatia)

Population
4.38 million (2004)

Ethnic make-up
Croats (90 per cent of the population), plus Serbs, Hungarians and Gypsies. The April 2001 census, the first since the 1991–95 war, indicated that Serbs made up 4.5 per cent of the population (the figure was 12 per cent in the early 1990s).

Religions
Predominantly Roman Catholic, with Christian Orthodox, Muslim and Jewish minorities, living mostly in Zagreb.

Education
Primary education is compulsory and free of charge. Secondary education is between the ages of 14–18. Vocational schools offer courses lasting for three or four years, including a period of practical instruction. There are four universities offering courses in science, engineering and medicine that meet international standards.

Public expenditure on education typically amounts to 5 per cent of annual gross national income.

Literacy rate: 98 per cent (World Bank 2004)
Compulsory years: Six to 14
Enrolment rate: 99 per cent; gross primary enrolment, of the relevant age group (including repetition rates), (World Bank).
Pupils per teacher: 19 in primary schools

Health
Total expenditure on health is 8–9 per cent of GDP, of which government spending is 84–85 per cent.

The healthcare system has recovered since the internal conflict ended in 1995, but national coverage remains patchy, notably in the Krajina and Eastern Slavonia regions.

HIV prevalence: 0.1 per cent aged 15–49 in 2003 (World Bank)
Life expectancy: 74 years (World Bank)
Fertility rate/Maternal mortality rate: 1.4 births per woman (2003); maternal mortality 6 per 100,000 live births (World Bank).
Infant mortality rate: 6 per 1,000 live births; 1 per cent of children under five years are malnourished (World Bank).
Head of population per physician/bed: 2.2 physicians and 5.9 hospital beds available per 1,000 people.

Welfare
The government faces a huge fiscal burden with an ageing population and a legacy of insufficient funds to pay retirees, particularly those who retired early following reforms of the late 90s. In 2002 the government introduced a dual social insurance and mandatory, privately managed, compulsory pension schemes, for all workers, with contributions that vary depending on the class of old age pension. Regular pensions require contributions of 10.75 per cent and 8.75 per cent (of payroll), from employee and employer respectively. Basic pensions require contributions of 8.75 per cent and 5.75 per cent (of payroll), from employee and employer respectively. Insurance contributions cover among other benefits, medical, disability and survivor's pensions. By 2020 projected pension fund assets should reach 25–30 per cent of GDP. In 2003 it was estimated there were over 50,000 Croatian refugees, of which 27,700 were internally displaced persons (IDP).

Main cities
Zagreb (capital, estimated population 685,500 in 2003), Split (173,600), Rijeka (142,500), Osijek (89,600), Zadar (68,900), Slavonski Brod (58,100), Pula (58,100), Karlovac (48,600), Dubrovnik (30,200, Vukovar (29,900).

Languages spoken
Croatian is written using the Latin alphabet. German and English are commonly used as second languages and business people are fluent in English. Bosnian and Serbian are also spoken and, near the Adriatic coast, Italian is spoken.

Official language/s
Croatian

Media
Press
Dailies: The most popular dailies mainly published in Croatian are *Vecernji List*, *Narodne Novine*, *Jutarnji List*, *Slobodna Dalmacija*, *Novi List* (Rijeka), *Vjesnik* and *Glas Slavojije* (Osijek). *Feral Tribune* (in English) is one of the rare independent voices of information in Croatia that has

been censored many times by the Zagreb government.

Weeklies: Some of the important weeklies include *Globus*, *ST* and *Nedjeljna Dalmacija*. *Croatia online weekly* (http://www.croatia.hr) is a weekly in English. *Nacional* is an independent political weekly in English/Croatian.
Hrvatski-Obzor is a political weekly in Croatian.
Business: *Privredni Vjesnik* (weekly) and *Informator*.
Periodicals: *Arkzin* is an independent monthly magazine.

Broadcasting
Radio: The state radio monopoly is RTH. Other than the RTH, Austrian, Italian and Slovenian radio and television broadcasts are also available in Croatia. Radio 101 pioneered independent media in Croatia like its Belgrade counterpart, B 92. Radio Rijeka was the first live Croatian radio channel on the Internet.
Television: The state-owned HTV commands a 95 per cent market share for its three channels.

Economy
Croatia was one of the most industrialised of the former Yugoslav republics in 1990 and enjoyed a relatively high standard of living. The nascent growth of a market economy was only just under way at the beginning of the first Croatian war in 1991, which had devastating results. Economic losses totalled over US$37 billion, in damaged infrastructure, particularly in the revenue earning tourism sector, lost output and the high costs in maintaining economically unproductive refugees from the region's major war zones.

Croatia has made significant attempts to rebuild and liberalise its economy since the collapse of Yugoslavia and the damage caused by the conflict.

President Ivo Sanader made EU membership along with creating a strong free-market economy government priorities. Croatia began official talks, in October 2005, to become an EU member. The negotiations had stalled in March 2005, when the EU declared that Croatia was not co-operating with the UN war crimes tribunal in The Hague and that wanted suspects had to be handed over for trial as a show of good faith. In September, Austria held up talks on entry negotiations with Turkey, on behalf of Croatia, saying that if Turkey was eligible for entry then so was Croatia.

In 2004, GDP growth was 3.8 per cent, which was, according to the IMF, expected as the government programme was designed to slow public consumption, while raising private consumption. The balance of payments was better than expected in 2004 with strong exports supporting a merchandise trade deficit, which fell to 24 per cent of GDP – 3 per cent down from 2003. The tourist sector added almost 20 per cent of GDP, returning it to its position as an economic leader. Inflation remained relatively low at 2.1 per cent while unemployment remained relatively high at 13.8 per cent – although this was a marked improvement on the 21.9 per cent in 2003. Industry contributed 30.1 per cent to GDP, of which manufacturing supplied 18.8 per cent, this represented 4.3 per cent and 4.0 per cent annual growth respectively. Agriculture contributed 8.2 per cent, and services 61.6 per cent of GDP in 2004. The government has begun to organise its macroeconomic programme to allow fiscal consolidation and maintain stability against the euro, in preparation for accession. In December 2004 a framework with ambitious fiscal targets – *Pre-Accession Economic Program* (PEP) was approved; external and public debt will be reduced, driven by government deficit and spending on health, social benefits and administration will be cut to lessen the tax burden. The PEP is expected to achieve its objectives by 2007.

External trade
The EU is Croatia's principal trading partner receiving almost 70 per cent of total exports, with Italy, Germany and Austria as its traditional markets.
Imports
Principal imports are machinery, transport and electrical equipment, chemicals, fuels and lubricants and foodstuffs.
Main sources: Italy (17.3 per cent total, 2004), Germany (15.7 per cent), Slovenia (7.1 per cent), Austria (7.1 per cent), Russia (7 per cent), France (4.3 per cent)
Exports
Principal exports are transport equipment, textiles, chemicals, foodstuffs and fuels.
Main destinations: Italy (23.1 per cent total, 2004), Bosnia and Herzegovina (14.7 per cent), Germany (11.5 per cent), Austria (9.6 per cent), Slovenia (7.7 per cent)

Agriculture
Farming
Almost half of the population live in rural areas where agriculture continues to be the traditional source of income. The government has prepared a Rural Development Plan 2005–06 with four principal measures: farm investment, processing and marketing of agricultural and fish products, improved rural infrastruture and technical assistance. This programme is intended to align agriculture with conditions necessary for accession to the EU. Of a total of 3.2 million hectares (ha) of arable land, 63 per cent is cultivated and the rest is pasture land. Only 68 per cent of agricultural land is privately owned. Agriculture contributed 8.2 per cent to GDP, and recorded growth of 4.2 per cent in 2004; it employed 16.2 per cent of the workforce.

Family farms with an average holding of 2.8ha per farm, contribute to the overall animal and horticultural production. Crop production is especially well developed, covering the needs for cereals, while cattle breeding accounts for almost 50 per cent of agriculture-generated GDP. The warm weather and mild winters suit grape-growing.

The government is committed to initiating agricultural market reform and promoting private farming. Reform in the agrarian production sector is accompanied by rising food imports, mostly from the EU. Agriculture within the country meets the domestic demand for wine, wheat, corn, eggs and poultry. Croatia's oil and sugar processing facilities are big enough to provide exports. However, with high production costs and a series of free trade agreements farm products cannot compete internationally.

Crop production in 2004 included: 3,267,855 million tonnes (t) cereals in total, 2,200,000t maize, 840,000t wheat, 180,000t barley, 330,000t potatoes, 5,167t treenuts, 19,930t pulses, 14,400t citrus fruit, 350,000t grapes, *71,400t tomatoes, 60,260t oilcrops, 10,200t tobacco leaves, *33,000t olives, 30,000t plums, 1,000,000t sugar beets, 58,000t apples, 35,000t chillies and peppers, 80,000t soya beans, 4,100t figs, 492,521t fruit in total, 440,823t vegetables in total. Livestock production included: 140,686t meat in total, 23,000t beef, 70,000t pig meat, 1,800t lamb, *42,570t poultry, *45,700t eggs, 768,500t milk, 1,616t honey, 2,286t cattle hides, 595t sheepskins.
* estimate
Fishing
There are rich marine resources concentrated on the Dalmatian Adriatic coast.
Forestry
Of a total of 1.7 million hectares (ha) of forest cover, nearly four-fifths of the forest is owned by the state, and the rest is in private hands. In 1990–2000, forest cover increased by an average of 0.11 per cent per annum, the equivalent of 2,000ha.

Croatia has a well-developed wood processing industry. Although a large amount of wood is reserved for domestic fuel consumption, the country manages to export industrial roundwood and sawnwood mainly to Slovenia and Italy respectively. Small volumes of wood pulp and panels are also exported, but paper is largely imported. In 2004, annual export of forest products amounted to US$328.1 million, while imports totalled US$347.9 million. Production in 2004 included 3,841,000 cubic metres (cum) roundwood, 2,887,000cum industrial roundwood, 582,000cum sawnwood, 2,074,000cum sawlogs and veneers, 558,000cum pulpwood, 103,000cum wood-based panels, 954,000cum wood fuel

Industry and manufacturing

The industrial sector contributed 30.1 per cent to GDP and recorded growth of 4.3 per cent in 2004, it typically employs around 30 per cent of the workforce. Manufacturing accounted for 18.8 per cent of GDP and recorded growth of 4.0 per cent in 2004.

State owned enterprises (SOE) are due to be restructured, in preparation for the expected competition within the EU. Privatisation of SOE has begun, although progress is slow. In 2005 government commitment to fiscal constraints, necessary for staff cuts, is still needed as SOE incur significant losses, particularly in the shipbuilding industry and the railway system.

Private enterprise in 2004, recorded a sizeable increase in its share of FDI, in retail and wholesale businesses; manufacturing, as a whole, attracted 24 per cent of FDI.

Investment in road infrastructure has resulted in an increased motorway network from 100km to 700km (1995–05).

Tourism

Tourism is one of the most important elements in Croatia's economy. It is the most important in foreign exchange earners, accounting for 20.6 per cent of GDP, slightly down on the 22.3 per cent in 2003.

It is expected to contribute US$3.3 billion in 2005, or 9.0 per cent of GDP and employ 22.9 per cent of the workforce.

The state still has a dominant position in tourism and the sector will have to be restructured in preparation for accession to the EU. It is expected that the travel and tourist sector will attract US$1 billion or 10.2 per cent of total capital investment in 2005.

There are approximately 190,000 beds in hotels and apartments, with an equal number of beds in private accommodation. The majority of visitors come from Germany, Italy, Slovenia, Czech Republic and Austria.

Hydrocarbons

Croatia was the former Yugoslavia's biggest oil producing region, however with around 50 per cent of total energy being thermal, consumption is correspondingly high; new energy efficiency initiatives are expected to reduce demand.

Oil fields are located in Slavonia and offshore, near the Dalmatia coast. In January 2004, Croatia had estimated oil reserves of 75 million barrels.

The 400,000bpd capacity Croatian Adriatic Oil (Adria) Pipeline, run by Jadranski Naftovod (JANAF) of Croatia takes oil that arrives by tanker at the Croatian Adriatic port of Omisalj into the interior of Croatia. There are currently negotiations between Transneft and Croatia to increase the capacity of the Adria pipeline. Croatia has two refineries and two lubrication production plants.

In January 2004, natural gas reserves stood at 24.6 billion cubic metres (cum), with an annual production of 1.75 billion cum. Imports total around 1.07 billion cum per year with consumption of 2.83 billion cum annually. Imported gas comes primarily from Slovenia via pipeline. Croatia has extensive coal reserves but production runs at less than 100,000 tonnes per annum, mostly for domestic power plant consumption.

Energy

Hydroelectric power is the largest source of domestic energy, accounting for approximately 35 per cent of local production and around 20 per cent of total energy consumption. Hydroelectric plants are mainly located along the Adriatic coastline (Obrovac, Senj, Zakucac). Imports of electricity account for around 10 per cent of total energy consumption. An important source of energy is the Krsko nuclear plant in Slovenia in which Croatia has a 50 per cent stake. Demand for electricity is increasing by around 5 per cent per year, creating an urgent need to increase generating capacity in Croatia. Croatia's first wind farm began generating electricity in January 2005. The cost of the installation was put at US$8.4 million and it is expected to generate 15 million kilowatts per year. Another wind farm is under construction close to Sibenik and two others are planned for the island of Vis, in the south, and the town of Obrovac.

Financial markets
Stock exchange
The Zagreb Stock Exchange (ZSE) began trading in 1994.

Banking and insurance

The central bank has general supervisory powers, endorsed by law, of the banking system. Legislation, since 2001, permits foreign investment in banks and since 2004 foreign banks may open branches in Croatia, although the EU is unimpressed about some of the restrictive stipulation necessary for this. Foreign exchange laws permit individuals opening foreign exchange accounts abroad and local banks offering foreign currency denominated loans.

There will be an amount of merging of supervisory authorities of the insurance, securities, investment funds and pensions into a financial services authority in line with EU requirements, before accession.
Central bank
Hrvatska Narodna Banka (HNB) (Croatian National Bank)
Main financial centre
Zagreb

Time

GMT plus one hour (GMT plus two hours from late March to late September)

Geography

The 56,538 square km of Croatia are shaped like a horse shoe, which swings around from the Pannonian plains of Slavonia, across the hills of central Croatia to the Istrian peninsular before going south along the Adriatic coast of Dalmatia. The country consists of two principal parts: the Slavonian or Danubian plains of the north and east, through which the River Sava flows, and the extended Mediterranean coastal region of the Istrian peninsula and Dalmatia to the south-west and south-east. The hinterlands of this coastal region are the Dinaric Alps, which also extend into Bosnia-Hercegovina. To the south-west of Zagreb, a narrow neck of territory connects the two elongated parts of the country. There are 1,185 islands and islets along the 1,778km Croatian coast. Croatia is bounded by Slovenia to the north-west, Hungary to the north-east and the Vojvodina area of Serbia to the east. Bosnia-Hercegovina abuts into Croatia, forming a southern border along the Sava River, and an eastern one inland from the Dalmatian coast, which stretches southwards. There is a short border with Montenegro at the southern tip of this narrowing stretch of Croatia (Dubrovnik area), beyond a short coastal strip of Bosnia-Hercegovina.

In the Adriatic Sea, Croatia also has maritime boundaries with Slovenia, Italy and Montenegro.

Climate

In northern Croatia, the climate is continental, on the Adriatic it is mediterranean, while in the mountainous regions, it is alpine. The coastal hinterlands have a colder climate with heavy snow in winter, but they can be very hot in summer. Temperatures inland average around 10 degrees Celsius (C), while average temperatures on the coastal areas are around 15 degrees C. During the summer months, temperatures along the coast are often in excess of 30 degrees C.

Precipitation is fairly constant country-wide throughout the year. The summer is the wettest season in the north, where the average annual rainfall in Zagreb is 890 millimetres. During the winter months, violent wind storms, known locally as the *Bora*, are common along the coast. A subsidiary sea of the Mediterranean, the Adriatic exercises a major influence on Croatia's climate, moderating the excesses of the continental climates of the north and east.

Dress codes
There is an increasing tendency towards formal dress in business in Croatia, particularly in Zagreb.

Entry requirements
Passports
A passport is required by all except citizens of Bosnia who need an identity card.
Visa
Required by all except many nationals of the Americas, Europe, Australasia, and some Asian countries, for stays of less than 90 days. Visitors will be issued with a border pass on arrival, and must keep the documentation until departure. For further details of extensions contact the consular section of the local embassy.
For those who require a business visa, they are issued to employees of foreign companies registered in Croatia; contact the Croatian Chamber of Economy e-mail:hgk@hgk.hr; website: www.hgk.hr for further information on company registration.
Prohibited entry
Nationals of Palestine, Taiwan and the Turkish Republic of Northern Cyprus.
Currency advice/regulations
The import and export of local currency is limited to K2,000 (in banknotes, up to K500). The import and export of foreign currency is unlimited. Foreign currency can be exchanged in banks, by authorised dealers and post offices; automated teller machines (ATMs) are common.
Travellers are advised to take travellers cheques in US dollars, UK pounds sterling or euros.
Customs
Goods for personal use up to the value of K300 can be imported free of duty.
Excise duties have to be paid on imports of oil derivatives, tobacco, beer, alcohol, non-alcoholic beverages and automobiles.
A foreign national can be exempt from paying customs duties on equipment imported on the basis of a foreign investment contract. Appeals for exemption from duty should be submitted to the Ministry of Finance.
Prohibited imports
The import of vehicles over seven years old is forbidden.

Health (for visitors)
There are no special requirements.

Credit cards
American Express, Diners' Club, Mastercard and Visa are accepted.

Public holidays
Fixed dates
1 Jan (New Year's Day), 6 Jan (Epiphany), 1 May (Labour Day), 22 Jun (Anti-Fascism Day), 5 Aug (Thanksgiving Day), 15 Aug (Assumption Day), 1 Nov (All Saints' Day), 25 Dec (Christmas Day), 26 Dec (St Stephen's Day).
Variable dates
Easter Monday

Working hours
Banking
Mon–Fri: 0800–1900; Sat: 0700–1200.
Business
Mon–Fri: 0830–1630.
Government
Mon–Fri: 0830–1630.
Shops
Food shops: Mon–Fri: 0700–2000, Sat: 0700–1500.
Non-food shops: Mon–Fri: 0800–1200, 1700–2000; Sat: 0800–1500.

Telecommunications
Mobile phones
There are GSM roaming facilities available in the 900 band width, the 1800 is planned. Coverage is virtually throughout the country.

Electricity supply
220V AC, 50 Hz

Weights and measures
Metric system

Social customs/useful tips
Although Croats are a rather gregarious people, there is a growing tendency to reserved formality in business contexts in order to give the impression of western-style efficiency, with punctuality norms beginning to take root. This image, however, is often belied by the inefficient manner in which businesses continue to operate in Croatia. On balance, foreigners should avoid informality with their business and other hosts and should observe western business standards. Foreigners should avoid all discussions of a political nature in Croatia.
Trade fairs are part of the regular business life in Croatia and are a useful way to meet potential partners and gain entry to the market. The principal venue is Zagreb, although Rijeka, Split and Osijek also host fairs.

Security
There is some street crime in Zagreb and other major cities.

Getting there
Air
National airline: Croatia Airlines
International airport/s: Zagreb Airport (ZAG), 17km from the capital; business centre, bank, post office, restaurants, bars, duty-free shopping.
Airport tax: None
Surface
Road: International buses connect Croatia with Austria, Italy, Hungary, France, Germany, Slovak Republic and Bosnia Hercegovina.
Rail: There are international rail routes to Zagreb from Munich, Vienna, Venice, Budapest and Graz.
Water: Ferry services connect Rijeka and Pula with Durres and Vlora (Albania).

Getting about
National transport
Air: There are regular routes from Zagreb-Rijeka, Zagreb-Split and Zagreb-Ljubljana (Slovenia).
The main domestic airports are Rijeka (RJK), 25km from Rijeka and Split (SPU), 24km from Split.
Road: The government plans construction of 700km of new roads by 2011, making a total of 1,220km of highways and superhighways. The last 33km of the 380km Dalmatian Motorway, joining Zagreb and Split was opened on 26 June 2005.
Buses: Intercity bus services are available across the country.
Rail: Major rail links run from Zagreb to Rijeka and Varazdin.
Water: Split and Rijeka are connected by a daily sea-ferry service, but domestic sea connections with Dubrovnik are less frequent.
City transport
Taxis: Good taxi services operate in all main cities. All taxis are metered with a basic charge. A 10 per cent tip is usual.
Buses, trams & metro: Trams in Zagreb and Osijek only; buses in other cities and towns. Services are generally cheap and regular.
Car hire
A national driving licence is usually acceptable, although there have been instances where hire companies also requested an international driver's licence. Traffic drives on the right. Speed limits are 130kph (81mph) on motorways, 100kph (62mph) on dual carriageways, 50kph (31mph) in built-up areas and 80kph (50mph) outside built-up areas. Right turns on red lights are strictly forbidden unless an additional green light (in the shape of an arrow) allows it. Right of way is always to the vehicle entering from the right.
Drink-driving is banned and subject to heavy penalties. The police also crack down on speeding and other road traffic

Nations of the World: A Political, Economic and Business Handbook

offences. Croatia has a poor road safety record.

BUSINESS DIRECTORY

The addresses listed below are a selection only. While World of Information makes every endeavour to check these addresses, we cannot guarantee that changes have not been made, especially to telephone numbers and area codes. We would welcome any corrections.

Telephone area codes
The international direct dialling code (IDD) for Croatia is +385, followed by area code and subscriber's number:

Zagreb	1	Split	21
Dubrovnik	20	Rijeka	51

Useful telephone numbers
Emergency road help and information (Croatian Automobile Association (HAK), English speakers): 987
Police: 92
Ambulance: 94

Chambers of Commerce
American Chamber of Commerce in Croatia, 1 Krsnjavoga, 10000 Zagreb (tel: 483-6777; fax: 483-6776; e-mail: info@amcham.hr).

Croatian Chamber of Economy, 2 Rooseveltov trg, PO Box 630, 10000 Zagreb (tel: 456-1555; fax: 482-8380; e-mail: hgk@hgk.hr).

Dubrovnik County Chamber, 6 Pera Cingrije, 20000 Dubrovnik (tel: 411-376; fax: 412-044; e-mail: hgkdu@hgk.hr).

Rijeka County Chamber, 23 Bulevar Oslobodjenja, 51000 Rijeka (tel: 209-111; fax: 216-033; e-mail: hgkri@hgk.hr).

Split County Chamber, 4 Obala A Trumbica, 21000 Split (tel: 321-100; fax: 346-956; e-mail: hgkst@hgk.hr).

Zagreb County Chamber, 45 Draskoviceva, 10000 Zagreb (tel: 460-6777; fax: 460-6803; e-mail: hgkzg@hgk.hr).

Banking
Croatian Bank for Reconstruction and Development, Trg J J Strossmayera 9, 10 000 Zagreb (tel: 459-1620; fax: 459-1721).

Privredna Banka Zagreb, Corporate Finance Division, Capital Markets, Rackoga 6, Zagreb (tel: 472-3124; e-mail: capital.markets@pbz.hr; internet site: http://www.pbz.hr).

Central bank
Hrvatska Narodna Banka (Croatian National Bank), Trg hrvatskih velikana 3, Zagreb 10002 (tel: 456-4555; fax: 455-0726; e-mail: info@hnb.hr).

Travel information
Croatian Chamber of the Economy, Director of Tourism, Rosseveltov Trg 2, 10000 Zagreb (tel: 456-1570; fax: 448-618).

Croatia Airlines, Savska 4A, 41000 Zagreb (tel: 616-0066; fax: 530-475).

Croatian Railways (HZ-Hrvatske Zeljeznice), Mihanoviceva 12, Zagreb (fax: 457-7597).

Tourist Community of Zagreb, Kaptol 5, 41000 Zagreb (tel: 426-411; fax: 272-628).

Tourist Information Centre, Trg bana Jelacicá 11, 41000 Zagreb (tel: 278-855; fax: 274-083).

Ministry of tourism
Ministry of Tourism, International Relations Department, Ulica grada Vukovara 78, 10 000 Zagreb (tel: 610-6300; fax: 610-9300).

National tourist organisation offices
Hrvatska turisticka zajednica (Croatian Tourist Board), Gunduliceva 3, 41000 Zagreb (tel: 424-637, 431-015; fax: 428-674).

Ministries
Government of the Republic of Croatia, Trg Svetog Marka 2, 10 000 Zagreb (tel: 456-9222; fax: 630-3023).

Ministry of Administration, Republike Austrije 16, Zagreb 10 000 (tel: 378-2111; fax: 378-2192).

Ministry of Agriculture and Forestry, Ulica grada Vukovara 78, 10 000 Zagreb (tel: 610-6111; fax: 610-9200).

Ministry of Culture, Trg Burze 6, 10 000 Zagreb (tel: 461-0477, 456-9022; fax: 461-0489).

Ministry of Defence, Trg Kralja Petra Kresimira 4 br 1, 10 000 Zagreb (tel: 456-7111; fax: 455-1105).

Ministry of Development and Reconstruction, Nazorova 61, 10 000 Zagreb (tel: 378-4500; fax: 378-4551).

Ministry of Economic Affairs, Ulica grada Vukovara 78, 10 000 Zagreb (tel: 610-6111; fax: 610-9120).

Ministry of Education and Sports, Trg Burze 6, 10 000 Zagreb (tel: 456-9000; fax: 456-9087).

Ministry of Environmental Protection and Zoning, Ul Republike Austrije 20, 10 000 Zagreb (tel: 378-2444; fax: 377-2822).

Ministry of European Integration, Ul grada Vukovara 62, 10 000 Zagreb (tel: 456-9335, 456-9336; fax: 469-8310).

Ministry of Finance, Kataneiaeva 5, 10 000 Zagreb (tel: 459-1333; fax: 492-2583).

Ministry of Foreign Affairs, Trg Nikole Subica Zrinskog 7–8, 10 000 Zagreb (tel: 456-9964; fax: 456-9988, 455-1795).

Ministry of Health, Ulica baruna Trenka 6, 10 000 Zagreb (tel: 459-1333, 460-7555; fax: 467-7076).

Ministry of Homeland War Veterans, Park Stara Tresnjevka 4, 10 000 Zagreb (tel: 365-7888; fax: 365-7852).

Ministry of Immigration, Savska cesta 41/12, 10 000 Zagreb (tel: 617-6011; fax: 617-6161).

Ministry of Internal Affairs, Savska 39, 10 000 Zagreb (tel: 612-2111; fax: 612-2036, 612-2452).

Ministry of Justice, Administration and Local Self-Government, Ul Republike Austrije 14, 10 000 Zagreb (tel: 371-0666; fax: 371-0772).

Ministry of Labour and Social Care, Prisavlje 14, 10 000 Zagreb (tel: 616-9111; fax: 616-9200).

Ministry of Maritime Affairs, Transportation and Communication, Prisavlje 14, 10 000 Zagreb (tel: 616-9111; fax: 615-6292, 619-6473).

Ministry of Physical Planning, Building Construction and Housing, Ulica Republike Austrije 20, Zagreb (tel: 378-2444; fax: 377-2555).

Ministry of Privatisation and Property Management, Gajeva 30a, 10 000 Zagreb (tel: 456-9103; fax: 456-9133).

Ministry of Public Works, Reconstruction and Construction, Ul Vladimira Nazora 61, 10 000 Zagreb (tel: 378-4500; fax: 378-4598).

Ministry of Science and Technology, Trg J. J. Strossmayera 4, 10 000 Zagreb (tel: 459-4444; fax: 459-4469; e-mail: office@science.hr; internet site: http://www.mzt.hr).

Ministry of Trades and Small and Medium Businesses, Ksaver 200, 10 000 Zagreb (tel: 469-8300; fax: 469-8310).

Parliament of the Republic of Croatia, Trg Sv Marka 6 i 7, 10 000 Zagreb (tel: 456-9222; fax: 492-0384).

Other useful addresses
Association of Croatian Hoteliers, Hotel Kvarner, Park 1 maja 4, 51410 Opatija (tel: 711-415; fax: 711-415).

British Embassy, Commercial Section, Vlaska 121 (3rd Floor), PO Box 454, 10000 Zagreb (tel: 455-5310; fax: 455-1685).

Croatian Embassy (USA), 2343 Massachusetts Avenue, NW, Washington DC 20008 (tel: 202-588-5899; fax: 202-588-8936; e-mail: webmaster@croatiaemb.org).

Croatia

Croatian Guarantee Agency, Ilica 49, 10 000 Zagreb (tel: 484-6622; fax: 484-6612).

Croatian Investment Promotion agency, World Trade Centre Building, Avenija Dubrovnik 15, 10000 Zagreb (tel: 655-4558; fax; 655-4563).

Croatian Privatisation Fund, Lueiaeeva 6, 10000 Zagreb (tel: 456-9119, 459-6377; fax: 456-9140, 611-5568; e-mail: croatia.eoi@hfp.hr; internet site: http://www.hfp.hr).

Croatian Securities Exchange Commission, Bogovieeva 3, 10 000 Zagreb (tel: 481-1407; fax: 481-1507).

Croatian Shipbuilding Co Ltd (Hrvatska brodogradnja-Jadranbrod), Av V Holjevca 20, 10020 Zagreb (fax: 652-8420).

Economic Development Corporations – see Ministry of Development and Reconstruction.

Information Department, Ilica 1a, 10000 Zagreb (tel: 455-6455; fax: 455-7827; internet site: http://www.hic.hr/english/index.htm).

Luka Ploce (second largest Croatian Port), Trg Kralja Tomislava 21, 20340 Ploce (tel: 067-9601; fax: 067-9836; email: luka-ploce@du.tel.hr).

State Agency for Deposit Insurance and Bank Rehabilitation, Jurisiceva 1, 10 000 Zagreb (fax: 481-3222: fax: 481-1907; e-mail: dragbank@zg.tel.hr).

State Bureau of Standards and Measures, Ul grada Vukovara 78, 10 000 Zagreb (tel: 610-6111; 610-9324; e-mail: pisarnica@dznm.hr).

State Bureau of Statistics, Ilica 3, 10 000 Zagreb (tel: 480-6111; fax: 481-7666; e-mail: ured@agram.dzs.hr).

Zagrebacki Velesajem (Zagreb fairs, exhibitions and conferences), Dubrovacka Avenija 2, Zagreb (fax: 520-6430).

Zagreb Stock Exchange, Ksaver 208, 41000 Zagreb (tel: 455-1866; fax: 455-1118; internet site: http://www.zse.hr).

Internet sites

Croatian Business Pages: http://www.hrvatska.com

Croatian Government: http://www.vlada.hr/english/contents.html

HINA, Croatian News Agency: http://www.hina.hr/nws-bin/ehot.cgi

Croatian Heritage Foundation: http://www.matis.hr/english/index.php

Hrvatska Radio Televizija: http://www.hrt.hr

Hrvatski Telekom: http://www.ht.hr

Cuba

KEY FACTS

Official name: República de Cuba (Republic of Cuba)

Head of State: President of the Council of State Dr Fidel Castro Ruz (since 1959; re-elected 6 Mar 2003)

Head of government: President of the Council of State Dr Fidel Castro Ruz

Ruling party: Partido Comunista de Cuba (PCC) (Cuban Communist Party)

Area: 110,860 square km

Population: 11.91 million (2004)

Capital: Havana

Official language: Spanish

Currency: Cuban peso (Cu$) and Cuban Convertible peso (CUC) both = 100 centavos (NB From 14 Nov 2004, the US dollar can only be used to convert to CUC)

Exchange rate: CUC0.92 per US$ (Oct 2005) (a further 10% surcharge is imposed on all US$ transactions converting to CUC, which was revalued by 8% in April 2005). It cannot be used for local payments.

GDP per capita: US$2,900 (PPP, 2004)

GDP real growth: 3.00% (2004)

Labour force: 5.72 million (2004)

Unemployment: 2.50% (2004)

Inflation: 3.00% (2004)

Balance of trade: -US$3.19 billion (2004)

Foreign debt: US$12.09 billion (2004)

Visitor numbers: 1.80 million (annually)*

* estimated figure

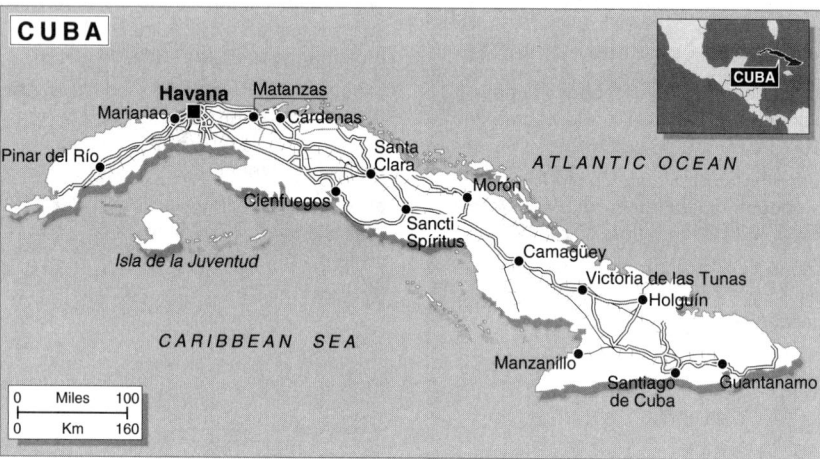

Two thousand and four saw Cuban President Fidel Castro Ruz fall. Not the fall that successive US governments had predicted in the 1960s and 1970s however. The 77-year old dictator, who has been in power for 46 years, underwent three hours and fifteen minutes of surgery to repair his knee-cap, which was fractured in eight places. Castro had fallen off stage during a rally in October 2004, but moved quickly to dampen speculation about his overall health. In a statement written by Castro himself, he assured the Cuban people that he was fine, adding 'I will not lose contact with you'. A further official government statement was issued soon after, in which the president was said to be in good form: 'his general health is good, and spirits are excellent'.

Still standing... but for how long?

Rumours of the Caribbean strong man's poor health have been circulating for years and the televised fall seemed merely to confirm such speculation. But in late 2004 Castro astonished many when he rose out of his wheelchair to stand with the aid of a metal cane during a meeting with President Hu Jintao of China. Then, the following month, apparently inspired by fellow leftist Hugo Chávez of Venezuela, he repeated the trick, this time remaining on his feet unaided for several minutes. Owing to his ultra-hands-on style in Cuba, rumours of his declining health continued to circulate on the island throughout 2005. The *Associated Press* (*AP*) recently reported that Castro has Parkinson's disease, reviving an old rumour.

Though Castro himself has continued to deny the speculation as press tittle tattle and the work of 'imperialist' plotters desperate to bring him down, attention has increasingly turned to his most likely successor, his brother Raúl. Raúl Castro Ruz, as second secretary of the Partido Comunista de Cuba (PCC) (Communist Party of Cuba), is first in the country's constitutional line of succession and first vice president of the governing Council of State and Council of Ministers.

Given that he is obviously being groomed for the role as eventual successor to his brother, his remarks in interviews are useful indicators of Cuba's future course, both in terms of domestic and foreign policy. Regarded as more of a hardliner than his older brother, he was quoted in 2005 as saying that 'the United States should normalise relations with Cuba while Fidel... is still alive' claiming that it could get 'more difficult' for Washington to do this at a later date: 'It would be in imperialism's interest to try, with our irreconcilable differences, to normalise relations as much as possible during Fidel's life'.

Domestic issues

In February 2005 Castro introduced a nationwide smoking ban in public places.

The new legislation is designed to raise life expectancy to 80 years by 2010, from the present 75–76 year average. A huge amount of government resources have been dedicated to non-smoking campaigns over the years. Even Castro himeslf, whose fondness for Cohiba cigars once prompted the US Central Intelligence Agency (CIA) to attempt to assassinate him by means of an expolding cigar, kicked the habit back in 1986. Smoking is now restricted to designated areas in nightspots and restaurants, but many Cubans have expressed their intention to violate the law. This is hardly surprising given that approximately 40 per cent of the 11.2 million population are believed to have a smoking habit.

Toward the end of 2005 Castro launched Operation July 26, a new resource-sharing project named after his successful political manoeuvering of the late 1950s. The new 'revolution' is aimed at exposing corrupt officials and members of the 'new rich'. Thoughout November thousands of young men and women were seen taking over petrol stations as the first tenet of the project, an overhaul of the fuel distribution system, began. Busloads of young people mobilised by the government were also reported to be operating in neighbourhoods across the island, to enforce energy saving regulations. Equipped with a clipboard and a set of energy saving lightbulbs the youngsters – of student age – distribute the lightbulbs while taking a census of the electrical appliances in each household, using a grading scale of 'well off', 'normal' and 'poor'.

Cubanomics

As a relic of an old ideological system, Cuba's economy remains unique. Prior to the collapse of the Soviet Union in the early 1990s Castro's Cuba relied upon exports of grain and other basic foodstuffs from its senior ally. When former Soviet Union president Mikhail Gorbachev cut economic aid and downsized a series of preferential trade deals with Cuba in the late 1980s however, the Caribbean country went into meltdown. But according to Castro and the president of the island's central bank, Francisco Soberón, Cuba's economy is back on the up: 'the most important sectors of the economy, with the exception of sugar, are doing well' he told the *Financial Times* of London (*FT*). Mr Soberón also claimed that the current account was positive in fiscal year 2004, for the first time since 1993, though he declined to provide figures to support his claim.

Government sources, not always the most reliable information source in Cuba, suggest that the surplus stood at US$176 million in 2004, as opposed to deficits of US$277 million (2002) and US$132 million (2003). Cuba remains heavily indebted to international creditors however, with debts of approximately US$13 billion outstanding. The country's short-term borrowing record is also poor. The government revalued the traditional peso by 7 per cent in March 2005, re-adjusting its value to 25 to the US dollar. The convertible peso (used for all foreign transactions, and by visitors), a remnant of the rejection of dollarisation in 2004, was also revalued, by 8 per cent in April.

Since 2003 the economy has become increasingly centralised under the auspices of the government in Havana, as market reforms instituted in the 1990s have been rolled back. However, a considerable number of external economic observers have critcised the government for chopping and changing its regulatory and monetary procedure, claiming that such policy shifts are depressing productivity in crucial areas of the economy. In line with such criticisms, the agricultural and sugar cane sectors struggled throughout 2005, as the country continued to endure a persistent drought.

On the surface, Cuba's macroeconomic fundamentals appear sound. Growth in real GDP has risen in every year since 2002 and stood at 3 per cent in 2004. Per capita GDP has also risen relatively swiftly throughout the decade of the 2000s, to reach US$2,900 by 2004. Inflation would also appear to be moving in the right direction. After rocky years of high upward pressure of 5.1 per cent in 2000 and 7.1 per cent (2003), a rate of 3 per cent per annum is good news. Beneath the veneer of improving economic statistics though, lurks a growing problem of bureaucratic paper trails and thick red tape induced by increasing centralisation, which has resulted in economic activity being held back. Consequently, crucial services such as medical care, pension provision and public transport have all suffered.

Foreign relations: a mixed bag

In January 2005 foreign minister Felipe Perez Roque announced that Cuba had resumed all formal diplomatic relations with Europe. High-level diplomatic correspondence had previously been severely limited for over a year and a half, following a clampdown on dissidents and a series of executions ordered by the Cuban government in the spring of 2003. Relations with France, Germany, Britain, Italy, Austria, Portugal and Sweden were normalised in the first week of January. Diplomatic ties were restored with the Czech Republic, Poland, Slovakia and the Netherlands soon after.

Historically poor, Cuba's relations with the United States took another jolt in May 2005, when Castro accused Washington of harbouring terrorist Luis Posada Carriles, supposedly 'Latin America's bin Laden'. Self-confessed militant Carriles' transfer by sea to Miami led the Cuban president to expose what he called the 'terrorist structure' operating in Florida. A thaw in relations appeared when Havana, for the first time in several decades, accepted a US aid package in the wake of destruction wrought by Hurricane Wilma. The US state department formally announced that a three-member disaster assessment team would visit the Cuban capital in October. After one step forward however, two were taken in the opposite direction. In November 2005 the *Financial Times* of London (*FT*) reported that the US government had established an office for reconstruction during transition within the State Department, co-ordinated with the Department of Defense. The *FT*

KEY INDICATORS — Cuba

	Unit	2000	2001	2002	2003	2004
Population	m	11.14	11.18	11.20	11.56	11.91
Gross domestic product (GDP)	US$bn	19.20	18.47	25.90	26.58	34.55
GDP per capita	US$	1,700	1,651	2,300	2,300	2,900
GDP real growth	%	5.6	3.0	1.4	2.6	3.0
Inflation	%	5.1	0.5	2.6	7.1	3.0
Exports (fob) (goods)	US$m	1,800.0	1,762.0	1,800.0	1,800.0	2,104.0
Imports (fob) (goods)	US$m	3,400.0	4,838.0	4,800.0	4,800.0	5,296.0
Balance of trade	US$m	-1,600.0	-3,076.0	-3,000.0	-3,000.0	-3,192.0
Exchange rate	per US$	1.00	1.00	1.00	1.00	1.00

also revealed that a 'nation-building exercise' may be employed during any future transition period following Castro's exit from the scene.

Castro has been active in securing natural resource deals with ideologically friendly nations over recent years and this trend continued in 2005. The Cuban president met with his foreign policy protégé Chávez, the man thought to be heir to Castro's title as chief irritant to Washington, in February. The two presidents completed an energy pact complete with discounted oil, of US$750 million. Cuba and China have also become more closely aligned, the latter having agreed to pump US$500 million into the Caribbean island's nickel industry.

Human rights: an empty bag?

Human rights in Cuba have been in a state of disrepair since Castro came to power in 1959. The status quo in the country was apparently confirmed in April by the decision of the United Nations' Human Rights Commission to keep Cuba under scrutiny.

But on 21 May, in what James Cason, head of the US diplomatic mission to Cuba called 'an exercise in grassroots democracy', some two hundred Cuban dissidents demonstrated in Havana. Given the swiftness usually employed by the authorities in crushing such demonstrations in previous years, May's gathering was unique in that it went ahead at all. Chants of 'freedom, freedom, freedom' echoed throughout a small area of the city as a 'victory for Cuba's democratic forces' was notched up, in the words of Martha Beatriz Roque, leader of the Assembly for the Promotion of Civil Society in Cuba.

Old habits die hard for the Cuban authorities, however. Prior to the gathering, Cuba denied visas to many European politicians and Cuban-American activists. Havana also expelled four European deputies who had entered the island a week before the meeting. The fact that the meeting was allowed to take place at all though is a positive development. In years gone by such an expression of dissatisfaction with the regime would have led to imprisonment for the perpetrators. One must wonder whether Castro's new approach is just a token gesture, designed to placate a small simmering of discontent in pockets of the country's population.

Castro's iron fist was in evidence in December 2005 when he barred the departure of three Cuban recipients of the EU Sakharov prize, awarded for 'freedom of thought'. The 'Ladies in White' as they came to be known, were refused permission to leave the country for the trip. The EU must have wondered just what 'constructive engagement' with Cuba entailed after the aging dictator went on to accuse European nations of being 'corrupt exploitative hypocrites' who established a preferential trade system based on colonialism which 'they keep in place today'. So much for the rapprochement earlier in the year!

Outlook

Cuba remains in the grasp of its ageing President Castro. How much time the eternal thorn in Washington's side has left at the helm of the Caribbean country remains to be seen. Despite a typically dramatic recovery from serious surgery, Castro is a frail old man, not the once dynamic, youthful figure capable of making three hour speeches in front of UN members. Until he departs however, Castro will no doubt continue to centralise, dictate and decide for all of Cuba's 11.9 million citizens. Barring ill health, the charismatic yet flawed leader will still be in power, his 47th year, come the end of 2006.

Risk assessment

Politics	Stable
Economy	Stable
Regional stability	Stable

COUNTRY PROFILE

Historical profile
1492 Christopher Columbus landed in Cuba and claimed the island for Spain.
1511 Diego Columbus, son of Christopher, settled the island. Spanish settlers established sugar plantations and exploited slaves from West Africa.
1514 The city of Havana was founded.
1607 Havana was named the capital of Cuba.
1762–64 Havana was captured by the British but was returned to Spain under the Treaty of Paris.
1868–78 The first war of independence ended in a truce after Spain promised reforms and greater autonomy – which were never fulfilled.
1886 Slavery was abolished.
1895–98 José Marti led a second war of independence; the US declared war on Spain.
1898 Spain was defeated and gave up all claims to Cuba, ceding it to the US.
1901 The constitution of the Republic of Cuba, modelled on the US constitution, was adopted.
1902 Cuba was officially granted independence from the US. Tomas Estrada Palma became its first president. However the US retained the right to intervene in Cuban domestic affairs.
1925 The Partido Comunista de Cuba (PCC) (Cuban Communist Party) was founded.
1933 Fulgencio Batista took power in a coup détat.
1934 The US abandoned its right to intervene in Cuban internal affairs.
1940 A new constitution was promulgated.
1944 Batista retired from office.
1952 Batista seized power again, backed by the US government. His regime was oppressive and corrupt.
1956 Fidel Castro began a guerrilla war against Batista's dictatorship.
1958 US backing for Batista was withdrawn.
1959 The Cuban revolution concluded when Castro's revolutionaries defeated the Cuban army and assumed power, founding a socialist state.
1960 All US owned businesses in Cuba were nationalised without compensation; the US broke off diplomatic.
1961 The US sponsored an unsuccessful military invasion, by Cuban exiles, at the Bay of Pigs. Cuba was declared a Communist state and Castro allied it to the USSR.
1962 Castro's fear of US aggression resulted in the Cuban missile crisis when he agreed to deploy USSR nuclear missiles on Cuba. The US blockaded Cuba, published evidence of the missiles and US President Kennedy gave an ultimatum that they be removed or the US would bomb Cuba. The crisis was resolved when the USSR agreed and withdrew the missiles, and in return the US closed its missile sites in Turkey. The US imposed a full trade embargo on Cuba.
1976 A new constitution created a National Assembly, which held its first session and elected Fidel Castro Ruz as president.
1989 The USSR began to breakdown and the trade in Cuban sugar for subsidised oil collapsed.
1991 Soviet troops left Cuba. The economy fell into depression.
1993 To ameliorate the economy some market reforms were adopted and the US dollar was made an official currency alongside the Cuban peso.
1998 US restrictions on remittances are eased.
2000 US approves the sale of food and medicines to Cuba.
2001 The first shipment in 40 years of US exported food arrived.
2002 The UN criticised Cuba for its poor civil rights. It was announced that at least 71 of Cuba's 156 sugar refineries were to be scrapped.
2003 A crackdown on dissidents resulted in international condemnation as 75

Cuba

people were imprisoned. The EU broke off diplomatic contacts.
2004 In January, the official exchange rate of Cu$1 per US$ replaced the convertible rate of Cu$21 per US$. In July, the US tightened restrictions on visits and money remittances to Cuba. From 8 November, the US dollar ceased to be legal tender and there was a 10 per cent commission for converting dollars to pesos.
2005 EU diplomatic relations with Cuba were re-established. In May, President Hugo Chávez of Venezuela and Fidel Castro signed a co-operation agreement; Cuba will supply doctors and medical treatment to Venezuela in exchange for crude oil at a preferential price.

Political structure
Constitution
The 1979 constitution gives all legislative power to the Asamblea Nacional de Poder Popular (National Assembly of People's Power) which runs local and central government. An amendment in 2002 made the Partido Comunista de Cuba (PCC) (Cuban Communist Party) the permanent party of government.
Form of state
Marxist-Leninist republic.
The executive
The president and the Consejo de Estado (Council of State) and council of ministers are appointed by the national assembly and drawn from the state (communist) party.
The council of state is the highest-ranking executive institution and is made up of a president, first vice president, and five vice presidents and 30 members. It has legislative powers when the national assembly is in recess. The council runs foreign trade and foreign relations, draws up the draft budget and is responsible for the general organisation of the revolutionary armed forces.
National legislature
The national assembly has 609 members elected for a five-year term from a closed list of PCC members. Its chief role is to approve laws put forward by the council of state.
According to the constitution the national assembly is the 'supreme organ of state power and represents and expresses the sovereign will of all the working people'. Its role includes approving laws, discussing and approving the state budget and supervising other official bodies.
Legal system
While the constitution provides for independent courts it explicitly subordinates the courts to state control. The national assembly chooses all judges. The People's Supreme Court is the highest judicial body; it oversees a system of regional tribunals and is accountable to the national assembly.
Last elections
March 2003 (presidential election by National Assembly); 19 January 2003 (parliamentary).
Results: Parliamentary: 609 pro-government candidates stood for exactly the same number of seats in the National Assembly and were elected unopposed; turnout was over 97 per cent.
Next elections
January 2008 (parliamentary); 2008 (presidential election by National Assembly).

Political parties
Ruling party
Partido Comunista de Cuba (PCC) (Cuban Communist Party)
Main opposition party
There is no opposition party.

Population
11.91 million (2004)
Ethnic make-up
The Cuban population is a product of the mix of four cultural groups: the indigenous people, Spaniards, Africans and Asians.
Mulatto (51 per cent), white (37 per cent), black (11 per cent), Chinese (1 per cent).
Religions
Many Cubans are agnostic or atheist, while unofficial estimates are of 75,000–100,000 practising Catholics. There is a smaller Protestant community. Practices based on African religions are reported to be increasing in popularity.

Education
Public expenditure on education amounts to 8.7 per cent of GDP. There is sustained investment in education with incentive rewards for excellence in pupils, teachers and schools. The education system promotes inclusively for learning outcomes and curriculum development between teachers and students.
Education is free at all levels. It is based on the Communist principle of combining learning with manual labour. Day nurseries and pre-school centres are available to all children after just six weeks. Primary schools are compulsory for six years until aged 12. Secondary schools are for 13- to 18-year-olds. State subsidies are available for workers returning to education to complete university courses.
Literacy rate: 97 per cent, adult rate (2003)
Compulsory years: 6 to 12.
Enrolment rate: 106 per cent gross primary enrolment, of the relevant age group (including re-enrolment); 81 per cent gross secondary enrolment, of the relevant age group (World Bank).
Pupils per teacher: 12 in primary schools.

Health
The total expenditure on health is around 7 per cent of GDP, of which government spending was typically about 90 per cent, There are approximately 260 hospitals and over 400 clinics that provide full and free medical services in all regions of the country. However, current US economic embargoes limit access to internationally purchased branded medical supplies.
In 2005 US$100 million was allocated to invest in the pharmaceutical industry. Generic medicines have become a major export item.
HIV prevalence: 0.1 per cent aged 15–49 in 2003 (World Bank)
Life expectancy: 76.9 years (2003)
Fertility rate/Maternal mortality rate: 1.6 births per woman (2003); maternal mortality 27 per 100,000 live births (World Bank).
Birth rate/Death rate: 12 births per 1,000 population; seven deaths per 1,000 population (2003).
Infant mortality rate: 6.5 per 1,000 live births (World Bank)
Head of population per physician/bed: 3.8 doctors per 1,000 people.

Welfare
In a 2005 economist reported to Castro that the minimum monthly income to survive in Cuba was Cu$300 (US$14.4). The minimum monthly wage was increased to Cu$225 (US$10.8), and monthly pension payments to CU$150 (US$7.2) benefiting 54 per cent of state employees. Wages in other sectors grew in line with these increases. Pensions and social assistance were also increased by 50 pesos a month. The 1976 constitution guarantees all Cubans the right and duty to have a job, while the state provides basic support for the aged, the disabled and others unable to work. Although the principle of full employment stands unchanged, the government has admitted that unemployment does indeed exist.

Main cities
Havana (estimated population 2.4 million in 2004), Santiago de Cuba (554,400), Camagüey (354,400), Holguín (319,300), Guantánamo (274,300), Santa Clara (251,800), Bayamo (191,100), Pinar del Río (180,400), Cienfuegos (171,500).

Languages spoken
The Spanish in use in Cuba is more Latin American than Castillian and many words are quite different from the Spanish used in Spain. Quite often the endings of words are dropped, shortened nouns are used and slang is prevalent. The further south

in Cuba, the more pronounced the accent.

English is quite widely spoken, as it is the main foreign language taught in schools.

Official language/s

Spanish

Media

The government runs all the media in Cuba and uses it as an important tool for reinforcing socialist ideals as well as for entertainment and education.

Cuba has two news agencies, the Agencia de Información Nacional (AIN) (National News Agency) for domestic news and Prensa Latina (PL), founded in 1959 to give what the government sees as the true picture of life in Latin America.

Press

Around 20 independent news agencies have sprung up since 1990 in spite of the interdiction by the constituion.

Law 88 criminalises the transfer of information to the US government indirectly or directly, or collaboration with foreign media. Additionally, the government strictly regulates Internet access. Only government officials, selected researchers, diplomats and tourists may access the web.

Dailies: There are many local and national newspapers published in both Spanish and English. The main newspapers include Havana *Granma Diario*, *Nueva Prensa Cubana*, *Granma Internacional*, *Tribuna de la Havana*, *Negocios en Cuba*, *Opciones*, *Juventud Rebelde*, *El Habanero* and *Cuba Ahora*. The two national daily tabloids are *Trabajadores* and the afternoon publication *Juventud Rebelde*.

Business: *El Economista de Cuba* published in Spanish.

Periodicals: Include *Marces*, *Orbe*, *Habanera* and *Cuba Internacional*.

Broadcasting

Services controlled by the Instituto Cubano de Radio Fusión (Cuban Institute of Radio).

Radio: Radio Rebelde, has a racy style for news, entertainment and sport and is considered the most popular, although there are no published audience surveys. Radio Reloj is possibly one of the most idiosyncratic radio stations in the world. Following a style which was established well before the 1959 revolution, it consists of short announcements, news headlines and time checks backed by the ticking of a metronome. Radio Havana Cuba, broadcasting on short-wave in Spanish, French, English, Portuguese, Guaraní, Quechua and Creole, carries Cuba's views to the Americas and Africa.

Television: Apart from Cuban programmes ranging from soap operas to university education, which account for 60 per cent of programming, the two television channels show a wide range of imported material including recent American films and serials.

Advertising

Advertising facilities are limited and state-controlled and generally not available to foreign companies.

Economy

Cuba began opening up its state-run economy to external investment after the collapse of the Soviet Union in 1991 as shortages of supplies, such as fuel, spare parts, fertilisers and herbicides, crippled Cuba's sugar production and the industrial sector, and caused a significant drop in GDP growth. The US trade embargo (in place since 1962), and politically inspired bureaucracy, have prevented sufficient foreign direct investment (FDI) for the economy to develop to its full potential. As a result, the economy has become increasingly reliant on tourism, which is subject not only to external and incidental forces but also internal political dogma. Since 2003 a severe drought, several hurricanes and the ongoing US-Cuban antagonism have impeded the sector's growth, while the government has reigned in joint foreign and Cuban domestic commercial initiatives in an attempt to lessen the effect of black-market dealings in foreign exchange.

Remittances, sent by Cuban exiles (mainly in Miami), which are estimated to bring the island over US$1 billion a year, were curtailed by US laws from August 2004. Cuban Americans are now only allowed to visit Cuba once every three years, this is to stem the outflow of money from America to Cuba. This has serious implications for Cuba's cash flow and economy, which was knocked further by an estimated US$2.4 billion worth of damage caused, between them, by Hurricanes Charley in August 2004 and Dennis in July 2005. Government figures show the economy grew by 7.3 per cent in the first half of 2005 and is projected to rise to 9.0 per cent by the end of the year. The growth is based on increases in several sectors including ferrous metallurgy at 15.5 per cent, non-ferrous metallurgy at 9.2 per cent, construction 8.2 per cent, communications sector 7.0 per cent and the food industry at 3.6 per cent.

Two currencies exist in Cuba; all local people use the Cuban peso (Cu$) while a convertible peso (CUC) is used for international trade and by foreign visitors. In March 2005 the convertible peso was re-valued by 8 per cent against foreign currencies and broke parity with the US dollar. The parity had existed since the convertible peso was created in 1994; the devaluation of the US dollar meant an increase in Cuba's expenses.

External trade

The balance of payments is reliant on foreign currency earnings from tourism, remittances from Cubans abroad and sugar. The US trade embargo continues to have a negative effect on trade in general, although Cuba has been bolstered in 2004–05 by trade agreements with China and Venezuela.

Cuba has a trade co-operation protocol with the 15-member Caribbean Community and Common Market (Caricom). In 2003, Cuba formally withdrew its application to join the EU's Cotonou trade accord.

Imports

Domestic companies require a licence to import certain goods, the number of which has decreased from 192 to 89 between 2003–05. The withdrawal of licences may be a way for the government to control imports, and its trade deficit, however the mechanism is also regarded as heavy-handed.

Imports comprise petroleum, machinery and equipment, food, chemicals.

Main sources: Spain (15.4 per cent total, 2004), Venezuela (13.7 per cent), US (11.5 per cent), China (8.0 per cent), Canada (6.6 per cent), Italy (6.5 per cent), Mexico (4.9 per cent), Germany (4.2 per cent)

Exports

Government figures show that exports of goods and services grew by 26.3 per cent in the first six months of 2005, compared with the same period in 2004.

Principal exports in 2005 included sugar, nickel, tobacco, fish, bio-technical medical products, citrus and coffee.

Main destinations: The Netherlands (23.5 per cent total, 2004), Canada (21.9 per cent), China (8.3 per cent), Russia (7.8 per cent), Spain (6.6 per cent)

Agriculture

Farming

The agricultural sector contributes approximately 7 per cent to GDP. Approximately 28 per cent of the total land area is cultivated. The economy has been affected by a severe drought that lasted from 2003–05 and cost the country an estimated US$1.2 billion. The drought caused the sugar harvest to drop by about a third from an average 34.8 million tonnes to 22.9 million tonnes. A recovery in 2004 was slow with a harvest of 24 million tonnes. In January 2005 it was announced that the growing season would be shorter than usual and that the expected harvest would be smaller than 2004.

Sugar is Cuba's most important export crop, however since its collapse as a top cash crop, there has been a concerted effort to diversify. The sugar industry is undergoing restructuring to make the production more efficient and identify new markets. In 2002 over 70 of the 156 sugar refineries in Cuba were decommissioned with some 100,000 workers laid off. Half of Cuba's 3.5 million hectares (ha) of sugar cane fields were re-utilised to produce other crops, particularly foodstuffs for domestic consumption and reduce the need for imports.

Two new cocoa processing plants with a capacity of 45,000 tonnes are planned to provide exports of high quality cocoa butter.

Approximately 95 per cent of Cuba's coffee plantations are the highly prized arabica bean. Coffee exports should be enhanced by the refurbishment of seven processing mills.

Cuba has begun developing organic farming, and there are over 100,000 small-to medium-sized organic farms reflecting the government's commitment to the 'greening of Cuba'.

Crop production in 2004 included: 24.0 million tonnes (mt) sugar cane, 1.0mt cereals in total, 716,000 tonnes (t) rice, 370,000t maize, 685,000t cassava, 330,000t potatoes, 490,000t sweet potatoes, 320,000t bananas, 800,000t plantains, 140,000t yams, 130,000t pulses, 110,595t coconuts, 16,000t green coffee, 1,600t cocoa beans, 808,000t citrus fruit, 645,000t tomatoes, 235,000t mangoes, 38,000t garlic, 17,377t oilcrops, 34,494t tobacco, 70,000t chillies & peppers, 125,000t papayas, 2.7mt fruit in total, 3.9mt vegetables in total. Livestock production included: 211,065t meat in total, 70,000t beef, 95,500t pig meat, 10,235t lamb & goat meat, 34,250t poultry, 79,000t eggs, 610,000t milk, 7,200t honey.

Fishing
Catches have fallen since the mid-1980s. The contraction of fin fish catches by the deep sea fleet, partly as a result of changes in fishing agreements, has been largely responsible. Cuba is investing considerable resources in shrimp farming, but production has not been commercially significant.

Forestry
Forests cover around 2.3 million hectares (ha), around 15 per cent of the total land area. Since 1990 forest cover has increased by an average of 1.27 per cent per annum or 28,000ha.

Exports of timber products in 2003 amounted to US$285,000 and imports amounted to US$55.1 million.

Timber production in 2003 included: 2,636,000 cubic metre (cum) roundwood, 808,000cum industrial roundwood, 181,000cum sawnwood, 400,000cum sawlogs and veneer logs, 149,000cum wood-based panels, 1,828,000 cum wood fuel, 60,200t charcoal.

Industry and manufacturing
The industrial sector contributes approximately 37 per cent to GDP.

Cuba's free trade zones, especially those of Wajay and Mariel have attracted a number of foreign companies. Mariel, located 48.2km west of Havana, is likely to play an important role in the future, especially if trade opens with the US.

The Hola processing plant in Havana toasts and grinds coffee beans for export to the UK, Ukraine, Bulgaria, the Bahamas and Spain.

The cigar industry is significant, with production increasing substantially in the late-1990s and generating annual revenues of an estimated US$150 million.

Tourism
Cuba has turned to tourism as a source of much-needed foreign earnings. Despite the US embargo, the sector, which had been neglected since 1959, has shown a steady growth since the early 1990s. Government figures show the annual growth in 2004 was 8 per cent and bookings for 2005 are expected to reach 2,300,000. The majority of tourists come from Canada and the EU.

Four new hotels began operation in 2005, adding 1,921 more rooms to the international tourist sector.

The US dollar was adopted as a legal currency, for tourists only, in 1993 and all visitors were expected to pay for goods and services in dollars, or a peso that was linked to the dollar. However international condemnation of Cuba's action in imprisoning dissidents led to increasingly strained relations with the US and the dollar was dropped as legal tender in November 2004. A Cuban Convertible peso (CUC), for use in international trade, was introduced instead of the dollar. Bank notes are printed locally and have to be used by visitors after exchanging at the official rate. Any dollar/peso conversation attracts a 10 per cent tax. The euro has been accepted in major tourist resorts since 2002, although the exchange rate is set by the US dollar.

Tourist assets are state-owned. Some competitiveness and joint ventures with foreign companies have been allowed, however these have not proved palatable to the regime and such schemes have been scaled back. In 2004, the government reinforced control over the sector, ostensibly to curb corruption, and structural reforms have been introduced.

Mining
Mining contributes around 6 per cent to GDP. The island's extensive nickel and cobalt ore reserves, among the largest in the world, offer attractive large-scale mining opportunities. Cuba's rich mineral resources are open to foreign exploration and development.

Exploration for gold, silver and base metals is carried out by more than a dozen foreign firms in concession areas covering nearly a third of Cuba's national territory. Cuba has updated its mining legislation, bringing it into line with most other Latin American countries.

Nickel production has been boosted by the injection of Canadian capital and technology. Government figures for 2004–05 showed nickel production reached 35,000 tonnes and overtook sugar as Cuba's biggest merchandise export, earning US$545 million. Since 2000 Cuba has supplied over half the nickel China uses in the production of stainless steel, and to maintain supplies China agreed, in November 2004, to invest US$500 million in the nickel industry. Cuba intends to modernise its processing plants and continue exploration for other base and precious metals. More than half the production comes from the Comandante Pedro Sotto Alba processing plant at Moa Bay, jointly operated since 1994 by Sherritt (Canada) and a Cuban company, Compania General de Niquel (General Nickel Company). Cuba's two other operating nickel plants are being modernised with the help of export-linked revolving credits from Dutch, German and other foreign banks and trade houses.

Hydrocarbons
Proven reserves of crude oil totalled 750 million barrels in 2003. Government figures show oil production increased in 2004 by over 9 per cent to just over 60,000 barrels per day (bpd) of mostly heavy crude oil, while fuel consumption has been held in check. The island imports over half of its oil needs, mainly from Mexico and Venezuela.

In an agreement made in August 2005 Venezuela will provide Cuba with 90,000 barrels of crude oil a day under favourable terms, in exchange for Venezuelan access to Cuban healthcare opportunities. Domestic oil production accounts for 80 per cent of the country's electricity needs. Most of Cuba's production is from oil fields on land, however following the first offshore rig, financed jointly by Cuba and Spain, more rigs are planned. The government plans to become self sufficient in energy produced by domestic oil.

Cuba has an estimated 70 billion cubic metres of natural gas reserves.

Cuba does not produce or import coal.

Energy
Cuba has installed hydropower capacity of some 57.3MW in 176 power stations,

with an estimated 400MW of total potential capacity.
Electricity supplies have been erratic, with power failures experienced intermittently throughout the island, as a result of equipment failure. In 2005 the government announced the investment of US$100 million in a programme of maintenance and US$282 million to be invested in new equipment and materials. A refurbished electricity plant, converted to utilise natural gas and new generators are expected to provide an extra one million kilowatts of electricity.
There is an emphasis on energy conservation, with an increased use of bagasse (residue of sugar cane, burned to produce energy) as an oil substitute, expansion of electricity capacity and re-use of old windmills.

Banking and insurance
The Cuban banking sector has been transformed from a closed and highly centralised Soviet-style model to a diversified two-tier banking system.
In a bilateral agreement signed in 2005 Cuba opened a subsidiary of the Foreign Bank of Cuba in Caracas, Venezuela, while a subsidiary of the Industrial Bank of Venezuela has been approved to open in Cuba.

Central bank
Banco Central de Cuba (BCC)

Time
GMT minus four hours in summer, GMT minus five hours in winter (October – March).

Geography
Cuba is the largest island in the Caribbean, lying 150km south of Florida. Together with offshore islands and an archipelago of about 1,600 coral cays surrounding the main island, the country has an area of 110,860 square km. The largest offshore island is the Isla de la Juventud, formerly known as the Isla de Pinos, which covers 2,200 square km. Most of the long, thin main island consists of plains and low ranges of hills. The highest mountains are in the Sierra Maestra in the extreme south-east, where the Pico Real de Turquina rises to 1,974 metres.

Climate
Subtropical, with an annual mean temperature of 25.7 degrees Celsius (C) the average summer shade temperatures can rise to 30 degrees C and higher. November–April is the cooler, dry season with maximum temperatures peaking at around 26 degrees C. Trade winds and sea breezes cool the air; there are sudden, short showers in summer. The months of June, September and October–November usually bring hurricanes.

The north is wetter than the south and the south, in particularly Santiago Province, is much hotter than the north.
There is rainfall of up to 250mm a year in the mountains.
It can be humid between May and October with some heavy rain. Humidity averages 62 per cent. However, during September and October, humidity can reach 95 per cent.

Dress codes
Dress since the 1959 revolution has been casual. Cubans wear lightweight and loose-fitting clothes, and formal dress, such as a tie, is an extremely rare sight.

Entry requirements
Passports
Required by all. Passports should be valid for six months beyond period of stay. Visitors must register with immigration officials the day after arrival.

Visa
Required by all, except nationals of countries who have reciprocal visa-free agreements.
Business visas, valid for 90 days from issue, are only obtained through sponsorship by an appropriate Cuban government organisation. For sponsorship contact the relevant State Trading Organisation or the commercial office of a Cuban embassy. Without a sponsor a visa will not be issued and a tourist card does not provide local firms with the opportunity to trade with business visitors.
Tourist cards are provided by airlines and tour operators who are registered with Cubatur. Exit visas are required for visitors staying more than 90 days.

Prohibited entry
In November 2003, the US Congress approved maintaining travel restrictions on US citizens to Cuba, even though both the Senate and the House of Representatives earlier passed separate measures lifting the 40-year-old ban.

Currency advice/regulations
From 8 November 2004, the US dollar is no longer legal tender.
Currency can be exchanged at the airport or hotel for 'convertible pesos'. When departing, they can be converted back again.
Visitors with only US dollars on arrival, can obtain 'convertible pesos' for a 10 per cent fee.

Health (for visitors)
Mandatory precautions
A yellow fever vaccination certificate is required if arriving from an infected area.

Advisable precautions
Vaccinations are recommended for typhoid, hepatitis 'A', tetanus and polio, as well as malaria prophylaxis – mosquitoes are a problem outside Havana.

The water supply in most upmarket hotels is excellent but elsewhere water precautions should be taken. Bottled water is readily available.
Medical services are good and free to visitors in an emergency. Insurance is advisable in case repatriation is required. Resorts and major cities have international clinics for tourists but the US embargo often means branded medicines may not be available. An adequate supply of regularly administered medication should be carried.
A visitor admitted to hospital is likely to be tested for HIV/Aids and will be deported if found to be a carrier.

Hotels
The best hotels can be found in Havana and Varadero beach. Foreign currencies should be exchanged at official Cadeca outlets.
The practice of tipping is growing – restaurants 5–10 per cent.

Credit cards
Only credit cards which are not issued in the US (Visa, Eurocard, MasterCard, Access) are accepted, generally only at tourist sites.

Public holidays
Fixed dates
1 Jan (Liberation Day), 1 May (Labour Day), 25 Jul (Rebellion anniversary, three days), 10 Oct (Anniversary of the War of Independence), 25 Dec (Christmas Day).

Variable dates
Carnival: Havana (Feb); Varadero (late Jan/Feb); Trinidad and Santiago de Cuba (Jun).

Working hours
Banking
Mon–Fri: 0830–1200, 1330–1500; Sat: 0830–1030.
Banks in resorts tend to stay open longer. Banks and post offices do not accept Eurocheques or 'American Express' travellers' cheques.

Business
Mon–Fri: 0830–1230 and 1330–1630; some offices open alternate Saturdays between 0800–1700.

Government
Mon–Fri: 0830–1230, 1330–1730.

Shops
Shops in Cuba generally open from 1230–1930. Shops usually close every other Saturday.
Shops are normally closed on Sunday, except those in tourist areas. Resort shops and supermarkets often open seven days a week and their hours vary according to demand.
Pharmacies are open daily 0800–2000; those with 'turno permanente' signs are open 24 hours.

Cuba

Telecommunications
Postal services
Cuba has very few official mail collection boxes, so visitors are advised to post mail in a hotel, or at the airport.
Mobile phones
GSM 900 service available in main tourist areas and cities only.

Electricity supply
110V AC, 60 cycles
Most plugs in hotels are two-pin, flat-pin type, although some are the two-pin, round-pin variety.
Some electric shaver points can be 220/240V.
Lighting is usually of the screw in, rather than bayonet, type.

Social customs/useful tips
Foreign residents say there are few restrictions on foreign visitors, however, they advise against vociferous public criticism of the government.
Cuba has placed great emphasis sports and baseball, originally imported from the US, is the national sport with boxing vying as the most popular spectator sport.
Cubans address each other, and often foreign visitors, as *compañero* or *compañera*, and the informal *tu* form is often used when speaking Spanish.
Photographing airports and sensitive sites is forbidden and permission should be sought before photographing public or religious buildings.

Security
Although Cuba is considered to be a generally safe country, the usual precautions should be followed.
Keep to the main busy areas in the cities. Keep valuables and money belt out of sight. Avoid going out alone if possible, especially at night.

Getting there
Air
National airline: Cubana (Empresa Cubana) de Aviación.
International airport/s: Havana-José Marti (HAV), 25km from city, with duty-free shops, bank, tourist information hotel reservation and car hire.
Other airport/s: Santiago de Cuba, Varadero-Juan Gualberto Gómez (VRA), 12km from Cuba's main beach resort.
Airport tax: International departures US$25, not applicable to transit passengers.
Surface
Main port/s: Antilla, Cienfuegos, Guayabal, Havana, Mariel, Matanzas, Nuevitas, Santiago de Cuba.

Getting about
National transport
Air: Cubana operates domestic services to main centres. Internal flights (limited) generally arranged through Cubatur.
Road: The Central Highway (Autopista Nacional) runs for over 1,100km, virtually from end to end of the island and gives access to a network of local roads. Total road system exceeds 30,000km, at least 40 per cent surfaced although some roads/tracks may not be passable in wet weather.
Buses: Cross-country buses are cheap but timetables are unreliable, and the buses can be overcrowded. Coaches link main centres, although difficulties with bookings have been recorded.
Rail: Around 3,442km of public service track; railcars operate between Havana-Cienfuegos, Cardenas-Jaguey, and also Havana-Santiago de Cuba – some services on this route offer refreshments and air-conditioning. Railway stations in Cuba are immaculately clean – but timetables are often unreliable.
Water: Hydrofoils run twice daily from the southern port of Surgidero de Batananó to the Isla de la Juventud. There are also slower boats sailing three times a week, but a day trip is not possible using these.
City transport
Taxis: There are state and private taxi services, usually ordered through a hotel. Turistaxis have stands at tourist centres and can also be flagged down in the street. Payment for these taxis is in hard currencies and it is advisable to agree payment beforehand on either the meter or fixed-rate system. Taxis can also be hired for the day; for travel outside Havana, taxis or cars with drivers are cheap but scarce.
Taxis are available at the international airport to take visitors to Havana. In Havana shared taxis offer low, flat fares.
Buses, trams & metro: Services in towns are generally considered erratic, inexpensive but invariably crowded. Cubanacan buses are available for tours of cities.
Car hire
Car hire is the most reliable form of transport for covering larger distances. Modern cars are available and can be booked in advance via the Internet through Cubatur (www.cubatur.cu). Hired locally, the price may rise sharply outside airport, city or tourist areas. Chauffeur-driven vehicles are also available.
A valid driver's licence is necessary. Traffic drives on the right; seat belts are not compulsory and the blood alcohol limit is 80mg/100ml.
Speed limits: autopista 100kph; paved roads 90kph; dirt roads 60kph; urban roads 50kph (40kph near schools).
Petrol is relatively easy to obtain and is charged in hard currencies. Petrol comes in two grades: *especial* and regular. Both are leaded and as a rule only the dearer *especial* is available to tourists. It is sold at 24-hour Servi-Cupet and Oro Negro petrol stations.

BUSINESS DIRECTORY
The addresses listed below are a selection only. While World of Information makes every endeavour to check these addresses, we cannot guarantee that changes have not been made, especially to telephone numbers and area codes. We would welcome any corrections.

Telephone area codes
The international direct dialling code (IDD) for Cuba is +53, followed by the area code and subscriber's number:

Camaguey	32	Matanzas	52
Ciego de Avila	33	Manzanillo	23
Cienfuegos	432	Santiago de Cuba	226
Florencia	335	Pinar del Rio	82
Havana	7	Villa Clara	42

Useful telephone numbers
There is an efficient, almost omnipresent, police service, but officers are unlikely to speak English.
Police: 116 can be dialled from any call box.
Havanautos (24-hour breakdown service): 338176 or 338177.

Chambers of Commerce
Cámara de Comercio de la República de Cuba, Calle 21, esq. A No 661, Vedado, Havana (tel: 551-321; fax: 333-042; e-mail: bic@camara.com.cu).

Banking
Banco de Inversiones SA, 5ta Ave No 6802 e/ 68 y 70, Miramar, Havana (tel: 243-374/5; fax: 243-373; e-mail: bdi@bdi.colombus.cu).

Banco Exterior de España, Línea esq. a 2, El Vedado, Havana (tel: 334-560; fax: 334-559).

Banco Financiero Internacional SA, Línea No 1, Vedado, PO Box 4068, Havana 4 (tel: 333-003, 333-148; fax: 333-006).

Banco Internacional de Comercio SA, 20 de Mayo y Ayestarán, Apartado 6113, Plaza de la Revolución, Havana 6 (tel: 335-482/5484; fax: 335-112; e-mail: bicsa@bicsa.columbus.cu).

Banco Metropolitano SA, (successor of the international branch of the Banco Nacional de Cuba), Línea No 63 esq a M, Vedado, Plaza, Havana (tel: 553-116/7; fax: 334-241; e-mail: banmet@nbbm.columbus.cu).

Casas de Cambio SA (CADECA), Calle Aguiar No 411, e/ Obrapia y Lamparilla,

Habana Vieja, Havana (tel: 335-673; fax: 335-673; e-mail: cadeca@cadeca.columbus.cu).

Grupo Nueva Banca SA (NB), Calle 1ra, No 1406 e/ 14 y 16, Miramar, Havana (tel: 247-564/67; fax: 245-674; e-mail: nbanca@nbanca.columbus.cu).

The Netherlands Caribbean Banking, 5ta Avenida No 6407 esq a 76, Miramar, Havana (tel: 240-419/21; fax: 240-472).

Central bank
Banco Central de Cuba, PO Box 746, Cuba 402, Habana Vieja, Havana (tel: 338-003; fax: 666-601; e-mail: webmaster@bc.gov.cu).

Travel information
Cubamar, Paseo 306 esq a 15, Vedado, Havana (tel: 662-523.4; fax: 333-111; e-mail: cubamar@cubamar.mit.cma.net).

Cubana, Calle 23, No 64 esq Infanta, Vedado, Havana (tel: 334-949/50; fax: 333-323; e-mail: eca@iacc.3.get.cma.net).

Havanatur/Infotur, Calle Obispo 358, (e/ Habana y Compostella), Old Havana (tel: 614-881); Plaza de Martí, Santiago de Cuba (tel: 23-302).

Ministry of tourism
Ministerio de Turismo Calle 19, No 710, Entre Paseo y A, Vedado, Havana (tel: 334 087; 334 318/9; fax: 334 086: Internet: www.cubatravel.cu; www.cubaweb.cu; www.ceniai.inf.cu).

National tourist organisation offices
Cubatur (Empresa de Turismo Nacional e Internacional), Calle F No 157 e/ Calzada y 9, Vedado, Havana (tel: 334-155/160; fax: 333-529, 333-104, 333-330; internet: www.cubatur.cu).

Ministries
Ministry of Agriculture, Avenida Independencia, entre Cornill y Sta Ana, Havana (tel: 845-770; fax: 335-086).

Ministry of Basic Industries, Avenida Salvador Allende 666, Havana (tel: 707-711; fax: 333-845).

Ministry of Communications, Plaza De la Revolucion 'José Martí', CP 10600, Havana (tel: 817-654).

Ministry of Construction, Avenida Carlos M de Cespedes y Calle 35, Havana (tel: 818-385; fax: 335-585).

Ministry of Construction Materials Industry, Calle 17,esq 0, Vevado, Havana (tel: 322-541; fax: 333-176).

Ministry of Culture, Calle 2, No 258, entre 11y 13, Vedado, Havana (tel: 399-945).

Ministry of Economy and Planning, 20 de Mayo y Ayestaran, Plaza de la Revolucion, Havana (tel: 816-444).

Ministry of Education, Obispo 160, Havana (tel: 614-888).

Ministry of Finance and Prices, Obispo 211, esq Cuba, Havana (tel: 604-111; fax: 620-252).

Ministry of the Fishing Industry, Avenida 5 y 248 Jaimenitas, Santa Fé, Havana (tel: 297-034).

Ministry of the Food Industry, Calle 41, No 4455, Playa, Havana (tel: 726-801).

Ministry of Foreign Affairs, Calzada 360, Vedado, Havana (tel: 324-074).

Ministry of Foreign Investment and Economic Co-operation, Calle 1, No 201, Vedado, Havana (tel: 736-661).

Ministry of Foreign Trade, Infanta 16, Vedado, Havana (tel: 786-230; fax: 786-234).

Ministry of Health, Calle 23, No 301, Vedado, Havana (tel: 322-561).

Ministry of Higher Education, Calle 23, No 565, esq aF, Vedado, Havana (tel: 552-314).

Ministry of the Interior, Plaza de la Revolucion, Havana (fax: 733-5261).

Ministry of Internal Trade, Calle Habana 258, Havana (tel: 625-790).

Ministry of Iron and Steel, Metallurgical and Electronic Industries, Avenida Rancho Boyeros y Calle 100, Havana (tel: 204-861).

Ministry of Justice, Calle 0, No 216, entre 23 y Humboldt, Vedado, Havana (tel: 326-319).

Ministry of Labour and Social Security, Calle 23, esq Calle P, Vedado, Havana (tel: 704-571).

Ministry of Light Industry, Empedrado 302, Havana (tel: 624-041).

Ministry of the Revolutionary Armed Forces, Plaza de la Revolución, Havana.

Ministry of Sugar, Calle 23, No 117, Vedado, Havana (tel: 305-061).

Ministry of Transport, Avenida Independencia y Tulipán, Havana (tel: 812-076).

Other useful addresses
British Embassy, Calle 34, No 702/4, Miramar, Havana (tel: 24-1049; fax: 24-9214).

CariFin (financial services Cuba), 311 and 313 22nd Street, Between 3rd and 5th Avanues, Mirimar, Havana (tel: 244-468/70; fax: 244-140; e-mail: havana@cdc.com.cu).

Compañía Fiduciaria SA (investments), Calle 36A No 121 apto, 2 e/ 1ra y 3ra, Miramar Playa, Havana (tel: 247-434/5; fax: 249-745; e-mail: nbfid@nbfid.columbus.cu).

Cuban Investment Company, PO Box 30003, North Vancouver, B.C. Canada V7H 2Y8 (tel: 00(1-604)929-9694; fax: 00(1-604)929-3694; e-mail: cubaninvestments@idmail.com).

Etecsa (Empresa de Telecomunicaciones de Cuba SA), Havana (tel: 452-221, 451-221; fax: 578-036).

Financiera Nacional SA (FINSA) (non-banking activities), Calle G No 301, esq a 13, Vedado, Havana (tel: 553-177, 338-863; fax: 662-232; e-mail: finsa@finsa.columbus.cu).

TIPS (Technological and Commercial Information Promotion System), National Office, No 302, Calle 30, Miramar, Havana (tel: 331-797/798; fax: 331-799).

Internet sites
Cubana: http://www.cubana.cu

Granma International (daily update in English, French, Spanish and Portuguese, with a summary in German): http://www.granma.cu

Cyprus

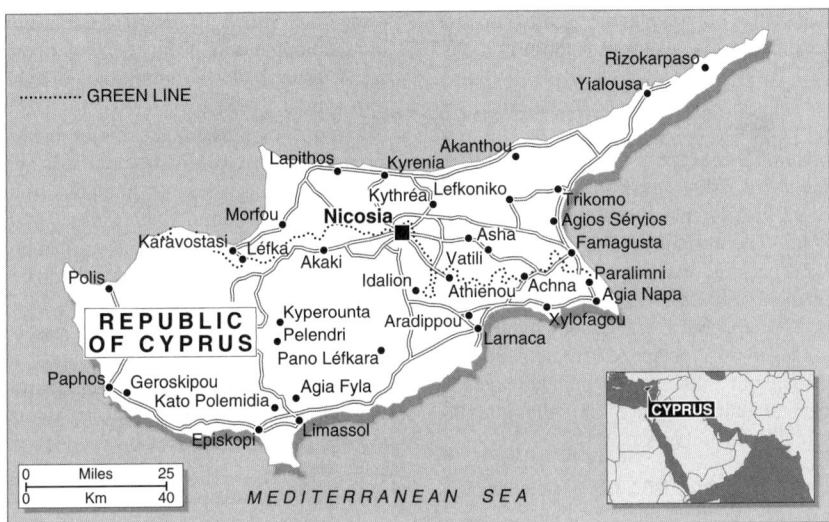

It was the Republic of Cyprus' (hereafter Cyprus) first full year as an EU member state in 2005, and despite its small size, it managed to play a significant role in one of the most contentious decisions to be made by the EU in decades – whether or not Turkey would be allowed to begin EU accession talks. Cyprus' first full year as an EU member was also marked by impressive progress in efforts to meet EU economic convergence targets. North of the Line of Control (LoC) dividing Cyprus from the self-declared independent Kuzey Kibris Türk Cumhuriyeti (Turkish Republic of Northern Cyprus) (TRNC) (hereafter northern Cyprus), it was a year of watershed elections.

Economic discipline and progress

It was a largely disciplined year for Cyprus, with GDP growth of around 4.0 per cent and inflation running at only 2.1 per cent. The budget deficit was also expected to come in under the 3.0 per cent ceiling prescribed by the EU. Generally, Cyprus' performance in its EU Convergence Programme, through which all new EU member states undertake economic reforms in order to bring their economies closer to existing EU norms, looked impressive.

EU diplomatic drama

In July 2005, Turkey signed a customs union with the EU, which theoretically paved the way for the beginning of accession talks later in the year. However, Turkey issued a caveat to the agreement, stating that its signature did not entail recognition of Cyprus. Moreover, Turkey refused to open its maritime and air ports to Cypriot traffic. Turkey had refused to recognise the Cypriot government since 1974 and in 1983 became the only country in the world to recognise the independence of Turkish northern Cyprus. Cyprus and some within the EU, including France, vocally took issue with this declaration. The customs union required that a joining country recognise all other signatory members. Cyprus demanded a robust response from the EU, including the setting of a deadline for Turkey to recognise its status as the only internationally recognised state on the island of Cyprus. Turkey protested in turn and it took the EU member states until September to publish an official response. The resultant communiqué stated that the EU 'regrets' Turkey's caveat and that it expected recognition of all member states as a 'necessary component of the accession process'. The Cypriot president, Tassos Papadopoulos, was reported to have been

KEY FACTS

Official name: Kypriaki Dimokratia-Kibris Cumhuriyeti (Republic of Cyprus)

Head of State: President Tassos Papadopoulos (DIKO) (elected 16 Feb 2003)

Head of government: President Tassos Papadopoulos

Ruling party: Coalition government: Dimokratikon Komma (DIKO) (Democratic Party), Anorthotikon Komma Ergazemenou Laou (AKEL) (Progressive party of the Working People) and Kinima Sosialdimokraton (KISOS) (Social Democrats Movement) (from Mar 2003)

Area: 9,251 square km

Population: 959,400 (2004)

Capital: Lefkosia (Nicosia); Greek spellings in use since 1995

Official language: Greek and Turkish

Currency: Cyprus pound (C£) = 100 cents

Exchange rate: C£0.48 per US$ (Oct 2005) (pegged to the euro; trades around C£0.58 per euro)

GDP per capita: US$19,202 (2004)

GDP real growth: 3.70% (2004); *4.0% (2005)

Labour force: 386,000 (2004)

Unemployment: 3.20% (2004)

Inflation: 2.30% (2004); *2.1% (2005)

Balance of trade: -US$4.04 billion (2004)

Foreign debt: US$7.33 billion (2004

* estimated figure

disappointed with the tone of the communiqué and the lack of a firm deadline for recognition. The attention of the EU's larger member states quickly transferred to other aspects of negotiations between the EU and Turkey over accession talks. The influence of smaller EU member states, even on an issue as emotive as territorial sovereignty, appeared to have found its natural limit.

Elections and embargoes in the north

There were two elections in Turkish northern Cyprus in 2005, one for a new parliament, the other for a president. It was the second time in 13 months that the parliament had faced the electorate, stemming from the collapse of Prime Minister Mehmet Ali Talat's coalition government in October 2004. Talat's broadly pro-European Cumhuriyeti Türk Partiyasi (CTP) (Republican Turkish Party) had campaigned in favour of Kofi Annan's re-unification plan, put to a referendum in April 2004. The CTP won a plurality of the votes in the February 2005 election but was forced to enter into another coalition with the nationalist Demokrat Parti (DP) (Democrat Party). In April, Talat won presidential elections with a decisive 55.6 per cent of the vote. Talat's election was a watershed in two respects. Firstly, it was the first time an election was not contested by Rauf Denktash, the dominant political figure in northern Cyprus for nearly 50 years. Secondly, as Denktash had been an adamant supporter of independence for northern Cyprus, his retirement allowed the rise of a new generation of leaders more inclined to favour re-unification as a means of gaining EU membership.

A small chink in the otherwise solid international trade embargo against northern Cyprus appeared in July. The unrecognised northern Cyprus government signed a deal with Azerbaijan, allowing for northern Cyprus aeroplanes to use Azeri airports and vice versa. The Cyprus government protested to the Azeri authorities but to no avail. Azerbaijan had long been close to Turkey and it is likely that Turkey facilitated the deal.

Progress on a promised aid package for northern Cyprus, granted by the EU as a reward for the Cypriot Turks' 'yes' vote in the April 2004 referendum on the UN re-unification plan, remained stalled in 2005. The eur259 million (US$312 million) package was meant to facilitate the opening of trade between northern Cyprus and the EU but the Cypriot government managed to postpone implementation throughout 2005, protesting that the aid deal amounted to breaking the international trade embargo.

Occupied land and an air crash

Having warned citizens of EU member states not to purchase land in northern Cyprus on the grounds that many of the original owners had been illegally dispossessed during the Turkish invasion of 1974, the Cypriot government carried out its threat to prosecute. Once inside the EU, from May 2004, Cyprus had warned that it would seek to confiscate properties belonging to EU citizens who had purchased 'occupied land'. One such case gained notoriety in December, when Cherie Blair, the wife of British prime minister, Tony Blair, agreed to represent a British couple who were being sued by Cypriots over a land purchase.

In August, a plane from Cyprus' partially state-owned national carrier, Helios, crashed en route to Athens, killing all 121 people on board.

Outlook

With GDP growth forecast to continue and the budget deficit thus far under control, Cyprus looks on course to join the euro zone in 2008.

In terms of achieving a major breakthrough on the re-unification of the island of Cyprus, things began optimistically in 2006 but almost immediately foundered. In January, Turkey suggested re-opening talks aimed at solving the deadlock between Cyprus' divided communities. It offered to open its ports to Cypriot vessels, ie implement the customs union signed in July 2005, in exchange for lifting Cypriot restrictions on trade with northern Cyprus. Cypriot foreign minister George Iakovou rejected the offer as 'reheated food'.

With northern Cyprus already administered by a pro-European government, it is probable that most resistance for a settlement will come from the south of the island. President Papadopoulos remains opposed to the UN-proposed peace plan of 2004, at least in its current form. With each EU member state possessing the right of veto over issues it considers of national importance, it therefore seems likely that until larger EU member states put serious pressure on Cyprus, it will simply continue to hold up confidence-building measures such as the aid package earmarked for northern Cyprus.

A review of Turkey's position on the customs union is meant to take place sometime in 2006. This will again throw the spotlight on Cyprus and its determination to wrest recognition of its international standing from Ankara.

Risk assessment

Politics	Stable
Economy	Improving
Regional stability	Problematic

COUNTRY PROFILE

Historical profile

Cyprus, traditionally the birthplace of the ancient goddess of love Aphrodite, has, in contrast, been the scene of political unrest for some 50 years. The tensions arise from the polarisation of the inhabitants into two political groups with diametrically opposed aspirations: the Greek Cypriots

KEY INDICATORS — Cyprus

	Unit	2000	2001	2002	2003	2004
Population	m	0.76	0.77	0.77	0.86	0.96
Gross domestic product (GDP)	US$bn	8.80	9.10	11.16	15.84	*15.42
GDP per capita	US$	13,060	13,412	14,504	18,326	19,202
GDP real growth	%	5.1	4.0	2.0	1.9	3.7
Inflation	%	4.1	2.0	2.8	4.2	2.3
Unemployment	%	3.4	3.0	3.2	–	–
Exports (fob) (goods)	US$m	951.0	970.0	1,000.0	1,030.0	1,175.0
Imports (fob) (goods)	US$m	3,556.5	4,040.0	4,200.0	3,900.0	5,217.8
Balance of trade	US$m	-2,605.5	-3,070.0	-3,200.0	-2,870.0	-4,042.8
Current account	US$m	-456.5	-320.0	-470.0	-450.0	-640.0
Total reserves minus gold	US$m	1,741.1	2,267.8	3,022.0	3,256.7	3,910.0
Foreign exchange	US$m	1,694.0	2,221.9	2,953.2	3,154.5	3,832.7
Exchange rate	per US$	0.59	1.56	0.60	0.51	0.47

* estimated figure

constituting 80 per cent of the population and the Turkish Cypriot minority. During the British colonial period, both communities had a common enemy – then upon independence seemingly intractable enmities surfaced. Over the years, the situation was further aggravated by the periodic, tacit intervention of both Turkey and Greece in Cyprus' affairs. As a colonial hangover, the UK retains two sovereign military bases on Cyprus; Turkey has around 30,000 troops in the north.

1878 After three centuries of rule, a weakening Ottoman empire ceded the island to the British in return for security guarantees against possible Russian expansion in the area. The origins of future problems lay in the composition of Cyprus' population – approximately 80 per cent Greek-speaking Christians, 18 per cent Turkish-speaking Muslims and 2 per cent others (Armenian, Latin and Maronite).
1925 Cyprus became a British crown colony.
1955 The Greek Cypriots of the Ethniki Organosis Kipriakou Agonos (Eoka) (National Organisation of Cypriot Combatants) launched a guerrilla war against the British. The Eoka wanted Cyprus to unify with mainland Greece.
1960 Cyprus was granted independence under President Makarios. Independence followed a compromise agreement between Greek and Turkish Cypriots, with Britain retaining sovereignty over two military bases.
1961 Cyprus joined the IMF and World Bank.
1963 Makarios upset the Turkish Cypriots when he proposed constitutional changes which would abrogate power-sharing arrangements. Inter-communal fighting erupted and the Turkish Cypriot community withdrew from the central government.
1964 A UN peace-keeping force was sent to the island.
1968–74 Talks on constitutional reform were inconclusive, as Turkish Cypriots sought separate municipalities in the five main towns.
1974 A brief Greek-sponsored coup by supporters of union with Greece toppled President Makarios, who escaped. Turkey invaded northern Cyprus and Greek Cypriots fled their homes in the north; 37 per cent of the island came under Turkish control, enforcing partition between north and south. The border between the two became known as the Green Line.
The coup failed and Glafcos Clerides took over as the Greek Cypriot president, until Makarios returned at the end of the year.
1975 Northern Cyprus declared the formation of the 'Turkish Federated State of Cyprus' with Rauf Denktash as president and with the aim of eventually gaining independence.
1977 President Makarios died and was succeeded by Spyros Kyprianou.
1980 UN-sponsored peace talks resumed.
1983 Rauf Denktash suspended talks and northern Cyprus officially declared its independence as the Kuzey Kýbrýs Türk Cumhuriyeti (KKTC) (Turkish Republic of Northern Cyprus) and introduced its own government and legal system. The independence move was rejected by the international community and only Turkey recognised it as a state.
1985 There was no agreement between Denktas and Kyprianou.
1988 Georgios Vassiliou was elected Greek Cypriot president.
1989 Talks between the two presidents were abandoned.
1992–93 Additional UN-sponsored talks with Rauf Denktash failed when the UN Security Council rejected Turkish demands for the recognition of separate sovereignty for the KKTC, including a right to secession.
1993 Glafcos Clerides defeated George Vassiliou in the presidential election.
1994 The European Court of Justice ruled that all direct trade between northern Cyprus and the EU was illegal.
1994–95 Talks continued between north and south with little progress. The Greek Cypriots and the UN pushed for a federal system, but this was rejected by the KKTC.
1996 Tension between the two sides increased and there was violence along the Green Line.
1997 UN-mediated talks between Clerides and Denktash failed.
1998 Clerides was narrowly re-elected for a second term. The EU listed Cyprus as a potential member.
1999 Further peace talks in the US failed to find a solution to Cyprus' division.
2000 Rauf Denktash was elected for a fourth five-year term as the KKTC president.
2001 The leaders of the two Cypriot communities held their first direct talks in four years and agreed to restart peace talks to pave the way for EU membership.
2002 The leaders of the Cypriot communities began UN-sponsored reunification talks. The UN reunification plan envisaged a federation with two constituent parts, presided over by a rotating presidency, but the KKTC would not agree, demanding international recognition. The EU summit in Copenhagen invited Cyprus to join in 2004, providing the two communities agreed to the UN plan by early spring 2003; without reunification, only the Greek Cypriot part of the island would gain membership.
2003 Tassos Papadopoulos won the presidential elections. The UN deadline for agreement on reunification passed without agreement. Crossing points between the two zones were temporarily opened and the government lifted 20-year-old trade sanctions against the KKTC, thus allowing farmers in the north to sell produce in the south and export to the EU, and permitting Turkish Cypriots to work in the south.
2004 On 24 April, in twin referenda on whether to accept the UN reunification plan and achieve a united EU entry, Greek Cypriots voted against unification with the north by 76 per cent, while in the north, 65 per cent voted in favour of the proposal. Internationally recognised Cyprus joined the EU on 1 May. Turkey agreed that it would recognise Cyprus as an EU member, before the start of its own accession talks in October 2005. In Northern Cyprus, Prime Minister Mehmet Ali Talat and his government resigned on 20 October.
2005 The European Commission (EC) received a letter on 29 March from Turkey, agreeing to extend a free trade accord with the EU, to include Cyprus and the nine other members that joined in May 2004. In April Mehmet Ali Talat won the Northern Cyprus presidential election, after President Denktash retired. Ali Talat won 55 per cent of the vote, compared to 23 per cent for runner-up Dervis Eroglu. In May UN diplomats began work with Greek Cypriots on peace talks. On 1 July, Cyprus became the eleventh EU member to ratify the EU constitution. In August, 121 people on board a Cypriot plane died in a crash as it approached Athen's airport. It was Cyprus' worst ever air accident.

Political structure
The government of southern Cyprus is internationally recognised as the sole administration of the Republic of Cyprus. Occupied by Turkish troops since 1974, northern Cyprus has its own government and calls itself the Kuzey Kýbrýs Türk Cumhuriyeti (KKTC) (Turkish Republic of Northern Cyprus). It is recognised only by Turkey.

Constitution
The constitution of the Republic of Cyprus was promulgated in 1960.
For the first time, at the 1998 presidential election, suffrage was extended to include all citizens of the republic above the age of 18 and subsequently, the legislative elections.
Northern Cyprus introduced its own constitution after declaring independence in 1983.

Form of state
Presidential republic

The executive
Executive power in the Republic of Cyprus is held by the president who is directly elected for a five-year term by universal suffrage. A Council of Ministers is appointed by the president, who convenes and presides over its meetings. Ministers may not sit in the House of Representatives, but may introduce bills.

National legislature
Legislative power is vested in an 80-member unicameral Vouli Antiprosópon (House of Representatives). Members are elected for a five-year term – 56 members of the House are Greek Cypriots, elected by the Greek Cypriot community; 24 seats are reserved for Turkish Cypriots, elected by the Turkish Cypriot community. The Turkish Cypriots seats have not been filled since 1963. In 1983, northern Cyprus introduced its own parliament, the 50-member Temsilciler Meclisi (House of Representatives).

Legal system
The Republic of Cyprus' legal system is embodied in the 1960 constitution and is based on British common law. The legal system in northern Cyprus is based on Turkish law.

Last elections
13 June 2004 (European Parliament); 24 April 2004 (referendum on unification); 14 December 2003 (Kuzey Kýbrýs Türk Cumhuriyeti (KKTC) (Turkish Republic of Northern Cyprus) parliamentary); 16 February 2003 (presidential); 27 May 2001 (parliamentary).
Results: European Parliament: Dimokratikos Sinagermos (DISI) (Democratic Coalition) won 28.2 per cent of the vote (two seats out of six), Anorthotikon Komma Ergazemenou Laou (AKEL) (Progressive party of the Working People) (Communist Party) 27.9 per cent (two), Dimokratikon Komma (DIKO) (Democratic Party) 17.1 per cent (one), For Europe 10.8 per cent (one) and Kinima Sosialdimokraton (KISOS) (Social Democrats Movement) 10.8 per cent (no seats); turnout 71.2 per cent.
Referendum: at least 76 per cent of Greek Cypriots voted against the referendum, while 65 per cent of Turkish Cypriots were in favour.
KKTC parliamentary elections: the Republican Turkish Party won 35.2 per cent of the vote (19 seats out of 50), the National Unity Party 32.9 per cent (18), the Peace and Democracy Movement 13.1 per cent (six) and the Democrat Party 12.9 per cent (seven).
Presidential: Tassos Papadopoulos won 51.5 per cent of the vote against 38.8 per cent for incumbent Glafkos Clerides and 6.6 per cent for Alekos Markidis; turnout was 90.5 per cent.

Next elections
May 2006 (parliamentary); 2008 (presidential).

Political parties
Ruling party
Coalition government: Dimokratikon Komma (DIKO) (Democratic Party), Anorthotikon Komma Ergazemenou Laou (AKEL) (Progressive party of the Working People) and Kinima Sosialdimokraton (KISOS) (Social Democrats Movement) (from Mar 2003)

Main opposition party
Dimokratikos Sinagermos (DISI) (Democratic Coalition)

Population
959,400 (2004)

Ethnic make-up
Greeks (84.1 per cent), Turks (11.8 per cent), Maronites (0.6 per cent), Armenians (0.3 per cent), Latins (0.1 per cent), foreign residents (mainly British and Greek) (3.1 per cent).

Religions
Christian Orthodox (77 per cent), Muslim (18 per cent).

Labour market and unemployment
Approximately 38 per cent of the workforce is female. The labour force is highly educated with an adult literacy rate of over 94 per cent.
Percentage of the population employed by sector: agriculture, forestry and fishing (10.2 per cent), mining and quarrying (0.2 per cent), manufacturing (14.2 per cent), electricity, gas and water (0.5 per cent), construction (8.7 per cent), wholesale and retail trade, restaurants and hotels (27.1 per cent), transport storage and communication (6.7 per cent), finance, insurance, real estate and business service (8.4 per cent), community, social and personal services (24.2 per cent).
Jobs are scarce in the north, where the public sector remains the biggest employer.

Education
Primary schooling lasts for six years between the ages of six and 12. Public general secondary education extends over six years. Almost 20,000 students, mostly from Turkey, Eastern Europe and the Middle East, attend six private universities in northern Cyprus.
Literacy rate: 97 per cent, adult rate (World Bank)
Compulsory years: Six to 15.
Enrolment rate: 100 per cent gross primary enrolment, of the relevant age group, (including repeaters), (World Bank)

Health
Total expenditure on health is 8–9 per cent of GDP, of which 54–55 per cent is government spending.
The government is looking for ways to persuade Greek-Cypriot medical specialists to return from overseas and offer high-quality healthcare services at a considerably lower cost than in Western Europe.
Life expectancy: 78.2 years (World Bank)
Fertility rate/Maternal mortality rate: 1.9 births per woman (World Bank)
Birth rate/Death rate: 8 deaths and 17 births per 1,000 people (World Bank)
Infant mortality rate: 4 per 1,000 live births (World Bank)

Welfare
Cyprus offers a statutory social insurance scheme securing decent pensions and allows pensioners to continue working without affecting their pensions. The Social Insurance Scheme provides insurance for all employees who contribute 16.6 per cent on the insured income. The employer deducts 6.3 per cent of the employees' income and contributes 6.3 per cent, while the remaining 4 per cent is paid by the state. There is provision for a non-contributory social pension for elderly people who are not entitled to a pension from any other source. There is also a complementary public assistance scheme for people whose resources are not sufficient to meet their basic and special needs. There is provision for unemployment and disability benefits. The National Social Security System allows women a paid 16-week maternity leave and a substantial birth allowance. Cyprus also offers crime victims a financial compensation programme.

Main cities
Nicosia municipal council voted to change the capital city's name to Lefkosia, Nicosia's Greek name, in 1995. The change was the result of a campaign to standardise place names according to their Greek pronunciation, although Nicosia is still the name in common use. Lefkosia (capital, estimated population 197,600 in 2003), Lemesos (Limassol) (149,100), Larnaka (Larnaca) (48,200), Pafos (Paphos) (32,700).
In Turkish-occupied northern Cyprus, cities include Lefkosa (the part under Turkish control – 45,800), Gazimagusa (35,700), Girne (19,000).

Languages spoken
Armenian and Arabic; English is widely spoken in tourist regions.

Official language/s
Greek and Turkish

Media
Press
Dailies: In southern Cyprus, there are nine dailies (eight in Greek, one in English) and eight weeklies (seven in Greek, one in English). In northern Cyprus, there are six daily papers in circulation, five weeklies and three periodicals.

Major national dailies and Sunday papers include *Cyprus Mail*, *Afrika* (formally known as *Avrupa*), IYenicag *Phileleftheros* and *Simerini*.

Weeklies: *Cyprus Weekly* is published weekly, with a diverse selection of political, business, environmental, arts and sports news. Other weeklies include *Kibris*, *Athlitiko Vima* (Sports Tribune) and *Economiki*, which provides economic news and information.

Business: Major business publications include *Euro Kerdos* (Euro Profit) and *Marketing*.

Periodicals: There are a number of periodicals (also available in English) covering general topics, current affairs and business. An official quarterly publication on Cypriot affairs is *Cyprus Today*. *Time Out* is read widely as an entertainment guide. Other periodicals include *To Periodiko*, *Cosmopolitan of Cyprus* and *Nicosia This Month*.

Broadcasting
Cyprus Broadcasting Corporation (CyBC) is the main broadcasting company on the island, providing both radio and television services.

Radio: There are a number of private radion stations, including *Radio Astra* and *Radio Proto*. Some radio programmes are broadcast in Arabic and Armenian.

Television: CyBC provides two terrestrial (RIK 1 TV and RIK 2 TV) and one satellite television station (Sat TV). There are also a number of private television stations. A number of Turkish television stations broadcast to northern Cyprus.

Economy
Since the 1960s, the economy has been transformed into a modern economy, with dynamic services, industrial and agricultural sectors and advanced physical and social infrastructure.

The economy is export-oriented with exports of goods comprising mainly manufactured products and, to a lesser extent, agricultural products. Tourism and other private services are the main factors in GDP growth.

The growing importance of the services industry, and in particular the offshore financial sector, is reflected in the contribution made to GDP growth of 74 per cent. The labour force is well-educated with a good level of English speakers.

Northern Cyprus, which uses the Turkish lira, suffers from high inflation. Financial aid from Turkey and remittances from the 200,000 Turkish Cypriots living abroad are vital sources of revenue.

Economic reforms made by Cyprus include abolishing the interest rate ceiling, granting the central bank legal independence, capital account liberalisation without jeopardising domestic and external stability and reform of the tax system. The European Council recognised these achievements and in December 2002, Cyprus was invited to join the EU, which it did officially on 1 May 2004.

Between 2004 and 2006, the 10 EU accession countries are to receive funding of up to eur25.1 billion (US$28.2 billion), which will include money for agriculture, infrastructure modernisation and regional aid. Cyprus will receive eur498.8 million (US$560 million). With the accession countries altogether expected to pay into the EU budget approximately eur14.8 billion (US$16.6 billion) during the first three years of membership, the total net cost of EU enlargement will be eur10.3 billion (US$11.5 billion). An additional eur15.7 billion (US$17.6 billion) is available for the accession countries if required.

Forecast at 4.0 per cent for 2005, real GDP growth comes from domestic demand, particularly from public and private consumption. Another contributing factor is the surge in construction, fuelled by demand for second homes.

Inflation has dropped over recent years to the current level of 2.3 per cent.

The fiscal deficit has shrunk from over 6 per cent of GDP in 2003 (caused by excessive public expenditure), to 4.1 per cent in 2004. This is predicted to fall further in 2005 to 2.8 per cent, just within the 3 per cent limit set by the EU. This prudent management resulted in approval for membership of the exchange rate mechanism (ERM2), which Cyprus entered in May 2005. Cyprus is expected to join the euro-zone in January 2008.

The concern caused in recent years by Cyprus' failure to meet the Maastricht Treaty's convergence criteria on account of the large deficit and public debt is now easing. A tax amnesty, consisting of a 5 per cent levy on illegally exported funds and covert savings, has paid dividends, raising funds worth 2 per cent of GDP. In addition, substantial cutbacks have been made in the defence budget, the retirement age has been raised from 60 to 63, and the unemployment rate has remained at an impressive 3.2 per cent. The government has agreed to control spending at a rate below any rise in GDP for the next three years. If Cyprus is to continue to succeed in tackling its deficit and join the euro-zone, it will have to address structural problems and refrain from public spending in the medium term.

External trade
The EU is Cyprus' biggest trading partner, primarily the UK, Greece, Germany and Italy.

Imports
Principal imports are consumer goods, petroleum and lubricants, intermediate goods, machinery and transport equipment. In 2004 total imports were valued at US$5.2 billion.

Main sources: Russia (30.2 per cent total, 2004), Italy (8.0 per cent), Greece (7.5 per cent), Germany (6.4 per cent), UK (6.1 per cent), Japan (5.8 per cent), France (4.2 per cent)

Exports
Major exports are agricultural products (potatoes, fresh vegetables, citrus fruits and wine), manufactured goods, clothing, cement, pharmaceuticals and cigarettes. In 2004 the export market was worth US$1.2 billion. Re-exports account for a significant share of total annual exports.

Main destinations: UK (20.2 per cent total, 2004), Greece (13.1 per cent), Israel (7.4 per cent), Germany (7.0 per cent), Belgium (4.6 per cent)

Agriculture
Farming
The agriculture sector contributes 5 per cent annually to GDP. Major crops are potatoes, grapes, citrus fruits and barley. Cattle, sheep and goats, swine and poultry are raised. Fresh pork, poultry meat and eggs satisfy local demand. Local production of beef, veal, mutton and lamb is supplemented by imports. Agriculture typically contributes 3.5 per cent to GDP and employs 7 per cent of the workforce.

The implentation of modern irrigation technologies has helped to address the sector's water shortage. A large-scale water development programme culminated in the Southern Conveyor Project that carries surplus water from the south-western part of the island to the central and eastern areas in an effort to broaden and boost agricultural production and alleviate water shortages.

Now a member of the EU, Cyprus is only eligible for full EU agricultural subsidies and rural development aid through the Common Agricultural Policy (CAP) by 2013.

During its transitional entry stage Cyprus has decided to implement the reform of the CAP on 1 January 2009. The reform was introduced throughout most of the EU on 1 January 2005, when subsidies on farm output, which tended to benefit large farms and encourage overproduction, were replaced by single farm payments not conditional on production. The change is expected to reward farms that provide and maintain a healthy environment, food safety and animal welfare standards. The changes are also intended to encourage market conscious production and cut the cost of CAP to the EU taxpayer.

Crop production in 2004 included: 107,450 tonnes (t) cereals in total, 13,000t wheat, 116,000t potatoes, 94,000t barley, 10,500t bananas, 886t pulses, 3,900t figs, 132,000t citrus fruit, 80,860t grapes, *38,200t tomatoes, 6,575t oilcrops, 360t tobacco, 2,255t treenuts, 27,500t olives, 11,000t apples, *2,600t taro, 259,020t fruit in total, 151,190t vegetables in total. Livestock production included: 108,248t meat in total, 4,500t beef, 53,000t pig meat, 4,900t lamb, 7,800t goat meat, 36,718t poultry, 12,300t eggs, *213,000t milk, 1,077t sheepskins.

* estimate

Fishing
The fishing industry largely consists of inshore and trawl fishing, as well as aquaculture. Annual fish production typically totals 4,000 tonnes.

Forestry
Forest and other wooded land accounts for less than a third of the land area. Industrial wood and paper products are largely imported. Exports in 2004 amounted to US$1.4 million while imports amounted to US$94.8 million.

Industry and manufacturing
The industrial sector contributes around 12 per cent to GDP and accounts for 16 per cent of the workforce.

Major growth industries, which are mainly export-based, include cement, food and drink, footwear and clothing. Chemical and pharmaceutical products, plastics and publishing are also expanding areas. Foreign investment is encouraged. Industrial activity in northern Cyprus is limited to food and textiles.

Industrial production was projected to climb 3.8 per cent in 2005.

Tourism
Tourism provides 54,000 jobs (15 per cent of the workforce) and contributes to approximately 20 per cent of GDP. Visitor arrivals totalled 2.7 million in 2004, an increase of 3 per cent on the previous year. However, visitor spending on the island is down and over one fifth of tourists are eschewing hotels for rented apartments. Hoteliers are losing revenue.

The UK is the principal market, accounting for 60 per cent of visitors, or 1.3 million annual visits. The majority of other arrivals come from other European countries and so the sector is expected to benefit from the 2004 EU accession. A Strategic Plan to improve the quality of tourism and increase visitor numbers by 2010 was adopted in November 2003. Competition from Turkish-occupied northern Cyprus has been limited in the past, as a result of the lack of direct air connections to that part of the island and restricted access from the south. However, visitor numbers to the north are increasing and have reached around 500,000. Most visitors come from Turkey. Restrictions on south-to-north visits have been reluctantly relaxed since EU accession, but only for daytrips. In summer 2005 an airliner flew from the Turkish Cypriot north to Baku, the capital of Azerbaijan. This was the first time a direct flight from the region has flown anywhere but Turkey.

Environment
The problems of water shortages, sewage disposal, industrial and agricultural pollution and waste disposal are acute. The government has introduced a programme of legislation incorporating the principle that the polluter pays.

Northern Cyprus is particularly badly affected by water shortages, a problem accentuated by the Turkish soldiers stationed on the island. Shortages have caused many to stop cultivating the land as low rainfalls mean water reserves are used faster than they are replenished. The Turkish government has proposed building a water pipeline to northern Cyprus, capable of carrying 70–100 million cubic metres a year to the island. Since the 1990s, giant plastic 'sacks' of water have been pulled across the Mediterranean from Turkey to northern Cyprus; there is a concern about a long-term shortage of water.

Mining
Cyprus was once famous for its enormous copper reserves. It has a 3,000 year tradition of copper mining, which was the biggest source of the nation's revenue. However after the 1974 Turkish invasion copper mining stopped. In 2005 East Mediterranean Resources obtained prospecting licences allowing access to 370 sq km. Test drillings were planned for late 2005.

Continued expansion in the construction industry has led to a boom in quarrying of construction materials and non-metallic minerals. Other quarried materials include marble, bentonite, umber, sienna, ochra and limonite.

Hydrocarbons
Cyprus has delimited its continental shelf to ward off encroachment by other countries. In March 2002, officials from Cyprus and Lebanon met to discuss marking out exclusive economic zones in the eastern Mediterranean Sea as a first step toward tapping offshore gas and oil deposits. In 2005 Egypt pledged to assist Cyprus in locating and exploiting its oil and gas reserves thought to be located off the southern and eastern edges of the country.

Cyprus does not produce or import natural gas, although it does import coal, typically 50,000 short tonnes per annum. A natural gas pipeline is being completed from Al-Arish in Egypt to Aqaba, Jordan and is planned to be extended to Cyprus by 2006. This would enable Cyprus to import natural gas and lower its dependence on oil.

Energy
Cyprus is almost completely dependent on imported petroleum. The Vassiliko electric power station was established in 2000. Four additional gas boilers will be installed by 2008, increasing the capacity from around 300MW to 778MW.

Cyprus is well suited to solar power with over 300 days of sunshine per annum. The government subsidies the implementation of solar technology to a maximum 55 per cent of the cost, and has now started to subsidise wind power.

Financial markets
Stock exchange

The Cyprus Stock Exchange (CSE) was transformed in 1996 from an over-the-counter market to an official stock exchange. The CSE became a fully computerised trading system in May 1999. The overall supervision of the stock exchange is assigned to the minister of finance and is exercised by the minister through the Securities and Exchange Commission.

Banking and insurance
The Bank of Cyprus, which was founded in 1899, leads the Cypriot banking sector. The Central Bank of Cyprus (CBC) oversees monetary policy. There are nine commercial banks. The abolition of the interest rate ceiling was part of a drive to reform banking practices in line with those of the EU.

Central bank

Central Bank of Cyprus

Time
GMT plus two hours (GMT plus three hours from late March to late September).

Geography
Cyprus is an island in the eastern Mediterranean Sea, about 100km south of Turkey. The landscape varies between rugged coastlines, sandy beaches, rocky hills and forest-covered mountains. The Troodos Mountains in the centre of the island rise to almost 1,950 metres.

Climate
Mediterranean. Summers are long and dry. Winters are changeable with occasional rain. Temperatures range from

Cyprus

0–27 degrees Celsius (C) (in the mountains), 5–40 degrees C (inland) and 9–35 degrees C (on the coast). Hottest months are July and August; coldest are January and February. Average annual rainfall is 500mm.

Entry requirements
Legal entry is only by Larnaka and Pafos airports and the ports of Pafos, Larnaka and Lemesos.
Since 1974, entry to northern Cyprus either via the Turkish mainland or through the ports of the occupied area, Famagusta (Ammaschostos), Karavostasi and Keryneia, or Ercan airport, is considered illegal by the government of the Republic of Cyprus. Tourists entering through these ports of entry are not permitted to cross the UN-patrolled Green Line and gain access to the south.

Visa
Required by all except citizens of most European, American and some Asian countries. Contact the local embassy or High Commission for a full list of exceptions. For a business visa, applications should include an introductory letter from the employer which gives details and the nature of business to be conducted.

Currency advice/regulations
The import of local currency is unrestricted, subject to declaration; foreign currency over US$1,000 (or the equivalent) must be declared. The export of local and foreign currency is limited to the amount declared on arrival. Local currency withdrawn from Cypriot banks may be exported, provided a holding certificate is obtained by the bank.
Visitors are advised to take travellers cheques in UK pounds sterling or Cyprus pounds.

Customs
Personal items may be imported duty-free. Unauthorised export of antiquities is prohibited; permission of the Cyprus Museum is required.

Health (for visitors)
Mandatory precautions
Compulsory vaccinations are not required.
Advisable precautions
Recommended immunisations incude tetanus and polio, while long-term visitors are advised to consider a hepatitis 'A' immunisation.
Tap water is safe to drink, but fruit, especially soft fruit, should be washed.

Hotels
There are over 400 hotels (one to five stars) and hotel apartments (A to C class) plus several other types of tourist accommodation. Visitors should book well in advance, especially during the peak holiday season (April–October). Cyprus Tourism Organisation (CTO) operates a rating system, both for hotels and any other licensed tourist accommodation. Tipping is not obligatory. A 10 per cent service charge and a 3 per cent tourism tax are included in the bill.

Credit cards
Most leading cards are accepted in the main hotels, restaurants and shops.

Public holidays
Fixed dates
1 Jan (New Year's Day), 6 Jan (Epiphany), 25 Mar (Greek National Day), 1 Apr (Greek Cypriot National Day), 1 May (Labour Day), 15 Aug (Assumption Day), 1 Oct (Cyprus Independence Day), 28 Oct (Greek National Day/Ochi Day), 24–26 Dec (Christmas Holiday).
Variable dates
Green Monday, Greek Orthodox Good Friday, Greek Orthodox Easter Monday, Pentecost (Festival of the Flood).

Working hours
Banking
Mon–Fri: 0830–1230 and (specially for tourists) 1515–1645.
Business
Mon–Fri: 0800–1300 and 1500–1800 (winter), 0730–1300 and 1600–1830 (summer); Wed and Sat half-day all year round.
Government
Mon–Fri: 0730–1430; Thu: 1500–1800.
Shops
Mon–Fri: 0800–1300 and 1430–1800 (winter), 0730–1300 and 1600–1830 (summer); Wed and Sat half-day 0800–1400.

Telecommunications
Telephone/fax
GSM 900/1800 and G3 services are available in Greek Cypriot areas

Electricity supply
240V AC. Socket outlets and sockets of flat three-pin type are used.

Weights and measures
The metric system is used.

Social customs/useful tips
It is considered impolite to refuse drinks offered at a first meeting. Cypriots customarily offer fruit preserves to guests. Between 1300–1600 hours is siesta time in the summer (May–September). Avoid shorts and wear suitable clothing when visiting churches and monasteries. There are restrictions on the photographing of military installations in both south and north Cyprus.

Getting there
Air
National airline: Cyprus Airways
International airport/s: Larnaka International (LCA), 8km from Larnaka (49km from Lefkosia); Pafos International (PFO), 10km east of Pafos (146km from Lefkosia).
Both airports offer tourist information, foreign exchange, hotel reservations and duty free shops.
Other airport/s: Northern Cyprus has an airport at Ercan with flights to and from Turkey. Flights are provided by a number of Turkish airlines and the northern Cypriot airline, Kibris Türk Hava Yollari (KYHY) (Cyprus Turkish Airlines). Visitors planning to arrive via Turkey are not allowed into southern Cyprus.
Airport tax: There is no airport tax.
Surface
Water: Access by ship from Greece, Syria, Israel, Italy, Lebanon and Egypt.
Main port/s: Lemesos (Limassol)

Getting about
National transport
Buses: Efficient 'intra-cud' (inter-town) bus service is available. All buses run from the central bus depots, connecting towns and villages. A rural bus operation is limited to once or twice a day, usually to the local market.
Urban buses operate frequently during the day. In certain tourist areas during the summer, buses extend their operations until midnight.
City transport
Taxis: An efficient service is operated throughout the island by metered taxis. The transurban service-taxis are shared taxis connecting all main towns. Prices are regulated. Between 2300–0600 an additional 15 per cent is charged. Tipping is standard practice.
Buses, trams & metro: There are few buses.
Car hire
Car hire is available in all parts of the island, particularly from airports and commercial centres. Rates vary depending on the size of the car and are also subject to seasonal variations. For a higher price, a prestige service is also available. Cheap rates are available for hire periods of more than one week. Visitors should book cars well in advance during the period June–September. A national or international driving licence is required. Driving is on the left. Road signs are in both Greek and English.

BUSINESS DIRECTORY

Telephone area codes
The international direct dialling code (IDD) for Cyprus is +357, followed by area code subscriber's number:

Larnaka	24	Lemesos	25
Lefkosia	22	Pafos	26

North Cyprus numbers are preceded by +90-392, in place of +357. Area code for Famagusta 366, Kyrenia 815.

Nations of the World: A Political, Economic and Business Handbook

Useful telephone numbers
Ambulance: 199.
Fire: 1991.
Police: 199.

Chambers of Commerce
Cyprus Chamber of Commerce and Industry, Chamber Building, 38 Grivas Dighenis Ave and 3 Deligiorgis Street, PO Box 21455, 1509 Lefkosia (tel: 889-600; fax: 667-433).

Famagusta Chamber of Commerce and Industry, 339 Ayiou Andreou Street, Andrea Chamber Bldg., PO Box 3124, Limassol (tel: 370-165, 370-167; fax: 370-291).

Larnaka Chamber of Commerce and Industry, 12 12 Gregoriou Afxentiou Str., Skourou Bldg., 4th Floor, PO Box 287, Larnaka (tel: 655-051; fax: 628-281).

Lefkosia Chamber of Commerce and Industry, 38 Grivas Dighenis Ave. and 3 Deligioris Str., Chamber Building, PO Box 1455, Lefkosia (tel: 449-500; fax: 367-433).

Limassol Chamber of Commerce and Industry, PO Box 347, 25 Spyrou Araouzou Street, Verengaria Building, PO Box 347, Limassol (tel: 362-556; fax: 371-655).

Pafos Chamber of Commerce and Industry, 32 Grivas Dighenis Avenue, Demetra Court, 2nd Floor, Flat 22, Pafos (tel:235-115; fax: 244-602).

Banking
Alpha Bank Ltd, Yiorkion Bldg, 1 Prodromou Street, 1095 Lefkosia (tel: 2277-3799, 2288-8888; fax: 2277-3744).

Bank of Cyprus Ltd, Box 1472, 86-90 Phaneromeni Street, Lefkosia (tel: 2246-4064; fax: 2246-4340).

Cyprus Development Bank, PO Box 1415, Alpha House, 50 Archbishop Makarios III Avenue, Lefkosia (tel: 2245-7575; fax: 2246-4322).

Cyprus Investment and Securities Corporation, 60 Digenis Akritas Avenue, PO Box 597, Lefkosia (tel: 2245-1535; fax: 2244-5481).

Cyprus Popular Bank Ltd, PO Box 2032, 39 Archbishop Makarios III Avenue, Lefkosia (tel: 2245-0000; fax: 2244-9169).

Federal Bank of the Middle East Ltd, J & P Building, 90 Archbishop Makarios III Avenue, 1077 Lefkosia (tel: 2288-8444; fax: 2288-8555).

Hellenic Bank Ltd, Corner 92 Dhigenis Akritas Ave & Cretes Str, 1061 Lefkosia (tel: 2286-0000; fax: 2276-507).

Sociéte Générale Cyprus Ltd, PO Box 25400, 7-9 Grivas Dighenis Ave, 1309 Lefkosia (tel: 2281-7777; fax: 2276-4471).

Central bank
Central Bank of Cyprus, 80 Kennedy Avenue, PO Box 25529, 1395 Lefkosia (tel: 714-100; fax: 378-153).

Travel information
Cyprus Airways, PO Box 1903, 21 Alkeou Street, Lefkosia (tel: 2244-3054, 2246-1800; fax: 2244-3167, 2236-0075; e-mail: marketing@cyprusair.com.cy; internet site: http://www.cyprusairways.com.cy).

Cyprus Hotel Association, PO Box 24772, Lefkosia (tel: 2237-4251; fax: 2236-5460).

Ministry of tourism
Ministry of Commerce, Industry and Tourism, 1421 Nicosia (fax: 375-120).

National tourist organisation offices
Cyprus Tourism Organisation (main office, for postal enquiries only), 19 Limassol Ave, PO Box 4535, Lefkosia (tel: 315-715; fax: 313-022); (for personal and telephone enquiries only, open every morning except Sun, and on Mon and Thurs afternoons) Laiki Yitonia, East of Eleftheria Sq, Lefkosia (formerly Nicosia) (tel: 444-264); (24-hour service) Larnaka International Airport (tel: 654-389).

Ministries
Ministry of Agriculture, Natural Resources and Environment, Loukis Akritas Avenue, Lefkosia (tel: 2230-0807; fax: 2278-1156).

Ministry of Commerce, Industry and Tourism, 2 A. Araouzos Street, Lefkosia (tel: 2230-3441, 2230-3456; fax: 2235-7120).

Ministry of Communication and Works, 28 Acheon Street, Lefkosia CY-1101 (tel: 2230-2830; fax: 2277-6272, 2246-5462, 2236-0578).

Ministry of Defence, 4 Emmanuel Roides Street, Lefkosia (tel: 2280-7528; fax: 2236-6225).

Ministry of Education and Culture, Gr Afxentiou Street, Lefkosia (tel: 2230-5188; fax: 2242-7559).

Ministry of Finance, Ex Secretariat Compound, Lefkosia (tel: 2280-3530; fax: 2236-6080).

Ministry of Foreign Affairs, Dem. Severis Avenue, Government House No. 18-19, Lefkosia (tel: 2230-0600; fax: 2245-1881).

Ministry of Health, Ex Secretarial Offices, Lefkosia (tel: 2230-9526; fax: 2236-8883).

Ministry of Interior, Dem. Severis Avenue, Ex Secretariat Offices, Lefkosia (tel: 2251-0222; fax: 2245-3465, 2236-6709).

Ministry of Justice and Public Order, 12 Helioupoleos, Lefkosia (tel: 2230-2355; fax: 2276-1427).

Ministry of Labour and Social Insurance, Byron Avenue, Lefkosia (tel: 2230-3481; fax: 2245-0993).

Presidential Palace, Lefkosia (tel: 2245-1333; fax: 2244-5016).

Other useful addresses
British High Commission, Alexander Pallis St, PO Box 1978, Lefkosia (tel: 2247-3131/7; fax: 2236-7198).

Central Post Office, Eleftheria Square, Lefkosia (tel: 2230-3219).

Cyprus Broadcasting Corporation, PO Box 4824, Lefkosia (tel: 2242-2231; fax: 2231-4050).

Cyprus Employers' and Industrialists' Federation, 30 Grivas Dhigenis Avenue, PO Box 1657, Lefkosia (tel: 2244-5102; fax: 2245-9459).

Cyprus News Agency, 7 Kastorias St, PO Box 3947, Lefkosia (tel: 2231-9009; fax: 2231-9006).

Cyprus Petroleum Refinery Ltd, PO Box 40275, 6302 Larnaka (fax: 2464-1401; e-mail: lambroug@cprl.com.cy).

Cyprus Telecommunications Authority, PO Box 4929, Lefkosia (tel: 2231-3111).

Department of Customs & Excise, Customs Headquarters, 29 Katsonis Street, Ay Omoloyitae, Lefkosia (tel: 2230-5404, 2230-5737; fax: 2235-5050).

Department of Statistics and Research, Ministry of Finance, 13 Andreas Araouzos Street, 1444 Lefkosia (tel: 2230-9305, 2230-3208; fax: 2237-4830, 2245-6712).

Embassy of the United States of America, Therissos St & Dositheos St, Lefkosia (fax: 2245-9571).

Press and Information Office, Apellis Street, Ay Omoloyitae, Lefkosia (tel: 2244-6430; fax: 2236-6123).

Internet sites
Bridge to Greece and Cyprus: http://www.greekvillage.com/bridge/bridge.htm

Central Bank of Cyprus: http://www.centralbank.gov.cy

Cyprus News: http://www.cyprusnews.com

Cyprus Telecommunications Authority: http://www.cytanet.com.cy

Cyprus Tourism Organisation: http://www.cyprustourism.org

Official Cyprus homepage: http://www.pio.gov.cy

Czech Republic

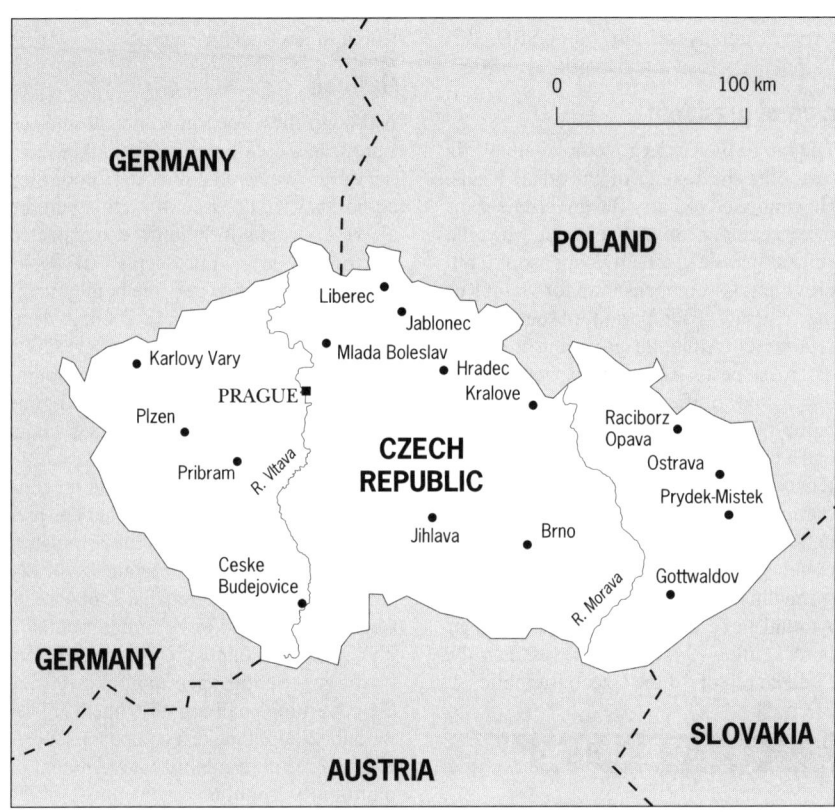

KEY FACTS

Official name: Ceská Republika (Czech Republic)

Head of State: President Václav Klaus (sworn in 7 Mar 2003)

Head of government: Prime Minister Jirí Paroubek (appointed 25 Apr 2005)

Ruling party: Coalition government from 25 Apr 2005: the Ceská Strana Sociálne Demokratická (CSSD) (Czech Social Democratic Party) and the Koalice (Coalition), comprising Krestanská a Demokratická Unie-Ceskoslovenská Strana Lidova (KDU-CSL) (Christian Democratic Union-Czechoslovak People's Party) and the Unie Svobody-Demokratická Unie (US-DEU) (Freedom Union-Democratic Union)

Area: 78,864 square km

Population: 10.29 million (2004); 10.20 million (OECD, 2003)

Capital: Prague

Official language: Czech

Currency: Czech koruna (Kc) = 100 hellers

Exchange rate: Kc24.56 per US$ (Oct 2005)

GDP per capita: US$10,480 (2004)

GDP real growth: 4.00% (2004); *5.0% (2005)

Labour force: 5.10 million (2004)

Unemployment: 8.30% (OECD, 2004)

Inflation: 2.80% (2004); *1.5% (2005)

Balance of trade: -US$1.68 billion (2004)

Foreign debt: US$45.30 billion (2004)

Annual FDI: US$41.00 billion (cumulative, 1995–2004, OECD); US$4.50 billion (OECD, 2004)*

* estimated figure

For a second year running, the Czech Republic managed to combine political fragility with economic stability. In April 2005, the Czech Republic's third prime minister in nine months was appointed. Nevertheless, in January 2006, a European Commission report was published indicating that the Czech Republic's economic performance was generally impressive in 2005.

A robust economy

Czech GDP grew by around 5 per cent in 2005 and inflation was held at 1.5 per cent. As a new EU member state, the Czech Republic is working towards economic goals laid out in a European Commission-monitored convergence programme. The Czechs, in 2005, managed to bring their budget deficit down to 3.2 per cent of GDP and public sector debt well below the 60 per cent of GDP reference value.

Euroscepticism rife

With economic indicators like these in 2005, the Czech Republic looks well on course to fulfil the minimum criteria for entering the euro-zone in the near future. However, widespread scepticism about the euro and about the proposed EU constitution was expressed in a series of public opinion polls in 2005. In May, a senior banker from the Ceska Národní Banka (CNB) (Czech National Bank) questioned the value of adopting the euro, pointing out that economic growth in the euro-zone was far less than that in the Czech Republic. This view found support with Czech president, Václav Klaus, a hardline eurosceptic long at odds with the relatively pro-EU integration policies of the government. President Klaus hails from the right-wing Obcanská Demokratická Strana (ODS) (Civic Democratic Party), which constitutes the country's official opposition. Previously, in April, President Klaus had called for a referendum on the EU constitution, at a time when opinion polls were showing that the constitution would be rejected. The government declined on this occasion and in June it announced that any referendum on the matter would be postponed until 2006 or 2007.

Another year, another PM

In April 2005, Czechs were introduced to their third prime minister in nine months, all three of them drawn from the same governing coalition. The latest turnover began in February, when a financial scandal started to gather pace, involving the prime minister, Stanislav Gross. An anti-corruption watchdog released a report questioning a property purchase by Gross dating back to 1999. Gross initially tried to ride out the political storm, despite losing a key coalition partner, the Krestanská a Demokratická Unie-Ceskoslovenská Strana Lidova (KDU-CSL) (Christian Democratic Union-Czechoslovak People's Party), over the issue. By April, the Gross government was in fact a minority government and faced a no-confidence motion. It was only able to survive due to tacit support from the Komunistická Strana Cech a Morava (KSCM) (Communist Party of Bohemia and Moravia), an unprecedented event since the fall of communism in 1989 and one which left many both inside and outside parliament feeling uneasy. On 25 April, Gross resigned as prime minister, after having only served in that role since July 2004. A new coalition, between Gross's Ceská Strana Sociálne Demokratická (CSSD) (Czech Social Democratic Party) and its former allies, including the KDU-CSL was forged. Gross's deputy within the CSSD, Jíri Paroubek, was sworn in as prime minister.

A vocal president

The fall of the Gross government did little to soothe the tongue of President Klaus. He continued to harry the government for the remainder of the year. In May, he signed into law an ODS-sponsored bill providing for compensation for victims of the Warsaw Pact period of occupation (1968–91). Although garnering a degree of cross-party support, the fact that the opposition drafted the new law drove home the fact that the government only had a one-seat majority. In July, President Klaus publicly lambasted Prime Minister Paroubek for suggesting that Germans expelled after the second World War who could prove that they were not Nazi sympathisers should be compensated. Around three million Germans lost their homes, after 1945, in what was then the Sudeten region of the Czech Republic.

The Roma community

In March 2005, Vera Dunkova, from the Czech Republic's minority Roma community, won a two-year court battle for compensation. Acting under cover for a Czech human rights group, Ms Dunkova had applied for a job in 2003 and had alleged that she had been discriminated against. There are approximately 300,000 Roma in the Czech Republic.

Outlook

Although the Czech government and the European Commission differ in their economic growth predictions for 2006, they agree that GDP growth will again be above 4 per cent. Inflation is also expected to remain low. Euroscepticism looks likely to continue to pervade both government and public opinion in 2006. A decision announced in September 2005 indicates that the government does not intend to seek membership of the euro-zone until January 2010 – the previous target had been 2009.

A general election is scheduled for June 2006, and will pit a coalition that has presented no less than three prime ministers since the last election against vocally eurosceptic and nationalist opposition. Considered a shoe-in by opinion polls in 2005, the ODS opposition vote has begun to soften, leaving open the prospect that the governing coalition of Prime Minister Paroubek might make a comeback. Whatever the result, a minority government or multi-party coalition is the most likely outcome.

Risk assessment

Politics	Fragile
Economy	Improving
Regional stability	Stable

COUNTRY PROFILE

Historical profile
1918 Czechoslovakia's independence was established. Before this, Moravia and Bohemia had been ruled by Austria, while Slovakia had been governed by Hungary.
1938 Czechoslovakia ceded its German-speaking areas of Sudetenland to Germany.
1939–45 The country fell under German control until the end of the Second World War.
1946 The Czechoslovak Communist Party (CPCz) formed a power-sharing government following national elections.
1948 After mass protests and strikes orchestrated by the Communists, a government crisis left the CPCz with a majority in government. Czechoslovakia became a

KEY INDICATORS — Czech Republic

	Unit	2000	2001	2002	2003	2004
Population	m	10.27	10.30	10.30	10.29	10.29
Gross domestic product (GDP)	US$bn	50.83	56.40	67.30	81.82	*107.05
GDP per capita	US$	4,949	5,484	6,552	7,951	10,480
GDP real growth	%	3.9	2.6	1.5	3.1	*4.0
Inflation	%	3.9	4.7	1.8	0.7	*2.8
Unemployment	%	8.9	8.5	9.0	7.5	8.3
Natural gas output	bn cum	3.7	3.9	4.0	4.0	0.0
Coal output	mtoe	23.2	25.8	24.3	70.8	23.5
Exports (fob) (goods)	US$m	29,019.0	33,349.0	38,000.0	40,800.0	66,510.0
Imports (fob) (goods)	US$m	32,115.0	36,477.0	41,700.0	43,200.0	68,190.0
Balance of trade	US$m	-3,095.0	-3,062.8	-3,700.0	-2,400.0	-1,680.0
Current account	US$m	-2,236.0	-2,638.0	-3,300.0	-4,300.0	-5,570.0
Foreign debt	US$bn	23.0	21.6	26.4	23.8	45.3
Total reserves minus gold	US$m	13,019.0	14,342.0	23,556.0	26,771.0	28,259.0
Foreign exchange	US$m	13,016.0	14,190.0	23,315.0	26,294.0	27,844.0
Foreign direct investment (FDI)	US$bn	4.5	4.8	7.9	–	–
Exchange rate	per US$	38.60	38.04	33.11	27.90	25.68

* estimated figure

Czech Republic

People's Republic, adopting a Soviet-style system.
1949–67 Stalinist-style rule, complete with party purges.
1968 Alexander Dubcek, the CPCz leader, introduced the policy of 'socialism with a human face' – a period known as the 'Prague Spring' – which ended with the crushing of the reformist movement by the Soviet army.
1969–88 There were on-going protests at occupation by the Soviet troops. Václav Havel and a group of dissidents called for the restoration of civil and political rights. Mass demonstrations in 1988 marked the anniversary of the 1968 invasion.
1989 The new spirit of *glasnost* was met with scepticism as the government initially resisted political and economic change. However, large public demonstrations in the major cities, the 'Velvet Revolution', led to the resignation of the Communist Party leadership. Václav Havel was elected president and a pluralistic political system and market economy were introduced.
1990 The country was renamed the Czech and Slovak Federative Republic. The first free elections since 1946 resulted in a coalition government involving all major parties, with the exception of the CPCz, and Havel was re-elected president.
1991 The Soviet forces completed their withdrawal.
1992 In elections, the Czech voters backed the centre-right, while the Slovaks supported Slovak separatists and left-wing parties. Vladimir Meciar (a supporter of Slovak separatism) became Slovak prime minister. He opposed the rapid privatisation of the public sector proposed by the Czech prime minister, Václav Klaus. Neither was prepared to compromise and agreed to the separation of Slovakia, despite President Havel's objections.
1993 Czechoslovakia divided into two independent countries, the Czech Republic (comprising the regions of Bohemia, Moravia and Silesia) and the Slovak Republic (Slovakia). Václav Havel was elected president of the Czech Republic and Václav Klaus continued as prime minister.
1996 Klaus was reappointed prime minister in a minority coalition government, following the Czech Republic's first parliamentary election.
1997 The Klaus government resigned following the collapse of the coalition over disagreements on the economic reform programme and allegations of financial corruption.
1998 Milos Zeman, leader of the Ceská Strana Sociálne Demokratická (CSSD) (Czech Social Democratic Party), became prime minister and Václav Havel was re-elected president.
1999 The Czech Republic joined NATO.
2000 In elections, a coalition of four small liberal parties, the '4Koalice', became the strongest force in the upper house.
2002 Torrential rain caused flooding in Prague when the river Vltava rose to its highest level since 1890. A state of emergency was declared. The CSSD won the parliamentary elections. President Václav Havel appointed Vladimír Spidla as prime minister and a coalition government was formed.
2003 Václav Klaus was elected president by parliament on 28 February and was sworn in on 7 March. Prime Minister Spidla survived a vote of no confidence on 11 March. In June, 77.3 per cent voted to join the EU; turnout was 55 per cent. On 26 September, Prime Minister Vladimír Spidla's government survived a second no-confidence vote.
2004 On 1 May, Czech Republic entered the EU. The government resigned on 30 June. The President asked Stanislav Gross to form a government; he appointed his cabinet on 4 August. The government won a vote of confidence on 24 August.
2005 Despite surviving a no-confidence vote on 1 April, Prime Minister Gross formally handed in the resignation of his government on 25 April and Jirí Paroubek was appointed prime minister; the new cabinet, unchanged in the key posts, was appointed the same day.

Political structure
Constitution
The constitution came into force on 1 January 1993. A majority of three-fifths of the members of parliament is required to change the constitution.
All citizens over the age of 18 are eligible to vote.
Form of state
Parliamentary democratic republic
The executive
The highest organ of executive power is the Council of Ministers, composed of the prime minister, the deputy prime ministers and ministers. It is answerable to the Chamber of Representatives.
The two legislative bodies together elect the president of the republic for not more than two five-year terms. The president's post is largely ceremonial but the president is the commander-in-chief of the armed forces. The president appoints the prime minister, and on the prime minister's recommendation, appoints the remaining members of the Council of Ministers.
National legislature
The Parliament (Parliament) is composed of two legislative bodies: the 200-member Poslanecká Snìmovna (Chamber of Deputies) (lower house), elected by proportional representation for a four-year term, and the 81-member Senát (Senate) (upper house), which is elected under a two-round majority system in 81 single-member constituencies. The Senate is partially renewed every two years, with one-third of the seats coming up for election. Senators serve a six-year term.
Legal system
The civil law system is based on Austro-Hungarian codes. Judicial power is exercised by independent courts.
Last elections
11–12 June 2004 (European Parliament); 28 February 2003 (third run-off presidential); 14–15 June 2002 (parliamentary).
Results: European Parliament: ODS won 30 per cent of the vote (nine seats out of 24); KSCM 20.3 per cent (six), Association of Independents/European Democrats 11 per cent (three), KDU-CSL 9.6 per cent (two), CSSD 8.8 per cent (two) and independents 8.2 per cent (two); turnout 28.3 per cent.
Parliamentary: the Ceská Strana Sociálne Demokratická (CSSD) (Czech Social Democratic Party) won 30.2 per cent of the vote (70 seats out of 200), the Obcanská Demokratická Strana (ODS) (Civic Democratic Party) 24.5 per cent (58 seats), the Komunistická Strana Cech a Morava (KSCM) (Communist Party of Bohemia and Moravia) and the coalition of the Krestanská a Demokratická Unie-Ceskoslovenská Strana Lidova (KDU-CSL) (Christian Democratic Union-Czechoslovak People's Party) and the Unie Svobody-Demokratická Unie (US-DEU) (Freedom Union-Democratic Union) 14.3 per cent (31 seats); turnout was 58 per cent.
Next elections
June 2006 (parliamentary); 2008 (presidential).

Political parties
Ruling party
Coalition government from 25 Apr 2005: the Ceská Strana Sociálne Demokratická (CSSD) (Czech Social Democratic Party) and the Koalice (Coalition), comprising Krestanská a Demokratická Unie-Ceskoslovenská Strana Lidova (KDU-CSL) (Christian Democratic Union-Czechoslovak People's Party) and the Unie Svobody-Demokratická Unie (US-DEU) (Freedom Union-Democratic Union)
Main opposition party
Obcanská Demokratická Strana (ODS) (Civic Democratic Party)

Population
10.29 million (2004); 10.20 million (OECD, 2003)

Nations of the World: A Political, Economic and Business Handbook

Ethnic make-up
The chief minorities are Slovaks (3 per cent of the population), Poles (0.6 per cent), Germans (0.5 per cent) and Silesians, Roma, Hungarians and Ukrainians.

Religions
Christianity is the principal religion, although 40 per cent of the population define themselves as atheist. Roman Catholicism is the main denomination (39 per cent of the population), followed by Protestant (5 per cent), Orthodox (3 per cent). There is a very small Jewish community, mainly in Prague.

The state and the church are linked, but there is growing pressure for their separation and the state no longer exercises control over church affairs.

Education
Compulsory education is free. Basic schooling is divided into two cycles with primary lasting for five years from aged six to 11; the second cycle lasts for four years until aged 15. Secondary schooling is offered in one of three designated institutions, a secondary general, technical or vocational school. Technical school programmes last up to six years, vocational courses last between three and four years and general secondary education last for four years and leads to higher education.

There are three universities, Prague's Charles' University (the oldest in Central Europe, founded in 1348), Masarykova University in Brno and Palacky University in Olomouc.

Public expenditure on education typically amounts to 5.1 per cent of annual gross national income.

Literacy rate: Virtually universal.
Compulsory years: Six to 15
Enrolment rate: 104 per cent gross primary school enrolment; 95 per cent gross secondary enrolment, of the relevant age group (including repetition rates) (World Bank).
Pupils per teacher: 18 in primary schools.

Health
Annual total expenditure on health is around 7.5 per cent of GDP. This is the highest proportion spent on health by any country in Central East Europe (CEE) of the OECD.

Since a market economy replaced the previously planned centralised economy healthcare has become more reative to local requirements, there are more clinics, many operated by foreign medical companies. Recently instituted heath insurance companies took in US$5.3 billion in 2004. The Czech constitution guarantees free health care for all citizens and sponsors health insurance through the General Health Insurance Company. Pure supplementary health care insurance is scarce and simply covers those items outside the mandatory state insurance. Some private companies cover four supplementary areas such as surgery, hospitalisation in the event of illness or accident, permanent disability and accidental death.

HIV prevalence: 0.1 per cent aged 15–49 in 2003 (World Bank)
Life expectancy: 75.2 years (World Bank)
Fertility rate/Maternal mortality rate: 1.2 births per woman; maternal mortality 9 per 100,000 live births (World Bank).
Infant mortality rate: 3.9 per 1,000 live births (World Bank)
Head of population per physician/bed: 3 physicians and 8.7 hospital beds per 1,000 people.

Welfare
The social security scheme provides old age pension insurance, sickness insurance, state social support benefits, and social care. Those registered in contracted employment, as self-employed (including farming personnel), and informal employment (employed for household duties), pay insurance premiums.

Pensions
A contribution not exceeding 3 per cent of the gross pay is regarded as a tax-deductible expense. The pension scheme significantly altered the conditions for retirement savings. The minimum retirement age for both men and women gradually increases to 63 years by 2012 and the government is proposing stricter criteria for early retirement.

Main cities
Prague (capital, estimated population 1.2 million in 2004); Brno (main city of Moravia) (376,400), Ostrava (Moravia) (317,700), Plzen (Pilsen) (164,900).

Languages spoken
The Czech and Slovak languages are mutually comprehensible. A large proportion of the population, particularly those engaged in industry and foreign trade, speak German. Hungarian, Romani and Polish are also spoken.

Official language/s
Czech

Media
Press
The Czech media enjoys freedom of expression and a reputation for irreverence. President Havel took one Czech newspaper to court in 1997 over articles relating to his marriage and has shown irritation concerning the intrusive and personal nature of media reporting. Czech newspapers have developed an irreverent, rather than investigative, style of reporting.

The Czech publishing sector has attracted significant foreign involvement since privatisation in 1991. By 1996, over half of the country's newspapers had non-Czech owners, mainly German and Swiss. Owing to the large size of the ex-patriate community in the Czech Republic, there are several English language newspapers and journals, of which *Prague Post* is best known.

Dailies: The largest national dailies include *Mladá fronta Dnes*, *Lidové Noviny*, *Blesk*, *Právo*, *ZN Zemské Noviny* and *Hospodárské Noviny*. *Blesk* tends to be sensationalist. *Právo* provides social-political analysis, *Lidové Noviny* carries intellectual commentary and analysis, *Hospodárské Noviny* economic and political news, *Haló Noviny* publishes political news.

Weeklies: The main weekly newspaper/magazine is *Blesk Magazin*. The weekly *Prague Post* is an English-language newspaper featuring general service, politics, economics and regular classifieds. *Prague Tribune* is a dual-language newspaper that is increasingly published in Czech rather than in English.

Business: *Czech Business Journal* is a weekly English-language publication. *Prague Business Journal* offers business, political and cultural news, as well as company and industry information. *The Prague Tribune* is a bi-monthly publication with an English-language electronic version available on the Internet (http://www.prague-tribune.cz).

Periodicals: There are around 800 magazines. The sector shows rapid changes, with new titles appearing and unsuccessful ones disappearing constantly. The main periodicals include *ABC Miadych Techniku Prirodovedcu*, published half yearly for youths, and *KDO JE KDO reveu* published bi-monthly caters to miscellaneous interests.

Broadcasting
Radio: Regional radio networks are being developed by the large number of independent stations as the sector begins to consolidate. There are 70 commercial radio stations.

Television: Ceská Televize (CT) (Czech Television), the only public broadcaster in the republic, has run at a loss in recent years. Czech TV was hit particularly hard by the rapid rise of TV Nova, the first national commercial channel launched in 1994.

Advertising
The Czech Republic has a well-developed advertising sector. Television and press media each typically take up over 40 per cent of adspend.

Czech Republic

Economy
The economy experienced substantial improvement in 2003 and 2004, with growth exceeding expectations. A surge in the last quarter of 2004 to 4.6 per cent accounted for the better outcome. The momentum was not maintained into the first quarter of 2005, but the growth for the year was projected to stay above 4 per cent. The main contributory factors were higher investment, mainly from abroad, and rising exports, which, stimulated by EU accession in May 2004, produced the best results since 2000 and substantially narrowed the trade deficit. Consumer spending, which was particularly important to growth in 2003, also continued to rise in 2004, although at a slower rate, a trend which, despite low inflation and rising incomes, seems set to continue. A negative factor is the unemployment rate, which is over 8 per cent.

Inflation, at 2.8 per cent, was lower than expected in 2004, despite some price rises and the uncertainties of EU accession. Inflation fell slightly in 2005 to 1.5 per cent. The Czech National Bank reduced its key interest rate to 1.75 per cent in April 2005.

Industrial output, especially in the metal, automotive and electrical sectors, has been strong. Cars and electrical appliances are manufactured by foreign-owned companies and target the export market.

External trade
Imports
The main classes of imports are machinery and transport equipment, raw materials and fuels, chemicals.
Main sources: Germany (36.2 per cent total, 2004), Austria (5.6 per cent), Italy (5.4 per cent), France (4.8 per cent), The Netherlands (4.7 per cent), Slovakia (4.7 per cent)

Exports
The modernisation of production facilities, resulting in the improved quality of exports have helped to promote export growth. Principal exports are machinery and transport equipment (52 per cent), chemicals, raw materials and fuel.
Main destinations: Germany (36.2 per cent total, 2004), Slovakia (9.1 per cent), Austria (6.1 per cent), Poland (5.5 per cent)

Agriculture
Farming
The agricultural sector accounts for around three per cent of GDP and 4.2 per cent of employment. Approximately 41 per cent of the country is arable land, 11 per cent permanent pasture and 2 per cent permanent crops. The most important crops are sugar beet, wheat, potatoes, maize, barley, rye and hops. The livestock industry is well developed with cattle, pigs, chickens and dairy products supplying the food processing industry.

Agriculture was collectivised during the communist period. Although production increased with the creation of large farms, soil erosion and the heavy use of machinery and chemicals have had a long-term detrimental effect on the landscape and environment. In 1991, parliament passed a law on land restitution, under which all land taken by the state after February 1948 was returned to its original owner or, if such a return was not possible, provided for the owner to be compensated. Large-scale operations still dominate the sector, with many of the same problems experienced during the communist era. Agriculture remains labour intensive, relying on inefficient techniques, outdated technology and a poor distribution system. EU membership should eventually help the sector to modernise and redevelop. The crop production in 2004 included: 8,769,193 million tonnes (t) cereals in total, 5,042,523t wheat, 2,330,582t barley, 934,674t rapeseed (canola), 29,000t poppy seed, 551,628t maize, 227,017t oats, 313,348t rye, 993,203t potatoes, 81,513t pulses, 69,733t grapes, 22,036t tomatoes, 421,747t oilcrops, 17,830t flax fibre, 6,311t hops, 4,976t treenuts, 3,579,278t sugar beet, 280,781t apples, 526,381t fruit in total, 336,884t vegetables in total. Livestock production included: 749,524t meat in total, 96,879t beef, 388,370t pig meat, 968t lamb, 38,500t rabbit, 223,692t poultry, 139.272t eggs, 2,614,062t milk, 7,738t honey, 11,753t cattle hides.

Fishing
The Czech Republic has a long tradition in freshwater fishing and aquaculture, owing to the thousands of man-made fish ponds dating from the middle ages. The principal catch is the common carp. The Czech Republic produces around 25,000 tonnes of freshwater fish per annum, of which around 13,000 tonnes are exported. Being landlocked, the country also imports over 200,000 tonnes of seafood per year. There are 12 processing plants.

Forestry
Forests cover around 2.6 million hectares (ha), about one-third of the total land area, with the growing stock volume per hectare considered among the highest in Europe. Coniferous species make up more than four-fifths of the stock volume. There is no other wooded land.

Three-quarters of forest land is publicly-controlled, mainly at national level; the remainder is privately-owned. Forest output is moderate and the industry depends largely on processing of domestic raw materials. Austria and Germany are important export markets for roundwood and sawn wood respectively.

The domestic wood industry satisfies the majority of industrial needs for newsprint, plywood, furniture and traditional woodworking.

The export of forest products in 2004 amounted to over US$1.4 billion, while imports were valued at over US$1.2 billion.

Production in 2004 included: 15,601,000 cubic metres (cum) roundwood, 14,411,000cum industrial roundwood, 3,940,000cum sawnwood, 8,428,000cum sawlogs and veneers, 5,593,000cum pulpwood, 1,390,000cum wood-based panels, 1,190,000cum woodfuel; 448,000 tonnes (t) recovered paper, 108,000t newsprint.

Industry and manufacturing
The industrial sector was among the most advanced in the world before the Second World War, with national GDP per capita the seventh highest in the world in 1938. The Communist takeover in 1948 led to the nationalisation of all enterprises and a concentration on heavy industry. Under communism there was insufficient capital investment, while a lack of management, marketing and financial skills handicapped the development of the sector. In common with its counterparts in other communist countries, Czech industry became characterised by outdated and inefficient technology, over-staffing and poor quality.

Since 1989, the Czech economy has diversified away from its heavy industrial base. Between 1986–98, industry's share of GDP fell from 60 per cent to 39 per cent as a flourishing services sector began to establish itself. In 2004, industry's share of GDP was 39.4 per cent, a drop from a high of around 40 per cent in 2001. The slowdown matched the global trend with manufacturing jobs increasingly being sourced in Asia.

Engineering is beginning to dominate the industrial sector. Automotive engineering accounted for 15.8 per cent of manufacturing exports in 2004.

Tourism
Tourism is a burgeonong sector, which has become a key contributor to the economy.The Czech Republic is one of the most popular tourist destinations in the world and Prague is one of Europe's favourite destinations. Over seven million visitor arrivals were recorded in 2004. A programme of renovation and modernisation has enhanced tourist facilities. Historic and cultural sites are the usual destinations for most visitors, but the health spas are increasingly popular. Tourism is expected to contribute 2.5 per cent to GDP in 2005.

Nations of the World: A Political, Economic and Business Handbook

Environment
One of the most lasting legacies of the communist era is pollution, with the Czech Republic one of the most despoiled corners of Europe. Not only is air pollution a major problem, water supplies have become infected and raw sewage has reportedly been dumped in waterways by individuals as well as factories. Although environmental awareness has grown since 1989, the government and the majority of the population have focussed on economic transformation and improving living standards rather than on the environment.

Hydrocarbons
The Czech Republic has proven oil reserves of only 17.3 million barrels, producing around 7,400 barrels per day. However oil companies are still interested in the region and currently the Western Carpathians are being explored for potential reserves. The Czech Republic currently imports oil from both Russia and Germany. There are three oil refineries with the Ceská Rafinérská being the largest. Natural gas reserves are around 3.1 billion cubic metres. Natural gas consumption increased by 35 per cent between 1993 and 2001 and is continuing to grow. The Czech Republic is reliant on imports to meet domestic demand with most of the natural gas coming from Russia and Norway.

The mining and hydrocarbons sector accounts for less than 5 per cent of GNP and employs a slightly smaller proportion of the workforce.

Energy
Electrical capacity is predominantly from thermal sources, with the remainder from hydroelectric and nuclear stations. The Czech Republic is a net exporter of electricity to Germany, Austria, Poland and Slovakia.

Strong emphasis is placed on the commissioning of new nuclear power stations and the upgrading of Chernobyl-style reactors to western safety standards. The country has two nuclear power plants, at Dukovany and Temelin.

Construction of the controversial Temelin nuclear power station began in the 1980s. The first reactor became operational in 2000, but was shut down several times due to technical problems. A second reactor became operational in January 2003, allowing Temelin to generate an extra 2,000MW of power. The power station will have to conform to EU safety standards by 2009.

Financial markets
Stock exchange
The Burza Cennych Papíru Praha (BCPP) (Prague Stock Exchange) was opened in 1993.

Banking and insurance
The country is suffering from high levels of public debt, approximately 18.8 per cent of GDP. Most of this debt can be attributed to government bail-outs in the banking sector. The IMF has estimated that continued bank restructuring will take up a large percentage of the Czech Republic's GDP.

Much of the bank restructuring has been as a result of the government attempting to ensure that there is compatibility between Czech and EU laws, following EU membership in 2004. This also includes continued privatisation, not least in the banking sector, where state-owned stakes in banks will gradually be eliminated.

The Foreign Exchange Act introduced partial liberalisation for capital account and full convertibility for current account transactions in Czech koruna. It also cleared the way for Czech membership of the Organisation for Economic Co-operation and Development (OECD), enabled companies to accept credit from non-resident banks and eased restrictions on direct investment.

The accumulation of bad domestic and international debt and non-performing loans, particularly to Russia, has reduced the attraction of Czech banking corporations to foreign investors. However, with the introduction of more stringent financial regulations and an improvement in accounting standards, bank privatisation will likely gain momentum.

Central bank
Ceska Národnì Banka (CNB) (Czech National Bank).

Time
GMT plus one hour (GMT plus two hours from late March to late September)

Geography
The Czech Republic is a landlocked country in central Europe, bordering Germany to the west, Poland to the north, Slovakia to the east, and Austria to the south. The landscape varies greatly from lowlands to Alpine-type mountains. It has numerous rivers (the Elbe (Labe), and its largest tributary, the Vltava, provide important links to sea ports).

With a total area of 78,864 square km the Czech Republic is slightly smaller than Austria and one-third the size of the UK. The country is split into two principal regions, Bohemia in the west and Moravia to the east. Surrounded by low mountains Bohemia is a plateau forming a basin drained by the Elbe and its tributary the Vltava. Prague is situated on the Vltava. The lowlands of Moravia are drained by the Morava which eventually flows into the Danube and by the Oder (Odra) which flows into the Baltic Sea.

Climate
The climate is continental with warm, showery summers and cold, snowy winters. June is the hottest month and January the coldest. February and March are the driest months and June, July and August the wettest. The average temperature in winter is -5 degrees Celsius (C) and in the summer around 20 degrees C.

Dress codes
Most people wear standard casual clothes. They do, however, dress up when eating out or going to the theatre or a concert. Some more exclusive restaurants do not admit people in casual wear and it is useful to enquire beforehand. For business, a suit and tie is advisable for men and a suit or dress for women.

Entry requirements
Passports
Passport required by all.
Visa
Required by all, except by most nationals of the Americas, Europe, Australasia, and some Asian countries; for stays of less than either 30 or 90 days. For these nationals, business trips are treated as tourism.

See http://czech.embassyhomepage.com for a full list of exceptions to visa controls. Business visas for nationals requiring visas require evidence of invitation from a local company and business letter of intention from employer.

Currency advice/regulations
Visitors must hold sufficient funds for the duration of their visit.

Major credit cards and travellers cheques are widely accepted. All hard currencies and Eurocheques are accepted. Note that commission rates on currency exchanges are very high. It is advisable to use your hotel, or the banks, many of which provide automated teller machine (ATM) services.

Health (for visitors)
Mandatory precautions
None
Advisable precautions
Immunisation for hepatitis 'A' and 'B' may be useful.

The Czech Republic has a reciprocal health agreement with the UK. Proof of UK residence is required before medical treatment can be received.

Credit cards
Credit cards are widely accepted.

Czech Republic

Public holidays
Fixed dates
1 Jan (New Year's Day), 1 May (Labour Day), 8 May (Liberation Day), 5 Jul (St Cyril and St Methodius Day), 6 Jul (Jan Hus Day), 28 Sep (Czech Statehood Day), 28 Oct (National Day), 17 Nov (Freedom and Democracy Day), 24–26 Dec (Christmas).
Variable dates
Easter Monday

Working hours
Banking
Mon–Fri: 0800–1800. There are also exchange offices in the main city centres, which operate seven days a week until 1900.
Business
Mon–Fri: 0800–1600.
Government
Mon–Fri: usually 0800–1600, but may vary.
Shops
Mon–Fri: 0800–1800; Sat: 0900–1200; some shops remain open late on Thursday evening.

Telecommunications
Mobile phones
GSM 900/1800 services are available throughout the country.

Electricity supply
Domestic: 220V, 50 cycles AC is almost universal, but there are still a few areas in Prague where 120V is supplied. Most of the better hotels have standard international two-pin plugs. Where these are not fitted, standard Czech sockets are used. Ordinary plugs will not fit, as they have an arrangement of two sockets and a grounding pin. Lamp fittings are screw-type. Industrial electricity supply is 360V, 50 cycles.

Weights and measures
The metric system is in use. In addition, the following measures are used: quintal or metric hundredweight = 100kg. Food is usually purchased by the decagram and kilogram.

Social customs/useful tips
A handshake is a traditional accompaniment to a greeting. Using a person's title is customary. Managing directors should be addressed as *reditel* and the chairman as *predseda*.
When visiting private homes it is customary to take flowers for the hosts. Visitors also generally leave their shoes in the hallway, partly as a mark of respect and partly because of pollution in the streets. As English was not widely taught in the Soviet era, many executives and officials do not have a working knowledge of the language. The use of a translator is, therefore, recommended.

The difference between a Slovak and a Czech may be difficult to spot; however mistaking one for the other can cause offence.
Tipping is appreciated in any restaurant, usually 5 to 10 per cent.
Drinking and driving is strictly forbidden. Illegally parked cars tend to be towed away by the police and it is advisable to park at attended car parks where the cost is relatively low.

Security
Street crime, especially in the centre of Prague, has increased since the 1989 revolution, as the police tend to keep a low profile. It is advisable to carry as little as possible in the way of valuables and cash. Car vandalism and theft have also increased.
Report any robberies in central Prague to the Central Police Office, Jungmannova 9, Prague 1 (tel: 6145-1760), where interpreters are available.

Getting there
Air
CSA Ceské Aerolinie (CSA Czech Airlines) flies to many capital cities in Western Europe. Regular shuttle flights fly from Prague to Bratislava and Kosice in Slovakia.
National airline: CSA Czech Airlines.
International airport/s: Prague-Ruzyne Airport (PRG), 15km from Prague.
Airport tax: None
Surface
Road: Entry is possible from Germany, Poland, Slovak Republic and Austria.
Rail: As part of the European intercity network there are convenient routes to the Czech Republic from Western Europe including the cities of Berlin, Frankfurt, Munich, Zurich and Vienna. The most famous and fastest trains include the Kafka, Goethe and the Einstein, which are operated by the state-owned Ceské Dráhy (CD) (Czech Railways).
The Vindobona Express operates daily from Vienna to Prague and on to Berlin. For more rail information call (tel: 2422-4200).
Water: As a landlocked country there are ferries only along the Vltava River from Germany.

Getting about
National transport
Air: CSA Ceské Aerolinie (CSA Czech Airlines) operates extensive low-cost domestic network.
There are regular daily flights from Prague to Brno, Ostrava, Presov, Holesov, Kosice, Piestany, Bystrica, Karlovy Vary and Poprad.
The approximate travel time from Prague to Brno is 45 minutes, one hour to Karlovy and 30 minutes to Karlovy Vary.

Road: There are several major highways linking Prague with the main towns (usually marked with an E). Motorways run from Prague to Plzen and Podebrady to Bratislava (Slovak Republic) via Brno. Users of the Czech motorways are required to purchase a vignette (season ticket) for each year.
Between 2000 and 2012, there are plans to build 987km of new highways.
Buses: The services of the national bus company, CAD, are faster and more comfortable than the train for many routes. The cost is equivalent to US$1 per hour of journey time, and tickets can be bought in advance from larger stations.
Rail: The rail service is efficient and coverage is comprehensive, composed of approximately 9,365km of track. It is advisable to book seats in advance on the main routes. Fares are low, although supplements may be charged for travel on express trains.
Water: There are many navigable waterways in the Czech Republic. The main river ports are located at Prague, Usti nad Labem and Decin.
City transport
Taxis: Legislation introduced in 1996, permitting drivers of official taxis to set their own rates for trips from the city centre to the airport and within the city confines, makes it advisable to negotiate prices before commencing travel. Higher charges are usually levied for night services.
Buses, trams & metro: The bus network is extensive, covering many areas not visited by rail. In addition to a flat-fare service, the buses are reliable and comfortable.
In Prague, tickets can be bought in advance from tabak shops and other shops displaying the sign Predprodej Jizdenek. On boarding the buses, insert your ticket into the top of the machines attached to the poles, then pull the handle towards you. Passes do not need to be punched. City buses operate predominantly on the outskirts of towns. City bus 119 leaves daily every five to seven minutes (peak times) or every 15 minutes (off-peak) for round trips from Dejvicka metro station to the airport. From the metro, follow the exit signs for Ruzyne Airport. An ordinary city transport ticket or pass is required before boarding. The CSA bus operates every 30 minutes from its terminal, off Revolucni near the river, to the airport. It also stops at Dejvicka metro station. Look for the sign that says 'Ruzyne'.
For more bus information (tel: 221-445).
Trams cover all the major streets and intersect with metro lines. There are tram services in Prague, Brno, Ostrava, Plzen and several other towns. Services usually operate between 0430–2400. After

midnight, night trams run approximately every 40 minutes. Blue badges on tram and bus stops denote an all night service. Tram 91, the 'historic tram', stops at most of the city's top sights, except for the castle. These trams run Saturdays, Sundays and during holidays, making hourly stops during the summer. Tickets should be punched in the appropriate machine on entering the tram. Note that a separate ticket is required when changing tram routes.

Car hire

Many of the international car hire companies, including Avis, Eurodollar and Hertz, operate in the Czech Republic. Speed limits are 60kph in towns and villages, 90kph on the main roads and 110kph on motorways. The speed limit is reduced to 80kph on motorways in built-up areas. It is advisable to avoid driving in the city centre as illegal parking will result in the use of car clamps.

Traffic drives on the right. Seat belts are compulsory and drink driving is strictly prohibited. An emergency road rescue service is available by calling 154. A valid national driving licence is required.

BUSINESS DIRECTORY

The addresses listed below are a selection only. While World of Information makes every endeavour to check these addresses, we cannot guarantee that changes have not been made, especially to telephone numbers and area codes. We would welcome any corrections.

Telephone area codes

The international dialling code (IDD) for the Czech Republic is + 420, followed by area code and subscriber's number:

Breclav	51	Ostrava	59
Brno	54	Plzen	37
Havirov	6994	Prague	2

Useful telephone numbers

Emergency calls:	158
Ambulance service:	155
Police:	158
	2121-1111
Traffic accidents:	154
	2121-3747
Emergency Medical Aid	298-341
(24-hours: doctors speak English and German):	290-651
Fire:	150
Directory enquiries: (Prague only):	120
International enquiries:	0135
Breakdown assistance:	154
	123
	777-521
Car repair service (24-hours):	733-351/3
Lost property office:	235-8887

Chambers of Commerce

American Chamber of Commerce in the Czech Republic, 10 Dusni, 11000 Prague 1 (tel: 2232-9430; fax: 2232-9433; e-mail: amcham@amcham.cz).

Breclav Chamber of Commerce, 10 namisti TG Masaryka, 69002 Breclav (tel: 932-6116; fax: 937-4126; e-mail: ohk@breclav.net).

British Chamber of Commerce - Czech Republic, 3 Pobrezni, 18600 Prague 8 (tel: 2483-5161; fax: 2483-5162; e-mail: britcham@britcham.cz).

Ostrava Regional Economic Chamber, 2224/8 Vystavni, 70900 Ostrava-Marianske Hory (tel: 747-9328; fax: 747-9324; e-mail: info@rhko.cz).

Banking

ABN AMRO Bank N.V. Amsterdam, Revolucni 1, 110 15 Prague 1 (tel: 22481-5141; fax: 22481-5100, 22481-5139).

Agrobanka Praha a.s. (largest private bank), Hybernska 18, 110 00 Prague 1 (tel: 22444-1111; fax: 22444-6199, 22444-1500).

Bankovni Asociace (Banking Association), Vodickova ulice 30, 110 00 Prague 1 (tel: 22422-5926; fax: 22422-5957).

BNP - Dresdner Bank, Vitezna 1, 150 000 Prague 5 (tel: 25700-6111).

Ceska Sporitelna a.s. (Czech Savings Bank), Na Prikope 29, 113 98 Prague 1 (tel: 22422-9268; fax: 22421-3455).

Ceskomoravska Stavebni, Ruzova 15, 110 00 Prague 1 (tel: 22407-2024; fax: 22407-2225).

Ceskomoravska Zarucni a Rozvojova Banks a.s., Jeruzalemska 4, 115 20 Prague 1 (tel: 22423-0734).

Ceskoslovenska Obchodni Banka a.s. (CSOB), Na Prikope 14, 115 20 Prague 1 (tel: 22411-1111; internet site: http://www.csob.cz).

Chase Manhattan, Karlova 27, 110 01 Prague 1 (tel: 22423-4313).

Citibank a.s., Evropska 178, 166 40 Prague 6 (tel: 22430-4243).

Commerzbank AG Frankfurt/Main, Pobocka Praha, Masarykovo Nabrezi 30, 110 00 Prague 1 (tel: 22491-5077, 22491-5329; fax: 22491-5850).

Credit Lyonnais Bank Praha, Ovocny trh 8-Myslbek Building, Prague 1 (tel: 22433-3543).

Creditanstalt a.s. Praha, Siroka 5, 110 01 Prague 1 (tel: 22110-2111; fax: 22481-2185).

Deutsche Bank AG, Pobocka Praha, Jungmannova 34, 110 00 Prague 1 (tel: 22421-2857; fax: 22422-5727).

Evropabanka a.s., Strosmayerovo nam 1, 170 01 Prague 7 (tel: 26671-2134).

GiroCredit Banka Praha a.s., Vaclavske nam 56, PO Box 749, 111 21 Prague 1 (tel: 22403-3333).

HVB Czech Republic, Prague (tel: 22111-2111; internet site: http://www.hvb.cz).

Interbanka a.s. Praha, Vaclavske nam. 40, 110 00 Prague 1 (tel: 22440-6111).

Komercni Banka a.s., Na Prikop 33, 114 07 Prague 1 (tel: 22402-1111; fax: 22424-3020).

Podnikatelska banka a.s., Rohacova 79, 130 79 Prague 3 (tel: 26121-6089; fax: 26121-6085).

Raiffeisenbank a.s. Praha, Vodickova 38, 110 00 Prague 1 (tel: 22423-1270; fax: 22423-1278).

Realitbanka a.s., Antala Staska 32, 146 20 Prague 4 (tel: 26104-5439).

Royal banka CS a.s., Krocinova 1, 110 00 Prague 1 (tel: 22422-8582; fax: 22422-4833).

Wustenrot - Stavebni Sporitelna s.a., Jugoslavska 29, 120 00 Prague 2 (tel: 22400-7200; fax: 22400-7204).

Zivnostenka Banka a.s., Na Prikope 20, 113 80 Prague 1 (tel: 22412-1111; fax: 22412-5555).

Central bank

Czech National Bank, Na Prikope 28, 110 08 Prague 1 (tel: 2441-8522; fax: 2421-7865; e-mail: info@cnb.cz).

Travel information

Cedok (travel and hotel corporation), Na Prikope 18, 111 35 Prague 1-Nove Mesto (tel: 22419-7111).

Czech Airlines (CSA), Airport Praha, Ruzyne 16008 (tel: 22480-6111; fax: 22481-5183; internet site: http://www.csa/cz/); City Service Centre, V Ceinici 5, 110 00 Prague 1 (underground line B, station Namesti Republiky) (tel: 22010-4111); sales and ticket reservations (tel: 22010-4310).

Buses (internet site: http://info.eunet.cz:5555/svt/abus_e.html).

Railway information: Hlavni nadrazi (the main station; serves most foreign destinations and many Czech cities and towns) general information (tel: 22461-1111); international tickets (tel: 22461-5108); reservations (tel: 22421-7654); Nadrazi Holesovice (Holesovice station; serves foreign destinations including Berlin, Vienna, Warsaw and Budapest) (tel: 22461-5865/6/7); (internet (information in English): http://www.cdrail.cz/ENGLISH/cd.htm).

National tourist organisation offices

Czech Tourist Authority Vinohradska 46 Praha 2 (tel: 2158-0411; internet:

Czech Republic

www.visitczechia.cz or www.cccr-info.cz); tourist information (tel: 22011-3229, between 0800 and 2000 hours; 22011-4512, 24 hours a day).

Ministries

Ministry of Agriculture, Tisnov 17, 117 05 Prague 1 (tel: 22181-2111; fax: 22481-0478).

Ministry of Culture, Milady Horakove 220, 160 41 Prague 6 (tel: 25708-5111; fax: 22431-8156; e-mail: minkult@mkcr.cz).

Ministry of Defence, Tychonova 1, 160 01 Prague 6 (tel: 22021-0255; fax: 22021-0257; e-mail: otevrenalinka@army.cz).

Ministry of Education, Youth and Sport, Karmelitska 8, 118 12 Prague 1 (tel: 25719-3111; fax: 25719-3790).

Ministry of the Environment, Vrsovicka 65, 100 10 Prague 10 (tel: 26712-1111; fax: 26731-0308: internet site: http://www.env.cz).

Ministry of Foreign Affairs, Loretanske namisti 5, 125 10 Prague 1 (tel: 22418-1111; fax: 22431-0017; e-mail: info@mzv.cz; internet site: http://www.czech.cz/).

Ministry of Health, Palackeho nam 4, 128 01 Prague 2 (tel: 22497-1111; fax: 22497 2111; e-mail: mzcr@mzcr.cz).

Ministry of the Interior, Nad Stolou 3, 170 34 Prague 7 (tel: 26142-1115; e-mail: dotazy@mvcr.cz; internet site: http://www.mvcr.cz).

Ministry of Justice, Vysehradska 16, 128 10 Prague 2 (tel: 22199-7111; fax: 22491-9927; e-mail: msp@msp.justice.cz: internet site: http://www.justice.cz).

Ministry of Labour and Social Affairs, Na Poøienim pravu 1, 128 01Prague 2 (tel: 22491-8391; fax: 22192-2664).

Ministry of Regional Development, Staromestske namisti 6, 110 15 Prague 1 (tel: 22486-1111; fax: 22486-1333).

Ministry of Transport and Communications, Naboei Ludvika Svobody 12, 110 15 Prague 1 (tel: 25143-1111; fax: 22481-0596; e-mail: utv0001@mdcr.cz).

Office of the Prime Minister, Naboei Eduarda Benese 4, 118 01 Prague 1 (tel: 22400-2111; fax: 22481-0231).

Office of the President, Prague Castle, 119 08 Prague 1 (tel: 22437-1111; fax: 22437-3300).

Other useful addresses

Asociace investicnich fondu (Association of Investment Companies and Funds), Tynska 21, 110 00 Prague 1 (tel: 22481-0063; fax: 22481-0063).

Asociace obchodnich spolecnosti a podnikatelu CR (Association of Trading Companies and Businessmen), Skretova 6, 120 59 Prague 2 (tel: 22421-5371/81; fax: 22423-0570).

Association of Czech Entrepreneurs, Skretova 6, 12059 Prague 2 (tel & fax: 22423-0580).

BBC (Radio), Na Porící 12, Prague 1 CZ-110 00 (tel: 22487-2545; fax: 22487-2546).

Board of Legislation and Public Administration, Vladislavova 4, PO Box 596, 117 15 Prague 1 (tel: 22419-1111; fax: 22421-5060).

British Embassy, Commercial Section, Palac Myslbek Na Prikope 21, 11719 Prague 1 (tel: 22224-0021/22/33; fax: 22224-3625).

Centrum vnejsich ekonomickych vztahu (Centre For Foreign Economic Relation), Politickych veznu 20, PO Box 791, 111 21 Prague 1 (tel: 22422-1586, 22406-2421; fax: 22422-1575).

Cesky statisticky urad (Czech Statistical Office), Sokolovska 142, 180 00 Prague 8 (tel: 26604-2414).

Confederation of Industry of the Czech Republic, Mikulandska 7, 11361 Prague 7 (tel: 22499-5679).

CzechInvest (Czech Agency for Foreign Investment), Stepanska 15, 120 00 Prague 2 (tel: 29634-2500; fax: 29634-2502; e-mail: marketing@czechinvest.org; internet site: http://www.czechinvest.org).

Czech Republic Embassy (USA), 3900 Spring of Freedom Street, NW, Washington DC 20008 (tel: 202-274-9100; fax: 202-966-8540; e-mail: amb_pol_washington@embassy.mzv.cz).

Czech Television (CTV) - Public Corporation, Kavcí Hory, Prague 4 CZ-140 70 (tel: 26113-1111).

Euro Information Centre, Network/Correspondence Centre, NIS Havelkova 22, 130 00 Prague 3 (fax: 22423-1114).

Fond narodniho majetku (National Property Fund), Rasinovo nabrezi 42, 120 00 Prague 2 (tel: 22491-1111; fax: 2206-618).

Nejvyssi soud CR (Czech Supreme Court), Buresova 20, 657 37 Brno (tel: 4132-1237; fax: 4121-3493).

NIS (National Information Centre of the Czech Republic), Havelkova 22, 130 00 Prague 3 (tel: 2421-5808/15, 2422-2026/9; fax: 2322-1484, 2422-3177).

Prazska informacni sluzba (Prague Information Service), Senovazne namesti 23, 110 00 Prague 1 (tel: 544-444; fax: 2421-1989).

Sdruzeni soukromych zemedelcu Cech, Moravy a Slezska (Association of Private Farmers of Bohemia, Moravia and Silesia), Tesnov 17, 117 05 Prague 1 (tel: 2491-3606; fax: 2491-0162).

Svaz prumyslu a dopravy CR (Confederation of Industry of the Czech Republic), Mikulandska 7, 113 61 Prague 1 (tel: 2491-5253).

UNIDO (Federation of Czech Industries), Mikulandska 7, 113 61 Prague 1 (tel: 22491-5679; fax: 22491-5253).

Ustavni soud CR (Czech Constitutional Court), Jostova 8, 660 83 Brno 2 (tel: 24216-1111).

Internet sites

Brno Trade Fairs and Exhibitions Co Ltd (press information): http://www.bvv.cz/bvv

Czech business directory: http://www.muselik.com/czech/cbd.html

Czech directory: http://www.inform.cz/def.asp

Czech Embassy in Washington DC: http://www.mzv.cz/washington

Czech Ministry of Finance: http://www.mfcr.cz

Czech Ministry of Industry and Trade: http://www.mpo.cz

Czech Office for Protection of Competition: http://compet.cz

Czech Republic (provides links to information about the country): http://www.muselik.com/czech/toc.html

Czech Telecommunications Office: http://www.ctu.cz

Czech Trade Promotion Agency: http://www.czechtrade.cz/

Czech Trade Promotion Agency (in English): http://www.czechtradeoffices.com/Global

Hotels and history: http://www.abaka.com/Czech/

IPB (Investicni A Postovni banka as): http://www.ipb.cz

Office of Czech Republic: http://vlada.cz

Denmark

KEY FACTS

Official name: Kongeriget Danmark (The Kingdom of Denmark)

Head of State: Queen Margrethe II

Head of government: Prime Minister Anders Fogh Rasmussen (V) (since 2001, re-elected Feb 2005)

Ruling party: Right-wing coalition government comprising the Venstre (V) (Liberal Party) and the Konservative Folkeparti (KF) (Conservative People's Party), supported by the Dansk Folkeparti (DF) (Danish People's Party) (coalition re-elected 8 Feb 2005)

Area: 43,080 square km

Population: 5.41 million (2004); 5.39 million (OECD, 2003)

Capital: Copenhagen

Official language: Danish

Currency: Danish krone (Kr) = 100 ore

Exchange rate: Kr6.19 per US$ (Oct 2005) (pegged through the original European Exchange Rate Mechanism; trades around Kr7.43 per euro)

GDP per capita: US$44,929 (2004)

GDP real growth: 2.30% (2004); *3.4% (2005)

Labour force: 2.85 million (2004)

Unemployment: 5.40% (OECD, 2004)

Inflation: 1.20% (2004)

Oil production: 394,000 bpd (2004)

Balance of trade: US$9.61 billion (2004)*

Foreign debt: US$348.96 billion (2004)

Annual FDI: US$71.20 billion (cumulative, 1995–2004, OECD)

* estimated figure

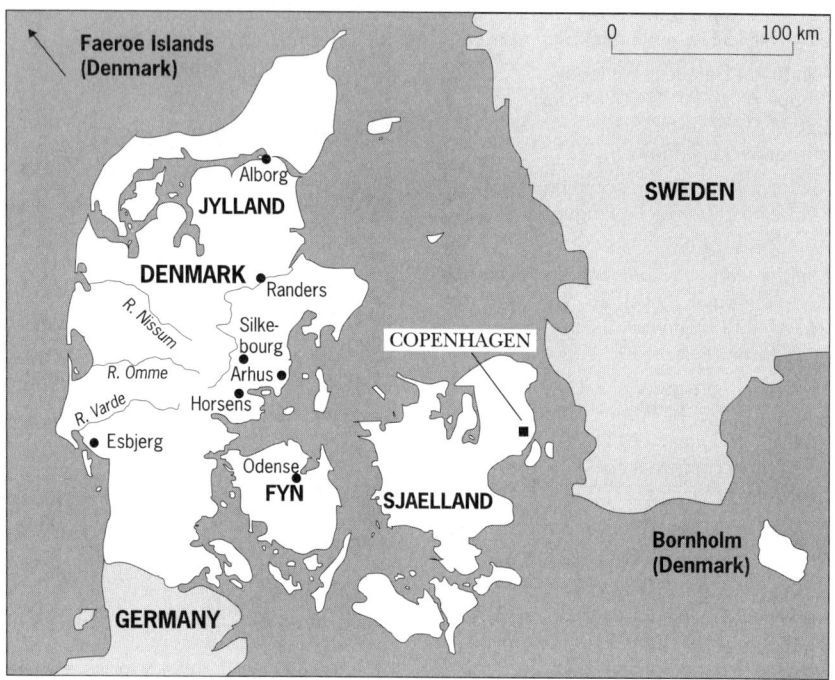

It was election year in 2005 for Denmark, with a general election in February and local elections in November. It was also a year in which the twin issues of Denmark's relationship with its Muslim minority and Denmark's relationship with Muslim-majority states were never far from the headlines.

High growth

In 2005, Denmark's GDP is estimated to have grown significantly, rising from 2.3 per cent in 2004 to 3.4 per cent in 2005. Denmark easily met most EU criteria for eligibility for entry into the euro-zone in 2005 but neither the government nor the populace appears keen to join – and despite the fact that the local currency, the krone, is pegged to the euro. Denmark rejected adopting the euro in a referendum in 2000.

A political year

In a bid to cash in on favourable opinion polls, Prime Minister Anders Fogh Rasmussen called an election for 8 February, nine months ahead of schedule. Rasmussen's Venstre (V) (Liberal Party) and his Konservative Folkeparti (KF) (Conservative Peoples' Party) allies subsequently emerged as the largest bloc in parliament. Drawing once again on the non-coalition vote the Dansk Folkeparti (DF) (Danish Peoples' Party) for a working majority, Rasmussen was duly sworn in as prime minister – the first Venstre prime minister ever to win a second term. Rasmussen's reaction, in December, to the findings of a two-year Velfærdskommissionen (Welfare Commission) suggested that the second Rasmussen government would differ little from its consensual style, particularly in relation to fiscal policy. The Velfærdskommissionen urged extra efforts to boost labour supply and reform the pension system but the government has said it will stick to Plan 2010, a fiscal strategy embraced by all mainstream political parties in 2001.

Local elections were held on 5 November, with Venstre defending a swag of mayoralties. The opposition Socialdemokratiet i Danmark (SD) (Social Democracy in Denmark) secured stunning

Denmark

victories across the country, including the mayoral offices in Denmark's four biggest cities. The results were hailed by SD officials and some analysts as the beginning of the SD's return to national power.

Immigration and Islam: a tricky year

Immigration, particularly from predominantly Muslim countries, once again rated as a key issue in Denmark's general election. Immigrants make up approximately 8 per cent of the country's population and of these nearly 50 per cent are Muslim. The 2001–05 Venstre-led government had imposed a number of restrictions on immigration into Denmark, producing, in 2002, what Rasmussen declared the toughest immigration laws in Europe. In pushing his 'tough on immigration' credentials, Rasmussen faced competition in the election campaign from the DF, which, among other things, advocated banning the use of non-Danish languages in Denmark.

A number of other incidents during 2005 reinforced the view that Denmark, once widely regarded as a bastion of tolerance, had adopted a less flexible attitude towards issues such as cultural diversity and race. In January, the supreme court ruled that a supermarket had the right to sack a Muslim employee who had refused a request that she not wear her headscarf to work. In April, Danish Queen, Margrethe II, was quoted as saying that Denmark had been too tolerant of Islamic radicalism, and that Muslim immigrants should improve their Danish so as to integrate better into society. In June, an anti-racist group claimed responsibility for an arson attack on the immigration minister's car. In August, a radio station had its licence revoked after calling for the extermination of Muslim immigrants. The temperature was further raised when ambassadors from 10 mainly Muslim countries demanded that Prime Minister Rasmussen take action against a Danish newspaper that had, in September, published cartoons depicting Mohammed as a terrorist. Rasmussen drew international criticism, in December, when he refused to meet with the ambassadors to discuss the issue.

The US alliance

By contributing troops to the US-led invasion and continuing occupation of Iraq, Denmark's relationship with the US has been close in recent years. In May 2005, US president George W Bush visited Denmark and publicly thanked the country for its assistance in both Iraq and Afghanistan. This alignment has not been without its critics, in Denmark and further afield.

The opposition SD leader pledged to withdraw Denmark's troops from Iraq if he won the election in February. A group of Danish citizens brought a lawsuit against Prime Minister Rasmussen in October, arguing that he contravened the constitution by going to war against Iraq. Worryingly, there have been threats by extremist groups to carry out attacks in Denmark similar to those in London in July, ostensibly in retaliation for Danish participation in the Iraq invasion. Also in October, six Muslim men were arrested in Denmark on suspicion of conspiracy to carry out a terrorist attack.

Hans off my Danish

A dispute between Denmark and Canada going back more than 30 years flared up again in July 2005. The Canadian defence minister paid a visit to the disputed Hans Island, lying between Greenland (Danish) and Ellesmere Island (Canadian). The Danish government protested the visit, stating that the island was Danish territory. Enthusiastic Danish and Canadian citizens subsequently traded insults, claims and counter-claims on the Internet. The Canadian foreign ministry sought to calm the atmosphere by insisting that it would continue to stock 'Danish pastries' in its canteen. A draft agreement was signed in September, setting out a path to resolve the dispute without rancour.

Royal headlines

For a country blessed (or cursed) with a relatively low-key monarchy, it was an unusually well-reported year for Denmark's royal family. Aside from the publication of Margrethe II's social engineering advice regarding Denmark's Muslim population, the royal family recorded its first divorce in 160 years. Margrethe's youngest son, Prince Joachim officially separated from his wife, Princess Alexandra. Crown Princess Mary, wife of Crown Prince Frederik, gave birth to a son, Christian. Also, in its first ever public financial report, the royal family was revealed to have overspent its annual allowance by some US$3 million.

Hans Christian Andersen

On 2 April 2005, Denmark celebrated the 200th anniversary of the birth of the widely loved fairy tale writer, Hans Christian Andersen. A concert was organised in Andersen's home town of Odense, with proceeds from ticket sales earmarked for literacy programmes in the developing world.

Outlook

Many analysts, including the OECD, warn that by ignoring the Velfærdskommissionen findings, the Rasmussen government might not be able to tackle Denmark's longer-term economic problems. GDP growth is forecast to slow in 2006, to around 2.9 per cent – still relatively healthy compared to other EU economies.

Given that the next general election isn't until 2009, SD claims of a revival may be a little premature. However, with Venstre

KEY INDICATORS — Denmark

	Unit	2000	2001	2002	2003	2004
Population	m	5.33	5.36	5.38	5.39	5.41
Gross domestic product (GDP)	US$bn	162.70	161.50	174.80	212.76	*243.04
GDP per capita	US$	30,530	30,240	32,491	39,453	44,929
GDP real growth	%	2.8	1.6	1.0	0.5	*2.3
Inflation	%	2.9	2.4	2.4	2.0	*1.2
Unemployment	%	5.3	5.2	5.0	5.5	5.4
Oil output	'000 bpd	359.0	342.0	371.0	368.0	394.0
Natural gas output	bn cum	8.1	8.4	8.4	7.9	9.4
Exports (fob) (goods)	US$m	50,703.0	50,943.0	56,800.0	67,887.0	73,060.0
Imports (fob) (goods)	US$m	43,946.0	43,983.0	49,230.0	58,749.0	63,450.0
Balance of trade	US$m	6,758.0	6,960.0	8,000.0	9,138.0	9,610.0
Current account	US$m	2,507.0	4,142.0	4,920.0	5,900.0	3,460.0
Total reserves minus gold	US$m	15,108.0	17,110.0	29,986.0	37,105.0	39,084.0
Foreign exchange	US$m	14,469.0	16,117.0	25,901.0	36,004.0	38,196.0
Exchange rate	per US$	8.08	8.32	7.75	6.52	5.99

* estimated figure

Nations of the World: A Political, Economic and Business Handbook

having been dealt its first real setback, in November, at a local level in years, it remains to be seen how well its party machine holds up.

The Rasmussen government can definitely expect pressure from several Muslim countries in 2006, over the issue of the cartoons depicting Mohammed. In January, Prime Minister Rasmussen welcomed an apology from the Danish newspaper at the heart of the dispute but refused demands from some Muslim governments for an official apology. Saudi Arabia recalled their ambassador in protest and Libya said it would close its embassy in Copenhagen, while in Palestine it provoked an extreme reaction when gunmen raided the Danish Red Cross offices in the Gaza Strip. The Danish government can also expect pressure from Danish businesses, especially those who stand to lose out in any 'boycott Danish' campaign in the Muslim world.

Risk assessment

Politics	Stable
Economy	Stable
Regional stability	Stable

COUNTRY PROFILE

Historical profile
Denmark is an ancient kingdom situated on an archipelago, which has historically served as a bridge between continental Europe and the Scandinavian peninsula. During the Napoleonic era, the Danes sided with the French and, as a result of their defeat, lost their dominance in Scandinavia.
1397 The Union of Kalmar united Denmark, Sweden and Norway under a single monarch.
1523 Denmark recognised Swedish independence.
1729 Greenland became a Danish province.
1814 Denmark ceded Norway to Sweden.
1849 Denmark became a constitutional monarchy with a bicameral parliament.
1903 Iceland was granted home rule from Denmark.
1918 Iceland became a sovereign state in union with Denmark.
1914–18 Denmark was neutral during the First World War.
1918 Denmark's transition to parliamentary government with universal suffrage was fully established after the First World War and has been suspended only during the Nazi occupation of the Second World War.
1939 Denmark signed a non-aggression pact with Nazi Germany.
1940 Germany invaded Denmark.
1945 The German occupation ended. Denmark recognised the independence of Iceland.
1948 The Faroe Islands were granted self-government within the Kingdom.
1949 Denmark was one of the founder members of NATO.
1953 A revision of the constitution allowed for female succession to the throne, abolition of the upper house of parliament and the introduction of proportional representation. Greenland became an integral part of Denmark.
1959 Denmark joined the European Free Trade Association (EFTA).
1972 Queen Margrethe ascended the throne.
1973 Denmark joined the European Economic Community (EEC).
1979 Greenland was granted home rule; Denmark retained control over Greenland's foreign affairs and defence.
1985 Parliament passed legislation to ban the construction of nuclear power plants.
1992 In a referendum, voters rejected the Maastricht Treaty on further European integration.
1993 Poul Schlüter, prime minister since 1982, resigned after a judicial enquiry criticised him for misleading parliament in 1989 over the Tamil visa scandal. A four-party coalition government was formed by Poul Nyrup Rasmussen. Denmark voted in favour of a revised Maastricht treaty.
1994 Rasmussen was returned to power after a general election.
1998 Danish voters endorsed the EU's Amsterdam treaty, which prepared the way for former eastern bloc countries to join the EU.
2000 In a referendum, Denmark voted against joining Europe's single currency.
2001 The Venstre (Liberal Party), led by Anders Fogh Rasmussen, won a slim majority in the parliamentary elections, he was only able to form a minority administration, in coalition with the Konservative Folkeparti (KF) (Conservative People's Party), relying on support from the far right-wing Dansk Folkeparti (DF) (Danish People's Party) in order to command a majority in parliament.
2002 New immigration rules sparked controversy. The EU-Russia summit was moved from Copenhagen to Brussels, when Russian President Putin threatened to boycott the summit if it was held in Copenhagen. A conference of Chechen exiles was also due to begin in Copenhagen at the same time.
2004 In May, Crown Prince Frederik married Australian-born Mary Donaldson, (their first son was born on 15 October 2005). Denmark and US agreed a deal to modernise the US Thule airbase in Greenland, over the objections of many local people.
2005 In the 8 February parliamentary elections, the ruling coalition retained power. The DF gained two more seats. A dispute with Canada over the ownership of Hans Islands, halfway between Greenland and Canada, erupted in July. In September the dispute was settled with a draft protocol to manage their dealings concerning the island.
2006 In January, Denmark ran into trouble when a boycott was threatened in the Middle East, over cartoons of Mohammed that has appeared in *Jyllands Posten* newspaper in Septermber 2005.

Political structure
Constitution
Denmark has a written constitution – *The Constitution Act* – adopted on 5 June 1953. It sets out the rights and requirements of the monarchy, state church, government, judiciary and the individual. The monarchy is governed by the *Succession to the Throne Act*, adopted 27 March 1953, whereby royal power is inherited. The Faroe Islands are a Danish external territory, electing two members to the Danish parliament, which maintains responsibility for constitutional, foreign and defence matters. A High Commissioner represents the Danish government and advises on joint affairs.
Greenland is a special cultural community in the Kingdom of Denmark. Only foreign policy, defence, police and monetary policy are Danish state affairs. Greenland elects two members to the Danish parliament.
Form of state
Constitutional monarchy
The executive
Executive power is vested in the monarch, and legislative power vested jointly in the monarch and parliament. The King appoints the prime minister and cabinet, who form the Council of State; they are responsible to the Folketing (parliament). All legislation is subject to the constitution.
National legislature
Since 1953, the Folketing has been a unicameral parliament of 179 members (175 members are elected for a four-year term, 135 of them by proportional representation in 17 districts and 40 others allotted in proportion to their total vote, plus two representatives each from the Faroe Islands and Greenland). Voting is not compulsory, and is open to all men and women over 18 years.
Legal system
Denmark's highest court is the Supreme Court in Copenhagen, made up of 15 judges. It hears appeals from two superior courts in Copenhagen and Viborg. These courts deal with appeals from the 84

Denmark

tribunals, or lowest courts of justice, around the country. They can also deal initially with cases of greater consequence.

Last elections
8 February 2005 (parliamentary); 13 June 2004 (European Parliament).
Results: Parliamentary: the ruling coalition retained power – the V Party won 29 per cent of the vote (52 seats out of 179), the SD 25.9 per cent (47), the Danish People's Party 13.2 per cent (24), the KF 10.3 per cent (18), the Radical Left-Social Liberal Party 9.2 per cent (17), the SF 6 per cent (11); The Greens 3.4 per cent (six) and two representatives each from the Faroe Islands and Greenland. Turnout is 84.4 per cent.
European Parliament: SD won 32.5 per cent of the vote (five seats out of 14), the V Party 19.4 per cent (three), KF 11.2 per cent (one), June Movement 9 per cent (one), SF 8.1 per cent (one), DF 6.8 per cent (one), Radical Left-Social Liberal Party 6.4 per cent (one) and People's Movement against EU 5.2 per cent (one); turnout 47.8 per cent.

Next elections
27 September 2005 (referendum on EU constitution); 2009 (parliamentary).

Political parties
Ruling party
Right-wing coalition government comprising the Venstre (V) (Liberal Party) and the Konservative Folkeparti (KF) (Conservative People's Party), supported by the Dansk Folkeparti (DF) (Danish People's Party) (coalition re-elected 8 Feb 2005)

Main opposition party
Socialdemokratiet i Danmark (SD) (Social Democracy in Denmark), Det Radikale Venstre (Radical Left (social liberal party)); Socialistisk Folkeparti (SF) (Socialist People's Party); De Grønne (The Greens).

Population
5.41 million (2004); 5.39 million (OECD, 2003)

Ethnic make-up
Danes make up the majority of the population, along with some 9,000 Greenlanders and around 12,000 Faroese. The largest immigrant groups from outside the kingdom are Turkish, British and Norwegian. There is a small German minority in southern Jutland.

Religions
The majority of the population (90 per cent) belong to the Lutheran Church although there are small groups of other Christian denominations.

Education
There are 10 years of compulsory schooling, although the average student attends school for 15 years.

The participation rate at primary and secondary levels is close to 100 per cent of the relevant age groups. Forty-six per cent of the relevant age group attend education at a tertiary level. The cost of university or post-high school further education is financed by a system of student grants supplemented by bank loans carrying a state guarantee.
Compulsory years: Seven to 16.
Pupils per teacher: 10 in primary schools.

Health
Total expenditure on health, is 8–9 per cent of GDP, of which 82–83 per cent is government spending.
Hospitalisation and treatment by general practitioners is free of charge, but there are part-charges for medicine prescribed by GPs. Treatment by dentists and opticians is subsidised but not free. Since 1988, several small private hospitals have opened, the fees for which can be covered by insurance schemes.
HIV prevalence: 0.2 per cent aged 15–49 in 2003 (World Bank).
Life expectancy: 77.1 years (World Bank)
Fertility rate/Maternal mortality rate: 1.8 births per woman; maternal mortality 0.1 per 1,000 live births: (World Bank)
Infant mortality rate: 4.4 per 1,000 live births (World Bank)
Head of population per physician/bed: 2.9 doctors and 5 hospital beds per 1,000 people.

Welfare
There is an extensive cradle-to-the-grave social security system, however the size of the welfare system has gradually been reduced since the 1990s. In 2005, the system came under close scrutiny and a government commissioned appraisal recommended that the pension aged should be raised and early retirement phased out, and charges set for some healthcare and educational services.
Currently welfare benefits include unemployment benefits, supplementary benefits and rent and heating grants.
Social security and welfare spending as a share of GDP is approximately 5.8 per cent.

Pensions
Denmark was the first country to introduce old age pensions in 1895, funded by two general taxes. To sustain the current pensions, there is a three pillar approach to provision. Pillar one is a basic, mandatory, publically administered scheme, maintained to provide for the poor in old age and may be supplemented by other allowances. Pillar two are mandatory, privately administered schemes and workplace pensions, which are devised to attract contributions as high as 16 per cent of wages. Pillar three are privately administered schemes with individual and voluntary contributions. Other schemes exist and fall within the rules of the three pillars.

Main cities
Copenhagen (capital, estimated population 1.1 million in 2004), Aarhus (220,700), Odense (144,600), Aalborg (120,600), Esbjerg (72,700).

Languages spoken
English and German are widely spoken in business and administration.
Official language/s
Danish

Media
The relationship between the Danish government and the press is very relaxed, and unhampered by government controls. A law enshrining the principle of openness in government, except for matters involving security, was passed in 1970. The newspaper press is not directly subsidised by the state, but it is exempt from the 25 per cent value added tax.

Press
There are nearly 400 newspapers in Denmark. Readership levels are high (85.6 per cent of all adults) and Sunday circulation is particularly strong. Market trends in recent years included the increasing popularity of broadsheets at the expense of evening tabloids and the fragmentation of the magazine readership, with family weeklies losing out to women's titles. Most publications are privately owned and tend to have fairly strong political leanings.
Dailies: There are almost 50 daily newspapers in Denmark, with Sunday readership particularly high. The leading newspapers are *Morgenavisen Jyllands Posten*, *Ekstra Bladet* and *Berlingske Tidende*.
Weeklies: The most popular Sunday newspapers include *Jyllands Posten*, *B.T.*, *Politiken*, *Ekstra Bladet*, *Berlingske Tidende*, *Jydske Vestkysten*, *Aktuelt.dk*, *Aktuelt* and *Børsen*. Other weeklies include *Kig Ind* and *Se og Hør*.
Business: *Børsen* is the leading business daily. Other popular business magazines include *Børsens Guldnr* (twice a year), *Børsens Nyhedsmagasin* (fortnightly), *Penge og Privaton Økonomi* (monthly), *Finansfokus* and *Nationaløkonomisk Tidsskrift*.
Periodicals: Periodicals on general interest, life-style, consumer and commercial interest include *Blender*, *Det Bedste fra Reader's Digest*, *En Skør Skør Verden*, *Social Demokraten* and the commercial quarterly *Ase Nyt*.

Broadcasting
Radio: The state radio service offers four radio channels: P1 (news and current affairs), P2 (classical music), P3 (for young people) and P4 (regional stations). DR Nyheder International broadcasts news in English. There are also a number of commercial radio stations throughout the country; two commercial networks, one national and one semi-national, were launched in 2003.
Television: There are six major TV channels broadcasting substantially in Danish and some minor channels such as TV6 and ZTV. The country's first national advertising-financed television station, TV2, introduced in 1988, is the market leader. The non-commercial public broadcaster, DR1, is second.

Advertising
The most widely used advertising media are the press and cinemas. Direct mail is also popular. TV2 is Denmark's advertising-financed television station. There is limited advertising on radio, and poster sites are heavily regulated.

Economy
Denmark has a balanced economy with a well-developed, export-based manufacturing sector, and an important agricultural sector. It is one of the wealthier EU countries on a per capita basis, benefitting from the development of offshore oil and gas reserves since the 1970s. The economy is heavily oriented towards export markets. The government has maintained a stable currency and successive foreign debt reductions. A large and comprehensive welfare state has helped keep Denmark's tax burden at the second highest level in the OECD after Sweden. Between 2004 and 2006, phased tax cuts are being introduced, to be offset by savings in public administration.

Denmark's GDP grew much faster than the EU average from 1994 to 2000, but in the unfavourable global economic climate from 2001, GDP fell for three years running. Recovery has been sluggish, but GDP grew by 2.3 per cent in 2004, as domestic expenditure and exports increased. The unemployment rate was 5.4 per cent in 2004.

External trade
Around 45 per cent of trade turnover is with other EU countries. Denmark has traditionally run up a healthy balance of trade surplus.

Imports
Principal imports are machinery and equipment, raw materials and semi-manufactures for industry, chemicals, grain and foodstuffs and consumer goods.
Main sources: Germany (22.9 per cent total, 2004), Sweden (12.4 per cent), The Netherlands (7.6 per cent), France (5.6 per cent), UK (5.4 per cent), Norway (5.0 per cent), Italy (4.3 per cent)

Exports
Principal export commodities include machinery and instruments, meat and meat products, dairy products, fish, chemicals, furniture, ships.
Main destinations: Germany (16.9 per cent total, 2004), Sweden (14 per cent), UK (6.9 per cent), US (5.4 per cent), France (5.2 per cent), The Netherlands (5.1 per cent), Norway (4.8 per cent)

Agriculture
Farming
The agricultural sector typically contributes around 3 per cent of GDP and employs 4 per cent of the labour force. The sector is organised into local co-operatives which are united in national federations. Agriculture benefits from the Common Agricultural Policy (CAP), which imposes import duties on products entering the EU from other countries in order to equalise the price of imported commodities with those produced within the union. Efforts to reform the CAP could have a significant impact on future production.

The government primarily acts as a regulator in the agricultural sector. It sets veterinary standards and lays down the rules for farm mergers and ownership. The government does not set production or export and import targets, and as a member of the EU, agriculture is subject to the EU agricultural production quota regime. Intensive farming is concentrated on livestock production, mainly pig-meat, beef, veal, poultry and dairy produce.

Denmark has large world market shares in products such as pig-meat, dairy products, seeds, mink pelts and fish products. The estimated crop production for 2004 included: 8,963,200 million tonnes (t) cereals in total, 4,758,500t wheat, 3,589,100t barley, 1,629,400t potatoes, 468,100t rapeseed (canola), 309,900t oats, 146,200t rye, 96,000t pulses, 177,897t oilcrops, 2,828,600t sugar beets, 30,000t apples, 62,799t fruit in total, 249,300t vegetables in total. Livestock production included: 2,120,994t meat in total, *148,000t beef, 1,762,000t pig meat, *1,500t lamb, 205,594t poultry, *81,000t eggs, 4,569,000t milk, 17,430t cattle hides.
* estimate

Fishing
Typical seafood catches total around 1.7 million tonnes per annum (tpy), yielding over 140,000 tpy of fish oils.

Denmark ranks fourth among the world's leading seafood exporters. It continues to export significant quantities of processed seafood, fish oil and meal mainly processed from imported raw material. Decreased Danish cod catches are putting pressure on prices and import substitutes. Cod and other fish imports from other countries have considerably increased.

Forestry
Forest and other wooded land accounts for only one-eighth of the land area, with forest cover estimated at 455,000 hectares (ha). Plantations constitute about 75 per cent of the forest area, with the remainder classed as semi-natural. Less than 25 per cent of the forest is under public ownership, with the rest shared between individuals and private institutions. Demand for forest products is high and is mostly met by imports. Most of the softwood logs are processed locally while high quality hardwood logs are increasingly imported. The furniture industry depends on imported raw materials and exports most of its production. Total imports of forest products in 2004 amounted to US$2.3 billion, while exports amounted to US$459.7 million. Production in 2004 included 1,626,940 cubic metres (cum) roundwood, 810,390cum industrial roundwood, 196,000cum sawnwood, 168,656cum pulpwood, 469,931cum sawlogs and veneers, 373,000cum wood-based panels, 816,550cum wood fuel; 430,000 tonnes (t) recovered paper, 140,299t printing and writing paper.

Industry and manufacturing
Denmark has a highly developed and diversified industrial sector, which is almost wholly under private ownership. The industrial sector contributes around 25 per cent of GDP and employs a quarter of the labour force.

As a country with a market economy and free external trade, government industrial policy plays a relatively minor role, especially as there is no significant state ownership in the industrial sector. The World Bank ranked Denmark at 8 for ease of doing business, and 15 for starting a business, out of 155 in 2005.

Government support for industry is largely confined to export credit arrangements and funds for research and development. The engineering, food processing and wood-paper industries are the economy's three biggest production areas.

Tourism
Tourism plays an important role in Denmark's economic life. It is a modern, highly developed country with extensive infrastructure and can cater for millions of tourist each year. As tourism is a combination of elements such as attractions, amenities, infrastructure and accompanying services, they are unlikely to be controlled by a single authority and the industry has an organic nature with growth dependent on local or individual stimulation. The industry is considering the

impact of tourisim on the environment and society, with schemes proposed that will manage its influence, both beneficial and harmful.

It is expected that travel and tourism in 2005 will generate US$11 billion, adding 3.5 per cent or US$10 billion to GDP. Around 9 per cent of the population is employed in the sector, which is expected to attract US$5.5 billion or 10 per cent of all capital investment in 2005.

Mining
The mining sector contributes under 1 per cent to Denmark's GDP. Denmark has no exploitable raw materials other than sand and gravel for construction.

In Greenland, there are substantial deposits of coal, iron ore, uranium, gold and diamonds, none of which are currently being exploited.

Hydrocarbons
Denmark is Western Europe's third-biggest oil and gas producer (after Norway and the UK).

In 2004 proven oil reserves amounted to 1.3 billion barrels of oil and production was 394,000 barrels per day (bpd). Proven reserves of natural gas were 90 billion cubic metres in 2004, and gas production was 9.4 billion cubic metres, 37 per cent of which is exported. Denmark has gas pipelines connecting its gas fields to its port of Kaergard in Jutland. Oil and gas production comes from 20 fields in the North Sea. Mærsk Olie and Gas is the operator of 16 of these fields, while DONG E&P is an operator of three and Amerada Hess ApS operates one. Denmark does not produce coal but imported 4.4 million tonnes oil equivalent (toe) in 2004, making it the second largest coal importer in Europe. Coal accounts for around a third of total primary energy supply. Primarily importing from South Africa, Columbia, Poland, the US and Australia, Denmark is hoping to replace coal energy with renewable sources.

Energy
Total electricity capacity amounts to around 1.3 million GW, most of which is from thermal power stations. Emphasis is on energy conservation and conversion of power stations from imported coal to locally produced gas. There is increased emphasis on developing renewable sources, such as wind, sun and biomass. Wind power has expanded rapidly, Denmark has the largest wind farm in the EU, producing 166MW of electricity, in Nysted; it went into operation in 2003. The target is to reach 50 per cent of capacity by 2030.

Financial markets
Stock exchange
The Københavns Fondsbørs (Copenhagen Stock Exchange) trades in the equity market, investment fund market, bond market and derivatives market.

Banking and insurance
Denmark has a healthy banking sector which is open to foreign competition. There are around 100 commercial banks in operation, although the two largest account for 60 per cent of total bank assets.
Central bank
Danmarks Nationalbank
Main financial centre
Copenhagen

Time
GMT plus one hour (GMT plus two hours from late March to late September).

Geography
Denmark is a low-lying country in northern Europe. It consists of the peninsula of Jutland, the islands of Zealand, Funen, Lolland, Falster and Bornholm and 401 smaller islands. The average height of the land above sea level is 30 metres and its highest point is only 173 metres above sea level. Denmark lies between the North Sea to the west and the Baltic Sea to the east. Its only land frontier is with Germany and totals 67.7km, while the coastline exceeds 7,300km. Nowhere is more than 52km from the sea. Norway lies to the north of Denmark, across the Skagerrak. Sweden lies to the north-east, its most southerly region being separated from Zealand by a narrow strait. Outlying territories of Denmark are Greenland and the Faeroe Islands in the North Atlantic Ocean.

Climate
Predominantly western winds bring warm, moist air from the west Atlantic, tempering the climatic influences from the east. In winter these can take the form of long periods of frost with ice-bound waters and, in summer, occasional high temperatures and drought. The average temperature in Denmark is 7.5 degrees Celsius (C); the temperature varies from - 0.1 degrees C in the coldest months to 16 degrees C in July. The average rainfall amounts to 664 mm and is distributed fairly evenly over the year, with August, harvest month, normally being the wettest.

Dress codes
Danes are generally informal about clothing. Businessmen usually wear jackets and ties at meetings and only adopt a dinner jacket (or long dresses for women) on very formal occasions.

Entry requirements
Passports
Required by all, except EU visitors travelling on national ID cards.
Visa
Required by all except nationals of EU and Schengen Accord signatory countries, North America, Australasia or Japan. For further exceptions contact the nearest consulate. Schengen visas cover all entry needs; for business trips, an original invitation from a business contact in Denmark is necessary when applying. A Schengen visa application (offered in several languages) can be downloaded on www.eurovisa.info/ApplicationForm.htm.
Currency advice/regulations
No restrictions on amount of foreign currency taken in or out of country, or on amount of Danish currency taken in.
Customs
Personal effects duty-free, plus duty-free allowance.

Health (for visitors)
Medical facilities are of international standards. EU nationals are covered for the cost of medical treatment in Denmark.
Mandatory precautions
None

Hotels
No official rating system. Bills include 15 per cent service charge. All usual credit cards accepted. Advisable to book accommodation in Copenhagen in advance especially during summer.

Public holidays
Fixed dates
1 Jan (New Year's Day), 5 Jun (Constitution Day), 24–26 Dec (Christmas).
Variable dates
Maundy Thursday, Good Friday, Easter Monday, Common Prayer Day, Ascension Day, Whit Monday.

Working hours
Banking
Mon–Fri: 0930–1600; Thu: 0930–1800.
Business
Mon–Fri: 0800/0830–1600/1630; offices frequently close early before the weekend or on the eve of public holidays.
Government
Mon–Fri: generally 0900–1700.
Shops
Mon–Thu: 0900–1730; Fri: 0900–1900/2000; Sat: 0900–1300/1400. First Saturday in each month most shops open: 0900–1600/1700.

Telecommunications
Mobile phones
The GSM 1800 and 900 networks operate throughout the country.

Nations of the World: A Political, Economic and Business Handbook

Social customs/useful tips
Shaking hands is the acceptable way to greet and depart from both business contacts and friends. Service is normally included on bills and further tipping is not necessary in hotels, restaurants or taxis. Punctuality is expected on all occasions.

Security
Apart from the occasional pickpocket, the streets of Copenhagen are generally safe after dark as well as during the day.

Getting there
Air
There are regular flights by most major international airlines. Maersk Air fly between London and the Faroe Islands via Billund in Denmark.
National airline: Scandinavian Airline System (SAS) – jointly owned with Sweden and Norway.
International airport/s: Copenhagen (CPH) at Kastrup, 8km south-east of capital. Business/conference centre, Internet access, duty-free shops, bars, restaurants, bank, post office, transfer hotel (maximum stay 18hrs), shower and sauna facilities. Car hire available. A new rail link between the airport and main railway station in Copenhagen takes 12 minutes. There are also regular bus services from the airport departing every 10–20 minutes taking 20 minutes.
Other airport/s: Aalborg (AAL), 6km north-west of city; Aarhus (Tirstrup) (AAR), 44km north-east of city; Billund (BLL), 2km east of city, Esbjerg (EBJ), 8km from city.
Airport tax: There is no airport tax.
Surface
Road: The new 18km toll Great Belt bridge and tunnel, linking Copenhagen to Funen, now provides the first seamless surface connection from the European continent to Copenhagen. It includes a 6.5km long suspension bridge, the world's second longest. A second bridge and tunnel, the Øresund connection, links Copenhagen with Malmö in Sweden consisting of an 8km bridge and an 8km tunnel connected by an artificial island. Tolls are applicable for both bridges. All other traffic crosses from Germany.
Rail: High-speed Intercity trains via Copenhagen airport connect to Funen (1 hour) and Jutland (2 hours) with additional connections to Malmö (Sweden) on a 30-minute journey via the Øresund link. Access from other European countries is via Germany.
Water: Regular ferry services from UK, Norway, Sweden, Poland, Iceland, the Faroe Islands and Germany.

Getting about
National transport
Air: The network of scheduled services radiates from Copenhagen. Domestic airports are generally situated between two or more cities which are within easy reach of each other. Domestic flights are usually of no more than 30 minutes duration.
Road: About 70,000km of roads including 593km of motorway. The road system in the Danish archipelago makes frequent use of ferries. Motorways are not subject to toll duty.
Buses: There are few private long-distance coaches.
Rail: Approximately 2,500km of railways are operated by Danish State Railway (DSB) and a few private companies, providing a very efficient service linked to the ferry services. Country bus network operates where there are no railways.
Water: Ferry services connect the islands of Zealand, Funen and Lolland and Jutland peninsula, operated by DSB. Also over 400km of inland waterways.
City transport
Taxis: There is a good service in all major towns. Taxis can be hailed in the street when they display their green 'Fri' sign, or by telephone or at ranks. Fare includes a tip.
Buses, trams & metro: Good bus service in Copenhagen, including night buses until 0230. Frequent, efficient services in other main towns. Flat-rate fares are usual.
Car hire
Hire cars are available throughout the country at main DSB stations and all airports. They can be booked in advance through stations, international car hire firms and travel agents. A valid driving licence is required, which must be carried when driving. Most firms stipulate a minimum age between 20–25. The speed limits are 50kph in built up areas, 80kph out of town and 100kph on motorways. Even for minor speed limit offences, drivers are liable to pay heavy fines on the spot. If payment cannot be made, the car may be detained. Avoid drinking and driving when in Denmark: apart from the obvious dangers, the laws are tough. The legal maximum is 0.8 promille of alcohol in the blood and offenders may face imprisonment for anything over 2.0 promille.

BUSINESS DIRECTORY
The addresses listed below are a selection only. While World of Information makes every endeavour to check these addresses, we cannot guarantee that changes have not been made, especially to telephone numbers and area codes. We would welcome any corrections.

Telephone area codes
The international direct dialling code (IDD) for Denmark is +45, followed by subscriber's number.

Useful telephone numbers
Fire, police, ambulance 112
Emergency dental treatment 3138-0251
24-hour chemist 3314-8266

Chambers of Commerce
American Chamber of Commerce in Denmark, 28 Christians Brygge, 1559 Copenhagen V (tel: 3393-2932; fax: 3313-0507; e-mail: mail@amcham.dk).

Danish Chamber of Commerce, Børsen, 1217 Copenhagen K (tel: 7013-1200; fax: 7013-1201; e-mail: hts@hts.dk).

Banking
Bikuben, Silkegade 8, DK-1113 Copenhagen K (tel: 3312-0133; fax: 3315-1133).

Bikuben Securities, 30 Finsbury Square, London EC2A 1NR (tel: (44) (0)171 628-5522; fax: (44) (0)171 256-5445).

Den Danske Bank AS (commercial bank), Holmens Kanal 2-12, DK-1092 Copenhagen K (tel: 3344-0000; fax: 3118-5873).

Den Danske Bank, 75 King William Street, London EC4N 7DT (tel: (44) (020)7410-4949, fax: (44) (020)7283-9526).

Finansradetr (bankers' association), Bankernes Hus, Amaliegade 7, DK-1256 Copenhagen (tel: 3312-0200; fax: 3393-0260).

Girobank, Girostoget 1, DK-2630 Tastrup (tel: 4371-4470; fax: 4358-4470).

Jyske Bank (Bank of Jutland), Vestergade 8-16, DK-8600 Silkeborg (tel: 8922-2222; fax: 8922-2499).

Jyske Bank, Jutland House, 119/120 Chancery Lane, London WC2A 1HU (tel: (44) (020)7831-2778; fax: (44) (020)7405-2257).

Sparekassen Nordjylland, Karlskogavej 4, DK-9000 Aalborg (tel: 9818-7311).

Sydbank, Peberlyk 4, DK-6200 Aabenraa (tel: 7463-1111; fax: 7463-1320).

Unibank AS, Kongens Nytorv 8, DK-1786 Copenhagen K (tel: 3333-3333; fax: 3395-5769).

Unibank Plc., 107 Cheapside, London EC2V 6DA (tel: (44) (020)7726-6000; fax: (44) (020)7726-4638).

Central bank
Danmarks Nationalbank, Havnegade 5, DK-1093 Copenhagen (tel: 3363-6363; fax: 3363-7103; e-mail: info@nationalbanken.dk).

Travel information
Copenhagen Airport, Kastrup, Amager (tel: 3154-1701; fax: 3151-1133).

Copenhagen Airtaxi, Copenhagen Airport Roskilde, DK-4000 Roskilde (tel: 391-114).

Denmark

Danish State Railways – train timetables (tel: 3314-1702). Reservations (tel: 3314-8800).

Forened Danske Motorejere (FDM) (the Danish motoring organisation), Blegdamsvej 124, DK-2100 Copenhagen Ø (tel: 3338-2112).

Scandinavian Airlines System (SAS), Frosundaviks Alle 1, Stockholm S-16187, Sweden (tel: (46-8)7970-000; fax: (46-8)858-741).

Ministry of tourism
Ministry of Business and Industry (including Communications and Tourism), Slotsholmsgade 10-12, 1216 Copenhagen K (tel: 3392-3350; fax: 3312-3778; e-mail: em@em.dk).

National tourist organisation offices
Danmarks Turistrad (tourist board), Vesterbrogade 6 D, 1620 Cogenhagen V (tel: 3311-1415; fax: 3393-1416).

Ministries
Ministry of Agriculture, Fisheries and Food, Holbergsgade 2, 1057 Copenhagen K (tel: 3392-3301; fax: 3314-5042; e-mail: fvm@fvm.dk).

Ministry of Business and Industry (including Communications and Tourism), Slotsholmsgade 10-12, 1216 Copenhagen K (tel: 3392-3350; fax: 3312-3778; e-mail: em@em.dk).

Ministry of Business and Industry, Invest in Denmark, Slotsholmsgade 10-12, Copenhagen K, DK-1216 (tel: 3392-3350; fax: 3312-3778; e-mail: Investdk@em.dk; internet site: http://www.investindk.com).

Ministry for Culture, Nybrogade 2, 1203 Copenhagen K (tel: 3392-3370; fax: 3391-3388; e-mail: kum@kum.dk).

Ministry of Defence, Holmens Kanal 42, 1060 Copenhagen K (tel: 3392-3320; fax: 3332-0655; e-mail: fmn@fmn.dk).

Ministry of Ecclesiastical Affairs, Frederiksholms Kanal 21, 1220 Copenhagen K (tel: 3392-3390; fax: 3392-3913; e-mail: km@km.dk).

Ministry of Economic Affairs, Ved Stranden 8, 1061 Copenhagen K (tel: 3392-3222; fax: 3393-6020; e-mail: oem@oem.dk).

Ministry for Education, Fredriksholms Kanal 21-25, 1220 Copenhagen K (tel: 3392-5000; fax: 3392-5547; e-mail: uvm@uvm.dk).

Ministry of Employment, Holmens Kanal 20, 1060 Copenhagen K (tel: 3392-5900; fax: 3312-1378; e-mail: am@am.dk).

Ministry for the Environment and Energy, Hojbro Plads 4, 1200 Copenhagen K (tel: 3392-7600; fax: 3332-2227; e-mail: mem@mem.dk).

Ministry of Finance, Christiansborg Slotsplads 1, 1218 Copenhagen K (tel: 3392-3333; fax: 3332-8030; e-mail: fm@fm.dk).

Ministry of Foreign Affairs, 2 Asiatisk Plads, 1448 Copenhagen K (tel: 3392-0000; fax: 3254-0533; e-mail: um@um.dk; internet site: http://www.um.dk/english).

Ministry for Health, Holbergsgade 6, 1057 Copenhagen K (tel: 3392-3360; fax: 3393-1563; e-mail: sum@sum.dk).

Ministry of Housing and Urban Affairs, Slotsholmgade 1, 3, 1216 Copenhagen K (tel: 3392-6100; fax: 3392-6104; e-mail: bm@bm.dk).

Ministry for the Interior, Christiansborg Slotsplads 1, 1218 Copenhagen K (tel: 3392-3380; fax: 3311-1239; e-mail: inm@inm.dk).

Ministry of Justice, Slotsholmsgade 10, 1216 Copenhagen K (tel: 3392-3340; fax: 3393-3510; e-mail: jm@jm.dk).

Ministry of Research, Bredgade 43, 1260 Copenhagen K (tel: 3392-9700; fax: 3332-3501; e-mail: fsk@fsk.dk).

Ministry for Social Affairs, Holmens Kanal 22, 1060 Copenhagen K (tel: 3392-9300; fax: 3393-2518; e-mail: sm@sm.dk).

Ministry for Taxation, Slotsholmsgade 12, 1216 Copenhagen K (tel: 3392-3392; fax: 3314-9105; e-mail: skm@skm.dk).

Ministry for Transport, Fredriksholms Kanal 27, 1220 Copenhagen K (tel: 3392-3355; fax 3312-3893; e-mail: trm@trm.dk).

Parliament, Christiansborg, 1240 Copenhagen K (tel: 3337-5500; fax: 3332-8536).

Prime Minister's Office, Christiansborg, Prins Jorgens Gard 11, 1218 Copenhagen K (tel: 3392-3300; fax: 3311-1665; e-mail: stm@stm.dk).

Other useful addresses
American Embassy, Dag Hammarskjolds Alle 24, DK-2100 Copenhagen Ø (tel: 423-144; fax: 430-223).

British Embassy, Kastelsvej 36, DK-2100 Copenhagen Ø (tel: 264-600; fax: 381-012, 431-400).

Central Telegraph Office, Købmagergade 37, DK-1150 Copenhagen K (tel: 3312-0903).

Copenhagen Stock Exchange, Nikolaj Plads 6, DK-1067 Copenhagen K (tel: 3393-3366).

Danish Convention Bureau, 27 Skindergade, 1159 Copenhagen K (tel: 3332-8601; fax: 3332-8803).

Danish Embassy (USA), 3200 Whithaven Street, NW, Washington DC 20008 (tel: (1)202-234-4300; fax: (1)202-328-1470; e-mail: wasamb@um.dk).

Danmarks Agentforening (association of commercial agents of Denmark), Børsen, DK-1217 Copenhagen K (tel: 3314-4941).

Danmarks Statistik, Sejrøgade 11, DK-2100 Copenhagen Ø (tel: 3917-3917; fax: 3118-4801).

Dansk Arbejdsgiverforening (employers' confederation), Vester Voldgade 113, DK-1503 Copenhagen V (tel: 3393-4000; fax: 3312-2976).

Det Okonomiske Rad (economic council), Kampmannsgade, DK-1604 Copenhagen V (tel: 3313-5128).

Grosserer Societetet, Børsen (royal exchange), DK-1217 Copenhagen (tel: 3391-2323).

Industriraadet (Confederation of Danish Industries), H C Andersen's Boulevard 18, DK-1790 Copenhagen V (tel: 3377-3377; fax: 3377-3410).

IPC (International Press Centre), Snaregade 14, DK-1205 Copenhagen K (tel: 131-615; fax: 911-613).

Regional Development Organisation (Copenhagen Capacity), Kongens Nytorv 6, 4, sal DK-1050 Copenhagen K (tel: 3333-0300; fax: 3333-7333).

Ritzaus Bureau 1/S (news agency), Mikkel Bryggersgade 3, DK-1460 Copenhagen K.

Royal Danish Embassy (USA), 3200 Whitehaven Street, NW, Washington DC 20008 (tel: (1)234-4300; fax: (1)238-1470; e-mail: wasamb@um.dk).

Teknisk Forlag AS (technical press-publishing house), Skelbaekgade 4, DK-1717 Copenhagen V.

Thomson Communications (Scandinavia) AS, Hestemøllestrede 6, Postboks 2181, DK-1017 Copenhagen K.

Internet sites
Danish web index: http://www.web-index.dk/

Statistical Office: http://www.dst.dk

Trade directory for Denmark: http://uhk.dk

White pages: http://infobel.com/denmark/default.asp

Yellow pages: http:// www.yellowpages.dk

Djibouti

KEY FACTS

Official name: République de Djibouti/Jumhouriyya Djibouti (Republic of Djibouti)

Head of State: President Ismail Omar Guelleh (since May 1999; re-elected 8 Apr 2005)

Head of government: Prime Minister Dileita Mohamed Dileita (appointed 4 Mar 2001)

Ruling party: Four-party Union pour la Majorité Présidentielle (UMP) (Union for a Presidential Majority) coalition, led by the Rassemblement Populaire pour le Progrès (RPP) (Popular Rally for Progress) (new government formed 22 May 2005)

Area: 23,200 square km

Population: 765,300 (2004)

Capital: Djibouti-ville

Official language: French/Arabic (Somali/Afar are the national languages)

Currency: Djibouti franc (Df) = 100 centimes

Exchange rate: Df174.25 per US$ (Oct 2005)

GDP per capita: US$793 (2004)

GDP real growth: 3.00% (2004)

Unemployment: 50.00% (2004)

Inflation: 3.00% (2004)

Balance of trade: -US$185.00 million (2003)

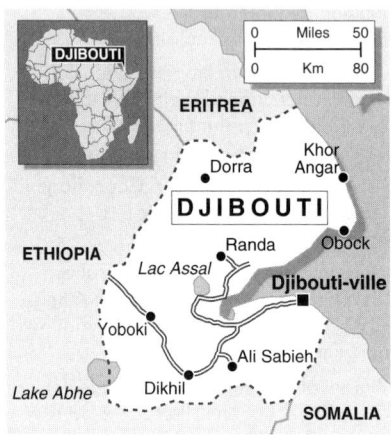

The economy of Djibouti is making the most of what the country has got – or rather where it is.

Location, location, location

Djibouti's location is the main economic asset of a country that is mostly barren. It is strategically located at the mouth of the Red Sea, close to the world's busiest shipping lanes and the Arabian oilfields; it is the terminus of rail traffic into Ethiopia. It serves as an important transshipment location for goods entering and leaving the east African highlands. Its transport infrastructure enables several landlocked African countries to fly in their goods for re-export. This earns Djibouti much-needed transit taxes and harbour fees. There are plans for a port at Doraleh and a new free trade zone.

The present leadership still favours close ties with France, which maintains a significant military presence in the country, but it has also developed increasingly stronger ties with the United States in recent years, which has been allowed to set-up the only US military base in sub-Saharan Africa. This has made Djibouti a front-line state in the US' global war on terrorism. It is a centre for US intelligence gathering.

Economy

Otherwise Djibouti is mostly wasteland. It has large salt deposits. The domestic economy is based on service activities connected with the country's strategic location – some of which will never be known – and status as a free trade zone in north-east Africa. Two-thirds of the inhabitants live in the capital city; the remainder are mostly nomadic herders. Scanty rainfall limits crop production to fruits and vegetables, and most food must be imported. Djibouti provides services as both a transit port for the region and an international transshipment and refueling center. The nation is heavily dependent on foreign assistance to help support its balance of payments and to finance development projects. An unemployment rate of at least 50 per cent continues to be a major problem.

Inflation is not a concern, the Djiboutian franc is tied to the US dollar; but the artificially high value of the franc adversely affects Djibouti's balance of payments. Per capita consumption dropped an estimated 35 per cent over the last seven years because of recession and civil war. Faced with a multitude of economic difficulties, the government has fallen into arrears on long-term external debt and has been struggling to meet the stipulations of foreign aid donors.

Djibouti has worked its way through a three-year International Monetary Fund (IMF) programme to reduce poverty and pay its debts through economic growth. Risks include weak institutional capacity, possible political opposition, and adverse regional unrest.

Sceptics say it should ask the West to pay. Controlling access to the Red Sea, Djibouti is of major strategic importance. During the Gulf War it was the base of operations for the French military. French troops, warships, aircraft and armoured vehicles stationed in Djibouti contribute directly and indirectly to more than half the country's income. The US has hundreds of troops in Djibouti – 2,000 of them (allegedly) man a highly secret high tech intelligence base controlled from a high tech command ship moored some distance off-shore.

Nevertheless, President Ismael Omar Guelleh has promised to tackle poverty by reducing Djibouti's dependence on imported food.

Djibouti

An IMF mission visited Djibouti in July 2005 to review economic developments as well as the country's short- and medium-term outlook. The IMF was encouraged by the government's determination since May the same year to check the sharp deterioration in the fiscal accounts noted at end-2004. Over the medium term, the authorities agreed with the IMF that expenditure must be cut and additional domestic revenues mobilised, including the adoption of a value added tax (VAT) to satisfy the need to increase spending on poverty-reduction and investment and accelerate economic growth.

The IMF said there should be formal safety net programmes to improve the targeting of public spending to the poor.

Politics

The French Territory of the Afars and the Issas became Djibouti in 1977. Hassan Gouled Aptidon installed an authoritarian one-party state and proceeded to serve as president until 1999. When Afar resentment erupted into civil war the rebels from the Afar party, the Front for the Restoration of Unity and Democracy (FRUD), were not allowed to participate. Unrest continued during the 1990s, leading to a civil war that ended in 2001 following the conclusion of a peace accord between Afar rebels and the Issa-dominated government. Djibouti's first multi-party presidential elections in 1999 resulted in the election of Guellah, Aptidon's nephew. A former head of security who worked for many years in his uncle's office, Guelleh supports Djibouti's traditionally strong ties with France.

Risk assessment

Economy	Improving
Politics	Fair
Regional stability	Fair

COUNTRY PROFILE

Historical profile
Djibouti was the last French colony on African soil. Until 1967 it had been known as French Somaliland. Then in 1977, as the French Territory of the Afars and Issas, it was granted independence and became the Republic of Djibouti. Its strategic importance at the foot of the Red Sea became internationally prominent following its adoption by the US as a military regional command and control centre in 2002.

The fear of a Somali takeover in Djibouti had been France's main excuse for continued rule. Ethiopia, which relies on the Addis Ababa-Djibouti railway for its maritime link, has long had close economic relations with Djibouti, and was not slow to draw attention to neighbouring Somalia's desire to recover all the territories traditionally inhabited by Somalis. At the time of Djibouti's independence in 1977, Somalia gave the Organisation of African Unity (now the African Union (AU)), France and Ethiopia assurances that it would respect the independence of a free Djibouti. France's hesitation in granting independence was further influenced by its decision to concentrate its Indian Ocean military presence on bases in Réunion and Mayotte.

1862 France reached agreements with local leaders which gave the French the right to settle in Djibouti. They also acquired the port of Obock. The country was called French Somaliland.

1888 Construction of Djibouti-ville began on the southern shore of Tadjoura Bay. At the end of the century, France signed an agreement with the Emperor of Ethiopia designating French Somaliland as the 'official outlet of Ethiopian commerce'. The agreement led to the construction of the vital Addis Ababa-Djibouti railway.

1892 Djibouti-ville became the capital of French Somaliland.

1917 The Addis Ababa-Djibouti railway was completed.

1946 French Somaliland was made an overseas territory, with its own parliament and representation in the French parliament.

1967 A referendum favoured continued French rule. French Somaliland was renamed the French Territory of the Afars and the Issas.

1977 The re-named Republic of Djibouti was granted independence by France after several years of growing protests and demonstrations. Hassan Gouled Aptidon of the Rassemblement Populaire pour le Progrès (RPP) (Popular Rally for Progress) was elected president.

1981 Djibouti became a one-party state, with the RPP as the only legal political party.

1991 The Front pour la Restauration de l'Unité et de la Démocratie (FRUD) (Front for the Restoration of Unity and Democracy) launched a civil war in northern Djibouti. The ethnic Afar organisation demanded multi-party elections.

1992 Following several months of fighting, Aptidon agreed to a referendum, which led to a limited, multi-party constitution. In the elections to the Chamber of Deputies only four parties are allowed to take part; the RPP won 72 per cent of the vote while a newly formed alliance led by the Parti du Renouveau Démocratique (PRD) (Party of Democratic Renewal) won the remainder.

1993 President Aptidon was re-elected for a fourth term.

1994 Despite the new constitution, FRUD did not end its armed struggle until December, when the government and FRUD signed a peace accord confirming the constitutional and electoral reforms of 1992.

1997 President Aptidon was re-elected for a fifth term. FRUD joined RPP in a coalition government.

1999 The 83-year-old president resigned after 22 consecutive years in power. Ismael Omar Guelleh was elected president.

2001 Dileita Mohamed Dileita replaced Barkat Gourad Hamadou as prime minister.

2002 The law limiting four parties to contest elections, passed in 1992, expired.

KEY INDICATORS — Djibouti

	Unit	2000	2001	2002	2003	2004
Population	m	0.64	0.64	0.66	0.71	0.77
Gross domestic product (GDP)	US$bn	0.55	0.60	0.60	0.67	*0.66
GDP per capita	US$	873	899	914	938	793
GDP real growth	%	0.7	3.0	2.5	3.0	3.0
Inflation	%	2.3	1.8	2.0	-2.2	3.0
Exports (fob) (goods)	US$m	72.0	78.0	86.0	70.0	–
Imports (fob) (goods)	US$m	272.0	284.0	295.0	255.0	–
Balance of trade	US$m	-200.0	-206.0	-208.0	-185.0	–
Current account	US$m	-43.0	-38.0	–	–	-70.0
Foreign debt	US$bn	0.3	0.3	0.3	0.4	–
Total reserves minus gold	US$m	67.8	70.3	73.7	100.1	93.9
Foreign exchange	US$m	66.0	68.8	70.2	98.4	91.2
Exchange rate	per US$	177.72	177.72	172.50	175.00	175.43

* estimated figure

US led coalition troops arrived, in preparation for military action in Afghanistan and against al Qaeda targets in the region.
2003 In January, the first fully multi-party elections held since independence were won by parties supporting President Guelleh. Large numbers of illegal immigrants – estimated at 15 per cent of the population – were deported.
2004 In October, the UN issued a famine early warning report for pastoral areas in the north-west and south-east. Low seasonal rain resulted in parched land unable to sustain the livestock on which people depend.
2005 In the 8 April presidential elections, Ismail Omar Guelleh, the only candidate, was re-elected with 100 per cent of the vote. A new government was formed on 22 May 2005.

Political structure
The executive
Executive power is vested in the Council of Ministers, headed by a prime minister, and responsible to the president, who is directly elected by absolute majority vote for a six-year term.
National legislature
The Assemblée Nationale (National Assembly) has 65 members, 33 Issa and 32 Afar, elected for a five-year term in multi-seat (four to 37 seats) constituencies.
Last elections
10 January 2003 (parliamentary) (the first full multi-party election since independence); April 2005 (presidential).
Results: Presidential: Ismail Omar Guelleh, the only candidate, was re-elected with 100 per cent of the vote; turnout was 78.9 per cent.
Parliamentary: the four-party Union pour la Majorité Présidentielle (UMP) (Union for a Presidential Majority) coalition won 62.7 per cent of the vote (all 65 seats in parliament).
Next elections
2008 (parliamentary).

Political parties
Ruling party
Four-party Union pour la Majorité Présidentielle (UMP) (Union for a Presidential Majority) coalition, led by the Rassemblement Populaire pour le Progrès (RPP) (Popular Rally for Progress) (new government formed 22 May 2005)
Main opposition party
Union pour l'Alternance Démocratique (UAD) (Union for a Democratic Alternative)

Population
765,300 (2004)
Ethnic make-up
About 60 per cent of the national total are Issas, of Somali origin and about 35 per cent are Afars who have links with Ethiopia; there are about 5 per cent European residents.
The population also includes refugees from the Ogaden and Eritrean wars in Somalia and Ethiopia.
The nomadic population (principally Afars) totals around 100,000.
Religions
Islam (94 per cent), Christianity (6 per cent)

Education
Literacy rate: 75.6 per cent men, 54.4 per cent women; adult rates (World Bank).
Enrolment rate: 45 per cent boys, 33 per cent girls, total primary school enrolment of the relevant age group (including repetition rates) (World Bank).

Health
Total expenditure on health is 7–8 per cent of GDP, of which 58–60 per cent is government spending.
The results of this spending appear limited, due mainly to poor management and the high costs of foreign staff and medicines.
HIV/Aids
This percentage is high enough to pose a significant threat to the country's future prosperity. Under a funding agreement in June 2004, US$12 million from the Global Fund to fight Aids, tuberculosis (TB) and malaria, will be spent on antiretroviral drugs to be supplied to Aids suffers until 2007. From an initial 200 patients it is expected that 4,000 patients will be treated, however the estimate of HIV positive cases in Djibouti is 9,000, with only 1,000 people registered – gaining them access to free treatment – though there has been an improvement in the numbers of people being tested.
HIV prevalence: 2.9 per cent aged 15–49 in 2003 (World Bank)
Life expectancy: 43.0 years (World Bank)
Fertility rate/Maternal mortality rate: 5.2 births per woman (World Bank)
Infant mortality rate: 97 per 1,000 live births; 18 per cent of children aged under five are malnourished (World Bank).

Welfare
The average unemployment rate in the country is about 45 per cent. Although poverty is more acute in the rural areas, 72 per cent of those defined as living in absolute poverty reside in urban areas. Djibouti has been severely affected by the large influx of refugees from Ethiopia, Somalia and Eritrea, putting great strain on its financial resources. In August 2003 thousands of refugees and illegal immigrants were given an ultimatum to leave the country. Most had fled the wars in Somalia and Ethiopia and their numbers were as high as 100,000, or 15 per cent of the Djibouti population. The reason given by the government for their expulsion was security. By February 2004, 3,361 had been repatriated to Somaliland, by the UN High Commission for Refugees (UNHCR), who provided food and other provisions for each person, to last for the first nine months. Other refugees ended up in camps in Ethiopia as internally displaced persons.

Main cities
Djibouti-ville (capital, estimated population 547,100 in 2003).

Languages spoken
English is understood by the larger trading houses. Cushitic languages, as well as Somali and Saho-Afar are widely spoken.
Official language/s
French/Arabic (Somali/Afar are the national languages)

Media
Press
Journalists have to generally avoid sensitive issues covering human rights, the army, FRUD, relations with Ethiopia and French financial aid. Numerous journalists have been expelled or detained for publications without government approval. There are also internal pressures on the media. Journalists are largely untrained and poorly paid.
The Djiboutian court enjoys 'an arsenal of laws' that permit it to ban any critical publication affecting the image of the regime. Although the constitution provides for a free press, circulation of information is highly restricted in practice. A law prohibits the dissemination of false information and regulates the publication of newspapers.
Dailies: The government owns the main Djiboutian newspaper, *La Nation de Djibouti*.
In 2001, the opposition paper *Le Renouveau* was temporarily suspended after it published an article criticising the destruction of the central market by the chief of police, Daher Ismael Kahin. The Editor of the newspaper, Ahmed Farah, was detained then released. *Le Renouveau* is the newspaper of the Parti Renouvellement Démocratique (PRD) (Democratic Renewal Party). Reporters Sans Frontières (RSF) (Reporters Without Borders), an international organisation fighting for press freedom, has repeatedly called on Djibouti to ratify the international covenant on civil and political rights.
Broadcasting
The government owns the radio and television stations, and the official media are generally uncritical of the government or government policy.

Djibouti

The Société de Telecommunications Internationales de Djibouti (STID), a commercialised company owned 75 per cent by the government and 25 per cent by France Cable & Radio (FCR), controls DJIBNET, which was set up in 1996 and is the sole provider of Internet services in the country. It operates via a link with France Telecom.

Radio: There are two AM and one FM radio stations. Radio service in French, Afar, Somali and Arabic. In May 2000 the British Broadcasting Corporation (BBC) was granted permission to broadcast its World Service in the country, in conjunction with the official government-owned station, Radio Télévision Djibouti (RTD). BBC and RTD broadcasts 24 hours a day in four languages.

In 2000, Radio France Internationale was granted a licence to continue broadcasting on the local FM band.

Television: There is one state-owned television station, broadcasting five hours per day.

Economy

Djibouti's economy is reliant on services. The agricultural sector is small and there is very little manufacturing. Economic activity centres on the port, the railway and other services, although the presence of foreign military directly and indirectly accounts for over half the country's income. The French military base, which once contributed around a quarter of Djibouti's GDP, has declined in importance since the French government decided to scale down its military presence in Africa. Since the 11 September 2001 terrorist attacks in the US, American and German troops have also used Djibouti as a military base from which to carry out the war on terrorism.

The 1991–94 civil war had a severe effect on the economy, hampering economic development and imposing a considerable burden on scarce government resources. Since 1994, the government has implemented a programme of economic reforms with assistance from multilateral and bilateral creditors and donors. The reforms were aimed at macroeconomic stabilisation, with control of public expenditure and reduction in the level of domestic and foreign debt. It has engaged in a programme of privatisation.

Around half the population live below the poverty line and the number is growing; rising unemployment is a significant problem with around 50 per cent of the population living without a job. Despite many social problems, growth of GDP has remained steady at around 3 per cent since 2001.

External trade

The large visible trade deficit is partly offset by net income from services and transport, aid flows and concessionary loans. There is a free trade zone near the port of Djibouti.

On 31 December 2002, the US approved Djibouti as being eligible for tariff preferences under the Africa Growth and Opportunities Act (AGOA). The legislation requires that countries are only eligible for greater access to US markets provided they have made continued progress toward a market-based economy, the rule of law, free trade, poverty reduction and the protection of workers' rights. This process is reviewed annually.

Imports

Principal imports are foods, beverages, transport equipment, chemicals and petroleum products.

Main sources: Saudi Arabia (21 per cent total, 2004), Ethiopia (9.9 per cent), India (8.2 per cent), China (7.8 per cent), US (6.1 per cent), France (6.0 per cent)

Exports

Principal exports are re-exports, live animals, skins, leather, coffee (in transit).

Main destinations: Somalia (63.9 per cent total, 2004), Yemen (22.6 per cent), Ethiopia (5.0 per cent)

Agriculture

Farming

The underdeveloped agricultural sector contributes only 3 per cent to GDP. Due to poor terrain (mostly desert), most agricultural producers are nomads engaged in herding goats, sheep and camels. Drought has severely affected the livelihoods of the herd owners. Around 95 per cent of food requirements are imported.

Projects under consideration include increasing the amount of arable land by irrigation schemes and rehabilitation of water dams and wells.

The estimated crop production for 2004 included: 13 tonnes (t) maize, 1,805t citrus fruit, 1,100 tomatoes, 1,500t pulses, 510t mangoes, 200t allspice, 3,493t fruit in total, 25,464t vegetables in total. Estimated livestock production included: 11,244t meat in total, 6,050t beef, 4,534t lamb and goat meat, 660t camel meat, 13,950t milk, 1,100t cattle hides, 420t sheepskins.

Industry and manufacturing

The industrial sector is limited to construction and small-scale concerns such as mineral water bottling, tanning, dairy and animal food plants. New industries set up in Djibouti include cement, tiles, paints and meat processing. Foreign investment is being encouraged and should be aided by renewed political stability in the region.

Tourism

Tourism is undeveloped, although its potential contribution to economic regeneration is acknowledged. Around 20,000 visitors were recorded in 2000, the majority from France.

Mining

Surveys have indicated the presence of minerals such as copper, gypsum and sulphur. No minerals are mined commercially. Salt is extracted and exported.

Hydrocarbons

Reported discoveries of gas reserves could make the country self-sufficient in gas and provide a surplus for export, although the exact amount is unknown. Chevron is engaging in oil exploration although so far there has been little success. The downstream industry serves as a supply centre for the export of petroleum products, mostly for Ethiopia. The Dubai Ports Authority hopes the new Doraleh terminal, which began construction in 2003, will double Djibouti's handling capacity, making it the largest transshipment point on the African continent, attracting inward investment. Djibouti relies entirely on refined oil product imports for its domestic demands.

Djibouti does not produce or import either natural gas or coal.

Energy

There is a geothermal power station; supply and distribution is overseen by the state-owned Electricité du Djibouti.

Banking and insurance

Central bank
National Bank of Djibouti
Main financial centre
Djiboutiville

Time

GMT plus three hours

Geography

Djibouti is in the Horn of Africa, at the southern entrance to the Red Sea. It is bounded on the north, west and south-west by Ethiopia, and on the south-east by Somalia. The land is volcanic desert.

Climate

Very hot and arid from April–August; average temperature 32 degrees Celsius (C) and can reach 45 degrees C. Slightly cooler from October–March, with occasional light rain.

Dress codes

Djibouti has a large Muslim population so visitors should dress modestly, especially in the city. However, it is far less strict than other Islamic countries.

Entry requirements

Passports
Required by all. Must be valid for six months beyond date of departure.

Visa
Required by all, except French nationals; valid for one month. For business visits, an employer's letter and a letter of invitation from a company in Djibouti are necessary. For further details visit the Djibouti website in Paris: http://www.ambdjibouti.org/. Transit visas, valid for 10 days, are also available for visitors who may obtain them at the border with proof of return/onward travel. Visitors also require evidence of a yellow fever vaccination.

Currency advice/regulations
No restrictions on import/export of local or foreign currency.

Health (for visitors)
Mandatory precautions
Yellow fever vaccination certificate if arriving from an infected area.
Advisable precautions
Yellow fever, typhoid, tetanus, hepatitis 'A' and polio vaccinations. Malaria prophylaxis recommended as risk exists throughout the country. There is a rabies risk. Water precautions should be taken.

Hotels
Available in Djibouti-ville – limited elsewhere. Service charge is normally included. Tipping is not usual.

Credit cards
Generally not accepted, except by airlines and Sheraton Hotel.

Public holidays
Fixed dates
1 Jan (New Year's Day), 1 May (Labour Day), 27 Jun (Independence Day), 25 Dec (Christmas Day).
Variable dates
Eid al Adha, Eid al Fitr, Islamic New Year, Birth of the Prophet.
The Islamic year contains 354 or 355 days, with the result that Muslim feasts advance by 10–12 days against the Gregorian calendar. Dates of feasts vary according to the sighting of the new moon, so cannot be forecast exactly. Islamic year 1426: 10 February 2005 to 30 January 2006.

Working hours
Banking
Sat–Thu: 0715–1145.
Business
Sat–Thu: 0630–1300.
Government
Sat–Thu: 0630–1300.
Shops
0730–1200, 1600–1900; closed Fri.

Electricity supply
220/380V AC, 50 cycles.

Getting there
Air
International airport/s: Djibouti-d'Ambouli (Code: JIB), 5km south of Djibouti-ville.
Airport tax: US$20
Surface
Road: There is a surfaced road from Addis Ababa (Ethiopia). Local advice should be taken as to when to travel by road as it can be difficult, with problems caused by the political situation.
Rail: There is a rail link with Ethiopia.
Main port/s: Djibouti-ville has 12 berths and a container terminal.

Getting about
National transport
Air: Djibouti Airlines operates a daily domestic service to Obock and Tadjoura from Djibouti. Dikhil and Ali-Sabieh can be reached by chartered aircraft.
Road: There are surfaced roads to the Ethiopian border and to Arta, and from Djibouti-ville to Tadjoura; most roads are in need of repair. Take local advice when planning to travel by road.
Rail: Some towns are served on the Djibouti– Addis Ababa railway.
Water: Ferry service linking Djibouti-ville with Tadjoura and Obock.
City transport
Taxis: They are available in main towns. Tipping is not usual as fares include gratuities; there is an official tariff, but it is usual for visitors to be charged 50 per cent more; there is a similar increase at night.
The journey from the airport to the centre of Djibouti-ville takes 10 minutes.
Car hire
Available in Djibouti-ville and at the airport. Valid international driving licence recommended. A temporary licence can be obtained on presentation of national licence. Traffic drives on right.

BUSINESS DIRECTORY
The addresses listed below are a selection only. While World of Information makes every endeavour to check these addresses, we cannot guarantee that changes have not been made, especially to telephone numbers and area codes. We would welcome any corrections.

Telephone area codes
The international dialling code (IDD) for Djibouti is + 253 followed by subscriber's number.

Useful telephone numbers
Police: 17
Fire: 18

Chambers of Commerce
Djibouti International Chamber of Commerce et Industry, Place de LaGuarde, PO Box 84, Djibouti (tel: 351-070; fax: 350-096; e-mail: cicid@intnet.dj).

Banking
Banque de Développement de Djibouti; PO Box 520, Angle Ave Georges Clémenceau et rue Pierre Curie, Djibouti-ville (tel: 353-391; fax: 355-022).

Banque Indosuez Mer Rouge; PO Box 88, 10 Place Lagarde, Djibouti-ville (tel: 353-016; fax: 351-638).

Banque pour le Commerce et l'Industrie-Mer Rouge; PO Box 2122, Place Lagarde, Djibouti-ville (tel: 350-857; fax: 354-260).

Central bank
Banque Centrale de Djibouti, Avenue Saint Laurent du Var, PO Box 2118, Djibouti-ville (tel: 352-751 fax: 356-288; e-mail: bndj@intnet.dj).

Travel information
Daallo Airlines (Airline of Horn of Africa), PO Box 1954, Djibouti-ville (tel: 353-401, 356-660; fax: 351-765).

Djibouti Airlines, Place Lagarde, PO Box 2240, Djibouti-ville (tel: 351-006; fax: 352-429).

Djibouti Airport, BP 204, Djibouti-ville (tel: 340-101 ext 300, 382-322; fax: 340-723).

Puntavia Airline de Djibouti, CP 2240, Djibouti-ville (tel: 351-036, 351-006; fax: 353-429, 356-660).

National tourist organisation offices
L'Office National du Tourisme et de l'Artisanat, BP 1938, place du 27 Juin, Djibouti-ville (tel: 352-800, 353-682, 353-790; fax: 356-322).

Ministries
Ministry of Agriculture and Rural Development, BP 453, Djibouti-ville (tel: 351-297).

Ministry of Commerce, Transport and Tourism, BP 121, Djibouti-ville (tel: 352-540).

Ministry of Foreign Affairs and Co-operation, BP 1863, Djibouti-ville (tel: 353-342).

Ministry of Industry and Industrial Development, BP 175, Djibouti-ville (tel: 350-340).

Other useful addresses
British Consulate, BP 81, Gellatly Hankey et Cie, Djibouti-ville (tel: 355-718; fax: 353-294); c/o Inchcape Shipping Office, Djibouti-ville (tel: 353-836/844).

Central Post Office, boulevard de la République, Djibouti-ville (tel: 350-669).

Compagnie du Chemin de Fer Djibouti-Ethiopien, BP 2116, Djibouti-ville (tel: 350-353).

Djibouti Embassy (USA), 1156 15th Street, NW, Washington DC 20005 (tel: 202-331-0270; fax 202-331-0302).

Office National d'Approvisionnement et de Commercialisation (ONAC), BP 75, Djibouti-ville (tel: 350-327).

Office of the Prime Minister, BP 2086, Djibouti-ville (tel: 351-494; fax: 355-049).

Radiodiffusion Télévision de Djibouti (RTD), BP 97, Djibouti-ville (tel: 352-294).

Service de Statistique et de Documentation, BP 1846, Djibouti-ville (tel: 353-331).

US Embassy, BP 185, Villa Plateau du Serpent, boulevard Maréchal Joffré, Djibouti-ville (tel: 353-995).

Internet sites

Africa Business Network: http://www.ifc.org/abn

AllAfrica.com: http://allafrica.com

African Development Bank: http://www.afdb.org

Africa Online: http://www.africaonline.com

Harambee Afrika (UK business club for traders with east, central and southern Africa; includes annotated web resource list): http://www.harambee.co.uk

Information on Horn of Africa: http://www.djibouti.com

Local online newspaper: http://www.djiboutipost.com

Mbendi AfroPaedia (information on companies, countries, industries and stock exchanges in Africa): http://www.mbendi.co.za

Dominica

KEY FACTS

Official name: The Commonwealth of Dominica

Head of State: President Nicholas Liverpool (from 1 Oct 2003)

Head of government: Prime Minister Roosevelt Skerrit (DLP) (sworn in 8 Jan 2004; re-elected 5 May 2005)

Ruling party: Dominica Labour Party (DLP) (since Feb 2000; re-elected 5 May 2005)

Area: 750 square km

Population: 70,400 (2004) Dominica has had negative population growth for over five years.

Capital: Roseau

Official language: English

Currency: East Caribbean dollar (EC$) = 100 cents

Exchange rate: EC$2.70 per US$ (fixed)

GDP per capita: US$3,643 (2004)

GDP real growth: 1.00% (2004)

Inflation: 2.30% (2004)

Balance of trade: -US$85.00 million (2003)

COUNTRY PROFILE

Historical profile
The British, French and native Carib population fought for control of the island during the seventeenth and eighteenth centuries before the British prevailed. Dominica formed part of the Leeward Islands Federation.
1940 Dominica was transferred to the Windward Islands.
1959 The island was separated from the Windward Islands and became governed by its own administrator.
1967 Dominica gained full control over its internal affairs.
1978 Dominica gained independence.
1995 The United Workers' Party (UWP), led by Edison James, won the general election, defeating the ruling Dominica Freedom Party (DFP).
2000 The UWP lost the election to a coalition composed of the Dominica Labour Party (DLP) and the DFP. Prime Minister Roosevelt Douglas died suddenly and Pierre Charles was appointed as his successor.
2002 Dominica ended the sale of passports under its economic citizenship programme.
2003 On 1 October, Dr Nicholas Liverpool became president, having been elected by parliament despite an opposition boycott of the sitting. Outgoing president, Vernon Shaw, did not seek re-election.
2004 On 6 January, Prime Minister Pierre Charles died; Roosevelt Skerrit was sworn in as prime minister on 8 January. The stabilisation levy was removed as part of Dominica's EC$302.00 million (US$111.85 million) June budget.
2005 Prime Minister Roosevelt Skerrit's DLP won the 5 May parliamentary elections; the DFP, the junior partner in the former coalition government, lost both of its seats – the first time in 35 years that the DFP had not won a seat.

Political structure
The executive
Executive power rests with the prime minister who acts on the advice of the cabinet.
The role of the president, as Head of State, is largely ceremonial. The president is nominated by the prime minister, in consultation with the leader of the opposition, and is then elected by the House of Assembly for five years, renewable once.

National legislature
The House of Assembly has five members nominated by the prime minister, four nominated by the leader of the opposition, one ex-officio member and 21 members directly elected by the 21 constituencies. Parliamentary terms run for five years.
The prime minister is the leader of the majority in the House of Assembly and the leader of the opposition is appointed by the president as leader of the main grouping outside the government.

Legal system
The legal system is based on English common law. There are three local levels of judiciary courts. The Eastern Caribbean Supreme Court, located in St Lucia, hears appeals. The Privy Council in the UK is the highest court of appeal.

Last elections
5 May 2005 (parliamentary)
Results: Parliamentary: The DLP won 12 seats out of 21, the UWP eight and independents one. The Dominica Freedom Party (DFP), the junior partner in the former coalition government, lost both of its seats – the first time in 35 years that the DFP had not won a seat.

Next elections
2010 (parliamentary)

Political parties
Ruling party
Dominica Labour Party (DLP) (since Feb 2000; re-elected 5 May 2005)
Main opposition party
United Workers' Party (UWP)
Political situation
Prime Minister Roosevelt Skerrit and the Labour Party won re-election in the May 2005 elections. Its coalition partner in the

previous government, the Dominica Freedom Party (DFP), failed to win any seats, but with 12 of the 21 parliamentary seats the Labour Party won a clear majority. Skerrit had campaigned on the growth bought to the island by an IMF funded programme. The programme had resulted in an increase in unemployment and taxes and was criticised by the opposition United Workers Party and its leader, Edison James.

Population
70,400 (2004) Dominica has had negative population growth for over five years.

Ethnic make-up
Black, mixed black and European, European, Syrian, Carib.

Religions
Roman Catholic (77 per cent), Methodist (5 per cent), Pentecostal (3 per cent), Seventh-Day Adventist (3 per cent), Baptist (2 per cent).

Education
Literacy rate: 94 per cent, adult rate (2003)
Compulsory years: Five to 16

Health
The total expenditure on health is around 6 per cent of GDP, of which government spending is over 70 per cent.

The country has experienced notable improvements with a decline in infant and maternal mortality and communicable diseases and an increase in life expectancy; chronic and other non-communicable diseases are now the leading causes of death and ill-health, even as new problems such as HIV/Aids present themselves.
Life expectancy: 76.7 years (World Bank)
Fertility rate/Maternal mortality rate: 1.9 births per woman (World Bank)
Birth rate/Death rate: 17 births per 1,000 population; seven deaths per 1,000 population (2003).
Infant mortality rate: 12 per 1,000 live births (2003)

Welfare
Dominica has a national insurance system in which employee contributions are 3 per cent of salary and employer contributions are 7 per cent.

Main cities
Roseau (capital, estimated population 20,000 in 2003), Berekua (3,900), Portsmouth (3,600).

Languages spoken
English and French-Creole.
Official language/s
English

Media
Press
There are no daily newspapers. Weekly publications include *The Chronicle* and *The Sun*. Online news is carried by News-Dominica.com and The Dominican.net.

Broadcasting
Radio: Government-operated radio service and two privately owned religious stations.
Television: Two local television companies provide 12 channels of cable television.

Economy
Dominica's precarious economic situation led to the government severing ties with Taiwan in April 2004, in favour of new relations with China, which promised, in turn, US$100 million for infrastructure improvements over the following five years. While opposition members of parliament and some commentators called into question the integrity of a government that could throw over old ties for such aid, the prime minister took the pragmatic view that without this aid the country would continue to be cash-strapped and unable to raise other investment funds from elsewhere.

Bananas provide about 40 per cent of export revenue. The state plays a significant part in both production and marketing of agricultural goods. The banana industry has weakened due to increased competition from other South American producers. The government has a Banana Production Recovery Plan in place to help the country cope when the market is fully liberalised in 2006.

The Dominican government relies heavily on loans from the National Commercial Bank to meet expenditure. Civil service wages consume around 60 per cent of government money earned from taxes. The Organisation of Eastern Caribbean States (OECS) shares a common currency and central bank. The seven OECS members are Antigua and Barbuda, Dominica, Grenada, Montserrat, St Kitts and Nevis, St Lucia and St Vincent and the Grenadines. The British Virgin Islands and Anguilla are associate members.

In early-2004, the IMF approved a US$11.4 million credit under the Poverty Reduction and Growth Facility (PRGF) arrangement.

The 2004/05 budget was presented in June 2004; it included the removal of the stabilisation levy, which had been in place since 2002. The budget noted a significant reduction in debt servicing as a result of the government's ongoing debt restructuring efforts.

The economic programme supported by the PRGF arrangement envisages a return to growth by addressing the country's debt and structural weaknesses. Growth rebound from -1.0 per cent in 2003 to 1.0 per cent in 2004.

External trade
Imports
Principal imports include manufactured goods, machinery and equipment, food and chemicals.
Main sources: US (36.6 per cent total, 2004), Trinidad and Tobago (18.1 per cent), UK (6.6 per cent), France (5.0 per cent), (Japan 4.7 per cent)

Exports
The principal exports include bananas (around 40 per cent), soap, bay oil, vegetables and citrus fruit.

KEY INDICATORS — Dominica

	Unit	2000	2001	2002	2003	2004
Population	m	0.07	0.07	0.07	0.07	0.07
Gross domestic product (GDP)	US$bn	0.27	0.26	0.25	0.38	*0.27
GDP per capita	US$	3,753	3,504	3,378	5,400	3,643
GDP real growth	%	0.5	-4.3	-3.6	-1.0	1.0
Inflation	%	1.9	1.9	-0.3	0.5	2.3
Exports (fob) (goods)	US$m	50.3	45.0	46.2	50.0	–
Imports (fob) (goods)	US$m	129.6	131.0	103.2	135.0	–
Balance of trade	US$m	-79.3	-86.0	-570.0	-85.0	–
Current account	US$m	-68.9	-43.0	-48.1	-45.0	-47.0
Foreign debt	US$bn	0.1	0.2	0.2	0.2	–
Total reserves minus gold	US$m	29.4	31.2	45.5	47.7	42.3
Foreign exchange	US$m	29.4	31.2	45.5	47.7	42.3
Exchange rate	per US$	2.70	2.70	2.70	2.70	2.70

* estimated figure

Main destinations: Jamaica (20.2 per cent total, 2004), UK (18 per cent), Antigua and Barbuda (10.0 per cent), France (9.6 per cent), Trinidad and Tobago (7.4 per cent)

Agriculture
The agriculture sector is the mainstay of the economy, accounting for around 18 per cent of GDP and employing 40 per cent of the labour force. About 25 per cent of the total land area is agricultural. Bananas are the main crop, with exports destined mainly for the UK. Banana exports are controlled through the Dominican Banana Marketing Board (DBMB), a government agency. Dominica's climate makes the banana crop highly vulnerable. Hurricanes occur periodically and in the past have wiped out as much as 95 per cent of the crop.

The government is trying to promote new crops as part of its diversification plan, for when the market is fully liberalised in 2006; these include coffee, mangos, and aloe vera.

Crop production in 2004 included: 180 tonnes (t) cereals in total, 25,220t citrus fruit, 120t potatoes, 1,850t potatoes, 1,000t cassavas, 4,550t yautia, 11,200t taro, 8,000t yams, 4,400t sugar cane, 11,500t coconuts, 29,000 bananas, 5,700t plantains, 1,900t mangoes, 380t green coffee, 220t cocoa beans, 188t assorted spices, 63,490t fruit in total, 1,495t oilcrops, 6,630t vegetable. Livestock production included: 1,364t meat in total, 540t beef, 420t pig meat, 64t lamb and goat meat, 340t poultry, 225t eggs, 6,100t milk.

Fishing
The typical annual fish catch is over 1,100t, plus 4t of other seafood. Forestry potential is not exploited.

Industry and manufacturing
Industry accounts for 24 per cent of GDP. The manufacturing sector is small-scale and centred on soap production, construction, agricultural processing (mainly coconut oil and copra), canned fruit juices, cigarettes, cigars and rum. Water bottling for export is also important.

Tourism
Tourism is an increasingly important sector of Dominica's economy, despite the lack of such attractions as white sand beaches. Tracts of rainforest cover a large area and the island is being developed as an eco-tourist destination. Boiling Lake, for instance, is among the top 25 nature experiences in the Caribbean. Cruise ship visitors are the largest and fastest-growing tourist group, followed by stay-overs and excursionists. The main markets are the Caribbean area and French West Indies, North America and UK. The sector is projected to contribute 9.6 per cent to GDP in 2005. It provides some 8,500 jobs, over 20 per cent of the total work force.

Hydrocarbons
Dominica does not produce oil, gas or coal. It relies on importing refined oil to meet domestic demand. The country needs fossil fuels to meet around half its energy consumption needs. Imports are mainly from other Caribbean islands and the US.

Trinidad and Tobago is planning to build a 600 mile undersea pipeline connecting islands on the way to Guadaloupe, which would give Dominica access to natural gas.

Energy
Around 80 per cent of Dominica's electricity needs are met by hydropower, of which there are plentiful resources. Dominica, St Lucia and St Kitts and Nevis are investigating the commercial development of geothermally-fueled electric power plants.

Banking and insurance
The seven members of the Organisation of Eastern Caribbean States (OECS), Antigua and Barbuda, Dominica, Grenada, Montserrat, St Kitts and Nevis, St Lucia and St Vincent and the Grenadines, share a common currency and central bank. The British Virgin Islands and Anguilla are associate members.

Central bank
Eastern Caribbean Central Bank, St Kitts and Nevis.

Offshore facilities
The offshore financial sector makes a significant contribution to Dominican GDP and it is an area that the government would like to see progress. The government introduced anti-money laundering legislation and in 2003 Dominica was removed from the OECD blacklist of non-compliant countries.

Time
GMT minus four hours

Geography
Dominica is situated in the Windward Islands group of the West Indies, lying between Guadeloupe to the north and Martinique to the south.

Climate
Sub-tropical with year-round tradewinds moderating the heat. Daytime temperatures range from 24–32 degrees Celsius; coolest from December–March. It is driest from January–May. The rainy season is from June–October; rainfall is much higher in mountain areas.

Entry requirements
Passports
Required by all; except nationals of North America holding proof of citizenship bearing a photo ID and return or onward tickets and French nationals with National Identity Cards (Carte d'Identité) for stays up to two weeks.

Visa
Tourist visas up to 21 days are valid for all visitors who can show proof of a return/onward ticket and sufficient funds for the duration of the stay. Longer visa-free stays are only granted to designated nationals of the Americas, Europe and Australasia. Business visas will be issued to visitors who represent foreign companies, who must present proof of employment.

Contact the nearest High Commission or embassy for further information and application form.

Currency advice/regulations
Export of foreign and local currency must not exceed the amount imported.

Health (for visitors)
Mandatory precautions
Yellow fever vaccination certificate required if arriving from infected area.

Advisable precautions
Immunisation for hepititis 'A' is useful. Other lesser risks include typhoid, bacillary and amoebic dysentery and occasional outbreaks of dengue fever as well as haemorrhagic dengue fever. Water precautions should be taken in rural areas. As visitors are required to pay up-front for treatment, it is strongly recommended to take out full medical insurance.

Hotels
Limited availability. Bills include a 10 per cent service charge and 5 per cent tax.

Public holidays
Fixed dates
1 Jan (New Year's Day), 3 Nov (Independence Day), 4 Nov (Community Service Day), 25 Dec (Christmas Day), 26 Dec (Boxing Day).

Variable dates
Carnival (Feb), Good Friday, Easter Monday, Whit Monday, Bank Holiday (first Mon in May), August Monday (first Mon in Aug).

Working hours
Banking
Mon–Thu: 0800–1400; Fri: 0800–1700.
Business
Mon–Fri: 0800–1600. Sat: 0800–1300.
Government
Mon–Fri: 0800–1600/1700.

Dominica

Telecommunications

Mobile phones
GSM 850 and 900/1900 services available throughout most of the island.

Electricity supply
220V AC, 50 cycles

Social customs/useful tips
Dominica's national dish is made from a large land frog, the *crapaud* or mountain chicken. In February 2004, a ban was placed on hunting the amphibians, which are facing extinction.

Getting there
Air
National airline: None
International airport/s: Melville Hall (DOM), 64km north-east of Roseau; Canefield (DCF), 5km north of Roseau. Both of these airports are too small for international jets; access by air is via Antigua, Barbados, Costa Rica, Martinique or Guadeloupe.
Airport tax: Departure tax: US$20 after a stay of more than 24 hours.
Surface
Main port/s: Roseau (Woodbridge Bay Deep Water Harbour). Portsmouth (Prince Rupert's Bay).

Getting about
National transport
Air: Regional airline Carib Express based in Barbados.
Road: The network is over 750km, most of which is classified as first class.
City transport
Taxis: Available at airports and through hotels. Fixed rate system.
Car hire
Temporary driver's permit required. Obtained on production of national driving licence.

BUSINESS DIRECTORY

The addresses listed below are a selection only. While World of Information makes every endeavour to check these addresses, we cannot guarantee that changes have not been made, especially to telephone numbers and area codes. We would welcome any corrections.

Telephone area codes
The international direct dialling code (IDD) for Dominica is +1 767, followed by subscriber's number.

Chambers of Commerce
Dominica Association of Industry and Commerce, 6 Cross Street, PO Box 85, Roseau (tel:448-2874; fax: 448-6868; e-mail: daic@marpin.dm).

Banking
Agricultural, Industrial & Development Bank (AID Bank), Charles Avenue, Goodwill (tel: 448-2853).

Bank of Nova Scotia, 28 Hillsborough Street, PO Box 520, Roseau (tel: 448-8580).

Banque Française Commerciale Antilles Guiyane, Queen Mary Street, PO Box 166, Roseau (tel: 448-4040).

Barclays Bank, 2 Old Street, PO Box 4, Roseau (tel: 448-2571).

Dominica Co-operative Credit Union, Great Marlborough Street, Roseau (tel: 82-191).

National Commercial Bank of Dominica, 64 Hillsborough Street, PO Box 271, Roseau (tel: 448-4401).

Royal Bank of Canada, Bay Front, PO Box 19, Roseau (tel: 448-2771).

Central bank
Eastern Caribbean Central Bank, Agency Office, PO Box 23, Dorsett House, Corner Old Street and Hodges Lane, Roseau (tel: 448-8001; fax: 448-8002).

Travel information
Cardinal Airlines, 26 King George V Street, PO Box 661, Roseau (tel: 449-8922; fax: 449-8923).

Ministry of tourism
Ministry of Tourism, Port and Employment, Government Headquarters, Kennedy Avenue, Roseau (tel: 82-401).

National tourist organisation offices
Dominica Tourist Board, National Development Corporation, PO Box 293, Roseau (tel: 82-045; fax: 85-840).

Division of Tourism (National Development Corporation), PO Box 73, Valley Road, Roseau (tel: 82-186, 82-351; fax: 85-840).

Ministries
Ministry of Agriculture and the Environment, Government Headquarters, Kennedy Avenue, Roseau (tel: 82-401; fax: 87-999).

Ministry of Communications, Works and Housing, Government Headquarters, Kennedy Avenue, Roseau (tel: 82-401; fax: 84-807).

Ministry of Community Development and Women's Affairs, Government Headquarters, Kennedy Avenue, Roseau (tel: 82-401; fax: 98-220).

Ministry of Education, Sports and Youth Affairs, Government Headquarters, Government Headquarters, Kennedy Avenue, Roseau (tel: 82-401; fax: 80-080).

Ministry of External Affairs, Legal Affairs and Labour, Government Headquarters, Kennedy Avenue, Roseau (tel: 82-401; fax: 85-200).

Ministry of Finance, Industry and Planning (The Economic Development Unit), Government Headquarters, Kennedy Avenue, Roseau (tel: 82-401; fax: 80-054).

Ministry of Health and Social Security, Government Headquarters, Kennedy Avenue, Roseau (tel: 82-401; fax: 86-086).

Ministry of Privatisation and Foreign Investment (National Development Corporation), PO Box 293, Valley Road, Roseau (tel: 82-045).

Ministry of Trade and Marketing, Government Headquarters, Kennedy Avenue, Roseau (tel: 82-401; fax: 86-103).

Office of the Prime Minister, Government Headquarters, Kennedy Ave, Roseau (tel: 82-406).

Other useful addresses
Co-operative Citrus Growers' Association, 21 Hanover St, Roseau (tel: 82-062).

Dominica Banana Marketing Corp (DBMC), Corner of Queen Mary St and Turkey Lane, Roseau (82-671).

Dominica Broadcasting Corporation, Victoria Street, Roseau (tel: 83-283; fax: 82-918).

Dominica Export-Import Agency (Dexia), PO Box 173, Roseau (tel: 82-780; fax: 86-308).

Dominica Hotel Association, PO Box 270, Roseau (tel: 84-436).

Dominica National Development Corporation (NDC), PO Box 293, Valley Road, Bath Estate, Roseau (tel: 82-045; fax: 85-840; internet site: http://ndcdominica.dm/index.htm).

International Business Unit, Ministry of Finance, Government Headquarters, Kennedy Avenue, Roseau (tel: 82-401; fax: 80-406; e-mail: ibu@cwdom.dm).

Dominican Republic

KEY FACTS

Official name: República Dominicana (Dominican Republic)

Head of State: President Leonel Fernández Reyana (PLD) (sworn in 16 Aug 2004)

Head of government: President Leonel Fernández Reyana

Ruling party: Partido Revolucionario Dominicano (PRD) (Dominican Revolutionary Party) since 2002

Area: 48,400 square km

Population: 8.79 million (2004)

Capital: Santo Domingo de Guzmán

Official language: Spanish

Currency: Dominican Republic peso (RD$) = 100 centavos

Exchange rate: RD$31.45 per US$ (Oct 2005); (devalued from RD$20 per US$ in Jan 2003)

GDP per capita: US$2,190 (2004)

GDP real growth: 2.00% (2004)

Labour force: 3.96 million (2004)

Unemployment: 17.00% (2004)

Inflation: 51.50% (2004)

Balance of trade: -US$2.65 billion (2004)

Foreign debt: US$7.75 billion (2004)

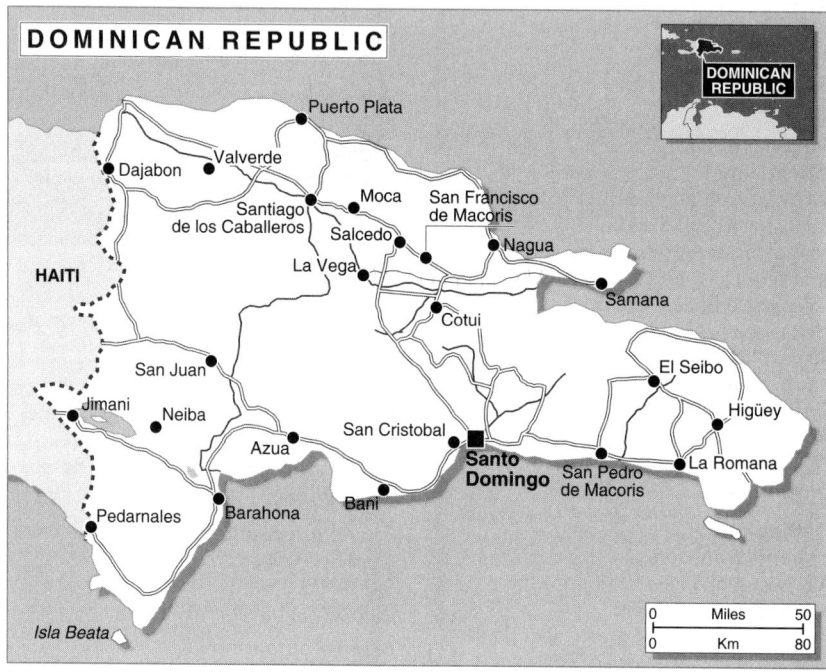

Immediately after he came to power in 2004, President Leonel Antonio Fernández Reyna of the Partido de la Liberación Dominicana (PLD) (Dominican Liberation Party) warned that his forthcoming term in office would be a long and difficult road. He even went as far as likening it to walking on a minefield or sitting on a burning stove, his inheritance was so poor.

The Dominican Republic has very few natural resources, but it does have a history of pervasive corruption. One of the major problems of Fernández' inheritance was the financially collapsed electricity sector. Also on the president's desk were the remnants of a wrecked IMF agreement in addition to an extremely volatile exchange rate. Per capita income had fallen US$398 dollars since 2001 to stand at US$2,190 by 2004, and Dominicans were generally dissatisfied and angry at the failure of their government.

An economic Houdini act

But thanks to his government's austere economic policy measures, the Dominican Republic under Fernández' presidency has begun to flourish, with healthy economic growth becoming the norm since he came to power. Astonishingly, the Fernández administration has knocked the economy into shape in virtually no time at all. Following stagflation (simultaneous negative growth and inflation) in 2003 and hyperinflation of 51.5 per cent in 2004, the rate of inflation has been reduced to just 3.7 per cent, according to the latest forecast by the IMF. At the same time a healthy growth rate has been maintained. In line with IMF predictions the economy is expected to expand by 4.5 per cent in 2005.

Though the overall economic picture for the country is looking much brighter, there are still serious sector-specific problems. Despite an upturn in the sector in the latter half of 2005, the travel and tourism industry remains in poor shape. Employment in the sector was down by 12.1 per cent on the level for 2004, while overall visitor exports declined by 22.5 per cent, despite a 3.5 per cent injection in capital investment. The woes in the tourism industry are especially damaging, as the

Dominican Republic

sector accounts for almost 20 per cent of the total workforce and constitutes 22.9 per cent of the Dominican Republic's total GDP.

In order for the economy to continue on its general upward trajectory increased levels of foreign direct investment are imperative. There was good news on this front in 2005 as Direct Expert of Nevada, USA, announced plans to invest RD$130 million (US$4.13 million) in the redevelopment – including the installation of casinos – of two state-owned hotels. The precious metals mining industry also received a boost when the Canadian company Placer Dome decided to go ahead with their US$1.35 billion Pueblo Viejo gold project. According to Placer Dome Chief Executive Peter Tomsett, the mine will produce approximately 12 million ounces over the next twenty years.

The Fernández government's sensible economic initiatives have been the bedrock of the nascent recovery. Tight monetary policy, coupled with the reopening of negotiations with the IMF has resulted in a stabilisation of the peso. The government has also managed to work closely with the United States Agency for International Development (USAID) and the World Bank to design a National Electricity Sector Revitalisation Programme in order to stabilise the flailing electricity generation and distribution sector and thereby partially relieve the government of its subsidy burden. The government's signing of the Central American Free Trade Agreement (Cafta) with the United States and five other Central American countries is expected to further increase the capacity of the economy and enhance prospects for future growth.

The perils of importing black gold

A major worry for the Dominican Republic is its reliance on imports of energy resources. The country's oil import bill was estimated to be US$2.57 billion in 2005, a sizeable increase from the US$1.66 billion total recorded in 2004. If crude oil prices continue to rise the country's oil bill could exceed US$3 billion by the end of 2006. Fernández, along with other high profile government figures, has expressed his concern at the increasing energy bill the country faces. Secretary of state for the presidency, Danilo Medina, has said that the government may need to tap into its stock of international reserves in order to foot the growing bill. This would almost inevitably mean a reduction in social spending and a downscaling of vital infrastructural investment programmes in education, drinking water and health.

The Dominican Republic is already a signatory of the Caracas Energy Accords, which facilitates the purchase of Venezuelan oil at reduced prices and also allows for extended credit in order to purchase energy supplies. As a means to ease the still growing problem of a high energy import bill, the government has initiated negotiations with other governments in the Latin American and Caribbean region. In August 2005 the government began talks with Trinidad and Tobago in an attempt to broker a natural gas import deal from the country. Also in the same month a delegation representing the Dominican government flew to Venezuela to conclude the Petrocaribe agreement. Petrocaribe is an initiative promoted by Venezuelan President Hugo Chávez designed at supplying oil at preferential rates to 13 countries in the Latin American and Caribbean region.

Outlook

The outlook for the Dominican economy looks healthier than it has down for several years. The Fernández government has worked wonders in a short space of time since coming to power and capital investment in the economy is beginning to increase after a long period of understandable wariness on the part of foreign investors. Despite a positive overall growth rate, sector-specific problems continue to exist, not least of all in the tourism industry, a vital component of the country's economy. The Dominican Republic's reliance on imported oil, coupled with rising international crude prices is a definite worry and further steps at addressing this problem need to be taken if the Dominican economic revival is to continue.

Risk assessment

Economic	Improving
Political	Good
Regional stability	Good

COUNTRY PROFILE

Historical profile
The island was inhabited by a group of Arauaco Indians known as Tainos.
1492 Land was sighted by Christopher Columbus. His brother Bartolomeo founded Santo Domingo and his son Diego was the first governor of the Spanish colony, who named the island Hispaniola.
1797 Ceded to France.
1808 Regained by Spain.
1821 Gained independence.
1822–44 Ruled by Haiti.
1844 Became independent as Dominican Republic.
1916–24 US armed forces invaded and occupied the island.
1930–1961 Rafael Trujillo ruled Dominican Republic directly as dictator between 1930–47 and indirectly until 1961 – through his brother and then close colleagues.
1962 Democratic election of Juan Bosch in the first free election for 38 years.
1965 Civil revolt caused another intervention of the US armed forces.
1966 The presidential election was won by Joaquín Balaguer (a president during the Trujillo era) of the Partido Reformista Social Cristiana (PRSC) (Social Christian Reform Party). Balaguer was re-elected in 1970 and 1974, during which period he survived several coup attempts.

KEY INDICATORS — Dominican Republic

	Unit	2000	2001	2002	2003	2004
Population	m	8.75	8.58	8.64	8.71	8.79
Gross domestic product (GDP)	US$bn	19.70	21.20	21.30	18.56	*18.67
GDP per capita	US$	2,290	2,588	2,587	2,400	2,190
GDP real growth	%	7.8	2.7	3.8	-0.4	2.0
Inflation	%	7.7	4.4	10.5	42.5	51.5
Unemployment	%	13.0	15.0	14.5	15.5	17.0
Exports (fob) (goods)	US$m	5,736.7	2,486.0	5,183.4	5,300.0	5,446.0
Imports (fob) (goods)	US$m	9,478.5	5,937.0	8,882.5	8,700.0	8,093.0
Balance of trade	US$m	-3,741.8	-3,540.0	-3,699.1	-3,400.0	-2,647.0
Current account	US$m	-1,026.5	-839.0	-875.2	1,010.0	1,130.0
Foreign debt	US$bn	4.6	5.1	4.9	4.8	7.7
Total reserves minus gold	US$m	625.5	1,099.5	468.4	253.1	798.3
Foreign exchange	US$m	625.1	1,099.0	468.1	253.0	796.7
Exchange rate	per US$	16.42	16.95	18.61	28.85	35.15

1978 Silvestre Antonio Guzmán of the Partido Revolucionario Dominicano (PRD) (Dominican Revolutionary Party) defeated Balaguer in the presidential election – the first time an elected president yielded power to an elected successor.
1994 The consitution was established, setting out the duties and powers of the president.
1996 Leonel Fernández Reyana of the Partido de la Liberación Dominicana (PLD) (Dominican Liberation Party) narrowly won the presidential election.
1998 The PRD won the majority of seats in both houses. In order to pass legislation, President Leonel Fernández had to reach agreement with the PRD.
2000 Rafael Hipólito Mejía Domínguez (PRD) won the presidential elections.
2002 The PRD won legislative elections.
2004 In January eight people died during a two-day general strike held to protest at the economic policies that included the peso's sharp devaluation, soaring inflation and persistent power cuts. The Dominican Republic acceded to the Central American Parliament in February. Leonel Fernández Reyana (PLD) won the 16 May presidential elections, and during his inaugural speech, in August, said he would promote fiscal austerity, fight corruption and support social concerns. Around 2,000 people died or were lost during severe flooding in May.
2005 On 6 September the Chamber of Deputies approved joining the Central American Free Trade Agreement (Cafta).

Political structure
In addition to their unicameral national parliaments, El Salvador, Guatemala, Honduras, Nicaragua, Panama and Dominican Republic, which acceded to the Central American Parliament in February 2004, also return directly elected deputies to the supranational Central American Parliament.

Constitution
The 1994 Constitution prevents the re-election of an individual as president for consecutive periods.

The executive
Executive power rests with the president, who is also head of government and commander-in-chief of the armed forces. The president is directly elected for a one-off four-year term. The cabinet is appointed and presided over by the president. The president, by constitutional decree, names the provincial governors, who are his representatives in each province.

National legislature
The legislature is the bicameral Congress. The 32-member Senate is elected for a four-year term, one member for each province plus one for the Distrito Nacional. The Senate elects the members of the judiciary.
The Chamber of Deputies (150 members) is elected under a system of proportional representation with members chosen on a provincial basis.

Last elections
16 May 2004 (presidential); 16 May 2002 (parliamentary).
Results: Presidential: Leonel Fernández Reyana (PLD) won 57.1 per cent of the vote, incumbent Hipólito Mejía (PRD) 33.7 per cent and Eduardo Estrella of the Partido Reformista Social Cristiano (PRSC) (Social Christian Reformist Party) 8.7 per cent; turnout was 72.8 per cent.
Parliamentary: PRD won 41.9 per cent of the vote, 73 deputies, 29 senators; PLD 29.1 per cent, 41and two; PRSC 24.3 per cent, 36 and one.

Next elections
2006 (parliamentary); 2008 (presidential).

Political parties
Ruling party
Partido Revolucionario Dominicano (PRD) (Dominican Revolutionary Party) since 2002
Main opposition party
Partido de la Liberación Dominicana (PLD) (Dominican Liberation Party)

Population
8.79 million (2004)
Ethnic make-up
Mixed race (73 per cent), white (16 per cent), black (11 per cent).
Religions
Roman Catholic (95 per cent). There is also a small Protestant community.

Education
Primary education lasts for six years and is free of charge. There are two systems of secondary education in operation, the traditional has six years of study divided into two-year then four-year cycles. The reform system has two cycles of three years. The emphasis of the former is academic and the latter scientific/technical. Both systems allow for specialised studies.
Secondary schooling is subsidised in private schools.
Literacy rate: 85 per cent, adult rate (2003)
Compulsory years: Seven to 17
Pupils per teacher: 28 in primary schools.

Health
Total expenditure on health is around 6 per cent of GDP, of which 36 per cent is government spending.
Seventy-nine per cent of the population have access to an improved water source. The HIV/Aids infection rates is one of the largest in the Caribbean.
HIV prevalence: 1.7 per cent aged 15–49 in 2003 (World Bank)
Life expectancy: 67.1 years (World Bank)
Fertility rate/Maternal mortality rate: 2.6 births per woman (World Bank)
Birth rate/Death rate: 24 births per 1,000 population; seven deaths per 1,000 population (2003).
Infant mortality rate: 29 per 1,000 live births (World Bank)

Main cities
Santo Domingo de Guzmán (capital, estimated population 2.2 million in 2004), Santiago de los Caballeros (501,800), La Romana (198,0000), San Pedro de Macoris (167,100), Puerto Plata (133,400), San Francisco de Macoris (131,300), San Cristobal (121,800).

Languages spoken
English is widely spoken.
Official language/s
Spanish

Media
Press
Dailies: There are five morning newspapers and two afternoon papers with nationwide circulation, all edited in Santo Domingo: El Caribe, El Nuevo Diario, El Siglo, Periódico Hoy, Listín Diario, El Nacional and Ultima Hora.
Weeklies: The Santo Domingo News is an English newspaper.
Periodicals: A magazine, Bohio Dominicano, with international coverage, specialises in tourism information. It is published in English and Spanish.
Broadcasting
There are around 180 AM-FM radio stations and 10 television stations, all private/commercial except for the government-owned Radio Televisión Dominicana, which accepts sponsored programmes, but is not fully commercial.
Radio: The main radio stations are Empresas Radiofónicas (owned by the Rodolfo Lama Jaar group), Radio Supra FM and a commercial radio station, Radio CNT.
Television: Main stations are: Radio Televisión Dominicana (state-owned), Color Visión, Circuito Independencia, Canal 6, Telesistema Dominicano and Teleantillas.
Advertising
Widely used in all forms of media except posters. The Santo Domingo Chamber of Commerce produces the weekly Comercio y Producción.

Economy
The economic situation had deteriorated badly in 2003. The collapse of the Banco Intercontinental (Baninter), and two other, smaller banks, led to a currency devaluation, along with a rapid increase in public debt and inflation. A nationwide energy crisis due to the surge in demand and

Dominican Republic

non-payment of bills resulted in periodic blackouts, which made the situation deteriorate further. Mejia, who was held responsible for the economic situation, was soundly beaten and replaced in 2004 by President Fernández. An IMF restructuring package was agreed and austerity measures implemented. The economy began focussing on trade and tourism to help reduce the country's debt. However, US observers have warned that corruption and cronyism in government could reduce the effectiveness of the IMF measures and prolong their execution.

The US signed the Central American Free Trade Accord (Cafta) in July 2005; over a 20-year period all tariffs and barriers to trade will be removed. The Dominican Republic is keen to supply goods to the US market although in return the US will now have unlimited access to Dominican markets for goods and services. Foreign direct investment (FDI) in 2004 is estimated to have been around US$100 million, somewhat lower than the US$309 million in 2003. FDI in 2004 was mainly directed at the tourism sector.

Government figures for remittances from overseas workers showed that the Dominican Republic received US$2.7 billion in 2004, of which the US (including Puerto Rico) accounted for US$1.84 billion. Around 1.5 million Dominicans live abroad, mostly in the US, and remittances have become one of the main hard currency earners for the country.

The result of the Central Bank guaranteeing 100 per cent of deposits in the three failed banks in 2003 tripled the national debt from around 18 per cent of GDP to over 50 per cent and short-term, high-interest loans were taken out to cover the cost. The new administration has addressed the fallout but with rising oil prices and the poor peso exchange rate the problems can still be exacerbated. It has been estimated that the 2005 oil bill was around US$2.4 billion.

External trade

The US signed a free trade agreement (FTA) with six Central America and Caribbean countries, including the Dominican Republic, on 3 August 2005. The Central American Free Trade Agreement (Cafta) with Dominican Republic, Costa Rica, El Salvador, Guatemala, Honduras and Nicaragua will remove all tariffs and barriers within 20 years.

The Dominican Republic also has an FTA with the 15-member Caribbean Community Common Market (Caricom) since 2000.

Imports
Foodstuffs, petroleum, cotton and fabrics, chemicals and pharmaceuticals.

Main sources: US (49 per cent total, 2004), Venezuela (13.8 per cent), Mexico (4.6 per cent), Colombia (4.2 per cent)

Exports
Ferro-nickel, sugar, gold, silver, coffee, cocoa, tobacco, meats and consumer goods.

Main destinations: US (79.7 per cent total, 2004), Canada (1.8 per cent), Haiti (1.7 per cent)

Agriculture
Farming

The agricultural sector employs 50 per cent of the workforce, produces two-thirds of all exports and contributes 25 per cent of GDP.

The principal commercial crop is sugar cane, production of which has fluctuated due to vagaries of weather, falling export demand and labour shortages.

The main agricultural exports – sugar, coffee, cocoa and tobacco – account for just under a half of the country's export earnings. Rice, vegetables and citrus fruits are grown for home consumption.

Cattle-raising has expanded considerably and commercial fishing is being developed.

Estimates of cultivated arable land vary between 18–25 per cent; pasture 17–30 per cent; woodland/forest 25–40 per cent. Soil is generally fertile and rainfall/water availability is adequate.

Agriculture is becoming more commercialised. The country benefits from agreements that provide it with duty free access to the US markets. These include the Generalised System of Preferences, the US Caribbean Basin Initiative.

Crop production in 2004 included: 5.2 million tonnes (t) sugar cane, 686,507t cereals in total, 41,305t maize, 639,785t rice, 154,000t tomatoes, 30,125t sweet potatoes, 20,355t yams, 76,379t yautia, 480,000t bananas, 192,500t plantains, 105,196t cassava, 41,509t potatoes, 29,000t chillies and peppers, 86,000t citrus fruit, 45,000t cocoa beans, 181,533t coconuts, 180,000t mangoes, 45,000t green coffee, 18,500t tobacco leaves, 53,909t oilcrops, 23,000t papayas, 1.2t fruit in total, 1,500t ginger, 366,050t vegetables in total. Livestock production included: 301,680t meat in total, 55,600t beef, 65,000t pig meat, 1,080t lamb and goat meat, 180,000t poultry, 83,000t eggs, 520,000t milk, 1,254t honey.

Forestry

Exports of forest materials in 2003 amounted to US$578,000 and imports were US$194 million.

Production in 2003 included 562,300 cubic metres (cum) roundwood, 6,300cum industrial roundwood, 3,600cum sawlogs and veneers, 556,000cum wood fuel, 70,000t charcoal.

Industry and manufacturing

The industrial sector contributes around a third of GDP and employs up to a quarter of the workforce.

Activity is centred on sugar refining (which is the dominant industry), cement production, the processing of foodstuffs, tobacco, beverages and textiles. The country is the largest exporter in the Caribbean region of apparel to the US. Some of the best known labels are manufactured in the Dominican Republic. The Caribbean Basin Initiative allows the country's textiles duty-free entry to the US market. However, with China now a member of the WTO this trade is threatened. Other light industries include plastics, rubber, chemicals and paper.

The emphasis is on encouraging joint ventures that utilise a high percentage of local materials, expanding facilities at the main industrial free zones (La Ramona, San Pedro de Macoris, Santiago) and overcoming the serious supply/energy problems. The free trade zone programme is the country's leading earner of foreign exchange.

Tourism

Tourism is the second-largest source of foreign exchange earnings, providing over 22.9 per cent of GDP and employing about 696,000. Tourism revenues totalled US$5.97 billion in 2004. Visitor arrivals, including an increased number of cruise ship visitors, exceeded 3.6 million in 2004.

Tourism in the first four months of 2005 registered a growth of 9.23 per cent on the same period in 2004. Two million visitors arrived, of which over 50 per cent were from the US. The exchequer earned over US$48,600 in air taxes alone, while tourist spending increased by just under 1 per cent.

Government spending has included the refurbishment of tourist facilities.

Mining

The mining sector as a whole typically accounts for 2 per cent of GDP and employs 3 per cent of the workforce.

Gold, silver and ferro-nickel are all mined in significant quantities. Gypsum, limestone and marble are mined for the domestic market. Deposits of copper, iron, titanium and platinum also exist.

In March 2003, Canada-based Placer Dome was given ownership of the Pueblo Viejo gold mine for 25 years, following a vote in the Senate. The mine, which has reserves of 15–30 million troy ounces, is set to see around US$350 million of investment between 2003–08.

The country's largest mining facility is operated by Falconbridge, a Canadian company, which exports 33,000 tonnes of nickel per year.

Some industry analysts believe that large deposits of nickel, copper and gold have yet to be discovered.

Hydrocarbons
Small deposits of oil are located at Charco Largo. However the Dominican Republic is heavily reliant on the import of petroleum products. Under the San José pact refined and unrefined oil from Mexico and Venezuela are imported under favourable terms. There are two oil refineries with a capacity of 48,300 barrels per day. Crude oil imports fill this capacity.
The Dominican Republic does not produce natural gas but imports liquefied natural gas from Trinidad and Tobago for power generation.
No coal is produced.

Energy
There is a heavy dependence on imported oil, most of which is used to generate electricity. Although power blackouts had become less common since the privatisation of the electricity sector in 1999, in 2003/04, the country's financial troubles led to many blackouts, sometimes lasting 20 hours. It was determined that price controls, high incidences of electricity theft and low collection rates contributed to the widespread distruption. Businesses have said that the high cost and poor provision of electricity has increased costs and lowered international competitiveness.

Financial markets
Stock exchange
The Bolsa de Valores de Santo Domingo (BVSD), the Dominican Republic's stock exchange, dates from 1991.

Banking and insurance
The foreign investment law of 1997 permits overseas banks to operate banks in the Dominican Republic.
The banking sector hit a crisis in 2003 when the Banco Intercontinental (Baninter) collapsed as a result of massive fraud. The Women's Development bank (Banmujer) began operations in 2001, lending small loans of around US$1,000 to women for entrepreneurial ventures.
Central bank
Banco Central de la República Dominicana.
Main financial centre
Santo Domingo.

Time
GMT minus four hours

Geography
The Dominican Republic occupies the eastern part of the island of Hispaniola, which lies between Cuba and Puerto Rico, in the Caribbean Sea. It has an international frontier with Haiti to the west.

Climate
Tropical with temperatures ranging from 27 degrees Celsius (C) during the dry season (November–April) to 37 degrees C from June–October when humidity is highest.

Entry requirements
Passports
Required by all, except nationals of US and Canada who require a notarised birth certificate and driving licence, and nationals of Germany, who require a National Identity Card. All passports must have over three months validation left from date of visit. No passport will be accepted if the applicant has visited, or intends to visit, Cuba.
Visa
Visit www.domrep.org/visas.htm for the list of countries where tourists may either visit for up to 60 days, without a visa or be able to purchase a tourist card upon arrival, although this can result in extended delays at port of entry. Business visitors and visitors from countries that may not use a tourist card should view the information at www.domrep.org/immigrant.htm.
Currency advice/regulations
Import of foreign currency must be declared and not be exceeded by export. Export of US dollars in cash or traveller's cheques is allowed up to a limit of US$10,000. Import/export of local currency is prohibited.
It is illegal to make payments in cash in a currency other than the Dominican Republic Peso (RD$).
Prohibited imports
Illicit drugs, weapons, plants and vegetables and pornographic material.

Health (for visitors)
Mandatory precautions
Yellow fever certificate if travelling from an infected area.
Advisable precautions
Vaccinations for meningitis, diphtheria and polio; other lesser risks include hepatitis 'A' and 'B' and occasional outbreaks of dengue fever. Bilharzia is endemic; use only well chlorinated and maintained swimming pools. Malaria precautions are recommended for visits to rural areas. A typhoid vaccination is recommended for longer stays. Water precautions are essential; use only bottled or boiled water. Eat only well cooked meals, preferably served hot. Pork, salad and mayonnaise may carry increased risk. Vegetables should be cooked and fruit peeled.
Health insurance (to include emergency repatriation) is strongly recommended, as medical care is limited and variable in quality. All personal medication should be carried with their prescription.

Hotels
Santo Domingo has a range of hotels, including good medium-priced rooms. Most small towns have acceptable, if basic, hotels.
Bills usually include 5 per cent government tax and 8 per cent service charge. Hotels are considerably more expensive during the winter. They are equipped with electricity generators, so guests do not suffer from the frequent power cuts.

Public holidays
Fixed dates
1 Jan (New Year's Day), 6 Jan (Epiphany), 21 Jan (Our Lady of Altagracia), 26 Jan (Duarte's Birthday), 27 Feb (Independence Day), 1 May (Labour Day), 16 Jul (Restoration Day), 24 Sep (Our Lady of las Mercedes), 6 Nov (Constitution Day), 25 Dec (Christmas Day).
Variable dates
Good Friday, Corpus Christi (May/Jun).

Working hours
Banking
Mon–Fri: 0830–1530.
Business
Mon–Fri: 0830–1230, 1430–1830.
Alternatively, Mon–Fri: 0930–1730.
Government
Mon–Fri: 0730–1430.

Electricity supply
110–120V AC, 60 cycles.

Weights and measures
The metric system has been adopted. However, certain other units are still in use, eg ounces and pounds are used in weighing solids, petrol and motor oils are measured in imperial gallons, cooking oil is retailed in pounds and fabrics are measured by the yard. Land surfaces in rural areas are generally measured by tarea – equal to 624 square metres.

Getting there
Air
International airport/s: Santo Domingo-Las Américas (SDQ), 30km east of city, duty-free shop, bar, restaurant, bank, post office, shops, hotel reservations, car hire; Gregorio Luperon International Puerto Plata (POP), 18km from city, bank, duty-free shop, restaurant, bar, car hire.
Airport tax: International departures US$10, excluding transit passengers.
Surface
Road: The main route runs from Haiti via Elias Pina.
Main port/s: There are 14 ports, including Santo Domingo (the largest) and Haina.

Getting about
National transport
Air: There are flights between Santo Domingo, Santiago, Samana, Punta Cana and Puerto Plata. These are

Dominican Republic

provided by Bavaro Sun Flight, Aerolineas Santo Domingo and Dorado Air.
Road: There are about 17,120km of roads. Highways link Santo Domingo-Hinguey, Montecristo, Dajabon, San Juan, Elias Pina. There is a direct route from Santo Domingo to Port-au-Prince in Haiti.
Buses: There are bus stations in all towns. Fairly numerous services from Santo Domingo to Puerto Plata, La Romana – journey times vary. Also to Barahona and Samana.
Rail: There are a number of freight-only railways.
City transport
Taxis: In Santo Domingo taxis are freely available in the main business districts. These are not metered and it is advisable to agree the price with the driver before setting out. Taxis which travel off these routes may be difficult to find, especially at night. No tip is expected.
Buses, trams & metro: Buses in Santo Domingo are cheap, though crowded.
Car hire
National or international licence required. Chauffeur-driven cars can be negotiated with taxi drivers outside main hotels. Car hire facilities are good, but fairly expensive.

BUSINESS DIRECTORY

Telephone area codes
This international direct dialling code (IDD) for the Dominican Republic is +1 809 followed by subscriber's number.

Useful telephone numbers
Santo Domingo
Emergency (Ambulance, Police): 911
Police: 682-3151
Police (radio patrol): 533-1074
Centro Médico Nacional
 (hospital): 682-0171
Fire Department: 682-2000
Red Cross: 682-4545

Chambers of Commerce
American Chamber of Commerce of the Dominican Republic, Avenida Sarasota 20, Torre Empresarial, PO Box 95-2, Santo Domingo (Tel: 381-0777; fax: 381-0286; e-mail: amcham@codetel.net.do).

British Chamber of Commerce of the Dominican Republic, Avenida San Martin 253, Edificio Santanita, PO Box 718-2, Santo Domingo (tel: 616-2335; fax: 616-2336; e-mail: britcham@tricom.net).

Santiago Cámara de Comercio y Producción, Avenida Las Carreras 7, Edificio Empresarial, Santiago (tel: 582-2856; fax: 241-4546; e-mail: csantiago@camarasantiago.com).

Santo Domingo Cámara de Comercio y Producción, Calle Arzobispo Nouel 206, PO Box 815, Santo Domingo (tel: 682-2688; fax: 685-2228; e-mail: camara.sto.dgo@codetel.net.do).

Banking
Banco Comercial BHD, Luis F Thomen Esq. Winston Churchill, Torre BHD, Santo Domingo (tel: 541-3232; fax: 566-9569).

Banco del Comercio Dominicano, Ave. 27 De Febrero Esq. Winston Churchill, Santo Domingo (tel: 545-5100; fax: 544-1298).

Banco del Exterior Dominicano, Ave Abraham Lincoln No. 756, Piantini, Santo Domingo (tel: 565-5540; fax: 565-5547).

Banco de los Trabajadores De La República Dominicana, Av México Esq Calle Altagracia, Santo Domingo (tel: 682-0171; fax: 685-6536).

Banco de Reservas de la República Dominica, Isabel La Catolica No. 72, Santo Domingo (tel: 688-2241; fax: 685-0602).

Banco Dominicano del Progreso, Ave John F Kennedy No. 3, Miraflores, Santo Domingo (tel: 563-3233; fax: 563-2451).

Banco Gerencial y Fiduciario Dominicano, Ave 27 de Febrero No 50, El Vergel, Santo Domingo (tel: 541-9400; fax: 567-6747).

Banco Latinoamericano, Gustavo Mejía Ricart Esq Agustín Lara, Ens Piantini, Santo Domingo (tel: 562-2662; fax: 562-1915).

Banco Mercantil, Ave Bolivar No. 308 Esq Jose Joaquín Pérez Gazcue, Santo Domingo (tel: 221-7151; 688-0608).

Banco Metropolitano, Ave Lope de Vega Esq Gustavo Mejía Ricart, Edif. Goico Castro, Ens Naco, Santo Domingo (tel: 562-4242; fax: 540-1566).

Banco Nacional de Crédito, John F Kennedy Esq Tiradentes, Ens Naco, Santo Domingo (tel: 540-4441; fax: 567-4698).

Banco Popular Dominicano, Av. John F Kennedy No 20 Esq Máximo Gómez, Torre Popular, 11 Avo. Piso, Santo Domingo (tel: 544-5900; fax: 544-5999).

Central bank
Banco Central de la República Dominicana, Calle Pedro Henríquez Ureña, Esq Leopoldo Navarro, Santo Domingo (tel: 221-9111; fax: 686-7488; e-mail: info@bancentral.gov.do).

Travel information
Aerolíneas Argo, Avenida 27 de Febrero 409, Santo Domingo (tel: 566-1844).

Dominicana de Aviación, Leopoldo Navarre, Edificio San Rafael, PO Box 1415, Santo Domingo (tel: 687-7111).

Santo Domingo-Las Américas International Airport, Santo Domingo (tel: 549-0450/0480).

Ministry of tourism
Secretaría de Estado de Turismo, César Nicholas Penson 59, Santo Domingo (tel: 685-2388; e-mail: dominicantourism@globalserve.net).

Other useful addresses
Asociación Dominicana de Empresas de Inversión Extranjera (ASIEX), Av Independencia Santo Domingo, RD (tel: 535-6165; fax: 535-1744).

Asociación Dominicana de Exportadores (ADOEXPO), Av W Churchill 5, Santo Domingo (tel: 532-6779; fax: 533-9734).

British Embassy, Floor 7, Edificio Corominas Pepín, Avenida 27 de Febrero No. 233, Santo Domingo (tel: 472-7111; fax: 427-7574).

Centro Dominicano de Promoción de Exportaciones (CEDOPEX), Av 27 de Febrero, Plaza de la Independencia, Santo Domingo, RD (tel: 530-5549; fax: 530-8208).

Consejo Nacional de Zonas Francas de Exportación, Leopoldo Navarro 61, Edif San Rafael 5ta Planta, Santo Domingo (tel: 686-8077; fax: 686-8079).

Corporación de Fomento Industrial, Av 27 de Febrero, Plaza de la Independencia, Santo Domingo, RD (tel: 530-1686; fax: 530-1303).

Public Enterprise Reform Committee, Gustavo Mejía Ricart No 73, Santo Domingo (tel: 683-3591; fax: 683-3964).

RCA Global Communications Inc, Edificio Diez, Calle Conde 203, Santo Domingo (tel: 682-3722).

Secretariat of State for Finance, Avda México, Santo Domingo, DN.

Secretariat of State for Industry and Commerce, Edif. de Oficinas Gubernamentales 7, Avda México, Santo Domingo, DN (tel: 685-171).

Internet sites
Dominican Republic One:
http://www.dr1.com/

Export promotion (in Spanish):
http://www.cedopex.gov.do/

Easter Island

KEY FACTS

Official name: Isla de Pascua (Easter Island)

Head of State: President of Chile

Head of government: Governor Jacobo Hey Paoa

Area: 180 square km

Population: 2,400 (2004)

Capital: Hanga Roa (only inhabited township)

Official language: Spanish

Currency: Chilean peso (CH$) = 100 centavos

Exchange rate: CH$528.75 per US$ (Oct 2005)

Visitor numbers: 15,000 (annually)*

* estimated figure

COUNTRY PROFILE

Historical profile
Easter Island, *Rapa Nui* in Polynesian, also known as *Te Pito O Te Henua* (the navel of the world), was settled in 400 AD by Polynesians from Asia. It is best known for the giant stone monoliths, known as moai, that dot the coastline. It is the most eastern point of the ancient Polynesian migrations.

The original population grew from a few hundred to about 20,000 at its peak, far exceeding the capabilities of the small island's ecosystem The islanders cut down the forests to make canoes and to transport and erect statues. Rats ate the seeds of the trees, preventing regeneration of the forests. The canoes needed repairs but there was a scarcity of wood, so deep-sea fishing became impossible, leading to food shortages. War between tribes ensued and the population declined. For many, Easter Island has become a metaphor for ecological disaster.

1680 Work on the *moai* ceased due to tribal wars induced by overpopulation and famine.
1722 The Dutch navigator, Jacob Roggeveen, came to the Island on Easter Sunday, hence its name.
1770 Spaniards came from Peru.
1774 Captain Cook visited the island.
1862–63 More than 1,000 islanders were kidnapped and despatched to Peru to work on the guano islands and plantations. Only 15 survived to be repatriated, but some were carrying infectious diseases which quickly decimated the population.
1866 Catholic missionaries converted the remaining population to Christianity.
1871 Conflict between the missionaries and a French settler who had established a sheep farm, forced the missionaries to leave with around 100 followers. Around 110 natives remained on the island.
1888 The island was annexed to Chile.
1966 The international airport opened.
2002 The first outbreak of dengue fever in Chile occurred on Easter Island. A 21-year-old woman was diagnosed with the fever after having lived on the island for two months.
2003 UNESCO awarded a German company a contract for US$11.5 million to restore the stone *moai*.

Political structure
Easter Island is administered as a province of Chile (part of the Valparaíso region), with a governor and locally elected council. Elections are held every four years for six councillors, who then elect the mayor. A Council of Elders was formed in 1983 to represent the interests of the native *Rapa Nuis* (Easter Islanders).

Form of state
Province of Chile

Political situation
There is a budding independence movement. Objections from locals concerning the immigration of Chileans has grown.

Population
2,400 (2004)
Religions
Christianity

Main cities
Hanga Roa is the only inhabited township.

Languages spoken
Rapa Nui, an Eastern Polynesian language, is spoken. English is not used.
Official language/s
Spanish

Media
Press
The Easter Island Foundation publishes the invaluable resource *Uncommon Guide to Easter Island* and *Rapa Nui Journal*, the premier source for Easter Island events and scientific studies. Rapa Nui news can be obtained from local internet sites (www.rapanui.cl) and *Te Rapa Nui* (www.rapanui.co.cl).
Broadcasting
Radio: There is radio reception from Chilean stations.
Television: Satellite television reception is available on Easter Island.

Economy
Tourism is the main economic resource.

External trade
Imports
Main imports are food, fuel, construction materials and machinery from Chile.
Exports
Main exports are tuna, avocados and pineapples to Chile.

Agriculture
Farming
Traditional subsistence farming is carried out.
Although the island is predominantly grassland, pine, eucalyptus and fruit trees have been planted.
The island's main crops are bananas, pineapples, sweet potatoes, yams, sugar cane, maize, potatoes, tomatoes, castor beans, melons, grapes and avocados.

Easter Island

Sheep farming has declined rapidly since the mid-twentieth century due to soil erosion. There are wild horses in addition to those used as draught animals and for riding. Poultry bred on the island includes pigeons, quail and ducks.

Fishing
Lobster, tuna and king fish are an important local source of protein.

Industry and manufacturing
There is a small manufacturing sector, based on the production of local handicrafts.

Tourism
Famous for its giant stone *moai* (statues), Easter Island is visited by around 40,000 tourists each year. Nearly a thousand of these ancient statues are strewn along its beautiful coastline and extinct volcano. There are also opportunities for hiking, horse-riding, cycling and swimming.

Banking and insurance
Central bank
Banco del Estado de Chile

Time
GMT minus six hours

Geography
Easter Island lies in the southern Pacific Ocean about 3,780km (2,350 miles) off the coast of Chile.

Climate
Subtropical, cooled by constant winds. Average rainfall is 1,250mm falling mainly in June–July; average temperature ranges from 16–27 degrees Celsius.

Entry requirements
Passports
Required by all.
Visa
As a province of Chile, the requirements are the same. Citizens of neighbouring countries or most EU states do not need visas. For further details contact the local embassy. Business visas are not required by those citizens who do not need a tourist visa; all others, including those who do not normally require them but who are visiting on short-term contracts or receive fees from a local company, do need a visa.
On arrival a 'tourist card' is issued and must be returned when leaving. Onward/return passage is necessary.

Health (for visitors)
Mandatory precautions
Vaccination certificates are required for yellow fever if travelling from an infected area.
Advisable precautions
Vaccinations for diphtheria, tuberculosis, hepatitis 'A' and 'B', polio, tetanus and typhoid are recommended. There is a risk of rabies.

Telecommunications
Telephone/fax
There is a limited telephone service available. There is no direct international dialling, although satellite links enable calls to be made through the international operator in Chile.
Internet/e-mail
There are internet bars in Hanga Roa.

Getting there
Air
National airline: Lan-Chile
International airport/s: Mataveri International (IPC), 1.6km south of Hanga Roa.
Surface
Main port/s: Hanga Roa.

Getting about
National transport
There are few surfaced roads. Four-wheel drive vehicles, motor cycles and horses are the main means of transportation. Minibuses are used by tourists.
Car hire
Make local enquiries regarding availability of car hire.

BUSINESS DIRECTORY
The addresses listed below are a selection only. While World of Information makes every endeavour to check these addresses, we cannot guarantee that changes have not been made, especially to telephone numbers and area codes. We would welcome any corrections.

Telephone area codes
The international direct dialling (IDD) code for Easter Island is +56 (Chile) followed area code 32 and Easter Island number 100 + subscriber's number.

Other useful addresses
Gobernación Provincial, Isla de Pascua.

Internet sites
General information: www.netaxs.com/~trance/rapanui.html

Ecuador

KEY FACTS

Official name: República del Ecuador (Republic of Ecuador)

Head of State: President Alfredo Palacio (sworn in 20 Apr 2005)

Head of government: President Alfredo Palacio

Ruling party: Coalition government led by the Movimiento Unidad Plurinacional Pachakutik-Nuevo País (MUPP-NP) (Pluri-National Pachakutik United Movement-New Country)

Area: 270,670 square km

Population: 13.18 million (2004)

Capital: Quito

Official language: Spanish

Currency: US dollar (US$) = 100 cents

GDP per capita: US$2,145 (2004)

GDP real growth: 6.60% (2004)

Labour force: 5.40 million (2004)

Unemployment: 11.10% (2004); 47.00% (2004, underemployment)

Inflation: 2.70% (2004)

Oil production: 535,000 bpd (2004)

Balance of trade: -US$90.00 million (2004)

Foreign debt: US$16.81 billion (2004)

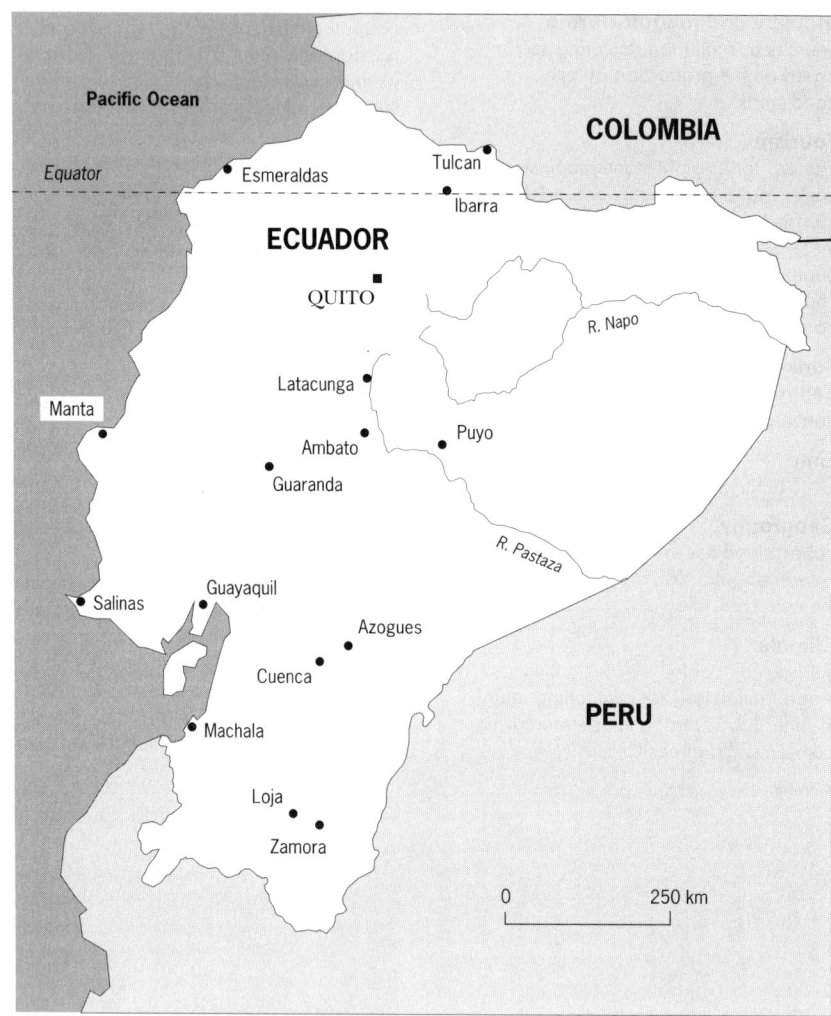

Never a stranger to political instability, Ecuador saw a continuation of the kind of domestic unrest in 2005 that has characterised the country's history. The country that had 86 governments and 17 different constitutions in its first 59 years of existence has had a rocky political year throughout 2005 with social upheaval and the dismissal of the president from office.

Complex politics

President Lucio Edwin Gutiérrez (Partido Sociedad Patriótica 21 de Enero) (PSP) (Patriotic Society Party of the Twenty First of January) had effectively ordered the dismissal of 27 of the Supreme Court's 31 judges in December 2004. The dismissals and the replacement of the justices with favourable candidates, which was carried out on the suspicion that the judges were in cahoots with the opposition Partido Social Cristiano (Social Christian Party), were vehemently opposed by much of the country's political elite. The controversy split the governing Movimiento Unidad Plurinacional Pachakutik–Nuevo País (MUPP–NP) (Pluri–National Pachakutik United Movement–New Country) and minister of the interior Jaime Damerval sided with the opposition in proposing the inception of an independent election council to oversee the appointment and dismissal of Supreme Court members. In response, Gutiérrez proposed a national referendum underlining his intention to lead the 'no' vote, which consequently forced the resignation of Damerval.

The mounting political crisis was intensified following the return of ex-president Abdalá Bucaram Ortiz. 'El Loco', as he is popularly known, was dismissed by Congress in 1997 for 'mental incapacity' and allegedly pocketing public funds, but remains very popular among the country's masses. Bucaram's first public pronouncement after his return, was delivered at a large rally, where he expressed regret at the death of the pope. He went on to assert, in his customary understated style that the Pope, who had perished just after Bucaram jetted in from Panama '...did not want to die until the leader of the Ecuadorian people returned to his homeland'! Mr. Bucaram was cleared by the Ecuadorian authorities of any wrongdoing soon after his return in what was most likely a political favour granted by Gutiérrez.

The political plot thickened on 13 April 2005 when Quito ground to a halt as opposition organised strikes were called in protest at Gutiérrez judicial purge. Violence erupted on the streets of the capital and police were forced to fire tear gas to break up mass protests. Gutiérrez at first appeared to stand firm, calling and then quickly lifting an official state of emergency. However, further strikes and protests ensued and the tidal wave of opposition to the incumbent was impossible to resist as protesters reached the presidential palace and the military withdrew its support. On 20 April 2005 Gutiérrez was removed from office by Congress on account of 'abandoning his post', with 62 of the 100 deputies supporting the motion.

Gutiérrez former vice-president Alfredo Palacio was quickly sworn in as President. The former cardiologist held a press conference in the ministry of defence – a direct nod to the military – and drew on his medical background to describe Ecuador's woes. Ecuador was 'in a coma' he said, and went on to deliver a stark warning to those '...who are trying to apply euthanasia'. In the wake of the crisis, both Gutiérrez and Bucaram – who was alleged to have been advising the president in his final hours- were attempting to flee the country. The former was granted political asylum by Brazil, while the latter fled to Panama. The political crisis had an immediate knock-on effect for Ecuador's negotiations in the Andean region trade talks in Washington. At the height of the crisis representatives from Colombia, Ecuador, Peru and the US were due to hold a press conference, but Ecuadorian officials, on hearing of their president's dismissal, staged a walk out.

Reduced economic growth

The Ecuadorian economy decelerated in 2005 having hit a growth peak of 6.6 per cent in 2004. Increased oil prices, the mainstay of the country's export base, were largely responsible for this growth and although crude oil prices have remained high in recent months the general slowdown is attributable to lower growth in private-sector oil production. Despite the increase in growth generated by oil exports, Ecuador remains badly exposed to a fall, though unlikely given the current geopolitical environment, in international crude oil prices. In a recent report the investment bank Credit Suisse First Boston highlighted the fact that Ecuador, excluding oil, would be running a fiscal deficit equivalent to 6 per cent of total GDP.

The government's generally austere macroeconomic policies have improved the overall health of the economy and inflation is now low and falling. The current rate of 2 per cent per annum is comparable to that of developed countries and is a marked improvement from the catastrophic 37.7 per cent recorded in 2001. In light of recent macroeconomic reforms and given the increasing appetite for risk for bonds in international capital markets the government sought to raise additional financing by means of debt issuance. Ecuador's debt sale in 2005 included a new government bond and was the first time the country had returned to international capital markets since its debt default in 1999. Following the debt issuance, Ecuadorian government bonds traded at relatively low prices, a direct consequence of the risk premium built into the bond price due to the unstable domestic political situation.

The political unrest and the accession to the presidency of Palacio has led to a general decline in foreign investor appetite for Ecuador. The appointment as finance minister of Rafael Correa, an economics professor plucked straight from academia with no practical experience of managing public finances, has heightened disquiet among external observers. Confidence in Correa was hardly strengthened when, shortly after assuming his new post, he labelled the 2000 dollarisation of the economy 'the greatest economic policy error', equivalent to confining the country to the status of a 'one-armed boxer in the ring'. Correa has since pledged the government to a reluctant continuation of the dollar economy however.

The IMF, EU and bananas

Following an announcement by Correa that the government would be abolishing an oil stablisation fund in a bid to devote a larger slice of the economic pie to social spending, the IMF suspended US$400 million in loans to Ecuador. The fund's move was denounced by Mr Correa who criticised the institution for acting 'outside any ethical or legal principle' in its

KEY INDICATORS — Ecuador

	Unit	2000	2001	2002	2003	2004
Population	m	12.65	12.79	12.98	13.08	13.18
Gross domestic product (GDP)	US$bn	18.00	18.00	24.30	27.20	*30.28
GDP per capita	US$	1,390	1,490	1,710	2,160	2,145
GDP real growth	%	2.3	5.6	3.0	2.0	6.6
Inflation	%	96.2	37.7	12.6	6.6	2.7
Unemployment	%	10.3	8.4	9.2	11.7	11.1
Oil output	'000 bpd	416.0	416.0	410.0	427.0	535.0
Exports (fob) (goods)	US$m	5,137.0	4,678.0	5,000.0	6,038.0	7,560.0
Imports (fob) (goods)	US$m	3,743.0	5,363.0	6,430.0	6,534.0	7,650.0
Balance of trade	US$m	1,395.0	-300.0	-1,000.0	-496.0	-90.0
Current account	US$m	928.0	-705.0	-1,220.0	–	-150.0
Total reserves minus gold	US$m	947.0	839.8	714.6	812.6	1,069.6
Foreign exchange	US$m	924.3	815.9	689.4	786.1	986.9
Exchange rate	per US$	1.00	1.00	1.00	1.00	1.00

* estimated figure

dealings with his country: 'they can keep their money' he said, 'Ecuador is not for sale'. Ecuador also clashed with the another major international institution throughout 2005. Along with five other Latin American banana producers, Ecuador sought WTO arbitration in their dispute with the EU over import regulations. The country's export-driven economy is significantly dependent on bananas and many of the country's growers would have been impoverished had the ruling been legitimised. However, the banana-producing nations were successful with their case and the WTO eventually ruled against the EU on 27 October, 2005.

Outlook

Given Ecuador's long history of political and social unrest it was hardly surprising that the country descended into crisis during 2005. There is always the possibility that this South American country may descend into some sort of state of unrest and as long as political instability is part of the country's make-up investors will steer clear of Ecuador, with the exception of the petroleum sector of course, which remains lucrative. The underlying macroeconomic conditions in the country do remain relatively strong however and it is important that the government, regardless of its political colour, maintains the macroeconomic structure of the country and keeps inflation to a low level.

Risk assessment

Politics	Poor
Economy	Stable
Regional stability	Good
Stock market	Stable

COUNTRY PROFILE

Historical profile
1530 Ecuador formed part of the Inca Empire until its conquest by the Spaniards.
1822 Antonio José de Sucre Alcalá defeated the monarchist forces of Spain at the battle of Pichincha. Ecuador gained its independence as part of the federation of Gran Colombia.
1930 Ecuador seceded from Gran Colombia and became an independent republic.
1941 Peru invaded the mineral-rich province of El Oro.
1942 Ecuador lost about 200,000 square kilometres of the disputed land to Peru.
1960s and 1970s A series of elected and appointed presidents (usually by the armed forces) ruled Ecuador. Few saw out their full terms of office.
1978 A new constitution was approved that provided for presidential elections.
1979 Jaime Roldós won the presidential election. The process of democratisation was encouraged and supported by US policy.
1981 Roldós was killed in an aircraft accident. Oswaldo Hurtado, his successor, was faced with the country's growing economic problems.
1984 The new president, Febres Cordero, introduced free-market economy measures. The drop in oil prices and an earthquake, which destroyed a long length of Ecuador's only pipeline, caused economic reforms to falter. Inflation reached over 50 per cent.
1992 Sixto Durán Ballén became president. Further measures were taken to stabilise and modernise the economy.
1997 President Abdala Bucarem, who won the mid-1996 presidential election, was removed from office by a coalition of opposition parties, the labour movement, business, the media and a group of ex-presidents. His administration was alleged to be corrupt and he was deemed mentally incompetant. Fabian Alarcón, became interim president.
1997 Popular protests called for a national assembly and new constitution.
1998 A new constitution and the presidency of Jamil Mahuad began in August. The Democracia Popular (DP) (Popular Democracy Party) became the single largest party in Congress.
2000 The economy was in recession and inflation ran at almost 60 per cent.
2000 Mahuad was ousted during widespread protests. Vice President Gustavo Noboa assumed the presidency. The US dollar was formally adopted as Ecuador's currency.
2002 Colonel Lucio Gutiérrez won the presidential run-off elections.
2003 In the Congreso Nacional (National Congress), no single political party held more than 26 seats (out of a total of 100) and the formal alliance of parties which supported Gutiérrez had only 22 seats.
2004 In April, hundreds of people were held hostage in several prisons around the country, some for over 10 days; demands for their safe release included better conditions and the release of prisoners whose remission was overdue. In December the congress dismissed and replaced most members of the Supreme Court. Gutiérrez accused the former court of bias towards the opposition.
2005 On 20 April, Congress voted (60–2) to remove President Lucio Gutiérrez; Vice President Alfredo Palacio was sworn in as president. In August, a state of emergency was declared in two provinces after protestors brought oil production to a halt. The crisis was diffused after oil companies operating in the country agreed to contribute to infrastructure costs. October saw the arrest and subsequent detention of former president Lucio Gutierrez on conspiracy charges following his return to Ecuador from exile in Colombia.

Political structure
Constitution
The constitution was promulgated in 1979, mandated by a popular referendum the previous year.
Ecuador comprises 21 provinces, including the Galapagos Islands, each administered by an appointed governor.
Form of state
Presidential democratic republic
The executive
Executive power rests with the president, elected by direct vote for a four-year term. The president cannot be re-elected. The cabinet is appointed by the president, who presides over it.
National legislature
The legislature is the unicameral Congreso Nacional (National Congress) which consists of 100 members.
Legal system
The Supreme Court heads the judiciary. Its judges are appointed by Congress for four-year, renewable terms.
Last elections
20 October/24 November 2002 (presidential); 20 October 2002 (parliamentary).
Results: Presidential run-off: Colonel Lucio Gutiérrez won 54.3 per cent of the vote and Álvaro Noboa 45.7 per cent. Parliamentary: Partido Social Cristiano (PSC) (Social Christian Party) 24 seats; Partido Roldosista Ecuatoriano (PRE) (Ecuadorian Roldosist Party) 15; Partido Izquierda Democrática (ID) Party of the Democratic Left) 13; Partido Renovador Institucional de Acción Nacional (PRIAN) (Institutional Renewal Party of National Action) 10; joint list of PSP and MUPP-NP six; Movimiento Unidad Plurinacional Pachakutik-Nuevo País (MUPP-NP) (Pluri-National Pachakutik United Movement-New Country) five.
Next elections
2006 (presidential); 2007 (parliamentary).

Political parties
Ruling party
Coalition government led by the Movimiento Unidad Plurinacional Pachakutik-Nuevo País (MUPP-NP) (Pluri-National Pachakutik United Movement-New Country)
Main opposition party
Partido Social Cristiano (PSC) (Social Christian Party)

Population
13.18 million (2004)

Ecuador

Ethnic make-up
Mestizo (mixed Indian and white) (65 per cent), Indian (25 per cent), white and others (7 per cent), black (3 per cent). The indigenous Indian population is composed of eight main groups, five in the Oriente and three on the coast, each with their own language. One of the Oriente groups, the Quechua, also live in the highlands (sierra).

Religions
Over 95 per cent of the population is nominally Roman Catholic, although Protestant churches have made inroads in recent years. There is freedom of worship.

Education
The education sector in Ecuador needs increased funding and technology.
Enrolment in primary schools has been increasing at an annual rate of 4.4 per cent per year, although many children drop out before the age of 15.
Public universities have an open admissions policy. The number of people entering university, however, has increased and this is putting a strain on resources, contributing to a decline in academic standards.
Literacy rate: 92.1 per cent, total; 90.6 per cent, female; adult rates in 2002 (World Bank).
Compulsory years: Six to 15
Enrolment rate: 117 per cent gross primary enrolment (including repeaters); 59 per cent gross secondary enrolment (World Bank).
Pupils per teacher: 25 in primary schools

Health
Total expenditure on health is around 2–3 per cent of GDP, of which government spending is just over 50 per cent.
Improved water sources and sanitation facilities are available to 71 per cent and 59 per cent of the population, respectively.
HIV prevalence: 0.3 per cent aged 15–49 in 2003 (World Bank)
Life expectancy: 71.0 years (World Bank)
Fertility rate/Maternal mortality rate: 2.7 births per woman (in 2003); maternal mortality 160 per 100,000 live births (World Bank).
Infant mortality rate: 24 per 1,000 live births; 14 per cent of children, aged under five, are malnourished (World Bank).
Head of population per physician/bed: 1.7 physicians and 1.6 hospital beds typically available per 1,000 people

Welfare
The Ecuadorian Social Security Institute operates under the ministry of social welfare and offers old-age benefits, sickness and maternity coverage, work, injury and unemployment benefits. The system covers only around 30 per cent of the working population. Coverage is particularly poor in rural areas.

Main cities
Quito (capital, estimated population 1.5 million in 2004), Guayaquil (2.0 million), Cuenca (285,700), Santo Domingo (206,700), Machala (204,400), Manta (188,900), Portoviejo (175,700).

Languages spoken
Quechua and Jarvo are spoken. There is pressure from indigenous groups for Quechua to be made an official language.
English, taught to all schoolchildren, is also widely spoken.
Official language/s
Spanish

Media
Foreign investment in the media is prohibited.
Press
Dailies: Principal dailies mostly in Spanish are *El Comercio* (Quito), *Diario El Universo* (Guayaquil), *Expreso* (Guayaquil), *El Diario Hoy* (Quito), *Diario El Mercurio* (on-line version is www.elmercurio.com.ec), *El Telegrafo*, *Diario El Universo*, *El Diario*, *Diario La Hora*, *Diario La Prensa* and *Vistazo*. US newspapers are also available in Quito and Guayaquil.
Business: *El Financiero* is a Spanish language business weekly.
Broadcasting
Radio: There are over 370 commercial stations, 10 cultural and 10 religious stations. Broadcasts are in numerous languages.
Television: There are 10 (commercial) stations and a cable network. Broadcasts are in Spanish and English.

Economy
The economy of Ecuador suffered greatly in the late 1990s and early 2000s, due to a combination of hazardous weather conditions and political unrest. However inflation has been brought under control and relatively strong GDP growth of 6.6 per cent was recorded in 2004. The IMF predicts a reduced growth rate of 2.7 per cent in 2005 and 2.8 per cent for 2006. The Ecuadorian economy was hit hard by the destruction of the *El Niño* weather system in 1997/98. A series of political crises also brought investment to a virtual halt. The economy has only just managed to maintain itself, largely as a result of the remittances sent from Ecuadorians living and working abroad and the rise in world oil prices.
The Ecuadorian authorities have been criticised by the IMF for poor fiscal management and large increases in the public wage bill. In September 2002, congress passed the Fiscal Responsibility and Transparency Law, which sets medium-term fiscal rules. The law was praised by the IMF, which urged the new government, appointed in January 2003, to continue efforts to lower the public debt in order to prevent crowding out of non-oil investment. The IMF also lauded the new government's commitment to a controversial public sector wage freeze, which should help maintain real exchange rate stability and generate investor confidence.

External trade
In addition to its membership of the Andean Community of Nations (CAN), Ecuador has also established a free trade area with Chile. Ecuador has also been a proponent of a Free Trade Area of the Americas and is a full member of the World Trade Organisation (WTO).
Imports
Principal imports are vehicles, medicinal products, telecommunications equipment and electricity.
Main sources: US (24.5 per cent total, 2004), Colombia (12.7 per cent), Venezuela (8.3 per cent), Brazil (5.8 per cent), Chile (4.9 per cent), China (4.8 per cent), Japan (4.3 per cent)
Exports
Principal exports are petroleum, bananas, cut flowers and shrimp.
Main destinations: US (48.3 per cent total, 2004), Colombia (5.5 per cent), Germany (4.8 per cent)

Agriculture
Farming
Prior to the rise in significance of the oil industry and other related economic activities, the agricultural sector was Ecuador's most prominent economic activity. In recent years output from the sector has fluctuated due to the adverse effects of the *El Niño* weather phenomenon and shifts in world cocoa and banana prices.
Virtually the whole of the country is suitable for some form of agricultural exploitation. However, the sector has suffered from low levels of mechanisation and irrigation, and lack of financial incentives.
In coastal regions the main crops are bananas, cocoa, coffee, oil palms, sugar cane, cotton, rice and maize, while the sierra produces legumes, maize, wheat, potatoes, rye and barley. Ecuador is the world's largest producer of bananas.
Cattle are mainly reared in the highlands. There is small-scale poultry farming in Manabi province.
Rose growing and cut-flower production started in the early 1980s and the country has a number of rose growing enterprises. The potential for rose exports from Ecuador is enormous since all-year-round

production is possible with no heating or cooling costs.

Temperate crops include blackberries, tamarillos (tree tomatoes), lemons, limes and avocados. In warmer regions, mangoes, pineapple, passion fruit, papaya, pepper, heart-of-palm and orito (kind of banana) thrive. In colder and temperate areas, broccoli, strawberry, asparagus, artichoke and peppers are grown. In addition, cucumbers, okra and melons are cultivated. The majority of the average annual pineapple harvest of 89,000 tonnes is sold to the US and to Europe.

Crop production in 2004 included: 1,801,714 million tonnes (t) cereals in total, 1,100,000t rice, 1,600,000t oil palm fruit, 5,900,000t bananas, 5,400,000t sugar cane, 651,000t maize, 125,000t cassava, 400,000t potatoes, 308,167t oilcrops, 652,000t plantains, 53,000t tomatoes, 246,200t citrus fruit, 83,000t green coffee, 88,000t cocoa beans, 1,400t tea, 109,000t soya beans, 68,353t pulses, 76,000t mangoes, 8,000t tobacco, 8,938t natural rubber, 7,381,275t fruit in total, 369,890t vegetables in total. Livestock production included: 594,844t meat in total, 212,000t beef, 150,400t pig meat, 8460t lamb, 2,475t goat meat, 212,693t poultry, 76,000t eggs, 2,508,910t milk, 31,722t cattle hides, 870t honey, 2,880t greasy wool.

Fishing

Over recent years the fishing industry has increased in importance. Both sea and shrimp fishing have become more economically significant, with shrimp now being the second most important foreign exchange earner in the agricultural sector, after bananas.

Government policy has concentrated on the development of sea food, including tuna, fish oil and fishmeal for export. The fisheries union in Ecuador has pressed for immediate reforms within the sector, asking for modernised management. The country's fishing legislation lacks organisation with poorly defined fishing rights.

In a typical year the annual fish catch is over 654,500mt, including 5,645mt freshwater fish and 64,200mt shellfish.

Forestry

Over 40 per cent of Ecuador's total land mass is forested; approximately 10.5 million hectares(ha). In a typical year exports of forest material amount to US$95.2 million, while imports amount to US$270.9 million.

Forests are mostly concentrated in the eastern Amazonian region characterised by lowland humid tropical rainforests. Forest plantations are mainly eucalyptus. Large quantities of sawn timber and wood based panels are produced, although exports remain limited. Production of hardwoods and balsa wood is dependent on the Andean market. Most of the paper and pulp demand is met by imports. According to some critics, there will be no forests left in Ecuador by 2030 and the government has been supporting a project which aimed to re-forest 500,000 hectares by the end of 2005, both for commercial and ecological reasons, with an emphasis on profitable exotic species.

Industry and manufacturing

Approximately 20 per cent of Ecuador's total GDP is generated by activity in the industrial sector, which is geographically concentrated in Quito and Guayaquil. The sector accounts for 15 per cent of the entire labour force in a typical year.

A free trade zone (FTZ), offering incentives for the manufacture of export products, was established at Esmeraldas.

Tourism

The tourism sector is playing an increasingly important role in the economy of Ecuador. The sector is the country's third most important economic activity, after petroleum and bananas. Travel and tourism employs 7.4 per cent of Ecuador's total labour force and constitutes 8.6 per cent of total GDP.

The mixture of environmental systems, including rain-forest and mountains, and especially the Galapagos Islands, favours eco-tourists as well as attracting trekkers, climbers, divers and backpackers. Ecuador converted to the US dollar in 2000, making it a more expensive country to visit than neighbouring countries. Visitor numbers have been rising steadily over recent years and the country hopes to attract one million visitors by 2007.

Mining

Mining concessions can be found over approximately 5.6 million hectares of Ecuador's total land mass. Approximately 36,000 miners make their living in the informal sector, which represents about 1 per cent of the country's labour force. Despite a growing foreign presence, Ecuador's mining industry is very much in its infancy, although it could become one of the economy's most dynamic sectors. The government is keen to make mining a high priority in view of its enormous production potential and the opportunity it offers to diversify the country's export base as an alternative to oil.

The most important mineral is gold, which is mined on a small-scale basis, although a number of foreign and local companies are negotiating with miners to take over their operations and introduce more technical expertise. Interest has been shown in gold, with a joint government and private mining venture in the Nambija region.

There are also major deposits of limestone, clay, plaster, barytine, feldspar, silica, phosphate, bentonite and pumice stone (Ecuador has one of the biggest reserves of pumice stone in the world). Kaolin, marble, puzzolan and gypsum are mined.

Hydrocarbons

Ecuador has significant proven oil reserves of 4.6 billion barrels and the country is the fifth largest crude oil producer in Latin America. The petroleum sector plays a driving role in the Ecuadorian economy, representing approximately 11 per cent of total GDP, some 52 per cent of export earnings and generating 35 per cent of total government revenues.

Oil production was 534,800 barrels per day (bpd) in 2004, with exports totalling 226,000bpd. Emphasis is on developing exploration and expanding refining capacity to increase the production of lighter products. However oil transportation has been a serious constraint for company investment until the recent construction of the Oleducto de Crudos Pesados (OCP) pipeline in September 2003.

Ecuador's natural gas reserves are relatively small, at approximately 12.18 billion cubic metres (cum) of natural gas reserves, located in Oriente and the Gulf of Guayaquil. However, a lack of infrastructure has inhibited the capacity to utilise these resources. Annual gas production is approximately 112 million cum. The long-awaited natural gas project in the Amistad Field in the Gulf of Guayaquil began drilling operations in 2000.

Ecuador is neither a producer nor consumer of coal. Although, there are small reserves of recoverable coal (lignite and sub-bituminous) estimated at 23.5 million tonnes, these remain unexploited.

Energy

Ecuador's installed electricity capacity stands at over 3,000MW. Hydroelectricity plays an important role in generation, as approximately two-thirds of electricity is generated from hydroelectric plants. The massive Paute hydro-plant generates more than 60 per cent of the country's electricity.

There are shortfalls in supply typically during the October–March dry season; two new hydroelectric dams and power plants, expected to be completed by 2007, should make up any shortfalls. Mazur is sited upstream of, and will also act as a reservoir for, the Paute power station; the San Francisco project is downstream from the existing Agoyan plant on the Pastaza river.

Ecuador has few reserves of natural gas or the infrastructure to exploit what does exist. There is a natural gas-fired power

Ecuador

plant near Machala, which, with a new pipeline linking it to a gas field, Amistad, in the Gulf of Guayaquil and an import deal with Peru agreed in late 2004, is forcast to have an energy capacity of 240MW.

The former state-owned electricity conglomerate (INECEL) has been broken up into single operating companies for either transmission or distribution. The reorganisation did not lead to any significant increase in efficiency or expansion. The government has been prevented from rationalising the industry by partisan interests and a lack of private investment.

Financial markets
Stock exchange
There are two stock exchanges in Ecuador: the Bolsa de Valores de Quito (BVQ) (the largest) and the Bolsa de Valores de Guayaquil.

Banking and insurance
Recent years have seen the virtual collapse of the banking sector in Ecuador, following a plethora of bad debts brought on by the *El Niño* weather phenomenon and economic decline in the late 1990s. Problems could be created if domestic borrowing increases to cover excessive government spending. This would make Ecuador's banking sector vulnerable to the kind of shocks seen in Argentina, where there was not enough US dollar liquidity to back depositors' withdrawals.

Central bank
Banco Central del Ecuador

Main financial centre
Guayaquil and Quito

Time
Mainland Ecuadorean time: GMT minus five hours; Galapagos Islands: GMT minus six hours.

Geography
Ecuador has three main regions – a low coastal strip, a high Andean cordillera with peaks rising to more than 6,000 metres, and a tropical lowland in the Amazon basin. The Andes, which here comprise two parallel ranges running north to south, form a barrier between 100 and 120km wide.

Chimborazo, an extinct volcano, is the highest mountain, at 6,310 metres, and there are several active volcanoes. Quito itself, which lies at 2,850 metres above sea level, is the second highest capital in South America, and visitors are advised to take things easy for a few days after arrival to avoid altitude sickness.

To the north, Ecuador is bordered by Colombia and to the east and south by Peru. To the west lies the Pacific Ocean. Of the Spanish-speaking nations of South America, only Uruguay is smaller in area.

Climate
Although the equator crosses the north of the country (and gives it its name), only the eastern lowlands (the Oriente) and the northern coastal region have a typically tropical climate, with abundant rains, high humidity and little seasonal change in temperature, which averages around 25 degrees Celsius (C). The port city of Guayaquil is in the tropical zone and has most rain between January and April. In the Andes, the climate varies from the cold of the high glaciers to the temperate zone of the central valley around Quito, where the mean annual temperature is between 13 degrees C and 19 degrees C. Days are warm and nights are cool all year round. The rainy season in the valley lasts from November–May.

Dress codes
In government offices and private businesses in Quito, dress is relatively formal. Women usually wear skirts, while the men wear suits or jacket and tie. Dress is generally less formal in Guayaquil, the largest city and Ecuador's major port.

Entry requirements
Passports
Passports are required by all. Passports must be valid for six months.

Visa
Most visitors do not need a visa for stays up to three months, however travellers should contact the local embassy for confirmation or visit www.ecuador.org/. Business visas must be applied for before departure, for all representatives of foreign companies, even those that do not need a tourist visa, a letter of introduction should be submitted giving full details and purpose of visit and the provision of an economical guaranty, before a public notary, stating that the representative will have sufficient funds for the visit. The Consul acts as public notary for Ecuador, and can issue certificates of 'Legal Existence of Companies' for use in Ecuador, plus authenticating documents and legalising translations of documents into Spanish. Documentation to be used in Ecuador must bear the consular stamp.

Currency advice/regulations
No restrictions on import or export of foreign or local currency.
International credit cards are generally accepted in Quito and Guayaquil. Travellers cheques can be difficult to exchange outside main towns. US dollar travellers cheques are the most easily negotiable.

Prohibited imports
Firearms, ammunition, narcotics, fresh or dry meat and meat products, plants and vegetables are prohibited/restricted unless previous permission is obtained.

Health (for visitors)
Mandatory precautions
A yellow fever certificate is required if arriving from infected areas, and for those intending to visit Pastaza province in the east.
A measles vaccination certificate is required by those arriving from Colombia, Venezuela, Germany or Italy.

Advisable precautions
Yellow fever, typhoid, polio, hepatitis 'A' and tetanus vaccinations are recommended. Malaria prophylaxis is advisable; the malaria risk is high and widespread all the year. There is a rabies risk.
Tap water is not safe to drink. Bottled mineral water is widely available.

Hotels
Wide range available in Quito and Guayaquil. A government tax of 10 per cent and a service charge of 10 per cent payable on all rates.

Credit cards
Major credit cards are generally accepted.

Public holidays
Fixed dates
1 Jan (New Year's Day), 1 May (Labour Day), 24 May (Battle of Pichincha Day), 10 Aug (Independence Day), 9 Oct^ (Foundation of Guayaquil), 12 Oct (Columbus Day), 2 Nov (All Souls' Day), 3 Nov^ (Foundation of Cuenca), 6 Dec^ (Foundation of Qito), 25 Dec (Christmas Day), 31 Dec (New Year's Eve).
^ Local holidays only.
If New Year's Day falls on a Sunday, 2 Jan becomes a holiday instead. Holidays falling on a Tuesday are observed on the preceding Monday, while those falling on Wednesday and Thursday are moved to Friday. The exceptions to the latter rule are 1 Jan, 1 May, 2 Nov and 25 Dec.

Variable dates
Carnival (two days), Maundy Thursday, Good Friday.
Carnival is celebrated on Shrove Tuesday and Ash Wednesday (six weeks before Good Friday).

Working hours
Banking
Mon–Fri: 0900–1330, 1430–1830; Sat: 0930–1400.

Business
Mon–Fri: 0800–1630.

Government
Mon–Fri: 0830–1630.

Shops
Mon–Fri: 0900–1300, 1500–1900. Sat: 1000–2000. (Shopping centres, Mon–Sat: 1030–2030; Sun: 1030–1830.)

Telecommunications
Mobile phones
GSM 850 service available in cities and large towns.

Nations of the World: A Political, Economic and Business Handbook

Electricity supply
110V AC, 60 cycles

Weights and measures
The metric system is in use.

Social customs/useful tips
When dealing with government or official bodies, be prepared for long negotiations. In addition, visitors may find that their appointments to see government officials or ministers are postponed at short notice, as they rarely work to exact times.
Although generally polite to visitors, revellers at carnival time are likely to throw water bombs or other types of liquid over the unwary.
Speak Spanish; if not, ensure that promotional material is in Spanish or has Spanish inserts. The British Embassy can help in finding a suitable translator and interpreter.
Quote prices FOB and CIF Ecuadorean port or airport in US dollars (insurance must be Ecuadorean).
Ecuadoreans prefer to deal with people they have spent time getting to know; lunches/business meetings can last from 1330 to 1800, dinners from 2000 onwards. Meetings often start late.
Ecuadoreans are polite and formal. Do not be discouraged by lack of enthusiasm; they like to be convinced. The use of the title Doctor, Engineer or Economist is common.

Security
Guayaquil has a serious street crime problem. Crime in Quito is on the increase, especially in the colonial centre of town, and police advise visitors to be wary of thieves and pickpockets and to watch luggage at all times.

Getting there
Air
National airline: Empresa Ecuatoriana de Aviación (Ecuatoriana).
International airport/s: Quito-Mariscal Sucre (UIO), 8km from city centre, duty-free shop, bar, restaurant, buffet, bank, post office, shops, car hire, tourist information. Guayaquil-Simón Bolivar (GYE), 5km north of city centre, duty-free shop, restaurant, buffet, currency exchange, post office, shops, car hire, tourist information;
Airport tax: International departures US$25, not applicable to 24-hour transit passengers; domestic departures US$1.50.
Surface
Access is possible from Colombia and Peru, although the quality of roads and railway services may vary.
Road: Buses run between Colombia and Ecuador via Tulcán, and between Peru and Ecuador via either Huaquillas or Macará.

Main port/s: Guayaquil, Manta and Esmeraldas.

Getting about
Passport checks are frequently made by the police, especially near the borders.
National transport
Air: Air transport is well developed. Several internal airlines including ANDES (freight), SAETA, SAN and TAME (military airline operating civilian schedules) operate domestic services to main towns. Air-taxi and charter services are available from Guayaquil and Quito.
With the exception of flying to the Galapagos Islands, internal flights are cheap.
Road: Most parts of the country are accessible by surfaced or all-weather roads. Major routes run north-south in the coastal lowlands and the sierra. The Pan-American Highway runs from Tulcan via Ibarra, Quito, Riobamaba, Cuenca, Loja to Macara. Good roads link the sierra to the coastal ports.
Buses: Bus services link main towns, including Quito-Esmeraldas, Quito-Manta, Guayaquil-Manta and Quito-Guayaquil. Most towns have a terminal terrestre (central bus terminal). Reservations in advance should be made for long-distance services. Timetables are changed frequently and not always adhered to.
Rail: Routes include Quito-Riobamba, Guayaquil-Bucay, Alausi-Huigra, Sibambe-Cuenca and Ibarra-San Lorenzo. Rail travel is generally uncomfortable and unreliable.
Water: Boats are a frequent mode of travel, particularly in the Oriente region, and on the north-west coast.
City transport
Taxis: Taxis are cheap. They can be hailed or found on ranks. It is best to ask the fare beforehand. At weekends and at night, fares are 25–50 per cent higher. Journey time from airport to city centre 20–30 minutes. Tips are not expected.
Car hire
Major companies operate from Quito and Guayaquil. An international permit is required. Traffic drives on the right. Police checks are common.

BUSINESS DIRECTORY

The addresses listed below are a selection only. While World of Information makes every endeavour to check these addresses, we cannot guarantee that changes have not been made, especially to telephone numbers and area codes. We would welcome any corrections.

Telephone area codes
The international direct dialling code for Ecuador is +593, followed by area code:

Ambato	3	Machala	7
Cuenca	7	Manta	4
Esmeraldas	6	Portoviejo	4
Guayaquil	4	Quito	2

Useful telephone numbers
Police: 101
Fire: 102
Ambulance (Quito): 131

Chambers of Commerce
American-Ecuadorian Chamber of Commerce, Avenida 6 de Diciembre y La Niña, Edificio Multicentro, Quito (tel: 250-7450; fax: 250-4571; e-mail: info@ecamcham.com).

British-Ecuadorean Chamber of Industry and Commerce, Avenida El Tiempo 464 y El Telegrafo, Quito (tel: 244-9239; fax: 225-7433; e-mail: info@egbcc.org).

Guayaquil Cámara de Comercio, Avenida Francisco de Orellana y Miguel H Alcivar, Centro Empresarial Las Cámaras, Guayaquil (tel: 268-2771; fax: 268-2725; e-mail: info@lacamara.org).

Quito Cámara de Comercio, Avenida Amazonas y República, Edificio Las Cámaras, Quito (tel: 244-3787; fax: 243-5862; e-mail: ccq@ccq.org.ec).

Banking
Banco Bolivariano, Junín 200 y Panamá, Guayaquil (tel: 562-777; fax: 565-025).

Banco de Guayaquil, Pichincha 105 y P Icaza, Guayaquil (tel: 514-209; fax: 512-427; e-mail: glasso@bankguay.com).

Banco del Pacifico, P Icaza 200 y Pedro Carbo, Guayaquil (tel: 566-010; fax: 564-636; e-mail: webadmin@bp.fin.ec).

Banco del Pichincha, Avenida Amazonas 4560 y Pereira, Quito (tel: 980-980; fax: 981-280).

Banco la Previsora, Avenida 9 de Octubre 100, Guayaquil (tel: 561-656; fax: 566-665; e-mail: blp@bprevisora.fin.ec).

BancoUnion, Cordova 916 y VM Rendon, Guayaquil (tel: 566-555; fax: 313-295; e-mail: info@banunion.com).

Filanbanco, Avenida 9 de Octubre 203 y Pichincha, Guayaquil (tel: 322-780; fax: 326-916).

Superintendencia de Bancos (Banking Supervisory Agency), Avenida 12 de Octubre 24-185, Quito (tel: 554-422).

Central bank
Banco Central del Ecuador, Avenida 10 de Agosto y Briceño, Plaza Bolivar, Quito (tel: 519-384, 571-807).

Travel information
Ecuatoriana Airlines, Reina Victoria y Colón, Edificio Torres de Almagro, Quito (tel: 563-003; fax: 563-920).

SAETA Airlines, Avenida Carlos Julio Arosemena Km 2.5, Guayaquil (fax:

Ecuador

201-153; e-mail: ehbuzon@saeta.com.ec).

TAME Airlines, Avenida Amazonas 13-54 y Colón, Quito (tel: 509-392; fax: 509-594).

Ministry of tourism

Ministry of Tourism, Av Eloy Alfaro N32-300 y Carlos Tobar, Quito (tel: 228-303, 507-560; fax: 507-564, 229-330; e-mail: mtur1@ec_gov.net; internet site: http://www.vivecuador.com).

National tourist organisation offices

Asociación Ecuatoriana de Agencias de Viajes y Turismo (ASECUT), Avenida Amazonas 2468, Quito (tel: 552-617; fax: 552-916).

Corporación Ecuatoriana de Turismo (CETUR), Reina Victoria 514 y Roca, Quito (tel: 527-002; fax: 568-198).

Ministries

Ministry of Agriculture, Avenida Amazonas y Eloy Alfaro, Quito (tel: 504-433; fax: 504-922).

Ministry of Defence, Exposición 208, Quito (tel: 512-803; fax: 569-386).

Ministry of Education, San Gregorio y Juan Murillo, Quito (tel: 583-337; fax: 580-116).

Ministry of Energy and Mines, Santa Prisca 223, Quito (tel: 552-533; fax: 502-092).

Ministry of the Environment, Avenida Eloy Alfaro y Amazonas, Quito (tel: 540-920; fax: 255-172).

Ministry of Finance and Public Credit, Avenida 10 de Agosto 1661 y Jorge Washington, Quito (tel: 503-328; fax: 500-702).

Ministry of Foreign Affairs, Avenida 10 de Agosto y Carrión, Quito (tel: 503-093; fax: 227-025; e-mail: dgproeco@mmrree.gov.ec).

Ministry of Foreign Trade, Avenida Amazonas y Eloy Alfaro, Quito (tel: 529-076; fax: 507-549).

Ministry of Government [Interior], Espejo y Benalcázar, Quito (tel: 584-919; fax: 580-067).

Ministry of Housing and Urban Development, Avenida 10 de Agosto 2270 y Cordero, Quito (tel: 238-060; fax: 566-785).

Ministry of Labour, Luis Felipe Borja y C. Ponce, Quito (tel: 566-148; fax: 503-122).

Ministry of Public Health, Juan Larrea 445, Quito (tel: 529-163; fax: 569-092).

Ministry of Public Works, Avenida Orellana y Juan León Mera, Quito (tel: 222-749; fax: 223-077).

Ministry of Social Welfare, Robles 850 y Páez, Quito (tel: 227-975; fax: 563-469).

Ministry of Tourism, Av Eloy Alfaro N32-300 y Carlos Tobar, Quito (tel: 228-303, 507-560; fax: 507-564, 229-330; e-mail: mtur1@ec_gov.net; internet site: http://www.turismo.gov.ec).

Other useful addresses

Bolsa de Valores de Quito (Stock Exchange), Avenida Amazonas 540 y Carrión, Quito (tel: 526-805; fax: 500-942; e-mail: informacion@ccbvq.com).

Bolsa de Valores de Guayaquil, 9 de Octubre 110 y Pichincha, Guayaquil (tel: 561-519; fax: 561-871; e-mail: earosemena@bvg.fin.ec).

British Embassy, Avenida Naciones Unidas y República de El Salvador, Quito (tel: 970-800/1; fax: 970-809).

Corporación Financiera Nacional, Juan León Mera 130 y Patria, Quito (tel: 564-900; fax: 223-823).

Ecuadorian Embassy (USA), 2535 15th Street, NW, Washington DC 20009 (tel: 202-234-7200; fax: 202-667-3482; e-mail: embassy@ecuador.org).

Empresa Estatel de Telecomunicaciones (EMETEL), Avenida 6 de Diciembre y Colón, Edificio Partenon, Quito (tel: 200-700; fax: 568-000).

Instituto Nacional de Estadística y Censos, Juan Larrea 534 y Riofrio, Quito (tel: 529-858; fax: 509-836).

National Bureau of Mines (DINAMI), Baquedano E7-13 y Reina Victoria, Edificio Araucaria, Quito (tel: 554-110; fax: 554-110; e-mail: dinami@accessinter.net).

National Council for the Modernisation of the State (CONAM), Edificio Corporación Financiera, Avenida Juan León Mera 130 y Patria, Quito (tel: 509-432; fax: 509-437).

Petroecuador, Avenida 6 de Diciembre y Paul Rivet, Edificio El Pinar, Quito (tel: 561-250; fax: 524-766).

Secretary General of the Administration, García Moreno 1043, Quito (tel: 580-750; fax: 580-751).

Superintendencia de Compañías del Ecuador (Companies Supervisory Authority), Roca 660 y Avenida Amazonas, Quito (tel: 529-960; fax: 565-685).

US Embassy, Avenida 12 de Octubre y Patria, Quito (tel: 562-890; fax: 502-052).

Internet sites

Economic Commission for Latin America (gateway site): http://www.eclac.cl/index1.html

Inter-American Development Bank: http://www.iadb.org

Latin Trade Online: http://www.latintrade.com

Latin World (directory of Internet resources): http://wwwlatinworld.com

Organisation of American States: http://www.oas.org

Egypt

KEY FACTS

Official name: Jumhuriyat Misr al Arabiya (Arab Republic of Egypt)

Head of State: President Hosni Mubarak (re-elected for fifth term Sep 2005)

Head of government: Prime Minister Ahmed Nazif (appointed by the President 9 Jul 2004)

Ruling party: National Democratic Party (NDP) (since 1996; re-elected Dec 2005)

Area: 1,001,499 square km

Population: 70.83 million (2004)

Capital: Cairo

Official language: Arabic

Currency: Egyptian pound (LE) = 100 piastres

Exchange rate: LE5.76 per US$ (Oct 2005); (Egyptian pound floated on Jan 2003)

GDP per capita: US$1,111 (2004)

GDP real growth: 4.10% (2004)

Labour force: 27.49 million (2004)

Unemployment: 10.90% (2004)

Inflation: 8.10% (2004)

Oil production: 708,000 bpd (2004)

Balance of trade: -US$8.21 billion (2004)

Foreign debt: US$29.70 billion (2003)

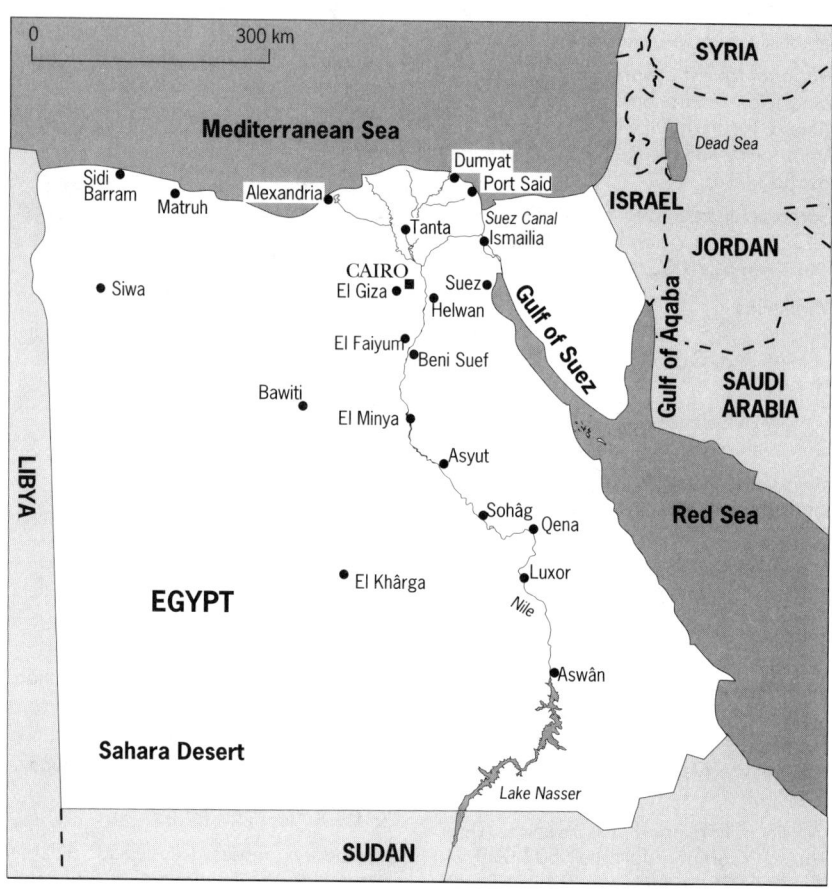

Driven by strong growth in export, real growth GDP advanced by 4.8 per cent in the first half of 2004/05. The stock market surged, the pound appreciated and a formal interbank market for foreign exchange was established. Egypt's external position strengthened: debt remained stable. There was more traffic in the Suez Canal and oil prices were higher. Strong current account flows enabled banks to strengthen their net foreign asset position; the Central Bank built up its reserve position.

All in all, a good time for Egypt and the recovery is likely to firm up. Preliminary data suggest a continuation of recent trends, yet the challenges ahead to build a dynamic, private sector-driven economy in Egypt remain considerable.

Economy

Output growth remains below the minimum required to absorb growth in the labour force, the financial sector is weak, and government borrowing and debt are still high. Egypt will have to maintain the current pace of structural reform while pursuing fiscal polices that will bring about robust responses from private investors and the growth needed to reduce unemployment and poverty.

Monetary policy needs to be more forward-looking and provide better guidance to the market and be more transparent. There are ongoing efforts to modernise Egypt's budget and improve treasury cash management which will enable the control of government expenditure and improve the fiscus, but they will not result in lower spending or borrowing unless there are concrete expenditure-reducing measures in place, such as pruning subsidies and the government wage bill. On borrowing, there must be specific targets to ensure that government debt follows a declining path.

A privatisation programme focuses on strengthening the banking system through the consolidation and privatisation of small joint venture and public sector banks; restructuring of public sector banks, including through recapitalisation; and resolution of the problem of non-performing loans.

The medium-term outlook for Egypt's balance of payments remains favourable. The ongoing development of Egypt's tourism potential, already at record levels, and vast gas resources bodes well. Five major projects are expected to raise Egypt's gas exports to approximately 21 billion cubic meters per annum by 2008. At current prices (US$126 per thousand cubic metres); this would result in gross annual inflows of US$2.7 billion (3.1 per cent of gross domestic product. The development of an export market for natural gas is a bright spot for future growth prospects, but improvement in the capital-intensive hydrocarbons sector does little to reduce Egypt's persistent unemployment, which relies on diversification to more labour intensive industry. A rapidly growing population (the largest in the Arab world), limited arable land, and dependence on the Nile all continue to overtax resources and stress society.

Lack of substantial progress on economic reform since the mid 1990s has limited foreign direct investment (FDI) in Egypt. However, the government has recently implemented several measures to boost FDI – customs reforms, income and corporate tax reforms, reduced energy subsidies and more privatisation.

Politics

President Muhammad Hosni Mubarak is Egypt's longest-serving ruler since Muhammad Ali in the early nineteenth century and one of the longest-serving leaders in the Arab world. Now 77, he gained a fifth consecutive term in presidential elections in September 2005. The poll was the first under a new system which allows multiple candidates to stand. In previous elections Egyptians voted yes or no for a single candidate appointed by parliament. The only opposition organisation which has broad public support, the Muslim Brotherhood, is outlawed and could not field a candidate. However, in elections to the parliament held in December 2005, the Muslim Brotherhood fielded 'independent ' candidates, 88 of whom were successful. These 88 are more than all the other opposition parties and independents combined.

Mubarak succeeded Anwar Sadat, who was assassinated in 1981. He himself has escaped no fewer than six assassination attempts. He is an economic liberal and his government has promised economic reforms. But Egypt remains plagued by high unemployment and low standards of living.

He has pursued friendly relations with the West and broke the isolation imposed on Egypt by Arab countries opposed to peace with Israel. As a military man he was credited with modernising the air force after Egypt's defeat in the six-day war with Israel in 1967. He helped to plan the 1973 Yom Kippur War – an Egyptian-Syrian attack on Israeli forces on the Suez Canal and in the Golan Heights.

The succession is hotly debated. Reports that Mubarak's younger son Gamal is being groomed for office have angered the opposition and have been denied by the president.

He was born in 1928. He and his wife Suzanne, who is part Welsh and part Egyptian, have two sons, Ala and Gamal.

Foreign relations

Egypt's three wars with Israel in 1948, 1967 and 1973, then its eventual peace with its adversary in 1979, have seen Egypt move from being a warring nation to become a key representative in the peace process. The historic step taken by President Anwar Sadat in the Camp David agreement with Israel saw the expulsion of Egypt from the Arab League until 1989, and in 1981 Sadat was assassinated by Islamic extremists angry at his moves to clamp down on their activities.

Mubarak has taken a more moderate line, but Islamic groups have continued their sporadic campaigns, being responsible for deadly attacks that have often targeted tourists and resort areas. Campaigners for political reform have become more vocal in recent times and have taken to the streets in defiance of an emergency law, in force since 1981. Activists say the law restricts political expression.

The regularity and richness of the annual Nile River flood, coupled with semi-isolation provided by deserts to the east and west, allowed for the development of one of the world's great civilizations. Egypt's ancient past and the fact that it was one of the first Middle Eastern countries to open up to the West means that it is seen by many as the intellectual and cultural leader in the region. The head of Cairo's Al-Azhar Mosque is one of the highest authorities in Sunni Islam.

Risk assessment

Political	Improving
Economic	Improving
Regional stability	Poor
Stock market	Improving

KEY INDICATORS — Egypt

	Unit	2000	2001	2002	2003	2004
Population	m	63.98	65.30	65.17	68.00	70.83
Gross domestic product (GDP)	US$bn	93.00	84.80	76.30	82.40	*75.15
GDP per capita	US$	1,360	1,299	1,143	956	1,111
GDP real growth	%	5.1	2.5	2.0	3.1	4.1
Inflation	%	2.7	2.3	2.5	4.2	8.1
Unemployment	%	11.5	12.0	12.5	10.7	10.9
Oil output	'000 bpd	781.0	758.0	751.0	750.0	708.0
Natural gas output	bn cum	18.0	21.0	22.7	25.0	26.8
Exports (fob) (goods)	US$m	7,061.0	7,078.0	6,640.0	8,205.0	11,000.0
Imports (fob) (goods)	US$m	15,382.0	16,432.0	14,640.0	14,821.0	10,210.0
Balance of trade	US$m	-8,321.0	-9,300.0	-7,800.0	-6,616.0	-8,210.0
Current account	US$m	-1,160.0	-30.0	610.0	1,940.0	3,420.0
Foreign debt	US$bn	29.2	28.1	28.7	29.7	33.8
Total reserves minus gold	US$m	13,118.0	12,926.0	13,242.0	13,589.0	14,273.0
Foreign exchange	US$m	12,913.0	12,891.0	13,151.0	13,400.0	14,108.0
Exchange rate	per US$	3.69	4.49	4.51	5.40	6.21

* estimated figure

Nations of the World: A Political, Economic and Business Handbook

COUNTRY PROFILE

Historical profile

Egypt is best known for its pyramids and ancient civilisations. It became part of the Ottoman Empire in the sixteenth century, although the Mamluk dynasty continued to govern after the conquest.

Egypt has the largest population in the Arab world and is, after Israel, the largest recipient of US aid worldwide. It has maintained a high profile not only within the Arab world, but also on the world stage, and despite being condemned by the other Arab nations, the country has changed its stance from being a warring nation to becoming a key representative in the Middle East peace process.

1811 Governor Mohammed Ali exterminated the Mamluks, the former ruling oligarchy, in the Citadel massacre.

Mohammed Ali was permitted hereditary rights to rule, providing Egypt remained a part of the Ottoman Empire.

1859–69 The Suez Canal was built.

1882 Britain occupied Egypt and although it still remained under Ottoman suzerainty, it became de facto a British colony.

1914 Britain eliminated the Ottoman suzerainty and the country became a British protectorate – the Egyptian Sultanate.

1922 Egypt was renamed Kingdom of Egypt and was officially independent, although Britain supervised until 1946.

1936 Signing of the Anglo-Egyptian Treaty, which restricted British military presence to the Suez Canal Zone.

1947–49 Egypt contributed to a pan-Arab military force that failed to occupy the newly-created state of Israel.

1952 The 23 July Revolution, led by the army, ousted King Fu'ad, who had just succeeded his father, King Faruq.

1953–56 Egypt was declared a republic in 1953, under President Mohammed Neguib. Neguib relinquished power in 1954 to Colonel Gamal Abdel Nasser, who was officially elected in 1956.

1956 Nasser nationalised the Suez Canal to fund the construction of the Aswan High Dam to regulate the annual flooding of the Nile River. After Egypt blockaded the Israeli Red Sea port of Eilat, Israeli forces attacked and occupied the Sinai peninsula, later being joined by Britain and France, which sought to regain control of the Canal Zone. In the face of strong international opposition, particularly from the US, all three withdrew their forces.

1967 Egypt again blockaded Eilat; Israel launched and won the Six Day War against Egypt, Jordan and Syria, taking control of the Sinai peninsular and the Gaza Strip, which had been Egyptian territory. Crucially, they also took control of the Golan Heights, overlooking Syria.

1968–70 The War of Attrition was a limited war fought between Egypt and Israel, initiated by Egypt as a way to recapture the Sinai peninsular from Israel; the war ended with frontiers at the same place as when the war started.

1970–73 Anwar al Sadat was elected president following the death of Nasser. He renamed the country the Arab Republic of Egypt and ruled it as a one-party state. The Aswan High Dam was inaugurated by the President. In the 6 October War (also known as the Yom Kippur War), Egypt and Syria invaded Israel to reclaim some of the land lost in the Six Day War, but despite early successful strategic gains for Egypt and Syria, Israel counter-attacked and repelled the invasion, re-conquering the Golan Heights from Syria.

1975 The Suez Canal reopened, having been closed since the 1967 war.

1978–84 Sadat visited Jerusalem, which led to the Camp David Peace Accords, the signing of the Egyptian-Israeli Peace Treaty and the eventual Israeli withdrawal from the Sinai peninsular in 1982. Egypt was expelled from the Arab League. Sadat was assassinated by Islamic extremists in 1981. A national referendum approved Hosni Mubarak as president and political opposition parties were allowed for the first time.

1989 Egypt rejoined the Arab League.

1991–94 Egypt contributed to the US-led military campaign against Iraq. The outcome of the Gulf War established the political and economic framework for an Arab-Israeli peace process. Egypt was a party to peace agreements between Israel and the Palestinians, which began negotiations on the status of the former Egyptian territory of Gaza.

1996–2000 The National Democratic Party (NDP) was re-elected in the 1996 and 2000 elections. Mubarak was re-elected president for a fourth term.

2003 Emergency powers established when Sadat was assassinated in 1981 were extended for another three years.

2004 Ahmed Nazif became prime minister. In November, the funeral of Palestinian leader, Yasser Arafat, was held in Cairo.

2005 In February, Egypt hosted the Sharm El Sheik summit, at which President Mahmoud Abbas and Prime Minister Ariel Sharon signed a truce; Isreal was to withdraw from Gaza and the Palestinian authorities curb the violence of militant groups opposed to Israel. Egypt resumed diplomatic ties with Israel. A constitutional amendment allowed multiple candidates in the presidential elections, which was won by incumbant Mubarak, for a fifth consecutive term. Three-stage parliamentary elections took place on 9 and 20 November and 1 December: the ruling National Democratic Party (NDP) won 311 of the 442 elective seats, the outlawed Muslim Brotherhood contested the elections as independents and won 88 seats, more than the other opposition parties and independents combined.

Political structure

Constitution

Under the 1971 constitution, amended in 1980, Egypt is an Arab Republic with a democratic socialist system. The constitution states that there should be no discrimination on the grounds of race or religion. The country is divided into 26 governorates, with governors appointed by the president. There is universal suffrage with a voting age of 18.

Form of state

Democratic socialist republic

The executive

Executive power rests with the president, who is elected by universal suffrage for a six-year term (and may be re-elected), having been nominated by at least one-third of the People's Assembly and approved by at least two-thirds. The president may choose one or more vice presidents, and appoints, and may dismiss, the prime minister and cabinet.

The president may take emergency measures, but these must be approved by a referendum within 60 days; he may also dissolve the People's Assembly (the legislative body) prematurely, but a referendum and elections must be held within 60 days.

The president is supreme commander of the armed forces and head of the police.

National legislature

The legislative body is the Majlis al Shaab (People's Assembly). Most members (444 out of the total 454) are elected every five years by universal suffrage. The remaining 10 representatives are appointed by the president.

A second 264-member chamber, the Majlis al Shura (Consultative Assembly), has no legislative powers and acts only in an advisory capacity. The term of office is six years, with half of the members standing for re-election every three years. Two-thirds of the members are elected by direct universal suffrage, with the provision that half are manual workers, including small farmers, and the remaining one-third are appointed by the president.

Legal system

The legal system is based on the constitution of 1971. Officially, Egyptian law is based on *Sharia* (Islamic law), although in practice it is based on English common law and the French Napoleonic code. Christians and Jews are subject to their own jurisprudence in personal status

Egypt

affairs. The Court of Cassation, consisting of five judges, is the highest court of appeal. Courts of appeal (three judges) sit in Cairo and four other cities. Assize courts (three judges) deal with serious crimes. Central tribunals (three judges) handle ordinary civil and commercial cases. Summary tribunals (one judge) deal with both civil and criminal cases and have the power to impose fines and decree three-year prison terms.

Last elections
October–December 2005 (legislative); September 2005 (presidential).
Results: Presidential: Incumbent, Hosni Mubarak (NDP) won 88.6 per cent of the vote, Ayman Nour, (al Ghad) 7.5 per cent. Turnout was low at 23 per cent of the electorate.
Parliamentary: the ruling National Democratic Party (NDP) won 331 of 432 elective seats, independents 112 seats (including 88 affiliates of the Muslim Brotherhood), New Wafd Party six seats, the Tagammu Party two seats and the al Ghad Party one seat. The president appointed 10 members to bring the total number of parliamentary members to 454. Turnout was 26.6 per cent and 12 seats were unallocated due to irregularities.

Next elections
By October 2010 (presidential); November 2005 (legislative).

Political parties
Ruling party
National Democratic Party (NDP) (since 1996; re-elected Dec 2005)
Main opposition party
New Wafd Party (NWP); The Tagammu Party (Progressive Unionist Party); al Ghad (Tomorrow Party).
The outlawed Muslim Brotherhood contested the parliamentary elections as independents and returned more candidates than the numbers of legitimate parties and other independents combined.

Population
70.83 million (2004)
Ethnic make-up
Eastern Hamitic (99 per cent); the remaining 1 per cent comprises minorities including Armenian, Italian and Greek.
Religions
Muslim (mostly Sunni) (92 per cent); Coptic Christian and others (8 per cent).

Education
Primary education is compulsory and free; followed by three years of intermediate school and two years of secondary school, which are also free, but not compulsory. University graduates have long been guaranteed employment by the state, and this has contributed to the growth of a bloated and overstaffed state bureaucracy. The desire by graduates for office-based professional employment has led to a shortage of skilled technical labour. The government is encouraging more students to go into technical education.
Literacy rate: 66.7 per cent men, 43.9 per cent women; adult rates (World Bank).
Compulsory years: 6 to 12
Enrolment rate: 101 per cent, total primary school enrolment of the relevant age group (including repetition rates); 78 per cent, total enrolment of the relevant age group, in intermediate and secondary schools, (World Bank).
Pupils per teacher: 23 in primary schools

Health
Total expenditure on health is around 4 per cent of GDP, of which 46 per cent is government spending.
Healthcare in the private sector has become increasingly popular in recent years, especially in Cairo, with the construction of a number of private hospitals that provide an alternative to the severely over-stretched public health service. However the general decline in living standards has placed many private sector healthcare institutions in financial difficulties.
Family planning is widely available and officially encouraged, although many religious leaders continue to preach that it is against Islam. The population continues to grow and the government expects it to double to 110 million over the next 30 years, even if the target of halving the average family size is achieved.
Improved water sources and sanitation facilities are available to 95 per cent and 94 per cent of the population, respectively.
HIV prevalence: 0.1 per cent aged 15–49 in 2003 (World Bank)
Life expectancy: 69.1 years (World Bank)
Fertility rate/Maternal mortality rate: 3.1 births per woman (2003); maternal mortality 170 per 100,000 live births (World Bank).
Infant mortality rate: 33 per 1,000 live births; 4 per cent of children aged under five were malnourished (World Bank).
Head of population per physician/bed: 2.0 physicians and 2.1 hospital beds per 1,000 people.

Welfare
Social security provisions include sickness benefits, pensions, health insurance, training and subsidies on basic goods, including pharmaceuticals. The government places particular stress on the improvement of rural living standards and has established rural social units to provide health, education and agricultural services. Social services include care for mothers and children, the aged, the handicapped and prisoners, family planning, cultural education and literacy courses. The government, employers and employees contribute to a national insurance scheme that covers pensions and sickness benefit. A social development fund provides retraining, unemployment insurance and assistance to people who lose their jobs as a result of reforms and the privatisation of public enterprises.

Main cities
Cairo (capital, estimated population 8.1 million in 2004); Greater Cairo, 10.6 million, is the largest city in Africa.
Other cities include Alexandria (4.0 million), Giza (2.7 million), Shubra al Khaymah (1.0 million), Port Said (548,900), Suez (488,200), Luxor (421,500), Asyut (401,600), El Faiyum (305,100), Ismailia (297,500), Aswan (256,100), El Minya (235,400).

Languages spoken
French and English are widely spoken, especially in business circles.
Official language/s
Arabic

Media
Cairo is the largest publishing centre in the Middle East. The state controls the main newspapers as well as the Egyptian Radio and Television Corporation (ERTC) and the Egyptian Television Organisation (ETO).
Press
Dailies: Usually published in Arabic language. These include *Al Ahram*, *Alalam Alyoum*, *Al Sha'ab*, *Al Akhbar*, *Al Gomhouriya* and *Al Wafd*. There are also daily French papers, *Progrès Egyptien* and *Le Journal d'Egypte*. *Egyptian Gazette* provides daily local information in English.
Weeklies: *Akhbar al Yom*, *Al Mussawar*, *Alahali Newspaper* and *Akher Sa'a* have the largest circulation. There are a large number of weekly magazines, including *Hawadeth Magazine*, *Riada Magazine* and the *Sayarat Magazine*. *The Cairo Times* is the best selling English language bi-weekly magazine reporting from Egypt and the region. The Egypt edition of *Middle East Times* provides independent weekly coverage of politics, culture and religion in the Arab and Islamic worlds.
Business: Daily financial newspaper, *Al Alam al Youm*. Business news is covered by *Egypt Today*, *Business Today Egypt* and the economic weekly *Al Ahram al Iqtisadi*. The main English-language commercial weekly *Middle East Observer* also provides financial information.
Periodicals: Monthly publications in Arabic language include *Al Manar Magazine* and *Al Murabeton*. English language

periodicals include the *Arab Ambassador*. IBA Media is Egypt's leading English-language publisher and publishes three monthly titles: *Egypt Today* (http://www.egypttoday.com), *Business Today Egypt* (businesstoday-eg.com) and *PC World Egypt* (pcworld.com.eg).

Broadcasting
Radio: The national service is broadcast by the ERTC. There are 12 stations operating. The state's radio programmes are in Arabic, but it has an FM foreign language programme with daily news bulletins in English, French, Italian, German and Greek.

Television: A number of channels are operated by ETO. Channel 1 specialises in Arab programming while Channel 2 has a larger selection of Western shows. More than 90 per cent of households have a television.

Egyptian broadcasters transmit 84 channels throughout the Middle East and Mediterranean via the Nilesat 101 satellite. Egypt broadcasts Egyptian programmes throughout the Arab World. Libya and Egypt have cable telecommunications and radio links between the two countries.

Advertising
Egypt's advertising sector is one of the fastest-growing in the region.

Economy
The most influential change to Egypt's economy in 2004 was the appointment of a pro-reform cabinet. It has begun essential structural reforms in taxes, trade and subsidies, as well as restructuring the financial system, modernising fiscal accounts and strengthening monetary policy, while speeding-up the sale of state entities.

International trade in goods and services staged a recovery in 2004 coupled with a rise in the stock market and an appreciation in the Egyptian pound. Egypt also moved to a system of unified, flexible exchange rates in December 2004 that has operated well since its inception.

The privatisation of 19 state businesses by 2004, including two financial entities, earned LE5.6 billion (US$896 million) with direct investment in non-petroleum sectors put in 2004/05 at US$1 billion. Traditionally the economy was driven by oil, tourism, Suez Canal tolls and expatriate workers' remittances, whereas in 2004 trade in cotton clothing accounted for US$1.2 billion to the US and EU – US$615 million to the US alone. Cotton exports between October 2004 and March 2005 reached 113,400 tonnes and were valued at US$231 million. This helped drive annual GDP growth at 4.1 per cent.

The government overhauled customs procedures and reduced import tariffs, predicting that the changes would generate a rise of around 1.5 per cent in GDP growth in 2005.

The promising start to Egypt's recovery has been monitored by the IMF who advocates that the bulk of the surplus to the budget should be used to retire government debts.

External trade
Imports
Principal imports are machinery and equipment, foodstuffs, chemicals, wood products and fuels. US goods to be imported during 2006 will be US$5.1 billion.

In September 2004 customs procedures and reduced import tariffs were overhauled.

Main sources: US (13.2 per cent total, 2004), Germany (7.2 per cent), Italy (7.1 per cent), France (6.1 per cent), China (5.5 per cent), UK (4.9 per cent), Saudi Arabia (4.4 per cent)

Exports
Principal exports are crude oil and petroleum products, cotton, textiles, metal products and chemicals. Other exports include refined sugar cane, raw cotton, potatoes, rice and oranges.

Main destinations: Italy (13.1 per cent total, 2004), US 11.6 per cent), UK (7.5 per cent), Germany (5.1 per cent), Spain (4.5 per cent), France (4.2 per cent)

Agriculture
Farming
The agriculture sector contributed 15.5 per cent to GDP in 2004 and employed around 30 per cent of the workforce. Its importance is declining in relation both to industry and to population growth.

Irrigation is supplied by the River Nile – the government is looking at ways to improve the efficiency of water use through the construction of lined canals and pipes. Problems surrounding the ecological effects of the Aswan High Dam persist. Fertile land is found in the Nile Valley and Delta – the cultivable area accounts for only 2.4 per cent of the total land area at around 3.1 million hectares.

The construction of the Aswan High Dam in the 1970s initially improved crop yields by providing a constant source of water for irrigation. However, the dam had a damaging long-term effect on agriculture. It has permanently raised the water table, causing serious drainage problems and high salinity as well as depriving the Nile valley of annual silt, a natural fertiliser, previously brought down by the river during the flood season. The silt has had to be replaced by costly chemical fertilisers. Virtually all water in Egypt comes from the River Nile, from which Egypt is allowed to take 55.5 billion cubic metres of water a year, under its agreement with nine other Nile basin countries. This imposes strict limitations on the expansion of agriculture.

A number of major irrigation schemes are under way. These are along the coast north-west of Alexandria, the Nile border with Sudan, East Oweinat in the desert and the largest project of them all, the Southern Valley Scheme. The cost of the Southern Valley Scheme is projected to reach US$85 billion by 2017. Saudi investment will build the largest farm in the world (six times bigger than Singapore) which will reach full production in 2010 and will employ 25,000 people permanently, as well as additional seasonal labour.

Agricultural production in Egypt is highly labour-intensive. Output suffers from crop infestation, price controls, fragmented land tenure, increased soil salinity and consumer preference for imported foods. Major subsistence crops include maize, sorghum, rice, wheat, beans and vegetables. Egypt's wheat consumption far outstrips local production, with Egyptian wheat crops supplying just 40 per cent of annual domestic demand. Some 65 per cent of food requirements are imported, making Egypt's annual food import bill around US$5.5 billion.

Cotton is a major export crop; however, WTO agreements, which came into force on 1 January 2005, removed tariffs and trade and will put enormous pressure on the industry as it attempts to compete with Asia that has lower production costs and lower prices. Egypt produces high-quality long staple cotton that has been traditionally exported to Europe, the US and Japan, and it may have to lose many jobs as it carves out a niche market in quality cotton rather than competing for the mass market.

Crop production in 2004 included: 20,260,855 million tonnes (t) 7,177,855t wheat, 5,800,000t maize, 6,150,000t rice, 1,950,000t potatoes, 6,780,000t tomatoes, 1,104,000t grapes, 1,100,000t dates, 2,561,600t citrus fruit, 16,335t sugar cane, 2,860,547t sugar beets, 320,000t olives, 740,000t seed cotton, 294,000t cotton lint, 239,444t oilcrops, 487,446t pulses, 950,000t sorghum, 880,000t bananas, 7,471,135t fruit in total, 14,873,500t vegetables in total. Livestock production included: 1,390,580tt meat in total, 297,500t beef, 230,000t buffalo, 69,840t rabbit, 40,000t camel meat, 76,000t lamb and goat meat, 664,240t poultry, 240,000t eggs, 5,319,681t milk, 8,710t honey, 117t cocoons, silk, 32,886t cattle hides.

Fishing
There are active fishing industries in the Mediterranean and the Red Sea, as well as more limited freshwater fishing on the

Nile and Lake Nasser. Egypt typically produces over 300,000 tonnes of seafood and 190,000 tonnes of freshwater fish per annum. Virtually all of this is used for domestic consumption. Eleven lakes used to provide an annual 173,000 tonnes of fish but this rate has declined in recent years due to overfishing, lack of investment and pollution.

Forestry

Forestry covers less than 1 per cent of Egypt's land area. As a result, industrial wood and paper products are largely imported.

Industry and manufacturing

Industrial production, with a growth rate estimated at 2.5 per cent in 2004, is an important component of the economy, providing 32.1 per cent of GDP, while manufacturing provides 18.2 per cent. However, individually they were both outperformed by the total services industry that provided 52.4 per cent of GDP in 2004, of which tourism represented the lion's share.

The government places emphasis on: industrial diversification and import substitution, the development of downstream chemicals, and of heavy industry such as the Helwan Iron and Steel Company, the Nag Hammadi aluminium plant and El Dikheila integrated steel works. Industry and manufacturing has been dominated by state-owned companies however there is a renewed interest by the government to sell off enterprises, including metallurgical, food, wood pulp, and chemical processing, and various smelting works.

A number of cotton concerns are also on the privatisation list, although these companies are at risk, not from the shift in economic rationalisation, by rather global trading dynamics. World Trade Organisation (WTO) rulings that came into practice on 1 January 2005 removed all global tariffs and subsidies on processed cotton. Egypt, as a major manufacture of cotton thread and cloths, could lose thousands of jobs and millions of dollars in export sales. However, a niche market is being formed, supplying cotton apparel to the US under the Qualified Industrial Zones (QIZ) protocol, whereby manufactured goods from nominated QIZ, which must contain 11.7 per cent Israeli input, will be given free access to US markets.

The petrochemical sector is a leading contributor to GDP and has a predicted 6 per cent annual growth.

Egypt has a growing automotive industry, supplying both vehicles and components. There are 18 vehicle manufacturers operating under joint trade agreements with foreign companies. BMW invested US$35 million in a new factory, providing jobs for 500 workers, which opened in May 2004.

There are plans to invest a further US$25 million in more facilities. Nissan will open a new assembly plant, geared to produce 3,800 cars a year, which is scheduled to be operational by 2007.

With an estimated labour force of 20.7 million and around 2 million unemployed in 2004, Egypt needs to find around 800,000 new jobs each year to sustain its growth.

Tourism

Tourism has become the single greatest foreign exchange earner and represents a significant component of Egypt's GDP at 15.4 per cent, contributing US$13 billion in 2005. The industry employed 13 per cent of all workers and earned US$7 billion from tourists alone, with a further US$2.6 billion in capital investment. Annual growth is predicted to increase by 5.4 per cent for 2006–15.

The industry has been able to weather a sequence of damaging events such as the bombings of the tourist resort at Sharm al Sheikh in July 2005, and those in the Red Sea resorts of the Sinai Peninsula in October 2004. This has been achieved by providing cheaper holidays, which has the drawback of impacting on the quality of the tourist base and level of spending. Archaeological attractions are the primary visitor attractions, although Egypt has increasingly enhanced its facilities by the development of resort tourism, especially on the Red Sea coast. More than 50 per cent of visitors are from Europe, nevertheless, in 2004 Gulf Arabs arrived in Cairo (by up to 32 per cent) in much larger numbers than before. They were particularly welcome as they are high-spending and longer visiting holidaymakers. These were tourists that had been deterred from visiting US and European destinations due to extra security and suspicion of middle-eastern travellers.

Mining

Government policy aims to encourage foreign and local companies to explore for and exploit raw materials. Agreements have been reached for exploration and production of sulphur, phosphate and gold. The government is keen to extend franchises for other minerals, especially titanium and silver. Among non-oil raw materials, only iron ore, phosphate rock and limestone is produced on a significant scale. Other minerals produced include baryte, clay, feldspar, fluorspar, gypsum, kaolin, quartz, salt, silica sand and talc. Manganese and chrome deposits have also been exploited, while commercial deposits of zinc, tin, lead and copper have been discovered in Sinai.

A contract to mine sulphur in Sinai is held by Freeport Egyptian Sulphur Company, a wholly owned subsidiary of US firm Freeport McMoran. The annual production capacity is thought to be around 250,000 tonnes per year (tpy). Egypt also has deposits of uranium.

Although Egypt has no bauxite, it has developed a significant aluminium industry based on electric power from the Aswan High Dam. Production was initially used for basic consumer goods but Egypt now exports a wide range of basic aluminium products.

Hydrocarbons

The upstream oil and gas industry generates around 10 per cent of GDP and represents an important source of foreign currency, with oil accounting for about 40 per cent of total export revenues.

Egypt's production in 2004 was 350,000 barrels per day (bpd), with proven oil reserves of 3.6 billion barrels. Increasing industrialisation and the rise in domestic oil consumption, has encouraged the government into continue with partnership deals for oil exploration. In July 2004 Egypt signed exploration deals with two prospecting firms, one from Tunisia and the other the US. In total, 14 wells will be drilled up to 2011.

BP's Saqqara oil field is expected to produce 40,000–50,000bpd annually from 2005. Other petroleum deposits have been discovered in the Qaran area of Egypt's Western Desert by the US-based Apache Corporation.

In view of limited oil reserves, interest has switched to gas exploration and proven reserves in 2004 were 1.85 trillion cubic metres (cum), which should last well into the twenty-first century at current annual rates of production of 26.8 billion cum. Egypt consumed 25.7 billion cum of natural gas in 2004 leaving a comparatively small amount for export. The completion of a small natural gas pipeline to Jordan has made the first natural gas exports possible; the pipeline is planned to extend to Syria, Turkey, Lebanon and Cyprus increasing the market still further.

Coal reserves at Maghara in Sinai total about 27 million tonnes, however, there is no commercial production.

Energy

Electricity is generated at thermal power stations throughout the country, and about a quarter of the total is supplied by the hydroelectric plant at the Aswan High Dam in Upper Egypt.

Around 98 per cent of all electricity needs is provided by the electricity sector but domestic demand is growing fast and to keep up with it Egypt has embarked on a major programme of capital investment. Not only are some current power stations being upgraded to produce more electricity but a number of new generating plants with the total capacity of 33,000MW are under construction. The OECD agreed a loan of US$20 million to fund the North Cairo Electricity Network, which should be operational by 2007, adding 750MW to the system.

There are a number of wind and solar power plants either newly opened or under construction with an expected total capacity of 297MW when they all become operational; the first began generating 93MW in 2004, in Za'farana.

Financial markets
Stock exchange
Egypt's stock market is considered the best of the emerging markets. After seven years of stagnation caused by a series of knocks starting with the Asian financial crisis, then the 2000 Palestinian *intifada*, followed by the terrorist attack on the US in 2001 and the devaluation of the Egyptian pound in 2003, the market has boomed on the back of rising oil prices, increased tourism and Arab money returning from the West.

Banking and insurance
The banking sector is dominated by four public-sector commercial banks – Banque Misr, Bank of Alexandria, Banque du Caire and the National Bank of Egypt – which hold about 60 per cent of deposits, 70 per cent of assets and 65 per cent of loans, and are the main conduit for public-sector trade, savings and financing. In February 2004, Egypt was removed from the OECD list of non-co-operative countries on money laundering after reforms had been implemented.

The Central Bank of Egypt (CBE) strengthened the monetary policy framework over 2004 which should aid it as it manages and limits inflationary pressures while stimulating market driven interest rates. The IMF in a 2005 report stressed that the CBE independence from political interference should be maintained.

As a whole, strong current account trading enabled banks to strengthen their net foreign assets in 2004 and 2005 and the CBE also took advantage of market conditions to build up its reserves. Total external debt remained stable at about US$29 billion (31 per cent of GDP) by the end of 2004.

As part of the privatisation programme under way by the government two state banks are in the process of being sold off to the commercial sector.

Central bank
Central Bank of Egypt

Main financial centre
Cairo

Time
GMT plus two hours (GMT plus three hours from May to September).

Geography
Most of Egypt is located in the north-east corner of Africa between the Mediterranean Sea, the Red Sea, Sudan and Libya. The Sinai peninsula, separated from the African continent by the Suez Canal and the Red Sea, borders Israel. The peninsula also faces Jordan and Saudi Arabia across the Gulf of Aqaba. About 95 per cent of Egypt is uninhabitable desert.

Climate
The climate is dry with very little rainfall, hot in summer and cool in winter. Temperatures in Cairo in the north vary from 43 degrees Celsius (C) maximum in summer to 18 degrees C maximum in winter. Sandstorms (the *khamsin* or *simoon* winds) can disrupt air traffic between March and May.

Rainfall is largely confined to the Mediterranean coast, with around 200 millimetres a year in Alexandria. Egypt is dependent on the Nile for nearly all its water needs. The government is pressing ahead with desert reclamation schemes, but these are also dependent on limited Nile waters as reserves of water under the desert have so far proved relatively insignificant.

Dress codes
Lightweight clothing is necessary for the hot summer months (May to September). Business dress is formal – suits are worn for all occasions. Men should not wear shorts, except at the beach and women should wear modest clothing in public, covering their arms and legs.

Entry requirements
Passports
Required by all except certain Palestinians and some merchant seamen. Passports must be valid for six months beyond the intended length of stay.

Visa
Required by all, except citizens of some adjacent countries, for full list of exceptions contact the local embassy or visit http://egypt.embassyhomepage.com. Business and tourist visas, valid for three months, available for most Europeans and North Americans, can be obtained at the point of entry.

All visitors, except those Europeans and US nationals on tourist visas, must register at the Office of Foreigners and Nationality within seven days of arrival. Hotels will normally undertake this on the visitor's behalf.

Currency advice/regulations
Import and export of local currency is restricted to LE1,000 per person. Import of foreign currency is unrestricted, but must be declared. Export of foreign currency is restricted to this declared amount.

Customs
It is permitted to import one bottle of alcohol and 200 cigarettes. Video equipment must be declared at customs.

Health (for visitors)
Mandatory precautions
A vaccination certificate against yellow fever is required if travelling from an infected area.

Advisable precautions
Typhoid, hepatitis 'A', tetanus vaccinations are recommended. Malaria exists from June–October in the El Faiyum area. There is also a rabies risk. Polio is endemic.

Avoid drinking tap water and use bottled water instead; water used for brushing teeth or making ice should be boiled first or otherwise sterilised. All fruit should be peeled and only well-cooked meat, vegetables and fish, served hot, should be eaten. Salad and mayonnaise may carry increased risk, except in top-class restaurants. Avoid food sold on the streets.

Hotels
There is a wide range available. Bills are quoted in US dollars and may be settled in Egyptian currency. A 20 per cent tax and service charge should be added to all prices.

Credit cards
Most credit cards are widely accepted. Excepting airline tickets, the free market exchange rate is used in calculating credit card transactions.

Public holidays
Fixed dates
7 Jan (Coptic Christmas Day), 25 Apr (Sinai Liberation Day), 1 May (Labour Day), 18 Jun (Evacuation Day), 23 Jul (Revolution Day), 6 Oct (Armed Forces' Day), 24 Oct (Suez Victory Day), 23 Dec (Victory Day).

Variable dates
Coptic Easter Monday, Eid al Adha, Eid al Fitr, Islamic New Year, Birth of the Prophet.

The Islamic year contains 354 or 355 days, with the result that Muslim feasts advance by 10–12 days against the Gregorian calendar. Dates of feasts vary according to the sighting of the new moon, so cannot be forecast exactly. Islamic year 1426: 10 February 2005 to 30 January 2006.

Working hours
As a Muslim country the official day off is Friday. Embassies and the offices of some foreign companies also close on Saturday and Sunday. Some companies treat Thursday as a half day. Hours may also vary between winter and summer.

Egypt

Banking
Sun–Thu: 0800/0830–1400. In cities centres also 1700/1800–1900/2000.
Business
Sat–Thu: 0900–1400.
Government
Sun–Thur: 0800–1400.
Shops
Sat–Thur: 0900–1300 and 1600–2000 (summer); 1000–1800 (winter). During Ramadan Sat–Thur: 0930–1530 and 2000–2200.
Department stores offer extended hours and local shops may vary their hours to suit.

Electricity supply
220–440V AC in most areas; in some rural districts 110–380V AC is still found.

Weights and measures
Metric system (local units also in use).

Social customs/useful tips
Hospitality is considered a prime virtue and it would be rude for visitors not to accept a token drink or other invitation. Many hosts will not allow a guest to pay for anything during his or her stay. Guests should therefore not squabble over paying at a restaurant, for example. In address, use the first name with the appropriate title (for instance Mr, Madame, Doctor, Engineer). Business cards in Arabic are appreciated.

Security
Violent crime against foreigners is rare. However, thieves operate in busy tourist areas such as Giza and Luxor. In these areas it is best to avoid wearing flashy or expensive jewellery.
Given its strategic position in the Middle East, Egypt is particularly sensitive regarding national security. Photographing bridges, railway stations and military installations is forbidden. Carrying a video camera can cause problems with the Egyptian authorities.

Getting there
Air
National airline: Egyptair
International airport/s: Cairo International (CAI), 22km from city; Alexandria International (ALY), 3km from city. Business centre, bank, post office, bars, restaurant, shops, pharmacy and car hire available.
Egypt is upgrading its international airports during 2005.
Other airport/s: Egypt is to build three new airports – at El Alamein (west of Alexandria), Dahab (south Sinai) and Mersa Alam (Red Sea). International airports are also being constructed at Taba and Suba Bay.
Improvements are planned at six international airports, including Sharm El Sheikh, Luxor and Aswan, as well as the development of three domestic airports, among them Port Said, to bring them up to the standards required to handle international flights.
Airport tax: There is no airport tax.
Surface
Road: There are road links from Libya and Israel.
A new road from Aswan to Port Sudan is under construction and is expected to be completed by April 2006. Until then no roads to Sudan are recommended.
Water: There are ferry services to Port Said and Alexandria from many destinations across the Mediterranean, run by Menatours. There are ferries between Aqaba in Jordan and Nuweiba on the Sinai peninsular and to Suez from Jeddah in Saudi Arabia. There are steamer services across Lake Nasser from Sudan, although these are suspended during periods of instability in Sudan.
Main port/s: Alexandria, Al Ghardaqah, Aswan, Bur Safajah, Damietta, Marsa Matruh, Port Said and Suez.

Getting about
National transport
Air: Egyptair operates domestic services from Cairo to Luxor, Aswan, Hurghada, Abu Simbel and Alexandria. Air Sinai operates services to North and South Sinai. If planning to fly south, book well in advance. Travel to certain areas of the Nile Delta is restricted.
Road: There is a 31,000km surfaced network which includes good roads linking Cairo-Alexandria, Cairo-Port Said, Ismailia-Suez-Sinai, Cairo-El Faiyum-Luxor-Aswan.
Buses: There are four intercity bus companies: luxury service Superjet, West Delta Bus Company, East Delta Bus Company, and Upper Egypt Bus Company. There are fast and comfortable services between most towns and cities, although they tend to be crowded, and tickets should be booked in advance where possible.
Rail: There are train services to all main cities and towns in Egypt, including express and through trains from Cairo to Alexandria, Luxor and Aswan. Four classes available; certain routes have air-conditioned sleeping cars and buffet service. Tickets must be reserved, sometimes up to two days in advance.
Water: Traditional sailboats (*felucca*) offer rides along the Nile river.
City transport
Taxis: Metered and unmetered taxis are readily available, but meters where fitted are often not used. Fares should be agreed in advance.
Air-conditioned limousines are available at airports and main hotels. Chauffeured taxis from Cairo airport to the city centre are recommended. Hotels have their own shuttle services. Hotel taxis or chauffeured hire cars are more efficient and can be hired by the day, subject to negotiation. Fares are usually listed in the major hotels.
City centre taxis are cheap, although often uncomfortable and never have air-conditioning. If you are travelling beyond the city centre, it is a good idea to carry a map to guide the taxi driver. The journey time from Cairo international airport to the city is about 40–60 minutes. Tipping is usually 10 per cent.
Buses, trams & metro: A bus service runs every 40–60 minutes from Cairo airport to the city centre, journey time 60 minutes. Local buses are numerous, cheap and crowded as are the few trams still in existence. The Cairo metro is fast, inexpensive and not too crowded, it has 43 stations, five of which run through central Cairo.
Ferry: Several routes run north and south of the city plied by waterbuses.
Car hire
An international driving licence and third-party insurance are needed. Hire charges should be negotiated in advance. The maximum speed limit on main roads is 90kph, rising to 100kph on the Cairo-Alexandria desert road; fines for speeding are substantial. Traffic in Cairo is heavily congested.

BUSINESS DIRECTORY
The addresses listed below are a selection only. While World of Information makes every endeavour to check these addresses, we cannot guarantee that changes have not been made, especially to telephone numbers and area codes. We would welcome any corrections.

Telephone area codes
The international direct dialling code (IDD) for Egypt is +20, followed by area code and subscriber's number:

Alexandria	3	Ismailiya	64
Ashara Ramadan	15	Kafr El Sheik	47
Aswan	97	Luxor	95
Asyut	88	Maeria	3
Benha	13	Mahalla	43
Beni Suef	82	Mansoura	50
Cairo	2	Marsa Matruh	3
Damanhur	45	Port Said	66
Damietta	57	Pyramids	2
El Arish	68	Sacheia	16
El Minya	86	Sohag	93
Fayoum	84	Suez	62
Giza	2	Tanta	40
Heliopolis	2	Zagazig	55

Useful telephone numbers
Cairo
Police 122
Fire 125

Ambulance 123
Police:
Aswan 22147
Alexandria 960-151-122
Suez 23-929

Chambers of Commerce
Alexandria Chamber of Commerce, 31 El-Ghorfa El-Togaria Street, Alexandria (tel: 809-339; fax: 808-993).

American Chamber of Commerce in Egypt, 33 Soliman Abaza Street, Doki-Giza, Cairo (tel: 338 1050; fax: 338-1060; e-mail: info@amcham.org.eg).

Aswan Chamber of Commerce, Abtal El-Tahreer Street, Aswan (tel: 323-084).

Cairo Chamber of Commerce, 4 Midan El-Falaki, Cairo (tel: 354-2943; fax: 355-7940).

Damietta Chamber of Commerce, Saad Zaghloul Street, Damietta (tel: 322-799; fax: 320-632).

Egyptian-British Chamber of Commerce, PO Box 4EG, 299 Oxford Street, London W1A 4EG (tel: 020-7499-3100; fax: 020-7499-1070; e-mail: info@theebcc.com).

Fayoum Chamber of Commerce, El-Nadi El-Reyadi Street, El Fayoum (tel: 322-148).

Federation of Egyptian Chambers of Commerce, 4 Midan El-Falaky, Cairo (tel: 795-1136; fax: 795-1164; e-mail: fedcoc@menanet.net).

Ismailia Chamber of Commerce, 163 Saad Zaghloul Street, Ismailia (tel: 221-663; fax: 322-515).

Port Said Chamber of Commerce, Benayet Souk El Goumla, Port Said (tel: 222-733; fax: 236-141).

Red Sea Chamber of Commerce, Old City Council Building, Hurghada (tel: 440-761).

Suez and South Sinai Chamber of Commerce, 47 Salah Eldin Elayoubi Street, Suez (tel: 227-783).

Banking
Alexandria Commercial and Maritime Bank, PO Box 2376, 85 El Horreya Avenue, 21519 Alexandria (tel: 392-1237, 392-1556, 392-9203; fax: 391-3706).

Arab African International Bank, 5 Midan Al-Saray Al Koubra, Garden City, Cairo (tel: 794-5094/5/6; fax: 795-8493).

Arab International Bank, 35 Abdel Khalek Sarwat Street, Cairo (tel: 391-8794, 391-6391; fax: 391-6233).

Bank of Alexandria, 49 Kasr El Nil Street, Cairo (tel: 393-6262, 391-1203; fax: 391-0481, 391-980).

Bank of Commerce & Development, 'Al Tegaryoon', PO Box 1373, 13 26th July Street, Sphinx Square, Mohandessin, Cairo (tel: 302-8156, 302-1623; fax: 302-3963).

Cairo Far East Bank, PO Box 757, 104 El Nil Street, Dokki, Cairo (tel: 336-2516/18; fax: 348-3818).

Crédit International d'Egypte, 46 El Batal Ahmed Abdel Aziz Street, Mohandessin, Cairo (tel: 336-1897, 336-1898; fax: 360-8673).

Delta International Bank, PO Box 1159, 1113 Corniche El Nil Street, Cairo (tel: 575-3492; fax: 574-3403).

Egyptian American Bank, PO Box 1825, 4 & 6 Hassan Sabri Street, Zamalek, Cairo (tel: 738-0126, 738-0136, 738-2661; fax: 738-0609, 738-0450).

Misr Exterior Bank; Cairo Plaza Building, Cornish El Nil, Boulaque, Cairo (tel: 778-701, 778-619, 766-381, 766-360; fax: 762-806, 578-0238).

Misr International Bank, PO Box 218, Embaba, 54 El Batal Ahmed Abdel Aziz Street, Mohandessin, Cairo (tel: 749-4424, 749-7091; fax: 700-928).

National Bank for Development (NBD), PO Box 647, 5(A) El Borsa El Gedida Street, 11511 Cairo (tel: 392-3245; fax: 390-5681).

National Bank of Egypt, PO Box 11611, National Bank of Egypt Tower, 1187 Corniche El Nil, Cairo (tel: 574-9101; fax: 576-2672).

Nile Bank, PO Box 2741, 35 Ramses Street, Abdel Moneim Riyad Sq, Cairo (tel: 574-1417, 574-3502, 575-1105; fax: 575-6296, 575-3640).

Suez Canal Bank, PO Box 2620, 11 Mohamed Sabri Abu Alam St, Cairo (tel: 393-1066, 393-1048, 393-1215; fax: 391-3522).

Central bank
Central Bank of Egypt, 31 Kasr el-Nil Street, Cairo (tel: 392-6211; fax: 392-6361; e-mail: general_secretary@cbe.org.eg).

Travel information
Cairo International Airport, Heliopolis, Cairo (tel: 291-4255; fax: 243-2522).

Egyptair, Cairo International Airport, Cairo (tel: 245-4400; fax: 418-3715).

Ministry of tourism
Ministry of Tourism, Misr Tourist Tower, Abbassiya Square, Abbassiya (tel: 282-8439; fax: 285-9551; e-mail: mot@idsc.gov.eg).

National tourist organisation offices
Egyptian Tourist Authority, Misr Building, Abbassia (tel: 482-0283; fax: 483-0844; internet: www.touregypt.net).

Ministries
Ministry of Agriculture, Animal and Fish Wealth and Land Reclamation, Nadi El Seid Street, Dokki, Giza (tel: 702-677; fax: 703-889; e-mail: capi@idsc.gov.eg).

Ministry of Cabinet Affairs and Administrative Development, 1 Magles El Shaab Street, Cairo (tel: 354-1722; fax: 355-6306; e-mail: cabinet1@idsc.gov.eg).

Ministry of Culture, 2 Shagaret El Dor St, Zamalek Cairo 03 (tel: 341-5568; fax: 340-6449; e-mail: mculture@idsc.gov.eg).

Ministry of Defence and Military Production, 5 Ismail Abaza Street, Cairo (tel: 355-3063; fax: 354-8739; e-mail: mod@idsc.gov.eg).

Ministry of Economy and International Co-operation, 8 Adly St, Cairo (tel: 390-6796; fax: 390-3029; e-mail: mineco@idscl.gov.eg; internet site: http://www.sis.gov.eg).

Ministry of Education, 4 Ibrahim Naguib St, Garden City, Cairo (tel: 355-7952; fax: 356-2952; E-mail: moe@idsc.gov.eg).

Ministry of Electricity and Energy, Ramses Street, Abbassia, Nasr City Cairo (tel: 261-6514; fax: 261-6302; e-mail: mee@idsc.gov.eg).

Ministry of Finance, Lazoughly Square, Justice and Finance Building, Cairo (tel: 354-1055; fax: 354-5433; e-mail: mofinance@idsc1.gov.eg).

Ministry of Foreign Affairs, Press and Information Department, Maspero, Corniche El Nil, Cairo 02 (tel: 354-1414; fax: 354-6285; e-mail: minexter@idsc1.gov.eg).

Ministry of Health and Population, Magles El Shaab St, Cairo (tel: 354-1076; fax: 355-3966; e-mail: moh@idsc.gov.eg).

Ministry of Higher Education, 4 Ibrahim Naguib Street, Garden City, Cairo (tel: 355-7952; fax: 356-2952; e-mail: mheducat@idsc1.gov.eg, info@sti.sci.eg).

Ministry of Housing, Reconstruction and New Urban Communities, 1 Ismail Abaza St, Cairo (tel: 355-3320; fax: 355-7836; e-mail: mhuuc@idsc1.gov.eg).

Ministry of Industry and Mineral Wealth, 2 Latin America Street, Garden City (tel: 355-7034; fax: 354-8362; e-mail: moimw@idsc.gov.eg).

Ministry of Information, Maspero, Corniche El Nil, Cairo (tel: 747-193; fax: 757-144; e-mail: rtu2@idsc.gov.eg).

Ministry of Insurance & Social Affairs, El Sheikh Rihan Street, Bab El-Louq, Cairo (tel: 337-0039; fax: 337-5390; e-mail: msi@idsc.gov.eg).

Egypt

Ministry of Interior, El Sheikh Rihan St, Cairo (tel: 355-7500; fax: 355-7792; e-mail: moi1@idsc.gov.eg).

Ministry of Justice, Justice and Finance Building, Lazoughli Sq, Cairo 15 (tel: 355-1176; fax: 355-8103; e-mail: mojeb@idsc1.gov.eg).

Ministry of Local Administration, Kasr El Aini St, Cairo 04 (tel: 355-3566).

Ministry of Manpower and Immmigration, 3 Youssef Abbas St, Nasr City, Cai (tel: 260-9363; fax: 260-9891; e-mail: mwlabor@idsc1.gov.eg).

Ministry of Petroleum, 16 El Mokhayyam El Da'em Street, Nasr City (tel: 262-2268; fax: 263-6060; e-mail: mopm@idsc1.gov.eg).

Ministry of Planning, Salah Salem Road, Nasr City (tel: 602-935; fax: 263-4747).

Ministry of Public Enterprises, Magles El Shaab Street, Cairo (tel: 355-8026; fax: 355-3606); PEO, 2 Latin America Street, Garden City, Cairo (tel: 794-3484; fax: 795-9233).

Ministry of Public Works and Water Resources, El Nil St, Embaba, Cairo 04 (tel: 354-5884; fax: 355-8008; e-mail: mpwwr@idsc.gov.eg).

Ministry of Rural Development, 4 Shooting Club Street, Dokki, Cairo (tel: 349-7470; fax: 349-7785).

Ministry of Shipping, 7 Abdel Khalek Sarwat St, Cairo, 01 (tel: 764-343).

Ministry of Social Affairs and Insurance, El Sheikh Rihan St, Bab El Louk, Cairo 06 (tel: 354-2900; fax: 917-799).

Ministry of State for Administrative Development and Environment and Ministry of the Public Enterprise, 1 Magles El Shaab Street, Lazoughli Square, CAI 06 (tel: 355-8026; fax: 355-5882; e-mail: mops3@idsc.gov.eg).

Ministry of State for Environmental Affairs, Helwan Road, Cairo (tel: 375-7306; fax: 378-4285; e-mail: eeaa@idsc.gov.eg).

Ministry of State for Military Production, 23 Kobri Al Kubba St, Cairo 36 (tel: 257-8697/2915).

Ministry of State for Planning and International Co-operation, Salah Salem Street, Nasr City (tel: 401-4615; fax: 401-4733; e-mail: miceu@idsx.gov.eg).

Ministry of State for Scientific Research Affairs, 101 Kasr El Aini St, Cairo 04 (tel: 355-7952).

Ministry of Trade and Supply, 99 Kasr El Aini St, Cairo 04 (tel: 355-0360; fax: 354-4973; e-mail: msit@idsx.gov.eg).

Ministry of Transport, Communications and Civil Aviation, 105 Kasr El Aini Street, Cairo (tel: 354-3623; fax: 355-5564; e-mail: garb@idsc.gov.eg).

Prime Minister's Office, 1 Magles El Shaab St, Lazoughli Square, Cairo 04 (tel: 354-7376; fax: 355-8048).

President's Office, Abdin palace, CAI 06 (tel: 391-0130).

Other useful addresses

Arab League, The Arab League Building, Corniche El Nil, Cairo (tel: 393-4499; fax: 775-626).

Arab Organisation for Industrialisation, 2D Abassiya Square, PO Box 770 (tel: 823-377; fax: 826-010).

Arab Republic of Egypt National Telecommunications Organisation (ARENTO), 26 Ramses Street (tel: 760-333; fax: 771-306).

British Embassy, 7 Ahmed Ragheb St, Garden City, Cairo (tel: 354-0852; fax: 354-0859).

Cabinet Office, 1 Maglis El Shaab Street, Lazoughli Square, CAI 04 (tel: 354-7376; fax: 355-8048).

Cairo Regional Center for International Commercial Arbitration, 3 Aboul Feda Street, Zamalek, Cairo (tel: 340-1330; fax: 340-1336).

Cairo Stock Exchange, 4 Sharia esh-Sherifein, Cairo (tel: 392-1402; fax: 392-8526).

Capital Market Authority, 20 Emad El Din Street, Sixth Floor, Downtown (tel: 777-774; fax: 755-339).

Central Agency for Public Mobilisation and Statistics (CAPMAS), Saleh Salem Street, Nasr City, Cairo (tel: 603-717; fax: 604-099).

Central Post Office, Ataba Square, Cairo.

Commercial International Investment Company (CIIC), 66-68 Mohie El-Din Abou El-Ezz St, Dokki, Cairo (tel: 335-8035, 335-7093, 337-6251; fax: 335-7095).

Commercial Representation Office, 96 Ahmed Orabi Street, Mohandiseen (tel: 347-1892; fax: 345-1840).

Commission of the European Communities Delegation in Egypt, 6 Ibn Zenki Street, Zamalek, Cairo (tel: 340-8388; fax: 340-0385).

Customs Information Centre, 4 El Tayaran Street, Nasr City (tel: 260-5711; fax: 261-2672).

Egyptian Electricity Authority, Abassia, Cairo (tel: 261-6537; fax: 261-6512, 401-1630).

Egyptian Embassy (USA), 3521 International Court, NW, Washington DC 20008 (tel: 895-5400; fax: 244-5131).

Egyptian General Petroleum Corporation (EGPCC), 4 Palestine Street, Fourth Sector, new Maadi (tel: 353-1438; fax: 353-1457).

Egyptian Radio and Television Corporation (ERTC), Radio and TV Building, Sharia Maspiro, Corniche en-Nil, PO Box 504, Cairo (tel: 749-508; fax: 746-989).

General Authority for Control of Imports and Exports, Atlas Building El Sheikh Maarouf and Ramses Streets (tel: 574-2830; fax: 766-971).

General Authority for Investment and Free Zones, 8 Sharia Adly, PO Box 1007, Cairo (tel: 390-6804).

General Organisation for Industrialisation (GOFI) 6 Khali Agha Street, Garden City (tel: 355-7005; fax: 354-4984).

General Organisation for International Exhibitions and Fairs (GOIEF), Exhibition Ground, Nasr City, Cairo (tel: 260-7811; fax: 260-7845, 260-7848).

International Finance Corp (IFC), 5 El Fallah Street, Mohandessin, Cairo (tel: 347-8081; fax: 347-3738).

International Group for Investments, 5 Zahraa Street, Dokko 12311, Cairo (tel: 361-1624; fax: 360-2178).

Internatinal Monetary Fund (IMF), 31 Kasr El Nil Street, Central Bank, Cairo (tel: 392-4257; fax: 351-7137).

Local Governorates, El-Islah El-Zerai Building, 10th Floor, 4 Nadi El-Seid Street, Dokki (tel: 349-4770; fax: 349-7788).

Sales Tax Authority, 4 El Tayaran Street, nasr City (tel: 260-7500; fax: 260-7501).

Taxation Authority, 5 Hussein Hegazi Street (tel: 355-7784; fax: 355-5438).

US Embassy, 5 Sharia Latin America, Garden City, Cairo (tel: 355-7371).

Internet sites

Africa Business Network: http://www.ifc.org/abn

AllAfrica.com: http://allafrica.com

Africa Online: http://www.africaonline.com

Arab Bank: http://www.arabbank.com

Egypt Business Directory: http://www.telefax.com.eg/default.htm

Egypt corporate information: http://www.corporateinformation.com/egcorp.html

Egypt economic indicators: http://www.economic.idsc.gov.eg/

Egypt www index: http://ce.eng.usf.edu/pharos/

El Salvador

KEY FACTS

Official name: República de El Salvador (Republic of El Salvador)

Head of State: President Antonio Saca (Arena) (sworn in 1 Jun 2004)

Head of government: President Antonio Saca

Ruling party: Coalition government: Alianza Republicana Nacionalista (Arena) (Nationalist Republican Alliance) and Partido de Conciliación Nacional (PCN) (National Conciliation Party) (elected Mar 2003)

Area: 21,400 square km

Population: 6.70 million (2004)

Capital: San Salvador

Official language: Spanish

Currency: US dollar (US$) adopted from 1 Jan 2001; the colón is no longer accepted as legal tender.

GDP per capita: US$2,335 (2004)

GDP real growth: 1.50% (2004)

Labour force: 2.90 million (2004)

Unemployment: 6.30% (2004) (additional underemployment)

Inflation: 4.50% (2004)

Balance of trade: -US$2.62 billion (2004)

Foreign debt: US$4.79 billion (2004)*

* estimated figure

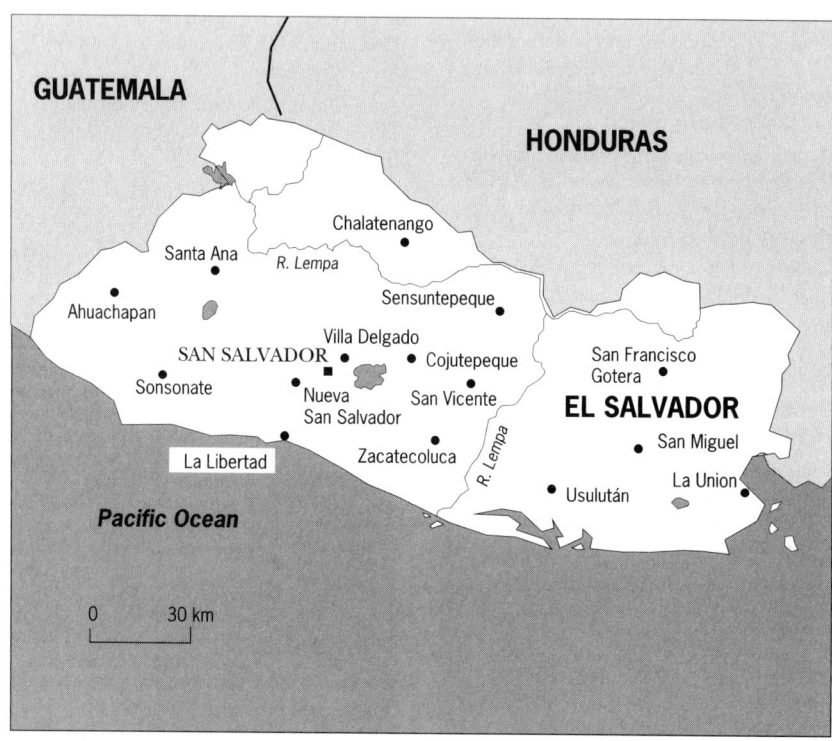

With a total land area of 21,400 square km coupled with a population of 6.7 million, El Salvador is the most densely populated of all the countries on the American mainland. The country has a history of political divisions, but in recent years political and social conflict has been minimised, though some tensions, naturally, still exist. One of the key reasons for the relatively placid atmosphere in El Salvador today is the successful reduction in the power of the military. El Salvador's constitution now prevents the military from intervening in matters of internal security. Furthermore, the military's manpower has also been reduced. At their peek during the civil war the armed forces numbered 63,000 men. Today, in early 2006, it is much less.

El Salvador is now a deomocratic republic, governed by the president as head of state. Both the office of the president (single five year term only) and each of the 84 deputies who make up the Legislative Assembly are elected by means of universal suffrage. Current President Elías Antonio Saca González, popularly known as Tony, was elected on 21 March 2004, by a clear margin of 22 per cent over leftist candidate Schafik Jorge Handal of the Frente Farabundo Martí para la Liberación Nacional (FMLN) (Farabundo Martí National Liberation Front). Saca was inaugurated as president on 1 June 2004, succeeding fellow Alianza Republicana Nacionalista (Arena) (National Republican Alliance) member and former president Francisco Flores. A Salvadorian national of Palestinian descent, Saca, prior to taking office, was a renowned businessman and radio sports commentator.

Economy

Saca was elected president on the back of his and Arena's commitment to free market reform, among other things. Over the years Arena has pursued a policy of prudent fiscal management and has privatised the banking system, the public pension provision, and the telecommunications industry. Import duties have also been reduced, intellectual property rights have

El Salvador

been better enforced and price controls have been abolished. GDP per capita income has increased year on year since 2002 and stood at US$2,335 in 2004. One of the negative consequences of the liberalisation of the economy has been uneven income distribution which has in turn resulted in a growing wealth gap.

Since dollarisation became an official reality in Salvadorian life on 1 January 2001, it is generally acknowledged that prices have risen in the country. As so often happens when a new currency is injected into the economy a rounding up of prices occurs – witness the effect of the introduction of the euro in many member countries in the late 1990s/early 2000s. Both currencies, the US dollar and the Salvadorian colón, circulated for three years, before the latter was abolished and the US dollar was officially adopted in 2004. Despite the displeasure felt by many Salvadorians at the loss of their currency and the consequent rise in prices, it is now generally acknowledged throughout the country, that a return to the former currency would be catastrophic for the economy as a whole.

Furthermore, the adoption of the dollar back in 2001 resulted in lower interest rates, thus facilitating increased opportunities for gaining short and long-term credit for Salvadorian citizens. The increase in liquidity in the economy brought about by more personal spending power and greater levels of disposable income led to an increase in consumer sales, as more Salvadorians purchased sizeable assets such as motor cars and residential property. Dissatisfaction with dollarisation often returns to the surface of public debate at the time of elections though. This was certainly the case in 2004, when the left made great play of Arena's alleged servitude to Washington.

El Salvador is one of the more stable economies in Central America and increased integration with the US economy looks set to continue. The country's trade deficit is large; one of the major sources of foreign income originates in the US, where Salvadorians working legally and illegally, send money back to family members in El Salvador. Home remittances sent back to the country from Salvadorians in the US are thought to constitute approximately 16 per cent of total GDP.

Cafta

El Salvador has a close relationship with the United States, owing to the Saca government's commitment to pro-US free trade policies. Indeed, Washington made little secret of its support for Saca during his electoral contest with left-wing candidate Schafik Jorge Handal in 2004. El Salvador was the first country to ratify the Central American Free Trade Agreement (Cafta), though it must be noted that the congressional hearing at which the agreement was confirmed was interrupted by protests.

The incumbent Arena administration has outlined its intention to pass fresh legisaltion designed to improve labour mobility, allowing workers in unproductive sectors to transfer more easily to lucrative industries. The Saca government argues that by passing such legislation, El Salvador will be better placed to take advantage of Cafta membership. In addition to Cafta, El Salvador also enjoys free trading relationships with Mexico, the Dominican Republic, Chile and Panama.

El Salvador's economy grew slowly in 2004, at a rate of 1.5 per cent, the lowest rate for 15 years and Saca is firmly committed to Cafta as a means of stimulating growth. Others disagree. William Pleitez, head of the UN Development Programme (UNDP) in the country, claims that Cafta 'would do nothing to change the competitiveness of the Salvadorean economy'. He has also urged the government to revise its growth strategy in order 'to take advantage of the unprecedented resources from migrants' remittances and the internal market' by investing much more in infrastructure and the educational system.

Outlook

El Salvador is more politically stable than it has been for many years. The endorsement of Saca as president by a comfortable margin in 2004 seemed to confirm the electorate's commitment to further economic integration with the US. Opposition to Cafta and other related policies is still evident however. Successive Arena administrations have pursued conservative fiscal policies and under Saca this course looks set to continue. Economic growth was slow in 2004 and will remain so in 2005 and 2006. According to the latest IMF forecast, growth in both years will be 2 per cent.

Risk assessment

Politics	Good
Economy	Stable
Regional stability	Good

COUNTRY PROFILE

Historical profile

1821 The Central American provinces (Costa Rica, Guatemala, Honduras, Nicaragua and El Salvador) declared independence from Spain.
1822 Central American confederation annexed itself to the Mexican Empire, under General Agustín de Iturbde, later Emporer Agustín I.
1823 Agustín I was overthrown and Mexico became a republic. The Central American states formed the United Provinces of Central America.
1825 Costa Rica, Guatemala, Honduras, Nicaragua and El Salvador formed the Central American Federation (CAF).
1838 The CAF was dissolved and El Salvador became an independent republic. By the twentieth century, the majority of the population was reduced to poverty and discontent, having been pushed off their land, and the land turned over to

KEY INDICATORS — El Salvador

	Unit	2000	2001	2002	2003	2004
Population	m	6.28	6.38	6.59	6.65	6.70
Gross domestic product (GDP)	US$bn	13.20	13.90	14.40	14.85	*15.82
GDP per capita	US$	2,127	2,223	2,181	2,234	2,335
GDP real growth	%	2.0	1.8	2.3	1.8	1.5
Inflation	%	2.3	–	1.9	2.1	4.5
Unemployment	%	6.6	7.5	10.0	6.8	6.3
Exports (fob) (goods)	US$m	2,971.6	1,249.0	1,300.0	1,357.0	3,329.6
Imports (fob) (goods)	US$m	4,690.2	3,866.0	4,050.0	3,926.0	5,948.8
Balance of trade	US$m	-1,718.7	-2,160.0	-2,700.0	-2,569.0	-2,619.1
Current account	US$m	-417.7	-211.0	-450.0	–	-700.0
Total reserves minus gold	US$m	1,922.4	1,741.0	1,622.8	1,942.9	1,927.2
Foreign exchange	US$m	1,889.8	1,709.6	1,588.8	1,905.8	1,888.4
Exchange rate	per US$	8.72	8.74	8.75	8.75	8.75

* estimated figure

crops for export. Most of El Salvador's income came from coffee exports.
1929 Coffee prices plummeted following the US stock market crash.
1932 Uprising of peasants and Indians. The military killed 30,000 people in *La Matanza* (the massacre).
1961 The right-wing Partido de Conciliación Nacional (PCN) (National Reconciliation Party) came to power following a military coup.
1969 Honduras and El Salvador fought what became known as the 'soccer war', which was prompted by land disputes and El Salvador's win in the World Cup play-offs between the two countries. Over 3,000 people died.
1970s There were demonstrations, civil disobedience and strikes. The *esquadrones de muerte* (death squads) were formed. Thousands of Salvadoreans were kidnapped, tortured and murdered.
1977 General Carlos Romero was elected president.
1979 Romero was ousted by reformist military officers, although this failed to stem the number of deaths at the hands of military-backed death squads.
1980 Napoleón Duarte became El Salvador's first civilian president since 1931.
1980s Civil war between the US-backed right-wing government and a leftist guerrilla group, Frente Farabundo Martí para la Liberación Nacional (FMLN) (Front for National Liberation), based largely in the countryside. Right-wing groups carried out indiscriminate street killings of 'subversives'. Some rural communities were targetted by the security forces for eradication.
1982 The far-right Alianza Republicana Nacionalista (Arena) (Nationalist Republican Alliance) came to power following violent parliamentary elections.
1984 Duarte won the presidential election and began to negotiate a settlement with the FMLN.
1989 Arena's Alfredo Cristiani was elected president.
1992 A formal cease-fire, under UN auspices, came into effect. An estimated 75,000 people had been killed in the 12-year war.
1994 Political killings and threats continued right up to the elections. Arena's Armando Calderón Sol was elected president.
1997 Arena won the Assembly elections.
1999 Francisco Flores (Arena) won the presidential election.
2000 The FMLN become the largest party in the National Assembly. Arena formed a coalition government with the PCN, giving the right-wing block a majority in the Assembly.
2001 El Salvador adopted the US dollar as its currency. The worst earthquakes for more than a decade resulted in almost 1,500 people dying and 1.5 million being made homeless.
2002 The government declared a state of emergency in response to an outbreak of dengue fever.
2003 In March parliamentary elections, Arena's number of seats fell by two and the PCN's increased by two, while the FMLN had no net gains, although it remained the largest party. A free trade agreement (FTA) with Panama came into effect in April.
2004 On March 21, Antonio Saca (Arena) won the country's presidential elections. In August 2004 the government of El Salvador along with that of the Dominican Republic, Costa Rica, Guatemala, Honduras and Nicaragua agreed to a proposed Central American Free Trade Agreement (Cafta) with the US.
2005 In March the OAS human rights court voted to re-open an investigation into the El Mozote massacre in 1981. Thousands of people fled the area surrounding the Ilamatepec volcano in October after it erupted. Just days later a tropical storm damaged the area and caused many deaths.

Political structure
In addition to their unicameral national parliaments, El Salvador, Guatemala, Honduras, Nicaragua, Panama and Dominican Republic, which acceded to the Central American Parliament in February 2004, also return directly elected deputies to the supranational Central American Parliament.

Constitution
The constitution came into effect in December 1983. It delineated the three arms of government – legislative, executive and judicial – granting them official autonomy. Executive power is held by the president who serves a non-renewable five-year term of office. Legislative power, formed of members elected on three-year terms is held by the unicameral National Assembly – which also holds the power to appoint a president if no candidate gains an absolute majority in the elections. In 1991 constitutional reforms strengthened the judicial and electoral systems. There are 14 *departamentos* (administrative divisions) which each have a governor and an elected local council headed by a mayor.

Form of state
Presidential democratic republic

The executive
Executive power is vested in the president (who is elected every five years in March), assisted by the vice president and council of ministers. A second round of elections must be held within 30 days of the declaration of the result of the first round if no candidate secures an absolute majority (51 per cent) at the first attempt. The presidential term begins on 1 June. The president is both the head of state and head of government.

National legislature
Legislative power is held by the unicameral Asamblea Legislativa (Legislative Assembly), which has 84 members elected for three years by proportional representation; 20 deputies serve in the Central American Parliament Parlacen. The term of office begins on 1 May.

Legal system
Since 1993, El Salvador has undergone a full-scale review of its judicial structure. In order to achieve a basic level of judicial independence, judicial appointments are the responsibility of the Legislative Assembly, and funding for the courts has been ensured. In 1996, El Salvador began a programme of judicial training, the renovation and expansion of efforts to educate juvenile offenders, and projects to strengthen administration and planning. The process of reform is continuing and is more autonomous and professional than at any time in El Salvador's history.

Last elections
21 March 2004 (presidential); March 2003 (parliamentary).
Results: Presidential: Antonio Saca (Arena) won 57.7 per cent of the vote against 35.6 per cent for Schafik Hándal (FMLN); Héctor Silva (CDU) 3.9 per cent. Parliamentary: the Frente Farabundo Martí para la Liberación Nacional (FMLN) (Front for National Liberation) 34 per cent of the vote, 31 seats; Arena 32 per cent, 27 seats; PCN 13 per cent, 16 seats; Partido Demócrata Cristiano (PDC) (Christian Democratic Party) 7.3 per cent, five seats; Centro Democratico Unido (CDU) (United Democratic Centre) 6.4 per cent, five seats.

Next elections
2009 (presidential)

Political parties
Ruling party
Coalition government: Alianza Republicana Nacionalista (Arena) (Nationalist Republican Alliance) and Partido de Conciliación Nacional (PCN) (National Conciliation Party) (elected Mar 2003)

Main opposition party
Frente Farabundo Martí para la Liberación Nacional (FMLN) (Farabundo Martí Front for National Liberation)

Population
6.70 million (2004)
Ethnic make-up
Approximately 94 per cent of the population are *mestizo*, 5 per cent Amerindian and 1 per cent white.

El Salvador

Religions
Predominantly Roman Catholic (75 per cent); most of the remaining 25 per cent belong to a number of Protestant churches.

Education
Low levels of literacy and educational skills are regarded by the government as a major impediment to foreign investment.
Literacy rate: 79.7 per cent, total; 77.1 per cent, female; adult rates in 2002 (World Bank).
Enrolment rate: 112 per cent gross primary enrolment of relevant age group, including repeaters; 56 per cent gross secondary enrolment; 17 per cent gross tertiary enrolment (World Bank).
Pupils per teacher: 33 in primary schools

Health
Total expenditure on health is about 9 per cent of GDP, of which 43 per cent is government spending.
Approximately 55 per cent of the population has access to safe water.
HIV prevalence: 0.7 per cent aged 15–49 in 2003 (World Bank)
Life expectancy: 70.4 years (World Bank)
Fertility rate/Maternal mortality rate: 2.8 births per woman (2003): maternal mortality 1.2 per 1,000 live births (World Bank).
Infant mortality rate: 32 per 1,000 live births; 11 per cent of children aged under five are malnourished (World Bank).
Head of population per physician/bed: 1.0 doctor per 1,000 people

Welfare
The state also operates a welfare system for benefits covering sickness, maternity and work injury. These are based on contributions by the employer and worker and subsidised by the state, but exclude casual workers and those involved in domestic work. Agricultural workers are denied sickness and maternity pay and teachers are excluded from work injury benefits.
Pensions
Old-age pensions are available to men aged over 60 and women over 55 with 25 years of contributions.

Main cities
San Salvador (capital, estimated population 504,700 in 2003), Soyapango (369,400), Santa Ana (167,200), Mejicanos (165,100), San Miguel (145,100).

Languages spoken
Nahua is spoken by some Amerindians. English is widely spoken in business circles.
Official language/s
Spanish

Media
Press
Dailies: In San Salvador there are six daily newspapers: *Diario Oficial*, *El Diario de Hoy* and *La Prensa Gráfica* (ultra-conservative), *Diario Latino* (El Salvador's most objective newspaper), *El Mundo* and *La Noticia*. *Diario de Oriente* is published in San Miguel and *Diario de Occidente* in Santa Ana.
Broadcasting
Radio: There are over 80 commercial radio stations in El Salvador, six commercially run television stations and two state run channels.
Television: There are approximately 11 television broadcast stations.
Advertising
Available in the press, cinemas, commercial TV and radio stations, periodicals and posters.

Economy
The economy has been experiencing slow growth throughout the 2000s and real GDP growth dropped below 2 per cent during 2003 and 2004. The IMF predicts modest growth for El Salvador again in 2005 and 2006 at 2 per cent year on year.
Unlike other Latin American countries, El Salvador's problem of economic dependence has been less a question of neglect and mismanagement of its assets by foreigners than one of battling unpredictable cycles of export commodities. For much of the post-colonial period, the economy remained relatively stagnant due to its lack of mineral wealth and the failure to break through the barriers of European protectionism to market its agricultural goods. Coffee exports have dominated the economic life of El Salvador since the second half of the nineteenth century. The joining of Cafta by El Salvador should spur growth by increasing investor interest and diversifying the economy further. It is hoped that long term results of joining the trade agreement will be an increase in income and reduction of poverty.
El Salvador has a poor economy, suffering from a weak tax collection system, factory closures, social inequality and falling world coffee prices. Current problems of dependency on the export of coffee and the marginal position of poor farmers continue to this day and remain a stumbling block in the development of El Salvador.
High levels of unemployment and underemployment still persist and remain a government priority. Although official unemployment was 6.3 per cent in 2004, underemployment was over 30 per cent. The country's ability to earn foreign exchange is hampered by its comparative disadvantage in terms of productivity due to low levels of capital. World prices for its main agro-export, coffee, have plummeted and it is doubtful whether government measures to boost productive capacity and protect farmers will have any effect.
Around a half of the population lives in poverty, indicating that the rise in the export sector is not leading to substantial benefits for the country's burgeoning poor. Few benefits are feeding through to the agricultural sector, which employs a third of the workforce, but contributes just 12 per cent to the nation's GDP. The government's emphasis on the development of the export-processing sector through the creation of a favourable investment climate and free zones is likely to attract more peasants into shanty towns which skirt the country's overcrowded urban areas, while failing to soak up surplus labour.
Remittances from Salvadoreans living abroad are the lifeblood of many Salvadoran families and represent one of the main pillars of the economy, helping to ease the country's balance of payments problems; annual transfers total US$2.5 billion, 16 per cent of GDP in 2004.

External trade
There has been an increase in non-traditional exports such as shrimps, sesame seeds, nuts, fruits and honey.
El Salvador, Guatemala, Costa Rica, Honduras, Nicaragua, Columbia and Venezuela have signed a free trade agreement to be completed in four stages; the last, creating a free market among the seven countries.
By August 2004, Dominican Republic, Costa Rica, El Salvador, Guatemala, Honduras and Nicaragua had agreed to a proposed Central American Free Trade Agreement (Cafta) with the US.
Imports
Principal imports include raw materials, consumer goods, capital goods, fuels, foodstuffs, petroleum and electricity. Machinery, raw material, work equipment and intermediate goods can be imported tax free.
Main sources: US (37.3 per cent total, 2004), Guatemala (9 per cent), Mexico (6.1 per cent)
Exports
Principal exports include offshore assembly exports, coffee, sugar, shrimp, textiles, handcrafts, chemicals and electricity.
Main destinations: US (57.9 per cent total, 2004), Guatemala (13.6 per cent), Honduras (7 per cent)

Agriculture
Farming
The agricultural sector of El Salvador's economy employs approximately a third of the country's total workforce. The sector

contributes about 12 per cent to total GDP. Approximately 34 per cent of total land is arable; 30 per cent permanent pastures.

Coffee is the most important crop. Other major crops are cotton, sugar cane, maize, beans and rice. There has been some diversification within the sector, with non-traditional exports such as sesame seeds, nuts, vegetables, fruits, honey and, above all, shrimps, taking an increasing share.

Crop production in 2004 included: 822,195t tonnes cereals in total, 5,280,400t sugar cane, 648,045t maize, 65,000t bananas, 75,709t plantains, 26,519t rice, 18,136t cassava, 13,000t potatoes, 147,631t sorghum, 10,814t chillies & peppers, 17,075t oilcrops, 25,416t tomatoes, 98,600t citrus fruit, 78,510t green coffee, 84,300t pulses, 83,686t roots and tubers, 284,948t fruit in total, 141,907t vegetables in total. Livestock production included: 126,580t meat in total, 26,500t beef, 7,850t pig meat, 92,111t poultry, 63,649t eggs, 412,602t milk, 2,362t honey, 6,665t cattle hides.

Fishing
The Gulf of Fonseca is regarded as one of Central America's greatest natural resources with rich fisheries and diverse marine life, which is shared by Honduras, Nicaragua and El Salvador. Typically, the annual catch is over 18,000mt per year.

Forestry
The forestry industry in El Salvador is relatively small. In a typical year forest material exports total approximately US$12 million. Imports of forest materials typically equate to US$160.2 million. Production in 2003 included 4,829,082 cubic metres (cum) roundwood, 682,000cum industrial roundwood, 68,000cum sawnwood, 682,000cum sawlogs & veneer logs, 4,147,082cum wood fuel, 19,622t charcoal.

Industry and manufacturing
Contributing approximately 28 per cent to total GDP and employing around a fifth of the total workforce, the industrial sector is a significant part of El Salvador's economy.

The national government has made efforts to shift the industrial sector towards manufacturing for export through the development of the *maquila* (in-bond manufacturing) sector and the creation of free zones. *Maquila* exports have accounted for the bulk of growth in the export sector since 1992. Investment incentives in the free zones include a 10-year income tax exemption, import duty exemptions or reduced exposure to taxes on equity or assets for 10 years.

Tourism
Tourism has traditionally played an insignificant role in El Salvador's economy. However, the travel and tourism sector is continuing to expand and now accounts for 7.8 per cent of total GDP, up from 2 per cent in 2000. The industry employs 6.8 per cent of the total labour force.

Mining
Mining has been a stable sector of the El Salvadorian economy for several years. Gold, silver, sea salt and limestone are mined or quarried and there are deposits of copper, iron ore, sulphur, mercury, lead, zinc and perlite. There are two gold mines, one at San Cristobal and the other near San Salvador which also mines silver. However, the mining sector is small and underdeveloped, contributing only 0.1 per cent to GDP. There are two cement works, the 240,000 tonnes per year (tpy) Cemento Mayan at Canton Tecomapa and the 684,000tpy Cemento de El Salvador at El Ronco.

Hydrocarbons
El Salvador has no proven reserves of oil, gas or coal. The country is totally reliant on imported petroleum products. Mexico and Venezuela are El Salvador's main suppliers; both nations offer preferential rates on their oil exports under the terms of the San José Pact.

Guatemala and Mexico signed a deal to create a 347mile, US$450 million, natural gas pipeline. There is a 17,000 barrel per day oil refinery operating at Acajutla.

Energy
El Salvador is the largest producer of hydroelectricity in Central America. Electric energy is produced by four hydroelectric installations (Guajoyo, Cerrán Grande, 5 de Novembre and 15 de Septembre) and one geothermal plant (Ahuachapan in the west of the country, with generating capacity of 95MW). Total installed capacity is about 650MW.

Financial markets
Stock exchange
The Bolsa de El Salvador was founded in 1964 and is situated in San Salvador.

Banking and insurance
The banking system of El Salvador remained under state ownership until 1991. Thereafter the government implemented market reforms that handed control to private investors. Interest rates are determined by the market.
Central bank
Banco Central de Reserva de El Salvador

Time
GMT minus six hours

Geography
El Salvador lies on the Pacific coast of Central America. Guatemala is to the west and Honduras to the north and east. The basins in the centre of the country rise to little more than 600 metres at San Salvador. Across this upland and surmounting it, run two more or less parallel rows of volcanoes, 14 of which are over 900 metres. Lowlands lie to the north and south of the high backbone. The ash and lava from the volcanoes have produced an ideal soil in which to grow coffee.

Climate
The climate is semi-tropical. The dry season is from November–April; temperature range 15–23 degrees Celsius (C); rainy season May–October; average temperature 28 degrees C. Generally, the temperature depends on the altitude; coastal areas are hotter and more humid than upland areas.

The driest month is February with just 5mm average rainfall. The wettest month is June with 328mm. The coldest month is December when the average daily temperature varies between 16 and 32 degrees C. In May, the hottest month, the variation is only slightly different, ranging between 19 and 33 degrees C.

Dress codes
Light cotton suits and ties are the generally accepted form of dress for businessmen, although some Salvadoreans will dress less formally in guyaberas (styled cotton shirts worn outside the trousers), particularly in the warmest months. Businesswomen should wear a light suit or equivalent. Dress as for business if invited to a social occasion unless suggested otherwise.

A sweater or light jacket will be required for evenings and for the highlands.

Entry requirements
Passports
Required by all. Passports must be valid for six months.
Visa
Required by all, except citizens of most Central American, EU and some Asian countries, (US nationals need a tourist card, issued by airlines or embassies) for a full list visit www.elsalvador.org or contact the local embassy. Business visas require further information: a letter of invitation from a El Salvadorian company, proof of financial solvency for the visitor and bank and commercial references for the foreign company being represented.
Currency advice/regulations
The US dollar was adopted from 1 January 2001.

Incoming tourists may import an unlimited amount of traveller's cheques, US dollars and Guatemala quetzals. Salvadoran

El Salvador

colónes can be exchanged for US dollars when leaving and any amount may be exchanged at the current exchange rate, at any bank branch office. US dollars are accepted almost everywhere.

Prohibited imports
Fruit, vegetables, plants and animals. It is illegal to import pornography into El Salvador, including *Playboy*.

Health (for visitors)
Mandatory precautions
A yellow fever vaccination certificate is required if arriving from an infected area.

Advisable precautions
Typhoid, polio, hepatitis 'A' and tetanus vaccinations. Dengue fever cases have risen, visitors should avoid exposing their skin during early morning and evening when the risk of being bitten by mosquitoes is highest. Malaria is not a virulent strain but prophylaxis should be taken as there is some risk in the Santa Anna province and rural locations. There is a high rabies risk. Water precautions are essential and only well-cooked food should be eaten. Milk is unpasteurised and should be boiled.

Hotels
The best hotels can be found in the capital. A 10 per cent tip is usual.

Public holidays
Fixed dates
1 Jan (New Year's Day), 1 May (Labour Day), 4 Aug (Transfiguration Bank Boliday), 5–6 Aug (San Salvador Festival (San Salvador only)), 15 Sep (Independence Day), 12 Oct (Columbus Day), 2 Nov (All Souls' Day), 24 Dec (Christmas Eve), 25 Dec (Christmas Day), 31 Dec (New Year's Eve).

Variable dates
Holy Wednesday, Maundy Thursday, Good Friday.

Working hours
Banking
Mon–Fri: 0900–1700. Sat: 0900–1300.
Business
Mon–Fri: 0900–1800.
Government
Mon–Fri: 0800–1730.
Shops
Mon–Sat: 0900–1200, 1400–1800. Supermarkets Mon–Sat: 0800–2200. The main shopping centres are open on Sunday.

Electricity supply
110V AC, 60Hz

Social customs/useful tips
Appointments should be made in advance. Salvadorans have a distinctly Latin sense of time and can be among the least punctual people in Central America, although many businessmen and bankers, particularly those with export experience, keep *horas inglesas* (punctual time). Business relationships and meetings tend to be formal in early stages. Use proper titles such as Licenciado (college graduate), Ingeniero (engineering graduate) and Doctor (physicians and lawyers), followed by the person's surname. Handshaking before and after meetings is important. First names should not be used until a business relationship has been consolidated. Upon introduction it is important to exchange cards; a supply of Spanish-printed cards is advisable.

Business is conducted in Spanish although some executives speak English. Some knowledge of spoken Spanish is much better than none.

Meetings over meals, including breakfast, are becoming common. Working lunches and dinners can be lengthy. Gratuities in restaurants and hotels are around 10 per cent.

Security
El Salvador has a poor personal security environment, with a homicide rate twice that of Los Angeles. Kidnappings, carjackings, and robbery are common and can occur anywhere. There is a risk of murder for those robbed, even if they do not resist. Downtown San Salvador should be avoided at all times, as should roads outside the city after dark. Reports indicate the border with Guatemala has been a site for attacks on vehicles. Jewellery or large amounts of cash should not be carried.

Business travellers should arrange to be met at the airport and be accompanied by a local representative, as this has been shown to reduce problems.

Getting there
Air
National airline: GRUPOTACA is the national airline (privately owned) and has the most extensive network in the region and is widely regarded as the most efficient Central American carrier.

International airport/s: San Salvador-El Salvador International (SAL), 35km south of San Salvador; car hire, restaurant, duty-free shops.

The airport and the highway that runs to it, are the most modern and developed in the region. It is expanding its services in order to become an international cargo warehousing and distribution centre.

Airport tax: International departure tax of US$24.65; not applicable to six-hour transit passengers.

Surface
Road: Roads run from Guatemala and Honduras. Duty is paid at the border when entering or leaving the country by land. It is advisable to carry small denomination notes to pay the border duties.

Rail: Lines run through El Salvador from Guatemala to Honduras.

Main port/s: Acajutla, La Unión/Cutuco, La Libertad (fishing only). Major ports on the Pacific are Puerto Barrios and Santo Tomás de Castilla.

Getting about
National transport
Air: Scheduled internal services from San Salvador to San Miguel, La Unión and Usulután. Charter flights are available.

Road: There is a network of 9,800km of paved roads. The Pan-American Highway (over 300km) runs through the country linking San Salvador with Santa Ana in the west and San Miguel in the east; Carretera Litoral runs south of the Pan-American Highway linking the capital with Sonsonate, Zacatecoluca and Usulatan. Many roads have fallen into considerable disrepair as a result of the war and cuts in government spending.

Buses: The bus system is excellent, with services between major towns. The buses are often crowded but do run frequently.

Rail: There are 602km of railway, including 429km of line from Guatemala to Honduras. A narrow gauge line links the western town of Ahuachpan and the port of Acajutia with San Salvador, which is in turn connected to La Union in the east. The railway is used largely for freight traffic.

City transport
The San Salvador roads project, completed in 1999, reduced a cross-town trip from north to south from over an hour to a few minutes.

Taxis: Taxis are bright yellow. The regular taxi line is Taxi Acacya. Taxis can be hailed or ordered by telephone. The fixed rate system is not rigidly followed – check before proceeding. No taxis have meters. Tipping is unusual but 10 per cent of fare is appreciated. Taxi from airport to city centre journey time is 25 minutes.

Car hire
A national or international permit valid for 30 days is required. Traffic drives on the right.

BUSINESS DIRECTORY
The addresses listed below are a selection only. While World of Information makes every endeavour to check these addresses, we cannot guarantee that changes have not been made, especially to telephone numbers and area codes. We would welcome any corrections.

Telephone area codes
Dialling code for El Salvador: IDD access code +503 followed by subscriber's number.

Useful telephone numbers
Emergency: 121

Information:	114
International enquiries/ calls (operator):	119, 120
For collect calls (US only):	190
Migration Office:	222-7328
Foreign Office:	222-6611

Chambers of Commerce
American Chamber of Commerce of El Salvador, Paseo General Escalón 5432, San Salvador (tel: 264-7609; fax: 263-3237; e-mail: contact@amchamsal.com).

El Salvador Cámara de Comercio e Industria, 9a Avenida Norte y 5a Calle Poniente, PO Box 1640, 1118 San Salvador (tel: 244-2000; fax: 271-4461; e-mail: camara@camarasal.com).

Banking
Ahorromet Scotiabank, Avenida Olímpica 129, Edificio Torre Ahorromet Scotiabank, San Salvador (tel: 245-1211; fax: 245-2884).

BANCASA (Banco de Construcción y Ahorro), 75 Avenida Sur 709, Colonia Escalon, San Salvador (tel: 263-5508; fax: 263-5506).

Banco Agrícola Comercial, Paseo General Escalón 3635, Colonia Escalón, San Salvador (tel: 224-0283; fax: 224-3948).

Banco de Comercio de El Salvador, 25 Avenida Norte y 23 Calle Poniente, San Salvador (tel: 226-4577; fax: 225-7767; e-mail: webmaster@banco.com.sv).

Banco Creditomatic, 55 Avenida Sur y Alameda Roosevelt, Centro Roosevelt, San Salvador (tel: 298-1855; fax: 224-4138).

Banco Cuscatlan, Km 10 Carretera a Santa Tecla, Edificio Pirámide Cuscatlán La Libertad (tel: 228-7777; fax: 228-9999).

Banco Hipotecario, Pje. Senda Florida Sur, Paseo General Escalón, San Salvador (tel: 223-3753; fax: 298-0447).

Banco Salvadoreño, Alameda Dr Manuel Enrique Araujo 3550, San Salvador (tel: 298-4444; fax 298-0102).

Grupo Capital, Alameda Dr Manuel Enrique Araujo, Edificio Century Plaza, San Salvador (tel: 245-6000; fax: 224-3303).

Unibanco, Alameda Roosevelt 2511, San Salvador (tel: 245-0651; fax: 298-5261).

Central bank
Banco Central de Reserva, Alameda Juan Pablo, entre 15 y 17 Avenida Norte, PO Box 106, San Salvador (tel: 281-8000; fax: 281-8013; e-mail: comunicaciones@bcr.gob.sv).

Travel information
Corporación Salvadoreña de Turismo (CORSATUR), Boulevard del Hipódromo 508, San Benito, San Salvador (tel: 243-7835; fax: 243-0427).

TACA International Airlines, Edificio Caribe, San Salvador (tel: 298-5055; fax:279-4345).

National tourist organisation offices
Instituto Salvadoreño de Turismo (ISTU) (El Salvador Tourist Board), Calle Rubén Darío 619, San Salvador (tel: 228-000, 222-8699, 222-8144, 222-9366; fax: 221-208).

Ministries
Ministry of Agriculture and Livestock, Final 1a Avenida Norte 13 Calle Oriente y Avenida Manuel Gallardo 704, San Salvador (tel: 279-1579; fax: 224-2944).

Ministry of Defence, Alameda Manuel Enrique Araujo, Carretera a Santa Tecla, San Salvador (tel: 223-0233; fax: 298-2005).

Ministry of Economy, Alameda Juan Pablo II Calle Guadalupe, Centro de Gobierno, San Salvador (tel: 281-7134; fax: 221-2797).

Ministry of Education, Alameda Juan Pablo II Calle Guadalupe, Centro de Gobierno, San Salvador (tel: 281-0256; fax: 281-0257).

Ministry of Environment, Alameda Roosevelt y 55 Avenida Norte, Torre El Salvador, San Salvador (tel: 260-8876; fax: 260-3092).

Ministry of Finance, Edificio Las Tres Torres, Avenida Alvarado, San Salvador (tel: 225-6500; fax: 225-7491).

Ministry of Foreign Affairs, Alameda Manuel Enrique Araujo 5500, San Salvador (tel: 243-3805; fax: 243-3710).

Ministry of Health, Calle Arce 827, San Salvador (tel: 271-0008; fax: 221-0985).

Ministry of Interior, Centro de Gobierno, San Salvador (tel: 221-8582; fax: 281-5959).

Ministry of Justice and Public Security, 6a Calle Oriente 42, Antiguo Local Policia Nacional, San Salvador (tel: 271-2655; fax: 245-2650).

Ministry of Labour, Paseo General Escalón 4122, San Salvador (tel: 263-5423; fax: 263-5272).

Ministry of Public Works, 1a Avenida Sur 603, San Salvador (tel: 293-6603; fax: 271-0163).

Other useful addresses
Asociación Nacional de la Empresa Privada (ANEP), 1a Calle Poniente y 71a Avenida Norte 204, Colonia Escalón, San Salvador (tel: 224-1236; fax: 223-8932; e-mail: anep@telesal.net).

Asociación Salvadoreña de Industriales (ASI), Calles Roma y Liverpool, Colonia Roma, San Salvador (tel: 279-2488; fax: 279-2070; e-mail: unatias@sv.cciglobal.net).

Bolsa de Valores de El Salvador, Alameda Roosevelt 3107, Edificio La Centroamericana, San Salvador (tel: 298-4244; fax: 223-2898; e-mail: webmaster@bves.com.sv).

British Embassy, Paseo General Escalón 4828, Edificio Inter-Inversiones, San Salvador (tel: 263-6527; fax: 263-6516; e-mail: britemb@sal.gbm.net).

Corporación de Exportadores de El Salvador (COEXPORT), Condominios del Mediterráneo A-23, Colonia Jardínes de Guadalupe, San Salvador (tel: 243-3110; fax: 243-3159; e-mail: service@coexport.com).

El Salvador Embassy (USA), 2308 California Street, NW, Washington DC 20008 (tel: 202-2265-9671; fax: 202-234-3834; e-mail: correo@elsalvador.org).

Fundación Salvadoreña para el Desarrollo Económica y Social (FUSADES), Urbanización y Boulevard Santa Elena, Edificio FUSADES, Antiguo Cuscatlán, La Libertad (tel: 278-3366; fax: 278-3369; e-mail: fusades@fusades.com.sv).

Superintendencia del Sistema Financiero, 7a Avenida Norte 240, San Salvador (tel: 281-24444).

Unión de Dirigentes de Empresas Salvadoreñas (UDES), Condominios del Mediterráneo C-22, Colonia Jardines de Guadalupe, San Salvador (tel: 243-2746; fax: 243-3145).

US Embassy, Boulevard Santa Elena Final, Antiguo Cuscatlán, La Libertad (tel: 278-4444; fax: 278-6011).

Internet sites
Bolsa de El Salvador (Stock Exchange) (Spanish): http://www.bolsavalores.com.sv/

El Salvador trade and investment: http://www.elsalvadortrade.com.sv/

Fundación Salvadoreña para el Desarrollo Económico e Social (Salvadorean Foundation for Social and Economic Development) (Spanish): http://www.fusades.com.sv/

Equatorial Guinea

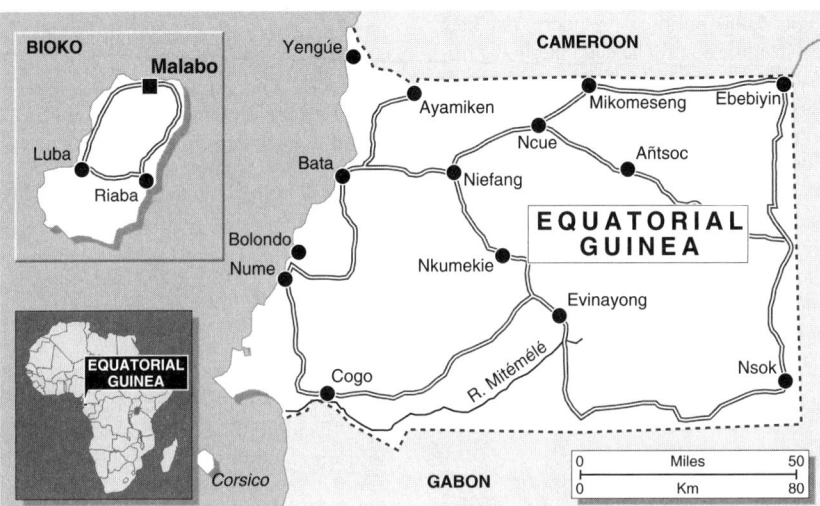

Oil revenues have pushed growth rates over the last five years in Equatorial Guinea from 16.9 per cent to 46.5 per cent. Since 1995, average annual growth has been 31 per cent – the world's fastest growing economy.

Oil and gas deposits were discovered off the island of Bioko, which also houses the capital Malabo, in the mid-1990s. Their exploitation will dominate economic development and continue to be the engine of growth in the foreseeable future, although revenues are now set to level out. Output in 2004 was 383,000 barrels per day; estimates for 2005 were for a four per cent increase, real economic growth was 34.2 per cent, 2005 expected 4.8 per cent.

The currency has appreciated 32 per cent in real terms since 2000, totally undermining any external competitiveness. Broad money has increased by 45 per cent owing to large foreign exchange inflows of government oil revenue and transfers from oil companies that contributed to the buildup of net foreign assets. Government spending failed to sterilise these inflows. Excess liquidity in the banking system rose without any significant impact on domestic prices because of limited lending opportunities.

There are persistent overruns in capital expenditure because of weak budgetary discipline, but usually stronger-than-expected revenues take care of it: in 2005 over 2003 the balance of payments surplus more than doubled.

Social imbalances

Unfortunately, the oil and gas wealth has not led to a measurable improvement in living conditions for the majority of the population. Forestry, farming and fishing are components of gross domestic product, where subsistence farming predominates. Pre-independence Equatorial Guinea counted on cocoa production for hard currency earnings, but the neglect of the rural economy has diminished potential for agriculture-led growth.

Equatorial Guinea is now better positioned to target these and other sectors while safeguarding macroeconomic stability, and to address the large social and development needs of its population. Undeveloped natural resources include titanium, iron ore, manganese, uranium, and alluvial gold. There are considerable inflows of foreign direct investment (FDI) but it is all into the hydrocarbon sector.

No more foreign aid

A number of aid programmes sponsored by the World Bank and the International Monetary Fund (IMF) have been cut off since 1993 because of corruption and mismanagement. Businesses in Equatorial

KEY FACTS

Official name: República de Guinea Ecuatorial (Republic of Equatorial Guinea)

Head of State: President Teodoro Obiang Nguema Mbasogo (PDGE) (since 1989; re-elected 1996 and Dec 2002)

Head of government: Prime Minister Miguel Abia Biteo Borico (named by the President on 11 Jun 2004)

Ruling party: Partido Democrático de Guinea Ecuatorial (PDGE) (Democratic Party of Equatorial Guinea) (re-elected 25 Apr 2004)

Area: 28,051 square km

Population: 486,800 (2004)

Capital: Malabo

Official language: Spanish and French

Currency: CFA franc (CFAf) = 100 centimes (Communauté Financière Africaine (African Financial Community) franc)

Exchange rate: CFAf544.07 per US$ (Oct 2005); CFAf655.95 per euro (pegged from Jan 1999)

GDP per capita: US$4,120 (2004)

GDP real growth: 34.20% (2004)

Labour force: 2.90 million (2004)

Inflation: 8.00% (2004)

Oil production: 350,000 bpd (2004)

Balance of trade: US$1.60 billion (2004)

Guinea are, for the most part, owned by government officials and their family members. The corruption watchdog Transparency International has Equatorial Guinea in the top 10 of its list of corrupt states.

No longer eligible for concessional financing because of large oil revenues, the government has now asked the IMF to put in place a 'shadow' poverty reduction programme. It has had to publicly recognise that the objectives of poverty reduction under its last National Development Plan (1997–2001) were not achieved.

The IMF has come up with what is very much a standard answer in such a situation: manage the oil money. Make oil revenues sustainable over a longer term, use the surplus money to fund sustainable secondary development that will create jobs and reduce poverty, budget conservatively, target spending. There was concern that over 2004 alone, a substantial increase in public spending had more than offset improved revenues. The World Bank has been asked to undertake a review of public expenditure in Equatorial Guinea. The government budgeted for growth in imports over 2005 to be seven per cent – in 2004 it was 103 per cent – and to reduce domestic spending by 32 per cent.

The government will now prepare an interim poverty reduction strategy paper that could serve as a roadmap and facilitate support from the country's development partners.

Politics

President Obiang Nguema came to power by overthrowing his uncle Macias Nguema in 1979. The two have been described by a variety of human rights organisations as among the worst abusers of human rights in Africa. The country became notorious when the widespread human rights abuses of Macias Nguema caused a third of the population to flee.

Obiang had his uncle tried and then executed him. The new president proclaimed an amnesty for refugees and released some 5,000 political prisoners, but kept the absolute control he had inherited. Officials said Nguema kept the presidency in the 2002 elections by winning more than 97 per cent of the vote. Opposition candidates had withdrawn from the poll, citing fraud and irregularities. Nguema was born in 1942 in mainland Equatorial Guinea. He received his military training in Spain and, after independence, served under his uncle-president, first as military governor of Bioko and then as presidential aide-de-camp.

A government-in-exile has been formed by opposition leaders living in Spain.

Risk assessment

Economic	Good
Political	Poor
Regional stability	Average

COUNTRY PROFILE

Historical profile

A former Spanish colony with a murky history of slavery and oppression, Equatorial Guinea was too small to make headline news until the 1990s when the discovery of oil turned it into the 'Kuwait of Africa'. However, as is the case with many 'oil-rich' countries, unless the oil revenues impact upon the still impoverished population of Equatorial Guinea, social problems will continue.

1470 The island of Anobon was first visited by the Portuguese, who subsequently settled it and the other islands in the Gulf of Guinea, including Bioko.
1477 Portugal ceded Bioko to Spain. Bioko became an important slave-trading base for several European nations up to the nineteenth century.
1844 Spanish began settling the mainland region of Río Muni.
1904 Río Muni and Bioko became the West African Territories, later named Spanish Guinea.
1968 Spanish Guinea was granted independence from Spain and renamed Equatorial Guinea. Macias Nguema became president.
1972 Nguema's presidency had degenerated into a tyranny as democratic institutions and practices were dismissed. The regime used terror to maintain power and up to one third of the population fled the country as the economy collapsed.
1979 Teodoro Obiang Nguema Mbasogo (the president's nephew) seized power in a *coup d'état*. Nguema was executed. Even though a ruling Supreme Military Council was established Obiang retained all effective power.
1984 and 1989 President Obiang was re-elected unopposed.
1993 The first multi-party elections were won by the president's Partido Democrático de Guinea Ecuatorial (PDGE) (Democratic Party of Equatorial Guinea); the main opposition parties boycotted the election.
1995 Zafiro, the country's largest oil field was discovered off Bioko Island.
1996 President Obiang won the presidential elections, which were described as 'a farce' by international observers.
1999 PDGE won 75 seats in the first fully contested parliamentary elections. Opposition parties alleged fraud and boycotted parliament.
2000 Equatorial Guinea and Nigeria signed a treaty agreeing to the demarcation of their maritime border.
2002 Opposition members accused the government of mass human rights abuse. President Obiang was re-elected.
2004 The ruling and allied parties won the 25 April parliamentary elections; foreign observers criticised both the poll and the results. Perpetrators of an alleged coup were arrested in Harare, Zimbabwe, when their plane landed for refueling. Nineteen mercenaries accused of the planned overthrow were convicted, including opposition leader, Severo Moto, who was sentenced to 63 years in prison
2005 In January, Sir Mark Thatcher, son of former UK prime minister, Margaret

KEY INDICATORS — Equatorial Guinea

	Unit	2000	2001	2002	2003	2004
Population	m	0.46	0.47	0.48	0.48	0.49
Gross domestic product (GDP)	US$bn	1.60	1.80	2.20	2.20	*3.23
GDP per capita	US$	3,478	3,448	4,104	2,700	4,120
GDP real growth	%	16.9	46.5	31.2	15.5	34.2
Inflation	%	6.0	12.0	12.0	6.0	8.0
Oil output	'000 bpd	113.0	181.0	237.0	249.0	350.0
Exports (fob) (goods)	US$m	767.0	927.0	2,500.0	2,500.0	2,771.0
Imports (fob) (goods)	US$m	170.0	148.0	600.0	562.0	1,167.0
Balance of trade	US$m	597.0	779.0	1,900.0	1,938.0	1,604.0
Current account	US$m	-300.0	-800.0	-1,220.0	-740.0	-650.0
Total reserves minus gold	US$m	23.0	70.8	88.5	237.7	945.0
Foreign exchange	US$m	22.9	69.9	87.9	237.7	944.3
Exchange rate	per US$	711.98	733.04	696.99	574.89	496.63

* estimated figure

Equatorial Guinea

Thatcher, was arrested in South Africa and pleaded guilty to financing the helicopter to be used in the 2004 attempted coup; he was fined US$500,000 and given a suspended gaol sentence. In December, Spain overturned the asylum status of opposition leader, Severo Moto, after receiving evidence he had been involved in a number of coup attempts.

Political structure
Constitution
A new constitution designed to usher in multi-party politics was adopted on 16 November 1991. It provided for the separation of powers between the president and prime minister and gave the president protection from impeachment, prosecution and *subpoena* before, during and after his term of office.

Form of state
Republic

The executive
The president is elected for a seven-year term by universal suffrage. The prime minister is appointed by the president.

National legislature
There is a 100-seat Cámara de Representantes del Pueblo (legislative assembly) elected for five years.

Legal system
Judges are appointed, transferred and dismissed for political reasons, even though the constitution provides for judicial independence. The judicial system does not appear to operate independently, thus undermining basic rights.

Last elections
25 Apr 2004 (parliamentary); December 2002 (presidential)

Results: Parliamentary: The ruling party, PDGE, and allied parties, won 98 seats out of 100. Foreign observers criticised both the poll and the results.
Presidential: President Teodoro Obiang Nguema Mbasogo (PDGE) was re-elected with 97.1 per cent of the vote against 2.2 per cent for Celestino Bonifacio Bacalé. Opposition parties withdrew their candidates about two hours after voting started, citing irregularities.

Next elections
2009 (presidential and parliamentary)

Political parties
Ruling party
Partido Democrático de Guinea Ecuatorial (PDGE) (Democratic Party of Equatorial Guinea) (re-elected 25 Apr 2004)

Main opposition party
Unión Popular (UP) (Popular Union); Convergencia para la Democracia Social (CPDS) (Convergence for a Social Democracy); Fuerza Democratiza Republicana (FDR) (Democratic Republican Front).

Population
486,800 (2004)

Ethnic make-up
The mainland region of Rio Muni is occupied by 75 per cent of the population, 90 per cent of whom belong to the Fang ethnic group. The island province of Bioko consists of Bubis, Fangs and Creoles.

Religions
Christianity (98 per cent, mostly Roman Catholic), traditional beliefs (2 per cent).

Education
Public expenditure on education typically amounted to 2.3 per cent of annual gross national income between 1994–1997 according to World Bank estimates.

Literacy rate: 83.2 per cent adult rate; 92.5 per cent male rate (Unesco).

Enrolment rate: 126 per cent gross primary enrolment of relevant age group (including repeaters); 115 per cent gross secondary enrolment.

Pupils per teacher: 41 in primary schools.

Health
The annual total expenditure on health is around 2 per cent of GDP, of which 60 per cent is government spending. Approximately 43 per cent of the total population is under 15 years. World Bank surveys show that 43 per cent of the population have access to improved water sources.

HIV/Aids
The government has failed in its commitments to eradicate the continuing epidemics of malaria and yellow fever, while allowing HIV prevalence to increase. There are an estimated 1,100 people living with HIV/Aids – most sufferers are over the age of 15.

Life expectancy: 52.2 years (World Bank)

Fertility rate/Maternal mortality rate: 5.4 births per woman (World Bank)

Infant mortality rate: 97 per 1,000 live births (World Bank)

Head of population per physician/bed: 0.2 doctor per 1,000 people.

Welfare
Welfare conditions in the country are virtually non-existent, with limited access to primary healthcare, education and job opportunities.
In 2003 the Government introduced a two-tier system that created a separate wage system for private sector workers inside and outside of the oil sector. The minimum monthly wage for all private sector workers was set at CFAf77,000 (approximately US$154), and an additional differential payment is made dependent on a worker's skills.
However the minimum wage law does not apply to public sector workers who are generally paid much less than their counterparts in the private sector.
Under-age youths perform both family farm work and street vending. The government does not enforce the legal minimum age for child employment.
Equatorial Guinea is also a destination and transit point for the trafficking in children (as unpaid workers) and women (for prostitution).
Human rights conditions in the country are considered, by Amnesty International, as 'alarming' as the security forces continue to harass civilians and political dissidents; imprisonment, torture and extrajudicial killings have been cited in all parts of the country.

Main cities
Malabo (capital, on island of Bioko, estimated population 92,900 in 2003), Bata (Rio Muni) (66,800).

Languages spoken
Fang, Bubi Ibo and Creole (pidgin English) are spoken.

Official language/s
Spanish and French

Media
Equatorial Guinea is a multi-party state with guaranteed freedom of the press. However, the government continues to use military courts, repressive laws and arbitrary arrests and prosecutions to restrict political freedom and civil rights. The rights to freedom of opinion, expression, sharing and publication of information are severely restricted, contrary to international standards.

Press
The Convergencia para la Democracia Social (CPDS) (Convergence for a Social Democracy), an opposition political party which was officially recognised in 1993, publishes *La Verdad*, a review issued two or three times a year. The AFP–Equatorial Guinea, a French news agency (www.wash.afp.com/english/home) is probably the most regular provider of news from Equatorial Guinea, with several articles a week. Other Spanish-language newspapers include *La Diaspora* and *Noticias de Guinea Ecuatorial*. The *Periódico en Español en Guinea Ecuatorial* published in Spanish, has its editorial offices in Germany, but its area of coverage is the Republic of Equatorial Guinea.

Periodicals: *La Diaspora* (Spanish) is published every other month.

Broadcasting
Radio: Two radio stations (one commercial) broadcast in Spanish and local African languages.

Television: There is a limited television service.

Economy

Government officials believe the oil industry has the capacity to transform Equatorial Guinea into an African Kuwait. However, the EU and World Bank have suspended their involvement in the country and the IMF's relations with the government remain at an *impasse*. Consequently, the government's high growth estimates are difficult to prove and independent analysts put growth at a far lower level. Nevertheless, even the more objective independent figures show extraordinary growth, spurred on entirely by oil production.

Buoyed by oil revenue, the government feels confident enough to dismiss the role of international financial institutions, which once kept the country afloat with substantial external financing. Before oil production came on stream, external aid accounted for about 25 per cent of GDP. Foreign oil companies – particularly ExxonMobil and TotalFinaElf have open access to one of the world's largest oil reserves.

Other than the oil sector, Equatorial Guinea's economy is underdeveloped. Equatorial Guinea is rich in timber, fishing and agricultural land and there is significant room for expansion in all these areas. Obiang has curtailed the fishing industry for fear that fishing boats might allow people to flee his regime. There are also undeveloped mineral resources of titanium, iron ore, manganese, uranium, and alluvial gold. The cocoa industry was troubled by falling world prices but, since 2000, cocoa commodity prices have been rising.

Growth in Equatorial Guinea has remained strong, even though it fell to 15.5 per cent in 2003; growth jumped back, to 34.2 per cent in 2004; inflation ran at 6 per cent in 2003 and only increased to 8 per cent in 2004. Nevertheless high unemployment rates of 30 per cent indicate a segmented employment pattern with the majority of the population dependent on primary industries and too few employed in valued-added secondary or tertiary industries.

Political instability did not occur following the attempted coup in 2004 and investment in the short term, remained steady. Growth is likely to remain strong in 2005, boosted by increasing oil revenues, even though oil production was capped in October 2004 as growing oil revenues threatened to destabilise the economy.

External trade

Around 90 per cent of all exports is crude oil.

Imports

Principal imports are petroleum sector equipment, other general equipment.

Main sources: US (32.1 per cent total, 2004), Côte d'Ivoire (16.9 per cent), Spain (13.7 per cent), France (8.6 per cent), UK (7.4 per cent)

Exports

Principal exports are petroleum, methanol, timber and cocoa.

Main destinations: US (34 per cent total, 2004), China (23.7 per cent), Spain (21.1 per cent), Canada (8.6 per cent)

Agriculture

Farming

Agriculture typically accounts for around 5 per cent of GDP, but employs 70 per cent of the workforce. The main cash crop, cocoa is grown on Bioko and Rio Muni, which also produces timber and coffee for export. Main food crops are cassava, sweet potatoes, bananas, palm oil and kernels.

The estimated crop production for 2004 included: 45,000 tonnes (t) cassava, 36,000t sweet potatoes, 20,000t bananas, 31,000t plantains, 105,000t roots and tubers, 6,000t coconuts, 35,000t oil palm fruit, 6,430t oilcrops, 2,422t cocoa beans, 3,500t green coffee, 51,000t fruit in total. Estimated livestock production included: 551t meat in total, 46t beef, 142t pig meat, 139t lamb and goat meat, 224t poultry, 190t eggs, 26t sheepskins.

Fishing

The fishing sector is a developing, and potentially lucrative, sector of the economy. The industry has been partially restored, since the 1970s when former President Nguema had banned fishing and destroyed the entire fishing fleet. Nevertheless, the industry is held back by low levels of investment and President Obiang's reluctance to permit a potential conduit that might allow access into the country by those opposed to his regime. The government is developing the 314,000 square kilometre exclusive maritime economic zone surrounding the island of Anobon, off the mainland territory coastline, which is one of the Atlantic's richest fishing fields.

An EU-Equatorial Guinea fisheries agreement, signed in 2001, gives EU trawlers the right to capture 5,500 tonnes of fish per year. Under the deal, the EU pays Equatorial Guinea eur412,500 (US$458,000) per year, much of which goes into expanding and improving local fishing production.

Forestry

Equatorial Guinea has 63 per cent forest cover and logging is an important economic sector. In 2004, the export of forest products amounted to US$96.58 million. Production in 2004 included 811,000 cubic metres (cum) roundwood, 364,000cum industrial roundwood, 364,000cum sawlogs and veneers, 447,000cum woodfuel.

Industry and manufacturing

The industrial sector used to contribute around 90 per cent of GDP but since the boom in oil exports industry and manufacturing have been reduced to minor elements in the economy. Most production is related to the oil sector although as of 2005 there is no refining capacity. The manufacturing sector is very small, contributing less than 2 per cent of GDP. The non-oil industrial sector is underdeveloped, with activity centred on very small-scale food and timber processing. The traditional industries of cocoa and coffee suffer from a lack of investment. Industrial production remains around 30 per cent.

Mining

Industrial production in mining is underdeveloped, activity is limited to artisan exploitation of alluvial gold. There are reserves of copper, iron ore, uranium, tantalum and manganese.

Hydrocarbons

The hydrocarbons sector accounts for around 60 per cent of GDP and 90 per cent of exports. Oil is the country's most important foreign exchange earner and Equatorial Guinea has become one of the largest oil producers in the Gulf of Guinea. Proven oil reserves were conservatively put at 1.28 billion barrels in 2004, with oil production capped at 350,000 barrels per day (bpd). With political stability, a liberal investment framework, few regulations and favourable Production Sharing Contracts (PSCs) (in which the government has a 25 per cent stake), oil companies are flocking to the small west African state.

There have been various disputes between Equatorial Guinea and its neighbours over the demarcation of maritime borders, however President Obiang adopted an equidistant line defining maritime boundaries and Nigeria, Cameroon and São Tomé and Príncipe have accepted this solution. Gabon and Equatorial Guinea agreed to joint exploration of sites of mutual interest until mediation finds a solution to their disagreement concerning ownership of three islands. The main oil and gas fields are found offshore in the Alba and Aafiro fields.

In 2004, proven gas reserves stood at 36.8 billion cubic metres (cum) and estimated reserves at 124.5 billion cum. Gas consumption has increased and a new state gas company Société Nationale de Gaz (Songaz) was launched in January 2005 to manage gas assets. The company will also have responsibility for developing the industrial and residential gas

Equatorial Guinea

market, as well as the exploitation, treatment, marketing, and distribution of natural gas.
Equatorial Guinea does not produce or import coal.

Energy
Equatorial Guinea's estimated installed electricity generating capacity is 131MW, but this is well below the potential of 11,000MW that could be produced through hydropower alone. Electricity is produced on Bioko Island by a combination of thermal and hydroelectric plants. Ageing equipment and past under investment in the system has left potential private investors reluctant to buy it from state control.
A new gas-fired power station with increased capacity is in operation but is constrained by its original supply lines. Increased capacity, of an expected 4–6MW, is due with the construction of another plant under construction in 2005.

Banking and insurance
Central bank
Banque des Etats de l'Afrique Centrale
Main financial centre
Malabo

Time
GMT plus one hour

Geography
Equatorial Guinea consists of the islands of Bioko, Corisco, Great Elobey, Small Elobey and Annobón and the mainland territory of Río Muni (Mbini) on the west coast of Africa. Cameroon lies to the north and Gabon to the east and south of Río Muni.
The mainland region of Rio Muni covers 26,000 square km while the island province of Bioko, which hosts the capital Malabo, is 2,000 square km. The island of Pagalu (17 square km), 600km south-east of Bioko, and three rocky outcrops – Elobey Grande, Elobey Chico and Corisco – close to the mainland, are all part of Rio Muni region.

Climate
Equatorial with heavy rainfall for most of the year except for slightly drier period from December–February. The mainland Rio Muni is drier and cooler than Bioko. Average temperature 26 degrees Celsius throughout the year, and generally very humid.

Entry requirements
Passports
Required by all.
Visa
Required by all. Business visas require a letter of invitation from a local company and proof of visitor's status and a letter of finance giving proof of sufficient funds for length of stay and a full itinerary.
International certificates of vaccination for smallpox, yellow fever and cholera are also required.
Currency advice/regulations
Visitors for business and tourism must declare any currency in excess of CFAf50,000 (approximately US$75) on arrival. Travellers who fail to declare excess currency, risk forfeiture of any amount over the CFAf50,000 limit when departing.
Cash in CFA francs is usually the only form of payment accepted in Equatorial Guinea.

Health (for visitors)
Mandatory precautions
A yellow fever vaccination certificate is required if arriving from an infected area.
Advisable precautions
Vaccinations against hepatitis 'A' and 'B', tetanus, diphtheria, polio, typhoid and meningitis are strongly recommended. Malaria prophylaxis is advisable as risk exists throughout the country. There is a rabies risk. Water precautions should be taken.
Medical facilities are limited so it is advisable to pack any personal medications required.

Hotels
Accommodation is very limited but there are hotels in Malabo and Bata. It is essential to book a hotel before travelling, preferably through local business contacts. Food is rarely available at the Bata Hotel and, in Malabo, air-conditioning is available only in some rooms in the Apartotel Impala.
When there is no service charge, gratuities are around 10 to 15 per cent.

Public holidays
Fixed dates
1 Jan (New Year), 8 Mar (Women's Day), 1 May (Labour Day), 25 May (Africa Day), 5 Jun (President's Day), 3 Aug (Armed Forces Day), 15 Aug (Constitution Day), 12 October (Independence Day), 10 Dec (Human Rights' Day), 25 Dec (Christmas Day).
Variable dates
Good Friday, Corpus Christi (May/Jun).

Working hours
Banking
Mon–Sat: 0800–1200.
Business
Mon–Fri: 0800–1500.
Government
Mon–Fri: 0830–1500; Sat: 0830–1200, (alternate Sat) 1000–1200.
Shops
(Mon–Sat) 0800–1300 and 1600–1900.

Electricity supply
220 V AC, 50 cycles

Social customs/useful tips
Corruption is endemic. Special permits from the Ministry of Information and Tourism are required for most photography, including the presidential palace and its environs, military installations, government buildings, airports, harbours and other areas.

Getting there
Air
There are three direct flights a week from Europe (Iberia).
International airport/s: Malabo international (SSG), 7km from the capital city on the island of Malabo.
Bata international, 7km from city, on the mainland of Equatorial Guinea, has recently been modernised.
Surface
Road: There is access by semi-surfaced road from Gabon to Mbini and Bata, although this route is not generally recommended.
Main port/s: Malabo, Bata, Luba, Mbini and Kogo.

Getting about
National transport
Air: Air Afrique Affaires, a private company based in Douala, Cameroon, operates air service between Bata and Malabo.
Road: On Bioko a surfaced road links major towns in the north. On mainland Rio Muni a surfaced road links Bata with Mbini and a partly surfaced road links Bata with Ebebiyin (near Gabon border). Other roads are unsurfaced and can be difficult.
Water: There is a weekly boat service between Malabo and Bata.

BUSINESS DIRECTORY
The addresses listed below are a selection only. While World of Information makes every endeavour to check these addresses, we cannot guarantee that changes have not been made, especially to telephone numbers and area codes. We would welcome any corrections.

Telephone area codes
The international direct dialling code (IDD) for Equatorial Guinea is +240 followed by area code and subscriber's number:
Bata   8   Malabo   9

Chambers of Commerce
Camara Oficiel de Comercio, Agricola y Forestal, 43 Avenida de la Indepencia, PO Box 51, Malabo (tel: 923-43; fax: 932-66).

Banking
Banco de Crédito y Desarrollo (credit and development bank), 1 Avenida de la Libertad, PO Box 39, Malabo (tel: 2146).

Banco Exterior de Guinea Ecuatorial, Carretera de Aeropuerto, Malabo (tel: 2001).

Banque Internationale pour l'Afrique Occidentale, Calle de Argelia No 6, PO Box 686, Malabo (tel: 2367, 2887).

Caisse Commune d'Epargne et d'Investissement en Guinée Equatoriale (CCEI-GE); PO Box 428, Malabo (tel: 2003, 2910; fax: 3311).

Société Générale de Banque GE; PO Box 686, Calle Argelia, Malabo (tel: 3337; fax: 2743).

Central bank
Banque des Etats de l'Afrique Centrale, Direction Nationale, PO Box 501, Malabo (tel: 20-10; fax: 20-06; e-mail: beacmal@beac.int).

Other useful addresses
Comite Sindical de Cacao (cocoa growers' organisation), Bioko.

Dirección General de Correos y Telecomunicaciones, Malabo.

Empresa Estatal de Comercio Interior y Exterior, Malabo.

Empresa General de Industria y Comercio (EGISCA), Malabo.

Empresa Guineano-Española de Petróleos (Gepsa), Malabo.

Internet sites
Equatorial Guinea oil: http://www.equatorialoil.com/

Africa Business Network: http://www.ifc.org/abn

AllAfrica.com: http://allafrica.com

African Development Bank: http://www.afdb.org

Africa Online: http://www.africaonline.com

Mbendi AfroPaedia (information on companies, countries, industries and stock exchanges in Africa): http://mbendi.co.za

Official site (in Spanish): http://www.guineaecuatorial.net/ms/main.asp

Eritrea

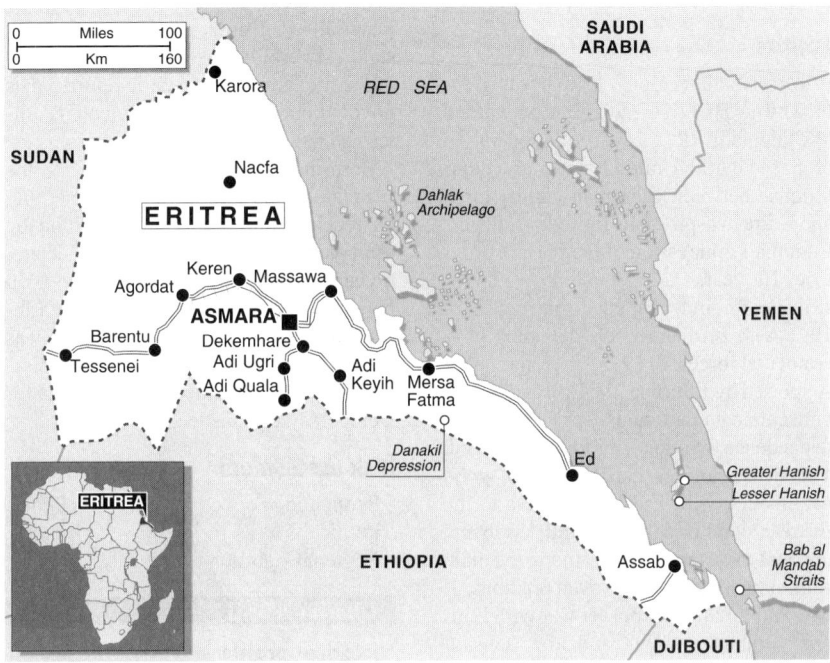

KEY FACTS

Official name: Hagere Ertra (State of Eritrea)

Head of State: President Issaias Afwerki (assumed power May 1991; elected president by the National Assembly 8 Jun 1993)

Head of government: President Issaias Afwerki

Ruling party: People's Front for Democracy and Justice (PFDJ) (formerly the Eritrean People's Liberation Front (EPLF))

Area: 125,000 square km

Population: 4.27 million (2004)

Capital: Asmara

Official language: There is no official language but the working languages are Tigrinya, Arabic and English.

Currency: Nakfa (Nk) = 100 cents

Exchange rate: Nk13.50 per US$ (Oct 2005) (From 26 Jan 2005, all transactions are to be conducted in the national currency, the nakfa)

GDP per capita: US$138 (2004)

GDP real growth: 1.80% (2004)

Labour force: 2.25 million (2004)

Inflation: 21.40% (2004)

Balance of trade: -US$557.56 million (2004)

Eritrea is one of the poorest countries in the world and its people live under a regime of political and religious repression. For its religious intolerance it has been blacklisted by the United States. It is a one party state, with the People's Front for Democracy and Justice (PFDJ) the only party allowed to operate. There are two opposition groups, which recently united and run the risk of being jailed for their efforts to promote a national dialogue with President Isaias Afwerki.

More than half of the population lives on less than US$1 per day and about one third lives in extreme poverty – consuming less than 2,000 calories per day. The authorities have produced a poverty and national food security strategy, which together set out plans aimed at increasing rural incomes and raising productivity.

Border conflict

The ongoing 'no war/no peace' impasse with Ethiopia after the 1998–99 border war, could continue indefinitely. Hostilities have officially ceased, both sides have declared victory, but the border is still (in early 2006) not accepted by either country.

In January 2006 the government refused to allow a United States' fact-finding mission to visit the border area. President Isaias Afwerki said there was no point to the visit. The issue involved nothing that was debatable. Afwerki has repeatedly warned that the resumption of the border conflict is inevitable.

Economy

Since independence from Ethiopia on 24 May 1993 Eritrea has faced the economic problems of a small, desperately poor country. Like the economies of many African nations, the economy is largely based on subsistence agriculture, with 80 per cent of the population involved in farming and herding. During the Ethiopian-Eritrea war in 1998–2000 growth fell to a negative 8.6 per cent in 2000. However, even during the war, Eritrea developed its transportation infrastructure, asphalting new roads, improving its ports, and repairing war damaged roads and bridges. Since the war ended, the government has maintained a firm grip on the economy, expanding the use of the military and party-owned businesses to complete Eritrea's development agenda.

The unresolved border issue compounds other pressing problems. These include Eritrea's inability to provide enough food; two thirds of the population receive food aid. Moreover, economic progress is hampered by the proportion of Eritreans who are in the army rather than the workforce.

There have also been four consecutive years of drought. Malnutrition has increased in many parts of the country. Macroeconomic imbalances have grown and overall performance has been weak. Monetary policy continues to be subservient to the government's financing requirements and budgeting is irregular.

The commercial banks remain profitable owing to income from their foreign exchange activities, and they appear to be in compliance with prudential regulations. However, they continue to hold a high proportion of non-performing loans, largely on account of the effects of the border war, and their core lending activities do not generate enough income to cover operational costs.

While saying they are committed over the long run to a return to market-based policies, the authorities have increasingly resorted to an administrative-controlled approach to economic management. National and defence spending, fiscal deficits and government debt are at unsustainable levels. In the period immediately ahead, priority will need to be given to curtailing non-priority outlays, stepping up efforts to collect tax arrears, and further strengthening tax administration. To improve fiscal transparency and strengthen investor confidence and donor support, the government needs to start publishing its budget regularly.

The country will continue to need technical assistance in a range of areas, and will have to take full and effective advantage of the assistance being made available by Eritrea's development partners, including those in East Africa.

Politics

A former Italian colony, Eritrea was occupied by the British in 1941. It was awarded to Ethiopia in 1952 as part of a federation proposed by the United Nations as a compromise between Ethiopian claims for it and Eritrean aspirations for independence. Ethiopia's annexation of Eritrea as a province 10 years later sparked a 32-year struggle for independence that ended in 1991 with Eritrean rebels defeating governmental forces. In 1993, in a referendum supported by Ethiopia, the Eritrean people voted almost unanimously in favour of independence, leaving Ethiopia landlocked. The two countries hardly became good neighbours, with Ethiopian access to the Eritrean ports of Massawa and Assab and unequal trade terms being among the main stumbling blocks to improved relations. A two-and-a-half-year border war with Ethiopia erupted in 1998 and after tens of thousands of people had been killed, was ended under UN auspices in December 2000. Eritrea currently hosts a UN peacekeeping operation that is monitoring a 25km-wide Temporary Security Zone on the border with Ethiopia. The independent commission at the Permanent Court of Arbitration in the Hague, empowered to resolve the border dispute, posted its findings in 2002 and in December 2006 ruled that Eritrea had launched unlawful attacks against Ethiopia in May 1998, starting the border war.

Issaias Afwerki was elected president of independent Eritrea by the country's national assembly in 1994. He had been the de facto leader before independence. Presidential elections, planned for 1997, never materialised. Eritrea remains a one-party state. Afwerki has been criticised for failing to implement democratic reforms. His government has clamped down on its critics and has closed the private press.

Born in 1946 in Asmara, he joined the Eritrean Liberation Front (ELF) in 1966. He received military training in China the same year, and then went on to be deputy divisional commander of the ELF. In 1970 he co-founded the Eritrean People's Liberation Front (EPLF) and in 1987 he was elected secretary general of the organisation. EPLF is now the People's Front for Democracy and Justice.

Risk assessment

Economic	Poor
Political	Poor
Regional stability	Poor

COUNTRY PROFILE

Historical profile
Since gaining independence from Ethiopia in 1993, Eritrea has had to weather constant political, economic and social upheaval. A two-year war with Ethiopia in 1998–99 left the economy in tatters with a peace agreement that left both sides disgruntled and unwilling to restore constructive relations. The optimism that surrounded independence has become disillusion, as the government has sidelined the democratic process and conducted widespread repression of any form of political or even religious dissidence.
1889–1941 Under Italian rule. Eritrea first emerged as a political entity following the Italian occupation of the Red Sea port of Massawa and other coastal enclaves in the 1880s. In 1889, Italy signed the Treaty of Ucciali with the Ethiopian Emperor, Menelik, and in 1890, named the country Eritrea.
1941 The UK defeated Italy during the Second World War and Eritrea became a British protectorate.
1952 UN-sanctioned federation with Ethiopia.
1962 Eritrea was annexed to Ethiopia as a province under Emperor Haile Selassie.
1991 The Eritrean People's Liberation Front (EPLF) overthrew Ethiopian Colonel

KEY INDICATORS — Eritrea

	Unit	2000	2001	2002	2003	2004
Population	m	4.00	4.20	4.19	4.23	4.27
Gross domestic product (GDP)	US$bn	0.78	0.59	0.64	0.63	*0.93
GDP per capita	US$	191	144	152	150	138
GDP real growth	%	-8.6	3.0	1.6	5.0	1.8
Inflation	%	19.9	15.0	18.8	18.8	21.4
Exports (fob) (goods)	US$m	35.0	20.0	54.0	20.0	64.4
Imports (fob) (goods)	US$m	471.0	490.0	520.0	500.0	622.0
Balance of trade	US$m	-436.0	-470.0	-460.0	-480.0	-557.6
Current account	US$m	-107.0	-87.0	-117.0	-152.0	-70.0
Total reserves minus gold	US$m	25.5	39.8	30.3	24.7	34.7
Foreign exchange	US$m	25.5	39.7	30.3	24.7	34.7
Exchange rate	per US$	8.22	8.46	8.38	8.43	8.58

* estimated figure

Eritrea

Mengistu's forces and liberated the territory; Issaias Afwerki assumed power.
1993 A vote resulted in a virtually 100 per cent acceptance of independence.
1994 Eritrea achieved nationhood and Afwerki was elected president by the National Assembly.
1998 Eritrea and Ethiopia resumed border warfare. The Permanent Court of Arbitration in the Hague ruled that Yemen should have the Red Sea island of Greater Hanish, fought over in 1995 by Eritrea and Yemen, and it was announced that Eritrea would return it to Yemen. The nakfa was introduced as Eritrea's national currency, to be used alongside the Ethiopian birr.
2000 UN peacekeepers opened a 1,000km cease-fire land corridor between Ethiopia and Eritrea and the two countries signed a peace deal in Algiers, ending the two-year war.
2001 The UN established a buffer zone along the border of Ethiopia and Eritrea.
2002 Eritrea and Ethiopia accepted a ruling on the border dispute, made by the Boundary Commission at the Permanent Court of Arbitration of The Hague. A new 1,000km boundary was established between the two countries.
2003 In March, the UN Mission in Ethiopia and Eritrea (UNMEE) mandate was extended until September.
2004 Eritrea suffered from a harsh drought in June, resulting in severe drinking-water problems both for humans and animals.
In July, implementation of the peace process that was to resolve the border conflict between Ethiopia and Eritrea remained stalled.
2005 From 26 January, all transactions are to be conducted in the national currency, the nakfa. Eritrea restricted the movement of UN peacekeepers along the Eritrea/Ethiopia border, leading to fears that the war would flare up again. In December the independent commission at the Permanent Court of Arbitration in The Hague, set up in December 2000 as part of the peace deal signed in Algiers in 2000 between Eritrea and Ethiopia, ruled that Eritrea had launched unlawful attacks against Ethiopia in May 1998, thereby triggering the border war between the two countries.

Political structure
A transition period is in effect until pluralist elections.
Constitution
A new constitution was adopted in May 1997.
A 150-member National Transitional Council was set up, with 75 seats allocated to the People's Front for Democracy and Justice (PFDJ), 60 to the Constitutional Assembly and 15 to overseas Eritreans.
The president governs with the help of his 24-member Consultative Council. The Consultative Council is composed of ministers and regional governors.
There are six administrative regions, each with regional, sub-regional (55) and village administrations (651). The regions enjoy a degree of autonomy.
Last elections
1994 (presidential)
Results: Presidential: Issaias Afwerki was elected by the National Assembly with 95 per cent of the vote.

Political parties
Ruling party
People's Front for Democracy and Justice (PFDJ) (formerly the Eritrean People's Liberation Front (EPLF))
Main opposition party
Opposition parties are not allowed.

Population
4.27 million (2004)
Ethnic make-up
There are nine ethno-linguistic groups.
Religions
Tigrigna-speaking Christians (mainly Orthodox), are the traditional inhabitants of the highlands, with some Protestant and Roman Catholic communities (49 per cent); Muslim communities of the western lowlands, northern highlands and east coast are 49 per cent. A small number of the population adhere to traditional beliefs.

Education
There are approximately 260 primary schools and over 50 secondary schools. It has been estimated by Oxfam that 93 per cent of children age 6–11 will enrol for school in 2015.
Literacy rate: 67 per cent men, 36 per cent woman; adult rates (World Bank 2002).
Enrolment rate: 53 per cent gross enrolment, of relevant age group, in primary education (World Bank 2001).
Pupils per teacher: 44 in primary schools.

Health
Total expenditure on health is 5–6 per cent of GDP, of which 65–66 per cent was government spending.
Access to an improved water source is available to 46 per cent of the population.
HIV/Aids
A survey published in 2001 revealed that 4.6 per cent of soldiers were HIV-positive and 22.8 per cent of female bar workers were affected as well. By 2002, more than 13,000 people had been registered as infected with HIV/Aids. The main incidences are in Asmara, the capital, and Assab, the sea port, where prostitution is rife. Up to 30 per cent of prostitutes are HIV positive.
HIV prevalence: 2.7 per cent aged 15–49 in 2003 (World Bank)
Life expectancy: 51.1 years (World Bank)
Fertility rate/Maternal mortality rate: 4.8 births per woman (2003); maternal mortality 10 per 1,000 per live births (World Bank).
Infant mortality rate: 45 per 1,000 live births (2003); 44 per cent of children aged under five were malnourished (World Bank).
Head of population per physician/bed: 0.03 doctors per 1,000 people.

Welfare
A post-war rehabilitation project, implemented by the UN Development Programme (UNDP), has put metal roofs, doors and windows back on houses that were deserted and ransacked during the border war with Ethiopia. An estimated 60,000 children were left crippled by the war, and another 45,000 orphaned. A large proportion of the population is dependent on food aid. UNICEF appeals in 2002 for refugee welfare raised a total of US$10.3 million, a large part of which was spent on establishing and rehabilitating water supplies in settlement areas, as well as setting up basic health and sanitation facilities.

Main cities
Asmara (capital, estimated population 400,000 in 2003), Assab (Aseb) (56,300), Keren (38,000), Massawa (Mitsiwa) (30,700).

Languages spoken
The principal language group in Eritrea is Afro-Asiatic; Arabic, Afar, Bilen, Hedareb, Kunama, Nara, Saho, Tigray and Tigrinya are spoken. English is rapidly becoming the language of business and is the medium of instruction at secondary schools and at university.
Official language/s
There is no official language but the working languages are Tigrinya, Arabic and English.

Media
Press
The government strictly controls the media. In 2001, the government imposed a ban on all private newspapers operating in the country. The editors of private publications were arrested, including the editors of *MeQaleh*, a private newspaper published in Tigrinya Asmara and *Keste Debena*. The move was designed to suppress criticism of the ruling People's Front for Democracy and Justice (PFDJ) before the next legislative elections, scheduled for 2003.

Weeklies: The government publishes *Hadas Eritrea* (New Eritrea) twice weekly in Tigrinya and Arabic.
Business: Asmara Chamber of Commerce publishes *Chamber News* in Tigrinya and English, and *Business* a quarterly publication in Tigrinya, Arabic and English.
Periodicals: *The Mirror* is an independent English-language monthly magazine published in Asmara. *The Eritrean Edition* is a quarterly publication.

Broadcasting
Radio: Voice of the Broad Masses of Eritrea (Dimtsi Hafash) broadcasts in Arabic, Tigrinya, Tigre, Afar and Kunama.
Television: The government television station is ERI-TV that broadcasts in Arabic, Tigrinya and Tigre. Transmissions are limited to Asmara and surrounding areas.

Economy
The main problems affecting the Eritrean economy are an inadequate and war-ravaged infrastructure, a lack of hard currency to pay for imports, a weak tax collection system and the predominance of unproductive subsistence agriculture. Eritrea is still reeling from the 1998–2000 border war, which cost the economy up to US$800 million. A long period of tension on the borders has not helped attract investment or promote macroeconomic stability. A series of droughts in recent years has exacerbated Eritrea's problems.

The government wants to diversify the economy (70 per cent of Eritreans are employed in agriculture), so that it can afford to buy abroad what it cannot grow itself. Some 70 per cent of the population depends on foreign aid for all or part of its food supply.

The country's economic future depends on its ability to eradicate major social and economic problems. These include widespread illiteracy, unemployment and poor levels of foreign investment. The border between Ethiopia and Eritrea, implemented after the Boundary Commission ruling in 2002, ought to have encouraged stability and allow Eritrea to focus on these problems, but relations between the two countries remain heated and continuing tensions are likely to deter investment until accord is reached.

In the long term, Eritrea may benefit from the development of offshore oil, fishing and tourism industries.

External trade
On 31 December 2002, the US approved Eritrea as being eligible for tariff preferences under the Africa Growth and Opportunities Act (AGOA). The legislation requires that countries are only eligible for greater access to US markets provided they have made continued progress toward a market-based economy, the rule of law, free trade, poverty reduction and the protection of workers' rights. This process is reviewed annually. On 1 January 2004, Eritrea's eligibility status was cancelled, because of its deteriorating human rights record.

Imports
Principal non-petroleum imports include machinery, food and manufactured goods.
Main sources: US (32.3 per cent total, 2004), Italy (15.5 per cent), Turkey (5.5 per cent), UK (4.6 per cent), Russia (4.4 per cent), Italy (6.4 per cent)

Exports
Principal exports include livestock, sorghum, textiles, food and small manufactures.
Main destinations: Malaysia (54.7 per cent total, 2004), Italy (8.8 per cent), France (3.7 per cent)

Agriculture
Farming
Crop production in 2004 included: 102,225 tonnes (t) cereals in total, 7,199t wheat, 2,291t maize, 11,554t millet, 16,000t potatoes, 56,743t sorghum, 16,864t barley, 40,286t pulses, 101,000t roots and tubers, 5,819t oilcrops, *2,000t fruit in total, *23,000t vegetables in total. Livestock production included: 32,135t meat in total, 16,650t beef, *732t camel meat, 6,700t lamb, 5,800t goat meat, 2,253t poultry, *1,978t eggs, *56,725t milk, 3,213t cattle hides, 670t sheepskins.
* estimate

Fishing
Fishing for sardines, anchovies, tuna, shark and mackerel is practised in the Red Sea on a very small scale. There are over 1,000 different species of fish off Eritrea's shores, with the stocks virtually untouched since the 1950s. The government believes there is potential for exporting 80,000 tonnes of fish annually. The sector has been badly affected by the closure of its market in Yemen as a result of a territorial dispute.

Forestry
Production in 2002 included: 2.3 million cubic metres (cum) roundwood, 1,924cum sawlogs and veneers, 2.3 million cum woodfuel, 152,473t charcoal.

Industry and manufacturing
The industrial sector contributes around 27 per cent of GDP and employs 10 per cent of the workforce.

The industrial base is traditionally centred on the production of glass, cement, footwear and canned goods, but most industrial enterprises have been badly damaged by war. All state-owned distribution and import/export enterprises established by the former government have been dissolved.

Major problems include outdated machinery and techniques, supply of energy, and the need for imports throughout the sector. With a lack of foreign currency and investment, industry is suffering from outdated machinery and intermediary goods which need to be imported.

Tourism
The tourism sector was badly affected by the war with Ethiopa. Around 165,000 tourists a year visited the country before hostilities broke out. Since the resumption of peace in 2000, arrivals have continued to increase year-on-year, rising from 40,000 in 2001 to over 100,000 by 2005. The continuing tensions between Eritrea and Ethiopia, as well as the need for improved infrastructure, may have held back faster growth. The government, with the support of UN agencies, is pursuing a 20-year development strategy, emphasising nature and heritage tourism and aiming for between 600,000 and 1 million visitors a year by 2020. The main markets are Italy and Germany.

Mining
Fighting along the border regions disrupted mining activities, although exploration continued elsewhere in Eritrea. The Phelps Dodge Exploration Corporation conducted exploration on the Debarwa copper-zinc deposits and identified up to four million tonnes of reserves, including at least two million tonnes of mineable high-grade copper and a large amount of gold.

Gold-bearing seams exist in highland areas. There are over 15 gold mines and a large number of prospects close to Asmara. The potential for new discoveries in the area is good. Substantial gold reserves have also been identified at Adi Nefas by LaSource Development SAS. Artisanal mining production is estimated to produce around 550kg per year. Despite Eritrea's mining potential, salt and marble remain the country's main exported minerals.

Hydrocarbons
Large offshore oil reserves beneath the Red Sea and substantial natural gas reserves in the Danakil depression have yet to be effectively exploited. Several oil companies have negotiated oil exploration contracts for the shallow waters off Eritrea's coast. Eritrea had a refining capacity of 18,000 barrels per day until the refinery in Assab was closed down in 1997 due to high maintenance costs, rendering Eritrea dependent on imports. Eritrea's economic plight and shortage of foreign currency has led to the suspension of petrol sales since October 2004 and a ban on private imports of oil since February 2005.

Eritrea

Energy
Electricity supply is available mainly to urban areas, leaving the majority of the population without access. Existing 66MW generating capacity was supplemented in 2003 by the completion of an 88MW plant funded by Saudi Arabia and the United Arab Emirates.

In July 2004, the World Bank approved an International Development Association (IDA) credit of US$29 million and an IDA grant of US$21 million in support of power distribution and rural electrification in Eritrea.

Some villages provide themselves with electricity from community diesel generators, while photovoltaic power is used to a limited extent for health centres, schools and water pumps.

Banking and insurance
Central bank
Bank of Eritrea

Time
GMT plus three hours

Geography
Eritrea extends inland from the Red Sea coast of eastern Africa. To the south, the country has a long frontier with Ethiopia, and a short frontier with Djibouti. Sudan lies to the north and west.

Climate
Coastal and lowland regions very hot and dry throughout the year. On the plateau, which includes Asmara, the dry season runs from October–May with temperatures ranging from as low as 6 degrees Celsius (C) in December to 26 degrees C in March (light rain from February–April). Temperatures can fall sharply at night during the dry season.

The rainy season runs from June–September with average temperature 21 degrees C. Rainfall is less than 500mm per year in lowland areas, increasing to 1,000mm in the highlands. The temperature gradient is similarly steep: average annual temperatures range from 17 degrees C in the highlands to 30 degrees C in Massawa. The Danakil depression in the south-east, which is more than 130 metres below sea-level in places, experiences some of the highest temperatures recorded, frequently exceeding 50 degrees C.

Entry requirements
Passports
Passports must be valid six months beyond intended length of stay.
Visa
Required by all except nationals of Kenya and Uganda. Business visas are valid for three months. A business letter giving proof of sufficient funds for length of stay, a full itinerary and copy of return/onward ticket should accompany application.

British nationals should register on arrival at the British Consulate in Asmara (tel: 112-0145).
Currency advice/regulations
There are no restrictions on import/export of local and foreign currency. From 26 January 2005, all transactions are to be conducted in the national currency, the nakfa.

Health (for visitors)
Mandatory precautions
A yellow fever vaccination certificate is required if travelling from or via an infected area.
Advisable precautions
Yellow fever, hepatitis A, tetanus, typhoid and polio vaccinations. Malaria prophylaxis recommended for visits outside Asmara. Water precautions should be taken. There is a rabies risk.

Hotels
Both Asmara and Massawa suffer from a severe shortage of hotel space; booking is advisable. Standards are low but are being improved. Service charge of 10 per cent and a small tip is usual in addition to service charge. Visitors are expected to pay bills at government-run hotels in US dollars or denominated traveller's cheques.

Credit cards
Credit cards are only accepted at a few outlets in Asmara.

Public holidays
Fixed dates
1 Jan (New Year's Day), 8 Mar (Women's Day), 24 May (Independence Day), 20 Jun (Martyrs' Day), 1 Sep (Start of the Armed Struggle).
Variable dates
Eid al-Fitr, Eid al-Adha, Easter.

Working hours
Banking
(Mon–Fri) 0800–1200, 1400–1800; (Sat) 0800–1230.
Business
Mon–Thu: 0700–1200, 1400–1800; Fri: 0700–1130, 1400–1800.
Shops
Mon–Fri: 0830–1300, 1430–2030.

Electricity supply
220V AC, 50 cycles.

Weights and measures
The metric system is in force.

Security
Street crime such as theft and robbery is rare in most cities. However it is advised not to walk around alone in any town, though particularly Asmara and Massawa, late at night. Valuables, in particular cameras and including passports, should be kept out of sight.

Getting there
Air
International airport/s:
Asmara-Johannes IV (ASM), 9km from city, restaurant, currency exchange, post office, duty-free.
Airport tax: International departures: US$15; domestic departures Nk5.
Surface
Road: There are no roads considered safe to enter the country. The 300km road from Kassala in Sudan, to Tessenai, is largely unsurfaced.
Main port/s: Massawa and Assab. Massawa's business was estimated to be 60 per cent down on pre-war projections. Assab has suffered concentrated Ethiopian attacks and its cargo levels are very low. It had previously relied on Ethiopia for 90 per cent of its trade.

Getting about
National transport
Road: The extensive road network is undergoing major rehabilitation with US$27m allocated by the government to road reconstruction.

There are 622km of asphalt roads. The Massawa-Asmara main route (107km) is finished. Other main routes (largely unsurfaced) are Asmara-Keren to Afabet-Nacfa in the north, and Asmara-Tessenai to the west, many bridges on this road were destroyed in a previous civil war.

In many parts of the country, roads are difficult or impassable during the rainy season. There are extensive mine fields in Eritrea, especially near the border with Ethiopia. Travelling on main roads outside of the border areas is generally safe but it is advised not to go off-road driving and do not travel after dark in rural areas.
Buses: Some bus services available, including one service to Addis Ababa.
Taxis: Taxis are available for trips outside the city, but the fares are higher.
Rail: The link from Asmara to the coast has been reopened.
City transport
Taxis: The journey time by taxi from the Asmara International Airport to the city is 15 minutes. Taxi drivers do not expect a tip.

BUSINESS DIRECTORY
The addresses listed below are a selection only. While World of Information makes every endeavour to check these addresses, we cannot guarantee that changes have not been made, especially to telephone numbers and area codes. We would welcome any corrections.

Telephone area codes
The international dialling code (IDD) for Eritrea is +291 followed by 1 and subscriber's number.

Chambers of Commerce
Eritrean National Chamber of Commerce, 46 Aboit Avenue, PO Box 856, Asmara (tel: 121-589; fax: 120-138; e-mail: encc@eol.com.er).

Banking
Commercial Bank of Eritrea; PO Box 291, 212 Liberty Avenue, Asmara (tel: 116-005, 121-844/48; fax: 124-8871, 121-849).

Eritrean Development & Investment Bank; PO Box 1266, 29 Atse Yohannes Street, Asmara (tel: 123-787, 114-520, 126-777).

Housing & Commerce Bank of Eritrea; PO Box 235, Bahti Meskerem Square, Asmara (tel: 120-350; fax: 120-401).

Central bank
National Bank of Eritrea, Zeraai Derres Square, PO Box 849, Asmara (tel: 123-033; fax: 122-091; e-mail: tekieb@eol.com.er).

Travel information
Ministry of tourism
Ministry of Tourism, PO Box 1010, Asmara (tel: 126-997).

Ministries
Ministry of Agriculture, PO Box 124, Asmara (tel: 181-499; fax: 181-415).

Ministry of Defence, PO Box 629, Asmara (tel: 113-349; fax: 114-920).

Ministry of Education, PO Box 5610, Asmara (tel: 113-044; fax: 113-866).

Ministry of Energy and Mines, PO Box 5285, Asmara (tel: 116-872; fax: 127-652); Department of Energy (fax: 112-339); Department of Mines (fax: 112-994).

Ministry of Finance and Development, PO Box 896, Asmara (tel: 113-633; fax: 117-947).

Ministry of Fisheries, PO Box 923, Asmara (tel: 114-271; fax: 112-185).

Ministry of Foreign Affairs, PO Box 190, Asmara (tel: 113-811; fax: 123-788).

Ministry of Health, PO Box 212, Asmara (tel: 112-877; fax: 112-899).

Ministry of Information, PO Box 242, Asmara (tel: 115-171; fax: 119-847).

Ministry of Justice, PO Box 241, Asmara (tel: 111-822).

Ministry of Local Government, PO Box 225, Asmara (tel: 113-006).

Ministry of Public Works, PO Box 841, Asmara (tel: 119-077).

Ministry of Trade and Industry, PO Box 1844, Asmara (tel: 118-386, 113-910; fax: 120-586).

Ministry of Transport and Communications, PO Box 204, Asmara (tel: 110-444; fax: 127-048).

Other useful addresses
African Minerals Inc (AMI), PO Box 3508, Asmara (tel: 120-280, 120-030; fax: 120-332).

British Consulate, 27 Lorenzo Tazaz Street, PO Box 997, Asmara (tel: 123-415; fax: 127-230).

Communications and Postal Authority, PO Box 234, Asmara (tel: 112-900; fax: 110-938).

Eritrean Association in London, UK (tel: (0)181-748-0547).

Eritrean Business Licence Office, PO Box 3045, Asmara (tel: 114-809, 114-752; fax: 126-694).

Eritrean Shipping Lines, PO Box 1110, Asmara (tel: 120-308/359/257; fax: 120-331).

Grain Board of Eritrea, PO Box 1234, Asmara (tel: 115-624; fax: 120-586).

Investment Promotion Centre, Asmara (tel: 118-822, 118-124; fax: 124-293).

Prima Eritrea Oil Company, Asmara (tel: 120-050; fax: 120-099).

Red Sea Trading Corporation (import/export services operated by the PFDJ), 29/31 Ras Alula Street, PO Box 332, Asmara (tel: 127-846; fax: 124-353).

US Embassy, PO Box 211, Asmara (tel: 120-004, 120-009; fax: 127-584).

Voice of the Broad Masses of Eritrea (Dimtsi Hafash), Ministry of Information, Radio Division, PO Box 872, Asmara.

Internet sites
Eritrean news: http://www.messelna.com

Africa Business Network: http://www.ifc.org/abn

AllAfrica.com: http://www.allafrica.com

African Development Bank: http://www.afdb.org

Africa Online: http://www.africaonline.com

Harambee Afrika (UK business club for traders with east, central and southern Africa; includes annotated web resource list): http://www.harambee.co.uk

Mbendi AfroPaedia (information on companies, countries, industries and stock exchanges in Africa): http://mbendi.co.za

Estonia

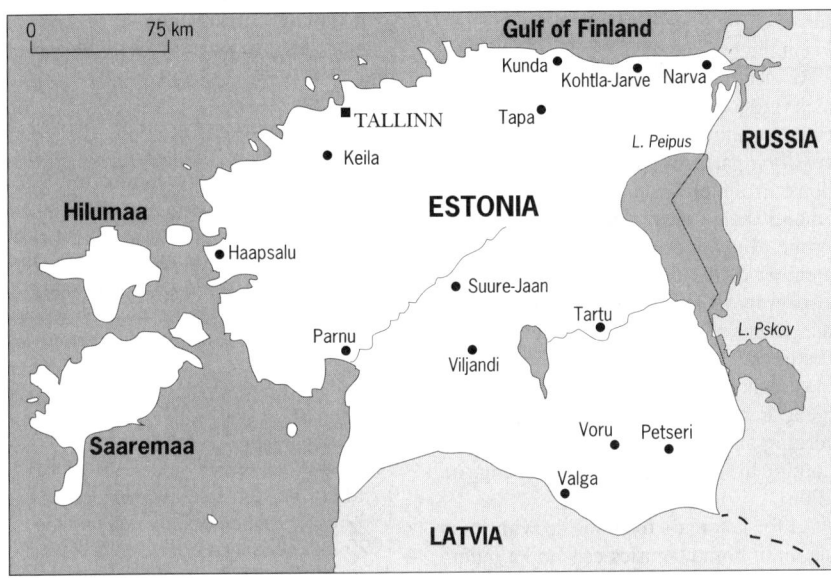

It was a run of the mill year for Estonia in 2005: it rowed with its Russian neighbour, recorded impressive economic growth and got itself a new government – Estonia's eighth in twelve years.

Baltic boom

Although forecasts vary, Estonian GDP grew by at least 6.5 per cent in 2005. Estonian finance ministry figures were at the bottom end of the spectrum (at 6.5 per cent) while the European Commission (EC) forecast a staggering 8.4 per cent. Either way, Estonia's economy was growing rapidly. Moreover, the external account deficit was reduced to less than 10 per cent of GDP in 2005 and unemployment fell to 8.1 per cent in August. Even though a supplementary budget in October increased spending by 1.3 per cent of GDP, the government was still on target to record an overall budget surplus of more than 1 per cent of GDP in 2005. The one economic indicator that told against the Estonian economy was a rise in inflation, up from 3.0 per cent in 2004 to 4.1 per cent in 2005, according to the EC.

Number eight

In April, Estonian president Arnold Rüütel, swore in Estonia's eighth government since 1993. The previous government, a broadly centre-right, three-party coalition led by Prime Minister Juhan Parts had been in office since March 2003. A vote of no-confidence in the government's justice minister, ostensibly over methods of tackling public sector corruption, led to Parts' resignation. Interestingly, the new prime minister, Andrus Ansip, was the leader of only the third biggest party in the parliament. Moreover, his newly-formed 3-party coalition consisted of two parties who had been members of the previous government. The new coalition government is considered by analysts to be more or less centre-right in political orientation, and is expected to lower taxes and accelerate privatisation.

Local elections in October made history. Estonia became the first EU state to allow e-voting on a large scale. According to officials, 80 per cent of those registered to vote had access to the new voting system. However, at 47 per cent, turnout was at its lowest in a decade. Results indicated approval for the new government, with all three coalition parties receiving around the same percentage of votes as they had gained in the 2003 general election. The only big loser was the Res Publica party of former prime minister Juhan Parts.

KEY FACTS

Official name: Eesti Vabariik (The Republic of Estonia)

Head of State: President Arnold Rüütel (since 2001)

Head of government: Prime Minister Andrus Ansip (RE) (appointed 12 Apr 2005)

Ruling party: Three-party coalition government sworn in 13 Apr 2005: Reformierakond (RE) (Reform Party); Eestimaa Rahvaliit (Rahvaliit) (ER) (Estonian People's Union); Eesti Keskerakond (Kesk) (EK) (Estonian Centre Party).

Area: 45,227 square km

Population: 1.24 million (2004)

Capital: Tallinn

Official language: Estonian

Currency: Kroon (plural krooni) (EEK)

Exchange rate: EEK12.98 per US$ (Oct 2005); (pegged at EEK15.65 per euro)

GDP per capita: US$8,287 (2004)

GDP real growth: 6.20% (2004);6.5% (2005)*

Labour force: 756,000 (2004)

Unemployment: 9.70% (2004)

Inflation: 3.00% (2004); 4.1% (2005)*

Balance of trade: -US$1.97 billion (2004)

Foreign debt: US$8.37 billion (2004)

* estimated figure

Nations of the World: A Political, Economic and Business Handbook

Russia: thaw then freeze

After 10 years of at times bitter negotiations, Estonia and Russia finally reached agreement on their mutual border. The agreement was struck in May and essentially it accepted the border that had existed in Soviet times. This was not without controversy in Estonia, as Soviet leader Joseph Stalin had annexed about 5 per cent of Estonia's territory to Russia. Acceptance of the Soviet border also meant that the Setu people, who speak a dialect of Estonian, were now permanently divided between Estonia and Russia. However, while Setu in Estonia expressed dissatisfaction with this arrangement, there does not appear to have been any major protest among Russian Setu.

While the border treaty appeared to signal a thaw in Estonian-Russian relations, this was all to change by the end of June. President Rüütel, like his Lithuanian counterpart, Valdas Adamkus, refused an invitation to attend celebrations in Moscow to mark the end of the Second World War Two in Europe. According to a local newspaper poll, 61 per cent of Estonians supported the refusal. Most Estonians still recall that Stalin's defeat of Hitler also brought with it nearly fifty years of annexation, deportation and Russification. If Russia were in any doubt that Estonians still felt strongly about deprivations suffered during the Soviet era, these were swept away in June. The Estonian parliament ratified the border treaty but only after inserting clauses referring to the Russian occupations of 1940–41 and 1945–91. Russia responded by stating that the treaty was null and void.

Outlook

Forecasts for the Estonian economy indicate that there will be a small reduction in growth in 2006, compared to 2005 levels. However, inflation is also expected to fall and the budget is also forecast to remain in surplus. The government is also expected to cut the flat tax rate.

An election is scheduled for early 2007, meaning a probable increase in government spending and the likelihood that the coalition partners will grow a little fractious in an effort to shore up support among their constituents. The fact that Prime Minister Ansip's party is a junior member of the governing coalition may also grow to rankle among members of the larger, Eesti Keskerakond (Kesk) (Estonian Centre Party). However, an almost rotating-door approach to government has not prevented Estonia from surging ahead economically and there is nothing to suggest that this will change in 2006.

As for Estonia's relationship with Russia, until both countries can find a mutually acceptable way to acknowledge and move on from the crimes of the Soviet era, border treaties and relations in general will remain strained.

Risk assessment

Politics	Fractious
Economy	Improving
Regional stability	Troubled

KEY INDICATORS — Estonia

	Unit	2000	2001	2002	2003	2004
Population	m	1.39	1.40	1.39	1.39	1.24
Gross domestic product (GDP)	US$bn	4.91	5.50	6.50	8.42	*10.81
GDP per capita	US$	3,409	3,811	4,648	6,060	8,287
GDP real growth	%	6.9	5.4	5.0	5.2	6.2
Inflation	%	4.0	5.7	4.3	1.5	3.0
Unemployment	%	13.7	12.7	12.5	9.9	9.6
Exports (fob) (goods)	US$m	3,291.6	3,338.0	3,500.0	4,181.0	5,970.3
Imports (fob) (goods)	US$m	4,080.5	4,125.1	4,600.0	5,867.0	7,936.3
Balance of trade	US$m	-788.9	-787.1	-1,141.0	-1,686.0	-1,966.1
Current account	US$m	-314.9	-353.4	-801.6	-1,200.0	-1,540.0
Foreign debt	US$bn	2.5	3.7	3.9	3.3	8.4
Total reserves minus gold	US$m	920.6	820.2	1,000.4	1,373.4	1,788.2
Foreign exchange	US$m	920.6	820.2	1,000.3	1,373.3	1,788.1
Exchange rate	per US$	16.97	17.56	16.31	13.72	11.85

* estimated figure

COUNTRY PROFILE

Historical profile

Around 3,000 BC the Finno-Ugric peoples began to migrate from Eastern Europe to the north-east coast of the Baltic Sea.
1219 Valdemar II of Denmark and the German Sword Brethren, a crusading order, conquered Estonia.
1346 The Danes sold their share of Estonian territory to the Livonian Order of Teutonic Knights (an alliance of the Sword Brethren and the German Order of Teutonic Knights).
1524–39 The State of Teutonic Knights, including Estonia, renounced religious allegiance to Rome and converted to Lutheranism.
1561 In the secularisation and partition of the State of Teutonic Knights, Estonia (now northern Estonia) became part of Sweden and Livonia (now Latvia and southern Estonia) and placed under Polish rule.
1721–1917 Estonia became a Baltic province of Russia.
1918–40 Independent republic.
1940–88 Constituent republic of USSR.
1988 Estonia declared its sovereignty.
1989 Economic autonomy was granted.
1990 Independence from the USSR was declared. The break-up of the Soviet Union led to a sharp decline in output.
1991 Independence was reaffirmed.
1992 Following the country's first free elections since independence, a coalition of various right-wing conservative parties, operating under the name Isamaa Pro Patria, was the heart of the government coalition, headed by Mart Laar as prime minister. Lennart Meri became president. Inflation soared to nearly 1,000 per cent as the Soviet energy and food supply system crumbled and hard currency was required for imports. Estonia introduced its own currency, the kroon, and a new post-Soviet constitution. The kroon was pegged to the Deutsche mark under a currency board system at a ratio of eight to one.
1994 GDP growth was registered for the first time since independence. Estonia joined the NATO Partnership for Peace programme (PfP). Laar lost a vote of no-confidence in the Riigikogu and Andres Tarand became caretaker prime minister until elections.
1995 The governing coalition parties lost ground in the parliamentary elections. A centre-left government was formed under Tiit Vähi as prime minister. Estonia applied to join the EU. The government collapsed when the ECP left.
1996–97 The re-formed coalition collapsed when six ministers resigned and the resulting minority government also

collapsed after Vähi's resignation. The ECP leader, Mart Siimann, became prime minister and formed a minority government with the Estonian Rural Union (EM) and independents.

1999 The Eesti Keskerakond (EK) (Estonian Centre Party) became the largest party in the Riigikogu after parliamentary elections; however, a coalition government was formed by the Erakond Isamaaliit (Isamaaliit) (Fatherland Union), the Reformierakond (RE) (Reform Party) and the Rahvaerakond Mõõdukad (Mõõdukad) (Moderate People's Party), having together a narrow majority of 53 seats. The government was again led by Mart Laar as prime minister. Estonia joined the World Trade Organisation (WTO).

2000 The economy recovered from the 1998 Russian crisis and foreign investment picked up.

2001 Arnold Rüütel was elected president by the electoral college.

2002 Mart Laar resigned over infighting within the coalition government. Siim Kallas, his replacement, formed a new government comprising the EK and RE.

2003 Following the March parliamentary elections Juhan Parts formed a coalition government comprising Uhendus Vabariigi Eest-Res Publica (ResP) (Union for the Republic-Res Publica), the RE and Eestimaa Rahvaliit (Rahvaliit) (Estonian People's Union). In April, the EU Accession Treaty was signed. In a September referendum, Estonians voted to join the EU.

2004 In April, Estonia acceded to NATO and entered the EU on 1 May.

2005 Juhan Parts resigned on 24 March and dissolved the coalition government after his justice minister lost a vote of no confidence in Parliament (54/47); the deputies were concerned about the minister's handling of a controversial anti-corruption plan. On 12 April, Andrus Ansip (RE) was appointed prime minister of a new three-party coalition government of RE, ER and EK. In March, the president declined an invitation to attend the ceremony in Moscow celebrating the end of the Second World War. A treaty delineating the border between Estonia and Russia was signed in May. However, the parliament amended the treaty to include reference the Soviet occupation; Russia suspended the treaty.

Political structure
Constitution
The constitution was adopted on 28 June 1992. It is based on the 1938 model, that provides legal continuity to the Republic of Estonia prior to Soviet occupation.

The constitution was adopted in 1992 when the country held its first post-independence elections. Only Estonian citizens are allowed to vote, leaving the 38 per cent non-Estonian population largely disenfranchised.

The constitution defines the areas of responsibility of the government as: 'to implement domestic and foreign policies; to direct and co-ordinate the work of government institutions; to organise and implement legislation, the resolutions of the Riigikogu (parliament) and edicts of the president; to submit draft laws and foreign treaties to the parliament; to prepare drafts of the state budget and to implement and report on the budget and to organise relations with foreign states'.

The constitution can only be amended by referendum and two successful passages through the Riigikogu.

Estonia is divided into 15 counties and six towns (the other 27 towns form part of the counties). The counties are divided into 193 parishes.

There is universal suffrage – for Estonian citizens only – from age 18.

Form of state
Democratic republic

The executive
Executive power is vested in the president who is directly elected for a five-year term by an electoral college consisting of 101 parliamentary deputies and 266 local government representatives. The winning candidate has to secure a majority within two rounds of voting otherwise the election returns to parliament.

The president nominates the prime minister who then forms a government. In case of the failure of the president's candidate(s) to form a government (the constitution permits the president two nominations), the parliament will name a prime minister to form a government. The prime minister alone nominates the ministers of his cabinet, who are formally appointed by the president and swear an oath before the parliament. Members of the government need not have any political party affiliation nor be members of the parliament.

National legislature
The Riigikogu (parliament) is a unicameral legislature, composed of 101 representatives elected by proportional representation for a four-year term. Its prime constitutional function is legislation, but it also has constitutional duties to review the activities of the executive and directly represent voters.

Legal system
Estonia's legal system is similar to that of continental Europe. The Civil Code underwent large-scale reforms in 2002, the most notable being the implementation of the Law of Obligations Act, which overhauled old contract laws that dated back to the Soviet era.

The Supreme Court has seventeen justices, of which the chief justice is appointed by the parliament after nomination by the president; the rest are appointed by the parliament after nomination by the chief justice. Justices are appointed for life. The Supreme Court can hear appeals, either in full session, or by means of a special *ad hoc* panel.

There are town and county courts where cases are heard by a judge and assistant judges, elected by popular vote.

Last elections
13 June 2004 (European Parliament); 2 March 2003 (parliamentary); 21 September 2001 (presidential).

Results: European Parliament: Eesti Sotsiaaldemokraatlik Tööpartei (Estonian Social Democratic Labour Party) won 36.8 per cent of the vote (three seats out of six), EK 17.5 per cent (one), RE 12.2 per cent (one) and Isamaa 10.5 per cent (one); turnout 26.9 per cent.

Parliamentary: the EK won 25.4 per cent of the vote (28 seats out of 101), ResP 24.6 per cent (28 seats), the Reform Party 17.7 per cent (19 seats), the ER 13 per cent (13 seats), Isamaa 7.3 per cent (seven seats) and the Mõõdukad 7 per cent (six seats); turnout was 58 per cent.

On 12 April 2005 Prime Minister Andrus Ansip formed a coalition government comprising the conservative ResP, centre-right RE and centre-left ER.

Presidential: Arnold Rüütel was elected president by the electoral college.

Next elections
2006 (presidential); 2007 (parliamentary).

Political parties
Ruling party
Three-party coalition government sworn in 13 Apr 2005: Reformierakond (RE) (Reform Party); Eestimaa Rahvaliit (Rahvaliit) (ER) (Estonian People's Union); Eesti Keskerakond (Kesk) (EK) (Estonian Centre Party).

Main opposition party
Uhendus Vabariigi Eest-Res Publica (ResP) (Union for the Republic-Res Publica); Erakond Isamaaliit (Isamaa) (Fatherland Union); Rahvaerakond Mõõdukad (Mõõdukad) (Moderate People's Party).

Population
1.24 million (2004)

Ethnic make-up
Estonians make up the majority of the population (62 per cent), followed by Russians (30 per cent), Ukrainians (3 per cent) and Belarussians (2 per cent). Russians are in the majority in many towns.

Religions
The main religious denominations are Lutheran, Russian Orthodox and Baptist, with Lutherans in the majority.

Nations of the World: A Political, Economic and Business Handbook

Education
Schools may be private, municipal or state run. The backbone of the education system is general comprehensive schooling, which caters for children of all ages and abilities. Pre-school attendance is high but is not a prerequisite for primary schooling. This is part of basic school education, lasting for nine years, starting from the age of seven.

On completion of basic education (aged around 16 – a student may choose to extend or abbreviate their study), a student may continue in an upper secondary or vocational school. The majority of schools offer a general curriculum. Some specialise in a branch of the humanities or sciences.

Compulsory years: 7 to 17
Enrolment rate: 95 per cent boys, 93 per cent girls, total primary school enrolment of the relevant age group (including repetition rates) (World Bank).
Pupils per teacher: 17 in primary schools.

Health
Total expenditure on health is 5–6 per cent of GDP, of which government spending is 77–78 per cent. Private healthcare provision is negligible.

Overall indices show an improvement in health in the general population. Life expectancy has increased by a half a year since 2000 and there has been 10–15 per cent more births registered in the first three months of 2004, stimulated perhaps by a large increases in maternity and paternity allowances, agreed in 2003. Infant mortality has seen a marked improvement down from 12 death per 1,000 live births to eight per 1,000 in 2003.

HIV prevalence: 1.1 per cent aged 15–49 in 2003 (World Bank)
Life expectancy: 71.2 years (World Bank)
Fertility rate/Maternal mortality rate: 1.4 births per woman; maternal mortality 50 per 100,000 live births (World Bank).
Infant mortality rate: 8 per 1,000 live births (World Bank)
Head of population per physician/bed: 3.1 physicians and 7.4 hospital beds typically available per 1,000 people.

Welfare
The guiding principle behind the government's social welfare development policy is the complete dismantling of the state-centred Soviet system. Government priorities include the establishment of an adequate social security system, funded by contributions from employers and employees.

Main cities
Tallinn (capital, estimated population 379,000 in 2003), Tartu (100,100), Narva (59,500), Kohtla-Järve (40,700), Pärnu (37,900).

Languages spoken
Estonian belongs to the Baltic-Finnic group of the Finno-Ugric languages, which also includes Hungarian and Finnish. The Latin alphabet is used. Various other languages spoken include Latvian, Lithuanian, Ukrainian, Belarusian, Russian, Finnish, Yiddish and German. English has replaced Russian as the primary business language.

By law, all transactions, contracts and company returns have to be in Estonian. Notarised transactions in English often accompany these.

Official language/s
Estonian

Media
Press
Under article 45 of the 1991 constitution, press censorship is not permitted in Estonia. All major newspapers are privatised. The Estonian Newspapers' Association includes 45 newspapers. In addition, there are other newspapers which are not part of the Association.

Dailies: Estonia's largest daily papers are *Postimees Eesti Sonumid, Monitor, Õhtuleht, Monitor, Tallinn-PM, Eesti Päevaleht* and *Sõnumileht*.

Weeklies: There is a wide range of weeklies, including *The Baltic Times* (in English) and *Eesti Ekspress*. *Delovoje Vedomosti* is a Sunday paper on business, *Maaleht* and *Sirp* are other popular weeklies.

Business: *Aripäev* is a business daily published by the Dagens Industri of Sweden. *Eesti Ekspress* is a weekly commercial newspaper.

Periodicals: *The Baltic Review* has general editorial features and those related to consumer interests. Other periodicals include *The Baltic Guide* and *Maakodu*, a monthly publication, features rural interest.

Broadcasting
The state-owned TV and radio has been transformed into two public service companies, regulated by a new broadcasting law and governed by a General Council, appointed by parliament. The two public service companies are members of the European Broadcasting Union (EBU).

Radio: Radio Estonia broadcasts in eight languages. There is also an independent radio station, Radio Kuku, broadcasting from Tallinn. Several local commercial radio stations broadcast all over Estonia. There are some 27 private radio stations operating in the country. Four are non-commercial, with three belonging to the Estonian Evangelical Christian and Baptist Congregations. Three private radio stations transmit Russian-language programmes.

Television: National TV broadcasts in Estonian and Russian. Three main private commercial TV channels, and some smaller ones, operate on two networks: ETV (state-owned), TV3 (private), Kanal 2, TV1 and ORT (Russian). It is also possible to receive Finnish programmes, and, in some parts of the country, Swedish transmissions.

Advertising
There are laws forbidding tobacco advertising and advertisements that promote the consumption of alcohol. It is forbidden to use newscasters or political commentators in advertising.

Economy
Estonia has restructured and stabilised its economy in a remarkably short period of time, achieving substantial progress in creating a market economy. It has one of the most liberal trading environments in Central and Eastern Europe (CEE). The World Bank ranked Estonia in its *Doing Business Economy Ranking* 16 for ease of doing business, and 43 for starting a business, out of 155, in 2005. In 2004 Estonia registered 'extraordinary' GDP growth of 6.2 per cent, and 8.5 per cent for the first six months of 2005, according to the IMF. These figures came on top of an already impressive 5.2 per cent in 2003. Robust domestic demand has been the main driving force of the economy, sucking in imports and causing the current account deficit to balloon. In 2005, IMF officials warned that this deficit could increase Estonia's external vulnerabilities. The painful macroeconomic reforms of the post-Soviet years have led to large productivity gains and suggest that the economy is capable of sustaining high levels of economic growth for a number of years. Inflation has increased since mid-2004, reaching 4.8 per cent by September, although for the year as a whole, it registered 3.0 per cent, up on 1.5 per cent in 2003. The unemployment rate has continued to fall, down to 9.6 per cent in 2004. The overall signs are of the beginnings of economy overheating as output is considered close to capacity and labour shortages are appearing in the construction industry.

Given the small size of the economy, the Estonian authorities regard early membership of the euro-zone as a priority, and as a means of protecting the economy – and the country in general – from global economic turbulence. Estonia joined the EU Exchange Rate Mechanism (ERM) – a centralised exchange rate that sets a margin within which a currency must remain – in June 2004 and unilaterally maintains its currency pegged to the euro.

The economy of Estonia since 2000 has impressed most analysts, with its strong and steady growth in GDP, however some are warning that things may now be beginning to self destruct, with inflation and personal credit running higher than expected. Nevertheless the government has firmly set it sights on the huge EU market, and membership of the European Monetary Union (EMU), to sustain Estonia's growth, exports of goods and services and the inflow of foreign and EU investment. The IMF has called for fiscal restraint and careful supervision of credit, while maintaining competitiveness, a call that seems to echo the government's strategy.

External trade
The Baltic Free Trade Agreement establishes a free trade area within the three Baltic States.

Imports
Principal imports are machinery and equipment (33.5 per cent), chemical products, textiles, foodstuffs and vehicle equipment.
Main sources: Finland (19.9 per cent total, 2004), Russia (13.2 per cent), Germany (11.6 per cent), Sweden (7.9 per cent)

Exports
Main exports include machinery and equipment (33 per cent), wood and paper, textiles, food products, furniture, metals, chemical products.
Main destinations: Finland (16.6 per cent total, 2004), Sweden (11.1 per cent), UK (8.6 per cent), Latvia (7.4 per cent), Germany (7.2 per cent), Russia (6.9 per cent), US (5.5 per cent), Lithuania (4.0 per cent)

Agriculture
Farming
The agricultural sector experienced a severe decline following independence until 2004 when it jumped by 2.5 per cent, from -1.5 per cent in 2003. The agriculture sector accounts for around 4.4 per cent of GDP – a fall from 9.9 per cent in 1994 – and employs 29 per cent of the workforce.

The agricultural reform programme has produced mixed results. Most large state-run farms have been dismantled but some co-operatives and state-owned farms persist.

Government agricultural policy is designed to provide affordable food for Estonians while balancing farm income and guaranteeing farm workers equivalent earnings to industrial workers.

Estonia is eligible for EU subsidies and rural development funds through the Common Agricultural Policy (CAP). However, like the other new EU member countries, it will only get the full amount by 2013. The EU decided to introduce CAP support funds gradually over a 10-year period.

During its transitional entry stage Estonia has decided to implement the reform of the CAP on 1 January 2009. The reform was introduced throughout most of the EU on 1 January 2005, when subsidies on farm output, which tended to benefit large farms and encourage overproduction, were replaced by single farm payments, not conditional on production. The change is expected to reward farms that provide and maintain a healthy environment, food safety and animal welfare standards. The changes are also intended to encourage market conscious production and cut the cost of CAP to the EU taxpayer.

Crop production in 2004 included: 599,701 tonnes (t) cereals in total, 184,730t wheat, 178,867t potatoes, 289,472t barley, 75,239t oats, 3,933t pulses, 3,700t tomatoes, 27,791t oilcrops, 17,700t apples, 26,830t fruit in total, 57,296t vegetables in total. Livestock production included: 68,076t meat in total, 13,783t beef, 38,542t pig meat, 312t lamb, 15,319t poultry, 13,070t eggs, 639,645t milk, 500t honey, 1,685t cattle hides.

Fishing
Some 130,000 tonnes of fish are caught per annum. The total catch has fallen dramatically as disputes with Latvia over territorial waters and falling investment have contributed to lower catches. Estonia has been a net fish importer since independence, although the value of exports has increased.

Forestry
Forest makes up 40 per cent of available land in Estonia. As with all sectors the forestry industry suffers from outdated machinery, equipment and a lack of finance and investment, yet despite this, total timber production has increased.

The government has established special credits for the forestry industry to develop technology. Traditionally most Estonian timber exports were of logs and for paper. A further increase in the overall value of timber exports is anticipated as paper related exports decline and the export of finished timber products increases.

The timber-processing industry has developed quickly, and the export potential for Estonian timber products is good, principally in Scandinavia, but also in Russia and Ukraine.

Estonia's only pulp mill at Kehra is owned by Horizon Pulp and Paper, part of the Singapore-based Tolaram group. In 2006, Estonian Cell, which is owned by Norway's Larvik Cell, will begin constructing a pulp mill at Kunda in northern Estonia. The mill, which will cost around US$184 million, will be partly financed by the European Bank for Reconstruction and Development (EBRD).

Exports in 2004 amounted to US$555 million, remaining somewhat constant on the 2003 figure, while imports were valued at US$305 million, an increase of one-third.

Production in 2004 included: 10,300,000 cubic metres (cum) roundwood, 8,300,000cum industrial roundwood, 2,000,000cum sawnwood, 4,300,000cum sawlogs and veneers, 2,850,000cum pulpwood, 2,000,000cum woodfuel, 387,825cum wood-based panels.

Industry and manufacturing
Industry contributed 29.3 per cent to GDP, of which 18.2 per cent was supplied by the manufacturing sector in 2004; both registered a 5 per cent growth rate.

During the Soviet era, the Estonian industrial sector was characterised by a high degree of concentration (20 per cent of enterprises produced two-thirds of industrial output), dependence on imports from the Soviet Union (80 per cent of all imports) and a reliance on the markets of the Soviet Union (90 per cent of exports). Since independence in 1990 industry has undergone much restructuring, with long-term investment following privatisation. Traditional industries such a furniture making are still thriving accounting for 9 per cent of exports in 2004, to modern advanced biomedical research and production with an emphasis on gene research and technologies. Electronics factories provide high-tech components for international corporations such as Nokia and Philips.

Estonia's relatively cheap labour, energy and raw materials are the main reasons for the country's industrial competitiveness, coupled with tax incentives for businesses and a well-educated and motivated workforce.

Tourism
Tourism is an important sector of the economy that is expected to contribute US$574 million or 4.9 per cent of GDP. In line with the lack of direct foreign investment, travel and tourism is expected to attract US$706 million, however this represents 21.3 per cent of total capital investment. The sector should generate US$1.5 billion in total exports and employ 17.7 per cent of the workforce.

Travel links, especially by air, and infrastructure continue to improve. The visitor attractions are mainly heritage-related, with Tallinn being the main destination, but other sectors, including rural and adventure tourism, are being developed. Visitor numbers in 2004 were 1.7 million; Finland continues to be the principal market, accounting for over 50 per cent of visitors.

Mining
Estonia has a limited range of mineral resources, principally for use in the construction industry. Mining and quarrying activities contribute less than 1 per cent of GDP.

Hydrocarbons
Estonia has no proven crude oil reserves, however there is a substantial amount of oil shale in the north-east. Estonian oil shale is produced by the state owned company Eesti Polevkivi (Estonian Oil Shale). Some 75 per cent of the country's energy needs are provided from oil shale. However due to the heavily polluting nature of oil shale the industry is under pressure from the EU to slow down and meet regulations. No new mines are scheduled to be built and it is predicted that in the next few years production targets will be lowered. Estonia remains important for the oil industry as Russian exports travel through the Estonian ports to be exported into the EU.

Estonia imports around 90 per cent of its oil needs. All Estonia's natural gas consumption is imported primarily through a 250-mile pipeline from Russia. The country produces no coal and relies entirely on imports, however coal consumption is expected to taper off as EU environmental regulations take effect.

Energy
Up to 75 per cent of Estonia's energy supply is derived from oil shale, but this is due to change by 2006 when the adoption of EU environmental regulations should have taken effect. The Narva Power Plants, which transform oil shale, supply some 90 per cent of the country's electricity. Natural gas, petroleum and by-products are all imported, mainly from Russia.

Financial markets
Stock exchange
The Tallinn Stock Exchange (TSE) is run by OMX Exchanges, a company that owns and operates the largest integrated and regulated Nordic and Baltic securities market in Northern Europe.

Banking and insurance
The commercial banking sector is licensed by the central bank. Foreign-owned banks are permitted to operate and bank shares are freely traded.
Central bank
Eesti Pank (Bank of Estonia)
Main financial centre
Tallinn

Time
GMT plus two hours; summer, GMT plus three hours

Geography
Estonia is situated in north-east Europe, the northernmost of the three Baltic States, bordering the Russian Federation to the east and Latvia to the south. Its northern coastline is on the Gulf of Finland and its western coastline in the Gulf of Riga and the Baltic Sea. From north to south the country measures 240km, from east to west 360km. With a total land area of 45,227 square km, Estonia is the smallest of the Baltic states and about the same size as Denmark.

Climate
The mildest areas are along the Baltic coast. Summer is short, with sunshine lasting up to nine hours a day, and an average temperature of 15 degrees Celsius (C). Winters are cold, with slush, ice and repeated light coverings of snow (average -4 degrees C). Spring and autumn are very short.

Dress codes
Warm clothes are required during winter, with a raincoat and umbrella necessary during the summer. Business dress is conservative but relatively informal, with a jacket and tie expected for meetings.

Entry requirements
Passports
Required by all.
Visa
Are required by all, except citizens of Europe, US, Australasia and some Asian countries. A full list can be found at www.visitestonia.com/.
Apart from the conditions of the tourist visas, further requirements for a business visa are necessary: a letter of invitation, a business letter declaring purpose of visit, a full itinerary and an undertaking of full financial security for the company representative. Accident and health insurance are also required.
For full details see www.estonia.com.
Currency advice/regulations
The import and export of local and foreign currency is limited to EEK80,000 or its equivalent.
Customs
There is a small duty-free allowance for personal goods. Declare all foreign currency and valuable items such as jewellery, cameras, computers and musical instruments.

Health (for visitors)
Mandatory precautions
No specific requirements.
Advisable precautions
Vaccinations may be advised for hepatitis 'A' and diphtheria.
Take mosquito lotion if travelling outside the towns. There is a risk of rabies.

Hotels
There are numerous good quality western style hotels in Tallinn. It is advisable to book a hotel before travelling.
For the peak period of June and July, the Estonian Tourist Board suggests the traveller books in January.
Bills must be paid in Estonian kroons if credit cards are not accepted.

Credit cards
Most major hotels and restaurants and a few shops accept American Express, Visa, Eurocard and Diners' Club.

Public holidays
Fixed dates
1 Jan (New Year's Day), 24 Feb (Independence Day), 1 May (Spring Day), 23 Jun (Victory Day, Anniversary of the Battle of Vonnu), 25 Jun (St John's Day, Midsummer), 25 Dec (Christmas Day), 26 Dec (Boxing Day).
Variable dates
Good Friday, Whit Sunday.

Working hours
Banking
Mon–Fri: 0930–1630.
Business
Mon–Fri: 0830–1830 (appointments best between 0900–1000). Lunch around 1300. Some offices stop work at 1630.
Government
Mon–Fri: 0900–1700.
Shops
Mon–Fri: 0930–1900, Sat: 0930–1600.

Social customs/useful tips
Estonians can be quite reserved and are not particularly talkative. Shaking hands is the normal form of greeting. Flowers are generally acceptable as a gift.
There is a service charge of 10 to 15 per cent, but a small tip in addition is appreciated.
Saunas are popular in Estonia, usually followed by a substantial meal washed down with liberal quantities of beer and vodka. Until you are sure of the ethnic background of your host avoid talking about Russians and the communist past. Many Estonians have relatives who were sent to Siberia, which has left strong feelings when it comes to Russia. Also avoid asking what your host did during the Soviet occupation – it may sound to them you are asking if they were a member of the Communist Party or even if they were sent to Siberia.
There is a strong sense of national pride and identity among Estonians and they do not appreciate being lumped together with Latvia and Lithuania as 'the Baltic states', or even being described as part of eastern Europe.

Security
Estonia is a safe place to visit compared to some of the other former Soviet republics, although muggings do occur in urban areas, especially at night. Car theft is also a problem.

Getting there
Air
National airline: Estonian Air
International airport/s: Tallinn (TLL) airport, 5km north-west of city. Includes a business centre, bank, post office, restaurant, bar, shops and car rental. Conference facilities also available. Bus no. 2 runs between the city and the airport, taking 15 minutes. A shuttle bus to the main hotels and the city centre meets all flights.
Airport tax: There is no airport tax.

Surface
Road: Foreign cars are flagged down at borders to examine the documents in an attempt to block the flow of stolen foreign cars. Check insurance before travelling and do not buy cheap insurance at the frontier. There are direct routes along the Baltic coast connecting Latvia and Lithuania and also the Russian Federation.
Rail: International lines run from surrounding countries, although rail travel between Estonia, Latvia and Lithuania is time-consuming.
Water: The Estline ferry service runs between Stockholm and Tallinn. A number of companies operate hydrofoil and ferry services between Helsinki and Tallinn. A once-a-week roll on/roll-off ferry line goes from Rostock (Germany) via Helsinki.
Main port/s: Muuga is Tallinn's port and is the most modern in the country.

Getting about
National transport
Air: There is limited domestic air travel with Baltic Aeroservis, which serves the islands of Kuressaare and Kärdla. Charter flights to other destinations can also be booked.
Road: Estonia has a high density of roads although there are few major highways. Signs are not illuminated and fairly small, so driving at night is best avoided. In winter roads can be icy and ungritted. The high level of car crime in the Baltic States means that border crossings can be very lengthy processes and insurance can be difficult to find.
Buses: Estonia has a very extensive bus network linking every area of the country. Tickets should be booked in advance.
Rail: The majority of major cities are covered. Tallinn and Tartu are connected by an express service.

City transport
Taxis: Taxis in Tallinn are relatively cheap. There is a good taxi service from Tallinn International Airport to the city centre, with a journey time of 10 minutes. Private services should display the name of the company and its number on the roof. Fares should be agreed upon beforehand. There are also minibuses called Marshrut-taxis, which operate on set routes, stopping at fixed destinations and seating up to 10 people.
Buses, trams & metro: All parts of the city can also be reached by bus, trolley-bus and tram. Tickets can be bought from stalls in the main shopping areas.

Car hire
Car hire can be arranged at the airport. Never drink and drive – no level of alcohol is permitted. Speed limit is 50km per hour in built-up areas, 90km per hour in the country and 110km per hour on motorways. Leaded petrol is easy to find and unleaded exists too. In towns there are parking permits, fines and wheel clamps. Driving is on the right. EU nationals should be in possession of a national driving licence.
The international car hire firms Avis, Hertz and Europcar all have bureaux in Estonia. Roads, although deteriorating, are of a reasonably good standard but can be dangerous in winter due to ice.

BUSINESS DIRECTORY
The addresses listed below are a selection only. While World of Information makes every endeavour to check these addresses, we cannot guarantee that changes have not been made, especially to telephone numbers and area codes. We would welcome any corrections.

Telephone area codes
The international direct dialling code (IDD) for Estonia is +372, followed by area code and subscriber's number:

Haapsalu	47	Rapla	48
Jõgeva	77	Tallinn	none
Narva	35	Valga	76
Pärnu	44	Viljandi	43
Polva	79	Voru	78

Useful telephone numbers
Fire brigade: 01
Police: 02
Ambulance: 03
Gas: 04
NB Numbers 01–04 cannot be dialled from mobile telephones; 112 should be dialled instead.

Chambers of Commerce
American Chamber of Commerce Estonia, Tallinn Business Centre, 6 Harju, 10130 Tallinn (tel: 631-0522; fax: 631-0521; e-mail: acce@acce.ee).

British-Estonian Chamber of Commerce, 21 Suur-Karja, 10148 Tallinn (tel: 640-5872; fax: 640-5873; e-mail: info@becc.ec).

Estonian Chamber of Commerce and Industry, 17 Toom-Kooli, 10130 Tallinn (tel: 646-0244; fax: 646-0245; e-mail: koda@koda.ee).

Banking
Eesti Forekspank (Estonian Forexbank), Narva mnt 9a, Tallinn (tel: 630-2100; fax: 630-2200; e-mail: bank@forex.ee); international settlements (tel: 640-6400).

Eesti Hoiupank (Estonian Savings Bank), Kinga 1, Tallinn (tel: 630-2600; fax: 630-2602; e-mail: mailbob@esb.ee).

Eesti Investeerimispank (Estonian Investment Bank), PO Box 26, Narva mnt 7, Tallinn (tel: 620-0800; fax: 620-0812/0801; e-mail: info@estib.ee); international settlements (tel: 620-0828).

Eesti Krediidipank (Estonian Credit Bank), Narva mnt 4, Tallinn (tel: 640-5000; fax: 631-3533; e-mail: krediidipank@ekp.ee).

Eesti Maapank (Land Bank of Estonia), Tallinna 12, Rakvere (tel: 43-821; fax: 43-617); in Tallinn (tel: 646-6295; fax: 646-6649/6313-720); international settlements (tel: 640-8321).

Eesti Pangaliit (Estonian Association of Banks), Pärnu mnt 19, Tallinn (tel: 245-5400; fax: 245-5401; e-mail: panagaliit@teleport.ee).

Eesti Uhispank (Union Bank of Estonia), Tartu mnt 13, Tallinn (tel: 610-4300, 631-2728; fax: 610-4302); international settlements (tel: 640-3516, 640-3519).

Hansapank, Liivalaia 8, EE0001 Tallinn (tel: 631-0311/310; fax: 631-0410; e-mail: webmaster@hansa.ee).

Merita Bank Ltd (foreign bank's branch), Harju 6, Tallinn (tel: 631-4040; fax: 631-4153; e-mail: merita@estpak.ee).

Tallinna Aripanga Aktsiaselts (Tallinn Business Bank), Estonia pst 3/5, Tallinn (tel: 245-5349; fax: 242-3322; e-mail: tbb@torn.ee).

Tallinna Pank, Parnu mnt 10, Tallinn (tel: 631-0100/0102, 640-5880; fax: 631-0111; e-mail: info@tp.ee); international settlements (tel: 640-5829).

Central bank
Eesti Pank (Bank of Estonia), Estonia Boulevard 13, Tallinn 15095 (tel: 668-0900; fax: 668-0954; e-mail: info@epbe.ee).

Travel information
Baltic Tours, Vene 23B, Tallinn (tel: 244-6331; fax: 244-0760).

Estonian Air, Vabaduse, Valjak 10, Tallinn (tel: 244-6383, 244-0295; fax: 631-2740).

Estonian Association of Travel Agents, Pikk 71, Tallinn (tel: 260-1705; fax: 242-5594).

Estonian Railways, 36 Pikk Str, Tallinn (tel: 240-1610; fax: 240-1710).

Finest Hotel Group, Parnu mnt 22, Tallinn (tel: 245-1510; fax: 244-6029).

Lufthansa Airport Office (tel: 638-8077; fax: 638-8077); Lufthansa city centre, Pärnu mnt 10, Tallinn (tel: 631-4444).

National tourist organisation offices
Estonian Tourist Board, 2-4 Kiriku Str, Tallinn (tel: 641-1420; fax: 641-1432; internet: http://www.visitestonia.com).

Ministries
Ministry of Agriculture, Lai 39/41, Tallinn (tel: 244-1166; fax: 244-0601).

Ministry of Citizenship and Immigration, Ministry of the Interior, Pikk 61, Tallinn (tel: 244-5080; fax: 260-2785).

Ministry of Culture and Education, Suur Karja 23, Tallinn (tel: 244-5077; fax: 244-0963).

Ministry of Defence, Pikk 57, Tallinn (tel: 239-9160/50; fax: 239-9165).

Ministry of Economic Affairs, Harju 11, Tallinn (tel: 244-0577; fax: 244-6860).

Ministry of Energy, Ministry of Economy, Kiriku 6, Tallinn (tel: 244-3941; fax: 244-8091).

Ministry of Environment, Toompuiestee 24, Tallinn (tel: 245-2507; fax: 245-3310).

Ministry of Finance, Suur Ameerika 1, Tallinn (tel: 268-3445; fax: 268-2097).

Ministry of Finance (Foreign Affairs Dept), Kohtu 8, Tallinn (fax: 245-2992).

Ministry of Foreign Affairs, Ravala 9, Tallinn (tel: 231-7091; fax: 277-1677, 231-7099; internet site: http://www.vm.ee).

Ministry of Industry and Energy, Gonsiori Str 29, Tallinn (tel: 242-3550; fax: 242-1133); Foreign Relations Dept (fax: 242-5468).

Ministry of the Interior, Pikk 61, Tallinn (tel: 266-3611; fax: 260-2785, 244-1112).

Ministry of Justice, Suur Karja 19, Tallinn (tel: 244-5120; fax: 224-6235).

Ministry of Reform, State Chancellery, Lossi Plats 1a, Tallinn (tel: 231-6730; fax: 244-0372).

Ministry of Social Affairs, Gonsiori 29, Tallinn (tel: 242-3434; fax: 242-1862).

Ministry of Trade and Commerce, Kiriku Tn 6, Tallinn (tel: 244-3941, 244-5921); Foreign Relations Dept (fax: 244-8091).

Ministry of Transport and Communication, Viru 9, Tallinn (tel: 239-7613; fax: 239-7606); Foreign Relations Department (fax: 244-9206).

Prime Minister's Office, Losi Plats 1a, Tallinn (tel: 231-6701; fax: 244-0372).

Other useful addresses
A/S Seesam Insurance, Kreutzwali 2/Narva mnt 24, Tallinn (tel: 243-3518; fax: 242-4886).

A/S Central (shipping agents), Hospidali 6, Parnu (tel: 244-0707).

Asker (building advice), Roosikrantsi 12, Tallinn (tel: 244-2165, 277-1304/124; fax: 277-1189).

Association of Construction Materials Producers of Estonia, Jaama 1A, Tallinn (tel: 251-2230; fax: 650-6178).

Baltic Insurance Co, Olevimagi 12, Tallinn (tel: 260-1384; fax: 260-1790).

Baltic Trade Company (commercial service organising exhibitions, seminars, joint ventures), Ravala Str 27, Tallinn (tel: 245-5089; fax: 244-5768).

Baltlink, Tartu mnt 13, Tallinn (tel: 242-1003; fax: 245-0893).

British Embassy, Kentmanni 20, 20001 Tallinn (tel: 631-3461/2; fax: 631-3354); commercial section (fax: 631-3463).

Business Advisory Services Centre, Lei 9, Tallinn (tel: 260-9675; fax: 631-3523).

Confederation of Estonian Industry, Gonsiori 29, Tallinn (tel: 242-2235; fax: 242-4962).

Department for Foreign Economic Relations, Suur Ameerika 1, Tallinn (tel: 268-3559; fax: 268-3622).

Department of Statistics, Endla 15, Tallinn (tel: 245-3889; fax: 245-3923; internet site: http://stat.vil.ee/K.E.S-ENGL.htm).

Eesti-Estline, Sadama 29, Tallinn (tel: 244-9051; fax: 242-5352).

Estonian Association of Construction Entrepreneurs, Ravala 8, Tallinn (tel/fax: 243-3213).

Estonian Business Advisory Services, Tallinn BAS Centre, Lai 0, Tallinn (tel: 260-9795; fax: 631-3523).

Estonian Embassy (USA), 1730 M Street, NW, Washington DC 20036 (tel: 202-588-0101; fax: 202-588-0108; e-mail: info@estemb.org).

Estonian Export Council, Kiriku 2/4, Tallinn (tel: 244-4703; fax: 244-3615).

Estonian Foreign Trade Association, Uus 32/34, Tallinn (tel: 260-1462; fax: 260-2184).

Estonian Institute for Market Research, Vaike-Karja 1, Tallinn (tel: 244-8605; fax: 244-1378, 277-1675).

Estonian Institute (information service), PO Box 3469, Tonismagi 8, Tallinn (tel: 244-0513; fax: 268-2057; e-mail: einst@einst.ee; internet site: http://www.einst.ee).

Estonian Investment Agency (EIA), Ravala Str 6 (room 602B), Tallinn (tel: 641-0166; fax: 641-0312).

Estonian Maritime Industry, Sadama 17, Tallinn (tel: 260-1723; fax: 244-4808).

Estonian Shipping Co, 3/5 Estonian Blvd, Tallinn (tel: 244-3802; fax: 242-4958, 243-1228).

Estonian State Energy Department, 29 Gonsiori Str, Tallinn (tel: 242-1579; fax: 242-5468, 242-1908); external department (tel: 242-1480).

Estonian Trade Council, Kiriku Str 2/4, Tallinn (tel: 244-4703; fax: 244-4615).

Hanson Insurance, Narva mnt 24, Tallinn (tel: 261-2440; fax: 242-5977).

Loksa Shipyard, Tallinn (tel: 257-5241; fax: 263-91230).

Municipality of Tallinn, Vabaduse Valjak 7, Tallinn (tel: 266-6146; fax: 244-1230).

National Customs Board, Ravala pst 9, Tallinn (tel: 231-7722; fax: 231-7727).

Port of Tallinn Authority, Sadama 25, Tallinn (tel: 242-7009; fax: 242-2950).

Radio Estonia – Foreign Service, Gonsiori 21, Tallinn (tel: 243-4282; fax: 243-4139).

Reklaam/Television Ltd, Tonismagi 2, Tallinn (tel: 243-4606; fax: 231-1077).

Ookean State Stock Corporation (Estonian Fishing Company), Paljassaare Str 28, Tallinn (tel: 247-1421, 249-7212; fax: 249-8190).

State Department of Foreign Trade, Komsomoli 1, Tallinn (tel: 268-3559; fax: 268-3097).

State Chancellery, Lossi Plats 1a, Tallinn (tel: 231-6730; fax: 244-0372).

Swiss Baltic Re-Advisers, Lai 27, Tallinn (tel: 244-8949; fax: 274-6469).

Tallink, PO Box 3495, Tallinn (tel: 244-0770; fax: 244-5224).

Tallinn New Port, Maardu tee 57, Tallinn (tel: 223-6500, 223-4313; fax: 223-8805).

Tallinn Stock Exchange, Tallinn (tel: 244-1920; fax: 244-9382).

Internet sites
Estonia Business: http://www.ee/www/Business/welcome.html

Estonia Country Guide: http://www.ciesin.ee/estcg/

Estonia Investment: http://www.investinestonia.com

Ethiopia

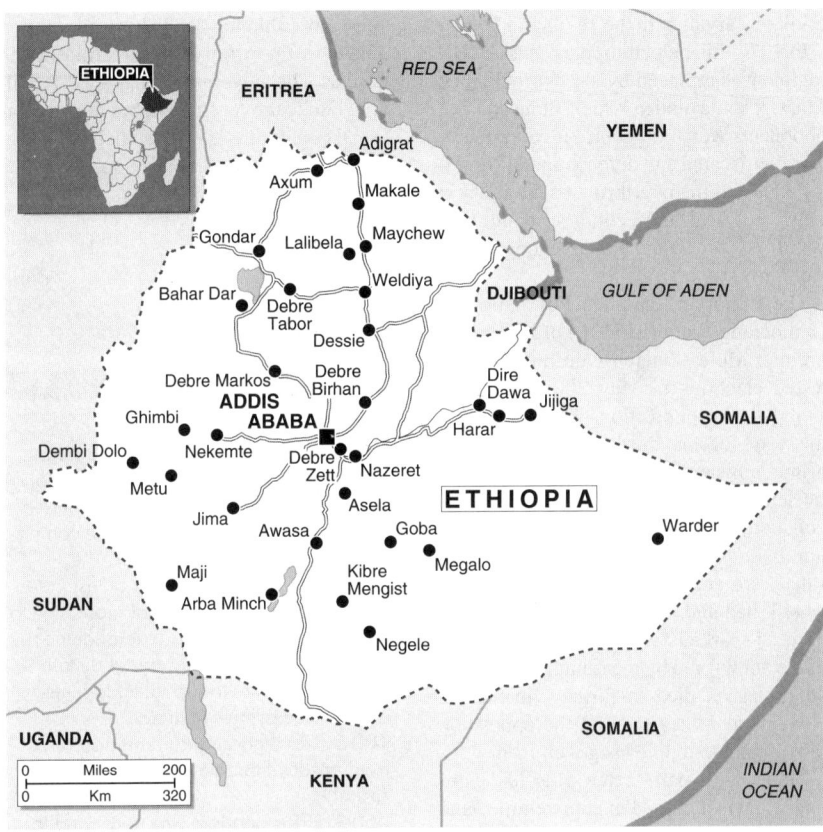

KEY FACTS

Official name: Ityopia (Federal Democratic Republic of Ethiopia)

Head of State: President Girma Wolde Giorgise (elected by parliament 8 Oct 2001)

Head of government: Prime Minister Meles Zenawi (leader of EPRDF) (since 1995; re-elected May 2005)

Ruling party: Ethiopian People's Revolutionary Democratic Front (EPRDF), an alliance led by the Tigray People's Liberation Front (TPLF)

Area: 1,251,282 square km

Population: 72.03 million (2004)

Capital: Addis Ababa

Official language: Amharic

Currency: Birr (Birr) = 100 cents

Exchange rate: Birr8.72 per US$ (Oct 2005)

GDP per capita: US$116 (2004)

GDP real growth: 11.60% (2004)

Labour force: 30.68 million (2004)

Inflation: 9.00% (2004)

Balance of trade: -US$1.54 billion (2004)

Foreign debt: US$3.00 billion (2004)

Ethiopia's poverty-stricken economy is based on agriculture, which accounts for half of gross domestic product, 60 per cent of exports, and 80 per cent of total employment. The agricultural sector suffers from frequent drought and poor cultivation practices. Coffee is critical to the Ethiopian economy, but historically low prices have seen many farmers switching to qat (a mildly narcotic leaf) to supplement their income.

Economy

Ethiopia remains one of Africa's poorest states, with a very low income per capita and a population that is almost two-thirds illiterate. Despite protestations from those being moved, its economy is highly dependent on agriculture, which in turn is almost entirely dependent on rainfall.

Many Ethiopians rely on food aid from abroad. In 2004 the government began a drive to move more than two million people away from the arid highlands of the east. Despite protestations from those being moved, authorities said the programme aimed to provide a lasting solution to food shortages.

The baseline development scenario takes into account four basic objectives:
- that there is a real growth rate average of 5.3 per cent for the period up to 2015
- annual inflation contained to 3 per cent
- foreign reserves at four months of imports
- a reducing ratio of total (domestic and foreign) debt to GDP.

The path of annual fiscal deficits excluding grants would need to be contained to about 10 per cent of GDP over the medium term. Assumed donor assistance would increase by US$5 billion per annum until 2015/16, before shifting to a downward trend.

A significant risk to successfully implementing the baseline scenario is the reoccurrence of a severe drought, which strikes about every third year, on average, and the creeping desertification apparent throughout northern Africa.

Taking into account the expected net foreign financing, the IMF has urged Ethiopia to limit domestic borrowing requirement to 1.5 per cent of GDP. There should be appropriate steps to ensure that all government borrowing decisions are only approved if consistent with the public debt strategy.

Over the period to 2006/07, the external current account deficit (excluding official grants) is projected to narrow progressively as a per cent of GDP. With export volume growing more strongly than import volume and some improvement in the terms of trade over the outer years, the trade deficit is also forecast to narrow somewhat. The current level of the exchange rate does not suggest a competitiveness problem. Services and non-coffee exports have been growing strongly and coffee export volumes have risen despite a decline in prices. Monetary and exchange rate policies will need to focus on achieving the government's inflation and international reserve targets. The case that the exchange rate should be weaker is not compelling.

Politics

Ethiopia is Africa's oldest independent country and, with the exception of a five-year occupation by Mussolini's Italy, has never been colonised. In the first part of the twentieth century Ethiopia forged strong links with Britain, whose troops helped evict the Italians in 1941 and put Emperor Haile Selassie back on his throne. During the 1960s and early 1970s British influence gave way to that of the US, which in turn was supplanted by the then-USSR.

Although relatively free from the coups that have plagued other African countries, Ethiopia's turmoil has been no less devastating. Drought, famine, war and ill-conceived policies brought millions to the brink of starvation in the 1970s and 1980s.

In 1974 this helped topple Selassie. His regime was replaced by a self-proclaimed Marxist junta under which thousands of opponents were purged or killed, property was confiscated and defence spending spiralled. With the overthrow of the junta in 1991, political and economic conditions stabilised somewhat, but not enough to restore investor confidence.

The Ethiopian People's Revolutionary Democratic Front (EPRDF) of incumbent premier Meles Zenawi won bitterly contested elections in May 2005, despite a swing to the opposition. The win paved the way for his third five-year stint as prime minister.

Claims of vote rigging accompanied the poll, and the EPRDF and the main opposition both claimed victory as the initial results were announced. Around 36 people were killed and hundreds were arrested in protests sparked by opposition allegations of electoral fraud by the ruling party. Some 46 protesters died in further violence in November. Meles accused the opposition of planning to topple his government.

Meles took part in the guerrilla campaign against the Mengistu regime, and was chosen as transitional head of state after the overthrow of the dictator in 1991. Once a Marxist-Leninist, by the 1990s he had become a champion of the free market and parliamentary democracy.

Ethiopia continues to face political uncertainties, largely related to the demarcation of its border with Eritrea. The Eritrea-Ethiopia Boundary Commission ruling that the town of Badme would be located within Eritrea ignited strong opposition in Ethiopia, leading to protracted delays in the official demarcation of the border. The government has said it will not go to war over Badme, but the international community's efforts, including a recent UN initiative, have not succeeded so far in resolving the impasse.

Risk assessment

Economic	Poor
Political	Poor
Regional stability	Poor

COUNTRY PROFILE

Historical profile

For millennia, Ethiopia has stood apart from the rest of Africa by virtue of its long history, rich religious and cultural heritage, unique ethnic and linguistic composition and style of government. The troubled passage of Africa's oldest independent country from feudal monarchy to something resembling a federal democracy, via two decades of brutal dictatorship, ran parallel to droughts, famines and the secession of Eritrea.
100 BC A kingdom including part of modern-day Ethiopia existed around Axum.
450 AD The kingdom was converted to Christianity and the Ethiopian church became part of the Coptic community.
1896 Italy tried to seize Ethiopia but lost the Battle of Adwa. The Italians held on to Eritrea on the Red Sea coast.
1916 Ras Tafari, later known as Emperor Haile Selassie, gained power over local lords but his appeal to the League of Nations for help against the occupying Italians went unheeded.
1936 Benito Mussolini's army invaded all of Ethiopia, which became part of Italian East Africa.
1941 British and Commonwealth troops along with the *arbegnoch*, Ethiopian resistance, fought the Italians.
1945 Emperor Haile Selassie returned to power after the Second World War.
1962 Eritrea was annexed by Ethiopia.
1974 Haile Selassie was deposed in coup led by Teferi Benti.
1975 Haile Selassie died in custody.
1977 Benti was killed and replaced by Colonel Mengistu Haile Mariam, who led a brutal regime known as the Dergue. At

KEY INDICATORS — Ethiopia

	Unit	2000	2001	2002	2003	2004
Population	m	63.49	65.40	64.80	68.42	72.03
Gross domestic product (GDP)	US$bn	6.30	6.10	6.00	6.23	*8.08
GDP per capita	US$	99	94	92	91	116
GDP real growth	%	4.5	7.3	5.0	-3.8	11.6
Inflation	%	6.2	-5.2	-7.2	15.1	9.0
Exports (fob) (goods)	US$m	486.0	441.0	467.0	433.0	562.8
Imports (fob) (goods)	US$m	1,131.4	1,558.0	1,600.0	1,630.0	2,104.0
Balance of trade	US$m	-645.4	-1,117.0	-1,131.0	-1,197.0	-1,541.2
Current account	US$m	-340.0	-230.0	-350.0	-180.0	-500.0
Total reserves minus gold	US$m	306.3	433.2	881.7	955.6	1,496.8
Foreign exchange	US$m	297.1	424.1	871.9	944.8	1,485.1
Exchange rate	per US$	8.22	8.46	8.38	8.43	8.58

* estimated figure

Ethiopia

least 100,000 opponents or critics were killed.
1977 Somalia tried to annex part of Ethiopia's Ogaden region, where most people are ethnic Somalis. Cuban and Soviet troops and tanks assisted Ethiopia in repelling the Somalian invasion.
1984 Drought led to a famine in which as many as one million people may have died.
1987 A Soviet-style constitution was adopted and the People's Democratic Republic of Ethiopia was formed. The regime was supported by the Soviet Union.
1991 Rebellions in Eritrea, led by the leftist Eritrean People's Liberation Front (EPLF) and, in Tigray province, by the Tigray People's Liberation Front (TPLF) ensued. Mengistu fled to Zimbabwe as the EPLF took control of Eritrea and a TPLF-led coalition, the Ethiopian People's Revolutionary Democratic Front (EPRDF), marched into Addis Ababa.
1995 A general election was held and won by the EPRDF. The country was officially renamed the Federal Democratic Republic of Ethiopia. Negaso Gidada became president.
1998 Border disputes resulted in Eritrea and Ethiopia resuming full-scale fighting in mid-year and sporadic clashes thereafter.
1999 Eritrea refused to withdraw from the disputed Badme area.
2000 The EPRDF parties won the legislative elections. UN Mission in Ethiopia and Eritrea (UNMEE) peacekeepers opened a 1,000km cease-fire buffer zone between Ethiopia and Eritrea after the two countries signed a peace deal in Algiers, ending the two-year war.
2001 President Gidada quit the ruling coalition but finish his term in office. Girma Wolde Giorgise was elected, by parliament, to the largely ceremonial position of president.
2002 Eritrea and Ethiopia accepted a ruling on their border dispute – by the international Boundary Commission in The Hague – and a new 1,000km frontier was established. Ethiopia, ravaged by drought, requested food aid for nearly six million people.
2004 A resettlement programme started to move over two million people away from parched, over-worked highlands to the pastural, but disease rife plains of south-west Ethiopia. Long-term drought in Afar region resulted in over 350,000 people receiving food aid, when livestock deaths became widespread.
2005 According to provisional results of the 15 May parliamentary elections, the ruling EPRDF and its allies won an overall majority, but election authorities are investigating episodes of fraud and vote rigging. In December the independent commission at the Permanent Court of Arbitration in The Hague, set up in December 2000 as part of the peace deal signed in Algiers in 2000 between Eritrea and Ethiopia, ruled that Eritrea had launched unlawful attacks against Ethiopia in May 1998, thereby triggering the border war between the two countries. The Ethiopian government has said that it will lodge a claim for compensation. On 28 December donors put on hold US$375 million of budget support because of a government crackdown on opposition supporters.

Political structure
Constitution
A constitution was adopted 8 December 1994 which established a federal system of government. The constitution formally came into force in August 1995 when the Federal Democratic Republic of Ethiopia was proclaimed.
Ethiopia comprises 11 semi-autonomous administrative regions organised loosely along major ethnic lines.
Form of state
Federal democratic republic
The executive
The role of president is largely a figurehead position. The prime minister, who is elected by parliament for a five-year term, has the most power.
The president is elected by parliament for a six-year term.
National legislature
The Federal Parliamentary Assembly has two chambers. The Yehizbtewekayoch Mekir Bet (Council of People's Representatives) has 527 members, elected for a five-year term in single-seat constituencies. The Yefederashn Mekir Bet (Council of the Federation) has 117 members, one each from the 22 minority nationalities and one from each professional sector of is remaining nationalities, designated by the regional councils which may elect them directly or provide their direct elections.
Last elections
15 May 2005 (parliamentary); October 2001 (presidential).
Results: Presidential: Girma Wolde Giorgise was elected by the Council of People's Representatives.
Parliamentary: the ruling EPRDF won 327 seats of 547 (with 59 per cent of the vote), CUD 109 seats, UEDF 52 seats, SPDP 24 seats, OFDM 11 seats, BGPDUF 8 seats, ANDP 8 seats, GPDM 3 seats, all others 1 seat.
Next elections
2005 (presidential); 2010 (parliamentary)

Political parties
Ruling party
Ethiopian People's Revolutionary Democratic Front (EPRDF), an alliance led by the Tigray People's Liberation Front (TPLF)

Main opposition party
Coalition of Unity and Democracy (CUD), United Ethiopian Democratic Forces (UEDF)

Population
72.03 million (2004)
Ethnic make-up
Oromo (40 per cent), Amhara and Tigrayan (32 per cent), Sidamo (9 per cent), Shankella (6 per cent), Somali (6 per cent), Afar (4 per cent), Gurage (2 per cent).
Religions
The Ethiopian Coptic Church is influential, particularly in the north. There is a large Muslim community in the south, made up mainly of Arabs, Somalis and Oromos. Ethiopian Orthodox (40 per cent), Muslim (40 per cent), animist and other (20 per cent).

Education
Ethiopia has one of the world's lowest school enrolment rates. The government aims to enrol 5.3 million children in primary schools by 2005. The pattern of enrolment shows large gender gaps with girls being more likely to drop out in the early stages. Oxfam estimates that fewer than one-third of boys and one-tenth of girls aged 6–11 start school and one quarter of these drop out during the first two grades. Female literacy rates are only 32 per cent and girls of primary school age work 14–16 hours a day on a variety of tasks, either helping out at home or earning an income. In regions where tuition fees have been abolished, school enrolment has increased by up to 20 per cent.
In secondary schools, English has replaced Amharic as the medium of instruction, although several local languages are also used.
Literacy rate: 43 per cent male, 32 per cent female; adult rates (World Bank).
Pupils per teacher: 43 in primary schools.

Health
The annual total expenditure on health is around 3.6 per cent of GDP, of which 40 per cent is government spending.
The government aims to reorganise health services through a twenty-year health development strategy, with a series of five-year investment programmes; the second phase began in 2003. The system provides access to health services for only about half of the population, mainly in the urban areas. Estimates suggests that 24 per cent and 15 per cent of the population respectively had access to improved water and sanitation facilities.
In February 2005 the World Health Organisation (WHO) launched an Africa-wide mass polio immunisation

programme, this coincided with the first case of the desease reported in four years appearing in Ethiopia. In August authorities reported a sharp increase in number of malaria cases in northern Ethiopia with 20,000 more cases in June 2005 than in June 2004.

HIV/Aids
There were 1.4 million people HIV positive in 2003, of which 770,000 were women, plus 120,000 children were HIV positive and 720,000 children were made orphans. There were 120,000 deaths due to aids in 2003.

The loss in annual GDP growth per capita was projected to be 0.6 per cent between 2002–10 due to the impact of the disease.

In Addis Ababa the prevalence rate of HIV/Aids has been falling from a high of 24 per cent in 1995 to 11 per cent in 2004.

HIV prevalence: 4.4 per cent aged 15–49 in 2003 (World Bank)
Life expectancy: 42.0 years (World Bank)
Fertility rate/Maternal mortality rate: 5.6 births per woman; maternal mortality 18 per 1,000 live births (World Bank).
Infant mortality rate: 112 deaths per 1,000 live births; 47 per cent of children aged under five were malnourished (World Bank).
Head of population per physician/bed: 0.05 physicians and 0.2 hospital beds per 1,000 people.

Welfare
Ethiopia is one of the poorest countries in the world, with annual income per capita below US$100. Following the end of the border conflict with Eritrea in 2000, the government of Ethiopia started to implement an ambitious adjustment and reform programme and renewed its commitment to poverty reduction.

Main cities
Addis Ababa (capital, estimated population 2.8 million in 2004), Dire Dawa (214,800), Nazret (166,600), Gondar (146,300).

Languages spoken
Oromigna and Tigrigna are widely spoken. English is taught in schools; as well as Arabic, French and Italian, it is used in business circles and understood in most hotels and major towns. Over 80 local languages are also spoken.
Official language/s
Amharic

Media
Press
In November 2001 the government resumed its harassment of Ethiopian journalists who began reporting news in the free press. Fana Democracy Publishing, that used to publish the weekly newspaper *Efoyta* was closed down in November 2001. The newspaper is no longer published.

Tamrat Zuma, the publisher and editor of the defunct newspaper *Atkurot* was released from nine months imprisonment in March 2002. Zuma announced his intention to restart the newspaper.

Dailies: *Addis Zemen* is a state-owned daily. *Ethiopian News Headlines* (http://www.ethiozena.net) provides daily on-line news service.

Weeklies: Several newspapers and periodicals are published in Amharic and English languages. There are several privately owned weeklies published from Addis Ababa including *Ilete Addis, Seifenebelbal, Tobya, Wonchif, Tomar, Mahlet* and the English language *Addis Tribune. Andenat* is a semi-monthly publication.

Broadcasting
Radio: Service by Voice of Ethiopia, chiefly in Amharic, but also in English, Arabic, Somali, French and local languages.
Television: The state-controlled commercial Ethiopian Television broadcasts to most of the country via a microwave link-up.

Economy
Ethiopia is one of the poorest countries in the world, despite a wealth of resources. Economic development has been retarded by various factors, including poor infrastructure, desertification, recurrent droughts, deterioration in the terms of trade and the effects of the war with Eritrea. Agriculture is the principal economic activity, accounting for around 40 per cent of GDP. The government is keen to diversify the economy.

The conclusion of peace with Eritrea brought with it the resumption of international support for the Ethiopian economy, which had been suspended due to the government's increased military expenditure and reports of human rights atrocities.

The drought of 2002–03, which caused a decline in agricultural output and water shortages, had a serious effect on the economy and necessitated a sharp increase in food aid. GDP growth contracted by -3.8 per cent in 2003, but by 2004, with better weather conditions, the economy was already improving and GDP grew by 11.6 per cent.

Despite a series of reform programmes to alleviate poverty, around 50 per cent of the population still live below the poverty line. Government plans of decentralisation, on IMF insistence, have had mixed success.

External trade
On 31 December 2002, the US approved Ethiopia as being eligible for tariff preferences under the Africa Growth and Opportunities Act (AGOA). The legislation requires that countries are only eligible for greater access to US markets provided they have made continued progress toward a market-based economy, the rule of law, free trade, poverty reduction and the protection of workers' rights. This process is reviewed annually.

Imports
Principal imports are food and live animals, petroleum and petroleum products, chemicals, machinery, motor vehicles, cereals, textiles, semi-manufactured goods and fertilisers.
Main sources: Saudi Arabia (25 per cent total, 2004), US (15.9 per cent), China (6.7 per cent)

Exports
Principal exports are coffee, khat, gold, leather products, live animals, oilseeds, marble and other minerals.
Main destinations: Djibouti (13.6 per cent total, 2004), Germany (9.7 per cent), Japan (9.0 per cent), Saudi Arabia (6.5 per cent), US (5.4 per cent), Italy (4.9 per cent), UK (4.3 per cent)

Agriculture
Farming
The agricultural sector is the mainstay of the economy, accounting for around 45 per cent of GDP, 85 per cent of employment and 62 per cent of exports. Only about two-thirds of Ethiopia's 122 million hectares of land is suitable for agriculture, of which around 15 per cent is actually cultivated. Large parts are affected by soil erosion. Intensive subsistence agriculture has depleted the soil and Ethiopia can no longer feed its population, even when the weather is good. Very little of the cultivated area is irrigated.

The chief cash crop is coffee, which accounts for around half of export earnings. Germany is the largest market for Ethiopian coffee. Falling world prices for coffee in recent years, together with severe droughts, has resulted in declining production and loss of revenues. Many growers have responded by switching to the production of qat. While coffee fell from 60 per cent of total exports to 35 per cent, export of qat increased to 15 per cent from 6 per cent.

Other cash crops include cotton and sugar. The main food crops are maize, sorghum, wheat, barley, millet and teff. Crop production in 2004 included: 9,280,044 tonnes t(t) cereals in total, 1.618,093t wheat, 2,743,881t maize, 1,784,282t sorghum, 1,087,374t barley, 2,454,276t sugar cane, 305,101t millet, 400,000t potatoes, 360,000t sweet potatoes, 1.044,205t pulses, 4,870,000t roots and tubers, 33,500t citrus fruit, 71,0000t garlic, 137,167t oilcrops, 259,980t green coffee, 135,000t mangoes, 116,000t allspice, 35,450t fibre crops, 74,000t treenuts, 310,000t yams, 230,000t papayas, 731,000t fruit in total, 884,800t vegetables in total. Livestock production included: 591,491t meat in total, 330,500t beef, 74,000t game meat, 4,500t camel meat, 55,130t lamb, 28,650t goat meat, 1,615t pig meat, 47,096t poultry, 36,624t eggs, 1,582,250t milk, 38,100t honey, 54,025t cattle hides, 9,825t sheepskins, 12,000t greasy wool.

Forestry
Only 4 per cent of Ethiopia's land area is forested. Since the mid-1970s, there has been extensive deforestation with up to 75 per cent of forest cover cleared or degraded, according to the UN's Food and Agriculture Organisation (FAO). Forest cover declined by an annual average of around 0.8 per cent or 40,000ha between 1990–2000. Ethiopia imported US$29.7 million of forest products in 2004. There is negligible export of forest products from Ethiopia.

Production in 2004 included 95.5 million cubic metres (cum) roundwood, 17,700cum sawnwood, 6,200cum sawlogs and veneers, 7,000cum pulpwood, 77,000cum wood-based panels, 93.0 million cum woodfuel, 3.2mt charcoal.

Industry and manufacturing
The industrial sector contributes 12.4 per cent of GDP and employs about 7 per cent of the workforce. Manufacturing of small handicrafts and other small industry sub-sectors make up around 7 per cent of GDP.

Industry is primarily based on the processing of agricultural raw materials. Principal among these is food processing, but textiles, handicrafts, and leather production are also significant.

Growth is constrained by a lack of raw materials, outdated machinery and techniques and the need for imports throughout the sector.

Tourism
Although visitor numbers have risen consistently each year since 1991, reaching around 200,000 in 2004, tourism is under-developed. The economic importance of the sector and Ethiopia's potential as a destination are recognised and priority is being given to improving the infrastructure and the country's image, which has suffered from the conflict with Eritrea and natural disasters. In November 2004, Ethiopia was selected by the World Tourism Organisation as one of the first beneficiaries of the Sustainable Tourism and Elimination of Poverty initiative, which will provide experise and attract funding for tourism proposals. Tourism is expected to contribute 4.5 per cent to GDP in 2005.

Mining
The mining sector accounts for around 6 per cent of GDP.

The government says there are at least 500 tonnes of proven gold reserves in the country. Activity is limited to small-scale gold mining.

The country has substantial reserves of iron ore and untapped reserves of platinum, tantalum (used in the electronics industry), nickel, phosphate, diatomite, copper, zinc, soda ash and potash. Tantalum reserves are estimated at 25,000 tonnes at one site alone.

The output of non-metallic minerals such as limestone and marble has increased significantly.

A number of foreign mining companies have been awarded exploration concessions.

Hydrocarbons
Ethiopia does not produce oil, but there is commercial potential and foreign interest in investment in the sector is high. An exploration deal between the Ethiopian government and Petronas (Malaysia) was signed in 2003, the first of potentially many inward investments into the oil industry. Ethiopia has had to rely on imports of refined oil to meet energy requirements since the closure of the Assab refinery in 1997. Sudan became an important source of supplies in January 2005, when shipment by tanker truck along a new road commenced.

Natural gas reserves are estimated at around 115 billion cubic metres.
Ethiopia does not produce or import coal.

Energy
Ethiopia has considerable hydroelectric capacity, although, so far, little has been used. Installed generating capacity is over 800MW. Only 4 per cent of the population has access to electricity.

Wood has always been a traditional source of energy, but it is hoped increased availability of electricity will reduce this, as many forests have become severely depleted.

The Tis Abay II hydroelectric power station, near Lake Tana in the north-west of the country, supplies 73MW to the Kaliti main power distribution station, operated by the Ethiopian Electric Power Corporation (EEPCO).

The construction of Ethiopia's first independent power project began in 2002. A 150MW hydroelectric facility will be built in western Ethiopia. The project is being managed by the Saudi Arabian company Mohammed International Development Research (Midroc) and when completed, output will be sold to EEPCO.

Banking and insurance
Central bank
National Bank of Ethiopia
Main financial centre
Addis Ababa

Time
GMT plus three hours
The Ethiopian day officially begins at 0600 (midnight elsewhere).

Geography
Ethiopia extends inland from the Red Sea coast of eastern Africa. The country has a long frontier with Somalia near the Horn of Africa. Sudan lies to the west, Djibouti to the east, Eritrea to the north and Kenya to the south.

Climate
Dependent on altitude. Lowland regions are very hot and dry throughout the year. On the plateau (including Addis Ababa) dry season from October–May with temperature range from as low as 6 degrees Celsius (C) in December to 26 degrees C in March (light rain from February–April). Temperatures can fall sharply at night during the dry season. Rainy season from June–September with average temperature 21 degrees C.

Entry requirements
Passports
Required by all. Must be valid for at least six months.
Visa
Required by all. For business visas, an application should be accompanied by a letter from a sponsoring organisation or company. For those self-employed, a letter from a solicitor, accountant or business registration authority should suffice. Visas are usually issued for a one month period; heavy penalties may be imposed for unauthorised extensions. If necessary, contact the Immigration Office for an Alien's Registration Card and an exit visa. Visa application forms can be downloaded from a number of Ethiopian embassy websites (see 'links' at www.ethioembassy.org.uk/).
An international certificates of vaccination, against yellow fever, is required when applying.
Foreign nationals are advised to register their arrival with the consular representative of their embassy.
Currency advice/regulations
Up to Birr100 can be imported and exported.
While there is no limit on the import of foreign currency, it must be declared on arrival. Export of foreign currency is allowed up to the amount declared.

Penalties for exchanging money on the black market range from fines to imprisonment.

Customs
Skins, hides and any antique articles require an export certificate. Laptop computers must be declared upon arrival and departure. Tape recorders require special customs permits.

Health (for visitors)
Health facilities are extremely limited in Addis Ababa and inadequate outside the city. Travellers should bring their own prescription drugs and a doctor's note describing the medication. If the quantity of drugs exceeds that expected for personal use, a permit from the ministry of health is required.

The altitude may cause health problems.

Mandatory precautions
A yellow fever inoculation certificate.

Advisable precautions
Visitors should be in date for the following vaccinations: yellow fever (within 10 years), polio (within 10 years), typhoid, tetanus (within 10 years), hepatitis A and B, meningitis. There is a rabies risk. Malaria prophylaxis recommended before visiting the lowlands. There is no malaria risk in Addis Ababa.

Water precautions should be taken.

Hotels
Hotels are available in Addis Ababa and other main centres. A service charge of 10 per cent and a tax of 2 per cent are added to bills but a small tip is usual in addition to the service charge. Payment is generally required in foreign currency.

Credit cards
Credit cards are accepted by airlines and the larger hotels only.

Public holidays
Fixed dates
7 Jan (Genna/Ethiopian Christmas Day), 19 Jan (Timket/Epiphany), 2 Mar (Victory of Adwa Day), 28 May (Downfall of the Dergue), 11 Sep* (Enkutatash/New Year's Day), 27 Sep (Meskel/Finding of the True Cross).

* 12 Sep in year before leap year.

Variable dates
Ethiopian Good Friday, Ethiopian Easter Day, Eid al Adha, Birth of the Prophet, Eid al Fitr.

Ethiopia follows the Julian calendar, instead of the Gregorian calendar used in most other parts of the world. The Ethiopian calendar year is divided into 13 months: 12 months of 30 days each and one month of five days (six in a leap year). The Ethiopian year commences on 11 September.

The Islamic year contains 354 or 355 days, with the result that Muslim feasts advance by 10–12 days against the Gregorian calendar. Dates of feasts vary according to the sighting of the new moon, so cannot be forecast exactly. Islamic year 1426: 10 February 2005 to 30 January 2006.

Working hours
Banking
Mon–Fri: 0800–1100, 1300–1600; Sat: 0800–1200.

Business
Mon–Thu: 0830–1230, 1330–1730; Fri: 0830–1130, 1330–1730. Most private businesses also work on Saturdays.

Government
Mon–Thu: 0830–1230, 1330–1730. Fri: 0830–1130, 1330–1730.

Shops
Mon–Sat: 0800–1300, 1400–2000. Local variations.

Telecommunications
Mobile phones
A GSM 900 service is available in large cities and towns only.

Electricity supply
220V, 50 cycles AC. Plugs are of the two-pin variety.

Social customs/useful tips
Handshaking is the usual mode of greeting. The first name is followed by that of the father – there are no family names. The words Ato, Woizero and Woizrity are the equivalents of Mr, Mrs and Miss respectively, and should be used when addressing people.

Smoking is not popular among traditional people, or in front of priests. Dress should be modest. Shoes are removed on entering churches/mosques. Private formal entertaining is common in Addis Ababa, and cocktail parties are not uncommon. Ethiopian law strictly prohibits the photographing of military installations, police/military personnel, industrial facilities, government buildings and infrastructure.

Security
Crime is an increasing problem in Addis Ababa. Normal precautions should be taken.

Exercise caution if travelling to the northern Tigray and Afar regions (within 50km of the Ethiopian/Eritrean border) because of landmines and unsettled conditions in the border area. Travel to the Ogaden Region is considered very dangerous and should not be attempted. Limit road travel outside major towns to daylight hours only.

Getting there
Air
National airline: Ethiopian Airlines (government-owned)
International airport/s: Addis Ababa-Bole International (Code: ADD), 8km from city, bar, buffet, restaurant, bank, post office, shops, car hire.
Airport tax: International departures US$20; excluding transit passengers.

Surface
Road: Entry by land into Ethiopia is possible, if difficult, via Dewale and Galafi (Ethiopia-Djibouti), Moyale (Ethiopia-Kenya), Humera and Metema (Ethiopia-Sudan), Jijiga (Ethiopia-Somalia). The road linking Nairobi and Addis Ababa forms part of the Trans-East African Highway.
Rail: The rail route from Djibouti to Addis Ababa is subject to disruption.
Water: Ethiopia has been landlocked since Eritrea gained independence.
Main port/s: Until the outbreak of hostilities with Eritrea in 1998, Ethiopia relied heavily on the Eritrean ports of Assab and Massawa. Djibouti has subsequently become Ethiopia's principal trading gateway.

Getting about
National transport
Air: Ethiopian Airlines operates domestic service to main towns.
Road: An all-weather road network connects principal towns. The road system is undergoing expansion.

There are border posts at Moyale on the Kenyan border, Adwa and Adigrat near the border with Eritrea, and Dewelle for Djibouti.

Roads are impassable to Lalibela from June to September.

Drivers bringing their own vehicles to Ethiopia will require a *carnet de passage*.
Buses: Coach services (liable to suspension) Addis Ababa-Gondar.
Rail: A line runs from Addis Ababa to Dire Dawa (and on to Djibouti). However, visitors are advised not to use this line for security reasons.

City transport
Taxis: In Addis Ababa, the National Tour Operations (NTO) provides taxis at the main hotels and the airport, although independent and communal cabs are available. It is advisable to check the fare and the destination before entering the cab. The most reliable taxis are available from the office of the Hilton Hotel. The taxi journey from the airport to the city centre takes about 30 minutes. Tipping is not usual.

Buses, trams & metro: Journey time from airport to city centre 30 minutes.
Car hire
Car hire (with or without driver) is available in the main centres. A valid international driving licence is required. Traffic drives on the right.

Payment for car rental is generally required in foreign currency.

Ethiopia

BUSINESS DIRECTORY

The addresses listed below are a selection only. While World of Information makes every endeavour to check these addresses, we cannot guarantee that changes have not been made, especially to telephone numbers and area codes. We would welcome any corrections.

Telephone area codes

The international dialling code (IDD) for Ethiopia is +251 followed by area code and subscriber's number.

Addis Ababa	1	Gondar	8
Awassa	6	Jimma	7
Bahir Dar	8	Mekelle	4
Dire Dawa	5	Nazareth	2

Chambers of Commerce

Addis Ababa Chamber of Commerce, PO Box 2458, Addis Ababa (tel: 515-055; fax: 511-479; e-mail: aachamber1@telecom.net.et).

Awassa Chamber of Commerce, PO Box 167, Awassa (tel: 200-375; fax: 205-197).

Bahir Dar Chamber of Commerce, PO Box 48, Bahir Dar (tel: 200-481; fax: 201-787).

Dire Dawa Chamber of Commerce, PO Box 198, Dire Dawa (tel: 113-082; fax 112-468; e-mail: luiji@telecom.net.et).

Ethiopian Chamber of Commerce, PO Box 517, Addis Ababa (tel: 518-240; fax: 517-699; e-mail: ethcham@telecom.net.et).

Gondar Chamber of Commerce, PO Box 50, Gondar (tel: 110-320; fax: 115-656).

Mekelle Chamber of Commerce, PO Box 503, Mekelle (tel: 402-529; fax: 408-914).

Nazareth Chamber of Commerce, PO Box 36, Nazareth (tel: 112-083; fax: 122-699).

Banking

Awash International Bank SC; PO Box 12638, Bole Road, Addis Ababa (tel: 614-482/83, 612-919; fax: 614-477).

Bank of Abyssinia SC; PO Box 12947, Addis Ababa (tel: 514-130, 514-752; fax: 511-575).

Commercial Bank of Ethiopia; PO Box 255, Unity Square, Addis Ababa (tel: 511-271, 515-004; fax: 514-522, 512-166).

Construction and Business Bank, PO Box 3480, Addis Ababa (tel: 512-300; fax: 515-103).

Dashen Bank SC; PO Box 12752, Garad Building, Debre Zeit Road, Addis Ababa (tel: 661-380, 655-525; fax: 661-640, 653-037).

Development Bank of Ethiopia, PO Box 1900, Josep Broz Tito, Addis Ababa (tel: 511-188; fax: 511-606).

Wegagen Bank SC; PO Box 1018, Addis Ababa (tel: 655-015; fax: 653-330).

Central bank

National Bank of Ethiopia, PO Box 5550, Addis Ababa, Ethiopia (tel: 517-430; fax: 514-588; e-mail: nbe.excd@telecom.net.et).

Travel information

Addis Ababa-Bole Airport, PO Box 978, Addis Ababa (tel: 180-455; fax: 612-533).

Ethiopian Airlines, PO Box 1755, Bole International Airport, Addis Ababa (tel: 612-222; fax: 611-474); town office (tel: 517-000; fax: 611-474; internet: www.flyethiopian.com).

National tourist organisation offices

Ethiopian Tourism Commission, PO Box 2183, Addis Ababa (tel: 517-470, 150-609, 513-962; fax: 513-899; internet: www.visitethiopia.com).

National Tour Operations (NTO), PO Box 5709, Addis Ababa (tel: 512-955; fax: 517-688).

Other useful addresses

Antiquities Authority, National Museum of Ethiopia, PO Box 76, Addis Ababa (tel: 117-150; fax: 553-188).

British Embassy, Commercial Section, Fikre Mariam Abatechan Street, Addis Ababa (tel: 612-354; fax: 610-588).

Central Statistical Office, PO Box 1143, Addis Ababa (tel: 113-010).

Department of Immigration and Refugee Affairs, PO Box 5741, Addis Ababa (tel: 553-899).

Djibouti–Ethiopian Railway Corporation, PO Box 1051, Addis Ababa (tel: 517-250; fax: 513-533).

Ethiopian Customs Office, PO Box 3248, Addis Ababa (tel: 513-100; fax: 518-355).

Ethiopian Embassy (USA), 3506 International Drive, NW, Washington DC 20008 (tel: 202-364-1200; fax: 202-686-9551; e-mail: ethiopia@ethiopianembassy.org).

Ethiopian Investment Authority, PO Box 2313, Addis Ababa (tel: 510-033; 514-396).

Ethiopian Privatisation Agency, PO Box 11835, Ethiopian Investment Authority Building, Bole Road, Addis Ababa (tel: 521-833; fax: 513-955).

Ethiopian Private Industries' Association, PO Box 8739, Addis Ababa (tel: 512-384; fax: 552-633).

Ethiopian Television, PO Box 5554, Addis Ababa.

Ethiopian Tourist Trading Enterprise, PO Box 8640, Addis Ababa (tel: 612-277; fax: 610-500).

Maritime and Transit Services, PO Box 1186, Addis Ababa (tel: 510-666; fax: 514-097).

Ministry of Culture and Information, PO Box 1364, Addis Ababa (tel: 551-011; fax: 551-609).

Ministry of Economic Development & Co-operation, PO Box 2428, Addis Ababa (tel: 519-684; fax: 517-988).

Ministry of Foreign Affairs, PO Box 393, Addis Ababa (tel: 517-345; fax: 514-300).

Ministry of Trade and Industry, PO Box 2559, Addis Ababa (tel: 518-200; fax: 514-288).

Organisation of African Unity (OAU), PO Box 3243, Addis Ababa (tel: 557-700; fax: 511-299).

Voice of Ethiopia, PO Box 1020, Addis Ababa.

Wildlife Conservation Department, PO Box 386, Addis Ababa (tel: 510-455; fax: 510-168).

Internet sites

Africa Business Network: http://www.ifc.org/abn

AllAfrica.com: http://www.allafrica.com

African Development Bank: http://www.afdb.org

ENA - Ethiopian News Agency: http://www.telecom.net.et/~ena

Ethiopian Mission to the UN: http://www.undp.org/missions/ethiopia

Ethiopian Privatisation Agency: http://www.undp.org/missions/ethiopia

Harambee Afrika (UK business club for traders with east, central and southern Africa): http://www.harambee.co.uk

Mbendi AfroPaedia (information on companies, countries, industries and stock exchanges): http://mbendi.co.za

Falkland Islands/Islas Malvinas

KEY FACTS

Official name: Falkland Islands

Head of State: Queen Elizabeth II

Head of government: Governor Howard J S Pearce (from 3 Dec 2002); Alan Huckle has been appointed to take over as governor in spring 2006

Area: 12,173 square km (including East and West Falkland and adjacent islands)

Population: 2,932 (2004)

Capital: Stanley

Official language: English

Currency: Falkland pound (Fl£) = 100 pence

Exchange rate: Fl£0.57 per US$ (Oct 2005); (pegged to pound sterling)

GDP per capita: US$25,000 (2003)

GDP real growth: 1.00% (2003)*

Inflation: 3.60% (2004)*

Balance of trade: -US$17.10 million (2003)

Visitor numbers: 30,000 (2003)*

* estimated figure

COUNTRY PROFILE

Historical profile
1592 First sighted by English mariners (Captain John Davis in ship *Desire* – the motto of the islands became Desire the Right).
1690 The first landing was by British Captain John Strong in the ship, *Welfare*. The Falkland Islands were named after the then Treasurer of the Navy, Viscount Falkland.
1764 French settlement was recorded. The islands were named Les Malouines after the French town of St Malo, hence the Argentine name of Malvinas for the islands.
1765 Captain John Byron (British) took formal possession of the islands at Port Egmont.
1767 The French settlement was sold to Spain and named Puerto de la Soledad.
1770 The Spanish ousted the British from Port Egmont.
1771 The British garrison was re-established.
1774 The garrison was withdrawn, leaving a plaque 'as a mark of possession' and a flag 'left flying'.
1820 The flag of the United Provinces of La Plata (Spanish) was hoisted at Puerto de la Soledad.
1823 The governor of the islands was nominated by the United Provinces Government (but did not visit).
1824 A German merchant, Louis Vernet, was given land by grant of the Buenos Aires government and a settlement of mixed nationalities, over the next few years, was established at Puerto de la Soledad.
1828 Vernet was appointed governor by the United Provinces. He attempted to stop sealing operations by other nations.
1831 The US protested about these actions and sent *USS Lexington* to sack Puerto de la Soledad (with the US president's approval). The islands were again unpopulated.
1833 Port Louis (Puerto de la Soledad) was taken over by the British, asserting full rights under naval superintendents until 1842.
1842 The first British governor, Richard C Moody, took up residence.
1982 Argentina invaded the Falkland Islands. The UK despatched a military force, composed of naval ships and troops. The UK recaptured the islands. South Georgia and the South Sandwich Islands became overseas territories of the UK.
1996 The UN Committee on Decolonisation rejected pressure from the UK and the Falklands for a self-determination clause. Argentina was opposed to any change due to their re-established diplomatic and trade links with the UK.
1999 In an effort to improve relations between the Falklands and Argentina, Argentine nationals were allowed to visit for the first time since 1982.
2001 The UK agreed to allow Argentinian private aircraft and shipping to visit the islands.
2002 Howard Pearce took office as governor.
2003 The 33rd General Assembly of the Organisation of American States (OAS) passed a statement of solidarity with Argentina's claim to the Falkland Islands. The OAS called on Britain and Argentina to resume negotiations over the South Atlantic archipelago as soon as possible.
2004 Relations between Argentina and the UK deteriorated during the first six months of the year: in February, Argentina banned charter flights to and from the Falklands crossing its airspace; there was a further dispute in March, when an Argentinian ice breaker, the *Almirante Irizar*, was present in a Falklands conservation zone for two days, challenging fishing vessels, demanding details of their permits – policing the zones contravenes the islands' jurisdiction; in June, Argentina gave permission for Aerolineas Argentinas to begin direct flights to the Falkland Islands but without a UK agreement.
2005 Council elections were held in November.

Political structure
Constitution
Defence and foreign affairs are the responsibility of the UK government.
Form of state
Overseas territory of the United Kingdom
The executive
Executive authority is vested in the British monarch and exercised by the governor. Under the constitution, the governor is advised by the Executive Council, over which he presides. The Executive Council is composed of three members of the Legislative Council, elected by the body to sit on the Executive Council for a period of 12 months, and two *ex-officio* members, the chief executive and the financial secretary.
National legislature
The Legislative Council is composed of eight members (three from Camp

constituency and five from the Stanley constituency) elected by universal adult suffrage and two *ex-officio* members – the chief executive and the financial secretary. The Legislative Council is empowered to pass laws for the government of the Islands, subject to the approval of the British monarch acting through the foreign affairs secretary of state.

Legal system
English common law

Last elections
November 2005 (parliamentary)
Results: Parliamentary: eight, non-partisans, were elected.

Next elections
2009 (parliamentary)

Political situation
There was an increase in tension between old adversaries Argentina and UK over the Falkland Islands in 2004. The president of Argentina, Néstor Kirchner, appears to have abandoned his predecessor's diplomatic dialogue, probably as a devise to enhance his own domestic political standing. In February 2004 Argentina refused to allow charter flights from Chile to overfly Argentina on their way to the Falklands. Then in March for two days an Argentine navel vessel challenged fishing vessels in Falkland Island waters, requesting their identity and demanding details of their permits. In June, it granted unilateral permission for Aerolineas Argentinas to operate two flights to the Falkland Islands. Although without UK permission to land this was a hollow gesture.

This increase in friction has damaged 10 years of steady progress to normalisation between the two countries.

Population
2,932 (2004)

Ethnic make-up
White, almost exclusively of British descent. Workers from St Helena make up about 10 per cent of the population.

Religions
Anglican, Roman Catholic, United Free Church, Evangelist Church, Jehovah's Witnesses, Lutheran, Seventh-Day Adventist.

Main cities
Stanley (capital, estimated population 2,100 in 2003), Goose Green (100).

Languages spoken
Official language/s
English

Media
Press
The two weekly newspapers are *Teaberry Express* and *Penguin News*.
The government publishes the magazine *The Gazette* covering current affairs and politics. The Falkland Islands News Area Network (http://www.sartra.com) provides a news agency service covering headlines from other regional newspapers such as *SAFIN Magazine*, *St.Helena News*, *The Islander Newspaper*, *Antarctic Sentinel* and the *United Kingdom Falkland Islands Trust*.

Broadcasting
Radio: One radio station is operated jointly by Falkland Islands Broadcasting Service and British Forces Broadcasting Service (BFBS). The radio station provides 24 hours/day listening on FM and MW and includes taped imported programmes, BBC World and local services.

Television: One TV station operated by Services Sound and Vision Corporation from Mount Pleasant Complex. A cable TV service, run by KTV, distributes seven channels including CNN, TNT, the Cartoon Network and BBC World island wide.

Economy
Until 1982, the islands were dependent on shrinking revenues from sheep farming. Following recommendations of the Shackleton Report big sheep farms were sub-divided and transferred into the hands of islanders instead of absentee landlords. With the collapse in world wool prices, only financial support from the government enabled many farms to survive.

The improvement in the standard of living has been financed by the sale of fishing licences – in 1986, an exclusive economic zone was set up around the islands.

There are indications that the zone is rich with oil and there remains cautious optimism following initial exploration in 1998. Tourism is becoming an increasingly important source of income and is being actively promoted by the Falkland Islands government.

The Falkland Islands Development Corporation (FIDC) assists with economic development and encourages and assists with the establishment of new businesses while acknowledging that the economy will remain single source for the immediate future.

Falkland Islands Company (owned by Falkland Islands Holdings plc) dominates local commercial activities. Main activities are retail and wholesale distribution, servicing the fishing industry, port, shipping, automotive and financial services and hotel and commercial accommodation.

In July 2004, for the first time since 1982, the Legislative Council ran a deficit – about US$18.6 million, the equivalent of 25 per cent of its total public expenditure budget. The main reason is that about 55 per cent of the government's annual revenue comes from the sale of fishing licences to mostly foreign vessels, but in 2004, for the second time in three years, the season had to be closed early, and nearly half the fees had to be returned, because of a collapse in stocks of ilex squid. The situation reiterates the urgent need for the Islands to develop more non-fishing activities as quickly as possible. The main areas of future development are organic farming, tourism and hydrocarbons.

External trade
Imports
Principal imports include fuel, food and drink, building materials and clothing.
Main sources: UK (62.7 per cent total, 2004), Spain (29.4 per cent), France (3.5 per cent)

Exports
Until the arrival of the fishery, wool and sheepskins, and hides were virtually the only exports. Squid, hake, finfish and mero (toothfish) together with wool, are the main exports. In 2003, exports totalled US$7.6 million.
Main destinations: Spain (79.4 per cent total, 2004), UK (8.7 per cent), Czech Republic (4 per cent)

Agriculture
Farming
Soil quality is generally poor – peat over clay (peat is used as fuel). Virtually all available land has been used for sheep farming although small areas of arable land are cultivated (eg potatoes, hay crops, vegetable crops grown by individual households).

A hydroponic garden facility constructed in Stanley yields good quality vegetable crops for local and shipping consumption. There is an indigenous tussock (or tussac) grass (*Poa Flabellata*), which will grow to a height of 3–4 metres) but because of its palatability for livestock, it has been over-grazed in most places.

Constant strong winds affect the suitability of all flora, and only the hardiest will survive. Indigenous grass covering large areas is known locally as 'whitegrass' (*Cortaderia Pilosa*) and a heather-like

KEY INDICATORS — Falkland Islands/Islas Malvinas

	Unit	2000	2001	2002	2003	2004
Fish production	tonnes	319,107.0*	265,018.0	100,630.0	120,000.0	–
Exchange rate	per US$	0.71	0.68	0.66	0.59	0.55

* estimated figure

plant 'diddle-dee' (*Empetrum Rubrum*) is common.

There are around 90 farms. The average size is 13,600ha, with an average of 8,200 sheep. Sheep stock are a Corriedale/Polwarth mixture with small admixture of other breeds, eg Romney. The average clip per sheep is over 3.55kg.

A small-scale wool processing and knitting plant at Fox Bay was established in 1985, and acquires local raw wool to produce high-quality yarns and garments. Up to 2.5 million kg of wool per year is exported to the UK market.

Certain sheep diseases found elsewhere (eg foot rot, skin complaints/parasites) are either absent or not considered a problem on the islands.

An abbatoir meeting EU standards was opened in 2001 and is an important part of the Islands' organic farming programme. Farmers are being encouraged to diversify. The Islands have accreditation as organic under the brand name, 'Falklands' Finest'. Mutton is the principal source of protein and is supplemented during winter by beef. A dairy farm on East Falkland provides an important proportion of the islands' milk. The pasture is improved by nitrogen fertiliser in quantities that would be uneconomic over a larger area.

Livestock production in 2004 included: 911t meat in total, 131t beef, 774t lamb, 105t pig meat, 7t poultry, 160t eggs 1,500t milk, 2,340t wool, greasy.

Fishing
As a result of the declaration of the Interim Conservation and Management Zone by the British government in 1986, the Falklands began managing and policing a fish reserve and generating significant revenues through the annual award of fishing licences.

Licence fees total more than US$40 million per year, which goes to support the islands' health, education and welfare system. Squid accounts for 75 per cent of the fish taken. The Fisheries Department monitors marine activity daily and restrictions have been imposed on seismic fleets, especially during the fishing season.

The total fish catch has been declining since 1999, when it reached a high of 377,038. The total fish catch in 2003 was 120,000 tonnes, up from 100,630 tonnes in 2002. The main species in the catch were red cod, Southern blue whiting, illex squid, kingclip, Patagonian squid, martialia squid, hake, skate, toothfish and hoki.

Industry and manufacturing
Small industrial units serve both onshore and offshore commitments. Hand-knitted local garments are produced for sale to visitors.

The Falkland Islands' largest private company, Falkland Islands Holdings plc, is quoted on the London Stock Exchange where it began trading in 1998. Activities are mainly retail trading and provision of services to the Falkland Islands. It controls about 80 per cent of retail sales, is the agent for Land Rover, the most popular vehicle, owns the Darwin Shipping Line and operates the port in Stanley.

Tourism
Tourism is a fast-growing industry, with the attraction of wildlife and also interest in the military aspects of the 1982 Falkland Islands conflict. As sheep production becomes increasingly uneconomic, tourism is seen as a possible means of maintaining some of the outlying communities. Cruise visitors have greatly increased in recent years.

Mining
There is speculation that the great blanket bogs which obscure much of the inland geology of the islands may hide some diamond-bearing kimberlites and exploration is under way. There has been some evidence of gold.

Hydrocarbons
In 1996, oil licences were granted by the UK government to a mixed group of international companies including Desire Petroleum, a group formed partly on behalf of the islanders. Potential reserves are estimated at up to 60 billion barrels.

The Falklands Islands Holdings company announced in June 2004 that it was forming a new oil exploration company called Falkland Oil and Gas (FOGL), in partnership with Global Petroleum and RAB Capital. With the mapping of 4,340km offshore leases FOGL believe that there is potentially 200–250 million barrels of oil in its operational areas.

Although there is potential in the oil sector in the Falkland Islands currently no oil is being produced and the islands rely on the import of petroleum products. Coal and gas is neither produced or imported.

Energy
The majority of households use oil. Stanley has a power station that generates 6.3MW of electricity at 240V/50Hz and a piped water supply. Outside Stanley settlements generate their own power and there is no public water supply.

There is a plentiful supply of peat (turf) although few houses still have peat stoves.

Time
GMT minus four hours (GMT minus three hours April–September)

Geography
The Falklands Islands, comprising two large islands and about 200 smaller ones, are in the south-western Atlantic Ocean, about 770km (480 miles) north-east of Cape Horn, South America. They are 500km (300 miles) from the South American mainland.

Climate
Temperatures range from minus 6–21 degrees Celsius (C) with occasional lows of minus 10 degrees C and highs of 25 degrees C. Rainfall is around 700mm per year. Strong to gale-force winds are frequent during spring and early summer.

In 2003, it was reported that the southernmost part of South America, the Falkland Islands and South Georgia are all likely to be affected by the ozone hole in future.

Entry requirements
Passports
Valid passports and return tickets are required.

Visa
Not required by citizens of EU, North America and most commonwealth countries. For further confirmation and exceptions contact Travel Co-ordinator in London (see Travel Information addresses). Booking forms for the flight from the UK include details and purpose of visit, and are required to be completed before, or on arrival.

Currency advice/regulations
The Falkland Islands has its own currency which is equivalent to UK sterling. The actual notes and coins are different, and these cannot easily be exchanged for sterling or other currencies outside the Islands.

Customs
If travelling from RAF Brize Norton in the UK, ensure that customs forms are endorsed at Brize Norton prior to departure if you wish to claim value-added tax (VAT) refunds on personal purchases. In the absence of a customs official at the time of check-in, completed claim forms can be placed in the 'drop box' for attention.

Prohibited imports
Uncooked or cured meat and plants are only allowed under licence. No livestock is allowed on any incoming aircraft.

Health (for visitors)
Mandatory precautions
None

Advisable precautions
Yellow fever vaccination in case of any stopover in Africa en route.

Radiation alerts are issued with local weather forecasts when the ozone hole stretches over the islands. Precautions against skin cancer should be taken with high factor suncream and clothing protection.

Credit cards
Credit cards are generally accepted at hotels and retail outlets.

Falkland Islands/Islas Malvinas

Public holidays
Fixed dates
1 Jan (New Year's Day), 21 Apr (Queen's Birthday), 14 Jun (Liberation Day), 25 Dec (Christmas Day), 26 Dec (Boxing Day), 28–29 Dec (Stanley Races).
Variable dates
Good Friday, Peat Cutting Day (first Mon in Oct).

Working hours
Government
Mon–Fri: (winter) 1100–1515, 1630–1930; (summer) 1200–1615, 1730–2030.

Telecommunications
Telephone/fax
Direct satellite telephone links are in operation throughout the Islands.
Postal services
The post code for the islands is: FIQQ 1ZZ.

Electricity supply
Voltage and plugs for electrical appliances are the same as in the UK, 240V 50Hz.

Getting there
Air
Flights to the Falkland Islands depart from RAF Brize Norton, Oxfordshire, UK, twice a week. All flights must be booked through Falklands Islands Government offices (tel +44 20-7222-2542). LanChile operate weekly flights from Punta Arenas. Punta Arenas connects to Santiago by commercial flights. Details from any travel agent or from International Tours and Travel in Stanley (tel +500-22041; fax +500-22042).
International airport/s: Mount Pleasant International Airport (MPN); 56km from Stanley.
Airport tax: Departure tax: £20.
Surface
Main port/s: Stanley. The main port is a floating system; the Falkland Interim Port and Storage System (FIPSS) was installed after the 1982 conflict by the army and is owned by the government. It is operated by the Falkland Islands Company which also operates a jetty in Stanley Harbour for retail and commercial operations.

Getting about
National transport
Air: The Falkland Islands Government Air Service (FIGAS) operates four nine-seater Britten-Norman Islander land-based aircraft to the majority of settlements according to bookings and weather conditions.
Road: There is a limited amount of surfaced road mainly around Stanley and Mount Pleasant. Gravel roads are a common feature.
Water: A coaster 'Tamar II' serves settlements and operates occasional voyages to Punta Arenas, Chile. Freight is transported locally in small coastal vessels run by Byron Marine.

City transport
Taxis: There is no taxi service from the airport to Stanley nor a car rental service. Prior arrangements should be made privately or from Stanley Cabs (+500-22600) or Lowes Taxis (+500-21381).
Buses, trams & metro: There is a bus service from the airport to Stanley, operated by Falkland Islands Tours & Travel (+500-21775, e-mail: astewart@horizon.co.fk).

BUSINESS DIRECTORY

Telephone area codes
The international dialling code (IDD) for the Falkland Islands is +500 followed by subscriber's number.

Chambers of Commerce
Falkland Islands Chamber of Commerce, PO Box 378, West Hillside, Stanley (tel: 22-264; fax: 22-265; e-mail: commerce@horizon.co.fk).

Banking
Standard Chartered Bank, Box 166, Ross Road, Stanley (tel: 27-220; fax: 27-219); UK contact (tel: +44(0) 20-7280-7500).

Travel information
Falkland Islands Company Travel Services, Stanley (tel: 27-633; fax: 27-603).

Falkland Islands Government Air Service (FIGAS), c/o Falkland Islands Government, Stanley Airport (tel: 27-219; fax: 27-309; e-mail: figas@horizon.co.fk).

Falkland Islands Tourist Board, Stanley (tel: 27-211; 22-281; fax: 27-210; e-mail: jfowler@FIDC.co.fk).

Falkland Islands Tourist Board, London, UK (e-mail: manager@tourism.org.fk) issues an accommodation guide.

Falkland Islands Tours & Travel (tel: 21-775; e-mail: astewart@horizon.co.fk).

RAF Brize Norton, Oxfordshire, UK (tel: +44 (0)1993-897-366).

Travel Co-ordinator, Falkland Islands Government Office, Falkland House, 14 Broadway, Westminster, London SW1H 0BH, UK (tel: +44 (0)20-7222-2542; fax: +44 (0)20-7222-2375; e-mail: travel@figo.u-net.com).

National tourist organisation offices
Falkland Islands Tourist Board, Shackleton House, Stanley (tel: 22-215; fax: 22-619; e-mail: jettycentre@horizon.co.fk; internet site: http://www.tourism.org.fk).

Ministries
Chief Executive, Thatcher Drive, Stanley (tel: 27-110; fax: 27-109).

Department of Agriculture and Mineral Resources, Stanley (tel: 27-355; fax: 27-352).

Department of Civil Aviation, Stanley Airport (tel: 27-300; fax: 27-302).

Department of Education, 23 Ross Road, Stanley (tel/fax: 27-292).

Department of Fisheries, PO Box 598, Stanley (tel: 27-260; fax: 27-265).

Department of Oil, Ross Road, Stanley (tel: 27-322; fax: 27-321).

Department of Public Works, Stanley (tel: 27-193; fax: 27-191).

Governor's Office, Government House, Stanley (tel: 27-433; e-mail: gov.house@horizon.co.fk).

Treasury, Falkland Islands Government, Thatcher Drive, Stanley (tel: 27-143; fax: 27-144).

UK Government Office, Falkland House, 14 Broadway, Westminster, London SW1H 0BH, UK (tel: +44 (0)20-7222-2542; fax: +44 0)20-7222-2375; e-mail: rep@figo.u-net.com).

Other useful addresses
Attorney General, PO Box 143, Stanley (tel: 27-273/4; fax: 27-276).

British Geological Survey, Petroleum Geology Group, Murchison House, West Mains Rd, Edinburgh, EH9 3LA (tel: +44(0)131 667-1000; fax: +44 (0)131 668-4930).

Customs & Immigration, Stanley (tel: 27-340; fax: 27-342).

Falkland Islands Development Corporation, Stanley (tel: 27-211; fax: 27-210).

Falklands Islands Co Ltd (FIC), Crozier Place, Stanley (tel: 27-600; fax: 27-603).

Medical Services/King Edward VII Memorial Hospital, Stanley (tel: 27-415; fax: 27-416).

Meteorological Office, RAF Mount Pleasant (tel: 73-557).

Overseas Territories Department, Foreign & Commonwealth Office, King Charles St, London SW1A 2AH (tel: +44(0)20-7270-3000; fax: (0)20-7270-2086).

The United Kingdom Falkland Islands Trust (administers the Shackleton Scholarship fund), c/o 14 Broadway, Westminster, London SW1H 0BH, UK (tel: +44 (0)20-7222-2542; fax: +44 (0)20-7222-2375).

Internet sites
Falkland Islands Government: http://www.falklands.gov.fk

Falkland Islands information: http://www.falklands-malvinas.com/

Falkland Islands web portal: http:/www.falklandislands.com

Falkland Islands News Network: http://www.sartma.com

Faroe Islands

KEY FACTS

Official name: Føroyar (Faroe Islands)

Head of State: Queen Margrethe II of Denmark

Head of government: Prime Minister Jóannes Eidesgaard (JF) (from 3 Feb 2004); Danish High Commissioner Søren Christensen (since 1 Aug 2005)

Ruling party: Coalition government of the Sambandsflokkurin (SF) (Union Party), the Javnaoarflokkurin (JF) (Social Democrats), and the Fólkaflokkurin (FF) (People's Party) (from 3 Feb 2004)

Area: 1,399 square km (18 islands)

Population: 48,200 (2004)

Capital: Tórshavn

Official language: Faroese, Danish

Currency: Faroese krone (FKr) (same value as Danish krone)

Exchange rate: FKr6.19 per US$ (Oct 2005)

GDP per capita: US$22,000 (2003)

GDP real growth: 10.00% (2003)

Labour force: 24,250 (2003)

Unemployment: 1.00% (2003)

Inflation: 5.10% (2003)

Balance of trade: -US$51.00 million (2003)

COUNTRY PROFILE

Historical profile
The first Norse settlers arrived in the Faroes from neighbouring Denmark and the Orkneys in the ninth century.
1380 Early administration was undertaken by a parliamentary body known as the Alting. The end of parliamentary procedures saw the Alting renamed the Løgting and becoming a royal court.
1397 The Faroes become a Danish province, with the political merger of Norway and Denmark into the Kalmar Union.
1849 The first Danish constitution included the Faroe Islands administered under the Danish county Roskilde.
1939–45 Although the Faroe Islands were occupied by the British during the Second World War, they were largely able to govern themselves, and the economy had never been better than in this period.
1946 The Faroe Islands returned to Danish control. In a referendum, a very small majority voted in favour of becoming an independent state. Negotiations and diplomacy led to a home rule arrangement instead.
1948 The Home Rule Act made the Faroes security, foreign and economic affairs the responsibility of Denmark.
1998 Anfinn Kallsberg replaced Edmund Joensen as prime minister.
2001 A referendum to be held for approval of legislative amendments to enable a gradual winding-down of Denmark's authority on the islands was shelved after Denmark's Prime Minister Poul Nyrup Rasmussen said that subsidies would stop after four years if the islanders voted for independence.
2002 In the parliamentary elections, Prime Minister Anfinn Kallsberg's coalition lost its majority but the Sambandsflokkurin (SF) (Union Party) did not get enough votes to form a government.
2004 After the parliamentary elections, Jóannes Eidesgaard (JF) became prime minister on 3 February, leading a coalition of the SF, the Javnaoarflokkurin (JF) (Social Democrats) and the Fólkaflokkurin (FF) (People's Party).

Political structure
Constitution
The Faroe Islands were administered as a Danish county until they achieved home rule in 1948. The Faroe Islands are a Danish external territory, electing two members to the Danish parliament, which maintains responsibility for constitutional, foreign and defence matters. A High Commissioner represents the Danish government and advises on joint affairs.

Form of state
Parliamentary democratic dependency

National legislature
Internal affairs are under the legislative control of the Løgting (parliament) which has 32 members elected by proportional representation (PR) in seven constituencies, with up to five supplementary seats dependent upon the numbers of people voting. Term of office is four years. All Faroese over the age of 18 years are eligible to vote.
The Landsstyri (a government of six members) is formed, based on the strength of the parties in the Løgting. The Løgmadur (prime minister) has to ratify all Løgting laws.
All Danish legislation must be submitted to the Landsstyri before becoming law.

Last elections
20 January 2004 (parliamentary)
Results: Parliamentary: the Sambandsflokkurin (SF) (Union Party) won 23.7 per cent of the vote (seven seats out of 32), the Social Democrats 21.8 per cent (seven), the Republicans 21.7 per cent (eight), the Fólkaflokkurin (FF) (People's Party) 20.6 per cent (seven), the Mioflokkurin (MF) (Centre Party) 5.2 per cent (two) and the Independence Party 4.6 per cent (one).

Next elections
2008 (parliamentary)

Political parties
Ruling party
Coalition government of the Sambandsflokkurin (SF) (Union Party), the Javnaoarflokkurin (JF) (Social Democrats), and the Fólkaflokkurin (FF) (People's Party) (from 3 Feb 2004)

Main opposition party
Tjóoveldisflokkurin (TF) (Republican Party)

Population
48,200 (2004)

Ethnic make-up
Scandinavian

Religions
Evangelical Lutheran Church of Denmark (85 per cent). The Faroe Islands are a diocese under the Danish national church. Of the various smaller religious communities the largest is the Plymouth Brethren.

Health
Life expectancy: 79 years: male 75 years; female 82 years (2003).
Fertility rate/Maternal mortality rate: Two births per woman (2003)

Faroe Islands

Birth rate/Death rate: 14 births per 1,000 population; nine deaths per 1,000 population (2003).
Infant mortality rate: Seven per 1,000 live births (2003)

Main cities
Tórshavn (Thorshavn), on the island of Streymoy (capital, estimated population 17,300 in 2003).

Languages spoken
Faroese (derived from Old Norse) and Danish. Icelandic, English, Norwegian and Swedish are also widely spoken and understood.
Official language/s
Faroese, Danish

Media
Press
Dailies: Dailies include *Sosialurin* and *Dimmalætting*.
Weeklies: Weeklies include the twice-weekly *Oyggjatidindi* and *Dagbladid*. *Tidindabladid* carries local and international news, and is published five times a week.
Business: The on-line newspaper, *faroeweb.com* (http://www.faroeweb.com) features contemporary Faroese topics.
Periodicals: Periodicals include *14 September* (twice a week), *Friu Føroyar* published weekly, *Nordlysid* published weekly and *Tingakrossur* (twice a week).
Broadcasting
The general broadcasting company is Útvarp Føroya (ÚF) and the television broadcasting company Sjónvarp Føroya (Svf).
Advertising
Most widely used media are the press and cinemas. Direct mail is also popular. There is no advertising on radio, and poster sites are heavily regulated.

Economy
The economy is heavily dependent on the fishing industry and is vulnerable to fluctuations in that sector. The collapse of the fishing industry in the early 1990s, due to falling world prices and catches, and the banking crisis from 1992 to 1996 devastated the Faroese economy, reducing GDP to two-thirds of its size in the 1980s. The unemployment rate was close to 20 per cent and 10 per cent of the population emigrated.
In 1998, the economy began to recove due to rising fish catches. Immigration was high, implying that many who left during the crisis have returned. Oil business activities have also improved the economic situation. Economic policy focussed on free market reform and public spending reduction.
The economy grew strongly for several years until 2002, since when it has stagnated. Fishing went into decline again in 2003 with a drop in prices and volume. A slight improvement of 0.7 per cent growth in GDP was forecast for 2005 and a little better for 2006, provided that inflation stays low.

External trade
Foreign trade is mainly with the EU countries, which receive around 80 per cent of exports. The EU accounts for around 58 per cent of imports, mainly consumer goods and raw materials.
Imports
Machinery and transport equipment, consumer goods, raw materials and semi-manufactures, fuels, fish and salt.
Main sources: Denmark (59.1 per cent total, 2004), Norway (18.8 per cent), Iceland (4.6 per cent)
Exports
Fish and fish products (94 per cent), stamps and ships.
Main destinations: Denmark (38.6 per cent total, 2004), UK (29.4 per cent), Norway (8.2 per cent), Nigeria (6.1 per cent)

Agriculture
Farming
Sheep-rearing is an important activity on the Faroe Islands. There are 70,000 sheep ranging free on the islands, providing meat and wool for the use of the inhabitants. Cattle are also kept for milk and meat. The islands have to import meat and other agricultural products, but have become self-sufficient in milk. Increasing co-operation among agricultural organisations has been fostered to make the islands as self-sufficient as possble. Potatoes are grown and also hay for the cows reared for milk production.
Crop and livestock production in 2004 included 1,500 tonnes (t) potatoes, 591,491t meat in total, 77t beef, 521t mutton and lamb, 119t sheepskins and 10t cattle hides.
Fishing
Fishing is the dominant economic activity, acounting for 97 per cent of exports. The main fish stocks are cod, haddock and coalfish. Typical annual catches include over 20,000mt crustacea and 400,000mt fish. The business is highly vulnerable to fluctuations in world prices and to the catches themselves. Sea farming of salmon and trout is an important sector, but has experienced a decline in production since a record year in 2003.

Industry and manufacturing
Most industrial activities are connected to the fishing sector. They include processing plants and shipyards, as well as the making of nets, ropes, etc. Small industries include breweries, building components, fibreglass boats, computer software, food and milk products, tinned fish and spun and wollen goods.

Tourism
Tourism is second in importance to fishing, but is not a major activity. Efforts have been made to develop its potential in order to help diversify the economy. Most foreign visitors come from Scandinavia.

Hydrocarbons
There is a possibility of offshore oil between the Faroe Islands and the Shetland Islands.
An agreement with the UK in 1999 established a boundary, paving the way for increased exploration activity on the Faroese side. The first exploration licences were awarded in August 2000. Subsequent oil exploration in the waters around the Faroe Islands have produced disappointing results, but a significant oil find in UK waters near the maritime border was announced in December 2002 by a consortium led by US-based Amerada Hess, which led to an increase in exploration in 2003 and 2004. The Faroese government does not expect any oil field development before 2007. A second licensing round was launched in August 2004 and the first licences issued in January 2005.
The Faroe Islands relies on imported petroleum products. It does not currently produce or import gas and coal.

Banking and insurance
Monetary policy and administration is headed by the Danish central bank (Danmarks Nationalbank).
When the banking crisis began in 1992, there were two big banks, one small private bank and savings banks in the Faroe Islands. One of the big banks was owned by Den Danske Bank. By the end of the crisis, the small bank had gone into bankruptcy, the two big banks had merged and were taken over by the Home Rule authorities and the savings banks were still in business. The savings banks and the merged bank function as banks under the same law.
Central bank
Danmarks Nationalbank

Time
GMT (GMT +1 hour end-March to end-September).

Geography
The Faroe Islands are a group of 18 islands (of which 17 are inhabited) in the North Atlantic Ocean, south-east of Iceland and north-west of the north coast of Scotland. The main island is Streymoy.

Climate
Mild winters and cool summers; usually overcast; can be foggy and windy.

Entry requirements
Visa
Even though a Danish territory, visas for Denmark are not valid for the Faroe Islands unless specified on the permit. For a business visa, an original letter of invitation from a local company or organisation, giving details about purpose of visit and duration of stay must accompany an application, along with evidence of hotel reservations.

Health (for visitors)
As for Denmark.

Public holidays
Fixed dates
1 Jan (New Year's Day), Apr 25 (Flag Day, afternoon only), 5 Jun (Constitution Day, afternoon only), 28 Jul (St Olav's Eve, afternoon only), 29 Jul (St Olav's Day), 24–26 Dec (Christmas Holiday), 31 Dec (New Year's Eve).

Variable dates
Maundy Thursday, Good Friday, Easter Monday, Prayer Day (Apr/May), Ascension Day, Whit Monday.

Working hours
Banking
Mon–Fri: 0930–1600 (Thu 1800).
Business
Mon–Fri: 0800–1600 or 0830–1630.
Government
Mon–Fri: generally 0900–1700.
Shops
Mon–Fri: 0800–1700 or 0900–1730, Sat: close at 1300 or 1400.

Telecommunications
A new underwater telecommunications cable laid between Scotland and Iceland, via the Faroe islands, has improved broadband communications.
Telephone/fax
To make international calls from the Faroe Islands, dial 009.

Getting there
Air
National airline: Atlantic Airways has regular flights to Denmark, Norway, Iceland, Scotland, England and Greenland.
International airport/s: Vágar airport on the island of Vágar, located near the town of Sørvágur, a ferry links the island to Streymoy.

BUSINESS DIRECTORY
The addresses listed below are a selection only. While World of Information makes every endeavour to check these addresses, we cannot guarantee that changes have not been made, especially to telephone numbers and area codes. We would welcome any corrections.

Telephone area codes
The international direct dialling (IDD) for the Faroe Islands is +298. There are no area codes.

Useful telephone numbers
Emergency services   000

Chambers of Commerce
Faroe Islands Trade Council, 12 Bryggjubakki, PO Box 259, Tórshavn 110 (tel: 353-100; fax: 353-101; e-mail: trade@trade.fo).

Banking
Central bank
Landsbanki Føroya, Müllers hús, í Gongini, PO Box 229, Tórshavn 110 (tel: 318-305; fax: 318-537; e-mail: landsbank@landsbank.fo).

Travel information
Atlantic Airways, Vagar Airport, FR-380 (tel: 333-700; fax: 333-380).

Maersk Air, Aarvegur 6, PO Box 3225, FO-110 Tórshavn (tel: 333-700; fax: 318-670; e-mail: ff@olivant.fo).

Smyril Line, Jonas Bronckgota 37, PO Box 370, FO-110 Tórshavn (tel: 315-900; fax: 315-707; e-mail: office@smyril-line.fo).

Air Iceland, Vagar Airport, FO-380 Sorvagur (tel: 332-755; fax: 332-280).

The Faroe Islands Tourist Board Copenhagen, Hovedvagtsgade 8, 2, DK-1103 Copenhagen K, Denmark (tel: (45)3314-8383; fax: (45)3393-8575).

Faroe Travel, PO Box 1199, FO-110 Tórshavn (tel: 312-600; fax: 319-200).

National tourist organisation offices
National Tourist Office, Tourist Information Centre, PO Box 118, FO-110 Torshaven, (tel: 316-055; fax: 310-858; e-mail: tourist@tourist.fo; internet site; http://www.tourist.fo).

Other useful addresses
British Consulate, Yviri vid Strond 19, PO Box 19, FR-3800 Tórshavn (tel: 313-510).

The Faroese Government, PO Box 64, FR-110 Tórshavn (fax: 314-942).

Faroese Press Agency, P/f Salvará, Tjarnardeild 12, Tórshavn.

Sjónvarp Føroya (television broadcasting), PO Box 21, FR-3800 Tórshavn (tel: 317-780).

Útvarp Føroya (general broadcasting), PO Box 328, FR-3800 Tórshavn (tel: 316-566).

Internet sites
Danish embassy with useful information on the Faroes: http://www.denmarkemb.org

Faroe business news: www.news.fo

Faroe Islands general site: www.faroe.com

Faroe Islands tourist site: www.http://tourist.fo

Fiji

Fiji expects to feel the effects of the loss of concessions to key markets for its textiles and sugar in 2005 and 2006. Growth in 2004 was 3.9 per cent, compared to 3.0 per cent in 2003, on the back of improvements in the agriculture, forestry and fisheries sector, and a jump of 7.5 per cent in industry, which had been driven by a surge in construction.

Economy

The sugar industry will need to become self-reliant if it is to survive the ending of EU sugar price subsidies, expected by 2007. The costs of restructuring are high; upgrading of the sugar mills is estimated at F$126 million (US$60 million), in addition to F$40 million (US$19 million) to pay small sugar cane farmers to leave the sector and F$40 million (US$19 million) for improving transport and handling systems.

Sugar cane growers claim that the government's restructuring programme is moving forward too rapidly and infrastructural problems, such as the decrepit railways, which have contributed to the sugar industry's plight, are being neglected.

Tourism should be Fiji's success story. Travel and tourism in 2005 is estimated to have contributed 12.0 per cent to GDP, provided over 95,000 jobs (around 1 in every 3.6 jobs, according to the World Travel and Tourism Council) and generated some US$545 million. Capital investments were estimated at US$140.2 million.

Market capitalisation on the South Pacific Stock Exchange topped F$1 billion (US$585 million) for the first time in 2005, with 16 listed companies. However, the Fiji Trade and Investment Board cancelled the investment certificates of 45 foreign investors in December 2005, maintaining that foreign investment approvals were being used by Chinese nationals to circumvent immigration procedures. The one-stop-shop investment concept is believed to be partly to blame for the situation. In the meantime, the Kava Council announced that kava could be exported to Europe again in 2006, after the ban on kava imports by Germany, placed three years ago, would be lifted.

Politics

Communal tensions in Fiji have improved after the coup in 2000. However, a rumour that President Josefa Iloilovatu may announce his retirement in 2006 could upset the delicate balance between indigenous Fijians and ethnic Indians. The president, who first came to power in July 2000 and was later re-appointed by the Great Council of Chiefs in 2001, has won the respect of many Fijians as he attempted to find common ground between the various racial and political groupings.

Risk assessment

Economic	Improving
Political	Stable
Regional stability	Improving

COUNTRY PROFILE

Historical profile

One of the largest islands in the Melanesian chain, Fiji was the first of the Pacific islands to achieve independence, in 1970. With over 800,000 people, it is also the most populous of the Pacific Island states. For many years it was also the region's most developed and diversified state. However, a coup by George Speight in 2000, which initially overthrew the country's first government to be led by an ethnic Indian, Mahendra Chaudhry, changed all that. In 2003 and 2004 Fiji continued to suffer from the controversies surrounding the coup despite the life sentence imposed on Speight in February 2002. In March 2003, a further two of the main figures in the coup, Ratu Timoci Silatolu and Jo Nata, were found guilty of treason by Fiji's High Court.

Polynesians, and later Melanesian migrants, settled in the Fijian islands. Polynesian influence is strong in the eastern regions.

At the beginning of the nineteenth century, European traders were attracted to the islands for the sandalwood, but by 1814 all the trees had been cut down.

1874 Fiji was pronounced a British colony.
1970 Fiji became independent and introduced a British-style political system. The constitution provided separate electoral rolls for each ethnic group.

KEY FACTS

Official name: Republic of the Fiji Islands

Head of State: President Josefa Iloilovatu Uluivuda (since Jul 2000; re-appointed by the Great Council of Chiefs and sworn in 15 Mar 2001)

Head of government: Prime Minister Laisenia Qarase (SDL) (sworn in 10 Sep 2001)

Ruling party: Coalition: Soqosoqo Duavata ni Lewenivanua (SDL) (Fijian People's Party) and Matanitu Vanua (MV) (Conservative Alliance Party) (since 2001)

Area: 18,333 square km (about 332 islands, 110 inhabited)

Population: 837,000 (2004)

Capital: Suva (on Viti Levu)

Official language: English, Fijian and Hindi

Currency: Fijian dollar (F$) = 100 cents

Exchange rate: F$1.71 per US$ (Oct 2005)

GDP per capita: US$2,143 (2004)

GDP real growth: 3.90% (2004)

Labour force: 355,000 (2004)

Inflation: 2.40% (2004)

Balance of trade: -US$617.51 million (2004)

Foreign debt: US$112.80 million (2004)

1987 Fiji had recognised the British sovereign as head of state, but after a series of coups, Lieutenant Colonel Sitiveni Rabuka overthrew the elected mixed Fijian and Indian government of Timoci Bavadra of the Labour Party, and declared the country to be a republic. Fiji was expelled from the British Commonwealth.

1990 President Ratu Sir Penaia Ganilau proclaimed and decreed a new constitution. This constitution created a bicameral legislature.

1994 The Soqosoqo Duavata ni Lewenivanua (SDL) (Fijian People's Party), led by Prime Minister Sitiveni Rabuka, won the election.

1997 Fiji was re-admitted to the Commonwealth, after a new, less ethnically biased constitution came into force.

1999 President Ratu Sir Kamisese Mara was sworn in for a five-year term. Prime Minister Mahendra Chaudhry (Fiji Labour Party) was elected and was Fiji's first prime minister of Indian descent.

2000 Prime Minister Chaudhry and his cabinet were held captive by an armed group seeking more power for ethnic Fijians. The Commonwealth suspended Fiji's membership. The hostages were freed and Ratu Josefa Iloilo became president. Laisenia Qarase was appointed prime minister of an interim government. The rebel leader, George Speight, rejected the interim government although it consisted almost entirely of indigenous Fijians. Australia imposed sanctions on Fiji and announced a substantial reduction in aid. The High Court ruled that the deposed government of Mahendra Chaudhry should be reinstated.

2001 The interim government was ruled illegal by the Court of Appeal, which stated that the 1997 multi-racial constitution should remain in place. Fiji was re-admitted to the Commonwealth. President Iloilo was re-appointed by the Great Council of Chiefs. He re-appointed Laisenia Qarase as prime minister to head a caretaker government. The general election, observed by the Commonwealth team, was won by Laisenia Qarase's SDL; since it failed to secure an outright majority, the SDL joined with the Matanitu Vanua (MV) (Conservative Alliance Party) in a coalition government. Qarase was sworn in as prime minister; his cabinet barred all ethnic Indians.

2002 Samisoni Speight Tikonasau, the brother of George Speight who was responsible for the coup in 2000, was elected to parliament, reflecting the extent of George Speight's support network among the voting public.

2003 In January, a cyclone destroyed homes and flooded parts of Fiji. The government declared wide areas of the north and east of the country a disaster zone. In November, the Great Council of Chiefs heard, for the first time, a presentation from the Girmit Council, which represents descendants of Indian indentured labourers brought to work in Fiji in the nineteenth century; it was hoped that the meeting would help to achieve some reconciliation between indigenous Fijians and Indo-Fijians. The High Court ruled that the FLP should be allowed its seats in the cabinet.

2004 Ratu Sir Kamisese Mara, who led Fiji to independence from Britain in 1970, died in April.

2005 Public consultation on legislation, the *Reconciliation, Tolerance and Unity Bill*, took place, including a threat by the army chief to overthrow the government if leaders of the 2000 coup were allowed to apply for amnesty under the legislation.

2006 In January, Prime Minister Qarase agreed to review the *Reconciliation, Tolerance and Unity Bill* to take account of the army's objections.

Political structure
Constitution
The constitution was promulgated on 25 July 1990 and amended on 25 July 1997 to allow non-ethnic Fijians more say in government and to make multi-party government mandatory. Bars against non-Fijians becoming prime minister and president were removed.

In a ruling on 1 March 2001, the Court of Appeal upheld the 1997 constitution.

The constitution states any political party with more than 10 per cent of the seats in parliament must be offered a cabinet position.

Voting: universal suffrage, over 21 years.

The executive
Executive authority is vested in the president, who is elected by the Great Council of Chiefs for a maximum of two five-year terms. A presidential council advises the president on matters of national importance. The president is the commander-in-chief of the military forces.

National legislature
There is a bicameral parliament – the Senate (upper house) (34 seats – 24 appointed by the Great Council of Chiefs, nine appointed by the president, and one appointed by the council of Rotuma) and the House of Representatives (lower house) (71 seats – 23 reserved for ethnic Fijians, 19 reserved for ethnic Indians, three reserved for other ethnic groups, one reserved for the council of Rotuma constituency encompassing the whole of Fiji and 25 open seats). Members serve five-year terms.

The prime minister is usually the leader of the majority party or coalition in parliament and is appointed by the president for a five-year term. The 18-member cabinet is appointed by the prime minister from among the members of parliament and is responsible to parliament.

The Great Council of Chiefs comprises the highest ranking members of the traditional chief system.

Legal system
Based on the British legal system.

Last elections
August/September 2001 (House of Representatives)

Results: Parliamentary: Fiji Labour Party (FLP) won 34.8 per cent of the vote (27 seats); Soqosoqo Duavata ni Lewenivanua (SDL) (Fijian People's Party) 26 per cent (32 seats); National Federation Party (NFP) 10.1 per cent (one seat); Matanitu Vanua (MV) (Conservative Alliance Party)

KEY INDICATORS — Fiji

	Unit	2000	2001	2002	2003	2004
Population	m	0.81	0.82	0.83	0.83	0.84
Gross domestic product (GDP)	US$bn	1.50	1.70	1.90	1.79	*2.63
GDP per capita	US$	1,595	1,994	2,242	2,151	2,143
GDP real growth	%	-2.8	2.6	4.4	3.0	3.9
Inflation	%	1.1	4.3	0.9	3.0	2.4
Exports (fob) (goods)	US$m	595.0	615.0	633.0	442.0	703.7
Imports (fob) (goods)	US$m	830.0	882.0	880.0	642.0	1,320.2
Balance of trade	US$m	-240.0	-267.0	-247.0	-200.0	-616.5
Current account	US$m	52.0	62.0	–	–	–
Foreign debt	US$bn	0.2	0.1	0.2	0.1	0.1
Total reserves minus gold	US$m	409.7	366.4	358.8	423.6	478.1
Foreign exchange	US$m	384.3	341.5	331.5	393.4	446.1
Exchange rate	per US$	2.13	2.28	2.19	1.90	1.72

* estimated figure

Fiji

9.9 per cent (six seats). A coalition government was formed between the SDL and the MV.

Next elections
2006 (House of Representatives)

Political parties
The 18-member cabinet includes two members of George Speight's party, Matanitu Vanua (MV) (Conservative Alliance), but shuts out all ethnic Indians, including Mahendra Chaudhry's Fiji Labour Party (FLP), which won 27 seats, entitling it to 38 per cent of the cabinet posts according to the multi-racial constitution. In July 2003, the High Court ruled that the FLP should be allowed to take up its seats in the cabinet. Prime Minister Laisenia Qarase accepted the ruling, but warned that the government may collapse.

Ruling party
Coalition: Soqosoqo Duavata ni Lewenivanua (SDL) (Fijian People's Party) and Matanitu Vanua (MV) (Conservative Alliance Party) (since 2001)

Main opposition party
Fiji Labour Party (FLP)

Population
837,000 (2004)

Ethnic make-up
Ethnic Fijians represent about 51 per cent of the population. Indians comprise about 44 per cent. There are also some Europeans, other Pacific islanders and Chinese.

Religions
Methodist (37 per cent), Roman Catholic (9 per cent), Hindu (38 per cent), Muslim (8 per cent).

Education
Fiji showed remarkable progress in access to basic education in the years following 1996. The biggest boost for basic education has been the introduction of tuition assistance for primary schools in 1994. Totalling about F$4.8 million (US$2.3 million) annually, this assistance has enabled primary schools to meet their annual development costs.

Primary schooling lasts for eight years; secondary education lasts for a possible seven years, with intermediate stages of four-year junior secondary, two-year senior secondary and one-year seventh form schooling. Progression through all stages culminates in examinations.

The University of the South Pacific, which serves 10 English-speaking territories in the South Pacific, is the main provider of higher education.

Government expenditure on education increased through the 1990s and typically amounts to 16.21 per cent of the national budget.

In September 2004, the EU announced a US$44 million programme aimed at improving the quality of education in Fiji. It will assist more than 70 per cent of primary schools and 50 per cent of secondary schools.

Literacy rate: 94 per cent, adult rate (2003)

Compulsory years: 6 to 14.

Enrolment rate: 110.45 per cent gross enrolment in primary education (including repitition rates).

Health
Total expenditure on health is 4 per cent of GDP, of which 67 per cent is government spending.

Health care facilities in Fiji are barely adequate for routine medical problems. Two major hospitals, the Lautoka Hospital and the Colonial War Memorial Hospital in Suva, provide emergency and outpatient services. Other hospitals and clinics provide only a limited range of health services.

Access to clean water is available to 47 per cent of the total population.

HIV prevalence: 0.1 per cent aged 15–49 in 2003 (World Bank)

Life expectancy: 69.7 years (World Bank)

Fertility rate/Maternal mortality rate: 2.6 births per woman (World Bank)

Birth rate/Death rate: 23 births per 1,000 population; six deaths per 1,000 population (2003).

Infant mortality rate: 16 per 1,000 live births (World Bank)

Head of population per physician/bed: 0.5 doctors per 1,000 people.

Main cities
Suva (capital, on Viti Levu, estimated population 177,300 in 2003), Lautoka (on Viti Levu, 45,700), Nadi (on Viti Levu, 32,600), Labasa (on Vanua Levu, 25,400), Nausori (on Viti Levu, 22,800).

Languages spoken
English is widely used in business circles. Fijian dialects are spoken by the indigenous Fijians (Bauan is the most spoken). The Indian community speaks Fiji-Hindi. Cantonese is also spoken.

Since 2003, compulsory classes teaching the Fijian and Hindi languages have been introduced in some primary and secondary schools in order to avert the threat of losing the ethnic languages of the country.

Official language/s
English, Fijian and Hindi

Media

Press
Dailies: The daily newspapers, including *Fiji Times* (Monday to Saturday), *Fiji Sun* and *Daily Post*, are published in Suva. A number of other papers are also published in Fijian and Hindi.

Weeklies: Weeklies in Fijian include *Nai Lalakai* and *Na Volasiga*, covering current affairs. *Shanti Dut* is a Hindi language publication featuring national and international news. *USP Bulletin* carries university news.

Business: Business publications include *Fiji Islands Business*, *Island Business* and *Construction and Commercial Trade News*.

Periodicals: Periodicals on current affairs and tourism and general interest magazines include *Pacific Islands Monthly*, *The Review*, *Islands* (quarterly), *PINA Nius* and *Spotlight on Nadi*. Other popular monthly tourism magazines are *Fiji Beach Press* and *Fiji Magic*.

Broadcasting
Radio: Fiji Broadcasting Commission, a government-funded body, broadcasts a fully commercial service on three wavebands; Fiji 1 in English and Fijian, Fiji 2 in English and Hindi, and Fiji 3 in English. FM96, a commercial radio station, broadcasts 24 hours in English.

Television: The government has set up a TV service for Fiji, Samoa and Tonga via satellite. In 2004, Pay TV brought television to more homes.

Fiji Television Limited acquired 100 per cent of Papua New Guinea's only television station EMTV in late 2004. The investment of A$2.1 million (US$2.72 million) marks a period of expansion for the parent company, Yasana Holdings (owned by, among others, the 14 provincial councils of Fiji).

Advertising
Advertising is available in local press, radio and cinema. Few sites are suitable for outdoor advertising.

Economy
The Fijian economy is highly dependent on sugar exports and tourism. However, the economy is relatively diverse with gold, silver and limestone mining contributing to Fijian exports. Confidence in Fiji as an investment destination has weakened due to the threat of social unrest following the 2000 coup, but growth returned to the country after the lifting of sanctions and the return of donor aid. In 2003, the EU agreed to resume development aid to Fiji, which had been frozen after the 2000 coup.

Increases in consumer spending and tourism spurred GDP growth in 2003 to 3.0 per cent, although this was lower than expected due to the downturn of gold and sugar production. Growth in 2004 fell to 3.9 per cent, against expectations, and is projected by the Asian Development Bank to decline in subsequent years – to 1.5 per cent in 2005 and further to 0.7 per cent in 2006, as the loss of protected sugar and textile exports takes effect.

External trade

Imports
Principal imports are manufactured goods, machinery and transport equipment, petroleum products, food and chemicals.

Main sources: Australia (27.7 per cent total, 2004), Singapore (24.8 per cent), New Zealand (17.8 per cent), Japan (4.2 per cent)

Exports
Principal exports are raw sugar, garments, gold, timber, fish, molasses and coconut oil. Exports totalled US$442 million in 2003.

Main destinations: US (23.6 per cent total, 2004), Australia (19.2 per cent), UK (12.8 per cent), Samoa (6.2 per cent), Japan (4.1 per cent)

Agriculture

Farming
The agricultural sector typically accounts for around 16 per cent of GDP and employs 40 per cent of the workforce. Historically, 85 per cent of land is granted to Fijian clans (*Mataqali*) and by law cannot be sold. This has led to underutilisation of some land. The soil is generally fertile and easily worked.

In 1997 the Native Land Trust Board (NLTB) refused to renew land-leases to Indo-Fijian farmers, forcing many off the land and into the towns. As a result, production of sugar fell and in 2004 over 30 per cent of these farms were vacant. NLTB admitted that rental income had dropped significantly and in 2003 it recorded a loss. An invitation to the ex-tenants to return was ignored as many had adapted to urban life, while young ethnic Fijians did not come forward to farm.

Sugar normally accounts for half agricultural output, but has declined both in quality and quantity. The sugar industry supports about 25 per cent of the working population, consumes around 12 per cent of all goods and services and earns more than 40 per cent of export income. The Fiji Sugar Corporation aims to diversify into ethanol and to encourage other uses for spare land, especially rice (50 per cent of which is imported).

Fiji's already ailing sugar industry suffered a devastating blow in August 2004, when the World Trade Organisation (WTO) decided in favour of a case brought by Brazil, Australia and Thailand, to prevent the EU from paying preferential prices for sugar imports from developing African, Caribbean and Pacific (ACP) countries like Fiji. For nearly 20 years, Fiji's sugar industry has been totally dependent on the EU's preferential prices, which are three to four times higher than world market levels. As a result, the sugar sector is in the process of restructuring in order to respond to the end of EU sugar subsidies in 2007. This has given impetus to the government's drive to find alternatives to sugar cane production.

Production in 2004 included: 16,330 tonnes (t) cereals in total, 15,000t rice, 1,300t maize, 33,000t cassava, 1,200t okra, 80t potatoes, 6,200t sweet potatoes, 38,000t taro, 6,500t bananas, 5,200t yams, 3,662t pineapples, 2,800t tomatoes, 1,634t papayas, 700t citrus fruit, t mangoes, 182,290t oilcrops, 140,000t coconuts, 3,300t ginger, 160t pepper spice, 385t tobacco, 22,821t fruit in total, 21,200t vegetables in total, 3,000,000t sugar cane. Livestock production included: 20,988t meat in total, 8,740t beef, 3,938t pig meat, 1,100t goat meat, 7,184t poultry, 2,600t eggs, 57,500t milk, 103t honey.

Fishing
Fishing for local consumption includes skipjack, yellowfin and commercial species. Prawns and oysters are raised in fish farms. Bêche-de-Mer, shark-fins, trochus, mother-of-pearl and turtle shells are collected and sold.

The typical annual fish catch is over 44,700t with over 14,000t of other seafood. One million pieces of coral are harvested annually as well as 160,000 units, pearls and shells.

Forestry
In addition to natural rain forest, large new plantations of pine and hardwood were established in the late 1970s. There are exports of pine chips to Japan and sawn pine to Australia. The clearing of forests has caused soil erosion.

Industry and manufacturing
The industrial sector as a whole accounts for 26 per cent of GDP and employs 15 per cent of the workforce. The manufacturing industry (excluding sugar milling) accounts for 13 per cent of GDP and sugar accounts for one-third of industrial output.

Sugar cane is crushed at local mills and exported as raw sugar and molasses. In June 2003, two mills were closed as part of the government's restructuring of the sector. Copra milling, which produces coconut oil and oil cake for export, is carried on at Suva and Savusavu. There are two breweries, a flour mill and a steel-rolling mill.

Tourism
Tourism is Fiji's most important economic activity and a vital contributor to the balance of payments. It accounts for 16 per cent of GDP, is the principal foreign exchange earner and gives employment to 40,000 people. The sector was seriously damaged by the coup in 2000, but recovered by 2003, when a record 430,800 visitors were recorded. Australia, from which a quarter of arrivals come, is the main market, followed by New Zealand, the US and the UK. Tourism in the rural areas and the outer islands, especially sustainable eco-tourism, is being developed. Expansion of the sector faces problems from shortage of skilled labour and pressure on available water and electricity provision.

Mining
The mining sector accounts for around 3 per cent of GDP and employs 2 per cent of the workforce.

Gold is Fiji's second largest export. Production is centred on one large mine, Vatukoula, owned by Emperor Gold Mines, which produces 120,000–160,000 ounces per annum and has reserves of around 3.5 million ounces. Accessible ore is expected to be exhausted within 10 years. Another smaller mine at Mount Kasai is operated by Pacific Island Gold and was reopened in 1997 following a 50-year closure.

Hydrocarbons
Fiji has no proven hydrocarbons reserves, but the outlook for oil exploration is optimistic. Fiji relies entirely on imports to meet energy requirements.

Energy
A mini-hydroelectric scheme in Vanua Levu supplies electricity to 40 villages and other processing industries.

Banking and insurance
Central bank
Reserve Bank of Fiji

Time
GMT plus 12 hours

Geography
Fiji comprises more than 300 islands, of which 100 are inhabited, situated about 1,930km (1,200 miles) south of the equator in the Pacific ocean. The four main islands are Viti Levu, Vanua Levu, Tavenui and Kadavu.

Climate
Hot and damp, tempered by cool winds from May–October. Maximum temperature during summer (December–April) 32 degrees Celsius (C), when hurricanes and cyclonic storms sometimes occur; rarely falls below 18 degrees C during the rest of the year.

Entry requirements
Passports
Required by all. Passports must be valid for six months beyond the the date of entry.

Visa
Visitor's visa (for stays up to four months) are issued on arrival to many citizens from 'exempt' countries, who possess sufficient funds and return/onward passage.

Fiji

Business visits, by representatives of overseas companies, may by undertaken using this visa.

Currency advice/regulations
In a review of currency designs in 2005 it was decided to retain the head of the British monarch on the currency, even though Fiji has been a republic since 1987.

No restriction on importation of currency. Foreign currency notes to a value equivalent to amount brought in and F$500 in Fijian currency notes may be taken out. The export of foreign currency exceeding US$2,326 should be declared at customs. Transfers of funds to accounts outside Fiji subject to Exchange Control legislation.

Customs
Personal effects allowed duty-free. Strict animal and plant quarantine regulations; fruit or plant material should not be brought in. Many agricultural and manufactured items subject to import embargoes and licensing and the list is subject to alteration. Details available from the Ministry of Commerce and Industry in Suva.

Health (for visitors)
Mandatory precautions
Vaccination certificates are required for yellow fever if travelling from an infected area.

Advisable precautions
Vaccination for diphtheria, tuberculosis, hepatitis 'A' and 'B', polio, tetanus, typhoid and dengue fever. There is a rabies risk.

In rural areas water should be boiled before drinking.

Hotels
There are around 223 tourist hotels of all types, frequently in scenic locations around the islands.

Tipping is not encouraged but visitors may give a gratuity for excellent service.

Credit cards
Most major credit cards accepted at hotels, restaurants, shops and rental car agencies, tours, cruises and travel agencies. American Express, Diners Club, Visa, JCB and Master Card have representatives in Suva.

Public holidays
Fixed dates
1 Jan (New Year's Day), 25–26 Dec (Christmas Holiday).

Variable dates
Good Friday, Easter Monday, National Youth Day (first Fri in May), Ratu Sir Lala Sukuna Day (last Mon in May), Queen's Official Birthday (Jun/Jul), Fiji Day (Oct), Diwali (Oct/Nov), Birth of the Prophet Mohammed.

Muslim and Hindu festivals are timed according to local sightings of various phases of the moon.

Working hours
Banking
Mon–Thu: 0930–1500; Fri: 0930–1600.
Business
Mon–Fri: 0800–1700.
Government
Mon–Thu: 0800–1300, 1400–1630; Fri: to 1600.
Shops
Mon–Fri: 0800–1700; Sat: 0800–1300.

Electricity supply
240/415V AC, with flat three-pin plug fittings and bayonet-type light fittings. Wiring rules of the Standard of Associations of Australia in use. Larger hotels have 110V conversion units for electric shavers.

Social customs/useful tips
Clothing may be casual, but should be modest: swimsuits are only acceptable on beaches and around hotel pools. On social occasions punctuality is appreciated, and dress should be formal – lightweight suit and tie for men and lightweight suit or equivalent for women. It is customary to shake hands on meeting and taking leave.

Getting there
Air
National airline: Air Pacific
International airport/s: Nadi International (NAN), 8km north of Nadi, 200km from Suva; duty-free shop, restaurant, buffet, bank, post office, car hire.
Other airport/s: Nausori (SUV), 21km from Suva with milk bar.
Airport tax: International departures and passenger service charge F$30 payable locally upon departure; not applicable to 24 hour transit passengers and children under 12 years.
Surface
Main port/s: Labasa, Lautoka, Levuka, Savusavu and Suva.

Getting about
National transport
Air: Air Fiji operates several daily flights between Nadi International and Nausori Airport and most other domestic services. Air Pacific operates the main route between Nadi and Suva. Sunflower Airlines and Turtle Island Airways operate on parts of Viti Levu and are available for charter. Helicopters can be chartered from Pacific Crown Aviation, Suva.
Road: A 3,300km road network, about one-third of which is tar-sealed. On Viti Levu, a 500km coastal highway links main centres. A trans-insular road on Vanua Levu connects Labasa with Savusavu.
Buses: Air-conditioned buses operate daily between Suva, Nadi and Lautoka; fares are cheap. Air-conditioned coaches for longer distances.
Rail: There were 597km of railways in 2003.
Water: Small inter-island vessels operate from Suva and Lautoka. A regular ferry service connects Suva and Labasa, Ovalau and Koro Island. Ferries also connect the majority of the major coastal areas of Viti Levu and Vanua Levu with all the major islands. It is also possible to charter boats.

City transport
Taxis: Metered taxis available in main centres. It is advisable to negotiate fares for long journeys in advance. Journey time for a taxi from the airport to the city centre is around 10 minutes.
Buses, trams & metro: Journey time from airport to city centre 20 minutes; buses operate 0700–1830.
Car hire
Chauffeur-driven and self-drive car hire available. Current overseas or international licence acceptable for six months. Driving on the left-hand side of the road, speed limits 50kph in towns and villages, 80kph on highways.

BUSINESS DIRECTORY
The addresses listed below are a selection only. While World of Information makes every endeavour to check these addresses, we cannot guarantee that changes have not been made, especially to telephone numbers and area codes. We would welcome any corrections.

Telephone area codes
The international dialling code (IDD) for Fiji is +679 followed by the customer number.

In 2002, all telephone and fax numbers changed from six to seven digits. All six-digit numbers in Suva which started with 2, 3 and 4, had the digit 3 added in front of the existing number. For further information, see the website: www.TelecomFiji.com.fj

Useful telephone numbers
Police, fire and ambulance: 000

Chambers of Commerce
Suva Chamber of Commerce, 7th Floor, Honson Building, Thomson Street, PO Box 337, Suva (tel: 331-3505).

Banking
Australia & New Zealand Banking Group Ltd, PO Box 179, ANZ House, 25 Victoria Parade, Suva (tel: 321-3000; fax: 330-0267).

National Bank of Fiji, 107 Victoria Parade, PO Box 1166, Suva (tel: 331-4400; fax: 330-2190, 330-2032).

Westpac Banking Corporation, 6th Floor, Civic House, Town Hall Road, Suva (tel: 330-0666; fax: 330-0718).

Central bank
Reserve Bank of Fiji, Private Mail Bag, Viti Levu Island, Suva (tel: 331-3611; fax: 330-1688).

Travel information
Air Fiji, 185 Victoria Parade, Suva (tel: 331-5055, 331-4495; fax: 330-0771, 337-0693).

Flight information (24 hours) (tel: 672-2599).

Hotel reservations (available 24 hours on arrival concourse) (tel: 672-2433).

Nadi International Airport, Civil Aviation Authority of Fiji, Private Mail Bag (tel: 672-2500, 672-1555; fax: 652-1500, 672-3795).

Tourist information (0800–1700 hours) (tel: 672-2433).

National tourist organisation offices
Fiji Visitors' Bureau, Thomson Street, PO Box 92, Suva (tel: 330-2433; fax: 330-0970, 330-2751; e-mail: infodesk@fijifvb.gov.fj; internet site: http://www.bulafiji.com).

Ministries
Ministry of Primary Industries and Co-operatives, PO Box 358, Rodwell Road, Suva (tel: 331-1233).

Prime Minister's Office (tel: 321-1201; fax: 330-6034).

Other useful addresses
Asian Development Bank (ADB), South Pacific Regional Mission, La Casa di Andrea, Fr. Dr. W. H. Lini Highway; PO Box 127, Port Vila (tel: +678 2 23-300; fax: +678 2 23-183; email: adbsprm@adb.org; internet: http://www.adb.org/SPRM).

Bureau of Statistics, PO Box 2221, Government Buildings, Suva (tel: 331-5144, 331-5822; fax: 330-3656).

Commonwealth Development Corporation, 371 Victoria Parade, Suva (tel: 330-2577).

Department of Information, PO Box 2225, Government Buildings, Suva (tel: 321-1250/1; fax: 330-0776).

Fiji Posts and Telecommunications Ltd, PO Box 40, Suva (tel: 321-0329; fax: 330-5591; internet site: http://www.TelecomFiji.com.fj).

Fiji Trade and Investment Board, PO Box 2303, Government Buildings, Suva (tel: 331-5988; fax: 331-5783).

Forum Secretariat, Ratu Sukuna Road, Suva (fax: 330-3069).

National Marketing Authority of Fiji, PO Box 5085, Raiwaqa, Suva (tel: 338-5888).

Pacific Islands News Association Secretariat (PINS), Private Mail Bag, Level II, Damodar Centre, 46 Gordon Street, Suva (tel: 330-3623; fax: 330-3943).

Internet sites
Fiji government: http://www.fiji.gov.fj

Tourism Council of the South Pacific: http://www.tcsp.com/destinations/fiji

Finland

KEY FACTS

Official name: Suomen Tasavalta: Republiken Finland (Republic of Finland)

Head of State: President Tarja Halonen (SDP) (since 2000)

Head of government: Prime Minister Matti Vanhanen (appointed 24 Jun 2003)

Ruling party: Three-party coalition from 15 Apr 2003: Suomen Keskusta (KESK) (Centre Party of Finland); Suomen Sosialidemokraatinen Puolue (SDP) (Social Democratic Party of Finland); Svenska Folkpartiet i Finland (SFP) (Swedish People's Party)

Area: 338,144 square km

Population: 5.22 million (2004); 5.21 million (OECD, 2003)

Capital: Helsinki

Official language: Finnish and Swedish

Currency: Euro (eur) = 100 cents (from 1 Jan 2002; previous currency markka, locked at M5.95 per euro)

Exchange rate: eur0.83 per US$ (Oct 2005)

GDP per capita: US$35,670 (2004)

GDP real growth: 3.70% (2004)

Labour force: 2.59 million (2004)

Unemployment: 8.90% (OECD, 2004)

Inflation: 0.10% (2004)

Balance of trade: US$12.82 billion (2004)

Foreign debt: US$226.51 billion (2004)

Annual FDI: US$49.50 billion (cumulative, 1995–2004, OECD); US$4.70 billion (OECD, 2004)*

* estimated figure

It was a difficult year for the Finnish economy in 2005, underscoring the predominance of the paper-manufacturing sector. Weeks of national strikes in Finland's paper mills, through May and June, had a substantial impact on the country's GDP growth. The Finns did their bit for conflict resolution in 2005, when they hosted successful peace talks between the Indonesian government and Acehnese separatists. Former Finnish president Martti Ahtisaari acted as chief mediator.

A paper weight on growth

A nation-wide strike over holiday pay and working conditions, affecting 24,000 employees in the paper-manufacturing sector, hit Finland hard in 2005. The strike, running through May and June, cost the industry an estimated 40 million euros a day. Paper accounts for approximately one third of Finland's exports and 40–50 per cent of manufacturing output. Finland only produces around 4 per cent of the world's paper but in Europe it supplies 60 per cent of magazine paper and 20 per cent of graphic paper. Financial analysts within Finland predicted that the strike would shave 0.3 per cent off the country's GDP for every month it continued. GDP contracted in the second quarter of 2005 by 1.6 per cent, compared to first quarter figures. Estimates for GDP growth over 2005 range between 1.6–2.2 per cent, a significant slowdown on 2004's 3.7 per cent.

Inflation remained remarkably low in 2005, declining slightly to 0.9 per cent. Unemployment also fell, to 8.4 per cent, compared to 8.9 per cent in 2004. Overall public finances remained in surplus.

Big polluter

In June, the European Environment Agency published a report that singled out Finland as one of the biggest emitters of carbon dioxide in the EU, second only to Italy. The EU is committed to reducing carbon dioxide emissions by 8 per cent of 1990 levels by 2012.

Italian charm

Also in June, comments by the Italian prime minister, Silvio Berlusconi, were published, in which he claimed to have used his 'playboy skills' on Finland's President Halonen, and insulted Finnish cuisine. The Italian ambassador to Finland was summoned by the Finnish government to discuss the comments.

Relations with Russia

With Russia set to become Finland's biggest trading partner over the next few years (it is already its third biggest, after Germany and Sweden), Finland invested a considerable amount of time on its Russian neighbour in 2005. Finnish president Tarja Halonen hosted her Russian counterpart, Vladimir Putin, in August, and visited Putin in St Petersburg in September. Trade and investment issues, particularly relating to Finnish investment in the neighbouring Russian Republic of Karelia, dominated talks. President Halonen politely rebuffed President Putin's efforts to garner Finnish support for Russia's quarrels with Estonia and Latvia. Russia has long complained that citizenship laws in these countries discriminate against their ethnic Russian minorities.

In August, after President Putin's visit to Finland, the Russian government announced that it was in no hurry to renew Finland's lease on the Saimaa Canal, half of which runs through Russian territory. The lease expires in 2013 and Finland has been pressing for an early extension. The canal runs through formerly Finnish territory forcibly annexed by Joseph Stalin in 1940. Opinion polls conducted in 2005 indicated that between a quarter and a third of Finns surveyed wanted the return of territories lost to Russia.

Peace in Aceh

Over the course of three negotiating rounds, conducted in January, February and April, Finland hosted peace talks between the Indonesian government and separatist rebels from the Indonesian province of Aceh. The two sides agreed to end their conflict, which began in 1976. Former Finnish president, Martti Ahtisaari brokered the talks, in his capacity as head and founder of the NGO Conflict Management Initiative (CMI).

Outlook

Analysts agree that Finland will experience accelerated economic growth in 2006, after 2005's strike-induced slowdown. The European Commission forecast for GDP growth in 2006 is 3.7 per cent. Inflation is expected to stay low and the budget to stay in surplus.

In January, President Halonen was re-elected to another 6-year term, after having to face a second round run-off, with 51.8 per cent of the vote. She had comfortably won a plurality of votes in the first round but was hard pressed in the second.

Risk assessment

Politics	Stable
Economy	Improving
Regional stability	Stable

COUNTRY PROFILE

Historical profile
Before independence in 1917, Finland was controlled by Sweden and later Russia. Prior to Sweden's conquest of Finland in the 1150s, the country had been a feudal and tribal society.
1150–1293 Sweden was in control of Finland.
1362 Finland was granted the full rights of a Swedish province.
1523 Treaty gave Russia part of Karelia (area between Finland and Russia).
1721 Russia took control of the whole of Karelia.
1809 Finland was conquered by Russia.
1905–06 Strikes were held by the population demanding rights and liberties. Parliamentary government and universal suffrage were established; in 1906, Finland became the first European country to give votes to women.
1917 Collapse of the Russian Empire. A Finnish declaration of independence was followed by a brief civil war.
1919 Establishment of a republic; Kaarlo Ståhlberg became Finland's first president. In the following 70 years, more than 60 governments, mainly minority coalitions, held power.
1939–41 The Soviet Union invaded Finland and after the bitter conflict of the 1939–40 'Winter War', Finland entered the Second World War on the side of Nazi Germany. In December 1940, German troops were invited by the Finnish government to occupy parts of the country and Finland joined Germany's invasion of the Soviet Union in 1941.
1944 Finland signed a peace treaty with the Soviet Union and its troops withdrew

KEY INDICATORS — Finland

	Unit	2000	2001	2002	2003	2004
Population	m	5.20	5.20	5.21	5.21	5.22
Gross domestic product (GDP)	US$bn	121.70	121.80	134.40	161.50	*186.60
GDP per capita	US$	23,440	23,420	25,848	31,773	35,670
GDP real growth	%	5.4	1.0	2.3	2.1	3.7
Inflation	%	3.4	2.6	2.2	1.3	0.1
Unemployment	%	9.8	9.1	9.3	9.2	8.9
Exports (fob) (goods)	US$m	45,703.0	42,980.0	45,040.0	52,834.0	61,083.0
Imports (fob) (goods)	US$m	32,019.0	30,323.0	33,230.0	41,312.0	48,262.0
Balance of trade	US$m	13,684.0	12,657.0	11,800.0	11,522.0	12,821.0
Current account	US$m	8,854.0	8,357.0	9,890.0	10,500.0	8,400.0
Total reserves minus gold	US$m	8,464.7	7,982.8	9,285.0	10,514.9	12,318.2
Foreign exchange	US$m	7,330.5	7,192.0	8,437.0	9,544.5	11,522.0
Exchange rate	per US$	6.14	6.34	1.04	0.88	0.80

* estimated figure

from Soviet territory. Finnish troops were then engaged in the 'Lapland War' in northern Finland against withdrawing German soldiers.

1945 Following the end of the Second World War, punitive reparations and the cession of Southern Karelia and its only Arctic port, Petsamo, were forced on Finland by the Soviet Union.

1948 The Treaty of Friendship, Co-operation and Mutual Assistance was signed by Finland and the Soviet Union. It lasted until 1992 after the Soviet Union's break-up.

1956–82 The powers of the strong executive presidency allowed for in the constitution were further enhanced by President Urho Kekkonen. He was succeeded by President Mauno Koivisto in 1982.

1987 The Suomen Keskusta (KESK) (Centre Party of Finland) was replaced after 50 years in government. Conservatives were in the coalition government for the first time in 21 years. Harri Holkeri was appointed Finland's first conservative prime minister since 1946.

1994 Martii Ahtisaari was elected as president. The Suomen Kristillinen Liitto (SKL) (Christian League of Finland), which opposed EU membership, withdrew from the coalition after Finland completed negotiations on joining the EU.

1995 Finland joined the EU. The Suomen Sosialidemokraatinen Puolue (SDP) (Social Democratic Party) won the parliamentary elections and formed a coalition government, with the SDP's Paavo Lipponen as prime minister.

1999 The SDP was again returned as the strongest party in the parliamentary elections; a five-party government coalition was formed. Lipponen was re-elected as prime minister.

2000 Tarja Halonen was elected as president – Finland's first female president. The powers of the president were reduced, following the introduction of a new constitution.

2001 Finland joined other EU states to support the US's military action in Afghanistan, following the 11 September terrorist attacks.

2002 The Vitireä Liitto (VIHR) (Green League) left the coalition government after parliament voted to proceed with plans to build Finland's fifth nuclear reactor.

2003 Anneli Jäätteenmäki became Finland's first female prime minister, heading a coalition of her own KESK, which won the March parliamentary elections, the SDP and the SFP/RKP. Jäätteenmäki resigned as prime minister in June and parliament elected the defence minister, Matti Vanhanen, as prime minister.

2004 In March, former prime minister Anneli Jäätteenmäki was acquitted of charges of illegally obtaining secret documents about the Iraq War while she was opposition leader.

2005 Former prime minister, Paavo Lipponen, stepped down as party leader of the SDP, in June; Eero Heinäluoma replaced him. A poll conducted in December showed that 49 per cent of Finns would vote 'no' to EU membership while 44 per cent would vote 'yes'.

2006 The incumbent president, Tarja Halonen, won 46 per cent of the vote in the 15 January elections. Although this was nearly twice the vote of her nearest rival, Sauli Niinisto, who won 24 per cent, the constitution demands a minimum of 50 per cent. The a run-off was won by Halonen with 51.8 per cent of the vote.

Political structure
Constitution
Finland's republican constitution, approved in 1919, was based on the principle of a unicameral parliament and a strong executive president.

In March 2000, a new constitution reduced the president's powers, and increased the role of the government – consisting of a prime minister and cabinet – who exercise power in conjunction with the president.

Form of state
Constitutional republic

The executive
The president is Head of State and is directly elected, by universal vote, for a six-year term, and is allowed to stand for office for two further consecutive terms. The president and government exercise executive power over matters of foreign policy and national security. The president is expected to approve or reject all measures adopted by the Eduskunta (parliament) within a period of three months, and if no decision is reached, a bill lapses.

National legislature
The 200-member unicameral parliament – the Eduskunta – is elected every four years by universal suffrage of all citizens aged from 18, using a system of proportional representation which takes into account the differing population densities in the 15 electoral districts. It usually meets for 120 days a year, starting in February, but can extend the session at its discretion. Any legislative proposal can be postponed until the next legislative session on a one-third vote in parliament.

The president is empowered to order elections, but the parliament decides when they are held. The parliament also appoints the prime minister and the 17 or 18 members of the Valtioneuvosto (Council of State/cabinet). Most of its members are drawn from within the parliament, but a few may come from outside. It is responsible to parliament for the general administration of the country. Because Finland has a loose, multi-party system, the cabinet always contains a coalition of parties and may be re-formed frequently.

Legal system
The legal system is based on Swedish civil law and is codified. The judicial system is divided between ordinary civil and criminal jurisdiction and special courts of litigation.

The president appoints a chancellor of justice who is not a cabinet member. His function is to oversee the Council of State and to submit an annual report on its legal conduct.

The Court of the Realm is supreme constitutional court, six of whose 13 members are elected by parliament for a term of four years. The final court for civil and criminal cases is the Korkein Oikeus (supreme court), whose president and 21 members are appointed directly by the state president; the supreme administrative court is the Korkein Hallinto-Oikeus. Composed of 21 presidentially-appointed judges, it is the highest tribunal of administrative appeal.

Last elections
13 June 2004 (European Parliament); 16 March 2003 (parliamentary); 16 January/6 February 2000 (presidential).

Results: European Parliament: KOK won 23.7 per cent of the vote (four seats out of 14), KESK 23.3 per cent (four), SDP 21.1 per cent (three), Greens 10.4 per cent (one), Vasemmistoliitto/Vänsterförbundet (Left Alliance of Finland) 9.1 per cent (one) and SFP 5.7 per cent (one); turnout 41.1 per cent.

Parliamentary: the KESK won 24.7 per cent of the vote (55 seats out of 200), the SDP 22.9 per cent (53), the KOK 18.5 per cent (40); Vasemmistoliitto (VAS) (Left League) 9.9 per cent (19); Vihreä Liitto (VIHR) (Green League) 8 per cent (14); Suomen Kristillisdemokraatit (KD) (Finnish Christian Democrats) 5.3 per cent (seven); the SFP 4.6 per cent (eight); Perussuomalaiset (PeruS/SannF) (True Finns) 1.6 per cent (three); För Åland i riksdagen (For Aland in Parliament) 0.2 per cent (one). Turnout was 69.6 per cent.

Presidential: Tarja Halonen was elected with 51.6 per cent of the vote.

Next elections
January 2006 (presidential); March 2007 (parliamentary).

Political parties
Ruling party
Three-party coalition from 15 Apr 2003: Suomen Keskusta (KESK) (Centre Party of Finland); Suomen Sosialidemokraatinen Puolue (SDP) (Social Democratic Party of Finland); Svenska Folkpartiet i Finland (SFP) (Swedish People's Party)

Nations of the World: A Political, Economic and Business Handbook

Main opposition party
Kansallinen Kokoomuspuolue (KOK) (National Coalition Party)

Population
5.22 million (2004); 5.21 million (OECD, 2003)

Ethnic make-up
Virtually all the population is of Finnish origin, apart from a small foreign population of around 20,000, a small number of Romany Gypsies, a Sámi (Lapp) minority in the north and a significant Swedish-speaking minority in the west.
The Estonians are close cultural relatives of the Finns. There are some small ethnic groups related to the Finns living in Russia.

Religions
Nearly 90 per cent of the Finnish population belongs to the Evangelical Lutheran Church. The Orthodox Church accounts for most of the remainder; there are Catholic, Jewish and Pentecostal minorities.

Education
Unesco reported, in 2004, that Finland achieved the highest overall scores in international tests for educational quality. Public expenditure on education amounts to 5.7 per cent of GDP. Universal primary education and gender parity, at this level and in secondary schools, have been achieved.

A sustained investment in education has resulted in high standards with the most rapid rise seen among those achieving a tertiary level qualification. The younger age groups are now more highly educated than their elders with about 83 per cent of people aged 25–34 having at least an upper secondary qualification in 1997, as against only 23 per cent of the population over the age of 65 achieving the same.

The education system consists of comprehensive secondary schools, post-comprehensive general and vocational education, higher education and adult education each lasting for three years. Vocational institutions provide initial apprenticeship training, in nearly all fields. A three-year vocational qualification gives access to all forms of higher education. The Finnish higher education system comprises polytechnics and universities. The polytechnic system is founded on a nationwide network of 29 regional polytechnics. There are 20 universities, all of which are in the public sector. In addition to degree programmes, universities also provide adult education and various research and consultant services.

Compulsory years: 7 to 16
Enrolment rate: 99 per cent, for both boys and girls, total primary enrolment of the relevant age group. Enrolment in secondary and tertiary levels of the relevant age group was 118 per cent and 74 per cent respectively (World Bank).
Pupils per teacher: 18 in primary schools.

Health
Total expenditure on health is 7 per cent of GDP, of which 67 per cent is government spending.
The national healthcare system is excellent and few take out private health insurance. Employers pay towards national health insurance through social security contributions. Health services have traditionally been free, but the 1990s saw changes and nominal charges introduced on a range of basic services.
HIV prevalence: 0.1 per cent aged 15–49 in 2003 (World Bank)
Life expectancy: 78.3 years (World Bank)
Fertility rate/Maternal mortality rate: 1.8 births per woman; maternal mortality 0.06 per 1,000 live births (World Bank).
Birth rate/Death rate: 10 deaths and 11 births per 1,000 people (World Bank).
Infant mortality rate: 3.1 per 1,000 live births (World bank)
Head of population per physician/bed: 2.9 doctors and 7.8 hospital beds per 1,000 people.

Welfare
Finland has a well-developed system of social welfare, and the high level of support has proved to be a stabilising factor in social terms. However, the government has been forced by a steadily rising budget deficit to seek ways of cutting its social spending. Welfare spending, despite cuts, typically totals over 50 per cent of GDP. Finland has an ageing population; those aged over 65 are expected to constitute over a quarter of the population by 2030, one of the highest proportions in the world. Pension regulations have permitted earlier retirement than in many other countries. These factors, combined with high life Most Finns receive health insurance, unemployment benefit, pension and family allowances.

Main cities
Helsinki (capital, estimated population 582,600 in 2003), Espoo (229,500), Tampere (201,200).

Languages spoken
Finnish belongs to the Baltic-Finnic group of the Finno-Ugric languages, which also includes Estonian and Hungarian and is also related to Sámi, the language of the indeginous people of northern Scandinavia.
English is widely understood in business circles; German and Russian are also spoken.

Official language/s
Finnish and Swedish

Media
Press
Penetration of newspapers among Finns is the third highest in the world, with 87 per cent of the population reading a daily newspaper. There is little foreign involvement in the print media sector.
Dailies: Finns tend to prefer local newspapers to the national press. The country has nearly 100 daily newspapers and over 100 local newspapers. The most popular are *Helsingin Sanomat*, *Ilta-Sanomat* (evening national), *Hämeen Sanomat*, *Aamulehti* (Tampere), *Turun Sanomat* (Turku), *Iltalehti* (evening national) *Tekniikka & Talous* and *Kaleva* (Oulu).
Weeklies: The most popular Sunday newspaper is *Helsingin Sanomat*. *Katso* features popular entertainment and *Apu* is a general interest weekly for most families.
Business: Prominent publications include *Kauppalehti* (daily), *Taloussanomat* (daily), and *Talouselama* (weekly), *Finnish Business Report*. *Pelit* caters to technologies and other consumer interests.
Periodicals: The most popular are general interest magazines, such as *Valitut Palat* (Reader's Digest, monthly) and *Seura* and illustrated news magazines, such as *Suomen Kuvalehti*. Popular women's magazines are *Eeva*, *Anna*, *Me Naise*, *Kauneus Ja Terveys* and *Kotiliesi*. Monthly entertainment and sports magazines include *Insider* and *Futari*.

Broadcasting
The state-controlled Finnish broadcasting company, Yleisradio (YLE), runs nationwide radio and television stations, but there is also a range of private commercial stations in operation.
Foreign involvement in the broadcast sector has grown in recent years as a result of Finland joining the EU and the arrival of cable, satellite and digital services. Finland's consumers can choose from some 200 private cable television networks and several satellite stations which operate in the private sector. Finland has linked up with the Swedish/Norwegian television networks to provide a unified teletext service offering faster news coverage in all three countries.
Radio: YLE operates four main channels, one of which caters to the Swedish-speaking minority, as well as a foreign service broadcasting to Europe, the Middle East, Africa, the Far East, and North and South America.
Radio Nova, a nationwide radio channel, began service in 1997 and covers 85 per cent of the population.
Television: The three state television channels, all run by YLE, transmit nearly 140 hours of programmes a week. Channel 3 is commercially operated and allows advertising. On the other two channels,

Finland

time is rented to a commercial television company, MTV.

Advertising
Direct mail advertising and direct response advertising via printed and broadcast media are steadily increasing in market penetration. Newspapers take the lion's share with 50 per cent of the total, television 19 per cent, periodicals 22 per cent, radio 1 per cent, and Internet 0.5 per cent.

Economy
Finland is a small market-oriented economy dependent on foreign trade; the record global high cost of hydrocarbons may have a dampening effect on the economy. Exports account for about 40 per cent of GDP so that international trade can have an adverse effect on the economy. In 2004, GDP growth was 3.7 per cent, and it is expected to achieve 3.0 per cent in 2005.

As the global economy begins to recover, Finnish output is up, while at the same time tax cuts worth 1 per cent of GDP are being phased in during 2005/06. Unemployment fell to 8.9 in 2004 and should fall further in 2005, wages and price inflation should remain stable due to an income policy agreement. Real household income is projected to rise by up to 4.8 per cent, with a corresponding rise in private consumption of about 3 per cent. Finland, in 2005, ran a budget surplus, one of the largest in the EU, partly in preparation for publicly funded pensions for its ageing population and healthcare in general.

Finland's exporters, principally paper manufacturers, have improved export order books and are experiencing an increase in growth, expected to be more than 10 per cent in 2005. Even so the most important sector of the Finnish economy is the services sector, which employs 68 per cent of the workforce.

The OECD 2005 *Economic Policy Reforms* makes a number of employment related recommendations including:
- reducing the high marginal tax rates on labour income
- reducing early retirement incentives a
- reducing the scale of state ownership of publicly funded services and entities and introduce competition and privatisation.

In 2005 a work economic forum survey ranked Finland first in its growth competitiveness index rankings, for the second year running. The World Bank ranked Finland in its *Doing Business Economy Ranking* 13 for ease of doing business, and 18 for starting a business, out of 155.

A mid-2005 strike, over holiday pay for 24,000 paper manufacturing sector workers cost Finland an estimated eur40 million (US$48 million) a day; strikes and lockouts lasted for several weeks.

External trade
Finland has concentrated on a policy of export-led growth since the early 1990s.

Imports
Main imports are foodstuffs, petroleum and petroleum products, chemicals, transport equipment, iron and steel, machinery, textile yarn and fabrics, grains.
Main sources: Germany (16.2 per cent total, 2004), Sweden (14.1 per cent), Russia (12.8 per cent), Netherlands (6.3 per cent), Denmark (5.3 per cent), UK (4.6 per cent), France (4.3 per cent)

Exports
Finland's economy is export-oriented, with over 40 per cent of production being shipped abroad.

Main exports are forestry products – timber, paper, pulp – (Finland is the world's second largest forestry exporter after Canada), mobile phones and wireless network technology, machinery and equipment, chemicals and metals.
Main destinations: Sweden (11 per cent total, 2004), Germany (10.6 per cent), Russia (8.9 per cent), UK (7.0 per cent), US (6.4 per cent), Netherlands (5.2 per cent), China (4.1 per cent)

Agriculture
Farming
The opening up of Finland's agricultural sector was a major issue in the negotiations for EU membership.

Finnish agriculture is based on small family farms, with the average agricultural area of a farm about 25 hectares (ha). Forests are an integral part of the country's farms, and the average forest area of farms is 43ha. About 43 per cent of the farms produce food crops. Wheat and rye are cultivated on about 10 per cent of the arable land, and about 9 per cent is used for growing other crops including potatoes and sugar beets.

Agriculture typically contributes 1.1 per cent of GDP, although active farms employ 5 per cent of the workforce. On average, only about half of the income of farm families is obtained from agriculture, while farm forestry usually provides 10 to 15 per cent of the income.

Production is based on livestock, and about 80 per cent of the agricultural area is used as pasture or for arable fodder cropping. About 33 per cent of the farms are dairy farms. Finland is 85 per cent self-supporting in food grains, dairy products and root crops.

Fundamental reform to the Common Agricultural Policy (CAP) was introduced throughout most of the EU on 1 January 2005. The subsidies paid on farm output, which tended to benefit large farms and encourage overproduction, were replaced by single farm payments not conditional on production. This is expected to reward farms that provide and maintain a healthy environment, food safety and animal welfare standards. The changes are also intended to encourage market conscious production and cut the cost of CAP to the EU taxpayer. Finland introduced this measure on 1 January 2006.

Crop production in 2004 included: 3,616,000 tonnes (t) cereals in total, 782,300t wheat, 619,400t potatoes, 1,724,700t barley, 35,000t tomatoes, 28,424t oilcrops, 1,063,500t sugar beets, 1,002,400t oats, 8,000t strawberries, 14,573t fruit in total, 229,035t vegetables in total. Livestock production included: 382,095t meat in total, 93,290t beef, 198,490t pig meat, 650t lamb, 86,970t poultry, 56,900t eggs, 25,181,530t milk, 1,700t honey, 10,500t cattle hides.

Fishing
Fishing, aquaculture and fish processing are a traditional part of Finnish industries. The food fishing industry is managed in accordance with the EU's Common Fisheries Policy (CFP), which covers resource, market and structural policies including inland waters and sea fishing as well as a monitoring system. The EU Commission has ratified the structural programme for the fisheries industry in Finland for 2000–06.

Fish farming is carried out both in the sea and in inland waters. The most important economic fish for sea fishing are Baltic herring and salmon. Although employment in the sector has dropped considerably, the catch remains stable due to the adoption of more efficient fishing techniques. The total catch is around 120,000 tonnes, of which less than a third is used for human consumption.

The annual production of farmed fish is around 17,500 tonnes consisting mainly of large rainbow trout.

Forestry
Nearly three-quarters of the country is covered by forest, estimated at 21.9 million hectares (ha). About two-thirds of the forest area is privately-owned, mainly by small-scale farmers. Timber products account for nearly a third of export products and nearly a third of manufacturing output. There is a high level of product specialisation, aided by the fact that the transport and machinery sectors tend to cater for the forest industry. The most common species of tree growing are Scots pine, spruce and birch.

Forest resources have been increasing steadily, as annual growth exceeds felling and natural losses. In 1990–2000, forest cover increased by an average of 0.04 per cent, the equivalent of 8,000ha per annum.

In 2004 exports amounted to US$13.1 billion, while imports were US$1.5 billion. Production in 2004 included: 53,799,662 cubic metres (cum) roundwood, 49,280,858cum industrial roundwood, 13,544,060cum sawnwood, 24,256,858cum sawlogs and veneers, 25,024,000cum pulpwood, 2,029,000cum wood-based panels, 4,518,804cum woodfuel. 1,002,400 tonnes newsprint, 9,021,600t printing and writing paper, 4,012,000t paperboard.

Industry and manufacturing
Industry in Finland is concentrated in three areas: paper and pulp production; machinery and other metal products; and hi-tech electronics (particularly mobile phone production). The metals, engineering and electronics sector account for over 50 per cent of the country's work force and exports. Finnish exports have underpinned its strong economy and only a severe global downturn could leave the country vulnerable, not only to industry-specific shocks affecting its three principal sectors, but also performance in its key markets.
Research and development (R&D) investment in Finland is one of the highest in the world.

Tourism
Travel and tourism is expected to contribute US$7.6 billion or 3.7 per cent of GDP in 2005, and employ 10.9 per cent of the workforce. Total exports generated are expected to reach US$5.3 billon and tourism is estimated to attract US$4.6 billion or 12.1 per cent of all captial investment. Visitors from Sweden are the most numourus at 608,765 in 2004; the next 16 countries together accounted for almost three million visitors.

Mining
The sector accounts for only 0.3 per cent of GDP.
There are around a dozen ore mines, producing mainly chromium, mercury, zinc, silver, copper and nickel.
Deposits are small. Prospecting is being intensified to curb imports; refining technology is a major focus of development work. Outokumpu, the mining and metals group, has modernised the production facilities at its Harjavalta plant through an investment programme. The programme includes the copper smelter and nickel production line located at Harjavalta and the copper refinery located at Pori, both towns in western Finland.

Hydrocarbons
Finland has no oil resources and there are no current exploration plans. All of its oil demands are imported primarily from the North Sea, Oman and Russia. Finland imported around 200,000 barrels per day (bpd) in 2004. There are two refineries in Finland with a joint capacity of 200,000bpd, both are located on the southern coastline and oil is brought to them by sea.
Finland has no gas resources and domestic demands are imported from Russia. Natural gas fulfils around 11 per cent of Finland's energy needs. There is interest from Finland to build a natural gas pipeline along the Baltic seabed although no terms have been made yet.
There are no coal reserves and Finland's needs are met by imports from Poland, Russia and the US. Finland consumed 5.8 million tonnes of oil equivalent in 2003.

Energy
Owing to the high proportion of energy-intensive industry, long distances between population centres and geographic situation with a cold climate, Finland's per capita energy consumption is one of the highest among International Energy Agency (IEA) countries.
There are four nuclear reactors – two Russian and two Swedish-built. Expansion of nuclear power has reduced dependence on imported coal and oil.
The fifth nuclear power plant, in Olkiluoto on the west coast, will begin construction in mid-2006, with completion and commercial electricity production of 1,600MW in 2009. The Finnish electricity company, Teollisuuden Voima Oy (TVO), will oversee construction. Nuclear power provides around 28 per cent of Finland's energy requirements.
Imatran Voima Oy (IVO), the state-owned power utility, has 12.5 per cent of the Nordic power market. Finland had two national grids which were merged in the late 1990s. The national grid operator is Fingrid. IVO and Industrial Power Group each own 30 per cent and the state 16 per cent.
Electricity demand is expected to increase at an estimated annual rate of 2–2.5 per cent by 2007, before levelling off.
Finland receives all its natural gas from Russia. To reduce its dependency on Russian supplies, one suggestion is to receive supplies from the Norwegian gas fields via a pipeline through Sweden, but the investment costs are currently too high.
Wood fuels provide Finland with around 10 per cent of the primary fuel for electricity generation and 15 per cent of the total energy requirement, one of the highest rates among the industrialised nations. Wood-based fuels can, however, have a moisture content of up to 60 per cent which can make them difficult to burn.

Financial markets
Stock exchange
The Helsinki Stock Exchange is part of the OMX Exchanges group that owns and operates stock exchanges in six Baltic region countries. OMX provides the exchanges and the software necessary to drive the largest integrated securities market in Northern Europe.
In 2004 the value of equities turnover was US$228 billion and the number was 19 million.

Banking and insurance
There are around 341 banks in Finland. Nordea, the largest bank in the Nordic region is Finnish. Other major banks in Finland include Oko Bank, Sampo Bank and Sweden's Svenska Handelsbanken AB.
Central bank
Suomen Pankki (Bank of Finland); European Central Bank (ECB).

Time
GMT plus two hours (GMT plus three hours from late March to late September).

Geography
Finland is the fifth-largest country in Europe, but also one of the most sparsely populated. The land frontier with Sweden to the north-west is 586km long, while the far northern border with Norway runs for 716km and the eastern border with Russia for 1,269km. Finland's western and southern shores are washed by the Baltic Sea.

Climate
Finland's climate varies widely across the country, with exceptionally strong differences between the summer and the winter norms. Temperatures average 5 degrees Celsius (C) in Helsinki and -0.4 degrees C in the north. January is the coldest of the long winter months, with an average -9 degrees C. Peak average temperatures in Helsinki are reached in July (18 degrees C).
Average annual rainfall in Helsinki is 675mm. Spring months are relatively dry, declining to 36mm in March, but higher rainfall starts in July, reaching a peak of around 70mm in the August–October period. Finland's snow season usually runs from November to April (although it runs up to May further north).

Dress codes
Formal dress, including dark-coloured suits for men, is normal for business purposes. In winter, heavy, warm clothing is essential for outdoor wear. A fur cap and winter boots or overshoes are also strongly recommended. Women should wear woollen suits or dresses, warm tights or stockings and ideally, fur-lined boots.

Finland

Entry requirements
Passports
Passports are required by all and must be valid for up to six months beyond the date of stay. Nationals of countries which are signatories of the Schengen Accord, may visit on national IDs.

Visa
Visas are required by all except nationals of Schengen Accord countries, North America, Australasia and some Asian countries, for up to three months. All visas issued will adhere to Schengen Accord requirements. For business visas a letter of invitation from a local business contact, stating nature and duration of stay, plus proof of return/onward ticket and travel insurance, with a minimum coverage of US$25,000, or other medical insurance that covers Finland, must accompany the application.
For further information see http://formin.finland.fi/doc/eng/services/entry/main.html or contact the consular section of the nearest embassy. A Schengen visa application (offered in several languages) can be downloaded on www.eurovisa.info.

Currency advice/regulations
There is unrestricted import of local and foreign currency, but export of either is limited to the amount imported.

Customs
Personal effects are duty free, plus duty free allowance for travellers from outside the EU.

Health (for visitors)
Mandatory precautions
No special requirements are necessary.

Hotels
In Helsinki and the surrounding area, hotels are classified into five price categories. Generally of a high standard. Rates vary depending on location, facilities and season. Accommodation should be booked well in advance, especially during summer. If accommodation is unobtainable, a place may be found through 'Hotellikeskus' (accommodation clearing-house) at the Central Railway Station in Helsinki. Gratuities are not expected, with the exception of porters. Service is included in restaurant bills, although a little extra can be added.

Credit cards
All major international credit cards are accepted.

Public holidays
Fixed dates
1 Jan (New Year's Day), 6 Jan (Epiphany), 1 May (May Day), 6 Dec (Independence Day), 24–26 Dec (Christmas Holiday).

Variable dates
Good Friday, Easter Monday, Ascension Day, Midsummer's Eve, All Saints' Day.

Working hours
Banking
Mon–Fri: 0915–1615. The post offices may close later than the commercial, savings and co-operative banks.

Business
Mon–Fri: 0800–1600; in summer businesses frequently close at 1530.
Finns tend to take fairly frequent holidays during the summer months. As a result, business visits between mid-June and mid-August should be undertaken only after making quite sure that the other party will be available. September to May is the favoured time for business visits. Some businesses and shops close from midday on the day before public holidays.

Government
Mon–Fri: 0800–1600.

Shops
Mon–Fri: 0900–1700; Sat: 0900–1300. Large department stores and supermarkets open Mon–Fri: 0900–2000; Sat: 0900–1800.

Telecommunications
Mobile phones
There are extensive GSM 900/1800 and G3 services available.

Electricity supply
220V AC, 50Hz. Continental two-pin plugs are standard.

Social customs/useful tips
Finns appreciate punctuality. A gift of flowers is usual when visiting a business partner's home for the first time. Guests should not start drinking before their hosts have proposed their health.
Tips are small, except for unusually good service.
Think twice before refusing to go to a sauna with a host, since such an invitation is seen as a gesture of confidence and friendship by your host. Business meetings are sometimes conducted in saunas. There are strict laws on drinking and driving.

Security
Street crime is a relative rarity in Finland; normal precautions apply.

Getting there
Air
National airline: Finnair
International airport/s: Helsinki-Vantaa (HEL), 19km north of capital; facilities include banks/bureaux de change, duty-free shops, car hire, hotel reservations, VIP lounge, conference rooms and restaurants.
Other airport/s: Jyväskylä (JYV), 21km from city; Kemi (KEM), 6km from city; Kokkola (KOK), 22km from city; Oulu (OUL), 15km south-west of city; Rovaniemi (RRVN), 10km from city; Tampere (TMP), 15km from city; Turku (TKU), 7km from city; Vaasa (VAA), 12km from city.
Airport tax: None

Surface
Road: The majority of road routes include sea ferry links from Sweden or Germany. There is a land link via Norway or Sweden to Finnish Lapland, involving travel through the Arctic Circle.
Rail: There are rail/sea links from Hamburg, Copenhagen and Stockholm to Helsinki or Turku. A rail connection to Stockholm is available from Haparanda/Tornio in the north. There are daily trains to Moscow and St Petersburg.
Water: Daily ferry services from Sweden, twice weekly from Germany and Poland. Reservations should be made in advance as these tend to be heavily booked, especially during summer and weekends. Also regular services to Estonia and St Petersburg.
Main port/s: Helsinki, Kotka, Hamina, Mariehamn, Vaasa, Turku, Pori, Sköldvik, Rauma and Oulu.

Getting about
National transport
Air: Finland has one of the densest internal networks in Europe. Finnair provides connections between Helsinki and Ivalo, Joensuu, Jyväskylä, Kajaani, Kemi, Kittilä, Kokkola, Kuopio, Kuusamo, Lappeenranta, Mariehamn, Mikkeli, Oulu, Pietarsaari, Pori, Rovaniemi, Saonlinna, Tampere, Turku, Vaasa and Varkaus.
Road: Finland's 77,000km network of public roads include 12,000km of high-grade national highway and 30,000km of secondary routes, but only 215km of motorways. Traffic is light but distances are great, the roads remain passable at all times of the year, although weight restrictions are imposed during April and May in southern Finland and May to June in northern Finland.
Buses: Efficient coach services cover the entire country, and are the main form of transport in Lapland.
Rail: Network of around 6,000km (including 1,600km electrified), operated by state railway company, Valtionrautatiet (VR). Relatively inexpensive and there are several passes available allowing travel over a set period. Seat reservation is obligatory on special express trains. Tickets are valid for one month. Sleeper services are available on the main connections.
Water: Important method of transport, owing to large number of lakes (187,888), which cover 31,500 square km.

City transport
Taxis: Taxis have a yellow 'taksi' sign, which is lit when the taxi is vacant. They can be hired at taxi ranks or signalled

Nations of the World: A Political, Economic and Business Handbook

City transport
Taxis: Taxis have a yellow 'taksi' sign, which is lit when the taxi is vacant. They can be hired at taxi ranks or signalled from the street. Fares are more expensive at night. Taxi drivers are not tipped.
Buses, trams & metro: An efficient and integrated bus, metro and tramway service, suburban rail lines and ferry services to Suomenlinna Islands, operates in Helsinki. A common fares system applies to all the modes (including the ferries) with a zonal flat fare and free transfer between services. Multi-trip tickets are sold in advance, as are various passes.
Regular bus services, including Finnair City Bus, operate from the airport to the city, taking 35 minutes. Some Helsinki hotels run courtesy coaches.

Car hire
Available in most major towns. Rates include maintenance and insurance. A minimum age limit (usually 19–23) and at least one year's driving experience is a requirement for all drivers. The speed limits are 50kph in built-up areas, 80kph on normal roads and 120kph on motorways. The wearing of seat belts is compulsory. The use of headlights at all times is obligatory. Traffic drives on the right. A national driving licence or International Driving Permit is required. Driving around Helsinki is not recommended due to the lack of parking spaces.

BUSINESS DIRECTORY

The addresses listed below are a selection only. While World of Information makes every endeavour to check these addresses, we cannot guarantee that changes have not been made, especially to telephone numbers and area codes. We would welcome any corrections.

Telephone area codes
The international direct dialling (IDD) code for Finland is +358, followed by area code and subscriber's number:

Hämeenlinna	3	Mikkeli	15
Helsinki	9	Oulu	8
Imatra	5	Pori	2
Joensuu	13	Rovaniemi	16
Jyväskylä	14	Tampere	3
Kotka	5	Tornio	16
Kuopio	17	Turku	2
Lahti	3	Vaasa	6

Useful telephone numbers
Ambulance, police, fire or medical help: 114

Chambers of Commerce
Central Chamber of Commerce of Finland, 17 Aleksanterinkalu, PO Box 1000, Helsinki 00101 (tel: 696-969; fax:650-303; e-mail: keskuskauppakamari@wtc.fi).

Central Finland Chamber of Commerce, 4 Sepänkatu, Jyväskylä 40100 (tel: 652-400; fax: 652-411; e-mail: info@centralfinlandchamber,fi).

Helsinki Chamber of Commerce, 12 Kalevakatu, Helsinki 00100 (tel: 228-601; fax: 2286-0228; e-mail: kauppakamari@helsinki.chamber.fi).

Kuopio Chamber of Commerce, 2 Kasarmikatu, Kuopio 70110 (tel: 282-0291; fax: 282-3304; e-mail: kauppakamari@kuopiochamber.fi).

Lapland Chamber of Commerce, 29 Maakuntakatu, Rovaniemi 96200 (tel: 318-877; fax: 318-885; e-mail: kauppakamari@lapland.chamber.fi).

Turku Chamber of Commerce, 1 Puolankatu, Turku 20100 (tel: 274-3400; fax: 274-3440; e-mail: kauppakamari@turku.chamber.fi).

Banking
Nordea Bank Finland, Aleksanterinkatu 36 B, Helsinki, Fin-00020 Helsinki (tel: 1651; fax: 1654-2838).

Nordic Investment Bank, Fabianinkatu 34, PO Box 249, Fin-00171 Helsinki (tel: 18-001; fax: 180-0210).

Oko Bank, PO Box 308, Fin-00101 Helsinki (tel: 4041).

Sampo Plc, Unioninkatu 22, Fin-00075 Helsinki (tel: 105-1515).

Suomen Pankkiyhdistys r y (Finnish Bankers' Association), Museokatu 8 A, Box 1009, Fin-00101 Helsinki (tel: 405-6120; fax: 4056-1291).

Suomen Säästöpankkiliitto (Savings Bank Association), Pohjoisesplanadi 35A, 00101 Helsinki 10 (tel: 13-341).

Central bank
Suomen Pankki (Bank of Finland), Snellmaninaukio, POB 160, 00101 Helsinki (tel: 183-1; fax: 174-872; e-mail: info@bof.fi); European Central Bank (ECB), Kaiserstrasse 29, D-60311 Frankfurt am Main, Germany (tel: +49(69)13-440; fax: +49(69)1344-6000).

Travel information
Finland Travel Bureau Ltd, Mail Department, PB319, 00101 Helsinki 10 (poste restante service).

Finnair, Tietotie 11A, Helsinki-Vantaa Airport (tel: 81-881; fax: 818-4401; internet site: http://www.finnair.com).

Finnish State Railways (internet site: http://www.vr.fi/e-index.htm).

Helsinki-Vantaa Airport (tel: 82-771).

Helsinki Tourist Office, Pohjoiiesesplanadi 19, Helsinki.

National tourist organisation offices
Finnish Tourist Board (Matkailun Edistamiskeskus), Töolönkatu 11, PO Box 625, SF-00100 Helsinki (tel: 4030-1211; fax: 4030-1301/1333; e-mail: mek@mek.fi; internet site: http://www.mek.fi).

Ministries
FINNIDA (Finnish International Development Agency), c/o Ministry for Foreign Affairs, Merikasarmi, Laivastokatu 22, 00160 Helsinki (tel: 134-151; fax: 629-840).

Ministry of Agriculture and Forestry, Hallituskatu 3 A, PO Box 232, 00171 Helsinki (tel: 1601 (exchange); fax: 160-2190).

Ministry of Defence, Et. Makasiinikatu 8 A, PO Box 31, 00131 Helsinki (tel: 16-161; fax: 653-254).

Ministry of Education, Meritullinkatu 10, PO Box 293, 00171 Helsinki (tel: 134-171; fax: 135-9335).

Ministry of the Environment, Kasarmikatu 25, PO Box 380, 00131 Helsinki (tel: 19-911; fax: 1991-9545).

Ministry of Finance, Aleksanterinkatu 3, PO Box 286, 00171 Helsinki (tel: 1601 (exchange); fax: 160-3120).

Ministry for Foreign Affairs, Merikasarmi, Laivastokatu 22, PO Box 176, 00161 Helsinki (tel: 134-151; fax: 1341-5070).

Ministry of the Interior, Kirkkokatu 12, 001070 Helsinki (tel: 1601; fax: 160-2927).

Ministry of Justice, Eteläesplanadi 10, PO Box 1, 00131 Helsinki (tel: 18-251; fax: 1825-7730).

Ministry of Labour, Eteläesplanadi 4, PO Box 524, 00101 Helsinki (tel: 18-561; fax: 1856-7950).

Ministry of Social Affairs and Health, Snellmaninkatu 4-6, PO Box 267, 00171 Helsinki (tel: 1601 (exchange); fax: 160-4716).

Ministry of Trade and Industry, Aleksanterinkatu 4, PO Box 230, 00171 Helsinki (tel: 1601; fax: 160-3666).

Ministry of Transport and Communications, Eteläesplanadi 16, 00130 Helsinki (tel: 1601 (exchange); fax: 160-2596).

Prime Minister's Office, Snellmaninkatu 1 A, Fin-00170 Helsinki (tel: 3589-1601).

Other useful addresses
American Embassy, Itäinin Puistotie 14B, 00140 Helsinki (tel: 171-931; fax: 635-332).

British Embassy, Itäinen Puistotie 17, 00140 Helsinki (tel: 2286-5100; fax: 2286-5262).

Finland

Confederation of Finnish Industries, Eteläranta 10, SF 00130, Helsinki 13 (tel: 661-665).

Council of State, Aleksanterinkatu 3 D, 00170 Helsinki (tel: 1601 (exchange); fax: 160-2163).

Finnish Embassy (USA), 3301 Massachusetts Avenue, NW, Washington DC 20008 (tel: 202-298-5800; fax: 202-298-6030; e-mail: info@finland.org).

Finnish Foreign Trade Association, Arkadiankatu 2, PO Box 908, 001001 Helsinki (tel: 69-591; fax: 694-0028).

Helsinki Stock Exchange, Fabianinkatu 14, 00100 Helsinki 10 (tel: 624-161).

Invest in Finland Bureau, Aleksanterinkatu 17, 00100 Helsinki (tel: 696-9125; fax: 6969-2530; internet site: http://www.investinfinland.fi).

Liiketyönantajain (Confederation of Commerce Employers), Eteläranta 10, 00130 Helsinki 13 (tel: 19-281).

Main Post Office, Mannerheimintie 11, 00100 Helsinki 10.

Meilahti Hospital Haartmanink 3, Helsinki (tel: 4711).

Nesté (largest industrial corporation), Keilaniemi, 02150 Espoo, Helsinki (tel: 4501).

Oy Suomen Tietotoimisto (news agency), Lönnrotinkatu 5, 00120 Helsinki 12 (tel: 646-224).

Statistics Finland, työpajakatu 13, Helsinki (tel: 17-341; fax: 1734-2279; internet site: http://tilastokeskus.fi/index_en.html).

Suomen Työnantajain Keskusliitto (Finish Employers' Confederation) Eleläranta 10, Helsinki 13 (tel: 17-281).

Tullihallitus (Board of Customs), Erottajankatu 2, 00120 Helsinki (tel: 6141).

Ulkomaankaupan Agenttiliitto (Finnish Foreign Trade Agents' Federation) Mannerheimintie 42A 00260 Helsinki 26 (tel: 446-768).

Internet sites

Virtual Finland: http://virtual.finland.fi

Finnish company information (top 100 Finnish companies): http://www.nedecon.fi

France

KEY FACTS

Official name: La République Française (The French Republic)

Head of State: President Jacques Chirac (RPR) (re-elected 5 May 2002)

Head of government: Prime Minister Dominique de Villepin (appointed by the President 31 May 2005)

Ruling party: Coalition government from 17 Jun 2002: Union pour un Mouvement Populaire (UMP) (Union for a People's Movement), comprising the Rassemblement pour la République (RPR) (Rally for the Republic) and Démocratie Libérale (DL) (Liberal Democracy); Union pour la Démocratie Française (UDF) (Union for French Democracy) and allies.

Area: 543,965 square km

Population: 60.30 million (2004)

Capital: Paris

Official language: French

Currency: Euro (eur) = 100 cents (from 1 Jan 2002; previous currency French franc, locked at Ff6.56 per euro)

Exchange rate: eur0.83 per US$ (Oct 2005)

GDP per capita: US$32,663 (2004)

GDP real growth: 2.30% (2004); 0.7% 3rd quarter 2005.

Labour force: 26.88 million (2004)

Unemployment: 9.60% (OECD, 2004); 9.7% Oct 2005

Inflation: 2.30% (2004)

Balance of trade: -US$7.94 billion (2004)

Foreign debt: US$2,797.77 billion (2004)

Annual FDI: US$356.00 billion (cumulative, 1995–2004, OECD); US$24.30 billion (OECD, 2004)*

* estimated figure

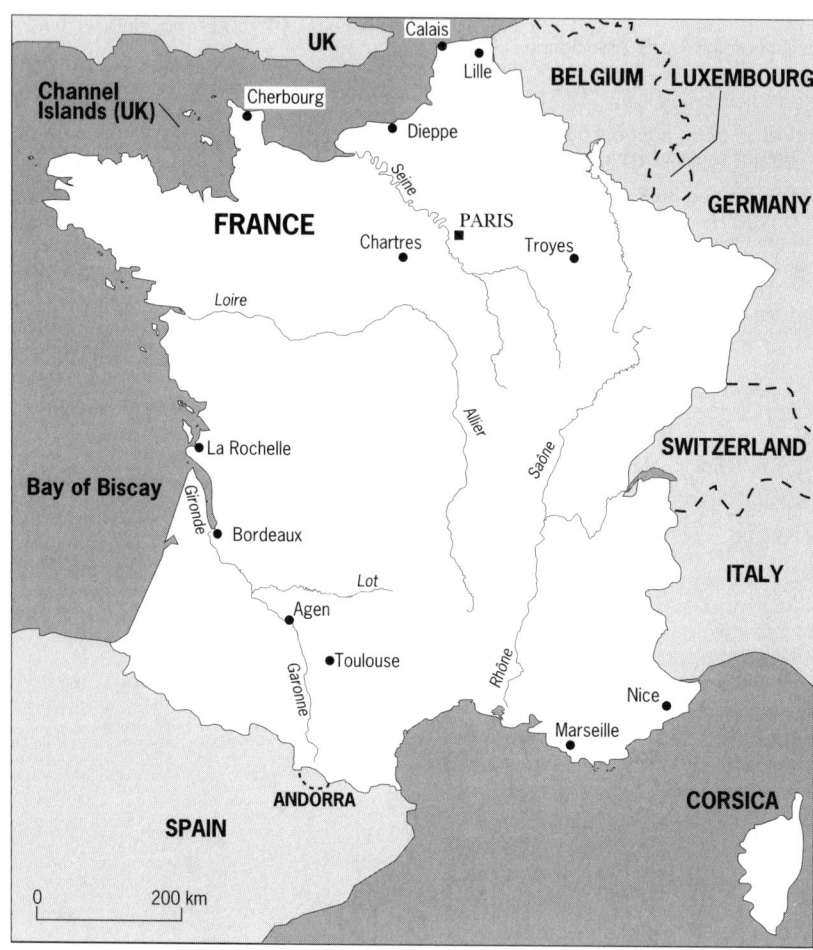

For France's ageing President Chirac, and his government, 2005 was a year best forgotten. The original scenario had been simple. The May referendum on the European Constitution was to produce a resounding endorsement not only of the Constitution, but *de facto* of the Union pour un Mouvement Populaire (UMP) (Union for a People's Movement, government's policies. This would be neatly followed by the announcement that Paris would host the 2012 Olympic Games. All that would then remain would be for Jacques Chirac to motor serenely onwards towards a third presidential term by winning the 2007 elections. This vision of events had started to go wrong with the government's embarrassing setbacks in both the regional and European parliamentary elections in 2004 which, in the true tradition of French politics eventually lead to the resignation of Prime Minister Raffarin.

The UMP government's defeat in the European referendum was not only a rejection of the EU Constitution, so carefully prepared by ex-President Giscard d'Estaing, but also of government policies and what was seen to be the threat of 'Anglo Saxon' work ethics that ran counter to the solidarity of state employment and of trades' union support. It was followed by July 2005's failure to secure the 2012 Olympic Games for Paris (a failure made worse by the fact that the victor was Paris's arch-rival, London). If this pattern of failures had made Jacques Chirac look like a lame-duck president, the figurative became a reality when, in September he suffered from a minor stroke. But all of these were minor set-backs, compared with what was to follow.

November heat

During the first three weeks of November alone, nearly 9,000 cars were destroyed by fire, and hundreds of public buildings vandalised in a wave of public unrest unseen since the 1968 student riots. For the government, the 2005 riots had a more worrying dimension: virtually all of the 5,000 or so people arrested and taken in to custody were of African or Caribbean origin; even more worryingly, a large proportion of them were Muslim.

The riots and related violence were largely confined to France's grim Hébergement de Loyer Moderé (HLM) (Low Cost Housing) suburban estates. Although many of these were in the *grand banlieu* (outlying suburbs) of Paris, the rioting spread to most of France's major cities, including Toulouse, Lille, Lyons and Strasbourg. The unrest was triggered by the apparently accidental electrocution in an electricity sub-station of two youths of African origin. The two were attempting to hide from the police, although they had not committed any crime. At the end of 2005 the results of the official report in to the incident was anxiously awaited by both sides. On the one hand it was hoped that the report would exonerate the police (a potentially pyrrhic victory as the report would then risk being seen as a whitewash of the police) while on the other it was felt that the report would find the police culpable of the violence and racism that many observers had long felt to be the case.

Responding to the situation, the government hastily announced a number of measures aimed at countering both unemployment and discrimination, while improving immigrant social conditions. 2006 was declared the year of equal opportunity, with businesses offered tax incentives to set up shop in 'difficult' areas, new apprenticeship schemes were introduced and state funding for non-governmental organisations (NGOs) re-introduced (it had been suspended in 2001). Although the latter measure was generally recognised as the easiest to activate quickly, at the end of 2005 NGOs were complaining that no funds had been received nor any concrete proposals for their re-introduction been tabled by the government. The haste with which the government announced its proposals was reminiscent of its response to the 'non' vote in May's referendum on the European constitution.

The 'Non' vote.

For France, one of the founder members of the EU and a leading architect of the constitution, to reject it was nothing less than a humiliation for an already beleaguered government seeking to break out of what had become a depressing litany of high unemployment and low productivity. The outcome was inevitably – and correctly – seen as an early move in the process of condemning the constitution to oblivion. Just as significantly, and as accurately, it was also seen as the first step in writing off Jacques Chirac's chances of a third term as president.

Before the referendum the government had already moved to assuage fears that the approval of the constitution would mean the adoption of ill-defined 'Anglo Saxon' business and employment practices. While still in office the lacklustre prime minister Jean-Pierre Raffarin had rejected the European Commission's proposed services directive, thereby hoping to secure support from French trades' unions, which saw the directive as a back door entrance for some form of globalisation.

The French electorate had a number of reasons for voting 'non'. The 'non' camp encompassed a wide spectrum of opposition, from the right-wing National Front, to essentially pro-European (but anti-constitution) socialists and the far left. Geographically the few départements that voted 'oui' included Lyons, southern Brittany, the area around Nantes, Lyons and the Jura; in the Parisian region only the western part of the Ile de France supported the constitution. What the government had failed to see was that the referendum offered a largely dissatisfied electorate a high profile opportunity of giving the government a bloody nose. Of which it took advantage.

Race and disaffection

France's long standing pre-occupation with the concepts of 'nation' and 'culture' have meant that national statistics do not take in to account race or religion. While this altruistic concern for these lofty concepts may have made sense in 1945, during several decades of immigration from France's former colonies little has been attempted or achieved by any of France's ruling governments – whatever their political characteristics – in terms of social and economic integration. The result has been large concentrations of largely immigrant populations where both levels of unemployment and petty crime are off the scale of organisations such as the Organisation for Economic Co-operation and Development (OECD), the 'rich man's club' of 30 major democratic countries, and the Council of Europe.

France's somewhat diffident, theoretical approach to racial integration and race relations is made even worse by the fact that as a result of its own policies, the

KEY INDICATORS — France

	Unit	2000	2001	2002	2003	2004
Population	m	59.30	59.56	59.85	60.08	60.30
Gross domestic product (GDP)	US$bn	1,286.30	1,307.40	1,462.30	1,749.30	*2,002.58
GDP per capita	US$	21,843	21,900	24,400	29,106	32,663
GDP real growth	%	4.2	2.1	1.1	0.5	2.3
Inflation	%	1.7	1.6	1.9	2.0	2.3
Unemployment	%	9.5	8.8	8.8	9.6	9.7
Coal output	mtoe	2.3	1.5	1.2	1.3	0.5
Exports (fob) (goods)	US$m	295,530.0	291,410.0	329,500.0	384,662.0	421,120.0
Imports (fob) (goods)	US$m	294,400.0	288,560.0	326,440.0	388,373.0	429,070.0
Balance of trade	US$m	1,130.0	2,850.0	3,000.0	-3,711.0	-7,940.0
Current account	US$m	20,430.0	21,360.0	28,060.0	39,200.0	-5,410.0
Total reserves minus gold	US$m	37,039.0	31,749.0	28,370.0	30,186.0	35,314.0
Foreign exchange	US$m	29,982.0	26,363.0	21,970.0	23,122.0	29,077.0
Exchange rate	per US$	7.10	7.00	1.04	0.88	0.80

* estimated figure

government lacks any accurate statistical tools for addressing – never mind solving – what had clearly become a major problem. In November 2005 the government found itself in a hopeless 'good cop – bad cop' situation. The tough, no nonsense policies and pronouncements of the diminutive interior minister Nicholas Sarkozy (Sarko to his friends and supporters) fly in the face of the more magisterial if somewhat vague and inevitably short term measures of his Prime Minister – and fellow presidential hopeful – the immaculately coiffeured and un-elected Dominic de Villepin. While Sarkozy, the often impulsive politician has a strong political power base, the non-elected de Villepin needs to rely on a direct appeal to France's already fragmented electorate. President Chirac distinguished himself by his absence from any public exposure at all in the days – or even weeks – following the riots, allowing his ministers to respond to the situation.

Creaking along

The riots were seen as characterising an 'old' European social and economic model, a major characteristic of which is the fact that France still has a disproportionately high number of those in employment working for the state. Even in partially privatised companies such as the power generation and distribution monopoly, Electricité de France (EDF), holidays, retirement age and pension expectations, not to mention the work ethic, have more in common with those of the civil service than the private sector.

In France, work has come to be seen almost as some form of punishment. While employment among those aged from 25 to 54 was at record levels in 2004, France still has a high level of youth unemployment and among those aged over 55. In company with the Germans, the French work less hours than other EU countries. In 2003 the French worked an average of 1,453 hours per annum (Germany's figure was even lower – 1,446 hours) compared to the 1,792 worked in the US. Within the EU the UK worked an average of 1,693 hours. The cost of an hour's work in France in mid-2004 was around eur27 (US$32), topped by Germany at eur29 (US$34). In the UK the figure was eur23 (US$27), in the United States US$22.

According to the OECD, France's unemployment rate of 9.6 per cent in 2004 was high. However, if the overall rate is high, of even greater concern to any French government is the fact that – again according to the OECD – more than 40 per cent of those 'actively seeking' work (in itself an optimistic description) have been doing so for more than one year, compared to an OECD average of 32 per cent. According to the OECD, France's archaic labour legislation, under which it is both difficult and expensive for employers to reduce payrolls and where hiring staff is similarly restrictive, result in high levels of unemployment. This had dropped from 9.8 to 9.7 per cent of the workforce in October 2005.

Economic growth showed signs of picking up in the third quarter of 2005. GDP grew by 0.7 per cent, well up on the 0.1 recorded in the second quarter of the year, confirming expectations of 1.5 per cent growth for the whole year. However, the riots and social unrest in November 2005 had severely dented consumer confidence and promised to do little to lower unemployment, despite the government's promised measures. Fears were also expressed by the business community that the riots would deter inward investors.

What had long been apparent was the growing divide between France's 'haves' and 'have nots'. A cosseted class of state employees appeared to have lost touch with those who create, or might continue to create, the wealth on which the whole edifice of French social ambitions rested.

In the run-up to the referendum the government was not operating from a position of strength. Its efforts to dilute the legislation on the 35-hour week simply antagonised both organised labour as well as many of those working for small businesses. In February 2005 finance minister Hervé Gaymard was forced to resign when it emerged that his monthly rent of US$17,000 was being paid by the taxpayer even though he owned a number of properties in Paris. His successor, Thierry Breton, found himself invited to approve pay rises designed to buy off voter opposition at a time when expenditure was supposedly being contained to control France's errant budget deficit and bring it within the EU norm of 3 per cent of GDP.

Within Europe, France's social structure, indeed its way of getting things done, is pretty unique. Well over half the population are civil servants or are closely related to a civil servant. Take away the one third of the population that is affected by unemployment – directly by being out of work, or indirectly because their family's income suffers as a result of their wife, husband, son or daughter being out of work, and there's not too many people left. This state of affairs has created a curious and contradictory 'nanny' state in which the *fonctionnaires* are totally dependent on the state for their income and social provisions, but are also the first to resist the extension of these provisions to other sectors of society – such as the young unemployed or deprived immigrants.

Olympic defeat – Chirac's decline

There was something symbolic about the outcome of Paris's bid for the 2012 Olympic Games, a bid very much the personal project of Chirac. Under his leadership France had already lost two Olympic bids. For the ageing Chirac, winning the Olympic Games for Paris had acquired talismanic status. It had also increasingly begun to look like a racing certainty, so much so that Chirac decided to attend only the July award ceremony in Singapore before proceeding to the G8 meeting in Scotland. The London bid turned out to be more professional, with UK premier Tony Blair spending two days in Singapore meeting each International Olympic Committee delegate before they voted. For Chirac the failure to clinch the vote was not only a personal disaster, it was seen as an affront to French *amour propre*. Coming as it did, not only just before the G8 meeting, but also only days before the 14 July Bastille Day celebrations, the timing, and the humiliation, could hardly have been worse for Chirac. To add insult to injury, across the Channel, the British were beginning the celebrations of the 200th anniversary of the Battle of Trafalgar, in which the British fleet under Lord Nelson defeated the French, ushering in a long period of British naval supremacy.

That the tide seemed to have turned against President Chirac was undeniable. As the year wore on, Chirac's approval ratings fell steadily, to the extent that by the end of 2005 it had become apparent that barring a miraculous comeback, any chances he once had of winning a third term in the 2007 elections had evaporated.

Economy drifts

The UMP government was elected in 2002 almost by default following the farcically poor showing of the socialist party in the first round of the elections. Since its election victory, the UMP has struggled to put the French economy back on track.

According to the Paris based OECD, after a weak performance in 2000–03, output growth appeared to recover in 2004, reaching 2.25 per cent although the forecast figure for 2005 was an optimistic 1.5 per cent. The French economy remained handicapped by out of date labour legislation, high minimum wage levels and inflexible employment protection legislation.

Since the 2002 elections some progress has been made in relaxing the 35-hour week legislation introduced by the socialist party. In February 2005 the government obtained a small victory with the amendment of the law governing the imposition of the 35-hour week. The amendment enabled private sector employees to choose whether to work longer hours if they reached a collective agreement with their employers. The original aim of the law had been simple – to reduce unemployment by encouraging older workers to limit their hours worked, thereby creating vacancies for France's unemployed young. In reality, the 35-hour week did little to create jobs and certainly created far less than might have been achieved by a small number of relatively minor improvements to France's outdated labour legislation and by facilitating the creation and establishment of new businesses and services.

In 2005 few of the government measures looked likely to produce the sought after savings or efficiencies. This was certainly the case with the proposed health reform measures, which took longer than expected to introduce, and failed to take in to account the health-care demands and needs of France's ageing population. Reductions in central government anticipated from lower levels of government employment also proved illusory; not only were the numbers involved modest, but according to the OECD increases in public service salaries eliminated most of the savings. Control of central government expenditure is expected to be reinforced by the introduction in 2006 of the much vaunted (and snappily named): *Loi organique relative aux lois de finances* (Organic law concerning finance legislation), or LOLF for short.

Agricultural cloud cuckoo land

Agriculture and its related social issues has long assumed a disproportionately high profile within the French economy and French society. France is the largest single beneficiary of the EU's farm subsidiaries which account for a whopping 40 per cent of total EU budget expenditure. French farmers benefited from eur9.4 billion (US$11 billion) in payments from the EU's Common Agricultural Policy (CAP) programme in 2004, over 20 per cent of all CAP payments. This meant that France received a net 8 per cent of all EU payments. The irony – not lost on those calling for further reform of the CAP – is that farmers only account for 3.5 per cent of France's population, barely registering as a group of economic significance within the EU. Unsurprisingly, however, support for the current CAP is manifested right across the French political spectrum, picturesquely painted by politicians as support for the small farmer. The reality is that over half of France's CAP payments go to the largest 10 per cent of farmers, while the smallest 75 per cent get barely 20 per cent of the handouts. But as one left-wing British politician once observed of the now defunct state-owned industry, 'that's more than our miners ever got'.

Foreign relations

Late 2005 saw the French government attempting to mount a rearguard offensive to restore an international image that had become increasingly tattered during the course of 2005. Central to this policy was French resistance to proposals put forward by France's *bete noire*, the UK's Tony Blair. These envisaged further reforms to the EU's contentious CAP which has traditionally favoured France and other EU agricultural economies. French diplomacy's surprising achievement in the weeks leading up to the December EU summit was an alliance with Poland's newly elected prime minister Kazimierz Marcinkiewicz, which did little to endear either country to the UK which had seen itself as the leading advocate of the interests of the ten new EU member countries. France's position was seen by many observers as simply opportunistic, Poland's as simply naïve. In 2003 President Chirac had done little to gain points with the ten accession countries by telling the to 'shut up' when they had the temerity to voice support for the US position over Iraq. Unlike the UK, Ireland and Sweden, France – faced by intractable unemployment – has declined to open its borders to EU workers from Eastern Europe, a position it shares with most EU member states including Italy, Germany and Spain.

A further element of France's diplomatic offensive was the announcement in December 2005 that the government's *Chaine Francaise d'information internationale* (CFII) would begin broadcasting in late 2006. Under an ambitiously grandiose scheme, the new broadcasting network will receive eur65 million (US$76.5 million) in funding from the French government, rising to eur70 million (US$82.5 million) annually until 2010. International news is a competitive field, long dominated by CNN and the BBC. CFII, which will broadcast in four languages, is unlikely to make much of a mark outside the francophone world, and much of that is already accustomed to relying on Paris for its news coverage.

Outlook

The period up to the 2007 presidential elections looks likely to be dominated by three principal currents. Of these, the most prominent will be the jockeying for position between prime minister Dominique de Villepin and interior minister Nicholas Sarkozy for the support of the centre-right. De Villepin succeeded in antagonizing both the US government and the British government by leading international opposition to a second UN resolution authorising force against Iraq. His time as prime minister has been dominated by the fall-out from the referendum reversal and the November riots. In each case he has carried the can for a tired president, seeking to outdo his close rival Sarkozy for political gain. Sarkozy was once Chirac's protégé, but has become his *bete noire*. As interior minister, the November riots allowed him to grab centre stage, which he did rather clumsily with references to the youth of the deprived suburbs as 'scum'. The ill-timed introduction of a law requiring French schools to teach the history of colonialisation in a positive light did little to help, revealing the insensitivity of a government again manifestly out of touch with popular sentiment.

The sidelined Socialist party looks likely to adopt former prime minister Laurent Fabius as its candidate. Its fortunes look likely to depend on the extent to which the centre right vote is divided between Chirac's would be heirs apparent. Following its dramatic success in the last elections, the right wing National Front is counting on the aftermath of November's riots, and any subsequent disturbances, boosting its already strong support.

Risk assessment

Economic	Worsening
Political	Good
Regional stability	Excellent
Stock market	Good

COUNTRY PROFILE

Historical profile

After the collapse of the Visigothic Merovingian kingdom, Gaul, in the eighth and ninth centuries, became the heart of an empire ruled by the Germanic Charlemagne (Charles the Great) and encompassing parts of Western Europe. After

Charlemagne's death in 814, parts of the West Frankish kingdom (most of modern-day France) were invaded by the Vikings and the Magyars before becoming a feudal lordship by the 10th century. The West Frankish kingdom eventually became the Royaume de France (Kingdom of France) and the lords appointed Hugues Capet as the first French King in 987.

1337–1453 The Hundred Years' War took place between the English and the French. The English were defeated in 1453 and driven out of Aquitaine in southern France.

1789 The lack of representation for the increasingly powerful middle class, opposition to France's absolute monarchy and economic problems led to the French Revolution and the overthrow of Louis XVI.

1792 The First Republic was declared.

1804 Napoléon Bonaparte declared himself emperor and launched a military campaign in Europe.

1815 Napoléon's defeat at Waterloo by the British, Belgians, Dutch and Prussians saw the end of his reign. Louis XVIII became King of France.

1848 An uprising led by students and workers, although quickly crushed, again led to the overthrow of the monarchy. Louis Napoléon (nephew of the first Napoléon) was elected president.

1852 Louis Napoléon declared himself emperor.

1871 France's defeat in the Franco-Prussian War resulted in the annexation of Alsace-Lorraine by the Germans.

1914 France was invaded by Germany.

1918 Following the end of the First World War and Germany's defeat, France regained Alsace-Lorraine.

1939 After Germany's invasion of Poland, France and the UK entered the Second World War by declaring war on Germany.

1940 France signed an armistice after Germany had invaded the country. The Germans installed a puppet government, the Vichy, led by Henri-Philippe Pétain. A Free French resistance movement was established in the UK under the leadership of General Charles de Gaulle.

1944 Following the liberation of France by the Allied powers, a provisional government took office under General de Gaulle.

1945 After the war in Europe ended in May, General de Gaulle retired from public office. The Fourth Republic was created with a constitution giving ultimate power to the Assemblé Nationale (National Assembly).

Between 1946 and 1958 France had 26 different governments, many including large communist elements.

1958 The Fifth Republic was created after the introduction of a new constitution, which allowed for the creation of a powerful presidency. In December, de Gaulle was elected president. France became a founder member of the forerunner of the EU, the European Economic Community (EEC), along with Belgium, Italy, Luxembourg, the Netherlands and West Germany.

1968 Discontent with low wages, lack of social reform and poor education policies led to a revolt by students and workers. The general strike was settled by the granting of generous wage rises and the student revolt collapsed, although de Gaulle's political position was fatally weakened.

1969 De Gaulle resigned from the presidency after losing a referendum on his programme for strengthening the regional government. He was succeeded by Georges Pompidou (1969–74) who was followed by Valéry Giscard d'Estaing (1974–81).

1981 François Mitterrand became the first socialist president since 1958 following Giscard d'Estaing's electoral defeat, governing with the first left-wing cabinet for 23 years.

1995 Jacques Chirac succeeded François Mitterrand as president.

2002 President Chirac defeated Le Pen in elections. Prime Minister Lionel Jospin resigned and Chirac appointed Jean-Pierre Raffarin of the Démocratie Libérale (DL) (Liberal Democracy) in his place. After legislative elections, a coalition government was formed, led by the UPM, UDF and allies.

2003 France was crippled by a series of public sector strikes over pension reform.

2004 Voting in the March regional elections showed national discontent with the government, resulting in the left-wing opposition carrying 21 out of the country's 22 mainland regions. Prime Minister Raffarin resigned, but was immediately re-installed by President Chirac, who instigated a major reshuffle of his government to carry it through the remaining three years of his term.

2005 France held a referendum on the European Constitution on 30 May in which almost 55 per cent voted 'Non', with 45 per cent in favour; turnout was about 70 per cent. Prime Minister Jean-Pierre Raffarin resigned the next day; Dominique de Villepin was appointed prime minister. Rioting broke out in the Paris suburb of Clichy-sous-Bois on 27 October, followed by disturbances elsewhere in the capital and in other towns and cities; the government declared a state of emergency on 8 November.

Political structure

Constitution

The 25 September 1958 constitution of the Fifth Republic maintained the original French republican ideals of liberty, fraternity and equality. It was designed to end post-war political deadlock by granting greater powers to the president. It guarantees the unity and indivisibility of the French state.

Since 1982 much administrative and financial power, traditionally held by the state, has been devolved to the 22 *régions* (regions) and 96 *départements* (departments) of metropolitan France. In March 2003, parliament approved constitutional amendments which allow all of the regions and departments a greater amount of autonomy.

In mid-2000, legislation was passed granting semi-autonomy to the island of Corsica as a single administrative unit, replacing its previous status as two standard *départements*. France's overseas territories are either classed as Département d'Outre-Mer (DOM) (Overseas Department) or Térritoire d'Outre-Mer (TOM) (Overseas Territory), depending on the level of autonomy.

Form of state

Semi-presidential democratic republic

The executive

Executive power is held by the president, elected by universal adult suffrage for a five-year term which can be renewed only once. A two-round voting system operates for presidential elections, with the second round a run-off between the two highest polling candidates from the first round. The president appoints the prime minister and other members of the government, can dissolve the Assemblée Nationale and can also veto laws. In practice, the president traditionally accepts as prime minister the leader of the largest party in the National Assembly, and approves the prime minister's choice of government ministers.

The presidential term of office was reduced from seven years to five with effect from the 2002 presidential elections.

National legislature

The legislature is a bicameral Parlement (Parliament) consisting of an upper house, the Assemblée Nationale (National Assembly), and a lower house, the Sénat (Senate). The Assemblée Nationale comprises 577 députés (deputies) elected by geographical constituencies (including 17 overseas representatives) for a five-year term while the Sénat has 321 seats, one-third of which are renewed every three years in indirect elections.

Legal system

The country has no supreme court but this role is filled by a nine-member Conseil Constitutionel (Constitutional Council). Its task is to ensure that law treaties and regulations are in keeping with the constitution and that elections are conducted in a regular manner. The highest court of appeal is the Cour de Cassation, which can overrule decisions in all lower courts, but not government legislation. Since the signing of the Single European Act in 1986, the European Court of Justice (ECJ) has been the highest authority in certain areas of French law. France also accepts International Court of Justice (ICJ) jurisdiction.

Last elections
13 June 2004 (European Parliament); 9 and 16 June 2002 (parliamentary); 21 April and 5 May 2002 (presidential).
Results: Referendum on EU constitution: 55 per cent voted against the constitution, 45 per cent in favour. Turn out was around 70 per cent.
European Parliament: PS won 28.9 per cent of the vote (31 seats out of 78), UMP 16.6 per cent (17), UDF 12 per cent (11), FN 9.8 per cent (seven), Greens 7.4 per cent (six), Mouvement pour la France (MPF) (Movement for France) 6.7 per cent (three) and PCF 5.3 per cent (two); turnout 43.1 per cent.
Parliamentary second round: the UMP (known during the election as the Union pour la Majorité Presidentielle (UPM) (Union for the Presidential Majority)), comprising the RPF and the DL, won 47.26 per cent of the vote (309 seats); PS 35.26 per cent (138); Front National (FN) (National Front) 11.3 per cent (no seats); Union pour la Démocratie Française (UDF) (Union for French Democracy) 3.92 per cent (23); Parti Communiste Français (PCF) (French Communist Party) 3.26 per cent (21).
Presidential: a poor turnout in the first round of the presidential elections resulted in incumbent Jacques Chirac and the extreme-right leader, Jean-Marie Le Pen qualifying for the run-off. Lionel Jospin finished third. In the run-off, Chirac defeated Le Pen, 82 per cent to 18 per cent; turnout was 80 per cent.

Next elections
2007 (presidential and parliamentary).

Political parties
Ruling party
Coalition government from 17 Jun 2002: Union pour un Mouvement Populaire (UMP) (Union for a People's Movement), comprising the Rassemblement pour la République (RPR) (Rally for the Republic) and Démocratie Libérale (DL) (Liberal Democracy); Union pour la Démocratie Française (UDF) (Union for French Democracy) and allies.

Main opposition party
Parti Socialiste (PS) (Socialist Party)

Population
60.30 million (2004)
Ethnic make-up
The population is predominantly Western European. North Africans form the principal ethnic minority, with smaller communities from former French colonies in Asia and sub-Saharan Africa.
Religions
There is no state religion, but Roman Catholicism predominates (90 per cent of population), with a significant Protestant minority concentrated in southern France (2 per cent) and Muslim and Jewish communities in major urban areas (1 per cent each).

Labour market and unemployment
The French labour force has high productivity rates and education levels are high. Regulations on working hours and conditions are extensive and many firms experience flexibility problems, although the introduction of a 35-hour working week in late 1999 to curb unemployment was actually used by many employers to enhance flexibility by increasing the amount of part-time employees.
In 2005, the government announced plans to allow employees to work longer than 35 hours.

Education
Compulsory education is provided for free. Primary schooling lasts to the age of 11, after which all pupils transfer to a four-year course in secondary school. At the age of 15 there are two options: either a three-year course leading to the *baccalauréate* examination or a two-year vocational course. An average of 80 per cent of schoolchildren are expected to achieve the *baccalauréate*, which is the minimum entry qualification to university. Educational expenditure is typically equivalent to 6 per cent of gross national income.
Compulsory years: Six to 16
Pupils per teacher: 19 in primary schools

Health
Annual total expenditure on health is around 9–10 per cent of GDP, of which approximately 76 per cent is government spending.
France's liberal state-subsidised medical system allows doctors and dentists to establish private practices. Patients, who are free to choose their own providers, are reimbursed by the state for up to 85 per cent of medical costs. The government makes full provision for people who are unable to make any contributions, by treating them as private patients covered by insurance. A survey by the Organisation for Economic Co-operation and Development (OECD) in mid-2000 showed the French healthcare system to be the best in the world in terms of diagnosis, cure and survival rates for major diseases. Official figures published in May 2004 indicated that the French health system was losing US$27,200 a minute. Proposed reforms to reduce the cost of the health system have met with vociferous opposition from doctors, nurses and health professionals. Fraud is estimated to cost the system more than US$980 million per year, and ease of access to prescription drugs is thought to be the principal reason for the fact that French consumption of drugs and medicine is more than three times the European average.
HIV prevalence: 0.4 per cent aged 15–49 in 2003 (World Bank)
Life expectancy: 79.3 years
Fertility rate/Maternal mortality rate: 1.9 births per woman; maternal mortality 0.1 per 1,000 live births (World Bank).
Infant mortality rate: 4.4 per 1,000 live births (World Bank)

Welfare
France's extensive social security system, including health insurance, family allowances and retirement insurance, covers 99.2 per cent of the population.
In common with other industrialised nations, France's ageing population is an increasing concern. The cost of pensions is set to escalate significantly from 9.8 per cent of GDP in 2001 to 13.5 per cent of GDP by 2030.

Main cities
Paris (capital, estimated population 2.1 million in 2004), Marseille (820,700), Lyon (443,900), Toulouse (411,800), Nice (332,000), Nantes (282,300).

Languages spoken
Breton is spoken in Brittany and Euskera (Basque) is spoken in the south-west, while in Alsace and Lorraine, in the east, German is widely spoken.
English is spoken in the business community, but an understanding of French is considered essential for visitors.
Flemish, Catalán, Occitan, Corsu, Arabic, Kabyle and Antillean are also spoken.
Official language/s
French

Media
Press
French newspapers are editorially free from government control and censorship, and cover the full political spectrum. There are around 870 newspapers and 2,300 magazines, reaching 47.7 per cent of adults. Regional newspapers have a larger readership than national titles.
Dailies: Some of the important dailies are *Le Parisien*, *L'Humanité*, *Libération*, *La Croix* (tabloid), *Les Echos*, *L'Equipe*, *La*

Nations of the World: A Political, Economic and Business Handbook

Voix du Nord, *Le Figaro*, *Sud Ouest*, and *Le Monde*.

Weeklies: The most popular Sunday newspapers are *Le Journal du Dimanche*, *France-Soir* (evening tabloid), and the Sunday tabloid *France Dimanche*. National weeklies covering financial interests include *Le Figaro Magazine*, *Le Figaro Economie* and *La Vie Financiére*. *Point de Vue-Images du Monde* features weekly international affairs and *Femme Actuelle* on women's issues.

Business: Business publications include the English-language daily *International Herald Tribune*, *Investir Magazine*, *Le Point*, *Les Echos*, *La Tribune de l'Expansion*, *L'Express* (weekly), *La Vie Française* (weekly), *Le Nouvel Economiste* (weekly), *Capital Finance* (weekly), and *L'Expansion* (bi-monthly).

Periodicals: *Entrevue* (monthly) covering general information, *Ca M'Intéresse* on current affairs; *Ca Se Passe Comme Ca* and *Actua Ciné* are monthlies for entertainment; *Astuces Beauté* and *Biba* for women's issues.

Broadcasting
Radio: There are over 1,200 radio stations, about half of which are commercial. Commercial stations operating outside France, such as Radio Luxembourg, Radio Monte Carlo, Sud Radio and Europe No 1, are also received.

Television: TF1 is the leading TV channel with 35 per cent audience share and almost 52 per cent of advertising revenues. France 2 and France 3, general channels from the public service, together have 40.9 per cent share of audience, but only 30 per cent of revenues. Cable and satellite television services are widely in use. Télédiffusion de France (TDF) operate six national networks.

Advertising
Numerous advertising agencies operate throughout the country. Television advertising is strictly controlled, by Régie Française de Publicité (RFP), and is expensive. There is limited advertising available on radio. All other media are widely used for advertising, although newspapers and magazines dominate.

Economy
France has a mixed economy with large agricultural, industrial and service sectors. In line with other mature economies, GDP is dominated by the services sector, followed by industry. The services sector annually contributes around 71 per cent to GDP. Although it accounts for a relatively low percentage of GDP (3.1 per cent), the country's agricultural heritage ensures that the sector remains politically important and can conflict with France's commitments to the EU.

The government has completed a major industrial restructuring and modernisation programme, placing particular emphasis on production for the home market and expanding export capacity. The government has traditionally played a very active role in the French economy. Although the state's influence has declined in recent years due to privatisation, the state sector continues to be important.

The economic situation improved in 2004, in the aftermath of the post-2001 downturn. GDP growth, which plummeted to 0.5 per cent in 2003, rebounded to 2.3 per cent in 2004, but the momentum was not sustained in 2005. Recent budget deficits have exceeded the 3 per cent limit agreed in the EU stability and growth pact, but it is hoped that privatisation will curb the deficit. Some much-needed reforms in the public finances, notably pensions, were carried through by the former government, but it is questionable whether the will remains to continue the process in other areas. A top priority of the government continues to be unemployment, which, at around 10 per cent, is a serious problem.

External trade
Manufacturing is the mainstay of France's impressive trade performance.

Imports
Principal imports are machinery and equipment, vehicles, crude oil, aircraft, plastics, chemicals

Main sources: Germany (19.2 per cent total, 2004), Belgium (9.8 per cent), Italy (8.8 per cent), Spain (7.3 per cent), UK (7.0 per cent), Netherlands (6.7 per cent), US (5.1 per cent)

Exports
Principal exports include machinery and transportation equipment, aircraft, plastics, chemicals, pharmaceutical products, iron, steel and beverages.

Main destinations: Germany (15 per cent total, 2004), Spain (9.4 per cent), UK (9.3 per cent), Italy (9.0 per cent), Belgium (7.2 per cent), US (6.7 per cent)

Agriculture
Farming
France is a major European food producer with self-sufficiency in dairy produce and is a substantial exporter of livestock produce, wine, fruit and vegetables. Agriculture contributes around 3.1 per cent to GDP and employs 5 per cent of the labour force. France is also the largest recipient of subsidies, financed through the EU's Common Agricultural Policy (CAP). Most of French agriculture is now governed by CAP. The CAP is based on three broad principles:
- the EU is treated as a single market for agricultural produce
- EU farmers are given preference over outside suppliers
- the cost of the CAP is met by EU member governments.

Fundamental reform to the CAP was introduced in January 2005. The subsidies paid on farm output, which tended to benefit large farms and encourage overproduction, were replaced by single farm payments not conditional on production. This is expected to reward farms that provide and maintain a healthy environment, food safety and animal welfare standards. The changes are also intended to encourage market conscious production and cut the cost of CAP to the EU taxpayer. France is due to introduce this measure in 2006.

The estimated crop production for 2004 included: 70,534,347 tonnes (t) cereals in total, 39,704,764t wheat, 11,040,214t barley, 16,391,359t maize, 7,254,221t potatoes, 30,554,256t sugar beets, 3,969,257t rapeseed (canola), 598,220t oats, 257,615t sorghum, 2,082,995t pulses, 26,863t citrus fruit, 7,542,036t grapes, 808,583t tomatoes, 2,167,411t oilcrops, 24,321t tobacco, 21,693t olives, 51,541t treenuts, 27,720t chillies & peppers, 2,216,940t apples, 90,700t fibre crops, 11,034,170t fruit in total, 8,808,293t vegetables in total. Livestock production included: 6,312,500t meat in total, 1,590,000t beef, 2,320,000t pig meat, 131,000t lamb and goat meat, 1,975,300t poultry, 1,010,000t eggs, 25,181,530t milk, 15,000t honey, 150,000t cattle hides, 11,000t horsemeat.

Fishing
Although oyster farming remains highly vulnerable to the risk of disease, France is the top European producer of oysters and among the first three producers of mussels (from both fishing and aquaculture). France is also the top European producer of fresh water trout and has remained competitive with European regions with more favourable environmental conditions. Sea bass and sea bream represent the majority of marine farm production with turbot farming expanding. Only part of the production is for domestic consumption, the remainder being exported.

Forestry
Forestry is France's richest natural resource with over a quarter (15 million hectares) of metropolitan France covered by forest, giving it the largest tree-covered area in the EU. The Office National des Forêts (ONF) (National Forestry Office) manages over a quarter of this area. Forestry is concentrated in the east, south and south-west of the country, with the largest area being the Landes, coastal forests south of Bordeaux. Deciduous forests account for 61 per cent of the total, while

38 per cent are coniferous or mixed. About 8 per cent of the wooded area is brushwood.

Although it is a net importer of sawn softwoods and pulp for its paper industry, France remains the largest producer of sawn hardwood in Europe.

The forestry industry supplies raw materials to several industries. About 60 per cent of French wood production is used in the construction industry.

Exports of forest products in 2004 amounted to US$7.1 billion, while imports amounted to US$9.0 billion. Production in 2004 included 34,594,000 cubic metres (cum) roundwood, 32,094,000cum industrial roundwood, 9,860,000cum sawnwood, 22,719,000cum sawlogs and veneers, 10,902,000cum pulpwood, 6,046,000cum wood-based panels, 2,500,000cum wood fuel; 5,942,000 tonnes (t) recovered paper, 1,118,000t newsprint, 3,475,000t printing and writing paper.

Industry and manufacturing

France has a broad industrial base incorporating a large capital-intensive state-owned sector, composed mainly of small- and medium-sized manufacturing enterprises, which together contribute around 25 per cent to GDP and employ 27 per cent of the labour force.

Industrial policy is generally aimed at developing the domestic market, promotion of 'new technology' sectors and internationalisation of state-owned companies. Government protection of industry is an important economic issue and one which threatens both to retard the efficiency of domestic markets and alienate France's European partners.

Leading sectors include agri-foodstuffs, telecommunications, aerospace, motor industry, metallurgy, chemicals, parachemicals and pharmaceuticals, textiles and clothing.

Tourism

France is the world's top destination for tourists with over 80 million visitors in 2004. France launched a major PR campaign in 2003 to promote the country to the US travelling public, but while the number of long-haul visitors increased, their main destination was Paris, and so regional centres did not benefit from these arrivals. China has designated France as an approved destination for its holidaying citizens; Chinese visitors could swell France's arrival numbers by several millions.

Mining

The mining sector typically contributes 7 per cent to annual GDP and employs less than 1 per cent of the workforce. France is a significant producer of iron ore, bauxite and potash. In an effort to reduce dependence on imported minerals, exploration for lead, zinc, barium and tungsten has been intensified.

Hydrocarbons

France has around 160 million barrels of estimated oil reserves. Crude oil production has declined since about 1990 from 67,000 barrels per day (bpd) to 23,300 bpd in 2004. France is a heavy consumer of oil, amounting to two million bpd, most of which has to be imported.

France has a crude oil refining capacity of 1.9 million bpd. The largest refinery, TotalFinaElf's at Gonfreville l'Orcher, has a capacity of 343,00 bpd. France will need substantial investment to upgrade the refining sector in order to meet the EU's stringent environmental regulations. France is a major player on world energy markets. TotalFinaElf is the fourth-largest company in the world and has assets in Africa, Latin America and the North Sea. It was created in 1999 when Total and Elf Aquitaine merged with Belgium's Petrofina.

France has around 14 billion cubic metres of estimated natural gas reserves, but production is negligible and declining. As with oil, France imports the bulk of the gas it consumes.

Coal reserves are small. Coal has gradually been replaced by nuclear power for electricity generation. The coal-mining industry ended with the closure of the last mine in 2004, but some coal is imported for the remaining coal-fired power stations and the steel industry.

Energy

Almost 80 per cent of French electricity is generated by nuclear power stations. There are 58 nuclear reactors in France. The government plans to expand the sector with the construction of a new generation of reactors as well as upgrading existing assets. France is one of the world's largest nuclear power producers and produces enough electricity to be a net exporter.

The state-owned monopoly, Electricité de France (EdF), owns the entire transmission network and supplies 95 per cent of all electricity in the country.

In 2000, France passed legislation that began the electricity sector's liberalisation. Since then, about 1,800 large industrial and commercial consumers comprising about 30 per cent of the market have been able to choose their electricity supplier.

The second-largest electricity group is the Compagnie Nationale de Rhône (CNR), which produces about 3 per cent of France's electricity, mostly from hydroelectric plants. The other producer is Société Nationale d'Electricité et de Thermique (SNET), a subsidiary of the French coal utility, Charbonnages de France.

Financial markets
Stock exchange

The Paris Bourse is part of Euronext, an integrated cross-border single currency stock, derivatives and commodities market composed of the Brussels, Paris and Amsterdam exchanges.

Euronext is the largest European exchange in terms of cash trading volume through the central order book. It is the second-largest exchange in Europe in terms of the number and total market capitalisation of listed companies.

Banking and insurance
Central bank

Banque de France; European Central Bank (ECB)

Time

GMT plus one hour in winter (GMT plus two hours in summer)

Geography

France is bordered to the north by the English Channel (La Manche), and to the north-east, east and south-east by Belgium, Luxembourg, Germany, Switzerland and Italy, respectively. The Mediterranean Sea forms the southern boundary, and Spain the south-western, while the west coast faces the Atlantic Ocean.

Climate

France has a moderate maritime climate in the north with a small temperature range and abundant rainfall. By contrast, southern France has a Mediterranean climate, with hot dry summers and mild, moist winters. Eastern France has a continental climate, with thunderstorms prevalent in summer. The average temperature in Paris in January is three degrees Celsius (C) and in July 18 degrees C. Annual rainfall in Paris is 573mm.

Dress codes

Western dress is the norm.

Entry requirements
Passports

Passports are required by all, expect nationals of EU countries with national ID cards. Passports must be valid for three months beyond the length of stay.

Visa

Required by all, except citizens of EU countries, North America, Australasia and Japan, for stays up to three months; this includes business trips by representatives of foreign entities with an invitation from a local company or organisation. Proof of adequate funds for stay, an itinerary, a guarantee of repatriation if necessary and return/onward ticket are also required. For further exceptions, full details and a copy of the application form visit www.diplomatie.gouv.fr/thema/dossier.gb.asp and follow the path (entering France) to the database. A Schengen visa application (offered in several languages) can be downloaded on www.eurovisa.info/ApplicationForm.htm.

Currency advice/regulations
There are no limits to the amount of local or foreign currency that may be imported or exported, although amounts exceeding US$7,452 should be declared.

Customs
Personal effects may be imported duty-free. French customs authorities enforce strict regulations concerning temporary importation into or export from France of items such as firearms, antiquities, medications, business equipment, sales samples.

Health (for visitors)
Mandatory precautions
None
Advisable precautions
There are no particular health hazards in France, although rabies is endemic in some areas.
Medical insurance is advisable for visitors to France if they are not covered by EU reciprocal arrangements as health care costs are high.

Hotels
Classified into deluxe and one- to four-star. Reservations (either direct or through centralised booking offices) should be made in advance during holiday seasons. Single rooms are rare and rates are usually quoted for double rooms. A tip of around 12–15 per cent of the bill is usual, provided no service charge has already been added.

Credit cards
All major credit cards are accepted.

Public holidays
Fixed dates
1 Jan (New Year's Day), 1 May (Labour Day), 8 May (Victory Day), 14 Jul (Bastille Day), 15 Aug (Assumption Day), 1 Nov (All Saints' Day), 11 Nov (Armistice Day) and 25 Dec (Christmas Day).
The months of July and August are traditionally when the French take their holidays.
Variable dates
Good Friday, Easter Monday, Ascension Day, Whit Monday.

Working hours
Banking
Mon–Fri: 0900–1200 and 1400–1600. Some banks close on Mondays and all close early on the day before a Bank Holiday.
Business
Mon–Fri: 0900–1200 and 1400–1800.

Anyone intending to visit France for business purposes should avoid the traditional holiday month of August, when most businesses and government departments keep only a skeleton staff at work.
Government
Mon–Fri: 0830–1800 (staggered nine-hour day with two-hour lunch break).
Shops
Mon–Fri: 0900–1830 (most shops are closed between 1200–1430). Some shops open on Sundays and some close on Mondays.

Electricity supply
220V AC

Social customs/useful tips
In France, strangers and acquaintances shake hands at the beginning and end of a meeting.
Most offices traditionally have a long lunch hour, lasting from 1200 until at least 1400. Lunchtime remains a popular time for doing business, with a number of restaurants in big cities catering expressly for business clients.
French nationals must carry identification at all times. Visitors should carry their passports. Spot identity checks are not uncommon and it is illegal to be without identification.

Security
Serious crimes represent only a tiny percentage of the total number reported, while there has been a big rise in delinquency, vandalism and petty theft. Pickpockets operate particularly in train stations and subways. Gangs of thieves prey on tourists on the rail link from Charles de Gaulle Airport to downtown Paris. One member of the gang distracts the traveller while another takes a piece of luggage, timing it so that they can quickly exit the train.
France has one of the highest road accident rates in Europe and the government has taken active steps to try and curb it.

Getting there
Air
France has a number of airports located in the various regions receiving international flights.
National airline: Air France
Air France and Koninklijke Luchtvaart Maatschappij (KLM) (Royal Dutch Airlines) joined forces in May 2004.
International airport/s: Charles de Gaulle (or Roissy) (PAR-CDG), 23km north-east of Paris. Facilities include a business centre, bank, post office, restaurants, bars, duty-free shopping, medical centre and pharmacy and hairdressers. Car hire is available.
Other airport/s: Orly (PAR-ORY), 14km south of Paris; Bordeaux (BOD), 12km from city; Lille (LIL), 15km from city; Lyon (LYS), 24km east of Lyon; Marseille (MRS), 24km north of city; Nice (NCE), 6km west of Nice; Toulouse (TLS), 10km from city; Biarritz (BIQ); Nantes (NTE); Perpignan (PGF) and Strasbourg (SXB).
Airport tax: None
Surface
France has good rail, road and sea connections with all surrounding countries.
Rail: The Eurostar service is provided by Belgium, UK and French railways, operating high speed rail connections between London, Paris and Brussels. Road vehicles are transported through the tunnel in Le Shuttle trains.
Water: There are regular cross channel ferries from the UK and Mediterrean ferries to Corsica, Spain (Balearic Islands) and North Africa.
Main port/s: Marseille (Europe's third-largest port), Boulogne, Nice, Calais, Dieppe, Dunkirk, Cherbourg, Le Havre, Rouen.

Getting about
National transport
Air: Paris is the most important business destination in France and is served by the two main airports, at Orly and Charles de Gaulle. Major cities are linked by Air France. Some services operate only during summer.
Road: France has the densest road network in the world. There are 806,000km of roads, including 7,100km of motorways, most of which are *autoroutes à péage* (toll roads).
Buses: There are good local bus services and some long-distance coach services.
Rail: French transport policy favours the railways. The Société Nationale des Chemins de Fer Français (SNCF) (French National Railroad Company) operates a nationwide network reaching to almost every part of the country. The most important rail lines radiate from Paris. Three high-speed train (TGV) lines link northern- and southern France. These trains are modern and comfortable; seats can be booked in advance.
Water: There are approximately 9,000km of inland navigable waterways. Major canal areas are situated in the north and north-east of Paris, where the majority of the navigable rivers, including the Seine, the Rhine, the Midi, Brittany and the Loire are connected with canals.

City transport
Paris has one of the best urban transport networks in the world. A *Carte Orange Hebdomadaire* allows unlimited travel for one week on most forms of public transport.
Taxis: From Charles de Gaulle and Orly airports to the city centre, limousines and taxis are available.
Taxis are only available from *stations de taxi* (taxi ranks). Day and night rates

should be displayed inside the vehicle. Note that extra charges are usually levied for journeys to racecourses, stations and airports. Tipping is usually 10–15 per cent.

Buses, trams & metro: In Paris, the same tickets may be used on buses and the metro; a carnet of 10 tickets is cheaper. Buses operate between 0600–2100; some exceptional routes operate until 0030.

Car hire

All major international hire companies have offices in Paris and other main towns. Drivers must carry at all times: a passport or national ID card, a valid driving licence, car ownership papers and proof of insurance.

Traffic drives on the right. *Priorité à droite* applies, particularly in built-up areas – cars coming out of a side turning on the right have priority, unless suspended where a sign indicates. Speed limits: 130kph on toll motorways, 110kph on dual carriageways, 90kph on other roads and 60kph in towns. Note that these limits are reduced when wet. Speed limits for drivers who have held their licence for less than two years are 110kph on motorways, 100kph on dual carriageways and 80kph on other roads.

Wearing of seat belts is compulsory in front seats.

BUSINESS DIRECTORY

The addresses listed below are a selection only. While World of Information makes every endeavour to check these addresses, we cannot guarantee that changes have not been made, especially to telephone numbers and area codes. We would welcome any corrections.

Telephone area codes

The International direct dialling (IDD) code for France is +33, followed by area code and subscriber's number:

Paris	1
North-west (Nantes, Rouen, etc)	2
North-east (Lille, Strasbourg etc)	3
South-east and Corsica (Lyon, Marseilles, etc)	4
South-west (Bordeaux, Toulouse, etc)	5

Useful telephone numbers

Police: 17
Fire: 18
Medical emergency and ambulance: 15

Chambers of Commerce

American Chamber of Commerce in France, 156 Boulevard Haussmann, 75008 Paris (tel: 5643-4567; fax: 5643-4560; e-mail: amchamfrance@amchamfrance.org).

Assemblée des Chambres Françaises de Commerce et d'Industrie, 45 Avenue d'Iéna, PO Box 3003, 75773 Paris Cedex 16 (tel: 4069-3700; fax: 4720-6128; e-mail: contactdie@acfci.cci.fr).

Boulogne-sur-Mer Chambre de Commerce et d'Industrie, 98 Quai Gambetta, 62204 Boulogne-sur-Mer (tel: 2199-6200; fax: 2199-6201; e-mail: ccibco@boulogne-sur-mer.cci.fr).

Bordeaux Chambre de Commerce et d'Industrie, 12 Place de la Bourse, 33076 Bordeaux (tel: 5679-5000; fax: 5569-5265; e-mail: bourse@bordeaux.cci.fr).

British-French Chamber of Commerce and Industry, 31 Rue Boissy d'Anglas, 75008 Paris (tel: 5330-8130; fax: 5330-8135; e-mail: information@francobritishchamber.com).

Calais Chambre de Commerce et d'Industrie, 24 Boulevard des Alliés, PO Box 199, 62104 Calais Cedex (tel: 2146-0000; fax: 2146-0099; e-mail: ccic@calais.cci.fr).

Grenoble Chambre de Commerce et d'Industrie, 1 Place André Malraux, PO Box 297, 38016 Grenoble Cedex 1 (tel: 7628-2828; fax: 7628-2747; e-mail: ccig@grenoble.cci.fr).

Loiret Chambre de Commerce et d'Industrie, 23 Place du Martroi, 45044 Orléans Cedex 1 (tel: 3877-7777; fax: 3853-0978; e-mail: direction@loiret.cci.fr).

Lorraine Chambre de Commerce et d'Industrie, 10 Viaduc J-F Kennedy, CS 4231, 54042 Nancy Cedex (tel: 8390-1313; fax: 8328-8833; e-mail: crci@lorraine.cci.fr).

Lyon Chambre de Commerce et d'Industrie, Palais du Commerce, Place de la Bourse, 69289 Lyon Cedex 2 (tel: 7240-5858; fax: 7837-5346; e-mail: info@lyon.cci.fr).

Nantes Chambre de Commerce et d'Industrie, 16 Quai Ernest Renaud, PO Box 90517, 44105 Nantes Cedex 4 (tel: 4044-6060; fax: 4044-6090; e-mail: administrator@nantes.cci.fr).

Nice Chambre de Commerce et d'Industrie, 20 Boulevard Carabaçel, PO Box 1259, 06005 Nice Cedex 1 (tel: 0820-422-222; fax: 9313-7399; e-mail: mde.nice.carabacel@cote-azur.cci.fr).

Rennes Chambre de Commerce et d'Industrie, 2 Avenue de la Préfecture, CS 64204, 35042 Rennes Cedex (tel: 9933-6666; fax: 9333-2428; e-mail: info@rennes.cci.fr).

Rouen Chambre de Commerce et d'Industrie, Palais des Consuls, Quai de la Bourse, PO Box 641, 76007 Rouen Cedex 1 (tel: 3414-3737; fax: 3514-3838; e-mail: ccir@rouen.cci.fr).

Strasbourg Chambre de Commerce et d'Industrie, 10 Place Gutenburg, 67081 Strasbourg Cedex (tel: 0388-752-525; fax: 0388-223-120; e-mail: direction@strasbourg.cci.fr).

Banking

Association Française de Banques, 18 Rue la Fayette, 75009 Paris (tel: 4246-9259).

Banque Française du Commerce Extérieur (BFCE), 21 Boulevard Haussmann, 75009 Paris (tel: 4800-4800; fax: 4800-3970).

Banque Indosuez, 96 Boulevard Haussmann, 75008 Paris (tel: 4420-2020; fax: 4420-1522).

Banque Nationale de Paris SA, 16 Boulevard des Italiens, 75009 Paris (tel: 4014-4546; fax: 4014-5599).

Banque Paribas, 3 Rue d'Antin, 75078 Paris Cedex 02 (tel: 4298-1234; fax: 4298-0433).

Caisse Centrale des Banques Populaires, 10-12 avenue Winston Churchill, 94677 Charenton Le Pont Cedex (tel: 4039-0000; fax: 4039-3940).

Caisse d'Epargne, 19 Rue du Louvre, 75001 Paris (tel: 4041-3031; fax: 4233-4518).

Compagnie Bancaire, 5 Avenue Kléber, 75798 Paris Cedex 16 (tel: 4525-2525; fax: 4501-7805).

Compagnie Financière de Crédit Industriel et Commercial (CIC Group), Rue de la Victoire 66, 75009 Paris (tel: 4280-8080).

Crédit Agricole, Boulevard Pasteur 91-93, 75015 Paris (tel: 4323-5202).

Crédit Commercial de France (CCF), 103 Avenue des Champs-Elysées, 75008 Paris (tel: 4070-7040; fax: 4070-7353).

Crédit Foncier de France, SA, 19 Rue des Capucines, 75001 Paris (tel: 4244-8000; fax: 4244-7822).

Crédit Local de France, 7-11 Quai André Citroen, 75015 Paris (tel: 4392-7777; fax: 4592-7672).

Crédit Lyonnais SA, Boulevard des Italiens 19, 75002 Paris (tel: 4295-7000).

Crédit Mutuel, 88 Rue Cardinet, 75017 Paris (tel: 4401-1010; fax: 4401-1227).

Société Générale, Boulevard Haussmann 29, 75009 Paris (tel: 4298-2000).

Union Européenne de CIC (CIC Group), 4 Rue Gaillon, 75107 Paris Cedex 02 (tel: 4266-7000; fax: 4266-7878).

Central bank

Banque de France, 39 rue Croix des Petits Champs, 75001 Paris (tel: 4292-4292; fax: 4292-3940; e-mail: cdoc@banque-france.fr).

European Central Bank, Kaiserstrasse 29, D-60311 Frankfurt am Main, Germany (tel: +49(69)13-440; fax: +49(69)1344-6000; e-mail: info@ecb.int).

Travel information

Air France (head office), 1 Place Max-Hymans, Paris 75757 Cedex 15 (tel: 4323-8181; internet site: http://www.airfrance.fr).

Airport office: 45 Rue de Paris, Roissy Charles de Gaulle, Paris 95747 (tel: 4156-7800).

Maison de la France (tourist office), 8 Avenue de l'Opéra, Paris 75001 (tel: 4296-1023; fax: 4286-8052).

Roissy Charles de Gaulle and Le Bourget airports, BP 20101, 95711 Roissy Charles de Gaulle Cedex (tel: 4862-1212, 4864-6807) (24 hours).

Ministries

Ministry of Agriculture, Fisheries and Food, 78 Rue de Varenne, 75700 Paris (tel: 4955-4955; fax: 4955-4039).

Ministry of Capital Works, Housing, and Transport, 246 bd. Saint-Germain, 75007 Paris (tel: 4081-2122; fax: 4081-3099).

Ministry of the Civil Service, Administrative Reform and Decentralisation, 72 Rue de Varenne, 75700 Paris (tel: 4275-8000; fax: 4275-8970).

Ministry of Culture and Communication, 3 Rue de Valois, 75042 Paris (tel: 4015-8000; fax: 4261-3577).

Ministry of Defence, 14 Rue Saint-Dominique, 75700 Paris (tel: 4219-3011; fax: 4505-4091).

Ministry for the Economy, Finance and Industry, 139 Rue de Bercy, 75572 Paris Cedex 12 (tel: 5318-4000; fax: 5318-9701; internet site: http://www.minefi.gouv.fr).

Ministry of Employment, Rue de Grenelle, 75700 Paris (tel: 4438-3838; fax: 4438-2010).

Ministry of the Environment, 20 Avenue de Segur, 75302 Paris 07 SP (tel: 4219-2021; fax: 4219-1120).

Ministry of Foreign Affairs, 37 Quai d'Orsay, 75700 Paris (tel: 4317-5353; fax: 4551-6012).

Ministry of Industry, the Post Office and Telecommunications, 101 Rue de Grenelle, 75700 Paris 9 (tel: 4319-3636; fax: 4319-3052).

Ministry of the Interior, Place Beauvau, 75800 Paris (tel: 4927-4927; fax: 4266-1280).

Ministry of Justice, 13 Place Vendome, 75042 Paris (tel: 4477-6060; fax: 4477-6000).

Ministry of Labour and Social Affairs, 127 Rue de Grenelle, 75700 Paris (tel: 4438-3838; fax: 4056-6710).

Ministry of National Education, Higher Education and Research, 110 Rue de Grenelle, 75700 Paris. (tel: 4955-1010; fax: 4955-1556).

Ministry for Relations with Parliament, 69 Rue de Varenne, 75700 Paris (tel: 4275-8000; fax: 4081-7300).

Ministry of Small- and Medium-Sized Enterprises, Trade and Artisan Activities, 80 Rue de Lille, 75700 Paris (tel: 4319-2424; fax: 4319-3767).

Ministry of Town and Country Planning, Urban Affairs and Integration, 35 Rue Saint-Dominique, 75700 Paris (tel: 4275-8000; fax: 4275-7755).

Ministry of Youth and Sport, Rue Olivier de Serres, 75015 Paris (tel: 5369-3000; fax: 5369-4370).

Prime Minister's Office, 57 Rue de Varenne, 75700 Paris (tel: 4275-8000; fax: 4544-1572).

Other useful addresses

Agence France Presse (news agency), 11–15 Place de la Bourse, 75002 Paris (tel: 4041-4646; fax: 4041-4632).

ANIT (public information service), 8 Avenue de l'Opéra, 75001 Paris (tel: 4260-3738).

La Bourse de Paris (Stock Exchange), 39 Rue Cambon, 75001 Paris (tel: 4927-7000; fax: 4289-7868).

Bureau International des Expositions (International Exhibition Bureau), 56 Avenue Victor-Hugo, 75116 Paris (tel: 4500-3863; fax: 4500-9615).

Caisse Centrale de Co-opération Economique (CCCE), 233 Boulevard Saint-Germain, Paris (tel: 4550-3220).

Centre Françaíse du Commerce Extérieur, 10 Avenue d'Iéna, 75116 Paris (tel: 4505-3000).

Direction Générale des Impôts, Centre des Non-Résidents, 9 Rue d'Uzés, 75094 Paris.

France Telecom, 6 Place d'Alleray, 75505 Paris Cedex 15.

French Embassy (USA), 4101 Reservoir Road, NW, Washington DC 20007 (tel: 202-944-6000; fax: 202-944-6166).

Institut National de la Statistique et des Etudes Economiques (INSEE), 18 Boulevard Adolphe Pinard, 75675 Paris Cedex 14 (tel: 4117-5050; fax: 4117-6666; internet site: http://www.insee.fr).

Invest in France Network/DATAR, 1 Avenue Charles Floquet, 75343 Paris Cedex 07 (tel: 4065-1006; fax: 4065-1240).

Service de la Répression des Fraudes et du Contrôle de la Qualité, 44 Boulevard de Grenelle, 75732 Paris.

Post Office, 52 rue du Louvre, Paris (tel: 4028-2000).

Internet sites

Les Echos: http://www.lesechos.fr

Le Figaro: http://www.lefigaro.fr

Le Monde: http://www.lemonde.fr

Ferry information: http://seafrance.com/ferries_to_france.html

France Bottin (provides market information on France's main companies): http://www.bottin.fr

French electronic phonebook (searches can be conducted by name or by regions): http://www.epita.fr:5000/11/english.html

Tourist information: http://www.francetourism.com/

French Guiana

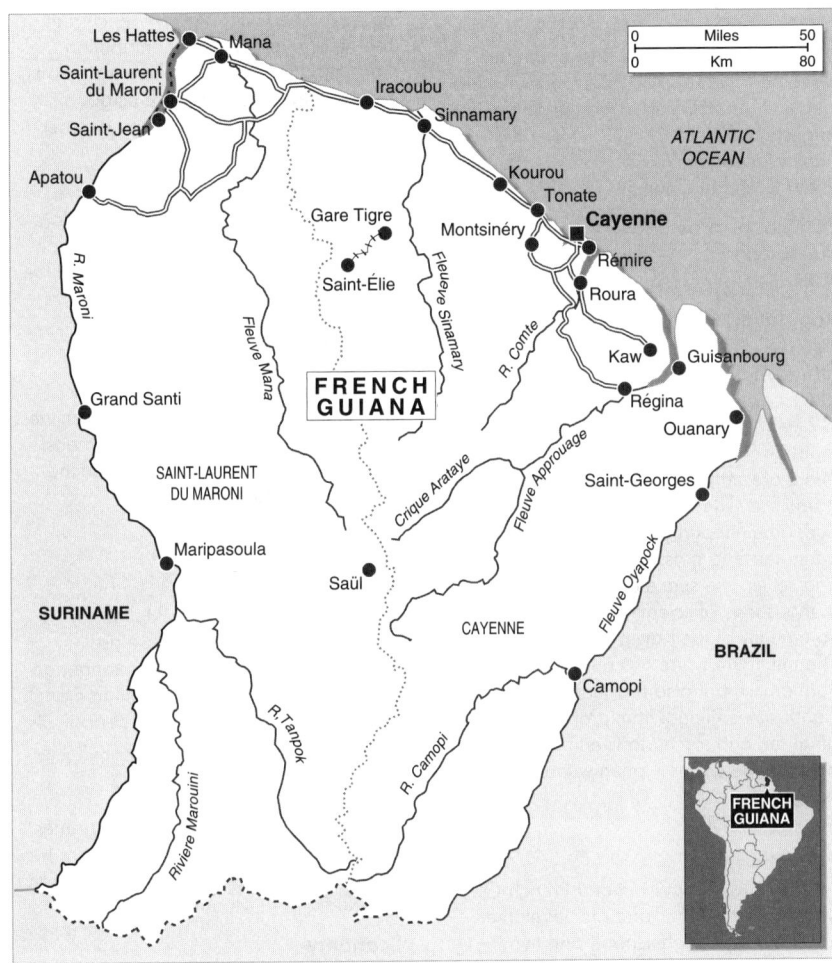

KEY FACTS

Official name: Guyane Française (French Guiana)

Head of State: President of France (Jacques Chirac)

Head of government: *Préfet* (Commissioner) Ange Mancini (from 31 Jul 2002)

Ruling party: Parti Socialiste Guyanais (PSG)

Area: 91,000 square km

Population: 196,800 (2004)

Capital: Cayenne

Official language: French

Currency: Euro (eur) = 100 cents (from 1 Jan 2002; previous currency French franc, locked at Ff6.56 per euro)

Exchange rate: eur0.83 per US$ (Oct 2005)

GDP per capita: US$6,000 (2003)

Labour force: 58,800 (2003)

Unemployment: 22.00% (2003)

Inflation: 1.50% (2003)

Balance of trade: -US$470.00 million (2003)

Foreign debt: US$1.20 billion (2003)

COUNTRY PROFILE

Historical profile
Carib and Arawak Indians were the original inhabitants of French Guiana.
1496 First reported European sighting.
1604 The French established their first settlement on French Guiana.
1654–1915 There were numerous changes in control between the French, British, Dutch, Brazilian and Portuguese, as well as border disputes. During this period the economy of the region came close to collapse, particularly after the abolition of slavery in 1848. Black African slaves had previously worked on French Guiana's sugar plantations.
1946 French Guiana became a French Département d'Outre-Mer (DOM) (Overseas Department).
1953 Closure of penal colony on Devil's Island.
1964 The Kourou Space Centre was established.
1974 French Guiana was further incorporated into the French political system and granted the status of region of France.
1983 French Guiana was granted devolution. A Regional Council was established under the French decentralisation policy.
1998 The Parti Socialiste Guyanais (PSG), remained the single largest party in the Regional Council after the elections.

2000 There were pro-independence demonstrations and French Guiana sought to alter its relationship as a DOM.
2002 French Guiana adopted the euro as its official currency. Arianespace launched Intelsat 904 into orbit from Kourou. The satellite will provide Internet, telecommunications and television services for Europe, Africa, Central Asia and Australia.
2003 In June, under a deal with the European Space Agency (ESA), Russia said that it hoped to start using, from 2006, the upgraded Kourou launch pad for its rockets.
2004 Seven ESA member states are involved in the Vega Programme to build a small single-body launcher with three solid propulsion stages and an upper stage powered by liquid propulsion. Vega is to be launched in 2006.
2005 Arianespace and the Russian Space Agency signed an agreement in April for construction of the Soyuz launch pad.

Political structure

Constitution
28 September 1958 (French Fifth Republic)
Under the 1946 constitution of the French Fourth Republic, French Guiana became a Département d'Outre-Mer (DOM) (Overseas Department) of France. In 1974, it was granted additional status as a region of France.
French Guiana is represented in the French National Assembly in Paris and in the Senate.
Administration is by a préfet appointed by the government in Paris.
Since 1983, following the French government's policy of decentralisation, regional councils have been elected with powers similar to those of the regions.
The local government comprises a Conseil Régional (Regional Council) of 19 members and a 31-member Conseil Général (General Council), both directly elected for six-year terms.

Form of state
Département d'Outre-Mer (DOM) (Overseas Department) of France, with additional status as a région (region) of France.

The executive
Executive power is vested in the president of France, represented by a Préfet (Commissioner), appointed by the president on the advice of the French Ministry of Interior.

National legislature
Local administration is through a directly-elected Conseil Général (General Council) of 19 members and an indirectly-elected 31-member Conseil Régional (Regional Council). Presidents of the General and Regional Councils are appointed by the members of those councils.
Two members are elected to the French National Assembly and one member to the Senate.

Legal system
French legal system

Last elections
March 2000 (General Council)
Results: Regional Council: the PSG won 11 seats but lost ground when three pro-independence candidates of the Mouvement de Décolonisation et d'Emancipation Sociale (Movement for Decolonisation and Social Freedom) were elected. The PSG remained the single largest party.

Next elections
2006 (General Council)

Political parties
Ruling party
Parti Socialiste Guyanais (PSG)

Population
196,800 (2004)

Ethnic make-up
Black or mixed race (66 per cent), white (12 per cent), East Indian, Chinese or Amerindian (12 per cent).
There are settlements of Hmong farmers from Laos. The troubles in neighbouring Suriname encouraged thousands of Surinamese to cross the border illegally and settle. The space centre has brought in thousands of scientists who live in a community of their own.
The minimum wage has attracted not only Surinamese but also Brazilians. These *clandestines* (illegal immigrants) are marginalised and forced to live in the poorest areas of the country, often without work.

Religions
Roman Catholic

Education
Schooling is compulsory and French Guiana has both public and private elementary schools, a high school, and two vocational schools. The condition of schools is, however, very poor, leading students to strike.
Literacy rate: 84 per cent, male; 82 per cent, female; adult rates (World Bank).

Health
Government health planning is seriously affected by the high prevalence of sexually transmitted diseases and an endemic level of dengue fever.
Health insurance is provided by the state-sponsored social security system, financed with compulsory contributions from salaries. People are usually reimbursed on the basis of rates negotiated between care providers and the social security.
Life expectancy: 77 years: male 74 years; female 80 years (2003)
Fertility rate/Maternal mortality rate: Three births per woman (2003)
Birth rate/Death rate: 21 births per 1,000 population; five deaths per 1,000 population (2003).
Infant mortality rate: 13 per 1,000 live births (2003)

Welfare
The official unemployment rate is 22 per cent with higher rates among young people. Jobs connected with satellite launching, combined with orderly French rule and an annual financial contribution amounting to US$500 million from Paris, have provided benefits such as good roads, decent health care, and a generous social security system.

Main cities
Cayenne (capital, estimated population 60,500 in 2003), St Laurent-du-Maroni (23,000), Kourou (main town around the space centre and rapidly growing, 22,900), Matoury (21,600), Rémire-Montjoly (18,600).

Languages spoken
French and French-Creole. Some business executives speak English, although business is generally conducted in French.

Official language/s
French

Media
Press
Daily papers are *Guyane-Matin*, *France-Guyane* and *La Presse de Guyane*. There are no English-language newspapers. US and metropolitan French papers are available. Several periodicals are in circulation but there are no trade publications.

Broadcasting
Radio-Télévision Française d'Outre-mer (RFO) broadcast in French. There are two independent radio stations: Cayenne FM and Radio Tout Mount.

Economy
The overall economy remains underdeveloped. Fishing and forestry are the main activities, but the space industry makes a vital contribution. Kourou space centre accounts for 25 per cent of GDP and half of tax revenues. An estimated 24 per cent of the population work directly or indirectly in jobs connected with the space industry. French Guiana is otherwise dependent on aid, technical assistance and imports from France.
As a department of France, French Guiana receives the same benefits as metropolitan France: a minimum wage, free education and health care, and a large, well-paid civil service.

External trade
There is heavy dependence on France for financial aid. The balance of trade deficit is mainly due to high imports of food and fuels, and undeveloped export potential.

French Guiana

Imports
Principal imports are food (grains, processed meat), machinery and transport equipment, fuels and chemicals.
Main sources: France (63 per cent), US, Trinidad and Tobago, Italy
Exports
Principal exports are shrimp, timber, gold, rum, rosewood essence and clothing.
Main destinations: France (62 per cent total), Switzerland (7 per cent), US (2 per cent)

Agriculture
Farming
Cultivation is limited to the coastal area. Only 0.18 per cent of the total land area is cultivated and production is dominated by crops for domestic consumption such as rice, maize and bananas, while sugar cane is grown for rum production.
A small number of cattle farms have also been established.
Crop production in 2004 included: 23,500 tonnes (t) rice, *10,400t cassava, 4,100t taro, *5,350t sugar cane, 3,770t tomatoes, 4,500t bananas, 3,170t plantains, 2,175t citrus fruit, 15,055t roots and tubers, 24,590t vegetables in total. Livestock production included: 1,908t meat in total, 320t beef, 1,100t pig meat, *28t lamb and goat meat, 460t poultry, *460t eggs, *270t milk.
* estimate
Fishing
The typical total annual fish catch is over 5,000mt. Shellfish, molluscs and cephalopods account for another 2,700mt per annum.
Forestry
The rainforest covers around 90 per cent of the land area. Poor infrastructure means the vast timber resources have not been fully exploited.

Industry and manufacturing
The sector includes construction, shrimp processing, forestry products, rum and gold mining. Manufacturing is virtually non-existent, except for small factories processing agricultural or seafood products and a few sawmills. A tile and brick-making plant, based on important fields of red clay, operates in the Cayenne neighbourhood. Production of rum from sugar cane has declined. Industrial activity is limited to the area around the Kourou space centre.

Tourism
Tourism is an important area of the economy. The sector suffered following the 11 September 2001 terrorist attacks in the US. The prospects for eco-tourism are good.

Mining
Bauxite deposits of 42 million tonnes and kaolin deposits of 40 million tonnes have been found, but extraction is not economically viable, although kaolin mining has begun in the Mana area. There are also reserves of silica, niobium and tantalite. Gold is mined, both legally and illicitly, the latter activity on a large scale and causing serious environmental damage. Significant exploitation of the mineral resources will come about only with further improvements in infrastructure.

Hydrocarbons
French Guiana does not produce oil, gas or coal. It is heavily dependent on imports of petroleum products to meet its energy needs, importing around 6,500 barrels per day. Gas and coal are not imported.

Energy
French Guiana relies to a large extent on petroleum imports from France.

Banking and insurance
The Banque Nationale de Paris Guyane Sa (BNP Guyane) is a major commercial bank offering a wide range of services. There are branches in Cayenne, Kourou and Rémire-Montjoly.
Central bank
European Central Bank

Time
GMT minus three hours

Geography
French Guiana lies on the north coast of South America, with Suriname to the west and Brazil to the south and east.

Climate
The climate is tropical. It is generally hot and humid with heavy rain. The dry season is August–December with an average temperature of 28 degrees Celsius (C). The rainy season is January–June with a temperature range of 22–32 degrees C.

Dress codes
For business meetings men should wear a lightweight or tropical suit and tie and women a lightweight suit or the equivalent.

Entry requirements
Passports
Passports are required by all except nationals of France and some francophone countries holding national identity cards. Passports should be valid for three months from the date of departure.
Visa
Required by all, except citizens of EU, North America, Australasia and Japan, for stays up to one month; this includes business trips by representatives of foreign entities with an invitation from a local company or organisation. Proof of adequate funds for stay, an itinerary, a guarantee of repatriation if necessary and return/onward ticket are also required. For further exceptions, full details and a copy of the application form visit www.diplomatie.gouv.fr/thema/dossier.gb.asp and follow the path (entering France) to the database.
Currency advice/regulations
There are no restrictions on the import of foreign currency but amounts should be declared, and the amount taken out must not exceed that taken in. It is recommended to check the latest regulations with the embassy/consulate as they can change at short notice.

Health (for visitors)
Mandatory precautions
A yellow fever certificate.
Advisable precautions
Hepatitis 'A', 'B' and 'D', typhoid and polio immunisations are recommended. Dengue fever is endemic. Malaria prophylaxis is advisable if travelling outside Cayenne. Water precautions should be taken, although tap water in Cayenne is safe. There is a rabies risk.

Hotels
There is a good standard of accommodation available in Cayenne, Kourou and St Laurent. Rates normally include service and taxes; if not, a 10 per cent tip is usual.

Public holidays
Fixed dates
1 Jan (New Year's Day), 1 May (Labour Day), 8 May (Victory Day), 10 Jun (Abolition Day), 14 Jul (Bastille Day), 15 Aug (Assumption Day), 15 Oct (Cayenne Festival, regional), 1 Nov (All Saints' Day), 2 Nov (All Souls' Day), 11 Nov (Armistice Day), 25 Dec (Christmas Day).
Variable dates
Carnival (two days Feb), Ash Wednesday, Good Friday, Easter Monday, Ascension Day, Whit Monday.

Working hours
Banking
Mon–Fri: 0730–1230, 1430–1730.
Business
Mon–Fri: 0800–1300, 1500–1800.
Government
Mon–Fri: 0730–1300, 1430–1830 (closed Wed and Fri afternoons).

Electricity supply
220V AC, 50 cycles

Social customs/useful tips
Appointments should be made in advance. It is customary to shake hands on meeting and taking leave. Business cards are exchanged after introduction.

Getting there
Air
International airport/s: Cayenne-Rochambeau (CAY), 15km from city; bar, post office, shops, hotel reservations, car hire.

Airport tax: There is no airport tax.
Surface
Road: There is a coastal road to Suriname but there is no road access to Brazil.
Water: Ferries run regularly to Suriname, and from St George to Oiapoque (Brazil).

Getting about
National transport
Air: Air Guyane, Guyane Aero Service and Heli-Inter Service serve main centres and the interior of the country. (Bookings can be made through Air France.)
Road: There are 356km of national routes and 366km of departmental roads. Cayenne district is served by a good road system, but the streets of Cayenne itself are inferior. The only major road runs from Cayenne, via Kourou, to St Laurent on Suriname border.
Buses: Scheduled services on Cayenne to St Laurent route.
Water: Major form of travel. Motor boat serves some coastal towns. River boats and small planes link interior centres with coast. 400km rivers are navigable by small ocean-going vessels and river and coastal steamers but interior connections are made by local craft.
City transport
Taxis: Taxis are available in main towns. Fares include gratuities.
Car hire
Car hire is available in Cayenne and at the airport. An international licence required.

BUSINESS DIRECTORY
The addresses listed below are a selection only. While World of Information makes every endeavour to check these addresses, we cannot guarantee that changes have not been made, especially to telephone numbers and area codes. We would welcome any corrections.

Telephone area codes
The international direct dialling (IDD) code for French Guiana is +594 followed by another 594 and the subscriber's (six digit) number.

Useful telephone numbers
Police: 17
Fire: 18
Talking clock: 3699
Times of tides: 378-300
Radio taxi: 307-305, 305-225
Bus service: 314-554

Chambers of Commerce
Guyane Chambre de Commerce et d'Industrie, PO Box 49, Hôtel Consulaire, Place de l'Esplinade, 97321 Cayenne (tel: 299-600; fax: 299-634; e-mail: contact@guyane.cci.fr).

Banking
Banque Française Commerciale, 8 Place des Palmistes, 97300 Cayenne (tel: 291-111; fax: 301-312).

Banque de la Guyane, PO Box 35, 2 Place Victor-Schloelcher, Cayenne (tel: 310-515).

Banque Nationale de Paris Guyane, 2 Place Victor-Schoelcher, Cayenne (tel: 396-300; fax: 302-308).

Crédit Agricole, Angle av L Héder et rue Damas, 97300 Cayenne (tel: 318-000; fax: 317-524).

Crédit Martiniquais, 76 Av Gal de Gaulle, 97300 Cayenne (tel: 315-700; fax: 314-801).

Crédit Populairé Caisse Crédit Mutuel, 93 rue Lalouette, 97300 Cayenne (tel: 301-523; fax: 301-765).

Central bank
European Central Bank, Kaiserstrasse 29, D-60311 Frankfurt am Main, Germany (tel: +49(69)13-440; fax: +49(69)1344-6000).

Travel information
Air France, Cayenne (tel: 379-899).

Air Guyane, Aéroport de Rochambeau, 97351 Matoury (tel: 356-555; fax: 356-506).

AOM (tel: 353-934).

Guyane Aero Services, Aéroport de Rochambeau, 97351 Matoury (tel: 356-162; fax: 358-450).

Héli-Inter Service Guyane, Aéroport de Rochambeau, 97351 Matoury (tel: 356-231; fax: 358-256).

Rochambeau International Airport, Cayenne (tel: 299-700).

Surinam Airways, c/o Atlas Voyages, 15 Rue Louis Blanc, 97300 Cayenne (tel: 317-298; fax: 305-786).

Syndicat Autonome des Hoteliers Restaurateurs et Cafétiers de Guyane, PK 9,2 Route de Rémire, 97354 Rémire Montjoly (tel: 354-100; fax: 354-405).

Syndicats d'Initiative Office du Tourisme, 7 Av du Président Monnerville, Cayenne 97300 (tel: 312-919).

TABA, PK 2,5 Route de Baduel, 97300 Cayenne (tel: 312-147; fax: 312-154).

Ministry of tourism
Agence Régionale de Développement du Tourisme et des Loisirs de la Guyane, 12 Rue Lallouette, BP 801, 97338 Cayenne (tel: 300-900; fax: 309-315).

Other useful addresses
Agence Régionale pour le Développement de l'Industrie Minière (ARDIM), 111 rue Christophe Colomb, 973000 Cayenne (tel: 294-575).

British Consulate, 16 Ave G. Monnerville, B.P. 211, 97324 Cayenne (tel: 311-034; fax: 304-094).

Centre Spatial Guyanais, Korou (tel: 326-123).

Direction Régionale de l'Industrie, de la Recherche et de l'Environnement, pointe Buzaré, PO Box 7001, 97307 Cayenne (tel: 297-530; fax: 290-734).

Ligue pour la Protection des Oiseaux (LPO), Fonds Mondial pour la Nature (WWF), Cayenne (tel: 309-189).

Radio-Télévision Française d'Outre-mer(RFO), 43 bis Rue du Dr Devèze, BP 336, 97305 Cayenne (tel: 311-500).

Internet sites
Latin world, commercial directory: http://www.latinworld.com

Centre Français du commerce exterieur (site in French): http://www.cfce.fr

French Guiana Consular Information: http://travel.state.gov/french_guiana.html

French Polynesia

COUNTRY PROFILE

Historical profile
French Polynesia consists of 118 islands and was settled by Polynesians betweeen 300 and 800 AD. From these islands, Hawaii, the Cook Islands and New Zealand were colonised.
1843 Tahiti, the largest island, and Moorea became French protectorates.
1880 Tahiti became a French colony. The other islands were annexed under the name Comptoirs Français de l'Océanie.
1957 The group of islands became the Territoire d'Outre-Mer (TOM, overseas territory) of French Polynesia, administered by a governor in Papeete on Tahiti.
1960 An international airport opened at Faa'a on Tahiti.
1963 French nuclear tests were conducted for the first time at Mururoa Atoll.
1977 Increased powers for the council of ministers was approved by the French government.
1984 New powers for the government, particularly in commerce were approved by the French government.
1983 Despite strong local protests, French authorities insisted that nuclear tests would continue for 'as long as necessary'.
1984 Jurisdiction over certain local affairs (local budget, health services, primary education, culture, social welfare, public works, agriculture and sports) was conferred on the council of ministers. Gaston Flosse became president of the governing council.
1986 The Tahoeraa Huiraatira-Rassemblement pour la République (TH-RPR) (People's Front-Rally for the Republic) won the Territorial Assembly elections.
1987 Following accusations of misappropriation of public funds, Flosse resigned as president.
1990 Aamendments to the constitution, augmented the president's and the Territorial Assembly's powers.
1996 Flosse was re-elected president. France ended nuclear testing. The French government relinquished control of all territory affairs except for defence, law enforcement, the judiciary and the local currency.
2002 An appeal court in Paris dismissed fraud accusations against President Flosse.
2004 President Jacques Chirac dissolved the Territorial Assembly as France changed French Polynesia's status to POM. In June, Oscar Temaru (UPLD) (Union for Democracy) was elected president of the new assembly. In October Temaru was ousted by Flosse (TH-RPR).
2005 Thirty seven seats in the May 2004 election were invalidated and by-elections were held in Tahiti and Moorea on 13 February. The final result of the assembly election was: 27 seats for the UPLD, 27 for the TH-RPR and three for the Alliance pour la Démocratie Nouvelle (ADN) (Alliance for a New Democracy). On 19 February, President Flosse (TH-RPR) was ousted in a no confidence vote. On 3 March, Oscar Temaru (UPLD), leader of the pro-independence movement and supported by the ADN, was elected president. Anne Boquet was appointed High Commissioner, taking up the post in September.

Political structure
Constitution
In 1996, the French government relinquished control over all the territory's affairs except for defence, foreign affairs, law enforcement, the justice system and the local currency. France is represented by a high commissioner who has a supervisory role. The territory is represented in the French Parliament by two deputies and a senator; it is due to get an extra senator following the 2007 elections.
The French Polynesian government has control over the territory's more than three million square kilometres of sea, as well as shipping, civil aviation, work permits, mineral exploration, foreign investment and local economic affairs. Under the Statute of Autonomy, French Polynesia has full control over its Exclusive Economic Zone.
In 2004, France approved a level of increased autonomy for French Polynesia that changed the region's political status from Térritoire d'Outre-Mer (TOM) (Overseas Territory) to a Pays d'Outre-Mer (Overseas Country). With the implementation of the 2004 statute the Assembly of French Polynesia will have 57 members instead of 49. There will also be six constituencies instead of five.
Under the 2004 autonomy law, the electoral list gaining the most votes in the elections wins a bonus of extra seats, amounting to a third of the seats in the local parliament.
Form of state
Autonomous Pays d'Outre-Mer (Overseas Country) of France

KEY FACTS

Official name: Territoire de la Polynésie Française (Territory of French Polynesia)

Head of State: President of France (Jacques Chirac), represented by High Commissioner Anne Boquet (from Sep 2005)

Head of government: President of the Territorial Government Oscar Temaru (UPLD) (elected 3 Mar 2005)

Ruling party: Union pour la Démocratie (UPLD)(Union for Democracy)

Area: 3,600 square km (35 islands and 83 atolls)

Population: 259,900 (2004)

Capital: Papeete (on Tahiti)

Official language: French and Reo Maohi (Tahitian)

Currency: Comptoirs Français du Pacifique franc (CFPf) = 100 centimes

Exchange rate: CFPf98.91 per US$ (Oct 2005); (pegged CFPf119.25 per euro)

GDP per capita: US$5,000 (2003)

GDP real growth: 4.00% (2003)

Labour force: 70,000 (2003)

Unemployment: 11.80% (2003)

Inflation: 1.50% (2003)

Balance of trade: -US$940.00 million (2003)

Visitor numbers: 212,767 (2003)

Nations of the World: A Political, Economic and Business Handbook

National legislature
The president of the council of ministers is elected by the 57-member Assemblée de la Polynésie Française (Assembly of French Polynesia) (Territorial Assembly), itself elected by proportional representation for a five-year term.

Last elections
3 March 2005 (President of the Territorial Assembly); 13 February 2005 (Territorial Assembly re-run); 23 May 2004 (Territorial Assembly).
Results: President of the Territorial Assembly: Oscar Temaru (UPLD) was elected with 29 votes out of 57 against 26 for Gaston Tong Sang from the Tahoeraa Huiraatira (TH) party.
Parliamentary: by-elections were held in Tahiti and Moorea after the previous election of 23 May 2004 was invalidated (37 seats out of the total 57).
Oscar Temaru's Union pour la Démocratie (UPLD) (Union for Democracy) won 46.9 per cent of the vote (25 seats), the ruling Tahoeraa Huiraatira-Rassemblement pour la République (TH-RPR) (People's Front-Rally for the Republic) of President Gaston Flosse 40 per cent (10) and the Alliance pour la Démocratie Nouvelle (ADN) (Alliance for a New Democracy) 10.6 per cent (two). Turnout was 79.8 per cent. The final result was: 27 seats for the UPLD, 27 for the TH-RPR, and three for the ADN.

Next elections
2010 (Territorial Assembly)

Political parties
Ruling party
Union pour la Démocratie (UPLD)(Union for Democracy)
Main opposition party
Tahoeraa Huiraatira-Rassemblement pour la République (TH-RPR) (People's Front-Rally for the Republic)

Political situation
The May 2004 general election for the assembly was a close-run competition. The ruling TH-RPR with only 28 seats did not reach the 29 needed for a majority, and the leading coalition parties, Union of Democracy, managed only 27 seats. While the leader of the pro-independence alliance, Oscar Temaru, held serious discussions with potential coalition partners, Gaston Flosse, the ex-president, attempted to have the results overturned through the courts. When this failed, Flosse appealed to the French Council of Paris to annul the election of office holders within the assembly, and halt the election for president. Not only did he fail, but by the time the debate and vote for president was under way he had lost his chance to put himself forward as a candidate.
With the votes of two independent assembly members and one from the TH-RPR, who crossed the floor, Temaru won by 30 votes to 27.
One of the first actions of the new president was a trip to France to see the minister responsible for POMs, Brigitte Girardin, to discuss the long term medical and environmental repercussions of the French nuclear testing on the Moruroa and Fangataufa atolls.

Population
259,900 (2004)
Ethnic make-up
Polynesian (78 per cent), Chinese (12 per cent), local French (6 per cent), metropolitan French (4 per cent).
Religions
Protestant (54 per cent), Roman Catholic (30 per cent), other (16 per cent).

Education
Enrolment rate: 116 per cent gross primary enrolment, of relevant age groups, (including repeaters) (World Bank).

Health
Life expectancy: 73.9 years
Fertility rate/Maternal mortality rate: 2.5 births per woman
Birth rate/Death rate: 18 births per 1,000 population; 4.5 deaths per 1,000 population.
Infant mortality rate: Nine deaths per 1,000 live births

Main cities
Papeete (capital, on Tahiti, estimated population 30,200 in 2003), Faa'a (on Tahiti, 30,600).

Languages spoken
English is spoken, especially in tourist and business circles.
Official language/s
French and Reo Maohi (Tahitian)

Media
Press
Dailies: There are are two daily newspapers in French *La Dépêche de Tahiti* (Tahiti's largest newspaper) and *Les Nouvelles de Tahiti*.
Weeklies: Weeklies include *Tahiti Sun Press* (in English), *La Tribune Polynesienne* (French) and *Tahiti Rama*.
Periodicals: Periodicals include *Les Cyber-Grognards* and a monthly publication *Tahiti-Pacifique Magazine*. *Tahiti Live* is an internet magazine (www.tahitilive.pf).
Broadcasting
Radio: In addition to the government-operated service, there are 10 private radio stations, including Radio Te Reo Tefana which broadcasts in Tahitian.
Television: The government operates a television service with two channels.
Advertising
Advertising is available in local newspapers. Correspondence and trade literature should be in French.

Economy
The main source of revenue is financial transfers from France, which represent 30 per cent of GDP.
A high proportion of the workforce is either employed by the military or supports the tourist industry, which is a change from the subsistence agricultural economy that it used to be. This is due to France stationing military personnel in the region since 1962. However, after French nuclear testing ended in 1996, the military contribution to the economy fell sharply. France agreed to contribute funds as compensation for a limited period, but has since agreed to make these payments for an indefinite period.
Aside from tourism and black pearls, the economy is based on smallholders growing fruit and vegetables and plantations providing copra and coconut oil for export.
The fisheries sector is growing. Deep-sea resources (mainly tuna) are fished mainly by Asian fleets under licence. French Polynesia owns the Pacific's largest exclusive economic zone.
Development of the remote archipelagos (Marquesas, Australs, Tuamotu and Gambiers) has begun with the

KEY INDICATORS — French Polynesia

	Unit	2000	2001	2002	2003	2004
Population	m	0.23	0.24	0.24	0.24	0.26
Gross domestic product (GDP)	US$bn	1.13	1.26	1.30	1.30	–
GDP per capita	US$	4,900	4,999	5,000	5,000	–
GDP real growth	%	4.0	2.5	–	4.0	–
Inflation	%	1.0	1.0	–	1.5	–
Exports (fob) (goods)	US$m	260.0	225.0	184.0	260.0	–
Imports (fob) (goods)	US$m	1,200.0	1,217.0	1,276.0	1,200.0	–
Balance of trade	US$m	-940.0	-992.0	-1,092.0	-940.0	–
Exchange rate	per US$	117.54	128.58	125.11	107.01	96.04

French Polynesia

construction of more airstrips and roads and improved port facilities and public services.

Development agreements with France have in particular strengthened social services and have helped create new businesses.

An objective for the government is a steady increase in the proportion of income generated in French Polynesia. The 2004 budget of CFPf164.30 billion (US$1.60 billion) focussed on economic development projects, social services, such as housing, employment and health, and local infrastructure. A new tax on fuel imports is to help fund an increase in old age pensions.

External trade
Imports
Main imports are fuels, foodstuffs, machinery and equipment.

Main sources: France (47.6 per cent total, 2004), New Zealand (8.6 per cent), Singapore (8.4 per cent), Australia (8.4 per cent), US (7.0 per cent)

Exports
Typically, the main exports are black pearls (90 per cent of total exports), coconut oil and its derivatives, copra, beer, vanilla, fish and shark meat.

Main destinations: France (41.2 per cent total, 2004), Japan (25.5 per cent), US (18.3 per cent), Thailand (4.6 per cent)

Agriculture
Farming
Accounts for 4 per cent of GDP and employs 13 per cent of the workforce. Its development is a central plank of government policy. Primary products are copra, vanilla, mother-of-pearl shells, taro and cultured pearls.

Weather permitting, local production supplies over 60 per cent of overall demand for some vegetables.

Local production supplies about 28 per cent of demand for dairy products and 83–87 per cent of demand for pork. Fruit is produced for export, for fruit juice factories, and for the local market.

Crop production in 2004 included: 88,000 tonnes (t) coconuts, 6,000t cassava, 11,440t oilcrops, 3,200t sugar cane, 3,500t pineapples, 1,150t citrus fruit, 900t potatoes, 7,210t vegetables in total, 7,620t fruit in total, 12,400t roots & tubers, 35t vanilla. Livestock production included: 1,921t meat in total, 200t beef, 950t pig meat, 78t goat and lamb, 693t poultry, 1,685t eggs, 1,200t milk, and 32t honey.

Fishing
Green mussel, prawn, live bait and freshwater shrimp aquaculture are under development. The fishing industry, in particular tuna, is growing. Typically, the annual catch is over 500,000mt including both fish and other seafood. The government aims to increase its commercial tuna-fishing fleet to around 150 vessels, which are to be built locally and overseas. Ship-building businesses in China and Fiji will probably be the main constructors.

Pearl farming is the second most important economic activity, after tourism, with over 800,000 harvested annually. Black pearls are the main merchandise export. They are mainly shipped to Japan and US.

Forestry
Although 70 per cent of the islands' land area is covered in forest, conditions limit exploitation to random felling, and almost all timber is imported. Plantations will yield productive forest of 11,250 hectares (ha) of Caribbean pine by 2025; 30ha of wood for local cabinet-making is planted per year.

Industry and manufacturing
The small manufacturing sector primarily processes agricultural products. It accounts for approximately 18 per cent of GDP and employs 19 per cent of the workforce.

The oil mill, Huilerie de Tahiti, purchases all copra produced and processes it into coconut oil and meal (for animal feed), soap-making and monoi (scented coconut oil). Other industries include breweries, soft drinks and fruit juice factories and power station. Several small concerns produce textiles and handicrafts.

Tourism
Tourism is the most important economic activity, accounting for a quarter of GDP, and is the primary earner of foreign income.

Visitor figures fell from around 250,000 in 2000 to 228,000 in 2001 and still further in 2002 as a consequence of the terrorist attacks of 11 September 2001 in the US. Recovery began in 2003, when 212,767 arrivals were recorded, a 13 per cent increase on the previous year. An increase in cruise ship passengers has contributed to the improvement and the authorities are actively encouraging cruise visits.

Mining
Reserves of phosphate are present but not exploited.

Hydrocarbons
French Polynesia does not produce oil, gas or coal. It relies on imports to meet its oil needs.

Energy
Solar energy is much used as a power source.

Banking and insurance
Although banking facilities in the principal urban centres are good, and include ATMs, financial service providers are scarce on some of the outlying islands.

Central bank
The Paris-based Institut d'Emission d'Outre-Mer (IEOM) provides all central banking services except foreign exchange reserves.

Time
GMT minus 10 hours

Geography
French Polynesia comprises several scattered groups of islands (120 islands in total) in the south Pacific Ocean, lying about halfway between South America and Australia. The Cook Islands are to the west and the Line Islands (part of Kiribati) to the north-west. The island groups in French Polynesia include the Iles du Vent (including the islands of Tahiti and Moorea) and the Iles Sous le Vent (about 160km north-west of Tahiti), which together constitute the Society Archipelago; the Tuamotu Archipelago which comprises 78 islands scattered east of the Society Archipelago in a line stretching north-west to south-east for about 1,500km; the Gambier Islands located 1,600km south-east of Tahiti; the Austral Islands lying 640km south of Tahiti; and the Marquesas Archipelago, 1,450km north-east of Tahiti.

Climate
French Polynesia is located in the tropical zone of the southern hemisphere. It has two seasons: warm and moist (Dec–Feb) average temperature 27 degrees Celsius (C); cool and dry (Mar–Nov), average temperature 21 degrees C. Rainfall varies, depending on relief of island and exposure to prevailing winds, but heaviest Nov–Mar. Most islands are mountainous (volcanic) and ringed with coral reefs; the Tuamotu and Gambier groups are mainly low-lying atolls.

Entry requirements
Passports
Required by all.
Visa
Required by all, except citizens of EU, North America, Australasia and Japan, for stays up to one month; this includes business trips by representatives of foreign entities with an invitation from a local company or organisation. Proof of adequate funds for stay, an itinerary, a guarantee of repatriation if necessary and return/onward ticket are also required. For further exceptions, full details and a copy of the application form visit www.diplomatie.gouv.fr/thema/dossier.gb.asp and select 'Entering France'.
Currency advice/regulations
Customs
Personal effects allowed duty-free. All baggage coming in from Fiji and Samoa, except hand luggage, is fumigated.

Travellers should carry clothing and toilet articles for an overnight stay in their hand luggage and arrange for their hotel to collect other baggage from the airport after fumigation.

Prohibited imports
Import of some plants, fruit, household pets, dangerous goods and drugs prohibited.

Health (for visitors)
Mandatory precautions
Vaccination certificate for yellow fever if travelling from an infected area.

Advisable precautions
Vaccination for diphtheria, tuberculosis, hepatitis 'A' and 'B', polio, tetanus, typhoid are recommended. There is a rabies risk.

Credit cards
American Express, Diners' Club, Master Card and Visa accepted throughout Tahiti.

Public holidays
Fixed dates
1 Jan (New Year's Day), 5 Mar (Gospel Day), 1 May (Labour Day), 8 May (Victory Day), 29 Jun (Internal Autonomy Day), 14 Jul (Bastille Day), 15 Aug (Assumption Day), 1 Nov (All Saints' Day), 11 Nov (Armistice Day), 25 Dec (Christmas Day).

Variable dates
Good Friday, Easter Monday, Ascension Day, Whit Monday.

Working hours
Banking
Mon–Fri: 0800–1530.
Business
Mon–Fri: 0800–1200, 1330–1730; Sat: 0800–1200.
Government
Mon–Fri: 0800–1200, 1330–1730; Sat: 0800–1200.
Shops
Mon–Fri: 0730–1130, 1400–1700; Sat: 0730–1130.

Telecommunications
Telephone/fax
Tahiti has an automatic telephone network, and the manual inter-island services are gradually being adapted to automatic.

Electricity supply
220V AC, 60 cycles (check with hotel before using appliances).

Weights and measures
Metric system

Social customs/useful tips
Tipping is not customary, and is contrary to traditional Tahitian hospitality.

Getting there
Air
National airline: Air Tahiti Nui is owned by the territorial government, the Tahiti Visitors' Bureau, the domestic airline, Air Tahiti, and private investors.

International airport/s: Papeete International de Tahiti-Faa'a (PPT), 6km from Papeete; restaurant, bank and car hire.
Airport tax: None.

Surface
Main port/s: Papeete (harbour installations can accommodate ships up to 35,000 tonnes).

Getting about
National transport
Air: Over 25 airfields in addition to Papeete International de Tahiti-Faa'a and some 45 small aircraft for local travel. Inter-island baggage limit is 10kg. Air Tahiti operates scheduled flights to Moorea, Huahine, Raiatea, Bora-Bora, Maupiti, Rangiroa, Manihi, Takapoto, Tubuai, Nuku-Hiva (Marquesas), Ua Huka, Hiva Oa, Ua Pou, Anaa, Makemo, Hao, Rurutu and Mangareva (Gambiers) and several other atolls. Air Moorea operates daily services between Tahiti and Moorea. Both airlines also offer air taxi services, charters, circle island flights and transportation to other islands. Other air operators include Tahiti Conquest Airlines (TCA), Tahiti Helicopters and Pacific Helicopter Services.

Road: There are approximately 200km of road on Tahiti, including a circular 120km asphalt road around the main part of the island, and 100km of road on Moorea.

Buses: 'Le Truck' runs an unscheduled transport service between Papeete and outlying districts, leaving approximately every half hour for nearby areas and daily for distant points.

Water: There is a scheduled boat service between Papeete and Moorea.

City transport
Taxis: Fares are controlled and should be displayed in each cab. In Tahiti, fares double between 2300 and 0500. Information on fares is available at GIE Tahiti Tourisme at the airport and in Papeete. The journey time from the airport to the city centre is 10 minutes.

Buses, trams & metro: Airport to city centre bus service operates 0400–2359 hours, every 15 minutes.

Car hire
There are numerous car hire establishments; rates include insurance. Drivers must hold a licence valid for at least one year and must be at least 21-years-old. Driving is on the right-hand side of the road.

BUSINESS DIRECTORY

The addresses listed below are a selection only. While World of Information makes every endeavour to check these addresses, we cannot guarantee that changes have not been made, especially to telephone numbers and area codes. We would welcome any corrections.

Telephone area codes
The international dialling code (IDD) for French Polynesia is + 689 followed by subscriber's number.

Useful telephone numbers
Police: 17
Fire: 18

Chambers of Commerce
French Polynesia Chamber of Commerce and Industry, PO Box 118, Rue Docteur Cassiau, 98713 Papeete (tel: 540-700; fax: 540-701).

Banking
Banque de Polynésie SA, PO Box 530, 355 Boulevard Pomare, Papeete (tel: 466-666; fax: 466-664).

Banque de Tahiti SA, PO Box 1602, Rue Cardella, Papeete (tel: 417-000; fax: 423-376).

Banque Socredo, PO Box 130, 115 rue Dumont d'Urville, Papeete (tel: 415-123; fax 433-661).

Central bank
Institut d'Emission d'Outre-Mer (IEOM), 5 rue Roland Barthes, 75598 Paris Cedex 12, France (tel : +33 1 5344-4141; fax : +33 1 4347-5134; e-mail: contact@ieom.fr).

Travel information
Air Moorea, BP 6019, Papeete (tel: 424-834).

Air Tahiti Nai, Blvd Pomare, BP 314, Papeete (tel: 422-333).

Service Territorial du Tourisme, BP 65 Papeete (tel: 505-700; fax: 481-275).

National tourist organisation offices
GIE Tahiti Tourisme, BP 65 Papeete (tel: 505-700; fax: 436-619; e-mail: tahiti-tourisme@mail.pf; internet site: http://www.tahiti-tourisme.com).

Other useful addresses
Institut Territorial de la Statistique, BP 395, Papeete, Tahiti (tel: 437-196; fax: 427-252).

Service des Affaires Economiques, BP 82, Papeete, Tahiti.

Syndicat des Importateurs et des Négociants, PO Box 1607, Papeete, Tahiti.

Syndicat d'Initiative de la Polynésie Française, BP 326, Papeete.

Internet sites
Tourism Council of the South Pacific: http://www.infocentre.com/spt.

Enterprise and development agency (in French): http://www.creation-entreprises.pf/

Gabon

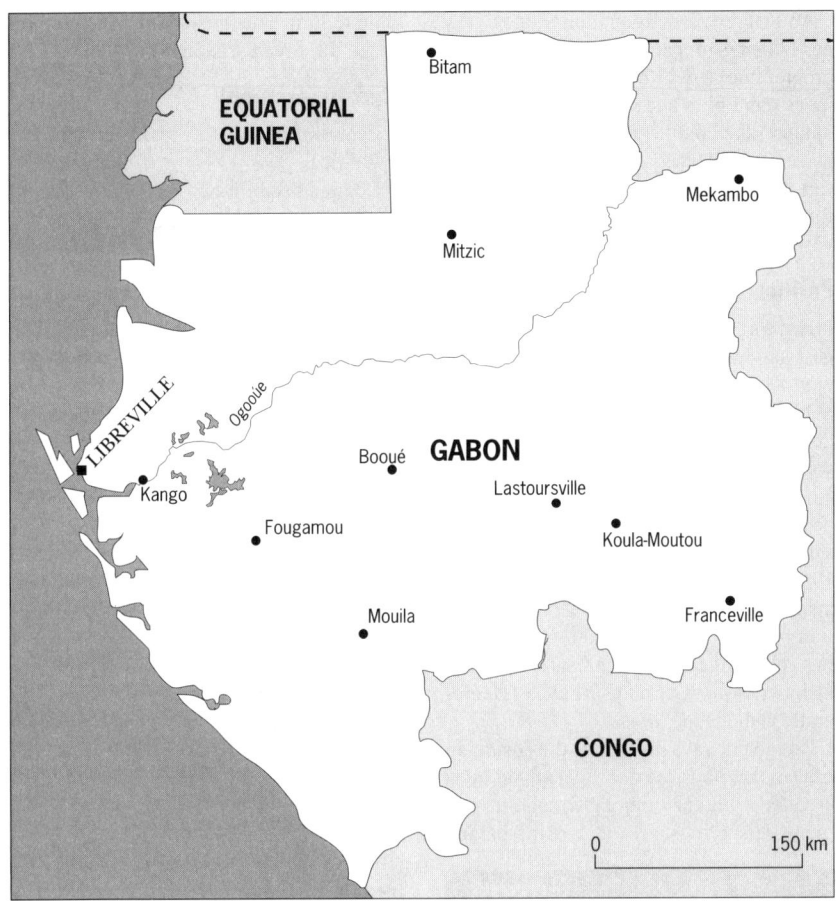

Gabon has one of Africa's highest incomes per capita – estimated at US$5,469 in 2004, it is well above the Sub-Saharan African average. Despite being made up of more than 40 ethnic groups, Gabon has escaped the strife afflicting many other West African states. Helping to maintain the stability of the country are French troops, deployed in 1964 after France reinstated President Leon M'ba after he had been overthrown in a coup. He gave way peacefully to Omar Bongo three years later.

Economy

Its wealth is due to oil. When oil prices began to fall in the late 1980s, opposition to incumbent President Omar Bongo increased, culminating in demonstrations in 1990. These ushered in political liberalisation, and in 1991 a new multi-party system. Bongo is still president. There is no constitutional restriction on how long he may serve. Despite these political conditions, a small population, abundant natural resources and considerable foreign support have helped make Gabon one of the more prosperous and stable African countries. It has maintained and conserved its pristine rain forest and rich biodiversity.

Despite the abundance of natural wealth, poor fiscal management hobbles the economy. The International Monetary Fund (IMF) has criticised the government for overspending on off-budget items, over borrowing from the central bank, and slipping on its schedule for privatisation and administrative reform. Nevertheless, the IMF provided a one-year stand-by

KEY FACTS

Official name: République Gabonaise (Gabonese Republic)

Head of State: President El Hadj Omar Bongo (PDG) (since 1967; re-elected 27 November 2005)

Head of government: Prime Minister Jean-François Ntoutoume-Emane (PDG) (since Jan 1999)

Ruling party: Parti Démocratique Gabonais (PDG) (Gabonese Democratic Party) (since 1960; in 2002, the PDG formed a coalition government with the opposition, the Rassemblement National des Bûcherons/Rassemblement pour le Gabon (RNB/RPG) (National Rally of Lumberjacks/Rally for Gabon)

Area: 267,667 square km

Population: 1.38 million (2004)

Capital: Libreville

Official language: French

Currency: CFA franc (CFAf) = 100 centimes (Communauté Financière Africaine (African Financial Community) franc)

Exchange rate: CFAf544.07 per US$ (Oct 2005); CFAf655.96 per euro (pegged from Jan 1999)

GDP per capita: US$5,469 (2004)

GDP real growth: 1.90% (2004)

Labour force: 607,000 (2004)

Inflation: 1.00% (2004)

Oil production: 235,000 bpd (2004)

Balance of trade: US$2.48 billion (2004)

Foreign debt: US$3.80 billion (2004)

arrangement in 1994–95, a three-year Enhanced Financing Facility at near commercial rates in late 1995, and stand-by credit of US$119 million in 2000. France provided additional financial support.

In 2004, Gabon signed a further US$105 million stand-by arrangement with the IMF and received Paris Club debt rescheduling later that year. However, Gabon's balance of payments has so improved that the 2005 disbursement of US$21 million was held back.

Fiscal discipline resulting from improved tax collection and strict expenditure control has helped to restore macroeconomic stability. Important structural reforms which could form the basis for the economic diversification needed to ensure long-term sustainable growth, have been launched.

Challenges

Looking ahead, significant challenges remain to reduce Gabon's dependence on oil, diversify the economy, and make decisive progress in poverty reduction. Multilateral donors are working with the government to direct Gabon's resources towards poverty alleviation, improved social outcomes, and better governance. Some progress has been made in terms of human development. For example, life expectancy remains relatively high (for Africa) at 56.6 years, while infant mortality remains low at 60 per 1,000, down from 88 in 1985, and 86 per cent of the population has access to safe water.

There will have to be sustained efforts to bolster non-oil revenue and improve the efficiency of public spending. By using the bulk of windfall oil revenues in the coming years to reduce domestic and external debt Gabon has the opportunity to place its public finances on a permanently sounder footing. At the same time, continued macroeconomic discipline needs to be accompanied by reinvigorating the structural reform process to accelerate the diversification of Gabon's economy and boost growth and employment in the non-oil sector.

An IMF Poverty Reduction Strategy Paper is being prepared for a medium-term programme. It will be a three-year public investment plan and reflected in the 2006 budget. The public expenditure reviews currently underway will assist in this effort. Gabon will almost certainly seek a further, but longer, stand-by arrangement with the IMF.

Politics

President Omar Bongo is Africa's longest-serving head of state, one of the world's longest serving leaders. He has led Gabon since he succeeded the post-independence leader Leon M'ba in 1967. He was re-elected for a further seven years in November 2005, receiving almost 80 per cent of the votes. International observers said the poll was largely free and fair. In 1968 he declared Gabon a one-party state, a status which it kept until 1991. Opposition parties have yet failed to pose a serious challenge to the president's Parti Démocratique Gabonois (PDG) (Democratic Gabonese Party).

Bongo portrays himself as the custodian of Gabon's political stability and has been credited with encouraging foreign investment. His critics accuse him of having authoritarian tendencies. Born in Franceville in 1935 as Albert-Bernard, Bongo served in the French air force from 1958 until independence, when he returned to join the foreign ministry. In 1973 he converted to Islam, assuming the name of Omar.

The Gabonese president appoints the country's prime minister, who is answerable to him. The president has the authority to dissolve parliament.

Risk assessment

Economic	Deteriorating
Political	Poor/stable
Regional stability	Average

COUNTRY PROFILE

Historical profile

Gabon's capital city, Libreville, (Freetown in translation) was founded as a settlement for freed slaves. The city is located on the site of a fort built in 1843 after a French officer succeeded in signing treaties with two local chiefs known as 'King' Denis and 'King' Louis. Libreville was later used as a base by another French officer, Pierre Savorgnan de Brazza, who set off in 1879 to spread French influence into the Congo.

The French government named a governor for Gabon in 1886 and two years later Libreville became the capital of the French Congo. In 1904 the capital was transferred to Brazzaville and Gabon became a colony in French Equatorial Africa in 1910. The northern part of the country, which was ceded to the Germans in the Cameroon in 1911, was recovered at the end of the First World War in 1918.

The region that is now Gabon was inhabited by the Omiéné by the sixteenth century. They were outnumbered by the Fang by the eighteenth century. Between the sixteenth and eighteenth centuries, Gabon was part of the Loango empire, which stretched from the Ogooué river to the Congo river.

1472 Portuguese navigators arrived in the Ogooué estuary and Gabon soon became an important centre for slave trading for the Portuguese, Dutch, British and French.

1839 Having gained a dominant position in the area and despite Fang resistance, Gabon became part of the French Congo. The French began work to abolish the slave trade.

1910 Gabon became part of French Equatorial Africa.

1939–1945 Gabon was held by the Free French.

1946 Gabon became a province of French Equatorial Africa. In gratitude for the support of the local population for the

KEY INDICATORS — Gabon

	Unit	2000	2001	2002	2003	2004
Population	m	1.21	1.30	1.33	1.36	1.38
Gross domestic product (GDP)	US$bn	4.90	4.30	5.00	5.64	*7.23
GDP per capita	US$	3,451	3,023	3,800	4,167	5,469
GDP real growth	%	-1.9	2.0	-0.1	2.6	1.9
Inflation	%	0.4	2.1	0.2	2.1	1.0
Oil output	'000 bpd	301.0	301.0	295.0	240.0	235.0
Exports (fob) (goods)	US$m	2,750.0	2,897.0	3,080.0	3,278.0	3,710.0
Imports (fob) (goods)	US$m	1,100.0	1,197.0	1,270.0	1,345.0	1,225.0
Balance of trade	US$m	1,612.0	1,700.0	1,800.0	1,933.0	2,485.0
Current account	US$m	1,000.0	520.0	260.0	580.0	750.0
Foreign debt	US$bn	3.3	3.8	3.8	3.8	3.8
Total reserves minus gold	US$m	190.1	9.8	139.7	196.6	443.4
Foreign exchange	US$m	189.8	9.6	139.4	196.3	436.9
Exchange rate	per US$	711.98	733.04	683.75	574.89	496.63

* estimated figure

Gabon

Free French, President Charles de Gaulle of France granted French citizenship to all the territory's people.
1957 Gabon gained internal autonomy.
1958 It achieved self-government within the French community.
1960 Gained full independence from France, under President Léon M'Ba. The Parti Démocratique Gabonais (PDG) (Gabonese Democratic Party) assumed power.
1964 French forces restored M'Ba to the presidency after an abortive military coup d'état.
1967 President M'Ba died. Vice President Albert-Bernard Bongo became president.
1973 Bongo was re-elected and converted to Islam, adopting the forename Omar.
1981–89 Political unrest grows as people call for more democracy.
1990 After demonstrations by students and strikes by workers, President Bongo legalised opposition parties.
1991 A new constitution was introduced that formalised the multi-party system.
1993 Bongo narrowly won the presidential election, although the opposition claimed massive electoral fraud.
1996 Parliamentary elections gave the PDG an overwhelming majority.
1998 President Bongo won another seven years in power with more than two-thirds of the vote.
1999 The country was plunged into a deep recession due to the fall in the world price of oil.
2001 The PDG won the parliamentary elections.
2002 The PDG formed a coalition with the opposition to form the government.
2003 Constitutional changes made in July allow presidents to run for office unlimited times.
2004 Gabon signed separate agreements to export around one billion tonnes of iron ore as well as oil to China.
2005 Presidential elections were held on 27 November, with military personnel voting two days earlier. Opposition candidates claimed this measure allowed vote rigging to take place. Incumbent El Hadj Omar Bongo Ondimba won 79.2 per cent of the presidential vote; Pierre Mamboundou 13.6 per cent and Zacharie Myboto 6.6 per cent. Turnout was 63.3 per cent.
2006 Omar Bongo was sworn in as president for a third seven-year term on 19 January. He has been in power for 38 years.

Political structure
Constitution
In 1991 a new constitution was introduced which restored multi-party elections and protected civil liberties. The constitution maintained a strong presidential role but allowed for a more influential prime minister.
In July 2003, the constitution was changed to allow presidents to run for office for unlimited number of times, and the number of presidential election rounds was reduced from two to one.

Form of state
Presidential democracy

The executive
Executive power is divided between the president, elected by universal suffrage every seven years, and the prime minister and Council of Ministers (Cabinet) who are appointed by the president.
Government members must be more than 35 years of age and have at least seven years' professional experience.
The president is head of state, head of administration and chief of the armed forces.

National legislature
Legislative power is vested in the 120-member Assemblée Nationale (National Assembly), with 111 members elected for five-year terms in single-seat constituencies and nine members appointed by the president.
Members of the 91-seat Sénat (Senate) are elected for six year terms by local and departmental councillors.

Legal system
The legal system is based on the French civil law system and customary law. There is judicial review of legislative acts in the Constitutional Chamber of the Supreme Court.

Last elections
9/24 December 2001 (National Assembly); 27 November 2005 (presidential).
Results: Parliamentary: the PDG won 53 out of 120 seats; in 2002, the PDG formed a coalition government with the opposition, the RNB/RPG.
Presidential: incumbent El Hadj Omar Bongo Ondimba won 79.2 per cent of the vote; Pierre Mamboundou 13.6 per cent and Zacharie Myboto 6.6 per cent. Turnout was 63.3 per cent.

Next elections
2006 (National Assembly); 2012 (presidential).

Political parties
Ruling party
Parti Démocratique Gabonais (PDG) (Gabonese Democratic Party) (since 1960; in 2002, the PDG formed a coalition government with the opposition, the Rassemblement National des Bûcherons/Rassemblement pour le Gabon (RNB/RPG) (National Rally of Lumberjacks/Rally for Gabon)

Population
1.38 million (2004)

Ethnic make-up
There are some 40 different ethnic groups, of which the Fangs are the largest (40 per cent of the total); the Bapounous (20 per cent) are also highly significant. There are some 25,000 Europeans, mainly of French nationality.

Religions
Christianity (59 per cent), mostly Roman Catholic; indigenous animist beliefs (40 per cent). There is a small Muslim community (less than 1 per cent).

Education
School is compulsory and free for all children up to the age of 16 years. Secondary education covers seven years, divided into a lower cycle lasting four years and an upper cycle lasting three years. On completion of the upper cycle, pupils take the examinations for the *Baccalauréat* for advancement to university. On completion of the lower cycle, pupils may opt to take a 'short' or a 'long' course of technical secondary education. The former leads to the *Brevet de Technicien* and the latter to the *Baccalauréat technique*.
Two universities – Omar Bongo University and the University of Science and Technology of Masuku (USTM at Franceville) – as well as various independent institutions provide higher education. Universities enjoy a certain degree of autonomy, even though higher education is financed exclusively by public funds.
Public expenditure on education typically amounts to 2.5 per cent of annual GDP.
Literacy rate: 79.8 per cent, male; 62.2 per cent, female; adult rates (World Bank).
Enrolment rate: 62 per cent total primary school enrolment of the relevant age group (World Bank).
Pupils per teacher: 56 in primary schools.

Health
Annual total expenditure on health is around 3–4 per cent of GDP, of which approximately 48 per cent is government spending.
Gabon is plagued by poor health conditions, which are aggravated by the hot and humid climate and is the country worst affected by malaria in sub-Saharan Africa.
Gabon faces a growing crisis of male impotence affecting 25 per cent of all adult men, blamed on high levels of alcohol and tobacco use.

HIV/Aids
HIV/Aids is a rapidly growing crisis the World Health Organisation (WHO) estimates that 30,000 people in Gabon are being infected with HIV each year and Gabon is beginning to experience the serious effects of the African pandemic. Around 8,600 children have been

orphaned by the disease. The main concentration of HIV/Aids cases is in the capital, Libreville. The government has launched a campaign to prevent the disease spreading further.
HIV prevalence: 8.1 per cent aged 15–49 in 2003 (World Bank)
Life expectancy: 53.0 years (World Bank)
Fertility rate/Maternal mortality rate: 4.0 births per woman; maternal mortality 600 per 100,000 live births (World Bank).
Birth rate/Death rate: 16 deaths to 36 births per 1,000 population,
Infant mortality rate: 60 per 1,000 live births (World Bank)

Welfare
Gabon's social welfare system, while deeply flawed, is one of the best in sub-Saharan Africa. It operates a social insurance system and healthcare system through separate funds administered by the National Social Security Fund (CNSS) and National Social Guarantee Fund (CNGS) for self-employed and state workers under contract through a pay-as-you-go system. As these funds have experienced financial difficulties and the government has undertaken to restructure them with a view to their long-term viability. Inadequate contributions have been blamed for the over-spending.

The social insurance system covers benefits including old age, disability, sickness, maternity and work injuries with provision for certain categories of self-employed workers. Old age pensions are available to men aged 55 with 20 years of insurance and 120 months of contribution during the last 10 years. It is set at a minimum of 40 per cent of average earnings during the last three or five years of pay. There is also provision for old-age settlement with a lump sum equal to 50 per cent of average monthly earnings for every six months of contribution, if the person is ineligible for pension.

Medical services are provided by hospitals and dispensaries operated by the CNSS, and by other establishments. Free maternity care is payable up to six weeks before, and eight weeks after, confinement. A family allowance law also offers benefits to employees with one or more children under the age of 16 years. Family Allowance Benefits provide a month income for each child and a year school allowances for primary, secondary and technical school students.

Main cities
Libreville (capital, estimated population 673,995 in 2004), Port-Gentil (118,940).

Languages spoken
French is used for all documentation. The main native language is Fang, with a number of other Bantu dialects spoken. It is essential that business visitors should be able to conduct business in French. Interpreters can be hired locally.

Official language/s
French

Media
Press
The official news agency is Agence Gabonaise de Presse (AGP).
Dailies: Gabon has two daily newspapers: *L'Union*, which is published by Sonapresse, owned jointly by the state, Sonadig, Multipresse Gabon and France Edition, and *Gabon-Matin*.
Periodicals: *L'Union* also publishes a monthly magazine, with a similar circulation. *M'Bolo* has three issues on holiday and travel.

Broadcasting
Gabon is developing as the centre of Francophone broadcasting for Central and West Africa, being the base of the radio service Africa No 1 and for the African operations of France's Canal Plus. The state has taken a financial interest in these broadcasting media, as well as in the main newspaper, directly and through parastatal groups. It therefore retains a degree of control.
Radio: Gabon is host to the radio service Africa No 1, broadcasting mostly programmes from Radio France Internationale (RFI). Africa No 1, which is 35 per cent state-owned, began transmissions in 1981. Africa No 1 broadcasts news from RFI, Radio Japan and Swiss Radio International to South America, the Middle East, Southern Africa, West Africa, as well as the whole of Central Africa.
Television: Gabon's state broadcaster is Radiodiffusion-Télévision Gabonaise (RTG), known as La Voix de la Rénovation. RTG has two television channels: RTG 1 is a national service, broadcast in Libreville and Franceville; while RTG 2 can be received only in the Libreville and the coastal area.
Téléafrica, a private commercial channel, began transmissions in 1988. Broadcasting 24 hours a day, it prepared the way for the establishment of Canal Plus Gabon, a subscription channel which will eventually serve the whole of Francophone Central Africa.

Advertising
Extremely limited facilities. The only active agency is Havas-Gabon.

Economy
Gabon has garnered criticism from the World Bank and the IMF for poor management of its economy. It is currently sub-Saharan Africa's fourth-largest oil exporter and revenue from oil has kept the economy afloat. Reserves of 39.1 billion barrels are running down with oil production in 2004 at 235,000 barrels per day. Assessing the economy and the end of oil, in a 2005 report, the IMF said that Gabon continues to face a 'lack of economic diversification, and weak non-oil growth'. Public sector employment and wages are considered an important inhibition on entrepreneurial enterprises, which constrains competitiveness in the non-oil tradable sector. Domestic growth in non-oil activities was modest and dependent on primary industries in timber production (around 80 per cent of total non-oil exports) and manganese (15 per cent). Both of these markets are privately exploited, are volatile and subject to external pressures. The agricultural sector remains largely underdeveloped.

The government has persistently failed to meet its privatisation targets. Future IMF assistance will depend on the privatisation of the remaining parastals. These include the agri-industries Agripoand, Agrogabon and Hevegab, the airline Air Gabon, Gabon Telecom and the ports of Owendo and Port Gentil. Privatisation in the telecommunications industry and the national airline have been slow, made more difficult by government mismanagement and corruption.

Gabon's GDP was 7.23 in 2004, and at US$4,469 its per capita GDP was significantly higher than the US$500 average of sub-Saharan Africa. However, income is distributed extremely unevenly with 90 per cent of the country's income and wealth held by 5 per cent of the population. Efforts to alleviate poverty, in partnership with international donors, are taking place.

External trade
Gabon is spearheading moves towards greater regional integration. In 1999, Gabon and five other African states that form the Central African Economic and Monetary Community (CAEMC) had agreed to converge their macroeconomic policies, stabilise their common currency, create a common market and harmonise their sectoral policies.

In 2002, the US approved Gabon as being eligible for tariff preferences under the African Growth and Opportunities Act (AGOA).

Imports
Principal imports are machinery and equipment, foodstuffs, chemicals and construction materials.
Main sources: France (46.1 per cent total, 2004), US (6.8 per cent), UK (6.0 per cent)

Exports
Principal exports are crude oil (77 per cent of total), timber, manganese and uranium

Main destinations: US (51.9 per cent total, 2004), China (9.1 per cent), France (7.7 per cent)

Agriculture

Farming
The agricultural sector in Gabon has been neglected, forcing the importation of a large percentage of the country's food needs. Only about 1 per cent of total land area is under cultivation and agriculture is further limited by the small size of the population. A shortage of cultivated lands has been the major problem facing the agricultural sector which, mostly through subsistence farming, supports a large portion of the population.

Principal cash crops are palm oil, cocoa and refined sugar, while subsistence crops are cassava, maize and plantains. Cocoa is grown mainly in Woleu Ntem province and coffee mainly in Ogooué-Ivindo, Ogooué-Lolo and Haut Ogooué provinces. Sugar cane is grown and refined by the Société Sucrérie du Haut-Ogooué (Sosuho). Annual sugar output is around 30,000 tonnes. Agrogabon set up three cattle ranches in the 1980s, importing tsetse fly-resistant cattle. They are located at Lekabi, Nyanga and N'Gounie. The only industrial-scale poultry farm is run by the Société Industrielle d'Agriculture et d'Elevage de Boumango (SIAEB).

The estimated crop production for 2004 included: 32,000 tonnes (t) cereals in total, 31,000t maize, 230,000t cassava, 155,000t yams, 2,800t sweet potatoes, 600t cocoa beans, 270,000t plantains, 446,800t roots and tubers, 13,118t oilcrops, 11,000t natural rubber, 235,000t sugar cane, 32,000t oil palm fruit, 59,000t taro, 294,000t fruit in total, 35,410t vegetables in total. Estimated livestock production included: 31,716t meat in total, 1,096t beef, 21,000t game meat, 3,080t pig meat, 960t lamb and goat meat, 3,600t poultry, 1,980t eggs, 1,575t milk.

Fishing
Gabon has well-stocked fishing grounds, which are only partially exploited. Domestic demand is estimated at around 36,000 tonnes. The typical annual catch is over 40,000 tonnes. Traditional fishing accounts for two-thirds of national fishing output. There are about a dozen fleets, most of which are foreign, engaged in industrial fishing in Gabonese waters.

Forestry
Exports of forest products amount to around US$320 million annually and timber is a source of employment for nearly a third of the working population outside the public sector. Forests cover almost 85 per cent of the land area, estimated at 21.8 million hectares (ha). Deforestation typically accounts for 0.05 per cent annually average decrease, or the equivalent of 10,000ha of forest cover.

The forestry industry is the second-largest industry in the country. Gabon commercially exploits and exports both soft and hard woods, but cultivation and processing of timber comprises the main portion of forestry activities. The country produces sawn timber, veneers and plywood. Tropical hardwood logs constitute the bulk of its roundwood exports. The potential commercial volume of live trees is estimated at 400 million cubic metres, 130 million of which is the much celebrated ebony gaboon wood.

Gabon is the fifth-largest world producer of timber, behind Finland, Canada, Sweden and New Zealand.

The forest is divided into three administrative zones. The coastal area is already fairly well exploited. The zone around Ngounie, Nyanga and Haut-Ogooué has the bulk of current activity. The Booue-Lastourville axis of the Transgabon railway is largely undeveloped. Seven large companies dominate okoume production. The largest is the majority state-owned Compagnie Forestière du Gabon (CFG).

Okoume, designated as the most important commercial timber, is selectively logged in a significant proportion of the country's forests. Exploitable forest potential is more than 300 million cubic metres. One-third of this is okoume, which is particularly suited to the production of plywood.

Timber production in 2004 included 4,088,000 cubic metre (cum) roundwood, 3,563,000cum industrial roundwood, 231,100cum sawnwood, 3,563,000cum sawlogs and veneer logs, 164,400cum wood-based panels, 525,353cum wood fuel, 17,400t charcoal.

Industry and manufacturing

The main industrial activities are oil refining and timber processing, although these activities are treated separately from other industry in the national accounts. The other main manufacturing sectors are food processing, drinks and tobacco, metal transformation (primarily connected with shipyard activities and supplying the oil and wood industries) and building materials. Small sub sectors include textiles and chemicals (lubricants, paints, varnishes and detergents).

A fair proportion of the very modest industrial sector has been based on a policy of import substitution. This is now being abandoned as part of structural adjustment measures. The outlook for industry is therefore bleak even though there are plans to develop a regional export market within the Union Douanière des Etats de l'Afrique Centrale (UDEAC) (Central African Customs and Economic Union) countries. In theory, this larger potential market would allow industry to develop economies of scale that the small domestic market does not justify. In practice, however, high labour costs are likely to frustrate efforts to promote the regional market. Gabon's labour costs are high due to the well-established social security system, most of the cost of which is borne by employers, offering benefits that are not found in many other West and Central African countries.

Tourism

Gabon receives around 120,000 foreign visitors annually. However, only around 1 per cent are tourists. Nevertheless this growing sector is expected to contribute US$1.5 million in 2005, or 3.3 per cent of GDP.

The ministry of tourism is beginning to market Gabon as an eco-tourist destination. La Lopée Reserve in south-east Gabon, covering 4,940 square km, was the country's first national park. The sector has yet to be fully developed with over US$226 million or 10.1 per cent of total capital investment expected to be spent on travel and tourism in 2005. However, the high local cost of living makes it difficult to compete internationally, even though Gabon has a good hotel infrastructure, marvellous sandy beaches, generally safe bathing and many wildlife attractions. There are about 6,000 hotel beds in the country. Gabon has five game reserves: La Lopée, Mouklaba, Wonga-Wonge, Sette-Cama and Iguela.

Mining

Mining and hydrocarbons together contribute around 50 cent to GDP and employ 10 per cent of the workforce.

Gabon is one of the world's leading producers of manganese and uranium. Other areas of interest are gold and iron ore. Activity is concentrated on extraction and export of manganese ore (reserves of 200 million tonnes) and uranium (reserves of 35,000 tonnes). Both are crudely refined before export, the manganese as a 51 per cent concentrate and the uranium as 74 per cent pure yellow cake. Manganese goes mainly to Europe, but also to the US and the Far East. Uranium goes mainly to France (about 10 per cent of France's requirements), the rest to Belgium and Japan. Manganese and uranium account for 10 per cent of merchandise exports. Manganese production is declining, while large deposits of iron ore, barytes (used in paint-making) and niobium, discovered

during construction of the Transgabon railway, have yet to be exploited.
There are 50 million tonnes of phosphate reserves.

Hydrocarbons

Gabon is sub-Saharan Africa's fourth-largest oil producer, after Nigeria, Angola and Equatorial Guinea. With income from oil exports representing around 40 per cent of GDP and 80 per cent of exports, Gabon's economy is highly dependent on this one commodity. The exports go primarily to Western Europe, although China has imported Gabonese crude for its growing market since February 2004.

In 2004, the proven oil reserves were 2.3 million barrels, with production at 235,000 barrels per day (bpd). Production is falling rapidly from the high of 370,000bpd in 1997.

The World Bank estimates that oil production is likely to decline by 50 per cent by 2007, which will strain government revenues. Exploration and production occurs both onshore and offshore. The country's downstream industry consists of the Sogara refinery, which has a capacity of 21,000bpd.

The government has consistently maintained a market-oriented policy towards its sizeable oil reserves and has one of the most attractive hydrocarbons codes in Africa. Under this law, the state has a minimum 25 per cent holding in all oil-producing companies operating in Gabon. Oil exploration permits are awarded under production-sharing agreements, which are individually negotiated. Natural gas reserves totalled approximately 33.9 billion cubic metres (cum) in 2004, down from 42 billion cum in 2003, with production at around 1 billion cubic metres per annum. All gas produced in Gabon is used for electricity or refinery fuel.

Gabon does not produce or import coal.

Energy

Gabon has a total electricity generating capacity of 300MW, more than two-thirds of which is hydroelectric with the potential of around 6,000MW when fully developed. The largest hydroelectric dams are Tchimbele (69MW) and Kinguele (58MW), on the M'Bei River.

Société d'Energie et d'Eau du Gabon (SEEG) is responsible for the production and distribution of electricity and water throughout the country – 51 per cent was sold to a French consortium in 1997, representing sub-Saharan Africa's first privatisation of a water and electricity utility. Consumption is principally concentrated in the regions of Libreville, Port-Gentil and Franceville.

Banking and insurance
Central bank
Banque des Etats de l'Afrique Centrale
Main financial centre
Libreville

Time
GMT plus one hour

Geography
Gabon is an equatorial country on the west coast of Africa, with Equatorial Guinea and Cameroon to the north, and the Republic of Congo to the south and east.

The eastern boundary lies along the watershed of the Democratic Republic of Congo (DRC), so that all rivers flow broadly west through Gabon into the sea. The sandy coastal strip consists of palm-fringed bays, lagoons and estuaries. The uplands are heavily eroded by river action, and there is a wide coastal plain, which is largely alluvial in nature. The natural vegetation is dense rain forest.

Climate
The climate is equatorial with an annual mean temperature of 28 degrees Celsius and high levels of humidity. The rainy seasons are between October and mid-December, and between mid-January and May. The dry season is from June to September.

Dress codes
Lightweight or tropical clothing is suitable, with rainwear for the monsoon season. Businessmen should wear a lightweight or tropical suit and women a lightweight suit or equivalent.

Entry requirements
Passports
Required by all. Passports must be valid for more than six months.
Visa
Required by all and to be applied for before travelling. Applications for business visas require a letter from the representative's company accepting responsibility for any expenses incurred, a full itinerary and a letter of invitation from a host company in Gabon.
Currency advice/regulations
There are no limits on the import of foreign or domestic currency, although any sum should be declared on arrival. Exports of local currency are controlled and there is a limit of CFAf200,000 for export to countries outside the franc zone. Visitors are advised to carry traveller's cheques in French francs.

Health (for visitors)
Mandatory precautions
A yellow fever vaccination certificate is required.

Advisable precautions
Immunisations are advisable for yellow fever, hepatitis 'A', tetanus, typhoid and polio. There is a rabies risk.

Malaria and Aids are prevalent and standard measures should be taken to avoid these diseases.

Dysentery can be caught from raw fruit and vegetables and unboiled water. Water which is used for drinking, brushing teeth or making ice should first be boiled. Dairy products made from local milk should be avoided. Meat and fish should be well cooked.

Hotels
Available in Libreville, Port Gentil, Lambaréné and other main centres. Service charge is usually included in bill, if not a tip of 10–15 per cent is usual.

Credit cards
Credit cards are not widely accepted.

Public holidays
Fixed dates
1 Jan (New Year's Day), 1 May (Labour Day), 6 May (Martyrs' Day), 15 Aug (Assumption Day), 16 Aug (Independence Day), 1 Nov (All Saints' Day), 25 Dec (Christmas Day).
Variable dates
Easter Monday, Whit Monday, Eid al Adha, Eid al Fitr.

The Islamic year contains 354 or 355 days, with the result that Muslim feasts advance by 10–12 days against the Gregorian calendar. Dates of feasts vary according to the sighting of the new moon, so cannot be forecast exactly.

Working hours
Banking
Mon–Fri: 0730–1130, 1430–1630.
Business
Mon–Fri: 0730–1200, 1430–1800.
Government
Mon–Fri: 0800–1200, 1500–1800; Sat: 0800–1300.
Shops
Mon–Sat: 0800–1200, 1500–1900.

Telecommunications
Telephone/fax
The network has modern and fully automated international exchanges.

Electricity supply
220-30V AC, 50 cycles. Round two-pin plugs are standard.

Social customs/useful tips
Business is conducted in French. Appointments should be made in advance. It is customary to shake hands when meeting and taking leave. Business cards are exchanged after introduction.

Gratuities are between 10–15 per cent if no service charged is included.

Gabon

The lifestyles of the middle classes in Libreville, Port-Gentil and Franceville have been heavily influenced by the French, and French etiquette has been largely adopted. As elsewhere in Africa, it is extremely unwise to attempt to photograph any military installations or troop movements, security checkpoints, etc.

Security
Crime is increasingly a problem with incidents of robbery and armed attacks, particularly around Libreville and Port-Gentil. Avoid carrying valuables or wearing jewellery in public and walking alone at night. Avoid travelling at night and always comply with the frequent police roadblocks.

Getting there
Air
National airline: Air Gabon (Compagnie Nationale Air Gabon).
International airport/s: Libreville-Léon M'Ba (Code: LBV), 12km from city; restaurant, currency exchange; Port Gentil (POG), 4km from city; Franceville.
Other airport/s: There are 65 other public and 50 private airfields linked mostly with the forestry and petroleum industries.
Airport tax: None

Surface
Road: The major routes are from the Republic of Congo, Cameroon or Equatorial Guinea. These are semi-surfaced but generally are in good condition and well maintained.
Water: There is a boat to and from São Tomé every five days.
Main port/s: The principal deep-water ports are Port Gentil, Owendo (Libreville). Mayumba and Nyanga are used for shipping timber. There is a fishing port in Libreville.

Getting about
National transport
Air: Air Gabon operates scheduled and charter flights to all main centres.
Road: There are an estimated 8,590km of roads, including 3,290km of main roads and 1,950km of secondary roads. Except for the routes Libreville-Ndende, Booué-Bitam, roads can be difficult in the rainy season. Travel by bush taxis and truck can be dangerous, especially in the rainy season.
Buses: Regular coach and minibus services link Libreville with Lambaréné, Oyem, Mouila and Bitam. Some services are subject to rainy season conditions.
Rail: Regular services operate on the Transgabon railway linking Libreville with Booué, Ndjolé and Franceville. There are two classes. The railcars are air-conditioned for some services but no refreshment or sleeping accommodation is scheduled. The rolling stock is generally new.

Water: The principal river is the Ogooué, navigable from Port-Gentil to Ndjole (310km), and serving the towns of Lambaréné, Ndjolé and Sindara.
A ferry service (taking two hours) operates between Libreville and Port-Gentil.

City transport
Taxis: Unmetered 'collective' and private taxis are available in main towns; tipping is not usual; rates vary according to the time of day. The journey from the airport to the Libreville city centre takes 10 minutes.

Car hire
Available in main towns, at airports and through hotels. International driving licence required. Charges are high.

BUSINESS DIRECTORY
The addresses listed below are a selection only. While World of Information makes every endeavour to check these addresses, we cannot guarantee that changes have not been made, especially to telephone numbers and area codes. We would welcome any corrections.

Telephone area codes
The international dialling code (IDD) for Gabon is + 241 followed by subscriber's number.

Useful telephone numbers
Police:	732-036	761-044
	760-950	720-951
Fire:	18	761-520
Ambulance:	732-771	762-344

Chambers of Commerce
Gabon Chamber of Commerce, Agriculture, Industry and Mines, PO Box 2234, Libreville (tel: 722-064; fax: 746-477).

Banking
Banque Gabonaise de Développement; PO Box 5, Rue Alfred Marche, Libreville (tel: 762-429, 762-489; fax: 742-699).

Banque Gabonaise et Francaise Internationale (BGFI) (BGFI), PO Box 2253, Blvd de l'Indépendance, Libreville (tel: 732-326, 764-035; fax: 740-894, 744-456).

Banque Internationale pour le Commerce et l'Industrie du Gabon SA, PO Box 2241, Avenue du Colonel Parant, Libreville (tel: 762-613, 763-811; fax: 746-410).

Banque Nationale du Crédit Rural, PO Box 1120, Avenue Bouët, Libreville (tel: 724-742, 766-144, 763-045; fax: 740-507).

Banque Populaire du Gabon, PO Box 6663, Blvd de l'Indépendance, Libreville (tel: 724-719; fax: 728-691).

Caisse Nationale d'Epargne, Siège Social, Libreville (tel: 766-509).

Centre de Chèques Postaux, Siége Social, Libreville (tel: 766-509).

Union Gabonaise de Banque SA, PO Box 315 & 2238, Avenue du Colonel Parant, Libreville (tel: 777-000; fax: 764-616).

Central bank
Banque des Etats de l'Afrique Centrale, Direction Nationale; PO Box 112, Libreville (tel: 761-352; fax: 744-563; e-mail: beaclbv@beac.int).

Travel information
ADL (Aeroport de Libreville), BP 363, Libreville (tel: 736-128).

Air Gabon (Compagnie Nationale Air Gabon), BP 2206, Aeroport International Léon M'ba, Libreville (tel: 730-027; fax: 731-156).

Eurafrique Voyages, BP 4026, Libreville (tel: 762-787; fax: 761-897).

Libreville Léon M'Ba International Airport, BP 363, Libreville (tel: 736-244/246/247; fax: 736-128).

Ministry of tourism
Ministry of Transport, Tourism and National Parks, BP 3974, Libreville (tel: 763-240).

Ministries
Ministry of Agriculture and Rural Development, BP 551, Libreville (tel: 721-579).

Ministry of the Arts, Culture and People Education, BP 1007, Libreville (tel: 724-028).

Ministry of Defence, Security and Immigration, BP 13493, Libreville (tel: 760-835).

Ministry of Economy, Finance, Budget and Privatisation, BP 9672, Libreville (tel: 721-571, 760-580; fax: 761-518).).

Ministry of Foreign Affairs and Co-operation, BP 2245, Libreville (tel: 762-251).

Ministry of Forestry and Environment, BP 199, Libreville (tel: 733-191).

Ministry of Higher Education, BP 3919, Libreville (tel: 763-252).

Ministry of Home (in charge of Local Collectivities and Mobile Security), BP 2110, Libreville (tel: 762-181).

Ministry of Housing, Land Registry and Town Planning, BP 512, Libreville (tel: 740-461).

Ministry of Justice, BP 547, Libreville (tel: 720-160).

Ministry of Labour and Human Resources, BP 2256, Libreville (tel: 732-739).

Ministry of Mining, Energy and Hydraulic Resources, BP 4041, Libreville (tel: 762-863).

Ministry of National Education and Professional Training, BP 6, Libreville (tel: 721-741).

Ministry of Public Health, BP 50, Libreville (tel: 762-522).

Ministry of Public Service and Administrative Reform, BP 496, Libreville (tel: 762-150).

Ministry of Shipping, BP 803, Libreville (tel: 733-210).

Ministry of Small and Medium Businesses, BP 4120, Libreville (tel: 720-636).

Ministry of Social Affairs, Family and Solidarity, BP 5684, Libreville (tel: 761-700).

Ministry of State Control, Decentralisation, Administration of Territory and Regional Integration, BP 178, Libreville (tel: 763-550).

Ministry of Trade Industry, BP 3906, Libreville (tel: 722-887).

Ministry of Youth and Sport, BP 3904, Libreville (tel: 763-576).

Other useful addresses

Compagnie Minière de l'Ogoué (COMILOG), BP 578, Libreville (tel: 722-474).

Conseil Economique et Sociale de la République Gabonais, BP 1075, Libreville (tel: 762-668).

European Development Fund, BP 321, Libreville (tel: 732-250).

Gabonese Embassy (USA), 2034 20th Street, NW, Washington DC 20009 (tel: 202-797-1000; faax: 202-332-0668).

Société de Développement de l'Agriculture au Gabon (AGROGABON), BP 2248, Libreville (tel: 764-082).

Société Equatoriale de Travaux Pétroliers Maritimes, BP 493, Libreville (tel: 753-509).

Société Gabonaise de Financement et d'Expansion, BP 2151, Libreville.

Société Gabonaise de Participation et de Développement, BP 1624, Libreville.

Société Gabonaise de Raffinage, BP 530, Libreville (tel: 752-365).

Société Nationale de Transports Maritimes (SONATRAM), BP 3841, Libreville (tel: 740-632; fax: 745-967).

US Embassy, Boulevard de la Mer, BP 4000, Libreville (tel: 762-002).

Internet sites

Africa Business Network: http://www.ifc.org/abn

AllAfrica.com: http://allafrica.com

African Development Bank: http://www.afdb.org

Africa Online: http://www.africaonline.com

Mbendi AfroPaedia (information on companies, countries, industries and stock exchanges in Africa): http://www.mbendi.co.za

The Gambia

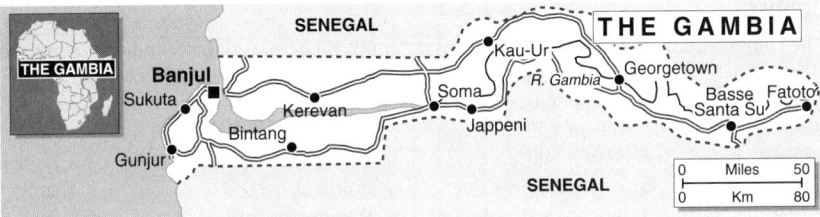

KEY FACTS

Official name: Republic of The Gambia

Head of State: President Yahya Alphonse Jamus Jebulai Jammeh (Chairman of APRC) (re-elected 18 Oct 2001)

Head of government: President Yahya Alphonse Jamus Jebulai Jammeh

Ruling party: Alliance for Patriotic Reorientation and Construction (APRC) (re-elected Jan 2002)

Area: 11,295 square km

Population: 1.42 million (2004)

Capital: Banjul

Official language: English

Currency: Dalasi (D) = 100 butut

Exchange rate: D28.30 per US$ (Oct 2005)

GDP per capita: US$276 (2004)

GDP real growth: 7.70% (2004)

Labour force: 746,000 (2004)

Inflation: 14.60% (2004)

Balance of trade: -US$66.50 million (2004)

Foreign debt: US$476.00 million (2003)

The Gambia's economic performance continues to be uneven owing to exogenous shocks, macroeconomic and structural policy slippage, poor governance, and weak institutions. Expansionary policies have increased the government's recourse to domestic bank financing, which, in turn, has raised real interest rates, increased the domestic debt burden, and tended to crowd out private investment. President Jammeh announced in 2004 that large reserves of oil had been discovered, but there have been no subsequent announcement of a 'new future' for The Gambia.

Economy

An International Monetary Fund (IMF) Poverty Reduction and Growth Facility (PRGF) was suspended by the IMF in 2003, because of weak policy implementation and governance problems, which in turn delayed the completion of the Gambia's first Poverty Reduction Strategy Paper (PRSP) implementation cycle of three years until the end of 2005 (instead of June 2003). The government had misreported net international reserves by US$38.8 million and failed to record US$28.5 million in government expenditures, while auditors had been unable to give an opinion on national accounts for several years because of the lack of documentation. The suspension of the PRGF meant that US$115 million of funds pledged by donors at the 2002 Geneva Round Table Conference were not disbursed in 2003 and 2004, further hampering completion of the PRSP.

In October 2005 a 6-month IMF Staff Monitored Programme was negotiated, for completion in mid-2006. If successful this should lead to a new PRGF for 2006–08, and pave the way for an HIPC completion point.

Although macroeconomic stability was restored in 2004 and 2005, policies weakened over 2005. Unbudgeted expenditures of Dalasi 100 million (US$3.5 million) (0.75 per cent of gross domestic product) led to a substantial increase in the net debt of the government. The Gambian Agricultural Marketing Corporation (Gamco), had been set up prior to the 2004/05 trade season, to market and process groundnuts. However, this has had a near disastrous effect on exports of processed groundnuts, as Gamco was unable to raise the finances to purchase what was a bumper harvest for groundnuts. The government's 1998 seizure of the private peanut firm Alimenta had eliminated the largest purchaser of Gambian groundnuts; the following two marketing seasons saw substantially lower prices and sales. Groundnut trading fully liberalised and it is hoped that other operators will meet the Regulatory Framework criteria in time for the 2005/06 season.

On the fiscal side, the National Emergency Fiscal Committee (NEFCOM) had some positive effects in ensuring greater control over expenditures. Steps are being taken to strengthen the public expenditure management system. A statistical strategy is being prepared for donors.

Donor suggestions include quarterly ceilings on discretionary expenditure, improved cash management, and enforcing the public enterprises' repayment of government loans. They welcomed a reduction in non-performing loans, and urged the further deepening of the financial sector, including by enhancing the legal framework and reinforcing creditor rights.

They have encouraged the acceleration of the privatisation programme.

Privatisation

A number of privatisations went through in 2005, including The Gambia Ports Authority's 80 per cent share in Banjul Shipyard to a Malaysian company and the government's 50 per cent shareholding in Senegambia Beach Hotel. The Gambia Divestiture Agency (GDA) is proceeding with the sale of The Gambia Groundnut Corporation (targetted for June 2006), and is in negotiation with various prospective purchasers for the government's stake in The Gambia Cotton Company Ltd (Gamcot) and Banjul Breweries Ltd.

Stability but little prosperity

Oil reserves or not, the first challenge for The Gambia is to make a decisive break from its past 'stop-go' policies and produce a meaningful development programme acceptable to the major donor nations. The country has no significant mineral or natural resource deposits and only a limited agricultural base, but unlike many of its West African neighbours it has enjoyed long spells of stability since independence. This stability has not so far translated into prosperity. Despite the presence of the Gambia River, which runs through the middle of the country, only one-sixth of the land is arable and the poor nature of the soil has led to the predominance of one crop – peanuts. About 75 per cent of the population depends on crops and livestock for its livelihood. Small-scale manufacturing activity features the processing of peanuts, fish, and hides.

Tourism is an important source of foreign exchange, as is the money sent home by Gambians living abroad. Most visitors are drawn to the resorts that occupy a stretch of the Atlantic coast. Re-export trade did constitute a major segment of economic activity, but a government-imposed preshipment inspection plan, and the instability of the Gambian dalasi curtailed that.

Politics

The Gambia gained its independence from Britain in 1965; it formed a short-lived federation of Senegambia with Senegal between 1982 and 1989. In 1991 the two nations signed a friendship and cooperation treaty. A military coup in 1994 overthrew the president and banned political activity, but a 1996 constitution and presidential elections, followed by parliamentary balloting in 1997, completed a nominal return to civilian rule. The country undertook another round of presidential and legislative elections in late 2001 and early 2002. Yahya Jammeh, the leader of the coup, has been elected president in all subsequent elections.

Soldier-turned-president Jammeh won a second five-year term in the October 2001 presidential elections in the Gambia. He gained 53 per cent of votes cast against less than 33 per cent for his main rival. Jammeh had joined the army in 1984 upon leaving school. After serving with the Gambian peace-keepers in Liberia he returned and, together with a group of veterans who had not been paid, ousted the elected president, Dawda Jawara, who had led the country since independence.

Upon taking power he set up bodies to investigate corruption and recover pilfered public funds. However, he has been criticised for harassing opposition activists and journalists.

Outlook

Unemployment and underemployment rates remain high; short-run economic progress depends on sustained bilateral and multilateral aid, on responsible government economic management, on continued technical assistance from the IMF and bilateral donors, and on expected growth in the construction sector.

Risk assessment

Economic	Poor
Political	Stable
Regional stability	Deteriorating

COUNTRY PROFILE

Historical profile
When independence came to The Gambia in 1965, there were many who doubted that Africa's newest state would hold on to her status for any appreciable length of time. The oldest and most northerly of Britain's former West African possessions, The Gambia is surrounded, except on her Atlantic seaboard, by the bigger and more populous Senegal. It is said that but for the river the country would not have existed.
1455 The Portuguese established trading stations along the River Gambia.
1889 The boundaries of The Gambia were agreed by the British and French.
1894 The Gambia became a British protectorate.
1965 Following independence, Dawda Jawara, as the head of the People's Progressive Party (PPP), became prime minister, with the British monarch as head of state.
1970 Following a referendum, The Gambia became a republic. Dawda Jawara was elected president.
1981 Around 500 people were killed when Senegalese troops intervened in support of Jawara and suppressed a coup.
1982 Senegal and The Gambia formed a confederation called Senegambia intended to integrate military, economic and political institutions.
1989 The Gambia, the subordinate partner, withdrew from Senegambia and the confederation collapsed.
1991 The Gambia and Senegal signed a treaty of friendship.
1994 President Jawara was deposed by a military coup and was replaced by Lieutenant Yahya Jammeh of the Alliance for Patriotic Reorientation and Construction (APRC). The 1970 constitution was suspended and all political parties banned.

KEY INDICATORS — The Gambia

	Unit	2000	2001	2002	2003	2004
Population	m	1.31	1.35	1.39	1.40	1.42
Gross domestic product (GDP)	US$bn	0.42	0.36	0.36	0.38	*0.41
GDP per capita	US$	318	307	265	246	276
GDP real growth	%	5.6	4.6	4.7	7.4	7.7
Inflation	%	0.9	4.5	8.6	17.0	14.6
Exports (fob) (goods)	US$m	133.0	146.0	160.0	138.0	114.4
Imports (fob) (goods)	US$m	202.0	216.0	252.0	225.0	180.9
Balance of trade	US$m	-69.0	-70.0	-90.0	-87.0	-66.5
Current account	US$m	-10.0	-10.0	-10.0	-20.0	-20.0
Total reserves minus gold	US$m	109.4	106.0	106.9	59.3	83.8
Foreign exchange	US$m	107.3	104.1	104.8	57.1	80.7
Exchange rate	per US$	12.79	16.47	19.91	25.95	27.31

* estimated figure

The Gambia

1996 A new constitution was approved giving multi-party democracy. Three political parties were prohibited from taking part in elections. Jammeh and the APRC were elected to the presidency and legislature, in what observers said were not free and fair elections.

2001 President Jammeh lifted the ban on opposition political parties. He was re-elected president.

2002 The centrist United Democratic Party (UDP) boycotted the parliamentary elections leaving the ruling APRC to win most seats unopposed.

2004 Transparency International, the corruption watchdog, ranked The Gambia in the bottom half at 90 out of 146 countries.

2005 In March over 30 senior officials were arrested and charged with corruption following a presidential report. They were later released and given two weeks to pay back the money owed to the government. Border tensions rose in August when Gambia doubled the price of ferry crossings and Senegalese haulage firms, in protest, blockaded access routes. Senegal was effectively split in two as goods were hauled around Gambia on roads that were not all-weather and were unsuitable for heavy loads. Gambia experienced a shortage of goods in the marketplace due to the loss of revenue and blockaded imports. Nigeria, as a representative of Ecowas, attempted to mediate between the protagonists.

Political structure
Constitution
The constitution was enacted in 1970, amended in 1982 and 1996.
Form of state
Democratic republic
The executive
Power rests with the president, who is elected by universal suffrage every five years. The president is both the head of state and head of government and appoints the cabinet.
National legislature
Legislative power is vested in the unicameral 53-member House of Representatives, comprising 48 members directly elected for a five-year term and five members appointed by the president.
Last elections
17 January 2002 (parliamentary); 18 October 2001 (presidential).
Results: Parliamentary: The ruling APRC won 45 seats, (of which 33 seats were unopposed by the UDP), the PDOIS won three seats.
Presidential: Yahya Alphonse Jamus Jebulai Jammeh won 53 per cent of the vote.
Next elections
2006 (presidential); 2007 (parliamentary).

Political parties
Ruling party
Alliance for Patriotic Reorientation and Construction (APRC) (re-elected Jan 2002)
Main opposition party
The United Democratic Party (UDP) is regarded as the main opposition party, although it boycotted elections.
The People's Democratic Organisation for Independence and Socialism (PDOIS) is the only opposition party represented in parliament.

Population
1.42 million (2004)
Ethnic make-up
Three major ethnic groups: Mandinka (42 per cent), Fula (18 per cent), Wolof (16 per cent). Other substantial ethnic groups: Jola, Serahule, Serere, Manjago, Bambara, Creole/Aku.
Religions
Muslim (90 per cent), Christian (9 per cent), animist beliefs (1 per cent).

Education
Primary schooling begins at aged seven and is free of charge and non-selective until aged 15. Secondary education is either vocational or academic. Basic vocational schools offer two-year courses and vocational secondary schools provide four-year courses. General secondary schools offer a three-year course leading to higher education provided by the University of The Gambia. The Gambia College offers vocational courses in agriculture, education, nursing, midwifery, and public health.
Literacy rate: Adult rates: 38.9 per cent, male; 31.9 per cent, female (World Bank).
Compulsory years: None
Enrolment rate: 77 per cent gross primary enrolment; 25 per cent gross secondary enrolment, of relevant age groups (including repeaters) (World Bank).
Pupils per teacher: 30 in primary schools.

Health
Annual government spending is around 49 per cent, and foreign spending 27 per cent, of the total expenditure on health, which is approximately 6 per cent of GDP. Improved water sources are available to 62 per cent of the population. Around 90 per cent of children are immunised against measles.
HIV/Aids
The Gambia has so far escaped much of the African pandemic. However, with 14 per cent of sex workers testing positive, there is a chance that the infection will spread.
HIV prevalence: 1.2 per cent aged 15–49 in 2003 (World Bank)

Life expectancy: 53.4 years (World Bank).
Fertility rate/Maternal mortality rate: 4.8 births per woman; maternal mortality 1,100 per 100,000 live births (World Bank).
Infant mortality rate: 90 per 1,000 live births (World Bank)
Head of population per physician/bed: 0.03 physicians and 0.6 hospital beds per 1,000 people.

Welfare
The Gambia has two important funds, the social security fund and the housing finance fund, that receive contributions from employers and employees either directly or indirectly. The Department of Social Welfare in Banjul has been restructured with four major units covering child care, adult, elderly and disabled services. The Gambia government and the Social Security and Housing Finance Corporation (SSHFC) initiated mass housing projects including a rural electrification programme covering all major towns and villages.

Main cities
Banjul (capital, estimated population 46,700 in 2003), Serekunda (344,100), Bakau (82,300), Brikama (80,400).

Languages spoken
Mandinka, Wolof and Fula are local languages. French is taught in some secondary and high schools. German, Italian, Dutch and the Scandinavian languages are also spoken by tourism staff.
Official language/s
English

Media
Press
Dailies: Daily newspapers include *Daily Observer* and *The Gambia Daily*.
Weeklies: Main weekly newspapers are *Weekend Observer*, *New Citizen* (formerly *Newsmonth*) and a bi-weekly publication, *The Point*.
Business: Business information is covered by *Business Weekly*, a weekly publication by The Gambia Communication Agency and Baroueli Enterprises.
Periodicals: Periodicals include *Gamco-op News* (quarterly), *Gambia Times* (monthly) and *The Nation* (irregular).
Broadcasting
Radio: Radio Gambia, a government non-commercial station, operates 19 hours daily in English and Gambian languages. The commercial station, Radio Syd, also broadcasts in English, French and African languages, and provides tourist information in German and Swedish.
Television: Senegalese transmissions are received.

Economy

The Gambia is classified by the World Bank as a low-income country. Although relatively stable, it has been characterised, by the IMF, as lacking economic diversification and having weak fiscal policies and poor governance. Even so, in a September 2005 report, the IMF identified improvements in the economy in 2004 that included strengthening financial policies that led to a basic primary fiscal surplus, reduced inflation, stabilised exchange rates and the rebuilding of international reserves.

Agriculture, forestry and fisheries remain the dominant sectors in the economy and have grown as a proportion of GDP, reflecting the country's industrial stagnation. Overall though, GDP growth was 7.7 per cent in 2004. Inflation reached 18 per cent by the end of 2003 and had fallen to 14.6 per cent in 2004.

The economy depends almost entirely on the cultivation and export of groundnuts in the form of nuts, oil and cattle cake. One policy that came in for criticism by the IMF was the government's decision in February 2005, to licence the Gambian Agricultural Marketing Corporation (Gamco), giving it a monopoly to market and process groundnuts. Gamco was unable to raise the finance to purchase the bumper harvest of the 2004/05 season groundnuts and a substantial proportion of the crop was lost.

The government's general policy is to diversify and broaden the productive base of the economy and foster economic growth and development. The Economic Recovery Programme (ERP) includes institutional reform, price liberalisation and the adoption of a flexible exchange rate regime. There is potential for tourism and re-exports, but political instability and poor infrastructure have hampered the development of these sectors.

Both the IMF and World Bank support The Gambia through the Heavily Indebted Poor Countries (HIPC) Initiative and Poverty Reduction and Growth Facility (PRGF) with funds worth a total of US$91 million, up to 2020.

The challenge for The Gambia is to make a crucial break from past piecemeal policies that inflated then depressed the economy, to diversify and establish the conditions that spark continued growth and reduce poverty. It is necessary to allow market forces to determine prices and interest rates while ensuring macroeconomic stability so that external shocks do not have a long lasting adverse effect on internal mechanisms.

External trade

Banjul is an important transit trade centre. In 2002, the US approved The Gambia as eligible for tariff preferences under the African Growth and Opportunities Act (AGOA).

Geographically, The Gambia presents itself as a long wedge separating the north and south of Senegal, and as a result haulage firms cross The Gambia to avoid the long and ardious route around it. Imports and re-exports, from goods traversing, have earned significant foreign exchange for the Gambian economy. So the closure of the border with Senegal in August 2005 had a severe effect on trade.

Imports

Imports which support transit trade are estimated at 34 per cent of total imports. Principal imports are foodstuffs, manufactures, fuel, machinery and transport equipment

Main sources: China (25.1 per cent total, 2004), Senegal (9.2 per cent), UK (6.3 per cent), Brazil (6.0 per cent), The Netherlands (4.9 per cent), US (4.8 per cent)

Exports

Principal exports are peanut products, fish, cotton lint, palm kernels and re-exports.

Main destinations: Thailand (16.6 per cent total, 2004), UK (15.5 per cent), France (14.2 per cent), India (12.3 per cent), Germany (9.2 per cent), (Italy 8.3 per cent), Malaysia (4.1 per cent)

Agriculture

Farming

Agriculture remains the main sector of the economy, typically contributing around 30 per cent to GDP and employing over 70 per cent of the workforce.

Approximately 17 per cent of the total land area is cultivated. Groundnuts are cultivated on about 60 per cent of the planted area, and provide 85 per cent of official export earnings. The Gambia is the second-largest producer of groundnuts in the world, after Senegal. Production of food crops (rice, maize, millet, sorghum, cassava) is insufficient to meet local needs, but receives a great deal of official encouragement. Small-scale fruit and cotton farming are also important while some livestock is exported to neighbouring countries for breeding.

The government, backed by international development agencies and donors, is attempting to increase agricultural production. The on-going US$2.5 million Lowlands Agricultural Development Project (LADEP) is aimed at developing 6,000 hectares for cultivation and the rehabilitation of 1,500 hectares in various lowland ecologies. US$2 million has been allocated to assist women's groups engaged in sheep, goat and poultry production while US$1.5 million is dedicated to an integrated rural development scheme.

The estimated crop production in 2004 included: 162,000 tonnes (t) cereals in total, 73,000t groundnuts (in shell), 25,000t maize, 22,000t rice, 3,200t pulses, 7,500t roots and tubers, 26,250t oilcrops, 90,00t millet, 35,000t oil palm fruit, 500t seed cotton, 150t cotton lint, 4,160t fruit in total, 9,000t vegetables in total. Estimated livestock production included: 6,677t meat in total, 3,180t beef, 444t pig-meat, 1,133t lamb and goat meat, 1,130t poultry, 748t eggs, 7,648t milk, 371t cattle hides, 1,000t game meat.

Fishing

Fishing has also increased in importance with the annual catch rising to over 22,000 tonnes. The government, with assistance from the UN Development Programme (UNDP), is encouraging improved methods and modernisation of boats. Illegal fishing by foreign trawler fleets remains a problem.

Forestry

Imports of forest products in 2004 amounted to US$2.3 million, while exports amounted to US$161,000.

Timber production in 2004 is estimated at 750,701 cubic metre (cum), 112,700cum industrial roundwood, 106,000cum sawlogs and veneer logs, 638,001cum wood fuel, 51,447t charcoal.

Industry and manufacturing

The industrial sector contributes around 6 per cent to GDP and employs 4 per cent of the workforce.

The manufacturing sector is small-scale and underdeveloped.

The main activities (most of which are centred around Banjul, particularly in the Kanifing Industrial Estate) include groundnut and fish processing, brewing, footwear, perfume, cement and brick production.

Tourism

The tourism sector is growing in importance in the Gambian economy with a US$132.5 million turnover estimated for 2005, showing a growth rate of 9.3 per cent and all other indicators for the sector show increases.

An increasing number of Europeans are arriving, of whom between 50–60 per cent are British; statistics in 2005 identified The Gambia as a particularly competitive destination for British visitors and overall growth was estimated at just over 10 per cent. The travel and tourist sector contributed 16.0 per cent (2004) to GDP and employed around 118,600 people in the industry. Capital investment in 2005, in tourism, is estimated at US$11.7 million or 16.6 per cent of total investment. The government has plans to see one million visitors arriving by 2013. A new tourist residential resort development, of 130 plots, is in the planning stages. Eco-tourism and historical sites are among the other tourist activities offered by The Gambia, although most tourists prefer the sea-and-sun holiday package. Six new hotels are scheduled for completion in 2005 and 2006. The Sheraton Hotel is due to open in mid-2006.

Environment
Concerns are mounting over the ecological effects of tourism on the local environment, particularly shore erosion and the depletion of water resources.

Mining
Most mining activity is centred on the production of industrial minerals for local consumption. The Australian Carnegie Corporation is investigating the Brufut deposits located along the coast and around 11,000 tonnes of zircon has been found. There are known deposits of kaolin, tin, ilmenite and rutile, mostly unexploited.

Hydrocarbons
The downstream industry is reliant on imported petroleum products, importing 1,940 barrels per day.
The Gambia does not produce or import gas.

Energy
There is total dependence on imported petroleum. Fuelwood is the main source of domestic energy. Hydroelectric resources are being developed on the River Gambia.

Banking and insurance
The banking sector is underdeveloped, but is growing as a result of increased economic activity and macroeconomic stability. The sector has seen consolidation, with two large mergers and privatisations.
It was announced in March 2005 that the introduction of the shared currency, the Eco, in The Gambia, Ghana, Guinea, Nigeria and Sierra Leone, which was due in July 2005, would be postponed. The currency was proposed to facilitate trade and growth with an ultimate plan to merge it with the CFA franc.
Central bank
Central Bank of The Gambia
Main financial centre
Banjul

Time
GMT

Geography
The Gambia is a narrow territory around the River Gambia on the west coast of Africa. The country has a short coastline on the Atlantic Ocean but is otherwise surrounded by Senegal.

Climate
Sub-tropical with distinct dry and rainy seasons. Dry season from November–May with average temperatures around 21–27 degrees Celsius (C). The dry Harmattan wind keeps the humidity low. Rainy season from June–October with high humidity and average temperatures around 26–32 degrees C.

Entry requirements
Passports
Required by all. Passports must be valid for three months from date of return.
Visa
Required by all, except citizens of countries with reciprocating visa-free entry for both tourism and business, (UK 30 days, others 90 days). For further details contact the nearest embassy for confirmation. All visitors must have onward/return tickets.
Currency advice/regulations
No restrictions on import or export of local and most foreign currency, although a declaration form must be completed on arrival. Exceptions: currency from Algeria, Ghana, Guinea, Mali, Morocco, Nigeria, Sierra Leone and Tunisia will not be accepted and cannot be exchanged.

Health (for visitors)
Mandatory precautions
Yellow fever vaccination certificate required only if travelling from an infected area.
Advisable precautions
Yellow fever, typhoid, hepatitis A and polio vaccinations are recommended. Malaria prophylaxis should be taken as risk exists throughout the country. There is a rabies risk.
In the Banjul and Fajara area, the water supply is fed from deep bore holes and is considered safe to drink. Bottled water is available from all hotels and most supermarkets. Water precautions are necessary outside these areas.

Hotels
Book well in advance, especially if arriving during tourist season (Nov–May). Many Gambian hotels are geared to package holidays. 10 per cent tip is usual.

Credit cards
Limited acceptance of credit cards. American Express is normally accepted in most hotels but this must be arranged at the beginning of your stay with the hotel management.

Public holidays
Fixed dates
1 Jan (New Year's Day), 18 Feb (Independence Day), 1 May (Labour Day), 22 Jul (Revolution Day), 15 Aug (Assumption Day), 25 Dec (Christmas Day).

Variable dates
Good Friday, Easter Monday, Eid al Adha, Birth of the Prophet, Eid al Fitr (two days).
The Islamic year contains 354 or 355 days, with the result that Muslim feasts advance by 10–12 days against the Gregorian calendar. Dates of feasts vary according to the sighting of the new moon, so cannot be forecast exactly.

Working hours
Banking
Mon–Thu: 0800–1330; Fri: 0800–1100.
Business
Mon–Thu: 0800–1600; Fri: 0800–1230.
Government
Mon–Thu: 0800–1600; Fri: 0800–1230.
Shops
Mon–Thu: 0900–1200, 1400–1700; (Fri–Sat) 0900–1300.

Electricity supply
220V AC, 50 cycles.

Social customs/useful tips
Handshaking is widely used as a form of greeting, whereas 'Salam alaikum' is the traditional greeting.
Many Gambians are Muslim and their religious customs and beliefs should be respected.

Getting there
Air
National airline: Gambia Airways.
International airport/s: Banjul-Bia International (Yundum International) (Code: BJL), 24km from city; bar, bank, post office, shop.
Airport tax: International departures D150; not applicable to transit passengers.
Surface
Road: Road access to Banjul is possible from Dakar (Senegal), by the Trans-Gambia Highway which crosses the River Gambia by ferry between Farafenni and Mansa Konko. There is an alternative car ferry crossing between Barra and Banjul. Government buses run between The Gambia and Senegal, via Barra, to Koalack and Dakar; there is also a high-class Gambian coach service.

Getting about
National transport
Road: Approximately 3,000km of roads, of which 450km are paved. Roads in and around Banjul are mostly bituminised, but unsealed roads often become impassable in the summer season.
Highways run along each bank of the River Gambia; the Trans-Gambia highway runs north to south, crossing the river at Farafenni-Mansa Konko (car ferry); other inland roads may become impassable in the rainy season.

Take care, there is a lack of adequate traffic signs.

Buses: The Gambia Public Transport Corporation (GPTC) operates cheap and reliable services linking Banjul with the coastal hotel area and other main centres. There are several commercial bus services, such as Amdalaye and Transgambia services.

Water: There are nearly a dozen ferry crossing points where people, livestock and vehicles cross the river. The Banjul-Barra ferry runs every 90 minutes (journey time 20–30 minutes) and there are small wooden ferries up-country which carry only three or four vehicles at a time. A boat travels from Banjul to Basse once a week. The journey takes about three days. It is possible to return overland by coach.

City transport
Taxis: Green (tourist) taxis have a diamond sign and a serial number on the side. They are licensed by the Gambia Tourism Authority and dedicated to serving tourists and other visitors. They are normally parked outside the hotels in the resort areas. The journey from the international airport to the city centre takes 30–40 minutes.

Yellow and Green taxis are mainly four-passenger saloon cars which run a shared taxi service between short distances or park by the roadside for individual hire.

The most common way of travelling is by Collective 'Bush' Taxis. These are mainly seven-passenger saloon cars, vans, minibuses and buses. They do not have a single colour and they operate a shared service between both short and long distances. It is advisable to agree the fare in advance when hiring collective taxis.

A 10 per cent tip is usual.

Car hire
International driving licence accepted for a period of three months. National licence can be used for a short visit. Traffic drives on the right.

Car hire facilities are somewhat limited and local enquiries through the tourist office are advised.

BUSINESS DIRECTORY

The addresses listed below are a selection only. While World of Information makes every endeavour to check these addresses, we cannot guarantee that changes have not been made, especially to telephone numbers and area codes. We would welcome any corrections.

Telephone area codes
The international dialling code (IDD) for The Gambia is + 220 followed by subscriber's number.

Useful telephone numbers
Police	17
Fire	18
Ambulance (Banjul)	16 or 18

Chambers of Commerce
Gambia Chamber of Commerce & Industry, 1-3 Ecowas Avenue, PO Box 333, Banjul (tel: 227-765; fax: 229-671; e-mail: gcci@qanet.gm).

Banking
Arab Gambian Islamic Bank Ltd, 7 Ecowas Avenue, Banjul (tel: 223-773; fax: 223-770).

First International Bank Ltd, PO Box 1997, 6 OAU Boulevard, Banjul (tel: 202-000/5; fax: 202-001, 202-000).

International Bank for Commerce (Gambia) Ltd, PO Box 211, 11a Liberation Avenue, Banjul (tel: 228-144, 228-145; fax: 229-312).

Standard Chartered Bank Gambia Ltd, PO Box 259, 8 Ecowas Avenue, Banjul (tel: 228-681/4; fax: 227-714).

Trust Bank Limited (TBL), PO Box 1018, 3-4 Ecowas Avenue, Banjul (tel: 225-777, 225-778/9; fax: 225-781).

Central bank
Central Bank of The Gambia, 1-2 Ecowas Avenue, Banjul (tel: 228-103; fax: 226-969).

Travel information
Banjul (Yundum) International Airport, PO Box 285, Banjul (tel: 473-000; fax: 472-190).

Gambia Airways, PO Box 268, 68-69 Wellington Street, Banjul (tel: 226-733, 227-778/9, 226-347; fax: 229-339).

Ministry of tourism
Department of State for Tourism and Culture, The Quadrangle, Banjul (tel: 229-563, 223-210; fax: 227-753).

National tourist organisation offices
Gambia Tourism Authority, Kololi, PO Box 4085, Bakau (tel: 462-491; fax: 462-487; internet site: http://www.visitthegambia.gm)

Ministries
Ministry of Agriculture and Natural Resources (MANR), The Quadrangle, Banjul (tel: 472-888; fax: 237-034).

Ministry of Finance and Economic Affairs, The Quadrangle, Banjul (tel: 227-221; fax: 227-954).

Other useful addresses
Central Statistics Office, Central Bank Building, Buckle Street, Banjul (tel: 228-105).

Gambia Embassy (USA), Suite 1000, 1155 15th Street, NW, Washington DC 20005 (tel: 202-785-1399; fax: 202-785-1430).

Gambia Hotel Association, c/o The Bungalow Beach Hotel, PO Box 2637, Serrekunda (tel: 465-288; fax: 466-180).

Gambia Investment Promotion and Free Zones Agency (GIPFZA), 5 Nelson Mandela Street, PO Box 757, Banjul (tel: 222-412, 222-836; fax: 222-829; e-mail: dipm.gipfza@qanet.gm; ceo.gipfza@qanet.gm).

National Investment Promotion Authority (NIPA), Independence Drive, Banjul (tel: 228-332; fax: 229-220).

Internet sites
Africa Business Network: http://www.ifc.org/abn

AllAfrica.com: http://allafrica.com

African Development Bank: http://www.afdb.org

Africa Online: http://www.africaonline.com

Gateway site: http://gambiagateway.tripod.com

Mbendi AfroPaedia (information on companies, countries, industries and stock exchanges in Africa): http://mbendi.co.za

The Gambia: http://www.gambia.com

The Gambia Tourism Authority: http://www.visitthegambia.gm

Georgia

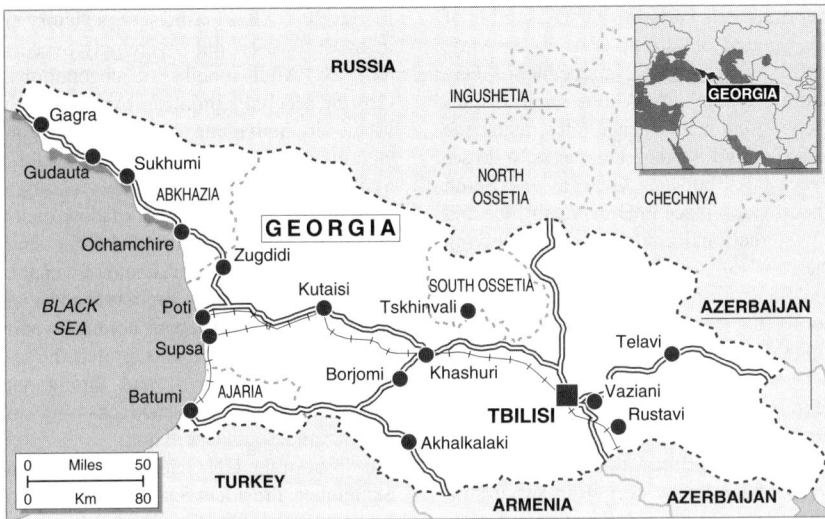

For Georgia, 2005 was a year of continuing aspirations and frustrations in terms of its economic and political goals. The completion of the Baku-Tbilisi-Ceyhan (BTC) oil pipeline, linking Azerbaijan-owned oil fields on the Caspian Sea with the outside world, cemented Georgia's position as a regional economic linchpin. However, stalemate was the order of the day in Georgia's attempts to bring back under its control two secessionist regions, Abkhazia and South Ossetia.

Georgia, transit king

With GDP growth of around 7.5 per cent in 2005, has Georgia continued to leave behind much of its post-Soviet economic blues. In December, Georgia became the proud owner of its first ever international credit rating – a B+ (long-term) from Standard & Poor's. Having contracted by nearly one half in 1992, the Georgian economy has grown rapidly since 2003. Foreign direct investment (FDI) has been the main engine of Georgian growth over the past couple of years. Although Georgia is itself resource poor, the BTC consortium has invested heavily in Georgia in order to facilitate oil shipments through Georgian territory. About 15 per cent of the BTC's length runs through Georgia and during construction, Georgians made up 75 per cent of the BTC's workforce. In May, the BTC was officially opened in Baku and Tbilisi currently earns US$50 million a year in transit fees. Environmentalists continue to criticise the BTC, particularly in relation to the pipeline's route through Georgia's Borjomi National Park. A second oil export route through Georgia also came online in July, the Baku-Supsa rail link, which ships Azeri oil from the Caspian to the Black Sea port of Batumi.

Economic diversification and reform

Georgia has around 55 per cent of its labour force engaged in the agricultural sector, and tried hard in 2005 to diversify and develop its economy. In July, the IMF gave Georgia a good report card with regard to macroeconomic reform and poverty reduction. By joining the flat tax brigade and promoting privatisation of government assets, Georgia hoped to improve its business climate. In this vein, in June, a National Anti-Corruption Strategy was launched by President Mikhail Saakashvili. In October, the Non-Governmental Organisation (NGO) Transparency International rated Georgia one of the most corrupt countries in the world (130th out of 158 countries surveyed, in descending order), although it also noted significant improvements. Tourism is viewed by the government and many

KEY FACTS

Official name: Sak'art'velos Respublika (Republic of Georgia)

Head of State: President Mikhail Saakashvili (sworn in 25 Jan 2004)

Head of government: Prime Minister Zurab Noghaideli (nominated by the President 8 Feb 2005)

Ruling party: Sak'art'velos Mokalaketa Kavshiri (SMK) (Union of Georgian Citizens) (since1995; last re-elected Mar 2004)

Area: 69,700 square km

Population: 5.32 million (2004)

Capital: Tbilisi

Official language: Georgian

Currency: Lari (L) = 100 tetri

Exchange rate: L1.79 per US$ (Oct 2005)

GDP per capita: US$866 (PPP, 2004)

GDP real growth: 8.50% (2004); *7.5% (2005)

Labour force: 2.63 million (2004)

Inflation: 5.70% (2004)

Balance of trade: -US$916.00 million (2004)

Foreign debt: US$1.90 billion (2004)

* estimated figure

businesses as a source of substantial economic growth, particularly with regards to Georgia's Black Sea coast. Soviet era elites once flocked to Georgia for its beaches, wine and cuisine. After years of decline, visitor numbers rose by 18 per cent in the first quarter of 2005 and the government is seeking to attract investment in tourist infrastructure.

Rose Revolution coalition wilts

Georgia experienced a potentially rocky start to the year when, in February, Prime Minister Zurab Zhvania was found dead, possibly having committed suicide. Despite losing one of its leading lights, the Rose Revolution team continued to dominate the political landscape for much of the year, under President Saakashvili and Zhvania's successor, Zurab Noghaideli. On 1 October, the ruling party easily defeated a newly re-organised opposition alliance in five by-elections. However, by the end of October there were signs that the Rose Revolution leadership was beginning to split. The high profile foreign minister, Salome Zurabishvili, was acrimoniously sacked, prompting speculation of a new political formation in the country.

Old problems

Fresh from reasserting central control over its wayward Ajaria Autonomous Republic (AAR) in May 2004, Georgia's government approached 2005 with cautious optimism regarding two other secessionist regions, Abkhazia and South Ossetia. The latter pair had broken away from Tbilisi in 1994 and 1992 respectively and, with Russian support, had resisted all efforts to reintegrate. With more than 200,000 ethnic Georgians expelled from their homes, from Abkhazia in particular, President Saakashvili was under pressure to re-unite Georgia. In January, Saakashvili presented a plan for the peaceful reintegration of South Ossetia into Georgia to the Parliamentary Assembly of the Council of Europe (PACE). In May, Saakashvili used his Independence Day address to call upon both separatist regions to enter into peace talks, using the Ossetian and Abkhaz languages to do so. Peace talks between Georgia and South Ossetia took place in Brussels in June and an international conference on resolving the stand-off was held in July. However, the South Ossetians boycotted the July conference and a series of shootings and abductions along the cease-fire line during the year stymied any real political progress. By September, Saakashvili was calling South Ossetia a 'criminal nest'.

Georgia's efforts to woo Abkhazia were, if anything, even less successful. The election of an opposition figure, Sergei Bagapsh, as president of breakaway Abkhazia in January temporarily raised hopes of diplomatic movement. However, talks on even basic issues, such as re-opening a rail-link between Georgia and Abkhazia broke down over an Abkhaz refusal to speak with Georgian negotiators. In May, Abkhazia began moves to confiscate all property vacated by ethnic Georgians who had fled the region, and in June began issuing independent passports. In July, Georgia stepped up its efforts to enforce a maritime blockade against Abkhazia, which resulted in the Abkhaz boycotting formal peace talks the following month, despite pressure from Georgia, the UN, France, Germany, the US and the UK to attend.

In the shadow of Russia

In May 2005, Georgia did score a victory in its quest to assert full sovereignty over its territory. After months of negotiations, Georgia secured a promise from Russia to vacate its remaining military bases on Georgian soil (in Batumi and Akhalkalaki), by the end of 2008. Nevertheless, Georgia very much remained in the shadow of its larger neighbour. Both Abkhazia and South Ossetia receive substantial financial, military and diplomatic support from Moscow. Russian peacekeepers, nominally part of multilateral deployments, protect the secessionists' front lines, and throughout 2005 Russia happily issued passports to Abkhaz and South Ossetians.

In front of the UN General Assembly in September, President Saakashvili went so far as to accuse Russia of trying to annex South Ossetia and Abkhazia. Despite professing respect for Georgia's territorial integrity, Russia also took care to maintain the status quo by resisting any attempt by Georgia to internationalise the conflict resolution process. In March, it moved to render toothless an agreement between Georgia and the EU over border monitoring, and in December it rejected a Georgian proposal to invite the US into the South Ossetia negotiation process. Restrictions on Georgia's freedom of movement also extended to its energy policy. In December, Russia refused to allow the transit of Kazakh natural gas through its territory into Georgia, despite willingness by Kazakhstan to facilitate the deal.

New horizons

In 2005, Georgia strove to diversify its relations, in an effort to counter Russian pressure. Georgia's post–9/11 romance with the US gathered pace, with a visit in May by President George W. Bush, the first by a US head of state. Referring to the Rose Revolution of November 2003, President Bush singled out Georgia as the catalyst for a global 'freedom movement'. In August, Georgia and the US conducted joint navy manoeuvres off Georgia's coast; and in September, President Saakashvili signed an agreement with the US granting Georgia US$295 million in funding for poverty reduction over five years.

KEY INDICATORS — Georgia

	Unit	2000	2001	2002	2003	2004
Population	m	5.27	5.40	5.40	5.37	5.32
Gross domestic product (GDP)	US$bn	3.00	3.20	3.30	3.34	*5.09
GDP per capita	US$	588	593	611	622	866
GDP real growth	%	2.0	4.5	5.4	4.7	8.5
Inflation	%	4.0	4.6	5.6	4.4	5.7
Unemployment	%	10.3	17.0	17.0	11.5	12.5
Exports (fob) (goods)	US$m	459.0	4,496.0	695.0	515.0	1,092.5
Imports (fob) (goods)	US$m	970.5	954.0	1,150.0	750.0	2,008.6
Balance of trade	US$m	-511.5	-458.0	-451.0	-235.0	-916.0
Current account	US$m	-269.0	-221.0	-211.7	-290.0	-340.0
Foreign debt	US$bn	1.6	1.7	1.8	1.7	1.9
Total reserves minus gold	US$m	109.4	159.4	197.6	190.7	382.9
Foreign exchange	US$m	106.1	155.4	194.6	185.8	371.7
Exchange rate	per US$	1.98	2.07	2.10	2.15	1.97

* estimated figure

Georgia also looked to its region for allies, particularly among countries who had recently thrown off Soviet and Russian hegemony. In what became known as the Borjomi Declaration, in August, President Saakashvili and Ukrainian president Viktor Yushchenko co-founded the Community for Democratic Choice (CDC), constituting a regional democratic coalition. In attendance at the CDC forum in December, were the presidents of Estonia, Latvia, Lithuania, Moldova, Romania, Macedonia, as well as Georgia and Ukraine.

Most ambitiously of all, President Saakashvili announced in September that Georgia would seek membership of both NATO and the EU. Already a signatory to NATO's Individual Partnership Action Plan (IPAP) since July, Saakashvili stated that full NATO membership was realistic by 2008. In November, Georgia commenced negotiations with the EU over a formal Action Plan, designed to bring Georgia into line with EU political and economic frameworks.

Outlook

Georgia's economy looks set for further growth in 2006, in the vicinity of 5 per cent. The prospect of the SCP being completed by the end of the year bodes well for FDI, and the tourism industry recovery will almost certainly gather pace. However, inflation reached double figures in 2005 and will require government attention.

Burned by failure to address its secessionist problems substantively in 2005, Georgia has set itself the task of presenting a formal peace plan to Abkhazia in 2006. However, as Russia views the Caucasus as part of its back yard and has proved reluctant to let Georgia stray too far, any progress will be dependent upon Tbilisi's ability to engage positively with Moscow.

Politically, Georgia will likely remain broadly stable in 2006. The fall-out from the sacking of Zurabishvili in October 2005 may yet prove more damaging for the alliance that led the Rose Revolution. However, with national elections not due until 2008, serious political upheaval is unlikely.

Risk assessment

Politics	stable
Economy	stable
Regional stability	stable

COUNTRY PROFILE

Historical profile
In the ninth century BC, the legendary Kingdom of Colchis was founded where Jason found the golden fleece and fell in love with Medea. Georgia is this mythical place. The country's Amirani legend parallels the Greek myth.

Georgia converted to Christianity in 330 AD.

The nineteenth century saw Georgia gradually incorporated into Russia.

1916 Georgia joined an alliance with Armenia and Azerbaijan.

1918–21 There was a brief spell of independence until Russia invaded in 1921 and Georgia was incorporated into the Soviet Union.

1940–45 An estimated 10 per cent of the population perished in the Stalin purges.

1989 The killing of 20 people by Soviet troops during a national demonstration in Tbilisi triggered the final disillusionment with communism.

1990 Following a referendum which called for independence from the Soviet Union, Zviad Gamsakhurdia was elected the first president in July. Racist policies caused problems.

1991 Independence from Russia was declared. Prime Minister Teniz Sigua resigned.

1992 Gamsakhurdia was overthrown in a coup and Eduard Shevardnadze assumed power. Parliamentary elections were held, at which Shevardnadze was elected Chairman of the State Security Council. Shevardnadze re-appointed Teniz Sigua as prime minister

After Georgian independence the northern region of Abkhazia declared itself independent of the new state. The subsequent war killed an estimated 10,000 and created 300,000 internally displaced persons (IDP).

1994 A cease-fire was signed.

1995 After surviving a car bomb assassination attempt, Shevardnadze was elected by popular vote, and the Sak'art'velos Mokalaketa Kavshiri (SMK) (Union of Georgian Citizens) secured a majority vote in the parliamentary elections. A constitution was adopted. The Abkhaz parliament rejected the proposed status of autonomous republic within Georgia.

1996 In accordance with the constitution, a National Security Council was established.

1997 A Civil Code, second only to the constitution in importance, was adopted. Capital punishment was abolished.

1998 Shevardnadze survived a second assassination attempt.

1999 Georgia became a member of the Council of Europe.

2000 President Shevardnadze won the presidential elections. He said that he would not stand for a third term.

2001 Fighting erupted between Georgian security forces and Abkhazia separatists, despite the signing of a peace agreement between the two sides. Mass demonstrations followed a raid on an independent television station by security forces after it criticised the government for corruption.

2002 US special forces arrived to help train and equip Georgian forces for counter-terrorist operations. Russia accused Georgia of harbouring Chechen militants in South Ossetia and the Pankisi Gorge. Russian President Putin warned of military action if Georgia failed to deal with them. President Shevardnadze promised to work with Moscow to fight the Chechen rebels.

2003 Work began in May on laying the Georgian section of the 1,760km Baku-Tbilisi-Ceyhan (BTC) oil pipeline. Opposition politicians claimed the 2 November parliamentary elections were rigged and on 14 November 15,000 people went to the President's office to demand his resignation. President Shevardnadze resigned on 23 November, a day after opposition forces had stormed parliament; he declared Nino Burdzhanadze acting president. On 25 November, the Supreme Court annulled the parliamentary election results.

2004 Mikhail Saakashvili was sworn in as president on 25 January. On 9 February, the President nominated Zurab Zhvania for the re-introduced post of prime minister. A bloc led by the President's party won all the seats in the 28 March parliamentary elections.

2005 On 3 February, Prime Minister Zurab Zhvania died from carbon monoxide poisoning from a faulty gas heater. President Saakashvili nominated finance minister, Zurab Noghaideli, as prime minister on 8 February. The BTC oil pipeline, which will carry one million barrels per day of Caspian oil to Western markets, opened on 25 May.

Political structure
Constitution
The 1995 constitution provides for a presidential republic with federal elements. The country is divided into nine districts and 64 regions.
Form of state
Presidential democratic republic
The executive
The president, who is head of state and head of government, is directly elected for five years and can serve no more than two terms. The head of state holds supreme executive power, together with the cabinet of ministers.
National legislature
The unicameral Sak'art'velos Parlamenti (Georgian Parliament) has 235 members who serve a four-year term (150 elected by party list, 75 in single-seat constituencies and 10 representing displaced persons from the separatist region of Abkhazia).

Nations of the World: A Political, Economic and Business Handbook

Legal system
The legal system is based on the civil law system.

Last elections
28 March 2004 (parliamentary); 4 January 2004 (presidential); 2 November 2003 (parliamentary) (the election results were annulled by the Supreme Court on 25 November 2003).
Results: Parliamentary: a bloc led by the President's party, Sak'art'velos Mokalaketa Kavshiri (SMK) (Union of Georgian Citizens), won all 150 seats elected by party list.
Presidential: Mikhail Saakashvili was elected with 96.3 per cent of the vote; Temur Shashiashvili 1.9 per cent; turnout 88 per cent.

Next elections
2008 (parliamentary); 2009 (presidential).

Political parties
Ruling party
Sak'art'velos Mokalaketa Kavshiri (SMK) (Union of Georgian Citizens) (since1995; last re-elected Mar 2004)
Main opposition party
Sruliad Sak'art'velos Aghordzinebis Kavshiri (SSAK) (All-Georgian Union for Revival)

Population
5.32 million (2004)
Ethnic make-up
There are over 100 different ethnic groups in the country, including Georgian (70 per cent), Armenian (8 per cent), Russian (6 per cent) and Azeri (6 per cent). Other significant ethnic groups include Abkhazians and Ossetians.
Religions
Greek Orthodoxy is the main religion. There are also Shi'ite and Sunni Muslims, Jehovah Witnesses, Jews, Armenian Gregorians, Catholics and Baptists. There is inter-communal strife between the Christian Georgians and the Ossetian and Abkhazian ethnic Muslim minorities.

Education
Elementary schooling lasts for six years followed by two years of basic education. Secondary school education lasts for three years. Technical and vocational upper secondary education takes another two to four years.
There are 26 public higher education institutions in Georgia including eight universities and 14 technical and specialised institutes. In addition, 209 private higher education institutions have been established.
Public expenditure on education typically amounts to 5.2 per cent of annual gross national income (World Bank). Loans of US$60 million from the World Bank helped reform Georgia's secondary education.
Compulsory years: 6 to 14.
Enrolment rate: 89 per cent boys; 88 per cent girls, total primary school enrolment of the relevant age group (including repetition rates) (World Bank).
Pupils per teacher: 18 in primary schools.

Health
Total expenditure is some 3–4 per cent of GDP, of which 67–68 per cent is government spending.
The population has 76 per cent and 99 per cent access to improved water and sanitation facilities, respectively.
HIV prevalence: 0.1 per cent aged 15–49 in 2003 (World Bank)
Life expectancy: 73.5 years (World Bank)
Fertility rate/Maternal mortality rate: 1.1 births per woman; maternal mortality rate 70 per 100,000 live births (World Bank).
Infant mortality rate: 41 per 1,000 live births; 3 per cent of children aged under five are malnourished (World Bank).
Head of population per physician/bed: There are 4.3 physicians and 4.8 hospital beds per 1,000 people.

Welfare
Georgia has to cope not only with 58.5 per cent of its people living below the official poverty line but also an increased influx of refugees in the Pankisi Valley, 150km north of Tbilisi, inhabited largely by ethnic Chechens, known as Kists. The US Agency for International Development (USAID) has funded Georgia to implement community level activities, which benefit refugees, internally displaced people and others affected by ethnic violence and the deterioration of the social welfare system.
The benefits system includes pensions, unemployment benefits and family allowance, all paid at flat rates. The government provides 100 per cent electricity tariff discounts for war veterans and 50 per cent discounts for tax, customs, defence and security personnel.
Increased poverty in the urban areas leads to high incidence of wage and social transfer arrears. UN reports suggest that the average minimum wage is still insufficient to ensure an adequate standard of living for large parts of the Georgian population.

Main cities
Tbilisi (population 1.2 million in 2004), Kutaisi (268,800); Rustavi (181,400), Batumi (145.400).

Languages spoken
Russian and English are spoken and in the territory of Abkhazia, Abkhazian is sometimes spoken.

Official language/s
Georgian

Media
Press
Dailies: Georgia declared the repeal of libel laws from the country's penal code in 2000. Local journalists, however, continue to complain about police harassment, while financial and technical constraints still limit the independent Georgian press.
Of the 100 registered newspapers in Georgia, only about 30 publish with any regularity. Even the daily newspapers that receive state subsidies, the Russian-language *Sakartvelos Respublika* and *Svobodnaya Gruziya*, face severe financial constraints. Links to major on-line news services are available at www.sakartvelo.com/Files/media.html.
Weeklies: Weeklies include the bi-weekly *The Georgian Times* in English and *Rezonansi* in Russian.
Business: The EU-funded *Georgian Economic Trends* published quarterly in English and Georgian is the best source of business news and information.
Broadcasting
Radio: There are a number of government-run radio stations, including Georgian Radio One (GR1) and Georgia Radio Two (GR2).
Television: There are nine major TV channels in Georgia. Rustavi2 is the most popular broadcasting company in Georgia, while 1st Channel is the official mouthpiece of the government.

Economy
Georgia's economy relies on agriculture and mining which make up around 40 per cent of total GDP and employ around 60 per cent of the work force. The export of primary products has left the economy susceptible to falling prices and global recession. The country is reliant on imports of fuel, food and pharmaceuticals to meet domestic demands.
Georgia was one of the earliest former Soviet republics to adopt market reforms, notably on prices and foreign investment. Political problems have slowed progress, and the ability to attract foreign investment and introduce further liberal reforms is governed by moves to stabilise the political situation. Sporadic fighting in the South Ossetia region has put pressure on the economy.

External trade
Imports
Imports typically include fuels, machinery and parts, transport equipment, grain and other foods and pharmaceuticals.
Main sources: US (14.8 per cent total, 2004), Turkey (13.6 per cent), Russia (11 per cent), Germany (7.5 per cent), UK

(6.5 per cent), Azerbaijan (6.2 per cent), Ukraine (5.3 per cent), Italy (4.1 per cent)

Exports
Merchandise exported includes scrap metal, machinery, chemicals, citrus fruits, tea and wine.
Main destinations: Turkey (28.1 per cent total, 2004), Russia (9.7 per cent), Spain (7.9 per cent), Turkmenistan (7.5 per cent), US (7.1 per cent), Armenia (5.3 per cent), Greece (5.0 per cent)

Re-exports
Fuel

Agriculture
Farming
The agricultural sector typically contributes over 30 per cent to GDP and employs about 50 per cent of the workforce. Georgia is a major agricultural producer and the warm climate favours the growing of a range of sub-tropical crops in the coastal region. Crops include tea, grapes, tobacco and fruit.
A great deal of Georgia's produce is exported to other former Soviet republics in return for much-needed supplies of manufactured goods.
Crop production in 2004 included: 662,850 tonnes (t) cereals in total, 185,800t wheat, 410,600t maize, 419,200t potatoes, 61,000t barley, 16,600t pulses, 38,000t citrus fruit, 180,000t grapes, 116,000t tomatoes, 9,443t oilcrops, 1,500t tobacco, 23,800t treenuts, 3,110t various spices, 24,000t tea, 60,000t apples, 379,500t fruit in total, 490,500t vegetables in total. Livestock production included: 109,300t meat in total, 47,200t beef, 36,800t pig meat, 8,000t lamb, 15,500t poultry, 27,866t eggs, 780,400t milk, 2,000t honey, 7,467t cattle hides, 1,170t sheepskins.

Forestry
Over two-fifths of the land is covered by forests and woodland, of which only a fifth is available for wood production and another fifth is classified as primeval forest untouched by man. Around 60 per cent of Georgia's trees are broadleafed, including beech, oak, hornbeam and chestnut, and the rest are coniferous, mainly spruce and pine. Forests are important to protecting soil and water. The state owns all forests by law.
Georgia produces and exports roundwood (typically 65 per cent of forestry exports) and sawnwood (27 per cent) from hardwood species. Total forest exports in 2004 amounted to US$17.9 million, while imports amounted to US$5.1 million.

Industry and manufacturing
Industry accounts for a quarter of GDP and employs about 20 per cent of the workforce. Light industrial activities include food-processing and drinks production, metallurgy, shipbuilding, car production, consumer durables, garment manufacturing and oil-processing. Other industries include mining, chemicals, heavy engineering and steel-making. Levels of self-sufficiency in the manufacturing sector are low and export manufacturing potential is limited. The sector is troubled by a periodic lack of finance, the slow pace of rehabilitation of enterprises and low levels of management.

Tourism
The tourism sector has considerable potential to expand, but is hindered by government inactivity and political instability. There were around 290,000 arrivals in 2004.

Mining
Georgia has major mineral deposits, notably manganese, copper and lead. Small quantities of iron ore are extracted. There are reserves of about 200 million tonnes of manganese ore in Chiatura, of which 60 per cent is recoverable through underground mining and 40 per cent through open-pit mining. The Madneuli mining plant at Kazreti in southern Georgia is the country's only producer of copper concentrate. The Madneuli deposit contains the bulk of copper reserves, with reserves of around 460,000 tonnes of ore.

Hydrocarbons
Georgia has limited oil reserves, estimated at 35 million barrels, but is believed to have greater potential. Exploration is taking place off the Black Sea coast as well as onshore. Georgia, which consumes 42,000 barrels per day (bpd), produces around 2,000 bpd and relies on imports from Russia and Azerbaijan. There are two refineries. Georgia has always been a natural transportation route for the oil from the Caspian Sea to the Mediterranean. The oil pipeline from Baku, Azerbaijan, to the Black Sea port of Supsa in Georgia, was opened in 1999. The initial capacity of the Baku-Supsa pipeline was 115,000bpd of Caspian Sea crude oil. The Baku-Tbilisi-Ceyhan oil pipeline, to carry one million barrels per day of Caspian oil to western markets, opened on 25 May 2005.
Georgia had proven natural gas reserves of 84.9 million cubic metres at the end of 2004. Georgia, whose production is small, is dependent on imports of natural gas from Russia.
Coal reserves are estimated at 800 million tonnes, of which over a half are located at Tkibuli-Shaorskoye.

Energy
Georgia has a generating capacity of 4.5GW, which is produced by 53 hydroelectric power stations and three thermal power plants. Fuel shortages and a deteriorating infrastructure means the electricity sector operates below capacity and there are frequent power cuts. In order to meet demand, Georgia imports electricity from Armenia, Azerbaijan and Russia and has run up considerable debt on these imports, resulting in disputes with the suppliers. Poor electricity supply and high rates have prompted widespread non-payment among Georgian electricity customers.

Financial markets
Stock exchange
The Georgian Stock Exchange (GSE) opened in August 1999. There are over 280 companies trading on the GSE. The GSE is part of the Federation of Euro-Asian Stock Exchanges (FEAS).

Banking and insurance
The banking sector has undergone reform since 1995 and the central bank, the National Bank of Georgia (NBG), has assumed a supervisory role. The NBG has concentrated on consolidating the banking sector to clamp down on poor management, corruption and non-performing loans. It has also progressively raised the minimum capital requirement, which has caused a dramatic fall in the number of banks operating in the country and forced many to seek foreign participation to survive.

Central bank
National Bank of Georgia (NBG)

Time
GMT plus three hours

Geography
Georgia is situated in west and central Transcaucasia on both sides of the Suram range. There are frontiers with Turkey and Armenia in the south, and with Azerbaijan in the south-east. The Black Sea coast is to the west. To the west of the Surams lies the more mountainous Kura basin. The Rion, which flows westwards into the Black Sea, and the Kura which flows eastwards through Azerbaijan into the Caspian Sea, are the country's two main rivers.

Entry requirements
Passports
Required by all. Passports must be valid for six months after date of departure.

Visa
Required by all and best applied for before travelling. If issued by the Consular section of the local Embassy of Georgia, a visitor does not have to register, and any stay in Georgia is subject to the validity of the visa. If not issued by the above, or when arriving at the airport and planning to stay longer than three days visitors are required to register with the Ministry of

Justice. On arrival, request an Immigration Card from the Immigration Officer, to be taken to the Ministry of Justice for registration.

Business visas require a letter of undertaking of financial responsibility for expenses incurred by representative, a full itinerary and an invitation from a local company or organisation.

Do not overstay the limit of the visa. The Georgian authorities can impose heavy penalties for non-compliance, including detention, fines and deportation, and all removals at the travellers expense.

Currency advice/regulations
No restrictions on import and export of local and foreign currency, but it must be declared on arrival.

Almost all payments are made in cash (US dollar notes are the most useful). Most foreign currency can be exchanged at special exchange shops in the streets of large towns.

Customs
Small amount of personal goods duty-free. On arrival declare all foreign currency and valuable items such as jewellery, cameras, computers and musical instruments.

Health (for visitors)
A reciprocal health agreement for urgent medical treatment exists with the United Kingdom. Some proof of UK residence will be required. Rabies is a health risk.

Mandatory precautions
A vaccination certificate is required for yellow fever if travelling from an infected area.

Advisable precautions
Water precautions are recommended (water purification tablets may be useful).

It is advisable to be 'in date' for the following immunisations: polio and tetanus (within 10 years), typhoid fever, hepatitis 'A' (moderate risk only), hepatitis 'B', meningitis.

Any required medicines should be carried by the visitor, and it could be wise to have precautionary antibiotics if going outside major urban centres.

A travel kit including a disposable syringe is a reasonable precaution.

Credit cards
Only one or two outlets in Tbilisi can handle credit cards.

Public holidays
Fixed dates
1 Jan (New Year's Day), 7 Jan (Orthodox Christmas Day), 19 Jan (Orthodox Epiphany), 3 Mar (Mothers' Day), 8 Mar (Women's Day), 9 Apr (National Day), 9 May (National Holiday), 12 May (National Holiday), 26 May (Independence Day), 28 Aug (Orthodox Assumption of the Virgin/Mariamoba), 14 Oct (Svetitskhovloba), 23 Nov (St George's Day/Giorgoba).

Variable dates
Orthodox Easter Monday

Working hours
Banking
Mon–Fri: 0930–1730.
Business
Mon–Fri: 0900–1800.
Shops
Mon–Sat: 0900–1700.

Electricity supply
220V AC 50Hz

Weights and measures
Metric system

Social customs/useful tips
Georgians are excellent hosts. Feasting is a central part of Georgian tradition. If you go to a dinner as the guest of honour, it is not unusual to be asked to sing a song or recite a romantic poem. When Georgians show friendship, it is sincere.

Security
There is a risk of terrorist activity, especially on the border with Chechnya. There has been an increase in the number of robberies, kidnappings and assaults involving foreigners, especially business people, in and around the capital, Tbilisi. Travellers should exercise caution in crowded places and markets, and when using public transportation. It is advisable not to walk alone at night and to avoid unofficial taxis.

Travellers should avoid unnecessary travel outside Tbilisi, especially at night. Train travel to Armenia, which is prone to incidents of theft and crime, should be avoided.

Getting there
Travellers intending to stay in Tbilisi for longer than three days must register with the Ministry of the Interior.

Air
National airline: Georgian Airways (Orbi) is a joint venture airline between Orbi Airline and the German airline, Germania.

International airport/s: Tbilisi-Novo Alexeevka (TBS), 18km from city centre.
Airport tax: There is no airport tax.

Surface
Road: Highways connect Georgia to the Russian Federation via the Caucasian Road Tunnel and the Georgian Military Highway to north Ossetia.
Rail: Tbilisi has railway connections with Azerbaijan, Armenia and Iran. The conflict in Abkhazia has affected the rail link with the Russian Federation.
Water: International connections to main ports from the Black Sea ports of Odessa, Sochi, Trabzon and Istanbul. Connections are also available with the Mediterranean ports of Genoa and Piraeus.

Main port/s: The main ports are Batumi (deals mainly with oil exports), Poti and Sukhumi.

Getting about
National transport
The European Bank for Reconstruction and Development's (EBRD) plans for the transport sector include improving the maintenance of existing rail, road, port and airport systems; promoting the commercialisation and privatisation of the transport industries; developing Georgian links with the Euro-Asian corridor; encouraging better co-ordination between the Georgian transport systems and those of the other states in the region; and providing technical co-operation for policy development, structural reform, economic analysis, project specification and preparation, and economic and environmental assessment.

Road: Difficult terrain and weather conditions restrict road links. Note that reliable road maps and signposts do not exist. Independent drivers should note that fuel can be difficult to obtain without specialist local knowledge. An international driving permit is required.

Buses: Buses operate between major towns and cities. There is a small underground system in Tbilisi.

Rail: There is approximately 1,583km of track with a double-track railway between Marelisi and Sagandzile. There are regular services between Tbilisi, Azerbaijan and Russia. Reservations are required for all trains.

City transport
There are many forms of cheap public transport in Tbilisi. A knowledge of the local language with its own script could be very helpful.

Taxis: Both official and unofficial taxis are plentiful.

Fares should always be agreed in advance as fares for foreigners can be set extremely high. It is advisable to use only official taxis and not share with strangers.

Car hire
Although the roads are severely pot-holed, hiring a car and driver through your guide or business associate is the quickest form of transport. It is not recommended to drive yourself.

BUSINESS DIRECTORY
The addresses listed below are a selection only. While World of Information makes every endeavour to check these addresses, we cannot guarantee that changes have not been made, especially to telephone numbers and area codes. We would welcome any corrections.

Georgia

Telephone area codes
The international direct dialling code (IDD) for Georgia is +995, followed by area code and subscriber's number:
Kutaisi 331   Tbilisi 32

Useful telephone numbers
Police: 02
Fire: 01
Ambulance: 03

Chambers of Commerce
American Chamber of Commerce in Georgia, 1 Nutsubidze Street, 380077 Tbilisi (tel: 251-436; fax: 250-495; e-mail: amcham@amcham.ge).

European Chamber of Commerce in Georgia, 33 Paliashvili Street, 380079 Tbilsi (tel: 253-494; fax: 225-600; e-mail: iccg@kheta.ge).

Georgian Chamber of Commerce and Industry, 11 Chavchavadze Avenue, 380079 Tbilisi (tel: 293-375; fax: 235-760; e-mail: ktm@ean.kheta.ge).

Banking
Bank of Georgia, 3 Pushkin Street, 380007 Tbilisi (tel: 997-726, 983-268, 933-230; fax: 983-262).

Export-Import Bank of Georgia (Eximbank), 5 Chorokhi Str, 380002 Tbilisi (tel: 999-394).

Central bank
National Bank of Georgia, 3/5 Leonidze Street, 380005 Tbilisi (tel: 996-505; fax: 999-346; e-mail: webmaster@nbg.gov.ge).

Travel information
Donavia (Donskie Avialinii), Sholokova Prospect 272, Rostov-on-Don 344009, Russia (tel: (7-8632)123-361; fax: (7-8632)520-567).

Georgian Airlines (Orbi), 112 Rustaveli Prospect, Tbilisi (tel: 995-318).

Ministries
Ministry of Agriculture and Food, Kostava 41, Tbilisi 380062 (tel: 996-261; fax: 933-300).

Ministry of Communications and Post, 2.9 April St, Tbilisi 380008 (tel: 999-528; fax: 934-419).

Ministry of Culture, 37 Rustaveli Ave, Tbilisi 380008 (tel: 937-433; fax: 999-037).

Ministry of Defence, 2 University St, Tbilisi 380007 (tel: 303-163; fax: 983-929).

Ministry of the Economy, 12 Czhanturia St, Tbilisi 380062 (tel: 230-925; fax: 982-743).

Ministry of Education, 52 Chkheixze St, Tbilisi 380002 (tel: 958-886; fax: 770-073).

Ministry of Environmental Protection and Natural Resources, 68a Kostava St, Tbilisi 380015 (tel: 230-664; fax: 983-425).

Ministry of Finance, 170 Barnovi, Tbilisi 380062 (tel: 226-805; fax: 292-368).

Ministry of Foreign Affairs, 4 Chitadze St, Tbililisi 380060 (tel: 989-377; fax: 997-249; internet site: http://www.mfa.gov.ge/).

Ministry of Health, 30 Gamsakhurdia Ave, Tbilisi 380113 (tel: 387-071; fax: 389-802).

Ministry of Industry, Ul K Gamsakurdia 28, Tbilisi 380060 (tel: 931-045, 386-558).

Ministry of the Interior, 10 D/Kheivnis St, Tbilisi 380014 (tel: 996-296; fax: 986-532).

Ministry of Justice, 19 Griboedov St, Tbilisi 380008 (tel: 989-252; fax: 990-225).

Ministry of Refugees and Accommodation, 30 Dadiani St, Tbilisi 380080 (tel: 663-302).

Ministry of Social Security, Labour and Employment, 7/2 Leonidze St, Tbilisi 380007 (tel: 938-989; fax: 936-150).

Ministry of State Property Management, 64 Czhavczhavadze Ave, Tbilisi 380062 (tel: 294-875; fax: 225-209).

Ministry of State Security, 4.9 April St, Tbilisi 380008 (tel: 982-383; fax: 932-791).

Ministry of Trade and Foreign Economic Relations, 42 Kazbegi Ave, Tbilisi 380062 (tel: 389-667; fax: 398-882).

Ministry of Transport, Tbilisi (tel: 364-682).

Ministry of Urbanisation and Construction, 16 V Pshavela Ave, Tbilisi 380060 (tel: 374-276; fax: 220-541).

Office of the President, 29 Rustaveli Avenue, Tbilisi 380004 (tel: 933-208, 931-561, 999-292).

Prime Minister's Office, Government House, Ul Ingorokva, Tbilisi 380034 (tel: 221-729, 984-464; fax: 932-727).

Other useful addresses
British Embassy, Metechi Palace Hotel, 380003 Tbilisi (tel: 955-497; fax: 001-065).

Business Communication Centre (BCC), 47 Kostava Street, Tbilisi 380079 (tel: 988-371; fax: 987-601).

Business Support Centre (BSC) Kutaisi, 124 Rustaveli Avenue, Kutaisi 384000 (tel: 310-1001; fax: 331-1001; e-mail: BSC@iberiapac.ge).

Caucasian Commodity Exchange, Tbilisi (tel: 380-946).

Committee for Socio-Economic Information of Georgia, 4 K Gamsahurdia Avenue, Tbilisi 380085 (tel: 361-450, 938-936; fax: 995-892, 995-622).

European Union Office, Tbilisi (tel: 999-602).

Georgian Embassy (USA), Suite 300, 1615 New Hampshire Avenue NW, Washington DC 20009 (tel: 202-387-2390; fax: 202-393-4537; e-mail: georgiaemb@hotmail.com).

Georgian Oil State Department, Kostava Str 65, 380015 Tbilisi (tel: 361-642; fax: 985-017).

Gruzimpex (Foreign Trade Organisation), 12 Georgiashvili Street, 380008 Tbilisi (tel: 997-090; fax: 997-313).

Gruzinform (State Information Agency), Tbilisi (tel: 933-340, 932-441).

Independent Agency for the Development of Municipal Services, 89/24 D Agmashenebeli Ave 3rd Floor, Tbilisi (tel: 951-003; fax: 986-950, 951-003).

Port of Batumi, 20 Gogebashvili Str, 384500 Batumi (tel: 76-260, 76-261; fax: 76-780).

Poti Sea Port, 52 David Agmashenebeli Str, Poti (tel: 20-630, 20-660; fax: 21-914, 20-688).

Press and Mass Media Committee, Ul Mardjanisthvili 5, Tbilisi (tel: 969-188).

Press Secretariat of the Head of State of the Republic of Georgia, 29 Rustaveli Avenue, Tbilisi (tel: 969-5181).

Sakenergo (state hydroelectricity company), 1 Vekua Street, Tbilisi (tel: 989-814; fax: 940-676, 983-197).

Saknavtoby (state oil company), 65 M Kestava Street, Tbilisi (tel: 331-642, 942-887; fax: 333-032, 332-509).

Saktransgasmretsvi (state gas company), 22 Delisi III Lane, Tbilisi (tel: 932-981, 996-683; fax: 536-193, 227-746).

SME Development Agency, Mr David Buadze, 7 Freedom Square, Suite 708, Tbilisi 380007 (tel: 999-077; fax: 933-539).

State Television and Radio, Ul Kostava 68, Tbilisi (tel: 362-460).

Telecom Georgia, Tbilisi (tel: 999-297; fax: 001-266).

Internet sites
Information on government, elected officials and economic information:
http://www.parliament.ge

Press office of the President of Georgia:
http://www.presidpress.gov.ge/

Georgian Investment Centre:
http://web.sanet.ge/gic/

Germany

KEY FACTS

Official name: Bundesrepublik Deutschland (Federal Republic of Germany)

Head of State: Federal President Horst Kohler (from 1 Jul 2004)

Head of government: Chancellor Angela Merkel (CDU/ CSU), leading a coalition government (10 Oct 2005)

Ruling party: Coalition led by: Christlich-Demokratische Union Deutschlands/ Christlich-Soziale Union Bayern (CDU/CSU) (Christian Democratic/Christian Social Union of Bavaria) and Sozialdemokratische Partei Deutschland (SPD) (Social Democratic Party of Germany)

Area: 357,041 square km

Population: 82.63 million (2004); 82.50 million (OECD, 2003)

Capital: Berlin

Official language: German

Currency: Euro (eur) = 100 cents (from 1 Jan 2002; previous currency Deutsche mark, locked at DM1.96 per euro)

Exchange rate: eur0.83 per US$ (Oct 2005)

GDP per capita: US$32,695 (2004)

GDP real growth: 1.70% (2004)

Labour force: 39.59 million (2004)

Unemployment: 9.50% (OECD, 2004)

Inflation: 1.80% (2004); *2.1% (2005)

Balance of trade: US$191.78 billion (2004)

Foreign debt: US$3,662.65 billion (2004)

Annual FDI: US$375.50 billion (cumulative, 1995–2004, OECD)

* estimated figure

In January 1871, in the Palace of Versailles, Wilhelm I was crowned Kaiser of the new German Empire, which then contained 39 million Germans. Quite apart from the grey areas, such as the tenuous position of Alsace Lorraine and the Saar Land under this arrangement, the concept of Germany as a nation state and a single body politic is, by European standards, relatively recent. It would still be true to say that by the end of the twentieth century significant differences – of outlook and approach – continued to persist between Germany's provinces. To this day the interests and attitudes of Bavarians are different in many respects from those of a Hamburger or a Stuttgarter. To this layer of diverging attitudes and views has been added a further, more recent, division: that between Germans originating from the old West Germany, and the so-called Ossies from the former East Germany. While unification may have taken place, integration at grass roots level certainly has not. In large part this is due to the fact that Germany's east can hardly be termed a success story: unemployment is high, investment is low, social – even racial – tensions run high.

On another, international level, Germany's business philosophy also differs in many respects from those of its international, particularly Anglo-Saxon, counterparts. In Germany, the interests of the employees and management of a company are often paramount. Take-over bids by foreign companies are generally viewed with suspicion, mistrusted and resisted rather than welcomed by both management and employees, often with scant regard for the interests of shareholders.

As unemployment continued its apparently inexorable rise throughout 2005, Germans began to ask themselves what it was their country, with its complex make-up, actually stood for. Years of post-war prosperity had resulted in a greater concern on the part of Germans over where to spend their often-extensive winter and summer holidays, rather than the direction in which Germany, Europe's largest economy, was pointed.

The landmark props of post-war German identity had, almost imperceptibly, fallen away. Prosperity, full employment and state benefits were no longer certainties. The Deutschmark, that solid symbol of Germany's economic strength had disappeared. Germany's currency, synonymous with Germany's post war *wirtschaftwunder* (economic miracle) had been replaced by the euro, a currency Germany's people now reluctantly shared with lesser economies. Worse, other euro countries such as Greece and Italy were known to be cooking the books in order to remain paid up members of the euro-zone. As if all that wasn't enough, Germany's outgoing Chancellor, Gerhard Schröder had succeeded in reducing relations with the US, Germany's most important ally and supporter, to an all-time low following his refusal to join the US coalition in Iraq or endorse US policy in the Middle East.

Germany's economic and political difficulties appear to have caused a *crise de confiance* within the German populace. The nation state that had for so long acted as nanny to its people, now appeared to have other concerns. This had lead to a peculiarly German period of introspection in an endeavour to analyse Germany's new problems and seek to account for the loss of its traditional values. Pessimism was certainly the prevailing mood in 2005.

Gloom, doom – and Mr Schröder

By late 2004 Chancellor Gerhard Schröder had become the victim of his own best intentions. The much heralded *Agenda 2010* package of reforms remained for the most part on the drawing board, as unemployment passed through the five million mark. Political concentration had moved from the pressing needs of the economy to the question of Mr Schröder's successor as Chancellor. The full effect of the *Agenda 2010* reforms went by default.

A mood of uncertainty surrounded Mr Schröder's decision, in mid-2005, to opt for early elections, triggered by a momentous defeat for his Sozialdemokratische Demokratische Deutschland (SPD) (Social Democratic Party), in the Nord-Rhein Westphalia regional elections. Mr Schröder's scheme was to bundle a nervous German electorate into a general election before the opposition, under the leadership of the Christlich-Demokratische Union (CDU) (Christian Democrats) newly appointed Angela Merkel, had been able to get their act together. The scheme depended on the orchestrated loss of a parliamentary vote of confidence. It was not originally clear how the desired early elections could be brought about, since the German constitution made no allowance for Mr Schröder's desired scenario. Only if a chancellor loses a vote of confidence can the president dissolve the Bundestag (lower house of Parliament) and call new elections. The last time this had happened was in 1982, when Helmut Kohl was elected chancellor by the Bundestag, deposing Chancellor Helmut Schmidt.

But he had wanted his position to be confirmed by a popular vote – so he called a confidence vote and got his own MPs not to support him. This enabled the Bundestag to be dissolved, and Mr Kohl to win the subsequent election. The Supreme Court raised serious criticisms of the procedure, doubting whether it was in line with Germany's constitution.

This time the outcome was uncertain, first because Mr Schröder's unpopular ruling coalition only enjoyed a thin majority in the Bundestag, second because Mr Schröder also risked having any such move blocked by the upper house, which was controlled by the opposition. To Mr Schröder's relief, the 1 July 2005 confidence motion failed, and President Köhler called for elections to be held on 18 September, a year earlier than planned. By persuading the SPD's parliamentary group to abstain, Mr Schröder had achieved his objective.

However, any popular enthusiasm shown before the elections for the untried and untested Mrs Merkel soon dissipated as the reality of the elections dawned. Despite the high poll ratings that she had achieved in mid-year following a makeover remarkably reminiscent of that undergone by the UK's Mrs Thatcher upon her election to party leadership, by the time of the election, the election results were less than conclusive. Mrs Merkel's CDU/CSU coalition obtained 226 seats, only four more than Mr Schröder's SPD, with 222 seats. The CDU/CSU coalition won 35.2 per cent of the vote, only one percentage point in front of the SPD with 34.2 per cent. This caused the already discredited Mr Schröder to announce that he would continue as chancellor, a move that did little for his popularity. The Freie

KEY INDICATORS — Germany

	Unit	2000	2001	2002	2003	2004
Population	m	82.17	82.20	82.12	82.38	82.63
Gross domestic product (GDP)	US$bn	1,878.00	1,847.70	1,976.20	2,400.70	*2,714.42
GDP per capita	US$	22,800	22,500	25,300	28,710	32,695
GDP real growth	%	3.1	1.0	0.1	-0.1	1.7
Inflation	%	1.9	10.7	1.3	0.9	1.8
Unemployment	%	10.7	10.7	8.7	9.5	9.5
Natural gas output	bn cum	16.9	17.0	17.4	17.7	16.4
Coal output	mtoe	56.4	54.2	54.8	54.1	54.7
Exports (fob) (goods)	US$m	549,840.0	569,950.0	612,240.0	750,000.0	909,700.0
Imports (fob) (goods)	US$m	492,330.0	481,440.0	493,320.0	600,000.0	717,920.0
Balance of trade	US$m	57,510.0	88,510.0	119,300.0	150,000.0	191,780.0
Current account	US$m	-20,390.0	2,440.0	12,800.0	53,513.0	96,410.0
Total reserves minus gold	US$m	56,890.0	51,309.0	51,170.0	50,694.0	48,823.0
Foreign exchange	US$m	49,667.0	43,615.0	42,495.0	41,095.0	39,899.0
Exchange rate	per US$	2.12	2.14	1.04	0.88	0.80

* estimated figure

Demokratische Partei (FDP) (Free Democratic Party) won 61 seats, followed by the LP/PDS coalition with 54 seats. Die Grünen (The Greens), which had played a significant role in Mr Schröder's government won only 51 seats. After weeks of negotiations, the CDU/CSU and the SPD agreed to form a Grand Coalition under the leadership of Angela Merkel as chancellor. Mrs Merkel and her cabinet were sworn in on 22 November 2005.

In terms of forcing the CDU's proposed economic reforms through the Bundestag, the outcome of the elections did not promise much. The SPD held on to the key portfolios of finance (Peter Steinbruck, SPD), labour and social affairs (Franz Josef Jung, SPD) and foreign affairs (Frank-Walter Steinmeier, SPD). Of the other major ministerial positions, apart from Mrs Merkel herself as chancellor, the CDU held the positions of Speker (President of the Bundestag, Norbert Lammert, CDU) and the interior ministry (Wolfgang Schaueble, CDU). Franz Josef Jung of the CDU coalition partner, the Bavarian-based Christlich-Soziale Union (CSU) (Christian Social Union), was appointed minister of defence. Germany's new government had all the appearances of compromise rather than confrontation with the key issues facing a troubled country.

After weeks of political bargaining between the CDU/CSU and the deposed SPD, what emerged in November 2005 was not what outgoing Chancellor Schröder had hoped for, not what the German electorate had sought, and certainly not what was needed. Inevitably, in the face of what was almost a political stalemate, concessions had been made. And concessions mean casualties. Probably the major casualty of this consensual approach was the deferment of long overdue changes to corporate tax and labour legislation, put off until 2008. Also deferred was the introduction of any changes to Germany's burdensome health and welfare funding. Angela Merkel had originally proposed a flat-rate premium for health care contributions, replacing those based on a proportion of wages. This, combined with subsidies for the very poor (a growing concern with five million unemployed), was seen as the sort of root and branch reforms Germany badly needed across the whole spectrum of government expenditure. But such fundamental reforms not only faced resistance from the opposition, but had soon lost the support of Mrs Merkel's own party in the face of popular opposition. By early 2006 it remained to be seen if the so-called Grand Coalition would be able to see through anything other than minor legislation. Mrs Merkel's original economic programme, originally agreed with the FDP that now found themselves in opposition, had set some store by its tax and labour reforms.

If the Grand Coalition had its problems, so too did the disgruntled and fragmented opposition, made up of the FDP and the Die Linkspartei (PDS) (the Left Party), formerly the Partei des Demokratischen Sozialismus (PDS) (the Party of Democratic Socialism), the descendants of the East German communist party, the Sozialistiche Einheitspartei Deutschland (SED) (Socialist Unity Party), that ruled communist East Germany until 1990. The Greens were disaffected by no longer being included in the ruling coalition, the FDP, as they had expected.

Schröder's dash for gas

Mr Schröder will be remembered for a number of things, not all of them positive. The lasting memory will probably be that of self-interest. He demonstrated a single-minded enthusiasm for concluding gas supply deals with Russia while Chancellor. As late as September 2005 he claimed that he was 'the German chancellor, and I have to represent German interests, particularly regarding energy security'. However prescient his remarks, in view of the Russian induced gas shortages that overtook Europe in early 2006, Mr Schröder may have been confusing Germany's interests with his own. Within 10 days of Chancellor Merkel's appointment, he selflessly accepted the position of chairman of the shareholder committee of the Russo-German pipeline project. The major shareholder in the project, which by-passes Poland, taking the gas straight to Germany, is the Russian state-owned Gazprom, with 51 per cent. The German shareholders are BASF and energy company EON.

The whole project offers an interesting insight into Russo-German business dealings. The chief executive of the 1,200km pipeline consortium is Matthius Warnig, chief executive of the Dresdner Bank in Russia. According to reports published in the *Wall Street Journal*, Mr Warnig (who is known to be a close friend of Mr Putin) was an officer in the former East German secret police, and knew Mr Putin when he was based in East Germany as a KGB officer. According to the German tabloid, *Bild am Sonntag*, Mr Schröder's salary for the job will be US$1 million. Germany lacks a code of behaviour for retired senior politicians. Despite this, Mr Schröder's seamless transition from politician to well-paid businessman created considerable anger in Berlin. In some legal circles he was considered to be in breach of the German criminal code by obtaining private gain from public office. Mr Putin – who speaks fluent German – and Mr Schröder developed a close personal relationship during the latter's time in office.

Economic stagnation

For some years, Germany has inherited (from the UK) the mantle of the 'sick man of Europe'. In December 2005 the annual inflation rate remained at 2.1 per cent, despite fears that it would begin to edge up again by the end of the year. These fears showed signs of being fulfilled, however, by January 2006's estimated rise to 2.2 per cent. However, the prestigious IFO (Institute for Economic Research, in Munich) forecast a lower rate of 1.7 per cent. Germany's newly appointed economics minister, Michael Glos of the CDU and a member of the Bundestag since 1976, was at pains to restrain any optimism generated by signs that German business confidence was at its highest for six years.

Germany's IFO index of the German business climate rose to 102 in January 2006, six points higher than the figure recorded in January 2005. The institute considered that the upswing in the German economy had gained in both breadth and momentum. Expectations in both manufacturing and exports had improved, as had those in the construction and retailing sectors. The only reservations expressed came from the wholesale sector. According to the IFO, in 2005 GDP was estimated to have grown by 0.9 per cent, well down on the modest growth of 1.7 per cent registered in 2004. This growth is being driven by foreign demand, boosted by increased world economic activity and a more favourable euro/dollar exchange rate. Investment is also beginning to pick up steam; in sharp contrast, however, private consumption is still not back on its feet.

According to the institute, the outlook for the German economy in 2006 remains good. As long as international economy continues to grow, exports will remain the most important factor of growth. Investment in plant and equipment looked likely to expand, not least due to improved depreciation allowances; and the decline in construction spending was expected to halt. Private consumption, which in Germany has stagnated dramatically, is expected to be stimulated in the second half-year by the pull-forward effect of the increase in VAT starting in 2007. Annual average growth in real GDP for 2006 is forecast at 1.9 per cent. Since trend growth of economic output is 1 per cent, capacity utilisation in the economy will increase perceptibly. Despite official forecasts putting inflation as high as 2.0 per cent, on a par with 2005, the IFO forecast, at 1.7 per cent, is expected to be somewhat lower than this year.

The labour market situation is expected to improve only hesitantly. The number of employed is expected to increase by only 215,000 in 2006; 100,000 of this will be from government inspired job creation schemes, about which doubts have been raised. The unemployed figure should drop by an annual average of 150,000; in the winter months, however, it was expected to remain above the five million figure.

The government's fiscal position certainly did not improve any in 2005. With a GDP/deficit ratio of 3.6 per cent, the Maastricht deficit ceiling of 3.0 per cent has now been exceeded for the fourth year in a row. The measures put forward by the Grand Coalition will not change much, meaning that the Stability and Growth Pact is also likely to be violated in 2006, with a deficit forecast to reach 3.2 per cent. Mr Schröder's swan song budget for 2006 had required the government to borrow eur22 billion (US$27 billion). This on top of a public debt figure estimated to have reached eur1.5 trillion (US$1.8 trillion) – 68 per cent of GDP – by the end of 2005. In a touching display of optimism in the face of adversity, former finance minister Hans Eichel had once promised to balance the budget by 2006.

Outlook

Germany's political malaise in 2005 was not remedied by the September elections. The stalemate that these created left the electorate dissatisfied and the politicians frustrated. Chancellor Merkel has already had to put a number of key reforms on the back-burner, raising doubts about the ability of the German economy to respond to the challenges facing it on a number of fronts. In foreign policy, although Mrs Merkel is able to distance Germany from Chancellor Schröder's antagonism of the US and cosy relationship with Mr Putin, unless she makes Germany's position within the enlarged EU clearer, there is every likelihood that the EU will remain bogged down in budgetary disputes. There is little future in devoting precious resources to outdated agricultural subsidies instead of to high tech research and development as China and India flourish.

Risk assessment

Economic	Weak
Political	Stable
Regional stability	Good

COUNTRY PROFILE

Historical profile

Prior to the nineteenth century, the area of modern-day Germany consisted of a series of city states forming part of the Holy Roman Empire. Following invasion by France and subsequent liberation in 1815, Prussia emerged as the most powerful state in the region.
1871 Germany was unified under the Prussian royal house of the Hohenzollerns. Wilhelm I was appointed Germany's first Kaiser. After defeating France in the Franco-Prussian War, Alsace-Lorraine was annexed by Germany.
1880–1900 After Germany became Europe's leading industrial power, it attempted to expand territorially and become a world power, establishing colonies in Africa and trying to influence politics in the Balkans.
1914–18 Germany invaded Belgium and then France. The UK intervened, but the war in France became attritional until 1917, when US troops joined British and French forces. The First World War ended in 1918 with Germany's defeat. Kaiser Wilhelm II went into exile in the Netherlands. The Weimar Republic, a federation of 19 states, was declared in November 1918.
1919 Friedrich Ebert was appointed Germany's first president. Germany was called on to make massive financial reparations and to cede Alsace-Lorraine to France and parts of the Saarland to Poland, as part of the Treaty of Versailles. The Rhineland was de-militarised and occupied by the Western European powers.
1920s Germany was gripped by an economic depression, suffering from hyper-inflation and high unemployment. As it could not afford to pay war reparations, France and Belgium occupied the industrialised Rhur as a protest.
1931 The instability of the economy and of democratic government led to the fascist National-Sozialistische Deutsche Arbeiterpartei (NSDAP) (Nationalist Socialist German Workers' Party) or Nazis, led by Austrian Adolf Hitler, becoming the largest party in the German parliament.
1933 Adolf Hitler was appointed chancellor of Germany.
1934 The Nazis consolidated their power. Hitler established himself as the führer (leader) of the Third Reich. The economy was rebuilt, all other political parties were banned and Hitler's opponents, Jews and other minorities were placed in concentration camps.
1936 German troops re-took the Rhineland and provided military aid to Spanish nationalists fighting the Spanish Civil War. Germany, Italy and Japan formed an alliance.
1938 Austria became part of the German Third Reich after its pro-Nazi chancellor, Arthur von Seyss Inquart, invited German troops into the country. Annexation of Sudetanland, Czechoslovakia.
1939 Germany signed a non-aggression pact with the Soviet Union. Britain and France declared war on Germany after German roops invaded Poland.
1940 Germany captured most of Western Europe while most of Eastern Europe had pro-German puppet governments installed.
1941 Germany invaded the Soviet Union. Following Japan's attack on Pearl Harbour, the US declared a state of war with Japan; three days later, Japan's allies, Germany and Italy, declared war on the US.
1944–45 The US, Britain and the Soviet Union liberated Nazi-occupied Europe. Adolf Hitler committed suicide in Berlin. Following the end of the Second World War, Germany was occupied by the Allied powers.
1949 The Federal Republic of Germany (FRG) was established in the western zone by unifying the British, French and American zones of control, and the German Democratic Republic (GDR) was established in the east, under the Sozialistische Einheitspartei Deutschlands (SED) (Socialist Unity Party), following failure of negotiations to establish a unified administration. Konrad Adenauer became federal chancellor. Waltar Ulbricht became general secretary of the GDR's ruling communist party until 1971 when Erich Honeker replaced him.
1951 The FRG and France merged their coal and steel industries through the European Coal and Steel Community (ECSC).
1953 Severe food shortages and the policy of 'sovietisation' in GDR led to uprisings and strikes, suppressed by Soviet troops, causing large numbers of refugees to begin fleeing to the West.
1954 The FRG was admitted to NATO.
1955 The GDR became a member of the Soviet Union's Warsaw Pact.
1957 The FRG declared Berlin its capital. Bonn became the seat of government until reunification.
1958 The FRG became a founding member of the forerunner of the EU, the European Economic Community (EEC).
1961 The GDR constructed the Berlin Wall between eastern and western sectors

to stem the flow of refugees to West Berlin.
1963–66 Ludwig Erhard succeeded Adenauer as federal chancellor.
1966–69 Federal Chancellor Kurt Georg Kiesinger's coalition comprised the two largest parties, Christlich-Demokratische Union (CDU) (Christian Democratic Union)/Christlich-Soziale Union (CSU) (Christian Social Union) and the Sozialdemokratische Partei Deutschland (SPD) (Social Democratic Party of Germany). He chose the mayor of Berlin, Willi Brandt, as his foreign minister.
1969 Willi Brandt (SPD) became chancellor, heading a coalition of SPD and Freie Demokratische Partei (FDP) (Free Democratic Party). He implemented a policy of *ostpolitik*, orienting FRG foreign policy towards Eastern Europe and détente with the GDR.
1971 Erich Honecker became leader of the GDR, which became one of the most hardline members of the Warsaw Pact. In the late 1980s, Honecker resisted calls for democratisation on the Russian *glasnost* pattern.
1973 The FRG and GDR joined the UN.
1974 Helmut Schmidt became federal chancellor after the fall of Brandt in a security scandal. Disputes over the deteriorating economic situation, nuclear power and defence policy led to coalition instability and the withdrawal of the FDP in 1982.
1982 The CDU leader, Helmut Kohl, became federal chancellor and formed a coalition government.
1989–90 The Soviet Union withdrew support for the Honecker regime, prompting his resignation, the dismantling of the Berlin wall, democratisation of the GDR and moves towards a market economy. The reunification of Germany took place in October 1990. Helmut Kohl won the first free German election since 1931.
1994 Federal elections resulted in a narrow victory for Chancellor Kohl and his CDU-led coalition.
1998 The SPD gained the largest share of the vote in the elections. Gerhard Schröder became chancellor and formed a coalition government with Bündis 90 (Alliance 90) and Die Grünen (Greens).
1999 Germany became a founding member of the European Economic and Monetary Union (Emu). Johannes Rau was elected as federal president.
2000 Helmut Kohl resigned as chairman of the CDU following revelations about illicit funding to the party during his time as chancellor. He was replaced by Angela Merkel.
2002 Euro currency replaced the deutsche mark. Gerhard Schröder was re-elected as chancellor by one of the narrowest margins in German election history.
2003 In March, the Constitutional Court rejected a government request to ban the neo-Nazi National Democratic Party, after accusations that state agents had infiltrated the party's ranks, acting as *agents provocateurs* to discredit it.
2004 On 1 July, Horst Köhler took office as federal president.
2005 In July Chancellor Schröder dissolved parliament in preparation for early elections. The 18 September elections were indecisive with the CDU/CSU winning 35.2 per cent of the vote and the SPD 34.2 per cent. Angela Merkel was named chancellor on 10 October, and confirmed by a parliamentary vote in November. She leads a coalition government of CDU/CSU and SPD and is Germany's first woman chancellor, as well as the first chancellor from the former communist eastern part of Germany.
2006 In January, a Russian dispute with Ukraine over gas supplies had a knock-on effect on Germay's supplies, sparking a debate over the nature of its relationship with Russia, particularly in terms of energy dependency.

Political structure
Constitution
Federal republic; under the 1949 *Grundgesetz* (constitution), Germany has a high degree of devolution.
The federal structure is formed from 16 *Bundesländer* (regional states), including the city of Berlin. Each state has its own constitution, an elected legislature and a government with responsibilities including education and public order.
Form of state
Federal parliamentary democratic republic
The executive
Executive authority is held by the Bundesregierung (federal government). The chief executive and head of government is the Bundeskanzler (federal chancellor), chosen by the Bundestag (lower house of the federal assembly) and usually the leader of the ruling party, who then appoints his own ministers. The Bundespräsident (federal president) is elected for a five-year term by the members of the Bundesversammlung (federal assembly), but has largely ceremonial duties.
National legislature
Federal legislative power is vested in the Bundesversammlung (federal assembly), which consists of the Bundestag (lower house) and Bundesrat (upper house). The Bundestag has 603 members elected for a four-year term to single-seat constituencies and by proportional representation, together with a speaker. The Bundesrat consists of 69 members chosen by the 16 Bundesländer (regional assemblies) and a speaker.
Legal system
The Federal Constitutional Court rules on constitutional issues, taking appeals from the lower courts. German law is largely code law that traces its roots to the Roman legal system. The court system below the Constitutional Court includes five branches: ordinary, labour, administrative, social and fiscal courts. Civil and criminal cases are normally in the jurisdiction of the ordinary court system, which is organised in local, regional and state tiers with a federal tribunal (Bundesgerichtshof), presiding over the system. Since the signing of the Single European Act in 1986, the European Court of Justice (ECJ) has been the highest court of appeal for rulings on matters affected by EU law.
Last elections
13 June 2004 (European Parliament); 23 May 2004 (presidential); 18 September 2005 (parliamentary).
Results: European Parliament: CDU/CSU won 44.5 per cent of the vote (49 seats out of 99), SPD 21.5 per cent (23), The Greens 11.9 per cent (13), PDS 6.1 per cent (seven) and FDP 6.1 per cent (seven); turnout 43 per cent.
Parliamentary: Angela Merkel as leader of the party with most seats became chancellor. CDU/CSU won 35.2 per cent of the vote, 226 seats, SPD 34.2 per cent, 222 seats, FDP 9.8 per cent, 61 seats, The Left Party 8.7 per cent, 54 seats, The Greens 8.1 per cent, 51 seats.
Presidential: Horst Köhler was elected as federal president.
Next elections
2009 (presidential).

Political parties
Ruling party
Coalition Christlich-Demokratische Union Deutschlands/Christlich-Soziale Union Bayern (CDU/CSU) (Christian Democratic/Christian Social Union of Bavaria) and Sozialdemokratische Partei Deutschland (SPD) (Social Democratic Party of Germany)
Main opposition party
Freie Demokratische Partei (FDP) (Free Democratic Party), Die Linkspartei (The Left Party), Die Grünen (The Greens).

Population
82.63 million (2004); 82.50 million (OECD, 2003)
Ethnic make-up
The majority of the population is Germanic. There is a small ethnic Slavonic (Sorbian) enclave in the south-east state of Saxony (approximately 60,000) and a Danish minority in the northern state of Schleswig-Holstein (approximately

Germany

50,000). There are an estimated 70,000 Sinti and Roma German nationals, mainly in the state's cities and towns. Some neighbourhoods in industrial cities are dominated by guest workers, mostly from Turkey, the Balkans and southern Europe.

Religions
The two principal religions are Roman Catholicism and Protestantism. The German Evangelical (Lutheran) church dominates in the overwhelmingly Protestant eastern, northern and central parts of the country. Members of the Catholic church form a majority in the south and west.

Education
Participation levels in primary and secondary education are almost 100 per cent, while 45 per cent attend some form of tertiary education. Approximately 4.8 per cent of GNP is spent on public education. The public school system is administered by the individual states. Primary education is free and grants are made available for secondary education in institutions where fees are charged.

A year of kindergarten is followed by four years of primary school (*Grundschule*). Pupils are then screened for later admission into either advanced study or specialised and vocational training. Those in the advanced track continue at a *Gymnasium* to the age of 19, and then take the *Arbitur* comprehensive academic examination for admission to university. The majority of pupils attend vocational college after the age of 16.

In June 2004, the German cabinet agreed to give 10 of the country's leading unversities and researsh centres an extra US$2.3 billion, over five years, from 2006.

Compulsory years: Six to 16
Pupils per teacher: 17 in primary schools

Health
Total expenditure on health is 10–11 per cent of GDP, of which 74–75 per cent is government spending.

There is no national health service, instead comprehensive healthcare is administered by the individual states. Per capita health expenditure typically averages an annual US$2,412.

Health insurance provides 100 per cent of workers' salary for six weeks then drops to 80 per cent for 78 weeks. Health insurance also covers maternity and death benefits. Health insurance premiums, split by worker and employer in the case of those with high salaries, average 12.5 per cent of gross earnings.

HIV prevalence: 0.1 per cent aged 15–49 in 2003 (World Bank)
Life expectancy: 78.3 years (World Bank)
Fertility rate/Maternal mortality rate: 1.3 births per woman (World Bank)
Birth rate/Death rate: 8.6 births per 1,000 population; 10.3 deaths per 1,000 population (2003).
Infant mortality rate: 4.2 per 1,000 live births (World Bank)
Head of population per physician/bed: 3.5 physicians and 9.3 hospital beds per 1,000 people.

Welfare
Germany's health and social security systems are among the most generous in the world. Health, unemployment and retirement insurance are mandatory for most ordinary wage-earners under a wide-ranging social insurance system that has developed over more than a century. The system operates on a payroll withholding plan with contributions from workers, employers and government.

The welfare system provides assistance for all needy people who are unable to fend for themselves. There are funds for the support of widows, orphans and disabled people. The state makes available housing allowances for the poor in addition to its subsidies to low-income housing construction. The annual budget for spending in 2005 is eur1.8 billion (US$1.5 billion), plus eur3.2 billion (US$2.6 billion) to be given to local authorities for their social programme spending.

Main cities
Berlin (capital, estimated population 3.4 million in 2004), Hamburg (1.7 million), Munich (1.2 million, Bavaria), Cologne (965,300, North Rhine-Westphalia), Frankfurt am Main (648,000, Hesse), Essen (588,800, North Rhine-Westphalia), Dortmund (587,600, North Rhine-Westphalia), Stuttgart (581,100, Baden-Württemberg), Düsseldorf (568,900, North Rhine-Westphalia), Bremen (527,900, Bremen), Hanover (516,300, Lower Saxony), Duisburg (513,400, North Rhine-Westphalia), Nürnberg (486,700, Bavaria), Leipzig (486,100, Saxony), Dresden (473,300, Saxony), Bochum (388,100, North Rhine-Westphalia), Wuppertal (365,400, North Rhine-Westphalia), Bielefeld (320,900, North Rhine-Westphalia).

Other cities include Bonn (307,500), Mannheim (306,100, Baden-Württemberg), Wiesbaden (Hesse), Kiel (Schleswig-Holstein), Magdeburg (Saxony-Anhalt), Erfurt (Thuringia), Mainz (Rhineland-Palatinate), Saarbrücken (Saarland), Potsdam (Brandenburg), Schwerin (Mecklenburg-Western Pomerania).

Languages spoken
English is widely spoken, especially in business circles; French is also spoken, particularly in the Saarland. In the north in Schleswig-Holstein, Danish is spoken by the Danish minority and taught in schools. Regional dialects often differ markedly from standard German. There is an ongoing debate on language reform in Germany. It is almost 100 years since language laws were last comprehensively reformed.

Sorbian, North and West Frisian, Romani, Turkish and Kurdish are also spoken.

Official language/s
German

Media
Press
Dailies: There are over 600 daily newspapers, dominated by private enterprises. Among the more influential daily newspapers are *Bild am Sontag* (tabloid), *Frankfurter Allgemeine Zeitung*, *Frankfurter Allgemeine Sonntagszeitung*, *Frankfurter Rundschau*, *Handelsblatt*, *Tageszeitung*, *Die Welt* and *Süddeutsche Zeitung*. The colourful tabloid *Bild* is the most widely read daily newspaper.

Weeklies: There are very few national Sunday papers. The magazine *Der Spiegel* contains issues of general interest. The weekly newspaper *Die Zeit* provides cultural and analytical commentary. *Welt am Sonntag* is the Sunday broadsheet newspaper. The *Euro Am Sonntag* is a Sunday paper for private investors.

Business: There are numerous trade and business publications. Influential business newspapers include the quarterly *BVW Zeitschrift für Vorschlagswesen* published by the German Institute of Business Management. *Börsen Zeitung* is a newspaper with detailed coverage of the financial market. Others are *Die Bank*, *Berliner Merkur*, *Börsen-Zeitung*, *Business Traveller*, *Finanzen*, *Business Magazine*, and a half-yearly publication on general economic matters, *Aktiv Wirtschaftszeitung*.

Periodicals: A monthly publication, *Deutscher Vertriebs-und Verkaufs-Anzeiger*, reports on trade, services and industry. Other publications, on current affairs and politics, include *Dialog* (quarterly), *Kommunalpolitische Blätter*, *Die Neue Gesellschaft/Frankfurter Hefte* and *Europäische Zeitung*. *Spiegel Kultur* is a monthly magazine for entertainment.

Broadcasting
Private radio and television have become more firmly established in competition with the publicly controlled stations and networks. The partial dismantling of the public broadcasting monopoly in the 1980s has resulted in the appearance of numerous, mostly local commercial radio stations and several commercial television stations beamed at German audiences.

Radio: There is an abundance of national and local radio stations in Germany.

Major stations include Deutsche Well-Radio and DeutschlandRadio. There are over 180 private radio stations.
Television: Among the private channels, RTL and SAT 1 dominate. Other private channels include Vox, RTL2, NTV, Tele 5 and Deutscher Fernsehfunk (east). State channels are ARD and ZDF.
About 26 million households in Germany (80 per cent) have cable connections or direct reception satellites. The average television household can receive 31 television channels (national, European, international television stations).
Advertising
Television, newspapers and consumer magazines are all major outlets in Germany's rich advertising market.

Economy
The Germany economy is more heavily based on industry than some of its EU partners, although the services sector is highly developed. The German economic system is described as a social market economy. Free enterprise is encouraged, but sometimes subordinate to political goals. Germany's economy typically accounts for 30 per cent of the output of the euro-zone.
The reunification process revealed a gulf between western and eastern Germany. There is a stark divide between the strong, technologically advanced and highly competitive western Germany and the less developed former communist economy of the east, which is in the throes of free market restructuring and continues to suffer simultaneously from high structural unemployment and skills shortages.
At a time when the global economy is recovering German growth is heavily dependent on foreign demand and has only been kept positive by its buoyant exports. Domestic demand has remained sluggish, so much so that the IMF has described the economy as 'fragile'. Germany's GDP contracted by 0.1 per cent in 2003 but expanded by 1.7 per cent in 2004. GDP growth was only 0.9 per cent in 2005 but is predicted to rise to 1.7 per cent in 2006.
OECD recommendations, in its 2005 publication, *Economic Policy Reforms*, to facilitate fiscal consolidation linked to fundamental reforms include:
- rationalising federal and state government responsibilities across different levels;
- reforming the social security system;
- reducing subsidies and tax expenditure;
- cutting statutory income tax rates.

Analysts predicted that the inconclusive federal election in September 2005 and the subsequent formation of a 'grand coalition' government between the CDU/CSU and the SPD might stymie economic reform. However, by December 2005 the economy began showing signs of recovery, with GDP growth rates for 2006 revised upwards from 1.2 per cent to 1.7 per cent. A decline in the German unemployment rate was also recorded in December 2005, falling to its lowest level in a year, at 11.2 per cent (adjusted for seasonal variations). Also in December 2005, Germany's business confidence index was measured at its highest level in five and a half years.

External trade
Germany is one of the world's leading exporters. But imports have been growing because of extra demand for capital equipment and consumer goods in eastern Germany. Western Germany's industrial sector has been transformed technologically to remain competitive in world markets, where it generally has a reputation for quality and reliable delivery. Tighter controls have been introduced on exports which might have military uses. As one of the world's main trading nations, Germany favours open markets. In international negotiations it is normally a strong advocate of trade liberalisation. Well over half of all German foreign trade is with EU countries.
Imports
Include machinery, vehicles, chemicals, foodstuffs, textiles and metals.
Main sources: France (9.2 per cent total, 2004), Netherlands (8.7 per cent), US (6.5 per cent), Italy (6.1 per cent), UK (5.8 per cent), Belgium (5.8 per cent), China (5.3 per cent), Austria (4.3 per cent)
Exports
Principal exports include machinery, vehicles, chemicals, metals and manufactures, foodstuffs and textiles.
Main destinations: France (10.2 per cent total, 2004), US (8.8 per cent), UK (8.2 per cent), Italy (7.2 per cent), The Netherlands (6.3 per cent), Belgium (5.7 per cent), Austria (5.4 per cent), Spain (5.0 per cent)

Agriculture
Farming
Germany has always provided incentives and subsidies for agriculture, which is generally regarded as a national resource.
Most of Germany's agriculture is now governed by the EU's Common Agricultural Policy (CAP). It is based on three broad principles:
- the EU is treated as a single market for agricultural produce
- EU farmers are given preference over outside suppliers
- the cost of the CAP is met by EU member governments.

Fundamental reform to the CAP was introduced on 1 January 2005 in Germany. The subsidies paid on farm output, which tended to benefit large farms and encourage overproduction, were replaced by single farm payments not conditional on production. This is expected to reward farms that provide and maintain a healthy environment, food safety and animal welfare standards. The changes are also intended to encourage market conscious production and cut the cost of CAP to the EU taxpayer.
Livestock production has long been the most important part of the sector, but is steadily declining.
In eastern Germany, restructuring continues, with attempts to replace large-scale, overmanned co-operatives with smaller, privately owned farms.
Cereal crop production in Germany (particularly wheat) was adversely effected in June and September of 2005, by unusually hot temperatures and late summer rains respectively. Estimates for total cereal production in 2005 were more than ten per cent lower than 2004 yields. The estimated crop production for 2004 included: 51,097,000 tonnes (t) cereals in total, 25,427,000t wheat, 3,830,000t rye, 12,993,000t barley, 13,044,000t potatoes, 4,200,000t maize, 1,186,000t oats, 29,000t hops, 12,000t tobacco, 2,041,345t oilcrops, 27,159,000t sugar beets, 1,120,000t grapes, 16,900t treenuts, 5,277,000t rapeseed (canola), 1,592,000t apples, 568,000t plums, 4,276,284t fruit in total, 3,947,500t vegetables in total. Livestock production included: 6,797,840t meat in total, 1,258,000t beef, 4,323,400t pig meat, 52,000t lamb, 28,152,000t milk, 1,038,400t poultry, 798,000t eggs, 16,000t honey, 141,000t cattle hides.
Fishing
West German sea fishing has experienced a sharp decline in recent decades. The government makes some subsidies available, but policy is largely an EU matter. The total seafood catch declined rapidly to just over 300,000 tonnes per annum during the mid 1990s. Since then catches have fallen to around 250,000 tonnes per year. Freshwater catches have also seen a drop in quantity of about one-fifth over the same period. Cuts in 2006 fishing quotas, agreed by the EU in December 2005, are expected to prolong this decline for the forseeable future.
The home ports of the east German deep-sea fishing fleets are Rostock-Marienehe and Sassnitz. The fleets work the waters off Iceland, Greenland, Labrador and Newfoundland and off the coast of West Africa. Inland fisheries account for only 4 per cent of the annual catch.
Forestry
Forest accounts for nearly a third of the land area estimated at 10.7 million hectares (ha) in 2000. These are located

mainly in the south, centre and east of the country, with relatively little on the northern plain. Most of the forest area is available for wood supply. The growing stock per hectare is high and has been increasing. About 50 per cent of forests are publicly owned.

Germany has a strong forest industry and is one of the leading producers of wood-based panels and paper in the global market. The large-scale engineered wood product industry is dependent partially on sawnwood imports. Paper production is also partly based on imported wood pulp. It is one of the largest exporters and consumers of recycled paper.

Forest exports in 2004 amounted to US$15.9 billion, while imports amounted to US$15.2 billion.

Production in 2004 included 54,504,000 cubic metres (cum) roundwood, 48,657,000cum industrial roundwood, 19,051,000cum sawnwood, 32,241,000cum sawlogs and veneers, 12,695,000cum pulpwood, 14,108,000cum wood-based panels, 5,847,000cum wood fuel; 13,219,000 tonnes (t) recovered paper, 2,403,000t newsprint, 7,880,000t printing and writing paper.

Industry and manufacturing

The industrial sector accounts for 36.2 per cent of GDP and employs approximately 36 per cent of the workforce.

Germany is a leading European producer of motor vehicles and accessories, industrial plant, machine tools, electrical goods, scientific instruments, chemicals, pharmaceuticals and consumer goods. Traditional industries (steel, shipbuilding) have contracted because of foreign competition and weaker demand.

Some companies have moved into entirely new industries in order to take advantage of government deregulation and growth in service industries.

Strenuous efforts are being made to modernise industry in western Germany through the use of electronics and more flexible production techniques, and to restructure industry in eastern Germany which has remained uncompetitive in terms of price and quality. Worst affected areas are steel, electronics, engineering and chemicals.

High production costs in eastern Germany are preventing the region's companies from competing with their western counterparts and are contributing to a high rate of insolvencies. The number of bankruptcies in Germany grew by a record 14 per cent in 2002 as more than 37,579 businesses filed for insolvency. In early 2002, several prominent German companies were affected, including the construction company Philipp Holzmann AG and the aircraft manufacturer Fairchild-Dornier, while 2003 bankruptcies included the electronics manufacturer, Grundig. Insolvencies were most marked in construction, the main growth sector in eastern Germany. In 2004, the car manufacturer Volkswagen (VW) recorded a large decline in profits and between June and July 2005 three senior VW officials were forced to resign amid accusations of bribery.

East German industry began to show improvements in growth and productivity in the late 1990s, particularly in the electronics, food processing, printing, engineering and automotive sectors.

Industrial production rose by 1.5 per cent in September 2005, and 1.1 per cent in October 2005.

Tourism

Tourism accounts for 8 per cent of GDP and is a major employer, providing work for 2.8 million people. The main market is Europe, principally the Netherlands, followed by the UK and Switzerland. The US, which comes second after The Netherlands, is the most lucrative market. The sector is not a significant net foreign exchange earner, because so many Germans travel abroad. Foreign visitor numbers were falling by more than a million each year from 2000, when 19 million were recorded, until 2003 when 18.4 million arrivals were recorded.

Mining

The mining sector accounts for around 1 per cent of GDP and 1 per cent of the workforce.

Hydrocarbons

Germany depends heavily on oil and gas imports (approximately 96 per cent for oil and 80 per cent for natural gas).

Total estimated oil reserves stood at 200–400 million barrels in 2005, situated mainly in the north and north-east of the country.

Most of the country's natural gas requirements are imported, although offshore gas fields in the North Sea, estimated to contain 12.7 billion cubic metres (cum), began to be developed in 2000. In 2004, proved natural gas reserves stood at 200 billion cum down from the 210 billion cum in 2003; production was 16.4 billion cum in 2004. Germany is the EU's second largest consumer of natural gas, after the UK, and fourth in the world, most of which is met by imports. Around 35 per cent of gas imports derive from Russia and in January 2006, when a Russian dispute over gas supplies with Ukraine led to a temporary reduction in supplies to Germany, the German government began exploring ways to diversify its imports. In September 2005 Germany signed an agreement with Russia to build a 1,200km gas pipeline underneath the Baltic Sea, which would transport Russian gas between the Russian town of Vyborg to the German town of Greifswald. The project is set to cost US$5billion; German companies control a 49 per cent stake in the pipeline, with the remainder in Russian hands. Work began on the pipeline in December 2005 amid complaints from Poland and the Ukraine that the project is designed to bypass its consumers. Also in December 2005, the former German chancellor Gerhard Schröder accepted a top position with the North European Gas Pipeline Company, the consortium overseeing the Vyborg-Greifswald pipeline. In response, spokespersons for Germany's main opposition parties accused the former chancellor of a conflict of interest.

Coal is Germany's main hydrocarbon resource. In 2004, coal reserves stood at 6.7 billion tonnes and production totalled 54.7 million tonnes oil equivalent (toe). Germany is the biggest coal producer in Europe and seventh in the world. Eastern Germany has huge deposits of lignite as well as significant deposits of anthracite, potassium salts and uranium ore. However, there are relatively few feasibly accessible natural resources other than large supplies of black and brown coal, so Germany is largely dependent on imports. High extraction costs mean that exploitation of small deposits of iron ore, copper, lead, tin and zinc is limited.

There is pressure to cut high-cost black coal output and jobs in the Ruhr and Saar basins as part of a drive for reduced government subsidies and more competition in energy markets.

In eastern Germany, brown coal production has been scaled back as supplies are used more efficiently in power stations and as efforts are made to curb pollution. Brown coal is regarded as a particularly dirty coal for carbon dioxide emissions and disruption of water levels would extend into The Netherlands.

Energy

There are over 2,800 power plants in Germany, including 19 nuclear reactors which provide nearly 30 per cent of Germany's electricity. Oil typically accounts for around two-fifths of energy consumption, coal for a quarter, natural gas for a fifth and nuclear energy for much of the remainder. Net energy imports account for over half of commercial energy. Pressure from environmental groups and the Greens led the government in June 2001 to announce the gradual phasing out of nuclear power by 2021. The decision is in line with Germany's developed use of renewable energy. Revenue from an energy tax is used to fund new renewable energy projects. In 2004, renewable energy accounted for 9.8 per cent of total electricity consumption in Germany, mainly from wind power.

Financial markets
Stock exchange
There are eight German stock exchanges – located in Frankfurt, Dusseldorf, Munich, Berlin, Hamburg, Stuttgart, Hanover and Bremen. The Frankfurt Stock Exchange is the dominant trading floor with more than half the volume traded. Combined volume on the eight German exchanges exceeds that of all other European financial centres except London.

Banking and insurance
A sophisticated banking system underpins the country's economic strength.
There are three main categories: central bank; multi-purpose banks, including commercial, co-operative and (publicly owned) regional Landesbanks and savings banks; and specialist banks, including mortgage banks and instalment credit houses.
Many banks have important shareholdings in industrial companies and bankers sit on the supervisory boards of many companies.
In 2003, Josef Ackermann, the chief executive of Germany's main bank Deutsche Bundesbank, was put on trial for corruption. Although initially cleared, a retrial was ordered in December 2005 and Ackermann is facing increasing calls for his resignation.
Central bank
Deutsche Bundesbank; European Central Bank (ECB)

Time
GMT plus one hour (GMT plus two hours from March to October)

Geography
The Alps form the southern border with Switzerland and Austria. Germany's southern and eastern borders facing the Czech Republic are also demarcated by mountain ranges. The eastern border with Poland follows the Oder and Neisse rivers. The north is a low, wide coastal plain along the North and Baltic seas, which are separated by Denmark's Jutland peninsula. Germany's western borders join (in an anti-clockwise direction) the Netherlands, Belgium, Luxembourg, France and Switzerland.
Picturesque, forested highlands dominate the central and southern regions. The country is drained by the Danube, Rhine, Elbe, Weser and Oder river systems.
The highest mountain, with an elevation of 2,962 metres, is an alpine peak called Zugspitze, straddling the border with Austria. The main centres of population are concentrated in the west, along the middle and lower Rhine from Karlsruhe, near the French border, and from there northward through the highly industrialised Ruhr conurbation, to the Netherlands border. The German segment of the Rhine is 865km long, all of it navigable. On the south-east side of Europe's continental divide or watershed, the Danube flows eastward from its source in the Black Forest, through 647km of west Germany, to leave the country at the Austrian border at Passau on its way to the Black Sea. There is an important canal system allowing ships to sail from the Oder to the Elbe (to Prague).

Climate
Moderate summers and rainy, bleak winters. Most of the country has a typical north-west coastal climate, heavily influenced by moist maritime air masses from the Atlantic. The eastern fringe of the country is sometimes influenced by the continental high pressure centre, making for somewhat colder winters and warmer summers. Prevailing winds are usually from the west.

Dress codes
It is customary to wear a suit and tie in banks, businesses and government offices.

Entry requirements
Passports
Required by all except citizens of Schengen agreement countries who may travel with national ID cards.
Visa
Required by all, except tourist and business visitors from EU, North America, Australasia and most of Europe for up to three months. For confirmation of exceptions visit the website of the consular section of the local embassy. All visas issued before arrival, will adhere to, and grant Schengen requirements and facilities. A Schengen visa application (offered in several languages) can be downloaded on www.eurovisa.info/ApplicationForm.htm.
Currency advice/regulations
No restrictions on the movement of local or foreign currency apply. Imports of money for investment are subject to German regulations.
Customs
Personal effects enter duty-free.

Health (for visitors)
EU nationals are covered for medical treatment.
Mandatory precautions
Vaccination certificates are not usually required, unless arriving from infected area.

Hotels
No official rating system. 10–15 per cent service charge. Advisable to book in advance, especially when trade fairs are being held. All major credit cards accepted.

Public holidays
Fixed dates
1 Jan (New Year's Day), 6 January (Epiphany), 1 May (Labour Day), 15 Aug (Assumption Day), 3 Oct (German Unity Day), 31 Oct (Day of Reformation), 1 Nov (All Saints' Day), 25 Dec (Christmas Day), 26 Dec (Boxing Day).
In some areas, Epiphany, Assumption Day, Day of Reformation and All Saints' Day are not observed.
Although not official holidays, many shops and businesses are also closed on Christmas Eve and New Year's Eve.
Variable dates
Good Friday, Easter Monday, Ascension Day, Whit Monday, *Corpus Christi (May/Jun), Repentance Day (Nov, Saxony only).
*In some areas, Corpus Christi is not observed.

Working hours
Banking
Mon–Fri: various hours between 0830 and 1530 (most open until 1800 on Thu).
Business
Mon–Fri: usually 0800–1730.
Government
Mon–Fri: usually 0800–1700.
Shops
Mon–Fri: 0900–2000; Sat: 0900–2000.

Telecommunications
Mobile phones
There are excellent facilities and widespread services.

Electricity supply
220V AC, 50 Hz. European-style round two-pin plugs are in use.

Social customs/useful tips
Handshaking is universal at the beginning and end of every social or business encounter. Germans acknowledge others, even strangers, with a standard greeting when entering or leaving a room, office, shop or railway compartment.
The focal point of German social life is frequently club membership. The thick web of traditional clubs, which are based on activities including pre-Lenten carnival and sports, card playing, animal husbandry and marksmanship, strongly contribute to social life. It is known as *Vereinsleben*, or club culture.
Germans are extremely aggressive drivers and politeness on the road is not rewarded. There is no speed limit on some parts of the *autobahn* (motorway network). Verbal public insults can result in lawsuits. There are also strict laws against racial slurs, especially anti-Semitism.

Do not try to pay bill if invited to a restaurant during business hours. If dining at a German's home, it is considered impolite to arrive late; a gift of flowers is a social 'must'; do not drink until the host has his or her glass. It is regarded as bad manners to keep your hands in your pockets when talking to someone.

Getting there
Air
National airline: Lufthansa
International airport/s: Berlin airports are small and do not receive intercontinental flights, arrivals are via intra-continental or connecting flights. A redeveloped airport accepting intercontinental flights will not be ready before 2009. Frankfurt Airport (FRA), the principal German airport, is 13km south-west of the city, facilities include banks, post office, duty-free, restaurants and business suites. Extensive access to the city and other German connections are provided by trains (including international rail links), buses and taxis. Car hire and limousine services are available.
Other airport/s: Bremen (BRE) 4km south of city; Berlin-Tempelhof (THF), Berlin-Tegel (TXL) and Berlin-Schönefeld (SXF); Cologne/Bonn-Konrad Adenauer (CGN) 20km north of Bonn and 14km south-east of Cologne; Düsseldorf (DUS) 8km north of city; ; Hamburg (HAM) 13km north of city; Hanover (HAJ) 11km from city; Leipzig/Halle (LEJ); Munich (MUC) 11km north-east of city; Nuremberg (NUE) 8km north of city; Stuttgart Echterdingen (STR) 14km south of city.
Airport tax: None.

Surface
Road: There are good quality motorways and main roads linking all surrounding countries; border controls have been withdrawn and visitors may enter without registration although the authorities reserve the right to stop travellers at their discretion.
Water: Ships provide regular passenger service and cruises on the Danube between Regensburg, Vienna, Bratislava and Budapest and from Passau via Austria, Slovakia, Hungary, Serbia, Bulgaria to Romania and the Black Sea.
Main port/s: Bremen, Bremerhaven, Hamburg, Kiel, Rostock, Stralsund, Wilhelmshaven and Wismar.

Getting about
National transport
Air: Frequent services link Berlin, Hanover, Cologne/Bonn, Düsseldorf, Frankfurt, Hamburg, Bremen, Munich, Nuremberg and Stuttgart. Early morning flights provide direct links between many of these centres. Domestic flights are not cheap, but competition is bringing down prices.
Road: There are over 487,000km of roads with a modern network of motorways (*autobahnen*) linking all cities. Secondary roads in eastern Germany may not be of comparable standard with the west.
Buses: Good nationwide coach services are operated by Deutsche Bahn (DB) and other companies.
Rail: DB runs reliable Intercity Express and Sprinter services, with high-speed trains between major cities which include faster east–west links. First and second class travel is available and it is advisable to book in advance. For long-distance travel, trains can often be a quicker option than flying.
Water: Seaports on the Baltic and North Sea coasts are linked to inland waterways and railways. Navigable inland waterways are used extensively.

City transport
Buses, trams, metro and electric railway services in many towns.
A Welcome Card entitles travellers to 48 hours of bus and rail travel. It can be bought at hotels or VBB (bus and train) offices. Otherwise, machines dispense tickets permitting three consecutive hours' travel on buses and trains.
Taxis: Good taxi services run in all main cities. In Berlin, the metered cabs are beige Mercedes with yellow taxi signs, available outside hotels or at well-signed ranks.

Car hire
Special weekend rates are available. Speed limits: built up areas 50kph, normal roads 100kph, *autobahns* 'recommended' top speed of 130kph. Information is available from automobile clubs such as Allgemeiner Deutscher Automobil Club eV (ADAC), Automobil Club von Deutschland eV (AvD) and Deutscher Touring Automobil Club eV. The wearing of seat belts is compulsory.

BUSINESS DIRECTORY
The addresses listed below are a selection only. While World of Information makes every endeavour to check these addresses, we cannot guarantee that changes have not been made, especially to telephone numbers and area codes. We would welcome any corrections.

Telephone area codes
The international direct dialling (IDD) code for Germany is +49 followed by the area code:

Berlin	30	Hamburg	40
Bonn	228	Hannover	511
Bremen	421	Leipzig	341
Cologne	221	Munich	89
Dortmund	231	Münster	251
Dresden	351	Nuremberg	911
Düsseldorf	211	Potsdam	331
Essen	201	Stuttgart	711
Frankfurt (Main)	69		

Useful telephone numbers
Police: 110
Fire: 112

Chambers of Commerce
American Chamber of Commerce in Germany, 12 Rossmarkt, 60311 Frankfurt am Main (tel: 929-1040; fax: 929-10411; e-mail: info@amcham.de).

Association of German Chambers of Industry and Commerce, 29 Breite Strasse, 10178 Berlin (tel: 203-080; fax: 203-081000; e-mail: dihk@berlin.dihk.de).

Berlin Chamber of Industry and Commerce, 85 Fasanenstrasse, 10623 Berlin (tel: 315-10666; fax: 315-10166; e-mail: service@berlin.ihk.de).

Bonn/Rhein-Sieg Chamber of Industry and Commerce, 17 Bonner Talweg, 53113 Bonn, (tel: 228-40; fax: 228-4170; e-mail: info@bonn.ihk.de).

British Chamber of Commerce in Germany, 60 Severinstrasse, 50678 Cologne (tel: 314-458; fax: 315-335; e-mail: info@bccg.de).

Cologne Chamber of Industry and Commerce, Unter Sachsenhausen 10-26, 50667 Cologne, (tel: 164-0551; fax:164-0129; e-mail: my@koeln.ihk.de).

Düsseldorf Chamber of Industry and Commerce, 1 Ernst-Schneider- Platz, 40212 Düsseldorf (tel: 355-70; fax: 355-7401; e-mail: ihkdus@duesseldorf.ihk.de).

Frankfurt am Main Chamber of Industry and Commerce, 4 Börsenplatz, 60313 Frankfurt am Main (tel: 219-70; fax: 219-71424; e-mail: info@frankfurt-main.ihk.de).

Hamburg Chamber of Industry and Commerce, 1 Adolphsplatz, 20457 Hamburg (tel: 361-38138; fax: 361-38401; e-mail: service@hk24.de).

Hannover Chamber of Industry and Commerce, 49 Schiffgraben, 30175 Hannover (tel: 31-070; fax: 310-7333; e-mail: schrage@hannover.ihk.de).

Munich Chamber of Industry and Commerce, 2 Max Joseph Strasse, 80333 Munich (tel: 511-6368; fax: 511-6290; e-mail: alberts@muenchen.ihk.de).

Münster Chamber of Industry and Commerce, 61 Sentmaringer Weg, 48151 Münster (tel: 707-0; fax: 707-325; e-mail: international@muenster.ihk.de).

Nuremberg Chamber of Industry and Commerce, 25–27 Am Hauptmarkt, 90403 Nuremberg (tel: 133-50; fax:

Nations of the World: A Political, Economic and Business Handbook

133-5200; e-mail: info@ihk-nuernberg.de).

Stuttgart Chamber of Industry and Commerce, 30 Jägerstrasse, 70174 Stuttgart (tel: 200-50; fax: 200-5354; e-mail: info@stuttgart.ihk.de).

Banking
Bayerische Landesbank, 18 Briennerstrasse, 80333 Munich (tel: 217-101; fax: 217-123579; e-mail: info@bayernlb.de).

Bremer Landesbank, 26 Domshof, 28195 Bremen (tel: 332-0; fax: 332-2322; e-mail: kontakt@bremerlandesbank.de).

Commerzbank, Kaiserplatz, 60261 Frankfurt am Main (tel: 136-20; fax: 285-389; e-mail: info@commerxbank.com).

Deutsche Bank, 12 Taunuslage, 60262 Frankfurt am Main (tel: 910-00; fax: 910-34225; e-mail: deutsche.bank@db.com).

Dresdner Bank, 1 Jürgen Ponto Platz, 60301 Frankfurt am Main (tel: 263-0; fax: 263-4831; e-mail: dresdner-bank@dresdner-bank.com).

DZ Bank, Platz der Republik, 60265 Frankfurt am Main (tel: 744-701; fax: 744-71685; e-mail: mail@dzbank.de).

Hamburgische Landesbank, 50 Gerhart Hauptmann Platz, 20095 Hamburg (tel: 333-30; fax: 333-32707; e-mail: info@hamburglb,de).

Hypovereinsbank, 16 Am Tucherpark, 80538 Munich (tel: 378-0; e-mail: info@hypovereinsbank.de).

Landesbank Baden-Württemberg, 2 Am Hauptbahnhof, 70173 Stuttgart (tel: 127-0; fax: 127-3278; e-mail: kontakt@lbbw.de).

Landesbank Berlin, 171 Bundesallee, 10889 Berlin (tel: 869-801; fax: 869-83074; e-mail: information@lbb.de).

Landesbank Hessen-Thuringen, 52-58 Neue Mainzer Strasse, 60311 Frankfurt am Main (tel: 913-201; fax: 291-517; e-mail: presse@helaba.de).

Landesbank Rheinland-Pfalz, 54-56 Grosse Bleiche, 55116 Mainz (tel: 113-01; fax: 113-2724; e-mail: lrp@lrp.de).

Landesbank Saar, 2 Ursulinenstrasse, 66111 Saarbrücken (tel: 383-01; fax: 383-1200; e-mail: service@saarlb.de).

Landesbank Schleswig-Holstein, 6 Martinsdamm, 24103 Kiel (tel: 900-01; fax: 900-2446; e-mail: info@lb-kiel.de).

Norddeutsche Landesbank, 10 Friedrichwall, 30159 Hannover (tel: 361-0; fax: 361-2502; e-mail: info@nordlb.de).

Westdeutsche Landesbank, 15 Herzogstrasse, 40217 Düsseldorf (tel: 826-2449; fax: 826-9683; e-mail: presse@westlb.de).

Central bank
Deutsche Bundesbank, Wilhelm Epstein Strasse 14, 60431 Frankfurt am Main (tel: 9566-3511; fax: 9566-4679; e-mail: presse-information@bundesbank.de).

European Central Bank (ECB), Kaiserstrasse 29, 60311 Frankfurt am Main (tel: 13-440; fax: 1344-6000; e-mail: info@ecb.int).

Travel information
Allgemeiner Deutscher Automobil Club (ADAC), 8 Am Westpark, 81373 Munich (tel: 767-60; fax: 767-62500; e-mail: adac@adac.de).

Automobil Club von Deutschland (AvD), 16 Lyoner Strasse 60528 Frankfurt am Main (tel: 660-60; fax: 660-6789; e-mail: avd@avd.de).

Deutsche Bahn (railway operator), 2 Potsdamer Platz, 10785 Berlin (tel: 297-0; fax: 297-1961; e-mail: info@bahn.de; internet site: http://www.bahn.de/index_e.html).

Lufthansa, 2-6 Von Gablenz Strasse, 50679 Cologne (tel: 696-0; fax: 696-3002; internet site: http://www.lufthansa.co.uk).

National tourist organisation offices
Deutsche Zentrale für Tourismus, Beethovenstrasse 69, 60325 Frankfurt am Main (tel: 757-20; fax: 751-903; e-mail: info@d-z-t.com).

Ministries
Office of the Federal Chancellor, 1 Schlossplatz, 10178 Berlin (tel: 400-0; fax: 400-01818; e-mail: internetpost@bundeskanzler.de).

Ministry of Consumer Protection, Food and Agriculture, Rochusstrasse 1, 53123 Bonn (tel: 529-05291; fax: 529-4262; e-mail: internet@bmvel.bund.de).

Ministry of Defence, 18 Stauffenbergstrasse, 10785 Berlin (tel: 200-400; fax: 200-48333; e-mail: poststelle@bmvg.bund.400.de).

Ministry of Economic Co-operation and Development, 40 Friedrich Ebert Allee, 53113 Bonn (tel: 535-0; fax: 535-3500; e-mail: poststelle@bmz.bund.de).

Ministry of Economy and Labour, 36 Scharnhorststrasse, 10115 Berlin (tel: 615-0; fax: 615-7010; e-mail: info@bmwa.bund.de).

Ministry of Education and Research, 2 Heinemannstrasse, 53175 Bonn-Bad Godesberg (tel: 57-0; fax: 573-601; e-mail:bmbf@bmbf.bund.de).

Ministry of the Environment, Nature Conservation and Nuclear Safety, 6 Alexanderplatz, 10178 Berlin (tel: 305-0; fax: 305-4375; e-mail: service@bmu.de).

Ministry of Families, Senior Citizens, Women and Youth, 42 Taubenstrasse, 10117 Berlin (tel: 206-550; fax: 206-551145; e-mail: poststelle@bmfsfj.bund.de).

Ministry of Finance, 97 Wilhelmstrasse, 10117 Berlin (tel: 682-0; fax: 682-4420; e-mail: poststelle@bmf.bund.de).

Ministry of Foreign Affairs, 1 Werderscher Markt, 10117 Berlin (tel: 500-000; fax: 500-3402; e-mail: poststelle@auswaertiges-amt.de).

Ministry of Health, 76a Am Propsthof, 53121 Bonn (tel: 941-0; fax: 941-4900; e-mail: info@bmg.bund.de).

Ministry of the Interior, 101 Alt-Moabit, 10559 Berlin (tel: 681-0; fax: 681-2926; e-mail: poststelle@bmi.bund.de).

Ministry of Justice, 37 Mohrenstrasse, 10117 Berlin (tel: 202-570; fax: 259-525; e-mail: poststelle@bmj.bund.de).

Ministry of Transport, Construction and Housing, 44 Invalidenstrasse, 10115 Berlin (tel: 200-80; fax: 200-81920; e-mail: buergerinfo@bmvbw.bund.de).

Other useful addresses
American Embassy, 4-5 Neustädtische Kirchstrasse , 10117 Berlin (tel: 830-50; fax: 238-6290).

Aussenhandelsvereinigung des Deutschen Einzelhandels (AVE) (foreign trade association of the German retail trade), 1 Mauritiussteinweg, 50676 Cologne 1 (tel: 921-8340; fax: 921-8346; e-mail: info@ave-koeln.de).

Ausstellungs- und Messe-Ausschuss der Deutschen Wirtschaft (AUMA) (trade fair industry association), 9 Littenstrasse, 10179 Berlin (tel: 240-000; fax: 240-00263; e-mail: info@auma.de).

British Embassy, 70-71 Wilhelmstrasse, 10117 Berlin (tel: 201-840; fax: 201-84123; e-mail: info@britischebotschaft.de).

Bundesagentur für Aussenwirtschaft (bfai) (German Office for Foreign Trade), 87-93 Agrippastrasse, 50676 Cologne (tel: 205-70; fax: 205-7212; e-mail: info@bfai.de).

Bundesanstalt für Arbeit (federal labour office), 106 Regensburger Strasse, 90478 Nuremberg (tel: 179-0; fax: 179-3600; e-mail: zentralamt@arbeitsamt.de).

Bundesverband der Deutschen Industrie (BDI) (industry federation), Haus der Deutschen Wirtschaft, 29 Breite Strasse,

10178 Berlin (tel: 202-80; fax: 202-82450; e-mail: info@bdi-online.de).

Bundesverband des Deutschen Gross- und Aussenhandels (wholesale and foreign trade federation), Haus des Handels, 1A Am Weidendamm, 10117 Berlin (tel: 590-09950; fax: 590-099519; e-mail: info@bga.de).

Bundesvereinigung der Deutschen Arbeitgeberverbände (BDA) (employers' associations federation),Haus der Deutschen Wirtschaft, 29 Breite Strasse, 10178 Berlin (tel: 203-30; fax: 203-31055; e-mail: info@bda-online.de).

Büro des Beauftragten für Auslandsinvestitionen in Deutschland (foreign investment in Germany), 34 Markgrafenstrasse, 10117 Berlin (tel: 206-570; fax: 206-57111; e-mail: office@fdin.de).

Deutscher Gewerkschaftsbund (DGB) (trades unions federation), 2 Henrietta Herz Platz , 10178 Berlin (tel: 240-600; fax: 240-60324; e-mail: info@bundesvorstand.dgb.de).

Deutsches Institut für Wirtschaftsforschung (DIW) (economic research institute), 5 Königin Luise Strasse , 14195 Berlin (tel: 879-890; fax: 897-89200; e-mail: postmaster@diw.de).

Deutsche Presse-Agentur (dpa) (news agency), 38 Mittelweg, 20148 Hamburg (tel: 411-30; fax: 411-32219; e-mail: info@hbg.dpa.de).

German Convention Bureau, 48 Münchener Strasse, 60329 Frankfurt am Main (tel: 242-9300; fax: 242-93026; e-mail: info@gcb.de).

German Embassy (USA), 4645 Reservoir Road, NW, Washington DC 20007 (tel: 202-298-4000; fax: 202-298-4249; e-mail: ge-embus@ix.netcom.com).

Industrial Investment Council (IIC), 57 Charlottenstrasse, 10117 Berlin (tel: 209-45660; fax: 209-45666; e-mail: info@iic.de).

Presse- und Informationsamt der Bundesregierung (government press office), 84 Dorotheenstrasse, 10117 Berlin (tel: 272-0; fax: 272-1365; e-mail: InternetPost@bundesregierung).

Statisches Bundesamt (federal statistical office), 11 Gustav Stresemann Ring, 65189 Wiesbaden (tel: 752-405; fax: 724-000; e-mail: pressestelle@stba.bund400.de; internet site: http://www.statistik-bund.de/e_home.htm).

Wirtschaftsförderung Berlin (Berlin Business Development Corpration), Ludwig Erhard Haus, 85 Fasanenstrasse, 10623 Berlin (tel: 399-800; fax: 399-80239; e-mail: info@wf-berlin.de).

Zentralverband der Deutschen Werbewirtschaft (ZAW) (advertising industry federation), 17 Villichgasse, 53177 Bonn (tel: 820-920; fax: 357-583; e-mail: zaw@zaw.de).

Internet sites

Gateway site to web directory (in German with translation facilities): http://www.dino-online.de/

German-British Chamber of Commerce: http://www.germanbritishchamber.co.uk

German Government Website: http://www.bundesregierung.de

Germany Business Finder: http://www.infospace.com/uk.telegr/intldb/bizfindint.htm?QO=DE

Germany Technical Corporation: http://www.gtz.de/home/english/index.html

Rentenbank: http://www.rentenbank.de

State Bank of Baden-Württemberg: http://www.l-bank.de

Tourist Board: http://www.germany-tourism.de

Yellow pages: http://english.branchenbuch.com

Ghana

KEY FACTS

Official name: Republic of Ghana

Head of State: President John Agyekum Kufuor (leader of NPP) (since 2001; re-elected 7 Dec 2004)

Head of government: President John Agyekum Kufuor

Ruling party: New Patriotic Party (NPP) (since 2000; re-elected 7 Dec 2004)

Area: 239,460 square km

Population: 20.35 million (2004)

Capital: Accra

Official language: English

Currency: Cedi (C) = 100 pesewas

Exchange rate: C9,062.50 per US$ (Oct 2005)

GDP per capita: US$434 (2004)

GDP real growth: 5.50% (2004)

Labour force: 10.60 million (2004)

Unemployment: 10.20% (2004)

Inflation: 12.60% (2004)

Balance of trade: -US$1.51 billion (2004)

Foreign debt: US$7.40 billion (2004)

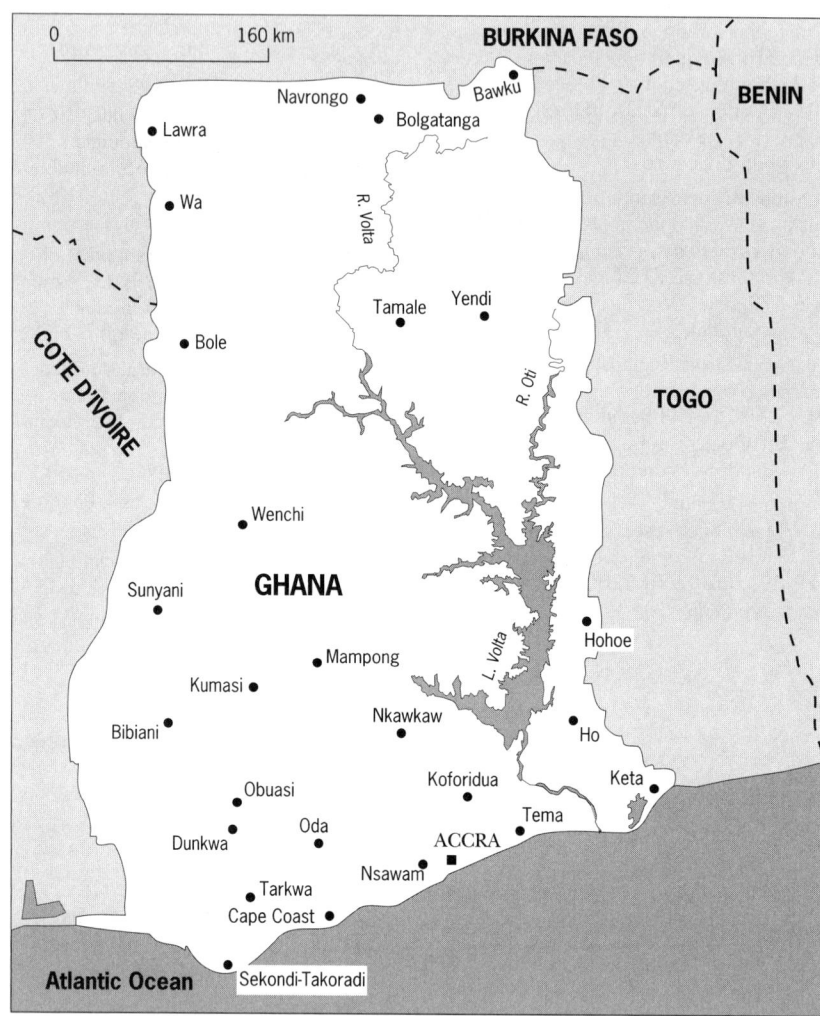

Ghana is one of several key African economies that are growing at an impressive rate, encouraged by growing political stability and financial prudence. Gold is the major export and foreign exchange earner, and agriculture the biggest employer. Trade and exchange rate liberalisation are designed to facilitate international investment and to achieve an economic climate that encourages business development. The increasing commitment from within the country is supported by several regional and global development agencies, all of which are committed to stimulating long-term business prospects.

Natural resources

Ghana is well-endowed with natural resources: gold, timber, industrial diamonds, bauxite, manganese, fish, rubber, hydropower, petroleum, silver, salt and limestone; but even so, Ghana remains heavily dependent on international financial and technical assistance. Gold, timber, and cocoa production are major sources of foreign exchange. The domestic economy continues to revolve around subsistence agriculture, which accounts for 34 per cent of gross domestic product and employs 60 per cent of the work force, mainly small landholders.

Ghana opted for debt relief under the Heavily Indebted Poor Country (HIPC) programme in 2002. And in December 2005, the International Monetary Fund (IMF) wiped out all outstanding debt incurred by Ghana to the fund before 1 January 2005, amounting to approximately US$381 million. Ghana qualified for this relief because of its 'overall satisfactory recent macroeconomic performance, progress in poverty reduction, and improvements in public expenditure management, freeing up resources for growth enhancing and poverty reducing spending'.

Economic priorities for Ghana include tighter monetary and fiscal policies, accelerated privatisation, and improvement of social services. Inflation should ease, but remain a major internal problem.

Ghana is allegedly an illicit producer of cannabis for the international drug trade; a major transit hub for south-west and south-east Asian heroin and, to a lesser extent, South American cocaine destined for Europe and the US. It has a widespread crime and money laundering problem, but the lack of a well-developed financial infrastructure limits the country's utility as a money laundering centre.

Politics

A well-administered country by regional standards, Ghana is widely regarded as a model for political and economic reform in Africa. It has a high-profile peacekeeping role; troops from Ghana have been deployed in Côte d'Ivoire, Liberia, Sierra Leone and the Democratic Republic of Congo.

Formed from the merger of the British colony of the Gold Coast and the Togoland trust territory, Ghana in 1957 became the first sub-Saharan country in colonial Africa to gain its independence, in this instance from Britain. Many years before, Ghana was the first place in sub-Saharan Africa where Europeans arrived to trade – first in gold, later in slaves.

Although Ghana has largely escaped the civil strife that has plagued other West African countries, in 1994–95 land disputes in the north erupted into ethnic violence, resulting in the deaths of 1,000 people and the displacement of a further 150,000.

In 1966 its first president and pan-African hero, Kwame Nkrumah, was deposed in a coup, heralding years of mostly-military rule. A series of coups resulted in the suspension of the constitution in 1981 and a ban on political parties. In 1981 Flight Lieutenant Jerry Rawlings staged a second and successful coup and the country began to move towards economic stability and democracy.

A new constitution, restoring multiparty politics, was approved in 1992 when Rawlings won presidential elections. He won again in 1996, but was constitutionally prevented from running for a third term. John Kufuor, who defeated former Vice President Atta Mills in a free and fair election, succeeded him.

President John Kufuor won a second term in December 2004, in a presidential poll internationally praised for being well-run and orderly. He is known as the 'Gentle Giant'. He came to power in the presidential ballot in December 2000, marking the first peaceful, democratic transfer of power in Ghana since independence. He succeeded the long-time ruler Jerry Rawlings. He has made economic growth a priority. During his first term, inflation and borrowing costs fell. He has also taken a leading role in mediating in regional conflicts, including those in Liberia and Côte d'Ivoire.

Born in 1938, he is a devout Roman Catholic. A lawyer who studied at Oxford, he held positions as deputy foreign minister and as secretary for local government before standing for the presidency.

Risk assessment

Political	Good/deteriorating
Economic	Satisfactory/vulnerable
Regional stability	Poor
Stock market	Satisfactory

COUNTRY PROFILE

Historical profile

The area of modern Ghana has been populated since the eighth century AD, but the main period of immigration seems to have taken place between 1200 and 1600. In 1482, the Portuguese built the first fort in the area, inaugurating an era of European competition along the entire Ghana coast, which continued into the eighteenth century until the British appeared to have established a degree of superiority. Almost uniquely, there emerged in the first half of the nineteenth century, a local community of lawyers, doctors, teachers and businessmen serving as a link between the European and African communities. Feeling that the British were insensitive to their interests, the indigenous community attempted to establish a modern state patterned on a Western model. The resultant Confederation, under the Ashanti King Ghartey IV was dismissed by the British government which rationalised the position by declaring the Gold Coast a Crown Colony. There followed a period of warfare with the Ashanti nation, that lasted until 1900.

1945–1957 An independence movement grew.

1957 Ghana (formerly the Gold Coast) was granted independence from British rule. English-speaking peoples of west Togoland voted for unification with Ghana.

1960 The country voted to become a republic. Dr Kwame Nkrumah of the People's Convention Party became president.

1964 Nkrumah declared the country a single political party state.

1966 The military overthrew Nkrumah and install the National Liberation Council, a transitional government.

1969 Dr Kofi Busia secured victory in the parliamentary elections and became prime minister.

KEY INDICATORS — Ghana

	Unit	2000	2001	2002	2003	2004
Population	m	18.41	19.70	20.15	20.25	20.35
Gross domestic product (GDP)	US$bn	5.00	5.30	5.80	7.70	*8.62
GDP per capita	US$	272	281	318	384	434
GDP real growth	%	3.7	4.3	4.5	4.7	5.5
Inflation	%	25.2	32.9	14.5	27.7	12.6
Exports (fob) (goods)	US$m	1,898.4	2,380.0	2,680.0	3,015.0	2,784.6
Imports (fob) (goods)	US$m	2,741.3	3,781.0	4,100.0	4,469.0	4,297.3
Balance of trade	US$m	-842.9	-1,400.0	-1,410.0	-1,454.0	-1,512.6
Current account	US$m	-42.0	-28.0	13.0	130.0	110.0
Foreign debt	US$bn	6.7	6.7	7.1	7.2	7.4
Total reserves minus gold	US$m	232.1	298.2	539.7	1,352.8	1,626.7
Foreign exchange	US$m	231.5	294.2	536.1	1,306.0	1,605.9
Exchange rate	per US$	5,455.06	7,170.76	7,869.75	8,625.00	8,930.04

* estimated figure

Nations of the World: A Political, Economic and Business Handbook

1972 After another military coup, Col Ignatius Acheampong took control of the country.

1978 Acheampong was deposed by the military and Lt-Gen F Akuffo, previously chief of the defence staff, became president.

1979 Akuffo's government was destabled in an unsuccessful coup launched by Flt-Lt Jerry J Rawlings. Dr Hilla Limann of the People's National Party (PNP) was later elected as president. A new constitution was promulgated.

1981 Jerry J Rawlings took power through a second military coup, disolved parliament and ruled through the Provisional National Defence Council (PNDC) .

1983–89 Discontent with the regime and its economic ineffectiveness led to a series of attempted coups, student unrest and alleged anti-government conspiracies. The government attempted to impose fiscal and monetary discipline and bring the economy into alignment with market trends and influences resulting in the cedi being devalued by 6,300 per cent in 1987. Over 1.1 million Ghanaians were expelled from Nigeria and returned home, placing great strain on limited resources.

1990 A national referendum on the restoration of multi-party politics was demanded.

1992 A referendum endorsed a new constitution to allow a multi-party system. Jerry Rawlings was elected president and his National Democratic Congress (NDC) secured an overall majority in legislative elections.

1993 The constitution entered into force and the Fourth Republic was inaugurated.

1996 Jerry Rawlings won the presidential election and his party, the NDC, won the legislative elections.

2000 John Kufuor won the presidential elections and his party, the New Patriotic Party (NPP), became the largest party in parliament. He became the first elected president in Ghana's history to succeed another elected president.

2002 The ruling NPP won a by-election in the northern constituency of Bimbilla, giving it a majority in parliament. Ethnic battles in the north led to the murder of Ghana's second most important tribal king, Ya Naa Yakubu Andani of the Dagbon people. His death led to the resignation of two senior government ministers.

2004 In February, former president, Jerry Rawlings, testified before the National Reconciliation Commission investigating human rights offences during the early years of his rule. Incumbent John Kufuor (NPP) was re-elected president in December and the ruling NPP won the parliamentary elections.

Political structure

Constitution
The constitution came into force on 7 January 1993. It is based on the US model. It allows for a multi-party system.
Ghana has 10 administrative regions which are subdivided into districts.

Form of state
Unitary republic

The executive
Executive power is vested in the president, vice president and Council of Ministers; both the vice president and the Council of Ministers are appointed by the president. The president is elected by universal suffrage for a maximum of two four-year terms.
If no candidate receives more than 50 per cent of votes in the presidential election, a new election between the two candidates with the highest number of votes is to take place within 21 days.

National legislature
Legislative power is held by a 200 member unicameral parliament, which is elected every four years by direct adult suffrage.

Legal system
The legal system is based on English common law and local customary law.

Last elections
7 December 2004 (presidential and parliamentary)
Results: Parliamentary: The NPP won 129 seats out of 230 and the NDC 88.
Presidential: John Agyekum Kufuor (NPP) was re-elected with 53 per cent of the vote, John Evans Atta Mills (NDC) 44 per cent.

Next elections
2008 (parliamentary and presidential)

Political parties
Ruling party
New Patriotic Party (NPP) (since 2000; re-elected 7 Dec 2004)
Main opposition party
National Democratic Congress (NDC)

Population
20.35 million (2004)

Ethnic make-up
Akan (including Ashanti) (44 per cent), Dagomba (16 per cent), Ewe (13 per cent), Ga-Adangbe (8.3 per cent), Guan (3.7 per cent), Gurma (3.5 per cent).

Religions
Christian (43 per cent), traditional religions (38 per cent), Muslim (12 per cent). There is complete freedom of worship in Ghana.

Education
The government's official medium-term strategy is to provide compulsory, free basic education for all. Government expenditure on education is about a quarter of total government spending. The Provisional National Defence Council (PNDC), the previous military government, introduced school fees and a loan scheme for tertiary education.
Some 50,000 literacy groups have been working to eliminate illiteracy in the country.
Ghana boasts the oldest university in sub-Saharan Africa – at Legon in Accra.
Literacy rate: Male; 61 per cent, female; adult rates (World Bank).
Pupils per teacher: 33 in primary schools.

Health
Annual total expenditure on health is around 4–5 per cent of GDP, of which 60 per cent is government spending.
In August 2004 the government imposed a 2.5 per cent levy on top of a 12.5 per cent VAT to be used in as a National Health Insurance.

HIV/Aids
The fragile infection rate trend was down from 3.6 per cent in 2003 to 3.1 in 2004. Officials will not laud the result as a victory until the trend shows a three-year steady decline. In the meantime infection rates of other sexually transmitter deseases (STD) are showing a rise among young people indicating unprotected sex. Authorities are planning to switch emphasis A survey in 2003 indicated there were over 350,000 people living with HIV (UNAIDS).
HIV prevalence: 3.1 per cent aged 15–49 in 2004. Prevalence in the north is lower averaging 1.8 per cent, while in the south it is 6.5 per cent (government figures).
Life expectancy: 54.4 years (World Bank).
Fertility rate/Maternal mortality rate: 4.4 births per woman (World Bank).
Infant mortality rate: 59 per 1,000 live births; 25 per cent of children aged under five are malnourished (World Bank).
Head of population per physician/bed: 0.06 doctors and 1.5 hospital beds per 1,000 people.

Welfare
The government's policies of structural adjustment have hit urban Ghanaians hard as the contraction of industry and the removal of state subsidies have led to increased unemployment, crime and poverty. In a bid to dampen the impact of reform, the government adopted a US$100 million Programme of Action to Mitigate the Social Costs of Adjustment (Pamscad) in the late 1990s to help cushion the shock of redundancies or redeployment as a result of the ERP. It involves 23 projects under five main categories: community initiatives, employment (including food-for-work schemes), redeployment (compensation for those made

redundant), basic needs (self-help schemes) and education. Medium-term strategies are centred on the provision of primary health care.

Main cities
Accra (capital, estimated population 1.7 million in 2004), Kumasi (645,100), Tamale (279,600) Tema (250,000), Obuasi (127,300), Teshi (121,600), Bolgatanga (93,100), Koforidua (89,200), Takoradi (88,000).

Languages spoken
There are over 25 major languages with numerous dialects. The principal languages spoken are Twi and Fante (spoken by the Akans), Ga, Hausa, Dagbani, Ewe and Nzema.
There is an official policy to encourage Ghanaians to be multilingual so French is also taught in most schools.
Official language/s
English

Media
Press
The Newspaper Licensing Law of 1989 (Provisional National Defence Council Law 211) regulates all newspapers and periodicals. It was passed largely to combat a spate of sensational fly sheets which had sprung up and which were said to have a combined circulation of 60,000. The government's stated policy is to introduce 'order and decency' into journalism. Licences are obtainable on application to the PNDC Information Secretary. A fee of C25,000 is payable and renewable annually. In-house publications and religious, educational, cultural, military and scientific newspapers or magazines may be exempted from the payment of the fee.
There is one official agency, the Ghana News Agency.
Dailies: English-language dailies include *The Mirror*, *The Independent*, *The Ghanaian Times*, and *The Daily Graphic*.
Weeklies: Weeklies include the *The Ghanaian Democrat*, *The Accra Mail*, *The Independent*, *The Statesman*, *Public Agenda*, *Ghanaian Chronicle*, *Crusading Guide*, *Christian Messenger*, *The Guide*, *Mirror*, *P&P*, *Pioneer* and *Weekly Spectator*.
Business: There are a number of weekly business newspapers including *Business and Financial Times*, *Business Chronicle*, *High Street Journal* and *The Financial Guardian*.
Periodicals: *Ghanaian Voice* is published irregularly.
Broadcasting
Radio: Ghana Broadcasting Corporation runs three radio stations. They include a radio service in English, Hausa and other African languages and an external radio service in English, French and Hausa.

There are also private radio stations. These include Atlantis Radio, Vibe FM, Joy FM, Choice FM, Radio Universe and Groove FM.
Television: Ghana TV (GTV) is a state-owned company operated by the Ghana Broadcasting Corporation. Metro TV is owned by both the government and a private company.

Economy
Ghana opted for debt relief under the Heavily Indebted Poor Country (HIPC) programme in 2002 and as a consequence undertook a regime to tighten fiscal policies, speed up privatisation of state entities and improve social services. Since then, the economy has shown a distinct improvement and on 13 July 2005 the IMF and the World Bank announced Ghana had been granted a total of US$3.5 billion in debt service relief, to run until 2020.
Ghana has achieved a stable macroeconomic environment, at 5.5 per cent GDP growth in 2004 up from 4.7 per cent in 2003. For this reason Ghana's sovereign credit rating was raised from B to B+ in 2004.
Rising world prices and record production of cocoa, which boosted revenue, and a 15.4 per cent growth rate in tourism have contributed to the country's healthy balance sheet. Only the impact of record global petroleum prices and unanticipated capital outlays could lessen the achievements, resulting in slowing growth and rising inflation in 2005. The government deregulated domestic fuel prices and eliminated subsidies in 2004, allowing the market to find its level while removing a drain on government expenditure. Inflation declined by half, falling to 12.6 per cent in 2004 and is expected to fall further into single digits in 2005. Consumer confidence has grown since 2003 and retail spending rose accordingly, with new service industries opening indicating a positive trend in businesses.
The government's dilemma is that it needs to limit increases to a relatively high tax burden, yet at the same time deliver the necessary public services. The IMF says this balancing act is vital to sustain the economy and provide for poverty reduction.
There is a Financial Sector Strategic Plan in place that provides direction for reform, particularly in regulatory and judicial restructuring, allowing for private property rights protection and competition. Further plans for the economy include the continued sale of parastatal enterprises, the removal of virtually all import restrictions and the elimination of exchange rate controls. The new inter-bank foreign exchange market has also increased access to foreign exchange.
Ghana is seen as a safe alternative by shipping traffic to the Côte d'Ivoire, which, since 2003, has been suffering internal strife. This increased Ghana's importance as a trading hub, and foreign investors became interested in developing Ghana's ports and improving trade relations. Ghana has to dramatically improve roads and port efficiency before it can take full advantage of Côte d'Ivoire's difficulties.
Ghana has much to look forward to and, as it has shown, has the capacity to grow and develop.

External trade
Ghana has a steadily growing trade deficit, with cocoa, gold and timber the principal export products. The government is trying to encourage the export of textiles, garments and processed goods with the aim of earning the country US$3.6 billion by 2006.
In 2002, the US approved Ghana as eligible for tariff preferences under the African Growth and Opportunities Act (AGOA).
Imports
Principal imports are capital equipment, petroleum and foodstuffs.
Main sources: Nigeria (12.8 per cent), China (10.1 per cent), UK (7.0 per cent), US (6.7 per cent), France (5.3 per cent), South Africa (4.2 per cent), The Netherlands (4.2 per cent), Germany (4.1 per cent)
Exports
Principal exports are gold (typically 40 per cent of total), cocoa timber, tuna, bauxite, aluminium, manganese ore and diamonds.
Main destinations: The Netherlands (11.1 per cent), UK (10.9 per cent), France (6.9 per cent), US (6.0 per cent), Belgium (4.8 per cent), Germany (4.4 per cent), Japan (4.3 per cent)

Agriculture
Farming
Agricultural land – around 14,600 hectares (ha) – accounts for almost 65 per cent of the total land area. There is over 6330ha of arable and permanently cultivated land and around 8350ha of pastureland.
Ghana is a leading cocoa producer in the world, providing 19 per cent of the total. Cocoa still has major importance to the economy providing around 60 per cent of export earnings. The monopoly of the Ghana Cocoa Board (GCB) was lifted in 1993, allowing private trading companies to purchase directly from farms. World prices in cocoa have risen since 2002 and farmers have invested in expanding cocoa production in order to take

advantage of the prices. However, in the first half of 2003, cocoa prices dropped by 30 per cent on international commodity markets when the harvest in Côte d'Ivoire was not so adversely affected by the civil war as had been anticipated. Nevertheless prices continued to rise generally and Ghana has profited from its earlier investment.

Other cash crops for export include bananas, kola nuts, limes, coffee, copra and palm kernels.

Crops grown for the local agribusiness include rubber, sugar, cotton, and oil palms.

Subsistence farming of food crops (cassava, plantains, rice, maize, sorghum, millet, yams) has been affected by prolonged drought and shortages of fertilisers, but there has been a recovery, particularly in maize and rice production. Crop production for 2004 included: 1,942,546 tonnes (t) cereals in total, 1,070,000t oil palm fruit, 1,157,621t maize, 9,738,812t cassava, 399,300t sorghum, 143,798t millet, 241,807t rice, 2,380,858t plantains, 15,521,171t roots and tubers, *330,000t citrus fruit, 311,760t oilcrops, 736,000t cocoa beans, 1,800t green coffee, 3,892,259t yams, 1,800,000t taro, 2,833,908t fruit in total, 642,450t vegetables in total. Livestock production included: 176,923t meat in total, 24,625t beef, 11,421t pig meat, 10,736t lamb, 11,867t goat meat, 47,096t poultry, 25,175t eggs, 35,490t milk, 2,827t cattle hides, 1,288t sheepskins.

Fishing
The annual domestic fish catch averages 300,000 tonnes, satisfying over 75 per cent of domestic demand. Fish farms have been set up in the north in an effort to achieve total fish self-sufficiency.

Tuna is one of Ghana's non-traditional exports, but the maximum sustainable yield from the 28,000 square km territorial waters is far from being realised.

Forestry
Ghana has around 39 per cent of forest cover in addition to 37 per cent of woodland. There are over 200 species of tropical hardwood.

Most commercial forestry is concentrated in the south. The extent of productive forest reserves is put at 1.2 million hectares, containing 190 million cubic metres of potential wood volume in trees over 30cm in diameter. Timber is Ghana's third-largest export commodity. The current export level of commercially viable species and sizes (trees with diameters of 70cm or more) can only be maintained if reliance on popular hardwoods is lessened and exploitation of lesser known species is increased. Domestic demand for wood for fuel is far greater than the permissible cut of one million cubic metres.

The National Forests Protection Strategy resulted in decreasing deforestation during the 1990s. The strategy plans to make the private sector responsible for the costs of forest depletion. The Environmental Protection Agency (EPA) monitors developments and policy affecting wildlife, forests and mining activities.

A local non-government body is developing a bamboo and rattan industry instead of available timber. The project plans to develop 20,000ha of bamboo by 2007.

Industry and manufacturing
The industrial sector accounts for approximately 27.2 per cent of annual GDP and accounted for 23.4 per cent of the country's growth achieved in 2004. Services are the second largest sector in the country and accounted for 32.4 per cent of the economy and was responsible for 25.9 per cent of overall growth in 2004. Manufacturing only contributes 9.0 per cent to GDP, electricity, gas and water 2.6 per cent and construction 8.5 per cent.

The privatisation and commercialisation of Ghana's public sector since the mid-1990s led to a severe contraction in manufacturing as jobs were shed, firms liquidated and the economy flooded by cheap imports. Officials believe foreign investment offers the key to the development of the sector.

Ghana's medium-sized manufacturing industries include aluminium smelting, paper and cement manufacturing and petroleum refining. The aluminium smelter at Tema, the Volta Aluminium Company (Valco), is the country's most capital-intensive enterprise. Potential production capacity is 200,000 tonnes, but only a fraction of this has been produced in recent years.

The government is seeking to expand important agri-based industries and textile manufacturing. It is also encouraging the establishment of more industries geared to processing local raw materials to replace imported inputs.

Tourism
Tourism has developed into a major foreign currency earner and the sector is one of the fastest-growing in Africa. It accounted for 4.8 per cent of GDP in 2004 and is forecast to contribute 5.4 per cent to GDP in 2005.

An ambitious 15-year development plan, exploiting tourism as a means of improving the economy, aims to increase arrivals to one million by 2010. If this target is to be achieved, more needs to be done to improve infrastructure and travel connections. Eco-tourism sites are being developed for European and the US markets, other amenities will cater for conventions, adventure holidays and the historical slave trade heritage sites.

Mining
Mining typically accounts for 18 per cent of GDP and employs 3 per cent of the workforce. Minerals resources include gold, manganese, diamonds, bauxite, iron ore, limestone, silica, columbite, tantalite and several rich clays.

Gold is the principal mineral export and Ghana is Africa's second-largest gold producer, after South Africa. Ashanti Goldfields Corporation (AGC) accounts for 85 per cent of total output. The other major producer is the State Gold Mines Corporation. Recoverable gold reserves are estimated at 57,000 tonnes. AGC has invested US$200 million in two new mines, while Newmont (the largest mining company globally) was given the go-ahead to begin the Ahafo South Project, a greenfields site, in April 2005. Diamonds and manganese each account for 1–2 per cent of export earnings. Diamonds (mostly industrial) are mined by Ghana Consolidated Diamonds Ltd in the Birim Basin. Ghana is the eighth-largest diamond producer in the world. Manganese ore is mined at Nsuta by the National Manganese Corporation. Manganese production averages 280,000 tonnes per annum.

Ghana has vast bauxite reserves near Kibi, but heavy transport/extraction costs have limited commercial development of local bauxite for use by the Valco aluminium smelter.

In 2003, Ghana granted mining licences in its protected forest reserves to attract new foreign investment.

Hydrocarbons
Ghana's oil reserves are less than 16 million barrels, which is generally too small for commercial exploitation. The substantial proportion of the one million tonnes per year domestic oil requirement is generally imported from Nigeria. Petroleum products account for about a quarter of the country's energy requirements. Arco and Petro Ghana, among other companies, are drilling offshore in the South Tano area in the west of the country. The Tema Oil Refinery (TOR) has a capacity of 45,000 barrels per day (bpd). A residual catalytic cracking (RCC) unit has been installed at TOR in order to boost productivity and produce petroleum and liquefied petroleum gas (LPG) for export. Natural gas reserves totalled 23.52 billion cubic metres (840 billion cubic feet), which are located primarily in the Tano fields.

The West African Gas Pipeline Project will link Nigeria, Ghana, Togo and Benin, supplying gas from Nigeria's gas fields. The projected was begun in 2003 with a consortium investing around US$500 million to construct the 1,000km pipeline; it is to be managed by Chevron Texaco. Construction in Ghana began in June 2005.

Ghana does not produce coal but imports minimal amounts of around 3,000 tonnes annually.

Energy

Hydroelectricity accounts for the majority of Ghana's domestic power.

The Volta River Authority (VRA) has responsibility for the development, generation and distribution of electricity. The 912MW Akosombo hydropower plant and the 160MW Kpong plant are run at capacity. There are plans to build an additional station (400MW) on the Black Volta River that could possibly export power to Burkina Faso, Côte d'Ivoire and Mali; however, by end-2005 no decision had been made.

The thermal power station near Takoradi produces 300MW and is due to be linked to the natural gas pipeline, under construction, from Nigeria. Ghana currently supplies electricity to the power grids in Benin and Togo from the Akosombo Plant on the Volta River.

Western Power Company, a subsidiary of the Ghana National Petroleum Corporation (GNPC) has secured funding for two barge-mounted gas turbines in the Western Region to add to overall production.

Several reforms have transformed Ghana's energy sector and, despite controversial price hikes for domestic and commercial consumers, consumption is growing as services improve.

Ghana has plans to install electricity service to every community of over 500 people by the year 2020. The National Electrification Scheme has proceeded since 1995 and is due to be completed, in five-year phases, by 2020.

Financial markets
Stock exchange
The Ghana Stock Exchange (GSE) has two main indices, the GSE All-Share Index and the Databank Stock Index (DSI).

The GSE has not only increased turnover significantly but also produced record returns of 87 per cent in 2003 and 142 per cent in 2004.

Banking and insurance

Stability in money markets and low inflationary expectations following petroleum deregulation, led to a reduction in the prime interest rate of 16.5 per cent on 30 May 2005, down from 18.5 per cent which had remained unchanged since May 2004.

It was announced in March 2005 that the introduction of the shared currency, the Eco, in Ghana, Guinea, Nigeria, Sierra Leone and The Gambia, which was due in July 2005, would be postponed. The currency was proposed to facilitate trade and growth with an ultimate plan to merge it with the CFA franc.

Central bank
Bank of Ghana
Main financial centre
Accra

Time
GMT

Geography

Ghana's southern border is the Gulf of Guinea. To the north, east and west lie the states of Burkina Faso, Togo and Côte d'Ivoire. From north to south the country extends a distance of about 680 km. The River Volta, which flows from the north to the south-east, is the most conspicuous landmark. There is a coastal area of thicket and mangrove which gives way in the east and north-east to more open plains and semi-deciduous forest. To the west and north-west of the coastal strip is high forest, which still covers the greater part of Ashanti and part of the Northern Region. The forest gives way in the north to Guinea savannah woodland; the extreme north-eastern corner of Ghana forms part of the drier Sudan savannah woodland.

Climate

Ghana lies entirely within the tropics. In the northern savannah the climate is hot and dry, with intermittent rainfall during March–September. In the hot and humid forest regions there are two rainy seasons, during March–June and September–November. At the coast, which is only 4.5 degrees from the Equator, the heat is intense.

The capital city, Accra, is only 65 metres above sea level. The capital's hottest month is March, with temperatures of 24–32 degrees Celsius (C); August is the coldest month, with temperatures of 21–27 C. The annual rainfall in the capital averages 865mm. The driest month is December when rainfall averages 18mm, and the wettest month is June when rainfall averages 235mm.

Dress codes

Western-style clothes are usually worn for business purposes, including shorts for outdoor occupations. On social or ceremonial occasions, traditional costume or Western-style clothes are equally acceptable.

Local dress includes the expensive, hand-woven Kente cloth for which Ghana is famous: this is worn by men like a toga. Wearing any military clothing, such as camouflage jackets or trousers, or any clothing or items that may appear military in nature, is strictly prohibited.

Entry requirements
Passports
Required by all, except by members of the Economic Community of West African States (ECOWAS,) who can obtain a Travel Certificate instead. Passports must be valid three months.

Visa
Required by all; citizens of Ecowas countries are granted visas gratis. Visas for both tourist and business trips are issued for three-month periods. An application for a business visa must contain a letter of confirmation from the representative's employer and itinerary, plus an invitation from a local host. All visitors must have return/onward passage.

Currency advice/regulations
It is advisable to check the latest currency regulations prior to visit.

It is easy to exchange US dollar bills for cedis. Visa cards can be used to withdraw cedis from Barclays Bank automatic teller machines (ATMs).

Unlimited import of foreign currency, but it must be declared. Foreign unused currency, travellers cheques, etc, declared on arrival, can be exported. Foreign currency must be exchanged with authorised dealers only. Keep the foreign exchange form. Import of local currency is prohibited and export is limited to C5,000, which must be recorded in passport.

Unused cedis can be re-exchanged into foreign currency by local banks or the Bank of Ghana, but the declaration form T.5 must show that the monies were obtained while in Ghana from an authorised dealer in foreign exchange.

Health (for visitors)
Mandatory precautions
A yellow fever vaccination certificate must be presented on arrival. A cholera vacination may be required, depending on local circumstances.

Advisable precautions
Cholera is seasonal. Typhoid, polio, tetanus, hepatitis 'A' and meningitis vaccinations are recommended. A hepatitis 'B' vaccination is recommended if staying in Ghana over six months. A vaccination for rabies is recommended if travelling to rural areas. Malaria prophylaxis should be taken as risk exists throughout the country. Water precautions are essential. There is a growing bilharzia risk and swimming in rivers is not advisable. Aids is present in Ghana. Guinea worm is rife and increasing in northern regions.

Emergency facilities are extremely limited. Insurance is vital and emergency evacuation should be included.

Hotels

Available in Accra, Kumasi, Takoradi and other regional capitals. Prices are high.

A 10 per cent government tax is added. Tipping is permitted in hotels, restaurants, etc. It is rarely added to the bill.

Credit cards
The most widely accepted credit cards are American Express, Diners' and Visa. They may be used for payment at nearly all airlines, leading hotels and major supermarkets.

Many restaurants and airlines prefer to be paid in cash.

Public holidays
Fixed dates
1 Jan (New Year's Day), 6 Mar (Independence Day), 1 May (Labour Day), 4 Jun (1979 Coup Anniversary), 1 Jul (Republic Day), 25 Dec (Christmas Day), 26 Dec (Boxing Day), 31 Dec (Revolution Day).

Variable dates
Good Friday, Easter Monday, Farmers' Day, Eid al Adha, Eid al Fitr.
The Islamic year contains 354 or 355 days, with the result that Muslim feasts advance by 10–12 days against the Gregorian calendar. Dates of feasts vary according to the sighting of the new moon, so cannot be forecast exactly. Islamic year 1426: 10 February 2005 to 30 January 2006.

Working hours
Banking
Mon–Thu: 0830–1400; Fri: 0830–1500.
Business
Mon–Fri: 0800–1200, 1400–1700. Sat: 0830–1200.
Government
Mon–Fri: 0800–1230, 1330–1700.
Shops
Mon–Tue and Thu–Fri: 0800–1200, 1400–1730. Wed and Sat: 0800–1300. Closed on Sundays.

Electricity supply
220V AC, 50 cycles

Social customs/useful tips
It is traditional to arrive with a gift when accepting private hospitality, particularly in rural areas. It is customary to use the right hand when presenting an object to another person, particularly in the case of food or a gift.

In northern Ghana, where the population tends to be Muslim, Islamic customs should be respected: it is considered unclean to eat or drink with the left hand; it is insulting to point the sole of your shoe at a Muslim. Older people are treated with special respect in Ghana.

It is inadvisable for foreigners to refer to tribalism or ethnic affiliations when discussing current affairs.

Body language differences include the custom of a greater degree of physical contact – touching and holding hands – between men and between women. Business people need patience when dealing with bureaucracy. There are regular power cuts in Accra and although the telephone system has improved, it may take several attempts to make an international call.

There are no unusual or particularly strict laws, but foreign visitors should observe all rules and regulations as Ghana does not take ignorance of the law as an excuse for non-observance. It is prudent to carry proof of identity.

Security
Violent crime has risen, particularly in and around Accra. Visitors are advised to exercise a high level of vigilance in public areas and when travelling in vehicles. If possible, avoid travelling alone in taxis after dark. Be wary when withdrawing cash from the few cash points in central Accra. Thefts of both luggage and travel documents occur at Kotoka International Airport. Ensure your documents are kept secured (particularly when leaving the airport) and never leave your baggage unattended.

Be wary of all offers of unsolicited assistance at the airport unless from uniformed porters or officials who, as with all other permanent staff, wear a current ID card bearing their name and photograph. ID cards without photographs are not valid. Taking photographs near sensitive installations, including military sites and government buildings, is prohibited. Permission should be obtained before taking photographs of anyone in uniform.

Getting there
Air
National airline: Ghana Airways
International airport/s: Accra-Kotoka International (ACC), 10km from city; duty-free shop, bar, buffet, restaurant, bank, post office, taxis.
Airport tax: The US$20 departure tax is payable in cedis or in US dollars.
Surface
Road: The coastal road runs from Lagos (Nigeria) through Cotonou (Benin) and Lomé (Togo) to Accra. The condition of this road is variable. A generally good road links Abidjan (Côte d'Ivoire) with Kumasi.
Main port/s: The main ports are Tema and Takoradi. Ships connect Tema, 25km east of Accra, with ports in Nigeria, Côte d'Ivoire, Cameroon and South Africa.

Getting about
National transport
Transport in northern Ghana can be more difficult than in southern Ghana.
Air: Sobel Air offers low-priced domestic flights from Kotoka Airport, 10km north-east of central Accra, to Kumasi and Tamale.
Road: There are over 30,000km of classified roads – 15,000km of these are trunk roads, the remainder being feeder roads. There are also around 6,000km of unclassified tracks. Of the total road network, approximately 6,000km are paved. There are reasonable roads between Accra and the main towns.
The main routes are Accra-Tema, Accra-Takoradi, Accra-Kumasi, Accra-Koforidua, Accra-Ho. Roads are often potholed and badly marked.
Buses: State-run bus services connect major centres. They are subject to delays and cancellation and are not recommended for business users.
Rail: The total network is about 1,000km, connecting Tema-Accra through Nsawam-Koforidua-Nkawkaw (Eastern Region) to Kumasi (Ashanti Region) through to Dunkwa and Prestea, Tarkwa and Sekondi-Takoradi (Western Region). Another line runs from Huni Valley (Western Region) to Kade (Eastern Region). Two classes; air-conditioning and restaurant cars not available; sleeping accommodation available on some services.
Water: The steamship, Yapei Queen, takes passengers daily across Lake Volta from Akosombo, 104km north-east of Accra at the base of Lake Volta, to Yeji, more than 200km away on the lake's north-western shore.

City transport
Taxis: There are cheap and reliable taxis in Accra.
Tipping is not usual; taxis are unmetered – fare is by negotiation; rates are often posted in hotels.
Buses, trams & metro: The bus services in Accra are run by the city authority and private operators.
Car hire
Car hire is expensive. An international driving licence is recommended; this must be endorsed by Police Licensing Office if stay exceeds 90 days. Traffic drives on the right.
The driving standards are poor. Driving at night is not advised.

BUSINESS DIRECTORY
The addresses listed below are a selection only. While World of Information makes every endeavour to check these addresses, we cannot guarantee that changes have not been made, especially to telephone numbers and area codes. We would welcome any corrections.

Telephone area codes
The international direct dialling code (IDD) for Ghana is +233, followed by area code and subscriber's number:
Accra 21 Takoradi 31

Ghana

Koforidua	81	Tamale	71
Kumasi	51	Tema	22

Useful telephone numbers
Police, fire and ambulance: 999.

Chambers of Commerce
Accra District Chamber of Commerce, Trade Fair Centre, PO Box 2325, Accra (tel: 662-427).

British-Ghana Chamber of Commerce and Industry, PO Box GP 21101, Accra (tel: 674-762; fax: 296-836; e-mail: info@ghanabritishchamber.com).

Ghana National Chamber of Commerce, 65 Kojo Thompson Road, PO Box 2325, Accra (tel: 662-427; fax: 662-210; e-mail: gncc@ncs.com.gh).

Banking
Agricultural Development Bank, PO Box 4191, Cedi House, Liberia Road, Accra (tel: 662-758, 662-762; fax: 662-912, 662-846).

Amalgamated Bank Limited, PO Box C1541, C131/3 Farrar Avenue, Accra (tel: 249-690; fax: 249-697; e-mail: amalbank@ighmail.com).

Barclays Bank of Ghana Ltd, PO Box 2949, Barclays House, High Street, Accra (tel: 664-901/4, 665-382; fax: 667-420).

CAL Merchant Bank Ltd, PO Box 14596, 45 Independence Avenue, Accra (tel: 221-056, 231-098, 222-345, 221-091, 231-912-7; fax: 231-104, 231-913).

Ecobank Ghana Ltd, 19 Seventh Avenue, Ridge West, Private Mail Bag, GPO, Accra (tel: 229-532, 228-812, 221-103, 667-109; fax: 667-127, 232-086).

First Atlantic Merchant Bank Ltd, PO Box C1620, Atlantic Place, No. 1 Seventh Avenue, Ridge West, Cantonments, Accra (tel: 231-433-5, 245-647, 245-660, 232-566; fax: 231-399).

Ghana Commercial Bank Ltd, PO Box 134, Accra (tel: 664-914 (5 lines), 664-911, 664-918; fax: 662-168).

International Commercial Bank Ltd, PO Box 20057, Accra (tel: 666-190, 665-779; fax: 668-221).

Merchant Bank (Ghana) Ltd, PO Box 401, Merban House, 44 Kwame Nkrumah Ave, Accra (tel: 666-331/2, 666-336; fax: 663-398).

Metropolitan and Allied Bank (GH) Ltd, PO Box C 1778, Valco Trust House, Castle Road Branch, Cantonments, Accra (tel: 232-770, 232-776; fax: 232-728).

National Investment Bank Ltd, PO Box 3726, 37 Kwame Nkrumah Avenue, Accra (tel: 240-001, 240-024; fax: 240-030/34).

Prudential Bank Ltd, PO Box 9820, Airport, Accra (tel: 226-322, 226-803; fax: 226-803).

SSB Bank Ltd, 1 Cola Avenue, Kokomlemle, Accra (tel: 222-564/223-375/222-136; fax: 222-136).

Stanbic Bank Ghana Limited, PO Box CT 2344, Valco Trust House, Castle Road, Ridge, Accra (tel: 234-683-4, 234-679, 250-066-7, 250-070-5; fax: 234-685).

Standard Chartered Bank Ghana Ltd, PO Box 768, 3rd Floor, Accra High Street Building, Accra (tel: 664-591-8, 672-210; fax: 667-751, 663-560).

The Trust Bank Ltd, PO Box 1862, Re-insurance House, 68 Kwame Nkrumah Avenue, Accra (tel: 240-049–052; fax: 240-056, 240-059).

Central bank
Bank of Ghana, PO Box 2674, Thorpe Road, Accra (tel: 666-174; fax: 662-996; e-mail: secretary@bog.gov.gh).

Travel information
Accra Kotoka International Airport, PO Box 87, Accra (tel: 776-171).

Ghana Airways, Ghana House, PO Box 1636, White Avenue, Accra (tel: 777-673; fax: 777-675).

Ghana Tourist Development Co Ltd, PO Box 8710, Accra (tel: 772-084; fax: 772-093).

Ministry of tourism
Ministry of Tourism, PO Box 4386, Accra (tel: 666-314, 666-426; fax: 666-826).

National tourist organisation offices
Ghana Tourist Board, PO Box 3106, Accra (tel: 238-330; fax: 231-779; e-mail: gtb@africa-on-line.com.gh).

Ministries
Ministry of Communications: PO Box M.41, Accra (tel: 229-870; fax: 229-786).

Ministry of Defence, Burma Camp, Accra (tel: 774-727; fax: 773-951).

Ministry of Education, PO Box M45, Accra (tel: 662-772; fax: 664-067).

Ministry of Employment and Social Welfare, PO Box M84, Accra (tel: 665-421; fax: 667-251).

Ministry of Environment, Science and Technology, PO Box M39, Accra (tel: 662-626; fax: 666-828).

Ministry of Finance and Economic Planning, PO Box M40, Accra (tel: 665-441, 665-587, 666-512; fax: 667-069; internet: www.finance.gov.gh).

Ministry of Food and Agriculture, PO Box M37, Accra (tel: 663-036, 665-421; fax: 663-250).

Ministry of Foreign Affairs, PO Box M53, Accra (tel: 664-008; fax: 665-363; internet: www.mfa.gov.gh/).

Ministry of Health, PO Box M44, Accra (tel: 665-323; fax: 663-810).

Ministry of Information, PO Box M41, Accra (tel: 228-0211).

Ministry of Interior, PO Box M42, Accra (tel: 665-421; fax: 662-688).

Ministry of Justice & Attorney General, PO Box M60, Accra (tel: 665-051).

Ministry of Land and Forestry, PO Box M212, Accra (tel: 665-949; fax: 666-801, 666-896).

Ministry of Local Government, Rural Development and Co-op, PO Box M50, Accra (tel: 664-763; fax: 667-911).

Ministry of Mines and Energy, PO Box 40, Stadium Post Office, Accra (tel: 667-090; fax: 668-262).

Ministry of Mobilisation (tel: 665-349; fax: 667-251).

Ministry of Roads and Transport, PO Box M43, Accra (tel: 666-465; fax: 667-911).

Ministry of Tourism, PO Box 4386, Accra (tel: 666-314; fax: 666-182; e-mail: MOT@ghana.com; internet site: http://www.estghana.gov.gh; www.africaonline.com.gh/Tourism).

Ministry of Trade and Industry, PO Box M47, Accra (tel: 663-327; fax: 665-114).

Ministry of Works and Housing, PO Box M43, Accra (tel: 662-242; fax: 663-268).

Ministry of Youth and Sports, PO Box M 252, Accra (tel: 664-71; fax: 663-927).

Other useful addresses
Accra International Conference Centre, PO Box C1054, Accra (tel: 669-600; fax: 669-825).

Ashanti Goldfields Co Ltd, Gold House, Patrice Lumumba Road, Roman Ridge, PO Box 2665, Accra (tel: 772-190, 776-224, 778-155; fax: 775-947).

Association of Ghanaian Industry, PO Box 8624, Accra (tel: 777-283; fax: 773-143).

Black Star Line, PO Box 2760, Accra (tel: 776-161; fax: 775-140).

British Diplomatic Mission, Accra (tel: 221-665).

Civil Aviation Authority, Kotoka International Airport, PO Box 87, Accra (tel: 773-283).

Coffee, Sheanuts Exporters' Association, c/o Mr J W Biney, Agrotrade Ltd., PO Box 226, Accra (tel: 224-820; fax: 224-564).

Customs, Excise and Preventive Service, PO Box 68, Accra (tel: 666-841; fax: 660-019).

Department of Co-operatives, PO Box M150, Accra (tel: 666-212).

Department of Urban Roads, Ministry of Roads and Transport, PO Box 38, Accra (tel: 230-381, 223-908; fax: 234-522).

Divestitute Implementation Committee, F35/5 Ring Road East, North Labone, PO Box CT102, Cantonments, Accra (tel: 772-049, 773-119, 760-281; fax: 773-126; e-mail: dicgh@ncs.com.gh).

Export Finance Company, Bank of Ghana, PO Box 2674, Accra (tel: 666-902; fax: 662-996).

Federation of Association of Ghanaian Exporters (FAGE), c/o Kiku Ltd., PO Box M378, Accra (tel: 223-215; fax: 776-755).

Finsap Implementation Secretariat, Private Mail Bag (PMB), Ministries Post Office, Accra (tel: 666-254, 664-976; fax: 667-448; e-mail: finsap@gh.com).

Ghana Assorted Foodstuffs Exporters Assocation, PO Box 16073, Airport - Accra (tel: 220-746; fax: 223-663).

Ghana Chamber of Mines, PO Box 991, Accra (tel: 665-355; fax: 662-926).

Ghana Civil Aviation Authority, Private Mail Bag, Kotoka International Airport, Accra (tel: 776-171; fax: 773-293; e-mail: centre-GCAA@ighmail.com; internet site: http://www.gcaa.com.gh).

Ghana Cocoa Board, PO Box 933, Accra (tel: 221-212; fax: 667-104, 665-076; e-mail: cocobod@africaonline.com.gh).

Ghana Export Promotion Council, Republic House, Tudu, PO Box M 146, Accra (tel: 228-813/830/623; fax: 668-263, 233-715; e-mail: gepc@ighmail.com).

Ghana Free-Zones Board, PO Box M626, Accra (tel: 670-532/5; fax: 670-536; e-mail: freezone@africaonline.com.gh; internet site: http://www.ghanaclassified.com.ghzb).

Ghana Furniture Producers/Exporters Association, PO Box 32, Trade Fair Centre, Accra (tel: 775-311).

Ghana Highway Authority, PO Box 1641, Accra (tel: 666-591; fax: 665-571).

Ghana Investment Promotion Centre (GIPC), PO Box M193, Accra (tel: 665-125/9; fax: 663-801; e-mail: gipc@ghana.com; internet site: http://www.gipc.org.gh).

Ghana Liaison Office, Cotecna Inspection S A, 10 Drake Avenue, Airport Residential Area, PO Box C2212, Cantonments, Accra (tel: 775-698; fax: 553-522).

Ghana National Petroleum Corporation (GNPC), Private Mail Bag, Tema (tel: 232-056; fax: 774-143).

Ghana National Procurement Agency, Ministries Post Office, Private Mail Bag, Accra (tel: 220-851; fax: 221-049).

Ghana Shippers Council, Private Mail Bag, Ministries Post Office, Accra (tel: 666-915; fax: 668-768).

Ghana Stock Exchange, Marketing Department, 5th Floor, Cedi House, Liberia Road, Accra (tel: 669-914; fax: 669-913; e-mail: stockex@ncs.com.gh; internet site: http://www.gse.com.gh).

Ghana Trade and Investment Gateway Project (GHATIG), PO Box M47, Accra (tel: 663-439, 664-074; fax: 665-423; e-mail: gateway1@ghana.com).

Ghana Yam Producers and Exporters' Association, PO Box 5233, Accra (tel: 775-311; fax: 668-263).

Ghanaian Embassy (USA), 3512 International Drive, NW, Washington DC 20008 (tel: 202-686-4520; fax: 202-686-4527; e-mail: hagan@cais.com).

Horticulturists' Association of Ghana, PO Box 9303, Accra (tel: 772-139; fax: 772-350).

Institute of Economic Affairs (tel: 776-641; fax: 776-724).

Internal Revenue Services, PO Box 2202, Accra (tel: 664-961; fax: 664-938).

Organisation for Export Development for Seafood, c/o Signotrade Ltd., PO Box 16851, Accra (tel: 712-762; fax: 668-263).

Precious Metals Marketing Corporation, PO Box M108, Accra (tel: 664-931; fax: 772-350).

Private Enterprises Foundation (PEF), PO Box C1671, Cantoments, Accra (tel: 222-313; fax: 231-487).

Registar-General's Department, PO Box 118, Accra (tel: 666-469).

US Diplomatic Mission, Accra (tel: 228-440).

Vegetables Exporters' Association, c/o Ghana Export Promotion Council, PO Box M146, Accra (tel: 221-212; fax: 668-263).

Volta River Authority, PO Box MB77, Accra (tel: 664-941, 221-124; fax: 662-610; e-mail: orgsrv@accra.vra.com).

Internet sites

Ghana Drum Magazine: http://www.erols.com/ghanadrm/Africa Business Network: http://www.ifc.org/abn

Ghana Forestry Commision: http://ghanatimber.org/

AllAfrica.com: http://allafrica.com

African Development Bank: http://www.afdb.org

Mbendi AfroPaedia (information on companies, countries, industries and stock exchanges in Africa): http://mbendi.co.za

Yellow Pages: http://www.ghanaforum.com/directory.htm

Gibraltar

For both the British and Spanish governments, Gibraltar is an anachronism that will not go away. For twenty-first century Britain it is more of a liability than an asset, for Spanish governments, it is an annoying irritation used by each of the major parties to highlight the shortcomings of the other. The 29,400 population crammed into 2.5 square miles (6.5 square km) on Spain's southernmost point is a mixture of Italian (mostly of Genoese ancestry), Moorish (from nearby Morocco), Jewish (who had been expelled from Spain), Maltese, Portuguese and Hindi cultures – everything, in fact except Spanish. There are relatively small numbers of British residents. This reflected the multicultural community that inevitably gravitates towards a garrison town as important as Gibraltar.

Spanish obstinacy

Spain lost control of the strategically important rocky outcrop wedged between the Spanish coast and the entrance to the Mediterranean in 1704, and formally ceded the territory to Britain under the 1713 Treaty of Utrecht. For the past 300 years Spain has been trying to get it back. However, with the colony's population almost unanimously opposed to any Spanish involvement in their affairs, talks launched by UK Foreign Secretary Jack Straw in 2001 were always going to be a non-starter.

While the 2002 referendum was not binding, an influential team of British observers said in December that the ballot was legitimate and London could ill afford to ignore the strength of feeling against any transfer of Gibraltar's sovereignty to Spain. The Rock's elected Chief Minister, Peter Caruana, said the vote represented a wake up call for Britain and the 'sheer contempt' of the Spanish government towards Gibraltar. Since becoming chief minister in 1996 (re-elected in 2000 and 2003), Peter Caruana's major preoccupation has been the future sovereignty of Gibraltar. Turnout in the referendum was close to 90 per cent on the 426 metre high rock, which has served as a British military base for much of its history. Of nearly 18,200 Gibraltarians who cast a vote, little more than 1 per cent voted in favour of a dual sovereignty arrangement.

Spanish relations

Following the March 2004 victory of Spain's socialist party in its general election, relations between the UK and Spain chilled. British prime minister, Tony Blair, had enjoyed a very close relationship with outgoing Spanish prime minister José María Aznar, which was not maintained under incoming socialist prime minister José Luis Rodriguez Zapatero. Spain's newly elected prime minister had reversed Spanish policy on Iraq, to the irritation of Downing Street. It was generally accepted by the British government that this new found frigidity would find an echo in the two countries' positions over Gibraltar, which even in a generally cordial climate had not proved easy.

In December 2004, however, an unprecedented meeting took place at Chevening, the official residence of UK Foreign Secretary Jack Straw. The meeting was attended by Gibraltar's Chief Minister Peter Caruana, two senior officials from the Spanish foreign office and British foreign office officials. The key change in the negotiations was the Spanish acceptance of a Gibraltarian presence at the discussions, something that Spain had hitherto resisted. Spain's change in attitude indicates an acceptance that any discussions that do not involve a direct Gibraltarian presence are doomed. The Chevening meeting followed subtle diplomacy by Mr Caruana, who – prompted by an article in the Spanish daily El País that appeared on August 4th, the anniversary of the capture of the rock – had first written to Spanish foreign minister Miguel Angel Moratinos. This initiative lead to a lunch meeting in the neighbouring Spanish town of Los Barrios between Mr Caruana and the Spanish foreign ministry's Director General for Europe, José María Pons.

300 years of sovereignty

The December meetings came at the end of a year in which Spanish irritation with Gibraltar had grown. The cause of the irritation was Gibraltar's celebration of 300

KEY FACTS

Official name: Gibraltar

Head of State: Queen Elizabeth II; Governor Sir Francis N Richards (from 27 May 2003)

Head of government: Chief Minister Peter Caruana (leader of GSD) (since May 1996; last re-elected 27 Nov 2003)

Ruling party: Gibraltar Social Democrats (GSD) (since May 1996; last re-elected 27 Nov 2003)

Area: 6 square km

Population: 29,400 (2004)

Capital: Gibraltar

Official language: English

Currency: Pound sterling (£) = 100 pence (the euro also circulates and is accepted informally)

Exchange rate: £0.57 per US$ (Oct 2005)

GDP per capita: US$17,500 (2003)

Unemployment: 2.00% (2003)

Inflation: 1.50% (2003)

Balance of trade: -US$410.90 million (2003)

Visitor numbers: 7.80 million (2003) (including non-Gibraltarian workers)

years of British sovereignty. On that day 17,000 Gibraltarians linked arms to encircle the Rock, dressed in the colony's colours of red and white. Relations had been strained by official visits by Britain's then defence minister, Geoff Hoon, the queen's daughter the Princess Royal and the on-going saga of the prolonged stay in Gibraltar of the nuclear submarine HMS *Tireless* for repairs. Despite this apparently deteriorating climate, the Spanish had made two apparently *simpático* gestures. One was the ending of the ban on the bad weather diversion of flights from Gibraltar to Málaga, the other was allowing cruise liners to sail between Spanish ports and Gibraltar.

The European Union

In June 2004, Gibraltar won a significant legal battle against the UK in the European Court of Human Rights. The verdict enabled Gibraltarians to vote in European parliamentary elections. Somewhat improbably, the British government decided that Gibraltar should become a part of the UK's South West region. One Gibraltarian candidate, representing Gibraltar's Reform Party – which is linked to the UK's Green Party – stood in the elections. However, in July 2005 the European Court of Justice became the stage for a dispute between Spain and the UK on the EU voting rights of commonwealth citizens living in Gibraltar. The Spanish government claimed that only EU citizens can vote in European parliamentary elections.

The Gibraltar government itself took the European Commission to court over the right to control its own corporate tax system. Although Gibraltar is a territory under British sovereignty, it does not formally constitute a part of the UK. Corporate tax is levied at 30 per cent of taxable profits in both Gibraltar and the UK, but Gibraltar would like to introduce lower rates, a move blocked in 2004 by the European Commission.

Thriving financial sector

Gibraltar's financial sector, both onshore and offshore, accounts for about 30 per cent of GDP, about the same proportion that comes from tourism. There are around 28,500 companies registered in Gibraltar, of which 8,000 are tax exempt, attracted to its special regime for international businesses.

The economy has held up well in view of the global economic slump and additional uncertainty caused by the 2003 Iraq War. Companies are attracted by its lightly taxed fiscal regime and stable currency – it uses the British pound, so monetary policy is effectively controlled by the UK.

Like many offshore centres, Gibraltar has been criticised by the Organisation for Economic Co-operation and Development (OECD), which is attempting to stamp out harmful tax practices, as well as by the EU. Under pressure from the EU, Gibraltar has made efforts to harmonise taxes and has unveiled detailed tax reform proposals to replace the tax-exempt status of some businesses, which are now awaiting EU approval. In 2002, Gibraltar had been removed from the OECD's black-list of unco-operative tax havens.

There are no exchange control restrictions and together with exemptions and concessions from domestic taxes for certain categories of companies, this has created substantial growth in the financial services sectors. This is especially true for trusts which can be sold to non-resident individuals who do not work in Gibraltar. A large number of expatriates work or simply reside in Spain and banks and insurance companies sell to this market.

Gibraltar does trade with Spain – they reopened their borders with each other in 1985 – but relations between the two are prickly despite inroads by the rock's offshore financial services centre into the Spanish market. Any relaxation would bring benefits to Gibraltar. Spain represents a huge market for its financial services and there would be the prospects of millions of euros of EU funding and benefits from free trade within the EU.

Outlook

Gibraltar's future is closely bound up with its relationship with Spain. Any relaxation on the part of the Spanish government is likely to benefit Gibraltar's stability and its economy. There is scant possibility of Gibraltarians voting in favour of adopting Spanish sovereignty, however the option may be dressed up. But in late 2005 closer commercial and transport links and increased opportunities for dialogue and co-operation seemed more possible than had been the case for some years.

Risk assessment

Economy	Good
Political	Satisfactory
Regional stability	Good

COUNTRY PROFILE

Historical profile
1704 The Rock was captured by the UK from Spain.
1713 Gibraltar was ceded to Britain in the Treaty of Utrecht. The Treaty stipulated that the Rock would become a part of Spain if Britain gave up sovereignty.
1830 Gibraltar became a crown colony.
1869 The opening of the Suez Canal increased Gibraltar's importance in guarding the route to India and the Far East.
1939–45 Gibraltar was a busy naval base in the Second World War. After the war, Spain continued to press for the return of Gibraltar, but rejected the UK's offer to refer the matter to the International Court of Justice.
1967 More than 12,000 Gibraltarians voted to remain British; only 44 opted for Spanish rule. The dispute continued to disrupt friendly relations between Spain and UK; for a while, Spain closed the frontier. Both countries sought a peaceful settlement, and the Gibraltarian people maintained their wish to remain British.
1969 Gibraltar adopted a new constitution.
1975 The death of Spain's dictator, General Franco, led to more friendly relations with Spain, but there was still no resolution of the sovereignty issue.
1984 The Brussels Agreement was signed between Spain and the UK, establishing a negotiating process over the issue of Gibraltar's sovereignty.
1996 Peter Caruana was elected chief minister.
1998 Spanish proposals for joint sovereignty were rejected by the UK.
2000 The UK and Spain reached an agreement over Gibraltar's administrative status, which allowed Spanish recognition of documents and passports issued in Gibraltar. The Royal Navy's nuclear submarine HMS *Tireless* arrived for repairs in Gibraltar, which sparked protests from the Spanish government and Gibraltar's civilians. The Gibraltar Social Democrats (GSD) won the elections.
2002 Spain and UK held talks to consider grounds for indefinitely sharing sovereignty of Gibraltar. An informal referendum rejected the talks by 95:1. However, both Spain and the UK said they would not recognise the vote.
2003 On 27 May, Sir Francis Richards took office as governor. Chief Minister Peter Caruana's GSD was re-elected in November.
2004 On 4 August, the 300th anniversary of the British occupation of Gibraltar was commemorated amid continued tensions with Spain over the issue of sovereignty. In December a trilateral forum, of the UK, Spain and Gibraltar, began talks on the territory's future.
2005 Cammell Laird announced it would invest US$34.9 million in its Gibraltar shipbuilding yard between 2006–08 to develop its market in superyacht building

and refitting. Gibraltarians took part in their first European elections. Formal discussion began with the UK on Gibraltar's constitutional relationship, which will end its status as a colony.

Political structure

Constitution
The constitution was promulgated in May 1969.

Gibraltar has a UK-appointed governor and a House of Assembly.

The Council of Ministers comprises the chief minister and not fewer than four, nor more than eight, other ministers appointed from the Assembly by the governor in consultation with the chief minister. The Council of Ministers deals with domestic matters.

The British government, through the governor, remains directly responsible for internal security, including police, defence and foreign affairs, and for ensuring financial and economic stability.

Form of state
British Crown colony

The executive
The governor does not take an active role in governmental affairs.

The Chief Minister is the head of the Gibraltar government and holds much of the power.

National legislature
The House of Assembly comprises a speaker (appointed by the governor), two ex-officio members and 15 elected members serving a four-year term. All legislation must be agreed by the governor.

Legal system
It is based on English common law coupled to statutes. The civil courts in Gibraltar are the Court of First Instance, the Supreme Court, the Court of Appeal and ultimately, the Privy Council in the UK.

Last elections
27 November 2003 (parliamentary)
Results: Parliamentary: Chief Minister Peter Caruana's Gibraltar Social Democrats (GSD) were re-elected with 51 per cent of the vote against the Gibraltar Socialist Labour Party (GSLP) with 40 per cent; turnout was 75 per cent.

Next elections
Before end-February 2008 (parliamentary).

Political parties
Ruling party
Gibraltar Social Democrats (GSD) (since May 1996; last re-elected 27 Nov 2003)
Main opposition party
Gibraltar Socialist Labour Party (GSLP)

Population
29,400 (2004)
Ethnic make-up
English, Italian, Maltese, Portuguese, Spanish.

Religions
Roman Catholic (77 per cent), Church of England (7 per cent), Muslim (7 per cent), Jewish (2 per cent).

Education
Gibraltar has a comprehensive system of education, based on the UK model. Bayside (merged with three separate schools), is the only secondary school for boys between the ages of 12 and 18. Westside School, the Gibraltar Girls' Comprehensive School caters for 900 students between the ages of 12 to 18. Many children are likely to receive third level education in the UK through several grant facilities, resulting in the high incidence of returning professional graduates.

Health
Health conditions are generally good and broadly comparable to most of Western Europe. Heart diseases and cancers account for most mortality. Gibraltar's health services are closely modelled on the UK's National Health Service, with which it maintains professional and service links. There is provision for a full range of primary care and secondary care services, available through the Primary Care Centre. Medical cases requiring tertiary care are usually referred to the UK or Spain. The St Bernard's Hospital is the only general hospital, with 170 beds providing outpatient services, emergency facilities and investigative facilities. Government expenditure towards healthcare amounted is around £30 million (US$45.2 million) per annum
Life expectancy: 79 years: male 76 years; female 82 years (2003)
Fertility rate/Maternal mortality rate: 1.7 births per woman (2003)
Birth rate/Death rate: 11 births per 1,000 population; nine deaths per 1,000 population (2003).
Infant mortality rate: Five per 1,000 live births (2003)

Welfare
A social insurance funds all state pensions and benefits, with contributions and other earnings on investments meeting the cost of the scheme. The government's investment in capital projects towards social and economic development is funded by the Improvement and Development Fund, 12 per cent of which is allocated for housing.

Languages spoken
Spanish, Italian, Portuguese and Malti; English is used in schools and for official purposes.
Official language/s
English

Media
Press
Dailies: The only daily newspaper is *Gibraltar Chronicle*.
Weeklies: There are some weekly publications including *Panorama*, *Vox* (which publishes a Spanish section) and *The New People*.
Broadcasting
Over 7,000 combined radio and TV licences are issued annually. Programmes and advertising are broadcast by Gibraltar Broadcasting Corporation (GBC). GBC-Radio broadcasts in English and Spanish, the British Forces Broadcasting Service in English only, GBC-TV in English only.
Advertising
All usual media are available to advertisers. Information on radio and TV advertising is available from GBC.

Economy
Gibraltar has few natural resources with almost no part of its land area capable of sustaining agriculture. There is also a significant absence of heavy manufacturing activity and the economy is dependent on imports of food, consumer goods, building materials, construction equipment and fuel. As such, the economy is service-based.

Traditionally, the services sector has been focussed on the UK's Ministry of Defence (MoD), alongside retail activity and tourism. Since the mid-1980s, Gibraltar's economic base has shifted from the public to the private sector as the MoD has scaled down its activities.

In 2005, three sectors, financial services, tourism and shipping and manufacturing, were driving the economy. E-commerce has become established since 2003, as Internet companies, particularly betting and gambling operations have relocated to Gibraltar to avoid gaming taxes elsewhere, most notably in the UK. In May 2005, the largest multi-player poker room on the Internet, PartyGaming Plc, was capitalised at US$9.1 billion, within days of being floated. Also, in May 2004 an independent trading firm, Mac Futures, opened a 100-desk trading facility in Gibraltar.

In late 2005, Cammell Laird (Gibralter) Ltd (who own and operate the former Royal Navy dockyard) announced that it had changed ownership and would be investing £20 million (US$35 million) over the next five years to target the superyacht market.

As Gibraltar diversifies its economy to take full advantage of it access to EU markets, it is acting as many small service orientated economies to compensate for its physical limitations and scale of production. How well it does may influence its ongoing negotiations with the UK government in determining its status as either a colony or independent nation.

External trade
A regular trade deficit is largely offset by invisible earnings.
Imports
Main imports are fuels, manufactured goods, and foodstuffs.
Main sources: Spain (22.6 per cent total, 2004), UK (12.8 per cent), Russia (11.8 per cent), Italy (9.8 per cent), Germany (7.6 per cent), France (4.7 per cent), US (4.6 per cent), Netherlands (4.4 per cent), Turkey (4.3 per cent)
Exports
Manufactured goods
Main destinations: France (21 per cent total, 2004), Spain (15.3 per cent), Turkmenistan (12.5 per cent), Germany (12.4 per cent), UK (10.0 per cent), Switzerland (8.9 per cent), Greece (7.4 per cent)
Re-exports
Petroleum (51 per cent of total), tobacco, manufactured goods and wine.

Industry and manufacturing
The shipbuilding company, Cammell Laird (Gibralter) Ltd ownes and operates the shipyard and dry dock. The port provides an important source of income. The Gibraltar government has encouraged the setting up of light industries there, by making available a package of incentives and other benefits to successful companies. Gibraltar also has a wine bottling plant and a satellite control system.
The New Harbours, a free-port zone where there are no duties or taxes on imported materials and low rates of tax on profits, comprises warehousing, industrial workshops and office space, available to rent or purchase for exporting companies.

Tourism
Tourism is a major sector of the economy and accounts for around a third of GDP. Gibraltar is known for its cheap shopping, military history, colonial architecture and beaches. Over seven million visitors arrive each year, mainly by the land route, although this number also includes non-Gibraltarian frontier workers.
Cross-border day visitors, who come primarily to shop, outnumber the traditional overnight visitors in both volume and value, resulting in a more robust economy. Cruise ship tourism is on the increase, and has been earmarked for encouragement by the authorities. Conference tourism is also being developed.

Hydrocarbons
Gibraltar does not produce oil, gas or coal. It imports petroleum products to meet its energies needs, around 4,000 barrels per day. However it does not import either gas or coal.

Banking and insurance
Gibraltar has a well-developed financial services sector, which has grown due to its independent jurisdiction under the EU's Treaty of Rome and its sound fiscal regime.
Gibralter is a signatory of a new EU tax agreement that was introduced in July 2005. It has agreed to pass on, to the tax department of an EU citizen's country, information concerning the amount of money in savings accounts, to allow tax to be levied from the account holder's home country.
There were 22 licensed banks and 18 insurance companies operating.
Offshore facilities
In 2003, the collapse of Rock Financial Services hit about 400 investors and was a blow to Gibraltar's reputation as a sound financial centre.

Time
GMT plus one hour (GMT plus two hours from late March to late September).

Geography
Gibraltar is situated at the southernmost tip of the Iberian Peninsula in southern Europe. The territory consists of a narrow peninsula running southwards from the south-west coast of Spain, to which it is connected by a sandy isthmus. About 8km (five miles) across the bay, to the west, lies Algeciras, the Spanish port, and 32km (20 miles) to the south, across the Strait of Gibraltar, is Morocco. The Mediterranean Sea is to the east.

Climate
Sub-tropical with hot and dry summers, and fairly mild rainy winters; temperatures vary between 10–29 degrees Celsius.

Entry requirements
Passports
Required by all.
Visa
As an overseas territory of the UK, visa requirements are the same. Visas are required by all, except nationals of North America, Australasia, Japan and other EU members. For further exceptions and advice visit www.ukvisas.gov.uk/ (includes application forms). All visas must be applied for before travelling.
Gibraltar is outside the Schengen Agreement area. Visitos should ensure they have the right to return to Spain on their Schengen visa before entering Gibraltar from Spain.
Currency advice/regulations
The currency is the pound sterling with locally issued notes guaranteed by the Bank of England.

Hotels
There is no official rating system. Reservations should be made in advance, especially during summer. Some hotels reduce rates between November and March.

Public holidays
Fixed dates
1 Jan (New Year's Day), 8 Mar (Commonwealth Day), 1 May (May Day), 10 Sep (Gibraltar National Day), 25 Dec (Christmas Day), 26 Dec (Boxing Day). Holidays occuring on Sunday are observed on the following Monday.
Variable dates
Good Friday, Easter Monday, Spring Bank Holiday (May), Queen's Official Birthday (Jun), Late Summer Bank Holiday (Aug).

Working hours
Banking
Mon–Thur: 0900–1530; Fri: 0900–1700.
Business
Mon–Fri: 0900–1700 (0800–1400, summer). Sat: 0900–1300.
Government
Mon–Fri: (winter) 0800–1615; (summer) 0730–1330.
Shops
Mon–Fri: Most shops open from 0900–1930 and some open from 0900–1300 and 1500–1900, Sat: 1000–1300.

Telecommunications
Mobile phones
GSM 900 is available throughout the territory.

Electricity supply
240V AC

Security
Violence and street crime is rare.

Getting there
Air
British Airways and Monarch Airlines operate direct services from the UK.
National airline: GB Airways
International airport/s: Gibraltar (GIB) is served by North Front, 1km from town centre.
Airport tax: None
Surface
Access is from Málaga, through the Spanish frontier at La Línea.
Water: There are regular ferry services from Tangier.

Getting about
National transport
Bus and taxi services are available. Taxi drivers are obliged by law to produce, on demand, a copy of the taxi fares. Gibraltar has a total of about 45km of roads. There is no railway network.
City transport
Taxis: Taxis are available from the airport to the town centre.

Gibraltar

Buses, trams & metro: There is a bus service 3/3B which operates from the airport to the town centre between 0830 and 2030, every 30 minutes, journey time 15 minutes.

Car hire
Car hire is available through local car hire firms and travel agents. A UK/international driving licence and evidence of insurance are required (third party). The British automobile clubs AA and RAC have agents in Gibraltar. Traffic drives on the right. The speed limit is 50kph (31mph), except where indicated. Dipped headlights are compulsory at night time.

BUSINESS DIRECTORY

The addresses listed below are a selection only. While World of Information makes every endeavour to check these addresses, we cannot guarantee that changes have not been made, especially to telephone numbers and area codes. We would welcome any corrections.

Telephone area codes
The international direct dialling code (IDD) for Gibraltar is +350 followed by subscriber's number. (The IDD for Gibraltar is not recognised by Spain).

Chambers of Commerce
Gibraltar Chamber of Commerce, Don House, 38 Main Street, PO Box 29, Gibraltar (tel: 78-376; fax: 78-403; e-mail: gichacom@gibnet.gi).

Banking
Abbey National (Gibraltar) Ltd, 237 Main Street (tel: 76-090; fax: 72-028).

ABN Amro Bank (Gibraltar) Ltd, PO Box 100, 2-6 Main Street (tel: 79-220/79-370; fax: 78-512).

Baltica Bank (Gibraltar) Ltd, 215a Neptune House, Marina Bay (tel: 42-670; fax: 42-676).

Banco Atlántico (Gibraltar) Ltd, Eurolife Building, 1 Corral Road (tel: 40-117; fax: 40-110).

Banco Bilbao Vizcaya International (Gibraltar) Ltd, 3rd Floor, Hadfield House, Library Street (tel: 79-420; fax: 73-870).

Banco Bilbao Vizcaya (Gibraltar) Ltd, 260/262 Main Street (tel: 77-797, 77-871, 77-896).

Banco Central Sa, 198/200 Main Street (tel: 73-625, 73-650, 73-675; fax: 73-707).

Banco Español de Crédito, 114 Main Street (tel: 76-518; fax: 73-947).

Banque Indosuez, 206/210 Main Street (tel: 75-090; fax: 79-618).

Barclays Bank plc, 84/90 Main Street (tel: 78-565; fax: 79-509).

Crédit Suisse (Gibraltar) Ltd, Neptune House, Marina Bay (tel: 76-606; fax: 76-027).

Gibraltar Private Bank Ltd, PO Box 407, 10th Floor, ICC, Casemates (tel: 73-350; fax: 73-475).

Hambros Bank Ltd, PO Box 375, 32 Line Wall Road (tel: 74-850; fax: 79-037).

Hispano Commerzbank (Gibraltar) Ltd, Suite 14, 30/38 Main Street (tel: 74-199; fax: 74-174).

Lloyds Bank plc, 323 Main Street (tel: 77-373; fax: 70-023).

Midland Bank Trust Corporation (Gibraltar) Ltd, PO Box 19, Hadfield House, Library Street (tel: 79-500; fax: 72-090).

National Westminster Bank, 57 Line Wall Road (tel: 77-737; fax: 74-557).

Republic National Bank of New York (Gibraltar) Ltd, Neptune House, Marina Bay, PO Box 5578 (tel: 79-374; fax: 75-684).

Royal Bank of Scotland (Gibraltar) Ltd, 1 Corral Road (tel: 73-200; fax: 70-152).

Varde Bank International (Gibraltar) Ltd, PO Box 476, Suite E, Regal House, 3 Queensway (tel: 42-455; fax: 42-456).

Travel information
GB Airways, Iain Stewart Centre, Beehive Ring Road, Gatwick Airport, West Sussex RG6 0PB, UK (tel: (1293)664-239; fax: (1293)664-218).

Gibraltar Information Bureau, Cathedral Square (tel: 76-400; fax: 79-980).

National tourist organisation offices
Gibraltar Tourist Board, Duke of Kent House, Cathedral Square (tel: 74-950; fax: 74-943; e-mail: gib1@gibnet.gi; internet site: http://www.gibraltar.gi).

Ministries
Government of Gibraltar, UK Office, 179 Strand, London WC2R 1EL, UK (tel: (0)20-7836-0777; fax: (0)20-7240-6612; e-mail: info@gibraltar.gov.uk; internet site: http://www.gibraltar.gov.uk).

Government Secretariat, 6 Convent Place (tel: 70-071; fax: 74-524).

Governor's Office, The Convent, Main Street (tel: 45-440; e-mail: convent@gibnet.gi).

Ministry of Tourism and Transport, Duke of Kent House, Cathedral Square (tel: 74-950; fax: 74-943).

Ministry of Trade, Industry and Telecommunications, Suite 771, Europort (tel: 52-052; fax: 71-406; e-mail: dticomm@gibnet.gi; internet site: http://www.gibraltar.gov.gi).

Other useful addresses
Economic Planning and Statistics Office, 6 Convent Place (tel: 75-515, 70-071).

Gibraltar Finance Centre, Suite 771, Europort (tel: 50-011; fax: 47-677; e-mail: fsc@gibnet.gi).

Gibraltar Information Bureau, Arundel Great Court, 179 Strand, London WC2R 1EH (tel: (0)20 7836-0777; fax: (0)20 7240-6612).

Gibraltar Telecommunications International Ltd, Mount Pleasant, 25 South Barrack Road (tel: 59-609; fax: 59-644).

Gibtelecom, Suite 942, Europort (tel: 52-200; fax: 71-673; internet site: http://www.gibtele.com).

Internet sites
Audio site – Talking about Gibraltar: http://www.gibnynex.gi/info/gibtalk

Business in Gibraltar: http://www.Gibraltarian.com/Gibraltar_business.asp

Government of Gibraltar: http://www.gibraltar.gov.gi

Gibraltar Broadcasting Corporation (GBC): http://www.gbc.gi

Offshore facilities: http://www.Gibraltaroffshore.com/

Greece

KEY FACTS

Official name: I Elliniki Dimokratia (The Hellenic Republic)

Head of State: President Karolos Papoulias (sworn in 12 Mar 2005)

Head of government: Prime Minister Costas Karamanlis (ND) (from 8 Mar 2004)

Ruling party: Nea Dimokratia (ND) (New Democracy) (sworn in 10 Mar 2004)

Area: 131,957 square km

Population: 11.07 million (2004); 11.04 million (OECD, 2003)

Capital: Athens

Official language: Greek

Currency: Euro (eur) = 100 cents (from 1 Jan 2002; previous currency drachma, locked at Dr340.75 per euro)

Exchange rate: eur0.83 per US$ (Oct 2005)

GDP per capita: US$18,722 (2004)

GDP real growth: 4.20% (2004);*3.5% (2005)

Labour force: 4.37 million (2004)

Unemployment: 10.50% (OECD, 2004)

Inflation: 3.10% (2004); *3.5% (2005)

Balance of trade: -US$38.78 billion (2004)*

Foreign debt: US$233.10 billion (2004)

Annual FDI: US$8.90 billion (cumulative, 1995–2004, OECD); US$1.40 billion (2004)*

* estimated figure

The afterglow of Greece's success in hosting the 2004 Olympic Games had very much burned low by 2005. The government strove, in 2005, to impose an economic austerity programme in order to combat serious current account and budget deficits. Despite widespread industrial unrest, the government managed to pass most of its programme as it commanded a comfortable parliamentary majority.

Deficits to cut

The Greek economy experienced a slowdown in 2005, partly in response to the end of Olympics-related investment and partly in response to the rise in world oil prices. GDP growth was nevertheless a respectable 3.5 per cent (OECD forecast). However, Greece's budget deficit was once again above the prescribed EU limit of 3.0 per cent, running at around 3.7 per cent in 2005 (European Commission forecast). Moreover, Greece's public sector debt was 107.9 per cent of GDP and inflation ran at 3.5 per cent in 2005.

In order to tackle rising deficits, the government initiated a series of public sector, pension and labour reforms. Fearing job losses and cuts to pensions, Greece's main union movements called a series of 24-hour strikes in March, June and December. After a promisingly consensual start to 2005, when Karolos Papoulias was overwhelmingly elected by parliament in March as the next president of Greece, politics soon became bitterly partisan again. The Nea Dimokratia (ND) (New Democracy) government faced a censure motion in parliament over the June strikes. In response, the prime minister, Kostas Karamanlis, called for and easily won a vote of confidence in his government. The Karamanlis government again faced down protesters and parliamentary opposition parties in December, when it passed an austere budget for 2006, designed to rein in the budget deficit.

Divisive issues (continued)

In December, an appeal against conviction on terrorism charges by 15 members of the terrorist organisation Epanastatiki Organosi dekaefta Noemvri (November 17) brought domestic terrorism back into the spotlight in Greece. Possible sympathisers with the November 17 movement bombed a number of public buildings in November and December. In October, Amnesty International published a report criticising Greece's treatment of its ethnic and religious minorities, particularly Roma, and asylum seekers. As if to underline the point, Greece was forced to cut short a presidential visit to Albania in the face of protests by members of the Cham community. The Chams, ethnically Albanian, had been deported en masse from northern Greece in 1944, allegedly for collaborating with the Nazis, and have since campaigned for the return of property rights in Greece. A potentially major political row broke in December when a local newspaper published claims that Greek and British intelligence services co-operated in the kidnapping of 28 Pakistani citizens in Athens, in connection with bombings in London in July. The abducted men claimed to have been tortured.

Regional issues

Since joining the EU in 1981, Greece has constituted Brussels' frontier with the Balkans and the Near East. For many years, Greece demonstrated a willingness to use its EU membership to pursue nationalist objectives in relation to its neighbours, including pressuring the Former Yugoslav Republic of Macedonia (FYROM) over its choice of name. However, in the late 1990s, Greece adopted a more conciliatory approach to its neighbours and has actively supported the European integration bids of former foes such as FYROM, Bulgaria and Turkey. In 2005, Greece continued this process of engagement by throwing its support behind the efforts of Bulgaria and Turkey to secure accession treaties with the EU – signed in April and October respectively. In April, the Greek government agreed to consider new UN proposals over which name FYROM could use at an international level. Also in April, the Greek parliament ratified the EU constitution.

However, a number of incidents in 2005 indicated that Greece's relations with its neighbours would always be complex. Greece claimed that Turkish jet fighters violated its airspace on several occasions during the year, and particularly in November and December. The Greek foreign ministry also felt the need, in November, to interject during a dispute between the Turkish authorities in Istanbul and the Ecumenical Patriarch of the Orthodox Church – the 'first among equals' in the world's Orthodox Church hierarchy, resident in Istanbul. Church matters also bizarrely saw Greece intervening in the politics of religion in Israel, when the Patriarch of Jerusalem was ousted from his position in May. Greece, along with Jordan and the Palestinian Authority (PA), supported the removal of Patriarch Irineos I against the wishes of the Israeli government. Greece then supported the candidacy of Irineos' eventual successor, Theophilos III, a Greek national.

Outlook

With Turkey now engaged in accession talks with the EU, it seems inevitable that Greece will be an important player, both publicly and privately, in shaping the future of EU enlargement. Although Greece will continue to support Cyprus' position vis à vis Turkey, Prime Minister Karamanlis also counts Turkey's prime minister Recep Erdoğan as a personal friend and, like his predecessors in government, sees Turkish membership as a strategic goal. As one of the first EU countries to report a case of avian flu (HVN1), Greece will also have to address its readiness to tackle serious health issues in 2006. Local (municipal) elections are due in October 2006, providing the government with its first real electoral test since passing a series of economic austerity measures. The opposition Panellino Socialistiko Kinima (Pasok) (Pan-Hellenic Socialist Movement) began to significantly narrow the gap between it and the government in opinion polls conducted at the end of 2005, suggesting that the Karamanlis administration may have a fight on its hands.

Risk assessment

Economic	Improving
Political	Stable
Regional stability	Good

COUNTRY PROFILE

Historical profile
Ancient Greece at one point ruled a substantial empire extending across the Middle East and Central Asia. Many features of Western civilisation can be traced to aspects of ancient Greek culture and institutions, including music, philosophy and democratic rule. The Greek monarchy later administered the eastern arm of the Roman empire. Following the fall of the Roman empire, Greece was initially ruled by the Byzantines from their capital in Constantinople (now Istanbul).
1454 After the fall of Constantinople to Suleiman the Magnificent, Greece and most of the eastern Mediterranean were occupied by the Ottoman empire.
1829 Following a war against the Ottomans lasting eight years, Greece declared its independence as a monarchy.

KEY INDICATORS — Greece

	Unit	2000	2001	2002	2003	2004
Population	m	10.94	10.97	11.00	11.04	11.07
Gross domestic product (GDP)	US$bn	112.60	116.40	132.80	172.80	*203.40
GDP per capita	US$	10,669	11,003	12,777	15,881	18,722
GDP real growth	%	4.5	4.3	3.6	4.5	4.2
Inflation	%	3.2	3.4	3.9	3.5	3.1
Unemployment	%	11.3	10.5	10.0	9.3	10.0
Coal output	mtoe	8.3	9.0	9.2	9.7	9.5
Exports (fob) (goods)	US$m	10,202.0	10,615.0	10,320.0	13,040.0	15,500.0
Imports (fob) (goods)	US$m	30,440.0	29,702.0	30,940.0	45,379.0	54,280.0
Balance of trade	US$m	-20,239.0	-19,087.0	-19,500.0	-32,339.0	-38,780.0
Current account	US$m	-9,820.0	-9,400.0	-5,200.0	-10,100.0	-8,420.0
Total reserves minus gold	US$m	13,424.3	17,564.8	8,083.0	4,361.4	1,191.0
Foreign exchange	US$m	13,115.5	16,314.1	7,629.0	3,843.3	743.7
Exchange rate	per US$	365.40	363.59	1.04	0.88	0.80

* estimated figure

1913 The London Conference reduced the amount of ethnic Albanian-dominated territory of the former Ottoman Empire, Cameria (Chamouria) was granted to Greece.
1917 Greece entered the First World War on the side of the Allies and made territorial gains.
1923 Greece signed the Lausanne Peace Treaty with Turkey. The Treaty outlined the territory of each country and provided Greece with a number of islands in the Aegean Sea.
1939 Greece rejected Italy's ultimatum seeking free passage for its troops in the Second World War and repelled its attack, but was occupied by Germany. The government and the King went into exile. Mass armed resistance grew out of various political groupings.
1944 Liberation from the Nazis. The returned National Unity government under George Papandreou fought a civil war against the Communists.
1949 Constitutional monarchy was re-established. There were territorial gains from the war, the last of which was the Dodecanese islands in the south-eastern Aegean Sea.
1967–72 A military coup led by right-wing army officers deposed King Konstantinos II. An attempted counter-coup by the King failed, and he went into exile. Colonel Georgios Papadopoulos appointed himself prime minister. The regime was brutal and repressive with all political activity banned.
1973 Greece was declared a republic with Papadopoulos as president. General Demetrios Ioannides led a bloodless coup; Papadopoulos was overthrown. Partial civilian rule was allowed. General Phaidon Gizikis was appointed president.
1974 Civil war in Cyprus and the Turkish invasion of the island brought Greece close to war with Turkey and caused the downfall of the military junta. Elections resulted in a decisive victory for Nea Dimokratia (ND) (New Democracy). A referendum rejected proposals for a return to constitutional monarchy.
1975 A republican constitution providing for a parliamentary democracy was promulgated and Konstantinos Tsatsos was elected president.
1977 The ND was re-elected with a reduced majority.
1980 In May, Constantine Karamanlis was elected president. Greece joined the EU.
1981 The Panellino Socialistiko Kinima (Pasok) (Pan-Hellenic Socialist Movement) gained an absolute majority in parliament in the elections. The Pasok government, led by Andreas Papandreou, was the first socialist government in Greek history.
1985 President Karamanlis resigned and Christos Sartzetakis became president. Pasok was returned to power and implemented proposed constitutional changes. The government's programme of economic austerity became very unpopular and resulted in widespread industrial unrest.
1986 Constitutional amendments limited the powers of the president.
1989 ND won the largest proportion of votes in the elections.
1993 The ND government was forced to resign after losing its one seat parliamentary majority. Pasok regained power.
1995 Costis Stephanopoulos was elected president.
1996 Prime Minister Papandreou resigned due to ill health and Costas Simitis became prime minister. Andreas Papandreou died, ending an era of authoritarian control over Pasok, which won the parliamentary elections.
2000 Incumbent president, Stephanopoulos, was re-elected. Pasok was re-elected, becoming the first party to win three successive elections. Greece's application to join the Economic and Monetary Union (Emu) was accepted.
2001 Greece officially joined the Emu.
2002 Euro currency replaced the drachma.
2004 The former opposition party, ND, led by Costas Karamanlis won the March parliamentary elections.
2005 On 8 February, Karolos Papoulias was elected president; he was sworn in on 12 March. Newly introduced labour laws ended 'jobs for life'.

Political structure
Constitution
The constitution of 1975 has been revised on several occasions in line with contemporary circumstances. It sets out the rights and responsibilities of the parliament, judiciary, people and church. The constitution is enshrined in law.
In March 1986, parliament ratified changes to the 1975 constitution, limiting the president's power in relation to parliament.
Form of state
Parliamentary democratic republic
The executive
The president of the republic is Head of State, and is elected by parliament for a five-year term, for a maximum of two terms. The president must be elected by a two-thirds majority, or on the third ballot by a three-fifths majority.
Since 1985 when presidential power was reduced, de facto executive power is wielded by the prime minister and cabinet. The cabinet is named by the prime minister.

National legislature
Legislative power rests with the 300-member unicameral Vouli ton Ellinon (parliament), elected for four years by universal and compulsory adult suffrage.
Legal system
Greek law is based on codified Roman law with the judiciary divided into civil, criminal, and administrative courts. Judicial independence is guaranteed under the constitution.
Last elections
8 February 2005 (presidential); 13 June 2004 (European Parliament); 7 March 2004 (parliamentary).
Results: Presidential: Karolos Papoulias was elected president, receiving 279 votes in the 300-seat parliament.
European Parliament: ND won 43.1 per cent of the vote (11 seats out of 24), Pasok 34 per cent (eight), KKE 9.5 per cent (three), SIN 4.2 per cent (one) and Laikos Orthodoxos Synagermos (LAOS) (Populist Orthodox Rally) 4.1 per cent (one); turnout 62.8 per cent.
Parliamentary: the ND won with 45.4 per cent of the vote (165 seats out of 300) against 40.6 per cent (116 seats) for Pasok. The KKE won 5.9 per cent (12) and the SIN 3.3 per cent (six). Turnout was 76.5 per cent.
Next elections
2008 (parliamentary); February 2010 (presidential).

Political parties
Ruling party
Nea Dimokratia (ND) (New Democracy) (sworn in 10 Mar 2004)
Main opposition party
Panellino Socialistiko Kinima (Pasok) (Pan-Hellenic Socialist Movement); Greek Communist Party (KKE); Sinaspismos tis Aristeras ke ti Proodu (SIN) (Coalition of Left and Progressive Forces).

Population
11.07 million (2004); 11.04 million (OECD, 2003)
Ethnic make-up
Greece is a very homogenous state and the vast majority of its citizens regard themselves as ethnic Greek. However, there are also small numbers of Turks, Pomaks, Gypsies, Vlaks and an increasing numbers of illegal Albanian economic refugees (some 300,000 are believed to live in Athens).
Religions
Over 95 per cent of the population are baptised in the Greek Orthodox Church. There are small Muslim, Catholic and Jewish communities.

Education
Primary education lasts for six years. Secondary education generally lasts for six years and is divided into two equal

Greece

periods. Approximately 47 per cent of the relevant age group participate in some form of tertiary education. Overcrowded classes at public high schools and a lack of facilities mean that students take private tuition or attend night school to improve their chances of going to university, for which entrance is fiercely competitive. Women comprise almost 60 per cent of Greek graduates.

Public education expenditure is equivalent to just over 3 per cent of GDP.

Literacy rate: 98 per cent, male; 96 per cent, female; adult rates (World Bank).

Enrolment rate: 93 per cent at primary level and 95 per cent at secondary level (of the relevant age groups).

Pupils per teacher: 14 in primary schools

Health

Annual total expenditure on health is about 9 per cent of GDP, of which around 56 per cent is government spending; private expenditure is approximately 44 per cent, of which pre-paid healthcare plans are 4 per cent.

Although basic healthcare is provided free of charge, many Greeks find standards unsatisfactory and prefer to go to private doctors and clinics, or even to pay the high cost of treatment abroad.

HIV prevalence: 0.2 per aged 15–49 in 2003 (World Bank)

Life expectancy: 78.0 years (World Bank)

Fertility rate/Maternal mortality rate: 1.3 births per woman (World Bank)

Infant mortality rate: 5.0 per 1,000 live births (World Bank)

Head of population per physician/bed: Four physicians and five hospital beds per 1,000 people

Welfare

Social security is handled by more than 350 state-run or state-supervised social insurance funds, which together cover almost all the Greek population. The largest of these funds is the general social security scheme, run by the Idryma Koinonikis Asfalisis (IKA) (Social Security Institute). The scheme covers 1.8 million wage earners, pays pensions and operates a network of hospitals and out patient clinics.

Parliament approved the restructuring of the debt-burdened and complex state pension system in June. Greece has a growing aged population, which will become problematic.

At 9 per cent of the total labour force, the proportion of Greek employees living in conditions of poverty is one of the highest in the EU.

Main cities

Athens/Piraeus (capital, estimated population 736,400 in 2003), Thessaloniki (361,200), Piraeus (179,300), Patras (167,000).

Languages spoken

Macedonian, Albanian, Turkish, Aroumanian, Bulgarian and Pomak are spoken by their resident populations. Most people in the business community also speak English, French or German.

Official language/s
Greek

Media

Press
Censorship is banned under the 1975 constitution, but a public prosecutor may stop circulation of an edition of a newspaper on the grounds that it is blasphemous, offends public decency, reveals military or state secrets or offends the Greek president.

There are about 280 newspapers and over 70 magazines in Greece, which reach over 50 per cent of adults.

Dailies: Most national dailies include a Sunday edition. *Athens News* is published daily in English. There are around 20 dailies, mostly published in Athens, and a few in Thessaloniki. Most popular are *To Vima*, *Eleftherotypia*, *Ta Nea*, *Eleftheros Typos*, *Adesmeftos Tipos* and *Apoyevmatini*. *Thessaloniki* is a popular regional daily. Other regional dailies include *Ethnos Kyriakis*, *Kathimerini Kyriakis*, *Makedonia*, *Naftemporiki*, *Eleftheri Ora*, and *Eleftheros*.

Weeklies: The most popular Sunday newspapers are *To Vima*, *Eleftherotypia*, *Kathimerini*, *Ethnos* and *Typos Kiriakis*. *7 Meres TV*, *Ego* (women's weekly) and *Kiriakatiki* are other popular weeklies of general interest.

Business: Some important financial and business publications include *Naftemporiki*, *Agora* and *Expendytis*. *Economicos Tachidromos* covers politics and economics; *Naftika Chronika* and *Naftiliaki* are of marine business interest.

Periodicals: *Gynaika* and *Praktiki* are women's monthlies and *Games* is a monthly magazine on sports.

Broadcasting
The state-supervised company, Elliniki Radiophonia Tileorassi (ERT) (Hellenic Radio and Television) operates two main television channels (ET-1 and ET-2) and a third in Thessaloniki as well as four radio channels.

Radio: There are 420 commercial radio stations. Local governments operate radio stations in Athens and Thessaloniki. The most popular are Sky 100.4 FM, 98.4 FM and Antenna 97.1 FM.

Television: A dozen satellite channels are available in the Athens area. Many of the private television stations are owned by Greek newspaper magnates and leading businessmen.

Advertising
Advertisements are aired on all state television channels as well as the private stations. Two of the four state-supervised radio stations accept advertising. Posters are widely used, under control of site owner. Cinemas are also popular, and direct mail is becoming increasingly important. Newspaper and magazine advertising is constrained by relatively low circulation figures. Key categories include food, retail, cigarettes, alcohol, clothing and electrical appliances. Advertising expenditure is equivalent to 2 per cent of annual GDP.

Economy

Greece has a mixed economy with a heavy dependence on tourism, agriculture and shipping. Since it adopted the euro in 2002 and the related decline in interest rates there has been sustained and robust growth. In 2004 GDP growth was 4.2 per cent, showing a slight fall from 4.5 per cent in 2003, due to the end of government spending on the Olympic games, and high global oil prices. Nevertheless household consumption rose on the back of increased credit sustained by the strength of shipping and good tourist receipts.

Unemployment is estimated to have risen from 9.3 per cent in 2003 to 10.5 per cent in 2004, partly as a result of workers finishing projects that had been under construction for the Athens Olympics until 2004. The country's high unemployment rate, particularly among the young, and large numbers of illegal immigrants remain major problems, as does the large underground economy, estimated at almost 30 per cent of total economic activity.

The government plans to reform the economy, including the tax system. The IMF has identified that the shortfall in budget forecasts is due to increased evasion of tax receipts, principally from VAT. The government plans to introduce more tax scrutiny, as well as reduce its expenditure in public sector wage and employment. It is hoped that the reforms will increase competitiveness, employment and investment activity.

Several large infrastructure projects were built for the 2004 Olympic Games, including an extension to the Athens subway system, an upgrading of its bus fleet and a new airport and toll highway. The EU co-financed some projects, including the new tram system, a suburban light railway, an extension of the metro to Athens airport and upgrades to health amenities. The costs of staging the Games were, however, far more than the original estimates, and pushed Greece's budget deficit above the 3 per cent of GDP ceiling permissible under the EU's Stability and Growth Pact.

General budget outlays increased by 12.7 per cent during the first half of 2004, compared with a target of 4.9 per cent; this increased the deficit for the first half of the year by 26 per cent over the same period in 2003 and by the end of 2004 it was 6 per cent of GDP. On the positive side, the improved infrastructure and success of the games have given investors the impression that Greece can compete in the competitive market for attracting investment.

Greece has benefited to the tune of around US$27 billion from the EU structural fund since 2000. The enlargement of the EU, and the mid-2005 row about the size of the 2007–13 EU budget, probably means that this will be cut by as much as a third by 2010.

According to the World Travel and Tourism Council (WTTC), in 2005 tourism, a major sector of the economy, is expected to directly account for 7.2 per cent of GDP, and 18.2 per cent of the total workforce. However, the majority of Greece's visitors are from western Europe (UK and Germany) and as long haul tourism becomes more popular and the Mediterranean less so, Greece will see a slackening of grown in the sector. To help counter this, the Ministry of Tourism is encouraging growth in non-traditional areas, such as golf courses, and is encouraging an upgrade in services offered.

External trade
The government is increasingly focussing its trade expansion policies to encompass central and eastern European countries.

Imports
Principal imports include raw materials, fuels and lubricants, chemicals, machinery and transport equipment, foodstuffs, basic manufactures and consumer goods.
Main sources: Germany (13.3 per cent total, 2004), Italy (12.6 per cent), France (6.6 per cent), Russia (5.4 per cent), The Netherlands (5.4 per cent), South Korea (4.6 per cent), US (4.4 per cent), UK (4.1 per cent)

Exports
Principal exports include manufactured goods, petroleum products, chemicals, textiles and agricultural products, fruit and vegetables, live animals, and tobacco.
Main destinations: Germany (13.3 per cent total, 2004), Italy (10.2 per cent), UK (7.6 per cent), Bulgaria (6.5 per cent), US (5.2 per cent), Cyprus (4.6 per cent), Turkey (4.6 per cent), France (4.2 per cent)

Agriculture
Farming
Agriculture is an important but diminishing sector of the economy, typically contributing, around 8.3 per cent to GDP and employing around 12 per cent of the labour force.

The government's agricultural policy is, to a large extent, shaped by EU farm policies, since the bulk of Greece's net benefits from EU membership arrive in the form of price supports for farmers. Greek farms are small by EU standards, averaging less than two hectares (ha).

Fundamental reform to the Common Agricultural Policy (CAP) replaced subsidies paid on farm output, which tended to benefit large farms and encourage over-production, with single farm payments not conditional on production. This is expected to reward farms that provide and maintain a healthy environment, food safety and animal welfare standards. The changes are also intended to encourage market conscious production and cut the cost of CAP to the EU taxpayer. Greece introduced this measure on 1 January 2006.

Main crops include wheat, barley, maize, fruit (especially olives), vegetables, oil seeds, tobacco, cotton and sugar beet. Traditionally, farm co-operatives have played a large role in agriculture as a source of purchasing seeds, renting machinery and selling products. Larger co-operatives also handle basic processing and marketing. Attempts to restructure the co-operatives have largely failed, with weak management and widespread corruption preventing their modernisation and development.

The sector is also handicapped by weak infrastructure, low levels of technology and generally poor soil. However, with the exception of meat, dairy products and animal feeds, Greece is self-sufficient in foodstuffs.

The estimated crop production for 2004 included: 4,584,200 tonnes (t) cereals in total, 1,800,000t wheat, 2,300,000t maize, 1,157,000t citrus fruit, 1,300,000t grapes, 850,000t potatoes, 220,000t barley, 1,800,000t tomatoes, 612,689t oilcrops, *121,000t tobacco, 2,300,000t olives, 2,300,000t sugar beet, 95,000t chillies & peppers, 78,000t treenuts, 1,100,000t seed cotton, 359,000t cotton lint, 4,080,600t fruit in total, 3,998,500t vegetables in total. Estimated livestock production included: 477,573t meat in total, 75,000t beef, 134,500t pig meat, 81,000t lamb, 44,000t goat meat, 134,373t poultry, 105,000t eggs, 1,970,045t milk, *15,000t honey, 12,250t cattle hides, *16,300t sheepskins, *9,600t greasy wool, *20t cocoons, silk.

* etimate

Fishing
Fish production is important for domestic consumption and export. The annual freshwater fish catch is around 25,000 tonnes, with a marine catch of approximately 270,000 tonnes. Coastal fish farms produce sea bass and gilthead bream.

Although Greece has an expanding aquaculture sector, its processing and marketing sector remains underdeveloped. Following the EU's common fisheries policy, the country benefits from the EU structural fund that covers the whole sector and also includes the development of the processing and marketing of products.

Forestry
Forest and other wooded land accounts for half of the land area, with forest cover estimated at 3.5 million hectares (ha). Most of the forest is in the northern and western part of the mainland and about 90 per cent is available for wood supply. Significant quantities of roundwood production are used for fuel consumption. More than three-quarters of the forest and other wooded land is under public ownership, and only about 20 per cent is privately owned. The forest sector is rather small and all types of forest products are imported, mainly comprising sawnwood and paper products.

Production in 2004 included 1,672,856 cubic metres (cum) roundwood, 599,248cum industrial roundwood, 527,772cum sawlogs and veneer logs, 195,805cum sawnwood, 1,073,608cum wood fuel.

Industry and manufacturing
Industry typically accounts for 25 per cent of GDP and employs 26 per cent of the labour force. Within the industrial sector, manufacturing accounts for 57 per cent of output and construction 32 per cent. The remaining 11 per cent of industrial output is accounted for by the minerals and utilities sectors.

Manufacturing, which contributes around 15 per cent to overall GDP, is dominated by small family-owned companies, most of which are situated around Athens or in export-oriented zones around the port of Thessaloniki.

The number of mergers and acquisitions of Greek firms by foreign investors has increased in recent years, with greater numbers of companies making initial public offerings (IPOs) on the Athens Stock Exchange. However, production has been sluggish and relatively few industries are competitive on a European level.

Greek industry is also less competitive compared to its EU neighbours because it has no land boundaries with the Union.

The aluminium sector, which is facing a shortage of domestic raw material, represents more than 1.5 per cent of GDP and employs approximately 40,000 workers.

Tourism
The tourist sector is Greece's biggest industry and principal source of foreign exchange earnings. In 2005 it should earn 38.6 per cent, or US$16.2 billion, in total exports. Travel and tourism is expected to generate US$23 billion, or 7.2 per cent of GDP and employ 18.2 per cent of the workforce, in 2005. The sector attracted US$5.7 billion or 10.7 per cent of total capital investment.

The government is seeking to improve quality by developing the conference and incentives market and upgrading hotels. Investment proposals for luxury leisure complexes are being encouraged.

Every year, there are around 12 million foreign visitors to Greece, with a boost of 4.52 per cent in 2004 when Greece hosted the Olympic Games in Athens.

Mining
There is a relative wealth of natural resources including large deposits of bauxite (aluminium ore), marble, lignite, magnesite, ferro-chrome, ferro-nickel, lead, zinc, uranium and manganese. Mining activity is small-scale and the sector typically contributes only 3 per cent to GDP and employs only 1 per cent of the workforce.

New gold resources have been found at Skouries (an ancient copper mine), estimated to contain five–seven million ounces of gold.

Hydrocarbons
Greece has oil reserves of around seven million barrels (2005), produces around 6,411 barrels per day (bpd) and consumes 429,000bpd annually and is, therefore, a net importer of oil; oil provides 65 per cent of the country's fuel source. However, its importance is beginning to decline, as natural gas becomes more important.

Most domestic oil production comes from the Prinos fields, which are exploited by North Aegean Petroleum Company (NAPC) consortium.

Greece's oil industry is dominated by the state owned Hellenic Petroleum (HP), for which the government has a 27.5 per cent stake.

Construction of a 280km oil pipeline linking the Bulgarian Black Sea port of Burgas with Alexandropoulis on the Mediterranean coast of Greece was agreed in April 2005. Greece may earn between US$30–50 million for this pipeline's siting. HP operates a 214km oil pipeline, with a capacity to carry about 50,200bpd, from the port of Thessaloniki to Skopje in Macedonia. HP also operates three oil refineries with a combined refining capacity of 301,400bpd and a private refinery with a 100,000bpd capacity.

Total natural gas reserves stood at 990 million cubic metres (cum) in 2005. Consumption has been low, since the mid-1990s when consumption was 28.3 million cum, to 2.4 billion cum in 2003, and is projected to triple by 2015. Over 60 per cent of gas is currently imported through a 320km pipeline from Russia and is in negotiation with other suppliers to allow diversification.

The Greek natural gas sector is controlled by the Greek Public Gas Company (DEPA). However, since 2004 market liberalisation has seen ownership opened to external competition.

In July 2005, construction of the Greece and Turkey 285km natural gas pipeline began.

Greece had coal reserves of 4.23 million tonnes in 2005. Reserves are comprised wholly of low quality lignite, with high extraction costs.

Energy
Greece generates approximately 50 million MW of electricity annually; around 90 per cent is thermal. Around 63 per cent of primary energy requirements are met by imported oil. Emphasis has been on developing indigenous oil resources (largely from the Prinos oil field) and expanding hydroelectric and geothermal power generation, but most future power plants will be entirely gas-fired. Growth in electricity has increased by 50 per cent since 1995 and the energy authorities estimate that it will need an extra 6,000MW of additional capacity by 2015.

The production, distribution and transmission of electricity in Greece was under the full control of the state-owned Public Power Corporation (PPC). However EU requirements for market liberalisation have compelled the government to open up ownership to competition. By 2005 state-control was 51 per cent of PPC. Although PPC has lost its monopoly it still produces 96 per cent of all electricity production.

The power network is connected to the networks of Albania, Bulgaria and Macedonia. Greece exports electricity to Kosovo in Serbia and Montenegro. Greece is the EU's second-largest solar collector (after Germany), with 20 per cent of households using solar powered water heaters.

Financial markets
Stock exchange
The Athens Stock Exchange (Athex) is home to the Helenic Exchange (Helex), Central Securities, Athens Derivatives Exchange and the Thessalonica Exchange (TSEC).

Athex has over 300 listed companies, with the Hellenic Telecom Organisation having the most traded shares in 2005.

Banking and insurance
Liberalisation of the banking system was initiated in 1987. Interest rates are fully freed and commercial banks permitted to handle forward dealing in foreign exchange. Companies can borrow in foreign exchange without restriction.
Central bank
Bank of Greece; European Central Bank (ECB).

Time
GMT plus two hours (GMT plus three hours from late March to late September)

Geography
Greece lies in south-eastern Europe. The country consists mainly of a mountainous peninsula between the Mediterranean Sea and the Aegean Sea. It is bounded by Albania, Macedonia (FYROM) and Bulgaria to the north, Turkey to the north-east, the Aegean Sea to the east, the Sea of Crete to the south and the Ionian Sea to the west. To the south, east and west of the mainland are many Greek islands, the largest being Crete.

Climate
Coastal regions and the islands have typical Mediterranean conditions, with mild, rainy winters and hot, dry, sunny summers. Rainfall comes almost entirely in the winter months, although amounts vary widely according to position and relief. Continental conditions affect the northern mountainous areas, with severe winters, deep snow cover and heavy precipitation, but summers are hot.

Athens: 8.6 degrees Celsius (C) (January); 28.2 degrees C (July); annual rainfall 414.3mm.

Dress codes
A suit and tie or formal clothing are necessary for business meetings, even during the hot summer months.

Women tend to dress smartly in the evening and men wear either suits or smart, casual clothes.

Entry requirements
Passports
Passports are not required by citizens of EU countries holding National Identity Cards. Passports must be valid for the intended length of stay.
Visa
Required by all, except nationals of Schengen agreement signatory countries and citizens of most of the Americas, Europe and many Asian countries. For confirmation of exceptions contact the consular section of the nearest embassy.

For those applying for a business visas, contact the consulate that administers your region before travelling to determine requirements. A Schengen visa application (offered in several languages) can be downloaded on www.eurovisa.info/ApplicationForm.htm.

Currency advice/regulations
The import of local and foreign currency is not restricted provided any amount exceeding eur10,000 is declared on arrival. The export of local and foreign currency is allowed although amounts over eur2,000 require an import declaration form issued on arrival.

Customs
Personal effects are allowed in duty-free. There are no restrictions on the import of goods from other EU member states. Strict regulations are enforced concerning the export from Greece of antiquities, including rocks from archaeological sites. Penalties range from large fines to prison terms.

Health (for visitors)
Mandatory precautions
Yellow fever vaccination certificate is required if travelling from infected area.

Advisable precautions
Long-term visitors should consider hepatitis 'A' immunisation. Drinking water is not always purified outside main cities. Comprehensive travel insurance is advisable, in case of medical or other emergencies.

Hotels
Numerous hotels in all main towns, classified as de luxe, A,B,C,D and E. There is a 15 per cent service charge. A small tip will be expected. It is advisable to make reservations well in advance, especially between May and September.

Credit cards
All major credit cards are accepted.

Public holidays
Fixed dates
1 Jan (New Year's Day), 6 Jan (Epiphany), 25 Mar (Independence Day), 1 May (Labour Day), 15 Aug (Assumption Day), 28 Oct (Ochi Day/National Day), 25 Dec (Christmas Day), 26 Dec (Boxing Day).

Variable dates
Greek Orthodox Shrove Monday, Greek Orthodox Good Friday, Greek Orthodox Easter Monday, Greek Orthodox Whit Monday.

Working hours
Banking
Mon–Fri: 0800–1400.

Business
Mon–Fri: generally 0800–1400 and 1700–2000; tend to close earlier during summer and on Mon and Wed afternoons.

Government
Mon–Fri: usually 0800–1500.

Shops
Mon, Wed and Sat: 0800–1500; Tue, Thu and Fri: 0800–1400 and 1730–2030, or 0900–1730.

Telecommunications
Mobile phones
There are GSM roaming facilities available in 900/1800 band widths, with coverage throughout the country, including the island territories.

Electricity supply
220V AC

Social customs/useful tips
Personal contact is the most important way of conducting business in Greece and many Greeks are wary of speaking frankly on the telephone.
Greek bureaucracy is very slow. Persistence and attendance in person at the office or ministry concerned is almost the only way of getting things done. Identification documents and various authorisation letters or seals are necessary.
It is forbidden to photograph military installations and aircraft. Penalties for breaking the law can be severe.

Security
Crime against tourists (pickpocketing and purse-snatching) is on the rise in tourist sites, particularly in Athens.

Getting there
Air
Greece has a strong holiday industry that relies on 80 per cent of international visitors arriving by air. Airports are located on the mainland as well as the islands.

National airline: Olympic Airways
International airport/s: Eleftherios Venizelos Airport (ATH), sited in Sparta, 27km north-west of Athens. Facilities include: business centre, shops, duty-free, restaurants and car hire. Further information can be obtained at www.aia.gr/. Six express bus routes carry passengers into Athens or the port of Piraeus.
Other airport/s: Alexandroupolis (AXD), 7km from city; Corfu (CFU), 1.6km from city; Heraklion (HER), 5km from city; Ioannina (IOA), 5km from city; Kos (KGS), 27km from city; Mykonos (JMK); Paros (PAS); Rhodes (RHO), 16km south-west of Rhodes; Thessaloniki Makedonia (SKG), 16km from city; Skiathos (JSI); Thira (JTR).
Airport tax: There is no airport tax.

Surface
Road: The Greek road network is accessible via Italy, Bulgaria and Macedonia (FYROM) (border crossing at Medzitlija, near Bitola).
Rail: The Greek rail network is connected to most European routes via Italy, Bulgaria and Macedonia (FYROM). There is a daily service between Athens and Istanbul.
Water: Frequent passenger ferry services operate from Italy to Piraeus. A car ferry service runs between Ancona and Brindisi (Italy) and Igoumenitsa and Patras. There is a ferry from Marmaris, Turkey, to the island of Rhodes.
Main port/s: Heraklion, Igoumenitsa, Patras, Piraeus, Rafina, Salonika and Volos.

Getting about
National transport
Air: As well as the international airports, there are a further 25 other airports all connected by regular services operated by Olympic Airways.
Road: There are 117,000km of roads in Greece, of which about 9,000km are unpaved. There are 470km of motorways, including a route from Athens to Thessaloniki.
Rail: Over 2,500km of track is operated by Hellenic Railways Organisation Ltd, with services to most towns.
Water: About 80km of navigable inland waterways are used, as well as several regular ferry services along the coast and connecting the various islands.

City transport
Taxis: Taxis are plentiful in Athens, but avoid rush hours. There is an extra charge for each piece of luggage, waiting time, journeys outside Athens/Piraeus and journeys after midnight. Yellow taxis run from the airport to downtown Athens.
Buses, trams & metro: There is a good, but often busy, bus network in Athens with a standard flat rate within city limits. Tickets are available at blue booths situated near the bus stops, or at many kiosks throughout the city. These tickets must be inserted into a machine inside the bus to be valid. Double-decker buses run between the airport and downtown Athens, operating every 20 minutes from 0600 until midnight.
The Attico Metro runs from 0530 to midnight daily, approximately every four minutes during rush hour and every 10 minutes at other times. Tickets must be purchased before entering the metro and must be cancelled upon entry.
An extension to the subway system was inaugurated in 2000 as part of the subway grid built for the 2004 Olympic Games. Most of the funding for the US$2.2 billion project was provided by the EU. Two additional subway extensions are planned for 2006.

Car hire
All major car hire companies have offices in Athens and some other main towns. Rates vary depending on size of car, length of hire and season. International driving licences are recognised, but UK, Belgian, Austrian and German full

licences are also accepted. International insurance Green Card is valid, provided Greece is mentioned. The wearing of seatbelts is compulsory. Traffic drives on the right .
Extreme care is necessary if riding a motorbike.

BUSINESS DIRECTORY

The addresses listed below are a selection only. While World of Information makes every endeavour to check these addresses, we cannot guarantee that changes have not been made, especially to telephone numbers and area codes. We would welcome any corrections.

Telephone area codes
The international direct dialling code (IDD) for Greece is +30, followed by area code and subscriber's number:
Athens 210 Samos 273
Heraklion 81 Thessaloniki 31

Useful telephone numbers
Police: 100
Fire: 199
Hospitals: 106
Emergency services (24-hours; information in English, French and Greek, to request ambulances, fire department, police and coastguard): 112

Chambers of Commerce
American-Hellenic Chamber of Commerce, 109 Messoghion Avenue, 11526 Athens (tel: 699-3559; fax: 698-5686; e-mail: info@amcham.gr).

Athens Chamber of Commerce and Industry, 7 Akademias Street, 10671 Athens (tel: 360-4815; fax: 361-6408; e-mail: info@acci.gr).

British-Hellenic Chamber of Commerce, 25 Vassilissis Sophia Avenue, 10674 Athens (tel: 721-0361; fax: 722-2119; e-mail: info@bhcc.gr).

Heraklion Chamber of Commerce and Industry, 9 Koronaiou Street, 71202 Heraclion, Crete (tel: 022-9013; fax: 022-2914; e-mail: info@ebeh.gr).

Samos Chamber of Commerce and Industry, 19 Koundourioti Street, 83100 Samos (tel: 087-970; fax: 022-784; e-mail: samcci@otonet.gr).

Thessaloniki Chamber of Commerce and Industry, 29 Tsimiski Street, 54624 Thessaloniki (tel: 037-0100; fax: 037-0166; e-mail: root@ebeth.gr).

Union of Hellenic Chambers of Commerce and Industry, 7 Akademias Street, 10671 Athens (tel: 363-2702; fax: 362-2320; e-mail: hellas@uhcci.gr).

Banking
Agricultural Bank of Greece SA, Panepistimiou 23, 105-64 Athens (tel: 939-9911; fax: 323-9611).

Alpha Bank, 40 Stadiou Street, 102-52 Athens (tel: 326-0000; fax: 326-5438).

Commerical Bank of Greece, 11 Sophocleous Street, 102-35 Athens (tel: 328-4000; fax: 325-3746).

Egnatia Bank, Omirou 22, 106-72 Athens (tel: 360-6914; fax: 362-7945).

General Bank, Panepistimiou 9, 105-64 Athens (tel: 324-1289; fax: 322-2271).

National Bank of Greece, Aeolou 86, 150-51 Athens (tel: 334-1000; fax: 321-3119; internet site: http://www.nbg.gr).

Post-Office Savings Bank, Pesmazoglou 2-6, 105-59 Athens (tel: 323-0621; fax: 323-1055).

Central bank
Bank of Greece, 21 E Venizelos Avenue, GR 102-50 Athens (tel: 320-1111; fax: 323-2239; e-mail: secretariat@bankofgreece.gr).

European Central Bank (ECB), Kaiserstrasse 29, D-60311 Frankfurt am Main, Germany (tel: +49(69)13-440; fax: +49(69)1344-6000; e-mail: info@ecb.int).

Travel information
Athens Airport (East), Helliniko, 167-00 Athens (tel: 969-9111; fax: 966-6162).

Athens Airport (West), Helliniko, 167-00 Athens (tel: 936-9111; fax: 936-3328).

Athens International Airport (Eleftherios Venizelos), 5th km Spata, Loutsa Ave, 190 04 Spata (tel: 369-8300; fax: 369-8883; internet site: http://www.aia.gr).

Hellenic Chamber of Hotels, 24 Stadiou Street, 10564 Athens (tel: 331-0022/33; fax: 323-6962, 322-5449).

Olympic Airways, Syngrou Ave 96-100, 117-41 Athens (tel: 926-9111; fax: 926-7154).

Ministry of tourism
Ministry of Tourism, Amerikis 2B, 105-64 Athens (tel: 322-3111; fax: 322-4148).

National tourist organisation offices
Ellinikos Organismos Tourismou (GNTO) (Greek National Tourist Organisation), Odos Amerikis 2, Athens 10564 (tel: 322-3111/9).

Ministries
Ministry of Aegean, Syngrou Ave 49, 117-43 Athens (tel: 923-7970; fax: 923-8200).

Ministry of Agriculture, Acharnon 2, 101-76 Athens (tel: 529-1111; fax: 524-0475).

Ministry of Commerce, Caningos Square, 106-77 Athens (tel: 381-6242; fax: 384-2642).

Ministry of Culture, Bouboulinas 20, 106-82 Athens (tel: 820-1100; fax: 820-1337).

Ministry of Education and Religious Affairs, Mitropoleos 15, 101-85 Athens (tel: 325-4221; fax: 324-8264).

Ministry of Environment, Town Planning and Public Works, Amaliados 17, 115-23 Athens (tel: 643-1461; fax: 644-7608).

Ministry of Finance, Karageorgi Servias 10, 101-84 Athens (tel: 331-3400; fax: 323-8657).

Ministry of Foreign Affairs, Academias 1, 106-71 Athens (tel: 361-0584; fax: 645-0028).

Ministry of Health, Welfare and Social Security, Aristotelous 17, 101-87 Athens (tel: 524-9010; fax: 522-3246).

Ministry of Industry, Energy and Technology, Michalakopoulou 80, 101-92 Athens (tel: 748-2770; fax: 770-8003).

General Secretariat for Energy and Technology, Mesogeion Ave 14-18, 115-10 Athens (tel: 775-2221; fax: 771-4153).

Ministry of Interior, Dragatsaniou 2, 105-59 Athens (tel: 322-3521; fax: 324-1180).

Ministry of Justice, Mesogeion 96, 115-27 Athens (tel: 775-7619; fax: 779-6055).

Ministry of Labour, Pireos 40, 101-82 Athens (tel: 523-3110; fax: 524-9805).

Ministry of National Defence, Papagou Camp, Mesogeion 227-229, 154-51 Athens (tel: 646-5201; fax: 646-5584).

Ministry of National Economy: Division for Foreign Capital and Attracting Investments, Syntagma Square, 101-80 Athens (tel: 333-2000; fax: 333-2130; internet site: http://www.dos.gr/welcome_en.htm).

Division for Private Investment Policy, Syntagma Square, 101-80 Athens (tel: 333-2252/3; fax: 333-2326).

Regional Development Divisions of Attica, Thiras 60, 112-52 Athens (tel: 862-9810; fax: 862-9742).

Ministry of Press and Mass Media, Zalokosta 10, 101-63 Athens (tel: 363-0911; fax: 360-6969).

Ministry of Prime Minister's Office, Vas Sofias, 106-74 Athens (tel: 339-3000; fax: 339-3020).

Ministry of Public Order, Pan Kanellopoulou 4, 101-77 Athens (tel: 692-8510; fax: 692-1675).

Ministry of Transport and Communications, Xenofontos 13, 105-57 Athens (tel: 325-1211; fax: 324-7400).

Prime Minister's Office, Maximos Mansion, Herod Atticus 19, 106-74 Athens (tel: 671-7071; fax: 671-5799).

Nations of the World: A Political, Economic and Business Handbook

Other useful addresses

Athenagence (ANA) (news agency), Odos Pindarou 5, Athens 10671 (tel: 363-9816).

Athens and Piraeus Electric Railways (ISAP), Athinas 67, 105-52 Athens (tel: 324-8311; fax: 322-3935).

Athens and Piraeus Trolleys (ILPAP), Admitou 17, 104-46 Athens (tel: 821-6305; fax: 883-7445).

Athens and Piraeus Water Company (EYDAP), Oropou 156, 111-46 Athens (tel: 253-3402; fax: 253-3124).

Athens Municipal Gas Corporation (DEFA), Orfeos 2, 118-54 Athens (tel: 346-1194; fax: 346-1400).

Athens Stock Exchange, Sofokleous 10, 105-59 Athens (tel: 321-1301; fax: 321-3938; internet site: http://www.ase.gr/).

British Embassy, I Ploutarchou Street, 106-75 Athens (tel: 727-2600).

Centre for Planning and Economic Research (KEPE), Ppokratous 22, 106-80 Athens (tel: 362-7321; fax: 361-1136).

Cotton Organisation (OBA), Syngrou Ave 150, 176-71 Athens (tel: 923-4314; fax: 924-3676).

'Democritus' Nuclear Research Centre, Ag Paraskevi, 153-10 Athens (tel: 651-8911; fax: 651-9180).

Department of Press and Information, Ministry to The Prime Minister's Office, Odos Zalokosta 10, Athens (tel: 363-0911).

Economic and Industrial Research Institute (IOBE), Tsami Karatasi 11, 117-42 Athens (tel: 924-1378; fax: 923-3977).

Export Promotion Organisation (OPE), Mar Antippa 86-88, 163-46 Athens (tel: 996-1900; fax: 991-5392).

Federation of Greek Industry (SEB), Xenofontos 5, 105-57 Athens (tel: 323-7325; fax: 322-2929).

Geological and Mineral Research Institute (IGME), Mesogion Ave 70, 115-27 Athens (tel: 779-8412; fax: 775-2211).

Greek Atomic Energy Commission, Ag Paraskevi, 153-10 Athens (tel: 651-8911; fax: 651-9180).

Greek Embassy (USA), 2221 Massachusetts Avenue, NW, Washington DC 20008 (tel: 202-939-5800; fax: 202-939-5824; e-mail: greece@greekembassy.org).

Greek Post Offices (ELTA), Apellou 1, 101-88 Athens (tel: 324-3311; fax: 324-1228).

Greek Radio and Television (ET 1), Mesogion Ave 432, 153-42 Athens (tel: 639-0772; fax: 639-0652).

Greek Radio and Television (ET 2), Mesogion Ave 136, 115-62 Athens (tel: 770-1911; fax: 777-6239).

Greek Railways Organisation (OSE), Sina 6, 106-72 Athens (tel: 362-4402; fax: 362-8933).

Hellenic Aerospace Industry (EAB), Mesogion Ave 2-4, 115-27 Athens (tel: 779-9679; fax: 779-7670).

Hellenic Centre for Investment (HCI), 3 Mitropoleos Str, GR-105 57 Athens (tel: 324-2070; fax: 324-2079).

Hellenic Organisation for Small- and Medium-Size Enterprises and Handicraft Undertakings (EOMMEX), Xenias 16, 115-28 Athens (tel: 771-5002; fax: 771-5025).

Hellenic Organisation for the Promotion of Exports (HOPE), 1 Mitropoleos Street, 10557 Athens (tel: 324-7011/16).

Hellenic Standardisation Organisation (ELOT), Acharnon 313, 111-45 Athens (tel: 201-5025; fax: 202-0776).

Hellenic Telecommunications Organisation (OTE), Kifissias 99, 151-24 Athens (tel: 611-7466; fax: 681-0899).

Hellenic Tobacco Organisation (EOK), Kapodistriou 36, 104-32 Athens (tel: 524-7311; fax: 524-7318).

National Statistical Service, Lykourgou 14-16, 101-66 Athens (tel: 324-85118; fax: 324-1098; internet site: http://www.statistics.gr/).

Panhellenic Confederation of Farmers' Co-operatives (PASEGES), Kifissias 16, 115-26 Athens (tel: 770-4737; fax: 777-9313).

Panhellenic Exporters' Association, Kratinou 11, 105-52 Athens (tel: 522-8925; fax: 522-9403).

Public Materials Administration Organisation (ODDY), Stadiou 60, 105-64 Athens (tel: 324-4231; fax: 324;2970).

Public Petroleum Corporation (DEP), Mesogion Ave 357-359, 152-31 Athens (tel: 650-1340; fax: 650-1383).

Public Power Corporation (PPC), Halkokondyli 30, 104-32 Athens (tel: 523-4301; fax: 523-5307).

Union of Commercial Agents, Voulis 15, Athens (tel: 322-3148).

Urban Transport Organisation (OAS), Metsovou 15, 106-82 Athens (tel: 883-6077; fax: 821-2219).

Internet sites

Bridge to Greece and Cyprus: http://greekvillage.com/bridge/bridge.htm

EFG Eurobank Ergasias: http://www.eurobank.gr

Greek telephone directory: http://www.hellasyellow.gr/

Greenland

COUNTRY PROFILE

Historical profile
Greenland first came under Danish rule in the fourteenth century.
1939–45 During the German occupation of Denmark in the Second World War, Greenland came under US protection.
1953 Greenland ceased to be a colony and became a county of the Danish Kingdom.
1973 Greenland joined the EEC (later EU) as part of Denmark.
1979 Home Rule was granted to Greenland.
1985 Greenland left the EEC. Greenland had voted 'no' to EEC membership in 1972 and again in 1982 and the Danish government had given the Greenlanders the right to decide about membership as the EEC was considered an economic arrangement, not a foreign policy question.
1987 A disagreement with Denmark over the presence of a US military radar system in Thule led to the fall of the coalition government.
1991 Parliamentary elections resulted in a coalition government composed of the Siumit party and the Inuit Ataqatigiit (IA) (Inuit Brotherhood).
1995 The IA receive the most votes in the elections, forming a coalition with Attásut.
Lars Emil Johansen became prime minister.
1997 Lars Emil Johansen was appointed Director of Royal Greenland Ltd and Jonathan Motzfeldt took over as prime minister.
1999 The Siumut (Forward) Party retained its position as the largest party in the Landstinget (parliament) in the elections. Siumut formed a coalition with Atassut (Community), a centre-right party, the loser of the election.
2000 The first offshore oil well drilled in 20 years was dry, dashing hopes for the development of Greenland's hydrocarbons industry. NASA scientists found that the ice sheet which covers 85 per cent of Greenland's territory is melting by one metre per year.
2001 Greenpeace campaigned in Greenland against US plans to develop its National Missile Defense (NMD), which would be dependent on radar facilities on the island. Lars Emil Johansen was elected for Siumut to the Danish parliament; the IA took the other seat and was represented in the Danish parliament for the first time.
2002 The Home Rule administration announced that it would begin the first licensing round for oil exploration off the coast of Greenland by the end of the year. After parliamentary elections, Hans Enoksen, leader of the social democratic Siumut party, became prime minister, leading a coalition government comprising the Siumut and IA parties.
2003 The month-old coalition government collapsed on 16 January after political disagreement over a top official's use of a healer to cleanse the government offices of evil spirits. On 17 January, the Siumut party formed a coalition with the Atassut party, without the involvement of the IA. In September, a budget miscalculation meant that the coalition faced defeat in a confidence vote; a new governing coalition was formed between the Siumut and IA parties.
2004 Scientists said that Greenland's huge ice sheet could melt within the next 1,000 years and swamp low-lying areas around the world if emissions of carbon dioxide and global warming are not reduced.
2005 Prime Minister Enoksen was returned to power in early elections in

KEY FACTS

Official name: Greenland (Kalaallit Nunaat)

Head of State: Queen Margrethe II (of Denmark)

Head of government: Prime Minister Hans Enoksen (leader of the Siumut party)

Ruling party: Coalition government between the Siumut and Inuit Ataqatigiit parties (from 2003, re-elected November 2005)

Area: 2,166,086 square km, of which 410,449 square km is not covered by ice

Population: 56,700 (2004)

Capital: Nuuk (Godthåb)

Official language: Greenlandic Inuit and Danish

Currency: Danish krone (Kr) = 100 ore

Exchange rate: Kr6.20 per US$ (Oct 2005)

GDP per capita: US$20,000 (2003)

GDP real growth: 1.80% (2003)

Labour force: 31,763 (2003)

Unemployment: 7.40% (2003)

Inflation: 1.60% (2003)

Balance of trade: -US$39.00 million (2003)

Foreign debt: US$25.00 million (2003)

Visitor numbers: 14,000 (2003)*

* estimated figure

November, called in response to allegations of misuse of public funds by ministers and failure of budgetary discussions.

Political structure
Constitution
The legislative basis for the Home Rule Administration is Act No 56 of 21 February 1979 which came into force on 1 May 1979 following a referendum in Greenland. According to the Act, Greenland is a special cultural community in the Kingdom of Denmark. Only foreign policy, defence, police and monetary policy are Danish state affairs. Greenland elects two members to the Danish parliament.

Form of state
Parliamentary democratic dependency

The executive
The strength of the parties in the Landstinget (parliament) determines the composition of the Landsstyre (government). There are seven Landsstyremaend (ministers) headed by the Landsstyreformanden (prime minister).

National legislature
The Landstinget (parliament) has 31 members elected by proportional representation and decides on the affairs transferred to the Home Rule administration, ie, domestic affairs and non-constitutional affairs.

Last elections
15 November 2005 (parliamentary)
Results: Parliamentary: the Siumut party won 30.8 per cent of the vote (10 seats out of 31), the Democrats 23 per cent (seven), IA 22.7 per cent (seven), Atassut 19.2 per cent (six) and turnout was 74.9 per cent.

Next elections
2006 (parliamentary)

Political parties
Ruling party
Coalition government between the Siumut and Inuit Ataqatigiit parties (from 2003, re-elected November 2005)

Main opposition party
Inuit Ataqatigiit (IA) (Inuit Brotherhood)

Political situation
With an economy dependent on grants from Denmark the Home Rule government in Greenland cannot afford to turn away any revenue earning project. In May 2004 an agreement between the US, Denmark and Greenland was signed allowing an upgrade of the US Air Base in Thule, northern Greenland, as part of the US ballistic missile defence shield. Greenland had been negotiating for cash in compensation but finally accepted less immediate benefits. Environmental and technological partnerships will be fostered including research, tourism, infrastructure and trade. US funding for Greenlandic students through scholarships will also be made available.

The residents from the location of Thule, who had been displaced in 1953 to make way for the air base, were not offered compensation and were aggrieved that they were not consulted before the agreement was signed. However a Home Rule minister pointed out that international agreements were the exclusive jurisdiction of the Home Land government.

Population
56,700 (2004)

Ethnic make-up
Eighty-eight per cent of the population are Inuit and Greenland-born whites and the remainder are primarily Danes.

Religions
Ninety-six per cent belong to the Evangelical Lutheran Church of Denmark.

Education
US$102 million was spent on education in 2002.
Pupils per teacher: 10 in primary schools.

Health
Life expectancy: 68.9 years (World Bank)
Fertility rate/Maternal mortality rate: 2.4 births per woman (World Bank)
Birth rate/Death rate: 16 births per 1,000 population; eight deaths per 1,000 population (2003).
Infant mortality rate: 17 per 1,000 live births (2003)

Main cities
Nuuk (Godthåb) (capital, estimated population 14,265 in 2003).

Languages spoken
Danish and Greenlandic Inuit, which is an eastern branch of the East-Eskimo language categorised by linguists as Inupik, which is spoken on the northern coasts of Canada and Alaska and the eastern-most tip of Siberia. Greenlanders connected with tourism often speak English.

Official language/s
Greenlandic Inuit and Danish

Media
Press
Dailies: There are no daily newspapers.
Weeklies:
Grønlandsposten/Atuagagdliutit and *Sermitsiak*.
Periodicals: *Grønland* is a general interest periodical, published 10 times a year.

Broadcasting
Kalaallit Nunaata Radioa (KNR) (Greenland Broadcasting Corporation) has overall responsibility for radio and television services.
Radio: Greenland Radio (KNR) broadcasts in Greenlandic and Danish to the entire country via Inuksat.
Television: Television programmes (mostly Danish in origin) are transmitted by KNR-TV, which also produces some programmes of its own. Each local community has one or more private TV stations which are allocated a 15-minute broadcast daily on KNR-TV (30 minutes on Sunday).

Advertising
The most widely used means of advertising are the press and direct mail. The one and only cinema in Greenland also shows advertising. There is no advertising on radio, and poster sites are heavily regulated.

Economy
Greenland has a small economy based on fishing and related industries. It is heavily dependent on subsidies from Denmark in the form of block grants. The total financial package received from Denmark is around US$500 million a year. Greenland entered a particularly difficult period in 2000 when fish production slowed due to stock depletion, falling international prices and the closure of fish plants on the island. Since then, Greenland has been looking at other ways to make the economy more diverse, including offshore oil exploration and tourism.

External trade
Imports
Imports include machinery and transport equipment, manufactured goods, food, petroleum products.
Main sources: Denmark (85.8 per cent total, 2004), Sweden (3.6 per cent), Norway (3.1 per cent)

Exports
Exports consist mainly of fish (halibut accounts for approximately 10 per cent) and other seafood, especially shrimp which makes up almost 90 per cent.
Main destinations: Denmark (65.2 per cent total, 2004), Japan (12.2 per cent), China (5.1 per cent)
The EU has an agreement allowing its vessels to fish in Greenland waters in exchange for Greenland fish products accessing to EU markets.

Agriculture
Farming
The agricultural sector, comprising around 60 farms, is largely confined to sheep farming in the south and small-scale reindeer farming. Livestock production in 2004 included 360 tonnes of mutton and lamb. The production of lamb and reindeer meat is mainly for domestic consumption. Arable areas mainly produce hay for fodder.

Fishing
Fishing is the mainstay of the economy, accounting for over 90 per cent of exports and giving employment to a quarter of the population. Principal products include shrimp, halibut, cod and seal. Typical annual catches include over 142,000 tonnes

Greenland

(t) shrimps and 197,000t fish. Halibut is increasingly important, while cod has declined in importance. Traditional sea mammal catches are typically over 2,500t whales and 115,000t seals annually. The fishing industry employs around 6,000 people. The principal export markets are the EU, especially Denmark, and Japan.

Forestry

Industry and manufacturing
Industry is centred on fish processing and packaging. Most of the sector is controlled by the government-owned Royal Greenland company, which manages factories and smaller plants in both GreenInd and Denmark. Some tanning and leatherworking takes place in the south. Infrastructure improvements have provided a boost to construction activity, in particular the development of new airstrips.

Tourism
Tourism offers good potential for expansion, despite being restricted by the short season and high costs. Greenland has a lot to offer tourists: icebergs, nature, wilderness, dog-sledging, whale watching, northern lights, etc. The sector has grown in recent years as a result of the home government's policy designed to promote economic diversification and reduce dependence on Denmark. Visitor numbers have risen to around 30,000 a year, mainly from Denmark.

Mining
There are known reserves of zinc, lead, copper, cobalt, uranium, iron ore, gold and diamonds. Mineral exploration is actively encouraged and the administration has reformed its mining regulations. Large quantities of two of the world's rarest metals, niobium and tantalum, exist in Greenland.

Hydrocarbons
Greenland still hopes that oil and gas might become one of the mainstays of the economy. Oil exploration began in the 1970s. By 2002, seven wells had been drilled offshore, with two detecting the presence of oil. The home rule government is encouraging further exploration offshore of West Greenland. Arctic climate and deep waters make the task difficult. At present, Greenland relies on imports.
Greenland does not produce or import gas and coal.

Energy
Greenland is almost totally dependent on Denmark for its energy supplies. There is a hydroelectric station in Buksefjorden, which supplies Nuuk, and other hydroelectric plants are under construction or being planned.

Banking and insurance
NUNA Bank A/S is an independent bank that was formerly a subsidiary of the Danish bank Sparekasse Bikuben AS. The two banks share a strong business relationship. The other major bank in Greenland is Grønlandsbanken, which is owned by Danish banks.

Central bank
Monetary policy and administration is handled by the Danish central bank (Danmarks Nationalbank).

Time
Scoresbysund: GMT minus one hour (GMT from last Sunday in March to last Sunday in September); East Greenland/Mesters Vig: GMT (GMT summer and winter); Qaanaaq & Thule: GMT minus four hours (GMT minus three hours from April to October); Angmagssalik and west coast: GMT minus three hours (summer and winter).

Geography
Greenland is the world's largest island. It lies in the North Atlantic Ocean, to the east of Canada and to the west of Iceland. Most of Greenland is permanently covered by ice, but 410,449 square km of coastland are habitable.

Climate
Arctic; temperatures at Nuuk/Godthåb vary between about -12 degrees Celsius (C) and 11 degrees C.

Entry requirements
Entry requirements are generally the same as for Denmark except that diplomats need a visa.
Approval must be obtained from the Greenland Home Rule administration, PO Box 1015, 3900 Nuuk, Greenland, for entry into the military defence areas including the gateways of Sondre Stromfjord and Thule (unless in direct transit to points outside the airport of Sondre Stromfjord) and entry for the purpose of mountain/glacier climbing or geological/archaeological research.

Visa
Even though a Danish territory, visas are not valid for Greenland unless specified in the permit. For a business visa, an original letter of invitation from a local company or organisation, giving details about purpose of visit and duration of stay must accompany an application, along with evidence of hotel reservations.

Health (for visitors)
Mandatory precautions
Vaccination certificates are not usually required.

Public holidays
Fixed dates
1 Jan (New Year's Day), 6 Jan (Epiphany), 21 Jun (National Day), 24–26 Dec (Christmas Holiday).
Variable dates
Maundy Thursday, Good Friday, Easter Monday, Great Prayer Day (Apr/May), Ascension Day, Whit Monday.

Working hours
Banking
Mon–Fri: 0930–1600 (Thu 1800).
Business
Mon–Fri: 0800–1600 or 0830–1630.
Government
Mon–Fri: generally 0900–1700.
Shops
Mon–Fri: 0800–1700 or 0900–1730, Sat: close at 1300 or 1400.

Electricity supply
220V AC, 50Hz.

Getting there
Air
National airline: Greenlandair
International airport/s: Nuuk, which is served from Canada by FirstAir, and a weekly connection to Reykjavík (Iceland). Frequency of services increases during the summer. Kangerlussuaq (Sondre Stromfjord (SFJ) international airport is served from Copenhagen by Greenlandair (GL). Other international airports include Narsarsuaq (UAK) and Kulusuk (KUS). The Icelandic airline Norlandair, Scandinavian Airlines and Air Iceland operates various flights to Greenland.
Airport tax: There is no airport departure tax for flights from Denmark.
Surface
Water: Local passenger lines operate on the west coast. It is the cheapest transportation, but low quality. Comfortable cruises are also offered in the summer season.
Main port/s: Nuuk/Godthåb

Getting about
National transport
Air: Greenlandair operates daily flights to Kangerlussuaq-Nuuk-Narsarísuaq, and twice a week to East Greenland. Other towns are linked by helicopter, as well as helistops at some settlements.
Greenlandair serves towns on the west coast. Regularity of departures is variable and reservations should be made well in advance.
Road: There are no roads connecting towns in Greenland. Only sea and air travel are available. Dog-sledges and snow mobiles can be hired for variable periods.
Water: Greenland Trade operates two passenger liners on the west coast.

Villages are served by local boats, some of which are for private hire.

BUSINESS DIRECTORY

The addresses listed below are a selection only. While World of Information makes every endeavour to check these addresses, we cannot guarantee that changes have not been made, especially to telephone numbers and area codes. We would welcome any corrections.

Telephone area codes

The international direct dialling (IDD) code for Greenland is +299, followed by the subscriber's number.

Banking

Central bank

Danmarks Nationalbank, Havnegade 5, DK-1093 Copenhagen (tel: (45) 3363-6363; fax: (45) 3363-7103; e-mail: info@nationalbanken.dk).

Travel information

Greenland Tourism Main Office, 29 Hans Egedesvej, PO Box 1615, Nuuk DK-3900 (tel: 342-820; fax: 322-877; e-mail: info@greenland.com).

National tourist organisation offices

Greenland Tourism a/s, Main Office, PO Box 1552, 3900 Nuuk (tel: 322-888; fax: 322-877; e-mail: info@visitgreenland.com).

Ministries

Grønlands Hjemmestyre (Greenland Home Rule administration), PO Box 1015, 3900 Nuuk (tel: 345-000; e-mail: info@gh.gl; internet site: http://www.gh.gl).

Greenland Home Rule Government Denmark Office, Sjaeleboderne 2, 1122 Copenhagen K, Denmark (tel: +45 3313-4224; fax: +45 3332-2024).

Prime Minister's Office, Greenland Department, 3 Hausergade, DK-1128 Copenhagen K, Denmark (tel: +45 3393-2200).

Other useful addresses

Greenland Trade Shipping Department, Grønlandshavnen, DK-9220 Aalborg Ost (tel: +45 9815-7677).

Kalaallit Nunaata Radioa (Grønlands Radio) (KNR) (Radio Greenland), H J Rinksvej 35, PO Box 1007, 3900 Nuuk (tel: 321-172; fax: 324-703).

Internet sites

Bureau of minerals and petroleum: http://bmp.gl/

Greenland Radio: http://www.knr.gl/

Greenland Tourism: http://www.greenland-guide.gl

Grenada

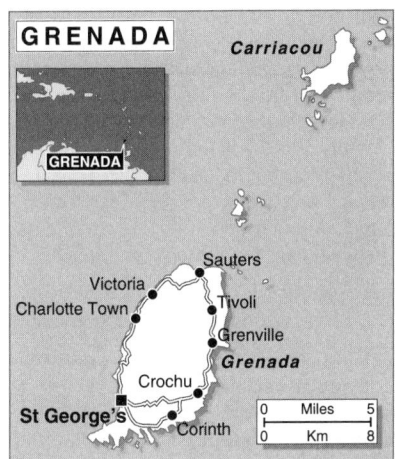

COUNTRY PROFILE

Historical profile
1762 Grenada was initially colonised by the French until captured by the British.
1783 British control of the islands was recognised.
1958 Grenada joined the Federation of the West Indies.
1967 Internal self-government was granted.
1974 Independence was granted.
1983 The US, backed by troops from Jamaica, Barbados and other members of the Organisation of Eastern Caribbean States (OECS), invaded the islands after a period of civil disturbances, anti-government protests, media restrictions and a power struggle within the left-wing government which resulted in the killing of Prime Minister Maurice Bishop and other ministers during the fighting. The rebel Revolutionary Military Council (RMC) was defeated and an interim government appointed until elections were held.
1984 The general election was won by the New National Party (NNP) led by Herbert Blaize.
1987 The National Democratic Congress (NDC) was formed.
1990 A coalition of NDC and Grenada United Labour Party (GULP) was elected, with Nicholas Braithwaite as prime minister.
1995 The NNP won the elections.
1996 Grenada signed anti-drug trafficking treaties with the US. The appointment of Sir Daniel Williams as governor general provoked controversy owing to his links with the NNP.
1999 The general election was won by the ruling NNP.
2001 Grenada was blacklisted by the OECD's Financial Action Task Force (FATF) for not doing enough to combat money laundering.
2002 The government revoked the licences of 36 offshore banks in an attempt to secure removal from the FATF blacklist. In September, Grenada was hit by tropical storm Lili, causing damage estimated at around 2 per cent of GDP.
2003 In July, Grenada was removed from the FATF's blacklist. Prime Minister Keith Mitchell's NNP was re-elected on 27 November. A new cabinet was sworn in on 3 December.
2004 Thirty years of independence were celebrated in February. Prime Minister Keith Mitchell was accused of taking a US$500,000 bribe from a German citizen. Hurricane Ivan struck Grenada in September, damaging 85 per cent of the island's housing.
2005 In April, Grenada-born, Private Johnson Beharry, received Britain's highest bravery awarded, the Victoria Cross, for his service in Iraq. Hurricane Emily struck the island in July, causing extensive damage.
2006 The EU granted eur9.3 million (US$11 million) for the rehabilitation of schools devastated by Hurricanes Ivan and Emily.

Political structure
Form of state
Independent state; it is a member of the Commonwealth.
The executive
The British monarch is the head of state, represented by the governor general appointed by the monarch. Executive power is vested in the cabinet, led by the prime minister. The cabinet is appointed by the governor general on the advice of the prime minister and is responsible to parliament. Following legislative elections, the leader of the majority party or the leader of the majority coalition is usually appointed prime minister by the governor general.
National legislature
The bicameral parliament consists of a 13-member Senate (10 senators appointed by the government and three by

KEY FACTS

Official name: Grenada

Head of State: Queen Elizabeth II; Governor General Sir Daniel C Williams (since Aug 1996)

Head of government: Prime Minister Keith C Mitchell (leader of NNP) (since Jun 1995; last re-elected 27 Nov 2003)

Ruling party: New National Party (NNP) (since Jun 1995; last re-elected 27 Nov 2003)

Area: 345 square km

Population: 94,200 (2004)

Capital: St George's

Official language: English

Currency: East Caribbean dollar (EC$) = 100 cents

Exchange rate: EC$2.70 per US$ (fixed)

GDP per capita: US$4,386 (2004)

GDP real growth: -3.20% (2004)

Inflation: 2.30% (2004)

Balance of trade: -US$202.30 million (2004)

Foreign debt: US$330.00 million (2004)

Nations of the World: A Political, Economic and Business Handbook

the leader of the opposition) and a 15-member House of Representatives (members are elected by popular vote to serve five-year terms).

Legal system
The legal system is based on English common law. Grenada is responsible for its own magistrate's courts. The regional Eastern Caribbean Supreme Court is responsible for the high court and the court of appeals. The final court of appeal is to the Privy Council in the UK.

Last elections
27 November 2003 (parliamentary)
Results: Parliamentary: Prime Minister Keith Mitchell's NNP was re-elected with eight seats out of 15 (47.7 per cent of the vote) against the NDC with seven seats (45.1 per cent); turnout was 57.7 per cent.

Next elections
2008 (parliamentary)

Political parties
Ruling party
New National Party (NNP) (since Jun 1995; last re-elected 27 Nov 2003)
Main opposition party
National Democratic Congress (NDC)

Political situation
Prime Minister Keith Mitchell was accused, in April 2004, of accepting US$500,000 from a German citizen in return for the post of general ambassador to Grenada and a diplomatic passport. The prime minister strenuously denied the allegation, although admitted to having been given US$15,000. In an official statement he said the German was a legitimate contact and the payment was 'above-board'. The opposition NDC leader, Kenneth Hobson, tabled questions in the House of Representatives and called for a full-scale, independent enquiry. A commission of enquiry was set up and commenced work in 2005.

Population
94,200 (2004)
Ethnic make-up
Black (82 per cent), mixed black and European (13 per cent), European and East Indian (5 per cent) and a small number of Arawak/Carib.
Religions
Roman Catholic (53 per cent), Anglican (13.8 per cent), other Protestants (33.2 per cent).

Education
Education in Grenada is based on the English GCSE and A level system. There are several excellent local schools and an international primary school.
In total, there are 79 schools, 59 primary, 19 secondary and one tertiary institution. TA Marryshow Community College has a school of agriculture and a teacher's training college.
The St George's University School of Medicine is run by a US firm and offers medical training as well as non-medical courses.
Compulsory years: Five to 16.
Enrolment rate: 95 per cent gross primary enrolment of relevant age groups (including repeaters) (World Bank 2003).

Health
Grenada is divided into seven health districts, six of which have a health centre responsible for primary care. In addition, there are several medical stations throughout the country.
Medical care is limited, but everyone has access to some form of healthcare, regardless of ability to pay.
Life expectancy: 73.1 years (World Bank)
Fertility rate/Maternal mortality rate: 3.0 births per woman (World Bank)
Birth rate/Death rate: 23 births per 1,000 population; 7.5 deaths per 1,000 population (2003).
Infant mortality rate: 18.0 per 1,000 live births (World Bank)
Head of population per physician/bed: 0.5 physicians per 1,000 people.

Welfare
The social welfare department of the ministry of labour administers social work programmes to families and gives financial aid to three private children's homes. There is also a women's shelter in the northern part of the island. There are a number of government social service agencies that monitor the welfare of children, women and those with disabilities.

Main cities
St George's (capital, estimated population 4,300 in 2003)

Languages spoken
English and French patois
Official language/s
English

Media
Press
Weeklies: Weeklies include *The Grenadan Voice*, *The Grenada Informer*, and *Grenada Today*.
Periodicals: *The Barnacle* is published monthly.
Broadcasting
Radio: GBC Radio is owned by the government of Grenada and operated by the Grenada Broadcasting Corporation (GBC), with a 20,000 watts transmission to the Caribbean on the medium-wave band.
Spice Capital Radio is a privately owned and operated 5,000 watts station, which transmits on both the FM and medium-wave band.
City Sounds FM (CSFM) Quality Radio operates out of Marrast Hill, St George's.
A new radio service – Radio Caricom, the Voice of the Caribbean Community – was officially launched at the 25th Meeting of the Conference of the Heads of Government in Grenada on 4 July 2004. Barbados, Belize, Grenada and St Lucia are 'pilot states' in the project, which will eventually be available to all member states.
Television: GBC Television is owned by the government and operated by the Grenada Broadcasting Corporation (GBC). The station transmits on channels seven and eleven.

Economy
In 2003, the economy began to recover quickly from the decline of the previous two years, driven by tourism, construction and agriculture. The trend continued

KEY INDICATORS — Grenada

	Unit	2000	2001	2002	2003	2004
Population	m	0.10	0.10	0.10	0.10	0.09
Gross domestic product (GDP)	US$bn	0.41	0.40	0.41	0.44	*0.44
GDP per capita	US$	4,210	4,000	3,837	5,000	4,241
GDP real growth	%	6.4	-4.7	-1.8	2.5	-3.2
Inflation	%	2.2	3.2	1.5	2.8	2.3
Exports (fob) (goods)	US$m	84.5	64.0	75.6	78.0	33.3
Imports (fob) (goods)	US$m	220.9	196.0	215.4	270.0	235.6
Balance of trade	US$m	-136.4	-132.0	-139.8	-192.0	-202.3
Current account	US$m	-90.0	-100.0	-130.0	-140.0	-50.0
Total reserves minus gold	US$m	57.7	63.9	87.8	83.2	121.7
Foreign exchange	US$m	57.7	63.9	87.8	83.2	121.7
Exchange rate	per US$	2.70	2.70	2.70	2.70	2.68

* estimated figure

Grenada

through 2004, until the island was struck by Hurrican Ivan in September with calamitous results. The positive GDP gains of 2.5 per cent in 2003 were turned to -3.2 per cent for 2004. The estimated damage amounted to US$815 million. In addition to extensive damage to buildings and infrastructure, tourism and agriculture, the principal foreign exchange earners and employers, were badly affected.

External trade
The widening trade deficit (due mainly to falling world prices for agricultural exports and the importation of construction equipment) is only partly offset by invisible earnings from tourism, workers' remittances from abroad and aid flows.

Imports
Main imports are food, manufactured goods, machinery, chemicals and fuel.
Main sources: US (27.7 per cent total, 2004), Trinidad and Tobago (25.4 per cent), UK (5.2 per cent)

Exports
Main exports are bananas, cocoa, nutmeg and mace, fruit and vegetables, clothing.
Main destinations: Saint Lucia (11.8 per cent total, 2004), US (11.6 per cent), Netherlands (8.1 per cent), Antigua and Barbuda (8 per cent), Germany (7.7 per cent), Saint Kitts and Nevis (7.2 per cent), Dominica (7.2 per cent), France (4.5 per cent)

Agriculture
Farming
The agricultural sector contributes around 8 per cent to GDP and accounts for around 65 per cent of exports.
Activity centres on the traditional farming of nutmeg/mace (the world's second-largest producer after Indonesia), cocoa and bananas. Nutmeg and cocoa exports have benefited from a decline in world supply due to political problems in global suppliers (Indonesia and Côte d'Ivoire), as opposed to improvements in output.
Agricultural development policy is geared towards the rehabilitation of the cocoa industry, the promotion of new export crops, greater provision of fertilisers and other inputs and privatisation of state farms. In 2002, the government announced that more land would be allocated for organic banana cultivation. Fruit jelly processing is also being developed.
The tropical storm which hit the island in 2002 was a great setback for the agricultural sector. The loss of earnings from the destruction of crops, in particular nutmeg, was estimated at about one-third of agricultural exports in 2002. By 2004, output of the main crops, including nutmeg and cocoa, was increasing once more. In September, the weather intervened again when Hurricane Ivan devastated the island. Nutmeg trees were uprooted, cocoa trees were damaged or destroyed and banana planatations were wrecked. The total output of fruits and vegetables was destroyed. Livestock was lost, while farm buildings and infrastructure suffered extensive damage.
Grenada will be adversely affected by the loss of export markets in 2007, when WTO-led legislation opens up the EU banana market to worldwide suppliers.
Crop production in 2004 included: 6,500 tonnes (t) coconuts, 4,380t citrus, 300t maize, 400t yams, 7,200t sugar cane, 4,100t bananas, 740t plantains, 1,900t mangoes, 1,500t avocados, 737t cocoa beans, 2,747t nutmeg, 200t other spices, 16,830t fruit in total, 4,000t roots and tubers, 2,649t vegetables in total. Livestock production included: 1,125t meat in total, 141t beef, 192t pig meat, 92t lamb & goat meat, 600t poultry, 920t eggs, 520t milk.

Fishing
There is a small fishing industry.
The typical total annual fish catch is over 2,247t. Shellfish, molluscs and cephalopods account for another 39t per annum.

Industry and manufacturing
The industrial sector accounts for around 20 per cent of GDP, of which manufacturing constitutes around 7 per cent. Manufacturing activities include the production of garments, beverages, flour, wheat-bran, animal feed, furniture, paints and varnishes, sugar, rum, coconut oil, lime juice and honey. Furniture, handicrafts and garments are also manufactured for export to the Caricom market. In 2002, cocoa processing operations were fully privatised.
The government is committed to achieving growth in the manufacturing sector and to this end is endeavouring to attract foreign firms to use Grenada as a base for exports to extra-regional markets. Joint ventures are encouraged between local private sector and foreign investors in order to assist local manufacturers to access capital, technology and marketing channels.

Tourism
Tourism, which accounts for around 5 per cent of Grenada's GDP and 5 per cent of the total labour force, is an increasingly important element in the economy, particularly in terms of its foreign exchange-earning capacity. After several difficult years, the sector saw recovery in 2003. Tourist arrivals increased by 3.36 per cent over the previous year, with 142,355 stay-over visitors and 146,925 cruise-ship passengers. The cruise market is being actively developed and a newly-constructed cruise terminal was opened on 16 December 2004 that is part of phase one of a redevelopment site for the city of St George. Visitor numbers, especially of cruise-ship passengers, continued to increase in 2004. The damage to accommodation caused by Hurricane Ivan in September resulted in an overall contraction of stay-over numbers for the year. The cruise-ship sector, on the other hand, recovered very quickly, recording 226,944 visitors for 2004.
The majority of visitors originate in the US, other Caribbean countries and the UK. An increasing number of visitors are coming from the UK and Germany due to the expansion of charter flights.

Hydrocarbons
Grenada does not produce oil and relies on imports of petroleum. In March 2004, the Grenada government asked the Commonwealth Fund for Technical Co-operation (CFTC) for advice on awarding contracts for oil and gas exploration. Grenada does not produce or import gas and coal. Trinidad and Tobago plans to build a 600 mile natural gas pipeline linking the eastern Caribbean islands, which would open possibilities of importing natural gas into Grenada.

Banking and insurance
The seven members of the Organisation of Eastern Caribbean States (OECS), Antigua and Barbuda, Dominica, Grenada, Montserrat, St Kitts and Nevis, St Lucia and St Vincent and the Grenadines, share a common currency and central bank. The British Virgin Islands and Anguilla are associate members.

Central bank
Eastern Caribbean Central Bank, St Kitts and Nevis.

Offshore facilities
The strengthening of the regulatory framework by the Grenada International Financial Services Authority (GIFSA) led to significant improvement and in 2003 Grenada was removed from the blacklist drawn up by the Organisation for Economic Co-operation and Development (OECD).

Time
GMT minus four hours

Geography
Grenada is a mountainous, heavily forested island. It is the most southerly of the Windward Islands in the West Indies. The country also includes some of the small islands known as the Grenadines, which lie to the north-east of Grenada, the largest of these being the low-lying island of Carriacou.

Climate
Tropical marine with an annual mean temperature of 28 degrees Celsius. Rain

occurs mainly from June–December. Driest from February–May.

Entry requirements
Passports
Required by all citizens except nationals of the US, UK and Canada provided they hold identification and a birth certificate. Passports should be valid for six months from the date of departure.

Visa
Not required by nationals of most of the Americas, Europe, Australasia and Japan, for both tourist and business trips, valid for three months. Business visitors should supply extra information: letter of introduction from foreign company and letter of invitation from a local host. For further details and exceptions contact the consular section of the nearest High Commission or Embassy.

Currency advice/regulations
Import of local currency unlimited subject to declaration. Export limited to amount declared on arrival.

Health (for visitors)
Mandatory precautions
Yellow fever certificate required if arriving from an infected area.

Advisable precautions
Immunisation against hepatitis 'A', 'B' and diphtheria may be recommended. Medical attention can cost several thousand dollars and doctors often expect immediate cash payments; insurance is advisable.

Hotels
Except for town hotels, most are located near beaches. An 8 per cent sales tax on food and beverages and 10 per cent service charge is added to the bill.

Public holidays
Fixed dates
1 Jan (New Year's Day), 7 Feb (Independence Day), 1 May (Labour Day), 25 Oct (Thanksgiving Day), 25–26 Dec (Christmas Holiday).

Variable dates
Good Friday, Easter Monday, Whit Monday, Corpus Christi (May/Jun), Emancipation Day (first Mon in Aug), Carnival (Aug).

Working hours
Banking
Mon–Thu: 0800–1400; Fri: 0800–1300, 1430–1700.

Business
Mon–Thu: 0800–1145, 1300–1600; Fri: 0800–1145, 1300–1700.

Government
Mon–Thu: 0800–1145, 1300–1600; Fri: 0800–1145, 1300–1700.

Shops
Mon–Fri: 0800–1145, 1300–1600; Sat: 0800–1145.

Electricity supply
220/240V AC, 50 cycles

Getting there
Air
International airport/s: Point Salines (GND), 8km from St George's; bureau de change, duty-free shop, restaurant, shops, car rental, taxis.
Airport tax: Departure tax: EC$50 per adult, payable in cash.

Surface
Water: Many shipping lines call at Grenada. Regular boat services from St Vincent, Martinique and Trinidad. There is a twice-weekly ferry service to Carriacou Island.
Main port/s: St George's.

Getting about
National transport
Road: There are approximately 980km of roads, of which 766km are suitable for motor traffic.
Buses: Public transport is provided by small private operators, with a system covering the entire country. Cheap but often slow and few run during the late afternoons, evenings and Sundays.

City transport
Taxis: Widely available. Fares are regulated.

Car hire
International licence required or local permit obtained (valid national licence must be presented to local Traffic Department). Traffic drives on the left.

BUSINESS DIRECTORY
The addresses listed below are a selection only. While World of Information makes every endeavour to check these addresses, we cannot guarantee that changes have not been made, especially to telephone numbers and area codes. We would welcome any corrections.

Telephone area codes
The international direct dialling code (IDD) for Grenada is +1 473, followed by subscriber's number.

Chambers of Commerce
Grenada Chamber of Industry and Commerce, PO Box 129, St George's (tel: 440-2937; fax: 440-6621; e-mail: gcic@caribsurf.com).

Banking
Bank of Nova Scotia, PO Box 194, Grand Anse, St George's (tel: 440-3274).

Barclays Bank, PO Box 37, Grand Anse, St George's (tel: 440-3232; fax: 440-3232).

Grenada Bank of Commerce, PO Box 4, Grand Anse, St George's (tel: 440-3521; fax: 440-4153).

Grenada Co-operative Bank, Church Street, St George's (tel: 440-2111, 440-3549; fax: 440-6600).

Grenada Development Bank, Halifax Street, St George's (tel: 440-2382/1620).

National Commercial Bank of Grenada, Halifax Street, St George's (tel: 440-3566/8).

Scotiabank, Halifax Street, St George's (tel: 440-3274).

Central bank
Eastern Caribbean Central Bank, Agency Office, Monckton Street, St George's (tel: 440-3016; fax: 40-6721).

Travel information
Grenada Hotel Association, Ross Point Inn, Lagoon Road, St George's (tel: 444-1353; fax: 444-4847).

Ministry of tourism
Ministry of Tourism, Civil Aviation, Social Security, Culture, Gender and Family, Ministerial Complex, 4th Floor, St. George's, (tel: 440-0366; fax: 440-0443).

National tourist organisation offices
Grenada Tourist Board, PO Box 293, The Carnage, St George's (tel: 440-2279/ 3371/2001/1346; fax: 440-6637).

Ministries
Ministry of Agriculture, Ministerial Complex, 2nd and 3rd Floors, St. George's (tel: 440-27008 fax: 440-4191).

Ministry of Carriacou and Petit Martinique Affairs, Beausejour, Carriacou (tel: 443-6026; fax: 443-6040).

Ministry of Communication & Works, Ministerial Complex, 4th Floor, St. George's (tel: 440-2181; fax: 440-4122).

Ministry of Education, Botanical Gardens, St George's (tel: 440-2166; fax: 440-6650).

Ministry of Finance, Trade, Industry and Planning, Financial Complex, St George's (tel: 440-2731; fax: 440-4115).

Ministry of Foreign Affairs and International Trade, Ministerial Complex, 4th Floor, St George's (tel: 440-2640; fax: 440-4184).

Ministry of Health and Environment, Ministerial Complex, 1st and 2nd Floords, St. George's (tel: 440-2649; fax: 440-4127).

Ministry of Housing, Social Services and Co-operatives, Ministerial Complex, 1st and 2nd Floors, St George's (tel: 440-6917; fax: 440-7990).

Ministry of Implementation, Ministerial Complex, 6th Floor, St George's (tel: 440-2255; fax: 440-4116).

Ministry of Labour and Local Government, Ministerial Complex, 3rd Floor, St. George's (tel: 440-2532).

Ministry of Legal Affairs, Attorney General's Office, Church Street, St. George's (tel: 440-2050; fax: 440-6630).

Ministry of Youth, Sports and Community Development, Ministerial Complex, 2nd Floor, St George's (tel: 440-6917; fax: 440-6924).

Office of the Prime Minister, Ministerial Complex, 6th Floor, St George's (tel: 440-2225; fax: 440-4116).

Other useful addresses

Export Development Unit, Ministry of Trade, Lagoon Road, St George's (tel: 440-2101; fax: 440-4115).

Grenada Cocoa Board, Scott St, St George's (tel: 440-2234).

Grenada Co-operative Banana Society, Scott St, St George's (tel: 440-2117).

Grenada Co-operative Nutmeg Association, PO Box 160, St George's (tel: 440-2097).

Grenada Industrial Development Corporation, Frequente Industrial Park, True Blue, St. George's (tel: 444-1035; fax: 444-4828; e-mail: gidc@caribsurf.com; internet site: http://www.grenadaworld.com).

Grenada International Financial Services Authority (GIFSA), Building 5, Financial Complex, Carenage (tel: 440-8717; fax: 440- 4780; e-mail: grenoffshore@caribsurf.com).

Grenada Manufacturers' Council, PO Box 129, St George's (tel: 444-4485/2937; fax: 440-6627).

Grenadan Embassy (US), 1701 New Hampshire Avenue, NW, Washington DC 20009 (tel: 202-265-2561).

Internet sites

Blue Horizons Cottage Hotel: http://www.cpscaribnet.com/ads/blue/blue.html

Calabash Hotel: http://www.cpscaribnet.com/ads/calabash/calabash.html

Coyaba Beach Resort: http://www.cpscaribnet.com/ads/coyaba/coyaba.html

Guadeloupe

KEY FACTS

Official name: Guadeloupe

Head of State: President of France (Jacques Chirac)

Head of government: *Préfet* (Commissioner) Paul Girot de Langlade (took office 17 Aug 2004)

Ruling party: Objectif Guadeloupe

Area: 1,780 square km

Population: 444,940 (2004)

Capital: Basse Terre

Official language: French

Currency: Euro (eur) = 100 cents (from 1 Jan 2002; previous currency French franc, locked at Ff6.56 per euro)

Exchange rate: eur0.83 per US$ (Oct 2005)

GDP per capita: US$9,000 (2003)

Balance of trade: -US$1.56 billion (2003)

COUNTRY PROFILE

Historical profile

Guadeloupe is situated within the Lesser Antilles. The first inhabitants were the Arawak Indians and Carib Indians. The Carib name for the island was Karukera (island of beautiful water).

1493–1600 Columbus was the first European visitor. Spain made two attempts to colonise the islands of Guadeloupe but was unsuccessful, due to strong indigenous resistance.

1635 France conquered the islands and established its first settlement.

1654 The French welcomed a small number of Dutch who settled in Guadeloupe. They proved vital to the turnaround of Guadeloupe's economy by developing its sugar industry. Black African slaves were brought to the island to work on plantations.

1674 Guadeloupe became part of the French Crown Colonies.

1700s Guadeloupe was the scene of many battles between the French and British, who repeatedly fought for possession.

1808–1814 Guadeloupe was occupied by the British.

1816 The islands were handed back to France by the Treaty of Vienna.

1854–1885 Following the abolition of slavery in 1847, workers were brought to Guadeloupe from India. During this period, blacks were allowed to participate in Guadeloupe's political sphere and Guadeloupe was allowed representation in the French parliament.

1946 Guadeloupe became a French Département d'Outre-Mer (DOM) (Overseas Department).

1974 Guadeloupe was further incorporated into the French political system and granted the status of region of France.

1983 Guadeloupe was granted devolution. A Regional Council was established under the French decentralisation policy.

1998 Hurricane Georges wreaked havoc on the islands

1999 The Basse Terre declaration of December by Guadeloupe, Martinique and French Guiana called for greater local control. The country was hit by hurricane Lenny.

2002 Guadeloupe adopted the euro as its official currency. In the French presidential elections, Guadeloupe's support for Jacques Chirac was overwhelming (91 per cent of the vote).

2003 In December, a referendum in Guadeloupe and Martinique rejected a French government-backed reform plan to streamline the system of local government and give the islands a new status.

2004 On 2 April, Victorin Lurel took office as president of the regional council. Paul Girot de Langlade took office as *préfet* on 17 August.

2005 A visit by French interior minister, Nicolas Sarkozy, was postponed following an announcement by President Chirac that a controversal law, passed in February 2005, and which had required the teaching of the French colonial era in a positive light, would be revoked. Sarkozy is a member of the conservative-led government that had passed the law. Protests by Guadeloupe islanders had been planned.

Political structure

Constitution

28 September 1958 (French Fifth Republic).

Under the 1946 constitution of the French Fourth Republic, Guadeloupe became a Département d'Outre-Mer (DOM) (Overseas Department) of France. In 1974, it was granted additional status as a region of France.

Guadeloupe is represented in the French National Assembly by four deputies and in the Senate by two senators.

Since 1983, following the French government's policy of decentralisation, regional councils have been elected with powers similar to those of the regions.

Administration is by a préfet appointed by the government in Paris.

The local government comprises a Conseil Régional (Regional Council) of 39 members and a 42-member Conseil Général (General Council), both directly elected for six-year terms.

Dependencies: Marie Galante, Les Saintes, Désirade, St Barthélémy and St Martin, Grand Bourg (on Marie Galante).

In a December 2003 referendum, voters from Guadeloupe and Martinique rejected a reform plan which would have streamlined the islands' local government and given them a new status. The change was rejected by 73 per cent of voters in Guadeloupe and 50.3 per cent in Martinique. (Voters on St Barthélémy and St Martin, approved the referendum, and are set to acquire the new status of 'overseas collective').

Form of state

Département d'Outre-Mer (DOM) (Overseas Department) of France, with additional status as a *région* (region) of France.

Guadeloupe

Legal system
French legal system

Political parties
Ruling party
Objectif Guadeloupe
Political situation
The number of Haitians arriving in Guadeloupe either as illegal immigrants or requesting asylum has challenged the authorities, with numbers rising from 135 in 2003 to 3,682 in 2004. The numbers are enough to overwhelm local resources and with few grounds to grant asylum appeals or leaves to remain, most are returned to their homeland. New measures to deal with human traffickers include seizing vehicles – aeroplanes, boats and cars – and rigorous scrutiny of identity papers.

Population
444,940 (2004)
Ethnic make-up
Black or mixed race (90 per cent), white (5 per cent), East Indian and others (5 per cent).
Religions
Roman Catholic (95 per cent), other: Hindu, African animist, Protestant (5 per cent).

Education
Many students pursue higher education in the islands or in France. The islands have a teacher's training college, a school of law, and a school of science.
Literacy rate: Over 90 per cent
Compulsory years: 6 to 17.

Health
In addition to several hospitals, Guadeloupe has a Pasteur Institute for the study of tropical diseases. The consumption of crack cocaine has increased steadily with a large number of drug addicts being treated regularly by the health and social services.
Life expectancy: 77.5 years: male 74 years; female 81 years (2003)
Fertility rate/Maternal mortality rate: Two births per woman (2003)
Birth rate/Death rate: 16 births per 1,000 population; six deaths per 1,000 population (2003).
Infant mortality rate: Nine per 1,000 live births (2003)
Head of population per physician/bed: 10.5 physicians per 10,000.

Welfare
The existence of a state homecare policy and a traditional lifestyle enable most people aged 60 and over to live at home. The people are highly dependent on French social welfare programmes and development funds. About one-third of children under the age of 17 are brought up in single-parent families. Financial assistance is often available to needy families for their children's basic needs and to enable children to attend school at an early age.

Main cities
Basse-Terre (capital, on the island of Basse Terre, estimated population 12,900 in 2003); Les Abymes (on Grande Terre, 65,700); Pointe-à-Pitre (commercial centre, straddles islands of Grande Terre and Basse Terre, 21,580); Capesterre (on Basse Terre, 20,400).
Dependencies include Marie Galante, Les Saintes, Désirade, St Barthélémy and St Martin, Grand Bourg (on Marie Galante).

Languages spoken
French (99 per cent); Creole patois is also spoken.
Official language/s
French

Media
Press
The main daily newspaper is *France Antilles*.
Other weekly and monthly publications include *L'Etincelle*, *7 Mag-Guadeloupe*, *Le Progrès Social*, *Combat Ouvrier*, *Jakata Magazine* and *Match*.
Broadcasting
Three radio and one television (France Région 3) stations operate.

Economy
Guadeloupe is heavily dependent on aid from France. The services sector dominates the economy and contributes typically 70 per cent to GDP. Most economic activity is undertaken by small businesses. Relatively high levels of external aid, from France and through EU regional and structural grants, have prevented any significant economic adjustment.
The economy is weakening. The tourism industry relies too heavily on visitors from France and is suffering from competition from Cuba and the Dominican Republic. The agricultural industry faces problems. Unemployment is high. The situation has resulted in many industrial disputes and strikes.

External trade
The rising trade deficit is only partially offset by earnings from tourism and aid flows from France aimed particularly at lowering the unemployment rate.
Imports
Principal imports are machinery and transport equipment, foodstuffs and live animals, basic manufactures, miscellaneous manufactures, road vehicles and parts, chemicals and related products.
Main sources: France (63 per cent total, 2004), Germany (4.0 per cent), US (3.0 per cent), Japan (2.0 per cent), The Netherlands Antilles (2.0 per cent)

Exports
Principal exports are bananas, machinery and transport equipment, rum, basic manufactures, sugar.
Main destinations: France (60 per cent total, 2004), Martinique (18 per cent), US (4.0 per cent)

Agriculture
Farming
Agriculture is the main sector of the economy, contributing 15 per cent to GDP and employing 15 per cent of the population. Guadeloupe is not self-sufficient, relying heavily on food imports from France.
An estimated 36 per cent of the total area is cultivated arable land, 10 per cent is pasture and 15 per cent woodland/forest (including national park land of around 3,000 hectares).
The export of bananas has been a prime acitivity accounting for around 50 per cent of foreign earnings. The future of the banana industry, which has relied on preferential access to the EU, is threatened by a World Trade Organisation (WTO) ruling that this access is illegal and will end. The EU has agreed new tariff quotas to be introduced from 2006. The number of banana producers fell from 1,000 to 400 in the period 1993–2003. In October 2003, banana producers in Martinique and Guadeloupe formed an association to seek to improve sales in France and in new markets.
Sugar, flowers and melons are also cultivated.
Crop production in 2004 included: 10,030 tonnes (t) yams, 2,895t citrus, 4,250t sweet potatoes, 820,000t sugar cane, 115,500t bananas, 9,150t plantains, 1,280t cassava, 3,070t tomatoes, 1,020t mangoes, 6,980t pineapples, 8t vanilla, 136,950t fruit in total, 34,944t vegetables. Livestock production included: 5,522t meat in total, 3,350t beef, 1,060t pig meat, 180t goat meat, 854t poultry, 1,656t eggs, 65t milk, 150t honey.
Fishing
Offshore fishing is a traditional source of food. The main fish catch includes lobsters, crab and octopus. The sector is underdeveloped, although demand is growing.
The typical total annual fish catch is over 10,114t. Shellfish, molluscs and cephalopods account for another 714t per annum.
Forestry
Exports of timber products in 2004 amounted to US$145,000 and imports amounted to US$30.6 million.
Timber production in 2004 included 15,300 cubic metres (cum) roundwood, 300cum industrial roundwood, 1,000cum sawnwood, 300cum sawlogs and 15,000cum wood fuel.

Industry and manufacturing
The industrial sector contributes around 17 per cent to GDP and employs 15 per cent of the workforce.
Manufacturing industries are small and centre on the processing of raw materials. Main activities include sugar refining, rum distilling, food processing, cement and brick manufacture, mineral water bottling and ship repair. The construction industry employs 12 per cent of the workforce and is the third-largest sector of activity.
There is an industrial freeport at Jarry.

Tourism
Tourism is estimated to account for 8.4 per cent per cent of GDP in 2005 and employ 25.5 per cent of the workforce, with revenue from travel and tourism expected to amount to US$657 million. The sector is predicted to grow by 7.2 per cent year-on-year between 2006–15 with economic activity doubling from US$1,046 million in 2005 to US$2,004 million in 2015.
About 81 per cent of Guadeloupe's tourists come from France, 12 per cent from other European countries and 7 per cent from US.

Mining
Guadeloupe has no mineral resources.

Hydrocarbons
Guadeloupe relies entirely on imported refined oil products. It does not import coal or natural gas.
A proposed pipeline from Trinidad and Tobago to Guadeloupe and Martinique opens possibilities for the future import of natural gas.

Banking and insurance
Central bank
Caisse Centrale de Co-opération Economique; European Central Bank (ECB)

Time
GMT minus four hours

Geography
Guadeloupe is the most northerly of the Windward Islands group in the West Indies. Dominica lies to the south, and Antigua and Montserrat to the north-west. Guadeloupe is formed by two large islands, Grande Terre (mountainous) and Basse Terre, separated by a narrow sea channel, with two smaller islands, Marie Galante, to the south-east, and La Désirade, to the east. St Barthélémy and the northern half of St Maarten (the remainder being part of the Netherlands Antilles) are dependencies.

Climate
Sub-tropical with annual mean temperature of 27 degrees Celsius. Levels of humidity and rainfall highest around Basse-Terre. Refreshing trade winds all year round. Humid season – hivernage – is between September and November.

Entry requirements
Passports
Required by all.
Visa
As an overseas region of France entry requirements are the same.
Required by all, except citizens of EU, North America, Australasia and Japan, for stays up to one month; this includes business trips by representatives of foreign entities with an invitation from a local company or organisation. Proof of adequate funds for stay, an itinerary, a guarantee of repatriation if necessary and return/onward ticket are also required. For further exceptions, full details and a copy of the application form visit www.diplomatie.gouv.fr/thema/dossier.gb.asp and follow the path (entering France) to the database.
Currency advice/regulations
There are no restrictions on the import and export of foreign currency but the amount imported must be declared. The amount of foreign currency, other than euros, that may be taken out must not exceed that imported.

Health (for visitors)
Mandatory precautions
A yellow fever vaccination certificate is required if travelling from an infected area.
Advisable precautions
Hepatitis, typhoid, tetanus and polio vaccinations. Water precautions should be taken.

Hotels
There is a good range of quality hotels in Guadeloupe, as well as more basic accommodation. If a service charge is not added, a 15 per cent tip is usual.

Credit cards
Credit cards are accepted in a large number of establishments.

Public holidays
Fixed dates
1 Jan (New Year's Day), 1 May (Labour Day), 8 May (Victory Day), 27 May (Abolition Day), 14 Jul (Bastille Day), 21 Jul (Schoelcher Day), 15 Aug (Assumption Day), 1 Nov (All Saints' Day), 2 Nov (All Souls' Day), 11 Nov (Armistice Day), 25 Dec (Christmas Day).
Variable dates
Carnival (two days Feb), Mid-Lent Thursday (half-way between Carnival and Lent), Ash Wednesday, Good Friday, Easter Monday, Ascension Day, Whit Monday.

Working hours
Banking
Mon–Fri: 0800–1200, 1430–1600.
Banks close at noon on the day preceding a bank holiday.
Government
Mon–Fri: 0800–1300, 1500–1800.
Shops
Mon–Sat: 0800–1200, 1430–1700.

Electricity supply
220/380V AC, 50 and 60 cycles

Getting there
Air
National airline: Air Caraibes; Air France.
International airport/s: Pointe-à-Pitre Le Raizet International Airport (PTP), 3km from Pointe-à-Pitre; duty-free shop, restaurant, buffet, bank, post office, shops, hotel reservations, car hire.
Airport tax: There is no airport tax.

Getting about
National transport
Air: Air Guadeloupe, Air St Barthélémy and Liat operate frequent services to all the dependent islands from Pointe-à-Pitre.
Road: The total network is around 3,000km – including about 500km of national highway; secondary roads can be tortuous.
Buses: There are several private bus lines that connect Pointe-à-Pitre or Basse Terre with all villages. There are no timetables; a hand gesture is needed to stop buses.
City transport
Taxis: Plentiful but generally regarded as expensive, particulary in rural areas.
Car hire
Reservations for car rental are advisable, especially between December and April. An international licence is required.

BUSINESS DIRECTORY
The addresses listed below are a selection only. While World of Information makes every endeavour to check these addresses, we cannot guarantee that changes have not been made, especially to telephone numbers and area codes. We would welcome any corrections.

Telephone area codes
The international direct dialling code (IDD) for Guadeloupe is +590, followed by another 590 and subscriber's number.

Chambers of Commerce
Basse Terre Chamber of Commerce and Industry, 6 Rue Victor Hugues, 97100 Basse Terre (tel: 994-444; fax: 812-117; e-mail: ccibt:ais.gp).

Pointe-à-Pitre Chamber of Commerce and Industry, Hôtel Consulaire, Rue Félix Eboué, 97159 Pointe-à-Pitre (tel: 937-600; fax: 902-187; e-mail: contacts@cci-pap.org).

Guadeloupe

Banking
Caisse Régionale de Crédit Agricole Mutuel de la Guadeloupe, BP 134, Zone Artisanale de Petit Perou, 97154 Pointe-à-Pitre (tel: 906-565).

Central bank
European Central Bank (ECB), Kaiserstrasse 29, D-60311 Frankfurt am Main, Germany (tel: +49(69)13-440; fax: +49(69)1344-6000).

Travel information
Air Guadeloupe, 97110 Abymes (tel: 822-835).

Air Martinique, Aéroport du Raizet, 97319 Les Abymes (tel: 211-342; fax: 890-247).

Ministry of tourism
Bureau Industrie et Tourisme, Préfecture de la Guadeloupe, Rue de Lardenoy, 97109 Basse Terre (tel: 817-681).

Direction de la Promotion Touristique, Préfecture de la Guadeloupe, Rue Lardenoy, 97100 Basse Terre (tel: 811-560).

National tourist organisation offices
Office Départemental du Tourisme (Guadeloupe Tourism Board), 5 Square de la Banque, PO Box 1099, 97181 Pointe-á-Pitre (tel: 894-689, 820-930; fax: 838-922).

Other useful addresses
Agence pour la Promotion Industrielle de la Guadeloupe (APRIGA), BP 1229, 97184 Pointe-à-Pitre (tel: 834-897; fax: 902-187).

Chambre d'Agriculture de la Guadeloupe, 27 rue Sadi-Carnot, 97110 Pointe-à-Pitre (tel: 821-130; fax: 918-873).

Port Autonome de la Guadeloupe, Boulevard Pointe Jarry, Zone de Commerce International, Basse Terre (tel: 213-971; fax: 213-979).

Port Autonome de Pointe-á-Pitre, Gare maritime, 97165 Pointe-á-Pitre Cedex (tel: 213-900; fax: 213-969; internet site: http://www.port-guadeloupe.com).

Syndicat des Producteurs-Exportateurs de Sucre et de Rhum de la Guadeloupe et Dépendances, Zone Industrielle de la Pointe Jarry, 97122 Baie Mahault, BP 2015, 97191 Pointe-à-Pitre (tel: 266-212).

Internet sites
Local government:
http://guadeloupe.pref.gouv.fr

Guam

KEY FACTS

Official name: Territory of Guam

Head of State: President of the USA, George W Bush

Head of government: Governor Felix Perez Camacho (Republican) (from 6 Jan 2003)

Ruling party: Republican Party (elected Nov 2004)

Area: 549 square km

Population: 164,500 (2004)

Capital: Agaña

Official language: Chamorro and English

Currency: US dollar (US$) = 100 cents

GDP per capita: US$21,000 (2003)*

Balance of trade: -US$127.30 million (2003)

Visitor numbers: 1,000,000 (2004)*

* estimated figure

COUNTRY PROFILE

Historical profile
Guam is the largest of the Marianas islands, which were occupied by the Chamorro Indians, a Malayo-Polynesian people, around 1500 BC.
1521 The Spanish seized control of Guam, which became a port of call for its galleons travelling between Mexico and the Philippines.
1898 Spain ceded Guam to the US after it lost the Spanish-American war. Guam was transformed into a strategic naval base.
1941 The US were forced out by the Japanese during the Second World War.
1944 US rule was reinstated after three years of fighting. Guam has remained an important military base since then.
1950 The Organic Act of Guam granted the island internal self-government and the islanders US citizenship, but not voting rights in US elections.
1962 The US passed the Naval Clearing Act which opened Guam's ports to foreign visitors.
1975 More than 100,000 evacuees from the fall of Vietnam were repatriated via Guam.
1996 Around 7,000 Kurdish refugees, fearing retaliation from Iraqi leader Saddam Hussein were housed on Guam.
1997 The strongest ever recorded typhoon ripped through Guam, leaving thousands homeless.
2002 Sino-Guamian economic ties were strengthened through visiting delegations to both countries. Felix Camacho (Republican) was elected governor. Super-typhoon Pongsona struck in December.
2004 In June, a state of emergency was declared after typhoon Tingting hit the island, leaving it almost completely inundated. Northern Marianas and Guam were struck by super-typhoon Chaba in August. In November, the Republicans won control of the legislature from the Democrats in the parliamentary elections.

Political structure
Constitution
Guam is represented by an elected non-voting delegate to the US House of Representatives; elections are every two years. Its inhabitants are US citizens but are not allowed to vote in US elections.

In June 2004, a new process for the island's primary elections was approved, which prevents voters from crossing over between political parties on the ballot; voters can, however, keep their political affiliations confidential.
Form of state
Although it is administered by the department of the interior, Guam is virtually a self-governing unincorporated territory of the US.
The executive
Local executive power rests with a governor, elected by popular vote to a four-year term, who heads a cabinet made up of departmental directors.
National legislature
The 15-member legislature is elected to a two-year term by popular vote. It passes legislation on local matters.
Last elections
4 November 2004 (parliamentary); November 2002 (gubernatorial).
Results: Parliamentary: the Republicans won control of the legislature from the Democrats.
Gubernatorial: Felix Camacho (Republican) was elected governor with 55 per cent of the vote over Robert Underwood (Democrat) with 45 per cent.
Next elections
2006 (gubernatorial); 2008 (parliamentary).

Political parties
Democratic Party and Republican Party.
Ruling party
Republican Party (elected Nov 2004)

Political situation
The up swing in Japan's economy coupled with the US military build-up has led to a revival in Guam's fortunes.
The US military presence on Guam includes two nuclear-powered submarines which were permanently stationed at the US naval base in early 2005, while the Andersen Air Force Base is being enlarged.
The tourist industry had been struggling to keep up visitor numbers after the devastating super-typhoons Pongsana, which struck in 2002, and Chaba in 2004 put off so many. Around a million tourists arrive each year, the bulk of which come from Japan, looking for sports, entertainment and scenic beauty. However in 2005 Japanese tour operators likened

Guam to a 'third world Asian country' as striptease clubs, massage parlours and prostitutes proliferated in the main tourist district. As an important source of foreign earnings the government could not afford to ignore the potential for such a reputation and the authorities began a series of crackdowns. Alternative sources of visitors are being sort, from Taiwan, China and Europe.

Population
164,500 (2004)
Ethnic make-up
Native Chamorros comprise 37 per cent of the population, Filipinos (26 per cent), white (10 per cent), Chinese, Japanese, Korean and others (27 per cent). There is tension between the Chamorros and guest workers from the Philippines and other Asian countries.
Religions
Roman Catholic (85 per cent)

Labour market and unemployment
About 31 per cent of local employment is with either US or territorial government while tourism accounts for a third of private sector employment. There are migrant workers from the Philippines and other Asian countries. Civilian pay by the military is typically twice that in the civilian economy.

Education
The education system is similar to that of the US but is poorly managed, with drop-out rates at around 50 per cent. Schools lack basic equipment and essential books.
Education is a high priority for parents and is considered the key to success in Chamorro life. Despite ongoing criticisms of the flaws in the system, the government has implemented no major reforms.
Compulsory years: Five to 16

Health
With a young and growing population the government is faced with the challenge of developing a health care system that will meet their needs. Health services are funded by the US government and the World Health Organisation (WHO). Health services are good but there is a shortage of adequately trained medical staff. Training of medical personnel was a government priority throughout 2002–05. There are high incidents of mental retardation and thyroid cancers, blamed on nuclear contamination when naval ships were sent for decontamination to Guam.
Life expectancy: 77.9 years (World Bank)
Fertility rate/Maternal mortality rate: 3.7 births per woman (World Bank)
Birth rate/Death rate: 23 births and four deaths per 1,000 population (2003)
Infant mortality rate: 6.5 per 1,000 live births (2003)

Welfare
Welfare is unevenly distributed among the population. The Chamorros are the main beneficiaries of welfare while Filipinos receive less than 10 per cent of government money, however in a 2005 a survey over 50 per cent found to be homeless were Chamorros.

Main cities
Agaña (capital, estimated population 3,900 in 2003), Tamuning (11,300), Mangilao (8,200).

Languages spoken
English, Chamorro, Chinese, Japanese and Korean.
Official language/s
Chamorro and English

Media
Press
Dailies: The *Pacific Daily News* is the English language newspaper.
Weeklies: There are several weeklies available in English, Japanese and Korean languages. The *Guam Kyodo News Service* provides a facsimile news service twice daily for the Japanese community and tourists. *Guam Shinbun* is a Japanese language weekly. English language weeklies are *Micro Call, Guam Shopper's Guide, Pacific Crossroads, Pacific Voice* (published on Sundays for the Catholic community), *Pacific Sunday News* and *Tropic Topics*. Korean language weeklies carrying news of Guam include *Korean Community News* and *Korean News*.
Business: *Guam Business News* is a monthly publication.
Periodicals: English language monthly publications include *Latte Magazine* featuring contemporary Guam and its multiculturalism; *Manila, Manila* is a glossy news and lifestyle magazine catering to the Filipino community.
Broadcasting
Several commercial radio services air programmes 24-hr/day. Commercial and public service TV includes cable service.

Economy
Guam remains one of the most prosperous islands in the Pacific and has the second highest GDP per capita of the region, Hawaii having the highest. About 60 per cent of Guam's income comes from US federal spending, particularly in defence facilities. Tourism is the leading area of the local economy. Most food and industrial goods are imported.
Although ties with the US are strong, Guam's economy is linked more directly with that of East Asia. The reliance on the Asian market makes the local economy vulnerable, particularly when tourist numbers fall, such as after 11 September 2001 terrorist attacks in the US and devastating typhoons, which caused widespread damage in 2002 and 2004. To revive the industry, the government is focussing on attracting more East Asian visitors, particularly from China.
There is some agriculture, with staple foods grown on smallholdings. Servicing of tuna boats also aids the economy. Around 350 US firms have established themselves as foreign sales corporations (FSCs) in Guam, with extensive assistance from the US. Small industries have grown with US encouragement. US military bases provide additional employment and around US$400 million annually to the government's revenues.
Aside from tourism, the only other significant source of income is the fishing industry, although the cement and construction industries have continued to prosper due to the constant ravaging of buildings and infrastructure by natural disasters.
Guam faces the problem of building up the civilian economic sector; it hopes to develop itself as a re-export centre and re-distribution hub for goods throughout the Pacific region. The territorial government is also looking into the possibility of developing an offshore financial centre, although the tax law environment is not favourable.
Following several years of stagnation and decline, the economy has been slowly recovering and growing. In 2004, economic recovery in Japan and more travellers from China benefitted the tourism sector. Increases in US defence spending, which include refurbishment of military bases, created more work. Recently announced projects include an US$18 million upgrade to the Navy water treatment facility, US$10.8 million for ammo wharf improvements, US$13 million for a Consolidated War Material Storage Facility at Andersen and US$20.2 million for improvements to Air Force family housing. However, the government continues to have serious financial challenges, as its deficit topped US$300 million in 2004, very close to its total annual budget.

External trade
Guam exports free of duty to a number of countries, including Australia, Japan and the US.
Imports
Main imports are petroleum and petroleum products, food and manufactured goods.
Main sources: Singapore (43 per cent total, 2004), Japan (20.6 per cent), South Korea (16.0 per cent), Hong Kong (9.8 per cent)
Exports
Main exports are onstruction materials, fish, food and beverage products.

Main destinations: Japan (55.4 per cent total, 2004), South Korea (27.3 per cent), Singapore (7.1 per cent)

Re-exports
Food re-exports for distribution throughout the Pacific provide the mainstay of export income. Re-exports of iron and steel scrap have been significant in the past currently most transshipments are of refined petroleum products.

Agriculture
Farming
The agriculture sector typically accounts for 7 per cent of gross island product (GIP). Most agricultural activity is part-time market gardening on smallholdings.
In March 2004, a fungus infected thousands of betel nut trees in the southern parts of Guam and scientists feared it could spread to other types of palm tree. More than 3,000 infected trees were destroyed.
Crop production in 2004 included: 53,000 tonnes (t) coconuts, 6,890t oilcrops, 5,164t vegetables in total, 2,760t melons, 2,350 roots & tubers, 100t sweet potatoes, 180t citrus fruit, 120t tomatoes, 2,685t fruit in total, 152t treenuts. Livestock production included: 202t of meat in total; 8t beef and buffalo meat, 11t goat meat, 140t pig meat, 43t poultry, 700t eggs and 12t honey.

Fishing
Fishing is an important source of protein. Future areas for growth include salmon and trout farming. Typical annual catches include 200t freshwater fish, 280t marine fish, and 28t of all other seafood.

Industry and manufacturing
Industry typically accounts for 15 per cent of GDP and employs about 3 per cent of the labour force. Most industrial goods are imported.
Main industries include US military, tourism, construction, transshipment services, concrete products, printing and publishing, food processing and textiles.
Government policy is attempting to focus on attracting foreign investment, particularly from Asian manufacturers, in order to develop the industrial base.

Tourism
Tourism is still Guam's most important economic activity. The government is seeking to expand into new markets in Europe and Asia, including China, and to diversify Guam's tourism product, especially into sports tourism.
Among Guam's natural attractions are it's unspoilt coral reefs, white sand beaches, lagoons and waterfalls. The brown tree snake, accidentally introduced in the 1940's has, however, decimated its bird-life and eradication programmes are carried out regularly. Guam is ideal for water sports including surfing, canoeing, jet skiing, and deep-sea fishing, in waters that are clear and warm. On the land, there are seven golf courses and good hiking tracks. It is one of the best diving destinations in the world with shipwrecks and coral reefs. On Cocos Island, two miles off the Southern tip of Guam there is a Spanish galleon wreck with billions of dollars worth of treasure that has still to be recovered.

Environment
In May 2005 a US research study confirmed that Guam had received measurable radioactive fallout during nuclear testing from 1946–62. The government confirmed that residents would be eligible under the Radiation Exposure Compensation Act. Radioactive polution was also acknowledged in Apra Habour, caused when military ships were decontaminated by washing down after testing.
Military expansion of the Andersen Air Force Base will cause the loss of some pristine native forest at a time when several endangered bird species are being reintroduced into the area.

Mining
Mining contributes less than 5 per cent to GDP. Rock and cement production supplies the construction industry.

Hydrocarbons
Guam does not produce or refine oil, it relies entirely on imports. Around 20,000 barrels per day of refined oil products, mainly jet fuel, gasoline and distillate are imported. Guam does not produce or import gas or coal.

Energy
A petroleum refinery has been in operation since the 1970s.

Banking and insurance
Central bank
Federal Reserve Bank of San Francisco

Time
GMT plus ten hours

Geography
Guam is the southernmost and largest of the Marianas, situated about 2,170km (1,350 miles) south of Tokyo, Japan, and 5,300km (3,300 miles) west of Honolulu, Hawaii.

Climate
Guam is warm and humid with temperatures averaging between 24–30 degrees Celsius. Dec–May is generally cooler and drier. Rainfall, up to 300mm/month and averages 2,000mm per annum. The heaviest rainfall is usually between Jul–Sep. There are occasional tropical storms. The tropical humidity is tempered somewhat by the prevailing north-westerly trade winds.

Entry requirements
Passports
Required by all except US citizens with proof of citizenship departing from US points.

Visa
US entry requirements apply. Visas required by all, except US citizens with proof of identity, and foreign nationals from countries that have visa free entry to the US and are in possession of machine readable passports under 'Visa Waiver Program' (VWP) due to be introduced in October 2005. All other visitors and passport holders must apply for a visa. Visits, for both tourism and business, and visas are valid for up to 90 days. A return/onward ticket is also required.
Further information can be found at http://travel.state.gov/ including information on temporary business visas. More detailed information can be found at http://uscis.gov/graphics/services/visa_info.htm.

Customs
Guam is a duty-free port.

Health (for visitors)
Mandatory precautions
Vaccination certificates required for yellow fever if travelling from infected area.

Advisable precautions
Vaccination for diphtheria, tuberculosis, hepatitis 'A' and 'B', polio, tetanus, typhoid. Rabies risk.

Public holidays
Fixed dates
1 Jan (New Year's Day), 4 Jul (Independence Day), 21 Jul (Liberation Day), 2 Nov (All Souls' Day), 11 Nov (Veterans' Day), 8 Dec (Lady of Camarin Day), 25 Dec (Christmas Day).

Variable dates
Martin Luther King Day (third Mon in Jan), President's Day (second Mon in Feb), Guam Discovery Day (first Mon in Mar), Good Friday, Memorial Day (last Mon in May), Labour Day (first Mon in Sep), Columbus Day (first Mon in Oct), Thanksgiving Day (fourth Thu in Nov).

Working hours
Banking
Mon–Thu: 1000–1500, Fri: 1000–1800. Automatic teller machines available.

Telecommunications
Telephone/fax
In September 2004, TeleGuam Holdings LLC purchased the Guam Telephone Authority (GTA) for the sum of US$150 million.
A mainly automatic telephone service has over 7,000 business lines and over 1,000

Guam

government lines. Overseas telecommunications facilities are available in Agaña.

Postal services
The Guam Main Facility branch is open 0900–1700 (Mon–Fri) and 0900–1200 (Sat). Branches at Agaña and Tamuning are open 0800–1600 (Mon–Fri) and 0900–1200 (Sat).

Mobile phones
Around 55,000 mobile phones are in use.

Electricity supply
110V AC, 60Hz

Weights and measures
US system

Getting there
Air
Korean Air, Continental Micronesia, All Nippon Airlines, Japan Airlines, Pacific Airlines and Paulau Micronesia Air all serve Guam.
International airport/s: The Antonio B Won Pat International Airport (GUM), 11km from Agaña; duty-free shop, first-class lounge, restaurant, currency exchange, hotel reservations and car hire.
Airport tax: There is no airport tax.
Surface
Main port/s: Apra Harbour; with services provided by Kyowa, Daiwa, Micronesia Transport, American President, Sea-Land Services and Austfreight shipping lines.

Getting about
National transport
Road: The roads and highways are third-rate and bumpy, with some 600km surfaced.
Buses: A reasonable service is connects almost all villiages, however services do not run on Sundays or public holidays.
Taxis: Fares are usually metered.
City transport
Car hire
Available through most major companies. In general, charges are based on time, mileage and insurance. An international driving licence is required.

BUSINESS DIRECTORY
The addresses listed below are a selection only. While World of Information makes every endeavour to check these addresses, we cannot guarantee that changes have not been made, especially to telephone numbers and area codes. We would welcome any corrections.

Telephone area codes
The international direct dialling code (IDD) for Guam is +1 671, followed by subscriber's number.

Chambers of Commerce
Guam Chamber of Commerce, 173 Aspinall Avenue, Ada Plaza Center, PO Box 283, Agana 96932 (tel: 472-6311; fax: 472-6202; e-mail: gchamber@guamchamber.com.gu).

Banking
Bank of Hawaii, PO Box BH, Agaña 96910 (tel: 4779-781; fax: 4777-533).

First Commercial Bank, 1st Floor, 330 Hernan Cortes ave, Agaña 96910 (tel: 4726-864/5; fax: 4778-921).

Union Bank of California NA, 194 Hernan Cortes Ave, Agaña 96910 (tel: 4778-811; fax: 4723-284).

Central bank
Federal Reserve Bank of San Francisco, 101 Market Street, San Francisco, California 94105, USA (tel: +1-415 974-2000; fax: +1-415 974-3341).

Travel information
Freedom Air, PO Box 1578, Agaña 96910 (tel: 649-1581; fax: 649-0729).

Guam Visitors Bureau, PO Box 3520, Agaña (tel: 646-5278; fax: 646-8861).

Other useful addresses
Guam Economic Development Authority, Suite 911, ITC Building, 590 South Marine Drive, Tamuning, Guam 96911 (tel: 649-4141; fax: 649-4146).

Internet sites
The Pacific Daily News:
http://www.guampdn.com

KUAM Broadcasting News:
http://www.kuam.com

US Office of Insular affairs:
http://www.doi.gov/oia

Guatemala

KEY FACTS

Official name: República de Guatemala (Republic of Guatemala)

Head of State: President Óscar Berger Perdomo (GANA) (sworn in 14 Jan 2004)

Head of government: President Óscar Berger Perdomo

Ruling party: Gran Alianza Nacional (GANA) (Grand National Alliance) (elected Nov 2003)

Area: 108,890 square km

Population: 12.39 million (2004)

Capital: Guatemala City

Official language: Spanish

Currency: Quetzal (Q) = 100 centavos

Exchange rate: Q7.65 per US$ (Oct 2005)

GDP per capita: US$1,953 (2004)

GDP real growth: 2.60% (2004)

Labour force: 4.76 million (2004)

Unemployment: 3.70% (2004)

Inflation: 7.00% (2004)

Balance of trade: -US$3.76 billion (2004)

Foreign debt: US$5.97 billion (2004)

Óscar José Rafael 'Berger' Perdomo defeated his rivals for the presidency in the national election in November 2003. The ruling Frente Republicano Guatemalteco (FRG) (Republican Front of Guatemala) selected dictatorial former president Efraín Ríos Montt as their candidate to replace outgoing president Alfonso Portillo Cabrera, also of the FRG. Berger, who ran on the Gran Alianza Nacional (Grand National Alliance) coalition ticket won the first poll, beating Álvaro Colom Caballeros (Unidad Nacional de la Esperanza, UNE, National Union of Hope) and Montt into second and third place respectively. In the subsequent run off between Berger and Montt, Berger won with 54 per cent of the vote.

Born into an upper class family of large sugar and coffee business interests, Berger read law at university before marrying Wendy Widmann, of a similar landed business elite background. The future president ran a very profitable skittles parlour in the 1970s before joining the successful Guatemala City mayoral campaign of Álvaro Arzú in 1985. Berger became an influential political player behind the scenes during Arzú's municipal reign in the mid- to late-eighties before becoming Mayor of Guatemala City himself in 1991. Berger served as Mayor until 1999 where he astutely built up his power base in anticipation of a presidential run. Just when he seemed perfectly poised for a bid for the highest office in the land, Berger apparently retired from politics to start a second career as a farmer. Allegedly, he had to be persuaded to run for president when the post became vacant in 2003.

Government policy

Since taking office in 2004 the Berger government has adopted the 1996 Peace Accords as the bedrock of its reform policy agenda. The Accords portray a broad national consensus on economic, social and security issues and as such the government's policy package is premised on three central tenets. The pillars of the policy are macroeconomic stability, structural economic reforms and financial sector restructuring.

One of the major policy targets for the Berger government is a limitation of the fiscal deficit to less than 2 per cent of total GDP. Simultaneously, the government is seeking to raise extra revenue so as to increase funding for public investment and social projects. The government has also taken steps to revamp monetary policy in a bid to reduce inflation to a rate of between 4 and 6 per cent. Also in 2005, in January, a legal mechanism for central bank intervention was put in place. This followed a series of foreign exchange interventions by the central bank over the prior twelve months. In addition, Guatemala's banking system has been reinforced by structural and regulatory reform legislation. One of the most important measures in this legislative package has been the incorporation of offshore banks into the main regulatory framework.

Berger has initiated a general package of structural reform called *Vamos Guatemala*, which is intended to promote and eventually create an environment of economic competitiveness and social advancement throughout the country. A Competitiveness Commissioner has been appointed and vital steps were taken in 2005 to increase corporate and business transparency. The Central American Free Trade Agreement (Cafta) was ratified by the Guatemalan Congress in 2005, despite protests by many domestic groups against the pact, which held up the Congressional deliberations for several days. The government is optimistic that Cafta, a free trade agreement including five other Central American countries and the US, will help underpin Guatemala's efforts at economic recovery.

Economic performance

Growth has been steady but slow over recent years in Guatemala. Real GDP growth hovered between 2 and 2.5 per cent during 2001–03. With the latest IMF growth forecast being 3.2 per cent for 2005 and 2006, the outlook for the next 24 months looks more promising. Inflation increased in 2004 and is now in the region of 5 per cent. But despite this increase, the annual inflation rate is currently at its lowest level since 2000.

The coffee industry is still the foundation of the Guatemalan economy though the country's travel and tourism industry performed well in 2005 and now accounts for a significant portion of total GDP (6.9 per cent). Tourism is undergoing expansion right across the industry. The sector employed 8.7 per cent more of the workforce than it did in 2004 and visitor exports shot up 13.8 per cent, to represent over 20 per cent of Guatemala's total exports. Capital investment, so vital to tourism sectors in many countries around the world, also increased, by almost 5 per cent. Nearly a tenth of Guatemala's total capital investment is now channeled into tourism and related areas.

The IMF has applauded the determination with which the government has set about achieving its primary goals of creating a stable macroeconomic environment and reducing the public deficit. Strong policies in the areas of fiscal deficit reduction and in streamlining the banking sector should help improve domestic confidence and consequently increase private investment levels.

Outlook

The political arena in Guatemala has been relatively stable since the 2003 elections, when social upheaval returned during the election campaign. Though protests were carried out during 2005 at the time of the Cafta ratification, mass social upheaval on the scale of the 1980s was not a prominent feature in the country during 2005. The Berger government has made a good start and has received congratulations from the IMF and other multilateral institutions for its reform-focused agenda. So long as Guatemala continues to remain relatively peaceful, and macroeconomic stabilisation continues to be the main objective of the government the economy should continue to grow at an unspectacular, yet healthy rate.

Risk assessment

Political	Improving/good
Economic	Improving
Regional stability	Good

COUNTRY PROFILE

Historical profile

1523–24 Pedro de Alvarado defeated the indigenous Mayan civilisation and created Guatemala as a Spanish colony.
1821 The Central American provinces (Costa Rica, Guatemala, Honduras, Nicaragua and El Salvador) declared independence from Spain.
1822 Central American confederation annexed itself to the Mexican Empire, under General Agustín de Iturbde, later Emperor Agustín I.
1823 Agustín I was overthrown and Mexico became a republic. The Central American states formed the United Provinces of Central America.
1825 Costa Rica, Guatemala, Honduras, Nicaragua and El Salvador formed the Central American Federation (CAF).
1838 The CAF was dissolved and Guatemala became a fully independent republic.

KEY INDICATORS — Guatemala

	Unit	2000	2001	2002	2003	2004
Population	m	11.42	11.73	12.04	12.22	12.39
Gross domestic product (GDP)	US$bn	19.10	20.50	21.70	24.70	*27.45
GDP per capita	US$	1,529	1,757	1,814	1,941	1,953
GDP real growth	%	3.6	2.1	2.4	2.4	2.6
Inflation	%	5.1	7.6	6.3	5.6	7.0
Exports (fob) (goods)	US$m	3,082.0	2,865.0	2,700.0	2,787.0	3,429.5
Imports (fob) (goods)	US$m	4,742.0	5,607.0	6,084.0	6,300.0	7,189.1
Balance of trade	US$m	-1,660.0	-3,190.0	-3,384.0	-3,513.0	-3,759.6
Current account	US$m	-1,049.5	-1,238.0	-1,190.0	–	-1,150.0
Total reserves minus gold	US$m	1,746.4	2,292.2	2,299.1	2,833.2	3,426.3
Foreign exchange	US$m	1,736.0	2,283.7	2,290.9	2,825.0	3,418.3
Exchange rate	per US$	7.76	7.85	7.85	7.91	7.94

* estimated figure

1844–65 Guatemala was ruled by conservative dictator Rafael Carrera.
1873–85 Liberal, Rufino Barrios, became president, he attempted to modernise the country by developing an army and introducing coffee plantations.
1930 General Jorge Ubico began his repressive dictatorship.
1941 Guatemala declared war on the Axis Powers.
1944 Ubico was overthrown in a popular revolution. Juan José Arevalo headed a new government that introduced social reforms, including a social security system and land redistribution.
1951 Jacobo Arbenz Guzmán became president and stepped up the reforms.
1954 A US-backed *coup d'état*, led by Colonel Carlos Castillo Armas and prompted by the US United Fruit Company when disused land it owned was nationalised overthrew the democratically elected government. A military dictatorship was installed.
1957 Castillo Armas was assassinated.
1958 Miguel Ramon Ydígoras Fentes took control and his autocratic rule led to a failed military revolt by junior officer in 1960. Most leaders of armed insurrection for the next 36 years of civil war were part of this group.
1963 Enrique Peralta became president following a coup and civilian administration was completely assumed by the military whose power and influence increased. Widespread repression of opposition groups increased as leaders were targetted for assassination or 'disappearance'. Insurgents countered with sabotage and violent guerrilla tactics.
1966 Civilian rule was restored when César Méndez, Revolucionario Partido (PR) (Revolutionary Party) was elected president. Nevertheless, the military launched a major counterinsurgency campaign, which crippled the guerrilla movement in the countryside.
1970 Carlos Arena, backed by the military and the US, was elected president.
1976 An earthquake struck just south-west of Guatemala City that killed around 27,000 people and left one million citizens homeless.
1978–1984 Over 90 per cent of all atrocities occurred during this time as government forces and insurgents battled. The most frequent victims were the ethnic Mayan population who were attacked by both sides and accused of being collaborators or sympathisers of the opposition.
1980 Thirty seven people died, in the Spanish Embassy siege in Guatemala City, when Mayan peasant farmers were protesting about military repression.
1981 Left-wing insurgent groups unified to become Unidad Revolucionaria Nacional Guatemalteca (URNG) (National Guatemalan Revolutionary Unit).
1982 General Efraín Ríos Montt seized power in a military coup. His dictatorship was in power during the bloodiest period of the civil war.
1983 Montt was ousted by General Mejía Victores, who declared an amnesty on guerrillas.
1985 Marco Vinicio Cerezo was elected president and Democracia Cristiana Guatemalteco (DCG) (Guatemalan Christian Democracy) won legislative elections.
1989 An attempt to overthrow Cerezo failed.
1991 Jorge Serrano Elias was elected president.
1993 Serrano's attempt to impose an authoritarian regime led to mass demonstrations and he was forced to resign. Ramiro de Leon Carpio was elected president by the legislature.
1994 Peace talks began between the government and the URNG.
1995 The URNG declared a cease-fire. The UN and the US criticised the government for widespread human rights violations and the deaths of more than 200,000 civilians during the civil war.
1996 After a civil war lasting 36 years, a peace treaty was signed. Alvaro Arzú and his Partido de Avanzada Nacional (PAN) (National Advancement Party) won the subsequent presidential and National Congress elections. Arzú began a purge on senior military officers implicated in human rights violations.
1999 A UN-sponsored investigation found that the security forces were responsible for 93 per cent of all human rights atrocities committed during the civil war and that the military had overseen 626 massacres in Mayan villages. Alfonso Portillo of the Frente Republicano Guatemalteco (FRG) (Guatemalan Republican Front) was elected president.
2000 Portillo was sworn in as president.
2001 A foreign exchange law allowed the free circulation of US dollars from May and citizens and companies were allowed to hold US dollar bank deposits without prior authorisation. The government paid US$1.8 million in compensation to the families of 226 victims killed by soldiers and death squads in the village of Las Dos Erres in 1982.
2003 Teachers, striking over demands for salary increases and improvements to the school system, disrupted international air travel and access to seaports. The ruling FRG was defeated by the Gran Alianza Nacional (GANA) (Grand National Alliance) in the parliamentary elections. Óscar Berger Perdomo (GANA) won the presidential run-off election on 28 December.
2004 Berger was sworn in as president on 14 January. Former dictator, Ríos Montt, was put under house arrest on charges of inciting a riot, and genocide relating to atrocities carried out when he was in power. The State accepted responsibility for more human rights violations during the civil war; US$3.5 million was paid out to victims in July. In September, 11 people were killed as demonstrators clash with police.
2005 In March, the government signed the Central American Free Trade Agreement (Cafta) with the US and five of the Central American and Caribbean states, amid anti-US demonstrations. Hurricane Stan hit the region in October causing 699 deaths, over 35,000 homes destroyed, landslides and extensive flooding. In the US, in November, Guatemala's top anti-drugs investigator was arrested on drug trafficking charges.

Political structure
In addition to their unicameral national parliaments, El Salvador, Guatemala, Honduras, Nicaragua, Panama and Dominican Republic, which acceded to the Central American Parliament in February 2004, also return directly elected deputies to the supranational Central American Parliament.

Constitution
The constitution, which came into effect in 1986 (replacing the 1966 constitution suspended in 1982), created a representative system of government in which power is exercised equally by the legislative, executive and judicial arms. Guatemala is divided into 22 provinces, subdivided into municipalities.

Form of state
Presidential democratic republic

The executive
Executive power is held by the president, directly elected for four years, assisted by a vice president and an appointed cabinet.

National legislature
Legislative power is vested in the 80-member unicameral Congreso de la República (Congress), elected every four years, of which 64 seats are elected in departmental congressional districts and 16 in a nationwide ballot. Electoral suffrage is universal for all aged 18 years or over. Congress approves laws by means of an absolute majority, except those involving constitutional change or any international treaty or agreement affecting the sovereignty of the state; these must secure a two-thirds majority. Congress is responsible for all electoral matters, for approving the budget and decreeing taxes and for conferring honours. Congress meets on 15 June each year and ordinary legislative sessions last four months.

Guatemala

Legal system
Guatemala has a civil law system with judicial review of legislative acts. The Supreme Court serves as the highest appeal court in the country; there is also a separate Court of Constitutionality and a Supreme Electoral Tribunal. The country does not accept the compulsory jurisdiction of the International Court of Justice.

Last elections
9 November 2003 (parliamentary); 9 November/28 December 2003 (presidential).
Results: Run-off presidential: Óscar Berger won 54.1 per cent of the vote and Álvaro Colom 45.9 per cent; turnout was 46.8 per cent.
Parliamentary: Gran Alianza Nacional (GANA) (Grand National Alliance) won 24.3 per cent of the vote (47 seats); Frente Republicano Guatemalteco (FRG) (Guatemalan Republican Front) 19.7 per cent (43); Unidad Nacional de la Esperanza (UNE) (National Union of Hope) 17.9 per cent (33) and Partido de Avanzade Nacional (PAN) (National Advancement Party) 10.9 per cent (17).

Next elections
2007 (presidential and parliamentary)

Political parties
Ruling party
Gran Alianza Nacional (GANA) (Grand National Alliance) (elected Nov 2003)
Main opposition party
Frente Republicano Guatemalteco (FRG) (Guatemalan Republican Front)

Population
12.39 million (2004)
Ethnic make-up
A high proportion of the population belongs to 22 Mayan ethno-linguistic groups, conserving the cultural heritage of their ancestors. Their numbers are disputed but they constitute at least 45 per cent of the population and possibly as much as 60 per cent. Many of the inhabitants of the Caribbean coast are of Afro-Caribbean origin.
Religions
The constitution guarantees freedom of worship. Catholicism is the most widespread religion, although large numbers of conversions have been made in recent years by Protestant churches, including mainstream non-conformists and US-based fundamentalist sects. Protestant leaders claim to have converted some 30 per cent of the population and are playing an increasingly active role in the country's politics. Some indigenous communities hold services combining Catholicism with pre-Columbian rites.

Education
Elementary education is free and lasts for six years and secondary education, which begins at age 13, for a further six years, divided into two three-year courses. There are five universities, three of which are private, located in Guatemala City and Quetzaltenango, the country's second-largest city.
Compulsory years: Seven to 14 in urban areas only.
Enrolment rate: 90 per cent total primary enrolment of the relevant age group; 26 per cent total enrolment in secondary schools, of the relevant age group; enrolment in tertiary education is less than 10 per cent.
Pupils per teacher: 35 in primary schools.

Health
Total expenditure on health is around 5 per cent of GDP, of which government spending is between 48–50 per cent. Healthcare remains inadequate with 80 per cent of spending and hospitals confined in the two major cities.
HIV prevalence: 1.1 per cent aged 15–49 in 2003 (World Bank)
Life expectancy: 66.1 years (World Bank)
Fertility rate/Maternal mortality rate: 4.3 births per woman; maternal mortality 2.9 per 1,000 live births (World Bank).
Infant mortality rate: 35 per 1,000 live births; 44 per cent of children aged under five are malnourished (World Bank).
Head of population per physician/bed: 0.9 doctors per 1,000 people and 1 hospital bed per 1,000 people.

Welfare
Social security, which is compulsory, covers health and hospital care as well as industrial accidents, disability and widowhood for registered workers. All employers with five or more workers are required by law to register with the State Institute of Social Security.

Main cities
Guatemala City (capital, estimated population 1.1 million in 2003), Mixco (287,600), Villa Nueva (138,900), Quezaltenango (124,200).

Languages spoken
Approximately 22 Indian languages are widely spoken throughout the highlands, including Quiché, Cakchiquel, Mam and Kekchi. About 40 per cent of all Guatemalan children enter school with no knowledge of Spanish.
English is spoken in almost all tourist areas.
Official language/s
Spanish

Media
Press
Most of Guatemala's media is privately owned. The independent newspapers such as *La Hora*, *Prensa Libre* and *El Periodico* freely criticise government policies. However many journalists face intimidation and some have even resorted to exile.
Dailies: Most dailies are published in Guatemala City. These include *Diario de Centroamérica*, *El Gráfico*, *Guatemala Daily*, *Diario de Hora*, *El Periódico*, *El Impacto*, *El Imparcial*, *Prensa Libre*, *Siglo Veintiuno*, and *La Tarde*.
Weeklies: *Guatemala Weekly* is also available for general interest.
Broadcasting
The government operates five radio stations. There are also six educational (with some broadcasts in English) and over 80 commercial stations, most of them provincial and many of them broadcasting at least part of the time in indigenous languages. The Catholic Church owns several radio stations which broadcast from rural areas. Five television stations are controlled by a mixture of outright state and private interests. The government controls one of the five television stations as well as the five main radio stations out of a total of over 100 radio stations.

Economy
The economy of Guatemala has grown steadily if somewhat slowly over recent years. The GDP growth rate hovered at 2.4 per cent during 2001–04. The outlook for the next two years is slightly better, with the IMF projecting growth of 3.2 per cent in 2005 and 2006. Despite an increase in inflation in 2004, to 7 per cent, the inflation rate in 2005 was around the 5 per cent mark, the lowest since 2000.
Coffee is the mainstay of the economy, followed by tourism, which has become the second most important source of revenue accounting for 6.9 per cent of GDP. The agricultural sector accounts for around a quarter of GDP and employs over half the workforce. This means however that Guatemala is heavily reliant on world demand and is sensitive to external shock.
The peace treaty reached in 1996 after 36 years of civil war set the conditions necessary for the renewal of Guatemala's basic infrastructure. In the 1990s the Guatemalan economy, which is the largest in Central America, grew at an average rate of 4.1 per cent per year. This is compared to an average of 0.9 per cent for the period 1981–90 when war, capital flight and deteriorating terms of trade severely restricted economic growth rates. The IMF has applauded the determination with which the government has set about achieving its primary goals of creating a stable macroeconomic environment and reducing the public deficit. Strong policies in the areas of fiscal deficit reduction and in streamlining the banking sector should

help improve domestic confidence, and through it increase private investment levels.

External trade
Guatemala is a full member of the Central American Common Market (CACM), along with Costa Rica, El Salvador, Honduras and Nicaragua.

By August of 2004, Costa Rica, the Dominican Republic, El Salvador, Guatemala, Honduras and Nicaragua had all agreed to a proposed Central American Free Trade Agreement (Cafta) with the US. In March 2005 the Guatemalan government signed the Central American Free Trade deal amid anti-US demonstrations.

Imports
Principal imports are foodstuffs, fuels, vehicles, clothing and other consumer goods, and construction materials.
Main sources: France (63 per cent total, 2004), Germany (4 per cent), US (3.0 per cent), Japan (2.0 per cent), Netherlands Antilles (2.0 per cent)

Exports
Principal exports are coffee (typically 38 per cent of annual total), sugar, rum, bananas and cardamom.
Main destinations: France (60 per cent total, 2004), Martinique (18.0 per cent), US (4.0 per cent)

Agriculture
Farming
Guatemala's most important economic sector is agriculture. The sector accounts for approximately 25 per cent of total GDP and employs about half of the country's total workforce. Despite the agricultural sector's high employment level, the number of jobs in the sector is falling due to increased mechanisation. Approximately 17 per cent of Guatemala's total land mass is cultivated arable land, 10 per cent pasture and 35 per cent forest. Throughout the 1990s, Guatemala was relatively successful in establishing agricultural diversification, in an effort to buttress export earnings against commodity price fluctuations. It also sought to encourage the development of processing and packaging plants so as to upgrade the value of farm exports. Most of this took place in the highland areas where there is a good supply of land and labour. The production of fresh and frozen vegetables and ornamental plants and flowers has been particularly successful.

Production is mainly export-oriented, the major cash crops being coffee (the largest single earner of foreign exchange), sugar cane, bananas, cotton, cardamom (Guatemala accounts for over 90 per cent of world trade in cardamom) and tobacco. Vegetables such as mangetout, broccoli and asparagus, as well as a wide variety of fruits, are exported to the US and Europe.

Coffee growers plan to double the country's production between 1998–2008. Coffee has suffered from poor global commodity prices, although rising output has helped offset some of the losses.

Maize is the main food crop, although rice and wheat are also grown. Agricultural produce also includes cocoa, beans and flowers.

Foreign investment has so far been limited as a result of the absence of a domestic land market. Land is regarded as an indication of wealth and most owners leave it fallow if they choose not to plant. Land distribution is uneven, with just under 80 per cent of all farms under 3.5 hectares (ha) and 1 per cent over 2,500ha. Most foreign participation is concentrated on the non-traditional agricultural crops now emerging as major export earners.

Crop production in 2004 included: 1,171,788 tonnes (t) cereals, 1,072,310t maize, 18,000,000t sugar cane, 282,923t potatoes, 580,000t oil palm fruit, 34,926t rice, 11,339t wheat, 1,000,000t bananas, *268,000t plantains, *252,877t citrus fruit, *187,000t mangoes, 102,299t pineapples, *20,540t tobacco, *187,229t tomatoes, 141,046t oilcrops, 132,105t pulses, 216,600t green coffee, 19,000t nutmegs, 35,049t sesame seeds, 390t pepper spice, *49,828t natural rubber, 1,995,469t fruit in total, *976,777t vegetables in total.
*estimate

Estimated livestock production included: 248,022t meat in total, 63,000t beef, 26,000t pig meat, 1,679t lamb and goat meat, 2,344t horsemeat, 155,000t poultry, 85,000t eggs, 270,000t milk, 1,500t honey, 8,880t cattle hides.

Fishing
Guatemala's typical catch is approximately 14,300 tonnes (t), 9,800t freshwater fish inclusive.

Forestry
Approximately 35 per cent of Guatemala's total land mass is covered by forests. Between 1990 and 2000 the country's total forest cover decreased by an average of 1.7 per cent per annum, the equivalent of 54,000ha. Some 20 per cent of Guatemala's land area is protected against industrial exploitation. Softwood conifers account for 22 per cent with broad-leaved species, including valuable hardwoods such as mahogany, cedar and rosewood, accounting for the rest. Other forest products include rubber and chicle, an important chewing gum base, which is extracted in the forested Petén region.

Some wood is available for fuel consumption, although a modest amount of sawnwood produced is also exported. Much of the domestic demand for paper is met by imports.

In a typical year, exports of forest materials amount to US$31.5 million while imports amount to US$197.3 million. Timber production in 2003 included 16,060,873 cubic metres (cum) roundwood, 509,000cum industrial roundwood, 366,000cum sawnwood, 492,000cum sawlogs & veneer logs, 43,400cum wood-based panels, 15,551,873cum wood fuel, 18,713t charcoal.

Industry and manufacturing
Guatemala has a well developed industrial sector and the sector as a whole contributes approximately one fifth to GDP in a typical year. Industry contributes around 20 per cent to GDP (manufacturing contributes around 14 per cent) and employs 15 per cent of the workforce. Industry is primarily involved in activities related to agricultural inputs for major firms involved in food and drink processing, rubber, textiles, pottery, paper and pharmaceuticals. Other important industries are the assembly of electronic products, manufacture of furniture, canned goods, oil refining, cement, metals (especially steel), electrical goods assembly, plastics, chemicals, fertilisers and cigarettes.

Social and industrial unrest, high energy costs, shortages of imported materials and a slump in private and public investment have severely hampered industrial production. However, major government house building and infrastructural repair plans since the end of the civil war seem to have given a signficant boost to the construction industry, although construction as a proportion of GDP has shrunk in recent years.

Tourism
The tourism industry of Guatemala has achieved steady growth in recent years. The sector now accounts for 6.9 per cent of total GDP and 6 per cent of total employment.

Guatemala relies on its ecology and Mayan ruins to attract visitors. Visitor numbers, which stood at 632,683 in 1998, two years after the end of the civil war, jumped to 818,645 the following year, reaching 884,190 in 2002. The following year saw a slight fall, attributed to signs of instability and lack of tourist events, but in 2004 the figure rose once more, to 1,004,000. The largest market for Guatemalan travel and tourism in recent years has been El Salvador, though the US and Canada overtook that country in 2003.

Mining
The Alta Verapaz copper mine represents the main mining operation in Guatemala. In addition to copper, tungsten and

antimony there are also exploitable reserves of marble and sulphur. Deposits of lead, zinc, gold and silver are also known to exist.
Lead is mined at Ballena and Penasco by Cía Minas de Oriente SA (Minersa). Reserves are estimated at 2.2 million tonnes and contain 86 grammes per tonne of silver. Minas de Guatemala operates the Annabella and Los Lirios antimony and tungsten mines, producing about 1,800 tonnes per month of ore (6 per cent antimony, 0.5 per cent lead). The Oxec copper mine, worked by Transmetales in Alta Verapaz, has a capacity of 150,000 tonnes per year. The country's major mineral resource is laterite, with the El Estor deposits estimated at 50 million tonnes. In August 2005 the World Bank was crtiticised for its role in funding a gold mining project in Guatemala. The Bank was criticised for not consulting the local community properly and for failing to evaluate the humanitarian or environmental implications of the proposed facility.

Hydrocarbons
Guatemala is the only oil producing country in Central America. The country's proven oil reserves stand at 526 million barrels, though actual reserves are thought to be as much as 1 billion barrels. Guatemala produces 19,800 barrels per day (bpd), a decrease on the 21,080 bpd figure recorded in 2003. The majority of production occurs in the northern jungle areas, near to the border with Mexico. Development of the industry has been slow due to the reluctance of foreign companies to invest in the area owing to political unrest and unfavourable terms. Guatemala refines oil imported primarily from Venezuela with favourable terms due to the San José pact.
Gas reserves amounted to 3.08 billion cubic metres in 2003. Although some areas are still to be properly surveyed. In December 1999, Guatemala and Mexico signed a protocol for the construction of a natural gas pipeline from southern Mexico to Guatemala. The pipeline is part of a wider Central America gas pipeline network and will meet the initial demand estimated at about 1.1 million cubic metres per day. It offers the potential to reduce the region's reliance on seasonally-dependent hydroelectric power. Guatemala does not consume or import natural gas. Guatemala typically imports over 220,000 tonnes of coal annually. Coal is mainly used for primary energy production. Guatemala does not produce coal.

Energy
Guatemala retains a total electricity generation capacity of approximately 1.3GW. The San José power station is Central America's largest coal-fired power plant. A 300MW thermal power plant owned by the Decasa consortium is under construction, the first phase of which was came on-line in 2003. A 165MW thermal plant owned by the US's Duke Energy was completed in mid-2003.

Financial markets
Stock exchange
A national stock exchange, the Bolsa de Valores Nacional (BVN), was established in Guatemala City in 1987. It is under common ownership with one share per associate, and trades mainly in government bonds and debt. Until the privatisation programme began in the 1990s, few private stocks and shares were traded, a reflection of how exclusive and restricted the business establishment in Guatemala was. The privatisation of state-owned assets has been carried out through the exchange. There is also an agricultural stock exchange (Bolsa Agrícola Nacional).

Banking and insurance
The Guatemalan banking and financial services sector is organised under a central banking system, above which is the higher authority of the Monetary Board. There are 35 private commercial banks in Guatemala, but the banking market is dominated by a handful of large institutions. Some 40 per cent of total assets are in the hands of the five largest banks. Guatemala is no longer on the OECD Financial Action Task Force (FATF) list of non-co-operative countries regarding money laundering.
Central bank
Banco de Guatemala

Time
GMT minus six hours

Geography
Guatemala has five distinct geographical zones. The first is the lowland Pacific strip running the length of the coastline, where the climate is tropical and summer rains are heavy. Most of the country's large sugar, banana and cotton farms are based here. Some 50km in from the coast the land rises to form the first of two mountain ranges running north-west to south-east. This range includes a string of volcanoes. A plateau formed by a series of volcanic basins at an average height of 1,500 metres above sea level forms the third zone; the capital, Guatemala City, and most of the country's population are to be found here.
Another mountain range with peaks of over 4,000 metres forms the basis of the north-west highlands, tapering down to the border with Honduras and El Salvador at its south-east extremity, where most of the country's more than four million indigenous people live. Beyond the mountains the land falls rapidly into a flat expanse of tropical forest. This area, which accounts for the northern part of the departments of Izabal, El Quiche, and Alta Verapaz and all the 36,400 square km of El Petén department, remains one of the region's last wildernesses.

Climate
The climate varies with altitude but is essentially sub-tropical with little variation between the seasons. The hottest month is May when the average daily minimum and maximum temperatures are 16 degrees Celsius (C) and 29 degrees C. The coldest month is January when the temperature varies between 12 degrees C and 23 degrees C. The driest month is February and the wettest June, when there is an average of 274mm of rainfall.

Dress codes
Guatemalans are generally conservative in dress. Tropical lightweight suits are the accepted dress in business circles in the capital. Extremes of fashion should be avoided.

Entry requirements
Passports
Required by all.
Visa
Visas are not required by most nationals of the Americas, EU, Australasia, and a few Asian countries, for between 1–3 months.
A business visa, requiring additional information to the visitor's visa, must be applied for before arrival. The application should include a company letter as proof of business intentions.
For further information and exceptions visit: www.guatemala-embassy.org/visas.asp.
Currency advice/regulations
No restrictions on import/export of foreign currency. There is free circulation of US dollars.

Health (for visitors)
Mandatory precautions
Cholera and yellow fever vaccination certificates are required from citizens of infected countries.
Advisable precautions
Malaria is prevalent in the low-lying areas outside the city, a prophylaxis is recommended. Dengue fever is endemic, although there is no preventive medication, mosquito repellent and clothing covering as much skin as possible should help. Inoculations are recommended against typhoid, hepatitis 'A' and 'B' typhoid and polio.
Guatemalan hospitals are reluctant to give medical treatment unless a patient has medical insurance, so evidence of insurance cover should be carried at all times. State-funded hospitals are regarded

as understaffed, ill-equipped and often unhygienic. Private clinics should be used where possible.

Bottled water should be used. Milk is often unpasteurised and should be boiled; avoid dairy products which are likely to have been made from unboiled milk. Only eat hot well-cooked meat and fish. Pork, salad and mayonnaise carry increased risk. Vegetables should be cooked and fruit peeled. There is a rabies risk.

Hotels
Most charge 10 per cent room tax.

Public holidays
Fixed dates
1 Jan (New Year's Day), 1 May (Labour Day), 30 Jun (Army Day), 15 Aug (Assumption Day (Guatemala City only)), 15 Sep (Independence Day), 20 Oct (Revolution Day), 1 Nov (All Saints' Day), 24 Dec (Christmas Eve, from mid-day), 25 Dec (Christmas Day), 31 Dec (New Year's Eve, from mid-day).
Variable dates
Good Friday

Working hours
Banking
Generally Mon–Fri: 0900–1500.
Business
Mon–Fri: 0800–1600. Private companies Mon–Fri: 0800–1200, 1400–1800.
Government
Mon–Fri: 0800–1600.
Shops
Shopping centres (Mon–Sun) 0900–2000.

Electricity supply
110V AC, 60 cycles

Social customs/useful tips
Customs and social mores tend to mirror those of Catholic Europe or the more conservative southern states of the United States. Punctuality is not one of most Guatemalans' strongest points, although Western propensity for good time keeping is recognised in their phrase 'English time'.

Security
Security in the capital has become much more of a problem in recent years as street crime and house break-ins have risen in the face of the growing socio-economic crisis. Armed mugging and gratuitous violence is now common and most companies have armed guards and watchmen.

Getting there
Air
National airline: Aerolíneas de Guatemala (Aviateca)
International airport/s: Guatemala City-Aurora (GUA), 6km from the city; duty-free shop, bar, buffet, restaurant, bank, hotel reservations, post office, shops, vaccination centre, car hire, tourist information and public telephones.
Airport tax: Passenger service charge for international departures US$30; not applicable to 24 hour transit passengers.
Surface
Road: The Pan-American Highway runs through the country from Mexico to El Salvador, stretching 511km. There are other roads from El Salvador, Honduras and Mexico and there is a route via Melchor de Mencos from Belize. Plans for any journey should be made in the light of current political and, in certain cases, road conditions.
Rail: It is possible to use scheduled train services but some of these are often subject to suspension.
Main port/s: Champerico, Puerto Barrios, San José, Santo Tomás de Castilla and the Quetzal Port.

Getting about
National transport
Air: Aviateca operates domestic service to major centres. Schedules are liable to change at short notice.
Road: Total network 13,238km, only 26 per cent of which is paved; using unpaved roads can be difficult. Paved roads are of fair quality.
Buses: Bus services connect major towns.
City transport
Taxis: There is a good taxi service in Guatemala City. Fares are generally negotiated but there are set rates for journeys from the airport to certain destinations. Tipping (5–10 per cent) is discretionary.
Buses, trams & metro: Numerous services within Guatemala City – said to be (outside usual rush hours) less crowded than some cities.
Car hire
Any valid licence is usually acceptable. Many of the international rental agencies have offices both at La Aurora airport and in Guatemala City centre.

BUSINESS DIRECTORY
The addresses listed below are a selection only. While World of Information makes every endeavour to check these addresses, we cannot guarantee that changes have not been made, especially to telephone numbers and area codes. We would welcome any corrections.

Telephone area codes
The international direct dialling code (IDD) for Guatemala is +502, followed by subscriber's number.

Chambers of Commerce
American Chamber of Commerce in Guatemala, Avenida las Americas 18-81, Zona 14, 01014 Guatemala City (tel: 363-1774; fax: 367-3414; e-mail: director@amchamguate.com).

Guatemala Chamber of Commerce, 10a Calle 3-80, Zona 1, 01001 Guatemala City (tel: 253-5353; fax: 220-9393; e-mail: info@camaradecomercio.org.gt).

Banking
Banco Nacional de Desarrollo Agrícola (BANDESA), 9 Calle 9-47, Zona 1, 01001 (tel: 535-222/9; fax: 537-927).

Banco Nacional de la Vivienda (BANVI), 6 Ave 1-22, Zona 4, 01004 (tel: 325-777/86).

Credito Hipotecario Nacional, 7 Ave 22-77, Zona 1, 01001 (tel: 500-112).

Banco de Occidente, 7 Ave 11-15, Zona 1, 01001 (tel: 531-333, 535-831; fax: 514-348).

Banco del Agro, 9 Calle 5-39, Zona 1, 01001 (tel: 514-026; fax: 300-322).

Banco del Café SA, Ave La Reforma 9-00, Zona 9, 01009 (tel: 311-311; fax: 311-1418).

Banco del Quetzal SA, Plaza El Robel, 7 Ave 6-26, Zona 9, 01009 (tel: 318-333; fax: 326-937).

Banco Granai & Townson SA, 7 Ave 1-86, Zona 4, 1004 (tel: 312-333/7; fax: 323-532).

Banco Industrial SA, 7 Ave 5-10, Zona 4, 01004 (tel: 312-323; fax: 319-437).

Citibank, Ave La Reforma 15-45, Zona 10, 01010 (tel: 336-574; fax: 336-860).

Lloyds Bank International, 6 Ave 9-51, Zona 9, 01009 (tel: 327-580/9; fax: 327-641).

Central bank
Banco de Guatemala, 7 Avenida 22-01, Zona 1, PO Box 365, 01001 Guatemala City (tel: 230-6222; fax: 253-4035; e-mail: webmaster@banguat.gob.gt).

Travel information
Asociación Guatemalteca de Agentes de Viajes (AGAV) (Guatemalan Association of Travel Agents), 6a Avenida 8-41, Zona 9, Apdo 2735, Guatemala City (tel: 310-320).

Aviateca-Aerolíneas de Guatemala, Avenida Hincapié 12-22, Aeropuerto La Aurora, Zona 13, Guatemala City (tel: 318-261, 318-222; fax: 347-846, 317-401).

Ministry of tourism
INGUAT (Instituto Guatemalteco de Turismo), 7A Avenida 1-17, Zona 4, Guatemala City (tel: 311-333; fax: 322-881).

National tourist organisation offices
Instituto Guatemalteco de Turismo (INGUAT) (Guatemalan Tourism Institute), 7a avenida 1-17, Zona 4, Centro Civico 01004, Guatemala City (tel: 331-1333;

Guatemala

fax: 331-8893; e-mail: inguat@guate.net).

Ministries

Ministry of Agriculture, Livestock and Food, Avenida Reforma 4-47, Zona 10, Guatemala City (tel: 253-6816/07; fax: 332-9995).

Ministry of Communications, Transport and Public Works, Avenida Reforma 4-47, Zona 10, Guatemala City (tel: 362-6051; fax: 362-6059).

Ministry of Culture and Sport, 5 Calle 4-33, Zona 1, Plaza Rabi, Guatemala City (tel: 230-1750/55/57; fax: 230-1754).

Ministry of Defence, Avenida Reforma 4-47, Zona 10, Guatemala City (tel: 221-4444, 360-9907; fax: 360-9909).

Ministry of Economy, 8 Avenida 10-43, Zona 1, Guatemala City (tel: 238-3331/2/3; fax: 251-5055).

Ministry of Education, Avenida Reforma 4-47, Zona 10, Guatemala City (tel: 221-4428).

Ministry of Employment and Social Security, 14 Calle 5-49, Zona 1, Edificio Nasa, Guatemala City (tel: 230-5592/4; fax: 251-3559).

Ministry of Energy and Mines, Diagonal 17, 29-78, Zona 11, Guatemala City (tel: 477-0382, 476-0680).

Ministry of Finance, Entre 8 Avenida y 21 calle, Zona 1, Centro Civico, Guatemala City (tel: 230-5180, 230-5202; fax: 251-6514).

Ministry of Foreign Affairs, Avenida Reforma 4-47, Zona 10, Guatemala City (tel: 331-8699, 331-9387, 332-1110).

Ministry of Health and Social Assistance, Avenida Reforma 4-47, Zona 10, Guatemala City (tel: 232-4509, 38 0258).

Ministry of the Interior, Avenida Reforma 4-47, Zona 10, Guatemala City (tel: 221-4444).

Other useful addresses

Agroindustrias de Exportación, 14 Calle 7-46, Zona 10, Guatemala City (tel: 336-052; fax: 335-277).

Asociación de Gerentes de Guatemala, 10a Calle 3-17, Zona 10, Edificio Aseguradora General, Nivel 70, Apartado Postal 2373, Guatemala City, 01010 (tel: 311-564, 311-664, 312-869; fax: 311-646).

Bolsa Agrícola Nacional, 4a Calle 6-55, Zona 9, Guatemala City (tel: 342-479; fax: 314-509).

Bolsa de Valores Global, Av La Reforma 9-76, Zona 9, Edificio SCI Centre, Nivel 70, Guatemala City, 01009 (tel: 314-115; fax: 326-121).

Bolsa de Valores Nacional, SA, 7a Av 5-10, Zona 4, Centro Financiero, Torre II, Nivel 20, Guatemala City, 01004 (tel: 311-752; fax: 315-542).

British Embassy, 7 Av 5-10, Zone 4, Edificio Centro Financiero, Torre II, Nivel 7, Guatemala City (tel: 321-601; fax: 341-904).

Centro de Investigaciones Económicas Nacionales (CIEN), 5 Av 15-45, Zona 10, Centro Empresarial, Torre 1, Of 302, Apartado Postal 260-C, Guatemala City (tel: 337-022; fax: 337-124).

Centro Nacional de Promoción de las Exportaciones, 6A Avenida Torre Profesional, Zona 14, Apdo 1237, Guatemala City.

Comité Co-ordinador de Asociaciones Agrícolas, Comerciales, Industriales y Financieras (CACIF), Ruta 6 9-21, Zona 4, Nivel 90, Guatemala City (tel: 310-651, 321-794; fax: 347-025).

Coperex (international marketing fair), 8 Calle 2-33, Zona 9, Parque de la Industria, Guatemala City (tel: 310-388/9; fax: 316-053).

Dirección General de Radiodifusión y Televisión Nacional, 5a Avenida Zona 1, Guatemala City (tel: 25-045).

Empresa Eléctrica de Guatemala (EEGSA), 8a Calle y 6a Avenida Esquina, Zona 1, Guatemala City (tel: 518-777).

Empresa Municipal de Agua (Empagua), 7a Avenida 1-20, Zona 4, Edificio Torre Café, Nivel 16, Guatemala City (tel: 315-164, 315-173; fax: 325-444).

Fundación para el Desarrollo de Guatemala (FUNDESA), Parque Gerencial Las Margaritas, Diagonal 6, 10-65, Zona 10, Of 402, Guatemala City (tel: 327-952, 327-957; fax: 327-958).

Guatemala–US Trade Association (GUSTA), 299 Alhambra Circle, Suite 207, Coral Gables, Florida 33134, USA (tel: (305)443-0343; fax: (305)433-0699).

Guatemalan Embassy (USA), 2220 R Street, NW, Washington DC 20008 (tel: 202-745-4952; fax: 202-745-1908; e-mail: info@guatemala-embassy.org).

Inforpress Centroamericana, 9a Calle A 3-56, Guatemala City 01001 (tel: 29-432; fax: 283-859).

Inguat, 7a Avenida 1-17, Zona 4, Guatemala City (tel: 311-333/9; fax: 318-893).

Instituto Centroamericano de Investigación y Tecnología Industrial (ICAITI), Avenida La Reforma 4-47, Zona 10, Guatemala City (tel: 340-213).

Instituto Nacional de Electrificación (INDE), 7a Avenida 2-29, Zona 9, Guatemala City (tel: 345-706, 345-711; fax: 345-811).

International Investment Securities Corporation, Edificio Galerías Reforma 8-60, Zona 9, Torre 1, Nivel 90, Guatemala City (tel: 324-432, 347-005; fax: 347-595).

Telgua (Empresa de Telecomunicaciones de Guatemala), 5 Calle Avenida Reforma, Zona 9, Guatemala City (tel: 331-8999/6599, 230-1050).

United States Department of Commerce, Guatemala Desk, Department of Commerce H3025, Washington DC 20230, USA (tel: (202)377-2627; fax: (202)377-3718).

US Embassy, Avenida La Reforma 7-01, Zona 10, Guatemala City (tel: 311-541; fax: 318-885).

Internet sites

Guatemalan portals:
http://mi-guatemala.tripod.com

Http://www.elcafecito.com/Zonas_geograficas/Paises/Guatemala

Business information:
http://www.tradepoint.org.gt

Guinea

KEY FACTS

Official name: République de Guinée (Republic of Guinea)

Head of State: President General Lansana Conté (PUP) (since 1984; re-elected 21 Dec 2003)

Head of government: Prime Minister Cellou Dalein Diallo (from 9 Dec 2004)

Ruling party: Parti de l'Unité et du Progrès (PUP) (Party of Unity and Progress) (since 1995; re-elected 30 Jun 2002)

Area: 245,857 square km

Population: 8.47 million (2004)

Capital: Conakry

Official language: French

Currency: Guinean franc (Gf)

Exchange rate: Gf4,025.00 per US$ (Oct 2005)

GDP per capita: US$403 (2003)

GDP real growth: 1.20% (2004)

Labour force: 4.00 million (2004)

Inflation: 17.50% (2004)

Balance of trade: US$37.20 million (2004)

Foreign debt: US$3.40 billion (2003)

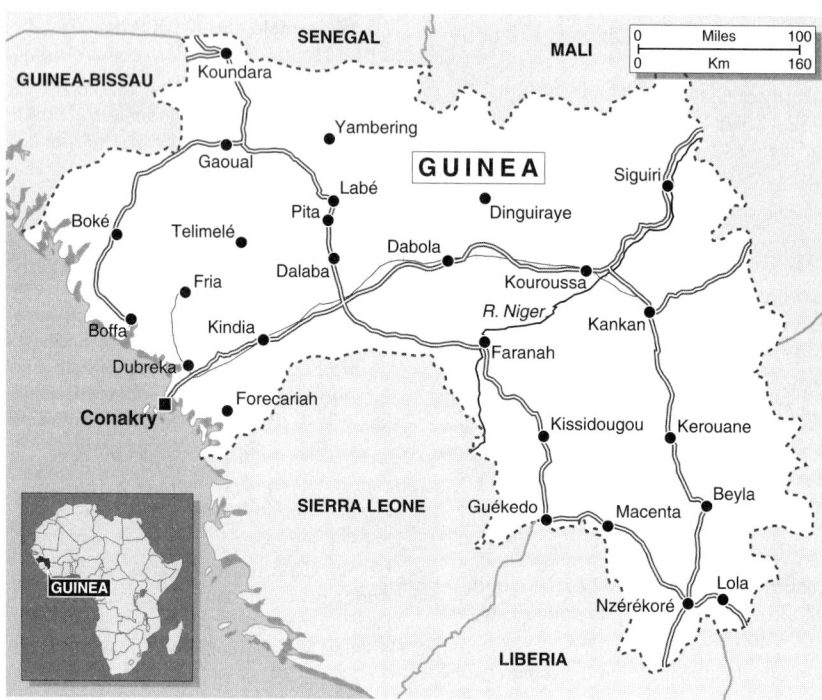

Guinea severed ties with France after independence in 1958 and turned to the Soviet Union. The first president, Ahmed Sekou Touré, pursued a revolutionary socialist agenda and crushed political opposition. Tens of thousands of people disappeared, or were tortured and executed, during his 26-year regime.

Economic mismanagement and repression culminated in riots in 1977. These led to some relaxation of state control of the economy. But it was only after the death in 1984 of Touré, and the seizure of power by Lansana Conte and other officers, that the socialist experiment was abandoned.

Although Guinea's mineral wealth makes it potentially one of Africa's richest countries, its people are among the poorest in West Africa. Acute economic problems, instability among its neighbours and uncertainty over a successor to its authoritarian president have prompted a European think-tank, the International Crisis Group, to warn that Guinea risks becoming a 'failed state'.

Economy

Guinea's economic situation has been characterised by weak economic growth and a sharp increase in inflation. In an unfavorable environment marked by on-going tensions in neighbouring countries, recurring electricity and water outages and interruptions to cement supplies, macroeconomic management proved to be inadequate and macroeconomic imbalances worsened.

The whole Gulf of Guinea region's tremendous potential is creating investment opportunities for the area from Gabon in the east to Guinea-Bissau in the west. Some of its resources, such as oil, minerals and forests, continue to attract significant investments whereas others, like natural gas, could be exploited to their full potential if necessary investments were undertaken. Nevertheless, the Gulf of Guinea has to cope with numerous challenges, both exogenous and endogenous, before it can fully benefit from its riches. One of these problems stems from the overwhelmingly weak institutions and governance, which add to the risks of 'natural resource curse' and can feed the theory of the 'Paradox of Plenty'.

Over 2006, the government of Guinea intends to implement an economic and financial programme to support assistance from the International Monetary Fund (IMF). The government has begun to implement tighter monetary and fiscal measures and the structural measures necessary to accelerate growth. The exchange rate regime has been liberalised.

Into 2006, the government's goal is to restore macroeconomic stability. Real GDP growth is expected to be a modest three per cent. Monetary policy will be targeted at reducing the inflation rate to slightly below 20 per cent on a year-on-year basis. The external current account deficit, excluding official transfers, should be approximately three per cent of GDP.

A primary objective is to increase the collection of domestic revenues by 1.7 per cent of GDP and to cut government expenditures by 2.7 per cent of GDP. This will make it possible to achieve a primary surplus of approximately three per cent of GDP, 3.5 percentage points better than in 2004, to limit the overall deficit (commitment basis, excluding grants) to 1.7 per cent of GDP.

Mining revenues should reach the equivalent of 3.1 per cent of GDP, based on an expected increase in volumes extracted and prices obtained. Non-mining revenue is expected to increase by about 0.4 per cent of GDP.

Primary current expenditure will be contained at 7.4 per cent of GDP by controlling non-priority spending, particularly transfers to the defence sector and expenditure involving missions abroad.

A budget deficit financing structure promotes auctions of treasury bills over direct financing by the central bank. The programme also calls for negative non-bank financing in order to gradually eliminate the government's domestic debt. Foreign borrowing will be limited to concessional financing only. Budget financing gaps are expected to be covered by assistance from development partners.

Structural reforms and privatisation

The government will pursue structural reforms to improve the quality and availability of public services and create an environment more conducive to sustainable growth, particularly by promoting the private sector. The supply of electricity and water and the telecommunications network will be improved, there will be focus on the restructuring and privatisation of public enterprises, fighting corruption, and improving the justice system.

The government has decided to revitalise its public enterprise privatisation programme to enable the private sector to participate more fully in the economic and social development of the country. First, the government will sell a portion or all of its holdings in seven companies: Banque Internationale pour le Commerce et l'Industrie de Guinée (BICIGUI), Banque Populaire Maroco-Guinéenne (BPMG), Union Générale des Assurances et Réassurances (UGAR), Société Mixte de Carburants Aéronautiques de Guinée (SOMCAG), Société Guinéo-Russe de Carrières Minières (SOGUIRUSSE), Société de Production d'Allumettes de Guinée (SOPRAG), and Société de Production Chimique (SOPROCHIM). It will also sell the assets of three enterprises: Société Mixte de Dragage (SOMIDRAT), a commercial enterprise (DIVERMA) and the movie theatres (ONACIG). The privatisation effort will be continued through to 2008 with the planned privatisation of some 20 enterprises. A third lot of 10 enterprises, primarily in the mining sectors, will be privatised after 2008.

Politics

President Lansana Conté seized power in a bloodless coup in 1984 and has ruled with an iron fist ever since. In 2003 he won a third term in a poll which was boycotted by the opposition. Voters in a referendum had backed the removal of a two-term limit which would have forced him to retire. Critics said the move was a constitutional coup which would ensure that he remained president for life.

Conté says he was born in the 1930s. After serving in the French army he returned home and became chief of staff in 1975. He seized power after President Sekou Touré's death in 1984, suspended the constitution, freed political prisoners and encouraged exiles to return. By 1992 he had organised a return to civilian rule, proceeding to win a presidential poll in 1993 and parliamentary elections in 1995.

Critics say he has lost popularity and has become increasingly isolated. Supporters say he has won a war against dissidents. Conté, who is a diabetic and a chain smoker, rarely makes public appearances. There is no obvious successor to the ailing leader.

Ruled by strong-arm leaders since independence, Guinea has been seen as a bulwark against instability in neighbouring Liberia, Sierra Leone and Côte d'Ivoire. However it has also been implicated in the conflicts that have ravaged the region.

Risk assessment

Economic	Unsatisfactory
Political	Unsatisfactory
Regional stability	Fair

COUNTRY PROFILE

Historical profile

Abandoned to its fate by France when it opted for immediate independence in 1958, Guinea struggled to sustain a revolutionary approach to independence. It remained isolated – even from its West African neighbours – for decades while its rulers sought to establish some form of

KEY INDICATORS — Guinea

	Unit	2000	2001	2002	2003	2004
Population	m	8.15	8.15	8.34	8.40	8.47
Gross domestic product (GDP)	US$bn	3.10	3.00	3.20	3.47	*3.51
GDP per capita	US$	380	368	385	413	403
GDP real growth	%	2.0	3.6	4.2	3.6	1.2
Inflation	%	6.8	5.4	3.0	12.9	17.5
Exports (fob) (goods)	US$m	695.0	731.0	886.0	835.0	725.6
Imports (fob) (goods)	US$m	555.0	562.0	668.4	670.0	688.4
Balance of trade	US$m	140.0	169.0	217.7	165.0	37.2
Current account	US$m	-201.0	-80.0	-140.0	-120.0	-190.0
Total reserves minus gold	US$m	147.9	200.2	171.4	–	–
Foreign exchange	US$m	147.6	199.3	169.6	–	–
Exchange rate	per US$	1,746.90	1,950.60	1,975.80	1,995.00	2,405.00

* estimated figure

representative democracy that worked in the African context. Nor has the ideological path followed by Guinea since independence been well received by its citizens, who only needed to look at neighbouring countries such as Senegal to see the more immediate and tangible attractions of *laissez-faire* capitalism.
From the thirteenth to fifteenth centuries Guinea was part of the Mali empire which covered a large part of West Africa.
1450s The coastal region began to be settled by European traders.
1849 The French declared the area around Boké a protectorate. France's influence grew as it took over most of the rest of the country calling it Rivières du Sud (rivers of the south),
1891 As French Guinea it was formally constituted a colony, separate from Senegal.
1956 In a referendum Guinea voted to opt out of the French Community.
1958 Guinea became independent under the leadership of Sekou Touré. France severed all financial and technical ties.
1960s Despite having the backing of the Soviet Union, Guinea expelled the Soviet ambassador for interference in internal matters. Guinea began to improve its relations with the West although it remained a non-aligned, Marxist, one-party state.
1977 Private trade had been banned until demonstrations by traders in the *market women's revolt*, led to a change in government policy.
1984 Touré died. In a bloodless coup, Colonel Lansana Conté became president and introduced IMF-backed austerity measures as well as a new currency, the Guinean franc, which replaced the syli.
1990 A new constitution was approved.
1993 Conté won the presidency in multi-party elections, which were marred by killings and alleged fraud.
1995 The Parti de l'Unité et du Progrès (PUP) (Party of Unity and Progress), led by President Conté, won the multi-party legislative elections.
1996 As much as a quarter of the army mutinied due largely to low pay.
1998 President Lansana Conté was re-elected.
1999 Lamine Sidime (PUP) was appointed prime minister.
2001 The government accused neighbouring Liberia and rebels from Sierra Leone of aiding its army mutineers and attempting to destabilise the country. The number of displaced peoples, locally and from abroad, grew. There were rebel attacks along the borders between Guinea and Liberia, and Sierra Leone. A constitutional referendum permitted Conté to retain the presidency and run for a third and extended term (from five to seven years).
2002 The ruling PUP won parliamentary elections, delayed by two years allegedly due to the fighting between Guinea and Sierra Leone, and Liberia.
2003 Incumbent Lansana Conté won the presidential elections. The National Assembly voted unanimously for an amnesty for those convicted of political crimes, allowing them to stand for positions in national politics.
2004 Cellou Dalein Diallol was named prime minister in December.
2005 The President escaped an assassination attempt when shots were fired at his motorcade in the capital, Conakry.

Political structure
Constitution
The constitution was promulgated in 1990. In 2001 a constitutional amendment revised the length of the presidential term from five years to seven, with no legal limit to the number of terms a president may sit.
Form of state
Republic
The executive
Prior to the constitutional amendments, made in 2001, the president was elected for a five-year term, renewable only once. Following the changes, the mandate increased to a seven-year term with no legal limit as to the number of times that it could be renewed.
The prime minister and the Council of Ministers are appointed by the president.
National legislature
The unicameral Assemblée Nationale Populaire (People's National Assembly) has 114 deputies serving five-year terms.
Legal system
The legal system is based on French civil law, customary law and decree.
Last elections
21 December 2003 (presidential); 30 June 2002 (parliamentary) (originally scheduled for November 2000).
Results: Presidential: incumbent Lansana Conté won 95.6 per cent of the vote and Mamadou Bhoye Barry 4.4 per cent; turnout was 82.8 per cent.
Parliamentary: the ruling Parti de l'Unité et du Progrès (PUP) (Party of Unity and Progress) won 61.5 per cent of the vote; Union pour le Progrès et le Renouveau (UPR) (Union for Progress and Renewal) 21.7 per cent; the opposition boycotted the election; the turnout was low.
Next elections
2010 (presidential)

Political parties
Political parties were legalised from April 1992.
Ruling party
Parti de l'Unité et du Progrès (PUP) (Party of Unity and Progress) (since 1995; re-elected 30 Jun 2002)

Main opposition party
Rassemblement du Peuple Guinéen (RPG) (Rally of the Guinean People).

Population
8.47 million (2004)
Ethnic make-up
Fulani (35 per cent), Malinke (30 per cent), Soussou (20 per cent).
Religions
Islam (85 per cent), a small number of Roman Catholics (8 per cent) and traditional beliefs (7 per cent).

Education
Guinea shows an upward trend in gross enrolment rate with increasing demand for teachers, school facilities, and other resources. The government has initiated the third phase of the project Basic Education for All (2001–2012) focussing on increased access, improved quality and efficiency through decentralisation processes. Despite significant urban/rural and gender disparities in enrolment ratios, there is overall improvement. The crisis in teacher supply persists despite the World Bank and the government's intensive teacher-training programme (FIMG), which had planned recruitment of approximately 6,000 teachers for the entire 1998-2001 period.
Government expenditure on education is about 25–26 per cent of the total national budget.
Enrolment rate: 45.2 per cent net enrolment in primary; 11.9 per cent net enrolment in secondary schooling (World Bank).
In rural areas the enrolment rate for girls remains at only 26 per cent.
Pupils per teacher: 49 in primary schools.

Health
Total expenditure on health is around 3.5 per cent of GDP, of which government spending is about 54 per cent.
Improved water sources and sanitation facilities are available to 48 per cent and 58 per cent of the population, respectively.
In August 2004 epidemeiologists of the Global Polio Eradication Initiative announced that new cases of polio had been confirmed in Guinea. The infection is believed to have spread from Northern Nigeria.
HIV/Aids
HIV/Aids infection is currently concentrated in urban areas. Overall 2.8 per cent of pregnant women, 42 per cent of sex workers and 2.5 per cent of young adults (aged 15–24) are HIV positive. With governmental initiatives and local education, it is hoped to avert a potential pandemic if the rates in rural areas follow the urban trend.

Guinea

HIV prevalence: 3.2 per cent aged 15–49 in 2003 (World Bank)
Life expectancy: 46.2 years (World Bank)
Fertility rate/Maternal mortality rate: 5.0 births per woman; maternal mortality 620 per 100,000 live births (World Bank).
Infant mortality rate: 109 per 1,000 live births; 23 per cent of children under aged five are malnourished (World Bank).
Head of population per physician/bed: 0.1 physicians and 0.6 hospital beds per 1,000 people.

Welfare

Guinea's social insurance system provides coverage for unemployed people, pensions, old-age benefits and survivor benefits (payable to widows, orphans and dependant relatives). Old age pensions are applicable to all those aged 55 and over. The system also provides sickness and maternity benefits as well as allowance for those families with children under the age of 17.

Main cities

Conakry (capital, estimated population 1.9 million in 2004), Nzérékoré (120,100), Kankan (112,200), Kindia (106,300).

Languages spoken

African languages are in daily use. English is seldom used.
Official language/s
French

Media

Press
Weeklies: Most newspapers in circulation are weeklies including *3P-Plus*, *La Lance*, *Le Lynx*, *Horoya* and *L'Indépendent*.
Broadcasting
Television and radio programmes in French, English, Arabic, Portuguese and local languages. Services operated by Radiodiffusion-Télévision Guinéenne (RTG) from Conakry and carry advertising.

Economy

Rich in minerals and fertile land, Guinea is a potentially wealthy country, but remains one of Africa's more underdeveloped economies.
Armed dissident activities and poor resource management have adversely affected the business environment in Guinea. The country possesses major mineral, hydropower and agricultural resources. It possesses over 30 per cent of the world's bauxite reserves and is the second largest bauxite producer.
Efforts to improve economic management under the terms of an IMF Poverty Reduction and Growth Facility (PRGF), which ran from May 2001 to May 2004, were only partially successful. The IMF suspended the PRGF in December 2002 because of the failure to meet key performance criteria. While there had been some growth in 2002, the economic situation deteriorated in 2003 with weakening GDP growth and rising inflation, which continued through 2004 and into 2005. Expenditure cuts frequently targeted non-defence expenditure, undermining the government's ability to reach its poverty alleviation targets. Continuing border security problems and political uncertainty have added to the government's difficulties. Further efforts to establish control of the econmy with tighter policies and reforms are being made in renewed co-operation with the IMF.
The situation is partly offset by donor support and debt relief.
Despite liberalising the investment environment, Guinea is still dependent on primary commodities and lacks the capital and infrastructure to diversify the country's export markets as well as provide for the domestic market. Moreover, the country's dependence on the export of bauxite and other minerals means the economy is highly vulnerable to fluctuations in global commodity prices, creating potential problems for sustainable economic development in the future.

External trade

Bauxite and alumina are Guinea's main export earners. Although diamond exports are rising, the balance of payments situation is precarious, despite large volumes of concessional assistance from the World Bank, IMF and foreign aid donors. Guinea does not belong to the West African Monetary Union (franc zone).
Guinea is eligible for tariff preferences under the African Growth and Opportunities Act (AGOA). The legislation requires that countries are only eligible for greater access to US markets provided they have made continued progress toward a market-based economy, the rule of law, free trade, poverty reduction and the protection of workers' rights. This process is reviewed annually.

Imports
Principal imports are petroleum products, metals, machinery, transport equipment, textiles, grain and other foodstuffs.
Main sources: France (14.6 per cent total, 2004), China (9.6 per cent), The Netherlands (6.8 per cent), Belgium (6.0 per cent), US (5.9 per cent), Italy (5.0 per cent), South Africa (4.6 per cent), Côte d'Ivoire (4.3 per cent), India (4.0 per cent)

Exports
Exports are dominated by bauxite and alumina (up to 90 per cent of total), gold, diamonds, coffee, fish, fresh fruit and vegetables.
Main destinations: South Korea (15.6 per cent total, 2004), Russia (13.1 per cent), Spain (12.3 per cent), Ireland (9.1 per cent), US (7.5 per cent), Germany (6.2 per cent), France (5.9 per cent), Ukraine (5.6 per cent), Belgium (5.2 per cent)

Agriculture

Farming
Traditional farming generates around 23 per cent of GDP and around 67 per cent of the population is engaged in subsistence farming.
Only 7 per cent of land is cultivated, although there is considerable potential for development.
Main cash crops are sugar cane, groundnuts, oil palm, cotton, citrus fruits and coffee. Main subsistence crops are rice (60 per cent of cultivated land), cassava, maize and vegetables.
Output has stagnated due to transport problems, low levels of mechanisation, poor marketing and a lack of vital inputs. Although infrastructural projects have rectified some problems, the country is in need of further investment to improve roads linking agricultural areas to domestic and foreign markets.
The fishing, forestry and livestock sectors are small. There is potential for lucrative fishing but the fishing fleet suffers from lack of funds.
The crop production in 2004 included: 1,142,000 tonnes (t) cereals in total, 900,000t rice, *90,000t maize, 1,350,000t cassava, 135,000T fonio, 60,000t sweet potatoes, 30,000t taro, *6,000t sorghum, *430,000t plantains, 150,000t bananas, *60,000t pulses, 1.3t roots and tubers, *210,000t citrus fruit, 169,877t oilcrops, 107,000t pineapples, *1,800t tobacco, *20,500t green coffee, 2,500t cocoa beans, 22,500t coconuts, 164,000t mangoes, 280,000t sugar cane, 40,000t yams, *830,000t oil palm fruit, 40,000t seed cotton, *15,000t cotton lint, 3,360t natural rubber, 1,106,000t fruit in total, 482,200t vegetables in total. Livestock production included: 56,017t meat in total, *35,483t beef, *1,911t pig meat, 4,276t lamb, 5,647t goat meat, *4,000t game meat, 4,700t poultry, 17,325t eggs, 91,500t milk, *600t honey, *6,262t cattle hides, 731t sheepskins.
* estimate

Forestry
The value of exports in 2004 amounted to US$6 million, while imports amounted to US$4.5 million.
The estimated production for 2004 included: 12.1 million cubic metres (cum) roundwood, 26,000cum sawnwood, 138,000cum sawlogs and veneers, 11.6 million cum woodfuel, 304,007t charcoal.

Industry and manufacturing
The industrial sector contributes around 4 per cent to GDP and employs 5 per cent of the workforce.

Apart from aluminium smelting, it is small-scale and designed to meet local requirements. Aluminium smelting from locally mined bauxite is being modernised with French aid.

The other main industries, textiles, food processing and plywood, are handicapped by supply bottlenecks and shortages of skilled labour.

The investment code and economic liberalisation are expected to attract more foreign capital.

Tourism
Tourism is undeveloped, lacking appropriate infrastructure and attracting only small numbers of visitors. The potential importance of the sector is recognised by the authorities who plan to develop it. Tourism is expected to contribute 5.7 per cent to GDP in 2005.

Mining
Mining is the most dynamic sector of the economy, accounting for around 30 per cent of GDP and almost all export earnings. Eight per cent of the workforce is employed in the sector. A mining code introduced in 1995 renewed foreign interest in the mining sector, offering a range of guarantees and tax incentives to foreign investors, who may own up to 85 per cent of any venture.

Bauxite accounts for around 20 per cent of GDP and around 90 per cent of exports. 650,000 tonnes of alumina are produced from the country's single refinery at Fria. The largest bauxite producer is the Sangarédi mine, operated by Compagnie des Bauxites de Guinée (CBG), a joint venture between the government and Halco. CBG has an annual production capacity of 14 million tonnes. Guinea is rich in uranium, titanium, copper, manganese, iron ore, gold and diamonds.

Diamond reserves are estimated at 40 million carats (93 per cent gem quality). The Aredor diamond mine, near Banankore, is 50 per cent owned by the government and 50 per cent by a consortium led by Bridge Oil of Australia and produces around 25,000 carats per year. Diamond mining capacity in Guinea is far lower than recorded exports. It is thought that many gems exported from Guinea have been smuggled from neighbouring countries into Guinea.

Key sites of precious stones include Siguiri, Mandiana, Dinguiraye, Kissidougou and Kérouané, and along the rivers of Baoulé, Milo and Diani.

Hydrocarbons
Oil is not produced in Guinea, but exploration for offshore petroleum is under way. Partners Houston's SCS Corp and US Oil Corp have obtained exclusive rights for exploration of offshore Guinea. Guinea relies on imports of refined oil products, importing 8,300 barrels per day.

Guinea does not produce or import natural gas or coal.

Energy
There is considerable potential for hydropower from several large rivers, as yet untapped.

The country imports oil to run power stations.

The Garafiri Dam, with power production capacity of 75MW, was built by France at a cost of US$211 million.

Banking and insurance
It was announced in March 2005 that the introduction of the shared currency, the Eco, in Guinea, Ghana, Nigeria, Sierra Leone and The Gambia, which was due in July 2005, would be postponed. The currency was proposed to facilitate trade and growth with an ultimate plan to merge it with the CFA franc.

Central bank
Banque Centrale de la République de Guinée

Main financial centre
Conakry

Time
GMT

Geography
Guinea lies on the west coast of Africa, with Sierra Leone and Liberia to the south, Senegal to the north, and Mali and Côte d'Ivoire inland to the east.

Climate
The climate is tropical and humid. South: rainy season falls in June–October, rainfall is particularly heavy in Conakry, average temperature range from 22–30 degrees Celsius (C). The dry season is from November–April, likely temperature range 24–35 degrees C. The north is generally cooler and drier.

Entry requirements
Passports
Required by all.

Visa
Required by all except nationals of some African countries. Before departure, visitors must have their return or onward tickets and visa certified by the Department de la Régulation Aérienne et Maritime. Business visas, applied for before arrival, should included a business letter with a full itenerary, and an invitation from a local company or organisation. Contact the nearest embassy for further details.

Currency advice/regulations
No restrictions on foreign currency and traveller's cheques. Exact amount should be declared on entry and declaration form produced on departure. The import and export of local currency is strictly forbidden.

Health (for visitors)
Mandatory precautions
Yellow fever vaccination certificate.

Advisable precautions
Typhoid and polio vaccinations. Malaria prophylaxis essential as risk exists throughout the country. Water precautions should be taken.

Hotels
Limited first-class accommodation available in Conakry and Kankan; good hotels are expensive. Hotel bills may be paid in foreign currency or by credit card. A service charge is usually included in the bill. Tipping is optional.

Public holidays
Fixed dates
1 Jan (New Year's Day), 1 May (Labour Day), 15 Aug (Assumption Day), 27 Aug (Anniversary of Women's Revolt), 28 Sep (Referendum Day), 2 Oct (Republic Day), 1 Nov (All Saints' Day), 25 Dec (Christmas Day).

Variable dates
Easter Monday, Eid al Adha, Birth of the Prophet, Ascension Day, Day after the Night's Vigil (Nov), Eid al Fitr.

The Islamic year contains 354 or 355 days, with the result that Muslim feasts advance by 10–12 days against the Gregorian calendar. Dates of feasts vary according to the sighting of the new moon, so cannot be forecast exactly. Islamic year 1426: 10 February 2005 to 30 January 2006.

Working hours
Banking
Mon–Sat: 0800–1300.

Business
Mon–Thu: 0800–1500; Fri: 0800–1300; Sat: 0800–1500.

Government
Mon–Thu: 0800–1500; Fri: 0800–1300; Sat: 0800–1500.

Electricity supply
220V AC, 50 cycles

Social customs/useful tips
Showing respect for people will enhance your regard. Always greet people and never go straight into conversation without pleasantries beforehand. It is considered polite to use people's titles.

Security
There is a risk of kidnapping in border areas.

Always carry an identity card or passport, if stopped you are obliged to show ID. Pickpocketing, muggings and armed break-ins occur in the city; avoid carrying valuables in public and remain vigilant. There are numerous confidence tricksters typically attempting to dupe foreigners into buying precious gems, gold and counterfeit goods.

Getting there
Air
National airline: Air Guinée
International airport/s: Conakry (Code: CKY), 13km from city, restaurant, bank, post office. Taxis are available to and from the city.
Airport tax: Domestic departures Gf3,000; international departures (destinations in Africa) US$20; international departures (non-African destinations) US$25; not applicable to transit passengers.
Surface
Road: Best route is the coastal road from Sierra Leone (Freetown) to Conakry. Roads from Ganta (Liberia) to N'zérékoré and from Mali (to Kankan and Siguiri) can be difficult.

Getting about
National transport
Air: Air Guinée operates regular domestic service between Conakry, Boké, Kankan, Kissidougou, Labé, Macenta, N'zérékoré, Siguiri.
Road: A few main roads are surfaced, eg from Conakry north to Kindia and Kissidougou, and parts of the road east to Freetown in Sierra Leone. Most roads are laterite and become impassable during the rainy season (May–Oct).
Buses: Coach services include Conakry-Kindia-Gaoual and Dabola-N'zérékoré.
Rail: Narrow-gauge railway from Conakry to Kindia and Kankan, which is in poor condition.
City transport
Taxis: Available in Conakry, limited availability elsewhere; can be hired from hotels by the hour or day. Standard fares apply within towns, but for longer journeys fares should be agreed in advance. Tipping is optional.
Car hire
International and national driving licence required. Driving outside city limits with chauffeur and special authorisation only.

BUSINESS DIRECTORY
The addresses listed below are a selection only. While World of Information makes every endeavour to check these addresses, we cannot guarantee that changes have not been made, especially to telephone numbers and area codes. We would welcome any corrections.

Telephone area codes
The international dialling code (IDD) for Guinea is + 224, followed by subscriber's number.

Chambers of Commerce
Guinea Chamber of Commerce, Industry and Handicrafts, PO Box 545, Conakry (tel: 454-216; fax: 452-951; e-mail: cciag@sotelgui.net.gn).

Banking
Banque Internationale pour le Commerce et l'Industrie de la Guinée SA; PO Box 1484, Avenue de la République, Conakry (tel: 414-515; fax: 413-962).

Banque Islamique de Guinee; PO Box 1247, 6è Avenue de la Republique, Conakry (tel: 415-086, 412-108; fax: 415-071).

Banque Populaire Maroco-Guineenne; PO Box 4400, Avenue de la Republique, Conakry (tel: 411-599, 419-0206, 412-360; fax: 413-261).

Ecobank - Guinee; PO Box 5687, Avenue de la Republique, Conakry (tel: 453-423; fax: 454-241).

International Commercial Bank; PO Box 3574, 4è Avenue Boulbinet, Conakry (tel: 412-590–592; fax: 415-450).

Société Générale de Banques en Guinée; PO Box 1514, Avenue de la République, Conakry (tel: 411-741, 411-746, 412-558; fax: 412-565).

Union Internationale de Banque en Guinée UIBG; PO Box 324, Angle 5è Boulevard, 6è Avenue de la République, Conakry (tel: 412-096, 414-309).

Central bank
Banque Centrale de la République de Guinée; PO Box 692, 3 Boulevard du Commerce, Conakry (tel: 412-651; fax: 414-898).

Travel information
Air Guinée (Compagnie Nationale Air Guinée), Route du Niger, BP 12, 12 Côte Commissariat Central, Conakry (tel: 444-602, 442-981 for reservations, 461-537 for airport, 444-614 for office).

Guinea Airlines, BP 3222, Conakry (tel: 443-246; fax: 412-491).

Other useful addresses
Agence Guinéenne de Presse, BP 191, Conakry.

Bureau Veritas, BP 1451, Conakry (tel: 441-841, 442-202; fax: 412-112).

Chambre Economique de Guinée, BP 609, Conakry.

Comité d'Etat pour la Co-opération avec l'Europe Occidentale, Conakry.

Direction Nationale des Marchés Publics et du Portefeuille de l'Etat (privatisation office), La Division du Portefeuille du Ministère des Finances, avenue de la République, face á l'hôpital Ignace DEEN, BP 2006, Conakry (tel: 413-957; fax: 414-220).

ENTRAT (state forwarding firm), BP 315, Conakry.

Entreprise Nationale Import–Export (Importex), BP 152, Conakry (tel: 442-813, 442-809).

French Commercial Department, Ambassade de France, BP 373, Conakry (411-605, 411-655; fax: 412-708).

Guinea Embassy (US), 2112 Leroy Place, NW, Washington DC 20008 (tel: 202-483-9420; fax: 202-483-8688; e-mail: emgui@sysnet.net).

Office National des Hydrocarbures (Onah), Conakry.

L'Office de Promotion des Investissement Privés – Guichet Unique (OPIP) (assistance for foreign investors), BP 2024, Conakry (tel: 451-830, 414-985; fax: 413-990; e-mail: dg@opip.org.gn).

Port Autonome, BP 805, Conakry (tel: 442-728, 442-737; fax: 414-564).

Radio-Télévision Guinéenne (RTG), BP 391, Conakry.

Statistical Office, Bureau du Premier Ministre, Conakry (tel: 442-148).

Internet sites
Africa Business Network: http://www.ifc.org/abn

AllAfrica.com: http://allafrica.com

African Development Bank: http://www.afdb.org

Africa Online: http://www.africaonline.com

Guinea: http://www.Boubah.com/

Mbendi AfroPaedia (information on companies, countries, industries and stock exchanges in Africa): http://mbendi.co.za

Guinea-Bissau

KEY FACTS

Official name: República da Guiné-Bissau (Republic of Guinea-Bissau)

Head of State: President João Bernardo Vieira (sworn in 1 Oct 2005)

Head of government: Prime Minister Aristides Gomes (sworn in 2 November 2005)

Ruling party: Coalition government from May 2004: the Partido Africano da Independência de Guiné e Cabo Verde (PAIGC) (African Independence Party of Guinea and Cape Verde) (45 seats) and the Partido para a Renovaçao Social (PRS) (Party for Social Renewal) (35 seats)

Area: 36,125 square km

Population: 1.38 million (2004)

Capital: Bissau

Official language: Portuguese

Currency: CFA franc (CFAf) = 100 centimes (Communauté Financière Africaine (African Financial Community) franc). New notes have been issued; old notes cease to be legal tender from Jan 2005.

Exchange rate: CFAf544.07 per US$ (Oct 2005); CFAf655.95 per euro (pegged from Jan 1999)

GDP per capita: US$208 (2004)

GDP real growth: 4.30% (2004)

Labour force: 695,000 (2004)

Inflation: 3.00% (2004)

Balance of trade: US$12.00 million (2003)

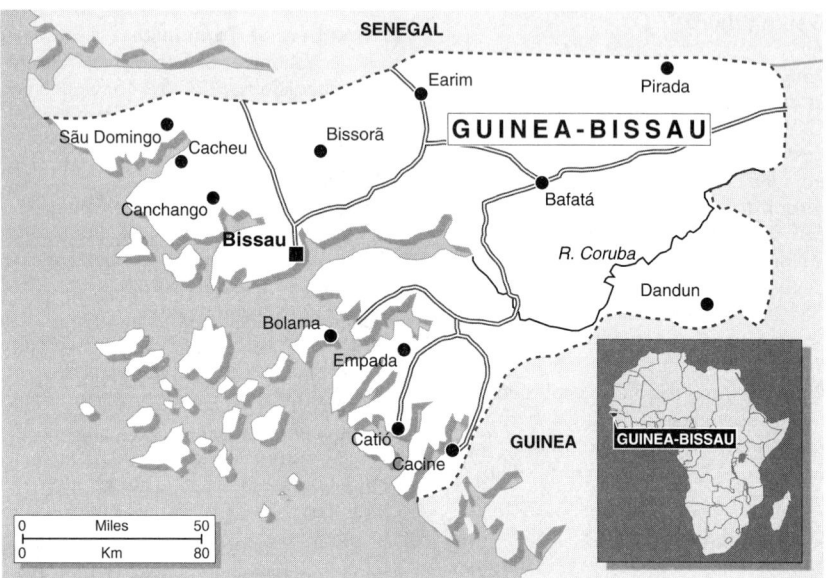

Guinea-Bissau is trying to overcome the effects of a long period of political instability and economic stagnation since the civil war of 1998–99. After a coup in 2003 and parliamentary elections in 2004, a new government was nominated in May 2004 and presidential elections were held in October 2005.

Economic situation

Guinea-Bissau ranks among the lowest 10 countries in the world on the human development index. More than two-thirds of the population of approximately 1.4 million lives below the poverty line, in a country where per capita GDP is US$200. The inequality of income distribution is one of the most extreme in the world.

There has been progress however. The leaders of the military have pledged allegiance to the constitution and elected government. Rules-based government has been largely restored and a start has been made on addressing the fiscal and economic problems. Importantly, fiscal control has been re-established, although the economic situation remains difficult, and the government has committed itself to a five-year development programme (2004-08). The country's industrial base was virtually destroyed in the war; enterprises remain severely undercapitalised because of confiscations and looting during the conflict, the infrastructure has deteriorated and electricity production has virtually ceased. As a result, there has been minimal private investment.

Most interim debt relief under the International Monetary Fund (IMF) Initiative for Heavily Indebted Poor Countries (HIPC) stopped after 2001 because of non-performance under the programme. Non-wage expenditure was cut and most external debt service also remained unpaid.

There is no short term fix for Guinea-Bissau. Because of high costs, the development of petroleum, phosphate and other mineral resources is not a near-term prospect. However, unexploited offshore oil reserves could provide much-needed revenue in the long run. The best that can be hoped for is a medium-term rally into longer-term slow, sustained, recovery. Donor assistance will be critical, which means the government will have to perform. During a meeting in Lisbon, donors pledged additional emergency budget support of CFAf1.3 billion (US$2.4 million) and several announced support to cover the costs of the elections (CFAf2.3 billion (US$4.2 million)). Substantial budget support, up to CFAf12 billion (US$22 million), was also expected from the European Union (EU).

The macroeconomic framework assumes that real growth will be around two per cent per annum, in line with population growth. The 2005 budget was in deficit by 28 per cent of GDP. Expenditure was up considerably over 2004, and is now at the level the government forecasts is the minimum necessary for it to operate. There is a strict day-to-day cash rationing system which limits new expenditure to available resources.

Additional revenue will have to come mainly from better administration and tax reform, for which there is considerable scope. A spin off, it is hoped, will be an improved investment climate. The government is also planning measures to protect and increase revenue from the fishing sector. Fishing licences accounted for one-third of revenue in 2004. However, surveillance of territorial waters has been minimal in recent years, leading to considerable illegal fishing and a decline in revenue.

High wage costs

The key element in reducing expenditure is to trim personnel costs. At about 70 per cent of revenue, high wage bills are the main reason for Guinea-Bissau's serious fiscal problems. Hiring policies loosened after the war and total public employees increased from about 17,900 in 1997 to an estimated 21,000 by end-2003. The size of the military increased sharply and is still above the pre-war level.

International aid

Improving the outlook for economic growth requires repairing the damage from the conflict. The EU is financing the rehabilitation of roads; the World Bank is to rehabilitate the electricity company. The starting point to improve the investment climate is an Action Plan for Simplifying Procedures for Trade and Investment, prepared under a World Bank-financed project for the Rehabilitation and Development of the Private Sector. Already identified are an investment code by the beginning of 2006 and early abolition of most licence fee requirements for the industrial and commercial sector, including for imports and exports.

Politics

Former military ruler of Guinea Bissau and recent exile, João Bernardo Vieira, was declared the winner of presidential polls in June 2005. Election officials said he won 52 per cent of a run-off vote, beating his rival, Malam Bacai Sanha. Vieira returned to Guinea-Bissau in April 2005 after six years of exile in Portugal. He said he had come back as a 'soldier of peace'. He ran as an independent candidate, campaigning among the country's young and unemployed.

Rival supporters clashed in the capital shortly after the initial results were announced and Sanha's party alleged fraud. However EU observers declared the poll to be free and fair and the new president took office in October, promising to promote reconciliation and national unity. The election – intended to cap years of coups and military dictatorships – marked the end of the caretaker government that took over after former president Kumba Yala was deposed in 2003.

Vieira, sometimes known as 'Nino', had previously ruled Guinea-Bissau for 19 years after taking power in a military coup in 1980. He liberalised markets and introduced multi-party politics; however, critics accused him of human rights abuses, crony capitalism, corruption and autocracy. Trained in China, he was a guerrilla commander in the country's campaign for independence from Portugal. He became head of the armed forces after independence in 1974.

Outlook

Once hailed as a potential model for African development, Guinea-Bissau is now one of the poorest countries in the world. It has massive foreign debt and an economy which relies heavily on foreign aid. If it is to fully recover, it has to maintain fiscal prudence and political stability.

Risk assessment

Economic	Poor
Political	Poor
Regional stability	Average

COUNTRY PROFILE

Historical profile

Guinea-Bissau and its sister state, Cape Verde, although tiny and more backward even than Angola and Mozambique, Portugal's other former African colonies, earned international renown following the outstanding successes of the political and guerrilla war waged by the Partido Africano para la Independéncia de Guiné e Cabo Verde (PAIGC) (African Party for the Independence of Guinea and Cape Verde).
The PAIGC had been founded in 1956 by Dr Amilcar Cabral, as a left-wing nationalist movement, which led an 11-year guerrilla struggle in mainland Guinea-Bissau from 1963 to 1974 for independence from Portuguese rule and was the first to liberate the majority of its mainland territory from Portuguese rule, demonstrating the inability of the Portuguese army to contain the guerrilla wars in its colonies.
For the next six years post-independence leader Cabral presided over a command economy. In 1980 he was overthrown by João Vieira. Four years later Vieira was ousted after he dismissed his army chief, triggering a crippling civil war. This ended after foreign mediation led to a truce, policed by West African peacekeepers, and free elections in January 2000. The victor in the poll, Kumba Ialá (Yala), was ousted in a bloodless military coup in September 2003. The military chief who led the coup said the move was, in part, a response to the worsening economic and political situation.

KEY INDICATORS — Guinea-Bissau

	Unit	2000	2001	2002	2003	2004
Population	m	1.12	1.20	1.23	1.51	1.38
Gross domestic product (GDP)	US$bn	0.22	0.20	0.22	0.28	*0.28
GDP per capita	US$	196	167	190	183	208
GDP real growth	%	7.5	0.2	-4.2	-1.2	4.3
Inflation	%	0.8	2.8	6.3	0.6	0.3
Exports (fob) (goods)	US$m	68.0	47.0	51.0	71.0	–
Imports (fob) (goods)	US$m	86.0	81.0	103.0	59.0	–
Balance of trade	US$m	-18.0	-34.0	-52.0	12.0	–
Current account	US$m	-150.0	-350.0	-690.0	-300.0	-240.0
Total reserves minus gold	US$m	66.7	69.5	102.7	164.4	227.2
Foreign exchange	US$m	66.7	69.3	102.3	163.2	226.6
Exchange rate	per US$	711.98	733.04	696.99	574.89	496.63

* estimated figure

1400s Until Portuguese traders first came to Guinea-Bissau, the country was part of the Mali empire.
1915 The Portuguese had colonised only the coastal regions until the nineteenth century but finally gained control of the interior. Unlike its other colonies, Portugal made little attempt to develop the then Portuguese Guinea.
1956 The liberation movement, PAIGC was founded.
1973 A unilateral declaration of independence was proclaimed on 24 September, by which time nearly all the necessary preparations for government had been made by the rebels. PAIGC dropped the name Portuguese Guinea in favour of Guinea-Bissau. Amilcar Cabral was assassinated
1974 Portugal long refused to relinquish power, extending Africa's longest war of independence, but finally granted it after the fall of Marcello Caetano, in Lisbon, in April. Luis Cabral, (brother of the PAIGC leader Amilcar Cabral), became president.
1980 PAIGC was committed to the unification of Guinea-Bissau and Cape Verde, but this aim was dropped when a military coup d'état led by João Bernardo Vieira, who replaced Cabral.
1990 Parliament revoked the PAIGC sole legitimate party status.
1994 Vieira was elected president in the first free elections and PAIGC won the parliamentary elections.
1997 Formal entry to the Communauté Financière Africaine when the CFA franc replaced the peso as national currency.
1998 A civil war began. General Ansumane Mane attempted a coup against Vieira following an army uprising, when Vieira had tried to sacked the general for smuggling arms into the neighbouring Senegalese province of Casamance. Senegalese and Guinea troops supported the government and after a month of fighting a cease-fire was agreed, in July.
1999 Ecowas forces arrived to keep the peace, but fighting broke out again and President Vieira was ousted. Malam Bacai Sanha became interim president. The Partido para a Renovaçao Social (PRS) (Party for Social Renewal) won the parliamentary elections.
2000 Kumba Ialá (Yala), leader of the PRS, was elected president.
2003 14 September, President Kumba Ialá was deposed in a bloodless coup. On 28 September, Henrique Rosa was sworn in as interim president and Antonio Artur Sanhá as interim prime minister. A caretaker government was sworn in on 3 October.
2004 The opposition, PAIGC, won the 28 March parliamentary elections. On 10 May, Carlos Gomes Júnior (PAIGC) was sworn in as prime minister.
2005 In July, former military leader and deposed president, João Bernardo Vieira (who had returned from exile in Portugal, in April), won the presidential election runoff and almost immediately sacked the government of Prime Minister Junior. Vieira was sworn-in as president on 1 October. Aristides Gomes was named as prime minister in November.

Political structure
Constitution
The 1984 constitution has been revised five times. The 1999 amendment reserves the highest posts in the country for 'native Bissau-Guineans'.
Form of state
Unitary republic
The executive
Executive power rests with the president, who is the head of state and serves a five-year term. The president appoints the prime minister, who presides over the Council of Ministers.
National legislature
The Assembleia Nacional Popular (National Assembly) has 102 seats and is elected for a five-year term.
Legal system
The legal system is based on the 1984 constitution, revised in 1993.
Last elections
24 July 2005 (presidential); 28/30 March 2004 (parliamentary).
Results: Presidential: former president João Bernardo Vieira was elected president with 52.4 per cent of the run-off vote. Malam Bacai Sanhá (PAIGC) was runner-up with 47.6 per cent. Turnout was 78.6 per cent.
Parliamentary: the former opposition, PAIGC, won 45 seats out of 100 and the PRS 35 seats.
Next elections
2009 (parliamentary).

Political parties
Ruling party
Coalition government from May 2004: the Partido Africano da Independência de Guiné e Cabo Verde (PAIGC) (African Independence Party of Guinea and Cape Verde) (45 seats) and the Partido para a Renovaçao Social (PRS) (Party for Social Renewal) (35 seats)

Population
1.38 million (2004)
Ethnic make-up
Balanta (30 per cent), Fula (20 per cent), Manjaca (14 per cent), Mandinga 13 per cent, Papel 7 per cent.
Religions
Some 65 per cent of the population are animist, 30 per cent Muslim and 5 per cent Christian.

Education
Literacy rate: 59 per cent, total; 26.2 per cent female adult rates (World Bank).

Health
Annual total expenditure on health is about 6 per cent of GDP, of which approximately 54 per cent is government spending.
Improved water sources are available to 49 per cent of the population.
HIV prevalence: 2.8 per cent (UNAIDS estimate 2004)
Life expectancy: 45.5 years (World Bank)
Fertility rate/Maternal mortality rate: 6.6 births per woman; maternal mortality 910 deaths per 100,000 live births (World Bank).
Infant mortality rate: 126 per 1,000 live births (World Bank).
Head of population per physician/bed: 0.2 physicians and 1.5 hospital beds per 1,000 people.

Main cities
Bissau (capital, estimated population 296,900 in 2003), Bafatá (20,000)

Languages spoken
Crioulo (a hybrid of medieval Portuguese and local words) is the common language. Balanta, Bijago and Fulani are also spoken. French is more widely spoken than English. All correspondence and documentation should be in Portuguese and French.
Official language/s
Portuguese

Media
The media has come under severe threat from the military operations in recent years. In April 2001, the opposition PAIGC accused a number of senior military officers of attempting to 'gag' the press. The Reporters sans Frontieres (RSF) also condemned the attacks against journalists by soldiers to the chief of staff of Guinea-Bissau's armed forces, Verissimo Correia Seabra. The RSF complained of other abuses against journalists, including the detention for one night of a journalist representing a private newspaper, *Diario de Bissau*.
Press
all Africa.com provides on-line news service on Guinea-Bissau's latest political and economic developments (http://allafrica.com/guineabissau/). The local weekly publication is *Correio-Bissau*.
Broadcasting
Radio: Radiodifusão Nacional da República da Guiné-Bissau broadcasts services in Portuguese.
Television: TV broadcasts are on Friday, Saturday and Sunday evenings.

Guinea-Bissau

Economy
The economy has been adversely affected by political unrest that disrupted business activities, and natural setbacks such as the locust infestation in January 2005. The military conflict of 1998–99 damaged the infrastructure, much of which has yet to be repaired, although several donors are providing assistance.

A bumper crop of the principal export, cashew nuts, and World Bank and African Development Bank (ADB) loans have helped to underpin the economy and GDP rose in 2004 to 4.3 per cent, from the negative growth of -1.2 per cent of 2003. Negative growth began in 2002, following the suspension of debt relief funds under the Heavily Indebted Poor Countries (HIPC) Initiative in 2001.

The country is one of the poorest in the world with all human-development indicators remaining low. GNI per capita is only US$208 and it is estimated that around 75 per cent of the population live below the poverty line. The informal (or black) economy has been estimated as larger that the legal market.

Guinea-Bissau is a member of the West African Economic and Monetary Union (WAEMU). Fiscal policies are key to regaining macroeconomic stability, mainly through increased tax revenue and reduced expenditures.

Central control of the economy was restored by the ministry of finance in 2004 but it was unable to restrain the wage bill which increased as the salaries of civil, security and political entities were harmonised; non-wage expenditure was cut instead. The single most important task, as far as potential donors and investors are concerned, is increasing transparency, a task underway in 2006.

External trade
Guinea-Bissau has a large trade deficit and heavy dependence on foreign aid and credits.

In 2002, the US approved Guinea-Bissau as eligible for tariff preferences under the African Growth and Opportunities Act (AGOA).

Imports
Principal imports are foodstuffs, transport equipment, fuels and lubricants, machinery and equipment.

Main sources: Senegal (23.4 per cent total, 2004), Portugal (20.4 per cent), China (8.2 per cent), The Netherlands (5.8 per cent)

Exports
Principal exports are cashew nuts, shrimp, peanuts, palm kernels, sawn timber and cotton.

Main destinations: India (54.9 per cent total, 2004), US (24.2 per cent), Nigeria (12.7 per cent), Italy (4.1 per cent)

Agriculture
Farming
The agricultural sector (including fishing) is the principal economic activity, accounting for around 60 per cent of GDP and over 70 per cent of total export earnings and employing 70 per cent of the workforce.

Only 9 per cent of total area is cultivated; inland areas are largely savannah, coastal areas are forest and mangrove swamps. Construction of a bridge on the Mansoa river between Dakar and Bissau improved links between Cacheu and Oio regions (which produce half of the country's agricultural output) and markets.

There are chronic food shortages, despite the emphasis on food self-sufficiency and co-operative farming.

The main food crop is paddy rice (19 per cent of cultivated land); other food crops include millet, sorghum, plantains, root crops, some maize and groundnuts.

Guinea-Bissau is one of the world's largest producers of cashew nuts. Other cash crops include palm kernels, coconuts, tobacco, sugar.

The crop production for 2004 included: 192,500 tonnes (t) cereals in total, *81,000t cashew nuts, 27,000t maize, 38,000t cassava, *15,000t sorghum, 127,000t rice, 39,000t plantains, *45,500t coconuts, 80,000t oil palm fruit, *8,200t citrus fruit, 20,527t oilcrops, 81,000t treenuts, *5,500t sugar cane, *1,500t cotton lint, *22,000t millet, 106,000t roots & tubers, 76,420t fruit in total, 25,500t vegetables in total. Livestock production included: 19,465t meat in total, 5,148t beef, 11,240t pig meat, 1,677t lamb and goat meat, 1,400t poultry, 1,164t eggs, 18,30t milk, 65t honey, 1,170t cattle hides, 189t sheepskins.
* estimate

Fishing
The fishing sector is important. Exports of fish and shellfish are expected to increase as the country's large marine resources are exploited. The European Development Fund gave US$35 million in aid to develop the fishing industry, including an ice-making plant. Fish worth between US$300–600 million are caught in the waters each year, but value added production on-shore is minimal.

More investment is needed to refurbish the main port, damaged during the civil war, to enable fish processing for export to Europe or to neighbouring countries for processing and re-export.

Industry and manufacturing
The industrial sector contributes around 12 per cent to GDP and employs 10 per cent of the workforce. Production is mostly agri-related: processing groundnuts, fish processing, rice dehusking, sugar refining. There is also a large brewery plant, a small Citroën assembly plant, brick making and textile industries. Since the end of the civil war, there has been a drive to modernise transport facilities.

Tourism
The sector is undeveloped, with only around 1,000 visitors per year, mostly for fishing or hunting.

Mining
There are some 200 million tonnes of bauxite reserves in the region of Boé, but exploration costs are too high to justify extraction. There are also known deposits of phosphate near Farim, as well as gold and possibly diamonds. The main barrier to investment in the mining sector is the country's poor infrastructure.

Test drilling at the Farim phosphate deposit indicated it was commercially viable with high phosphate recovery rates (84.1 per cent).

Hydrocarbons
Guinea-Bissau imports all its petroleum needs. Offshore oil exploration has been undertaken recently and while some oil deposits have been found they are not yet commercially viable. More test drilling will be carried out in 2006.

Gas and coal are neither produced or imported.

Energy
Electricity generating capacity stands at around 15MW following investment in four 1MW generators from China and three small generators from Libya since 2002. The country has an electricity deficit that may be eased by a proposed Ecowas plan to create an electricity network incorporating regional producers.

Guinea-Bissau is dependent on imported oil while hydroelectric potential remains largely untapped.

Banking and insurance
Central bank
Banque Centrale des Etats de l'Afrique de l'Ouest
Main financial centre
Bissau

Time
GMT

Geography
Guinea-Bissau lies on the west coast of Africa, with Senegal to the north and Guinea to the east and south.

Climate
Tropical with rainy season from mid-May to November and dry season from December–April. Average temperatures range from 20–38 degrees Celsius (C) in April–May, and from 15–33 degrees C in December–January. High humidity from July–September.

Nations of the World: A Political, Economic and Business Handbook

Entry requirements
Passports
Required by all.
Visa
Required by all except nationals of all Ecowas countries. Business visas should be applied for before arrival. Applications should include a letter from the visitor's company accepting responsibility for any expenses incurred, and a full itinerary. For further details, contact the nearest embassy.
An exit visa, obtainable from the central police station in Bissau, is necessary before leaving. Visa extensions are also available from the central police station.
Currency advice/regulations
Import/export of local currency is prohibited. Foreign currency import is unlimited, but amounts should be declared; export is allowed up to the declared amount.

Health (for visitors)
Medical facilities are limited.
Mandatory precautions
Yellow fever vaccination certificate.
Advisable precautions
Typhoid and polio vaccinations. Malaria prophylaxis should be taken as risk exists throughout country. Water precautions are necessary.

Hotels
Accommodation is very limited and difficult to obtain at short notice. Reservations should be made well in advance, preferably through business contacts. Hotel tariffs are liable to change at short notice, therefore confirmation of booking is recommended.

Credit cards
Credit cards cannot be used.

Public holidays
Fixed dates
1 Jan (New Year's Day), 20 Jan (Death of Amilcar Cabral), 8 Mar (Women's Day), 1 May (Labour Day), 3 Aug (Assassination of Pidjiguoiti), 24 Sep (National Day), 25 Dec (Christmas Day).
Variable dates
Eid al Adha, Eid al Fitr.
The Islamic year contains 354 or 355 days, with the result that Muslim feasts advance by 10–12 days against the Gregorian calendar. Dates of feasts vary according to the sighting of the new moon, so cannot be forecast exactly. Islamic year 1426: 10 February 2005 to 30 January 2006.

Working hours
Banking
Mon–Fri: 0830–1430.
Business
Mon–Fri: 0830–1430.

Government
Mon–Fri: 0830–1430.
Shops
Mon–Fri: 0730–1230, 1430–1830.

Telecommunications
Telephone/fax
Communications are poor.
Mobile phones
There is no mobile phone service.

Getting there
Air
International airport/s: Bissau (Code: BXO), 8km from city. Taxis and minibuses are available to take visitors to the city.
Airport tax: International departures US$20
Surface
Road: The road from Guinea is mostly paved; however, that which is not, from the border to Labé, gets boggy in the rainy season. Petrol is readily available only in the cities.
A 720-metre bridge over the Mansoa river has improved the traffic flow on the trans-African coastal road between Dakar, Senegal, and Bissau.
Water: There are weekly sea links between Cape Verde and Guinea-Bissau.
Main port/s: Bissau

Getting about
National transport
Air: There are no mainland internal flights. Flights go between Bissau and Bubaque Island and a small plane flies to Orango Island from Bissau.
Road: Total road network is over 3,250km, of which about a third is all-weather.
Buses: Minibuses operate on the main roads.
Taxis: Long-distance taxis leave from the market square in Bissau.
Water: Boats serve most towns on the coast and up-river. Tickets available from the Guinémar Office.
City transport
Taxis: Taxis are available in Bissau and serve all main towns.

BUSINESS DIRECTORY
The addresses listed below are a selection only. While World of Information makes every endeavour to check these addresses, we cannot guarantee that changes have not been made, especially to telephone numbers and area codes. We would welcome any corrections.

Telephone area codes
The international dialling code (IDD) for Guinea-Bissau is + 245 followed by subscriber's number.

Chambers of Commerce
Guini-Bissau Associação Comercial, Industrial e Agricola, PO Box 88, Bissau (tel: 222-276).

Guini-Bissau Camara do Comercio, Industria e Agricultura, PO Box 361, Bissau (tel: 212-844; fax: 201-602).

Banking
Central bank
Banque Centrale des Etats de l'Afrique de l'Ouest, Direction Nationale, Avenue Amilcar Cabral 124, PO Box 38, Bissau (tel: 215-548; fax: 201-305).

Ministries
Ministry of Economy and Finance, Rua Justino Lopes 74A, Bissau (tel: 203-495; fax: 203-496).

Ministry of Finance, Avenue Domingos Ramos, Caixa Postal 67, Bissau (tel/fax: 201-037).

Ministry of Mines and Energy, Caixa Postal 387, Bissau.

Other useful addresses
Empresa Nacional de Comércio Geral, CP 5, Bissau (tel: 212-925).

Empresa Nacional de Pesquisas e Exploração Petroliferas e Mineiras (Petrominas), 58 Rua Eduardo Mondlane, Bissau (tel: 212-279).

Guinea-Bissau Embassy (USA), 15929 Yukon Lane, Rockville MD 20855 (tel: 202-947-3958).

Guinémar Office, 21A Rua Guerra Mendes, Bissau.

Petroguin, Caixa Postal 387 Bissau (tel: 221-155, 222-625; fax: 221-155, 222-625).

Radiodifusão Nacional da República da Guiné-Bissau, CP 191, Bissau.

Internet sites
Africa Business Network: http://www.ifc.org/abn

AllAfrica.com: http://allafrica.com

African Development Bank: http://www.afdb.org

Africa Online: http://www.africaonline.com

Harambee Afrika (UK business club for traders with east, central and southern Africa; includes annotated web resource list): http://www.harambee.co.uk

Mbendi AfroPaedia (information on companies, countries, industries and stock exchanges in Africa): http://mbendi.co.za

Guyana

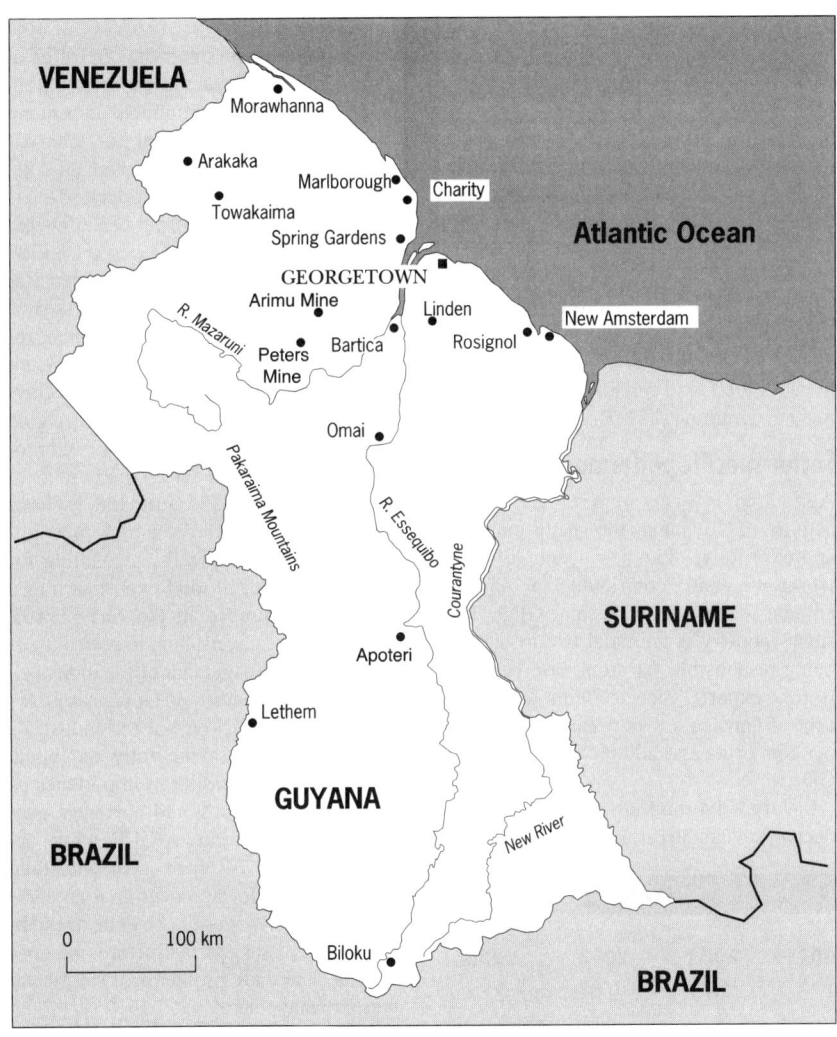

KEY FACTS

Official name: Co-operative Republic of Guyana

Head of State: President Bharrat Jagdeo (PPP/Civic) (since Aug 1999; re-elected 19 Mar 2001)

Head of government: Prime Minister Samuel A A Hinds (since 1997)

Ruling party: People's Progressive Party/Civic (PPP/Civic) Coalition (re-elected 19 Mar 2001)

Area: 214,970 square km

Population: 869,100 (2004)

Capital: Georgetown

Official language: English

Currency: Guyana dollar (G$) = 100 cents

Exchange rate: G$190.00 per US$ (Oct 2005)

GDP per capita: US$1,024 (2004)

GDP real growth: 1.60% (2004)

Labour force: 334,000 (2004)

Inflation: 4.70% (2004)

Balance of trade: -US$79.90 million (2004)

Foreign debt: US$1.08 billion (2004)

Ethno-politics remain prominent in Guyana. It is fair to say that in this racially divided country, electoral results have been premised more on ethnicicity than anything else since the multiracial People's Progressive Party (PPP) fractured in the 1950s. From 1964 until 1992 the once socialist People's National Congress (PNC) governed Guyana and at one point attempted to fully turn the country into a non-aligned Communist state, with the party superseding all legislative process.

President Jagdeo

The country's political system remains strictly a two party affair. The PPP, which draws the majority of its support from rural rice and sugar farmers in addition to Indo-Guyanese citizens, has been in power since 1992. The PNC, the main opposition party, draws predominantly on the support of black Guyanese living in urban areas.

Bharrat Jagdeo of PPP became President of Guyana in 1999 at the age of 35 having succeeded Janet Jagan, of who's cabinet he was a member. The youngest head of state among the Caribbean Community and Common Market (Caricom) group of states, Jagdeo's administration has been plauged by allegations of corruption, electoral malpractice, incompetence and nepotism.

However, it is important to bear in mind, that in the rough and tumble environment of Guyanese politics, such accusations are often made and were in fact continually made by the PPP against the PNC when the latter was in office prior to 1992. In 2001 Jagdeo's bid for re-election was successful as his party triumphed at the polls once more to give him a second term in office. Guyana's ever present racial tensions were again in evidence leading up to and after the poll as many Afro-Guyanese citzens protested against the victory of the Indo-Guyanese Jagdeo, claiming that the PNC had been the victim of electoral malpractice.

Economic overview

The economy of Guyana has performed erratically throughout the 2000s. Growth rates have generally been low, interspersed with contractions in 2000 and 2003. The IMF forecasts a contraction of 2.6 per cent in 2005, though the outlook for 2006 is more positive, with projected positive growth of 3.4 per cent.

Despite the government priority of promotion of foreign investment and membership of the Caricom inward investment has been slow. Social and political unrest between ethnic divisions of the country has proved a deterrent to foreign investors. A credit to Guyana of US$413.6 million under the Heavily Indebted Poor Countries (HIPC) initiative was approved in 2003. It supported Guyana's efforts in stimulating economic growth, increasing productivity in key sectors such as sugar, improving the accountability and transparency of the public sector and the delivery of public services, including health, education and the water supply. Raising the standards of living in the region is an important issue, with around 40 per cent of the population living below the poverty line.

Owing to the low international market prices of Guyana's main exports, the country has experienced persistent trade deficits. This factor, combined with a high debt service burden has had a serious effect on Guyana's balance of payments position. In 2004, the government and the Inter-American Development Bank (IDB) signed a US$28 million soft loan agreement for the Fiscal and Financial Management Programme (FFMP).

Sector specific performance

Agriculture is a very important economic activity in Guyana as the sector employs approximately 35 per cent of the workforce and contributes a similar amount to the country's total GDP. The sugar industry is a crucial export earner, being responsible for around 46 per cent of total exports. Rice accounts for 12 per cent of Guyana's export earnings and 19 per cent of its agricultural contribution to GDP.

In July 2004 the European Union (EU) decision to cut the price of imported sugar, by up to 20 per cent in 2005 and 33 per cent in 2007, sparked demonstrations against visiting EU delegation. The EU proposal would mean a cut of US$0.10 per pound and could cost Guyana over US$37 million. Ironically the changes come in a year of a bumper sugar crop, when Guyana Sugar Corporation (GuySuCo) reported that 324,940 tonnes, the second highest production in 15 years, had been harvested.

Both mining and quarrying are of great importance to Guyana's economy. Both activities combined, amount to 25 per cent of total GDP and account for approximately 12 per cent of the country's total work force. Annual gold production averages 440,000 ounces, 70 per cent of which comes from Omai Gold Mines, a US$300 million venture. Cambior and Golden Star Resources – Canadian companies – own 65 per cent and 30 per cent of Omai, respectively, and the Guyana government owns 5 per cent. Royalties paid to Guyana's Gold Board are linked to world gold prices. An estimated one-fifth of gold production is smuggled across the borders to Venezuela, Brazil and Suriname by local miners. Bauxite is the country's most important mineral, typically accounting for around a quarter of total export earnings. Production slumped in the early 1980s, prompting the government to seek outside help for the management of the industry.

The tourism industry in Guyana is growing relatively quickly, but the industry's potential remains to be fully exploited. The sector is increasing in importance as an economic activity and currently contributes 9.3 per cent to GDP while accounting for 7.7 per cent of total employment. Development is at an early stage with much work to be done to establish the necessary infrastructure and conditions. There are problems of safety and waste management.

Outlook

Guyana's economy performed poorly in 2005, registering a contraction of over 2 per cent, according to the latest forecast by the IMF. The Jagdeo government has been plagued by allegations of electoral fraud and general incompetence, allegations that are usually banded about regardless of the party in power. As such, Guyana remains politically unstable and likely to erupt socially at any point in the near future. Racial divisions and correlating poverty levels remain a real problem. Though positive growth is forecast for the economy in 2006 a great deal needs to be done to reach a political consensus in the

KEY INDICATORS — Guyana

	Unit	2000	2001	2002	2003	2004
Population	m	0.76	0.77	0.79	0.83	0.87
Gross domestic product (GDP)	US$bn	0.71	0.70	0.71	0.85	*0.79
GDP per capita	US$	824	955	1,007	1,029	1,024
GDP real growth	%	-0.7	1.9	1.8	0.2	1.6
Inflation	%	6.1	1.5	4.3	5.8	4.7
Exports (fob) (goods)	US$m	505.0	490.0	494.9	500.0	570.2
Imports (fob) (goods)	US$m	585.0	584.0	563.1	575.0	650.1
Balance of trade	US$m	-80.0	-96.8	-68.2	-75.0	-79.9
Current account	US$m	-109.0	-131.0	-110.6	–	-90.0
Foreign debt	US$bn	1.3	1.4	1.5	1.2	1.1
Total reserves minus gold	US$m	305.0	287.3	284.5	276.4	231.8
Foreign exchange	US$m	295.8	284.8	279.8	271.6	224.7
Exchange rate	per US$	182.40	187.30	190.70	179.00	179.00

* estimated figure

Guyana

country so that Guyana may begin to implement macroeconomic policy as a united country rather than being split down ethno-centric lines.

Risk assessment

Economic	Poor
Political	Poor
Regional stability	Stable

COUNTRY PROFILE

Historical profile
The area before European settlement was inhabited by semi-nomadic, hunter-gatherer Amerindian tribes, notably Arawaks and Caribs.
1498 Christopher Columbus first sighted Guyana.
1616 The Dutch built the first fort.
1640 The first African slaves arrived to work on sugar plantations. Settlements grew up in Essequibo, Demerara and Berbice and were sustained by trade through the Dutch West India Company.
1763 The Berbice slave rebellion began on one plantation and spread to others along the Berbice river.
1781–1803 The Three colonies of Essequibo, Demerara and Berbice, passed into the hands of the English, briefly to the French, back to the Dutch, then the English, then the Dutch and lastly back to the English.
1814 After the Napoleonic Wars the colonies of were ceded to Britain.
1831 The British administration merged the three colonies into British Guiana, but retained the Dutch administrative, legislative and legal system.
1834 Britain abolished slavery in all its territories. Many Indian and smaller numbers of Chinese and Japanese indentured labourers were brought to work on the estates.
1920 Indentureship ended.
1953 The General election was won by the People's Progressive Party (PPP), led by Cheddi Jagan and Forbes Burnham. The British government deemed the government as pro-Communist and suspended the constitution. The PPP spilt and Burnham founded the People's National Congress/Reform PNC/R party.
1957 and 1961 The PPP won both general elections. Support began to grow for independence.
1964 Guyana's political system was generally viewed as fraudulent with Guyana a de facto one-party state and an 'administrative dictatorship'.
1965 The PPP won most seats in the general election, however a coalition of PNC and another minor, conservative, party formed a government. Burnham became prime minister and stayed in post in an increasingly authoritarian manner, until 1980
1966 Guyana gained independence.
1971 A UN tribunal convened to try and resolve the long-standing border dispute with neighbouring Venezuela concerning the oil-rich Essequibo region.
1980 A new constitution introduced the post of executive president, and Forbes Burnham became the first.
1985 President Burnham died. Desmond Hoyte became president. The one-party state and radical socialism was gradually replaced by a market economy. Austerity measures introduced in the late 1980s resulted in great civil unrest.
1992 The National Assembly and Regional Council were elected in the first free and fair general elections. Hoyte lost the presidency to former Marxist, Dr Cheddi Jagan, (PPP).
1997 A coalition PPP/Civic won the election, but PNC refused to accept the election results. Cheddi Jagan died in March. Samuel Hinds became president until December when Jagan's widow Janet was elected president.
1998 After boycotting parliament since the 1997 election, the PNC returned to the National Assembly, following intervention by the Caribbean Community (Caricom), which carried out an independent audit of the election results and brokered an accord with the PNC, which also catered for a new constitution and fresh elections.
1999 Janet Jagan resigned the presidency due to ill-health; she was succeeded by Bharrat Jagdeo.
2000 Guyana had an agreement with the Canadian oil company CGX Energy to drill within waters also claimed by neighbouring Suriname. Suriname gunboats raided the exploration oil-rig sparking international tension; diplomatic proposals for joint exploration and exploitation failed.
2001 The general election was won by President Jagdeo's ruling PPP/Civic.
2002 A high-profile television presenter, Mark Benschop, was charged with treason after he was accused of inciting demonstrators to storm the presidential offices compound. The demonstrators were complaining of discrimination against Afro-Guyanese.
2003 A UN tribunal convened and tried, without success, to resolve the maritime border dispute with Suriname.
2004 CGX Energy announced it had begun exploration of inshore waters along the Cortenyne Coast, with drilling in the disputed Berbice area to start by September. A key witness in the trial of home affairs minister Ronald Gajraj was shot dead before he could testify about allegations of extra-judicial killings. The minister had stepped down after several months of procrastination and opposition inquiry. Guyana joined 12 South American countries in the launch of an economic and political bloc called the South American Community of Nations.
2005 Severe flooding in January affected half the country's population. By March, the economic effect was shown to be a 2.2 per cent reduction in the year's economic growth, costing the nation about US$65 million. In April Ronald Gajraj was reinstated as home affairs minister, following a ruling by a presidential commission acquitting him of any wrongdoing, however the decision to reinstall the minister provoked international criticism. In May, Gajraj resigned his position.

Political structure
Constitution
The constitution was enacted in 1980, a decade after Guyana became a co-operative republic and 14 years after joining the Commonwealth.
Guyana is divided into 10 regions, each headed by a chairman who presides over a regional democratic council. Local communities are administered by village or city councils.
Form of state
Co-operative republic
The executive
Executive power rests with the president, who appoints and supervises the prime minister and other ministers. The president is the presidential candidate chosen by the major party in the National Assembly. Most cabinet ministers are also members of the National Assembly; the constitution limits non-member technocrat ministers to five. Technocrat ministers serve as non-elected members, allowing them to debate, but not to vote.
National legislature
The unicameral National Assembly comprises 40 members chosen on the basis of proportional representation from national lists named by the political parties and an additional 25 members, who are elected by regional administrative districts. The president may dissolve the Assembly and call new elections at any time, but no later than five years from its first sitting.
Legal system
Guyana's legal system is based on Roman Dutch law modified by English common law. The country has a series of magistrates' courts and further appellate courts, a Court of Appeal, headed by a chancellor of the judiciary, and a High Court, presided over by a chief justice. The chancellor and the chief justice are appointed by the president.
An ombudsman investigates complaints against government departments or other authorities.

Last elections
19 March 2001 (general)
Results: Parliamentary: People's Progressive Party/Civic (PPP/Civic) Coalition 53.1 per cent of the vote, 34 seats; People's National Congress/Reform (PNC/R) 41.7 per cent, 27 seats.
Next elections
2006 (general)

Political parties
Ruling party
People's Progressive Party/Civic (PPP/Civic) Coalition (re-elected 19 Mar 2001)
Main opposition party
People's National Congress/Reform (PNC/R)

Population
869,100 (2004)
Ethnic make-up
East Indian (51 per cent) (resident mostly in agricultural areas) and Afro-Guyanese (30 per cent) (resident mostly in towns) make up the majority. The remainder are of Chinese and European heritage, or Amerindians, most of whom live in the west and south or on reserves.
The main groups of Amerindians are Arawak, Carib, Wapisiana and Warao. The Caribs include Akawaio, Macushi, Patamona and Waiwai.
Religions
Christian (approximately 50 per cent), Hindu (35 per cent) and Muslim (10 per cent).

Education
Education includes primary school, four to six years of secondary school and between three to four years of higher academic or practical education. Students are usually expected to remain in the school system until the age of 16. There are around 900 schools in Guyana.
Literacy rate: 98.7 per cent, total; 98.3 per cent, female: adult rates in 2002 (World Bank).
Compulsory years: Five to 14
Enrolment rate: 97.4 per cent net primary enrolment (World Bank).

Health
Total expenditure on health is around 5.3 per cent of GDP, of which some 80 per cent is government spending.
The government has stepped up provisions for drugs and medical supplies in all hospitals and health centres including facilities in the Georgetown Public Hospital Corporation (GPHC).
Improved water sources are available to 48 per cent of the population.
HIV/Aids
By 2001 46 per cent of sex workers were living with HIV/Aids and the probability of the virus passing into the wider population is considered by UNAID/WHO as high.
HIV prevalence: 3.2 per cent aged 15–49 in 2003 (World Bank)
Life expectancy: 62.2 years (World Bank)
Fertility rate/Maternal mortality rate: 2.3 births per woman (World Bank)
Birth rate/Death rate: 9 deaths and 18 births, per 1,000 population (World Bank).
Infant mortality rate: 52 deaths per 1,000 live births; 12 per cent of children aged under five are malnourished (World Bank).

Welfare
The government has been developing new housing schemes, including distributing over 20,000 housing lots for a Low Income Settlement Project. The private sector has also been encouraged to assist in the development of the housing sector.

Main cities
Georgetown (capital, estimated population 227,700 in 2003), Linden (44,300), New Amsterdam (32,500).

Languages spoken
Guyana is the only English-speaking country in South America. Urdu, Hindi, Amerindian languages and Creole are also spoken. Along the Brazilian border, many Guyanese also speak Portuguese.
Official language/s
English

Media
Press
Full press freedom is not guaranteed by the constitution. The government exercises indirect control over the press through restrictions on imported newsprint.
Dailies: There is one state-owned daily newspaper *Guyana Chronicle*, affiliated to the People's National Congress (PNC).
Weeklies: These publications include the independent bi-weekly newspaper *Stabroek News*. Other weeklies are *New Nation*, *Mirror* (People's Progressive Party, Sunday), *Catholic Standard* and *Sunday Chronicle*.
Business: The *Official Gazette* of Guyana is published weekly by the ministry of information. *Guyana Business* is published quarterly by the Chamber of Commerce and Industry, Georgetown. Professional periodicals include *Sugar News* (Guyana Sugar Corp, monthly) and *Guymine News* (Guyana Mining Enerprise Ltd).
Periodicals: Those covering local political news are *Dayclean* and *Guyana Review*.
Broadcasting
Radio: Guyana Broadcasting Corporation (GBC) operates two radio stations (Radio Rorima and Voice of Guyana) on behalf of the government.
Television: Most television reception is from neighbouring countries. Two local television services broadcast channels received by satellite from the US.

Economy
Despite achieving independence in 1966, Guyana has found it difficult to move away from a typical colonial dependency on agriculture and mining as the mainstays of its economy. Sugar, gold, bauxite, lumber and rice are the dominant export commodities. Although efforts have been made to diversify the economic base, government involvement in the economy has traditionally been an obstacle to dynamic growth. As Guyana's main exports are highly susceptible to world price fluctuations the country is sensitive to external shock. Despite the government priority of promotion of foreign investment and membership of the Caribbean Community (Caricom) inward investment has been slow. Social and political unrest between ethnic divisions of the country has proved a deterrent to foreign investors.
A credit to Guyana of US$413.6 million under the Heavily Indebted Poor Countries Initiative (HIPCI) was approved in 2003. It supports Guyana's efforts in stimulating economic growth, increasing productivity in key sectors such as sugar, improving the accountability and transparency of the public sector and the delivery of public services, including health, education and the water supply. Raising the standards of living in the region is an important issue, with around 40 per cent of the population living below the poverty line.
In 2004, the government and the Inter-American Development Bank (IDB) signed a US$28 million soft loan agreement for the Fiscal and Financial Management Programme (FFMP).

External trade
Owing to the low international market prices of Guyana's main exports, the country has experienced persistent trade deficits. This factor, combined with a high debt service burden has had a serious effect on Guyana's balance of payments position.
Guyana is one of the original founder members of the Caribbean Community, or Caricom.
Imports
Fuels and lubricants (typically up to 40 per cent of total), machinery and transport equipment, consumer goods, food and chemicals.
Main sources: US (26.2 per cent total, 2004), Trinidad and Tobago (21.6 per cent), UK (6.4 per cent), Cuba (5.9 per cent), China (4.7 per cent)
Exports
Sugar (typically 46 per cent of total), bauxite/alumina, shrimps, rice, molasses, rum, timber and gold.
Main destinations: Canada (22.8 per cent total, 2004), US (19 per cent), UK (12.1 per cent), Portugal (8.2 per cent),

Jamaica (6.6 per cent), Belgium (6.3 per cent)

Agriculture
Farming
Agriculture is a very important economic activity in Guyana. The sector employs approximately 35 per cent of the workforce and contributes a similar amount to the country's total GDP.

The sugar industry is an important export earner, responsible for around 46 per cent of total exports. Rice accounts for 12 per cent of Guyana's export earnings and 19 per cent of its agricultural contribution to GDP.

About 2 per cent of the total land area is under cultivation. Cultivation of cash crops is confined to the alluvial coastal plain.

The main cash crops are sugar, rice and shrimps. In July 2004 the European Union (EU) decision to cut the price of imported sugar, by up to 20 per cent in 2005 and 33 per cent in 2007, sparked demonstrations of the visiting EU delegation. The EU proposal would mean a cut of US$0.10 per pound and could cost Guyana over US$37 million. Ironically the changes come in a year of a bumper sugar crop, when Guyana Sugar Corporation (GuySuCo) reported that 324,940 tonnes, the second highest production in 15 years had been harvested.

Guyana is self-sufficient in sugar, rice, vegetables, fish, meat and fruit and increased government investment in the sector has improved production of many other products. Cassava is the principal crop grown in the interior.

Emphasis is also being placed on the cultivation of oil palms, soya beans and corn, and on the development of dairy farming. There is a national herd of livestock of between 200,000–250,000 head which are ranched on the Rupununi savannah in the south-east.

The estimated crop production in 2004 included: 3,000,000 tonnes (t) sugar cane, 501,500t rice, 29,000t cassava, 45,000t coconuts, 12,200t citrus fruit, 17,000t bananas, 1,300t pulses, 40,300t roots and tubers, 6,420t oilcrops, 68,371t fruit in total, 41,812t vegetables in total. Estimated livestock production included: 26,635t meat in total, 1,750t beef, 675t pig meat, 520t lamb, 260t goat meat, 23,430t poultry, 465t eggs, 30,000t milk, 74t honey.

Fishing
The fishing industry represents a valuable source of income to the economy of Guyana. Produce is sold on both domestic and international markets and the industry employs approximately 5 per cent of the country's total workforce.

Guyana is the region's largest exporter of shrimp, which make up 14 per cent of total exports. Government initiatives in the fishing sector include the improvement of fisheries management and the encouragement of investment in unexploited marine stocks. The typical annual fish catch is over 55,000mt, of which 27,000mt is shellfish.

In January 2004, Guyana obtained certification to export fishery products to European countries.

Forestry
Guyana is one of the most densely forested countries in the world. Approximately 95 per cent of the country's total land mass is covered by forest and woodland.

All the forests are state-owned. Sawnwood and plywood are the principal forest products; pulp and paper, however, are imported.

In a typical year the import of forest products amounts to US$3.8 million, while exports of forest products amount to approximately US$30 million.

Estimated production in 2004 included 1,161,635 cubic metres (cum) roundwood, 292,000cum industrial roundwood, 38,000cum sawnwood, 112,000cum pulpwood, 165,000cum sawlogs & veneer logs, 51,000cum wood-based panels, 869,635cum wood fuel, 21,516t charcoal.

Industry and manufacturing
The expansion of the industrial sector has traditionally been hampered by a lack of domestic energy supplies together with a dearth of technical and managerial personnel. At present the sector contributed roughly 10 per cent of total GDP and employs approximately 10 per cent of the total work force.

Previously, a serious shortage of foreign exchange had also caused the closure of many firms relying on imported inputs. However, the government is trying to expand the country's industrial base with a policy of diversification and greater encouragement of foreign investors to work with the predominant state sector.

Guyana's manufacturing industry is dominated by the processing of raw materials. Activity related to the mining sector (predominantly bauxite, gold and diamonds) and the processing of agricultural products such as sugar, rice, coconuts and timber, together account for about three-quarters of manufacturing activity. The remainder is accounted for by small-scale import substitution production for the local market. A shortfall in investment is a recurring problem.

In December 2003, Guyana and Trinidad and Tobago concluded an agreement to import raw sugar from Guyana in 2004, to meet the additional requirements of the sugar refinery operated by the Sugar Manufacturing Company Limited (SCML).

Tourism
The tourism industry in Guyana is growing relatively quickly, but the industry's potential remains to be fully exploited. The sector is increasing in importance as an economic activity and currently contributes 9.3 per cent to GDP while accounting for 7.7 per cent of total employment. Development is at an early stage with much work to be done to establish the necessary infrastructure and conditions. There are problems of safety and waste management. Eco-tourism is seen as the way forward. Visitor numbers declined sharply in the 1990s and did not recover until 2000. Numbers are still struggling to return to the 1994 level of 113,000 arrivals. There were 100,911 visitors in 2003 and this figure rose again to 126,200 in 2004. Most visitors are overseas Guyanese and Caribbean nationals.

Environment
In mid-January 2005 severe rains and flooding caused extensive damage to Guyana's infrastructure, killing dozens and leaving around 20,000 people temporarily homeless as they waited for flood waters to subside.

Mining
Both mining and quarrying are of great importance to Guyana's economy. Both activities combined, amount to 25 per cent of total GDP and account for approximately 12 per cent of the country's total work force.

Annual gold production averages 440,000 ounces, 70 per cent of which comes from Omai Gold Mines, a US$300 million venture. Cambior and Golden Star Resources – Canadian companies – own 65 per cent and 30 per cent of Omai, respectively, and the Guyana government owns 5 per cent. In mid-2003, residents of western Guyana began legal action against Omai for allegedly allowing a dam to collapse on the Essequibo river in 1995, pouring 2.9 million cubic metres of cyanide-tainted slurry into the river. Around 23,000 residents supporting the writ want Omai to pay US$2 billion in damages and are demanding an end to the dumping of toxic waste into the river. A similar writ was issued in 2000, but was thrown out by the courts on technical grounds.

Royalties paid to Guyana's Gold Board are linked to world gold prices. An estimated one-fifth of gold production is smuggled across the borders to Venezuela, Brazil and Suriname by local miners. There is also inefficient alluvial mining by some 10,000 miners using dredgers and suctions.

Bauxite is the country's most important mineral, typically accounting for around a quarter of total export earnings. Production slumped in the early 1980s, prompting the government to seek outside help for the management of the industry. There are known deposits of kaolin, molybdenum, uranium, copper, semi-precious stones, talc, soapstone and high-silica sand, which the government would like to develop.

In a typical year, Guyana's gold production is estimated to be 384,000 ounces.

Hydrocarbons
In June 2004, a UN tribunal was empowered to settle a dispute over potentially oil-rich territory clamed by both Guyana and Suriname. The disputed maritime area includes an oil-rich concession granted to a Canadian company. At present Guyana imports oil, primarily from Venezuela under preferential terms. It is estimated, that if the border dispute is settled in Guyana's favour, the country's oil output would double that of Trinidad and Tobago.

Gas and coal are neither produced nor imported.

Energy
Guyana continues to be heavily dependent on imported oil from both Venezuela and Trinidad and Tobago in order to meet its energy needs. The country does have considerable potential for hydroelectric power generation however.

The International Development Association (IDA) has financed a project to evaluate Guyana's petroleum reserves, and a licence has been given to Petrel USA, to explore for offshore oil.

Guyana Electricity Corporation (GEC) is government-subsidised, and much of its financing is from the Inter-American Development Bank (IDB). A number of the GEC's existing thermal stations are being rehabilitated.

The GEC's commissioning of the US$17 million 22MW Wartsila generating plant has brought total capacity in the Demerara system up to 94MW, which is sufficient to meet peak demand.

Banking and insurance
Guyana's banking and financial services industry is concentrated in the capital Georgetown. The Central Bank of Guyana regulates the industry.

Central bank
Bank of Guyana

Main financial centre
Georgetown

Time
GMT minus four hours.

Geography
A plain about 15km wide runs along the 320km northern (Atlantic) coast and extends west into Venezuela and east into Suriname. This strip, which lies some 1.5 metres below sea level and is protected by a system of dykes, is intensively farmed and contains 90 per cent of the population. To the south of this area the land is mountainous, heavily forested and covered with a network of fast-flowing rivers with numerous rapids and falls, including the Kaietur Falls on the Potaro River which is seven times higher than Niagara. There are substantial reserves of bauxite, gold and diamonds in this area. To the south-west along the border with Venezuela is a region of upland savannah, the Rupununi, where the rest of the population, predominantly Amerindian, engages in limited agriculture and cattle-raising.

Climate
The climate is tropical, with a mean monthly temperature of 26–28 degrees Celsius (C) throughout the year on the coast (28 degrees C in the interior). Temperatures of above 32 degrees C or below 24 degrees C at any time of day or any season are rare. Rainfall is between 200–280mm per year on the coast, mainly in two sharply defined wet seasons, May to August and November to January. In the south there is a single rainy season from April to September, but rainfall is lower – averaging 150mm per year.

Dress codes
Among local businessmen the *shirtjac suit* – based upon a civilian version of the bush jacket – is widely worn in preference to the traditional business suit. It is perfectly acceptable to wear an open-necked shirt without a jacket on all but the most formal of occasions, but shorts are frowned upon.

Entry requirements
Passports
Required by all. Passports must be valid for at least six months after arrival and a return/onward ticket is required.

Visa
Visas are required by all except nationals of North America, Western Europe, Australasia, some Asian and all Caricom countries. For full details see: www.guyana.org/govt/visa_requirements.html. Business visas require a letter of invitation from a local company and full itinerary.

Currency advice/regulations
The import and export of local currency is limited to G$200. The import of foreign currency is unlimited.

Health (for visitors)
Mandatory precautions
A yellow fever vaccination certificate is required if arriving from an infected area.

Advisable precautions
Vaccination against yellow fever is encouraged for travellers to rural areas. There is a risk of malaria in some areas of the interior, and adequate precautions should be taken. Water in urban areas is chlorinated, but typhoid is a risk in rural areas so drinking water should be boiled; bottled water is widely available. Dairy products are likely to be made from unpasteurised milk.

Various hepatitis strains are common. 'B' and 'D' stains are endemic in the Amazon basin and precautions are necessary. Tropical parasites, TB, and dengue fever all occur in certain areas. Professional advice concerning precautions should be sort before travelling to Guyana.

Hospital conditions may not match those in developed countries; health insurance, including repatriation is recommended. Travellers should carry enough prescription and medical supplies for the duration of their stay.

Snakes, scorpions and other venomous creatures often lurk in folded clothing, shoes and bathroom fittings and visitors should be alert.

Hotels
Hotels are available in Georgetown, Linden and New Amsterdam. Rooms are generally in short supply. A 10 per cent tip is usual.

Public holidays
Fixed dates
1 Jan (New Year's Day), 23 Feb (Republic Day), 1 May (Labour Day), 26 May (Independence Day), 25 Dec (Christmas Day), 26 Dec (Boxing Day).

When a public holiday falls on a Sunday, the following Monday is taken as the holiday.

Variable dates
Holi (Hindu, Mar), Good Friday, Easter Monday, Caricom Day (first Mon in Jul), Liberty Day (first Mon in Aug), Diwali (Hindu, Oct/Nov), Eid al Adha, Birth of the Prophet.

Hindu and Muslim festivals are timed according to local sightings of various phases of the moon.

Working hours
Banking
Mon–Thu: 0800–1230; Fri: 0800–1230, 1500–1700.

Business
Mon–Thu: 0800–1600; Fri: 0800–1200.

Government
Mon–Thu: 0800–1200, 1300–1630; Fri: 0800–1200, 1300–1530.

Shops
Mon–Fri: 0800–1130, 1300–1600; Sat: 0800–1130.

Guyana

Electricity supply
Electricity supply is not standardised; Georgetown generally 110V AC 60Hz, but some supplies are 220V AC, 50Hz. Elsewhere supply is 110V AC at either 50 or 60 cycles.

Weights and measures
The metric system is official, but imperial measures are often preferred.

Social customs/useful tips
Business is often conducted in a relaxed atmosphere and an emphasis is placed upon personal contact. At the same time, careful observance of polite formalities such as handshaking and formal use of titles (such as Mr, etc) is appreciated. All officials should be treated with careful respect. Attention to detail in the making and keeping of appointments is also appreciated, although punctuality may not be reciprocated.
Invitations to the homes of business contacts are regularly offered since Guyanese pride themselves upon their hospitality. It is customary for visitors to return the invitation in a hotel or to a restaurant.
Hotel and restaurant staff and taxi drivers customarily receive a 10 per cent tip; airport porters are tipped by the bag and cinema usherettes and cloakroom attendants not at all.

Security
The streets of Georgetown can be unsafe after dark due to street robbery, and the use of taxis is recommended. Ostentatious display of wealth such as expensive wristwatches or jewellery and the carrying of large amounts of cash should be avoided. As in all cities, it is unwise to leave articles unattended in parked cars or hotel rooms.

Getting there
Air
National airline: Guyana Airways.
International airport/s: Cheddi Jagan International Airport, Timehri (GEO), 40km from city; bank, duty free and bar. Ogle Airport is being upgraded to become Guyana's second international airport, to be completed by 2008.
Airport tax: G$2,500 for international departures; not applicable to transit passengers departing within 24-hours.
Surface
Road: A coastal road runs from the Suriname border to Georgetown, via a ferry across the Berbice River at New Amsterdam.
Entry from Brazil is possible at Lethem where international border controls are in place. A new bridge across the river Takutu was under construction in January 2005. When completed it will connect Bonfim in Roraima State (Brazil) to Lethem. A new Lethem-Linden road was begun in 2004, completion dates by January 2005 had not been announced. There are unsealed road in current use. A domestic flight to Georgetown is a feasible alternative to driving. There are no road connections to Venezuela.
Water: There is a ferry service between Guyana-Suriname.
Main port/s: Georgetown, New Amsterdam and Springlands.

Getting about
National transport
Air: Air travel is the only efficient method of reaching the interior of the country. Trans Guyana Airways operates both regional and interior flights, but occasionally permits are needed from the ministry of the interior for non-nationals. Early booking is essential.
Charter facilities are available at Georgetown. Larger towns and mining companies have airports or landing strips.
Road: There are all-weather, asphalt roads along the coast and some brick roads inland. A coastal road links Georgetown, Rossignol, New Amsterdam and the Suriname border. Another coast road runs west from Georgetown, via the Demerara River, to Parika. A sealed highway to the Brazilian border via Lethem is in the initial stage of construction; only unsealed roads exist currently.
Buses: Buses are operated privately and run regularly and are generally reliable (although crowded). Services run along the coast. Private tapir minibuses, mine buses and bush buses (into the interior) are also available.
Rail: There is no passenger rail service, although some mining companies have private goods lines.
Water: Passenger and cargo vessels travel up the Demerara, Essequibo and Berbice rivers, and also along the coast between the rivers. Ferries link Parika-Bartica on the Essequibo River; Rosignol-New Amsterdam on the Berbice River; Corriverton-Suriname on the Corentyne River. These services include New Amsterdam-Ituni, Georgetown-Bartica, Rosignol-New Amsterdam. River taxis (small wooden boats) service the same areas as the ferries. The taxis are faster and more expensive, they may also be chartered.
City transport
Taxis: Taxis are widely available in major towns and can be found on ranks. They have standard fares for inner city journeys; fares for longer trips should be negotiated in advance. A 10 per cent tip is usual. For early morning flights from Timehri, make taxi arrangements the previous day.
Buses, trams & metro: Minibuses are a cheap mode of transport. They connect Timehri airport with Georgetown and are safe in the day. At night it is wiser to use a taxi.

Car hire
Car hire facilities are limited. They are available in Georgetown but must be booked well in advance. An international driving licence is required. Traffic drives on the left.

BUSINESS DIRECTORY

Telephone area codes
The international dialling code (IDD) for Guyana is +592, followed by subscriber's number:

Chambers of Commerce
Berbice Chamber of Commerce, 17-18 Strand, New Amsterdam, PO Box 18, Berbice (tel: 33-873; fax: 35-642).

Georgetown Chamber of Commerce and Industry, PO Box 10110, 156 Waterloo Street, North Cummingsburg, Georgetown (tel: 55-864; fax: 63-519; e-mail: chamber@sdnp.org.gy).

Banking
Bank of Baroda, Avenue of the Republic & Regent Street, Georgetown (tel: 640-056).

Bank of Nova Scotia, Regent & Hinck Streets, Georgetown (tel: 640-312; fax: 57-985).

Citizens Bank Guyana Ltd, 201 Camp & Charlotte Sts, Georgetown (tel: 61-705/6; fax: 61-719).

Demerara Bank Ltd, 230 Camp St & South Rd, Georgetown (tel: 50-610/9; fax 50-601).

Guyana Bank for Trade & Industry, 47-48 Water Street, Georgetown (tel: 68-430/9; fax: 71-612).

Guyana Co-operative Agricultural & Industrial Development Bank, 126 Barrack & Parade Streets, Kingston, Georgetown (tel: 58-806/9; fax: 68-260).

Guyana National Co-operative Bank, Lombard & Cornhill Streets, Georgetown (tel: 57-810/9).

National Bank of Industry & Commerce, 38-40 Water Street, Georgetown (tel: 64-091/5; fax: 72-921).

Central bank
Bank of Guyana, 1 Avenue of the Republic, PO Box 1003, Georgetown (tel: 226-3250; fax: 227-2965; e-mail: comminications@solutions2000.net).

Travel information
Air Services Ltd, Wights Lane, Kingston, Georgetown (tel: 61-767, 65-759).

Guyana Airways Corporation, 32 Main Street, PO Box 10223, Georgetown (tel: 68-195, 68-095; fax: 60-032).

Guyana Overland Tours, PO Box 10173, 6 Avenue of the Republic, Robbstown, Georgetown (tel: 69-876).

Roraima Airways, 101 Cummings Street, Georgetown (tel: 59-647, 42-834; fax: 59-646).

Tourism Association of Guyana, 228 South Road, Lacytown, Georgetown (tel: 50-807; fax: 50-817).

Ministry of tourism
Ministry of Trade, Tourism and Industry, 229 South Road, Georgetown (tel: 62-392; e-mail: mtti@sdnp.org.gy).

National tourist organisation offices
The Tourism and Hospitality Association of Guyana, (THAG), 157 Waterloo Street, Georgetown (tel: 50-807; fax: 50-817; e-mail: tag@solutions2000.net; internet site: http://www.exploreguyana.com).

Ministries
Ministry of Agriculture, Regent & Vlissengen Roads, Georgetown (tel: 67-863; fax: 73-638; guyagr@sdnp.org.gy).

Ministry of Amerindian Affairs, New Garden Street, Georgetown (tel: 65-167; fax: 63-395).

Ministry of Culture, Youth and Sports, 71 Main Street North, Georgetown (tel: 64-190; fax: 55-067).

Ministry of Education, 26 Brickdam, Georgetown (tel: 63-891; fax: 55-570).

Ministry of Finance, Main Street, Georgetown (tel: 73-992 fax: 73-420).

Ministry of Fisheries, Crops & Livestock, Regent & Vlissengen Roads, Georgetown (tel: 61-565; fax: 72-928; e-mail: minfci@sdnp.org.gy).

Ministry of Foreign Affairs, 254 South Road & New Garden Street, Georgetown (tel: 58-683; fax: 59-192; e-mail: minfor@sdnp.org.gy).

Ministry of Health and Labour, Brickdam, Georgetown (tel: 65-861; fax: 56-985).

Ministry of Home Affairs, Brickdam, Georgetown (tel: 62-444; fax: 62-740).

Ministry of Housing and Water, Homestretch Avenue, Georgetown (tel: 57-192).

Ministry of Human Services and Social Security, 1 Water and Cornhill Streets, Georgetown (tel: 50-655; fax: 71-308; e-mail: nrdocgd@sdnp.org.gy).

Ministry of Information, Area B Homestretch Avenue, Georgetown (tel: 68-996; fax: 64-003; e-mail: gis@sdnp.org.gy).

Ministry of Labour, Brickdam, Georgetown (tel: 65-861; fax: 56-985).

Ministry of Legal Affairs, 95 Carmichael Street, Georgetown (tel: 62-616; fax: 69-721).

Ministry of Local Government, Fort Street, Kingston, Georgetown (tel: 65-071; fax: 58-619).

Ministry of Public Service, 64 Waterloo Street, Georgetown (tel: 71-193; fax: 57-899).

Ministry of Public Works and Communications, Wight's Lane, Georgetown (tel: 55-540; fax: 55-539).

Ministry of Transport and Hydraulics, Battery Road, Kingston (tel: 59-350; fax: 56-954).

Office of the President, New Garden Street, Georgetown (tel: 51-330; fax: 63-395).

Office of the Prime Minister, Wight's Lane, Georgetown (tel: 66-955, 73-101; fax: 67-573).

Other useful addresses
Association of Non-Traditional Exporters of Guyana (ANTEG), (tel: 60-779; fax: 61-063),

Bauxite Industry Development Co, 71 Main Street, Georgetown (tel: 57-780; fax: 67-413).

British High Commission, 44 Main Street, PO Box 10849, Georgetown (tel: 65-881; fax: 53-555, 68-818).

Caribbean Community Secretariat, Bank of Guyana Building, PO Box 10827, Avenue of the Republic, Georgetown (tel: 69-281/9; fax: 67-816, 37-127; e-mail: carisec2@caricom.org).

Consultative Association of Guyanese Industry, East Street, PO Box 10730, Georgetown.

Forest Products Association of Guyana (tel: 69-848).

Forestry Commission, 1 Water Street, Georgetown (tel: 67-271; fax: 68-956; e-mail: forstry@sdnp.org.gy).

Geology and Mines Commission, PO Box 1028, Brickdam, Georgetown (tel: 53-047; fax: 52-274; e-mail: ggmc@sdnp.org.gy).

Guyana Broadcasting Corporation, PO Box 10760, Georgetown (tel: 69-231).

Guyana Embassy (USA), 2490 Tracy Place, NW, Washington DC 20008 (tel: 202-265-6900; fax: 202-232-1297; e-mail: guyanaemb@aol.com).

Guyana Export Promotion Council, Sophia National Exhibition Park, Sophia, Georgetown (tel: 59-443, 73-394, 68-526; fax: 63-400).

Guyana Manufacturers' Association (GMA), 62 Main Street, Georgetown (tel: 74-295; fax: 70-670).

Guyana Mining Enterprise Ltd, Linden, Georgetown.

Guyana News Agency, Lama Ave, Bel Air Park, Georgetown (tel: 53-105).

Guyana Office for Investment, Go-Invest, 190 Camp & Church Streets, Georgetown (tel: 50-658, 70-653; fax: 50-655).

Guyana Rice Producers' Association (tel: 64-411, 76-957).

Guyana Rice Board, 1-2 Water Street, Georgetown (tel: 66-822).

Guyana State Corporation, 45-47 Water Street, Georgetown (tel: 60-530).

Guyana Sugar Corporation, 201 Camp Street, Cummingsburg, PO Box 10547, Georgetown (tel: 60-571; fax: 57-274).

Institute of Private Enterprise Development, (IPED), Georgetown (tel: 58-949, 53-067, 64-765).

New Guyana Marketing Corporation, Robb Street, Georgetown.

Omai Gold Mines Limited, 176-D Middle Street, Cummingsburg, Georgetown (tel: 68-129, 65-898; fax: 66-468).

Private Sector Commission (PSC), Georgetown (tel: 57-170, 64-603; fax: 70-725).

Public Corporations Secretariat, PO Box 1020, 45-7 Water Street, Georgetown (tel: 60-536/9).

Shipping Association of Georgetown, 28 Main and Holmes Streets, Georgetown (tel: 62-632).

State Planning Commission, 229 South Street, Lacytown, Georgetown (tel: 68-093; fax: 72-499).

United States Embassy, 31 Main Street, Georgetown (tel: 54-900; fax: 58-497).

Internet sites
Berbice online newspaper: http://www.berbicenews.com

Guyana News and Information: http://www.guyana.org/

Economic Commission for Latin America and the Caribbean: http://www.eclac.cl/index1.html

Inter-American Development Bank: http://www.iadb.org

Organisation of American States: http://www.oas.org

Latin World: http://www.latinworld.com

Latin Trade Online://www.latintrade.com

Local web directory: http://sdnp.org.gy/guylink.html

Haiti

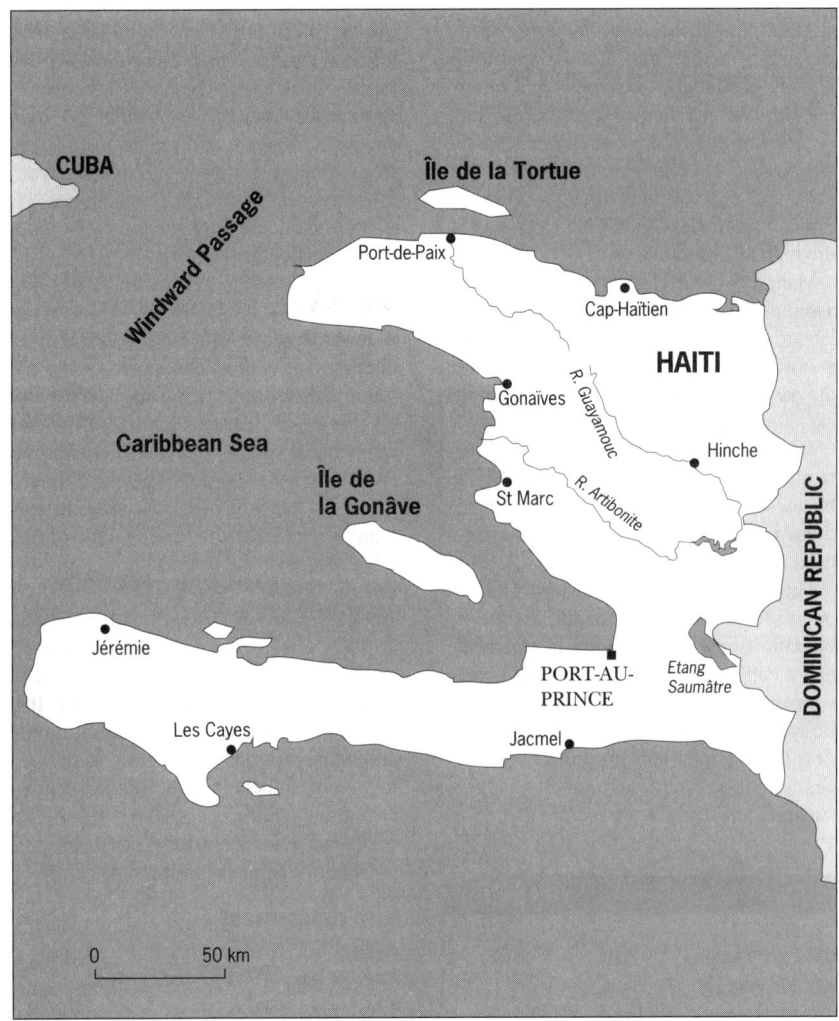

KEY FACTS

Official name: République d'Haiti (Republic of Haiti)

Head of State: Interim President Boniface Alexandre (sworn in 29 Feb 2004)

Head of government: Prime Minister Gérard Latortue (sworn in 13 Mar 2004)

Ruling party: Government of national unity (13 ministers with no party affiliations; sworn in 17 Mar 2004)

Area: 27,750 square km

Population: 8.67 million (2004)

Capital: Port-au-Prince

Official language: French and Creole

Currency: Gourde (G) = 100 centimes

Exchange rate: G42.15 per US$ (Oct 2005)

GDP per capita: US$419 (2004)

GDP real growth: -3.50% (2004)

Labour force: 3.77 million (2004)

Inflation: 27.10% (2004)

Balance of trade: -US$747.00 million (2004)

Foreign debt: US$1.20 billion (2004)

Haiti's political arena remained in a fragile state during 2005 in the run up to elections in the country in 2006. Gérard Latortue is currently Prime Minister and Boniface Alexandre is President. Their respective appointments occurred after former president Jean-Bertrand Aristide was overthrown in a military coup launched on 29 February 2004. The date for the 2006 elections has been pushed back on numerous occasions and the first round of the contest now looks set to take place on 7 February 2006.

There are several candidates currently in the running for the presidency including René Préval, Charles Henri Baker, Leslie François Manigat, Guy Philippe and Marc Bazin. Those that have had their candidacy ruled as ineligible include Gérard Jean-Juste and Dumarsais Siméus. According to opinion polls published in Haiti toward the end of 2005 and in early 2006 independent René Préval possesses a comfortable lead over the other candidates in the crowded field.

Economy

Poverty is Haiti's biggest problem. Three-quarters of the population live below the poverty line, subsisting on less than US$2 a day. Unemployment is high, in the region of 65 per cent, illiteracy is estimated at around 50 per cent, epidemics and malnutrition are widespread and population growth is running at 2 per cent per year. Haiti's public sector is in disarray and the country's infrastructure network is badly fragmented and in need of significant investment. Without economic growth, it is unlikely that there will be any significant improvement in Haiti's existing levels of poverty.

The key to Haiti's future economic development lies in the government's ability to implement the structural changes necessary to satisfy the international community's prerequisite for releasing millions of US dollars in aid. Political infighting and uncertainty have delayed the implementation of important structural reforms, perpetuating existing poverty levels. Economic recession over 2001–03 led to a decline in social indicators and a deterioration in Haiti's political situation.

An Inter-American Development Bank loan of US$25 was forthcoming in November 2003 to help with public finance reform, but, following President Aristide's departure in February 2004, it was discovered that Haiti was totally bankrupt. The situation was made worse by devastating floods and mudslides in 2004. This increased the pressure on the transitional government and foreign aid was necessary to alleviate the problems. Despite instability, international donors promised Haiti US$1.09 billion in reconstruction aid. This, along with the arrival of UN forces on 1 June 2004, has assisted political and economic stability.

Economic recovery has continued to be elusive, but inflation has declined slightly since the high of 32.2 per cent in 2003, the exchange rate was stabilised and a number of structural measures have been implemented.

Industry and agriculture

Besides the traditional food processing, construction and textile industries, there is an important artisan manufacturing sector producing handicrafts. Haiti is the world's leading producer of baseballs and one of the Caribbean's largest suppliers of garments and electronic components to the US market. There is very little production for local consumption and workers are typically paid less than US$3 per day in the industrial sector.

Many US-owned light manufacturing and assembly plants operate as offshore 'cheap labour' industries (mainly assembling sports goods, toys, electrical components) and in the past significantly contributed to foreign exchange earnings.

Manufacturing output in Haiti continues to suffer from the uncertain political and business climate and the resulting international pressures for massive internal structural reforms.

The manufacturing industry consists largely of an assembly sector. Assembly operations are concentrated in electronic and electrical equipment, sporting goods, toys and garments. There is also a domestic manufacturing sector which is mainly devoted to import substitution and the processing of agricultural products such as sugar and fruit, although there is an important artisan manufacturing sector producing handicrafts such as baskets, leather goods, brushes, and rugs.

Agriculture accounted for around 27 per cent of GDP in 2004 and employs two-thirds of the working population. The main cash crops are coffee, sisal and sugar. An estimated 47 per cent of the total land area is cultivated and 20 per cent is pasture. Subsistence farming and animal husbandry predominate. Only 10 per cent of cultivation is carried out on large plantations. Maize, rice, sorghum, millet, beans, fruit and vegetables are grown. Production is largely outside the cash economy. Recurrent drought, insufficient irrigation, low producer prices and a weak infrastructure have kept production levels down and necessitated the import of foodstuffs, particularly cereals.

Outlook

A tense political stand off is currently in operation in Haiti, leading up to the national elections in early 2006. The date for elections is 7 February 2006, but such arrangements can only be considered provisional until the election has actually taken place, as the poll has been pushed back many times since the original date of October 2005 was given. Economic growth remains slow, but at least it is positive. The IMF forecasts growth of 1.5 per cent in 2005 and 2.5 per cent in 2006, respectively. If the economy is to continue to grow however, it is absolutely vital that political disruption is kept to a minimum and whoever wins the election is allowed to govern on behalf of the Haitian people, free from interference. Given Haiti's recent and distant history however, this eventuality is far from likely.

Risk assessment

Politics	Poor
Economy	Poor/improving
Regional stability	Good

COUNTRY PROFILE

Historical profile
1492 Christopher Columbus landed and named the island Hispaniola, or 'little Spain'.
1496 The Spanish established the first European settlement in the western hemisphere at Santo Domingo, now the capital of the Dominican Republic.
1697 The island of Hispaniola was divided between France and Spain. The western half became Haiti.
1801 A former black slave, Toussaint Louverture, led a guerrilla rebellion, conquering Haiti, abolishing slavery and proclaiming himself governor general of all

KEY INDICATORS — Haiti

	Unit	2000	2001	2002	2003	2004
Population	m	7.96	8.00	8.10	8.38	8.67
Gross domestic product (GDP)	US$bn	3.90	3.70	3.80	2.70	*3.54
GDP per capita	US$	475	463	444	440	419
GDP real growth	%	0.9	-1.7	-1.5	0.7	-3.5
Inflation	%	11.5	14.2	8.7	32.3	27.1
Exports (fob) (goods)	US$m	327.0	317.0	298.0	298.0	338.1
Imports (fob) (goods)	US$m	1,078.0	1,057.0	1,140.0	1,140.0	1,085.0
Balance of trade	US$m	-751.0	-743.0	-842.0	-842.0	-746.9
Current account	US$m	-249.0	-177.0	–	–	20.0
Foreign debt	US$bn	1.2	1.3	–	1.2	1.2
Total reserves minus gold	US$m	183.1	141.6	81.7	62.0	114.4
Foreign exchange	US$m	183.0	141.0	81.1	61.6	114.4
Exchange rate	per US$	21.17	24.43	29.25	38.00	38.88

* estimated figure

Hispaniola. He was captured by the French and died in their custody.
1804 Independence was declared by former slave Jean-Jacques Dessalines, who declared himself emperor. There were various monarchical periods until 1859.
1806 Dessalines was assassinated and Haiti became divided into the black-controlled north and the mulatto-controlled south.
1818–43 Pierre Boyer unified Haiti, but excluded blacks from power.
1915 The US invaded Haiti claiming it was protecting its property and investments threatened by clashes between blacks and mulattos.
1934 The US withdrew its troops.
1956 François 'Papa Doc' Duvalier, a voodoo physician, seized power in a military coup and became president in the following year.
1964 Duvalier declared himself president-for-life and established a dictatorship with the help of the violent Tontons Macoute militias.
1971 Duvalier died and was succeeded by his son, the 19-year-old Jean-Claude 'Baby Doc' Duvalier, who declared himself president-for-life.
1986 Baby Doc fled Haiti amid riots and a multitude of coup attempts. Lieutenant General Henri Namphy assumed power as the head of a governing junta.
1988 Leslie Manigat became president but was overthrown in a coup led by Brigadier General Prosper Avril, who installed a civilian government under military control.
1990 Jean-Bertrand Aristide was elected president.
1991 Aristide was expelled from the country following a military coup. The new junta promised elections at a future date. The US, France and Canada suspended aid to Haiti and refused to recognise the new government.
1993 The UN imposed sanctions on Haiti after the military regime rejected an accord designed to facilitate Aristide's return to power.
1994 After US forces removed the military government of General Raoul Cedras, Aristide returned from exile and was reinstalled as president. He was not permitted by law to stand for re-election in 1995.
1995 René Preval was elected to replace Aristide.
1997 US troops left Haiti. Prime Minister Rosny Smarth resigned.
1999 President Préval dissolved the legislature and a Provisional Electoral Council (CEP) was created to organise elections; Jacques Eduard Aléxis was appointed prime minister and a government was sworn in.
2000 The Fanmi Lavalas (FL) (Lavalas Family) party won control of the Senate and Jean-Bertrand Aristide won the controversial presidential election.
2001 President Aristide was sworn in; he appointed Jean-Marie Chéréstal as prime minister. Aristide agreed to hold new parliamentary elections in return for the OAS helping Haiti to obtain US$500 million of suspended aid.
2002 Prime Minister Chéréstal resigned amid allegations of corruption and incompetence. Aristide appointed Yvon Neptune as prime minister.
2004 The escalating violent protests in Haiti stemmed from disputed elections in 2000, which the opposition says were rigged. The opposition rebels, led by Guy Philippe, gained control of several towns, and on 29 February, President Jean-Bertrand Aristide resigned and left the country; Chief Justice Boniface Alexandre was sworn in as caretaker president. The UN approved a multi-national security force to restore law and order. On 9 March, Gérard Latortue was named as prime minister and on 17 March, a government of national unity was sworn in. The hurricane that struck in May devastated the island of Hispaniola, shared between Haiti and Dominican Republic, with a death toll in Haiti of around 2,000. A UN force assumed Haiti peacekeeping duties in June. In August, the US made available US$9 million to Haiti to assist in election preparations for 2005; an agreement was signed between Haiti, the UN and the Organisation of American States (OAS) for the organisation of the elections.
2005 UN peacekeepers cracked down on violence between supporters and opponents of ousted president Jean-Bertrand Aristide. In December the presidential and legislative elections were again postponed, to 8 January 2006, but in early January they were delayed for the fourth time; no date was proposed although the UN Security Council called for elections to be held before 7 February 2006.
2006 Gen Urano Teixeira Da Matta Bacellar, head of the UN peacekeeping force, was found dead in his hotel room. On 7 January the electoral authorities set 7 February as the election date, with the second round scheduled for 19 March.

Political structure
Constitution
Under the 1987 constitution, executive power is held by an elected president, serving a five-year term, and a cabinet of ministers.
Form of state
Republic
The executive
The president is elected for a five-year term by universal suffrage. A president may be elected for a maximum of two, non-continuous terms. The prime minister is appointed by the president whose decision is ratified by the senate.
National legislature
The bicameral National Assembly consists of an 83-member House of Representatives, elected every four years in single-seat constituencies, and a 27-member Senate, elected for six years (one-third renewed every two years) in single-seat constituencies.
Legal system
Haiti's judicial system is based on the French Napoleonic Code. Judges are appointed by the president. The supreme court is the Court de Cassation, which may make rulings on constitutional matters. There is a court of appeal and civil courts in the major administrative centres.
Last elections
26 November 2000 (presidential); May 2000 (parliamentary) (results disputed).
Results: Presidential: Jean-Bertrand Aristide won the election, which was boycotted by the opposition.
Parliamentary: the Fanmi Lavalas (FL) (Lavalas Family) party won control of the Senate, but opposition politicians complained of fraud and intimidation.
Next elections
7 February 2006 (presidential and parliamentary). These elections have been postponed four times. The second round will be held on 19 March.

Political parties
Ruling party
Government of national unity (13 ministers with no party affiliations; sworn in 17 Mar 2004)
Main opposition party
Convergence Démocratique (CD) (Democratic Convergence) (15-party opposition coalition)

Population
8.67 million (2004)
Ethnic make-up
Approximately 95 per cent are Afro-Caribbean; the remainder are white or of mixed race.
Religions
Roman Catholic (80 per cent), Protestant (16 per cent). Around half the population also practices voodoo, an African-derived belief.

Education
Only 20 per cent of the population complete primary schooling which is theoretically compulsory and the pass rate for secondary school exams is 7–8 per cent. Secondary education is provided by the state and *lycées* (private secondary schools). There are also vocational training and domestic science establishments. There is a state-run university and an administration and management institute

(which offers courses in medical subjects, agricultural and veterinary sciences, law, economics and ethnology) and an Institute of Administration and Management.
Literacy rate: 52.9 per cent adult rates (World Bank)
Compulsory years: 6 to 15.
Enrolment rate: 64 per cent total primary school enrolment of the relevant age group (including repetition rates) (World Bank).
Pupils per teacher: 35 in primary schools.

Health
Total expenditure on health is around 5 per cent of GDP, of which some 60 per cent is government spending.
The vaccination coverage for children has been irregular and accounts for only 25 per cent. In May 2002, a nationwide campaign was organised to inoculate two million children under the age of 10 years; 53 per cent of all children had been vaccinated by 2002. Improved water sources and sanitation facilities are available to 46 per cent and 28 per cent of the population, respectively.

HIV/Aids
HIV/Aids has become a leading cause of death, and urban infection rates are over twice the number of rural population infection rates.
For the first time, in June 2004, a joint mission was undertaken by the UN and UNAids, who have sent teams into the field with peacekeepers, in an attempt to limit HIV in a conflict zone. This initiative is designed to pre-empt the spread of the desease before the main contingent of peacekeepers arrive. There are fears that as 1 in 20 Haitians are HIV positive and with the arrival of a peacekeeping force with an almost inevitable sex-industry that will develop, Haiti could become a flashpoint of transmission. UNAids provides condoms, education and testing services to the peacekeepers.
HIV prevalence: 5.6 per cent aged 15–49 in 2003 (World Bank).
Life expectancy: 51.9 years (World Bank)
Fertility rate/Maternal mortality rate: 4.2 births per woman (World Bank)
Birth rate/Death rate: 34 births per 1,000 population; 13.4 deaths per 1,000 population (2003).
Infant mortality rate: 76 per 1,000 live births (World Bank)
Head of population per physician/bed: There are 0.08 physicians and 0.7 hospital beds available per 1,000 people.

Welfare
Since 80 per cent of Haiti's population live below the poverty line and its social and economic indicators remain far lower than the average for Latin America and the Caribbean, the country is not eligible for the IMF's Heavily Indebted Poor Countries (HIPC) debt relief initiative.
In the public sector, still only 20 per cent of resources go to rural areas, where approximately two-thirds of the people live. Poor welfare provision is one factor which causes migration both from the countryside to the capital and out of the country. As many as 330,000 Haitians are thought to be living in the US.

Main cities
Port-au-Prince (capital, estimated population 1.2 million in 2004), Carrefour (384,400), Delmas (325,700), Cap Haïtien (126,100).

Languages spoken
Official language/s
French and Creole

Media
Freedom of the press has been a casualty of political instability in Haiti. The government licenses radio and TV stations through the Conseil National des Télécommunications.
Press
Dailies: Dailies are *Le Nouvelliste*, *Le Matin*, *Le Nouveau Monde* (government-owned), *Panorama* and *Le Progressiste Haitien*. On-line French publications include *Haiti Online* (http://www.haitionline.com/).
Weeklies: Publications include *Haiti Observateur* and *Haiti Progrès* (www.haiti-progres.com) in English, French and Creole.
Business: Weekly business news is covered by *Haiti en Marche* (www.haitienmarche.com) and *Journal du Commerce*.
Broadcasting
Radio: The government also operates its own radio station, Radio Nationale. There are five independent radio stations, Radio Cacique, Radio Lumière (Protestant), Radio Metropole, Radio MBC and Radio Soleil.
Television: The government owns one TV station, Télévision Nationale, which serves areas outside the capital through relay stations. There is one private TV station, Télé-Haiti, which is a cable station relaying captured satellite signals on four channels.

Economy
Poverty is Haiti's biggest problem. Three-quarters of the population live below the poverty line, subsisting on less than US$2 a day. Unemployment is high, in the region of 65 per cent, illiteracy is estimated at around 50 per cent, epidemics and malnutrition are widespread and population growth is running at 2 per cent per year. Haiti's public sector is in disarray and the country's infrastructure network is badly fragmented and in need of significant investment. Without economic growth, it is unlikely that there will be any significant improvement in Haiti's existing levels of poverty.
The key to Haiti's future economic development lies in the government's ability to implement the structural changes necessary to satisfy the international community's prerequisite for releasing millions of US dollars in aid. Political infighting and uncertainty have delayed the implementation of important structural reforms, perpetuating existing poverty levels.
Economic recession over 2001–03 led to a decline in social indicators and a deterioration in Haiti's political situation.
An Inter-American Development Bank loan of US$25 was forthcoming in November 2003 to help with public finance reform, but, following President Aristide's departure in February 2004, it was discovered that Haiti was totally bankrupt. The situation was made worse by devastating floods and mudslides in spring 2004. This increased the pressure on the transitional government and foreign aid was necessary to alleviate the problems. Despite instability, international donors promised Haiti US$1.09 billion in reconstruction aid. This, along with the arrival of UN forces in June 2004, has assisted political and economic stability. Economic recovery has continued to be elusive, but inflation has declined, the exchange rate was stabilised and a number of structural measures have been implemented.

External trade
Imports
Main imports are food, manufactured goods, machinery and transport equipment, fuels and raw materials.
Main sources: US (52.9 per cent total, 2004), Dominican Republic (6 per cent), Japan (2.9 per cent)
Exports
Main exports are coffee, clothing, mangoes, manufactures, leather and raw hides, seafood and cocoa.
Main destinations: US (81.8 per cent total, 2004), Dominican Republic (7.2 per cent), Canada (4.2 per cent)

Agriculture
Farming
Agriculture accounted for around 27 per cent of GDP in 2004 and employs two-thirds of the working population. The main cash crops are coffee, sisal and sugar.
An estimated 47 per cent of the total land area is cultivated and 20 per cent is pasture. Subsistence farming and animal husbandry predominate. Only 10 per cent of cultivation is carried out on large plantations. Maize, rice, sorghum, millet, beans, fruit and vegetables are grown. Production is largely outside the cash economy.

Haiti

Recurrent drought, insufficient irrigation, low producer prices and a weak infrastructure have kept production levels down and necessitated the import of foodstuffs, particularly cereals.
Crop production in 2004 included: 1,050,000 tonnes (mt) sugar cane, 199,000t yams, 398,000t cereals in total, 198,000t maize, 340,000t cassava, 11,500t potatoes, 175,000t sweet potatoes, 105,000t rice, 95,000t sorghum, 300,000t bananas, 283,000t plantains, 261,000t mangoes, 68,100t pulses, 29,000t green coffee, 65,650t citrus fruit, 12,385t oilcrops, 25,500t coconuts, 1,014,150t fruit in total, 204,350t vegetables in total. Livestock production included: 95,265t meat in total, 42,500t beef, 28,200t pig meat, 6,780t lamb & goat meat, 5,600t horse meat 8,635 poultry, 5,000t eggs, 69,200t milk, 850t honey.

Fishing
The total annual fish catch is typically around 5,000 tonnes, three-quarters of which is through marine fishing. Around 10 per cent is exported.

Forestry
Forests cover around 88,000 hectares (ha) or 1 per cent of the total land area. This compares to around 40 per cent of land area in 1940. Deforestation is causing serious soil erosion and desertification. The rapid decline of the forests is partly due to the demand for fuel wood. There are no large-scale forest industries. The local demand for industrial wood and paper products is mainly met by imports. Imports of timber products in 2004 amounted to US$16.2 million.
Timber production in 2004 included: 2.2 million cubic metres (cum) roundwood, 239,000cum industrial roundwood, 13,800cum sawnwood, 224,000cum sawlogs and veneer logs, 2.0 million cum wood fuel, 28,000t charcoal.

Industry and manufacturing
Industry accounted for around16 per cent of GDP in 2004 and employed 10 per cent of the workforce. It is concentrated in Port-au-Prince.
Besides the traditional food processing, construction and textile industries, there is an important artisan manufacturing sector producing handicrafts, such as baskets, leather goods, brushes, and rugs. Manufacturing operations are concentrated in electronic and electrical equipment, sporting goods, toys and garments. Haiti is the world's leading producer of baseballs and one of the Caribbean's largest suppliers of garments and electronic components to the US market. There is very little production for local consumption.
Manufacturing output in Haiti continues to suffer in an uncertain political and business climate and international pressures for massive internal structural reforms.

Tourism
Tourism continues to be hurt by Haiti's unsettled conditions. The importance of the once-thriving sector to the economy is recognised and efforts are being made to revive it. Cruise ship arrivals account for the majority of visitors. Tourism is expected to contribute around 2.2 per cent to GDP in 2005.

Mining
The mining and export of bauxite ceased in 1983 with the closure of Reynolds mine at Miragoane. There are known, but not commercially viable, deposits of copper, silver, gold, marble, lignite and natural asphalt.

Hydrocarbons
Haiti relies on the import of petroleum products to meet domestic demand. Most of this is supplied by Mexico and Venezuela, which sell oil to 11 Caribbean and Central American countries on favourable terms under the San José Pact of 1980. Haiti does not import gas or coal.

Energy
The electricity supply is restricted to main towns. Haiti experiences power cuts on a regular basis.
Local wood provides three-quarters of total energy and is a major cause of deforestation and soil erosion.

Banking and insurance
The banking sector is underdeveloped and in disarray. The crowding out of private sector credit has undermined the banks' ability to function as an important part of the economy. Few people have bank accounts and the large informal sector and black market tends to keep the savings ratio and therefore banks' capital at low levels.

Central bank
Banque Nationale de la République d'Haiti.

Main financial centre
Port-au-Prince

Time
GMT minus five hours.

Geography
Haiti occupies the western part of the Caribbean island of Hispaniola (the Dominican Republic occupies the remaining two-thirds), and some smaller offshore islands. Cuba is to the west and is less than 80km away.
Much of Haiti's land area is covered by mountains, which rise up to about 3,000 metres. Environmental damage caused primarily by population pressure has reduced the area of forests to about 6–8 per cent of land area. A number of rivers flow vigorously during the rainy season only, and there are large lakes in the centre of the country close to the border with the Dominican Republic.

Climate
Year-round temperature in Port-au-Prince varies only slightly from 24–27 degrees Celsius (C). The rainy season is from May–November. The climate is tropical, with the rainy seasons in October–November and May–June. May is the wettest month (231mm average rainfall) and December to February the driest and coldest. Temperatures vary from around 22 degrees C on the coast in January to 34 degrees C in July.

Dress codes
Jackets (tropical weight) and ties are normally worn for formal business. Swimwear is only worn at beaches and pools. Dresses of at least knee-length are recommended for women.

Entry requirements
Passports
Passports are required by all except nationals of USA and Canada with proof of identity.

Visa
Business and tourist visas are not required by citizens of North America or Argentina. Business visitors from other destinations should supply proof of sufficient funds for length of stay and possess return/onward passage. For further information contact the nearest embassy.

Currency advice/regulations
There are no restrictions on imports or exports of foreign or local currency. Traveller's cheques are widely accepted. It is difficult in banks and almost impossible in hotels and shops to exchange foreign currency other than US dollars.

Health (for visitors)
The rate of HIV sero-positivity is high and precautions should always be taken.

Mandatory precautions
Yellow fever vaccination is required if arriving from an infected area.
Anti-malaria precautions are essential. Tap water is not safe to drink, and therefore ice, salads, raw vegetables and unpeeled fruits are suspect.

Advisable precautions
Inoculations against typhoid, polio and tetanus are recommended. Malaria prophylaxis and a mosquito net to cover a double bed may be necessary. Drink only bottled water and be wary of ice in restaurants.
Medical facilities are very limited and offer a poor standard of care. Adequate supplies of essential medicines should be carried by visitors, with their prescription details accompanying. Local emergency

services are inadequate, so full travel insurance, which includes emergency medical evacuation, should be obtained.

Hotels
Five per cent tax and 10 per cent service charge are usually added to the bill.

Credit cards
Major credit cards are accepted.

Public holidays
Fixed dates
1 Jan (Independence Day), 2 Jan (Ancestors' Day), 14 Apr (Pan American Day), 1 May (Labour Day), 18 May (Flag and University Day), 15 Aug (Assumption Day), 17 Oct (Death of Sessalines), 24 Oct (United Nations Day), 1 Nov (All Saints' Day), 2 Nov (All Souls' Day), 18 Nov (Vertières Battle Day), 25 Dec (Christmas Day).

Variable dates
Carnival (two days, Feb), Ash Wednesday, Good Friday, Ascension Day, Corpus Christi (May/Jun).

Working hours
Banking
Mon–Fri: 0900–1300.

Business
Mon–Fri: 0800–1200, 1330–1700. (Exceptions May–Sep 0700–1200, 1330–1600).

Government
Mon–Fri: 0800–1400.

Electricity supply
110-220V AC

Weights and measures
Officially the metric system is in force but many US measures are also used.

Social customs/useful tips
Careful observance of polite formalities such as handshaking, direct eye contact, formal use of titles such as Monsieur, etc, is essential, and offence may be taken if they are not observed. All officials should be treated with careful respect.

Security
Crime is widespread and often violent. The kidnapping of foreign nationals for ransom money is increasingly common. Random shootings, during robbery, has become more common, and pickpockets are numerous. Do not leave property in vehicles and always travel with doors locked and windows up. Armed hold-ups of vehicles take place, even in daylight, in busy parts of Port-au-Prince.
Some areas of Port-au-Prince should be avoided at all times. Wherever possible you should avoid going out after dark. Where possible leave documents in a safety deposit box.

Getting there
Air
National airline: Haiti Trans Air (Hanair)
International airport/s: Port-au-Prince International Airport (PAP), 10km from city; duty-free shop, bar, buffet, bank, car hire.
Airport tax: G100, excluding transit passengers.

Surface
Road: Access is possible from Dominican Republic, although sometimes, bureaucratic delays can occur.
Main port/s: Port-au-Prince, Cap Haitien, Gonaives.

Getting about
National transport
Air: Caribintair flies to Cap Haitien. Other towns can be reached from Port-au-Prince by charter flights.
Road: The total road network is around 4,000km, although not all passable/practicable in wet weather. Surfaced roads from Port-au-Prince to Cap Haitien, Port-au-Prince to Jacmel and Port-au-Prince to Les Cayes.
Camionettes (large out-of-town taxis) are available.
Buses: Unscheduled services operate from Port-au-Prince to Les Cayes, Jacmel, Jérémie, Hinche, Port de Paix and Cap Haitien.
Rail: There is no railway, except for transporting sugar cane.

City transport
Taxis: Publiques (shared taxis) can be identified by red ribbon in the window and registration number beginning 'P'. Tipping is not usual.
Car hire
Cars can be hired in Port-au-Prince, at the airport and in Petionville. International licence is required. Hire cars have registration numbers beginning with 'L'.

BUSINESS DIRECTORY
The addresses listed below are a selection only. While World of Information makes every endeavour to check these addresses, we cannot guarantee that changes have not been made, especially to telephone numbers and area codes. We would welcome any corrections.

Telephone area codes
The international direct dialling code (IDD) for Haiti is +509, followed by subscriber's number.

Chambers of Commerce
Haiti Chamber of Commerce and Industry, Boulevard Harry Truman, PO Box 982, Port-au-Prince (tel: 222-8661; fax: 222-0281; e-mail: ccih@acn2.net).

Banking
Banque Commerciale d'Haiti, Champ de Mars, Port-au-Prince (tel: 23-931).

Central bank
Banque de la République d'Haiti, Rues des Miracles et du Magasin de l'Etat et, PO Box 1570, Port-au-Prince (tel: 299-1200; fax: 299-1045; e-mail: webmaster@brh.net).

Travel information
Air Haiti, 35 ave Marie-Jeanne, Port-au-Prince (tel: 62-722).

Association Hotelière et Touristique d'Haiti, Hotel Montana, rue F. Cardozo, route de Pétionville, BP 2562, Port-au-Prince (tel: 71-920; fax: 76-137).

National tourist organisation offices
Office National du Tourisme d'Haiti, Avenue Marie Jeanne, Port-au-Prince (tel: 21-729).

Ministries
Ministry of Economy and Finance, Palais des Ministères, Port-au-Prince (tel: 21-628).

Ministry of Information and Co-ordination, 300 Route de Delmas, Port-au-Prince.

Other useful addresses
Association des Industries d'Haiti (ADIH), Delmas 31 et 33, Etase Galeria 128, BP 2568, Port-au-Prince (tel: 64-509; fax: 62-211).

Association des Producteurs Agricoles (APA), c/o Chambre de Commerce et d'Industrie d'Haiti, blvd Harry S. Truman, Cite de l'Exposition, Port-au-Prince (tel: 20-281; fax: 34-717).

Centre de Promotion des Investissements et des Exportations Haitiennes (PROMINEX), Angle rue Lamarre et ave John Brown, Port-au-Prince (tel: 26-381).

Haitian Embassy (USA), 2311 Massachusetts Avenue, NW, Washington DC 20008 (tel: 202-332-4090; fax: 202-745-7215; e-mail: embassy@haiti.org).

Haitian International Business Center, 444 Brickell Avenue, Brickell Suite 650, Miami, Florida 33131, USA (tel: (305)374-8300).

Internet sites
Embassy of Haiti: http://www.haiti.org

Haiti Business Directory: http://www.ascnet.net/haiti/directory.htm

Haiti website (in French): http://www.haitiwebs.com/

Latin America Network Information Center: http://www.lanic.utexas.edu

Honduras

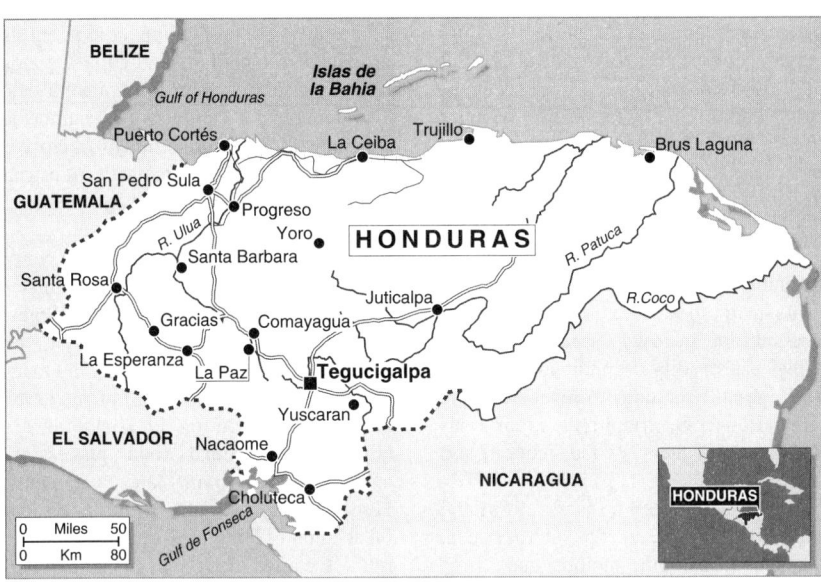

On 1 May 2005 former president Ricardo Rodolfo Maduro Joest's plane crashed into the Caribbean Sea just off the coast of Tela, Atlántida. Had he died, it would have marked a tragic end to a political career that was actually prompted by a different tragedy. Maduro only decided to run for president after his son, Ricardo Ernesto, was kidnapped and killed in 1997. Inspired by a need to prevent a repeat of his son's tragic death, he successfully ran for the highest office in the land on a platform of anti-gang crime measures.

Following the crash Maduro, who was remarkably only slightly injured, was taken to hospital in Comayagua, where he made a successful recovery. Maduro's Partido Nacional de Honduras (PNH) (National Party of Honduras) did not disply the same kind of survival instincts, however, as they were defeated in the presidential poll in November 2005.

Zelaya's triumph

José Manuel Zelaya Rosales, popularly known as Mel Zelaya was inaugurated as president on 27 January 2006 having won the presidency on the night of 27 November 2005. Zelaya became the fifth Partido Liberal de Honduras (PLH) (Liberal Party of Honduras) president in the history of Honduras, after he defeated the ruling PNH party candidate Porfirio Pepe Lobo Sosa.

One of Zelaya's most effective campaigners is said to be his mother. She watched her son train as a civil engineer in his younger life before entering politics and rising to become the minister for investment. Mother and son then embarked on the campaign trail around Honduras where the younger Zelaya sold his policies to the Honduran electorate. Zelaya campaigned on a platform of tough measures to combat crime, including a doubling of police numbers from 9,000 to 18,000.

But as well as promising to be tough on crime he also pledged to be tough on the causes of crime through his advocacy of a re-education programme for the country's gang members, particularly the notorious *Mara Salvatrucha* (*MS-13* or *MS*) criminals. Zelaya's embrace of rehabilitation policies, in contrast to Pepe's strigent advocacy of the death penalty for murderous gang members, put clear blue water between the two candidates. Zelaya's promotion of the rehabilitation strategy also ensured his candidacy was protrayed in a more positive and forward looking light by many of the country's newspapers.

KEY FACTS

Official name: República de Honduras (Republic of Honduras)

Head of State: President Ricardo Maduro Joest (inaugurated 27 Jan 2002); Manuel Zelaya (Partido Liberal de Honduras (PLH) (Liberal Party of Honduras)) won the 27 Nov 2005 elections and will be inaugurated on 27 2006.

Head of government: President Ricardo Maduro Joest (inaugurated 27 Jan 2002); Manuel Zelaya (Partido Liberal de Honduras (PLH) (Liberal Party of Honduras)) won the 27 Nov 2005 elections and will be inaugurated on 27 2006.

Ruling party: Partido Nacional (PN) (National Party) (elected 25 Nov 2001)

Area: 112,088 square km

Population: 6.94 million (2004)

Capital: Tegucigalpa

Official language: Spanish

Currency: Lempira (L) = 100 centavos

Exchange rate: L18.86 per US$ (Oct 2005)

GDP per capita: US$1,035 (2004)

GDP real growth: 4.20% (2004)

Labour force: 2.67 million (2004)

Unemployment: 28.50% (2004)

Inflation: 8.10% (2004)

Balance of trade: -US$1.27 billion (2004)

Foreign debt: US$5.37 billion (2004)*

* estimated figure

The economy in 2005

Honduras is finding ways of extricating itself from the control of US fruit companies and an arrogant once-powerful military command. Economic restructuring is a priority for Honduras, one of Latin America's poorest nations, as it attempts to diversify its export markets away from dependency on agriculture and remain in favour with multilateral organisations and international financiers. This has involved an increasingly unpopular privatisation programme in which prices have risen while incomes dropped.

The Honduran economy has grown steadily over the past few years. Inflation is gradually coming under control, being forecast at 7.8 per cent for 2005 by the IMF, a decrease from the 8.1 per cent level recorded in 2004. The IMF forecasts growth of 4.2 per cent in 2005 and 4.5 per cent for 2006.

Most companies in Honduras are small and family-owned, with the dominant sectors being commerce, hotels and restaurants, manufacturing and financial services. Many of these firms are operating to the limits of their capacity and company financial problems are often due to corruption and bad management. Successive governments have tried to promote private investment, but have been hampered by tortuous bureaucracy, an overvalued national currency and civil wars in each of the three neighbouring countries.

The approval of the Central American Free Trade Agreement should encourage the growth of foreign investment in Honduras. In May 2005 US President George W Bush pledged US$215 million in aid to Honduras. The aid endowment is designed to help reduce Honduras's impoverished rural communities and increase the country's capacity for trade.

Sector highlights

Agriculture is one of the most important economic activities in Honduras. The sector accounts for around 80 per cent of total exports, constitutes 20 per cent of total GDP and employs 57 per cent of the country's workforce. Sugar cane, bananas (grown on the northern lowland) and coffee are the main agricultural exports. The government is encouraging the growth of new banana varieties but it is likely to be a number of years before new crops become profitable exports.

The main food crops are maize, rice, sorghum and beans. Production of these staples has steadily risen, though food imports are still required to meet domestic demand. Other agricultural exports include frozen meat, wood, cotton and tobacco.

Emphasis has been on land reform and the cultivation of new crops such as cocoa, allspice, cardamom, melons and citrus fruits.

Honduras's industrial sector is the smallest in Central America and contributes in the region of 27 per cent to total GDP. Approximately 15 per cent of Honduras' workforce is employed in the sector. Government responsibility for the industrial sector has traditionally been divided between the ministry of economy's general directorate of industry, the central bank and various other official institutions. In the late 1980s, the government of the day introduced policies aimed at stimulating Honduran labour-intensive industries, especially agri-industry, while boosting investment and exports to combat high unemployment. The authorities since then have continued to try and release Honduras from dependency on certain commodities such as bananas and coffee.

Virtually no production equipment is produced in Honduras and capital goods must be imported from foreign suppliers. The demand for capital goods cannot be funded without the government's help and the need to expand the country's industrial base is being frustrated by financial constraints.

Manufacturing remains heavily dependent on imports of capital goods, raw materials and foreign technology; the biggest growth in the sector has been the *maquiladora* (in-bond assembly and manufacturing) industries. The four main areas of manufacturing in Honduras are concentrated around food processing, agro-export, *maquila* and chemicals. However, capacity utilisation is still low on account of Honduras' narrow domestic market and lack of international competitiveness.

The government has successfully assisted the growth of the Honduran industrial sector by designating free trade zones (FTZ) and privately funded Export Processing Zones (EPZs). The vast majority (90 per cent) of all merchandise currently manufactured in the zones is clothing. Cloth is manufactured in the US and exported to Honduras from where it is then re-exported as garments, often duty free, to the US.

Outlook

Honduras' economy is growing nicely but the country still remains very poor in terms of the number of people living below the poverty line. The Maduro presidency succeeded in steadying the Honduran macroeconomic ship but much work remains to be done. Growth is healthy while inflation is falling, but the latter is still at a higher rate than desired by policy makers in the country. With fresh political capital, the Zelaya administration will seek to continue the progress made under its predecessor government. If macroeconomic stability and a commitment to cutting crime – thereby improving the investment climate and increasing levels of foreign direct investment (FDI) – remain dual policy objectives, then the Honduran economy looks set to continue its upward trajectory in the immediate future.

KEY INDICATORS — Honduras

	Unit	2000	2001	2002	2003	2004
Population	m	6.46	6.62	6.78	6.86	6.94
Gross domestic product (GDP)	US$bn	5.90	6.40	6.60	7.00	*7.37
GDP per capita	US$	897	872	977	997	1,035
GDP real growth	%	5.0	2.5	2.0	2.0	4.2
Inflation	%	11.0	9.7	7.7	6.8	8.1
Exports (fob) (goods)	US$m	2,039.2	1,379.0	1,440.0	1,396.0	2,411.2
Imports (fob) (goods)	US$m	2,697.6	2,250.0	2,980.0	2,994.0	3,678.5
Balance of trade	US$m	-658.4	-850.0	-1,136.0	-1,598.0	-1,267.3
Current account	US$m	-509.7	-656.0	-450.0	–	-430.0
Foreign debt	US$bn	5.2	5.1	5.4	5.4	–
Total reserves minus gold	US$m	1,313.0	1,415.6	1,524.1	1,430.0	1,970.4
Foreign exchange	US$m	1,301.7	1,404.4	1,511.9	1,417.1	1,956.9
Exchange rate	per US$	14.84	15.47	16.44	17.43	18.20

* estimated figure

Honduras

Risk assessment

Politics	Improving
Economy	Improving
Regional stability	Good

COUNTRY PROFILE

Historical profile
1821 The Central American provinces (Costa Rica, Guatemala, Honduras, Nicaragua and El Salvador) declared independence from Spain.
1822 Central American confederation annexed itself to the Mexican Empire, under General Agustín de Iturbde, later Emperor Agustín I.
1823 Agustín I was overthrown and Mexico became a republic. The Central American states formed the United Provinces of Central America.
1825 Costa Rica, Guatemala, Honduras, Nicaragua and El Salvador formed the Central American Federation (CAF).
1838 The CAF was dissolved and Honduras became a fully independent republic.
1840–1957 Honduras was ruled by a military and civilian élite.
1957 The first democratic presidential election was won by Ramon Villeda Morales, a popular moderate reformist.
1963 Morales was ousted by Colonel Osvaldo Lopez Arellano in a military coup. Military rule continued until 1980.
1969 Honduras and El Salvador fought what became known as the 'soccer war', which was prompted by land disputes and El Salvador's win in the World Cup play-offs between the two countries. Over 3,000 people died.
1981 Presidential elections were won by Roberto Suazo Cordova of the Partido Liberal de Honduras (PLH) (Liberal Party of Honduras), although real power remained in the hands of the army under General Gustavo Alvarez.
1985 José Azcona Hoyo (PLH) won the presidential election, following a change in the constitution which limited the presidency to a maximum of one term.
1989 Rafael Leonardo Callejas Romero of the Partido Nacional (PN) (National Party), the right-wing opposition party, was elected president.
1993 Carlos Roberto Reina Idiáquez (PLH) won the presidential election.
1997 Carlos Roberto Flores Facussé (PLH) was elected president.
1998 Honduras was severely affected by Hurricane Mitch – around 11,000 people were killed and 1.3 million left homeless.
1999 The constitution was amended to make the president the commander-in-chief of the armed forces.
2001 Ricardo Maduro Joest (PN) was elected president and the PN won the legislative elections.
2002 In January, Honduras renewed diplomatic ties with Cuba, with whom it had broken relations in 1961. Persistent drought and the decline in world coffee prices left around 300,000 Hondurans suffering from hunger.
2003 After prisoners rioted, the government was accused of overcrowding prisons without solving the crime epidemic.
2004 In May, more than 100 prisoners, many of them gang members, were killed in a fire at San Pedro Sula.
2005 The 27 November presidential election was won by Manuel Zelaya Rosales, who will take power on 27 January.

Political structure
In addition to their unicameral national parliaments, El Salvador, Guatemala, Honduras, Nicaragua, Panama and Dominican Republic, which acceded to the Central American Parliament in February 2004, also return directly elected deputies to the supranational Central American Parliament.

Constitution
The constitution was promulgated in 1982 and amended in 1999, making the president the commander-in-chief of the armed forces.
Voting is by secret ballot and is compulsory for all citizens aged 18 or over. Members of the security forces are barred from voting. Municipal elections and elections of representatives in the 18 departments are held every two years.

Form of state
Presidential democratic republic

The executive
Power is divided between a strong executive, a unicameral national assembly and an independent judiciary. The president, three vice presidents and members of the national assembly serve parallel four-year terms. Presidents are not allowed to stand for re-election to a second term in office.

National legislature
Limited legislative functions are vested in the 128-member National Congress, elected by proportional representation every four years. Seats are distributed according to a complex system of proportional representation. The National Assembly appoints supreme court justices, who administer the judiciary.

Legal system
The legal system is based on Roman and Spanish civil law. Honduran laws are set out in the 'Cordigoes' or codes. The civil code covers dealings between people. The business code covers all matters relating to business while the penal code covers crime and punishment. The legal system is in desperate need of reform.

Last elections
27 November 2005 (presidential and legislative)

Results: Presidential: Manuel Zelaya (PLH), won around 51 per cent, Porfirio Lobo Sosa (PN) about 45 per cent. Parliamentary: THIS IS THE 2001 RESULT: Partido Nacional (PN) (National Party) 46.5 per cent of the vote, 61 seats; Partido Liberal de Honduras (PLH) (Liberal Party of Honduras 40.8 per cent, 55 seats.

Next elections
2006 (presidential and legislative)

Political parties
Ruling party
Partido Nacional (PN) (National Party) (elected 25 Nov 2001)
Main opposition party
Partido Liberal de Honduras (PLH) (Liberal Party of Honduras)

Population
6.94 million (2004)
Ethnic make-up
Around 90 per cent are *mestizos*, with minorities of Indians, blacks, whites and others. The largest indigenous group is the Garifuna, descendants of African slaves and Arawak Indian women from San Vicente, who live along the north coast. The Miskitos live in the Mosquitia – wetland, rainforest country – and the Lencas live around Copan.
Religions
More than 90 per cent of the population are Roman Catholics. There is freedom of worship.

Education
Primary education is compulsory and free of charge. Secondary education, from 13 years to 17 years, is not compulsory.
Literacy rate: 74.3 per cent total adult rate (World Bank)
Compulsory years: Seven to 12
Enrolment rate: 110 per cent gross primary enrolment, of the relevant age group (including repetition rate); 32 per cent gross secondary enrolment; 9 per cent gross tertiary enrolment (World Bank).
Pupils per teacher: 35 in primary schools

Health
In Honduras the quality of, and access to, healthcare is directly tied to income levels. Adequate health care is available to those able to pay the high cost. Health care for the urban and rural poor is limited.
Total expenditure on health is some 6 per cent of GDP, of which government spending is 53–54 per cent.
The ministry of health manages 28 hospitals with 4,093 beds. There are also 31 hospitals managed by the private sector. The private sector generally concentrates on individual care and does not participate in general public sector health activities. A national policy was formulated to make sure people have access to safe,

quality drugs. This policy however, has not been implemented.

The relatively young population places an extra burden on health facilities. Nearly two-thirds of the population have no access to essential drugs.

Infectious and parasitic diseases are the leading causes of death. Gastroenteritis and tuberculosis are serious problems. Approximately one-third of the population has no access to safe water or sanitation facilities.

HIV/Aids
The disease is spread predominantly through heterosexual intercourse. A study showed that the HIV prevalence in female sex workers was over 10 per cent (USCF – Centre for HIV Information, 2005).
HIV prevalence: 1.8 per cent aged 15–49 in 2003 (World Bank)
Life expectancy: 66.1 years (World Bank)
Fertility rate/Maternal mortality rate: 4.0 births per woman; maternal mortality 110 per 100,000 live births (World Bank).
Infant mortality rate: 32 per 1,000 live births; 25 per cent of children aged under five are malnourished (World Bank).
Head of population per physician/bed: 9 physicians, 3 nurses and 3 dentists per 10,000 population.

Welfare
Honduras is classified as a low-income country by the World Bank – 50 per cent of its inhabitants live below the poverty line. Social security benefits, mainly for pensions and health care, cover around 12 per cent of the Honduran population and account for around 1 per cent of GDP. Social security is mainly limited to urban centres. About 80 per cent of those covered live either in the capital, Tegucigalpa, or in the northern city of San Pedro Sula.

Organised social security started operations in 1962. Contributors are covered for general illness, maternity, accidents at work, professional illnesses, invalidity, old age and funeral expenses. There is no unemployment benefit.

Dependants, who account for 60 per cent of those covered, get some access to health care and pensions. Children under five years get free health treatment and wives of contributors receive maternity care in hospitals run by the social security institute. The widows of contributors receive pensions and there are more restricted pensions for widowers. Orphans, usually up to the age of 14 years, receive some support.

Main cities
Tegucigalpa (capital, estimated population 1.3 million in 2003), San Pedro Sula (505,200), La Ceiba (116,700).

Languages spoken
English is common in some parts of the north coast and the Caribbean Islas de la Bahía.
Official language/s
Spanish

Media
The constitution guarantees freedom of expression. Although there are no formal limits on what can be published by the media, editors have been known to complain that they are under pressure to play down issues judged sensitive by the authorities. The media generally avoids criticism of the military and coverage of human rights issues.
Press
Dailies: The daily newspapers are mainly in Spanish. These include *El Heraldo* and *La Tribuna* in Tegucigalpa; *Diario El Tiempo* and *La Prensa de Honduras* in San Pedro Sula. *El Nuevo Día* is also available.
Weeklies: The government publishes decrees in the weekly *La Gaceta*. *Honduras This Week* is an English language weekly paper covering Central America.
Periodicals: There are also several periodicals and a number of trade papers. The *Coconut Telegraph* is a periodical on holiday and travel.
Broadcasting
Radio and television play a key role in Honduras, where literacy is around 60 per cent. Television is dominated by Emisoras Unidas, which controls three channels. It also owns HRN, a major radio station. Roughly 90 per cent of homes in the capital, Tegucigalpa, have radios and 87 per cent have television. There are an estimated 330,000 television sets in Honduras.

The government has little direct participation in the media. All television stations and 80 per cent of newspapers are owned by private business interests.
Radio: There are over 280 commercial radio stations and one official station, Radio Honduras, run by the government.
Television: Nine television channels and 12 cable television stations operate from Tegucigalpa and San Pedro Sula.

Economy
The Honduran economy has grown steadily over the past few years. Inflation is gradually coming under control, forecast at 7.8 per cent for 2005, a decrease from the 8.1 per cent level recorded in 2004. The IMF forecasts growth of 4.2 per cent in 2005 and 4.5 per cent for 2006.

The archetypal 'banana republic', Honduras is finding ways of extricating itself from the control of US fruit companies and an arrogant once-powerful military command. Economic restructuring is a priority for Honduras, one of Latin America's poorest nations, as it attempts to diversify its export markets away from dependency on agriculture and remain in favour with multilateral organisations and international financiers. This has involved an increasingly unpopular privatisation programme in which prices have risen while incomes dropped.

Most companies in Honduras are small and family-owned, with the dominant sectors being commerce, hotels and restaurants, manufacturing and financial services. Many of these firms are operating to the limits of their capacity and company financial problems are often due to corruption and bad management. Successive governments have tried to promote private investment, but have been hampered by tortuous bureaucracy, an overvalued national currency and civil wars in each of the three neighbouring countries. Almost two-thirds of Honduras' population lives below the poverty line, with income inequality increasing. Hurricane Mitch strained the economy considerably after 1998 and cost an estimated US$2 billion. The economy is currently in a period of growth, although the changes in GDP remain too sluggish to support major improvements to poverty. However, public spending on health and education has alleviated some problems in the country.

The joining of the Central American Free Trade Agreement (Cafta) should encourage the growth of foreign investment in Honduras. The World Bank is making special loans to the country to increase competitiveness of its domestic industries and to assist immediate problems caused by the agreement.

In May 2005 US President George W Bush pledged US$215 million in aid to Honduras. The aid endowment is designed to help reduce Honduras's impoverished rural communities and increase the country's capacity for trade.

External trade
In 2004, Honduras, along with Costa Rica, the Dominican Republic, El Salvador, Guatemala and Nicaragua agreed to a proposed Central American Free Trade Agreement, known as Cafta.
Imports
Principal imports are machinery and transport equipment, industrial raw materials, chemical products, fuels and foodstuffs.
Main sources: US (51.3 per cent total, 2004), El Salvador (3.3 per cent), Mexico (2.9 per cent)
Exports
The government is currently trying to cultivate new crops and turn them into profitable exports. Honduras exports coffee, shrimp, bananas, gold, palm oil, fruit, lobster and timber.

Honduras

Main destinations: US (63.3 per cent total, 2004), El Salvador (2.8 per cent), Guatemala (2.6 per cent)

Agriculture

Farming

Agriculture is one of the most important economic activities in Honduras. The sector accounts for around 80 per cent of total exports, constitutes 20 per cent of total GDP and employs 57 per cent of the country's workforce.

Sugar cane, bananas (grown on the northern lowland) and coffee are the main agricultural exports. The government is encouraging the growth of new banana varieties but it is likely to be a number of years before new crops become profitable exports.

Hurrican Mitch devastated the agricultural sector in 1998 and just about wiped out the banana and coffee plantations. Further damage to the coffee sector occurred due to low world prices and ongoing drought. The price of a pound of robusta fell to around US$0.17 cents, the lowest for 30 years. By the end of December 2004 prices were back at over US$1 per pound.

Other agricultural exports include frozen meat, wood, cotton and tobacco.

The main food crops are maize, rice, sorghum and beans. Production of these staples has steadily risen, though food imports are still necessary to meet domestic demand.

Emphasis has been on land reform and the cultivation of new crops such as cocoa, allspice, cardamom, melons and citrus fruits.

Crop production in 2004 included: 5,362,753 tonnes (t) sugar cane, 1,135,000t oil palm fruit, 514,152t maize, 29,194t rice, 178,140t green coffee, 2,000t cocoa beans, 52,553t sorghum, 18,000t potatoes, 965,066t bananas, 260,000t plantains, 192,515t oilcrops, 195,936t citrus fruit, 53,000t tomatoes, 5,150t tobacco, 1,531,451t fruit in total, 418,365t vegetables in total. Livestock production included: 138,840t meat in total, 54,000t beef, 10,000t pig meat, *278t lamb and goat meat, 74,000t poultry, 40,015t eggs, 598,000t milk, *175t honey, 9,520t cattle hides.
* estimate

Fishing

Honduras' annual fish catch is typically over 18,000mt, of which approximately 12,000mt is shellfish. The country's main fish export is lobster, harvested by divers who spend up to seven hours a day on the sea bed. The lobsters are mainly exported to the US. Legislation requires all divers to undergo specific instruction and boat owners to hold licences to carry trained divers only. The government is expected to promote the potential of Honduras' fishing industry in order to attract investment and curtail growing unemployment along the country's coasts which has forced fishermen to dive for lobsters. Improved regulation would benefit the lobster colonies which are in danger of being depleted. Honduras also has a well-established shrimp farming industry.

Forestry

Honduras does not have a great deal of energy resources and consequently wood is widely used as an inexpensive form of fuel. This has led to a widespread problem of deforestation in Honduras.

During 1990–95, the average rate of deforestation was 2.3 per cent, the third highest rate in the Western hemisphere after Haiti and Paraguay. Although it is estimated that 7.4 million hectares of land were covered by forest in 1987, annual deforestation in the 1980s was thought to be in the region of 70,000 hectares. Since then the government has been keen to redress the rate of deforestation through education and development programmes.

The government has promoted the protection of Honduras' forests by agreeing with foreign companies such as Stone Container Corporation (US), to establish a comprehensive forestry management plan enabling Honduras to increase the size of its forest coverage.

In a typical year, exports of forest materials amount to US$43.1 million, while imports amount to US$100 million. Production in 2003 included 9,504,428 cubic metres (cum) roundwood, 801,000cum industrial roundwood, 421,000cum sawnwood, 801,000cum sawlogs & veneer logs, 9,000cum wood-based panels, 8,703,428cum wood fuel, 3,000mt charcoal.

Industry and manufacturing

Honduras's industrial sector is the smallest in Central America and contributes in the region of 27 per cent to total GDP. Approximately 15 per cent of Honduras' workforce is employed in the sector. Government responsibility for the industrial sector has traditionally been divided between the ministry of economy's general directorate of industry, the central bank and various other official institutions. In the late 1980s, government introduced policies aimed at stimulating Honduran labour-intensive industries, especially agro-industry, while boosting investment and exports to combat high unemployment. The authorities since then have continued to try and release Honduras from dependency on certain commodities such as bananas and coffee.

Virtually no production equipment is produced in Honduras and capital goods must be imported from foreign suppliers. The demand for capital goods cannot be funded without the government's help and the need to expand the country's industrial base is being frustrated by financial constraints.

Manufacturing remains heavily dependent on imports of capital goods, raw materials and foreign technology; the biggest growth in the sector has been the *maquiladora* (in-bond assembly and manufacturing) industries. The four main areas of manufacturing in Honduras are concentrated around food processing, agro-export, *maquila* and chemicals. However, capacity utilisation is still low on account of Honduras' narrow domestic market and lack of international competitiveness.

The key to helping the growth of the Honduran industrial sector has been the government-backed free trade zones (FTZ) and privately funded Export Processing Zones (EPZs). Roughly 90 per cent of all merchandise currently manufactured in the zones is clothing. Cloth is manufactured in the US and exported to Honduras from where it is then re-exported as garments, often duty free, to the US.

Tourism

The tourism industry of Honduras continues to expand. The sector now constitutes 10.4 per cent of the country's total GDP and accounts for 8.5 per cent of total employment.

Travel and tourism is an increasingly important economic activity, with the environment and Mayan remains as major attractions. Despite the 11 September 2001 terrorist attacks in the US and local problems, visitor numbers continued to rise annually. 549,500 arrivals were recorded in 2002, compared with 517,914 in 2001, a trend which continued in 2003. In 2004, the total rose once again, with 688,200 people visiting Honduras. Over half of the visitors come from other Central American countries.

Mining

At present the mining sector employs approximately 2 per cent of Honduras' total workforce. The country has large reserves of tin, iron, copper and coal. There are small reserves of gold, silver, lead and zinc that are extracted for export.

Hydrocarbons

Honduras does not produce oil at present, despite extensive offshore exploration aimed at locating deposits. Purchases of foreign oil are the country's main import. Apart from wood, primary energy output is limited to hydroelectric energy and vegetable residues, mainly bagasse (the waste left over from sugar cane once the juice is extracted). The first oil exploration licensing round was started in 2001. The area of a border dispute between Honduras and Nicaragua has possible large oil reserves. The area was opened for bidding by Nicaragua in 2002 without the dispute being resolved. Honduras imports all its oil needs and has no refining capacity.

Honduras is neither a producer nor an importer of natural gas.

Energy
In recent years, emphasis has been placed on offshore oil exploration and the development of Honduras' significant hydropower potential. At present, approximately a quarter of the country's energy requirements are imported.

The 292MW El Cajón hydroelectricity plant, and a second hydroelectric dam at Río Lindo/Yojoa, are meeting all the country's electricity needs as well as exporting power to Nicaragua, Costa Rica, El Salvador and Guatemala.

The electricity grids of Honduras and El Salvador have been linked in order to increase export trade in power.

Banking and insurance
The regulators of the banking and financial services sector of Honduras retain tight restrictions on bank ownership of fixed assets and limits on buying corporate shares. Foreign banks wishing to set up in Honduras must obtain approval from the president. Domestic and foreign-owned banks operate under identical rules, and historically there has been little difference in the type of business they conduct.

Central bank
Banco Central de Honduras
Main financial centre
Tegucigalpa

Time
GMT minus six hours

Geography
Honduras is in the middle of the Central American isthmus. It has a long northern coastline on the Caribbean Sea and a narrow southern outlet to the Pacific Ocean. Guatemala is to the west, El Salvador is to the south-west and Nicaragua to the south-east. Covering 112,088 square km, Honduras is the second largest country in Central America after neighbouring Nicaragua. Much of the country is covered by thick forests and mountains, while around a quarter of the land is suitable for farming. Apart from a low coastal plain in the north-east, the country is crossed by numerous ranges of mountains and hills. The highest peak is the Cerro de las Minas at 2,866 metres in the western Sierra de Celaque.

Climate
Honduras has a tropical climate on the coast and a temperate climate in the mountainous interior. Temperatures in the capital Tegucigalpa, at 960 metres, are usually between 15 degrees Celsius (C) and 30 degrees C. Rain falls throughout the year on the north coast, while the rest of the country has heaviest rains between May and November. The average rainfall is 3037mm per year. During the rainy season, May–November, the climate is temperate; in March and April the warm days are punctuated by cool nights; and in December–February it is cool and dry during the day, but chilly at night. The best time to visit is April–May.

Entry requirements
Passports
Passports are required by all and must be valid for six months upon arrival.
Visa
Visas are not required by nationals of most of the Americas and Europe (excluding Schengen agreement states), Australisia, Japan and some other Asian countries. Business visas should be accompanied by a company letter as proof of business intentions and a full itinerary. For confirmation and requirements, contact the local embassy.
Currency advice/regulations
There are some restrictions on the import and export of most foreign currencies. US dollars must be declared on arrival, and re-export is allowed up to the declared amount.

Health (for visitors)
Mandatory precautions
A yellow fever vaccination certificate is required if arriving from an infected area.
Advisable precautions
Typhoid, tetanus and polio vaccinations are advisable. There is a risk of malaria, especially in rural areas – prophylaxis is recommended. Water precautions are essential throughout the country. In 2003, Honduras, Guatemala and El Salvador reported serious outbreaks of dengue fever.

Hotels
Hotel standards are reasonable in Tegucigalpa and San Pedro Sula. Hotel bills are subject to 5 per cent sales tax.

Public holidays
Fixed dates
1 Jan (New Year's Day), 14 Apr (Americas Day), 1 May (Labour Day), 15 Sep (Independence Day), 3 Oct (Morozán Day), 12 Oct (Columbus Day), 21 Oct (Armed Forces Day), 25 Dec (Christmas Day).
Variable dates
Maundy Thursday, Good Friday.

Working hours
Banking
Mon–Fri: 0900–1500.
Business
Mon–Fri: 0800–1200, 1330/1400–1700; Sat: 0800–1100.
Government
Mon–Fri: 0800–1200, 1330/1400–1700; Sat: 0800–1100.

Electricity supply
110 or 220V AC, 60 cycles.

Social customs/useful tips
Men are very possessive of women. Avoid being familiar, looking at or giving a greeting kiss to women. Handshaking is the main form of greeting. Embracing is frowned upon by both men and women. Mothers are regarded as the leading family figures. It is a grave offence to insult someone's mother. Women rather than men are often the principal family breadwinners. Grandparents and elders are highly respected. The extended family plays an important social role by providing a sense of unity.

It is customary to send flowers to the hostess if invited to dinner or as a guest to someone's home.

Professional persons should be addressed by their title. Graduates are known as *Licenciados,* and correspondence to them should open with: *Estimado Señor Licenciado,* and close with: *Atentamente.*

Security
There is widespread petty and violent crime, including armed robbery, car hijacking, burglary and sexual assaults. Exercise vigilance, particularly in the poorer areas of Tegucigalpa, and do not carry large amounts of money, take only what is necessary and keep the rest deposited at the hotel. Do not travel by road at night.

Getting there
Air
National airline: There is no national carrier, but Grupo Taca and Lineas Aereas National de Hondura (LAN) regularly fly from Tegucigalpa to other destinations in the Americas, Caribbean and Europe.
International airport/s: Tegucigalpa-Toncontín (TGU), 4.8km from city; duty-free shop, bar, restaurant, bank, post office, vaccination centre, shops, car hire.
Airport tax: US$25 for international departures; not applicable for transit passengers departing the same day. There is an airport user fee L5 for domestic departures to Mosquitia and L10 to other destinations, and US$10 for international departures. It does not apply to transit or transfer passengers.
Surface
Road: It is possible to reach Tegucigalpa via the Pan-American Highway from

Goascorán (on the border with El Salvador) and from El Espino and Guasaule (on the border with Nicaragua). Bus services run from most Central American countries. Entry from Guatemala is possible via the Western Highway.
Main port/s: Ampala, La Ceiba, Puerto Cortés, Roatan, San Lorenzo, Trujillo/Castilla, Tela.

Getting about
National transport
Air: There are 190 usable airfields, of which two have long runways. Isleñas Airlines, Sosa Airlines and Rollins Air are the three local airlines, operating numerous flights between Tegucigalpa, San Pedro Sula, Roatan, La Ceiba, Trujillo and Tela. To reach more remote areas using other services, local enquiries should be made.
Road: Network of 10,468km, concentrated along coast (roughly San Pedro Sula to Trujillo) and the area between San Pedro Sula and Tegucigalpa and the Guatemalan border. The main highways are paved, although roads are of varying quality. Travel on unpaved roads is not recommended.
Buses: Frequent services San Pedro Sula to Tegucigalpa; also linking with Juticalpa, Danlí, Choluteca. In general services and extent of network between main centres are favourably reported.
Rail: There are passenger train services in the north, running between San Pedro Sula, Puerto Cortés and Tela, although they are somewhat ramshackle and the service is slow.
Water: Water transport is commonly used to travel between Honduras, the Caribbean islands and the bay islands. In Mosquitia almost all transport is along the waterways due to poor road infrastructure.
City transport
Taxis: Can be hailed, ordered by telephone or found at ranks; also possible to hail and share a taxi; fares by negotiation (sometimes a flat rate). Tipping is not usual.
Buses, trams & metro: Buses stop outside the entrance to the Toncontín international airport. All buses in and around the capital operate between 0500 and 2100.
Car hire
A national or international licence is required. Rental cars are available in Tegucigalpa, San Pedro Sula, La Ceiba and on the island of Roatán. Budget, Hertz and National all operate in Honduras.

BUSINESS DIRECTORY
The addresses listed below are a selection only. While World of Information makes every endeavour to check these addresses, we cannot guarantee that changes have not been made, especially to telephone numbers and area codes. We would welcome any corrections.

Telephone area codes
The international direct dialling code (IDD) for Honduras is +504 followed by the customer number.

Chambers of Commerce
American-Honduran Chamber of Commerce, Hotel Honduras Maya, PO Box 1838, Tegucigalpa (tel: 232-7043; fax: 232-2031; e-mail: amcham@t.hn2.com).

Cortes Camará de Comercio e Industrias, 17 Avenida Circunvalación, PO Box 14, San Pedro Sula (tel: 553-0761; fax: 533-3777; e-mail: ccic@ccichonduras.org).

Honduras Federación de Camarás de Comercio e Industrias, Edificio Castañito, Bulevar Morazan, Tegucigalpa, PO Box 3393 (tel: 232-6083; fax: 232-1870; e-mail: fedecamara@sigmant.hn).

Tegucigalpa Camará de Comercio e Industrias, Bulevar Centramérica, PO Box 3444, Tegucigalpa (tel: 232-4200; fax: 232-0159; e-mail: infoccit@ccit.hn).

Banking
Banco Atlantida SA, PO Box 3164, Plaza Bancatlan, Tegucigalpa (tel: 321-742; fax: 321-273).

Banco CentroAmericano de Integración Económico, Edificio Midence Soto, Nivel 10, PO Box 772, Tegucigalpa, M D C Honduras (tel: 372-230; fax: 311-906).

Banco Continental SA, PO Box 390, San Pedro Sula, Cortes (tel: 531-310; fax: 522-750).

Banco del Comercio SA (Bancomer), PO Box 160, San Pedro Sula, Cortes (tel: 533-600; fax: 533-128).

Banco de El Ahorro Hondureño SA, PO Box 3185, Tegucigalpa (tel: 375-161; fax: 374-638).

Banco de Honduras SA, PO Box 3434, Tegucigalpa (tel: 326-122; fax: 326-164).

Banco de la Exportación SA (Banexpo), PO Box 3988, Tegucigalpa (tel: 394-256; fax: 394-265).

Banco de las Fuerzas Armadas SA (Banffaa), PO Box 877, Tegucigalpa (tel: 312-051; fax: 313-832).

Banco de Los Trabajadores SA, PO Box 3246, Tegucigalpa (tel: 379-501; fax: 378-422).

Banco de Occidente SA, PO Box 3284, Tegucigalpa (tel: 370-310; fax: 370-486).

Banco del País SA, PO Box 314, San Pedro Sula, Cortes (tel: 525-202; fax: 525-229).

Banco Hondureño del Café (Banhcafe), PO Box 583, Tegucigalpa (tel: 328-370; fax: 328-332).

Banco Financiera Centroamericana SA (Ficensa), PO Box 1432, Tegucigalpa (tel: 381-661; fax: 381-630).

Banco La Capitalizadora Hondureña SA (Bancahsa), PO Box 344, Tegucigalpa (tel: 371-171; fax: 372-775).

Banco Mercantil SA (Bamer), PO Box 116, Tegucigalpa (tel: 320-006; fax: 323-137).

Banco Sogerín SA, PO Box 440, San Pedro Sula, Cortes (tel: 533-888; fax: 572-001).

Lloyds Bank, PO Box 3136, Tegucigalpa (tel: 366-864; fax: 366-417).

Central bank
Banco Central de Honduras, Barrio El Centro, Avenida Juan Ramón Mollna, PO Box 3165, Tegucigalpa MDC (tel: 372-270; fax: 382-879; e-mail: usbi@mail.bch.hn).

Travel information
National tourist organisation offices
Honduras Tourism Bureau, PO Box 3261, Tegucigalpa (tel: 383-974; fax: 382-102).

Ministries
Ministry of Agriculture, Boulevard Miraflores, Tegucigalpa, MDC (tel: 32-8394; fax: 325-375).

Ministry of Culture, Arts and Sport, Ave La Paz, Tegucigalpa, MDC (tel: 369-738; fax: 369-738).

Ministry of Defence, 4c, 5a Tegucigalpa, MDC (tel: 380-065; fax: 380-238).

Ministry of Education, 1C 2-3A Comaguela (tel: 228-517; fax: 374-312).

Ministry of External Relations, Antigua Casa Presidencial, Centro Civico Gubernamental, Tegucigalpa, MDC (tel: 343-297; fax: 341-484).

Ministry of Health, 3C 4A Tegucigalpa, MDC (tel: 228-518; fax: 384-141).

Ministry of Industry, Trade and Tourism, 5A, 4C Edif Salame, Tegucigalpa, MDC (tel: 382-025; fax: 372-836).

Ministry of Labour and Social Security, 7C 2-3 Ave Comayaguela (tel: 379-778; fax: 223-220).

Ministry of Natural Resources and Environment, Barrio la Fuente, Tegucigalpa, MDC (tel: 375-664; fax: 375-726).

Ministry of Public Works, Transport and Housing, Barrio la Bolsa, Comayaguela (tel: 33-7690; fax: 252-227).

Presidential Office, Palacio José Cecilio del Valle, Bd Juan Pablo II, Tegucigapa, MDC (tel: 326-282; fax: 31-0097).

Other useful addresses

Asociación Nacional de Industriales, Boulevard los Proceres, 4a Avenida, Colonia Lara, Tegucigalpa.

Asociación Hondureña de Productores de Café (Coffee Producers' Association), 10a Avenida, 6a Calle, Apdo 959, Tegucigalpa.

British Embassy, Edif Palmira, 3rd Floor, Colonia Palmira, Tegucigalpa (tel: 320-612, 320-618; fax: 325-480).

Consejo Hondureño de la Empresa Privada, Barrio la Plozuela, 5th Floor, Edificio San Miguel, Tegucigalpa.

Corporación Nacional de Inversiones (CONADI), Apdo 842, Tegucigalpa (tx: 1192).

División Estudios Económicos, Banco Atlántida, Apdo 57-C, Boulevard Centroamérica, Tegucigalpa.

Home Office, Palacio Nacional, 2o Piso, Tegucigalpa, MDC (tel: 228-604; fax: 37-1121).

Honduran Embassy (US), 3007 Tilden Street, NW, Washington DC 20008 (tel: 202-966-7702; fax: 202-966-9751; e-mail: embassy@hondurasemb.org).

Honduras Stock Exchange, PO Box 161, San Pedro Sula (tel: 534-410; fax: 534-480).

Secretary of the Treasury, 3C, 5A Tegucigalpa, MDC (tel: 220-111; fax: 382-309).

Secretaria de Planificación y Presupuesto (SECPLAN), 2 Avenida 9 y 10 Calle Comayaguela, Tegucigalpa.

US Embassy, Avenida La Paz, Apdo 26-C, Tegucigalpa (tel: 323-120; fax: 320-027).

Internet sites

Cámara de Comercio e Industrias de Cortes (Cortes Chamber of Commerce and Industry) (local, national and international business issues in Spanish only): http://www.123.hn/

Honduras yellow pages: http://www.only-honduras.com

Latin America Network Information Center: http://www.lanic.utexas.edu/

Hong Kong

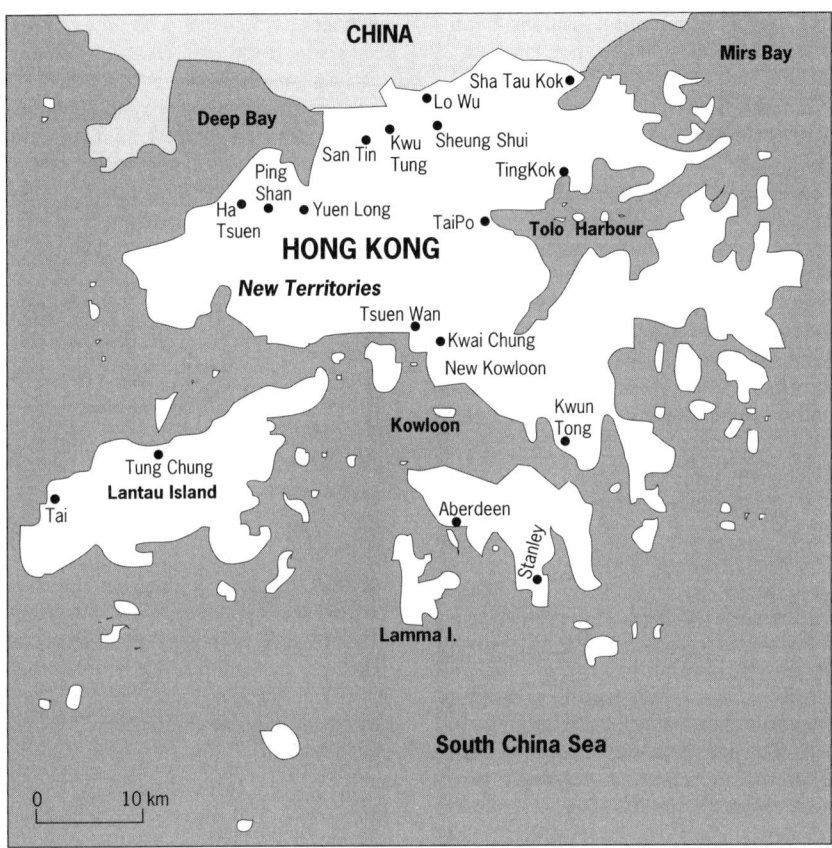

KEY FACTS

Official name: Xianggang Tebie Xingzhengqu (Hong Kong Special Administrative Region (SAR) of China)

Head of State: State President Hu Jintao (elected 15 Mar 2003)

Head of government: Chief Executive Donald Tsang (from 21 Jun 2005)

Ruling party: There is no official ruling party; all candidates and parties must receive official approval from the Zhongguo Gongchandang (Chinese Communist Party).

Area: 1,070 square km (including 235 islands)

Population: 7.84 million (2004)

Capital: There is no capital city as such, but the Legislative Council building is situated in the central district of Victoria, on Hong Kong Island

Official language: Chinese, English

Currency: (HK$) = 100 cents

Exchange rate: HK$7.76 per US$ (Oct 2005)

GDP per capita: US$23,667 (2004)

GDP real growth: 8.10% (2004)

Labour force: 3.71 million (2004)

Unemployment: 6.70% (2004)

Inflation: -0.40% (2004)

Balance of trade: -US$9.31 billion (2004)

Foreign debt: US$59.21 billion (2004)

The Hong Kong and China partnership – 'one country, two systems' – since the 1997 British hand-over, has seen a small pocket of unregulated capitalism operate within the world's largest communist nation. China's growth has been good news for Hong Kong business, with its economy in the ascendancy. However, powerful Chinese rule has strangled hopes for democracy in the supposedly autonomous region, at least for the foreseeable future. In 2005 one Chinese-controlled chief executive was replaced by another, and Disneyland set up camp in the region.

Leadership change

In March 2005 the Hong Kong Chief Executive Tung Chee-hwa declared his resignation of the leadership two years before his term expired. The public confidence this former shipping magnate inspired on his arrival in 1997 eventually faded and he came to be seen as a pawn of Beijing. He had been chosen by the Beijing administration for his acceptance of Chinese interference. Tung encountered much popular protest, most of all on the subject of his anti-subversion laws, about which 500,000 people turned out to demonstrate. This high turnout encouraged democracy activists and led to eyebrows being raised in alarm in Beijing. Donald Tsang, former financial secretary, immediately became the stand-in chief executive on his predecessor's resignation. Tsang is a Harvard graduate and was knighted by the British Queen Elizabeth II in 1997. He is highly experienced in the civil service and has a trusted reputation.

In March 2005 the Hong Kong government announced that the next chief executive would rule for only two years, in contravention of the Basic Law which sets each term at five years. China also discounted the possibility of direct elections for 2007 or 2008. Both these decisions were signs that China is setting out to determine Hong Kong law and seeking to step up control over the region. China is reacting to the building momentum for democratic reform by resolutely blocking progress.

Three men, Chim Pui-ching, Lee Wing-tat as well as Donald Tsang sought the leadership. However, candidates have to be nominated by 100 members of the election board to enter the running. If only one person generates enough nominations, no election is held. Tsang garnered 710 nominations out of a possible 800, and so he took up the two-year post unchallenged. In October 2005 a University of Hong Kong poll put public approval of Tsang at 62 per cent, the highest level of public confidence in leadership since 1997. This is slowly on the wane, however.

Democracy and protest

In 1997 when Hong Kong and the New Territories were handed back to the Chinese, the resident population were led to expect they were to get democracy and self-determination. The country's mini–constitution, the Basic Law, assures Hong Kong 'a high degree of autonomy' from China, and eventual democracy. Article 45 of the law states that 'the ultimate aim is the selection of the Chief Executive by universal suffrage'. Tsang, a stronger and more independent figure than the easily-manipulated Tung, was the focus of much expectation. He entered office with promises of establishing a more representative government, involving middle-class as well as purely business interests. However, Tsang too has shown much deference towards Beijing, not insisting upon the autonomy to which the region is legally entitled. China's tight grip on the province and its stifling of the democratic process has made universal voting look like a remote possibility – and has led to disappointment and frustration among the Hong Kong populace.

In January 2005 2,000 pro-democracy activists lined the streets of Hong Kong to demand political reform and the holding of elections in 2007 and 2008. They also protested about the excessive influence of business tycoons in the running of the country and the lack of concern for the poor. Business influence had been put into the spotlight by official plans for one company to develop the so-called West Kowloon Cultural District, a hub of shops, housing and museums in a waterside spot. There was concern about the granting of a virtual monopoly for such a large area and, after the protests, the government agreed to break up the development among different investors.

In September 2005, 60 Hong Kong democracy activists were permitted entry to mainland China for the first time in 10 years. They had been banned since 1989, when they had helped organise protests in support of the Tiananmen Square protestors. Meetings between the visitors and Chinese Communist party officials were arranged to discuss the political structure of Hong Kong and the fate of the Tiananmen Square demonstrators. Tsang praised the dialogue as being 'a very good start' – the meeting, allowing the democrats' freedom of expression, was certainly a historic first. It signals Chinese realisation that they cannot completely ignore the growing calls for democracy in Hong Kong.

In December 2005 Tsang's electoral reforms were blocked by pro-democracy lawmakers, who denounced the proposed changes as inadequate. The chief executive had announced plans to expand the Legislative Council from 60 to 70 people and increase the electoral committee from 800 people to 1,600, rather than to introduce suffrage to all citizens. This distinctly weak offering was thought to be the result of Chinese pressure. Tsang lamented the setback, and declared that he would not submit any new reforms in the next year. China also condemned the outcome of the vote, claiming it to be a betrayal of the people's wishes.

In apparent contradiction to the Chinese view, thousands of people organised a march to demonstrate for real democratic change and to protest against Tsang's weak offerings. The turnout was estimated to be 63,000 by police but 250,000 by the marchers themselves. The former head of the civil service, Anson Chan, was a significant figure among the protesters. The marchers wanted at least to be told when voting rights will be extended to all – the Basic Law states no time scheme for this. They stand some hope of success, considering that past marches precipitated the downfall of Tung.

In December 2005 Hong Kong hosted the latest meeting of the World Trade Organisation which characteristically generated significant levels of anti-globalisation violence. Nearly 1,000 people were arrested and 70 people injured when policemen attacked the protestors. The violence was the fiercest in the region for over fifteen years. Many of the protesters were South Korean farmers concerned about an end to their high rates of subsidies.

Economy

Hong Kong is one of the most unregulated, laissez faire markets in the world. The territory retained its title of world's freest economy in the *2005 Index of Economic Freedom*. However, despite seeming freedom, some businesses, especially in the utilities sector, have become monopolistic. A lack of legislation has prevented the flourishing of economic competitiveness. Hong Kong is reliant on trade with few natural resources and a declining manufacturing sector.

KEY INDICATORS — Hong Kong

	Unit	2000	2001	2002	2003	2004
Population	m	6.80	6.87	6.94	7.39	7.84
Gross domestic product (GDP)	US$bn	166.10	161.90	161.50	158.60	*163.01
GDP per capita	US$	24,426	23,566	24,000	23,125	23,667
GDP real growth	%	10.5	0.1	2.3	2.1	8.1
Inflation	%	-3.7	-1.6	-3.0	-2.6	-0.4
Unemployment	%	5.1	4.9	7.3	7.8	6.7
Exports (fob) (goods)	US$m	202,698.0	190,926.0	200,620.0	224,040.0	260,263.0
Imports (fob) (goods)	US$m	210,891.0	199,257.0	208,600.0	208,100.0	269,575.0
Balance of trade	US$m	-8,193.0	-8,331.0	-8,000.0	15,940.0	-9,312.0
Current account	US$m	8,915.0	11,968.0	12,600.0	16,180.0	15,870.0
Total reserves minus gold	US$m	107,540.0	111.2	111.9	118.4	123.5
Foreign exchange	US$m	107,540.0	111.2	111.9	118.4	123.5
Exchange rate	per US$	7.79	7.80	7.80	7.70	7.79

* estimated figure

Hong Kong

In March 2005 Hong Kong announced that it would achieve a balanced budget before its target date and generate the first surplus in 5 years. This financial success was achieved by means of a property boom, cuts in public spending and a large bond issuance. The expanding services industry also contributed to the upward trend. Hong Kong has benefited from the rise of China with its 2005 exports rising by 16 per cent on 2004/05. Stock markets, one third of which are made up of Chinese companies, also performed very well in 2005. This in turn led to the best ever year for initial public offerings (IPOs). Unemployment has reached its lowest levels for three years, helped in part by a tourism surge.

Uncharacteristically Hong Kong weighed up the idea of new economic restrictions and regulations in 2005.

The government began to consider the introduction of a national minimum wage early in 2005 as salaries have been stagnating and falling for three years. This would be set at around HK$4,500 (US$580) per month. As the demand for low-cost labour in the region has been almost entirely swallowed up by China, factory workers in Hong Kong have lost their jobs or suffered wage cuts. Other topics in discussion were overtime pay and an introduction of maximum working hours. Most people work Saturdays and a 50 hour working week is not unusual. Business is naturally opposed to the proposed changes. The IMF has recommended the financial authorities introduce a goods tax to increase government revenue, prompting more complaints from businesses. In January 2005 new measures were announced to crack down on the publication of false accounts. Those who produce dishonest figures will be subject to US$1.3 million fines or 10 years imprisonment.

The end of the global Multi-Fibre Agreement on 1 January 2005 which set quotas on the textile trade led to a substantial rise in Chinese cloth exports. The US and the EU are concerned by this rise and are looking for ways to re-introduce limits on Chinese goods. This led garment manufacturers to consider relocating some of their factories in Hong Kong, and bringing Chinese workers into the province to work in them. However, there are not only legal barriers preventing the import of workers, but costing problems – Chinese factory hands would qualify for higher wages if based in Hong Kong. There is not significant demand for factory work in Hong Kong, where standards of living are higher. People prefer to take office and service jobs. Despite these disincentives to Hong Kong investment there is a real likelihood of future expansion of the textile sector in the region.

Disneyland and pollution worries

In September 2005 Hong Kong DisneyLand opened its gates to the new wave of wealthy Chinese leisure-seekers. The US$1.8 billion project is 57 per cent owned by the government and should be a huge boost to the tourist sector. Disney songs and entertainment in the park will be performed in Cantonese.

The park has generated negative publicity about Hong Kong's environmental problems. The investment bank CLSA warned of a 'constant haze' over the attraction due to pollution wafting over from Chinese factories, power stations and transport. Hong Kong borders China's Guangdong region, the workshop of the world, home to tens of thousands of factories. Hong Kong has taken measures to curb sulphur emissions but unregulated southern China has contributed to its smaller neighbour's poor air quality and visibility.

Plans for China and Hong Kong to jointly develop the Pearl River delta by building a colossal 20km bridge raised environmental concerns. The bridge, expected to be complete in 2010, will cut journey times between the two areas from four hours to less than half an hour and bring significant economic benefits to the area. However increased traffic will bring further air and water pollution to the area and threaten the river's wildlife. China does not have a good record in environmental legislation and Hong Kong is known to be under the influence of wealthy businessmen.

In August 2005 a carcinogenic chemical, malachite green, was found in Chinese fish imported to Hong Kong. The chemical is an illegal industrial dye. It has fostered mistrust in Hong Kong of the food industry and of Chinese regulation. It is the latest in a chain of misfortunes, including Sars, avian 'flu and pig 'flu.

Outlook

The economy looks set to have another good year. The democracy lobby will continue to push for change in 2006 and is likely to be joined by a growing camp demanding progress on environmental improvements after a noticeable decline in local air and water quality and visibility. Tsang faces a difficult task trying to reconcile Chinese demands with domestic pressure.

Risk assessment

Economic	Good
Political	Fair
Regional Stability	Good
Stock Market	Good

COUNTRY PROFILE

Historical profile

Hong Kong offers one of the safest harbours in the region and has been a useful anchorage for European traders from the fifteenth century. The Chinese Emperor limited foreign traders to designated enclaves and limited their access to the Chinese domestic market. Trade between China and Europe became distorted when huge quantities of tea, silks and porcelain – through Hong Kong, one of the designated trading centres – was not reciprocated in foreign imports. Those goods that were imported were subject to high import tariffs – thus creating a serious European trade deficit. It was regrettable that the easiest product European merchants could find to trade with the Chinese was opium, much of it grown in the Indian subcontinent under British influence. The East India Company shipped many tons into China before the Emperor banned its sale.

1839 China impounded opium stocks and blocked further shipments. Major traders, Jardine Matheson, called on the British government to exert its right to trade. The Royal Navy blockaded Chinese ports, sparking the first Opium War.
1842 China ceded Hong Kong to Great Britain under provision of the *Treaty of Nanking*, following defeat in the first Opium War, which it fought to wipe out the illicit smuggling of opium into the country. Hong Kong was already a sizeable local fishing community with 3,000 inhabitants and 2,000 fishermen. Hong Kong became an important British naval base and attracted merchants from mainland China allowing the colony to become an important regional entrepôt.
1856–60 The second Opium War was fought in which the British and French defeated China.
1860 The Kowloon Peninsula was acquired under the *Convention of Peking*.
1898 The New Territories were leased from China for a period of 99 years.
1900s Immigration from the mainland increased as social turmoil due to the Boxer rebellion and general insecurity in China grew, while the prospects of employment in Hong Kong's light industries increased.
1937 Outbreak of the Sino-Japanese War. As the Japanese army advanced further into China, more Chinese fled to Hong Kong. It is estimated that over

500,000 Chinese entered the territory at this time.
1941 Hong Kong fell to the Japanese.
1945 After Japan's defeat in the Second World War, Britain resumed control of the territory.
1984 The UK conceded that from July 1997, on the expiry of the lease on the New Territories, China would regain sovereignty over the whole of Hong Kong. The Sino-British Joint Declaration contained detailed assurances on the future of Hong Kong.
1997 Hong Kong became a Special Administrative Region (SAR) of the People's Republic of China in an arrangement to last for 50 years. The Hong Kong stock market crashed; a fear that currency speculators would trade the Hong Kong dollar down in value prompted authorities to raise interest rates.
1998 Only 23 per cent of eligible voters turned out to choose an 800-member election committee with powers to nominate the chief executive and 10 legislators. The election process was criticised as complicated and undemocratic. Hong Kong International Airport on Lantau Island, the largest civil engineering project in history, was opened.
1999 Beijing redefined the constitution, ruling who had the right to live in Hong Kong. This constitutional change sparked protests.
2000 There was a low turnout in the elections which saw the Democratic Party (DP) lose a seat to the pro-Beijing Democratic Alliance for the Betterment of Hong Kong (DAB) in the Legislative Council (LegCo).
2001 Chief Secretary Anson Chan, holder of the SAR's second most powerful office, resigned, amid concerns that pressure from Beijing had made her position unsustainable. Donald Tsang replaced Chan as chief secretary.
2002 Chief Executive Tung Chee Hwa was appointed for a second five-year term.
2003 The flu-like killer disease, Severe Acute Respiratory Syndrome (Sars), spread to Hong Kong from mainland China. Around 500,000 people protested over a proposed anti-subversion law, which many believe threatened basic rights; another demonstration of 50,000 people called for universal suffrage and the dismissal of Chief Executive Tung Chee-hwa.
2004 In April, Chinese legislators ruled out direct elections for a Hong Kong leader in 2007.
2005 On 10 March, Chief Executive Tung Chee-hwa resigned due to ill health; Chief Secretary Donald Tsang became acting chief executive. Henry Tang became acting chief executive on 1 June after the State Council approved the resignation of Donald Tsang. On June 16 a 796-member electoral college chose Tsang as chief executive; he was declared elected as the only valid candidate. He was officially appointed to the post on 21 June and sworn in on 24 June. In December Hong Kong's legislators rejected an electoral reform package proposed by Tsang, saying the reforms did not go far enough towards democracy. Main proposals included expanding the committee responsible for electing the chief executive and increasing the size of the legislature.

Political structure
Constitution
The Basic Law, promulgated by the People's Republic of China (PRC) in 1990, effectively became Hong Kong's constitution after sovereignty of the former British colony was handed over to mainland China in July 1997. The Basic Law pledges to maintain Hong Kong's economic, social and political distinctiveness for a period of 50 years after the handover to the PRC, under the principle of 'one country, two systems'. Foreign affairs and defence are the responsibility of the central government in Beijing.

Form of state
Special Administrative Region (SAR) of the People's Republic of China

The executive
Hong Kong is administered by a Beijing-appointed chief executive, who represents the Chinese Politburo. Tung Chee Hwa was appointed chief executive by a 400-member Selection Committee in 1996, assuming the role in July 1997. The 13-member Executive Council (ExCo) serves in an advisory role for the Chief Executive. Under the terms of the Basic Law, an 800-member 'election committee', mostly selected from the business community via functional constituencies, will nominate future chief executives.

National legislature
The 60-seat unicameral LegCo comprises 24 members directly elected by geographical constituency, 30 members indirectly elected to represent professional and other functional constituencies, and six indirectly elected by the 800-member 'election committee'.
The first term was two years from 1998 to 2000; subsequent terms are four years.

Legal system
Under the Basic Law, Hong Kong's legal system is guaranteed independence from the Chinese judiciary. A Hong Kong Court of Final Appeal replaced the Privy Council in the United Kingdom as the highest court. The autonomy of this institution was seriously undermined in 1999 after a bitter dispute between the executive and the court over the migration of dependants from mainland China, in which China's legislature, the National People's Congress (NPC), overruled the Court of Final Appeal. However, the government in Beijing declared that recourse to the NPC would be kept a rare and exceptional act, and has not been invoked since.

Last elections
September 2004 (LegCo)
Results: Legislative Council (third term): the number of members returned by geographical constituencies through direct elections rose from 24 to 30, accounting for half of all the LegCo members.

Next elections
2008 (LegCo)

Political parties
Ruling party
There is no official ruling party; all candidates and parties must receive official approval from the Zhongguo Gongchandang (Chinese Communist Party).

Main opposition party
There is no formal opposition. The largest single party in the Legislative Council is the Democratic Party (DP) (liberal).

Population
7.84 million (2004)

Ethnic make-up
Approximately 98 per cent of the population is of Chinese descent. There are Caucasian, Indian and Filipino minorities, perhaps totalling more than 200,000, but many of these are seasonal migrant workers.

Religions
Buddhism and Taoism (74 per cent); Confucianism, Islam and Hinduism (17 per cent); Christianity (9 per cent). There are places of worship for most other religious groups. Falun Gong, the sect banned in mainland China, is legal in Hong Kong.

Education
Primary education is provided free in all government schools and in most government-assisted schools from the ages of six to 11 years. Secondary schools are divided into junior and senior levels, for 12–14-year-olds and 15–16-year-olds, respectively. The secondary school system consists of Anglo-Chinese grammar schools, Chinese middle schools, secondary technical schools and pre-vocational schools. There are a number of universities, several of which used to be technical colleges. After the British handover in 1997, 24 of Hong Kong's 124 secondary schools which taught in English were ordered to change to Cantonese. Government expenditure on education amounts to over 20 per cent of the SAR government budget. The largest proportion of the budget is spent on basic education, accounting for 68.8 per cent of total spending on education.

Hong Kong

Literacy rate: 93.8 per cent total, 90.1 per cent female; adult rates (World Bank).

Health
Government efforts have been mainly geared to the continuous development of the primary health care services. Eighteen health centres and 18 visiting health teams provide services to the elderly and their carers. There are three types of hospital in Hong Kong: public, government-assisted and private. Provision of hospital service at nominal cost is made universally accessible to all people. Hong Kong's health care service faces a huge financial strain due to its ageing population and escalating medical costs.

Life expectancy: 80.1 years (World Bank)

Fertility rate/Maternal mortality rate: 1.0 birth per woman; maternal mortality 5.6 per 100,000 total births (World Bank).

Birth rate/Death rate: 7.9 births and 5 deaths and per 1,000 people (World Bank)

Infant mortality rate: 2.7 per 1,000 live births (World Bank)

Welfare
The social security schemes available in Hong Kong cover a broad range of developmental, support and remedial services, and financial assistance to those in need. The Comprehensive Social Security Assistance Scheme is means-tested and non-contributory. The Scheme provides cash assistance to individuals and families to meet their basic and essential needs. The recipients are also helped through various initiatives to establish self-reliance. The Social Security Allowance Scheme aims to meet the special needs of the elderly and people with disabilities. The Accident Compensation Schemes provide short-term assistance to families or individuals in cases of reduced or lost earnings.

Main cities
Victoria (Hong Kong Island) (estimated population 2.4 million); Kowloon (two million); New Territories (1.3 million); outlying islands (60,000).

Languages spoken
Cantonese is the Chinese language spoken at home by more than 90 per cent of the population. Mandarin Chinese (Putonghua), the official language of the People's Republic of China, is widely understood.
English is universally understood in business and commerce.

Official language/s
Chinese, English

Media
The branch offices of China's official Xinhua state news agency in Hong Kong and Macao were renamed from 18 January 2000 as the Liaison Offices of the Central People's Government for their respective Special Administrative Regions (SARs).

Press
Hong Kong enjoys greater press freedom than many other Asian countries. It does not impose prior censorship on its newspapers or television and radio news reports, although it does censor motion picture and television films.

Dailies: English-language dailies include *South China Morning Post*, *Hong Kong Standard*, and *Hong Kong Commercial Daily*. There are around 50 Chinese-language dailies, *Oriental Daily News* having the largest circulation. Others include *Ming Pao*, *Ming Pao Daily News*, *Sing Tao Daily* and *Ta Kung Pao*.

Weeklies: The leading weeklies are *Asia Week*, *Far Eastern Economic Review*, and *Hong Kong This Week*, a weekly newspaper published in co-operation with the Hong Kong Tourist Association (listing events and items of interest to visitors).

Business: There are numerous trade and technical publications in English and Chinese. *Asia Times*, a regional daily business newspaper, was first published in 1995. Monthly business magazines include *Asia Incorporation*, *Asian Business* and *Cargo News Asia*. Quarterly magazines on trade issues are *Asian Furniture News* and *Business and Technology Information Quarterly*. Financial, banking and investment news can be obtained from *Finance Asia*. Technologies magazines are *PC World Hong Kong* and *Nikkei Electronics Asia*.

Periodicals: There are over 500 periodicals in circulation in Hong Kong. *Adweek Asia* caters to marketing and public relations and *Sun* (monthly) features issues of ethnic interest. Other popular monthly entertainment magazines include *BC Magazine* and *Beat Magazine*.

Broadcasting
Radio: There are 15 different radio channels in English and Chinese.

Television: There are two commercial television stations, Hong Kong TVB and Asian Television. Both broadcast Chinese and English-language services. Individual foreign holdings in broadcasting companies are limited to 10 per cent and total overseas interests to 49 per cent. There is also one satellite broadcaster based in Hong Kong – Star TV – and one cable television operator.

Advertising
Advertising is available in the press, on commercial radio and TV, in cinemas and on poster sites, with some direct mail. Advertising expenditure is equivalent to 1.4 per cent of GDP.

Economy
Hong Kong's economy is concentrated around its services industry, which should enable it to capitalise on the enhanced trade flows between China and the wider world, leading to growth in demand for Hong Kong's financial, insurance and shipping services.

The 1997–98 Asian financial crisis led to a deep recession and a collapse of the property market. A second recession came with the global downturn of 2001–02, and the 2003 outbreak of Sars also aggravated the situation.

Hong Kong has enjoyed a remarkable recovery since the Sars crisis. GDP increased from around two per cent in 2003 to over eight per cent in 2004. A boom in tourism from the mainland as a result of China's easing of travel restrictions, a return of consumer confidence and a rise in exports contributed to the revival. Rising unemployment was a problem for several years, but by 2005, in response to the expansion of the financial and tourism sectors, employment figures began to improve.

China's decision to put the Pearl River Delta area at the forefront of its development strategy for the twenty-first century should shore up Hong Kong's position as a trading intermediary, whether through passage of physical goods or as a provider of key services.

External trade
Imports
Main imports are raw materials and semi-manufactures, consumer goods, capital goods, foodstuffs and fuels, (most is re-exported).

Main sources: China (43.5 per cent total, 2004), Japan (12.1 per cent), Taiwan (7.3 per cent), US (5.3 per cent), Singapore (5.3 per cent), South Korea (4.8 per cent)

Exports
Trade between Hong Kong and China represent the SAR's main market. Exports include electrical machinery and appliances – telecommunications, sound recording and reproducing apparatus – textiles, apparel, footwear, watches and clocks, toys, plastics, precious stones and printed material.

Main destinations: China (44 per cent total, 2004), US (17 per cent), Japan (5.3 per cent)

Re-exports
The country re-exports large volumes of goods to China and US. Typically, 31 per cent are in the form of raw materials and 53 per cent consumer goods. The volume of re-exports handled by the SAR is expected to decline.

Agriculture

Farming
Agriculture accounts for around 0.1 per cent of GDP. The land area is mountainous, with fertile soils when they are watered. Agricultural land, including 600 hectares of orchards, accounts for 7 per cent of the total land area.

Main crops include sweet potatoes, yams, taro, sugar cane, white cabbage, flowering cabbage, lettuce, chinese kale, radishes and watercress.

Fishing
Hong Kong has a fishing fleet of about 4,900 vessels, most of which are mechanised. The fishing sector employs about 24,000 fishermen, who are provided with training organised by the Agriculture and Fisheries Conservation Department (AFCD) in order to enhance the competitiveness of the sector. Pond and marine fish farming in the New Territories accounts for 3 per cent of total production. Seafood production can reach up to 200,000 tonnes per annum. Freshwater fish production is more limited, typically 4,000 tonnes or less per annum. In addition, Hong Kong imports in the region of 60,000 tonnes of freshwater fish per annum and some 500,000 tonnes of seafood, of which 300,000 tonnes are typically re-exported.

Industry and manufacturing
Industry accounts for around 11 per cent of GDP and employs 18 per cent of the workforce. The relocation of manufacturing operations from Hong Kong to mainland China is causing a long-term decline in the sector. The re-export sector, in contrast, has grown due to growing consumer demand and industrial production on the mainland.

Tourism
Tourism is the most important sector of the economy. It was affected by the Sars outbreak in 2003, which reduced visitor numbers, particularly from mainland China, its largest market. A prompt, vigorous and imaginative strategy quickly reversed the initial impact to such effect that the sector boomed in 2004 with a 40.4 per cent increase in visitor numbers. The impetus was mainly due to an increase in tourists from mainland China, who comprised 56 per cent of the 21,810,630 arrivals. The upward trend increased in 2005.

Infrastructure and attractions are being expanded, especially in connection with the new Disneyland opened in September 2005. Tourism is expected to contribute two per cent to GDP in 2005.

Environment
Hong Kong is suffering air pollution as a result of pollution from southern China; visibility has declined over the past 30 years and continues to worsen. Although Hong Kong has sharply reduced its own emissions, it lies at the southern end of a vast industrial conurbation that includes Guangzhou and Shenzhen.

Mining
Mining accounts for less than 0.05 per cent of GDP, producing mainly kaolin (around 44,500 tonnes) and feldspar (around 5,500 tonnes).

Hydrocarbons
Hong Kong relies entirely on imports of hydrocarbons.

Natural gas is brought to Hong Kong via the pipeline from the South China Sea offshore gas field and is used for power generation.

Annual coal imports of around nine million tonnes meet 20 per cent of energy consumption.

Financial markets

Stock exchange
The Hong Kong Stock Exchange is the world's seventh largest in terms of capitalisation and the second largest in Asia, ranking only behind Japan.

Banking and insurance
Domestic banks in Hong Kong have tended to rely on the property sector for their earnings. Mortgages and other property-related lending still account for 40 to 50 per cent of total loans. Banking practice codes were revised in 2001 to make banking more transparent and consumer friendly. In 2002, some of the criteria for entry to the banking sector were relaxed. The aim was to attract a wider range of domestic and international banks to become involved in the SAR.

Hong Kong is an excellent location for insurers and has the largest number of insurance companies in Asia. Mainland Chinese insurers are linking up with foreign insurers in Hong Kong to cater for China's insurance market. By 2003, there were around 7,000 insurance establishments in the SAR with a total premium income of US$7 billion. French AXA group, the world's biggest insurance company, has its regional headquarters in Hong Kong.

Central bank
Hong Kong has no finance ministry or official central bank. The Hong Kong Monetary Authority (HKMA) oversees the monetary and banking system.

Main financial centre
Central District

Time
GMT plus eight hours (GMT plus seven hours in summer)

Geography
Hong Kong comprises some 235 islands and islets and a portion of the Chinese mainland, adjoining China's southern province of Guangdong. It consists of three areas: Hong Kong Island, the Kowloon Peninsula and the New Territories, which account for 92 per cent of the territory. About 75 per cent of Hong Kong's land is unsuitable for food production, consisting of hills that rise from sea level to 900 metres.

Climate
Hong Kong is subtropical and monsoonal. Summer (May to mid-September) is hot and humid with a risk of typhoons. July and August can be very hot. Autumn (September to December) is generally sunny, but drier, and the most pleasant time of year. Winter (December to February) is dry, but can get uncomfortably cold, with an average temperature of 15 degrees Celsius (C). Spring (March and April) is moderately warm and damp. The average annual temperature is about 23 degrees C, while rainfall averages 2,224mm per year, and humidity is often above 83 per cent.

Dress codes
Business dress is formal as appearance is taken seriously. Very smart dress is also *de rigueur* for ladies; skirts are advisable, rather than trousers.

Entry requirements

Passports
A valid passport is required by all. Passports must be valid for six months after arrival.

Visa
Regulations regarding entry into Hong Kong are extensive owing to the high level of illegal immigration. Travellers are advised to obtain up-to-date information before any journey.

Visas are not required by all. A full list of exceptions and periods of stay (usually 90 days) can be found on www.immd.gov.hk/ehtml/hkvisas_4.htm. Business and tourist visas are considered the same, up to the minimum time allowed to visit. For further clarification email: enquiry@immd.gov.hk; or contact the local Chinese embassy.

Currency advice/regulations
There are no currency restrictions.

Customs
Personal effects, one litre of alcohol and 200 cigarettes are allowed in duty-free. There is strict enforcement of anti-drug laws and this can sometimes lead to delays at the airport, with spot checks on departing as well as incoming passengers. Visitors wishing to purchase ivory products in Hong Kong will need an export licence from the Hong Kong authorities, and will

Hong Kong

also need to show an import licence for their final destination.

Prohibited imports
Narcotics, fireworks, firearms, mace sprays or stun guns, textiles, ivory products, animals and plants, game, meat and poultry. Visitors entering from China should expect searches for fireworks.

Health (for visitors)
Mandatory precautions
Cholera certificates are sometimes required for individuals coming from an infected area. Yellow fever inoculation is needed for travellers from countries where the disease is known to exist.

Advisable precautions
Vaccinations are recommended for diphtheria, tuberculosis, hepatitis 'A' and 'B', polio, tetanus and typhoid. Malaria precautions should be taken. Tap water is safe to drink.

Hotels
A 10 per cent service charge and 5 per cent tax are added to hotel bills.

Credit cards
Major international credit cards are widely accepted, although cash prices may be lower.

Public holidays
Fixed dates
1 Jan (New Year's Day), 5 Apr (Ching Ming/Tomb Sweeping Day), 1 May (Labour Day), 1 Jul (HKSAR Establishment Day), 1 Oct (National Day), 25 Dec (Christmas Day), 26 Dec (Boxing Day).

Variable dates
Good Friday, Easter Monday, Chinese New Year (Jan/Feb, three days), Birth of Buddha (May), Chinese Mid-Autumn Festival (Sep/Oct), Chung Yeung Festival (Oct).

Working hours
Shopping and services may be restricted during Chinese New Year, but less so during the Christmas period.

Banking
Mon–Fri: 0900–1630; Sat: 0900–1230.

Business
Mon–Fri: 0900–1700; Sat: 0900–1300.

Government
Mon–Fri: 0900–1300, 1400–1700; Sat: 0900–1230.

Shops
Central District 1000–1900; Causeway Bay and Wanchai 1000–2130; Tsimshatsui East 1000–1930; Tsimshatsui, Yaumatei and Mong Kok 1000–2100. Most department stores and shops open Sundays. Some Japanese stores close one day per week, and street markets operate all day and into the night.

Telecommunications
Mobile phones
GSM 900/1800 services are available throughout the islands and territories.

Electricity supply
200V AC, 50Hz. No uniformity in plug design.

Weights and measures
Metric system (Imperial system and local units also in use).

Social customs/useful tips
Western influence in Hong Kong has produced ways of doing business that are similar to other major business capitals. However, behind the facade of modern office blocks and neon-lit shopping malls, ancient Chinese customs still survive and have become part of the life of the foreign community.
Business cards are handed out liberally as a method of developing a network of professional contacts. A Chinese translation on the reverse side is a worthwhile addition. Use both hands when offering a business card, as passing it with one hand is seen as impolite.
Appearances of wealth are considered important in a territory that is dedicated to making money. Business contacts are ostentatiously wined and dined. Most entertaining is done in restaurants. It is considered bad manners to divide the bill after a meal. If you go to a dinner as the guest of honour, you should rise and thank the host briefly for his hospitality. Personal friendships and family ties oil the wheels of business. The wealthy keep a high social profile, donating large sums of money to charity.
Punctuality is helpful as most people have packed days, although some allowances are made for the heavy traffic.
Policemen who speak English have a red shoulder badge.

Security
The level of crime against visitors is relatively low. Theft, mainly by pickpockets, is a problem on the streets.

Getting there
Air
National airline: Cathay Pacific Airways
International airport/s: Hong Kong International (HKG), 34km from the centre. Post office, bank, bureau de change, restaurants/cafeterias, duty free shop, taxis.
Airport tax: HK$120, excluding children under 12 years.

Surface
The business district and commercial centre of Hong Kong is located on Hong Kong island. Kowloon and the new territories across the harbour are part of the Asia mainland, with road links providing connections.

Road: Bus services link Guangzhou to the Hong Kong border.
Rail: The Kowloon-Canton Railway Corporation (KCR) is the main carrier of passengers to and from China, with express trains serving Kowloon-Guangzhou and Kowloon-Lowu.
Water: Hovercraft services operate four times a day to and from Guangzhou and several times daily to and from Zhuhai. There are frequent daily services to and from Macao by hovercraft (75 minutes), jetcats (75 minutes), high speed ferry (90 minutes) and jetfoil (60 minutes).
Main port/s: Victoria Harbour (Hong Kong Island) and Tolo Harbour (New Territories).

Getting about
National transport
Air: Dragon Airlines (Dragonair) is the regional airline.
Hong Kong maintains separate immigration and customs policies from the mainland and flights between them are treated as international and not domestic flights.
Road: Hong Kong's road network is extensive and of high quality but often congested in central areas.
Buses: Bus services are inexpensive and convenient. There are three main private bus companies, China Motor Bus (CMB), Citybus and Kowloon Motor Bus (KMB, Kowloon only), and private minibus services.
Rail: There are three rail systems which operate outside urban areas. The KCR runs a passenger service between Kowloon and Guangzhou (China) and a suburban service to the new towns of the north-eastern New Territories; KCR also operates the Light Rail Transit network in the north-western New Territories; a cable-hauled funicular railway operates on Hong Kong Island between Garden Road in the Central District to Victoria Gap on the Peak.
The Airport Express is a dedicated high-speed train link, with a journey time of 23 minutes from central Hong Kong to the airport.
Water: There are extensive ferry, hovercraft, hydrofoil and coastal services between the islands of Hong Kong.

City transport
Taxis: Metered taxis are readily available in most areas of the territory. They carry four to five passengers. Cabs are painted green and silver in the New Territories, and red and silver in town. Hong Kong taxis are reasonably priced. It is advisable to have the destination written in Chinese. Tips are discretionary. Taxi drivers retain odd cents of change as a matter of course. Meters calculate time and distance. A ride from the airport to Central

Nations of the World: A Political, Economic and Business Handbook

District will include a charge for the cross-harbour tunnel, double the actual toll.
Buses, trams & metro: There are regular shuttle buses to and from the airport to both Central District (Hong Kong Island) and Tsimshatsui (Kowloon). They are about 20 per cent cheaper than taxis and serve five routes every 12–15 minutes. Airport bus routes A11 and A12 operate 0600–2359 hours to Central District, journey time 70 minutes.
Trams: A flat fare system operates on Hong Kong Island's double-decker five-line tram system. The trams are crowded at rush hour, but afford good views of Hong Kong at other times.
Trains: Airport Express Train link takes 23 minutes to Hong Kong Station, operates 0600–0100 hours.
Ferry: There are regular ferry services across the narrow strip of water from Star Ferry terminal at the north of Hong Kong Island to Kowloon.
Car hire
A valid driving licence issued in the country of origin may be used for up to 12 months. Parking difficulties and traffic congestion should be taken into account when planning to drive in Hong Kong. Chauffeur-driven and self-drive car hire is available.

BUSINESS DIRECTORY

The addresses listed below are a selection only. While World of Information makes every endeavour to check these addresses, we cannot guarantee that changes have not been made, especially to telephone numbers and area codes. We would welcome any corrections.

Telephone area codes
The international direct dialling code (IDD) for Hong Kong is +852, followed by subscriber's number.

Useful telephone numbers

Emergencies	999
Directory enquiries	108
Problems	109
International calls	010
Calls to China	012
Collect calls (reversed charge)	011
Tourist information	2801-7177
International direct dialling code enquiries	013

Chambers of Commerce
American Chamber of Commerce in Hong Kong, 1904 Bank of America Tower, 12 Harcourt Road, Central (tel: 2526-0165; fax: 2810-1289; e-mail: amcham@amcham.org.hk).

British Chamber of Commerce in Hong Kong, Emperor Group Centre, 288 Hennessy Road, Wan Chai (tel: 2824-2211; fax: 2824-1333; e-mail: info@britcham.com).

Banking
Bank of East Asia Ltd, GPO Box 31, 10 Des Voeux Road, Central (tel: 2842-3200; fax: 2845-9333).

Chekiang First Bank Ltd, Chekiang First Bank Centre, 1 Duddell Street (tel: 2922-1222; fax: 2866-9133).

The China State Bank Ltd; 39-41 Des Voeux Road, Central (tel: 2841-9333; fax: 2845-0584).

Dao Heng Bank Ltd, 11th Floor, The Center, 99 Queen's Road, Central (tel: 2218-8822; fax: 2285-3822).

DBS Kwong on Bank Ltd, 139 Queen's Road Central, Central (tel: 2815-3636; fax: 2167-8222).

Hang Seng Bank Ltd, Hang Seng Bank Headquarters, 83 Des Voeux Road, Central (tel: 2825-5111; fax: 2845-9301).

Hong Kong and Shanghai Banking Corp, 1 Queen's Road, Central (tel: 2822-1111; fax: 2868-1646).

Hua Chiao Commercial Bank Ltd, Hua Chiao Commercial Building, 88-98 Des Voeux Road, Central (tel: 2542-9888; fax: 2543-4035).

Nanyang Commercial Bank Ltd, 151 Des Voeux Road, Central (tel: 2852-0888; fax: 2815-3333).

Overseas Trust Bank Ltd, 11th Floor, The Center, 99 Queen's Road, Central (tel: 2218-2706; fax: 2285-3313).

Shanghai Commercial Bank Ltd, 12 Queen's Road, Central (tel: 2841-5415).

Wing Lung Bank Ltd, 45 Des Voeux Road, Central (tel: 2826-8333; fax: 2810-0592).

Central bank
Hong Kong Monetary Authority, 3 Garden Road, Central (tel: 2878-8196; fax: 2878-8197; e-mail: hkma@hkma.gov.hk).

Travel information
Cathay Pacific Airways, Swire House, 9 Connaught Road, Central (tel: 2747-5000; fax: 2810-6563).

Hong Kong Automobile Association, March Road, Wanchai (tel: 2574-3394).

Star Ferry Concourse, Kowloon; Shop 8, Basement Jardine House, Central (tel: 2801-7177 (visitor hotline); fax: 2810-4877).

National tourist organisation offices
Hong Kong Tourist Association (HKTA), 9-11th Floor, Citicorp Centre, 18 Whitfield Road, North Point (tel: 2807-6543, 2807-6177 (tourist information); fax: 2807-6582; internet site: http://www.hkta.org).

Other useful addresses
Agriculture and Fisheries Department, 13/F Canton Road Government Offices, 393 Canton Road, Kowloon (tel: 2733-2174; fax: 2311-3731).

Banking, Securities, Insurance & Companies Division, 24th Floor Admiralty Centre, Tower II, Central (tel: 2527-8337; fax: 2865-6146).

Buildings Department, 3-12/F Murray Building Garden Road, Central (tel: 2848-2327; fax: 2840-0451).

Business & Industrial Trade Fairs Ltd, 18F First Pacific Bank Centre, 51 Gloucester Road, Wanchai (tel: 2865-2633; fax: 2866-1770, 2865-5513).

Census and Statistics Department, Wanchai Tower 1, 12 Harbour Road, Wanchai (tel: 2823-4807).

Chinese Manufacturers' Association of Hong Kong, 3rd and 4th Floor CMA Bldg, 64 Connaught Road, Central (tel: 2545-6166).

Civil Aviation department, 46/F Queensway Government Offices, 66 Queensway (tel: 2867-4332; fax: 2869-0093).

Consumer Council, 22/F, K Wah Centre, 191 Java Road, North Point (tel: 2856-3113; fax: 2856-3611).

Department of Health, 17 & 21/F Wu Chung House, 213 Queen's Road East, Wan Chai (tel: 2961-8989; fax: 2836-0071).

Environmental Protection Department, 24-28/F Southorn Centre, 130 Hennessy Road, Wan Chai (tel: 2835-1018; fax: 2838-2155).

Exchange Fund Division, 24th Floor Admiralty Centre, Tower II, Central (tel: 2529-0024; fax: 2865-6146).

Federation of Hong Kong Industries, 4/F Hankow Centre, 5-15 Hankow Road, Kowloon (tel: 2723-0818).

Finance Branch, Government Secretariat, Central Government Offices, Lower Albert Road, Central (tel: 2810-2540; fax: 2810-1530).

Hong Kong Convention & Incentive Travel Bureau (trade fairs), 35th Floor Jardine House, Central (tel: 2801-7111; fax: 2810-4877).

Hong Kong Exporters' Association, Room 825 Star House, 3 Salisbury Road, Tsim Sha Tsui, Kowloon (tel: 2730-9851).

Hong Kong Government Industry Department, 'One-Stop' Unit, 14th Floor, Ocean Centre, 5 Canton Road, Kowloon (tel: 2737-2434; fax: 2730-4633).

Hong Kong Government Office, Investment Promotion Unit, 6 Grafton Street,

Hong Kong

London W1X 3LB (tel: (020) 8499-9821; fax: (020) 8495-5033).

Hong Kong Industrial Estates Corporation, 107 Estate Centre Building, 19 Dai Cheong Street, Tai Po Industrial Estate, Tai Po, New Territories (tel: 2664-1183).

Hong Kong Productivity Council, 78 Tat Chee Avenue, HKCP Bldg, Kowloon (tel: 2788-5678).

Hong Kong Standards and Testing Centre, 10 Dai Wang Street, Tai Po Industrial Estate, Tai Po, New Territories (tel: 2667-0021).

Hong Kong Telecom Association, GPO Box 13461 (tel: 2881-2333; fax: 2881-2332).

Hong Kong Trade Development Council, Research Department, 36-39/F Office Tower, Convention Plaza, 1 Harbour Road, Wan Chai (tel: 2584-4333; fax: 2824-0249; internet site: http://www.tdc.org.hk/).

Industry Department, 14/F Ocean Centre, 5 Canton Road, Tsim Sha Tsui (tel: 2737-2216; fax: 2377-0730).

Labour Department, 16/F Harbour Building, 38 Pier Road, Central (tel: 2852-3511).

Securities & Futures Commission, 38/F Two Exchange Square, 8 Connaught Place (tel: 2840-9202; fax: 2845-9553).

Stock Exchange of Hong Kong Ltd, 1/F, 1 and 2 Exchange Square, 8 Connaught Place, PO Box 8888 (tel: 2522-1122; fax: 2868-1308).

Telecommunications Authority, 29th Floor, Wu Chung House, 213 Queens Road East, Wan Chai (tel: 2961-6333; fax: 2803-5110).

Trade Department, Ocean Centre, 5 Canton Road, Kowloon (tel: 2722-2333).

US General Consulate, 26 Garden Road (tel: 2523-9011; fax: 2845-1598).

Visa Office, Ministry of Foreign Affairs, 5th Floor, Lower Block, 26 Harbour Road, Wanchai (tel: 2835-3794).

Internet sites

Economic Services Bureau: http://www.info.gov.hk/esb/content.htm

Hong Kong Airport: http://www.hkairport.com

Hong Kong Shipping directory: http://www.info.gov.hk/mardep/sdfiles/shipdir.ht

Hong Kong Statistics: http://www.info.gov.hk/censtatd/eindex.htm

Hungary

KEY FACTS

Official name: Magyar Köztársaság (Republic of Hungary)

Head of State: President László Sólyom (took office 7 Aug 2005)

Head of government: Prime Minister Ferenc Gyurcsány (MSzP)

Ruling party: Coalition government: Magyar Szocialista Párt (MSzP) (Hungarian Socialist Party) and Szabad Demokratak Szovetsege (SzDSz) (Alliance of Free Democrats) (since May 2002)

Area: 93,033 square km

Population: 10.12 million (2004); 10.12 million (OECD, 2003)

Capital: Budapest

Official language: Hungarian (Magyar)

Currency: Forint (Ft)

Exchange rate: Ft207.05 per US$ (Oct 2005); (from 9 May 2001, the forint has been free to float against the euro within a 15 per cent band)

GDP per capita: US$10,129 (2004)

GDP real growth: 4.00% (2004); *4.2% (2005)

Labour force: 4.12 million (2004

Unemployment: 5.90% (OECD, 2004)

Inflation: 6.80% (2004); *3.7% (2005)

Balance of trade: -US$2.92 billion (2004)

Foreign debt: US$74.92 billion (2004)

Annual FDI: US$35.20 billion (cumulative, 1995–2004, OECD); US$4.20 billion (OECD, 2004)*

* estimated figure

The year 2006 will mark the fiftieth anniversary of the bloody Hungarian revolution. In 1956 Hungarians were struggling against Soviet control; in 2005 their government was battling EU budget directives. EU accession, secured in 2004, has helped Hungary attract greater international interest, both political and financial. With a population of only 10 million, Hungary is a country sometimes in danger of being overlooked – but 2005 propelled it into the limelight with a visit from the UK premier, Tony Blair, and a prime ministerial meeting with the US President, George Bush. Ferenc Gyurcsány, the Prime Minister, seized on this 50-minute conversation to bolster his international image and exhorted Bush to join Hungary for its imminent anniversary celebrations.

Economy

EU membership has brought palpable benefits to Hungary, boosting agricultural incomes, helping GDP growth and pumping regional and structural aid into the country. The economy grew at an estimated rate of 4.2 per cent in 2005, maintaining its strong status among the new EU states. Inflation fell to an estimated 3.7 per cent, while the Budapest Stock Exchange, the Bux index, rose 58 per cent. The Organisation for Economic Co-operation and Development (OECD) has said it is satisfied with Hungarian growth but has condemned government policy which it claims is thwarting the country's future economic prospects.

Despite some very positive developments, 2005 was characterised by unrelenting criticism from Brussels. In 2004 Hungary generated the second highest deficit in Europe, at 5.4 per cent of GDP. This only got worse in 2005, climbing to 6.1 per cent. These figures seriously flout the EU stability and growth pact, which lays down a deficit limit of 3 per cent of GDP as a prerequisite to entering the euro-zone. Hungary had planned to convert to the single currency in 2010. However, there are real concerns that it will not meet the deficit targets for entering the Exchange Rate Mechanism II (ERM II) by 2008. Hungary must spend two years in the ERM II before converting to the euro in 2010. A significant factor in the imbalance was the demand by Eurostat, the

EU's statistical information service, that Hungary incorporate its expensive motorway construction figures into the budget. It had cunningly tried to isolate these figures, exploiting the project's status as a public/private partnership. This factor alone raised the 2005 deficit by 1.9 per cent of GDP. The true arithmetic only emerged when the national bank revealed that the government had been massaging the figures. In turn, the government accused the bank of politicking.

This spat notwithstanding, the bloated deficit is deep-rooted and stems back to the previous prime minister. The Socialist ruler, Péter Medgyessy, and his finance minister, Tibor Draskovics, triggered the problems with their over-generous spending on welfare and social security. This tendency of liberality has never really been halted. Gyurcsány is rejecting calls made by the European Commission (EC) to halt investment in social security and development. He justified his fiscal policy, insisting that the growing economy should by rights be financing an upgrade of second-rate Hungarian living standards. In an interview with the *Financial Times* of London, he asked defiantly, 'What the hell would Europe like to have from us?' In November, Gyurcsány was similarly outspoken about the gulf in prosperity between east and western Europe. He warned that if regional aid to poorer nations was restricted, as mooted during the UK's EU presidency, the resultant waves of migration could threaten social stability.

The appointment of a new finance minister, Janos Veres, in April 2005 seemed to signal official recognition that state spending had to be reined in. However, such measures have not materialised. EU commissioner for economic and monetary affairs, Joaquin Almunia, has taken a dim view of the Hungarians' failure to control their budget. With others, he has warned that tight fiscal discipline will be the only way to regulate the books. Hungary not yet being a member of the euro-zone, it is not liable for formal sanctions. However, other punishments are possible, such as withholding structural funds: Almunia has not ruled this out.

Similarly, the EC has expressed exasperation at Veres' planned tax cuts, instead recommending that any deductions come only after the deficit target has been achieved. Veres has promised serious reforms in order to regulate budgetary imbalances after the forthcoming election. However, not only is there disquiet over the far-off timing of these changes, but cynicism over whether they will be enacted at all. National Bank governor, Zsigmond Jarai, has predicted that any delay in economic reforms would necessitate a postponement to euro-zone entry. This could be by as much as three years. The government, meanwhile, will not formally admit that there will be any rescheduling of the initial timetable.

Business

In 2005, the biggest airport privatisation in the world was undertaken in Hungary when BAA (formerly known as British Airports Authority) purchased the majority stake of Budapest airport. The sale was completed at eur1.84 billion and BAA is planning to invest further in developing the airport between 2006–11. The developers hope the site will equal the size of London Stansted by 2020. Already Budapest has become one of the most important entry points into mainland Europe thanks to its new status as an EU member state and the proliferation of low cost airlines. Numbers using the airport were expected to rise 23 per cent in 2005. The government will invest eur1.6 billion of the total revenue from the sale in lowering the national debt, which in turn will assist the problem of the budget deficit.

Hungary made its transition from communist state to democratic free-market society in a relatively short space of time, in the 1990s. This recent selling of Budapest airport marks the near-completion of privatisation in Hungary, with 80 per cent of financial activity now operating privately.

Gyurcsány's efforts to make Hungary more attractive to investors by offering tax incentives and a simplification of bureaucracy, looks like it is paying off. Exports and investments are now flourishing, and in turn are bumping up GDP growth. Not only has the country's most lucrative privatisation just gone through, but in October, Hankook, a South Korean company, announced plans for a huge tyre manufacturing plant. The factory will be sited in Dunaujvaros, 65 miles from the Hungarian capital. The project is worth a total of eur500 million, is expected to generate 1,500 jobs and has a completion date of 2007. The Hungarian finance minister lauded this as 'the deal of the decade'. Furthermore, in 2005 Tata Consultancy Services (TCS) decided to enlarge its operations in Hungary. TCS is the biggest software company in India and over the coming three years will recruit another 700 staff to join its existing 300 in Hungary.

For now, Hungary is reaping great rewards from foreign investors who appreciate the relatively low labour costs, relatively skilled workforce and sound infrastructure that the country has to offer. Since 2004 foreign investment has been responsible for the creation of over 14,000 jobs. However, the country cannot afford to be complacent, as other eastern

KEY INDICATORS — Hungary

	Unit	2000	2001	2002	2003	2004
Population	m	10.02	10.00	9.96	10.04	10.12
Gross domestic product (GDP)	US$bn	45.60	51.90	63.30	83.04	*99.71
GDP per capita	US$	4,549	5,137	6,356	8,272	10,129
GDP real growth	%	5.2	3.8	3.5	2.9	4.0
Inflation	%	9.8	9.1	5.3	4.6	6.8
Unemployment	%	6.4	5.7	5.7	5.9	5.9
Coal output	mtoe	3.8	2.8	2.7	2.8	2.9
Exports (fob) (goods)	US$m	25,366.0	28,071.0	31,900.0	40,000.0	55,368.0
Imports (fob) (goods)	US$m	27,472.0	30,089.0	35,200.0	44,500.0	58,290.0
Balance of trade	US$m	-2,106.0	-2,018.0	-3,300.0	-4,500.0	-2,922.0
Current account	US$m	-1,494.0	-1,097.0	-2,800.0	-3,600.0	-8,930.0
Foreign debt	US$bn	30.8	30.3	35.0	31.5	74.9
Total reserves minus gold	US$m	11,190.0	10,727.0	10,348.0	12,737.0	15,908.0
Foreign exchange	US$m	10,915.0	10,302.0	9,721.0	12,015.0	15,312.0
Foreign direct investment (FDI)	US$bn	1.1	2.4	0.9	–	–
Exchange rate	per US$	282.18	286.49	250.10	216.92	202.52

* estimated figure

European countries are hot on Hungary's heels, eager to offer even greater savings to overseas companies. Hungary particularly has to look out for Slovakia, Romania, Poland and the Czech Republic. Competition for labour is focussed not only on cost but on the quality of the workforce. The president of the American Chamber of Commerce in Hungary, Les Nemethy, has signalled the limited numbers of skilled workers in Hungary as being a problem.

The Roma

In 2004 Hungary took one step towards tackling one of its most entrenched social problems: the widespread discrimination experienced by its Roma population. Livia Jaroka was elected as the first Romany MEP. It was a fitting move considering that Europe has just entered the Decade of Roma Inclusion (2005–15), in which eight nations are participating: Hungary, Romania, Croatia, Bulgaria, the Czech Republic, Slovakia, Serbia and Montenegro, and Macedonia. Roma people, who account for 7 per cent of Hungary's population and over 10 million people in Europe, are often forced to live in utterly wretched conditions. They suffer astronomically high levels of joblessness: in some areas unemployment rates have reached 100 per cent. The average jobless figure among Roma is seven times the Hungarian average. Roma suffer discrimination and segregation in education, housing and healthcare. One in five Roma children is written off as having learning difficulties and relegated in sink classes. Jaroka has raised the profile of this persecuted minority and in 2005 some progress was made. In Miskolc, in the east of the country, the Chance for Children organisation proposed to the courts that the segregation of white and Roma children in the school system was illegal. The local administration was acquitted but publicity from the case contributed to the amendment of the Education Act, passed in December 2005. This change will prevent schools selecting pupils along ethnic lines, and will prioritise places for disadvantaged children, predominantly Roma. In the same month, the Roma Rendôrök Országos Egyesülete, or National Roma Police Association, was inaugurated. This is the first such organisation in the world and hopes to break down the deep mutual distrust that exists between the legal authorities and Hungary's ethnic minorities.

Outlook

This year's election promises to be lively, possibly too much so. The last campaign, in 2002, was bitter and slanderous, with former communists and nationalists exercising historic mutual hatreds. The ballot raised temperatures not only in debating chambers but in homes and workplaces: turnout nudged 80 per cent. In December 2005, the incumbent Magyar Szocialista Párt (MSzP) was even with the centre-right Fiatal Demokraták Szövetsége-Magyar Polgári Párt (Fidesz Party) in the opinion polls. The Fidesz Party has declared that if it is to win the spring elections, it will review the country's recent privatisations and possibly even cancel them. The prospect of the election will ensure that no austerity measures will be taken in the immediate term while both parties focus on populist vote-winning measures such as tax cuts and investment.

Risk assessment

Economy	Good
Political	Good
Regional stability	Good
Stock market	Good

COUNTRY PROFILE

Historical profile

The Hungarians (Magyars) are a Turkic or Finno-Ugrian people who settled on the Hungarian plains in the seventh century AD.
From the mid-eighteenth century, Hungary, together with Austria and a large area of central and eastern Europe, was part of the dual monarchy ruled by the Habsburgs.
1914–18 After the assassination of Archduke Ferdinand, the heir to the Austro-Hungarian throne, Austro-Hungary declared war on Serbia in June 1914, with the support of Germany. In November 1918, after the Austro-Hungarian empire was defeated in the First World War, Hungary declared its independence, King Karl IV stood down as head of state of Hungary and the Entente powers carved-up Hungary as a punishment for its role in the First World War, taking two-thirds of its territory and nearly 60 per cent of its pre-war population.
1919 Communists seized power and declared the Hungarian Soviet Republic but were defeated by Admiral Miklos Horthy, who governed as Regent from 1920 until 1944.
1920 Hungary signed the Treaty of Trianon, confirming its territorial losses to Romania, Yugoslavia, Czechoslovakia and Austria.
1939–45 Hungary allied with Germany and acquired territory through the partitioning of Czechoslovakia and the Axis invasion of Yugoslavia. Having sought to break the alliance, Hungary was occupied by Germany in 1944 before being invaded by the Soviets later in the same year. Following the end of the Second World War, Hungary's territory was reduced to pre-war boundaries and severe reparations exacted.
1947 Communists were the largest single party in the general election.
1949 The People's Republic was established. With Matyas Rakosi as prime minister, purges and political trials on the Stalinist model followed. Agriculture was reorganised on the Soviet pattern and industry was nationalised.
1953 The more liberal Imre Nagy became prime minister, before being replaced by communist András Hegedüs in 1958.
1956 Support for liberals grew among the population but turned into violence. Nagy became prime minister for eleven days before the Soviet Union intervened militarily. The communist Magyar Szocialista Mukaspart Partja (MSzMP) (Hungarian Socialist Workers' Party), returned to power with János Kádár as prime minister.
1958 Nagy was executed in Romania for his part in the 1956 Hungarian uprising. Árpád Szákasits, as chairman of the Presidential Council, became the head of state.
1960s Kádár introduced a number of minor liberal reforms such as dismantling collective farms, raising wages and introducing some intellectual freedom.
1988 Dissatisfaction among party members with the remoteness of the leadership led to the resignation of Kádár and moves towards 'Socialist Pluralism'.
1989 The MSzMP was re-named the Magyar Szocialista Párt (MSzP) (Hungarian Socialist Party). Mátyás Szürös became Hungary's interim president.
1990 First free multi-party parliamentary elections for 43 years resulted in the formation of a coalition government led by József Antall of the Magyar Demokrata Fórum (MDF) (Hungarian Democratic Forum).
1994 The general election resulted in a coalition government led by Gyula Horn of the MSzP.
1998 The centre-right Fiatal Demokraták Szövetsége-Magyar Polgári Párt (Fidesz-MPP) (Federation of Young Democrats-Hungarian Civic Party), led by Viktor Orbán, unexpectedly won the general election and formed a coalition government with the MDF and the Függietian Kisgazda, Foldmunkas és Polgári Párt (FKGP) (Independent Smallholders' Party).
1999 Hungary became one of the first former Soviet satellite states to join NATO.

Hungary

2000 Ferenc Mádl was elected president by parliament, replacing Árpád Göncz who had been president since 1990.
2001 The government introduced the Status Law, providing the four million ethnic Hungarians in neighbouring countries the right to work and study in Hungary.
2002 After parliamentary elections, Péter Médgyessy (leader of MSzP) was sworn in as prime minister of a coalition government, comprising MSzP and Szabad Demokratak Szovetsege (SzDSz) (Alliance of Free Democrats).
2003 In the April EU membership referendum turnout out was only 46 per cent; 84 per cent of voters said yes to membership.
2004 Hungary entered the EU on 1 May. After the ruling MSzP withdrew support from him, Prime Minister Péter Medgyessy resigned. On 29 September, parliament endorsed Ferenc Gyurcsány as prime minister.
2004 A proposal to grant citizenship to ethnic Hungarians born overseas was approved by 51.5 per cent in a referendum. However the vote was invalidated by low turn-out.
2005 László Sólyom was sworn in as president on 7 June. He took office on 5 August.

Political structure
Constitution
In 1989 the 1949 constitution was amended so that Hungary was formally re-titled the Hungarian Republic, concluding 40 years as a People's Republic.
Under the amended constitution, Hungary has a multi-party system.
Supreme power is vested in parliament. The Constitutional Court has the power to overturn decisions or decrees that are considered unconstitutional.
Form of state
Parliamentary democratic republic
The executive
The prime minister is chosen by the National Assembly and heads the executive Council of Ministers or cabinet. The prime minister's control of the cabinet has been enhanced by the creation of a minister for the prime minister's office.
The president is also elected by the National Assembly for a five-year term. The president has no executive power, and is not able to dissolve parliament.
National legislature
Legislative power is vested in the unicameral Országgyüles (National Assembly), elected every four years, which enacts the constitution and laws, determines the state budget and elects the president of the republic, the prime minister and the Council of Ministers. The Országgyüles contains 386 deputies, of whom 176 are elected from single-member constituencies.

Legal system
The legal system is based on the amended 1949 constitution.
Civil and criminal cases are brought before district and county courts and the Supreme Court in Budapest. District courts are courts of first instance whereas county courts may act either as courts of first instance or as appeal courts. The Supreme Court is usually an appeal court, but can also take cases submitted to it by the Public Prosecutor and act as a court of first instance. All courts of first instance have one professional judge and two lay assessors. Appeal courts have three professional judges. The district and county judges are elected by district or county councils. All members of the Supreme Court are elected by parliament.
Last elections
6 June 2005 (presidential); 13 June 2004 (European Parliament); 7/21 April 2002 (parliamentary).
Results: Presidential: László Sólyom won in the third round (with a simple majority sufficient), with 185 votes against 182 for Katalin Szili his opponent.
European Parliament: Fidesz-MPP won 47.4 per cent of the vote (12 seats out of 24), MSzP 34.3 per cent (nine), SzDSz 7.7 per cent (two) and Magyar Demokrata Fórum (MDF) (Hungarian Democratic Forum) 5.3 per cent (one); turnout 38.5 per cent.
Parliamentary: Magyar Szocialista Párt (MSzP) (Hungarian Socialist Party) (178 seats) and the Szabad Demokratak Szovetsege (SzDSz) (Alliance of Free Democrats) (20 seats) against Fiatal Demokraták Szövetsége-Magyar Polgári Párt (Fidesz-MPP) (Federation of Young Democrats-Hungarian Civic Party) (188 seats).
Next elections
2006 (parliamentary); 2010 (presidential).

Political parties
Ruling party
Coalition government: Magyar Szocialista Párt (MSzP) (Hungarian Socialist Party) and Szabad Demokratak Szovetsege (SzDSz) (Alliance of Free Democrats) (since May 2002)
Main opposition party
Fiatal Demokraták Szövetsége-Magyar Polgári Párt (Fidesz-MPP) (Federation of Young Democrats-Hungarian Civic Party)

Population
10.12 million (2004); 10.12 million (OECD, 2003)
Ethnic make-up
The population is almost entirely made up of ethnic Hungarians. Small groups of Germans, Slovaks, Romanians, Serbs and Gypsies (Roma) make up about 4 per cent of the population. Roma are not recognised as an official ethnic group, although they are estimated to number between 360,000 and 600,000.
Religions
There is no official national religion. Roman Catholic (67.5 per cent), Calvinist (20 per cent) and Lutheran (5 per cent). There are approximately six million Roman Catholics, two million Calvinists, 430,000 Lutherans, and 80,000 Jews in Hungary.

Education
Compulsory education starts at six years of age and most children complete secondary education. There are four types of secondary school, offering either academic or vocational education. Apprentice training schools are attached to factories and agricultural co-operatives. There are 57 higher education institutes, including 10 universities and nine technical universities. Some privatisation of education is taking place as church and other private schools are created. Public expenditure on education is equivalent to around 5 per cent of annual gross national income (GNI), and includes subsidies to private education at the primary, secondary and tertiary levels.
Literacy rate: 99.4 per cent total, 99.2 per cent female, adult rates in 2002 (World Bank).
Compulsory years: Six to 18
Enrolment rate: 89.7 per cent net primary enrolment, 84.9 per cent net secondary enrolment (World Bank 2003).
Pupils per teacher: 12 in primary schools.

Health
The health system is run by the State Health Fund, an entity with substantial operational autonomy and no effective accountability. It is financed by payroll taxes of 15 per cent from employers and 4 per cent from employees, although transfers from the budget have been necessary due to a large funding gap.
Service delivery remains poor. Although healthcare is free in Hungary, patients regularly hand over cash bribes to poorly-paid medical staff in order to gain proper access. There are reports of doctors recommending dangerous treatments in exchange for bribes. A major area of concern is the heavy subsidisation of medicine, which patients often obtain freely and then sell on.
The total expenditure on health is 6–7 per cent of GDP, of which government spending is 75 per cent.
HIV prevalence: 0.1 per cent aged 15–49 in 2003 (World Bank)
Life expectancy: 72.6 years (World Bank)
Fertility rate/Maternal mortality rate: 1.3 births per woman (2003); maternal mortality 15 per 100,000 live births (World Bank).

Infant mortality rate: 7.7 per 1,000 live births (World Bank)
Head of population per physician/bed: 3.5 physicians and 8.3 hospital beds per 1,000 people.

Welfare
Economic reforms have included a pioneering reorganisation of the pension system, with a new 'multi-pillar' system launched in 1996, supported by a World Bank US$150 million loan. Employees make mandatory contributions to the existing pay-as-you-go (PAYG) system and to a fully funded second pillar, based on a system of personal savings accounts held in privately managed pension funds. Those joining the work force after June 1998 were obliged to participate in the new system. In 2001, the government made both systems voluntary. The new scheme has proved highly popular. The largest private pension fund is managed by Nationale-Nederlanden (NN), with 257,000 members and Ft4 billion (US$16.4 million) in managed assets. Social security contributions on salaries are paid by the employer (39 per cent) and by the employee (10 per cent). Employer contributions must also be made to the unemployment solidarity fund (4.5 per cent) and by the employee (1.5 per cent).

Main cities
Budapest (capital, estimated population 1.7 million in 2004), Debrecen (210,500), Miskolc (182,600), Szeged (173,200), Pécs (163,900), Györ (134,600), Nyíregyháza (121,400), Székesfehérvár (112,200).

Languages spoken
Slovak, Croatian, Serbian, Slovene, Romani are also spoken.
The main foreign language is German, followed by English, Russian and French.
Official language/s
Hungarian (Magyar)

Media
The national news agency is Magyar Távirati Iroda (MTI) (Hungarian News Agency).

Press
As with other Central European countries, the Hungarian media sector was transformed with the advent of democracy. New titles continue to appear regularly and the market is very fluid. Unlike the broadcasting sector, the printed media market has experienced a swift transition to private control with several foreign publishing houses quickly making themselves felt. Axel Springer Verlag, from Germany, owns 10 regional titles and the Dutch VNU Group owns the daily *Magyar Hirlap*, the tabloid *Mai Nap* and several business titles.

The tabloid sector, which developed quickly after 1989, is dominated by foreign organisations. The market-leading *Blikk* is owned by Ringier of Switzerland and the American Gannett Corporation. The Austrian publisher Deton has a minority stake in *Kurir* and the Canadian Hebdo Mag purchased *Expressz* in mid-1995.
Dailies: Dailies include *Békés Megyei Nap*, *Népszabadság Nemzeti Sport*, *Kisalfold*, *Mai Nap*, *Zalai Hírlap*, *Vas Nepe*, *Magyar Hírlap*, *Magyar Nemzet*, *Vilggázderág*, *Népszava* and *Blikk*. The MTI Hungarian News Agency publishes the *Daily News* in English.
Weeklies: The largest circulation belongs to *Szabad Fold*. International publications include *Budapest Week*, (in English) published on the Internet, *Budapester Rundschau* and *Neue Zeitung* (both in German).
Popular magazines include *TVR HIT*, *Kiskegyed*, *Tele Magazin*, *Reform* and *HVG*.
Business: Leading dailies include the *Napi Gazdaság* and *Világgazdaság*. The *Budapest Business Journal*, published weekly in English, offers daily business news, along with comprehensive industry and company information. *Budapest Sun* includes business-related information. *Heti Világgazdaság* also focusses on economic issues. Foreign language periodicals of financial and business interests include the *Hungarian Market Report*, *Hungarian Observer*, The Hungarian Chamber of Commerce publishes the quarterly *Hungarian Business Herald* and *Hungarian Economic Review*.
Periodicals: The *Közéleti Krónika* is a monthly periodical of general interest. Other periodicals include the *Hungarian Travel Magazine*, *Hungarian Digest*, *Hungarian Book Review*, *New Hungarian Quarterly*, *Invest in Hungary* and the *Hungarian Trade Journal*. Foreign magazines can be bought in large hotels and at some news-stands.

Broadcasting
The state's broadcasting monopoly finally ended in 1995, when legislation was passed liberalising the sector. The bill released two television channel frequencies and several radio frequencies on 10-year concessions to private operators. TV1, with two channels, remains under state control and has experienced trouble since the 1990s competing in the new environment.
Radio: There are seven commercial radio stations. The first independent Romany radio station, Radio C, began broadcasting in October 2001. The station has broadcast only music since April 2003.
Television: Hungarian Television's Channel One and Channel Two remain in state hands. Hungarian Television, also known as Antenna Hungaria, must by law remain 50 per cent state-owned.
There are nine commercial TV stations in all, and only a few private regional broadcasting channels, mainly in the Budapest area. Approximately 60 per cent of households receive cable or satellite stations.

Advertising
Advertising is usually conducted through national agencies such as Magyar Hirdetö, Hungexpo, Magyar Média and Interpress. Advertising space can be purchased directly on television and radio, in cinemas, newspapers, magazines and posters. Radio and television advertisements for alcohol and tobacco products have been permitted since 1996.

Economy
Hungary has a market economy with a large industrial base and heavy dependence on foreign trade. In the mid-1990s Hungary, which had originally been the economic jewel in the transitional crown, encountered severe economic problems, notably large government deficits. The tough austerity measures that were imposed in 1995 and 1996 were impressively successful, as GDP growth grew, inflation fell and the budget deficit narrowed. Increased privatisation followed, as did praise from international financial institutions.

Since the mid-1990s, Hungary has boasted one of the most successful growth rates in Central Europe. Unemployment has fallen from the 9.7 per cent recorded in 1999, to a forecast 7.1 per cent in 2005 while the Bux index has climbed 58 per cent.

The main driving force behind this economic growth has been an unsustainable change in government policy. Since the beginning of 2001 the government has increased public spending and pushed wages sharply upwards. Households added to the economic expansion by borrowing heavily. Consequently, consumer expenditure and domestic demand replaced export-oriented manufacturing as the mainspring of the economy. Increased wages and the strength of the forint reduced Hungary's international competitiveness in the midst of a global economic downturn.

By the first months of 2004, exports and investment began to replace domestic consumption as the main drivers of growth. 2004 saw a 15 per cent leap in exports, in turn expected to rise by another 10 per cent in 2005. Such success on the exports front is underpinning growth and creating good investment prospects. During 2004–05, over 14,000 jobs were generated in Hungary by overseas investors. GDP growth was forecast at 4.2 per cent in 2005, amounting to 62 per cent of the EU average – an upsurge of 10 per cent over the past five years. Inflation, which began to fall in mid-2004, is expected to continue falling with rates projected at around 3.7 per cent for 2005. Macroeconomic policies have improved recently, nevertheless further progress is necessary to meet the 2010 target date for joining the European Monetary Union (EMU). Fiscal consolidation, including more structural spending measures should be adopted. Employment rates remain low at 62 per cent, and rank near-bottom among OECD members. Meanwhile the cost of labour is escalating. A reform of the arguably over-generous disability benefit scheme should be replaced by increased work incentives.

The OECD 2005 publication, *Economic Policy Reforms*, makes a number of recommendations including:

- reducing state control on the operations of network industries, so that deregulation of prices and retail gas and electricity markets are liberalised
- reducing the tax wedge for low-income workers to allow more earnings to remain within the wage packet and reduce activity in the grey-market
- reducing administrative burdens when businesses start-up, including online registration, standardised documents, reduced fees and simplified legal procedures.

Between 2004 and 2006, the 10 EU accession countries will receive funding of up to eur25.1 billion (US$28.2 billion), which will include money for agriculture, infrastructure modernisation and regional aid. Hungary should receive eur3.0 billion (US$3.3 billion). However, Joaquin Almunia, EU commissioner for economic and monetary affairs, is displeased about Hungary's mounting budget deficit. This currently stands at 6.1 per cent of GDP, in contrast to the EU deficit limit of 3 per cent. The government has been roundly condemned for massaging figures in line with this target. Punitive measures, such as a reduction in aid allowances, could follow.

The government has postponed its target date for joining the euro-zone until 1 January 2010 after it realised it was unlikely to meet its original 2008 target, because it was unable to achieve the necessary fiscal readjustment. However, there are now concerns that Hungary's euro-zone joining date could be delayed further, until 2013.

External trade

The majority of foreign trade was conducted through state monopolies until 1990 and since then there has been a considerable rise in the number of joint companies which have the right to engage in foreign trade on their own.

In 1992, Poland, Slovakia, the Czech Republic and Hungary (the Visegrad Four) established a regional trading zone designed gradually to eliminate tariff barriers. Many measures aimed at liberalising trade have been unrolled.

In 1995, Hungary signed an agreement with the other members of the Central European Free Trade Agreement (CEFTA) to work towards creating a common market. However, now Hungary has exchanged membership of CEFTA for that of the EU, it hopes to capitalise on new markets while maintaining close links with its old Eastern and Central European trading allies. Its biggest trading partner is Germany.

Imports

Principal imports are machinery and equipment (51.6 per cent), other manufactures, fuels and electricity, food products, raw materials.

Main sources: Germany (29.2 per cent total, 2004), Austria (8.3 per cent), Russia (5.7 per cent), Italy (5.5 per cent), The Netherlands (4.9 per cent), China (4.8 per cent), France (4.7 per cent)

Exports

Principal exports are machinery and equipment (61.1 per cent), other manufactures, food products, raw materials, fuels and electricity.

Main destinations: Germany (31.4 per cent total, 2004), Austria (6.8 per cent), France (5.7 per cent), Italy (5.6 per cent), UK (5.1 per cent)

Agriculture

Farming

The agricultural sector contributes 7 per cent to GDP and employs around 12 per cent of the workforce. Agriculture and animal husbandry dominate in the Great Plain in central and eastern Hungary. The western region of Transdanubia – which includes Lake Balaton, the largest lake in Central Europe – is dominated by intensive agriculture and animal husbandry. Farming is largely socialised; co-operatives are the dominant form of production. The agriculture and food industry produces on average 50 per cent more food than is consumed domestically. Principal crops include wheat, maize, barley, sugar beet and potatoes. The livestock sector is also important. Crop cultivation, especially wheat, maize, potatoes, fruit and vegetables, accounts for around half of Hungary's agricultural output. Processed and unprocessed meat, dairy products and wine are the other main products. The agriculture and food industry produces, on average, 50 per cent more than is needed for domestic consumption. After EU accession in 2004, Hungary is eligible for EU agricultural subsidies and rural development through the Common Agricultural Policy (CAP). However, it will only receive the full amount by the end of a 10-year transition period in 2013. During its transitional entry stage Hungary has decided to implement the reform of the CAP on 1 January 2009. The reform was introduced throughout most of the EU on 1 January 2005, when subsidies on farm output, which tended to benefit large farms and encourage overproduction, were replaced by single farm payments, not conditional on production. The change is expected to reward farms that provide and maintain a healthy environment, food safety and animal welfare standards. The changes are also intended to encourage market conscious production and cut the cost of CAP to the EU taxpayer.

Crop production in 2004 included: 16,749,350 tonnes (t) cereals in total, 6,020,000t wheat, 8,317,000t maize, 1,423,000t barley, 125,000t rye, 767,000t potatoes, 650,000t grapes, 231,600t tomatoes, 110,000t chillies & peppers, 621,127t oilcrops, 287,000t rapeseed (canola), 9,000t tobacco, 60000 various herbs and spices, 3,130,000t sugar beets, 680,000t apples, 216,000t oats, 1,531,000t fruit in total, 1,854,500t vegetables in total. Livestock production included: 1,120,000t meat in total, 51,000t beef, 600,000t pig meat, 2,600t lamb, 448,600t poultry, 189,000t eggs, 1,990,000t milk, 16,000t honey, 300t sheepskins, 4,000t greasy wool, 7,000t cattle hides.

Fishing

Hungary is a landlocked country and although there is some fishing from lakes and rivers, most of the country's consumption needs are met through imports. Fish production in Hungary is mostly concentrated in the available 140,000 hectares (ha) of natural water and 20,000ha of man-made fishponds. The fish production sector primarily involves common carp and African catfish and remains a small and special sub-sector of agriculture. The sector traditionally supports less than 0.5 per cent of the total labour force and contributes below 2 per cent of the total for agricultural production. Annual consumption per capita is typically less than 3kg.

Forestry

Forests account for a fifth of Hungary's land area but the industry amounts to only 0.3 per cent of GDP. Forestry agriculture largely concentrates on production using hardwood species of trees, mostly being used for energy purposes. Oak and black locust are most prevalent. The state owns about 58 per cent of forests and and employs 20,000 workers on this land. Hungary is a net importer of all primary forest

products as a result of not undertaking softwood and pulp production.
Exports of forest products in 2004 amounted to US$582.3 million, while imports were valued at US$963.8 million. Production in 2004 included: 5,660,300 cubic metres (cum) roundwood, 2,988,300cum industrial roundwood, 1,575,000cum sawlogs and veneers, 204,800 cubic metres (cum) sawnwood, 653,300cum pulpwood, 2.672,000cum woodfuel.

Industry and manufacturing
Mechanical engineering, chemicals, pulp and paper industries, as well as the iron and steel industry and metal processing are particularly successful sectors. Other industries include building materials, food processing and textiles. One of the fastest growing sectors in Hungary, as the country moves away from heavy industry, is motor vehicle components and assembly. Foreign direct investment (FDI) has contributed greatly to industrial output in Hungary, concentrating in areas such as machinery, vehicles, computers, telecommunications equipment, electrical and electronic goods. These successes have been concentrated in a relatively small number of capital-intensive companies. Analysts warn that Hungary could be in danger of developing a two-tier economy, with a prosperous, predominantly foreign-owned sector of larger enterprises and a struggling, locally-owned sector of small- and medium-sized enterprises (SMEs).
In the past, government policy focussed on the development of heavy industry and agriculture. In the late-1990s, this shifted towards the development of SMEs. These account for 45 per cent of GDP and represent 69 per cent of employment. The main problem facing smaller enterprises is the growing black market. This is due to a constantly changing and, thus far, largely unfavourable tax system in which evasion is widespread. Law-abiding SMEs are finding it difficult to compete with black market labour. In order to help compensate for this, the government has tried to promote entrepreneurial SMEs through tax cuts and better access to credit.
In 2002, the government launched its 'Smart Hungary' programme to improve SME access to investment funding and to help improve human capital. The purpose of the programme is to improve productivity levels, which will go some way to addressing Hungary's high labour costs. In early 2003, the government announced at least US$680 million in grants and subsidised loans for SMEs, US$180 million to help SMEs combat liquidity constraints and US$110 million towards farm restructuring. At the end of 2003, the SME programme was incorporated into a development programme designed to respond to Hungary's EU membership in 2004.
Industrial production increased by 3.1 per cent in 2003.

Tourism
Since 1988, Hungary has seen an unprecedented tourist boom as package tourists and international convention delegates take advantage of competitive prices, relatively crime-free streets and a rich and varied cultural scene. Most visitors are from Germany and Austria, but there are increasing numbers from Poland, America and Japan. The sector accounts for almost 10 per cent of GDP and employs 10–13 per cent of the workforce. The sector has traditionally played an important role in Hungary's foreign exchange revenues.
Emphasis is on three fields of tourism – conference, spa, and exclusive tourism, particularly equestrian tourism.
Tourist arrivals numbered 3 million in 2004, up slightly from the previous year.

Mining
The mining sector accounts for 5 per cent of GNP and employs 3 per cent of the workforce.
Hungary is a major European producer of bauxite, and also a small-scale producer of lignite and manganese ore. In the Northern Hills, iron ore and copper are mined.

Hydrocarbons
Hungary is a small-scale producer of coal, oil and natural gas. In the Great Plain in central and eastern Hungary, there are natural gas and oil deposits and brown coal is mined in the Northern Hills region. Hungary has 102.5 million barrels of oil reserves, producing around 41,000 barrels per day (bpd) Hungry is the largest oil producer in North Central Europe. Hungry has one oil refinery with a capacity of 161,000 bpd, US$59 million has been invested to create a new hydrodesulfurisation unit in line with EU standards for low sulphur gasoline and diesel.
Proven reserves of natural gas stand at around 1.2 trillion cubic feet. Hungary relies heavily on imports of natural gas from Russia. Domestic consumption and production of natural gas are projected to rise 30 per cent and fall 20 per cent respectively by 2010. Gas storage capacity is well developed and can hold 120 days of peak winter imports.
Coal reserves totaled 3.3 billion tonnes in 2004; coal production was 2.9 million tonnes oil equivalent. Hungarian coal tends to be high in sulphur and ash, making it difficult to expand coal production and conform to EU environmental norms. Only the country's lignite reserves offer any possibility for an expansion in domestic production.

Energy
Hungary is around 50 per cent dependent upon imported oil and gas from Slovakia and, to a lesser extent, the Middle East. Electricity is imported via a grid from Vinnitsa in Ukraine. Hungary has one nuclear power plant near Paks in central Hungary. The plant provides 40 per cent of domestic energy needs and is dependent on enrichment and processing facilities from the Russian Federation. There are also three privately-owned small hydroelectric power plants in Hungary, based at Hernádviz, Kisköre and Tiszalök, although these provide limited electricity. There are plans to implement geothermal energy in addition to the wind generators which have been operating since 2000.

Financial markets
Stock exchange
The Budapest Stock Exchange (BSE), the first of the former socialist Central and Eastern European exchanges to reopen, was formally re-established in 1990.

Banking and insurance
Hungary has the most developed financial sector in Eastern Europe, with the Magyar Nemzeti Bank (MNB) (National Bank of Hungary) (central bank) playing an important role in economic and financial management of the economy. The country privatised banking services from 1994–97 in order to attract foreign investment. About 30 of the 38 banks in Hungary are foreign-owned and are led by the OTP Bank (formely known as the National Savings Bank). Foreign-owned banks control 90 per cent of the country's total banking assets. OTP Bank, with an extensive branch network, offers banking for the general public, and also foreigners needing foreign exchange accounts.
Foreign trade and currency transactions are conducted by the Magyar Külkereskedelmi Bank (MKB) (formerly the Hungarian Foreign Trade Bank) and by some other banks.
The Central-European International Bank is an internationally active offshore bank owned by the central bank and six foreign banks.
Hungary adopted a German model for the banking system in 1999, allowing banks to engage in both commercial and investment banking.
Central bank
Magyar Nemzeti Bank (MNB) (National Bank of Hungary)
Main financial centre
Budapest

Hungary

Time
GMT plus one hour in winter, GMT plus two hours in summer.

Geography
Hungary is a landlocked country in Central Europe surrounded by the Alps, the Carpathians and the Dinaric Mountains. The Danube and Tisza rivers run through the country, which is bounded by Slovakia to the north, Ukraine to the north-east, Romania to the east, Serbia and Montenegro, Croatia and Slovenia to the south and Austria to the west.
The River Danube forms Hungary's north-western border with Slovakia and then flows south through Budapest, bisecting the country. More than half of the land surface consists of plains less than 200 metres above sea level. The highest point is Kekes at 1,015 metres in the Matra hills to the north, while the lowest point is on the southern edge of Szeged along the River Tisza (the longest tributary of the Danube) at 77 metres.
The major regions of the country are: the Pannonian or Great Hungarian Plain (central and eastern Hungary), east of the River Danube and also drained by the Tisza; Transdanubia (western Hungary, including Lake Balaton, the largest lake in Central Europe); the Little Hungarian Plains in the north-west between the mountains and the Danube; and along Hungary's northern border are the Matras, foothills of the Carpathian Mountains.

Climate
The temperate continental climate of Hungary is under the varying influence of three climatic zones: continental, Atlantic and Mediterranean. The annual median temperature in Budapest is 10.8 degrees Celsius (C). The warmest month is July, with an average of 21.7 degrees C, the coldest January, with minus 1.2 degrees C. Averaging 1,988 hours of sunshine a year, Hungary experiences more sun than most of the countries in Western Europe. Average annual rainfall is 630mm, but distribution is unpredictable. Most rain usually falls in May and June, but the south-west regions may have more in October. May is the wettest month, and September the driest. The central parts of the Great Plains are the driest with 200–500mm, the hilly western area of Koeszeg and Sopron the wettest with 900–1,000mm.

Dress codes
Hungarians used to dress more formally than West Europeans, but blazers, sports coats and flannels are as acceptable as lounge suits for visiting businessmen. Do not be offended if Hungarians ask where you bought your clothes or how much they cost.
Advisable clothing: medium to heavy-weight and heavy topcoat for winter; lightweight clothing for summer. A raincoat will be needed in spring and autumn.

Entry requirements
Passports
Passport required by all; must be valid for six months.
Visa
Required by all, except nationals of Europe (for 30 days). Business trips may be made visa-free, or on short-term visas. For terms and conditions see: www.mfa.gov.hu/Kulugyminiszterium/en. Transit passengers must have onward/return passage.
Currency advice/regulations
The import and export of local currency is limited to Ft200,000, provided the amount is declared on arrival. The import and export of foreign currency is unlimited, provided amounts greater than Ft50,000 are declared. There is no compulsory money exchange and the Forint can be re-exchanged for up to 50 per cent of the officially exchanged sum (but not more than US$450, and on producing the exchange receipts) at any authorised office or branch of the National Savings Bank.

Health (for visitors)
Mandatory precautions
There are no special requirements.
Advisable precautions
There are no specific precautions necessary although a hepatitis 'A' immunisation might be useful.

Hotels
The majority of large hotels are operated by the three big hotel chains, Hungar Hotels, Pannonia and Danubius. Reservations should be made in advance directly or through IBUSZ.
Tipping usually 10–15 per cent.
All Budapest hotels charge a 2 per cent tourism tax for guests staying more than one night.
Good hotels are concentrated in Pest, the business half of Budapest.

Credit cards
Credit cards are accepted and can be used for cash advances.

Public holidays
Fixed dates
1 Jan (New Year's Day), 15 Mar (Anniversary of 1848 Revolution), 1 May (Labour Day), 20 Aug (National Constitution/St Stephen's Day), 23 Oct (Republic Day), 1 Nov (All Saints' Day), 25–26 Dec (Christmas Holiday).
Variable dates
Easter Monday, Whit Monday.

Working hours
Banking
Mon–Fri: 0800–1300 or 0800–1500.
Business
Mon–Thu: 0800–1700; Fri: 0800–1500.
Government
Mon–Fri: 0800–1630.
Shops
Mon, Tue, Wed & Fri: 1000–1800, Thu: 1000–2000, Sat: 1000–1300.
Shops may have varied opening hours. Food shops open at 0600–0700 and may not close until 2000.

Telecommunications
Mobile phones
There is a GSM dual band of 900 and 1800 with coverage throughout the country.

Electricity supply
220V AC, 50 cycles

Social customs/useful tips
Business people are expected to dress smartly. Local business people are generally friendly and hospitable and it is usual for visitors to be invited to lunch or dinner in a restaurant. Business cards are widely distributed and visitors are advised to have a supply available in Hungarian. Best months for business visits are September to May and appointments should always be made. Interpreter and translation services may be booked through travel agents.
Punctuality is appreciated.
If you are invited to a Hungarian home, take flowers for the hostess and wine or liquor for the host.
In business Hungarians expect people to speak their mind. Giving and receiving gifts is very common; take promotional gifts with you. If a meeting gets heated ask for a coffee, and revert to small talk until calm returns.
Carry some form of identity at all times.

Security
There has been an increase in street crime in Budapest, although levels are still below those in many Western capitals. Bag-snatching and pickpocketing are common in Budapest. Criminals at times pose as police officers, and credentials should be requested for inspection. 'Incidents' are sometimes contrived on the Budapest–Vienna motorway and other major routes, designed to stop motorists and expose them to robbery.
Hungarian law requires visitors to carry passports at all times.

Getting there
Air
National airline: Magyar Legikozlekedesi (Malev Hungarian Airlines) (Malev)
International airport/s: Budapest-Ferihegy (BUD, 16km from city;

duty-free shop, restaurants and bar, bank/bureaux de change, tourist information centre, post office and car hire. Scheduled bus services run to the city centre; minibuses run to and from any address in the city. The 93 bus runs an express service between the underground terminus at Kobánya-Kispest and the Ferihegy terminals; a pre-purchased or season ticket is required. Taxis are available at all times.

Airport tax: None

Surface
Hungary has good international road and rail connections, with access from Vienna, Prague, Graz and Ljubljana.

Water: A hydrofoil service is available on the Danube between Vienna and Budapest in the summer. Ships provide regular passenger service and cruises starting at Passau and Regensburg (Germany) to Budapest, passing through Austria and Slovakia. There are also links with the rivers Rhine and Main and the Black Sea.

Getting about
National transport
Road: Generally the road system is good. Tolls are payable on some roads and all motorways for which season tickets can be purchased. There are eight arterial roads: all but the M8 start from central Budapest. From Budapest the two main highways are the M1 to Györ (then to Austria) and the M7 along Lake Balaton. The M3 connects Budapest with eastern Hungary.

Buses: Budapest is linked to all major towns. Tickets are available from Volán offices throughout the country.

Rail: Services are operated by MÁV. All cities are linked by efficient services, but facilities are often inadequate. Supplements are payable on intercity (IC) and express trains and reservations are compulsory on IC trains and recommended for express trains, particularly in summer. Tickets and seat reservations can be bought 60 days in advance at domestic railway stations.

Water: Ferries run several times daily between Budapest and Visegrád over the summer; one service extends to Esztergom.

City transport
Most government offices, business centres and main hotels are located in Pest, on the eastern side of the Danube. The public transport system is good and it is rarely necessary to take a taxi, especially as the city centre is quite compact.

Buda, the hilly, western part of the city, is more difficult to get around without a car.

Taxis: Locals favour the Fotaxi company (pronounced furtaxi, red and white check logo). Taxis are available from ranks, by telephone or can be hailed in the street. Taxis are metered. Avoid all unmarked cabs as they not only demand payment for mileage covered, but also for the return journey to their starting point.

A taxi from the airport to the centre of Budapest takes between 40 minutes and one hour; always agree your fare in advance. Be warned that airport taxi drivers have a reputation for rudeness and overcharging. Non-airport taxis are plentiful and inexpensive although rates vary widely (watch out for meters being on the 'night' rate during the day). Tipping of 15–20 per cent is expected.

Buses, trams & metro: There is good public transport in all the main towns, including tramways in some.

Budapest has bus, trolleybus, tramway, suburban railway (HEV), a three-line metro and boat services. The metro has ticket barriers at all stations. The bus–trolleybus–tramway system has pre-purchase flat fares with ticket puncher on board. Day passes and season tickets are available for all the transport modes in the city. Trams and buses generally run from 0430–2300. Some night services also operate. The metro runs from 0430–2310; stations are identified by a large 'M'.

Trains: Main railway stations: Déli Pu (Southern RW Terminal), Krisztina krt 37/a, Budapest I.
Keleti Pu (Eastern RW Terminal), Baross Tér (tel: 142-9150).
Nyugati Pu (Western RW Terminal), Teréz krt 111 (tel: 122-7860).

Ferry: The Danube provides a ready highway for ferries and sightseeing cruises.

Car hire
Hire cars are available from the IBUSZ travel company, from hotels and from companies at Ferihegy airport. Speed limit in built up areas 50kph, on main roads 110kph and motorways 130kph. There is an absolute ban on drinking and driving. Seat belts are compulsory. Price rates are set at German levels. An international driving licence is recommended.

For travel on the M1 and M3 motorways, drivers require a motorway vignette, obtainable from the Hungarian Auto Klub, petrol stations, post offices, and some motorway access points. Without one, drivers may be fined.

BUSINESS DIRECTORY

Telephone area codes
The international direct dialling code (IDD) for Hungary is +36, followed by area code and subscriber's number:

Budapest	1	Pecs	72
Debrecen	52	Szeged	62
Gyor	96	Szekesfehervar	22
Miskolc	46	Szombathely	94
Nyiregyhaza	42		

Useful telephone numbers
Ambulance: 04
Police: 07
Fire department: 05
24-hour emergency service (English-speaking): 118-8212
24-hour multi-lingual crime reporting service: 0800–2000: 438-8080; after hours: 06-80-660-044
Fotaxi (tel: 222-2222)
City Taxi (tel: 211-1111)
Volantaxi (tel: 166-6666)

Chambers of Commerce
American Chamber of Commerce in Hungary, 10 Deak Ferencu utca, 1052 Budapest (tel: 266-9880; fax: 266-9888; e-mail: info@amcham.hu).

Borsod-Abauj-Zemplen County Chamber of Commerce and Industry, 1 Szentpali u, 3530 Miskolc (tel: 328-539; fax: 328-722; e-mail: bokik@mail.bokik,hu).

British Chamber of Commerce in Hungary, 6 Bank utca, 1054 Budapest (tel: 302-5200; fax: 302-5201; e-mail: bcch@bcch.com).

Budapest Chamber of Commerce and Industry, Krisztina krt 99, 1016 Budapest (tel: 488-2000; fax: 488-2119; e-mail: bkik@bkik.hu).

Czongrad Chamber of Commerce and Industry, 2-4 Tisza Lajos krt, 6701 Csongrád (tel: 426-343; fax: 426-149; info@csmkik.hu).

Fejér County Chamber of Commerce, 4-6 Hosszusetater, 8000 Székesfehérvár (tel: 510-310; fax: 510-312; e-mail: fmkik@mail.fmkik.hu).

Gyor-Moson-Sopron County Chamber of Commerce and Industry, 10/A Szent Istvan ut, 9021 Gyor (tel: 520-202; fax: 520-291; e-mail: kamara@gymskik.hu).

Hajdu-Bihar County Chamber of Commerce and Industry, 10 Petofi ter, 4025 Debrecen (tel: 500-721; fax: 500-720; e-mail: info@hbkik.hu).

Hungarian Chamber of Commerce and Industry, 6-8 Kossuth Lajos ter, 1055 Budapest (tel: 474-5101; fax: 474-5105; e-mail: mkik@mkik.hu).

Pecs-Baranya Chamber of Commerce and Industry, 36 Majorossy I ut, 7625 Pécs (tel: 507-149; fax: 507-152; e-mail: pbkik@pbkik.hu).

Pest County Chamber of Commerce and Inustry, 40 Vaci utca, 1051 Budapest (tel: 317-7666; fax: 317-7755; e-mail: titkarsag@pmkik.hu).

Sopron Chamber of Commerce and Industry, 14 Deak ter, 9400 Sopron (tel: 523-570; fax: 523-581; e-mail: k-kamara@sopron.hu).

Vas County Chamber of Commerce and Industry, 2 Honved ter, 9700 Szombathely

Hungary

(tel: 312-356; fax: 316-936; e-mail: vmkik@vmkik.hu).

Veszprem Chamber of Commerce, 3 Budapesti u, 8200 Veszprém (tel: 429-008; fax: 412-150; e-mail: vkik@iveszpremikamara.hu).

Zala County Chamber of Commerce and Industry, 24 Petofi Sandor ut, 8900 Zalaegerszeg (tel: 550-514; fax: 550-525; e-mail: zmkik@zmkik.hu).

Banking

General Banking and Trust Co Ltd, Markó ut 9, H-1055 Budapest (tel: 269-1450; fax: 260-1440).

Magyar Külkereskedelmi Bank (commercial bank), St István ter 11, H-1821 Budapest (tel: 269-0922; fax: 269-0959).

OTP Bank, Nádor ut 16, H-1876 Budapest (tel: 153-1444; fax: 112-6858).

Raiffeissen Bank, PO Box 173, H-1054 Budapest (tel: 484-4400; fax: 484-4444).

Central bank

Magyar Nemzeti Bank (National Bank of Hungary), 1054 Szabadság tér 8-9, 1850 Budapest (tel:428-2752; fax: 302-3000).

Travel information

Ferihegy International Airport flight enquiries (tel: 157-7155); passenger service (tel: 157-8555; fax: 157-8993).

Hungarian Automobile Club, Francis ut 38, Budapest XIV (tel: 691-8310).

IBUSZ – Hungarian Travel Agency (main Budapest office), Tanács krt 3/c, Budapest VII (tel: 142-3140).

Lufthansa Airport Office (tel: 157-0290, 157-6506; fax: 157-6192); town office, V ci utca 19-21, Budapest (tel: 266-4511; fax: 266-8669).

Malev Hungarian Airlines (Magyar Legikozlekedesi), Roosevelt ter 2, Budapest H-1051 (tel: 266-9033; fax: 266-2759).

Police Tourinfo Office (service in English and German), Vigado Utca 6, 1051 Budapest.

Secretariat of the Hungarian Tourist Council, 6th floor, Margit krt 85, H-1024 Budapest (tel: 1175-1682; fax: 1175-38190).

National tourist organisation offices

Tourinform (Hungarian Tourist Board), Suto ut 2, H-1052 Budapest (tel: 117-9800; fax: 117-9578; e-mail: tourinform@mail.hungarytourism.hu; internet site: http://www.hungarytourism.hu).

Ministries

Ministry of Agriculture and Regional Development, Kossuth Lajos tér 11, H-1055 Budapest (tel: 302-0000; fax: 302-0402).

Ministry of Defence, Balaton ut 7-11, H-1055 Budapest (tel: 332-2500; fax: 311-0182).

Ministry of Economic Affairs, Honved U 13-14, H-1055 Budapest (tel: 302-2355; fax: 302-2394; internet site: http://www.gm.hu/english).

Ministry of Education, Szalay U 10-14, H-1055 Budapest (tel: 302-0600; fax: 302-2002).

Ministry of Environmental Protection, Fo ut 44-50, H-1011 Budapest (tel: 457-3300).

Ministry of Finance, József Nádor tér 2-4, H-1051 Budapest (tel: 118-2066, 138-2633; fax: 118-2570).

Ministry of Foreign Affairs, Bem rkp 47, H-1027 Budapest (tel: 458-1000; fax: 155-9693).

Ministry of Health, Arany János u 6-8, H-1051 Budapest (tel: 332-3100; fax: 302-0925).

Ministry of Home Affairs, József Attila u 2-4, H-1051 Budapest (tel: 331-3700, 332-5790; fax: 118-2870).

Ministry of Justice, Kossuth Lajos ter 4, H-1055 Budapest (tel: 268-3003).

Ministry of Transport, Telecommunications & Water Management, Dob ut 74-81, H-1077 Budapest (tel: 322-0220, 341-4300; fax: 322-8695).

Office of the President, Kossuth Lajos Ter 3-5, Budapest (tel: 268-4000).

Pressinform (information bureau for foreign journalists), Budakeszi ut 41, H-1021 Budapest (tel: 175-1890; fax: 175-1178).

Prime Minister's Office, Kossuth Lajos tér 1-3, H-1055 Budapest (tel: 268-3000; fax: 268-3050).

Other useful addresses

Allami Biztositó (state insurance company), Ullöi ut 1, H-1813 Budapest (tel: 117-8566).

Amex, Deak Ferenc ut 10, 1050 Budapest (tel: 117-8008).

British Embassy, 6 Harmincad utca, Budapest 1051 (tel: 266-2888; fax: 266-0907).

Budapest Stock Exchange, Deak Ferenc ut 5, H-1052 Budapest (tel: 117-5226; fax: 118-1737; internet site: http://www.fornax.hu/fmon/index.html).

Central Statistical Office, International Relations Department, Keleti Károly utca 5–7, , PO Box 51, H-1525 Budapest (tel: 212-6136; fax: 212-6378; internet site: http://www.ksh.hu/eng/index.htm).

Federation of Scientific and Technical Societies (MTESZ), Kossuth Lajos tér 6–8, Budapest V (tel: 153-3333).

Hungarian Aluminium Industrial Co Ltd (HUNGALU), Privatisation Directorate, Room 419, 85 Margit krt, Budapest 1024 (tel: 175-6528; fax: 175-5802).

Hungária Biztositó (Hungária Insurance Company), Bánk ut 17–6, H-1115 Budapest (tel: 182-0750).

Hungarian Embassy (USA), 3910 Shoemaker Street, NW, Washington DC 20008 (tel: 202-362-6730; fax: 202-686-6412; e-mail: office@huembwas.org).

Hungarian Foundation for Enterprise Promotion, Etele ut 68, Budapest H-1115 (tel: 203-0348/60; fax: 203-0377).

Hungarian Investment and Trade Development Agency (ITD), Euro Information Correspondence Centre, Dorottya ut 4, 1051 Budapest (tel: 118-1712/6064; fax: 118-6198; e-mail: itdheicc@mail.datanet.hu; internet site: http://www.itd.hu/index.htm).

Hungarian Privatisation and Foreign Investment, APV, Pozsonyi ut 56, H-1133 Budapest (tel: 269-8600; fax: 267-0079).

Hungary EU Energy Centre (Thermie), Konyves Kalman Krt 76, 1087 Budapest VIII (tel: 269-9067, 133-1304; fax: 269-9065).

Hungexpo International Fair Centre, Dobi Istvan ut 10, Budapest X.

Magyar Tavirati Iroda (Hungarian news agency) (MTI), Fem utca 507, 1016 Budapest (tel: 155-6722).

Mineralimpex Hungarian Oil and Gas Co, Benczur u 13, 1068 Budapest (tel: 131-6720; fax: 153-1779, 142-3584).

US Embassy, Szabadsag ter 12, 1054 Budapest (tel: 267-4400; fax: 269-9326 or 269-9337 (Consular Section).

Internet sites

British Chamber of Commerce in Hungary: http://www.bcch.com/

Hungary Network: http://www.hungary.com/

Virtual Hungary: http://virtualhungary.com/

Budapest Network: http://www.budapestnetwork.com

Budapest Sun: http://www.budapestsun.com

Iceland

KEY FACTS

Official name: Lyoveldio Island (Republic of Iceland)

Head of State: President Ólafur Ragnar Grímsson (since 1996; re-elected 26 Jun 2004)

Head of government: Prime Minister Halldór Ásgrímsson (FSF) (from 15 Sep 2004)

Ruling party: Coalition of Sjálfstaeðisflokkurinn (SSF) (Independence Party) and Framsóknarflokkurinn (FSF) (Progressive Party)

Area: 103,100 square km

Population: 299,815 (2005)

Capital: Reykjavík

Official language: Icelandic

Currency: Icelandic krona (Ikr) = 100 aurar

Exchange rate: Ikr60.96 per US$ (Oct 2005)

GDP per capita: US$43,576 (2004)

GDP real growth: 5.70% (2004)

Labour force: 161,000 (2004)

Unemployment: 3.10% (2004)*; 3.30% (2003)

Inflation: 3.10% (2004)

Balance of trade: -US$519.00 million (2004)

Annual FDI: US$1.70 billion (cumulative, 1995–2004, OECD); US$400.00 million (OECD, 2004)*

* estimated figure

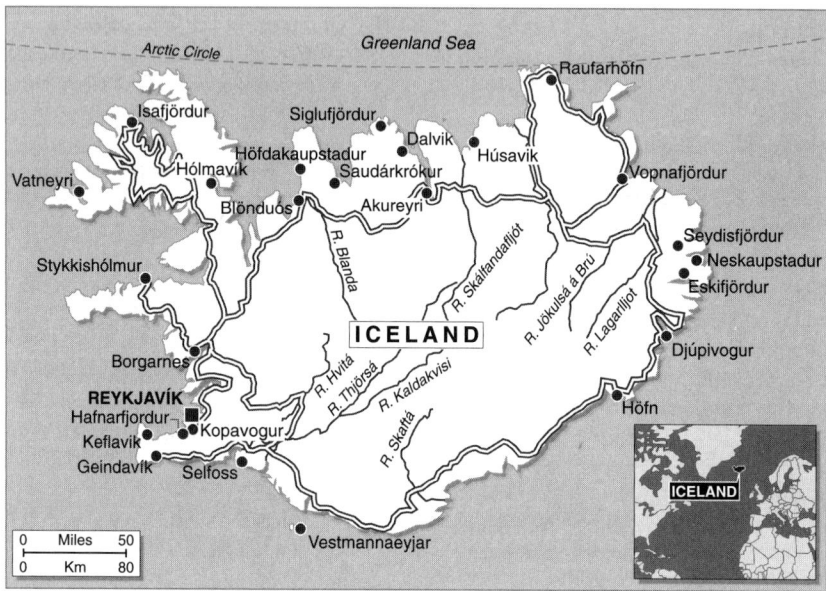

In March 2005 the Icelandic parliament held a vote as to whether one time chess champion and US national Bobby Fischer should be granted Icelandic citizenship. Fischer has been a fugitive since 1992 for playing a chess match against the Soviet Boris Spassky, in defiance of UN economic sanctions. The US promised to send Fischer to jail for a decade and slap a US$250,000 fine on him if he were to return to his country of birth. Politicians voted unanimously to grant the chess hero an Icelandic passport.

EU relations

Halldor Ásgrímsson, former foreign minister and leader of the the Framsóknarflokkurinn (FSF) (Progressive Party), is known to be well disposed to Iceland's European Union membership. The Icelandic people themselves are not overwhelmingly enthusiastic. Nevertheless, pressure on Iceland could emerge if Norway, Iceland's geopolitical buttress, were to join the EU. Analysts believe that Norway's EU membership could end the European Economic Area (EEA), which was established in 1992 as a trading bloc between the then 12-member European Community (EC) and the six member states of the European Free Trade Association (EFTA). Iceland would not find it problematic if the EEA was dissolved, as over 60 per cent of its trade is already done with the EU.

Baugur

A political feud in mid-2004 provided Icelanders with some of the most entertaining politics they have experienced for years. Former prime minister Oddsson's long-standing feud with Baugur – Iceland's biggest commercial group – concerning its predatory media interests, were, for him, a bridge too far. The Baugur group, under its high profile chief executive and majority shareholder, 37-year old Jon Asgeir Johanneson, already had significant business interests in Iceland, controlling an estimated 45 per cent of Iceland's food retailing industry. The UK supermarket Somerfield escaped a Baugur takeover bid in February 2005 while Whittards of Chelsea, the specialist tea retailers, was successfully snapped up in December 2005. Baugur already controls the supermarket chain Iceland, the fashion retailers Karen Millen, Oasis and Whistles, and the toy store Hamley's.

Iceland

In an interview with the UK *Financial Times*, Oddsson said that Baugur's media interests would be like Tesco (the UK's largest supermarket group) owning half the television channels and two-thirds of the national press as well. To counter the threat, Oddsson introduced new legislation intended to prohibit ownership of both print and broadcast media, and also prevent a company that was dominant in any particular sector of the Icelandic economy – Baugur, for example – from owning more than 5 per cent of a broadcasting company.

The proposed legislation was vetoed by Iceland's president, Ólafur Ragnar Grímmson, who saw it as more of a feud between Messrs Oddsson and Johanneson than as a matter of public interest. Mr Johanneson, it later emerged, was a key player in Grímmson's presidential re-election campaign. This was the first time in over 60 years that the presidential veto had been used, and left the proposed legislation to be decided by referendum vote.

In September 2005 an Icelandic court dismissed all 40 charges of embezzlement and dodgy accounting levelled at the conglomerate by the Oddsson government. This put an end to a three-year long legal process, and the threat of a six-year prison sentence for Jon Asgeir Johanneson. The businessman issued a statement saying the criminal charges had political roots.

Whaling and cod

Iceland is stubbornly refusing to acknowledge the benefits of conservation and the environment in its persistence with commercial whaling. Iceland rejoined the 2002 International Whaling Commission (IWC), only to announce that it would resume commercial whaling. In August 2003, Iceland recommenced whaling, although it claimed that it was for research purposes only. Iceland has expressed fears that over-abundant whale numbers may further deplete the country's important cod stocks. Like Norway and Japan, Iceland does not consider itself bound by the IWC moratorium on whaling, which has been in place since 1986.

Iceland's open market economy is still largely based on the fishing industry. The pattern of economic growth is therefore heavily determined by the size of the fish catch and world prices of fish products.

Iceland's long standing gloom and pessimism over the depletion of cod stocks had reached crisis levels by 2004. Overfishing in Iceland's waters has seriously threatened the fish-dependent economy. The fishing industry accounts for around 60 per cent of exports.

Iceland has the capacity to produce large quantities of relatively inexpensive hydro-electricity, although its isolated geographic position is an obstacle to the prospects of making energy an export industry. GDP growth in 2005 was forecast at a much-improved 5.8 per cent, which is set to drop slightly to 4.9 per cent in 2006. The economy is in danger of overheating, however, thanks in part to investment projects in the aluminium sector and high domestic consumption. Inflation was 3.5 per cent in 2005, above the EU's official limit of 3 per cent, although no formal sanctions can be brought because Iceland is not an EU member. Unemployment is generally low and in 2005 reached 3.1 per cent. Wages in Iceland are 37 per cent higher than those in EU states while construction workers receive almost two-thirds more than their continental neighbours. The cost of living is high, however.

In order to reduce further its dependency on fishing, Iceland is actively developing tourism, bio-technology and information technology. In September 2005 Iceland Telco was sold for US$0.9 billion, in a record payment for the Treasury. The cash injection will be used to repay government debt and invest in housing and transport.

Outlook

Iceland should continue to prosper in the long-term despite the weakened state of the fishing industry. Investment opportunities in Iceland are few. In principle, the construction of the Alcoa Fjaroaal aluminium smelter plant and Kárahnjúkar hydroelectric dam should double GDP growth in the long-term.

Risk assessment

Economic	Good
Political	Good
Regional Stability	Good
Stock Exchange	Good

COUNTRY PROFILE

Historical profile

Settled by Norwegians and Celtic (Scottish and Irish) immigrants during the late ninth and tenth centuries, Iceland boasts the world's oldest parliament, the Althingi. Iceland was under Norwegian, then Danish, rule from the thirteenth century. The severity of Iceland's terrain was frequently compounded by natural disasters leading, in the nineteenth century, to large-scale emigration to the USA and Canada. The island was granted its own constitution in the 1840s.
1903 Iceland was granted Home rule from Denmark.
1918 Iceland became a sovereign state in union with Denmark.
1940 Germany invaded Denmark. British troops were stationed in Iceland.
1944 Iceland terminated the convention linking it with Denmark and declared itself a republic.
1948 Iceland joined the International Whaling Commission (IWC).
1949 Iceland joined NATO and the Council of Europe. A large US airbase was established at Keflavík.
1953 Iceland became a founding member of the Nordic Council.
1959–71 The Coalition of Independence and Social Democratic Parties remained in power.

KEY INDICATORS — Iceland

	Unit	2000	2001	2002	2003	2004
Population	m	0.28	0.28	0.28	0.29	0.29
Gross domestic product (GDP)	US$bn	8.80	7.00	8.60	9.67	*12.38
GDP per capita	US$	28,343	24,936	28,648	33,317	43,576
GDP real growth	%	5.7	2.2	-0.5	4.1	5.7
Inflation	%	5.2	6.5	4.8	2.0	3.1
Unemployment	%	1.4	1.4	2.5	3.3	3.1
Exports (fob) (goods)	US$m	1,901.0	1,990.0	2,260.0	2,520.0	2,897.0
Imports (fob) (goods)	US$m	2,377.0	2,295.0	2,290.0	2,900.0	3,415.0
Balance of trade	US$m	-476.0	-305.0	-10.0	-380.0	-519.0
Current account	US$m	-849.0	-699.0	-601.0	-571.1	-670.0
Total reserves minus gold	US$m	388.9	338.3	440.1	792.3	1,046.0
Foreign exchange	US$m	364.6	314.8	414.7	764.6	1,017.3
Exchange rate	per US$	78.62	97.43	91.58	75.99	70.14

* estimated figure

Nations of the World: A Political, Economic and Business Handbook

1960s–70s Iceland's unilateral extensions of its territorial waters to protect its fishing grounds led to the 'Cod Wars' with the UK, and in 1976, caused a temporary break in diplomatic relations, the first such break between NATO members.
1980 Vigdís Finnbogadóttir was elected president, the world's first popularly elected female head of state.
1985 Iceland was declared a nuclear-free zone, barring entry to all nuclear weapons.
1987 Thorsteinn Pálsson was appointed prime minister.
1991 Davíd Oddsson became prime minister of the coalition government. In the same year, Iceland quit the International Whaling Commission (IWC) after the organisation refused to consider Icelandic proposals for moderate catch quotas.
1995 Oddsson was re-elected prime minister.
1996 Ólafur Ragnar Grímsson, a left-wing former finance minister, was elected president, replacing Vigdís Finnbogadóttir, who stepped down after 16 years in office.
1999 The elections again returned a centre-right coalition of Sjálfstaeðisflokkurinn (SSF) (Independence Party) and Framsóknarflokkurinn (FSF) (Progressive Party) under the leadership of Prime Minister Davíd Oddsson.
2000 Ólafur Ragnar Grímsson was unopposed in the presidential elections.
2002 Iceland's bid to rejoin the IWC, without signing up to the moratorium on commercial whaling, was rejected.
2003 Prime Minister Oddsson's SSF won the May parliamentary elections.
2004 Incumbent Ólafur Ragnar Grímsson was re-elected in the 26 June presidential elections. In September, Halldór Ásgrímsson (FSF) became prime minister, as Davíd Oddsson stepped down and became foreign minister. The exchange of posts will not alter policies within the coalition government.
2005 The government granted Bobby Fischer, the chess grandmaster and US fugitive of 10 years, Icelandic citizenship.

Political structure
Constitution
The constitution was adopted 17 June 1944.
The parliament and office of president jointly exercise legislative power, with due adherence to the constitution. The judiciary is guaranteed independence.
Elections are by proportional representation with universal direct suffrage over the age of 18.
The constitution recognises the Evangelical Lutheran Church as the state church.
Form of state
Parliamentary democratic republic

The executive
Executive power is vested jointly in the offices of the president as Head of State, and prime minister as head of government (appointed by the president) and the cabinet (appointed by the prime minister and approved by parliament).
Any citizen aged over 35 may become president, by popular vote (if more than one candidate stands for the post; without a challenge a candidate is duly elected without a vote).
National legislature
Legislative power is held jointly by the president and the 63-member Althingi (parliament). Members are elected for a four-year term by proportional representation.
The president is head of state, directly elected for a four-year term.
Legal system
The legal system is based on the 1944 constitution; the civil law system is based on Danish law.
Last elections
26 June 2004 (presidential); 10 May 2003 (parliamentary).
Results: Presidential: incumbent Ólafur Ragnar Grímsson was re-elected with 85.6 per cent of the vote; Baldur Ágústsson received 12.5 per cent and Ástthór Magnússon 1.9 per cent; turnout was 62.6 per cent.
Parliamentary: the SSF won 33.7 per cent of the vote (22 seats out of 63), Alliance 31 per cent (20 seats), the FSF 17.7 per cent (12 seats), the Vinstrihreyfing - Grænt framboð (VG) (Left-Green Alliance) 8.8 per cent (five seats) and the Frjálslyndi Flokkurinn (FF) (Liberal Party) 7.4 per cent (four seats); turnout was 87.7 per cent.
Next elections
2007 (parliamentary); 2008 (presidential).

Political parties
Ruling party
Coalition of Sjálfstaeðisflokkurinn (SSF) (Independence Party) and Framsóknarflokkurinn (FSF) (Progressive Party)
Main opposition party
Samfylkingin (Alliance)

Population
299,815 (2005)
Ethnic make-up
Almost the entire population are descendants of Norwegians and Celts.
Religions
Lutherans (96 per cent), Protestants and Catholics (3 per cent).

Education
Pre-schooling is offered to children aged between one and six years when compulsory primary education begins. This leads into lower secondary school until aged 16 when students choose upper secondary education – either academic grammar or comprehensive schooling or vocational industrial or specialised training. Upper secondary education covers four years and is open to anyone who has completed compulsory school. Grammar and comprehensive attainment leads to higher education facilities at age 20.
Icelandic municipalities are responsible for delivering education in different regions.
The total public expenditure in education is typically 5–6 per cent of GDP.
Compulsory years: Six to 16.
Enrolment rate: 99 per cent net primary enrolment; 85.3 per cent net secondary enrolment (World Bank 2003).

Health
Annual total expenditure on health is around 9 per cent of GDP, of which approximately 84 per cent is government spending.
The country is divided into health care regions, each with their own primary health care centres, some of which are run jointly with the local community hospital; hospitalisation is free of charge. The number of Icelandic physicians has increased steadily during the last decade.
HIV prevalence: 0.2 per cent aged 15–49 in 2003 (World Bank)
Life expectancy: 79.9 years (World Bank)
Fertility rate/Maternal mortality rate: 2.0 births per woman (World Bank)
Infant mortality rate: 3.0 per 1,000 live births (World Bank)
Head of population per physician/bed: 3.2 doctors per 1,000 people.

Welfare
Iceland follows the Nordic social security system, which aims to provide universal social welfare and health services.
The social security system covers pension, occupational injury, health and maternity insurance. Most pensions are covered by private pension funds. There is generous coverage for maternity leave for both men and women.

Main cities
Reykjavík (capital, estimated population 114,800 in 2003), Kópavogur (25,900), Hafnarfjörður (21,300), Akureyri (15,900).

Languages spoken
The Icelandic language belongs to the North Germanic branch of the Indo-European family.
Official language/s
Icelandic

Media
Press
Dailies: The most popular dailies published in Reykjavík are *Morgunbladid*,

Iceland

Dagbladid Visir, *Tíminn* and *Daily News* from Iceland.

Weeklies: *Vikurfréttir* is published weekly in Sudurnes, Iceland. *Sed og Heyrt* is a weekly magazine featuring entertainment.

Business: *Iceland Business* is a quarterly publication from Reykjavik. Other business interests are covered by *Aegir* on marine issues, *Fiskifrettir*, *Sjavarfrettir*, *Freyr* and *Farmers Magazine*.

Periodicals: There are several monthly and bi-monthly magazines. *Iceland Reporter* is a monthly newspaper in English. *Iceland Review* is published quarterly in English. *Mannliff* and *Bleikt og Blatt* are general consumer magazines.

Broadcasting

Radio: Six main radio stations broadcast nationally: Icelandic State Broadcasting Service (RUV) – Channel One and Two, plus Radio Bylgjan/Stjarnan/Adalstodin. Channel One broadcasts on medium and long wave as well as on FM. Islenska utvarpsfelagid runs private radio stations.

Television: Programmes broadcast by Icelandic State Broadcasting Service – Television (RUV) and Channel Two (Stod 2). There are five television stations in Iceland.

Advertising

Newspaper, radio and television advertising are the most effective. The quality of locally produced television advertising material is very high by international standards. Information can be obtained from Samband islenskra auglysingastofa (Association of Icelandic Advertising Companies), Hateigsvegur 3, 105 Reykjavík (tel: 562-9588; fax: 562-9585).

Economy

Iceland has an open market economy based largely on fishing (although cod stocks are diminishing), tourism (expanding fast) and aluminium smelting (based on abundant geothermal power and water). It has a small population (299,815 in 2005) and one of the highest per capita GDP rates in Europe. Despite interest rates of 9 per cent by mid-2005, a number of high profile investments have been made by Icelandic investors in the UK and northern Europe.

The fishing industry made up almost 60 per cent of exports in 2004 and 9.4 per cent of GDP. However, the level of cod catches are falling, and having a knock-on effect for the processing industry. The large fish processing company, Samherji, will be moving its operations from Dalvík to Grimsby, UK, by March 2006. Its modern plant in Dalvík is being dismantled and moved to an EU member-state with wages lower by 30–40 per cent and with transport costs at half Samherji's current expenditure, but most particularly to dissipate the negative effect of the strong krona on exports.

The Alcoa Fjaroaal aluminium smelter plant is due to become operational in 2007. The national power company, Landsvirkjun, is building a number of dams to supply the water for the plant and has had to counter the opposition from environmentalists. The employment opportunities created by the plant are considered to outweigh environmental considerations. Once exports of aluminium start in 2007 it is expected that fish related exports and aluminium will be 50 per cent of exports each.

The economic recovery has been stronger than anticipated with GDP growth at 5.7 per cent in 2004 and expected to be over 5 per cent in 2005. Inflation did not reach the central bank's upper limit of 4.0 per cent, running at 3.1 per cent in 2004; it is possible that interest rates may have to rise again to prevent a wage and price spiral from developing. Unemployment was low at 3.1 per cent in 2004 and is unlikely to rise by much in 2005.

External trade

Over 60 per cent of trade turnover is conducted with the EU, of which UK, Germany, France, Denmark and The Netherlands are the principal traders. Other main trading partners are US, Japan, Eastern Europe and Sweden.

Export trade grew by 4.3 per cent, while imports grew by 33.3 per cent in 2004.

Imports

Principal imports include machinery and equipment, petroleum products, foodstuffs and textiles.

Main sources: Germany (12.3 per cent), US (10 per cent), Norway (9.8 per cent), Denmark (7.6 per cent), UK (6.9 per cent), Sweden (6.4 per cent), The Netherlands (5.7 per cent)

Exports

Marine products (70 per cent), agricultural products, manufactured goods and minerals: aluminium, ferro-silicon, diatomite.

Main destinations: UK (19.1 per cent), Germany (17.1 per cent), The Netherlands (11 per cent), US (10.2 per cent), Spain (6.9 per cent), Denmark (4.6 per cent)

Agriculture

Farming

Some 20 per cent of Iceland's land area is suitable for the raising of livestock and for fodder production. Only 6 per cent of the area is used for the cultivation of, principally, hay and potatoes, and the rest is used for livestock.

Arable land is scarce, but good grazing allows for self-sufficiency in meat (mostly lamb), milk, poultry, eggs, cheese and butter.

The sector is small-scale, heavily subsidised and organised into co-operatives. High import tariffs protect domestic production from foreign competition. Estimated crop production in 2004 included: 7,500 tonnes (t) potatoes, 1,000t tomatoes, 1,100t cucumbers, 558t cabbages, 20t fruit in total, 3,745t vegetables in total. Livestock production included: 26,950t meat in total, 3,650t beef, 5,800t pig meat, 8,700t lamb, 5,600t poultry, *2,600t eggs, 109,000t milk, 695t cattle hides, *1,920t sheepskins, *1,060t horsemeat, 498t greasy wool.
* estimate

Fishing

Fishing replaced farming early in this century as the dominant sector of the economy. The fishing industry (including processing) is the single most important export earner, accounting for 60 per cent of Iceland's exports. The large modernised trawler fleet supplies over 110 freezing plants, which produce white fish fillets, frozen shrimps, capelin, scampi, scallops, fish oil and fish meal.

The Icelandic Freezing Plants Corporation and Iceland Seafood Ltd are the leading fish exporters.

There is rapid growth of inland and offshore fish farming.

Forestry

Forest exports in 2004 amounted to US$430,000, while imports amounted to US$76.4 million.

Industry and manufacturing

The industrial sector contributes 26 per cent to GDP and employs 30 per cent of the workforce.

It is centred on fish and food processing. A salmon fish processing plant on Iceland's east coast is the first to use state-of-the-art technology to process salmon for export to the EU and US.

Other major industrial activity focusses on aluminium smelting, ferro-silicon alloys, diatomite production and light manufacturing. The demands of the fishing industry have lead to developments in the country's computer, software and electronics industries and have also encouraged developments in biotechnology and pharmaceuticals.

The relatively cheap supply of electrical power in Iceland has lead to power-intensive industries, the largest of which is aluminium smelting. In 2003, the government approved the construction of the Alcoa Fjaroaal aluminium smelter plant in eastern Iceland. The US's Alcoa Inc is funding the construction of the plant, which is expected to be completed in 2007.

Tourism

Tourism is an increasingly important sector, accounting for 13 per cent of foreign exchange earnings and 4.5 per cent of GDP. A growing proportion of arrivals are winter visitors. The Nordic countries, North America and particularly the UK are the main markets. The industry is well organised and expanding, catering largely to adventure and eco-tourists. Whale-watching, which attracts around 25 per cent of tourists, is growing in popularity. The decision to resume whale-hunting in 2003 hurt Iceland's image abroad and has given rise to fears that it could undermine the more lucrative tourist sector.

Travel and tourism is expected to provide US$1.8 billion or 7.1 per cent of GDP and employ over 20 per cent of the workforce, in 2005. The sector is expected to attract US$659 million or 18.7 per cent of total capital investment for 2005.

Hydrocarbons
Iceland does not produce any hydrocarbons. It consumes both coal and oil to meet domestic energy demands. Iceland does not consume natural gas. It consumes around 15,760 barrels per day (bpd) of refined oils. Iceland is dependent on these oils to fuel its cars, transportation system and fishing trawlers. Iceland also consumes approximately 139,700 tonnes of coal annually. With the government having an official policy to replace fossil fuels with hydrogen fuels, the consumption of oil and coal is likely to decrease as this industry grows.

Energy
Rapid development of cheap hydroelectric and geothermal power has led to self-sufficiency in energy requirements. Geothermal energy accounts for 54 per cent of Iceland's energy consumption while hydro-energy accounts for 17 per cent. Imported energy (oil and coal) serve 29 per cent of domestic energy needs. It is estimated that only 12 per cent of Iceland's energy potential has been harnessed. Iceland aims to become the first fossil-fuel free economy by 2020 and plans to develop a fully hydrogen-powered transport system by 2035. Around 85 per cent of homes have geothermal heating. The fishing fleet remains dependent on imported oil.

Financial markets
Stock exchange
The Iceland Stock Exchange (ICEX) has benefited from joining the Norex Alliance. Its trading system has been upgraded in order to cope with increased demand.

Banking and insurance
In addition to the central bank, there are four commercial banks operating: the Búnadarbanki Íslands (Agricultural Bank), Icebank Ltd, Islandsbanki Ltd and Landsbanki Íslands (National Bank of Iceland) are privately owned.
Kaupthing, an investment bank, and the Búnadarbanki merged in May 2003 to form the Kaupthing Búnadarbanki.
Central bank
Sedlabanki Íslands (Central Bank of Iceland)

Time
GMT

Geography
Iceland comprises one large island and numerous smaller ones, situated near the Arctic Circle in the North Atlantic Ocean. The main island lies about 300km (190 miles) south-east of Greenland, about 1,000km (620 miles) west of Norway and about 800km (500 miles) north of Scotland. The Gulf Stream keeps Iceland warmer than might be expected.

Climate
Temperate, with mild but stormy winters and cool summers. Rainy in the south. Average temperatures vary between about -1 and 12 degrees Celsius.

Dress codes
Medium-weight throughout year, plus a topcoat and raincoat for winter.

Entry requirements
Passports
Passports must be valid three months after date of departure. Not required by nationals of countries which are signatories of the Schengen Accords, which includes most EU member states.
Visa
Visas are required by all except nationals of most EU countries, the Americas, Australasia and some Asian countries. For a full list of exceptions visit: www.utl.is/english and follow link to Schengen. Business trips may be made visa-free, or on short-term visas. A Schengen visa application (offered in several languages) can be downloaded on www.eurovisa.info/ApplicationForm.htm.
Currency advice/regulations
Import and export of local currency is limited to Ikr8000. There are no restrictions on the import of foreign currency.
Customs
Fishing equipment (including waders and rubber boots) and riding equipment must be accompanied by a certificate of disinfection issued by an authorised veterinary authority.

Health (for visitors)
Free or reduced-cost state-provided emergency health treatment is available.
Mandatory precautions
There are no compulsory vaccinations.
Advisable precautions
Travellers should have up-to-date tetanus and polio immunisations.

Hotels
Most towns have hotels and guest houses available. Between June and September university hostels and boarding schools are also used as hotels. Some hostels and many farms provide bed and breakfast service. The rating system is one-star (basic) to five -star (luxury). Tipping is not customary.

Public holidays
Fixed dates
1 Jan (New Year's Day), 1 May (Labour Day), 17 Jun (National Day), 24 Dec (Christmas Eve, from mid-day), 25 Dec (Christmas Day), 26 Dec (Boxing Day), 31 Dec (New Year's Eve, from mid-day).
Variable dates
Maundy Thursday, Good Friday, Easter Monday, First Day of Summer, Ascension Day, Whit Monday, Commerce Day (first Mon in Aug).

Working hours
Banking
Mon–Fri: 0915–1600 (winter), 0800–1600 (summer), plus 1700–1800 on Thu (Co-operative Bank, National Bank, Agricultural Bank (Kringlam).
Business
Mon–Fri: usually 0900–1700.
Government
Mon–Fri: usually 0900–1700.
Shops
Mon–Fri: 1000–1800. Most also open Sat 1000–1400/1600 (winter only, Oct to end May). Kiosks remain open until 2330 or even later.

Telecommunications
Mobile phones
GSM 900/1800 services are available in populated areas.

Electricity supply
220V AC

Social customs/useful tips
Icelanders are generally self-confident, self-reliant and reserved. However, once the initial contact has been made people are more than likely to be friendly. Handshaking is customary on arrival and departure.

Getting there
Air
National airline: Flugleidir (Icelandair)
International airport/s: Reykjavík (REK)/Keflavík (KEF), 51km south-west of Reykjavík. Buses and taxis available, 40–50 minute drive to capital.
Airport tax: There is no airport tax.
Surface
Water: Ferry services to Seydisfjóedur (in the east) from several north European ports during summer.

Iceland

Getting about
National transport
Air: Icelandair, Air Iceland and Ilandsflug run domestic services throughout the island to 10 major destinations which link with regional carriers in the west, north and east of the country. There are 12 local airports. Light aircraft readily available for charter and sightseeing.

Road: There are approximately 12,000km of roads. Main highways (approximately one quarter of total) follow coastline and are hard-surfaced, the rest are gravel-surfaced. Regular coach services link even the remote inland areas.

Water: Passenger and car ferries sail several times a day between Reykjavík and Akranes and between Thorlakshöta and Vestmannaeyian.

City transport
Taxis: These are used extensively and usually summoned by telephone, although they can be hailed in the street. The journey time from the airport to the city centre is about 40 minutes.

Buses, trams & metro: There are excellent regular services covering the centre and suburbs of Reykjavík. There is a standard fare for any length of journey, even if it involves more than one bus route. Journey time from the airport to the city centre is about 45 minutes.

Car hire
Car hire is available in Reykjavík and several other towns. Rates vary depending on the type of car. Minimum age 20 years, and an international driving licence is usually required. Advance reservations are necessary between June and August. Self-drive cars not recommended as a method of national transport as road surfaces tend to be poor.

BUSINESS DIRECTORY

Telephone area codes
The international direct dialling code (IDD) for Iceland is +354, followed by subscriber's number.

Chambers of Commerce
Iceland Chamber of Commerce, House of Commerce, Kringlan 7, 103 Reykjavík (tel:510-7100; fax: 568-6564; e-mail: info@chamber.is).

Banking
Kaupthing Búnadarbanki, Austurstraeti 3, 101 Reykjavík (tel: 525-6000; fax: 525-6209).

Íslandsbanki (Bank of Iceland), Kringlunni, 155 Reykjavík (tel: 560-8000; fax: 560-8150).

Landsbanki Íslands (National Bank of Iceland), Laugavegur 77, 155 Reykjavík (tel: 560-6400; fax: 552-9882; internet site: http://www.landsbanki.is).

Central bank
Sedlabanki Íslands, Kalkofnsvegi 1, 150 Reykjavík (tel: 569-9600; fax: 569-9605; e-mail: sedlabanki@sedlabanki.is).

Travel information
Airport Authority, Leifur Eiriksson Passenger Terminal, Keflavík Airport, 235 Keflavík.

BSI Travel (buses), Umferdarmidstödin v/Hringbraut, 101 Reykjavík.

Icelandair, Reykjavík Airport, Reykjavík IS-101 (tel: 505-0200; fax: 505-0300; internet site: http://www.icelandair.com).

National tourist organisation offices
Icelandic Tourist Board (Ferdamalarad Islands), Laekjargotu 3, 101 Reykjavík (tel: 552-7488; fax: 562-4749; e-mail:info@icetourist.is; internet site: http://www.icetourist.is).

Ministries
Ministry of Agriculture, 4th Floor, Sölvhólsgötu 7, 150 Reykjavík (tel: 560-9750; fax: 552-1160).

Ministry of Commerce and Industry, Arnarhváli, 150 Reykjavík (tel: 560-9070, 560-9420; fax: 562-1289).

Ministry of Communication, Hafnarhúsinu vio Tryggvagötu, 150 Reykjavík (tel: 560-9630; fax: 562-1702).

Ministry of Culture and Education, Sölvhólsgötu 4, 150 Reykjavík (tel: 560-9504; fax: 562-3068).

Ministry of the Environment, Vonarstraeti 4, 150 Reykjavík (tel: 560-9600; fax: 562-4566).

Ministry of Finance, Arnarhválli, 150 Reykjavík (tel: 560-9200; fax: 562-8280).

Ministry of Fisheries, Skúlagötu 4, 150 Reykjavík (tel: 560-9670; fax: 562-1853).

Ministry for Foreign Affairs, Rauoarásti\01g 25, 150 Reykjavík (tel: 560-9900; fax: 562-2373, 562-2386).

Ministry for Foreign Affairs, Trade Department, Hverfisgata 115, 105 Reykjavík (tel: 560-9930; fax: 562-4878).

Ministry of Health and Social Security, Laugavegi 116, 150 Reykjavík (tel: 560-9700; fax: 551-9165).

Ministry of Industry, Arnarhváli, 150 Reykjavík (tel: 560-9420; fax: 562-6859).

Ministry of Justice, Arnarhváli, 150 Reykjavík (tel: 560-9010; fax: 552-7340).

Ministry of Social Affairs, Hafnarhúsinu vio Tryggvagötu, 150 Reykjavík (tel: 560-9100; fax: 552-4804).

Office of the Prime Minister (Stjórnarráoshúsinu vio Laekjargötu), 150 Reykjavík (tel: 560-9400, 560-9403; fax: 562-4014, 562-8626).

Other useful addresses
Association of Icelandic Importers, Exporters & Wholesale Merchants, (Félag Islands Storkaupmanna), Húsi verslunarinnar, 103 Reykjavík (tel: 567-8910; fax: 468-8441).

British Embassy, Laufásvegur 31, PO Box 460, 101 Reykjavík (tel: 550-5100; fax: 550-5105; e-mail: britemb@centrum.is).

Customs Department, Tolhusid, Tryggvagata 19, 150 Reykjavík (tel: 560-0300; fax: 562-5826).

Embassy of the United States of America, Laufásvegur 21, Reykjavík (tel: 629-100; fax: 29-139).

Export Council of Iceland, Lagmuli 5, Box 8796, 129 Reykjavík (tel: 568-8777; fax: 568-9197).

Federation of Icelandic Co-operative Societies (Samband of Iceland), Import Division, v/Holtavegur, 104 Reykjavík (tel: 568-1266; fax: 568-0290).

Icelandic Embassy (USA), Suite 1200, 1156 15th Street, NW, Washington DC 20005 (tel: 202-265-6653; fax: 202-265-6656; e-mail: icemb.wash@utn.stjr.is).

Icelandic Energy Marketing Agency, Haaleitisbraut 68, 103 Reykjavík (tel: 515-9000; fax: 515-9003; e-mail: landsvirkjun@lv.is).

Iceland Management Association, Ananaust 15, 121 Reykjavík (tel: 562-1066).

Invest in Iceland Bureau (privatisation and foreign investment), Hallveigarstigur 1, PO Box 1000, IS-121 Reykjavík (tel: 511-4000; fax: 511-4040; internet site: http://www.invest.is/us/index.htm; e-mail: Invest@icetrade.is).

National Economic Institute (for information on economic development corporations), Thjodhagsstofnun, Kalkofnsvegi 1, Reykjavík (tel: 569-9500; fax: 562-6540).

Retailers' Association of Iceland, Hus Verslunarinnar, Kringlan 7, 103 Reykjavík (tel: 568-7811; fax: 568-5569).

Statistical Bureau in Iceland, Hagstofa Islands, Skuggasund 3, 150 Reykjavík (tel: 560-9800; fax: 562-8865; internet site: http://www.statice.is/).

Internet sites
Iceland Reporter:
http://www.centrum.is/icerev/

Iceland websites:
http://www.iceland.vefur.is/

The Trade Council of Iceland:
http://www.icetrade.is/

India

KEY FACTS

Official name: Republic of India (also known as Bharat, local-language name)

Head of State: President Aavul Pakkiri Jainulabidin Abdul Kalam (elected by the national and state parliaments, sworn in 25 Jul 2002)

Head of government: Prime Minister Manmohan Singh (sworn in 22 May 2004)

Ruling party: Coalition government led by the Indian National Congress (Congress) (elected Apr/May 2004)

Area: 3,287,590 square km

Population: 1.09 billion (2004)

Capital: New Delhi

Official language: Hindi and English; 15 other languages are recognised for official use in regional areas.

Currency: (Rs) = 100 paisa

Exchange rate: Rs43.97 per US$ (Oct 2005)

GDP per capita: US$608 (2004)

GDP real growth: 7.30% (2004)

Labour force: 482.42 million (2004)

Unemployment: 9.20% (2004)

Inflation: 3.80% (2004)

Oil production: 819,000 bpd (2004)

Balance of trade: -US$20.15 billion (2004)

Foreign debt: US$117.20 billion (2004)

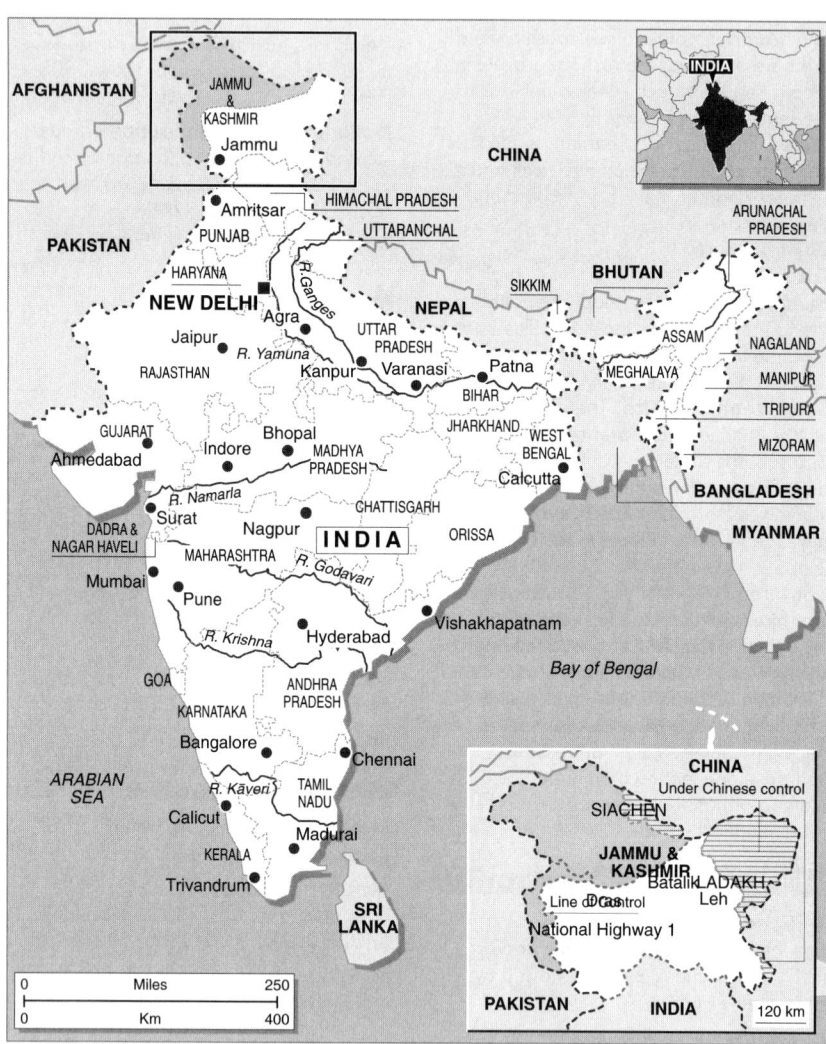

India is a teeming, diverse, ex-colonial, secular, democratic nuclear state. It has the second biggest population in the world, 1.1 billion people, but only the seventh greatest land area. A 2005 report compiled by the UN forecasts that India will become the most populous nation by 2030, five years earlier than previous estimates. Its middle classes, already numbering 200 million people, are growing thanks to some extent to a booming software and IT sector. Hundreds of millions, however, remain in devastating poverty.

India and Pakistan

The two countries have gone to war three times since partition and independence in 1947, twice over the border area of Kashmir. The disputed Kashmir region has been the site of a 15-year violent uprising in which over 40,000 people have been killed. In early 2005 an election was held there for the first time in nearly 30 years. Turnout was high despite widespread intimidation and five deaths. Pakistan has said that it wants a referendum to be held on the position of Kashmir, but India has resisted these calls.

A peace process started in 2004 saw progress in February 2005 when officials announced the future opening of a civilian bus service to ferry passengers across the line of control (LOC) that divides the two sides. Those using the service need to attain entry permits, rather than passports, which India initially sought. It is the first bus service to travel this route since before the partition and has mostly symbolic weight. The announcement was significant in generating confidence among locals, who finally would be able to travel to meet separated family members. The ceasefire also agreed at this time has survived, reflecting popular fatigue with continued violence.

Shortly after the bus service was announced General Pervez Musharraf, the Pakistani president, agreed to attend a cricket tour in India, for the first time for years. This was not all plain sailing as Pakistan diplomats objected to the official match itinerary, requesting that the Ahmedabad match be re-located outside of Gujarat, for fears about the security of the Muslim side. This state had been the scene of a massacre in 2002 which left almost 2,000 Muslims dead. Attacks on Muslims have allegedly been state-sponsored: Human Rights Watch carries reports of Indian policemen telling dying Muslims 'we have no orders to save you'. Muslim girls were subject to a huge wave of sexual violence and rape. The Indian authorities claim that the massacre was a spontaneous response to the Muslim torching of a train carrying Hindu worshippers. However, observers have noted that the events bore the hallmarks of careful planning – by nationalists who seek to create an official Hindu state.

In July 2005 six extremists, suspected Islamic militants, attacked a temple under construction in Ayodhya in the worst terrorist violence for several years. The temple is on ground claimed by both Hindus and Muslims – the site originally housed a mosque, which was torched by Hindu militants, and replaced with a temple. Water bombs and tear gas had to be used to break up Hindu anti-government protests. The attack posed a serious threat to the peace negotiations with Pakistan.

In October 2005, a catastrophic earthquake occured on the India-Pakistan border, killing members of both nationalities. However, in the event this marked another stage in relations between the rival states. India provided aid to afflicted Kashmiris and Pakistanis although Pakistan barred Indian troops' involvement in search and rescue missions. India could have provided significant resources, in so doing generating confidence in the peace process. General Musharraf cited security concerns as the reason for restrictions on foreign involvement.

New Delhi suffered multiple bomb attacks in October 2005, which killed 60 people shopping at busy market stalls, preparing for the impending Hindu celebration of Diwali. Despite the bombing however, India and Pakistan made further diplomatic progress with a relaxation on travel rules, allowing relatives to travel over five crossing points to see family affected by the earthquake.

A subsequent bombing, this time in November 2005 in Indian-controlled Kashmir, did not help relations. Five people died in a car bomb attack, which was carried out by suicide bombers from Jaish-e-Mohammed, a large Islamic group in the region which India claims is sponsored by the Pakistani government.

In December 2005 terrorists tried new tactics, bombing a university in Bangalore, the Silicon Valley of India. A gunman killed conference guests with an automatic rifle. Previously militants have tried to maximise death tolls by operating in crowded areas.

US relations

Bilateral co-operation and agreements characterised US-India relations in 2005 with Bush declaring in July that 'our relationship has never been stronger'. In March 2005 US secretary of state Condoleezza Rice visited the Indian prime minister to push for further confidence-building and peace measures with Pakistan, and to discuss nuclear issues and arms sales. India had joined the club of nuclear nations in 1998 and the US had applied sanctions in response. Washington officials pressed India to sign the nuclear non-proliferation treaty, something Indians were not prepared to do. Now that India is clearly on its way to being a major world power, America has taken notice and relations have become closer. Rice agreed to sell the country jet fighters and share nuclear and space technology, which many Indians felt the US had been unfairly withholding. The agreement was widely interpreted as a sign of US trust of the Indian nuclear strategy. The US's diplomacy was highly strategic as it needs to boost leverage in the negotiations about Indian plans for a pipeline to Iran. Two thirds of Indian oil is sourced from the Gulf region, something with which the US is uncomfortable.

Legislation was passed by the Indian parliament in May 2005, formalising its non-proliferation stance. The Weapons of Mass Destruction and their Delivery Systems Bill tightens the restrictions on exports and transit of weapons of mass destruction technology. The transparent

KEY INDICATORS — India

	Unit	2000	2001	2002	2003	2004
Population	m	1,000.00	1,030.00	1,049.00	1,068.50	1,088.06
Gross domestic product (GDP)	US$bn	456.00	484.50	504.00	603.30	*691.88
GDP per capita	US$	456	470	480	539	608
GDP real growth	%	4.0	5.1	5.8	7.4	7.3
Inflation	%	4.0	3.7	5.1	4.6	3.8
Unemployment	%	10.6	9.2	8.8	9.1	9.2
Oil output	'000 bpd	778.0	782.0	793.0	793.0	819.0
Natural gas output	bn cum	26.1	26.4	25.4	30.1	29.4
Coal output	mtoe	154.3	161.1	168.4	172.2	188.8
Exports (fob) (goods)	US$m	43,132.0	44,894.0	50,000.0	62,952.0	69,180.0
Imports (fob) (goods)	US$m	55,325.0	59,264.0	57,620.0	79,658.0	89,330.0
Balance of trade	US$m	-12,193.0	-5,800.0	-7,300.0	-16,706.0	-20,150.0
Current account	US$m	-4,198.0	1,410.0	7,060.0	6,850.0	2,050.0
Foreign debt	US$bn	103.0	103.7	97.1	100.6	117.2
Total reserves minus gold	US$m	37,902.0	45,870.0	67,665.0	98,938.0	126,593.0
Foreign exchange	US$m	37,264.0	45,251.0	66,994.0	97,617.0	125,164.0
Exchange rate	per US$	44.94	47.19	48.09	46.81	45.26

* estimated figure

bill is a substitute for signing the non-proliferation treaty and will, it is hoped, strengthen India's stance as a 'responsible' nuclear power, as one with a 'no first use' policy. July saw the first defence agreement struck with the US since they went nuclear in 1998, which US defence minister Donald Rumsfeld called a 'new era' for the allies. It provides for closer ties and sharing of technology and weapons manufacture. The pact has been seen as part of a US strategy for curbing Chinese power in Asia. India is uncomfortable with this assumed function as it is eager to be on good economic and political terms with China.

In July 2005 Prime Minister Singh told US President George W Bush that 'India's track record in nuclear non-proliferation is impeccable' in negotiations about civilian nuclear technology. Despite the trust India has gained, without signing the nuclear non-proliferation treaty it was legally barred in the US from involvement in nuclear deals. Bush promised to ask Congress to bypass the law and technicalities to sell nuclear reactors to New Delhi. Bush faced opposition to this plan – by people who felt it would weaken the US case against Iran. However, others are pushing tighter ties with India, a strategic ally in the light of the rise of China. US senior officials agreed on 'full civil nuclear energy co-operation and trade' with the nuclear power, if Prime Minister Singh agreed to certain international inspections and controls.

However despite all the deal-doing with Prime Minister Singh, Indians were notably aggrieved when Bush sanctioned the sale of F-16 fighter jets to Pakistan, a reward for Musharraf's role in the US-led war on terrorism. Pakistan's military build-up is seen by India as a direct threat.

The US has been surprisingly co-operative in helping to solidify the Indian nuclear sector – except it has not backed the country's claim for a seat on the UN Security Council.

In August 2005 India and Pakistan reached a nuclear accord promising to give notice to the other before launching ballistic missile tests. The pact will formalise an up-to-now informal notification system and tighten links between the two countries.

Economy

The prime minister has solid financial credentials which have helped allay investor fears in the wake of the 2004 election. There had been concerns that a Congress-lead government would reverse the privatisation programme of the previous Bharatiya Janata Party (BJP) government. However, Manmohan Singh is a former senior IMF economist and the architect of the reform programme of the early 1990s. He appointed pro-reform Palaniappan Chidambaram as finance minister. Both are credited with rescuing India from a balance of payments crisis in 1991 and then nearly doubling the rate of economic growth and have the trust of the domestic and international business communities.

In 2005 the economy grew 7.13 per cent, driven by the tourism, manufacturing and financial sectors. Prime Minister Singh pushed for a target of 10 per cent growth in coming years.

In early 2005 the stock market reached near record highs, sending a signal to foreign investors across the world that India was not to be overlooked in the race to capitalise on the Chinese surge. Goldman Sachs, the investment bank, predicted that in 2015 India's growth could outpace that of China. The country is cruising past European nations and is set to become the third biggest world economy by 2030. In China the state has a far greater presence in business and there is a lack of transparency: it is on these issues that India has the edge in Asia. UK bank Lloyds TSB has an Indian workforce of over 1,000 and over three-quarters of non-US IT services are based in India. The IT sector is showing year-on-year growth of over 30 per cent and is expanding beyond Bangalore (soon to become Bengaluru) to other major cities such as Chennai.

McKinsey, the management consultants, said in September 2005, 'we expect foreign direct investment to increase exponentially'. This is in spite of the fact that communist party members in November blocked further privatisation and economic reforms which would have opened floodgates to 100 per cent FDI in key sectors such as energy and airports. The Common Minimum Programme (CMP), agreed by the coalition partners in May 2004, had shown a strong left-wing influence in economic policy-making with increased spending on education and agriculture, a slowdown of reforms and the introduction of value added tax. At the moment India receives only US$5 billion a year – a tenth of the level of FDI ploughed into China.

In January 2005 the Multifibre Arrangement (MFA) production quotas, which had in effect guaranteed India a role in the global market, were removed. This legislation had been introduced in the 1970s and its removal is one of the most significant recent events in the global economy. Retailers are now free to find the cheapest markets without restrictions. This deregulation puts great pressure on prices and China was initially expected to dominate the market. However, ten months after the change, it was clear that India, with its low labour costs and skilled workforce, was also faring well. Before the removal of quotas the Indian market was worth US$320 billion – this is set to rise. Indian exports to the EU increased by a quarter in the first six months of 2005.

Banking

The banking sector is in need of liberalisation and its inefficiency is a significant barrier to national prosperity. The government controls 40 per cent of banking resources leaving banks with enough only to lend to major corporations. Smaller businesses do not get a chance and much of the country is alienated from banking services and credit. About 70 per cent of Indian peasants have no bank account.

Interest rates have been liberalised and a credit culture encouraged but the public sector is still the dominant presence, slowing growth and reform. World Bank specialist Priya Basu analyses the sector thus: 'the banking system has traded efficiency for stability'. Banking reforms will to a significant extent determine India's future growth.

Manufacturing

The international consensus is that India reigns over the IT outsourcing industry and China is the manufacturing workshop of the world. However, India has not been content to leave all manufucuturing to its Asian arch rival. This is because India's lack of serious industry is the only thing stopping it from being one of the most mighty global economies. India has fallen behind in the industry stakes partly due to lower investment levels, but also because its electricity and transport is far more expensive than in China. Indian factories are not the sleek and modern operations that China's have become. However, in the first half of 2005 the manufacturing sector grew 9.8 per cent and business confidence was at a ten year peak. India is channelling its energy into the mobile telecommunications sector as it is the world's fastest growing market for mobile phone use. Motorola set up in India in December 2005 and Nokia is due to follow in 2006. A serious focus on manufacturing in India could go a long way towards alleviating problematic unemployment figures.

Reform is necessary to attract further FDI, although the very idea of FDI is challenged by the communist presence within the government, trade unoins, and some industry magnates. Though analysts are keen to play up the potential rivalry of China and India, while China churns out masses of cheaply produced goods, India will seek to dominate a technology-based corner of the market.

The National Manufacturing Competitive Council recommended in September 2005 a range of measures that would enable India to compete on a world scale in industrial production. These included facilitating the sacking of staff, reform of import tariffs, investment in infrastructure and reducing the many layers of bureaucracy.

Class system

Yet farmers remain the poorest and most vulnerable people in Indian society, rural unemployment is on the rise and there has been an alarming rise in farmers' suicides due to increasing hardship. As the rich got richer on the back of growth in services, economic inequalities increased. Surveys suggested that India was shining for just 250 million middle-income earners, who saw a moderate increase in income. The 325 million people in the 'poor' socio-economic category, whose income is below Rs3,750 (US$80) per month and those 350 million classified as lower-middle income, living on Rs3,750–7,500 (US$80–160) per month, have had no increase in living standards. Moreover, those living on fixed savings, such as middle-income pensioners, saw their income diminish due to high negative interest rates.

The 'India Shining' campaign drew attention to this growth in inequality, with India's poor feeling neglected by the development boom.

Political affairs

The president of the Hindu nationalist Bharatiya Janata Party (BJP) (Indian People's Party Lal Krishna Advani) has been seeking to moderate, the image at least, of right-wing Hindu extremism which has been the party's main campaign platform.

The government coalition has been at loggerheads, largely due to left-wing factions; this has threatened the authority of the prime minister. There have been no shortages of corruption scandals, either. In October 2005 Indian foreign minister Natwar Singh was accused of receiving bribes from the Saddam Hussein regime. He is one of the most high profile individuals to be implicated in the scandal.

In December 2005 11 members of parliament were dismissed after video evidence of their corruption was released. The disgraced MPs are from both the Congress and the BJP as well as local parties and had received cash payments in return for asking questions in parliament.

Tsunami

On 26 December 2004 an earthquake in the Indian ocean caused a huge *tsunami* (tidal wave), which swept across Southeast Asia for seven hours. The death toll was estimated at over 12,500, with 6,000 people dying in Tamil Nadu state alone, and 647,600 people displaced. The global response was an outpouring of donations, pledges of aid and support – but also criticisms of the lack of any kind of early warning system. However Prime Minister Singh told the international donor community that India would not need any financial assistance and could pay fully for reconstruction itself. India rushed to Sri Lanka's assistance, in a turnaround indicative of a new globalised modern world. India, for so long seen as the subject of international aid packages, had now turned donor. India is pouring US$28 million into its own national *tsunami* early warning system rather than collaborating on regional-wide technology.

One of the biggest concerns in India was the loss of so many women and children: they accounted for 75 per cent of the dead, making a replenishing of the population somewhat difficult. The government announced support for women wishing to reverse sterilisation operations.

Eventually, the Indian government did allow some foreign assistance, in the shape of Unicef, which officials said they regarded as a 'stakeholder' rather than a charity.

Outlook

To attract FDI, the government will have to work on improving the country's crumbling transport infrastructure and low levels of human development – problems that threaten to put the country at a competitive disadvantage to China. Such public investment could also help lift the heavy industry and agriculture sectors, which form the bulk of formal employment. Apart from short-lived spurts of growth, these sectors have lagged behind the high-value and capital intensive services and hi-tech sectors. Restrictions on business and reams of red tape are also problems that need government attention.

Overall, the Indian economy is set to perform well, on the back of a general upward trend in the business cycle. The services sector has become the largest sector of the economy, in terms of its share of GDP. As services are more economically stable than the industrial and agricultural sectors, annual GDP growth is likely to remain stable at around 7 per cent and India will continue to be one of the world's fastest growing economies.

Risk assessment

Economic	Good
Political	Good
Regional Stability	Good
Stock Market	Good

COUNTRY PROFILE

Historical profile

1200 The start of five-and-a-half centuries of Muslim rule over the region, beginning with the Sultanate era.
1757 The region gradually came under the influence of British rule after the battle of Plassey.
1858 India came under the direct rule of the British crown after a failed mutiny.
1885 The Indian National Congress was founded by Indian nationalists.
1920s Nationalist leader, Mohandas Karamachand Gandhi, launched a campaign of civil disobedience against British rule.
1942 Congress launched its 'Quit India' campaign.
1947 The Union of India was granted independence by Britain. Hundreds of thousands died during communal violence following independence. Jawaharlal Nehru of the Congress became India's first prime minister. The Hindu ruler of Muslim-majority Jammu and Kashmir joined secular India rather than Islamic Pakistan when the subcontinent was partitioned at the end of British rule. India and Pakistan went to war in Kashmir. A peace agreement was signed.
1948 Gandhi was assassinated by a Hindu fundamentalist.
1950 India became a republic. It remained a member of the Commonwealth. The constitution of India was adopted. France transferred sovereignty of Chandernagore to India.
1954 France ceded its four remaining Indian settlements (Pondicherry, Yanam, Mahe and Karaikal).
1961 Indian forces overran the Portuguese territories of Goa, Daman and Diu and they were annexed by India.
1962 India lost a border war with China.
1964 Nehru died and was succeeded by Lal Bahadur Shastri.
1965 India and Pakistan fought a second war over Kashmir.

1966 Shastri died and Nehru's daughter, Indira Gandhi, became prime minister.
1971 India-Pakistan war over East Pakistan (later Bangladesh). A Treaty of Friendship was signed with the Soviet Union.
1972 The Simla peace agreement set a new Line of Control (LoC) in Kashmir, separating India- and Pakistan-controlled areas.
1974 India exploded its first nuclear device in underground tests.
1975 Indira Gandhi was found guilty of instigating electoral malpractice and was barred from office.
1977 Congress lost elections for the first time.
1980 Indira Gandhi was reinstated as prime minister heading a Congress splinter group, Congress (Indira). There followed years of widespread political and religious disturbances in several states.
1984 Indira Gandhi was assassinated by her Sikh bodyguard after troops stormed the Golden Temple, the Sikhs' most holy shrine, to arrest Sikh separatists. Her son, Rajiv Gandhi, was sworn in as prime minister. Widespread violence continued.
1987 India deployed peace-keeping troops in Sri Lanka.
1989 After an election in which over 100 people died, VP Singh was sworn in as prime minister. His government was the first minority government in Indian history.
1990 The Indian army opened fire in Srinagar during a protest against a crackdown on separatism, killing 38 and giving impetus to rebel campaigns. Singh resigned in November. Chandra Shekhar was sworn in as prime minister. Indian troops withdrew from Sri Lanka. Muslim separatists, trained and armed by Pakistan, began a campaign of violence in Kashmir.
1991 Shekhar resigned, and the reformist government of PV Narashima Rao came to power. Rajiv Gandhi, the former prime minister, was assassinated by Sri Lankan Tamil separatists while electioneering.
1996 Following the general elections, the post-independence Nehru/Gandhi dynasty came to an end with the defeat of Congress. The largest single party in parliament became the Hindu fundamentalist Bharatiya Janata Party (BJP) (Indian Nationalist Party), which attempted and failed to form a government, after which the United Front (UF), a 13-party coalition, succeeded.
1997 Kocheril Raman Narayanan became India's tenth president, after five years as vice president. He was the first Dalit (untouchable) to become president. The UF government was toppled after Congress withdrew its support in the lower house.
1998 A coalition government led by the BJP was formed and Atal Behari Vajpayee was appointed prime minister. India and Pakistan each conducted underground nuclear tests, leading to widespread international condemnation and US sanctions.
1999 Prime Minister Vajpayee made a historic bus ride to Pakistan for a peace summit with Prime Minister Nawaz Sharif. Vajpayee lost a confidence vote, but was reaffirmed, following general elections. Pakistan and India fought a brief war in Kargil in Indian-controlled Kashmir.
2000 India celebrated the birth of its one billionth citizen. New states – Chattisgarh (part of Madhya Pradesh), Uttaranchal (in the north) and Jharkand (part of the eastern state of Bihar) – were created.
2001 The US lifted sanctions on Pakistan and India as a reward for supporting its attacks on Afghanistan. There was an unsuccessful terrorist attack on India's parliament, which India blamed on Pakistan and imposed sanctions.
2002 Rebels thought to be from Pakistan attacked an Indian army camp in Kashmir, killing more than 30 people. India threatened retaliation and moved troops to the border. The tension eased when India lifted its five-month ban on direct flights to Pakistan and ordered its naval battleships back to port. A P J Abdul Kalam was sworn in as president.
2003 India and China reached a *de facto* agreement over the status of Tibet and Sikkim in a cross-border trade agreement. The Indian and Pakistani armies began a cease-fire across the LoC dividing the disputed state of Kashmir and the Himalayan glacier of Siachen.
2004 Prime Minister Vajpayee visited Pakistan in January on his first visit since 1999, for a meeting with President Musharraf. In their first talks with the Indian government, Kashmiri separatist leaders agreed on 22 January that all violence in the Himalayan region should stop. The Indian National Congress (Congress) won the April/May parliamentary elections. On 22 May, Manmohan Singh was named as prime minister. On 26 December, an earthquake off the island of Sumatra caused a *tsunami* that devastated coastal areas in the region. The final toll for India was estimated to be 12,407 dead or missing, 647,599 displaced.
2005 The first bus-link for 57 years between divided Kashmir began on 8 April. In May, in the first tour of India in six years, the Pakistani touring cricket team was victorious; diplomatic relations were boosted by the tour. India, along with Bangladesh, Bhutan, Maldives, Nepal, Pakistan and Sri Lanka, signed the South Asia Free Trade Agreement (SAFTA), to come into effect on 1 January 2006. In December, former prime minister Vajpayee (BJP) announced his interntion to stand down from active politics at the next general election. L K Advani resigned as president of the opposition BJP on 31 December; he was replaced by Rajnath Singh.
2006 The third bus link between India and Pakistan was launched in January – the service (Lahore-Amritsar) is the first direct link across divided Punjab since partition in 1947. 'Bus diplomacy' is proving popular and successful and will include a rail link between Rajastan state and Sindh province when it is relaunched in February; it was last run in 1965.

Political structure
Constitution
The Constitution of India was inaugurated on 26 January 1950. The Preamble declares that the people of India solemnly resolve to constitute a 'sovereign socialist secular democratic republic' and to secure to all its citizens, justice, liberty, equality and fraternity. India has 28 self-governing states and seven union territories with a federal form of government. Any citizen aged 18 years and over is eligible to vote. India is the world's largest democracy.

Form of state
Secular, democratic republic

The executive
Executive power lies with the prime minister, who is appointed by the president, who has a largely ceremonial role and serves a five-year term. The prime minister nominates a 20-member Council of Ministers (cabinet).

National legislature
Parliament consists of two houses, the 545-member Lok Sabha (House of the People) (lower house), and the 245-member Rajya Sabha (Council of States) (upper house).
Members of the Lok Sabha are directly elected for a maximum five-year term by universal adult suffrage, except for two who are nominated by the president. Members of the Rajya Sabha are elected by the state assemblies for six years (one-third being replaced every two years), except for 12 who are nominated by the president.
The legislative field is divided between the Union (central government) and the states. The Union possesses exclusive powers to make laws with respect to matters grouped under 97 headings in the constitution, including foreign affairs, defence, citizenship and trade with other countries. The Union territories are administered by the federal government based in New Delhi. Major legislation requires passage through both houses of parliament.

Each state has its own governor and elected state assembly, with a chief minister and council of ministers. Policy in areas such as agriculture, education and law and order are determined at the state level.

Legal system
The legal system is based on English common law. There is limited judicial review of legislative acts.

The judiciary is independent and known for delivering verdicts which may not necessarily please the government in power. The Chief Justice presides over the Supreme Court, which is the highest court in the land. Each state has its own high court.

Last elections
20 April/10 May 2004 (parliamentary); 18 July 2002 (presidential).

Results: Parliamentary: the INC (Congress), led by Sonia Gandhi, won 145 seats out of 542 (26.8 per cent of the vote), its allies 74 (8.3 per cent); the BJP 138 (22.6 per cent), its allies 47 (12.5 per cent); the Communist Party of India (Marxist) 43 (5.5 per cent), the Samajwadi Party 36 (4.3 per cent), the Bahujan Samaj Party 19 (5.3 per cent) and the Communist Party of India 10 (1.4 per cent).

Presidential: A P J Abdul Kalam received 89.6 per cent of the 4,896 votes cast by members of the national and state parliaments.

Next elections
2009 (parliamentary)

Political parties
Ruling party
Coalition government led by the Indian National Congress (Congress) (elected Apr/May 2004)

Main opposition party
Bharatiya Janata Party (BJP) (Indian Nationalist Party)

Population
1.09 billion (2004)

Ethnic make-up
Indo-Aryan (72 per cent), Dravidian (25 per cent), Mongoloid and others (3 per cent).

Religions
Hindu (84 per cent), Muslim (13 per cent), Christian, Sikh, Buddhist, Jain.

Education
A Constitutional Amendment act passed in 2001 made education for all children aged six to 14 a fundamental right. The government earmarked 8 per cent of GNP for education, of which at least 50 per cent would be allocated to primary education. The government is also aiming for universal elementary education by 2010. Accordingly, the department of elementary education and literacy was allocated Rs4,900 crore (US$1,067 million) for 2002/03.

Primary education up to the age of 14 is compulsory in most states and lasts for eight years. Lower primary education between aged six and 11 is free in all states, but upper primary education from 11 to 14 years is free in only 12 states.

Secondary and higher education spending is forecast at Rs49.5 billion (US$1 billion) in 2003/04, of which, Rs17.7 billion (US$388 million) is allocated to higher education spending.

Gender differences, ethnic minorities, caste discrimination and regional disparities have contributed largely to wide inequalities in the development of basic education between Indian states. Independent surveys at the grassroots level show that despite the rhetoric of policy makers, expenditure in the education sector has been falling and typically 6,600,000 working children are still denied the right to primary education. Micro-level strategies for basic education in rural areas are developed through concerted co-operation between local communities, NGOs, government, and international donors.

Literacy rate: 58.8 per cent total, 47.3 per cent females, adult rates in 2002 (World Bank).

Compulsory years: Six to 14. Compulsory education is enforced in eight States/Union Territories (UT) when it covers entirely primary schooling; in four States/UT compulsory education is only enforced between ages six to 11; while in March 2003, the ministry of education confirmed that as many as 20 States/UT had not introduced any measure of compulsion.

Enrolment rate: 92 per cent gross primary enrolment; 58 per cent for upper primary enrolment.

Pupils per teacher: 62 in primary schools.

Health
The size and complexity of the Indian population renders universal healthcare difficult to achieve. Health expenditure in 2003/04 was forecast at Rs25 billion (US$549 million), of which, Rs8.39 billion (US$184 million) was to be spent on public health. The breakdown includes Rs49.5 billion (US$1 billion) on family welfare, which includes Rs4.48 billion (US$98 million) on reproductive and child health programmes.

With 70 per cent of the world's registered leprosy patients living in India in 2002, the government embarked on a Leprosy control programme with support from the World Bank. The 2003/04 budget allocated Rs750 million (US$16.4 million) to the programme.

Polio, which is endemic in some states, has been targetted for eradication. For the five months to May 2004 only eight cases were recorded – the lowest number ever – as against 225 in 2003. In May 2004 a programme of vaccination for about 120 million children was under way, ahead of the summer season which brings most infections, and is directed at the large state of Uttar Pradesh and other isolated hot spots. World health agencies hope that if polio can be eradicated from India it will help break a critical link in the global transmission chain.

In September 2004 a new drug treatment, the first in 40-years, for Tuberculosis, which kills one million suferers in India and 10 million worldwide, was announced. The medication was develop, and will be manufactured, in India as part of its positioning as a major location of cost-effective, bio-medical research.

HIV/Aids
The World Bank warned India that without greater measures to prevent the spread of HIV through the use of condoms, infections rates and subsequent deaths from Aids could surpass all other pathogens. Indian authorities say infection rates are falling, though critics claim that the factors that lead to high rates in sub-Saharan Africa are all present in India: large pools of migrant labour, large numbers of prostitutes and stigma about sex and the Aids disease. Condom use has levelled out at 50 per cent and without an increased use new infections could grow by 3 million before 2013. Nationwide policies to tackle the disease are not apparent, with each state tackling the threat locally and some seemingly unable to change old habits. The 2003/04 budget allocated Rs2 billion (US$43 million) to the National Aids Control Organisation (Naco), which was launched in 1999.

In April 2005 the head of the UN backed Global Fund to Fight Aids, Tuberculosis and Malaria, Richard Feacham, said official Indian statistics on the disease were wrong. Stating that Indian had more infections than registered, due to underreporting and that India's infection rates had surpassed that of South Africa. He rejected India's estimate of 5.1 million HIV sufferers, saying that the etimate was a 'conservative figure based on limited data', and he did not believe that India had adequate surveillance measures. The Global Fund has contributed US$265 million for Aids control (2004–09). The government increased the Naco spending to US$95.8 million, however it is estimated that per capita spending on Aids control in India is only US0.29, half the rate spent in Thailand.

While India's infection rate is only 1 per cent, in some of its most populous states the infection rates are up to 20 per cent. The UK endorsed the Naco assertion that more foreign aid would be spent on HIV/Aids sufferers. Of the £123 million (US$219), donated by the UK to fight the disease, £95 million (US$169 million) still remains to be spent by March 2007.

HIV prevalence: 0.9 per cent aged 15–49 in 2003 (World Bank)

Life expectancy: 63.4 years (World Bank)

Fertility rate/Maternal mortality rate: 2.9 births per woman (2003); maternal mortality 410 per 100,000 live births (World Bank).

Birth rate/Death rate: 9 deaths to 27 births per 1,000 head of population.

Infant mortality rate: 63.0 per 1,000 live births; 45 per cent of children aged under five are malnourished (World Bank).

Welfare

The between 60–115 million children toiling as bonded workers in India. Most are agricultural labourers while others work in factories or as domestics. The majority of these children are *Dalit* caste (the untouchables) and may be bound to their employer for years to pay back loans incurred by their parents. While these children are working they do not attend school which perpetuates their deprivation in later life.

The are estimates of between 60–115 million children toiling as bonded workers in India. Most are agricultural labourers while others work in factories or as domestics. The majority of these children are *Dalit* caste (the untouchables) and may be bound to their employer for years to pay back loans incurred by their parents. While these children are working they do not attend school, which perpetuates their deprivation in later life.

Homeless children, widows, the elderly, and the disabled (who often occupy the strata of the most destitute people in India) do not have any explicit protection in the constitution, and consequently not enough demand for any government - (whether local, state or national) to extend care to them. The National Nutrition Mission, distributes food grains at subsidised prices to poor families.

World Bank estimates that India has 40 per cent of the World's poor. The government estimates that 85 per cent of the population is in need of some form of welfare support; 25 per cent of the population belongs to either scheduled castes (SC) or scheduled tribes (ST) and these people have been ascribed special welfare measures. The National SC and ST Finance and Development Corporation provides funds for developing entrepreneurial and other skills.

The central government's expenditure on social services accounts for 1.66 per cent of GDP. India's population suffers periodic problems of floods, droughts and other natural disasters.

Pensions

The 2003/04 budget planned a massive overhaul of the pension system. From 1 January 2004, new employees in the public and private sector stopped paying into state pensions and were made to pay into privately managed funds.

The public sector finance organisation, Life Insurance Corporation of India (LIC), also ran a new pension scheme, the The state-subsidised scheme will be available to workers above the age of 55, guaranteeing an annual return of 9 per cent and a maximum pension of Rs2,000 (US$43) per month.

An assurance scheme called *Janaraksha* has been designed by the LIC to provide life insurance for farmers and workers with irregular incomes.

Main cities

New Delhi (capital, estimated population 10.4 million in 2004); Mumbai, capital of Maharashtra state (12.6 million) (name changed from Bombay in November 1995); Kolkata, capital West Bengal state (4.9 million) (name changed from Calcutta August 1999); Bangalore (name changing to Bengaluru 1 Nov 2006), Karnataka state (4.6 million); Chennai, capital of Tamil Nadu state (4.5 million) (name changed from Madras in November 1995); Ahmadabad, Gujarat state (3.7 million); Hyderabad, capital of Andhra Pradesh state (3.7 million); Kanpur, Uttar Pradesh state (2.7 million); Pune, Maharashtra state (2.7 million), Sûrat (2.6 million), Jaipur (2.5 million), Lakhnau (2.3 million), Nâgpur (2.2 million).

Languages spoken

Hindi is spoken by almost a third of the population. English is widely spoken and is often the main language of business, with over 350 million Indians using it as the *lingua franca*. Most central government documents are in both Hindi and English. Government policy is to encourage wider use of Hindi.

There are 15 local official languages in the various states, of which the most widely spoken are Punjabi, Telugu, Bengali, Marathi, Tamil, Urdu and Gujarati. There are 1,652 languages spoken throughout the country.

Official language/s

Hindi and English; 15 other languages are recognised for official use in regional areas.

Media

Except during the emergency imposed from 1975 to 1977, the print media in India has had considerable freedom. Television and radio are both state-run, although output on the cable network is operated privately. In 2002, *Tehelka.com*, an on-line investigative publication which revealed top-level corruption, closed down after advertisers and editorial staff were subjected to months of intimidation by the authorities. It plans to relaunch in 2004 as a subscription service.

Press

India has four national news agencies, all independent of the government: in English, the Press Trust of India and United News of India, in Hindi and other Indian languages, Samachar Bharati and Hindustan Samachar.

Dailies: There are a large number of daily regional newspapers, publishing in either English or in Indian languages. The main national English language daily newspapers are *The Hindu* (www.hinduonline.com), *Hindustan Times* (www.hindustantimes.com), *Asian Age*, *India Daily*, *Indian Express*, *Telegraph* and *Times of India*.

Weeklies: There are no major national weeklies, but a huge number are published at local level.

Business: The main daily financial newspapers published in English are the *Economic Times* (New Delhi, Mumbai and Kolkata editions), *Financial Express* (Delhi, Chennai and Mumbai), *Hindu Business Line* and *Business Standard* (Kolkata). Among business publications, the internet edition of *The Economic Times* (www.economictimes.com) provides comprehensive coverage of corporate, economy, stock markets, and politics. It also provides features, news and analysis, weekly magazines comprising of Investors guide, corporate Dossier & Brand Equity.

Periodicals: Business periodicals include *Capital* (Kolkata), *Commerce*, *Business India*, *Business World* and *Update* (Mumbai). There are numerous trade publications covering most industries including plastics, engineering, the motor trade, paints, chemicals and textiles. *Industrial Economist* (www.indeconomist.com) covers south India's economic and corporate scene. *Tribune India* provides news on Indian and world politics, sports, entertainment, art and culture, business and stock market.

Broadcasting

Radio: In mid-1999, the government began offering FM licences around the country to the private sector, although they are not allowed to provide current affairs or news programmes.

Television: An estimated 51.8 per cent of the country's area and 73.7 per cent of the population are covered by the television network. There are 50 television stations in India.

India has 22 million cable television households. It is expected that this will provide a big potential market for Internet usage when technology to use the cable infrastructure to connect to the Internet becomes widely available.

Advertising

Advertising is available on commercial radio and television, in the press, in cinemas and outdoors subject to certain restrictions.

Economy

India's huge population and size are both a strength and a weakness. There is great potential for increased productivity in almost all sectors, but the physical infrastructure is poor and illiteracy is widespread. With the population projected to reach 1.8 billion by 2050, economic growth needs to remain strong in order for GDP per capita to increase beyond its 2004 level of around US$608 per annum. Radical changes to the agricultural sector are needed to sustain growth as farming remains almost completely reliant on good monsoon rains. Modernisation of this sector would improve living conditions in the agriculture-based states and reduce income inequalities.

The founders of modern India believed that a dynamic public sector was the engine for industrialising an essentially agricultural economy. Massive investment was poured into basic industries like steel, while strict licensing and controls on imports and foreign exchange were imposed as the tools of a centrally planned economy.

Since the mid-1990s, India has moved some way towards greater flexibilty, including a degree of foreign ownership in some sectors and privatisation of industrial enterprises. Foreign direct investment has been encouraged, but attracts only around US$5 billion a year. The economy has averaged 6.8 per cent growth since 1994. Growth has exceeded seven per cent since 2003 and reached eight per cent in 2005. Tourism and financial services, together with strong manufacturing activity, have contributed to the improving results, but the government recognises that to reach ten per cent growth, agriculture and infrastructure would have to be improved.

The services sector is responsible for over half of GDP, with agriculture accounting for a declining share and industry's contribution remaining static at around 27 per cent.

External trade

Rules governing trade are slowly being rationalised and simplified. Rules restrict the import of most consumer goods without a special licence; these include electronic goods, telecommunication equipment (except cellphone handsets), watches, fabrics and alcoholic beverages.

Imports

Main imports include crude oil, machinery, gems, fertiliser and chemicals,
Main sources: US (7.0 per cent total, 2004), Belgium (6.1 per cent), China (5.9 per cent), Singapore (4.8 per cent), Australia (4.6 per cent), UK (4.6 per cent), Germany (4.5 per cent)

Exports

Principal exports include textile goods, gems and jewellery, engineering goods, chemicals and leather manufactures.
Main destinations: US (18.4 per cent total, 2004), China (7.8 per cent), UAE (6.7 per cent), UK (4.8 per cent), Hong Kong (4.3 per cent), Germany (4.0 per cent)

Agriculture

Farming

Agriculture accounts for around 21 per cent of GDP. Main crops are wheat, rice, pulses, tea, sugar cane, cotton, jute, coffee, oilseeds, tobacco, rubber and potatoes. The southern state of Kerala accounts for 93 per cent of the natural rubber production. Dairy farming has made India self-sufficient in milk powder and butter (*ghee*).

Domestic demand and consumption patterns within the country have shifted from cereals to non-cereals including oilseeds, pulses, fruits, vegetables and dairy products. This shift calls for diversification of agricultural production and rural development to sustain future growth. While emphasis on minimum price support for rice and wheat has been beneficial, crop diversification and removal of restrictions on stock limits allowing greater flexibility in marketing are some of the key issues requiring more attention.

Of the 181 million hectares (ha) of agricultural land available, 162 million ha is arable and 11 million ha is permanent pasture. Land legislation has ensured that agriculture remains a fragmented sector, with the typical holding about one hectare. The land ceiling does not extend to farmland used for the cultivation of plantation crops, such as tea, coffee and rubber. Other problems for the sector include a lack of technological modernisation and infrastructural bottlenecks related to irrigation and rural electrification.

Use of improved seed varieties, irrigation and fertilisers has made India self-sufficient in most grains. Land for extending cultivation is limited, but there is scope for productivity improvements in other crops. The sector is dependent on annual monsoon levels and if rains are poor during the July sowing season production can suffer.

Crop production ('000) in 2004 included: 233,360 tonnes (t) cereals in total, 72,060t wheat, 129,000t rice, 244,800t sugar cane, 5,500t soya beans, 6,800t rapeseed, 1,370t barley, 14,000t maize, 9,400t millet, 7,530t sorghum, 6,700t cassava, 25,000t potatoes, 900t sweet potatoes, 9,021t oilcrops, 9,000t seed cotton, 9,500t coconuts, 10,800t mangoes, 7,600t tomatoes, 14,500t pulses, 4,750,000t citrus fruit, 1,200t grapes, 275t green coffee, 851t tea, 1,053t various spices, 762 natural rubber, 51,000t pepper spice, 5,100t fibre crops, 3,000t cotton lint, 1,900t jute, 598t tobacco, 16,820t bananas, 47,031t fruit in total, 80,529t vegetables in total. Livestock production included: 6,032t meat in total, 1,483t beef, 1,483t buffalo, 497t pig meat, 239t lamb, 475t lamb and goat meat, 1,715t poultry, 1,890t eggs, 92,000t milk, 52,000t honey, 77,000t silk cocoons, 56t sheepskins, 408t cattle hides.

Fishing

India's share in the world seafood market largely depends on its shrimp exports. The crustacea catch is typically around 600,000 tonnes, and the fish catch is typically around six million tonnes, the export value of which is approximately US$65 million and US$80 million respectively. The government has given increased attention to the development of other fishery resources including squid, cuttlefish and fin fish. Export of frozen items has enabled India to penetrate into markets of Western Europe, North America and South-east Asia.

About a third of exports comprise low-value fin fish varieties and another third are frozen shrimp. Japan remains the largest importer of Indian sea food, although the emergence of the South-east Asian market due to import liberalisation has boosted the industry. The US is also a major buyer of frozen seafood, accounting for around 15 per cent of the value of marine products exported.

The sector is likely to witness steady growth as the organised corporate sector has become increasingly involved in the preservation, processing and export of coastal fish. The introduction of several resource specific vessels will enlarge the scope of marine fish landings.

Forestry

India has vast and diverse forest resources, comprising around 22 per cent of the total land area and ranging from tropical moist and dry deciduous types to evergreen, alpine, thorn and mangrove forests. Forest cover is estimated at 64 million hectares (ha). India has more than 12 million ha of forest plantations, used mainly for fuel consumption. There are about 80 national parks and around 450 wildlife sanctuaries.

Wood is an important source of fuel: India is the world's largest consumer of fuelwood. India has a very low level of industrial wood consumption in per capita terms. The forestry industry consists of small production units with low operating efficiency. There is an acute shortage of raw material, particularly for the manufacture of pulp and paper.

Total imports of forest products in 2004 amounted to US$1.17 billion, while exports amounted to US$91.9 million.

Industry and manufacturing

Industry contributed 27 per cent to GDP in 2004. Heavy industry has traditionally been dominated by large state-controlled enterprises. With the steady removal of protection by the state since the early 1990s, these lost some ground to smaller enterprises. Main heavy industries include steel, chemicals, cement and heavy engineering. Further developments in petrochemicals and fertilisers are expected. Textiles account for 35 per cent of India's export earnings.

Small companies are moving into high-technology products including computers, as well as traditional light engineering and textiles. Import controls have been relaxed on raw materials and services necessary for increased export trade. The entire system of industrial licensing has been revised to promote freer competition and many companies are now turning to private capital markets for expansion funding.

Tourism

Tourism is the third-largest foreign exchange earner and is growing at more than 6 per cent per year. The sector accounted for 4.9 per cent of GDP in 2004. About six per cent of the workforce is employed in the sector.

There were 3.91 million arrivals in 2005, an increase of 13.2 per cent on 2004, despite the impact of the December 2004 *tsunami* on the region.

Mining

India is well-endowed with mineral resources, mainly iron ore, manganese, uranium, good-quality bauxite (an estimated 2.65 billion tonnes of reserves, the world's fourth largest) and chromite, but they are not fully exploited. Other minerals present include lead, zinc, tin, silver, mercury and cobalt.

Most of India's raw materials are for domestic consumption. The only exports of any significance are iron ore, mica and manganese ore. India's major markets for iron ore are Japan, South Korea and China. India's reserves of copper, zinc and lead are of relatively low quality.

Hydrocarbons

India had 5.4 billion barrels of oil reserves in 2005 and produced 837,000 barrels per day (bpd). Most of the oil reserves are located in the Mumbai High, Upper Assam, Cambay, Krisha-Godavari and Cauvery basins. Oil consumption, which averaged around 2.5 million bpd in 2005, is expected to grow to 3.9 million bpd by 2010, requiring net imports of at least 3 million bpd. Oil accounts for around a third of total energy consumption. In an effort to reduce dependence on imports, India is encouraging further exploration and production. India has a refinery capacity of 2.3 million bpd.

India had natural gas reserves of 920 billion cubic metres in 2004 and produced 29.1 billion cubic metres. Over two-thirds of India's gas reserves are located in the Mumbai High basin and Gujarat. Total gas consumption was 32.1 billion cubic metres and is projected to rise by around five per cent a year. Much of this increase is attributed to increased use of gas in electricity power generation. Consumption could be higher, but problems in financing liquefied natural gas (LNG) import projects have led to downward revisions of forecasts. The government is improving and expanding the infrastructure to meet the growing demand for natural gas.

India had total coal reserves of 92.4 billion tonnes in 2004 and produced 189 million tonnes oil equivalent (mtoe). India is the world's third-largest coal producer after China and the US. The main coal fields are in Bihar, West Bengal and Madhya Pradesh. Around 90 per cent of coal is produced by Coal India Ltd (CIL). Consumption was around 205 mtoe in 2004. Power generation accounts for around 70 per cent of coal consumption; the second-largest consumer is heavy industry. Consumption is forecast to rise to around 387 million tonnes by 2010.

Energy

India has installed electricity generating capacity of 126GW (78GW thermal, 26GW hydroelectric and 2.5GW nuclear). 80 per cent of the population has access to electricity, but supplies are unreliable and interruptions are frequent. Government policy is to increase capacity by 100GW by 2012 to keep pace with rapid industrialisation and bring electricity to the whole country.

More efficient stoves, solar cookers and biogas plants are being developed to address the problem of energy shortages. Other renewable sources are being explored, including wind and solar generators.

Financial markets
Stock exchange

India has 24 stock exchanges. The main ones are The Stock Exchange, Mumbai and the National Stock Exchange, both of which are fully automated.

Banking and insurance

Indian banking has traditionally been strongly directed from the centre; even private sector banks (excluding foreign banks) are required to lend to national priority projects. In February 2005 the remaining 27 banks in government hands were given freedom to manage themselves, including the ability to acquire foreign assets and close down unprofitable accounts. The government had nationalised the country's 14 major domestic banks in 1969. Since the mid-1980s there has been a relaxation and improved profitability due to the deregulation of interest rates and the removal of credit allocation obligation, except for quotas for priority sectors. Reforms made since the mid-1990s have led to a growth in private sector banking activity.

Financial reforms implemented in 2001 focussed on tightening regulations on capital adequacy, income recognition, non-performing assets (NPAs), disclosure and transparency in accounting and risk management. The 2002 budget allowed foreign banks to establish subsidiaries in India for the first time, and sector caps on portfolio investments made by foreign institutional investors were eased.

Central bank

The Reserve Bank of India (RBI) controls India's financial system on a day-to-day basis.

Main financial centre

Mumbai is the main financial centre; New Delhi, Kolkata and Chennai are also important.

Time

GMT plus five hours 30 minutes

Geography

India has three main regions: the Himalayas to the north, which border Bhutan, Nepal and Tibet; the Indo-Gangetic Plain, a large alluvial tract, which separates the Himalayas from the south; and the Peninsular Shield in the south, where India neighbours Sri Lanka and the Maldives. India also borders Bangladesh, Myanmar, China and Pakistan.

Climate

India's winter is January–February, with hot weather increasing from March–May, south-western monsoons from June–September, and post monsoons or north-east monsoons in the southern peninsula from October–December. Temperatures vary from sub-zero in the far north during winter to constant tropical heat in southern

India

regions. Average summer temperatures on the plains are approximately 27 degrees Celsius.

Dress codes

Dress is mostly informal in India except in winter months in New Delhi, where suits and coats are more usually worn. Women are expected to dress with modesty even in very hot weather. Businessmen can expect to wear suits and ties to meetings all year as most buildings have air conditioning.

Entry requirements

Passports

Required by all.

Visa

Required by all, and must be obtained before travelling as visas cannot be issued on arrival. Foreign nationals arriving on long-term, multiple, visas are required to register with the nearest Foreigners Regional Registration Officer within 14 days of arrival. Those overstaying their visa entitlement will be fined and may be prosecuted.

For business visas a letter, issued by the local host company or organisation, giving details of itinerary, and traveller's company, a summary of purpose of trip, and the acceptance of full responsibility for any expenses incurred during the term of stay, should be submitted with the application. Business visas, valid for 10 years with multiple entries, are available to foreign businessmen who have set up or intend setting up joint ventures in India. For further details of various visas and restrictions see www.indianembassy.org or www.hcilondon.net. Nationals of Pakistan and Bangladesh are advised to seek further advice before travelling to, or via, India.

Prohibited entry

Nationals of Afghanistan if holding a passport or ticket which shows evidence of boarding in Pakistan.

Currency advice/regulations

Import of local currency is prohibited. Import of foreign currency is unlimited, although amounts over US$2,500 must be declared on arrival. Export of local currency is prohibited. Foreign currency may be exported up to the amount imported and declared. Foreign exchange receipts should be retained.

Traveller's cheques are accepted. Currency may only be exchanged at banks or authorised money changers.

Customs

Personal effects are duty-free, although high-value items may require a written undertaking to re-export them. Usual quota permitted includes 200 cigarettes and one litre of alcohol.

Health (for visitors)

Mandatory precautions

Vaccination certificates for yellow fever if travelling from an infected area.

Advisable precautions

Vaccinations for diphtheria, tuberculosis, hepatitis 'A' and 'B', Japanese B encephalitis, meningitis, tetanus, typhoid. Anti-malarial precautions should be taken. There is a risk of rabies. Polio is endemic. Locally manufactured Western proprietary medicines are easily obtainable, but visitors on regular medication should bring their own supplies.

Hotels

International-standard accommodation is widely available. Hotel bills must be paid in foreign exchange or in rupees proved to have been purchased in India with foreign exchange, which can be a lengthy procedure. Hotels in main cities are usually heavily booked, and it is advisable to book well in advance. It may be necessary to carry bedding when visiting up-country hotels and rest-houses.

Credit cards

Major credit cards are accepted by larger hotels, travel agencies and airline offices, as well as some larger stores. The Central Card is issued by the Reserve Bank of India and is widely accepted.

Public holidays

Fixed dates

1 Jan (New Year's Day, regional), 26 Jan (Republic Day), 15 Aug (Independence Day), 2 Oct (Mahatma Gandhi's Birthday), 26 Nov (Guru Nanak's Birthday), 25 Dec (Christmas Day).

The numerous public holidays observed in India tend to vary from state to state, and are usually declared at the beginning of the year in which they fall. Individual states also have their own religious festivals.

Variable dates

Good Friday, Mahavira's Birthday (Feb/Mar), Holi (Hindu, Mar), Sri Rama's Birthday (Apr), Buddha Purnima (May), Vijaya Dasami/Dussera (Sep/Oct), Diwali (Hindu, Oct/Nov), Eid al Adha, Eid al Fitr, Islamic New Year, Birth of the Prophet Mohammed.

Hindu, Muslim and Buddhist festivals are timed according to local sightings of various phases of the moon.

Working hours

Banking

Mon–Fri: 1000–1400; Sat: 1000–1200, in New Delhi, Kolkata and Chennai. Mon–Fri: 1100–1500; Sat: 1100–1300 in Mumbai.

Business

Mon–Fri: 1000–1700, in New Delhi and Chennai; 0930–1700 in Kolkata; 1000–1730 in Mumbai.

Government

Mon–Fri: 1000–1730, in New Delhi, Kolkata and Chennai; 0930–1630 in Mumbai.

Shops

Mon–Fri: 0930–1930 in New Delhi; 1000–1830 in Kolkata; 1000–1830 in Mumbai; 0900–1930 in Chennai.

Electricity supply

Usually 220V AC, 50Hz; some areas have a DC supply for domestic use. Plugs used are of the round two- and three-pin type.

Weights and measures

Metric system

Social customs/useful tips

Namaste is the usual greeting (palms together as in prayer). Visiting cards are exchanged – use the right hand when giving or receiving items. It is not customary for business associates to be entertained at home.

Business and official contacts are addressed by the last name – *Sri* (Mr), *Srimati* (Mrs or Ms).

Cows are sacred to Hindus, and many Hindus are vegetarian. Sikhs and Parsees do not smoke tobacco. Muslims do not eat pig's flesh in any form, and orthodox Muslims do not drink alcoholic beverages. Officially the government follows a strictly secular policy, with religion considered a private affair.

Hotels, which provide virtually the only bars in India, require non-resident foreigners to pay their bills in foreign currency.

Security

Generally, travel in India is quite safe, but travel to Jammu and Kashmir regions is not recommended. Mumbai is the safest city in India. Its police force is known to be the most efficient in the country. It is reasonably safe to travel by taxi until midnight anywhere in the city except slums and red-light districts.

Getting there

Air

In January 2004, the airline service between Pakistan and India was restored.

National airline: Air India.

International airport/s: There are six international airports: Babatpur (VNS), 22.5km from Varanasi; Sahar International (BOM), 36km north of Mumbai, with duty-free shop, bar, restaurant, currency exchange, post office; Netaji Subhas Chandra Bose International (CCU), 27km north-east of Kolkata, with duty-free shop, bar, restaurant, buffet, bank, hotel reservations, post office shops; Meenambakkam (MAA), 14km south-east of Chennai, with duty-free shop, restaurant, buffet, bank, hotel reservations, post office, shops; Indira Gandhi

International (DEL), 20km south of Delhi, with duty-free shop, restaurant, buffet, bank, post office; Patna (PAT), 8km from Patna. Dabolim airport has been upgraded to international standards.
Airport tax: None.
Surface
Road: Overland access is possible through Pakistan, Nepal and Bangladesh, but status and opening hours of border crossings should be checked.
Rail: Rail connections exist between India and Bangladesh, although the journey is difficult.
The train service between Pakistan and India was restored in January 2004 – one train a week between Lahore in Pakistan and Attari in India.
Main port/s: India has 12 major ports: five on the east coast, Kolkata-Haldia, Paradip, Visakhapatnam, Chennai and Tuticorin and seven on the west coast, Kandla, Mumbai, Jawaharlal Nehru, Mormugao, New Mangalore and Cochin.

Getting about
National transport
Air: The only time-efficient way to get between the large cities and even some smaller ones is by plane. The cost of air travel is reasonable and there are several domestic carriers. Airline tickets may now be bought at least one hour before flights, from the airport.
Smoking and drinking are banned on air services and it is advisable to get an executive class seat.
Bangalore, Jaipur and Varanasi airports are open to charter flights.
Road: There are two million kilometres of road, including 833,000km of surfaced roads and 35,000km of national highways connecting main cities. Chauffeur driven cars can be hired in the big cities.
Buses: A number of long-distance express bus services operate, and air conditioning is becoming increasingly available. Poor roads make travel uncomfortable.
Rail: The Indian rail network covers over 64,000km and is the main form of domestic transport. Rail connections are available between all major towns and cities, with air-conditioned coaches and sleeper accommodation available on some routes. Some train journeys take 24 hours or more.
Water: There are coastal shipping and ferry services.
City transport
Taxis: Local taxis of varying standards are usually available. In main cities, metered taxis may not always show current rates, and fares should be negotiated in advance.
Tipping is officially discouraged, but is in practice discretionary.

Other transport includes motorised trishaws.
Buses, trams & metro: The New Delhi metro network which will eventually cover 60km, is due to be completed by 2010. The first section of elevated tracks was opened in 2002 and in July 2005 another 11km stretch of underground lines, from the government areas of the capital, via the commercial area, to the old city, was opened. The next 32km section is due to open in December 2005. When completed it is expected to cut a journey across the city from one hour at rush-hour, to 15 minutes.
There are surburban metro systems in Mumbai, Kolkata and Chennai (a monorail rapid transit system).
Car hire
Self-drive hire cars are available in Mumbai and chauffeur-driven car hire is available in main cities.

BUSINESS DIRECTORY
The addresses listed below are a selection only. While World of Information makes every endeavour to check these addresses, we cannot guarantee that changes have not been made, especially to telephone numbers and area codes. We would welcome any corrections.

Telephone area codes
The international direct dialling (IDD) code for India is +91, followed by area code and subscriber's number:

Ahmedabad	79	Jammu	191
Amritsar	183	Kolkata	33
Bangalore	80	Lucknow	522
Bhopal	755	Madurai	452
Chandigarh	172	Mumbai	22
Chennai	44	Nagpur	712
Cochin	484	New Delhi	11
Goa	832	Patna	612
Hyderabad	40	Pune	212
Jaipur	141	Rajkot	281
Jallunder	181	Varanasi	542
Kanpur	512	Vishakhapatnam	891

Useful telephone numbers
Police:	100
Ambulance:	102
Fire:	101
Operator:	199
Directory enquiries:	197
International enquiries:	187
Call booking:	186

Chambers of Commerce
American Chamber of Commerce in India, Maurya Sheraton Hotel, Sardar Patel Marg, New Delhi 110021 (tel: 2302-3102; fax: 2302-3109; e-mail: usamcham@bol.net.in).

Associated Chambers of Commerce and Industry of India, 147B Gautam Nagar, Gulmohar Enclave, New Delhi 110049 (tel: 2651-2477; fax: 2651-2154; e-mail: assocham@sansad.nic.in).

Bengal National Chamber of Commerce and Industry, 23 RN Mukherjee Road, Kolkata 700001 (tel: 248-2951; fax: 248-7058; e-mail: bncci@bncci.com).

Bombay Chamber of Commerce and Industry, Mackinnon Mackenzie Building, Shoorji Vallabhdas Road, Mumbai 400001 (tel: 2261-4681; fax: 2262-1213; e-mail: bcci@bombaychamber.com).

Cochin Chamber of Commerce and Industry, Bristow Road, PO Box 503, Cochin 682003 (tel: 266-8650; fax: 266-8651; e-mail: chamber@md2.vsnl.net.in).

Federation of Indian Chambers of Commerce and Industry, Federation House, Tansen Marg, New Delhi 110001 (tel 2373-8760; fax@ 2332-0714; e-mail: ficci@ficci.com).

Goa Chamber of Commerce and Industry, Goa Chamber Building, Rua de Ormuz, Panaji-Goa 403001 (tel: 222-4223; fax: 242-9010; e-mail: gcci@sancharnet.in).

Gujarat Chamber of Commerce and Industry, Ashram Road, PO Box 4045, Ahmedabad 380009 (tel: 658-2301; fax: 658-7992; e-mail: gcci@gujaratchamber.org).

Indian Chamber of Commerce and Industry, Indian Chamber Road, Mattancherry, PO Box 236, Cochin 682002 (tel: 222-4335; fax: 222-4203; e-mail: mail@iccicochin.com).

Madras Chamber of Commerce and Industry, Karumuttu, 634 Anna Salai, Chennai 600035 (tel: 2434-9452; fax: 2434-9164; e-mail: mascham@md3.vsnl.net.in).

Mahratta Chamber of Commerce, Industries and Agriculture, 14 Tilak Road, Pune 411002 (tel: 444-0371; fax: 444-7902; e-mail: mccipune@vsnl.com).

PHD Chamber of Commerce and Industry, PHD House, opposite Asian Games Village, New Delhi 110016 (tel: 685-2416; fax: 686-3135; e-mail: phdcci@del2.vsnl.net.in).

Rajasthan Chamber of Commerce and Industry, Chamber Bhawan, MI Road, Jaipur 302003 (tel: 256-163; fax: 256-1419; e-mail: info@rajchamber.com).

Banking
Allahabad Bank, 2 Netaji Subhas Road, Kolkata 700 001 (tel: 220-0283; fax: 221-4598; email: homktg@allahabadbank.co.in).

Bank of Baroda, Suraj Plaza-1, Sayaji Ganj, Baroda 390 005 (tel: 361-852; 362-395).

Bank of India, Express Towers, Nariman Point, Mumbai 400 021(tel: 2202-3020; fax: 2202-3167; email: cmdboi@bom5.vsnl.net.in).

Canara Bank, Canara Bank Buildings, 112 Jayachamarajendra Road, PO Box 6648, Bangalore 560 002 (tel: 222-1581; fax: 222-2704; email: canbank@blr.vsnl.net.in).

Central Bank of India, Chandermukhi, Nariman Point, Mumbai 400 021 (tel: 2202-6428).

Corporation Bank, Mangalore 575 001 (tel: 426-416; fax: 441-208; email: corpho@corpbank.com).

ICIC, 163 Backbay Reclamation, Mumbai 400 020 (tel: 2202-5115; fax: 2204-6582).

Oriental Bank of Commerce, Harsha Bhawan, E-Block, Connaught Place, New Delhi 110 001 (tel: 2332-3444; fax: 2371-3244; email: obc@obcindia.com).

Punjab National Bank, 5 Sansad Marg, New Delhi 110 066 (tel: 2371-6032; fax: 2332-1305; email: pnbibd@ndf.vsnl.net.in).

State Bank of India, Madame Cama Road, PO Box 10121, Mumbai 400 021 (tel: 2202-2059; fax: 2204-0073).

Union Bank of India, Union Bank Bhavan, 239 Vidhan Bhavan Marg, Nariman Ponit, Mumbai 400 021 (tel: 2202-4647, 2202-6049; email: ibdhelpdesk@unionbankofindia.co).

Central bank
Reserve Bank of India, Central Office Building, Shahid Bhagat Singh Road, Mumbai 400 001 (tel: 286-1602; fax: 266-2105; e-mail: helpprd@rbi.org.in).

Travel information
Indian Airlines, Airlines House, 113 Gurdwara Rakabganj Road, New Delhi 110 001 (tel: 2335-7307; fax: 2371-9484).

Ministry of tourism
Department of Tourism of the Government of India, Ministry of Tourism, Transport Bhawan, 1 Parliament Street, New Delhi 110001 (tel: 371-0379; fax: 371-0518).

National tourist organisation offices
India Tourism Development Corporation Ltd, SCOPE Complex, Core VIII, 6th Floor, 7 Lodi Road, New Delhi 110003 (tel: 436-0303; fax: 436-0233).

Ministries
Ministry of Agriculture, Krishi Bhavan, Dr Rajendra Prasad Road, New Delhi 110 001 (tel: 2378-2691; fax: 2338-8006).

Ministry of Chemicals and Fertilisers, Shastri Bhavan, Dr Rajendra Prasad Road, New Delhi 110 001 (tel: 2338-6519; fax: 2338-6364).

Ministry of Civil Aviation, Rajiv Ghandi Bhavan, Safdarjung Airport Complex, New Delhi 110 003 (tel: 2463-2991; fax: 2461-0354; e-mail: secy@civilav.delhi.nic.in).

Ministry of Commerce and Industry, Udyog Bhavan, Rafi Marg, New Delhi 110 001 (tel: 2301-0261; fax: 2301-4418; e-mail: commerce@hub.nic.in).

Ministry of Communications, Dak Bhavan, Parliament Street, New Delhi 110 001 (tel: 2371-0350; fax: 2371-2333).

Ministry of Consumer Affairs, Food and Public Distribution, Krishi Bhavan, Dr Rajendra Prasad Road, New Delhi 110 001 (tel: 2338-5723; fax: 2378-2213).

Ministry of Defence, South Block, New Delhi 110 011 (tel: 2301-6220; fax: 2301-5403).

Ministry of the Environment and Forests, Paryavaran Bhavan, CGO Complex, Lodhi Road, New Delhi 110 003 (tel: 2436-1896; fax: 2436-2222; e-mail: secy@menf.delhi.nic.in).

Ministry of External Affairs, South Block, New Delhi 110 011 (tel: 2301-6660; fax: 2301-0700).

Ministry of Finance, North Block, New Delhi 110 001 (tel: 2301-2810; fax: 2301-3289; internet site: http://wwwmnic.in/finmin/).

Ministry of Health and Family Welfare, Nirman Bhavan, Maulana Azad Road, New Delhi 110 011 (tel: 2301-4751; fax: 2301-6648).

Ministry of Heavy Industries and Public Enterprises, Udyog Bhavan, Rafi Marg, New Delhi 110 001 (tel: 2301-4598; fax: 2301-3086; e-mail: nic-dpe@hub.nic.in).

Ministry of Home Affairs, North Block, New Delhi 110 001 (tel: 2301-1011; fax: 2301-5750).

Ministry of Human Resource Development, Shastri Bhavan, Dr Rajendra Prasad Road, New Delhi 110 001 (tel: 2378-2698; fax: 2338-1355; e-mail:ksm@sb.nic.in).

Ministry of Information and Broadcasting, Shastri Bhavan, Dr Rajendra Prasad Road, New Delhi 110 001 (tel: 2338-4782; fax: 2378-3513).

Ministry of Labour, Shram Shakti Bhavan, Rafi Marg, New Delhi 110 001 (tel: 2371-7515; fax: 2371-1708; e-mail: labour@lisd.delhi.nic.in).

Ministry of Law, Justice and Company Affairs, Shastri Bhavan, Dr Rajendra Prasad Road, New Delhi 110 001 (tel: 2338-7557; fax: 2338-4241; e-mail: lawmin@caselaw.delhi.nic.in).

Ministry of Mines, Shastri Bhavan, Dr Rajendra Prasad Road, New Delhi 110 001 (tel: 2338-3082; fax: 2338-6402; e-mail: dom@sb.nic.in).

Ministry of Ocean Development, Mahasagar Bhavan, CGO Complex, Lodhi Road, New Delhi 110 003 (tel: 2436-0874; fax: 2436-0779).

Ministry of Parliamentary Affairs, Parliament House, New Delhi 110 001 (tel: 2301-7798; fax: 2301-7726; e-mail: parlmin@sansad.nic.in).

Ministry of Petroleum and Natural Gas, Shastri Bhavan, Dr Rajendra Prasad Road, New Delhi 110 001 (tel: 2338-3100; fax: 2338-6550).

Ministry of Power, Shastri Bhavan, Dr Rajendra Prasad Road, New Delhi 110 001 (tel: 2371-4168; fax: 2371-7519).

Ministry of Railways, Rail Bhavan, Parliament Street, New Delhi 110 001 (tel: 2338-2323; fax: 2330-3871).

Ministry of Science and Technology, Technology Bhavan, New Mehrauli Street, New Delhi 110 016 (tel: 2301-4999; fax: 2686-3847).

Ministry of Space, Lok Nayak Bhavan, New Delhi 110 003 (tel: 2469-7130; fax: 2461-7377).

Ministry of Surface Transport, Transport Bhavan, Parliament Street, New Delhi 110 001(tel: 2371-4095; fax: 2373-1270).

Ministry of Textiles, Udyog Bhavan, Rafi Marg, New Delhi 110 001 (tel: 2301-3779; fax: 2301-3711).

Ministry of Tourism, Transport Bhawan, Parliament Street, New Delhi 110 001 (tel: 2338-4173; fax: 2338-5115).

Ministry of Urban Development and Poverty Alleviation, Nirman Bhavan, Maulana Azad Road, New Delhi 110 011 (tel: 2301-8495; fax: 2301-4459; e-mail: muae@urban.delhi.nic.in).

Ministry of Water Resources, Shram Shakti Bhawan, Rafi Marg, New Delhi 110 001 (tel: 2371-4200; fax: 2371-0253; e-mail: webmaster@mowr.delhi.nic.in).

Ministry of Youth Affairs and Sport, Shastri Bhavan, Dr Rajendra Prasad Road, New Delhi 110 001 (tel: 2338-4183; e-mail: web.yas.@sb.nic.in).

Prime Minister's Office, South block, New Delhi 110 011 (tel: 2301-2312; fax: 2301-6857).

Other useful addresses
Asian Development Bank, India Resident Mission, 37 Golf Links, New Delhi 110 003 (tel: 2469-2578; fax: 2463-6175; e-mail:adbinrm@mail.asiandevbank.org).

Nations of the World: A Political, Economic and Business Handbook

British Deputy High Commission, Maker Chambers IV, 222 Jamnalal Bajaj Road, PO Box 11714, Nariman Point, Mumbai 400021 (tel: 2283-0517, 2283-2330, 2283-3602; fax: 2202-7940).

British Deputy High Commission, 1 Ho Chi Minh Sarani, Kolkata 700016 (tel: 242-5171; fax: 242-3435).

British Deputy High Commission, 24 Anderson Road, Chennai 600006 (tel: 827-3136/7; fax: 826-9004).

British High Commission, Shanti Path, Chanakyapuri, New Delhi 110 021 (tel: 2687-2161; fax: 2687-2882).

British Trade Office, 37/7 Cunningham Road, Bangalore 560052 (tel: 2220-4844; fax: 2220-4855).

Delhi Stock Exchange Association Ltd, 3 and 4/4B Asaf Ali Rd, New Delhi 110 002 (tel: 2327-9000/1302; fax: 2332-6182).

Delhi Tourism and Transport Development Corporation Ltd, 18A DDA, SCO Complex, Defence Colony, New Delhi 24 (tel: 2461-4354; fax: 2469-7352).

Department of Atomic Energy, South Block, New Delhi 110 011 (tel: 2301-1773; fax: 2301-3843).

Department of Electronics, Electronics Niketan, 6 CGO Complex, New Delhi 110 003 (tel: 2436-3101; fax: 2436-3083).

Federation of Indian Exports Organisation (FIEO), 56 Asiad Village, New Delhi 110 016 (tel: 2649-3220).

Foreign Investment Promotion Board, Prime Minister's Office, South Block, New Delhi 110 011 (tel: 2301-7839; fax: 2301-6857).

India Investment Centre, Jeewan vihar Building, Sansad Marg, New Delhi 110 001 (tel: 2373-3673; fax: 2373-245).

Indian Airlines, Stores and Purchases Department, Safdarjung Airport, New Delhi 110 003 (tel: 2461-1293; fax: 2462-1776; e-mail: sinha.ial@gems.vsnl.net.in).

Indian Embassy (USA), 2107 Massachusetts Avenue, NW, Washington DC 20008 (tel: 202-939-7000; fax: 202-265-4351; e-mail: indembwash@indiagov.org).

Infrastructure Leasing and Financial Services, East Court, Zone VI, 4th Floor, India Habitat Centre, Lodhi Road, New Delhi 110 003 (tel: 2463-6637/41/42).

Power Grid Corporation of India Ltd, 10th Floor, Hemkunt Chambers 89, Nehru Place, New Delhi 110 019 (tel: 2622-2995, 2646-6806; fax: 2647-3332, 2642-8357).

Silk and Rayon Export Promotion Council, Resham Bhavan 78, Veer Nariman Rd, Mumbai 400020 (tel: 2294-792).

State Trading Corporation of India, Jawahar Vyapar Bhavan, Tolstoy Marg, New Delhi 110 001 (tel: 2331-3177; fax: 2332-6741).

The Stock Exchange (BSE), Phiroze Jeejeebhoy Towers, Dalal Street, Mumbai 400001 (tel: 2272-1233/4; fax: 2272-1552; e-mail: info@bseindia.com; internet site: http://www.bseindia.com).

Trade Development Authority, PO Box 767, Bank of Baroda Building, Parliament St, New Delhi 110 001 (tel: 2332-0214).

US Embassy, Shanti Path, Chanakyapuri, New Delhi 110 021(tel: 2687-6500; fax: 2687-6579, 2687-0031 (Consular Section)).

Internet sites

Explore India:
http://www.exploreindia.com

General Information:
http://www.hcidhaka.org

India Department of Commerce:
http://www.nic.in/eximpol/

India On-line:
http://indiaonline.com/index.html

Indian business:
http://www.indiamart.com/allindia/

Indian company information:
http://www.tradeaccess.com/general.htm

Indian Economy and Business links:
http://www.ib-net.com/links/economy.htm

India Opportunity:
http://www.DocuWeb.ca/India

Indian Press Information Bureau:
http://www.nic.in/India-Image/PIB/

Indonesia

Indonesia, a country of over 17,000 islands, is the world's largest Islamic democratic state with a Muslim population of 200 million. It experienced thirty years of stable, if authoritarian rule under President Suharto, lasting until 1998 when he was forced to resign in May, despite having been re-elected just three months earlier. Since then there have been four presidents. 1998 was also the year of the Asian financial collapse, which enveloped Indonesia among others.

Former army general, President Susilo Bambang Yudhoyono, won a landslide victory in October 2004. He is the first directly elected leader and his populist touch helped generate a significant level of optimism in the country. Yudhoyono promised first and foremost to tackle corruption and has made notable inroads since his accession, launching lawsuits against several high profile personalities.

Tsunami

On 26 December 2004 an earthquake off the coast of Sumatra caused a huge *tsunami* (tidal wave), which swept across South-east Asia, with Indonesia's isolated Aceh province being the worst hit region. Some parts in the north of the island of Sumatra lost nearly 70 per cent of their population. Around 167,000 people died and over half a million were displaced or are missing. The local economy took a battering: the port of Banda Aceh was almost completely destroyed, 10 per cent of fishermen were killed in the impact and nearly all boats destroyed. The global response was an outpouring of donations, pledges of aid and support – but also criticisms of the lack of any kind of early warning system. By 2006 Banda Aceh had benefited from an almost complete reconstruction but other devastated regions are likely to remain undeveloped for years to come.

In March 2005 another earthquake, 8.7 on the Richter scale, struck the region, leaving an estimated 2,000 people dead. However, showing that lessons have been learned since the fateful 26 December 2004, this time there were tidal wave warnings.

Peace

The natural disaster brought hope as well as destruction. The *tsunami* precipitated a peace agreement with Aceh rebels, who offered a ceasefire in the wake of the waves and volunteered soldiers to contribute to aid efforts. The national army was initially reluctant to stop military operations against the rebels, fuelling international concern over the excessive control they exert in Aceh. However, by the end of 2005, all 25,000 Indonesian troops had quit the province, leaving behind only local law-enforcers. The Gerakan Aceh Merdeka (GAM) (Free Aceh Movement) surrendered their arms after thirty years of violent disturbances and 15,000 fatalities. Four hundred rebels were set free from imprisonment. The Helsinki peace agreement stipulates some measure of self-determination for Aceh, without granting it independence. Ballots in the province are due to be held in 2006 and former rebels, granted amnesty in the deal, are to form a political party. A truth and reconciliation committee is to be set up.

Foreign relations

Indonesia's formerly close relations with the US had broken down in the late 1990s. By 2005 relations were definitely frosty and American relief efforts in the wake of the *tsunami* were not welcomed. Indonesia was angry with the US for waging war on Iraq, a fellow Muslim nation, but pleased when the US ended its arms ban on Indonesia in a move to strengthen a counter-terrorism partnership between the two nations. The embargo had been levied in response to Indonesian human rights atrocities in Timor Leste in 1999.

Indonesia is also hostile towards the UN, whom it blames for the relinquishing of Timor Leste in 2002. For the same reason Indonesia has had cool relations with Australia. Not only this, but Jakarta resents the bullish stance John Howard, the Australian Prime Minister, has taken towards terrorism – promoting the use of pre-emptive strikes – and towards asylum-seekers. However, Australian aid after the *tsumani* helped build bridges between the two estranged nations. The EU enjoys more trust among Indonesians – and is to monitor the Aceh peace deal with a team of 220 inspectors. This arrangement should be mutually beneficial, restoring credibility to the EU's foreign affairs reputation. Indonesians have warned however that 220 white faces might be seen to represent unwelcome Western interference.

KEY FACTS

Official name: Republik Indonesia (Republic of Indonesia)

Head of State: President Susilo Bambang Yudhoyono (sworn in 20 Oct 2004)

Head of government: President Susilo Bambang Yudhoyono

Ruling party: Coalition between the Partai Demokrasi Indonesia Perjuangan (PDI-P) (Indonesian Party of Democratic Struggle) and Partai Kebangkitan Bangsa (PKB) (National Awakening Party).

Area: 1,919,443 square km (17,508 islands)

Population: 221.78 million (2004)

Capital: Jakarta, on Java

Official language: Bahasa Indonesia

Currency: Rupiah (Rp) = 100 sen

Exchange rate: Rp10,290.00 per US$ (Oct 2005)

GDP per capita: US$1,165 (2004)

GDP real growth: 5.10% (2004); *7.0 (2005)

Labour force: 108.99 million (2004)

Unemployment: 9.20% (2004)

Inflation: 6.10% (2004)

Oil production: 1.13 million bpd (2004)

Balance of trade: US$24.79 billion (2004)

Foreign debt: US$141.50 billion (2004)

* estimated figure

Nations of the World: A Political, Economic and Business Handbook

In March 2005 Indonesia and Malaysia clashed over rights to oil near Borneo. Indonesia had contracted Unocal, an American company, to exploit the area, while Malaysia had given rights to Royal Dutch/Shell. Anti-Malaysian protests took place in Jakarta. Tensions were inflamed but officials resolved to settle the issue by negotiation. Also closer to home, in April 2005 Timor Leste and Indonesia agreed their land borders. This was an important step on the road towards reconciliation.

Terrorism

Jemaah Islamiah (JI) is the major terrorist group in Indonesia, with links to al Qaeda. Abu Bakar Bashir, spiritual leader of the JI, was jailed for 30 months, later reduced by 4 months and 15 days, in 2005 on charges related to the bombing of a nightclub on Bali in 2002. In October 2005 Bali was again the victim of a terrorist strike, which killed 20 people and was carried out by three suicide bombers. It is the latest realisation of the continued terrorist threat in the area. The news will impact heavily on the tourist industry, one of the most important sectors for the local economy. Three men were convicted of planning the attacks and sentenced to death.

In November 2005 Indonesian authorities announced the death of Azahari Bin Husin who had blown himself up moments before police storming his house could arrest him. Husin, a Malaysian citizen, studied at Reading University, England, in the 1980s. He is believed to have been a key figure in the 2002 Bali attacks, the 2003 bombing of the Marriott hotel and the 2004 targeting of the Australian embassy, both in Jakarta.

Corruption

Indonesia has a reputation for being one of the most corrupt countries in the world – it was joint 137 (out of 158) on the Transparency International corruption perception index in 2005. Corruption, and red tape, hampered relief efforts in the aftermath of the tsunami. Boxes of aid festered in Sumatra ports, not cleared by customs due to reams of red tape and misplaced documentation.

Investors have become wary of an investment climate mired in litigation, bureaucracy and delays. Where Western countries are becoming more cautious, Chinese companies, however, are stepping in to fill the gap. China has already aquired Indonesia's Repsol YPF and Devon Energy.

It was the culture of inveterate corruption and inefficny that President Yudhoyono pledged to tackle on taking office in late 2004. In January 2006 the former chief of Bank Umum Serita, David Nusa Wijaya, was arrested and accused of embezzling huge amounts of emergency funds during the 1998 Asian financial crisis. He faces eight years in jail for stealing US$14.6 billion. The capture is significant as the case of Wijaya was one of the most high-profile in the country.

In April 2005 Abdullah Puteh, once governor of Aceh, was condemned to ten years imprisonment on corruption and embezzlement charges. Bank Mandiri, one of Indonesia's largest companies, was also placed under investigation in April 2005. The company is accused of accepting bribes from big-name clients.

These arrests are significant, marking the determination of the president and sending a reassuring message to the business community.

Economy

The first half of 2005 brought GDP growth of 5.9 per cent with a projected rate of 5.9 per cent for 2006. A surge in FDI has generated both this growth in GDP as well as historic highs in the stock market. Increased FDI is a sign that investors are gaining in confidence following high-profile anti-corruption measures. Progress has been particularly good in the transport and communications sectors.

However, one threat to further economic expansion is the inflation rate of 7 per cent in 2005, a six year high. The rise is in part a response to fuel price surges. Unemployment is over 10 per cent while the rupiah is at the lowest level in four years. The decision to increase short-term interest rates was intended to stabilise the currency.

Indonesian finance officials declared their intentions in January 2005 of selling off government stakes in six banks. These sales are expected to generate US$800 million, money which is likely to be used to tackle debt amassed during the 1998 Asian financial crisis. When completed these sales will be significant in the privatisation process. The national bank, Bank Indonesia, has suggested that the 130 banks in the country be cut to 60.

Contracts and disputes

FDI is crucial to the Indonesian economy, yet in 2005 there were several long-running business disputes involving Indonesian and foreign firms. These include the Mexican cement company, Cemex, an American firm, Karaha Bodas, a Singapore supermarket, Dairy Farm, and Total, the French oil company. The president has expressed a desire to resolve these protracted squabbles as they have had an unfavourable impact on the business climate and FDI levels.

In March 2005 American cigarette manufacturers Philip Morris took over HM Sampoerna at a cost of US$5.2 billion, bringing a significant boost to the Indonesian economy. This was the biggest takeover in Indonesian history. In the same month the global oil company BP started work on a US$5 billion contract involving three gas fields in Papua. Production of liquefied natural gas, an expected 7.6 million tonnes annually, will begin in 2008.

Asia Pulp and Paper (APP) has expressed an interest in purchasing the Kiani Kertas paper mill in Borneo. The mill is likely to attract bids of around US$600 million. Also interested are JP Morgan and United Fiber Systems (UFS). The proposed project has attracted criticism for its likely destructive impact on Borneo's rainforests, with advisor Deutsche Bank considering withdrawing its involvement.

Settlement was finally reached in 2005, after four years of wrangling, between ExxonMobil and the national oil provider, Pertamina, over a contract renewal and proposed US$2 billion oil exploration project in the Cepu field, Java. Pertamina was seeking more favaourable returns in addition to a sharing of operation rights. In August the government stepped into the fray with promises to sack the head of Pertamina, who had been a stumbling block to negotiations.

Fuel prices

Fuel is a sensitive issue in Indonesia. It was riots over fuel prices which precipitated the fall of the former president, Suharto, ruler for three decades. The present president cut fuel subsidies by half and raised petrol prices by a third in March 2005 in efforts to encourage economic growth. The cost of subsidies would have reached about US$13 billion per year and finance officials pledged to pour the saved cash into welfare payments, education and infrastructure. The subsidies were tackled so as not to penalise the poor who are the primary consumers of kerosene. The decision risked the president's popularity and was a test of his political bravery. In September prices were increased again by a huge and unexpected 126 per cent in reaction to the continued rise in global oil prices. There were threats of mass disturbances, which in the event did not materialise.

Bird 'flu

Four people have died since the beginning of 2005 from the H5N1 strain of avian 'flu, although chickens had been found with the disease as early as August 2003. There was international criticism that the country did not react swiftly and decisively enough to the outbreak. Indonesian officials opted to vaccinate birds rather than slaughter them on masse, which would be an expensive, but more effective, option.

Outlook

The president has made a good impression in his first year of office. In 2006 he is expected to make further efforts to drive out corruption which in turn will help economic growth.

Indonesia became a net importer of oil in 2005. Output dwindled to below Opec quotas of 1.4 million bpd, partly due to a lack of modernisation of production facilities. This has prompted speculation that the country might quit Opec in 2006.

Risk assessment

Economic	Good
Political	Good
Regional Stability	Stable
Stock Market	Good

COUNTRY PROFILE

Historical profile
It is thought that Negroid peoples came to Irian Jaya, from East Africa around 30,000 years ago. Melanesians arrived later; the resultant population migrated throughout the islands of what is now Indonesia. Later settlers arrived from India, Burma and China. Islam spread to Indonesia as a result of the strong trading links with the Arabian Peninsula.
1511 The Portuguese arrived in Indonesia, looking for spices. The Spaniards followed, bringing Christianity to the region.
1799 The Dutch gained control of the territory through the United East India Company. They gradually extended their control throughout the entire region. The Portuguese maintained East Timor.
1924 The Partai Kommunis Indonesia (PKI) (Indonesian Communist Party) was established. It was first active among trade unionists and rural villagers. The rural areas came to be the PKI's main power base.
1942–45 The islands of the Dutch East Indies were occupied by the Japanese. After the Second World War the Dutch regained control. Nationalist leader Ahmed Sukarno returned from internal exile and organised the fight for independence from Dutch colonial rule.
1945 In a speech in July Sukarno urged the adoption of the *Panca Sila* (Five Principles) as the ideological basis of the new state. The five principles were nationalism, internationalism (or humanitarianism), democracy, social justice, and belief in God.
1949 After four years of insurgency The Netherlands recognised the independence of Indonesia. A federal constitution was introduced, giving limited self-government to the 16 constituent regions. Ahmed Sukarno as leader of the Partai Nasional

KEY INDICATORS — Indonesia

	Unit	2000	2001	2002	2003	2004
Population	m	210.49	213.86	217.72	219.75	221.78
Gross domestic product (GDP)	US$bn	153.30	145.30	184.60	208.30	*257.64
GDP per capita	US$	730	690	848	946	1,165
GDP real growth	%	4.8	3.3	3.7	3.4	5.1
Inflation	%	3.8	11.5	11.9	6.6	6.1
Unemployment	%	13.0	9.5	10.3	10.5	9.2
Oil output	'000 bpd	1,456.0	1,410.0	1,278.0	1,179.0	1,126.0
Natural gas output	bn cum	63.9	62.9	70.6	72.6	73.3
Coal output	mtoe	47.3	56.9	63.3	70.5	81.4
Exports (fob) (goods)	US$m	65,406.0	57,365.0	58,820.0	61,053.0	69,860.0
Imports (fob) (goods)	US$m	40,366.0	31,328.0	35,810.0	32,551.0	45,070.0
Balance of trade	US$m	25,040.0	23,600.0	25,400.0	28,502.0	24,790.0
Current account	US$m	7,986.0	6,900.0	7,450.0	–	7,280.0
Foreign debt	US$bn	141.8	133.1	130.0	131.0	141.5
Total reserves minus gold	US$m	27,939.0	27,246.0	30,971.0	34,962.0	34,952.0
Foreign exchange	US$m	27,736.0	27,048.0	30,754.0	34,742.0	34,724.0
Exchange rate	per US$	8,421.80	10,260.90	9,672.50	8,674.50	8,934.84

* estimated figure

Indonesia (PNI) Indonesian Nationalist Party, assumed the presidency. The Dutch retained control of West Papua; the Portuguese retained control of East Timor.

1950 The constitution was dissolved and the country adopted a unitary political structure. Sukarno was elected president.

1955 Sukarno won Indonesia's first general election. Political instability prompted Sukarno to dissolve parliament and a period of autocratic rule ensued.

1962 Dutch authority for West Papua was passed to UN administration.

1963 Authority for West Papua was transferred to Indonesia.

1964 Indonesia laid claim to areas of Borneo which had been granted to Malaysia on its independence, leading to a three-year guerrilla conflict on the Malaysian border, which severely damaged the Indonesian economy.

1965 A failed *coup d'état* by the PKI resulted in the deaths of hundreds of thousands of left-wing activists.

1967 Sukarno transferred full emergency power to General Suharto, commander of the Indonesian armed forces.

1968 General Suharto became president.

1975 Portugal granted independence to its colony of East Timor.

1976 East Timor was invaded by Indonesia and became a province. This annexation was never officially recognised by the UN.

1985 Australia recognised Indonesia's incorporation of East Timor.

1997 The South-East Asian economic crisis caused the rupiah to plummet in value.

1998 Suharto, re-elected in March, was forced to resign on 21 May after accusations of corruption and widespread public disturbances as the country's economy reached near collapse. He was succeeded by Bacharuddin Jusuf Habibie.

1999 A UN sponsored referendum on independence was supported by the population of East Timor. Anti-independence militia rampage through East Timor until UN administration is imposed and the Indonesian government agreed to grant it independence. Abdurrahman Wahid was elected president of Indonesia by the People's Consultative Assembly.

2000 Ex-president Suharto's legal trial, on corruption charges, collapsed. Ethnic, religious and separatist violence in several provinces grew.

2001 The IMF halted further loans citing the government's inability to tackle corruption. Wahid was voted out of office for his alleged involvement in two financial scandals. Vice President Megawati Sukarnoputri was sworn in as president.

2002 Indonesia, Malaysia and the Philippines signed a pact to counter terrorism. The government and separatist rebels in Aceh province signed a peace agreement giving greater autonomy and free elections to Aceh in exchange for disarmament by rebels. Constitutional changes included the posts of president and vice president to be by popular vote. A bomb planted by Islamic fundamentalists on the island of Bali, and targetted at Western tourists, killed 202 people. The International Court of Justice awarded the disputed islands of Sipadan and Ligitan to Malaysia.

2003 The Aceh peace accord failed; martial law was imposed. Three Bali bomb suspects were found guilty and sentenced to death.

2004 Susilo Bambang Yudhoyono won the presidential elections, and was sworn in on 20 October. On 26 December, an earthquake off the island of Sumatra caused a *tsunami* that devastated coastal areas in the region, particularly the peninsula of Aceh on Sumatra island. The final estimate for Indonesia was 167,000 dead or missing, 572,126 displaced.

2005 In March warships were dispatched to the Ambalat region of the Sulawesi Sea off the east coast of Borneo when Royal Dutch/Shell, under an agreement with Malaysia, started to explore for oil. Indonesia not only claims the region as its own, but had also signed a similar deal in 2004 with US Unocal Corp for hydrocarbon exploration. An agreement was signed on 8 April between the leaders of Indonesia and Timor-Leste, recognising the location of their shared land border. On 29 December, the government withdrew the last of its troops from Aceh province, thereby fulfilling the most important condition of the peace agreement signed with the separatist rebels. The withdrawal followed the disbanding of the military wing of the Gerakan Aceh Merdeka (GAM) (Free Aceh Movement) a few days earlier.

Political structure
Constitution
The system of government is based on the 1945 constitution which underlines the unity of Indonesia as a republic, supplemented by the General Elections Law of 1969.

The constitution provides for five branches of government: the president, the Dewan Perwakilan Rakyat (DPR) (House of People's Representatives), the Supreme Audit Board, the Supreme Court and the Supreme Advisory Council. Despite geographic diversity and the limited reach of the political centre, Indonesia has not implemented a federal system, an option tarnished by association with the colonial era under Dutch rule. Instead, each of the 27 provinces is headed by a governor who is responsible to the president through the minister of home affairs, and represents the central government in his province. The north Sumatran province of Aceh, the territory of Jogjakarta in central Java, and the capital, Jakarta, have a special status.

Since 1985, by law, all major organisations, including political parties, religious groups and trade unions, must include acknowledgement of *Pancasila* (the Five Principles) as their sole guiding ideology in their constitutions. It emphasises tolerance among different religious groups and a political system based on consensus.

All Indonesian citizens over the age of 17 are eligible to vote, as well as those citizens under the age of 17 who are married. To stand for election, a citizen must be at least 21 years old.

In August 2002, 14 amendments were made to the constitution, to take effect with the next elections. The revisions included the abolition of the reservation of 38 parliamentary seats for military personnel.

In July 2003, parliament passed legislation setting the parameters for the first direct presidential election.

Form of state
Democratic republic

The executive
Executive power rests with the president, who serves a five-year term. Under the constitutional amendments introduced in August 2002, the president and the vice president are to be directly elected by the people, rather than being appointed by the Majelis Permusyawaratan Rakyat (MPR) (People's Consultative Assembly). The president is also head of government and can deploy direct legislative powers. The cabinet is appointed by the president; it may be partisan or largely composed of technocrats without an independent power base.

National legislature
The MPR has 700 members, comprising 135 regional representatives, 65 representatives of professional groups and the 500 members of the DPR.

The MPR is to be restructured in 2004. Within the DPR, the 500 members are elected via proportional representation for a five-year term. The constitutional reforms agreed in 2002 will mean that after the 2004 elections, the armed forces will no longer appoint any members of parliament and all members will be directly elected.

All statutes and the state budget must be approved by the DPR, which has the right to initiate legislation. Draft legislation is submitted to the DPR by the government, and passes through four stages: an explanation of the proposed legislation, a general debate, discussions between the appropriate commission of the DPR and

Indonesia

the government, and a final debate and vote. Legislation that is approved is sent to the president for enactment. The Supreme Audit Board is responsible for auditing the state's finances and reporting the results of its investigations to the DPR.

Legal system
The judicial powers of the state are exercised by the Supreme Court.

Last elections
20 September 2004 (presidential run-off); 5 July 2004 (first round presidential); 5 Apr 2004 (parliamentary).
Results: Presidential run-off: Susilo Bambang Yudhoyono won 60.6 per cent of the vote, defeating incumbent Megawati Sukarnoputri, 39.4 per cent. Parliamentary: Partai Demokrasi Indonesia Perjuangan (PDI-P) (Indonesian Party of Democratic Struggle) won 37.4 per cent (154 seats); Partai Golongan Karya (Golkar) (Party of the Functional Groups) 20.9 per cent (120 seats).

Next elections
2009 (parliamentary and presidential)

Political parties
Ruling party
Coalition between the Partai Demokrasi Indonesia Perjuangan (PDI-P) (Indonesian Party of Democratic Struggle) and Partai Kebangkitan Bangsa (PKB) (National Awakening Party).

Main opposition party
Partai Golongan Karya (Golkar) (Party of the Functional Groups); Partai Persatuan Pembangunan (PPP) (United Development Party).

Population
221.78 million (2004)
Ethnic make-up
Although 95 per cent of the population are of Malay origin, there are some 300 minorities, including Melanesian, Proto-Austranesian, Polynesian and Micronesian; there are approximately four million ethnic Chinese. Indonesia encompasses the Islamic people of Aceh on the northern tip of Sumatra, the densely populated main island of Java, the tourist resorts of Bali, the island of Flores and the primitive tribes of Irian Jaya in the east.

Religions
Islam (87 per cent), Christianity (10 per cent), Hinduism (mainly in Bali) (2 per cent) and Buddhism (1 per cent). Indonesia has the world's largest Muslim population, although Hindu-derived and indigenous religious variations are common. Religious violence has spread in line with political uncertainty. Animist beliefs are held in remote areas.

Education
Free universal primary education has been a long-term aim of the government. Almost 100 per cent of eligible children attend such schools, compared to only 40 per cent when President Suharto came to power in 1968. The overall literacy rate has increased by 31 per cent, up from 54 per cent in 1970.

Secondary education consists of two three-year cycles; over 50 per cent of eligible students are in secondary education. Tertiary education has also expanded, with 11 per cent of eligible students in school, up from 1 per cent in the late 1960s. The vast majority of tertiary institutions are privately owned, although there is a network of state institutions around the country. The quality of these universities and colleges varies enormously and large numbers of Indonesian students go overseas for their tertiary education. Despite improvements, the Indonesian education system is not supplying enough technicians and scientists for the country's ambitious plans.

Public expenditure on education typically amounts to 1.4 per cent of annual GDP. In April 2003, the Islamic Development Bank approved a US$31 million loan to Indonesia to finance university expansion.

Literacy rate: 87.9 per cent total, 83.4 per cent female; adult rates in 2002 (World Bank).
Compulsory years: 7 to 16
Enrolment rate: 113 per cent gross primary enrolment of the relevant age group (including repeaters); 56 per cent gross secondary enrolment (World Bank).
Pupils per teacher: 22 in primary schools.

Health
Total expenditure on health is 2–4 per cent of GDP, of which 25–26 per cent is government spending.

While basic healthcare has improved immeasurably over the past 30 years, it remains an urban rather than rural phenomenon. Inadequate numbers of trained staff remain the rule. Expatriates and wealthier Indonesians usually go to Singapore or Australia for operations. State healthcare is rudimentary. According to government figures, there are about 1,350 hospitals in Indonesia with 110,200 beds. There are approximately 0.7 hospital beds per 1,000 people, which is low even by regional standards (India has 0.8 beds per 1,000). Improved water sources are available to 74 per cent of the population.

HIV prevalence: 0.1 per cent aged 15–49 in 2003 (World Bank)
Life expectancy: 66.9 years (World Bank)
Fertility rate/Maternal mortality rate: 2.4 births per woman (2003); maternal mortality 230 per 100,000 live births (World Bank).
Infant mortality rate: 31 per 1,000 live births; 27.3 per cent of children aged under five are malnourished (World Bank).

Welfare
Although poverty has been greatly reduced, the decline in living standards during the economic contraction of 1998 has yet to be reversed. The government has no plans to provide comprehensive welfare for the country's population of over 200 million. Instead, the government attempts to subsidise the cost of living of the poor through price controls, although these are being phased out in line with IMF commitments on goods such as kerosene. The state-run Workers' Accident Insurance and Provident Fund (*Jamsostek*) is the only form of social security in Indonesia. The insurance covers accident, sickness, pensions, unemployment, health and housing benefits. Outside *Jamsostek* there are other welfare programmes provided by private insurance companies, but they are not compulsory.

Main cities
Jakarta (capital, on island of Java, estimated population 9.0 million in 2004); Surabaya (3.1 million); Bandung (2.8 million); Medan (2.2 million) on Sumatra; Palembang (1.5 million) on Sumatra; Tangerang (1.3 million), Semarang on Java (1.3 million); Ujung Pandang (Makassar) on Sulawesi (Celebes) (1.3 million); Banjarmasin (568,800); Samarinda (508,900) and Pontianak (506,300) on Kalimantan (Borneo); Denpasar on Bali (502,100); Jogjakarta on Java (484,200).

Languages spoken
Bahasa Indonesia has existed as an official language for the past 70 years, and is still in the process of developing, with new words constantly being added. For simplicity's sake, the use of English words is common, particularly in the banking, insurance and technology sectors. However, the government wishes to promote Indonesian language development and reduce the use of foreign words.

English is widely spoken in government and business circles and by the younger generation. Many older Indonesians speak Dutch as a second language.

Each ethnic group has its own language. Altogether, more than 580 languages and dialects are spoken, including Javanese, Sundanese, Arabic and Chinese.

Official language/s
Bahasa Indonesia

Media
Press
Dailies: Daily newspapers are licensed by the government and restricted to 12 pages a day, with the option of 16 pages twice a week.

The government has the power to revoke licences of newspapers and magazines if they fail to report in a 'healthy, free and responsible manner'. Foreign newspapers are censored by the information ministry before they go on sale.

English-language dailies which circulate widely in West Java are *The Indonesia Times*, *Indonesia Observer* and *The Jakarta Post*. Indonesian-language dailies include *Kompas*, *Pos Kota*, *Suara Pembaruan*, *Suara Karya* and *Suara Merdeka*, *Surabaya Post*, *Pikiran Rakyat* (from Bandung and Jawa Bharat) and *Republika* (from Jakarta, Java).

Weeklies: Publications include *Tempo*, *DeTik*, *Editor* and *Fokus*.

Business: *Indonesian Commercial Newsletter* is a bi-monthly, bilingual business publication. Other publications include *Economic and Business Review Indonesia*, *Standard Trade and Industry Directory of Indonesia* and *Waspada*.

Periodicals: *Intisari* is a widely read periodical.

Broadcasting
Radio: In 2002 there were 60 radio stations in Jarkarta. The main stations are Radio Republik Indonesia, Indonesia Radio Network and Voice of Indonesia.

Television: Metro TV, a 24-hour news channel began broadcasting in November 2000. It broadcasts in Mandarin. Other stations inlude TVRI 1 and 2 (government owned) Suraya Citra Televisi Indonesia (SCTV), Rajawali Citra TV Indonesia and Televisi Pendidikan Indonesia.

Advertising
Advertising is available in newspapers, where it is limited by government regulations on size of papers. It is also available in a wide range of magazines, in cinemas and on public and private commercial radio. Outdoor advertising on bus exteriors, hoardings and bus stop shelters is popular. Advertising expenditure is equivalent to approximately 0.4 per cent of annual GDP.

Economy
Prior to 1997, the Indonesian economy had been growing at approximately 8 per cent per annum for almost three decades. This growth was powered primarily by oil and gas findings in the 1970s, leading to wider industrialisation. With the collapse of oil and gas prices in the 1980s, Indonesia engaged in a progressive liberalisation of its economy, with massive inflows of foreign investment increasingly targetted at the non-traditional export sector. This, in turn, has been driven by the need for Japanese, South Korean and Taiwanese industries to find more competitive production centres.

Since 1969 the economy has been managed through a series of five-year plans known as *Repelita*. The oil price collapse and currency realignments of the mid-1980s provoked a government drive to increase production of value-added items for export. Indonesia earns around three-quarters of its export income from non-hydrocarbon sources – a combination of manufacturing and agricultural commodities.

The level of external debt stood at US$14.51 billion in 2004. Financing this debt is a signficant financial burden for the government, hampering its economic reform plans.

Indonesia's economy is one of the least reformed in the South-east Asian region, with a high level of debt in the banking sector, an ineffective legal system and lack of clear, coherent policy. These failings have deterred foreign participation in the economy, hence the lack of expertise and professional management skills needed for Indonesia to upgrade.

Growth in the economy continues, GDP increasing by 5.1 per cent in 2004. Unemployment is a problem with around 10 per cent of the population jobless, but further economic diversification is likely to bring new jobs.

External trade
The variety of resources and a competitive industry have led to continual trade surpluses.

Imports
Main imports include machinery and equipment, chemicals, fuels and foodstuffs.

Main sources: Japan (19.3 per cent total, 2004), China (11 per cent), Singapore (9.2 per cent), Thailand (6.8 per cent), Malaysia (6.5 per cent), US (5.7 per cent), Australia (5.0 per cent), Germany (4.2 per cent)

Exports
One of the most successful export sectors has been consumer electronics and home appliances, resulting from greater investment.

Major exports include oil and gas, electrical appliances, plywood, textiles and rubber.

Main destinations: Japan (21.8 per cent total, 2004), US (13.5 per cent), China (7.5 per cent), Singapore (7.4 per cent), South Korea (5.9 per cent), Malaysia (4.9 per cent)

Agriculture
Farming
Agriculture accounts for around 15 per cent of GDP and employs 48 per cent of the labour force. Agricultural products make up 25 per cent of non-oil export earnings.

After planting more high-yield varieties, investing in irrigation systems, doubling the use of fertilisers and trebling the use of pesticides, Indonesia has achieved self-sufficiency in rice. Poor harvests can still result in rice and other cereals having to be imported to rebuild stocks.

Cassava, maize, sugar, sweet potatoes, bananas and many other fruits and vegetables are grown for local consumption. Self-sufficiency in sugar is a government goal.

It is estimated that there are 1.2 million clove farmers. Indonesia consumes 95 per cent of worldwide clove production, used in the manufacture of *kretek* (clove/tobacco mix) cigarettes. The clove cigarette industry is one of the country's major employers and the government has tariffs in place to restrict the import of cloves, mainly from Madagascar and Zanzibar, in an attempt to maintain its sustainability when over 80 per cent of the cloves consumed is home grown.

Large estates that have undergone rehabilitation produce coffee, tea, rubber, coconuts and palm oil nuts, mostly for export.

Indonesia is the world's largest producer of coconuts and the second-largest of palm oil, copra and natural rubber. It is the third-largest in rice, coffee and cocoa. Crop production ('000) in 2004 included: 65,416 tonnes (t) cereals in total, 54,061t rice, 11,355t maize, 19,264t cassava, 1,376t sweet potatoes, 905t potatoes, 9,000t seed cotton, 4,394t bananas, 105t fibre crops, 22,395t roots and tubers, 16,289t coconuts, 60,400t oil palm, 872t citrus fruit, 613t tomatoes, 463t pineapples, 16,135t oilcrops, 141t tobacco, 430t cocoa beans, 702t green coffee, 24,600t sugar cane, 1,006t mangoes, 2,766t natural rubber, 24,600t sugar cane, 3t vanilla, 90t cloves, 260t kapok, 177t avocados, 629t chillies & peppers, 173t tea, 672,439t soya beans, 65t pepper spice, 12,207t fruit in total, 6,280t vegetables in total. Livestock production included: 2,312t meat in total, 380t beef, 46t buffalo meat, 567t pig meat, 35t lamb, 70t goat meat, 1,164t poultry, 1,051t eggs, 850,990t milk.

Fishing
Foreign aid organisations have assisted the government in rehabilitating the fishing sector. Foreign fishing trawlers are not permitted to operate in Indonesian waters, as these would obstruct traditional coastal fishermen.

Indonesia's fishing industry is plagued by corruption and illegal fishing methods, such as the use of bottle bombs to increase the size of the catch. Ineffective monitoring of fishing techniques means that these practices are likely to continue. Shrimp and tuna fish are important exports. Other species include scad, Indian mackerel and sea catfish. Indonesia is the fifth largest producer of tuna in the world and has become one of the world's biggest exporters of shrimps and prawns.

Forestry

Forest products are the third most important export earner. Indonesia has some of the world's largest remaining reserves of tropical hardwoods. Legislation aims to reduce the rate of felling and to ban the export of logs, and has increased the proportion used locally in timber processing. Illegal logging remains a problem and has doubled the deforestation rate. It is estimated that Indonesia is losing up to two million hectares (ha) of forest annually. It was estimated that 300,000cum of hardwood is illegally felled each year in the state of New Guinea and shipped to China for processing. Indonesia's decentralisation programme could worsen the situation since local governments do not have the ability to manage their resources effectively. The military have also been implicated in the illegal logging trade with corruption and entrenched interests underpinning the activity. Indonesia is under pressure from international organisations to reform its forestry policy to control the unprecedented rate at which the forests are depleting.

Exports in 2004 totalled to US$4.6 billion, while imports amounted to US$958.6 million.

Production in 2004 included 109,060,284 cubic metres (cum) roundwood, 3,248,500cum industrial roundwood, 6,250,000cum sawnwood, 26,000,000cum sawlogs and veneers, 3,248,000cum pulpwood, 7,329,000cum wood-based panels, 79,563,784cum wood fuel, 74,452 tonnes charcoal.

Industry and manufacturing

Industry contributes around 44 per cent of GDP and employs 15 per cent of the workforce.

In the oil-rich 1970s, Indonesia operated a highly protected industrialisation policy with heavy state involvement on both a regulatory and investment front. Declining export revenues from oil and gas in the mid-1980s led to a reversal of this policy. Industry was progressively deregulated and foreign investment encouraged in previously protected areas. Non-traditional export industries were promoted – initially garments and shoes, later electronics, chemicals and minerals. The government also successfully encouraged investment in automobile manufacturing, air and sea transportation, power, communications and highways.

Tourism

The tourist sector, which grew to 5.1 million visitors in 2000, was hit by a series of disasters which reversed the upward trend. Following the 11 September 2001 terrorist attacks in the US came the Bali bombing in October 2002. The impact especially of the latter event promised to be less damaging than was expected, but signs of recovery in early 2003 were negated by the Iraq war, the Sars outbreak and the terrorist attack on the Marriott Hotel in Jakarta. Visitor numbers, which stood at around five million in 2002, fell to 4.4 million in 2003. The setback was temporary. Despite the introduction of a new visa policy in February 2004, the sector recovered quickly, recording 5.3 million arrivals in 2004. Then, in October 2005, another bomb in Bali set back the industry yet again. The government, which recognises the importance of tourism to the economy and actively promotes the sector, aims to attract 10 million visitors by 2009.

The biggest market is Singapore, which accounted for 1.6 million arrivals, followed by Malaysia, Japan, Australia and Taiwan.

Tourism had been expected to contribute 3.1 per cent to GDP in 2005.

Environment

Indonesia is ranked first in the world for its range and variety of corals, and together with the Philippines, Australia, Papua New Guinea and Solomon Islands for coral reef fish species.

Mining

The archipelago of Indonesia produces tin, copper and chromium ore. Indonesia is the world's second-largest producer of tin (after China), producing typically 46,000 tonnes of tin concentrate. In addition to other precious metals, it is also a major producer of copper, bauxite and nickel. Mining and quarrying typically account for around 13 per cent of GDP. Mining's share of GDP has fallen continuously in recent years as production has dropped in response to depressed world prices. Increasing world demand for copper and rising prices have encouraged mines to be restarted and new mines opened.

The government is eager to increase investment in gold, copper and nickel exploitation, although complex issues are involved in mineral exploitation throughout the archipelago. Indonesia is by far the largest gold producing nation in Asia and one of the top 10 producers in the world. Gold is mined at Lebong Tandai in Sumatra and is produced as a by-product from the Freeport copper mine in the highlands of Irian Jaya. Most of Indonesia's gold mines have a short life span. Instability, particularly in separatist areas such as Aceh and Papua, has halted exploration projects in the past. The majority of gold comes from PT Freeport's mining facility in Irian Jaya.

Nickel is mined from new, large deposits in central Sulawesi and Irian Jaya; much of it becomes ferro-nickel and nickel matte, primarily for export. Bauxite production is carried out at Asahan in north Sumatra, for export to Japan.

Tin mining is carried out by state-owned PT Tambang Timah and joint-venture company PT Koba Tin (25 per cent owned by PT Tambang Timah and 75 per cent owned by Iluka Mining Corporation). PT Tambang Timah is the world's largest tin producer, producing tin from Bangka Island, including dredging operations at Karimun and Kundur islands in the Riau Province. The company has tin reserves estimated at around 382,000 tonnes, of which 60 per cent is located offshore.

Hydrocarbons

The role of oil and gas peaked in the early 1980s when it contributed over four-fifths of total exports. Although oil and gas earnings are still significant, their contribution to GDP is declining.

The oil sector remains very important and Indonesia is the major oil producer in South-east Asia. Oil accounts for 17 per cent of exports. In March 2004, Indonesia became a net importer of crude oil, which could continue if investment levels remain low.

Indonesia had proven reserves of 4.7 billion barrels in 2004 and produced 1.26 million barrels per day. The state-owned oil company, Pertamina, dominates the sector, although foreign involvement has steadily increased. In the downstream sector, Indonesia has eight refineries with a combined capacity of 1,056,000bpd. Indonesia had proven natural gas reserves of 2.56 trillion cubic metres in 2004 and produced 73.3 billion cubic metres. Natural gas is supplied from two very large fields at Arun in North Sumatra and Badak in East Kalimantan, although large offshore discoveries have been made around the Natuna Islands in the South China Sea; nearly all is liquefied.

Large-scale systematic coal operations began in 1980 and Indonesia is now the world's third-largest coal producer. Indonesia had coal reserves of 5.0 billion tonnes in 2005. Coal output was around 81.5 million tonnes. Coal is one of the top 10 non-oil exports.

Lower grade lignite prevails (59 per cent) followed by sub-bituminous (27 per cent) and bituminous and anthracite (14 per cent). The state-owned PT Tambang Bukit Asam produces around nine million tonnes per year from four open cast mines. The rest is produced by private coal companies.

Energy

Indonesia has installed electricity-generating capacity of around 25GW, generated mainly by oil-fired plants and some hydro-power. Projects are planned to develop coal and gas-fired and hydro-electric power generation in order to preserve oil for export.

The sector has suffered from under-investment in generating equipment, with the result that, while demand continues to increase, supply is erratic

Financial markets
Stock exchange
The Jakarta Stock Exchange (JSE) is small by regional standards and has attracted little attention from global investors. It has around listed 300 companies, all domestic.

Banking and insurance
The fragile political climate of early 2001 distracted the government from reforming its banking system, which is in a parlous state. Former president, Sukarnoputri, promised international aid donors that she would restructure and privatise Indonesia's banks. The sale of Bank Central Asia (BCA), Indonesia's largest bank, which took place in 2002, restored the credibility of the Indonesia Bank Restructuring Agency (IBRA) and enhanced public confidence in the banking industry.

The IMF has since commended the government's restructuring policies, which have restored solvency to the banking system with net earnings becoming positive for the first time since the 1998 crisis. However, the IMF pointed out that profitability remains low and the large state-sector banks suffer from illiquidity. It has advised the government to divest the large state shareholdings acquired during the course of the crisis while strengthening standards of corporate governance within the sector.

Indonesia was removed from the OECD Financial Action Task Force (FATF) list of non-co-operative countries on money laundering in early 2005.

Central bank
Bank Indonesia

Main financial centre
Jakarta

Time
Indonesia spans three time zones, from GMT plus seven hours (West Zone – Java, Sumatra, west and central Kalimantan and Madura) to GMT plus eight hours (Central Zone – Bali, south and east Kalimantan, Sulawesi and Timor) and GMT plus nine hours (East Zone – Aru, Kai, Moluccas, Tanimbar, Irian Jaya).

Geography
The Indonesian archipelago has 17,508 islands and is the largest in the world, extending about 5,150km (3,200 miles) from Sumatra in the west to Irian Jaya, the western half of New Guinea, in the east. The main islands are Sumatra, Java, Bali, Sulawesi (the Celebes) and Timor. Kalimantan, the Indonesian part of Borneo island shared with Malaysia and Brunei, forms a major part of Indonesian territory. Now independent, the former Portuguese colony of East Timor became the youngest province in 1976. Indonesia's neighbours are Malaysia, Singapore, Papua New Guinea, the Philippines and Australia.

Part of the so-called volcanic 'ring of fire' on the Pacific rim, Indonesia has hundreds of volcanoes, 70 of them still active, and hardly a year passes without a major eruption. Earthquakes are also frequent, but rarely cause significant damage.

The country has the world's second largest area of primary rainforest after Brazil, with species of plant and animal life as diverse as anywhere on the planet.

Climate
All of the islands in the archipelago lie within the tropical zone, with average temperatures of 26 degrees Celsius (C). The dry season usually lasts from May to September, the wet season from October to April. In the hill regions west of Jakarta, average temperatures drop to a pleasant 21 degrees C. Indonesia straddles the equator and days are all the same length and rain is frequent. Yearly rainfall in Jakarta is about 300mm and humidity is more than 80 per cent. The islands east of Bali have a much drier climate, and tropical vegetation and jungles give way to rocky savannahs.

Dress codes
Foreigners are expected to dress for business as they would at home, despite the heat, although men can get away without ties and jackets during the day. Formal attire includes suits, or traditional *batik* shirts. Women are advised to dress conservatively as do their Indonesian counterparts. Although Indonesia is Muslim, there is little of the radicalism found elsewhere. At least in Jakarta, the only women wearing veils will be strict Islamic schoolgirls. The dress traditionally worn by men and women, is the *sarong*. This length of fabric wraps around the waist and is topped by elaborate blouses or shirts. Halter tops and shorts are frowned upon in most places except around sports facilities or on the beach. Proper decorum should especially be observed when visiting places of worship.

Entry requirements
Passports
Required by all. All visitors must be in possession of passports valid for at least six months with proof of onward passage, either return or through tickets.

Visa
Required by all, except nationals of many American countries, EU, Australasia and Asean passport holders, for up to 60 days. Visit www.dfa-deplu.go.id/ for further information and list of exceptions. Business travellers (from the above mentioned countries) arriving on visa-free, short-term visits need to supply a letter of business intent from the employing foreign company or the sponsor in Indonesia.

Currency advice/regulations
The maximum amount of Indonesian currency which may be imported or exported is Rp50,000 per person. Import and export of foreign currency is unlimited. Exchange rates for foreign currency are generally the same at both banks and money changers. Major currencies or travellers cheques may be exchanged at most banks, except in the provinces. It is advisable to carry rupiahs in sufficient amount before travelling to outer provinces or minor towns.

Customs
Personal effects are allowed entry; electrical goods are subject to customs duty. Cars, photographic equipment and typewriters are admitted, provided they are taken out on departure. They must be declared.

Prohibited imports
These include narcotics, arms, ammunition, TV sets, radio, radio cassette, pornography, fresh fruit, information printed in Chinese characters and Chinese medicine. All movies and films must be censored by the film censor board.

Health (for visitors)
Mandatory precautions
Vaccination certificates for yellow fever if travelling from infected area.

Advisable precautions
Vaccinations for diphtheria, tuberculosis, hepatitis 'A' and 'B', Japanese 'B' encephalitis, polio, tetanus, typhoid. Anti-malarial precautions should be taken. There is a high risk of catching dengue fever. Rabies is a risk. All water should be boiled before drinking.

Hotels
International-standard hotels have air-conditioning and often business centres, where translation and secretarial services are normally available. A 10 per cent service charge is normally added to the bill, so tipping with small change is usual. Where no service charge has been added, a tip of 5–10 per cent would be appropriate.

Credit cards
American Express and Visa cards are accepted at international standard hotels, but are not accepted for domestic air fares. International car hire companies,

Indonesia

such as Avis and Hertz, will also accept credit cards. Also Master Card in major hotels and shops.

Public holidays
Fixed dates
1 Jan (New Year), 17 Aug (Independence Day), 25 Dec (Christmas Day).
Variable dates
Chinese New Year (Jan/Feb), Nyepi (Hindu New Year, Mar/Apr), Waisak Day (Birth of the Lord Buddha, May), Good Friday, Ascension Day of Jesus Christ, Eid al Adha, Islamic New Year, Birth of the Prophet Mohammed, Ascent of Prophet Mohammed, Eid al Fitr.
The Islamic year contains 354 or 355 days, with the result that Muslim feasts advance by 10–12 days against the Gregorian calendar. Dates of feasts vary according to the sighting of the new moon, so cannot be forecast exactly. Islamic year 1426: 10 February 2005 to 30 January 2006.

Working hours
Banking
Mon–Fri: 0800–1500; Sat: 0800–1100. Hotel banks may remain open longer.
Business
Mon–Fri: 0800–1600; Sat: 0830–1230. Fri: it is difficult to make an appointment after 1100 although businessmen sometimes meet people in the late afternoon and early evening.
Government
Mon–Thu: 0800–1500; Fri: 0800–1130; Sat: 0800–1400.
Shops
0800/1000–2100/2200 (some close at 1730).

Electricity supply
Generally 220V 50Hz, with two-pronged plug. However, some hotels in the provinces may still be using 110V AC, 50Hz. It is better to check before using an appliance.

Weights and measures
Metric system

Social customs/useful tips
Indonesia is predominantly Muslim and alcohol is not considered essential to social intercourse. Care should be taken to respect Muslim, Hindu and other religious conventions. Footwear should be removed before entering places of worship and temples and sometimes also private homes.
Handshaking with the right hand is customary both for men and women. It is conventional to shake hands and give a slight bow with the head on meeting and taking leave. Punctuality is appreciated on social occasions.
Pork is forbidden for the Muslim population and beef for the Balinese Hindus. Do not start to consume food or drink until invited by the host to do so.
Pribumi is used to describe anything indigenous or native to Indonesia, and occurs in commercial or business contexts with reference to local participation, local capital investment or local loans.
In Indonesia, Western-style beckoning is considered rude; instead, turn your hand palm down, and waggle your fingers – like an upside-down wave. Putting your hands on your hips is considered an overt sign of aggression or contempt.
The word 'no' is regarded as impolite; often people use the word *belum*, which means 'not yet'.

Security
Indonesia has a high crime rate and credit card fraud is a growing problem. Pickpocketing and thefts occur in popular tourist sites.
New residents in a neighbourhood are required to report to the chairman of their neighbourhood association (RT), who is responsible for all activities and concerns in the neighbourhood. Each neighbourhood also has its own civilian security force, called *Hansip*, who patrol at night. Since 2000, Indonesia has been experiencing unrest and violence. There has been sectarian and ethnic strife in Aceh, Irian Jaya, Central and West Kalimantan, Maluku, North Maluku, Central and South Sulawesi and tension in West Timor. Since October 2002, terrorist attacks have deliberately targetted Western tourists.

Getting there
Air
National airline: Garuda Indonesia (GA) and Merpati Nusantara Airlines (MZ).
International airport/s: Soekarno-Hatta International (CGK), 28km north-west of Jakarta, banks/bureaux de change, a post office, duty-free shops, gift shops, 24-hour restaurants, snack bars, car hire and 24-hour medical/vaccination facilities; Denpasar Bali Ngurah Rai International (DPS), 13km south-west of the city, is the main airport on Bali; Bandung Husein (BDO); Cirebon Penggung (CBN); Ketapang (KTG); Pontianak Supadio (PNK); Semarang Uani (SRG); Surabaya Juanda (SUB).
Airport tax: International departures: Rp100,000.
Surface
Water: High-speed ferries run between Sumatra and Malaysia. Routes are either Medan–Penang or Dumai–Melaka. There are also services between Mandalo (Sulawesi) and the Philippines. Maritime piracy is a problem in some Indonesian waters.
Main port/s: Tanjung Priok, Jakarta; Tanjung Perak, Surabaya; Belawan, on Sumatra.

Getting about
National transport
Air: Garuda Indonesia operates extensive domestic services, including daily services between Jakarta, Surabaya and Medan. Other routes are also served by Sempati Air and Merpati Nusantara Airlines.
Road: Extensive road network includes over 220,000km of road, 25 per cent of which is surfaced. A 525km highway links key areas in Jambi and South Sumatra. Toll roads are good, but roads are narrower and poorly maintained in rural areas and remote regions. Secondary roads are frequently impassable in the rainy season. Driving outside major cities at night can be hazardous.
Buses: Express coach services link the main cities. Local bus services are inexpensive, but their use is complicated, they are often crowded, and service may be interrupted in the rainy season.
Rail: The rail network, limited to Java, Sumatra and Madura, comprises 8,600km of track. Java and parts of Sumatra have air-conditioned express rail services with sleeping and dining cars only between major cities. Fares are comparatively cheap but higher on air-conditioned trains. There are several trains daily from Jakarta to Bandung and Surabaya. Ordinary services can be slow, with many stops.
Water: There are extensive scheduled and non-scheduled inter-island sailings.
City transport
Roads in major cities are good.
Taxis: Taxis are plentiful but in various states of disrepair. Wherever possible, opt for Blue Bird or Silver Bird taxis and check the driver switches on the meter before starting the journey.
Taxis can be obtained at hotels, airports and railway stations. From Sukarno-Hatta airport to Jakarta, taxis add a surcharge and toll.
There are metered taxis only in Jakarta, Surabaya, Bandung, Solo, Semarang and Jogjakarta, but it may be necessary to insist on the use of the meter. Fares are very reasonable. Taxis may also be hired by the hour, which is less expensive for longer journeys.
In Jakarta it can be difficult to hail taxis, so engage one at the hotel and retain it until returning. A 10 per cent tip is usual. There are also minicabs for two passengers, the *bemo* (small bus) which plies regular routes, and the *becak*, all of which need advance bargaining to come to a mutually accepted fare.
From city centre to Jakarta Soekarno-Hatta airport taxi journey times are about 45 minutes.
Buses, trams & metro: Journey time on the bus from city centre to Jakarta

Soekarno-Hatta International Airport is about 60 minutes.

Car hire
Car hire, mostly chauffeur-driven, is available in major towns and cities. Except for international car hire operators which accept credit cards, full payment for car hire is made up-front. Traffic drives on the left. Driving at night can be dangerous outside major urban areas as it is common to encounter drivers who do not use their lights.

BUSINESS DIRECTORY

The addresses listed below are a selection only. While World of Information makes every endeavour to check these addresses, we cannot guarantee that changes have not been made, especially to telephone numbers and area codes. We would welcome any corrections.

Telephone area codes
The international direct dialling (IDD) code for Indonesia is +62, followed by the area code and subscriber's number:

Balik Papan	542	Manado	431
Bandung	22	Medan	61
Banjarmasin	511	Padang	751
Denpasar	361	Palembang	711
Jakarta	21		

Useful telephone numbers
Jakarta
Police: 510-110
Ambulance: 118
Fire: 371-309, 113
Directory (local): 108
Directory (other Indonesian): 106
International information: 102
International operator: 101
Domestic connections: 100

Chambers of Commerce
American Chamber of Commerce in Indonesia, World Trade Centre, Jalan Jend Sudirman Kav 29-31, Jakarta 12920 (tel: 526-2860; fax: 526-2861; e-mail: info@amcham.or.id).

Bali Chamber of Commerce and Industry, Gedung Merdeka, Jalan Surapati 7, Denpasar 80232 (tel: 233-053; fax: 227-020; e-mail: kadin_bali@balinetwork.com).

British Chamber of Commerce in Indonesia, World Trade Centre, Jalan Jend Sudirman Kav 31, Jakarta 12920 (tel: 522-9453; fax: 527-9135; e-mail: bisnis@britcham.or.id).

Indonesian Chamber of Commerce and Industry, Menara Kadin Indonesia, Jalan HR Rasuna Said X-5 Kav 2-3, Jakarta 12950 (tel: 916-5535; fax: 527-4485; e-mail: info@kadin.net.id).

Jakarta Chamber of Commerce and Industry, Majapahit Permai B21-23, Jalan Majapahit 18-22, PO Box 3077, Jakarta 10160 (tel: 380-8091; fax: 384-4549; e-mail: kadin_jkt@indosat.net.id).

Banking
Bank Dagang Nasional Indonesia (BDNI), Jl Hayam Wuruk No 8, Jakarta (tel: 231-1221/0530/0886; fax: 380-5725).

Bank Danamon, Jl Kebon Sirih No 15, Jakarta 10340 (tel: 231-1331, 230-1901/2; fax: 230-1883/5).

BankExim, Jl Lapangan Setasiun No 1, Jakarta 11110 (tel: 692-3122, 690-0991; fax: 692-3047, 690-5328).

Bank Internasional Indonesia (BII), Jl MH Thamrin Kav 22 No 51, Jakarta Pusat (tel: 230-0888/0666; fax: 230-1426).

Bank Mandiri, Jakarta (e-mail: corp.communications@bankmandiri.co.id; internet site: http://www.bankmandiri.co.id).

Bank Negara Indonesia (BNI), Jl Jend Sudirman Kav 1, Jakarta 10220 (tel: 251-1946; fax: 251-1214).

Bank Umum Nasional, 135 Jl Senen Raya, Jakarta 10410 (tel: 231-2828; fax: 231-2929).

Indonesian Bank Restructuring Agency, Komplek Bank Indonesia, Jl Budi Kemuliaan, Building D, 10th Floor, Jakarta (fax: 231-1478).

PT Bank Pembangunan Indonesia, JL RP Soeroso No 2-4, Jakarta 10011 (tel: 230-1908; fax: 230-1242/3, 230-0154).

PT Bank Bali Tbk, 17th Floor, Gedung Bank Bali, Jalan Jenderal Sudirman Kav 27, Jakarta 12920 (tel: 523-7899; fax: 250-0811).

PT Bank Buana Indonesia, Jalan Asemka 32-36, Jakarta 11110 (tel: 260-1051, 260-1055; fax: 260-1014).

Central bank
Bank Indonesia, 2 Jalan MH Thamrin, Jakarta 10110 (tel: 381-7187; fax: 350-1867; e-mail: humasbi@bi.go.id).

Travel information
Bouraq Indonesia Airlines, PO Box 2965, Jalan Angkasa 1-3, Kernayoran, Jakarta 10720 (tel: 629-5289; fax: 629-5364).

Garuda Indonesia, Jl. Merdeka Selatan 13, Jakarta 10110 (tel: 380-1901; fax: 380-6652; internet site: http://www.garuda-indonesia.com).

Ikatan Motor Indonesia (IMI), Gedung KONI, Pusat Senayan, Kotakpos 609, Jakarta (tel: 591-102).

Merpati Nusantara Airlines, PO Box 323, Jalan Angkasa 2, Jakarta 10013 (tel: 413-608; fax: 420-7311).

Sempati Air Transport, Jalan Medan Merdeka Timur No 7, PO Box 2068, Jakarta 13610 (tel: 348-760; fax: 809-4420).

National tourist organisation offices
Direktorat Jenderal Pariwisata Indonesia (Directorate-General of Tourism), 16/19 Jalan Medan Merdeka-Barat, Jakarta 10110 (tel: 386-0934; fax: 386-0828; internet site: http://www.tourismindonesia.com).

Ministries
Ministry of Agriculture, Jalal Harsono RM 3, Ragunan, Pasar Minggu, Jakarta 12550 (tel: 781-5380; fax: 781-6385).

Ministry of Defence, Jalal Medan Merdeka Barat 13-14, Jakarta 10110 (tel: 384-0889; fax: 384-5178).

Ministry of Economy, Jalal Lapangan Banteng Timur 2-4, Jakarta 10310 (tel: 319-01152; fax: 319-01151).

Ministry of Education, Jalal Jend Sudirman, Senayan, Jakarta (tel: 573-1618; fax: 573-6870).

Ministry of Energy and Mineral Resources, Jalal Medan Merdeka Selatan 16, Jakarta 10110 (tel: 380-4242; fax: 384-7461).

Ministry of Finance, Jalall Lapangan Banteng Timur 2, Jakarta 10170 (tel: 344-9230; fax: 381-4324).

Minstry of Fisheries and Maritime Affairs, Jalal Veteran, 3rd Floor, Jakarta (tel: 385-7009; fax: 344-6733).

Ministry of Foreign Affairs, Jalal Taman Pejambon 6, Jakarta 10111 (tel: 344-1508; fax: 385-1193).

Ministry of Forestry and Estate Crops, Jalal Jend Gatot Subroto, Senayan, Jakarta (tel: 573-1820; fax: 570-0226).

Ministry of Health, Jalal HR Rasuna Said Blok X-5 Kav 4-9, Jakarta 12950 (tel: 520-1590; fax: 520-1591).

Ministry of Home Affairs, Jalal Medan Merdeka Utara 7, Jakarta 10110 (tel: 384-2222; fax: 385-1193).

Ministry of Justice and Human Rights, Jalal HR Rasuna Said Kav 4-5, Kuningan, Jakarta (tel: 525-3006; fax: 525-3090).

Ministry of Manpower and Transmigration, Jalal Taman Makam Pahlawan 17, Jakarta (tel: 798-9912; fax: 799-2629).

Ministry of Political, Social and Security Affairs, Jalal Medan Merdeka Utara 7, Jakarta 10110 (tel: 384-9453; fax: 345-0918).

Ministry of Religious Affairs, Jalal Lapangan Banteng Barat 3-4, Jakarta 10710 (tel: 381-1679; fax: 381-1436).

Ministry of Resettlement and Regional Infrastructure, Jalal Pattimura 20, Kebayoran Baru, Jakarta 12110 (tel: 720-3962; fax: 726-0769).

Ministry of Social Affairs, Jalal Rasuna Said blok X-5 Kav 4-9, Jakarta 12950 (tel: 310-3781; fax: 310-3783).

Indonesia

Ministry of Trade and Industry, Jalal Jend Gatot Subroto Kav 52-53, Jakarta 12950 (tel: 525-6548; fax: 522-9592).

Ministry of Welfare, Jalal Salemba Raya 28, Jakarta 10430 (tel: 310-3781; fax: 310-3783).

Other useful addresses

Asean Investment Promotion Agency, The Investment Co-ordinating Board (BKPM), Jalan Gatot Subroto No 44, PO Box 3186, Jakarta (tel: 512-008, 515-041, 517-022, 510-023; fax: 514-945).

Asean Secretariat, 70 A Jalan Sisingamangaraja, Jakarta 12110 (tel: 726-2991, 724-3372; fax: 724-3504, 739-8234; e-mail: asean.or.id).

Asian Development Bank, Indonesia Resident Mission, Gedung BRI II, 7th Floor, Jl. Jend Sudirman Kav. 44-46, Jakarta 10210 (tel: 251-2721; fax: 251-2749; e-mail: adbirm@mail.asiandevbank.org).

Badan Ko-ordinasi Penanaman Modal (BKPM) (Co-ordinating Board for Capital Investment), Jalan Jend Gatot Subroto 44, Jakarta Selatan (tel: 525-4981, 525-4619; fax: 525-4945).

Badan Pelaksana Bursa Komoditi (ICEB) (Indonesian Commodity Exchange Board), Bursa Building, 2nd and 4th floors, Jalan Medan Merdeka Selatan 14, Jakarta 10110 (tel: 371-921; fax: 380-4426).

Badan Pelaksana Pasar Modal (BAPEPAM) (Capital Market Operation Board), Jalan Medan Merdeka Selatan 14, Jakarta 10110 (tel: 365-509).

British Consular enquiries: British Embassy, Deutsche Bank Building, 19th Floor, 80 Jalan Imam Bonjol, Jakarta 10310, Indonesia (tel: (62 21) 390-7484; fax: (62 21) 316-0850; internet site: www.britain.in.indonesia.or.id).

Business Advisory Services, Kuningan Plaza Building, Jalan Rasuna Said Kav C-11-14, Jakarta (tel: 517-7295).

Central Bureau of Statistics, Jl Dr Sutomo 18, Jakarta (tel: 372-808; internet site: http://www.bps.go.id).

Commander-in-Chief of the Armed Forces, ABRI Headquarters, Mabes ABRI Cilangkap, Jakarta Timur (tel: 384-2679, 840-1243; fax: 380-6711).

Indonesia-British Business Association, C/O Ernst & Young International, Jakarta Stock Exchange Building 23rd Floor, J1 Jenderal Sudirman, Kav 52-53, Jakarta 12190 (tel: 515-1984; fax: 515-1985).

Indonesia Science Institute, Jl Jend. Gatot Subroto No. 10, Jakarta 12710 (tel: 525-1831).

Indonesian Bank Restructuring Agency, Komplek Bank Indonesia, JL Budi Kemuliaan, building D, 10th Floor, Jakarta (fax: 231-1478).

Indonesian Embassy (USA), 2020 Massachusetts Avenue, NW, Wasahington DC 20036 (tel: 202-775-5200; fax: 202-775-5365; e-mail: indonesia@dgs.dgsys.com).

Jakarta Stock Exchange (JSE), Jalan Mendeka Selatan 14, Jakarta Pusat (internet site: http://www.jsx.co.id).

Office of the National Land Agency (BPN), Jl Sisingamangaraja 2, Jakarta Selatan (tel: 722-2420, 739-3939).

Subroto, Kav 52-53, Jakarta (tel: 520-1613; fax: 520-1606).

US Embassy, Medan Merdeka Selatan 5, Jakarta (tel: 344-2211; fax: 386-2259; e-mail: jakconsul@state.gov; internet site: http://www.usembassyjakarta.org).

Internet sites

IndonesiaNet Business Centre: http://www.indonesianet.com/

Yellow pages: http://www.yellowpages.co.id/

Iran

KEY FACTS

Official name: Jomhoori e Islami e Iran (Islamic Republic of Iran)

Head of State: Wali Faqih (Supreme Leader) Sayed Ali Khamenei (since 1989)

Head of government: President Mahmoud Ahmadinejad (elected 24 Jun 2005, took office 6 Aug)

Ruling party: Conservative coalition, led by the Combatant Clergy Society (elected 7 May 2004)

Area: 1,648,195 square km

Population: 67.42 million (2004)

Capital: Tehran

Official language: Farsi (Persian)

Currency: Rial (IR) 10 rials = 1 toman

Exchange rate: IR9,035.00 per US$ (Oct 2005); (managed float rate from 21 Mar 2002)

GDP per capita: US$2,473 (2004)

GDP real growth: 6.60% (2004)

Labour force: 24.55 million (2004)

Unemployment: 11.20% (2005)

Inflation: 15.60% (2004)

Oil production: 4.08 million bpd (2004)

Balance of trade: US$7.49 billion (2004)

Foreign debt: US$13.40 billion (2004)

For Iran, 2005 was a year in which nuclear technology featured prominently. Having agreed to suspend its uranium enrichment programme in November 2004, Iran spent 2005 fencing with the US, the EU and the UN's International Atomic Energy Agency (IAEA) over its future plans. It was also an election year in Iran. Mohammed Khatami, in office since 1997, had reached the end of his two-term limit, meaning that Iran had to choose a new president. The little-known Mahmoud Ahmadinejad surprised everyone by defeating former president Hashemi Rafsanjani in a second round run-off on 24 June.

Strong growth, difficult future

The IMF forecasts that Iran's GDP grew by a robust 6 per cent in 2005. Iran benefited from strong oil export earnings in 2005, when prices soared above US$60 per barrel. Iran sits on 10 per cent of the world's known oil reserves.

Official unemployment remained at around 11 per cent in 2005. This was sobering news for young Iranians. Approximately half of Iran's 70 million people are under the age of 25 and Iran needs to generate around a million new jobs every year just to ensure that the unemployment rate doesn't increase beyond 11 per cent.

The World Trade Organisation (WTO) opened membership negotiations with Iran in May 2005.

In with the new

After eight years of reformist president Mohammed Khatami, Iranians went to the polls in June to pick a new head of government. Surprising all the pundits, the ultra-conservative mayor of Tehran and newcomer to national politics, Mahmoud Ahmadinejad, triumphed over political veteran Hashemi Rafsanjani, president of Iran 1989–97. Although beaten by Rafsanjani in the first round, Ahmadinejad was the runaway victor in the second, with 62 per cent of the vote.

The election was branded a 'sham' by US president George W Bush and US secretary of state Condoleezza Rice. Of over 1,000 candidates registering to run in the election, the ultra-conservative and un-elected Guardian Council of the Constitution approved only 7. Moreover, women are barred from running for president.

As president, Ahmadinejad promised to crack down on moral and political corruption and to take a hard-line against anything that resembled foreign, and in particular US, interference in Iranian affairs. Other clues as to Ahmadinejad's views emerged between October and December, when he stated that Israel should be 'wiped off the map' and that the Holocaust was a hyped up 'myth'. With a conservative-dominated Majlis (parliament) in place, the president may have expected a sympathetic ear. However, apart from general agreement on Israel and Iran's controversial nuclear programme, the Majlis and the president were at loggerheads from August to December. The Majlis rejected three consecutive presidential nominations for oil minister and opened impeachment proceedings against the president's defence minister.

A familiar face?

Austria and the US launched separate investigations into President Ahmadinejad in July. The US stated that it suspected Ahmadinejad of involvement in the 1979 US Embassy hostage drama in Tehran, and Austria announced that it was investigating claims that Ahmadinejad was involved in the assassination of Iranian Kurdish exiles in Vienna in 1989.

Nuclear high stakes

Whichever way you turned in 2005, there was a story about Iran's activities, ambitions or intent regarding nuclear technology. At stake was Iran's claim, reiterated by President Ahmadinejad before the UN General Assembly in September, that it had the right to develop nuclear power. Iran first began its nuclear programme in 1974, froze it in 1979 and resumed operations in 1992. The stated intent has been since 1974 that Iran wants to build nuclear power stations, not nuclear weapons. The US, EU and the IAEA point out that, as a signatory of the Nuclear non-Proliferation Treaty (NPT), Iran is bound to open its facilities to international inspection. This inspection regime was instituted with the intent of preventing the development of nuclear arsenals by states other than the 'official' nuclear states – the US, Britain, France, China and Russia.

In November 2004, Iran agreed to suspend its uranium enrichment programme and enter into negotiations with the EU over a permanent solution to Iran's nuclear ambitions. This followed months of pressure from the US to refer Iran to the UN Security Council. The US alleged that Iran was trying to manufacture a nuclear bomb, with uranium enrichment being a key stage in the process, and argued that only the Security Council could wave a big enough stick to deter Iran. The EU deal meant that the US had to cool its heels until diplomacy ran its course. The scene was therefore set for both Iran and the EU to deliver a deal in 2005, with the US having suffered a diplomatic setback.

Negotiations were rocky from the start, with an IAEA inspection team claiming that it had only been given partial access to an Iranian nuclear facility at Parchin. In February, Iran rejected an EU offer to give Iran a light-water nuclear reactor in exchange for closing down Iran's efforts to develop a heavy-water reactor. The latter type of reactor is capable of producing plutonium for use in a nuclear bomb. In March, the US, EU and IAEA presented a united front in demanding full 'transparency' from Iran regarding its nuclear programme. Iran-EU talks broke down again in March and definitively in June. In August, the IAEA accused Iran of having conducted illegal experiments with plutonium in 1995 and 1998, when Iran revealed that it had effectively lied in earlier assurances given to the UN body.

Matters came to a head in September, when the IAEA officially paved the way for Iran's nuclear activities to be referred to the UN Security Council. A caveat was that there was no date set for the referral to take place. The key reason for this was that the IAEA felt room should be allowed for an alternative proposal to deal with Iran. Russia proposed that it enrich uranium of Iran's behalf and keep any nuclear waste generated in the process. Thus Iran would not be in possession of an enrichment process or the materials needed to produce a nuclear bomb. In November, the IAEA agreed to delay any referral to the Security Council until Iran considered Russia's proposal.

Iran and Iraq

A war of words broke out between Iran and Britain in October 2005 over events in Iraq. British prime minister Tony Blair publicly suggested that Iran had been providing material support to insurgents in the south of Iraq. A number of British soldiers had been killed in this part of Iraq earlier in 2005. Iran angrily denied the claim and in turn accused Britain of fomenting unrest in its Khuzestan province. US officials had on several occasions previously accused Iran of supplying weapons and training to Iraqi militants operating in the south of the country.

Iranian and Iraqi leaders hailed 2005 as a turning point in relations between the two countries. Iran hosted Iraqi prime minister Ibrahim Jaafari and Iraqi president Jalal Talabani in 2005 – the highest level contacts between the former enemies in decades.

Unrest in the provinces

Iran experienced serious unrest in its western Khuzestan province. Sharing a border

KEY INDICATORS — Iran

	Unit	2000	2001	2002	2003	2004
Population	m	63.66	64.68	65.10	66.26	67.42
Gross domestic product (GDP)	US$bn	67.20	83.90	112.20	137.10	*162.71
GDP per capita	US$	1,054	1,299	1,724	1,853	2,473
GDP real growth	%	4.9	4.7	5.0	4.5	6.6
Inflation	%	12.6	11.4	17.3	16.0	15.6
Oil output	'000 bpd	3,772.0	3,688.0	3,336.0	3,852.0	4,081.0
Natural gas output	bn cum	–	–	–	–	85.5
Exports (fob) (goods)	US$m	28,345.0	26,000.0	25,760.0	28,283.0	38,790.0
Imports (fob) (goods)	US$m	15,207.0	21,600.0	26,450.0	29,547.0	31,300.0
Balance of trade	US$m	13,138.0	4,400.0	1,000.0	-1,264.0	7,490.0
Current account	US$m	12,645.0	4,754.0	3,730.0	–	8,740.0
Foreign debt	US$bn	8.0	7.2	7.3	8.7	13.4
Exchange rate	per US$	1,764.43	1,753.56	5,746.00	8,137.00	8,545.00

* estimated figure

Nations of the World: A Political, Economic and Business Handbook

with Iraq, Khuzestan is home to most of Iran's Arab population. Arabs constitute a majority in Khuzestan's capital, Ahwaz. In April, June, July, October and November, bombings and riots wracked Ahwaz. Iranian authorities launched a crackdown and banned the pan-Arab satellite TV station *al Jazeera*, blaming it for fomenting the unrest. Some Arabs in Khuzestan accuse Tehran of sponsoring a campaign to dilute Ahwaz's Arab population with Iranian settlers.

Riots also broke out in July in Iran's Azarbayjan-e Gharbi province. A leader from the province's Kurdish population was arrested and allegedly tortured to death, apparently on the grounds that he had advocated autonomy for Iranian Kurds. The killing sparked unrest in the cities of Oshnavieh and Mahabad.

Outlook

Negotiations between Iran and the IAEA continued into 2006, in an effort to persuade the Iranians to accept a Russian offer to undertake uranium enrichment on its behalf. However, Iran rejected the proposed deal in January 2006 and on 4 February 2006 the IAEA voted 27–3 (with five abstentions) to refer Iran to the UN Security Council. Iran responded by stating that it would resume full-scale enrichment of uranium and ban IAEA inspections. Iran also protested that the IAEA had, by calling for a vote, abandoned its usual consensus approach to disputes. The IAEA's original referral vote in September 2005 was unprecedented at the time.

Although events in February indicate that the nuclear dispute has entered a new and potentially dangerous phase, it must be acknowledged that both sides have left some room for compromise. Iran has since suggested that the Russian proposal warrants further negotiations and the IAEA itself put off the act of referral until the IAEA head hands down a formal report on Iran's nuclear programme on 6 March 2006.

Risk assessment

Politics	Combative
Economy	Improving
Regional stability	Fragile

COUNTRY PROFILE

Historical profile
Formerly one of the greatest empires of the ancient world, in the seventh century, Persia (renamed Iran in 1935) was one of the first countries to be occupied by Islamic armies. It has since maintained a distinct cultural identity within the Islamic world by retaining its own calendar, language and distinctive styles in arts and literature, and adhering to the Shi'a interpretation of Islam. The poet, Omar Khayam, whose poems have been translated into many languages, was born in Persia in the latter part of the eleventh century.

1907 A constitution was introduced, which limited the royal absolutism of the ruler. An Anglo-Russian agreement (annulled after the First World War) divided Iran into spheres of influence, one Soviet and the other British.

1909–13 Following the discovery of a large oil field in Masjet Soleiman, the Anglo-Persian Oil Company (APOC) was founded in 1909. A licence to search for, refine, produce and export oil, was granted to the APOC in 1913. (The APOC changed its name to the Anglo-Iranian Oil Company (AIOC) in 1935; the AIOC was a British enterprise, owned jointly by the private sector and the British government. Later, the company was renamed British Petroleum (BP)).

1921–26 A Cossack officer, Reza Khan, carried out a military coup, becoming prime minister in 1923. Parliament subsequently proclaimed him the Shah, to be called Reza Shah Pahlavi, ushering in the Pahlavi era. His eldest son, Mohammed Reza was proclaimed crown prince.

1935 Persia was renamed Iran.

1941 In the Second World War, after Reza Shah demonstrated allegiance to Germany, the British and Soviets entered Iran and removed him from power. They permitted his son, Mohammad Reza Shah Pahlavi, to succeed to the throne.

1949 The power of the Shah was increased following an attempted assassination by the Tudeh communist party, which was then banned.

1950 Mohammed Mosaddeq, a leading advocate of oil nationalisation, was installed as prime minister, following the assassination of his predecessor.

1951 Iran's Assembly approved the nationalisation of the oil industry, which was formerly controlled by Britain. As a result, Britain boycotted the purchase of Iranian oil. A contest for control of the government began between the young Shah and the nationalistic Mosaddeq.

1953–54 Mainly due to oil interests, the British persuaded the US to help the Shah remove Mosaddeq. Large sectors of Iranian public opinion condemned the US and Britain for this coup and Mosaddeq became a folk hero of Iranian nationalism. Drilling concessions were granted to eight foreign oil companies.

1963 The Shah assumed complete control of the government and launched a programme of land reform and social and economic modernisation. He used the Secret Police (SAVAK) to control opposition to his reforms.

1978 Following several years of growing opposition to the Shah's rule, martial law was imposed.

1979 The Shah was overthrown by forces loyal to the exiled religious leader, Ayatollah Khomeini, who became *Valy e Faqih* (supreme spiritual leader) of Iran. The Shah and his family were forced into exile in Egypt. The Islamic Republic of Iran was proclaimed following a referendum. Fifty-two staff members at the US Embassy in Tehran were taken hostage by Islamic militants, who demanded the extradition of the Shah from the US, where he was having medical treatment.

1980 Abolhassan Beni Sadr was elected president. The former shah died of cancer.

1980–88 The Iran-Iraq War broke out after Iraq invaded Iran over disputed border areas.

1981 The US Embassy hostages in Tehran were released.

1989 After Ayatollah Khomeini's death, Ali Akbar Hashemi Rafsanjani was sworn in as president, a post which had previously been largely ceremonial, and Khomeini's position as Supreme Leader was taken by the former president, Ayatollah Ali Khamenei.

1990 A peace agreement with Iraq was signed.

1995 Oil and trade sanctions were imposed by the US, which alleged that Iran had sponsored terrorist groups throughout the region, had sought to acquire nuclear arms and destabilise the Middle East peace process.

1996 In the general election, the Combatant Clergy Society (CCS) retained its position as the largest single group.

1997 Many people were surprised when Mohammad Khatami, a moderate cleric, was elected president.

2000 Elections to an expanded Majlis returned a majority for reformist candidates. Ayatollah Ali Khamenei halted a bill that would have revived Iran's banned reformist newspapers.

2001 President Khatami was re-elected for a second term. Saudi Arabia and Iran signed a security accord to combat terrorism, drug trafficking and organised crime.

2002 Iran released nearly 700 Iraqi prisoners held since the 1980–88 war. President Bush included North Korea with Iran and Iraq in an 'axis of evil' due to their supposed development of Weapons of Mass Destruction (WMD). Iran began construction of its first nuclear reactor.

2003 Student-led protests were held in Tehran against the clerical establishment. Parliament passed a bill guaranteeing free parliamentary elections. Iran came under pressure from the International Atomic Energy Agency (IAEA) over its nuclear energy programme. Subsequent IAEA inspections concluded there was no evidence of a weapons programme. A major earthquake hit the city of Bam in the south-east, killing 40,000 people and leaving the city in ruins.

2004 Over a third of parliament resigned in February after the Council of Guardians upheld the disqualification of more than 2,000 prospective reformist candidates hoping to stand in the elections. In March, President Bush extended sanctions for another year. Iran failed to fully co-operate with an IAEA enquiry into its nuclear activities. Run-off parliamentary elections held in May were won by the conservatives. As part of a deal with the EU, Iran agreed to suspend most of its uranium enrichment programme.

2005 Three villages were destroyed and 40 badly damaged when an earthquake struck central Iran in February. Mahmoud Ahmadinejad was elected president in the run-off elections on 24 June; he took office in August. He promised to pursue the country's nuclear power programme, increasing tension with the US and EU. In Octoer he caused international concern when he suggested that Israel should be wiped off the map. In December he described the Holocaust as a myth. A new natural gas pipeline between Iran and Azerbaijan was inaugurated on 20 December.

Political structure
Constitution
Iran became an Islamic Republic in April 1979, having previously been a monarchy under the Shah. The constitution of the Islamic Republic was formally adopted in December 1979. The constitution also provides for representation in the Majlis Shura-e-Islami (Islamic Consultative Assembly) of non-Islamic minorities, Zoroastrians, Jews and Christians. However, power is wielded mainly by the Shi'a clergy.

Form of state
Islamic republic

The executive
The Wali Faqih (Supreme Leader of the Islamic Revolution) retains overall control of all branches of government, including the judiciary and the revolutionary guard. He declares war and peace and can veto presidential nominations. His role combines spiritual leader, theological protector and supreme authority. The structure of the constitution is effectively split between the president, who is elected every four years, and the Supreme Leader, who has overall control. The Supreme Leader, in his role as theological protector, appoints the Council for the Protection of the Constitution. All legislation adopted by the Majlis Shura-e-Islami is scrutinised by the council to ensure that it is in keeping with Islamic principles and laws. The council consists of six religious lawyers.

The Council of Guardians, composed of 12 jurists and clerics, has supervisory powers over elections and a right of veto over all legislation if it does not conform with Islamic law and the constitution. It is independent of the Supreme Leader.

In 1986, the Expediency Council was established to mediate between the Majlis and the Council of Guardians. It is designed to resolve political decisions which cannot be solved through the main channels, but it is controlled by the spiritual leader.

A further adjunct to the Supreme Leader's power is the Assembly of Experts which consists of 83 clerics who elect the next Supreme Leader, interpret the constitution and approve Majlis decisions. The cumulative effect of this plethora of legislative institutions is that despite the enhancement of the president's power, following reform in 1989, he remains tightly constrained by these institutional checks and balances.

National legislature
The 290-member Majlis Shura-e-Islami is elected every four years. Although MPs are technically independent, the Majlis is now very loosely divided along party political lines between the conservative clergy groupings and the reformist May 23 Front, named after the day of President Khatami's victory in 1997. The Majlis is elected by universal suffrage, with a voting age of 15.

Legal system
The judiciary is organised independently of the other branches of government. There are two types of courts: public and special. The Penal Courts, Special Civil Court and Islamic Revolution Courts adjudicate on the basis of Islamic laws, fixed since 1979 for a wide range of crimes.

Last elections
24 June 2005 (run-off presidential); 20 Feb/7 May 2004 (parliamentary).
Results: Presidential (run-off): Mahmoud Ahmadinejad was elected with 61.5 per cent of the vote against 35.9 per cent for Ali Akbar Hashemi Rafsanjani. Turnout was about 60 per cent. Ahmadinejad is to take office in August.
Parliamentary run-off: conservatives won 40 seats out of 57 seats, reformists eight and independents nine.

Next elections
2008 (parliamentary); 2009 (presidential).

Political parties
Ruling party
Conservative coalition, led by the Combatant Clergy Society (elected 7 May 2004)

Main opposition party
May 23 Front, of which the largest grouping is the Mosharekat (Participation) Front

Population
67.42 million (2004)

Ethnic make-up
The population is predominantly Persian (55 per cent), with the second largest group being Azeris, concentrated in the north-west. There are also Afghans (approximately two million Afghan refugees were repatriated by the UN refugee organisation in 2002), Kurds, Baluchis, Lurs, Turkmen, Arabs and nomads.

Religions
Islam of the Twelver Shi'a sect is dominant. A Sunni Muslim minority is concentrated in fringe areas of Iran. There are also small Baha'i, Christian, Jewish and Zoroastran communities.

Education
Government expenditure on education was 37.2 per cent of the annual budget in 1999/2000, with 7.4 per cent for higher education and 4.0 per cent for research. Education is compulsory for eight years from the ages of six. This is not fully effective in rural areas. Primary education is free and lasts for five years. Secondary education begins at 11 years and lasts for up to seven years, with a first course of three years and a second course of four years.

Secondary education is split between intermediate (or 'guidance') schools and secondary schools. There are also technical, business and other specialised vocational schools.

Iran has 116 higher education institutes, 23 of which are full universities.
Literacy rate: 78.1 per cent total; 71.4 per cent female, adult rates in 2002 (World Bank).
Compulsory years: 6 to 14.
Enrolment rate: 98 per cent total primary enrolment of relevant age group; 77 per cent total secondary enrolment (World Bank).
Pupils per teacher: 30 in primary schools.

Health
Total expenditure on health is around 5 per cent of GDP, of which 46 per cent is government spending.

Drug abuse is a serious problem in Iran, due to imports of cheap heroin and opium from Afghanistan, and there are an estimated two million drug addicts.

HIV/Aids
Intravenous drug users in Iranian prisons accounted for 65 per cent of HIV infections in the country. A programme has been implemented, by non-governmental agencies, working to reduce the harm of HIV/Aids among this group.

Rates of HIV/Aids infection among tuberculosis patients also rose and reached 4.2 per cent by mid-2001 (UNAID/WHO).
HIV prevalence: 0.1 per cent aged 15–49 in 2003 (World Bank)
Life expectancy: 69.4 years (World Bank)
Fertility rate/Maternal mortality rate: 2.0 births per woman (2003); maternal mortality 37 deaths per 100,000 live births (World Bank).
Infant mortality rate: 33 per 1,000 live births; 11 per cent of children aged under five are malnourished (World Bank).
Head of population per physician/bed: 0.85 doctors and 1.2 hospital beds per 1,000 people.

Welfare
A large number of organisations, usually autonomous, are responsible for social welfare. Various foundations manage sequestered property worth billions of US dollars. They are responsible for the care of families of men killed in the war with Iraq, for war refugees and for rural development. At the local level in the cities and towns, mosque committees (*komitehs*) have funds, which are made available for poorer families. The country's rationing system, that includes giving coupons for limited quantities of staple foods and other items at heavily subsidised prices, is also run through mosques.
Iran's Social Security Organisation (SSO) provides a list of services, including survivor's pension, subsidies to large families, retirement, unemployment and disability benefits.

Main cities
Tehran (capital, estimated population 8.0 million in 2004), Mashhad (2.1 million), Esfahan (1.4 million), Tabriz (1.2 million), Shiraz (1.2 million), Karaj (1.1 million), Ahvaz (1.0 million).

Languages spoken
Azeri Turkish is the second most popular language. English and Arabic are widely taught in high schools. In the cities, French and German are also spoken.
Official language/s
Farsi (Persian)

Media
Press
The Iranian press has changed rapidly since the revolution in 1979. From 1981, the war with Iraq led to drastic changes, with many closures of newspapers, magazines and journals, and purges of editors with liberal, conservative or radical views. Since then the press has been restrained further.
President Khatami's election resulted in a more independent press and the establishment of reformist publications. The emergence of a freer press has increased the tension between conservatives and reformers. The courts have taken an increasingly harsh stance towards reformist journalists and many publications have been banned by the Council of Guardians.
All newspapers and magazines must be licensed; insults to senior religious figures are a criminal offence. The constitution guarantees freedom of the press but contains strict sanctions against publishing material contrary to public morality or that would insult religious beliefs or libel individuals. As a result, reformist newspapers have been closed down and repressed by the religious authorities.
The official news agency is the Islamic Republic News Agency (IRNA).
Dailies: The principal publications include *Al Vefagh Daily*, *Kayhan*, *Ettela'at*, *Khorassan*, *Risala'at*, *Abrar* and *Jomhoori Islami*. None are truly independent, being broadly pro-regime and uncritical of the Islamic revolution. However, there are differences in their political sympathies, with different editors and proprietors supporting different government factions.
Risala'at has been more critical of the government than other newspapers. Iran's leading pro-reform daily newspaper, *Neshat*, was suspended in 1999, for propagating against the state.
In Tehran there are three English-language publications *Tehran Times*, *Iran Daily* and *Kayhan International*.
Weeklies: Weekly newspapers tend to be special interest publications. The leading weeklies are *Kayhan Varzeshi*, *Donyaye Varzesh* (both sport), *Kayhan Bacheha* (children's interest), *Zan-e-Ruz*, *Ettela'at Banovan* (both women's interest) and the general interest *Ettela'at Haftegi*.
Business: *World Economy* is published daily, and is the most popular business publication, although distribution is generally limited to Tehran.
Periodicals: Weekly publications covering political organisations and politics in general include *Iran Weekly Digest*, *Iran-e-Javan* (weekly magazine) and *Weekly Press digest*.
Broadcasting
Radio: There are three national radio channels, Radio Networks 1 and 2 and Radio Quran. Regional and local radio programmes are broadcast in Arabic, Armenian, Assyrian, Azerbaijani, Baluchi, Bandari, Dari, Farsi, Kurdish, Mazandarani, Pashtu, Turkoman, Turkish and Urdu. The external radio service broadcasts in English, French, German, Spanish, Turkish, Arabic, Kurdish, Urdu, Pashtu, Armenian, Bengali, Russian and Farsi. The radio company is the Voice of the Islamic Republic of Iran.
Television: Broadcasting is tightly controlled by the state and there have been many purges of editors whose views were not approved of. The state-run television network, Vision of the Islamic Republic of Iran, has 28 local channels.

Economy
There are serious concerns about the sustainability of Iran's economic growth because of its high dependence on oil prices. The economy is protected by high external tariffs, price controls, subsidies and a banking system which lacks liquidity. There are also concerns at the government's apparent willingness to print money to finance state-owned industries' deficits.
Politically-run state conglomerates called *bonyad* dominate the economy, particularly the non-oil sector. They are allocated two-thirds of the budget each year and own or control all the country's transport, oil, petrochemical and mining companies. Despite this, the private sector remains surprisingly resilient. Many new private sector companies have been formed since the revolution. The government hopes that Iranian expatriates will form the spearhead of 'foreign' private-sector investment in the development of manufacturing capacity. The government also hopes to increase Iran's industrial competitiveness and exports by encouraging privatisation. After he was elected president in 1997, Khatami inherited the Second Five-Year Economic Development Plan (FYEDP) (1996–2000) which was financed by spiralling debt and plagued by problems of low international oil prices and a widening trade deficit. By 2000, Iran's economic growth was averaging half that envisaged in the Second FYEDP, currency reserves were depleted, the rial's market rate had depreciated by around 75 per cent and the budget deficit had gone out of control.
The problems faced by Khatami led to a significant change in policy direction under the Third FYEDP (2000–04). By targetting the overbearing power of the state, it aimed at removing obstacles to foreign and domestic investment, privatisation, increasing the role and diversity of the private sector, export-oriented growth and the development of non-oil sectors. The plan's launch coincided with a rise in oil export prices, which reversed declining oil revenues and the growing trade deficit. In an effort to avoid the economic problems associated with fluctuating oil prices, the government diverted excess revenue into an oil stabilisation fund managed by the Central Bank of Iran (CBI).
Real GDP growth in 2004 was 6.6 per cent and it is expected to slow down a little in 2005 to around 5.8 per cent. Although Iran received higher oil export revenues in 2003 and 2004, its budgetary pressures continued. There is a high level

of poverty and unemployment (11.2 per cent in 2005) and over-dependence on oil revenues, despite efforts to diversify the economy. Government attempts to reduce the public sector to around 10 per cent of GDP have failed and most of the economy remains in public sector hands.
In 2005, US President Bush extended sanctions for another year.

External trade
Shortages of foreign currency have produced a boom in counter (barter) trade, which obscures the extent of foreign trade; Iran is also understandably reluctant to declare the full extent of its oil traffic in the Gulf, but oil revenues are thought to exceed US$15 billion per annum.

Imports
Main imports include industrial raw materials and intermediate goods, capital goods, foodstuffs and other consumer goods, technical services and military supplies.

Main sources: Germany (13 per cent total, 2004), France (8.9 per cent), Italy (8.0 per cent), China (7.7 per cent), UAE (6.4 per cent), South Korea (6.3 per cent), Russia (4.9 per cent)

Exports
Crude oil (typically 80 per cent of total), petroleum products, non-oil items, which include carpets, pistachio nuts, dates and caviar.

Main destinations: Japan (20 per cent total, 2004), China (9.9 per cent), Italy (6.3 per cent), South Africa (6.3 per cent), Taiwan (4.8 per cent), Turkey (4.7 per cent), South Korea (4.7 per cent), France (4.3 per cent), The Netherlands (4.3 per cent)

Agriculture
Farming
Since the 1979 revolution, land ownership has been in dispute. Meanwhile, people have moved from the countryside to the city. This has left a shortage of agricultural labour, despite high unemployment in the economy as a whole. On many farms, particularly those in the private sector near Tehran, immigrant Afghan workers have replaced Iranians.
Since it was set up in the 1980s, the Bonyad-e Mostazafin (Foundation for the Oppressed and Deprived) has brought new facilities, especially water, electricity and roads, to thousands of rural villages. Government efforts to stimulate sluggish private investment in agriculture have made little headway. As half of Iran's farmers belong to 3,000 rural co-operatives, grouped into 180 unions and benefiting from cheap credit made available by the state, they are reluctant to embrace private sector competition.
The government wants to reduce the import bill for food and agricultural inputs.

Iran imports large quantities of meat, rice, vegetables, oil, sugar and tea, as well as cattle fodder, fertilisers, machinery and tractors. It is encouraging the expansion of cotton and sugar cane plantations, livestock production and downstream processing industries for these products.
The crop production ('000) for 2004 included: 21,610 tonnes (t) cereals in total, 14,000t wheat, 4,180t potatoes, 2,700t barley, 3,400t rice, 6,500t sugar cane, 6,050t sugar beets, 1,500t maize, cassava, 310t seed cotton, 105t cotton lint, 695t pulses, 519t treenuts, 3,825t citrus fruit, 275t pistachios, 2,800t grapes, 4,200t tomatoes, 105t chillies & peppers, 94t oilcrops, 21t tobacco, 40t olives, 135t soya beans, 52t tea, 2,400t apples, 880t dates, 90t figs, 13,143t t fruit in total, 13,495t vegetables in total. Livestock production included: 1,646t meat in total, 320t beef, 12t buffalo meat, 348t lamb, 105t goat meat, 846t poultry, 610t eggs, 5,980t milk, 29,000t honey, 41t cattle hides, 58t sheepskins, 75,000t greasy wool, 6,000t cocoons, silk.

Fishing
There are few river systems in Iran, and most freshwater fishing is for subsistence purposes. There is commercial fishing on the Persian Gulf and the Caspian Sea. Iran produces around 444,000 tonnes of seafood per year. Main species are sturgeon, tuna, mackerel, shrimps, lobsters and crayfish. Iran produces around 90 per cent of the world's caviar. Fish farming is an increasingly important activity.

Forestry
There is some forestation in the north of the country, near the Caspian Sea, but limited commercial exploitation is generally for domestic purposes only.

Industry and manufacturing
The government's goal in the past has been to build up basic industries as a means of import substitution and to develop a broad industrial base to reduce reliance on oil. The government has also given priority to the development of downstream industries in the oil and gas sectors and to the development of mining and metals processing.
Tehran and Isfahan are the main industrial centres. The largest industrial conglomerate is the National Iranian Industries Organisation (NIIO), a state-owned group which is directly responsible for 90 companies in manufacturing, engineering and trading. The NIIO companies are in nine industrial groups: textiles and leather, chemicals, pharmaceuticals, food, electrical goods, construction and cellulose. Industry accounted for 41 per ecnt of GDP in 2004.

Tourism
Iran's potential as a major tourist destination has been impeded by inadequate accommodation standards and travel restrictions, as well as a generally poor image abroad. Nevertheless, visitor numbers have grown in recent years. The authorities recognise the value of tourism and in 2004 announced a long-term programme to develop the sector, while reducing state involvement. An integrated tourism body was created in May 2004. Obstacles to visitors are being eased and pricing differentials eliminated. Tourism is expected to contribute 3.6 per cent to GDP in 2005.

Mining
Iran is one of the world's 15 major mineral-rich countries and the mining sector employs directly over 107,000 workers. Production has a market value of over US$4 billion. The government is trying to encourage private investment in mineral exploration and production.
The majority of the large-scale mines and major industries, including steelworks, copper, lead and zinc, are partially or totally state-owned. The government has sought to develop the country's abundant mineral resources as an alternative to oil- and gas-based industrial development. However, as in other sectors, expansion of mineral production has suffered from shortages of foreign currency for machinery and spare parts, power cuts, and the lack of mining experts. Consequently, Iran is still obliged to import many raw materials, which it could produce from its own resources, given appropriate investment and manpower skills.
The Iranian government has strongly encouraged foreign investment on 'buy-back' terms that enables foreign investors to recoup capital through receipt of the project's output. Substantial improvement is targetted for the non-ferrous metals sector including aluminium, copper and zinc. Iran has 60 lead and zinc mines, 30 coal mines, 20 copper mines and 40 deposits of chromite, fluorene and sulphur. It also has an important industrial mineral sector, and is the third largest producer of gypsum in the world.

Hydrocarbons
The ministry of oil is responsible for state companies which control the oil, gas and petrochemicals sectors. They are the National Iranian Oil Company (NIOC), the National Iranian Gas Company (NIGC) and the National Petrochemical Company (NPC). Iran's total oil reserves were estimated at 132.5 billion barrels in 2004, 11.1 per cent of the world's total. At current rates of production, Iran's oil reserves should last until at least the middle of the 21st century and there are hopes of

finding new oil fields in Iranian territorial waters in the Caspian Sea; Iran's Caspian oil reserves could amount to around 15 billion barrels, although this is dependent on an agreement on boundaries by the littoral states. The government hopes to attract foreign investment in order to raise production capacity to 5.6 million bpd by 2010 and 7.3 million bpd by 2020. Iran's Opec quota was 3.96 million bpd in 2005. Iran exports 2.5 million bpd, around half of which goes to Asia, with the rest destined for Europe and Africa. The constitution prohibits granting oil licences on a concessionary basis or in the form of a direct equity stake. International oil companies are involved in developing Iran's oil fields on a buyback basis. This entails the contractor funding all investments in an oil field in return for an allocated production share from the state-owned NIOC. The operation of the oil field is transferred to the NIOC once the contract is completed.

In the downstream sector, petrochemicals are being developed as part of the government's strategy to add value to hydrocarbon exports. Iran is the second largest petrochemical producer in the region, after Saudi Arabia, with output of 20 million tonnes in 2005, expected to rise to 27 million tonnes by 2007. Iran is encouraging foreign investment into the petrochemical industry.

Proven gas reserves were 27.5 trillion cubic metres in 2003, with production at 85.5 billion cubic metres. Natural gas accounts for around 50 per cent of Iran's total energy consumption. The government is keen to expand export markets, particularly in Asia. The massive South Pars gas field, which is shared with Qatar, is being developed in 25 stages over 25 years. Iran produces around one million tonnes per year (tpy) of coal and consumes approximately 1.6 million tpy.

Iran's first mechanised underground coal mine is at Tabas. It produces around 1.5 million tonnes of coking coal for steel production each year.

Energy
Iran has an electricity generating capacity of 31GW, over 90 per cent of which is produced by thermal power stations and the remainder by hydroelectricity. Iran's demand is growing rapidly at around 7.5 per cent per annum and this will require a doubling of electricity generating capacity by 2012. The government has set up a number of build-operate-transfer (BOT) contracts to generate foreign investment in the electricity sector. However, it appears unwilling to break up or privatise the state-controlled Tavanir organisation, which operates as a monopoly in the power sector.

In 1998, the Russian government announced that it would honour a contract worth US$780 million to build two nuclear reactors near the Iranian port of Bushehr. Ukraine had previously pulled out after US pressure. In 2001, Russia agreed to help develop Iran's nuclear generating capacity, particularly the continuing development of the first Bushehr reactor. The US has raised strong objections over the development of nuclear power in Iran, claiming that it will be used for military purposes and the construction of nuclear warheads. The Iranian government insists the Bushehr reactors are for domestic energy consumption and has stood by the terms of the Nuclear Non-Proliferation Treaty, of which Iran is a signatory.

Financial markets
Stock exchange
The Tehran Stock Exchange (TSE) was established in 1968.

Banking and insurance
Before the revolution, Iran's banking system was handicapped by the small number of banks, by heavy indebtedness (both to the central bank and to foreign creditors) and by the high levels of non-performing assets, a legacy of the virtual absence of regulatory controls under the Shah's regime. After the reorganisation in 1979, the sector's weakness was further aggravated by economic recession, the freezing of Iranian assets held abroad and the long war with Iraq.

The government recognises that the state-owned banking system is unable to provide sufficient credit for economic growth. Non-banking credit institutions (NBCIs) will legally do what *bazaaris* have been doing for two decades. Foreign banks, a number of which have a representative office in Tehran, became more active as oil exports revived and financing became available for the reconstruction programme. Reconstruction requires imported goods and services. French banks are keen to regain the dominance they enjoyed in foreign trade financing in Iran before 1983, when France's supply of weapons to Iraq caused a breakdown in relations between France and Iran. Several French banks are on the approved list of the National Iranian Oil Company (NIOC). The most active are Banque Paribas, Société Générale and Banque Nationale de Paris.

As part of the 2000–04 economic development programme, the banking sector is being opened up to foreign participation and in 2002, Bank Markazi (the central bank) agreed to license the first fully foreign-owned banks since the 1979 revolution.

Central bank
Bank Markazi Jomhouri Islami Iran
Main financial centre
Tehran

Time
GMT plus three and a half hours

Geography
Iran is a large and varied country. Much of it is desert wilderness, with mountainous regions along the western borders with Iraq and in the north with Turkey. Around 11 per cent of Iran is forested, notably in the northern regions of the Caspian Sea and Zagros mountains.

By the early part of the twentieth century, the majority of the population were villagers living in fertile fringes of Iran's great central plateau, which is made up of vast sand and salt deserts. However, rapid urbanisation, especially the growth of the capital Tehran, has changed the distribution of the population and the activities in which it is engaged.

Water is scarce in most of Iran and its availability dictates the density of the population in settled areas. There are very few towns of any size in central and eastern Iran, although there are lush oases scattered across the sand and salt deserts. There is a traditional system of subterranean water channels, cut from the water tables in mountains for irrigation.

Climate
The climate for most of the country is dry and hot in summer before abruptly changing to a bitterly cold winter. The best season for visiting is around the Persian New Year ('Nowruz', 21–24 March). Temperatures range from 51 degrees Celsius (C) in summer at the head of the Gulf to -14 degrees C in winter in the interior. The mean temperatures are 3 degrees C in January and 29 degrees C in July. The Gulf area becomes unbearably hot and humid in summer.

Dress codes
Since the 1979 Islamic Revolution, ties are shunned by Iranians but suits are acceptable. Informal dress is acceptable for men (not shorts). The Islamic dress code for women has relaxed recently to includes loose trousers, long skirts, long sleeves, long coats and a headscarf; avoid make-up. Women should always dress discreetly in public.

Entry requirements
Passports
Required by all except certain seamen.
Visa
An independent traveller can visit Iran but there may be difficulties in obtaining a visa. It is easier and often cheaper to travel as part of an organised group tour.

Iran

Visas are required by all and are valid for 30 days. Business visas must have an invitation letter from a local, sponsoring company, to be submitted to the foreign ministry in Tehran for approval. When authorised, the host company can obtain a reference number which is forwarded to the applicant. After one week, the visitor should contact the consulate quoting the reference number, and confirm the approval. Once confirmed, the application and documents can be submitted to the consular section for further action.

Prohibited entry
Israeli citizens or anyone with Israeli stamps in their passport will be rejected.

Currency advice/regulations
There is no restrictions for the import of foreign currency, declared on arrival (on a customs form or at the Tehran (Mehrabad) airport branch of the Bank Melli), export is limited, however, to US$10,000. The US dollar, sterling, yen and the euro are the most easily traded. Be prepared to be given large quantities of low-denomination notes from money changers.

Customs
The export of all antiques (over 50 years old) is prohibited, including gems, coins, handwritten manuscripts and other artifacts.

Prohibited imports
The import of all alcohol, firearms and ammunitions, video tapes and obscene publications is strictly prohibited.

Health (for visitors)
Mandatory precautions
A yellow fever certificates is required if travelling from an infected area. An AIDS certificate is required if staying more than three months.

Advisable precautions
Cholera is a high risk and precautions are required. Typhoid, dysentery and typhoid fever are common.

Hotels
The situation and status of hotels should be carefully checked. The use of the name of an international management chain does not imply a current connection with the chain, but may indicate only a previous link or the usual name by which the hotel is known. Most hotels are utilitarian. Evening entertainment is very rare.

Credit cards
Mastercard and visa are accepted in major locations.

Public holidays
Fixed dates
11 Feb (Victory of the 1979 Islamic Revolution), 19 Mar (Oil Nationalisation Day), 21–25 March (Now Ruz/Persian New Year), 1 Apr (Islamic Republic Day), 2 Apr (Public Outing Day), 4 Jun (Death of Imam Khomeini), 5 Jun (Anniversary of Uprising against the Shah).

Iran uses the solar Persian calendar, which differs from the Gregorian calendar: there are 31 days in each of the first six months of the Persian calendar, 30 days in each of the next five months and 29 days in the last month, except in leap year when it has 30 days.

The Persian calendar dates from the Arab/Muslim invasion and the introduction of Islam into the country. The calendar (known as the *Hejrieh Shamsi*) is very precise; it was devised by the renowned Persian mathematician, Omar Khayyam. The months are: Farvardin, Ordibehesht, Khordad, Tir, Mordad, Shahrivar, Mehr, Aban, Azar, Day, Bahman, Esfand. The Iranian calendar year was briefly changed in commemoration of the 2,500th anniversary of the Persian Empire in 1971. The year was changed from 1350 Hejrieh Shamsi to 2530 Melli (national). This calendar was unpopular and the nation reverted to the old calendar soon afterwards.

Persian year 1384: from 21 March 2005 to 20 March 2006.

Variable dates
Eid al Adha, Islamic New Year, Ashura, Death of Prophet Mohammed and Martyrdom of Imam Hassan (Apr), Birthday of the Prophet Mohammed and Imam Sadeq (Apr), Birthday of Imam Ali (Aug), Ascent of the Prophet, Birthday of Imam Mahdi (Sep), Martyrdom of Imam Ali (Sep), Qds Day (Nov), Eid al Fitr, Martyrdom of Imam Sadeq (Nov), Birthday of Imam Reza (Dec).

The Islamic year contains 354 or 355 days, with the result that Muslim feasts advance by 10–12 days against the Gregorian calendar. Dates of feasts vary according to the sighting of the new moon, so cannot be forecast exactly.

Working hours
Friday is the Muslim day of religious observance (weekly holiday).

Banking
Sat–Wed: 0800–1700; Thu: 0800–1200; closed on Friday.

Business
Sat–Wed: 0700/0800–1300, 1600–1900. Closed on Thursday and Friday.

Government
Sat–Wed: 0700/0800–1300, 1600–1900. Closed on Thursday and Friday.

Shops
Sat–Wed: 0800–2000; Thu: 0800–1200; most bakeries and some food shops stay open on Fridays while the rest close.

Electricity supply
220V AC, 50 cycles

Weights and measures
Metric system

Social customs/useful tips
Visitors for business engagements are expected to arrive on time for appointments. However, it is by no means uncommon to be kept waiting, or even for appointments to be cancelled without notice.

The Gulf is never called Arabian, but is usually identified as Persian.

Normal Muslim customs prevail within most areas of the country. Alcohol is forbidden, although tolerance is shown to non-Muslims who may drink it at home. Women must sit at the back of buses. Men and women who are not married must not touch, therefore a business deal with a woman may not be sealed with a handshake.

Business negotiations can take a long time. A good lawyer and a detailed contract are essential.

Prostitution, casual sex and especially homosexual sex, are punishable with death or long prison sentences. Foreign visitors are not exempt from these laws.

Security
There is little violent street crime in Tehran, but visitors should take great care of their wallets and bags. Keep passports separate from other valuables. Bogus policemen are an increasing hazard for the unwary business traveller. Their technique is to demand to see proof of identification and then make off with a visitor's wallet.

Getting there
Air
National airline: Iran Air (Homa)
International airport/s: Mehrabad (THR), 5km west of Tehran, with duty-free shop, restaurant, bank, post office, shops; Shiraz (SYZ), 15km from city, with currency exchange, post office, shops.
Airport tax: Departure tax: IR70,000.

Surface
Road: There are roads from Iraq, Turkey, Afghanistan and Pakistan, although these routes are not always passable. A 192-metre road bridge over the Araks river, linking Armenia with Iran, was opened in 1996.
Rail: There is a link with Turkey and Syria, and since 1996, a rail route into Turkmenistan that runs nearly 300km from the Iranian Silk Road city of Mashhad, crossing the Turkmen border at Sarakhs to join the Soviet-era Turksib railway at Tedzhen.
Water: Ferries run between Iran and United Arab Emirates, Manama (Bahrain) and Kuwait City.
Main port/s: The large ports on the Gulf include the country's main oil terminal at Kharg Island, the largest port Khorramshahr, Bandar Shahid Rajai,

Bushehr, Bandar Khomeini and Chah Bahar. The main ports on the Caspian Sea are Bandar Anzali and Bandar Nowshahr.

Getting about
National transport
Air: Iran Air runs frequent services between most cities and Tehran. Internal flights are cheap. Seats can be difficult to acquire without booking well in advance.
Road: Surfaced roads serve main centres; condition of secondary roads may vary.
Buses: There is an extensive, comfortable and cheap bus network that runs throughout the country. Scheduled long-distance coach services vary in their routes, but usually travel between all the main towns.
Rail: Rail services on the 5,500km network may vary, but there are usually various classes of service, with sleeping accommodation, air-conditioning and restaurant services available.

City transport
Taxis: Taxis are not metered and frequently shared. Those hired by telephone or by hotels are more expensive. Tipping is not expected.

Car hire
An international driving licence (along with two photographs) is required.

BUSINESS DIRECTORY

Telephone area codes
The international direct dialling (IDD) code for Iran is +98, followed by the area codes:

Abadan	631	Isfahan	31
Ahvaz	61	Kerman	51
Arak	2621	Mashad	51
Babol	11	Shiraz	71
Bakhtaran	431	Tabriz	41
Hamadán	261	Tehran	21

Useful telephone numbers
Police: 110
Ambulance: 123
Fire: 125
General emergencies: 123
Traffic accidents: 197

Chambers of Commerce
British-Iranian Chamber of Commerce, Industries and Mines, 254 Taleghani Avenue, Tehran 15814 (tel 881-0525; fax: 881-0526; e-mail: ibccim@mftmail.com).

Iran Chamber of Commerce, Industries & Mines, 254 Taleghani Avenue, Tehran 15814 (tel: 884-6031; fax: 882-5111; e-mail: info@iccm.org).

Shiraz Chamber of Commerce, Industries and Mines, Zand Street, Shiraz 71356-53564 (tel: 230-4415; fax: 233-1220; e-mail: info@sccim.com).

Tehran Chamber of Commerce, Industries and Mines, 254 Taleghani Avenue, Tehran 15814 (tel: 884-6031; fax: 882-5111; e-mail: info@tccim.com).

Banking
Bank Maskan (Construction Bank), Ave Ferdowsi, Tehran (tel: 675-021/9; fax: 673-262, 673-667).

Bank Mellat, Head Office Bldg, 327 Taleghani Ave, 15817 Tehran (tel: 829-2710).

Bank Melli Iran, PO Box 11365-171, Ferdowsi Avenue, Tehran (tel: 3231; fax: 391-2813).

Bank Refah Kargaran, 40 Northern Shiraz Ave, Mollasadra Ave, 19917 Tehran (tel: 804-2875; fax: 804-1392).

Bank Saderat Iran, PO Box 15745-631, Bank Saderat Tower, 43 Somayeh Avenue, Tehran (tel: 830-6091; fax: 883-9539).

Bank Sepah, PO Box 11364-9569, Imam Khomeini Square, Tehran (tel: 311-1091/9).

Bank Tejarat, PO Box 11365-5416, 130 Taleghani Avenue, Nejatoullahie, 15994 Tehran (tel: 882-6690; fax: 889-3641).

Export Development Bank of Iran, PO Box 15875-5964, 129 Khaled Eslamboli Str, 15139 Tehran (tel: 872-5140; fax: 871-6979).

Central bank
Bank Markazi Jomhouri Islami Iran, PO Box 11365-8551, Ferdowsi Avenue, Tehran, Iran (tel: 311-0101; fax: 311-5674; internet site: http://www.cbi.ir/e/).

Travel information
Exodus, 9 Weir Road, London SW12 0LT, UK (tel: +44(0)20-8675-5550; tour brochures: +44(0)20-8673-0859).

Iran Air (Homa), Iran Air Building, Mehrabad Airport, Tehran 13185 (tel: 600-9111; fax: 600-3248).

Tourist Information Office (tel: 892-212/215); (Mehrabad airport) (tel: 667-785); (railway station) (tel: 555-067).

Ministry of tourism
Ministry of Culture and Islamic Guidance, Baharestan Square, Avenue Kamalolmolk, Tehran (tel: 303-581/5; fax: 311-7535, 311-0840).

National tourist organisation offices
Iran Tourist Co, 257 Motahari Avenue, Tehran 15868 (tel: 873-6762/5; fax: 873-6158; e-mail: info@irantouristco.com; internet site: http://www.irantouristco.com).

Ministries
Ministry of Commerce (internet site: http://www.iran-export.com).

Ministry of Foreign Affairs (internet site: http://mfa.gov.ir).

Ministry of Oil, Taleghani Street, Tehran (tel: 615-118).

Ministry of Science, Research and Technology, Unit 2, Ostad Nejatollahi Street, Teheran (tel: 896-395; fax: 893-310; e-mail: msrt@mche.or.ir).

Other useful addresses
Export Promotion Centre of Iran, PO Box 11-48, Tajrish, Tehran (tel: 821-911; internet site: http://www.tpo.ir).

International Institute for Commercial Relations Development of Continents, No 7 Third Floor, Bazar Abbassi, Ferdowsi Square, PO Box 11, 365-3963, Tehran (tel: 820-697).

Iran International Fair and Exhibition Corporation, PO Box 98, 22 Tadjrish, Tehran.

Iran Water and Power Resources Development Company (IWPC), Building No 1, Sixth Floor, No 212 Nejatollahi Street, Tehran (tel: 880-1038/9; fax: 897-635).

Iranian Interests Section (USA), 2209 Wisconsin Avenue, NW, Washington DC 20007 (tel: 202-965-4990; fax: 202-965-1073; e-mail: requests@daftar.org).

National Iranian Oil Company (NIOC), Taleghani Avenue, Tehran (tel: 646-7432; fax: 646-4281).

Planning and Budget Organisation (Sazman-e-Barnameh va Budje), Meidan-e Baharestan, Tehran.

Statistical Centre of Iran, Dr Fatemi Ave, Tehran 14144 (tel: 655-061/9).

Tehran Stock Exchange, Building No 9 of Bank Markazi, Hafez Avenue, Tehran 11389 (tel: 670-309/219; internet site: http://www.tse.or.ir/tse2/default.asp).

Internet sites
Customs:
http://www.irica.gov.ir/LHomeIE.htm
General information:
http://www.salamiran.org
General political information:
http://www.netiran.com
Iran tourist organisation:
http://www.itto.org/index.asp
Islamic Republic News Agency:
http://www.irna.ir

Iraq

KEY FACTS

Official name: Al Jumhouriya al Iraqia (The Republic of Iraq)

Head of State: President Jalal Talabani (took office 7 Apr 2005)

Head of government: Prime Minister Ibrahim Jaafari (named 7 Apr 2005)

Ruling party: United Iraqi Alliance (sworn in 3 May 2005) The Kurdistan Alliance (in the Kurd-held, semi-autonomous north)

Area: 434,924 square km

Population: 25.39 million (2004)

Capital: Baghdad

Official language: Arabic and Kurdish

Currency: New Iraqi dinar (ID) 1,000 fils

Exchange rate: ID1,469.60 per US$ (Oct 2005); (Iraqi Central Bank auction rate) (New Iraqi dinar introduced 15 Oct 2003)

GDP per capita: US$1,303 (2004)

GDP real growth: 37.30% (2004)

Labour force: 7.23 million (2004)

Unemployment: 27.50% (2004)*

Inflation: 7.00% (2004)

Oil production: 2.03 million bpd (2004)

Balance of trade: US$200.00 million (2004)

Foreign debt: US$125.00 billion (2004)

* estimated figure

It was an historic year for Iraq in 2005, with the populace voting, in January, in the country's first multi-party elections in 50 years. The vote was for a transitional parliament and government to replace the interim government appointed in June 2004. The election of a new parliament in January paved the way for the writing of a new Iraqi constitution, which was approved by a referendum in October, and the election, in December, of Iraq's first full-term parliament and government. It was also one of the most violent 12-month periods in Iraq since the US-led invasion in March 2003. Thousands of Iraqi civilians, members of the Iraqi security services, US-led occupation forces and insurgents were killed in fighting across the country.

Oil dependency

In August 2005, the IMF published its first report on Iraq in 25 years. It warned of a looming economic crisis if Iraq did not manage to secure debt relief. In December, the IMF endorsed a US$685 million loan to Iraq and praised macroeconomic reforms undertaken by the government. The loan approval triggered a positive response among other credit agencies, including the Paris Club of creditor nations, which agreed to write off 80 per cent of Iraq's US$38.9 billion debt over the next four years.

In October, Iraq's oil exports temporarily ground to a halt due to a combination of sabotage and bad weather. Oil exports make up nearly 97 per cent of the

699

Iraqi government's total revenues. GDP grew by an estimated 16.7 per cent in 2005.

Historic elections

Iraqis went to the polls no less than three times in 2005. On 20 January, Iraqis voted for a transitional government. Sunni leaders called for a boycott although with national turnout at 58 per cent, it was evident that some Sunnis ignored this call. A Shi'a-dominated coalition – the United Iraqi Alliance (UIA) – won 48 per cent of the vote and 140 seats in the new, 275-seat transitional parliament. A Kurdish coalition – the Kurdish Alliance (KA) – took 75 seats and a party led by the outgoing interim prime minister Iyad Allawi – the Iraqi National List (INL) – won 40 seats. The UIA and the KA formed a coalition that commanded a two-thirds majority in the parliament and proceeded to dominate the carve-up of government and parliamentary posts. After months of haggling, the first elected post-Ba'athist government was sworn in on 3 May. Ibrahim Jaafari, a Shi'a, was sworn in as prime minister; his cabinet included a mix of Shi'a, Sunni and Kurdish politicians. Earlier, on 7 April, Jalal Talabani was sworn in as Iraqi president – the first Kurd to hold this office in Iraq and the first Kurd ever to serve as head of state in the Arab world. This government was the first non-Sunni dominated government since the 1920s.

Work began in May on drafting a new constitution, although Sunni leaders boycotted the process until July. The committee charged with drafting the constitution missed the original deadline for completion on 15 August but by the end of the month a draft was brought before parliament and approved. Provisions of note were:

- the establishment of a loose, federal-style Iraqi state that recognised the autonomous Kurdish region that had existed in the north of the country since 1991
- an agreement to hold a referendum in the oil-rich city of Kirkuk on the question of whether or not Kirkuk would join the Kurdish region
- recognition of the right of Shi'a-dominated provinces in the south to group together into 'super-regions', subject to referenda
- the recognition of Islam as the source of all laws, provided that these do not contradict democratic principles.

Last minute concessions were granted to Sunni participants in the drafting committee, including a promise to revisit the content of the constitution after national elections scheduled for December.

Sunni leaders urged their followers to vote against the constitution on the grounds that its federalist approach paved the way for the break-up of Iraq. Shi'a and Kurdish leaders called for a 'yes' vote. The referendum, held on 15 October, resulted in a 'yes' vote, 79 per cent to 21 per cent, but not without controversy. Three Sunni-dominated provinces voted against the proposed constitution but not in sufficient numbers to constitute a two-thirds majority in each province – the required threshold for rejection. Some Sunnis subsequently claimed that the vote had been rigged although international observers generally approved the process. Turnout was 63 per cent.

Kurdish Iraqis went to the polls in June to elect a new parliament and president. With Jalal Talabani taking up residence in the presidential palace in Baghdad, Iraqi Kurdistan's other senior leader Massoud Barzani swept the field. Talabani and Barzani had previously struck a deal in which each would back the other, in Baghdad and Iraqi Kurdistan respectively.

Iraqis again went to the polls on 15 December, to elect their first full (ie non-transitional) government since the US-led invasion. The blocs dominating the outgoing transitional government, the UIA and the KA won most seats again – 128 and 53 respectively – down slightly on their performance in January. Smarting from their lack of influence in the previous parliament and constitutional committee, Sunni leaders urged their community to mobilise and vote. Two Sunni-dominated parties took 55 seats between them. The INL of former interim prime minister Iyad Allawi lost nearly half of its seats, taking only 25. Some Sunnis complained that the ballot had been rigged, particularly in the Baghdad area, although international observers generally praised the conduct of the election.

A violent year

It was one of the most violent 12-month periods in Iraq since March 2003. US Joint Chiefs of Staff chairman, General Richard Myers said in April that the insurgents were as strong as they were a year ago but insisted that his forces were winning the war. US and Iraqi forces conducted numerous major operations, particularly in the west of the country, aimed at flushing out insurgents. However, insurgents continued to inflict horrendous losses on civilians and soldiers alike through the use of roadside bombs and suicide bombs. In September alone, suicide bombers killed nearly 200 Iraqi civilians in Baghdad. The US non-governmental organisation Iraqi Coalition Casualty Count (ICCC) estimates that nearly 6,000 Iraqi civilians were killed between April and December 2005. It also estimates that nearly 3,000 Iraqi security personnel were killed in the course of 2005. The ICCC also quotes US Defense Department figures stating that the US armed forces suffered over 6,700 casualties in Iraq in 2005, including more than 800 killed. The number of US forces operating in Iraq rose to an all-time high of 150,000 in 2005. Outgoing prime minister Jaafari has called for their withdrawal, although he did not suggest a timetable.

Outlook

Results for the 15 December election were only announced in January 2006 and negotiations over what the new government

KEY INDICATORS — Iraq

	Unit	2000	2001	2002	2003	2004
Population	m	22.95	23.60	24.00	24.70	25.39
Gross domestic product (GDP)	US$bn	31.80	27.90	25.50	21.58	33.70
GDP per capita	US$	1,376	1,184	1,054	844	1,303
GDP real growth	%	4.0	-6.0	-2.0	-9.5	37.3
Inflation	%	70.0	60.0	70.0	90.0	7.0
Oil output	'000 bpd	2,583.0	2,371.0	2,030.0	1,344.0	2,027.0
Exports (fob) (goods)	US$m	21,800.0	11,040.0	13,300.0	16,543.0	10,100.0
Imports (fob) (goods)	US$m	13,800.0	5,190.0	8,000.0	21,680.0	9,900.0
Imports	US$m	8,000.0	–	–	–	–
Balance of trade	US$m	–	5,850.0	5,300.0	-5,137.0	200.0
Exchange rate	per US$	0.31	0.30	0.31	0.31	^61,450

^ New Iraqi dinar introduced 15 Oct 2003

might look like are on-going. The Shi'a and Kurdish alliance that dominated the previous parliament has an outright majority but there is talk of forming a national unity coalition, encompassing other groups and interests. However, some newly elected Sunni politicians are refusing to participate and are calling for the formation of an official opposition bloc. Thus far the UIA has insisted upon retaining the prime ministerial office and all of the security ministries, including defence and the interior. The Kurds have called for a renewal of incumbent president Talabani's mandate. Senior Sunni leaders have said that they will not tolerate Shi'a dominance of the security ministries, and want the constitution revisited – particularly the federalism clause. They have also threatened a campaign of civil disobedience if their demands are not met.

Shi'a and Kurdish leaders hope that by bringing Sunnis into government, many of the insurgent groups, most of whom are Sunni, could be persuaded to give up their arms – or at least cease fire. This hope will probably override the temptation on the part of the Shi'a and Kurds, who theoretically could form a government on their own, to offer compromises on the thorny issue of the constitution and control of the security ministries. International pressure is certainly being brought to bear to produce this outcome.

Risk assessment

Politics	Formative
Economy	Improving
Regional stability	Fragile

COUNTRY PROFILE

Historical profile
Prior to the First World War, Iraq was part of the Ottoman Empire and was known as the province of Mesopotamia. The Ottomans sided with Germany in the War and after they were defeated, the country was administered by the British under a League of Nations mandate from 1920 until independence in 1932. As the British colonial administrators discovered, Iraq is not one body politic, but three. First, a Sunni Arab minority, long used to ruling the country, largely emanating from what has become known as the 'Sunni Triangle' – the 150km stretch of country from Baghdad north to Tikrit, former president Saddam Hussein's hometown. Secondly, the predominantly southern, Shi'a Arab majority, who felt that they were oppressed and inadequately represented in Baghdad under Saddam Hussein. The third component, the Kurds, long wanted self-rule in northern Iraq. They gained some self-autonomy after the first Gulf War. The creation of an independent Kurdistan could lead to intervention by Turkey, which fears that an independent Kurdish state would eventually encompass parts of southern Turkey. The Kurdish minority has little in common with its Arab compatriots and, if allowed, would happily go its own way.

1920 Iraq was placed under British mandate.
1921 Amir Faisal ibn Hussain (a member of the Arab Hashemite dynasty) was proclaimed Iraq's first King.
1932 Iraq became an independent state.
1933 King Faisal died and was succeeded by his son, Ghazi.
1939 King Ghazi was killed in a car crash and was succeeded by the infant Faisal II, whose uncle, Prince Abd al Ilah, acted as regent.
1953 King Faisal II assumed full powers.
1958 A military coup overthrew the monarchy and a republic was proclaimed.
1963 Pan-Arab elements in the armed forces staged a coup and formed a government under Colonel (later Field Marshal) Abd as Salem Muhammad Aref
1966 Aref was killed in an airplane crash and was succeeded by his brother.
1968 Major General Abd ar Rahman Muhammad Aref was removed from office in a coup organised by the Hizb al Ba'ath al Arabiyah al Ishtiraki (Ba'ath) (Socialist Arab Rebirth Party). The Ba'ath government was headed by Major General Ahmad Hassan al Bakr (a former prime minister) and supreme authority was vested in the Revolutionary Command Council (RCC).
1970 The RCC and the leader of the Kurdistan Democratic Party (KDP) signed a peace agreement.
1972 Iraq nationalised the Iraq Petroleum Company (IPC).
1979 The vice president of the RCC, Saddam Hussein (already the real power in Iraq), replaced Al Bakr as president.
1980–88 The Iran-Iraq War broke out after Iraq invaded Iran over a disputed border area.
1988 A chemical attack ordered by Saddam Hussein on the northern Kurdish town of Halabja, killed 5,000 people.
1990 The Iraqi invasion of Kuwait was condemned by the international community which, led by the US, deployed armed forces to Saudi Arabia. Following the invasion, the United Nations Security Council (UNSC) imposed an arms embargo and economic sanctions on Iraq (Resolution 661) and passed Resolution 678, which authorised member states to use force if Iraq had not withdrawn from Kuwait by 15 January 1991.
1991 The Gulf War started on 16 January. Coalition forces launched an aerial bombing campaign against Iraqi forces in Kuwait and Iraq and US-led ground forces (from around 30 countries, including Syria, Egypt and Morocco) liberated Kuwait.

The UN maintained the arms embargo and economic sanctions on Iraq after the end of the War in an attempt to force it to disarm of weapons of mass destruction (WMD). After a Kurdish and Shi'a Muslim-led uprising was brutally quashed by Saddam Hussein's regime, the US, UK and France imposed 'no-fly zones' on Iraq to protect the Kurds in the north and the Shi'as in the south. The UN adminstered the three northern provinces of Dahuk, Arbil and As Sulaymaniyah, which allowed the Kurds to develop their own semi-autonomous Kurdish enclave, with its own parliament.
1993 The US launched 24 cruise missiles at targets in Baghdad after an alleged Iraqi plot to assassinate former US president George Bush was uncovered.
1994 Saddam Hussein appointed himself prime minister as well as president.
1995 The population voted in a referendum on Saddam Hussein's presidency and, inevitably, supported him. The Iraq oil-for-food programme, administered by the UN, began.
1996 Saddam Hussein's son-in-law, his brother and their families, were granted asylum in Jordan; the two men were subsequently promised a pardon by Saddam Hussein, but were killed on their return to Baghdad. Saddam Hussein's eldest son, Uday, survived an assassination attempt.
1998 Various disputes arose between Iraq and the UN over UN inspections to verify the termination of Iraq's WMD programme; Saddam Hussein excluded the weapons inspectors from Iraq. As a result, the US and the UK launched their largest military attack against Iraq since the Gulf War, bombing installations throughout Iraq.
1999 The spiritual leader of the Shi'a community, Ayatollah Mohammed Sadiq al Sadr, was assassinated in Najaf.
2000 In his capacity as head of the Organisation of the Petroleum Exporting Countries (Opec), President Hugo Chávez Frías of Venezuela travelled overland to Baghdad – the first democratically elected head of state to enter Iraq since the Gulf War.
2001 Five UN officials working for the UN oil-for-food programme were expelled by Iraqi authorities on charges of spying.
2002 A presidential referendum extended Saddam Hussein's rule for another seven years. US President Bush received evidence of terrorist links with Iraq; he demanded that Hussein must prove to the UN weapons inspectors that he disposed of his WMD, as stipulated in the UN

resolution after the Gulf War, the US would launch a war against Iraq. Tony Blair, the UK prime minister confirmed his support for the US. UN weapons inspectors were allowed into Iraq for the first time in four years, however the information they were shown was not sufficient to convince the US that there were no WMD. President Bush included Iraq, North Korea with Iran and a list of countries that supported terrorism as an 'axis of evil'.
2003 After diplomatic efforts to force Iraq to disarm failed and the expiry of an US ultimatum giving Hussein and his sons 48 hours to leave the country, US-led coalition forces invaded Iraq. With central Baghdad under US control, Hussein's government collapsed; the Ba'ath party was abolished, together with institutions of the former regime. The UN Security Council lifted economic sanctions against Iraq. A 25-member Iraq Governing Council (IGC) was appointed with a rotating nine-member presidency. Hussein's sons, Uday and Qusay, were killed in a battle with US troops attempting to arrest them. The leader of the Shi'as, Ayatollah Mohammed Baqr al Hakim, was killed in Najaf. An amended US resolution on Iraq, legitimising the US-led administration, was approved by the UN, which stressed early transfer of power to the Iraqis. The security situation deteriorated as guerrilla warfare intensified. At the end of the year, Saddam Hussein was captured in Tikrit.
2004 After the president of the IGC was killed in a car bomb attack, Iyad Allawi (a Shi'a) was designated prime minister on 28 May and Ghazi al Yawar (a Sunni tribal leader) was chosen as president. An interim 36-member cabinet was appointment to governed Iraq until elections for a fully independent government could be held; it had power-sharing responsibilities with the US-led multinational forces in matters of security. In June, the US handed over sovereignty to the Iraqi interim government. Hussein was transferred into Iraqi legal custody. In August, there was heavy fighting for more than a week in an uprising against coalition troops by Shi'a militia loyal to radical cleric, Moqtada al Sadr, in the holy city of Najaf.
2005 An estimated eight million people voted in the 31 January elections for a Transitional National Assembly. Many Sunni Moslems boycotted the elections, and the Shi'a United Iraqi Alliance won most seats. On 16 March, Iraq's first freely elected parliament in half a century began its opening session after a series of explosions targetted the gathering. Kurdish leader Jalal Talabani was named President, to take office on 7 April. Previous president, and Sunni leader, Ghazi al Yawar, and Shi'ite leader, Adel Abdul Mahdi, were named as deputies. On 7 April, Shi'a leader, Ibrahim Jaafari, was named Prime Minister of the new government, which was sworn in on 3 May. The Kurdish parliament unanimously elected Massoud Barzani as president of the autonomous region of Kurdistan; he was sworn in on 14 June.
The trial of former president, Saddam Hussein, opened on 19 October. He is accused, along with seven others, of murduring 148 people in 1982 in the Shi'a town of Dujail. It was adjourned for 40 days after defence lawyers said they needed more time to examine the prosecution's documents. It was resumed on 28 November but adjourned again, until 5 December, after one of the defendants said that he had been unable to replace his original attorney, who had been murdered.
2006 The chief judge, Rizgar Amin, in the trial of Saddam Hussein tendered his resignation on 15 January. Judge Raouf Adbul Rahman was appointed to replace him on an interim basis.

Political structure
Constitution
A public referendum approved a new permanent constitution on 15 October 2005. It came into effect when the elections for the Council of Representatives took place on 15 December 2005.
The constitution declares that the Republic of Iraq is an independent, sovereign nation, and its system of governance is democratic, federal, and representative (parliamentary). Islam is the official religion of the state and is a basic source of legislation. Iraq is part of the Arab nation and the Islamic world.
Universal suffrage begins at aged 18.
The country is divided into 18 provinces (*muhafazat*, singular *muhafazahW0*): al Anbar, al Basrah, al Muthanna, al Qadisiyah, An Najaf, Arbil, As Sulaymaniyah, At Ta'mim, Babil, Baghdad, Dahuk, Dhi Qar, Diyala, Karbala', Maysan, Ninawa, Salah ad Din and Wasit.
Form of state
Republic, federal
The executive
Executive authority consists of the Presidency Council, the Council of Ministers, presided over by the prime minister.
The Presidency Council consists of the president and two deputies; they are elected by the national assembly.
National legislature
The unicameral Majlis al Watani (National Assembly), with 275 members elected in January 2005, convened for the first time on 16 March 2005.
There is a 115-seat Kurdish parliament in the semi-autonomous northern governorates.

Legal system
Under the constitution the Judiciary is independent and represented by courts of different kinds and levels, issuing their rulings according to law. No authority can interfere in the judiciary or in the affairs of justice.
The Federal Judiciary includes the Supreme Judiciary Council, and the Supreme Federal Court. The Iraqi court system is divided into the Civil Courts, Courts of Personal Status, and Criminal Courts.
Last elections
31 January 2005 (parliamentary); 27 March 2000 (elections to 220 seats in the 250-seat National Assembly).
Results: Parliamentary: the Shiite religious list, known as the United Iraqi Alliance, received 48 per cent of the votes (about 132 seats out of the 275 seats in the National Assembly); the main Kurdish alliance 25 per cent (about 70 seats); Interim Prime Minister Iyad Allawi's group under 14 per cent (about 38 seats) and the largest Sunni-Arab-led ticket, topped by Interim President Ghazi al Yawar, less than 2 per cent (four or five seats).
Next elections
December 2005
Political parties
Ruling party
United Iraqi Alliance (sworn in 3 May 2005) The Kurdistan Alliance (in the Kurd-held, semi-autonomous north)
Main opposition party
The National Iraqi List, is a coalition of secular nationalists made up of Sunni and Shi'a Moslems; Iraqi Accord Front is an alliance of three Sunni parties.

Population
25.39 million (2004)
Ethnic make-up
Arabs comprise 75 per cent of the population, with Kurds representing a further 20 per cent (mostly located in northern Iraq) and Turkmen, Assyrian and other minorities making up the remaining 5 per cent.
Religions
Shi'a (also known as Shi'ite, Shiite, Shi'is) Muslims are the largest religious group, comprising 54 per cent of the population. Sunni Muslims were politically dominant in the Saddam Hussein period, although accounting for only 42 per cent of the total. There is a significant number of Christians and a small number of Yazidis and others.

Education
After the 2003 Iraq War, attempts began to re-build Iraq's education system. In June 2003, the US Agency for International Development (USAID) granted

US$2 million to provide immediate educational needs.

Free education is provided for children between the ages of six and 18.

Literacy rate: 40.1 per cent total, 24.1 per cent female, adult rates in 2002 (World Bank).

Compulsory years: Six and 12

Pupils per teacher: 20 in primary schools.

Health

By August 2004, safe drinking water was available to only 54 per cent of the population and only 37 per cent of households were connected to a sewage system. The CPA allowcated US$2.8 billion to improve the water system.

HIV prevalence: 0.1 per cent aged 15–49 in 2003 (World Bank)

Life expectancy: 63.1 years (World Bank)

Fertility rate/Maternal mortality rate: 4.0 births per woman (World Bank)

Infant mortality rate: 102 per 1,000 live births (World Bank)

Head of population per physician/bed: 32,000 hospital beds and over 6,000 doctors (World Bank).

Looting following the collapse of Saddam Hussein's regime left hospitals without adequate supplies and facilities.

Welfare

Iraq is struggling to repair its social infrastructure, welfare and pensions are being administered in an *ad hoc* manner until the newly elected government can get to grips with the economy and implement nationwide policies.

All political parties, during the January 2005 election campaign, advocated the introduction of comprehensive state subsidies and welfare measures and to aleviate the widespread poverty the government may have to invest heavily in its welfare programmes.

Main cities

Baghdad (capital, estimated population 6.0 million in 2004), Mosul (1.9 million), Basra (1.5 million), Arbil (864,900), Kirkuk (755,700), Sulaymaniyah (662,600).

Languages spoken

French and English are spoken in business.

Official language/s

Arabic and Kurdish

Media

The media has been liberated from the official sanctions of censorship however it is now under physical threat from terrorist activities that have targetted reporters and media personnel.

Press

Dailies: Publications include *Al Mada*, *Al Mashriq*, *Al Dustur* and *Al Ittihad* (Kurdish newspaper).

In 2003, the London-based *Al Zaman* newspaper was made available in southern Iraq, providing Iraqi and international news.

Weeklies: Included are *Al Iqtisadi Al Jadidand* (The New Economist), *Al Zawra* (official journal of the Iraqi National Union of Journalists), *Al Iraq Al Riyadhi* (sports) and *Al Siyasah Al Yawm* (Politics Today). The IWN publishes *Al Sabah* twice weekly, providing news on the CPA.

Periodicals: The English language *Baghdad Observer* was a relatively popular periodical before 1991, but its circulation has subsequently fallen sharply.

Broadcasting

Radio: The domestic service is in Arabic, Kurdish and other minority languages; external service is in numerous languages. The main station is the *Republic of Iraq Radio*; since 2003 more than 20 radio stations began operations.

Television: The US and UK took over state television frequencies and began broadcasting the first Iraq-based television channel in May 2003.

A private station *Al Sharqiya* broadcasts by terrestrial and via satellite.

Economy

It is inevitable that an economy so badly ground down by years of distortion and exploitation has only one way to go once liberated and the Iraqi economy showed this when growth jumped by 37.3 per cent in 2004, from a negative growth of 9.5 per cent in 2003.

Recovery in the oil sector was the primary reason for the growth. The IMF has cautioned that the state of the economy under the Emergency Post Conflict Assistance (EPCA) programme intended to help with the necessary economic restructuring, post-Saddam Hussein, is not as healthy as it was expected to be. The security situation is hampering efforts to repair the infrastructure with contractors and donors stating that insurance outlays ranged from 30–50 per cent of total costs. Violence has deterred trade and investment, while the political conditions are slowing down administrative changes needed to affect institutional capacities.

Unemployment is high with various rates quoted, from the most pessimistic at 70 per cent (Baghdad University) to 28 per cent (ministry of planning). The UN Development Programme, using the International Labor Organisation (ILO) methodology, calculated a rate of 10.5 per cent (excluding discouraged workers) in 2004, however there was a disproportionate rate among young, educated workers of 37 per cent (including discouraged workers).

Inflation from June–May 2004–05 was 37 per cent, exceeding the 15 per cent EPCA programme projection for the end 2005. Government spending on goods and services was larger than budgeted due to greater outlays for defence and security. Structural reforms to the economy have been slow with delays including the commitment to increase domestic prices for refined oil products.

The IMF recommended that foreign debt rescheduling had to be addressed as a priority. On 1 November 2004 the Paris Club of international sovereign lenders agreed to reschedule 80 per cent, of the debt held by them, in three stages. Iraq's debt, after the first stage of debt reduction, was estimated to be around US$78 billion (reduced from US$114 billion before the rearrangement) or the equivalent of three times the GDP. Without the two further stages of Paris Club rescheduling Iraq's debt will be unsustainable. A meeting with private creditors was also held in Dubai in May 2005.

The balance of payments is dominated by oil. There were large current account deficits in 2004/05, funded largely by assets held abroad and frozen during the period of sanctions.

The medium-term outlook appears satisfactory, providing the expansion of oil production continues uninterrupted and world prices for oil remain buoyant. Growth in GDP is expected to reach 17 per cent in 2006 and then decline to 7 per cent by 2010. Non-oil growth should remain strong, sustained by much public investment as the country rebuilds itself. Inflation is expected to fall as shortages end.

Analysts are agreed that security is the key to Iraq's success. With a large reserve of oil, it has the potential to provide much for its citizens, but the political situation, as violent acts attempt to drive a wedge between the different communities, will determine whether the success can be sustained.

External trade

Iraq has an open trade investment regime whereby a customs duty of 5 per cent is levied on all import goods, except primary commodities such as food, medicines, clothing and humanitarian items.

The Trade Bank of Iraq (TBI) was established to provide financial and related services to facilitate imports and exports.

Iraq applied the WTO for membership in 2004.

Imports

Imports include food, medicines and manufactured goods. US goods to be

imported during 2006 will be US$2.2 billion.
Main sources: Turkey (25.0 per cent total, 2004), US (11.1 per cent), Jordan (10.0 per cent), Vietnam (7.7 per cent), Germany (5.6 per cent), Australia (4.8 per cent)

Exports
Main exports include crude oil (83.9 per cent), crude materials excluding fuels, food and live animals.
Main destinations: US (55.8 per cent total, 2004), Spain (8.0 per cent), Japan (7.3 per cent), Italy (6.5 per cent), Canada (5.8 per cent)

Agriculture
Farming
The area of cultivatable land in Iraq is estimated to be around 12 million hectares (ha). About four million ha of this arable land consists of rain-fed agriculture and the remaining eight million depends on irrigation. Less than 50 per cent of this land is actually cultivated. However, irrigation systems are badly in need of repair and salinity is increasingly affecting large areas of arable land.
The most important crops are barley and wheat (yields of each exceed one million tonnes in a good year) and rice; and after cereals, which account for most of the arable land, cotton, dates, vegetables and fruit.
Historically, dates were the most valuable exports after oil (with an annual value of around US$75 million). Production plummeted due to the war with Iran (1980–88), and to pollution which affected millions of trees in the south, following the 1991 Gulf War.

Fishing
There is a small fishing industry, mostly based on the Tigris and Euphrates rivers. Without import and export activities it will remain insignificant.

Forestry
Forests cover around 800,000ha, or 1.8 per cent of the land area and are mainly confined to the northern part of the country. There is no significant commercial exploitation.

Industry and manufacturing
Iraq's major industries centre on the petroleum, chemical, textile, construction and food processing sectors. Much of Iraq's industrial base was affected by war and sanctions. Before the 1991 Gulf War, Iraq was second only to Saudi Arabia in terms of oil production and reserves.
Iraq's oil industry was boosted and re-invested into by the UN oil-for-food programme, although it was far from pre-1991 levels. During 2004 and 2005 there were efforts to re-build Iraq's industrial and manufacturing base, particularly in oil production.

Tourism
Tourism could bring a great deal of revenue into the economy. Since August 2003, the Baghdad Institute for Tourism and Hotels is offering a graduation class to the country's travel industry.

Mining
The mining sector contributes about 8 per cent to GDP and employs 4 per cent of the working population.
Iraq has huge resources of phosphates and its sulphur reserves are among the world's largest; there is significant potential for sulphur exports.
Other minerals include glass sand, raw materials for the construction industry, and modest quantities of iron ore, lead, copper and gypsum.

Hydrocarbons
Iraq has proven oil reserves of 15.5 billion tonnes of oil in 2004; production was 2.0 million barrels per day (bpd), an increased of 50.8 per cent on 2003. The IMF estimated that crude oil exports accounted for 76.7 per cent of GDP in 2004. Increased production is being planned with 3.3 million bpd projected for 2009.
In 2003, the UN granted the US permission to control Iraq's oil revenues through a specially created development fund, which is monitored by an international advisory board.
There are also proven natural gas reserves of 3.1 trillion cubic metres (cum) in 2004, just under 15 per cent of global reserves. About 70 per cent of Iraq's natural gas supplies are by-products of oil production. Prior to the 1991 Gulf War, Iraq was producing up to 20 billion cum of natural gas per annum, but this fell sharply during 1991–2002.The largest gas fields are in the north at Kirkuk, and in Rumaila and Zubair in the south.
Iraq has some small low-grade coal deposits, with some limited exploitation before 1990 suppling the domestic chemicals industry. These mines are thought to have fallen into disuse following the destruction of industrial capacity and imposition of UN sanctions.

Energy
Much of Iraqi's national power grid, including 20 power stations, was destroyed or damaged by coalition bombing in the 1991 Gulf War. Further damage was done during the 2003 Iraq War when the Baghdad power grid was badly damaged. By July 2003, it was estimated that no more than 3,600MW of electricity was being generated. Another 2,000MW is required to meet the country's needs in the short-term. By December 2005 5 per cent of the population had electricity for 24 hours/7 days a week, 40 per cent had more than eight hours per day and 15 per cent had only 2–4 hours per day. As an indicator of the quality of modern life, more has to be done to improve the service for most of the population to benefit.

Financial markets
Stock exchange
The Iraq Stock Exchange (ISX), was re-opened on 24 June 2004. It is an independent, self-regulating institution with the Iraq Securities and Exchange Commission overseeing proceedings.
The initial plan was to relist 10–15 stocks per month. Companies have to have their accounts verified and international auditors and major shareholders have to be vetted to exclude former regime members. The exchange processed the 589 million shares traded on the first day manually and will continue to do so until the contract for new electronic equipment is fulfilled.

Banking and insurance
The banking systems, according to the IMF in 2005, is weak and barely functioning. It comprises the Central Bank of Iraq and 26 chartered banks. Two state-owned banks, the Rafidain and Rashid Banks, account for over 90 per cent of the commercial banking assets and 75 per cent of the local branch network. These institutions are heavily over-staffed with too many staff under-skilled and the government may invite foreign involvement in restructuring them. It may also amalgamate four of the smaller, and specialised banks into two regional development banks and well establishing new Islamic banks.
In 2003, the Trade Bank of Iraq (TBI) was established to provide financial and related services to facilitate imports and exports. It is independent of the Central Bank of Iraq.
The authorities will be implementing international accounting and auditing standards, and improving disclosure requirements, to adhere to recognised practices in good governance.
Central bank
Central Bank of Iraq

Time
GMT plus three hours (GMT plus four hours April–September)

Geography
Iraq is bounded by Turkey to the north, Iran to the east, Kuwait to the south-east, and Saudi Arabia, Jordan and Syria to the west. There is also a neutral zone between Iraq and Saudi Arabia administered jointly by the two countries with Iraq's portion covering 3,522 square km. The country's most fertile area and heartland is the flood plain of the Tigris and Euphrates rivers, which flow in parallel for most of their length from the Turkish and Syrian

Iraq

borders respectively, to the Gulf. The north-east of Iraq is mountainous while the large western desert area is sparsely populated and undeveloped.

Climate
There is an excessively hot sub-tropical period with no rainfall from May–September (38–49 degrees Celsius (C)). Dry and pleasantly warm from October–April (20–25 degrees C), with occasional heavy rain. Continental conditions affect the northern mountainous areas which experience severe winters, but the southern plains have warm winters with some rain and very hot, dry summers. The temperature in Baghdad ranges from between 4 degrees C and 16 degrees C in January, to between 24 degrees C and 33 degrees C in July and August. Average annual rainfall is 300mm.

Dress codes
Conservative and modest dress should be worn in public in conformity with local Islamic traditions. Safari suits or short-sleeved suits are acceptable for men at work or at informal meetings; lounge suits in light materials are worn for formal meetings and in the evening.

Entry requirements
All requirements are subject to change and should be thoroughly checked before departure.
Passports
Passports are required by all.
Visa
All advice on obtaining visas should be made through the consular section of the visitor's own representative embassy.
Prohibited entry
Nationals of Israel and holders of passports with evidence of travel in Israel are denied entry.
Currency advice/regulations
A currency declaration form must be completed on arrival and departure.
Customs
Before the war, personal effects were duty-free. Customs duty was imposed on a motor vehicle after two months. Certain 'non-essential' goods are prohibited. The export of antiques and artefacts is prohibited.

Health (for visitors)
Travellers should be aware of the poor capacity of Iraqi hospitals to extend medical care and that communications and essential services, including power and water cannot be relied upon.
Mandatory precautions
A certificate of vaccination against yellow fever, if travelling from an infected area.
Advisable precautions
Precautions should include vaccinations against cholera, typhoid, tetanus, polio, hepatitis 'A' and 'B' and TB, as well as malaria prophylaxes. All water should be regarded as being potentially contaminated. Water used for drinking, brushing teeth or making ice should be boiled or otherwise sterilised. Dairy products are likely to be unpasteurised and should be avoided. Eat only well-cooked meat and fish, preferably served hot. Vegetables should be cooked and fruit peeled. Pork, salad and mayonnaise may carry increased risk.

Comprehensive medical insurance covering repatriation is essential. There are severe shortages of essential drugs. Detailed health advice should be sought before visiting Iraq.

Hotels
Payment in hard currency is required.

Credit cards
Not in use.

Public holidays
Fixed dates
1 Jan (New Year's Day), 6 Jan (Army Day), 8 Feb (Ramadan Revolution), 17 Apr (FAO Day), 1 May (Labour Day), 14 Jul (National Day), 17 Jul (Republic Day), 8 Aug (End of Iran-Iraq War).
Variable dates
Eid al Adha, Islamic New Year, Ashura, Birth of the Prophet, Eid al Fitr.
The Islamic year contains 354 or 355 days, with the result that Muslim feasts advance by 10–12 days against the Gregorian calendar. Dates of feasts vary according to the sighting of the new moon, so cannot be forecast exactly. Islamic year 1426: 10 February 2005 to 30 January 2006.

Working hours
The weekly closing day is Friday.
Banking
Summer hours: Sat–Wed: 0800–1200; Thu: 0800–1100. Winter hours: Sat–Wed: 0900–1300; Thu: 0900–1200.
Business
Sat–Wed: 0800–1400; Thursday: 0800–1300.
Government
Summer hours: Sat–Wed: 0800–1200; Thu: 0800–1100. Winter hours: Sat–Wed: 0830–1430 Thu: 0830–1330.
Shops
Small shops tend to open very early, close during the middle of the day and then re-open from around 1600–1900 or later. Food markets open around 0900 and close at mid-day or when supplies are exhausted.

Telecommunications
Mobile phones
Satellite telephones provide the only reliable means of communications..

Electricity supply
220V AC, 50 cycles

Weights and measures
Metric system.

Social customs/useful tips
Traditional Islamic culture predominates, with Quranic law playing an active role in the day-to-day life of the country. Visitors should be careful to respect this and act accordingly. They should always address their hosts by full name and title. Traditional Arab hospitality is generally offered. In business meetings formal courtesies are expected. Visiting cards are regularly exchanged and these should be printed in Arabic as well as English. Meetings may not always be on a one-to-one basis and it is often difficult to confine conversation to the business in hand, as many topics may be discussed in order to assess the character of potential business partners. Patience and good humour are required. Always refer to the stretch of water south of Iraq as the Arabian Gulf or the Gulf – never the Persian Gulf.

It is unwise to discuss religion or politics, and desirable to have an informed view on contemporary issues (such as Israel) in case such subjects arise.

During the Ramadan fasting month, both smoking and drinking in public are forbidden.

Security
Although major combat operations have ended, the security situation in Iraq remains dangerous. Guerillas have been targetting coalition interests and personnel as well as international agencies, such as the UN and the Red Cross.

Getting there
Air
National airline: Iraqi Airways. In September 2004, Iraqi Airways resumed international flights to Syria and Jordan, twice a week.
International airport/s: Baghdad International Airport (BGW), 18km west of Baghdad; Basra International Airport.
Other airport/s: Smaller airfields exist at Hadithah, Kirkuk and Mosul.
Airport tax: ID2000
Surface
Road: The only two borders open are the highway from Amman, Jordan, to Baghdad (2,331km across the desert) and from Turkey via the road through Zakho and Mosul; this crosses Iraqi Kurdistan territory and the Kurds sometimes impose taxes on goods carried.
Travel by road remains hazardous and is not recommended.
Rail: The line between Mosul and Aleppo, Syria was reopened, although the service was suspended.
Main port/s: Umm Qasr and Khor al Zubair are the major commercial ports.

Nations of the World: A Political, Economic and Business Handbook

Getting about
National transport
Air: Services are subject to US military restrictions. Prior to 2003 Iraqi Airways flew from Baghdad to Basra. There are domestic airports at Mosul and Kirkuk.

Road: Despite the Iraq War, the country's 40,800km road system is in relatively good condition with 84 per cent paved.

Rail: The rail network includes some three-class services with sleeping accommodation, restaurant cars and air-conditioning. Rail links between most major centres include Baghdad-Mosul, Baghdad-Arbil and Baghdad-Basra.

City transport
Taxis: Taxis are available in major cities and at hotels. There are shared and regular taxis. There is a standard fare system, but inflation overtakes it. Taxis have meters, but it is legal to charge double the amount shown on the clock. A surcharge is made after 2200 hours. Fares should be clearly agreed in advance. Tipping is not expected.

Car hire
Cars are available for hire in Baghdad, but visitors require valid national and international driving licences. Third-party insurance is compulsory. International traffic signs are used.

BUSINESS DIRECTORY
The addresses listed below are a selection only. While World of Information makes every endeavour to check these addresses, we cannot guarantee that changes have not been made, especially to telephone numbers and area codes. We would welcome any corrections.

Telephone area codes
The international direct dialling code (IDD) for Iraq is +964, followed by area code and subscriber's number:

City	Code	City	Code
Baghdad	1	Mosul	60
Basra	40	Najaf	33
Erbil	66	Nasiriya	42
Kirkuk	50	Sulayimaniya	53
Kut	23	Tikrit	21

Useful telephone numbers
Police: 104
Directory enquiries: 102
Operator: 537-2191
International operator: 105
Fire: 115
Ambulance: 122
Speaking clock: 106
Emergency hospital: 719-5191

Chambers of Commerce
Federation of Iraqi Chambers of Commerce, Sadoon Street, PO Box 3388 Al-Alwia, Baghdad (tel: 718-7348; fax: 718-1115; e-mail: union@uruklink.net).

Baghdad Chamber of Commerce, Mustansir Street, PO Box 24168 Almsarif, Baghdad (tel: 887-6111; fax: 887-9563).

Basrah Chamber of Commerce, Al-Azizyah Street, Alashad, Basrah (tel: 211-343; fax: 212-478).

Mosul Chamber of Commerce, Khalid Ibn Al-Waleed, PO Box 35, Mosul (tel: 774-771; fax: 771-359).

Banking
Bank of Baghdad, PO 3192, Alawiyah (tel: 822-7083).

Credit Bank of Iraq, PO Box 3420, Baghdad (tel: 360-0494).

Dar Es Salaam Investment Bank, PO Box 3067, Alawiyah (tel: 360-4646).

Industrial Bank of Iraq, al Khullani Square, PO Box 5825, Baghdad (tel: 887-2181).

Iraq Middle East Investment Bank, PO Box 10379, Baghdad (tel: 360-4242).

Rafidain Bank, New Banks' Street, Massarif, PO Box 11360, Baghdad (tel: 887-0522: fax: 415-8616).

Rashid Bank, PO Box 7177, Tourism Building, Haifa Street, Baghdad (tel: 884-5287, 885-3433; fax: 882-62001).

Central bank
Central Bank of Iraq, PO Box 64, Rashid Street, Baghdad, Iraq (tel: 886-5171; fax: 886-6802).

Travel information
Baghdad International Airport, Baghdad (tel: 887-2500, 886-3999; fax: 887-5808).

Ministries
Directorate of Foreign Economic Relations, Ministry of Trade, Khulafa Street, al Khullani Square, Baghdad (tel: 887-2682).

Ministry of Industry and Military Industrialisation, Nidhal Street, near Sa'adoun Petrol Station, Baghdad (tel: 887-2006).

Ministry of Oil, al Mansour, PO Box 6178, Baghdad (tel: 541-0031).

Other useful addresses
Iraq National Oil Company, al Khullani Square, PO Box 476, Baghdad (tel: 887-1115).

Iraqi Federation of Industries, Iraqi Federation of Industries Building, al Khullani Square, Baghdad.

Iraqi Interests Section (USA), 1801 P Street, NW, Washington DC 20036 (tel: (1)202-483-7500; fax: (1)202-462-5066).

Internet sites
Coalition Provisional Authority: www.cpa-iraq.org

Iraq Stock Exchange: www.isx-iq.net

Ireland

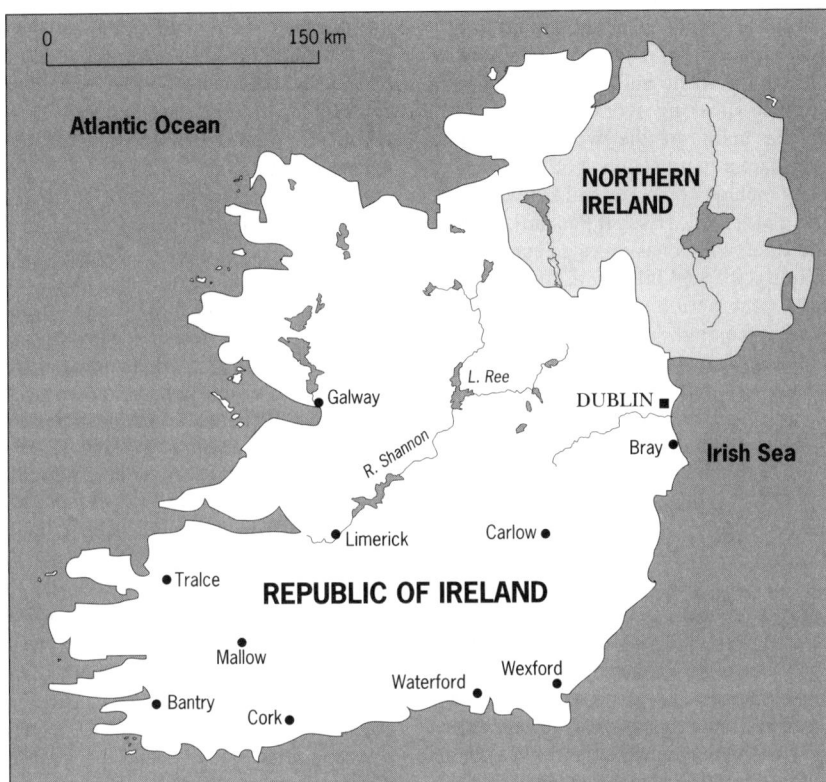

Ireland's President Mary McAleese, re-appointed in October 2004, succeeded former leader Mary Robinson seven years previously. This was the first time in history that a woman has succeeded another woman as an elected head of state anywhere in the world. Economic growth remained successful in 2005 and there was a breakthrough in the IRA peace process.

What a difference a decade makes

In 1984, Ireland was described as 'overtaxed, over-borrowed and underutilised'. A rising tax burden, inflation and growing unemployment, living standards which had fallen by over 10 per cent in five years all added up to a pretty gloomy picture. The then minister of finance summed up the position 'consumption has declined, investment has fallen and growth has been stifled'.

In 2005 Ireland's macroeconomic prospects could not have looked much better. Better, in fact than the wildest dreams of the politicians who were running Ireland 20 years earlier. The IMF in 2005 said that they believed Ireland to have virtually full employment. In 2004 the Organisation for Economic Co-operation and Development (OECD) ranked Ireland ahead of the United Kingdom in terms of price adjusted GDP per capita. Ireland was also ranked second to Luxembourg in terms of wage-earners' spending power in 2003. These two countries have something else in common. In an European Commission survey carried out in December 2005 it was the Luxembourg and Irish citizens who gave the EU the highest approval rating – at 82 and 73 per cent respectively, compared to only 33 per cent of British citizens.

Ireland's economic development and rapid transformation owes a lot to its low levels of taxation, introduced by the architect of recovery, former finance minister Charlie McCreevy. He is now the EU internal market commissioner.

KEY FACTS

Official name: Éire (Ireland)

Head of State: President Mary McAleese (elected 30 October 1997; was returned unopposed to a second seven-year term 1 Oct 2004)

Head of government: Prime Minister Bertie Ahern (leader of Fianna Fáil) (since 1997; re-appointed 6 Jun 2002)

Ruling party: Coalition government led by Fianna Fáil (Soldiers of Destiny) (since Jun 2002)

Area: 70,283 square km

Population: 4.02 million (2004); 3.95 million (OECD, 2003)

Capital: Dublin

Official language: Irish (Gaelic) and English

Currency: Euro (eur) = 100 cents (from 1 Jan 2002; previous currency, punt, locked at IR£0.79 per euro)

Exchange rate: eur0.83 per US$ (Oct 2005)

GDP per capita: US$44,888 (2004)

GDP real growth: 5.10% (2004)

Labour force: 1.90 million (2004)

Unemployment: 4.50% (OECD, 2004)

Inflation: 2.30% (2004)

Balance of trade: US$39.56 billion (2004)*; US$39.91 billion (2003)

Foreign debt: US$944.95 billion (2004)

Annual FDI: US$139.30 billion (cumulative, 1995–2004, OECD); US$14.10 billion (OECD, 2004)*

* estimated figure

In April 2005 the Irish Stock Exchange introduced the Irish Enterprise Exchange (IEX), specifically designed to benefit small- and medium- sized companies. There is a minimum market capitalisation but otherwise no other admission criteria, unlike the main stock exchange.

The benefits of Ireland's spectacular macroeconomic turnaround are not, however, evenly spread. According to the United Nations, Ireland has the highest levels of inequality of all Western countries except the US. The OECD puts Ireland's poverty level at 15.3 per cent, one of the highest in the EU. The Roman Catholic Church, local councillors and newspaper commentators have all criticised the government for underspending on welfare. In December 2005, the finance ministry went some way to addressing the problem of the country's image as a tax haven. The exemptions for pop stars and racehorse owners will be tightened and a lot of the high earners' tax breaks and tax relief available for property investment have been scrapped. These reforms will be helpful in reducing the gulf between the highest and lowest earners, and the widespread perception of the unfairness of the tax system.

McCreevy had also managed to alienate a large proportion of Ireland's 103,000 civil servants by proposing that half of them should be re-located from the capital, Dublin, by 2007. The government justified the re-location proposals as part of a wider regional development plan. Around 25 per cent of Ireland's population live in or around Dublin. While the containment of public expenditure was welcomed by EU officials in Brussels, some economists considered it overly cautious in an economy with regular growth levels of 5 per cent.

On McCreevy's watch Ireland's corporation tax was cut to 12.5 per cent (compared to 30 per cent in the UK), a move that attracted criticism from the unreformed economies of fellow EU members France, Germany and Italy. Low taxation, a relatively stable political environment and a well-educated English speaking workforce have attracted many of the world's leading manufacturers to set up shop in Ireland. They include computer and software giants IBM, Dell, Hewlett Packard, Apple and Intel, which has invested some eur7 billion (US$8.64 billion) in Ireland over a 14 year period. In September 2005 Wyeth, the tenth largest global pharmaceutical company, opened a new US$2 billion production facility in South County Dublin. It is one of the largest biotech plants in the world and employs more than 1,000 people.

Another major investment project underway is Shell's US$1.1 billion natural gas project off the western coast of the country. The development will meet 60 per cent of Irish gas needs and will come on stream in 2007. Work was held up in 2005, however, by disputes over the laying of a gaspipe. Five Rossport farmers refused to allow the pipe to run through their land and were jailed after ignoring a court ruling supporting the gas company. The case has generated bad publicity for the investment climate in Ireland. FDI inflows fell dramatically from 2003 to 2004 however, from US$27 billion to US$9 billion. This can be explained by a downturn in inward equity investment.

End of an era?

After 2003, Ireland ceased to receive structural funding from Brussels, regarded by many economists as a key catalyst in the republic's dramatic growth since EU membership. Ireland will continue to benefit from the Common Agricultural Policy (CAP). Despite the loss of funding and its contribution to GDP, the OECD still forecast a 5 per cent growth rate in 2005 and 4.9 per cent for 2006.

Although the services sector continues to be Ireland's most important, generating almost 50 per cent of GDP, the manufacturing sector, thanks to FDI, now accounts for almost one-third of GDP and 80 per cent of exports. Ireland's economy is highly dependent on international trade and in 2005 invisible trade – from services – improved. The UK remains Ireland's biggest export market.

Ireland's sustained economic strength and regular budget surpluses up until 2002, have enabled it to reduce its external debt from 95.2 per cent of GDP in 1990 to a more acceptable 30 per cent of GDP in 2005, now one of the lowest rates in the EU.

Like many other Western countries Ireland has to face the prospect of an ageing population. However, Ireland is better placed to deal with this social change than most, with good workplace conditions for the over-60s and a high effective retirement age.

External relations

By 2004 Ireland's relations with the UK, its biggest trading partner, had improved beyond recognition from the dark days of the 1970s when the Northern Ireland issue had polarised the two governments. The Irish *Taoiseach* (prime minister) Bertie Ahern had worked closely with the UK's Prime Minister Tony Blair to establish some sort of normality in the province under the aegis of the Good Friday Agreement of 1998.

In December 2004 the IRA was suspected of carrying out a multimillion pound bank robbery from Northern Bank. The IRA denied involvement but a former Sinn Fein politician was among the arrested suspects. Following the robbery, Tony Blair warned Sinn Fein would have to stop all violent and criminal activity otherwise it would be barred from the power sharing government in Northern Ireland. The Irish defence minister, Willie

KEY INDICATORS — Ireland

	Unit	2000	2001	2002	2003	2004
Population	m	3.78	3.80	3.84	3.93	4.02
Gross domestic product (GDP)	US$bn	95.30	103.40	119.90	148.60	*183.56
GDP per capita	US$	25,340	27,140	31,190	39,030	44,888
GDP real growth	%	9.9	6.0	6.1	3.6	5.1
Inflation	%	5.6	4.9	4.7	4.1	2.3
Unemployment	%	4.3	3.8	4.4	4.8	4.5
Exports (fob) (goods)	US$m	73,433.0	78,371.0	88,470.0	92,695.0	98,745.0
Imports (fob) (goods)	US$m	48,017.0	48,369.0	51,940.0	52,789.0	59,183.0
Balance of trade	US$m	25,416.0	30,003.0	32,000.0	39,906.0	39,562.0
Current account	US$m	-593.0	-1,043.0	-176.0	-2,990.0	-2,660.0
Total reserves minus gold	US$m	5,360.0	5,587.0	5,415.0	4,079.0	2,831.0
Foreign exchange	US$m	4,983.0	5,196.0	4,879.0	3,425.0	2,324.0
Exchange rate	per US$	0.85	0.86	1.04	0.88	0.80

* estimated figure

O'Dea, stated that Dublin could 'no longer now turn a blind eye to criminality'. The bank heist along with the highly publicised murder of Robert McCartney, a Belfast Catholic man, both combined to the dwindling of sympathy for the IRA, both domestically and in the US. In April 2005 the president of Sinn Fein, Gerry Adams, instructed the IRA to reject 'armed struggle', and to 'fully embrace and accept' peaceful means. The link between the IRA and Sinn Fein, the political wing, appeared to be broken. Tony Blair called the announcement 'significant'.

Outlook

Ireland's economic prospects in an enlarged EU remain good. The loss of EU structural funding will slow down infrastructural development, much of which is still urgently needed if the economy is to maintain its rapid growth rate. Ireland's next elections are not due until 2007, which leaves the Fianna Fáil and its coalition partners, the Progressive Democrats, time to focus more on social reforms and improvements, an essential step if they are to recover popularity and have a realistic prospect of re-election.

Risk assessment

Economic	Good
Political	Good
Regional Stability	Good
Stock Market	Good

COUNTRY PROFILE

Historical profile

In the twelfth century, the Norman invasion began a long period of foreign domination. Over the centuries, Irish Catholic hostility increased along with English control, following the seizure of land, the Protestant Reformation and the loss of religious and political freedoms.
1801 Ireland was united with Great Britain through the Act of Union.
1840s The potato crop was blighted over several years, leading to severe famine. Combined with emigration, this reduced the population by one-third. The decade also saw the beginnings of a republican movement.
1916 The British army suppressed the republican Easter Rising, provoking the formation of Sinn Féin (Ourselves alone).
1919–21 The Anglo-Irish War was fought against British troops and police by the military arm of Sinn Féin, the Irish Republican Army (IRA).
1921 Partition saw 26 southern counties form the Irish Free State under the British crown, while the six north-eastern counties remained part of the UK.
1922 The Dáil Eireann (Irish parliament) ratified the treaty establishing the Free State, sparking a civil war with nationalists, who advocated full independence, led by Eamonn De Valera.
1927 De Valera entered parliament as the head of the newly-created Fianna Fáil (Soldiers of Destiny).
1932 Fianna Fáil won the elections. De Valera began to work towards full independence from Britain.
1937 The constitution was promulgated, abolishing the Free State and declaring Ireland as an independent state.
1938 Douglas Hyde became the country's first president, with De Valera as prime minister.
1939–45 Ireland remained neutral during the Second World War, but many Irishmen fought in the British Army acting on behalf of the Irish state.
1948 Fianna Fáil lost the election and De Valera was replaced by John Costello.
1949 A republic was proclaimed and Ireland left the Commonwealth. Partition remained contentious and the IRA mounted a terrorist campaign for reunification with the six northern counties.
1955 Ireland joined the UN.
1957 De Valera was voted back into office as prime minister; he said that the union of Northern Ireland with the Republic could not be achieved through violence.
1959 De Valera became president.
1973 Ireland joined the forerunner of the EU, the European Economic Community (EEC). Fianna Fáil, the traditional party of government, lost power in the general election and Jack Lynch resigned. Liam Cosgrave formed a coalition between his party, Fine Gael, and the Labour Party. The IRA became active again after a long period of decline as fighting intensified in the North due to oppression of Catholics under the Unionist-run regime and later, direct rule from London.
1977 Fianna Fáil won the general election and Jack Lynch again became prime minister.
1980s None of a succession of elections produced a single-party majority government.
1985 The Ango-Irish Agreement established regular participation by the Irish government in political, legal, security and cross-border matters in Northern Ireland.
1990 The first left-winger and the first woman, Mary Robinson, was elected to the presidency.
1992 In a referendum, Irish voters agreed to loosen the abortion laws, enabling women to travel abroad to have an abortion.
1993 The Downing Street Declaration by the Irish and British governments offered talks to all parties in Northern Ireland if they renounced political violence.
1995 A referendum to change the 1937 constitution narrowly approved the lifting of the ban on divorce.
1997 Mary McAleese, who lives in Northern Ireland, became the first British subject to be elected president of the Irish Republic.
1998 In a referendum, nearly 95 per cent of voters approved the Good Friday Agreement, which entailed Ireland giving up its constitutional claim to Northern Ireland.
2001 In a referendum, Ireland voted against the Treaty of Nice, which proposed enlargement of the EU to include up to 13 new member states.
2002 Euro currency replaced the punt. After parliamentary elections, Bertie Ahern was confirmed as prime minister and formed a coalition government led by Fianna Fáil. At the second attempt, Ireland voted 63 per cent in favour of the EU's Treaty of Nice, on a turnout of 48 per cent.
2004 As holder of the EU presidency, it hosted ceremonies to welcome the EU's 10 new member states. On 1 October, President Mary McAleese was returned unopposed for a second term.
2005 Irish was adopted as an official working language of the EU. In the Irish-speaking, mainly western, districts (*Gaeltacht*), English has been removed from road signs and official maps.

Political structure
Constitution

The constitution was drawn up in 1937. The Uchtarán na Eireann (president), directly elected every seven years, is guardian of the constitution, and may submit a bill to the people in a referendum or to the Supreme Court if it is felt that legislation might contravene the constitution. The constitution was amended three times by referendum in the 1990s, to loosen anti-abortion laws, legalise divorce and give up Ireland's territorial claim to Northern Ireland in favour of the principle of unity by consent.

Form of state

Parliamentary democratic republic

The executive

Executive power is exercised by the cabinet, led by the *Taoiseach* (prime minister) who is appointed by the president on the recommendation of the Dáil Eireann (House of Representatives).

National legislature

Legislative power is vested in the bicameral Oireachtas (National Parliament), consisting of the Seanad Eireann (Senate) and the Dáil Eireann.
The Dáil is the main legislative body and has the responsibility of electing the cabinet, which must consist of not less than seven and no more than 15 members.

There are 166 members of the Dáil, who are elected by proportional representation every five years.

The Seanad, with 60 members, is elected by a system of electoral colleges, its periods corresponding with that of the Dáil. It can delay a bill for up to 90 days or suggest changes, but cannot block it permanently. The *taoiseach* nominates 11 Seanad members, 43 are elected by panels representing vocational and cultural interests and six are elected by Ireland's universities.

Legal system
The Irish constitution declares that every person living in Ireland has certain fundamental personal rights, listed in articles. Every constitutional right has the same status and value, however when a conflict arises between constitutional rights the courts have the prerogative to adjudicate which constitutional right is more important in which particular case. Much civil and criminal law is derived from English common law and remains in force if it is consistent with the Constitution.

The courts are made up of District, Circuit and the High Court. District Courts deal with summary offences and minor civil cases. Circuit Courts deal with civil cases of a more serious nature and criminal cases are presented before a judge with a jury of 12 citizens.

The High Court, has full jurisdiction in civil and criminal cases and can act as an appeal court from the Circuit Court. When exercising criminal jurisdiction, it is called the Central Criminal Court. Under the Offences Against the State Act 1939, Special Criminal Courts were set up; these sit without a jury.

The Supreme Court, the court of final appeal, consists of a Chief Justice and five other judges who can hear appeals on all High Court decisions. It is also the final arbiter on the interpretation of the constitution.

Last elections
October 2004 (no presidential elections were held as Mary McAleese was the only candidate); 11 June 2004 (European Parliament); 17 May 2002 (parliamentary).
Results: European Parliament: Fianna Fáil won 29.5 per cent of the vote (four seats out of 13), Fine Gael (United Ireland Party) 27.8 per cent (five), Sinn Féin 11.1 per cent (one), Labour 10.6 per cent (one), Green Party 4.3 per cent (no seats) and independents 16.7 per cent (two); turnout 59.7 per cent.
Parliamentary: Fianna Fáil won 80 seats out of 166, Fine Gael 31, Labour 21, Progressive Democrats eight, Green Party six and Sinn Féin five.

Next elections
2007 (parliamentary); 2011 (presidential).

Political parties
Ruling party
Coalition government led by Fianna Fáil (Soldiers of Destiny) (since Jun 2002)
Main opposition party
Fine Gael (United Ireland Party)

Population
4.02 million (2004); 3.95 million (OECD, 2003)
Ethnic make-up
Ireland is predominantly white. Only recently has it seen non-white immigration.
Religions
Roman Catholic (95 per cent); Church of Ireland (2.8 per cent); Presbyterian (0.4 per cent) Jewish (0.1 per cent); others (0.3 per cent); no religion (1.2 per cent).

Education
Education is divided into three levels: primary, secondary and tertiary. Primary schooling (including, although not compulsory, infant pre-schooling from age four), lasts for eight years. Secondary schooling starts age 12 for either five or six years, and includes a junior and a senior cycle with examinations at the end of each. About 81 per cent of Irish students complete the senior cycle and almost 50 per cent go on to tertiary education, which can be either academic or vocational. Ireland has a higher proportion of graduates with scientific skills in the 25–34 age group than any other OECD member, except Japan.
Compulsory years: Six to 15.
Enrolment rate: 105 per cent gross primary enrolment of relevant age group; 118 per cent gross secondary enrolment (including repeaters) (World Bank).
Pupils per teacher: 22 in primary schools.

Health
Annual total expenditure on health is around 6–7 per cent of GDP, of which government spending is about 76 per cent.

Eight regional health boards administer Ireland's health system, which is funded by the central government, through the department of health, which in turn is under the control of the minister of health. Various community welfare services operate for the chronically sick, the elderly and the disabled. Almost 38 per cent of the population – those on lower incomes – receive medical services free of charge. The remainder receive public hospital services for a minimum charge. Charges are also made to the better-off for visits to the family doctor and to hospital consultants.
HIV prevalence: 0.1 per cent aged 15–49 in 2003 (World Bank)
Life expectancy: 77.7 years (World Bank)

Fertility rate/Maternal mortality rate: 2.0 births per woman; maternal mortality, 5 per 100,000 live births (World Bank).
Infant mortality rate: 5.1 per 1,000 live births (World Bank)
Head of population per physician/bed: 2.2 physicians and 3.7 hospital beds available for 1,000 people.

Welfare
Social insurance is compulsory for employees and the self-employed. The principal benefits are unemployment, disability and maternity payments plus pay-related benefits to supplement those on low incomes, invalidity pension (for those on disability benefit), widows' payments (contributory and non-contributory), orphans' payments, deserted wives' payments, old age pensions (contributory and non-contributory), medical treatment benefits, including dental and optical, an occupational injuries scheme and certain free schemes for the elderly. Employees in the private sector contribute at the highest rate.

Main cities
Dublin (capital, estimated population one million in 2004), Cork (193,400), Limerick (84,900), Galway (67,200), Waterford (47,800).

Languages spoken
Official documents are printed in both English and Irish.
Five per cent of the population speak Irish as their first language.
Official language/s
Irish (Gaelic) and English

Media
Press
There are over 50 newspapers, which reach 59 per cent of adults, and over 100 magazines. Over five million national newspapers are sold in Ireland every week.
Dailies: Top dailies include *Irish Independent*, *Irish Times*, *The Star*, *Ireland Today*, *Star* and *Cork Evening Echo*. All British dailies are available.
Weeklies: *Foinse* is a national weekly newspaper in Gaelic. *An Phoblacht Republican* is a weekly newspaper with an Irish Republican perspective that includes news and analysis on national and international affairs. Other weeklies include *Socialist Worker*, *Sunday Independent*, *Sunday World*, *News of the World*, *Sunday Tribune*, *Donegal News*, *Galway Advertiser*, *Waterford*, *Limerick Post* and *Sunday Times*.
Business: Dublin has a small number of business publications. The weekly newspaper *Sunday Business Post* provides Ireland's financial, political, and economic news. *Unison Ireland* also offers business news. *Marine Times Online*

Ireland

(http://www.marinetimes.ie) is the electronic version of the newspaper *Marine Times* that covers the Irish fishing and aquaculture industries and communities. Most UK trade publications are also available.

Periodicals: Periodicals of general interest include *History Ireland*, *Irish Roots Magazine* and *Skerries News*. Those featuring entertainment include *GV Magazine* and *Hotpress*.

Broadcasting

Broadcasting laws lay down rules regarding the balance of news and current affairs and culture in broadcasting, in addition to the prohibition of matters which the minister for telecommunications considers likely to promote or incite crime. Radio Telefís Éireann (RTE) has responsibility for operating the national radio and television services in Ireland.

Radio: There are 23 commercial radio stations. Approximately 88 per cent of the adult population listen to radio.
RTE provides two radio channels, Radio 1 and 2FM. It also transmits *Radio na Gaeltachta*, a radio service in Irish Gaelic, which shares a third radio network with classical music service FM3.

Television: There are two commercial TV stations. RTE provides two television channels (RTE 1 and Network 2).
Broadcasts from the UK can also be received in many parts of the country.
One-third of homes are cabled. All cable systems carry the UK channels and a number of them also carry satellite channels.

Advertising

Promotion of tobacco products is banned, and the advertising of alcohol is strictly controlled. Commercials on TV and radio are limited to 10 per cent of transmission time. Newspapers, magazines, posters and films are also widely used. Information is available from the Advertising Standards Authority in Dublin.

Economy

From an admittedly low base, Ireland has achieved impressive economic growth since it joined the EU (then called the European Economic Community) in 1973. Per capita GDP increased from almost 60 per cent of the EU average to over 100 per cent in 2004. Ireland has an open economy with principle exports in goods and services producing 50 per cent of GDP, of which tourism, as the major service industry, typically contributes over 4 per cent of GDP. The economy is highly integrated into the global economy through trade and investment links, so that external forces affect its performance, not least, the appreciation of the euro against the US dollar. Nevertheless exports in 2004 amounted to almost eur84 billion (US$66 billion) while imports amounted to just over eur50 billion (US$39 billion).

The past decade has seen a slowdown from double-digit growth, in the mid-1990s, to a comparatively sedate 5.1 per cent, in 2004. The economy has been driven by a young and rapidly expanding labour supply, government pursuit of 'pragmatic and innovative' policies, the opening up of markets to international trade in goods and services, strategic use of EU Structural and Cohesion Funds and investment in education and technological innovation.

Juxtaposed with high-tech industries is an agricultural sector that accounts for 8 per cent of GDP, 7 per cent of exports and employs 7.5 per cent of the workforce. Ireland has a highly skilled labour pool. A national development plan is focussed on IT, life-sciences, medical technologies, engineering, financial and international services, Internet based activity and digital business. Of the more than 1,100 foreign-owned companies operating in Ireland around 50 per cent are US based, and the combined number of UK and German companies make up around 25 per cent. Those industries that have shown most growth in exports are computers and electrical machinery and chemical and pharmaceuticals products.

It is expected that growth will continue at a rate of around 5 per cent. Domestic demand should expand rapidly, stimulated by strong income growth and government spending. Although wages will grow, inflation is projected to remain relatively low at around 2 per cent in 2005 and edging up to 2.75 by 2006.

External trade

Ireland's impressive economic growth has been accompanied by dramatic increases in imports and exports due to the expansion of international trade.

Imports
Imports consist of data processing equipment, other machinery and equipment, chemicals, petroleum and petroleum products, textiles and clothing.
Main sources: UK (35.2 per cent total, 2004), US (13.5 per cent), Germany (8.9 per cent), France (4.3 per cent), The Netherlands (4.3 per cent)

Exports
The value of Ireland's exports has shown significant growth. Most of this expansion has occurred in the industrial sector. Exports consist mainly machinery and equipment, computers, chemicals, pharmaceuticals, live animals and animal products.
Main destinations: US (20.2 per cent total, 2004), UK (17.5 per cent), Belgium (14.8 per cent), Germany (7.5 per cent), France (5.9 per cent), Italy (4.5 per cent), Netherlands (4.4 per cent)

Agriculture

Farming
Agricultural earnings equate to over 8 per cent of annual GDP and around 7 per cent of export earnings. The sector employs 7.5 per cent of the labour force. With its temperate climate and relatively high levels of rainfall, Ireland is suited to stock raising, with the result that there is a predominance of livestock production in Irish agriculture. Approximately 70 per cent of all land is devoted to pasture while 10 per cent is tilled. Irish farms tend to be owner-occupied, with an average size of just over 25 hectares.

Agriculture policy is dominated by the EU and its Common Agricultural Policy (CAP). Ireland is a major beneficiary of EU farm subsidies. Fundamental reform to the Common Agricultural Policy (CAP) was introduced on 1 January 2005 in Ireland. The subsidies paid on farm output, which tended to benefit large farms and encourage overproduction, were replaced by single farm payments not conditional on production. This is expected to reward farms that provide and maintain a healthy environment, food safety and animal welfare standards. The changes are also intended to encourage market conscious production and cut the cost of CAP to the EU taxpayer.

Ireland is a net exporter of agricultural goods. Main exports include meat, vegetables, milk, butter and alcoholic beverages. Main agricultural imports include rice and maize.

The crop production in 2004 included: 2,142,400 tonnes (t) cereals in total, 1,159,000t barley, 1,500,000t sugar beets, 849,000t wheat, *500,000t potatoes, *7,500t pulses, 10,000t tomatoes, *2,660t oilcrops, 15,000t apples, 134,000t oats, 22,700t fruit in total, 221,660t vegetables in total. Livestock production included: 993,305t meat in total, 570,000t beef, 223,000t pig meat, 63,000t lamb, *132,680t poultry, 32,000t eggs, 5,500,000t milk, *197t honey, 64,750t cattle hides.
* estimate

Fishing
The sea fishing industry makes an important contribution to the agricultural economy. Mackerel accounts for about 35 per cent of total catch, and is the most important species landed.

Forestry
With forest cover estimated at 659,000 hectares (ha), it occupies less than a tenth of the total land area. Though Ireland is traditionally one of Europe's least forested countries, massive afforestation programmes have contributed to an

annual average increase of 3.03 per cent, the equivalent of 17,000ha of forest cover. Private ownership in new planting areas has been rising with around two-thirds of the forest remaining under state ownership. Employment in the forest and wood products industry is about 13,000.

Most of the forest is available for wood supply. Roundwood production has considerably increased with the expansion of forest cover. Much of the production consists of softwood logs for the domestic sawn wood and panel industry. Ireland imports most of its paper and sawn wood. Exports of forest materials in 2004 amounted to US$424.5 million, while imports amounted to US$845.8 million. Production in 2004 included 2,499,306 cubic metres (cum) roundwood, 2,479,760cum industrial roundwood, 1,676,348cum sawlogs and veneers, 938,959cum sawnwood, 704,387cum pulpwood, 19,546cum woodfuel.

Industry and manufacturing
The industrial sector accounts for 24 per cent of GDP, 80 per cent of the value of annual exports and approximately 27 per cent of employment.

Ireland's indigenous manufacturing base is relatively small. Traditional industries, such as food and beverages, textiles, paper, non-metallic minerals and machinery, dominate, although there has been rapid growth in new export-oriented chemicals as well as electronic engineering industries. Most of the new capital and skill-intensive industries are subsidiaries of large US and European multinationals and are heavily reliant on imported primary and intermediate inputs.

US Wyeth Pharmaceuticals is investing US$1 billion in a factory in the world's largest integrated biotechnology campus at Grange Castle in Dublin, which opened in September 2005. Wyeth will produce infant vaccines, antibiotics and an arthritis treatments.

Tourism
Tourism has grown at a rapid rate since 1990, the number of visitors doubling to 6.6 million by 2004. The sector contributes around 4.5 per cent of GDP and gives employment to 140,000 people. All parts of the Republic benefit from the expansion of tourism, which has become an important factor in regional development, bringing employment and business to otherwise economically-deprived areas. Dublin has become a major short city-break destination. The UK is the main source of visitors. US tourists is the next largest and the most lucrative market. Vastly improved air connections, as well as sea links, have assisted Ireland's tourist explosion. The authorities are concerned about the cost and quality of the tourism product and are seeking to sharpen the sector's competitiveness.

Mining
Mining accounts for about 1 per cent of GNP and 1 per cent of the workforce. Europe's largest zinc and lead deposits are located at Navan, County Meath, and are operated by Tara Mines. Production has continued since the mid-1970s.

Ireland is Europe's leading producer of zinc. There are also reserves of gypsum, barytes, dolomite, silica sand, limestone, coal, marble and small amounts of silver. Gypsum is extracted from an open-pit at Knocknacran, Co Monaghan. Gold and base metals have been discovered at Clontibret, County Monaghan.

A zinc mining project at Lisheen, county Tipperary, began production in 2000. The US$280.5 million project is a joint venture between Ivernia West, an Irish exploration company, and Anglo-American, the South African company. The two ore deposits, containing 19 million tonnes of recoverable reserves, have been producing 1.5 million tonnes of ore or 160,000 tonnes of zinc a year since 2000.

Hydrocarbons
Dependence on imported petroleum has been reduced due to the exploitation of domestic gas and peat reserves. No significant hydrocarbon reserves have been found. In 2003, the Irish government adjusted the regulations for exploration and production in a bid to encourage new investment in the oil industry.

Natural gas represents around 23 per cent of primary energy consumption. Ireland's total proven gas reserves amounted to 19.8 billion cubic metres in 2004. However, Ireland still continues to import around 80 per cent of its gas demand, primarily from Britain. The government plans to become self sufficient in gas by 2007; this will be when the Corrib and Sevens Head gas field comes online. Indigenous reserves of natural gas are located in the Kinsale Head gas field and the smaller Ballycotton field off the Cork coast.

Coal is not produced in Ireland but is imported.

Energy
Ireland has the only stand-alone electricity and gas grid in the EU, although new projects will increase the country's interdependence with the UK and the rest of Europe. It has an installed capacity of 4,600MW, with peak demand of 3,800MW. It is one of the fastest growing energy markets in Europe, with demand increasing by 5 per cent a year from the mid-1990s.

A natural gas pipeline project linking the country to the UK will provide security of supply and meet growing demand from industry and power generation. Dependence on imported petroleum has been reduced due to the exploitation of domestic gas and peat reserves. Peat continues to provide around 550MW of generated electricity and is also used in significant quantities as a domestic fuel.

Financial markets
Stock exchange
The Irish Stock Exchange (ISE) has faced severe constraints on growth as, like many small markets in the euro-zone, Irish equities have suffered as institutions re-locate assets. This reduced the weighting of Irish stocks as they no longer had to match their liabilities with assets, but bought euro-based equities which no longer represent a currency risk.

The ISE launched the Irish Enterprise Exchange (IEX) in April 2005, designed to offer a trading forum for local and smaller companies within Ireland.

Banking and insurance
The two top Irish banks, Allied Irish Banks (AIB) and the Bank of Ireland, dominate the domestic market.

There is evidence of intensified competition within the domestic Irish market, with domestic and international newcomers. Domestically, certain building societies and banks have been looking to increase their value to shareholders through mergers and diversification of services. Banking competition from abroad is mainly from the UK. However, the Irish banking system is widely regarded as overcrowded and may be in need of consolidation if its long-run competitiveness is to be sustained. Higher inflation and worries about European interest rates have dampened the short-term outlook for Irish equities.

Central bank
Central Bank of Ireland; European Central Bank (ECB).

Time
GMT (GMT plus one hour from late Mar to late Oct).

Geography
Ireland is situated in the extreme north-west of Europe, bounded in the east by the Irish Sea, in the west by the Atlantic Ocean and in the south by the Celtic Sea. The landmass is bounded by mountains and has a low-lying central plain.

The island of Ireland consists of 32 counties, of which six, in the north east, belong to Northern Ireland, part of the United Kingdom.

Ireland

Climate
Ireland lies in an area of moderate south-westerly winds and its climate is influenced by the warm waters of the Gulf Stream, assuring it of a mild climate with almost uniform temperatures throughout the country, although in general the climate along the east coast tends to be warmer and dryer than areas in the west and on higher ground.

The coldest months are January and February, when temperatures average between 4 and 7 degrees Celsius (C); the warmest months are July and August, when temperatures average between 14 and 17 degrees C. There is rain throughout the year, with annual rainfall varying between 800 and 1,200mm. The driest months are May and June.

Dress codes
While dress tends to be informal, business people normally wear suits, and evening social events can be quite formal. A medium-weight raincoat is advised throughout the year.

Entry requirements
Passports
Required by all except UK-born nationals, but may need to produce some form of identification. Other EU visitors require national ID cards.

Visa
Visas are not required by nationals of the EU, the Americas, Australasia and many Asian countries. For confirmation see www.irlgov.ie/iveagh/. Other business travellers should contact the consular section of the nearest Irish Embassy before visiting.

Currency advice/regulations
There are no currency regulations.

Customs
Personal effects are duty-free.

Health (for visitors)
Mandatory precautions
There are no requirements.

Advisable precautions
Travel insurance for those not entitled to free emergency cover.

Hotels
Classified into three categories: Star A, Star B and Star C. Single room prices vary depending on season and facilities offered. Prices are cheaper outside the capital. Tipping: 10 per cent is customary.

Credit cards
All usual credit cards are widely accepted.

Public holidays
Fixed dates
1 Jan (New Year's Day), 17 Mar (St Patrick's Day), 25 Dec (Christmas Day), 26 Dec (St Stephen's Day).

Variable dates
Good Friday, Easter Monday, May Bank Holiday (first Mon in May); June Bank Holiday (first Mon in Jun), Summer Bank Holiday (first Mon in Aug), Halloween Bank Holiday (last Mon in Oct).

Working hours
Banking
Mon–Fri: 1000–1600 (open on Thursdays until 1700 in Dublin and in all principal cities and towns).

Business
Mon–Fri: 0900–1700.

Government
Mon–Fri: 0915–1300, 1415–1715.

Shops
Mon–Fri: 0900 or 0930–1730. Supermarkets normally stay open until 2100 on Thursday and Fridays.

Telecommunications
Mobile phones
GSM 900/1800 services operate throughout the country.

Electricity supply
220V AC

Social customs/useful tips
The hold of the Catholic Church over Ireland has diminished in recent years and the country now has an air of moderate social liberalism, although there are more conservative attitudes in rural areas. Homosexuality was decriminalised in 1993 and divorce was legalised in 1995, bringing Irish law into line with the rest of the EU as well as the liberal ideas of most of the Irish people.

Getting there
Air
National airline: Aer Lingus
International airport/s: Dublin (DUB), 10km north of city, facilities include duty-free, car hire, bank, bureau de change, bars, restaurants, tourist information centre and chemist. Airport express coaches and taxis are available to the city centre.
Shannon (SNN), 26 km from Limerick, facilities include duty-free, bank, bureau de change, bar, restaurant and tourist information centre. Bus services are available every hour to and from both Limerick and Clare, (60 minutes duration). A daily express coach travels between both Shannon and Limerick, or Galway. A taxi service is also available to Limerick.
Other airport/s: Cork (ORK), 5 km from city; Horan (NOC) at Knock, Co Mayo, Connaught Province.
Airport tax: None

Surface
Road: Bus Éireann and National Express operate services from London, and many other UK centres, to Dublin, Belfast and other destinations.

Rail: The most comfortable and reliable train/ferry services to Ireland depart from London.

Water: In addition to conventional ferry crossings, there are now high-speed services as well as upgraded, quality boats sailing on many Irish sea routes. Routes include links with Scotland, England and Wales to alternative destinations in the Republic of Ireland as well as Northern Ireland. Continental connections include routes to north-western France.
Rail links provide connections from the major seaports.
Main port/s: The main ports are Dun Laoghaire, Dublin, Rosslare and Cork. (Northern Ireland: Belfast and Larne).

Getting about
National transport
Air: Daily services between Dublin and Shannon, and Dublin and Cork operated by Aer Lingus. Also one flight daily between Dublin and Horan Airport, Knock. Charter services are available. Domestic airports include Waterford (WAT), Galway (GWY), Sligo (SXL), Carrickfinn (CFN) and Kerry (KIR). In addition, there are also various small airstrips which receive passenger services.

Road: The Irish road network carries the overwhelming part of Irish imports and exports. A good highway system links all cities.

Buses: Bus Éireann is the national bus line, with services all over the south and north. Winter bus schedule is often drastically reduced and many routes simply disappear after September.

Rail: Ireland's rail network is not extensive. Iarnród Éireann (Irish Rail) is the main operator, with routes which fan out from Dublin. Iarnród Éireann, in partnership with Northern Ireland Railways, operates a high-speed service between Dublin and Belfast.

Water: There are many boat services to outlying islands off the west coast and across rivers.

City transport
Taxis: Taxis in Ireland tend to be expensive. There are metered taxis in Cork, Dublin, Galway and Limerick, but in other places one needs to agree on the fare beforehand. If you book a taxi by telephone there may be a small pick-up charge.

Buses, trams & metro: There are comprehensive bus services in all towns and cities, combined in Dublin with DART suburban trains (fast, surburban rail service). Two new tram services – the Luas – were inaugurated in 2004. The red line runs from Connelly Street in Dublin's city centre, west then south-west, to Tallaght. The green line runs from St Steven's Green, in the administrative district of Dublin, south to Cherrywood.

Car hire
Available in all main towns, but heavy demand during tourist season. All international hire companies are represented in Ireland. Drivers must be aged between 21 and 75. A national or international driving licence is required and the driver is generally required to have had at least two years experience. Speed limits 30mph (48kph) in built-up areas and 60mph (96kph) on main roads. Driving is on the left.

BUSINESS DIRECTORY

Telephone area codes
The international direct dialling (IDD) code for Ireland is +353 followed by area code and subscriber's number:

Cork	21	Mullingar	44
Donegal	73	Shannon	61
Dublin	1	Sligo	71
Galway	91	Tipperary	62
Kilkenny	56	Waterford	51
Killarney	64	Wexford	53
Limerick	61	Wicklow	404

Chambers of Commerce
American Chamber of Commerce Ireland, 6 Wilton Place, Dublin 2 (tel: 661-6201; fax: 661-6217; e-mail: ifo@amcham.ie).

Chambers of Commerce of Ireland, 17 Merrion Square, Dublin 2 (tel: 661-2888; fax: 661-2811; e-mail: info@chambersireland.ie).

Cork Chamber of Commerce, Fitzgerald House, Summerhill North, Cork (tel: 450-9044; fax: 450-8568; e-mail: info@corkchamber.ie).

Dublin Chamber of Commerce, 7 Clare Street, Dublin 2 (tel: 644-7200; fax: 676-6043; info@dublinchamber.ie).

Dun Laoghaire Rathdown Chamber of Commerce, Kilcullen House, 1 Haigh Terrace, Dun Laoghaire (tel: 284-5066; 284-5034; e-mail: info@dirchamber.ie).

Dundalk Chamber of Commerce, Hagan House, Ramparts Road, Dundalk (tel: 933-6343; fax: 933-2085; info@dundalk.ie).

Limerick Chamber of Commerce, 96 O'Connell Street, Limerick (tel: 415-180; fax: 415-785; e-mail: info@limchamber.ie).

Mullingar Chamber of Commerce, ACC House, Dominick Street, Mullingar (tel: 44-044; fax: 44-045; e-mail: info@mullingar-chamber.ie).

Sligo Chamber of Commerce and Industry, 16 Quay Street, Sligo (tel: 916-1274; fax: 916-0912; e-mail: sligochamber@eircom.net).

Waterford Chamber of Commerce, Georges Street, Waterford (tel: 311-136; fax: 876-002; e-mail: info@waterfordchamber.ie).

Wexford Chamber of Industry and Commerce, The Ballast Office, Crescent Quay, Wexford (tel: 22-226; fax:241-70; e-mail: info@wexchamber.iol.ie).

Banking
Allied Irish Bank Ltd, Bankcentre, PO Box 452, Ballsbridge, Dublin 4 (tel: 660-0311; fax: 668-2508).

Allied Irish Investment Bank plc, Bankcentre, Ballsbridge, Dublin 4 (tel: 660-4733).

Bank of Ireland, Lower Baggot Street, Dublin 2 (tel: 661-5933; fax: 661-5671).

The Institute of Bankers in Ireland (banking association), Nassau House, Nassau Street, Dublin 2 (tel: 679-3311).

Investment Bank of Ireland Ltd, 26 Fitzwilliam Place, Dublin 2 (tel: 661-6433; fax: 661-6433).

National Irish Bank, 7/8 Wilton Terrace, Dublin 2 (tel: 678-5066; fax: 661-3324).

Central bank
Central Bank of Ireland, PO Box 559, Dame Street, Dublin 2 (tel: 434-4000; fax: 671-6561; e-mail: enquiries@centralbank.ie).

European Central Bank (ECB), Kaiserstrasse 29, D-60311 Frankfurt am Main, Germany (tel: +49(69)13-440; fax: +49(69)1344-6000; e-mail: info@ecb.int).

Travel information
Aer Lingus, Head Office Block, Dublin Airport (tel: 705-2222; fax: 705-3832; internet site: http://www.aerlingus.ie/).

Cork Airport (tel: 313-131).

Dublin Airport (tel: 844-4900).

Ryanair, Corporate Head Office Building, Dublin Airport (tel: 844-4489, 844-4400; fax: 844-4402).

Shannon Airport (tel: 471-666).

Facts and maps on Ireland: http://alison.citeweb.net/irlande.htm

Ministry of tourism
Department of Tourism, Sport & Recreation: http://www.irlgov.ie/tourism-sport

National tourist organisation offices
Irish Tourist Board, Baggot Street Bridge, Dublin 2 (tel: 676-5871, 661-6500; fax: 676-4764, 676-4765; internet site: http://www.irland.travel.ie/home/index.asp).

Other useful addresses
Central Statistics Office, Skehard Road, Cork (tel: 359-000; fax: 359-090; internet site: http://www.cso.ie).

Confederation of Irish Industry, Confederation House, Kildare Street, Dublin 2 (tel: 660-1011).

Department of Agriculture, Food and Forestry, Kildare Street, Dublin 2 (tel: 678-9011; fax: 661-6263).

Department of Defence, Colaiste Caoimhin, Mobhi Road, Glasnevin, Dublin 9 (tel: 637-9911; fax: 637-7993).

Department of Enterprise and Employment, Kildare Street, Dublin 2 (tel: 661-4444; fax: 676-2654).

Department of Finance and Department of the Public Service, Government Bldgs, Upper Merrion Street, Dublin 2 (tel: 676-7571; fax: 676-7335).

Department of Foreign Affairs, 80 St Stephen's Green, Dublin 2 (tel: 478-0822; fax: 478-1484).

Department of Taoiseach, Government Buildings, Upper Merrion Street, Dublin 2 (tel: 668-9333; fax: 678-9791).

Department of Tourism and Trade, Kildare Street, Dublin 2 (tel: 662-1444; fax: 676-6154).

Department of Transport, Energy and Communications, Clare Street, Dublin 2 (tel: 671-5233; fax: 677-3169).

Enterprise Ireland, 11 Whitehall, Dublin (tel: 857-0000; fax: 808-2020; internet site: http://www.irish-trade.ie).

IDA Ireland (Industrial Development Agency), Wilton Park House, Wilton Place, Dublin 2 (tel: 668-6633; fax: 660-3703).

Irish Business and Employers' Confederation, 84 Lower Baggot Street, Dublin 2 (tel: 660-1011; fax: 660-1717).

Irish Embassy (USA), 2234 Massachusetts Avenue, NW, Washington DC 20008 (tel: 202-462-3939; fax: 202-232-5993; e-mail: embirlus@aol.com).

Provincial Newspapers' Association of Ireland, 33 Parkgate Street, Dublin 8 (tel: 679-3679).

The Stock Exchange, 24-28 Anglesea Street, Dublin 2 (tel: 677-8808; fax: 677-6045).

Internet sites
Access Ireland: http://www.visunet.ie/

Business information: http://www.factfinder.ie/

Doras web directory: http://www.doras.ie/

Ireland On-Line: http://www.home.iol.ie/

Irish Government website: http://irlgov.ie/

Irish Times: http://www.irish-times.com/

Irish trade web (information on Irelands top 1000 companies): http://www.itw.ie/

Israel

KEY FACTS

Official name: Medinat Israel (State of Israel)

Head of State: President Moshe Katsav (Likud) (elected by parliament Jul 2000)

Head of government: Prime Minister Ariel Sharon (Likud) (elected 6 Feb 2001; re-elected 28 Jan 2003)

Ruling party: Likud (right-wing)-led coalition government from 10 Jan 2005, including Labour and a small orthodox party

Area: 20,700 square km (excluding occupied territories)

Population: 6.70 million (2004)

Capital: Jerusalem (Israel regards the entire city as its capital although it is not recognised by the UN.)

Official language: Hebrew

Currency: New shekel (NIS) = 100 agorot

Exchange rate: NIS4.60 per US$ (Oct 2005)

GDP per capita: US$17,695 (2004)

GDP real growth: 4.30% (2004)

Labour force: 2.99 million (2004)

Unemployment: 10.70% (2004)

Inflation: -0.40% (2004)

Balance of trade: -US$2.40 billion (2004)

Foreign debt: US$74.46 billion (2004)

It was a year of upheaval in Israel, particularly in its domestic politics and its conflict with the Palestinians. In February, the government approved plans to evacuate Israeli settlements in the Palestinian Occupied Territories – the first such evacuation since the withdrawal from Israeli settlements in the Sinai as part of a 1978 peace agreement with Egypt. The evacuations were duly carried out in August and September, in the Gaza Strip and the northern West Bank. A political earthquake took place in November, when Prime Minister Ariel Sharon announced his resignation from the ruling Likud party and his intent to contest upcoming national elections at the head of the newly formed Kadima (Forward) party.

Economic recovery continues

Since 2003, when Israel's economy finally emerged from a two-year recession, Israelis have experienced rapid economic growth. In 2005, this trend continued, with GDP growth estimated to have been 4–5 per cent. Unemployment fell to 10 per cent and rises were recorded in the tourism sector, consumer confidence and foreign direct investment (FDI). The Israeli stock market reacted nervously to two events in 2005, the resignation of finance minister Binyamin Netanyahu in August and Prime Minister Sharon's stroke in December, but managed to recover.

Bulldozer demolishes own work (1)

Nicknamed 'the bulldozer' by many in Israel, Prime Minister Sharon had shocked the country in December 2003 when he first flagged the idea of withdrawing Israeli settlers and soldiers from the occupied Gaza Strip. Having spent three decades providing military, political, moral and financial support for the settlement movement, it appeared that 'the bulldozer' was going to bulldoze at least some of his own handiwork. The 'disengagement plan' was refined and gathered pace in 2005, passing Sharon's cabinet in February. The final plan envisaged the evacuation of all 21 settlements from the Gaza Strip, consisting of around 8,500 people, and four settlements in the northern West Bank, comprised of about 630 people. Israeli Defense Force (IDF) personnel would also be withdrawn. The estimated bill for the withdrawal was US$2.2 billion, with one third earmarked for the relocation of Israeli army bases and half for settler compensation.

Sharon had had a tough time of it in 2004 and 2005 securing the numbers within his governing coalition for the disengagement plan, particularly from his own Likud party. In May 2004, he lost an internal Likud referendum calling for a rejection of the disengagement and although he ignored the result, a group of rebels within the Likud party parliamentary bloc coalesced. This group, fluctuating between 8 and 15 members, proceeded to make life difficult in the Knesset (parliament) for Sharon throughout 2004 and 2005.

Facing down parliamentary attempts to sabotage his disengagement plan in March and a rally by up to 40,000 pro-settlers in April, Sharon executed his plan. During August and September, Israel conducted its first evacuation of settlers since 1982, as stipulated in a land for peace deal with Egypt in 1978. Ironically, Sharon had also played a key role in dismantling settlements in the Sinai.

Relations with the Palestinians

A key problem for the government was how to withdraw from occupied territory without appearing to have retreated in the face of Palestinian, and in particular Hamas (Islamic Resistance Movement), attacks. The problem within the problem was that this was a unilateral withdrawal, formulated without discussion with the Palestinians' official governing body, the Palestinian Authority (PA). Israel had unilaterally withdrawn its forces from southern Lebanon in 2000 and was sensitive to criticism from politicians on the right and some within the military establishment that Israel risked a new propaganda defeat. In 2000, Israel's chief Lebanese foe Hezbollah (Party of God), had presented Israel's withdrawal as a military defeat and had paraded through formerly occupied territory as liberators.

Palestinian presidential elections in January, in which the late President Yasser Arafat's long-serving deputy Mahmoud Abbas emerged victorious, presented both Israel and the Palestinians with an opportunity to start relations anew. Abbas was known to favour renewed peace negotiations and Sharon seized his chance. In January, Israel allowed Palestinian police units to deploy unhindered in the Gaza Strip for the first time in years, and pledged not to launch attacks in PA territory. On 8 February, at a summit in Sharm al Sheikh, Egypt, Sharon and Abbas declared a truce between their peoples. Sharon offered Abbas prisoner releases, security control over five West Bank cities and the right to be consulted over the execution of the disengagement. In exchange, Abbas promised to tackle militants within his own camp and to enforce calm in the Palestinian territories. In March, most Palestinian factions, including Hamas, agreed to extend a *hudna* (temporary truce) with Israel.

In practice few of these undertakings were implemented in full, either by Israelis or Palestinians, much like during the previous period of *hudna*, originally declared in 2003. Although the number of attacks, including suicide bombings, against Israelis diminished in some respects, Hamas and the smaller Palestinian Islamic Jihad group (PIJ) continued to shell and launch rocket attacks from the Gaza Strip against civilian and military targets in Israel, and Israel continued to raid the Occupied Territories, by land and air, resulting in civilian and militant casualties.

Nonetheless, there was a degree of co-ordination between Israel and the PA over the disengagement plan, with the PA assuming control of the evacuated territories. The IDF experienced some difficulty in extracting several thousand settlers and their supporters from the Gaza Strip, who had refused to leave voluntarily. After a brief period of calm, violence between the IDF and Gaza-based militants resumed.

In September, Israel implemented an agreement with Egypt, in which 750 Egyptian border guards were allowed to deploy on the Egypt-Gaza border. This marked a significant departure from demilitarisation clauses within Israel's 1978 peace treaty with Egypt but was considered necessary by the government in order to prevent weapons-smuggling into the Gaza Strip. In November, Israel acceded to a US-brokered deal with the PA, allowing for direct transport links between the Gaza Strip and the West Bank. This deal highlighted the fact that despite Israel's August-September withdrawal, it had maintained a virtual siege of the Strip, cutting it off from the outside world. The PA was also permitted to assume control of the Gaza-Egypt border crossing at Rafah for the first time on 25 November, although Israel suspended, in December, the operation of the Gaza-West Bank link. Moreover, also in December, Israel unilaterally declared a no-go zone in the northern Gaza Strip and proceeded to launch artillery and air strikes in the area. This was in response to the continued firing of Qassam rockets into Israel by the PIJ.

Old habits and new realities

In 2005, Israel accelerated efforts to secure its core territorial interests in the West Bank, with a view to unilaterally establishing its eastern frontier. Numerous reports in 2004–05 fuelled the government's fear that Israel was losing its grip over the territory known in the pre-independence period as Mandate Palestine (comprising Israel and the Palestinian Occupied Territories). The basis of this slippage was demography – Jews in Israel and the Occupied Territories had lower fertility rates than Arabs. Both Prime Minister Sharon and leaders in the main opposition party Avoda (Labour) shared the view that steps must be taken to ensure a Jewish majority in Israel, even if this required losing some territory in the West Bank. Efforts to secure 'core territorial interests' included the continuation of the controversial separation barrier and settlement expansion.

The government stepped up its efforts to complete a barrier it had begun erecting in

KEY INDICATORS — Israel

	Unit	2000	2001	2002	2003	2004
Population	m	6.04	6.40	6.51	6.61	6.70
Gross domestic product (GDP)	US$bn	110.40	110.40	103.60	109.04	*117.55
GDP per capita	US$	17,662	17,158	15,895	16,501	17,695
GDP real growth	%	6.4	-0.6	-1.0	0.9	4.3
Inflation	%	1.1	1.1	5.7	1.6	-0.4
Unemployment	%	8.8	9.3	10.3	11.3	*10.0
Exports (fob) (goods)	US$m	30,837.0	27,395.0	29,470.0	29,320.0	36,167.0
Imports (fob) (goods)	US$m	34,187.0	30,944.0	35,240.0	32,270.0	38,564.0
Balance of trade	US$m	-3,350.0	-3,549.0	-6,800.0	-2,950.0	-2,397.0
Current account	US$m	-1,700.0	-2,090.0	-1,820.0	150.0	140.0
Total reserves minus gold	US$m	23,281.2	23,378.6	24,082.9	26,315.1	27,094.4
Foreign exchange	US$m	23,163.0	23,179.1	23,665.0	25,778.4	26,616.0
Exchange rate	per US$	4.08	4.21	4.63	4.60	4.48

* estimated figure

June 2002, despite a ruling against it by the International Court of Justice (ICJ) in July 2004. According to the government, the barrier was designed to prevent Palestinian suicide bombers from entering Israel. However, in many sections of its 670km length, the barrier extends deep into the West Bank, expropriating 6–8 per cent of Palestinian land. The government was forced to revise small sections of the barrier in 2005, after rulings against it in the Israeli Supreme Court. In November, a confidential EU report, which was leaked, accused Israel of using the barrier to seize Palestinian land, particularly in the Jerusalem area. The report asserted that the government was deliberately sealing off Arab East Jerusalem, which the Palestinians want as their future capital, from the rest of the West Bank, effectively annexing it to Israel.

Throughout 2005, Israel announced or approved new plans to expand several of its settlements in the West Bank. These included towns near the Green Line, such as Beitar Ilit and Elkana, but also Ariel and Maale Adumin, which cut deep into the West Bank. These came despite numerous statements from US officials calling for Israel to honour previous commitments to halt such expansion.

On 8 March, an official report was submitted (the Sasson Report) to the government documenting the expansion of illegal settlement outposts in the West Bank over the last 15 years. The report castigated the government and its various predecessors for clandestinely assisting in the establishment of the outposts. Many of these had been erected after March 2001, drawing attention to a promise given by Prime Minister Sharon to US President George W Bush. Israel had undertaken to dismantle all outposts built after this time but had in fact only removed a tiny proportion. Although the government agreed to act on the findings, little action was taken in 2005.

Bulldozer demolishes own work (2)

Some political commentators had, in recent years, predicted a big bang in Israeli politics, whereby significant parts of the two major parties, Likud and Avoda, would merge to form a new, centrist faction. On 21 November, Prime Minister Sharon announced that he was quitting the Likud – a party he had helped found in 1973. Sharon subsequently announced the formation of a new political party, Kadima, which he intended to lead into early national elections, later called for 28 March. The purpose of Kadima, stated Sharon, was to capture the centre ground of Israeli politics and to reach a lasting agreement with the Palestinians. Fourteen Likud and two Avoda parliamentarians immediately defected to Kadima, as did a member of a small religious party. In the following weeks, other members of parliament including former Avoda prime minister Shimon Peres and Likud defence minister in Sharon's out-going government, Shaul Mofaz, defected to Kadima. Dozens of other public figures, including mayors and academics, also joined.

The immediate catalyst for the big bang had been the victory of Amir Peretz in an Avoda leadership contest, on 10 November. However, Sharon's problems with his own party, the Likud, lay at the heart of his dramatic split. Peretz had defeated acting leader Peres. Peres had taken Avoda into a coalition with Sharon's Likud the previous January and was a long-time personal friend of Sharon. Sharon feared, correctly, that Avoda under Peretz would dissolve the coalition, leaving him without counterpoint to dissidents within his own party. Beginning in June 2004, rebels within the Likud party worked to change Sharon's policies regarding the Palestinians, particularly the disengagement plan, and failing in this set about inflicting a series of embarrassing parliamentary defeats on the prime minister. A new coalition, forged in January 2005, including Likud, Avoda and two small religious parties failed to alleviate Sharon's problems. In August, the pressure mounted again when Sharon's right-wing rival within the Likud, Binyamin Netanyahu, resigned from the government to launch a leadership challenge. Although Sharon fended off Netanyahu in September, after nearly a year and a half of Likud infighting it was evident that his patience with his own party had worn thin.

Opinion polls taken in the weeks immediately following Kadima's birth indicated that the new party would easily win the most seats in the upcoming election.

War of words

Israel entered into a war of words with Iran in 2005. In January, Israel warned that Iran was only three years off from producing its own nuclear bomb. The government denied that Israel would attack Iran to prevent such a development but urged the international community to pressure Iran to stay its course. In October, Iranian president Mahmoud Ahmadinejad called for Israel to be 'wiped off the map' and, in December, publicly questioned the occurrence of the Holocaust.

Outlook

Israel's domestic order was again thrown into turmoil when Prime Minister Sharon suffered a major stroke on 4 January 2006. Sharon had suffered a minor stroke on 18 December 2005 but had appeared to recover fully. Sharon remains in a coma, despite several operations to alleviate his condition. Sharon's long-term deputy in government, Ehud Olmert became acting prime minister and acting leader of Kadima.

Although both strokes had stressed the nerves of some who saw Sharon and his new party as the best means of achieving peace and stability for Israel, opinion polls still indicated that Kadima, stroke or no, was heading for a stunning electoral victory. Indeed, Kadima's position improved in the polls taken after 4 January.

The political scene was complicated further by Hamas' landslide victory in PA elections on 25 January. The US and many other countries joined Israel in its proclamation that it would refuse to negotiate with a Hamas-led PA, unless it renounced violence and recognised the state of Israel.

If, as expected, Olmert leads Kadima to victory on 28 March, it is likely that he will form a coalition with Avoda and one or more of the religious parties. Based on his campaign announcements to date, as well as his previous statements, Olmert is expected to renew Israel's efforts to finalise Israel's eastern border and to secure an agreement with the Palestinians. Even with the PA in the hands of Hamas, Olmert will still be able to conduct negotiations with non-Hamas Palestinian representatives, including President Mahmoud Abbas and/or the Palestine Liberation Organisation (PLO). Failing this, Olmert has indicated that more unilateral withdrawals are possible, without reference to the Palestinians. However, such a development would likely put at risk both the short and long-term stability of the region, as the Palestinians have their own minimum expectations regarding a future state.

Risk assessment

Politics	Stabilising
Economy	Improving
Regional stability	Tense

COUNTRY PROFILE

Historical profile
The struggle between the Israelis and the Palestinians over historic claims to land is one of the most enduring of all the world's conflicts.

1917 The Balfour Declaration suggested the establishment in Palestine of a national home for the Jewish people.
1922 The Council of the League of Nations assigned to Britain a mandate for the Ottoman Arab territory of Palestine, a region that covered present-day Israel and Jordan, plus the Golan Heights region (claimed by Syria). The British divided the mandate into two parts, designating all lands west of the Jordan River as Palestine and those east of the river as Transjordan. The League of Nations mandate also addressed the goal of restoring a Jewish homeland in Palestine.
1929 Riots in Jerusalem between Arab Palestinians and Jews were sparked by a dispute over the use of the western wall of the Al Aqsa Mosque (the site is sacred to Muslims, and Jews claim it as part of their temple).
1936–39 The Arab Higher Committee opposed Jewish immigration to Palestine and the Peel Commission concluded that the mandate in Palestine was unworkable. Legislation limiting the number of Jewish immigrants into Palestine was introduced by the British government.
1945–46 Many Jews who had survived the Nazi German Holocaust arrived in Palestine and Jewish extremists began to oppose Britain's immigration legislation. Transjordan became independent and was later re-named Jordan.
1947 Britain decided to leave Palestine and called on the UN to make recommendations. The UN adopted Resolution 181, which called for the establishment of both Jewish and Arab states within Palestine. A partition plan was drawn up, based solely on population, with Jerusalem as an international zone under UN jurisdiction. The Jews agreed to the partition; the Arabs refused.
1948 Conflict ensued between Arabs and Jews. Jewish leaders announced the formation of the State of Israel, open to the immigration of Jews from all countries. Egypt, Iraq, Lebanon, Syria and Jordan joined Palestinian and other Arab guerrillas and invaded Israel. The armistice agreements extended the territory under Israel's control beyond the UN partition boundaries. Many Arabs fled Israel to become refugees in the surrounding Arab countries, ending the Arab majority in the new Jewish state.
1956 Egypt blockaded the Red Sea port of Eilat and Israeli forces attacked and occupied the Sinai peninsula, later being joined by Britain and France, which sought to regain control of the Canal Zone. In the face of strong international opposition, particularly from the US, all three withdrew their forces.
1967 After Egypt again blockaded Eilat, Israel launched and won the Six Day War against Egypt, Jordan and Syria, taking control of the Sinai peninsular and the Gaza Strip, which had been Egyptian territory, together with the Golan Heights, formerly claimed by Syria, and the West Bank, including East Jerusalem, which had been united with Jordan since 1950. Around 300,000 Palestinian Arabs fled to Jordan.
Israel's settlement policy started; it occupied the Sinai peninsular, the Golan Heights, the Gaza Strip and the West Bank, including East Jerusalem, re-unifying the city; the Jews transferred to these areas became known as settlers and the territories became known as the occupied territories.
1968–70 The War of Attrition was a limited war fought between Egypt and Israel, initiated by Egypt as a way to recapture the Sinai from Israel. The war ended with frontiers at the same place as when the war started.
1973 Lebanon was used by the Palestinians as a base for activities against Israel. In retaliation, Israeli commandos raided Beirut, killing three associates of Palestine Liberation Organisation (PLO) chairman, Yasser Arafat. In the 6 October War (also known as the Yom Kippur War), Egypt and Syria invaded Israel to reclaim some of the land lost in the Six Day War, but despite some early strategic gains by Egypt and Syria, Israel counter-attacked and repelled the invasion, re-conquering the Golan Heights from Syria.
1978 Prime Minister Menachim Begin and Egyptian Prime Minister Anwar Sadat signed peace accords at Camp David in the US. Israel agreed to withdraw from the Sinai.
1981 Israel annexed East Jerusalem and the Golan Heights.
1982–85 The Sinai peninsular was returned to Egypt in 1982. Israel launched a full-scale invasion of Lebanon. Despite subsequently withdrawing from most of the territory, Israel maintained some troops in Lebanon in order to help secure its own northern border. 1987 The Palestinians launched an *intifida* (uprising) against the Israelis.
1988 The Harakat al Muqawama al Islamia (Hamas) (Islamic Resistance Movement) was formed and began armed resistance to Israeli rule in the occupied territories of the West Bank and Gaza Strip.
1989 Mass immigration, of Jews from the Soviet Union, began; many settled in the occupied territories.
1991–93 Israel and the PLO conducted secret negotiations in the Norwegian capital of Oslo, crafting an interim peace accord, which was signed in the US. The Oslo Peace Accords laid the basis for transfer of authority from the Israeli military administration to the PLO in the Gaza Strip and an undefined area around the town of Jericho in the West Bank. President Ezer Weizman took office.
1995–96 A follow-up treaty, Oslo II, (known collectively, with the first, as the Accord), was signed. It envisaged Palestinian autonomy, with Israeli troop units withdrawn from the West Bank. Yasser Arafat was elected president of the Palestinian Legislative Council (PLC), the assembly of the Palestinian National Authority (PNA).
2000 President Ezer Weizman resigned three years before the end of his second term; Moshe Katsav, (Likud party), was elected president. Israel withdrew its forces from southern Lebanon without reaching an agreement with Syria on the future of the Golan Heights. The Camp David summit aimed a pushing forward the Accord failed when no agreement could be reached; the Palestinians claimed sovereignty over all of east Jerusalem, including Judaism's holiest place Temple Mount. The right-wing opposition leader, Ariel Sharon, made a provocative visit to Palestinian controlled Temple Mount (called al Haram as Sharif by Arabs) and the second *intifada* was launched. A total blockade was imposed by Israel on the West Bank and Gaza.
2001 Ariel Sharon was elected prime minister. He declared the PNA a terrorist-supporting organisation and launched Operation 'Defensive Shield', invading the PNA-controlled West Bank and Gaza Strip, attacking its institutions and besieging Yasser Arafat's headquarters.
2002 Saudi Arabia proposed a peace initiative, whereby Israel could have normal relations, peace and security with the Arab world if Israel withdrew from captured territories and agreed to recognise a Palestinian state. Israel began building a 640km security barrier, claiming it was the only way to control the infiltration of militant terrorists.
2003 US President Bush unveiled the Middle East Road Map to Peace, to run between 2003–05, with a cease-fire, an end to Jewish settlements in the occupied territories and the creation of an independent Palestinian state. However neither side kept to its timetable and it, *de facto*, failed.
2004 In February, it was announced that all Jewish settlements in the Gaza Strip would be removed. On 3 May, Sharon's government survived a no-confidence vote. The International Court of Justice ruled that the West Bank security barrier was illegal, and that construction should halt. In December, Sharon's minority coalition was on the brink of collapse after he dismissed four Shinui ministers who had voted against the 2005 budget bill. President Yasser Arafat died in November.

2005 Israel's parliament approved Sharon's new coalition government on 10 January. On 8 February, Sharon and the newly elected Palestinian president, Mahmoud Abbas, signed a truce that planned to bring to an end four years of violence between the two countries. Egypt and Jordan agreed to return their ambassadors to Israel. On 20 February, the cabinet approved the removal of Jewish illegal settlers from the Gaza Strip and part of the West Bank. Hamas bombed targets in Israel claiming it was not party to the truce. Abbas ordered a crackdown and sacked senior security chiefs. On 21 August Israeli troops began clearing Jewish settlements from Gaza. Most commercial buildings were left standing but some homes and synagogues were destroyed. In November Sharon left the Likud, a party he had helped found, to form a centrist party, Kadima, which would be aligned between the right-of-centre Likud and Labour on the left. Sharon suffered a minor stroke on 18 December. On 19 December, Binyamin Netanyahu was elected to replace him as leader of Likud.

2006 Ariel Sharon suffered a massive stroke on 4 January; his deputy, Ehud Olmert, took over as acting prime minister. He will remain as acting prime minister until the elections scheduled for 28 March are held. Olmert was asked by the Kadima party to stand in as party chairman. The four Likud party ministers were ordered to resign by Mr Netanyahu – three resigned on December 12.

Political structure
Constitution
Israel passed the Law and Administration Ordinance on attaining independence, in 1948. In the Declaration of the Establishment of the State of Israel that embodied the principals of law, it was recognised that these principals would evolve in time and circumstances.
Basic laws set out the powers of the executive, legislative and judicial branches. The country functions without a written constitution as Israel's founders wanted to avoid creating problems between religious and secular Jews and between Jews and the non-Jewish minority.
Form of state
Parliamentary democracy
The executive
Executive power rests with the government (a cabinet of ministers), headed by a prime minister as head of government. The government may determine its own agenda and executive procedures.
The prime minister is directly elected for four years and cannot be deposed from office without fresh elections.
The prime minister chooses members of the cabinet from either inside or outside the Knesset (parliament). The cabinet is responsible to the Knesset.
The president is Head of State and has a largely ceremonial role; elected every five years for a maximum of two terms.
National legislature
The 120-seat unicameral Knesset is elected by proportional representation for a maximum of four years. The country is divided into six *mezoh* (administrative districts).
Legal system
The law is based on English common law, components of Jewish religious law and some features of other systems, as appropriate.
The judiciary has constitutionally guaranteed independence. The court system has three levels: the Supreme Court, district courts and magistrates' courts. The court system does not employ juries in Israel. There is also a separate system of limited and specific tribunals that deal with military, labour law and religious, civil matters.
Last elections
28 January 2003 (parliamentary); 6 February 2001 (prime minister); 31 July 2000 (presidential).
Results: Parliamentary: the Likud party won 38 seats out of 120, Avoda 19, Shinui 15, Shas 11, National Union Party (NUP) seven, Meretz six, National Religious Party (NRP) six, United Torah Judaism (UTJ) five and smaller parties 13; turnout was 68.5 per cent.
The Likud-led coalition government, which includes the centre-right secular Shinui party, the far-right NRP and the NUP, gives Prime Minister Sharon an eight-vote majority in the Knesset.
Presidential: Moshe Katsav, the Likud party candidate, was elected president by parliament.
Next elections
28 March 2006 (parliamentary).

Political parties
Ruling party
Likud (right-wing)-led coalition government from 10 Jan 2005, including Labour and a small orthodox party
Main opposition party
Avoda (socialist coalition)

Population
6.70 million (2004)
Ethnic make-up
European, Middle Eastern and North African Jews, Arabs and Druze.
Religions
The Jewish, Muslim, Catholic, Greek Orthodox, Druze, Protestant and Baha'i faiths are all represented. Non-Jews make up 18 per cent of the population. They include 635,000 Muslims, 105,000 Christians (almost all Arabs) and 78,000 Druze. The ultra-orthodox Jewish, or charedi, population has nearly doubled since 1990 to about 600,000, or 10 per cent of Israel's population.

Education
Education is provided free of charge and is organised by the state. Primary schooling lasts until aged 11.
Secondary schools are divided into four groups: state schools, which are attended by the majority, state religious schools, Arab and Druze schools and Torah schools for ultra-orthodox Jews. Youth Aliya schools specialise in educating new immigrants.
Demand for tertiary education consistently outstrips domestic supply, so that more Israelis study at universities abroad than at home, giving the country a ratio of graduates that is one of the highest in the world. Public expenditure on education typically amounts to around 8 per cent of GDP.
Literacy rate: 95.3 per cent total; 93.4 per cent female, adult rates in 2002 (World Bank).
Compulsory years: Five to 16
Enrolment rate: 98 per cent total primary enrolment, of relevant age group (including repeaters); 88 per cent total secondary enrolment (World Bank).
Pupils per teacher: 14 in primary schools

Health
Total expenditure on health is 8–9 per cent of GDP, of which 70 per cent is government spending.
The ministry of health, the large municipalities, private, non-profit institutions and health insurance funds cater to different medical facilities. Companies are required to contribute to insurance for their employees to cover hospital treatment. The Histadrut (General Federation of Labour) whose members include 90 per cent of Jewish workers, provide sickness benefits and medical care. About 95 per cent of the population are covered by a health insurance plan.
Smoking is prevalent among 45 per cent of men and 30 per cent of women causing health hazards. It is estimated that 99 per cent of the population have access to safe water and sanitation facilities are universal. By 2002, 95 per cent of children aged under 12 years were immunised.
HIV prevalence: 0.1 per cent aged 15–49 in 2003 (World Bank)
Life expectancy: 78.8 years (World Bank)
Fertility rate/Maternal mortality rate: 2.7 births per woman; maternal mortality 5 per 100,000 live births (World Bank).
Birth rate/Death rate: 6 death and 21 births per 1,000 people (World Bank)
Infant mortality rate: 5.0 per 1,000 live births (World Bank)
Head of population per physician/ bed: 4.6 physicians and 6 hospital beds available per 1,000 people.

Welfare

There is a state-sponsored social welfare system, the National Insurance Institute, which covers the entire population. It is largely financed by compulsory monthly fees collected under the National Insurance Law, with the government providing the remaining funds. The system provides pensions, general disability payments, work injury compensation, child support and other allowances. The Institute also reimburses employers for salaries paid to employees during annual military reserve duty. Citizens disabled during military service are entitled to additional benefits from the defence ministry.

Main cities

Jerusalem (capital, estimated population 695,500 in 2003). Israel regards the entire city as its capital, but its claim to East Jerusalem, captured by Arab forces in 1948 but recaptured by Israel in 1967, is disputed by Palestinians and a number of other countries.

Most embassies are located in Tel Aviv (estimated population 365,300 in 2003). Other cities include Haifa (280,200) and Bersheva (186,900).

Languages spoken

English and European languages are widely spoken. Arabic is the most common language among non-Jews.

Official language/s
Hebrew

Media

Press
There are three press agencies in Israel. Itim, the Hebrew-language news agency, is an independent Israeli newspaper co-operative. There is also the Jewish Telegraphic Agency. The Palestine Press Service is the only Arab agency in the occupied territories.

The Israeli Press Council was set up in 1963 to supervise matters regarding the press. It issued a code of professional ethnics which is mandatory for all journalists.

The Daily Newspaper Publishers' Association conducts negotiations between publishers and the government, sets contract terms for employees, and purchases and distributes newsprint.

Dailies: Most Hebrew newspapers and journals are published from Tel Aviv. The English-language *Jerusalem Post* is published in West Jerusalem. Most Arabic newspapers are published in East Jerusalem, with the exception of *Al Ittihad*, which is published in Haifa. The important dailies include *Al Ayam, Al Quds, Ha'aretz, Yediot Aharonoth* and *Ma'ariv*. Gamla is an on-line newsletter (http://www.gamla.org.il/english/index1.htm) carrying news and commentary on the political issues of the Middle East.

Business: Business publications include the English language monthly *Israel Economist* and the weekly publication *Globes* (www.globes.co.il), which is in Hebrew and English. I-Biz runs a regularly updated business news site: www.i-biz.co.il.

Broadcasting
Radio: Israel Radio broadcasts nationally on five stations, one of which is in Arabic. There are external services broadcasts in Hebrew and a handful of other Middle Eastern and European languages.

Television: Colour service is in Hebrew and Arabic, with controlled advertising, transmitted by Israel Broadcasting Authority (IBA). There are daily news bulletins in English. Educational service is provided by the Instructional Television Trust. A second channel has been transmitting since 1989. The first commercial television station began in 1993. Programmes can be received from neighbouring countries.

Advertising
Besides television, radio and press, there is cinema screen advertising, as well as limited poster and illuminated sign facilities. Newspapers account for around 46 per cent of adspend but revenues are falling; television expenditure has swelled to 23 per cent of total national advertising spending; radio accounts for 9 per cent of total advertising revenue.

Economy

The Israeli economy seems to have turned a corner with growth in 2004 at 4.3 per cent, up from a modest 0.9 per cent growth in 2003, which had followed two years of contraction. Global growth and a better state of security, coupled with economic reforms that have tightened fiscal conditions plus an easing of monetary policies have contributed to the improvement. Exports and private consumption were the leaders and growth has continued, although not so strongly. While unemployment is still high at around 10 per cent, the trend shows it falling.

The economy has been severely damaged by the Palestinian conflict estimated, by the Tel Aviv-based Adva Centre, to have caused US$7– US$12 billion in losses between 2000–04. The Israeli government has had to face the harsh task of cutting public debt by postponing infrastructure improvement and reducing social programmes and limiting future expenditure growth.

The security barrier between Israeli and Palestinian territories has sparked international controversy and could restrict foreign aid, on which the country is reliant. Agriculture contributes around 2 per cent to GDP, industry 17 per cent and the services sector 81 per cent. The country has become a centre for the production of high technology products, especially software, for global markets. The state participates in all industries and services except agriculture but has said it will reduce its role. There is a significant co-operative sector, involved in industry, agriculture and construction and a considerable number of joint ventures between firms in different sectors.

External trade

Israel has a free trade agreement with the US and signed an EU trade and co-operation accord to bolster stability and trade in the Euro-Mediterranean region.

Imports
Principal imports include raw materials, military equipment, investment goods, rough diamonds, fuels, grain, consumer goods.

Main sources: US (15 per cent total, 2004), Belgium (10.1 per cent), Germany (7.5 per cent), Switzerland (6.5 per cent), UK (6.1 per cent)

Exports
Principal exports are machinery and equipment, software, cut diamonds, agricultural products, chemicals, textiles and apparel.

Main destinations: US (36.8 per cent total, 2004), Belgium (7.5 per cent), Hong Kong (4.9 per cent)

Agriculture

Farming
The agricultural sector contributes around 2 per cent to GDP and employs 5 per cent of the working population.

Israel is largely self-sufficient in food, importing some cereals, sugar beet and animal feeds. Food, beverages and tobacco are exported.

Farms are relatively small but mostly part of *kibbutzim* (larger co-operatives) or *moshavim* (co-operative smallholder villages), sharing machinery etc. The *kibbutz* and *moshav* movement formed the backbone of early Jewish settlement in Palestine before the State's creation in 1948. The *Keren Kayemeth Le Yisrael* (Jewish National Fund) was created in 1901 to buy land for the settlers. Since 1948 it has become involved in land development, especially land reclamation and forestry.

Israel's agricultural miracle of the 1950s and early 1960s, with annual growth levels of around 12 per cent, was based on intensive irrigated farming, the rise in domestic demand from new immigrants and the expansion of export markets. From the late 1960s, growth slowed to stagnation by the 1980s. Many blamed the bureaucratic marketing organisations for stifling incentives and others blamed an overemphasis on heavily irrigated cash crops, such as cotton, which have become

increasingly costly to produce and are vulnerable to international competition.
The major crops are fruits (30 per cent of total production), vegetables (14 per cent) and livestock (42 per cent).
About 40 per cent of farm produce is sold locally, 26 per cent to industry for processing and another 26 per cent is exported directly.
Of the total cultivated land area (4,400 square km), over half is under irrigation. The general trend in agriculture is towards greater mechanisation and many agricultural workers have transferred to industry. Crop production in 2004 included: 293585 tonnes (t) cereals in total, 165,635t wheat, 80,000t maize, 570,777t potatoes, 21,301t sweet potatoes, 36,850t sorghum, 10,700t barley, 95,000t bananas, 14,805t pulses, 240,000t citrus fruit, 14,300t dates, 95,000t grapes, 405,000t tomatoes, 65,000t avocados, 29,965t oilcrops, 50,000t olives, 335,000t watermelons, 5,201t treenuts, 125,000t apples, 47,500t seed cotton, *20,000t cotton lint, 118,000t chillies & green peppers, 1,170,300t fruit in total, 1,669,895t vegetables in total. Livestock production included: 581,244t meat in total, 81,537t beef, 18,030t pig meat, 5,400t lamb, 2,567t goat meat, 473,630t poultry, 90,720t eggs, 1,208,119t milk, 3,200t honey, *80t camel meat, 810t sheepskins, *880t greasy wool, 6,200t cattle hides.
* estimate

Fishing
There is some fish farming; approximately 85 per cent of the total catch of fish is consumed locally.

Forestry
Between 60,000–70,000 tonnes of timber are harvested annually. Imported forest products amounted to US$760 million in 2003, while exports were US$45 million.

Industry and manufacturing
The sector contributes around 17 per cent to GDP and employs 28 per cent of the working population.
The growth sectors are the capital intensive, science-based industries, such as aircraft (executive jets and fighters), electronics (telecommunications equipment), biotechnology, agricultural technology, chemicals and mining.
A wide range of goods are made or assembled for the domestic market, including cars, commercial vehicles, electrical goods, paper and paper products.
Israeli governments have historically worked with trade unions and employers to plan economic policy. Key policy elements have been to build up basic industry with state or trade union funds and high-tech industries that are either state-owned (a spin-off from the important arms industry) or privately-owned, but which benefit from government incentives aimed specifically at attracting foreign technology. Industry has long been supported with protective tariffs and subsidies, but Israel is progressively exposing its domestic market to competition from abroad as a result of growing trade with the EU and the US. Exports are vitally important to Israeli industry on account of the small size of the domestic market.
The strength of the Israeli manufacturing industry is increasingly in high technology. Traditional industries, such as food processing, textiles, metals, rubber and plastics and chemicals, are well developed but the future manufacturing base is likely to be in heavy and hi-tech industries, particularly the defence industry. Government policy is to shift from low value labour intensive industries to high value hi-tech industries. These have become increasingly important as labour-intensive industries such as the textile industry relocate to more competitive economies such as Jordan, Egypt and Turkey where labour costs are lower.
In 2005 the government embarked on its largest privatisation programme since the late 1990s. A stake of 30 per cent of Bezeq Israel Telecom was sold to a private consortium headed by media mogul Haim Saban, for US$970 million.

Tourism
The tourism industry is affected by the ongoing domestic terrorism since 2000. It has been estimated that up to 2 out of 3 anticipated visitor arrivals failed to arrive. Luxury hotels, built in anticipation of the greater numbers, have been standing empty as the industry restructures itself. Numbers are increasing as the focus of marketing has turned to Jewish and Christian pilgrims, cultural tourists and secular visitors who now see the destination as a country with localised violence.
In 2003 Israel joined the Euromed Heritage Programme, a computerisation project, sponsored by the EU, which focusses on cultural tourists of archaeology, arts and history, promoting sites through the internet. Israel and Jordan have a joint marketing arrangement to package resorts for overseas visitors, such as cruise ships visiting the Gulf of Aqaba.
Travel and tourism is expected to add US$3 billion or 2.4 per cent of GDP in 2005 and employ 8.3 per cent of the total work force. Tourism should generate US$3.6 billion in total exports and is part of the reason that in 2005 it is estimated to have attracted US$2.7 billion or 13.3 per cent of total investment.

Mining
The mining sector typically contributes 1 per cent to GDP and employs 1 per cent of the workforce.
There are vast reserves of potash, bromine and periclase in the area of the Dead Sea, the world's most saline lake, and deposits of 600 million tonnes of phosphate rock in the Negev Desert. These evaporites are produced for fertilisers and industrial minerals. Phosphates are mined at Oron (around 1.2 million tonnes per annum); potash is extracted from the Dead Sea at Sodom (approximately 3.5 million tonnes per annum). Israel is the world's second-largest producer of bromine and produces 20 per cent of world output.

Hydrocarbons
Israel does not produce oil and for political and security reasons is reluctant to obtain its hydrocarbons from one single source, particularly one from the Middle East. Currently Israel obtains the majority of its oil from Russia and central Asia – Turkmenistan and Kazakhstan. Other sources include Mexico, Egypt, Angola and the UK. It imports around 300,000 barrels per day (bpd) and it is estimated to have around four million barrels of oil reserves located underneath gas reserves. There has been significant oil exploration onshore and in the Mediterranean (with the drilling of over 350 wells). In May 2004 a deposit to the east of Kfar Saba was discovered with an estimated billion barrels of oil. Israel has two oil refineries, at Haifa and Ashdod, with a joint capacity of 220,000bpd, this supplies all of the country's refined oil needs. If the Israeli-Palestinian conflict is resolved then Israel could provide an alternative route for oil exports from the Gulf to the West. At present, oil exports travel through the Suez canal or around southern Africa. Israel has an estimated 600 million tonnes of recoverable oil shale, producing around 9,000bpd. This reserve is located mainly in the Rotem basin region.
Natural gas reserves are estimated at 90–141 billion cubic metres (cum), found in deposits off the Israeli coast and Gaza Strip coast.
Israel has plans to increase the percentage of natural gas in its energy mix. The Yam Thetis group, constructed a gas production and distribution facility delivering gas from the Mari field (offshore) to the coast and production began in December 2004.
Approximately 32 per cent of Israel's energy requirements is met by coal. Israel does not produce coal but imports it primarily from South Africa, Columbia, Australia and Indonesia.

Nations of the World: A Political, Economic and Business Handbook

Energy
The Israel Electric Corporation (IEC) is the public utility company responsible for generating and supplying energy to the country. Israel has 9.1GW of installed electricity generating capacity, 70 per cent of which comes from coal-fired power stations, 25 per cent from oil-fired stations and the remainder by gas-oil and independent power producers (IPPs). Approximately 97 per cent of fuel requirements are met from imports.

The government forecasts that the country will need to expand capacity to 15.3GW by 2010. This will require an estimated US$1.3 billion investment in the sector. To do this, the government hopes to increase the participation of the private sector, with the aim of 10 per cent of electricity to be generated by IPPs.

The IEC has begun the process of converting diesel-powered generators to natural gas. It hopes to generate 40 per cent of its energy from gas by 2006. It is also in the process of acquiring new gas turbines, which will increase generating capacity by 650MW.

A new coal-fired power station in Ashkelon with sophisticated anti-pollution measures is expected to come online by 2009 and add 1,220MW to total generating capacity.

Solar power is widely used for domestic hot water heating, but not for the commercial generation of electricity.

Financial markets
Stock exchange
Israel's stock market is the Tel Aviv Stock Exchange (TASE).

Banking and insurance
The government introduce structural reforms to the banking system in 2005 with the legislation to break the dominance of the largest banks over capital markets. It is intended to open up the banking sector to foreign competition. The top two banks, Hapoalim and Leumi, will be required to sell their mutual funds before 2009 and provident funds by 2008. Smaller institutions have longer to do the same.

Central bank
The Bank of Israel (BOI), Jerusalem. It has the sole right to issue currency, create and implement monetary policy, regulate and supervise commercial and other banks, control foreign exchange, maintain foreign currency reserves and publish the only representative exchange rate for the shekel versus foreign currencies.

Main financial centre
Tel Aviv

Time
GMT plus two hours in winter (September to April); GMT plus three hours in summer (April to September).

Geography
Israel is at the eastern end of the Mediterranean Sea, with a coastline of about 270 km from the Lebanese border in the north to the north-eastern tip of the Sinai Desert in the south.

Topography is varied. The southern coastline is fairly straight, while the northern coast is characterised by indentations and inland hills. There is only one true bay, at Haifa, with a small bay opposite at Akko. The narrow, level coastal plain is the most densely populated and intensively cultivated part of the country and contains most industry.

The northern Galilee region receives more rainfall than the south, but is hilly and less developed agriculturally. The Negev Desert dominates more than half the southern part of the country, extending to the Gulf of Aqaba in the south. It is sparsely populated, and its arid soils require intensive irrigation. The Jordan Rift dominates the eastern boundary of the occupied West Bank, extending from the Sea of Galilee south to the Dead Sea and the Gulf of Aqaba. In the north-east, the Golan Heights, seized from Syria in 1967, contain Mount Hermon, the highest point in Israeli-controlled territory.

Climate
The climate is subtropical, with summer temperatures reaching 44 degrees Celsius (C), especially in the south. Winter temperatures dip to zero degrees C in Jerusalem and the north.

Dress codes
Basking in warm weather most of the year, Israelis have an antipathy for ties, except on formal occasions. Jackets are rarely required, but have become more popular. Much of the country has a desert climate, with hot days and cool evenings. In hilly Jerusalem, temperature differences can be dramatic and even in the height of summer a sweater is often necessary at night. Warm sweaters are recommended in winter as central heating in private homes is rare in Tel Aviv and often inadequate in Jerusalem. Tel Aviv, along the coast, is far more humid and evenings are warmer. For women, modest clothing is recommended in Muslim, Christian or Jewish religious shrines and in most Arab areas, particularly in the occupied territories and East Jerusalem as well as in the ultra-orthodox Jewish section of Jerusalem, Mea She'arim. Women wearing trousers or sleeveless tops in these areas risk being hissed at. Elsewhere, dress for women is usually casual.

Entry requirements
Passports
All travellers require passports with at least six months validity from the date of entry to Israel.

The Israeli Ministry of the Interior insists that Israeli citizens holding dual nationality must enter and leave Israel on their Israeli passport.

Israeli exit tax at land borders: US$16. NB When crossing into Israel from any border other than the West Bank, it is important to note that an Israeli stamp, or exit stamp from any of the neighbouring countries, will mean entry is barred to almost any other Arab country. It is possible to request that the passport should not be stamped and a separate form is stamped instead and attached to the passport; the form can be removed when exiting the country.

Visa
Israel has agreements with 65 countries for visa-free travel, including most citizens from Europe, the Americas, Australasia and some Asian countries; transit passengers with onward passage within 24 hours.

Prohibited entry
Persons carrying a Palestinian identity number will not be permitted to enter Israel through Ben Gurion International Airport if their last departure was through the Allenby Bridge or Rafah border crossings.

Currency advice/regulations
There is no limit to the amount of foreign or Israeli currency taken in by visitors. Up to US$100 worth of Israeli currency may be converted to other currencies on departure without proof of foreign exchange transactions during stay. There are temporary restrictions for foreign citizens of Palestinian origin. Most foreign exchange transactions are carried out by banks but licensed money-changers operate openly in Arab East Jerusalem, offering a better rate. Most hotels offer currency exchange.

Customs
Video cameras and other electronic items must be declared upon entry.

Health (for visitors)
Mandatory precautions
There are no vaccinations required.
Advisable precautions
Precautions are advised against typhoid and polio. Mains water is normally safe to drink but readily available bottled water is advised for the first few weeks of a visit.

Hotels
Plenty of hotels in business and tourist centres. Service charge of 15 per cent usually added to bill. Settlement of bills in foreign currency will avoid payment of local taxes. Many hotels quote prices in US dollars.

Credit cards
American Express, Diners Club, Visa and Mastercard/Access are widely accepted. The latter can be used to withdraw funds from affiliated banks.

Israel

Public holidays
Variable dates
Purim (banks only) (Mar), First day of Passover (Apr), Last day of Passover (Apr), Yom Ha'atzmaut (Israel Independence Day) (May), Shavuot (Pentecost) (Jun), Tisha B'Av (ninth of Av fast) (banks only) (Aug), Rosh Hashanah (Jewish New Year) (Sep/Oct), Yom Kippur (Day of Atonement) (Oct), First day of Succoth (Feast of Tabernacles) (Oct), Last day of Sukkot (Feast of Tabernacles) (Oct), Shemini Atzeret (Celebration of Renewal and Thanksgiving) (Oct), Chanukah (Feast of the Lights) (Dec).

The Jewish religious day is Saturday – *Shabbat* – and begins at nightfall on Friday until nightfall on Saturday. Most public services and shops close early on Friday.

Muslim and Christian holidays are also observed by the respective populations. Thus, depending on the district, the day of rest falls on Friday, Saturday or Sunday. 2005 begins in the Jewish year 5765 and ends in 5766; 2006 begins in 5766 and ends in 5767.

Working hours
Banking
Sun–Tue and Thu: 0900–1700. All banks are closed on Saturday, and the afternoons of Wednesday and Friday. Foreign banks are open up to 1900.

Business
Sun–Thu: 0800–1730. On Fridays, some businesses stay open until 1230, but most close all day.

Government
Sun–Thu: 0730–1430 (Jun–Oct); 0730–1300, 1345–1600 (Nov–May). All government offices close on Friday afternoon and all day on Saturday.

Shops
Sun–Fri: 0800–1900; some shops close 1300–1600. Jewish shops observe closing time near sunset Friday evenings; Arabic stores are closed on Friday; Christian shops are closed on Sunday. Shops in hotels are often open until midnight.

Telecommunications
Mobile phones
There are GSM 900/1800 roaming facilities available, with coverage throughout Israel and the West Bank.

Electricity supply
220V AC, 50 cycles. Most sockets are round and three-pronged so a European adaptor is necessary.

Weights and measures
Metric system, but area is usually measured in dunam (1,000 sq metres).

Social customs/useful tips
People are hospitable and informal and culturally diverse. Jewish traditions and customs are generally adhered to.

Israel is largely secular in character and Mediterranean in style. The Jewish Sabbath, from Friday dusk until Saturday dusk is, however, widely observed. Shops close on Friday by 1400 and do not open again until Sunday morning. Most cinemas and restaurants are closed on Friday night. In most cities over the Sabbath there is no public transport (except for taxis), postal service, or banking service. Some religious sections in Jerusalem and the Tel Aviv suburb of Bnei Brak, as well as Tel Aviv's main street, Rehov Dizengoff, are closed to traffic. The same is true on six Jewish religious holidays.

Punctuality is not a strong point and business visitors should not be surprised to be kept waiting. Business meetings are less formal in character than in northern Europe but the normal courtesies are observed.

It is considered a violation of the Sabbath (Saturdays) to smoke in public places such as restaurants and hotels.

Security
Security is tight owing to the threat of terrorist activity, and delays in the ongoing peace process have increased tensions somewhat. Business travellers often encounter delays because of security alerts. Prolonged questioning and detailed searches may take place at the time of entry and/or departure. Do not leave bags unattended.

In Jerusalem, tourists should exercise caution at religious sites on holy days. Visitors are advised to avoid demonstrations and areas where large crowds are gathering. The theft of passports, credit cards and valuables from public beaches is commonplace. Visitors should carry passports at all times as a form of identity. Money and valuables should be kept out of sight.

Getting there
Air
National airline: El Al Israel.
El Al has an intensive security check and passengers are advised to arrive for flights in plenty of time.
International airport/s: Ben Gurion International (TLV), 20km south-east of Tel Aviv (50k west of Jerusalem); duty-free shop, bar, buffet, restaurant, hotel reservations, post office, shops, car hire.
Other airport/s: Eilat Central Airport (ETH)
Airport tax: None
Surface
Road: Tourists from Jordan can cross into Israel after obtaining a 'bridge pass' from the Jordanian Interior Ministry in Amman. It is also possible to cross the border at Eilat on the Red Sea coast. The road and bus route, via Cairo and Rafa (Gaza Strip), has been closed.
There is an exit tax of US$16 at all land border crossings.
Water: There are sailings between Larnaca (Cyprus) and Haifa three times a week.
Main port/s: Haifa, Ashdod and Eilat.

Getting about
National transport
Air: Arkia operate daily services from Tel Aviv to Jerusalem, Haifa, Eilat, and other major cities.
Road: Main roads are good. Maximum speed 90km per hour.
Buses: Buses connect all centres of population; they are frequent and cheap but can be crowded. Buses do not operate from sunset on Friday to sunset on Saturday.
Rail: Services between Tel Aviv and Haifa (hourly). Seats can be reserved. No service Friday evenings or Saturday.
City transport
Taxis: Taxis are metered but flat rates often apply so it is advisable to check with your hotel concierge before setting off on any long trips.
From Ben Gurion airport to Tel Aviv centre takes about 30 minutes.
Many offices close on Fridays and consequently traffic flows are better.
For inter-city travel (including Saturdays), *sherut* (share taxis) run between central points in main cities and are not expensive. Some *sherut* companies, including Arieh and Aviv, will accept advance bookings.
Car hire
International companies have offices in main cities and at Ben Gurion airport. Drivers must be over 21 years and have an international credit card and national or international licence. Seat belts are compulsory for drivers and front-seat passengers. Most road signs on major roads are in English.

BUSINESS DIRECTORY
The addresses listed below are a selection only. While World of Information makes every endeavour to check these addresses, we cannot guarantee that changes have not been made, especially to telephone numbers and area codes. We would welcome any corrections.

Telephone area codes
The international direct dialling (IDD) code for Israel is +972, followed by area code and subscriber's number:

Afula	4	Kfar Saba	9
Ashdod	8	Natanya	9
Ashkelon	8	Nazareth	4
Beersheva	8	Raanana	9
Briei Brak	3	Ramat Gan	3
Eilat	8	Rehovot	8

Haifa	4	Safed	4
Holon	3	Tel Aviv	3
Jerusalem	2		

Useful telephone numbers
International operator	188
Directory enquiries	144
Collect calls	142
Overseas operator	188
Ambulance	101
Fire	102
Police	100
Correct time	155

Chambers of Commerce
America-Israel Chamber of Commerce and Industry, 35 Shaul Hamelech Boulevard, PO Box 33174, Tel Aviv 61333 (tel: 695-2341; fax: 695-1272; e-mail: amcham@amcham.co.il).

British-Israel Chamber of Commerce, 29 Hamered Street, PO Box 50321, Tel Aviv 61502 (tel: 510-9424; fax: 510-9540; e-mail: isrbrit@bezeqint.net).

Federation of Israeli Chambers of Commerce, 84 Ha'ashmonaim Street, PO Box 20027, Tel Aviv 61200 (tel: 563-1020; fax: 561-9027; e-mail: chamber@chamber.org.il).

Haifa and the North Chamber of Commerce and Industry, 53 Ha'atzmaut Road, PO Box 33176, Haifa 31331 (tel: 862-6364; fax: 864-5424; e-mail: main@haifachamber.org.il).

Banking
Bank Hapoalim BM, 50 Rothschild Blvd, Tel Aviv 66883 (tel: 567-5777; fax: 567-6015; internet site: http://www.bankhapoalim.co.il).

Bank Leumi Le-Israel BM, 24-32 Yehuda Halevi St, Tel Aviv 65546 (tel: 514-8111; fax: 566-1872).

The First International Bank of Israel Ltd, Shalom Tower, 9 Ahad Haam St, Tel Aviv 65251 (tel: 519-6111; fax: 510-0316).

Investec Bank (Israel) Ltd; PO Box 677, 38 Rothschild Boulevard, Tel Aviv 61006 (tel: 564-5645; fax: 564-5210).

Israel Discount Bank Ltd, 27-31 Yehuda Halevi Street, Tel Aviv 65136 (tel: 514-5555; fax: 514-5346; internet site: http://www.discountbank.net).

Union Bank of Israel Ltd, 6-8 Ahuzat Bayit Street, Tel Aviv 65143 (tel: 519-1111; fax: 519-1421).

Central bank
Bank of Israel, PO Box 780, Kiryat Ben-Gurion, Jerusalem 91007 (tel: 655-2211; fax: 652-8805; e-mail: webmaster@bankisrael.gov.il).

Travel information
Arkia Israeli Airlines Ltd. (Charter Airline), Sde Dov, PO Box 39301, Tel Aviv, 61392 (tel: 690-2222; fax: 699-1512).

Automobile and Touring Club of Israel (MEMSI), 20 Harakevet Street, PO Box 65144, Tel Aviv 65117 (tel: 564-1122; fax: 566-0493).

Bus Station, Levinsky and Levanda intersection, Nava Sha'anan, Tel Aviv.

Dan Co-operative Society for Public Transport Ltd. (City buses), 39 Shaul Hamelech Blvd., Tel Aviv, 64928 (tel: 693-3333; fax: 693-3511).

Egged Israel Transport Co-operative Ltd. (Intercity buses), 142 Petach Tikvah Road, Tel Aviv, 64921 (tel: 692-2211; fax: 696-5354).

El Al Israel Airlines Ltd., Ben Gurion Airport, Lod, 71285 (tel: 971-6111; fax: 972-1442; internet site: http://www.elal.co.il).

Israel Airports Authority, Ben Gurion Airport (tel: 971-2804; fax: 971-2436). For information on taxes and tarrifs (tel: 971-5596).

Israel Ports and Railway Authority, 74 Derech Petach Tikva, POB 20121, Tel Aviv, 61201 (tel: 565-7000; fax: 512-1048).

Israel Railways, PO Box 18085, Tel Aviv, 61180 (tel: 542-1515; fax: 695-8176).

Municipal Information Offices: maps and information about Israel – Jaffa Gate, Jerusalem (tel: 280-382); information about Jerusalem only – Jaffa Road, Jerusalem (tel: 258-844); also offices at Nazareth and Bethlehem.

Ministry of tourism
Ministry of Tourism, 24 King George Street, PO Box 1018, Jerusalem 94262 (tel: 675-4811; fax: 625-3407; e-mail: doar@tourism.gov.il; internet site: www.travelnet.co.il).

Ministries
Prime Minister's Office, 3 Kaplan Street, PO Box 187, Kiryat Ben-Gurion, Jerusalem 91919 (tel: 670-5555; fax: 651-2631; e-mail: markal@pmo.gov.il).

Ministry of Agriculture, Agricultural Centre, PO Box 50200, Bet-Dagan (tel: 948-5555; e-mail: pniot@moag.gov.il).

Ministry of Communications, 23 Jaffa Street, Jerusalem 91999 (tel: 670-6320; fax: 670-6372; e-mail: intmocil@moc.gov.il).

Ministry of Construction and Housing, Kiryat Hamemshala, PO Box 18110, Jerusalem 91180 (tel: 584-7211; fax: 581-1904).

Ministry of Defence, Kaplan Street, Hakirya, Tel-Aviv 61909 (tel: 569-2010; fax: 691-6940).

Ministry of Education, 34 Shivtei Israel Street, PO Box 292, Jerusalem 91911 (tel: 560-2222; fax: 560-2223; e-mail: info@education.gov.il).

Ministry of the Environment, 5 Kanfei Nesharim Street, Givat Shaul, PO Box 34033, Jerusalem 95464 (tel: 655-3777; fax: 653-5934).

Ministry of Finance, 1 Kaplan Street, Kyriat Ben-Gurion, PO Box 13195, Jerusalem 91008 (tel: 531-7111; fax: 563-7891; e-mail: webmaster@mof.gov.il).

Ministry of Foreign Affairs, Hakirya, Romema, Jerusalem 91950 (tel: 530-3111; fax: 530-33367; e-mail: markal@mofa.gov.il; internet site: http://www.israel.org/indexfr.html).

Ministry of Health, 2 Ben-Tabai Street, PO Box 1176, Jerusalem 91010 (tel: 670-5705; fax: 623-3026).

Ministry of Industry and Trade, 30 Agron Street, PO Box 299, Jerusalem 91002 (tel: 622-0220; fax: 624-5110).

Ministry of the Interior, 2 Kaplan Street, PO Box 6158, Kiryat Ben-Gurion, Jerusalem 91061 (tel: 670-1411; fax: 670-1628).

Ministry of Justice, 29 Salah A-din Street, Jerusalem 91010 (tel: 670-8511; fax: 628-8618; e-mail: feedback@justice.gov.il).

Ministry of Labour and Social Welfare, 2 Kaplan Street, PO Box 915, Kiryat Ben-Gurion, Jerusalem 91008 (tel: 675-2311; fax: 675-2803).

Ministry of National Infrastructure, 216 Jaffa Street, Jerusalem 91130 (tel: 500-6777; fax: 500-6888).

Ministry of Public Security, Kiryat Hamemshala, PO Box 18182, Jerusalem 91181 (tel: 530-9999; fax: 584-7872).

Ministry of Religious Affairs, 236 Jaffa Street, PO Box 13059, Jerusalem 91130 (tel: 531-1171; fax: 531-1183; e-mail: tsibor@religinfoserv.gov.il).

Ministry of Science, Culture and Sport, Kiryat Hamemshala Hamizrahit, POB 49100, Jerusalem 91181 (tel: 541-1111).

Ministry of Transport, 97 Jaffa Street, Jerusalem 91000 (tel: 622-8211; fax: 622-8693).

Other useful addresses
Administration of Rabbinical Courts, 9 Koresh Street, Jerusalem 91012 (tel: 624-8603; fax: 624-5019).

British Embassy, 192 Hayarkon Street, Tel Aviv 63405 (tel: 524-9171; fax: 524-3313).

Central Bureau of Statistics, 3 Kaplan Street, PO Box 187, Kiryat Ben-Gurion, Jerusalem 91919 (tel: 655-3553; fax: 655-3325).

Israeli Academy of Sciences and Humanities, Albert Einstein Square, Talbieh, PO Box 4040, Jerusalem 91040 (tel: 563-6211).

Israel Airports Authority, Ben Gurion Airport (tel: 971-2804; fax: 971-2436). For information on taxes and tarrifs (tel: 971-5596).

Israel Convention Bureau (ISCOB), Israel Tourism Administration, PO Box 1018, Jerusalem.

Israeli Broadcasting Authority, Klal Building, 97 Jaffa Street, PO Box 6387, Jerusalem 91063 (tel: 529-1888).

Israel Chemicals Ltd., 123 Hahashmonaim Street, Tel Aviv, 67133 (tel: 563-0232; fax: 561-5391).

Israel Electric Corporation Ltd., 2 Hahagana Boulevard, Haifa, 35254 (tel: 854-8548; fax: 853-8149).

Israel Fuel Corporation Ltd. (Delek), Prof. Y. Kaufman Street, PO Box 50250, Tel Aviv, 61500 (tel: 591-5555; fax: 510-2072).

Israel Land Administration (part of the National Infrastructure Ministry), 6 Shamai Street, POB 2600, Jerusalem 94631 (tel: 520-8422; fax: 523-4960).

Israel Shipyards Ltd, Po Box 10630, Haifa Bay, 26118 (tel: 846-0245; fax: 841-0572).

Israel Telecommunication Corporation, PO Box 1088, Jerusalem, 91010 (tel: 539-5333; fax: 625-2506).

Israel Trade Fairs Centre/Israel Convention Centre, PO Box 21075, 61210 Tel Aviv (tel: 422-422).

Israeli Embassy (US), 3514 International Drive, NW, Washington DC 20008 (tel: 202-364-5500; fax: 202-364-5560; e-mail: ask@israelemb.org).

The Knesset, Kiryat Ben-Gurion, Jerusalem 91950 (tel: 675-3333; fax: 652-1599).

Manufacturers' Association of Israel, Industry House, PO Box 50022, 29 Hamered Street, Tel Aviv (tel: 650-121).

National Coal Supply Corporation Ltd., 155 Bialik Street, Ramat Gan, 52523 (tel: 751-2261; fax: 751-0119).

National Insurance Institute, 13 Weizmann Blvd, Jerusalem 91909 (tel: 670-9211; fax: 670-9792).

National Water Company (Mekorot), 9 Lincoln Street, Tel Aviv, 67134 (tel: 623-0555; fax: 623-0833).

Office of the President, 3 Hanassi Street, Jerusalem 92188 (tel: 670-7211; fax: 561-0037).

Oil Refineries Ltd., PO Box 4, Industrial Zone, Haifa, 31000 (tel: 878-8111; fax: 872-8319).

Ormat Industries Ltd., Po Box 68, Szydlowksi Road, New Industrial Area, Yavne, 70650 (tel: 433-777; fax: 439-901).

Pama Development for Energy and Sources, PO Box 20118, 14 Kalman Magen Street, Tel Aviv, 61200 (tel: 695-8129; fax: 695-8131).

Paz Oil Company Ltd., PO Box 434, 4 Hagefen Street, Haifa, 31003 (tel: 856-7111; fax: 852-2390).

Postal Authority, 237 Jaffa Street, Jerusalem 91999 (tel: 629-0800; fax: 629-0921).

State Comptroller, POB 1081, Jerusalem 91010 (tel: 531-5111).

Tahal Consulting Engineers Ltd (Water), PO Box 11170, 54 Ibn Gvirol Street, Tel Aviv, 61111 (tel: 692-4434; fax: 696-9969).

The Tel Aviv Stock Exchange Ltd (TASE), 54 Ahad Ha'am Street, Tel Aviv 65202; postal address: PO Box 29060, Tel Aviv 61290 (tel: 567-7411; fax: 510-5379; internet site: http://www.tase.co.il).

Zim Israel Navigation Co. Ltd., 7-9 Pal Yam Avenue, Haifa, 31000 (tel: 865-2111; fax: 865-2956).

Internet sites

Mercantile Discount Bank: http://www.mercantile.co.il

Yellow and White Pages: http://www.yellowpages.co.il

Italy

KEY FACTS

Official name: Repubblica Italiana (Italian Republic)

Head of State: President Carlo Azeglio Ciampi (since May 1999)

Head of government: Prime Minister Silvio Berlusconi (FI) (since 2001; sworn in again 23 Apr 2005)

Ruling party: Centre-right coalition from 23 Apr 2005: Forza Italia (FI) (Italian Force), Alleanza Nazionale (AN) (National Alliance), Lega Nord (LN) (Northern League) and Unione dei Democratici Cristiani e dei Democratici di Centro (Union of Christian and Centrist Democrats) and allied parties

Area: 301,277 square km

Population: 57.31 million (2004); 57.48 million (OECD, 2003)

Capital: Rome

Official language: Italian

Currency: Euro (eur) = 100 cents (from 1 Jan 2002; previous currency lira, locked at L1,936.27 per euro) (Campione d'Italia, an Italian enclave near Lake Lugano in Switzerland, uses the Swiss franc, although the euro also circulates)

Exchange rate: eur0.83 per US$ (Oct 2005)

GDP per capita: US$29,219 (2004)

GDP real growth: 1.20% (2004)

Labour force: 24.27 million (2004)

Unemployment: 8.00% (OECD, 2004)

Inflation: 2.30% (2004)

Oil production: 104,000 bpd (2004)

Balance of trade: US$7.10 billion (2004)*

Foreign debt: US$1,639.05 billion (2004)

Annual FDI: US$100.60 billion (cumulative, 1995–2004, OECD); US$16.80 billion (OECD, 2004)*

* estimated figure

In May 2005 Italy's four-party coalition government headed by billionaire media-magnate, and the country's richest man, Silvio Berlusconi, completed three years in power. This made it the longest serving government in Italy's post-war history. Since 1945, Italy has had 58 different governments each lasting, on average, less than a year.

Berlusconi's problems

Throughout his premiership, Berlusconi has been fighting a rearguard action against a number of legal actions and investigations, including three convictions for dishonesty, which have done little to create the image of probity and integrity he has sought to acquire. Taking a leaf out of French President Jacques Chirac's book, Berlusconi has succeeded in introducing legislation rendering Italy's prime minister and other senior officials immune from prosecution during their time in office.

In August 2003 the respected UK current affairs weekly magazine, *The Economist* went so far as to submit an open letter to Berlusconi challenging him to answer allegations about conflicting interests in his business and political career. In 2005 the journal still unapologetically asserted him to be 'unfit to govern'. The allegations included charges of bribing judges in a case relating to Berlusconi's holding company, Fininvest, of exerting political pressures on disgraced former prime minister, Bettino Craxi, and 'judicial interference' in the privatisation of the electricity utility SME. One of the magazine's main grievances against the tycoon is the fact that he holds sway over 90 per cent of mainstream television channels, stifling the potential for coverage of political opposition. Berlusconi's libel case against *The Economist* was dismissed by the Italian courts.

Fortunately for Berlusconi, his government appeared to be absolved of any direct involvement in Italy's biggest financial scandal, the collapse of the Parmalat group in 2003. Following the collapse, with debts estimated at eur14 billion (US$17.5 billion) it emerged that politically motivated payments had been made to Christian Democrat politicians, but these went back so far that they pre-dated Berlusconi's political debut in 1994. Thousands of Italian investors lost money, in many cases their life savings, by investing in Parmalat bonds. Parmalat executives had, it seemed, agreed on occasion to purchase bankrupt companies to avoid political embarrassment for their Unione dei Democratici Cristiani e dei Democratici di Centro (UDC) (Union of Christian and Centrist Democrats) cronies. Former finance minister Giulio Tremonti was quoted as saying that the Parmalat affair had cost the government eur11 billion, a figure which neatly approximated to the budget deficit shortfall.

In December 2005 after months of condemnation Antonio Fazio finally resigned from his post as governor of the Bank of Italy. He is being investigated by the European Commission for blocking a Dutch takeover of the Italian bank, Banca Antonveneta, in favour of domestic company Banca Popolare Italiana.

Immigration

A prominent topic in Italy in recent years has been the question of immigration, or more specifically, illegal immigration. As boatloads of illegal immigrants attempt to cross to Sicily or Lampedusa (an Italian island in the southern Mediterranean) the question of immigration has risen to the top of the political agenda. Italy has, in the past, been accused by the United Nations of maltreating immigrants and failing to observe due legal process in asylum applications. Its location inevitably makes Italy a popular destination for immigrants, not only from North Africa, but also from Central Europe, notably Albania, Romania and Moldova.

Disguising the deficit

Italy is Western Europe's fourth-largest economy, although a lower growth rate in the size of the working population and a history of low domestic investment have meant that both productivity and GDP growth have lagged behind its continental partners for some time. Over the past 15 years, Italy's economic growth has been rock-bottom in the league of EU countries.

Italy is a large industry-based economy with a heavy dependence on imported energy. Traditionally, the government has been significantly involved in industry through large state holding companies. However, a somewhat haphazard privatisation programme, started in 1992, has continued to reduce the government's role in the economy. Privatisation, or partial privatisation in the form of 'sell-offs' has been seen by the government as an opportunistic means of dressing up the national accounts when necessary. The progress of privatisation in Italy can be judged by the catastrophic state of the national airline, Alitalia, which has an estimated accumulated debt of some eur1.72 billion.

The investment climate is poor with very low levels of FDI. Italy was ranked 47th, slightly higher than Botswana, in the September 2005 World Economic Forum's competitiveness league. Productivity is low while labour costs are not. The cost of living has risen since the adoption of the single currency in 2002. Social indicators, such as holidays taken, new clothes bought and supermarket consumption, all add up to a picture of declining living standards.

The service sector, particularly tourism, is important to overall economic performance. Tourism is Italy's third biggest source of foreign income, after machinery and textiles and clothing (which are dangerously under threat from the rise of Chinese manufacturing). Florence alone receives over seven million visitors a year. The country's south, the *Mezzogiorno*, has much lower per capita income levels and higher unemployment rates than the more industrialised north, despite many years of heavy government subsidies. The severe regional imbalances in Italy's labour market are also a serious problem for the economy.

To improve growth, the government is trying to bolster consumer confidence with a number of measures and reforms, notably the proposed tax cuts that are due to take effect in 2006, which were given qualified backing by Domenico Siniscalco, the new finance minister. But try as the government might, the hoped-for rise in consumer confidence has failed to materialise. The new measures form part of a four-year economic plan that optimistically forecast a steady rise in economic growth.

KEY INDICATORS — Italy

	Unit	2000	2001	2002	2003	2004
Population	m	57.60	57.50	57.10	57.48	57.31
Gross domestic product (GDP)	US$bn	1,077.00	1,089.70	1,220.00	1,470.00	*1,672.30
GDP per capita	US$	18,620	18,950	21,240	25,137	29,219
GDP real growth	%	3.2	1.7	0.4	0.4	1.2
Inflation	%	2.5	2.8	2.6	2.8	2.3
Unemployment	%	10.5	9.5	9.0	8.9	8.0
Oil output	'000 bpd	88.0	79.0	103.0	107.0	104.0
Natural gas output	bn cum	16.8	15.5	15.1	13.7	13.0
Exports (fob) (goods)	US$m	238,736.0	242,430.0	252,000.0	290,231.0	336,400.0
Imports (fob) (goods)	US$m	228,019.0	226,568.0	241,090.0	289,017.0	329,300.0
Balance of trade	US$m	10,717.0	15,862.0	8,200.0	1,214.0	7,100.0
Current account	US$m	-5,670.0	-650.0	-7,120.0	-21,940.0	*-24,820.0
Total reserves minus gold	US$m	25,566.0	24,419.0	28,603.0	30,366.0	27,859.0
Foreign exchange	US$m	22,423.0	20,905.0	24,588.0	26,056.0	24,011.0
Exchange rate	per US$	2,096.78	2,115.24	^1.04	0.88	0.80

* estimated figure

^ From 1 Jan 2002; previous currency lira, was replaced by the euro

In 2005 Italy recorded GDP of 0.0 per cent – it was merciful that the economy did not actually contract. However, 2006 is set to bring 1.4 per cent growth. The parlous state of the Italian economy has meant that government revenues have fallen well below expectations, making it difficult, if not impossible, for the government to balance its books. Italy's budget deficit in 2006 is expected to be 5 per cent of GDP and well above the 3 per cent ceiling imposed by the EU's Stability and Growth Pact. Joaquin Alumnia, the EU commissioner for economic affairs, called the Italian deficit 'very worrying' in April 2005 and threatened sanctions.

In response to EU concerns over the possible scale of Italy's budget deficit, the Berlusconi government is planning a series of expenditure cuts totalling some eur10 billion (US$12 billion), to be followed by further cuts of eur12 billion (US$14.5 billion). The expenditure cuts were an essential counterpart of the government's plan to cut taxes by as much as eur12 billion in 2005/06, to be followed by further cuts in 2007/08. The first series of tax cuts had been ostensibly introduced to boost the flagging economy, although the timing of their introduction – to be shortly before Italy's next general election – did not go unnoticed.

At the end of 2005 Italy's public debt was some 120 per cent of GDP, the highest level in the EU, and on the rise. Italy's debt 'stock' is also the third highest in the world. While lower interest rates have reduced the cost of debt servicing, sustained budget deficits have made it difficult to reduce the figure; any sustained debt reduction programme would require the government to generate budget surpluses averaging 5 per cent of GDP, a surreal figure for the Italian economy. Under Berlusconi budget surpluses have become budget deficits, as government expenditure has grown at an average of 11.5 per cent annually, well above the recent minimal GDP growth rate.

Ripe for reform is Italy's antiquated pension regime, which costs the equivalent of 15 per cent of GDP annually. This figure is set to rise as Italy's negative demographics – a low birth-rate combined with increasing longevity – create greater financial imbalance. In mid-2004 the government proposed raising the retirement age from 57 to 62 by 2008, a measure calculated to save 0.7 per cent of GDP.

The country's birth rate is minimal, at only 1.3 children per family. The population is in decline and employment rates are among the lowest in western Europe, especially among young people. Forty per cent of Italians in their early thirties are living with their parents, unable to get a foot on the property ladder, nor a stable job.

External relations

Berlusconi has on occasion been quite nationalistic in his dealings with the EU, promising (but failing) to make the Italian economy, Europe's fourth largest, one of the most competitive in Western Europe and wanting to end the domination of the French and Germans in EU politics. The EU, which has already had to cope with the rise of right-wing parties in Austria, Belgium, France and the Netherlands, has become alarmed by the tone of Berlusconi's statements and the appointment of many anti-EU and right-wing politicians to his cabinet. The Berlusconi government's relations with the EU have been coloured by the fact that the outgoing President of the European Commission, Romano Prodi, is not only a former Italian prime minister, but is also a long standing political opponent of Berlusconi.

The left-leaning Prodi returned to Italy in late 2004 to resume a domestic political career. Berlusconi's approval ratings are at an all time low, while in October 2005, in primary elections, Prodi won 73.5 per cent of a vote to decide the next leader of the Olive Tree party. The high proportion of the vote means Prodi has secured a convincing mandate to challenge the incumbent in the 2006 elections.

In November 2005 Berlusconi announced voting reforms, to re-introduce proportional representation (PR) in time for the May 2006 poll. PR had been discarded in 1993 after a series of corruption scandals but has re-entered favour possibly because Berlusconi believes he has more chance of winning in this, rather than a first-past-the-post system. Also, the Senate will become a federal style house and regional authorities will get more power.

In general, Italians have shown themselves to be ardent Europeans, albeit for different reasons. In the relatively prosperous north, EU membership has been seen as a seal of approval for Italy's economic and political achievements. In the less prosperous south, EU membership has been seen as the source of substantial investment and aid. Both North and South share the commonly held conviction that the less importance Italian politicians have and the more that power moves to Brussels, the better.

Berlusconi has attempted to increase Italy's international profile, particularly in the run-up to the 2003 Iraq War, meeting with both US President George W Bush and Russian President Vladimir Putin. Italy supported the US-led coalition, but did not provide any troops, although they did send police officers (*carabineri*) to help in the post-war effort.

Berlusconi has also sought to increase Italy's influence within the EU. In particular, Berlusconi has made it known that he wants to end Franco-German domination of the EU. This has strengthened relations between Italy and the UK. Some observers believe that the strengthened Anglo-Italian relationship is the first step towards creating a new axis in EU politics.

However, this theory seemed to be discredited in 2004 when the government expressed its concern over the apparent formation of an EU 'directorate' between France, Germany and the UK following two EU 'summit' meetings between France's Jacques Chirac, Germany's Gerhard Schröder and the UK's Tony Blair, to which the Italians were not invited. Berlusconi described the second meeting, held in Berlin, as a 'big mess'. The UK has, however, generally been supportive of any EU member state when it has held a similar view or policy to its own. Historically, Italy has been more supportive of Western European political and economic integration. In 1957, it was one of the founder members of the predecessor of the EU, the European Economic Community (EEC). The UK has generally been lukewarm to Western Europe's integration and, unlike Italy, it is not a member of the euro-zone. The UK has also been looking for allies to help it increase its influence in the EU and end Franco-German domination.

Outlook

Following Forza Italia's reversals in the June 2004 elections, in the run-up to the next elections, which have to take place by May 2006, much will hinge on Romano Prodi's return to Italian politics. The polls suggest that Prodi's Olive Tree Coalition could obtain one-third of the vote from a seriously disillusioned Italian electorate. Were this to happen, by gaining the support of other left-wing parties – including the communists – Prodi could become prime minister again. It is doubtful whether the bundle of reforms proposed by Berlusconi will have had any noticeable effect on the economy before the elections. This would leave the new prime minister with the unattractive inheritance of a declining, unreformed and almost insolvent economy. Forza Italia indeed!

Italy

Risk assessment

Economic	Poor
Political	Fair
Regional Stability	Good
Stock Market	Fair

COUNTRY PROFILE

Historical profile

By the 400s BC the Roman state – comprising several cities in close association – had begun its expansionist policy that transformed it from a vigorous republic to an empire that encompassed most of Europe, North Africa, the Middle East and some of Asia Minor. It eclipsed all previous empires and influenced the peoples of Europe for many centuries.

By the fifth century AD, little of the Roman Empire survived and the peninsula became a feudal society before being conquered by invading armies.

The prestige of the Roman Empire lingered on and endowed the leaders of the Christian Church with a status that probably would have been lacking otherwise. The city states of Italy in the Middle Ages were vibrant, rich and centres of education and industry. Pre-eminent among them were Venice and Genoa (powerful maritime trading centres), Florence (a centre for trade and artistic merit) and Rome (the seat of the Pope). With divided loyalties and rivalries the independent states on the peninsular were unable to resist concerted invasion by predatory outsiders.

1796–1806 The French, under Emperor Napoléon Bonaparte, occupied Italy. The country was carved up to be ruled by Napoléon, his relatives and Pope Pius VII.

1814–15 Following Napoléon's defeat by the Austrians, British, Prussians and Russians, Italy returned to its feudal status under the terms of the Congress of Vienna. Regions of northern Italy were also handed to Austria.

1848 A rise in nationalism and rebellion against Austrian rule began, known locally as the Risorgimento (Revival). A key figure in this process was Giuseppe Garibaldi.

1859–61 A partly unified Italy was created under the King of Sardina (Sardina, Piedmont, Genoa, Savoy), Vittorio Emmanuelle II.

1870. Italian nationalists liberated Rome from French rule and proclaimed it the capital of a unified Italy under Vittorio Emmanuelle II.

1889–90 Italy established colonies in Africa through military conquest, namely in Somalia and Eritrea.

1901 Italy secured a territorial concession in the Chinese city of Tientsin

1911–12 Italy gained Tripolitania and Cyrenaica (later Libya) and the Dodekanesa (Dodecanese) Islands from the Ottoman Empire.

1916–18 Italy eventually fought alongside the Allies in the First World War. Ensuing disorder and economic weakness fostered the rise of Benito Mussolini and the Partito Nazionale Fascista (PNF) (National Fascist Party).

1919 Italy gained Trentino-Südtirol (South Tyrol), the Istrian peninsula and Trieste, which had been parts of the Austro-Hungarian Empire, under the terms of the Treaty of Versailles. Italian nationalists later seized control of the former Austro-Hungarian city of Fiume (now Rijeka), in the face of Yugoslav claims.

1922 After Italian fascists marched on Rome, Mussolini and the PNF were invited to form a government by the Italian King, Vittorio Emmanuele III.

1924–26 Mussolini increased his prime ministerial powers, effectively making his rule a dictatorship.

1929 Three Lateran Treaties granted Roman Catholicism special status in Italy. The Vatican City state, under the rule of the Pope, was created within Rome.

1935–36 Italy invaded Abyssinia (now Ethiopia).

1936 Italy supported General Franco's nationalists in the Spanish Civil War until he won in 1939.

1940–42 Italy was part of the Axis powers, assisting Nazi Germany's military campaigns in Europe and Africa. It also invaded British Somaliland in East Africa in 1940.

1943 Allied forces invaded southern Italy and its African colonies. Mussolini was removed from government, imprisoned, and Pietro Badoglio was appointed prime minister. After escaping from prison, Mussolini declared the creation of the Repubblica Sociale Italiana (Social Republic of Italy) in German-controlled northern Italy.

1945 The fascist regime collapsed as the allies liberated the whole of Italy. Mussolini was executed by Italian partisans.

1946 In May, Vittorio Emmanuele III abdicated from the Italian throne and was temporarily replaced by Umberto II. After a referendum the Italian monarchy was abolished and a republic was declared. Enrico De Nicola was appointed as temporary head of state.

1948 De Nicola was elected the Republic's first president. The constitution, which established a parliament, was promulgated.

1949–82 There followed a succession of short-lived coalitions involving the Democrazia Cristiana (DC) (Christian Democrats) and up to four other major parties, frequently producing several regroupings and new cabinets in a year.

1978 Former prime minister and then president of the DC, Aldo Moro, is assassinated by the Red Brigades.

1983–87 Bettino Craxi, of the Partito Socialista Italiano (PSI) (Italian Socialist Party), headed what was then the longest-running post-war Italian government.

1989 The DC returned to government and Giulio Andreotti became prime minister for the third time.

1992–93 Italy had two prime ministers in two years, Giuliano Amato and Carlo Azeglio Ciampi. Both were forced to resign after political and corruption scandals.

1994 Silvio Berlusconi, of the Forza Italia (FI) (Go Italy!) – a party he largely created and funded, was elected prime minister in March and resigned in December. A transitional government was formed led by independent Lamberto Dina.

1996 The centre-left Ulivo (Olive Tree) coalition won the parliamentary elections and the coalition's leader, Romano Prodi, was appointed prime minister.

1997 A constitutional reform commission, drawn from both houses of parliament, altered the Italian political system by introducing direct elections for the office of president.

1998 The Democratici di Sinistra's (DS) (Democrats of the Left) Massimo d'Alema succeeded Romano Prodi, who resigned after parliament rejected the budget.

1999 The government fell and d'Alema resigned. He was reinstated by the newly-elected president, former prime minister Ciampi.

2000 D'Alema resigned and was replaced by Giuliano Amato, heading a new centre-left 12-party coalition government.

2001 In May, the Casa delle Libertà (House of Freedom) coalition won the elections and Silvio Berlusconi became prime minister for a second time. Voters approved a referendum on constitutional changes to give more power to the regions.

2002 Euro currency replaced the lira. A controversial bill, allowing Berlusconi to retain control of his media empire, is passed in parliament.

2003 Berlusconi went on trial on corruption charges for allegedly bribing judges. In June, a bill was passed that granted the five most senior figures in government immunity from prosecution while in office. The Parmalat dairy food-manufacturing giant – one of Italy's blue-chip companies – was declared insolvent when a US$11 billion-plus accountancy fraud was discovered. In November, a national day of mourning was declared after nineteen Italian servicemen are killed in Iraq by a suicide bomber.

2004 In January, the Constitutional Court threw out the immunity from prosecution law and the prime minister's trial resumed in April.

2005 In March an Italian secret service agent was shot dead in Iraq by American troops during a hostage rescue operation, prompting massive street demonstrations in Italy. On 20 April, Prime Minister Silvio Berlusconi handed in his resignation, pledging to form a new government. On 23 April, at the request of President Carlo Azeglio Ciampi, Berlusconi formed his government with the key ministries unchanged; the government won a vote of confidence in the Chamber of Deputies on 27 April (334–240).

In October a bill was passed by the lower house of Parliament that would reform the electoral system. The reform would change the system, in force since 1993, whereby 75 per cent of seats are held by constituency winners and 25 per cent are distributed by proportional representation, to a system where all seats will be determined by proportional representation. Only parties that win a minimum of 2 per cent of the vote will be allocated seats. The opposition are concerned that this will favour Premier Berlusconi's coalition government and that the small centre-left parties in particular will fall under the 2 per cent level needed to win seats. Also in October, former prime minister and European Commission head, Romano Prodi, won the right to head the renamed centre-Left bloc, L'Unione (The Union), formerly Ulivo, in the April 2006 general election. In December Antonio Fazio, governor of the Bank of Italy, resigned and was replaced by Mario Draghi. Also in December, the upper house of Parliament passed Prime Minister Berlusconi's electoral reform bill.

Political structure
Constitution
Under the terms of the 1948 constitution, Italy's legislative power is held by a bi-cameral parliament.

Italy is divided into 20 regions which enjoy a large degree of autonomy. Each region has a regional council elected every five years by universal suffrage.

In October 2001, the constitution was amended by the federalist reform bill. This bill increases the decision-making power of the regions.

In October 2005 a bill was passed by Parliament that would, if passed by the upper house, reform the electoral system. The reform would change the system, in force since 1993, whereby 75 per cent of seats are held by constituency winners and 25 per cent are distributed by proportional representation, to a system where all seats will be determined by proportional representation. Only parties that win a minimum of 2 per cent of the vote will be allocated seats.

Form of state
Parliamentary democratic republic

The executive
Executive power is held by the prime minister, who is usually the leader of the largest party in the lower house of the parliament, and by a cabinet of ministers chosen by him.

The president, who must be more than 50 years old, holds a seven-year term of office and is elected by an electoral college consisting of both chambers of parliament and regional representatives. From the presidential term due to start in 2006, presidents will be directly elected. The president nominates a number of Supreme Court judges and has the power to dissolve parliament but has no other executive powers.

National legislature
Parliament consists of the *Camera dei Deputati* (Chamber of Deputies) and the *Senato della Repubblica* (Senate of the Republic). The Chamber of Deputies comprises 630 directly elected deputies. The Senate, with 315 elected members and seven life senators, is selected regionally.

Legal system
The legal system is based on the constitution of 1948.

The Constitutional Court, set up in 1955, is the final arbiter of the constitutionality of laws and decrees. It defines the powers of the state and regions and passes judgements in disputes between them. It can also try the president and government ministers. The court consists of 15 judges. Five are appointed by the president, five by parliament and the remainder by the highest law and administrative courts.

The highest court of cassation is divided into 23 appeal court districts, with three other sections. These are then further divided into 159 tribunal districts which, together, are divided into 899 magistracies. There are 90 first degree assize courts and 26 assize courts of appeal.

Last elections
12–13 June 2004 (European Parliament); 13 May 2001 (parliamentary); 13 May 1999 (presidential).

Results: European Parliament: Ulivo won 31.1 per cent of the vote (25 seats out of 78), Forza Italia (FI) (Italian Force) 21 per cent (16), Alleanza Nazionale (AN) (National Alliance) 11.5 per cent (nine), Rifondazione Comunista (RC) (Refounded Communist Party) 6.1 per cent (five), Unione dei Democratici Cristiani e dei Democratici di Centro (UDC) (Union of Christian and Centrist Democrats) 5.9 per cent (five), Lega Nord (LN) (Northern League) 5 per cent (four), Federazione dei Verde (Green Federation) 2.5 per cent (two), Partito dei Comunisti Italiani (PdCI) (Party of Italian Communists) 2.4 per cent (two) and Lista Bonino (LB) (Bonino List) 2.3 per cent (two); Occhetto (SCDO/ELDRP) 2.1 per cent (two); Socialists United for Europe (SUE/ELDRP) 2 per cent (two); Fiamma Tricolore (FT) 0.7 per cent (one); Popular Alliance-Democrats' Union for Europe (AP-UDEUR/EPP-ED) 1.3 per cent (one); Social Alternative (AS) 1.2 per cent (one); Pensioners' Party (PP/EPP-ED) 1.1 per cent (one). Turnout was 73.1 per cent.

Parliamentary: the Casa delle Libertà (House of Freedom) coalition won the elections.

Presidential: Carlo Azeglio Ciampi was elected president by the Electoral College with 70 per cent of the vote.

Next elections
9 April 2006 (presidential and parliamentary)

Political parties
Ruling party
Centre-right coalition from 23 Apr 2005: Forza Italia (FI) (Italian Force), Alleanza Nazionale (AN) (National Alliance), Lega Nord (LN) (Northern League) and Unione dei Democratici Cristiani e dei Democratici di Centro (Union of Christian and Centrist Democrats) and allied parties

Main opposition party
The centre-left Ulivo (Olive Tree) coalition includes Democratici di Sinistra (DS) (Democrats of the Left), Partito Popolare Italiano (PPI) (Italian People's Party), Unione Democratica per l'Europa (UDEUR) (Democrats Union for Europe), Partito dei Comunisti Italiani (PCI) (Italian Communist Party) and Federazione dei Verdi (Verdi) (Green Federation). In 2005, most members of Ulivo joined L'Unione, a new centre-left coalition headed by former prime minister Prodi.

Population
57.31 million (2004); 57.48 million (OECD, 2003)

Ethnic make-up
Centuries of colonisation have meant that Italy has many ethnic heritages and groups, including Arberesh (Albanian) (around 100,000, mainly in southern Italy), French (around 100,000, mainly in Valle d'Aosta), German (around 290,000, mainly in Trentino-Alto Adige), Friulian (around 600,000, mainly in Friuli-Venezia Giulia), and Greek (around 4,000, mainly in Calabria). The country has been a destination for immigrants from all over the world. There are an estimated one million foreigners residing in Italy.

Religions
97.5 per cent Roman Catholic.

Education
Schooling is free of charge and compulsory from age six. Primary schooling lasts until age 11 years, and lower secondary schools from age 11 to 14 years. Only the first year of upper secondary schooling is compulsory.

Higher secondary schools, from age 14, provide five-year courses in the arts, sciences and teacher training. Specialised secondary schools run four-year courses, and vocational and professional training programmes lasting for three and five years, respectively.

Graduation from higher secondary school automatically gives a student a place at university. Besides universities, a wide range of professional training establishments also provide higher education. Most of the existing universities were directly established by the state, although some private institutions are recognised. There are 51 state universities and three technical universities.

Public expenditure on education typically amounts to 4.9 per cent of annual gross national income.

Literacy rate: 98.5 per cent total; 98.2 per cent female, adult rates (World Bank).
Compulsory years: Six to 15
Enrolment rate: 101 gross primary enrolment of relevant age group (including repeaters); 95 per cent gross secondary enrolment (World Bank).
Pupils per teacher: 11 in primary schools

Health
Annual total expenditure on health is about 8 per cent of GDP, of which government spending is around 75 per cent. The healthcare system is regionally based, providing universal coverage free of charge at the point of service. There are deep regional inequalities in healthcare expenditure and in supply and utilisation of healthcare services.

Healthcare is financed through general taxation collected centrally, various other regional taxes and users' payments, which replaced the previous system of social health insurance contributions. In 2000, the National Health Fund was replaced by the National Solidarity Fund, which was developed to transfer funds to the regions unable to raise sufficient resources. The Fund was authorised to spend 10 per cent of the overall regional funding.

HIV prevalence: 0.5 per cent aged 15–49 in 2003 (World Bank)
Life expectancy: 79.8 years (World Bank)
Fertility rate/Maternal mortality rate: 1.3 births per woman; maternal mortality 11 per 100,000 live births (World Bank).
Birth rate/Death rate: 10 deaths to nine births per 1,000 people (World Bank)
Infant mortality rate: 4.3 per 1,000 live births (World Bank)

Welfare
Italy has a fully comprehensive social security system with benefits covering unemployment, retirement pensions, disability, family allowances and health services. The social security system is financed by contributions made by the state, employers and employees, and forms part of the government's overall budget.

The pension system is contribution-based calculated on the basis of the social security contributions paid over the course of working life. The system assures equal benefits for both public and private sector employees. There is increasing government expenditure on old-age pensions and survivorship annuities due to its ageing population.

There have been promising developments in the regulation of family allowances and income maintenance programmes. The Family Allowance fund, replaced by the Family Unit Allowance, differentiates the allowance in relation to the number of members of the family and the make-up of the family unit's income.

Pensions
The long-awaited pension reform bill was passed in July 2004. Italy was spending 14 per cent of GDP on pensions and the bill is expected to save 0.7 per cent of GDP annually from 2013–30.

The requirements for employees will be that they must pay 40 years of contributions into the fund before receiving benefits at aged 57, or retire later at aged 60 with a minimum 35 years contributions. This reform will be implemented by 2008.

Main cities
Rome (capital, estimated population 2.5 million in 2004), Milan (1.2 million), Naples (991,700), Turin (856,000), Palermo (651,500), Genoa (602,500), Bologna (369,300), Florence (351,600), Bari (311,900), Catania (305,900), Venice (265,700).

Languages spoken
German is spoken in South Tyrol on the Austrian border. Slovene is spoken by a minority in Trieste. French is spoken in the Val d'Aosta, bordering France and Switzerland. Albanian is spoken in some areas of Basilicata, Calabria and Sicily. An increasing number of business people also speak English, replacing French as the second commercial language.

Official language/s
Italian

Media
The national news agency is the Rome-based Agenzia Nazionale Stampa Associata (ANSA), which was founded in 1954.

Since 1993, groups have not been allowed to own more than three national television networks or more than 20 per cent of total daily newspaper circulation. Those owning two television networks are limited to 8 per cent of newspaper circulation, while for those with one television channel the ceiling is 16 per cent. The legislation also restricts advertising to a maximum of 11 minutes per hour.

Press
There are approximately 125 newspapers, which reach 42.5 per cent of the adult population, and an estimated 10,000 magazines. Much of the press is controlled directly or indirectly by major industrial groups.

Leading political parties publish their own newspapers. Many others are financially controlled by big business. The Agnelli family (which owns Fiat) controls the Turin-based La Stampa, Milan's Corriere della Sera and the sports daily Gazzetta dello Sport. The Ferruzzi group owns Il Messagero in Rome and the business daily Italia Oggi. Fininvest controls the Milan daily Il Giornale. Carlo de Benedetti, chairman of Olivetti, controls the biggest publishing company Mondadori, La Repubblica and over 12 regional newspapers.

Dailies: Italy's top dailies are Sette Corriere della Sera, Il Corriere della Sera, La Repubblica, La Gazzetta dello Sport, La Stampa (multi-regional), Il Sore 24 Ore, Corriere dello Sport/Stadio Il Messagero (regional), Il Giornale, Il Resto del Carlino and Il Gazzettino.

Weeklies: There are 51 weekly magazines, with an average of 14.8 million copies produced. The widest read weekly is Sorrisi e Canzoni. General interest weeklies and special interest magazines include Gente, Oggi, Panorama, Famiglia Cristiana (Roman Catholic), L'Espresso (news), Avvenimenti, Chi, Specchoi Della Stampa and Visto.

Business: There are many specialised trade magazines, mostly published in Milan. Major economic and business publications include Espansione and Tempo Economico, both monthly, and Il Mondo and Mondo Economico, both weekly. Business dailies include Il Sole 24 Ore. Milano Finanza is Italy's daily financial newspaper.

Periodicals: There are around 100 monthly magazines with an average 12.3 million copies produced. General periodicals on life-style, consumer, entertainment and commercial interests include: L'Automobile, Messaggero di San Antonio, L'Opinione, Il Mundo, La Padania, Airone, Capital, Città Nuova, Focus, Gente Mese, Italian Life, L'Incontro, Max and Rocca.

Nations of the World: A Political, Economic and Business Handbook

Broadcasting
Italy's main radio and television channels are controlled by Radiotelevisione Italiana (Rai-TV).
Radio: There are around 2,500 radio stations; 250 commercial radio stations are monitored by Audiradio. There are three national Rai-TV networks and over 4,000 private stations. There are over 15 million licensed radio receivers.
Television: There are over 14.8 million licensed television receivers. There are almost 1,000 television stations, including the three Rai-TV networks, three Fininvest and the rest private stations, of which about a quarter are affiliates to national networks. On average 94.8 per cent of the population watch television, 87.6 per cent of these every day.
Mediaset, a company set up and owned by Prime Minister Silvio Berlusconi, controls three of Italy's biggest television stations. Mediaset and Rai-TV together command 90 per cent of the television audience.

Advertising
Legislation enacted in the late 1990s has restricted the amount of advertising television and radio stations can broadcast. Newspapers account for around 35 per cent of all advertising, magazines a further 35 per cent, radio and television 22 per cent and cinemas 2 per cent. Billboards and other forms account for the remainder. All three state-owned TV networks and two of the three Rai radio networks carry advertising, as do all the private stations.

Economy
Italy is Western Europe's fourth-largest economy, although a lower growth rate in the size of the working population and a history of low domestic investment have meant that GDP growth has lagged behind its continental partners for some time.
Italy is a large industry-based economy with a heavy dependence on imported energy. Traditionally, the government has been significantly involved in industry through large state holding companies. However, a privatisation programme started in 1992 continues to reduce the government's role in the economy.
The services sector, particularly tourism, is important to overall economic performance. Tourism is Italy's third biggest source of foreign income after machinery and textiles and clothing. Florence alone receives over seven million visitors a year. The country's south, the Mezzogiorno, has much lower per capita income levels and higher unemployment rates than the more industrialised north, despite many years of heavy government subsidies. The severe regional imbalances in Italy's labour market are a serious problem for the economy.
Italy's decision to join the euro improved investor confidence significantly.
In July 2004, the economy minister, Giulio Tremonti, resigned after a showdown with coalition allies over how to tackle Italy's fragile economy and contain a growing budget deficit, which has run at around 4.3 per cent since 2001. Tremonti had been adept at keeping the Italian budget within strict EU parameters, but he could not find a way to revive the economy, which has persistently underperformed, particularly in terms of low productivity and export levels.
To improve growth, Prime Minister Silvio Berlusconi is trying to bolster consumer confidence by announcing proposed tax cuts to take effect in 2006. These are backed by Domenico Siniscalco, the new economics minister, but the hoped-for rise in consumer confidence has not materialised.
Italy's GDP growth is below the euro-zone average – growth flatlined in 2005 (0.0 per cent), down from 1.3 per cent in 2004, although the IMF projects that it will grow by 1.4 per cent in 2006. Inflation was 2.3 per cent in 2004 and although Italy has successful employment growth figures, its traditional industries such as textiles and white goods are threatened by cheaper imports from the Far East, especially China.
In December 2005 China overtook Italy as the world's sixth largest economy.

External trade
Italy conducts most of its trade with other EU members, which account for approximately 57 per cent of exports and 60 per cent of imports.

Imports
Main imports are engineering products, chemicals, transport equipment, energy products, minerals and non-ferrous metals, textiles and clothing, food, wine and tobacco.
Main sources: Germany (18.1 per cent total, 2004), France (10.7 per cent), Netherlands (5.8 per cent), Spain (4.7 per cent), Belgium (4.4 per cent), UK (4.3 per cent), China (4.1 per cent)

Exports
Main exports are engineering products, textiles and clothing, production machinery, motor vehicles, transport equipment, chemicals; food, beverages and tobacco; minerals and non-ferrous metals.
Main destinations: Germany (13.7 per cent total, 2004), France (12.1 per cent), US (8 per cent), Spain (7.3 per cent), UK (6.9 per cent), Switzerland (4.1 per cent)

Agriculture
Farming
Italian farming is characterised by substantial regional differences. Farms in the north are closer to their counterparts in north European countries – in terms of technology, culture and economy – than Italian farmers in the south. Italy's programme for developing the south of the country includes drainage and irrigation schemes, and building up co-operatives and integrated agribusiness ventures to improve trading opportunities.
The country has gradually adapted and delegated much of its farm policy to the EU, through the Common Agricultural Policy (CAP). Fundamental reform to the CAP was introduced on 1 January 2005 in Italy. The subsidies paid on farm output, which tended to benefit large farms and encourage overproduction, were replaced by single farm payments not conditional on production. This is expected to reward farms that provide and maintain a healthy environment, food safety and animal welfare standards. The changes are also intended to encourage market conscious production and cut the cost of CAP to the EU taxpayer.
Only 20 per cent of Italy is fertile arable land and farms are mostly small-scale. Regions with the most labour intensive farms are Sicily and Apulia. Capital intensive farms are most common in the northern province of Emilia Romagna, but the overall proportion of agricultural employment is the same in the north and south. In mountain areas, which stretch throughout the peninsula and on the islands, agricultural activity concentrates on forestry and livestock. The climate is ideal for vineyards and Italy vies with France as one the world's biggest wine producers.
The plains of the north and of Apulia, the heel of Italy, are also important areas for wheat, olives and fruit. Half of total agricultural income is generated in the Po valley and the plains in the north. The area produces the entire rice crop, cereals such as wheat and corn, fodder and livestock. In central Italy, wine-making and wheat-growing are the main activities. Most citrus fruit and olives are grown in the south, where vegetables and cereals are also grown.
Crop production in 2004 included: 22,863,890 tonnes (t) cereals in total, 8,628,758t wheat, 10,983,080t maize, 1,166,877t barley, 1,496,000t rice, 215,008t sorghum, 1,809,097t potatoes, 21,260t sweet potatoes, 126,081t pulses, 3,233,739t citrus fruit, 8,691,970t grapes, 7,496,997t tomatoes, 959,069t oilcrops, 102,762t tobacco, 294,161t treenuts, 3,300,000t olives, 10,100,000t sugar beets, 362,461t chillies & peppers, 26,507t garlic, 491,998t soya beans,

Italy

2,069,243t apples, 336,316t oats, 17,672,632t fruit in total, 16,128,969t vegetables in total. Livestock production included: 4,132,400t meat in total, 1,142,000t beef, 1,400t buffalo meat, 1,618,000t pig meat, 56,000t lamb, 4,000t goat meat, 1,019,000t poultry, 222,000t rabbit meat, 693,000t eggs, 11,790,000t milk, 8,000t honey, *132,000t cattle hides, 13,300t sheepskins, *45,000t horsemeat, *11,000t greasy wool, *60t cocoons, silk.
* estimate

Fishing
The fishing industry has a turnover of around US$4 billion, but it remains a neglected sector of the economy. Sicily and the Adriatic coast produce 76.4 per cent of the country's fish. The most important fish commercially are sardines and anchovies.

Forestry
Forest and wooded land account for less than 40 per cent of land area. Sixty per cent of the forest is available for wood supply. Broadleaved species account for 66 per cent of the growing stock, the main species being beech, deciduous and evergreen oaks, poplars and chestnut. Common coniferous species include pine, Norway spruce and European larch.
Italy is one of the major consumers, producers and traders of forest products in the EU. It accounts for nearly ten per cent of EU total paper and wood-based panel production.
Exports of forest material in 2004 amounted to US$4.3 billion, while imports amounted to US$9.5 billion. Production in 2004 included 8,697,393 cubic metres (cum) roundwood, 2,883,316cum industrial roundwood, 1,448,398cum sawlogs and veneers, 1,580,000cum sawnwood, 533,175cum pulpwood, 5,596,000cum wood-based panels, 5,814,077cum woodfuel; 5,474,000 tonnes (t) recovered paper, 193,000t newsprint, 3,110,000t printing and writing paper.

Industry and manufacturing
The industrial sector contributes approximately 32 per cent to GDP and employs 33 per cent of the labour force. Subdivided by sector, manufacturing contributes approximately 26 per cent to annual GDP, with construction accounting for a further 6 per cent.
Problems in the sector include growing competition in traditional products from developing countries, and the small share of the export market taken by value added high technology products. Efforts to attract industrial investment to the depressed southern region have met with only partial success, despite large subsidies.

Industrial production grew by only 0.7 per cent in 2004 and is estimated to have declined by 1.7 per cent in 2005.

Tourism
Italy's important tourist sector, which accounts for 6.2 per cent of GDP and gives employment to around two million people, was badly hit by the 11 September 2001 terrorist attacks in the US. Recovery was obstructed by the Iraq war and the SARS outbreak in 2003. The strengthening of the euro vis-a-vis other currencies has added to the sector's difficulties, deterring US and Japanese tourist in particular. Arrivals from Germany, the biggest market, have also shown a decline.
China has designated Italy as an approved destination for its holidaying citizens and it has already become one of the top three in Europe; Chinese visitors could swell Italy's arrival numbers by millions.

Mining
The mining sector accounts for only 0.5 per cent of GDP and employs a similar percentage of the workforce. Italy has relatively poor mineral resources, although large quantities of iron ore and pyrites, mercury, lead, zinc, bauxite, aluminium, sulphur, gravel, alabaster and marble exist.
Sardinia (Cagliari, Sassari and Iglesias) is the main mining area and holds the only large sulphur deposit in Europe, but mining it is not economically viable. Bauxite is mined mainly in Abruzzi, Campania and Apulia, though output has dropped due to falling demand from the aluminium industry. Output of lead, zinc and particularly copper have all increased. Quarrying activity is strong, with marble and gravel much in demand for the construction and road building industries.

Hydrocarbons
Italy relies heavily on energy imports (85 per cent of domestic requirements). However, a plan is under way to develop indigenous resources, as well as the use of coal and natural gas.
Proven oil reserves stood at 700 million barrels in 2004, producing 107,000 barrels per day (bpd). Italy consumes 1.9 billion bpd and is one of the largest oil importers in Europe with 90 per cent of its consumption dependent on imports. It imports approximately 1.8 million bpd, mostly from Libya (28.3 per cent of oil imports) and Iran (17.2 per cent). Italy also has a refining capacity of 2,292,000bpd. Italy, one of the largest per capita oil consumers in Europe, sought to decrease its reliance on oil imports by developing other fuel sources in the 1990s. To promote this diversification the government adjusted fuel taxes, with the duty on oil rising by between 33–61 per cent. Domestic taxes on natural gas will increase by only 5 per cent, with petrol replacement gas tax actually set to fall by 23 per cent.
Italy produces 13.0 billion cubic metres of gas annually (2004) from reserves of 170 billion cubic metres (2004), most of which are in and off Sicily. At current rates of consumption this is only enough to supply Italy's needs for another twenty years. Natural gas use has increased significantly since the 1990s and accounts for 30 per cent of the country's total energy consumption. According to Snam, the company responsible for supplying and transporting methane gas throughout Italy, natural gas will generate 60 per cent of the country's electricity by 2010. Domestic production meets 40 per cent of domestic demand, with the remainder imported under long-term contracts from the countries of the former Soviet Union, Algeria and the Netherlands. Future supplies are likely to be diversified as plans to build a US$5.5 billion gas pipeline between Libya and Sicily become reality. The 600km pipeline, which opened in October 2004, will deliver a total of 10 billion cubic metres per year to Italy. Snam also signed a 25-year contract with Norway in October 2001 to receive six billion cubic metres of natural gas per year through existing pipelines.
Most domestic coal production is used in electricity generation, although coal accounts for only 8 per cent of total domestic energy consumption. Italy consumed 17.1 million tonnes of oil equivalent in 2004.
Russia's decision to cut off gas supplies to Ukraine on 1 January 2006 caused alarm in Italy, as a sizeable portion of its import network is dependent upon Ukrainian transnational pipelines.

Energy
Ente Nazionale per L'Energia Elettrica (Enel), the former state-owned energy monopoly, was privatised in November 1999.
It owns 85 per cent of Italy's electrical generating capacity, although the government restructured the company in 2002. Enel also sold off some of its regional electricity distribution networks to municipal companiess.
Italy has four nuclear power stations, all of which are owned by Enel. Following a public vote in 1987, which decided against the use of nuclear power, none of the plants are currently in operation. They are not expected to be reopened.
Electricity needs are met by buying extra power generated by France's nuclear reactors.

Nations of the World: A Political, Economic and Business Handbook

Banking and insurance
Scandal hit the Central Bank in July 2005 when the governor, Antonio Fazio, refused to allow a cross-border banking takeover and was subsequently placed under investigation in two criminal inquiries. He refused to resign for several months, receiving strong support from one of Italy's governing parties, the Lega Nord, and the Catholic Church, but was eventually replaced by Mario Draghi in December. Unlike Mr Fazio, who held an open-ended mandate, Mr Draghi will serve a six-year term, renewable once.
Central bank
Banca d'Italia; European Central Bank (ECB).

Time
GMT plus one hour in winter; GMT plus two hours in summer.

Geography
Italy consists of a peninsula stretching from southern Europe into the Mediterranean and a number of adjacent islands, including Sicily in the south-west and Sardinia in the west. The country stretches 1,200km from north to south and has 7,456km of coastline.

The distinctive boot-shaped peninsula is dominated by two extensive mountain ranges, accounting for about 75 per cent of the land area. The Alps form a natural barrier separating Italy from Slovenia in the north-east, Austria and Switzerland in the north and France in the north-west. The Apennines form the backbone of the peninsula.

Italy experiences frequent minor earthquakes, especially in the south, and its active volcanoes include Vesuvius in the Naples district, Etna in Sicily and Stromboli in the Aeolian Islands.

Two autonomous countries lie within Italy's frontiers, the Vatican City in Rome, home of the Holy See, and the tiny republic of San Marino in the north-east.

Climate
While Italy lies in a temperate zone, the climates of the north and south vary. Summers are uniformly hot, although summers in the south can be extremely hot and dry. In the winter, the south is generally mild, while the north can be extremely cold – particularly near the Alps and Po Valley. Temperatures range from about 4–30 degrees Celsius.

Dress codes
Particular attention is paid to dress, although dress codes are not rigid. Most businessmen wear suits and ties during business hours.

Entry requirements
Passports
Passports must be valid for six months upon arrival.
Visa
No visa requirements for citizens of most of Europe, the Americas, Australasia and some Asian countries, visiting for up to 90 days. For a full list, and further information for those citizens not included on the list of visa-free travel, visit www.italyemb.org/Visti.htm. A Schengen visa application (offered in several languages) can be downloaded from www.eurovisa.info/ApplicationForm.htm.

Business travel is also allowed for those enjoying visa-free travel. Those who do not have visa-free arrangements must provide a letter from their employer guaranteeing travel expenses, including full itinerary and purpose of the trip. Letters of invitation from all Italian companies to be visited, and a current (not over 90 days) *Visura Camerale* issued by the Italian Chamber of Commerce should be attached; a return/onward ticket must be produced before collection of the passport and visa from the issuing Consular Office; who may request any additional documents at its discretion.

Within eight days of arrival in Italy the visa traveller must appear before local police authorities to receive a 'Residency Permit' and will also need to show proof of health insurance.
Currency advice/regulations
Import and export of local and foreign currency up to eur10,329 (US$11,350) is permitted. Importing an amount larger than this must be declared on form V2, completed and validated on arrival, and not exceeded by the amount taken out.
Customs
Personal effects are duty-free.

Health (for visitors)
Under EU healthcare arrangements, all EU nationals are entitled to emergency treatment. Insurance is advised for specialist treatment.
Mandatory precautions
None
Advisable precautions
No special immunisations are needed. Pharmacists are usually open from 0830 to 1300 and 1600 to 2000.

Hotels
Classified into five star categories. Rates are fixed with the Provincial Tourist Board, and vary according to class, season, services available and locality. All major credit cards are accepted in the large, top-category hotels in major cities but not widely elsewhere.

Public holidays
Fixed dates
1 Jan (New Year's Day), 6 Jan (Epiphany), 25 April (Liberation Day), 1 May (Labour Day), 2 Jun (Anniversary of the Republic), 15 Aug (Assumption Day), 1 Nov (All Saints' Day), 8 Dec (Immaculate Conception), 25 Dec (Christmas Day), 26 Dec (St Stephen's Day).
Variable dates
Easter Monday

Working hours
Business travellers would do best to avoid August when Italians desert the stifling heat of the big cities for the beaches and mountains. The mass exodus usually begins in mid-July and lasts at least until after the *Ferragosto* festival (August 15). Most factories, government offices, shops and restaurants close for all of August or are run by minimal staff.

The afternoon siesta is still very much part of the Italian way of life in Rome and the south. In northern Italy, there is a growing trend towards standard European business hours of 0900 to 1700, at least in offices.
Banking
Mon–Fri: 0830–1400, many are also open from 1445–1545 in Rome and Milan.
Business
Northern Italy: 0930–1300 and 1400–1800.
Central and southern Italy: 0830–1245 and 1630–2000.
Government
Post offices: Mon–Fri: 0830–1345 and Sat: 0830–1200; central post offices stay open until 2100.
Government offices: Mon–Sat: 0830–1345; a few open Mon–Fri: 1730–2000.
Shops
Mon–Sat: 0830–1230 and 1530–1930. Hours differ from town to town and in summer. All shops have one half-day closing each week.

Electricity supply
220V AC, 50Hz

Social customs/useful tips
Italians always shake hands on meeting and leaving. Exchanging business cards is also normal practice as it helps to reinforce the informal network of personal contacts which permeates Italian business. Businessmen prefer that written communication, either by e-mail, facsimile or letter, be sent prior to telephoning, so they know who they are dealing with in advance. Personal titles are considered important, although often more prestigious than professionally accurate. Small luxury goods are frequently exchanged as gifts in business. Smoking is still fashionable, with

Italy

fewer restrictions than in many other Western countries.
Italians are required to carry identification on them at all times and foreigners are recommended to do likewise.

Security
Handbag snatching and pickpocketing are widespread, particularly in popular tourist spots in Rome and Naples. It is advisable not to wear conspicuous jewellery or carry personal valuables. In general the level of violent crime is low, but drug-related crime is on the increase in Milan, Rome and Naples. With this in mind, visitors to Rome are advised to avoid the streets around the Termini area at night.

Getting there
Air
National airline: Alitalia
International airport/s: Rome Fiumicino (FCO) 35km south-west of Rome, facilities include duty-free, car hire, bank and 24-hour bureau de change and 24-hour bar/restaurant. There is a direct rail link to Termini Station in central Rome and a bus service every 15 minutes. Taxis are also available to the city.
Milan Malpensa (MXP) 46km north-west of Milan.
Other airport/s: Pisa (PSA), 2km from city, (an hour by train from Florence); Turin International (TRN), 16km north-west of city; Venice Marco Polo (VCE), 13km north-west of city; Bologna G. Marconi (BLQ); Milan Linate (LIN); Naples Capodichino (NAP); Genoa Cristoforo Colombo (GOA); Palermo (PMO).
Airport tax: There is no airport tax.
Surface
Road: Italy can be entered by road from France, Switzerland, Austria and Slovenia. However, several passes are closed during winter. In addition to the Riviera coastal motorway, access from France and Switzerland is maintained via the St Bernard, Mont Blanc and Fréjus tunnels.
Rail: The quickest way to Italy is by Eurostar or Rail Europe, through the Channel Tunnel to Paris or Brussels, and from there to Italy. There are also daily services run by Ferrovie dello Stato (FS) (Italian State Railways) which carry cars, particularly during the summer season. Routes include Milan-Genoa-Naples-Villa San Giovanni; Bologna-Naples-Villa San Giovanni. These services are available from special stations and tickets can be booked at the departure station. Owners are required to travel on the same train.
In 2002, France and Italy began construction work on a 52km tunnel and high-speed rail link under the Alps. The line will run from Lyon and Turin and will carry passengers and freight and will halve the journey time between the two cities. It is expected to be completed by 2012.
Water: Ferry services connect Trieste, Ancona, Brindisi and Bari with Durres and Vlora in Albania. Plus Sicily and Malta, and Brindisi to Corfu in Greece.
Main port/s: Genoa, Trieste, Augusta, Taranto, Leghorn, Savona, Ancona, Bari, Brindisi, Civitavecchia, Venice, La Spezia, Naples, Palermo (Sicily), and Cagliari and Porto Torres (Sardinia).

Getting about
National transport
Air: Alitalia and Aero Transporti Italiani (ATI) operate services connecting Rome to most major towns. Alisarda operate services connecting Rome, Milan and Turin with Sardinia.
Road: Total length of roads approximately 317,000km, including a toll motorway system (*autostrade*) which connects most cities.
Buses: Extensive bus services, operated by several companies, link all major towns.
Rail: Efficient and fairly cheap network operated by FS and several small private companies, over half of which is electrified. Advisable to book 'express' tickets in advance. There are many reduced tickets available, offering unlimited travel over fixed periods for individuals and groups. These include the Italy Flexicard, the Kilometric card and the Italy railcard. Prices vary according to first- or second-class travel.
Water: Ferryboat and hydrofoil services linking the mainland with Sicily, Sardinia and the smaller islands are operated by several lines including the State Railways.
City transport
Taxis: Available in all towns and tourist resorts, usually in ranks at railway stations, or can be called by phone. Fares vary considerably, and unmetered cabs should be avoided. Drivers round up their fares; gratuities are not necessary.
Buses, trams & metro: All major cities have bus services with one standard fare. Day and monthly tickets are available. Bus tickets can also be bought in packs of five and then fed into a machine upon boarding.
Metro in Rome and Milan with standard single fare as for buses. In Milan tickets last for 70 minutes and can be used on both metro lines and all bus routes. A daily or monthly ticket usable for all Rome services is available. The metro journey from Malpensa international airport, Milan, to the city centre takes around 30 minutes.
Tram services are available in Milan, Naples and Turin.
Car hire
Self-drive cars are available; the daily rate depends on the engine size, plus an additional charge per kilometre. Special weekly tariffs are available. VAT is charged. Official translation of driving licence required. Air and rail travellers can get special deals including car hire. Drive on the right. Maximum speed is 50kph in towns, 90/110kph on country roads and 130kph on motorways. Seat belts are obligatory by law.
Road signs are international. Many petrol stations are closed between 1200–1500.

BUSINESS DIRECTORY
The addresses listed below are a selection only. While World of Information makes every endeavour to check these addresses, we cannot guarantee that changes have not been made, especially to telephone numbers and area codes. We would welcome any corrections.

Telephone area codes
The international direct dialling code (IDD) for Italy is +39, followed by area code:

Bologna	051	Pisa	050
Capri	081	Rome	06
Florence	055	Trieste	040
Genoa	010	Turin	011
Milan	02	Venice	041
Naples	081	Verona	045

Useful telephone numbers
Police, fire and ambulance: 113

Chambers of Commerce
American Chamber of Commerce in Italy, 1 Via Cantù, 20123 Milan (tel: 869-0661; fax: 805-7737; e-mail: amcham@amcham.it).

Bergamo Camera di Commercio, 16 Largo Belotti, 24121 Bergamo (tel: 422-5111; fax: 226-023; e-mail: info@bg.camcom.it).

Bologna Camera di Commercio, Palazzo Mercanzia, 4 Piazza Mercanzia, 40125 Bologna (tel: 609-3111; fax: 609-3451; e-mail: segreteria.generale@bo.camcom.it).

Brescia Camera di Commercio, 3 Via Orzinuovi, 25125 Brescia (tel: 351-41; fax: 351-4222; e-mail: brescia@bs.camcom.it).

British Chamber of Commerce for Italy, 12 Via Dante, 20121 Milan (tel: 877-798; fax: 8646-1885; e-mail: bcci@britchamitaly.com).

Ferrara Camera di Commercio, 11 Via Borgoleoni, 44100 Ferrara (tel: 783-711; fax: 240-204; e-mail: cciaa.ferrara@fe.camcom.it).

Florence Camera di Commercio, 3 Piazza dei Giudici, 50122 Florence (tel: 2795-1; fax: 2795-259; e-mail: info@fi.camcom.it).

Genoa Camera di Commercio, 4 Via Garibaldi, 16124 Genoa (tel: 270-41; fax: 270-4300; e-mail: camera.genova@ge.camcom.it).

Mantua Camera di Commercio, 28 Via Pietro Fortunato Calvi, 46100 Mantua (tel: 234-1; fax: 234-234; e-mail: mantova@mn.camcom.it).

Milan Camera di Commercio, 9b Via Meravigli, 20123 Milan (tel: 8515-1; fax: 8515-4232; e-mail: infohighway@mi.camcom.it).

Naples Camera di Commercio, 2 Via S Aspreno, 80133 Naples (tel: 760-7111; fax: 552-6940; e-mail: segretaria.generale@na.camcom.it)

Padua Camera di Commercio, 34 Via E Filiberto, 35122 Padua (tel: 820-8111; fax: 820-8290; e-mail: info@pd.camcom.it).

Parma Camera di Commercio, 2 Via Verde, 43100 Parma (tel: 210-11; fax: 282-168; e-mail: segretaria.generale@pr.camcom.it).

Pavia Camera di Commercio, 27 Via Mentana, 27199 Pavia (tel: 393-1; fax: 304-559; e-mail: pavia@pv.camcom.it).

Rome Camera di Commercio, 147 Via De' Burrò, 00186 Rome (tel: 520-2630; fax: 520-82617; e-mail: info@rm.camcom.it).

Siena Camera di Commercio, 30 Piazza Matteotti, 53100 Siena (tel: 202-511; fax: 270-981; e-mail: cciaa@si.camcom.it).

Treieste Camera di Commercio, 14 Piazza della Borsa, 34121 Trieste (tel: 670-1111; fax: 670-1321; e-mail: info@ts.camcom.it).

Turin Camera di Commercio, 24 Via San Francesco da Paola, 10123 Turin (tel: 571-6405; fax: 571-6404; e-mail: urp@to.camcom.it).

Unione Italiana delle Camere di Commercio, Industria, Artigianato e Agricoltura, 21 Piazza Sallustio, 00187 Rome (tel: 470-41; fax: 470-4240; e-mail: segretaria.generale@unioncamere.it).

Venice Camera di Commercio, 2032 Via XXII Marzo, San Marco, 30124 Venice (tel: 786-111; fax: 786-330; e-mail: segretaria.generale@ve.camcom.it).

Verona Camera di Commercio, 96 Corso Porta Nuova, 37122 Verona (tel: 808-5011; fax: 594-648; e-mail: cciaavr@vr.camcom.it).

Banking
Banca Commerciale Italiana, Via del Corso, 226 C.A.P. 00186 Rome (tel: 67-121; fax: 6712-4925).

Banca di Napoli, Via Toledo 177–188, 80132 Naples (tel: 791-1111).

Banca Nazionale del Lavoro, Via Vittorio Veneto 119, 00187 Rome (tel: 47-021; fax: 4702-6263).

Banca Nazionale dell'Agricoltura SPA, Via Salaria 231, 00199 Rome (tel: 85-881; fax: 8588-3396).

Banca Popolare Commercio E Industria Scarl, Via Casifina 1790, 00132 Rome (tel: 207-1712; fax: 207-2676).

Banca di Roma, Via del Corso 320, 00186 Rome (tel: 67-071; fax: 6707-3783).

Cassa di Risparmio delle Provincie Lombarde, Piazza Barberini 21, 00167 Rome (tel: 46-781; fax 486-884).

Cassa di Risparmio di Roma, 320 Via del Corso, 00186 Rome (tel: 67-071; fax: 6707-3783).

Cassa di Risparmio di Torino, 31 Via XX Settembre, 10121 Torino (tel: 57-661; fax: 638-203).

Credito Italiano, 00144 Piazzale dell'Industria 46 (tel: 54-631; fax: 5423-7006).

European Investment Bank, via Saroagna 36, 100187 Rome (tel: 47-191; fax: 487-3438).

Istituto Centrale Delle Banche Di Credito Cooperativo, Via Torino 146, 00184 Rome (tel: 47-161; fax: 4716-5583).

Istituto Di Credito Delle Casse Di Rigparmio Italiane, Via San Basilio 15, 00187 Rome (tel: 47-151; fax: 4715-3579).

Mediocredito Centrale, Via Piemonte 51, 00187 Rome (tel: 47-911; fax: 479-1626).

Monte dei Paschi di Siena, Piazza Salimbeni, Siena (tel: 294-111).

Nuovo Banco Ambrosiano, Piazza Paolo Ferrari 10, 20121 Milan (tel: 85-941).

UBAE Arab Italian Bak SpA, Piazza Venezia 11, 00187 Rome (tel: 67-5921; fax: 678-4606).

Central bank
Banca d'Italia, Via Nazionale 91, 00184 Rome (tel: 47-921; fax: 479-22983).

European Central Bank (ECB), Kaiserstrasse 29, D-60311 Frankfurt am Main, Germany (tel: +49(69)13-440; fax: +49(69)1344-6000; e-mail: info@ecb.int).

Travel information
Alitalia (Linee Aeree Italiane), Centro Direzionale, Viale Alissandro Marchetti, 111, Rome 100148 (tel: 709-2780; fax: 709-3065).

Ministry of tourism
Ministry of Industry and Tourism, Via Molise 2, 00187 Rome (tel: 47-051; fax: 4705-2215).

National tourist organisation offices
Ente Nazionale Italiano per il Turismo (ENIT), Via Marghera 2-6, 00185 Rome (tel: 49-711; fax: 446-3379; email: sedecentrale.enit@interbusiness.it; internet: www.enit.it).

Ministries
Ministry of Agriculture and Forests, Via XX Settembre 20, 00187 Rome (tel: 46-651; fax: 592-314).

Ministry of Defence, Via XX Settembre 8, 00187 Rome (tel: 488-2126; fax: 474-7775).

Ministry of Education, Viale Trastevere 76/A, 00153 Rome (tel: 58-491; fax: 580-3381).

Ministry of Employment and Social Welfare, Via Flavia 6, 00187 Rome (tel: 46-831; fax: 4788-7174).

Ministry of the Environment, Piazza Venezia 11, 00187 Rome (tel: 70-361; fax: 678-3844).

Ministry of Equal Opportunities, c/o Presidenza del Consiglio dei Ministry, Palazzo Chigi, 00187 Rome (tel: 67-791; fax: 678-3998).

Ministry of Finance, Viale Europa 242, 00144 Rome (tel: 59-971; fax: 501-5714).

Ministry of Foreign Affairs, Piazzale della Farnesina, 00194 Rome (tel: 36-911; fax: 323-6258).

Ministry of Foreign Trade, Viale America 341, 00144 Rome (tel: 59-931; fax: 5964-7504).

Ministry of Health, Viale dell'Industria 20, 00144 Rome (tel: 59-941; fax: 5964-7649).

Ministry of Industry and Tourism, Via Molise 2, 00187 Rome (tel: 47-051; fax: 4705-2215).

Ministry of the Interior, Piazzale del Viminale, 00184 Rome (tel: 6451; fax: 482-5792).

Ministry of Justice, Via Arenula 71, 00186 Rome (tel: 68-851; fax: 5227-8550).

Ministry of Posts and Telecommunications, Viale America 201, 00144 Rome (tel: 59-581; fax: 594-274).

Ministry of Public Administration, Palazzo Vidoni, Corso Vittorio Emanuele 116, 00186 Rome (tel: 680-031).

Ministry of Public Works, Piazza Porta Pia 1, 00198 Rome (tel: 44-121; fax: 4426-7275).

Italy

Ministry of Transport, Piazza della Croce Rossa 1, 00161 Rome (tel: 84-901; fax: 4424-1539).

Ministry of the Treasury and Budget, Via XX Settembre 97, 00187 Rome (tel: 47-611; fax: 488-2146).

Ministry for University, Scientific and Technological Research, Piazzale Kennedy 20, 00144 Rome (tel: 59-911; fax: 591-5493).

Office of the President, Palazzo del Quirinale, 00187 Rome (tel: 4699).

Prime Minister's Office, Palazzo Chigi, Piazza Colonna 370, 00187 Rome (tel: 67-791; fax: 678-3998).

Other useful addresses

Agenzia Nazionale Stampa Associata (news agency), Via della Dataria 94, 00187 Rome (tel: 678-6161).

Borsa Valori di Milano, Piazza Degli Affari, 20100 Milan (tel: 8534).

British Embassy, Via XX Settembre 80/A, 00187 Rome (tel: 482-5551, 482-5441; fax: 487-3324).

Commissione Nazionale per le Società e la Borsa (Commission for Companies and the Stock Exchange), Milan (tel: 877-841).

Confederazione Generale dell'Industria Italiana (General Confederation of Italian Industry), Viale dell'Astronomia 30, 00144 Rome (tel: 59-031).

Confederazione Generale Italiana del Commercio (General Confederation of Italian Commerce), Piazza G.C. Belli 2, Rome (tel: 588-783, 580-192).

Ente Nazionale Idrocarburi (ENI), Piazzalo E. Mattei, 00144 Rome (tel: 59-001).

Ente Partecipazioni e Finanziamento Industria Manifatturiera (EFIM), Via XXIV Maggio 43–45, 00187 Rome (tel: 47-101).

Istituto Nazionale di Statistica (ISTAT) (national statistics office), Via Cesare Balbo 16, 00100 Rome (tel: 46-731; fax: 4673-4177).

Istituto per la Ricostruzione Industriale (IRI) Via Vittorio Veneto 85, 00187 Rome (tel: 47-271).

Istituto Nazionale per il Commercio Estero (Italian government agency for promotion of foreign trade), 21 Via Liszt, 00100 Rome (tel: 59-921).

Italian Embassy (US), 3000 Whitehaven Street, NW, Washington DC 20008 (tel: 202-612-4400; fax: 202-518-2154; e-mail: stampa@itwash.org).

US Embassy, Via Vittorio Veneto 119A, 00187 Rome (tel: 46-741; fax: 4674-2356).

Internet sites

Gateway site of servers listed by city (launches into Italian language sites): http://www.cilea.it/WWW-map/

Italian Central Bank: http://www.bancaditalia.it/

Italian Statistics: http://www.istat.it

Italian Embassy in the US (includes economic and trade data) http://www.italyemb.org

Ministry of Foreign Affairs: http://www.esteri.it/eng/index/htm

Yellow pages Online: http://www.paginegialle.it

Jamaica

KEY FACTS

Official name: Jamaica

Head of State: Queen Elizabeth II (since 1952); represented by Governor General Howard Cooke (since 1991)

Head of government: Prime Minister Percival James Patterson (since 1992)

Ruling party: People's National Party (PNP) (since 1989)

Area: 10,989 square km

Population: 2.68 million (2004)

Capital: Kingston

Official language: English

Currency: Jamaican dollar (J$) = 100 cents

Exchange rate: J$62.53 per US$ (Oct 2005)

GDP per capita: US$3,237 (2004)

GDP real growth: 2.50% (2004)

Labour force: 1.36 million (2004)

Unemployment: 15.00% (2004)

Inflation: 11.50% (2004)

Balance of trade: -US$1.94 billion (2004)

Foreign debt: US$4.84 billion (2004)

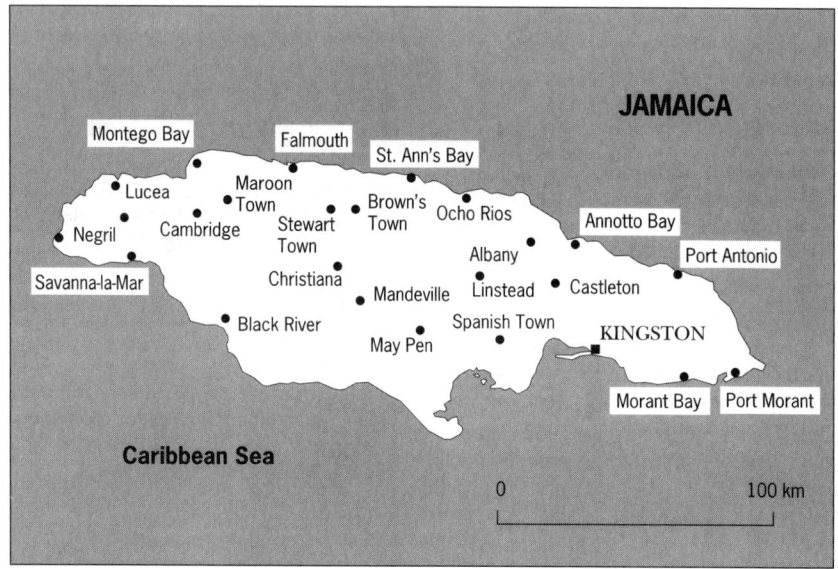

Owing to its status as a Commonwealth country, Jamaica's head of state is Queen Elizabeth II. A governor general represents the monarch's interests in the country and is appointed on the recommendation of the serving prime minister. Nowadays, the governor general's role is purely symbolic in nature and executive power is exclusively invested in the prime minister and his/her cabinet. The country's overall system of representative democracy is closely modeled on the British Westminster system.

The political arena in 2005

Jamaica's electoral politics are dominated by the two largest parties in the country – the Jamaica Labour Party (JLP), which at present is the main opposition, and the governing Peoples' National Party (PNP). Other minor parties include the conservative Jamaican National Democratic Movement (NDM) and the United Peoples' Party. Prime Minister Percival Noel James Patterson is the longest serving premier in the country's history, having come to power in 1992 following former Prime Minister Michael Manley's retirement owing to poor health.

Patterson is now viewed as a respected statesman in the Caribbean region and he shot to international prominence in 2004 when he announced that his government, along with that of Venezuela and St Kitts and Nevis, did not intend to recognise Gérard Latortue as prime minister of Haiti. Patterson's stand in allowing deposed Haitain president Jean-Bertrand Aristide refuge in Jamaica while he launched a lawsuit against the US and France for allegedly kidnapping him, won the Jamaican prime minister much praise throughout the region and beyond.

In January 2005 former prime minister Edward Seaga stepped down as leader of the JLP having served in the position for almost 29 years. His departure from the political scene after so long is a significant development in Jamaican politics where longevity is something of a buzzword. Seaga was succeeded by former government minister Bruce Golding. The possibility of Golding's return to the JLP as leader would have been considered fantastical after he split from the party to form the NDM in 1995. However, Golding's rehabilitation in JLP party circles was completed in January when he seized the leader of the opposition post.

Jamaica

Economic developments

Slow growth has been a feature of the Jamaican economy over recent years, and the IMF projects increased growth of just 0.7 per cent for 2005. Inflation has risen in recent years, but took a downturn from January to March 2005 when the rate was almost zero. Agriculture, tourism and the bauxite/alumina industry have dominated Jamaica's economy for a number of years. More recently the services sector has gained in importance. Sugar, and later banana production, used to produce much of Jamaica's earnings during the pre-independence era, but with diversification it now exports bananas, coffee, citrus fruit, onions, peppers and other vegetables as well as beverages including rum, beer and carbonated drinks. A plan to double the refining capacity of the Jamalco Aluminium Refinery to 2.8 million tonnes was announced in July 2005. The cost of US$1.2 billion includes a power station as well as high hurricane-wind and earthquake defences.

Jamaica is an open and import-dependent economy, vulnerable to the effects of oil and commodity prices on its balance of trade. Like other Caribbean countries, it can suffer from periodic hurricanes and flooding. Hurricane Ivan that devastated many areas and crops in 2003 is estimated to have cost Jamaica US$362 million and the effect on the economy in 2004 was to limit growth to 1–2 per cent. Remittance earnings, particularly from emigrants in the US, Canada and UK, have become an important source of foreign exchange with over US$300 million typically injected into the economy each year.

The sharp rise in the price of oil in 2005 highlights the country's vulnerability to forces beyond its control. An agreement signed with Venezuela in August 2005 (the PetroCaribe Energy Co-operation Agreement) guarantees a supply of 21,000bpd of favourably priced crude oil, refined products or LPG. Meanwhile, the business environment continues to be negatively affected by high levels of petty and organised crime, with observers monitoring the murder rate as closely as more orthodox indicators.

There is a heavy reliance on commodity exports. Dependence on energy imports continues to cause severe balance of payments difficulties although the PetroCaribe Energy Co-operation Agreement with Venezuela will help to ease these difficulties.

Natural resources

The mining sector generates around half of export earnings and contributes approximately 9 per cent to GDP. Mining and quarrying employs approximately 1 per cent of the workforce. Activity is centred on the extraction of bauxite and alumina refining. Known reserves of bauxite are around two billion tonnes, although most is of relatively low quality. Other minerals exploited include gypsum, marble, silica and clays.

On 20 June 2005 a bilateral agreement was signed between China and Jamaica to establish a bauxite mining and alumina refinery facility, projected to process 1.4 million tonnes of alumina a year.

Jamaica derives around 96 per cent of its energy requirements from imported oil. Early attempts, in the 1970–80s, to find commercially exploitable deposits of oil and gas were unsuccessful; any deposits found were too costly to retrieve. However in November 2004 the government launched an offer for licences to explore four onshore and 22 offshore blocks in Jamaica's exclusion zone. New technology and more experience has led to the belief that any viable deposits may now be exploitable.

Outlook

The main objective for the Patterson government continues to be that of increasing the rate of growth in the economy, which has been under-performing for several years. Simultaneously, the economy must be managed in such a way as to reduce the demon of rapidly rising inflation. Jamaica has been plagued by upward price pressures throughout the 2000s and controlling this potential problem remains the name of the economic game in the country. The rising level of crime, a problem throughout the Caribbean, also needs to be reduced and kept in check if further foreign investment and tourists are to be attracted to the island. An economic upturn is expected in 2006 with the IMF forecasting increased growth of 3.7 per cent.

Risk assessment

Politics	Stable
Economy	Stable
Regional stability	Good

COUNTRY PROFILE

Historical profile

1494 Jamaica was sighted by members of an expedition led by Christopher Columbus.
1509 Jamaica was occupied by Spaniards. Most of the indigenous Arawak community died from exposure to European diseases. African slaves were brought in to work on the sugar plantations.
1655 The British captured the island. Jamaica became a slave-based economy producing sugar and some coffee for export.
1692 Jamaican capital, Port Royal, sunk into the sea after an earthquake and Spanish Town became the new capital.
1834 Abolition of slavery.
1865 A major revolt against Jamaican landowners among freed slaves living in hardship was brutally put down by the British. The local legislature surrendered its powers and Jamaica became a crown colony.
1870 Plantations began to replace sugar cane with banana production, due to increased sugar beet production in Europe.
1884 A new constitution marked the revival of Jamaican autonomy.

KEY INDICATORS — Jamaica

	Unit	2000	2001	2002	2003	2004
Population	m	2.57	2.60	2.63	2.66	2.68
Gross domestic product (GDP)	US$bn	7.40	8.00	7.40	8.10	*8.03
GDP per capita	US$	2,800	2,771	2,730	2,763	3,237
GDP real growth	%	1.1	1.7	1.0	1.9	2.5
Inflation	%	6.4	7.0	6.5	16.7	11.5
Exports (fob) (goods)	US$m	1,554.6	1,436.0	1,500.0	1,368.0	1,586.1
Imports (fob) (goods)	US$m	2,908.1	2,949.0	3,600.0	3,813.0	3,525.9
Balance of trade	US$m	-1,353.5	-2,080.0	-2,100.0	-2,445.0	-1,939.8
Current account	US$m	-274.6	-587.0	-680.0	-975.0	-1,150.0
Total reserves minus gold	US$m	1,053.7	1,900.5	1,645.1	1,194.9	1,846.5
Foreign exchange	US$m	1,053.6	1,899.0	1,644.2	1,194.8	1,846.4
Exchange rate	per US$	42.70	46.00	48.50	54.83	60.52

* estimated figure

1930s The worldwide economic depression and greater international competition undermined the Jamaican sugar industry.
1938 Popular uprisings caused by unemployment and resentment of racial British policies led to the establishment of the People's National Party (PNP) by Norman Manley.
1944 Universal adult suffrage was introduced and a new constitution allowed for the election of the House of Representatives.
1958 Jamaica became part of the attempted West Indies Federation.
1962 At the insistence of Prime Minister Alexander Bustamante, Jamaica left the West Indies Federation and gained separate independence as a member of the British Commonwealth. Kingston became the capital city.
1968–69 Protests against poor housing conditions turned into serious riots in Kingston.
1972 Michael Manley became prime minister and pursued a policy of economic self-reliance.
1976 The PNP won another term following elections marked by violence and proceeded to nationalise businesses and build closer ties with Cuba.
1980 Edward Seaga became prime minister and reversed the nationalisation policies of the previous government. The US granted the Seaga government substantial aid after it distanced itself from Cuba.
1988 Hurricane Gilbert caused an estimated US$3 billion damage to much of the island.
1989 The PNP ousted the JLP in elections, returning Michael Manley as prime minister. Manley, however, chose to continue Seaga's policy.
1992 Manley retired on health grounds and was succeeded by Percival Patterson.
1993 The PNP was returned to office with an increased majority.
1997 The PNP won a third term in office.
1999 Protests against a new fuel tax spilled over into rioting in several areas. The Jamaican Defence Force (JDF) was ordered onto the streets to tackle the high rate of crime.
2001 Violence broke out in Kingston. There were gun battles between the police and gangs with political links. The army was called out after 25 people had been killed.
2002 The ruling PNP won parliamentary elections.
2004 Extra police were drafted into St James, the island's tourism capital, in July, to tackle the escalating crime wave. The business community pledged J$200,000 (US$3,289) worth of petrol each month to aid the police. Ivan, the worst hurricane since 1988, struck Jamaica on 12 September, damaging thousands of homes and killing 15 people.
2005 Jamaica and Venezuela signed a US$200 million agreement on 23 August to modernise and expand the Petrojam oil refinery in Kingston.

Political structure
Constitution
Jamaica is a parliamentary democracy and independent state within the Commonwealth. The British monarch is the titular head of state and is represented by a governor general appointed on the advice of the prime minister. The governor general's role is mainly ceremonial and is guided in most cases by the prime minister, who as head of government effectively exercises executive power. Duties include appointing the leader of the opposition from among members of parliament who do not support the government. The governor general must have no affiliation with any political party while holding office. Local governments in the 14 parishes are due for election every three years. The minimum voting age is 18. Voting is by secret ballot and the candidate who wins the most votes in each constituency is elected in a first-past-the-post electoral system.

Form of state
Constitutional monarchy

The executive
The head of state is the British monarch who is represented by the Governor General of Jamaica. The prime minister is selected by the governor general from the House of Representatives as the member best able to command the support of the House. Executive power rests with the cabinet – made up of the prime minister and at least 11 ministers. Cabinet ministers are chosen by the prime minister.

National legislature
The legislature is a bicameral parliament. It consists of a 60-member House of Representatives, elected every five years, and a 21-member Senate, appointed to a parallel term. The prime minister, who is also leader of the majority in the House of Representatives, appoints 13 senators, while the remaining eight are named by the leader of the opposition. The Senate mainly reviews legislation passed by the House of Representatives, although it can also initiate legislation, except on financial matters.

Voting must be held within three months of the dissolution of parliament. There have been eight parliaments since 1962, when Jamaica became the first English-speaking West Indian island to gain independence from the UK.

Legal system
The judiciary is headed by a Supreme Court and a Court of Appeal. The governor general, acting under the guidance of a six-member Privy Council based in London, UK, can grant pardons to convicted criminals. The final appeal is to the Judicial Committee of the Privy Council in the UK.

Last elections
16 October 2002 (parliamentary)
Results: Parliamentary: the ruling People's National Party (PNP) won 52 per cent of the vote (35 seats out of 60) and the Jamaica Labour Party (JLP) 47.3 per cent (25 seats); turnout was 56.3 per cent.

Next elections
2007 (parliamentary)

Political parties
Ruling party
People's National Party (PNP) (since 1989)
Main opposition party
Jamaica Labour Party (JLP)

Population
2.68 million (2004)
Ethnic make-up
Afro-Caribbean (90.9 per cent), East Indian (1.3 per cent), European (0.2 per cent), Chinese (0.2 per cent), mixed (7.3 per cent) and other (0.1 per cent).
Religions
Jamaica is home to a number of Christian denominations, mostly Protestant (over 61 per cent of the population). These include the Church of God (21 per cent), Baptist (9 per cent), Anglican (6 per cent) and Seventh-Day Adventist (9 per cent) churches. Roman Catholics (4 per cent) and spiritual cults (35 per cent) make up the other principal religious groups.

Education
The quality of schooling has slowly deteriorated over the last 20 years as debt reduction and other fiscal issues take higher priority. Jamaica's education system is based on the British system. Schooling consists of a two year pre-primary from aged 4, then a compulsory primary cycle of six years. Secondary schooling is divided into three phases, at the end of each, students either leave or move up to the next grade. They enter a 'first cycle' secondary school for three years, then a sixth form education of two-years and finally a 'second cycle' secondary school of two years; GSE 'O' and 'A' level examinations conclude the latter two. The education system accommodates a variety of public and private schools.

The main beneficiary of the government's spending on education is the primary school system, which enjoys a higher per capita expenditure than secondary and tertiary education.

Free places are offered in secondary schools through an annual common entrance examination, but a shortage of places has meant that not all children who qualify can be accommodated.

Post-secondary education is available at three universities and a number of community and teacher-training colleges. Opportunities for tertiary education remain limited, with only 8 per cent of high school graduates going to university or other higher institutions.

The primary and secondary education system was affected by the structural adjustment programme agreed with the IMF during the 1990s, which resulted in general cutbacks in social services expenditure. However, education has also benefitted from direct support from multilateral institutions. In 1996, the World Bank initiated a US$28 million student loan project, and has sponsored reform of secondary education. In 2000, the Inter-American Development Bank (IDB) approved a US$31 million loan to support the development of the primary school system.

Literacy rate: 88 per cent, adult rate (2003)
Compulsory years: Six to 12
Enrolment rate: 101 per cent gross primary enrolment, of relevant age group (including repeaters) (World Bank)
Pupils per teacher: 31 in primary schools.

Health
Total expenditure on health is around 7 per cent of GDP, of which government spending is about 42 per cent.

Jamaica's health care is affordable and improving dramatically; increasing life expectancy and lowering infant mortality rates to some of the best figures in the Caribbean. Unfortunately, money has been taken out of the funding for the public education system.

Improved water sources and sanitation facilities are available to 71 per cent and 84 per cent of the population, respectively.

HIV prevalence: 1.2 per cent aged 15–49 in 2003 (World Bank)
Life expectancy: 75.8 years (World Bank)
Fertility rate/Maternal mortality rate: 2.3 births per woman (World Bank)
Birth rate/Death rate: 17.4 births per 1,000 population; 5.4 deaths per 1,000 population (2003).
Infant mortality rate: 17 per 1,000 live births (World Bank)
Head of population per physician/bed: 1.3 physicians and 2.1 hospital beds available per 1,000 people.

Welfare
Welfare is provided under the National Insurance Scheme (NIS) and the Social Assistance Programme. The NIS is contributory and provides protection against loss of income for men aged 18 to 70 years and women aged 18 to 65 years. There has also been multilateral involvement in welfare provision, including a US$20 million Jamaica Social Investment Fund (JSIF) initiated by the World Bank in 1996. JSIF is part of a national programme aimed at eliminating poverty and generating social funds. The Bank has initiated a social assessment programme for the inner cities, to allow the JSIF to target poverty more effectively. The Jamaican government has mobilised support from several non-governmental organisations and other charities towards the administration of social security and welfare measures. It is open to collaboration and partnership with stakeholders, both locally and abroad to improve the quality of services delivered to the poor. Such organisations include, Food for the Poor, which was involved in a massive programme to build 2,000 homes for poor families across Jamaica.

Main cities
Kingston (capital, estimated population 590,500 in 2003), Spanish Town (133,400), Portmore (113,400), Montego Bay (93,500).

Languages spoken
English and a local patois, influenced by Elizabethan English.

Official language/s
English

Media
The media is free from censorship. Although the government has wide involvement in television, it has little control over radio and none in the print media.

Press
Dailies: The island's major daily newspapers are published by the Gleaner Company Ltd and Jamaica Record Ltd. The major English language dailies are *The Star* (an afternoon tabloid), *The Jamaica Gleaner*, *The Jamaica Observer* and *The Jamaica Record*.
Weeklies: Several weeklies, periodicals and fortnightly community papers are published in towns and parishes. Some of the popular weeklies include the *Jamaica Herald*, *Western Mirror* and the *North Coast Times*.
Business: Business publications include an economic and business newsletter *Insight* (twice monthly) and the monthly *Investor's Choice Magazine*.

Broadcasting
Radio: Radio broadcasting is operated by a number of companies including the commercial Radio Jamaica Ltd, KLAS FM (Mandeville), IRIE FM (Ocho Rios) and Radio Waves (Montego Bay). Altogether there are eight major stations.
Television: Jamaica has two major networks, TVJ (formerly the Jamaica Broadcasting Corporation (JBC)) and Videomax Mediamix (CVM). The government has licenced island-wide zones for cable television providers since 1998.

Advertising
Radio, television, the press and billboards are the major advertising media in Jamaica. Radio, with eight authorised stations, is perhaps the most wide-ranging medium. Local TV networks TVJ and CVM also offer slots for advertisers. Internet service providers (ISPs) that offer advertising opportunities include CWJamaica (Cable and Wireless), InfoChannel, Colis, Jamweb, World Telenet and Jamaica on Line, among others. There are a number of advertising agencies with national coverage. Direct marketing through the postal system and via telephone marketing have been successfully used by some companies.

Economy
Agriculture, tourism and the bauxite/alumina industry have dominated Jamaica's economy for a number of years. More recently the services sector has gained in importance. Sugar, and later banana production, used to produce much of Jamaica's earnings during the pre-independence era, but with diversification it now exports bananas, coffee, citrus fruit, onions, peppers and other vegetables as well as beverages including rum, beer and carbonated drinks. A plan to double the refining capacity of the Jamalco Aluminium Refinery to 2.8 million tonnes was announced in July 2005. The cost of US$1.2 billion includes a power station as well as high hurricane-wind and earthquake defences.

Jamaica is an open and import-dependent economy, vulnerable to the effects of oil and commodity prices on its balance of trade. Like other Caribbean countries, it can suffer from periodic hurricanes and flooding. Hurricane Ivan that devastated many areas and crops in September 2003 is estimated to have cost Jamaica US$362 million and the effect on the economy in 2004 was to limit growth to 1–2 per cent.

Remittance earnings, particularly from emigrants in the US, Canada and UK, have become an important source of foreign exchange with over US$300 million typically injected into the economy each year.

The Patterson government has worked hard to reverse Jamaica's disappointing economic growth of the 1990s, with steady improvement in primary production and industry. The tourist industry provides over 10 per cent of GDP and almost 10 per cent of employment but tourist numbers are directly effected by natural disasters. Successful tourist promotions after Hurricane Ivan saw numbers rise in 2004, outstripping the record-breaking numbers of 2003. The 2005 sharp rise in the price of oil highlights the country's vulnerability to forces beyond its control. An agreement signed with Venezuela in August 2005 (the PetroCaribe Energy Co-operation Agreement) guarantees a supply of 21,000bpd of favourably priced crude oil, refined products or LPG

Inflation in January–March 2005 was almost zero. Inflation in 2004 had been falling steadily from the 16.7 per cent in 2003, but hurricane damage caused it to average out at 11.5 per cent for the year. Meanwhile, the business environment continues to be negatively affected by high levels of petty and organised crime, with observers monitoring the murder rate as closely as more orthodox indicators. Projected growth for 2005 is 2–3 per cent.

External trade

Strong export growth in 2004 resulted in an overall improvement of US$170 million in the trade deficit.

Traditional exports in 2004 grew by 24.3 per cent, or US$995 million from the US$800 million in 2003, while non-traditional exports grew by 22.2 per cent or US$183 million from the US$33 million in 2003. Agricultural exports grossed US$43.3 million over that of 2003, although Jamaica's agricultural exports had been severely effected by Hurricane Ivan that had devastated large areas in September 2004.

There is a heavy reliance on commodity exports. Dependence on energy imports continues to cause severe balance of payments difficulties although the PetroCaribe Energy Co-operation Agreement with Venezuela will help to ease these difficulties.

Imports

Principal imports are food and other consumer goods, industrial supplies, fuel, parts and accessories of capital goods, machinery and transport equipment and construction materials. Total imports (fob) in 2004 were US$3.53 billion.

Main sources: US (38.3 per cent total, 2004), Trinidad and Tobago (10.3 per cent), Venezuela (5.6 per cent), France (5.5 per cent), Japan (4.6 per cent)

Exports

Principal exports are alumina, bauxite, sugar, bananas, rum, coffee, yams, beverages, chemicals, wearing apparel and fuels. Total exports (fob) in 2004 were US$1.59 billion.

Main destinations: US (17.2 per cent total, 2004), Canada (14.3 per cent), France (12.6 per cent), China (11.4 per cent), UK (8.6 per cent), The Netherlands (7.0 per cent), Norway (5.8 per cent), Germany (5.6 per cent)

Re-exports

Re-exports including chemicals, machinery, transport equipment and miscellaneous manufactures represent 3.5 per cent of total value.

Agriculture

Farming

The agricultural sector, including forestry and fishing, typically contributes 6.9 per cent to GDP and employs approximately 19 per cent of the workforce. Agricultural production is often affected by adverse weather conditions. Blue Mountain coffee, one of the most expensive in the world, is grown in Jamaica.

Crop production in 2004 included: 22,000 tonnes (t) sweet potatoes, 221,000t citrus fruit, 4,000t potatoes, 130,000t bananas, 20,189t plantains, 20,571t pineapples, 15,000t cassava, 1,000t maize, 2,700t green coffee, 1,150t cocoa beans, 23,121t oilcrops, 148,000t yams, 170,000t coconuts, 19,395t tomatoes, 10,400t pimento & allspice, 1,800t tobacco leaves, 467,093t fruit in total, 196,586t vegetables in total, 2,100,000t sugar cane. Livestock production included: 102,923t meat in total, 14,500t beef, 5,490t pig meat, 1,568t lamb and goat meat, 81,321t poultry, 5,765t eggs, 28,500t milk, 1,000t honey.

Fishing

Although most fishing is for domestic consumption, inland commercial fishing could be developed. The local freshwater fish industry has been able to increase production of fish in smaller ponds and cut its production cost by 30 per cent, thanks to new technology. Traditional ponds which occupy vast acreages, produce a negligible 6.25 fish per square metre. Latest technology put to use at the Longville Park fish farm, which consists of four concrete-lined ponds approximately 250 square metres in size with automated systems to monitor oxygen levels in the water and feeding, is likely to increase production up to 125 fish per square metre. Estimates show that annual output could increase to 6.6 million pounds of freshwater fish, enabling Jamaica to compete on the world market.

The typical annual marine fish catch is 4,660mt and 560mt shellfish.

Forestry

Exports of timber products in 2003 amounted to US$81,000 and imports amounted to US$66.8 million.

Production in 2003 included 859,519 cubic metres (cum) roundwood, 285,400cum industrial roundwood, 66,200cum sawnwood, 132,400cum sawlogs and veneers, 577,119cum wood fuel, 8,741t charcoal.

Industry and manufacturing

Overall performance of the manufacturing and processing sectors was estimated to have increased by 4.4 per cent from January to September 2004 over the same period in 2003. The industrial sector typically contributes 35 per cent to GDP, of which manufacturing contributes 12 per cent. The sector employs around 8 per cent of the workforce.

The growth in cement production, in line with increased construction, and food processing were 2004 production leaders. Agro-industries dominate the manufacturing sector, particularly textiles, sugar refining, paper products, cigarettes and alcohol, particularly rum and beer. Of these the textile industry has declined under the impact of competition from producers with freer trade links to the US, such as Mexico.

Other important manufacturing industries (most of which are foreign-owned and heavily dependent on imported materials and components) include chemicals, machinery and tools, glass, cement and metal products. Industry in Jamaica has suffered from difficulty in competing with more efficiently produced imports. Other problems include the high cost of security due to instances of drug contamination of exports by smugglers.

The main capital-intensive industries are petroleum refining at Kingston (capacity 34,200 barrels per day), and the refining of bauxite for export. The emphasis of industrial policy during the 1990s was on expanding facilities at the Kingston and Montego Bay free zones, encouraging foreign investment in export-based manufacturing and exploiting opportunities offered under the Caribbean Basin Initiative (CBI). In 2003, Alcoa Inc, the world's leading supplier of alumina, completed a 250,000 tonne expansion project at the Jamalco refinery at a cost of US$115 million. The revised tax arrangements, along with the expansion, lowered costs at the refinery by approximately 30 per cent. Further expansion of the Jamalco's Clarendon refinery was announced in July 2005 when a plan was agreed by Alcoa and the Jamaica government. This will add 1.5 million tonnes per year (mtpy) of capacity at a cost of US$1.2 billion, bringing the total capacity to 2.8 mtpy. The construction costs include a new power station and high hurricane wind and earthquake protection.

Total bauxite and alumina production in Jamaica for 2004 was 13.25 million tonnes and 4.02 million tonnes respectively.

Tourism
Tourism is Jamaica's principal economic activity. Outstanding tourist numbers in 2003 were surpassed in 2004 with over 1.28 million visitors arriving. Of these over 70 per cent were from the US and 17 per cent from Europe. Cruise shipping fell slightly with 414 ships arriving between January–September 2004, disembarking almost one million visitors. Tourist growth in 2005 registered 8 per cent for the first four months of the year. China has designated Jamaica as an approved destination for its holidaying citizens; Chinese visitors could swell arrival numbers by many thousands.

Mining
The mining sector generates around half of export earnings and contributes approximately 9 per cent to GDP. Mining and quarrying employs approximately 1 per cent of the workforce.
Activity is centred on the extraction of bauxite and alumina refining. Known reserves of bauxite are around two billion tonnes, although most is of relatively low quality. Other minerals exploited include gypsum, marble, silica and clays.
On 20 June 2005 a bilateral agreement was signed between China and Jamaica to, establish a bauxite mining and alumina refinery facility, projected to process 1.4 million tonnes of alumina a year.

Hydrocarbons
Jamaica derives around 96 per cent of its energy requirements from imported oil. Early attempts, in the 1970–80s, to find commercially exploitable deposits of oil and gas were unsuccessful; any deposits found were too costly to retrieve. However in November 2004 the government launched an offer for licences to explore four onshore and 22 offshore blocks in Jamaica's exclusion zone. New technology and more experience has led to the belief that any viable deposits may now be exploitable.
Jamaica does not produce coal but imports around 54,000 tonnes per annum.

Energy
Almost all the country's energy needs are imported. Oil is supplied at concessionary rates by Mexico and Venezuela. There is a strategy to move from oil to liquefied natural gas as the country's main source of energy for electricity generation. The major consumer is the alumina industry, where energy accounts for up to 40 per cent of production costs.
The potential for hydroelectric schemes is small and most electricity is generated in oil-fired power stations.

Banking and insurance
The banking sector has undergone extensive restructuring since 1997, when the government intervened to prevent a complete collapse of the country's financial institutions. The sector's problems arose from a lack of proper risk management which created inherent weaknesses. These were exposed when the monetary authorities raised interest rates to stem the tide of inflation causing asset values to plummet. The restructuring of the financial sector was completed by the Financial Sector Adjustment Company (Finsac) in March 2002 at an estimated cost of around 30 per cent of GDP. In the restructuring process, Finsac merged banks and sold them to the Royal Bank of Trinidad and Tobago. Consequently, foreign banks have a high presence in Jamaica, controlling around 80 per cent of total bank deposits.
Central bank
The Bank of Jamaica

Time
GMT minus five hours

Geography
Jamaica, with an area of 10,989 square km, is the third largest island in the Caribbean. Covered with dense tropical vegetation, it is 234km long and 82km across at the widest point. The island lies about 145km south of Cuba and 160km west of Hispaniola. Mountain ranges snake across the island from south-east to north-west, with many long spurs to north and south. The highest summits are at the eastern end of the island, with the Blue Mountain Peak the tallest at 2,256 metres. The longest river, the Rio Minho, flows south from its source in the centre of the country, and is 92km long.

Climate
Jamaica is around 5 degrees south of the Tropic of Cancer and has a maritime tropical climate characterised by warm trade winds. Average coastal and lowland temperatures are around 27 degrees Celsius, with little seasonal variation. Mean annual rainfall is about 200mm, with the main rainy season in October and a second one in May. Jamaica may be subject to the tropical storms and hurricanes typical of the Caribbean basin weather system.

Dress codes
Dress codes are mainly informal. Officials wear a jacket and tie or loose-fitting lightweight clothes when the climate is hot and humid. A sweater is rarely needed, even on cooler evenings. Light rainwear is useful. On social occasions, dress as for business meetings unless otherwise indicated.

Entry requirements
Passports
A passport valid for six months from date of departure is required by all except citizens of the US, who require only proof of identity and nationality and a return ticket for stays under six months.
Visa
No visa requirements for citizens of EU, Australasia, and some American and Asian countries. Some nationals may be issued with tourist visas at port of entry, for full list of exceptions see http://www.jhcuk.com/newguide-fr.html. Business visas require a business letter of intent.
Currency advice/regulations
The import and export of local currency is prohibited. The import and export of foreign currency is allowed. Amounts in excess of US$10,000 must be declared.
Prohibited imports
Firearms, explosives (unless accompanied with the prescribed permit issued in Jamaica), plants and flowers (unless accompanied by a Ministry of Agriculture permit), fruits, rum, vegetables (unless canned), honey, coffee and illicit drugs.

Health (for visitors)
Mandatory precautions
A yellow fever vaccination certificate is required if arriving from an infected area.
Advisable precautions
Hepatitis 'A' and 'B', tetanus, TB, typhoid and polio vaccinations are recommended. Drinking water from the public supply is safe.
Foreigners visiting the island can use public health services, but are advised to seek private medical attention. Insurance to cover the latter which can be expensive is highly recommended.

Hotels
Around 145 hotels and guest houses are available, all graded and mostly geared towards holidaymakers. There are also numerous resort villas and apartments.

Public holidays
Fixed dates
1 Jan (New Year's Day), 6 Aug (Independence Day), 25–26 Dec (Christmas Holiday).
Variable dates
Ash Wednesday, Good Friday, Easter Monday, National Labour Day (fourth Mon in May), Emancipation Day (first Mon in Aug), National Heroes' Day (third Mon in Oct).

Working hours
Banking
Mon–Thu: 0900–1400; Fri 0900–1500. Branches of some banks open on Sat.
Business
Mon–Fri: 0830–1630/1700. Some offices open Sat.

Government
Mon–Fri: 0830–1630/1700. Some offices open Sat.
Shops
Mon–Sat: 0900–1600/1700. (Exception: Wed and Thu 0900–1200/1300 downtown and uptown Kingston respectively).

Electricity supply
110/220V AC, 50 cycles

Social customs/useful tips
Appointments should be made in advance. Punctuality is appreciated. An additional 10 per cent tip is usual, even where a 10–15 per cent service charge is billed automatically. Penalties for drug offences are severe, with possession of even small quantities possibly leading to imprisonment. Luggage should be packed without the help of others and only your own should be carried through customs.

Security
It is advisable not to walk around after dark due to street crime. Some parts of Kingston are considered dangerous even during the daytime, avoid exploring nightlife away from main hotels and restaurants, unless accompanied by Jamaican friends. Only taxis, authorised by the Jamaica Union of Travellers Association (Juta) should be used and preferably ordered through hotels.
Beaches, more isolated villas and smaller establishments with fewer security arrangements can also be dangerous. Poor neighbourhoods, such as West Kingston, Grant's Pen, August Town and Harbour View should be avoided at all costs. These areas may be subject to curfew and are prone to organised gang violence, often using semi-automatic weaponry. Visitors should not offer resistance to carjackers or robbers.
Murder rates are very high in Jamaica and the situation is upsetting business sentiment. However, attacks on tourists along the popular northern coast have declined, thanks to a system of mobile police patrols.

Getting there
Air
National airline: Air Jamaica.
International airport/s: Kingston-Norman Manley International (KIN), 17km south-east of city, JTB information office, duty-free shop, bar, restaurant, buffet, bank, post office, car-hire.
Other airport/s: Montego Bay-Sangster International (MBJ), 3km north of Montego Bay, duty-free shop, bar, restaurant, bank, post office, shops, JTB information office, car hire (restricted hours in some instances).
Airport tax: J$1,000 on international departures (tax may be included in ticket price); not applicable to transit passengers.
Surface
Water: The island has several ports catering for international shipping and local ferries.
Main port/s: Kingston, Montego Bay, Ocho Rios and Port Antonio.

Getting about
National transport
Air: Air Jamaica Express links Kingston, Ocho Rios, Port Antonio and Negril.
Road: There is an extensive network of surfaced, all-weather roads (over 3,800km) plus some 11,300km of secondary roads, half of which are suitable for motor traffic. Upgrading of the road system is planned.
Buses: Minibuses in towns are generally cheap but crowded; in country often considered slow, crowded and sometimes dangerous. There are regular, scheduled services over longer distances (eg Kingston-Montego Bay; journey time varies, to some extent dependent on route).
Rail: Jamaica has 473km of track. A twice-daily service runs between Kingston and Montego Bay.
City transport
Taxis: All taxis have red PPV plates. It is advisable to negotiate fares (J$) in advance. Taxis in Kingston no longer use meters. A 10 per cent tip usual.
Car hire
Widely available. International or national licence accepted; traffic drives on the left.

BUSINESS DIRECTORY
The addresses listed below are a selection only. While World of Information makes every endeavour to check these addresses, we cannot guarantee that changes have not been made, especially to telephone numbers and area codes. We would welcome any corrections.

Telephone area codes
International direct dialling code (IDD) for Jamaica is +1 876, followed by subscriber's number.

Chambers of Commerce
American Chamber of Commerce of Jamaica, Le Méridien Jamaica Pegasus Hotel, 81 Knutsford Boulevard, Kingston (tel: 929-7866; fax: 929-8597; e-mail: info@amchamjamaica.org).

Jamaica Chamber of Commerce, 85a Duke Street, Kingston (tel: 922-0150; fax: 924-9056; e-mail: jamcham@cwjamaica.com).

Montego Bay Chamber of Commerce and Industry, 4-7 Overton Plaza, PO Box 213, Montego Bay (tel: 952-6045; fax: 952-2784).

Banking
National Investment Bank of Jamaica, 32 Trafalgar Road, Kingston 10 (tel. 929-9050).

Bank of Nova Scotia Jamaica, Scotia Centre, Port Royal Street, Kingston (tel: 922-1000).

CIBC Jamaica, 23-27 Knutsford Boulevard, Kingston 5 (tel: 929-9310).

Citibank N.A., 63-67 Knutsford Boulevard, Kingston 5 (tel: 926-3270/3285; fax: 929-3745).

National Commercial Bank of Jamaica, The Atrium, 32 Trafalgar Road, Kingston 10 (tel: 929-9050).

RBTT Bank Jamaica, 17 Dominica Drive, Kingston 5 (tel: 960-2340; e-mail: rbtt@cwjamaica.com).

The Financial Sector Adjustment Company, PO Box 54, 76 Knutsford Boulevard, Kingston 5: (tel: 906-1809; fax: 906-1822; info@FINSAC.com).

Trafalgar Commercial Bank, 60 Knutsford Boulevard, Kingston 5 (tel: 929-3383, 929-3511, 929-3521; fax: 929-3654).

Central bank
Bank of Jamaica, Nethersole Place, P.O. Box 621, Kingston (tel: 922-0750; fax: 922-0854; e-mail: info@boj.org.jm).

Travel information
Air Jamaica Ltd, 72–76 Harbour St, Kingston (tel: 922-3460; fax: 922-0107).

Jamaica Hotel and Tourist Association, 2 Ardenne Road, Kingston 10 (tel: 926-3635; fax: 91-054).

National tourist organisation offices
Jamaica Tourist Board, Dominica Drive, Kingston (tel: 929-9200/19; fax: 929-9375).

Ministries
Office of The Prime Minister, Jamaica House, 1 Devon Road, Kingston 6 (tel: 927-9941/3; fax: 929-0005).

Ministry of Agriculture, Hope Gardens, Kingston 6 (tel: 927-1731/45; fax: 927-1904).

Ministry of Education and Culture, 2 National Heroes Circle, Kingston 4 (tel: 922-1400/19; fax: 967-1837).

Ministry of Finance and Planning, 30 National Heroes Circle, Kingston 4 (tel: 922-8600/15; fax: 922-7097).

Ministry of Foreign Affairs and Foreign Trade, 21 Dominica Drive, Kingston 5 (tel: 926-4220/8; fax: 929-5112; e-mail: mfaftjam@cwjamaica.com).

Ministry of Health, Oceana Hotel Complex, 2 King Street, Kingston (tel: 967-1092; fax: 967-7293).

Ministry of Industry, Commerce and Technology, 36 Trafalgar Road, Kingston 10

Jamaica

(tel: 929-8990/9; fax: 960-1623; e-mail: gojmii@infochan.com).

Ministry of Labour and Social Security, 1f North Street, Kingston (tel: 922-9500, 967-1900; fax: 922-6902).

Ministry of Land and Environment, 2 Hagley Park Road, Kingston 10 (tel: 926-1590, 926-7008; fax: 926-2591; e-mail: mehsys@hotmail.com).

Ministry of Local Government, Youth & Community Development, 85 Hagley Park, Kingston 10 (tel: 754-0994; fax: 960-0725).

Ministry of Mining and Energy, 36 Trafalgar Road, Kingston 10 (tel: 926-9170/7; fax: 968-2082; e-mail: hmme@cwjamaica.com).

Ministry of National Security and Justice, Mutual Life Building, North Tower, 2 Oxford Road, Kingston 5 (tel: 906-4908/33; fax: 906-1724; e-mail: inform@infochan.com).

Ministry of Tourism and Sports, 64 Knutsford Boulevard, Kingston 5 (tel: 920-4956; fax: 920-4944; e-mail: opmt@cwjamaica.com).

Ministry of Transportation and Works, 1c-1f Pawsey Place, New Kingston (tel: 754-1900; fax: 927-8763).

Ministry of Water and Housing, 7th Floor, Island Life Building, 6 St Lucia Avenue, Kingston 5 (tel: 754-0973; fax: 754-0975; e-mail: prumow@cwjamaica.com).

Attorney General's Department, Mutual Life Building, North Tower, 2 Oxford Road, Kingston 5 (tel: 906-2416/7) and 79-83 Barry Street, Kingston (tel: 922-6140; fax: 922-5109).

Other useful addresses

All-Island Jamaica Cane Farmers' Association, 4 North Ave, Kingston 4 (tel: 922-3010; fax: 922-077).

Banana Export Co (BECO), 10 South Ave, Kingston 4 (tel: 922-5490).

British High Commission, Trafalgar Road, PO Box 575, Kingston 10 (tel: 926-9050; fax: 929-7869).

Cabinet Office, 1 Devon Road, Kingston 10 (tel: 927-9941/3; fax: 929-8459).

Cocoa Industry Board, Marcus Garvey Drive, PO Box 68, Kingston 15 (tel: 923-6411).

Coffee Industry Board, Marcus Garvey Drive, Kingston 15 (tel: 923-7211).

Jamaica Bauxite Institute, Hope Gdns, PO Box 355, Kingston 6 (tel: 927-2073; fax: 927-159).

Jamaica Exporters' Association (JEA), 13 Dominica Drive, PO Box 9, Kingston 5 (tel: 929-1292; fax: 929-831).

Jamaica Information Service, Kingston (tel: 926-3740, 926-3590; fax: 926-715).

Jamaica Manufacturers' Association, 85a Duke Street, Kingston (tel: 922-8880/2).

Jamaica Promotion Corporation (Jampro Limited), 35 Trafalgar Road, Kingston 10 (tel: 929-9450, 929-9452/6; fax: 924-9650; e-mail: jamprouk@investjamaica.com).

Jamaica Stock Exchange, Nethersole Place, Kingston (tel: 922-0806).

Jamaican Embassy (USA), 1520 New Hampshire Avenue, NW, Washington DC 20006 (tel: 202-452-0660; fax: 202-452-0081; e-mail: emjam@sysnet.net).

Kingston Free Zone, Lot 27, Shannon Drive, Kingston 15 (tel: 923-5274).

The Planning Institute of Jamaica, 39 Barbados Ave, Kingston 5 (tel: 926-1480; fax: 926-4670).

US Embassy, Mutual Life Centre, 2 Oxford Road, Kingston 5 (tel: 929-4850).

Internet sites

Export Jamaica:
http://www.exportjamaica.org

Jamaica Stock Exchange:
http://www.jamstockex.com

CVM Television:
http://www.cvmtv.com/top_news1.htm

Jamaica and Jamaican Top 5 Sites:
http://www.top5jamaica.com

Jamaicamarket (business gateway):
http://www.jamaicamarket.com

Jamaica Promotions Corporation (Jampro) (export and investment promotion agency):
http://www.investjamaica.com

Japan

KEY FACTS

Official name: Nippon or Nihon (Japan)

Head of State: Emperor Tsegu no Miya Akihito (since 1989)

Head of government: Prime Minister Junichiro Koizumi (leader of LDP) (since Apr 2001); re-elected Sep 2005

Ruling party: Coalition government: Liberal Democratic Party (LDP) and New Komeito (Clean Government) Party (since Jun 2000; re-elected Sep 2005).

Area: 377,728 square km (3,900 small islands)

Population: 127.94 million (2004); 127.62 million (OECD, 2003)

Capital: Tokyo

Official language: Japanese

Currency: Yen (¥)

Exchange rate: ¥113.34 per US$ (Oct 2005)

GDP per capita: US$36,575 (2004)

GDP real growth: 2.60% (2004)

Labour force: 66.66 million (2004)

Unemployment: 4.70% (OECD, 2004)

Inflation: -0.70% (IMF 2005)

Balance of trade: US$132.13 billion (2004)

Foreign debt: US$1,544.83 billion (2004)

Annual FDI: US$57.40 billion (cumulative, 1995–2004, OECD); US$7.80 billion (OECD, 2004)*

* estimated figure

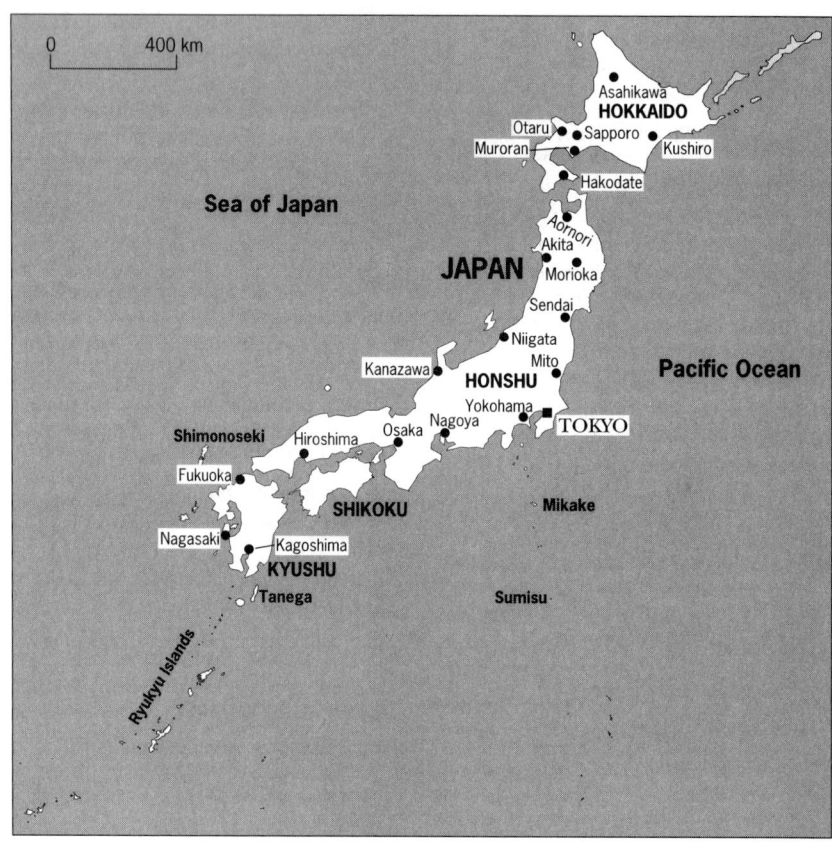

The Japanese existed in peaceful isolation for over 260 years, until they unbolted their doors with the Meiji Restoration of 1853. Traces of this closed-off period remain in Japan: economically and socially an insular and protective approach prevails. This has not always led to economic competitiveness, nor to friendly relations with its East Asian neighbours. In 2005 the world kept a wary eye on mounting Sino-Japanese animosity, generated in part by the re-elected Japanese Prime Minister, Junichiro Koizumi's, unapologetic visits to a controversial war shrine.

Japan has been modernising, with proposals to privatise its post office and railways – but not necessarily westernising. Working hours are longer than in the West and the suicide rate – not unrelated – is particularly high. In 2004, 30,000 took their own lives.

Economic gloom

At the beginning of 2005 Japan was in the economic doldrums. 2004 had brought a technical recession to the country, with two quarters of negative growth. Deflation had been steady for a decade, and in 2005 was encouraged by price falls in utility bills as a result of deregulation. Deflation, however, was just one part of a grim picture. There was also a slowdown in manufacturing output, falls in the value of land and property, problematic levels of bad debt and low levels of bank lending. Japan is an export-reliant economy and suffered from a lack of robust export demand. The fall of the euro against the dollar meant that Japan's foreign reserves shrunk steadily.

One of the prime setbacks for Japanese growth in 2005 was the high price of oil. This affected truckers, transport companies, wholesalers and fishing companies particularly badly. The rising cost of oil contributed to a 60 per cent shrinking of the trade surplus.

The emergent China has been an unsettling spectre in East Asia, threatening to wrest lucrative electronics and exports contracts away from its first world neighbour. At the same time, Japan's biggest market, the US, cannot be wholly relied upon in its current state to prop up Japanese exports. Japan has the highest level of debt among global economies, amounting to 170 per cent of GDP. The budget is drawn equally from taxation and government bond issuance. While tax revenue has been flat since the 1980s, spending has climbed. Prolific government bond issuances have compensated for excessively low tax rate – 80 per cent of workers pay taxes of only 10 per cent. This is not a healthy balance. Koizumi's government, recognising the need for spending cuts and a boost in taxation revenues, has expressed a desire to reform income tax by widening the criteria for eligibility. However, this stops short of the necessary hike in consumption tax. The incumbent Liberal Democratic Party (LDP) is reluctant to raise taxes before Koizumi's expected exit in 2006 or before the 2007 elections in the upper house. Budget savings are likely to come out of welfare payments, pay for civil servants and pensions allowances.

Slow recovery

However, despite a very gloomy start to 2005, the economy recovered month-on-month. Deflation, a major worry, was curtailed and reversed by the close of the year. Unemployment is now much reduced while bankruptcies are at their lowest level for years. The Nikkei, the stock market index for the Tokyo Stock Exchange (TSE) has risen to a four-year high. Foreign direct investment (FDI) doubled during 2004/05 and for the first ever time, more investment was ploughed into the country than was directed outwards. This is particularly significant when compared to the 1990s figures, when investment in Japan was one tenth of outward investment. Corporate profits had been healthy during deflation, but there was no trickle down to wage-earners. Profits came at the expense of the Japanese workforce, which lacks influential and aggressive labour unions. Without adequate representation, workers incomes were declining, with households resorting to savings accounts to fund living expenses. The resulting sluggish domestic consumption was a primary factor in the stagnation of the economy. However, by the end of 2005 these profits began to feed down into the pockets of workers and consumers. This led to the strongest retail sales figures for eight years, signalling that at last domestic demand is recovering. Rising wages have enabled a climb in the consumer price index (CPI).

Not only the prices of goods, but also the value of land has strengthened. In Tokyo, house prices climbed for the first time in 13 years – though admittedly the rest of Japan is still suffering from the 1990s crash. Non performing loans (NPL) have been brought under control. Annual growth of the Nikkei was 23 per cent while the Topix climbed 30 per cent. Machinery production has picked up. All this explains why business confidence, measured by the Tankan survey, increased consistently until reaching the highest level in over a decade. It is important to remember, however, that Japan's economy still has certain weaknesses and the improvements beginning to materialise are gradual and slow.

Quasi-foreign firms and fat fingers

While the Japanese economy was slowly recuperating, three big incidents preoccupied the newspapers. One was the argument between the finance ministry and the Bank of Japan (BoJ) over the Bank's ultra-loose monetary policy. Another was the decision to tighten up the rules surrounding 'quasi-foreign' companies. The third item of news was the 'fat finger' debacle in December, which cost Mizuho Securities, a banking company, dearly and also highlighted flaws in the TSE.

The government sanctioned changes in Article 821 of the revised commercial code legislation in 2005. This relates to 'quasi-foreign' companies, who primarily do business in Japan, but are incorporated overseas. The new laws would require these companies to shift entirely to Japan, which would have serious repercussions for contracts, taxation and pension arrangements. Not just this, but hostile takeovers (by foreign firms) would be banned – which could inhibit FDI. Hundreds of companies would be affected by these proposals. Some businesses have threatened to complain to the World Trade Organisation (WTO). After protests by the American Chamber of Commerce in Japan (ACCJ) and others, it was agreed in a Diet meeting that banks would be immune from the changes, and also that talks on the issue would be postponed.

The BoJ has followed an ultra-loose monetary stance since 2001, which works by flooding the market with liquidity while keeping interest rates at zero. The Bank wants to be liberated from this strategy of quantitative easing, and be free to raise interest rates whenever it deems fit. The finance ministry, however, does not trust the Bank – it demands that interest rates do not rise and has threatened to bring the independent BoJ back under state control. This debate raged throughout the latter half of 2005. The government fears that a hasty rise in interest rates would jeopardise economic recovery and

KEY INDICATORS — Japan

	Unit	2000	2001	2002	2003	2004
Population	m	126.74	127.10	127.35	127.65	127.94
Gross domestic product (GDP)	US$bn	4,677.10	4,146.30	4,370.0	4,330.0	*4,623.40
GDP per capita	US$	36,915	32,700	31,700	32,859	36,575
GDP real growth	%	2.8	0.4	-0.3	2.5	2.6
Inflation	%	-0.1	-0.7	-0.9	-0.2	-0.7
Unemployment	%	4.7	5.0	5.4	5.3	4.7
Coal output	mtoe	–	–	–	–	0.7
Exports (fob) (goods)	US$m	459,500.0	383,590.0	415,990.0	471,934.0	539,000.0
Imports (fob) (goods)	US$m	342,800.0	313,380.0	336,390.0	382,959.0	406,870.0
Balance of trade	US$m	116,720.0	70,210.0	80,000.0	88,975.0	132,130.0
Current account	US$m	116,900.0	87,800.0	124,600.0	136,215.0	171,810.0
Total reserves minus gold	US$m	356,009.0	395,155.0	461,186.0	663,289.0	833,891.0
Foreign exchange	US$m	348,583.0	387,727.0	451,458.0	652,790.0	824,264.0
Exchange rate	per US$	107.77	121.53	125.72	113.48	108.14

* estimated figure

consumer spending. The ultra-loose policy is therefore likely to continue until at least early 2006.

In December an unfortunate typing mistake, made by a so-called 'fat finger' trader, cost Mizuho Securities US$300 million. The trader mistakenly entered the value of one share as Y610,000 rather than Y1. He also sold over 40 times as many shares as existed. This error, swiftly identified, grew into a fiasco when it emerged that the TSE computer system did not have the capacity to stop trading.

China and Japan

This year Sino-Japanese tensions were stoked by both sides and rose significantly. Early in 2005 Chinese ire was centred around Japanese school textbooks. Controversial nationalist schoolbooks published in 2001 were followed up in 2005 with similar volumes. They offer a highly subjective and bitterly disputed account of the 1931–45 period in which Japan invaded and ruled China. The so-called Rape of Nanjing in 1937, in which Japanese troops entered the walled city and raped thousands of women, is not truthfully addressed. Neither are the Japanese experiments with germ warfare, carried out on Chinese captives in Unit 731. Angered by Japanese denial of their own past brutality, thousands of Chinese demonstrators poured into the streets in April, vandalising the Japanese consulate along with shops and restaurants. Consumers vowed to boycott Japanese goods. Both sides tried to extract apologies from the other while nationalist sentiment swelled. In April, Koizumi duly apologised for the 'tremendous damage and suffering' the Japanese army wreaked during its occupation of China – not the first national apology. He said he wanted 'friendship, friendship, friendship, friendship' with the president of China, Hu Jintao. The two countries have agreed to each nominate historians who will study the disputed historical events together with the hope of arriving at some level of consensus. Japan's diplomatic efforts were doubtless made with the coveted membership of the UN Security Council in mind. China is disputing Japan's claim to a permanent seat, believing that Japan has undermined its credibility for such a post by its past atrocities, and its failure to fully come to terms with this history.

As the textbooks dispute died down, Koizumi's visit to Japan's most controversial war shrine provoked another flare-up. The memorial glorifies 14 class A war criminals, alongside ordinary soldiers. The prime minister would have been criticised domestically if he did not go; and internationally if he did. The Nippon Izokukai, the Japan War-Bereaved Association, represent an important sector of the electorate, and one which currently supports Koizumi's LDP.

Although Koizumi did appear at the shrine, he did make some concessions to Chinese outrage by not entering the inner shrine, not clapping at the shrine and not wearing traditional mourning attire. It is also significant that he declined to worship at the shrine on 15 August, the sixtieth anniversary of Japanese surrender. Japanese officials are considering the possible creation of a separate shrine, or the deletion of the names of war criminals from the existing memorial. China reacted to Koizumi's visit by withdrawing from a planned diplomatic meeting with Japan on the subject of North Korean nuclear proliferation.

In late 2004 Japan, backed by the US, declared its aim to seek peace and security for Taiwan. This riled China, who called this announcement an 'abominable act.' Many Taiwanese consider themselves to be independent, while China considers the island to belong firmly to them.

Another phase in the Sino-Japanese relationship started with the proposals to jointly develop gas resources in the East China Sea near the border between the two countries. China had been accused of underhand activities in disputed areas of the sea. Inflammatory accusations flew in both directions.

Japan-US relations

Relationships with the US are generally good, and have been buoyed by continued Japanese support for Bush's Iraq strategy. One niggling glitch was resolved when Japan agreed to resume imports of US beef, which had been suspended for two years due to fears of BSE. Another source of tension between the two global economies has been the situation of American troops in Japan. Bush wanted numbers to be cut, but bases to be technologically developed. While Japan supported these proposals, underpinned by the growth of and threat posed by China, it dragged its heels in negotiations, frustrating the Americans. Debate lasted for nine years before being finally resolved in October 2005.

As part of Japan's support for the US-led war on terror, it also ended its seven-year long sanctions against Pakistan in 2005.

Japan and the rest of the world

Japan has been engaged in talks with neighbouring states to try to convince North Korea to give up nuclear developments. Allegations of North Korean abductions of Japanese citizens resurfaced during the nuclear debate.

Meanwhile South Korea and Japan have been disputing control of a set of islands located between the two countries. The islands are variously called Takeshima (Japanese name) and Dokdo (South Korean). Relations became heated and were not helped by Koizumi's insistence on visiting the Yasukuni war shrine, offensive to Koreans as well as the Chinese.

Japan plans to double official development assistance (ODA) to Africa and to increase the proportion of GDP which ODA represents. This percentage, 0.2 per cent, is low considering Japan's status as the second largest world economy. Koizumi's offers of increased aid have, however, been challenged by his finance ministry.

Domestic politics

When Koizumi encountered opposition to his plans to privatise the Japanese post office, he quickly called a general election for 11 September 2005. His plans are ambitious: when carried through they will create the world's biggest bank with savings and assets of US$3,190 billion and 25,000 branches. 85 per cent of Japanese hold their savings in the post office. Koizumi won a landslide victory, with 61.7 per cent of seats, which duly vindicated his plans for reform. However, these will not, by any means, be easy to accomplish. His undoubted charisma, his promotion of female candidates in the media, and some say, his unorthodox haircut, all also contributed to his win. The turnout, at 67.51 per cent, was strong.

The privatisation of the post office has aroused strong passions on both sides as it encapsulates the debate about a role the state should play in the economy. The election was billed as a referendum on post office reform: the majority voted for neo-liberalism and a smaller role for the state. The Japanese system is traditionally protective: some desire, while others fear, a slide towards the ruthless capitalism of the US. There is also concern about the seeming inevitability of post office closures, especially of small and rural branches. From 2007 the post office will be broken down into quarters: postal delivery, counter service, savings and insurance. The government will hold just a one-third stake by 2017.

The fact that the Japanese imperial family has not produced a son for forty years means that calls have been made to sanction succession through the female line. The alternative to Princess Aiko being crowned emperor would be the introduction of concubines into the imperial bedroom. Several commentators have recommended this step.

Outlook

A concern that Japan shares with most of the western world is its ageing population and depleting workforce. A quarter of the Japanese population is over sixty years old and in the first half of 2005 there were 30,000 more deaths than births. Thanks to a healthy diet and a plummeting birthrate, currently 1.26 children per family, Japan is set to have one of the oldest populations in the world in coming years.

The economy should continue to improve. Provided zero interest rates are maintained for the short term, wage increases should ensure sustained growth in consumer spending. The success of negotiations about gas exploration in the East China Sea will be a determining factor in relations with China.

Koizumi has already indicated that he will retire in September 2006. His cabinet reshuffle in November 2005 gave some suggestion of who is likely to be his heir. Shinzo Abe, the chief cabinet secretary, Taro Aso, the foreign minister and Sadakazu Tanigaki, the finance minister, all seem to be in the running.

Risk assessment

Economic	Improving
Political	Good
Regional Stability	Some tension
Stock Market	Stable

COUNTRY PROFILE

Historical profile
1600 The unification of Japan began in the Tokugawa period (1600–1868), during which a national administrative hierarchy was formed.
1868 The restoration of the imperial family from political obscurity ended the Tokugawa shogunate and began the Meiji era. Key reforms were initiated to orient Japan to the West and end centuries of isolation.
1894 Japan defeated imperial China in a brief war.
1895 China ceded Taiwan to Japan and allowed Japan to trade in China.
1904–05 Japan went to war with Russia and won.
1910 After three years of fighting, Japan annexed Korea.
1914–19 Japan had limited participation in the First World War on the side of Britain and the allies. The Treaty of Versailles gave Japan some territory in the Pacific.
1920–32 Since the late 1920s, extreme nationalism had increased. In 1931, Japan invaded Manchuria, renaming it and installing a puppet regime. The Japanese prime minister was assassinated in 1932 by ultra-nationalists. The military held increasing influence in the country.
1938–41 Japanese forces occupied large parts of China and south-east Asia, forcing the British out of Singapore, Malaysia and Hong Kong.
1945 Following its defeat in the Second World War, the subsequent armistice ceded control over many of Japan's outer islands, and the country was placed under US military occupation.
1947 A new democratic constitution was enacted, renouncing all military activity outside Japan.
1951 Following the signing of the peace treaty, Japan regained its sovereignty. Sovereignty over the Tokara Archipelago and the Amami islands were also restored.
1955 The Liberal Democratic Party (LDP) was formed by a coalition of centre-right groups.
1956 Japan joined the UN.
1964 Prime Minister Hayato Ikeda was succeeded by Eisaku Sato, who was to become the longest-serving prime minister in Japanese history, remaining in office until 1972.
1972 The Bonin Islands and the remainder of the Ryukyu Islands (including Okinawa), which had been under US administration since 1945, were finally returned to Japan.
1976 Following the resignation of Sato's successor, Kakuei Tanaka, in 1974, Tanaka was arrested on charges of accepting bribes. The scandal damaged the LDP, which, in the elections, lost its overall majority for the first time.
1983 Following seven years of judicial proceedings, Kakuei Tanaka was found guilty of accepting bribes. Tanaka began appeal proceedings and refused to resign his legislative seat, forcing a premature general election.
1986 The LDP recovered its absolute majority in the *Diet*.
1987 The high court upheld the 1983 decision, finding Tanaka guilty of accepting bribes.
1989 The Showa era ended with the death of Emperor Hirohito, who had reigned since 1926. He was succeeded by his son, Akihito, beginning the Heisei era.
1993 The LDP lost its majority in the lower house in the national election and a coalition government was formed.
1994 Tomiichi Murayama, leader of the Social Democratic Party of Japan (SDPJ), became Japan's fourth prime minister in a year.
1996 The LDP won the general election.
1997 Ryutaro Hashimoto of the LDP returned for his second term as prime minister. The economy entered a severe recession.
1998 Keizo Obuchi succeeded Hashimoto, who resigned following his party's defeat in the upper house election.
2000 Obuchi died and was replaced by Yoshiro Mori. The LDP lost its parliamentary majority, forcing Prime Minister Mori to rely on coalition partners. Mori survived the first in a series of votes of no-confidence.
2001 Mori was rocked by scandals and an unpopular image, he resigned as prime minister and party leader. Junichiro Koizumi was elected as the LDP's new president and became prime minister. He helped turn around the fortunes of the LDP as it won Tokyo's metropolitan elections. The LDP coalition won the upper house elections.
2002 Koizumi's opinion poll ratings plummeted as his 'reform' agenda prove unpopular.
2003 The LDP was re-elected in the parliamentary elections.
2004 The opposition won the House of Councillors partial elections on 1 July; however, the LDP-led coalition retained its majority in both houses. Japanese non-combat troops are sent to Iraq. Huge earthquakes killed 30 people in the north.
2005 Parliament was dissolved and an early election called for 11 September, after the prime minister's proposals to privatise Japan Post was defeated in the upper house. The LDP won an increased majority in the Diet, gaining 47 seats, while the main opposition, DPJ, lost 63 seats. Turnout was 67.51 per cent. Relations with China were strained as a result of controversial Japanese textbooks, Koizumi's visits to a war shrine commemorating war criminals and China's exploration of disputed areas of the East China Sea.
100 people are killed in Amagasaki in a rare but severe train crash.

Political structure
Constitution
The Japanese constitution came into force in 1947. It may be amended only if the proposed alteration is passed with a two-thirds majority by the Diet (parliament) and then submitted to the people for ratification, either in a referendum or election.

Japan is a parliamentary democracy based on universal adult suffrage. Religion and state are constitutionally separate.

Since the crown prince and his siblings have no male children, in November 2004, the ruling Liberal Democratic Party (LDP) had begun to consider constitutional changes that would allow a woman to ascend to the imperial throne.

Form of state
Constitutional monarchy

The executive
Executive power is vested in the cabinet, which consists of the prime minister and not more than 20 ministers of state (including ministers without portfolio and the chief cabinet secretary) and is collectively responsible to the Diet.

By convention, the chosen president of the majority party becomes prime minister; the Emperor appoints the prime minister, who must already have been approved by the Diet. The prime minister appoints the cabinet, the majority of whom must be members of the Diet; the cabinet remains collectively responsible to the Diet.

The Emperor is the head of state under the constitution, but has only formal powers related to government.

National legislature
The Diet (parliament) is the highest organ of state power and the sole lawmaking authority, comprising two houses: the 480-member House of Representatives (lower house) and the 242-member House of Councillors (upper house).

The House of Representatives is the stronger and has precedence in the enactment of laws, passage of the budget, approval of treaties and choice of the prime minister. The House of Representatives has a four-year term. Three hundred of the members are elected from single seat constituencies, the other 180 members being elected by proportional representation.

House of Councillors members are elected for six-year terms, with half the seats filled by election every three years.

Legal system
The judiciary is independent, but the role of bureaucratic interpretation and the reluctance of the Japanese to get involved in litigation mean that judges are less influential than in Western democracies. All judicial power is vested in the Supreme Court and four types of inferior court – High, District, Family and Summary Courts.

The judges of the Supreme Court, except the chief judge, who is appointed by the Emperor, are appointed by the cabinet. The judges of inferior courts are also appointed by the cabinet, but only from a list of persons nominated by the Supreme Court.

Last elections
1 July 2004 (second half of the seats House of Councillors); 9 November 2003 (House of Representatives); 29 July 2001 (half the seats of the House of Councillors).

Results: Parliamentary (July 2004): for the first time since 1989, the opposition won the partial elections, with the ruling LDP winning only 49 seats out of 121 contested; however, the LDP-led coalition retained its majority in both houses. Parliamentary (House of Representatives): the Liberal Democratic Party (LDP) was re-elected, winning 237 seats out of 480 in the House of Representatives, its coalition partners 38 (New Komeito 34, New Conservative Party four), Minshuto Democratic Party of Japan (DPJ) 177, Japanese Communist Party (JCP) nine, Social Democratic Party (SDP) six, Jiyu Rengo (Liberal League) one, Mushozoku-no-kai (Independents' Party) one and non partisans 11. Turnout was 52 per cent.

Next elections
11 Sep 2005 (House of Representatives, snap election called by Prime Minister Koizumi after the House of Councillors voted down his postal privatisation bill); 2007 (House of Councillors).

Political parties
The government moved from being a three-party coalition to a two-party government when the New Conservative Party was disbanded in November 2003 and absorbed into the dominant Liberal Democratic Party (LDP).

Ruling party
Coalition government: Liberal Democratic Party (LDP) and New Komeito (Clean Government) Party (since Jun 2000; re-elected Sep 2005).

Main opposition party
The Minshuto (Democratic Party of Japan (DPJ) – amalgamation of four parties, of which the original Minshuto is the largest).

Population
127.94 million (2004); 127.62 million (OECD, 2003)

Ethnic make-up
Japan is generally recognised to be racially homogenous, however there are small numbers of Ainu (indigenous people) and almost one million Koreans. The 1980s saw an influx of illegal immigrants into Japan, notably from the Philippines. Immigration levels have remained low relative to other industrialised countries, with non-Japanese making up only 2 per cent of the population.

Religions
Shintoism and Buddhism (majority), Christianity (minority). Many people profess both Shintoism and Buddhism, observing Shinto rites for birth and marriage and Buddhism for funerals. Both religions continue to play a significant role in cultural, philosophical and even business and political spheres. There are approximately 1.7 million Christians.

Education
Japan follows the American educational cycle of 6-3-3-4 years, where the six, elementary (primary) years and three junior high school years are free of charge and mandatory.

Even though competition is fierce, 97 per cent of students enrol for non-compulsory high school at aged 15. Valued places in prestigious high schools virtually guarantee a direct path into universities and other institutes of higher education. High school lasts for three years. There are a number of private international schools. At 62.6 per cent, Japan has the highest rate, of any industrialised country, for students going into higher education. There are three types of institutes of higher education: university, junior college and technical college.

There are also kindergartens for pre-school children, and miscellaneous schools for vocational and practical training, and special education schools for the physically and mentally handicapped. Admission is highly competitive at every stage of schooling and there have been many critics who question whether the intensive school curriculum enables students to confront a dynamic, modern world. Changes have been introduced to encourage a greater flexibility in both teaching and learning. The academic year has been amended to five days a week and 210 days a year.

Public expenditure on education typically amounts to 3.6 per cent of annual gross national income.

Compulsory years: Six to 15
Enrolment rate: 101 per cent gross primary enrolment, 103 gross secondary enrolment; of the relevant age groups (including repeater) (World Bank).
Pupils per teacher: 19 in primary schools

Health
Total expenditure on health is 8 per cent of GDP, of which government spending is some 77–78 per cent.

Medical facilities in Japan are excellent, with around 97 per cent of all medical services covered by plans such as National Health Insurance, which is also available to foreigners with residence or work visas.

Japan has a low fertility rate reflecting trends in all developed countries as its population ages rapidly. In a February 2005 study the recorded number of Japanese men fell by 0.01 per cent, as the population rose by 0.05 per cent, these figures are the smallest seen (apart from

Japan

the war years when statistics of military deaths were withheld) since records began in 1920. The fall in the number of men could be explained by many working abroad, however what is sure is the number of Japanese aged over 65, in 2004, reached a record high of 19.5 per cent, as those aged under 14 fell to an all-time low of 13.9 per cent. The concerns in the changing demographics has prompted reform of the state pension where amendments implemented in 2004 steadily reduce benefits, as premiums increase.

HIV/Aids
There are signs that the sexual behaviour of youth in Japan could be changing significantly and putting this group at greater risk of HIV infection.
HIV prevalence: 0.1 per cent aged 15–49 in 2003 (World Bank)
Life expectancy: 81.7 years (World Bank). Japan has the highest life expectancy in the world.
Fertility rate/Maternal mortality rate: 1.3 births per woman; maternal mortality eight per 100,000 live births (World Bank)
Birth rate/Death rate: 9.61 births per 1,000 people; 8.55 deaths per 1,000 people (2003).
Infant mortality rate: 3.1 per 1,000 live births (World Bank)
Head of population per physician/bed: 1.9 physicians and 16.5 hospital beds typically available for 1,000 people.

Welfare
Japan's social security system is divided into five parts: public assistance, welfare services, social insurance (medical care, pensions, child allowances, unemployment insurance and workers' accident compensation), public health, public service pensions and assistance for war victims.
There are some 26,000 social welfare institutions (excluding day nursery facilities), of which around 16,600 are public and 9,400 private.

Pensions
The falling birth rate and ageing population has increased the pressure on the pension scheme, which relies on contributions paid by those working, too many of whom have opted out, so that in 2002/03 the payment on pensions exceeded contributions and the Social Insurance Agency was forced to release assets to make up a ¥38.2 billion (US$304.7 million) shortfall. The welfare ministry estimates that social security costs will increase fourfold by 2025, from ¥65 trillion (US$608 billion) in 1995 to ¥274 trillion (US$2.6 trillion) in 2025. To compound the problem, the stagnating economy in the 1990s resulted in a huge pension liabilities gap – underfunded pension liabilities are thought to total ¥419 trillion (US$3.9 trillion). To fill the gap, the government has raised corporate taxes and scaled back the benefits.

The pension reform bill was opposed by those who claimed that the underlying assumptions on which it was based were flawed. About 40 per cent of self-employed workers are said to have failed to pay contributions, many believe they would be unlikely to see any retirement benefits. Without a unified pension, which covers all workers, the funding remains problematic, although a sales tax has been proposed to add to the funding.

Family support
A social security reform bill was passed in June 2004, in which corporate tax will be increased gradually from 13.58 per cent in 2004 to 18.3 per cent in 2017, while benefits will be reduced, with payments at only 50 per cent of the average take-home pay. Opposition say increased tax will encourage employers to hire part-time workers who are covered by another scheme.

Main cities
Tokyo, on Honshu, (capital, estimated population 8.3 million in 2004); Yokohama, (3.5 million); Osaka (2.6 million) Nagoya, (2.2 million), Sapporo (1.9 million), Kobe (1.5 million), Ome (1.5 million), Kyoto (1.5 million), Fukuoka (1.4 million), Kawasaka (1.3 million), Hiroshima (1.1 million), Sendai (1.0 million), Kitakyushu (1.0 million).

Languages spoken
It is hard to operate in Japan without some knowledge of Japanese or the services of an interpreter.
Pupils are taught English in school for seven years but this involves a formal grammatical knowledge rather than spoken English.

Official language/s
Japanese

Media
Press
Dailies: Japan has the highest newspaper circulation and readership in the world; 70 million copies are printed daily.
The major national dailies are *Yomiuri*, *Asahi Shimbun*, *Mainichi* and *Sankei*.
The four English-language dailies are: *Japan Times*, *Mainichi Daily News*, *Daily Yomiuri* and *Asahi Evening News*.
Weeklies: Weeklies including regional Sunday newspapers are *Aera*, *Asahi Graph*, *Asahi Shimbun* and *Asahi Weekly*. *Japan Update* is an English-language weekly with news, movie listings and classifieds.
Business: A trade-press of 7–8,000 publications covers most aspects of business and the economy. *Nihon Keizai Shimbun* is the leading financial daily. It also publishes a weekly edition in English, *Japan Economic Journal*. *Daily Yomiuri* mainly targets businesses. Some of the major industrial dailies are *Nikkan Kogyo*, *Nihon Kogyo*, *Nikkei Business* and *Nikkei Sangyo*. *Diamond Weekly* has weekly coverage on business matters.
Toyo Keizai, the main economic monthly, also publishes an English version, *Oriental Economist*. *Business Tokyo* (monthly, in English) gives a useful summary of business developments in Japan. *Agora (Japan)* is a monthly business magazine. *Tokyo Business* is a news magazine in English. *Forbes Nihonban* carries in-depth business features.
Periodicals: The English language *Tokyo Journal* includes a monthly guide to what's on in the capital.

Broadcasting
Radio: There are numerous radio broadcasting services, both government and commercial. The English-language Far East Network, the radio station of the US forces, is available 24 hours on both medium wave and FM. Another English language station, KYTO, is available.
Television: Of the numerous TV networks, the major national ones are the Nippon Television Network (NTV), the Tokyo Broadcasting System (TBS), Fuji Television and TV Asahi. Nippon Hoso Kyokai (NHK) is the non-commercial public network. Certain Tokyo hotels have closed-circuit English language TV. Some TV programmes including news are available in English through a bilingual converter.
Cable television is avaiable in the majority of hotels.

Advertising
Advertising is available in the press, commercial radio, TV and in cinemas. Outdoor advertising is widely available.

Economy
2004 had brought a technical, if minimal, recession to the country and deflation seemed entrenched. The exports market, Japan's main driver of growth, was not doing well: rising global oil prices did not help. There had been little good news to come out of the Japanese economy since the bubble burst in 1991. However the tide of misfortune began to turn in 2005. Domestic demand, underpinned by strong corporate profits, plus an increase in employment and wages, have all encouraged the expansion. Deflation has been reversed. Although export growth has slowed from the high of 14.5 per cent in 2004, the economy is expected to expand by 1.5–2.0 per cent in 2005. The unemployment rate has fallen to 4.4 per cent. Non performing loans (NPL) have been brought under control. Annual growth of the Nikkei was 23 per cent while the Topix

climbed 30 per cent. Production has picked up. All this explains why business confidence, measured by the Tankan survey, increased in 2005, reaching the highest level in over a decade.

However, restrictions and protectionist measures still curtail Japan's global competitiveness. Japan's prime minister presents himself as a reformist – the privatisation of the post office will be his defining accomplishment – and corporate Japan has restructured, particularly by reducing its 15 banks to a 'big four'. Bad debts have been slashed from over 20 per cent to less that 5 per cent. Despite progress, further liberalisation is necessary for a full economic recovery.

The OECD, in its 2005 *Economic Policy Reforms* publication, recommended:
- liberalising services through enforcement of competition laws and imposing heavier sanctions
- reducing agriculture subsidies so that such support shifts its composition from market price support to direct payments
- easing employment protection measures to reduce dualism in the labour market and aid restructuring.

The IMF have warned that pensions and welfare payments for what is set to be one of the world's oldest populations will be substantial.

External trade
Rising oil prices were to blame for a deceleration in trading in 2005.

Imports
Principal imports are machinery and equipment, fuels, foodstuffs – fish products, meat products, chemicals, textiles and raw materials.
Main sources: China (20.7 per cent total, 2004), US (14 per cent), South Korea (4.9 per cent), Australia (4.3 per cent), Indonesia (4.1 per cent), Saudi Arabia (4.1 per cent), UAE (4.0 per cent)

Exports
Principal exports are transport equipment, vehicles, semiconductors, electrical machinery and chemicals. Japanese economic growth has traditionally been driven by its exports market. In 2005, however, China outpaced Japan, to become the world's third largest exporter.
Main destinations: US (22.7 per cent total, 2004), China (13.1 per cent), South Korea (7.8 per cent), Taiwan (7.4 per cent), Hong Kong (6.3 per cent)

Agriculture
Farming
The agricultural sector accounts for approximately 1.5 per cent of GDP and employs around 7 per cent of the workforce (down from 50 per cent at the end of the Second World War). Most people in farm employment supplement their income with non-farm employment.

Only about 15 per cent of the land area is available for agriculture and stock-rearing and this is constantly in demand for residential use. Agriculture is highly intensive, making considerable use of technology and capital investment.

Wet cultivation of rice is the main activity (virtually self-sufficient), with a trend toward production of beef, citrus fruits and tobacco. Wheat, barley, soya beans, potatoes, sweet potatoes, vegetables, fruit, tea and silkworms are also produced. The price of rice has declined and it is difficult for the paddy farmers to make a profit. In addition, consumers' tastes have changed and they are eating more potatoes, bread, pasta and noodles instead of rice.

Japanese farming is heavily protected by government subsidies and high import tariffs, despite the fact that Japan is dependent on food imports. The political influence of farmers has frequently stalled free trade negotiations with other countries which are deemed as competitors to the Japanese farming sector.

Crop production in 2004 included: 12,041,460 tonnes (t) cereals in total, 10,912,000t rice, 2,839,000t potatoes, 860,000t wheat, 26,800t buckwheat, 1,009,000t sweet potatoes, 198,500t barley, 118,900t pulses, 4,310,000t roots and tubers, 1,470,000t citrus fruit, 2,300,000t cabbages, 205,800t grapes, 740,000t tomatoes, 57,037t oilcrops, 52,659t tobacco, 1,350,000t sugar cane, 4,656,000t sugar beets, 280,600t soya beans, 95,000t tea, 881,100t apples, 3,705,840t fruit in total, 11,699,400t vegetables in total. Livestock production included: 3,031,358t meat in total, 513,100t beef, 1,270,400t pig meat, 1,237,686t poultry, 2,471,912t eggs, 8,334,000t milk, *3,300t honey, 7,000t horsemeat, 32,000t cattle hides, 650t cocoons, silk.

* estimate

Fishing
Japan is one of the world's great fishing nations and there are some 3,000 fishing ports dotted around its coasts. Its methods of driftnet fishing, which drags up sea fauna indiscriminately from the ocean, have been criticised throughout the world. The establishment of 200-mile economic zones at sea by a number of countries has meant that Japan has had to go further afield for fishing grounds: half the catch now comes from outside Japanese waters and Japanese boats have increasingly been accused of predatory practices. Fishing contributes substantially to domestic food supply and export earnings. Japanese fishermen catch pollack, pilchards, cod, salmon, mackerel and other fish throughout the north and central Pacific, and are second only to the former USSR in whaling. The total annual marine catch can be up to seven million tonnes per year, with a further 5 per cent of demand imported. Aquaculture is well developed and there are inshore fisheries for squid, clams, crustaceans, shallow-water fish and dolphins.

Japan remains a whaling nation and has been criticised for using overseas aid to manipulate countries into voting in favour of maintaining whaling in international waters. The typical import value of aquatic mammals amount to over US$176 million yearly, while total fish imports average over US$2 billion.

Forestry
Japan is heavily forested, with forests covering around 66 per cent of the total land area. The variation in climate across Japan means that the country enjoys a diverse range of forests. Plantations account for around 44 per cent of total forested area. About 42 per cent of forests are in public ownership.

Japan is a major consumer of wood and paper products. Despite being heavily forested, Japan is one of the world's largest importers of forest products and by far the largest importer of tropical logs and wood products. The production costs involved in the extraction of Japanese wood are high, so the country is forced to rely on imports. Exports of forest materials typically amount to around US$950 million, while imports amount to over US$10 billion.

Industry and manufacturing
The industrial sector contributes approximately 40 per cent of GDP. Manufacturing employs nearly 24 per cent of the workforce, compared to 16 per cent in the US and an average of 18 per cent in OECD countries. In the past, industry has benefited from innovative technology and, in some less competitive sectors such as chemicals, aircraft and software, from considerable financial backing from the government. Japan has also traditionally led the world in automated production processes, which has helped to reduce the industrial workforce and redeploy workers into the tertiary sector.

One of the main long-term problems in Japanese industry is its productivity. The Nikkei-300 non-financial companies have typically had a return on equity of just 4 per cent, compared to 20 per cent in the US. Since the mid-1990s, Japanese industry has failed to produce a positive spread between cost of capital and return on capital.

Part of the root cause of inefficiency is the prevailing culture. The Japanese are admired for their discipline and patience, but these qualities have not resulted in increased productivity; and whereas Japanese product innovation and development is excellent, sales and marketing have lagged behind. In uncompetitive, protected sectors, firms have paced their development to keep step with the slowest. Although the government, as well as companies themselves, is coming round to seeing the benefit of alliances with foreign firms in order to compete on the international stage, the process is slow. Moreover, communication issues surrounding Japan's complex corporate culture can act as something of a barrier to merger and acquisition activities between Japanese and foreign firms.

Nevertheless, as the cross-holding structure typical of Japan's famous *keiretsu* groups (business networks which own stakes in one another as a means of mutual security) unravels, Japanese firms in general are coming under pressure to prioritise profits over their traditional relationships. Firms kept alive by their banks after they have lost all hope of financial viability – often termed the 'zombies' by Asian business journalists – will need to be closed or merged in order to restore investor confidence in the industrial sector.

Tourism
Taiwan and Korea are the main sources of tourists to the country. Tourist arrivals in 2004 numbered 5,702,400. The tourism sector was worth 3.5 per cent of GDP in 2005, providing 2,737,000 jobs and involving 4.3 per cent of the workforce.

Mining
Mining accounts for 0.5 per cent of GDP and 1 per cent of total employment. There are few exploitable mineral resources. Molybdenum, manganese, zinc, copper and iron are mined on a small scale. Japan is self-sufficient in sulphur and limestone.

Hydrocarbons
Japan has the thid highest oil consumption in the world and relies heavily on imports, particularly from the Middle East. In 2005 talks were held with Russia on arrangements to transport oil via a new pipeline, from Eastern Siberia to the Pacific Ocean and Japan. The first stage of construction is due to be completed in 2008 with no timetable yet agreed for the second and final phase. There is some dispute over the exact routing of the pipeline, with Japan aggrieved at Chinese involvement. Capacity is expected to reach 1.6 million bpd.

Japan and China are also locked in talks about exploration of gas fields in the East China Sea. This could boost reserves and contribute to sourcing Japan's annual gas consumption of 72.2 billion cubic metres. In 2002 Japan closed its coal mines. It is a large coal importer, using the fuel for 20 per cent of its energy needs. Japan produced a mere 0.7 million tonnes oil equivalent in 2004, while it used 120.8 million tonnes. In 2004, it had only 359 million tonnes of proven coal reserves.

Energy
Japan is reliant on imported energy and is among the top five biggest energy users in the world. Japan has a total generating capacity of around 230GW. Around 60 per cent of total generation is produced by thermal plants, 30 per cent by nuclear reactors, 8 per cent by hydroelectric dams and the rest from geothermal, solar and wind power. Japan is already the third largest nuclear consumer and is set to increase its reliance on nuclear energy even further. The government plans to build up to 12 additional nuclear reactors by 2010 to add to the current total of 52. There are plans to expand nuclear power generation by 30 per cent.

Liquefied natural gas (LNG) is also likely to become an important source of energy for electricity generation in the long-term. Japan's electricity prices are among the highest in the world, but prices are falling due to cuts in capital investment. The country is served by 10 vertically integrated utility companies which have monopolies over different regions; Japan has no national grid. The regional organisation of grids is an impediment due to the limited number of inter-connections. In 2005 the utilities market was deregularised and made more efficient, leading to significant price cuts.

The Japanese government is committed to energy efficiency.

Financial markets
Stock exchange
The Tokyo Stock Exchange's (TSE). The Nikkei index rose by 23 per cent over 2005, while the topix (Tokyo Stock Price Index) rose by 30 per cent.

Banking and insurance
In the 1990s the bubble burst in the Japanese economy and banks were the major casualties. They became burdened with huge amounts of non-performing loans (NPL) and bad debt.

In efforts to bounce back and also to prevent future risk, a series of mergers and takeovers took place in the banking sector. The fifteen banks that had existed during the financial crash were reduced to four. The biggest bank, Mizuho Bank, was created when Dai-Ichi Kangyo Bank, Fuji Bank and the Industrial Bank of Japan merged. The other three are: Mitsubishi Tokyo Financial Group, Sumitomo Mitsui Banking and the United Financial of Japan Group (UFG). However, the biggest 'bank' in the world is the Japanese post office, which is in the process of privatisation.

The Bank of Japan (BoJ) was granted independence from the government in 1998. However, in 2005 the government applied acute pressure to the BoJ to ensure that it did not raise interest rates above zero before economic growth was proven to be steady. The finance ministry reacted to the BoJ's reluctance by threatening to rescind its independence. The government's distrust of the Bank's monetary policy stems from 2000 when the Bank prematurely raised interest rates against the will of domestic finance officials and the IMF.

Central bank
Bank of Japan.
Main financial centre
Tokyo, Osaka and Nagoya.

Time
GMT plus nine hours

Geography
Japan lies off the north-east coast of Asia and consists of four main islands – Hokkaido, Honshu, Shikoku and Kyushu – and thousands of smaller islands running in an arc from north (latitude 45 33'N) to south (latitude 24 25'N). Japan is mainly mountainous with only 29 per cent of the national land area consisting of plains and basins. It has about 10 per cent of the world's active volcanoes and its highest mountain, Mount Fuji (3,776 metres), is a dormant volcano. Japan occupies less than 0.3 per cent of the earth's total land area: it is only 4 per cent of the size of the United States and one and a half times bigger than the United Kingdom.

Climate
The general climate is temperate, except for part of Hokkaido in the north and some of the southernmost islands. Spring is March–May, with average temperatures of 6.1 degrees Celsius (C) (minimum) and 20.6 degrees C (maximum). The rainy season is mid-June–mid-July. Summer is June–August, with temperatures between 20 degrees C and 27.9 degrees C. Autumn is September–November, with temperatures ranging from 10.3 degrees C to 23.9 degrees C. Rainfall is heaviest June and August–September. Winter is December–February, with temperatures from -5.1 degrees C to 15.8 degrees C. Annual rainfall is 1,000–2,500mm. South and central Japan can be subject to typhoons in late summer and early autumn.

Dress codes
Traditional Japanese dress consisted of kimonos for both men and women. In modern Japan, dark business suits and Western dress are the normal rule. For formal occasions women often wear kimonos, while men usually wear morning dress, but occasionally also wear kimonos for weddings etc.

Nations of the World: A Political, Economic and Business Handbook

Entry requirements
Passports
Required by all. Passports must be valid for the duration of stay.
Visa
No visa requirements for citizens of most of Europe, the Americas, Australasia and some Asian countries, visiting for up to 90 days. For a full list, and application form, plus further information for those citizens not included on the list of visa-free travel, see www.mofa.go.jp/j_info/visit/visa/index.html.
Business travel is allowed for those enjoying visa-free travel for the minimum period. Those who do not must provide business letters, itinerary and invitations from Japanese hosts.
Currency advice/regulations
There are no restrictions on currency import or export. However, amounts in excess of Y1 million (about US$8,560 as of end-May 2003) must be declared. All money exchanged must be through authorised banks and money changers. The money exchange counter at Narita airport is open from 0900–2300.
Customs
Personal effects duty-free. Visitors may purchase souvenir items (pearls, cameras, transistor radios) free of sales tax at designated shops, but they must be taken out of the country within six months.

Health (for visitors)
There are no mandatory precautions. Japan has extensive health facilities with high standards, although medical services are expensive and insurance is essential. The International Association of Medical Assistance to Travellers provide English speaking doctors.
Advisable precautions
Inoculations may be useful for the occasional occurrence of typhoid hepatitis 'A' and 'C' and TB.

Hotels
Hotels should be booked well in advance. Service charges and taxes are added to the bill, and tipping is not customary. In addition to Western-style hotels, there are traditional Japanese-style inns (ryokan) in Tokyo and Osaka.

Credit cards
Foreign cards may not be accepted at bank ATMs, but post office and Citibank ATMs usually accept them.

Public holidays
Fixed dates
29 Dec–3 Jan government offices and many manufacturers and firms are closed. Avoid visits during Golden Week (Apr–May) and the Obon festive season (late Jul–third week in Aug), when everywhere is very crowded.
1 Jan (New Year's Day), 2 Jan (Bank Holiday), 3 Jan (Bank Holiday), 11 Feb (Foundation Day), 29 Apr (Greenery Day), 3 May (Constitution Day), 4 May (Citizens' Day of Rest), 5 May (Children's Day), 20 Jul (Marine Day), 21 Sep (Navy Day), 15 Sep (Respect for the Aged Day), 23 Sep (Autumnal Equinox), 3 Nov (Culture Day), 23 Nov (Labour Thanksgiving Day), 23 Dec (Emperor's Birthday), 31 Dec (New Year's Eve).
With the exception of New Year's Day, if a holiday falls on a Sunday, the following day is treated as a holiday instead. When there is a single day between two national holidays, it is also taken as a holiday.
Variable dates
Coming of Age Day (Seijin-no-hi) (Jan), Vernal Equinox (Shunbun-no-hi) (Mar), Physical Fitness Day (Oct).

Working hours
Banking
Mon–Fri: 0900–1500.
Business
Mon–Fri: 0900–1700; Sat: 0900–1200 (most companies close on Saturdays).
Government
Mon–Fri: 1000–1700; Sat: 1000–1200.
Shops
1000–1900 (many closed on Wed or Thu).

Telecommunications
Mobile phones
3G services are available in city areas.

Electricity supply
100V AC, 60 cycles in west Japan (Osaka) and 100V AC, 50 cycles in east Japan (Tokyo), with flat two-pin plug fittings.

Weights and measures
Metric system

Social customs/useful tips
The Japanese are a polite and reserved people. They do not expect overseas visitors to understand or adopt their customs – but they do value courtesy and friendliness and efforts to follow their customs are appreciated. The suffix san is added to the surname (i.e. Suzuki-san instead of Mr Suzuki) in polite conversation.
In most Japanese homes, in Japanese-style inns and frequently in traditional restaurants, it is taboo to wear outdoor shoes; instead slippers are provided. It is considered bad etiquette to step on the door sill or the borders of the 'tatami' mats.
Japan has become thoroughly Westernised on the surface but the people still celebrate numerous traditional festivals. These range from the informal – cherry blossom viewing in the spring and kite flying – to formal festivals such as celebrating a person's coming of age.
The Japanese insist on punctuality and punctiliousness in business behaviour. It is essential to carry *meishi* or name cards (preferably with your name in Japanese on the reverse). When receiving name cards at formal meetings, the correct procedure is to study them carefully and then place them in front of you on the table. Seating arrangements are particularly important in Japan. The place of honour is generally that furthest from the door.
Gift giving is a pleasant Japanese custom and for Japanese businessmen the exchange of gifts at New Year is very important. Ideally, gifts should consist of something personal, and be given, unopened, at the start of meetings. Whisky is now so widely sold and discounted in Japan that it is not a particularly attractive gift. When receiving gifts the Japanese practice is to treat them as objects of great reverence, but never to open them in front of the donor.
Late night business entertainment is common, but being invited to a Japanese home is rare. Restaurants are the usual venue for private social entertaining. Drinking has its own rituals: it is bad manners for a visitor to pour a drink for himself. It is impolite to blow your nose in public. Kissing in public, standing too close to someone while talking and eating while walking down the street are also considered impolite. Do not point with your index finger – use the whole hand, palm turned upwards, in a flowing movement.

Security
Japanese cities are safe despite recent increases in crime. Burglaries are uncommon. Late night travel is usually perfectly safe, even for single women, though drunks are to be avoided.

Getting there
Air
National airline: Japan Airlines (JAL); Japan Air System (JAS); All Nippon Airways (ANA)
International airport/s: Tokyo International, Narita (NRT), 60km east of Tokyo, with duty-free shops, bank/bureau de change (0900–2300), car hire, restaurants and tourist information centres with multilingual staff. There is a free shuttle bus connecting the two terminals.
Osaka Kansai International (KIX), 50km south-west of city; duty-free shops, car hire, banks/bureaux de change, tourist information (0900–2100) and bar/restaurant. Travel time by Nankai Express to Nama station in central Osaka 29 minutes. Tickets for these smart, liveried royal blue trains, which connect with the Shinkansen Bullet train network must be pre-booked.

Fukuoka, Itazuke (FUK), 10km from city; Nagoya, Komaki (NGO), 18km from city; Kagoshima (KOJ), 6km from city; Kumamoto (KMJ), 8km from city; Okinawa (OKA) 3km from Naha; Osaka International (OSA); Kobe; Kyoto.

Limousine bus services link Kansai International Airport with Osaka city centre and various other points including Kobe, Hikone and Nara.

Other airport/s: Haneda (HND), the former international airport, serves largely as a domestic airport, 19km south of Tokyo. China Airlines flights from Taipei, Taiwan, arrive here.

Airport tax: Tokyo Narita International Airport levies a tax of ¥2,040, which is usually included in the ticket price. Kansai International Airport at Osaka levies a passenger service facility charge of ¥2,650 for adults departing on international flights (usually included in the ticket price).

There is no departure tax from Haneda airport.

Getting about
National transport

Air: Most domestic flights from Tokyo to Osaka and other Japanese cities are from Haneda, 19km from Tokyo. Extensive air services provided by a number of local airlines link all main cities and provincial towns. Tickets can be purchased by automatic machines at Tokyo and Osaka International Airports' domestic departure counters.

Road: Road transport is the main form of domestic access. The network consists of 1.2 million km of road. There are good motorways linking Tokyo, Osaka, Kobe, Hiroshima, Yamaguchi, Shimonoseki, Moji, Fukuoka, Kumamoto and Morioka. Tolls are payable on certain roads. Long-distance travel by road is not recommended (travel time from Tokyo to Nagasaki by car is 18 hours, by train 9 hours and by plane 1.40 hours), road signs are in Japanese and roads are frequently very crowded outside main cities.

Buses: An extensive network of frequent coach services link main centres via express motorways, but visitors are advised against coach travel in view of language difficulties and the complexity and number of routes available.

Rail: Japan Railways run national routes from the terminal located beneath the airport.

It is easy to travel by rail to all regions. Express and 'limited express' trains are best for intercity travel with very frequent services run on the main routes. *Shinkansen*, the 'Bullet Trains', are the fastest, with compartments for wheelchair passengers, diners and buffet facilities. Supplements are payable on the three classes of express train and in 'Green' (first-class) cars of principal trains, for which reservations must be made well in advance; two pieces of ordinary luggage may be carried free, but there are restrictions on size and weight. Other types of train include *Tokkyu* (Limited Express), *Kyuko* (Express), *Kaisoku* (Rapid Train) and *Futsu* (Local Train). For short-distance trains, tickets can only be bought at vending machines outside train stations.

Long-distance one-way tickets generally do not permit stopovers and ticket refunds are not made after the time of the planned journey. Foreign visitors can make considerable savings by buying a Japan Rail exchange voucher, which is sold only outside Japan.

All Japan Railways (JR) stations display station names in both Japanese and Roman letters. The station's name is at the top centre of the signboard, in large letters; the names of the previous station and the next station are at the bottom of the signboard, in smaller letters.

Water: Jetfoil services to Kobe. There is also a jetfoil from Kansai International Airport to Osaka Port, with a journey time of around 40 minutes.

City transport

Taxis: Metered taxis can be easily hired in large cities at hotel entrances or by flagging them down in the street, but do not try to open or close the driver-controlled passenger door. Tipping is not required. Journey times: from Narita International Airport to Tokyo city centre around 90 minutes; from Kansai International Airport to Osaka city centre about 60 minutes. There is a surcharge after 2200 and an additional time charge is levied for traffic jams. Taxis are five times more expensive than trains.

Few taxi drivers understand foreign languages or read Roman lettering, so it is advisable to have your destination, including the name of a nearby landmark, written down in Japanese, along with the telephone number if possible. Hotels can often help with this. A map showing the location of the destination is also helpful.

Buses, trams & metro: Limousine buses depart several times an hour from Narita airport to city-centre hotels; journey time is about two hours. There is also a bus to the Tokyo City Air Terminal (TCAT). Tickets for all services can be bought in the terminals.

Buses can be confusing and are best used with someone who knows the system. Efficient underground railway services operate in Tokyo, Yokohama, Osaka, Kyoto, Kobe, Nagoya, Sapporo and Fukuoka, with station names displayed in Roman as well as Japanese lettering. Visitors are advised to take a minimum fare ticket and go to the Fare Adjustment Window at their destination with sufficient coinage to pay any excess fare.

Tokyo also has a good network of trams. The Tokyo rush hour can be a daunting prospect and is not recommended for the frail or faint-hearted.

Trains: JR and Keisei railway lines provide frequent services from Narita airport to the city centre, journey time 60–90 minutes.

Car hire

An international driving licence is required. Driving is on the left. Chauffeur-driven cars are often recommended for visitors without command of Japanese and knowledge of the area, as traffic and navigation can be difficult. Symbolic road signs have the expected international meanings, but few signs are written in the Roman alphabet. A red triangle with white script means 'stop', while a white triangle with a red border and blue script means 'proceed slowly'.

BUSINESS DIRECTORY

The addresses listed below are a selection only. While World of Information makes every endeavour to check these addresses, we cannot guarantee that changes have not been made, especially to telephone numbers and area codes. We would welcome any corrections.

Telephone area codes

The international direct dialling (IDD) code for Japan is +81, followed by area code and subscriber's number:

Fukuoka	92	Nagoya	52
Hiroshima	82	Okayama	862
Kawasaki	44	Osaka	66
Kobe	78	Sapporo	11
Kyoto	75	Tokyo	3
Nagasaki	958	Yokohama	45

Useful telephone numbers

Emergency
Police: 110.
Ambulance/Fire: 119
Overseas calls
Tokyo to south-east Asia: 3211-4211.
Tokyo operator: 0051.
Tokyo telegraph office: 3211-5588.
Nagoya telegraph office: 203-3311.
Osaka telegraph office: 228-2151.

Chambers of Commerce

American Chamber of Commerce in Japan, Masonic 39 MT Building, 2-4-5 Azabudai, Minato-ku, Tokyo 106-0041 (tel: 3433-5381; fax: 3433-8454; e-mail: info@accj.or.jp).

British Chamber of Commerce in Japan, Kenkyusha Eigo Centre Building, 1-2, Kagurazaka, Shinjuku-ku, Tokyo 162-0825 (tel: 3267-1901; fax: 3267-1903; e-mail: info@bccjapan.com).

Nations of the World: A Political, Economic and Business Handbook

Fukuoka Chamber of Commerce and Industry, 2-9-28 Hakata-ekimae, Hakata-ku, Fukuoka 812-8505 (tel: 441-1110; fax: 474-3200; e-mail: fksomu@fukunet.or.jp).

Kobe Chamber of Commerce and Industry, 6-1 Minato-jima Naka-machi, Chuo-ku, Kobe 650-8543 (tel: 303-5801; fax: 303-2312; e-mail: info@kcci-iic.ne.jp).

Nagoya Chamber of Commerce and Industry, 2-10-19 Sakae, Naka-ku, Nagoya (tel: 223-5611; fax: 231-6768; e-mail: info@nagoya-cci.or.jp).

Yokohama Chamber of Commerce and Industry, 2 Yamashita-cho, Naka-ku, Yokohama 231-8524 (tel: 671-7400; fax: 671-7410; e-mail: info@yokohama-cci.or.jp).

Banking
Mitsubishi Tokyo Financial Group, 1-3-2 Nihonbashi-Hongkucho, Chuo-ku, Tokyo (tel: 3245-1111; fax: 3246-1708); 7-1 Marunouchi 2-chome, Chiyoda-ku, Tokyo 100 (tel: 3240-1111; fax: 3211-6645).

Mizuho Bank, 1-1-5 Uchisaiwaicho, Chiyoda-ku, Tokyo 100 (tel: 3596-111).

Sumitomo Mitsui Banking Corporation, 1-2 Yurakucho, 1-chome, Chiyoda-ku, Tokyo 100-0006 (tel: 2501-1111).

Central bank
Bank of Japan (Nippon Ginko), 2-1-1 Nihonbashi-Hongokucho, Chuo-ku, Tokyo 103 (tel: 3279-1111; fax: 3277-1473).

Travel information
Japan Airlines (JAL), Tokyo Building, Marunouchi 2-7-3, Chiyoda-ku, Tokyo 100 (tel: 3284-2610; fax: 3284-2659; internet site: http://www.spin.ad.jp/jal/home-e.html).

Japan Automobile Federation, Shiba-Koen, 3-5-8 Minato-ku, Tokyo 105 (tel: 3436-2811).

Tourist Information Centre, 1-6-6 Yurakucho 1-chome, Chiyoda-Ku, Tokyo 100 (tel: 3502-1461); Kyoto Tower Building, Higashi-Shiokojicho, Shimogyo-ku, Kyoto 600 (tel: 371-5649).

Japan Travel Phone is a nationwide telephone service for English-language assistance and travel information. Available from 0900–1700 daily, the service is toll-free from outside Tokyo or Kyoto: information on eastern Japan: 0088-222-800 (or 0120-222-800); information on western Japan: 0088-22-4800 (or 0120-444-800). Tokyo: 3503-4400. Kyoto: 371-5649. Tokyo; French-language assistance: 3503-2926.

Tokyo: Japan Railways (JR) English-language information service, (Mon–Fri, except holidays) 1000–1800; reservations cannot be accepted by telephone service: 3423-0111. (Narita Express has a free phone connection to this service).

National tourist organisation offices
Japan National Tourist Organisation, 2-10-1 Yuraku-cho, Chiyodaku, Tokyo (tel: 3201-3331; fax: 3201-3347; internet: www.jnto.go.jp).

Ministries
Ministry of Agriculture, Forestry and Fisheries, 1-2-1 Kasumigaseki, Chiyoda-ku, Tokyo 100-8950 (tel: 3502-8111; fax: 3592-7697; e-mail: white56@maff.go.jp).

Ministry of Education, Culture, Sports, Science and Technology, 3-2-2 Kasumigaseki, Chiyoda-ku, Tokyo 100-8959 (tel: 3581-4211; fax: 3595-2017).

Ministry of the Environment, 1-2-2 Kasumigaseki, Chiyoda-ku, Tokyo 100-8975 (tel: 3581-3351; e-mail: MOE@eanet.go.jp).

Ministry of Foreign Affairs, 2-2-1, Kasumigaseki, Chiyoda-ku, Tokyo 100-8919 (tel: 3580-3311; fax: 3581-2667; e-mail: webmaster@mofa.go.jp).

Ministry of Health, Labour and Welfare, 1-2-2 Kasumigaseki, Chiyoda-ku, Tokyo 100-8916 (tel: 5253-1111; fax: 3501-2532).

Ministry of Justice, 1-1-1 Kasumigaseki, Chiyoda-ku, Tokyo 100-8977 (tel: 3580-4111; fax: 3592-7011; e-mail: webmaster@moj.go.jp).

Ministry of Land, Infrastructure and Transport, 2-1-3 Kasumigaseki, Chiyoda-ku, Tokyo 100-8918 (tel: 5253-8111; fax: 3580-7982; e-mail: webmaster@mlit.go.jp).

Ministry of Public Management, Home Affairs, Posts and Telecommunications, 2-1-2 Kasumigaseki, Chiyoda-ku, Tokyo 100-8926 (tel: 5253-5111; fax: 3504-0265; e-mail: feedback@mpt.go.jp).

Defence Agency, 5-1 Ichigaya, Honmura-cho, Shinjuku-ku, Tokyo 162-8801 (tel: 3268-3111; e-mail: info@jda.go.jp).

National Public Safety Commission, 2-1-2 Kasumigaseki, Chiyoda-ku, Tokyo 100-8974 (tel: 3581-0141).

Prime Minister's Office, 1-6-1, Nagata-cho, Chiyoda-ku, Tokyo 100-8914 (tel: 3581-2361; fax: 3593-1784).

Other useful addresses
Asian Development Bank, Japanese Representative Office, Second Floor, Yamato Seimei Building, 1-7 Uchisaiwaicho 1-Chome, Chiyoda-ku, Tokyo 100 (tel: 3504-3160; fax: 3504-3165; E-mail: adbjro@mail.asiandevbank.org).

Association for the Promotion of International Trade, Nihon Building, 6-2 Otemachi 2-chome, Chiyoda-ku, Tokyo (tel: 3245-1561).

British Embassy, No 1 Ichiban-cho, Chiyoda-ku, Tokyo 102 (tel: 3265-6340; fax: 5275-0346).

Council of All-Japan Exporters' Association, Kikai Shinko Kaikan Building, 5-8 Shibakaen 3-chome, Minato-ku, Tokyo.

Defence Agency, 9-7-45 Akasaka, Minato-ku, Tokyo 107-0052 (tel: 3408-5211; fax: 3408-6480).

Economic Planning Agency, 3-1-1 Kasumigaseki, Chiyoda-ku, Tokyo 100-0013 (tel: 3581-0261; fax: 3581-0838).

Environment Agency, 1-2-2 Kasumigaseki, Chiyoda-ku, Tokyo 100-0013 (tel: 3581-3351; fax: 3502-0308).

Fair Trade Commission, 2-2-1 Kasumigaseki, Chiyoda-ku, Tokyo 100-0013 (tel: 3581-5471; fax: 3581-1963).

Federation of Economic Organisations (Keidanren), 9-4 Othe-machi 1-chome, Chiyoda-ku 100, Tokyo (tel: 3279-1411; fax: 5255-6250).

Hokkaido Development Agency, 3-1-1 Kasumigaseki, Chiyoda-ku, Tokyo 100-8922 (tel: 3581-9111; fax: 3581-1208; e-mail: info1@had.go.jp).

House of Councillors, 1-7-1 Nagata-cho, Chiyoda-ku, Tokyo 100-0014 (tel: 3581-3111; fax: 3581-2900).

House of Representitives, 1-7-1 Nagata-cho, Chiyoda-ku, Tokyo 100-0014 (tel: 3581-5111; fax: 3581-2900).

Imperial Household Agency, 1-1 Chiyoda, Chiyoda-ku, Tokyo 100-0001 (tel: 3213-1111; fax: 3282-1407).

Japan Commercial Arbitration Association, Tosho Building, 2-2 Marunouchi 3-chome, Chiyoda-ku, Tokyo (tel: 3214-0641).

Japan Committee for Economic Development, Kogo Club Building 4-6 Marunouchi 1-chome, Chiyoda-ku, Tokyo (tel: 3211-1271).

Japan External Trade Organisation (JETRO), 2-5 Toranomon 2-chome, Minato-ku 105, Tokyo (tel: 3582-5511).

Japan Federation of Economic Organisations (Keidanren), 9-4 Otemachi 1-chome, Chiyoda-ku, Tokyo (tel: 3279-1411).

Japan Federation of Economic Organisations (Keidanren), 9-4 Otemachi 1-chome, Chiyoda-ku, Tokyo (tel: 3279-1411).

Japan Federation of Importers' Organisation, Nihombashi Daiwa Building, 1-6-1 Nihombashi Hon-Cho, Chuo-ku, Tokyo (tel: 3270-2020).

Japan Federation of Smaller Enterprise Organisation, 8-4 Nihonbashi Kayaba-cho 2-chome, Chuo-ku 103, Tokyo (tel: 3669-6862; fax: 3668-2957).

Japan Foreign Trade Council, World Trade Centre Building, 4-1 Hamamatsu-cho 2-chome, Minato-ku 105, Tokyo (tel: 3435-5952; fax: 3435-5979).

Japan Guide Association (interpreter and translation services), Shin Kokusai Building, 4-1 Marunouchi 3-chome, Chiyoda-ku, Tokyo (tel: 213-2706).

Japan International Co-operation System, 5th Floor, Shinjuku Sanshin Bldg, 4-9 Yoyogi 2-chome, Shibuya-ku, Tokyo 151 (tel: 5981-5988; fax: 5981-5994).

Japan Productivity Centre, 1-1 Shibuya 3-chome, Shibuya-ku 150, Tokyo (tel: 3409-1111; fax: 3409-4128).

Japan Securities Dealers Association, 5-8 Nihombashi Kayabacho 1-chome, Chuo-ku, Tokyo (tel: 3667-8459; fax: 3666-8009).

Japanese Embassy (USA), 2520 Massachusetts Avenue, NW, Washington DC 20008 (tel: 202-238-6700; fax: 202-328-2187).

Kansai Economic Federation, Nakanoshima Centre Bldg, 2-27 Nakanoshima 6-chome, Kita-ku, Osaka 530 (tel: 253-2351; 253-1678).

Management and Co-ordination Agency, 3-1-1 Kasumigaseki Chiyoda-ku, Tokyo 100-0013 (tel: 3581-6361; fax: 3593-1620).

Okinawa Development Agency, 1-6-1 Nagata-cho, Chiyoda-ku, Tokyo 100-0014 (tel: 3581-2361; fax: 3581-4783).

Science and Technology Agency, 2-2-1 Kasumigaseki, Chiyoda-ku, Tokyo 100-8966 (tel: 3581-5271; fax: 3593-1371; e-mail: www@sta.go.jp).

Statistics Bureau & Statistics Centre Management & Coordination Agency, 19-1 Wakamatsu-cho, Shinjuku-ku, Tokyo 162 (tel: 3202-1111; fax: 5273-1180).

Supreme Court, 4-2 Hayabusa-cho, Chiyoda-ku, Tokyo 102-0092 (tel: 3264-8111; fax: 3221-8975).

Tokyo International Trade Fair Commission, 7-24 Harumi 4-chome, Chuo-ku, Tokyo 103 (tel: 3666-0141, 3531-3371; fax: 3663-0625).

Tokyo Stock Exchange, 2-1 Nihombashi Kabutocho 1-chome, Chuo-ku, Tokyo (tel: 3666-0141; fax: 3663-0625, 3666-0141; internet site: http://www.tse.or.jp).

West Japan Railway Company, 4-24 Shibata 2-chome, Kita-ku, Osaka 530-8341 (tel: 375-8981; fax: 375-8919).

World Trade Centre of Japan, 4-1 2-chome Hamamatsu-cho, Minato-ku, Tokyo (tel: 3435-5651).

Internet sites

Asahi Shimbun: http://www.adv.asahi.com/english

Japan access: http://www.keidanren.or.jp/A2J/index.html

Japan Company Record: http://www.japancompanyrecord.com/

Japan Hotel Association: http://www.j-hotel.or.jp

Japan Information Network: http://jin.jcic.or.jp

Japan Statistics: http://www.stat.go.jp/1.htm

JETRO Homepage (Japanese Trade Promotion): http://www.jetro.go.jp

Sanwa Bank: http://www.sanwabank.co.jp

Jordan

KEY FACTS

Official name: Al Mamlaka al Urduniya al Hashemiya (The Hashemite Kingdom of Jordan)

Head of State: King Abdullah II (crowned Feb 1999)

Head of government: Prime Minister Marouf Bakheet (from 24 Nov 2005)

Ruling party: National Constitutional Party (NCP) (pro-monarchy coalition formed from a union of nine centrist parties)

Area: 91,860 square km

Population: 5.80 million (2004)

Capital: Amman

Official language: Arabic

Currency: Jordanian dinar (JD) = 1,000 fils

Exchange rate: JD0.71 per US$ (Oct 2005)

GDP per capita: US$1,947 (2004)

GDP real growth: 6.70% (2004)

Labour force: 1.80 million (2004)

Unemployment: 15.00% (official, 2004); 30.00% (unofficial, 2004)

Inflation: 3.40% (2004)

Balance of trade: -US$4.40 billion (2004)

Foreign debt: US$7.32 billion (2004)

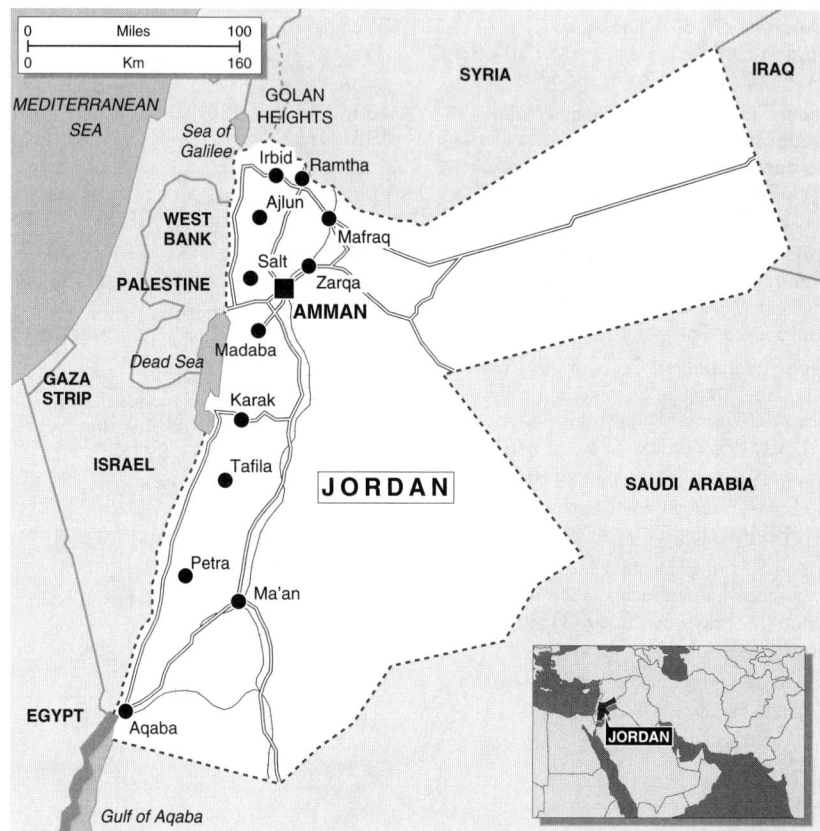

Jordan suffered from a severe case of 'jihad blowback' in 2005, with two major terrorist incidents in the country. Since the US-led invasion of Iraq in March 2003, hundreds, possibly thousands, of Jordanian citizens have crossed the border into Iraq in order to fight the occupation forces and their allies – the most notorious of these being Abu Musab al-Zarqawi, leader of al Qaeda in Iraq. In 2005, militants claiming allegiance to Zarqawi staged attacks in Amman and Aqaba. Jordan's King Abdullah II was forced to act to try and heal the growing rift with his US allies and the rift within his own country.

A growing economy

Although higher oil prices hit Jordan especially hard in 2005, due to the country's almost total lack of indigenous hydrocarbon resources, GDP still grew by 7.6 per cent in the first half of the year. Analysts state that Jordan must maintain growth above 6 per cent if it is to accommodate its rapidly expanding labour force and keep unemployment down. Construction of a gas pipeline between Jordan and Egypt continued apace in 2005, with the intent of reducing Jordan's dependency on oil imports. Privatisation of state assets was accelerated in 2005 and an economic reform package, praised by the IMF, was announced in July. A key component of this package was a commitment to significantly reduce a state fuel subsidy by 2007.

The jihad comes home

After more than two years of fighting US-led forces in Iraq, Jordanian militants associated with Zarqawi's al Qaeda organisation carried out attacks on home soil. In August, Jordanian militants launched a missile attack on a US navy ship docked in Jordan's port city of Aqaba. A missile was also launched into Israel, targeting the port and resort of Eilat. Although little damage was done to the chosen targets a Jordanian soldier was killed in the attack. On 9 November, a series of co-ordinated suicide bomb attacks in the Jordanian capital of Amman killed 59 people. Most of the dead were Jordanian citizens, many of them of Palestinian descent, killed while attending wedding celebrations in two hotels.

The November attacks in particular caused widespread revulsion in Jordan, from the government to the street. King Abdullah declared a relentless war against terrorism and 100,000 people marched through Amman on 18 November, protesting against the attacks. Previously, some Jordanians had expressed sympathy with Zarqawi's views, if not his methods. However, an audio tape purported to be from Zarqawi himself, in which Zarqawi defended his actions and threatened to kill King Abdullah, was widely derided in the Jordanian press and appeared to attract little public support.

A difficult balancing act

Since its independence in 1946, Jordan has been the region's perennial tightrope walker – wedged as it is between much larger and at times predatory neighbours. There was no let-up in 2005 for Jordan. Jordan had been experiencing significant pressure to undertake political and economic reform from its US ally since the assassination in Amman of a US aid official in October 2002. However, Jordan's relations with its most powerful ally deteriorated markedly in 2005. A Jordanian citizen was blamed for a particularly horrific suicide bombing in Hilla, Iraq in February. This led to renewed US scrutiny of Jordan and the flow of Jordanian militants into Iraq. The attack on a US navy ship in August only heightened US dissatisfaction with Jordan.

In an effort to address another pressing regional problem, King Abdullah returned Jordan's ambassador to Israel in March. This brought to an end a boycott imposed in 2000, in protest against Israel's policies towards the Palestinians. However, a Jordanian attempt to float a new peace plan at the Arab League summit in Algiers in the same month resulted in an embarrassing diplomatic defeat. The Jordanian delegation appeared to offer Israel normalisation of relations between it and the Arab states before any peace settlement with the Palestinians. Jordan, unsurprisingly, found itself virtually disowned.

King Abdullah responded to these challenges, from both within and outside the kingdom, by sacking the government in April and sacking its replacement in November. These were the fourth and fifth government's respectively since 1999, when Abdullah ascended to the throne.

Outlook

The Hashemite dynasty moved through 2005 with the sense and appearance of permanent crisis. Allies and neighbours regularly voiced their disappointment with Jordan, scores of Jordanian citizens were killed in terrorist attacks and the country had three governments in one year. Although Jordan's 'jihad blowback' is nothing like that faced by Saudi Arabia, 2006 will undoubtedly throw up serious challenges to the monarchy. Jordan can also be expected to step up its efforts to forge a closer relationship with Iraq, in order to recreate the intimate trade and political relations the two countries enjoyed prior to 1991. Jordan was the first Arab country to send a senior leader to Iraq, in September 2005. However, the new Iraqi government is likely, at the very least, to demand more robust efforts to curb the flow of Jordanian fighters into Iraq.

Risk assessment

Politics	Fragile
Economy	Improving
Regional stability	Fragile

COUNTRY PROFILE

Historical profile
The Turkish Ottoman Empire entered the First World War on Germany's side. After the defeat, the British and French agreed a division of spheres of influence in the Middle East. The territory constituting present-day Jordan and Israel was awarded to Britain as a mandate by the League of Nations. The British divided the mandate into two parts, designating all lands west of the Jordan River as Palestine and those east of the river as Transjordan. The population at that time was made up largely of bedouin tribesmen; today, these families – known as East Bank Jordanians – are outnumbered by the descendants of Palestinian refugees from Israel and the West Bank. This imbalance of refugees and nationals puts Jordan in an invidious position. Jordan, with no oil and few other natural resources of its own, relies on the good will of its neighbours. King Hussein, father of the present King Abdullah II, ever the pragmatist, wove a delicate path between his Western aid-giving allies, Iraq and its subsidised oil, and Israel and Jordan's volatile Palestinian refugees.

The Israeli-Palestine conflict was made worse by the Iraq War, during which Jordan supplied discreet support to the US, allowing US special forces to operate from the country. This was in contrast to its position during the Gulf War, when Jordan had openly sided with Iraq.

1928 Transjordan obtained qualified independence in a treaty with Britain.

1946 Transjordan achieved full independence as the Hashemite Kingdom of Jordan under the Emir, who took the title of King Abdullah.

1948 Jewish leaders announced the formation of the State of Israel in British-mandate Palestine and thousands of Palestinian Arabs fled to Jordan and the West Bank.

KEY INDICATORS — Jordan

	Unit	2000	2001	2002	2003	2004
Population	m	5.04	5.18	5.33	5.56	5.80
Gross domestic product (GDP)	US$bn	8.30	9.00	12.60	10.13	*11.20
GDP per capita	US$	1,249	1,728	1,786	1,820	1,947
GDP real growth	%	3.9	4.2	4.9	3.1	6.7
Inflation	%	0.7	1.8	1.8	2.5	3.4
Exports (fob) (goods)	US$m	1,897.0	2,293.0	2,520.0	3,085.0	3,200.0
Imports (fob) (goods)	US$m	4,540.0	4,812.0	5,300.0	5,480.0	7,600.0
Balance of trade	US$m	-2,643.0	-2,519.0	-2,770.0	-2,395.0	-4,400.0
Current account	US$m	59.0	32.0	-113.0	429.0	-90.0
Foreign debt	US$bn	7.9	7.9	8.1	8.2	7.3
Total reserves minus gold	US$m	3,331.3	3,062.2	3,975.9	5,194.3	5,266.6
Foreign exchange	US$m	3,330.6	3,061.0	3,975.0	5,193.1	5,246.8
Exchange rate	per US$	0.71	0.71	0.71	0.71	0.71

* estimated figure

1950 A post-war agreement united Jordan with the part of Palestine remaining in Arab hands (the West Bank, including East Jerusalem, but excluding the Gaza Strip).
1951 King Abdullah was assassinated and was succeeded by his son, Talal bin Abdullah.
1952 Hussein bin Talal formally took power as King Hussein after his father, Talal bin Abdullah, stepped down due to mental illness.
1956 King Hussein banned political parties.
1957 British troops completed their withdrawal from Jordan.
1967 Six Day War. Israel occupied the West Bank and Gaza Strip and re-unified Jerusalem; around 300,000 Palestinian Arab refugees entered Jordan.
1970 Civil war (Black September) between the Jordanian army and Palestinians followed airplane hijackings by the Palestine Liberation Organisation (PLO) resistance group. The PLO was forcefully expelled from its bases in Jordan and moved to Lebanon
1972 An attempted military coup was thwarted.
1974 Jordan and other Arab countries recognised the PLO as the sole legitimate representative of the Palestinian people.
1978–84 The House of Representatives (parliament) was temporarily replaced during these years by a National Consultative Council appointed by the King.
1986 King Hussein severed political links with the PLO and ordered its main offices to shut.
1988 The House of Representatives was dissolved, prior to King Hussein's announcement of the severance of all administrative and legal ties with the West Bank. The King publicly backed the Palestinian *intifada* against Israeli rule.
1989 The first general elections since 1967 were contested only by independent candidates.
1992 Parliament authorised political parties for the first time since they were banned by King Hussein 36 years previously.
1993 Multi-party elections were held.
1994 The Jordan-Israel Peace Treaty was signed at Wadi Araba, Jordan, following the opening of the first border crossing between Aqaba (Jordan) and Eilat (Israel).
1997 The parliamentary elections were boycotted by nine opposition parties, led by the Islamic Action Front (IAF). The Islamists said the electoral law favoured the rural constituencies, where support for the King was strong, over the towns, where nearly half of Jordan's population lived. The elections were won by the National Constitutional Party (NCP), a pro-monarchy coalition formed from the union of nine centrist parties.

1999 King Hussein appointed his eldest son, Abdullah bin Hussein, as crown prince and heir, replacing Prince Hassan, the King's brother, who had been appointed crown prince in 1965. King Hussein, who had been treated for cancer for many years, died, and Abdullah bin Hussein was sworn in as King.
2000 King Abdullah II made a historic visit to the state of Israel. Jordan joined the World Trade Organisation (WTO).
2002 Senior US diplomat, Laurence Foley, was shot dead outside his home in Amman. Many political activists were arrested.
2003 King Abdullah II ratified an amended law adding six women members to the women's share in parliament. Independent candidates, allies of the King, won two-thirds of the seats in the parliamentary elections. The King appointed Faisal al Fayez as prime minister and three female ministers.
2004 In February, King Abdullah and Syrian President Bashar al Assad launched the Wahdah Dam project. Israel and Jordan agreed a joint project to build a desert science centre on their shared border. Eight Islamic militants were sentenced to death for killing an American, Laurence Foley, in 2002. Cars filled with explosives were seized and suspects arrested, thought to be linked to Al Qaeda.
2005 Egypt and Jordan agreed to return their ambassadors to Israel after the Sharm El Sheikh summit in Egypt, at which a truce was signed by Israel and Palestine. On 5 April, Prime Minister Faisal al Fayez's government resigned; King Abdullah II named Adnan Badran as the new prime minister. There were a series of bomb blasts at three hotels in Amman on 9 November, killing at least 59 people and injuring over 100. After a wide government shake up in the wake of the bombings, King Abdullah appointed Marouf Bakheet prime minister on 24 Nov.

Political structure
Constitution
Under a revised constitution of January 1952, the throne passes by male descent to heirs above the age of 18. A Regent or Council of Regency exercises power on behalf of the heir if he is below the age of 18 on succeeding to the throne. King Hussein's youngest brother, Prince Hassan, was Crown Prince between 1964–99, but in January 1999, a change was made to the constitution. The constitution previously required the meeting of a 'family council' to discuss a change of succession. Under the revision, King Hussein directly appointed his eldest son, Abdullah bin Hussein, as the new Crown Prince.

Jordan is divided into eight governorates, each headed by a governor and consisting of districts, sub-districts and counties. At local government level there are 152 municipalities, including Greater Amman, and 340 village councils. Local affairs are managed by city or village councils. Councils are under the supervision of the ministry of municipal and rural affairs.
A national charter, published by King Hussein in 1991, enshrined the principle of political freedom. It also underscored the ultimate power of the monarchy.
In February 2003, King Abdullah II ratified an amended law adding six women members to the parliament.
Form of state
Monarchy with limited parliamentary democracy.
The executive
The King is head of state and commander-in-chief of the armed forces. The King has the power to declare war or conclude peace treaties, order elections, inaugurate, adjourn and prorogue the lower house of parliament as well as to appoint the prime minister, cabinet and speaker of the upper house of parliament.
National legislature
Legislative power rests with the al Ayan council (Senate/upper house), – 50 members appointed by the King – and the House of Representatives (lower house) – 110 members elected by universal suffrage for a four-year term.
Eighteen seats in the House of Representatives are reserved for Christians, Circassians and Bedouins. Six seats are reserved for women.
Individual ministers or governments may be removed from office on a vote of no-confidence by the House of Representatives.
Legal system
Judges are appointed by royal decree and are independent of the legislature and the executive. The King has the right of clemency and must confirm death sentences.
Last elections
17 June 2003 (parliamentary) (postponed from November 2001)
Results: Parliamentary: Allies of King Abdullah II won 62 seats out of 110 and the Islamic Action Front (IAF) 18 seats; turnout was 58.9 per cent.
Next elections
2007 (parliamentary)

Political parties
Ruling party
National Constitutional Party (NCP) (pro-monarchy coalition formed from a union of nine centrist parties)
Main opposition party
Islamic Action Front (IAF) (the political wing of the Muslim Brotherhood)

Jordan

Population
5.80 million (2004)

Ethnic make-up
The population is predominantly Arab, with small minorities of Circassians, Armenians and Kurds. No official figures are kept but it is generally accepted that Palestinians constitute 60 to 70 per cent of Jordan's population.

Religions
Over 80 per cent of the population are Sunni Muslims. There is a Christian minority, mainly Roman Catholic, Coptic and Greek Orthodox, and smaller numbers of other Muslims.

Education
The government has instituted a programme to revise and upgrade the state school system, involving teacher retraining, new curricula and substantial school construction. University students tend to concentrate on science, mathematics and computer programming. Consequently, Jordan has a steady supply of young people with the necessary skills in computer programming, as well as those with training in basic technical education.

Literacy rate: 90.9 total; 85.9 females; adult rates, in 2002 (World Bank).

Compulsory years: 6 to 14; elementary aged 6–11 and preparatory 12–14.

Enrolment rate: 70 per cent for boys and 72 per cent for girls total primary school enrolment, (including repetition rates) of the relevant age group (World Bank estimates 1994–2000).

Pupils per teacher: 21 in primary schools.

Health
Total expenditure on health is around 10 per cent of GDP, of which government spending is 47 per cent.

Improved water sources and sanitation facilities are available to 99 per cent and 96 per cent of the population, respectively.

HIV prevalence: 0.1 per cent aged 15–49 in 2003 (World Bank)

Life expectancy: 72.1 years (World Bank)

Fertility rate/Maternal mortality rate: 3.5 births per woman (2003); maternal mortality 41 per 100,000 live births (World Bank).

Birth rate/Death rate: 4 deaths and 30 births per 1,000 population.

Infant mortality rate: 23 per 1,000 live births (World Bank)

Head of population per physician/bed: 1.6 doctors per 1,000 people.

Welfare
Social security in Jordan has few beneficiaries relative to contributing workers and it only first started paying benefits in 1995.

All workers in non-government establishments that employ more than five persons are obliged to contribute to the state social security fund. Those in smaller establishments may contribute voluntarily. Lump-sum payments and hospital expenses are made in the case of work-related injury, death and retirement pensions. The Social Security Corporation (SCC) provides two types of insurance – old age disability and work-related injuries insurance. It collects revenues directly from wages and is not reliant on the government budget. It covers both the private sector and any public employees hired after 1995.

Main cities
Amman (capital, estimated population 1.3 million in 2004), Zarqa (512,200), Irbid (267,200), Aqaba (100,700), Salt (66,200), Mafraq (67,400).

Languages spoken
English is the second language and is widely spoken; most people in business can both speak and correspond in English. French is spoken to a lesser extent.

Official language/s
Arabic

Media

Press
A press and publications law was passed in late 1992. The law banned a wide range of items including those which harm the King or his family or reveal information about the armed forces. The ban on hurting national unity, insulting Arab or Muslim heads of state or transgressing so-called 'public ethics' caused the most controversy.

The law also forced all Jordanian journalists to become members of the Jordan Press Association and denies them the right to protect their sources. The law came as media activity surged with a dozen newspapers licensed or applying for licences and the legalisation of domestic satellite dishes opening Jordanians to uncensored world television.

The Jordan News Agency (Petra) provides news to local and foreign media. The Ministry of Information, which Petra had been a part of, ceased to exist in early 2002. A new media policy is being drawn-up by the Jordanian Media Higher Council, which was established in December 2001.

Dailies: Jordan has both Arabic and English dailies, all published nationally. The Arabic newspapers are *Sawt al Shaab*, *al Ra'i Daily* (both government-owned), *al Dustour*, *al Aswaq* and *al Arab Alyawm*. The English newspapers are *Arab Daily*, *Assabeel Jordan Times* and *Jordan Times*.

Weeklies: There are several weeklies in Arabic, including *Akhbar al Usbu*, *Amman al Masa*, *Assabeel Weekly* and *al Hawadith*. English language weeklies include *The Star* and there is also a French weekly supplement to *The Jordan Times*.

Broadcasting
Broadcasting is run by state bodies and the press is licensed by the government. Restrictions on the press eased considerably in the early 1990s and many areas have been opened to active discussion. A certain amount of self-censorship remains and some subjects – including information on military and security establishments and criticism of the royal family – are strictly taboo.

Radio: The state radio service broadcasts domestic and external programmes in Arabic and English.

Television: The state television service runs one Arabic channel and one foreign channel which broadcasts programmes in English, French and Hebrew.

Advertising
Advertising is handled through the private sector, and appears in newspapers and on the television and radio.

Economy
Jordan has hardly any oil and is poor in water. The country's geographic location at the centre of the Middle East means that its fortunes are strongly influenced by regional circumstances. Unlike many Arab states, Jordan has strong trade links with its neighbours. Intra-Arab trade and remittances from overseas workers, especially those in the Gulf states, make a significant contribution to the economy. Furthermore, Jordan has long served as a transit route for goods destined for Iraq, from where it formerly received subsidised oil. The consequences of the 2003 Iraq War on the Jordanian economy from lost export opportunities, a higher oil import bill and reduced foreign direct investment were estimated as high as US$1.5 billion.

Since 2000, the country has adopted a strategy of diversifying its economic base. The government launched a five-year reform programme at the end of 2001, the chief priorities of which are improvements in welfare services, education and water resources.

A privatisation programme was cautiously initiated in the 1990s, particularly in the hotel and tourism sector. With a budget deficit that reached US$609 million in 2002, there was a serious need for fiscal prudence and the government turned to privatisation and careful negotiation with its international creditors as the primary methods of balancing the budget. Jordan secured financial loans from the US and the EU to support its economic reform and development programmes during 2002–04.

Economic policies are designed to strengthen economic growth, maintain financial stability and a solid external reserve position and reduce public indebtedness through continued fiscal consolidation.

There are good signs of Jordan's recovery from the disruptions caused by the war in Iraq, with GDP growing by 6.7 per cent in 2004, compared with 3.1 per cent in 2003. Jordan's economy will continue to be vulnerable to external shocks and regional unrest.

External trade

In view of declining GDP per capita and Jordan's limited natural resources, trade is crucial to Jordan. King Abdullah has approached the idea of economic integration between Jordan, Syria and the Lebanon in a practical fashion with the proposal to unify customs classifications and rules of origin between the three countries. This will not only facilitate trade between the three countries, but will also help trade negotiations with the EU. The unified rules will simplify tariff negotiations with third countries and co-operation will strengthen the collective bargaining position of Jordan and its Middle East partners. Until the economic embargo was imposed in 1990, Iraq was Jordan's main trading partner.

Jordan has a free trade agreement with the US.

Imports

Main imports are crude oil, textile fabrics, machinery, transport equipment and manufactured goods.

Main sources: Saudi Arabia (19.9 per cent total, 2004), China (8.4 per cent), Germany (6.8 per cent), US (6.7 per cent)

Exports

Main exports are clothing, phosphates, fertilisers, potash, vegetables, manufactures and pharmaceuticals.

Main destinations: US (25.8 per cent total, 2004), Iraq (18.4 per cent), India (6.4 per cent), Saudi Arabia (5.2 per cent)

Agriculture

Farming

Agriculture contributed around two per cent to GDP in 2004, compared with around five per cent in 1994. Jordan became a net importer of foodstuffs when it no longer had access to its principal growing areas on the West Bank of the River Jordan. More than 91 per cent of the total land area is classified as desert and only 6 per cent is cultivable. The sector is vulnerable to drought. Extreme variations in seasonal rainfall in the highland areas lead to severe fluctuations in yields from year to year. Highland farmers are one of the poorest groups in the country. Irrigated farming in the Jordan Valley has been a success in production terms, but marketing has suffered from periods of overproduction and fluctuations in exports.

Jordan has two distinct agricultural zones: the irrigated Jordan Valley and the rain-fed highlands. Government policy has been to encourage intensive fruit and vegetable growing in the Jordan Valley, both for local consumption and as a major export earner, and to boost cereal and fodder production in the highlands in an effort to reduce a high food import bill. Farming is a private sector activity, but the state-owned Agricultural Marketing and Processing Company (AMPC) plays a regulatory role in fresh produce imports. The government buys cereal and fodder crops at fixed prices, with prices of other crops set according to supply and demand. Since 1986, state land in southern Jordan has been leased to private farmers for sophisticated irrigation projects conceived at a time when the Arab world was placing heavy emphasis on food self-sufficiency. The projects rely on ground water reserves and there is increasing concern that the benefits of increased production are outweighed by the depletion of scarce water supplies.

Crop production in 2004 included: 90,650 tonnes (t) cereals in total, 50,000t wheat, 10,000t maize, 120,000t potatoes, 30,000t barley, 51,000t bananas, 42,000t apples, 3,030t tobacco, 120,000t olives, 147,300t citrus fruit, 28,000t grapes, *415,000t tomatoes, 4,200t pulses, 26,434t oilcrops, 307,350t fruit in total, 1,036,300t vegetables in total. Livestock production included: 125,742t meat in total, 4,700t beef, *250t camel meat, 3,900t lamb, *1,600t goat meat, 115,100t poultry, *34,100t eggs, 194,900t milk, 200t honey, 60,000t sheepskins.
* estimate

Fishing

Jordan's only seaboard is in the south at Aqaba, on the Red Sea. The number of fishermen and vessels is negligible and the catches are consumed locally for the most part. A number of fish farming projects have been started, but with little success. The level of the Jordan river is frequently very low, contributing to the difficulties of fish farming. The majority of Jordan's fish for consumption is imported.

Forestry

Active afforestation programmes are under way in some areas in an effort to control soil erosion and desertification.

Exports in 2004 amounted to US$24 million largely based on paper pulp, while imports of most forest materials amounted to US$167 million. There is little commercial exploitation of forests.

Industry and manufacturing

Jordan's geographical location has affected its trade and industrial development. The Iran-Iraq war (1980–88) and the Gulf War (1991), as well as the Israeli-Palestinian crisis, have restricted Jordan's trade. It is therefore understandable that the government believes that industrial expansion depends on developing new overseas markets beyond the region. The minerals sector has successfully developed secure markets in the Indian sub-continent and in South-East Asia. Most other Jordanian industry relies on highly volatile Arab markets. State industries have become a particular burden, with the Jordanian Water Authority accumulating debts of US$113 million.

With the loss of exports of manufactured goods to Iraq, there was a 6 per cent drop in output in 2003.

Tourism

Tourism is the most important sector of the economy. The sector accounts for about 10 per cent of GDP and is the second highest earner of foreign exchange. Jordan has been experiencing a growth in tourism inspite of the regional conflicts. New resorts are being built along the Dead Sea and Gulf of Aqaba with luxury hotels, international retail outlets, sports facilities, entertainment centres and private residences. The resort of Ras al Yamaniya in Aqaba has been designated a duty-free zone to attract both visitors and investment. Urban regeneration has also been included in plans, by the antiquities ministry, to market Jordan, with Amman and Petra rivalling its coastal resorts as top holiday destinations.

In 2003 Jordan joined the Euromed Heritage Programme, a computerisation project, sponsored by the EU, which focuses on cultural tourists of archaeology, arts and history, promoting sites through the internet.

There were 2.8 million visitors in 2004, compared with 2.3 million in 2003.

Environment

Water is the single greatest challenge to Jordan's long-term well-being. The available figures on supply and demand present a disturbing picture. Agriculture remains the largest consumer of water resources, accounting for over 70 per cent of total water use. The acute water shortage means that Jordan is heavily reliant on ground water, of which 45 per cent is irreplaceable. In the long-term, water consumption at the present rates cannot be sustained. With an increasing population rate in Jordan, the government has estimated that per capita water supply will fall from the current 200 cubic metres per person to only 91 cubic metres by 2025.

A programme of dam building has improved supply but it is clear that a solution to the problem will have to come from better regional arrangements for water sharing. Jordan receives 215 million cubic metres annually from Israel through dams and pipelines. The Israeli-Palestinian conflict has not disrupted these water supplies and the government has done its utmost not to offend Israel over the conflict in order to prevent a repeat of Israel's decision in 1999 to cut water supplies to Jordan . The building of the Wahdeh (formerly known as Maqarin) dam on the Jordanian-Syrian border cannot proceed without the agreement of Israel, which stands to lose water as a result of the project. The water and irrigation ministry has invested some US$5billion to boost supply, which will be invested in a number of projects until 2010.

Mining

The Jordanian government earmarked the mining and minerals industry as a priority sector for investment and development. The Natural Resources Authority (NRA) is the main policy-making body in the mineral sector, which promotes investment and undertakes operations. The agency has benefited from the UN Conference on Trade and Development's (Unctad) technical assistance and is able to attract foreign investment into the sector. The NRA has identified a range of metallic and non-metallic minerals, of which Jordan has substantial reserves. The EU is funding a project to identify the economic potential of non-oil mineral resources, including copper, a granitoid complex and ornamental stone.

The phosphate and potash industries in Jordan are key contributors to the economy. The Eshidiya deposit owned by Jordan Phosphate Mining Corporation (JPMC) has a proved phosphate reserve of 1,200 million tonnes. The Arab Potash Company (APC), which accounts for 4.4 per cent of the world's total potash production, produces 1.8 million tonnes of potash annually in Jordan. Almost 1.4 million tonnes is exported to 28 countries (mostly Asian).

The Jordan Safi Salt Company (Jossco) produces 1.2 million tonnes per year of industrial salt. Jordan is also an important exporter of calcium carbonate to other Middle Eastern states. Mineral production is largely of industrial minerals derived from the overlying sediments and volcanics. The most important mineral resources, which merit development and provide investment opportunities, are silica sand, tripoli, gypsum, ornamental stone (Ajlun limestone) and zeolite.

Hydrocarbons

Jordan, unlike its neighbours Iraq and Syria, is not blessed with huge gas or oil reserves and has to import the bulk of its oil requirements to meet domestic demand. The country is untypical of the Middle East in that its economy is not directly linked to the fluctuations of the international oil market.

Proven oil reserves are small and there is no oil production. The government encourages foreign oil companies to undertake exploration. Long-held hopes of a good oil find that could bring prosperity have not been achieved so far, but there are indications of a sizeable reserve in the Azraq area. The rising oil prices are an added inducement to the government and the industry to step up exploration of Jordan's potential.

Jordan has 6.5 billion cubic meters (cum) of natural gas reserves. Jordan currently produces around 849,000cum per day of natural gas from the Risheh field. The Risheh field provides gas to a thermal power station, which generates around 12 per cent of Jordan's electricity. Jordan is already receiving natural gas from Egypt through a pipeline which will connect Egypt, Jordan, Syria, Lebanon, Iraq and Europe when completed.

Jordan does not produce or import coal.

Energy

Government policy has been to restrain energy consumption while increasing efforts to develop domestic energy sources and lessen dependence on oil imports. Domestic oil production falls well below energy demand estimated to be equivalent to two million barrels per year.

The state-owned Jordan Electricity Authority (JEA) is the main electricity producer, with two major plants: the Hussein Thermal Power Station outside Amman and the Aqaba Thermal Power Station in the south. Total installed capacity is around 1600MW. Responsibility for distribution of electricity lies with the Jordan Electric Power Company (Jepco) and the Irbid District Electricity Company (Ideco).

In 2001, Jordan, Syria and Egypt inaugurated a US$300 million electricity line linking the grids of the three countries. Gas finds in the Risha area of north-eastern Jordan in the early 1990s have enabled the country to reach 25 per cent self-sufficiency in electricity generation, equivalent to 6,570MWH. The Risha field itself produces around 12 per cent of Jordan's electricity needs through two 30MW gas turbines connected to the national grid. Major expansion in Jordan's power generating capacity will continue to depend on imported oil.

Financial markets
Stock exchange
The Amman Stock Exchange (ASE) was established in 1976 and is claimed to be one of the most efficient in the Middle East.

Banking and insurance
Central bank
Central Bank of Jordan (CBJ)
Main financial centre
Amman

Time
GMT plus two hours in winter; GMT plus three hours in summer.

Geography
Jordan is bounded by Syria to the north, Iraq to the east, Saudi Arabia to the south and Israel, the West Bank and Gaza Strip to the west. The only access to the sea is at Aqaba at the northern tip of the Gulf of Aqaba and about 400km south of the capital Amman.

There are three major geographical regions – the Jordan Rift Valley, the Eastern Uplands and the desert. Settlement is concentrated in northern and central sections of the uplands which run in a narrow strip from the Syrian border in the north to the Shubak/Petra area in the south.

Climate
The climate is Mediterranean with dry, warm to hot summers and wet, mild to cool winters. There are noticeable variations due to altitude with temperatures in the Jordan Valley and Aqaba region around 10 degrees Celsius (C) higher on average than the highlands area throughout the year. Daytime temperatures in the highlands range from 25 to 32 degrees C in summer and from 7 to 15 degrees C in winter. Rainfall ranges from 40cm annually in the northern highlands to 10cm in the south and 20cm in the Jordan Valley.

Dress codes
Lightweight clothing is needed during the hottest months and warm clothing in winter when snow is not uncommon. Both men and women should dress discreetly in public.

Entry requirements
Passports
Required by all (with a few exceptions, mainly for neighbouring states and service personnel). There must be at least six months validity on a passport from date a visa is issued.
Visa
Required by all, except most citizens of the Middle East. Many nationals may obtain a visa at the port of entry (for stays up to 14 days) and all others must apply in advance. Visit www.mfa.gov.jo/pages.php?menu_id for a full list of each category. Business visas

should be applied for in advance and require a business letter outlining purpose of visit and an itinerary.

Visas are not issued at the King Hussein Bridge across the Jordan River from Israel.

Currency advice/regulations
There are no restrictions on the import or export of foreign or Jordanian currency. In addition to the banks, there are licensed money-changers supervised by the Central Bank of Jordan (CBJ), but free to set their own exchange rates and commission fees, which generally makes them more competitive than the banks.

Prohibited imports
Table salt. Diesel for vehicles or other non-petrol passenger cars.

Health (for visitors)
Mandatory precautions
There are no automatic health checks at entry points, but travellers arriving from areas with infectious diseases such as cholera are expected to have had appropriate vaccinations. Travellers coming from an infected area require a yellow fever vaccination certificate.

Advisable precautions
Vaccination against typhoid, polio and hepatitis is advisable. Tap water is generally of a good standard, but short-stay visitors may prefer bottled water.

Hotels
There is a good selection of hotels in Amman. A number of new hotels are being built in Amman, around the Dead Sea and in Aqaba. The main tourist centres are Aqaba and the ancient city of Petra. A service charge of 10–12 per cent is usually added to the bill plus a government tax of 10 per cent on all services at three-, four- and five-star hotels and restaurants.

Extra tips are discretionary. Porters' and drivers' tips are about 8 per cent.

Credit cards
Major credit cards are accepted at hotels and restaurants.

Public holidays
Fixed dates
1 Jan (New Year's Day), 30 Jan (King Abdullah II's Birthday), 1 May (Labour Day), 25 May (Independence Day), 10 Jun (Army Day), 5 Jul (Arab Solidarity Day), 14 Nov (King Hussein's Birthday), 25 Dec (Christmas Day).

Friday is the official weekly holiday.

Variable dates
Eid al Adha (four days), Islamic New Year, Birth of the Prophet, Ascent of the Prophet, Eid al Fitr (three days).

The Islamic year contains 354 or 355 days, with the result that Muslim feasts advance by 10–12 days against the Gregorian calendar. Dates of feasts vary according to the sighting of the new moon, so cannot be forecast exactly.

Working hours
Banking
0830–1230 (Sat–Thu); some banks open for two hours in the afternoon, generally from 1500–1700.

Business
Summer: 0800–1300, 1500–1900 (Sat–Thu); winter: 0800–1330 (Sat–Thu). During Ramadan, most firms operate only from 0900–1600. Christian businesses may close on Sunday afternoon.

Government
0800–1400 (Sat–Thu).

Shops
0800–2000/2100 or 0930–1330, 1530–1800 daily. Some shops close Fridays and public holidays.

Electricity supply
Domestic 220V, 50 cycles AC. Industrial 220–380V 50 cycles AC.

Lamp sockets are screw-type, and there is a wide range of wall sockets. Bring a universal adapter.

Weights and measures
Metric system. Land is measured in dunums (1,000sq metres).

Social customs/useful tips
Jordanian society operates a mixture of traditional and modern attitudes and habits, and a foreigner needs to be aware which apply in any given situation. Business appointments are usually respected, though most people keep an open door and interruptions must be expected. All meetings are prefaced by an extended exchange of pleasantries allowing both sides the chance to assess each other. Tea and coffee are offered in all offices, and should be accepted; however, on the third or fourth appointment during a morning it is acceptable to excuse oneself and accept just a glass of water. It is still not customary to refer directly to a man's wife unless you have actually met her; it is safer to enquire after the welfare of 'the family'. It is forbidden to eat, drink or smoke in public in daylight hours during Ramadan.

Handshaking is the customary form of greeting. Jordanians are proud of their Arab culture and are hospitable and courteous. A small gift is quite acceptable in return for hospitality.

Islam plays an important role in society. Be discreet when drinking alcohol and do not drink in public places. Women are expected to dress modestly, and for both women and men beachwear must only be worn on the beach or by the poolside.

Security
Street crime is rare in Jordan, with mugging virtually unheard of. However, housebreaking and car theft is on the increase and reasonable precautions must be observed. There are occasional small-scale bomb attacks against cinemas and nightclubs in Amman. Women do not usually walk alone in Amman after about 2200, but driving alone is safe. A woman alone wanting a taxi late at night is advised to telephone a taxi office with which she is familiar.

Getting there
Air
National airline: Royal Jordanian Airlines

International airport/s: Amman-Queen Alia International (AMM), 32km east of Amman (35 minutes from city centre).

Airport tax: Departure tax for foreign visitors: JD10 (US$13) (2003).

Surface
Road: King Hussein Bridge is the only way to cross the Jordan river from Israel, and only the official minibus services are allowed to cross it. There are also buses and taxis from Syria, where the only border crossing point is at Ramtha/Der'a. There are a number of routes into Jordan from Jeddah and Riyadh in Saudi Arabia.

Rail: Cross-border rail links are largely for freighting purposes.

Water: There are ferry services, including car ferries, between Aqaba and Nuweiba in Egypt.

Main port/s: Aqaba is the country's only port.

Getting about
National transport
Air: The only internal air route is between Amman and Aqaba. Royal Jordanian Airlines operate regular flights. Arab Wings offer a charter service.

Road: The road network is good, with well-surfaced main roads connecting all the major towns and cities.

Buses: The Jordanian Express Tourist Transport Company (Jett) runs extensive services.

Rail: The rail network is generally used for cargo, although there are initiatives under way to provide tourist services, in particular between Amman and Aqaba.

Water: There are no passenger services along the Jordan river.

City transport
Taxis: Metered taxis are readily available in Amman and other cities (do not let your driver forget to switch on his meter). Can be hired for the journey or the day for an agreed sum. Do not use a taxi without a meter before agreeing the fare with the driver. There are also many service taxis offering a standard charge for any journey. Since there are few street names outside Amman, destinations are generally described in relation to landmarks. Tipping is approximately 10 per cent.

Jordan

Car hire
National or international driving licence required. Driver must be at least 25 years old and not over 60. Speed limit is 100kph. Insurance is compulsory.

BUSINESS DIRECTORY

The addresses listed below are a selection only. While World of Information makes every endeavour to check these addresses, we cannot guarantee that changes have not been made, especially to telephone numbers and area codes. We would welcome any corrections.

Telephone area codes
The international direct dialling (IDD) code for Jordan is +962 followed by the area code:

Amman	6	Madaba	8
Aqaba	3	Mafraq	4
Balga (Salt)	5	Zarqa	9
Irbid	2		

Chambers of Commerce

American Chamber of Commerce in Jordan, 23 Salem Al-Hindawi Street, Shmeisani, PO Box 840817, Amman 11184 (tel: 565-1860; fax: 565-1862; e-mail: mail@jaba.org.jo).

Amman Chamber of Commerce, Al-Sharif Shaker Bin Zaid Street, PO Box 287, Amman 11118 (tel: 566-6151; fax: 566-6155; e-mail: info@ammanchamber.org.jo).

Amman Chamber of Industry, 2nd Circle Amman, PO Box 1800, Amman 11118 (tel: 464-3001; fax: 464-7852; e-mail: aci@aci.org.jo).

Aqaba Chamber of Commerce, PO Box 12, Aqaba 77110 (tel: 201-2235; fax 201-3070; e-mail: ask@index.com.jo).

Federation of Jordanian Chambers of Commerce, Al-Sharif Shaker Bin Zaid Street, PO Box 7029, Amman 11118 (tel: 566-5492; fax: 568-5997; e-mail: fjcc@nets.com.jo).

Irbid Chamber of Commerce, PO Box 13, Irbid (tel: 724-2077; fax: 724-2072; e-mail:icc@go.com.jo).

Jerash Chamber of Commerce, PO Box 195, Jerash (tel/fax: 635-1278).

Madaba Chamber of Commerce, PO Box 120, Madaba (tel: 544-120; fax: 545-878).

Mafraq Chamber of Commerce, PO Box 21, Mafraq (tel: 623-4197; fax: 623-1135).

Zarqa Chamber of Commerce, PO Box 77, Zarqa (tel: 385-3307; fax: 385-4617).

Banking

Arab Bank Plc, PO Box 950545, 11195 Amman (tel: 560-7231; fax: 560-6793; e-mail: international@arabbank.com.jo).

Arab Banking Corporation (Jordan), PO Box 926691, 11190 Amman (tel: 5 66-4183; fax: 568-6291; e-mail: info@arabbanking.com.jo).

Arab Jordan Investment Bank, PO Box 8797, 11121 Amman (tel: 560-7126; fax: 568-1482; e-mail: info@ajib.com).

Bank of Jordan, PO Box 2140, 11181 Amman (tel: 569-6277; fax: 569-6291; boj@go.com.jo).

Cairo Amman Bank, PO Box 950661, 11195 Amman (tel: 461-6910; fax: 464-2890; e-mail: cainfo@ca_bank.com.jo).

Export and Finance Bank, PO Box 941283, 11194 Amman (tel: 569-4250; fax: 569-2062; e-mail: info@efbank.com.jo).

Housing Bank for Trade and Finance, PO Box 7693, 11118 Amman (tel: 560-7315; fax: 567-8121; e-mail: quality@hbtf.com.jo).

Jordan Gulf Bank, PO Box 9989, 11191 Amman (tel: 5 60-3931; fax: 566-4110; e-mail: jgb@jkbank.com.jo).

Jordan Investment and Finance Bank, PO Box 950601, 11195 Amman (tel: 566-5145; fax: 568-1410; e-mail: jifbank@jifbank.com.jo).

Jordan Kuwait Bank, PO Box 9776, 11191Amman (tel: 568-8814; fax: 569-5604; e-mail: webmaster@jkbank.com.jo).

Jordan National Bank, PO Box 3103, 11181 Amman (tel: 562-2282; fax: 562-2281; ingo@inb.com.jo).

Union Bank for Saving and Investment, PO Box 35104, 11180 Amman (tel: 560-7011; fax: 566-6149; e-mail: info@unionbankjo.com).

Central bank
Central Bank of Jordan , PO Box 37, 11118 Amman (tel: 463-0301; fax: 463-8889; e-mail: banksuper@cbj.gov.jo).

Travel information
Royal Jordanian Airlines, PO Box 302, Amman (tel: 672-872 (head office)).

Ministry of tourism
Ministry of Tourism & Antiquities, PO Box 224, Amman (tel: 464-2311/4; fax: 464-8465; e-mail: tourism@mota.gov.jo).

National tourist organisation offices
Jordan Tourism Board, PO Box 830688, Amman 11183 (tel: 567-8294; fax: 567-8295; e-mail: jtb@nets.com.jo; internet: http://www.see-jordan.com).

Ministries

Ministry of Agriculture, University of Jordan Street, PO Box 2099, Amman (tel: 568-6431, 568-6151; fax: 568-6310).

Ministry of Awqaf and Islamic Affairs, POB 659, Amman (tel: 566-141; fax: 560-2254).

Ministry of Communications and Postal Affairs, PO Box 35214 (tel: 560-7111; fax: 560-6233).

Ministry of Culture, PO Box 6140, Amman (tel: 463-6392/3569-6588; fax: 569-6598).

Ministry of Defence, PO Box 80, Amman (tel: 464-1211, 462-2131; fax: 464-2520).

Ministry of Development Affairs, PO Box 1577, Amman (tel: 464-361; fax: 464-8825).

Ministry of Education, PO Box 1646, Amman (tel: 847-671; fax: 566-6019).

Ministry of Energy and Mineral Resources, PO Box 2310 (tel: 586-3326/9; fax: 586-5714, 581-5615).

Ministry of Finance, PO Box 85, Amman (tel: 463-6321, 463-6502, 463-7781/2; fax: 464-3132, 464-3121).

Ministry of Foreign Affairs, 3rd Circle, PO Box 35217, Amman (tel: 464-4361, 464-4311; fax: 464-8825; internet www.mfa.gov.jo/).

Ministry of Health, PO Box 86, Amman (tel: 566-5131; fax: 568-8373).

Ministry of Industry and Trade, PO Box 2019, Amman (tel: 560-7191; fax: 560-3721).

Ministry of Information, PO Box 1794, Amman (tel: 464-1467; fax: 464-8895).

Ministry of the Interior, PO Box 100, Amman (tel: 463-8849, 566-3111, 569-1141; fax: 560-6908).

Ministry of Justice, PO Box 6040, Amman (tel: 566-3101; fax: 568-0238).

Ministry of Labour, PO Box 9052, Amman (tel: 560-7481; fax: 566-7193).

Ministry of Municipal, Rural and Environmental Affairs, 3rd Circle, PO Box 1799, Amman (tel: 464-1393/7; fax: 467-2135).

Ministry of Parliamentary Affairs, Jabal, Amman (tel: 464-1211; fax: 464-2520).

Ministry of Planning, PO Box 555, Amman (tel: 464-4466/7; fax: 464-9341).

Ministry of Public Works and Housing, PO Box 1220, Amman (tel: 585-0470, 585-0479; fax: 585-7590).

Ministry of Social Development, PO Box 6720, Amman (tel: 593-1391; fax: 567-3198).

Ministry of Supply, PO Box 830, Amman (tel: 560-2121, 560-2135; fax: 560-4691).

Ministry of Tourism & Antiquities, PO Box 224, Amman (tel: 464-2311/4; fax: 464-8465; e-mail: tourism@mota.gov.jo).

Ministry of Trade and Industry, PO Box 2019, Amman (tel: 663-191; fax: 603-721).

Ministry of Transport, PO Box 35214, Amman (tel: 551-8111; fax: 552-7233).

Ministry of Water and Irrigation, PO Box 2412, Amman (tel: 568-0100, 568-0117; fax: 567-9143).

Ministry of Youth, PO Box 1794 (tel: 604-701; fax: 604-717).

Prime Minister's Office, PO Box 80, Amman (tel: 641-211; fax: 642-520).

Other useful addresses

Amman Financial Market (AFM), PO Box 8802, Amman (tel: 660-170; fax: 686-830).

Amman World Trade Centre, PO Box 962140, Amman (tel: 560-5791/2; fax: 560-5793).

Arab Potash Company (APC), PO Box 1470, Amman (tel: 566-6165; fax: 567-4416).

British Embassy, PO Box 87, Abdoun, Amman (tel: 592-3100; fax: 592-3759; e-mail: british@nets.com.jo).

British Embassy, Commercial Section, PO Box 6062, Amman (tel: 592-3100; fax: 592-3759; e-mail: becommercial@nets.com.jo).

Chief of the Royal Court, PO Box 80, Amman (tel: 464-1211, 462-7421; fax: 464-2520).

Civil Aviation Authority, PO Box 7547, Amman (tel: 92-282; fax: 891-653).

Customs Department, PO Box 90, Amman (tel: 463-8358; fax: 464-7791; internet site: http://www.customs.gov.jo).

Indo-Jordan Chemicals Company, PO Box 926787, Amman (tel: 568-5732; fax: 568-5730).

Institution for Standards and Metrology, PO Box 941287, Amman 11194 (tel: 568-0139; fax: 568-1099).

Investment Promotion Council, PO Box 893, Amman 11821 (tel: 553-1081/2/3; fax: 552-1084; e-mail: ipc@amra.nic.gov.jo).

Jordan Dead Sea Industries Company (JODICO), PO Box 941260, Amman (tel: 569-941; fax: 569-5939).

Jordan Europe Business Association, PO Box 910751, Amman (tel: 568-5433; fax: 566-6550).

Jordan Export Development and Commercial Centres Corporation (JEDCO), PO Box 7704, Amman (tel: 560-3507; fax: 568-4568; internet site: http://www.jedco.gov.jo).

Jordan Fertilisers Industrial Company, PO Box 409, Aqaba (tel: 201-4156; fax: 201-7008).

Jordan Magnesia Company (JORMAG), PO Box 941260, Amman (tel: 569-5941; fax: 569-5939).

Jordan Phosphate Mines Company (JPMC), PO Box 30, Amman (tel: 560-7141; fax: 568-2290).

Jordanian Business Association, PO Box 926182, Amman (tel: 568-0855; fax: 566-0663).

Jordanian Embassy (USA), 3504 International Drive, NW, Washington DC 20008 (tel: 202-966-2664; fax: 202-966-3110; e-mail: hkjembassydc@aol,com).

National Electric Power Company (NEPCO), PO Box 2310, Amman 1181 (tel: 558-615; fax: 518-336).

Nippon Jordan Fertilisers Company Ltd., Po Box 926861, Amman (tel: 569-1708; fax: 568-4127).

US Embassy, PO Box 354, Jabal, Amman 11118 (tel: 592-0101; fax: 592-0163).

Internet sites

Arabia On-line: http://www.arabia.com

ArabNet: http://www.arab.net/

Global Chamber of Commerce: http://www.gcc.net

Kazakhstan

This country, which neighbours both China and Russia, is the size of India but with a population of only 13.89 million. In admittedly less than free and fair conditions, the vast majority of voters opted for the status quo in the 2005 general election. Kazakhstan is saved from the poverty and instability of some of its central Asian neighbours by virtue of its plentiful oil and gas reserves. It is Kazakhstan's possession of desperately sought after resources that has led to world leaders refraining from too strong criticism of a virtually authoritarian regime.

Domestic politics

In January 2006 Nursultan Nazarbayev embarked upon another seven year term after winning the December 2005 presidential elections. Russian President Vladimir Putin attended victory celebrations along with seven other central Asian prime ministers and Chinese Vice President, Zeng Qinghong. The 65-year old Nazarbayev has been in charge since 1989 and has pursued an exemplary financial policy. He has also brought political stability to a region recently characterised by popular upheaval. Nazarbayev's share of the vote in the last three elections since 1991 has been 99, 80 and 91 per cent. He called the 2005 election 'unprecedentedly democratic'. The campaign leader of the opposition candidate, Zharmakhan Tuyakbai, begged to differ, calling the latest results 'just absurd'.

There has been international criticism that the election did not meet standards of democracy – except from Russia, who certified the election as being fair. Otherwise, there is widespread recognition that opposition members were intimidated. The leader of the opposition party Democratic Choice, Galymzhan Zhakiyanov, was imprisoned throughout the electoral process serving a seven year sentence for alleged abuse of power during his time as a local governor. In November 2005 a strong critic of the president died in uncertain and suspicious circumstances. The official verdict of suicide was vehemently disputed by the man's widow. Rallies and campaigning were temporarily banned from April – December 2005 in response to revolutionary uprisings in neighbouring states such as Georgia and Kyrgyzstan. Students and new police recruits were warned they had only one choice in the election – unless they wanted to be expelled. The media was skewed towards the incumbent, with some channels devoting up to 75 per cent of coverage to Nazarbayev alone and only 12 per cent to his rival. A new electronic voting system was received with mistrust and there were reports of multiple voting. Opposition leader Tuyakbai warned 'the

KEY FACTS

Official name: Kazakstan Respublikasy (Republic of Kazakhstan)

Head of State: President Nursultan Äbishuly Nazarbayev (re-elected 4 Oct 2005)

Head of government: Prime Minister Daniyal Akhmetov (appointed Jun 2003)

Ruling party: Otan (Fatherland) party (since Oct 1999; re-elected 19 Sep 2004)

Area: 2,717,300 square km

Population: 13.89 million (2004)

Capital: Astana (seat of government) (renamed May 1998; formerly called Akmola; inaugurated as the new capital Dec 1997); Almaty (formerly Alma Ata, commercial capital)

Official language: Kazakh

Currency: Tenge (T) = 100 tein (introduced Nov 1993)

Exchange rate: T133.69 per US$ (Oct 2005)

GDP per capita: US$2,715 (2004)

GDP real growth: 9.40% (2004); 8.8% (2005)*

Labour force: 7.60 million (2004)

Unemployment: 8.00% (2004)

Inflation: 6.90% (2004)

Oil production: 1.29 million bpd (2004)

Balance of trade: US$6.79 billion (2004)

Foreign debt: US$26.03 billion (2004)

* estimated figure

authoritarian regime of Nazarbayev is taking a totalitarian turn'.

Tuyakbai also expressed concern that a sharply polarised society was evolving with growing extremes of wealth and poverty. Democracy and social welfare have been sidelined in the race for oil exploitation and wealth. With wealth Nazarbayev is seeking glory and international acceptance. The latter may be hard to come by. However, he has glorified himself in the construction of a new purpose–built capital in Astana, 1000km north of the former capital Almaty.

Economy

Since breaking away from Soviet control the economy has been rapidly liberalised. The IMF praised Kazakhstan's sound macroeconomic management, which has ensured strong growth and a rise in living standards. In 2005 annual GDP growth was 8.8 per cent, largely helped by oil sales. Inflation for 2005 stood at a projected 6.9 per cent, some improvement on 1990s' figures of 1,000 per cent.

Privatisation is virtually complete and much liberalising reform has been carried out in order to align the country with World Trade Organisation (WTO) standards. An area still requiring attention is the country's insufficient competitiveness.

FDI has been coming in thick and fast – US$28 billion has been invested in the past 10 years, 80 per cent of which was oil related. Real wages were bumped up 14 per cent in 2005 while unemployment dropped to 8.4 per cent. In recognition of the country's increased revenues and the stabilisation of the economy, in November 2005 the finance minister announced plans to repay US$849 of national debt.

Oil resources

Nazabayev's success rests upon the economy, which depends on the oil market. Oil makes up 25 per cent of GDP and 50 per cent of exports. Nazabayev has plans for the construction of new oil pipes to avoid future transportation through Russia and for large-scale sales to the Ukraine. Kazakhstan is a key oil source and for this reason the US and others have not risked alienating the country by condemning its electoral practices. The stability of the Kazakh government satisfies world energy markets nervous about the prospects of future oil supply.

The Kashagan oil field, unearthed 5 years ago, was the most significant oil discovery in recent history.

In August 2005 China National Petroleum Corporation (CNPC) entered a bid for PetroKazakhstan worth US$4.18 billion. Shareholders approved the deal in October. The completed sale would be the region's biggest oil takeover and would add 2 per cent to the Chinese group's reserves. The acquisition would be an important victory in China's race for resources.

The site is 1,000km from Chinese soil and there are plans to build a pipeline to transport output to China.

However in October the Kazakh government made a statement announcing that they wanted control of the assets and strategic control of the petrol company. Negotiation is expected to drag on into 2006. One snag in the PetroKazakhstan deal is the company's constant wrangling with the government. Long–running litigation and the Kazakh government's introduction of new taxes explain why Western companies did not bid for the company. The Indian energy minister Mani Shankar Aiyar accused Goldman Sachs in October 2005 of failing to ensure that PetroKazakhstan was sold fairly and of facilitating the lower–value Chinese bid.

The Caspian sea harbours a lot of oil potential and India's ONGC looks to be a favoured competitor in the selling off of the area. America and Europe have already netted sizeable Kazakh oil assets. The country is conveniently located between China and Europe and has pipelines going both west and east.

In November 2005 Kazatomprom, the national uranium miner, announced they had plans for domination of the world market, seeking to overtake the Canadian firm Cameco to become the largest global supplier. Production will nearly quadruple from 4,000 tonnes a year to 15,000 tonnes by 2010. The government added that the company would stay under national control until it had expanded, and funding for the expansion had already been secured.

Copper

In December 2005 the copper mining company, Kazakhmys, entered the London FTSE 100 valued at around US$4 billion. In 2004 the company generated sales of US$1.2 billion and profits of US$441 million, 50 per cent higher than the previous year. First, however, Kazakhmys was interrogated about its habit of investing its pension assets into its own shares – at odds with UK governance standards and best practice. Kazakhmys employed JP Morgan Cazenove and 200 Ernst and Young accountants to examine company accounts and make sure it would meet London regulations. It was the first company from the former Soviet Union to be

KEY INDICATORS — Kazakhstan

	Unit	2000	2001	2002	2003	2004
Population	m	14.95	14.80	14.90	13.50	13.89
Gross domestic product (GDP)	US$bn	18.30	22.40	24.20	29.70	*40.74
GDP per capita	US$	1,225	1,510	1,650	1,948	2,715
GDP real growth	%	9.8	13.2	9.5	9.5	9.4
Inflation	%	9.8	8.4	5.9	6.1	6.9
Unemployment	%	6.0	8.9	9.4	8.6	8.0
Oil output	'000 bpd	744.0	828.0	989.0	1,106.0	1,295.0
Natural gas output	bn cum	10.7	10.8	12.3	12.9	18.5
Coal output	mtoe	38.4	40.6	37.6	43.2	44.4
Exports (fob) (goods)	US$m	9,615.4	9,119.7	9,680.0	13,233.0	20,603.1
Imports (fob) (goods)	US$m	6,849.8	8,224.1	8,890.0	91,440.0	13,817.6
Balance of trade	US$m	2,765.6	895.6	780.0	-78,207.0	6,785.6
Current account	US$m	743.2	-1,749.0	-1,820.0	-69.0	920.0
Foreign debt	US$bn	12.5	14.4	17.5	6.6	26.0
Total reserves minus gold	US$m	1,594.1	1,997.2	2,555.3	4,236.2	8,473.1
Foreign exchange	US$m	1,594.1	1,997.2	2,554.2	4,235.0	8,471.9
Foreign direct investment (FDI)	US$bn	1.2	2.7	2.6	2.1	4.3
Exchange rate	per US$	142.13	146.74	153.86	149.55	136.41

* estimated figure

accepted into the main FTSE market. On entering the listings, the company announced that they would sell 120 million shares, over 25 per cent of the company.

Outlook

The IMF called Kazazhstan's economic outlook 'highly favourable'. Areas of potential concern are interest rates and an insufficiently diversified economy.

The oil market would seem dependable for the short term at least. By 2015 oil production will triple, according to forecasters, to three million barrels a day. Kazakhstan is determined to become one of the world's top ten oil producers.

Nazarbayev has ambitions to launch his nation onto the world stage. He is seeking membership of the WTO and has voiced plans to turn Kazakhstan into one of the world's 50 most developed countries. One way he hopes to achieve this is through an ambitious space programme, costing US$350 million.

The other major route to prominence is via the temporary leadership of the Organisation for Security and Co-operation in Europe, for which Kazakhstan is pencilled in for 2009. There are calls, however, that the country should be stripped of this privilege in light of its undemocratic electoral process.

Risk assessment

Economic	Good
Political	Fair
Regional Stability	Fair
Stock Market	Good

COUNTRY PROFILE

Historical profile

For centuries Kazakh nomads, a Turkic people ethnically close to the Uighurs of Xinjiang in China, dominated the vast steppe between Russia and northern China. In the eighth century, Arabs invaded the region and introduced Islam. Mongol tribes led by Genghis Khan invaded Central Asia in the thirteenth century and became assimilated into the Turkic tribes that made up the majority in their empire. The Kazakhs sprung from the descendants of Mongols, Turkic and other peoples and went on to form one of the world's last great nomadic empires. From the eighteenth century, the khans of the three main Kazakhi Zhuzes, or Hordes, increasingly sought Russian protection against Oryat raiders from Xinjiang, rendering the Kazakhs susceptible to the Russian expansion of the nineteenth century.
1822–1915 Tsarist Russia deposed the khans, took control of the Kazakh tribes and established the garrison town of Verny, now Almaty. Russian and Ukrainian peasants were brought in to settle the Kazakh lands and the first industrial enterprises were set up.
1916–17 The population joined the other Central Asian republics in a violent uprising against Russian rule, which was suppressed. After the October Revolution in Russia, the Russian ruler, Lenin, gave the peoples of Central Asia the right of self-determination.
1920s–30s Kazakhstan was granted autonomous status as part of the USSR in 1920. Soviet nationalities policy under the direction of Joseph Stalin saw Soviet rule enforced from Moscow by Red Army troops who put down Muslim revolts throughout Central Asia after the Russian civil war. Industrialisation and collectivisation of agriculture began. One million mainly nomadic Kazakhs died of starvation in the central government's campaign to enforce permanent settlements and build collective farms.
1930s–40s Kazakhstan was granted full Soviet Socialist Republic status in 1936. The country was transformed into a major producer of non-ferrous metals, coal and oil, as well as a region of developed agriculture.
1940s–50s Koreans, Crimean Tatars, Germans and others were forcibly moved to Kazakhstan. The first nuclear test explosion was carried out in 1949 at Semipalatinsk in eastern Kazakhstan.
1950s–60s Russian President Nikita Khruschev's 'Virgin Lands' scheme began. It brought agriculture to much of the Kazakh steppe and made the Kazakhs a minority in their own republic, as Russian and Ukrainian settlers were sent to run the collective farms. In 1961, the first manned spacecraft took off from Baykonur cosmodrome in central Kazakhstan.
1986 Riots in Almaty over the replacement of Dinmukhamed Kunayev (an ethnic Kazakh) with Gennady Kolbin (an ethnic Russian) as head of the Kommunisticheskaya Partiya Kazakhstana (KPK) (Communist Party of Kazakhstan) were the first signs of ethnic and nationalist unrest in Central Asia.
1989 Nursultan Nazarbayev, an ethnic Kazakh, was appointed leader of the KPK. Kazakh was declared an official language and Russian a language of inter-ethnic communication.
1990 Kazakhstan's Supreme Soviet appointed Nazarbayev as the country's first president and declared state sovereignty.
1991 Nazarbayev won uncontested presidential elections. President Nazarbayev had supported Gorbachev's efforts to keep the Soviet Union intact and Kazakhstan was the last Soviet Republic to declare full independence. Kazakhstan joined the Commonwealth of Independent States (CIS), an association which grew out of the remnants of the Soviet Union. The President signed a decree closing the Semipalatinsk nuclear testing ground.
1992 Kazakhstan became a member of the UN.
1993 A programme of national privatisation began.
1994 The first multi-party parliamentary elections were held for a full-time professional legislature, the Kenges (parliament). Results returned a predominantly pro-Nazarbayev assembly. Uzbekistan signed an economic, military and social co-operation treaty with Kazakhstan and Kyrgyzstan.
1995 President Nazarbayev dissolved parliament following a ruling by the Constitutional Court that the 1994 parliamentary elections were invalid. The president's term of office was extended to 2000 and a referendum endorsed the introduction of a new constitution.
1996 Uzbekistan, Kazakhstan and Kyrgyzstan agreed to create a single economic market.
1997 Oil agreements were signed with China. Kazakhstan's capital was moved from Almaty to Akmola, formerly known as Tselinograd.
1998 The new capital was renamed Astana. The constitution was amended to extend the presidential term from five to seven years and to remove the upper age limit for a president.
1999 Presidential elections were brought forward from 2000; Nazarbayev was re-elected after his main rival was barred from standing. International observers claimed there were serious irregularities in the parliamentary elections. An attempt by ethnic Russians in north-east Kazakhstan to form a separate state failed.
2000 A law was passed granting Nazarbayev life-long powers and privileges. Belarus, Kazakhstan, Kyrgyzstan, Russia and Tajikistan (formerly the Customs Five) established the Eurasian Economic Community (EEC). Internal security and border controls were increased following incursions by Islamic militants from Kyrgyzstan and Uzbekistan.
2001 The country's first major pipeline running from the large Tengiz oil field to the Black Sea was opened. Nazarbayev purged the government of officials accused of joining the newly formed Democratic Choice reform movement. Pope John Paul II paid his first visit to Kazakhstan. Tajikistan, China, Russia, Kazakhstan, Kyrgyzstan and Uzbekistan formed the Shanghai Co-operation Organisation (SCO) and agreed to fight ethnic and religious militancy, while promoting investment and trade.
2003 A bill allowing private ownership of land was passed. Russia, Ukraine,

Kazakhstan and Belarus signed an economic union treaty.

2004 A deal was signed with China on the construction of an oil pipeline to the Chinese border. Nazarbayev's Otan (Fatherland) party was re-elected in the 19 September Majlis elections; international observers considered them flawed.

2005 In January, Democratic Choice, one of the main opposition parties, was ordered by the court to be dissolved because it had encouraged protests against the parliamentary election results.
Nursultan Nazarbayev was re-elected president on 4 December.

2006 Opposition leader, Galymzhan Zhfakiyanov, was released from prison. He is one of the founders of the Democratic Choice Party.

Political structure
Constitution
A referendum endorsed the introduction of a new constitution on 30 August 1995, replacing the first constitution of January 1993.

In 1998, the constitution was amended to extend the presidential term of office from five to seven years, the Majlis (lower house) deputies' term from four to five years, and the upper house senators' term from five to six years; the upper age limit for a president was also removed.

A law passed in 2000 granted President Nazarbayev life-long powers and privileges.

Form of state
Secular democratic republic

The executive
Power is concentrated in an executive presidency. The president is elected by the people for a seven-year term. The prime minister and the Council of Ministers are appointed by the president. The 1995 constitution gave the president wide powers, such as the ability to dissolve the two-chamber parliament if the president's nominee for prime minister was rejected twice, or if a vote of no-confidence was held. Moreover, only the president can initiate constitutional amendments, call referenda at his discretion and appoint administrative heads of regions and cities.

National legislature
A two-chamber kenges (parliament) was created by the 1995 constitution, replacing the old 177-seat Supreme Kenges. With the president ruling by decree, the kenges' power is limited. Neither body has the power to initiate legislation.
The Majlis, or lower house, has 77 seats. Members are popularly elected for five-year terms, 67 in single-seat constituencies and 10 by proportional representation.
The upper house (Senate) has 39 members (previously 47); seven senators are appointed by the president; other members are popularly elected, two from each of the 14 oblasts. Senators serve six-year terms.

Legal system
The legal system is based on the civil law system. The country has a Supreme Court (44 members), and a Constitutional Council (seven members).

Last elections
19 September 2004 (Majlis); 1999 (Senate); 4 December 2005 (presidential).
Results: Parliamentary (Majlis): President Nursultan Nazarbayev's Otan (Fatherland) party won 33 seats in the 77-seat lower house, the pro-presidential Aist (Stork) bloc 10, the Asar (All Together) party three, the Ak Zhol (Bright Path) party one and independents eight.
Presidential: Nursultan Äbishuly Nazarbayev was re-elected with 91.07 per cent of the votes, Zharmakhan Tuyakbai won 6.6 per cent. Turnout was 75 per cent.

Next elections
2009 (parliamentary); 212 (presidential).

Political parties
Ruling party
Otan (Fatherland) party (since Oct 1999; re-elected 19 Sep 2004)
Main opposition party
Kommunisticheskaya Partiya Kazakhstana (KPK) (Communist Party of Kazakhstan); Respublikanskoye Nardonoye Partiya Kazakhstana (RNPK) (Republican People's Party of Kazakhstan); Agrarian Party (AP); Civic Party (CPK).

In January 2005, Democratic Choice, one of the main opposition parties, was ordered by the court to be dissolved because it had encouraged protests against the parliamentary election results.

Population
13.89 million (2004)
Ethnic make-up
Kazakh (Qazaq) (45 per cent, principally in the south), Russian (36 per cent, principally in the north), Ukrainian (5 per cent), German (4 per cent), Uzbek (2 per cent), Tartars (2 per cent), Uighur (1 per cent), Korean (0.6 per cent).
Religions
Muslim (47 per cent), Russian Orthodox (44 per cent), Protestant (2 per cent) and other (7 per cent). Kazakhstan is officially a secular state along Turkish lines. Kazakhs are predominantly Islamic (Sunni), while Russians belong to the Orthodox Church. Islam, not of a fundamentalist nature, is strongest in the countryside. North American and European evangelical organisations are very active throughout the country.

Education
Although the 99 per cent literacy rate claimed by the Soviet authorities for Central Asia was exaggerated, particularly in rural areas, education in Central Asia surpasses that of neighbouring countries to the south.

Primary education starts from the age of six and lasts for four years followed by basic secondary education for five years and general secondary, which is not compulsory, lasting for another two years. Secondary professional education is offered in special professional or technical schools, lyceums or colleges and vocational schools. The Academy of Sciences in Almaty is the republic's principal college of higher education. Several private institutions offering higher education have been licensed. The Academy of Sciences is the republic's principal college of higher education.

Compulsory years: Six to 15
Enrolment rate: 89 per cent, total primary school enrolment of the relevant age group, including repetition rates (World Bank estimates 1994–2000).
Pupils per teacher: 18 in primary schools.

Health
The total expenditure on health is just over 3 per cent of GDP, of which 60 per cent is government spending.

Kazakhstan's healthcare system is highly decentralised with a separate development model for every region. Public funds available for reforming the system are limited and do not cover the basic needs of the population, including access to primary healthcare services.

The healthcare services sector consists of public and private providers, including hospitals, offices and clinics of medical doctors, other specialised healthcare facilities and health insurance providers. The number of public hospitals has fallen leaving 63.8 beds available per 10,000 people. This reduction corresponded to a growth of small out-patient facilities (so-called family healthcare units); with the network numbering 1,752 facilities. The number of private hospitals has increased by over 30 per cent since 2000. More than half of private clinics and hospitals concluded contracts with regional healthcare departments to provide certain medical services to be paid from regional state budgets.

HIV prevalence: 0.2 per cent aged 15–49 in 2003 (World Bank)
Life expectancy: 61.3 years (World Bank)
Fertility rate/Maternal mortality rate: 1.8 births per woman; maternal mortality 70 per 100,000 live births (World Bank).

Infant mortality rate: 63 per 1,000 live births; 4.2 per cent of children aged under five are malnourished (World Bank).

Welfare
Kazakhstan has emerged as a role model in pension reform in the Commonwealth of Independent States (CIS). In January 1998, a pay-as-you-go (PAYG) system was replaced with a privately managed and fully-funded system (similar to that introduced by Chile in the 1980s). Under the new system, employees pay a compulsory 10 per cent of their wages into a personal retirement account. This is in addition to existing pension liabilities funded through a 15 per cent payroll tax which will be cut to 5 per cent by 2009.

Main cities
Astana (capital, estimated population 288,200 in 2004); Almaty (commercial capital, 1.0 million); Karaganda (404,600); Shymkent (333,500); Taraz (305,700); Pavlodar (299,500).

Languages spoken
Kazakh (Turkic) is only spoken by around 40 per cent of the population. Russian is the language of inter-ethnic communication, spoken by two-thirds of the population and used in everyday business.
Official language/s
Kazakh

Media
Government interference in the workings of the media remains prevalent and the introduction of broadcasting licences has resulted in the closure of a number of private media companies.
Press
There are over 650 newspapers and 150 magazines published in Kazakhstan. President Nazarbayev tends to manipulate the media during elections, while members of his family exercise considerable control over sections of the press.
The National Agency of Press and Mass Media is a governmental department that acts as the founder of state newspapers and magazines. It is financed by the national budget and owns the national news agency, Kazakh Akparat Agenttigi (KazAAG) (Kazakh Information Agency).
Dailies: There are several daily and weekly newspapers in both Russian and Kazakh including: *Kazakhstanskaya Pravda*, *Karavan*, *Panorama* and *Kazakhstanskaya Vecher*. *Almaty Herald* (http://www.herald.kz/) is the online English-language newspaper in Kazakhstan.
Business: *Business Club* carries information for investors.
Broadcasting
State-owned channels and commercial stations are broadcast in Kazakhstan alongside Russian and Chinese television channels. The Turkish Radio and Television Corporation (TRT) also broadcasts programmes for Kazakhstan.
A satellite launched in 1996 broadcasts five television and several radio stations. The joint US-Kazakh company, Alma TV, launched the first cable television station in Almaty in 1996. Kazakhstan has a city TV channel called *Almaty-Yuzhnaya Stolitsa* (Almaty-Southern Capital). Programmes are distributed via the Alma-TV cable television network. The channel's operation is financed by the Almaty city council.
A law was introduced in January 2002 requiring that at least 50 per cent of all television and radio broadcasts be in the Kazakh language.

Economy
During the Soviet era, Kazakhstan's economy was based on the production of agricultural products and raw materials for the energy sector which were then processed in the other republics. The collapse of the Soviet Union in 1991 left Kazakhstan without a market for its produce and largely without the wherewithal to process the raw materials itself. Kazakhstan's attempt to introduce a free market economy as well as political instability initially left the economy in turmoil in 1992–98. Energy shortages were commonplace and the reliance on Russian export routes stifled oil and gas earnings.
Macroeconomic and currency stability began to be achieved by 2000 due to oil revenue windfalls. GDP growth climbed from 9.8 per cent in 2000 to 13.2 per cent in 2001, before falling to 9.5 per cent in 2002 and 2003 and steadying at 9.4 per cent in 2004. There are fears that Kazakhstan's economy may become skewed and suffer from 'Dutch disease', where the economy becomes overwhelmed by the oil sector.
Despite a strong macroeconomic performance, the IMF has criticised delays in the privatisation programme and land and social sector reform. It has also warned against excessive currency appreciation and urged the government to promote greater saving, open up trade and continue to maintain a strict monetary regime. Corruption, bureaucracy and Soviet-style administration continue to pose problems for foreign investment. Per capita income remains lower than it was during the Soviet period and a significant number of people are emigrating.
Since 2003, there there have been several improvements in Kazakhstan. Manufacturing grew as a result of the government's efforts to diversify the economy, unemployment decreased and living standards improved. The banking sector remained strong, which contributed to growing public confidence.
Enhancing living standards remains a key government objective. It is continuing to implement poverty reduction and rural development programmes and encouraging private sector development with a view to creating more jobs. With diversification and strong foreign direct investment inflows, particularly in the oil sector, the economic outlook remains positive.

External trade
Since 1996, Kazakhstan has been working towards membership of the World Trade Organisation (WTO), but will have to introduce large-scale trading reforms before membership is granted.
The Commonwealth of Independent States (CIS) Customs Union was transformed in 2000 into the Eurasian Economic Community (EEC), comprising Kazakhstan, Kyrgyzstan, Tajikistan, Russia and Belarus. The stated aims of this development were to provide a common payments system, equal access to foreign investment and co-ordination of activities in international economic organisations. The main priority of the EEC is to combat smuggling and increase border security. This may restrict rather than liberalise trade between the member states.
Kazakhstan's trade was boosted with China, Kyrgyzstan, Russia, Tajikistan and Uzbekistan following the formation of the Shanghai Co-operation Organisation (SCO) in June 2001.
Imports
Principal imports include machinery and equipment (41 per cent), metal products and foodstuffs.
Main sources: Russia (33.9 per cent total, 2004), China (13.6 per cent), Germany (9.6 per cent), France (6.8 per cent)
Exports
Principal exports include oil and oil products (58 per cent), ferrous metals, chemicals, machinery, grain, wool, meat and coal.
Main destinations: Russia (13.5 per cent total, 2004), Bermuda (13.4 per cent), China (10.4 per cent), Germany (9.2 per cent), Switzerland (9.1 per cent), France (6.7 per cent)

Agriculture
Farming
Agriculture contributes approximately 8.5 per cent to GDP and employs a quarter of the working population.
Kazakhstan's farming area constituted 16 per cent of the former Soviet Union's farm land. The cultivation of the 'Virgin Lands' in the north during the Soviet period introduced a high level of mechanisation and Kazakhstan used to provide around 14 per cent of Soviet grain.
There are still many problems in the agricultural sector, including weaknesses in input supply (such as fertilisers), poor

incentives for farm production and failure to restructure farm enterprises.

Privatisation is proceeding slowly. Small-scale private farming has been introduced in the south, while production in the north remains more centralised. While agricultural land may be leased long-term, attempts to introduce private land ownership is unpopular.

Irrigated land in the south and east produces fruit, vegetables, sugar beet, rice, tobacco, mustard and natural rubber. Wheat, cotton and oilseeds are the main crops produced. Dairy farming, horse breeding and sheep breeding are also undertaken.

Crop production in 2004 included: 12,347,161 tonnes (t) cereals in total, 9,942,300t wheat, 1,534,000t barley, 2,243,300t potatoes, 276,661t rice, 300,000t maize, 140,000t oats, 28,000t grapes, 175,681t oilcrops, 27,000t pulses, 480,000t tomatoes, 397,900t sugar beets, 50,000t chillies & peppers, *16,000 tobacco, 467,100 seed cotton, 142,000t cotton lint, 140,000t apples, 267,000t fruit in total, 2,739,800t vegetables in total. Livestock production included: 732,350t meat in total, 340,000t beef, 195,000t pig meat, 99,000t lamb, 7,500t goat meat, 37,000t poultry, 53,000t horsemeat, 129,792t eggs, 4,515,000t milk, *1,000t honey, 41,800t cattle hides, 10,940t sheepskins, 26,600t greasy wool.

* estimate

Fishing
In the north-eastern part of Kazakhstan cold water fish are found in the River Ob catchment area, including the Altai Mountains drainage of the Irtysh River, mountain rivers of the Tien Shan range and in Lake Balkhash, which has a mix of cold water and temperate water fish stocks. The fishing of streams and rivers is largely unmanaged, but considerable effort has been put into maintaining reasonably high fish catches in some lakes and reservoirs. Kazakhstan has concentrated largely on the exploitation of indigenous fish stocks. The typical annual fish catch is over 31,000mt.

Forestry
Forest and other wooded land account for a small part of the total. Forests cover around 12.1 million hectares, which has increased by an average of 2.22 per cent per annum.

The increasing demand for forest products is met by imports, mainly from the Russian Federation, with imports valued at US$159 million and exports at US$5 million, in 2004.

Industry and manufacturing
The share of industry, including mining, in GDP in 2004 was estimated at 39.5 per cent. The sector grew by 10.6 per cent in 2004.

Kazakhstan inherited a well-developed industrial base from the Soviet era. The principal activities are in minerals, petrochemicals, food processing, machinery and light industry.

Tourism
Kazakhstan's considerable tourist potential is being actively developed by the government, which has accorded it priority status. A Law on Tourism Activities was promulgated and a five-year Tourist Development Plan adopted in 2001, with the object of presenting a positive image of the country, building essential infrastructure and ensuring visitor safety. Visitor numbers and revenues have risen. There were 106,486 arrivals in 2004, an increase of 19.2 per cent over the previous year. Tourism contributed 1.6 per cent to GDP in 2004. Attractions include the Silk Road, adventure and eco-tourism. Air connections are being improved – Air Astana has opened direct routes to major European cities as well as Seoul and Bangkok.

Environment
The Aral Sea is drying up due to the overuse of water from the two main rivers which feed into it. This has resulted in desertification of the surrounding land. A UN study published in 2004 reported that there was no possibility of restoring the water and the need must be on preserving what was is left.

The government has endorsed a 2004 joint strategy to resolve the demands of its water requirements with its neighbours.

Mining
Mining contributes around 15 per cent to GDP and employs 8 per cent of the workforce.

Rich in mineral resources, Kazakhstan produces 40 per cent of the world's chrome ore, second only to South Africa. There are also important deposits of iron ore, nickel, cobalt, vanadium, titanium, copper, lead, wolfram, zinc, gold, silver, tin, tungsten, molybdenum, uranium, cadmium, bismuth, pyrophyllite, barite, phosphorites, magnesium, phosphorous, asbestos, rare earths and sizeable manganese deposits in eastern and northern Kazakhstan. There are significant bauxite reserves in southern Kazakhstan.

Hydrocarbons
Kazakhstan was the Soviet Union's second-largest oil producer after Russia and is believed to have the world's largest untapped oil and gas reserves. Since independence the government has concentrated its efforts on attracting foreign investment to this sector.

Kazakhstan has proven oil reserves of 9.0 billion barrels. Total reserves are thought to be far higher. Foreign investment has flooded into the booming oil sector and since 1992, oil production has increased by over 50 per cent to 1.2 million barrels per day (bpd). Around 75 per cent of production is exported and accounts for around a quarter of GDP. There are three major refineries at Pavlador, Atyrau and Shymkent with a joint capacity of 345,093 bpd. The downstream sector, which is unattractive to foreign investors, continues to be state-controlled.

Kazakhstan has proven natural gas reserves of 1.9 trillion cubic metres and produces 16.2 billion cubic metres a year. A lack of sufficient pipeline infrastructure has meant that Kazakhstan has not reached its full potential in natural gas exploitation. The government has targeted the sector for expansion. The completion of the 635km Karachaganak-Atyrau pipeline in 2003 allows Kazakhstan to export limited quantities of gas and other hydrocarbons.

Kazakhstan has recoverable reserves of coal of 37.5 billion tonnes and produces 95 million tonnes per year. Coal is the largest domestic source of energy. Output and consumption of coal have declined since independence. Around 28 million tonnes of coal are exported, mainly to Russia and Ukraine. Many of the high-cost underground coal mines have been closed, and its more competitive surface mines have been purchased and are operated by international energy companies.

Energy
Kazakhstan has a total electricity generating capacity of 17.4GW produced mainly by coal-fired power plants, but with an increasing proportion from five hydroelectric power stations. The sector is faced with large amounts of inefficient or redundant equipment and needs considerable investment if it is to reverse the decline in output and halt the frequent power stoppages experienced since independence.

Kazakhstan closed down its only nuclear station in 1999. The government is considering the construction of a new 1,500MW nuclear power plant in the south-east near Lake Balkash by 2012.

Financial markets
Stock exchange
The Kazakhstan Stock Exchange (KSE) was launched in September 1997.

Banking and insurance
In the early 1990s, Kazakhstan had a liberal banking policy which allowed the emergence of many banks which were under-capitalised and badly managed.
Central bank
National Bank of Kazakhstan

Kazakhstan

Following the National Bank of Kazakhstan's transition to international accounting standards, it announced on 29 January 2003 that it will no longer set the exchange rate for the tenge for accounting purposes.

Time
GMT plus six hours (winter); GMT plus seven hours (summer).

Geography
Kazakhstan, in Central Asia, is a landlocked country but with a coastline on the Caspian Sea, (the largest lake in the world). It is the second-largest country in the region, extending some 1,900km (1,200 miles) from the Volga river in Europe, in the west, to the Altai mountains, in the east, and about 1,300km (800 miles) from the Siberian plain in the north to the Central Asian deserts in the south. Kazakhstan's 2.7 million square km are equivalent to the size of Western Europe and comprise rolling steppes to the north, desert to the south and part of the western edge of the Tien Shan mountains to the south-east.

Kazakhstan is bordered by the Russian Federation to the north, China to the east, Kyrgyzstan, Uzbekistan and Turkmenistan to the south. In the south-west there is almost a 1,000km coastline on the Caspian Sea. Half of the Aral Sea lies within Kazakhstan, the other half in Uzbekistan.

Climate
The temperature varies greatly from temperate steppe in the north to desert in the south. Temperatures in southern Kazakhstan average -3 degrees Celsius (C) in January and 29 degrees C in June. Average temperatures in Almaty range from -5 degrees C to 35 degrees C. Rainfall averages 200–300mm per annum in the north of the country and 400–500mm in the south.

Dress codes
Not overly formal during business hours, although women must dress modestly. Formal wear may be expected when visiting the theatre or attending a dinner party. Shorts should not be worn except in a sporting environment.

Entry requirements
Passports
Required by all visitors, valid for three months beyond intended length of stay.
Visa
Required by all and should be obtained in advance. Business visas are issued after an invitation from a local company has been registered with the consular department of the Ministry of Foreign Affairs in Kazakhstan. When authorised, the host company obtains a reference number which is forwarded to the applicant who submits the application form along with a business letter of intent, a full itinerary and an undertaking of financial responsibility for expenses incurred by the representative. Details of these requirements can be obtained from the consular section of the nearest embassy.

Tourist visits, over three days, require registration by the local authorities, on arrival.

There is no agreement allowing visas issued in one Commonwealth of Independent State (CIS) country to be used to transit Kazakhstan. If intending to visit two or more CIS countries, contact the relevant embassies for advice before travelling.

Currency advice/regulations
Import and export of the national currency is forbidden. Import of foreign currency is allowed without limitations but must be declared on arrival. When leaving refund of exchanged currency is possible against exchange receipt. It is advisable to take US dollars and euros; often only hard currencies are accepted.

Customs
A customs declaration form must be completed and retained until departure. Such items that should be declared are those valuables intended for personal use (jewellery, cameras, computers etc). These belonging must be exported when leaving and it is advisable to keep receipts for goods purchased locally.

Prohibited imports
Military weapons and ammunition; illicit drugs; pornography; live animals; photographs or printed material detrimental to the image of Kazakhstan; loose pearls or anything couriered for a third party.

Health (for visitors)
A reciprocal health agreement for urgent medical treatment exists with the UK. Proof of UK residence is required.
Mandatory precautions
Vaccination certificates are required for yellow fever if travelling from an infected area. For stays over one month and applications for visas for stays over three months, an AIDS certificate is required.
Advisable precautions
It is advisable to be 'in date' for the following immunisations: polio (within 10 years), tetanus (within 10 years), typhoid fever, TB, hepatitis 'A', tick-borne encephalitis. Anti-malarial precautions advisable. Any medicines required by the traveller should be taken by the visitor, and it could be wise to have precautionary antibiotics if going outside major urban centres. A travel kit including a disposable syringe is a reasonable precaution. Water precautions recommended: water purification tablets may be useful or drink bottled water. Rabies is a health risk.

Hotels
Advisable to book at least a month in advance through Intourist or other specialist travel agents. There are many luxury Western-style hotels in Almaty. Gratuities are becoming more customary, particularly in international hotels.

Credit cards
More widely accepted than anywhere else in Central Asia; as well as being welcomed in shops and hotels, they can be used for cash advances.

Public holidays
Fixed dates
1–2 Jan (New Year), 8 Mar (Women's Day), 21 May (Nauryz Meyrami/Traditional Spring Holiday/Persian New Year), 1 May (Unity Day), 9 May (Victory Day), 30 Aug (Constitution Day), 25 Oct (Republic Day), 16 Dec (Independence Day).
Variable dates

Working hours
Banking
Mon–Fri: 0900–1300; Sat: closed.
Business
Mon–Fri: 0900–1800.
Shops
Mon–Sat: 0900–1700.

Electricity supply
220V AC.

Social customs/useful tips
Kazakhistanis are very hospitable and courteous. It is best to book appointments for meetings in the morning. Cancellation, even at the last minute, is fairly common. Russian is the everyday business language. Business and politics are intertwined, with negotiations and deals often 'arranged'.

Security
It is unwise to venture out on the streets alone at night. Dress inconspicuously as wealthy-looking foreigners can be a target for muggers.

It may be preferable to travel by intercity bus rather than train, as robberies are making rail travel increasingly hazardous.

Getting there
Air
Almaty is the principal gateway to the country and well-served, with the most developed air routes through Turkey and Russia.
National airline: Air Kazakhstan.
International airport/s: Almaty (ALA), 10km, north-east of the city; facilities include car hire, duty-free, restaurant and post office. Buses (travel time 20 minutes) and taxis connect to the city centre.
Astana (TSE), 17 km from city; facilities include duty-free and restaurant. Buses and taxis connect to the city centre.

Other airport/s: There are fifteen other airports.
Airport tax: None

Surface
Road: There are generally good international road connections to the surrounding countries. The north-east area is well served by roads to the Urals and the North Caucasus.
Rail: A railway line was completed in 1991 between Almaty and Urumchi in China. There are also rail connections to Russia, Kyrgystan and Turkmenistan. A new railway line is being built to connect Iran and Turkey with Kazakhstan. Foreign visitors should use caution when traveling by train, other than the Almaty-Moscow line as violent crime against westerners is on the increase.
Main port/s: Aktau (formerly Shevchenko) on the Caspian Sea is the main oil port and trans-shipment centre.

Getting about
National transport
Air: There are fifteen domestic/local airports located around the regions and are served by scheduled internal flights. However it should be noted that maintenance procedures for aircraft on internal flights may not conform to internationally accepted standards.
Planes and helicopters can be chartered for nominal prices provided you have a good local contact.
Road: Primary and secondary roads are of poor quality, particularly in desert and semi-desert regions. However, the Oral region is well served by road links to the Urals, European Russia and the North Caucasus. Road transport is subject to cancellation and delay. Passengers are advised to travel in groups. Petrol supplies are adequate. Kazakhstan has 189,000km of paved and gravelled roads, 108,100km of unpaved roads and 80,900km of earth roads.
Buses: There are regular bus services between all the main cities.
Rail: Rail links are extensive but slow. There are 14,460km of railway, excluding industrial lines, in Kazakhstan. The Turksib railway connects Almaty with the Trans-Siberian line to the north at Novisibirsk, while the principal rail connection with Moscow runs through Chimkent and Uralsk.

City transport
Taxis: Unless Russian or Kazakh is spoken, ensure any taxi taken is booked through the hotel reception desk and that the price is agreed beforehand.
Buses, trams & metro: Swift and cheap trolley-bus and bus network in Almaty.

Car hire
A national driver's licence with an authorised translation or an international driving permit is required.

BUSINESS DIRECTORY
The addresses listed below are a selection only. While World of Information makes every endeavour to check these addresses, we cannot guarantee that changes have not been made, especially to telephone numbers and area codes. We would welcome any corrections.

Telephone area codes
The international direct dialling code (IDD) for Kazakhstan is +7, followed by area code and subscriber's number:

Almaty	3272	Shymkent	3252
Astana	3172	Uralsk	3112
Karaganda	3212	Ust-Kamenogorsk	3232
Petropavlovsk	3152	Zhezkazgan	3102

Useful telephone numbers
Police: 02
Fire: 01
Ambulance: 03

Chambers of Commerce
Almaty Chamber of Commerce and Industry, 45 Tole bi Street, Almaty 480091 (tel: 620-301; fax: 611-404; e-mail: alcci@nursat.kz).

American Chamber of Commerce in Kazakhstan, 531 Seifullina Prospect, Almaty 480091 (tel: 587-938; fax: 587-939; e-mail: information@amcham.kz).

East Kazakhstan Chamber of Commerce and Industry, PO Box 177, 3 Novatorov Street, Ust-Kamenogorsk 492000 (tel: 265-310; fax:267-247; e-mail@cci@ustk.kz).

Kazakhstan Union of Chambers of Commerce and Industry, 26 Masanchi Street, Almaty 480091 (tel: 920-052; fax: 507-029; e-mail: tpprkaz@online.ru).

North Kazakhstan Chamber of Commerce and Industry, 112 Mira Street, Petropavlovsk 642015 (tel: 460-568; fax: 465-443; e-mail: tpp@petropavl.kz).

Semipalatinsk Chamber of Commerce and Industry, 92/22 Abai Street, Semipalatinsk 490050 (tel/fax: 627-887; e-mail: tpp@relcom.kz).

South Kazakhstan Chamber of Commerce and Industry, 31 Tauke khan Street, Shimkent 486050 (tel: 211-405; fax: 211-403).

West Kazakhstan Chamber of Commerce and Industry, 67 Kuibyshev Street, Uralsk 417000 (tel: 504-440; fax: 513-537; e-mail: zktpp@kaznet.kz).

Banking
ATF Bank, 100 Furmanov Str, 480091 Almaty (tel: 503-765; fax: 501-995).

Bank Centercredit, 100 Shevchenko Street, 480072 Almaty (tel: 634-605, 680-140; fax: 507-813).

Central Asian Bank for Co-operation and Development, 115-a Abay Ave, Almaty (tel: 422-737; fax: 428-627).

Demir Kazakhstan Bank, 61A Kurmangazy Street, 480091 Almaty (tel: 508-550, 508-527; fax: 508-525).

Export-Import Bank of Kazakhstan, 118 Pushkin Street, 480021 Almaty (tel: 622-815, 633-767, 634-300; fax: 631-985).

Halyk Savings Bank of Kazakhstan; 97 Rozybakieva St, 480046 Almaty (tel: 509-991; fax: 679-738).

Kazkommertsbank, 135 Gagarin Avenue, 480060 Almaty (tel: 585-101; fax: 585-281; internet site: http://www.kkb.kz).

Temirbank, 68/74 Abay Ave, 480008 Almaty (tel: 587-888; fax: 590-529; e-mail: board@temirbank.kz; internet site: http://www.temirbank.kz).

Central bank
National Bank of Kazakhstan, 21 Koktem-3, 480090 Almaty (tel: 504-631; fax: 506-090; e-mail: info@nationalbank.kz).

Travel information
Aeroflot, 111 Zhibek Zhola Street, Almaty (tel: 390-594).

Air Kazakhstan, 59 Mira Street, 480003 Almaty (tel: 335-518; fax: 335-506).

Flight information (24 hours) (tel: 541-555).

Intourist, Hotel Ostrar, Gogolya 65, Almaty (tel: 330-045, 330-076).

Almaty Airport, Mailin Street 2B, 480040 Almaty (tel: 571-300; fax: 571-281).

Astana International Airport, PO Box 1968, 473026 Astana (tel: 333-709; fax: 333-741).

Kazakhstan Tourist Agency, 22 Kosmonautov Street, 480083 Almaty (tel: 390-318; fax: 390-257).

Travel Bureau, Hotel Irtysh, Ulitsa Abai 97, Semipalatinsk, Almaty (tel: 447-529, 447-531).

National tourist organisation offices
Department of Tourism, 4 Republic Square, Almaty 4860065 (tel/fax: 620-030; e-mail: dep_tour@nursat.kz; internet: www.kaztour.kz).

Ministries
Ministry of Agriculture, 49 Abai Street, 473000 Astana (tel: 323-763; fax: 324-541).

Ministry of Culture, Information and Public Accord, 22 Beibitshilik Street, 473000 Astana (tel: 322-495; fax: 326-203).

Ministry of Defence, 49 Auezova Street, 473000 Astana (tel: 337-845;fax: 337-892).

Ministry of Economy and Trade, 2 Beibitshilik Street, 473000 Astana (tel/fax: 333-003).

Ministry of Education and Science, 83 Kenesary Street, 473000 Astana (tel: 322-540; fax: 326-482).

Ministry of Employment and Social Security, 2 Manasa Street, 473000 Astana (tel: 153-602; fax: 341-270).

Ministry of Energy and Mineral Resources, 37 Beibitshilik Street, 473000 Astana (tel: 337-133; fax: 337-164).

Ministry of Finance, 60 Republic Avenue, 473000 Astana (tel: 334-186;fax: 280-321).

Ministry of Foreign Affairs, 10 Beibitshilik Street, 473000 Astana (tel: 327-669; fax: 327-667).

Ministry of Internal Affairs, 4 Manasa Street, 473000 Astana (tel: 343-601; fax: 341-738).

Ministry of Justice, 45 Pobeda Street, 473000 Astana (tel: 391-213; fax: 321-554).

Ministry of Natural Resources and Environmental Protection, 81 Karl Marx Street, 475000 Kokshetau (tel: 54-265; fax: 50-620).

Ministry of State Revenues, 48 Abai Avenue (tel: 326-951;fax: 326-963).

Ministry of Transport and Communications, 49 Abai Street, 473000 Astana (tel: 326-277; fax: 321-058).

Prime Minister's Office, 11 Beibitshilik Street, 473000 Astana (tel: 320-985;fax: 152-028).

Other useful addresses
Atomic Energy Agency, 13 Republic Square, 480013 Almaty (tel: 637-626; fax: 633-356).

Board for Investment Projects, Department of Transport, Room 124, Gogol Str 86, 480091 Almaty (tel: 323-661, 324-769; fax: 322-679, 324-449).

Business Communication Centre, 89 Michurina Street, Almaty 480059 (tel: 476-803, 347-549; fax: 347-798).

Central Asia Research Forum, School of Oriental and African Studies, Thornhaugh Street, London WC1H 0XG, UK (tel: (0)20-7323-6300; fax: (0)20-7436-3844).

Centre for Economic Reforms, 4 Republic Square, Almaty (tel: 621-836).

Committee for the use of Foreign Capital, 152 Bogenbai Batyr, 3rd Floord, Ablay Khan Street 97, 480091 Almaty (tel: 627-326; fax: 696-152).

Embassy of the Republic of Kazakhstan,1401 16th Street, NW, Washington, DC 20036, USA (tel: (202) 232 5488. Fax: (202) 232 5845; e-mail: kazak@imtr.net; internet: http://www.kazakhstan-embassy-us.org)

Kazakh Centre of Business Co-operation 'Atakent', 42 Timiryazeve Street, Almaty 480058 (tel: 473-113; fax: 509-238).

Kazakh Embassy (USA), 1401 16th Street, NW, Washington DC 20036 (tel: 202-232-5488; fax: 202-232-5845; e-mail: kazakhembus@verizon.net).

Kazakhgas, 521 Seifullin Street, Almaty (tel: 324-288; fax: 325-442).

Kazakhstan Caspishelf, 211 Mukhanov Street, Almaty (tel: 416-034; fax: 416-430).

Kazakhstan Commerce (import-export), Zhibek Zholy 64, 480002 Almaty (tel: 333-871; fax: 331-483).

Kazakhstan Foreign Trade Organisation, v/o Kazakhintorg, Gogolya 111, Almaty (tel: 328-381).

Kazakhstanmunaigas (oil and gas refining), 458 Seifullin Street, Almaty (tel: 695-800; fax: 626-630).

Kazakh Academy of Sciences Engineering Institute, 80 Bogenbay Batyr Street, Almaty 480100 (tel: 541-281; fax: 695-769).

Kazakhstan Stock Exchange, Ulitsa Timipiazeva 42, Almaty (tel: 441-043; fax: 447-809).

Kazakh State TV and Radio, Ulitsa Mira 175, Almaty (tel: 633-716).

Kazchrome Transnational Corporation, 56 Kunaev Street, Almaty, 480002.

KazMunayGaz, 142 Bogenbai Batyr Street, 470091 Almaty (tel: 626-080; fax: 695-405).

Kazpisprom (a joint-stock company representing food producers), 92 Internatsionalnaya Street, Almaty (tel: 629-482; fax: 628-652).

Kaztag (state news agency), 77 Ablai Han Street, Almaty (tel: 625-037).

Kazvetmet (represents metal producers), 111 Gogol Street, 480003 Almaty (tel: 622-318; fax: 328-488).

Market Economy Group (privatisation committee), President's Office, Government House, Almaty (tel: 621-022).

State Property and Privatisation Committee, Ministry of Finance, 36 Auezov Street, 473024 Astana (tel: 334-397; fax: 320-937).

Union of Manufacturers and Businessmen, 4/450 Republic Square, Almaty (tel: 622-307; fax: 665-490).

Internet sites
Kazakhstan local navigator: http://reenic.utexas.edu/reenic/countries/kazakhstan/kazakhstan/html

Kazakhstan government website: http://www.president.kz/

Kenya

KEY FACTS

Official name: Jamhuri ya Kenya (Republic of Kenya)

Head of State: President Mwai Kibaki (Narc) (sworn in 30 Dec 2002)

Head of government: President Mwai Kibaki

Ruling party: National Rainbow Coalition (Narc) (elected 27 Dec 2002)

Area: 582,646 square km

Population: 33.52 million (2004)

Capital: Nairobi

Official language: KiSwahili and English

Currency: Kenyan shilling (Ksh) = 100 cents (convertible with currencies of Tanzania and Uganda)

Exchange rate: Ksh74.00 per US$ (Oct 2005)

GDP per capita: US$482 (2004)

GDP real growth: 3.10% (2004)

Labour force: 16.94 million (2004)

Inflation: 11.50% (2004)

Balance of trade: -US$1.60 billion (2004)

Foreign debt: US$6.79 billion (2004)

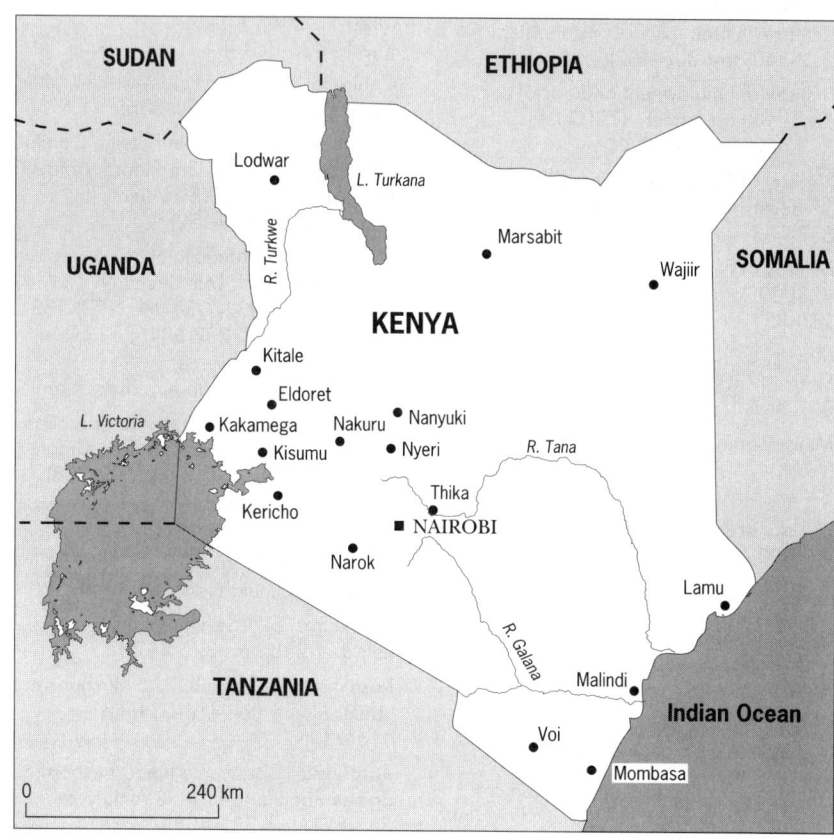

In 2004/05, two and a half years after the ousting of Jomo Kenyatta's Kenya African National Union (Kanu), the National Rainbow Coalition (Narc) of Mwai Kibaki continued to rebuild Kenya. It was supported by donor institutions and nations who had welcomed an end to the corruption and misrule of first Kenyatta and later Daniel arap Moi. Kibaki is being watched carefully to see if he will eventually deliver on promises of a new constitution under which the rulers will be accountable, and move to tackle macro-economic vulnerabilities and impediments to economic growth and poverty reduction.

Kibaki's constitutional plans suffered a surprising setback when a referendum rejected the proposed new constitution in late 2005. Kibaki had urged Kenyans to endorse the document, which he portrayed as a modernising measure, but the charter did little more than create bitter divisions, with critics saying it left too much power in the hands of the president.

Delays in economic reforms

So far, when tackled on a perceived slowness of economic reform, Kibaki's government has pleaded the large amount of time devoted to constitutional reform, capacity constraints in key ministries, and the slow resumption of donor budgetary assistance. Progress in implementing structural reforms has been mixed.

There have been delays in implementing reforms in the areas of public expenditure, the financial sector and parastatals. The lack of progress in moving toward a comprehensive medium-term expenditure framework and instituting a more robust expenditure management system is attributable to organisational and capacity constraints at the ministry of finance. Parastatal reforms suffered from a lack of consensus on the objectives and modalities for privatisation.

The medium-term macroeconomic framework has been modified to take account of the more difficult environment now foreseen for the medium-term. The terms of trade are now projected to deteriorate moderately instead of producing the modest gains envisaged earlier. Donor assistance will fall significantly short of earlier expectations and key reforms in the financial and parastatal sectors have been crowded out of the legislative agenda by constitutional reform deliberations.

Economy

The domestic revenue effort has been strengthened and expenditure restructuring and management reforms accelerated. Domestic borrowing targets have been relaxed somewhat. Although these changes will result in a moderate increase in domestic budgetary resources and in an improvement in the productivity of public spending, public investment will be scaled down over the medium-term compared to original assumptions.

Projected real growth at 2.7 per cent over 2004/05 was lower than the 3.1 per cent originally expected, but a moderate pickup in economic activity is foreseen. The tourism sector is projected to continue to perform strongly as it recovers from the adverse effects of the Western travel ban after the terror bomb attacks in Nairobi in 1998 and Mombasa in 2002. The drought and high oil prices are expected to contribute to a pickup in overall consumer price inflation to well above earlier projections.

The eventual lowering of the domestic debt ratio to GDP remains the key focus of the economic programme. To preserve some essential social and economic programme in the face of slow donor support, domestic borrowing will exceed expectations, but in the short-term be broadly unchanged at 22 per cent of GDP compared with the original target of 24.7 per cent. Some crowding out of private activity is expected, as the public sector will absorb a sizeable proportion of projected financial savings. The domestic debt-ratio is expected to decline thereafter.

The coming into effect on 1 January 2005 of the East African Community (EAC) Customs Protocol involving a lowering of the top tariff rate from 35 per cent to 25 per cent is projected to result in revenue losses of 0.3 per cent of GDP. The programme includes several measures aimed at raising compliance and expanding the tax base.

Public service reforms have been stepped up. There are new wage-setting guidelines, terms and conditions of service for top management are being streamlined, and merit will be the key determinant for promotion. The monetary programme is designed to reduce underlying inflation to 3.5 per cent largely through reserve money targeting, with broad money as the intermediate target and open market operations as the main instrument. The programme is consistent with targeting a growth rate of reserve money of 3.8 per cent. The government will continue to implement a flexible exchange rate system, while the Central Bank's intervention in the foreign exchange market will be limited to meeting net foreign assets targets and smoothing disruptive short-term fluctuations.

Corruption in high places

Reflecting Kibaki's election platform, anti-corruption measures dominate political and structural reform. Three pieces of major legislation cover:

- the full enforcement of the ant-corruption measures in line with guidelines of the United Nations and the African Union ensuring the effectiveness of anti-corruption investigative agencies
- the adequate prosecution capacity for handling an expected expansion in corruption-related case-loads.
- systems for the annual declaration and verification of wealth, assets, and liabilities of ministers and senior public officials.

In early 2006 finance minister David Mwiraria resigned after being accused, with other senior officials, of being involved in a scam to received money for security contracts. Former anti-corruption ombudsman, John Githongo, who fled to exile in the UK in February 2005, was asked by parliament to return to Nairobi to give evidence. His report on corruption, which was leaked to the press, said that his attempts to investigate the Anglo-Leasing scandal had been blocked by four ministers, including Mr Mwiraria.

Politics

Leading the opposition to the long-time ruling Kanu, Mwai Kibaki and his Narc won a landslide victory in the December 2002 elections. The constitution barred his predecessor, Kanu leader Daniel arap Moi, from standing for re-election. Kibaki came to power on promises to fight corruption, but two years into his presidency, crime and corruption were widespread and the economy remained weak. A poll suggested that many Kenyans thought that life was worse under the Narc government than under Moi. An economist, Kibaki served as finance minister and vice president in the 1970s and 1980s. He left Kanu in 1991 and founded the Democratic Party. His victory marked the end of almost 40 years of uninterrupted rule by Kanu, and it was third time lucky for Kibaki, who lost two elections in the 1990s.

He was born in 1931 and is a member of Kenya's largest tribe, the Kikuyu. He studied in Uganda and Britain before

KEY INDICATORS — Kenya

	Unit	2000	2001	2002	2003	2004
Population	m	29.30	30.80	31.26	32.39	33.52
Gross domestic product (GDP)	US$bn	8.82	10.20	10.40	14.30	*15.60
GDP per capita	US$	301	337	331	385	482
GDP real growth	%	-0.3	1.2	1.2	1.9	3.1
Inflation	%	6.2	0.8	2.0	3.6	11.5
Exports (fob) (goods)	US$m	1,733.4	1,879.0	1,740.0	2,411.0	2,589.0
Imports (fob) (goods)	US$m	3,044.0	3,393.0	3,140.0	3,564.0	4,190.0
Balance of trade	US$m	-1,270.6	-1,514.0	-1,390.0	-1,153.0	-1,601.0
Current account	US$m	-23.8	-359.0	-243.0	-25.0	-580.0
Foreign debt	US$bn	6.3	6.0	6.2	5.7	6.8
Total reserves minus gold	US$m	897.7	1,064.9	1,068.0	1,481.9	1,519.3
Foreign exchange	US$m	881.2	1,048.1	1,050.0	1,461.0	1,499.0
Exchange rate	per US$	76.18	78.56	77.99	76.79	77.37

* estimated figure

joining the push for Kenya's independence in the 1960s. He became an MP in 1963.

Risk assessment

Economic	Poor, improving
Political	Poor, improving
Regional stability	Stable
Stock market	Negligible

COUNTRY PROFILE

Historical profile
Following the troubled Mau Mau years of the 1950s and the struggle to win independence from a then reluctant Britain and an even more reluctant white settler minority, Kenya managed to establish some sort of economic and political stability, despite a number of crises. Since independence, Kenya was run mostly by a Kikuyu hierarchy with one or two non-Kikuyus taking leading roles from time to time, perhaps the most notable being former President Daniel arap Moi, who demonstrated remarkable political durability.

From the mid-nineteenth century British interest in the region grew, in 1895 Kenya was declared a British protectorate, and a crown colony in 1920. White settlers established large farms from early in the twentieth century.
1944 The Kenyan African Union (KAU) was formed to voice local demands for the return of native lands.
1947 KAU was led by Jomo Kenyatta, a prominent member of the Kikuyu tribe.
1952 A state of emergency was announced in response to guerrilla activity by the Kikuyu-led secret society, the Mau Mau. More than 13,500 Africans were killed during the uprising, compared to less than 100 Europeans.
1953 The KAU was suspended. Kenyatta was detained.
1957 Africans were elected to the Legislative Council and offered ministerial posts.
1960 A new constitution gave Africans a majority in the Legislative Council. The KAU split: the Kenya African National Union (Kanu) (which had a strong Kikuyu and Luo membership) and the Kenya African Democratic Union (Kadu) were established.
1961 Kenyatta was freed and became president of Kanu and leader of an all-party African government.
1963 The Republic of Kenya was proclaimed and Kenyatta became president.
1964 Kadu was dissolved.
1978 Jomo Kenyatta died and was succeeded as president by Daniel arap Moi.
1979, 1983 and 1988 Only Daniel arap Moi stood in the presidential elections and was elected unopposed.
1992 After a lengthy period in, effectively, a one-party state, multi-party elections were held and President Moi was re-elected.
1997 President Moi and Kanu won the presidential and parliamentary elections.
1998 Terrorists blew up the US embassy in Nairobi, 244 people were killed and over 4,000 people were injured.
2001 President Daniel arap Moi appointed the opposition National Development Party (NDP) leader, Raila Odinga, to his 26-member cabinet, forming Kenya's first coalition government. International aid was withheld by the IMF when the government failed to implement anti-corruption measures.
2002 The NDP and Kanu announced a merger in the run-up to the general election. Uhuru Kenyatta became Kanu's presidential candidate, leading to a wave of defections, including Raila Odinga. Emilio Mwai Kibaki of the opposition, National Rainbow Coalition (Narc), won the presidential elections with 62.3 per cent of the vote.
2003 A draft constitution was presented to parliament, proposing a number of reforms.
2004 The deadline for the enactment of the long-awaited new constitution, which proposed restricting presidential powers and creating a post of prime minister, was missed. In a corruption survey Kenya was rated 129 worst, out of 146, by the watchdog, Transparency International, which said the problem remained 'rampant'.
2005 A referendum on constitutional changes held on 22 November was lost by the government. On 23 November, President Kibaki dismissed his entire cabinet. President Kibaki named a new cabinet on 7 December. On 21 December Justice and Constitutional Affairs minister, Martha Karua, was asked to prepare a bill for a new constitution.

Political structure
Constitution
The constitution was promulgated in 1963. In 1997, a number of constitutional changes took place; these allowed the formation of a coalition government, the review of the constitution by an independent commission and increased the number of directly elected seats in the Kenyan National Assembly from 188 to 210. A further 12 seats are nominated by the government.

A constitutional amendment affirming the National Assembly's supremacy and curbing the powers of the presidency was approved in November 1999. This removed the president's right to appoint the clerk of the house, enabling the legislature to appoint and dismiss the clerk, who is no longer answerable to the president's office. The clerk manages everything from the National Assembly's agenda to its budget.

The country is divided into seven provinces run by provincial commissioners appointed by the president. The provinces are divided into districts run by district commissioners. Towns and districts have municipal and country councils, which are partly elected and partly nominated, but the commissioner has wider powers than the councils. The Nairobi area has a separate government-appointed city commission.

As of October 2004, the draft constitution awaits enactment.
Form of state
Republic
The executive
Executive power in Kenya is in the hands of the president, assisted by the vice president and cabinet, both named by the president.
National legislature
The unicameral Bunge (National Assembly) has 222 members: 210 elected in single-seat constituencies for a five-year term and 12 members appointed by the president.
Legal system
Kenya's legal system is based on English common law, Islamic law and tribal law, with a High Court and Court of Appeal. The Chief Justice of the Court of Appeal is appointed by the president.
Last elections
27 December 2002 (presidential and parliamentary)
Results: Presidential: Mwai Kibaki was elected with 63 per cent of the vote, Uhuru Kenyatta 30 per cent.
Parliamentary: the opposition, Narc, won 124 seats out of 210, Kanu 64 and Ford-People 14; turnout was 55.9 per cent.
Next elections
December 2007 (presidential and parliamentary)

Political parties
Ruling party
National Rainbow Coalition (Narc) (elected 27 Dec 2002)
Main opposition party
Kenya African National Union (Kanu)

Population
33.52 million (2004)
Ethnic make-up
Kenya is a multi-cultural society. Most of Kenya's people belong to 13 ethnic groups although there are a further 27 smaller groups. The majority of Kenyans belong to Bantu tribes such as the Kikuyu (22 per cent), Luhya (14 per cent) and Kamba (11 per cent). The Luo (13 per cent) are of Nilotic origin, as are the

smaller Kalenjin (12 per cent), Maasai, Turkana and others.

The Kikuyu live in the central highlands and have traditionally been dominant in commerce and politics, although this is changing. A small European settler population remains in the highlands, involved in farming and commerce. In the north live the Somalis and the nomadic Hamitic peoples (Turkana, Rendille and Samburu); Kamba and Maasai peoples are concentrated in the south and eastern lowlands, and the Luo live around Lake Victoria.

Religions
Protestant (38 per cent), Roman Catholic (28 per cent), animist (26 per cent), Muslim (6 per cent), others (including small Hindu, Sikh and Jain minorities) (2 per cent).

Education
Education has expanded rapidly since independence in 1963. The number of primary schools has more than doubled, while that of secondary schools has increased eighteen-fold. Enrolment at primary schools has declined by 20 per cent since 1980, when the gross enrolment rate was 115 per cent (including repeaters).

Primary education begins at the age of six and is provided free of charge at state schools, however the lack of state funds compels schools to charge fees for books, electricity, water and upkeep, forcing children of poor families to either abandon learning early on or develop an erratic attendance record.

It has been estimated by Oxfam that 75 per cent of children aged six to 11 will enrol for school by 2015.

Secondary school enrolment has grown since 1980, when it was 20 per cent, but still covers only a small proportion of the relevant age group.

The present government, elected in December 2002, has pledged to introduce universal, free and compulsory primary education, an aim which will require higher levels of expenditure then currently spent.

Literacy rate: 88 per cent and 75 per cent, adult male and female rates respectively; adult rates (World Bank).

Enrolment rate: 85 per cent gross primary enrolment of the relevant age group (including repetitions); 24 per cent gross secondary enrolment (World Bank).

Pupils per teacher: 31 in primary schools.

Health
Annual total expenditure on healthcare by government amounts to 1.2 per cent of GDP.

Improved water sources are available to 48 per cent of the population.

HIV/Aids
The strategy to limit the impact of HIV/Aids in Kenya has become embroiled in non-medical issues concerning the allegations of government corruption and the prerequisites imposed by international donors before funds can be spent. In February 2005 the health ministry acknowledged that US$54 million of the US$70 million offered by the US had not been spent on HIV/Aids programmes as intended. Together with the US, other donors have wanted an agency to monitor and audit spending before funds are spent; the health ministry said that the agency was now operational. US funding is also predicated on the purchase of brand-named anti-retroviral drugs – at three-times the price of their generic counterparts.

The number of HIV positive cases have fell from a high of 4.5 million in 2000 to 2.1 million in 2004, and deaths from Aids dropped from 800 per day to 300 per day. HIV testing also improved with a 10-fold increase between 2002–04. Kenyan businesses were rated as best in the region for having HIV prevention programmes and providing their workers with condoms.

However the picture is not wholly positive, while rates of infections in urban areas have declined, infection figures for rural areas have yet to peak.

The annual loss in terms of GDP per capita growth are projected to be 1.3 per cent per annum between 2000–10. Households, in which one family member dies of Aids, are estimated to lose between 49–78 per cent of their annual income.

Kenya's Population Council has reported that many women surveyed, knowing they were HIV positive had not disclosed their condition to their partners for fear of violence or abandonment.

The Kenyan government's annual expenditure on HIV/Aids amounts to 6.5 per cent of the annual healthcare budget.

HIV prevalence: 6.7 per cent aged 15–49 in 2003 (World Bank)
Life expectancy: 45.4 years (World Bank)
Fertility rate/Maternal mortality rate: 4.8 births per woman; maternal mortality 590 per 100,000 live births (World Bank).
Infant mortality rate: 79 per 1,000 live births (World Bank)
Head of population per physician/bed: 0.13 doctors per 1,000 people.

Welfare
Approximately 47 per cent of the total population is under 15 years. Around 50 per cent of the population is thought to live on less than US$1 a day. Around 80 per cent of the population is at risk from drought, famine and HIV/Aids.

A social security system, administered separately from the government budget, covers only government employees and workers in the small modern sector of the economy. The welfare system is financed by the National Social Security Fund (NSSF), set up in 1965. The NSSF has approximately 2.7 million members. In theory, social security contributions are compulsory and are deducted from wages at source. Deductions range from one-thirtieth to one-tenth of earnings. The employer pays half of each employee's contribution. In practice, few families or small businesses enrol their servants or workers. In November 2001, President Moi announced the establishment of a mandatory National Social Health Insurance (NSHI) scheme that would cover all Kenyans.

Social security benefits are limited to survivor's benefit (paid on the death of contributor), invalidity benefit, withdrawal benefit (a fixed sum paid on retirement) and an emigration grant. There is no unemployment benefit. Every Kenyan is entitled to supplementary health benefit under the National Hospital Insurance scheme, founded in 1966.

Main cities
Nairobi (capital, estimated population 2.5 million in 2004, some 1,650 metres above sea-level), Mombasa (712,600), Nakuru (333,800), Kisumu (275,100), Eldoret (246,900), Nyeri (218,800).

Languages spoken
KiSwahili is the lingua franca. In addition, most tribes have their own language. English is universally used in business and spoken by most people in the tourist industry. Other languages are Gikuyu, Kiluhya, Dholuo, Kikamba, Maasai and Somali.

Official language/s
KiSwahili and English

Media
Press
Newspaper distribution is limited to large towns and a low level of literacy means that readership is small.

Dailies: The principal daily newspapers are *Daily Nation* (owned by the Aga Khan), *East African Standard*, *Taifa Leo*, *Kenya Times* and *Mombasa Times*.
Weeklies: Weeklies and Sunday newspapers include *Sunday Nation*, *Sunday Standard*, *Sunday Times*, *Post on Sunday*, *Star*, *Herald*, *Dispatch*, *The East African* and *Kenya Leo*.
Business: Business publications are *Business Africa* and *Business Chronicle*.
Periodicals: There are a number of general and specialised periodicals.

Broadcasting

Radio: State-run Kenya Broadcasting Corporation (KBC) operates extensive national services in KiSwahili, English, Hindi and numerous African languages. Radio is listened to by over 66 per cent of adults.

Television: KBC operates one channel for 126 hours per week. The commercial service is in KiSwahili and English.

A satellite channel, Kenya Television Network (KTN) was launched by Kenya Times Media Trust in 1990. KTN operates 24 hours per day and can only be viewed in the Nairobi area.

Television is watched by only around a sixth of households.

Advertising

Advertising in Kenya is widespread and sophisticated. It is available in print, on television and the radio and outdoor posters.

Economy

Kenya is a predominantly rural, low income economy, and heavily indebted to international lenders. Seventy-five per cent of its land area is arid or semi-arid, leading to high concentrations of population, notably in the large shanty towns that skirt the major cities such as Nairobi. Agriculture dominates employment, with at least 60 per cent of the population engaging in subsistence farming yet only contributing around 2 per cent to total GDP. Available arable land is scarce and output depends on a climate which frequently brings drought, as in 2005.

Despite this, Kenya probably has the most developed economy in East Africa and is well placed to take advantage of the successful Structural Adjustment Programmes (SAPs) taking place in Tanzania and Uganda. Industrial activity is more diversified and includes more private sector involvement than in neighbouring countries. Industries include food processing, tobacco, beverages and transport. There is a strong service sector, mainly tourism and financial services, which contributes the bulk of GDP and is a major source of employment and foreign exchange.

The economy has made moderate progress, aided by a domestic austerity programme, but population growth threatens to overtake economic advances. Large current account deficits have been partly funded by foreign borrowing.

After a sluggish period, the economy has begun to pick up, with GDP increasing from 1.9 per cent in 2003 to 3.1 per cent in 2004 and expected to grow further in 2005.

Kenya's biggest problem for several years has been the level of corruption, in both government and business. This has resulted in several suspensions of aid from international donors (the latest by the UK and US in early 2006).

External trade

On 31 December 2002, the US approved Kenya as being eligible for tariff preferences under the African Growth and Opportunities Act (AGOA). The legislation requires that countries are only eligible for greater access to US markets provided they have made continued progress toward a market-based economy, the rule of law, free trade, poverty reduction and the protection of workers' rights. This process is reviewed annually.

Imports

Principal imports are machinery and transport equipment, petroleum products, motor vehicles, iron and steel, resins and plastics.

Main sources: UAE (13.2 per cent total, 2004), Saudi Arabia (9.6 per cent), South Africa (9.3 per cent), US (8.0 per cent), UK (7.2 per cent), China (6.7 per cent), Japan (5.4 per cent), India (4.9 per cent)

Exports

Principal merchandise exports are tea (typically 28 per cent of total), horticultural products and coffee. Other exports include petroleum products, fruit and vegetables, cement and sisal.

Main destinations: Uganda (12.8 per cent total, 2004), UK (11.6 per cent), US (10.4 per cent), The Netherlands (8.3 per cent), Pakistan (5.1 per cent), Egypt (4.7 per cent), Tanzania (4.3 per cent)

Agriculture

Farming

Agriculture accounted for around 16 per cent of GDP in 2004. The sector generates 60 per cent of export earnings and gives employment to 62 per cent of the workforce. Less than 20 per cent of Kenya's land surface is arable. There is an acute shortage of arable land and uneven distribution has resulted in most farmers working plots of two hectares or less. Population growth and rapid urbanisation place increasing pressure on food production and distribution to meet demand at affordable prices. In addition, there is an ecological risk to some of the most fertile areas of western and central Kenya, which are already severely overpopulated. Given the pressure on the land, increased food production depends on the development of new high-yielding crops.

The principal cash crops are tea, coffee (mainly arabica grown by smallholders), sugar, cotton, pyrethrum, sisal, tobacco, pineapples and wattle. Kenya produces high quality coffee, an average of one million bags per annum. In 2005 the government relaxed the rules under which coffee farmers could sell their crops to agents rather than to national auction houses. Production of coffee has dropped from 118,000 tonnes in 1987 to 50,000 tonnes in 2003 and the changes are expected in increase competition and farmer's income. Horticultural produce is increasingly important and it is the second-largest export earner after tea with flowers making up the largest share (close to 40,000 tonnes).

Primary and processed agricultural products account for over 55 per cent of export earnings. Subsistence farming comprises more than half of output. Maize is the most important food crop. Sorghum, cassava, beans and fruit are also grown. Inadequate storage facilities, little irrigation, recurrent drought and lack of incentives and land have restricted growth.

The government's goal during the 1990s was to maintain at least 5 per cent annual growth in agricultural output to the end of the century. However, production has been consistently behind these targets, achieving only 2.9 per cent in the decade since 1995. Population has outpaced food production, the shortfall having to be met through imports mainly fro Asia. The estimated crop production for 2004 included: 2,708,925 tonnes (t) cereals in total, 2,138,425t maize, 4,660,995t sugar cane, 300,000t wheat, 630,000t cassava, 1,000,000t potatoes, 580,000t sweet potatoes, 120,000t sorghum, *210,000t bananas, *830,000t plantains, 560,000t pulses, 2,230,000t roots and tubers, *40,390t citrus fruit, *260,000t tomatoes, *39,262t oilcrops, *20,000t tobacco, *64,500t green coffee, 295,000t tea, 118,000t mangoes, 600,000t pineapples, *5,000t cotton lint, 21,500t treenuts, 2,091,040t fruit in total, 1,218,200t vegetables in total. Livestock production included: 497,335t meat in total, 318,655t beef, 19,800t camel meat, 18,525t pig meat, 34,200t lamb, 36,300t goat meat, *54,000t poultry, *60,720t eggs, 2,965,700t milk, 21,500t honey, 40,950t cattle hides, 6,840t sheepskins.

* estimate

Fishing

Fishing resources remain underexploited. Kenya has a coastline of 680km as well as territorial waters in Lake Victoria and Lake Takana. The annual marine catch is around 4,000 tonnes per year (tpy) while the freshwater catch is around 155,000tpy. The sector is operating well under capacity. Analysts believe that the sustainable level of tuna fishing alone is 200,000tpy.

Forestry

Kenya has only 2 per cent of forest cover. Deforestation is a major problem. There was an annual average decrease of 93,000ha of forest cover between 1990 and 2000. A Permanent Presidential

Kenya

Commission on Soil Conservation and Afforestation was created in 1980 to correct the situation.

Fuelwood and charcoal meet more than 75 per cent of the domestic energy requirement. The government is attempting to protect timber resources which are being depleted because of wood fuel demands. The need for land is placing increasing pressure on Kenya's forestry reserves. The government estimates that only 70 per cent of Kenya's wood fuel demands are met by regenerative growth.

Industry and manufacturing

Industry accounted for around 20 per cent of GDP in 2004, with manufacturing contributing over 13 per cent.

Foreign investment, particularly from the UK, Japan and US, plays a significant role. Emphasis is on developing joint venture, export-oriented industries and encouraging greater utilisation of local raw materials and other inputs. Large sections of industry continue to operate well below full capacity as a result of import controls, rising costs and marketing difficulties. Rainfall can also have an impact on the sector's performance, with power shortages and reduced agricultural production during drought causing knock-on effects for manufacturing.

The manufacturing sector has been affected by power shortages, a fall in the growth of foreign direct investment (FDI) and rising costs of fuel imports. However, it remains the most developed manufacturing sector in East Africa.

Principal industries include food and tobacco processing, beverages, chemicals, machinery and transport equipment, textiles, glass, vehicle assembly and construction materials.

Tourism

Tourism is the country's largest foreign exchange earner and is expected to contribute 5.3 per cent to GDP in 2005. Kenya's tourist assets are its wildlife, mostly accessible through a system of parks and reserves, extensive white sand beaches protected by coral reefs, and dramatic scenery from deserts to tropical rain forest. Tourism is recognised as a means of poverty reduction and private sector growth. To this end, Kenya and the EU formed the Kenya Trust Fund in 2002 to finance tourism development and the marketing and promotion of tourism.

Since 2004, the sector has recovered from the damage it suffered as a result of terrorist attacks in 1998 and 2002. Vigorous promotion, together with the lifting of warning alerts by other governments, has resulted in an escalation in the number of visitors mainly from Europe and Asia in 2004 and 2005. The growth of the market has exceeded the availability of accommodation. Attention is being turned to developing Kenya from a mass market to a high-value destination.

Mining

Mining accounts for just 1 per cent of GDP. The sector is dominated by the production of industrial minerals such as soda ash, flourspar, kaolin and some gemstones. Gold is also produced in small quantities by artisanal gold miners. The government's policy is to encourage private sector participation in further exploration, prospecting and development of the mineral resources sector.

The most promising mining prospects are within the licences held by the Canadian mining company Tiomin Resources for deposits covering four areas – Mambrui, Sokoke, Vipingo and Kwale – which hold 12 per cent of the world's rutile and ilmenite resources.

Hydrocarbons

Kenya oil requirements are met by imports, which accounted for around 22.5 per cent of total imports in 2005. Kenya imports about two million tonnes of crude oil per year, mainly from the United Arab Emirates, but recovers some foreign exchange by exporting refined productsto Uganda, Rwanda, Zambia and Tanzania. Kenya has a 90,000bpd capacity oil refinery at Mombasa, but even after investment in improvements the refinery still produces around 60 per cent below capacity.

There has been limited exploration for oil since 1954, mainly in the Rift Valley and the north-eastern provinces, without tangible results. Interest has been ignited by discoveries in Sudan, which shares Kenya's geology, and by the rise in world oil prices. Companies from a number of countries, including China, are becoming increasingly involved in the possibility of locating reserves of oil and also gas and the search is also being extended offshore to the Lamu basin.

Kenya does not produce or import natural gas.

Kenya has plans to diversify its fuel sources for electricity generation and is searching for coal in the Mui and Mutitu basins in Mwingi and Kitui districts.

Energy

Kenya has a total generating capacity of 1,032MW. A further 423MW by 2006 is planned to meet increasing demand caused by a growing economy. Hydroelectric and geothermal power supplies around 25 per cent of energy needs. Electricity is supplied inland by hydroelectric plants in the Tana river basin, by the geothermal station at Olkaria, and at Kipevu, on the coast, by a 75MW oil-fired plant which was opened in 1999. This is irregularly supplemented by a bulk supply of 30MW from Owen Falls in Uganda, under a 50-year agreement signed in 1958.

In July 2004, the World Bank approved a credit of US$80 million for Kenya's energy sector recovery project, which aims to support efficient expansion of power generation capacity to meet the economy's projected supply deficits by 2006/07and to improve access to electricity to the urban poor.

Financial markets
Stock exchange

In 2005 the Nairobi Stock Exchange (NSE) had 48 equity listings with a market capitalisation of US$6 billion. The NSE is small and somewhat speculative. It was established in 1954 and is sub-Saharan Africa's fourth-largest bourse. It originally operated as an association of stockbrokers with no trading floor until October 1991. The introduction of the trading floor has led to a substantial increase in trading volumes and dramatic upward movement in the various indexes. In 1995, foreign investors were allowed back into the NSE for the first time in 30 years. The NSE has been instrumental in enabling the public and private sectors in Kenya to raise large amounts of capital for expansion projects and for the financing of new businesses.

Banking and insurance

Kenya contains a thriving community of foreign banks, which were attracted during the 1970s and 1980s by its reputation for political and commercial stability, good telecommunications infrastructure and the large number of multinationals based in the country. However, the sector is plagued by high levels of non-performing loans which threaten to undermine banking liquidity, affecting the wider economy.

Central bank
Central Bank of Kenya
Main financial centre
Nairobi

Time

GMT plus three hours

Geography

Kenya lies almost exactly astride the equator on the east coast of Africa. It is bounded by Ethiopia and Sudan to the north, Uganda and Lake Victoria to the west, Tanzania to the south and Somalia and the Indian Ocean to the east.

From the Indian Ocean, the land rises gradually through dry bush to the arable land of the highlands. The highest peak is Mount Kenya at 5,200 metres. The west of the country is dissected by the Great Rift Valley, partly filled by a chain of lakes.

Climate
The climate is tropical in low-lying districts, especially along the coast, but is more temperate on the plateau and in the highlands. Kenya has two rainy seasons when temperatures can fall sharply: the long rains from April to June and the short rains in October and November. The hottest month is February, with temperatures of 20–30 degrees Celsius (C), while the coolest month is July, with temperatures of 11–22 degrees C. Nairobi, at an altitude of 1,661 metres, has a mean annual temperature of 17 degrees C and annual rainfall averaging 864mm.

Dress codes
A lightweight suit, collar and tie or other formal clothing should be worn for business meetings. Despite a hot tropical climate, nights can be cool and it is advisable to have a sweater to cover day wear, which should be light cotton casual at the coast. Warmer clothing is needed especially in June and July. Evening dress should normally be smart casual. Nairobi is considerably cooler than Mombasa.

Entry requirements
Passports
Required by all, except holders of *Kinderausweis* Identity Card with photograph, issued by Germany. Passports must be valid for six months from date of entry.
Visa
Required by all. Some exceptions are allowed and some foreign nationals may obtain a visitor's visa at the port of entry, while others must apply well in advance. Visit www.kenyaembassy.com/consular/visa.htm for further information and a full list of each category. Business visitors require a business letter of intent with a full itinerary and an invitation from a local company or organisation to be submitted with the application.
Currency advice/regulations
Import of local currency up to Ksh200 is allowed. No restrictions on foreign currency imports.
Export of local currency is prohibited. Unlimited foreign currency can be exported. Tanzanian and Ugandan currency is only negotiable in the form of traveller's cheques. US dollar or other hard currency traveller's cheques are recommended.

Health (for visitors)
Mandatory precautions
Yellow fever vaccination certificate if arriving from an infected area.
Advisable precautions
Yellow fever, typhoid, tetanus, hepatitis A, meningitis and polio vaccinations. Malaria prophylaxis necessary for coastal and other lower altitude regions. Water precautions should be taken – bilharzia is present. Vaccinations for rabies are recommended if travelling to rural areas.

Hotels
There is a wide range available in main centres. It is advisable to book well in advance during peak season (November–April).

Credit cards
Major cards are widely accepted.

Public holidays
Fixed dates
1 Jan (New Year's Day), 1 May (Labour Day), 1 Jun (Madaraka Day), 10 Oct (Moi Day), 20 Oct (Kenyatta Day), 12 Dec (Independence/Jamhuri Day), 25–26 Dec (Christmas Holiday).
Holidays falling on a Sunday are observed the following Monday.
Variable dates
Good Friday, Easter Monday, Eid al Fitr.

Working hours
Banking
Mon–Fri: 0900–1400. Open first and last Sat in each month 0900–1100.
Barclays Bank, Kenyatta Avenue, Nairobi, open daily for foreign exchange until 1600.
Airport banks are open until midnight every day.
Business
Mon–Fri: 0800–1300, 1400–1700; Sat: 0830–1200/1230. Mombasa offices normally open and close half-an-hour earlier.
Government
Mon–Fri: 0800–1300, 1400–1700; Sat: 0830–1200/1230. Mombasa offices normally open and close half-an-hour earlier.
Shops
Sat: 0830–1300. Many shops open outside these hours.

Electricity supply
230/240V AC, 50 cycles. Subject to power surges outside main centres. Sockets are usually three-pin square (British type).

Social customs/useful tips
Personal contact is an important way of doing business in Kenya.
Bureaucracy can be frustratingly slow, although persistence pays. Going in person to the relevant office is often the best way of getting things done. Government and commercial offices are within easy walking distance of the main hotels.
Outside the major towns local customs vary from place to place. In the game parks and bush, some tribes do not like being photographed, although in areas where tourism is more developed, some tribe members will allow photographs for a fee. Visitors to game parks should not leave their vehicles without permission from the guide. There is a large Arab influence on the coast and most hotels display government signs saying nudity is banned. Topless bathing for women is, however, tolerated in areas where there are large concentrations of hotels. Kenyans are friendly and open, and the greeting, *jambo*, will be returned with a smile.
The purchase or export of ivory is banned. When the president is driving past, all bystanders along the road are required to stand still until he has passed. It is prohibited to photograph the president or his residence, military, police or related installations.

Security
Security is not a problem in the major towns during the day but flashy displays of jewellery are not recommended. Do not carry large amounts of cash.
Nairobi is practically deserted after 2200. Walking around the African quarters of town without a guide or in the shanty towns around the capital is not advised. Visitors are advised to avoid political meetings and demonstrations.
Incidents of armed car-hijacking are prevalent in Nairobi and Mombasa.
Do not attempt to escape from hijackers or resist their demands.

Getting there
Air
Kenya Airways announced in January 2006 that it would start direct flights to Paris in July.
National airline: Kenya Airways (privatised)
International airport/s: Nairobi – Jomo Kenyatta International (NBO), 17km from city, duty-free shop, bar, restaurant, buffet, bank, post office, shops, car hire.
Other airport/s: Mombasa – Moi International (MBA), 13km south-east of city, duty-free shop, bar, restaurant, bank, post office, shops, car hire. Medium-sized airports have also been developed at Eldoret, Kisumu and Malindi.
Airport tax: There is no airport tax.
Surface
Road: An all-weather road links Nairobi to Addis Ababa, Ethiopia, and there is a 590km road link between Kitale and Juba (Sudan).
In rural areas, some of the unsurfaced roads can be difficult in wet weather.
You can travel by road to Uganda, Ethiopia, Sudan and Tanzania. Entry by these routes can be difficult. Regulations and conditions should be checked with Kenyan authorities before travelling.
Rail: The Kenya Railways system comprises approximately 1,920km of one metre gauge single track. A 1,085km main line runs from the port of Mombasa through Nairobi, Nakuru and Eldoret to the Ugandan border. There are departures daily, offering modern, first- and

second-class service from Nairobi-Mombasa; the overnight service is popular. The journey time is approximately 14 hours.

Trains often run late, but are fairly comfortable. It is advisable to book sleeping compartments in advance.

Main port/s: Mombasa

Getting about

National transport

Air: Kenya Airways operates an extensive and regular service linking Mombasa, Malindi, Kisumu and other major centres with Nairobi.

Local light aircraft companies, such as Airkenya Aviation and Eagle Aviation, fly regular services to smaller airfields, such as Lamu, a tourist attraction on the coast. Charter flights are also available to game reserves, such as Maasai Mara, and main centres. The major charter companies include Africair, Caspair, Pioneer, Sunbird, Air Kenya, operating from Nairobi's Wilson Airport.

Road: The growth in road transportation has led to overloading of some highways, and both the maintenance and improvement of these routes have been neglected. This also applies to roads which come under the jurisdiction of town authorities. Nearly all main towns are connected by good surfaced roads. In rural areas some of the unsurfaced roads can be difficult in wet weather.

Long-distance (Peugeot) taxi service operates between towns. Cars can be shared, although it is not generally recommended.

Buses: Several major bus companies operate fast coach services on all major routes, centred on Nairobi.

Rail: There are departures daily, with modern, first- and second-class service from Nairobi-Mombasa; the overnight service is popular. Journey time is approximately 14 hours. Trains often run late, but are fairly comfortable. It is advisable to book sleeping compartments in advance.

In May 2003, it was estimated that US$500 million would be needed to rehabilitate the railway track.

City transport

Taxis: Available in most major towns. Some licensed taxis are metered and often shared, with fares according to time and distance. However, fares for long trips should be agreed in advance. Taxis cannot be hailed in the street. A 10 per cent tip is usual. The taxis of companies that run fleets, such as Kenatco, are the most reliable. Most of the older yellow band taxis are unmetered and fares must be negotiated.

Buses, trams & metro: Good and fairly cheap services operate in Nairobi and Mombasa. Also the Matatu – minibuses and vans; these are unregulated and can be overcrowded – not recommended for visitors.

Car hire

Can be hired from travel operators and hotels in Nairobi, Mombasa and Malindi. International driving licence accepted, or national driving licence endorsed at a Kenyan police station or at the Registrar of Motor Vehicles in Nairobi (valid for 90 days).

BUSINESS DIRECTORY

The addresses listed below are a selection only. While World of Information makes every endeavour to check these addresses, we cannot guarantee that changes have not been made, especially to telephone numbers and area codes. We would welcome any corrections.

Telephone area codes

The international direct dialling (IDD) code for Kenya is +254, followed by area code and subscriber's number:

Eldoret	53	Malindi	42
Garissa	46	Mombasa	41
Kajiado	45	Nairobi	20
Kericho	52	Naivasha	50
Kisumu	57	Nakuru	51
Kwale	40	Voi	43

Chambers of Commerce

Kenya National Chamber of Commerce & Industry, Ufanisi House, Haile Selassie Avenue, PO Box 47024, Nairobi (tel: 220-866; fax: 340-664; e-mail: kncci@swiftkenya.com).

Banking

African Banking Corporation Ltd, PO Box 46452, Mezzanine Floor, ABC-Bank, Koingange Street, Nairobi (tel: 223-922, 251-540/1, 226-712, 248-978; fax: 222-437).

Barclays Bank of Kenya Ltd, PO Box 30120, Barclays Plaza, Loita St, Nairobi (tel: 214-270, 313-405; fax: 213-915, 215-418).

The Co-operative Bank of Kenya Ltd, PO Box 48231, Union Towers, Kenya-Re Plaza - Taifa Rd, Moi Ave, Nairobi (tel: 225-579, 228-453/7, 251290/9; fax: 229-38, 246-635, 227-747).

Commercial Bank of Africa Ltd, Commercial Bank Building, Standard/Wabera Streets, Nairobi (tel: 228-881; fax: 335-827, 340-157).

Development Bank of Kenya Ltd, PO Box 30483, Finance House, Loita Street, Nairobi (tel: 340-401, 340-402, 340-403; fax: 338-426).

Imperial Bank Ltd, PO Box 44905, 8th Floor, IPS Bldg, Kimathi St, Nairobi (tel: 252-175/6/7/8, 252-184/5, 225-060; fax: 230-994, 250-137).

Investments & Mortgages Bank Ltd, PO Box 30238, I & M Bank House, 2nd Ngong Avenue, Nairobi (tel: 711-994-8, 310-105-7; fax: 713-757, 716-372).

Kenya Commercial Bank Ltd, PO Box 48400, Moi Avenue, Nairobi (tel: 339-441; fax: 215-565).

National Bank of Kenya Ltd, PO Box 72866, National Bank Building, Harambee Avenue, Nairobi.

Standard Chartered Bank Kenya Ltd, PO Box 30003, Stanbank House, Moi Avenue, Nairobi (tel: 330-200, 331-210; fax: 214-086).

Central bank

Central Bank of Kenya, PO Box 60000, Haile Selassie Avenue, 00200 Nairobi, Kenya (tel: 246-000; fax: 219-719; e-mail: info@centralbank.go.ke).

Travel information

AA of Kenya, PO Box 40087, Nairobi.Kenya Aviation, PO Box 30357, Wilson Airport, Nairobi (tel: 502-421, 501-601; fax: 500-845).

Kenya Airways, Kenyatta International Airport, PO Box 19002, Nairobi (tel: 822-171; fax: 822-707).

Kenya Railways, PO Box 30121, Nairobi (tel: 221-211).

Ministry of tourism

Ministry of Tourism and Wildlife, Utali House, Uhuru Highway, PO Box 30027, Nairobi (tel: 331-030; fax: 217-604).

National tourist organisation offices

The Chief Tourist Officer, Ministry of Tourism, PO Box 54666, Nairobi.

Ministries

Ministry of Agriculture, Livestock Development and Marketing, Kilimo House, Cathedral Road, PO Box 30028, Nairobi (tel: 718-870; fax: 725-774).

Ministry of Commerce and Industry, Co-operative House, Haile Selassie Avenue, PO Box 30430, Nairobi (tel: 340-010, 340-224; fax: 218-845).

Ministry of Energy, Nyayo House, Kenyatta Avenue, PO Box 30582, Nairobi (tel: 333-551).

Ministry of the Environment and Natural Resources, Kencom House, Moi Avenue, PO Box 30126, Nairobi (tel: 229-261).

Ministry of Finance, Treasury House, Harambee Avenue, PO Box 30007, Nairobi (tel: 338-111; fax: 330-426).

Ministry of Information and Broadcasting, Jogoo House 'A', Taifa Road, PO Box 30025, Nairobi (tel: 334-688; fax: 340-659).

Ministry of Planning and National Development, PO Box 3007, Nairobi (tel: 338-111; fax: 330-426).

Ministry of Transport and Communications, Transcom House, Ngong Road, PO Box 52692, Nairobi (tel: 729-200; fax: 726-362).

Office of the President, Harambee House, Harambee Avenue, PO Box 30510, Nairobi (tel: 227-411; fax: 723-666).

Other useful addresses

Africa Growth Fund, PO Box 34045, Nairobi (tel: 721-566; fax: 722-240).

African Project Development Facility, International House, PO Box 46534, Nairobi.

Agricultural Development Corporation, PO Box 30367, Nairobi (tel: 338-530).

Attorney-General's Office, State Law Office, Harambee Avenue, PO Box 40112, Nairobi (tel: 227-461; fax: 211-082).

British High Commission, Bruce House, Standard Street, PO Box 30465, Nairobi (tel: 335-944; fax: 333-196); Commercial Section, Upper Hill Road, PO Box 30133, Nairobi (tel: 714-699; fax: 719-082; e-mail: bhctrade@users.africaonline.co.ke).

Capital Markets Authority (CMA), Re-Insurance Plaza, Taifa Rd, PO Box 74800, Nairobi (tel: 221-910/869; fax: 216-681).

Central Police Station, University Way, Nairobi (tel: 222-222).

Central Reference Library, Ministry of Information, Department of Information, PO Box 8053 or 30025, Nairobi (tel: 223-201).

Communications Commission of Kenya (CCK), 5th Floor, Longonot Place, Kijabe Street, PO Box 14448, Nairobi 00800 (tel: 240-165, 250-173, 310-083/4; fax: 252-547; internet site: http://www.cck.go.ke).

Customs and Excise, PO Box 40160, Nairobi.

Development Finance Company of Kenya, Finance House, Loita Street, PO Box 30483, Nairobi (tel: 340-401; fax: 338-246).

East African Report on Trade and Industry, PO Box 30339, Nairobi.

Economic Development for Equatorial and Southern Africa, PO Box 56038, Nairobi (tel: 822-920/4; fax: 822-925/907).

Executive Secretariat and Technical Unit (ESTU), Anniversary Towers, University Way, 7th Floor, PO Box 34542, Nairobi (tel: 222-127/57/68; fax: 216-945).

Export Processing Zones Authority (EPZA), British American Centre, Mara Rd, PO Box 50563, Nairobi (tel: 712-800/6; fax: 713-704).

Export Promotion Council (EPC), Anniversary Towers, 1st Floor, University Way, PO Box 40247, Nairobi (tel: 228-534/5; fax: 218-013).

Federation of Kenya Employers (FKE), Argwings Kodhek Road, PO Box 48311, Nairobi (tel: 721-929; fax: 721-948).

General Post Office, Kenyatta Avenue, Nairobi.

Horticultural Crops Development Authority (HCDA), Uniafric House, Koinange St, PO Box 42601, Nairobi (tel: 337-381/3).

Industrial and Commercial Development Corporation, Uchumi House, Nkrumah Avenue, PO Box 45519, Nairobi (tel: 229-213; fax: 333-880).

Industrial Promotion Services Ltd, IPS Building, PO Box 30500, Nairobi (tel: 228-026, 728-207; fax: 214-563).

International Finance Corporation, View Park Towers, PO Box 30577, Nairobi (tel: 224-726; fax: 219-980).

Investment Promotion Centre, National Building, 8th Floor, Harambee Avenue, PO Box 55704, Nairobi (tel: 221-401/4; fax: 336-663).

Kenya Association of Manufacturers (KAM), Mpaka Rd, Westland, PO Box 30225, Nairobi (tel: 746-005/7; fax: 746-028).

Kenya Association of Tour Operators (for information on conference facilities throughout Kenya), PO Box 48461, Nairobi (tel: 227-005).

Kenya External Trade Authority, PO Box 43137, Nairobi (tel: 226-016).

Kenya Power Company Limited, Stima Plaza, Kolobot Road, PO Box 47936, Nairobi (tel: 741-181/9; fax: 337-351).

Kenya Revenue Authority, Tax Programmes and New Business Initiatives, Nairobi (tel: 715-428; fax: 715-432).

Kenya Tea Development Authority, Commonwealth House, Moi Avenue, Nairobi (tel: 221-441).

Kenyan Embassy (USA), 2249 R Street, NW, Washington DC 20008 (tel: 202-387-6101; fax: 202-462-3829; e-mail: info@kenyaembassy.com).

Kenyatta International Conference Centre, PO Box 30746, Nairobi (tel: 332-383).

Nairobi Stock Exchange, Kimathi Street, IPS Building, 2nd Floor, PO Box 43833, Nairobi (tel: 230-692; fax: 224-200).

US Embassy, Corner Moi and Haile Selassie Avenues, PO Box 30137, Nairobi (tel: 334-141; fax: 340-838).

Internet sites

Africa Business Network: http://www.ifc.org/abn

AllAfrica.com: http://allafrica.com

African Development Bank: http://www.afdb.org

Africa Online: http://www.africaonline.com

Harambee Afrika (UK business club for traders with east, central and southern Africa; includes annotated web resource list): http://www.harambee.co.uk

KenyaWeb: http://www.kenyaweb.com/

Mbendi AfroPaedia (information on companies, countries, industries and stock exchanges in Africa): http://mbendi.co.za

Kiribati

COUNTRY PROFILE

Historical profile
Micronesians from the South Pacific settled Kiribati between 200 and 500 AD. Kiribati (pronounced Kiribas) is made up of 33 low-lying coral atolls and is sub-divided into three main groups known as the Gilbert Islands, the Phoenix Islands and the Line Islands.
1892 Kiribati became part of the British colony of the Gilbert and Ellice Islands and was administered by the West Pacific High Commission in Fiji.
1942 The islands were occupied by the Japanese during World War II.
1963 Transition to independence began, with the formation of legislative and executive councils under the supervision of a British governor general.
1975 Ellice Islands seceded and formed the separate entity of Tuvalu.
1979 Became the fully independent Republic of Kiribati.
1982–91 Iremia Tabai won the first three post-independence presidential elections in 1982, 1983 and 1987. Constitutional restrictions prevented Tabai contesting the 1991 elections which were won by Teatao Teannaki.
1994 Teburoro Tito of the Mwaneaaban te Mauri Party (MMP) was elected president.
1997 China built a satellite tracking base on Kiribati's main atoll on a 15-year lease.
1998 Teburoro Tito was elected to his second term.
2001 The Pacific Islands Forum, of which Kiribati is a member, completed its negotiations to bring 14 Pacific island countries into a free trade agreement, known as the Pacific Islands Countries Trade Agreement (PICTA). The government of President Tito suffered heavy losses in the second round of parliamentary elections.
2002 Parliament passed newspaper registration laws, giving powers to ban the publication of newspapers that face complaints.
2003 Teburoro Tito won the February presidential elections. On 28 March, President Tito lost a no-confidence motion in which the opposition won 21 out of 40 votes. The ruling party, MMP, was re-elected in the general elections in May for all the seats in the House of Assembly, following its premature dissolution in March. On 4 July, Anote Tong (Boutokaan te Koaua Party) (BTK) (Pillars of Truth) was elected president. In November, Kiribati established diplomatic relations with Taiwan, but also offered to honour the lease of the satellite tracking station to China, although the possible military use of the Chinese base has divided Kiribati since its installation. China rejected Kiribati's offer and on 29 November, severed diplomatic relations with Kiribati.
2004 In January, President Anote Tong invited visiting Taiwanese Minister of Foreign Affairs, Eugene Chien, to his native Maiana, an island located east of the country's capital, Tarawa, for a festival attended by local village chiefs and tribal leaders.

Political structure
Formerly the UK Dependent Territory of the Gilbert Islands, Kiribati gained independence in 1979.

Constitution
The 1979 constitution provides for free and open elections. Kiribati elections run in two phases with a general election for MPs in the first round and then the elected members are required to put forward three candidates for a presidential election.

Form of state
Independent democratic republic; it is a member of the Commonwealth.

The executive
Executive power is exercised by a twelve-member cabinet chosen by the beretitenti (president) from the Maneaba (house of assembly). The cabinet is composed of a president, vice president and 10 ministers.
The beretitenti is head of state and head of government and is elected by the people from among three candidates nominated by the Maneaba from its ranks. The president does not act on behalf of a political group and serves a four-year term; the limit is three terms.

National legislature
The Maneaba consists of 42 representatives elected by universal adult suffrage to a four-year term and one nominee representing Banaba (most of whose inhabitants now live on the island of Rabi in Fiji). The attorney general is an ex officio member (if not already an elected member).

Last elections
4 July 2003 (presidential); 9/16 May 2003 (parliamentary).
Results: Parliamentary: the ruling MMP, won 24 seats; BTK, 16 seats.
Presidential: Anote Tong (BTK) was elected with 47.4 per cent of the vote,

KEY FACTS

Official name: Ripaberikan Kiribati (Republic of Kiribati) (pronounced Kiribas)

Head of State: President Anote Tong (Boutokaan te Koaua (BTK)) (elected 4 Jul 2003)

Head of government: President Anote Tong

Ruling party: Mwaneaban te Mauri Party (MMP)

Area: 810 square km (33 islands and atolls)

Population: 99,079 (2004)

Capital: Bairiki (on Tarawa)

Official language: I-Kiribati, English

Currency: Australian dollar (A$) = 100 cents)

Exchange rate: A$1.31 per US$ (Oct 2005)

GDP per capita: US$760 (2004)

GDP real growth: 1.80% (2004)

Inflation: 2.30% (2004)

Balance of trade: -US$38.00 million (2003)

Foreign debt: US$15.70 million (2003)

followed by his brother Harry Tong (MMP) with 43.5 per cent and Banuera Berina (Maurin Kiribati Pati (MKP)) with 9.1 per cent.

Next elections
2007 (presidential and parliamentary)

Political parties
Ruling party
Mwaneaban te Mauri Party (MMP)
Main opposition party
Boutokaan te Koaua Party (BTK)

Population
99,079 (2004)
Ethnic make-up
Predominantly Micronesian, with some Polynesian.
Religions
Roman Catholic (52 per cent), Protestant (Congregational) (40 per cent), Seventh-Day Adventist, Islam, Baha'i Faith, Latter-day Saints and Church of God.

Education
The Junior Secondary School (JSS) programme aims to provide universal access to basic secondary education. Almost all the outer islands (except Teraina and Tabuaeran) and South Tarawa have junior secondary schools.
Higher education, including both university level programmes and post-secondary vocational/technical training, is provided by the government and the regional institution, University of the South Pacific (USP). The government also operates two tertiary institutions on South Tarawa: Tarawa Technical Institute and Kiribati Teachers College.
Literacy rate: 92.2 per cent, adult rate.
Compulsory years: six to 15
Enrolment rate: 67.8 per cent gross school enrolment.

Health
Total expenditure on health is some 8.0 per cent of GDP, nearly all of which, 98.8 per cent, was government spending.

The government has collaborated with the World Health Organisation (WHO) to strengthen its primary healthcare services. WHO's technical support has brought down the infant mortality rate and increased life expectancy.
Improved water sources are available to 47 per cent of the population.
There is one general hospital in Tarawa and a number of health centres in the more populated islands. There are few doctors. Medical facilities are of the most basic kind and there are no pharmacies. Excessive alcohol consumption has become a very severe problem both socially and medically. Diabetes linked to a western diet is widespread.

HIV/Aids
There has been a significant increase in infections on Tarawa.
Life expectancy: 63.1 years (World Bank)
Fertility rate/Maternal mortality rate: 3.6 births per woman (World Bank)
Birth rate/Death rate: 31 births per 1,000 population; 8.6 deaths per 1,000 population (2003).
Infant mortality rate: 49 per 1,000 live births (World Bank)
Head of population per physician/bed: 0.3 doctors per 1,000 people. There are 165 nurses in addition to 29 medical assistants.

Welfare
The government has instituted a bonding system requiring all trained personnel to serve the country for at least the same number of years that it has funded their training. The retirement age, which was previously 50 years for all government employees, has been increased to 60 years for doctors and 55 for other categories.

Main cities
Bairiki, (capital, on Tarawa, estimated population 26,600 in 2003), Bikenibeu (on Tarawa, 7,400).

Languages spoken
English is used for official communications and is widely understood in the capital, Tarawa. It is used less on the outer islands where i-Kiribati is the norm. In the i-Kiribati language the letters 'ti' are pronounced 's' (Kiribati is pronounced Kiribas).
Official language/s
I-Kiribati, English

Media
Press
In October 2002, the Newspaper Registration Amendment Bill was passed, giving powers to a registrar to deregister and stop the publication of newspapers that face complaints.
Weeklies: *Te Uekera* is a weekly newspaper published by the Kiribati Broadcasting and Publications Authority (KBPA). The present KBPA is controlled by an independent board and is not a printing and broadcasting arm of government. The weekly publication is 90 per cent in the vernacular and is sold on the street. This newspaper is the successor to *Atoll Pioneer*, which was published by the government.
An independent weekly, *Newstar*, began publication in April 2004.
Business: *Kiribati Business Link* is published locally. Some regional business news is available from *Business Pacific* and *Islands Business*.
Periodicals: There are no newsagents and only limited copies of overseas papers and magazines are sold in shops. These include *Marshall Island Journal* and *Pacific Islands Monthly*. The Catholic Mission of Kiribati publishes regular magazines including *Te Itoi ni Kiribati*. The Kiribati Protestant Church publishes *Kaotan te Ota* which is generally irregular.
Broadcasting
Radio: The government-operated Radio Kiribati is a division of the Broadcasting and Publications Authority. It broadcasts daily for one-and-a-half hours in the morning and at lunchtime and three-and-a-half hours in the evening in the local languages.

Economy
Kiribati lacks both human and natural resources; the infrastructure is weak, the islands remote and the soil is poor and droughts frequent and this, together with a traditional land tenure structure, makes the islands unconducive to large-scale agricultural activity. However, it used to export phosphate from Banaba Island until the deposits were exhausted in 1979 and

KEY INDICATORS — Kiribati

	Unit	2000	2001	2002	2003	2004
Population	m	0.09	0.09	0.10	0.10	0.10
Gross domestic product (GDP)	US$bn	0.04	0.04	0.04	0.08	*0.06
GDP per capita	US$	571	546	609	727	760
GDP real growth	%	-1.6	1.8	1.0	2.5	1.8
Inflation	%	0.4	6.0	3.2	1.4	2.3
Exports (fob) (goods)	US$m	5.8	3.9	–	6.0	–
Imports (fob) (goods)	US$m	35.0	31.8	–	44.0	–
Balance of trade	US$m	-29.2	-27.9	-31.7	-38.0	–
Current account	US$m	4.8	1.8	-3.0	-10.0	-10.0
Exchange rate	per US$	1.66	1.82	1.86	1.55	1.28

* estimated figure

the Revenue Equalization Reserve Fund (RERF), which was financed by phosphate earnings, continues to be important to Kiribati and held over US$400 million in 2004. Income from the RERF enables the government to cover fiscal deficits and to buffer year-to-year movements on the current account. Almost all manufactured goods are imported, and with only small exports of copra, the annual trade balance is consistently in deficit (US$51.1 million in 2004). Despite this, thanks to the large foreign holdings in the RERF, official reserves remain high at some US$359.6.

Kiribati's large (around 3.5 million square kilometres – some six times the area of France) Exclusive Economic Zone (EEZ) is a major source of fishing licence revenue. Although it fell in 2002, it was still over a third of GDP in 2003. GDP growth fell in 2004 to 1.8 per cent, from 2.5 per cent in 2003, but inflation was low, copra prices were high and income from the RERF went up to A$25 million (US$34 million).

Official development assistance amounts to between US$15 million and US$20 million per year, mainly donated by Japan, the UK, Australia and New Zealand. Kirimati (Christmas) Island has been used for landings of unmanned space shuttles operated by the Japan Aerospace Exploration Agency (previously the National Space Development Agency). Japan is leasing land on Kirimati to build a spaceport, and according to the agreement will spend US$12.9 million over the period 1999–2012. Japan is also funding the building of a storage and handling area at the island's fishing port. Game fishing and birdwatching have also been attracting visitors to the island.

Kiribati's development strategy, as set out in its National Development Strategy 2004–07, covers six key sectors: economic growth, fair distribution, public sector performance, conservation of physical assets, equipping the population to manage change and the sustainable use of financial reserves by ministries. According to the Asian Development Bank (ADB), Kiribati's prospects in the medium term will be hampered by lack of private sector development, overdependence on the government, pressures of population growth and associated low youth employment opportunities. GDP is forecast to be 1.5 per cent in 2005.

External trade
Trade deficits have occurred every year since the cessation of phosphate mining in 1979.

Imports
Principal imports are fuel, machinery and transport equipment, food, manufactured goods, miscellaneous manufactures, chemicals. Imports totalled US$44 million in 2003.

Main sources: Australia (36.0 per cent total, 2004), Fiji (24.8 per cent), Japan (11 per cent), New Zealand (8.7 per cent), France (4.4 per cent)

Exports
Principal exports are copra (62 per cent), coconuts, fish, dried shark fins and seaweed. Exports totalled US$6 million in 2003.

Main destinations: France (45.1 per cent total, 2004), Japan (28.9 per cent), US (9.0 per cent), Thailand (5.4 per cent)

Agriculture
Farming
The agricultural sector accounts for about 15 per cent of GDP and around 60 per cent of exports.

Agricultural development is limited by poor soil quality. There are commercial and government-owned copra plantations on Teraina (Washington) and Tabuaeran (Fanning) islands, but peasant smallholdings are more usual. Most copra is exported to Europe by the Copra Co-operative Society (CCS).

Flour, sugar and rice are replacing the traditional breadfruit and taro in the national diet, increasing reliance on imports. Crop production in 2004 included: 103,000 tonnes (t) coconuts, 13,390t oilcrops, 2,000t taro, 5,000t bananas, 5,900t vegetables in total, 6,300t fruit in total, 9,800t roots and tubers and 230t treenuts. Livestock production included: 1,359t meat in total, 900t pig meat, 459t poultry and 240t eggs.

Fishing
There are programmes to upgrade subsistence fisheries to small commercial enterprises.

Deep-sea fishing is carried out by foreign fleets under licence in the immense Kiribati Exclusive Economic Zone (EEZ). In May 2003, Kiribati and the EU completed a deal under which Spanish, French and Portuguese purse seine and long-line fishing boats are to be allowed to catch tuna in the EEZ.

Typically, the annual catch for home consumption is over 32,000t including both fish and other seafood.

Industry and manufacturing
Small-scale manufacturing industries include clothing, furniture and handicrafts.

Tourism
Tourism plays a minor role in the Gilbert Islands but in the northern Line Islands tourism has a high priority. A growing number of tourists visit the rare seabird colonies situated on Kirimati (Christmas Island).

Attractions include World War Two battle sites, game fishing, ecotourism, and the Millennium Islands, situated just inside the International Date Line and the first place on earth to celebrate the New Year. There are also opportunities for fishing, surfing and diving, although there are not many organised activities.

Access to Kiritimati has been aided by a weekly charter flight from Honolulu.

Environment
The South Pacific Regional Environment Programme (SPREP) reported in 1999 that, due to global warming, two uninhabited islands in the Kiribati group, Tebua Tarawa and Abanuea, had disappeared beneath the waves, others have almost gone, and the main islands suffer severe floods from high tides.

Lagoon pollution has occurred on the main island of Tarawa.

Hydrocarbons
Kiribati does not produce any hydrocarbons and does not import natural gas or coal. It relies entirely on imports of distillate, jet fuel and gasoline to meet its fuel requirements.

Energy
Annual electricity production and consumption is about 6.5 million kW.

Banking and insurance
There is no central bank in Kiribati and the sole commercial bank is the Bank of Kiribati. The government does not buy and sell foreign exchange.

Time
GMT plus twelve hours

Geography
Kiribati comprises 33 atolls in three principal groups, within an area of about 3.6 million square km (two million square miles) in the mid-Pacific Ocean. The country extends about 3,870km (2,400 miles) from east to west and about 2,050km (1,275 miles) from north to south. Nauru lies to the west and Tuvalu and Tokelau to the south.

Climate
Temperatures range from 25–33 Celsius. The wet season extends from Dec–May and rainfall variation is high in most of the islands. A gentle breeze from the easterly quarter is predominant. The westerly gale (Oct–Mar) can be unpleasant.

Entry requirements
Passports
Required by all; also onward air ticket and proof of sufficient funds while staying in the country.

Visa
Required by all, except citizens of UK and most commonwealth countries and Pacific islanders, for up to either 20 or 30 days,

dependent on business, tourist and nationality criteria. Contact the nearest consulate for further information (some details are given at www.embassy-avenue.jp/kiri/visa/index.html). Citizens of Australia, Japan and US require visas.

Currency advice/regulations
There is no restriction on the importation of currency into Kiribati via travellers cheques expressed in Australian currency; Australian currency in notes may also be imported without restriction.

Customs
Personal effects are allowed duty-free. Firearms, ammunition, explosives and indecent publications are prohibited imports. Strict quarantine laws govern the import of plants, or parts of plants, vegetable matter or soil, clay or earth, animals and/or animal products. Visitors are not allowed to take out of the country human remains, artefacts over 30 years old, traditional fighting swords, traditional tools, dancing ornaments or suits of armour.

Health (for visitors)
Mandatory precautions
Vaccination certificate for yellow fever is required if travelling from an infected zone.

Advisable precautions
Vaccination for diphtheria, tuberculosis, hepatitis A and B, polio, tetanus, typhoid are recommended. There is also a rabies risk. It is advisable to boil water before drinking. Dengue fever is occasionally reported.

Hotels
In addition to the islands' four hotels, there are rudimentary rest houses. All hotels provide laundry services. Travellers cheques are seldom accepted. A 10 per cent services charge is added to all hotel bills. Tipping is not customary.

Public holidays
Fixed dates
1 Jan (New Year's Day), 18 Apr (Health Day), 12 Jul (Independence Day), 7 Aug (Youth Day), 25 Dec (Christmas Day), 26 Dec (Boxing Day).

Variable dates
Good Friday

Working hours
Banking
Mon–Fri: 0930–1500 for all branches of Bank of Kiribati except Bikenibeu which opens from 0900–1400 and Kiritimati Island branch which opens between 1230 and 1330.

Business
Mon–Fri: 0800–1230, 1330–1615.

Government
Mon–Fri: 0800–1230, 1330–1615.

Shops
Shopping on Tarawa is very limited. Mon–Sat: 0700–1900 (some shops open until 2030).

Electricity supply
240V AC, 50 cycles. Appliances with the standard Australian type three-pin plug will operate within South Tarawa.

Weights and measures
Metric system (Imperial units also used).

Social customs/useful tips
In official correspondence i-Kiribati adopt the western convention of signing their names with initials and surname, but it is customary (and more polite) to address people by their first name.
Women should not go out in shorts or short dresses especially on the outer islands. Bikinis should not be worn.

Getting there
Air
National airline: Air Kiribati
International airport/s: Bonriki International (TRW) on Tarawa.
Airport tax: Departure tax A$10; not applicable to transit passengers not leaving the airport and continuing their journey by the same aircraft.

Surface
Cargo services operate from Australia, New Zealand, Japan and US. Large ships anchor offshore and are offloaded by barge. Government ships operate between Fiji and Kiribati. The remoteness of the islands restricts the number of large vessels which call. The international ports are Betio (on Tarawa), Banaba and Kirimati.

Getting about
National transport
Air: Air Kiribati provides Trislander and Casa inter-island plane connections several times a week to most of the islands. Charter flights can be arranged.
Road: There are 30km of asphalt road on Tarawa. The majority of vehicles are motorcycles able to travel beyond the confines of the limited road network.
Buses: A large fleet of privately owned buses operates an efficient and inexpensive mode of public transport from the airport to the main centres on South Tarawa. They may be flagged down anywhere on the main road; users may get off anywhere they wish. Buses operate daily from Betio to Buota 0600–2100.
Water: Ships operate from Betio to all the outer islands transporting cargo and vehicles as well as passengers.

City transport
Taxis: Taxis are available on Tarawa but cannot be booked, nor do they have meters. Charges are high.

Car hire
Overseas driving licences and international driving permits are recognised in Kiribati for a maximum period of two weeks after arrival. Persons hiring a rental car should be at least 17-years-old. Driving is on the left side of the road and the speed limit is 45kph in towns/villages, 65kph on the open highway. In general, car hire is available on urban Tarawa and Kiritimati only.

BUSINESS DIRECTORY

The addresses listed below are a selection only. While World of Information makes every endeavour to check these addresses, we cannot guarantee that changes have not been made, especially to telephone numbers and area codes. We would welcome any corrections.

Telephone area codes
The international direct dialling (IDD) code for Kiribati is +686, followed by subscriber's number.

Useful telephone numbers
Fire, police, ambulance: 999
Tungaru Central Hospital, Nawerewere, South Tarawa: 28-100.

Chambers of Commerce
Kiribati Chamber of Commerce, PO Box 550, Betio, Tarawa (tel: 26-351; fax: 26-332; e-mail: kcc@tski.net.ki).

Banking
Bank of Kiribati Ltd, PO Box 66, Bairiki, Tarawa (tel: 21-095; fax: 21-200; e-mail: bankofkiribati@tksl.net.ki).

Development Bank of Kiribati, PO Box 33, Bairiki, Tarawa (tel: 81-224; fax: 81-444; e-mail: bokxmas@tksl.net.ki).

Travel information
Air Kiribati, PO Box 274, Bikenibeu, Tarawa (tel: 28-088/093; fax: 26-204).

Air Marshall, PO Box 104, Bairike, Tarawa (tel: 21-578; fax: 21-579).

Air Nauru, Tobaraoi Travel, Tarawa (tel: 26-567; fax: 26-000).

Air Tungaru Corporation, PO Box 274, Bikenibeu, Tarawa (tel: general 28-088; reservations 21-214).

Authentic Atoll Tours, PO Box 296, Bangantebure, Bikenibeu, Tarawa (tel and fax: 28-454).

Tarawa Agency, PO Box 274, Bikenibeu, Tarawa (tel: 28-088, 28-165; fax: 28-216).

National tourist organisation offices
Kiribati Visitors Bureau, PO Box 261, Bikenibeu, Tarawa (tel: 28-287/288; fax: 26-193).

Kiribati

Ministries

Ministry of Commerce, Industry and Tourism, PO Box 510, Betio, Tarawa (tel: 26-157, 26-158; fax: 26-233).

Ministry of Education, Bikenibeu, Tarawa (tel: 28-091; fax: 28-222).

Ministry of Environment, Bairiki, Tarawa (tel: 21-099; fax: 21-120).

Ministry of Finance and Economic Planning, PO Box 67, Bairiki, Tarawa (tel: 21-082; fax: 21-307).

Ministry of Foreign Affairs, PO Box 68, Bairiki, Tarawa (tel: 21-342; fax: 21-466).

Ministry of Health and Family Planning, Bikenibeu, Tarawa (tel: 28-081; fax: 28-152).

Ministry of Line and Phoenix Group, Bairiki, Tarawa (tel: 21-449).

Ministry of Trade, Industry and Labour, Bairiki, Tarawa (tel: 21-097; fax: 21-167).

Ministry of Transport and Communications, Betio, Tarawa (tel: 26-435; fax: 26-193).

Ministry of Works and Energy, Betio, Tarawa (tel: 26-192; fax: 26-343).

Other useful addresses

Abamakoro Trading Ltd, PO Box 492, Betio, Tarawa (tel: 26-568; fax: 26-415).

Asian Development Bank (ADB), South Pacific Regional Mission, La Casa di Andrea, Fr. Dr. W. H. Lini Highway; PO Box 127, Port Vila (tel: +678 2 23-300; fax: +678 2 23-183; email: adbsprm@adb.org; internet: http://www.adb.org/SPRM).

British High Commission, PO Box 61, Bairiki, Tarawa (tel: 21-327; fax: 21-488).

Broadcasting and Publications Authority, PO Box 78, Bairiki, Tarawa.

General Post Office, Bairiki (tel: 21-080). Kiribati Co-operative Wholesale Society (tel: 26-092; fax: 26-224).

Kiribati National Library and Archives, PO Box 6, Bairiki, Tarawa (tel: 21-245; fax: 28-222).

Kiribati Shipping Corporation, PO Box 495, Betio, Tarawa (tel: 26-195; fax: 26-204).

Office of the Attorney General, Bairiki, Tarawa (tel: 21-242).

Philatelic Bureau, Ministry of Transport and Communications, PO Box 494, Betio, Tarawa (tel: 26-515; fax: 26-193).

Telecom Kiribati Ltd, PO Box 72, Bairiki, Tarawa (tel: 21-287; fax: 21-010).

Tungaru Central Hospital, Bikenibeu, Tarawa (tel: 28-081).

Internet sites

South Pacific Tourism Organisation: http://www.tcsp.com/kiribati/index.html

Kiribati homepage: http://www.trussel.com/f_kir.htm

Government site: http://www.tskl.net.ki/kiribati/

North Korea

KEY FACTS

Official name: Chosun Minchu-chui Inmin Konghwa-guk (Democratic People's Republic of Korea) (DPRK)

Head of State: Kim Jong-il formally assumed power and was elected General Secretary of the KWP in Oct 1997. In Sep 1998, his father, Kim il-Sung, who died in 1994, was named President of North Korea for life.

Head of government: Prime Minister Pak Pong Ju (from 3 Sep 2003)

Ruling party: Chosun Rodongdang (Korean Workers' Party) (KWP)

Area: 122,400 square km

Population: 22.69 million (2004)

Capital: Pyongyang

Official language: Korean

Currency: Won (W) = 100 chon)

Exchange rate: W900.00 per US$ (Nov 2004) (based on central bank dealing; floating exchange rate from mid-2003)

GDP per capita: US$800 (2003)

GDP real growth: 1.00% (2004)

Labour force: 11.70 million (2004)

Balance of trade: -US$900.00 million (2003)

Foreign debt: US$12.00 billion (2003)

North Korea celebrated the 60-year anniversary of freedom from Japanese rule in 2005. Celebrations would have been more energetic without the mass malnutrition and the spectre of starvation. While also rousing patriotism and national unity, Kim Jong-il urged the farmers to boost production, focussing on rice and potatoes. Kim himself, however, was more concerned about the manufacture of nuclear arms.

The Bush victory came as bad news for Kim, who had been praying for a Democrat victory.

Under Japanese rule from 1910 to 1945, the Korean peninsula was controlled by the police and the army. Nationalist movements were suppressed ruthlessly, doing little to foster a love of the Japanese on the part of the Korean people. At the end of the Second World War, Russian troops entered Korea from the north and American troops from the south, each establishing its own, rival, government. The Russians brought with them a resistance leader, Kim il-Sung, father of the current President Kim Jong-il, who became head of the Democratic People's Republic of Korea (North Korea) in September 1948. From June 1950 the communist régime in the north attempted to reunite Korea by force, but the fighting – in which Chinese 'volunteers' arrived in numbers to oppose US-led United Nations forces – achieved nothing. An armistice signed at Panmunjon in July 1953 left the border in much the same state – along the 38th parallel – as it had been at the beginning of what later became known simply as the Korean War.

North Korea originally adopted Marxism-Leninism as its ruling philosophy. In 1972, however, the ruling philosophy was refined into the so-called *Juche* ideology, based on somewhat nebulous tenets of self reliance largely inspired by the rambling writings of Kin il-Sung. *Juche*, it was claimed, was a people centred ideology aimed to 'realise the independence of the masses'. However, the people the new ideology appeared to be centred around were North Korea's ruling family and its cronies.

The dynasty continues

There are reports that the 'Dear Leader' Kim Jong-il's personal credibility is in ruins and the regime is teetering on the edge. This is in part for personal reasons – in 2004 his favoured mistress died of breast cancer – and economic. Food levels are minimal. The Japanese foreign ministry compiled an analysis which concluded that they were 'signs of instability' and that the fight to succeed Kim would be explosive. The leader is thought to prefer his 24-year old son with his favourite mistress, Kim Jong-chol and has been grooming him for succession. Jong-chol went to school in Switzerland under an assumed name. There have been rumours of gun battles between the Kim family, specifically between the heir and Kim il-Sung's illegitimate son, contesting the succession.

Economic mess

North Korea has not disclosed official economic data since 1965, although South Korea's figures for North Korean GDP indicate a rise of 2.2 per cent in 2004. However, the economy has been shrinking for over ten years since collapse in the 1990s and is in a fragile state, kept alive only by aid donations. The country has been crippled by industrial stagnation and famine, exacerbated by its vast defence spending and an intensification of military exercises. Goods are mass produced at low quality and rationed. The concentration of economic policy on the development of heavy industry reflected the continued implementation of outdated former Soviet-style priorities, wholly unsuited to present conditions.

Foreign investment in industry, construction, technology and tourism is officially encouraged, but there have been few firms willing to invest in North Korea.

In 2001 Chinese finance officials invited North Koreans to view their rapid factory lines and miracle economy in a bid to stop the flow of impoverished North Koreans over the border to China. In 2002 Kim Jong-il responded by pushing through a series of economic reforms, modernising and decentralising the tightly controlled economy a little. Prices were liberalised and some private markets opened for business while foreign investment was sought. Reform led to spiralling inflation of 100 per cent, although the price of rice rocketed 55,000 per cent. Civil servants suffered as their wages did not rise in line with prices. People's savings were wiped out by such high inflationary rates. Kim's reforms benefited the rich because they could afford to buy the more plentiful goods but plunged everyone else deeper into economic misery. The yawning gap between the poorest and richest is opening up even wider. Some are surviving on 35 cents a month. 2002 did mark a shift however from a purely ideological economy based on national need, to a marginally more outward looking market approach.

In 2005 finance officials pushed for further modernisation of national companies and discussed ways to bring in more foreign direct investment to the failing economy. Exports between the two Koreas, for the first six months of 2005, have grown 40 per cent, to a level of US$453 million. These financial exchanges, a large part of which comprise aid, is politically motivated – southern businesses operate at a loss thinking to pave the way to reunification of the peninsula. Fibre optic cables were laid to link the two Koreas in 2005, facilitating communication between divided families, and it was agreed that plans for two linking roads and two railways would also be unveiled. There is some evidence of North Korea's modernisation – internet access, a few bars and restaurants and even the sight of one or two hamburgers for sale. A middle class market is emerging.

Food aid

Some estimates put the number of North Koreans who starved to death in the 1990s as high as two million, 10 per cent of the population. Malnutrition is still rife and children have stunted growth. Food aid programmes have been tentatively and grudgingly received by the North Korean government but after ten years of aid, in 2005 Kim claimed that there were enough food resources and foreign aid workers should quit the country.

In May 2005 the UN World Food Programme made a global appeal for increased funds saying that food was getting ever-more scarce in the region. The programme currently feeds 6.5 million in North Korea but only has enough aid now to feed 3.6 million on half rations. The price of key commodities was becoming too high for cash-strapped pockets. Political tussles have complicated food aid provision with the US slashing donations by half from 2003 to 2004. Japanese donors also became hesitant in the face of reawakened tensions about Japanese hostages captured during the Cold War by North Korea years ago.

After Kim Jong-il conceded to re-engage in disarmament talks, the South Korean government gave the go-ahead for 500,000 tonnes of rice. Though South Korean aid was given in what a spokesperson called 'brotherly love and humanitarianship', with all other countries food for the starving is becoming a political bargaining tool.

Bird 'flu

The Pyongyang outbreak of avaian 'flu in March 2005 was an unwelcome setback for the impoverished economy. South Korea banned imports of its neighbour's chickens and imposed quarantines, as did Japan. The dictatorship did not come clean about its discovery and culls of thousands of poultry until it was confronted by a suspicious World Health Organisation.

KEY INDICATORS — North Korea

	Unit	2000	2001	2002	2003	2004
Population	m	21.60	22.00	22.22	22.47	22.69
Gross domestic product (GDP)	US$bn	16.35	16.65	16.89	10.13	–
GDP per capita	US$	757	757	760	800	–
GDP real growth	%	-3.0	-3.0	1.2	1.0	2.2
Exports (fob) (goods)	US$m	–	–	–	1,200.0	–
Imports (fob) (goods)	US$m	–	–	–	2,100.0	–
Balance of trade	US$m	–	–	–	-900.0	–
Exchange rate	per US$	2.20	2.20	2.20	2.20	2.20

The loss of so many chickens, a prime protein source, hit the starving.

Optimism or pessimism?

Two theories are advanced as to why North Korea persists in maintaining and developing an expensive nuclear arsenal and missile system. The optimists view is that if rice was Kim il-Sung's idea for the formation of socialism in North Korea, missile development was its means of survival. The late 'great leader' had decreed that 'Rice is Socialism' and that North Korea as a Socialist country would triumph only when its people were well fed. Under Kim il-Sung, North Korea's hills and small mountains were deforested to plant rice. Agricultural experts dared not challenge the great leader's policy, even though the North Korean climate was ill-suited for rice farming. Meanwhile, instead of building up conventional military and weaponry, Kim il-Sung concentrated on developing means of mass destruction, which would be more effective for his brinkmanship policy

In 2000, a local South Korean newspaper reported that three North Koreans, including a father-and-son missile development team, had defected to the US. According to the report, which Washington refused to confirm, the former North Korean missile researcher, known only as Lim, testified that North Korea's missile technology was first-class and that it had a 6,000km range rocket that was ready to fly. He was also quoted as remarking that Pyongyang had endured great difficulties and poverty in order to develop nuclear and missile technology and that it would never give them up, despite pressure from the international community. The optimistic view is that Pyongyang will continue to make food aid a condition for de-militarisation and normalisation in the Beijing meetings. A more pessimistic theory, prevailing since the Iraq war is that the investment in nuclear weapons is an end in itself, a non-negotiable deterrent and guarantor of the régime's continued hegemony over its starving people.

Kim il-Sung's strategy to develop weapons of mass destruction, however, may prove to be an ineffective and costly one after all. If the US goes ahead with its plan to deploy laser weapon technology in the Korean peninsula by 2007, Pyongyang's missile would be rendered ineffective as a major threat or as a leverage tool for negotiations.

Any significant de-militarisation programme would create problems of another kind for North Korea. The de-mobilisation of its million strong armed forces – in 2004 one of the largest armies in the world – would have disastrous social consequences. Redundant soldiers would have no jobs to go to, creating the risk for the government of widespread social unrest and a reduced capability to maintain control. A US based human-rights group has estimated that there are already some 20,000 political prisoners in North Korea.

External pressures

The Bush victory came as bad news for Kim, who had been praying for a Democrat victory. In February 2005 North Korea announced to the world that it had produced nuclear weapons. It also refused to co-operate in six-party disarmament talks that have been in motion for several years. The country's foreign office stated that the nuclear technology had been manufactured in response to 'the Bush administration's ever more undisguised policy to isolate and stifle' the communist regime. The world acted with surprise, fear and to some extent, cynicism, seeing the bold statement as a tactical ploy to prepare the ground for further multilateral negotiations.

Disarmament talks were abandoned in June 2004 but in 2005 were resumed with new US negotiators: Condoleezza Rice, secretary of state, and Christopher Hill, chief negotiator. These figures are more amenable than their inflammatory predecessors, although the Chinese were the most constructive, key facilitators. Chinese motives include peace in the region and a reduction of North Korean refugees, and improved relations with the US. The crunch point in the Korea negotiations was whether or not North Korea would agree to surrender its nuclear arsenal in return for certain conditions. After 20 days in September it did – in return for light water reactors for electricity generation, to be given at an 'appropriate' time, and energy and security assurances.

The next talks, the fifth round, were held in November 2005, when North Korea agreed to delay atomic testing and dismantle its nuclear weaponry. In December progress slowed, however, with North Korea refusing to co-operate on the nuclear issue until the US had displayed its confidence in the regime by removing economic sanctions. North Korea also demanded 'respect' from the Americans in return for diplomatic re-engagement. The US rather than acceding to these demands seemed to toughen its approach, while North Korea then announced it would build light water reactors themsevles. Though this plan may not be feasible in light of North Korea's financial siuation, the announcement is a hostile one and does not bode well for the next round of talks.

Outlook

North Korea's nuclear arsenal is a cause for concern and talks in 2006 will not be starting from a good base. The nuclear technology is the country's bargaining tool in securing enough food for its starving people – but it is doubtful how far an unsympathetic US and Japan will go with financial aid.

North Korea remains something of an international enigma, with scant prospect of an improvement in its economic prospects. The chasm between the richest and poorest is likely to widen as some liberalisation is undertaken. Economic sanctions from the West will be rendered ineffective if China and South Korean step in to fill the gap. Once infrastructure is restored, the DPRK, with its low-cost, relatively educated and very well disciplined workforce, might conceivably become a centre for competitively priced exports to Russia and China. A priority for the country would be forge economic and investment ties with neighbouring countries to get a foot in the door of the world economy.

Risk assessment

Economic	Poor
Political	Poor
Regional Stability	Poor

COUNTRY PROFILE

Historical profile
The northern kingdom of Koguryo (from which the modern 'Korea' is derived) achieved unification of the peninsula in the tenth century. In the thirteenth century, it was invaded and ruled by Mongolians. The Mongolians were eventually overthrown by the Ming dynasty who called the country 'Chosun'.

1910 Japan formalised its annexation of Korea after gaining responsibility for its security following victory in the Russo-Japanese war of 1905.

1919 Japan suppressed the mass March First movement for self-determination.

1930s–1940s Japan imposed measures designed to assimilate the Korean population, including the outlawing of the Korean language and family names. Korea suffered under military occupation but gained the benefits of forced industrialisation.

1945 Liberation at the hands of Allied forces was a prelude to partition of the peninsula as the victorious powers

encouraged friendly governments north and south of the 38th parallel. The US occupied the south while the north was taken over by the Soviet Union. As the two powers did not wish to give independence to Korea, feeling that the Korean people needed political and social re-education, a line of demarcation was established.
1947 The Chosun Rodongdang (Korean Workers' Party) (KWP) was established by Kim il-Sung (known as the 'Great Leader').
1948 The Democratic People's Republic of Korea (DPRK) was established as an independent communist state.
1950 North Korea, backed by Soviet and Chinese Communist forces, invaded South Korea. War ensued.
1953 A cease-fire was signed on 27 July; a peace treaty was never signed.
1972 A constitution was laid down.
1994 Kim il-Sung, who spent his last two decades in power, died. He was succeeded by his son Kim Jong-il (known as the 'Dear Leader').
1995–96 Floods destroyed 16 per cent of arable land.
1997 Kim Jong-il formally assumed power. He was elected general secretary of the KWP.
1998 Kim il-Sung, who died in 1994, was named president of North Korea for life.
1999 The head of UN World Food Programme (WFP) warned of imminent famine.
2000 Australia, the Philippines and Italy restored diplomatic ties with North Korea. South Korea President Kim Dae-Jung visited Pyongyang and met Kim Jong-il in an unprecedented and much fêted meeting of the two Koreas' leaders. The then US secretary of state, Madeleine Albright, visited Kim Jong-il. North Korea and the UK established diplomatic relations.
2001 An EU delegation held talks with Kim Jong-il. Talks started by the US administration in 2000 were suspended. Talks on opening the first land route between the Republic of Korea and Korea DPR broke down. After the worst winter in 50 years and a summer drought harvests were devastated, the UN WFP called for over US$300 million in food aid.
2002 US President George W Bush included North Korea with Iran and Iraq in an 'axis of evil' due to their development of Weapons of Mass Destruction (WMD). There were real developments in inter-Korean relations – the two sides agreed to resume the engagement process after the South Korean envoy, Lim Dong-won visited North Korea. The accord included plans for economic co-operation, continuing family reunions and a revival of a cross-border railway project linking the two countries. At the height of the famine, UN estimates one-third of the population received food aid and half the population were malnurished.
2003 Talks were held in Beijing, China, between US and North Korean representatives, in order to try to persuade North Korea to end its nuclear arms programme. The 687 candidates chosen by the ruling KWP, standing unopposed, won 100 per cent of the votes each in the 3 August parliamentary elections to the National Assembly. On 3 September, Pak Pong Ju became premier. Harvests improved but 6.5 million people were still considered vulnerable, as food aid continued.
2004 In May, a train carrying explosive materials was ignited by a stray electric wire and at least 161 people were killed and more than 1,000 injured. South and North Korea agreed to open cross-border roads and to make test runs on two railways in October. Japan resumed its food aid in August.
2005 In May, fears about North Korea's missile and nuclear ambitions were revived when a short-range missile was test-fired in the general direction of Japan. International talks to defuse the nuclear weapons issue continued throughout the year. In November, North Korea proposed a five-step plan to abandon its nuclear weapons programme.
2006 Kim Jong-il visited China, touring hi-tech facilities and Yantian container port.

Political structure
Constitution
Under the terms of the 1972 constitution, nominal political authority is held by a unicameral Supreme People's Assembly (SPA).
Local government is vested in nine provincial and three municipal elected people's assemblies.
Government at all levels is dominated by the Chosun Rodongdang (Korean Workers' Party) (KWP).
The executive
The head of state holds executive power and governs in conjunction with a Central People's Committee and an appointed Administrative Council (cabinet).
The head of state is no longer president since the title was given to Kim il-Sung, after he had died, for life.
Kim Jong-il was given administrative powers in 1994 and formally assumed power as head of state after being elected general secretary of the ruling KWP in 1997.
National legislature
The SPA exercises legislative power. Its 687 members are elected every four years from a single list of candidates.
The SPA, which elects a standing committee to represent it when not in session, also elects the head of government.

Legal system
The legal system is based on the German civil law system with Japanese influences and Communist legal theory.
Last elections
3 August 2003 (parliamentary)
Results: 687 candidates chosen by the ruling Chosun Rodongdang (Korean Workers' Party) (KWP), standing unopposed, won 100 per cent of the votes each; turnout was 99.9 per cent.

Political parties
No political parties, other than the KWP, are permitted to operate.
Ruling party
Chosun Rodongdang (Korean Workers' Party) (KWP)

Population
22.69 million (2004)
Ethnic make-up
The Korean DPR (DPRK) has a highly homogeneous population descended from migratory groups who entered the Korean Peninsula from Siberia, Manchuria and inner Asia. There is a small Chinese community and a few ethnic Japanese.
Religions
The constitution provides for 'freedom of religious belief' but, in practice, organised religious activity is discouraged, except for certain government-sponsored religious groups. Traditional religions are Buddhism, Confucianism, Daoism, Shamanism and Chondogyo.

Education
The is a national Education for All Forum (EFA) that organises consultations with organisations such as the Youth League, the Women's Union and the Academy of Educational Science.
Education in Korea consists of six years of elementary education, three years of junior high school, three years of senior high school, and four years of college education. The government has established a free educational system and plans to extend this to the remote areas of the country. However, school attendance in some areas has reportedly dropped to between 60–80 per cent, due to extreme economic hardship not only, in families through lack of food, but also in school facilities with inadequately trained teachers, poor heating and scarce learning materials.
Competition for college entry is fierce. There are three universities. These are the Kim il-Sung, Kim Chaek Polytechnic and Korryo-Songgyungwan. There are also around 280 colleges.
It is common for students to opt for military service after graduation. This is not compulsory, but can positively affect an individual's future career.
Literacy rate: 95–99 per cent, adult rate.

Health
There is an extensive, free medical care system, but the quality of care has declined.
Total expenditure on health is 2.5 per cent of GDP, of which 73–74 per cent is government spending. Water and sanitation sector, one of the key priority areas, remains poorly funded at only 18 per cent of the requirement.
A nutrition survey conducted by Unicef, in 2002, indicated that 40 per cent of children under five were chronically malnourished or stunted (a fall from the previous high of 45 per cent in 2000) and in 2003 nationwide, 5 million people, especially children, the elderly and pregnant females were dependent on foreign food aid. The mortality rate for those aged under 5 was 55 per 1,000 children; maternal mortality continues to increase as estimates show that the nutritional status of some 480,000 pregnant and nursing women is poor.
Life expectancy: 62.4 years (World Bank 2004)
Fertility rate/Maternal mortality rate: 2.1 births per woman (World Bank 2004)
Birth rate/Death rate: 17.6 births per 1,000 population; seven deaths per 1,000 population (World Bank 2003).
Infant mortality rate: 42 per 1,000 live births (World Bank 2004)

Welfare
A large segment of the civilian population rely on the government-run public distribution system. In 2003 the meagre food ration was further reduced to 250–380 grammes per person daily – half the minimum daily energy requirement. People are required to rely on independently procured supplements; families in urban, industrial areas have fared worst.

Main cities
Pyongyang (capital, estimated population 2.8 million in 2004), Hamhung (834,200), Ch'ongjin (684,600), Namp'o (665,500), Sinuiju (383,200), Wonsan (352,800).

Languages spoken
English, amoung other international languages, is used in business.
Official language/s
Korean

Media
Press
Dailies: These include *Rodong Shinmun*, *Minju Choson*, *Rodong Chongnyon* and *Pyongyang Times*. The Korean News Service in Tokyo also provides an internet service *Korean News* at www.kcna.co.jp/index-e.htm.
Business: The Foreign Trade Publishing House publishes a monthly journal, *Foreign Trade of the DPRK*, which includes listings of specialised corporations, giving telegraphic and telex addresses.
Periodicals: A semimonthly, Tokyo-based unofficial mouthpiece of the Korea DPR government, *The People's Korea*, reports on Korean affairs.
Broadcasting
Radio: National and locally-produced programmes are widely disseminated (factory, outdoor loudspeakers); there are external services in several languages.
Television: There are two stations, plus a third channel at weekends. Viewing foreign channels is illegal for Korean DPR nationals.

Economy
North Korea has probably the world's most highly centralised planned economy. The concentration of economic policy on the development of heavy industry reflects the continued implementation of outdated Soviet-style priorities, wholly unsuited to present conditions. The country is crippled by industrial stagnation and famine, which have been exacerbated by vast defence spending and an intensification of military exercises. North Korea relies on foreign food aid and energy supplies for survival. Foreign investment in industry, construction, technology and tourism is officially encouraged, but there have been few firms willing to invest in North Korea. Rapprochement with South Korea could help rescue the economy. Once infrastructure is restored, North Korea, with its low-cost, relatively educated workforce, could become a centre for competitively-priced exports to Russia and China. Joint venture projects are in operation, mostly with Japan-based Koreans.
Two-way trade between the two Koreas, which was legalised in 1988, increased from US$18.8 million in 1989 to US$697 million in 2004. Only about half consisted of commercial trade, the rest comprising aid and co-operative projects.

External trade
North Korea's foreign trade accounts for less than 10 per cent of GDP – some is on a barter basis. Barter trade with China ended in 1993. Rajin-Sonbong is a special economic zone, on the north-eastern border with China and Russia, allowing free trade access in return for investment.
Imports
Main imports are oil, coke, crude rubber, alloying elements, coking coal, sulphur, halite, grain, cotton, sugar and palm oil. Food and energy staples such as wheat and fuel oil are granted in aid by foreign countries.
Main sources: China (32.9 per cent total, 2004), Thailand (10.7 per cent), Japan (4.8 per cent)

Exports
Main exports are clothing, iron and steel, armaments, machinery and equipment, non-ferrous metals, manufactured goods, fireproof bricks, anthracite, magnetite cakes, cement, magnesia clinker and machine tools. The trade in illicit drugs is thought to be an important source of foreign currency for North Korea.
Main destinations: China (29.9 per cent total, 2004), South Korea (24.1 per cent), Japan (13.2 per cent)

Agriculture
Farming
The agriculture sector accounts for an estimated 30 per cent of GDP and is thought to employ 43 per cent of the workforce.
Agriculture is mostly practised on large-scale collective and state farms, which have been fatally mismanaged. Main crops are rice, maize and potatoes. Other crops include wheat, barley, rape, sugar, millet, sorghum, pulses, sweet potatoes, vegetables, tobacco and silkworms. Extra grain supplies are necessary. Since the mid-1990s, North Korea has been affected by adverse climatic conditions, with a series of floods and droughts destroying crops. Other problems affecting the sector include severe deforestation, which has caused silting of rivers, a lack of fertilisers and pesticides and low levels of mechanisation. This has led to a serious food deficit at a time when North Korea's increasing political isolation has affected aid flows.
Crop production in 2004 included: 4,456,000 tonnes (t) cereals in total, 2,370,000t rice, 1,727,000t maize, 2,052,000t potatoes, 175,000t wheat, *350,000t sweet potatoes, *680,000t cabbages, *300,000t pulses, *19,200t treenuts, *71,000t tomatoes, *90,000t garlic, *68,640t oilcrops, *64,000t tobacco, 24,800t fibre crops, *660,000t apples, 36,000t seed cotton, *12,000t cotton lint, *59,000t chillies & peppers, *360,000t soya beans, 1,401,500t fruit in total, 3,938,100t vegetables in total. Livestock production included: 227,742t meat in total, 21,000t beef, 147,100t pig meat, *990t lamb, 11,205t goat meat, 46,526t poultry, *135,000t eggs, *94,000t milk, 1,500t cocoons, silk.
* estimate

Industry and manufacturing
The industrial sector accounts for an estimated 20 per cent of GDP and is thought to employ a similar percentage of the workforce.
Major manufacturing activities have been diversified to include production of steel, iron, non-ferrous metals, machinery and equipment, fertilisers, plastics and cement. Light industrial products include silk,

cotton and rayon textiles, chemicals, processed food, machine tools, hardware and machinery.

Development projects in western and eastern industrial zones have included a vinalon factory in Sunchon with productive capacity of 100,000 tonnes per annum, a potash fertiliser complex in Sariwon, a coal mining complex in Anju, steel complexes in Nampo and Chongjin and synthetic rubber plants in Hamhung and Namhung.

Two production centres are planned at the port cities of Nampo and Wonsan to supplement a free-trade zone in the Rajin-Sonbong area bordering China and Russia, which has little infrastructure to support its industry. The new centres will specialise in consumer product exports by foreign companies and will be located near population centres.

Hyundai, South Korea's largest conglomerate, has developed North Korea's largest industrial complex, costing US$5 billion and located in Kaesong.

Tourism

Tourism is recognised as a means of earning foreign exchange and visitors, with the exception of Americans, are allowed into the country. The sector is undeveloped. Infrastructure is lacking, entry procedures are protracted, the cost, which includes mandatory minders, is high, and movements are tightly controlled. Arrivals, organised as package tours, are mainly by cruise ships, but a land route, via the Demilitarised Zone, opened in 2003. The main markets are South Korea, China and Japan. Around 2,000 visitors come from western countries. South Korea is actively engaged in consolidating tourism between the two countries for political reasons.

Mining

The mining sector is thought to account for some 10 per cent of GDP and to employ 5 per cent of the workforce. North Korea is well-endowed with mineral resources, including refractory clays, phosphates, sulphur and graphite and ores of iron, magnesium, tungsten, copper, lead, zinc, silver, gold, magnesite and nickel. Non-ferrous metals are an important foreign exchange earner, with 70 per cent of zinc, lead and copper production in the Hamhung district.

Hydrocarbons

North Korea has no proven reserves of oil or natural gas. North Korea relies on imports of oil for its requirements, mainly for transportation purposes, but does not import natural gas.

North Korea has coal reserves conservatively estimated at around 1.0 billion tonnes, with annual production at over 100 million tonnes. Small amounts of coal are imported. Coal supplies over 85 per cent of domestic primary energy consumption.

Energy

Electrical generating capacity is 9.5GW, two-thirds of which is provided by hydropower and the rest by coal-fired plants. Capacity is under-utilised and consumption has declined over the years. Infrastructure, including power plants and the transmission grid, have deteriorated. Blackouts and supply shortages are frequent. Construction of the first reactor to replace an existing plant, said to be capable of producing plutonium, was expected to begin in late 2002, but following opposition from the US after it was reported that North Korea had not discontinued its nuclear weapons programme, plans for two reactors were shelved.

Banking and insurance

There are no private banks in North Korea. The euro replaced the US dollar as the official foreign exchange currency in 2002; the Japanese yen is an unofficial exchange currency.

Central bank
Central Bank of the Peoples' Repubic of Korea

Main financial centre
Pyongyang

Time
GMT plus nine hours

Geography
North Korea occupies the northern part of the Korean peninsula, bordered to the north by the People's Republic of China and to the south by the Republic of Korea. Over two-thirds of the land area is mountainous.

Climate
Winters are cold, with temperatures ranging from -3 degrees Celsius (C) to -8 degrees C in January and falling as low as -20 degrees C at night. Summers are warm and humid, with an average temperature in August of 25 degrees C. Most rainfall is from June–September.

Entry requirements
Passports
Required by all.
Visa
Required by all. Applications for visas should be made well in advance. It is impossible to visit Korea DPR except by official invitation or by joining group tours from certain countries. Contact the nearest embassy for further details.
Currency advice/regulations
Import and export of local currency is prohibited. Import and export of foreign currency is unlimited, but must be declared. The euro replaced the US dollar as the official foreign exchange currency in 2002; the Japanese yen is also accepted.
Customs
All import-export transactions are carried out through state agencies and subject to controls.
Prohibited imports
Documents, literature, audio and videotapes, compact discs and letters may be deemed as pornographic, political or intended for religious proselytising. Mobile telephones and global positioning satellite systems are not permitted and must be deposited on entry and collected on departure at the Customs checkpoint.

Health (for visitors)
Mandatory precautions
No compulsory vaccinations.
Advisable precautions
Malaria and cholera are a risk and precautions are essential. Vaccinations against diphtheria, hepatitis 'A' and 'B', Japanese 'B' encephalitis, polio, tuberculosis, tetanus and typhoid. Rabies is a risk. Hospitals often lack heat, medicine, and supplies, and suffer from frequent power loss and outbreaks of infection. Hospitals do not generally provide food for patients. Visitors with known serious, medical conditions should avoid visiting and those in good health should avoid any invasive surgery. All medication necessary should be taken (in their original packaging) in sufficient quantities, as it is not possible to purchase supplies locally.

Drink only bottled or sterilised water, avoid dairy products, which are probably unpasturised. Eat only hot, cooked meat, fish and vegetables, or peeled fruit, and avoid pork, salads and mayonnaise.

It is strongly recommend that visitors obtain comprehensive medical insurance before travelling to DPRK.

Hotels
Booking is normally through government agencies.

Credit cards
The main hotels in Pyongyang will take credit and debit cards (Visa and Mastercard but not American Express). Travellers' cheques are not accepted. Hotels generally insist on full payment in advance when checking-in.

Tipping is officially frowned upon, but is increasingly expected by some hotel staff.

Public holidays
Fixed dates
1 Jan (New Year's Day), 16–17 Fob (Kim Jong-il's Birthday), 15 Apr (Kim il-Sung's Birthday), 15 Apr (Army Day), 1 May (Labour Day), 27 Jul (Victory Day), 15 Aug (Liberation Day), 9 Sep (Foundation of the Democratic People's Republic of Korea (DPRK)), 10 Oct (Foundation of the

Korean Workers' Party (KWP)), 27 Dec (Constitution Day).

Working hours
Banking
0900–1700. The Trade Bank of the DPRK situated near Kim Il-Sung Square in Sungni Street, Pyongyang, is open in the morning every day except Sunday.
Business
0800–1200, 1300–1700.
Government
0800–1200, 1300–1700.
Shops
1000–1800.

Telecommunications
Mobile phones
In 2004, the use of mobile phones was banned.

Electricity supply
The electric current on the national grid is 220V AC and 60Hz. 220V and 110V power points are available in hotels.

Weights and measures
Metric system

Social customs/useful tips
Koreans give a short bow or nod as a sign of respect when greeting or departing, although foreigners are usually greeted with a handshake.
When anything is handed over to or received from another person, including business cards, it is polite to use both hands. The card should be read and not immediately put away.
The surname precedes the given name in Korean, but may be transposed for the benefit of foreigners.
Chopsticks should never be placed upright in rice: this is only done at funerals.
In homes and traditional restaurants, shoes are removed and slippers worn.
The Korean word for 'four' is similar to that for death and considered unlucky. Many public buildings and all hospitals omit the fourth floor.
Names should never be written in red ink, a traditional symbol of death.

Security
Government agencies closely supervise visitors to North Korea. Hotel rooms, telephones and fax machines may be monitored, and personal possessions in hotel rooms may be searched. Photographing roads, bridges, airports, railway stations, or anything other than designated public tourist sites may be perceived as espionage and could result in confiscation of cameras and film or even detention.

Getting there
Air
An aviation accord between the two Koreas opened North Korea's airspace to international flights from early 1998.
It is essential to reconfirm ticket bookings for a return journey some days in advance, as an issued air ticket does not guarantee a seat, unless it has been confirmed and endorsed prior to travel. For most travellers this will be done by their travel agents or inviting organisation in the DPRK.
National airline: Air Koryo (formerly Chosonminhang Korean Airways).
International airport/s: Sunan (FNJ), 24 km from Pyongyang.
Other airport/s: Sunan (FNJ), 24km from Pyongyang.
Airport tax: None.
Surface
Rail: Rail services operate to/from Beijing and Moscow. In 2002, the rail link between South Korea and the North Korean border re-opened.
Main port/s: Chongjin, Haeju, Hungnam, Najin, Nampo, Wonsan. The two Koreas are discussing expansion of shipping routes. Nampo and Wonsan may become special import-export zones.

Getting about
National transport
It can be difficult to reach many areas of the interior, although the system is developing.
Air: Air Koryo (formerly Chosonminhang Korean Airways) operates domestic services.
Road: The road network (75,112km) includes motorways between Pyongyang and Wonsan and Pyongyang and Nampo.
Buses: There are no inter-city buses.
Rail: The rail network is estimated at 8,533km, 89 per cent of which is electrified, with two classes of accommodation. Rail travel is slow.
City transport
Taxis: Taxis are available and should be booked through the hotel.
Buses, trams & metro: There is a four-line underground system in Pyongyang.

BUSINESS DIRECTORY

Telephone area codes
The international direct dialling (IDD) code for PDR Korea is +850, followed by area code and subscriber's number.
Pyongyang 2

Banking
Changgwang Credit Bank Chukzen 1-dong, Mangyongdae District, Pyongyang (tel: 316-74; fax: 381-4793).

Credit Bank of Korea, Chongryu 1-Dong, Munsu Street, Otan-dong, Central District, Pyongyang (tel: 381-8285; fax: 381-7806).

Foreign Trade Bank of the Democratic People's Republic of Korea, FTB Building, Jungsong dong, Central District, Pyongyang (tel: 381-5270; fax: 381-4467).

The International Industrial Development Bank, Mansu-dong, Central District, Pyongyang (tel: 381-8610).

Korea Daesong Bank, Segori-dong, Gyongheung Street, Pyongyang (tel: 818-221; fax: 814-576).

Korea Joint Bank, Ryugyong 1 dong, Pothonggang District, Pyongyang (tel: 381-8151; fax: 381-4410).

Koryo Bank, Pong-Hwa Dong, Potonggang District, Pyongyang (tel: 381-8168; fax: 381-4033).

Central bank
Central Bank of the Democratic People's Republic of Korea, Mansu-dong, 58-1 Sungri Street, Central District, Pyongyang, (tel: 333-8196; fax: 381-4624).

Travel information
Koryo Group, (UK company in Beijing, China, arranging tourism to North Korea): www.koryogroup.com

Kumgangsan International Tourist Company, Central District, Pyongyang (tel: 31-562, 35-431; fax: 812-100).

Tourist Advertisement and Information Agency, Songuja-dong, Mangyongdae District, Pyongyang (tel: 73-525, 73-675).

Ministry of tourism
State General Bureau of Tourism Democratic People's Republic of Korea, Central District, Pyongyang (tel: 817-201; fax: 817-607).

Other useful addresses
Committee for the Promotion of International Trade of the Democratic People's Republic of Korea, Central District, Pyongyang (tel: 34-801).

Foreign Languages Publishing House, Sosong District, Pyongyang (tel: 51-863).

Foreign Trade Publishing House, Pyongyang District, Pyongyang.

Korea-Europe Technology & Economy Services, 15 Sojae-chon, Konguk-dong, Potonggang District, Pyongyang (e-mail: ketes@ketes.org).

Korean Central News Agency (KCNA), Potonggang District, Pyongyang.

Korean General Company for Economic Co-operation, Central District, Pyongyang.

Korean General Merchandise Export and Import Corporation, Central District, Pyongyang.

Korean Publications Exchange Association, PO Box 222, Pyongyang 20691 (tel: 32-356).

Korean Publications Export and Import Corporation, Central District, Pyongyang.

South Korea

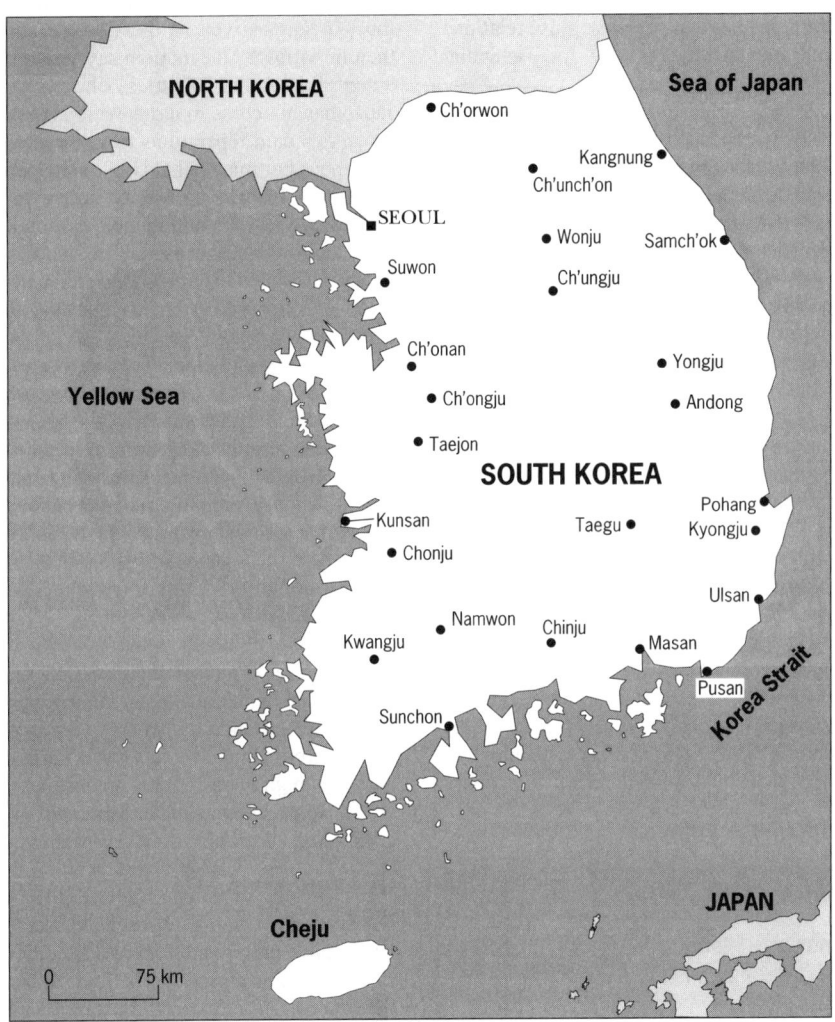

KEY FACTS

Official name: Daehan Min-kuk (Republic of Korea)

Head of State: President Roh Moo Hyun (UD) (inaugurated 25 Feb 2003)

Head of government: Prime Minister Lee Hai Chan (UD) (from 30 Jun 2004)

Ruling party: Uri Dang (UD) (Our Party) (from 15 Apr 2004)

Area: 99,091 square km

Population: 47.72 million (2004)

Capital: Seoul

Official language: Korean

Currency: Won (W) = 100 chon

Exchange rate: W1,041.50 per US$ (Oct 2005)

GDP per capita: US$14,098 (2004)

GDP real growth: 4.60% (2004)*; 3.8% (2005)*

Labour force: 22.92 million (2004)

Unemployment: 3.70% (OECD, 2004)

Inflation: 3.60% (2004)

Balance of trade: US$38.16 billion (2004)

Foreign debt: US$166.67 billion (end 3rd qtr 2004)

Annual FDI: US$48.60 billion (cumulative, 1995–2004, OECD); US$8.20 billion (OECD, 2004)*

* estimated figure

South Korea has been revelling in something of a boom in neighbouring East Asian countries thanks to the cosmetic good looks of its soap and film stars. In the arena of politics or science, however, Korean celebrities have not been quite so successful. Relations with North Korea have not moved on much in five years and there is still tension with old colonial master Japan.

North and South

Communist North Korea and booming South Korea are technically warring enemies: the Korean war ended in 1953 with an armistice not a peace agreement. The border separating the states has the highest military presence of any border in the world. South Korea is increasingly keen to resolve tensions and engage with the reclusive communist leader Kim Jong-il, with its so-called 'sunshine policy', while the US has tried to freeze the state out of the international community. In 2000 a milestone was reached with a historic handshake between the two leaders taking place; but this has not accelerated progress, however.

In response to North's Korea's declaration of nuclear weapons manufacture in February 2005, South Korea requested military negotiations, claiming a need to discuss the country's disputed maritime boundary.

Talks between the two Koreas were held in May – with the biggest achievement being North Korea's actual involvement rather than any progress on the nuclear situation during the talks. 500,000 tonnes of South Korean fertiliser was dependent on North Korean involvement. The South's incentive, meanwhile, was to press the North to re-engage in multilateral disarmament talks.

In July 2005 President Roh Moo Hyan made the laying of new power lines and 2 million kilowatts of increased energy supplies to North Korea dependent on Kim Jong-il's diplomatic engagement on the nuclear issue. North Korea's grave energy shortage gave them little option but to accede, despite their lack of interest in disarmament.

South Korea is also pursing a policy of economic engagement: in Kaesong, North Korea, factories employ 400 South Koreans alongside North Koreans and elsewhere Fiat car manufacture is engaging workers from both sides of the border. Kim Jong-il has been given the honour of naming the newly produced cars – he has chosen 'whistle' and 'cuckoo' to date.

In July 2005 fibre optic cables were laid to link the two countries, the first communications links for 60 years. The technology will facilitate the holding of online video reunions between families divided by the Korean war and subsequent travel restrictions. Businesses will also be able to use the cables.

In November 2005 the South Korean premier agreed in talks with US President George W Bush that it was time for a formal peace agreement to be reached between the two Koreas. North Korea is likely to insist upon conditions before signing, such as the issue of the 30,000 US soldiers stationed in South Korea, which the North want to see sent home. A treaty, it is hoped, would improve tense relations and pave the way for eventual reunification.

South Korea and Japan

2005 was South Korea and Japanese friendship year, forty years after the restoration of diplomatic relations between the two countries. However it was also the year the two neighbours vehemently disputed control of a set of islands located between the countries. The islands are variously called Takeshima (Japanese name) and Dokdo (South Korean) and around them are thought to be 600 million tonnes of natural gas resources. Shimane, a western Japanese prefecture, announced the creation of a Takeshima Day to be held in February. This was greeted with angry protest with some commentators citing the Japanese decision tantamount to an act of war. The Japanese, meanwhile, intended no such thing. Outside the Japanese embassy in Seoul a mother and child severed their own fingers in protest. The South Korean National Security Council declared: 'The series of recent Japanese actions make us fundamentally doubt whether Japan intends to co-exist with its neighbour.'

These recent tensions can be seen to stem in part from the Japanese Prime Minister Junichiro Koizumi's insistence on visiting the Yasukuni war shrine, which commemorates 14 class A war criminals alongside rank and file fallen soldiers. These criminals exerted great suffering on the Koreans as well as the Chinese and their honoring by the modern day leader is a sign, East Asian countries believe, that Japan has not come to terms with its past. Japan has paid reparations to its slighted neighbour but financial aid has not helped win trust. This war shrine, and all it symbolises, is a major stumbling block in Japanese ambitions for a seat in the UN Security Council. South Korea, alongside China and North Korea, vowed in April to contest the Japanese bid.

South Korea and Japan have been wrangling over trade agreements for 18 months. The Japanese ministry of agriculture issued a point-blank refusal to relinquish protectionist measures on rice imports, and severely restricted debate on other crops and fishing produce: the South Koreans expressed exasperation and annoyance about the lack of progress in June 2005.

In December 2005 the International Crisis Group (ICG) recommended that the East Asia area institute a regional body to co-operate on military, energy, security and environmental issues. While Europe enjoys a high level of inter-involvement, North Korea, Japan and China are not incorporated into such a tight organisation.

US relationship

Differences in approach towards North Korea have precipitated some difficulties in the relationship between the US and South Korea. South Korea has contributed troops to missions in Iraq with the third largest quota of soldiers, despite domestic resistance. In November 2005, one day after a meeting between Roh Moo Hyun and US President George W Bush, however, the country declared its intention to remove one third, or 1,000, of these troops. The development constituted an embarrassment to the US who was not consulted about the reduction.

Mass amnesty

In August 2005 4.2 million Korean criminals were granted mass amnesty. Though this seems like a lot of people, it is only the fourth biggest official pardon since South Korea won its independence from Japan. The reason there are so many petty

KEY INDICATORS — South Korea

	Unit	2000	2001	2002	2003	2004
Population	m	46.84	47.14	47.43	47.57	47.72
Gross domestic product (GDP)	US$bn	456.70	423.00	460.70	605.30	*679.67
GDP per capita	US$	9,656	8,870	9,630	10,641	14,098
GDP real growth	%	8.5	3.8	7.0	3.1	4.6
Inflation	%	2.3	4.3	2.8	3.3	3.6
Unemployment	%	4.1	3.7	3.0	3.4	3.7
Coal output	mtoe	2.2	1.7	1.5	1.5	1.4
Exports (fob) (goods)	US$m	175,948.0	151,371.0	161,966.0	193,817.0	257,745.0
Imports (fob) (goods)	US$m	159,076.0	137,979.0	154,535.0	178,827.0	219,584.0
Balance of trade	US$m	16,872.0	13,392.0	7,431.0	14,990.0	38,161.0
Current account	US$m	11,405.0	8,617.0	6,090.0	12,321.0	26,820.0
Total reserves minus gold	US$m	96,130.5	102,753.3	121,345.2	155,284.2	198,996.6
Foreign exchange	US$m	95,855.1	102,487.5	120,811.4	154,508.8	198,175.3
Exchange rate	per US$	1,130.96	1,290.99	1,253.28	1,194.23	1,145.47

* estimated figure

criminals stems from an inappropriate, over-criminalising judicial system. A Seoul-based attorney explained: 'much of what is a civil matter in the UK or US is a crime in South Korea,' such as, for example, going back on a promise to marry someone. Courts have a staggeringly high conviction rate and requests from prosecutors, for search warrants, for instance, are granted by the courts without much questioning.

In March 2005 plans were announced for the family register to be restructured. Since the fourteenth century, the male has been the head of the household and wives and children are defined in relation to him. Females are registered under their father, then their husbands, and back to their fathers if they divorce – a rapidly increasing occurrence. Women's rights groups hope that the overhaul of the registration system might contribute to an adjustment in the patriarchal Korean mindset, and pave the way towards a more democratic, equal society.

Economy

The UK investment company Alliance Trusts predicted in July that South Korea was set to be the world's eighth largest economy by 2050. The IMF has called it one of the most open and liberal economies in the region. It is still, however, a country with a large number of strikes – 400 in 2004 – powerful unions and a largely unmodernised market. The unions pose a significant threat to competition. GDP growth in 2005 was projected at an underperforming 3.8 per cent.

Thanks to increased foreign ownership and international profits from Korean enterprise – over 40 per cent of the stock market is foreign-controlled – it appears there has been some level of protective, nationalist backlash in the business world. Foreign firms have reported being penalised in sometimes arbitrary or untransparent ways. In April 2005 a bill was proposed curbing foreign presence on banking boards. All board members must have lived in Korea for over 12 months and half the board must be Korean citizens. The EU challenged the proposals.

In the same month Korean investigators looked into allegations of tax avoidance on the part of US firms such as Newbridge Capital and Lone Star. In June 2005 Deutsche Bank was suspended from trading for three months on the grounds that it had not warned state companies about known risks in currency swaps.

Businesses are in turn becoming unhappy about the level of regulation and the unpredictability of the business climate. This is illustrated by the substantial drop in foreign direct investment in 2004 and 2005.

Export growth, at a rate of 11 per cent, was not as furious as in recent years – 31 per cent in 2004 – thanks to the value of the won, dangerously high against the dollar. Industrial manufacturing, especially of mobile phones, declined. In June South Korea began to plough foreign exchange reserves into domestic companies in a bid to encourage them to invest abroad. Domestic demand had been undergoing something of a slump until an upward turn in July. Spending was encouraged by tax cuts and low interest rates.

In March 2005 regulating authorities agreed to reform the competition climate in Korea, curbing the power of the old boy network conglomerates, or *chaebol*. From April, the largest *chaebol* was able to invest only 25 per cent of their assets into other companies. This will reduce the problem of cross-shareholding and the excessive influence of relatively few individuals. Companies can avoid the legislation by meeting certain criteria such as excellence in corporate governance. By the end of 2005 however it seemed that the *chaebol* reforms have been minimal or token.

Stem cell debacle

One of the year's biggest embarrassments for South Korea was the admission of Hwang Woo-suk, biologist at the Seoul National University, that he had faked stem cell research. Hwang's declarations in 2004 and 2005 that he had created stem cell lines from cloned embryos and had developed customised stem cells was greeted with rapture in the scientific community. The research had encouraging implications for Parkinson's disease and Alzheimers patients. His research was groundbreaking and it cast South Korea into the spotlight as a modern, scientific, progressive nation. Hwang had become a national celebrity, inspiring postage stamps and widespread adulation.

However, in December 2005 allegations began to emerge casting doubt on the credibility of Hwang's work and with mounting pressure he was forced to admit that most of his claims were fabrications. He resigned from his post at the university, blaming researchers and junior colleagues for untrustworthy work. Not only this, but it emerged that two junior scientists donated their own eggs for Hwang's research: this contravenes ethical guidelines. Now there are calls in the international community for the imposition of tighter legislation and monitoring of research laboratories. It has been suggested that Hwang's motive was nationalism. National pride did indeed surge in the midst of the celebrations, but now South Koreans are despondent and defensive in equal measure.

Outlook

South Korea's dullish reputation has been transformed into something modern and vibrant. The economy has great potential but the country is not maximizing its opportunities, partly due to resistance to foreign influence. It needs to open up further and push through liberalising reforms.

Risk assessment

Economic	Fair
Political	Good
Regional stability	Fair

COUNTRY PROFILE

Historical profile

The peninsula of Korea developed a society and culture heavily influenced both by contact with imperial China and links to Japan. From the fourth century, Buddhism influenced an indigenous artistic and intellectual life.

The northern kingdom of Koguryo (from which the modern 'Korea' is derived) achieved unification of the peninsula in the tenth century. In the thirteenth century, it was invaded and ruled by Mongolians. The Mongolians were eventually overthrown by the Ming dynasty who called the country 'Chosun'.

1910 Japan formalised its annexation of Korea after gaining responsibility for its security following victory in the Russo-Japanese war of 1905.

1919 Japan suppressed the mass March First movement for self-determination.

1930s–1940s Japan imposed measures designed to assimilate the Korean population, including the outlawing of the Korean language and family names. Korea suffered under military occupation but gained the benefits of forced industrialisation.

1945 Liberation at the hands of Allied forces was a prelude to partition of the peninsula as the victorious powers encouraged friendly governments north and south of the 38th parallel. The US occupied the south while the north was taken over by the Soviet Union. As the two powers did not wish to give independence to Korea, feeling that the Korean people needed political and social re-education, a line of demarcation was established.

1948 Political divisions in the peninsula deepened. In the south, the Republic of

Korea became independent after UN-supervised elections were held. Dr Syngman Rhee, leader of the Liberal Party, became the country's first president. The declaration of the Democratic People's Republic of Korea in the North followed, with Kim il-Sung becoming premier and head of state.
1950 North Korea invaded the South with backing from China and the Soviet Union, prompting US-led intervention under a UN mandate.
1953 A cease-fire was signed on 27 July; a peace treaty was never signed.
1960 President Rhee was forced to resign.
1961 The government was deposed by a military coup led by General Park Chung-Hee.
1963 After years of military leadership, a new constitution was enacted. Park became president.
1980 Demonstrations by students led to martial law being imposed throughout the country. The National Assembly was closed and all political activity banned.
1981 Martial law was lifted and political parties were formed.
1985 The election results transformed the political scene with the emergence for the first time of a relatively powerful parliamentary opposition.
1986 The opposition launched a campaign demanding constitutional reform.
1987 Roh Tae-Woo was elected president.
1988 The Constitution of the Sixth Republic was adopted, following sustained popular unrest during 1987.
1993 President Roh was succeeded by Kim Young-Sam.
1997 The Asian financial crisis in July precipitated the near collapse in South Korea's economy. Within 14 days South Korea's credit rating plunged from A1 to Baa2. It was only saved by the devaluation of the won and a US$57 billion loan by the IMF and G-7 countries. The political upheaval from the economic crisis resulted in defeat for the Hannara Dang, (Grand National Party) (GNP) and opposition leader Kim Dae-Jung was elected president.
2000 President Kim Dae-Jung visited Pyongyang in North Korea and met President Kim Jong-il, in an unprecedented and much-fêted meeting of the two Korean leaders. President Kim Dae-Jung won the Nobel peace prize.
2001 The government resigned after a vote of no-confidence threatened Lim Dong-Won, the unification minister and chief architect of the sunshine policy promoting engagement with North Korea. The president subsequently returned Lim to government as a presidential advisor, appointed five new ministers and retained Lee Han-Dong as prime minister.
2002 Key inter-Korean relations developed after the South Korean envoy Lim Dong-Won visited North Korea and an accord was signed that included plans for economic co-operation and a revival of a cross-border railway project linking the two countries. Parliament rejected the president's choice of prime minister – Chang Sang, who could have been the first female premier – appointing Chang Dae-Whan instead. In a by-election, the opposition party, the GNP won 11 seats out of 13. The GNP attained 139 seats in the 273-member National Assembly. Kim Suk Soo became prime minister. Roh Moo Hyun won the presidential elections.
2003 Roh Moo Hyun became president on 25 February. Goh Kun became prime minister on 26 February. President Roh left the ruling Saecheonnyeonminju Dang (SMD) (Millennium Democratic Party) in October. The Uri Dang (UD) (Our Party) was formed by members in the SMD loyal to the President. The President called a referendum to re-affirm his leadership.
2004 On 12 March, President Roh was suspended after a vote of the National Assembly to impeach him (193–192). Prime Minister Goh Kun took over as acting president. The UD won the 15 April National Assembly elections; for the first time since 1985 left-leaning liberals gained control of parliament. On 14 May, the Constitutional Court overturned the impeachment motion against President Roh, who resumed his duties. Prime Minister Goh Kun resigned and Lee Hai Chan became prime minister. South and North Korea agreed to open cross-border roads and to make test runs on two railways.
2005 On 30 December the National Assembly voted 110 to 31 to extend South Korea's troop deployment in the northern Iraqi region of Arbil until the end of 2006, although troops would be cut from 3,200 to 2,300 however.

Political structure
Constitution
A new constitution, allowing direct presidential elections and thus providing a framework for civilian rule, took effect in 1988 after receiving overwhelming approval in a referendum. The constitution removed the president's sweeping emergency powers that included the right to dissolve parliament. It also enhanced the authority of the legislature and judiciary. It provided for more civil liberties, including restoration of *habeas corpus*, while the National Assembly was empowered to supervise and investigate state affairs. Free presidential elections replaced the electoral college system, which had favoured the ruling party candidate. In addition, the constitution requires that the armed forces must maintain political neutrality. The constitution provides for greater checks and balances among the executive, legislative and judiciary powers. A Board of Audit and Inspection was set up to monitor all government expenditure, revenue and agencies. The chairperson is appointed by the president but only with the National Assembly's approval.
A constitutional court has judgement on the constitutionality of any legislation.

Form of state
Democratic republic

The executive
Executive power is held by the president, who is popularly elected for a single term of five years and governs with the assistance of the State Council, normally composed of 15–30 ministers and headed by the prime minister. The State Council is appointed by the president on the advice of the prime minister. It does not have to be composed entirely of members of the National Assembly. No active member of the armed forces may serve on the State Council.
The president has veto power over legislation, but the National Assembly can override this by a two-thirds vote.
Other presidential powers include the appointment of officials such as judges, ministers, the mayors of five cities (Seoul, Pusan, Taegu, Inchon and Kwangu) and the governors of nine provinces.

National legislature
Legislative power is exercised by the unicameral Kuk Hoe (National Assembly), which, under the 1988 constitution, must have no fewer than 200 members, serving four-year terms.

Legal system
There is a three-tier legal system, headed by a Supreme Court. This Court is composed of a chief justice (for a six-year term) and 13 justices (on recommendation by the chief justice), all appointed by the president, with the consent of the National Assembly. Below the Supreme Court are High Courts (intermediate appelate courts) and, below these, District Courts. High Courts and District Courts are divided into geographic districts. Korea also has a number of specialised courts, such as a Family Court and an Administrative Court.

Last elections
15 April 2004 (National Assembly); 19 December 2002 (presidential).
Results: Parliamentary: Uri Dang (UD) (Our Party) won 152 seats out of 299; Hannara Dang (HD) (Grand National Party) 121; Minjunodong Dang (MDD) (Democratic Labour Party) 10; Saecheonnyeonminju Dang (SMD) (Milennium Democratic Party) nine; Jayu Minju Yonmaeng (JMY) (United Liberal Democrats) four, NA21 one. Turnout was 60.6 per cent.

South Korea

Presidential: Roh Moo Hyun won 49.0 per cent, Lee Hoi Chang 46.5 per cent and Kwon Young Ghil 3.9 per cent.
Next elections
2007 (presidential); 2008 (National Assembly).

Political parties
Ruling party
Uri Dang (UD) (Our Party) (from 15 Apr 2004)
Main opposition party
Hannara Dang (HD) (Grand National Party)

Population
47.72 million (2004)
Ethnic make-up
Koreans, although apparently homogeneous, have complex ethnic origins, with much genetic input from the nomadic tribes of Mongolia and Central Asia. There are over 25,000 Chinese, the only major foreign ethnic community besides the 37,000 US troops stationed in South Korea. In addition, there are some 230,000 migrant labourers from a variety of countries such as Kazakhstan, Morocco and China. There is also a growing number of refugees who have escaped from the harsh conditions of North Korea.
Religions
There is no state religion and the country is tolerant of various religious faiths. Although census and churchgoing data conflict, the most recent information available indicates that up to 49 per cent of the population professes to be Christian, 47 per cent Mahayana Buddhist, 3 per cent Confucianist.

Education
Public expenditure on education amounts to 3.6 per cent of GDP. Universal primary education and gender parity, at this level and in secondary schools, have been achieved.
Primary schooling lasts until a child is 12, middle secondary schooling lasts for three years, these constitute compulsory education. Upper secondary high schools offer either, an academic, special purpose (combined academic and vocational courses), or a wholly vocational programme, lasting for three years.
There are five types of public and private teriary institutions including junior colleges and universities.
Literacy rate: 98 per cent, male; 96.8 per cent, female; adult rates (World Bank).
Compulsory years: 6 to 15
Enrolment rate: 110 per cent, gross primary enrolment, of relevant age group (including repeaters); 102 per cent, gross secondary enrolment (World Bank).
Pupils per teacher: 31, in primary schools

Health
There are around 19,500 private clinics complementing the country's hospitals, of which a significant number are university-affiliated. Improved water sources and sanitation facilities are available to 92 per cent and 63 per cent of the population resectively.
Life expectancy: 73.9 years (World Bank)
Fertility rate/Maternal mortality rate: 1.5 birth per woman; maternal mortality 20 deaths per 100,000 live births (World Bank).
Birth rate/Death rate: 6 deaths and 14 births per 1,000 population (World Bank estimates).
Infant mortality rate: 5 per 1,000 live births (World Bank)

Welfare
The National Basic Livelihood Protection Law makes social assistance a legal right for the unemployed, based on a concept of 'productive welfare' which combines means-testing with self-support plans to facilitate re-entry to the workforce. Public pensions provision, introduced in 1988, is set to increase as the system confronts an ageing population with a 12-fold increase in the expected number of beneficiaries by 2010. Contributions will have to double to 18 per cent of salary to maintain an actuarial balance, according to the Organisation for Economic Co-Operation and Development (OECD). The South Korean government may consider alternative options, such as privately-managed pensions funds, paid into by the allowances firms are obliged to award departing employees.

Main cities
Seoul (capital, estimated population 9.6 million in 2004), Pusan (3.5 million), Inch'on (2.5 million), Taegu (2.4 million), Taejeon (1.4 million), Kwangju (1.4 million), Seongnam (1.2 million), Pucheon (1.0 million).
In 2007, the government will start building a new administrative capital in Chungcheongnam-do province, to the south of Seoul; the first ministries and government departments will move in 2012; the city should be complete by 2030.

Languages spoken
The Korean language is a member of the Altaic family with origins in Mongolia. Approximately 60 per cent of the vocabulary is borrowed from Chinese. The written language employs its own phonetic character system, Hangul.
English is spoken to a limited extent in government and business circles. The older generation often speak Japanese.

Official language/s
Korean
Media
The Korean media, reputedly notorious for their appetite for influence, are thought, by civic campaigners, to be a constituency in need of urgent reform. Efforts made in the past to curtail publishers and their various backers have not succeeded. The sector has a long tradition of collaborating with South Korea's authoritarian regimes and is sensitive about criticism of bias.
Press
Dailies: The 'Big Three' national dailies are *Chosun Ilbo*, *Joong-Ang Ilbo* and *Donga Ilbo*. Other Korean language newspapers are *Hankook Ilbo*, *Han-Kyoreh Shinmun*, *Kyunghyang Shinmun*, *The Pusan Ilbo Daily News*, *The Maeil Shinmun*, *The Korea Daily News*, *The Munhwa Ilbo* and *Yonhap News*. Bi-lingual publications include *Joong-Ang Ilbo* (Korean, English), and *Korea Times* (Korean, English). *The Korea Herald* is an English language publication (www.koreaherald.co.kr).
Weeklies: News magazines include *Korea Newsreview* (English). The *Courrier de la Corée* (French) is published by the *Korea Herald* and provides a summary of major events.
Business: Business publications include *Korea Business World*, *Business Korea*, *Maeil Economic Daily* and *Korea Economic Daily*.
Periodicals: *Dong-A Herald* is a bi-monthly student newspaper. *The Granite Tower* is a monthly English language tabloid.
Broadcasting
Radio: There are educational, religious, commercial and public external broadcasts (by the state-run Korea Broadcasting System) on four channels in 12 languages.
Television: There are over 30 television stations run by the country's networks, of which the most senior are Korea Broadcasting System (KBS) and Munwha Broadcasting Corporation (MBC). The longest-running stations are KBS 1, 2, 3 (an educational station), MBC and AFKN-TV (operated by the US military for its personnel and their dependants). Other networks operating in South Korea include Asia-Pacific broadcaster Arirang TV, which provides English-language programming, the youth-oriented Mnet, Korea Music Television, Seoul Broadcasting System (SBS) and the News Channel of Korea.
Advertising
Commercial advertising may be placed with the daily press, radio and television stations and cinemas. Advertising standards are defined and controlled by the

Korea Broadcasting Ethics Committee and the Korea Newspaper Ethics Committee. The Korea Broadcasting Advertising Corporation (Kobaco) grants recognition to advertising agencies for television and radio. Advertising expenditure is typically equivalent to 1.2 per cent of GDP.

Economy

Economic growth over the past 30 years has been spectacular. South Korea had the 11th-largest economy in the world in 2004 and is now the US's seventh-largest trading partner. It managed to avoid most of the shocks that hit many other East Asian economies in 2001/02 due to its highly diversified industrial base and large domestic market. The economy recovered somewhat from weak consumption after the large household debt levels of 2002 and an increase in exports to China helped to pull the economy out of a brief recession at the end of 2003. By 2004 GDP had recovered slightly to 4.6 per cent and was forecast to be 3.8 per cent in 2005 and to reach 5.0 per cent in 2006.

South Korea is performing better than some other newly industrialised Asian economies, and the reforms put in place since the 1997–98 Asian financial crisis are addressing some of the issues that adversely affected the economy, especially the hold of the *chaebols* (industrial conglomerates) over the financial sector. Structural problems and a rapidly aging population are problems for the future. Among structural concerns are the rigid labour market, underdeveloped financial markets and a general lack of regulatory transparency. Bank privatisation and creating a more liberalised economy with a mechanism for bankrupt firms to exit the market are also important tasks. Korean industry is increasingly worried about diversion of corporate investment to China. In the meantime, two-way trade between North and South Korea has increased from US$18.8 million in 1989 to US$697 million in 2004.

South Korea's total lack of hydrocarbons will always be a concern and means that all oil and natural gas have to be imported, making the economy vulnerable to oil price rises.

Growth rates of GDP and of labour productivity are above most other OECD countries, which is helping narrow the income gap relative to the average OECD level.

The OECD, in its 2005 *Economic Policy Reforms* publication, recommends:
- Easing employment protection for regular workers by relaxing the conditions on collective dismissals, at the same time developing the social safety net by improving unemployment insurance.
- Continuing to shift the support payments to agricultural producers (which currently represents 60 per cent of total farm receipts) from market price support to direct payments; and eliminate the remaining restrictions on farm size so as to improve productivity.
- Further liberalising services by accelerating the restructuring of network industries and establishing independent regulators to promote competition.
- Removing ownership, procedural and regulatory barriers to foreign direct investment (FDI), already fairly low, and extend the incentives offered in the three Free Economic Zones to the rest of the country.
- Improving the functioning of the financial sector, including privatising the banks, and generally moving towards a more pre-emptive approach to financial supervision.

External trade

Negotiations have begun with China, Japan and India to achieve free trade areas (FTA).

Imports

Principal imports are machinery, electronics and electronic equipment, oil, steel, plastics, transport equipment and organic chemicals.

Main sources: Japan (21.6 per cent total, 2004), US (12.7 per cent), China (12.3 per cent), Saudi Arabia (5.1 per cent)

Exports

Principal exports are semi-conductors, wireless telecommunications equipment, motor vehicles, computers, steel, ships and petrochemicals.

Main destinations: China (22.4 per cent total, 2004), US (17.8 per cent), Japan (8.3 per cent), Hong Kong (4.8 per cent)

Agriculture

Farming

The agricultural sector accounts for around 3.7 per cent of GDP and employs 15 per cent of the workforce. Farming remains essentially subsistence-based and is inherently uncompetitive. While, by comparison, farmers are richer than their counterparts elsewhere in Asia, the average farm holding is big enough to support only a small family and the disparity in incomes between the urban and rural populations is growing.

Price-support policies for farmers are being reduced in line with South Korea's international commitments. Increasing the average size of farms and decoupling production decisions from government aid are likely to be vital in promoting efficiency in farming.

The main crops grown are rice, sweet potatoes, barley, soya beans and a wide range of fruit and vegetables. Despite considerable efforts, the country depends on imports for animal feed grains. Ginseng, tobacco, pears and processed noodles are among South Korea's exports. Crop production in 2004 included: 7,152,561 million tonnes (t) cereals in total, 6,800,000t rice, 2.6t cabbages, 12,000t wheat, 550,000t potatoes, 268,733t sweet potatoes, 260,000t barley, 340,000t chillies & peppers, 378,846t garlic, 15,919t pulses, 73,756t treenuts, 621,000t citrus fruit, 360,000t grapes, 269,918t tomatoes, 38,247t oilcrops, 35,666t tobacco, 135,570t soya beans, 1,500t tea, 350,000t apples, 2,440,802t fruit in total, 11,022,330t vegetables in total. Livestock production included: 1,716,903t meat in total, 187,000t beef, 1,100,000t pig-meat, 2,475t goat meat, 420,024t poultry, 526,000t eggs, 2,304,950t milk, 26,000t honey, 3t cocoons, silk, 31,200t cattle hides.

Fishing

The fishing industry is an important source of export earnings but international restriction of fishing zones has limited potential growth. South Korean fishing vessels are mostly active in the South Pacific. The annual catch, of which some 60 per cent is marine fish, totals up to 2.6 million tonnes.

Forestry

Forests, around half of which are conifer, cover some 65 per cent of the total land area. Much of the forest owes its existence to large-scale replanting programmes implemented after the Second World War and since the end of the Korean War in 1953. The latter conflict, together with logging under the Japanese occupation, and demand for fuelwood, badly degraded the native forest.

South Korea and Indonesia have an agreement for forestry co-operation. This involves projects such as tree planting, fighting forest fires, skills development and eco-tourism investment.

Exports of forest materials in 2004 amounted to US$1.6 billion, while imports amounted to US$3.6 billion. Production in 2004 included 4,136,202 cubic metres (cum) roundwood, 1,673,000cum industrial roundwood, 4,380,000cum sawnwood, 3,720,000cum wood-based panels, 289,000cum sawlogs & veneers, 1,017,000cum pulpwood, 714,000cum veneer sheets, 2,463,202 cum wood fuel, 29,292 tonnes charcoal.

Industry and manufacturing

Korea's industrialisation programme made it the world's eleventh richest economy during the 1990s, when it became the world's largest shipbuilder and producer of DRAM memory chips, the fourth biggest car exporter and the sixth largest steelmaker. The industrial sector accounts for around 40 per cent of GDP and employs around a fifth of the workforce. The manufacture of iron and steel products, the automobile industry, shipbuilding, petrochemicals and electronics continue to be central to export-led growth. Other main products include fertilisers and other industrial chemicals, rubber, synthetic and natural textiles, garments, footwear and processed foods. The industrial structure continues to be haunted by the legacy of rapid state-guided industrialisation protected from overseas competition. The government has struggled to limit the economic power of the 30 largest leading companies (*chaebol*), which still dominate national industry.

Tourism
Tourism is an important and growing industry. New hotels, both de luxe and budget class, have opened and more are being built throughout the country. New resort complexes are under construction. There were 5.8 million visitor arrivals in 2004. Tourism is expected to contribute 1.6 per cent to GDP in 2005.

Mining
There are no significant mineral resources. South Korea relies mainly on imports to meet its increasing domestic demand. The major mineral imports are iron ore, copper and zinc ore concentrates. Cement is a major export commodity to the US, as there is surplus in the domestic market.
LG-Nikko Copper Incorporated, a joint venture established by LG and Japan Korea Joint Smelting Company, a Japanese consortium, is the only copper smelting and refining operation in South Korea. Each company was obliged to invest US$20 million in the joint venture that took control of LG's Changhang and Onsan copper smelting and refining operations, which had an estimated value of US$830 million.
Domestic iron ore supplies only about one per cent of South Korea's needs. The Pohang Iron and Steel Company (Posco), the largest crude steel producer in South Korea and the only integrated iron and steel producer, formed a strategic alliance with Nippon Steel Corp, to expand research and development, and also encouraged other Asian companies to join the alliance. Posco employs more than 5,000 employees at production plants in Pohang and Kwangyang, producing more than 23.4 million tonnes of steel products annually for customers in over 60 countries. Its products range from electrical steel sheets to stainless steel products.

The only lead and zinc mine, at Kumba, supplies about 10 per cent of the demand for lead and zinc concentrates. Korea Zinc, which is one of the largest primary zinc producers in the world, completed the expansion of its zinc plant complex at Onsan, and is able to produce over 350,000 tonnes per year. Young Poong Corporation, its parent company, increased zinc metal output at the Sukpo zinc refinery, in the North Kyongsang Province, by over 198,300 tonnes per year.
The non-metal mineral sector accounts for 51.9 per cent of the total mining industry. Other industrial mineral production includes limestone, silica stone, kaolin, serpentine, feldspar and zeolite. Major imports consist of potash, asbestos and manganese ores and concentrates.

Hydrocarbons
South Korea has no domestic oil reserves. Oil consumption was 2.1 million bpd in 2004, making it the world's seventh largest consumer and fourth largest importer. The country has built up strategic petroleum reserves which cover 90 days of imports, in order to offset any disruption to supply. The state-owned Korea National Oil Corporation (KNOC) has, in an effort to secure the country's oil supply, bought up stakes in oil companies throughout the world and is involved in 18 foreign exploration and production projects. South Korea has an oil refining capacity of 2.6 million barrels per day (bpd).
Domestic gas production began in November 2003 with KNOC's development of a small natural gas field, located offshore in the south-east. The development supplies just 2 per cent of the country's total demand for natural gas. South Korea has relied on imports of liquefied natural gas (LNG) to provide it with gas since 1985, when the Korea Gas Corporation (Kogas) was formed. Consumption of natural gas, which has increased in recent years, typically amounts to 18.7 billion cubic metres. Indonesia and Malaysia provide most of South Korea's LNG, other sources being Brunei, Australia and Qatar. LNG is the fastest growing energy source in South Korea.
Coal supplies around 21 per cent of South Korea's energy needs. Domestic production has declined from 10 million tonnes in the mid-1980s to less than 4 million tonnes in 2004. Domestic coal production is of low-quality anthracite used in residential heating and small boilers. Steam coal for power supply and metallurgical coal for steelmaking come mainly from China and Australia, where the Korean Electric Power Corporation (Kepco) has invested in a number of mines.

Energy
South Korea has over 50GW of generating capacity, supplied mainly by thermal and nuclear power. The government projects electricity demand will rise by an average annual rate of 3.4 per cent between 2002 and 2015.
The privatisation of the state-owned electricity utility, Korean Electric Power Corporation (Kepco), has moved at a slow pace due to strong opposition from the trade unions.

Banking and insurance
The 1997/98 financial crisis revealed underlying structural problems in South Korea's banking system. The crisis led to the creation of the Financial Restructuring Committee (FRC), which reported a large ratio of non-performing loans (NPLs) to total loans and poor accounting standards. The government was forced to nationalise the country's five largest banks so that by 2002/03 at 7.5 per cent, South Korea had the second-lowest NPL ratio in East Asia after Hong Kong. The estimated recovery rate on South Korean NPLs is 35 per cent, compared to Singapore and Hong Kong at 75 per cent and 50 per cent respectively.
Although the financial system is in better health, controversies linger over bank privatisation. Arguments also surround banking regulation, with President Roh reluctant to allow the *chaebol* to regain their influence over the sector. Roh favours increasing the powers of independent directors and shareholders as well as encouraging greater foreign ownership, although there is little foreign interest in South Korea's banking sector which is seen as risky.
Another pressing concern for the government is consolidating the banking sector into three or four large banks.

Central bank
Bank of Korea

Main financial centre
Seoul

Time
GMT plus nine hours. Summer time: April–October (add one hour).

Geography
South Korea forms the southern part of the Korean peninsula, in north-east Asia, with the Democratic People's Republic of Korea to the north. To the west is the Yellow Sea, the East China Sea is to the south and the Sea of Japan is to the east. The Korea Strait separates the peninsula from Japan in the south-east. The country's portion of the peninsula is dominated by rugged terrain and mountains, culminating in the T'aebaek-sanmaek mountain range which runs from north to south along the eastern coast. Both major rivers

originate in this range, the Naktong flowing to the Korea Strait and the Han river to the Yellow Sea. Plains are few and far between, mostly concentrated in the west, with the coastal strips in the east and south typically narrow. There are a number of islands off the southern and western coasts. Of these the largest is Cheju, over 1,800 square km in size and home to South Korea's highest peak, Mount Hallasan (1,950 metres).

Climate
Winters are dry and very cold, with temperatures well below 0 degrees Celsius (C) between December–February. Korean summers are typically hot and humid, with monsoon rains, tropical storms and occasional typhoons from June to September. The average July temperature range is 22–29 degrees C. The narrow southernmost coastal plain has the mildest climate and is home to vegetation such as bamboo and evergreen oak.

Entry requirements
Passports
Required by all except certain UN personnel. Passports should be valid for six months from the date of departure.
Visa
Required by all, except nationals of North America, Japan, Australia and most EU citizens, who may enjoy visa-free stays for up to three months. Others may also enjoy visa-free visits and it is advisable to check with consular officials.
Currency advice/regulations
Import and export of won is limited to US$10,000. Local currency is not convertible outside South Korea. Foreign currency is not restricted, but must be declared on arrival and departure. Exchange receipts should be retained.
Customs
Personal effects are duty free. High-value items (cameras, watches etc) should be recorded on arrival on your passport to ensure re-export. Visitors may be liable for import duty and tax on items lost or stolen while in the country. Apply for customs clearance prior to importing an automobile. A certificate from the Cultural Properties Preservation Bureau is necessary for exporting antiques. Permission for trade imports or exports must be obtained from the trade and industry ministry or from authorised foreign exchange banks, and certain items may be restricted or prohibited (such as ginseng and cuttlefish).
Prohibited imports
Japanese-made automobiles, narcotics and certain plant types.

Health (for visitors)
Health facilities in South Korea are generally good. The high level of pollution may be a serious problem for those suffering from respiratory conditions.
Mandatory precautions
An HIV/Aids-free certificate is required for stays of over three months.
Advisable precautions
Vaccinations are recommended for diphtheria, tuberculosis, hepatitis 'A' and 'B', Japanese B encephalitis, polio, tetanus and typhoid. There is rabies risk and travellers should avoid stray animals.

Hotels
Western-style hotels include a 10 per cent service charge in the bill. Tipping is not usual, although it is on the increase in Western-style hotels.

Credit cards
Major hotels accept credit cards, but check when booking which ones are accepted for settlement of hotel bills. Also accepted in major department stores, supermarkets etc.

Public holidays
Fixed dates
1 Jan (New Year's Day), 1 Mar (Independence Movement Day), 5 Apr (Arbor Day), 5 May (Children's Day), 6 Jun (Memorial Day), 17 Jul (Constitution Day), 15 Aug (Liberation Day), 3 Oct (National Foundation Day), 25 Dec (Christmas Day).
The summer vacation is the last week in July and the first week in August.
Variable dates
Sollal (Lunar New Year, Jan/Feb), Birth of Buddha (May), Chu'sok (Harvest Moon Festival, Sep/Oct).

Working hours
Sunday is the weekly closing day. Service establishments open as late as 2200 over weekends and on public holidays.
Banking
Mon–Fri: 0930–1630; Sat: 0930–1330.
Business
Mon–Fri: 0900–1200, 1300–1800 or later; Sat: 0900–1300.
Government
Mon–Fri: 0900–1200, 1300–1800; Sat: 0900–1300 (Mar–Oct).
Mon–Fri: 0900–1200, 1300–1700; Sat: 0900–1300 (Nov–Feb).
Shops
Mon–Sat: 1030–1930. Small shops open from early morning till late evening every day of the week.

Electricity supply
110V and 220V AC, 60 cycles, with two-pin square plug fittings and screw-type lamp fittings (gradually switching to 220V AC).

Weights and measures
Metric system used in commerce; local system also in use, especially relating to land and buildings.

Social customs/useful tips
Korean surnames precede given names, and given names are never used alone, except by intimates. The family names, 'Kim', 'Lee' and 'Park', cover more than half the population and may have variant spellings. Business associates are normally addressed by title (e.g. Director Kim or Manager Lee).

Business entertaining usually takes place in restaurants and wives do not participate. Business visitors should carry a good supply of business cards, which are exchanged on introduction. Hotels can provide bilingual business cards overnight. Note the official romanisation of Korean words has been altered to more accurately reflect pronunciation (e.g. Gimpo international airport rather than Kimpo, Busan instead of Pusan and Gimchi instead of Kimchi, Korea's signature spiced cabbage dish). However, the former romanisations are still widely used, with some major newspapers declaring a complete boycott of the new system.

Business etiquette is very formal. Punctuality and a smart appearance are important. Jackets and ties are required, even in summer. However, the ritual of getting drunk with a potential business partner may be expected. You should appear respectful at all times and keep smiling even if negotiations are slow. Business associates like to spend time getting to know you. Confirm agreements in writing. It is impolite to refuse food or drink. Use the right hand when giving or receiving. Outdoor shoes should never be worn inside a house.

There are certain areas, particularly near the demilitarised zone, where entry and photography are forbidden.

Getting there
Air
National airline: Korean Air (KAL); Asiana Airlines.
International airport/s: Inchon International Airport (ICN), 40km west of Inchon and 52km from Seoul. Facilities include car hire, bank, restaurant, duty free and business suite. Connected to the city by rail, taxi (30–60 mins) buses and ferry. Pusan (PUS) 27km from city, with flights arriving mainly from Japan. Cheju (CJU) on the island of Cheju.
Airport tax: 10,000 won, not applicable to transit passengers.
Surface
Rail: In 2002, the rail link between South Korea and the North Korean border re-opened, however, access is strictly limited.
Water: There is a daily ferry service between Pusan and Shiminoseki, Japan.
Main port/s: Pusan, Inchon, Masan, Ulsan, Mokpo, Kunsan, Yosu.

South Korea

Getting about
National transport
Air: Gimpo Airport, located close to Gimpo, west of Seoul, is used for all domestic flights. Korean Air operates daily services between Seoul and Pusan (50 minutes), Taegu, Cheju, Ulsan and Kwangju, with less frequent services to other centres. Other services are provided by Asiana Airlines. Expect to be searched for firearms when embarking on internal flights.

Road: The road network contains more than 60,000km of highways and lesser roads. More than half of roads are paved. Major cities are linked by motorways, but minor roads may be poorly maintained. Pusan is over five hours distant from Seoul by road, compared to four hours by rail.

Buses: Air-conditioned express *Chwasok* buses operate between major cities, in competition with trains. Villages are often connected by a network of local buses.

Rail: Korean National Railroads offers normal and super-express trains between major cities. The super-express train (*Saemaul-ho*) runs between Seoul and Pusan, Chongju, Yosu and Inchon. Timetables and station signs are often in English. Many trains have sleeping and dining cars.

Water: Various services are available. Mokpo and Pusan are linked by a steamer service twice weekly. The *Angel Line*, a hydrofoil service, runs between Pusan and Yosu five times daily, via Chongmy. The island of Cheju is linked to the mainland by daily ferries, including car ferries, three times per week.

City transport
Public transport in Seoul is well-developed, but as in other metropolises can become crowded at rush-hour.

Taxis: Registered taxis carry meters and are clearly marked on the roof. Taxis are plentiful, and available at ranks, by telephone (Seoul (2)414-0150/5) or can be hailed. Call taxis are more comfortable than smaller taxis, but more expensive. Standard fares are charged for shorter distances, sharing is common and tipping is unusual. In Seoul and Pusan light brown-coloured taxis are rated more highly, but are more expensive. A 20 per cent surcharge applies between midnight and 0400. Taxi drivers suspend use of meters for journeys outside town, so negotiate the fare for such trips in advance. If cabs are proving hard to hail, the number of fingers held out can indicate the premium the traveller is willing to pay (two fingers signifies two times the metre fare, and so on).

It is advisable to carry written instructions in Korean if possible.

Buses, trams & metro: The Korean Air limousine shuttle bus calls at 20 Seoul locations, including major hotels.

City buses, though cheap and convenient, are crowded. Purple and white buses have few seats. Green and beige 'seat buses' make fewer stops and are more comfortable and air-conditioned. Tokens are available at most stops. There are English-language signs on city-centre buses only.

Trains: Taking the subway rather than taxi for any medium or long range city trips can save hours. Seoul has excellent subway systems – Line 1 runs from the Seoul railway station to Chongnyangni, NE of the city; Line 2 is a 48.8 km circle connecting downtown with major points south of the Han-gang river and also serves the Seoul Sports Complex; Line 3 runs southeast across the Han-gang river; Line 4 runs south-west.

Subway fare system is divided into zone one and zone two.

Signs are in English and Korean.

Pusan is also developing a subway system.

Car hire
International driving licences are acceptable, but chauffeur-driven car hire is recommended in the main cities.

BUSINESS DIRECTORY

The addresses listed below are a selection only. While World of Information makes every endeavour to check these addresses, we cannot guarantee that changes have not been made, especially to telephone numbers and area codes. We would welcome any corrections.

Telephone area codes
The international direct dialling (IDD) code for the Republic of Korea, is +82, followed by area code and subscriber's number:

Inchon	32	Seoul	2
Pusan	51	Taegu	53

Useful telephone numbers
Police: 112
Fire/ambulance: 119
Directory: 114
International calls: 1035/1037

Chambers of Commerce
American Chamber of Commerce in Korea, 4501 Trade Tower, 159-1 Samsung-dong, Kangnam-gu, Seoul 135-729 (tel: 564-2040; fax: 564-2050; e-mail: info@amchamkorea.org).

British Chamber of Commerce in Korea, 21/F Seoul Finance Centre, 84 Taepyoung-ro 1-ga, Chung-gu, Seoul 100-101 (tel: 720-9406; fax: 720-9411; e-mail: bcck@bcck.or.kr).

European Union Chamber of Commerce in Korea, Kyobo Building, 1 Chongro 1-ga, Chongro-gu, Seoul, 110-714 (tel: 725-9880; fax: 725-9886; e-mail: eucck@eucck.org).

Inchon Chamber of Commerce and Industry, 447 Nonhyon-dong, Namdong-gu, Inchon 405-300 (tel: 810-2800; fax: 810-2807; e-mail: ebiz@incci.co.kr).

Korea Chamber of Commerce and Industry, 45 Namdaemunro 4-ga, Chung-gu, Seoul 100-743 (tel: 316-3114; fax: 771-3267; e-mail: info@korcham.net).

Pusan Chamber of Commerce and Industry, 853-1 Pomchon-dong, Pusanjin-gu, Pusan 614-021 (tel: 645-7771; fax: 645-3003; e-mail: julyjang@pcci.or.kr).

Taegu Chamber of Commerce and Industry, 107 Sinchon 3-dong, Tong-gu, Taegu 701-023 (tel: 755-0041; fax: 795-5774; e-mail: mrlee@dcci.or.kr).

Banking
Bank of Seoul, 10-1, 2-ka, Namdaemun-ro, Chung-gu, Seoul (tel: 77-160; fax: 756-6389).

Cho Hung Bank Ltd., 14, 1-ka, Namdaemun-ro, Chung-gu, Seoul (tel: 733-2000; fax: 732-0835).

Citizens National Bank, 9-1, 2-ka, Namdaemun-ro, Chung-gu, Seoul (tel: 77-140; fax: 757-3679).

Commercial Bank of Korea, 111-1, 2-ka, Namdaemun-ro, Chung-gu, Seoul (tel: 754-3920; fax: 754-9203).

Export-Import Bank of Korea, 16-1, Yoido-dong, Youngdungpo-gu, Seoul 150-010 (tel: 779-6114; fax: 784-1030).

Hanil Bank, 130, 2-ka, Namdaemun-ro, Chung-gu, Seoul (tel: 77-120; fax: 754-0479).

Hana Bank, 101-1, 1-ga Ulchiro, Chung-gu, Seoul 100-191 (tel: 754-2121; fax: 756-6358).

Korea Development Bank, 10-2, Kwanchul-dong, Chongro-gu, Seoul (tel: 398-6369; fax: 720-0015).

Korea Exchange Bank, 181, 2-ka, Ulji-ro, Chung-gu, Seoul (tel: 77-146).

Korea First Bank, 100 Kongpyong-dong, Chongro-gu, Seoul (tel: 733-0070; fax: 736-8092).

Shinhan Bank, 120, 2-ga, Taepyung-ro, Chung-gu, Seoul (tel: 756-0505; fax: 774-7013).

Central bank
Bank of Korea, 110, 3-KA Namdaemun-ro, Chung-ku, Seoul 100-794 (tel: 759-4114; fax: 759-4060; e-mail:bokdplp@bok.or.kr).

Travel information
Asiana Airlines (internet site: http://www.us.flyasiana.com/).

Gimpo Airport (internet site: http://www.airport.co.kr/eng/dba/airport/gimpo/index.html).

Incheon International Airport (internet site: http://www.airport.or.kr/Eng/home.jsp).

Korea Automobile Association, 1, PO Box 2008, Seoul (tel: 785-5051).

Korean Air, 41-3 Seosomun-Dong, Chung-gu, Seoul (tel: 755-2221; fax: 751-7799; internet site: http://www.koreanair.com/).

Korean Travel (internet site: http://english.tour2korea.com/).

Ministry of tourism
Ministry of Culture and Tourism, 82-1 Sejongno, Chongno-gu, Seoul (tel: 736-7946; fax: 736-8513).

National tourist organisation offices
Korean National Tourism Organisation (KNTO), 40 Cheongyecheonmo, Chung-gu, Seoul 100-180 (tel: 729 9497; fax: 319 0086; e-mail: webmaster@mail.knto.or.kr; internet site: www.tour2korea.com or www.knto.or.kr/english/index.html).

Ministries
Ministry of Agriculture and Forestry, 1 Jungang-dong, Kwachon, Kyongki-do 427-760 (tel: 500-1587; fax: 503-7249; e-mail: webmaster@maf.go.kr).

Ministry of Construction and Transportation, 1 Jungang-dong, Kwachon, Kyongki-do 427-712 (tel: 504-9031; fax: 504-6825; e-mail: webmaster@moct.go.kr).

Ministry of Culture and Tourism, 82-1 Sejongno, Jongno-gu, Seoul 110-703 (tel: 3704-9114; fax: 3704-9119; e-mail: webmaster@mct.go.kr).

Ministry of Defence, 1 Yongsan-dong, Yongsan-gu, Seoul 140-701 (tel: 795-0071; fax: 703-3109; e-mail: cyber@mnd.go.kr).

Ministry of Education and Human Resources Development, 77-6 Sejong-no, Jongno-gu, Seoul 110-760 (tel: 3703-2114; fax: 2100-6133; e-mail: webmaster@moe.go.kr).

Ministry of Environment, 1 Jungang-dong, Kwachon, Kyongki-do 427-729 (tel: 2110-6546; fax: 504-9206; e-mail: shinae@me.go.kr).

Ministry of Finance and Economy, 1 Chungang-dong, Kwachon City, Kyonggi-Do, Seoul (tel: 503-7171; fax: 502-0193; internet site: http://www.mofe.go.kr/mofe/eng).

Ministry of Finance, Jungang-dong, Kwachon, Kyongki-do 427-725 (tel: 503-9032; fax: 503-9033; e-mail: fppr@mofe.go.kr).

Ministry of Foreign Affairs and Trade, 95-1 Doryean-dong, Jongno-gu, Seoul 110-787 (tel:3703-2114; fax: 2100-7999; e-mail: webmaster@mofat.go.kr).

Ministry of Gender Equality, 77-6 Sejong-no, Jongno-gu, Seoul 110-760 (tel: 3703-2500; fax: 2106-5145; e-mail: webadmin@moge.go.kr).

Ministry of Government Administration and Home Affairs, 77-6 Sejong-no, Jongno-gu, Seoul 110-760 (tel: 3703-2114; fax: 3703-5502; e-mail: webmaster@mogaha.go.kr).

Ministry of Government Legislation, 77-6 Sejong-no, Jongno-gu, Seoul 110-760 (tel: 3703-2114; fax: 738-2649; e-mail: lawinfo@moleg.go.kr).

Ministry of Health and Welfare, 1 Jungang-dong, Kwachon, Kyongki-do 427-760 (tel: 503-7524; fax: 504-6418; e-mail: m_mohw@mohw.go.kr).

Ministry of Information and Communication, 100 Sejong-no, Jongno-gu, Seoul 110-777 (tel 750-2114; fax: 750-2915; e-mail: webmaster@mic.go.kr).

Ministry of Justice, 1 Jungang-dong, Kwachon, Kyongki-do 427-760 (tel: 503-7023; fax: 2110-3079; webmaster@moj.go.kr).

Ministry of Labour, 1 Jungang-dong, Kwachon, Kyongki-do 427-716 (tel: 2110-2114; fax: 503-9772; e-mail: webmaster@molab.go.kr).

Ministry of Maritime Affairs and Fisheries, 50 Chungjeongno, Saedaemun-gu, Seoul 120-715 (tel: 3148-6114; fax: 3148-6044; e-mail: webmaster@momaf.go.kr).

Ministry of Planning and Budget, 520-3 Banpo-dong, Seocho-gu. Seoul 137-756 (tel: 3480-7990; fax: 3480-7600; e-mail: nara@mpb.go.kr).

Ministry of Science and Technology, 2 Jungang-dong, Kwachon, Kyongki-do 427-715 (tel: 503-7600; fax: 503-7673; e-mail: webadmin@most.go.kr).

Ministry of Trade, Industry and Energy, 1 Jungang-dong, Kwachon, Kyongki-do 427-760 (tel: 2110-5061; fax: 503-9496; e-mail: webmocie@mocie.go.kr).

Ministry of Unification, 77-6 Sejong-no, Jongno-gu, Seoul 110-760 (tel: 3703-2433; fax: 739-5047; e-mail: webmaster@unikorea.go.kr).

Other useful addresses
Association of Foreign Trading Agents in Korea (AFTAK), 218 Hangangro 2-ka, Youngsan-gu, Seoul (tel: 792-1581; fax: 749-1830).

Board of Audit and Inspection, 25-23 Samchong-dong, Jongno-gu, soul (tel: 721-9114; fax: 721-9299).

British Embassy, 4 Chung-dong-Chung-gu, Seoul (tel: 735-7341/3; fax: 736-6241).

Customs Administration, 71 Nonhyun-dong, Kangnam-gu, Seoul (tel: 512-0011; fax: 512-2322).

Economic Planning Board, 1 Chungang-dong, Kwach'on City, Kyonggi, Seoul (tel: 503-7171).

Emergency Planning Committee, 1 Chungang-dong, Kwachon-City, Kyonggi-Do (tel: 503-7723; fax: 503-7727).

Fair Trade Commission, 1 Chungang-dong, Kwachon-City, Kyonggi-Do (tel: 503-7171; fax: 504-5144).

Foreign Investment Policy Division, Rm 203, Complex No 3, 1 Chungang-dong, Kwacheon City, Kyongki-do (tel: 503-9276/7; fax: 503-9324).

Institute of Foreign Affairs and National Security, 1376-2 Seocho-dong, Seocho-gu, Seoul (tel: 571-1020; fax: 571-1019).

Invest Korea, Kotra Bldg 300-9 Yomgok-dong, Seocho-gu, Seoul 137-70 (tel: 3460-7545; fax: 3460-=7946; internet site: http://www.investkorea.org).

Korean Exhibition Centre, 65 Samsung-dong, Gangnam-gu, Seoul (tel: 553-7907/8; fax: 557-5784).

Korean Foreign Trade Association, TCPO Box 100, Seoul (tel: 551-5114; fax: 551-5100/5200).

Korean Information Service, 82-1 Sejongno, Jongno-gu, Seoul 110-703 (internet site: http://www.korea.net).

Korean Republic Embassy (US), 2450 Massachusetts Avenue, NW, Washington DC 20008, USA (tel: 202-939-5600; fax: 202-797-0595; e-mail: information_usa@mofat.go.kr).

Korea Stock Exchange, 33, Yoido-dong, Youngdeungpo-gu, KR-Seoul 150-010 (tel: 780-2271; fax: 786-0263; internet site: http://www.kse.or.kr/e_index.html).

Korean Trade Promotion Corporation (KOTRA), CPO Box 1621 10-1, 2-ka Hoehyun-dong, Chung-gu, Seoul (tel: 753-4180/9; internet site: http://www.kotra.or.kr/eng/index.php3).

Meteorological Administration, 1 Songwall-dong, Jongno-gu, Seoul (tel: 738-0345; fax: 723-8731).

National Statistical Office, Hanta Building, 645-15 Yoksam-dong, Kangnam-gu, Seoul (tel: 222-1901; fax: 538-3874;

South Korea

internet site: http://www.nso.go.kr/eindex.htm).

National Tax Administration, 108-4 Susong-dong, Jongno-gu, Seoul (tel: 397-1200; fax: 720-0278).

Overseas Aircargo Service Inc, 1–6 Fl. Daishin Bldg, 93–62 Bukchang-dong, PO Box 2757, Chung-gu, Seoul (tel: 753-8374/6; fax: 756-9400).

Rural Development Administratin, 250 Socun-dong, Suwon-City, Kyonggi-Do (tel: 292-4370; fax: 292-4163).

Securities Exchange Commission, 28-1 Yoido-dong, Yongdongpo-gu, Seoul (tel: 785-7593; fax: 785-3475).

Small and Medium Business Administration, 2 Chungang-dong, Kwachon-City, Kyonggi-Do (tel: 509-7114; fax: 503-7941).

Internet sites

EC21 (Internet trade site): http://www.ec21.net

Korea Asset Management Corporation: http://www.kamco.or.kr/eng/index.htm

Korea Infogate: http://www.koreainfogate.co.kr

Samsung Economic Research Institute: http://www.koreaeconomy.org

Kuwait

KEY FACTS

Official name: State of Kuwait

Head of State: Sheikh Sabah al Ahmad al Jabir al Sabah (since 19 January 2005)

Head of government: Prime Minister Sheikh Nasser Muhammad al Ahmed (from 7 February 2006)

Ruling party: 16-member Council of Ministers (appointed 2003)

Area: 17,818 square km (including neutral zone)

Population: 2.39 million (2004)

Capital: Kuwait City

Official language: Arabic

Currency: Kuwaiti dinar (KD) = 1,000 fils

Exchange rate: KD0.29 per US$ (Oct 2005)

GDP per capita: US$19,559 (2004)

GDP real growth: 7.20% (2004); *5.8% (2005)

Labour force: 1.12 million (2004)

Unemployment: 2.20% (2004)

Inflation: 1.80% (2004)

Oil production: 2.42 million bpd (2004)

Balance of trade: US$19.30 billion (2004)

Foreign debt: US$15.02 billion (2004)

* Estimate figure

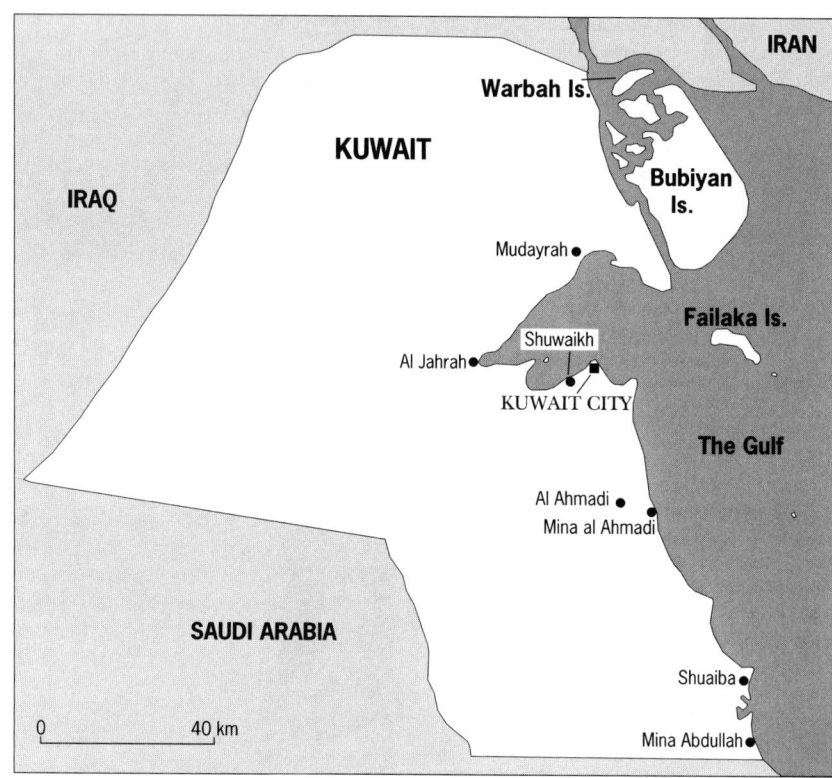

There were a number of developments in Kuwait that generated headlines in 2005 but all of these paled in comparison to the constitutional upheaval sparked by the death of the country's reigning emir, Sheikh Jabir al Ahmed al Sabah, on 15 January 2006. Under Kuwait's constitution, Sheikh Sa'ad al Abdullah al Sabah, the Crown Prince since 1978, had automatically succeeded to the throne on the death of Sheikh Jabir, who had ruled Kuwait for 29 years. In a move unprecedented not only in Kuwait, but also throughout the region, in January 2006 Kuwait's parliament voted unanimously to depose Sheikh Sa'ad on the grounds that his ill health made it impossible for him to rule. Prime Minister Sheikh Sabah al Ahmad al Jabir al Sabah, who had in reality been running the country for several years, was named Emir in his stead. Since independence in 1961, Kuwait's successions have been orderly affairs, alternating between the two branches of the 250-year old al Sabah dynasty.

Oil surge

2005 was one of Kuwait's best returns on oil exports in a decade. The growth in oil revenues meant that the economy as a whole surged forward, with GDP growing by an estimated 5.8 per cent in 2005. Kuwait continues to rely very much on its oil, which still accounts for between 90 and 95 per cent of all export earnings and some 40 per cent of GDP. However, non-oil GDP has been growing in recent years due to the resumption of normal trade relations with Iraq.

Kuwait's oil reserves represent over 8 per cent of the world's total, almost 100 billion barrels. The bulk of Kuwait's oil – around 60 per cent – is exported, principally to Asia. Kuwait also possesses natural gas but in less dramatic quantities. The government proposes to use natural gas

Kuwait

Kuwait's 'jihad blowback'

Kuwaitis received reminders in 2005 that some of its citizens were active participants in al Qaeda-linked attacks around the world. In January, al Qaeda affiliated militants fought several gun battles with Kuwaiti police in and around the capital, Kuwait City. The militants were opposed to the presence of US troops in the emirate and were accused by the government of plotting to kidnap US personnel. In January and November, US authorities released several Kuwaiti nationals from detention in Guantañamo Bay. All were to be retried in Kuwait on charges of undermining Kuwaiti security and fighting against an ally of Kuwait – the US.

Political reform

In May 2005, parliament approved constitutional amendments granting women full political rights, including the right to vote and the right to stand for election. Women will be allowed to participate in the next general election, scheduled for 2007. In June, Kuwait's first female cabinet minister was appointed. Massouma al Mubarak was sworn in as planning minister and minister for administrative development. Also in June, Kuwait held its last all-male poll – elections to Kuwait's municipal councils. Women will be allowed to stand and vote in the next local elections, scheduled for 2009.

Political dissent

A Kuwaiti minister, health minister Muhammad Jarallah, was forced to resign in April after a no-confidence motion in parliament. This was only the third such occasion when the parliament had forced a change in an otherwise unassailable government. Tensions between parliament and government heightened further in October, when an MP called for Crown Prince Sheikh Sa'ad to be set aside in any future succession – a rare attack on a member of the royal family.

Constitutional moves

In June 2005, Crown Prince Sheikh Sa'ad was admitted to hospital, sparking concerns over the future of the succession in the emirate. The Emir, Sheikh Jaber, had been in declining health since 2001 and died on 16 January 2006. Kuwait's cabinet moved swiftly. The resort by the cabinet to a formal constitutional solution to what risked becoming a succession impasse marked a first for the emirate and for its Gulf neighbours. Sheikh Sa'ad, who was 76, was reported to be suffering from Alzheimer's disease and deemed to be incapable of even uttering the one sentence oath of office. The Kuwaiti cabinet found itself with little alternative but to invoke clause three of the Kuwaiti succession law, which requires the new emir to be 'sound of mind'. This gives parliament the final say on the succession. The cabinet decision paved the way for a parliamentary vote in which its 65 members unanimously voted to oust Sheikh Sa'ad – who had only been ruler for 9 days – on health grounds.

On 24 January, the cabinet nominated Sheikh Sabah al Ahmad al Sabah to become Kuwait's new ruler. Sheikh Sabah, who has been Kuwait's prime minister and de facto ruler for nine years, comes from a different branch of the ruling branch to Sheikh Sa'ad. His appointment breaks with the tradition of the ruler coming from alternate branches of the family, a departure which had already caused some friction within the ruling family. Sheikh Sabah was sworn in as the fifteenth al Sabah Emir of Kuwait on 29 January 2006. Sheikh Sabah is himself no spring chicken. Aged 76, he has been fitted with a pacemaker. He is, however, recognised to be an experienced political figure. He has served as Kuwaiti foreign minister (1963–2003) and prime minister (2003–06).

Outlook

With the accession of Sheikh Sabah, Kuwaiti politics can be expected to settle down for the time being. The new emir is widely respected and renowned for his governmental experience. Although reportedly in good health, Sheikh Sabah, at the age of 76, cannot be expected to reign for long. He is yet to appoint a crown prince. Any movement on this front is likely to be closely watched as Sheikh Sabah's own succession broke with family tradition, in that he is the second successive emir to be from the Jaber branch of the al-Sabah dynasty. Members of the Salem branch of the family will expect that the emirate return to their control after Sheikh Sabah dies. Moreover, the Emir has yet to appoint a prime minister and some MPs have urged him to again break with tradition and draft in someone from outside the al-Sabah family.

If the price of oil remains constant, analysts predict that Kuwait could post a surplus for 2005/06 of more than US$20 billion.

Risk assessment

Politics	Stable
Economy	Stable
Regional stability	Fragile

COUNTRY PROFILE

Historical profile

Kuwait became part of Ottoman Empire during the sixteenth century. In the mid-eighteenth century, the Al Khalifa family (now rulers of Bahrain) helped their relatives, the Al Sabah, to establish power in Kuwait, which became semi-autonomous in the later years of Ottoman rule, under the Sheikh of the Al Sabah family. Kuwait was the first Gulf country to have an elected parliament. In 1999, Sheikh Jabir issued a decree giving women full

KEY INDICATORS — Kuwait

	Unit	2000	2001	2002	2003	2004
Population	m	2.19	2.30	2.35	2.37	2.39
Gross domestic product (GDP)	US$bn	37.80	32.80	35.30	38.85	41.75
GDP per capita	US$	17,138	14,202	13,704	16,388	19,559
GDP real growth	%	1.7	-1.0	-0.9	2.7	7.2
Inflation	%	1.7	1.7	2.0	2.1	1.8
Oil output	'000 bpd	2,169.0	2,142.0	1,871.0	2,238.0	2,424.0
Natural gas output	bn cum	9.6	9.5	8.7	8.3	9.7
Exports (fob) (goods)	US$m	19,576.0	16,173.0	16,100.0	21,794.0	30,221.0
Imports (fob) (goods)	US$m	6,846.0	6,932.0	8,230.0	9,882.0	10,920.0
Balance of trade	US$m	12,730.0	9,241.0	8,000.0	11,912.0	19,301.0
Current account	US$m	14,865.0	8,566.0	7,230.0	6,846.0	15,100.0
Total reserves minus gold	US$m	7,082.4	9,897.3	9,208.1	7,577.0	8,241.9
Foreign exchange	US$m	6,504.4	9,191.1	8,357.0	6,640.5	7,347.4
Exchange rate	per US$	0.30	0.31	0.30	0.30	0.29

political rights, but the move was narrowly defeated in the National Assembly; a new bill passed its second reading in June 2005, which will enable women to vote in the 2007 elections, providing they abide by Islamic Law.

Kuwait took a front-line role in the 2003 Iraq War, with thousands of coalition troops based in the emirate. The Iraqi occupation of the emirate during 1990–91 had inflicted deep psychological scars on Kuwaiti society and most of the population were glad to see the back of Saddam Hussein, Iraq's dictator.

1899 The Sheikh accepted British protection in order to counter the spread of Turkish influence. It also granted control of external relations to Britain.
1918 The end of the First World War saw the finish of what was already only nominal Turkish control over Kuwait.
1938 Oil was first discovered in Kuwait. Further exploration was interrupted by the Second World War.
1940s–50s Drilling resumed after the War and Kuwait soon developed into a thriving commercial centre. The government began using oil revenues to develop the country's infrastructure and a modern and comprehensive welfare system.
1961 Kuwait's status as a British protectorate ended and it became an independent country. The ruling Sheikh became the Emir and assumed full executive power. Iraq claimed Kuwait as part of its territory, but backed down after British military intervention.
1963 The constitution was promulgated and National Assembly elections were held.
1976 The Emir suspended the National Assembly; he said it was not acting in the country's interests.
1977 In December Sheikh Jaber al Ahmad al Sabah succeeded his cousin, Sheikh Sabah al Salem al Sabah as Emir.
1980 In the Iran-Iraq War, Kuwait supported Iraq.
1981 The National Assembly was recalled, but was again dissolved in 1986.
1985 The Emir survived an assassination attempt.
1990 Iraq invaded Kuwait and the Emir and cabinet flet to Saudi Arabia. The invasion was condemned by the international community which, led by the US, deployed armed forces to Saudi Arabia. UN Resolution 678 authorised member states to use force if Iraq did not withdraw by 15 January 1991.
1991 Iraq did not withdraw its forces when required. The Gulf War commenced with an airborne bombing campaign against Iraqi positions in Kuwait. US-led alliance ground forces entered Kuwait and force Iraq to retreat. Iraq agreed to accept all UN resolutions concerning Kuwait. A demilitarised zone between Iraq and Kuwait was established, to be monitored by the UN. The Emir returned and imposed a three-month period of martial law.
1992 The Emir was pressurised into allowing National Assembly elections, in which the opposition fared well.
1994 Following UN pressure and Russian mediation, Iraq officially recognised Kuwait's independence and the UN-demarcated borders.
1999 Islamists and liberals swept to victory in parliamentary elections. A draft law granting women full political rights, including the right to vote, was narrowly rejected by parliament. The National Assembly was suspended by the Emir, following a dispute over the misprinted state edition of the Qur'an.
2001 The Constitutional Court refused to grant women the vote.
2002 The Emir suffered a brain haemorrhage; he received treatment in London.
2003 Prior to the US-led invasion of Iraq, 150,000 US troops and allies massed in the border area of Kuwait. Islamist and pro-government candidates were successful in parliamentary elections; liberal candidates had major losses. Emir Sheikh Jaber appointed his brother, foreign minister Sheikh Sabah al Ahmad al Jabir al Sabah, as prime minister, separating the post from the role of heir to the throne for the first time since independence.
2005 The constitution was amended, giving women the right to vote and stand for parliament. For the first time, two women were named as members of the national assembly in June and because of a change in the law, women will be able to take part in parliamentary elections in 2007, providing they abide by Islamic law.
2006 The Emir of Kuwait, Sheikh Jaber al Ahmad al Sabah, died on 14 January. Crown Prince Sheikh Sa'ad al Abdullah al Sabah had been chosen as heir apparent in 1978, but had been unwell for some time. Although initially becoming Emir, on 24 January the cabinet nominated Sheikh Sabah al Ahmad al Sabah as Emir in his stead.

Political structure
Constitution
The constitution was enacted on 29 January 1963. It authorises the ruling al Sabah family to choose an Emir, who holds executive power and can proclaim legislation by decree.
The constitution ascribes the political system as democratic, with sovereignty residing in the people. Impartial personal liberty and equality of rights and duties before the law are guaranteed.
The Emir or one-third of the national assembly may propose amending the Constitution by deleting or adding new ones, except for the Emiri System and the principles of liberty and equality unless to increase provisions. Approval by a two-thirds majority is required for such a bill to succeed.
Males aged over 21 may vote; to include women aged over 21 from 2007.

Form of state
Constitutional monarchy (Emirate)

The executive
Executive power resides with the Emir, who is Head of State and appoints a prime minister, acceptable to the national assembly. In consultation with the prime minister the Emir appoints the Council of Ministers, who may not be members of parliament, although they assume *ex officio* membership during their term of office.
The Emir rules by decrees agreed by the Council of Ministers and, approved by parliament. He is also supreme commander of the armed forces.
Since 2003, the office of prime minister has been separated from the office of the Crown Prince, allowing greater independence of the legislature.

National legislature
The parliament is the unicameral Majlis al Umma (national assembly) of 50 elected members for four-year terms, plus 15 appointed *ex officio* cabinet ministers.

Legal system
The Judiciary is based on Egyptian laws, derived from French law. The legal system is a mix of *Sharia* (Islamic law) and Napoleonic law.
In 1960, a unified judicial system was adopted, establishing different levels of courts. There are three separate divisions including the Courts of First Instance subdivided into criminal, commercial and civil boards, the Constitutional Court and the Court of State Security. The judiciary is administered by a council of seven senior judges and minister.

Last elections
5 July 2003 (parliamentary)
Results: Parliamentary: the Islamists won 21 seats out of 50, government supporters 14, liberals three and independents 12.

Next elections
2007 (parliamentary)

Political parties
No political parties are allowed, although informal groupings exist.
The largest such groupings are the Islamic Patriotic Coalition (a Shi'a fundamentalist group), two Sunni fundamentalist groups, the Islamic Constitutional Movement and the Islamic Popular Grouping (also known as the Salafi). The Kuwait Democratic Forum is the largest secular political group

Kuwait

and has liberal and Arab nationalist opinions.

Ruling party
16-member Council of Ministers (appointed 2003)

Population
2.39 million (2004)

Ethnic make-up
Kuwaiti (37 per cent), other Arab (35 per cent), south Asian (9 per cent) and Iranian (4 per cent).

Religions
Sunni Muslim (45 per cent), Shi'ite Muslim (30 per cent), other Muslims (10 per cent); others, including Christian, Hindu and Parsi (15 per cent).

Education
There is state and private education at all levels; state schools are single-sex and only private schools may be co-educational. Tuition in the state sector is in Arabic.

Compulsory schooling begins at aged six and lasts until students have completed two four-year cycles in, first, elemental then intermediate schools. The last four-year cycle is not compulsory; as with the previous two stages, it is free of charge.

Pre-primary schools (also funded by the state) cater for four- to six-year-olds. Public expenditure on education is typically equivalent to around 5 per cent of annual GNP and included subsidies to private education at primary, secondary and tertiary levels. Average public expenditure was estimated at 39.6 per cent of GNP per capita for primary level students, 5.5 per cent for secondary level and a higher expenditure of 87.9 per cent for tertiary level students.

Literacy rate: 82.9 per cent total; 81 per cent female, adult rates in 2002 (World Bank).

Compulsory years: Six to 14

Enrolment rate: 77 per cent gross primary enrolment of relevant age group (including repeaters); 65 per cent gross seconday enrolment (World Bank).

Pupils per teacher: 14 in primary schools

Health
Total expenditure on health is around 4 per cent of GDP, of which government spending amounts to some 80 per cent. Kuwait offers free, high quality health services through its clinics and hospitals, but charges for certain medical services for some residents and expatriates. The Ministry of Public Health (MPH) manages the health system and provides care on a referral basis through a network of local clinics, general and specialised services.

Life expectancy: 77 years (World Bank)

Fertility rate/Maternal mortality rate: 2.5 births per woman (2003); maternal mortality 5 per 100,000 live births (World Bank).

Birth rate/Death rate: 3 deaths and 20 births per 1,000 people (World Bank)

Infant mortality rate: 8.0 per 1,000 live births; 2 per cent of children aged under five years are malnourished (World Bank).

Head of population per physician/bed: 19 physicians and 28 hospital beds per 10,000 people.

Welfare
The social insurance system was set up as a basic scheme to include all employees with an addition supplementary scheme covering only those employees with an average monthly income above KD1,250. Disability benefits are provided up to 60-years of age. The survivor pension amounts to 33.3–100 per cent of the deceased person's earnings according to number of widows and family dependants. A widow or widower receives a minimum monthly benefit.

Pensions
The old age pension is calculated on the number of years of contribution, the age at retirement and average earnings. It is set at a minimum of 65 per cent, and by a maximum benefit of 95 per cent, of the last monthly earnings.

Main cities
Kuwait City (capital, estimated population 32,600 in 2003), As-Salimiya (146,900), Jalib As-Suyuh (115,200).

Languages spoken
English is widely spoken, especially in business circles.

Official language/s
Arabic

Media
Press
The Ministry of Information issues licences to newspaper publishers. Kuwait has a reputation for having one of the most liberal press in the Gulf region. Generally speaking, there is no pre-publication censorship, with the government often using 'leaks' to the press to test public responses to its policies. However, the press is dependent on the government-owned Industrial Bank of Kuwait (IBK) for the financing of new plant and equipment purchases and strong criticism of the ruling Al Sabah family is not taken lightly. The official news agency is the Kuwait News Agency (KUNA), an independent public corporate body.

Dailies: Five Arabic dailies are *Al Qabas*, *Al Anbaa*, *Al Siyassah*, *Al Watan* and *Al Rai al Aam*. Daily publications guided by government officials include *Sawt al Kuwait* (also published in London) and *Al Fajr al Jadid*.

Arab Times is a national and Sunday English-language newspaper. *Kuwait Times* is a national daily and Sunday newspaper published in English, Malayalam and Urdu.

Weeklies: Weeklies include *Iqra'a* (political weekly), *Al Dostoor*, *Al Yaqaza*, *Almouasher* and *Azzamen Magazine*.

Business: Business news is covered by *The Kuwaiti Digest*, *Al Iktissad Wal Aamal* and *Majallat al Oloom*.

Periodicals: *Al Arabi* (monthly) and *New Arabia* (fortnightly newsletter in English from London) are also directly influenced by government officials.

Broadcasting
Radio: Radio Kuwait is state-run, with programmes in English and Arabic. The BBC World Service is available on FM in Kuwait City.

Television: Kuwaiti TV is state-run. There are three networks and a satellite channel. Times of broadcasts change during Ramadan.

Advertising
Foreign firms are not allowed direct access to the Kuwaiti market, except via local agents and distributors, or joint ventures. Direct marketing can take place through various channels – newspaper advertising is a traditional staple of the market, and direct marketing through the mail has become popular. Satellite television is an effective tool for reaching conservative Kuwaiti and expatriate women in the privacy of their own homes.

Economy
Once described as 'an oil well masquerading as a country', Kuwait is vastly wealthy. The Kuwait Investment Company (KIC) is one of the most respected global financial institutions and other state organisations, such as the Kuwait Petroleum Corporation (KPC), are recognised as major global investors.

The economy is centred on the oil and natural gas industries. In 2004, proven oil reserves were 99 billion barrels, or 8.3 per cent of the world's total reserves. Production was 2.4 million barrels per day (bpd), an increase of only 200,000 bpd on the 2003 output but, due to the record high oil prices, export revenue jumped by over 30 per cent from US$21.8 billion in 2003 to US$30.2 billion in 2004 and Kuwait's balance of trade surplus was US$15 billion.

The volatility of Kuwait's neighbour, Iraq, as well as legal and administrative barriers to investment, have discouraged large-scale foreign undertakings in Kuwait's upstream oil operations. The overt presence of the state in the economy (80 per cent) distorts the country's macroeconomic adjustment and has led to sharp imbalances.

The economy in 2004 was strengthened considerably by oil revenue. GDP growth was 7.2 per cent, while inflation was kept down to 1.8 per cent. The leading risk to the economy, and it has been judged by analysts as unlikely, is a sharp fall in the price of oil, which is projected to fall only gradually. Kuwait's macroeconomic performance has been strong, it has begun structural reforms to foster non-oil growth and generate Kuwaiti employment while limiting public sector expenditure. Unemployment remained steady at 2.2 per cent in 2004, at a time when the labour force was growing.

The government is managing an economy, in the short- to medium-term, with large fiscal and external current account surpluses, growing national savings and improved trading, both with Iraq and other Gulf states, with non-oil sector growth at 5.5 per cent in 2004. In 2005, Kuwait was ranked 47 out of 155 for ease of doing business, by the World Bank Group.

Savings – 10 per cent of all government revenue and any fiscal surpluses – are being set aside in the Reserve Fund for Future Generations (RFFG). The reserves are managed by the state-run Kuwait Investment Authority.

External trade
Imports
Food, construction materials, vehicles and parts and clothing. US goods to be imported during 2006 will be US$2.3 billion.
Main sources: US (13.1 per cent total, 2004), Germany (12.7 per cent), Japan (8.2 per cent), China (5.9 per cent), Italy (5.4 per cent), UK (5.4 per cent), Saudi Arabia (4.7 per cent), France (4.6 per cent)
Exports
Petroleum, refined oil-related and related products (95 per cent of the annual total), and fertilisers.
Main destinations: Japan (22.6 per cent total, 2004), US (13.4 per cent), South Korea (13.4 per cent), Singapore (12.4 per cent), Taiwan (8.4 per cent), The Netherlands (4.1 per cent)

Agriculture
Farming
Kuwait remains dependent on food imports. The sector as a whole accounts for only 0.4 per cent of GDP.
Crop production in 2004 included: 7,800 tonnes (t) cereals in total, 5,000t wheat, *33,000t potatoes, *2,000t barley, 10,500t dates, 36,000t tomatoes, 16,000t eggplants, 11,500t cauliflower, 6,800t chillies & peppers, 11,695t fruit in total, 185,620t vegetables in total. Livestock production included: 81,975t meat in total, 2,000t beef, 490t camel meat, 36,900t lamb, 42,000t poultry, 25,000t eggs, 45,136t milk, 319t cattle hides, *13,020t sheepskins.
* estimate

Fishing
Fish stocks have recovered after war-related pollution reduced stocks in the early 1990s. Fish forms a relatively major part of the national diet, and domestic production can satisfy only 40 per cent of domestic requirements.

Industry and manufacturing
Industrial areas are located in Shuaiba, Mina Abdullah (both in south Kuwait) and Shuwaikh. Efforts to foster growth of non-oil industries have been hindered by the small size of the domestic market and a lack of natural resources other than hydrocarbons. Industry has been growing very slowly as a proportion of GDP, to between 11 and 13 per cent of total output.

Tourism
Kuwait adopted a long-term strategy in 2004 to develop tourism as part of its economic diversification objectives. The sector has been dominated by official and business visitors and entry has been difficult. The priority is to improve domestic tourism (73 per cent of Kuwait residents travel abroad each year) and increase arrivals from other Gulf states. Visa regulations were eased in March 2004 to make Kuwait more accessible to overseas tourists. Kuwait has few tourist attractions, but is engaged on an ambitious programme to expand resort and leisure facilities, including the development of Failaka Island and the Sulaibikhat coast.

Travel and tourism is estimated to have contributed 1.5 per cent of GDP and employ 7.6 per cent of the work force. It was set to attract US$433.8 million or 10.9 per cent of total capital investment in 2005. The sector generates around US$2.6 billion in export revenue.

Hydrocarbons
Kuwait is the third largest oil producer in the Middle East. In 2004, it had 99 billion barrels of proven oil reserves, more than 8 per cent of the world total and output was 2.42 million barrels per day (bpd). Reserves are sufficient to last 100 years at current rates of extraction. Kuwait invested some US$15 billion over the period 1995–2005 to increase its crude oil output to 3.5 million bpd. Kuwait's Opec quota was 2.207 million bpd in March 2005; it has plans to increase its output to 4.0 million bpd.

In 2005 Kuwait signed agreements with two consortia to develop refining and marketing ventures in China and India, and Project Kuwait, a plan to revitalise a group of oil fields, at an estimated US$9 billion.

Kuwait has let a contract to Hyundai to build storage tanks for 11 million barrels of crude oil for export and refining. The contract is worth US$1.25 billion. There are also plans to modernise three refineries to increase total domestic processing capacity to 1.0 million bpd from 800,000bpd and to allow for environmentally cleaner products.

Natural gas reserves stood at 1.57 trillion cubic metres (cum) in 2004 and gas production totalled 9.7 billion cum. Although all gas produced is 'associated gas' produced alongside oil, Kuwait possibly found its first gas field in 2004. However it may take several years before production can begin. Currently all natural gas production (9.7 billion cum in 2004) is consumed domestically. With the proposed Qatar-Kuwait gas pipeline project expecting completion in early 2006, Qatar expects to be able to sell 15 million tonnes of gas per year to Kuwait.

Kuwait does not produce or import coal.

Financial markets
Stock exchange
The Kuwait Stock Exchange (KSE).
The stock price index increased by 34 per cent in 2004 due to the buoyant economy and abundant liquidity.

Banking and insurance
The IMF, Financial System Stability Assessment (FSSA), reported that the banking system was well capitalised with no immediate threat of instability. The capital adequacy ratio (CAR) was positive and quality assets were improving profits and returns on equity, which were increasing significantly. The financial institutional framework has been strengthened.

Central bank
Central Bank of Kuwait
Main financial centre
Kuwait City

Time
GMT plus three hours

Geography
Kuwait lies at the north-west corner of the Persian Gulf. To the south and south-west it shares a border with Saudi Arabia, and to the north and west with Iraq.

Kuwait is mainly flat desert with a scattering of oases. From east to west, the country is about 208km and from north to south, 185km. The al Mutla ridge is the only significant geographic feature. The desert is generally gravelly.

Climate
Kuwait is less humid than other Gulf countries. However, the coast is more humid than inland, although the temperatures are lower.

Kuwait has four seasons. Mid-February to mid-April is spring; April to September

Kuwait

(summer) is very hot (up to 49 degrees Celsius (C) in the shade); autumn is around mid-September to mid-November. The winter months are usually pleasant, with daytime temperatures around 18 degrees C and cold nights. Sandstorms occur, particularly in spring. Kuwait has an annual rainfall ranging from 10mm to 370mm which falls almost entirely between the months of November and April.

Dress codes
Lightweight or tropical clothes are worn in the summer, although in winter months a medium-weight jacket and a jumper are advisable. Women should dress modestly. A long-sleeved shirt and tie should be worn at business meetings but a jacket may be carried. On social occasions dress as for business meetings, unless otherwise indicated.

Entry requirements
Passports
Passports are required by all, and they must be valid for six months from date of entry.
Visa
Required by all, except citizens of Oman, Qatar, Saudi Arabia and UAE.
Business visas require an invitation from a sponsor in a local company or organisation which should be submitted to the issuing embassy, along with a business letter from the employer giving an account of the visitor's position and role within the foreign company, and full itinerary with purpose of visit and length of stay.
Since 2004, visas can be obtained on arrival for nationals of the US, Western Europe, South East Asia, Australia and New Zealand. Visitors from other countries must obtain visas prior to departure.
Currency advice/regulations
No restrictions on currency imports or exports.
Customs
Household and personal effects, tobacco and perfume may be imported without restriction; 4 per cent duty may apply on some items; International Car Certificate (Triptyque) required for cars imported for personal use for three-month period; guarantor or guarantee is required in other cases.
Prohibited imports
Alcoholic beverages and any materials used for making them (ie hops, malt extracts, wine kits); pornographic and/or politically subversive materials; pork products in any form; all goods of Israeli origin. Prohibition of alcoholic beverages strictly enforced. Other prohibited items include binoculars, rubber balloons and canned meat.

Health (for visitors)
Health facilities are excellent.
Mandatory precautions
There are no compulsory vaccinations.
Advisable precautions
Recommended immunisations are hepatitis 'A', polio and tetanus. There is a risk of rabies.

Hotels
Most visitors are business travellers. Five-star hotels have swimming pools and exercise/gymnasium facilities. Small tip for porters is customary. There is usually a 15 per cent service charge.

Credit cards
Major credit cards (American Express, Diners Club, Visa and Mastercard or Access) accepted at all hotels and many restaurants and shops.

Public holidays
Fixed dates
1 Jan (New Year's Day), 25 Feb (National Day), 26 Feb (Liberation Day).
Variable dates
Eid al Adha (four days), Islamic New Year, Birth of the Prophet, Ascent of the Prophet, Eid al Fitr (three days).
The Islamic year has 354 or 355 days, with the result that Muslim feasts advance by 10–12 days against the Gregorian calendar each year. Dates of the Muslim feasts vary according to sightings of the new moon, so cannot be forecast exactly. Islamic year 1426: 10 February 2005 to 30 January 2006.

Working hours
Friday is a weekly holiday, when government offices, embassies and banks are closed. Office hours are liable to change during month of Ramadan.
Banking
Sun–Thu: 0800–1200; Sun–Thu, Ramadan: 0900–1230.
Business
Sat–Wed: 0700–1400.
Government
Sat–Wed, winter: 0730–1330; Thu, summer: 0730–1130; Sat–Wed: 0700–1300; Thu: 0700–1100; Sat–Thu, Ramadan: 0900–1300.
Shops
Sat–Thu: 0800–1230, 1630–2100.

Telecommunications
Mobile phones
There are GSM roaming facilities available, with coverage throughout the country.

Electricity supply
240V AC; plug fittings normally three-pin flat type (British).

Weights and measures
Metric system (local units are also in use).

Social customs/useful tips
Appointments should be made in advance. Punctuality is appreciated. Personal introductions are advantageous. If the visiting executive is a woman, this must be clearly stated in initial correspondence. On the street, women should not respond to approaches by men and should avoid eye contact.
Men shake hands on meeting and taking leave. Conference visits are an accepted way of doing business and other visitors may be present. The host may hold several conversations at the same time. It is not customary to start talking business immediately. Business cards should have an Arabic translation on the reverse side. Islamic conventions apply. At meetings it is polite to drink coffee or tea when offered. It is the convention to use the right and not the left hand when shaking hands, eating, and passing or receiving anything. Almost everything may stop five times a day for prayers. Some people prefer not to shake hands with those of the opposite sex. When sitting cross-legged on sofas or cushions, soles of the feet must not be shown. A man should not enquire about another man's wife, only about the children. Pork and alcohol are forbidden.
Gratuities are around 10 per cent. Bargaining is not as common as in other countries. There are many restrictions on photography.

Security
Kuwait is relatively safe but take normal travel precautions. Like the rest of the Middle East, there is a threat to westerners from possible terrorist attacks. Mines remain a problem outside Kuwait City.

Getting there
Air
National airline: Kuwait Airways.
International airport/s: Kuwait International (KWI), 16km south of city; hotel accommodation for transit passengers, duty-free shop, buffet, restaurant, bank, hotel reservations, post office, shops.
Airport tax: There is no airport tax.
Surface
Road: There are excellent roads from the Saudi Arabian and Iraqi borders.
Main port/s: Several commercial shipping lines call in at Kuwait City.

Getting about
National transport
Road: A network of 3,800km of good paved roads and expressways link towns.
Buses: Nationwide service operated by Kuwait Transport Company, generally rated good and inexpensive.
City transport
Taxis: Taxis are not metered. Both private and shared taxis, which are orange and operate on set routes, are available. Taxis are more expensive from hotel ranks. There is a standard taxi fare in Kuwait City

and drivers do not expect a tip. If hiring a taxi for a day or half-day agree the fare in advance. Call taxis are reliable and widely used.

Car hire
Locally approved/inspected international driving licence (valid for duration of entry permit) and insurance with Gulf Insurance Company or Kuwait Insurance Company are essential. Driving is on the right.

BUSINESS DIRECTORY

The addresses listed below are a selection only. While World of Information makes every endeavour to check these addresses, we cannot guarantee that changes have not been made, especially to telephone numbers and area codes. We would welcome any corrections.

Telephone area codes
The international direct dialling code (IDD) for Kuwait is +965, followed by subscriber's number.

Useful telephone numbers
Fire, Police, Ambulance: 777
Telephone enquiries: 101
Directory enquiries: 023 or 244-4777

Chambers of Commerce
American Business Council of Kuwait, PO Box 29992, Safat 13159 (tel: 564-3149; fax: 563-8012; e-mail: abckuwait@hotmail.com).

Banking
Al-Ahli Bank of Kuwait KSC, PO Box 1387 Safat-13014, Mubarak Al-Kabir St, Kuwait City (tel: 241-1101/2; fax: 242-4557).
Commercial Bank of Kuwait SAK, PO Box 2861 Safat-13029, Mubarak Al-Kabir St, Kuwait City (tel: 241-1001; fax: 245-0150).
Gulf Bank KSC, PO Box 3200 Safat-13032, Raed Centre next to Awadi Tower, Kuwait City (tel: 244-9501; fax: 244-5212).
Industrial Bank of Kuwait KSC, PO Box 3146, Safat 13032, Kuwait City (tel: 245-7661; fax: 246-2057).
National Bank of Kuwait SAK, PO Box 95 Safat-13001, Ali Awadi Tower, Ahmed Al-Jaber St, Kuwait City (tel: 242-2011; fax: 246-4156).

Central bank
Central Bank of Kuwait, PO Box 526, Abdulla Al-Salem Street, Safat 13006, Kuwait City (tel: 244-9200; fax: 244-0887; cbk@cbk.gov.kw).

Travel information
Gulf Automobile Association, PO Box 827, Safat, Kuwait City (tel: 242-3864, 243-8640).

Kuwait Airways, PO Box 394, Safat, Kuwait International Airport, Safat 13004, Kuwait (tel: 434-5555; fax: 431-9204; internet site: http://www.kuwait-airways.com).
Kuwait International Airport (tel: 473-3625).

Ministry of tourism
Tourism Department, Ministry of Information, PO Box 193, Safat, Kuwait City (tel: 242-7141).

Ministries
Ministry of Awqaf and Islamic Affairs, PO Box 13, 13001 Safat, Kuwait City (tel: 248-0000; fax: 243-3750).
Ministry of Communications, PO Box 318, 13004 Safat, Kuwait City (tel: 481-9033; fax: 484-7058).
Ministry of Defence, PO Box 1170, 13012 Safat, Kuwait City (tel: 484-8300; fax: 483-7244).
Ministry of Education, PO Box 7, 13001 Safat, Kuwait City (tel: 483-6800; fax: 483-7829).
Ministry of Electricity and Water, PO Box 12, 13001 Safat, Kuwait City (tel: 537-1000; fax: 537-1420).
Ministry of Foreign Affairs, PO Box 3, 13001 Safat, Kuwait City (tel: 242-5141; fax: 241-2169; e-mail: info@mofa.org).
Ministry of Health, PO Box 5, 13001 Safat, Kuwait City (tel: 246-2900; fax: 243-2288).
Ministry of Higher Education, PO Box 27130, 13132 Safat, Kuwait City (tel: 240-1300; fax: 245-6319).
Ministry of Information, PO Box 193, 13002 Safat, Kuwait City (tel: 241-5300; fax: 241-9642; e-mail: info@moinfo.gov.kw).
Ministry of Interior, PO Box 12500, 71655 Safat, Kuwait City (tel: 243-3804; fax: 243-6570).
Ministry of Justice, PO Box 6, 13001 Safat, Kuwait City (tel: 248-0000; fax: 243-3750).
Ministry of Oil, PO Box 5077, 13051 Safat, Kuwait City (tel: 241-5201; fax: 241-7088).
Ministry of Planning, PO Box 15, 13001 Safat, Kuwait City (tel: 242-8200; fax: 240-7326).
Ministry of Public Works, PO Box 8, 13001 Safat, Kuwait City (tel: 538-5520; fax: 538-0829).
Ministry of Social Affairs & Labour, PO Box 563, 13006 Safat, Kuwait City (tel: 248-0000; fax: 241-9877).

Other useful addresses
British Embassy, PO Box 300, 13003 Safat (tel: 240-3334; fax: 240-7395).
Central Tenders Committee, PO Box 1070, 13011 Kuwait City (tel: 243-1719; fax: 241-6574).
Council of Ministers, PO Box 1397, 13014 Safat (tel: 245-5333; fax: 245-5002).
General Secretariat, PO Box 1397, Safat 13014 (tel: 245-5333; fax: 245-5002).
Kuwait Foreign Trading, Contracting & Investment Co, PO Box 5665, Kuwait 13057 (tel: 244-9031).
Kuwait International Fair Co, PO Box 656, Safat, Kuwait City (tel: 245-8560/1/2/3/4/5).
Kuwait National Industries Co, PO Box 417, Safat, Kuwait City (tel: 815-466, 812-455).
Kuwait National Petroleum Company, PO Box 70, 13001 Safat (tel: 326-2616; fax: 326-0280).
Kuwait Oil Company (KOC), PO Box 9758, 61008 Ahmadi (tel: 398-9111; fax: 398-3661).
Kuwait Parliament, The National Assembly (tel: 245-5422; fax: 243-9032).
Kuwait Petroleum Corp, PO Box 26565, Safat, Kuwait City (tel: 245-5455; fax: 246-7159).
Kuwaiti Embassy (USA), 2940 Tilden Street, NW, Washington DC 20008 (tel: 202-966-0702; fax: 202-364-2868).
National Housing Association, PO Box 23385, 13094 Safat (tel: 471-7844; fax: 242-8801).
Petrochemical Industries Board Co, PO Box 1084, Safat, Kuwait City (tel: 242-2141; fax: 246-0224).
Shuaiba Area Authority, PO Box 4690, Safat (tel: 960-903).

Internet sites
Business News, Arabia online: http://www.arabia.com
Gulf Business Explorer: http://www.igulf.com
Kuwait Information: http://www.kuwait-info.org

Kyrgyzstan

In 2005, Kyrgyzstan became the third former Soviet republic to experience a 'colour revolution', in which long-serving Soviet era elites were pushed out of office by a popular uprising. The so-called 'tulip revolution' ousted Kyrgyz president Askar Akayev on 24 March, following a week of protests against parliamentary elections widely considered to be fraudulent. Subsequent presidential elections, in July, brought to power leading opposition figure Kurmanbek Bakiyev.

A rebounding economy

Despite political upheaval in 2005, according to the IMF the Kyrgyz economy managed to grow by around 3 per cent. The Kyrgyz finance ministry puts 2005 GDP growth closer to 5 per cent. Inflation also stayed relatively low, at around 4.5 per cent. In August, the new Kyrgyz government accepted considerable assistance from the IMF in the formation of economic policy for 2006 and 2007. The IMF forecasts 5–6 per cent growth over the next two years.

The 'tulip revolution'

On 24 March 2005, President Akayev, in office since 1991, fled the country. On April 4, from exile in Russia, he formally resigned. This followed people power-based revolutions in two other former Soviet republics, in Ukraine (December 2004) and Georgia (November 2003). Protests had been building since the second round of parliamentary elections on 13 March. The first round, held on 27 February, had been declared 'neither free nor fair' by international observers. Demonstrations were initially confined to the south of the country, traditionally under-represented in Kyrgyz power structures. Protesters seized control of two cities in the south, Jalal-Abad and Osh, before unrest broke out in the capital Bishkek.

After the flight of President Akayev, Kyrgyzstan was left with two rival parliaments – the parliament in place before the marred elections in February and March and the parliament elected by those polls. After an impasse lasting several days, the old parliament agreed to suspend itself and both groups of MPs agreed to appoint leading opposition figure Kurmanbek Bakiyev as acting prime minister. Bakiyev had previously served as a regional governor and as prime minister (2001–02) but had since fallen out with President Akayev. Bakiyev promptly appointed Felix Kulov, a former vice president (1992–93) and mayor of Bishkek (1998–99) as national security csar. Kulov had been serving a jail sentence for corruption but had been freed by protesters on 24 March.

Building a new government

With a new presidential election agreed for 10 July, the newly empowered

KEY FACTS

Official name: Kyrgyz Respublikasy (Kyrgyz Republic)

Head of State: President Kurmanbek Bakiyev (elected 10 Jul 2005)

Head of government: President Kurmanbek Bakiyev (from 28 Mar 2005)

Ruling party: Government formed 25 Mar 2005.

Area: 198,500 square km

Population: 5.32 million (2004)

Capital: Bishkek (formerly Frunze)

Official language: Kyrgyz, Russian

Currency: Som (S) = 100 tyin

Exchange rate: S40.85 per US$ (Oct 2005)

GDP per capita: US$425 (2004)

GDP real growth: 6.00% (2004)

Labour force: 2.36 million (2004)

Unemployment: 18.00% (2004)

Inflation: 4.10% (2004)

Balance of trade: -US$128.40 million (2004)

Foreign debt: US$1.97 billion (2004)

opposition had to act fast if it were to agree on an orderly succession. Some of the splits exposed in the tulip revolution continued to influence events, particularly in terms of regionalism. Acting Prime Minister Bakiyev, a southerner by birth, declared his intention to run for president early on and received enthusiastic backing from the south of country. Bakiyev's main potential rival was Kulov, a northerner, who had quickly resigned from the national security position to which Bakiyev had appointed him in March. Observers feared a renewed power struggle along north-south lines but the two leaders struck a deal in May, by which Bakiyev would run for president and, in the event of a Bakiyev victory, Kulov would be duly appointed prime minister.

In the 10 July election, Bakiyev won 89 per cent of the vote on a turnout of nearly 75 per cent. He was inaugurated in August and set about forming a new government headed by Kulov.

The post-Akayev era

Politics have been tough and at times fatal in the post-Akayev era. A number of MPs and public figures were assassinated between the March 2005 overthrow of Akayev and the end of the year. In June, protesters returned to the streets in Osh and Bishkek. The demonstrations were unrelated but underscored the fragile grip of the post-Akayev authorities. Moreover, weeks of rioting and hostage taking in Moldavanovka prison just outside Bishkek led to demonstrations against the Kulov government during October and November.

The regional balance

Following the Andijan Massacre in neighbouring Uzbekistan in May, Kyrgyzstan's regional importance increased significantly. Smarting from US criticism of its handling of the uprising in Andijan, the Uzbek authorities announced the imminent closure of a US airbase on its territory. In need of bases in Central Asia as part of its war on terrorism in Afghanistan, the US government opened negotiations in July with the new government in Kyrgyzstan over the fate of its airbase at Manas, near Bishkek. In October, the two governments sealed a new agreement, allowing the US to keep the base until the completion of its operations in Afghanistan.

This development was viewed with suspicion in the region, particularly by Russia, China and Uzbekistan. These states do not welcome any further extension of the US presence in Central Asia and had been lobbying for a withdrawal via the 6-nation Shanghai Co-operation Organisation (SCC). The SCC, comprised of Russia, China, Uzbekistan, Tajikistan, Kazakhstan and Kyrgyzstan, had demanded in July that the US give a timetable for the dismantling of its remaining bases in the region. In a sign of its displeasure at the prospect of yet another 'colour revolution' on its doorstep, Russia had initially condemned the protests that led to the overthrow of former president Akayev and had then provided him with political asylum.

Outlook

Kyrgyzstan heads into 2006 with a new and relatively shaky administration in place. Although President Bakiyev's grip on office looks durable, Prime Minister Kulov's government faces a range of challenges, from the street and from parliament. On top of protests in Bishkek and Osh, the Kulov government suffered a setback at the hands of parliament in September 2005. Kulov's nomination for foreign minister, Roza Otunbayeva, was rejected – despite that fact that she was a widely respected, both inside and outside the country, for her previous stints in the same office (1992, 1994–97, 2005). In a by-election scheduled for 9 April 2006, Otunbayeva is expected to enter parliament, setting up a renewed showdown between Kulov and his parliamentary foes. The killing of public figures has continued into 2006, suggesting that many scores from the 'tulip revolution' era and the previous Akayev era remain unsettled.

In January 2006, scores of non-governmental organisations (NGOs) in Kyrgyzstan protested against government moves to increase state supervision over them. The government argues that it is trying to stamp out Islamic militancy and suspects that some NGOs have links with such militants.

Risk assessment

Politics'	Fragile
Economy	Improving
Regional stability	Fragile

COUNTRY PROFILE

Historical profile

In the eighth century, Arabs invaded Central Asia and introduced Islam. The Kyrgyz are a Turkic people, thought to be descended from tribes on the Yenisey River on the Siberian steppe, whose different clans fought over pastoral land in the Tian Shan mountains to secure grazing for their livestock.

Kyrgyzstan was the first of the Central Asian states to declare independence from the Soviet Union. The US's war on terrorism towards the end of 2001 catapulted the region back onto the world stage. Kyrgyzstan played a part in the war by providing the US with its bases, from which to undertake military operations in Afghanistan. The US's involvement in Central Asia comes at a time when Kyrgyzstan has to fight its own war on terrorism, against Islamic militants from

KEY INDICATORS — Kyrgyzstan

	Unit	2000	2001	2002	2003	2004
Population	m	5.00	5.00	5.01	5.16	5.32
Gross domestic product (GDP)	US$bn	1.30	1.50	1.60	1.80	*2.21
GDP per capita	US$	260	300	320	1,600	425
GDP real growth	%	5.1	5.3	-0.5	5.2	6.0
Inflation	%	9.6	6.9	2.1	3.3	4.1
Unemployment	%	7.5	8.3	8.7	7.2	18.0
Exports (fob) (goods)	US$m	510.9	480.0	501.0	590.0	646.7
Imports (fob) (goods)	US$m	502.1	472.0	590.0	717.0	775.1
Balance of trade	US$m	8.8	8.0	-54.0	-127.0	-128.4
Current account	US$m	-60.0	-20.0	-40.0	-50.0	-70.0
Foreign debt	US$bn	1.8	1.7	1.8	1.5	2.0
Total reserves minus gold	US$m	239.0	263.5	288.8	364.6	548.7
Foreign exchange	US$m	238.3	262.2	288.2	354.3	528.8
Exchange rate	per US$	47.70	48.38	47.04	44.99	42.56

* estimated figure

Tajikistan who have undertaken incursions into the Ferghana Valley.

1700s–1800s After being invaded by the Arabs, Mongols and the Chinese, Kyrgyzstan was ruled by the Khanate of Kokand (part of modern-day Uzbekistan).

1876 Tsarist troops conquered Kokand and incorporated Kyrgyzstan into the Russian empire.

1916–17 Following the suppression of rebellion in Central Asia against Russian rule and the outbreak of civil war after the October Revolution in Russia, many Kyrgyz crossed the eastern border into China.

1918 Parts of Kyrgyzstan were absorbed into Russian-controlled Turkestan.

1920s–30s Soviet nationalities policy under the direction of Joseph Stalin saw Soviet rule enforced from Moscow by Red Army troops who put down Muslim revolts throughout Central Asia after the Russian civil war. All arable and grazing lands were consolidated into large state-owned farms, upsetting the traditional Kyrgyz way of life, based on nomadic livestock-herding. The Kyrgyz Communist Party was established as the sole legal party.

1924 Kyrgyzstan was designated the Kara-Kyrgyz Autonomous Region (renamed Kyrgyz Autonomous Region in 1925) and absorbed into the Russian Socialist Federated Soviet Republic (RSFSR).

1926 The Kyrgyz Autonomous Region was upgraded to an Autonomous Soviet Socialist Republic (ASSR).

1936 Kyrgyzstan became a constituent republic within the Union of Soviet Socialist Republics (USSR).

1940s–80s Kyrgyzstan was an important source of raw materials to the Soviet Union.

1990 The Kyrgyz and Uzbek population rioted in ethnically-divided Osh in southern Kyrgyzstan. Askar Akayev was appointed chairman of the Kyrgyz Socialist Republic.

1991 Kyrgyzstan was the first Central Asian republic to declare independence from the USSR. Akayev stood alone in the country's presidential elections. Kyrgyzstan joined the Commonwealth of Independent States (CIS).

1992 An economic reform programme was launched.

1993 Kyrgyzstan adopted its first post-Soviet constitution allowing for a parliamentary system of government. The som replaced the rouble as the unit of currency.

1994 Akayev won a resounding referendum victory, giving him the mandate to make the legislature a bicameral body. Uzbekistan signed an economic, military and social co-operation treaty with Kazakhstan and Kyrgyzstan.

1995 Akayev was re-elected for a second five-year term.

1996 A referendum to give the president the authority to appoint all top officials was approved by 94.5 per cent of voters; parliamentary approval is only required for prime ministerial candidates. Uzbekistan, Kazakhstan and Kyrgyzstan agreed to create a single economic market.

1998 A referendum on a package of constitutional changes was overwhelmingly approved. The changes included the introduction of private land ownership – a first by a Central Asian state. Kyrgyzstan became a member of the World Trade Organisation (WTO), the first country in the former Soviet Union to join.

1999 Troops were sent in after Islamic militants crossed the border from Tajikistan and seized hostages.

2000 Government forces engaged Islamic fighters who seized hostages again. President Akayev was elected for a third term, contrary to the constitution and amid allegations of electoral irregularities. The elections were followed by the harassment and imprisonment of opposition leaders and the closure of opposition newspapers. The presidents of Belarus, Kazakhstan, Kyrgyzstan, Russia and Tajikistan (formerly the Customs Five) established the Eurasian Economic Community (EEC).

2001 Akayev announced that he would not stand for re-election in the 2005 presidential election. Tajikistan, China, Russia, Kazakhstan, Kyrgyzstan and Uzbekistan formed the Shanghai Co-operation Organisation (SCO) and agreed to fight ethnic and religious militancy, while promoting investment and trade.

2002 Prime Minister Kurmanbek Bakiyev's government resigned; First Deputy Prime Minister Nikolai Tanayev was named prime minister and formed a government. Opposition protesters marched in the capital, demanding the President's resignation.

2003 A constitutional referendum was held, in which 80 per cent of voters backed President Akayev's proposed changes, which the opposition said restricted civil liberties; the referendum extended the president's term of office. A bill was passed which granted President Akayev and two other Soviet era Communist leaders lifelong immunity from prosecution.

2004 In January, opposition parties joined in a coalition to fight the next elections.

2005 Numerous independent and opposition candidates were barred from standing in the February/March parliamentary elections. President Akayev was ousted from power by a popular uprising when widespread allegations of government interference in the parliamentary elections, fuelled by poverty and corruption, sparked a revolt. On 24 March opposition demonstrators forced Akayev to flee to Moscow; he resigned in April. The Supreme Court cancelled the results of the parliamentary elections, although later elected members took their seats. Acting president, Kurmanbek Bakiyev, won the July presidential elections and was sworn in on 6 August. Feliks Kulov was approved by parliament as prime minister. A new cabinet was sworn in on 20 December.

Political structure
Constitution

The constitution was adopted in 1993 (amended in 1998 and 2003). It defines Kyrgyzstan as a sovereign, unitary, democratic and secular republic. All land, airspace and natural resources are the property of the state unless assigned for private usage. Discrimination on the grounds of language is forbidden. There is universal direct adult suffrage by secret ballot.

There are six administrative *oblasts* (regions): Chu, Issyk-Kul, Osh, Talas, Jalal-Abad and Naryn. The capital, Bishkek, has special status and is not included in any oblast.

The February 2003 consitutional referendum gives local authorities more power.

Form of state
Republic

The executive

The directly elected president is constitutionally limited to a maximum of two consecutive five-year terms. However, President Akayev, who had already served two terms in office, was able to stand in the presidential elections of October 2000. Akayev was granted a third term by the Constitutional Court on the grounds that he first became president before the introduction of the present constitution. The constitutional referendum held on 2 February 2003 extended the president's term of office until 2005.

The constitution states that the president must be able to speak the Kyrgyz language. The president has the authority to appoint all top officials, except the prime minister, for whom parliamentary approval is needed.

National legislature

The Jogorku Kenesh (Supreme Council), established in 1994, has two chambers. The upper house, Myizam Chygaruu Jyiyny (Legislative Assembly), has 60 members, elected for a five-year term, 45 in single-seat constituencies and 15 by proportional representation. The lower house, El Okuldor Jyiyny (People's Representatives Assembly), has 45 members, elected for a five-year term in single-seat constituencies.

In accordance with a 2003 referendum, the parliament is slated to become unicameral with 75 deputies after the 27 February 2005 elections.

Legal system
The legal system is based on a civil law code. There are three ultimate legal authorities: the Constitutional Court, the Supreme Court and the Higher Arbitration Court. All are composed of judges with a 15-year term of office who must be approved by the national legislature and the executive. The Constitutional Court rules on the constitutionality of central and local government legislation and on the validity of elections. The Supreme Court is the highest court of appeal for civil, criminal and administrative cases previously heard in oblast, district, city and military courts. The Higher Arbitration Court oversees and rules on the operation of the regional and City of Bishkek arbitration courts.

Last elections
10 July 2005 (presidential); 13 March 2005 (second round parliamentary).
Results: Presidential: Kurmanbek Bakiyev with 88.9 per cent of the vote; Tursunbai Bakir uulu came second with 3.8 per cent. Turnout was 74.6 per cent.
Parliamentary (second round): 39 seats were allocated; one seat remained undecided because a majority voted against all candidates. Most of those elected were nonpartisans, many had supported President Akayev; the opposition had six seats. Turnout was 60 per cent.

Next elections
2010 (presidential and parliamentary)

Political parties
Ruling party
Government formed 25 Mar 2005.
Main opposition party

Population
5.32 million (2004)
Ethnic make-up
Kyrgyz (54.0 per cent, originally a nomadic people of Turko-Mongolian origin who still dominate in rural areas), Russians (12.0 per cent), Ukrainians (2.5 per cent), Germans (2.0 per cent), Kazakh, Uighurs and others (29.5 per cent).
Religions
Predominantly Muslim (Sunni) (70 per cent of the population). There are also Russian Orthodox and Baptist churches.

Education
Primary education lasts for three years between the ages of seven and 10. Secondary education comprises of compulsory basic secondary (five years) and non-compulsory complete secondary (two years) which gives access to higher education. Vocational education is provided by professional schools which lasts for one-and-a-half years for those with complete secondary education.
There are 51 higher education institutions, of which 26 are run by the government. There are 13 non-governmental and 12 private higher education institutions.
Compulsory years: Seven to 15
Enrolment rate: 104 per cent gross primary enrolment of relevant age group (including repeaters); 79 per cent gross seceondary enrolment (World Bank).
Pupils per teacher: 20 in primary schools.

Health
Annual total expenditure on health is around 4 per cent of GDP, of which government spending is about 49 per cent. The healthcare system in Kyrgyzstan continues to be based on practices developed in the Soviet era, which concentrate on primary care and are cost-inefficient. The primary health sector has been supported by international donors, including the International Development Association (IDA), Asian Development Bank (ADB) and the German and Swiss governments, to resist the tide of an overall decline.
A mandatory medical health insurance fund provides for 70 per cent of the population, covering 65 hospitals and 350 groups of family doctors. In-patient treatment is provided through a system of referrals throughout several levels of the system. Patients are entitled to essential drugs free of charge. Medical equipment supplies only 20 per cent of the needs of medical institutions. Kyrgyzstani clinics and hospitals use outdated equipment, 75 per cent of which needs to be replaced or upgraded. There is a shortage of affordable drugs and vaccines and most of the drugs are imported by small traders who do not conform to strict safety rules.
HIV prevalence: 0.1 per cent aged 15–49 in 2003 (World Bank)
Life expectancy: 65.0 years (World Bank).
Fertility rate/Maternal mortality rate: 2.4 births per woman; maternal mortality 65 per 100,000 live births (World Bank).
Infant mortality rate: 59 per 1,000 live births; 7 per cent of children aged under five are malnourished (World Bank).
Head of population per physician/bed: Three doctors per 1,000 people.

Welfare
Like many other former Soviet countries, Kyrgyzstan has a large and complex social benefit system. Social spending, including expenditures of the social fund, makes up 28 per cent of the government budget and 7 per cent of GDP. Although the government budget subsidises the social fund, the payroll tax and the total costs of pensions are high. Pensions are often below subsistence level and the government believes that the current pension system is financially unsustainable. It is looking at cutting costs, preferably by reducing the number of beneficiaries, and aims to move to a system with a minimal state pension and a service pension based on payments into a pension insurance scheme.
Around 44.5 per cent of the population live below the poverty line. The aim of the Participatory Poverty Alleviation Programme (PPAP), set up by the UN Development Programme (UNDP), in co-operation with President Akayev's administration, is to reduce poverty in the country by 10 per cent by 2010.

Main cities
Bishkek (formerly Frunze) (capital, estimated population 824,900 in 2003); Osh (225,600).

Languages spoken
Kyrgyz is a Turkic language. Russian is widely spoken, even among ethnic Kyrgyz.
Official language/s
Kyrgyz, Russian

Media
There is relative media freedom, although some opposition politicians have complained about press censorship and bias.
Press
Several daily and weekly newspapers include *The Times of Central Asia*, *Info Pyramida*, *Vecherni Bishkek*, *Slovo Kirgyzstana*, *Kriminal*, *Res Publica* and *Dzany Muun (New Generation)*.
Broadcasting
Kyrgyz National TV and Radio Broadcasting Corporation is state-run, two networks.
Radio: Several international organisations started Radio Salaam in 2001. Broadcasting in Russian and Kyrgyz from Batken in the Ferghana Valley, it is the country's first independent station.
Television: There are Russian TV and radio services from Moscow. Osh TV is an independent TV company broadcasting in the southern regions of the country mostly in the Uzbek language.
Advertising
There is an active advertising sector using print media and billboards in particular, but services are also available in broadcast media.

Economy
The economy is principally agricultural. Kyrgyzstan is one of the poorer countries of the former Soviet Union and was affected more than most by the loss of subsidies from Russia following independence. Prior to independence, Kyrgyzstan was an important source of raw materials for the Soviet Union. Upon independence, demand from Russia for

raw materials decreased dramatically and Kyrgyzstan had to create new markets. Economic reform spearheaded by President Akayev has led to considerable support from Western countries and from the International Finance Institutions (IFIs). Kyrgyzstan is a recipient of international funds from the World Bank and the Asian Development Bank (ADB) and also receives assistance from the EU and bilateral aid from Japan, US, Germany and other EU countries.

Kyrgyzstan has received a number of IMF loans, as part of a US$102 million Poverty Reduction and Growth Facility (PRGF) agreement.

In 2003, the economy rebounded from -0.5 per cent growth in 2002 to 5.2 per cent. In 2004 GDP growth continued at 6.0 per cent. Foreign direct investment (FDI) rose by 27 per cent and there was a recovery in gold production.

Although the government is committed to the formation of a market economy, the central economic planning system is proving hard to dismantle. Industry is plagued by debt and needs to develop its processing facilities to add value to the country's raw materials if it is to survive. Kyrgyzstan is struggling under the burden of its huge US$1.50 billion foreign debt. Indicators over the medium term have been the main cause for concern and show that strong adjustment would be required. The IMF and the Paris Club agreed to write off US$500 million of debt between 2004–05.

Although the economy is proceeding towards achieving macroeconomic stability and poverty levels have fallen, some 44.5 per cent of the country's population still lives in poverty, mainly in rural areas.

In the period 2004–06, the ADB is to loan US$90 million to Kyrgyzstan to promote private sector-led growth and human development.

External trade
In 1994, Kyrgyzstan entered an economic union with Uzbekistan and Kazakhstan, in the form of the Central Asian Union (CAU). The leaders met in 1997 to discuss ways to improve regional co-operation. However, economic integration within the Union has been limited due to the different speed of reforms in the states. In 2000, the CIS Customs Union was transformed into a Eurasian Economic Community (EEC) composed of Kyrgyzstan, Kazakhstan, Tajikistan, Russia and Belarus. The aims of this development were to provide a common payments system, equal access to foreign investment and co-ordination of activities in international economic organisations. However, the first priority of the group, to combat smuggling and increase border security, may restrict rather than liberalise trade between the member states.

A Partnership and Co-operation Agreement was signed with the EU in 1995 and came into force in 1999. Kyrgyzstan's trade has been further boosted with China, Kazakhstan, Russia and Uzbekistan, following the formation of the Shanghai Co-operation Organisation (SCO) in June 2001.

Imports
Main imports are food, oil and gas, machinery and equipment, chemicals and foodstuffs.
Main sources: Russia (23.1 per cent total, 2004), China (22.9 per cent), Kazakhstan (19.3 per cent), Turkey (7.2 per cent), Germany (4.5 per cent), Uzbekistan (4.4 per cent), US (4.2 per cent)

Exports
The main exports are cotton, wool, meat, tobacco; gold, mercury, uranium, natural gas, hydropower, machinery and shoes. Exports totalled US$488 million in 2003.
Main destinations: UAE (23.8 per cent total, 2004), Switzerland (16.9 per cent), Russia (16.9 per cent), Kazakhstan (10.1 per cent), China (9.8 per cent)

Agriculture
Farming
Agriculture is one of Kyrgyzstan's main sources of wealth, accounting for around 37 per cent of GDP and employing approximately 48 per cent of the labour force.

The total area of agricultural land is 10 million hectares (ha), but only 7 per cent is cultivated.

The main products are tobacco (55,000 tonnes per annum), wool, cotton, leather, silk, meat, grain (especially barley), fruit and vegetables.

Livestock production accounts for about 60 per cent of gross agricultural income. Kyrgyzstan is the third-largest wool producer in the former Soviet Union. Only 15 per cent is processed locally. Vegetable oil, milk products and baby foods are imported.

There are no price regulations and there is no duty on export products. Since the amendment of the constitution in 1998 to allow for the full private ownership of land, the government has worked on a plan to auction land under the Land Redistribution Fund (which administers about 25 per cent of all arable land) and to implement a scheme to eliminate the state monopoly on seed production. The government lifted the moratorium on free land sales in 2001.

Crop production in 2004 included: 1,708,938 tonnes (t) cereals in total, 998,200t wheat, 1,362,500t potatoes, 18,300t rice, 233,400t barley, 452,900t maize, 71,000t tomatoes, 48,564t oilcrops, 642,400t sugar beets, 121,700t seed cotton, 48,000 cotton lint, 15,000t tobacco, 37,700t pulses, 21,200t garlic, 14,600t grapes, 190,860t fruit in total, 831,200t vegetables in total.

Livestock production included: 189,200t meat in total, 96,000t beef, 37,000t lamb, 7,200t goat meat, 25,300t pig meat, 4,800t poultry, 16,743t eggs, 1,186,700t milk, 1,500t honey, 150t silk cocoons, 9,975t cattle hides, 5,850t sheepskins, 10,013t greasy wool.
* estimate

Fishing
Fishing remains important for domestic consumption, but fish stocks have been drastically reduced by irrigation, pollution and a lack of investment. The typical annual catch is 200million tonnes.

Forestry
Forests cover four per cent of Kyrgyzstan's land area, or 7,000 square km. Conifers account for 40 per cent of forest composition. Almost half of the forests are mature and over-mature stands. All forests are state-owned. Despite commercial potential, there are no significant forest industries, although Kyrgyzstan has a co-operation agreement with Switzerland for forestry development.

The total forested area has remained stable for several decades and could probably absorb higher levels of exploitation, but the World Bank indicated in 2000 that forest cover in mountain foothill areas is vital to prevent excess water run-off causing flooding problems.

The government aims to increase production, both to meet domestic needs and to export to other Central Asian countries.

Industry and manufacturing
The industrial sector contributes around 21 per cent to GDP, with manufacturing accounting for 13.6 per cent.

Prior to independence, Kyrgyzstan was a significant producer of agricultural machinery, military equipment and medical supplies. Since fundamental manufacturing inputs came from other parts of the former Soviet Union, independence severely impacted upon the size of the industrial base.

Tourism
The geographical remoteness of Kyrgyzstan is an immediate obstacle to growth in the tourist sector, but the country's attractions should encourage international tourist demand. In 2001, the government initiated measures to develop the potentially lucrative tourist sector, but has been slow to build on them. Internal unrest and unsatisfactory infrastructure and services have also impeded significant progress. Despite its immediate shortcomings, Kyrgyzstan tourism should

benefit from the country's natural beauty, historical sites and some of the highest mountains in the world.

Mining

Kyrgyzstan has deposits of gold, mercury, antimony, wolfram, tungsten, lead, zinc, uranium, rock salt and gypsum. Uranium oxide and molybdenum are produced at the Kara-Balta combine (Chu Valley). Metallic antimony (7,800 tonnes per year (tpy)) and antimony oxide (6,000 tpy) produced at the Kadamzhay combine (Osh Region), account for 13 per cent of world supply. Mercury is produced at the Khaidarkan combine (Osh Region), accounting for 21 per cent of world output. Kyrgyzstan has impressive reserves of tin and tungsten, which are concentrated in the Sary-Dzhaz river basin, in the east of the country, and have been prospected and prepared for commercial development.

Kyrgyzstan attracts foreign mining and metallurgical companies due to its lax environmental laws. Large mining and metallurgical plants have failed to take into account the hazards of mercury, cyanide, acids and other toxic substances used in the ore refining and enrichment process. This has caused environmental disasters and poses a threat to the health of workers and the local population.

Antimony manufactured at the Kadamzhay combine suffers from high production costs and is unable to compete with relatively cheap antimony available from Chinese producers. Three other undeveloped reserves include Nichkesu (with estimated reserves of 100,000 tonnes), Savoyardy (90,000 tonnes) and Aktyub (30,000 tonnes).

The Russian, Kyrgyzstani and Kazakhstani governments have co-operated to step up the extraction and processing of raw uranium. The state-owned Khaidarkan combine in the Osh region is the only mercury producer in Kyrgyzstan. It is responsible for the improvement of ore enrichment technology and the development of the Novoye deposit, which has a high concentration of mercury, antimony and fluoride.

Most of the gold reserves are concentrated in lode deposits. With substantial deposits in the Talas mountains in the north and the Batken region in the south, together with relatively low production costs, gold is a key export for Kyrgyzstan. The Kumtor gold mine is one of the 10 largest in the world, accounting for around 30 per cent of exports and 11 per cent of GDP. Kumtor has reserves of 514 tonnes of gold. The mine typically has an annual production of 18.9 tonnes of gold; this level of production will be sustainable until 2010–13. The Kumtor Gold Company, a joint venture between Canada's Cameco and state-owned Kyrgyzaltyn, provides around 95 per cent of Kyrgyzstani gold.

Hydrocarbons

Kyrgyzstan has proven oil reserves of 40 million barrels and estimated reserves of over 2 billion barrels. Kyrgyzstan produces around 4,400 barrels per day (bpd). Domestic consumption is 11,000bpd. The downstream industry consists of one crude oil refinery at Dzhalal-abad, south of Bishkek, which was built in 1997 and has a capacity of 10,000bpd, although supplies of crude are unreliable and the refinery operates below capacity.

Kyrgyzstan has estimated gas reserves of 7.1 billion cubic metres. Gas exploitation is small due to the difficulties involved in recovering reserves. Annual domestic production of 100 million cubic metres only supplies a fraction of the 1.9 billion cubic metres consumed annually. Most gas is imported by Uzbekistan.

Coal reserves are estimated at 1.3 billion tonnes. There are sizeable coal deposits in Shurab, Kyzyl-Kiya, Naryn and Kok-Yangak. Further coal could be extracted from the Kara-Keche deposit in northern Kyrgyzstan, but it would need foreign investment to cover the US$52 million required for development.

Energy

Kyrgyzstan has an electricity generating capacity of 3.6GW. Hydropower stations account for around 80 per cent of electricity generated. There are 18 hydropower stations and two thermal power stations.

Kyrgyzstan supplies small quantities of electricity to Kazakhstan and Uzbekistan, in return for oil, gas and coal imports.

Financial markets
Stock exchange

Central Asia's second stock exchange, the Kyrgyzstan Stock Exchange (KSE), was established in 1995. Despite trading being very thin, it is playing a growing role in ensuring that scarce financial resources are directed towards areas of highest economic return. The KSE was accepted into the Federation of Euro-Asian stock exchanges in the same year

Banking and insurance

During the final years of the Soviet Union, the banking sector was one of the first economic activities to be liberalised.

Upon independence in 1991, Kyrgyzstan had a large number of small banks, many of which offered limited services and had poor ratios of reserves to deposits. Of the Central Asian countries, Kyrgyzstan has made the best progress towards tighter regulation and supervision of banks, although it continues to fall short of the progress made by the Baltic states and Eastern European countries.

Kyrgyzstan adopted the Basle capital requirements in 1995, since when the minimum capital requirement has been increased in stages. As regulation of the system has tightened, so the number of banks has fallen. Simultaneously, privatisation has progressed in Kyrgyzstan to the extent that less than 10 per cent of the banking market is controlled by state banks. Furthermore, 16–17 per cent of the market is controlled by the three foreign banks with a presence in the country. The largest investment bank is the Kairat Bank.

Central bank

National Bank of the Kyrgyz Rebublic
The Law on Banks and Banking Activity, enacted in 2003, strengthened the regulatory powers of the central bank to ensure good management and corporate governance in banks, improve financial disclosure, and control insider dealing.

Time

GMT plus five hours

Geography

Kyrgyzstan is a relatively small, landlocked country situated in eastern Central Asia. There are border crossings with the People's Republic of China to the east and south-east, Kazakhstan to the north, Tajikistan to the south and south-west and Uzbekistan to the west.

The Tian Shan mountains, with glaciers, fast flowing rivers and deep lakes, account for most of the country's high alpine terrain, except for the eastern edge of the steppe bordering Kazakhstan and the fertile Osh Valley to the west. Lake Issyk-Kul in the north-east of the country is the second deepest crater lake in the world.

Climate

Temperature varies from the temperate steppe to sub-zero temperatures in the mountains (Bishkek: minus 5–35 degrees Celsius). Depending on terrain, annual rainfall varies from 170mm and 265mm.

Dress codes

Dress in the business community is in formal, European style.

Entry requirements
Passports

Passports are required by all and must be valid for a minimum of six months at the time of entry.

Visa

Required by all except some nationals of former communist states. For tourist purposes, it is advisable to obtain visas in advance even though some nationals including UK, can pick up a visa from the embassy or on arrival, without a letter of

Kyrgyzstan

invitation. Business visas require an invitation from a sponsor in a local company or government organisation, with confirmation of the contacts to be met and their business addresses and telephone numbers. These should be submitted to the issuing embassy, along with a business letter from the employer giving an account of the visitor's position and role within the foreign company, and full itinerary with purpose of visit and length of stay. For individual business travellers, visa support is required from the Ministry of Foreign Affairs. More information is supplied at www.kyrgyzstan.org/ or should be gathered from the nearest consulate.

CIS transit visas are no longer valid to enter neighbouring countries; a visa for each state should be obtained in advance.

Currency advice/regulations
There are no restrictions on the import or export of local currency, but due to foreign exchange shortages, receipts must be shown for the re-export of foreign currency. Traveller's cheques are accepted.

Customs
On arrival, declare all foreign currency and valuable items such as jewellery, cameras, computers, etc.

Health (for visitors)
A reciprocal health agreement for urgent medical treatment exists with the UK. Proof of UK residence will be required.

Mandatory precautions
Vaccination certificates are required for yellow fever if travelling from an infected area.

Advisable precautions
Water precautions are recommended: water purification tablets may be useful or drink bottled water. It is advisable to be 'in date' for the following immunisations: polio (within 10 years), tetanus (within 10 years), typhoid fever, tuberculosis, hepatitis 'A' (moderate risk only), hepatitis 'B', tick-borne encephalitis.

Any medicines required by the traveller should be stocked by the visitor, and it would be wise to have precautionary antibiotics if going outside major urban centres. A travel kit including a disposable syringe is a reasonable precaution. There is a risk of rabies.

Hotels
It is advisable to book in advance through specialist travel agents. Tips are becoming more customary.

Credit cards
Credit cards are accepted.

Public holidays
Fixed dates
1 Jan (New Year's Day), 7 Jan (Orthodox Christmas Day), 8 Mar (Women's Day), 21 Mar (Noruz/Persian New Year), 1 May (Labour Day), 5 May (Constitution Day), 9 May (Victory Day), 31 Aug (Independence Day).

Variable dates
Eid al Adha, Eid al Fitr.
The Islamic year contains 354 or 355 days, with the result that Muslim feasts advance by 10–12 days against the Gregorian calendar. Dates of feasts vary according to the sighting of the new moon, so cannot be forecast exactly. Islamic year 1426: 10 February 2005 to 30 January 2006.

Working hours
Banking
Mon–Fri: 0930–1730.
Business
Mon–Fri: 0900–1800.
Government
Mon–Fri: 0900–1800.
Shops
Mon–Fri: 0900–1700.

Electricity supply
220V AC

Social customs/useful tips
There are many customs and traditions to be understood. Alcohol is available and smoking is widespread. Gratuities are becoming more customary, particularly in international hotels.

Security
Western nationals have been advised to be vigilant if staying in Kyrgyzstan. Close proximity to Afghanistan and the presence of Western troops in the country could make foreign travellers a target of Islamic rebels. Travellers have been particularly advised to stay away from the southern provincial capital of Osh and especially the surrounding area.

It is unwise to venture out on the streets alone at night. Keep expensive jewellery, watches, cameras, etc, out of sight. Avoid parks at night and use registered taxis only.

Getting there
Air
National airline: Kyrgyz Aba Zholdoru (Kyrgyzstan Airlines)
International airport/s: Bishkek-Manas airport (FRU), 30km north of city, exchange office, duty-free shops, post office, restaurants.
A wider range of direct connections to Europe and Russia are available from the commercial centre Alma Ata (Almaty) of neighbouring Kazakhstan, than from Bishkek Manas airport itself, however it is a four hour drive away.
Airport tax: US$10
Surface
Road: There are roads and border crossings with China, Kazakhstan, Tajikistan and Uzbekistan. Roads can be hazardous in winter. The border crossings in the south-west of the country are considered insecure due to the activity by Islamic rebels.
Rail: Bishkek is linked by rail to Central Asia's transport hub, Tashkent, in Uzbekistan.
Kyrgyzstan and China agreed to construct a transit railroad in 2001, connecting the two countries, with completion by 2005–06.

Getting about
National transport
Air: Kyrgyz Aba Zholdoru operates domestic services. There are regular flights from Bishkek to Osh.
Road: There are 21,000km of roads, only about 50 per cent of which are in reasonable condition. Travel by road is generally difficult because of the terrain and in spring, landslides are common in mountain areas, especially around Osh. Travel by horseback in the mountains. There are no garage facilities on the main roads to and from Bishkek. Care should be taken when travelling by road, especially if a breakdown is involved. Driving during the winter months in private vehicles can be hazardous and some routes could be closed at times. Taxis and private drivers are often willing to provide inter-city services at reasonable prices.
Buses: There are regular and convenient bus services between major towns and cities.
Rail: The only line in use for passenger services is the 340km line in the north of the country, which connects to the Kazakhstani border at both ends and passes through Bishkek. The service is unreliable and is not widely used.
City transport
Taxis: Few taxis have meters and a price should be agreed beforehand. It is sometimes possible to hire private cars, but visitors are recommended to travel only in official taxis.
Buses, trams & metro: Cheap trolley-buses. Service 153 from Bishkek-Manas airport to city centre, every 15 minutes.
Car hire
A national licence with authorised translation or an international driving permit is required. A rented car is often accompanied by a driver.

BUSINESS DIRECTORY
The addresses listed below are a selection only. While World of Information makes every endeavour to check these addresses, we cannot guarantee that changes have not been made, especially to telephone numbers and area codes. We would welcome any corrections.

821

Nations of the World: A Political, Economic and Business Handbook

Telephone area codes
The international direct dialling (IDD) code for Kyrgyzstan is +996, followed by area code and customer's number:
Bishkek 312 Osh 322

Useful telephone numbers
Fire: 101
Police: 102
Ambulance (free): 103
Ambulance (private): 151

Chambers of Commerce
Bishkek Chamber of Commerce, Industry and Hanicraft, 539 Jibek-Jolu, Bishkek (tel: 670-113; fax: 660-048; e-mail: bishkekchamber@netmail.kg).

Kyrgyzstan Chamber of Commerce and Industry, 107 Kievskaya Street, Bishkek 720001 (tel: 210-565; fax: 210-575; e-mail: cci-kr@imfiko.bishkek.su).

Banking
Bakai, 75 Isanov Street, Bishkek 720001 (tel: 660-610; 660-612; e-mail:bank@bakai.kg).

Demir Kyrgyz International, 245 Chui Boulevard, Bishkek 720040 (tel: 610-610; fax: 610-444; e-mail: dkib@demirbank.com.kg).

Eridan, 57 Kalyk-Akieva Street, Bishkek 720001 (tel: 650-610; fax: 650-654; e-mail: eridanbank@infotel.kg).

Kairat, 390 Frunze Street, Bishkek 720033 (tel: 218-932; fax: 218-955; e-mail: kairat@kairatbank.kg).

Kurulush, 28 Manas Street, Bishkek 720391 (tel: 219-736; fax: 219-743; e-mail: kurulush@bank.kg).

Kyrgyzstan, 54 Togolok Moldo Street, Bishkek 720001 (tel: 219-598; fax: 610-220; e-mail: akb@elcat.kg).

Central bank
National Bank of Kyrgyz Republic, 101 Umetalieva St, 720040 Bishkek (tel: 253-933; fax: 255-237; e-mail: mail@nbkr.kg).

Travel information
Airport 'Manas', Bishkek 720062 (tel: 313-593; fax: 313-040; e-mail: manas@ch2m.bishkek.su).

AKC Kyrgyz Concept, 1000 Razzakova Street, Bishkek 720001 (tel 210-556; fax: 660-220; e-mail: akc@mail.elcat.kg).

Kyrgyzstan Aba Joldoru (national airline), Airport 'Manas', Bishkek 720062 (tel: 257-755; fax: 257-162; e-mail: mana@ch2m.bishkek.su).

Kyrgyzstan Airlines (domestic services), Airport 'Manas', Bishkek 720062 (tel: 696-600).

National tourist organisation offices
Kyrgyz State Agency for Tourism and Sport, 17 Togolok Moldo Street, Bishkek 720033 (tel: 220-657; fax: 212-845).

Ministries
Ministry of Agriculture and Water Resources, 96a Kievskaya Street, Bishkek 720040 (tel: 221-435; fax: 226-784).

Ministry of Environmental Protection, 131 Isanova Street, Bishkek 720033 (tel: 219-737; fax: 216-763).

Ministry of Finance, 58 Erkindik Boulevard, Bishkek 720002 (tel: 228-922; fax: 227-404, 620-955).

Ministry of Foreign Affairs, 59 Razzakopva Street, Bishkek 720040 (tel: 220-545; fax: 263-639).

Ministry of Foreign Trade and Industry, 106 Chui Boulevard, Bishkek 720002 (tel: 223-866; fax: 220-793, 252-747).

Ministry of Justice, 37 Orozbekova Street, Bishkek 720040 (tel: 228-489; fax: 261-115).

Ministry of Transport and Telecommunications, Isanova Street, Bishkek 720017 (tel: 216-672; fax: 213-667).

Other useful addresses
British Embassy, 173 Furmanova Street, Alma Ata, Kazakhstan (accredited to Kyrgyzstan) (tel: (7-3272) 506-191; fax: (7-3272) 506-260).

Free Economic Zone General Directorate, 303 Manas Street, Bishkek 720026 (tel: 670-511; fax: 670-512).

Goskominvest (State Committee on Foreign Investments and Economic Co-operation), 58A Erkindik Boulevard, Bishkek 720002 (tel: 223-292; fax: 620-017; e-mail:satc@imfiko.bishkek.su).

Kyrgyzstan Embassy (USA), 1732 Wisconsin Avenue, NW, Washington DC 20007 (tel: 202-338-5141; fax: 202-338-5139; e-mail: embassy@kyrgyzstan.org).

Kyrgyzvneshtorg (Foreign Trade Association), 276 Abdymomunova Street, Bishkek 720033 (tel: 215-701; fax: 620-836).

National Statistical Committee of the Kyrgyz Republic, 374 Frunze Street, Bishkek 720033 (tel: 226-363; fax: 220-759; e-mail: zkudabaev@nsc.bishkek.su).

State Property Fund, 57 Erkindik Boulevard, Bishkek 720002, (tel: 227-706; fax: 660-236; e-mail: spf@imfiko.bishkek.su).

Stock Exchange, 172 Moskvskaya Street, Bishkek 720010 (tel:665-059; fax: 661-595; e-mail: kse@kse.kg).

US Embassy, 171 Mira Boulevard, Bishkek 720016 (tel: 551-241; fax: 551-264; e-mail: mukambaevaibx@state.gov).

Internet sites
The Times of Central Asia: http://www.times.kg

Government of Kyrgyzstan (list of departments in Cyrillic script, email addresses in Latin script): http://kenesh.bishkek.gov.kg/

Laos

KEY FACTS

Official name: Saathiaranarath Prachhathipatay Prachhachhon Lao (Lao People's Democratic Republic)

Head of State: President General Khamtai Siphandon (since 1998)

Head of government: Prime Minister Boungnang Vorachith (appointed 27 Mar 2001)

Ruling party: Lao People's Revolutionary Party (LPRP)

Area: 236,800 square km

Population: 5.69 million (2004)

Capital: Vientiane

Official language: Lao (English is the business language of the Lao government)

Currency: New kip (Nk) = 100 at

Exchange rate: Nk10,425.00 per US$ (Oct 2005)

GDP per capita: US$416 (2004)

GDP real growth: 6.00% (2004); 2.3% (2005)*

Labour force: 2.93 million (2004)

Inflation: 11.20% (2004)

Balance of trade: -US$214.00 million (2004)

Foreign debt: US$3.00 billion (2004)*

* estimated figure

The communist nation of Laos is landlocked and one of the poorest regions in south-east Asia. Hmong anti-communist fighters, veterans of the Vietnam War, emerged from the jungles in which they had hidden in fear for 30 years in 2005 and the World Bank approved the construction of a hydroelectric dam.

Economy

In 2005 GDP growth was projected at a good 7.3 per cent with inflation falling to below the 10 per cent mark. The Asian Development Bank recommended that the Lao government do more to encourage private enterprise, and reform the banking sector. Infrastructure is scant and shaky and 80 per cent of the workforce are involved in subsistence agriculture, mostly rice. However, the services and tourism sectors have been growing in recent years. Government revenues have risen while poverty has fallen to a third of the population, from 39 per cent in 2003.

Dam

After ten years of negotiations with the government, the World Bank agreed in April 2005 to fund the Nam Theun Two hydroelectric dam, at a cost of US$1.3

billion. French, Australian and Thai investors are also involved. The *raison d'être* for the dam is the revenue it would generate from the sale of electricity to Thailand: an estimated annual sum of US$2 billion, from 2009–34. The World Bank's chief economist for the region commented 'only projects like this offer any possibility for development in the country'. There is precious little industry in Laos and poverty is endemic.

However, there are concerns about the social and environmental impact the dam will have on people and wildlife. Around 6,000 people will have to be re-housed and it will affect about 40,000 people who depend on fishing in the Xe Bang Fai river. It will also put at risk a population of endangered elephants The Lao government has a poor record on transparency – it was only recently that they began to publish an annual budget. There is mistrust of the management of this project and the future fate of the displaced peoples.

US relations

In June 2005 two Hmong Americans and two Californians were apprehended in Laos; three of them were deported, accused of 'liaising illegally' with Hmong rebels. The Laos government said that they were 'making trouble'. The Americans belong to the US NGO, the Fact Finding Commission (FFC), whose stated aims are to publicise the fate of Laos fighters who supported the CIA in their war in south-east Asia. When the Communists came to power in 1975 their opponents were left unprotected by the US – they have lived a fugitive existence in the jungles for 30 years ever since, terrified of revenge from the Laos government. In June 2005 170 anti-communist fighters left their jungle hideouts and gave themselves up.

Thousands of ethnic Hmong fled to Thailand claiming persecution from their Communist government, and likely death if they return. They are living in poor conditions in Thailand with temporary shelters not sufficient for the monsoon season. Pneumonia and bronchitis are widespread and drinking water is in short supply. The United Nations High Commission for Refugees (UNHCR) designated the Hmong group as refugees and instructed the Thai government to assess their claims on an individual basis. However, the Thai military are not sympathetic to these requests and want to deport them collectively.

Drugs

US authorities have been pushing for an elimination of the opium trade in Laos for years but with increased urgency from 2000. Their efforts, combined with those of the EU, have helped result in a 73 per cent reduction in poppy cultivation in the past five years. However, what is good news for the American government has been bad news for the Lao poor. Hill tribes have lost their source of incomes and 65,000 have been displaced to new areas without enough food to sustain them. Malaria and dysentery outbreaks have led to reports of a 4 per cent mortality rate, which normally indicates a war-zone. Despite US$80 million dollars of UN aid, there have been few steps taken towards offering and implementing alternatives to the drugs trade.

Outlook

GDP growth for 2006 has been estimated at 7 per cent, which will be driven by the building of the new hydroelectric dam. With the lucrative opium trade all but obliterated, Laos urgently needs a new major source of revenue if it is to reduce dependence on foreign aid.

Risk assessment

Economy	Fair
Politics	Fair
Regional Stability	Good

COUNTRY PROFILE

Historical profile

Between the fourth and eighth centuries, communities along the Mekong river began to form into townships, called muang.

1353 This development culminated in the formation of the Lane Xang (million elephants) Kingdom by King FaNgum and established Xieng Thong, now known as Luang Prabang as capital of Lane Xang Kingdom.

1548–71 During the reign of King Setthathirat, the capital was moved to Vientiane. During this period the That Luang Stupa, a venerated religious shrine and a temple to house the Phra Keo, the Emerald Buddha, were constructed.

1641 A Dutch merchant of the East India Company, Geritt Van Wuysthoff established the first European contact with the Kingdom. Later, Italian missionaries visited.

1893 Laos was put under French administration.

1945 Laos was briefly occupied by the Japanese towards the end of the Second World War.

1950 Laos was granted semi-autonomy as an associated state within the French union.

1954 Laos gained independence and became a constitutional monarchy. Civil war began between monarchists and communists of the Pathet Lao.

1960s Laos was subjected to intensive bombing by the US in its war against the North Vietnamese in one of the worst aerial bombardments in world history.

1973 The Vientiane cease-fire agreement led to renewed divisions between royalists and communists.

1975 The Pathet Lao (the Lao Communist movement) won the civil war. The Lao People's Democratic Republic (LDPR) was proclaimed by a National Congress of People's Representatives. Pathet Lao was renamed the Lao People's Revolutionary Party (LPRP), which became the sole legal

KEY INDICATORS — Laos

	Unit	2000	2001	2002	2003	2004
Population	m	5.20	5.30	5.44	5.57	5.69
Gross domestic product (GDP)	US$bn	1.70	1.80	1.70	1.81	*2.41
GDP per capita	US$	315	333	312	325	416
GDP real growth	%	5.9	5.0	5.7	5.5	6.0
Inflation	%	27.1	7.8	10.6	15.5	11.2
Exports (fob) (goods)	US$m	393.0	350.0	300.0	345.0	365.5
Imports (fob) (goods)	US$m	591.0	558.0	499.0	555.0	579.5
Balance of trade	US$m	-190.0	-208.0	-199.0	-210.0	-214.0
Current account	US$m	-20.0	-70.0	-100.0	-120.0	-200.0
Foreign debt	US$bn	2.5	2.5	2.7	2.5	*3.0
Total reserves minus gold	US$m	139.0	130.9	191.6	208.6	223.3
Foreign exchange	US$m	138.9	127.5	185.5	189.5	207.9
Exchange rate	per US$	7,887.64	8,954.58	7,600.00	7,741.00	7,862.00

* estimated figure

political party. Kaysone Phomvihane was appointed prime minister and began a policy of socialist transformation of the economy.
1979 The government modified its approach following widespread food shortages and an exodus of Laotian refugees to Thailand.
1986 Laos introduced market reforms, encouraged by Soviet leader Mikhail Gorbachev.
1989 The first elections since 1975 were held, although all candidates had to be vetted by the LPRP. The LPRP retained power.
1991 A security and co-operation pact was signed with Thailand. A new constitution was promulgated. Kaysone Phomvihane became president and General Khamtai Siphandon became prime minister.
1992 President Phomvihane died. Siphandon became head of the LPRP.
1995 The US lifted its 20-year aid embargo.
1997 Laos became a member of the Association of South-east Asian Nations (Asean). The Asian financial crisis undermined the value of the kip.
1998 Khamtai Siphandon became president.
2000 Anti-government demonstrations erupted and a series of bomb blasts were detonated by terrorists, possibly based in the US. In December, Laos celebrated 25 years of communist rule.
2001 Boungnang Vorachith was appointed prime minister. Laos agreed a three-year Poverty Reduction and Growth Facility (PRGF) with the IMF. Parliament introduced a death penalty for the possession of more than 500 grammes of heroin. The UN's World Food Programme (WFP) launched a three-year programme to feed 70,000 malnourished children in Laos.
2002 The LPRP was re-elected. Khamtai Siphandon was re-elected president by the National Assembly.
2003 As part of reforms pledged to foreign donors three years ago, Laos' one-party parliament is in the process of amending its constitution, in a move towards decentralisation.
2004 Russia said it would help upgrade Laos' military hardware.
2005 In April the World Bank approved funds for the construction of the Nam Theun Two hydroelectric dam and the foundation stone was laid in November.

Political structure
Constitution
The first constitution was endorsed in August 1991, enshrining the single-party rule of the Lao People's Revolutionary Party (LPRP).

The country is divided into provinces, municipalities, districts and villages. Each of these has a local administrative structure that is subject to the laws and policies of the national government.
Laos' one-party parliament is in the process of amending its constitution in a move towards decentralisation.
The executive
The president, elected by the National Assembly every five years, is the head of state.
The head of government is the prime minister, who is appointed by the president. The Council of Ministers is also appointed by the president.
National legislature
The legislature is unicameral. The Sapha Heng Xat (National Assembly) has 99 members, directly elected for a five-year term.
The Lao People's Revolutionary Party (LPRP) Congress meets every five years. The last Congress was held in March 2001.
Last elections
24 February 2002 (parliamentary and presidential)
Results: Parliamentary: the Lao People's Revolutionary Party (LPRP) (the only party in the parliament) won 108 seats out of 109.
Presidential: President General Khamtai Siphandon was re-elected by the National Assembly.
Next elections
2007 (parliamentary and presidential)
Political parties
Effective political power is exercised by the leadership of the sole legal political organisation, the Lao People's Revolutionary Party (LPRP).
Ruling party
Lao People's Revolutionary Party (LPRP)
Population
5.69 million (2004)
Ethnic make-up
There are three main ethnic groups: the Lao Loum (lowlanders), the Lao Theung (semi-nomadic people who live mainly on the mountain slopes) and the Lao Soung (hill tribes and minority elements).
Religions
The Lao Theung and the Lao Soung are animist, but the great majority of Lao are Theravada Buddhists; there are some Christians.
Education
Nearly 60 per cent of teachers in primary and secondary schools are underqualified.
Secondary education starts at the age of 11 and is divided into three-year lower secondary school and three-year upper secondary school. Higher education is

provided by the National University of Laos, which has merged with 10 higher education institutions located in Vientiane. There are also higher technical institutes and teacher training colleges.
Public expenditure on education typically amounts to 2.1 per cent of annual gross national income. In October 2001, the Asian Development Bank approved a US$20 million loan to support a project partly that will enable over 550,000 children, especially girls and ethnic minorities to receive better primary education. The government is expected to fund the balance with the help of other international donors and complete the project by end-2007.
Literacy rate: 63 per cent male, 32 per cent female; adult rates (World Bank).
Compulsory years: six to 11.
Enrolment rate: 112 per cent gross primary enrolment of the relevant age group (including repeaters); 29 per cent gross secondary enrolment (World Bank).
Pupils per teacher: 30 in primary schools.

Health
Annual total expenditure on health is about 3 per cent of GDP, of which government spending is around 55 per cent. Improved water sources and sanitation facilities are available to 90 per cent and 46 per cent of the population, respectively.
HIV/Aids infection is one of the major public health challenges in the country, affecting almost all provinces and populations and is expected to triple in the next 20 years, unless preventive measures are undertaken.
HIV prevalence: 0.1 per cent aged 15–49 in 2003 (World Bank)
Life expectancy: 54.7 years (World Bank).
Fertility rate/Maternal mortality rate: 4.8 births per woman; maternal mortality 650 per 100,000 live births (World Bank).
Infant mortality rate: 82 deaths per 1,000 live births; 40 per cent of children under aged five are malnourished (World Bank).
Head of population per physician/bed: 0.24 physicians and 2.6 hospital beds per 1,000 people.

Welfare
About 40 per cent of the population live in poverty. The country is covered under the Asian Development Bank (ADB's) poverty reduction strategy that focusses on rural development, regional integration, human resource development, sustainable environmental management and private sector development. To achieve this, the ADB has lent Lao PDR about US$45–55 million annually on concessional terms for the period 2002–2004, in addition to

other technical assistance grants. Another US$1 million grant is provided by the Japan Fund for Poverty Reduction to help the landless poor increase their participation in farm-based production.

Main cities
Vientiane (capital, estimated population 194,200 in 2003), Savannakhet (58,200).

Languages spoken
The adopted business language of the Lao government is English. Widely spoken languages other than Lao are: Thai, English, Vietnamese, Chinese, Russian, German, and to a much lesser extent, French; plus tribal languages.

Official language/s
Lao (English is the business language of the Lao government)

Media
Press
Dailies: Lao-language dailies include *Pasason* and *Vientiane Mai*.
English-language foreign Internet services covering daily news include *Lan-Xang.com* (www.lan-xang.com), with news articles from the pro-royal Laotians living outside, *Laos Globe* (www.laosguide.com) and *Laos News* (www.laosnews.net).
Weeklies: *Vientiane Times* is a biweekly English-language newspaper.
Business: Weekly business paper is *Khao Tulakit*.
Periodicals: *Lao Vision* is a magazine published by Laotians in the US.
Broadcasting
State-run TV and radio (Lao National Radio). Radio Free Asia Lao (RFA) (www.rfa.org/) covering local news is a private, non-profit corporation broadcasting news and information in nine languages to listeners in Asia who do not have access to full and free news media.

Economy
Laos is one of the poorest countries in the world. A third of the population exists outside the money economy and 85 per cent depend on subsistence agriculture.
Throughout the 1980s, Laos relied mainly on funding from the former Soviet bloc, Sweden and Vietnam, but the importance of Western aid, both bilateral and multilateral, increased during the 1990s. Laos remains heavily dependent on aid, with the largest multilateral donor, the Asian Development Bank (ADB), lending around US$80 million annually and the World Bank providing US$40 million. Total foreign assistance amounts to approximately US$250 million a year and accounts for over 20 per cent of GDP.
Laos moved away from a centrally controlled economy to a market orientated system in 1986, with the introduction of the New Economic Mechanism (NEM), which aimed to stimulate private activity. Accelerated privatisation has seen a rapid reduction in state-owned enterprises since 1988.
The main sectors receiving foreign direct investment are services and industry and the key investors are China, Thailand, Singapore, Malaysia, Norway and France.

External trade
Transit cargo is transferred along an east-west, cross-border highway since a 1999 agreement between Laos, Vietnam and Thailand was signed.
Imports
Principal imports are machinery and equipment, vehicles, fuel and consumer goods.
Main sources: Thailand (60.5 per cent total, 2004), China (9.2 per cent), Vietnam (8.7 per cent)
Exports
Principal exports are electricity (typically 40 per cent of total), garments, wood products, coffee and tin.
Most of the increase in exports was associated with the very rapid growth in non-traditional exports, especially garments, the country's leading foreign exchange earner.
Main destinations: Thailand (19 per cent total, 2004), Vietnam (16.4 per cent), France (7.9 per cent), Germany (5.6 per cent), UK (4.9 per cent)

Agriculture
Farming
Agriculture contributes around 47 per cent of GDP and employs over 80 per cent of the workforce.
Rice, the main crop, is cultivated in irrigated lowland paddies and on drier hill farms.
Other crops include maize, sweet potatoes, cassava, pulses, groundnuts, fruit, vegetables, sugar cane, coffee, tobacco and cotton. Livestock raised includes cattle, buffaloes, pigs, goats and poultry.
Crop production in 2004 included: 2,732,500 tonnes (t) cereals in total, 2,529,000t rice, 203,500t maize, 55,500t cassava, *36,000t potatoes, *194,000t sweet potatoes, 46,000t bananas, 36,000t pineapples, *17,100t pulses, 68,500t citrus fruit, 9,148t oilcrops, 33,300t tobacco, 32,100t green coffee, 223,300t sugar cane, 261t tea, 3,900t fibre crops, 6,603t seed cotton, 2,200t cotton lint, 201,000t fruit in total, 783,506t vegetables in total. Livestock production in 2004 included: 81,732t meat in
total, 21,000t beef, 18,425t buffalo meat, 27,160t pig meat, 497t goat meat, 14,650t poultry, 6,000t milk, 12,300t eggs, 1,944t cattle hides.
* estimate

Industry and manufacturing
The industrial sector accounts for around 27 per cent of GDP and employs over 10 per cent of the workforce.
There is no heavy industry. The production of tin concentrates is the main industrial activity. Other major industries include textiles, bricks, cement, minerals and hydroelectricity.
Small-scale manufacturing industries produce beer, cigarettes, detergents, rubber footwear, plywood, matches, salt, animal feed, veterinary products, handicrafts, alcoholic beverages and soft drinks.
The growth sectors are garments, wood products, handicrafts and light industry, including vehicle assembly.

Tourism
Tourism is an increasingly important contributor to GDP and the balance of payments. The sector has strengthened steadily since the mid-1990s. There were 894,000 arrivals in 2004, an increase of 33 per cent over 2003. Around three-quarters of visitors came from the region, with Thailand in the lead. Tourism is expected to contribute 5.5 per cent to GDP in 2005.

Mining
Mining together with hydrocarbons contributes around 5 per cent to GDP. The sector employs 1 per cent of the workforce.
As with other economic sectors in Laos, resources have not been optimised because of bureaucracy, lack of infrastructure and inefficiency.
Principal minerals include tin, high-grade iron ore, gold, copper, potash, limestone, manganese, lead, zinc, gypsum and bauxite.
There is great potential for the extraction of gold, and explorations have been conducted by Pan Australian and CRA Exploration of Australia (a subsidiary of Rio Tinto Zinc), both in joint ventures with the Laos government. Commercial interest in gold mining has surged following the success of the Sepon project – 80 per cent Oxiana Resources and 20 per cent Rio Tinto – which started gold and copper production in 2003.

Hydrocarbons
Laos does not produce any hydrocarbons. It relies on imports of petroleum products to meet domestic consumption levels. Laos does not import either coal or natural gas. Several Thai companies are developing open-cast lignite mines.

Energy
Laos has installed electricity generating capacity of 700MW, supplied mainly by hydropower. Supply is restricted mainly to the capital. Laos exports electricity to its neighbours, mainly Thailand and China.

The government envisages expansion of capacity by constructing more dams around Laos over time as a means of earning revenue from increased exports of electricity. In 2005, construction began on the World Bank-supported but controversial Nam Theu Two hydropower project, which will add 1,070MW to capacity, much of which will be exported to Thailand; it is expected to be completed by 2009.

The Asian Development Bank puts Laos' hydropower potential at 18,000MW, which could earn around US$20 billion a year.

Banking and insurance

Since the early 1990s, the number of banks in Laos has more than doubled, with a corresponding rise in business. There are eight state-run commercial banks, two joint venture banks, seven foreign banks and 32 private non-bank foreign exchange bureaux operating in Laos. Banks are gradually adopting commercial lending practices. Restructuring from September 2002 includes the phased recapitalisation of the state commercial banks, the merger of two smaller banks and a rationalisation of banking operations.

Central bank
Banque de la RDP Lao (Bank of Lao PDR)

Time

GMT plus seven hours

Geography

Laos is a landlocked country in south-east Asia, bordered by the People's Republic of China to the north, Vietnam to the east, Cambodia to the south, Thailand to the west and Myanmar (Burma) to the northwest.

Climate

Most of the year is hot and humid. The climate is monsoonal and has three distinct seasons. The hot dry season begins in February, with temperatures up to 40 degrees Celsius (C), only broken by the odd shower of rain. A build-up of storm activity in April–May with increasing humidity heralds the wet season during June–October, typified by a more consistent pattern of rain and cloudy days through June, July and August. There can be as much as 250mm rainfall per month. Temperatures average 29 degrees C. During this time, the Mekong River rises and flooding of the surrounding area is not uncommon. The dry season arrives in November with cooler weather and reduced humidity. Average temperature may drop to 14–15 degrees C. The cool weather can continue until February. Always cooler in the mountains, especially at night.

Entry requirements

Passports
Required by all. Must be valid for 15 days, and can only be extended for 15 days.

Visa
Required by all. Tourist visas, issued to accredited tour operators in advance of a visit, or directly through embassies, are authorised for 15 days without extension. Business visas must be arranged in advance by a sponsor in Laos, and only when approval has been given will the issuing embassy give permission for visits up to one month, with extensions possible to complete the business. Without local contacts, applications may be made through the Foreign Investment Management Committee (FIMC). The approval process takes about two weeks, but visas are collected from the Lao Embassy in Bangkok.

All further information should be sought through the nearest embassy.

Exit visas are also required by all and are obtainable from the police or Immigration Department, Vientiane.

Currency advice/regulations
Import and export of local currency is prohibited; no restrictions on foreign currency. American Express and US dollar traveller's cheques are easiest to cash.

Customs
It is forbidden to take any antiques or Buddha images over 50-years-old out of the country. Such items brought into Laos from other countries have to be declared at Customs.

Health (for visitors)

Laos has few hospitals and medical facilities.

Mandatory precautions
Vaccination certificates for yellow fever if travelling from an infected area.

Advisable precautions
Anti-malaria precautions; malaria is endemic in many areas of Laos but is not found in Vientiane. Mosquito repellent is recommended as dengue fever can be caught in Vientiane all year round. Immunisations against diphtheria, hepatitis 'A' and 'B', Japanese 'B' encephalitis, TB, tetanus, polio and typhoid. Rabies is a health risk.

Comprehensive health insurance, including provision for air evacuation, is strongly advised.

Credit cards

Major credit cards are accepted by main hotels and some restaurants. The handling fee of 1.5–3.0 per cent is generally passed on to the customer.

Public holidays

Fixed dates
1 Jan (New Year's Day), 6 Jan (Pathet Lao Day), 20 Jan (Army Day), 8 Mar (Women's Day), 22 Mar (Lao People's Party Day), 13–15 Apr (Lao New Year), 1 May (Labour Day), 1 Jun (Children's Day), 13 Aug (Day of the Free Laos), 12 Oct (Day of Liberation), 2 Dec (National Day).

Variable dates
Chinese New Year (Feb), Birth of Buddha (May), Buddhist Fast begins (Jun), Buddhist Fast ends (Jul/Aug).

Working hours

Local government offices, commercial companies and banks are likely to be closed on some or all of the following days: 20 Jan (Army Day), 22 Mar (Party Day), 15 Aug (Constitution Day).

Banking
Mon–Fri: 0900–1600.

Business
Mon–Sat: 0800–1200, 1400–1700.

Government
Mon–Sat: 0800–1200, 1400–1700. Some ministries close at 1130 for lunch; others work a half-day Saturday.

Shops
(Mon–Sun) 0900–1700.

Electricity supply

220V 50Hz. Power outlets are two-prong round or flat sockets.

Weights and measures

Metric system (local units also in use).

Social customs/useful tips

The generally accepted form of greeting among Lao people is the nop, performed by placing one's palms together in a position of praying at chest level, but not touching the body. The higher the hands, the greater the sign of respect. Nonetheless, the hands should not be held above the level of the nose. The nop is accompanied by a slight bow to show respect to persons of higher status and age. It is also used as an expression of thanks, regret or saying goodbye. But with Western people, it is acceptable to shake hands.

Since the head is considered the most sacred part of the body and the soles of the feet the least, one should not touch a person's head nor use one's foot to point at a person or any object. It is forbidden for a woman to touch a Buddhist monk.

Men and women rarely show affection in public.

Getting there

Air
Advance reservations should be made for flights from Bangkok.

National airline: Lao Aviation.
International airport/s: Vientiane-Wattay International Airpirt (VTE), 4km from city centre.
Airport tax: International departures US$10; domestic departure Nk100.

Surface

Road: Opened in 1994, the Mitraphap Bridge/Friendship Bridge over the Mekong River, situated 14km east of Vientiane, provides the first modern road link with Thailand. It also gave Laos road access to a port for the first time.

It is possible to cross into Laos from Thailand at Chiang Kohong. The border can also be crossed at Houeixay in Bokeo province.

From Boten in Luang Namtha Province, there is a road to China.

Border crossings have been set up at Lak Sao on road No 8, in Borikhamsay Province, and at Dan Savanh, in Avannakhet Province, on road No 9.

Rail: Entry via the rail line running from Bangkok is subject to special permission.

Water: From Kunming or Xishuangbanna, China, it is possible to travel by boat along the Mekong river south into Bokeo Province.

Getting about
National transport

It is relatively easy to travel in northern Laos but in the south, public transport is extremely erratic.

Air: Travel by air is the most convenient means of transportation within Laos. Lao Aviation flies daily from Vientiane to Luang Prabang, Savannakhet, Xieng Khouang, Pakse and Oudomsay. There are several flights a week to Luang Namtha, Sayaboury, Houeixay, Sam Neua, Saravane, Lak Xao, Muangkhong and Attapeu.

Road: Laos has 18,153km of national roads, 2,500km of which are paved. The most important road is route No 13 which runs north-south from China to Cambodia. It links Pak Mong in the north with Khong in the south, passing through major urban areas of Luang Prabang, Vientiane, Savannakhet and Champassack. Road No 1 runs from Thailand, through Laos, to China; road No 9 runs from Thailand, through Laos, to Vietnam. Construction has faltered on the Chiang Rai-Kunming Road Improvement Project, total cost US$594.3 million. When regional economies recover, the project is expected to recommence and, when complete, will involve over 1,220km of road along the north axis of the subregion, and will provide road links from Yunnan Province, Laos, to Bangkok in Thailand.

Buses: There are services between main centres.

Rail: A line from Vientiane to Nong Khai is operating, including air-conditioned coaches.

Water: River transport is important, especially on the Mekong River, which flows through 1,865km of Laos.

City transport

The easiest way to travel around town is with a car and driver, usually arranged through your hotel.

Taxis: Three-wheeled tuk-tuk (motorcycle taxis) are easily found.

Taxis are available in Vientiane, but often operate along certain routes in the manner of buses. Individual hire may require negotiation. Tipping is discouraged.

Car hire

Arrangements are generally made through hotels.

BUSINESS DIRECTORY

The addresses listed below are a selection only. While World of Information makes every endeavour to check these addresses, we cannot guarantee that changes have not been made, especially to telephone numbers and area codes. We would welcome any corrections.

Telephone area codes

The international dialling code (IDD) for Laos is +856 followed by area code (Vientiane only) and subscriber's number:
Vientiane 21

Useful telephone numbers

Police: 191
Police (Immigration Office) emergency number: 212-520
Fire: 190
Ambulance: 195
International Medical Clinic: 214-018, 214-022, 214-025

Chambers of Commerce

Lao National Chamber of Commerce and Industry, Sihom Road, Chanthabury, PO Box 4596, Vientiane (tel: 219-224; fax: 219-223; e-mail: laocci@laotel.com).

Banking

Banque de la République Democratique Populaire Lao, PO Box 19, Rue Yonnet, Vientiane (tel: 213-109, 213-110; fax: 213-108).

Banque Pour Le Commerce Exterieur La; PO Box 2925, N 1 Pang Kham Rd, Vientiane (tel: 213-200; fax: 213-202).

Joint Development Bank Ltd; 75/15 Lane Xang Ave, Vientiane (tel: 213-536; fax: 213-530).

Lane Xang Bank Ltd; 6-80 Setthathiilath, Vientiane (tel: 213-400, 212-186, 212-108, 212-105; fax: 213-404).

Vientiane Commercial Bank Ltd; 33 Lane Xang Ave, Hatsady, Chanthaboury, Vientiane (tel: 222-700; fax: 213-513).

Central bank

Banque de la République Democratique Populaire Lao, PO Box 19, Rue Yonnet, Vientiane (tel: 213-109; fax: 213-108; e-mail: bol@pan-laos.net.la).

Travel information

Lao Aviation, 2 Pangkham Road, PO Box 4169, Vientiane (tel: 212-055; fax: 212-056).

Ministry of tourism

Ministry of Trade and Tourism, Vientiane (tel: 412-003, 412-436; fax: 412-434).

National tourist organisation offices

National Tourism Authority of Lao PDR, PO Box 3556, PO Box 3556, Lane Xang Avenue, Vientiane (tel: 212-248, 212-251; fax: 212-769).

Ministries

Department of Foreign Trade, Ministry of Industry and Commerce, Vientiane.

Ministry of Agriculture and Forestry, Vientiane (tel: 412-358).

Ministry of Commerce and Tourism, Vientiane (tel: 107-484).

Ministry of Communications, Transport, Post and Construction, Vientiane (tel: 412-281); Foreign Relations Department (tel: 412-267).

Ministry of Defence, Vientiane (tel: 412-803); Foreign Relations Departments (tel: 412-805, 412-810).

Ministry of Education, Vientiane (tel: 216-000); Foreign Relations Department (tel: 216-005).

Ministry of External Economic Relations, Foreign Investment Adviser, Vientiane (tel: 169-804).

Ministry of Finance, Vientiane (tel: 412-142, 412-404, 412-417).

Ministry of Foreign Affairs, Vientiane (tel: 414-002, 414-003).

Ministry of Industry and Handicrafts, Vientiane (tel: 413-000, 413-004, 413-006); (Electricity Division) (tel: 413-010; fax: 413-013); (Industry Division) (tel: 414-332); (Geology and Mines Division) (tel: 212-080, 212-082; fax: 222-539).

Ministry of Information and Culture, Vientiane (tel: 212-898, 212-402); (Foreign Relations Director) (tel: 212-409).

Ministry of the Interior, Vientiane (tel: 212-503, 212-501); (Foreign Relations Division) (tel: 212-554).

Ministry of Justice, Vientiane (tel: 414-101).

Ministry of Labour and Social Welfare, Vientiane (tel: 213-001, 213-002).

Ministry of Public Health, Vientiane (tel: 412-985, 214-046).

Other useful addresses

ASEAN Investment Promotion Agency, Foreign Investment Management Committee in charge of Promotion Administration and Investment Services, Luang Prabang

Road, Vientiane (tel: 216-663; fax: 215-491).

ASEAN Secretariat, 70 A J1 Sisingamangaraja, Jakarta 12110, Indonesia (tel: 62(21)726-2991, 724-3372; fax: 724-3504, 739-8234; e-mail: asean.or.id).

British Embassy, Commercial Section, 1031 Wireless Road, Bangkok 10330, Thailand (tel: (662)253-0191; fax: (662)255-8619).

British Trade Office, Vientiane, Pandit J Nehru Road, PO Box 6626, Vientiane (tel: 413-606; fax: 413-607).

Foreign Investment Management Committee, Luang Prabang Road, Vientiane (tel: 216-662, 216-663, 217-009, 217-018); fax: 215-491, 217-007, 217-013).

Lao Embassy (USA), 2222 S Street, NW, Washington DC 20008 (tel: 202-332-6416; fax: 202-332-4923).

Lao Import-Export Company, 43-47 Lanexang Road, Vientiane.

Lao National Radio, Vientiane (tel: 212-428, 212-429, 212-431, 212-430).

Lao National Television Channel 9, Vientiane (tel: 412-182).

Lao Water Authority, Commercial Division, Vientiane (tel: 412-885; fax: 414-378).

United Nations Development Programme (UNDP), Phon Kheng Road, PO Box 345, Vientiane (tel: 4101, 5605; fax: 5001).

US Embassy, Thatdam Bartholonie Road, Bane Thatdam, Vientiane (tel: 213-966, 212-581, 212-582, 212-585).

Internet sites

Asian Development Bank: http://www.adb.org/lrm

Laos Business Centre: http://www.asiadragons.com/

Laos website: http://laos.asiaco.com/

Web directory: http://www.angelfire.com/ca/laoscom/

Web directory: http://www.laoworld.com/

Worldwide Gazeteer – Laos: http://www.c-allen.dircon.co.uk/Countries/Laos.htm

Latvia

KEY FACTS

Official name: Latvijas Republika (Republic of Latvia)

Head of State: President Vaira Vike-Freiberga (since Jul 1999; re-elected 20 Jun 2003)

Head of government: Prime Minister Aigars Kalvitis (nominated by the President 24 Nov 2004)

Ruling party: Coalition government, comprising Tautas Partija (TP) (People's Party), Jaunais Laiks (New Era), Latvijas Pirmâ Partija (LPP) (Latvia's First Party) and Zaïo un Zemnieku Savienîba (ZZS) (Green and Farmers' Union) (approved by parliament 2 Dec 2004)

Area: 64,589 square km

Population: 2.26 million (2004)

Capital: Riga

Official language: Lettish

Currency: Lats (Ls) = 100 santims

Exchange rate: Ls0.58 per US$ (Oct 2005)

GDP per capita: US$5,822 (2004)

GDP real growth: 8.00% (2004); *7.3% (2005)

Labour force: 1.30 million (2004)

Unemployment: 8.80% (2004)

Inflation: 6.30% (2004); *6.0% (2005)

Balance of trade: -US$1.68 billion (2004)

Foreign debt: US$7.37 billion (2004)

* estimated figure

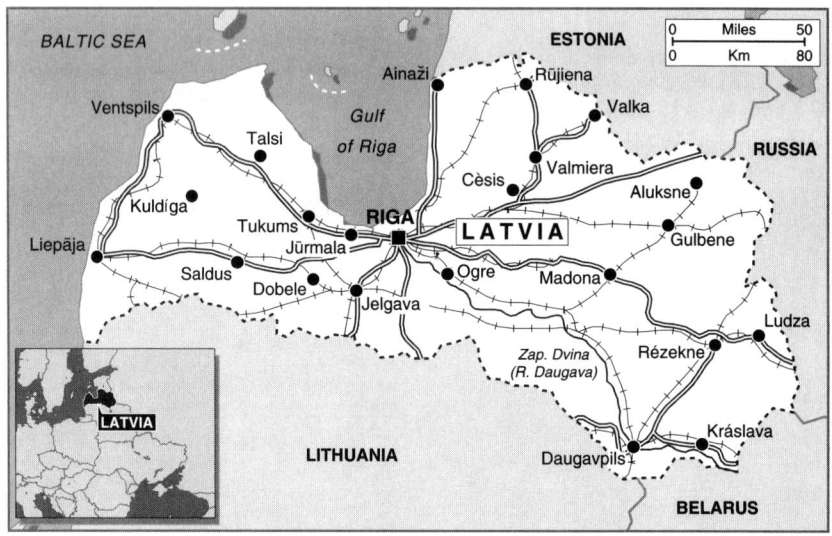

Latvia in 2005 began to reap the benefits of having joined both NATO and the European Union in the previous year. Membership of these two coveted clubs signifies acceptance into the international community and is the culmination of Latvia's successful transition to a free market economy. 2005 was also the year of continued tensions between this Baltic state and its mighty Russian neighbour. They clashed over borders, minority Russian speakers in Latvia, schools legislation, SS veteran marches and the sixty-year anniversary of the end of the Second World War. Latvia briefly commanded the attention of the global media when US President George W Bush dropped by for a day visit and a show of solidarity.

Politics

Latvia had the first Green premier in Europe, Indulis Emsis – until he resigned in late 2004, two weeks after the previous prime minister had quit. From December 2004 the country has been led by Aigars Kalvitis, of the centre right Tautas Partija (TP) (People's Party).

Economy

Latvia is one of a small cluster of the fastest growing economies in the EU with estimated growth of 7.3 per cent in 2005. Accession facilitated new markets for Latvia's booming export sector, although domestic demand is also responding positively to wage increases. The stock market is very strong with shares surging by 22 per cent in 2005. The basis for such success has been structural reform, prudent financial policy and efforts to contain fraud. Latvia entered the Exchange Rate Mechanism II in 2005 in preparation for entry into the euro-zone on 1 January 2008.

However, strong inflation could hinder progression to the single currency, with rates for 2005 forecast at 6 per cent. The Maastricht treaty sets maximum inflation levels at 1.5 per cent more than the average of the bottom three inflation rates among EU countries. Currently, this would equate to about 3.5 per cent. Inflation, along with rising wages, could also jeopardise the country's competitiveness. Levels of external debt are problematic and rising energy prices are a concern.

Foreign affairs

2005 marked fifteen years since Latvia achieved independence from the USSR. The BBC recently quoted a high ranking Russian official as saying 'There's no country in the world that Russia has worse

Latvia

relations with than Latvia'. The Soviets ruled this small Baltic nation for nearly fifty years. This half-century left a legacy of unresolved issues and mutual hostilities. The Russians present themselves as liberators; the Latvians define them as invaders and illegal occupiers. A Latvian foreign affairs official, Andrejs Pildegovics, said, 'We are still on the front line… I tell ambassadors coming to Latvia, "You have been sent to the battlefield"'.

2005 was also the 60-year anniversary of the conclusion of the Second World War. This was observed in Moscow in May with patriotic ritual. Latvia, Estonia and Lithuania were invited to send representatives to the commemorative events. Estonia and Lithuania consider attendance of the Russian ceremony as tantamount to sanctioning Soviet occupation post-second world war. Latvia, however, did attend, dismissing its reservations in the hope that such diplomacy could lead to a resolution of border disputes. Not only this, but the official attendance pleased minority Russian-speakers, of whom there are many more in Latvia than in the other Baltic states.

In fact, up to 40 per cent of Latvian residents are Russian speakers. National hostility aimed at Russia significantly impinges upon this group. About half of Russian speakers, 450,000 people, are precluded citizenship and the right to vote, be a teacher or civil servant, because they have not passed, or have refused to sit, an official language and history test. One of the questions in this test requires the candidate to acknowledge that Latvia was occupied by Russia.

In late 2004, new laws were instituted curbing the use of Russian in Latvian classrooms. Over half of senior school lessons must now be conducted in Latvian. The laws were greeted with notable levels of angry protest, with the Russians defining them as a human rights abuse. The legislation is variously seen as an attempt to integrate the Russian speaking section of the population; or as a punishment directed at Russian sympathisers.

Another event antagonistic towards the Russian minority, and indeed, Latvian Jews, is the annual nationalist march of one hundred SS veterans and their families. Latvia had a very high rate of membership of the SS and has never really come to terms with its Nazi past, with not a single Nazi criminal being prosecuted since the country won independence. In March 2005 troops who had fought for Hitler clashed with pro-Soviet protesters in the capital Riga. Twenty five people were arrested, including almost all the anti-SS protesters.

In 2005 George Bush demonstrated his allegiances in the rift by visiting Riga to meet the Latvian president, Vaira Vike-Freiberga. In a letter to the leader, Bush mentioned how 'the war marked the Soviet occupation and the annexation of Estonia, Latvia and Lithuania and the imposition of communism'. Bush's visit was significant for both political and economic reasons. The US is an important ally for a country with a population of only 2.4 million. Meanwhile, the international media coverage is good for Latvia's prospects of attracting foreign investment. The EU, however, has maintained a distanced stance towards Latvia, not wishing to jeopardise its relations with Russia.

Society

In December 2005, Latvian politicians opposed the wishes of the president and prime minister by passing legislation disallowing gay marriages. The move also attracted criticism from the EU. In fact there is now conflict between Latvian national law and EU law on this issue, out of which has arisen some confusion. The amendment to the law followed a gay pride demonstration in the summer – a historic first for a country in which homosexuality is still taboo. The prime minister had said on television that it was 'unacceptable' for homosexuals to march past the Doma cathedral in the centre of town. Hundreds appeared to agree, turning out to protest against and outnumber the few marchers.

Outlook

In early 2006 Latvia will represent the EU Presidency in Belarus. The British Queen Elizabeth II is expected to visit the country later in the year. The IMF has recommended a tax reduction for those on low incomes, and also a controlling of inflation. This will have to be a priority for the coming years if Latvia is to stick to the timetable for adoption of the euro.

Risk assessment

Economic	Good
Political	Good
Regional Stability	Stable
Stock Market	Good

COUNTRY PROFILE

Historical profile

Before being occupied by the Germans in the thirteenth century, Latvia had been an important Baltic trading route and was a largely feudal and tribal society.
1561 Latvia came under Polish rule after the Livonian Order appealed to Poland-Lithuania for protection from Russia's Ivan the Terrible.
1620s Following the Polish-Swedish war, most of Latvia came under Swedish rule, except Courland in western Latvia where the dukes of Jelgava maintained allegiance to Poland until 1709.
1700–21 Russia's Peter the Great destroyed Swedish power in the Great Northern War. Latvia became part of the Russian empire.
1795 Apart from a brief period of French occupation in 1812, Courland was under

KEY INDICATORS — Latvia

	Unit	2000	2001	2002	2003	2004
Population	m	2.43	2.40	2.42	2.30	2.26
Gross domestic product (GDP)	US$bn	7.10	7.60	8.30	9.70	*13.63
GDP per capita	US$	3,008	3,186	3,452	4,078	5,822
GDP real growth	%	6.6	7.6	5.0	7.5	8.0
Inflation	%	2.7	2.5	1.9	2.7	6.3
Unemployment	%	13.2	7.7	8.0	8.7	8.8
Exports (fob) (goods)	US$m	2,058.0	2,216.0	2,350.0	2,743.0	4,185.0
Imports (fob) (goods)	US$m	3,116.0	3,566.0	3,650.0	3,921.0	6,935.0
Balance of trade	US$m	-1,058.0	-1,351.0	-1,300.0	-1,178.0	-2,749.0
Current account	US$m	-485.0	-758.0	-568.0	-771.0	-1,680.0
Foreign debt	US$bn	4.7	4.4	4.4	3.4	7.4
Total reserves minus gold	US$m	850.9	1,148.7	1,241.4	1,432.4	1,912.0
Foreign exchange	US$m	850.8	1,148.6	1,241.3	1,432.2	1,911.7
Exchange rate	per US$	0.61	0.63	0.61	0.56	0.52

* estimated figure

Nations of the World: A Political, Economic and Business Handbook

Russian control until 1915 when the Germans occupied the province.

1914–18 During the First World War, Latvia alternated between Russian and German control five times. It was under Bolshevik Russian control in late 1918 by which time Latvian independence had been declared by nationalists.

1919 Joint British and German forces expelled Bolshevik Russian forces and democratic rule was introduced.

1922 A constitutional parliament, with proportional representation, was adopted.

1934–39 Prime Minister Karlis Ulmanis declared a state of emergency, suspended parliament and banned all political parties. In 1936, he assumed the title of president, becoming an autocratic ruler.

1939 Through the German and Soviet Ribbentrop-Molotov pact, Latvia was forcibly incorporated back into the Soviet Union.

1940 Latvia was incorporated as a constituent republic of the USSR.

1941 The Germans invaded and occupied Latvia.

1944 The Soviet Union liberated Latvia from German rule.

1945–80s The mass deportation to Siberia of Latvian citizens by Stalin, following the war, resulted in an influx of Russian nationals as the Soviet Union introduced collective farming and developed heavy industries in the country.

1991 Soviet troops were deployed in Riga after multi-party elections had removed the Latvijas Komunistiska Partija (LKP) (Latvian Communist Party) from office the previous year. Following the Soviet Union's withdrawal due to international pressure, Latvia declared its independence. Anatolijs Gorbunov of the Latvijas Tautas Fronte (LTF) (Latvian Popular Front) became head of state as chairman of the Latvian Supreme Council. Ivars Godmanis, also of the LTF, became head of government as the chairman of the Council of Ministers.

1993 A coalition led by Latvijas Cels (LC) (Latvia's Way) formed a government with the Latvijas Zemnieku Savienia (LZS) (Latvian Farmers' Union). The 1922 Satversme (constitution) was fully reinstituted. Guntis Ulmanis of the LZS was elected the first post-Soviet Latvian president. The LC's Valdis Birkavs was appointed prime minister.

1995 Parliamentary elections led to political turmoil as the ruling LC lost its dominant position and no single party held a majority. A six-party coalition government was eventually formed, dominated by the two largest parties, the centrist LC and the left-wing Democrâtiskâ Partija 'Saimnieks' (DPS) (Democratic Party 'Master'). After wrangling and negotiation, Andris Skele of the LC was appointed prime minister.

1996 President Ulmanis was re-elected by the Saeima (parliament) for a second term of four years.

1998 Latvians narrowly backed the liberalisation of the country's citizenship laws in a referendum held alongside general elections. A centre-right coalition was formed, with Vilis Kristopans of the LC as prime minister.

1999 Latvia became a member of the World Trade Organisation (WTO), the first of the Baltic states to join. Independent Vaira Vike-Freiberga was elected president. The minority centre-left coalition headed by Vilis Kristopans fell and a majority coalition government was formed under Prime Minister Andris Skele.

2000 Skele's coalition collapsed over plans to privatise the Latvian Shipping Company (Lasco) and the dismissal of economics minister, Vladimir Makarovs. A majority coalition government was formed by former Riga mayor, Andris Berzin of the LC. Formal accession talks with the EU began.

2001 The Organisation for Security and Co-operation in Europe (OSCE) completed a six-year mission in Latvia.

2002 After parliamentary elections, Einars Repše formed a coalition government comprising Jaunais Laiks (JL) (New Era), Latvijas Pirmâ Partija (LPP) (Latvia's First Party), Zaïo un Zemnieku Savienîba (ZSS) (Green and Farmers Union) and the Apvienîba 'Tçvzemei un Brîvîbai'/Latvijas Nacionala Konservativa Partija (TB/LNNK) (Union for the Fatherland and Freedom/Latvian National Conservative Party). NATO invited Latvia to join the alliance by 2004.

2003 On 20 June, President Vaira Vike-Freiberga was re-elected by a vote of 88–6 in the 100-seat parliament. In a September referendum, Latvians voted by 67 per cent to 32 per cent to join the EU in 2004.

2004 The LPP withdrew from the coalition on 28 January, leaving the coalition without a majority. Prime Minister Repše's government resigned on 5 February and Indulis Emsis (ZZS) was designated as prime minister on 20 February. Emsis' minority coalition government, comprising Tautas Partija (TP) (People's Party), LPP and ZZS was approved by parliament on 9 March. In April, Latvia acceded to Nato and on 1 May it entered the EU. The Emsis minority coalition government resigned in October and on 24 November, President Vaira Vike-Freiberga nominated Aigars Kalvitis as prime minister.

2005 In March several Latvian SS veterans and young nationalists were arrested in public confrontations with anti-fascist demonstrators in Riga. In May US President George Bush made an official visit to the capital. In June the proposed EU constitution was approved by parliament.

Political structure

Constitution
In 1993, the Constitutional Law supplemented the 1922 constitution. The constitution provides for basic rights and freedoms.

Latvian citizens 18 years and over and those resident in Latvia before 27 June 1940, are eligible to vote.

Form of state
Parliamentary democratic republic

The executive
Executive powers are vested in the Cabinet of Ministers, nominated by the prime minister and appointed by and accountable to, parliament. The Cabinet of Ministers is led by the prime minister, who is appointed by the president.

The president is elected by parliament for a four-year term.

National legislature
Legislative authority is vested in a 100-member unicameral Saeima (parliament), directly elected for a four-year term by proportional representation.

Parties must receive at least 5 per cent of the national vote to gain seats in the Saeima.

Legal system
The legal system is based on a civil law system. The appointment of judges to the Supreme Court is confirmed by the Saeima.

Last elections
12 June 2004 (European Parliament); 20 June 2003 (presidential); 5 October 2002 (parliamentary).

Results: European Parliament: TB/LNNK won 29.8 per cent of the vote (four seats out of nine), JL 19.7 per cent (two), PCTVL 10.7 per cent (one), TP 6.6 per cent (one) and Latvijas Ceis (LC) (Latvia's Way) 6.5 per cent (one); turnout 41.2 per cent.
Presidential: President Vaira Vike-Freiberga was re-elected by a vote of 88–6 in the 100-seat parliament.
Parliamentary: Jaunais Laiks (JL) (New Era) won 23.9 per cent of the vote (26 out of 100 seats), Par Cilvçka Tiesîbâm Vienotâ Latvijâ (PCTVL) (For Human Rights in a United Latvia) 18.9 per cent (25 seats); Tautas Partija (TP) (People's Party) 16.7 per cent (20 seats); Zaïo un Zemnieku Savienîba (ZZS) (Green and Farmers Union) 12 seats; Latvijas Pirmâ Partija (LPP) (Latvia's First Party); Apvienîba 'Tçvzemei un Brîvîbai/LNNK (TB/LNNK) (Alliance Fatherland and Freedom-LNNK) seven; turnout was about 55 per cent.

Next elections
2006 (parliamentary)

Political parties

Ruling party
Coalition government, comprising Tautas Partija (TP) (People's Party), Jaunais Laiks (New Era), Latvijas Pirmâ Partija (LPP) (

Latvia

Latvia's First Party) and Zaïo un Zemnieku Savienîba (ZZS) (Green and Farmers' Union) (approved by parliament 2 Dec 2004)

Main opposition party
Apvienîba 'Tçvzemei un Brîvîbai'/LNNK (TB/LNNK) (Alliance Fatherland and Freedom-LNNK)

Population
2.26 million (2004)

Ethnic make-up
Latvian (56 per cent), Russian (32 per cent), Belarussian (4 per cent), Ukrainian (3 per cent), Polish (2 per cent), Lithuanians (1 per cent). The Latvian parliament revised naturalisation laws in 1998 to speed up the integration of Latvia's 680,000 non-citizens, mostly ethnic Russians. Citizenship is granted to stateless children, even if their parents are not citizens, provided they have lived in Latvia for at least five years. Most ethnic Russians must still pass language examinations to become citizens.

Religions
Predominantly Protestant (Lutheran), with a Roman Catholic minority in the east of the country. Orthodox Christianity is the most common religious denomination among Russians in Latvia.

Education
Education has traditionally been important in Latvia and a high level of education enabled Latvia to become a centre of the Soviet communications and electronics industries.

For those who live in rural Latvia, educational opportunities are limited. About 25 per cent in the 18–24 age group receive only a basic education.

Basic education lasts for nine years. From this, students are channelled into either 1) a basic vocational school for a two-year course from age 16; or 2) a vocational school from age 15 for three years; or 3) a vocational secondary school at age 15 for four years. Each vocational school course has its relevant qualifications. Students undertaking academic study progress to a general secondary school from age 16 for four years. Students who graduate from either the general or vocational secondary school may undertake higher education.

There are four universities and a number of other higher education institutions in Latvia. All universities and 17 other higher education institutions are state-run. In addition, there are a number of private institutions of which 10 are state-recognised. Higher education institutions confer academic degrees and professional higher education qualifications.

Annual total expenditure on education is around 7 per cent of GDP.

Literacy rate: 98 per cent adult male and female rates; adult rates (World Bank).
Compulsory years: Seven to 18.
Enrolment rate: 96 per cent gross primary enrolment of the relevant age group (including repeaters); 84 per cent gross secondary enrolment (World Bank).
Pupils per teacher: 13 in primary schools.

Health
Annual total expenditure on health is around 7 per cent of GDP, of which government spending is about 53 per cent. The Latvian healthcare system is set to become more expensive with the introduction of more payment-based services. However, the country has one of the highest ratios of doctors to population in the world.

Healthcare has largely deteriorated in Latvia. This has been due to a lack of primary healthcare provision, an over-stretched network of small hospitals, overstaffing and over-specialisation, the lack of modern management systems and the use of hospitals as dumping grounds for people with social rather than medical problems.

HIV prevalence: 0.6 per cent aged 15–49 in 2003 (World Bank)
Life expectancy: 70.7 years (World Bank)
Fertility rate/Maternal mortality rate: 1.3 births per woman; maternal mortality 45 per 100,000 live births (World Bank).
Infant mortality rate: 10 per 1,000 live births (World Bank)
Head of population per physician/bed: 3.4 physicians to 10.3 hospital beds per 1,000 people.

Welfare
The social security system provides a state pension. There is provision for a social insurance fund. The pension system is a fund-based one, with three tiers composed of a modified pay-as-you-go (PAYG) system stronger links with contributions, a mandatory state-funded system of privately managed savings accounts and voluntary privately managed pensions.

A private pension fund law came into effect at the beginning of 1998. The legislation regulates private pension funds, which are supervised by the state insurance inspection department. Banks, life insurance companies, brokerages and investment companies are permitted to operate private pension funds, which allow saving in addition to the state pension scheme.

Main cities
Riga (capital, estimated population 706,200 in 2003), Daugavpils (111,700), Liepaja (82,300), Jelgava (56,600), Jurmala (52,000), Ventspils (40,700), Rezekne (37,500).

Languages spoken
Russian, English and German are widely spoken (over 80 per cent of Latvians speak both Lettish and Russian); Lettish is required for citizenship. Belarusian, Ukrainian, Polish and Yiddish are also spoken. Some 150,000 Latvians speak Latgalian. A law passed in February 2004 requires at least 60 per cent of teaching at minority schools to be in Latvian.

Official language/s
Lettish

Media
Press
After spectacular growth, developments in recent years have been towards consolidation.

Dailies: *Diena* is an independent daily published six days a week in Latvian. Other important dailies include *Lauku Avize*, *Rigas Vilni*, *Zemgales Zinas*, *Chas*, *Latvijas Vestnesis* and *Neatariga Rita Avize*.

Weeklies: *The Baltic Times* is an independent English-language weekly, that carries general news and business information on Estonia, Latvia and Lithuania. *Tovary Optum* is another weekly business publication in Russian.

Business: Business publications include *Dienas Bizness* in both Russian and Latvian languages, representing a joint business venture between Dagens Industri of Sweden and the Latvian daily *Diena*. Other important publications are *Bizness-Shans* and *Biznez I Baltya*.

Periodicals: *Lilit* and *Santa* are popular women's monthly magazines.

Broadcasting
Radio: Radio is an important part of the Latvian media; there are around 12 mainstream radio stations.

Television: Four Latvian television channels broadcast in the republic. The two state-owned stations, LTV1 and LTV2, are less popular than the privately owned LNT and TV3. Russian-based channels, although popular with large parts of the population, have increasingly faced opposition as the government – through its control of transmission rights – attempts to limit Russian influence on Latvia. Despite this, there are still signs of an increase in viewing of Russian-language channels.

Advertising
Latvia has the largest advertising market among the Baltic states. Television accounts for a third and newspapers over 40 per cent of adspend.

Economy
With one of the highest growth rates among new EU members over the past decade, Latvia became a member of the

World Trade Organisation (WTO) in 1999. GDP growth in 2005 was 7.3 per cent, down slightly from 8.0 per cent in 2004. The average yearly growth since 2000 is 7 per cent. General trends in the economy are positive as growth is driven by both strong domestic demand and by a robust export market. In the first half of 2005 Latvian shares surged 22 percentage points. Despite healthy growth, however, per capita GDP remains the lowest in the EU.

According to the International Labour Organisation (ILO), unemployment in 2004 stood at 10.1 per cent, down from 14.6 per cent in 2000. The IMF figure for unemployment in 2004 is 8.8 per cent. The average monthly wage is low but the government has implemented a six-year project to increase wages by 42 per cent. The minimum wage is scheduled to reach eur146 in 2006 and eur210 in 2010. The figures were conceived with budgetary stability in mind and the government will refuse to go ahead with increases if stability is under threat. Unlike developed Western economies, public sector wages are on average 25 per cent higher than those in the private sector.

Inflation is predicted to rise to 6.0 per cent in 2005, threatening Latvia's expected 2008 accession into the eurozone. Latvia joined the Exchange Rate Mechanism II (ERMII) in April 2005 and will only be able to progress to the single currency if inflation is controlled. Mounting external debt has reached problematic levels. The IMF's Executive Board advised the closure of capital gains tax loopholes which are thought to be behind a recent flurry in house-buying. The Board also expressed concern that growth and competitiveness could be hindered by wage increases. Latvia has recently taken measures against money laundering.

Between 2004 and 2006, the 10 EU accession countries will receive funding of up to eur25.1 billion (US$28.2 billion), which will include money for agriculture, infrastructure modernisation and regional aid. Latvia will receive eur879.5 million (US$988 million). With the accession countries altogether expected to pay into the EU budget approximately eur14.8 billion (US$16.6 billion) during the first three years of membership, the total net cost of EU enlargement will be eur10.3 billion (US$11.5 billion). If enlargement proves to be more costly during 2004–06, the EU could spend an extra eur15.7 billion (US$17.6 billion).

External trade

Following the Soviet occupation of the Baltic states in 1940, the centrally planned economy ensured that the bulk of Latvia's trade was redirected to other republics of the Soviet Union. Since independence, however, the balance has moved back to the West and the EU in particular, which accounts for 55 per cent of Latvian imports. Reforms carried out in Latvia were with membership of the EU in mind. Latvia has a liberal trde policy and is a member of the World Trade Organisation.

Imports
Principal imports are machinery and equipment, chemicals, fuels and vehicles.
Main sources: Germany (16.1 per cent total, 2004), Russia (14.4 per cent), Lithuania (7.6 per cent), Finland (6.5 per cent), Sweden (5.6 per cent), Estonia (5.1 per cent), Italy (4.2 per cent), Poland (4.0 per cent)

Exports
Principal exports are timber (typically 37 per cent of total), and timber products, machinery and equipment, metals, textiles and foodstuffs.
Main destinations: UK (22.1 per cent total, 2004), Germany (9.9 per cent), US (8.2 per cent), Sweden (7.3 per cent), France (6.6 per cent), Lithuania (6.4 per cent), Estonia (5.2 per cent), Denmark (4.2 per cent), Russia (4.1 per cent)

Agriculture
Farming
Latvia's agricultural sector still has remnants of the old Soviet central planning system and has suffered during the transition to a capitalist economic environment. With the majority of output going to the food processing sector, demand has fallen considerably. With agriculture employing over 15 per cent of the workforce, its problems are becoming increasingly significant politically. The agriculture sector is also hugely disadvantaged by the subsidies that the EU pays to its own farmers under the Common Agricultural Policy (CAP). Latvia itself is not due to benefit from CAP policies until 2013.

During its transitional entry stage Latvia has decided to implement the reform of CAP on 1 January 2009. The reform was introduced throughout most of the EU on 1 January 2005, when subsidies on farm output, which tended to benefit large farms and encourage overproduction, were replaced by single farm payments, not conditional on production. The change is expected to reward farms that provide and maintain a healthy environment, food safety and animal welfare standards. The changes are also intended to encourage market conscious production and cut the cost of CAP to the EU taxpayer.

The sector is dominated by dairy farming, pig-breeding, grain production and potatoes. Latvia is self-sufficient in the production of cattle and dairy products, pork, sugar beet, flax and potatoes. Any surplus is exported to Russia, other republics of the CIS and the EU.

The reform of the agricultural sector has proceeded at a faster rate than in either Lithuania or Estonia and 95 per cent of agricultural production comes from the private sector. Crops cover about 28 per cent of the total land area and permanent pastures about 13 per cent.

Decreases in agricultural output have been caused by the structural reforms in the sector, a lack of modern technology and the money to buy it, problems in the distribution of produce – particularly from the small private farms – and an absence of bank credit combined with high interest rates.

Stock-breeding contributes over 50 per cent of gross agricultural production; however, this means that large amounts of fodder must be imported. Consequently the structure of the agricultural sector is changing with greater emphasis placed on grain production.

Crop production in 2004 included: 1,060,000 tonnes (t) cereals in total, 530,000t wheat, 628,400t potatoes, *275,000t barley, 100,000t rye, 103,600t rapeseed (canola), 4,500t pulses, 800t fibre crops, 12,000t tomatoes, 39,883t oilcrops, 505,600t sugar beets, 45,000t apples, 88,000t oats, 62,000t fruit in total, 180,800t vegetables in total. Livestock production included: 73,400t meat in total, 21,800t beef, 37,000t pig meat, *400t lamb, 14,000t poultry, 31,630t eggs, 788,400t milk, 650t honey, 2,584t cattle hides, 13,200t sheepskins.
* estimate

Fishing
Latvia's extensive coastline provides large fish catches. Principal catches include sprat, Baltic Sea pilchards, Riga Gulf pilchards, cod and salmon. Typical annual catches amount to some 145 million tonnes per year (tpy).

Thirty per cent of total fish production is used domestically while 70 per cent is exported. In October 2005, Latvia held discussions with Joe Borg, EU Commissioner for Fisheries, about conservation methods to protect overexploited and depleted cod stocks in the Baltic Sea.

Forestry
With forests covering approximately 40 per cent of total land area, forestry has the potential to become one of the most important sectors of the economy. About 60 per cent of the forest is classified as soft wood (66 per cent pine forest and 34 per cent spruce) with the remaining hardwood mainly birch. Reforestation following cutting is compulsory.

Latvia's rich and extensive forests are mainly in areas of low population, making

Latvia

the felling, processing and export of timber relatively easy. There is potential to harvest 8.3 million cubic metres of timber a year, half of which would be available for pulp production. The timber and furniture industry accounts for about 8 per cent of GDP and employs around 51,000 people. Timber and furniture exports grew substantially in the 1990s and currently comprise around 25 per cent of total exports. In particular, growth in exports to the EU is the result of higher wood exports.

There are about 2,500 forest industry companies in Latvia, all but a few in private ownership; the majority concentrate on sawn wood milling, wood panel production and furniture. Progress in the timber industry has been made since independence, although there is still a lack of finance, management and design skills and many production techniques remain inefficient. Pulp and paper production does not meet domestic demand. Even though Latvia is one of the top five countries in Europe in terms of forest resources per capita, it lacks a large processing plant for pulp and paper production, and consequently a large proportion of raw timber produce is exported to the pulp mills of Sweden.

Exports of forest material in 2004 amounted to US$1.0 billion, while imports amounted to US$299.0 million. Production in 2004 included 12,419,987 cubic metres (cum) roundwood, 11,449,987cum industrial roundwood, 7,753,987cum sawlogs and veneers, 3,920,000cum sawnwood, 3,096,000cum pulpwood, 970,000cum woodfuel.

Industry and manufacturing
The industrial sector accounts for 25.3 per cent of GDP and employs around 30 per cent of the work force.

Total manufacturing output declined in the late 1990s with food-processing hit particularly. Many Latvian food producers do not yet meet EU specifications and are therefore limited to less lucrative domestic or CIS markets such as Russia. Machinery and equipment manufacture also suffered. Latvia is one of the most heavily industrialised areas of the former Soviet Union. A well-developed infrastructure and a broadly diversified industrial base includes both light and heavy industries including high-technology manufacturing and shipbuilding. Main industries are mechanical engineering, metal working, textiles and the food industry. Forestry, paper, chemicals, petrochemicals and communications are also important. The textiles sector is successful and export-focussed (82 per cent).

The manufacturing industry is concentrated on the production of railway carriages, buses, mopeds, washing machines and telephone systems. Mineral fertilisers are also produced. Riga, Liepaja and Ventspils are the principal industrial centres.

Industrial production increased by an estimated 8.5 per cent in 2004.

IT and telecommunications are expanding sectors, with a growth rate averaging 25 per cent over the past ten years. Banking, transport and logistics services also contribute significantly to the ecomony.

Tourism
Interest in tourism grew again after Latvia's independence in 1991 and there has been substantial investment. However, the sector is still underdeveloped, comprising only 1.3 per cent of GDP in 2005. The sector employs 14,000 people, which amounts to 1.2 per cent of the total workforce. The short summer season is a barrier to development. Tourist arrivals numbered 850,000 in 2004, up from 509,000 in 2000.

Mining
Mineral resources include limestone, clay for cement industry, dolomite, gypsum, sand for glass, clay for pottery, sand for silicate products, sand and gravel. The few minerals found in Latvia are used as building materials.

Mining and the quarrying of mineral resources account for approximately 0.5 per cent of annual GDP and have a negligible impact on the economy.

Hydrocarbons
Latvia is reliant on hydrocarbons imports, receiving most of its needs from Belarus, Russia and Lithuania. As it has no refining capacity it imports petroleum products. Latvia's Ventspils port was Russia's primary northern crude oil export terminal. However, Russia has constructed its own terminal in order to avoid the transit fees. This will probably decrease Latvia's Russian export volumes.

Latvia does not have any natural gas resources and is reliant on Russian imports of gas to meet domestic demand. In 2005 Gazprom, Russia's huge state-owned gas company, announced plans to significantly increase prices to Ukraine and other Baltic states including Latvia. This led to temporary disruptions in supply. Latvia does not produce coal but does produce around 500,000 tonnes of peat per annum. Coal imports come mostly from Poland.

Energy
Hydroelectric power provides 68 per cent of Latvia's power needs. However, its hydroelectric and thermal power plants do not provide the country with enough power to meet requirements.

The government adopted an energy development plan in the mid-1990s which should make Latvia 85 per cent energy self-sufficient by 2010, through modernising existing plants and building new thermal and hydroelectric capacity. However, much of the development is dependent on foreign investment. Most of Latvia's main hydroelectric stations are based on the Daugava River. State-owned Latvenergo is the operator of all of Latvia's hydro and thermal power plants.

Some 40 per cent of Latvia's electricity needs is imported from Estonia and Lithuania. The Baltic states are seeking to create a single Baltic electricity market, to integrate with Western European markets. In April 2003, power companies from Latvia, Estonia and Finland signed an agreement to lay a 315-MW underwater electricity cable between Finland and Estonia. The line, known as 'Estlink', is intended to supply Nordic countries with secure and efficient electricity generated in the Baltic states. The project is expected to cost US$117 million and to be ready by the close of 2006. Once the project is completed, Latvia should benefit from enough electricity to meet its rising needs, and enable better electricity integration of the Baltic and Nordic regions. The cable should reduce dependency on Russian supplies.

Latvia has the largest wind energy station in the Baltics, with a peak output of 2.5 million kilowatt hours of electricity per year (enough for over 1,500 households). The German energy company Preussen Elektra funded 70 per cent of the plant, which has a minimum operating life of 20 years. Over 500MW of wind energy is technically possible in the country, with only 20MW installed so far. National legislation facilitates investment in renewable energy.

Financial markets
Stock exchange
The Riga Stock Exchange (RSE) was officially re-opened in 1995. The official RSE index is known as the DJRSE.

Banking and insurance
The Bank of Latvia, the national central bank, is independent and manages the monetary supply and instigates governmental financial policy. The Financial Capital Markets Commission audits commercial banks. In the early 1990s most state banks were privatised and the sector proliferated. 1995 and 1998 saw major crises in the sector, involving mass insolvency and closures. Since then, regulation has been improved to stabilise Latvian banking and encourage investment by the West. Western owned banks control much

of the country's finances. There are over 20 banks in operation.
Central bank
Latvijas Banka (Bank of Latvia)
Offshore facilities
Riga is popular with Russians seeking safe dollar accounts. Russian-linked banks have become influential in the sector.

Time
GMT plus two hours (GMT plus three hours from late March to late September)

Geography
Latvia is situated in north-eastern Europe on the east coast of the Baltic Sea. It is slightly larger than Switzerland at 64,589 sq km and is bordered by Estonia to the north, the Russian Federation to the east, Belarus to the south-east and Lithuania to the south and south-west. With rolling plains and gentle hills, half the country is less than 90 metres above sea level. There are over 2,300 lakes and 12,000 rivers; the longest is the River Daugava. The largest lake is Lake Lubans which stretches over 81 square km. Latvia's highest point is in the south-east of the country where Latgale Upland reaches 289 metres.

Climate
Temperate climate, but with considerable temperature variations. Mildest areas along the Baltic coast. Summer is warm with relatively mild weather in spring and autumn. Summer sunshine may be nine hours a day. Winter, which lasts from November to mid-March, can be very cold. Rainfall is distributed throughout the year with the heaviest rainfall in August. Snowfalls are common in winter months.

Dress codes
Warm clothing is essential in winter as are a raincoat and umbrella during spring and summer. Business dress is conservative but relatively informal, with a jacket and tie expected for meetings.

Entry requirements
Passports
Required by all and must be valid for at least six months. For identification purposes, a photocopy of the passport should be carried at all times.
Visa
Required by all and valid for 90 days. Some exceptions include citizens of Europe, North America, Australasia, and Japan for visits up to three months. Business visits for those from visa-free states are included within the exceptions. For further exceptions contact the nearest consulate or visit www.am.gov.lv/en/?id=136 for a full list. All visitors must have valid travel health insurance including emergency repatriation cover.

Currency advice/regulations
There are no restrictions on import and export of local and foreign currency. All freely convertible currencies, preferably US dollars and euros, are accepted. Eurocheques are accepted in hotels and restaurants, but traveller's cheques are not normally accepted in restaurants and shops.
Customs
It is advisable to declare valuable items such as jewellery, cameras, computers and musical instruments. Ensure that the declaration is stamped by the customs officials.
A certificate must be obtained to export religious art over 50 years of age.
Prohibited imports
Narcotics; guns and ammunition (without a police import permit); fresh meat.

Health (for visitors)
Mandatory precautions
There are no special requirements.
Advisable precautions
It is advisable to be 'in date' for the following immunisations: tuberculosis, hepatitis 'A' and diphtheria.
Any medicines required by the traveller should be taken by the visitor, and it could be wise to have precautionary antibiotics if going outside major urban centres. Rabies is endemic.
A travel kit including a disposable syringe is a reasonable precaution. It is recommended to drink bottled water. The tap water is occasionally yellow.

Hotels
Riga has business-class hotels. Tips are included in restaurant bills.

Credit cards
Credit cards are accepted in most hotels and restaurants.

Public holidays
Fixed dates
1 Jan (New Year's Day), 1 May (Labour Day), 23 Jun (Ligo Day/Midsummer's Eve), 24 Jun (St John's Day/Summer Solstice), 18 Nov (National Day), 25–26 Dec (Christmas/Winter Solstice), 31 Dec (New Year's Eve).
Variable dates
Good Friday, Easter Monday.

Working hours
Banking
Mon–Fri: 0900–1600. Some banks are open between 0900–1230 on Saturdays.
Business
Mon–Fri: 0900–1800. Appointments are best made between 0900–1000.
Government
Mon–Fri: 0900–1700.
Shops
Mon–Fri: 1000–1900, Saturday: 1000–1600. Grocery and department stores are usually open from 0800 until 1900. There are quite a few food stores in Riga that provide 24-hour service.

Telecommunications
Mobile phones
GSM 900/1800 services are available throughout most of the country.

Electricity supply
220V AC, 50 Hz. European-style two-pin plugs are in use.

Social customs/useful tips
Latvians can be reserved and formal, but hospitable. When meeting, shake hands and slightly nod your head. If invited to a private home, it is usual to bring flowers for the hostess. Business cards are widely used.
The informal custom of overcharging foreigners (particularly by taxi-drivers) has developed since 1991.
Taxi fares do not usually include a tip, whereas restaurant bills usually do. Tipping is generally expected. Carry small-denomination US dollar bills as well as local currency for tips, taxis etc. Reference to Russia and Russians should be avoided, at least until you are sure of the ethnic background of your host. Many Latvians have strong feelings about Russia as many have relatives who were sent to Siberia during the Soviet period. It is also wise not to ask your host what they did before independence, as they may think you are asking whether they were in the Communist Party or even if they were sent to Siberia.

Security
As living standards have dropped, so the crime rate has risen since independence. Care should be taken not to display valuables when walking around the city. When walking, travellers should be alert to the threat of pickpocketing and other forms of theft. Always avoid unlit streets and parks at night, and be extra vigilant if walking alone.
Car theft is rife. Wherever possible, guarded car-parks should be used and valuables kept out of sight.

Getting there
Air
National airline: Air Baltic (ABC)
International airport/s: Riga International (RIX) 8km west of Riga; facilities include currency exchange, car hire, post office, business lounge and duty-free stores. The number 22 bus links the airport with the city centre and tickets are available from the post office; alternatively taxis are located in front of the terminal building, and the journey takes about 15 minutes.
Airport tax: There is no airport tax.

Latvia

Surface
Road: There are roads leading from all the surrounding countries, however not all have customs control and it is advisable to determine which border crossing has this facility before undertaking a fruitless journey. Visit http://www.transit.lv/ for details of the country's road network.
Rail: The Berlin to St Petersburg service passes through Daugavpils in south-eastern Latvia. Trains also link Riga with Moscow, St Petersburg and Minsk.
Water: There are direct ferries to Riga from Travemünde in Germany and Stockholm in Sweden.
Main port/s: Warm-water ports at Riga and Ventspils and Liepaja, (designated a Special Economic Zone (SEZ)).

Getting about
National transport
Air: There are two air taxi, and one helicopter hire, companies operating from Viga airport.
Road: Latvia has a good road network, although secondary roads are in a variety of conditions.
Buses: The extensive bus network is a better form of transport than trains.
Rail: Riga is connected to all major towns and there are some cross country services. The railway terminal in Riga is Stacijas Laukums.
City transport
Most of the sights in Riga are within walking distance.
Taxis: Taxis accept both US dollars and lats. They are generally cheaper if summoned by the hotel concierge. Taxi fares do not include a tip, but one is usually expected.
Buses, trams & metro: Riga Transport Authority provides an economic and extensive bus system, including buses, trams and trolley buses operating between 0530–2400. In addition, some routes have an hourly night service. Each service requires a separate, flat fee ticket, which can only be purchased from the on-board conductor. Routes are displayed on the Riga city map, available from most kiosks. Bus No 22 leaves for the city centre from the airport every 20–30 minutes, and an express bus service goes to vartious hotels in the city. Guests staying at the De Rome, Metropole and Eurolink hotels can pre-book a minibus transfer from the airport or hire a private limousine.
Metro: There is a service into the suburbs between 0500–2300.
Car hire
European nationals require a new European Licence (i.e. Pink UK licence, an International licence or a Green Card). Third party insurance is compulsory and the car registration documents must be carried at all times. The speed limit is 50kph in towns and 90kph on the open road, unless otherwise marked.
Hertz, Avis and Europcar have desks in the arrivals hall of Riga International Airport.
Remember, shiny western cars are a magnet for thieves, so make sure the car is fitted with an alarm and steering lock.
It is illegal to drive after consuming any amount of alcohol.

BUSINESS DIRECTORY
The addresses listed below are a selection only. While World of Information makes every endeavour to check these addresses, we cannot guarantee that changes have not been made, especially to telephone numbers and area codes. We would welcome any corrections.

Telephone area codes
The international direct dialling (IDD) code for Latvia is +371, followed by area code

Daugavpils	54	Rezekne	46
Jelgava	30	Riga	not required
Liepaja	34	Ventspils	36

Useful telephone numbers
Fire brigade: 01
Police: 02
Ambulance: 03
Gas leakages: 04
Road accidents: 737-7000
Lost and found: 708-6628
Information service: 118, 722-2222, 777-0777
Accidents on railway, water, air transport: 226-343, 203-948
National telephone operator: 116
International telephone operator: 115

Chambers of Commerce
American Chamber of Commerce in Latvia, 4 Torna iela, Riga 1050 (tel/fax: 721-2204; e-mail: amcham@amcham.lv).

British Chamber of Commerce in Latvia, Valdemara Centrs, 21 Kr. Valdemara iela, Riga 1010 (tel: 703-5216; fax: 703-5318; e-mail: info@bccl.lv).

Latvian Chamber of Commerce and Industry, 35 Kr Valdemara iela, Riga 1010 (tel: 722-5595; fax: 782-0092; e-mail: info@chamber.lv).

Banking
Hansabank, 26 Kalku Street, Riga LV-1050 (tel: 702-44444; fax: 702-4400; e-mail: info@hansabanka.lv).

Latvijas Krâjbanka, 1 Palasta Street, Riga LV-1954 (tel: 709-2020; fax: 721-2083).

Parex Banka, 3 Smilsu Street, Riga LV-1522 (tel: 701-0000; fax: 701-0001; e-mail: inquiry@parex.lv).

Saules Bank, 16 Smilsu Street, Riga (tel: 702-0500; fax: 702-0505; e-mail: office@saules.com).

Unibanka, 23 Pils Street, Riga (tel: 721-5555; fax: 721-5566; e-mail: atsauksmes@unibanka.lv).

Central bank
Latvijas Banka, K Valdemara iela 2a, LV-1050, Riga (tel: 702-2300; fax: 702-2420; e-mail: info@bank.lv).

Travel information
Air Baltic Corporation (ABC), Riga International Airport, Riga LV-1053 (tel: 207-777; fax: 207-505); Kalku iela 15, Riga LV-1050 (tel: 207-777; fax: 722-8284).

Latvian Tourism Development Agency, Pils laukums 4, Riga (tel: 722-9945; fax: 750-8468; e-mail: tda@latviatourism.lv).

Lidosta Airport flight enquiries (tel: 207-009; fax: 348-654).

Lufthansa Airport Office (tel: 207-183; fax: 207-026); city centre, Kr Barona iela 7-9, Riga LV-1442 (tel: 728-5614; fax: 782-8199).

Polish Airlines, Maza Pils iela 5, Riga LV 1863 (tel: 724-2870; fax: 724-2869).

Riga International Airport Information (tel: 720-7009; internet site: http://www.riga-airport.com).

Riair (Rigas Aeronavijas), 1 Melluzu Street, Riga LV-1067 (tel: 720-7325; fax: 786-0189).

Riga Bus Station (Autoosta) (tel: 721-3611, 721-3826).

Riga Tourist Information Bureau, 22 Skarnu iela (tel: 722-1731; fax: 722-7680).

SAS, Kalku iela 15, Riga LV 1050 (tel: 721-6139; fax: 722-4282).

Ministry of tourism
Ministry of Environmental Protection and Regional Development, Peldu iela 25, Riga (tel: 702-6492; fax: 782-0442; e-mail: tourism@varam.gov.lv).

National tourist organisation offices
Latvian Tourist Board, Riga 800 Office, Torna iela 4, 1B-103, Riga LV-1050 (tel: 732-0550; fax: 732-0609; e-mail: ltboard@latnet.lv; internet: www.latviatourism.lv).

Ministries
Department of Citizenship and Immigration, 6 Raina Blvd, Riga LV-1181 (tel: 721-9181; fax: 782-0156).

Latvian Customs Department Kr Valdemara iela 1a, Riga LV-1841 (tel: 732-0928; fax: 732-2440).

Ministry of Agriculture, Republikas Laukums 2, Riga LV-1981 (tel: 702-7107; fax: 702-7512).

Ministry of Culture, Kr Valdemara iela 11a, Riga LV-1364 (tel: 722-4772; fax: 722-7916).

Ministry of Defence, Kr Valdemara iela 10-12, Riga LV-1010 (tel: 721-0124; fax: 783-0236).

Ministry of Economics, Brivibas Boulevard 55, LV 1519 Riga (tel: 701-3109; fax: 728-0882); Department of Energy Development (tel: 728-7730, 722-0151; fax: 733-8026, 722-4794).

Ministry of Education, Vajnu iela 2, 1098 Riga (tel: 722-2415; fax: 721-3992; e-mail: vetpmu@com.latnet.lv).

Ministry of Environmental Protection and Regional Development, Peldu St 25, 1494 Riga (tel: 722-3612; fax: 782-0442; e-mail: Saule@varam.gov.lv).

Ministry of Finance, Smilsu iela 1, Riga LV-1919 (tel: 722-6672; fax: 721-1140); World Bank Technical Unit (tel: 722-0348; fax: 782-0168).

Ministry of Foreign Affairs, 36 Brivibas bulv, Riga LV-1395 (tel: 701-6210; fax: 728-2121; e-mail: info@info.gov.lv; internet site: http://www.mfa.gov.lv).

Ministry of the Interior, Raina bulv 6, Riga LV-1533 (tel: 728-7260; fax: 721-2255).

Ministry of Justice, Brivibas bulv 34, Riga LV-1536 (tel: 728-2607; fax: 728-5575).

Ministry of Transport, Gogola iela 3, 1743, Riga (tel: 702-8214; fax: 721-7180).

Ministry of Welfare, Skolas iela 28, Riga LV-1331 (tel: 729-2800; fax: 727-6445).

State Property Fund (privatisation), Ministry of Economics, 36 Brivibas Boulevard, LV 1519 Riga (tel: 213-501; fax: 280-882); external department (tel: 722-5426; fax: 828-223).

Other useful addresses
Association of Insurers, Valnu iela 1, Riga LV-1912 (tel: 722-4375, fax: 724-3286).

Baltic Data House Ltd (marketing research), Akas iela 5/7, Riga LV-1050 (tel: 227-6144; fax: 227-6246, 934-6442).

British Council, Blaumena iela 5a, LV-1050 Riga (tel: 232-0468; fax: 883-0031).

British Embassy, 5 Alunana iela, Riga LV-1010 (tel: 733-8126/31; fax: 733-8132).

Business Centre (to use fax, telex, xerox, e-mail, typing, international telephone) 55 Elizabetes, Hotel 'Latvia' (tel: 722-2211).

Central Statistical Bureau of Latvia, Lacplesa Str, 1 Riga (tel: 727-0126; fax: 782-0166; internet site: http://www.csb.lv/avidus.cfm).

Commercial Port of Riga, Eksporta iela 6, Riga LV-1242 (tel: 732-5350; fax: 783-0051).

Commercial Port of Ventspils, Dzintaru iela 22, Ventspils LV-3602 (tel: 22-821; 21-231).

Committee for Television & Radio Broadcasting, Doma Laukums 8, Riga LV-226935 (tel: 227-906; fax: 200-025).

Consular Department, Elizabetes iela 57, Riga (tel: 728-6815; 928-7398 (24 hours); fax: 782-8274).

Department of Customs, K. Valdemara iela 1a, Riga LV-1181 (tel: 721-9639; fax: 733-1123; e-mail: pmlp@pmlp.gov.lv).

Enterprise Support Centre, Perses Str 2, 1011 Riga (tel: 722-7623, 728-9328; fax: 782-0442); External Adviser (tel: 701-3161; fax: 782-8251, 728-0882).

Fire Protection Agency, 5 Maskavas Street, Riga (tel: 220-1322).

Government Information Agency, 36 Brivibas bulv, Riga LV-1070 (tel: 728-2828; fax: 728-4450).

Interlatvija Foreign Trade Association, Komunaru Bulv 1, 226010 Riga (tel: 332-952, 333-597; fax 226-070).

International Advertising Association, Liela Pils iela 9, Riga LV-1755 (tel: 722-8361; fax: 722-9252).

Komunalprojekts AS, 148A Brivibas Blvd, Riga LV 1012 (tel/fax: 237-6920).

Latvian Association of Civil Construction Engineers, 22/24 Grecinieku Street, Riga LV 050 (tel: 721-2661; fax: 722-4832).

Latvian Association of Traders, Kr Barona 48/50, LV-1011 Riga (tel: 721-7372; fax: 782-1010).

Latvian Business Consultants' Association, Jauniela 24, Riga LV-1050 (tel: 722-0320, 782-0076; fax: 722-8926).

Latvian Business Union (commercial information), Bungada PO Box 475, 226001 Riga (tel: 320-888; fax: 217-633).

Latvian Development Agency, Business Information Institute, 2 Perses Street, Riga LV-1442 (tel: 728-3425; fax: 782-0458; e-mail: invest@lda.gov.lv; internet site: http://www.lda.gov.lv/investo/osshop.htm).

Latvian Embassy (USA), 4325 17th Street, NW, Washington DC 20011 (tel: 202-726-8213; fax: 202-726-6785; e-mail: embassy@latvia-usa.org).

Latvian Foreign Trade Centre, 2 Elizabetes Street, Riga (tel: 732-0619, 732-1818, 732-2816; fax: 783-0035, 732-3313).

Latvian Privatisation Agency, Kr Valdemara Street 31, Riga LV-1887 (tel: 732-2281, 733-2082; fax: 783-0363; e-mail: lpa@mail.bkc.lv).

Latvian Retailers' Association, Kr Barona iela 48/50, Riga LV-1011 (tel: 721-7372; fax: 782-1010).

Latvian State Radio, 8 Doma Laukums (tel: 720-6722; fax: 720-6709, 782-0216).

LETA News Agency, Palasta 10, 226947 Riga (tel: 223-462; fax 320-5920).

Liepaja Special Economic Zone Authority, 4 Feniksa iela, LV-3401 Liepaja (tel: 26-605; fax: 80-252).

Main Post Office, Brivibas Bulvaris 21, Riga (tel: 224-155; fax: 733-1920).

National Environmental Health Centre, 7 Klijanu Street, Riga (tel: 237-7473; fax: 237-5940).

Port of Liepaja, Feniksa iela 4, Liepaja LV-3400 (tel: 342-5887; fax: 789-3418).

Public Investment Unit, Brivibas Blv. 36, 1519 Riga (tel: 701-3122; fax: 782-0458).

Riga City Council, 3 kr Valdemara Street, Riga LV-1539 (tel: 232-0680; fax: 222-0785).

Riga Fairs, Conferences & Exhibitions (tel: 213-637).

Riga Commercial Port, 5a Katrinas Street, Riga LV-1227 (tel: 732-9224; fax: 783-0215; e-mail: rto@mail.bkc.lv).

Rigas Ostas Parvalde (Riga Port Authority), 6 Eksporta St, Riga LV-1010 (tel: 732-2644; fax: 783-0051).

Riga Stock Exchange, Doma Laukums 6, Riga LV-1885 (tel: 721-2431, 722-9449; fax: 722-4515).

Saeima (Parliament), 16 Jekaba (tel: 732-2938; fax: 721-1611).

Statistical Committee, 1 Lacplesa iela (tel: 727-0126; fax: 783-0137).

US Embassy, Raina Bulvaris 7, LV-1050 Riga (tel: 721-0005, 722-0367, 722-9709; fax: 722-6530).

Ventspils Free Port Authority, 8 Uzavas Str, Ventspils LV3601 (tel: 362-2586; fax: 362-1297).

Ventspils Tirdznecibas Osta (Ventspils Commercial Port), 20a Dzintaru Street, Ventspils LV-3602 (tel: 366-8778; fax: 362-1231).

World Trade Centre, Elizabetes iela 2, Riga LV-1340 (tel: 322-242; fax: 7830-0385).

Internet sites
Baltic News Service: http://www.bns.ee

Business in the Baltic States: http://www.binet.lv/english/database

Latvian information: http://www.ciesin.ee/LATVIA/

Pirma banka: http://www.rkb.lv

Trasta Komercbanka: http://www.tkb.lv

Lebanon

KEY FACTS

Official name: Jumhouriya al Lubnaniya (Republic of Lebanon)

Head of State: President General Émile Lahoud (since Oct 1998; in 2004, the President's six-year term was extended by three years)

Head of government: Prime Minister Fouad Siniora (since 30 Jun 2005)

Ruling party: Hariri-Jumblatt Alliance (since May 2005)

Area: 10,452 square km

Population: 4.43 million (2004)

Capital: Beirut

Official language: Arabic

Currency: Lebanese pound (LL) = 100 piastres

Exchange rate: LL1,503.50 per US$ (Oct 2005)

GDP per capita: US$5,225 (2004)

GDP real growth: 5.00% (2004)

Labour force: 1.73 million (2004)

Inflation: 3.00% (2004)

Balance of trade: -US$6.38 billion (2004)

Foreign debt: US$15.84 billion (2004)

It was the year of the 'cedar revolution' in Lebanon in 2005. After 29 years of occupation, Syrian troops and intelligence corps withdrew from Lebanese soil. Throughout this period, Syria had dominated Lebanese politics and Lebanon's economy. The withdrawal, called a 'redeployment' by Syria, was precipitated by the assassination of former prime minister Rafik Hariri on 14 February 2005. Hariri had been expected to do well in elections scheduled for May. Although Hariri had accommodated himself to Syrian hegemony in the past, he had recently taken a more nationalistic line, calling for an end to Syria's domination. This change had been precipitated by a Syrian-orchestrated extra-constitutional extension of Lebanese president Emile Lahoud's term, due to expire in 2004. After Hariri's assassination, hundreds of thousands of Lebanese, from the country's often divided Muslim and Christian communities, took to the streets in Beirut, demanding an end to the Syrian presence and calling for justice. Most Lebanese suspected that Hariri had been assassinated on orders from Damascus, either by Syrian agents or members of the pro-Syrian Lebanese security services.

The economy survives

As prime minister 1992–98 and 2000–04, Rafik Hariri was credited by many with Lebanon's 'economic miracle' – the booming recovery of the country after nearly two decades of civil war. Although Hariri's policies substantially increased Lebanon's public debt and he himself attracted criticism for virtually combining his roles as business magnate and prime minister, his assassination led many to fear that Lebanon's economy might collapse. However, after some initial tremors in the finance sector, Lebanon's economy rode out the rest of 2005 reasonably well.

An economic slowdown that had begun prior to Hariri's murder meant that GDP growth was negligible in 2005. Inflation was stable at around 1 per cent.

The 'cedar revolution'

Taking its cue from recent regime changes in Ukraine and Georgia, Lebanese turned out in their hundreds of thousands in the wake of Hariri's assassination to demand the resignation of the pro-Syrian government of Prime Minister Omar Karami and President Lahoud. Although a large pro-Syrian rally, mainly made of up of Lebanon's Shi'a community, took place, the Karami government fell on 28 February. President Lahoud again appointed Karami on 10 March but continuing demonstrations and pressure from opposition MPs forced a second resignation on 13 April.

The second key demand of the anti-government protestors was the removal of Syrian influence from Lebanon, including Syrian troops and intelligence agents. Syria had already undertaken a minor withdrawal in December 2004, already under pressure from UN Security Council Resolution 1559, sponsored by the US and France. The resolution, passed in September 2004, called for free and fair elections in Lebanon and respect for its sovereignty. President Bashar Assad announced a second partial redeployment in March. However, pressure from demonstrators in Beirut and pressure from the US, the EU, Russia and Syria's own Arab allies, Saudi Arabia and Egypt, forced Assad to announce a full withdrawal. Moreover, the US and the EU demanded that all Syrian troops be withdrawn before the Lebanese general election, scheduled for May and June. The US and the EU argued that elections could not be free and fair while taking place under occupation. The last Syrian soldiers left Lebanese soil on 26 April. UN inspectors confirmed this withdrawal on 23 May, and that of the Syrian intelligence services. The US continues to accuse Syria of deploying its intelligence apparatus in Lebanon – denied by Syria.

The second stage of the cedar revolution was the stripping away of pro-Syrian elements within Lebanon itself. Pressure mounted on President Lahoud to resign, particularly when bishops from his Maronite community began to distance themselves from him. Three Lebanese intelligence chiefs and the commander of the presidential guard were taken into custody in September. Key to this process was the formation of an anti-Syrian electoral bloc, the Rafik Hariri Martyr List (RHML). This included the Tayyar Al Mustaqbal (Current for the Future), recently formed by Hariri's son, Sa'ad, and the Hizb al Taqadummi al Ishtiraki (Progressive Socialist Party) of veteran Druze community leader Walid Jumblatt. Matters were complicated by the unexpected return from exile of Michel Aoun, the former Lebanese prime minister and army chief, weeks before elections. Although a veteran of anti-Syrian politics, Aoun refused to join the RHML and insisted upon running his own electoral list. Nevertheless, the RHML won a landslide in elections staggered over four weekends, from 29 May to 19 June, taking 72 of 128 seats. Aoun's Alliance took 21 seats and the pro-Syrian Shi'a list, comprised of Hezbollah (Party of God) and Harakat Amal (Amal) (Hope Movement), took 35.

Forming a government

Because of the formalised sectarian nature of Lebanese politics, forming a government was no easy task – even with an overwhelming majority in parliament. In practice, the largest bloc had to satisfy both the president and the other parties that all of Lebanon's communities were being represented – whether Maronite Christian, Shi'a or Sunni Muslim. A government was finally formed on 19 July, led by the late Rafik Hariri's former finance minister, Fouad Siniora. Only non-MPs were awarded cabinet posts so as to reduce political tension. For the first time, a senior Hezbollah official was included within the government, despite the fact that many countries, including the US, consider Hezbollah to be a terrorist group. The US was thus reminded that even though the cedar revolution, which it had openly backed, had removed the formal architecture of Syrian control, Hezbollah and, to a degree, pro-Syrian sentiment, was part of Lebanon's political landscape.

Almost post-Syrian politics

The post-Syrian era has in many respects been dominated by two issues: the fact that pro-Syrian sentiment still runs deep in parts of the country and the UN investigation into the assassination of Rafik Hariri. Soon after the former prime minister's murder, the Lebanese government agreed to allow the UN to carry out an official investigation. Reports by the investigators, released in October and December, implicate high-ranking Syrian officials as well as pro-Syrian members of the Lebanese security forces.

Lebanon's early experience of post-Syrian politics has been difficult and not

KEY INDICATORS — Lebanon

	Unit	2000	2001	2002	2003	2004
Population	m	3.50	3.60	3.65	4.04	4.43
Gross domestic product (GDP)	US$bn	16.50	16.80	17.90	19.62	*21.77
GDP per capita	US$	4,486	4,663	4,907	4,858	5,225
GDP real growth	%	-0.5	0.8	1.0	1.0	5.0
Inflation	%	-1.0	0.5	4.0	2.5	3.0
Exports (fob) (goods)	US$m	715.0	798.0	894.0	971.0	1,783.0
Imports (fob) (goods)	US$m	6,230.0	7,290.0	6,180.0	6,525.0	8,162.0
Balance of trade	US$m	-5,515.0	-6,492.0	-5,280.0	-5,554.0	-6,379.0
Current account	US$m	-3,065.0	-3,775.0	-3,990.0	-3,587.0	-3,130.0
Foreign debt	US$bn	–	–	–	–	15.8
Total reserves minus gold	US$m	5,943.7	5,013.8	7,243.8	12,519.4	11,734.6
Foreign exchange	US$m	5,895.4	4,965.8	7,190.9	12,460.8	11,672.4
Exchange rate	per US$	1,507.50	1,507.50	1,507.38	1,507.50	1,515.04

* estimated figure

without danger. From March, Lebanon has experienced a series of bombings, many without claims of responsibility. Most of the bombings have taken place in Christian areas – the Christian community traditionally being the most anti-Syrian in Lebanon. Several public figures known for their anti-Syrian views have been targeted, including former Communist Party leader George Hawi (assassinated in June) and journalist and MP Gibran Tueni (assassinated in December).

A political crisis broke out in December due to a cabinet boycott by Shi'a members, which, due to the consensus-based safeguards in the Lebanese constitution, in effect paralysed government. The Hezbollah and Amal took issue with the government's request to the UN investigative committee to extend its remit to cover the various politically motivated murders taking place after the assassination of Hariri. The Shi'a parties also took issue with the UN's continued reference to their armed wings as 'militias', arguing instead that they were 'national resistance' movements.

Outlook

The cabinet boycott was resolved in January 2006 but only after the government agreed to Shi'a demands that Shi'a armed groups not be referred to as militias. The government therefore continues to face the reality of thousands of armed men, based in the south of the country, not under its control. Hezbollah can be expected to continue pressing, by force of arms, Lebanese claims to the disputed Shebaa Farms, currently occupied by Israel. While the government also supports this claim, the ensuing violence has and will cause it headaches, particularly as retaliatory Israeli airstrikes often do not distinguish between Hezbollah and state targets. Further progress in disarming Palestinian militias in the east of the country and near Beirut can be expected as these groups have little local support.

With its first post-Syrian government little more than 6 months old, it remains to be seen how Prime Minister Siniora copes with events. Regardless of the 'redeployment', Syria remains Lebanon's nearest and most influential neighbour. Lebanon has accused Syria of continuing to hold Lebanese political prisoners and has demanded compensation for the 29-year occupation, but Prime Minister Siniora has also stressed the need to achieve good neighbourly relations. Given Lebanon's tiny size relative to Syria, it is unrealistic to expect otherwise.

The issue of President Lahoud's tenure will likely resurface in 2006. The anti-Syrian bloc that dominates parliament has always insisted that the pro-Syrian Lahoud resign as soon as possible. Technically, Lahoud's term in office does not expire until 2007. However, he is currently serving out a term extension forced upon the parliament at a time when Syrian influence was still overwhelming. Lahoud's position is untenable but any resignation on his part could upset Lebanon's sectarian balance – Lebanon's president must be from the Maronite Christian community. Lebanon will therefore face difficult times in 2006, due to the complex interplay between pro- and anti-Syrian feeling, sectarian loyalties, effectively smothered by the Syrian occupation, the national desire for reclaiming the Shebaa Farms, and the continuing role of the UN in determining responsibility for Rafik Hariri's murder.

In a report published in October, the IMF expressed fears that government debt was on course to 'snowball' if the public deficit was not reined in. GDP growth is expected to accelerate significantly in 2006.

Risk assessment

Politics	Fragile
Economy	Improving
Regional stability	Tense

COUNTRY PROFILE

Historical profile
Lebanon became part of the Turkish Ottoman Empire in the sixteenth century and remained so until the end of the First World War. In 1920, the League of Nations granted the mandate for Lebanon and Syria to France and the state of Greater Lebanon was proclaimed, including the former autonomous province of Mount Lebanon and the provinces of north Lebanon, south Lebanon and the Biqa, historically part of Syria. The foundations of the state were laid down in 1943. The president would be a Maronite Christian, the prime minister a Sunni Muslim and the speaker of the Chamber of Deputies (later the National Assembly) a Shi'a Muslim. The census of 1932 (in which Christians were in a majority of 54 per cent) was used as the basis for the distribution of seats.

By the 1960s, Lebanon had become the region's dominant financial, business and tourism centre. Its capital, Beirut, was known as the 'Paris of the east', the main street, Al Hamra, boasting not only smart cafés and restaurants, but excellent bookshops and fashionable boutiques. But religious and political divisions threatened the country. By 1975, these had been magnified by income inequalities and the failure of the dominant Christians to update the 1932 census in favour of the faster-growing Muslim population. These tensions fuelled a 15-year-long civil war, which destroyed not only the glamour and sophistication, but also deprived Lebanon of its true independence as – under the terms of the Ta'if Accord, the peace agreement between the warring factions – Syrian domination became the order of the day until 2005, when they withdrew their troops.

1926 The constitution was approved and the Lebanese Republic declared.
1940 Lebanon came under the control of the Vichy French government.
1941 After occupation by Free French and British troops, independence was declared.
1943 France agreed to the transfer of power to the Lebanese government with effect from 1944.
1948 A major influx of Arab refugees from Palestine built tensions between Christian Maronites and Muslim Shi'as.
1958 The first civil war erupted between Muslim and Christian groups
1964 Yasser Arafat established a Palestine Liberation Organisation (PLO) stronghold in Lebanon.
1970 Anti-Israeli terrorist attacks from Lebanese bases increased after the PLO was expelled from Jordan. Israeli retaliations further alienated leftist Muslims from conservative Maronites (the largest Christian sect) and undermined governmental legitimacy, with nine changes in three years.
1975 Full-scale civil war erupted between Muslims (with PLO aid) and Christians. Southern Lebanon and the western half of Beirut became bases for the PLO and other Muslim militias, while the Christians controlled East Beirut and the Christian section of Mt Lebanon.
1976 A 30,000-strong Arab Deterrent Force was established to restore peace.
1978 In reprisal for an attack by Palestinians based in Lebanon, Israel invaded and occupied the south of the country; the UN called on Israel to withdraw its troops; it handed over the territory to the mainly Christian Lebanese militia.
1982 Hizbollah (Party of God) was formed by Muslim clerics, backed by Iran and Syria, to respond to the Israeli invasion of Lebanon and to advocate the establishment of an Islamic government (it became a political movement in 1985 and entered parliament in 1992). Israel launched a full-scale invasion after an assassination attempt on Shlomo Argov, its ambassador to the UK. Syria, which maintained a large army in Lebanon,

unsuccessfully fought Israel. Christian Phalangist militiamen, with Israeli compliance, massacred more than 1,000 Palestinian refugees in the Sabra and Shatila camps. A Western multinational force monitored the evacuation of the PLO to Tunis.
1983 Hostilities between Israel and Lebanon ended. Syrian forces remained in Lebanon.
1985 Despite withdrawing from most of the territory, Israel maintained some troops to support the mainly Christian South Lebanon Army (SLA) (a militia set up and supported by Israel) in order to help secure its own northern border.
1986–90 Factional conflict worsened as various efforts at national reconciliation failed. Lebanon had two governments – one mainly Muslim in West Beirut, headed by Salim al Huss, the other, Christian, in East Beirut, led by the Maronite Commander-in-Chief of the Army, General Michel Aoun.
1989 Under the Ta'if Accord, a government of national reconciliation was formed with an equal number of Christian and Muslim members. Elias Hrawi was elected president.
1990 The civil war ended and General Aoun fled.
1992 President Hrawi appointed Rafik al Hariri as prime minister, heading a cabinet of technocrats. Al Hariri, a rich businessman, born in Sidon but with Saudi Arabian nationality, became the mastermind behind the reconstruction of Lebanon.
1993–97 The Oslo Peace Accords laid the basis for transfer of authority from the Israeli military administration to the PLO in the Gaza Strip and an undefined area around the town of Jericho in the West Bank. A follow-up treaty, Oslo II, envisaged Palestinian autonomy, with Israeli troop units withdrawing from the West Bank. Yasser Arafat was elected president of the Palestinian Legislative Council (PLC), the assembly of the Palestinian National Authority (PNA). Attacks and reprisals continued between Hizbollah and Palestinian guerrillas, and Israel.
1998 The National Assembly elected army chief of staff, General Émile Lahoud, as president, replacing Elias Hrawi. Following the resignation of Prime Minister al Hariri, Salim al Huss was appointed to the post.
2000 The Israeli army withdrew from southern Lebanon and the SLA disbanded. Sporadic clashes continued between Hizbollah and Israeli forces. Rafik al Hariri won convincingly at the elections and was re-appointed prime minister.
2003 Israeli warplanes and artillery attacked suspected Hizbollah positions in the disputed Shebaa Farms area in south Lebanon in retaliation for guerrilla attacks.
2004 On 3 September, parliament approved extending pro-Syria President Émile Lahoud's six-year term by three years.
In September, UN Security Council resolution 1559 demanded that Syrian soldiers leave Lebanon and that Hizbollah disarm. Rafik al Hariri opposed the extension of Lahoud's term and stood down as prime minister; Omar Karami was nominated for the post.
2005 On 14 February, former prime minister Rafik al Hariri was assassinated in a car bomb attack. Syria was accused of supporting the perpetrators. On 28 February, thousands of protesters gathered in Beirut, demanding the withdrawal of Syrian troops; the pro-Syrian government of Prime Minister Omar Karami resigned. The presidents of Lebanon and Syria agreed that Syrian troops would withdraw to the Bekaa valley in eastern Lebanon. A protest held in Beirut on 8 March, organised by Hizbollah to show loyalty to Syria, countered weeks of anti-government and anti-Syrian protests. President Lahoud reappointed Karami as prime minister but he resigned again on 13 April, after failing to form a new government. On 15 April, Najib Mikati became the new prime minister and named a cabinet on 19 April, in which both pro-Syrian and anti-Syrian ministers held important posts. The last Syrian troops pulled out of Lebanon on 26 April.
In parliamentary elections, held between 29 May–3 July, Hariri-Jumblatt, the bloc led by Sa'ad al Hariri (son of Rafik al Hariri), won 72 seats, the Shi'a Muslim bloc of Amal and Hizbollah won 35 seats and the anti-Syrian Michel Aoun and allies won 21 seats. Fouad Siniora became prime minister on 30 June.
On 1 September four pro-Syrian generals were charged with assassination of Rafiq al Hariri, following the findings of the UN's chief investigator.

Political structure
Constitution
The constitution was enacted in May 1926, and has since been amended on five occasions. A key amendment agreed under the Ta'if Agreement of 1989 reduced the authority of the president by transferring executive power to the cabinet. The prime minister must be a Sunni Muslim, with the cabinet made up of equal numbers of Muslims and Christians.
Form of state
Republic
The executive
As head of state, the president is elected for a single six-year term by parliament and should be a Maronite Christian. Since 1990, however, Syria has effectively chosen the president and thereby alienated large parts of the Christian community. Under the consitution, the president chooses the prime minister upon recommendation from the parliament. In reality, Syria decides who is appointed to the position. The prime minister, who must be a Sunni Muslim, is responsible for choosing members of the 30-member Council of Ministers (cabinet). Ministers may be selected from inside or outside parliament. President General Émile Lahoud's six-year term of office, due to end in November 2004, was extended by parliament by three years.
National legislature
The Majlis al Nuwab (unicameral National Assembly) has 128 members, elected for a term of five years by the religious communities: Maronites (34), Sunnites (27), Shi'ites (27), Greek Orthodox (14), Greek Catholics (eight), Druzes (eight), Armenian Orthodox (five), Alaouites (two), Armenian Catholics (one), Protestants (one), Christian Minorities (one).
Legal system
The legal system is based on the 1926 constitution and the Commercial Code, the Civil Procedure Code, the Criminal Procedure Code and the Penal Code. French law has had a lasting impact on local legislation, while Ottoman law and Islamic law have also influenced Lebanon's legal system. Civil law is based on the Code of Obligations and Contracts and the Land Ownership Law. Various branches of the legal framework are being revised and updated. Lebanon has an independent judiciary.
Last elections
29 May–3 July 2005 (parliamentary); 15 October 1998 (presidential).
Results: Parliamentary: The Harriri-Jumblatt alliance won a total of 72 seats out of 128, an alliance of Amal and the Hizbollah won 35 seats, and Aoun's Free Patriotic Movement and its allies won 21 seats.
Presidential: General Émile Lahoud was elected president by the National Assembly. In 2004 Lahoud's term in office was extended until 2007 at the insistence of the Syrians.
Next elections
2007 (presidential); 2010 (parliamentary).

Political parties
Ruling party
Hariri-Jumblatt Alliance (since May 2005)

Population
4.43 million (2004)
Ethnic make-up
The Lebanese belong to a single ethnic grouping, Levanto Arab, which encompasses the people of the Levant coast

Lebanon

from northern Syria to southern Palestine. Armenians and Kurds have settled in Lebanon and there are Syrian troops and many Syrian workers.

Religions
There are 17 recognised religious groupings in Lebanon. Five predominate: Shi'a Muslims, Sunni Muslims, Maronite (Catholic) Christians, Greek Orthodox Christians and Druze.

Education
Education is mainly run by private enterprises and the religious sector. State schools exist and are free of charge. Primary education lasts for nine years. The civil war severely disrupted state education at all levels and by the end of the civil war in 1990, 1,270 schools throughout the country needed rehabilitation at an estimated cost of US$65 million. Public expenditure on education is equivalent to approximately 2.5 per cent of annual GNP.
There is a government-run Lebanese National University, but the major universities continue to be operated by the US, France and Egypt. There are over 10 universities in Beirut.
Literacy rate: 86.1 per cent total, 81.4 per cent female, adult rates (World Bank).
Compulsory years: None
Enrolment rate: 111 per cent total primary enrolment of the relevant age group (including repetition rates); 81 per cent total secondary enrolment (World Bank).

Health
Annual total expenditure on health is about 12 per cent of GDP, of which government spending is approximately 28 per cent.
A Social Security Fund covers the health expenses of workers.
HIV prevalence: 0.1 per cent aged 15–49 in 2003 (World Bank)
Life expectancy: 70.9 years (World Bank)
Fertility rate/Maternal mortality rate: 2.2 births per woman; maternal mortality 100 per 100,000 live births (World Bank).
Infant mortality rate: 27 per 1,000 live births; 3 per cent of children aged under five are malnourished (World Bank).
Head of population per physician/bed: 2.1 physicians and 2.7 hospital beds per 1,000 people.

Welfare
Since 1963, Lebanon has operated a social insurance system offering lump sum benefits only. Social insurance covers employees in industry, commerce and agriculture, but excludes temporary agricultural employees and those previously entitled to special benefits under the labour code.

In 1999, old age pensions were available to men aged over 60, but compulsory for those aged over 64. The benefit included a lump sum amount equivalent to the average monthly earnings during the last 12 months or the final month. The rate for disability benefit is a lump sum equal to the final month's earnings multiplied by the number of years in service. Widows receive 25 per cent of their former spouse's benefit. There are no sickness or maternity benefits. Workers receive medical benefits for up to 26 weeks or 52 weeks in special cases. Family allowances are employment-related and are available to employees with a non-working wife or with one to five children. The maximum monthly allowance is equivalent to 75 per cent of the minimum wage.

Main cities
Beirut (capital, estimated population 1.2 million in 2004), Tripoli (212,900), Sidon (149,000), Zahlé (76,600).

Languages spoken
French and English are widely spoken in business circles.
Official language/s
Arabic

Media
Press
Dailies: There are many daily newspapers in Arabic, and one in French. *L'Orient-Le Jour* is published in French and is the country's fifth-largest newspaper. *An Nahar* and *Al Anwar* are published in Arabic. Another popular political daily is *As Safir*. *Lebanon Daily Star* survived the civil war years. *Beirut Times*, an English-language newspaper, was launched in 1997.
Weeklies: Weeklies are available in both Arabic and French languages. Arabic weeklies include *Tripoli Lebanon*, *Annabaa Magazine*, *Al Ahed Magazine*. English-language weeklies are *Monday Morning*, *Eco News*, *Al Aman Magazine* and *Al Afkar magazine*. *La Revue du Liban* is a French-language weekly.
Periodicals: Periodicals include *Hitek Magazine* in English.
Broadcasting
The Lebanese Broadcasting Company (LBCI) is privately owned. In 1996, Lebanon banned broadcasts of political programmes and news by about 50 private television stations and 150 radio stations and ordered them to close. Political broadcasting is restricted to four TV stations and three radio outlets controlled by the pro-government establishment.
Radio: Most radio stations in the country are operated along sectarian lines.
Television: There are five TV stations among which some are commercial. A satellite channel was launched in 1996.

Advertising
The local advertising and marketing industry is well developed. Television accounts for 58 per cent of adspend; print media accounts for 30 per cent, with the majority being channelled into national newspapers; radio accounts for 7 per cent; billboards 4 per cent and cinema advertising 1 per cent.

Economy
Before the outbreak of civil war in 1975, Lebanon was one of the region's strongest and most developed economies, with a large banking and commercial sector, expanding industry and basic agriculture. The post-war reconstruction of the devastated infrastructure has made huge demands on resources. Inadequate investment in essential services, such as energy supply, has added to the problems of revival. Public debt stands at 180 per cent of GDP.
Recovery has been further impeded by Syria's occupation of Lebanon. Syria exploited its presence in Lebanon for its own economic advantage and to the detriment of Lebanon, draining away billions of dollars through expatriate workers, smuggling and other activities, and by interference in Lebanese business affairs. To help strengthen the economy, the authorities initiated a low income tax schedule to provide investment incentives, increase disposable income and expand the tax base. The Horizon 2000 reconstruction programme has been extended from 10 to 13 years (to 2007) with US$17.7 billion of public expenditure planned, together with US$42 billion from the private sector. The government's aim is to re-establish Lebanon as a financial and commercial centre, although this depends as much on external factors as it does on the reconstruction programme. The government has attempted to reduce total debt by introducing tax reforms and privatisation. In February 2002, 10 per cent VAT on all consumer goods was introduced. The 2003 budget created social discord as spending on services was poor, while taxes were increased to help manage the budget deficit which stood at around 14 per cent of GDP.

External trade
The Social and Economic Co-operation Agreement between Lebanon and Syria provides for the abolition of customs duties on trade between the two countries, free circulation of individuals, labour, goods and capital within their borders, as well as the co-ordination of labour and social security legislation and industrial policy.
The EU signed a Euro-Mediterranean association agreement with Lebanon in January 2002. Once fully in force, the

agreement will develop political and economic relations between EU member states, Lebanon and states in the Mediterranean basin. It will also create a free-trade zone.

Imports
Major imports include petroleum products, vehicles, medicine, clothing, meat and live animals, consumer goods, paper, textile fabrics, tobacco.
Main sources: Italy (12.2 per cent total, 2004), France (11.2 per cent), Germany (8.9 per cent), China (6.3 per cent), US (6.0 per cent), Syria (5.1 per cent), UK (5.0 per cent)

Exports
Principal exports are jewellery, inorganic chemicals, miscellaneous consumer goods, fruit, tobacco, construction minerals, electricity, machinery and switch gear, textile, paper.
Main destinations: Switzerland (10 per cent total, 2004), UAE (9.5 per cent), Turkey (9.3 per cent), Saudi Arabia (7.1 per cent), France (5.1 per cent), US (5.1 per cent)

Agriculture
Farming
The agricultural sector has still not recovered from the effects of the civil war. In 2004, it accounted for around seven per cent of GDP, compared with 12 per cent in 1994. Annual output is less than a fifth of pre-war levels, with only about 30 per cent of domestic demand for food and food products being met.

While agricultural exports have shown signs of recovery, they earn only around US$233 million compared with expenditure of US$1.5 billion on imports of agricultural produce. Main goods for export are surplus products such as apples, citrus fruit and potatoes.

Agricultural and farming activities are in private hands. The land tenure system and difficult terrain have resulted in the majority of farmland being divided into small relatively uneconomic units. This has acted as a disincentive to investment in irrigation and mechanisation. The government provides little aid to the sector, which has had to compete with heavily subsidized produce from other countries. Lebanon's membership of the Greater Arab Free Trade Agreement (Gafta), which came into effect in January 2005, could expose the sector to further pressures.

The relatively mild climate allows for diversified agricultural production. Main crops: wheat, barley, maize, vegetables, potatoes, fruit, olives, tobacco. Farmers have started the cultivation of advanced cash crops, such as avocados and flowers.

Goats, cattle and sheep are the main types of livestock raised in Lebanon. One-third of Lebanon's land is cultivable with 400,000 hectares of arable land, of which 25 per cent is irrigated. The main agricultural areas are the Beka'a valley, the Akkar plain, the coastal plain and the foothills of the central mountain range. Most of these areas were badly affected by war. Agriculture in the south and in the Beka'a valley was particularly affected. Agriculture remains an important source of income in rural areas, and although it is difficult to estimate the number of full-time farmers, most families conduct or participate in agriculture as a part-time activity.

The estimated crop production for 2004 included: 144,600 tonnes (t) cereals in total, 120,000t wheat, 350,000t potatoes, 13,950t pulses, 59,000t cabbages, 24,000t pumpkins, 329,000t citrus fruit, 110,000t grapes, 218,000t tomatoes, 41,889t oilcrops, 66,000t bananas, 10,000t tobacco, 10,000t figs, 180,000t olives, 26,040t treenuts, 4,500t chillies and peppers, 140,000t apples, 849,100t fruit in total, 810,900t vegetables in total. Estimated livestock production included: 201,403t meat in total, 52,500t beef, 1,903t pig meat, 14,300t lamb, 2,700t goat meat, 130,000t poultry, 46,500t eggs, 309,900t milk, 750t honey, 4,500t cattle hides, 1,950t sheepskins, 1,750t greasy wool, 50t cocoons, silk.

Fishing
Despite Lebanon's extensive coastline, commercial fishing remains a minor activity, contributing less than one per cent to GDP annually.

Forestry
Forest cover amounts to less than 8 per cent of total land area.

Industry and manufacturing
Industry and manufacturing is small to medium scale. The sector accounts for around 12.6 per cent of GDP and employs 18 per cent of the workforce. The main products are building materials, textiles and clothing, food processing and furniture.

Construction employs about 6 per cent of the workforce. Industry provides more than 40 per cent of Lebanon's merchandised export earnings.

Tourism
Tourism has recovered from the devastation of the civil war and Lebanon's popularity as a destination has been restored. By 2003, despite the Iraq War, visitor numbers were returning to pre-war levels. Around 1 million arrivals were recorded and the rising trend continued into 2004, when 1,278,000 arrivals were recorded. The sector's contribution to GDP continues to increase, although, at 12 per cent, it is still short of the 19.4 per cent attained in 1974.

The sector suffered a setback in 2005, precipitated by the assassination early in the year of Rafik al Hariri and the subsequent political instability. Year-on-year visitor numbers fell by around 14 per cent for the period January to September. There were signs of recovery in September. The longer-term prospects for the sector are not expected to be damaged by the events of 2005, although there is a growing need for lower-cost accommodation and better air connections.

The main market is Saudi Arabia, followed by Kuwait and Jordan, but increasing numbers of Europeans are rediscovering Lebanon. Asia is another growing market for the Lebanon.

The sector is concentrated on Beirut and the surrounding region. The attractions and infrastructure of the rest of the country remain to be developed.

The sector gives employment to around 24,000 people, double the pre-war level.

Mining
Lebanon has few natural resources. There are minor deposits of high-grade iron ore, asphalt, coal, lignite, phosphates and salt, all of which are exploited for internal consumption. There are also quarries for building-stone, and sand and lime suitable for use in construction.

Hydrocarbons
Lebanon relies on the import of refined oil to meet domestic demand. Initial studies indicate the presence of offshore oil and gas reserves. Several international companies have shown interest, but exploration has not been initiated yet. With the surge in fuel costs due to growing world demand in 2005, the search for hydrocarbons is likely to accelerate. With its eyes on this prospect, the government is drafting legislation to regulate the sector. It has been speculated that Lebanon could recover up to 90,000 barrels per day from any reserves.

Lebanon does not produce natural gas. A gas pipeline from Syria to Lebanon was completed in March 2005, which is intended to feed a major power station in northern Lebanon; the supply of gas by Syria did not commence in mid-2005 as scheduled.

Lebanon does not produce coal, importing around 221,0000 short tonnes per annum.

Energy
Electricity supply is highly inefficient and expensive. Outages are a regular feature of life. Electricité du Liban (EDL), the state-owned electricity provider, operates at an annual loss of US$400 million a year. Electricity is produced using

imported fuel oil, which accounts for around 70 per cent of EDL's total costs. A kilowatt is three times more expensive in Lebanon than in Egypt, Syria or Turkey. EDL is scheduled to be partially privatised under a law passed in 2002.

Lebanon is seeking to convert from fuel oil to natural gas for electricity generation. Like oil, natural gas has to be imported. A pipeline giving access to Syrian gas at preferential prices was completed in March 2005, but commencement of supply has been held up. Other sources under discussion in 2005 were Egypt, through the Arab natural gas pipeline, and Qatar.

Financial markets
Stock exchange
The Beirut Stock Exchange (BSE) is one of the smallest in the region and its performance is poor compared to other emerging markets.

Banking and insurance
Before the civil war, Lebanon was the unrivalled financial centre in the Middle East. Lebanon's free exchange system, strict secrecy laws, and strong currency all served to attract regional and international institutions and customers. Favourable economic and financial conditions following the end of the civil war initially led to an improved monetary and banking situation. However, lack of dynamism in the sector has since discouraged most foreign investors.

Central bank
Banque du Liban (BDL) (Bank of Lebanon)
Main financial centre
Beirut

Time
GMT plus two hours (winter); GMT plus three hours (summer).

Geography
Lebanon stretches approximately 140km along the eastern shore of the Mediterranean, bounded by Syria to the north and east and Israel to the south. Its terrain is mountainous, dominated by the parallel ranges of the Lebanon in the west and the Anti-Lebanon in the east, which run north-east to south-west. Between these ranges lies the Beka'a valley, broad in the north, narrowing in the south. The coastal plain is defined by the Lebanon range which in places plunges into the sea, dividing the coastal strip into segments. The major cities are: Tripoli in the north, Beirut on one of the wider segments halfway down the coast and Sidon and Tyre in the south.

Climate
In the summer, temperatures range between 20–30 degrees Celsius (C); Beirut average 27 degrees C. The coastal region is humid in the summer months. In the winter, temperatures in the coastal region range between 10–16 degrees C and it becomes colder inland. Snow is usual on mountains. Most rain falls between November and March. Lebanon enjoys an essentially Mediterranean climate with mild, rainy winters and long warm summers. It almost never rains between June and October, and there is an average of 300 sunny days every year. In summer it is possible to escape the heat and humidity of the coast and go to the mountains. Average annual rainfall is 893mm in Beirut, mostly occurring in winter.

Dress codes
Formal clothing is required for business meetings. Women should dress modestly.

Entry requirements
Passports
Passport valid for six months are required by all except nationals of Syria arriving from their country with a valid national ID.
Visa
Required by all, with a few exceptions. Contact the nearest consulate for confirmation. Those who apply for a business visa must submit a business letter from the visitor's company with a letter or fax from a local business contact stating the purpose of the trip.
Prohibited entry
Entry is refused to holders of Israeli and Palestinian passports, holders of passports containing a visa for Israel, valid or expired, used or unused, and passports with entry stamps to Israel.
Currency advice/regulations
There are no restrictions on the import and export of local or foreign currencies.
Customs
There are restrictions on the amount of imported cigarettes and spirits allowed.

Health (for visitors)
Mandatory precautions
Vaccination certificates for yellow fever are required if travelling from an infected area. There are no other mandatory vaccinations required to enter Lebanon.
Advisable precautions
It is recommended that visitors have preventative vaccinations for polio, typhoid, tetanus and hepatitis 'A'.
Lebanon's medical services are generally modern, with most doctors speaking French or English. The private hospitals are the best, but more expensive, and it is recommended that insurance is taken out by all visitors.

Hotels
A 16 per cent service charge is usually added to the bill, with additional tipping extra.
There are fashionable hotels on the shores of the Mediterranean in Beirut. All hotels arrange free transport to and from the airport.

Credit cards
International credit cards are accepted throughout the capital, and in the more developed areas across the country.

Public holidays
Fixed dates
1 Jan (New Year's Day), 6 Jan (Armenian Christmas, Armenian community only), 7 Jan (Orthodox Christmas Day), 9 Feb (Feast of St Maroun), 1 May (Labour Day), 6 May (Martyrs' Day), 15 Aug (Assumption Day), 1 Nov (All Saints' Day), 22 Nov (Independence Day), 25 Dec (Christmas Day).
Variable dates
Good Friday, Orthodox Good Friday, Eid al Adha (three days), Islamic New Year, Ashura (two days), Birth of the Prophet, Eid al Fitr (three days).
The Islamic year contains 354 or 355 days, with the result that Muslim feasts advance by 10–12 days against the Gregorian calendar. Dates of feasts vary according to the sighting of the new moon, so cannot be forecast exactly.

Working hours
Banking
Mon–Fri: 0800–1230; Sat: 0800–1200.
Business
Mon–Fri: 0900–1600.
Government
Mon–Fri: 0800–1400; Sat: 0800–1300.
Shops
Mon–Sat: 0800–1900. Some shops open on Sundays.

Electricity supply
110V or 220V AC, 50 cycles. Supply is subject to fluctuations and blackouts. It is advisable to use a stabiliser when operating more advanced electronic equipment.

Weights and measures
Metric system

Social customs/useful tips
Punctuality is expected for business appointments but is less strictly observed for social engagements. The usual form of greeting is to shake hands. It is the custom to offer coffee or tea to visitors and it is considered rude to refuse. Muslim traditions are observed.
During Ramadan (the four weeks prior to the Eid al Fitr holiday) employees tend to work shorter hours. It is advisable to avoid business trips at this time.

Security
Security in Lebanon is likely to remain hostage to the regional tensions over the Israeli-Palestinian and Iraqi conflicts. Visitors are advised to carry their passports.

Nations of the World: A Political, Economic and Business Handbook

Getting there
Air
There are daily flights between Beirut and most European and Middle Eastern capitals. Lebanon's flag carrier, Middle East Airlines (MEA), connects Beirut with most European capitals, other parts of the Middle East, some African capitals and Singapore.
National airline: Middle East Airlines (MEA).
International airport/s: Beirut International (Code: BEY), 16km from city, with duty-free shop.
Airport tax: There is no airport tax.
Surface
The only way into Lebanon by land is through Syria. Entry by road via Israel is prohibited.
Road: Land entry via the northern coastal road or through the Bekaa Valley.
Water: A catamaran operates between Larnaca in Cyprus and Beirut.
Main port/s: Beirut, Tripoli, Saida (Sidon), Jounieh, Tyre and Byblos.

Getting about
National transport
Air: There are no domestic air services.
Road: Some 6,000km of roads and highways, excluding municipal roads. There are two international motorways with a total length of 570km. Some 40 per cent of the road network is in poor condition. New routes are being constructed all the time.
Buses: Buses travel between Beirut and other major towns around the country. There are only limited daily departures.
Rail: There is no passenger railway network in Lebanon.
City transport
Taxis: There are taxis available throughout Beirut and most of the country. Service taxis usually follow established routes where one person will often share the taxi with up to four other passengers. Share taxis will stop on request. Ordinary taxis are not restricted to a set route and will take passengers anywhere in the country. The government has fixed charges for airport taxis.
Buses, trams & metro: A few buses are available to certain destinations. Not recommended for foreign visitors.
Car hire
There are several international car hire companies in Beirut, usually offering competitive rates. Rental companies can also provide drivers with their cars.

BUSINESS DIRECTORY
The addresses listed below are a selection only. While World of Information makes every endeavour to check these addresses, we cannot guarantee that changes have not been made, especially to telephone numbers and area codes. We would welcome any corrections.

Telephone area codes
The international direct dialling (IDD) code for Lebanon is +961, followed by area code:

Grand Beirut	1	Tripoli	6
Kerswan and Jbeil	9	Tyre	7
Sidon	7	Zahle	8

Chambers of Commerce
American Lebanese Chamber of Commerce,1153 Foch Street, PO Box 175093, Beirut (tel: 985-330; fax: 985-331; e-mail: amchamlb@cyberia.net.lb).

Beirut and Mount Lebanon Chamber of Commerce, Industry and Agriculture, Sanayeh, 1 Justinien Street, PO Box 11-1801, Beirut (tel: 353-390; fax: 353-395; e-mail: info@ccib.org.lb).

Federation of the Chambers of Commerce, Industry and Agriculture in Lebanon, Sanayeh, 1 Justinien Street, PO Box 11-1801, Beirut (tel: 745-288; fax: 341-328; e-mail: fccial@cci-fed.org.lb).

Sidon and South Lebanon Chamber of Commerce, Industry and Agriculture, Boulevard Maarouf Saad, PO Box 41, Saida (tel: 720-123; fax: 722-986; e-mail: chamber@ccias.org.lb).

Tripoli and North Lebanon Chamber of Commerce, Industry and Agriculture, Bechara Khoury Street, PO Box 47, Tripoli (tel: 425-600; fax: 442-042; e-mail: comindeg@adm.net.lb).

Banking
ABN-AMRO Bank Lebanon, ABN AMRO Tower, Charles Malek Avenue, Achrafieh, Beirut (tel: 219-200; fax: 217-756/7).

Arab African International Bank, Riad El Solh, beirur (tel: 980-162/3, 980-264/5; fax: 633-912).

Bank of Beirut; PO Box 11-7354, Bank of Beirut sal Bldg, Foch Street, Beirut Central District, Beirut (tel: 738767/68; fax: 602166).

Banque Audi, Banque Audi Plaza, Bab Idriss, 2021 8102 Beirut (tel: 200-250, 331-600; fax: 339-220).

British Arab Commercial Bank Ltd, ARESCO Centre, Banque du Liban Street, PO Box 113-5495, Hamra, Beirut (tel: 602-437; fax: 602-438).

British Bank of the Middle East, PO Box 11-1380, 9/F SNA Building, Ashrafieh, Tabaris Square, Beirut (tel: 647-611/5; fax: 425-295).

Banque Libano-Française, PO Box 11808, Beirut Liberty Plaza Bldg, Roma Street, Ras Beirut, Beirut (tel: 791332; fax: 340355).

BLOM Bank, BLOM Banks's Bldg, Rashid Karami St, Verdun, Beirut, Lebanon (tel: 743-300, 738-938; fax: 738-946).

Banque de la Méditerranée; Méditerranée Group Building, Clemenceau Street, Kantari Beirut, 2022 9302 Beirut (tel: 373-937; fax: 362-706).

Central bank
Banque du Liban, PO Box 11-5544, Masraf Loubane Street, Beirut (tel: 750-000; fax: 478-2740; e-mail: bdlit@bdl.gov.lb).

Travel information
Middle East Airlines, PO Box 206, Beirut International Airport.

Tourist Police (343-209).

Trans Mediterranean Airways, PO Box 11-3018, Beirut International Airport.

Ministry of tourism
Ministry of Tourism, Information Services, 550 Central Bank Street, PO Box 11-5344, Beirut (tel: 354-764; fax: 343-279; e-mail: mot@lebanon-tourismgov.lb).

Ministries
Ministry of Agriculture, Georges Jaber Building, Badaro Street, Beirut (tel: 455-613; fax: 455-475; e-mail: ministry@agriculture.gov.lb).

Ministry of Defence, Yarzé, Beirut (tel: 452-963; fax: 457-920).

Ministry of the Displaced, Old Sidon Road, Damour (tel: 840-474; fax: 840-476; e-mail: mod@dm.net.lb).

Ministry of Economy and Trade, Assaf Building, Rue Artois, Beirut (tel: 340-504; fax: 354-640; e-mail: postmaster@economy.gov.lb).

Ministry of Education and Higher Education, Rue Georges Piko, Beirut (tel: 744-251; fax: 371-079).

Ministry of Electricity and Water Resources, Shiah, Beirut (tel: 565-040; fax: 449-639).

Ministry of the Environment, 550 Central Bank Street, Beirut (tel: 524-999; fax: 524-555).

Ministry of Finance, MOF Building, Riyad el Solh Square, Beirut (tel: 981-001; fax: 642-762; e-mail: infocenter@finance.gov.lb).

Ministry of Foreign Affairs, Rue Sursock, Beirut (tel: 334-400; fax: 584-098).

Ministry of Health, Museum Street, Beirut (tel: 615-701; fax: 645-099).

Ministry of Industry, Rue Sami Solh, Beirut (tel: 427-247; fax: 427-112).

Ministry of Information, Rue Hamra, Beirut (tel: 351-032; fax: 423-189).

Lebanon

Ministry of the Interior, Rue des Arts et Métiers, Sanayeh, Beirut (tel: 981-270; fax: 751-622).

Ministry of Justice, Rue Sami Solh, Beirut (tel: 425-670; fax: 422-957).

Ministry of Labour, Shiah, Beirut (tel: 556-831; fax: 556-832).

Ministry of Posts and Telecommunications, Rue Sami Shoh, Beirut (tel: 888-100; fax: 423-005; e-mail: webmaster@mpt.gov.lb).

Ministry of Public Works and Transport, Fiyadieh, Hazmieh, Beirut (tel: 458-975; fax: 459-434)..

Ministry of Social Affairs, Rue Badaro, Beirut (tel: 395-561; fax: 396-148).

Ministry of Sports and Youth, Campus of UNESCO, Beirut (tel: 790-529; fax: 840-440).

Ministry of Tourism, 550 Central Bank Street, Beirut (fax: 340-940; e-mail: mot@lebanon-tourism.gov.lb).

Office of the President, Presidential Palace, Beirut (tel: 220-0000; fax: 425-395).

Office of the Prime Minister, Riyad el Sol Square, Beirut (tel: 862-001; fax: 869-630).

Other useful addresses

Assocation of Lebanese Industrialists, PO Box 1520, Chamber of Commerce and Industry Building, Justinian Street, Beirut (tel: 350-280; fax: 351-167).

Board for Foreign Economic Relations, PO Box 11-5344, Beirut (tel: 483-391/5

British Embassy, Commercial Section, PO Box 60180, Coolrite Building, Autostrade, Jal El Dib, Beirut (tel: 406-330, 405-033, 402-035; fax: 402-033).

Council for Development and Reconstruction (CDR), Tallet El Serail, Beirut Central District (tel: 643-981; fax: 647-947, 864-494, 865-630).

Electricité du Liban, Nahr Street, Beirut (tel: 442-720; fax: 583-084).

Higher Council for Privatisation, Grand Serail, Beirut Central District, Beirut (tel: 987-500; fax: 983-061).

International Fairs and Promotions, SARL, PO Box 55576, Beirut.

Investment Development Authority of Lebanon, Presidency of the Council of Ministers, Liberty, Lyon Street, PO Box 113-7251, Sanayeh, Beirut (tel: 344-676, 344-403; fax: 344-463, 347-397).

Lebanese Embassy (USA), 2560 28th Street, NW, Washington DC 20008 (tel: 202-939-6300; fax: 202-939-6324; e-mail: info@lebanonembassy.org).

Solidére (development company for rebuilding Beirut), Industry and Labour Bank Building, Riyadh El-Solh Street, PO Box 11-9493, Beirut (tel: 346-891, 646-137/8/9; fax: 646-136).

Internet sites

Investment Development Authority of Lebanon (IDAL): http://www.idal.com.lb

Lebanon Online: http://www.lebanon.com

Ministry of Economy and Trade: http://www.economy.gov.lb

Ministry of Tourism: http://www.lebanon-tourism.gov.lb

Lesotho

KEY FACTS

Official name: Kingdom of Lesotho

Head of State: King Letsie III (sworn in Feb 1996; crowned Oct 1997)

Head of government: Prime Minister Bethuel Pakalitha Mosisili (LCD) (since 1998)

Ruling party: Lesotho Congress for Democracy (LCD) (re-elected May 2002)

Area: 30,355 square km

Population: 2.59 million (2004)

Capital: Maseru

Official language: Sesotho and English

Currency: Loti (maloti, plural) (L) = 100 lisente; has parity with the South African rand, which is legal tender.

Exchange rate: L6.36 per US$ (Oct 2005)

GDP per capita: US$652 (2004)

GDP real growth: 2.30% (2004)

Labour force: 770,000 (2004)

Inflation: 5.50% (2004)

Balance of trade: -US$246.40 million (2004)

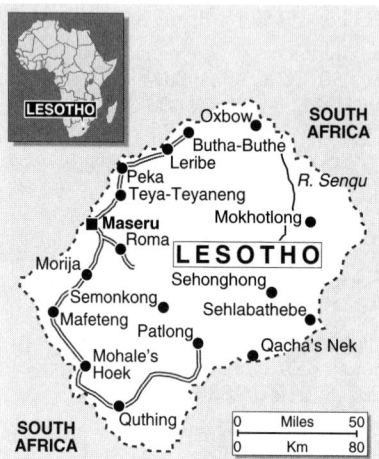

The Kingdom of Lesotho is made up mostly of highlands where many of the villages can be reached only on horseback, by foot or light plane. During the winter shepherds have to contend with snow. While much of the tiny country, with spectacular canyons and thatched huts, remains untouched by modern machines, developers have laid down roads to reach its mineral and water resources. Major construction work was undertaken to create the Lesotho Highlands Water Project.

Because of scarce resources, attributable to the harsh environment on the highland plateau and the limited agricultural space in the lowlands, Lesotho has been heavily dependent on the country which completely surrounds it - South Africa.

Over the decades thousands of workers have been forced by the lack of employment opportunities to find jobs on South African mines. Poverty is deep and widespread, with the UN describing 40 per cent of the population as 'ultra-poor'.

Economic prospects

Lesotho has made considerable gains in macroeconomic stability since 2004. The government's fiscal position and the external current account have improved markedly, the inflation rate has slowed, and net international reserves have increased. However, poverty remains widespread. Growth has been weakened by the cumulative impact of several shocks: a substantial real appreciation of the exchange rate of the South African rand, to which the Lesotho loti is pegged; the removal of textile quotas by industrial countries; a continuing decline in the terms of trade; and persistent drought.

Lesotho's economic prospects could be affected by further trade preference erosion, a declining trend in revenue receipts from the Southern African Customs Union (Sacu) - essentially a free trade area comprised of Botswana, Lesotho, Namibia, South Africa and Swaziland - and falling remittances from Lesotho workers in South Africa as the South Africans seek to have more of their nationals employed in the mines. The number of Basotho mine workers in South African mines fell from an average of 96,000 in 1997 to 62,000 in 2002 and have continued to fall. Lesotho is facing the challenge of restoring external competitiveness and promoting rapid and broad-based growth to reduce poverty. With the country's commitment to keep the loti pegged to the rand, the burden of safeguarding macroeconomic stability will necessarily fall on fiscal policy and accelerating structural reforms to restore competitiveness.

Regional trade

Lesotho is a small, open, low-income economy with very close financial and commercial ties to South Africa. It is a member of SACU and the (Southern Africa) Common Monetary Area (CMA). Trade among SACU countries is free of tariffs and duties. Trade with South Africa accounts for about two-thirds of Lesotho's external trade, and foreign direct investment (stock) from South Africa is about 20 per cent of Lesotho's gross domestic product. Lesotho's banking system comprises four banks, three of them South African. Workers' remittances from South Africa and receipts of Lesotho's share of SACU revenue constitute a significant part of national income.

Lesotho has achieved moderate growth since the early 1990s, strongest during 1991–95, reflecting the impact of substantial public investment in the Lesotho Highlands Water Project to divert water it

Lesotho

was pumping from the highlands to the central areas of South Africa, to the Johannesburg industrial areas. Since 2000, garment exports to the United States under the US African Growth and Opportunity Act (AGOA) have become the main engine of growth, but these are now in jeopardy as the US liberalises the import of textiles. In the second half of 2004/05, factory closures accounted for the loss of about 10,000 jobs - 20 per cent of the jobs in the sector. Nonetheless, overall real growth has been driven by factor accumulation of capital, with a minimal contribution from growth in productivity. Per capita GDP was US$652 in 2004.

The authorities have reformed public expenditure management and the financial sector and privatised public enterprises. The introduction of value added tax (VAT) and the creation of the Lesotho Revenue Authority (LRA) have helped to raise non-SACU revenue. On the upside, diamond exports are projected to rise further with the opening of two more mines, supported by foreign investment. On balance, GDP is forecast to decline in 2005/06 by about 0.75 per cent, the average annual inflation is expected to be somewhat higher, and the external current account deficit projected to widen.

Under the baseline scenario for 2005/06–2007/08, real GDP growth remains weak because the dampening effect of the trade shock on growth is only partially offset by increases in non-garment manufacturing and diamond mining. This scenario assumes that public investment and implementation capacity improve beginning in 2005/06 and that private investment remains at about 24 per cent of GDP. Assuming some improvement in the marginal output-capital ratio, annual real GDP growth is projected to pick up to about 2 per cent/per annum over the medium term. The fiscal surplus (including grants) is projected to decline in 2005/06 and switch to a deficit in subsequent years. This fiscal weakening reflects both a downward trend in revenues (after 2005/06) and a sharp rise in total expenditures in 2005/06 followed by gradual reductions relative to GDP in subsequent years.

Musical thrones

Once head of state in one of the last countries in the world to be ruled by an absolute monarch, King Letsie III now has no legislative or executive powers. The monarchy is now hereditary, under the terms of the constitution, which came into effect after the March 1993 election. The monarch is a 'living symbol of national unity'; under traditional law the college of chiefs has the power to determine who is next in the line of succession, and who shall serve as regent in the event that the successor is not of mature age.

Letsie III succeeded his father, King Moshoeshoe, who was dethroned and exiled in 1990, but returned to Lesotho in 1992. Letsie III abdicated and his father was reinstated as monarch in 1995, but already there was a strong movement towards constitutional government. Letsie III was restored as king in 1996 after his father died in a car accident.

Basutoland was renamed the Kingdom of Lesotho upon independence from the UK in 1966 under King Moshoeshoe. In 1998, violent protests and a military mutiny following a contentious election prompted a brief but bloody intervention by South African and Botswana military forces under the aegis of the Southern African Development Community. Constitutional reforms have since restored political stability; peaceful parliamentary elections were held in 2002. The leader of the majority party in the Assembly automatically becomes prime minister.

Bethuel Mosisili won a second five-year term as prime minister in the 2002 elections. His Lesotho Congress for Democracy (LCD) won a majority in the 120-seat parliament. Mosisili first came to power in May 1998. Opposition members protested against the results and protests sparked the unrest which brought South African and Botswana peacekeepers to the country.

Before entering parliament Mosisili worked as an academic and a teacher. He studied in Africa and the US.

Risk assessment

Economic	Satisfactory
Political	Satisfactory
Regional stability	Satisfactory

COUNTRY PROFILE

Historical profile

A fight for survival brought the African nation-state of Basutoland into existence in the nineteenth century; the fight for survival still characterises the Kingdom of Lesotho. When the Zulu-Mfecane swept over South Africa in the early nineteenth century the mountain fastness of present-day Lesotho offered a defensive position to its inhabitants and a refuge to people of very diverse origins up-rooted from elsewhere. A local chief, Moshoeshoe 1 (1831–70), took his chance to prove himself as one of the outstanding empire-builders of nineteenth century Africa. Through shrewd diplomacy and military ability, but especially as a gifted administrator, creating a reform model for traditional government. Moshoeshoe succeeded in defending his people and expanding his domain. For some time he could even defend his state against the advancing Boers, but at last, against their never ending land hunger, broke down. An unjust peace after military defeat in 1866 forced the Basuto to hand over half their agricultural lands to the Orange Free State.

When Britain responded to Moshoeshoe's pleas for British rule and protection a part of the lost territory was restored, but a disappointingly small portion. It needed another desperate fight, the Gun War of 1880, to convince the British government that rule by South Africa's whites was not acceptable to Moshoeshoe's nation and London arranged for direct rule through

KEY INDICATORS — Lesotho

	Unit	2000	2001	2002	2003	2004
Population	m	2.16	2.20	2.23	2.41	2.59
Gross domestic product (GDP)	US$bn	0.99	0.81	0.78	0.88	*1.38
GDP per capita	US$	458	367	354	364	652
GDP real growth	%	2.4	3.2	4.2	4.2	2.3
Inflation	%	6.2	6.9	11.2	7.6	5.5
Exports (fob) (goods)	US$m	211.1	286.0	354.8	422.0	484.5
Imports (fob) (goods)	US$m	727.6	675.0	736.0	738.0	730.9
Balance of trade	US$m	-516.5	-389.0	-381.2	-316.0	-246.4
Current account	US$m	-151.4	-90.0	-140.0	-150.0	-20.0
Total reserves minus gold	US$m	417.9	386.5	406.4	460.3	502.8
Foreign exchange	US$m	412.6	381.5	400.9	454.4	496.7
Exchange rate	per US$	6.94	8.61	10.54	7.56	6.19

* estimated figure

its representative in South Africa, the High Commissioner in Cape Town.
1600s Modern-day Lesotho was settled by the Sotho people; the area was already home to the San people.
1800s European traders and missionaries arrived in the area, and were soon followed by the Boers on their Great Trek. The Boer trek coincided with the expansion of the Zulu state. King Moshoeshoe the Great ensured the survival of his people by taking them to a mountain stronghold in about 1820. The policy of assisting refugees on condition that they help in defence proved successful – by 1842 the King's people numbered around 40,000 and were protected by outlying refugee settlements.
1870 By the time King Moshoeshoe died, a Basuto nation of 150,000 had been established.
1910 After annexing Basutoland, the British established the Basutoland National Council comprising members nominated by chiefs.
1960 After a new constitution was introduced, elections were held, which were won by the Basutoland Congress Party (BCP) ahead of the Basutoland National Party (BNP) led by Chief Leabua Jonathan.
1965 The BCP lost the election to the BNP; Chief Jonathan became the first prime minister of the Kingdom of Lesotho. King Moshoeshoe II was stripped of most of his powers.
1966 Independence was granted.
1970 The constitution was suspended and opposition political parties banned.
1986 The government of Chief Leabua Jonathan was overthrown in a military coup by Major General J M Lekhanya. A military government chaired by Lekhanya ruled Lesotho in co-ordination with King Moshoeshoe II and a civilian cabinet appointed by the King. The new regime was more amenable to South Africa's wishes.
1990 A constituent assembly was set up to frame a new constitution; a timetable was announced for a return to civilian rule. King Moshoeshoe II was stripped of his executive and legislative powers and exiled by Lekhanya.
1991 Lekhanya was overthrown by a group of military officers led by Major General Elias Ramaema who took control. Because Moshoeshoe II initially refused to return under the new rules of the government in which the King was given only ceremonial powers, Moshoeshoe's son was installed as King Letsie III.
1992 King Moshoeshoe returned from exile as a common citizen, in a deal with the military regime.
1993 A new constitution was adopted leaving the King as ceremonial head of the country. Elections signalled a return to democracy; the BCP won a convincing victory. King Letsie III became a purely constitutional monarch.
1994 After growing unrest, King Letsie III suspended the constitution. King Moshoeshoe, in collaboration with military supporters staged a coup but it was thwarted within a month. The settlement eventually negotiated allowed for both the re-establishment of parliamentary rule and King Letsie abdicated in favour of King Moshoeshoe.
1996 King Moshoeshoe II was killed in a road accident and was again succeeded by his son, who was sworn in as King Letsie III.
1997 King Letsie III was formally crowned.
1998 The Lesotho Congress for Democracy (LCD) won the elections. The result was rejected by opposition groups. After riots broke out in Maseru and reports circulated of an imminent military coup, 800 South African and Botswanan soldiers entered Lesotho with the aim of restoring order. The Interim Political Authority (IPA) was created to work alongside the government to prepare for elections.
2000 King Letsie III married Karabo Motsoeneng.
2001 President Thabo Mbeki of South Africa visited Lesotho to mend diplomatic relations and develop economic links. Twenty-seven LCD members of parliament quit the party to form the Lesotho People's Congress (LPC).
2002 The ruling LCD won the parliamentary elections.
2003 Families displaced by the Lesotho Highlands Water Project (LHWP), and resettled in the Maseru district, won a ruling that improvements to their schools should be made by the project's authority.
2004 In February, Prime Minister Mosisili declared a state of emergency and appealed for food aid. In March, the first phase of the LHWP was officially opened.

Political structure
Constitution
A new constitution was adopted in 1993, which redefined the role of the monarchy and altered the legislative branch of the government.
The King, who is head of State, has no executive or legislative authority.
Form of state
Constitutional monarchy
The executive
Executive power is vested in the prime minister, leader of the majority parliamentary party, and the cabinet appointed by the prime minister.
National legislature
Legislative power is held by a bi-cameral National Assembly.
The first chamber was enlarged from 80 seats to 120 for the 2002 elections. The voting system is a combination of proportional representation (40 seats) and first past the post (80 seats). Elections are called every five years.
The second chamber (Senate) is made up of 22 principal chiefs and 11 members appointed by the King with advice from the prime minister, with a term of five years.
Legal system
The legal system is based on English common law and Roman-Dutch law.
Last elections
25 May 2002 (parliamentary) (held under a new voting system)
Results: Parliamentary: the ruling LCD won an outright majority, with 54.9 per cent of the vote, taking 77 seats, the opposition BNP won 22.4 per cent and 21 seats out of 40.
The Lesotho People's Congress (LPC) and National Independent Party (NIP) each won five seats and minor parties the rest.
Next elections
2006 (parliamentary)

Political parties
Ruling party
Lesotho Congress for Democracy (LCD) (re-elected May 2002)
Main opposition party
Basotho National Party (BNP)

Population
2.59 million (2004)
Ethnic make-up
The Basotho nation is an amalgam of mainly Sesotho-speaking people. Some 45 per cent of the population is of Nguni origin. A number of smaller groups, including San Griqua, Indian and European, have also become naturalised Basotho.
Religions
Christianity (approximately 80 per cent, mainly Roman Catholic), various traditional beliefs and others (20 per cent).

Education
Primary education is free from the age of six.
Public expenditure on education typically amounts to around 8.5 per cent of gross national income (GNI). Lesotho has one university, located in the capital, Maseru.
Literacy rate: 72 per cent male, 93 per cent female; adult rates (World Bank).
Compulsory years: Six to 13.
Enrolment rate: 108 per cent gross primary enrolment, of the relevant age group (including repeaters); 31 per cent gross secondary enrolment (World Bank).
Pupils per teacher: 46 in primary schools.

Health
Annual total expenditure on health is about 5–6 per cent of GDP, of which

approximately 79 per cent is government spending.
HIV/Aids
The HIV prevalence is among the highest in the world.
HIV prevalence: 28.9 per cent aged 15–49 in 2003 (World Bank)
Life expectancy: 37.2 years (World Bank)
Fertility rate/Maternal mortality rate: 4.3 births per woman; maternal mortality 530 per 100,000 live births (World Bank).
Infant mortality rate: 79 per 1,000 live births; 16 per cent of children aged under five are malnourished (World Bank).
Head of population per physician/bed: 0.05 doctors per 1,000.

Main cities
Maseru (capital, estimated population 173,700 in 2003), Maputsoa (35,000), Mafeteng (32,900).

Languages spoken
English becomes the medium of instruction from the fifth year of primary education.
Official language/s
Sesotho and English

Media
Press
Dailies: *Public Eye Daily* (www.publiceye.co.ls) is an important newspaper with on-line edition.
Weeklies: There are several weeklies including *Lentsoe la Basotho*, *Leselinyana la Lesotho* (bi-weekly), *Lesotho Today*, *Makatolle*, *Mirror*, *Mphatlalatsane* and *Setsomi Sa Litaba*. *Mopheme* is the most popular semi-weekly newspaper in Lesotho.
Periodicals: Monthly periodicals include *Southern Star* and *Thebe*. *Leseli ka sepolesa* is published irregularly from Maseru.
Broadcasting
Radio: Radio Lesotho broadcasts in English and Sesotho.

Economy
For a small, rural, land-locked country, with few significant resources, almost any activity can have an effect on the economy and Lesotho is no exception. The economy in 2004 benefited from clothing exports to the US of over US$450 million, as the manufacturing sector provided 21 per cent of GDP; remittances from miners working in South Africa also increased by 8.1 per cent and increased government revenue from Southern African Customs Union (SACU) import duties helped sustain an overall GDP growth rate of 2.3 per cent, however this was a fall on the 4.2 per cent of 2003.
The IMF appreciated the sustained growth, with its accompanying declining inflation and stronger external current account as well as increased international reserves. However it also identified external shocks to the economy that reduced growth, in manufacturing and agriculture, including the elimination of textile quotas under WTO rulings, the declining agricultural output due to a three-year prolonged drought, and structural weaknesses from poor farming techniques, soil erosion and lack of agri-finance, and job losses as South African mines laid off Lesotho workers. Lesotho lost over 20,000 textile jobs between June 2004 and January 2005 as factories closed and owners relocated to other places where lower costs and better infrastructure offered them higher returns. To achieve the Millennium Development Goals the government has to undertake measures and accept a heavy burden to reduce the harm being done by HIV/Aids. There is almost one in three people suffering from Aids and it is adversely affecting private and public economies. The loss of manpower and farming skills has led to a drop in agricultural output. Social indicators remain poor with around two-thirds of the population living below the poverty line. In 2005 the World Food Programme estimates 500,000 people are in need of food aid.
The US$8 billion Lesotho Highlands Water Project (LHWP) is one of the largest and most ambitious multi-purpose water schemes anywhere in the world, in addition to being one of Africa's biggest civil engineering projects. Once complete, the LHWP will provide South Africa with 79 cubic metres of water a second, by diverting the flow of the Senqu and its tributaries northwards to South Africa. By 2044, revenues are predicted to contribute some 5 per cent to Lesotho's annual GDP. The LHWP is due to be fully completed in 2020. However, construction is slowing, thereby reducing economic activity. The first phase of the LHWP was officially opened in March 2004.

External trade
As a member of the SACU (together with South Africa, Namibia, Swaziland and Botswana), Lesotho, as a land-locked country, was allowed to impose customs duties of other member states' goods. In 2005 this right is under threat of withdrawal and Lesotho risks losing 54.7 per cent of its total tax receipts – more than income tax and value added tax combined.
Lesotho is also a member of the Southern African Development Community (SADC), which is reducing trade barriers within the region allowing for greater movement of goods and services.
In 2002, the US approved Lesotho as eligible for tariff preferences under the African Growth and Opportunities Act (AGOA). Through this, textile exports to the US were virtually duty-free, however the 1 January 2005 WTO elimination of textile quotas ruling has impeded this trade and Lesotho is left looking for investment to fill the void.
Imports
Principal imports include food, building materials, vehicles, machinery, medicines and petroleum products.
Main sources: Hong Kong (34.2 per cent total, 2004), Taiwan (33.9 per cent), China (11.2 per cent), Germany (9.2 per cent)
Exports
Principal exports are manufactures (75 per cent) (clothing, footwear, vehicles), wool and mohair, food and live animals.
Main destinations: US (96 per cent total, 2004), Canada (1.5 per cent), Belgium/Luxembourg (1.1 per cent)

Agriculture
Farming
The agricultural sector has traditionally been a major contributor to the economy. A series of programmes were implemented from 1996 to boost agricultural development through commercialisation and privatisation. Progress has been slow and the IMF reported in 2005 that agriculture suffered from structural weaknesses that included poor farming techniques, soil erosion, lack of water in lowland areas and lack of access to agri-finance.
There are a number of factors constraining development such as the government's heavy involvement in production, marketing and processing of the sector. This involves controlling commodity prices as well as containing imports and exports. These policies have deterred private sector involvement and hampered growth. The country also faces a severe lack of land suitable to arable farming as well as poor soil fertility and unreliable rainfall. Poverty is widespread in rural areas, where households rely on miners' remittances to remain in operation. As more workers are being laid off in South African mines the agricultural sector is finding it hard to maintain production levels enough to feed the population.
Moreover, the construction of the Mohale dam as part of the Lesotho Highlands Water Project (LHWP) has meant flooding the most fertile land area, the only region producing a food surplus. The World Bank maintains that the US$55 million earned from water sales to South Africa will far exceed the US$2 million value of Mohale valley crops. Farmers from the Katse Dam area have been given food aid and skills training and communities have been resettled. Environmental organisations expressed concern over

increased unemployment, food insecurity and water shortages downstream due to dams.

The estimated crop production for 2004 included: 247,550 tonnes (t) cereals in total, 51,000t wheat, 150,000t maize, 90,000t potatoes, 46,000t sorghum, 11,400t pulses, 13,000t fruit in total, 18,000t vegetables in total. Estimated livestock production included: 22,220t meat in total, 8,710t beef, 2,775t pig meat, 3,900t game meat, 3,100t lamb, 1,935t goat meat, 1,800t poultry, 1,512t eggs, 23,750t milk, 1,876t cattle hides, 620t sheepskins, 3,900t game meat, 2,600t greasy wool.

Industry and manufacturing
The industrial sector as a whole typically contributes around 40 per cent of GDP and employs around 26 per cent of the labour force.

Most firms are small and are in joint ventures with the Lesotho National Development Corporation (LNDC). Production is largely for export (clothing, footwear, textiles) or import substitution (food processing, bricks). Other enterprises include handicrafts, ceramics and furniture making. Pharmaceuticals and leather/hide processing are under development. Industrial production grew by 2.6 per cent and manufacturing by 3.0 per cent in 2004.

Tourism
The Lesotho Tourism Development Corporation (LTDC) provides the direction for the tourism sector. It's strategy is to develop village based facilities where visitors can experience traditional customs and lifestyles. The country is also being marketed for the eco-tourist and those enjoying activity holidays.

The Lesotho highlands are the main tourist attraction as well as the world heritage site of Maloti/Drakensberg, which has been given a US$15 million grant, by the World Bank, to protect its bio-diversity. Travel and tourism is expected to contribute over US$223 million, or 2.6 per cent of GDP in 2005 and employ around 27,000 workers. The sector is estimated to attract over 11 per cent of total capital investment, at almost US$70 million in 2005.

Mining
The diamond industry is mainly based on the Letseng la Terae mine. Letseng Diamonds and the New Mining Corporation each have a 38 per cent share in the project while the government retains a 24 per cent share. The mine produces just three carats per 100 tonnes, compared to the global average of 50–100 carats per 100 tonnes. Production costs are at least 10 times greater than the world average. However, Letseng la Terae continues to be in operation due to the high number of large diamonds produced.

Hydrocarbons
Lesotho does not produce any hydrocarbons. Explorations for oil took place in 1970 however this proved unsuccessful and no further attempts have been made. Currently it imports refined oil, primarily from South Africa.

Coal consumption makes up for 87 per cent of Lesotho's energy requirements and is also imported from South Africa.

Energy
The electricity supply is the responsibility of the Lesotho Electricity Corporation (LEC), and most of its power requirements are supplied by South Africa.

The first phase of an ambitious US$8 billion Lesotho Highlands Water Project (LHWP) should produce enough hydro-electricity to meet almost all Lesotho's needs.

Banking and insurance
Restructuring of the banking sector in the 1990s has strengthened the position of Lesotho's banking sector by improving asset management and the capital base of domestic banks. Along with the liberalisation of interest rates, restructuring has enabled domestic banks to respond to interest rate movements in South Africa and strengthened the Central Bank's ability to influence the money supply.

Central bank
Central Bank of Lesotho

Time
GMT plus two hours

Geography
Lesotho is a landlocked country, entirely surrounded by South African territory. It is a mountainous land situated at the highest part of the Drakensberg escarpment on the eastern rim of the South African plateau. To its west, the land falls through foothills to a lowland area where the majority of the population lives. Three large rivers, the Orange, the Caledon and the Tugela, rise in the mountains and flow through it.

Climate
Temperate climate with well-marked seasons.

More than 85 per cent of the country's rainfall – averaging 700mm in mountain areas – falls from October to April. Spring comes in August. Summer from November–January with average temperature 27 degrees Centigrade (C), rising to 32 degrees C in lowland areas.

Autumn days are warm. Winter from May–July with temperatures as low as -7 degrees C in lowlands and -18 degrees C in highlands.

Snowfalls can occur on the highlands at any time of the year.

Dress codes
In summer, light, loose clothing is most comfortable, but include a raincoat. Spring and autumn clothing should include a jersey for the cool evenings. Heavy woollens, vests, windcheaters, socks and jackets are a must in winter. Warm clothing is also essential for a journey into the Maloti where severe weather conditions can be encountered any time of the year.

Entry requirements
Passports
Required by all. Passports must be valid for six to 12 months beyond length of stay.

Visa
Required by all, except those (mostly Commonwealth) countries listed at the consular section – visas of www.lesotholondon.org.uk/. Further information may be requested through the consulate, or application forms downloaded from consulate websites, within applicant's country.

Currency advice/regulations
There is no restriction on foreign currency, but all transactions must be conducted in Maseru.

The Lesotho maloti is at parity with the South African rand, which is also accepted as legal currency.

Traveller's cheques are acceptable.

Health (for visitors)
Mandatory precautions
Yellow fever vaccination for visitors from infected areas.

Advisable precautions
Immunisations for hepatitis 'A', polio, tetanus and typhoid. There is a rabies risk.

Hotels
There are a number of comfortable, international-class hotels in Maseru.

Throughout the rest of the country, accommodation ranges from medium-sized hotels to smaller tourist lodges.

Bills are subject to tax of 12 per cent. Tip of 10 per cent is usual.

Credit cards
Major credit cards are accepted.

Public holidays
Fixed dates
1 Jan (New Year's Day), 11 Mar (Moshoeshoe's Day), 4 Apr (Heroes' Day), 1 May (Workers' Day), 17 Jul (King Letsie III's Birthday), 4 Oct (Independence Day), 25 Dec (Christmas Day), 26 Dec (Boxing Day).

Variable dates
Good Friday, Easter Monday, Ascension Day.

Working hours

Banking
(Mon, Tue, Thu, Fri) 0830–1530; (Wed) 0830–1300; Sat: 0830–1100.

Business
Mon–Fri: 0800–1245, 1400–1630; Sat: 0800–1300.

Government
Mon–Fri: 0800–1245, 1400–1630.

Shops
Mon–Fri: 0800–1700; Sat: 0800–1500.

Telecommunications

Telephone/fax
Automatic services are available.

Getting there

Air
National airline: International flights are via Johannesburg, with regular air services operated by South African Airways.
International airport/s: Maseru-Moshoeshoe I (MSU), 18km south of Maseru.
Airport tax: International departures L20; transit passengers are exempt.

Surface
Road: Good tarred roads from South Africa into the south and west of the country. With the implementation of the Highlands Water Project, the road network is being expanded.
There are 12 border control posts from South Africa.
Rail: Lesotho does not have its own rail system, although Maseru is linked to the South African system for freight traffic only.

Getting about

National transport
Air: Air Lesotho's domestic air services were terminated on 31 January 1999. Charter companies in Lesotho are Highlands Air and Senqu Air.
Road: Over 3,500km of tarred, gravel and dirt roads. Approximately 500km are tarred.
Roads are being continuously upgraded, and tarred roads connect main towns in seven out of 10 districts. A spin-off of the Highlands Water Project is the opening-up of the interior of the country to all vehicles.
Buses: A good service provided by mainly privately owned buses. Coach services operate Maseru-Welkom; Maseru-Qacha's Nek.

Car hire
Driving licences issued in most countries are valid in Lesotho for a period of up to six months, provided they are printed in English or are accompanied by a certified translation. International driving permits are also recognised.
Seat belts are compulsory. The driver of the car must carry a valid international licence at all times. Traffic drives on the left.
In winter, antifreeze is a wise precaution for all cars with watercooled engines. Chains are useful in mud and snow. Petrol can be obtained in all District Headquarter towns but is not easily obtainable elsewhere.
For visitors using their own vehicles information should be obtained from Lesotho Tourist Board Information Office.

BUSINESS DIRECTORY

The addresses listed below are a selection only. While World of Information makes every endeavour to check these addresses, we cannot guarantee that changes have not been made, especially to telephone numbers and area codes. We would welcome any corrections.

Telephone area codes
The international dialling code (IDD) for Lesotho is +266 followed by the subscriber's number.

Useful telephone numbers
Queen Elizabeth II Hospital: 312-501
Police: 123
Fire brigade: 122
Ambulance: 121

Chambers of Commerce
Lesotho Chamber of Commerce & Industry, PO Box 79, Fairways Centre, Kingsway Avenue, Maseru 100 (tel: 323-482; fax: 310-414; e-mail: lcci@lesoff.co.za).

Banking
Lesotho Bank Ltd; PO Box 1053, Kingsway, Maseru 100 (tel: 314-333; fax: 310-348).
Barclays Bank plc, PO Box 115, Kingsway, Maseru (tel: 312-423; fax: 310-068).
Lesotho National Development Bank, PMB A96, Maseru (tel: 312-012; fax: 310-038).
NedBank, 1st Floor, Standard Bank Bldg, Kingsway, PO Box 1001, Maseru 100 (tel: 322-696; fax: 310-025).

Central bank
Central Bank of Lesotho, PO Box 1184, Corner Airport and Moshoeshoe Roads, Maseru 100 (tel: 314-281; fax: 310-051; email: cbl@centralbank.org.ls/).

Travel information
Air Lesotho (reservations), PO Box 861, Mejametalana Airport, Maseru (tel: 317-317; fax: 310-126).

Ministry of tourism
Ministry of Tourism, Sports and Culture, PO Box 52, Maseru 100 (tel: 313-034).

National tourist organisation offices
Lesotho Tourist Board, PO Box 1378, Maseru 100 (tel: 312-896, 313-760; fax: 310-108).

Ministries
Minister to the Prime Minister, PO Box 527, Maseru 100 (tel: 311-000; fax: 310-102).
Ministry of Agriculture, Co-ops, Marketing and Youth Affairs, PO Box 24, Maseru 100 (tel: 323-561; fax: 310-349).
Ministry of Defence and Public Service, PO Box 527, Maseru 100 (tel: 311-000; fax: 310-102).
Ministry of Education and Manpower Development, PO Box 47, Maseru 100 (tel: 313-045; fax: 310-206).
Ministry of Finance and Economic Planning, PO Box 395, Maseru 100 (tel: 311-101; fax: 310-157).
Ministry of Foreign Affairs, PO Box 1378, Maseru 100 (tel: 311-150; fax: 311-150).
Ministry of Health and Social Welfare, PO Box 514, Maseru 100 (tel: 324-404; fax: 310-467).
Ministry of Home Affairs and Local Government, Rural and Urban Development, PO Box 174, Maseru 100 (tel: 323-771; fax: 310-319).
Ministry of Information and Broadcasting, PO Box 36, Maseru 100 (tel: 323-561; fax: 310-003).
Ministry of Justice, Human Rights, Law and Constitutional Affairs, PO Box 402, Maseru 100 (tel: 322-683).
Ministry of Labour and Employment, Private Bag A116, Maseru 100 (tel: 322-565).
Ministry of Natural Resources, PO Box 426, Maseru 100 (tel: 313-632).
Ministry of Tourism, Sports and Culture, PO Box 52, Maseru 100 (tel: 313-034).
Ministry of Trade and Industry, PO Box 747, Maseru 100 (tel: 322-138; fax: 310-326).
Ministry of Transport and Telecommunications, PO Box 413, Maseru 100 (tel: 323-691).
Ministry of Works, PO Box 20, Maseru 100 (tel: 311-362; fax: 310-125).

Other useful addresses
British High Commission, PO Box 521, Maseru 100 (tel: 313-961; fax: 310-120).
Lesotho Embassy (USA), 2511 Massachusetts Avenue, NW, Washington DC 20008 (tel: 202-797-5533; fax: 202-234-6815).

Lesotho National Development Corporation, Private Bag A96, Maseru 100 (tel: 312-012; fax: 310-038; internet site: http://www.lndc.org.ls/).

Lesotho National Insurance Corporation, Private Bag A96, Maseru 100 (tel: 313-031; fax: 310-007).

Livestock Marketing Corp, PO Box 800, Maseru (tel: 322-444) (sole marketing concern for all livestock and products, including mohair).

Multilateral Investment Guarantee Agency (MIGA), 1818 H Street NW, Washington DC 20433, USA (tel: (1 202)473-1079; fax: (1 202)334-0265).

Radio Lesotho, PO Box 552, Maseru (tel: 323-561).

Statistics Bureau, PO Box 455, Maseru (tel: 323-852).

Trade Promotion Unit, Ministry of Trade and Industry, PO Box 747, Maseru (tel: 323-414; fax: 310-121).

Internet sites

Africa Business Network: http://www.ifc.org/abn

AllAfrica.com: http://allafrica.com

African Development Bank: http://www.afdb.org

Africa Online: http://www.africaonline.com

Harambee Afrika (UK business club for traders with east, central and southern Africa; includes annotated web resource list): http://www.harambee.co.uk

Public Eye (on-line edition of daily newspaper): http://www.publiceye.co.ls

Lesotho news agency: http://www.lena.gov.ls/news.htm

Mopheme newspaper: http://www.lesoff.co.za/news/

Lesotho Council of Non-Governmental Organisations (LCN): http://www.lecongo.org.ls/

Liberia

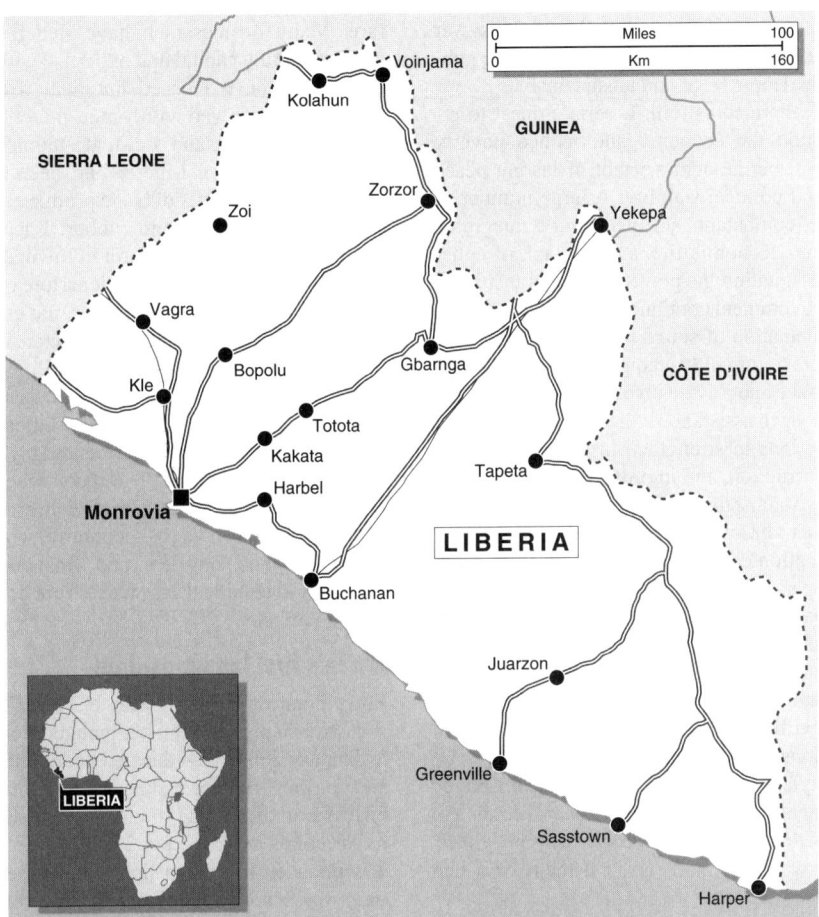

KEY FACTS

Official name: Republic of Liberia

Head of State: Ellen Johnson-Sirleaf (since Nov 2005)

Head of government: Chairman Gyude Bryant

Ruling party: National Transitional Government (from Oct 2003 until Jan 2006)

Area: 111,370 square km

Population: 3.85 million (2004)

Capital: Monrovia

Official language: English

Currency: Liberian dollar (L$) = 100 cents (new Liberian $ banknotes introduced Mar 2000)

Exchange rate: L$57.00 per US$ (Oct 2005); (parallel market rate from 23 Feb 2004)

GDP per capita: US$127 (2004)

GDP real growth: 21.80% (2004)

Labour force: 1.33 million (2004)

Unemployment: 80.00% (2004)*

Inflation: 7.80% (2004)

Balance of trade: -US$86.70 million (2004)

Foreign debt: US$3.00 billion (2004)*

* estimated figure

Liberia is Africa's oldest republic, but it became better known in the 1990s for its long-running, ruinous civil war and its role in a rebellion in neighbouring Sierra Leone. The West African nation was relatively calm until 1980 when William Tolbert was overthrown by Sergeant Samuel Doe after food price riots. By the late 1980s, arbitrary rule and economic collapse culminated in civil war when Charles Taylor's National Patriotic Front of Liberia (NPFL) militia overran much of the countryside, entering the capital in 1990. Doe was executed. The respite was brief, with anti-government fighting breaking out in the north in 1999. Taylor accused Guinea of supporting the rebellion. Meanwhile Ghana, Nigeria and others accused Taylor of backing rebels in Sierra Leone.

Matters came to a head in 2003 when Taylor – under international pressure to quit and hemmed in by rebels – stepped down and went into exile in Nigeria. The signing of a peace agreement in 2004 ended 15 years of intermittent civil wars.

Peace at last?

Over 2004 there was an intensification of internal hostilities, followed by the introduction of the National Transitional Government of Liberia tasked with steering the country towards elections in 2005. International aid was resumed. The gross domestic product rebounded. Prices stabilised and the exchange rate returned to preconflict levels, reflecting a return of private capital, donor inflows, and an increase in the demand for local currency. Official reserves increased modestly, but from low levels. Once the transitional government took office, co-operation with the International Monetary Fund (IMF) on policy implementation and payments significantly strengthened. The IMF decided to allow a resumption of the fund's technical assistance to Liberia in March 2004, but stressed that a continued track record of co-operation and policy implementation would be required to pave the way for a gradual removal of the IMF's remedial measures. (Liberia had been in continuous arrears to the IMF since 1984 and a declaration of non-cooperation had been issued by the fund in 1986, and the country's voting and related rights suspended in 2003. At end-August 2004, Liberia's arrears to the IMF amounted to US$750 million or 711 per cent of quota.)

Economy

Although a domestically funded fiscal deficit was quickly rolled back, there was a large buildup of arrears – despite the introduction of a cash-management committee to avoid the recurrence of a cash deficit, significant expenditures were still made without authorisation. Collections slowed, largely reflecting delays in extending preshipment inspections to all imports and exports.

Over 2005, the economic recovery was expected to strengthen, underpinned by continued consolidation of the security situation and reconstruction activities. Real growth was projected to grow by 8.5 per cent, led by agriculture, domestic manufacturing, and services. With higher imports and increased production, domestic prices are expected to moderate further. The trade deficit is projected to narrow on a further moderate increase of exports and decline of donor-funded imports for humanitarian assistance.

The resulting pick-up in donor-related and reconstruction activities has led to a rebound of economic activity, stabilisation of prices and the exchange rate, and a modest increase in official reserves. However, the macroeconomic position is still fragile, activity is still below the pre-war level, poverty is widespread, and the public debt is large and unsustainable.

A prerequisite in Liberia's quest to rebuild the economy and reduce poverty will be the achievement of lasting peace and political stability. A large number of ex-combatants still need to be integrated into economic life, and the lack of cohesion within the power-sharing transitional government continues to hinder the implementation of sound policies and reforms. Libya urgently requires external assistance and private investment, and the flow of such assistance will depend on decisive actions to strengthen institutions, reduce corruption, and improve governance.

Against this background, fiscal management has weakened. There is an anti-corruption commission which must be made operational as quickly as possible. Investigations into the circumstances surrounding sales of iron ore and the alleged disappearance of a large number of import and export permits should be conducted swiftly, and the outcomes of the investigations made public. Declaring her own-style war on corruption and mismanagement, new President Ellen Johnson-Sirleaf in January dismissed her entire government and replaced them with her own nominees.

Economic woes

Civil war and government mismanagement had destroyed much of Liberia's economy, especially the infrastructure in and around Monrovia, while continued international sanctions on diamonds and timber exports will continue to limit growth prospects for the foreseeable future. Many businessmen have fled the country, taking capital and expertise with them. Some have returned, but many will not. Richly endowed with water, mineral resources, forests, and a climate favourable to agriculture, Liberia had been a producer and exporter of basic products – primarily raw timber and rubber. Local manufacturing, mainly foreign owned, had been small in scope. The departure of former president, Charles Taylor, the establishment of the all-inclusive Transitional Government, and the arrival of a United Nations' mission were all necessary for the eventual end of the political crisis, but have done little to encourage economic development. The reconstruction of infrastructure and the raising of incomes in the ravaged economy will largely depend on generous financial support and technical assistance from donor countries.

Africa's first lady president

Ellen Johnson-Sirleaf became Africa's first woman president on her inauguration in January 2006. US-educated economist and former finance minister Johnson-Sirleaf won the second round of presidential elections in November 2005. The poll was intended to draw a line under Liberia's war. Known in Liberia as the 'Iron Lady', Johnson-Sirleaf drew much of her support from women voters and Liberia's small educated elite. One of her priorities is to reintegrate into society former child soldiers. She has declared a 'zero tolerance' of corruption. She served as finance minister under President William Tolbert in the late 1970s and fled the country after the Tolbert government was overthrown. She has worked for the UN and the World Bank.

Some of the opposition to Johnson-Sirleaf stems from her one-time association with former Liberian leader Charles Taylor. She briefly supported the then warlord in his quest to overthrow military leader Samuel Doe. Since her election she has said that bringing Taylor to justice is not one of her major concerns. Born in 1938, Johnson-Sirleaf is a widowed mother-of-four.

KEY INDICATORS — Liberia

	Unit	2000	2001	2002	2003	2004
Population	m	2.92	3.20	3.20	3.53	3.85
Gross domestic product (GDP)	US$bn	0.52	0.56	0.56	0.42	*0.45
GDP per capita	US$	176	176	122	120	127
GDP real growth	%	–	–	2.0	-5.0	21.8
Inflation	%	–	–	14.0	15.0	7.8
Exports (fob) (goods)	US$m	–	–	1,079.0	–	4.7
Imports (fob) (goods)	US$m	–	–	5,051.0	–	91.4
Balance of trade	US$m	–	–	3,972.0	–	-86.7
Foreign debt	US$bn	2.0	2.0	1.5	3.0	–
Total reserves minus gold	US$m	0.3	0.5	3.3	7.4	18.7
Foreign exchange	US$m	0.2	0.4	3.3	7.3	18.7
Exchange rate	per US$	40.95	48.58	61.75	54.35	54.50

* estimated figure

Liberia

Risk assessment

Economic	Poor
Political	Poor
Regional stability	Poor

COUNTRY PROFILE

Historical profile
Like Sierra Leone's capital (Freetown), Liberia's capital (Monrovia) was established (in 1821) as a settlement for freed slaves. But while most of Freetown's early inhabitants were released from slave ships before they had crossed the Atlantic, the early Liberian settlers came directly from slavery in the United States – hence the American names, customs and institutions (including the presidential system of government). Monrovia itself was named after President Monro.

Also like Sierra Leone, Liberia grew to its present size gradually as inland tribal areas were added to the original coastal settlements, whose Americo-Liberian people established a kind of colonial rule over these areas. Although English is the only language of the descendants of the settlers, there are a number of separate languages in the interior, where chiefs still play a role in government. Liberia's frontiers, the result of long wrangling with Britain and France, sometimes divide tribes, part of which are in Sierra Leone, or in Guinea or Côte d'Ivoire, Liberia's other two neighbours. The Vai, which invented a written language of its own, is one such tribe.

1822 Liberia was created by a number of US philanthropists with the idea that freed slaves would be resettled in Africa. Many refused to go and those who did were met with hostility from the indigenous population.

1847 Liberia was established as an independent state. The US did not formally recognise this status until 1862.

1944–71 Under President William Tubman of the True Whig party (which monopolised power from early in Liberia's existence), the country received massive foreign investment, but this only exacerbated tension between the descendants of the settlers and the indigenous people.

1963 The local people were enfranchised – around 97 per cent of the total population.

1971 Tubman was succeeded by William Tolbert.

1980 Following protests against the government the previous year, Tolbert's government was overthrown in a coup led by Master Sergeant Samuel Doe, who survived several coup attempts and won an 'election' held in 1985. His government proved widely unpopular.

1984 New multi-party constitution.

1990 Opposition groups, led by Prince Johnson and Charles Taylor overran most of Liberia and captured Monrovia. With Johnson and Taylor both claiming the presidency, the West African peacekeeping force, the Economic Community of West African States Monitoring Group (Ecomog), installed Amos Sawyer as head of an Interim Government of National Unity (IGNU). Taylor's National Patriotic Front of Liberia (NPFL) controlled around 90 per cent of Liberia; the remnants of Doe's supporters and Johnson's forces were both encamped within the capital.

1993 After a period of heavy fighting, a UN-sponsored peace accord was signed, calling for the creation of a six-month transitional government representing the IGNU, the NPFL and Doe's supporters and the United Liberation Movement for Democracy (Ulimo).

1994–95 Several agreements were reached, none of which brought a final peace.

1996 An attempt to arrest one faction leader for breaking the truce led to two weeks of serious street fighting in Monrovia until Ecomog regained control. Following the renewed conflict, both the faction leaders and Ecowas agreed to hold elections in 1997.

1997 Charles Taylor and his NPFL won a landslide victory.

1999 The Ghanaian and Nigerian troops, who were part of Ecomog, withdrew from Liberia.

2000 President Charles Taylor announced that his government was forming a new army.

2001 There were rebel attacks on the border between Guinea and Liberia and Liberia closed its border with Sierra Leone.

2002 A state of emergency was declared after rebels (Liberians United for Reconciliation and Democracy (LURD)) attacked a town near the capital, Monrovia.

2003 The UN Security Council extended its arms embargo against Liberia for 12 months and added an export ban on unsawn timber. In June, foreign nationals were evacuated from Monrovia amid fighting by LURD rebels in their campaign against President Taylor, who, despite pressure from the US, initially refused to resign. President Taylor eventually accepted Nigeria's asylum offer. West African peacekeepers entered Monrovia and on 8 August President Taylor submitted his resignation and named his vice president Moses Blah to take over on 11 August when he left for Nigeria. The government and two rebel groups selected Gyude Bryant, chairman of the Liberia Action Party (LAP), to head Liberia's interim post-war administration; he was sworn in on 14 October.

2004 In February, international donors pledged more than US$500 million in reconstruction aid. The UN Security Council voted in March to freeze the assets of former president Charles Taylor.

2005 The first elections since the end of the civil war were held in October. The run-off between former finance minister Ellen Johnson-Sirleaf and former international footballer George Weah was held on 8 November. The result was declared on 23 November – Johnson-Sirleaf 59.4 per cent, Weah 40.6 per cent. Johnson-Sirleaf thus became the first woman president in Africa. Weah initially challenged the results, alleging fraud, but withdrew his case from the Supreme Court on 20 December, allowing the inauguration of the new president to go ahead. On 21 December the UN Security Council extended its ban on arms sales to Liberia for a further 12 months, and the sale of diamonds and timber for a further six months.

2006 The Secretariate of the ACP countries lifted sanctions against Liberia in January. This makes the country eligible for direct aid and funds from the EU. Edwin Snowe was elected Speaker of the House of Representatives.

Political structure
Constitution
The multi-party 1984 constitution, approved by referendum, replaced the 1847 constitution which was suspended in April 1980.

The executive
Executive power rests with the president, elected by universal adult suffrage for a term of six years; the maximum number of terms is two. The president is head of state, head of government and commander-in-chief of the armed forces. The president must be a natural-born Liberian citizen of not less than 35 years of age, the owner of unencumbered property valued at not less than US$25,000 and resident in Liberia 10 years prior to the elections.

National legislature
Formerly, legislative power was held by the 26-member Senate (elected for a term of nine years) and the 64-member House of Representatives (elected for a term of six years).

The National Transitional Legislative Assembly (NTLA), installed in October 2003, comprises 76 members.

Legal system
Liberia has a dual system of statutory law based on Anglo-American common law for the modern sector and customary law based on unwritten tribal practices for the indigenous sector.

Last elections
2005 (first round presidential; run off 8 Nov); 2005 (House of Representatives and Senate).
Results: First round presidential: George Weah (CDC) 28.3 per cent, Ellen Johnson-Sirleaf (UP) 19.8 per cent, Charles Brumskine (LP) 13.9 per cent, Winston Tubman (NDPL) 9.2 per cent, Varney Sherman (Cotol) 7.8 per cent. Run-off: Ellen Johnson-Sirleaf 59.4 per cent, George Weah 40.6 per cent..
House of Representatives: CDC 15 seats (out of 64), LP 9 seats, UP 8 seats, Cotol 8 seats, APD 5 seats, NPP 4 seats.
Senate: Cotol 7 seats (out of 30), NPP 4 seats, CDC 3 seats, LP 3 seats, UP 3 seats, APD 3 seats.

Political parties
Liberia Action Party (LAP); Liberian People's Party (LPP); United People's Party (UPP); Unity Party (UP); Citizens' Development Party (CDP); National Patriotic Party (NPP).

Ruling party
National Transitional Government (from Oct 2003 until Jan 2006)

Population
3.85 million (2004)

Ethnic make-up
Indigenous tribes (95 per cent), Americo-Liberians (5 per cent).

Religions
Christianity (68 per cent), traditional beliefs (18 per cent), Muslim (14 per cent).

Education
Primary education lasts for six years ending at age 12. Junior secondary school last for three years before successful students can progress onto senior secondary school for a further three years.
Higher education is provided principally by the Uninversity of Liberia in Monrovia, the African Methodist Episcopal University and Cuttington University College.
Literacy rate: 54 per cent male, 24 per cent female, adult rates (Government statistics).
Compulsory years: Six to 16.

Health
Annual total expenditure on health is around 4 per cent of GDP, of which government spending is approximately 76 per cent.
Liberia's healthcare system is virtually non-existent, with few doctors, nurses or medicine.

HIV/Aids
Altogether there were 96,000 adults, of which 54,000 women, and 8,000 children under the age of 15, living with HIV/Aids in 2003. Deaths from Aids totalled 7,200 and there were 36,000 orphans aged 0–17 created in 2003 (UCSF).

HIV prevalence: 5.9 per cent aged 15–49 in 2003 (World Bank)
Life expectancy: 47.1 years (World Bank).
Fertility rate/Maternal mortality rate: 5.8 births per woman (World Bank).
Infant mortality rate: 157 per 1,000 live births (World Bank).
Head of population per physician/bed: 0.02 doctors per 1,000 people.

Main cities
Monrovia (capital, estimated population 550,200 in 2003), Zwedru (35,300), Buchanan (27,300).

Languages spoken
English is the business language. There are three main Liberian dialects – Golla, Bassa, Kpelle, Kru and Vai.

Official language/s
English

Media
Media freedom was severely restricted and the police closed newspapers and radio stations critical of President Taylor's regime.

Press
Since the former president Taylor's departure, several independent newspapers have started publication.
Dailies: The Liberia Communications Network (LCN), owned by former president Charles Taylor, published two dailies *The Patriot* and *Newsbeat*. Other dailies published mainly from Monrovia include *The News*, *Daily Times*, *The Inquirer* and *The National Chronicle*.
Weeklies: Weeklies published from Monrovia are *By Monrovia Weekend* (biweekly), *Eye* and *New Democrat Weekly*.

Broadcasting
State-owned TV and radio suffered particularly from looting in the civil war and lost its TV and FM radio transmitters in 1991. The Liberia Broadcasting System (LBS) has one FM small transmitter that can reach only Monrovia, and no television.
The LCN controls a TV and radio network which uses the frequency 89FM, previously used by LBS, and which, by law, belongs to the state.
Radio: There is no domestic radio outside of the greater Monrovia area, but international stations can be heard.

Economy
The economy has been severely damaged by years of conflict, instability and corruption, resulting in displacement of large sections of population, unemployment in excess of 80 per cent, the destruction of infrastructure and the collapse of production of traditional commodities, including diamonds, iron, rubber, coffee and timber. The once-prosperous country has been reduced to one of the poorest in the world. More than three-quarters of the population live below the poverty line, while utilities, such as running water and electricity, are practically non-existent. The foreign debt amounts to over US$3 billion.
The challenges of reconstruction are enormous, but Liberia has considerable resources which, given the right conditions of peace and stability, should enable the country, with foreign aid, advice and investment, to embark on recovery.
Since 2004, when a transitional government was formed and with the return of IMF and World Bank involvement in Liberia, there has been some growth. Prices and exports were stabilised and the exchange rate improved, despite the continuation of UN economic sanctions, especially on timber exports, because of misuse of the income. In 2005, the IMF found that, despite good omens for the year, the government's fiscal management was unsatisfactory. There has been a tentative return of donor aid and private capital, which is expected to increase substantially if the new government elected in 2005 can restore stability and good governance.

External trade
Increased outflow of foreign company remittances, debt repayments and falling exports have kept the current account in deficit.

Imports
Principal imports include fuels, chemicals, machinery, transportation equipment, manufactured goods and foodstuffs.
Main sources: South Korea (38.1 per cent total, 2004), Japan (21.9 per cent), Singapore (12.6 per cent), Croatia (4.8 per cent)

Exports
Principal exports rubber, timber, iron, diamonds, cocoa and coffee.
Main destinations: Germany (36.9 per cent total, 2004), Poland (18.6 per cent), US (11.4 per cent), Greece (10.6 per cent)

Agriculture
Farming
Hit by hostilities and migration from rural areas, production has been reduced from pre-war levels. Agriculture is still the most important sector of the economy, contributing approximately 35 per cent to GDP and employing 55 per cent of the workforce.
One of the country's principal cash crops is rubber, which provides a large proportion of exports. Although mostly grown in foreign-owned plantations, smallholders are responsible for over half the total acreage planted.
Coffee, cocoa and timber are also grown for export, but, as with rubber, earnings have been reduced due to falling world

prices. Palm oil is produced mostly for the domestic market. The main food crops are rice, cassava and sweet potatoes, followed by eddoes and yams. The government had attempted to improve production to reduce the need for imports of rice which have become necessary to meet domestic demand.

The estimated crop production for 2004 included: 110,000 tonnes (t) rice, 490,000t cassava, 25,500t taro, 20,000t yams, 19,000t sweet potatoes, 110,000t bananas, 42,000t plantains, 3,500t pulses, 543,500t roots and tubers, 7,000t citrus fruit, 49,950t oilcrops, 174,000t oil palm fruit, 1,500t cocoa beans, 3,200t green coffee, 115,000t natural rubber, 255,000t sugar cane, 20,000t yams, 169,200t fruit in total, 76,000t vegetables in total. Estimated livestock production included: 21,416t meat in total, 1,000t beef, 4,400t pig meat, 6,500t game meat, 1,316t lamb and goat meat, 8,200t poultry, 4,520t eggs, 715t milk.

Fishing
Commercial ocean fishing is a growing activity, particularly shrimps.

Forestry
Timber is normally an important export, but, because of misuse of revenues, has been subject to UN economic sanctions since 2001. The largest timber concession is the Oriental Timber Corporation (OTC), which is Indonesian-owned.

Industry and manufacturing
The small industrial sector contributes 4.9 per cent to GDP. The manufacturing sector is relatively underdeveloped, contributing 4 per cent to GDP. Activity is mainly confined to textiles, food and rubber processing, wood products, cement and chemicals.

The sector has been weakened by the country's upheavals, which damaged infrastructure and deterred investment. Growth in the sector is in any case constrained by the small size of the domestic market, the need to import practically all raw materials, shortage of skilled labour and financial problems.

Tourism
In April 2003, Liberia requested the UN Scientific and Cultural Organisation (UNESCO) to add two Liberian sites, Sarpo National Park and Providence Island, to The World's Cultural Heritage.

Mining
Prior to the civil war, Liberia was one of the world's major producers of iron ore (mainly extracted from mines at Mount Nimba, Mano River and Bong), which accounted for around 30 per cent of GDP. Production ceased completely as a result of the war. Efforts are being made to revive the sector. In August 2005, an agreement was entered into with the Mittal Steel Company to develop reserves and associated infrastructure in western Liberia.

Diamonds are mined, previously earning Liberia an estimated US$300 million annually. During the war, factions exploited production. Current production figures are hard to gauge due to the allegations of diamond smuggling with Sierra Leone, Guinea and Côte d'Ivoire. Liberia's diamond exports, along with timber, have been subject to UN economic sanctions since 2001, because of misuse of the revenues. Foreign investors, anticipating future stability, are showing interest in the sector.

Hydrocarbons
There are no known oil or gas reserves in Liberia. There is potential in the territorial waters in the Gulf of Guinea. Investigation is at an early stage. The National Oil Company of Liberia has signed several exploration agreemnents since 2004, but with small and sometimes obscure companies. Liberia relies on imports from neighbouring countries for its petroleum requirements. The sole refinery at Monrovia was mothballed in 1984. Liberia does not produce or import gas and coal.

Energy
The electricity generation and supply infrastructure was wrecked early in the civil war. Privately-owned generators are the only source of electricity for those who can afford them. It is not expected that grid supplies will be available for at least five years. The state-owned Liberian Electricity Corporation (LEC) estimates that it will need in excess of US$100 million to repair the system. As a step towards reconstruction of the sector, the LEC is undergoing a process of liberalisation, including staff restructuring, under the auspices of the EU.

Banking and insurance
The civil war has led to a virtual collapse of the banking system and lending services have declined dramatically. The country's five commercial banks have found it hard to attract capital savings, as the public and businesses have tended to hoard money rather than put it in banks due to a general crisis of confidence in the banking system. The subsequent lack of liquidity in the banking sector has led to a wide spread between the average deposit and lending rates. Lack of affordable bank credit has hampered growth across the economy, particularly the agricultural sector. Unless the government can ensure political stability and security and a policy is instituted to increase bank savings, Liberia's banking sector will remain in the doldrums.

Central bank
In October 1999 the National Legislature enacted a law creating the Central Bank of Liberia, which replaced the National Bank of Liberia. Monetary authority functions are undertaken by the central government.

Main financial centre
Monrovia

Time
GMT

Geography
Liberia lies on the west coast of Africa, with Sierra Leone and Guinea to the north and Côte d'Ivoire to the east.

Climate
Hot and tropical with high levels of humidity (85–90 per cent) and there is little temperature variation throughout the year. Average temperatures range between 20–22 degrees Celsius (C) at night and 28–32 degrees C during the day. Wet season lasts from May–October with especially heavy rain June–July.

Entry requirements
Passports
Required by all. Passports must be valid for six months from date of entry.

Visa
All governments recommend that their citizens do not travel to Liberia until the security situation is stabilised.

All requirements for visas are those set out by the former administration and cannot be verified. Contact both the nearest embassy of Liberia and your own ministry of foreign affairs for current and relevant information.

Currency advice/regulations
There are no restrictions on import and export of local or foreign currency. US dollars are legal tender.

Health (for visitors)
Mandatory precautions
Yellow fever vaccination certificate is required.

Advisable precautions
Typhoid, hepatitis 'A', tetanus and polio vaccinations are recommended. Malaria prophylaxis should be taken as risk exists throughout the country. There is a rabies risk. Drinking water should be boiled and filtered.

Hotels
The airport hotel and other major hotels in Monrovia should be booked in advance. Rates are expensive and tipping is optional.

Credit cards
There is limited acceptance of credit cards.

Public holidays
Fixed dates
1 Jan (New Year's Day), 11 Feb (Armed Forces Day), 8 Mar (Decoration Day), 15 Mar (J J Roberts' Birthday), 12 Apr (National Redemption Day), 14 Apr (Fast and Prayer Day), 6 May (Samuel K Doe's Birthday), 14 May (National Unification Day), 25 May (Africa Day), 26 Jul (Independence Day), 24 Aug (Flag Day), 29 Oct (Youth Day), 29 Nov (President Tubman's Birthday), 25 Dec (Christmas Day).
Variable dates
Thanksgiving Day (Nov)

Working hours
Banking
Mon–Thu: 0900–1200; Fri: 0800–1400.
Business
Mon–Fri: 0800–1200, 1400–1600.
Government
Mon–Fri: 0800–1200, 1300–1600.
Shops
Mon–Sat: 0800–1300, 1500–1800.

Telecommunications
Telephone/fax
The service is 100 per cent automatic but very limited outside Monrovia.

Weights and measures
Imperial system

Security
Crime is high in the capital, Monrovia, with theft and assault prevalent, particularly at night.

Getting there
Air
International airport/s: Monrovia-Robertsfield International (Code: ROB), 60km from city; duty-free shop, bar, restaurant, buffet, post office, shops.
Airport tax: International departures US$20; not applicable to children under 12 years and transit passengers.
Surface
Road: The Monrovia-Sierra Leone road is paved. Routes from Côte d'Ivoire and Guinea are not generally recommended during rainy season.

Getting about
National transport
Air: Air Liberia operates a domestic service between Monrovia and main towns. Air taxi companies charter planes between Monrovia and airfields throughout the country.
Road: A network of 10,000km covers most areas, although many roads are untarred. Main highways are: Monrovia-Sanniquellie (with a branch Ganta-Harper) and Monrovia-Buchanan.
Rail: There are no passenger railways, but the LAMCO mining company accepts passengers on the mineral line between Buchanan and Nimba county.

Water: Freight/passenger services between Monrovia and Buchanan.
City transport
There are buses and taxis available from the airport to the city centre.
Taxis: Zoning system in operation. Negotiate fares in advance for long-distance journeys. Tipping is not usual.
Car hire
Chauffeur-driven or self-drive cars are available in Monrovia. International driving licence or national driving licence with permit (valid for up to 30 days) accepted. Traffic drives on the right. Self-drive cars are not generally recommended.

BUSINESS DIRECTORY
The addresses listed below are a selection only. While World of Information makes every endeavour to check these addresses, we cannot guarantee that changes have not been made, especially to telephone numbers and area codes. We would welcome any corrections.

Telephone area codes
The international dialling code (IDD) for Liberia is +231, followed by subscriber's number.

Chambers of Commerce
Liberia Chamber of Commerce, Capitol Hill, PO Box 92, Monrovia (tel: 223-738).

Banking
Liberian Bank for Development and Investment (LBDI), Corner of Randall and Ashmun Streets, PO Box 547, Monrovia (tel: 227-140; fax: 226-939).

International Bank (Liberia) Limited; 64 Broad Street, Monrovia (tel: 227-438; fax: 226-092/3).

Liberian Trading and Development Bank Ltd, PO Box 293, Tradevco Building, Ashmun Street, 1000 Monrovia 10 (tel: 226-072, 226-074; fax: 226-471).

Central bank
Central Bank of Liberia; PO Box 2048, Warren and Carey Streets, Monrovia (tel: 227-928; fax: 226-144).

Travel information
Air Liberia, PO Box 2076, Monrovia (tel: 222-144, 226-404).

Ministries
Ministry of Commerce, Industry, PO Box 10-9041, 1000 Monrovia 10 (tel: 226-283).

Ministry of Finance, Bureau of Customs and Excise, PO Box 10-9013, 1000 Monrovia 10.

Ministry of Foreign Affairs, PO Box 10-9002, 1000 Monrovia 10 (tel: 226-763, 221-029, 221-751).

Ministry of Information, Culture and Tourism, PO Box 10-9021, Capitol Hill, 1000 Monrovia 10 (tel: 226-045, 226-269, 227-349; fax: 226-045).

Ministry of Justice, Bureau of Immigration, PO Box 10-9006, Broad Street, 1000 Monrovia 10.

Ministry of Lands, Mines and Energy, PO Box 10-9024, 1000 Monrovia 10 (tel: 226-281, 221-580, 221-488, 221-460).

Ministry of Planning and Economic Affairs, PO Box 10-9016, 1000 Monrovia 10 (tel: 226-962, 227-987, 222-121, 222-331, 223-208, 221-971).

Ministry of Information, Cultural Affairs and Tourism, PO Box 10-9021, UN Drive, 1000 Monrovia 10 (tel/fax: 226-078).

Ministry of Youth and Sports, PO Box 10-9040, 1000 Monrovia 10 (tel: 226-284).

Other useful addresses
Commonwealth Development Corporation, PO Box 2015, Monrovia.

ELTV (Liberian television system), PO Box 594, Monrovia.

Liberian Development Corporation, PO Box 9043, Monrovia.

Liberian Embassy (USA), 5201 16th Street, NW, Washington DC 20011 (tel: 202-723-0437; fax: 202-723-0436; e-mail: info@liberiaemb.org).

Liberian News Agency (LINA), Ministry of Information, PO Box 9021, Capitol Hill, Monrovia (tel: 222-229).

National Investment Commission, PO Box 10-9043, 1000 Monrovia 10 (tel: 226-685, 226-575).

National Ports Authority, PO Box 14, Monrovia.

Statistics Bureau, PO Box 9016, Monrovia (tel: 222-622).

Internet sites
Africa Business Network: http://www.ifc.org/abn

African Development Bank: http://www.afdb.org

Africa Online: http://www.africaonline.com

AllAfrica.com: http://allafrica.com

Harambee Afrika (UK business club for traders with east, central and southern Africa; includes annotated web resource list): http://www.harambee.co.uk

Mbendi AfroPaedia (information on companies, countries, industries and stock exchanges in Africa): http://mbendi.co.za

Libya

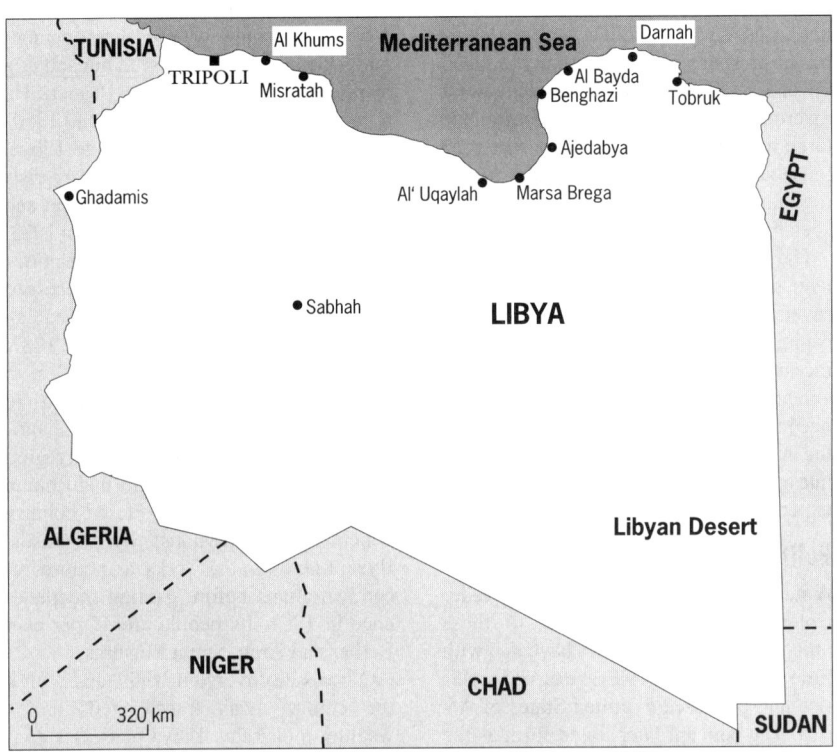

KEY FACTS

Official name: Al Jamahiriya al Arabiya al Libiya ash Shabiya al Ishtirakiya al Uzma (The Great Socialist People's Libyan Arab Jamahiriya)

Head of State: Leader of First of September Revolution, Colonel Muammar al Qadafi

Head of government: Secretary General of the General People's Committee, Shokri Ghanem (from 14 Jun 2003)

Ruling party: There are no official political parties

Area: 1,775,500 square km

Population: 5.81 million (2004)

Capital: Tripoli

Official language: Arabic

Currency: Libyan dinar (LD) = 1,000 dirhams

Exchange rate: LD1.33 per US$ (Oct 2005) (In 2003, Libya unified its exchange rate system which comprised official, commercial and black-market rates; this amounted to a devaluation of the dinar.)

GDP per capita: US$5,121 (2004)

GDP real growth: 0.90% (2004)

Labour force: 1.98 million (2004)

Unemployment: 30.00% (2004)

Inflation: -1.00% (2004)

Oil production: 1.61 million bpd (2004)

Balance of trade: US$11.43 billion (2004)

Foreign debt: US$4.07 billion (2004)

The Libyan economy depends primarily upon revenues from the oil sector, which contribute practically all export earnings and about one-quarter of GDP. These oil revenues and a small population give Libya one of the highest per capita GDPs in Africa, but little of this income flows down to the lower orders of society.

Economy

The economy remains largely state controlled. The country faces a long road ahead in liberalising the socialist-oriented economy, but initial steps – including applying for membership of the World Trade Organisation (WTO), reducing some subsidies, and announcing plans for privatisation – are laying the groundwork for a transition to a more market-based economy. The non-oil manufacturing and construction sectors, which account for about 20 per cent of gross domestic product (GDP), have expanded from processing mostly agricultural products to include the production of petrochemicals, iron, steel, and aluminum. Climatic conditions and poor soils severely limit agricultural output, and Libya imports about 75 per cent of its food.

Since the lifting of the UN and US Libya-specific trade sanctions in 2003 and 2004, the pace of economic and structural reforms has picked up somewhat, with the implementation of measures aimed at enhancing the role of the private sector in the economy. However, these reforms continue to be implemented in an ad hoc and non-transparent manner. To help attract investors, leader Colonel Muammar Abu Minyar al Qadafi has asked the United States to remove Libya from the list of countries alleged to sponsor terrorism. US oil firms have started investing in the country.

The fiscal stance continued to be expansionary in 2005, with a non-oil fiscal deficit widening to 36 per cent of GDP. However, reflecting higher hydrocarbon revenues, the overall consolidated surplus remained stable at about 10.5 per cent of

GDP. Non-oil revenue share of GDP declined by three per centage points as a result of widespread tax evasion and low efficiency in tax collection. While capital expenditures were compressed to make room for the payment of US$1.1 billion of the Lockerbie settlement, current expenditure, excluding the Lockerbie payment, remained high at 30 per cent of GDP.

The overall fiscal surplus is estimated to have reached about 19 per cent of GDP, with oil revenue estimated at 52.4 per cent of GDP. However, the non-oil revenue share is estimated to have declined by about one per centage point to 7 per cent of GDP, partly owing to reduced tax revenue in connection with the new tax law provisions.

Some progress has been made on the reform front. Measures taken include the adoption of laws to encourage domestic and foreign private investment, the adoption of a new tax law, the removal of customs duty exemptions enjoyed by public enterprises, the reduction in tariff rates, and the preparation of a new banking law that gives the Central Bank of Libya greater independence. A privatisation plan (not including the utilities, the oil and gas sector, and the air and maritime transportation sectors) has been initiated. It involves the sale of 360 economic units.

The Libyan government has withdrawn its participation in IMF's Heavily Indebted Poor Countries (HIPC) Initiative on grounds of insufficient political support for ratification. It is preparing its own debt relief plan.

The fiscal and external current account balances register large surpluses and international reserves have risen sharply. There is an increased effort to reform the economy through measures to encourage foreign investment, enhance the role of the private sector, and liberalise the exchange system and external trade.

Much remains to be done to transform Libya's economy into one that is market-based and Libya's large fiscal surpluses present a good opportunity to speed up economic reforms while maintaining macroeconomic stability. To control the large non-oil deficit, the non-oil tax base must be strengthened, including by reducing tax exemptions and streamlining spending.

The substantial oil windfall projected over the medium term should be largely saved, or partly used to finance human capital investment and structural reform measures, including restructuring public enterprises and the civil service. There is a need to address the rigidities arising from the mechanical distribution of oil revenues between capital and current expenditures.

Politics

A staunch Arab nationalist, Libyan leader Colonel al Qadafi's attempts to forge unity with other Arab states have met with little success. In the 1990s he turned to Africa and proposed a United States of Africa. The concept later found form as the African Union, replacing the by then somewhat tarnished Organisation of African Unity.

From the earliest days of his rule following his 1969 military coup, Colonel al Qadafi has held absolute power. He espouses his own political system, the Third Universal Theory. This is a combination of socialism and Islam derived in part from tribal practices and is supposed to be implemented by the Libyan people themselves in a unique form of 'direct democracy'. Qadafi has always seen himself as a revolutionary and visionary leader. He used oil funds during the 1970s and 1980s to promote his ideology outside Libya, supporting subversives and terrorists abroad to hasten the end of Marxism and capitalism. In addition, beginning in 1973, he engaged in military operations in northern Chad's Aozou Strip – to gain access to minerals and to gain influence in Chadian politics – but was forced to retreat in 1987. Libya claims more than 32,000sq km in south-eastern Algeria and 25,000sq km in Niger in currently dormant disputes; various Chadian rebels from the Aozou region reside in southern Libya. A former Roman colony, Libya is a mostly desert country which saw invasions by Vandals, Byzantines, Arabs, Turks and more recently Italians before gaining independence in 1951. Its people are 97 per cent Berber and Arab, Sunni Muslims.

Oil was discovered in 1959, and with it the country was transformed into a wealthy monarchy. Libya possesses considerable reserves of oil and gas. Ten years later the king was overthrown in a coup led by the 27-year-old Qadafi, and the country embarked on a radically new chapter in its history. Over the years he has supported a broad range of militant groups, including the Irish Republican Army and the Palestine Liberation Organisation. His son Sayf al Islam Qadafi is said to be behind the drive to break Libya's isolation. Sayf has denied reports that he is being groomed to succeed his father.

Risk assessment

Economic	Improving
Political	Improving
Regional stability	Uncertain

COUNTRY PROFILE

Historical profile
Libya's coastal plain has hosted permanent settlements since at least 8000BC. Berber tribes began to migrate to the area in 3000BC. The people of what is now Libya came under the influence of several empires, including the Egyptian Pharaohs,

KEY INDICATORS — Libya

	Unit	2000	2001	2002	2003	2004
Population	m	5.24	5.34	5.44	5.63	5.81
Gross domestic product (GDP)	US$bn	39.20	27.50	16.88	14.53	*29.12
GDP per capita	US$	6,939	5,082	3,015	2,583	5,121
GDP real growth	%	6.5	3.1	1.7	3.3	0.9
Inflation	%	-2.9	-8.8	-9.9	-2.1	-1.0
Oil output	'000 bpd	1,475.0	1,425.0	1,376.0	1,488.0	1,607.0
Natural gas output	bn cum	5.5	5.4	5.7	6.4	7.0
Exports (fob) (goods)	US$m	13,900.0	13,100.0	11,700.0	14,527.0	18,650.0
Imports (fob) (goods)	US$m	7,600.0	8,700.0	4,200.0	6,663.0	7,224.0
Balance of trade	US$m	6,300.0	4,400.0	7,500.0	7,864.0	11,426.0
Current account	US$m	7,750.0	3,680.0	*120.0	3,640.0	7,450.0
Total reserves minus gold	US$m	12,461.0	14,800.0	14,307.0	19,584.0	25,689.0
Foreign exchange	US$m	11,408.0	13,749.0	13,159.0	18,310.0	24,336.0
Exchange rate	per US$	0.51	0.59	1.27	1.27	1.27

* estimated figure

the Phoenicians, the Greeks, the Romans, the Byzantines and the Ottomans, and in recent times, the Italians. Colonel Muammar al Qadafi, who seized power in 1969, exercises absolute authority in his role as Leader of the First of September Revolution. Libya, which was isolated by much of the international community over the 1988 bombing of a PanAm flight over Lockerbie in Scotland, formally took responsibility for the incident in 2003, and relations with the West were further improved when Libya later renounced weapons of mass destruction (WMD).

1510 During the struggle between Hapsburg Spain and the Ottoman Turks for supremacy in the Mediterranean, Spanish forces captured and largely destroyed Tripoli.

1524 Tripoli was entrusted to the Knights of St John of Malta.

1551 The Knights were driven out of Tripolitania by the Turks who began consolidating their control over the Maghreb region. The three provinces of Tripolitania, Cyrenaica and Fezzan were joined into one regency in Tripoli by the Ottomans.

1711–1835 Although nominally part of the Ottoman empire, the Turks in effect gave way to the local Karamanli dynasty until 1835, when the Turks strengthened their control again. The local rulers levied a toll on every Christian fleet using the Mediterranean.

1870–1911 The area was dominated by the Sanusi religious order, although the Turks and the Italians continued to invade periodically.

1911–42 By the time of the First World War in 1914, an Italian force had taken control of the coastal towns. After the War, Italy captured the Libyan nationalist hero, Omar Mukhtar, hanging him in 1931. Italy introduced an Italianisation programme.

Italy's colonisation of Libya ended when the Italians and Germans lost the war in the Western Desert. The British took over Tripolitania and Cyrenaica and the French took over the Fezzan.

1951 Libya was granted independence under King Idris (originally Mohammed Idris al Sanusi, a member of the Sanusi religious order).

1955 Oil exploration started.

1959 Oil was discovered.

1961 King Idris opened a 167km pipeline, which linked important oil fields in the interior to the Mediterranean Sea, making it possible for Libya to export oil.

1969 As pan-Arabism swept the Arab world, Colonel Muammar al Qadafi seized power as Leader of the Revolution. Most economic activities were nationalised, including the oil industry.

1970 The government closed the British airbase in Tobruk and the US Air Force base in Tripoli. Property belonging to Italian settlers was nationalised.

1971 The Federation of Arab Republics (FAR), comprising Libya, Egypt and Syria, was approved by national referendum, but was never realised.

1972 Libya and Egypt agreed to merge into a single state; the plans were abandoned.

1973 Qadafi announced a cultural revolution in which people's committees were established throughout the country. Libyan forces invaded the Aozou Strip in northern Chad.

1974 A plan to unify Libya and Tunisia was agreed, but never implemented.

1977 Qadafi set up the General People's Congress (GPC) and the country was renamed the Great Socialist People's Libyan Arab Jamahiriya.

1980 An agreement to merge Libya and Syria was made, but failed to materialise.

1981 The US shot down two Libyan aircraft which challenged its warplanes over the Gulf of Sirte, claimed by Libya as its territorial waters.

1984 Police Constable Yvonne Fletcher was killed during demonstrations outside the Libyan embassy in London. The UK suspended diplomatic relations with Libya.

1986 In an unsuccessful attempt to bring down the Qadafi regime, the US launched a major airstrike on Tripoli, causing substantial damage. The US claimed its raids were in response to an alleged Libyan involvement in the bombing of a nightclub in Berlin, which was used by US military personnel. The US imposed economic sanctions against Libya.

1988 Libyan terrorists were blamed for the bomb which destroyed a Pan Am passenger aircraft over Lockerbie in Scotland.

1989 Algeria, Libya, Mauritania, Morocco and Tunisia formed the Arab Maghreb Union.

1992 UN sanctions were imposed on Libya for refusing to hand over two men suspected of the Lockerbie bombing.

1994 Libya returned the Aozou Strip to Chad.

1995 Qadafi ordered the expulsion of 30,000 Palestinians in protest at the Oslo accords signed by the Israeli government and the Palestine Liberation Organisation (PLO).

1999 UN and EU sanctions were suspended after Libya agreed to arrest and extradite Lockerbie bombing suspects. The UK re-established diplomatic links with Libya.

2000 Qadafi visited Arab states in North Africa and the Middle East, seeking to promote Arab co-operation. Libya was one of the key signatories to the creation of the African Union (AU).

2001 Abdelbaset Ali Mohmed al Megrahi, a Libyan intelligence agent, was found guilty of the Lockerbie bombing in a Scottish court based in The Netherlands, while his co-accused, al Amin Khalifa Fhimah, was acquitted. The US imposed a five-year extension to sanctions against Libya.

2002 Megrahi's appeal failed and he was sentenced to life imprisonment in a Scottish jail.

2003 Libya was chosen to chair the UN Human Rights Commission. The Libyan government and lawyers representing families of Lockerbie bombing victims signed a compensation agreement worth US$2.7 billion. Libya formally took responsibility for the bombing before the UN Security Council. The UN Security Council voted to lift the 11-year-old sanctions against Libya (already suspended). Libya announced that it would abandon its programmes to develop weapons of mass destruction (WMD).

2004 Libya agreed to compensate families of victims of the 1989 bombing of a French passenger aircraft and to pay US$35 million to victims of the bombing of a Berlin nightclub in 1986. The UK prime minister, Tony Blair, met Colonel al Qadafi, the first visit of this kind since 1943. UN sanctions were finally lifted in February, and in April, US President Bush eased sanctions against Libya as a reward for giving up WMD. On 29 June, the US and Libya restored diplomatic relations after a break of 24 years, and US economic sanctions were lifted in September. President Chirac of France visited Libya, the first visit by a French president since 1951.

2005 Libya officially opened to tourism on 26 February. By October leases on 26 oil fields had been allocated to foreign companies.

Political structure
Constitution
Libya has no constitution. In 2000, 14 ministries were abolished and their powers devolved to provincial committees or other bodies.

Form of state
Jamahiriya, or state of the masses.

The executive
Libya has no official head of state, but Colonel Muammar al Qadafi exercises absolute authority in his role as Leader of the First of September Revolution. Federal executive power is exercised by the General People's Committee (GPC) (council of ministers). The Secretary General of the GPC is a post broadly equivalent to that of prime minister.

National legislature
Political power is vested in the General People's Congress (GPC).

Libya is officially run by popular committees and congresses. Each sends delegates to the GPC, which approves laws and sets policy guidelines. There are 300 congresses, each having an executive popular committee, which can effectively take some decisions at a local level.

Legal system
The Libyan legal system is based on *Sharia* (Islamic law) and the Italian civil law system. There are separate religious courts and no constitutional provision for judicial review of legislative acts. The judicial system consists of the Supreme Court, courts of appeal, courts of first instance and summary courts. Libya has not accepted compulsory International Court of Justice (ICJ) jurisdiction.

Political parties
Ruling party
There are no official political parties
Main opposition party
The two most active internal opposition movements are the Islamic Liberation Party and the Muslim Brotherhood. The main exiled opposition is the US-based National Front for the Salvation of Libya (NFSL).

Population
5.81 million (2004)
Ethnic make-up
Berber-Arab (97 per cent). There are small communities of Greeks, Maltese, Italians, Egyptians, Pakistanis, Turks, Indians and Tunisians.
Religions
Sunni Muslim (97 per cent). A third of Libya's Muslims are affiliated to the Sanusi religious sect, which had fought against European colonialism in the first half of the twentieth century.

Education
Libya has paid particular attention to its education system, with the aim of reducing illiteracy and improving the education available to women.
Education is free for all children during the compulsory years. Secondary schooling begins at aged 15 and the curriculum is divided into three- or four-year courses and comprises a number of secondary school types including both academic and specialised or vocational centres. English and Arabic are the main languages for instruction.
Higher education is offered in 14 universities and 54 higher vocational institutes.
Literacy rate: 81.7 per cent total, 70.7 per cent female; adult rates (World Bank 2004).
Compulsory years: 6 to 15.

Health
Total expenditure on health is around 3 per cent of GDP; private, out-of-pocket expenditure on health as a percentage of total spending on health is some 56 per cent.
The government provides free health services to all its citizens. UN sanctions had a detrimental impact on the quality and access to healthcare provision and many medical services and pharmaceutical products became unavailable. With the lifting of sanctions in 2004, it is expected that these shortcomings will be overcome quickly. Many Libyans have typically sort medical treatment in Tunisia, Egypt or in Western Europe. There are two large hospitals in Tripoli and Benghazi.
HIV prevalence: 0.3 per cent aged 15–49 in 2003 (World Bank)
Life expectancy: 72.7 years (World Bank)
Fertility rate/Maternal mortality rate: 3.3 births per woman (2003); maternal mortality 0.75 per 1,000 live births (World Bank).
Infant mortality rate: 13 per 1,000 live births; 5 per cent of children aged under five are malnourished (World Bank).
Head of population per physician/bed: 1.3 physicians and 4.3 hospital beds typically available per 1,000 people.

Welfare
The government is theoretically committed to full provision of welfare services to all Libyan nationals. In reality, parts of the population are often not covered by welfare provisions. The most common welfare benefit is housing to those in need. The government provides a national social security system covering pensions and other social insurance, but the availability of such services regularly depends on annual oil receipts, which make up a large proportion of total government revenues.

Main cities
Tripoli (capital, estimated population 1.3 million in 2004), Benghazi (734,900), Al-Khums (Homs) (195,000), Misratah (Misurata) (175,200), Al-Marj (164,700), Tobruk (152,200).

Languages spoken
Italian and English are spoken and there are also pockets of native Berber speakers.
Official language/s
Arabic

Media
Press
Newspapers and periodicals are published by the official Jamahiriya News Agency (Jana) and Trades Unions. The main newspapers are *Al-Fajr Al-Jahid* and *Shu'un Libiyah*. A number of weekly, fortnightly, monthly and occasional periodicals are also produced. These include *Al Sidra Magazine*, *Ath-Thaqafa Al-Arabiya (Arab Culture)*, *Ad-Daawa Al-Islamia (Islamic Call)* and the monthly *Risala Al-Jihad (Holy War Letter)* in Arabic, English and French.
Broadcasting
The broadcast media is controlled by the state-owned Great Socialist People's Libyan Arab Jamahiriya Broadcasting Corporation.
Radio: Programmes are broadcast in Arabic and English from Tripoli and Benghazi.
Television: The television service broadcasts in Arabic, but there are also channels which broadcast in Italian, English and French.

Economy
Libya's economy depends heavily on revenues from its oil sector which provided 52.4 per cent of GDP in 2004. With rising oil prices since 1999, and the further steep increase in 2005, export revenues have given Libya a fiscal surplus of 19 per cent of GDP and a deflation rate of -1 per cent.
Libya has, since late 2003 and the lifting of UN trade sanctions imposed in response to Libya's refusal to hand over two security agents suspected of the Lockerbie bombing of 1988, begun structural reforms to enhance the role of the private sector. The IMF has advised that the expansionary fiscal stance adopted should be maintained, although such reforms are being implemented in an informal and non-transparent manner. Reform measures in financial and banking matters have included increased banking supervision. The Central Bank of Libya was given greater freedom to conduct monetary policies, such as bank-lending rates reduced to encourage private sector demand and the modernisation of the payment system. New laws have been introduced to provide for domestic and foreign investment, plus a new tax law and the removal of customs duty exemptions. However, non-oil revenue in 2004 declined by 3 per cent of GDP due to widespread tax evasion and weak tax collection.
The government has sold 42 small entities with another 360 due to be privatised, although utilities and the oil and gas sectors will be exempt from these sales.
Import restrictions and inefficient resource allocations have led to periodic shortages of basic goods and foodstuffs. The non-oil manufacturing and construction sectors, which account for about 20 per cent of GDP, have expanded from processing mostly agricultural products to include the production of petrochemicals, iron, steel, and aluminium. Climatic conditions and poor soils severely limit agricultural output, and Libya imports about 75 per cent of its food requirements.
In the short- to medium-term, the economy can rely on the hydrocarbon sector to

achieve economic growth. The country offers vast potential, with only 25 per cent of the land area offered for exploration in 2004–05.

Libya has indicated a desire to attract US$10 billion worth of foreign direct investment (FDI) in the hydrocarbon sector by 2010.

Libya needs to produce more water and to reduce its dependence on food imports. Phase 3 of the Great Man-Made River (GMR) project to bring water from underground aquifers beneath the Sahara to the Mediterranean coastal areas is scheduled for expansion in early 2006.

External trade
Libya has pioneered economic integration, actively encouraging the free movement of labour and capital among African states, particularly with the formation of the African Union (AU). It is a member of the Arab Maghreb Union (AMU) with Algeria, Mauritania, Morocco and Tunisia. The easing of tensions between Algeria and Morocco has enabled these countries to consider further regional integration.

Imports
Goods imported include machinery, transport equipment, semi-finished goods, food and consumer products.

Main sources: Italy (28.2 per cent total, 2004), Germany (11.1 per cent), Tunisia (6.0 per cent), UK (5.8 per cent), Turkey (5.0 per cent), France (4.1 per cent)

Exports
Crude oil accounts for 95 per cent, refined petroleum products and natural gas.

Main destinations: Italy (37.7 per cent total, 2004), Germany (16.7 per cent), Spain (11.6 per cent), Turkey (7.5 per cent), France (6.5 per cent)

Agriculture
Farming
Agriculture is estimated to account for 5 per cent of GDP and to employ 18 per cent of the labour force.

The cultivated land is only 1.2 per cent of the total land area and over 80 per cent of all agricultural production is concentrated around oases and the northern coastal regions, especially near Benghazi and Tripoli. Less than 1 per cent of land is irrigated.

Climatic conditions and irrigation problems limit output. Over 70 per cent of food requirements are imported. Libya is self-sufficient in fruit and vegetables, dairy products and poultry. The main crops are potatoes, wheat, barley, dates, tomatoes, almonds, oats, olives, citrus fruits and groundnuts.

The huge Great Man-Made River (GMR) phased project delivers 3.68 million cubic metres of water from underground reservoirs in the Sahara to Libya's main cities and 135,000 hectares of cultivable land. Further phases for the expansion of the system were under construction by 2005 and expected to be completed within 41 months.

The estimated crop production in 2004 included: 213,465 tonnes (t) cereals in total, 125,000t wheat, 195,000t potatoes, 190,000t tomatoes, 80,000t barley, 19,375t pulses, 25,000t treenuts, 150,000t dates, 71,350t citrus fruit, 30,000t grapes, 46,500t oilcrops, 180,000t olives, 345,700t fruit in total, 869,900t vegetables in total. Estimated livestock production included: 142,170t meat in total, 6,300t beef, 27,370t lamb, 6,000t goat meat, 3,700t camel meat, 98,800t poultry, 60,000t eggs, 203,408t milk, 800t honey, 5,635t sheepskins, 9,487t greasy wool.

Fishing
The total annual catch is typically 33,000 tonnes, of which up to 6,000 tonnes are exported with a total value of between US$15–30 million. Most of the catch is taken by artisanal boats with nets or hooks. There is negligible freshwater fishing, although the government has attempted to stock reservoirs with fish. Libya has a number of fish canning plants, which can tuna and sardines. Fishmeal is also produced.

Small quantities of fish are exported to Greece, Malta and Tunisia. There is a tuna cannery at Zanzur, and sardine canneries at Zuara and Khoms.

Forestry
Libya is very lightly forested, with less than 1 per cent of total land area covered by forest and woodland, from which small quantities of sawn timber and paper are produced. The majority of domestic demand for industrial wood products is met by imports. Experiments have been undertaken into tree planting, to halt the advance of the desert, but with mixed success; there has been some development of orchards.

Industry and manufacturing
The industrial sector is estimated to contribute 18 per cent to GDP and to employ 15 per cent of the workforce. Virtually all industry was state-owned until the privatisation of state entities – excluding utilities and the gas and oil sectors – began in 2004.

Traditionally the industrial sector was limited to small-scale processing operations, mostly in food, wood and paper, textiles and soap. However, traditional small-scale agri-allied industries have given way to the growth of import substitution industries (such as building materials manufacture) and heavy industries (such as petrochemicals, iron and steel, concrete pipes and vehicle assembly). The National Petrochemicals Company (Napectco) has built up a substantial petrochemicals capacity since the late 1970s using local feedstock. The large Marsa Brega complex is owned by Napectco which hosts a number of plants producing petrochemicals, ethanol, ammonia and urea. Much industrial investment has gone into expanding capital intensive chemicals capacity as a means of increasing the value added content of exports.

Major metal smelting projects have been impeded by low incomes and depressed world prices in recent years. Other constraints to development are insufficiently trained Libyan manpower and the small domestic market.

Tourism
After the rapprochement with the West achieved in 2003 and the lifting of US sanctions in February 2004, Libya officially opened to tourism on 26 February 2005.

Travel sanctions and political isolation was an obstacle to the revival of Libya's tourism sector. Its tourist infrastructure was neglected for many years and, while new resort and hotel projects have been initiated, more investment is needed to upgrade old resources. The Mediterranean beaches and ancient historical sites, together with its proximity to Europe and other developed North African tourist destinations, provide the country with good potential for expanding visitor numbers. Capital investment in travel and tourism is expected to reach US$1.2 billion or 31.2 per cent of total capital investment, and the sector's share of GDP is growing, from a low 1–2 per cent of GDP in 2004 to an estimated 3.2 per cent in 2005.

Mining
Major mineral deposits include iron ore (which supplies the steel complex at Misurata), potassium, magnesium, sulphur, gypsum and phosphate. There are also potential uranium deposits. Commercial exploitation of minerals is restricted by high development costs.

Salt and construction materials are produced, but large reserves of iron ore at Wadi Shatti remain undeveloped, although this is being reconsidered.

Hydrocarbons
Libya is Africa's third-largest oil producer after Nigeria and Algeria, it is ninth in the world and is one of Europe's biggest African suppliers. Italy, Germany, Spain and France are the main export markets. However, the oil fields operated by the government are estimated to be undergoing a natural 8 per cent per annum production decline. This has made Libya increasingly reliant on foreign companies and their skilled workers.

Proven oil reserves stood at 39.1 billion barrels in 2004, or approximately 3.3 per cent of the world's total reserves. Production was around 1.6 million barrels per day (bpd) in 2004 of which 1.34 million bpd are exported; there are plans for production to increase to two million bpd by 2010 and three million bpd by 2015.

In 2005, the Libyan government sold, by competition, rights to 26 oil fields to various international companies. An initial US$103 million for the leases will be followed by a percentage of the production of recovered oil.

Libya has three domestic refineries, with a combined capacity of approximately 343,000bpd, nearly twice the volume of domestic oil consumption.

Libya's gas reserves were estimated at 1.49 trillion cubic metres (cum) in 2004. Annual gas production was 7.0 billion cum in 2004. Further expansion in gas production remains a high priority for the authorities. The government appears to favour more gas consumption domestically, which could in turn make more oil available for exports. Moreover, with the increasing attractiveness of gas as a source of fuel, Libya's vast gas reserves are widely seen as a major export commodity to European countries.

Libya does not produce coal.

Energy
Electricity production capacity is 4.6GW with an added 3.3GW for peak periods. The vast majority of electricity is provided by oil-fired power plants.

Power demand is growing rapidly at 6–8 per cent per annum. The government hopes to double generating capacity by 2020.

Several plans to add generating stations and upgrade and extend the supply system have all been hampered by funding problems encountered by the state power supplier General Electricity Company (GECOL).

Banking and insurance
Libya's banking sector was in the early stages of privatisation in 2005. Initially five, state-owned, banks will have 50 per cent of their stock offered to foreign banks that may participate as minority shareholders, although being allowed to influence management. Foreign banks will also be permitted to begin retail operations in Libya.

Central bank
Central Bank of Libya

Main financial centre
Tripoli

Time
GMT plus one hour (GMT plus two hours April–September).

Geography
Libya is the fourth-largest country in Africa. It extends along the Mediterranean coast of North Africa with Tunisia and Algeria to the west, Niger and Chad to the south, Egypt to the east, and Sudan to the south-east. Most of the country is part of the Sahara Desert. Only the narrow coastal strip receives sufficient rainfall to be suitable for agriculture and it is here that 90 per cent of the population live.

Climate
The coastal areas enjoy a temperate Mediterranean climate. Summer (May–September) temperatures are up to 40 degrees Celsius (C), while winter (November–April) temperatures reach 25–32 degrees C during daytime but can fall to 4–5 degrees C at night. Otherwise, with 90 per cent of the country desert, very hot days (to 50 degrees C), cold nights and sandstorms are likely in May–June. There is low rainfall, mainly between October and March in the highlands and semi-desert.

Dress codes
A lightweight suit or jacket and trousers are advised. A tie and a long-sleeved shirt should be worn at business meetings, but a jacket is not essential. Women should dress modestly, covering their arms and knees.

Entry requirements
Passports
Required by all.
Restrictions on US passport holders were lifted in February 2004.

Visa
Required by all and valid for three months. Exceptions granted for citizens of most Middle East Arab, and a few other, states. For further information contact the nearest Libyan consulate. All documentation must have Arab translations.
Business visitors should be sponsored by a Libyan company which will organise the issue of a business visa. Nevertheless travellers on a business visa will be refused entry if they do not possess at least US$500, or the equivalent, for living expenses.

Prohibited entry
Nationals of Israel and passport holders with Israeli visas.

Currency advice/regulations
Passengers arriving in Tripoli are required to have a minimum of US$500 (this amount can change, so it is advisable to check). This requirement is subject to a border check and the passenger faces possible deportation if the requirement is not met. Import of foreign currency is subject to declaration while export of foreign currency is limited. All currency must be declared.

Traveller's cheques are often hard to cash. Carrying cash is the only realistic option, and the favoured currency is the US dollar. Penalties for the use of unauthorised currency dealers are severe.

Customs
There are strict customs regulations about the import or export of firearms, religious materials, antiquities and medications.

Prohibited imports
Alcohol, pork and certain other items that may be considered offensive; for clarification contact the nearest embassy.

Health (for visitors)
The hospital with the best reputation is the Oil Clinique-NOC.

Mandatory precautions
Yellow fever and cholera vaccination certificates are required if travelling from infected areas.

Advisable precautions
Visitors should have typhoid and polio vaccinations. Malaria prophylaxis is recommended for visits to certain areas. Avoid drinking tap water.
It is advisable to pack necessary medication as some medicines may not be available in Libya.

Hotels
Limited availability and usually expensive.

Credit cards
Credit cards are not accepted.

Public holidays
Fixed dates
3 Mar (Declaration of the People's Authority Day), 11 Jun (Evacuation Day), 1 Sep (Revolution Day), 26 Oct (Day of Mourning).

Variable dates
Eid al Adha, Eid al Fitr.
The Islamic year contains 354 or 355 days, with the result that Muslim feasts advance by 10–12 days against the Gregorian calendar. Dates of feasts vary according to the sighting of the new moon, so cannot be forecast exactly.

Working hours
Friday is the Muslim holy day and all offices, businesses and banks are closed. The oil industry is also closed on Saturday.

Banking
Mon, Wed and Sat: 0730–0800, 1230–1300 and about 1500–1700; Fri: closed. Hours may vary between winter and summer and be reduced during Ramadan.

Business
Sat–Thu: 0700–1400 summer, 0730–1430 winter.

Government
Sat–Thu: 0700–1400 summer, 0730–1430 winter.

Shops
Shops are mainly open 0800–1800, often closing for a few hours during the middle of the day.

Electricity supply
110 or 220V AC

Social customs/useful tips
Alcohol is banned throughout Libya and visitors arriving with alcohol will have it confiscated. Women often do not attend Arab social or business meetings, despite gender equality enshrined in the constitution.

Photography of public buildings and anything of military or security interest is not permitted. It is best to avoid criticism of the country, its leadership or Islam while in Libya since this could potentially result in a heavy-handed response from the authorities.

During Ramadan, eating, drinking and smoking in public is banned throughout the hours of daylight. Islamic and Arab customs prevail and must be respected by visitors. Pork is forbidden by Muslim law. Food is traditionally eaten with the right hand only.

Security
Crime is growing in Libya. The most common crimes are car theft and theft of items left in vehicles. Muggings have occurred on the beaches. Travel to remote areas is best undertaken in groups.

Getting there
Air
National airline: Jamahiriya Libyan Arab Airlines.
International airport/s: Benina International (BEN), 29km from Benghazi; Sebha (SEB), 11km from town; Tripoli International (TIP), 34km from city.
Airport tax: LD6 departure tax.

Surface
Road: There are entry points via Tunisia and Egypt by the main coast road, Algeria (via Sabhah and Ghat) and Niger and Chad (via Sabhah).
Water: There are ferry services from Malta to Tripoli. There also occasional services from Casablanca (Morocco) and Alexandria (Egypt).
Main port/s: Benghazi, Misratah, Marsa Brega and Tripoli (established as a free port in 1999). Libya aims to resuscitate its trading role using the free port as the nucleus for trade between Africa and Europe.

The air embargo led to an expansion of Libya's port facilities.

Getting about
National transport
Air: Travel between western and eastern provinces is generally by air. Libyan Arab Airlines operates a domestic service between main centres.
Road: There is a surfaced road system comprising an estimated 32,000km linking all main centres. The main roads include the 1,820km national coast road from the Tunisian to the Egyptian border; Sabhah-Ghat; Tripoli-Sabhah; Agedabia-Kufra; Sabhah-Chad and Niger borders. The maintenance of rural roads is generally poor and many are unpaved.
Buses: There are services between main centres.
Rail: There has been no railway in operation since 1965 when the network was broken-up. There are plans to construct a new east-west railway line from the Tunisian border to Tripoli, extending it along the coast to Misratah and then on to Egypt via Tobrok. Another railway line is planned to run north-south from Misratah to Sabhah, and then on to Chad, however these projects are still little beyond their planning stages and may take several years before fruition. Meanwhile Libya has let contracts with private foreign companies to supply crossing and pointwork for the proposed east-west line.

City transport
Taxis: Yellow government taxis are generally cheaper than private taxis. It is advisable to negotiate the fare in advance. Taxis are often on a shared basis.
Buses, trams & metro: State-run bus services operate in Benghazi and Tripoli. They can be unreliable and overcrowded.

Car hire
There are car hire agencies in Tripoli and Benghazi, although rates can be quite high.

BUSINESS DIRECTORY
The addresses listed below are a selection only. While World of Information makes every endeavour to check these addresses, we cannot guarantee that changes have not been made, especially to telephone numbers and area codes. We would welcome any corrections.

Telephone area codes
The international direct dialling code (IDD) for Libya is +218, followed by area code and subscriber's number:

Benghazi	61	Tobruk	87
Misratah	51	Tripoli	21

Chambers of Commerce
Benghazi Chamber of Commerce, Trade, Industry and Agriculture, Issabri Street, PO Box 208, Benghazi (tel: 80-971; fax: 80-761; e-mail: benghaziccia@netscape.net).

Misurata Chamber of Commerce, Trade, Industry and Agriculture, Souweihli Street, PO Box 84, Misurata (tel: 616-497; fax: 620-340; e-mail: info@ccimisrata.org).

Tobruk Chamber of Commerce, Industry and Agriculture, Alfadel Abu Omar Street, PO Box 868, Tobruk (tel/fax: 24-835).

Tripoli Chamber of Commerce, Trade, Industry and Agriculture, 6 Najd Street, PO Box 2321, Tripoli (tel: 333-6855; fax: 333-2655).

Union of Chambers of Commerce, Trade, Industry and Agriculture, PO Box 12556, 26 Bandong Street, Tripoli (tel: 444-1613; fax: 444-1457; e-mail:unionchamber@hotmail.com).

Banking
Libyan Arab Foreign Bank, PO Box 2542, That al-Imad Administrative Complex, Tripoli (tel: 335-0155, 335-0160, 335-0086/7; fax: 335-0164/8).

Sahara Bank, PO Box 270, 10 First of September Street, Tripoli (tel: 333-9804; fax: 333-7922).

Wahda Bank, PO Box 452, Sharia Gamal Abd an-Naser, Benghazi (tel: 222-4122; fax: 222-4122, 222-4709).

Umma Bank Sal, PO Box 685, 1 Giaddat Omar El-Mokhtar Street, Tripoli (tel: 333-4031/35, 444-2541, 444-2544; fax: 333-2505, 444-2476).

Central bank
Central Bank of Libya, PO Box 1103, Tripoli (tel: 333-3591; fax: 444-1488; e-mail: info@cbl-ly.com).

Other useful addresses
General National Organisation for Industrialisation, PO Box 4388, Tripoli (tel: 44-680, 34-995).

Kufrah & Serir Authority, Council of Agricultural Development, Benghazi.

National Oil Corporation, PO Box 2655, Tripoli (tel: 46-180).

National Trade Union Federation, PO Box 734, Tripoli.

Internet sites
Qadafi's official website:
http://www.algathafi.org

Africa Business Network:
http://www.ifc.org/abn

African Development Bank:
http://www.afdb.org

Africa Online:
http://www.africaonline.com

AllAfrica.com: http://allafrica.com

Libya on the Web:
http://www.libyaweb.com/news.htm

Libyans Online:
http://www.libyaonline.com

Libyan Mission at United Nations:
http://www.un.int/libya/

Azar Libya Travel and Tour Company:
http://www.angelfire.com/az/azartours/index.html

Liechtenstein

KEY FACTS

Official name: Fürstentum Liechtenstein (The Principality of Liechtenstein)

Head of State: Prince Hans-Adam II (since 1989; on 15 Aug 2004, he handed over day-to-day responsibility for running the county to his son, Prince Alois, while remaining head of state)

Head of government: Prime Minister Otmar Hasler (FBP) (since Apr 2001)

Ruling party: Fortschrittliche Bürgerpartei (FBP) (Progressive Citizens' Party) (since Feb 2001; re-elected 13 Mar 2005)

Area: 160 square km

Population: 35,000 (2004)

Capital: Vaduz

Official language: German

Currency: Swiss franc (Swf) = 100 centimes/rappen (the euro also circulates informally)

Exchange rate: Swf1.29 per US$ (Oct 2005)

GDP per capita: US$25,000 (2004)*

Labour force: 29,000 (2004)*

Unemployment: 1.30% (2004)*

Inflation: 1.00% (2004)*

Balance of trade: US$1.55 billion (2003)

* estimated figure

COUNTRY PROFILE

Historical profile
Independence in 1719 was followed in the early nineteenth century by a period of French domination, then close connection with Austria until 1918.
1938–70 Fortschrittliche Bürgerpartei (FBP) (Progressive Citizens' Party) was the majority party in the coalition government.
1970–74 Vaterländische Union (VU) (Fatherland Union) was the majority party in coalition, followed by FBP in the 1974 elections.
1978 Liechtenstein was admitted to the Council of Europe. A VU-led coalition was formed.
1984 Prince Hans-Adam II took over executive power from his father. Women were granted the vote in national elections, but not in local elections.
1986 Women were allowed to vote in all elections.
1989 The VU gained a majority of one seat.
1993 FBP became the largest party
1997 The VU gained an outright majority, the first by any party for over 60 years, and Mario Frick became prime minster.
2001 FBP was elected and Otmar Hasler became prime minister.
2002 Liechtenstein concluded an agreement with Monaco over the prevention of money laundering and terrorist financing.
2003 Voters in a referendum held in March gave Prince Hans-Adam II more power, including the right to dismiss any government deemed incompetent. The vote followed a long-standing dispute between parliament and the monarch, who had threatened to leave the country if his constitutional reform proposals were not adopted.
2004 Liechtenstein adopted a new aubergine-coloured flag. On 15 August, Prince Hans-Adam II handed over day-to-day responsibility for running the country to his son, Prince Alois. Prince Hans-Adam II remains head of state. The International Court of Justice dismissed Liechtenstein's claim for compensation from Germany over a dispute over Germany's handling of assets in 1945.
2005 In parliamentary elections on 13 March, Otmar Hasler of the ruling Fortschrittliche Bürgerpartei (FBP) (Progressive Citizens' Party) was re-elected with 48.7 per cent of the vote (12 seats out of 25). The government will be in coalition with the Vaterländische Union (VU) (Fatherland Union) 38.2 per cent (10 seats). The Freie Liste (Free List) got 13 per cent (three seats). Turnout was 86.5 per cent.

Political structure
Constitution
The constitution dates from 1921.Voting rights for women on national issues were granted in 1984, and on local matters two years later.
In March 2003, a constitutional referendum gave Prince Hans-Adam II more political powers. Just over 64 per cent of voters were in favour of the changes. The referendum conferred on him the power to veto the decisions of parliament and to sack the government, and powers over the appointment of judges, but it took away his right to rule by emergency decree for an unlimited period and to nominate government officials.
Form of state
Absolute monarchy; following a referendum in March 2003, which gave Prince Hans-Adam II power to appoint and dismiss governments.
The executive
The head of state is the monarch. The March 2003 referendum conferred on the monarch the power to veto the decisions of parliament and to sack the government
National legislature
The constitution provides for a unicameral parliament (Landtag, 25 seats elected for a four-year term), which elects a five-member government, which is thereafter officially approved by the head of state. Elections are held every four years on the basis of proportional representation.
Legal system
The monarch appoints the country's judges.
Last elections
13 March 2005 (parliamentary); March 2003 (constitutional referendum).
Results: Parliamentary: the ruling FBP was re-elected with 48.7 per cent of the vote (12 seats out of 25), the VU 38.2 per cent (10), and the Freie Liste (Free List) 13 per cent (three). Turnout was 86.5 per cent.
Constitutional referendum: 64 per cent of voters were in favour of constitutional changes.

Liechtenstein

Next elections
2009 (parliamentary)

Political parties
Ruling party
Fortschrittliche Bürgerpartei (FBP) (Progressive Citizens' Party) (since Feb 2001; re-elected 13 Mar 2005)
Main opposition party
Vaterländische Union (VU) (Fatherland Union)
Political situation
Prince Hans-Adam II gave his country an ultimatum in March 2003, either agree to amend the 1921 constitution and make Liechtenstein an absolute monarchy, or he would remove himself and his billions to Austria; his subjects overwhelmingly agreed. As part of his powers the Prince has the right of veto over any parliamentary bills and the right to dismiss a government and govern alone.

The 45-country strong Council of Europe, of which Liechtenstein has been a member since 1978, considered this a potentially undemocratic move and sent a two-man inspection team. Although the team considered Liechtenstein should be monitored for long-term effects, this would have put the country on the same footing as Turkey, Azerbaijan and Armenia and so Liechtenstein mounted a strong lobbying campaign for acceptance of membership under an absolute monarchy, which succeeded by January 2004.

In August 2004 Prince Alois became his father's deputy, assuming the tasks, but not the power, of Head of State.

Population
35,000 (2004)
Ethnic make-up
Alemannic (87.5 per cent), Italian, Turkish and other (12.5 per cent).
Religions
Roman Catholic (80 per cent), Protestant (7.4 per cent).

Education
Primary education lasts for five years. Secondary education, starting at aged 12, is provided through three school types: *Oberschule, Realschule* and *Gymnasium*. Each is geared to the attainment outcomes expected of their students.

On completing four years (compulsory) secondary education, a lower secondary school certificate is awarded. *Realschule* students either undertake a one year technical or vocational course leading to specialised schools of further education, or an academic course to attain the lower level Matura Certificate. Students of the *Gymnasium* complete a four year academic course, attaining the higher grade Matura Certificate which is recognised for university entrance either at home or in Switzerland, Austria and Germany.

Compulsory years: Seven to 16.

Health
Life expectancy: 79 years
Infant mortality rate: 10 deaths per 1,000 live births.

Main cities
Vaduz (capital, estimated population 5,300 in 2003), Schaan (5,700), Triesen (4,700), Balzers (4,300).

Languages spoken
Allemannish – a dialect of German – is also spoken.
Official language/s
German

Media
Press
Dailies: Two main dailies include the *Liechtensteiner Vaterland* (Vaduz) and *Liechtensteiner Volksblatt* (Schaan).
Weeklies: *Liechtenstein News* is the official weekly newspaper, providing tourist and hotel information in the principality.
Broadcasting
Swiss, German and Austrian TV and radio broadcasts can be received (with commercials).
Advertising
There are no restrictions on newspaper advertising.

Economy
Liechtenstein has a highly industrialised, export-based economy with a well-developed banking sector. It ranks as one of the wealthiest countries per capita in the world. There is close economic interdependence with Switzerland through a customs and currency union. The tourism sector is an important earner of foreign exchange and the services sector also enjoyed rapid expansion during the latter part of the 1990s. Over half of the workforce is employed in the services and commerical industry while 40 per cent of GDP is generated by industry and manufacturing. 3,000 businesses are registered in Liechtenstein, which is equivalent to one business per 11 residents. There is an extremely high ratio of self-financing enjoyed by domestic businesses plus their ability, if necessary, to fall back on private wealth. A number of companies are research-focussed and are considered world leaders in their particular specialisms.

In 2000, the Organisation for Economic Co-operation and Development (OECD) named Liechtenstein as an unco-operative tax haven.

In June 2004, Switzerland, Andorra, Monaco, San Marino and Liechtenstein agreed to put in place equivalent measures to those to be applied by the EU's member states as regards the taxation of income from savings.

External trade
Financial services and tourism make significant contributions to balance of payments. Liechtenstein joined the European Economic Association (EEA) in 1995. Liechtenstein is also one of the four members of the European Free Trade Association (EFTA).
Imports
Imports of agricultural products, raw materials, machinery, metal goods, textiles, foodstuffs and vehicle.
Main sources: EU, Switzerland
Exports
There has been rapid growth in exports of small speciality machinery, connectors for audio and video, parts for motor vehicles, dental products, hardware, prepared foodstuffs, electronic equipment and optical products.

Overall exports are valued at 4.6 billion Swiss francs.
Main destinations: EU (62.6 per cent in total) – Germany (24.3 per cent) Austria (9.5 per cent), France (8.9 per cent), Italy (6.6 per cent), UK (4.6 per cent), US (18.9 per cent), Switzerland (15.7 per cent)

Agriculture
Farming
Agriculture is small-scale, employing only about 1.7 per cent of the population (350 workers). Activity is concentrated on dairy farming and farming of fodder cereals although vegetable cultivation and wine production are also undertaken. Utilising methods such as technical rationalisation and intensive cultivation, yields have been steadily increasing. Production typically includes 150 tonnes (t) grapes and 12,000t milk.

KEY INDICATORS — Liechtenstein

	Unit	2000	2001	2002	2003	2004
Population	m	0.03	0.03	0.03	0.03	0.04
Gross domestic product (GDP)	US$bn	1.06	1.07	1.09	0.82	*0.88
GDP per capita	US$	33,088	33,000	33,000	25,000	*25,000
Exchange rate	per US$	1.69	1.69	1.56	1.32	1.24

* estimated figure

Forestry
42 per cent of the principality is forested land. The forestry industry has grown since the late 1990s, doubling production to 22,167 cubic metres (cum) industrial roundwood and 18,000cum sawlogs and veneer logs by 2002, and maintaining production of 4,000cum fuel wood annually. 0.3 per cent of the agicultural sector are employed in forestry.

Industry and manufacturing
Industry and trade employs about 45 per cent of the workforce. Owing to lack of raw materials and a small domestic market, the sector is export-based and centred on specialised and high-technology production. Manufacturing is centred on machine building, precision engineering and metal working industries. There are also traditional industries such as chemicals (mainly pharmaceuticals), textiles, ceramics and food processing. The production of materials for dental medicine, of microsections for optics and electronics, the manufacture of preserves and deep-frozen products, upholstery, and varnishes, have all attained growing importance. Liechtenstein is the world's largest exporter of false teeth.

Tourism
Liechtenstein receives around 50,000 tourist arrivals each year, mainly from Germany and Switzerland. There has been a steady decline in number of arrivals, down from 78,000 in 1990 and 59,000 in 1995. In recent years stays in the towns have risen, while those in the mountains have fallen. The Prince's art collection includes over a thousand works including some by Van Dyck and Rubens. A portion of the £300 million collection is on display to the visiting public.

Hydrocarbons
Liechtenstein does not produce any hydrocarbons and relies entirely on imports, primarily from the EU. Liechtenstein imports around 90 per cent of its total energy needs. 46 per cent of Liechtenstein's primary energy consumption is met by oil imports. Gas contributes 27 per cent of energy consumption.

Energy
Liechtenstein is dependent on imported energy, which supplies 90 per cent of its needs. The remainder is sourced from domestically generated hydropower (75 per cent) and wood (25 per cent). The country has ratified the Kyoto Protocol. The government has pledged to source 10 per cent of domestic energy requirements from renewable sources particularly biomass and solar.

Banking and insurance
Three main banks are in operation: Liechtensteinische Landesbank, LGT Bank in Liechtenstein and Verwaltungs und Privat-Bank (VP Bank) AG. These have a close association with the Swiss banking system. Secrecy laws are strict although new legislation has put an end to the old anonymous numbered accounts.
There is a total of 17 banking institutes in operation.
Liechtenstein is a signatory of an EU tax agreement introduced in July 2005 in a number of non-EU countries. Liechtenstein will impose a withholding tax, up to 35 per cent, to be passed to the tax department of an EU citizen's country, but retaining the anonymity of the saver. This means that the relevant EU country will not be informed about the amount of money in its citizens' bank accounts. Liechtenstein has also agreed to supply information on tax fraud, for criminal or civil trials, and notify EU member states about additional malpractices.
In April 2005, a banking ombudsman was appointed in Liechtenstein, ending years of reliance on the Swiss banking ombudsman.
The insurance sector is a recent development. Eight companies make up the Liechtenstein Insurance Association, formed in 1998.
Central bank
Centrum Bank AG
Offshore facilities
Liechtenstein is a major international offshore financial centre, and the largest single supplier of fiduciary funds in Europe.

Time
GMT plus one hour (GMT plus two hours from late March to late September).

Geography
Liechtenstein is in central Europe. It lies on the east bank of the Upper Rhine river, bordered by Switzerland to the west and south and by Austria to the north and east.

Climate
Varies with altitude, generally mild and often windy. Average summer temperature 17 degrees Celsius (C). Average winter temperature 1 degree C.

Dress codes
Medium-weight throughout the year, with a topcoat for winter.

Entry requirements
Visa
All regulations match those of Switzerland. Visas are required by all. However some exceptions exist and length of stays vary, visit www.swissemb.org/ for details. Business visas for those that need one: i.e. non visa-free states, should have a letter of invitation from a Liechtenstein company and/or a letter from the visitor's company stating reason for visit and guarantee that all expenses will be covered, to accompany the application.
A visa is not required by EU nationals.
Currency advice/regulations
No currency restrictions (currency union with Switzerland). Travellers cheques must be endorsed by companies, not private persons.
Customs
Restricted amounts of alcoholic beverages, tobacco and gifts (up to value of Swf100) may be imported duty free.

Health (for visitors)
Mandatory precautions
None
Advisable precautions
Up-to-date tetanus and polio immunisations.

Hotels
Tips are included in hotel and restaurant bills.

Public holidays
Fixed dates
1 Jan (New Year's Day), 2 Jan (St Berchtold's Day), 6 Jan (Epiphany), 2 Feb (Candlemas), 19 Mar (Feast of St Joseph), 1 May (Labour Day), 15 Aug (Assumption Day), 8 Sep (Nativity of Our Lady), 1 Nov (All Saints' Day), 8 Dec (Immaculate Conception), 25 Dec (Christmas Day), 26 Dec (St Stephen's Day), 31 Dec (New Year's Eve).
Variable dates
Shrove Tuesday, Good Friday, Easter Monday, Ascension Day, Whit Monday, Corpus Christi (May/Jun).

Working hours
Banking
Mon–Fri: 0800–1630.
Business
Mon–Fri: 0800–1200 and 1330–1730.
Government
Mon–Fri: 0800–1630.
Shops
Mon–Fri: 0800–1200, 1330–1830; Sat: 0800–1600.

Getting there
Air
International airport/s: The nearest international airport is Kloten, Zürich (ZRH), Switzerland, approximately 130km from Vaduz. Travel to Liechtenstein can then be continued by road, rail or bus; an autoroute connects Zürich with Liechtenstein.
Surface
Road: Good road access from Switzerland and to a lesser extent Austria. Autoroute (A13) extends along Liechtenstein's Rhine border to Lake Constance, Austria and Germany in the north, and

Liechtenstein

continuing southwards towards St Moritz. In the west there are autoroutes to Zürich, Bern and Basel.

Motorway connections: Balzers, Vaduz, Schaan, Bendern, Ruggell.

Rail: The nearest rail stations to Vaduz are at Sargans and Buchs, in St Gallen, Switzerland. Another rail station is at Feldkirch in Austria.

Getting about
National transport
Buses: All villages can be reached by bus service.
Rail: Restricted rail network, with stations at Nendelny and halts at Schaan and Schaanwald.
Nearest main rail stations are at Buchs and Sargans in St Gallen, Switzerland, and Feldkirch in Austria.

City transport
There are regular and inexpensive bus services, and easily obtainable taxi services. Tipping is not customary.

Car hire
Service offered by Hertz AG and Beck Taxi in Vaduz. Driver must have held a valid driving licence for at least one year and be over 20 years of age. Speed limit 50 kph in city, 80kph outside. Traffic drives on the right.

BUSINESS DIRECTORY

The addresses listed below are a selection only. While World of Information makes every endeavour to check these addresses, we cannot guarantee that changes have not been made, especially to telephone numbers and area codes. We would welcome any corrections.

Telephone area codes
The international direct dialling (IDD) code for Liechtenstein is +423, followed by subscriber's number.

Chambers of Commerce
Liechtenstein Chamber of Commerce and Industry, 11 Josef Rheinberger-Strasse, 9490 Vaduz (tel: 237-5511; fax: 237-5512; e-mail: info@lihk.li).

Banking
Centrum Bank AG, Heiligkreuz 8, FL-9490 Vaduz (tel: 235-8585; fax: 235-8686).

LGT Bank in Liechtenstein AG (prior to Jan 1996, known as BIL GT Group), Herrengasse 12, FL-9490 Vaduz (tel: 235-1122; fax: 235-1522).

Verwaltungs und Privat-Bank AG, Im Zentrum, Aeulestrasse 6, FL-9490 Vaduz (tel: 235-6655; fax: 235-6500).

Central bank
Liechtensteinische Landesbank, 44 Städtle, PO Box 384, 9490 Vaduz (tel: 236-8811; fax: 236-8822; e-mail: llb@llb.li).

Travel information
National tourist organisation offices
Liechtenstein National Tourist Office, Städtle 38, Postfach 139, FL-9490 Vaduz (tel: 392-1111; 66-460); Tourist Office, FL-09497 Malbun (tel: 26-577).

Other useful addresses
Amt fuer Volkswirtschaft (national statistics office), Kirchastrasse 7, FL-9490 Vaduz (tel: 236-6871; fax: 236-6889).

Liechtenstein Embassy (USA), 633 Third Avenue, 27th Floor, New York, NY 10017 (tel: 202-599-0220; fax: 202-599-0064).

Postillion-Reisen AG, Landstrasse 9, FL-9494 Schaan (tel: 26-565; fax: 27-037).

Presse-und Informationsamt, Regierungsgebäude, FL-9490 Vaduz (tel: 236-6111; fax: 236-6460).

Internet sites
Liechtenstein News: http://www.news.li

Tourism information: http://www.tourismus.li/

Lithuania

KEY FACTS

Official name: Lietuvos Respublika (Republic of Lithuania)

Head of State: President Valdas Adamkus (inaugurated 12 Jul 2004)

Head of government: Prime Minister Algirdas Brazauskas (LSDP) (since 5 Jul 2001; re-appointed 11 Oct 2004)

Ruling party: A coalition government from 14 Dec 2004: including Lietuvos Socialdemokratu Partija (LSDP) (Social-democratic Party of Lithuania), Darbo Partija (DP) Labour Party), Naujoji Sajunga (NS) (New Union) and independent members of parliament.

Area: 62,500 square km

Population: 3.49 million (2004)

Capital: Vilnius

Official language: Lithuanian

Currency: Litas (plural Litai) (Lt) = 100 cents

Exchange rate: Lt2.86 per US$ (Oct 2005); the litu was pegged to the US$ until Feb 2002, when it was re-pegged to the euro at a rate of Lt3.4528.

GDP per capita: US$6,404 (2004)

GDP real growth: 6.60% (2004)

Labour force: 1.83 million (2004)

Unemployment: 8.00% (2004)

Inflation: 1.20% (2004)

Balance of trade: -US$2.32 billion (2004)

Foreign debt: US$10.01 billion (2004)

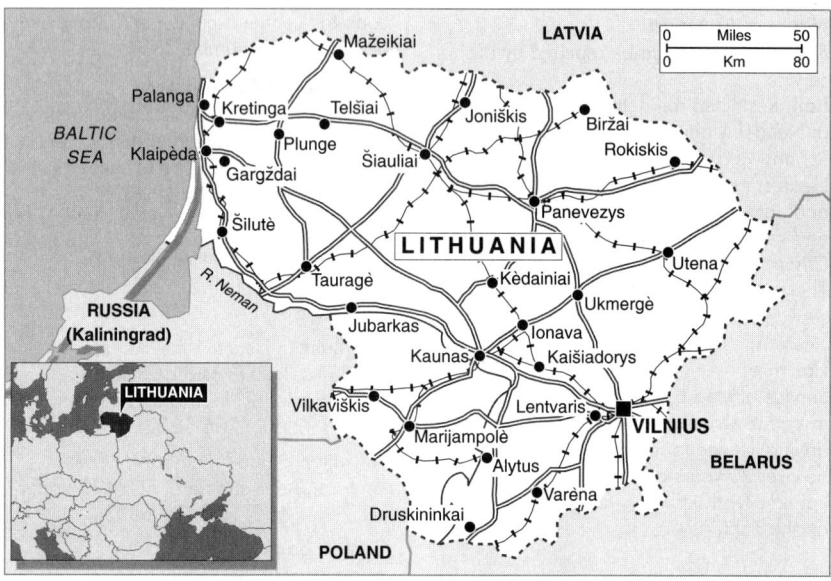

Lithuania was the first of the Soviet republics to breakaway from the then USSR, declaring its independence first in March 1990, and then again in 1991 when a referendum was held, overwhelmingly in favour of independence. Moscow refused to recognise the new state until after its own change of government in 1991. The last Russian troops finally withdrew from Lithuania in 1993. Lithuania has subsequently restructured its economy and joined both NATO and the European Union (EU) in the 2004. A slow starter in the westernising of its economy, it has caught up rapidly.

Economic success

The EU in December gave Lithuania a development budget for the period 2007–13 of US$15 billion, 56 per cent up on the budget for 2004–06. Confirming the budget, Prime Minister Brazauskas told President Adamkus that for every one litas Lithuania puts into EU budget it will get back five.

Lithuania will also get EU structural aid of eur220 million and eur50 million to assist in the closing of its nuclear station Ignalina – the eur50 million was largely at the insistence of UK Prime Minister Tony Blair, the then EU president.

The country has rebounded from the 1998 Russian financial crisis. Unemployment dropped from 10.5 per cent in 2003 to 8.0 per cent in 2004 and is forecast to be around 5.0 per cent in 2005 – below the EU25 average. Since joining the EU labour migration has contributed to the decline in unemployment. However, structural imbalances in the labour market persist. Long-term unemployment remains a serious problem – it was at 55.7 per cent at the end of the first quarter of 2005. High taxes to fund social insurance benefits hamper job creation and contribute to unemployment and tax avoidance. Gross average wages rose significantly, reflecting a combination of a shortage of qualified labour, higher profitability in the private sector, and government efforts to attract and retain a skilled public sector labour force.

Growing domestic consumption and increased investment have furthered recovery. Trade has been increasingly oriented toward the West. Privatisation of the large, state-owned utilities, particularly in the energy sector, is nearing completion. More than 80 per cent of enterprises have been privatised. Foreign government and business support have helped in the transition from a Soviet-style command economy to a market economy.

Lithuania is an upper middle-income country with a gross national income (GNI) per capita of US$6,404 in 2004. Almost 30 per cent of the country is covered with forests. Lithuania's major exports are refined oil products (about one quarter of total exports), machinery and equipment (12.7 per cent), and textiles (11.4 per cent). Close to 70 per cent of the country's trade is with the EU.

Foreign direct investment (FDI) from EU member states, the Nordic countries in particular, is rising. However, despite remarkable progress over recent years the country is still among the poorest of EU members with less than half (48 per cent) of the EU25 average purchasing power.

Despite an unfavourable external environment, notably stagnating markets in the EU, Lithuania's real growth remained robust at 6.6 per cent in 2004, making the country the second fastest-growing economy in the EU.

After almost two years of deflation, consumer prices surged in 2004 because of record-high oil prices and the one-time effect of EU accession. As of May 2005, Lithuania's 12-month average inflation was higher than the EU reference value, which is the average of the three lowest rates adjusted by an extra 1.5 per centage points.

Keeping inflation under control is crucial for Lithuania's adoption of the euro in early 2007. The rest of the convergence criteria are not of particular concern. However, if external imbalances persist, inflation may be a significant obstacle for Lithuania to join the euro-zone.

Lithuania has made visible progress in improving its business climate. According to the World Bank, Lithuania was among the top 10 reformers of an investment climate and in the top 20 in terms of creating a business environment. However, in addition to improving its business climate and adopting competitive tax rates, Lithuania has to make substantial efforts to attract foreign investments to sustain sufficient financing of the current account.

The current account deficit widened in 2004, reaching 7.2 per cent of GDP, mostly due to accelerating imports of consumer goods. Restructuring in the industrial sector has led to an increase in imports of capital goods. However, in the first quarter of 2005, the external account deficit narrowed, reflecting brisk exports – a benefit of Lithuania's accession to the EU.

Tension with the big bear

Tension between Lithuania and Russia remains high, not least because of alleged interference by politicians in Kaliningrad, the Russian-controlled coastal enclave in Lithuania, in Lithuanian affairs. On holiday in Kalingrad's resort town of Sochi, Russian President Vladimir Putin in December 2005 praised the Kaliningrad governor's idea of inviting ethnic Russians from the Baltic countries to resettle in the enclave, saying once he officially heard of it he would support it.

Putin is well aware that Lithuania's declaration of independence in 1990 helped set off the collapse of the USSR. The Baltic states were the key advocates of human rights in Russia. For several years Lithuania has been known as a venue for Russian dissidents to express their dissatisfaction with the Russian government. There have been negative interviews in the media, along with their unflattering assessments of Putin and Russia.

Then in 2005 President Adamkus declined an invitation to attend celebrations in Moscow marking the end of the Second World War.

Politics

President Valdas Adamkus was re-elected in June 2004 (after his predecessor, Rolandas Paksas, was accused of having links with Russian organised crime). Algirdas Mykolas Brazauskas first became prime minister in July 2001 and was re-appointed by the president in October 2004. The next presidential election will be in June 2009.

Liberal democrats are seeking the re-election of former president Rolandas Paksas, who was in office until 2004, when parliament tried to impeach him. He had allegedly told his biggest financial supporter Russian businessman Yuri Borisov that his phone was bugged. Impeachment was sought on the grounds that Paksas had revealed a state secret. No one seemed to deny that the state was eavesdropping on Borisov, or say for what reason it might have been, and the Supreme Court threw out the case for lack of evidence.

This leaves the field clear for Paksas, spoken of as 'the daredevil of Lithuanian politics', to make a political comeback, something the liberal democrats are urging him to do. Still in his forties, he is politically a youngster compared to septuagenarians Adamkus and Brazauskas.

Risk assessment

Economy	Good
Politics	Good
Regional stability	Good

COUNTRY PROFILE

Historical profile
The Grand Duchy of Lithuania was in union with Poland from 1569; it was annexed by Russia between 1772 and 1795. 1795–1914 Lithuania became part of the Russian empire.
1914–18 The Russians were driven out of Lithuania by the Germans in the First World War.

KEY INDICATORS — Lithuania

	Unit	2000	2001	2002	2003	2004
Population	m	3.50	3.48	3.47	3.48	3.49
Gross domestic product (GDP)	US$bn	11.20	12.00	14.20	17.95	*22.26
GDP per capita	US$	3,037	3,446	4,081	5,156	6,404
GDP real growth	%	3.9	5.9	4.2	6.0	6.6
Inflation	%	1.0	1.2	0.3	-0.4	1.2
Unemployment	%	11.5	12.5	12.0	10.5	8.0
Exports (fob) (goods)	US$m	4,050.4	4,889.0	6,028.4	7,906.0	9,273.8
Imports (fob) (goods)	US$m	5,154.1	5,997.0	7,343.3	9,600.0	11,590.4
Balance of trade	US$m	-1,103.8	-1,108.0	-1,314.9	-1,694.0	-2,316.6
Current account	US$m	-674.9	-573.6	-720.7	-1,011.0	-1,910.0
Foreign debt	US$bn	4.9	5.3	*10.5	8.3	9.1
Total reserves minus gold	US$m	1,311.6	1,617.7	2,349.3	3,372.0	3,512.6
Foreign exchange	US$m	1,310.2	1,599.3	2,295.9	3,371.9	3,512.5
Foreign direct investment (FDI)	US$bn	0.4	0.4	0.8	0.2	–
Exchange rate	per US$	4.00	4.00	3.64	3.03	2.62

* estimated figure

1918 Lithuania declared independence.
1922 A constitution declared Lithuania a parliamentary republic with the Seimas as the parliamentary organ.
1926 In a military coup, Antanas Smetona came to power as the head of an authoritarian regime.
1940 Lithuania was invaded and occupied by the Soviet Union.
1941 Lithuania was occupied by the Germans, until it was re-annexed by the Soviets in 1944.
1988 A nationalist movement, the Lithuanian Reform Movement (Sàjudis), was set up by a group of writers and intellectuals; at a mass rally in Vilnius, the leaders declared that the USSR occupied Lithuania illegally.
1989 Parliament approved the declaration of Lithuanian sovereignty, stating that Lithuanian laws take precedence over Soviet laws.
1990 Sàjudis won the elections (the first free elections for 50 years). Vytautas Landsbergis was elected chairman of parliament, which declared Lithuania's independence. Fearing the impact that this would have on nationalist demands in the other Baltic republics, the Soviet Union immediately imposed an economic blockade; Lithuania agreed to suspend independence, pending talks.
1991 Talks with Moscow failed and the economy faced turmoil; Landsbergis ended the suspension of the declaration of independence. A referendum was held, resulting in an overwhelming vote for independence. Following a failed coup in Moscow, the USSR recognised Lithuania's independence. Lithuania, together with Latvia and Estonia, were admitted to the UN.
1992 A new constitution introducing a presidency was adopted by referendum. The Lietuvos Demokratine Darbo Partija (LDDP) (Democratic Labour Party of Lithuania) won more seats than Sàjudis in the elections – the LDDP was the first former communist party to return to power in central and eastern Europe.
1993 Algirdas Brazauskas, the former Lietuvos Komunistu Partija (LKP) (Lithuanian Communist Party) first secretary, won direct presidential elections and appointed Adolfas Slezevicius prime minister. Following the defeat of the Sàjudis organisation in the 1992 elections, the Homeland Union was established.
1996 Allegations of corruption led to the removal of Slezevicius and Mindaugas Stankevicius was appointed prime minister. After elections, the Tevynes Sajunga (TS) (Homeland Union) formed a centre-right coalition government with the Lietuvos Kricioniu Demokratu Partija (LKDP) (Lithuanian Christian Democratic Party) and the Lietuvos Centro Sajunga (LCS) (Centre Union of Lithuania). Gediminas Vagnorius was appointed prime minister.
1998 Valdas Adamkus was elected president.
1999 Vagnorius resigned in April; Rolandas Paksas was appointed prime minister, but he later resigned in August. A new government, under the leadership of Andrius Kubilius, came to power.
2000 Following the parliamentary elections, a minority coalition government was established, which included the Lietuvos Liberalu Sajunga (LLS) (Lithuanian Liberal Union), LCS and the Modernuju Kriscioni Demokratu Sajunga (MKDS) (Modern Christian-Democratic Union) with the support of other smaller parties. Rolandas Paksas, leader of the LLS, was again appointed prime minister.
2001 Prime Minister Rolandas Paksas' coalition government was brought down over differences about energy sector privatisations. A coalition government was formed, led by the Lietuvos Socialdemokratu Partija (LSDP) (Social-democratic Party of Lithuania). The LSDP's Algirdas Brazauskas was appointed prime minister.
2002 The litas was re-pegged from the US dollar to the euro.
2003 Rolandas Paksas won the presidential election. Algirdas Brazauskas was re-appointed prime minister on 4 March. In a referendum on membership of the EU, 90 per cent voted in favour; turnout was 60 per cent.
2004 In March, Lithuania acceded to NATO, and to the EU on 1 May. On 6 April, parliament impeached the president, Rolandas Paksas, following an inquiry that concluded his alleged links with Russian organised crime was a threat to national security. Valdas Adamkus was re-elected president in June and inaugurated on 12 July. In the two stage parliamentary elections, the Darbo Partija (DP) (Labour Party), won most with 39 seats, however this did not reached the necessary 71 for an absolute majority. A coalition government was formed including the DP, LSDP, Naujoji Sajunga (NS) New Union and non-aligned members of parliament; Algirdas Brazauskas was re-appointed prime minister, by the president.
2005 In March, the president declined an invitation to attend the ceremony in Moscow, celebrating the end of the Second World War. In September a Russian fighter plane crashed into Lithuanian territory and sparked diplomatic tensions. It was later discovered to have been caused by a technical malfunction and human error.

Political structure
Constitution
The constitution was adopted on 25 October 1992.
The written constitution has precedence over all subsequent laws unless amended by referendum. The office of the president, parliamentary democracy and an independent judiciary are all guaranteed under the constitution, along with specific citizens' rights.
Form of state
Parliamentary democratic republic
The executive
The head of state is the president, who is directly elected for a maximum of two five-year terms. The president can dissolve parliament if it refuses to appoint a new government or, at the latter's request, if the parliament passes a vote of no confidence. The president cannot use this power during the last six months of the presidential term of office, or if an early election has taken place during the previous six months.
The prime minister is appointed or dismissed by the president, with the approval of the Seimas. Ministers are appointed and dismissed by the president on the recommendation of the prime minister.
National legislature
The 141-member Seimas (parliament) is elected on a partly proportional, partly constituency system for a four-year term. The Seimas, on a two-to-three majority vote of its members, can decide to hold early elections.
Universal suffrage is from aged 18.
There are 56 municipalities, of these, 44 are districts and 12 are towns or cities. They are managed by municipal councils, elected for a three-year terms, and by a mayor appointed by the relevant council.
Legal system
The Lithuanian legal code is based on civil law system with no judicial review of legislative acts. The court system consists of district and county courts, the Court of Appeal and the Supreme Court as well as the Administrative Court. The president participates in the process of appointment and dismissal of judges. Moreover, the president has the right to apply to the Constitutional Court concerning the conformity of the legal acts passed by the government. Judges are independent in administering justice.
Last elections
13/27 June 2004 (first and second round presidential); 13 June 2004 (European Parliament); 10/24 October 2004 (first and second round parliamentary).
Results: Presidential second round: Valdas Adamkus won 52.6 per cent, against 47.4 per cent for Kazimiera Prunskiene; turnout was 52.4 per cent.

Lithuania

European Parliament: Darbo Partija (DP) (Labour Party) won 30.4 per cent of the vote (five seats out of 13), Lietuvos Socialdemokratu Partija (LSDP) (Social-democratic Party of Lithuania) 14.4 per cent (two), Vytautas Landsbergis (Homeland Union) (VL) (Conservative Party) 12.4 per cent (two), Liberalu ir Centro Sajunga (LCS) (Liberal and Centre Union) 11.2 per cent (two), Valstieciu ir Naujosios Demokratijos Partiju Sajunga (VNDPS) (Union of Farmers and New Democratic Party) 7.4 per cent (one) and Liberalu Demokratu Partija (LDP) (Liberal Democratic Party) 6.9 per cent (one); turnout 48.2 per cent.

Parliamentary: the opposition DP, established in 2003 and led by a Russian, Viktor Uspaskich, won 28.46 per cent of the vote (39 seats out of 141), Algirdas Brazauskas' coalition 'Working for Lithuania' 20.65 per cent (31), the Homeland Union 14.73 per cent (25), former president Rolandas Paksas' coalition 'For the Order and Justice' 11.36 per cent (10), the Liberal and Centre Union 9.18 per cent (18), and the Union of Farmers' Party and New Democracy Party 6.6 per cent (10); turnout was 45.9 per cent.

Next elections
2009 (presidential)

Political parties
Ruling party
A coalition government from 14 Dec 2004: including Lietuvos Socialdemokratu Partija (LSDP) (Social-democratic Party of Lithuania), Darbo Partija (DP) Labour Party), Naujoji Sajunga (NS) (New Union) and independent members of parliament.

Main opposition party
Naujosios Demokratijos Partija (NDP) (New Democratic Party), Vytautas Landsbergis (Homeland Union) (VL) (Conservative Party), Liberalu ir Centro Sajunga (LCS) (Liberal and Centre Union) and Lietuviu Valstieciu Partija (LVP) (Lithuanian Peasant Party).

Population
3.49 million (2004)
Ethnic make-up
Lithuanian (80.1 per cent), Russian (9.1 per cent), Polish (7 per cent), Belarussian (1.5 per cent) and others (2.3 per cent). There are long-standing cultural and political links with Poland, and many Poles live in the southern Vilnius region where they are in the majority, and have their own schools and newspapers.

Religions
Roman Catholic (primarily), Lutheran, Russian Orthodox, Protestant, Evangelical Christian Baptist, Muslim, Jewish.

Education
Primary school starts at age seven and is compulsory. There are three types of school, run by the state: primary (attended for four years), middle (five years) and secondary (three years). There are 17 higher education institutions in Lithuania. Vilnius University, founded in 1579, is the oldest university in Eastern Europe and also the largest in Lithuania.

Literacy rate: 99 per cent male and female; adult rates (World Bank).

Compulsory years: Seven to 14

Enrolment rate: 98 per cent gross primary enrolment of relevant age group (including repeaters); 86 per cent secondary enrolment and 31 per cent at tertiary level (World Bank).

Pupils per teacher: 16 in primary schools.

Health
Annual total expenditure on health is around 6 per cent of GDP, of which 71 per cent is government spending. Lithuania is suffering from a lack of primary healthcare provision and an overstretched network of small hospitals and large polyclinics. Over-specialisation of staff, low-quality equipment and a lack of investment have also put a strain on the health system.

The private sector accounts for only 2–3 per cent of total healthcare in Lithuania. Private clinics can charge 60 per cent more for any treatment than those funded by the state. The Lithuanian government sees these clinics as a threat to the state health care system.

HIV prevalence: 0.1 per cent aged 15–49 in 2003 (World Bank)

Life expectancy: 71.9 years (World Bank)

Fertility rate/Maternal mortality rate: 1.3 births per woman; maternal mortality 18 per 100,000 live births (World Bank).

Infant mortality rate: 8.0 per 1,000 live births (World Bank).

Welfare
The government is introduced a multi-pillar pension system, with voluntary public pension contributions for workers in 2004. A 2000 law enforces private voluntary pension funds.

The social security system provides pensions, sickness allowance, maternity and child care benefits and unemployment benefit. Small family grants are also provided that are not subject to means-testing. Contributions to the Lithuanian Social Insurance Fund are tax deductible. Employers contribute 30 per cent of the payroll of the company and employees pay 1 per cent of their wages.

Main cities
Vilnius (capital, estimated population 543,500 in 2003), Kaunas (379,800), Klaipeda (193,400), Siauliai (134,200), Panevezys (120,000).

Languages spoken
By law, all transactions, contracts and company returns must be in Lithuanian. English is widely spoken by business people. Other languages spoken include Russian, Polish, Belarusian, Ukrainian, German and Yiddish.

Official language/s
Lithuanian

Media
Press
The state-owned news agency ELTA serves the local press in Lithuanian and Russian. The Baltic News Service provides an English-language news service to the three Baltic republics.

Dailies: Dailies include *Lietuvos Rytas* (Lithuania's Morning), *Kauno Diena*, *Klaipeda*, *Siauliu Krastas*, *Vakarines Navjienos* and *Respublika* (Republic).

Weeklies: English-language weeklies include *The Baltic Times* and *Lithuanian Weekly*. Other Lithuanian language publications include the national weekly *7 menodienos*, *Kalba Vilnius* for entertainment and *Lietuvos Sportas* is published three times in the week.

Business: Business publications include a fortnightly economics magazine *Lietuvos Ukis* and the business paper *Verslo Zinios*.

Broadcasting
The state-owned enterprise Lietuvos Radio ir Televizijos Centras (LRTC) is responsible for the broadcasting of state and commercial television and radio programmes. There are three national commercial channels and one state-owned national channel in Lithuania, as well as seven regional stations.

Television: The privately owned TV channel LNK leads the market with an estimated 29.2 per cent audience share, followed by TV3 (27.5 per cent) and LTV (23.6 per cent). Baltijos TV (BTV) is a private channel with national coverage which is gaining in popularity.

Economy
The economy in 2004 was marked by clear indications of healthy growth and all due to the structural reforms begun in the 1990s. The GDP growth in 2004 was 6.6 per cent, and if the expected rate of 6.5 per cent in 2005 is fulfilled it will have shown three years of level high growth. The growth is due largely to consumer spending in not only consumer goods but also investment in residential properties. The confidence in the economy is due to Lithuania's efforts to achieve higher standards of living through its transition to an open market economy. Accession to the EU, on 1 May 2004, and the country's commitment to the EU Exchange Rate Mechanism (ERM) – a centralised exchange rate that sets a margin within which a currency must remain – has set a

modus operandi, around which the government can unify policies. Success in the ERM is a key indicator on a currency's suitability to join the European Monetary Union (EMU), which Lithuania has declared its intentions of joining in early 2007.

Analysts are agreed that the continued health of the economy is dependent on further structural reforms to improve the business environment that will enhance the prospects of exporters and investors. EU funds are expected, from accession, and these are due to be invested in restructuring the agricultural sector and improve the supply side of the economy. The viability of the welfare and healthcare systems are also dependent on a sound financial structure and the reforms necessary to achieve them should be maintained. It has also been noted that if EU funds are not made available on schedule the reforms under way and those planned may be blighted.

The economic growth in 2004 did not come at the expense of inflation that remained at 1.2 per cent. However there has been some concern about the expansion of credit. In 2004 low interest rates encouraged rapid growth in personal credit which briefly reached 70 per cent, on an annual basis, before falling back to 40 per cent. Nevertheless, the majority of the credit is being absorbed by productive enterprises. Industry in 2004 grew by 7.0 per cent and provided 33.6 per cent of GDP, of which manufacturing was 20.8 per cent.

Lithuania has shown that it can reform and now has the challenge of competing within a larger marketplace. Its success to date is due to the objectives its people adopted in the 1990s and if they remain focussed are likely to achieve much more.

External trade
As a member of the EU Lithuania applies all customs treaties both intra- and international.
Lithuania is a member of the WTO.

Imports
Principal imports include mineral products (21 per cent), machinery and equipment, transport equipment, chemicals, textiles and clothing and metals.
Main sources: Russia (23.1 per cent total, 2004), Germany (18.1 per cent), Poland (4.7 per cent), Italy (4.6 per cent)

Exports
Principal exports are mineral products (23 per cent), textiles and clothing, machinery and equipment, chemicals, wood and wood products and foodstuffs.
Main destinations: Switzerland (10.7 per cent total, 2004), Latvia (10 per cent), Germany (9.5 per cent), Russia (7.9 per cent), France (7.5 per cent), US (5.2 per cent), UK (5.1 per cent), Estonia (4.5 per cent), Denmark (4.3 per cent)

Agriculture
Farming
Agricultural land constitutes 53.4 per cent of total land area, estimated at 3.4 million hectares (ha). The industry employs about 18 per cent of the total labour force and contributed 6.2 per cent of GDP in 2004. Main products include grain, potatoes, sugar beet and dairy products, meat and silk.

Land restitution began soon after independence in 1990, with the creation of 104,000 private family farms. The break up of state-owned farms into small plots, the limited availability of capital and a lack of business skills have slowed the recovery and development of the agricultural sector.

The agriculture ministry has embarked on the EU's Special Accession Programme for Agriculture and Rural Development (SAPARD) programme covering the period to 2007 and is intending to utilise EU funds to restructure the sector. Lithuania will not be eligible for full EU agricultural subsidies and rural development aid through CAP until 2013. During its transitional entry stage Lithuania has decided to implement the reform of the CAP on 1 January 2009. The reform was introduced throughout most of the EU on 1 January 2005, when subsidies on farm output, which tended to benefit large farms and encourage overproduction, were replaced by single farm payments, not conditional on production. The change is expected to reward farms that provide and maintain a healthy environment, food safety and animal welfare standards. The changes are also intended to encourage market conscious production and cut the cost of CAP to the EU taxpayer.

Lithuania's European and transatlantic integration will significantly increase competitive pressures on its agriculture, with a large proportion of exports heading to the US. It has adopted the Swedish model of organic farming with policies that draw heavily on bilateral international projects. Environmental factors continue to affect agricultural reforms – 50 to 70 per cent of nitrogen and 10 to 20 per cent of phosphorus found in surface waters originated in farming activities.

Crop production in 2004 included: 2,859,400 tonnes (t) cereals in total, 1,315,000t wheat, 1,021,400t potatoes, 970,000t barley, 180,000t rye, 204,500t rapeseed (canola), 57,500t pulses, 78,854t oilcrops, 904,900t sugar beets, 115,000t oats, 45,000t fruit in total, 379,400t vegetables in total. Livestock production included: 221,670t meat in total, 60,000t beef, 114,000t pig meat, 800t lamb, 46,000t poultry, 52,000t eggs, 1,863,000t milk, 1,100t honey, 7,600t cattle hides.

Fishing
The opportunity to export fishery products to the EU market without any tariff barriers has attracted the interest of its seafood processing industry.

Redfish, mackerel, cod, red plaice, black halibut and shrimp are caught in the high seas. Baltic Sea catches include cod, sprat, Baltic sprat, plaice, turbot, salmon and smelt.

Forestry
Forest and other wooded land accounts for a third of the land area, with forest cover estimated at 1.9 million hectares (ha). Most of the forest is available for wood supply. About 80 per cent of the forest area is owned by the state, although private ownership has been rising since the early 1990s. Consumption of forest products per capita is below the European average level.

The sawmill industry, which exports half of its production, contributes largely to the national economy. Large volumes of roundwood, comprising mostly pulpwood, are exported mainly to Sweden and Germany. Although pulp and paper production is one of the oldest industries in Lithuania, most of the internal demand for high quality paper is met by imports. Chemical timber, furniture, wood-fibre and wood-chipboards are also produced, with chipboard materials in particular having strong export potential. Sawn hardwood is also used in the domestic furniture industry.

Exports of forest material in 2004 amounted to US$335.7 million, while imports amounted to US$320.1 million. Production in 2004 included 6,120,000 cubic metres (cum) roundwood, 4,860,000cum industrial roundwood, 3,420,000cum sawlogs and veneers, 1,450,000cum sawnwood, 1,430,000cum pulpwood, 1,260,000cum woodfuel.

Industry and manufacturing
The industrial sector accounted for 33.6 per cent of GDP of which, 20.8 per cent was manufacturing in 2004; it employs around 40 per cent of the workforce. Main industries are shipbuilding, consumer electronics, metalworking, machine building, machine tools, scientific instruments, sulphuric acid, paper, meat, dairy products, food processing, textiles, clothing and furniture. One of Lithuania's priorities is the development of light industry, particularly furniture, using natural wood products.

The principal branches of existing light industry in Lithuania are textiles and knitwear, with the largest leather and footwear enterprises in Vilnius, Kaunas and Siauliai. Other areas offering potential for growth include electronics.

The EU has stressed the need for Lithuania to speed-up restructuring of the industrial sector, particularly food processing and agricultural industries.

In 2005, the World Bank ranked Lithuania in its *Doing Business Economy Ranking* 15 for ease of doing business and 37 for starting a business, out of 155.

Industrial production increased by 7 per cent in 2004.

Tourism
Lithuania's tourist facilities are improving and around 1.2 million tourists visit Lithuania annually. Travel and tourism is expected to contribute US$431 million, or 1.6 per cent to GDP. While total exports in tourism is expected to earn US$1 billion, it is only expected to attract US$656 or 10 per cent of total capital investment. The country's main foreign tourism markets are neighbouring countries from the former Soviet bloc – Russia, Latvia and Poland. The fastest growing markets are Latvia, Germany, Scandinavian and Asian countries.

There are a number of tourist centres, including Trakai, the medieval capital of Lithuania, in the country's lake district. Apart from the castle, there is potential for watersports. The coastal resort of Palanga boasts sandy beaches as well as health and spa facilities. Birstonas on the bank of the Nemunas River is also a centre for spa treatments. Five national and nearly 30 regional parks are classified as protected areas.

Mining
Lithuania is famous for its high quality deposits of amber which supply the local jewellery industry. Amber deposits have been found in the coastal region of Curonian Bay and Juodkrante. The Juodkrante site covers 82 hectares; amber deposits are estimated at 112 tonnes. Lithuania also has large reserves of high-quality iron ore in the south, but extraction is not economically viable.

Other raw materials found in small quantities include limestone, dolomite, gypsum, clay, sand and gravel.

Hydrocarbons
Lithuania's oil reserves have been falling since the 1990s. However exploration is under way and Lithuania estimates that it has 55.5 million cubic metres (cum) of oil onshore, and 36–72 million cum offshore. In 2004, production dropped by 21.1 per cent on the 469,800cum in 2003. This was due to the limited reserves, maturing fields and difficulties putting new fields online. The oil in production and the reserves found so far are high quality, light crude, which is easy to convert into refined products.

The country imports most of its domestic consumption oil needs of approximately 67,000 barrels per day (bpd) from Russia, via the Druzhba pipeline.

Lithuania is home to the only oil refinery in the Baltics – the Mazeikiu refinery which has a capacity of 263,000bpd and is one of the most efficient in the former Soviet Union. On 2002, 27 per cent of the Mazeikiu refinery was sold to Russia's second largest oil company, Yukos.

Lithuania's natural gas situation is similar to that of oil: the country has scarce reserves and is heavily dependent on Russian imports to meet the country's domestic consumption demand of 3.2 billion cubic metres per annum. In September 2005 Germany and Russia announced an agreement for a gas pipeline, to supply Russian gas to Western Europe, to be build under the Baltic Sea and bypassing Lithuania. Relations between Russia and Lithuania have been strained and West European countries are keen that their supplies of gas are not impeded by any such strain. For Lithuania's part, any plan to become the hub for gas supplies to the EU is threatened by this arrangement, as well as the implicit risk to its own supplies from Russia.

Nevertheless major infrastructure upgrading projects are under way at several Lithuanian ports.

Lithuania has reduced consumption, but still imports small quantities of coal from Poland and Russia.

Energy
The Lithuanian energy sector is dominated by Lietuvos Energija, the largest electric power company in the country. The company is 96.2 per cent state-owned, with a minority stake held by Sweden's Vatenfall. The company is structured into separate companies, responsible for generation, distribution and transmission. A privatisation programmed began in January 2004, paving the way for the complete privatisation of the electricity sector by 2010.

The ageing Ignalia nuclear power plant, similar in construction to the Chernobyl facility is being decommissioned as part of the EU accession agreement. Almost US$200 million in international grants was raised to help finance the closing down of the first reactor in January 2005. The closure date for the second reactor is 2009.

Financial markets
Stock exchange
The Nacionaline Vertybiniu Popieriu Birza (NVPB) (National Stock Exchange of Lithuania) is in Vilnius. The NVPB is a non-profit organisation with 136 shareholders, modelled on the French system.

Banking and insurance
Lithuania has a two-tier banking system whereby the commercial and central bank functions of the state bank are separated. Foreign-owned banks may operate in the country. Commercial banking operations have been removed from the central bank, which has assumed the government's responsibility for setting interest policy. The Lietuvos Zemes Ukio Bankas (LZUB) (Lithuanian Agricultural Bank) was sold by the government in early-2002 – the end of state involvement in commercial banking.

Central bank
Lietuvos Banka (LB) (Bank of Lithuania)
Main financial centre
Vilnius

Time
GMT plus one hour (GMT plus two hours from late March to late September). In 1998, Lithuania joined the Central European time zone – it is now one hour behind both Latvia and Estonia.

Geography
Lithuania is the largest of the three Baltic states, situated on the eastern coast of the Baltic Sea in north-eastern Europe. It is bordered by Latvia to the north, Belarus to the south-east, Poland to the south-west and the Russian Federation to the west. There is a dense network of waterways, the main river being the Nemunas, which flows south to north into the Baltic Sea. There are many lakes in the northern regions of the Baltic Highlands. The highest point is Juozapine Hill (294 metres) in the east of the country.

Climate
Lithuania enjoys one of the mildest climates along the Baltic coast. Summer sunshine may last nine hours a day, but winters can be very cold. Annual rainfall averages 490mm and humidity 80 per cent.

Dress codes
Warm clothing is necessary in winter. Business dress is conservative but relatively informal, with a jacket and tie expected for meetings. A raincoat is useful during spring and autumn.

Entry requirements
Passports
Passports are required by all.
Visa
Required by all, except citizens of EU, North America, Australasia and some Asian countries for tourist and business visits up to 90 days.
For a full list of visa-free citizens visit www.ltembassyus.org/

consular_info/visa_information.htm or contact the nearest consulate.
Business visas for all others must be applied for with an invitation from a local company or organisation and certified by the migration authorities in Lithuania (stamped and signed by a migration officer). A business letter, by the visitor's company, giving purpose of visit and full itinerary should also be included.

Currency advice/regulations
Import and export of national currency is not allowed. A refund is possible against exchange receipt.
Import of foreign currencies is unlimited, but a declaration is required for amounts over the equivalent of Lt10,000. Export is allowed up to the amount declared, less amounts exchanged or spent. Export exceeding the equivalent of Lt100,000 is not permitted.
Lithuania is still primarily a cash economy. Visitors can change money in banks, shops, kiosks and hotels. Traveller's cheques are more widely accepted than elsewhere in the Baltic states.

Customs
A small amount of personal goods may be brought into Lithuania duty-free. On arrival, declare valuable items such as jewellery, cameras, computers and musical instruments.

Health (for visitors)
Most medical supplies are available, including disposable needles, anaesthetics, antibiotics and other pharmaceuticals.

Mandatory precautions
Vaccination certificates are required for cholera or yellow fever if travelling from an infected area.

Advisable precautions
It is advisable to be 'in date' for the following immunisations: polio (within 10 years), tetanus (within 10 years), typhoid fever, hepatitis 'A' (moderate risk only). It is recommended that bottled water is used for drinking; tap water is occasionally brown.

Hotels
There are many hotels in Vilnius. Some have been restored or taken over. Most ask for payment in hard currency. Tipping is not widely practised.

Credit cards
An increasing number of hotels, restaurants and other businesses accept major credit cards.

Public holidays
Fixed dates
1 Jan (New Year), 16 Feb (Independence Day), 11 Mar (Restoration Day), 6 Jul (Statehood Day), 15 Aug (Assumption Day), 1 Nov (All Saints' Day), 25–26 Dec (Christmas Holiday).

Variable dates
Easter Monday

Working hours
Banking
Mon–Fri: 0900–1700.
Business
Mon–Fri: 0900–1300 and 1400–1800 (appointments best between 0900–1000); lunch break 1300–1400.
Shops
Mon–Fri: 1000–1400 and 1500–1900; Sat: 1000–1600.

Telecommunications
Mobile phones
A GSM network covers the republic's eight largest cities.

Electricity supply
220V AC, 50Hz. European plugs are required.

Social customs/useful tips
Social behaviour is fairly informal. Lithuanians are open and hospitable. Straight professional questions receive straight answers. Business cards are used widely and shaking hands is the common form of greeting and farewell. Most Lithuanians are punctual – being late for a meeting can be a bad start.
Tipping has become more widespread, with waiters often expecting generous tips from westerners – avoid leaving hard currency.
Lithuanian-Russian relations are not as tense as those between Estonians and Latvians and Russians, although care should be taken when discussing Russia and its role in the region. Lithuanians also dislike being described as members of the Baltic states, rather than Lithuanian.

Security
Compared to other European capitals, the crime rate in Vilnius is relatively low, but street crime does occur. Make use of hotel safe deposit boxes and be careful not to show valuables when walking around the city. Car theft is common.

Getting there
Air
National airline: Lithuanian Airlines
International airport/s: Vilnius International (VNO), 5km from city; post office, bureau de change, cafetarias/bars, duty free shop.
Airport tax: Departure tax Lt60
Surface
Road: Lithuania has a good network of interconnecting roads, providing links to neighbouring countries. There are bus services from destinations in Lithuania to other Baltic cities, Kaliningrad and some services to Western Europe.
Rail: Lithuania has a well developed rail network and Vilnius is the major city for rail connections in the region. There are train connections with Poland through Grodno in Belarus (Belarus visa required). There are regular trains to Russia (Moscow and St Petersburg). Rail travel between Lithuania, Latvia and Estonia is slow. Passengers to destinations outside Lithuania are asked to pay in hard currency.
Water: Between Hull (UK) and Klaipeda there is a fortnightly shipping service. Two ferry lines link Klaipeda to Germany. It is advisable to book at least one month in advance.

Getting about
National transport
Road: Lithuanian roads are the best in the Baltic countries. Modern four-lane motorways connect Vilnius with Kaunas, Laipeda and Panaeveys. There are potholes and open sewers on secondary roads and on some roads in town. Avoid driving at night when it is difficult to see the road.
Buses: Buses are convenient and the cheapest way to travel as trains do not serve every town and village.
Rail: The rail system is being upgraded. Twice daily trains connect Vilnius with the Baltic coast.
Water: There is a dense network of rivers in Lithuania. The longest river is the Nemunas – total length 973km, 475km of which is in Lithuania – which is suitable for navigation in parts. Lakes cover 1.5 per cent of the total land area.
City transport
Taxis: Fares are negotiated but are always more expensive from the airport, railway station, cathedral and Vilnius Department Store. Avoid paying in hard currency and insist that the meter is used. Flagging down a taxi in the street is not easy; there are taxi-stands and taxis can be booked by telephone.
Buses, trams & metro: There is a choice of buses and trolley buses within the city. Tickets can be purchased from kiosks (spaudos kioskas) and drivers; they must be inserted into a validating machine on board. Services operate from 0600 to 0030 or 0100.
The Vilnius railway station is a cosmopolitan marketplace and terminus, but it is not safe for visitors at night.
Car hire
Many of the major car rental companies operate in Lithuania. The speed limits are 110kph (68mph) on motorways, 90kph (56mph) on country roads and 60kph (38mph) inside towns. Traffic drives on the right. National driving licences are required.
If hiring a vehicle, make sure it has an alarm and steering lock.
Drivers must pay a fee to use any road leading to Vilnius old town.

Lithuania

BUSINESS DIRECTORY

The addresses listed below are a selection only. While World of Information makes every endeavour to check these addresses, we cannot guarantee that changes have not been made, especially to telephone numbers and area codes. We would welcome any corrections.

Telephone area codes

The international direct dialling code (IDD) for Lithuania is +370, followed by area code and subscriber's number:

Kaunus	37	Panevezys	45
Klaipeda	46	Siauliai	41
Palanga	460	Vilnius	5

Useful telephone numbers

Directory enquiries: 09
International operator: 8-194
Fire: 01
Police: 02
Ambulance (greitoji pagalba): 03
Vilnius City Road Police, Giraites 3: 631-168

Chambers of Commerce

American Chamber of Commerce in Lithuania, 5 Lukiskiu Street, 2600 Vilnius (tel: 261-1181; fax: 212-6128; e-mail: acc@acc.lt).

Association of Lithuanian Chambers of Commerce, Industry and Crafts, 9 J Tumo-Vaizganto Street, 2001 Vilnius (tel: 261-2102; fax: 261-2112; e-mail: info@chambers.lt).

British Chamber of Commerce in Lithuania, 21 T Sevcenkos Street, 2009 Vilnius (tel: 239-2316; fax: 239-2301; e-mail: info@bccl.lt).

Kaunas Chamber of Commerce, Industry and Crafts, PO Box 2111, 8 K Donelaicis Street, 3000 Kaunas (tel: 229-212; fax: 208-330; e-mail: chamber@chamber.lt).

Klaipeda Chamber of Commerce, Industry and Crafts, 17 Danes Street, 5800 Klaipeda (tel: 390-861; fax: 410-626; e-mail: klaipeda@chambers.lt).

Panevezys Regional Chamber of Commerce, Industry and Crafts, 34 Respublikos Street, 5319 Panevezys (tel: 463-687; fax: 462-227; e-mail: panevezys@chambers.lt).

Siauliai Regional Chamber of Commerce, Industry and Crafts, 88 Vilniaus Street, 5400 Siauliai (tel: 525-504; fax: 523-903; siauliai@chambers.lt).

Vilnius Regional Chamber of Commerce, Industry and Crafts, 31 Algirdo Street, 2600 Vilnius (tel: 213-5550; fax: 213-5542; e-mail: vilnius@chambers.lt).

Banking

Bankas Snoras, 7A Vivulskio Street, 2600 Vilnius (tel: 216-2770/216-2771; fax: 310-155).

Lietuvos Zemes Ukio Bankas (Lithuanian Agricultural Bank), Totoriu 4, 2600 Vilnius (tel: 628-842/927; fax: 226-047).

Lithuanian Commercial Banker's Association, Vilniaus 4/35, Vilnius 2001 (tel: 227-063; fax: 227-065).

Lithuanian Development Bank, Stulginskio 4-7, 2600 Vilnius (tel: 225-259; fax: 227-360).

Lietuvos Taupomasis Bankas (Lithuanian Savings Bank), Savanoriu pr 19, 2015 Vilnius (tel: 232-379; fax: 232-431).

Lietuvos Valstybinis Komercinis Bankas (Lithuanian State Commercial Bank), Jogailos 14, 2001 Vilnius (tel: 626-872; fax: 615-428).

Vilniaus Bankas (commercial bank), Gedimino pr 12, 14, 2600 Vilnius (tel: 610-723; fax: 626-557).

Central bank

Lietuvos Bankas (Bank of Lithuania), 6 Gedimino Avenue, 2001 Vilnius (tel: 268-0029; fax: 262-8124; e-mail: info@lb.lt).

Travel information

Air Lithuania, 132 Veiveriu Street, Karmelava Airport, Kaunas 3010 (tel: 295-203, 291-681; fax: 226-030).

Airport (Aerouostas) information (tel: 630-201, 635-560); international information (tel: 669-481).

Austrian Airlines, SAS & Swissair, 2nd Floor, Vilnius Airport (tel: 662-000, 660-202; fax: 660-139).

Ferry (Klaipeda – Kiel) information (tel: 826-157-849; fax: 826-153-466; advance booking tel: 826-155-549); (Klaipeda – Mukran) information (tel: 826-117-825; advance booking tel: 826-199-936; fax: 826-116-681).

GT International Travel Consultants, Kalvariju 223, Vilnius (tel: 778-392; fax: 350-115).

Lithuanian Airlines, 8 Radunes, Vilnius Airport, Vilnius 232038 (tel: 630-116; fax: 266-828).

Lithuanian Tourism Association, Pylimo 6, 2001 Vilnius (tel: 750-803; fax: 227-550).

Travel Bureau, Lietuva Hotel, Ukmerges 20, Vilnius (tel: 356-225).

Ministry of tourism

State Tourism Department, Gedimino Ave 30/1, 2694 Vilnius (tel: 622-610; fax: 226-819).

National tourist organisation offices

Lithuanian Tourist Board, Ukmergès 20, 2600 Vilnius (tel: 726-558; fax: 226-819).

Ministries

Ministry of Agriculture, Gedimino Avenue 19, LT-2025 Vilnius (tel: 391-001; fax: 224-440; e-mail: zum@zum.lt).

Ministry of Culture, J Basanaviciaus Street 5, LT-5683 Vilnius (tel: 610-458; fax: 220-886 ; e-mail: culture@muza.lt).

Ministry of Defence, Tortoriu 25/3, LT-2001 Vilnius (tel: 735-501; fax: 226-082; e-mail: vis@kam.kam.lt).

Ministry of the Economy, Gedimino Avenue 38/2, LT-2600 Vilnius (tel: 622-416; fax: 623-974; e-mail: pr@po.ekm.lt).

Ministry of Education and Science, A Volano Street 2/7, LT-2691 Vilnius (tel: 622-929; fax: 612-077; e-mail: smmin@smm.lt).

Ministry of the Environment, A Jaksto Street 4/9, LT-2694 Vilnius (tel: 610-558; fax: 220-847; e-mail: info@aplinkuma.lt).

Ministry of Finance, J Tumo-Vaizganto Street 8a/2, LT-2600 Vilnius (tel: 390-005; fax: 791-481; e-mail: finmin@finmin.lt).

Ministry of Foreign Affairs, J Tumo-Vaizganto Street 2, LT-2600 Vilnius (tel: 362-401; fax: 313-090; e-mail: urm@urm.lt).

Ministry of Health, Vilniaus Street 33, LT-2001 Vilnius (tel: 621-625; fax: 224-601; e-mail: ministerija@sam.lt).

Ministry of the Interior, Sventaragio Street 5, LT-2600 Vilnius (tel: 717-2301; fax: 698-380; infoskyrius@vrm/lt).

Ministry of Justice, Gediminio Avenue 30/1, LT-2600 Vilnius (tel: 624-670; fax: 625-940).

Ministry of Social Welfare and Labour, A Vivulskio Street 11, LT-2693 Vilnius (tel: 603-773; fax: 603-813; e-mail: post@socmin.lt).

Ministry of Transport, Gediminio Avenue 17, LT-2679 Vilnius (tel: 393-911; fax: 224-335; e-mail: transp@transp.lt).

Office of the President, S Daukanto Square 3, LT-2008 Vilnius (tel: 625 542; fax: 225-382; e-mail: info@president.lt).

Office of the Prime Minister, Gedimino Avenue 11, LT-2039 Vilnius (tel: 622-101; fax: 227-452; e-mail: kanceliarija@lrvk.lt).

Other useful addresses

Association of Light Industry Enterprises of Lithuania, Saltonishkiu 29/3, 2677 Vilnius (tel: 751-877, 738-131; fax: 351-127).

Association of Lithuanian Entrepreneurs, A Jakshto 9, 2600 Vilnius (tel: 614-963, 628-702; fax: 220-448).

BNS (English-language Baltic news service), Konarskio 49, Vilnius (tel: 660-253, 660-526).

Central Telegraph Office, Vilniaus 33-2, Vilnius (tel: 619-614).

British Embassy, Antakalnio 2, Vilnius 2055 (tel: 222-070/1; fax: 727-579; e-mail: BE-VILNIUS@post.omnitel.net).

Central Post Office, Gedimino 7, Vilnius (tel: 616-759).

Commercial Court of the Republic of Lithuania, Gedimino pr 39/1, 2640 Vilnius (tel: 622-843; fax: 619-927).

Confederation of Lithuanian Industrialists, Saltonishkiu 19, 2600 Vilnius (tel: 751-278; fax: 723-320).

Construction Production Certification Centre, Linkmenu 28, 2600 Vilnius (tel: 728-077; fax: 728-075).

Department of Customs, A. Jaksto 1/25, 2600 Vilnius (tel: 226-415, 617-310; fax: 224-948; internet site: foreign trade database: http://www.cust.lt/).

Department of Forestry (tel: 621-514).

Department of Statistics, Gedimino pr 29, 2746 Vilnius (tel: 619-556; fax: 223-545).

ELTA Lithuanian News Agency, Gedimino Ave 21/2, Vilnius 2600 (tel: 628-864; fax: 629-507).

Energy Agency, A Vienuolio 8/4, 2600 Vilnius (tel: 226-158; fax: 225-208).

Lithuanian Builders' Association, Vytauto 14/2, 2000 Vilnius (tel: 225-568; fax: 225-901).

Lithuanian Building Industry Association, Sevcenko 19, 2000 Vilnius (tel: 233-479; fax: 635-641).

Lithuanian Commercial Bankers' Association, Vilniaus 4/35 (tel: 227-063; fax: 227-065).

Lithuanian Construction Association, Raugyklos 15, 2600 Vilnius (tel: 622-553; fax: 226-178).

Lithuanian Development Agency, Investment, Marketing and Public Relations Departments, Sv Jono Str 3 2600 Vilnius (tel: 627-438; fax: 220-160; e-mail: lda@lda.lt; internet site: http://www.lda.lt/); Export Department, Algirdo 31, 2600 Vilnius (tel: 233-822; fax: 233-626; e-mail: lda@lda.lt).

Lithuanian Economic and Foreign Investment Development Agency (FIDA), J Jasinskio 9, 4th floor, 2600 Vilnius (tel: 614-942, 618-181; fax: 618-181).

Lithuanian Embassy (USA), 2622 16th Street, NW, Washington DC 20009 (tel: 202-234-5860; fax: 202-328-0466; e-mail: info@ltembassyus.org).

Lithuanian Export Promotion Agency, J.Tumo-Vaizganto 8a/2, 2739 Vilnius (tel: 225-758; fax: 225-756; e-mail: lepa.epd@post.omnitel.net).

Lithuanian Free Market Institute, Birutes 56, 2600 Vilnius (tel: 727-584; fax: 721-279).

Lithuanian Information Institute, Kalvariju 3, 2659 Vilnius (tel: 727-968; fax: 723-017).

Lithuanian International Trade Agency, V Kudirkos st 18, 2600 Vilnius (tel: 620-883; fax: 610-663; e-mail: LAITA@post.omnitel.net).

Lithuanian Investment Agency (LIA), Sv Jono 3, 2600 Vilnius (tel: 623-870; fax: 220-160).

Lithuanian Manufacturers' Confederation, Saltonishkiu 19, 2687 Vilnius (tel: 751-278; fax: 723-320).

Lithuanian Privatisation Agency, Gedimino 38/2, 2600 Vilnius (tel: 624-671; fax: 623-510).

Lithuanian Road Administration, State Property and Service Division, 36/2 Basanaviciaus Street, Vilnius LT-2009 (tel: 235-849, 637-565; fax: 231-362).

Lithuanian-Russian Commercial Information Centre (consulting, marketing and general assistance to companies seeking to do business in Lithuania), Vilnius (tel: 357-903, 353-010; fax 624-872).

Lithuanian Standardisation Board, A Joksto g 1/25, 2600 Vilnius (tel: 226-962; fax: 226-259).

Lithuanian Television & Radio Broadcasting, Konarskio 49, 2674 Vilnius (tel: 660-637).

Privatisation Agency, Gedimino Prosp 38/2, Vilnius (tel: 624-671; fax: 623-510).

Securities Commission, Ukmerges g 41, 2600 Vilnius (tel: 724-091).

State Competition and Consumer Protection Office, Gedimino pr 38/2, 2600 Vilnius (tel: 627-797; fax: 226-419).

State Patent Bureau, Algirdo g 31, 2600 Vilnius (tel: 233-349; fax: 233-357).

State Quality Inspectorate, Gedimino pr 19, 2600 Vilnius (tel: 621-758; fax: 623-127).

State Tax Inspection, Sermuksniu st 6, 2600 Vilnius (tel: 620-060).

Vilnius City Administration, Gedimino ave 9, 2600 Vilnius (tel: 620-160).

Internet sites

Lithuania on-line page provides access to major Lithuanian web sites: http://www.aiva.lt/lol

Luxembourg

KEY FACTS

Official name: Groussherzogtom Lëtzebuerg, Grossherzogtum Luxemburg, Grand-Duché de Luxembourg (The Grand Duchy of Luxembourg)

Head of State: Grand Duke Henri of Luxembourg (acceded 7 Oct 2000)

Head of government: Prime Minister Jean-Claude Juncker (CSV) (appointed by the Grand Duke in 1995)

Ruling party: Coalition government: Chrëschtlich Sozial Volkspartei (CSV) (Christian Social People's Party) and Demokratesch Partie (DP) (Democratic Party) (since 4 Aug 1999; the CSV was re-elected 13 Jun 2004)

Area: 2,586 square km

Population: 457,700 (2004)

Capital: Luxembourg-Ville

Official language: Lëtzebuergish (Luxembourgish); French and German are the administrative languages.

Currency: Euro (eur) = 100 cents (from 1 Jan 2002; previous currency Luxembourg franc, locked at Lf40.34 per euro)

Exchange rate: eur0.83 per US$ (Oct 2005)

GDP per capita: US$69,929 (2004)

GDP real growth: 4.40% (2004)

Labour force: 301,000 (2004)

Unemployment: 4.20% (OECD, 2004)

Inflation: 2.20% (2004)

Balance of trade: -US$3.16 billion (2004)

Annual FDI: US$57.00 billion (OECD, 2004)*

* estimated figure

This green grand duchy with a population of only 230,000 people enjoys considerable prosperity and an outward looking mindset. Luxembourgish, German and French are the official languages, although many speak English too. The country was one of six founders of the European Economic Community in 1957, later to become the European Union. It is fitting, therefore, that the current prime minister is such a revered European statesman.

EU relations

Jean-Claude Juncker of the Christian Social People's Party retained his position as prime minister and finance minister after the June 2004 elections, to become the EU's longest serving prime minister. He also held the presidency of the EU from January to July 2005. He is hugely respected figure both domestically and in Europe, a talented negotiator and an excellent linguist, fluent in five languages. Juncker was one of the chief architects of the Maastricht Treaty, especially the Economic and Monetary Union sections. Thanks to the personal qualities and depth of economic understanding of this leading personality Luxembourg has enjoyed a greater platform in European affairs than would be usual for a country of its size. However, with characteristic eloquence, Juncker tells the Continent why his grand duchy matters: 'institutional life of Europe is a bit like in the animal kingdom – a flea can drive a lion crazy, but there is no known example of a lion driving a flea crazy. That shows how important it is to find the right balance between great and small.'

In June 2005, on the verge of handing over the EU leadership baton to British prime minister, Tony Blair, Juncker lashed out at the UK, commenting 'some delegations, who shall remain nameless, lacked the political will to reach an agreement'. Juncker was frustrated at the lack of progress on the future EU budget discussions, with Blair insisting that the UK rebate was not up for negotiation, and poorer countries offering to relinquish funds in order to break the deadlock. In a forceful display of rhetoric, Juncker proclaimed himself 'disheartened, disappointed, basically sad', and declared that he had 'no comment, no opinion and no advice' for the uncompromising Blair.

There was better EU news for Juncker to come, however. On 10 July Luxembourg held a referendum, in which all 230,000 citizens were legally required to vote, on whether the EU constitution should be approved. Fifty-six per cent of voters endorsed the constitution – just as well, because another 'no' vote following the Dutch and French rejections would have sounded the death knell for the document. It was also just as well because Juncker had promised to resign if his electorate threw out the constitution. The relieved leader celebrated the result, which he described as 'the popular will of a small state but a great nation'.

In another round of personal success Juncker was appointed as 'Mr Euro' in late 2004, and took office in January 2005. President of the Eurogroupe committee of finance ministers, Juncker is the political face of Europe's single currency. This new elected position replaces the old system of rotating leadership. 'Mr Euro' will govern until 31 December 2006 although his term can be extended once.

Economy

With growing political and economic integration in the EU, Luxembourg could potentially benefit from European regionalism, as it is located in the centre of the European geographical area with the highest economic activity. However, future developments in EU policy in regard to financial operations could also deprive Luxembourg of substantial earnings which are an integral part of its economy.

After several years of sluggish growth the Luxembourg economy is enjoying a recovery. Economic growth (GDP) was forecast at 3.1 per cent in 2005, expected to rise to 3.2 per cent in 2006. Growth will be generated by increased exports and corporate investment. The manufacturing sector is enjoying the return of lost business confidence and orders look to be high. Although Luxembourg's record of attracting foreign direct investment is good, it has been advised that it should tackle labour market reform, to help attract new businesses. In 2004 net inflow of FDI was US$57.4 billion, almost half of the previous year.

Unemployment appears to be growing steadily, rising to 4.6 per cent in 2005 and forecast to rise to 5.1 per cent in 2006 and up to 5.6 per cent by 2007. The labour market is in need of reform to render it more flexible. High energy prices in 2005 had a negative impact on domestic private consumption and exports were affected by weak foreign markets.

The steel industry since 2000 has fallen from its prominence as one of the primary revenue earners but this has been offset by the emergence of Luxembourg as a financial centre. Services in 2004 were estimated at 83.1 per cent of GDP and industry 16.3 per cent. In 2005 financial services led growth, followed by business services, industry, transportation and communications. The banking sector did particularly well and there were some 167 banks in Luxembourg, providing employment for over 23,300 employees.

Monetary policy

The European Central Bank (ECB) took over responsibility for Luxembourg's monetary policy from the Banque Centrale du Luxembourg (BCL) (Central Bank of Luxembourg) when the country joined the European Economic and Monetary Union (Emu) in January 1999. The ECB's main role is to encourage price stability of the euro currency, aiming for low inflation and low interest rates. To maintain price stability of the euro, the ECB aims for an inflation rate of 2.0 per cent across the euro-zone. The ECB has had a difficult time trying to maintain the euro-zone annual inflation rate at the 2 per cent target. Luxembourg's inflation in 2005 was 2.2 per cent, which is not predicted to change in 2006, according to the Paris-based Organisation for Economic Co-operation and Development (OECD).

Banking laws

Luxembourg has faced increasing international pressure to reform its banking secrecy laws over recent years, an issue which has had the potential to sour relations with a number of international allies. Alongside other EU and key non-EU financial centres, Luxembourg has yielded to US pressure to reform its banking secrecy laws in order to provide the US Internal Revenue Service (IRS) with information regarding interest paid to US citizens. Luxembourg has in principal agreed to relax its secrecy laws from 2010. Final approval of the directive is conditional on similar action being undertaken in other EU states and dependencies (principally the British Channel Islands and

KEY INDICATORS — Luxembourg

	Unit	2000	2001	2002	2003	2004
Population	m	0.44	0.44	0.45	0.45	0.46
Gross domestic product (GDP)	US$bn	17.80	19.50	20.10	25.64	*31.14
GDP per capita	US$	40,355	43,413	45,902	56,754	69,929
GDP real growth	%	7.5	5.1	0.5	1.2	4.4
Inflation	%	3.1	2.7	2.1	2.5	2.2
Unemployment	%	2.7	2.6	2.8	3.8	4.2
Exports (fob) (goods)	US$m	8,506.0	8,791.0	9,609.0	10,000.0	13,714.0
Imports (fob) (goods)	US$m	10,727.0	11,158.0	11,772.0	13,600.0	16,871.0
Balance of trade	US$m	-2,222.0	-2,367.0	-2,163.0	-3,700.0	-3,157.0
Current account	US$m	1,149.0	884.0	1,636.0	3,400.0	2,250.0
Total reserves minus gold	US$m	76.6	105.6	151.7	279.9	298.4
Foreign exchange	US$m	72.3	99.2	142.4	178.7	139.3
Exchange rate	per US$	43.68	44.07	1.04	0.88	0.80

* estimated figure

Luxembourg

French and Dutch overseas territories) and by key non-EU states such as Andorra, Liechtenstein, Monaco and Switzerland. Under the directive, EU countries will have to exchange information about savings accounts held by non residents so they cannot avoid demands made by their national tax authorities. Withholding taxes on income from investment accounts held by EU citizens in other EU countries will gradually be introduced.

International pressure for reform is likely to continue; while the OECD does not list Luxembourg as an international tax haven, it remains listed as a country with a potentially harmful tax regime.

Outlook

With one of the world's highest GDP per capita, continuous economic growth over the past ten years and low inflation, Luxembourg's economy is strong and diversified. Luxembourg is undergoing growing political and economic integration in the EU. However, future developments in EU policy in regard to financial operations could also deprive Luxembourg of substantial earnings which are an integral part of its economy. The IMF is confident of good economic growth in Luxembourg into 2006.

Risk assessment

Economic	Good
Political	Good
Regional Stability	Good

COUNTRY PROFILE

Historical profile

Modern-day Luxembourg was occupied by the Burgundians, Prussians, Spanish and French until the nineteenth century, when it came under German and Dutch control.
1867 Luxembourg was granted independence.
1914–18 Luxembourg was occupied by the Germans.
1921 The Belgian-Luxembourg Economic Union (BLEU) was formed.
1940–45 Nazi Germany occupied Luxembourg.
1948 The Benelux Economic Union (Benelux) was inaugurated between Belgium, Luxembourg and the Netherlands and became effective in 1960, establishing the three countries as a single customs area in 1970.
1949 Luxembourg became a founding member of NATO.
1957 Luxembourg became one of the founder members of the forerunner to the EU, the European Economic Community (EEC).
1964 Grand Duchess Charlotte abdicated after a reign of 45 years and was succeeded by her son, Prince Jean.
1974 After being in power since 1918, the Chrëschtlich Sozial Vollekspartei (CSV) (Christian Social People's Party) was defeated by the Demokratesch Partie (DP) (Democratic Party) in general elections.
1979 The CSV regained power.
1990 Luxembourg was an original signatory of the Schengen Agreement to remove all border controls.
1994 Jean-Claude Juncker became prime minister.
1999 A CSV/DP coalition government was formed after the CSV failed to win enough seats in the parliamentary elections to have an outright majority. Juncker remained as prime minister.
2000 Grand Duke Jean abdicated and was succeeded by his son, Prince Henri.
2002 Euro currency replaced the Luxembourg franc. Luxembourg was named by a French parliamentary committee as a haven for tax evasion and money laundering.
2003 After EU talks on new rules for the taxation of savings invested abroad, in January, Luxembourg won the right to decide when they would drop the withholding tax and begin exchanging information.
2004 The Chrëschtlich Sozial Vollekspartei (CSV) (Christian Social People's Party) was re-elected in the parliamentary elections on 13 June.
2005 On 10 July, voters in Luxembourg approved the European constitution by 57 per cent to 43 per cent.

Political structure
Constitution
The constitution was adopted in 1868 and has been amended on four occasions (1919, 1994, 1996 and 1998). It can be amended when at least two thirds, of a minimum 75 per cent of parliamentary members, vote in agreement. A plebicite must ratify the amendment.
The constitution sets out the role of the hereditary crown as Head of State, and the rights of citzens before the law. Universal direct suffrage for all those registered and over the age of 18.
Form of state
Parliamentary democratic monarchy
The executive
Executive power is vested in the Grand Duke and exercised through the constitution and the law.
The Council of Ministers is led by the prime minister, who is chosen by the Grand Duke, and must have the support of the Chamber of Deputies.
National legislature
Legislative power is exercised by a unicameral 60-member Châmber vun Députéirten / Chambre des Députés (Chamber of Deputies), which is elected for a five-year term by proportional representation in four multi-seat constituencies. A 21-member Council of State, chosen by the Grand Duke, acts as an advisory body and has some legislative functions.
Legal system
Loosely based on Napoleonic code, of inquisitorial justice. The highest court is th Superior Court of Justice. Justices of the peace, district court judges and members of the Superior Court are appointed for life by the Grand Duke. Special laws regulate military tribunals. Administrative courts have jurisdiction over tax and administrative matters. There is a Constitutional Court that decides on the conformity of laws within the constitution. The Grand Duke has the authority to revoke or reduce penalties awarded by judges.
Last elections
13 June 2004 (parliamentary); 13 June (European Parliament).
Results: Parliamentary: the ruling CSV was re-elected with 36.1 per cent of the vote (24 seats out of 60), LSAP/POSL 23.4 per cent (14), DP 16.1 per cent (10), Déi Gréng (Green Party) 11.6 per cent (seven) and Aktiounskomitee fir Demokratie an Rentengerechteekeet (ADR) (Action Committee for Democracy and Pensions Justice) 10 per cent (five). European Parliament: CSV won 37.1 per cent of the vote (three seats out of six), LSAP/POSL 22.1 per cent (one), Green Party 15 per cent (one), DP 14.9 per cent (one) and ADR 8 per cent (no seats); turnout 90 per cent.
Next elections
10 July 2005 (referendum on the EU constitution); 2009 (parliamentary).

Political parties
Ruling party
Coalition government: Chrëschtlich Sozial Vollekspartei (CSV) (Christian Social People's Party) and Demokratesch Partie (DP) (Democratic Party) (since 4 Aug 1999; the CSV was re-elected 13 Jun 2004)
Main opposition party
Lëtzeburger Sozialistesch Arbechterpartei or Parti Ouvrier Socialiste Luxembourgeois (LSAP/POSL) (Luxembourg Socialist Workers' Party)

Population
457,700 (2004)
Ethnic make-up
The inhabitants of Luxembourg are mostly of German and French origin, but have a distinct national consciousness. From just under 20 per cent in 1970, the percentage of foreign residents has risen to over 30 per cent. The Portuguese, who account for over 10 per cent of the total population, form the largest foreign

community. The second largest immigrant community comes from Italy (5 per cent).
Religions
Approximately 97 per cent of the population is Roman Catholic.

Education
Primary education lasts for six years, until the age of 12. Instruction is initially given in German, and French is added in the second year. Secondary education can be obtained through either a ILycé, or *Lycé Technique*. The first offers general and technical schooling, for up to seven years with an initial period of three years then an advanced (and non-compulsory) programme of four years. The *Lycé Technique* offers complete seven-year courses. French replaces German in the classroom at secondary schooling.
Higher education in the Grand Duchy is limited in scope. Approximately 4,000 students attend foreign universities, predominantly in Belgium and France.
Compulsory years: Six to 15.
Enrolment rate: 85 per cent net primary enrolment (Unicef).

Health
Luxembourg has one of the highest levels of GDP per capita in the world and is well resourced to retain the high level of healthcare that the country's small population currently enjoys.
Annual total expenditure on health is around 6 per cent of GDP, of which government spending is approximately 90 per cent.
HIV prevalence: 0.2 per cent aged 15–49 in 2003 (World Bank)
Life expectancy: 78.3 years (World Bank)
Fertility rate/Maternal mortality rate: 1.6 per woman (World Bank)
Infant mortality rate: 4.9 per 1,000 live births (World Bank)

Welfare
The social security system was built in several stages. It has been extended to include both the socio-professional categories and at risk groups. The minimum wage, which functions as a mechanism to guarantee resources, consists of a supplementary benefit paid up to a threshold determined according to the composition of the household. The benefit is awarded irrespective of the causes of the situation of need. Sickness benefits, in which patients pay only a small part of medical costs, as well as birth, family and unemployment payments, are included in the plans. Housing conditions are generally comparable to those found in other Western European countries. There has been some difficulty in assimilating the many thousands of foreign workers and their families.

Luxembourg conforms to the EU provisions dealing with social security based on the principle of free movement of workers within the EU that enables its workers to accept a job in another member state without suffering any inequality with regard to social security. The EU social security arrangements aim to co-ordinate the national social security schemes in all the member states of the EU and the European Economic Area (EEA).
The social security system covers benefits for sickness and maternity, pensions, insurance against accidents at work and occupational diseases, unemployment benefits and family allowances. The scheme is compulsory and covers all persons in paid employment as well as self-employed workers in the country. Half of the contribution due is payable by the worker and half by the employer. There is no contribution towards industrial accident insurance, family benefits or unemployment benefit. Contributions are payable for sickness and maternity insurance, disability insurance, old-age and survivor's pension, amounting to a certain percentage of his/her remuneration.

Main cities
Luxembourg-Ville (capital, estimated population 78,800 in 2003), Esch-sur-Alzette (27,900), Dudelange (17,800).

Languages spoken
Official language/s
Lëtzebuergish (Luxembourgish); French and German are the administrative languages.

Media
Press
Dailies: Principal dailies include *Luxemburger Wort* (*La Voix du Luxembourg*), *Tageblatt-Zeitung fir Letzeburg*, *Lëtzebuerger Journal* and *Zeitung vum Letzebuerger Vollek*. The French *Le Républicain-Lorrain*, which has an extensive Luxembourg section, is also widely read.
Weeklies: Include *Télécran* (entertainment), *Contacto* and *Revue* covering issues of general interest.
Business: There are numerous journals and magazines including *d'Letzebuerger Land*, *l'Echo de l'Industrie*, *De Letzeburger Merkur*, *Luxembourg Business* and *Luxemburg News*.
Periodicals: Those featuring general interest, current affairs and women's issues include *Foyer de la Femme*, *Gaart an Heem*, *Grénge Spoun* and *Select Magazine*.
Broadcasting
Compagnie Luxembourgeoise de Télédiffusion, the operator of Radio-Télé Luxembourg (RTL), operates 14 television channels in six countries and 18 radio stations across eight countries.
Advertising
There is commercial advertising on radio, TV and billboards.

Economy
The economy was running at an impressive GDP average of 6 per cent in 2000 and 2001, until a sudden drop to 0.5 per cent in 2002. Since then recovery has been progressive with a GDP rise to 4.4 per cent in 2004 and inflation remained fairly constant between 2.7–2.2 per cent 2001–04.
The steel industry since 2000 has fallen from its prominence as one of the primary revenue earners but this has been offset by the emergence of Luxembourg as a financial centre. Services in 2004 were estimated at 83.1 per cent of GDP and industry 16.3 per cent. In 2004 financial services led growth, followed by business services, industry, transportation and communications. The banking sector did particularly well and there were some 167 banks in Luxembourg, providing employment for over 23,300 employees. Although Luxembourg's record of attracting foreign direct investment (FDI – US$57.4 billion, 2004) is good, it has been advised that it should tackle labour market reform, to help attract new businesses. Luxembourg is well situated at the heart of the EU and could benefit from European regionalism. It is a member of the euro-zone.
The agricultural sector is small, mostly dairy and meat. It provides employment for under 2.0 per cent of the work force. Forecasts for 2005 were that activity would slow, but pick up again in 2006. The OECD made a number of recommendations including welfare and tax reforms, and strengthening the financial sector.

External trade
Over two-thirds of Luxembourg's trade is with EU member states. Luxembourg and Belgium operate the Belgian-Luxembourg Economic Union (BLEU).
Luxembourg's merchandise trade is perennially in deficit because of its narrow economic base and consequent dependence on imports. The shortfall is outweighed by the surplus on invisibles accounts.
Imports
Imports are minerals, metals, foodstuffs and quality consumer goods.
Main sources: Belgium (30.0 per cent total, 2004), Germany (21.8 per cent), France (12.5 per cent), China (11.9 per cent), The Netherlands (4.5 per cent)
Exports
Luxembourg's dependence on exports of goods and services has made it

favourable to open borders and free-flowing commercial activity. Most trade is with Luxembourg's immediate neighbours. Despite increased specialisation in intermediate products, the range of products exported has been growing steadily. The more traditional products (including agri-foodstuffs, steel products, rubber tyres, glass, plastics and textiles and ceramics) are joined by others, including glass, steel, non-ferrous metals (copper and aluminium), paper-based media and computer media. Despite profound change in the composition of the goods exported, intermediate products still account for some 80 per cent of total products.

Main destinations: Germany (21.8 per cent total, 2004), France (20.1 per cent), Belgium (10.5 per cent), UK (9.3 per cent), Italy (7.1 per cent), Spain (5.6 per cent), The Netherlands (4.3 per cent)

Agriculture
Farming
The country has gradually adapted and delegated much of its farm policy to the EU, through the Common Agricultural Policy (CAP). Fundamental reform to the CAP was introduced on 1 January 2005 in Italy. The subsidies paid on farm output, which tended to benefit large farms and encourage overproduction, were replaced by single farm payments not conditional on production. This is expected to reward farms that provide and maintain a healthy environment, food safety and animal welfare standards. The changes are also intended to encourage market conscious production and cut the cost of CAP to the EU taxpayer.

Farming is concentrated on barley, oats and potatoes in the north, and fruit and grapes in the east.

Although agricultural output has tripled since the 1980s, its contribution to GDP has in the same period declined from 4 per cent in mid-1970s to around 1 per cent in late 1990s. The number of farms declined from 5,173 in 1980 to 2,950 in 1998 as high agricultural production costs and high employment in Luxembourg caused more people to leave the farming industry and farmland has subsequently been converted to other uses. This trend slowed in 2003 and 2004 as the economy slowed and jobs were not so readily available. Three-quarters of the land is cultivated. Pasture accounts for 55 per cent of all cultivated farmland.

Food and wine account for about 1.9 per cent of exports.

Crop production in 2004 included: 180,000 tonnes (t) cereals in total, 80,000t wheat, 16,000t rapeseed (canola), 3,000t maize, 8,000t rye, 22,000t potatoes, 55,000t barley, 2,100t pulses, 4,000t apples, 17,000t grapes, 6,080t oilcrops, 150t treenuts, 23,000t oats, 23,645t fruit in total, 16,110t vegetables in total. Livestock production included: 45,350t meat in total, 17,500t beef, 11,500t pig meat, 70t lamb & goat meat, 15,950t poultry, 265,000t milk, 3,200t cattle hides, 280t horsemeat.

Fishing
Luxembourg does not have any significant freshwater fishing industry.

Forestry
Largely driven back to the least productive soil and escarpments where viable development is precluded, woods cover some 89,000 hectares or around a third of the country. Extending over 4,500 hectares, the forest of Gruenwald is the largest continuous wooded area in the Grand Duchy. Forestry only plays a very modest role in the overall economy, the commercial exploitation of private forests and those subject to the system of forest tenure only represent on average between 0.1 per cent and 0.2 per cent of GDP.

Industry and manufacturing
As with the agricultural sector, Luxembourg's industrial base has declined in proportion to the dominant services sector and accounts for only 30 per cent of GDP. The country's principal industries include steel, chemicals, rubber, plastics, processing, glass, aluminium, metalworking and vehicle spares manufacture.

Tourism
Tourism is becoming a most important area of the economy and is being actively promoted by the government. In 2005 travel and tourism is expected to contribute US$1.2 billion or 3.4 per cent of GDP and employ over 12 per cent of the workforce. It should also attract US$496 million, or 6.4 per cent of total capital investment.

The Dutch have traditionally been the main visitors followed by the Belgians, Germans, French and British. Luxembourg receives the largest number of tourists in the region, followed by the Ardennes and Mëllerdall.

Mining
Iron ore, discovered around 1850, made the fortune of modern Luxembourg's economy. The steel industry still serves as one of the most important sector of the economy, although its share of GDP fallen has since the early 2000s.

Hydrocarbons
Luxembourg does not have any oil, natural gas or coal reserves. The country imports all its hydrocarbons, totalling 52,300 barrels per day (bpd) of refined oil products, 1.2 billion cubic metres of natural gas and 127,000 tonnes of coal. These imports come primarily from the EU.

Energy
There is heavy dependence on imported energy, mainly from Belgium and Germany. Luxembourg has a hydroelectric dam at Vianden, but still imports electricity. There are no nuclear power plants. Of the 6.1 billion KW hours consumed annually, only 648 million KW is generated in Luxembourg.

Financial markets
Stock exchange
The principal source of growth in the domestic economy has been the financial services sector. The main activities are banking and investment fund management.

The Luxembourg Stock Exchange trades every working day.

Banking and insurance
Luxembourg has a large banking sector. Activity is oriented towards wholesale banking services, with a large concentration of German and Scandinavian banks serving corporate customers in Europe. Private banking has rapidly increased. Banking accounts for around 16 per cent of GDP and employs 10 per cent of the workforce. Luxembourg's banking secrecy laws were a source of complaint abroad, however new rules allow authorities to investigate as necessary. There is concern that EU requirements for the deduction of a withholding tax from all foreign accounts will adversely affect the sector.

Central bank
The European Central Bank (ECB) acts as the central bank, issuing notes and coins and determining interest rates.

Time
GMT plus one hour (GMT plus two hours from late Mar to late Sep).

Geography
Luxembourg is a landlocked country in Western Europe, bounded by Belgium on the north and west, Germany to the east and France to the south. Luxembourg consists mainly of the upper basins of the Sauer (Sûre) and Alzette rivers. The highest point is Buurgplaatz (559 metres), in the Ardennes Plateau in the north. The southern two-thirds of the country is a rolling plateau, the Bon Pays.

Climate
Luxembourg's climate is temperate, without extremes. Sea winds (south-west and north-west) shed a great part of their moisture before reaching the Luxembourg frontiers. May to mid-October is suitable for vacations; July and August are the warmest; May and June are the sunniest months; in September and October there is often an 'Indian summer'.

Dress codes
Medium-weight clothing is required throughout the year. A raincoat is useful.

Entry requirements
Passports
Passports are required by nationals of most countries. Exceptions include holders of national identity cards issued to nationals of some European countries.
Visa
Required by all, except nationals of Europe, North America, Australasia, or Japan. For a full list of visa-free citizens visit www.luxembourg-usa.org/consindex.html. Schengen visas cover all entry needs; for those requiring a business visa, a letter of business references and proof of sufficient funds to cover the cost of your intended stay should accompany the application. A Schengen visa application (offered in several languages) can be downloaded on www.eurovisa.info/ApplicationForm.htm.
Currency advice/regulations
There are no restrictions on the movement of local or foreign currency.
Customs
Personal effects and goods up to a specified value are duty-free. Passengers carrying weapons and transiting through Luxembourg must hold an Autorisation de Transit d'Armes certificate issued by the Luxembourg Ministry of Justice.

Health (for visitors)
Mandatory precautions
None
Advisable precautions
It is recommended that travellers have up-to-date tetanus and polio immunisations.

Hotels
A one-to five-star rating system is partially in operation. Bills include the service charge. Tipping is optional.

Credit cards
All main credit cards are accepted.

Public holidays
Fixed dates
1 Jan (New Year's Day), 1 May (May Day), 23 Jun (National Day), 15 Aug (Assumption Day), 1 Nov (All Saints' Day), 25 Dec (Christmas Day), 26 Dec (St Stephen's Day).
If a holiday falls on a Sunday, the Monday following is usually a holiday as well (maximum two per annum).
Variable dates
Carnival (Feb), Easter Monday, Ascension Day, Whit Monday, Luxembourg City Fair Day (Luxembourg City only, Sep).

Working hours
Banking
Mon–Fri: 0900–1630.
Business
Mon–Fri: 0800–1800, lunch 1200–1400.
Government
Mon–Fri: 0800–1800, lunch 1200–1400.
Shops
There are large variations in shop hours, but they are generally open 0900–2000, closed Mon morning.

Electricity supply
220V AC

Weights and measures
Metric system

Social customs/useful tips
Punctuality is appreciated. Business people are expected to wear suits. It is advisable to make prior appointments and business cards are widely used.

Security
Luxembourg has a low crime rate. However, during the tourist season pickpocketing and theft from vehicles do occur.

Getting there
Air
National airline: Luxair
International airport/s: Findel (LUX), 5km east of capital.
Airport tax: None
Surface
Road: There are good road links with Brussels, Trier, Paris, Frankfurt and Saarbrücken. Luxembourg has open borders with all its immediate neighbours, namely Germany, France and Belgium.
Rail: There are rail connections with Brussels, Frankfurt, Amsterdam, Basle and Paris.

Getting about
National transport
Road: Luxembourg has around 2,900km of roads, of which 120km are motorways.
Buses: There are state-run bus services between most towns.
Rail: There are 280km of railway track. State-run railway services link the capital with most main towns.
Water: A canal service operates on the Mertert.
City transport
Taxis: There is a metered taxi service with a minimum charge. Tipping is usually 15 per cent.
Buses, trams & metro: Regular flat-fare bus service operates within greater Luxembourg-Ville. Network tickets are valid for one day from punching until 0800 the next day. For small trips you can buy short distance tickets valid for one hour.
Car hire
Car hire is available from the airport and hotels.

BUSINESS DIRECTORY

Telephone area codes
The international direct dialling (IDD) code for Luxembourg is +352, followed by subscriber's number.

Chambers of Commerce
American Chamber of Commerce in Luxembourg, 31 Boulevard Konrad Adenauer, 1115 Luxembourg (tel/fax: 431-756; e-mail: info@amcham.lu).

British Chamber of Commerce for Luxembourg, 6 Rue Antoine de Saint Exupéry, 1432 Luxembourg (tel: 465-466; fax: 220-384; e-mail: info@bcc.lu).

Luxembourg Chamber of Commerce, 7 Rue Alcide de Gaspari, 2981 Luxembourg (tel: 423-939; fax: 438-326; e-mail: chamcom@cc.lu).

Banking
Association des Banques et Banquiers (Banking Association), Luxembourg BP 13, L-2010 (tel: 29-501, 463-6601; fax: 460-921).

Bacob Bank Luxembourg SA, 47 Boulevard Prince Henri, PO Box 11, L2010 Luxembourg (tel: 461-3411; fax: 469-063).

Banque Continentale du Luxembourg SA, 2 Boulevard Emmanuel Servais, L-2535 Luxembourg (tel: 474-491; fax: 477-688-333).

Banque de Luxembourg SA, 80 Place de la Gare, BP 2221, L-1022 Luxembourg (tel: 499-241; fax: 494-820).

Banque et Caisse d'Epargne de l'Etat (state and savings bank), 1 Place de Metz, L-2954 Luxembourg (tel: 40-151; internet site: http://www.bcee.lu).

Banque Générale du Luxembourg, Boulevard JF Kennedy, L-2951 Luxembourg (tel: 47-991, 42-421; fax: 4799-2579).

Banque Internationale à Luxembourg SA BIL, 2 Boulevard Royal, L-2953 Luxembourg (tel: 45-901; fax: 4791-2010).

Banque Nationale de Paris SA, 22-24 Boulevard Royal, L-2952 Luxembourg-Ville (tel: 47-641; fax: 26-480).

Caisse Centrale Raiffeisen SC, 28 Boulevard Royal, BP 111, L-2011 Luxembourg (tel: 462-151).

Deutsche Bank Luxembourg SA, 25 Boulevard Royal, BP 586, 2449 Luxembourg-Ville (tel: 468-181).

Deutsche Girozentrale International SA, 16 Boulevard Royal, L-2449 Luxembourg (tel: 462-471; fax: 462-477).

Fortuna, Société Co-opérative de Credit et d'Epargne, 128-132 Boulevard de la Pétrusse, BP 1203, L-1012 Luxembourg (tel: 488-888).

Luxembourg

Kredietbank SA Luxembourgeoise, 43 Boulevard Royal, L-2953 Luxembourg (tel: 47-971; fax: 472-667).

Republic National Bank of New York, 32 Boulevard Royal, Luxembourg (tel: 470-711; fax: 479-331, 479-226).

Société Générale Bank and Trust, 11-13 Avenue Emile Reuter, L-2420 Luxembourg.

Société Nationale de Credit et d'Investissement, 7 Rue du St Esprit, BP 1207, L-1012 Luxembourg (tel: 461-9711).

Central bank
Banque Centrale du Luxembourg 2Boulevard Royal, L-2983 Luxembourg (tel: 4774-1; fax: 4774-4901; e-mail: direction@bcl.lu).

European Central Bank (ECB), Kaiserstrasse 29, D-60311 Frankfurt am Main, Germany (tel: +49(69)13-440; fax: +49(69)1344-6000; e-mail: info@ecb.int).

Travel information
Convention Bureau (tel: 227-565; fax: 467-073).

Luxair, Luxembourg Airport, 2987 Luxembourg-Ville (tel: 798-2311/2221; fax: 443-2482, 436-344).

Luxembourg Airport (tel: 400-808).

Luxembourg Station, Place de la Gare (tel: 481-199).

Syndicat d'Initiative et de Tourisme, Place d'Armes, L-1136 Luxembourg (tel: 222-809; fax: 474-818).

Ministry of tourism
Ministère des Classes Moyennes et du Tourisme, 6 Avenue Emile Reuter, L-2137 Luxembourg (tel: 4656-1406; fax: 474-011).

National tourist organisation offices
Office National du Tourisme, 77 Rue d'Anvers, Box 1001, L-1010 Luxembourg (tel: 400-808; fax: 404-748).

Ministries
Ministère des Affaires Etrangères, du Commerce Extèrieur et de la Coopèration, 5 Rue Notre-Dame, L-2913 (tel: 4781; fax: 461-720).

Ministère de l'Agriculture, de la Viticulture et du Developpement Rural, 1 Rue de la Congrègation, L-2913 (tel: 4781; fax: 464-027).

Ministère de l'Amenagement du Territoire, 18 Montée de la Pètrusse, L-2946 (tel: 4781; fax: 408-970).

Ministère de la Culture, 20 Montée de la Pétrusse, L-2912 Luxembourg (tel: 4781; fax: 402-427).

Ministère de l'Economie, 19-21 Boulevard Royal, L-2914 (tel: 478-4100; fax: 460-448).

Ministère de l'Education Nationale et de la Formation Professionnelle, 29 rue Aldringen, L-2926 (tel: 4781; fax: 478-5113).

Ministère de l'Education Physique et des Sports, 66 route de Treves, L-2916 (tel: 4781; fax: 434-599).

Ministère de l'Energie, 19 Boulevard Royal, L-2449 (tel: 4781).

Ministère de l'Environnement, 18 Montèe de la Pètrusse, L-2918 (tel: 4781; fax: 400-410).

Ministère de la Famille, 14 Avenue de la Gare, L-2919 Luxembourg (tel: 4781; fax: 478-6570).

Ministère des Finances, 3 rue de la Congregation, L-2931 (tel: 4781; fax: 475-241).

Ministère de la Fonction Publique et de la Réforme Administrative, Plateau du St Esprit, L-2011 (tel: 4781; fax: 478-3122).

Ministère de la Force Publique, Plateau du St Esprit, Bâtiment Vauban, L-2915 (tel: 4781; fax: 462-682).

Ministère de l'Intèrieur, 19 Rue Beaumont, L-2933 (tel: 4781; fax: 418-46).

Ministère de la Jeunesse, 26 Rue Zithe, L-2943 Luxembourg (tel: 4781; fax: 467-454).

Ministère de la Justice, 16 Boulevard Royal, L-2934 Luxembourg (tel: 4781; fax: 227-661).

Ministère du Logement, 6 Avenue Emile Reuter, L-2942 (tel: 4781; fax: 478-4840).

Ministère de la Promotion Féminine, 33 Boulevard Prince Henri, L-2919 Luxembourg (tel: 4781; fax: 41-886).

Ministère de la Santé, 57 et 90 Boulevard de la Pétrusse, L-2320 Luxembourg (tel: 4781; fax: 484-903).

Ministère de la Sécurité Sociale, 26 Rue Zithe, L-2936 Luxembourg (tel: 4781; fax: 478-6328).

Ministère des Transports, 19-21 Boulevard Royal, L-2938 Luxembourg (tel: 4781; fax: 464-315).

Ministère des Travail et de l'Emploi, 26 rue Zithe, L-2939 (tel: 4781; fax: 478-6325).

Ministère des Travaux Publics, 4 Boulevard FD Roosevelt, L-2940 Luxembourg (tel: 4781; fax: 462-709).

Other useful addresses
Bourse de Luxembourg SA (stock exchange), 11 Avenue de la Porte-Neuve, L-2227 Luxembourg (tel: 477-9361; fax: 22-050; internet site: http://www.bourse.lu/).

Board of Economic Development, 19-21 Boulevard Royal, L-2914 Luxembourg (tel:478-4135/4141; fax: 460-448).

Confédération du Commerce Luxembourgeois, 23 Allée Scheffer, L-2520 Luxembourg (tel: 473-125).

Fédération des Industriels Luxembourgeois, 7 Rue Alcide de Gasperi, L-1615 Luxembourg (tel: 435-366; fax: 438-326).

Foires Internationales de Luxembourg, L-2088 Luxembourg (tel: 043-991; fax: 0439-9315).

Groupement des Industries Sidérurgiques Luxembourgeoises (Federation of Iron and Steel Industries in Luxembourg), 3 Rue Goethe, BP 1704, 1637 Luxembourg-Ville (tel: 480-001).

Luxembourg Embassy (USA), 2200 Massechusetts Avenue, NW, Washington DC 20008 (tel: 202-265-4171; fax: 202-328-8270; e-mail: info@luxembourg-usa.org).

Offshore Company Registration Agents (Luxembourg) SA, PO Box 878, 19 Rue Aldringen, L-1118 Luxembourg (tel: 224-286; fax: 224-287).

Press and Information Service of the Government, 43 Boulevard Roosevelt, L-2450 Luxembourg (tel: 478-224, 478-321; fax: 470-285, 20-090).

Radio Télé-Luxembourg (RTL), Villa Louvigny, L-2850 Luxembourg (tel: 476-6242; fax: 4766-2737).

Service Central de la Statistique et des Etudes Economiques (STATEC), 6 Boulevard Royal, L-2013 Luxembourg (tel: 4781; fax: 464-289; internet site: http://statec.lu/).

Société Européenne des Satellites (SES), Château de Betzdorf, L-6815 Luxembourg (tel: 710-725/1; fax: 725-227; internet site: http://www.astra.lu).

Internet sites
Complete list of banks in Luxembourg: http://www.bank.lu

Government statistics: http://statec.gouvernement.lu

Luxembourg weekly publication (in English): http://www.352.lu

Luxembourg government: http://gouvernement.lu

The Station Network, online information (in English): http://www.station.lu

Web directory: http://Luxembourg.lu/

Macao (China)

KEY FACTS

Official name: Macao Special Administrative Region of China (Macao SAR)

Head of State: State President Hu Jintao (elected 15 Mar 2003)

Head of government: Chief Executive Edmund Ho Hau Wah (appointed Dec 1999; re-elected 29 Aug 2004)

Ruling party: There are no political parties: there are 12 popularly elected seats in the legislature, an additional 10 seats are filled by business and special interest groups, and 7 seats are appointed by Macao's chief executive.

Area: 26 square km (Macao peninsula, Taipa and Coloane islands)

Population: 451,000 (2004)

Capital: Macao City

Official language: Chinese and Portuguese

Currency: Pataca (Pa) = 100 avos

Exchange rate: Pa7.99 per US$ (Oct 2005); (the pataca is pegged to the Hong Kong dollar at Pa1.03)

GDP per capita: US$18,096 (2004)

GDP real growth: 28.00% (2004)

Unemployment: 4.80% (2004)

Inflation: 1.10% (2004)

Balance of trade: -US$610.00 million (2004)

Visitor numbers: 16.67 million (2004)

COUNTRY PROFILE

Historical profile

The former Portuguese colony of Macao has grown rapidly since the mid-1980s. Like Hong Kong, Macau once had hopes of establishing itself as a regional service centre for business relations between southern China and overseas investors. But China's entry into the WTO largely renders the need and the role for middlemen obsolete and Hong Kong's services sector has always been more developed and sophisticated. For decades, Macao's economy has traditionally relied on gambling, tourism and the export of textiles and clothing. When textile and clothing manufacturers relocated to China, Macao was left with a definite need to diversify its economy. This need became more acute with the end of the multi-fibre agreement in 2005. As land supply is limited, mass production facilities are not viable. Therefore incentives to attract high-technology manufacturing and investment have been implemented. These include specifically, a new legal framework allowing for the development of offshore services; job creation schemes; applications for the immigration of technical workers simplified; and intellectual property rights protection.

1513 The first group of Portuguese arrived at the entrance to the Pearl River, the area that is now Macao.
1557 The colony of Macao was founded by the Portuguese with the apparent approval of the Chinese authorities.
1845 After years of Chinese rule, the Portuguese expelled the Chinese and announced Macao a free port. The territory enlarged to include the islands of Taipa and Coloane.
1860 The Portuguese introduced gambling licences to the territory.
1887 Macao's status was recognised by the Treaty of Amity and Commerce, signed between Portugal and China.
1939–45 Macao remained neutral during the Second World War and its economy prospered.
1976 The Portuguese government declared Macao a special territory and granted it a high degree of independence.
1987 The Sino-Portuguese Joint Declaration on the Question of Macao was signed.
1999 China resumed control over the territory. Edmund Ho Hau Wah became the first chief executive, as Macao became a Special Administrative Region (SAR) of China.
2001 The Associação de Novo Macau Democrático (ANMD) (New Democratic Macao Association), won two of the 10 directly-elected seats in the legislature.
2002 As part of the move to liberalise the gambling sector, Macao issued three casino licences to private operators. This broke the monopoly of self-made billionaire and the world's most successful casino operator, Stanley Ho Hung San.
2003 Severe Acute Respiratory Syndrome (Sars) spread around the region early in the year.
2004 On 29 August, Edmund Ho was re-elected chief executive.
2005 In the 25 September parliamentary elections the pro-democracy group, ANMD, won 18.8 per cent of the votes.

Political structure
Constitution

The Basic Law, promulgated by the People's Republic of China (PRC) in 1993, effectively became Macao's Constitution after sovereignty of the former Portuguese Special Territory was handed over to mainland China in December 1999. The Basic Law pledges to maintain Macao's economic, social and political distinctiveness for a period of 50 years after the handover to the PRC, under the principle of 'one country, two systems'.
Under the Basic Law, members of the executive and legislature must be permanent Macao residents. Private property, free speech and freedom of conscience are guaranteed.

Form of state

Special Administrative Region (SAR) of the People's Republic of China.

The executive

Under the terms of the Basic Law of Macao SAR (MSAR), executive power is vested in the chief executive, except in foreign affairs and defence, which are the responsibility of the Chinese government. The chief executive, appointed by China after local consultation and who must have been a resident for at least 20 years, serves a five-year term, and cannot serve more than two consecutive terms. An Executive Council of 10, appointed by the chief executive, consists of five MSAR departmental heads, three MSAR legislators and two other representatives.

National legislature
The Legislative Assembly of Macao is composed of 29 members, of whom seven are government appointees, 10 are indirectly elected by business associations, and 12 are directly elected. Membership rose to 29, under the terms of the Basic Law, with the elections in 2005. The chief executive has the power to remove members and dissolve the Legislative Council under conditions of political deadlock.

Last elections
25 September 2005 (parliamentary)
Results: Parliamentary: Associação de Novo Macao Democrático (ANMD) (New Democrat Macao Association) won 18.8 per cent of the votes (two seats), Associação dos Cidadãos Unidos de Macao (ACUM) (United Citizens Association of Macao) 16.58 per cent (two seats), União para o Desenvolvimento (UPD) (Union for Development) 13.29 per cent (two seats), União Promotora para o Progresso (UNIPRO) (Union for Promoting Progress) 9.6 per cent (two seats). Other parties one seat each. Turnout was 58.4 per cent.

Next elections
September 2006 (parliamentary)

Political parties
There are no formal political parties. However, pro-Chinese associations control a majority of the Assembly's elective seats. A number of civic associations exist. The Associacao de Novo Macao Democratio (ANMD) (New Democratic Macao Association) has a significant presence in the Assembly.

Ruling party
There are no political parties: there are 12 popularly elected seats in the legislature, an additional 10 seats are filled by business and special interest groups, and 7 seats are appointed by Macao's chief executive.

Population
451,000 (2004)

Ethnic make-up
Approximately 96 per cent of the territory's inhabitants are Chinese (mostly Cantonese from Guangdong province); the remainder are Mavanese (mixed Portuguese and Chinese).

Religions
Chinese Buddhism (45 per cent), Christianity (Roman Catholicism) (15 per cent).

Education
Primary education begins at age six and lasts until age 12. There are three stages to secondary schooling, beginning with junior, lasting for three years, then senior for two years and finally a pre-university one-year course. The first 10 years of education are free of charge.

Teaching may be given in Chinese, English or Portuguese.

Some 25 per cent of Macao's inhabitants attend any of 83 primary schools, 40 secondary schools, nine vocational technical colleges or nine institutes of higher education. The University of Macao has approximately 3,500 students in 80 undergraduate and post-graduate degree subjects.

Literacy rate: 94.3 per cent total, 91.7 per cent female, adult rates (World Bank).
Enrolment rate: 84.9 per cent net primary enrolment; 62.3 per cent net secondary enrolment (World Bank).

Health
Macao's population is young, with around 60 per cent between the ages of 15 and 50. Approximately 9 per cent of the government budget is allocated to healthcare.
Life expectancy: 79.3 years (World Bank)
Fertility rate/Maternal mortality rate: 1.2 births per per woman (World Bank)
Infant mortality rate: Six per 1,000 live births (World Bank).
Head of population per physician/bed: One doctor per 439 patients and one hospital bed per 474 head of population. The country has one public hospital, the Kiang Wu, and some 311 private clinics.

Welfare
Unemployment benefits, old age pensions and invalid benefits are administered by the Social Security Fund, which is financed through employer and employee contributions as well as government subsidies. Public assistance centres are co-ordinated by the Macao Social Welfare Institute in conjunction with the Church and other civilian organisations.

Main cities
Macao City (capital, estimated population 427,100 in 2003).

Languages spoken
Only 1.8 per cent of the population speak Portuguese. English is widely spoken and used in business and tourist circles.

Official language/s
Chinese and Portuguese

Media
The branch offices of China's official Xinhua state news agency in Hong Kong and Macao were renamed from 18 January 2000 as the Liaison Offices of the Central People's Government for their respective Special Administrative Regions (SAR).

Press
Dailies: The main Portuguese language dailies are *Gazeta Macaense*, *Jornal de Macau* and *Macau Hoje*. Chinese language dailies are *Ou Mun*, *Si Man*, *Va Kio*, *Tai Chung* and *Seng Pou*. *Jornal Va Kio* and *Macao Daily News* are two Cantonese dailies.
Weeklies: Weeklies include *O Clarim*, *Comercio de Macau*, *Ponto Final* and *Tribuna de Macau*.
Periodicals: English language periodicals include the monthly *Macao Travel Talk*, the biennial *Macao Image* and the quarterly *Welcome to Macao*.

Broadcasting
Radio: TDM SARL broadcasts in Portuguese and Cantonese, with some commercial programming. Hong Kong commercial radio is also available.
Television: Local television station Teledifusao de Macao (TDM) broadcasts 1800–2300. Macao Cable TV also

KEY INDICATORS — Macao (China)

	Unit	2000	2001	2002	2003	2004
Population	m	0.41	0.42	0.43	0.44	0.45
Gross domestic product (GDP)	US$bn	6.20	6.20	6.31	6.76	*8.16
GDP per capita	US$	14,225	14,195	14,190	18,500	18,096
GDP real growth	%	4.6	2.1	9.5	9.0	28.0
Inflation	%	-1.6	-2.0	-2.6	-2.6	1.0
Unemployment	%	6.8	6.4	6.4	6.3	4.2
Exports (fob) (goods)	US$m	2,510.0	2,306.0	2,349.0	2,360.0	2,506.0
Imports (fob) (goods)	US$m	2,240.0	2,392.0	2,524.0	2,530.0	3,115.0
Balance of trade	US$m	270.0	86.9	-175.0	-170.0	-610.0
Total reserves minus gold	US$m	3.3	3,510.0	3.8	4.3	5.4
Foreign exchange	US$m	3.3	3,510.0	3.8	4.3	5.4
Exchange rate	per US$	8.03	8.03	8.03	7.98	8.00

* estimated figure

operates. Transmissions are received from Hong Kong.

Economy

Macao has grown rapidly since the mid-1980s. Most of its income is derived from the services sector, including gambling- related activities and tourism. China has established its second-largest Special Economic Zone in Zhuhai (on the mainland adjacent to Macao), which has powerful business links with Macao.
Macao offers tax and other incentives for investment in tourism and hotels, electronics manufacturing industry, fishing industry and property development. It has certain competitive advantages over Hong Kong. For example, wage costs, factory rentals, office space and residential accommodation cost about half – in some cases a third – of Hong Kong equivalents. Lower operating costs in Zhuhai, particularly in labour-intensive processes, have led to a migration of many enterprises, particularly textile manufacturers, to Zhuhai, but more sophisticated, capital-intensive processes have tended to remain in Macao.
Shipping facilities have been upgraded with the construction of the Ka Ho port which has a container terminal and an oil terminal.
Air transit services depend heavily upon demand from Taiwan and could be affected if Taiwan's relations with the mainland improve.
Following the gambling sector's liberalisation in 2002, gambling and tourism continue as Macao's leading industries, providing the territory with extra revenue of US$2 billion per annum.
The Mainland/Macao Economic Partnership Arrangement (CEPA) came into force on 1 January 2004, removing tariffs on 272 categories of goods going from Macao into China and facilitating bilateral trade and co-operation on industrial projects.

External trade
Imports
Principle imports include raw materials and semi-manufactured goods, foodstuffs, tobacco, capital goods, mineral fuels and oils and alcohol.
Main sources: China (44.4 per cent total, 2004), Hong Kong (10.6 per cent), Japan (9.6 per cent), Taiwan (4.9 per cent), Singapore (4.1 per cent), US (4.1 per cent)
Exports
Principal exports include clothing, textiles, footwear, toys, electronics, machinery and parts, and textile yarns.
Main destinations: US (48.7 per cent total, 2004), China (13.9 per cent), Germany (8.3 per cent), Hong Kong (7.6 per cent), UK (4.4 per cent)

Agriculture
Farming
The agriculture and fishing sectors typically account for 0.1 per cent of GDP and 0.2 per cent of the workforce.
Soils are generally meagre and there is little agricultural production. Macao imports its food and water requirements, mainly from China.
Fishing
Fish, prawns and other sea foods are trawled for local consumption and export.

Industry and manufacturing
The textile and garment industries provide the bulk of Macao's exports, although they are subject to limitations such as EU quotas and some producers have been moving to Zhuhai. Other main products include toys, printing and packaging, leather products, electronics and opticals, food and beverages, furniture, woodware and ceramics.

Tourism
Tourism is enjoying a boom, buoyed by the influx of mainland Chinese and the liberal gambling regime. The relaxation by the Beijing authorities on travel to Macao and Hong Kong under the Individual Visit Scheme in July 2003 resulted in mainland China overtaking Hong Kong as the main market. The policy enabled Macao to weather the impact of the Sars outbreak. Visitor numbers held up in 2003, even increasing slightly to 11.9 million, while in 2004 arrivals increased by 40 per cent to 16.7 million and in 2005 by a further 12 per cent to 18.7 million. The main attractions are the casinos, especially since the de-monopolisation of gaming in 2002, and the race-tracks. Cultural, leisure and business tourism, underpinned by major infrastructure work, are being developed. Tourism and gaming account for over 50 per cent of GDP and employ around 40 per cent of the workforce.

Hydrocarbons
Macao does not produce any hydrocarbons. Macao relies on the import of refined oil to meet its domestic demand. It does not import natural gas.
Macao consumes small quantities of imported coal.

Energy
Companhia de Electricidade de Macao (Macao Electricity Company) is the concessionary for production, transmission and distribution of electricity. Two thermal power stations on Coloane Island meet about 80 per cent of the total requirements, the remainder being imported from neighbouring Zhuhai City in mainland China.

Banking and insurance
Since China took control of Macao in 1999, new banking laws intended to attract more foreign banks and allow a full range of offshore banking services have been enacted to ensure participation in financing the development of southern China. Macao enjoys some of the most liberal financial systems in the world.
Central bank
There is no central bank. The Monetary Authority of Macao (known as Autoridade Monetária e Cambial de Macao until 2000) is the monetary and foreign exchange authority of the territory.
Main financial centre
Macao City

Time
GMT plus eight hours

Geography
Macao comprises the peninsula of Macao and two nearby islands: Taipa, linked to the mainland by a bridge, and Coloane, which is connected to Taipa by a causeway. The territory lies opposite Hong Kong on the western side of the mouth of the Xijiang (Sikiang) river.

Climate
Subtropical and monsoonal. Winter (November–April) is cool and dry, with an average temperature of 14–23 degrees Celsius (C). Summer (May–September) is hot, humid and rainy, with an average temperature of 27 degrees C. October and November are somewhat less humid. Average annual rainfall ranges from 1,000–2,000mm; monsoon rains from May–October.

Entry requirements
Passport and visa regulations are liable to change at short notice.
Passports
Valid passport required by all except holders of a Hong Kong Identity Card (HKIC) and nationals of China with a China Identity Card.
Visa
Required by all, except citizens of many European and Asian countries, North America and Australasia, arriving as tourists. For a full list of exceptions and lengths of stay, visit www.dsi.gov.mo for details. Requirements for business visas should be obtained from the nearest Chinese consulate, well in advance of a business visit.
Currency advice/regulations
There are no restrictions on the amount of local and foreign currency that may be imported or exported.
Customs
Personal effects are allowed duty-free. Macao is a free port and there are no import duties, except on electrical appliances and equipment, which are subject

Macao (China)

to a 5 per cent *ad valorem* duty. Registration is required for all imports and an import licence for goods subject to consumption tax, such as beverages, coffee, rice, salt, sugar, wheat, matches, tobacco, bricks, cement and mineral oils, gases, vehicles. There are no export duties on articles purchased in Macao.

As inward and outward travel is generally through Hong Kong, export/import regulations of Hong Kong must be observed.

Health (for visitors)
Mandatory precautions
No compulsory vaccinations are required.
Advisable precautions
Vaccinations for diphtheria, tuberculosis, hepatitis 'A' and 'B', Japanese 'B' encephalitis, polio, tetanus and typhoid. Rabies is a risk.

Hotels
The majority of the small hotels available are air-conditioned. There are around 9,000 hotels rooms. A 10 per cent service charge and 5 per cent tax are added to the bill. It is customary to leave a small tip.

Credit cards
Most major credit cards are widely accepted.

Public holidays
Fixed dates
1 Jan (New Year's Day), 5 Apr (Ching Ming Festival), 1 May (Labour Day), 1 Oct (National Day of China), 2 Nov (All Souls' Day), 8 Dec (Immaculate Conception), 20 Dec (Macao Special Administrative Region Establishment Day), 22 Dec (Winter Solstice), 24–25 Dec (Christmas Holiday).
Variable dates
Chinese New Year (Jan/Feb), Good Friday, Birth of Buddha (Apr/May), Dragon Boat Festival (May/Jun), Mid-Autumn Festival (Sep/Oct), Chung Yeung Festival (Oct).

Working hours
Banking
Mon–Fri: 0930–1600; Sat: 0930–1230.
Business
Mon–Fri: 0900–1300, 1500–1730; Sat: 0900–1230.
Shops
Mon–Sat: 1000–1900.

Electricity supply
220V AC, 50Hz in new buildings and 110V AC for most domestic supply, with various types of plug fittings.

Weights and measures
Metric system

Social customs/useful tips
It is customary to shake hands on meeting and taking leave.

Getting there
Air
National airline: Air Macao
International airport/s: Macao International (MFM), on Taipa Island, south of Macao City.
The airport is linked to Macao and mainland China via a four-lane motorway and bridge. A rail link to connect it with Guangzhou is planned. Estimated travelling time into central Macao is 10 minutes, and 20 minutes to the Chinese border.
Airport tax: Pa80 per person for destinations in China, and Pa130 for other destinations. Payment is required in local currency.
Surface
Road: Macao is connected to mainland China by a short causeway. Two bridges, the Friendship and Lotus, and a six-lane highway, link the islands of Taipa and Coloane with the Zhuhai Special Economic Zone.
Water: Most visitors enter via Hong Kong. There are over 100 scheduled sailings each way throughout the day, and jetfoils operate round the clock (journey time 55 minutes). It is advisable to book in advance.
Main port/s: Macao City; new container port and plans for a deep water harbour.

Getting about
National transport
Buses: Bus services operate 0700–2400, with services between the ferry pier and the city centre and Taipa-Coloane Island.
Rail: The proposed light rail system will connect all major ports and tourist attractions along the coast of the Macao Peninsula and the new town, Cotai, terminating at Macao International Airport. The light rail system will also connect to the inter-city express railway transport system proposed by mainland China.
City transport
Central Macao is tiny and easily walkable. It is possible to hire three-wheeled, two-passenger rickshaws, although they are forbidden to cross the bridge and unsuitable for negotiating hills. It is best to negotiate the fare before starting the journey.
Taxis: Taxis are inexpensive and readily available. Licensed, metered taxis are mostly painted black with cream-coloured tops. Radio taxis are painted yellow.
Buses, trams & metro: Good local bus services. Transmac AP1 service from airport to city centre every 30 minutes, journey time 30 minutes, and STCM service 21, every 20 minutes, journey time 30 minutes.

Car hire
Car hire is available. Driving is on the left. An international driving permit is required. The minimum driving age is 21.

BUSINESS DIRECTORY
The addresses listed below are a selection only. While World of Information makes every endeavour to check these addresses, we cannot guarantee that changes have not been made, especially to telephone numbers and area codes. We would welcome any corrections.

Telephone area codes
The international direct dialling code (IDD) for Macao is +853, followed by subscriber's number.

Useful telephone numbers
Police, fire and ambulance: 999

Chambers of Commerce
Macao Chamber of Commerce, Edificio ACM, 175 Rua de Xangai, Macao (tel: 576-833; fax: 594-513; e-mail: acm@macauweb.com).

Banking
Banco Comercial de Macau SA, Rua da Praia Grande No 22, PO Box 545, Macao (tel: 569-622; fax: 580-967).

Banco Delta Asia SARL, 79 Avenida Conselheiro Ferreira de Almeida, Macao (tel: 559-898; fax: 570-068).

Banco Weng Hang SARL, 241 Avenida de Almeida Ribeiro, Macao (tel: 335-678; fax: 576-527).

Luso International Banking Ltd, 47 Avenida Dr Mário Soares, Macao (tel: 378-977; 378-977; fax: 578-517).

Tai Fung Bank Ltd, Tai Fung Bank Headquarters Building, 418 Alameda Dr. Carlos d'Assumpção, Macao (tel: 322-323; fax: 570-737).

Central bank
Monetary Authority of Macao, Calçada do Gaio 24-26, Macao City (tel: 568-288; fax: 325-432; e-mail: general@amcm.gov.mo).

Travel information
Administração de Aeroportos (tel: 711-808; fax: 711-803).

Air Macao (tel: 396-5555; fax: 396-6866).

East Asia Airlines (tel: 790-7040).

Far East Jetfoils (tel: 790-7093).

Flight information (24 hours) (tel: 861-111).

Macao International Airport, R Dr Pedro Jose Lobo, 1–3, Edif Luso Internacional, 26 o andar, Macao (e-mail: aacm@aacm.gov.mo; internet site: http://www.macau-airport.gov.mo).

Sociedade de Turismo e Diversoes de Macao, 9 Largo do Senado, Macao (tel: 315-566; fax: 510-104).

National tourist organisation offices
Macau Government Tourist Office, PO Box 3006, 9 Edifício Largo do Leal Senado (tel: 375-156, 561-167, 555-424, fax: 510-104).

Other useful addresses
Coastal International Exhibition Co Ltd, Room 3808, China Resources Building, 26 Harbour Road, Wanchai, Hong Kong (tel: +852 2827-6766; fax: + 852 2827-6870; e-mail: general@coastal.com.hk).

Macao Business Support Centre (tel: 728-212; fax: 727-123, 728-213; e-mail: mbsc@ipim.gov.mo).

Macao Commercial Association (Associacão Comercial de Macão), Edifício ACM, Rua da Xanghai, 5th Floor (tel: 576-833; fax: 594-513).

Macao Export Promotions Department, 1-3 Rua Pedro José Lobo, International Building (tel: 78-221).

Macao Importers and Exporters' Association, Av do Infante D Henrique No 60-62, 30 o andar, Centro Comercial Central, Macao (tel: 553-187, 375-859; fax: 512-174; e-mail: aeim@macau.ctm.net).

Macao Industrial Association, PO Box 70, Travessa da Praia Grande No. 56 (tel: 574-125; fax: 578-305).

Macao Statistics Department, PO Box 3022, Ground Floor, Rua Inácio Baptista, 4D-6, Seaview Garden (tel: 550-935; fax: 307-825; internet site: http://www.dsec.gov.mo).

Macao Trade and Investment Promotion Institute, 1–3 Rua Dr Pedro Jose Lobo (7th/8th Floor) (e-mail: ipim@ipim.gov.mo); Investment Promotion (tel: 340-090, 712-660; fax: 712-659; internet site: http://www.ipim.gov.mo); Trade Promotion: (tel: 378-221, 710-528; fax: 590-309).

Internet sites
Macao Environment Council: http://www.ambiente.gov.mo

Macao government: http://www.macau.gov.mo

Macao Tower Convention and Entertainment Centre: http://www.gaming-exhibition.com

Macedonia

Macedonia seemed to receive praise from all directions in 2005, both for economic and political achievements. Taken to the brink of full-scale civil war in 2001, Macedonia ended 2005 with celebrations, having been accepted as a candidate for EU membership on 17 December. Macedonia is only the third former Yugoslav republic to achieve this, after Slovenia and Croatia.

Sound economic indicators

Macedonia's GDP grew by 3.6 per cent in 2005 and inflation ran at only 0.5 per cent. The budget deficit also fell, to 4 per cent of GDP. However, unemployment remained stubbornly high, at 37.5 per cent, which, in September, elicited a warning from the United Nations Development Programme (UNDP).

Political progress against the odds

When the Macedonian government and ethnic Albanian rebels signed up to the Ohrid Peace Agreement in August 2001, it was agreed that dozens of changes to Macedonia's law code and constitution would have to be made in the interests of inter-communal harmony. Many of these, some of them potentially explosive, were addressed in 2005. In March, local elections were held – the first within new electoral boundaries drawn up under the Ohrid framework. The new boundaries were designed to accurately reflect Albanian majorities in many western towns and the March elections threatened to inflame nationalist sentiment within the titular Macedonian community. However, the election was generally violence-free and earned praise from the EU. The Organisation for Security and Co-operation (OSCE) noted some problems but approved overall conduct. A second potentially divisive issue was overcome in July, when parliament passed a law allowing for the flying of the Albanian flag in majority Albanian districts. However, in November, the government postponed a bill that would have comprehensively institutionalised the use of the Albanian language.

Regional issues

In 2005, Macedonia unexpectedly became embroiled in disagreements with two of its

KEY FACTS

Official name: Republika Makedonija (Former Yugoslav Republic of Macedonia) (FYROM)

Head of State: President Branko Crvenkovski (sworn in 12 May 2004)

Head of government: Prime Minister-designate Vlado Buckovski (from 18 Nov 2004)

Ruling party: Za Makedonija Zaedno (For Macedonia Together) multi-ethnic 10-member coalition led by the Socijaldemockratski Sojuz na Makedonija (SDSM) (Social Democratic Alliance of Macedonia) (from 1 Nov 2002; re-shuffled May 2004)

Area: 25,713 square km

Population: 2.13 million (2004)

Capital: Skopje

Official language: Macedonian and Albanian.

Currency: Macedonian dinar (Md)

Exchange rate: Md50.76 per US$ (Oct 2005); (pegged to the euro; trades around Md60 per euro)

GDP per capita: US$2,295 (2004)

GDP real growth: 2.30% (2004); *3.6% (2005)

Labour force: 974,000 (2004)

Unemployment: 36.70% (2004); *37.5% (2005)

Inflation: -0.30% (2004); *0.5% (2005)

Balance of trade: -US$1.05 billion (2004)

Foreign debt: US$1.86 billion (2004)

* estimated figure

former Yugoslav co-republics, Croatia and Serbia. In November, Croatian prosecutors launched an investigation into the activities of Macedonia's Chief of Staff, General Miroslav Stojanovski. It was alleged that he had played a role in the Serbian-led siege of the Croatian city of Vukovar in 1991, and may have been involved in subsequent atrocities.

A long-running dispute between the Macedonian Orthodox Church and the Serbian Orthodox Church came to a head in 2005, dragging in the respective national governments. In September, a Macedonian court confirmed a jail sentence for the Archbishop Jovan of the Ohrid archdiocese in Macedonia. Jovan had attempted to negotiate a deal with the Serbian Church that would partially recognise the Macedonian Church's autonomy from the former. However, activists within the Macedonian Church condemned Jovan as a traitor and, backed by the Macedonian government, launched a criminal case against him. The Serbian government has backed its own national Church in the dispute.

Macedonia in Europe

Several obstacles on Macedonia's road to European integration were overcome in 2005. In March, two Macedonians wanted for war crimes, allegedly committed during 2001's civil conflict, were extradited to stand trial at the International Criminal Tribunal for the former Yugoslavia (ICTY) in The Hague. Resolving outstanding arrest warrants against suspected war criminals has often been cited by EU representatives as a minimum requirement for progress towards European integration. In November, the European Commission delivered a positive report on Macedonia's EU membership prospects, and recommended that EU leaders accept it as a candidate state. The UN Special Envoy to neighbouring Kosovo also lavished praise on Macedonia, citing it as a shining example of conflict resolution and post-conflict recovery. In December, EU leaders formally accepted Macedonia as a candidate state for membership, despite French reservations over the EU's capacity to absorb new members. Fears that Greece might veto Macedonia's candidature due to its long-running dispute with Macedonia over the right to use the name 'Macedonia' proved unfounded.

In a boost for Macedonia in its dispute with Greece, EU member Poland agreed in August to recognise Macedonia by its constitutional name, Republika Makedonija. Poland became the second EU member state to do so, after Slovenia.

US relations

Macedonia continued to enjoy close relations with the US government in 2005, building upon the diplomatic coup of November 2004, when the US granted recognition of Macedonia's constitutional name in the face of Greek opposition. While hosting Macedonian prime minister Vlado Buckovski in October, US president George Bush Jnr offered support for Macedonia's quest to join NATO. In December, the Macedonian government stated that it would maintain its current contingent of troops in Iraq and increase the number of personnel serving in Afghanistan.

Outlook

After its successes in 2005, Macedonia now faces a relatively difficult year ahead. Chronic high unemployment threatens to detract from Macedonia's efforts to stabilise its post-conflict politics. The postponed language bill, which is supposed to help solve the issue of the Albanian language's status in Macedonia once and for all, will have to be addressed. With talk of an election in September, the governing coalition will come under pressure from its Albanian members, who will want a tangible 'win' to present to their supporters. Moreover, there will be pressure from the Macedonian nationalist opposition to further postpone or even sideline the bill permanently. One encouraging sign for the expected election is that in August 2005, opposition parties from both the Macedonian and Albanian communities opened talks on an informal electoral alliance. This bodes well for future co-operation between the communities, whatever the make-up of the next government.

Further difficulties are predicted in Macedonia's judicial sphere. The NGO, the International Crisis Group (ICG), points to the risks involved in a decision by the ICTY to allow, in 2006, the Macedonian courts to deal with pending war crimes charges against four Macedonian nationals. The ICG suggests that the Macedonian judiciary is at present incapable of dealing with the trials, a point foreshadowed by the EU Commission in November 2005. Such trials, in an election year, could present an welcome fillip to the anti-government nationalist forces.

In 2006, the long delayed Albania-Macedonia-Bulgaria-Oil (AMBO) pipeline should show signs of progress, bringing some US$20–30 million per year to Macedonia in transit fees.

Risk assessment

Politics	stable
Economy	stable
Regional stability	stable

COUNTRY PROFILE

Historical profile

Macedonia has been occupied by the Greeks, Romans, Bulgarians, Byzantines, Serbs and the Ottoman Turks. It is jokingly known as the home of both the fruit salad of the same name, and Alexander the

KEY INDICATORS — Macedonia

	Unit	2000	2001	2002	2003	2004
Population	m	2.11	2.12	2.13	2.13	2.13
Gross domestic product (GDP)	US$bn	3.56	3.40	3.70	4.70	*5.25
GDP per capita	US$	1,685	1,700	1,737	1,900	2,295
GDP real growth	%	4.6	-4.6	0.3	3.0	2.3
Inflation	%	9.2	5.2	3.3	2.5	-0.3
Unemployment	%	38.0	42.0	43.0	37.0	36.7
Exports (fob) (goods)	US$m	1,317.1	1,155.0	1,110.5	1,358.0	1,629.0
Imports (fob) (goods)	US$m	1,875.2	1,688.0	1,880.0	2,324.0	2,677.0
Balance of trade	US$m	-558.0	-600.0	-767.6	-966.0	-1,048.0
Current account	US$m	-107.2	-353.0	-325.3	-284.0	-280.0
Foreign debt	US$bn	1.6	1.4	1.6	1.3	1.9
Total reserves minus gold	US$m	429.4	745.2	722.0	897.7	905.0
Foreign exchange	US$m	428.7	742.9	715.9	897.4	904.2
Exchange rate	per US$	65.90	68.04	63.71	53.91	47.00

* estimated figure

Great (known in Iran as Alexander of Macedonia).
1371 The Ottoman Turks conquered the area and retained control until the nineteenth century.
1893 The Vnatrešno-Makedonska Revoluciona Organizacija (VMRO) (Internal Macedonian Revolutionary Organisation) was founded to gain independence from the Ottoman Empire.
1912–13 During the Balkan conflicts, the Turks were driven out and the area was divided between Serbia and Greece, with a small section being retained by Bulgaria.
1918 Macedonia became part of the new Kingdom of Serbs, Croats and Slovenes along with parts of Bosnia-Hercegovina, Croatia, parts of Dalmatia, Montenegro, Serbia, Slavonia and Slovenia.
1929 The Kingdom was renamed Yugoslavia.
1941–45 Macedonia was occupied by Bulgaria, under German direction. The Partisans, led by Josip Broz Tito – also leader of the Communist Party of Yugoslavia (CPY) – eventually liberated the whole of Yugoslavia.
1945 Following the end of the Second World War, Macedonia became one of the constituent republics of a federated Yugoslavia. Tito assumed power and a Soviet-style constitution was adopted. The other republics were Bosnia-Hercegovina, Croatia, Slovenia, Montenegro, Serbia and the two autonomous regions of Vojvodina and Kosovo.
1953 Constitutions adopted in 1953, 1963 and 1974 increased the autonomy extended to the constituent republics.
1990 Following the collapse of communism in Yugoslavia, Macedonia held its first multi-party elections and the VMRO became the largest party in parliament.
1991 The first multi-party National Assembly was officially constituted. After a referendum in which the people voted overwhelmingly in favour of Macedonian sovereignty and independence, Macedonia declared its independence.
1992 Kiro Gligorov, the former communist leader, was elected president.
1993 Greece showed consternation over Macedonia's choice of name and flag which the Greek government argued were a claim on its northern province of Macedonia. To accommodate Greek concerns, Macedonia eventually agreed to join the UN with the temporary prefix of 'Former Yugoslav Republic' and an alternative national flag design was introduced.
1994 Kiro Gligorov was re-elected president. Greece imposed a partial trade embargo on Macedonia.
1995 An accord resulting in a normalisation of relations between Greece and Macedonia ensured that Macedonians had access to the northern Greek port of Thessaloniki, their nearest outlet to the sea.
1998 A coalition government under the leadership of Ljubco Georgievski was formed after elections.
1999 Amid accusations of electoral irregularities from the opposition, Boris Trajkovski of the Vnatrešno-Makedonska Revoluciona Organizacija-Demokratska Partija za Makedonsko Nacionalno Edintsvo (VMRO-DPMNE) (Internal Macedonian Revolutionary Organisation-Democratic Party for Macedonian National Unity) was elected president.
2000 A coalition government was formed and led by Prime Minister Georgievski.
2001 There were clashes between ethnic Albanian guerrillas and police in Tetovo and other parts of Macedonia. A cease-fire was brokered and a NATO force was sent to Macedonia to supervise the collection of arms handed in by ethnic Albanian rebels. The Ohrid Agreement was signed in August, paving the way for political reforms to enhance the status of the ethnic Albanian population within Macedonia. In April, the Macedonian government signs a Stabilisation and Asociation Agreement (SAA) with the EU, aimed at bringing Macedonia into line with EU political, economic and social norms.
2002 After parliamentary elections, the Socijaldemockratski Sojuz na Makedonija (SDSM) (Social Democratic Alliance of Macedonia) leader, Branko Crvenkovski, became prime minister, heading a multi-ethnic, 10-member coalition government.
2003 The EU took over NATO's military mission in Macedonia in March to oversee implementation of the Ohrid Agreement. On 4 April, Macedonia joined the World Trade Organisation (WTO).
2004 President Boris Trajkovski died in a plane crash on 26 February; Parliament Speaker Ljupco Jordanovski became acting president. On 22 March, Macedonia formally submitted its application to join the EU. In the first round of presidential elections on 14 April, Prime Minister Branko Crvenkovski won 42.9 per cent of the vote; he went on to win the second round on 28 April and was sworn in as president on 12 May. On 14 May, he asked Hari Kostov to form a new government. In November, an opposition-backed referendum designed to repeal the laws giving minority Albanians in Macedonia greater autonomy, failed after a low turnout; the unexpected announcement by the US to recognise Macedonia by its constitutional name, the Republic of Macedonia, just prior to the referendum was widely credited with helping to defeat the referendum; Prime Minister Hari Kostov resigned as a result of disputes within the ruling coalition and on 26 November, Vlado Buckovski was named as prime minister.
2005 In March, local elections were held, the first under redrawn electoral boundaries, as stipulated in the Ohrid Agreement. Despite fears of inter-communal tension, EU oberservers reported a high turnout and few irregularities. In November, The EU Commission recommended that Macedonia be granted EU candidate status. The leaders of the EU member states endorsed this decision in December.

Political structure
Constitution
Under the constitution, adopted on 17 November 1991, the Former Yugoslav Republic of Macedonia (FYROM) is a sovereign, independent, democratic and socially responsive state. There is universal suffrage from age 18. The constitution guarantees the free expression of national identity, the rule of law (including international law) and the legal protection of property. The principles of a free commercial market, urban and rural planning and environmental protection are also enshrined in the constitution.
Constitutional amendments to give the ethnic Albanian minority more rights were endorsed by parliament in November 2001.
Form of state
Parliamentary democratic republic
The executive
The executive is headed by the president, directly elected every five years. The prime minister appoints a cabinet of 20 ministers, who must be approved by a majority of the country's national assembly.
National legislature
The national legislature is the unicameral Sobranje (National Assembly). The Sobranje has 120 members elected every four years, 85 by direct election and 35 by proportional representation.
Legal system
Judicial powers are vested in courts which are nominally independent of government under the terms of the 1991 constitution. In practice, the judiciary remains politicised, especially in cases involving ethnic Albanians and other minorities. All civil and criminal cases are dealt with by courts of general jurisdiction. The Supreme Court is the highest court. Elected by parliament, the Judicial Council appoints and dismisses all judges and other judicial officials. The judicial system is the administrative responsibility of the justice ministry. There is a public prosecutor. The Constitutional Court decides on the conformity of national legislation with the 1991 constitution.

Macedonia is aiming to harmonise its laws and judicial standards with those of the EU and the Council of Europe, but progress is slow.

Last elections
28 and 14 April 2004 (presidential); 15 September 2002 (parliamentary).
Results: Presidential: in the first round of elections, Prime Minister Branko Crvenkovski won 42.9 per cent of the vote, Sasko Kedev 34.5 per cent and Gzim Ostreni 14.3 per cent; turnout was 55.4 per cent. Branko Crvenkovski went on to win the second round.
Parliamentary: Za Makedonija Zaedno (For Macedonia Together) coalition led by the Socijaldemockratski Sojuz na Makedonija (SDSM) (Social Democratic Alliance of Macedonia) won 60 of 120 seats in the National Assembly; the former ruling party, VMRO-DPMNE, and the Liberalna Partija na Makedonije (LPM) (Liberal Party of Macedonia) 33 seats. SDSM leader, Branko Crvenkovski, became prime minister, heading a multi-ethnic 10-member coalition government.
Presidential: Boris Trajkovski was elected president. The opposition complained of electoral irregularities.

Next elections
2006 (parliamentary); 2009 (presidential).

Political parties
Ruling party
Za Makedonija Zaedno (For Macedonia Together) multi-ethnic 10-member coalition led by the Socijaldemockratski Sojuz na Makedonija (SDSM) (Social Democratic Alliance of Macedonia) (from 1 Nov 2002; re-shuffled May 2004)

Main opposition party
Vnatrešno-Makedonska Revoluciona Organizacija-Demokratska Partija za Makedonsko Nacionalno Edintsvo (VMRO-DPMNE) (Internal Macedonian Revolutionary Organisation-Democratic Party for Macedonian National Unity)

Population
2.13 million (2004)
Ethnic make-up
Macedonian (63 per cent), Albanian (30 per cent), Turkish (4 per cent), Romanian (3 per cent). The Albanians are concentrated in Tetovo, Gostivar and other parts of the north-west.

Religions
The official religion is Macedonian Orthodox Christianity, which is practised by approximately two-thirds of the population. Muslims (over a quarter of the population) and Roman Catholics practise openly.

Education
The educational system is entirely state-controlled. During the 1990s, independence from Yugoslavia meant an end to federal subsidies, resulting in declining educational provision in Macedonia. Politically, the issue of ethnic Albanian access to higher education in the Albanian language has been the cause of great controversy and even violence in Macedonia. Primary schooling lasts for eight years and is followed by attendance at either a general secondary school for academic students or at a variety of technical, specialist or vocational schools. After four years, in whichever mode of school, students must undertake examination before advancement to the second, three-year stage. Courses may last until students are aged 19.
There are three universities in Macedonia: Skopje, Bitola and Tetovo. The Albanian-language University at Tetovo is legalised and classified by parliament as an accredited private institution.
Compulsory years: Seven to 15.
Enrolment rate: 99 per cent total primary enrolment of relevant age group (including repetition rates); 63 per cent total secondary enrolment (World Bank).

Health
The standard of state healthcare is low compared to the rest of the former Yugoslavia, the basic healthcare infrastructure has declined mainly due to the lack of funds to replace essential equipment and retain doctors in the state sector.
Healthcare provision has increasingly involved extra charges, notably for medication, leading to a large black market in healthcare services. Most healthcare professionals are either in semi-private or private practice and some parts of the healthcare system have been privatised. Externally, Macedonia received considerable international aid for local healthcare during the 1990s.
Improved water sources and sanitation facilities are available to 99 per cent of the population.
HIV prevalence: 0.1 per cent aged 15–49 in 2003 (World Bank)
Life expectancy: 73.6 years (World Bank)
Fertility rate/Maternal mortality rate: 1.8 births per woman; maternal mortality three per 100,000 live births (World Bank).
Infant mortality rate: 10 per 1,000 live births; and 5.9 per cent of children aged under five are malnourished (World Bank).

Welfare
Welfare provision was heavily subsidised by budgetary transfers from outside Macedonia during the Yugoslav period, when retirement pensions and other welfare benefits were relatively generous at around 80 per cent of average monthly income. Consequently, the state pension fund experienced major financial problems after independence. Welfare benefits declined sharply, aggravated by spells of high inflation. The IMF and other official creditors have made loans available in recent years for the state pension fund and unemployment benefit outlays. The foreign exchange remittances of emigrants plays a major role in the economic support of many Macedonians.

Main cities
Skopje (capital, estimated population 452,500 in 2003), Bitola (84,400), Kumanovo (78,900), Tetovo (60,800).

Languages spoken
Macedonian (Slavic) is written using the Cyrillic alphabet.
The Albanian minority campaigned successfully to have its language officially recognised as the country's second language. Turkish, Serbian, Croatian and Romani are also spoken.
English, French and German are often understood.

Official language/s
Macedonian and Albanian.

Media
Press
Dailies: Nearly all newspapers are privately-owned. The most widely-read dailies, *Nova Makedonija*, *Dnevnik*, *Vecer*, the Albanian-language *Flaka e Vellazerimit* and the Turkish-language *Birlik* are 33 per cent state-owned. Other national newspapers include *Denes*, *M-Express*, *Nova* and *Utrenski Vesnik*.
Major daily news services in Macedonia are available online from the *Macedonian Media* (http://www.makedonija.com), *Macedonian Information Center* (http://www.makedonija.com/mic/index.html) and the *Macedonian Information and Liason Service* (http://www.soros.org.mk/mn/mils.html).
Weeklies: During the 1990s, there was a proliferation of new weekly and periodical titles, but the finances of many are extremely precarious. Some have had to turn to foreign funding sources, notably the Soros Foundation, which has also provided economic aid to the Macedonian government. Weekly publications include *Economic Press* featuring economics and finance. Other weekly publications include the bi-weekly *FORUM* magazine, *Makedonsko Sonce* (English/Macedonian) and *Start* in Macedonian.
Periodicals: The government has provided resources for a number of high quality English-language titles, notably *Balkan Forum*.

Broadcasting
Makedonska Radio Televizija (MKRTV) (Macedonian Radio and Television) is the state broadcasting monopoly. As in other former Yugoslav republics, government control of TV and radio broadcasting is

tight. However, radio broadcasting has been liberalised and a number of smaller privately-owned broadcasters have been established.

Other than MKRTV, Bulgarian, Serbian, Albanian, Turkish and Greek broadcasting output is easily available in Macedonia. Satellite dish and VCR ownership is also growing very fast.

Economy
The most economically underdeveloped area of Yugoslavia during 1929–41, Macedonia made relatively limited socio-economic progress during 1945–91, when it was by far the poorest and least developed constituent republic of the Yugoslav federation. There was, however, considerable socio-economic change in Macedonia during the communist Yugoslav era, notably through forced industrialisation based on capital goods, rapid urbanisation focussed on Skopje and, from the 1960s onwards, a high rate of emigration from the republic. At the same time, Macedonia's continued underdevelopment, relative to the more economically advanced Yugoslav republics, meant that it remained a net beneficiary of financial and other economic transfers from the federal government in Belgrade throughout the period. Local economic development was heavily concentrated in the Skopje area.

Macedonia's economic decline during the 1990s was further aggravated by the lack of real macroeconomic stabilisation of the local economy until 1993–94. In 1994, following the successful introduction of the dinar the previous year, macroeconomic stabilisation was largely achieved.

However, economic stability was hampered by two developments in particular. In February 1994, the Greek government imposed a trade embargo on Macedonia (on all items except food) in a dispute over national symbols. Macedonia's inability to use the Greek port of Thessaloniki, Macedonia's closest outlet to the sea, disrupted Macedonia's exports to the rest of the world. The embrago was lifted in October 1995. Moreover, hostilities between the Macedonian government and ethnic Albanian guerrillas in 2001 brought to a temporary halt further economic growth.

GDP growth began its recovery in 2002 at 0.3 per cent and reached 3.0 per cent in 2003, but fell back in 2004 to 2.3 per cent. Unemployment continues to be a major problem for Macedonia with around 37 per cent of the working population out of work in 2003 and 2004.

In April 2001, Macedonia signed a Stabilisation and Association Agreement (SAA) with the EU, which committed the Macedonian government to bringing the economy into line with EU economic norms. The SAA came fully into force in April 2004.

In March 2002, an international donors conference, organised by EU and the World Bank, pledged US$275 million to assist the Macedonian economy, primarily the budget deficit and structural reforms. In August 2004, the IMF approved a US$11.7 million disbursement after completing the final review of Macedonia's economic performance under the April 2003 US$29.4 million stand-by arrangement. The IMF emphasised that although Macedonia had achieved fiscal sustainability by putting in place a sound macroeconomic policy framework, in order to strengthen and diversify the sources of growth, structural reforms were necessary for the health sector, banking and financial sectors, governance and business environment.

In November 2005, the EU Commission recommended that Macedonia be granted EU candidate status, with one of the conditions being the continuation of economic reforms. EU member states ratified this decision in December 2005.

External trade
Macedonia acts as a trading crossroads, linking Greece and Turkey with the northern states. Germany is the main market for 21 per cent of Macedonian exports. Serbia and Montenegro is the market for 18 per cent of exports, many of them low quality.

Imports
Principal imports are machinery and equipment, chemicals, fuels, foodstuffs and automobiles.
Main sources: Greece (18 per cent total, 2004), Germany (14.4 per cent), Serbia and Montenegro (9.3 per cent), Slovenia (8.1 per cent), Bulgaria (7.6 per cent), Turkey (7.0 per cent)

Exports
Principal exports are food, beverages, tobacco; miscellaneous manufactures, iron and steel.
Main destinations: Serbia and Montenegro (30.8 per cent total, 2004), Germany (20.1 per cent), Greece (9.0 per cent), Croatia (7.0 per cent), US (4.8 per cent)

Agriculture
Farming
The agricultural sector accounts for 13 per cent of GDP and employs 30 per cent of the workforce.

Agricultural land totals 1.3 million hectares (ha), of which approximately half is cultivable and half is pasture. Macedonia has propitious conditions for agriculture and is nearly self-sufficient in food production. The private sector accounts for over 75 per cent of agricultural production.

The government has allowed a systematic break-up of the old *agrokombinats*, or collectivised farms. As a result, privately owned farms now account for 90 per cent of annual output, although each farm is rarely more than 25ha. New private company formation in agriculture is also growing rapidly.

On the negative side, the state still directly controls 30 per cent of all arable land, or around 300,000ha. Markedly less productive than the private sector, state farms and co-operatives are scheduled to be privatised in due course, although this remains politically controversial. Local agriculture is one of the few sectors of interest to potential foreign investors due to the cultivation of higher value cash crops (particularly tobacco) with ready markets in the EU, and cheap labour costs. Economically, the government now regards agriculture as a major area for future growth and development, including increased foreign direct investment (FDI). Crop production in 2004 included: 683,541 tonnes (t) cereals in total, 358,351t wheat, 146,105t maize, 10,273t rye, 199,000t potatoes, 149,963t barley, 14,676t rice, 27,714t pulses, 5,247t treenuts, 247,673t grapes, 116,837t tomatoes, 6,490t oilcrops, 21,140t tobacco, 14,000t olives, 52,199t sugar beets, 82,409t apples, 4,091t oats, 110,000t chillies and peppers, 394,333t fruit in total, 521,486t vegetables in total. Livestock production included: 28,416t meat in total, 8,824t beef, 9,373t pig meat, 7,030t lamb, 3,189t poultry, 18,700t eggs, 264,774t milk, 916t honey, 1,340t cattle hides, 3,176t greasy wool.

Fishing
Macedonia has a small fishing industry, which catches freshwater fish for domestic consumption.

Forestry
Forest and other wooded land account for about two-fifths of the land area, equivalent to approximately 906,000ha. More than four-fifths of the forest is available for wood supply. Forest resources supply an active forestry industry producing approximately 774,000 cubic metres (cum) of timber per annum.

Forest wood is mainly used for fuel, while hardwood processed in local sawmills is largely exported. Domestic demand for softwoods and paper is met by imports. Annual exports of forest products amount to US$7.5 million while imports amount to US$64.9 million in 2004.

Production in 2004 included 812,000cum roundwood, 124,000cum industrial roundwood, 20,852cum sawnwood, 118,000cum sawlogs and veneers, 688,000cum woodfuel.

Industry and manufacturing
Industry and manufacturing account for nearly 35 per cent of GDP. Macedonia retains a relatively industrialised economy inherited from the Yugoslav period. During the 1990s, the collapse of the Yugoslav market and subsequent regional conflict, the loss of former Soviet markets, the Greek economic blockade and resultant energy shortages all had devastating consequences for Macedonian industrial output.

Although privatisation of smaller industries has been largely completed, sell-offs of larger industries are still at an early stage. State industries suffer from overstaffing, slow growth, a slow rate of change in the structure of production and ailing technology. Industrial production in 2004 was stagnant at 0.0 per cent.

Tourism
Macedonia's nascent tourist industry is primarily based at the lakeside town of Ohrid. Summer tourism is concentrated around the lakes and the national parks. Lakes Ohrid, Prespa, Dojran and Mavrovo cover a total water surface of 679 square km.

Winter tourism is developing in several ski resorts; there are 14 mountain massifs with peaks over 2,000 metres and perpetual Alpine climatic conditions. Both summer and winter tourism offer good potential for development.

Interesting archaeological sites exist, as well as numerous mosaics, frescoes and icons, the earliest dating from Roman times, in monasteries, churches and mosques. The old part of Ohrid town is a UN Educational, Scientific and Cutural Organisation (Unesco)-protected World Heritage Site, as is the lake itself. Macedonia's tourism sector suffered heavily during the war in Kosovo (1999) and inter-ethnic fighting within Macedonia itself (2001). Tourist arrivals increased by 6.8 per cent in 2003, compared to 2002.

Environment
The Vardar, Macedonia's main river, collects the waste from several towns with no treatment facilities before flowing through Greece to the Aegean Sea. A system for monitoring the waterways and a project for communal water treatment for six towns have been initiated by the Macedonian government.

Macedonia and Albania participate in the Lake Ohrid Conservation Project (LOCP) which is a bilateral project supported by the World Bank.

Mining
Macedonia is an important producer of metals and mines significant quantities of copper and lead-zinc ores, ferroalloys and some silver. There is also some chromium production from reserves that overlap with those of nearby Albania. The aluminium and copper ore production is centred on Alumina AD in Skopje and 'Bucim' Radovis DM in Radovis respectively. There is also significant quarrying of decorative and architectural building stone.

The mining sector in Macedonia has had little chance for growth due to regional instability and depressed market conditions. The various conflicts in the former Yugoslavia have created a regional dislocation of transportation of cargoes on the Danube river, shifting the route of exports through the port of Thessaloniki in Greece at a huge cost. This financial burden has diminished Macedonia's production of hot and cold rolled steel to about 30 per cent of capacity, and the export of finished products by Balkan Steel International (BSI). However, it was not regional dislocation that affected some companies that have traditionally exported through Greece. Their production fell or ceased due to shortage of foreign investment and adverse market conditions. Foreign investment and participation has been restricted to the steel industry (Duferco and BSI), petroleum refining (Hellenic Petroleum) and cement (Titan Cement and Holderbank Financiere Glaris).

Hydrocarbons
Macedonia has no significant domestic production of oil, requiring imports to supply domestic consumption. The oil distribution network is largely state-run. The refining company Okta runs the country's oil refineries. Hellenic Petroleum owns 54 per cent of Okta while the other 46 per cent is state owned. Russian oil companies have expressed an interest in purchasing Macedonia's oil refineries with the 2004 privatisation plan. In December 2004, Macedonia signed a US$1.2 billion agreement with Bulgaria and Albania that provided for the construction of a trans-Balkans oil pipeline. The pipeline will connect the Black Sea with the Adriatic, via the Bulgarian port of Burgas and the Albanian port of Vlores, and will transport Russian and Caspian oil that would otherwise flow through the Bosphorus. The pipeline is expected to be completed by 2008.

The country does not produce or import significant quantities of natural gas. However Macedonia is planning to use natural gas as its main source of energy in the future, so it is interested in improving natural gas transportation. The reconstruction of the existing Skopje-Oblic (Pristina) gas pipeline is planned to meet the growing natural gas demand. Macedonia has a gas pipeline of 100km in length from Deve Bair to Skopje with a connection to the international gas pipeline in Bulgaria that supplies Greece with natural gas. The pipeline transfers over 800 million cubic metres per annum as part of a wider Russian gas export pipeline network in the Balkan region.

Macedonia has large reserves of coal, estimated at more than one billion tonnes, which should last for the foreseeable future at the annual production rate of 8.9 million tonnes. Most local coal output is low grade lignite which is used extensively for domestic energy production. Higher quality anthracite coals and coke (approximately 130,000 tonnes per annum) have to be imported for some primary electricity generation and the local metallurgical industry.

Energy
Four-fifths of energy needs are satisfied by domestic production of thermoelectric and hydroelectric power; the deficit is imported from Serbia and Montenegro and Bulgaria.

A number of new hydroelectric power plants are being built and plans are being considered by the government to modernise some of Macedonia's older power plants.

Financial markets
Stock exchange
The Macedonia Stock Exchange (MSE) was co-founded by eight commercial banks and two new brokerage companies in 1995. Its significance has grown thanks to privatisation, but it remains a limited source of investment.

Banking and insurance
There are seven major public lending and savings banks in Macedonia, as well as several smaller private commercial credit banks. The sector is dominated by Stopanska Banka, which has approximately 65 per cent of domestic banking assets and 50 per cent of banking deposits.

The republic has a tiered banking structure. The Narodna banka na Republika Makedonija (NBRM) (National Bank of the Republic of Macedonia) is responsible for the money supply, the liquidity of financial institutions and foreign currency transactions and reserves. The banking system requires a major overhaul. Competition is being introduced with the emergence of private credit institutions such as Uniprokom. International institutions are providing loans.

Central bank
Narodna banka na Republika Makedonija (NBRM) (National Bank of the Republic of Macedonia)

Time
GMT plus one hour (GMT plus two hours from late March to late September).

Macedonia

Geography
Situated in south-eastern Europe on the Balkan peninsula, Macedonia, or Vardar Macedonia, is part of a wider historical and geographical region of the same name. Part of this ancient territory, known as Pirin Macedonia, is situated in modern-day Greece. Roughly rectangular in shape, Macedonia is bordered by Serbia and Montenegro to the north (Kosovo to the north-west and Serbia to the north-east), Albania to the west, Bulgaria to the east and Greece to the south. Geographically, the republic is dominated by the Balkan Mountains and the Vardar River, which flows north-west to south-east.

Macedonia's strategic importance is out of all proportion to its small size, population and economic resources. On the negative side, its small size and lack of direct access to the sea makes Macedonia very vulnerable to its stronger neighbours in the southern Balkans.

Macedonia's major geographic characteristics are two large inland lakes, Ohrid and Prespa, which are shared with Albania and Greece. Lake Ohrid is a Unesco-designated World Heritage Site.

Climate
The river valleys of Vardar and Strumica are temperate Mediterranean, as is the eastern region. Western and northern regions are temperate continental. However, temperatures may vary from 40 degrees Celsius (C) in the summer to minus 30 degrees C in the winter. Rainfall averages 742 millimetres annually, but around 450 millimetres in Skopje which has about 100 days of rain annually. Skopje can be very hot in the summer and shrouded in mist in the winter.

Dress codes
Informal dress is tolerated in Macedonia, but should be avoided in business contexts, notably in Skopje.

Entry requirements
Passports
Required by all.
Visa
Required by all, except citizens of most European, and some Asian countries. For a full list of exceptions visit www.mnr.gov.mk/consular/vizaEN.htm Business visas require a letter of invitation from a local company, submitted with the application.

Advice from the government of Macedonia suggests visitors should contact the nearest consulate to confirm their visa status and requirements before travelling.
Currency advice/regulations
Currency can be exchanged without limitation at banks, hotels and licensed money-changers, although the cashing of travellers' cheques tends to be restricted to banks.

Health (for visitors)
Medical care in private facilities or by private practitioners is not covered by insurance and must be paid for in full. All foreigners in Macedonia are entitled to medical care in every state medical facility and foreigners staying for a year or more have a right to full medical coverage. Temporary visitors and those in transit are entitled to basic necessities and emergency first-aid treatment.
Mandatory precautions
None
Advisable precautions
There are no special requirements, but the local tap water should not be drunk. Public health is poor in certain parts of Macedonia.

Hotels
Some restaurants add a surcharge of 20 per cent for live music. Tipping not expected, but loose change or more is usually left depending on quality of service.

Public holidays
Fixed dates
1–2 Jan (New Year), 7 Jan (Orthodox Christmas Day), 14 Jan (Orthodox New Year's Day), 1 May (Labour Day), 2 Aug (Iliden Day), 8 Sep (Independence Day), 11 Oct (Antifascism Day).
Variable dates
Orthodox Easter Monday, Eid al Adha, Eid al Fitr.

Working hours
Banking
Mon–Fri: 0730–1930; Sat: 0800–1300.
Business
Mon–Fri: 0800–1600 or 0830–1630.
Government
Mon–Fri: 0700–1500 or 0730–1530.
Shops
Mon–Fri: 0800–1200 and 1700–2000/2100, but many shops open throughout day; Sat: 0800–1500.

Telecommunications
Telephone/fax
There are over 470,000 fixed telephone lines registered in Macedonia. MakTel will be the monopoly operator until January 2006.
Mobile phones
Services are provided by MobiMak, a subsidiary of MakTel, and coverage is good in most urban areas, except in the centre of the country around Brod and Krusevo.

Electricity supply
220V AC 50Hz with two large round prongs.

Weights and measures
Metric system.

Social customs/useful tips
Macedonians are a friendly people, although less gregarious then their Serbian neighbours in the Balkans. Similar to the Bulgarians, they are also practically minded. Western-style efficiency, however, is notable only by its absence. Although things are changing for the better, notably in Skopje, punctuality norms are not widely respected.

Political discussions of any sort are best avoided altogether by foreigners. There are strict laws against drinking and driving, speeding and other traffic offences. They are rigorously enforced, although the ubiquity of police corruption means that penalties can take the form of bribes rather than official fines.

Security
While some degree of stability has come to Macedonia since August 2001, parts of the country remain dangerous. In the north and west of the country, there have been sporadic outbursts of fighting and the area is heavily mined. In Skopje, street and other crimes have also become a serious problem. Car theft is very common. Local ownership of firearms is high. Visitors are advised to keep themselves informed of political developments.

Getting there
Air
National airline: Makedonski Aviotransport (MAT) (Macedonian Airlines)
International airport/s: Skopje (SKP), 6km from city; Ohrid (OHD, 10km from city.
Air traffic control systems are not up to European standards and the airports are by-passed by many international carriers and used primarily by regional airlines.
Airport tax: There is no airport tax.
Surface
Road: Bus services operate along the main routes connecting Albania, Bulgaria, Greece and Serbia. In September 2000, a new border crossing to Greece was opened at Medzitlija, near Bitola.
Rail: Intercity trains provide connections between Skopje and Serbia and Greece. Access from Bulgaria is via Belgrade. Construction of a 55km connecting link across the border to the Bulgarian network, begun in 1994, has yet to be completed.

Getting about
National transport
Air: There are no regular scheduled flights, although occasional flights between Ohrid and Skopje are available.
Road: There are 4,876km of modernised roads. The main road is between Ohrid and Tetovo.
Rail: There are 922km of railway lines, of which 231km are electrified. The main

terminals are at Skopje, Bitola and Gevgelija on the Greek border, Kicevo in the west of the country and Kriva Palanka on the Bulgarian border.

City transport

Taxis: Good service operating in all main cities. All taxis are metered, but there is no basic charge. A 10 per cent tip is usual. The journey from Skopje airport to the city centre is approximately 20–25 minutes.

Buses, trams & metro: Most city centres are served by trams, and the suburbs by buses. The service is generally cheap and regular.

Car hire

Limited availability in Skopje, but very expensive. Special insurance is required for travel to certain parts of the country. An international driving licence is required. Hired cars generally have to be paid for in foreign exchange.

BUSINESS DIRECTORY

The addresses listed below are a selection only. While World of Information makes every endeavour to check these addresses, we cannot guarantee that changes have not been made, especially to telephone numbers and area codes. We would welcome any corrections.

Telephone area codes

The international direct dialling code (IDD) for Macedonia is +389 followed by the area code:

Gostivar	42	Prilep	48
Kicevo	45	Skopje	2
Kochani	33	Tetovo	44
Kumanovo	31	Veles	43

Useful telephone numbers

Police: 92
Fire: 93
Ambulance: 94
Time: 95
Telegrams: 96
Telephone service: 977
Report emergencies: 985
Emergency road service: 987
Telephone information: 988

Chambers of Commerce

American Chamber of Commerce in Macedonia, 13 Juli Street 20, 1000 Skopje (tel: 123-873; fax: 123-872; e-mail: contact@amcham.com.mk).

Economic Chamber of Macedonia, Dimitrie Cupovski Street 13, PO Box 324, 1000 Skopje (tel: 118-088; fax: 116-210; e-mail: ic@ic.mchamber.org.mk).

Skopje Regional Chamber, Partizanski Odredi Boulevard 2, PO Box 509, 1000 Skopje (tel: 112-511; fax: 116-419; e-mail: regkomsk@regkom.org.mk).

Banking

Balkanska Banka, 6 Maksim Gorki, Skopje (tel: 127-155; fax: 132-186).

Eksport Import Banka, Dame Gruev 14, PO Box 836, Skopje (tel: 133-411; fax: 112-744; e-mail: info@eximpb.com.mk).

Invest Banka, Makedonija 9/11, Skopje (tel: 114-166; fax: 135-528).

Izvozna i Kreditna Banka, 11 Oktomvri 8, Skopje (tel: 122-207; fax: 122-393).

Komercijalna Banka, Kej Dimitar Vlahov 4, PO Box 563, Skopje (tel: 112-077; fax: 111-780; e-mail: international@kb.com.mk).

Kreditna Banka Skopje, Dame Gruev, Skopje (tel: 116-433; fax: 116-830).

Makedonska Banka, Bul. VMRO 12/2-3, Skopje (tel: 117-111; fax: 117-191; e-mail: info@makbanka.com.mk).

Radobank, Jurij Gagarin 17, Skopje (tel: 393-300; fax: 380-453; e-mail: radobank@radobank.com.mk).

Sileks Banka, Gradski Zid, Blok 9, Lokal 5, Skopje (tel: 115-288; fax: 114-891).

Stopanska Banka, 11 Oktomvri 7, Skopje (tel: 191-191; fax: 114-503; e-mail: sbank@stb.com.mk).

Teteks Bank, Naroden Front 19a, Skopje (tel: 127-449; fax: 131-419).

Tutunska Banka, 12 Udarna brigada bb, PO Box 702, Skopje (tel: 105-600; fax: 164-068; e-mail: tbanka@tb.com.mk).

Zemjodelska Banka, Vasil Glavinov 28/2, Skopje (tel: 112-699; fax: 224-844).

Central bank

National Bank of the Republic of Macedonia, PO Box 401, Kompleks banki, 1000 Skopje (tel: 108-108; fax: 108-357).

Travel information

Avioimpex (Macedonian Airways), Dimitrija Chupovski 10, Skopje (tel: 114-344; fax: 117-516; e-mail: axx@avioimpex.com.mk).

Macedonian Airlines (MAT), Vasil Glavinov 3, Skopje (tel: 292-333; fax: 229-576; e-mail: mathq@mat.com.mk).

Ohrid Airport, PO Box 134, Ohrid (tel: 31-656; fax: 33-616; e-mail: ohdap@airports.com.mk).

Skopje Airport, Skopje (tel: 148-333; fax: 148-300; e-mail: skpap@airports.com.mk).

Tourist Association of Skopje, Gradski Zid Blok 3, PO Box 399, Skopje (tel: 118-498; fax: 230-803).

Ministries

Ministry of Agriculture, Forestry and Water, Leninova 2, Skopje (tel: 134-477; fax: 211-997).

Ministry of Culture, Bul. Ilinden bb, Skopje (tel: 118-022; fax: 127-112).

Ministry of Defence, Orce Nikolov bb, Skopje (tel: 119-872; fax: 221-808; e-mail: info@morm.gov.mk).

Ministry of Economy, Bote Bocevski bb, Skopje (tel: 113-705; fax: 111-541; e-mail: ms@mt.net.mk).

Ministry of Education and Science, Dimitrija Chupovski 9, Skopje (tel: 117-277; fax: 118-414; e-mail: contact@mofk.gov.mk).

Ministry of Environment and Urban Planning, Drezdenska 52, Skopje (tel: 366-930; fax:366-931; e-mail: info@moe.gov.mk).

Ministry of Finance, Dame Gruev 14, Skopje (tel: 117-288; fax: 117-280).

Ministry of Foreign Affairs, Dame Gruev 6, Skopje (tel: 110-330; fax: 115-790; e-mail: mailmnr@mnr.gov.mk).

Ministry of Health, Vodnjanska bb, Skopje (tel: 147-147; fax: 113-014).

Ministry of Internal Affairs, Dimce Mircev bb, Skopje (tel: 117-222; fax: 112-468).

Ministry of Justice, Dimitrija Chupovski 9, Skopje (tel: 117-277; fax: 226-975).

Ministry of Labour and Social Policy, Dame Gruev 14, Skopje (tel: 117-288; fax: 118-242).

Ministry of Local Self-Government, Dimitrija Chupovski 9, Skopje (tel: 117-288; fax: 211-764)

Ministry of Transport and Communications, Crvena Skopska Opstina 4, Skopje (tel: 128-200, 145-0538, 145-513, 123-292; fax: 118-144).

Prime Minister's Office, Bul. Ilinden bb, Skopje (tel: 115-389; fax: 113-512).

Other useful addresses

Bank Rehabilitation Agency, Kompleks banki bb, Skopje (tel: 126-323; fax: 121-250).

British Embassy, Dimitrija Chupovski 26, 4th Floor, Skopje (tel: 116-772; fax: 117-005; e-mail: beskopje@mt.net.mk).

Customs Administration, Lazar Licenovski 13, Skopje (tel: 224-467; fax: 237-832).

Fund for National and Regional Roads, Dame Gruev 14, Skopje (tel: 118-044; fax: 220-535; e-mail: tanjam@.mpt.net.mk).

Macedonia Telecommunications, Orce Nikolov bb, Skopje (tel: 141-000; fax: 120-244).

Macedonian Embassy (USA), 3050 K Street, NW, Washington DC 20007 (tel: 202-337-3063; fax: 202-337-3093; e-mail: rmacedonia@aol.com).

Macedonian Stock Exchange, Mito Hadzivasilev 20, Skopje (tel: 122-055;

Macedonia

fax: 122-069; e-mail: mse@unet.com.mk).

Privatisation Agency of the Republic of Macedonia, PO Box 410, Nikola Vapcarov 7, Skopje (tel: 117-564; fax: 126-022; e-mail: agency@mpa.org.mk).

Skopje Fair, Belasica bb, PO Box 356, Skopje (tel: 118-288; fax: 117-375; e-mail: skfair@mt.net.mk).

Skopje Free Economic Zone, Salvador Allende 73, Skopje (tel: 176-170; fax: 177-101; e-mail: sfez@mol.com.mk).

US Embassy, Bul. Ilinden bb, Skopje (tel: 116-180; fax: 117-103).

Internet sites

Privatisation Agency of the Republic of Macedonia: http://www.mpa.org.mk

Economic Chamber of Macedonia: http://www.mchamber.org.mk

Government of FRY Macedonia: http://www.gov.mk/english

Agency of Information: http://www.sinf.gov.mk/defaulten.htm

National Bank of the Republic of Macedonia: http://www.nbrm.gov.mk

Macedonian Stock Exchange: http://www.mse.org.mk

Republic of Macedonia News Collection: http://b-info.com/places/Macedonia/republic/news/

Madagascar

KEY FACTS

Official name: Repoblikan'i Madagasikara (Republic of Madagascar)

Head of State: President Marc Ravalomanana (TIM) (sworn in 6 May 2002)

Head of government: Prime Minister Jacques Sylla (appointed 16 Jun 2002)

Ruling party: Tiako i Madagasikara (TIM) (I Love and Care for Madagascar)

Area: 592,000 square km (the fourth-largest island in the world)

Population: 17.66 million (2004)

Capital: Antananarivo

Official language: Malagasy, French

Currency: Franc Malgache (Mf) = 100 centimes

Exchange rate: Mf2,087.00 per US$ (Oct 2005)

GDP per capita: US$251 (2004)

GDP real growth: 5.30% (2004)

Labour force: 8.31 million (2004)

Inflation: 13.80% (2004)

Balance of trade: -US$278.80 million (2004)

Madagascar has made significant progress in terms of macroeconomic stabilisation and structural reform. Political stability has been broadly restored following the disputed 2001 presidential elections and the ensuing political crisis. Since that time, the authorities have taken measures to re-establish investor confidence and re-invigorate private sector growth.

The economy

Key structural reforms have been implemented, albeit with significant delays, in particular in the area of public enterprise reform and the fight against corruption. However, the economy remains vulnerable to shocks, including cyclones, and policy slippages. Progress in domestic revenue mobilisation and in strengthening the budget process also remained modest, reflecting in part the country's limited institutional capacity.

In the medium term, real growth is expected to average six per cent per annum and fiscal consolidation is projected to continue, driven by an improvement of the revenue performance and modest expenditure increases. The current account position should also improve over the medium-term. While remaining fragile, the external debt position should remain sustainable, provided the authorities continue to limit new external financing to grants and to highly concessional loans. There are several risks to this outlook however, especially in the external sector, where the impact of the expiry of preferential agreements on textiles exports could turn out to be larger than currently expected.

The government is committed to contain inflation, preserve Madagascar's competitiveness, and gradually build-up official reserves. This, together with accelerated progress on structural reforms and the assistance of the donor community, will be crucial for Madagascar to attain macroeconomic stabilisation.

Containing inflation hinges on the steadfast and timely implementation of tight monetary and fiscal policies as well as on the evolution of the world prices of oil and rice. Madagascar's revenue performance remains weak – reflected in a relatively low revenue-to-GDP ratio.

The International Monetary Fund (IMF) has encouraged the central bank to take further steps to improve the effectiveness of monetary policy and to be more proactive in managing liquidity. It has endorsed the authorities' flexible exchange rate policy, which limits exchange market intervention to smoothing operations, and agreed that the current exchange rate appears to be broadly appropriate.

The expiration of the Agreement on Textiles and Clothing in 2005 and the expected end of the third-party apparel provision of the US African Growth and Opportunity Act in 2007 reinforce the importance of strengthening competitiveness.

Madagascar's limited absorptive and institutional capacity has adversely affected the implementation of structural reforms. Shortcomings in economic and social data hamper policy formulation and implementation. It will be important to continue

Madagascar

to build national ownership of policies through a close dialogue with civil society. Better alignment of technical assistance with policy priorities will be crucial.

Having discarded past socialist economic policies, Madagascar now follows a World Bank and IMF led policy of privatisation and liberalisation. This strategy has placed the country on a slow and steady growth path from an extremely low level. Agriculture, including fishing and forestry, is a mainstay of the economy, accounting for more than one-fourth of gross domestic product and employing 80 per cent of the population. Deforestation and erosion, aggravated by the use of firewood as the primary source of fuel are serious concerns. Poverty reduction and combating corruption will be the centerpieces of economic policy for the next few years.

Politics

Millionaire businessman turned president Marc Ravalomanana has implemented free-market reforms which have been welcomed by donors and investors. Aid has increased and foreign debt has been cancelled. But poverty remains endemic and protesters have taken to the streets over rising prices. When he claimed victory in presidential elections in December 2001 a bitter six-month struggle for power with his predecessor, veteran leader Didier Ratsiraka, ensued. After the US and France recognised Ravalomanana as the legitimate leader, Ratsiraka flew to France and his forces on the island switched sides.

Ravalomanana was born in the village of Imerikasina, near Antananarivo. In true rags-to-riches fashion, he began his working life selling home-made yogurt off the back of a bicycle. His dairy and oil products business is now the largest non-foreign-owned company on the island.

Formerly an independent kingdom, Madagascar became a French colony in 1896, but regained its independence in 1960.

Risk assessment

Economic	Improving
Political	Fair
Regional stability	Satisfactory

COUNTRY PROFILE

Historical profile

A French protectorate was established in Madagascar in 1895 and a colony in 1896. During the Second World War – in 1942 – British troops landed on the island, to prevent it falling to the Japanese. The pace towards independence quickened after the 1939–45 war with the formation of modern political parties, which co-operated with the French authorities in implementing constitutional reforms. In a 1958 referendum, Madagascar voted to become an autonomous republic within the French African community.
1500 The first Europeans landed in Madagascar.
1790s King Andrianampoinimerina unified the Merina tribe which soon became the island's dominant tribe, controlling nearly half of Madagascar.
1820 Britain signed a treaty recognising Madagascar as an independent state under Merina rule.
1890 An Anglo-French treaty gave control of the island to France.
1894 Queen Ranavalona III was forced to abdicate and Madagascar was declared a French colony.
1947 After several decades of growing resentment and resistance to French rule, an insurrection was crushed by France with the loss of several thousand lives.
1960 The Republic of Madagascar (known between 1960–72 as the Malagasy Republic) gained full independence. Philibert Tsiranana became president.
1972 Tsiranana was forced from office; he was replaced by General Gabriel Ramantsoa.
1975 After a short tussle between pro- and anti-government forces a military coup replaced Ramantsoa with Didier Ratsiraka. The country was renamed the Democratic Republic of Madagascar.
1992–93 Following three years of protests and civil disturbances after Ratsiraka's third presidential election victory, a referendum endorsed a multi-party constitution which enshrined a unitary state and reduced the powers of the president. In the presidential election Ratsiraka was defeated by Albert Zafy.
1997 Didier Ratsiraka beat Albert Zafy in the presidential election.
2000 Ratsiraka and his party retained considerable political power, after 70 per cent of the electorate boycotted local elections.
2001 Both candidates, Ratsiraka and Marc Ravalomanana, declared themselves winners in the presidential election.
2002 Civil disturbance accompanied the heated debate about the prospective winner of the presidential election. Ravalomanana was declared the winner by the Constitutional High Court in April, following a recount. Ravalomanana was recognised by the US as Head of State. Didier Ratsiraka fled to the Seychelles. President Marc Ravalomanana's Tiako i Madagasikara (TIM) (I Love and Care for Madagascar) won the parliamentary elections.
2003 On 27 January, Prime Minister Jacques Sylla announced a new cabinet.
2004 The IMF agreed to write off debts of US$2 billion. In August, Madagascar joined the Southern African Development Community (SADC).

Political structure
Constitution
Constitutional reforms in 1995 and 1998 gave the president the power to appoint or dismiss the prime minister and presidential terms in office were limited to three.
Form of state
Republic
The executive
Under the constitution the prime minister is head of government and exercises virtually all executive power. The president is directly elected for five years.

KEY INDICATORS — Madagascar

	Unit	2000	2001	2002	2003	2004
Population	m	15.97	16.40	16.90	17.28	17.66
Gross domestic product (GDP)	US$bn	3.90	4.70	4.50	4.74	*4.36
GDP per capita	US$	243	286	266	274	251
GDP real growth	%	4.8	6.7	-11.9	9.6	5.3
Inflation	%	11.9	7.0	14.8	1.0	13.8
Exports (fob) (goods)	US$m	824.0	947.0	55.0	700.0	868.2
Imports (fob) (goods)	US$m	997.0	1,095.0	68.0	985.0	1,147.0
Balance of trade	US$m	-174.0	-148.0	-13.0	-285.0	278.8
Current account	US$m	-283.0	-170.0	-298.0	-228.0	-370.0
Total reserves minus gold	US$m	285.2	398.3	363.3	414.3	503.5
Foreign exchange	US$m	285.1	398.2	363.2	414.2	503.3
Exchange rate	per US$	6,767.50	6,588.50	6,832.00	6,040.00	7,562.50

* estimated figure

Nations of the World: A Political, Economic and Business Handbook

National legislature
Legislative power is vested in a 160-member Antenimieram-Pirenena (Assemblée Nationale) (National Assembly), elected for five years by proportional representation. The Senate, has 90 members, two-thirds of which are appointed by an electoral college, and the remainder nominated by the president, all serving six years.

Last elections
15 December 2002 (parliamentary); 16 December 2001/24 February 2002 (presidential).
Results: Parliamentary: President Marc Ravalomanana's Tiako i Madagasikara (TIM) (I Love and Care for Madagascar) won 102 seats out of 160, the Firaisankinam-Pirenena (FP) (National Union) coalition 23, independents 22 and minor parties 13; turnout was 67.6 per cent.
Presidential: there was no clear winner; the High Constitutional Court declared that a recount of the election showed Marc Ravalomanana was the winner with 51.5 per cent of the vote, over Ratsiraka with 35.9 per cent.

Next elections
2006 (parliamentary); 2007 (presidential).

Political parties
Ruling party
Tiako i Madagasikara (TIM) (I Love and Care for Madagascar)
Main opposition party
Andry sy Riana Enti-Manavotra an'i Madagasikara (Arema) (Association for the Rebirth of Madagascar), Firaisankinam-Pirenena (FP) (National Union), Rassemblement pour le socialisme et la democratie (RPSD) Party for Socialism and Democracy, Leader-Fanilo (Torch) Democratic Action for Reconstruction Party.

Population
17.66 million (2004)
Ethnic make-up
The population comprises 18 separate ethnic groups, all deriving in varying degrees from Malayo-Indonesian origin, with African and Arab influences a particular feature in coastal areas. The Merinas (central highlands) represent about 26 per cent of the total, while the Betsimisaraka on the east coast account for 15 per cent and the Betsileo (southern highlands) 12 per cent. The other main groups are the Antankarana (north), Sakalava (west) and Mahafaly and Antandroy (far south). There is long-standing rivalry between the highland groups (particularly the Merina) and those of the coastal regions.
Religions
Traditional beliefs (45 per cent), Christianity (about 45 per cent), Islam (7 per cent).

Education
Primary education lasts for five years. Secondary schooling is divided into two, beginning with a four-year programme. When completed students may continue in either an acedemic or technical programme, for a further three years. Education may be given in either French or Madagasy.
The majority of those who do not attend school or who withdraw early come from the poorest sections of the population and those living in rural areas; illiteracy rates in women are a higher among the youngest; and nearly half of school age children are not enrolled in schools.
Public expenditure is around 3 per cent of GDP, of which around 40 per cent is spent on primary and 35 per cent on secondary education. Higher education expenses amount to only 0.5 per cent of GDP.
Literacy rate: 68.1 per cent total, 61.6 per cent female; adult rates (World Bank).
Compulsory years: Six to 11.
Enrolment rate: 120 per cent gross primary enrolment of relevant age group (including repeaters), World Bank.
Pupils per teacher: 47 in primary schools.

Health
About 60 per cent of the population live within 5km of, or about one hour's walk from, a public health centre.
Total expenditure on health is around 2 per cent of GDP, of which government spending is about 66 per cent.
Vaccination facilities remain poor with only 61 per cent of children immunised against measles, before aged one year. More than three-quarters of the people have no ready access to drinking water.
HIV/Aids
The government has a national Aids policy that covers all economic sectors.
HIV prevalence: 1.7 per cent aged 15–49 in 2003 (World Bank)
Life expectancy: 55.7 years; although nearly one-third of the population's life expectancy is below 40 (World Bank 2002).
Fertility rate/Maternal mortality rate: 5.2 births per woman; maternal mortality 488 per 100,000 live births (World Bank).
Infant mortality rate: 78 per 1,000 live births (World Bank)
Head of population per physician/bed: One doctor per approximately 10,000 people; most health officers work in urban areas.

Welfare
In 2004, three separate cyclones, including Cyclone Gafilo, estimated to have been the worst cyclone in 20 years, killed over 100 people and damaged more than 117,000 hectares of farmland as well as many schools and healthcare centres. Total damage from Cyclone Gafilo was estimated, by Government, at US$250 million.

Main cities
Antananarivo (capital, and principal business centre, estimated population 1.3 million in 2004); Toamasina (Tamatave), on the east coast, the island's main port and the centre of the main area for producing cloves (173,700); Antsirabé (158,900); Fianarantsoa, a rich agricultural region (137,700); Mahajanga (Majunga), the west coast's main port (134,600); Toliara (formerly Tuléar), port on the south-west coast (101,900); Antsiranana (formerly Diégo-Suarez), port in the extreme north of the island (74,400).

Languages spoken
French is the usual business language and the medium for all documentation. Very little English is spoken.
Official language/s
Malagasy, French

Media
Press
Dailies: The 1990 law on press freedom was followed by a boom in privately-owned newspapers and encouraged more critical political reporting by the print media. Daily newspapers in French include the privately owned *Midi Madagasikara* and *Madagascar Tribune* and the Antananarivo daily *L'Express de Madagascar*. Other popular dailies are *Gazetiko* and *Maresaka*.
Weeklies: Weeklies include a Roman Catholic publication *Lakroa* (Cross) covering rural and remote areas and a bi-weekly *Telo Nohorefy*. *Dans les media demain* (In The Media Tomorrow) is a privately-owned Antananarivo weekly news digest with a large circulation in the Madagascan diaspora. *Feon'ny Merina* (Voice of the Merina) promotes the interests of Merina people of Malay origin.
Periodicals: Monthly magazines are *Jureco* and the news magazine *Revue de l'Ocean indien* covering other Indian Ocean islands.
Broadcasting
State monopoly of radio and television has been abolished. Radio-Télévision-Antenne 2 Malagasy (RTM) and Radio Madagasikara broadcast in Malagasy and French. There are several private stations as well as state radio and television.
Radio: *Echo du Capricorne* is a weekly radio broadcast dealing with Madagascar in general, presented in both Malagasy and French.

Economy
Agriculture is the predominant sector in the economy, although textile

Madagascar

manufacturing became a major export in 2004. It has yet to be seen what the elimination of textile quotas under a WTO ruling will have on the sector. The government is attempting to minimise the impact by diversifying the export base.

Since coming to power in 2002 the government has introduced a liberalised foreign exchange, removed import licences and ended some state monopolies. The IMF advises that, to maintain the buoyant 5–6 per cent GDP growth, other measures should be encouraged such as a reform of the taxation system, to be consistent and predictable and avoids *ad hoc* exemptions. These reforms should be transparent and include a consensus on the reform's goals and strategies.

Macroeconomic development and reforms have resulted in progress as investor confidence and private investment has grown. Nevertheless external shocks can still have an adverse effect; vanilla volume sales dropped in 2004, and inflation rose as the current account deficit widened, particularly with the record high price of imported oil.

The economy still needs help through loans and grants from international donors and has taken advantage of niche opportunities in aid-funded areas such as infrastructure, education, health, mining, energy, tourism, agriculture (including cotton and non-traditional exports) and consumer goods.

In one of the world's poorest countries, around 70 per cent of the population live below the poverty line. The IMF drew attention to the Poverty Reduction and Growth Facility (PRGF) programme that should be used to its full at a time when the economy is strong and not left until a time of weakness that would render progress less effective. Madagascar has reached the set conditions for aid under the enhanced Heavily Indebted Poor Countries (HIPC) Initiative, which will allow it to borrow funds backed by the Initiative's guarantee.

The progress in macroeconomic policies have seen a marked improvement and it is for the government to maintain tight fiscal policies and allow the market to evolve while minimising the shocks of higher import prices.

External trade

Regular trade and current account deficits are largely financed by aid flows and external borrowing.

In 2002, the US approved Madagascar as being eligible for tariff preferences under the Africa Growth and Opportunities Act (AGOA).

Imports
Principal imports are capital goods, petroleum, consumer goods and food. Control and inspection of goods with FOB value above US$5,000 are obligatory.

Main sources: France (17.6 per cent total, 2004), China (11.1 per cent), Hong Kong (6.7 per cent), Iran (6.2 per cent), South Africa (5.8 per cent)

Exports
Principal exports are coffee, vanilla, shellfish, sugar; cotton cloth, chromite and petroleum products.

Main destinations: US (35.7 per cent total, 2004), France (30.7 per cent), Germany (7.1 per cent), Mauritius (4.4 per cent)

Agriculture
Farming

The agricultural sector dominates the economy. With a growth rate of 3.1 per cent in 2004, it contributed 28.8 per cent to GDP and employs around 75 per cent of the working population. Madagascar has a wide range of soil types.

Main cash/export crops are prawns, coffee, cotton, cloves and vanilla, production of which has fluctuated due to recurrent droughts and cyclones. Vanilla used to be the country's main export crop but increased competition worldwide has reduced exports.

Main food crops are rice, maize, bananas and sweet potatoes. Groundnuts, pineapples, coconuts and sugar are also grown, mostly for internal use. The decline in coffee prices led to many growers switching production to rice, increasing production by 5 per cent, and making Madagascar self-sufficient in rice (the staple diet of the country) for the first time since the mid-1970s, with annual production at around 3.0 million tonnes per year. Divestiture of vanilla, cotton and sugar parastatals is expected to encourage greater foreign investment.

The livestock sector is dominant in the west and south of the country.

Crop production in 2004 included: 3,390,646 tonnes (t) cereals in total, 200,000t taro, 349,646t maize, 2,191,420t cassava, 280,500t potatoes, 542,234t sweet potatoes, 3,030,000t rice, *290,000t bananas, 101,610t pulses, 3,214,154 t roots and tubers, *84,500t coconuts, *97,900t citrus fruit, 29,182t oilcrops, 1,326t tobacco, 4,500t cocoa beans, 65,000t green coffee, 3,000t vanilla, *15,500t cloves, *1,600t pepper spice, *4,790t other spices, 39,170t groundnuts in shells, 2,459,705t sugar cane, 17,000t sisal, 36,800t fibre crops, *210,000t mangoes, *890,600t fruit in total, *343,610t vegetables in total.

* estimate

The estimated livestock production or 2004 included: 297,067t meat in total, 146,625t beef, 4,000t game meat, 70,000t pig meat, 8,616t lamb and goat meat, 67,160t poultry, 19,436t eggs, 535,000t milk, 3,930t honey, 20,700t cattle hides, 416t sheepskins, 50t cocoons, silk.

Fishing
Since 1996, prawns have been the number one export earner, with around 7,000 tonnes of prawn exports earning revenues of over US$60 million per annum.

Forestry
Only 15 per cent of Madagascar's ancient forest remains. Deforestation has left the hills exposed to the wind and rain which strips away the soil. Forest preservation and the creation of national parks are receiving large-scale international support.

Exports of timber production in 2004 was US$16.4 million while imports amounted to US$5.7 million.

Estimated production in 2004 included 10,866,866 cubic metres (cum) roundwood, 97,000cum industrial roundwood, 95,000cum sawnwood, 74,000cum sawlogs and veneers, 5,000cum wood-based panels, 10,789,866cum woodfuel, 871,934t charcoal.

Industry and manufacturing

The industrial sector contributes around 16 per cent of GDP and employs around 9 per cent of the workforce.

Industry is dominated by food processing and the manufacture of textiles for international markets. Other major sectors include rice milling, sugar refining, distilling, oil-seed crushing, meat, fruit and vegetable canning, processing of cashew nuts, fruit juices, milk products and jams, cigarettes, soap and rope manufacturing, cotton spinning and brewing. Major capital-intensive industries are oil refining, fertiliser and cement production.

There are 150 firms based in industrial free zones, representing mainly textile, food processing and information technology, and creating 6,000 jobs in the Antananarivo area alone. Many textile companies in Mauritius are relocating to Madagascar due to the cheaper labour rates.

Tourism

Tourism is the second most important foreign exchange earner, after textile exports. The sector is expected to earn US$152.7 million, contribute 3 per cent of GDP in 2005, and attract 11.6 per cent of all capital investment. Travel and tourism is predicted to employ over 450,000 people, or provide one in every 18 jobs. France is the main market and adventure and eco-tourism are the main attractions. There is considerable potential for expansion of the sector in these and other activities, such as coastal resorts, but inadequate infrastructure and low investment are a hindrance to becoming truly competitive with more established Indian Ocean destinations.

Environment
Madagascar has plants and wildlife found nowhere else on earth, and growth of both tourism and mining needs to be controlled to protect the fragile ecosystems.

Mining
Excluding gold and gem production by artisinal miners, mining contributes less than 1 per cent of GDP and employs 1 per cent of the workforce. If the informal sector is included, the contribution to GDP is around 3 per cent.
Madagascar is rich in mineral resources, although it is still only a minor mineral producer by regional standards. There are sizeable deposits of a number of minerals, industrial ores and precious and semi-precious gemstones including chrome ore, mica, graphite, gold, bauxite, uranium, iron ore, ilmenite/titanium, quartz, nickel, copper, lead, platinum, labradorite, rock-crystal, rhodolite, marble, garnets, emeralds, rubies and sapphires. There are known deposits containing 100 million tonnes of bauxite and 400 million tonnes of iron ore, although these have not been developed due to the country's poor infrastructure.
Only chrome, mica and graphite have been exploited to any great extent, and export earnings from these are limited due to lack of demand. The world's largest known emerald cluster was discovered in Madagascar in 1996.
Small quantities of semi-precious stones (garnets and amethysts) are mined for export.
The state-owned Société Kraomita Malagasy (Kraoma) is Madagascar's main chromite producer. It extracts around 40,000 tonnes of concentrates and 80,000 tonnes of lumpy ore per year from the Andriamana complex and a further 20,000 tonnes from the Behandrinana mine.
There are some 100,000 individual gold miners and small syndicates. Although the government tolerates this form of mining, it is worried about its ecological effects which include a high level of mercury leaking into streams and rivers.
The country also produces graphite, 66 per cent of which comes from the Gallois mine. It exports up to 15,000tpy, mostly to UK, US and Germany.

Hydrocarbons
Madagascar does not produce oil, however exploration has shown that deposits of oil are evident. There are eight international oil companies exploring offshore blocks, including ExxonMobile, Norsk-Hyfro and Aminex.
There is one refinery in Toamasina with a capacity of around 15,000 barrels per day (bpd).
Madagascar relies on importing both crude and refined oil and a small amount of coal; it does not import natural gas.

Energy
The majority of the country's energy needs are supplied by imported fuel.
Besides fuelwood, hydropower is the main domestic energy source. Some mines and factories have their own small diesel or stream-powered generators. Construction of the country's second dam, at Ankorahotra, has been suspended pending evaluation of the oil fields.

Banking and insurance
Moves to strengthen banking supervision have been enhanced through the IMF backed Financial Sector Assessment Program.
Central bank
Banque Centrale de la République Malgache

Time
GMT plus three hours

Geography
The Democratic Republic of Madagascar comprises the island of Madagascar, the fourth-largest in the world, and several much smaller offshore islands, in the western Indian Ocean, about 500km (300 miles) east of Mozambique, in southern Africa.

Climate
Tropical, cooler in highlands. The summer period spans the months of November to April. Numerous areas have their own micro-climates – the highlands are subject to mild freshness in the winter, while the eastern parts of the island experience high temperatures and humidity, with barren and arid conditions dominating the western sector.
In Antananarivo hottest month December (15–28 degrees Celsius), coldest July (9–19 degrees Celsius). The wettest month is January. Winter in the capital lasts from April to October, when it is cold and dry. Madagascar falls within the cyclone belt and cyclones tend to occur during the rainy season December–March, which is hot. It is rainy until June or July on the east coast and is hotter throughout the year. It is drier but hotter on the west coast.

Dress codes
In Antananarivo, in the winter months, normal weight clothing is suitable, with a woollen sweater/cardigan recommended. In the summer men should wear tropical suits and women, cotton dresses. On the coast, tropical clothing is recommended all year round.

Entry requirements
Passports
Required by all. Passports must be valid for six months beyond visa issue date.
Visa
Required by all, along with proof of return/onward passage. Short-term visas, up to three months, can be obtained at a port of entry. Business visas require a letter of invitation from a local company, and a letter of recommendation from a business or organisation willing to assume financial responsibility for the visitor, to be submitted with an application.
Currency advice/regulations
Local currency: up to Mf5,000 may be imported and exported.
No limit on import of foreign currency, but amounts over Mf50,000 in value must be declared on arrival, and export is allowed up to the declared amount.

Health (for visitors)
Mandatory precautions
Yellow fever vaccination certificate required if arriving from an infected area.
Advisable precautions
Typhoid, polio, tetanus and hepatitis A vaccinations recommended. Malaria risk exists throughout the country and prophylaxis is necessary. There is a rabies risk. Water precautions should be taken.

Hotels
Good hotels are available in Antananarivo, Toamasina, Nosy Be, Ste Marie and Taolanaro. A service charge is added to bills at some hotels. Discretionary tipping is usual.

Credit cards
Credit cards are of limited use in Madagascar and few establishments accept them.

Public holidays
Fixed dates
1 Jan (New Year's Day), 29 Mar (Commemoration Day – 1947), 1 May (Labour Day), 26 Jun (Independence Day), 15 Aug (Assumption Day), 27 Sep (St Vincent de Paul's Day), 1 Nov (All Saints' Day), 25 Dec (Christmas Day), 30 Dec (Anniversary of the Republic of Madagascar).
Variable dates
Good Friday, Easter Monday.

Working hours
Banking
Mon–Fri: 0800–1500.
Business
Mon–Fri: 0800–1630.
Government
Mon–Fri: 0800–1200, 1400–1800.
Shops
Mon–Fri: 0800–1200, 1400–1800.

Madagascar

Electricity supply
110 or 220V AC, 50 cycles; also 380V AC, 50 cycles

Getting there
Air
National airline: Air Madagascar
International airport/s: Antananarivo (Code: TNR), 14km south-east of city; restaurant, currency exchange.
Airport tax: None. Any departure tax is usually included in the price of the ticket.
Surface
Water: There are few scheduled sea passages.
Main port/s: Toamasina (Tamatave), on the east coast, is the island's main port. It is used by numerous foreign shipping lines. Mahajanga (Majunga) is the west coast's main port. Antseranana (Diégo-Suarez) is in the extreme north of the island, and Toliara (Tuléar) is on the south-west coast.

Getting about
National transport
Air: Air Madagascar and TAM airlines fly more than 60 domestic routes. There are connections between all major towns, apart from Antsirabe. Air travel is the most used and generally recommended form of transport. There are over 100 airfields on the island, although many are just airstrips.
Road: Generally poor and in need of repair, and only passable in good weather (the dry season).
Three main roads leave Antananarivo – (RN4) to Mahajanga (Majunga), (RN2) to Toamasina (Tamatave), and the plateau route south to Fianarantsoa (RN7).
Rail: Two classes; light refreshments may be available; air-conditioning available on first-class trains.
Routes are: between Toamasina and Antsirabe, via Antananarivo, incorporating a connection between Moramanga and Lake Alaotra; and between Fianarantsoa and Manakara on the east coast. Daily services operate on most routes.
City transport
Taxis: Flat fare system for short journeys in most towns, otherwise by negotiation; tipping is not usual.
Car hire
Available in main centres. International driving licence required.

BUSINESS DIRECTORY

The addresses listed below are a selection only. While World of Information makes every endeavour to check these addresses, we cannot guarantee that changes have not been made, especially to telephone numbers and area codes. We would welcome any corrections.

Telephone area codes
The international dialling code (IDD) for Madagascar is +261 followed by operator and area codes and subscriber's number:

Antananarivo	22	Nosy-Be	86
Antsiranana	82	Toamasina	53
Fianarantsoa	75	Toliara	18
Mahajanga	62		

Useful telephone numbers
Police: 17
Fire: 18
Ambulance: 2235-753

Chambers of Commerce
Antananarivo Chamber of Commerce, Industry and Agriculture, 20 Rue Paul Dussac, PO Box 166, 101 Antananarivo 101 (tel: 202-11; fax: 20213).

Antsiranana Chamber of Commerce, Industry and Agriculture, 3 Rue Colbert, PO Box 76, Antsiranana 201 (tel: 223-72; fax: 294-03).

Madagascar Federation of Chambers of Commerce, Industry and Agriculture, 20 Rue Paul Dussac, PO Box 166, Antananarivo 101 (tel: 20-211; fax: 20-213).

Mahajanga Chamber of Commerce, Industry and Agriculture, Boulevard Poincaré, PO Box 52, Mahajanga 401(tel: 226-21).

Nosy-Be Chamber of Commerce, Industry and Agriculture, Cours de Hell, PO Box 11, Nosy-Be 207 (tel: 610-26; fax: 610-56).

Toamasina Chamber of Commerce, Industry, Handicrafts and Agriculture, 4 Rue de Commerce, PO Box 108, Toamasina 501 (tel: 323-45; fax: 320-25).

Banking
BNOI (linked with Banque Nationale de Paris), PO Box 25 bis, 101 Antananarivo (tel: 2234-609; fax: 2234-610).

Bank of Africa-Madagascar, PO Box 183, 2 Place de L'Independance, Antananarivo 101 (tel: 2239-100/2239-250, 2223-641; fax: 2229-408).

Banque SBM Madagascar, 1 Rue Andrianary Ratianarivo Antsahavola, Antananarivo 101 (tel: 2266-607/2266-646-47; fax: 2266-608).

BFV-Société Générale, PO Box 196, 14 Lalana Jeneraly Rabehevitra, Antananarivo 101 (tel: 2220-691; fax: 2234-554).

BNI-Crédit Lyonnais Madagascar, PO Box 174, 74 Rue du 26 Juin 1960, Antananarivo 101 (tel: 228-00/239-51; fax: 337-49).

Investco Southern Investment Bancorp, PO Box 8510, Immeuble NIAG, 8 Lalana Rainizanabololona, Antanimena, Antananarivo 101 (tel: 2264-820/2229-114; fax: 2261-329).

Union Commercial Bank SA, PO Box 197, 77 Rue Solombavambahoaka Frantsay, Antsahavola, Antananarivo 101 (tel: 2227-262; fax: 2228-740, 2232-282).

Central bank
Banque Centrale de Madagascar, Avenue de la Révolution Socialiste, PO Box 550, Antananarivo (tel: 217-51; fax: 345-32; e-mail: banque-centrale@ banque-centrale-madagascar.mg).

Travel information
Air Madagascar, BP 437, 31 Avenue de l'Indépendance, Analakely, Antananarivo 101 (tel: 2222-222, 2222-200; fax: 2233-760, 2225-728); Ivato Airport, Antananarivo (tel: 2244-222, ext 5200).

Association des Agences de Voyages de Madagascar, BP 541, Antananarivo (tel: 2222-364).

Air Mauritius, 77 Ialana Solombavabahoaka, Frantsay, Antsahavola, Antananarivo (tel: 2235-900; fax: 2235-773).

Réseau National des Chemins de Fer, (Railway network), BP 259, Soarano, Antananarivo (tel: 2220-521).

Ministry of tourism
Direction du Tourisme de Madagascar, Tsimbazaza, BP 610, Antananarivo (tel: 2226-298).

National tourist organisation offices
Maison du Tourisme de Madagascar (Madagascar Tourist Office), Place de l'Indépendance, Antaninarenina, PO Box 3224, Antananarivo (tel: 2232-529; fax: 2232-537).

Ministries
Ministry of Private Sector Development and Privatisation, Comité de Privatisation, Zone III 1er étage, Ampefiloha, Antananarivo (fax: 2260-138).

Ministry of Tourism, PO Box 610, Tsimbazaza, Antananarivo (tel: 2226-298).

Ministry of Transport and Meteorology, Anosy, Antananarivo (tel: 2224-604, 2222-719).

Other useful addresses
Agence Nationale d'Information 'Taratra' (ANTA), 3 rue du R P Callet, BP 386, Antananarivo (tel: 2221-171).

Association of the Hotel Industry of Madagascar (SIHM), c/o Sofitrans – Soarano, Antananarivo (tel: 2222-330).

British Embassy, Commercial Section, First Floor, Immeuble 'Ny Havana', Cité des 67 Ha, BP 167, 101 Antananarivo (tel: 2227-749, 2227-370; fax: 2226-690).

Civil Aviation Management, Antananarivo (tel: 2227-715).

Comité de Privatisation, Secrétariat Technique á la Privatisation Immeuble FIARO, Zone III 1er étage, Ampefiloha, 101 Antananarivo (fax: 2260-138).

Customs Services, Ivato Airport, Antananarivo (tel: 2244-032).

Institut National de Géodésie et Cartographie/FTM, BP 323, Antananarivo (tel: 2222-935).

Institut National de la Statistique et de la Recherche Economique (DGBDE), Direction Générale, BP 485, Antananarivo (tel: 2221-652).

Madagascan Embassy (US), 2374 Massachusetts Avenue, NW, Wasghington DC 20008 (tel: 202-265-5525; fax: 202-265-3034; e-mail: malagasy@embassy.org).

Office Militaire National pour les Industries Stratégiques (monitors major industrial projects), 21 Lalana Razanakombana, Antananarivo.

Société d'Etude et de Réalisation pour le Développement Industriel, BP 3180, Antananarivo (tel: 2221-335).

Syndicat de l'Industrie Hôteliére de Madagascar, BP 341, Antananarivo (tel: 2220-202).

Internet sites

Africa Business Network: http://www.ifc.org/abn

African Development Bank: http://www.afdb.org

Africa News Online: http://www.allafrica.com

Africa Online: http://www.africaonline.com

Harambee Afrika (UK business club for traders with east, central and southern Africa; includes annotated web resource list): http://www.harambee.co.uk

Mbendi AfroPaedia (information on companies, countries, industries and stock exchanges in Africa): http://mbendi.co.za

Malawi

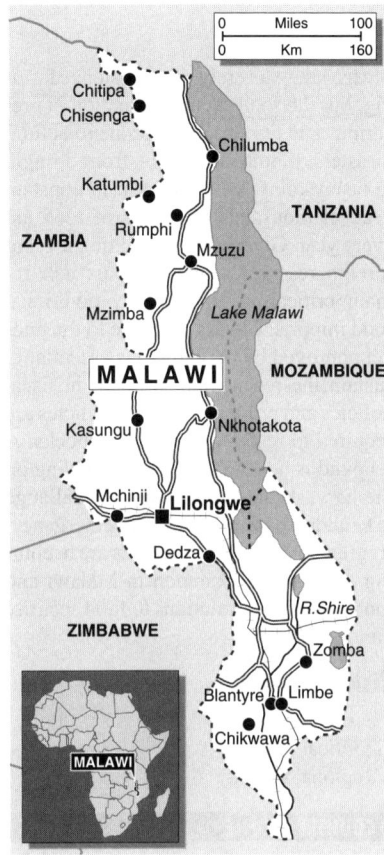

For three decades the destiny of Malawi was tied to the whims of its totalitarian self-elected-president-for-life, Kamuzu Banda, who enjoyed being surrounded by dancing women and who encouraged people to betray relatives who criticised his rule. In the mid-1990s he buckled under popular pressure to hold elections, and lost – finally giving Malawians a taste for multi-party democracy.

Landlocked Malawi ranks among the world's least developed countries. The single major natural resource, agricultural land, is under severe pressure from rapid population growth – agriculture accounted for nearly 36 per cent GDP and 80 per cent of export revenues in 2005. The performance of the tobacco sector is key to short-term growth as tobacco accounts for over 50 per cent of exports. The economy depends on substantial inflows of economic assistance from the International Monetary Fund (IMF), the World Bank, and individual donor nations, and has been urged by world financial bodies to free up its economy. Since the mid-1990s it has privatised many loss-making state-run corporations.

When the elephants fight ...

Bingu wa Mutharika, who had been hand-picked by former president Bakili Muluzi (after parliament refused to accept an amendment to the constitution allowing Muluzi to stand for a third term) as the candidate of the ruling United Democratic Front (UDF), was sworn in as President of Malawi on May 24, 2004. Perceived as a relative outsider, Mutharika's nomination surprised many UDF members and led to several defections. The run-up to the poll was overshadowed by opposition claims of irregularities. European Union and Commonwealth observers said although voting passed peacefully, they were concerned about 'serious inadequacies' in the poll. Less than a year later Mutharika resigned from the UDF, accusing the party and his predecessor Muluzi of opposing his high-profile anti-corruption campaign. He formed a new grouping, the Democratic Progressive Party (DPP). Donor countries warned in 2005 that long-running impeachment proceedings against Mutharika arising from a power struggle between the president and his predecessor were diverting the government's attention from pressing problems, including food shortages.

In his New Year's Eve speech, President Muthrika said he would be willing to talk to the opposition, provided they dropped their impeachment charges. The UDF has said it would be ready to take up his offer to break the political impasse, provided he improved relations with parliament. However, political analysts say it is unlikely the opposition would join a government of national unity and that all they can do is wait for the 2009 elections.

... the grass gets trampled under foot

Malawi's economic performance has been disappointing. Although GDP real growth in 2004 was 4.3 per cent, in 2005 growth

KEY FACTS

Official name: Dziko la Malawi (Republic of Malawi)

Head of State: President Bingu wa Mutharika (UDF) (sworn in 24 May 2004)

Head of government: President Bingu wa Mutharika

Ruling party: A coalition led by United Democratic Front (UDF) with the Republican Party (RP), Movement of Genuine Democratic Change (MGODE), National Democratic Alliance (NDA), Alliance for Democracy (AFORD) and 38 non-partisan parliamentary members (elected 20 May 2004)

Area: 118,484 square km

Population: 11.65 million (2004)

Capital: Lilongwe

Official language: English

Currency: Kwacha (K) = 100 tambala

Exchange rate: K124.10 per US$ (Oct 2005)

GDP per capita: US$151 (2004)

GDP real growth: 4.30% (2004); *2.0% (2005)

Labour force: 5.35 million (2004)

Inflation: 11.60% (2004)

Balance of trade: -US$17.70 million (2004)

Foreign debt: US$3.13 billion (2004)

* estimated figure

was setback by an agricultural slump and high international oil prices. In addition, weak governance and programme implementation has led to an unstable macroeconomic situation. Malawi began a three-year Poverty Reduction and Growth Facility (PRGF) programme in June 2005, the first six months of which are due to be evaluated in February 2006. Depending on the results of this assessment, Malawi may qualify for total debt relief from the IMF – Malawi had not been among the 19 poor countries which had had their debt written off by the IMF in December 2005.

The overarching medium-term objective will be to reduce poverty through private sector-led growth. Fiscal policy will aim to reduce the government's domestic debt, while allowing for increases in pro-poor and pro-growth spending.

There is a need for several fundamental economic challenges. The uneven implementation of policies in the past has left the country with a high debt burden that is consuming a large share of government revenue and is diverting resources from private investment.

The main objectives over the period 2005–08 are: to raise economic growth to near six per cent a year, with an emphasis on rural incomes; increase health services and educational opportunities; reduce core inflation to the 5–8 per cent range; run a fiscal surplus to reduce the government's domestic debt to less than 15 per cent of gross domestic product from more than 24 per cent; build international reserves to at least two months of imports.

The possible elimination of the European Union sugar regime in 2008 would have a significant adverse impact on exports, as would drought in the tea and tobacco producing regions. The government is assessing ways to diversify the economy, and faces many impediments – but the major ones are being addressed.

The National Road Authority is working with the European Union to repair and expand the existing road network. Rail links to ports in Nacala and Beira (both in Mozambique) are being repaired with the co-operation of the government of Mozambique. These improvements will significantly reduce the cost of key imports, in particular, fertiliser. The repair and construction work in rural areas will provide a source of income for farmers.

Completion of an interconnector from the hydroelectric dam in Cahorra Bassa, will significantly expand the supply of electricity by 2007. The sale of Malawi Telecom is being reviewed following problems identified during the due diligence phase of the sales agreement.

By increasing fiscal transparency, improving budget procedures, and providing full independence to the central bank, the authorities are expecting to strengthen the institutional framework from fiscal 2006/07.

Past expenditure overruns often reflected a lack of firm commitment and a deterioration in expenditure management. The turnaround in spending control in 2004/05 demonstrated the authorities' commitment to live within the approved budget, but management systems can still be improved.

The country faces a health crisis worsened by the effects of brain drain. The spread of HIV/AIDS has increased the demand for health services: life expectancy has declined to 39 years, and child mortality remains at 189 per 1,000 live births. The medium-term programme accommodates a sizable increase in health expenditure – US$40 million will be disbursed in 2005/06, with a total of US$200 million committed over six-years.

Outlook

Most Malawians rely on subsistence farming, but the food security situation is precarious and the country is prone to natural disasters of both extremes – from drought to heavy rainfalls – putting it in constant need of thousands of tonnes of food aid every year. Given the constraining level of foreign reserves, donor support will remain critical to finance any additional food imports. Close adherence to the budget approved by parliament is essential to sustain the recent improvement in fiscal policies and prudent monetary policies are required to respond to external shocks. A rebound is possible in 2006 depending on the harvest, but the paramount challenge is to address the food security emergency. Regrettably, food emergencies are becoming increasingly common in Malawi and more permanent solutions to food security are needed.

Risk assessment

Economic	Poor
Political	Poor
Regional stability	Poor

COUNTRY PROFILE

Historical profile

In the wake of Scottish missionaries Britain declared a protectorate over the country called Nyasaland in 1891. It succeeded in subduing the local clans in a series of campaigns ending in 1897. The respite was brief: in 1915 the population rose in a brief attempt to displace the colonial power – led by mission-educated John Chilembwe, who was shot during the rising. The British during this time were attempting to develop a cash economy based on coffee plantations and cash crop production in the southern and central parts of the country began. The planters grew rich, peasant farmers were ruined and the pattern of migration to the south in search of work, which has since become a major part of Malawi's economy, began. The movement which brought the country to independence began after the Chilembwe revolt, developed in the inter-war years and culminated in the formation of the Nyasaland African National Congress in

KEY INDICATORS — Malawi

	Unit	2000	2001	2002	2003	2004
Population	m	11.31	11.40	11.65	11.65	11.65
Gross domestic product (GDP)	US$bn	1.50	1.70	1.80	1.70	*1.81
GDP per capita	US$	150	165	186	146	151
GDP real growth	%	1.7	-1.5	1.8	4.9	4.3
Inflation	%	29.6	27.2	14.2	9.6	11.6
Exports (fob) (goods)	US$m	431.0	441.0	421.0	435.0	503.4
Imports (fob) (goods)	US$m	600.0	566.0	796.0	505.0	521.1
Balance of trade	US$m	-169.0	-125.0	-375.0	-70.0	-17.7
Current account	US$m	-90.0	-120.0	-220.0	-180.0	-140.0
Foreign debt	US$bn	2.5	2.7	2.9	2.9	–
Total reserves minus gold	US$m	246.9	206.7	165.2	126.5	133.3
Foreign exchange	US$m	243.5	203.1	162.0	122.6	128.6
Exchange rate	per US$	59.54	72.20	77.15	96.83	107.50

* estimated figure

1944. Britain was eventually unable to resist the pressures for independence, which after lengthy negotiations, was finally achieved in 1964.
In the eighth century, the Bantu people of Nyasaland began trading with Portuguese merchants on the east African coast.
1891 The British declared the area a protectorate and in the wake of David Livingstone's explorations, an increasing number of Europeans went to Nyasaland, particularly missionaries. The settlers expropriated land and imposed taxes which led to ever growing numbers of Africans working in settler plantations or emigrating to the then Rhodesia or South Africa.
1950s Opposition to colonial rule, which had begun in the southern highlands, became more widespread. The Nyasaland African Congress was established to oppose the planned Central African Federation (CAF) with Northern and Southern Rhodesia, and the heavy-handed interference by white settlers in traditional agricultural methods.
1954 The Nyasaland African Congress grew rapidly upon the return from Britain of Dr Hastings Kamuzu Banda; within a year the colonial authorities had jailed him and other leaders.
1961 The authorities released Dr Banda and invited him to London for a constitutional conference, at which Nyasaland was promised eventual independence regardless of constitutional developments in the rest of the CAF. Elections followed, which Dr Banda's Malawi Congress Party (MCP) won.
1963 The CAF was officially dissolved, paving the way for independence in Nyasaland a year later, with Dr Banda as Prime Minister.
1966 Nyasaland became a republic and was renamed Malawi; Dr Banda became president.
1971 Banda declared himself president for life.
1978 Dr Banda and the MCP won the first election since independence.
1992 Catholic bishops condemned Banda and the one-party state and sparked mass demonstrations; humanitarian aid to the country was cut off.
1993 A referendum overwhelmingly backed a multi-party option and political parties began to develop.
1994 The United Democratic Front (UDF) beat the MCP in multi-party legislative elections and Bakili Muluzi became president. Dr Banda retired.
1995 Banda was acquitted of ordering the murder of three government ministers, he later apologising for any suffering he may have 'unknowingly caused'.
1997 Hastings Banda died in South Africa, where he was being treated for pneumonia.
1999 The UDF won the parliamentary elections and Muluzi retained the presidency for the last, five-year term.
2000 Corruption scandals began to threaten aid flow. Muluzi was forced to dismiss his government.
2002 Malawi's bishops condemned Muluzi's rule, warning that it was becoming a dictatorship. International aid was suspended due to a lack of reform and transparency. A drought caused widespread hunger; food aid was supplied by the UN.
2004 The government offered anti-retroviral drugs to HIV/Aids sufferers, free of charge. The 20 May presidential elections were won by Bingu wa Mutharika (UDF), while the Malawi Congress Party (MCP) won most seats in the parliamentary elections. The elections were not considered free and fair by observers. A coalition government was formed led by the UDF.
2005 Mutharika resigned from the UDF and formed a new group, the Democratic Progressive Party (DPP). Parliament began impeachment proceedings against the president for corruption. A UN humanitarian appeal for US$88 million for food aid had, by October, reached only US$28 million. The president declared a nationwide disaster in response to the food crisis.

Political structure
Constitution
The constitution dates from 1966. A multi-party political system was adopted in 1994.
Malawi is divided into 24 administrative divisions.
Form of state
Republic
The executive
The president is both the head of state and the head of government. The president names the 36-member Cabinet and is elected by popular vote for a five-year term.
National legislature
The unicameral 193-member National Assembly is elected by popular vote to serve a five-year term.
Legal system
The legal system is based on English common law.
Last elections
20 May 2004 (presidential and parliamentary)
Results: Presidential: Bingu wa Mutharika (UDF) won with 35.9 per cent of the vote, followed by John Tembo (MCP) with 27.1 per cent, Gwanda Chakuamba of the Mgwirizano Coalition with 25.7 per cent and Brown Mpinganjira (NDA) with 8.7 per cent.
Parliamentary: the MCP won 60 seats out of 193, the UDF 49 and the Mgwirizano Coalition 28, the National Democratic Alliance (NDA) 8, Alliance for Democracy (AFORD) 6, non-partisans 38.
Next elections
2009 (presidential and parliamentary)

Political parties
Ruling party
A coalition led by United Democratic Front (UDF) with the Republican Party (RP), Movement of Genuine Democratic Change (MGODE), National Democratic Alliance (NDA), Alliance for Democracy (AFORD) and 38 non-partisan parliamentary members (elected 20 May 2004)
Main opposition party
Malawi Congress Party (MCP)

Population
11.65 million (2004)
Ethnic make-up
Chewa (60 per cent), Lomwe (18 per cent), Yao (13 per cent), Ngoni (7 per cent).
Religions
Christianity (80 per cent), Islam (13 per cent), traditional beliefs (7 per cent).

Education
Primary education lasts for eight years. Junior secondary school follows, and if successful, students may progress to the senior secondary school, of which each stage lasts for two years. Instruction is given in English.
Educational attainment, defined as completion of standard eight (at the end of primary school), is only 11.2 per cent. While education is free, provision has not kept up with demand. In some rural areas children have to walk up to 13km to the nearest school. The government's decision to provide free primary education has brought a crisis in the system, placing severe restrictions on its education budget. Secondary schools have less than half the teachers they need and about two-thirds of these are not trained to teach at secondary level. The government proposes to convert Malawi Distance Education Centres (DECs) into Community Day Secondary Schools (CDSS) in order to alleviate the shortage of secondary school teachers.
The University of Malawi typically has approximately 3,000 students, with roughly 1,000 new enrolments every year.
Literacy rate: 64.1 per cent total, (49 per cent female, 72 per cent male); adult rates (World Bank).
Compulsory years: 5 to 13.
Enrolment rate: 134 per cent gross primary enrolment, of relevant age group (including repeaters); 29 per cent gross secondary enrolment (World Bank).

Pupils per teacher: 59 in primary schools; in some classes the ratio has increased to 96:1 due to Aids related illness among teachers.

Health

Malaria is endemic; around four million new cases are reported each year. Malaria accounts for 18 per cent of all hospital deaths and 40 per cent of all outpatients visits. A programme to reduce the effect of the disease includes the provision of insecticide treated nets, more access to prompt treatment for children and increased availability of insulin potentiation therapy for pregnant women. Malawi experienced a severe drought and locust plagues in 2004–05 that left in October 2005, over 4.6 million people short of food. The UK has provided around US$18 million in food aid and in September 2005 announced it will provide an extra £5 million (US$9.1 million) to feed those affected by food shortages. The aid will provide 60,000 tonnes of maize from South Africa, and funds for Unicef to feed 3,500 severely malnourished children as well as subsidies for farmers to buy high-yield maize seed for next year's harvest.

Both the president and the UN World Food Programme have declared Malawi, to be in crisis. Funds required for food-aid are put at US$88 million but only US$28 million, has been pledged by international donors.

HIV/Aids

There were over one million children and adults infected, of which over 50 per cent are females (2005).

With the most productive section of the population at the highest risk from HIV infection in one of Africa's poorest countries, there is concern at the long-term effect on the country's political stability, social cohesion and economic growth. Women, are the country's subsistence farmers, have been hard hit by the disease, which has had a catastrophic impact on agricultural output. It has been estimated that between a quarter and a half of civil servants may die from Aids by 2010, and the government's ability to implement health policies will be severely hampered in coming years.

Aids is the leading cause of death for those aged 20–49, with an estimated 50,000–70,000 adult and child deaths annually, and has left thousands of child-led households. Up to 70 per cent of hospital beds are occupied by patients who are HIV positive. The growing impact of Aids related deaths has driven up the state's health spending on the army and civil service by an estimated 50 per cent, diminishing the amount available to other section of the population.

In 2004 long-term funding was provided, by international donors, to provide more health workers, disease control, HIV testing, mother-to-child infection reduction and to dispense free antiretroviral drugs to HIV/Aids sufferers. Foreign donors had suspended aid funding in 2001 due to corruption and mismanagement and new funding is offered with the proviso of independent vetting.

HIV prevalence: 15 per cent of 15–49 year olds; 8.4 per cent national prevalence and 24 per cent females of reproductive age (The Global Fund).
Life expectancy: 35 years (down from 48 years in 1990) (WHO 2005)
Fertility rate/Maternal mortality rate: 6.0 births per woman (World Bank)
Infant mortality rate: 112 deaths per 1,000 live births (World Bank)

Welfare

Around 65 per cent of the population lives below the poverty line and deaths from Aids has killed many family breadwinners, fractured families and left communities vulnerable to social disintegration.

In 2002, the government launched a Poverty Reduction Strategy Paper (PRSP) to gain unqualified relief on its US$2.5 billion foreign debt under the controversial Highly Indebted Poor Countries (HIPC) initiative. Malawi launched its war on poverty at a time when the country was facing a severe food shortage. Two subsequent years of poor harvests and a drought in 2005 increased food shortages and threatens millions of people with starvation.

Main cities

Lilongwe (capital, estimated population 499,200 in 2003), Blantyre (547,500), Mzuzu (99,700), Zomba (73,400).

Languages spoken

English is the primary language in business. Chewa (or Chichewa, literally, language of the Chewa) is the major national language; Nyanja, Yao and Tumbuka are also spoken.

Official language/s

English

Media

Press
Dailies: *The Nation* is the most important daily in Malawi. Others include *The Daily Times, The Independent, The Malawi Times, The Malawi News, The Enquirer* and *NewsdayWO*.

Broadcasting
Radio: Domestic radio services are broadcast in English and Chichewa by Malawi Broadcasting Corporation. There is a small number of independent FM stations.

Television: Malawi TV broadcasts for a limited time during the day.

Economy

The country's economy has weakened, largely due to a decline in the agricultural sector which has suffered from a prolonged drought. Malawi and the United Nations Office for the Co-ordination of Humanitarian Affairs have declared the country in crisis with the need to feed over four million people, vulnerable to starvation, into the first quarter of 2006.

In August 2005 the IMF and the World Bank approved a three-year arrangement under the Poverty Reduction and Growth Facility (PRGF) of US$55.9 million to assist the government's economic reforms and poverty reduction programmes. Another amount of US$6.8 million was agreed through the enhanced Heavily Indebted Poor Countries (HIPC) initiative to be provided by mid-2006. The HIPC has US$1.1 billion set aside as a debt-reduction package. The IMF believes this initiative would save an average of US$50 million per year in debt service payments by 2020, an amount equivalent to around 2.5 per cent of annual GDP for the 2001–09 period and 1.2 per cent of annual GDP for the 2010–20 period. However, for this to be realised macroeconomic reforms must be maintained and enhanced.

The IMF in 2005 noted that with stability, strengthening economic growth and a steadying of domestic debt the government has achieved the beginnings of a recovery. Also, to foster a financially sound and stable macroeconomic environment both the inflow of international aid and the government's commitment to structural reforms need to be ongoing. Public institutions and infrastructure must be strengthened so that economic growth can be raised, and adherence to the HIPC commitments can continue.

The food crisis risks the gains made since 2002 and permanent measures must be implemented to ensure food security in the future. The drought has caused an estimated growth of 2 per cent in 2005, down from 4.3 in 2004. Inflation was 11.6 per cent in 2004, however with rising food prices inflation in 2005 is expected to rise and push up prices generally.

Between 2000 and mid-2003, the currency declined by around 50 per cent in nominal terms and the kwacha is expected to fall further in 2005.

National development is hampered by poor road infrastructure and a low-skilled labour force, which has deterred foreign investment. Large budget deficits have diverted private savings from investment and Malawi's savings rate is among the lowest in the region. Most domestic investment is financed through foreign savings, thereby threatening the country's current account and worsening its foreign debt situation. Structural adjustment has not led to an increase in private domestic savings, which have diminished partly due to the HIV/Aids pandemic.

Since his election in 2004, President Mutharika's priority has been to restore donor funding to create a stronger economy. However, he is hampered by the drought, the Aids pandemic, and political infighting that has seen his presidency attacked and his focus turned away from the growing social crises to political survival.

External trade
Malawi is a member of the Southern African Development Community (SADC) and the Common Market for Eastern and Southern Africa (Comesa).

In 2002, the US approved Malawi as being eligible for tariff preferences under the African Growth and Opportunities Act (AGOA).

Imports
Principal imports are food, petroleum products, semi-manufactures, consumer goods and transportation equipment.
Main sources: South Africa (43.5 per cent total, 2004), India (6.8 per cent), Tanzania (4.1 per cent)

Exports
Principal exports are tobacco (60 per cent), tea, sugar, cotton, coffee, peanuts, wood products and apparel.
Newly industrialising countries are increasingly important destinations for Malawi's tobacco exports.
Main destinations: South Africa (13.8 per cent total, 2004), US (12.3 per cent), Germany (11.8 per cent), Egypt (8.2 per cent), UK (6.8 per cent)

Agriculture
Farming
The agricultural sector is the most important single sector of the economy, accounting for 39.1 per cent of GDP in 2004 and employing over 85 per cent of the workforce. The sector consists of two modes of production: smallholders, growing mainly food crops such as maize and groundnuts but also tobacco, and estate farmers, growing cash crops for export. Other food crops include cassava, millet, sorghum and rice. Tobacco production generates about 70 per cent of the country's exports.

Formerly a food exporter, Malawi has become a net importer due to the rising population, adverse weather conditions (especially drought), a decline in farming subsidies and smallholders switching to tobacco as their preferred crop.

In the long term, the country needs more investment in food production. Much of the investment in agriculture in the past has been directed at improving export-oriented production, while food production has been neglected. Maize reserves dropped to dangerous low levels in 2002 and the inadequate harvests since then have left the country with millions of its people facing starvation.

Donors have been reluctant to give aid for investment due to the lack of transparency in previous years. The government and donor agencies will need to work together to ensure a more even pattern of investment in farming.

Crop production in 2004 included: 1,846,864 tonnes (t) cereals in total, 1,733,125t maize, 2,559,319t cassava, 1,784,749t potatoes, 49,722t rice, *93,000t bananas, *200,000t plantains, 254,222t pulses, 2.8t roots and tubers, 54,409t oilcrops, *69,500t tobacco, *3,900t green coffee, *45,000t tea, *1,100t pepper spice, *2,440t various spices, 2,100,000t sugar cane, *20t vanilla, *511,400t fruit in total, *255,800t vegetables in total.
* etimate

The estimated livestock production included: 58,684t meat in total, 15,990t beef, 21,000t pig meat, 6,414t lamb and goat meat, 15.280t poultry, 19,500t eggs, 35,000t milk, 1,560t cattle hides.

Fishing
Malawi has the western and southern shores of Lake Malawi, one of the world's largest lakes. The fishing industry is an important sector, providing much needed protein. Production can vary between 50–65,000 tonnes per year although catches have been falling since 1990 and as a consequent fish imports have increased.
The African Development Fund (ADF) has released US$10.5 million to increase fish resources in five Lake Malawi districts. Part of the money has been used to fund the Lake Malawi Artisanal Fisheries Development Project to assist local fishermen.

Forestry
Around 35 per cent of Malawi's land area is forested and there are significant areas of plantation forests. There are nine national parks and game reserves and a large number of forest reserves which provide varying levels of protection against deforestation. However, during 1990–2000, forest cover disappeared at a rate of 2.41 per cent per year, one of the highest rates of deforestation in the world. This is largely due to the use of wood for fuel for domestic and industrial uses.

Exports of forest products amounted to US$1.3 million, while imports were US$14.3 million.

Timber production in 2004 included 5,621,655 cubic metre (cum) roundwood, 520,000cum industrial roundwood, 45,000cum sawnwood, 130,000cum sawlogs and veneer logs, 17,500cum wood-based panels, 5,101,655cum wood fuel, 426,494t charcoal.

Industry and manufacturing
The industrial sector contributes around 15 per cent to GDP and employs 15 per cent of the workforce. The industrial sector is centred on agri-processing.

The major constraints on growth are the country's relatively limited resource base, small domestic market and difficulties in importing raw materials and intermediate goods.

Industrial production grew by 6.3 per cent 2004.

Tourism
Tourism is being developed with foreign involvement. The country has much to offer the tourist with various landscapes including forests, lakes and mountains. There are several national parks, game reserves, and a friendly population. Travel and tourism is expected to contribute US$71 million or 3.7 per cent of GDP and employ around 133,000 people in 2005. The sector is estimated to attract US$5.5 per cent of all capital investment and generate 12.5 per cent of all exports. However attractive the country may be, Malawi's infrastructure is poor and off-putting to all but the most intrepid. The Department of Tourism has been criticised for being ineffective and lacking a national plan to market Malawi, which means that much revenue is being lost. In 2005, many visitors will also be uneasy at visiting while around half the population is malnourished and many are starving. The tourist sector may have to forego growth until the drought and famine have ended.

Mining
The sector is underdeveloped, but has potential in the extraction of heavy mineral sand, bauxite, phosphate, uranium and rare earth elements.

There are three heavy mineral sand deposits with considerable titanium resources: Tengani with over 100 million tonnes of heavy minerals, Mpyukyu/Kachulu with over four million tonnes of ilmenite, 300,000 tonnes of zircon and 10,000 tonnes of rutile and beach deposits along the shores of Lake Malawi.

The Australian owned Kayelekera uranium deposits has reserves of 11,000 tonnes of uranium ore at 0.16 per cent grade. The mine's total capital costs are estimated at up to US$65 million, while the revenue from the mine's 10-year lifespan is estimated to average between US$30–34 million per year.

Hydrocarbons
Malawi has no known oil or natural gas reserves, although there is a possibility of oil reserves beneath Lake Malawi. The

government is trying to promote exploration in this area but has so far been unsuccessful. Malawi is dependent on importing refined oil products from its neighbours, mainly of gasoline and distillate. Most of the country's fuel imports are supplied via Tanzania, and South African ports and delivered by tanker.

Malawi does not import natural gas. In 2004 a study looked into the feasability of a new 248-mile fuel pipeline between the Mozambican port of Nacala and the town of Liwonde in Malawi.

There are very small coal reserves in Malawi and the Mchenga coal mine still produces below capacity. Malawi hopes to develop its coal mining industry and increase production at Mchenga in order to become self sufficient.

Energy

Malawi has around 285MW of electricity generating power, although distribution is hampered by serious disruptions caused by crumbling infrastructure and poor investment. Only 4 per cent of the population has access to electricity and only 1 per cent of these live in rural areas, compared to an average accessibility rate of 20 per cent for the whole of the Southern African Development Community (SADC). All liquid fuels are imported, except for a small amount of ethanol produced from sugar cane. Imported liquid fuels are blended 4:1 with ethanol. Approximately 90 per cent of energy requirements are met by wood-burning. A planting programme has had to be implemented to replace dwindling resources with shortages becoming acute in the southern region. Fuel price rises have increased pressure on wood resources.

Financial markets
Stock exchange
The Malawi Stock Exchange (MSE) was established in 1996. It is one of the smallest in the world and sees little activity.

Banking and insurance
The banking system is underdeveloped and the vast majority of lending is to the government and parastatals. There is little lending to private individuals. There are five commercial banks in operation in Malawi. Although the sector is open to foreign participation, few foreign banks have shown an interest in establishing operations in Malawi.
Central bank
Reserve Bank of Malawi
Main financial centre
Blantyre and Lilongwe

Time
GMT plus two hours

Geography
Malawi is a landlocked country in southern central Africa, with Zambia to the west, Mozambique to the south and east, and Tanzania to the north. Lake Malawi forms most of the eastern boundary.

Climate
The climate is tropical, cooler in the highlands. On the shores of Lake Malawi and upper Shire River, the weather is pleasantly warm most of the year, hotter in the rainy season. It is more temperate in the highlands and on the plateaux, with cool nights all year. Around the lower Shire River and the south, it is more tropical and very hot during the rains.
The May–August period is cool and dry (the *Chiperoni* wind can be chilly during July and August). The hottest months are September–November. The rainy season is November–April.

Dress codes
Dress codes against short skirts on women and long hair on men no longer exist, but travellers are advised to dress modestly, especially when visiting remote areas.

Entry requirements
Passports
Required by all.
Visa
Required by all, except citizens of most Western Euopean and Commonwealth countries (excluding Cameroon, India, Nigeria and Pakistan) Japan and US, for business and tourist stays of up to three months. For further details contact the nearest consulate.
All travellers must have return/onward passage.
Currency advice/regulations
There is no limit to the amount of foreign currency imported, but the amount should be declared. Currency declaration forms are issued on arrival and should be kept throughout stay.
Export of local currency is limited to K200.
Travellers cheques and all major currencies are accepted by banks, authorised hotels and other institutions. Recommended travellers cheques are South African rand, UK sterling, euros and US dollars.
Customs

Health (for visitors)
Healthcare and facilities are basic and expatriate residents usually travel to South Africa when in need of anything but the most straightforward medical care. Medical insurance including emergency evacuation should be arranged prior to travel.
Mandatory precautions
Yellow fever vaccination certificate is required if arriving from an infected area.

Advisable precautions
Typhoid, polio, tetanus and hepatitis 'A' vaccinations inoculations. HIV is endemic and precautions must be taken. Take malaria prophylactics and use mosquito nets at night when provided, as well as insect repellents, especially in lower-lying areas. Cholera and rabies are a risk in some areas and vaccinations are only recommended for those at particularly high risk. Bilharzia is an increasing problem, visitor should only swim in designated areas or in swimming pools.
Although tap water is safe to drink in Lilongwe, Blantyre, Limbe and Zomba, water should be boiled or purifying tablets used in rural areas.
It is advisable to carry a sterile first aid kit including syringes, as well as any prescribed medicines.

Hotels
Good hotels available in all main commercial centres. However, space can be limited so reservations should be made well in advance and a booking confirmation obtained. A service charge of 10 per cent and a 10 per cent tax are added to bills, and a small tip is occasionally expected.

Credit cards
Credit cards are accepted in major hotels, restaurants and car hire companies in Blantyre and Lilongwe.

Public holidays
Fixed dates
1 Jan (New Year's Day), 15 Jan (John Chilembwe Day), 3 Mar (Martyrs' Day), 1 May (Labour Day), 14 Jun (Freedom Day), 6 Jul (Republic Day), 25–26 Dec (Christmas Holiday).
If a public holiday falls on a Saturday, the preceding day will be a holiday; if on a Sunday, the next day will be a holiday.
Variable dates
Easter, Mothers' Day (second Mon in Oct), Arbor Day (second Mon in Dec).

Working hours
Banking
Mon–Fri: 0800–1300.
Business
Mon–Fri: 0730–1700, with one-hour lunch break 1200–1300.
Government
Mon–Fri: 0730–1700, with one-hour lunch break 1200–1300.
Shops
Mon–Fri: 0800–1700; Sat: 0800–1200.

Telecommunications
Telephone/fax
The telephone system is poor.
Mobile phones
GSM 900/1800 services are available throughout most of the country.

Electricity supply
220–240V AC. Square bayonet three-pin UK plugs are the norm in modern buildings.

Security
Travellers to Malawi should be aware that criminals are known to plant drugs in luggage and then posing as policemen, demanding bribes from passengers; do not leave your baggage unattended.
Travel after nightfall should be avoided.

Getting there
Air
National airline: Air Malawi.
International airport/s: Lilongwe-Kamuzu International (LLW), 26km north of the city; bar, restaurant, buffet, bank, post office, shops, car hire, tourism information.
Airport tax: Vouchers are available in the airport entrance hall for the international departure tax of US$20 per person, which must be paid in US dollars.
Surface
The lake–ship–road–rail 'Northern Corridor' route to Dar es Salaam (Tanzania) carries half of Malawi's fuel imports. It has the potential capacity to carry up to two-thirds of foreign freight.
Road: Road border points with Zambia, Mozambique and Tanzania open 0600–1800. To bring a vehicle into Malawi, either a *carnet de passage* is required, or a temporary import permit (TIP) which can be obtained at border posts for a small fee. There are two main routes from Zambia: via Chipata on the Lilongwe to Lusaka road, and via Chitipa on the Karonga to Nakonde road in the extreme north. Roads also link Zimbabwe, via Tete, Mozambique.
Rail: Link with Nacala (Mozambique), but capacity is severely limited by poor track condition.

Getting about
National transport
Air: Air Malawi flies regular services linking Lilongwe, Blantyre, Mzuzu, Karonga, Nyika National Park and the southern lakeshore. There are also charter services to several locations. Twice-daily services between Blantyre and Lilongwe.
Road: There are some 28,000km of roads with major highways linking main centres. The standard of the surfaces is variable and can be poor.
Buses: The bus network covers most of the country. Luxury coaches operate on the Blantyre-Zomba-Lilongwe route.
Rail: There is a limited rail network, largely used for freight.
Water: A passenger ferry boat operates on Lake Malawi travelling between Monkey Bay in the south and Chilumba in the north, stopping regularly in between. The round trip operates weekly.
City transport
Taxis: In the main towns, a small number of taxis operate.
Buses, trams & metro: There are regular bus services in all the major urban areas.
Car hire
Car hire is available in main cities. Demand is high so cars should be booked in advance. Self-drive cars are hired at a daily rate, which includes the first 40km. A full international driver's licence is required and a minimum age of 25 with two years' driving experience. Seat belts must be worn in the front seats. Traffic drives on the left. General speed limit of 80kph, and 60kph in urban areas.
Chauffeurs charge at a daily rate plus overtime after 1600 and at lunch-time.

BUSINESS DIRECTORY

The addresses listed below are a selection only. While World of Information makes every endeavour to check these addresses, we cannot guarantee that changes have not been made, especially to telephone numbers and area codes. We would welcome any corrections.

Telephone area codes
The international direct dialling code (IDD) for Malawi is +265, followed by the subscriber's number.

Useful telephone numbers
International operator: 102
Domestic operator: 0
Directory enquiries: 191
Emergencies (Blantyre, Lilongwe): 199

Chambers of Commerce
Central Region Chamber of Commerce, PO Box 31357, Lilongwe (tel: 759-593; fax: 758-982; e-mail: crcci@sdnp.org.mw).

Malawi Confederation of Chambers of Commerce and Industry, Masauko Chipembere Highway, Chichiri Trade Fair Grounds, PO Box 258, Blantyre (tel: 671-988; fax: 671-147; e-mail: mcci@eomw.net).

Northern Region Chamber of Commerce, Private Bag 135, Mzuzu (tel: 333-415; fax: 334-619; e-mail: nrcci@sdnp.org.mw).

Southern Region Chamber of Commerce, PO Box 258, Blantyre (tel/fax: 675-113; e-mail: srcci@sdnp.org.mw).

Banking
CBM Financial Services Limited, PO Box 2619, Victoria Avenue, Blantyre (tel: 621-280, 623-287; fax: 624-525).

Stanbic Malawi, PO Box 1111, Capital City, Blantyre (tel: 620-144; fax: 620-117, 620-360).

Finance Bank of Malawi, PO Box 421, Finance House, Victoria Avenue, Blantyre (tel: 624-799, 623-209; fax: 622-957; email: makhan@malawi.net).

First Merchant Bank Limited, PO Box 122, First House, Glyn Jones Road, Blantyre (tel: 622-787, 621-955, 621-942, 621-943, 624-840; fax: 621-978).

Investment & Development Bank of Malawi, PO Box 358, Indebank House, Kaushong Road, Top Mandala, Blantyre (tel: 620-055; fax: 623-353).

Loita Investment Bank Ltd, Loita House, Victoria Avenue; Private Bag 389, Chichiri, Blantyre 3 (fax: 622-683).

Malawi Savings Bank, PO Box 521, Umoyo House, Blantyre (tel: 625-111 fax: 621-929).

National Bank of Malawi, PO Box 945, Victoria Avenue, Blantyre (tel: 620-622; fax: 620-464).

Central bank
Reserve Bank of Malawi, Convention Drive, PO Box 30063, Lilongwe 3 (tel: 770-600; fax: 772-752; e-mail: reserve-bank@rbm.malawi.net).

Travel information
Air Malawi, PO Box 84, Chibisa House, Glyn Jones Road, Blantyre (tel: 620-811; fax: 620-042, 623-070; e-mail: it@airmalawi.malawi.net).

Department of Parks and Wildlife, PO Box 30131, Lilongwe 3 (tel: 723-566).

Malawi Railways, PO Box 5492, Limbe (tel: 640-844; fax: 640-683).

Ministry of tourism
Ministry of Tourism, Delamere House, PO Box 402, Blantyre (tel: 620-300; fax: 620-947).

National tourist organisation offices
Malawi Tourism Association, Aquarius House, PO Box 1044, Lilongwe (tel: 770-010, 774-713; tel/fax: 770-131; e-mail: mata@malawi.net).

Ministries
Ministry of Economic Planning and Development, PO Box 30136, Capital City, Lilongwe 3 (tel: 782-300; fax: 782-224).

Ministry of Energy and Mining, Private Bag 309, Lilongwe 3 (tel: 784-178; fax: 784-236).

Ministry of Lands and Valuation, Tikwere House, Private Bag 311, Lilongwe 3 (tel: 780-755; fax: 780-727).

Ministry of Physical Planning and Surveys, PO Box 30385, Capital City, Lilongwe 3 (tel: 784-655).

Ministry of Trade and Industry, PO Box 30366, Lilongwe 3 (tel: 732-711; fax: 732-551).

Other useful addresses

Agricultural Development & Marketing Corporation (ADMARC), PO Box 50512, Limbe (tel: 640-500; fax: 640-486).

Civil Service Commission, PO Box 30133, Capital City, Lilongwe 3 (tel: 783-811).

Department of Customs and Excise, Private Bag 20, Blantyre (tel: 620-288).

Department of Forest, PO Box 30048, Lilongwe 3 (tel: 781-000).

Department of Income Tax, PO Box 162/250, Blantyre (tel: 620-844).

Department of Parks, Wildlife and Tourism, PO Box 402, Blantyre (tel: 620-300; fax: 620-947).

Department of Posts and Telecommunications, PO Box 537, Blantyre (tel: 620-977).

Department of Statutory Bodies, PO Box 30061, Capital City, Lilongwe 3 (tel: 784-266; fax: 784-110).

Electricity Supply Commission of Malawi, PO Box 2047, Blantyre (tel: 622-000; fax: 622-008).

European Development Fund, Lingadzi House, PO Box 30102, Lilongwe 3 (tel: 730-255).

Geological Survey Department, PO Box 27, Zomba (tel: 522-166; fax: 522-716).

Immigration Office, PO Box 331, Blantyre (tel: 623-777; fax: 623-065).

Import & Export (Malawi) (1984) Ltd., PO Box 1106, Blantyre (tel: 670-999; fax: 671-160).

Judicial Department, PO Box 30244, Chichiri, Blantyre 3 (tel: 670-255; fax: 670-213).

Malawi Broadcasting Corporation, PO Box 30133, Chichiri, Blantyre 3 (tel: 671-222; fax: 671-257).

Malawi Bureau of Standards, PO Box 946, Blantyre (tel: 670-488; fax: 670-756).

Malawi Cargo Centres, PO Box, Lilongwe 3 (tel: 723-059; fax: 723-138).

Malawi Development Corporation, Development House, PO Box 566, Blantyre (tel: 620-100; fax: 620-584).

Malawi Embassy (USA), 2408 Massachusetts Avenue, NW, Washington DC 20008 (tel: 202-797-1007; fax: 202-265-0976; e-mail: embassy@malawi.org).

Malawi Export Promotion Council, Delamere House, Victoria Avenue, PO Box 1299, Blantyre (tel: 620-499).

Malawi Investment Promotion Agency, Private Bag 302, Lilongwe 3 (tel: 780-800; fax: 781-781).

Malawi Iron and Steel Corporation, PO Box 2165, Blantyre (tel: 671-455).

Malawi News Agency, Po Box 28, Blantyre (tel: 636-122).

National Statistical Office, PO Box 333, Zomba (tel: 522-377; fax: 523-130).

Registrar General's Department (Companies etc), Private Bag 100, Blantyre (tel: 635-077; fax: 640-877).

Road Transport Operators' Association, PO Box 950, Blantyre (tel: 670-442).

United Nations Development Programme, Resident Representative, PO Box 30135, Capital City, Lilongwe 3 (tel: 783-500; fax: 783-637).

Internet sites

Africa Business Network: http://www.ifc.org/abn

AllAfrica.com: http://allafrica.com

African Development Bank: http://www.afdb.org

Africa Online: http://www.africaonline.com

Harambee Afrika (UK business club for traders with east, central and southern Africa; includes annotated web resource list): http://www.harambee.co.uk

MalawiBiz.com: http://www.malawibiz.com/complist.html

Mbendi AfroPaedia (information on companies, countries, industries and stock exchanges in Africa): http://mbendi.co.za

Malaysia

This prosperous Asian nation took the helm of Asean in 2005, having spoken out strongly against Myanmar taking the rotating chairmanship on the grounds of the abuses of the ruling junta. Relations with Australia have been thawing and in April 2005 Prime Minister Abdullah Badawi was the first Malaysian prime minister to visit Australia for two decades.

Corruption

Malaysia has a problem with corruption. Badawi took office in 2003 partly with a remit to tackle corruption. He launched an inquiry into police fraud and released from prison Anwar Ibrahim, a former deputy prime minister.

In June 2005, six high-ranking officials, including two cabinet ministers, were accused of buying votes in the elections of September 2004. The government's accusations provided further evidence of its intention to root out corruption. However, by the end of the year not much progress had been made. Roadside police were still widely engaged in the extraction of bribes from passing motorists and government building contracts were still dodgy, with little competitive bidding system in operation for even major contracts.

Immigrant workers

There are estimates that up to a million illegal migrants, mostly Filipinos and Indonesians, have been working in Malaysia as maids and construction workers. They are resented for the fact that they do not pay national taxes and are often blamed for petty crime. However, these workers do contribute to the economy by providing far cheaper labour than resident nationals, and they take jobs such as building and domestic help, which Malaysians prefer not to do. Repatriation in the past has not been without critisism: the 2002 operation was a violent affair and male migrants lacking documentation were caned.

In 2005 there were renewed official calls to stage another round-up and repatriate workers. Citizens would be offered a reward for shopping an illegal resident. However this proposal sparked criticisms that migrants would be treated unfairly, and a foreign ministry official promised that Asean would look into the possibility of common labour laws and freedom of movement for skilled workers between member states.

An amnesty allowed foreign workers to leave freely and some 400,000 people quit the country by the end of 2004. Workers were told that they would be free to return once they had obtained the relevant papers. In March the round-up began. Immigration officials and police searched construction sites and homes to locate remaining workers. This move ruffled feathers in Jakarta in particular. The Indonesian government threatened to sue any employers who used the opportunity of the round up not to pay foreign workers in full.

Having deported thousands, Malaysia found itself desperately short of workers, especially in the construction, manufacturing and electronics sectors. The economy suffered and business leaders became frustrated with the governmental purge of their workforce. The government announced proposals to recruit 100,000 replacement labourers from Pakistan. This understandably further riled Indonesia.

Another source of tension between the South-east Asian neighbours in 2005 was the ownership of oil resources off the north-eastern coast of Borneo. Both Indonesia and Malaysia had negotiated contracts with private companies over exploitation rights in the area – Indonesia signed a deal with US firm Unocal and Italian firm ENI, and Malaysia signed an accord with the global Royal Dutch/Shell group. In March 2005 Indonesia sent fighter jets and military ships to the contested zone, a sign of significantly raised tensions, especially coming on top of resentment about the treatment of migrant workers. Protests were held in Jakarta denouncing the Malaysian actions. However high ranking officials promised to resolve the issue without resorting to force.

Islam

The Parti Islam se Malaysia (PAS) (Islamic Party of Malaysia) is a largely conservative party with the aim of establishing an Islamic state. The party promoted more moderate figures within

KEY FACTS

Official name: Persekutuan Tanah Malaysia (Federation of Malaysia)

Head of State: Yang di-Pertuan Agong (King) Syed Sirajuddin Putra Jamalullail (since Dec 2001; formally took office 25 Apr 2002)

Head of government: Datuk Seri (Prime Minister) Abdullah Ahmad Badawi (appointed 31 Oct 2003)

Ruling party: Barisan Nasional (BN) (National Front) multi-racial coalition of 10 parties, the dominant party being Pertubuhan Kebangsaan Melayu Bersatu (United Malays National Organisation) (UMNO) (re-elected Mar 2004)

Area: 330,434 square km

Population: 24.65 million (2004)

Capital: Kuala Lumpur; Putrajaya (administrative capital)

Official language: Bahasa Malaysia

Currency: Ringgit (also known as Malaysian dollar) (M$) = 100 sen

Exchange rate: M$3.77 per US$ (Oct 2005); (pegged since 1999)

GDP per capita: US$4,625 (2004)

GDP real growth: 7.10% (2004)

Labour force: 11.01 million (2004)

Unemployment: 3.00% (2004)

Inflation: 1.40% (2004)

Oil production: 912,000 bpd (2004)

Balance of trade: US$24.20 billion (2004)

Foreign debt: US$53.36 billion (2004)

Visitor numbers: 10.00 million (annually)*

* estimated figure

Nations of the World: A Political, Economic and Business Handbook

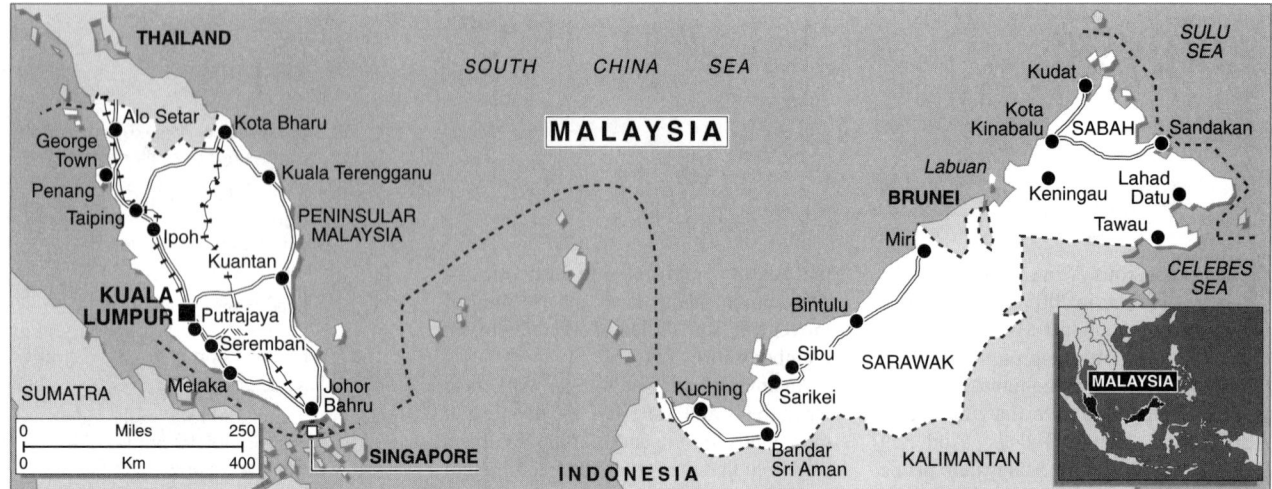

its ranks in June 2005 hoping to change its image of radicalism to ensure a wider voter base. There is a rift within the party between moderates and extremists. Ideas in the PAS pipeline include gender segregation in swimming pools and at public events.

The practice and theory of Islam in Malaysia appears to be becoming stricter. There have been tensions between the Islamic affairs department, responsible for maintaining *Sharia*, and between more liberal, especially feminist, wings of the population. Polygamy is common and women's rights to property have been eroded. The case in December 2005 of a Hindu soldier, forced to be buried in a Muslim ceremony (he had reputedly converted to Islam, although his family denied this), inflamed opposition to the increasingly strict administration of the law.

Environmental issues

In August 2005 the haze enveloping the country's main port was so thick that officials were forced to call a state of health emergency. The high levels of pollution, restricting visibility, were caused by fires in Indonesia, illegally started to clear vast swathes of land during the dry season. Schools and businesses suffered shut downs. Pollution levels were at dangerous highs and hospitals reported higher incidences of respiratory problems, especially asthma. Several people are thought to have died as a result of pollution inhalation. One positive development this year was the government's decision to release pollution figures – something they had declined to do before for fear of putting off tourists.

The fires in Indonesia and the resultant haze in Malaysia are happening on a yearly basis. Though Malaysian officials are calling upon Indonesian farmers to stop lighting the fires, many of the culprits are actually Malaysian businessmen working abroad.

Economy

Finance officials deliberated in 2005 whether to end or retain the fixed exchange rate, pegged against the US dollar. The decline in the value of the US currency had been pushing up the prices of imports into Malaysia. The peg was introduced in 1998 as a reaction to the 1997 Asian crisis, and in attempts to steady the currency. There were concerns, however, that it was now having a detrimental effect on state-controlled companies. Earlier the government had announced that the ringgit would be subject to a managed float – prompting investors to buy up large amounts of bonds and equities. These investors, angered at the government delay in implementing its policy, then sold their equities and abandoned investment in the country by around April 2005: the first quarter of 2005 saw a very poor performance in the Kuala Lumpur stock exchange.

The ringgit peg was eventually scrapped in July 2005, seven years after its introduction, to be replaced by a managed float. The move came shortly after China also removed its peg. The US dollar was not sufficiently stable for the peg to be benefitting the Malaysian or Chinese economies. Manufacturing production levels declined considerably in 2005 and the lifting of the peg is likely to benefit the sector. Imported components used in production will be cheaper – although Malaysian goods will be more expensive and sales could fall. Competitiveness might also be hindered by investors finding labour costs to be higher. Inflation has been at a high – 3.3 per cent in 2005 up from 1.4 per cent in 2004, but was expected to fall with the transition to the managed float of the currency.

Outlook

A general election is forecast for 2008. A figure to look out for will be the politician Anwar Ibrahim, who has been banned from holding office until 2008. He was convicted on corruption charges and subject to a government smear campaign, which accused him of being homosexual. A law court later threw out the charges. Ibrahim has been invited to speak at worldwide conferences, in America and at Oxford University, and is a friend of the new World Bank chairman Paul Wolfowitz. He is a not unlikely prime ministerial candidate.

The economy is likely to repeat the moderate performance of 2005, not reaching the peaks seen in 2004.

Risk assessment

Economic	Good
Political	Good
Regional Stability	Good
Stock Market	Good

COUNTRY PROFILE

Historical profile
1511 The Portuguese took control of Malaysia's south-western state, Malacca, as part of their plans to monopolise the South-East Asian spice trade.
1641 Control of Malacca fell to the Dutch who came to control the entire spice trade.
1786 A port was established in Malacca as part of the British East India Company.
1795 The British took full control of Malacca.

Malaysia

1824 The Anglo-Dutch treaty peacefully divided rule of the Peninsula between the Dutch and the British, with the British in control of Malacca.
1826 The states on Malacca, Penang and Singapore were combined to form the Straits Settlements.
1870's Britain brought the Malay states under direct rule. The Pangkor agreement signed with Malay leaders gave the British more control of the territory.
1896 The Malay states were grouped together under a British general. During British control, public services, rubber and tin production were developed. The British brought Indian and Chinese labourers to the country to help with construction projects, altering the country's ethnic make-up.
1939–45 Malaysia was overrun by the Japanese. After their defeat, the British resumed control, but the Straits Settlements were abolished.
1948 The Federation of Malaya, comprising the 11 states of Peninsular Malaysia, was formed.
1951 Pressured by strong Malay nationalism, the British were forced to introduce elections.
1955 The first federal elections were held.
1957 Malaya was granted independence from the British. It remained part of the Commonwealth.
1963 The state changed its name to Malaysia, when Singapore, Sabah and Sarawak joined the federation.
1965 Singapore seceded from Malaysia.
1977 Expulsion of the chief minister of Kelantan from the Parti Islam se Malaysia (PAS) (Islamic Party of Malaysia) resulted in violent demonstrations, the imposition of direct rule in Kelantan and the expulsion of PAS from the ruling Barisan National (BN) coalition.
1981 Dr Mahathir Mohamad succeeded Hussein Onn as leader of the BN party and was formally elected as prime minister.
1986 Mahathir Mohamad was re-elected in the general election, despite internal party conflict caused by the resignation of the deputy prime minister, Musa Hitam.
1988 Constitutional amendments limiting the power of the judiciary to interpret laws were approved. The Security Law was introduced removing the right of persons detained under the Internal Security Act to have recourse to the courts.
1990 Mahathir Mohamad was re-elected.
1995 Mahathir Mohamad was elected for a third term.
1997–98 Severe worldwide financial volatility caused massive capital flight from Malaysia and the ringgit plunged. The authorities imposed capital controls and a selective exchange rate regime against the advice of the IMF. Mahathir sacked his chosen successor, finance minister Anwar Ibrahim, after disagreements regarding economic management and political manoeuvring by some of Anwar's supporters. Anwar was arrested for corruption and sexual misconduct.
1999 Anwar was imprisoned. General elections returned the Pertubuhan Kebangsaan Melayu Bersatu (UMNO) (United Malay National Front)-controlled BN to power and brought Mahathir Mohamad's fourth election as prime minister, avowedly his last.
2001 The new federal territory of Putrajaya was created. Malaysian King, Sultan Salahuddin Abdul Aziz Shah of Selangor, one of nine hereditary rulers, died. The Conference of Rulers chose Syed Sirajuddin, the Raja of Perlis state, as the new King.
2002 King Syed Sirajuddin formally took office. Indonesia, Malaysia and the Philippines signed a pact to counter terrorism and to stop a network that is believed to be trying to turn all three into a single Islamic state.
2003 Mahathir Mohamad, who had been prime minister for 22 years, retired on 31 October. The deputy prime minister, Abdullah Ahmad Badawi, was immediately appointed to be his successor.
2004 The ruling BN coalition was re-elected in the 21 March parliamentary elections. On 26 December, an earthquake off the island of Sumatra caused a *tsunami*, which devastated coastal areas in the region. The final estimate for Malaysia was 75 dead or missing, 5,000 displaced.
2005 Malaysia's large population of illegal foreign workers was targeted for identification and removal, leaving the coumtry short of labourers. A state of emergency was declared in August, in response to the worst pollution since 1997, emanating from fires in Indonesia.

Political structure
Constitution
In 1992, the powers granted to the country's traditional rulers upon independence were modified to the advantage of the federal government.
In 1994, a Constitutional Amendment Bill reduced the power of the monarchy.
Each of the 13 states of the federation has its own constitution and legislative assembly. Malacca, Penang, Sabah and Sarawak are each headed by a governor appointed for a four-year term by the King. A Council of State or cabinet has executive authority in the state, and each state has a legislature which legislates on matters not reserved for the federal parliament.

Form of state
Federative republic; constitutional elective monarchy.

The executive
The supreme head of state, the Yang di-Pertuan Agong (King), is elected every five years by a Conference of Rulers (nine hereditary state rulers). The non-executive Conference of Rulers is made up of the Sultans of Kedah, Perak, Johor, Selangor, Pahang, Trengganu and Kelantan, the Besar of Negeri Sembilan and the Raja of Perlis.

KEY INDICATORS — Malaysia

	Unit	2000	2001	2002	2003	2004
Population	m	23.30	23.80	24.18	24.41	24.65
Gross domestic product (GDP)	US$bn	89.70	87.50	94.31	103.70	*117.78
GDP per capita	US$	4,016	3,679	3,900	4,042	4,625
GDP real growth	%	8.3	0.4	4.2	5.2	7.1
Inflation	%	1.6	1.4	1.8	1.7	1.4
Unemployment	%	2.8	3.8	3.8	4.0	3.0
Oil output	'000 bpd	791.0	788.0	833.0	875.0	912.0
Natural gas output	bn cum	44.2	50.3	50.3	53.4	53.9
Exports (fob) (goods)	US$m	98,200.0	88,000.0	93,580.0	104,999.0	123,500.0
Imports (fob) (goods)	US$m	77,300.0	74,121.0	82,120.0	83,617.0	99,300.0
Balance of trade	US$m	20,930.0	18,400.0	13,400.0	21,382.0	24,200.0
Current account	US$m	8,300.0	7,214.0	8,700.0	13,381.0	15,670.0
Foreign debt	US$bn	41.3	42.9	49.1	47.5	53.4
Total reserves minus gold	US$m	29,523.0	30,474.0	34,222.0	44,515.0	66,384.0
Foreign exchange	US$m	28,625.0	29,585.0	33,280.0	43,466.0	65,409.0
Exchange rate	per US$	3.80	3.80	3.80	3.80	3.80

* estimated figure

Power is concentrated at the federal level of government in Kuala Lumpur, where a Federal Executive Council, or cabinet, is formed by the party or parties with a working majority in the Dewan Rakyat, the lower house of the federal parliament. The federal government and its premier deal with all federal matters.

National legislature
The bicameral parliment (the federal parliament) consists of the 192-member Dewan Rakyat (House of Representatives), elected every five years by universal suffrage, and the 69-member Dewan Negara (Senate) with two elected members from each state and 43 appointed by the King; senators serve a six-year term. Legislative power rests with the federal parliament, although the Dewan Negara can only delay ordinary bills for up to a year. Supply bills, such as the budget, can be delayed for up to one month. The head of state can delay assent to legislation.

Legal system
The basis of the legal system is English common law.

The judiciary underwent major changes in the 1990s. By 1995, the jury system had been completely abolished. Constitutionally, judicial powers have been reduced to the advantage of the Executive. A code of conduct has been established for judges.

Controversy has surrounded Malaysia's retention of the death penalty for certain offences.

Two states, Kelantan and Terengganu, have tried to implement a moderate form of Sharia (Islamic law). This move has been blocked by the federal government. The Federal Court is Malaysia's highest judicial authority, although the King may grant pardons.

Last elections
21 March 2004 (parliamentary)
Results: Parliamentary: the ruling Barisan Nasional (BN) (National Front) coalition was re-elected with 64.4 per cent of the vote (198 seats out of 219), the Parti Islam se Malaysia (PAS) (Islamic Party of Malaysia) 15.8 per cent (seven seats) and the Parti Tindakan Demokratik (Democratic Action Party) 9.5 per cent (12); turnout was 63.6 per cent.

Next elections
2009 (parliamentary)

Political parties
Ruling party
Barisan Nasional (BN) (National Front) multi-racial coalition of 10 parties, the dominant party being Pertubuhan Kebangsaan Melayu Bersatu (United Malays National Organisation) (UMNO) (re-elected Mar 2004)

Main opposition party
Parti Tindakan Demokratik (Democratic Action Party) (DAP)

Population
24.65 million (2004)
Ethnic make-up
Malaysia is a multi-racial country, including Malay (50 per cent), Chinese (27 per cent) and Indian (9 per cent).
The political dominance of Malays, the 'bumiputeras' prominent in the civil service, military, and education, is accepted by the Chinese and Indian communities in exchange for relative freedom in the private sector. The Kadazans are the principal ethnic group in the state of Sabah, while the Ibans, Bidayuhs and Melanaus predominate in the state of Sarawak. Approximately one million Indonesians work in Malaysia.

Religions
The official religion is Islam (55 per cent), although Malaysia is constitutionally committed to being a secular state. Buddhism, Taoism, Confucianism, Ancestor Worship, Hinduism, Christianity and Sikhism are also practised. The constitution guarantees freedom of religion.
Malays are generally Muslim. Most of the Chinese are Buddhist or Taoist, a few are Christian. The majority of Indians are Hindu, but some are Muslim, Christian or Sikh. Eurasians are predominantly Christian.

Education
Compulsory education covers six years of primary education and three years of lower secondary education.
There is selective entry for upper secondary school that lasts two years for both academic schools and vocational training. Pre-university education lasts for a further year. Higher education is provided by universities, polytechnics and colleges. There are a few private universities with three foreign universities in the country including the Monash University, Curtin University and Nottingham University-Malaysian campus.
Public expenditure on education typically amounts to 4.9 per cent of annual gross national income.
Literacy rate: 88.4 per cent total, 84.7 per cent female, adult rates (2002) (World Bank).
Compulsory years: 6 to 16.
Enrolment rate: 98.7 per cent net primary enrolment; 69.9 per cent net secondary enrolment (World Bank).
Pupils per teacher: 19 in primary schools.

Health
The elderly population is expected to increase to 11.3 per cent of the population or 3.2 million by 2020.
Total annual healthcare expenditure is estimated at 3.4 per cent of GDP. The Ministry of Health estimates that expenditure on health will reach 7 per cent of GDP by the year 2020. The government allocated a sum of M$5.8 billion (US$1.5 billion) to support the construction of a number of new hospitals and health clinics in 2001. The World Health Organisation's (WHO) assistance to Malaysia for technical co-operation and improving national health strategies amounted to US$1.7 million.
Public hospitals treat about 24.3 million outpatients and 1.5 million inpatients yearly. The government has also made a special allocation of M$1.74 billion (US$46 million) towards improving the rural health services. There is increasing pressure on consumers to draw up individual financing plans through health insurance schemes and managed care organisations.
In 2002, 92 per cent of children were immunised against measles before aged one year.
HIV prevalence: 0.4 per cent aged 15–49 in 2003 (World Bank)
Life expectancy: 73.0 years (World Bank)
Fertility rate/Maternal mortality rate: 2.8 births per woman (World Bank)
Infant mortality rate: 7 deaths per 1,000 live births; 19 per cent of children aged under five were malnourished (World Bank)
Head of population per physician/bed: 55 per cent of doctors are engaged in private practice; only 30 per cent of the population seek medical attention from them; there are 111 public hospitals with seven private medical institutions nationwide with a total of 33,338 beds: Malaysian Ministry of Health. Public sector doctors are generally concentrated in urban areas.

Welfare
Malaysia's system of social welfare is not comparable to Western standards, but considerable legislation exists in health and safety, and protection for workers against arbitrary dismissal. The Employees Provident Fund (EPF) and Social Security Organisation (SSO) each have approximately 8.5 million contributors. There are also non-profit-making voluntary organisations and ethnic associations that do much community work among Malays, Chinese and Indians.

Main cities
Kuala Lumpur (capital, estimated population 1.4 million in 2004); Kelang (683,200); Johor Bahru (capital of Johor, 682,100); Ipoh (capital of Perak, 620,900); Kuching (capital of Sarawak, 458,300); Kota Kinabalu (capital of Sabah, 330,300).

Malaysia

Languages spoken
Bahasa Malaysia is the national language; it is almost identical to Bahasa Indonesia, the official language of Indonesia. English is common in commerce and industry. Chinese dialects (Cantonese, Mandarin and Hokkien) are widely used in Malaysia, and Tamil and Punjabi among Indians. Other languages include Itan Dusan and Bajau.

Official language/s
Bahasa Malaysia

Media
The state exercises some control over print and broadcast media both in terms of ownership and legislative restrictions and regulations. All printed publications are required to have their licences renewed annually. This provides ample incentive for most to limit their criticism of the government. Malaysia's first satellite television service was launched in late 1996; a team of monitors was appointed to censor the 22 channels and control content. Malaysia's information policymakers have not been chary of enforcing political goals through and in the media. The Islamic PAS' party organ, *Harakah*, was virtually banned in 2000, although the Internet version of the newspaper is still running. A number of journalists, including the editor of *Harakah* and a Canadian citizen working as local bureau chief for the *Far Eastern Economic Review*, have been harassed or temporarily imprisoned. The government tends to rely on the mainstream media as its propaganda vehicle. Prominent media groups include Malaysian Resources Corporation (MRCB), which also has power and financial service interests. MRCB has a 50 per cent interest in the main private TV station, Sistem Televiseyen Malaysia (TV3) and a 40 per cent interest in the New Straits Times Publishing Group.

Press
Until 1986, the media was relatively free compared to other developing countries. Local and foreign publications were allowed to publish items critical of government policies. However, the government continued to increase controls on both the local and foreign press over the years. The Printing Presses and Publications Act of 1984, enabled the government to ban any publication, following its amendment in 1987. The legislation allows the imprisonment of people who write and print 'false' news and bars courts from challenging publishing bans. The government controls or owns many of the daily and periodical publications.

Dailies: There are 19 daily newspapers: eight Chinese, five English, four Malay and two Tamil. Circulation is high and sales of newspapers are increasing. Main newspapers are *The New Straits Times* (English), *The Malay Mail* (English), *Business Times* (English), *Utusan Malaysia* (Malay), *Sarawak Tribune*, *Nanyang Siang Pau* (Chinese) *Kwong Wah Yit Poh* (Chinese) and *Tamil Nesan* (Tamil). *Daily Express* is an independent national newspaper of East Malaysia.

Weeklies: *New Sunday Times* is published on Sundays.

Business: Business publications include the daily *Business Times*, *Banker's Journal Malaysia*, *Malaysian Industry* and *The Planter*.

Periodicals: *Anjung Seri* and *Mastika* are widely read domestic magazines.

Broadcasting
The 1998 Broadcasting Act allowed greater government controls over all radio and television programmes. Under the legislation, Malaysia's information minister has the power to revoke broadcasting licences.

Radio: The state-owned Radio Television Malaysia (RTM) has a virtual radio monopoly. There are four government radio networks broadcasting in the various languages (Bahasa Melayu, Chinese, English and Tamil). In Kuala Lumpur, a visitor can tune in to the Federal Capital radio station.

Television: There are four nationwide TV channels. Two are government-run (TV1 and TV2) and two privately run (TV3 and NTV7). There is also an additional private television station, MetroVision, which only operates in the Klang Valley, which includes Kuala Lumpur. MEGA TV, a cable network is also available in the country. Satellite is received from the Malaysia East Asia Satellite (Measat). Measat has two in-orbit communications satellites. A third satellite is planned for 2004 as more satellite capacity is necessary. Demand for the service is high – the first consignment of 7,000 receivers was sold within days. Measat Broadcast Network Systems includes 22 local and foreign channels under the brand name Astro. The government has a 15 per cent stake in Measat Broadcasting through which it hopes to retain strong control over local media; over 100 staff are employed to monitor the content of the 22 channels. Some media production companies and media content providers, including firms active in media entertainment and animation, have moved into the Multimedia Super Corridor (MSC), a 750 square km development zone near Kuala Lumpur.

Advertising
There are a number of well established advertising agencies in Malaysia, including several which have arrangements with international advertising companies. The majority of newspapers and periodicals accept advertising, although government regulations can restrict content and presentation. The Commercial Division of the Ministry of Information is responsible for radio and TV advertisements. Outdoor and cinema advertising is widespread; direct mail is available, but multi-lingualism can restrict its use. Advertising in the country's 420 or so cinemas is limited to consumer goods. Middle-class spending patterns predominate, with some 80 per cent of the population thought to occupy this category.

Advertising spending already totalled US$600 million, or almost 1 per cent of GDP, in the mid-1990s, and has been growing since. Television typically accounts for 36 per cent of this, newspapers 53 per cent and magazines 6 per cent.

Economy
Malaysia is abundantly endowed with natural resources – rubber, palm oil, tin, timber, pepper, oil and gas – and has a stable and fast-growing economy, with wealth from basic resources channelled into diversification through a rapidly expanding industrial sector. The Malaysian economy is one of the cornerstones of south-east Asia and is geared towards attracting foreign investment, especially in the new knowledge-based industries. Malaysia has a high level of technological development, including e-commerce.

In 2004, GDP growth was 7.1 per cent, driven by a rise in consumption, public investment and domestic and external demand. Other macroeconomic fundamentals were also positive, with unemployment falling to 3 per cent and inflation to 1.4 per cent. Sustained economic recovery will be underpinned by improvements in the banking sector. Restructuring and consolidation has brought down the level of non-performing loans, which had generated a banking crisis in the late 1990s.

Retaining investor interest will depend on the extent that the government is able to make the business climate more transparent and reliable. Part of developing a more favourable environment will be reducing the protection given to *bumiputera*-owned (indigenous ethnic Malay) businesses, something the government is reluctant to do since it might override Malay supremacy in the business world.

The objective of the government's national development policy (NDP) is for Malaysia to become a fully developed nation by the year 2020, not only economically, but also in all other aspects. The government's main priority is to improve its human capital in order to remain regionally competitive. Economic diversification is also being encouraged. Five-year development plans have transformed the economy over the last decade from a low-technology commodity-based environment to one where manufacturing and the services sectors are employing higher and more sophisticated technology.

External trade
Malaysia is heavily dependent on foreign trade; since the 1990s the country has traded more than it produces. The country has been aiming to eclipse Singapore as a regional centre for re-exports.

Imports
Main imports include electronics, machinery, petroleum products, plastics, vehicles, iron and steel products and chemicals.
Main sources: Japan (16.1 per cent total, 2004), US (14.6 per cent), Singapore (11.2 per cent), China (9.9 per cent), Thailand (5.6 per cent), Taiwan (5.5 per cent), South Korea (5.0 per cent), Germany (4.5 per cent), Indonesia (4.0 per cent)

Exports
Main exports are electronic equipment, petroleum and liquefied natural gas, wood and wood products, palm oil, rubber, textiles and chemicals.
Main destinations: US (18.8 per cent total, 2004), Singapore (15 per cent), Japan (10.1 per cent), China (6.7 per cent), Hong Kong (6.0 per cent), Thailand (4.8 per cent)

Agriculture
Farming
Agriculture contributes around 9.5 per cent to GDP. Labour shortages and migration from rural to urban areas are contributory factors in the decline of the sector in recent decades. Over 20 per cent of the total land area is cultivated. Malaysia is the world's largest producer of palm oil and natural rubber, the latter accounting for around 25 per cent of world production. Most rubber production (97 per cent) occurs in Peninsular Malaysia. Smallholders account for 69 per cent of output. The government is looking to upgrade the sector from small-scale farming to high-scale farming involving the use of technology.

The government has encouraged diversification away from rubber, the colonial-era staple export, into palm oil production; Malaysia now accounts for over half of world output. World Bank aid has supported government initiatives to improve productivity, increase diversification and alleviate poverty in the agricultural sector. In line with the government's emphasis on new sources of growth within the sector, the production of selected Malaysian tropical fruits and flowers has made a particular contribution. Production and export of cocoa and pepper have increased, as newly planted areas have improved yields. Other main crops are coconuts, sugar cane, tobacco, vegetables, coffee, tea, maize and groundnuts. Sugar cane and tea are grown as plantation crops; for the rest, smallholders account for most cultivation.

The government is trying to encourage higher yields in rice, the main subsistence crop. The formerly state-owned Bernas group, a monopoly rice importer, has entered into joint ventures with Marditech, the commercial arm of the Malaysian Agricultural Research and Development Institute (Mardi), in a drive to produce high-class rice that could rival Thai varieties. The dominance of smallholdings in rice cultivation remains the biggest barrier to advanced rice cultivation.

The state-run Palm Oil Research Institute of Malaysia (Porim) is attempting to genetically modify the oil palm, in order to create more palm olein, used as refined cooking oil in India and China.

Crop production in 2004 included: 2,183,664 tonnes (t) rice, 1,200,000t sugar cane, 75,000t maize, 430,000t cassava, 530,000t bananas, 710,000t coconuts, 69,881,000t oil palm fruit, 30,700t citrus fruit, 320,000t pineapples, 15,789,529t oilcrops, 13,850t tobacco, 33,423t cocoa beans, *39,200t green coffee, 4,250t tea, 19,570t mangoes, 1,190,000t natural rubber, 22,000t pepper spice, 5,700t various spices, 2,500t ginger, 1,297,350t fruit in total, 510,565t vegetables in total. Livestock production included: 1,158,467t meat in total, 4,666t buffalo meat, 21,254t beef, 203,497t pig meat, 1,320t lamb and goat meat, 927,490t poultry, 441,999t eggs, 45,125t milk, 3,374t cattle hides.
* estimate

Fishing
Malaysia typically produces 1.5 million tonnes of fish and other aquatic life per year. It imports about 100,000 tonnes and exports over twice this amount, but the bulk of production is destined for domestic consumption. The main species of fish catch are freshwater fish, marine fish, squid, cuttlefish, octopus, shrimps and prawns. Malaysia is also experimenting with fish-farming.

Forestry
Around 58 per cent of Malaysia is covered by natural forest. Some 14 million hectares (ha), or 43 per cent of total land area, are within designated Permanent Forest Estates, designed to ensure sustainable forestry. Of these some 10.5 million ha are productive forest, the remainder being protected. More than three million ha are designated as conversion forests, which will eventually be cleared and put into alternative use.

Malaysia is one of the world's largest exporters of tropical hardwood; Sarawak is the most important timber-producing area. New markets have been found in the Middle East. The sector is moving away from upstream operations into operations with more value added, including furniture (25 per cent of total exports), plywood (23 per cent), and sawn timber (17 per cent).

Malaysia is a member of the International Tropical Timber Organisation (ITTO) and is committed to sustainable forest management. Rattan, rubber and bamboo are alternatives to logging.

Production in 2004 included 21.3 million cubic metres (cum) roundwood, 4.7 million cum sawnwood, 18.2 million cum sawlogs and veneers, 3.1 million cum woodfuel, 27,480 tonnes charcoal.

Industry and manufacturing
Manufacturing makes the largest contribution to the economy, accounting for over 30 per cent of GDP and 80 per cent of export earnings. Heavy industries based on the country's natural resources have been developed. The promotion of small- and medium-sized firms has been ephasised and measures taken to disperse industries to less developed states. Conglomerate groups, often politically well-connected, used to control large parts of Malaysian industry.

The recession tamed some of the excesses of this system. Many have been restructured and the old management replaced.

Tourism
Tourism is expected to contribute 5.3 per cent to GDP in 2005. The sector is the second most important foreign exchange earner, after industry. Tourism has been accorded priority status by the government to improve foreign exchange earnings, and to provide employment opportunities. Visitor numbers fell sharply from 13.3 million in 2002 to 10.6 million in 2003 in the wake of the Sars scare, but rebounded in 2004 to 15.7 million. The majority of visitors to Malaysia traditionally come from other Asean nations. The government wants to attract more long-haul tourists from Europe and Australia.

Mining
The leading minerals mining firm, the Malaysia Mining Corporation (MMC), is trying to diversify away from tin and is prospecting for base and precious metals on the east coast of peninsular Malaysia. Gold mining has been revived and the Penjom mine accounts for 70 per cent of annual gold production. Malaysia produces around 4,000kg of gold per year. Other resources mined include iron ore, bauxite and copper.

There are undisclosed reserves of gold and antimony in Bau in Sarawak. MMC has also found reserves of copper, silver, gold and bismuth in Pahang state and deposits of alluvial gold in Kelantan state. The mining sector output is declining, mainly as a result of falling tin, copper and petroleum output.

Hydrocarbons
Malaysia has proven oil reserves of three billion barrels and production of around 775,000 barrels per day (bpd) of crude oil. Domestic consumption is estimated at 519,000bpd. Malaysia exports 270,000bpd, mainly to Japan, Singapore, South Korea and Thailand. There are six refineries with a total refining capacity of 545,000bpd. Oil reserves are in decline. Most oil production is concentrated in offshore activities around the Malaysian peninsula. A new deep water discovery will help boost reserves and increase production in the near future.

Malaysia has natural gas reserves totalling 2.41 trillion cubic metres and production of 53.4 billion cubic metres per annum, more than double domestic consumption. Most of the surplus gas is converted into liquefied natural gas (LNG) and exported to Japan, South Korea and Taiwan. Malaysia accounts for almost a fifth of global exports of liquefied natural gas (LNG). Malaysia has proven coal reserves of 275 million tonnes, mainly located on Sarawak.

Energy
Malaysia's total installed generating capacity is 14GW, of which 86 per cent is supplied by thermal plants and the rest by hydropower. Around 52 per cent of demand comes from the industrial sector, 25 per cent from transportation, 12 per cent from commercial sectors and 11 per cent from residential users. It is estimated that demand will have risen by over 8 per cent per annum between 2002 and 2005. Development of the coal reserves and hydropower potential is intended to diversify sources of energy and reduce the use of gas in thermal generation. Reducing the number of national blackouts Malaysia suffers is a priority.

Five independent power producers (IPPs) supply power alongside the established utilities in Sarawak, Sabah and Peninsular Malaysia.

Financial markets
Stock exchange
Since 1996, foreign companies have been able to list shares on the Kuala Lumpur Stock Exchange (KLSE), which is one of the world's most important commodity trading centres.

The Malaysia Monetary Exchange (MME) trades interest rate and currency futures, and is distinct from the Kuala Lumpur Options and Financial Futures Exchanges (Kloffe).

The Malaysian Exchange of Securities Dealings and Automated Quotations (Mesdaq) is an over-the-counter market designed to generate venture capital for high-technology companies.

Banking and insurance
Bank Negara Malaysia ordered a major consolidation programme in 2001. This involved creating 10 institutions from 31 commercial banks, 19 financial companies and 12 merchant banks. By end-2001, 51 financial institutions had successfully merged. As a result, Malaysia's banking system is well-capitalised to meet future demands for capital expenditure.

Central bank
Bank Negara Malaysia

Offshore facilities
Measures to enhance development of Labuan island, Malaysia's offshore banking centre, are planned. Approximately 1,000 financial institutions already have a presence in Labuan.

Time
GMT plus eight hours

Geography
Malaysia comprises 13 states in the Malay Peninsula situated south of Thailand, including Sabah and Sarawak states on the north coast of the island of Borneo, which is separated from the Peninsula by the South China Sea. Peninsular Malaysia extends 740km from Perlis state in the north to Johor state in the south. Sabah and Sarawak stretch some 1,120km from Tanjung Datu (Sarawak) in the west to Hog Point (Sabah) in the east.

Malaysia has a land frontier with Thailand to the north, is bordered by the Republic of Singapore to the south and by the Indonesian island of Sumatra across the Straits of Malacca to the west. Other important neighbours are the Philippines and Brunei which separates Sabah and Sarawak.

Climate
The climate is tropical with high temperatures and high humidity throughout the year. Relative humidity averages about 80 per cent annually.

Average daily temperatures 21–32 degrees Celsius (C) in the lowlands; in the hill resorts they average 18–24 degrees C but can be as low as 16 degrees C. November–February is the rainy season for the east coast of Peninsular Malaysia, the north-eastern part of Sabah and western part of Sarawak. In some years, rainfall is concentrated in short periods and some flooding can occur.

During the months of April, May and October, the west coast of the peninsula experiences occasional thunderstorms in the afternoons. Showers are heavy but they clear up as quickly as they come. Rainfall averages around 2,300mm a year.

Dress codes
Lightweight clothing is worn all year. The dress code tends to be conservative and although jackets are not usually worn in offices, a tie and long-sleeved shirt are normal. For formal meetings, a full suit is required. Government officials often wear a safari-style short-sleeved suit. In deference to the Islamic culture, western business women should dress modestly at all times.

Entry requirements
Passports
Passports are required by all, and they must be valid six months from date of departure. Visitors must have an onward or return ticket and enough money to finance their stay in Malaysia.

Visa
Required by all; some visitors can obtain visas, for business and tourist purposes, on arrival but only from airports. For a detail list of requirements see www.kln.gov.my.

A visitor's pass issued for entry into the Malaysia peninsular is not valid for entry into Sabah and Sarawak.

Visitors arriving in Singapore can obtain a visa for Malaysia from the offices of Fascinating Holidays travel agents. The process takes up to three days and the charge in August 2004 was S$20, this service is offered between Monday–Friday, (except public holidays).

Prohibited entry
Holders of Israeli passports.

Currency advice/regulations
All visitors must declare amounts over M$1,000, or equivalent, on a Travellers Declaration Form (TDF), which can be obtained at the airport. On departure, the TDF must be filled in prior to immigration clearance.

The import and export of local currency is limited to M$1,000. The import of foreign currency is unlimited. The export of foreign currency is limited to the amount imported on arrival.

Customs
Personal items and a limited amount of tobacco (200 cigarettes or 50 cigars) and alcoholic beverages (one litre of wine, spirits or whisky) may be imported duty-free.

Prohibited imports
Items include firearms and ammunition, daggers and knives and pornographic materials. Malaysia enforces a very strict drug abuse policy that includes the death sentence for convicted drug traffickers.

Health (for visitors)
Mandatory precautions
Valid certificate of vaccination against yellow fever if travelling from infected area.
Advisable precautions
Vaccinations are advisable for diphtheria, tuberculosis, typhoid, hepatitis 'A' and 'B', Japanese 'B' encephalitis, tetanus and polio. Tap water is boiled by many people before drinking, although it is generally regarded as safe.
There is a malaria risk in Sabah (northern Malaysia) and the eastern province of Sarawak There is a rabies risk.
Visitors with respiratory problems, may be put at risk from the poor air quality caused by pollution.

Hotels
A 5 per cent tax and 10 per cent service charge is added to hotel and restaurant meals. Tipping is not encouraged.

Credit cards
Extensive acceptance of all major cards, particularly in urban centres and hotels. Travellers cheques are also widely accepted.

Public holidays
Fixed dates
1 Jan (New Year's Day), 1 May (Labour Day), 31 Aug (National Day), 25 Dec (Christmas Day).
Holidays falling on Sunday are celebrated on the following Monday.
Malaysia's multi-ethnic and multi-religious population celebrates a variety of holidays – federal, Muslim, Christian, Buddhist, Hindu and others.
In addition to federal holidays, each state has 3–4 additional holidays, one of which is the birthday of its ruler.
1 Feb (City Day) is a holiday in the Federal Territory of Kuala Lumpur.
Variable dates
Chinese New Year (two days, Jan/Feb), Birth of Buddha (Apr), The King's Birthday (first Sat in Jun), Divali (Hindu, Oct/Nov), Eid al Adha, Islamic New Year, Birth of the Prophet Mohammed, Eid al Fitr (two days).
The Islamic year contains 354 or 355 days, with the result that Muslim feasts advance by 10–12 days against the Gregorian calendar. Dates of feasts vary according to the sighting of the new moon, so cannot be forecast exactly.

Working hours
As well as Friday, the Muslim weekly holiday on Thursday afternoon is observed in the states of Johor, Kedah, Kelantan, Perlis and Terengganu. Other states have a Saturday–Sunday weekend.
Banking
Mon–Fri: 1000–1500, Sat: 0930–1200 in Peninsular Malaysia; Mon–Fri: 0800–1200, 1400–1500; Sat: 0900–1100 in Sabah; Mon–Fri: 1000–1500; Sat: 0930–1130 in Sarawak. In Kedah, Perlis, Kelantan and Terengganu, banks are open from 0930–1130 on Thursday and are closed on Friday.
Business
Mon–Thu: 0730–1645; Fri: 0730–1215, 1445–1645; Sat: 0730–1315; some variation in Sabah and Sarawak.
Government
Mon–Thu: 0800–1245, 1400–1615; Fri: 0800–1215, 1445–1615; Sat: 0800–1245. In Johor, Kedah, Perlis, Kelantan and Terengganu, government offices are open from 0800–1245 on Thursday and are closed on Friday.
Shops
Usually 1000–2200 (department stores and supermarkets), 0930–1900 (shops) in Peninsular Malaysia; Mon–Sat: 0800–1830 in Sabah; Mon–Fri: 0900–1800, Sat: 0900–1300 in Sarawak.

Electricity supply
220V AC, 50Hz. Three-pin square plug fittings and bayonet-type light fittings are generally used.

Weights and measures
Metric system

Social customs/useful tips
Appointments must be made in advance and punctuality is important. It is customary to shake hands on meeting and taking leave, although Muslim women avoid shaking hands with men and vice versa. Business cards are exchanged after introduction. By tradition, Malaysians are hospitable, open people and prefer to avoid arguments, which are seen as distasteful. Avoiding loss of face is an important consideration in business negotiations.
Malaysians place great importance on the correct use of titles. *Tunku* or *Tengku* indicates hereditary royalty; *Tun* denotes membership of a high order of chivalry. *Tan Sri an Datuk* (or *Datuk Seri* or *Dato*) indicate knighthood. *Tuan* or *Encik* is the equivalent of Mr, *Puan* of Mrs, *Cik* of Miss.
Visitors should be aware of the conventions of Muslims, Buddhists and Hindus, and other religious and ethnic groups. Muslims are not permitted to drink alcohol or eat pork. The fasting month of Ramadan is strictly observed. Use right hand only for receiving anything (food, drink, money etc) and for eating. Refusal of offered refreshment is considered discourteous. It is customary to bargain when shopping, except in department stores. Tipping is officially discouraged but is seen in the capital.
The authorities have a very strict attitude to drug abuse and there can be a mandatory death sentence for anyone, including foreigners, who is convicted of possession of even a very small amount of narcotics. Other punishments include whipping, in addition to any custodial sentence. Warning notices about *dadah* (drugs) are prominently displayed at the airport.

Security
Street crime is low compared with European cities, but is increasing. Bag snatching is becoming common generally, as is passport theft on aircraft and in airport buildings. Possessions should not be left unattended, even in vehicles with a locked boot. Credit card fraud is becoming more common, and care should be taken when paying by this method.
Visitors are advised to avoid street gatherings and demonstrations which could place them at risk, especially if gatherings lack police permission.
The UK Foreign Office advises extreme caution if visiting north-east Sabah from Kudat eastwards because of the risk of kidnapping by the Abu Sayyaf, a Philippines-based terrorist group.

Getting there
Air
National airline: Malaysian Airlines (MAS).
International airport/s: Kuala Lumpur International Airport (KUL), 55km south of Kuala Lumpur, near Putrajaya, duty-free shop, bar, restaurant, buffet, bank, business facilities, post office, shops, car hire. Taxis must be pre-paid in the airport arrivals area; (travel time – 40 minutes). KL City Buses operate a 24-hour Express Bus Service to the Airport Bus Terminal–Hentian Duta–Kuala Lumpur city centre, leaving every 15 minutes (luxury coach) or every hour (semi-luxury coach). The journey takes about 1 hour.
Other airport/s: Penang (Bayan Lepas) (PEN), 16km south of Georgetown, capital of small island off the north-west coast of the peninsula, duty-free shop, bar, restaurant, currency exchange, hotel reservations, shops, car hire; Kota Kinabulu (BKI), 6.5km from city, situated on the northern coast of Sabah state (the north-eastern part of Borneo Island); Kuantan (KUA), 16km from city; Kuching (KCH), 11km from the city, situated in the west of Sarawak on the island of Borneo.
Airport tax: International departure tax M$40; domestic M$10.
Surface
Road: The state of Johor is linked to Singapore by a causeway, with coach services to Kuala Lumpur and Malacca (and on to Thailand). A second causeway is operated by the private sector. It is also possible to cross the land border between Malaysia and Indonesia between Pontianak in Kalimantan and Kuching in Sarawak. A daily express bus runs between Pontianak and Kuching.

Malaysia

Rail: A railway line runs from Singapore to Kuala Lumpur, Butterworth, and on into Thailand.

Water: The main ferry crossing from Singapore is between North Changi and Tanjung Belungkor. High-speed ferries run between Sumatra and Malaysia; routes are either Medan–Penang or Dumai– Melaka. A ferry from Port Kelang, Kuala Lumpur's port, goes to Belawan, on Sumatra. Yachts sail irregularly between Langkawi in Malaysia and Phuket in Thailand.

Getting about
National transport
Air: There are over 20 domestic airports. MAS operates extensive network services to main centres and, particularly in Sabah and Sarawak, smaller towns.

Road: About 80–90 per cent of the 43,818km road network in Peninsular Malaysia is paved. In the monsoon season driving can be difficult.

In almost every town there are long-distance taxi offices or *teksi* (taxi) ranks. They wait for the full complement of four passengers before leaving.

Buses: Most long-distance bus services operate from the Puduraya bus and taxi station on Jalan Pudu in Kuala Lumpur. The buses are fast, economical and reasonably comfortable. Seats can be reserved. On many routes buses are air-conditioned, which cost a little more than the regular buses. In Sabah and Sarawak rural services are provided by four-wheel-drive vehicles.

Rail: The capital city is the hub of the national railway system, which is modern, comfortable and economical. Day and night services link major cities in Peninsula Malaysia.

There is a line which branches off the Singapore-Kuala Lumpur-Butterworth-Thailand line at Gemas and runs through Kuala Lipis up to the north-east corner of Malaysia, near Kota Baharu. There are other branch lines which are not used very much.

There are express and ordinary trains. Express trains are air-conditioned and are generally first- and second-class only, and on night trains there is a choice of sleepers or seats.

Rail passes are only available to foreigners and can be purchased at a number of main railway stations.

Water: The Straits Steamship Company operates a passenger service between Port Kelang and Sabah and Sarawak every nine to 10 days. There are frequent ferry services between Penang and Butterworth. There are boats between the Peninsula and offshore islands, and along the rivers of Sabah and Sarawak.

City transport
Taxis: Travel vouchers for airport taxis are available at the airport counters at fixed rates.

Between midnight and 0600, an extra surcharge of 50 per cent applies. There is an extra charge for telephone bookings. Taxi coupons at fixed prices to various destinations in the city and its vicinity are available at Platform Four of the Kuala Lumpur railway station.

It is advisable to ask your hotel to order a taxi in advance, or hire a taxi by the hour, or hire the hotel limousine.

There are bicycle rickshaws in many towns.

Buses, trams & metro: Construction of Kuala Lumpur's light rail driverless metro system was divided into two: Section 1, from Subang Depot to Pasar Seni Station, commenced operation in September 1998 and Section 2, from Pasar Seni Station to Terminal PUTRA, started up in June 1999.

Trains: The express rail link between central Kuala Lumpur and the international airport opened in April 2002.

Car hire
Car hire is available in all main cities. Driving is on the left-hand side of the road, and the use of seat belts in front seats is obligatory. International driving licences are required. Chauffeur-driven cars are available.

BUSINESS DIRECTORY

The addresses listed below are a selection only. While World of Information makes every endeavour to check these addresses, we cannot guarantee that changes have not been made, especially to telephone numbers and area codes. We would welcome any corrections.

Telephone area codes
The international direct dialling (IDD) code for Malaysia is +60, followed by area code and subscriber's number:

Ipoh	5	Melaka	6
Johor Bahru	7	Penang	4
Kota Kinabalu	88	Port Dickson	6
Kuala Lumpur	3	Sandakan	89
Kuantan	9	Sibu	84
Kuching	82	Taiping	5

Useful telephone numbers
Emergency	999
Operator	102
Directory	103
International service	108
Tourist Police	243-5522

Chambers of Commerce
American Malaysian Chamber of Commerce, Amoda Building, 22 Jalan Imbi, 55100 Kuala Lumpur (tel: 2148-2407; fax: 2148-8540; e-mail: info@amcham.com.my).

British Malaysian Chamber of Commerce, c/o British High Commission, 185 Jalan Ampang, 50450 Kuala Lumpur (tel: 2163-1784; fax: 2163-1781; e-mail: britcham@bmcc.org.my).

Kuala Lumpur Chamber of Commerce, 79 Kompleks Damai, Jalan Datuk Haji Eusoff, Kuala Lumpur (tel: 4042-4711; fax: 4042-1540; e-mail: dpmmbkl@tm.net.my).

Malay Chamber of Commerce Malaysia, Plaza Pekeliling, 2 Jalan Tun Razak, 50400 Kuala Lumpur (tel: 4041-8522; fax: 4041-4502; e-mail: wmaster@dpmm.org.my).

Malaysian International Chamber of Commerce and Industry, Plaza Mont' Kiara, 2 Jalan Kiara, 50480 Kuala Lumpur (tel: 6201-7708; fax: 6210-7705; e-mail:micci@micci.com).

Banking
Affin Merchant Bank Berhad, PO Box 1124, 27th Floor, Menara Boustead, 69 Jalan Raja Chulan, 50200 Kuala Lumpur (tel: 242-3700; fax: 242-4982).

Arab-Malaysian Merchant Bank Bhd, Level 18, Menara Dion, Jalan Sultan Ismail, 50250 Kuala Lumpur (tel: 206-3939; fax: 206-6172).

Aseambankers Malaysia Bhd, 33rd floor, Menara Maybank, 100 Jalan Tun Perak, Kuala Lumpur (tel: 238-4211, 238-4233; fax: 238-4194).

Bank Pembangunan, Jalan Sultan Ismail, PO Box 12352, Kuala Lumpur (tel: 291-3399; fax: 292-8520).

Bank Islam Malaysia Bhd, 10th Floor, Darul Takaful, Jalan Sultan Ismail, 50250 Kuala Lumpur (tel: 269-35842; fax: 269-22153).

Bank of Commerce Bhd, 6 Jalan Tun Perak, Kuala Lumpur (tel: 293-1722, 298-3022; fax: 298-6628).

Chung Khiaw Bank Ltd, Chung Khiaw Bank Building, Jalan Raja Laut, Kuala Lumpur (tel: 292-4511; fax: 291-0281).

Citibank Bhd, 28 Medan Pasar, Peti Surat 10112, Kuala Lumpur (tel: 232-8585; fax: 202-1101).

D & C Mitsui Merchant Bankers Bhd, 22nd floor, Wisma On-Tai, 161B Jalan Ampang, Kuala Lumpur (tel: 261-2444; fax: 261-9241).

Development and Commercial Bank Bhd, Wisma On-Tai, 161B Jalan Ampang, Kuala Lumpur (tel: 261-9077).

Hong Leong Bank Bhd, Aras 2, Wisma Hong Leong, 18 Jalan Perak, Kuala Lumpur (tel: 264-2828; fax: 925-8623).

HSBC Bank Malaysia Bhd, 2 Leboh Ampang, Kuala Lumpur (tel: 230-0744, 230-9022; fax: 232-1146).

Kwong Yik Bank Bhd, 75 Jalan Bandar, Kuala Lumpur (tel: 232-5633; fax: 238-7227).

Malayan Banking Bhd, Menara Maybank, 100 Jalan Tun Perak, Peti Surat 12010, Kuala Lumpur (tel: 230-8833; fax: 230-2611).

MUI Bank Bhd, 21st floor, MUI Plaza, Jalan P Ramlee, Kuala Lumpur (tel: 241-1533; fax: 241-6306).

Public Bank Bhd, 146 Jalan Ampang, Peti Surat 12542, Kuala Lumpur (tel: 263-8888, 263-8899; fax: 232-0607).

Sabah Development Bank, SDB Tower, Wisma Tun Faud Stephens, KM 2.4, Jalan Tuaran, Sabah (tel: 232-177; fax: 222-852).

Southern Bank Bhd, Wisma Genting, Jalan Sultan Ismail, Peti Surat 12281, Kuala Lumpur (tel: 263-7000; fax: 232-5008).

Standard Chartered Bank, 2 Jalan Ampang, Kuala Lumpur (tel: 232-6555; fax: 238-3295).

United Malayan Banking Corp Bhd, Bangunan UMBC, Jalan Sultan Sulaiman, PO Box 12006, Kuala Lumpur (tel: 230-5833/9866; fax: 232-2627).

United Overseas Bank, Chung Khiaw Bank Bldg, Jalan Raja Laut, Kuala Lumpur (tel: 292-7722; fax: 291-1608).

Central bank
Bank Negara Malaysia, Jalan Dato' Onn, PO Box 10922, Kuala Lumpur 50929 (tel: 2698-8044; fax: 2691-2990; e-mail: info@bnm.gov.my).

Travel information
Automobile Association of Malaysia, 30 Djalan Datuk Sulaiman, Taman Tun Dr Ismail, Kuala Lumpur (tel: 262-5777).

Kuala Lumpur International Airport (KLIA) (internet site: http://www.jaring.my).

Kuala Lumpur Tourist Association (KLTA) and KL Visitors Centre, 3 Jalan Sultan Hishamuddin, 50050 Kuala Lumpur (tel: 238-1832).

Malaysian Airlines (MAS), 33rd Floor, Bangunan MAS, Jalan Sultan Ismail, Kuala Lumpur, 50250 (tel: 261-0555; fax: 261-3472; internet: www.malaysianairlines.com).

KL Airport (tel: 746-3000/1014); DCA Information (tel: 746-1235).

Malaysia Tourist Information Complex (MATIC), 109 Jalan Ampang, Kuala Lumpur (tel: 243-4929).

Railway Station (tel: 274-7435).

National tourist organisation offices
Tourist Development Corporation Malaysia (TDC), HQ 24th-27th Floors, Menara Dato'Onn, Putra World Trade Centre, 45 Jalan Tun Ismail, 50480 Kuala Lumpur (tel: 293-5188; fax: 293-5884, 293-0207; e-mail: tourism@tourism.gov.my).

Information Centre: Level 2, Putra World Trade Centre, Jalan Tun Ismail (tel: 441-1295); Terminal 1, Subang Airport, Arrival Hall (tel: 746-5707); Information Counter, Railway Station (tel: 274-6063); KL Tourist Information Centre, Jalan Parlimen (tel: 293-6664).

Ministries
Ministry of Agriculture, Wisma Tani, Jl Sultan Salahuddin, 50624 Kuala Lumpur (tel: 298-2011; fax: 291-3758).

Ministry of Culture, Arts and Tourism, Peti 5-7, Tingkat 21, 34-36 Menara Dato' Onn (PWTC), 45 Jl Tun Ismail, 50694 Kuala Lumpur (tel: 293-7111; fax: 291-0951).

Ministry of Defence, Jl Padang Tembak, 50634 Kuala Lumpur (tel: 292-1333, 230-1033; fax: 298-4662, 298-5372).

Ministry of Domestic Trade and Consumer Affairs, Tingkat 22-24, Putra Place, 100 Jl Putra, 50622 Kuala Lumpur (tel: 232-9955; fax: 238-9558).

Ministry of Education, Level 7, Block J, Pusat Bandar Damansara, 50604 Kuala Lumpur (tel: 255-6900; fax: 255-6910).

Ministry of Energy, Telecommunications and Post, Tingkat 1, Wisma Damansara, Jl Semantan, 50668 Kuala Lumpur (tel: 256-2222; fax: 256-2286, 255-7901).

Ministry of Entrepreneur Development, Tingkat 24, Medan MARA, Jl Raja Laut, 50652 Kuala Lumpur (tel: 298-5022; fax: 291-7623).

Ministry of Finance, Block 9, Kompleks Pejabat Kerajaan, Jl Duta, 50592 Kuala Lumpur (tel: 258-2000; fax: 255-6264, 254-2636).

Ministry of Foreign Affairs, Wisma Putra, Jl Wisma Putra, 50602 Kuala Lumpur (tel: 248-8088; fax: 242-4551).

Ministry of Health, Jl Cenderasari, 50590 Kuala Lumpur (tel: 298-5077; fax: 298-5964).

Ministry of Home Affairs, Jl Dato' Onn, 50546 Kuala Lumpur (tel: 230-9344, 293-6122; fax: 230-1051).

Ministry of Human Resources, Block B, Utara, Jl Damanlela, Pusat Bandar Damansara, Bukit Damansara, 50530 Kuala Lumpur (tel: 255-7200; fax: 255-4700).

Ministry of Housing and Local Government, Paras 4 & 5, Block K, Pusat Bandar Damansara, Peti Surat 12579, 50782 Kuala Lumpur (tel: 254-7033; fax: 255-4066, 254-7380).

Ministry of Information, Angkasapuri, Bukit Putra, 50610 Kuala Lumpur (tel: 282-5333; fax: 282-1255).

Ministry of International Trade and Industry, Block 10, Kompleks Pejabat Kerajaan, Jl Duta, 50622 Kuala Lumpur (tel: 254-0033/6022; fax: 255-0827).

Ministry of Land and Co-operative Development, Tingkat 5 & 6, Wisma Tanah, Jl Semarak, 50574 Kuala Lumpur (tel: 292-1566; fax: 291-8641).

Ministry of National Unity and Community Development, Tingkat 20, Wisma Bumi Raya, Jl Raja Laut, 50562 Kuala Lumpur (tel: 292-5022; fax: 293-7353).

Ministry of Primary Industries, Tingkat 6-8, Menara Dayabumi, Jl Sultan Hishamuddin, 50654 Kuala Lumpur (tel: 274-7511; fax: 274-5014).

Ministry of Rural Development, Tingkat 5-10, Kompleks Kewangan, Jl Raja Chulan, 50606 Kuala Lumpur (tel: 261-2622; fax: 261-1339).

Ministry of Science and Technology, Tingkat 14, Wisma Sime Darby, Jl Raja Laut, 50662 Kuala Lumpur (tel: 293-8955; fax: 293-6006).

Ministry of Transport, Tingkat 5-7, Wisma Perdana, Jl Dungun, Bukit Damansara, 50616 Kuala Lumpur (tel: 254-8122; fax: 255-7041).

Ministry of Works, Jl Sultan Salahuddin, 50580 Kuala Lumpur (tel: 291-9011/1011; fax: 298-6612).

Ministry of Youth and Sports, Aras 6 & 7, Block K, Pusat Bandar Damansara, Bukit Damansara, 50570 Kuala Lumpur (tel: 255-2255; fax: 255-6521).

Prime Minister's Department, Jl Dato' Onn, 50502 Kuala Lumpur (tel: 232-1957/37; fax: 298-4172, 232-9227).

Other useful addresses
Advertising Standards Authority of Malaysia, c/o Coopers and Lybrand, Hong Kong Bank Building, Leboh Pasar, Kuala Lumpur.

Asean Investment Promotion Agency, Malaysian Industrial Development Authority, 6th Floor, Wisma Damansara, Damansara Heights, PO Box 10618, 50720 Kuala Lumpur (tel: 255-3633; fax: 255-0697).

Asean Secretariat, 70 A Jl Sisingamangaraja, Jakarta 12110, Indonesia (tel: 62(21)726-2991, 724-3372; fax: 724-3504, 739-8234; e-mail: asean.or.id).

British Consul, 3rd Floor, Bangunan Rugayah, Jalan Song Thain Cheok, 93100 Kuching, Sarawak (tel: 231-320; fax: 418-019).

Malaysia

British Council, Jalan Bukit Aman, PO Box 10539, 50916 Kuala Lumpur.

British High Commission, PO Box 11030, 185 Jalan Ampang, 50732 Kuala Lumpur (tel: 248-2122; fax: 244-7766, 244-9692 (Consular Section).

British Malaysian Industry & Trade Association (BMITA), PO Box 12574, 50782 Kuala Lumpur.

Capital Issues Committee, Kementerian Kewangan, 11th Floor, Block 9, Khazanah Malaysia, Jl Duta, Kuala Lumpur (tel: 254-0011; fax: 254-2636).

Federal Land Development Authority, (FELDA), Jl Maktab, Kuala Lumpur (tel: 293-5066; fax: 292-0089).

Federation of Malaysian Manufacturers, Tingkat 17, Wisma Sime Darby, Jl Raja Laut, 50350 Kuala Lumpur (tel: 293-1244; fax: 293-5105).

Foreign Investment Committee, Economic Planning Unit, Prime Minister's Dept, Jl Dato' Onn, Kuala Lumpur (tel: 230-0133).

Kuala Lumpur Stock Exchange, Tingkat 4, Block A, Exchange Sq, off Jl Semantan, Bukit Damansara, 50490 Kuala Lumpur (tel: 254-6433; fax: 255-7463).

Malaysian Embassy (US), 2401 Massachusetts Avenue, NW, 20008 (tel: 202-328-2700; fax: 202-483-7661; e-mail: mwwashdc@erols.com).

Malaysian Export Trade Centre, Ministry of Trade and Industry, Wisma PKNS, Jl Raja Laut, 50350 (tel: 292-8122).

Malaysian Industrial Development Authority (MIDA), 3rd-6th Floor, Wisma Damansara, Jl Semantan, PO Box 10618, 50720 Kuala Lumpur (tel: 255-3633; fax: 255-0697).

Perbadanan Nasional Berhad (PERNAS), 16th Floor, Menara Tun Razak, Jl Raja Laut, Kuala Lumpur (tel: 242-5022).

Sarawak Economic Development Corporation, 1st Floor, Bangunan Yayasa Sarawak, Jl Masjid, PO Box 400, Kuching.

Securities Commission, 3 Jl Semantan, Bukit Damansara, 50490 Kuala Lumpur (tel: 253-9988; fax: 253-6184).

Suruhanjaya Dagangan Kommoditi, Tingkat 5, City Point, Kompleks Dayabumi, Jl Sultan Hishamuddin, 50050 Kuala Lumpur (tel: 293-6644).

Internet sites

Malaysia Homepage:
http://www.jaring.my/

Information on the economy, news, education, tourism, government, politics and research and development:
http://www.jaring.my/msia/welcome.html

Malyasia yellow and white pages:
http://www.tpsb.com.my/thome.htm

Maldives

KEY FACTS

Official name: Divehi Raajjeyge Jumhooriyyaa (Republic of Maldives)

Head of State: President Maumoon Abdul Gayoom (since 1978; 90 per cent voted for him in 17 Oct 2003 referendum)

Head of government: President Maumoon Abdul Gayoom

Ruling party: There are no political parties.

Area: 298 square km (1,190 tiny atoll islands) – Malé: 1.5 square km

Population: 292,000 (2004)

Capital: Malé, on Malé Island

Official language: Dhivehi (Maldivian)

Currency: Rufiyaa (MRf) = 100 laari

Exchange rate: MRf12.80 per US$ (Oct 2005)

GDP per capita: US$2,318 (2004)

GDP real growth: 8.80% (2004)

Labour force: 128,000 (2004)

Inflation: 6.40% (2004)

Balance of trade: -US$285.00 million (2003)

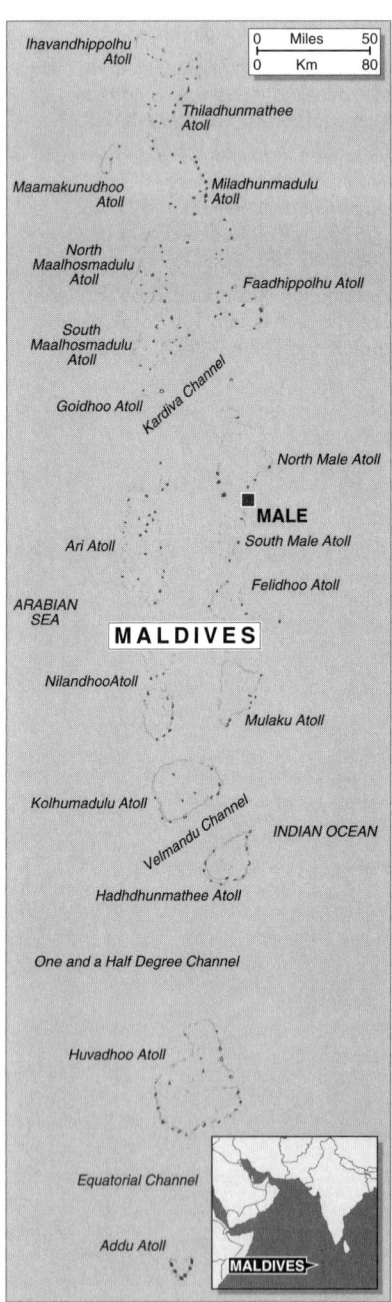

COUNTRY PROFILE

Historical profile

1887 The islands were placed under British protection, with internal self government.
1932 The first democratic constitution was proclaimed. The sultanate became an elected position.
1953 The Maldives became a republic and a member of the Commonwealth as the sultanate was abolished. However, the sultanate was restored within months.
1965 Gained full independence as a sultanate and left the Commonwealth.
1968 Following a referendum, the country reverted from a sultanate back to a republic.
1975 The UK pulled out of its military base on Addu atoll. A proposal from the USSR to take over the base was rejected.
1978 Maumoon Abdul Gayoom was elected president.
1981 An industrial zone was established on Gan.
1982 Rejoined the Commonwealth.
1988 An attempt by Sri Lankan Tamil mercenaries to depose the government was thwarted with the help of Indian army forces.
1994 Non-party elections to the Majlis (parliament) were held.
1997 A new constitution was passed.
1998 President Maumoon Abdul Gayoom was re-elected for a fifth consecutive five-year term.
1999 Forty non-partisan members were elected to the Majlis.
2001 The Maldivian director for the environment condemned the US decision to reject the Kyoto Protocol, saying that it would leave the Maldives vulnerable in the face of rising sea levels. The Kyoto Protocol is designed to halt global warming by enforcing strict hydrocarbon emission levels for major countries.
2002 The Maldivian and Indian governments began working together to implement a plan for poverty reduction in the Maldives.
2003 The health minister announced that the uninhabited island of Feydhoofinolhu would be used as isolation quarters to treat any suspected Severe Acute Respiratory Syndrome (Sars) cases. There were riots in Malé in September when prison inmates protested at alleged torture; government buildings and the election office were burned. President Maumoon Abdul Gayoom won a sixth term with over 90 per cent of the vote in the 17 October referendum, confirming his re-election by parliament.

Maldives

2004 In June, the President outlined proposed changes to the constitution, which would limit his powers. Opponents of the regime are sceptical, since the changes were proposed after human rights abuses in the Maldives were highlighted by the media. On 26 December, an earthquake off the island of Sumatra caused a *tsunami* that devastated coastal areas in the region. Twenty of the Maldives' inhabited islands were devasted by the *tsunami*. The final toll in the Maldives was estimated at 108 dead or missing and 29,577 displaced.

2005 In the 22 January parliamentary elections, all candidates for the 42 seats ran officially as independents. On 2 June, parliament voted in favour of introducing multi-party politics. Maldives, Bhutan, Bangladesh, India, Nepal, Pakistan and Sri Lanka signed the South Asia Free Trade Agreement (Safta), to come into effect on 1 January 2006.

Political structure

Constitution
The Republic of Maldives is a former sultanate. The constitution dates from November 1997.
Voting: universal suffrage over 21 years. Local authority is vested in atoll chiefs and island headmen appointed by the president.
In June 2004, President Maumoon Abdul Gayoom outlined proposed changes to the constitution: the president would not be able to serve more than two five-year terms; he would lose the right to appoint eight members of the Majlis; the office of prime minister would be created; the powers of the executive and legislature would be separated; there would be freedom of association.

The executive
Executive power is held by the president, who is head of state and head of government. The president is nominated by the legislature and directly elected for a renewable five-year term. The president is also commander-in-chief of the armed forces, minister of defence and national security, and minister of finance and treasury.

National legislature
The Majlis (parliament) has 50 members. Each of the 20 administrative atolls has a quota of two members, and the capital island Malé is also given two seats. Among the 50 members, 42 are elected and eight members are selected by the president. Term of office is five years.
The president has the sole power to summon the Majlis which can alter the constitution by majority vote. A cabinet is appointed and chaired by the president; cabinet ministers are not required to be members of the Majlis.

Legal system
The legal system is based on Islamic law with admixtures of English common law, primarily in commercial matters.

Last elections
22 January 2005 (parliamentary); 17 October 2003 (referendum confirming the President's re-election by parliament).
Results: Parliamentary: all candidates for the 42 seats ran officially as independents.
Presidential referendum: President Gayoom won more than 90 per cent of the vote; turnout 77 per cent.

Next elections
2009 (parliamentary)

Political parties
Although the constitution does not ban the formation and functioning of political parties, an opposition party, the Maldivian Democratic Party (MDP), formed in 2003, was banned.

Ruling party
There are no political parties.

Political situation
With what many democratic countries would consider an overwhelming mandate to govern, President Abdul Gayoom was returned to power in September 2003 with 90 per cent of the vote, on a 77 per cent turnout. Such a margin cannot be explained, if his detractors are to be believed. Some have called his presidency a 'despotic totalitarian regime' with opposition activists prone to arbitrary arrests, torture and detention without trials. Others have noted that 15 of the senior posts in his cabinet are occupied by family members and the rest by close associates; since coming to power in 1978 he has maintained a grip on the special majlis, which is the only body that nominates a single candidate for presendent.

Unprecedented civil unrest preceded the election of Gayoom, and as a result constitutional reforms have been proposed including presidential terms of office limited to two, separate executive and legislature, office of prime minister to be created and freedom of association. However, some say the omission of a mention of a bill of rights or freedom of expression was significant.

Population
292,000 (2004)

Ethnic make-up
The majority of the population are Sinhalese or Dravidian, with significant Arab and smaller African minorities.

Religions
Islam (Sunni majority)

Education
Primary education is provided through either private or state schools; lessons are given in English, Arabic and Dhivehi.
The curriculum, for segregated (by gender) secondary education, is based on the British system and many schools prepare students to sit the General Certificate of Education at 'O' level and a few for 'A' level examinations. Students have to travel abroad for higher education.
President Gayoom has made improving education levels his top priority. There is an ongoing teacher training programme due to the shortage of qualified teachers. Typically 2.4 per cent of the GNP is spent on primary education.
Literacy rate: 97.2 per cent total; adult rates (World Bank).
Enrolment rate: 98 per cent net primary enrolment (Unicef).
Pupils per teacher: 24 in primary schools.

KEY INDICATORS — Maldives

	Unit	2000	2001	2002	2003	2004
Population	m	0.27	0.27	0.28	0.28	0.29
Gross domestic product (GDP)	US$bn	0.56	0.62	0.62	1.25	*0.75
GDP per capita	US$	2,060	2,220	2,220	3,900	2,318
GDP real growth	%	5.6	2.1	4.3	8.4	8.8
Inflation	%	-1.1	0.6	2.0	-1.5	6.4
Exports (fob) (goods)	US$m	108.7	116.0	133.6	110.0	–
Imports (fob) (goods)	US$m	342.0	349.0	344.7	395.0	–
Balance of trade	US$m	-233.3	-233.0	-211.1	-285.0	-285.0
Current account	US$m	-52.0	-59.0	-36.0	-30.0	-90.0
Total reserves minus gold	US$m	122.8	93.1	133.1	159.5	203.6
Foreign exchange	US$m	120.5	90.8	130.7	156.7	200.7
Exchange rate	per US$	11.77	12.24	12.80	12.78	12.80

* estimated figure

Health

The Maldives has significantly improved health services and severe diseases such as malaria, childhood tuberculosis and leprosy have been eradicated. Government spending was 83.5 per cent, and foreign spending 16.5 per cent, of the total expenditure on health in 2001, which was 6.7 per cent of GDP.

There are two hospitals on the main island and six regional hospitals serving all the remaining islands. In addition, there are 45 health centres and 36 health posts serving the islands.

By 2002, 99 per cent of children were immunised against measles before aged one year.

HIV/Aids

The first Maldivian with HIV was identified in 1991. There have been six deaths as a result of Aids. Although the HIV rate is very small, the Maldives is particularly vulnerable to the spread of the virus due to the high number of migrant workers that pass through the islands. Drug usage among young people is also on the rise.

Life expectancy: 69.5 years (World Bank)
Fertility rate/Maternal mortality rate: 4 births per woman (World Bank)
Infant mortality rate: 55 per 1,000 live births; 45 per cent of children aged under five are malnourished (World Bank).
Head of population per physician/bed: There are 436 physicians per 100,000 people; around 60 per cent of the population do not have access to a hospital (World Bank).

Welfare

Due to the highly dispersed character of the country, it is difficult for the government to ensure that everyone receives benefits. The ministry of women's affairs and social welfare has responsibility for administering the welfare programme that covers women, children, the disabled and unemployed.

Main cities

Malé (capital, estimated population 81,600 in 2003).

Languages spoken

The Maldivian language is Indo-Aryan.
Official language/s
Dhivehi (Maldivian)

Media

Press
Dailies: The major daily newspapers include *Haveeru Daily* and *Miadhu Daily*. *Aafathis Daily News* is one of the oldest local newspapers.
Business: The *South Asian Business Analyst* is in circulation here.

Economy

The main economic activities are fishing, tourism and shipping. The high population growth rate has led to shortages of land and housing.

Development of the tourism industry has required investment in infrastructure and modern passenger boats. Government policy has been to set up resorts on uninhabited islands, preserving a desert island atmosphere.

On all islands, water supply is a critical problem. Sanitary conditions have been improved since a project in 1984 to provide drinking water for Malé. The project included development of mosque wells and construction of public and private collection tanks, a sewage system and a desalination plant. It was funded in part by loans from the Saudi Fund for Development. Other plans include construction of housing and land reclamation.

The government's open market policy has generally proved successful. With low inflation, further strong growth appears sustainable.

As an Islamic nation, the Maldives receives aid from Kuwait and Saudi Arabia. President Gayoom has also managed to harness a steady flow of Japanese aid. In addition, development funding comes from the UK and Australia.

Neither the war in Iraq nor Severe Acute Respiratory Syndrome (Sars) appeared to have an adverse effect on the economy in 2003, which grew by 8.4 per cent – the tourism sector contributed more than half of GDP growth. Growth continued in 2004 at 8.8 per cent.

The largest project undertaken by the Maldives is the ongoing Hulhumalé infrastructure project, reclaiming land and developing a new town on an island close to Malé, the capital city. Reclamation began in 1997. Hulhumalé's hospital and Fareediyya School were opened in April 2004 and the ferry terminal is under construction.

External trade

The Maldives is one of the 32 developing nations designated in 1985 to receive exemption from US competitive trade requirements in accordance with the Generalised System of Preferences.

Imports

Main imports are electronics, machinery, petroleum products, plastics, vehicles, iron and steel products and chemicals.
Main sources: Japan (16.1 per cent total, 2004), US (14.6 per cent), Singapore (11.2 per cent), China (9.9 per cent), Thailand (5.6 per cent), Taiwan (5.5 per cent), South Korea (5.0 per cent), Germany (4.5 per cent), Indonesia (4.0 per cent)

Exports

Main exports include electronic equipment, petroleum and liquefied natural gas, wood and wood products, palm oil, rubber, textiles and chemicals.
Main destinations: US (18.8 per cent total, 2004), Singapore (15 per cent), Japan (10.1 per cent), China (6.7 per cent), Hong Kong (6.0 per cent), Thailand (4.8 per cent)

Agriculture

Farming

Agriculture, including fishing, accounts for around 15 per cent of GDP and employs 40 per cent of the labour force. Farming is at subsistance level on small-holdings, confined to field crops and fruit trees, with no livestock. Main crops are water melon, sweet potato, cucumber, cassava pumpkin, cabbage and yam. Approximately 6 per cent of the total land area is under cultivation. The soil is shallow and highly alkaline, with poor water-retaining properties.

Crop production in 2004 included: 35,000 tonnes (t) coconut, 12,500t groundnuts, 200t sweet potatoes, 350t taro, 4,550t oilcrops, 8,340 roots & tubers, 2,300t treenuts, 30,165t vegetables in total, 3,500t bananas and 13,500t fruit in total. Meat production is about 1,000t per annum.

Fishing

The fishing sector is second to tourism in importance in the economy. Fish provide the main source of protein for the population with a 126,000mt annual catch. Fishing employs over 20 per cent of the workforce.

Tourism

Tourism is the main economic activity. It contributes around 30 per cent of GDP and is the principal source of foreign exchange and revenue. The most important market is Italy, with around a quarter of visitors, followed by the UK, Germany and Japan. Tourist arrivals have risen at an annual average rate of 17 per cent. Receipts from tourism have not kept pace with the increased numbers, due to decline in spending per visitor. In 2003, there were 563,593 visitors, compared with 484,680 in 2002. While by 18 December 2004 visitor arrivals reached a record 600,000, six days later, the Asian *tsunami* struck, wrecking much infrastructure, causing an estimated US$10 million worth of damage and impacting severely on visitor numbers in 2005.

Environment

It has been reported that the beaches of one-third of the Maldives' 200 inhabited islands could be swept away by rising sea levels, as global warming melts the fringes of polar ice caps. Another issue affecting the Maldives is the depletion of fresh water aquifiers which threatens water supply.

Maldives

Hydrocarbons
The Maldives do not produce any oil and rely on imports of refined oil products, mainly of distillate and jet fuel, to meet domestic energy requirements.
The Maldives do not produce or import natural gas or coal.

Energy
The Maldives has installed generating capacity of around 106MW, supplied by oil. Around half the capacity is concentrated in resort areas. The State Electricity Company (Stelco) generates a third of the supply; the rest is supplied by Island Development Committees and private generators.

Banking and insurance
Central bank
Maldives Monetary Authority

Time
GMT plus five hours

Geography
The Republic of Maldives is one of the smallest countries in the world. It consists of 1,190 small coral islands (202 being uninhabited) grouped in 19 atolls that form a chain 764km long and 129km wide in the Indian Ocean, about 675km (420 miles) south-west of Sri Lanka. The northern tip of the Maldives is about 600km south of India. These tropical islands cover a total of only 298 square km.

Climate
There is year-round sunshine, with temperatures ranging 26–30 degrees Celsius. Most rainfall occurs during the south-west monsoon season from April–October.

Entry requirements
Passports
Required by all.
Visa
All business and tourist visas are issued free, on arrival, to all visitors, at the airport in Malé, for visits of up to 30 days, proof of return/onward passage is necessary. A work permit must be obtained if visitor is employed by a local company (see: www.humanresources.gov.mv/).
Currency advice/regulations
No restrictions.
Customs
Personal effects are allowed duty-free. Tortoise and articles produced using tortoise shells may not be exported.
Prohibited imports
Alcohol, pork, pharmaceuticals and goods at variance with Islamic culture are prohibited or subject to restrictions. Pornographic material may not be imported.

Health (for visitors)
Mandatory precautions
Vaccination certificate required for yellow fever if travelling from an infected area.
Advisable precautions
Anti-malarial precautions, outside Malé. Diphtheria, hepatitis 'A' and 'B', polio, TB, tetanus and typhoid. There is a rabies risk.
Dengue fever is rife, although there is no preventive medication, visitors are advised to use mosquito repellent, a mosquito net at night, and wear clothing covering as much skin as possible to reduce the risk. Symptoms match those of sever flu with high fever and muscle aches.

Hotels
There are two hotels in Malé, 36 guest-houses and 64 island resorts, mostly in Malé Atoll, and in more distant atolls.

Credit cards
All major credit cards, including American Express, Visa and MasterCard, are widely accepted on the islands.

Public holidays
Fixed dates
1 Jan (New Year's Day), 21 Apr (National Day), 26–27 Jul (Independence Days), 3 Nov (Victory Day), 11–12 Nov (Republic Day).
Variable dates
Hajj Day (Jan), Eid al Adha, Islamic New Year, Birth of the Prophet, Start of Ramadan, Eid al Fitr (End of Ramadan), Huravee Day (Jul), Martyrs' Day (Sep). The Islamic year contains 354 or 355 days, with the result that Muslim feasts advance by 10–12 days against the Gregorian calendar. Dates of feasts vary according to the sighting of the new moon, so cannot be forecast exactly. Islamic year 1426: 10 February 2005 to 30 January 2006.

Working hours
Banking
Sun–Thu: 0800–1330.
Business
Sun–Thu: 0730–1430. During the month of Ramadan 0900–1300.
Government
Sun–Thu: 0730–1430.
Shops
Sat–Thu: 0930–2300; Fri: 1400–2300.

Weights and measures
Metric system

Social customs/useful tips
Alcohol can only be consumed in holiday resorts.

Getting there
Air
National airline: Air Maldives

International airport/s: Malé International Airport (MLE), on Hulule Island, 2km north-east of Malé.
Airport tax: US$10 for all passengers departing for international travel, excluding transit passengers.
Surface
Main port/s: Gan, Uligamu and Malé. There are no deep-water ports. Cargo is off-loaded into lighters.

Getting about
National transport
Air: Air Maldives operates regular domestic flights. Government charter planes are also available. Hummingbird Helicopters offers a shuttle service to the islands.
Water: There is a public boat service from the airport to Malé city centre, with a journey time of 15 minutes. Resort islands have regular ferry services. Local boats can be hired; rates are negotiable. Charter vessels are available.
City transport
Taxis: Taxis cannot be hailed in the street, but there are many taxi ranks.
Car hire
Due to the small size of the islands, there is little need for transportation. It is possible to walk to all places within the small area of Malé.

BUSINESS DIRECTORY
The addresses listed below are a selection only. While World of Information makes every endeavour to check these addresses, we cannot guarantee that changes have not been made, especially to telephone numbers and area codes. We would welcome any corrections.

Telephone area codes
The international direct dialling code (IDD) for the Maldives is +960, followed by subscriber's number.

Useful telephone numbers
Police: 119
Fire: 118
Ambulance: 102

Chambers of Commerce
Maldives National Chamber of Commerce and Industry, G Viyafaari Hiya, Ameenee Magu, PO Box 92, Malé 2004 (tel: 326-634; fax: 310-233; e-mail: mncci@dhivehinet.net.mv).

Banking
Bank of Ceylon, Orchid Magu, Male (tel: 30-45/6; fax: 32-0575).

Bank of Maldives (PLC) Ltd, 11 Boduthakurufaanu Magu, Male 20-05 (tel: 32-2948; fax: 32-8233).

Habib Bank Ltd, Ground Floor, 1/6 Orchid Magu Ship Plaza, Male (tel: 32-2051/2; fax: 32-6791).

State Bank of India, Boduthakurufaanu Magu, Male (tel: 32-0860, 31-6773; fax: 32-3053).

Central bank
Maldives Monetary Authority, 3rd Floor, Umar Shopping Arcade, Chandhanee Magu, Malé 20-02 (tel: 312-343; fax: 323-862; e-mail: mail@mma.gov.mv).

Travel information
Air Maldives, 26 Ameer Ahmed Magu, Malé (tel: 322-436; fax: 325-056).

Malé International Airport, Maldives Airports Authority, Malé (tel: 322-211, 326-763; fax: 325-034).

Tourist Information Unit, Marine Drive, Malé (tel: 5528).

Ministry of tourism
Ministry of Tourism, 2/F Ghazi Building, Orchid Magu, Henveiru, Malé (tel: 313-461).

Ministries
Ministry of Atolls Administration, Malé (tel: 323-070; fax: 327-750).

Ministry of Constructions and Public Works, Malé (tel: 323-234; fax: 328-300).

Ministry of Defence and National Security, Malé (tel: 322-607).

Ministry of Education, Malé (tel: 323-261; fax: 321-201).

Ministry of Finance and Treasury, Malé (tel: 318-472, 3235-908; fax: 324-432, 324-432).

Ministry of Fisheries and Agriculture, Malé (tel: 322-625; fax: 326-558).

Ministry of Foreign Affairs, Marine Drive, Malé 20-25 (tel: 323-400; fax: 323-841).

Ministry of Health, Malé (tel: 328-887; fax: 327-909).

Ministry of Home Affairs and Housing, Malé (tel: 321-752; fax: 324-739).

Ministry of Information, Arts and Culture, Malé (tel: 323-838; fax: 326-211).

Ministry of Justice, Malé (tel: 323-941; fax: 324-103).

Ministry of Planning, Human Resources and Environment, Malé (tel: 320-776, 323-919; fax: 327-351).

Ministry of Tourism, Malé (tel: 323-224; fax: 322-756, 322-512).

Ministry of Trade, Industries and Labour, Malé (tel: 323-668; fax: 323-756).

Ministry of Transport and Communications, Malé (tel: 323-993; fax: 323-994).

Ministry of Women's Affairs and Social Welfare, Malé (tel: 317-165; fax: 316-237).

President's Office, Malé (tel: 323-701; fax: 325-500).

Other useful addresses
Attorney General's Office, Malé (tel: 321-106; fax: 314-109).

Maldives National Ship Management Ltd, 2/F, Ship Plaza, Male (tel: 323-871; fax: 324-323).

Maldives Association of Tourism Industries, H.Mahi, Malé (tel: 318-708; fax: 326-641).

Maldives Traders' Association, G. Viyafaari, Wmeenee Magu, Malé (tel: 326-634; fax: 321-889).

State Trading Organisation, Haveeree Higun, Malé (tel: 323-279; fax: 325-218).

Internet sites
Maldives Consular Information: http://www.travel.state.gov/maldives.html

Maldives news online: http://maldivesculture.com

Maldives Yellow Pages: http://www.maldivesyellowpages.com

Mali

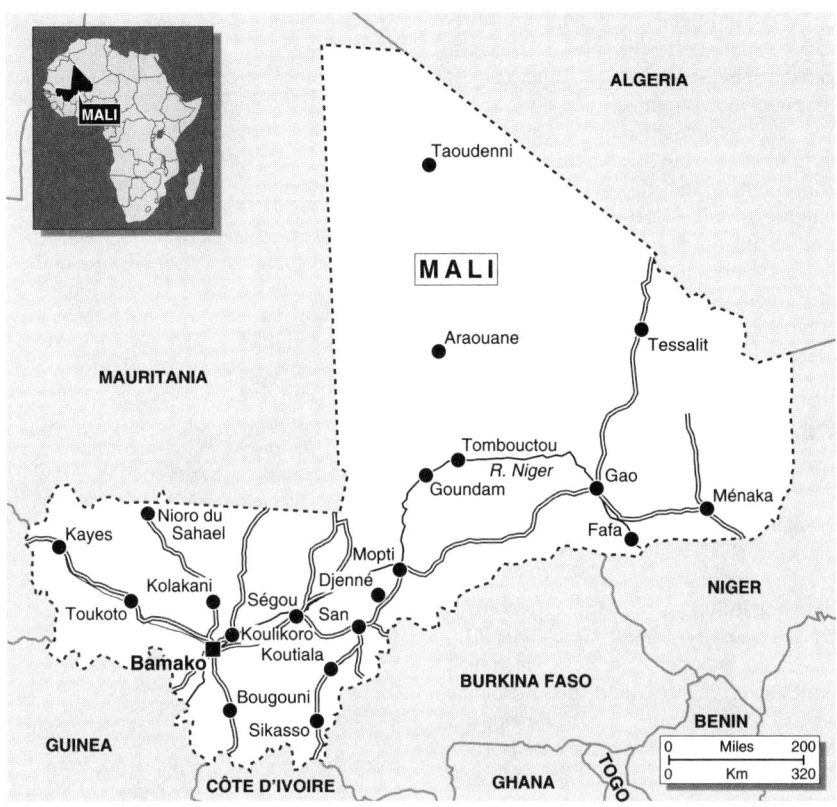

KEY FACTS

Official name: République du Mali (Republic of Mali)

Head of State: President Amadou Toumani Touré (sworn in 8 Jun 2002)

Head of government: Prime Minister Ousmane Issoufi Maïga (appointed 29 Apr 2004)

Ruling party: Espoir 2002 (Hope 2002) Coalition: Rassemblement pour le Mali (Rally for Mali), Congres Nationale pour la Initiative Démocratie (National Congress for Democratic Initiative)

Area: 1,241,238 square km

Population: 11.79 million (2004)

Capital: Bamako

Official language: French

Currency: CFA franc (CFAf) = 100 centimes (Communauté Financière Africaine (African Financial Community) franc). New notes have been issued; old notes cease to be legal tender from Jan 2005.

Exchange rate: CFAf544.07 per US$ (Oct 2005); CFAf655.95 per euro (pegged from Jan 1999)

GDP per capita: US$404 (2004)

GDP real growth: 2.20% (2004)

Labour force: 5.75 million (2004)

Inflation: -3.10% (2004)

Balance of trade: US$50.00 million (2003)

The core of ancient empires going back to the fourth century, Mali was conquered by the French in the middle of the 19th century. In 1958 it was proclaimed the Sudanese Republic and the following year it became the Mali Federation, after uniting with Senegal. However, Senegal seceded and Mali became independent in 1960.

In 1985 Mali fought a brief border war with Burkina Faso, and relations continue to be strained. In the early 1990s the army was sent to the north to quell a rebellion by Tuareg tribes over land, cultural and linguistic rights. Mali remains relatively peaceful.

The International Monetary Fund (IMF) in December 2005 granted Mali 100 per cent relief on US$108 million it owed to the Fund at the beginning of the year. This, said the IMF, was because of its overall satisfactory recent macroeconomic performance, progress in poverty reduction, and improved public expenditure management. Mali has continued to implement sound macroeconomic policies and maintain macroeconomic stability.

The relief will substantially reduce the risk of debt distress over the medium term. In view of the country's continued vulnerability to shocks and substantial external financing needs, preserving debt sustainability will require limiting new borrowing to highly concessional loans.

Economy

The outlook for 2006 and for the medium term is encouraging. Agricultural production, particularly cereals, should rebound following adequate rainfall, resulting in a reversal of recent inflation. The terms of trade have begun to improve, notably with respect to gold prices. Mali has told the IMF it remains fully committed to completing the privatisation of its textile development company by 2008 and attaches high priority to financial sector reforms.

To sustain growth at an average of approximately six per cent per annum over the medium term, Mali will focus its policies and reforms on improving efficiency and competitiveness, particularly through structural reforms in the cotton and banking sectors and the strengthening of public finances and public institutions. The current account deficit is expected to narrow as the terms of trade gradually improve and gold exports increase as a result of the opening of new mines.

Projected gross financing from external grants and loans will increase substantially in 2006, largely on account of a shift toward sectoral budget support (1.6 per cent of GDP). Total aid support is projected to reach 11.1 per cent of GDP, including the equivalent of 2.8 per cent of GDP in general budget support linked to implementation of the economic reform programme.

A revised timetable for reform of the cotton sector, postponing privatisation until 2008, has been approved. The issues centre on whether to sell assets by zoning or equity in new subsidiary companies, creating a regulatory framework, and strengthening the role of cotton producers in downstream activities. By end-September 2006, a detailed technical operational plan for privatisation will be ready.

The privatisation of other non-financial sector companies is proceeding, albeit with some technical delays: in June 2005, the sale of the bulk of the government's shares in its cottonseed mill was finalised.

Restructuring of the electricity sector will see the government taking a controlling stake, but Mali remains committed to private management of the company and by May 2006 there will be a management audit, an assessment of the financial situation, and a review of the pricing mechanism.

Mali is among the poorest countries in the world, with 65 per cent of its land area desert or semi-desert. Economic activity is largely confined to the riverine area irrigated by the Niger. About 10 per cent of the population is nomadic and some 80 per cent of the labour force is engaged in farming and fishing. Industrial activity is concentrated on processing farm commodities. Mali is heavily dependent on foreign aid and vulnerable to fluctuations in world prices for cotton, its main export, along with gold. Worker remittances and external trade routes for the landlocked country have been jeopardised by continued unrest in neighbouring Côte d'Ivoire.

Politics

Amadou Toumani Touré, the army general credited with rescuing Mali from military dictatorship and handing it back to its people, won presidential elections in May 2002.

Touré first came to power in 1991, overthrowing military ruler Moussa Traoré after his security forces killed over 100 pro-democracy demonstrators. He gained widespread respect, and the nickname 'soldier of democracy', for handing power to elected civilians the next year. Born in 1948, Touré belongs to no official party but went into the first round of the elections with the backing of numerous support groups and 22 minor parties.

Risk assessment

Economic	Poor
Political	Satisfactory
Regional stability	Deteriorating

COUNTRY PROFILE

Historical profile

Mali takes it name from one of the ancient empires of West Africa. The earliest of these was the empire of Ghana, which reached its height in the tenth century. It was succeeded by the empire of Mali in the thirteenth century. In the nineteenth century, the whole area gradually fell under the influence of the French who had established their first fort in the Upper Volta in 1792. The French conquest of the country was achieved by 1892 when it became the colony of Upper Senegal and Niger (later to be called French Soudan). Mali was given regional autonomy as the Soudan Republic in November 1958 and became independent in 1960.

900 Modern-day Mali was part of the empire of Ghana.
1250s Sundiata Keita, leader of the Mandinka people, established the Empire of Mali, which stretched from the Atlantic to the present-day borders of Nigeria and controlled most trans-Sahara trading routes by the fourteenth century.
1464 The Songhai Empire, centred around Gao, overwhelmed the Mali Empire and began to conquer the Sahel.
1591 After a Moroccan invasion, the Songhai Empire collapsed.
1890s Mali became a French colony.
1960 Mali gained independence from France as part of the Federation of Mali, which was dissolved a few weeks later when Senegal broke away. The Republic of Mali was established and Modibo Keita became the country's first president.
1968 Keita was overthrown by a military coup, led by Moussa Traoré, who became president.
1977 Protests erupted following Keita's death in prison.
1979 A new constitution provided for elections in which Traoré was elected as president.
1985 A border war erupted between Mali and Burkina Faso, but was ended after intervention by other African states.
1991 Following pro-democracy demonstrations, Traoré was deposed by a military coup. A 25-member military/civilian Transitional People's Salvation Committee came to power, led by Lieutenant Colonel Amadou Toumani Touré.
1992 Touré resigned and did not stand in the elections he organised. Alpha Oumar Konaré was democratically elected president.

KEY INDICATORS — Mali

	Unit	2000	2001	2002	2003	2004
Population	m	11.22	11.30	11.57	11.68	11.79
Gross domestic product (GDP)	US$bn	2.50	2.60	3.20	3.69	*4.86
GDP per capita	US$	223	230	276	316	404
GDP real growth	%	4.6	1.4	9.6	5.6	2.2
Inflation	%	-0.7	5.2	4.9	-0.8	-3.1
Exports (fob) (goods)	US$m	518.0	739.0	766.0	680.0	–
Imports (fob) (goods)	US$m	909.0	952.0	429.0	630.0	–
Balance of trade	US$m	-391.0	-213.0	337.0	50.0	–
Current account	US$m	-270.0	-310.0	-100.0	-210.0	-230.0
Total reserves minus gold	US$m	381.3	348.9	594.5	908.7	1,040.7
Foreign exchange	US$m	369.7	337.4	582.4	894.6	1,026.2
Exchange rate	per US$	711.98	733.04	696.99	574.89	496.63

* estimated figure

1995 A peace agreement with Tuareg rebels led to the return of thousands of refugees from neighbouring African states.
1997 President Konaré was re-elected..
1999 Traoré was sentenced to death for corruption, but his sentence was commuted to life imprisonment by Konaré, who announced that he would not contest the next presidential election
2000 Mande Sidibe, a former IMF official, was appointed prime minister.
2001 Konaré announced the indefinite postponement of a constitutional referendum which proposed granting him immunity from prosecution.
2002 Amadou Toumani Touré won the run-off presidential election and named Ahmed Mohamed Ag Hamani as prime minister. The Constitutional Court reversed the outcome of the parliamentary elections. The government resigned without public explanation and a new government of national reconciliation took over.
2003 In March, the IMF announced that Mali was to benefit from debt relief amounting to approximately US$675 million under the enhanced Heavily Indebted Poor Countries (HIPC) initiative.
2004 On 28 April, Prime Minister Hamani and his government resigned. Ousmane Issoufi Maïga was appointed prime minister.

Political structure
Constitution
A referendum held in January 1992 approved a constitution establishing multi-party rule.

A two-round voting system for electing parliamentarians was established.

In 1997, a new electoral code introduced an Independent National Electoral Commission (CENI) comprising 34 members: 10 representatives of government services, 10 from civil society and 14 from the political parties (seven from the opposition and seven from the parliamentary majority).

Other changes included the authorisation of independent candidacies, the reduction in the number of voters per polling station to 700 and an increase in the number of deputies in the National Assembly from 116 to 147. The principle of sponsoring presidential candidates was ended, and correspondence or proxy voting and eligibility for other African nationals were annulled.

Administratively, Mali is divided into eight regions and the capital district of Bamako, each under the authority of an appointed governor.

Form of state
Republic

The executive
The directly-elected president serves a five-year term, with a limit of two terms. The president is head of state and commander-in-chief of the armed forces. The president appoints the prime minister and chairs the Council of Ministers.

National legislature
Mali has a 147-member National Assembly with a five-year term. Election is direct and by party list. The head of government is the prime minister.

Legal system
The legal system is based on the French civil law system and customary law. There is judicial review of legislative acts in the Constitutional Court, which was formally established on 9 March 1994.

Last elections
28 April/12 May 2002 (presidential); 14/28 July 2002 (legislative).
Results: Presidential: Amadou Toumani Touré 64.4 per cent of the vote, Soumaila Cisse 35.6 per cent.
Parliamentary: the Alliance for Democracy in Mali won 57 seats and the Hope 2002 coalition 37 seats; turnout was 25.7 per cent.

The Constitutional Court later reversed the outcome of the parliamentary elections, giving the Espoir 2002 coalition 66 of the 147 seats, compared to 51 for the Alliance for Democracy in Mali.

The government resigned without public explanation and a new Government of National Unity took over.

Next elections
2007 (presidential and parliamentary)

Political parties
Ruling party
Espoir 2002 (Hope 2002) Coalition: Rassemblement pour le Mali (Rally for Mali), Congres Nationale pour la Initiative Démocratie (National Congress for Democratic Initiative)

Main opposition party
Alliance pour la Démocratie en Mali-Parti Pan-Africain pour la Liberté, la Solidarité et la Justice (ADEMA) (Alliance for Democracy in Mali)

Population
11.79 million (2004)
Ethnic make-up
Mande (50 per cent), Peul (17 per cent), Voltaic (12 per cent).
Religions
Muslim (90 per cent), indigenous beliefs (9 per cent), Christian (1 per cent).

Education
Primary schooling is divided into two stages, with the first and compulsory stage lasting until aged 13, followed by three years of basic education. At age 16 students may follow either an academic path in a general secondary school, for three years, or specialised education through a technical secondary school, for either two or three years. Four year vocational courses are also available.

Mali has one of the highest pupil-teacher ratio in the world, with an average of around 80 pupils per teacher.
Literacy rate: 27.2 per cent total, 17.3 per cent female, adult rates (World Bank).
Compulsory years: Seven to 13
Enrolment rate: 29 per cent net primary enrolment (Unicef)
Pupils per teacher: 80 in primary schools.

Health
Total expenditure on health is about 4.5 per cent of GDP, of which government spending is 40 per cent and foreign spending is about 20 per cent.

Improved water sources and sanitation facilities are available to 65 per cent and 30 per cent of the population respectively. In August 2004 epidemiologists of the Global Polio Eradication Initiative announced that new cases of polio had been confirmed in Mali. The infection is believed to have spread from Northern Nigeria.

HIV/Aids
There are an estimated 100,000 people living with HIV/Aids in Mali – 5,000 are under the age of 15. Mali has so far escaped much of the African pandemic. The African Development Fund (ADF) provided US$12.1 million for a programme to reduce the prevalence rate from 1.9 per cent in 2003 to 1 per cent by 2008. The money will be used to improved testing for the disease, antiretroviral drugs and training medical and research workers to monitor and manage the pandemic.
HIV prevalence: 1.9 per cent aged 15–49 in 2003 (World Bank)
Life expectancy: 40.6 years (World Bank)
Fertility rate/Maternal mortality rate: 6.4 births per woman (World Bank)
Infant mortality rate: 122 per 1,000 live births; 25 per cent of children aged under five are malnourished (World Bank).
Head of population per physician/bed: 1 doctor and two hospital beds per 10,000 people (World Bank 2002).

Welfare
In the mid-1990s, it was estimated that 72.8 per cent of the population lived on less than US$1 per day and over 90 per cent lived on less than US$2 per day. The distribution of wealth in Mali is highly unequal and the highest 10 per cent of the population owns 56.2 per cent of the wealth.

In over 70 districts in Mali, one million people were affected by swarms of locust and suffered acute food shortages. Emergency food aid was provided from reserves while government officials estimated over 440,000 tonnes of the 2004 harvest to have been destroyed.

Main cities
Bamako (capital and main business centre, estimated population 935,400 in 2003); Sikasso (125,500); Mopti (112,700).

Languages spoken
Tamazight (the Berber language) is recognised as a national language. Tamazight belongs to the Afro-Asiatic family and is related to ancient Egyptian and Ethiopian. Arabic, Bambara, Fulani, Senoufo and Dogon are commonly spoken. Very little English is spoken.

Official language/s
French

Media
Press
Dailies: Dailies include *L'Essor*, *Info-Matin*, *Le Soir de Bamako* and *Sud-info*.
Weeklies: Eighteen opposition parties launched a weekly paper, *La Voix de l'Opposition* in 1998. Other weeklies published from Bamako include *Aurore*, *Carcan*, *Carrefour*, *Les Echos*, *Independent*, *Scorpion*, *Le Malien Magazine*, *Soudanais*, *Tambour*, *Temps* and *Le Zenith*.
Periodicals: Periodicals include the bi-monthly *Cauris* and *Courrier* (irregular).

Economy
Mali is one of the world's poorest countries and is heavily dependent on foreign aid. Before 1991, the Soviet Union was the country's main source of aid. Since then, the country has looked increasingly toward international financial institutions (IFIs). China has taken an increasingly important role in infrastructural projects and joint venture companies.

The economy is vulnerable to price fluctuations in the world price of cotton, its main export. In co-operation with the IMF, the government has implemented various structural adjustment programmes to diversify the economy and the country's export markets. Gold mining has attracted an increasing number of foreign investors. Under the auspices of the IFIs, the Malian authorities continue to reduce budget deficits, cut the operating losses of state enterprises and liberalise the economy.

Mali's economy is susceptible to climatic change and is reliant on the economic state of neighbouring countries. Although Mali saw strong growth of 9.6 per cent in 2002, this dropped to 5.6 per cent in 2003, due to political and economic instability in neighbouring Côte d'Ivoire. Subsequently, poor rainfall and locust attacks have contributed to further decline to 2.2 per cent in 2004. A recovery to 6 per cent growth is forecast for 2005, encouraged by non-cotton agriculture and gold.

External trade
A significant amount of foreign trade goes unrecorded. The large current account deficit is partly funded by workers' remittances and official transfers.

On 31 December 2002, the US approved Mali as being eligible for tariff preferences under the African Growth and Opportunities Act (AGOA). The legislation requires that countries are only eligible for greater access to US markets provided they have made continued progress toward a market-based economy, the rule of law, free trade, poverty reduction and the protection of workers' rights. This process is reviewed annually.

Imports
Principal imports are petroleum products, machinery and equipment, construction materials, foodstuffs and textiles.
Main sources: France (15.4 per cent total, 2004), Senegal (7.2 per cent), Côte d'Ivoire (6.6 per cent), Germany (4.1 per cent)

Exports
The main exports are cotton, gold and livestock.
Main destinations: China (32 per cent total, 2004), India (10.3 per cent), Italy (7.6 per cent), Bangladesh (6.8 per cent), Thailand (5.9 per cent), Germany (5.2 per cent), Taiwan (4.0 per cent)

Agriculture
Farming
Agriculture is the mainstay of the economy, contributing around 35 per cent of GDP, employing 73 per cent of the workforce (largely at subsistence levels) and accounting for about 45 per cent of agricultural exports. Only about 2 per cent of the total land area is cultivated, but approximately 20 per cent of the total land area along the Niger River is suitable for cultivation, with the most productive areas lying between Bamako and Mopti. Principal food crops are millet, sorghum, paddy rice, maize and groundnuts. Supported by foreign aid, the government has co-ordinated a programme to expand production of rice as a staple food. There is a regular food deficit due to recurrent drought, crop smuggling and an inefficient marketing and distribution system. The main export crops are cotton, groundnuts, cereals, fresh fruit and vegetables. Mali is Africa's second-largest cotton producer. Livestock exports have experienced growth in recent years following the abolition of export taxes on livestock. The livestock sector is a mainstay of the economy in the northern half of the country and contributes 20 per cent to GDP. Recent desertification caused by deforestation and global warming has shifted herding activity southwards.

In 2004, the worst locust plague for 15 years attacked crops across much of west Africa and the Sahel region of southern Sahara. The UN has organised a nine-country response group with Morocco and Algeria sending aid of vehicles and pesticide but, a year after the warning was first given, it has been estimated that only 3 per cent of the 4.3 million hectares that required spraying has been treated. Mauritania is the hatching ground for the largest swarms although the insects are breeding elsewhere in the region. In Mali, the damage caused by locust swarms, together with poor rainfall, decimated livestock herds in 2004.

Crop production in 2004 included: 2,728,274 tonnes (t) cereals in total, 7,000t wheat, *365,174t maize, 24,200t cassava, 74,500t sweet potatoes, *650,000t sorghum, 877,000t rice, 113,300t pulses, 146,437t roots and tubers, 50,000t tomatoes, 100,340t oilcrops, 1,004t tobacco, 350,000t sugar cane, 239,499t cotton lint, 47,800t yams, *815,000t millet, 32,000t fruit in total, 333,000t vegetables in total. Livestock production included: 247,417t meat in total, 97,760t beef, 2,176t pig meat, 36,000t lamb, 18,000t game meat, 48,454t goat meat, 34,800t poultry, *9,900t eggs, 601,770t milk, 300t honey, 15,040t cattle hides, 8,352t sheepskins, 7,552t camel meat
* estimate

Fishing
Fishing is an important livelihood along the Niger River. The annual fish catch is around 100,000 tonnes.

Inland fisheries have been targeted for development as part of the national poverty reduction strategy. Fish processing and packaging centres and 10,000ha fish ponds plus supporting developments are among the undertakings. A US$22 million package of support was provided in October 2004 by the African Development Bank.

Forestry
The estimated production of timber for 2004 included: 5.4 million cubic metres (mcum) roundwood, 12,800cum sawnwood, 3,900cum sawlogs and veneers, 4.9 million cum woodfuel, 109,796mt charcoal.

Industry and manufacturing
The industrial sector is growing, contributing around 26 per cent to GDP in 2004. Manufacturing is concerned mainly with agricultural processing for domestic consumption and export. Other industries include soft drinks, textiles, soaps, plastics, cigarettes, cement, bricks and agricultural tools and equipment. Activity is concentrated in Bamako.

Around 90 per cent of production is accounted for by state enterprises, although rationalisation and privatisation plans are likely to continue.

Tourism
Toursim is an increasingly important sector of the economy, third only to gold and cotton. It is expected to contribute 3.5 per cent to GDP in 2005. Around 200,000 visitors arrive each year. Infrastructure is being expanded to cater for the industry.

Mining
The mining sector typically contributes around 10 per cent to GDP and employs 0.5 per cent of the workforce. Gold is Mali's principal mineral resource and since the late 1990s has replaced cottojn and livestock as the country's largest export earner.

Following the introduction of new mining laws in 1991, which helped expand gold production, Mali has become Africa's third largest gold producer after Ghana and South Africa. Total gold reserves are estimated at up to 700 tonnes and geologists claim there is potential for further discoveries. However, commercial exploitation is hampered by the lack of adequate physical infrastructure. Gold represents 80 per cent of the country's total mineral production.

The first privately owned gold mine was opened by BHP-Utah at Syama in 1990, but following operational difficulties it was sold to Randgold of South Africa in 1996. The mine underwent an investment programme and production peaked at 6.1 tonnes in 1999. However, in January 2001, Randgold decided to mothball Syama after extensive flooding led to financial losses.

Opened in 1997, the Sadiola Hill open-cast mine, owned by AngloGold, IAMGold and the Mali government, has estimated reserves of around 130 tonnes. With average annual production estimated at around 10 tonnes per annum until 2010, it is the second largest gold mine in Africa and one of the biggest and lowest cost gold mines in the world.

The Yatela gold mine – owned jointly by AngloGold (40 per cent), IAMGold (40 per cent) and the Mali government (20 per cent) – lies 35km to the north of Sadiola, and was officially opened in September 2002. It has reserves of over 72 tonnes with estimated average annual production of 6 tonnes over a period of 12 years. In 2002, it produced 6.8 tonnes of gold.

The Morila gold mine, opened in early 2001, is forecast to produce an average of 10 tonnes per year over a period of 14 years and is jointly owned by Rangold (40 per cent), AngloGold (40 per cent) and the Mali government (20 per cent). In 2002, Morila produced 15.2 tonnes of gold. Feasibility studies are being conducted on the re-opening of the Kalana gold mine which could produce an estimated 430kg per annum. There are also large unexploited deposits at Kodieran (43 tonnes), Loulo (30.1 tonnes), Segala (15.4 tonnes) and Tabakto (1 tonne). Artisanal gold mining has been practised in Mali for around 1,000 years and represents 0.6 per cent of GDP and employs around 150,000 seasonal workers. Much of this kind of mining is performed without permits and is generally dangerous. Phosphate production is around 10,000 tonnes per annum. Small quantities of salt, limestone and uranium are also mined. There are known deposits of bauxite, manganese, iron and tin, and prospecting for lithium, diamonds and copper is under way. Lack of adequate infrastructure has deterred commercial exploitation.

Hydrocarbons
There are no known oil or gas resources in Mali. Petroleum products are imported from the SIR refinery at Abidjan, Cote d'Ivoire, and the SAR refinery at Dakar, Senegal. Typically 4,000 barrels per day (bpd) of refined oil are imported. Mali has no refining capacity.

Energy
Mali is reliant on imported petroleum, although sufficient electricity is produced to meet local demand. Bamako is supplied with hydroelectric power from the dam at Selingué. Most other towns rely on diesel generators.

The Manantali dam in south-west Mali began producing hydroelectricity in 2002, 13 years after it was completed.

Financial markets
Stock exchange
Malian shares are listed on the regional stock exchange (bourse) which opened in Abidjan, Côte d'Ivoire, in 1998. The exchange also lists shares from companies registered in Benin, Burkina Faso, Côte d'Ivoire, Niger, Senegal and Togo. The seven members of the bourse are also members of the Economic and Monetary Union of West Africa (UEMOA) as well as being members of the Economic Community of West African States (Ecowas).

Banking and insurance
Mali has an undeveloped banking sector with just nine banks and two financial institutions. Three of the banks are majority owned by the state while the state owns a minority share in three others. There are three privately owned banks. In recent years, the sector has undergone liberalisation.

Central bank
Banque Centrale du Mali

Main financial centre
Bamako

Time
GMT

Geography
Mali is a landlocked country in West Africa, with Algeria to the north, Mauritania and Senegal to the west, Guinea and Côte d'Ivoire to the south, and Burkina Faso and Niger to the east.

Climate
There is considerable variation between southern, central and northern areas, rain being rare and sporadic in the far north, Sahara region. Bamako's rainy season runs from June to October with humidity reaching 80 per cent and temperatures ranging from 20 degrees Centigrade (C) to 36 degrees C. The warm, dry season runs from November to February followed by a hot, dry season between February and May with average temperatures of 35 degrees C.

Entry requirements
Passports
Required by all. Passport must be valid six months from date of entry.

Visa
Required by all except citizens of Ecowas countries. For further details and exceptions visit www.maliembassy-usa.org/. Business visas also require a covering company letter declaring the purpose of the trip and proof of return/onward passage.

Currency advice/regulations
No restrictions on import/export of local currency. Unlimited import of foreign currency but it must be declared. Foreign currency up to equivalent of CFAf250,000 in bank notes can be exported.

Health (for visitors)
Mandatory precautions
Yellow fever vaccination certificate is required by all.

Advisable precautions
Typhoid, tetanus, hepatitis A and polio vaccinations are recommended. Malaria prophylaxis should be taken as risk exists throughout country. There is a rabies risk. Water precautions must be taken.

Hotels
There are only a few good hotels available and these can be expensive.

Credit cards
Only accepted in main hotels.

Public holidays
Fixed dates
1 Jan (New Year's Day), 20 Jan (Armed Forces Day), 26 Mar (Day of Democracy), 1 May (Labour Day), 25 May (Africa Day),

22 Sep (Independence Day), 25 Dec (Christmas Day).
Variable dates
Easter Monday, Eid al Adha, Birth of the Prophet, Eid al Fitr.
The Islamic year contains 354 or 355 days, with the result that Muslim feasts advance by 10–12 days against the Gregorian calendar. Dates of feasts vary according to the sighting of the new moon, so cannot be forecast exactly.

Working hours
Banking
Mon–Thu: 0730–1200, 1315–1500. Fri: 0730–1230.
Business
Mon–Thu: 0730–1230, 1300–1600. Fri: 0730–1230, 1430–1730.
Government
(Mon–Thu, Sat) 0730–1430, Fri: 0730–1230.

Electricity supply
220V AC, 50 cycles.

Getting there
Air
National airline: Air Mali.
International airport/s: Bamako (BKO), 15km from city.
Airport tax: CFAf2,500 is payable on domestic flights; CFAf8,000 on international flights within Africa; and CFAf10,000 is payable for flights outside Africa. The airport tax may be collected at time of ticket sale and does not apply to transit passengers on the same flight and for children under two years.
Surface
Road: Good road from Niger (Niamey); condition of routes from Côte d'Ivoire and Burkina Faso varies; those from Senegal and Algeria are not generally recommended.
Rail: A regular twice weekly rail service from Senegal (Dakar) to Bamako (with sleeping and restaurant cars and facility for conveying vehicles). Journey takes up to 29 hours.
Main port/s: River ports of Bamako, Mopti, Tombouctou and Gao on the Niger.

Getting about
National transport
Air: There are no scheduled services between Bamako and other towns. Charter of light aircraft available from Société des Transports Aériens (STA). Tombouctou Air Service provides domestic flights.
Road: Main roads run from Sikasso and Bougouni in the south to Bamako, and from Bamako to Mopti and on to Gao via a new tarred road. Condition of roads are variable and secondary roads can be difficult.
Buses: Cheap but generally uncomfortable. Services run from Bamako to all main towns.
Rail: Main routes: Bamako-Koulikoro (59 km) leaves Bamako daily at 1100 and 1700; Bamako-Kayes (494km) leaves Bamako daily at 0945. There are two classes: sleeping and restaurant facilities. Some air-conditioned cars are available.
Water: Three river steamers operate up and down the River Niger betwen August and late December, linking Koulikoro, Mopti, Tombouctou and Gao. Four classes are available, but first-class cabins must be booked in advance through SMERT, the tourist organisation.
City transport
Taxis: Cheap and widely available but not metered. Official standard fare system in Bamako. Tipping is not usual.
Car hire
International driving licence recommended. Hired cars are usually Renaults or Peugeots.

BUSINESS DIRECTORY

Telephone area codes
The international dialling code (IDD) for Mali is +223, followed by subscriber's number.

Useful telephone numbers
Police: 17
Fire: 18
Ambulance: 225-002

Chambers of Commerce
Mali Chamber of Commerce and Industry, Place de la Liberté, BP 46, Bamako (tel: 222-9645; fax: 222-2120; e-mail: ccim@cefip.com).

Banking
Bank of Africa Mali, BP 2249, 418 Avenue de la Marne, Bamako (tel: 224-672, 224-088; fax: 224-653).

Banque Commerciale du Sahel; BP 2372, 127 Rue, Bozola, Bamako (tel: 210-195/97, 225-536; fax: 225-543).

Banque de Développement du Mali, BP 94, Ave Modibo Keita, Quartier du Fleuve, Bamako (tel: 222-050, 224-088; fax: 225-085, 224-250).

Banque de l'Habitat du Mali, BP 2614, Rue de Métal Soudan, Quartier du Fleuve, Bamako (tel: 229-190; fax: 229-350).

Banque Internationale du Mali; BP 15, Blvd de l'Indépendance, Bamako (tel: 225-111, 225-066; fax: 224-566).

Banque Internationale pour le Commerce et l'Industrie du Mali; BP B72, Bd du Peuple, Immeuble Nimagala, Bamako (tel: 233-370; fax: 233-373).

Banque Malienne de Crédit et de Dépôts, BP 45, Avenue Modibo Keïta, Bamako (tel: 225-336; fax: 227-950).

Banque Nationale de Développement Agricole - Mali; BP 2424, Immeuble Dette Publique, Bamako (tel: 226-464, 226-611 fax: 222-961).

Ecobank-Mali; BP 1272, Quartier du Fleuve, Place de la Nation, Bamako (tel: 233-300; fax: 233-305).

Central bank
Banque Centrale des Etats de l'Afrique de l'Ouest, Direction Nationale, PO Box 206, Avenue Moussa Travele, Bamako (tel: 222-3756; fax: 222-4786).

Travel information
Air Mali, Immeuble Scif, Square Lumumba, BP 27, Bamako (tel: 225-741/42; fax: 222-349).

Commissariat au Tourisme, BP 191, Bamako (tel: 225-673).

Delta Voyages SA, Immeuble Gamby (ex BNDA), BP 5005, Bamako (fax: 231-272).

Timbuctours, BP 222, Bamako (tel: 225-315).

Ministry of tourism
Ministry of Crafts Industry and Tourism, BP 2211, Bamako (tel: 223-6344, 223-6450; fax: 223-8201).

Ministries
Ministry of Foreign Affairs, Bamako (fax: 230-327, 225-226).

Ministry of Public Works and Transport, BP 17759, Rue 214 Hippodrome, Bamako (tel: 222-901; fax: 220-874; e-mail: ssimpara@cefib.com).

Ministry of Rural Development and Water, Bamako.

Other useful addresses
Direction Nationale du Plan et de la Statistique, Koulouba, Bamako (tel: 222-753).

Direction Nationale de la Sécurité des Services de l'Immigration, Avenue de la Nation, Bamako.

Radiodiffusion-Télévision Malienne, BP 171, Bamako (tel: 222-474).

Mali Embassy (USA), 2130 R Street, NW, Washington DC 20009 (tel: 202-332-2249; fax: 202-332-6603; e-mail: info@maliembassy-usa.org).

Internet sites
Africa Business Network: http://www.ifc.org/abn

African Development Bank: http://www.afdb.org

AllAfrica.com: http://www.allafrica.com

Africa Online: http://www.africaonline.com

Malta

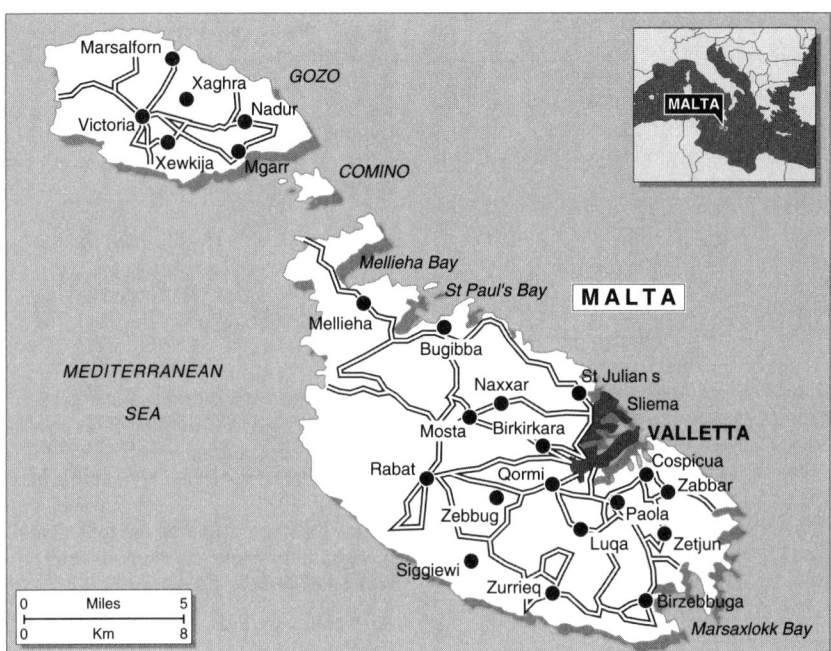

KEY FACTS

Official name: Republic of Malta

Head of State: President Eddie Fenech Adami (from 4 Apr 2004)

Head of government: Prime Minister Lawrence Gonzi (sworn in 23 Mar 2004)

Ruling party: Partit Nazzionalista (PN) (Nationalist Party) (elected Sep 1998; re-elected 12 Apr 2003)

Area: 316 square km

Population: 396,329 (2004)

Capital: Valletta

Official language: Malti and English

Currency: - (Lm) = 100 cents

Exchange rate: Lm0.36 per US$ (Oct 2005)

GDP per capita: US$13,734 (2004)

GDP real growth: 1.50% (2004)

Labour force: 153,000 (2004)

Unemployment: 5.70% (2004)*

Inflation: 2.70% (2004)

Balance of trade: -US$871.30 million (2004)

* estimated figure

Malta, positioned as it is between Europe (Sicily) and Africa, astride the great trade route from the eastern Mediterranean to the exit to the Atlantic at Gibraltar, has seen many rulers come and go. The Phoenicians were there around 1000 BC, the Greeks came in 736 BC, when it was named Melita. There was a period of Byzantine rule from the fourth to the ninth century, and then a long period of Arab rule when most of the population became Muslims and spoke Arabic. The Arabs were followed by the Sicilian Normans (who restored Christianity), the Angevines, Hohenstaufen and the Aragonese towards the end of the thirteenth century. Spain gave the islands to the Knights of St John who built the city of Valletta, named after Jean Parisot de la Valette. The French under Napoleon captured the islands in 1798, and the British took the islands two years later when Malta became a British protectorate, and then part of the British Empire in 1814 (as part of the Treaty of Paris); it became fully independent in 1964. It is no wonder that the Maltese are now an adaptive, tough people.

An European economy

International trade, and in particular export activities, represent Malta's economic lifeline. Measures designed to increase the competitiveness of Maltese exports and to widen the range of incentives available to the industrial investor are given priority. Malta's economy is closely interlinked with the EU, which it entered on 1 May 2004.

Since the 1990s, economic development has been led by the tourism sector, which accounted for over a quarter of GDP. The semi-conductor manufacturing sector has also become a major contributor to the Maltese economy, accounting for around three-quarters of manufacturing exports. Transport-related services, such as transshipment and ship repair, are important to the economy, although less so than ten years ago when the economy depended on ship repairing. Incentives have been introduced to attract foreign investment and to encourage offshore business and financial houses to use Malta as a base for operations in Europe and the Mediterranean.

In per capita terms, Malta is one of the most affluent EU members, although it is the smallest.

The narrow range of foreign exchange earning sectors and the small domestic market make Malta vulnerable to external shocks.

A key requirement for Malta to be able to adopt the euro by 2008 (it entered the exchange rate mechanism (ERM II) in May 2005) is the reduction of the budget deficit from 6.3 per cent of GDP in 2003 to below 3 per cent of GDP by 2006. Despite crackdowns, tax evasion still contributes to loss in government revenues. The government must also reduce the size of the public sector and labour costs, which remain high, compared to the general level of productivity.

The Maltese economy is heavily dependent on tourism, which is expected to contribute around 32 per cent to GDP in 2005. The impact of the 2001 terrorist attacks in the US, compounded by the Iraq War and the Sars outbreak in 2003, resulted in a decline in visitor numbers, but there were signs of recovery in 2004. The UK is the main market and continues to show growth, although this has been offset by falling numbers from the next most important sources of visitors, Germany, Italy and France. Niche tourism, in particular diving, English-language learning and conferences, is being developed. The majority of tourists arrive by air, but cruise ship visits have risen and a terminal is under construction to foster this trend.

Risk assessment

Economy	Fair
Politics	Fair
Regional stability	Good

COUNTRY PROFILE

Historical profile
1814 Malta became a crown colony of the UK, with limited self-government.
1942 The islanders were awarded the George Cross for heroism during a three-year siege and severe bombing by Germans and Italians in the Second World War.
1947 Malta was granted full internal self-government.
1956 In a referendum, a majority voted in favour of integration with the UK as proposed by the Partit Laburista (PL) (Labour Party) under Dominic Mintoff.
1959–62 Disturbances followed the rejection of Mintoff's integration proposals by the British, leading to his resignation. The British reinstated direct rule.
1964 Malta was granted full independence within the Commonwealth, reinforced by defence and aid treaties with UK.
1971 A Labour government was elected under Mintoff, who signed co-operative treaties with Eastern and Western countries and established close relations with Libya.
1974 Malta declared itself a republic.
1981 The PL gained more seats but fewer votes than the Partit Nazzionalista (PN) (Nationalist Party), which mounted a campaign of civil disobedience and boycotted the House of Representatives for over a year.
1987 The PN, under Eddie Fenech Adami, came to power following constitutional amendments. The government's aim was to maintain non-aligned status, while seeking closer ties with the West.
1990 Malta applied to join the EU.
1996 The EU application was frozen by Alfred Sant when he took office as prime minister in the new PL government.
1998 Prime Minister Eddie Fenech Adami renewed the island's application to join the EU after the PN was returned to power in early elections.
2000 At the EU summit in Nice, Malta was placed in the first wave of accession candidates.
2002 An independent survey revealed that over 60 per cent of Maltese were happy with the government's actions to prepare the country for EU membership.
2003 A March referendum produced a 53.6 per cent vote in favour of EU membership in a turnout of 91 per cent. The ruling PN won the parliamentary elections.
2004 On 23 March, Prime Minister Eddie Fenech Adami stepped down and Lawrence Gonzi was sworn in as prime minister. On 4 April, Eddie Fenech Adami took office as president. Malta entered the EU on 1 May.
2005 The Maltese parliament ratified the European constitution in a unanimous vote on 6 July.

Political structure
Constitution
The independence constitution of 1964 was amended on 13 December 1974, to provide for the creation of the office of president to replace that of governor general.
Form of state
Parliamentary democratic republic; it is a member of the Commonwealth.
The executive
The House of Representatives elects the president as constitutional head of state for a five-year term. The president appoints the prime minister and, on the latter's advice, the cabinet, which holds executive power.
National legislature
Legislative power is vested in the unicameral House of Representatives (65 members elected for five years by universal adult suffrage on a plurality basis). Should a party polling a majority of votes fail to gain a majority of seats in the House, extra seats are allocated until a majority of one seat is achieved.
Legal system
The judiciary is independent. Public law is based on English common law.
Last elections
12 June 2004 (European Parliament); 4 April 2004 (presidential, by House of

KEY INDICATORS — Malta

	Unit	2000	2001	2002	2003	2004
Population	m	0.39	0.39	0.40	0.40	0.40
Gross domestic product (GDP)	US$bn	3.72	3.71	4.60	4.64	*5.39
GDP per capita	US$	9,538	9,409	11,197	11,705	13,734
GDP real growth	%	6.4	-1.2	1.2	2.8	1.5
Inflation	%	2.4	2.9	2.0	2.0	2.7
Unemployment	%	5.0	5.1	5.6	5.6	*5.7
Exports (fob) (goods)	US$m	2,475.9	2,317.0	2,500.0	2,000.0	2,688.3
Imports (fob) (goods)	US$m	3,097.6	3,157.0	3,000.0	2,800.0	3,559.6
Balance of trade	US$m	-621.7	-840.0	-500.0	-800.0	-871.3
Current account	US$m	-521.0	-193.8	-172.4	-280.0	-560.0
Total reserves minus gold	US$m	1,470.2	1,666.2	2,209.3	2,728.7	2,699.7
Foreign exchange	US$m	1,385.8	1,582.4	2,115.2	2,624.5	2,589.4
Exchange rate	per US$	0.42	0.44	0.43	0.37	0.34

* estimated figure

Malta

Representatives); 12 April 2003 (parliamentary).
Results: European Parliament: PL won 49 per cent of the vote (three seats out of five), PN 40 per cent (two) and Alternattiva Demokratika (AD) (Democratic Alternative, also known as the Green Party) 10 per cent (no seats); turnout 82.4 per cent.
Parliamentary: the ruling PN won 51 per cent of the vote and the Partit Laburista (PL) (Labour Party) 47 per cent; turnout was 97 per cent.
Next elections
2008 (parliamentary); 2009 (presidential, by House of Representatives).

Political parties
Ruling party
Partit Nazzionalista (PN) (Nationalist Party) (elected Sep 1998; re-elected 12 Apr 2003)
Main opposition party
Partit Laburista (PL) (Labour Party)

Population
396,329 (2004)
Ethnic make-up
Most Maltese are descendants of Phoenicians, with strong elements of Italian and other Mediterranean influences.
Religions
Roman Catholic (98 per cent).

Education
Primary education lasts for six years; secondary schooling lasts for five years, divided into a three-year orientation cycle and a two-year cycle of specialisation. There are two types of secondary education schools – junior Lyceums and area secondary schools; following either of these leads to a choice between academic or technical courses. Over 54 per cent of students continue with their education and training after the age of 16. Church schools are funded through the government and tuition is free.
Higher education is mainly provided by the University of Malta. The quality of education in Malta is high and attracts students from the Mediterranean and the Middle East.
Literacy rate: 92.6 per cent total; 93.4 per cent female, adult rates (World Bank).
Compulsory years: Five to 16.
Enrolment rate: 108 per cent (boys); 107 per cent (girls) gross primary enrolment of the relevant age group (including repetition rates) (World Bank).

Health
Public hospital services are adequate although there have been concerns over the long waiting times. Total bed capacity is around 2,000. An increasing number of doctors are resigning due to poor working conditions and wages. Due to the low numbers of doctors, some health centres have stopped operating on a 24-hour basis.
In 2002, a programme of refurbishment and modernisation was undertaken in all government hospitals.
HIV prevalence: 0.2 per cent aged 15–49 in 2003 (World Bank)
Life expectancy: 78.5 years (World Bank)
Fertility rate/Maternal mortality rate: 1.4 births per woman (World Bank)
Infant mortality rate: 5.0 per 1,000 live births (World Bank).

Welfare
The Maltese welfare system is poised for reform. There is a significant welfare gap in society.
The social security contribution rate paid by every Maltese employer is 10 per cent. The self-employed pay a rate of 15 per cent. In January 2002, a Care Allowance was introduced for children living in institutions. This allowance was extended to foster parents.

Main cities
Valletta (capital, estimated population 9,210), Birkirkara (21,600), Qormi (18,100), Mosta (17,900).

Languages spoken
Malti, English and some Italian; most business correspondence is in English.
Official language/s
Malti and English

Media
Press
Dailies: The major dailies include *The Malta Independent* (English), *The Times* (English), *In-Nazzjon* (Maltese), *L-orizzont* (Maltese).
Weeklies: *The Malta Independent on Sunday* (English), *The Sunday Times* (English), *Il-Mument* (Maltese), *It-Torca* (Maltese).
Business: *The Malta Business Weekly* (English, published every Thursday).
Broadcasting
Supervised by Malta Broadcasting Authority. Xandir Malta (part of TeleMalta Corp) broadcasts two radio services (Radio Malta) and a TV service (Television Malta). Private broadcasting services have been introduced following a liberalisation of media laws. Six private radio stations are already in operation. Over 20 Italian TV stations are received in Malta, and many satellite stations are available through a cable television network.
Advertising
Advertisements can be placed on radio and TV through Xandir Malta in Gwardamangia. Newspapers, periodicals, cinemas and poster sites also available.

Economy
International trade, and in particular export activities, represent Malta's economic lifeline. Measures designed to increase the competitiveness of Maltese exports and to widen the range of incentives available to the industrial investor are given priority. Malta's economy is closely interlinked with the EU, which it entered on 1 May 2004. Since the 1990s, economic development has been led by the tourism sector, which accounted for over a quarter of GDP. The semi-conductor manufacturing sector has also become a major contributor to the Maltese economy, accounting for around three-quarters of manufacturing exports. Transport-related services, such as transhipment and ship repair, are important to the economy. Incentives have been introduced to attract foreign investment and to encourage offshore business and financial houses to use Malta as a base for operations in Europe and the Mediterranean. In per capita terms, Malta is one of the most affluent EU members, although it is the smallest.
The narrow range of foreign exchange earning sectors and the small domestic market make Malta vulnerable to external shocks.
A key requirement for Malta to be able to adopt the euro by 2007 is the reduction of the budget deficit from 6.3 per cent of GDP in 2003 to below 3 per cent of GDP by 2006. Despite crackdowns, tax evasion still contributes to loss in government revenues. The government must also reduce the size of the public sector and labour costs, which remain high, compared to the general level of productivity.

External trade
Regular trade deficits are partly offset by invisible earnings, mainly from tourism and overseas investment. Germany, Italy and the UK account for around 60 per cent of total trade turnover.
Imports
Principal imports consist mainly of foodstuffs, machinery and equipment, fuels, beverages and tobacco
Exports
Major exports include copra cake, coconut oil, handicrafts and fish.
Main destinations: US, Japan, Australia, China

Agriculture
Farming
The agricultural sector accounts for around 2.5 per cent of GDP and employs less than 2 per cent of the population. Agricultural production supplies only about 20 per cent of Malta's food needs. There is a limited area of land available for agriculture and freshwater supplies are scarce. Potatoes and onions are the largest vegetable crops; potatoes are also the largest export crop. Grapes are the largest fruit crop and flower cultivation is flourishing.

Malta has decided to implement the reform of the EU Common Agricultural Policy (CAP) on 1 January 2007. The reform was introduced throughout most of the EU on 1 January 2005, when subsidies on farm output, which tended to benefit large farms and encourage overproduction, were replaced by single farm payments, not conditional on production. The change is expected to reward farmers who provide and maintain a healthy environment, food safety and animal welfare standards. The changes are also intended to encourage market conscious production and cut the cost of CAP to the EU taxpayer.

The estimated crop production for 2004 included: 11,700 tonnes (t) cereals in total, 9,500t wheat, 23,000t potatoes, 2,200t barley, 1,150t pulses, 1,000t citrus fruit, 1,240t grapes, 250t figs, 9,000t tomatoes, 6,555t fruit in total, 46,150t vegetables in total. Livestock production included: 20,288t meat in total, 1,410t beef, 9,800t pig meat, 138t lamb and goat meat, 7,547t poultry, 6,140t eggs, 46,760t milk, 1,350t rabbit.

Fishing
Around 1,000 tonnes of marine fish are landed annually, while acquaculture produces 2,000 tonnes. Around 370 people are registered as full-time fishermen, with 300 registered fishing vessels in operation. Another 1,500 boats are owned by part-time fishermen.

Forestry
Exports of forest material in 2004 amounted to US$913,000, while imports amounted to US$85 million.

Industry and manufacturing
The industrial sector contributes approximately 30 per cent to GDP and employs 35 per cent of the labour force. Manufactures include textiles, clothing, synthetic fibres, footwear, wines and beer, furniture, electronic goods, automobile components, measuring/controlling equipment and tobacco products.

Ship-repairing is an important foreign exchange earner, but the Malta Drydocks company suffered falling revenues during the 1990s as worldwide shipping activity declined. As a result, the government has decided to end subsidies to both the Malta Drydocks and Malta Shipbuilding companies by 2008.

Tourism
The Maltese economy is heavily dependent on tourism, which is expected to contribute around 32 per cent to GDP in 2005. The impact of the 2001 terrorist attacks in the US, compounded by the Iraq War and the Sars outbreak in 2003, resulted in a decline in visitor numbers, but there were signs of recovery in 2004. The UK is the main market and continues to show growth, although this has been offset by falling numbers from the next most important sources of visitors, Germany, Italy and France. Niche tourism, in particular diving, English-language learning and conferences, is being developed. The majority of tourists arrive by air, but cruise ship visits have risen and a terminal is under construction to foster this trend.

Mining
Malta has no exploitable natural resources.

Hydrocarbons
Malta does not possess any natural energy resources and all energy sources have to be imported. Malta has, over the years, built up a preferential arrangement with Libya for the import of crude petroleum. Energy-related imports account for some 7 per cent of total imports. Exploration for oil and gas has been conducted offshore for a number of years, but no commercial reserves have been identified.

Financial markets
Stock exchange
The Malta Stock Exchange (MSE) was set up in 1992 to encourage private investment in a range of commercial and government stocks. It has grown rapidly as a result of strong domestic and offshore investment interest, with total market capitalisation of over US$3.7 billion.

Banking and insurance
There are two major commercial banks – Bank of Valletta and the HSBC Bank Malta plc.
Central bank
Central Bank of Malta

Time
GMT plus one hour (GMT plus two hours from March to September).

Geography
The largest and only inhabited islands of the Maltese archipelago in southern Europe are Malta, Gozo and Comino in the central Mediterranean Sea. The main island, Malta, lies 93km (58 miles) south of the Italian island of Sicily and 290km (180 miles) north of the Libyan coast, with Tunisia to the west.

Climate
Mediterranean, with hot summers and warm winters. Temperatures range from about 29 degrees Celsius (C) down to about 10 degrees C. January and February are the coldest months, July and August the hottest. August and September tend to be hot and humid, but usually with sea breezes in evening.

Dress codes
European clothing is suitable for winter, spring and autumn; tropical weight for summer.

Entry requirements
Passports
A passport is required by all except nationals of Austria, Belgium, France, Germany, Greece, Italy, Luxembourg, Netherlands, Portugal, Spain and Switzerland for visits of up to three months.
Visa
Visa are required by all except citizens of Europe, North America, Australasia and a few Asian and other countries; for a full list visit www.foreign.gov.mt/london/hc.htm, the site also includes generic visa application forms. Only business travellers from countries that require visas, and staying for less than 91 days, need apply and should use the tourists visa form.
Currency advice/regulations
No limit on foreign currency taken in, but amount should be declared on entry, then up to this amount may be taken out. The import of local currency is limited to Lm50 and the export of local currency limited to Lm25.
Customs
Personal effects duty-free, plus duty-free allowance.

Health (for visitors)
Vaccination certificates are not required unless travelling from an infected area. Water supplies are filtered and tap water is safe to drink.

Hotels
Classified from five-star to one-star. All hotel staff speak English and many are multi-lingual.

Credit cards
All major credit cards are accepted.

Public holidays
Fixed dates
1 Jan (New Year's Day), 10 Feb (St Paul's Shipwreck), 19 Mar (St Joseph's Day), 31 Mar (Freedom Day), 1 May (Labour Day), 7 Jun (Commemoration of the 1919 Uprising), 29 Jun (Feast of St Peter and St Paul), 15 Aug (Assumption Day), 8 Sep (Our Lady of the Victories Day), 21 Sep (Independence Day), 8 Dec (Immaculate Conception), 13 Dec (Republic Day) and 25 Dec (Christmas Day).
Variable dates
Good Friday

Working hours
Banking
Mon–Fri: 0830–1230, Fri: 1700–1900, Sat: 0830–1200.
Business
Mon–Fri: 0830–1245 and 1430–1730.
Government
Mon–Fri: 0745–1230 and 1315–1715; (from Jun to Sep) 0730–1330 only.
Shops
Mon–Sat: 0900–1300 and 1600–1900.

Malta

Electricity supply
240V AC

Weights and measures
The metric system is the main one in use. Sometimes, the imperial system is also used and, on rare occasions, the old local measures.

Getting there
Air
Regular flights from most major international airports in Europe and North Africa.
National airline: Air Malta.
International airport/s: Malta (MLA) at Luqa, 5km from Valletta.
Airport tax: None
Surface
Water: There are regular car ferry services from Sicily and the Italian mainland.

Getting about
National transport
Air: Internal flights (by helicopter) operate between Malta and Gozo.
Buses: Regular bus services run from Valletta to most towns and villages on Malta and Gozo.
Water: Gozo Channel Company operates a regular round-the-clock daily ferry service between Malta and Gozo.
City transport
Metered taxis are available.
Car hire
Self-drive cars are available at daily, weekly and monthly rates with unlimited mileage and fully comprehensive insurance. A national or international driving licence is required, which must be endorsed at the Police Licensing Office, Floriana. Speed limits are 40kph in built-up areas and 64kph elsewhere. Driving is on the left.

BUSINESS DIRECTORY

The addresses listed below are a selection only. While World of Information makes every endeavour to check these addresses, we cannot guarantee that changes have not been made, especially to telephone numbers and area codes. We would welcome any corrections.

Telephone area codes
The international direct dialling (IDD) code for Malta is +356 followed by subscriber's number.

Useful telephone numbers
Police: 191
Ambulance: 196
Fire brigade: 199
Directory enquiries: 190
Overseas operator: 194
Time check: 195

Chambers of Commerce
Malta Chamber of Commerce and Enterprise, Exchange Buildings, Republic Street, Valletta VLT 05 (tel: 2123-3873; fax: 2124-5223; e-mail: admin@chamber.org.mt).

Maltese-American Chamber of Commerce, Exchange Buildings, Republic Street, Valletta VLT 05 (tel: 2124-7233; fax: 21245223; e-mail: president@malta-uschamber.com).

Banking
APS Bank ltd, 275 St Paul Street, Valletta VLT 07 (tel: 247-547; fax: 238-698).

Bank of Valletta Ltd, 58 Zachary Street, Valletta VLT 04 (tel: 243-261/7; fax: 230-894).

Bank of Valletta Group, BOV Centre, High Street, Sliema, SLM 16 (tel: 336-224; fax: 346-160; internet site: http://www.bov.com).

HSBC Bank Malta plc, 233 Republic Street, Valletta VLT 05 (tel: 485-713; fax: 489-425).

HSBC Bank Malta (Overseas) plc, 15 Republic Street, Valletta VLT 05 (tel: 249-801/4; fax: 249-805).

Investment Finance Bank Ltd, 168 Strait Street, Valletta VLT 07 (tel: 232-017, 233-349; fax: 242-014).

Lombard Bank (Malta) Ltd, Lombard House, 67 Republic Street, Valletta VLT 05 (tel: 248-411/8; fax: 246-600).

Valletta Investment Bank Ltd, 144 St Christopher Street, Valletta VLT 02 (tel: 235-246; fax: 234-419).

Central bank
Central Bank of Malta, Castille Place, Valletta CMR 01 (tel: 2550-2500; fax: 2550-2500; e-mail: info@centralbankmalta.com).

Travel information
Air Malta, Head Office, Malta International Airport, Gudja (tel: 2299-9984, 2299-9885; fax: 2299-9368; internet site: http://www.airmalta.com).

Malta International Airport Ltd, Luqa LQA 05 (tel: 249-600; fax: 243-042; internet site: http://www.maltairport.com).

National tourist organisation offices
Malta Tourism Authority, 280 Republic Street, Valletta CMR 02 (tel: 224-444, 225-048/9; fax: 220-401; e-mail: info@visitmalta.com; internet site: http://www.visitmalta.com).

Ministries
Ministry of Economic Affairs, Auberge d'Aragon, Independence Square, Valletta (tel: 239-898).

Ministry of Foreign Affairs, Palazzo Parisio, Merchants Street, Valletta (tel: 242-853).

Ministry of Finance, Maison Demandols, South Street, Valletta CMR 02 (tel: 232-646; fax: 224-667).

Other useful addresses
British High Commission, 7 St Anne St, PO Box 506, Floriana (tel: 233-134/8; fax: 622-001).

Department of Industry, St George's, Canon Road, St Venera (tel: 446-259).

Department of Information, Auberge de Castille, Valletta (tel: 225-241, 224-901; fax: 237-170).

Department of Trade, Lascaris, Valletta (tel: 224-411).

Embassy of the United States of America, PO Box 535, Valletta (tel: 23-560/5; fax: 243-229).

Hotels and Restaurants Association, 7 Frederick Street, Valletta (tel: 336-843; fax: 237-253).

Malta Broadcasting Authority, National Rd, Blata 1-Bajda (tel: 221-281).

Maltacom (telecommunications), Spencer Hill, Marsa HMR12 (postal address: PO Box 40, Qormi, QRM01) (tel: 240-000; fax: 246-369; e-mail: mcintrel@maltacom.com; internet site: http://www.maltacom.com).

Malta Development Corporation, PO Box 141, Marsa GPO 01; head office: Triq I-Industrija, Qormi (tel: 441-888; fax: 441-887; e-mail: info@mdc.com.mt; internet site: http://www.investinmalta.com).

Malta Drydocks, The Docks (tel: 822-451, 822-491; fax: 800-021).

Malta Export Trade Corporation, Trade Centre, PO Box 8, San Gwann SGN 01 (tel: 446-186/7/8; fax: 496-687; internet site: http://www.metco.com.mt/main.htm).

Malta Federation of Industry, Development House, St Anne Street, Floriana VLT 01 (tel: 222-074, 234-428; fax: 240-702).

Malta Financial Services Centre (MFSC), Attard (tel: 441-155; fax: 441-188).

Malta Freeport Corporation Ltd, Freeport Centre, Port of Matrsaxlokk, Kalafrana BBG 07 (tel: 650-200; fax: 684-814).

Malta Investment Management Co Ltd (MIMCOL), Trade Centre, San Gwann Industrial Estate, Birkirkara SGN09 (tel: 497-970; fax: 499-568).

Malta Maritime Authority, Maritime House, Lascaris Wharf, Valletta VLT 01 (tel: 250-360/4; fax: 250-365).

Malta Shipbuilding Co Ltd, Marsa (tel: 220-051, 237-297; fax: 240-930).

Malta Stock Exchange, Pope Pius V Street, Valletta VLT 11 (tel: 244-051/5; fax: 244-071).

Malta Trade Fairs Corporation, The Fair Grounds, Naxxar NXR 02 (tel: 410-371/4; fax: 414-099).

Maltese Embassy (US), 2017 Connecticut Avenue, NW, Washington DC 20008 (tel: 202-462-3611; fax: 202-387-5470; e-mail: malta_embassy@compuserve.com).

Parliamentary Secretariat for Maritime and Offshore, House of Four Winds, Valletta (tel: 241-570).

Privatisation Unit, Ministry of Finance and Economic Affairs, Trade Centre, San Gwann Industrial Estate, San Gwann SGN 09 (internet site: http://www.maltacom.com).

Sea Malta Co Ltd, Sea Malta Building, Flagstone Wharf, Marsa HMR 12 (tel: 232-230/9; fax: 225-776).

Internet sites
Malta Government: http://www.magnet.mt/

Marshall Islands

COUNTRY PROFILE

Historical profile
The Marshall Islands comprise over a thousand flat coral islands of white sand beaches and lagoons.
1788 The Marshall Islands were named after Captain John Marshall, who visited the islands on his way to China from Botany Bay.
1886 Germany established a protectorate over the Marshall Islands.
1914 The islands were captured from Germany by Japan.
1935 The Japanese transformed the islands into a military base.
1944 Allied occupation of the islands.
1945 After the end of the Second World War, control of the Marshall Islands was granted to the US.
1946 The Marshall Islands were used as a nuclear testing ground by the US.
1947 Marshall Islands became one of six entities in the Trust Territory of the Pacific Islands (TTPI) established by the UN with the US as the Trustee.
1962 The US ended nuclear testing on the islands.
1965 The Congress of Micronesia was established, with representatives from all TTPI islands.
1978 The Marshall Islands Constitutional Convention adopted the nation's first constitution.
1979 The government of the Marshall Islands was officially established and the islands became self-governing. Amata Kabua was elected president.
1982 The official title of the islands became the Republic of the Marshall Islands (RMI).
1983 Marshall Island voters approved the Compact of Free Association (CFA) with the US.
1986 The US Congress approved the CFA. The RMI was granted sovereignty, aid and US defence, in return for continued US military missile testing.
1990 The UN Security Council formally ended the trusteeship.
1991 The RMI joined the UN.
1995 President Amata Kabua was re-elected for the fourth time.
1996 Amata Kabua died on 20 December. He was succeeded by his cousin, Imata Kabua, who was.elected on 14 January 1997.
1999 The United Democratic Party (UDP) won the general election.
2000 Kessai Note (UDP) was elected president.
2001 Former inhabitants of Bikini and the Enewetak atolls were awarded over US$1 billion in compensation for hardship suffered when they were evacuated and re-settled in the 1940s to allow US nuclear tests on the islands.
2003 In April, the RMI concluded negotiations with the US on the provisions of the CFA. Parliamentary elections were held on 17 November.
2004 On 5 January, Kessai Note was re-elected as president.

Political structure
Constitution
The constitution was adopted in 1979. Under the Compact of Free Association (CFA), the Marshall Islands have control over all domestic and foreign affairs with the exception of defence which is the responsibility of the US.
There are 25 administrative divisions.
Form of state
Self-governing territory in free association with the US.
The executive
Executive power rests with the president and the cabinet. The president is both head of state and head of government, elected by parliament for a four-year term. The president appoints the cabinet from members of the Nitijela (parliament).
National legislature
The system of government is bicameral. The Nitijela has 33 members elected for a four-year term.
Each inhabited atoll is represented in the Nitijela; Majuro and Ebeye have five and three representatives respectively, being the most populated.
The 12-member Iroij (council of chiefs) serves a four-year term. The council of chiefs is composed of traditional leaders, with consultative authority on matters relating to land and custom.
Last elections
5 January 2004 (presidential); 17 November 2003 (parliamentary).
Results: Presidential: Kessai Note was re-elected with 20 votes, against nine for Justin de Brum.
Parliamentary: parliament was elected without the participation of parties, although some of the MPs may be members of the United Democratic Party (UDP).
Next elections
2007 (parliamentary); 2008 (presidential).

Political parties
Ruling party
United Democratic Party (UDP)

KEY FACTS

Official name: Republic of the Marshall Islands

Head of State: President Kessai H Note (UDP) (elected by the *Nitijela* on 10 Jan 2000; re-elected 5 Jan 2004)

Head of government: President Kessai H Note

Ruling party: United Democratic Party (UDP)

Area: 183 square km consisting of 29 atolls and 1,225 islets

Population: 56,429 (2004)

Capital: Majuro (on Majuro atoll)

Official language: Marshallese, English

Currency: US dollar (US$) = 100 cents)

GDP per capita: US$1,800 (2004)

GDP real growth: -1.50% (2004)

Inflation: 2.40% (2004)

Balance of trade: -US$45.00 million (2003)

Visitor numbers: 1,380 (2003)

Main opposition party
Aelon Kein Ar

Political situation
Negotiations over the renewal of the Compact of Free Association (CFA) were concluded in late 2003; the US president signed the bill in December 2003. The new agreement includes a halt to unmonitored adoption of RMI children by US citizens, and a limit on immigration to the US, although RMI citizens retain the right to travel to the US without a visa. The US military missile testing base on Kwahalein Atoll caused much dissension between the Marshall Islands government and the Kwahalein Negotiation Commission (KNC), a loose alliance of landowners. Rental payments were the prime motivator for the KNC. The government was already in negotiations with the US concerning CFA funds paid to the islands. Each year the US provides 55 per cent of the national government's budget and millions of dollars more are added through US federal funds, and the government had to balance the aims of both sides to channel the negotiations. An initial claim for US$2 billion was rejected by the US and later proposals resulted in a KNC alliance disintegration, leaving the government to agree to US$16.6 million rising to US$19.9 million for leases up to 2066. KNC members rejected the agreement and their supporters in parliament did not join in the CFA signing ceremony held in April 2004.

Population
56,429 (2004)
Ethnic make-up
Micronesian
Religions
Christian (mostly Protestant).

Education
Enrolment rate: 134 per cent (boys); 133 per cent (girls), gross primary enrolment of the relevant age group (including repetition rates) (Unicef).

Health
Over 80 per cent of children are immunised against measles. Total expenditure on health is around 10 per cent of GDP, of which government spending is typically 65 per cent and foreign spending 25 per cent.
Life expectancy: 69 years: male 67 years; female 71 years (2003).
Fertility rate/Maternal mortality rate: Four births per woman (2003)
Birth rate/Death rate: 34 births per 1,000 population; five deaths per 1,000 population (2003).
Infant mortality rate: 53 per 1,000 live births (World Bank)

Main cities
Majuro (capital, on Majuro atoll, Dalap-Uliga-Darrit Municipality, estimated population 20,500 in 2003), Ebeye, on Kwajalein, (11,000).

Languages spoken
There are two main Marshallese dialects from the Malayo-Polynesian family. Marshallese is used by the government. English is taught in the schools and is widely spoken. Japanese is also spoken.
Official language/s
Marshallese, English

Media
Press
The *Marshall Islands Journal* containing items in both Marshallese and English, is published every Friday.
Broadcasting
Government-owned radio broadcasts at least 18 hrs/day in English and Marshallese. TV coverage is fairly widespread, and there is some cable relay. Alele Museum Foundation television station broadcasts educational programmes; the Marshall Broadcasting Company TV station is privately owned.

Economy
Marshall Islands' largest single private sector employer and contributor to government revenues (the tuna loining plant jointly owned by Pacific Micronesia and Orient Line, the government and Star Kist) closed in August 2004, putting over 500 people, mostly women, out of work. Exports from the plant had been US$4.3 million in 2003, over half the islands' exports (excluding re-exports). The government had been guarantor of a US$2 million loan and acquired control after the closure. It has been investigating alternative interests to reopen the plant. On top of this, revenue from fishing licences fell by 47 per cent in 2004.

This double blow to the economy has been partly off-set by the new financial agreement with the US under the Compact of Free Association (CFA) which came into effect in 2004. Under the agreement the US committed to long-term financial support, allowing the Marshall Islands' government to increase allocations for recurrent and capital expenditures by 20 per cent. However, a number of government projects fell behind in 2004, principally due to departments having difficulty in adopting new procedures that were intended to improve accountability and increase value for money. Education had been allocated US$12 million (60 per cent of the annual capital budget) for four new high schools and one elementary school, but failed to complete the construction, resulting in a large carry-over of work into 2005.

Visitor arrivals fell in 2004, while on the positive side copra exports rose by 16 per cent to US$1.2 million, approximately 1 per cent of GDP. Copra is important as a cash crop for the peoples of the outer islands. Inflation was 2.4 per cent, up slightly as a result of higher fuel costs. Terms of the revised financial assistance package under the CFA cover a 20-year term (2004–23) of economic assistance to the key sectors of education, health, infrastructure and private sector development and environment protection. A large increase in capital expenditures for 2004 and 2005 was made necessary by the previous 5–6 years when the government was re-paying government bonds and saving for the Intergenerational Investment Fund (IIF).

The IIF had been set up in 1999 to provide for the time when the US would no longer be contributing to the budget. In 2002 US$14 million was set aside for the fund, and in 2003 a further US$15 million, both traunches came from the capital improvement funding provided for under the CFA, leaving the government without the necessary funds for infrastructure improvements and maintenance. The US will be contributing US$7 million a year to the IIF until 2023, and together with government contributions the Fund should be able to provide for the islanders' future.

The use of the US dollar as the country's currency acts as a partial shield to major macroeconomic fluctuations, and compliance with CFA guidelines has helped promote responsible economic policies.

KEY INDICATORS — Marshall Islands

	Unit	2000	2001	2002	2003	2004
Population	m	0.05	0.05	0.06	0.06	0.06
Gross domestic product (GDP)	US$bn	0.10	0.10	0.11	0.12	*0.11
GDP per capita	US$	1,861	1,863	1,821	1,600	1,800
GDP real growth	%	0.7	0.6	4.0	2.0	-1.5
Inflation	%	-1.9	2.0	2.0	2.5	2.4
Balance of trade	US$m	-51.0	-52.0	–	-45.0	–

* estimated figure

Marshall Islands

In June 2003, the Organisation for Economic Co-operation and Development (OECD) removed the Marshall Islands from its list of countries it monitors as being an unco-operative tax haven.
The public sector will continue driving the economy over the medium term. Over the long term, the government has the fiscal challenge of managing the adjustment to a decline in CFA funds and placing government revenues on a sustainable basis.

External trade
Goods part-manufactured in the Marshall Islands enjoy preferential access to US markets under the Compact of Free Association.
Imports
Principal imports, far outstripping exports, are foodstuffs, machinery and equipment, fuels, beverages and tobacco
Main sources: US, Japan, Australia, NZ, Singapore, Fiji, China, Philippines
Exports
Principal exports are copra cake, coconut oil, handicrafts and fish
Main destinations: US, Japan, Australia, China

Agriculture
Farming
Subsistence farming of taro, breadfruit, bananas, yams, sweet potatoes and vegetables, along with pig and poultry raising, is the main occupation. Large areas of potentially arable land remain uncultivated.
Crop production in 2004 included: 15,000 tonnes (t) coconuts and 1,950t oilcrops; livestock production is only adequate to maintain families.
Fishing
Fishing, particularly tuna, is important, supplying the principal source of protein as well as export revenues. A dozen longline tuna boats built with Asian Development Bank money almost doubled the fleet in the mid-1990s. Tuna is supplied to the country's tuna processing factory, located at Majuro.
A Hawaiian company, Black Pearl Inc, noted after extensive research the potential for breeding black pearl oysters. Some farms have opened but it will be several years before they can compete with world market leaders. Seaweed farming may offer an alternative. Typical pearl and shell harvest production is 100,000 units per annum.

Industry and manufacturing
Small-scale industries include handicrafts, fish processing, copra processing, bakeries and boat building and repairs. A tuna processing factory which opened in 1999 was a significant addition to industry. The Marshall Islands Ports Authority agreed with the Ching Fu Shipyard of Taiwan to locate a floating drydock in Majuro in 2005, which is the largest ship repair facility in the central Pacific.

Tourism
Tourism is relatively undeveloped, although there is potential for growth. Visitor numbers are negligible – less than 1,400 tourists in 2004; business visitors numbered around 2,250. In general, there was a slow but steady growth in the number of holidaymakers until 2001, peaking at 1,483, but falling to 1,380 in 2003. The main market is Japan, followed by the US.

Mining
Small mineral deposits exist, but exploitation is hampered by a shortage of land to accommodate the displaced population and doubts about economic viability. Extraction of phosphate occurs at Ailinglaplap.

Hydrocarbons
The Marshall Islands rely entirely on the import of hydrocarbons from the US and Australia. Fossil fuels make up 99 per cent of the Marshall Island's total energy production.

Banking and insurance
Growth in the Marshall Islands' banking sector is limited by the size of its population. Commercial bank lending in 2004 was some US$45 million while deposits were substantially greater at US$81 million.

Time
GMT plus twelve hours

Geography
Two groups of islands make up the Marshall Islands – the Ratak and Ralik chains, comprising 29 atolls and covering about 183 square km (70 square miles) of land. The territory lies within the area of the Pacific Ocean known as Micronesia (which includes Kiribati, Tuvalu and other territories). The islands lie about 3,200km (2,000 miles) south-west of Hawaii and about 2,100km (1,300 miles) south-east of Guam.

Climate
Tropical climate. Warm and humid, temperatures 23–30 degrees Celsius, humidity around 80 per cent. High temperatures are cooled by trade winds. Rainfall variable, minimum 250mm per year, can occur in downpours. Hurricanes are remotely possible.

Entry requirements
Passports
Required by all
Visa
Required by all, except US citizens. Tourist and business visas are issued on arrival for stays up to three months.
All visitors must have proof of adequate funds and return/onward passage. Special regulations may apply to some non-tourist destinations. Further information can be obtained through www.rmiembassyus.org/.

Health (for visitors)
Mandatory precautions
Cholera immunization is required if arriving from infected areas.
Advisable precautions
Vaccinations for hepatitis 'A' and 'B' and typhoid are recommended; those for tetanus and diphtheria should be updated as needed.

Hotels
Comfortable tourist accommodation can be found in Majuro and Ebeye.

Credit cards
Visa, Mastercard and American Express are accepted by most major businesses.

Public holidays
Fixed dates
1 Jan (New Year's Day), 1 Mar (Memorial and Nuclear Victims' Remembrance Day), 1 May (Constitution Day), 21 Oct (Compact Day), 17 Nov (President's Day), 25 Dec (Christmas Day).
Some dates vary from island to island.
Variable dates
Fishermen's Day (first Fri in Jul), Rijerbal/Labour Day (first Fri in Sep), Manit/Custom Day (last Fri in Sep), Gospel Day (first Fri in Dec).

Working hours
Banking
Mon–Fri: 1000–1500; Fri: 1000–1800.
Business
Mon–Fri: 0800–1700.
Government
Mon–Fri: 0800–1700.
Shops
Mon–Sat: 0800–2000; (Sun) 0800–1800.

Telecommunications
Telephone/fax
International satellite links provide fax and Internet facilities. Communication with the outer islands is by radio.
Postal services
There are US Postal Service offices on Majuro and Ebeye.
Mobile phones
Cellular service is available on Maburo, Ebeye and Kwajalein.

Social customs/useful tips
In business an informal attitude prevails. Appointments should be made. Business cards are exchanged. Business is usually conducted in English. Permission should be sought before taking photographs of people. The minimum drinking age is 21 years. Swimsuits, shorts or short skirts

should not be worn in urban areas. Tipping is optional.

Getting there
Air
National airline: Air Marshall Islands.
International airport/s: Majuro International (MAJ). There are buses, taxis and hotel transport form the airport to the city centres.
Airport tax: Departure security fee of US$20 on international flights.
Surface
Majuro and Ebeye are the main ports.
Main port/s: Majuro

Getting about
National transport
Air: Regular scheduled flights by Air Marshall Islands service 10 of the 24 atolls.
Road: The main roads on the major islands are paved. Others are stone-, coral- or laterite-surfaced roads and tracks.
Water: Frequency of inter-island services is governed by weather conditions; there are trips to inhabited islands at least every 30–45 days. Four government operated field ships connect the islands within the Marshalls on a regular schedule. Inter-island cruises are available.
City transport
Taxis: Taxis are plentiful and relatively cheap, but usually operate on a shared basis.

Car hire
There are many car hire operators. Driving is on the left. The minimum age is 18.

BUSINESS DIRECTORY

The addresses listed below are a selection only. While World of Information makes every endeavour to check these addresses, we cannot guarantee that changes have not been made, especially to telephone numbers and area codes. We would welcome any corrections.

Telephone area codes
The international direct dialling (IDD) code for Marshall Islands is +692 followed by area code and subscriber's number:
Ebeye 329 Majuro 625.

Chambers of Commerce
Majuro Chamber of Commerce, PO Box 1318, Majuro 96960 (tel: 625-3051; fax: 625-3343; e-mail: majurochamber@hotmail.com).

Banking
Bank of Marshall Islands, PO Box J, Majuro 96960 (tel: 625-3636; fax: 625-3661; e-mail: bankmar@ntamar.com).

Travel information
Air Marshall Islands, PO Box 1319, Majuro 96960 (tel: 625 3731; fax: 625 3730).

Chief of Immigration, Ministry of Foreign affairs, Majuro 96960 (tel: 625 3181; fax: 625 3685).

Division of Trade and Industry, Majuro 96960.

Marshall Islands Visitors' Authority, PO Box 1727, Majuro 96960 (tel: 625 3206); (fax: 625 3218).

Ministry of tourism
Ministry of Resources and Development, Tourism Office, PO Box 1727, Majuro 96960 (tel: 625 3206).

Other useful addresses
Division of Trade and Industry, Majuro 96960.

Marshall Islands Embassy (USA), 2433 Massachusetts Avenue, NW, Washington DC 20008 (tel: 202-234-5414; fax: 202-232-3236; e-mail: info@rmiembassyus.org).

Ministry of Resources and Development, Tourism Office, PO Box 1727, Majuro 96960 (tel: 625 3206).

Internet sites
Website of the Marshall Islands: http://www.rmiembassyus.org/

The Pacific business centre: http://cba.hawaii.edu/pbcp/

Martinique

COUNTRY PROFILE

Historical profile
Martinique is situated within the Windward Islands. Its name is said to be derived either from Martinica (given in honour of St Martin) or a corruption of Madinina, meaning 'island of flowers' (the name given by the Carib Indians, the first inhabitants).
1493 Columbus was the first European visitor.
1635 The island was settled by the French – in the face of indigenous Indian hostility.
1700s The island was seized by the British several times.
1763 Marie-Josephe Rose Tascher de la Pagerie – Napoleon's Empress Josephine – was born at Les Trois Ilets.
1814 The British gave up their attempts to control the island and it became a French possession under the Treaty of Paris.
1848 The Emancipation Proclamation abolished slavery in the West Indies.
1902 St Pierre was destroyed by an eruption of Mount Pelée.
1946 Martinique became a French Département d'Outre-Mer (DOM) (Overseas Department).
1974 Martinique was further incorporated into the French political system and granted the status of region of France.
1983 Martinique was granted devolution. A Regional Council was established under the French decentralisation policy.
1999–2001 The presidents of the regional assemblies of Martinique, Guadeloupe and French Guiana called for more autonomy from France.
2002 Martinique adopted the euro as its official currency.
2003 In December, a referendum in Guadeloupe and Martinique rejected a French government-backed reform plan to streamline the system of local government and give the islands a new status.
2004 Cunard's newest, and largest, cruiseship, *Queen Mary II* first called in to Martinique on 4 February. It will continue to call regularly and is expected to boost the island's tourism. On 8 February, Yves Dassonville took over as *préfet*, replacing Michel Cadot.
2005 The visit by French interior minister, Nicolas Sarkozy, was postponed following the announcement by the French president that a controversal law, passed in February 2005, which required the teaching of the French colonial era from a positive standpoint would be revoked.
Sarkozy is a member of the conservative-led government that passed the law. Protests, by Martinique islanders, were planned.

Political structure
Constitution
28 September 1958 (French Fifth Republic)
Under the 1946 constitution of the French Fourth Republic, Martinique became a Département d'Outre-Mer (DOM) (Overseas Department) of France. In 1974, it was granted additional status as a region of France.
Martinique is represented in the French National Assembly by four deputies and in the Senate by two senators.
Administration is by a préfet appointed by the government in Paris.
Since 1983, following the French government's policy of decentralisation, regional councils have been elected with powers similar to those of the regions.
Local administration is through a Conseil Régional (Regional Council) of 41 members and a 45-member Conseil Général (General Council), both directly elected for six-year terms.
In a December 2003 referendum, voters from Guadeloupe and Martinique rejected a reform plan which would have streamlined the islands' local government and given them a new status. The change was rejected by 73 per cent of voters in Guadeloupe and 50.3 per cent in Martinique. (Voters on St Barthélémy and St Martin, approved the referendum, and are set to acquire the new status of 'overseas collective').

Form of state
Département d'Outre-Mer (DOM) (Overseas Department) of France, with additional status as a région (region) of France.

The executive
The island is administered by a *préfet* (commissioner), appointed by the government in Paris.

National legislature
Legal system
French law applies. The country has no supreme court but this role is filled by a nine-member Conseil Constitutionel (Constitutional Council). Its task is to ensure that law treaties and regulations are in keeping with the constitution and that elections are conducted in a regular manner. The highest court of appeal is the Cour de Cassation, which can overrule decisions in all lower courts, but not government legislation. Since the signing of

KEY FACTS

Official name: Martinique

Head of State: President of France (Jacques Chirac)

Head of government: Préfet (Commissioner) Yves Dassonville (from 8 Feb 2004)

Ruling party: L'Alliance Mouvenent pour l'Indépendance de la Martinique (MIM)/Conseil National des Comités Populaires(CNCP)(since 2004)

Area: 1,100 square km

Population: 424,804 (2004)

Capital: Fort-de-France

Official language: French

Currency: Euro (eur) = 100 cents (from 1 Jan 2002; previous currency French franc, locked at Ff6.56 per euro)

Exchange rate: eur0.83 per US$ (Oct 2005)

GDP per capita: US$10,700 (2003)

Labour force: 136,200 (2004)

Balance of trade: -US$1.75 billion (2003)

Visitor numbers: 655,300 (2003)

the Single European Act in 1986, the European Court of Justice (ECJ) has been the highest authority in certain areas of French law.

Last elections
28 March 2004 (*Conseil Régional*).
Results: L'Alliance Mouvenent pour l'Indépendance de la Martinique (MIM)/Conseil National des Comités Populaires(CNCP) won 21 seats out of 41; Convergence Martiniquaise (nine seats); Les Forces Martiniques de Progrès (4 seats).

Next elections
2007

Political parties
Ruling party
L'Alliance Mouvenent pour l'Indépendance de la Martinique (MIM)/Conseil National des Comités Populaires(CNCP)(since 2004)
Main opposition party
Convergence Martiniquaise
Political situation
The referendum held in Martinique in 2003 seemed straightforward. The French government's proposal was twofold. First, it would streamline the local government apparatus and reduce the number of elected offices. The second effect would be an alteration in Martinique's relationship with France, which would effectively reduce its standing as a region of France. The proposal was made in response to a call for more independence in 1999–2000.
However, the proposal was rejected and the failure was thought to be due to voters' worry that any change in their status would ultimately result in a withdrawal of French central government funds needed, most particularly, for social security.

Population
424,804 (2004)
Ethnic make-up
African and mixed race (90 per cent), white (5 per cent), East Indian and others (5 per cent).
Religions
Roman Catholic (85 per cent), Protestant (10 per cent), Islam, Hindu, pagan African (5 per cent).

Education
There is 42 per cent enrolment in education for the 20- to 24-year age groups with a high rate of unemployment among them.
Literacy rate: 98 per cent, adult rate (2003)

Health
Water for consumption is subject to intensive controls and is of high quality.
There are three public hospitals including one teaching hospital, and three private clinics.

HIV/Aids
Martinique has a departmental Aids control scheme.
Life expectancy: 78.7 years: male 79.3 years; female 78.2 years (2003).
Birth rate/Death rate: 15 births per 1,000 population; 6.4 deaths per 1,000 population (2003).
Infant mortality rate: 7.4 per 1,000 live births (2003)
Head of population per physician/bed: 20 physicians available per 10,000 people.

Welfare
With unemployment ranging between 30 and 35 per cent among the youth, there has been a noticeable increase in the number of people calling for independence from France. The French social security system guarantees a high minimum wage, a 35-hour working week, five-week vacations, a 40 per cent incentive on salary and other social benefits.

Main cities
Fort-de-France (capital (prefecture), estimated population 96,400 in 2003), Le Lamentin (36,400), Le Robert (21,800), Schoelcher (21,400), Sainte Marie (20,600, Le Francois (19,000).

Languages spoken
French and Creole patois (developed from French, English, Spanish and some African languages). English is widely understood.
Official language/s
French

Media
Press
France Antilles is the major daily. Weekly publications include *Le Progressiste, Aujourd'hui Dimanche, Justice, Le Naif* and *Antilla*.
Broadcasting
There are two main radio and one television (Radio France d'Outre-Mer) stations.

Economy
France continues to subsidise Martinique and has modernised its infrastructure. The local economy represents no more than 25 per cent of GDP, while France accounts for the remaining 75 per cent. Martinique has a substantial market economy, primarily based on sugar cane, bananas, tourism and light industry.
A French government 15-year economic development plan for the dependent territories, published in 2002, has led to further improvements to infrastructure and improved the island's investment climate. One of the improvements is the construction of a land and sea transportation terminal next to Pointe Simon Cruise Terminal, which allows water taxis and public transporters to depart from and arrive at the same area.
Tourism, especially the cruise industry, is increasingly important to Martinique's economy.

External trade
The large trade deficit is only partly offset by invisible earnings from tourism, workers' remittances from abroad, and French aid aimed at developing the tourist trade and reducing unemployment.
Imports
Principal imports are petroleum products, crude oil, foodstuffs, construction materials, vehicles, clothing and other consumer goods.
Main sources: France (62 per cent), Venezuela (6.0 per cent), Germany (4.0 per cent), Italy (4.0 per cent), US (3.0 per cent)
Exports
Principal exports are refined petroleum products, bananas, rum and pineapples.
Main destinations: France (45 per cent), Guadeloupe (28 per cent)

Agriculture
Farming
Once the mainstay of economy, the agricultural sector has declined in recent years. It employs 10 per cent of the workforce and contributes 7 per cent to GDP. Around 48 per cent of total land area is cultivated, 25 per cent is forest and 19 per cent savannah. The majority of farms are privately run by smallholders. Activity is centred on the production of sugar cane, pineapples and bananas, mainly for industrial processing and export.
Crops such as sweet potatoes, yams, manioc, beans, cabbages and tomatoes are grown primarily for domestic consumption. Small quantities of aubergines and limes are exported. Virtually all the island's meat requirements are met by imports.
The future of the important banana industry, which has relied on preferential access to the EU, is threatened by a World Trade Organisation ruling that this access is illegal and must end. The EU has agreed new tariff quotas to be introduced from 2006. The number of banana producers fell from 1,200 to 750 in the period 1993–2003. In October 2003, banana producers in Martinique and Guadeloupe formed an association to seek to improve sales in France and in new markets. Estimated crop production in 2004 included: 7,500 tonnes (t) yams, 1,200t sweet potatoes, 207,000t sugar cane, 310,000t bananas, 16,000t plantains, 1,300t citrus, 1,130t coconuts, 1,350t cabbages, 2,240t melons, 20,800t pineapples, 850t lentils, 349,000t fruit in total, 22,300t roots and tubers, 32,200t

Martinique

vegetables in total. Livestock production included: 5,400t meat in total, 2,300t beef, 1,660t pig-meat, 260t lamb, 1,050t poultry, 1,500t eggs, 2,200t milk.

Fishing
Fishing (lobster, crayfish, crab, clams) is undertaken all year round. The typical total annual fish catch is over 6,250t. Shellfish, molluscs and cephalopods account for another 909t per annum.

Industry and manufacturing
Major industries include an oil refinery (capacity 17,000 barrels per day (bpd)), a cement works, rum distilling, sugar refining, dairy produce, fruit canning, soft drinks manufacture, mineral water bottling and a polyethylene plant.
Industrial development has been poor and centres mainly on the manufacture of consumer goods for the local market. Five industrial zones have been set up and tax exemptions introduced to encourage light industrial development.

Tourism
Tourism is an increasingly important sector of the economy. Demand is expected to grow by 4.2 per cent per annum between 2002 and 2012. Visitors come mainly from France, Europe and Canada. Following a fall in visitor numbers over several years, 2003 saw a recovery, especially in cruise passenger numbers. Arrivals in 2003 totalled 721,702. The momentum was not maintained in 2004, due to a 40 per cent fall in cruise passengers, resulting in total arrivals of 630,307. Arrivals by air continued to show a modest increase. The sector's projected contribution to GDP in 2005 is 2.0 per cent

Mining
Martinique has no mineral resources.

Hydrocarbons
Martinique does not produce any hydrocarbons and relies on imports of crude oil. In 2001 Martinique imported 17,840 barrels of oil per day (bpd), of which 16,300 bpd was crude oil for the refining plant. Most of this is used for domestic consumption, although some is re-exported.
Martinique does not produce or import coal or natural gas. A proposed pipeline from Trinidad and Tobago to Martinique and Guadeloupe opens possibilities for the future import of natural gas.

Energy
Electricity production: 585 million kW. There is one refinery and two thermal power stations. Together, SARA (Société Anonyme de Raffinerie des Antilles) and EDF (Electricité de France) employ 900 people.

Banking and insurance
Central bank
Caisse Centrale de Co-opération Economique; European Central Bank (ECB)

Time
GMT minus four hours

Geography
Martinique is one of the Windward Islands in the West Indies, with Dominica to the north and St Lucia to the south. The volcanic peak of Mont Pelée dominates the island.

Climate
Sub-tropical with an annual mean temperature of 26 degrees Celsius. Rain heaviest in the north. Rainy season from June–October. The island's temperature is moderated by trade winds.

Entry requirements
Passports
Required by all and must be valid for at least three months from the date of departure.
Visa
As an overseas region of France entry requirements are the same.
Required by all, except citizens of EU, North America, Australasia and Japan, for stays up to one month; this includes business trips by representatives of foreign entities with an invitation from a local company or organisation. Proof of adequate funds for stay, an itinerary, a guarantee of repatriation if necessary and return/onward ticket are also required. For further exceptions, full details and a copy of the application form visit www.diplomatie.gouv.fr/thema/dossier.gb.asp and follow the path (entering France) to the database.
Currency advice/regulations
There are no restrictions on the import and export of foreign currency, but the amount must be declared on arrival. The amount of foreign currency that may be taken out must not exceed that taken in.

Health (for visitors)
Mandatory precautions
A yellow fever vaccination certificate is required if travelling from an infected area.
Advisable precautions
Hepatitis, typhoid, tetanus and polio vaccinations. Water precautions should be taken.

Hotels
There is a 5 per cent room tax. If service charge is not added, 15 per cent tip is usual.

Public holidays
Fixed dates
1 Jan (New Year's Day), 1 May (Labour Day), 8 May (Victory Day), 22 May (Abolition of Slavery), 14 Jul (Bastille Day), 21 Jul (Schoelcher Day), 15 Aug (Assumption Day), 1 Nov (All Saints' Day), 11 Nov (Armistice Day), 25 Dec (Christmas Day).
Variable dates
Carnival (four days, Feb), Good Friday, Easter Monday, Ascension Day, Whit Monday.

Working hours
Banking
(Mon–Fri) 0800–1200, 1430–1700. Banks close at noon on day preceding a bank holiday.
Business
(Mon–Fri) 0800–1200, 1430–1700 (Sat) 0800–1200.
Government
(Mon–Fri) 0730–1300, 1500–1730.
Shops
(Mon–Fri) 0900–1300, 1500–1800; (Sat) 0900–1300.

Electricity supply
220/380V AC, 50 cycles

Getting there
Air
National airline: CTA Air Martinique
International airport/s:
Fort-de-France-Lamentin (FDF), 14km from city; restaurant, car hire, shops.
Airport tax: There is no airport departure tax.
Surface
Main port/s: Fort-de-France is the only commercial port but there are other ports at St Pierre, Trinité and Le Marin.

Getting about
National transport
Air: Charter flights and helicopter trips provided by Air Martinique.
Road: Well-developed network of more than 1,600km, with 1,200km paved and the rest gravel and earth.
Water: There are regular ferry services from Fort-de-France to Pointe de Bout and Anse Mitan.
Car hire
International licence required, supported by valid foreign licence for periods after 20 days.

BUSINESS DIRECTORY
The addresses listed below are a selection only. While World of Information makes every endeavour to check these addresses, we cannot guarantee that changes have not been made, especially to telephone numbers and area codes. We would welcome any corrections.

Telephone area codes
The international direct dialling code (IDD) for Martinique is +596, followed by 596 and subscriber's number.

Useful telephone numbers
Fire brigade: 18.
Police: 17.
Life-saving: 725-656.
Information: 12.
Weather: 510-626, 612-626.
Voice clock: 593-699.
Police station: 553-000.
Gendarmerie: 635-151.
Préfecture: 681-861.
Taxis: 636-362, 631-010.
Ambulance: 755-980, 751-575.
Regional hospital: 552-000.

Chambers of Commerce
Martinique Chamber of Commerce and Industry, 50 Rue Ernest Deproge, PO Box 478, Fort-de-France 97241 (tel: 552-839; fax: 606-668; e-mail: info@martinique.cci.fr).

Banking
Banque des Antilles Françaises, 34 rue Lamartine, BP 582, 97200 Fort-de-France (tel: 739-344; fax: 635-894).

Banque Française Commerciale, 6-10 rue Ernest Deproge, 97200 Fort-de-France (tel: 638-257).

Banque National de Paris, Avenue des Caraibes, 97200 Fort-de-France (tel: 737-111).

Chase Manhattan Bank, Place de Monseigheur Romero, 97200 Fort-de-France (tel: 602-424).

Crédit Martiniquais, rue de la Liberté, Fort-de-France (tel: 701-240).

Institut d'Emission des DOM (IEDOM), Boulevard General de Gaulle, BP 512, 97206 Fort-de-France (tel: 594-400; fax: 594-404).

Société Générale de Banque aux Antilles, rue de la Liberté, BP 408, 97200 Fort-de-France (tel: 716-983).

Central bank
European Central Bank (ECB), Kaiserstrasse 29, D-60311 Frankfurt am Main, Germany (tel: +49(69)13-440; fax: +49(69)1344-6000).

Travel information
Agence Régionale pour le Développement du Tourisme de la Martinique (ARDTM), Anse Goureaud (tel: 616-177).

Air France, Bord de Mer, Fort-de-France (tel: 637-552, reservations 716-997).

Air Martinique, Aéroport du Lamentin, 97232 Le Lamentin (tel: 510-809, 421-658; fax: 515-927, 421-658).

Délégation Régionale au Tourisme, 41 rue Gabriel Péri, 97200 Fort-de-France (tel: 631-861).

Lamentin Airport, 97232 Le Lamentin (tel: 421-600, 421-985).

National Tourist Board (for information and booking rooms) (tel: 421-805/6).

Tourist information: Pointe Simon Terminal, 97200 Fort-de-France (tel: 717-591); Quai des Tourelles, Port, 97200 Fort-de-France (tel: 733-533); Aéroport, Aérogare arrivée, 97232 Lamentin (tel: 421-805/6; fax: 421-807).

Ministry of tourism
Office Départemental du Tourisme de la Martinique (ODTM), BP 520, Pavillon du Tourisme, blvd Alfassa, 97206 Fort-de-France (tel: 637-960; fax: 736-693).

National tourist organisation offices
Office du Tourisme, 76 rue Lazare Carnot, 97200 Fort-de-France (tel: 602-773, 602-785; fax: 602-795).

Other useful addresses
Agence pour le Développement Economique de la Martinique, Immeuble Nayaradou, Plateau de Cluny, 97233 Schoelcher (tel: 734-581; fax: 724-138).

Bureau del'Industrie de l'Artisanat, Préfecture, 97262 Fort-de France (tel: 713-627).

Chambre Départementale d'Agriculture, Place D'Armes, BP 312, 97286 Lamentin Cedex (tel: 517-575; fax: 519-342).

Chambre des Métiers, 2 Rue du Temple, Morne Tartenson, BP 1191, 97249 Fort-de-France (tel: 713-222; fax: 704-730).

Post Office, 132 boulevard Pasteur, Fort-de-France (tel: 599-600).

Préfecture, rue Victor Severe, BP 647-648, 97262 Fort-de-France (tel: 631-861; fax: 714-029; internet site: http://www.martinique.pref.gouv.fr/pages/somangl.html).

Internet sites
Regional Council of Martinique: http://www.cr-martinique.fr/anglais/accueil_anglais.html

Martinique Promotion Bureau: http://www.martinique.org

Martinique Shipping Services: http://www.marship.fr

Mauritania

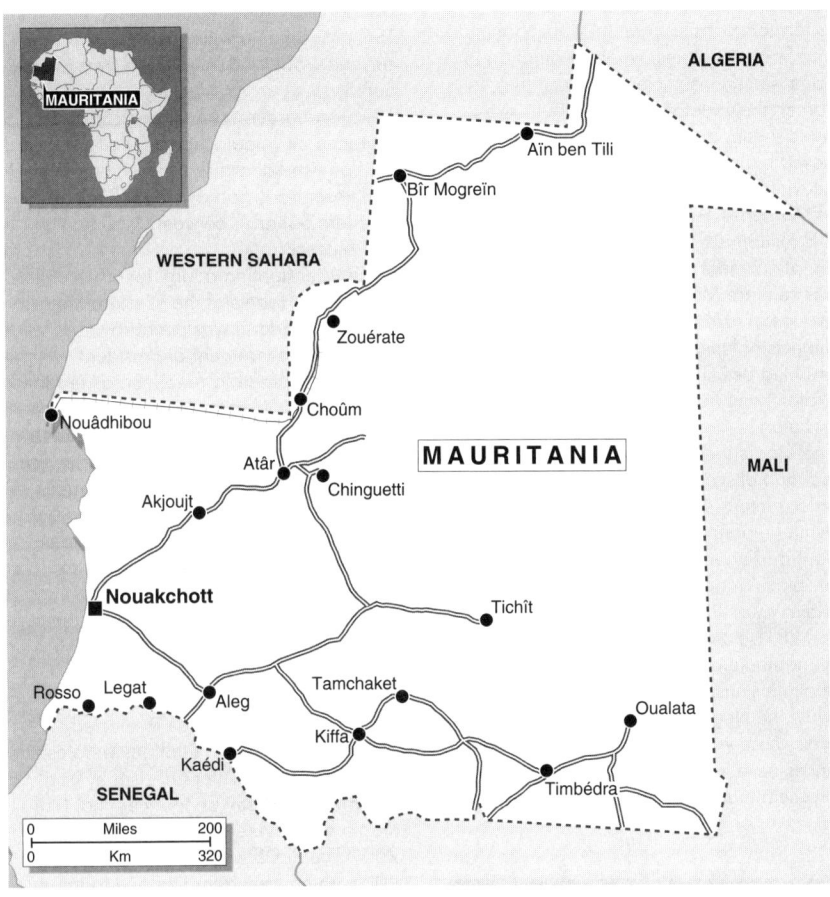

Mauritania is eligible for debt relief from the International Monetary Fund (IMF), but is not in a position to qualify for disbursements immediately, because its macroeconomic performance and the management of public finances have substantially deteriorated.

The IMF is now working with the government to remedy the issues, which include budgeting formation and execution, and reporting. An initial disbursement under a poverty reduction programme was voluntarily repaid as a result of inaccurate information provided to the IMF. The programme was found to be irretrievably off-track. The arrangement was cancelled.

Economy

Half the population still depends on agriculture and livestock for a livelihood, even though many of the nomads and subsistence farmers have been forced into the cities by recurrent droughts. Mauritania has extensive deposits of iron ore, which account for nearly 40 per cent of its total exports. The decline in world demand for this ore, however, has led to cutbacks in production.

The nation's coastal waters are among the richest fishing areas in the world, but overexploitation by foreigners threatens this key source of revenue. Drought and economic mismanagement has resulted in a buildup of foreign debt which now stands at more than three times the level of annual exports.

Exploratory oil wells in tracts 80km offshore indicate potential extraction at current world oil prices. Mauritania has an estimated one billion barrels of proved reserves. The Chinguetti and Tiof fields are

KEY FACTS

Official name: République Islamique Arabe et Africaine de Mauritanie (Islamic Republic of Mauritania)

Head of State: Colonel Ely Ould Mohamed Vall (leader of Junta following coup of 3 Aug 2005 which overthrew Colonel Maaouya Ould Sid'Ahmed Taya (PRDS) who had been president since 1984; last re-elected 7 Nov 2003)

Head of government: Prime Minister Sidi Mohamed Ould Boubacar (named by Junta leader, Col Ely Ould Mohamed Vall, 7 Aug 2005)

Ruling party: The Military Council for Justice and Democracy, headed by Colonel Vall

Area: 1,030,700 square km

Population: 2.83 million (2004)

Capital: Nouakchott

Official language: Hassani Arabic and Wolof

Currency: Ouguiya (UM) = 5 khoums

Exchange rate: UM268.17 per US$ (Oct 2005)

GDP per capita: US$462 (2004)

GDP real growth: 5.20% (2004)

Labour force: 1.27 million (2004)

Unemployment: 20.00% (2004)

Inflation: 10.40% (2004)

Balance of trade: -US$5.00 million (2003)

Foreign debt: US$2.50 billion (2003)

Nations of the World: A Political, Economic and Business Handbook

expected to yield millions more barrels of oil. Substantial oil production and exports are scheduled to begin in early 2006 and may average 75,000 barrels per day. Meantime the government emphasises reduction of poverty, improvement of health and education, and promoting privatisation of the economy.

Politics

Military leader Ely Ould Mohammed Vall seized power in August 2005 in a bloodless coup while President Taya was out of the country for the funeral of the Saudi King. Many Mauritanians welcomed the coup. Vall said the army had acted to end a 'totalitarian' regime and promised to hold presidential elections within two years. It appointed veteran politician Sidy Mohamed Ould Boubacar as prime minister.

One of Vall's first acts was to free 21 Islamists, jailed by the previous government. He also granted an amnesty for Mauritanians accused of political offences. Col Vall says Mauritania will continue to honour a commitment to combat terrorism.

Despite its current military head of state, Mauritania is a highly-centralised republic dominated by a strong presidency. The 1991 constitution provides for a civilian government composed of a dominant executive branch, a senate and a national assembly. It remains an autocratic state, and the country continues to experience ethnic tensions among its black population and different Moor (Arab-Berber) communities.

Risk assessment

Economy	Fair
Politics	Poor
Regional stability	Fair

COUNTRY PROFILE

Historical profile

Mauritania is a country of contrasts. While its territory consists mainly of vast Sahelian and Saharan plains, where vegetation in parts is even insufficient to graze the camel, the vegetation in the south supports sheep, goats, cattle and cultivation based mainly on the seasonally flooded alluvial zone along the river Senegal and its tributaries. And while the population of 2.8 million is bound by a common Muslim attachment to the Malekite sect, 75 per cent are Moors, heterogeneous groups of Arabo-Berber stock, speaking dialects of Hassaniya, and 25 per cent are Negroes (Toucouleurs, Sarakoles, Wolofs) and light skinned nomads (Peulh or Fulani).

The Moors themselves are divided on social and descent criteria rather than skin colour into a superior group, the Bidan or 'white' moors (55 per cent of the population) and an inferior group, the Harattin or 'black' moors, who were once slaves (slavery was finally banned in Mauritania in 1981). Both of these groups are nearly all nomadic pastoralists, living a patriarchal life similar to the Arab Bedouins, while the Negroes are sedentary cultivators. These wide cultural and ethnic differences have led to racial clashes, a problem that is found right across Africa where the Saharan peoples adjoin Africa peoples in the same country.

1800s France gained control of Mauritania, ruling it from Senegal.
1957 Limited self-government was granted under the Loi cadre.
1960 Mauritania gained full independence from France under the regime of the Mauritanian People's Party. Mokhtar Ould Daddah became president.
1974 Mauritania withdrew from the CFAf currency zone and introduced the ouguiya.
1975 An agreement between Mauritania, Morocco and Spain led to the division of the Spanish Sahara (a Spanish colony and the present-day Sahrawi Arab Republic (Western Sahara)) between Mauritania and Morocco.
1978 After fighting a largely unsuccessful war against rebels of the Western Sahara, President Daddah was overthrown.
1979 The government of President Haidallah agreed to renounce all territorial claims to Western Sahara.
1981 Slavery was banned in Mauritania.
1984 Haidallah was removed from office by Colonel Maaouya Ould Sid'Ahmed Taya.
1992 Multi-party elections were held in which President Taya was returned to office.
1996 The governing Parti Républicain Démocratique et Social (PRDS) (Social and Democratic Republican Party) won the elections.
1997 President Taya was re-elected.
1999 Full diplomatic relations were established with Israel. After criticism by Iraq, the foreign ministry announced that Mauritania had severed its relations with Iraq.
2001 The PRDS was re-elected.
2002 An emerging famine due to three years of drought.
2003 The OPEC Fund for International Development donated US$300,000 to support an emergency operation by the World Food Programme (WFP) in Mauritania. A coup attempt by rebels in Nouakchott was foiled by the President's troops on 9 June. On 6 July, President Maaouya Ould Sid'Ahmed Taya named Sghair Ould M'Bareck as the new prime minister. Incumbent Maaouya Ould Sid'Ahmed Taya was re-elected president in the 7 November elections. On 12 November, Prime Minister Sghair Ould M'Bareck was re-appointed.
2004 In January, a team of US military experts began training the Mauritanian army.
2005 Mauritania lost its crop production, which had been attacked by the locust swarms in 2004. The UN called for food aid. On 3 August, while President Taya was out of the country, a military coup overthrew his regime. Colonel Ely Ould

KEY INDICATORS — Mauritania

	Unit	2000	2001	2002	2003	2004
Population	m	2.64	2.72	2.81	2.82	2.83
Gross domestic product (GDP)	US$bn	0.90	0.90	0.98	1.04	*1.36
GDP per capita	US$	322	313	339	370	462
GDP real growth	%	5.2	4.6	4.2	5.4	5.2
Inflation	%	3.3	4.7	3.9	5.5	10.4
Exports (fob) (goods)	US$m	345.0	345.0	321.0	355.0	–
Imports (fob) (goods)	US$m	329.0	357.0	388.0	360.0	–
Balance of trade	US$m	16.0	-110.0	-20.0	-5.0	–
Current account	US$m	-30.0	-11.0	20.0	-110.0	-290.0
Foreign debt	US$bn	2.5	1.8	2.5	2.5	–
Total reserves minus gold	US$m	279.9	284.5	396.2	415.3	–
Foreign exchange	US$m	279.5	284.3	396.0	415.2	–
Exchange rate	per US$	238.92	255.25	271.74	266.42	265.93

* estimated figure

Mohamed Vall (leader of the military Junta) was declared president and head of the Military Council for Justice and Democracy.

Political structure
Constitution
The constitution was approved in July 1991.
Form of state
Islamic republic
The executive
The president is the head of state and is elected by universal suffrage for six-year terms. The president appoints the prime minister and presides over the Council of Ministers, who are recommended by the prime minister and appointed by the president. The president is the supreme chief of the armed forces.

The president, after consultation with the prime minister and the presidents of the assemblies, may pronounce the dissolution of the National Assembly.
National legislature
Legislative power is vested in a bicameral legislature, with the 81-member al Jamiya al Wataniyah (national assembly, the lower house) being directly elected every five years, and a 56-member Majlis al Shuyukh (senate, the upper house), indirectly elected every six years.

The prime minister, under the authority of the president, defines the policy of the government, divides the tasks among the ministers and directs and co-ordinates the action of the government.
Legal system
The legal system is based on the 1991 constitution and is strongly influenced by *Sharia* (Islamic law).
Last elections
7 November 2003 (presidential); 9 October 2001 (parliamentary).
Results: Presidential: Incumbent Maaouya Ould Sid'Ahmed Taya was re-elected with 66.7 per cent of the vote, followed by former president Mohammed Khouna Ould Haidalla with 18.7 per cent, Ahmed Ould Daddah with 6.9 per cent and Messaoud Ould Boulkheir with 5 per cent; turnout was 60.8 per cent.
Parliamentary: The PRDS won 51 per cent of the votes (64 seats).
Next elections
2006 (parliamentary); November 2009 (presidential).

Political parties
Political parties were legalised in July 1991 but were forbidden to be organised on racial or regional lines, or to be opposed to Islam.
Ruling party
The Military Council for Justice and Democracy, headed by Colonel Vall

Main opposition party
Limited information exists following the August 2005 coup.
The Parti Républicain Démocratique et Social (PRDS) (Social and Democratic Republican Party) held power until the coup. Other political parties formed the main opposition to the previous admininistration. Union des Forces Démocratiques–Ère Nouvelle (UFD–EN) (Union of Democratic Forces–New Era). Action pour Changement (AC) (Action for Change) was the largest opposition party in parliament after the 2001 elections, but was banned in 2002.

Population
2.83 million (2004)
Ethnic make-up
The population comprises a majority of Arabised Moors. The rest are ethnically linked with the peoples of Senegal and Mali. Moor-black (40 per cent), Moor (30 per cent), black (30 per cent).
Religions
Islam (99 per cent) is the state religion.

Education
Primary schooling lasts for six years. Progression to secondary education is through a competitive entrance examination. Secondary schooling lasts for six years, divided into two three-year cycles. Each stage requires further examination and students may graduate from either with academic or technical qualifications. Public expenditure on education typically amounts to around 5 per cent of gross national income (GNI).
Literacy rate: 41.2 per cent total; 31.3 per cent female, adult rates in 2002 (World Bank).
Compulsory years: Six to 16.
Enrolment rate: 87 per cent (boys); 82 per cent (girls) gross primary enrolment of the relevant age group (including repeaters), (Unicef).
Pupils per teacher: 50 in primary schools.

Health
Total annual expenditure on health is around 3–4 per cent of GDP, of which government spending is about 72–73 per cent, while foreign spending is around 23 per cent.
By 2002, 81 per cent of children were immunised against measles. Improved water sources and sanitation facilities are available to 37 per cent and 33 per cent of the population, respectively.
HIV prevalence: 0.6 per cent aged 15–49 in 2003 (World Bank)
Life expectancy: 51 years (World Bank)
Fertility rate/Maternal mortality rate: 4.6 births per woman (World Bank)

Infant mortality rate: 77 per 1,000 live births; 32 per cent of children aged under five are malnourished (World Bank).
Head of population per physician/bed: Seven doctors per 10,000 patients.

Main cities
Nouakchott (administrative capital, estimated population 661,400 in 2003); Nouadhibou (formerly Port-Etienne, 80,400).

Languages spoken
French is usually spoken in business circles; English is rarely spoken. Hassani Arabic, Pulaar, Soninke and Wolof are the major languages in everyday use.
Official language/s
Hassani Arabic and Wolof

Media
Press
The only daily newspaper is *Ach-Chaab* printed in both Arabic and French. There are a large number of weekly papers. Issues of weekly newspapers are routinely seized under Article 11 of the 1991 Press Law, which allows government to censor arbitrarily publications that attempt any open criticism of state action. Pre-publication censorship, the arrest of journalists and bans of newspapers are very common government actions in Mauritania. The weekly *Rajoul al-Chari* has been under attack and the independent weekly *Le Calame* has faced suspension. Other newspapers targetted by the government include *La Tribune* and the weekly *Al Alam*.

Agence Mauritanienne d'Information (http://www.mauritania.mr/ami) in Nouakchott is the official government press agency that publishes the daily editions of *Chaab* newspapers (circulated in Arabic), *Horizons* (French) and the official *Bulletin* of the Agency.
Broadcasting
Office Mauritanien de Radiodiffusion et de Télévision (OMRT) broadcasts in Arabic and French.
Advertising
Radio Mauritanie accepts advertisements. TV advertising rates are reasonable.

Economy
Before the August 2005 military coup the economy was given mixed praise and caution by the IMF. Mauritania had completed an arrangement to become a recipient of the Heavily Indebted Poor Counties (HIPC) Initiative and had, from 2003, embarked on a three-year programme, however after fiscal and monetary figures were analysed it was found that the programme was 'irretrievably off-track' and the arrangement was cancelled. The problems were traced to the government's response to poor harvests from the 2002 drought and civil

unrest, which were dealt with by government spending. The fiscal deficit from January 2003 to June 2004 exceeded 50 per cent of GDP in that period, and currency in circulation and broad money tripled so that by 2004 inflation was 10.4 per cent. In July 2004 measures were undertaken to limit the excesses. Non-budget spending was halted and the central bank imposed stricter controls on bank deposit reserves, while reducing its investment in government operations.

Structural reforms progressed slowly during which major weaknesses in fiscal, monetary and exchange rate management were identified. Steps were taken to tighten them and further reforms were undertaken.

Mauritania is due to be an oil producer in 2006 and has begun to organise the necessary oil revenue management and tracking frameworks that included measures for transparency and governance. The IMF advised that funds should be used in accordance with Mauritania's own poverty reduction stratergy plans.

Since the coup the new prime minister has not rejected the IMF analyses of the economy. A new committee will monitor efforts for good governance and an inspector general has been appointed to oversee public spending. The new regime signed the Extractive Industries Transparency Initiative (an anti-corruption measure, giving greater accountability in resource-rich developing countries) in September 2005.

External trade
Mauritania belongs to the Arab Maghreb Union (UMA), together with Algeria, Libya, Morocco and Tunisia.

In 2002, the US approved Mauritania as being eligible for tariff preferences under the African Growth and Opportunities Act (AGOA).

Imports
Principal imports are machinery and equipment, petroleum products, capital goods, foodstuffs and consumer goods.

Main sources: France (14.5 per cent total, 2004), US (7.7 per cent), China (7.4 per cent), Spain (5.9 per cent), Belgium (4.3 per cent), UK (4.3 per cent)

Exports
Principal exports are fish and fish products (typically 45 per cent of total value), iron ore and gold.

Main destinations: Japan (13 per cent total, 2004), France (10.9 per cent), Spain (9.6 per cent), Italy (9.5 per cent), Germany (8.7 per cent), Belgium (7.4 per cent), China (5.8 per cent), Russia (4.8 per cent)

Agriculture
Farming
Production of food crops is restricted to irrigated land in the south along the north bank of the Senegal River. Three years of drought created serious food shortages as yields for millet and sorghum dropped by over 60 per cent in 2002; agricultural growth in 2003 was only 0.2 per cent. This rose to 3.7 per cent in 2004 as harvests improved. International aid and imported cereals have been vital in supplementing the main food crops – millet, sorghum, rice, maize, potatoes and dates.

Most of Mauritania consists of arid and semi-arid land and although it is unsuitable for crops, livestock rearing is an important sector. Nomadic herders comprise around 10 per cent of the population, although their numbers are dwindling. In 2005 Oxfam stated intermittent droughts since 2000 have affected nomadic herders and northern farming families, leading to food crises and a need of food and farming aid.

In late 2004 large plagues of locust attacked crops across much of west Africa and the Sahel region of southern Sahara. Initial fears of widespread destruction of harvests did not occur however food prices had spiralled during the threat and only returned to expected norms after early rains in May 2005.

The estimated crop production for 2004 included: 152,600 tonnes (t) cereals in total, *6,000t maize, *2,200t potatoes, *2,000t sweet potatoes, *68,000t sorghum, 77,000t rice, *24,000t dates, 44,500t pulses, *6,700t roots and tubers, *1,500t oilcrops, *2,500t yams, *27,100t fruit in total, 4,200 vegetables in total. Livestock production included: 89,349t meat in total, 23,000t beef, 22,000t camel meat, 24,750t lamb, 13,800t goat meat, 4,320t poultry, 5,270t eggs, 348,575t milk, 3,420t cattle hides, 3,300t sheepskins.

* estimate

Fishing
Fishing contributes up to 10 per cent of GDP and provides around 45 per cent of export earnings as well as being an important source of food for Mauritanians. The coastal waters are among the richest in the world and joint venture fishing is one of the most important foreign exchange earners. The catch is mainly deep sea species and shellfish – particularly shrimp for the Japanese market.

Industry and manufacturing
The industrial sector contributes around 10 per cent to GDP and employs 5 per cent of the workforce.

The most important activities are fish freezing and processing and the treatment of locally mined iron ore. There are also various small import substitution industries (brewing, footwear, dairy processing etc), oil refining and a sugar refinery in Nouakchott.

Industrial production increased by 2 per cent in 2003.

Tourism
The tourism sector is underdeveloped. Revenues from the sector are estimated at an annual US$20 million. Most foreign visitors are business travellers to Nouakchott, drop-in visitors crossing the border from Senegal or occasional desert safari enthusiasts.

Mining
The mining sector contributes around 13 per cent to GDP, employs 5 per cent of the working population and generates 42 per cent of export earnings.

The annual output of iron ore is around 12 million tonnes, of which about 11 million tonnes is exported – 36 per cent to France, 26 per cent to Italy, 16 per cent to Belgium, 8 per cent to Germany, 4 per cent to Spain and 4 per cent to the UK. The iron mines are located in the Tiris region in the north and are owned and operated by Société Nationale Industrielle et Minière (SNIM). Other mineral resources include copper (at Akjoujt); gold (also near Akjoujt); phosphates (deposits at Bofal), diamonds and uranium.

Hydrocarbons
Currently Mauritania does not produce hydrocarbons but this will change in 2006 when the Chinguetti oil field begins production. It is expected to produce around 75,000 barrels per day (bpd) and the field should last for eight years.

Other oil and gas fields will come online before 2008, including the Tiof oil field, with reserves of 350 million barrels, the Banda field with 85–140 billion cubic metres, and the Pelican field with 28–42 billion cubic metres, of gas reserves. More exploration of offshore sites is underway.

A new ministry of oil and energy was set up in March 2005.

Mauritania has one refinery, the Somir Refinery, at Nouadhibou. This runs on Algerian crude and is operated by an Algerian company.

Mauritania imports small amounts of coal.

Energy
Primary energy resources consist of non-commercial biomass, mostly fuel wood. Over half of the installed generating capacity is provided by hydroelectric dams. There is small-scale thermal electricity (generating capacity 110MW), the majority of which is provided by isolated diesel generators.

Completion of work on the Manantali dam, on the Senegal river, has led to an increase in hydroelectric power supply to Mauritania, Senegal and Mali, with five generators supplying around 40MW each.

The Société Mauritanienne d'Electricité (Maurelec) is responsible for electricity generation, transmission and supply. The electricity network serves only a few people in urban areas.

Banking and insurance
In recent years, Mauritania's banking sector has undergone liberalisation with the government selling its equity stake in commercial banks, making the sector more competitive. Reform of the banking sector has led to limits on bank lending and to new laws on debt recovery.

Domestic confidence in the banking sector remains low and 60 per cent of cash is still not placed in banks. However, this represents an enormous opportunity for the banking sector to increase savings and improve liquidity. An increase in the number of bank branches and the introduction of micro-banking schemes may transform the sector in coming years.

Central bank
Banque Centrale de Mauritanie
Main financial centre
Nouakchott

Time
GMT

Geography
Mauritania lies in north-west Africa, with the Atlantic Ocean to the west, Algeria and Western Sahara to the north, Mali to the east and south, and Senegal to the south. The north is mainly desert.

Climate
The climate is hot and dry. The hottest month in Nouakchott is September (24–34 degrees Celsius (C)); the coldest is December (12–29 degrees C); the wettest month is August.

Entry requirements
Passports
Required by all.
Visa
Required by all, except citizens of neighbouring states, contact the consular section of the nearest embassy for confirmation of exclusions. Business travellers may visit with a tourist visa, obtained in advance. An application should include a bank letter showing sufficient funds for the length of trip, an employer's letter of accreditation and an invitation from a local company or organisation.

All travellers must have return/onward passage.

Currency advice/regulations
Unlimited foreign currency may be imported, but the amount must be declared on arrival. Unexchanged foreign currency may be exported. Declaration forms must be produced on departure. Import and export of local currency is strictly forbidden. Controls are constantly subject to modification.

Health (for visitors)
Mandatory precautions
Yellow fever vaccination certificate required if arriving from an infected area.
Advisable precautions
Yellow fever, hepatitis A, tetanus, typhoid and polio vaccinations. Malaria prophylaxis should be taken.

Water precautions are advisable. There is a rabies risk.

Hotels
Accommodation is limited and visitors should book well in advance. A service charge is normally included in the bill, otherwise a 15 per cent tip is usual.

Credit cards
Only accepted in main hotels.

Public holidays
Fixed dates
1 Jan (New Year's Day), 1 May (Labour Day), 25 May (Africa Day), 10 Jul (Armed Forces Day), 28 Nov (Independence Day).
Variable dates
Eid al Adha, Islamic New Year, Birth of the Prophet, Eid al Fitr.

The Islamic year contains 354 or 355 days, with the result that Muslim feasts advance by 10–12 days against the Gregorian calendar. Dates of feasts vary according to the sighting of the new moon, so cannot be forecast exactly. Islamic year 1426: 10 February 2005 to 30 January 2006.

Working hours
Banking
(Sun–Wed) 0800–1115; 1430–1630; Thu: 0800–1500.
Business
Sat–Wed: 0800–1500; Thu: 0800–1300. Some stop for a lunch-time break (usually 1200–1300 or 1500).
Government
Sat–Wed: 0800–1500; Thu: 0800–1300.
Shops
Sat–Thu: 0800–1200; 1430–1800.

Electricity supply
127/220V AC, 50 cycles. Plugs and sockets mostly two-pin (round).

Getting there
Air
National airline: Air Mauritanie
International airport/s: Nouadhibou (NDB), 4km from city; Nouakchott (NKC), 4km from city.
Airport tax: International departures to Africa UM560; all other international departures UM860; excluding transit passengers.

Surface
Road: Routes include crossings from Morocco, Algeria, Senegal and Mali. The Mali and Morocco borders may present greater trouble in crossing. A surfaced roads exists from Dakar (Senegal) to Nouakchott.
Main port/s: Nouadhibou and Nouakchott

Getting about
National transport
Air: Air Mauritanie provides a daily service between Nouakchott, Nouadhibou and Zouerate, while flying bi-weekly to other towns such as Kaédi.
Road: There is a paved road between Rosso (on the Senegal River, where a ferry connects with the road to Dakar) and Akjoujt, via Nouakchott. Other roads linking major centres are adequate, although 4x4 vehicles are recommended, minor roads are usually impassable after the rainy season.
Buses: Limited service.
Rail: A track runs inland from the coast (Nouakchott-Zouerate), mainly for freight, but there are some passenger services (single-class) scheduled; motor vehicles are sometimes carried.
City transport
Taxis: Taxis are numerous in the main towns. Fares are standardised but not metered. A small tip is usual. Taxis can also be rented by the hour.
Car hire
An international or national driving licence is required. It is advisable to have a driver as finding one's way around is difficult. Out of town, a four-wheel drive with chauffeur, although expensive, is recommended.

BUSINESS DIRECTORY
The addresses listed below are a selection only. While World of Information makes every endeavour to check these addresses, we cannot guarantee that changes have not been made, especially to telephone numbers and area codes. We would welcome any corrections.

Telephone area codes
The international dialling (IDD) code for Mauritania is +222, followed by subscriber's number.

Chambers of Commerce
Mauritania Chamber of Commerce, Industry and Agriculture, Avenue de la République, PO Box 215, Nouakchott (tel: 525-2214; fax: 525-3895; e-mail: ccia@mauritel.mr).

Banking
Banque Mauritanienne pour le Commerce International, PO Box 622, Immeuble Afarco, Avenue Gamal Abdel Nasser, Nouakchott (tel: 254-353, 252-826,

252-469, 252-826, 254-353; fax: 252-045).

Banque Nationale de Mauritanie; PO Box 614 & 291, Avenue Gamal Abdel Nasser, Nouakchott (tel: 251-262, 252-707, 252-602, 252-934; fax: 253-397).

Central bank
Banque Centrale de Mauritanie, PO Box 623, Avenue de l'Indépendance, Nouakchott (tel: 525-2206; fax: 525-6525).

Travel information
Air Mauritanie, BP 41, Nouakchott 174, (fax: 53-815).

Société Mauritanienne de Tourisme et d'Hôtellerie, BP 552, Nouakchott.

National tourist organisation offices
Direction du Tourisme, BP 246, Nouakchott (tel: 53-337).

Ministries
Ministry of Commerce, Artisans and Tourism, BP 182, Nouakchott (tel: 51-057).

Ministry of Economy and Finance, BP 197, Nouakchott (tel: 54-395; fax: 53-114).

Ministry of Fishing and Maritime Economy, BP 137, Nouakchott (tel: 52-476).

Ministry of Foreign Affairs and Co-operation, BP 230, Nouakchott (tel: 52-682).

Ministry of Health and Social Security, BP 169, Nouakchott (tel: 52-052).

Ministry of Industry and Mines, BP 183, Nouakchott (tel: 51-318).

Ministry of the Interior, Post and Telecommunications, BP 195, Nouakchott (tel: 52-020).

Ministry of Planning, BP 238, Nouakchott (tel: 51-612).

Ministry of Transport, BP 237, Nouakchott (tel: 53-337).

Ministry of Rural Development, BP 180, Nouakchott (tel: 51-500; fax: 57-574).

To contact other ministries (tel: 53-337).

Other enquiries: Budget (tel: 52-666), Customs (tel: 51-404), Finance (tel: 53-337), Hydraulics (tel: 51-611), Imports (tel: 52-093), Industry (tel: 53-337), Information (tel: 51-931), Marine market (tel: 57-893), Post and Telecommunications (tel: 51-649), Statistics (tel: 53-070), Treasury (tel: 51-462).

National Statistics Office, BP 240, Nouakchott (tel: 51-477).

Prime Minister's Office, BP 184, Nouakchott (tel: 53-337).

Other useful addresses
Bureau d'Achats pour la République Islamique de Mauritanie (BARIM), BP 272, Nouakchott (deals with imports of food, textiles etc).

Exploitation des Mines d'Or de l'Inchin (MORAK), Akjoujt (tel: 61-263; fax: 61-079); Nouakchott (tel: 56-423, 57-499; fax: 56-320).

Fédération des Banques et Services, Nouakchott (tel: 58-343; fax: 53-301).

Fédération des Industries et Armement de Pêche (FIAP), Nouadhibou (tel: 45-089; fax: 45-430).

Fédération des Industries et des Mines (FIM), Nouakchott (tel: 52-160, 51-990; fax: 53-301).

Fédération du Commerce (FC), Nouakchott (tel: 52-160, 51-990; fax: 53-301).

Fédération Nationale des Transports (FNT), Nouakchott (tel: 57-936, 54-738; fax: 57-935).

La Confédération Générale des Employeurs de Mauritanie (CGEM), Nouakchott (tel: 52-160, 51-990; fax: 53-301).

Mauritanian Embassy (USA), 2129 Leroy Place, NW, Washington DC 20008 (tel: 202-232-5700; fax: 202-319-2623).

Mauritanienne d'Entreposage des Produits Pétroliers (MEPP), Nouakchott (tel: 52-646; fax: 54-608).

Société Arabe des Mines d l'Inchin (Samin), Akjoujt (tel: 61-104; fax: 61-279).

Société Mauritanienne de Commercialisation de Produits Pétroliers (SMCPP), Nouakchott (tel: 52-651; fax: 52-542).

Société Nationale d'Importation et d'Exportation (SONIMEX), BP 290, Nouakchott (tel: 51-472, 52-224; fax: 53-014).

Société Nationale d'Eau et d'Electricité (SONELEC), Nouakchott (tel: 52-308; fax: 53-995).

Société Nationale Industrielle et Miniére (SNIM), Nouadhibou (tel: 45-174; fax: 45-396); Nouakchott (tel: 53-689; fax: 53-689).

Société Nationale pour le Développement Rural (SONADER), Nouakchott (tel: 51-800; fax: 53-286).

Internet sites
Africa Business Network: http://www.ifc.org/abn

AllAfrica.com: http://allafrica.com

African Development Bank: http://www.afdb.org

Africa Online: http://www.africaonline.com

Mbendi AfroPaedia (information on companies, countries, industries and stock exchanges in Africa): http://mbendi.co.za

Mauritius

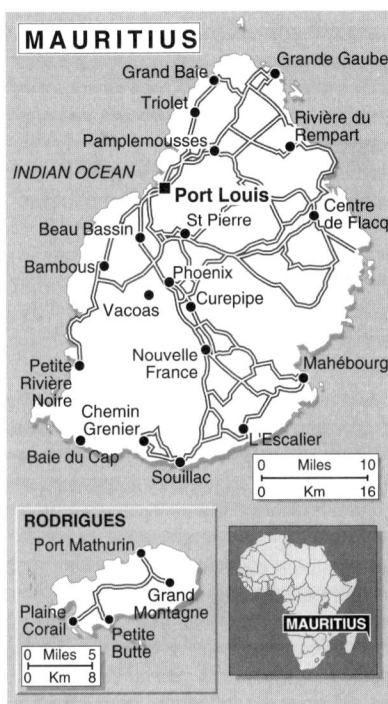

Mauritius has been increasingly affected by the phasing out of external trade preferences for its textile exports and, more recently, by higher prices for petroleum product imports. Growth has slowed to 3.5 per cent in 2004/05 and is expected to remain subdued during the next two fiscal years. The surplus on the external current account has recently turned into a deficit, owing to a decline in exports and a price-related surge in petroleum product imports. The real effective exchange rate has depreciated and net foreign official reserves have dropped, although they remain at relatively comfortable levels.

Economy

The slowdown of economic activity and the suspension of periodic adjustments of retail petroleum prices have negatively affected Mauritius' fiscal position. While the central government deficit was kept at about 5 per cent of GDP during 2004/05, the State Trading Company (STC) incurred a rising deficit owing to the lack of adjustment of retail petroleum prices since early 2005. Unless corrective action is taken, the overall fiscal position during 2005/06 is expected to deteriorate further, owing to lower than originally projected revenue collections associated with lackluster activity and a further increase of the STC's deficit as the gap between retail prices and import costs of petroleum products widens.

A deteriorating external economic environment, particularly for the sugar and textile sectors, has recently led to a slowdown of economic activity, an increase in the external current account deficit, and a loss of international reserves.

Remarkably, Mauritius's development has been financed almost entirely from domestic savings, which have been intermediated through an efficient domestic banking system. Foreign direct investment (FDI) has played a minor role. A volcanic island of lagoons and sandy beaches in the Indian Ocean, Mauritius has a reputation for stability and racial harmony among its mixed population of Asians, Europeans and Africans. The island has maintained one of the developing world's most successful democracies and has enjoyed years of constitutional order.

Annual growth has been in the order of five per cent to six per cent. This remarkable achievement has been reflected in more equitable income distribution, increased life expectancy, lowered infant mortality, and a much-improved infrastructure.

The government's development strategy centers on expanding local financial institutions and building a domestic information telecommunications industry. Mauritius has attracted more than 9,000 offshore entities, many aimed at commerce in India and South Africa, and investment in the banking sector alone has reached over $1 bln.

Mauritius's immediate and medium-term challenges are threefold. First, there is a need to diversify and transform the economy, especially in light of the expected loss of trade preferences in the sugar and textile sectors. Second, Mauritius must undertake structural reforms to increase labour market flexibility. Third, persistent budget deficits need to be reduced if medium-term fiscal sustainability and macroeconomic stability are to be preserved.

KEY FACTS

Official name: Republic of Mauritius

Head of State: President Karl Offman (elected by the National Assembly Feb 2002)

Head of government: Prime Minister Navin Ramgoolam (from 5 Jul 2005)

Ruling party: Alliance Sociale (AS) (Social Alliance) (elected 3 Jul 2005)

Area: 1,865 square km

Population: 1.26 million (2004)

Capital: Port Louis

Official language: English and French

Currency: Mauritian rupee (MR) = 100 cents

Exchange rate: MR30.30 per US$ (Oct 2005)

GDP per capita: US$4,829 (2004)

GDP real growth: 4.40% (2004)

Labour force: 546,000 (2004)

Unemployment: 10.80% (2004)

Inflation: 4.40% (2004)

Balance of trade: -US$233.00 million 2004

Foreign debt: US$2.40 billion (2003)

Nations of the World: A Political, Economic and Business Handbook

Tourism

Notwithstanding prevailing uncertainties, the government is optimistic about the growth prospects for the tourist sector. Plans are being implemented to construct about 20–25 hotels (representing additional capacity of about 40 per cent) in the next three years.

This increase in capacity, however, is coming at a time when the hotel occupancy rate has declined. More generally, a consistent strategy needs to be developed to market Mauritius as a tourist destination, since the envisaged rapid expansion may conflict with preserving the country's image as an 'upper-end' tourism product. Moreover, issues related to the expansion of air access may need to be resolved in order to increase tourist arrivals.

Politics

Mauritius has a multiparty democratic system. Former Prime Minister Navin Ramgoolam of the Social Alliance returned to power after defeating Paul Bérenger of the Mauritian Militant Movement in elections in July 2005. The new premier promised to tackle rising inflation and unemployment. To this end, he advocates trade agreements that give preference to Mauritian exports, including sugar and textiles.

Born in 1947, Ramgoolam first served as prime minister between 1995 and 2000. He is a doctor and lawyer.

Outlook

Mauritius is one of the key regional economies that are growing at an impressive rate, encouraged by growing political stability and financial prudence. Since independence in 1968, it has experienced a significant transformation, moving from an economy that was almost entirely dependent on sugar cane cultivation and sugar manufacturing to one that has benefited from an export-led growth strategy.

Industry, in particular clothing and textile manufacture, now forms a cornerstone of the economy, while rapid growth of the tourism and financial services sectors during the past decade have further diversified the economy. Small-businesses in particular are thriving in this environment, accounting for an ever-greater proportion of available jobs.

The government is setting its sights firmly on making the country a cyber-island and to position Mauritius as a regional ICT hub. With investment in quality telecommunication infrastructure, high-tech business park facilities and appropriate legal framework, Mauritius is fast making information and communication technology the fifth pillar of the economy.

Risk assessment

Economic	Good
Political	Fair
Regional stability	Good
Stock market	Encouraging

KEY INDICATORS — Mauritius

	Unit	2000	2001	2002	2003	2004
Population	m	1.18	1.20	1.21	1.24	1.26
Gross domestic product (GDP)	US$bn	4.60	4.50	4.50	5.51	*6.06
GDP per capita	US$	3,914	3,812	4,010	4,447	4,829
GDP real growth	%	3.6	5.6	5.3	4.8	4.4
Inflation	%	5.3	5.4	5.0	5.6	4.4
Unemployment	%	8.0	8.6	8.8	9.8	–
Exports (fob) (goods)	US$m	1,559.4	1,633.0	1,830.2	1,600.0	2,012.0
Imports (fob) (goods)	US$m	1,953.3	2,056.0	2,018.3	1,800.0	2,245.0
Balance of trade	US$m	-393.9	-423.0	-188.1	-200.0	-233.0
Current account	US$m	-240.0	-90.0	100.0	100.0	30.0
Foreign debt	US$bn	2.4	1.7	2.0	2.4	–
Total reserves minus gold	US$m	897.4	835.6	1,227.4	1,577.3	1,605.9
Foreign exchange	US$m	857.1	796.3	1,184.5	–	–
Exchange rate	per US$	26.25	29.13	29.96	27.55	27.50

* estimated figure

COUNTRY PROFILE

Historical profile

Mauritius, which had previously been visited by Arabs and Malays, was first sighted by a European, the Portuguese Pereira, in 1511. In 1695, the Dutch seaman Wybrandt Van Warwijk, took possession of the island for Holland and named it Mauritius after Prince Maurice of Nassau. Evacuated by the Dutch in 1715, Mauritius was taken by the French who renamed it Bourbon. Under the French, sugar plantations were set up and thousands of African slaves shipped to the island to work in the fields.

Blockaded by the British during the Napoleonic Wars, the island was ceded to Britain by the treaty of Paris in 1814. It remained a British colony for a century and a half until independence in 1968. In 1835, slavery had been abolished in the island and as a source of alternative labour Indians were recruited to work in the sugar cane fields.

1598 A Dutch squadron landed at Grand Port and named the island Mauritius.
1638 Mauritius was settled by the Dutch. The island became an important port of call for Dutch, English and French trading ships. The Dutch introduced sugar cane and imported slaves to harvest it.
1710 The Dutch abandoned their settlement.
1721 France claimed the island; it also imported large numbers of slaves to harvest sugar cane, cotton and other crops.
1810 Britain defeated a French naval squadron and the island was ceded to Britain at the end of the Napoleonic Wars.
1835 Slavery was abolished. Most freed slaves left the plantations and settled in coastal towns; workers had to be imported from the Indian sub-continent to take their place, most of whom opted to remain on the island at the end of their contracts.
1936 The Labour Party (LP) was formed and organised strikes and protests between 1937–45.
1953 A group of Mauritians under Seewoosagur Ramgoolam rose to the leadership of the LP, which won the elections to the Legislative Council. Most Creoles joined the Parti Mauricien Social-Démocrate (PMSD) (Social Democratic Party of Mauritius).
1959 New political parties emerged including the Muslim Committee of Action (CAM). CAM formed an alliance with the LP.
1968 Mauritius gained independence from Britain.
1969 Ramgoolam's LP-CAM (Muslim) ruling alliance was strengthened when a coalition with the PMSD was formed. In response, the Mouvement Militante

Mauritius

Mauricien (MMM) (Mauritian Militant Movement) was established.

1982 The LP lost power as the MMM, in alliance with the Parti Socialiste Mauricien (PSM), gained power under the premiership of Aneerood Jugnauth.

1983 The MMM split and Jugnauth formed the Mouvement Socialiste Mauricien (MSM) (Mauritian Socialist Movement) which formed a government with the LP.

1990 The MMM and the MSM formed a political alliance and aimed to transform Mauritius into a republic.

1995 An alliance of the LP and the MMM, led by Navinchandra Ramgoolam and Paul Berenger, won the parliamentary elections. Ramgoolam became prime minister.

1997 The LP-MMM coalition broke up when the MMM left government and became the official opposition. Even so, the LP continued to hold an outright majority in the legislature and for the first time since independence, Mauritius was governed by a single party.

2000 The opposition, MSM/MMM, won the parliamentary election. Aneerood Jugnauth, leader of the MMM, became prime minister for the second time. Mauritius revived a claim to sovereignty over Diego Garcia, British Indian Ocean Territory.

2001 The WTO trade policy review encouraged Mauritius to further liberalise and diversify its economy. A constitutional amendment was introduced, allowing Rodrigues Island to have two representatives in the National Assembly and its own regional assembly.

2002 President Cassam Uteem resigned and Vice President Angidi Chettiar became interim president, but he also resigned. Both resigned having refused to sign into law controversial anti-terrorism legislation. The National Assembly elected Karl Offman as president.

On Rodrigues Island, the Rodrigues People's Organisation (RPO) won 10 seats out of 18 and the Mouvement Rodriguais (MR) (Rodrigues Movement) won eight seats in the first Rodrigues Regional Assembly election. The Rodrigues Regional Assembly opened with Jean Daniel Spéville as chief commissioner.

2003 On 4 February, Serge Clair became chief commissioner of Rodrigues Island. Prime Minister Sir Aneerood Jugnauth stepped down in September, handing over the post to his deputy, Finance Minister Paul Bérenger.

2004 In May, the IMF praised the economic performance of Mauritius, suggesting that its success was due to the quality of the country's institutions.

2005 In the 3 July parliamentary elections the opposition Alliance Sociale (AS) (Social Alliance) won 49 per cent of the vote (38 out of 62 constituencies) and the incumbent coalition MSM and MMM won 43 per cent (22). Turnout was 81.5 per cent.

Political structure

Constitution
Mauritius is a republic with a president as head of state.
The president is elected by a simple majority of all the members of the National Assembly for a five-year term. The National Assembly is the supreme body that votes laws. The president's agreement and signature is required to sign legislation into law.

Form of state
Republic

The executive
Executive power is vested in the prime minister, leader of the majority parliamentary party.
There is a Council of Ministers consisting of the prime minister and not more than 24 other ministers.

National legislature
The unicameral National Assembly has 62 seats elected by universal adult suffrage for five years.
For the purpose of electing members of the National Assembly, the island of Mauritius is divided into 20 three-member constituencies.
The island of Rodrigues returns two members.
The official language of the National Assembly is English but any member may address the Chair in French.

Last elections
3 July 2005 (parliamentary); February 2002 (presidential).
Results: Presidential: the National Assembly elected Karl Offman as president. Parliamentary: Alliance Sociale (AS) (Social Alliance) won 49 per cent of the vote (38 out of 62 constituencies) and the coalition of MSM and MMM won 43 per cent (22). Turnout was 81.5 per cent. Condidates for the remaining eight seats in the 70-member National Assembly were nominated by the electoral board, giving representation in parliament to showing high but unsuccessful placings.

Next elections
2007 (presidential); 2010 (parliamentary).

Political parties

Ruling party
Alliance Sociale (AS) (Social Alliance) (elected 3 Jul 2005)

Main opposition party
Coalition of Mouvement Socialiste Mauricien (MSM) (Mauritian Socialist Movement) and Mouvement Militante Mauricien (MMM) (Mauritian Militant Movement)

Population
1.26 million (2004)

Ethnic make-up
Indentured workers were brought from India to work on sugar estates and their descendants form a majority of the population, followed by Creoles (of mixed, predominantly African, origin), Muslim Indians, Chinese and Europeans. Hindu Indo-Mauritian (51 per cent), Creole (27 per cent), Muslim Indo-Mauritians (17 per cent), Chinese (2 per cent).

Religions
Hinduism (51 per cent), Christianity (Roman Catholic) (31.3 per cent), Muslim (16.6 per cent).

Education
Education is modelled on the English school system. Primary schooling lasts for six years until the age of 12; lower secondary schooling lasts for five years and upper secondary schooling for a further two years. Examinations are undertaken at each transition.
The expenditure allocated to education by central government was 16 per cent (Unicef estimates 1992–1999).
Literacy rate: 85.3 per cent total; 82.3 per cent female, adult rates (World Bank).
Compulsory years: Five to 12.
Enrolment rate: 93.6 per cent net primary enrolment, of the relevant age group; 62.9 per cent net secondary enrolment (World Bank).
Pupils per teacher: 24 in primary schools.

Health
By 2002, 84 per cent of children were immunised against measles, before aged one year.
Total expenditure on health is 3–4 per cent of GDP, of which government spending is 60 per cent.
Life expectancy: 72.3 years (World Bank)
Fertility rate/Maternal mortality rate: 2.0 births per woman (World Bank)
Infant mortality rate: 16 deaths per 1,000 live births; about 15 per cent of children aged under five are malnourished (World Bank).

Main cities
Port Louis (capital, estimated population 143,800 in 2003), Beau Bassin/Rose Hill (108,900), Vascoas-Phoenix (103,300), Curepipe (79,700), Quatre Bornes (76,400).

Languages spoken
Creole and Bhojpuri are the predominant languages in everyday life.
Official language/s
English and French

Nations of the World: A Political, Economic and Business Handbook

Media

Press
Several daily newspapers including *Le Mauricien*, *l'Express*, *The Sun* and some weekly newspapers and periodicals are in circulation.

Broadcasting
Mauritius Broadcasting Corporation (MBC) operates two TV and three radio channels. Broadcasts in English, French, Creole, Hindi, Tamil, Telegu, Marathi, Urdu, Chinese, Gujarati and Bhojpuri. French pay-TV station Canal Plus and Sky News from the UK British Sky Broadcasting Corporation have been transmitting programmes since 1995.

Radio: Radio Sugar FM is the main station, operated by MBC.

Economy
Mauritius has a stable, prosperous economy, but changes are taking place due to World Trade Organisation (WTO) requirements to liberalise trade and diversify the economy. The government hopes to model the island on Singapore based on the free port, expansion of offshore banking, manufacturing base and modernisation of traditional industries as well as its well-placed geographical situation between Asia and Africa. Despite growing financial and tourism sectors, sugar cane continues to make up around a quarter of all export earnings, but this industry is likely to decline as the economy diversifies.

In 2004, the IMF praised the economic performances of Botswana and Mauritius, compared to those of other African countries, suggesting that their success was due to the quality of the two countries' institutions.

External trade
The Cotonou Agreement, which replaced the Lomé Convention in 2000, gave preferential treatment to Mauritius on European markets and supports its sugar industry. However, these preferences have been revoked on some exports (sugar and textiles), which will mean competing with China and other lower waged economies in future.

The textile industry grew up as unexploited textile import quotas with the US made Mauritius an attractive production location for Indian and Chinese companies, whose own national quotas had been filled.

On 31 December 2002, the US approved Mauritius as being eligible for tariff preferences under the African Growth and Opportunities Act (AGOA). The legislation requires that countries are only eligible for greater access to US markets provided they have made continued progress toward a market-based economy, the rule of law, free trade, poverty reduction and the protection of workers' rights. This process is reviewed annually.

Imports
Principal imports are manufactured goods, capital equipment, foodstuffs, petroleum products and chemicals.

Main sources: France (13.1 per cent total, 2004), South Africa (10.8 per cent), India (7.6 per cent), China (5.9 per cent), Germany (4.5 per cent), Singapore (4.0 per cent)

Exports
Principal exports are clothing and textiles, sugar, cut flowers and,, molasses.

Main destinations: UK (30.6 per cent total, 2004), France (22.7 per cent), US (13.7 per cent), Madagascar (7.7 per cent)

Agriculture

Farming
The agricultural sector contributes around 6 per cent to GDP and employs 13 per cent of the workforce.

Sugar cane cultivation dominates the sector. Approximately 70 per cent of all cultivated land is devoted to the crop, and the sugar industry as a whole employs the majority of the workforce and accounts for 3 per cent of GDP. Cultivation is undertaken both on large plantations and by smallholders.

The other major export crop is tea, grown by tenant farmers. Mauritius is the fourth-largest producer of tea per capita in the world. Around 75 per cent of tea production (green leaf) is controlled by the Tea Development Authority, whose commercial activities are privately run.

Tobacco is grown for the home market. Main food crops include potatoes and other vegetables, output of which is sufficient to meet domestic demand.

Much of the island's meat requirement is imported. Around 75 per cent of food requirements are also imported.

Crop production in 2004 included: 190 tonnes (t) maize, *130t cassava, 175t taro, 12,300t potatoes, *500t sweet potatoes, 12,100t bananas, *410t citrus fruit, 13,200t tomatoes, *4,560t pineapples, 516t oilcrops, 480t tobacco, 673t various spices, 5,200,000t sugar cane, *1,436t tea, *17,820t fruit in total, 72,727t vegetables in total. Livestock production included: 30,467t meat in total, 500t beef, *825t pig meat, *232t lamb and goat meat, *28,279t poultry, *5,200t eggs, *4,000t milk.

* estimate

Fishing
All fish-farming production and 90 per cent of marine fishing provides about 40 per cent of the nutritional requirement of the Mauritian population. Commercial aquaculture includes cultivation of giant freshwater prawns and oysters. Mauritius is a hub for longline tuna fishing fleets that dock to offload their cargo on to freezer ships for transhipment and provides the local economy with foreign currency.

Total fish catches amount to over 10,000 tonnes per year with another 70 tonnes of other sea food. Over 70,000 cultivated oysters are produced each year.

Sports fishing has become a major influence, along with reef diving, which not only drives the local tourist industry but also employs boats and crews formerly used in fishing that were less capable of competing with modern replacement ships and mechanisation.

Forestry
The annual value of exports in 2004 amounted to US$1.5 million, while imports amounted to US$52 million. Annual estimated production: 13,500 cubic metres (cum) roundwood, 3,000cum sawnwood, 5,000cum sawlogs and veneers, 6,000cum woodfuel, 100mt charcoal.

Industry and manufacturing
The industrial sector contributes around 30 per cent to GDP and employs 28 per cent of the workforce.

The industrial sector is based on the Export Processing Zones (EPZ) which were opened in the 1970s to take advantage of the preferential treatment which Mauritius receives under the Cotonou Agreement. Production of textiles, and in particular knitwear, has become the most significant EPZ industry, and Mauritius is the world's third-largest exporter of pure new wool products. The EPZ textiles industry employs 91 per cent of the industrial workforce, accounts for 68 per cent of EPZ enterprises and 80 per cent of EPZ exports. The EPZs generate 23 per cent of GDP. In 2001, the knitwear industry moved towards high-fashion apparel as part of the effort to modernise.

Diversification is being encouraged to help get over the loss of preferential treatment in textiles. Other industries include the manufacture of watches and clocks, jewellery, spectacle frames and leather goods.

Informatics Park for foreign companies specialising in information technology was opened in 1994. Mauritius has plans to develop into a 'cyber island' and will receive assistance from the IMF as part of its upgrade.

Tourism
Tourism is the third most important source of foreign exchange. The sector is expected to account for 14.5 per cent of GDP in 2005.

There are around 105 registered hotels with around 11,000 total room capacity. Twenty new hotels are planned by 2016 at the total cost of US$450 million. Saturation point is near and there is a risk of environmental damage if development is not managed and contained accordingly. There were 718,861 visitor arrivals in 2004, compared with 702,018. Europe is the main market, especially France, which accounts for more than a quarter of visitors, followed by South Africa.

Hydrocarbons

There are no known oil or gas reserves in Mauritius, which is reliant on imports to meet its energy needs. Refined oil products supply 84 per cent of Mauritius' energy needs and 19,600 barrels per day (bpd) were imported in 2001. Imports of petroleum products are handled by the State Trading Corporation. Mauritius does not import natural gas.

Mauritius does not produce coal, but imports it to meet 5 per cent of its energy requirements. In 2001 it imported 383,000 short tonnes.

Energy

Local electricity supply is largely from diesel powered thermal stations. There has been rapid development of electricity generation from bagasse (refuse produced in sugar-making). Hydroelectricity plants produce 25 per cent and bagasse 15 per cent of electricity.

Financial markets

Stock exchange

The Stock Exchange of Mauritius (SEM) was established by the government in July 1989 with five companies listed.

The stock market was opened to international investors in 1994.

There are ambitions to become a regional exchange, supplemented by offshore funds and listings from mainland Africa. In 1996 a central depository and settlement system was introduced. A new Securities Act also brought the framework up to world standards.

A weighted index, the SemDex, was introduced in 1998. In June 2003, market capitalisation was US$1.6 billion, with 38 listed companies. Foreign investors do not need approval to trade shares unless investment is for the purpose of management of a Mauritian company or for a holding over 15 per cent of a sugar company.

Banking and insurance

In 1989 tax and duty incentives were introduced for foreign banks licensed to engage in offshore banking. Mauritius launched Africa's first offshore banking centre at the end of 1989 which continues to expand.

Central bank

Bank of Mauritius.

Main financial centre

Port Louis.

Time

GMT plus four hours

Geography

Mauritius lies in the Indian Ocean. The principal island from which the country takes its name, lies about 800km (500 miles) east of Madagascar. The other main islands are Rodrigues, the Agalega Islands and the Cargados Carajos Shoals (St Brandon Islands).

Climate

Maritime – tropical in summer (November–April), and sub-tropical for rest of year. High humidity especially in inland areas. Summer temperatures average 25–30 degrees Celsius (C) with maximum 35 degrees C in February. Highest rainfall occurs in summer (and cyclones are likely). From May–November, drier and warm with temperatures 19–27 degrees C. Lowest rainfall from September–November. Inland areas generally 5 degrees C lower than coast with higher rainfall.

Entry requirements

Passports

Passports must be valid for six months from date of entry.

Visa

Required by all except citizens of most Commonwealth countries, plus EU, US and others. For a full list and to download a visa application form see www.maurinet.com/embvisa.html. Business travellers may visit with a tourist visa, obtained in advance. An application should include details of sufficient funds for the length of trip, an employer's letter of accreditation and an invitation from a local company or organisation.

All travellers must have return/onward passage.

Currency advice/regulations

No limits on import and export of local currency. Any amount of foreign currency may be imported, subject to declaration, and any unused balance may be exported.

Health (for visitors)

Mandatory precautions

Yellow fever and cholera vaccination certificates are required if arriving from infected areas.

Advisable precautions

Typhoid, tetanus, hepatitis A and polio vaccinations. Water precautions should be taken.

Hotels

Wide choice available but relatively expensive. Ten per cent tax surcharge added to bills (10 per cent tip is usual except where service charge is included). Business visitors staying longer than a day or two generally prefer beach hotels.

Public holidays

Fixed dates

1–2 Jan (New Year), 1 Feb (Abolition of Slavery Day), 12 Mar (National Day), 1 May (Labour Day), 15 Aug (Assumption Day), 2 Nov (Arrival of Indentured Labourers), 25 Dec (Christmas Day).

There is a diversity of cultures in Mauritius, each with its own set of holidays.

Variable dates

Thaipoosam Cavadee (Jan/Feb), Chinese New Year (Jan/Feb), Maha Shivaratri (Feb/Mar), Ougadi (Mar/Apr), Ganesh Chaturthi (Aug/Sep), Diwali (Oct/Nov), Eid al Fitr.

Hindu festivals are timed according to local sightings of various phases of the moon.

Working hours

Banking

Mon–Fri: 0930–1430; Sat: 0930–1130.

Business

Mon–Fri: 0830–1630, Sat: 0900–1200.

Government

Mon–Fri: 0845–1600.

Electricity supply

220V AC, 50 cycles.

Weights and measures

The metric system is in general use, but certain obsolete French measures are still used in connection with the measurement of land.

Getting there

Air

National airline: Air Mauritius.

International airport/s: Sir Seewoosagur Ramgoolam International (Code: MRU) 3km from Mahébourg, 48km south-east of Port Louis; buffet, currency exchange, post office, shops, car hire, banks, duty-free shop.

Airport tax: International departures MR500.

Surface

Main port/s: Port Louis is the island's only commercial port. It has five deep water quays, an eight hectare container park, with an annual throughput of 85,000 TEUs and provision for refrigerated containers. Its free port status underpins the island's offshore banking system.

Getting about

National transport

Air: Air Mauritius operates inter-island service between Mauritius and Rodrigues and Réunion. Two Air Mauritius Bell Jet helicopters are available for transfer from airport to hotel and tours.

Road: There is an extensive network throughout the island. About 93 per cent of the road network is paved. Occasional congestion. A dual highway links Port Louis and Phoenix, Port Louis and Mapou/Pamplemousses.

Nations of the World: A Political, Economic and Business Handbook

Buses: Good bus services cover the main island.

City transport
Taxis: Operate in all towns, villages and resorts. Generally unmetered so it is advisable to agree a fare before starting the journey. Tipping is not usual.

Car hire
Widely available. International or foreign licence accepted; traffic drives on the left.

BUSINESS DIRECTORY

The addresses listed below are a selection only. While World of Information makes every endeavour to check these addresses, we cannot guarantee that changes have not been made, especially to telephone numbers and area codes. We would welcome any corrections.

Telephone area codes
The international dialling code (IDD) for Mauritius is +230, followed by subscriber's number.

Chambers of Commerce
Mauritius Chamber of Commerce and Industry, 3 Royal Street, Port Louis (tel: 208-3301; fax: 208-0076; e-mail: mcci@intnet.mu).

Banking
African Asian Bank Limited, Office 5, 8th Floor, Max City Building, Corner Louis Pasteur & Remy Ollier Streets, Port Louis (tel: 240-7002, 240-7350; fax: 240-7009).

Bank of Baroda, African Asian Bank Limited, PO Box 553, Sir William Newton Street, Port Louis (tel: 208-1504; fax: 208-3892).

Bank of Mauritius, PO Box 29, Sir William Newton Street, Port Louis (tel: 202-3800; fax: 208-9204).

Banque Nationale de Paris Intercontinentale, 1 Sir William Newton Street, Port Louis (tel: 208-4147/8/9, 208-4151/2; fax: 208-8143).

Delphis Bank Limited, 16 Sir William Newton Street, Port Louis (tel: 208-5061; fax: 208-5388).

Development Bank of Mauritius Ltd, PO Box 157, Chaussée, Port Louis (tel: 208-0241; fax: 208-8498).

Indian Ocean International Bank Ltd, 34 Sir William Newton Street, Port Louis (tel: 208-0121; fax: 208-0127).

Mauritius Commercial Bank Ltd, 9-15 Sir William Newton St, Port Louis (tel: 202-5000; fax: 208-7054).

South East Asian Bank Ltd, 26 Bourbon Street, PO Box 13, Port Louis (tel: 208-8826/7/8, 212-2884/6/7; fax: 208-8825).

State Bank of Mauritius Ltd, PO Box 152, State Bank Tower, 1 Queen Elizabeth II Ave, Port Louis (tel: 202-1111; fax: 202-1234).

Central bank
Bank of Mauritius, Sir William Newton Street, Port Louis (tel: 208-4164 fax: 208-9204; e-mail: bomrd@bow.intnet.mu).

Travel information
Air Mauritius, Rogers House, 5 President John F. Kennedy Street, PO Box 441, Port Louis (tel: 208-7700; fax: 208-8331).

Ministry of tourism
Ministry of Tourism, Emmanuel Anquetil Bldg, Sir Seewoosagur Ramgoolam St, Port Louis (tel: 201-2286).

National tourist organisation offices
Mauritius Tourism Promotion Authority, 11th Floor, Air Mauritius Centre, President John Kennedy Street, Port-Louis (tel: 210-1545; fax: 212-5142; e-mail: mtpa@intnet.mu; Internet: www.mauritius.net).

Ministries
Ministry of Agriculture and Natural Resources, NPF Bldg, 9th Floor, Port Louis (tel: 212-7946; fax: 212-4427).

Ministry of Arts, Culture, Leisure and Reform Institutions, Government Centre, Port Louis (tel: 201-2032).

Ministry of Civil Service Affairs and Employment, Government Centre, Port Louis (tel: 201-1035; fax: 212-9528).

Ministry of Co-operatives and Handicraft, Life Insurance Corporation of India Bldg, 3rd Floor, John Kennedy St, Port Louis (tel: 208-4812; fax: 208-9265).

Ministry of Economic Planning and Development, Emmanuel Anquetil Bldg, Sir Seewoosagur Ramgoolam St, Port Louis (tel: 201-1576; fax: 212-4124).

Ministry of Education and Science, Sun Trust Bldg, Edith Cavell St, Port Louis (tel: 212-8411; fax: 212-3783).

Ministry of Energy, Water Resources and Postal Services, Government Centre, Port Louis (tel: 201-1087; fax: 208-6497).

Ministry of the Environment and Quality of Life, Barracks St, Port Louis (tel: 212-8332; fax: 212-9407).

Ministry of External Affairs, Government Centre, Port Louis (tel: 201-1416; fax: 208-8087).

Ministry of Finance, Government Centre, Port Louis (tel: 201-1145; fax: 208-8622).

Ministry of Fisheries and Marine Resources, Port Louis.

Ministry of Health, Emmanuel Anquetil Bldg, Sir Seewoosagur Ramgoolam St, Port Louis (tel: 201-1910; fax: 208-0376).

Ministry of Housing, Lands and Town and Country Planning, Moorgate House, Port Louis (tel: 212-6022; fax: 212-7482).

Ministry of Industry and Industrial Technology, Government Centre, Port Louis (tel: 201-1221; fax: 212-8201).

Ministry of Information, Government Centre, Port Louis (tel: 201-1278; fax: 208-8243).

Ministry of Internal and External Communications, Emmanuel Anquetil Bldg, 10th Floor, Sir Seewoosagur Ramgoolam St, Port Louis (tel: 201-1089; fax: 212-1673).

Ministry of Justice, Jules Koenig St, Port Louis (tel: 208-5321).

Ministry of Labour and Industrial Relations, Ming Court, cnr Eugène Laurent and GMD Atchia Sts, Port Louis (tel: 212-3049; fax: 212-3070).

Ministry of Local Government, Government Centre, Port Louis (tel: 201-1215).

Ministry of Manpower Resources and Vocational and Technical Training, Jade House, Remy Ollier St, Port Louis (tel: 242-1462).

Ministry for Rodrigues Island, Fon Sing Bldg, Edith Cavell St, Port Louis (tel: 208-8472; fax: 212-6329).

Ministry of Social Security and National Solidarity, cnr Maillard and Jules Koenig Sts, Port Louis (tel: 212-3006).

Ministry of Trade and Shipping, Government Centre, Port Louis (tel: 201-1067; fax: 212-6386).

Ministry of Women's Rights, Child Development and Family Welfare, Rainbow House, cnr Edith Cavell and Brown Sequard Sts, Port Louis (tel: 208-2061; fax: 208-8250).

Ministry of Works, Treasury Bldg, Port Louis (tel: 208-0281; fax: 212-8373).

Ministry of Youth and Sports, Emmanuel Anquetil Bldg, Sir Seewoosagur Ramgoolam St, Port Louis (tel: 201-1242; fax: 212-6506).

Prime Minister's Office, Government Centre, Port Louis (tel: 201-1001; fax: 208-8619).

Other useful addresses
British High Commission, Commercial Section, 7th Floor, Les Cascades Building, Edith Cavell Street, Port Louis (tel: 208-9850/1; fax: 212-8470).

Export Processing Zone Development Authority, 5th Floor, Les Cascades, Edith Cavell St, Port Louis (tel: 212-9760; fax: 212-9767).

Mauritius Embassy (USA), Suite 441, 4301 Connecticut Avenue, NW, Washington DC 20008 (tel: 202-244-1491; fax: 202-966-0983; e-mail: mauritius.embassy@prodigy.net).

Mauritius Employers' Federation, Cerné House, Chausse, Port Louis (tel: 212-1599; fax: 212-6725).

Mauritius Export Processing Zone Association, 42 Sir William Newton St, Port Louis (tel: 208-5216; fax: 212-1853).

Mauritius Free Port Authority, 2nd Floor, Deramann Tower, Sir William Newton St, Port Louis (tel: 212-9627; fax: 212-9629).

Mauritius Industrial Development Authority, Level 2, BAI Bldg, 25 Pope Hennessy St, Port Louis (tel: 208-7750; fax: 208-5965; e-mail: mida@media.intnet.mu).

Mauritius Offshore Business Activities Authority, 1st Floor, Deramann Tower, 30 Sir William Newton St, Port Louis (tel: 212-9650; fax: 212-9459).

Mauritius Standards Bureau, Ministry of Industry and Industrial Technology, Réduit (tel: 454-1933; fax: 464-7675).

Internet sites

Africa Business Network: http://www.ifc.org/abn

AllAfrica.com: http://allafrica.com

African Development Bank: http://www.afdb.org

Business Directory: http://www.mauritius.co.uk/

Harambee Afrika (UK business club for traders with east, central and southern Africa; includes annotated web resource list): http://www.harambee.co.uk

Mbendi AfroPaedia (information on companies, countries, industries and stock exchanges in Africa): http://mbendi.co.za

Mexico

KEY FACTS

Official name: Estados Unidos Mexicanos (United Mexican States)

Head of State: President Vicente Fox (PAN) (since Dec 2000)

Head of government: President Vicente Fox

Ruling party: Partido Acción Nacional (PAN) (National Action Party) (since Dec 2000, despite being in a minority in the Chamber of Deputies)

Area: 1,958,201 square km

Population: 102.80 million (2004)

Capital: Mexico City (DF)

Official language: Spanish

Currency: Mexican peso (Mex$) = 100 centavos

Exchange rate: Mex$10.78 per US$ (Oct 2005)

GDP per capita: US$6,506 (2004)

GDP real growth: 4.40% (2004)

Labour force: 40.74 million (2004)

Unemployment: 3.20% (2004)*; 25.00% (underemployment, 2004)*; 3.00% (2003)

Inflation: 4.70% (2004); 4.60% (2005)*

Oil production: 3.82 million bpd (2004)

Balance of trade: -US$8.81 billion (2004)

Foreign debt: US$165.90 billion (2004)

Annual FDI: US$147.90 billion (cumulative, 1995–2004, OECD); US$16.60 billion (OECD, 2004)*

* estimated figure

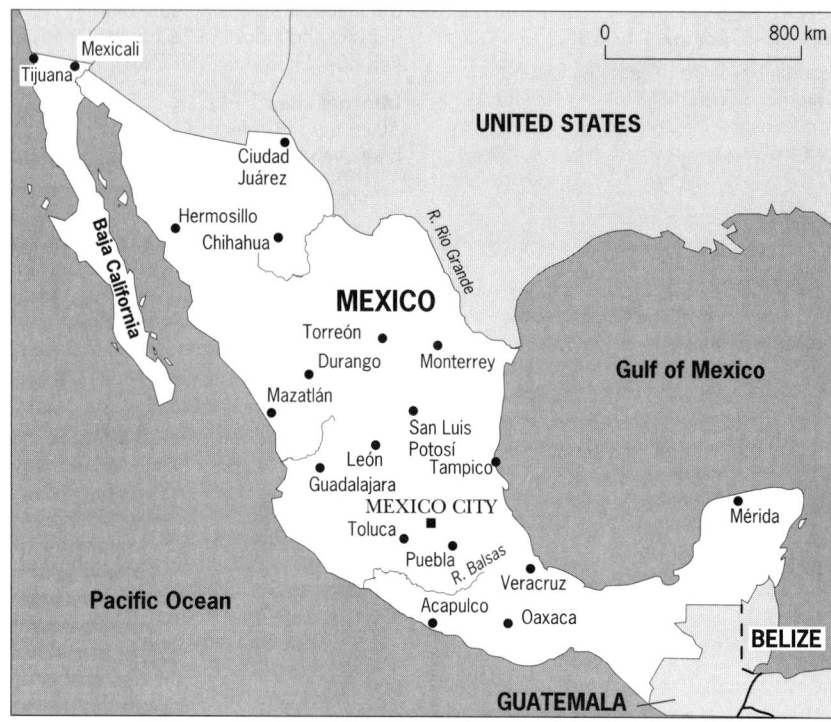

President Vicente Fox Quesada's (Partido Acción Nacional (PAN) (National Action Party) first and only term in office, which expires in 2006, may be described as one of failed expectations. Having been elected to the presidency in 2001, as the first non-Partido Revolucionario Institucional (PRI) (Institutional Revolutionary Party) president in 70 years, the whole of Mexico held its breath in anticipation of the dawning of a new era. Victorious with 43 per cent of the vote, Fox was presented with a minority in Congress. Opposition forces were already baying for the new president's blood, as he had run a particularly ruthless electoral campaign, never afraid to dish the dirt on the personal activities of his political opponents.

As if facing wounded and vengeful enemies was not bad enough, Fox further antagonised his opponents and raised the expectations of his supporters when he pledged to solve Mexico's southern guerrilla conflict 'in fifteen minutes'. An unrealistic promise to achieve economic growth of 7 per cent in each of his six years in office didn't help either. Fox was still seen as a political saviour by the population at large until the 2003 mid-term elections though, in which his party suffered several high profile losses. Increasingly over the years Fox even succeeded in alienating his own supporters by means of his cabinet appointments. His original cabinet in 2000 did not include a single PAN member and the subsequent creation of *el gabinetazo* (the super cabinet), composed of prominent members of the business elite, did nothing to endear him further.

The lamest of lame ducks

The incumbent's final full year in office has been nothing short of a political and public relations disaster. January began with reports of complete disarray within the country's prison infrastructure after inmates serving drug-related offences took over the maximum security La Palma prison, apparently planning a mass breakout. The army was later sent in to regain control amid sensational reports of prisoner co-operation with civilian drug lords outside of the prison. Things got even worse for Fox in May when, following controversial remarks concerning Hispanic immigrants and African-American citizens at a business convention in Texas, he was rebuked by US civil-rights campaigner, Reverend Jesse Jackson.

Regional elections

A number of sub-national elections took place in Mexico in 2005, including Baja California Sur, Guerrero, Quintana Roo and Hidalgo in February, Colima in April, Nayarit and Estado de México in July and Coahuila in September. PAN candidates generally performed poorly and Fox's anti-midas touch was evident on other occasions during 2005. The day after Foxistas had come out in force at a pre-arranged Day of Democracy event their candidate in the Estado de México, Rubén Mendoza Ayala, was defeated. Luis Ernesto Derbez, Fox's foreign minister and Washington's preferred candidate for the head of the Organisation of American States (OAS) was also defeated in his quest for the top diplomatic role in Latin America. Then, following comments by Fox on the inappropriateness of campaigning for political office while holding government office, Secretary of the Interior Santiago Creel (the president's favoured successor), lost his bid for the presidential candidacy to Felipe Calderón.

Mexico's first lady

Rumours of President Fox's wife Marta 'Sahagún' de Fox's (also known by her maiden name: Marta Sahagún Jiménez) future political ambitions have been common knowledge among Mexico's political elite for years. Though the position or title of First Lady does not officially exist under the Mexican constitution, Sahagún is commonly acknowledged to be an influential member of the president's inner circle, having previously been Fox's official spokesperson. Fox himself has frequently used the phrase *la pareja presidencial* (the presidential couple) to describe their working relationship, to the chagrin of the Mexican media.

The plot had thickened for *la pareja presidencial* in 2004 when the *Financial Times* of London (*FT*) unearthed evidence that Sahagún's charitable foundation, Vamos Mexico, had been receiving illicit funds from the state-run national lottery. These funds were allegedly earmarked to finance a future presidential run for Sahagún, potentially in 2006 after her husband's term finished. A follow up report was later published by the *FT* in the final days of 2004, in which it was alleged that only 35 per cent of Vamos Mexico's funds were dedicated to charitable work and the organisation's accounting standards were criticised. A Congressional investigation was launched and it subsequently emerged that Sahagún had amassed US$7.5 million in an American bank account, which she later claimed was a donation from the Coca-Cola Corporation, her husband's old employer. Fox's political secretary then resigned, stating that he could no longer stay in his position so long as the president continued to act as patron to his wife's presidential ambitions. Following the alleged scandal Sahagún's presidential ambitions fell into a state of disrepair, having damaged her popularity and credibility severely.

Race for the Presidential Palace

On 2 July 2006 Mexicans will choose a new president to serve a single six-year term. A variety of different parties, eight in total, will contest the election. The majority of parties have selected their presidential candidates for 2006 already. Candidates include Felipe Calderón of PAN, the controversial Andrés Manuel López Obrador of the Partido de la Revolución Democrática (PRD) (Party of the Democratic Revolution) and Roberto Madrazo Pintado (PRI). The PAN, having succeeded in being the first opposition party to win a presidential election are looking weary and appear to be tarnished by Fox's lacklustre presidency. While the PRI, their pride wounded so severely in 2000, are keen to regain the keys to the presidential palace.

The recent surge in support for PRD candidate López Obrador, has raised the prospect of a third party wining the presidency in the space of three elections. Such a development would represent the true commencement of competitive multi-party politics in the country. But there remains a lot of work for López Obrador to do before he can safely call the presidential residence his home. Despite a substantial lead for the Mexico City Mayor, Calderón has clawed back some ground in recent weeks. A poll published on 26 January 2006 by the *El Universal* newspaper put López Obrador on 33 per cent and Calderón on 27 per cent with Madrazo trailing in third position with only 20 per cent.

López Obrador's current lead in the polls caps a resurgence for this comeback-kid of Mexican politics. The Mexico City mayor was the subject of a politically motivated attempt by his opponents to impeach him, which culminated in April 2005. The impeachment case, which was launched for a relatively minor offence by Mexican political standards, if passed, would have effectively eradicated López Obrador's immunity from prosecution and thus barred him from the 2006

KEY INDICATORS — Mexico

	Unit	2000	2001	2002	2003	2004
Population	m	99.02	101.00	102.40	102.60	102.80
Gross domestic product (GDP)	US$bn	575.00	618.00	644.00	626.10	*676.50
GDP per capita	US$	5,600	6,160	6,320	6,006	6,506
GDP real growth	%	6.6	-0.1	0.7	1.3	4.4
Inflation	%	9.5	6.4	5.0	4.5	4.7
Unemployment	%	4.0	2.5	2.7	3.0	–
Oil output	'000 bpd	3,450.0	3,560.0	3,585.0	3,789.0	3,824.0
Natural gas output	bn cum	35.8	34.7	34.8	36.4	37.1
Coal output	mtoe	5.3	5.7	5.7	5.0	4.3
Exports (fob) (goods)	US$m	166,455.0	158,443.0	160,810.0	164,240.0	187,999.0
Imports (fob) (goods)	US$m	174,458.0	168,398.0	168,950.0	169,634.0	196,810.0
Balance of trade	US$m	-8,003.0	-9,955.0	-8,200.0	-5,394.0	-8,811.0
Current account	US$m	-18,157.0	-17,708.0	-14,060.0	-11,030.0	-8,710.0
Foreign debt	US$bn	154.7	154.4	151.0	151.0	–
Total reserves minus gold	US$m	35,509.0	44,741.0	50,594.0	58,956.0	64,141.0
Foreign exchange	US$m	35,142.0	44,384.0	49,895.0	57,740.0	62,778.0
Exchange rate	per US$	9.46	9.34	9.79	10.81	11.29

* estimated figure

presidential race. In a vote by the Chamber of Deputies on 7 April, the members of the chamber voted 360 to 127 to remove López Obrador's constitutional immunity from prosecution.

Mobilising his supporters in an attempt to reverse the decision, a peaceful march was scheduled for 24 April through Mexico City, where reports suggested over a million people turned out to show their support for his cause. In what appeared to be the beginnings of a climb down President Fox announced a cabinet reshuffle effective from 27 April. The new Attorney General announced on 4 May that charges against López Obrador would be dropped on the basis of a constitutional loophole, thus freeing him to participate in the 2006 election. Opposition parties voiced their disgust at the ruling, most notably the PRI.

Economy

President Fox's economic policy has at times been criticised for being poorly thought out. Slow growth has been the predominant feature of the Mexican economy since 2001. Following an inheritance of real GDP growth equivalent to 6.6 per cent, a contraction of 0.1 per cent was recorded in 2001. An expansion of just 0.7 per cent was recorded in 2002, followed by a 1.3 per cent increase in 2003, before a jump to 4.4 per cent in 2004. Many observers claim that this slow rate of growth has led to a marked increase in migration to the United States, as the number of jobs available in the economy has fallen. According to data released in September 2005, as reported by *El Universal*, there are now 180,000 fewer jobs in the economy than there were in 2001. The latest data released by the IMF and the World Bank put Mexico in 11th and 12th positions respectively, in rating the world's largest economies by total GDP.

An alternative school of thought points to the Fox administration's implementation of macroeconomic stabilisation in Mexico. When measured in terms of GDP per capita the economy is healthier than in 2000. Per capita income among Mexicans now averages approximately US$900 more than when PAN came to power. Furthermore, the increase in personal wealth has been achieved within an environment of decreasing inflation. Having been 9.5 per cent per annum in 2000 the rate now stands at 4.7 per cent. Indeed, the Fox government deserves credit for generally steadying the economy, a feat that is especially important when Mexico's recent history of economic crisis (1994–95) is factored in. Though growth has been sluggish in recent years, there is a case to be made that the economy may now have turned the corner and is on the way to more dynamic expansion. The latest IMF forecast suggests an augmentation of 3 per cent in 2005 and 3.5 per cent in 2006.

Foreign relations

In November 2005 Fox vehemently criticised several other Latin American governments for their refusal to participate in the proposed Free Trade Area of the Americas (FTAA). Fox is steadfastly committed to the FTAA on the grounds that it will be of huge material benefit to the Mexican economy. He has also shared a generally warm personal relationship with US president George W Bush, despite having opposed Washington's policy of regime change in Iraq. In fact, in recent months Fox's prominent advocacy of the FTAA has displeased the press in his own country, resulting in allegations of subservience to Washington.

Outlook

The presidential elections scheduled to take place in July 2006 will make for exciting viewing. Victory for López Obrador will mean that Mexico's party political system will be more or less consolidated, as multi-party competition will become a true reality for the first time. A victory for the Mexico City Mayor would also mean a shift to the left, with likely increases in public spending. Economic growth, though sluggish over recent years, did pick up in 2004 and 2005, but whether this will prove momentary or permanent remains to be seen.

Risk assessment

Economy	Stable/Improving
Politics	Stable
Regional stability	Good

COUNTRY PROFILE

Historical profile

The Olmecs inhabited the country around 3,500 years ago, their civilisation reaching its peak about 1200 BC. By AD 500–600, the Mayas had risen to prominence and Teotihuacan, (where Mexico City now stands) was thriving, with 200,000 inhabitants.
1519 The Spanish, and Hernan Cortés, arrived. The Aztecs were the dominant culture.
1810–21 The Spanish colony became independent. Conflicts with the US and France ensued.
1876–1910 The Porfirio Díaz dictatorship, known as the *Porfiriato*, led to a series of revolutions and coups.
1911 Díaz resigned and was replaced by Francisco Madero, one of the revolutionary leaders.
1911–17 A period of civil war, with revolutionary peasant leaders Francisco Villa and Emiliano Zapata refusing to back the government.
1914 General Venustiano Carranza seized power, preventing the re-emergence of the *Porfiriato*.
1917 The institution of Mexico's modern liberal constitution which enshrined land reform and labour rights.
1920 Carranza was assassinated. Civil war broke out.
1929 President Plutarco Elías Calles created the Partido Nacional Revolucionario (PNR) (National Revolutionary Party), a multi-class party that developed institutionalised mechanisms which enabled and controlled popular participation in government.
1934 General Lázaro Cárdenas became president and restructured the PNR, renaming it the Partido de la Revolución Mexicana (PRM) (Party of the Mexican Revolution). He also created official unions for workers and peasants, which were controlled by the official party.
1939 Disenchanted middle-class conservatives launched the Partido de Acción Nacional (PAN) (National Action Party).
1940 Leon Trotsky was assassinated in Mexico.
1946 Miguel Alemán became president and renamed the ruling party the Partido Revolucionario Institucional (PRI) (Institutional Revolutionary Party), signifying the final transition from the ideals of the revolution to liberal capitalism and a corporatist state.
1968 Growing disenchantment with authoritarian politics and rising urban poverty led to a series of mass demonstrations, culminating in a massacre of several hundred peaceful demonstrators, most of them young students.
1970 Luis Echeverría Alvarez became president, seeking to calm political turbulence through increased state spending and bolstering the power of trade unions.
1976 José López Portillo was appointed president. Oil revenues were used to borrow additional capital to initiate a rapid transition towards industrial development.
1982 An economic recession in the US, high international interest rates and falling oil prices sparked a debt crisis in which Mexico was unable to obtain enough loans to service existing debts and ran out of money. A programme of economic stabilisation and structural adjustment was initiated under the administration of President Miguel de la Madrid, creating divisions within the PRI.
1988 The PRI split. The left-wing *corriente democrática* joined a coalition of minor

parties to back the candidacy of Cuauhtémoc Cárdenas, son of former president, Lázaro Cárdenas, in the presidential elections. Despite massive electoral fraud, Cárdenas still managed to come second behind the PRI's Carlos Salinas de Gortari.
1992 As part of Mexico's commitments in the run-up to the signing of the North American Free Trade Agreement (Nafta), Salinas effectively repealed Article 27 of the Mexican Constitution which had guaranteed land reform.
1994 The Zapatistas led an uprising in Chiapas in response to the treatment of indigenous peasants and neo-liberal economic policy. The Zapatistas attracted worldwide sympathy and attention was fixed on the effects of economic policy and Nafta on the growing number of Mexico's poor. The PRI's presidential candidate, Luis Donaldo Colosio, was murdered; many believed the killing was carried out by members of his own party.
1994 Ernesto Zedillo of the PRI won the presidential election amid accusations of dirty tricks and vote-buying.
1997 Mid-term congressional elections left the PRI as the biggest single party in the lower house of Congress, but denied it an absolute majority. A deal was struck between the left-wing Partido de la Revolución Democrática (PRD) (Party of the Democratic Revolution) and the traditionally conservative Partido Acción Nacional (PAN), as well as two smaller parties, giving the opposition its first taste of real power.
2000 PAN won the elections, and the PRI lost the presidency and its majority in the Senate, as well as its status as the party with the largest number of seats in the lower house. The break with PRI rule was historic as the party, including its previous incarnations, had enjoyed continuous office since 1929.
2001 The Senate unanimously approved a constitutional bill granting autonomy to indigenous people, opening the way for peace talks with the Zapatista rebels, although this fell short of the demands of the Zapatistas.
2002 Roberto Madrazo won the elections for the leadership of PRI.
2003 An earthquake in January, estimated at 7.6 magnitude, was the strongest to hit Mexico in seven years.
2004 In January a federal investigation was ordered into the unsolved murder of 250 women, over a ten year period, in the border town of Ciudad Juarez. In July, some 250,000 people demonstrated in the capital, Mexico City, against the ineffectiveness of the city and national governments in the face of violent crime and kidnappings.
2005 Six prisoners were murdered in January and all high security jails were put on high alert, following an escalation of tension between the authorities and drug gangs. In April, Mexico City mayor Andres Manuel Lopez Obrador was stripped of his immunity from prosecution by Congress in a land expropriation dispute. The case was later dropped by the national government. Hurricane Wilma hit the Yucatan peninsula in October, leading to property damage and severe flooding.

Political structure
Constitution
The political system established by the 1917 constitution emphasises presidential power.
Mexico is a federal republic of 31 states and one federal district (Mexico City). States are divided into municipalities. State governors are directly elected every six years. Deputies of state legislatures hold office for three years. The states are empowered to raise taxes and introduce and enforce state laws.
In order to register for federal elections, political parties must have a total of at least 65,000 party members and must have 3,000 supporters per state in at least 16 states or 300 party members per constituency in at least half of the constituencies which return deputies elected by majority vote. Alternatively, a party may be allowed conditional registration if it has been active for four years. This conditional registration can be converted to official registration if the party then obtains at least 1.5 per cent of the vote. In 1989, a law was adopted giving a party obtaining 35 per cent of the vote in a general election an absolute majority in the chamber of deputies.

Form of state
Federal presidential democratic republic

The executive
The president is directly elected by majority vote for a period of six years and takes office on 1 December of the election year, but is unable to stand for a second term. The president is assisted by a cabinet (usually 19 members), one of whom is the governor of the Federal District (the administrative area which includes the capital, Mexico City), the attorney general for the country as a whole and the attorney general for the Federal District. The cabinet is appointed by the president.
The president also appoints the judges of the supreme court and higher courts of justice, the senior officers of the armed forces and diplomats, but these appointments are subject to approval by the Senate.

National legislature
The Congress is a bicameral legislature consisting of the 500-member Chamber of Deputies, elected for a three-year term, and the 64-member Senate, whose members are elected every six years.
The Senate is elected by majority vote and is composed of two members for each of the 31 states and two members for the Federal District.
Of the deputies, 300 are elected by majority vote and 200 by proportional representation.
The permanent committee, composed of 15 deputies and 14 senators, acts in place of the Congress when the Congress is in recess. Members of both chambers are ineligible for immediate re-election.

Legal system
Under the 1917 constitution, the judiciary is independent of the executive and legislative bodies, but in practice the judiciary tends not to oppose the president.
The judicial system is divided into federal and state judiciaries.
The federal system has both ordinary and constitutional jurisdiction. It consists of the 21-member supreme court (which deals with penal, administrative, civil and labour cases), collegiate circuit courts (cases regarding an individual's constitutional rights) and unitary circuit courts (appeals). There are 12 collegiate circuits and nine unitary circuits. There are 68 district courts.

Last elections
6 July 2003 (congressional: Chamber of Deputies); 2 July 2000 (presidential and congressional (Chamber of Deputies and Senate)).
Results: Congressional: the ruling party, Partido Acción Nacional (PAN) (National Action Party), lost seats, winning only 153 seats; the Partido Revolucionario Institucional (PRI) (Institutional Revolutionary Party) became the largest party in Congress with 224 seats; there was a low turnout (42 per cent).
Presidential: Vicente Fox won with 43.43 per cent of the vote.

Next elections
2006 (presidential and congressional)

Political parties
Ruling party
Partido Acción Nacional (PAN) (National Action Party) (since Dec 2000, despite being in a minority in the Chamber of Deputies)

Main opposition party
Partido Revolucionario Institucional (PRI) (Institutional Revolutionary Party)

Population
102.80 million (2004)
Ethnic make-up
Mestizo (mixed Indian-European) (55 per cent), Amerindian (29 per cent), European origin (16 per cent).

Nations of the World: A Political, Economic and Business Handbook

Religions
Roman Catholic (89 per cent), Protestant (6 per cent).

Education
Compulsory education is provided free of charge. Primary schooling lasts for six years; secondary education (which begins at age 12), is divided into two cycles of three years. Students either follow an academic or technical programme of education, which can lead on to higher education or specialised training.
In 1985, the government reorganised state education with priority given to literacy.
Literacy rate: 91.7 per cent total; 89.8 per cent female, adult rates in 2002 (World Bank).
Compulsory years: Six to 16
Enrolment rate: 106 per cent gross primary enrolment of relevant age group (including repeaters); 64 per cent gross secondary enrolment; 16 per cent in tertiary education (World Bank).
Pupils per teacher: 27 in primary schools (World Bank)

Health
Total expenditure on health is around 6 per cent of GDP, of which government spending is 44 per cent.
By 2002, 96 per cent of infants aged less than one year had been immunised against measles. Access to clean drinking water is available to over 80 per cent of the population.
About half of the hospitals belong to the Instituto Mexicano del Seguro Social (IMSS) (Mexican Institute for Social Security).
HIV prevalence: 0.3 per cent aged 15–49 in 2003 (World Bank)
Life expectancy: 73.6 years (World bank)
Fertility rate/Maternal mortality rate: 2.2 births per woman (World Bank)
Infant mortality rate: 23 per 1,000 live births; about 7.5 per cent of children aged under five are malnourished (World Bank).
Head of population per physician/bed: With 1.3 doctors per 1,000 of the population, Mexico has more physicians per head than any other state in Central America with the exception of Panama.

Welfare
Social welfare is administered primarily by the IMSS and financed by contributions from employees, employers and the government. Some institutions, such as Petróleos Mexicanos (Pemex) (Mexican Petroleum), the military and the Federal Electricity Commission, have their own systems. About half of the working population is covered by social security. There is no unemployment benefit.

Main cities
Mexico City (capital, estimated population 8.7 million in 2004; 2,240 metres above sea-level), Ecatepec (1.8 million), Guadalajara (1.7 million), Puebla (1.4 million), Ciudad Juárez (1.3 million), Tijuana (1.3 million), Nezahualcóyotl (1.3 million), Monterrey (1.1 million), León (1.1 million), Zapopan (943,800), Naucalpan (859,700), Tlalnepantla (734,200), Guadalupe (700,500).

Languages spoken
Native American languages spoken include Náhuati, Maya and Zapoteco. Some English is spoken in business centres.
Official language/s
Spanish

Media
Press
Dailies: There are several Spanish language dailies published from Mexico City and other regions, the most influential being *Excélsior*, *La Crónica de Hoy*, *El Debate*, *Diario de Chihuahua*, *El Diario de Yucatan*, *Frontera*, *El Heraldo de Chihuahua*, *El Heraldo de México*, *El Imparcial*, *El Día*, *El Independiente*, *El Informador*, *La Jornada*, *Kesher Editorial*, *La Mañana*, *El Mañana*, *Mural*, *Reforma*, *El Universal*, *Uno más uno*, *El Norte* and *Novedades*. English language publications include a daily colour tabloid *El Nacional*, *Diario de Juárez*, *Público*, *The News* and the bi-lingual *Novedades Quintana Roo* (Spanish, English).
The sport papers *Esto* and *Ovaciones* have the largest circulations.
Weeklies: *Gringo Gazette* is an English language bi-weekly newspaper covering local news, recreation, entertainment, and community events in southern Baja.
Business: Business publications include *El Financiero* and the daily *El Economista*.
Broadcasting
Radio: Over 800 commercial and 45 cultural radio stations. Radio VIP in Mexico City broadcasts in English.
The largest radio station is Radio Centro. Approximately a third of the population owns a radio set.
Television: Most Mexicans have access to a television set. There are over 400 television stations. The largest is Televisa, a private company, which closely follows the government line but operates independently. It has four channels, one of which is broadcast nationally. The company estimates that its main news programme, 24 Hours, reaches an average of 14 million viewers. The second largest station, Channel 13, estimates that its main news programme, 7 Days, is watched on average by six million people.

Advertising
Annual advertising expenditure is equivalent to 1.2 per cent of GDP. Most international advertising companies have offices in Mexico City. Television advertising dominates the sector, but billboards are popular. This is partly because restrictions on tobacco and alcohol advertising do not apply to billboards, and partly owing to the high population density in the three main cities, especially Mexico City, which contains half the country's 15,000 billboards.

Economy
Mexico's economy has performed somewhat erratically during the 2000s. Real GDP growth was as low as 0.6 per cent in 2002 and 1.6 per cent in 2003, but in recent years the level of growth has picked up. In 2004, the economy grew by 4.4 per cent and the IMF forecasts a reduced level of 3 per cent for 2005 and 3.5 per cent for 2006. The rate of inflation in the economy has fallen from 9.5 per cent in 2000 and now stands at 4.6 per cent. Mexico is a large oil producer with exports accounting for just under one-third of government revenue. Remittances from Mexicans working in the US are Mexico's second most important source of income, overtaking the tourist sector. One-tenth of the population live and earn in the US and the impact on the economy of the increasing number of families being left without a main bread-earner has not yet struck.
Mexico's membership of the North American Free Trade Agreement (NAFTA) since 1994 has encouraged massive inflows of foreign direct investment, which in turn have transformed Mexico into a manufacturing base serving its large domestic market as well the US market. Virtually all the world's major companies are now present in Mexico. Asian electronics companies, for instance, proliferate in the state of Baja California, which is host to a multitude of operations run by companies based in the Far East. Despite this, the services sector has steadily risen – by 4.1 per cent in the first quarter of 2005, compared to a fall of 0.2 per cent for the industry sector. The rise of Chinese exports to the US is beginning to have an adverse affect on Mexican exports.
Mexico has largely decoupled its economy from Brazil, and has much stronger ties with the US. Underpinning this has been a shift from an oil-based economy to a manufacturing-based economy, driven by the initial growth of the *maquiladoras* (in-bond assembly lines) and the development of import-export business, particularly in the car and light manufacturing industries.

The overall expansion of the Mexican economy has increased jobs in the formal sector and bolstered disposable income. Together with a strong peso, this has led to a surge in imports, although high oil export prices have limited the deterioration of the trade deficit. Sluggish growth in 2003 and 2004 was largely due to the economic slowdown in the US. Industrial output continued to decline due to a contraction in the *maquiladora* sector. The OECD 2005 Economic Policy Reforms makes a number of employment related recommendations including: making the school system more effective, eliminating barriers to the telecommunications sector, easing restrictions on FDI, reforming the tax system and improving the 'rule of law'.

External trade

Mexico is a member of the Organisation for Economic Co-operation and Development (OECD). The country is a signatory of the North American Free Trade Agreement (Nafta) along with the United States and Canada. Mexico has also signed free trade agreements with Costa Rica, Venezuela and Colombia.

Imports

Principal imports are metalworking machines, steel mill products, agricultural machinery, electrical equipment, car parts for assembly, repair parts for motor vehicles, aircraft, and aircraft parts.

Main sources: US (65.8 per cent total, 2004), Germany (3.8 per cent), China (3.7 per cent)

Exports

Principal exports are manufactured goods, oil and oil products, silver, fruits, vegetables, coffee and cotton.

Main destinations: US (81 per cent total, 2004), Canada (5.9 per cent), Japan (1.1 per cent)

Agriculture

Farming

Approximately 5 per cent of Mexico's total GDP is attributable to the agricultural sector. Despite this relatively low percentage contribution to GDP, the labour intensive nature of the agricultural sector ensures that it employs up to a quarter of the total workforce.

Farming is small-scale and frequently inefficient. About 50 per cent of total cultivatable land (estimated at 19 million hectares) is held by *ejidos*, rural communities farming on small individual/collective lots. There are few large commercial farms except in export-oriented vegetable-producing regions of the north-west. The principal food crops are maize (over 50 per cent of harvested area and 60 per cent of total grain production), sorghum, wheat, rice, barley, potatoes, soya beans and dry beans. The production of basic foodstuffs can be severely affected by drought, insufficient irrigation (less than 30 per cent of cultivated land is irrigated) and underdeveloped marketing and infrastructural back-up. Supplies of food grain in particular have not kept up with the demands imposed by rapid population growth. Principal export crops are coffee, cotton, fresh fruit, honey, sugar, tobacco and tomatoes. Exports of cattle are also important.

Mexico's membership of the North American Free Trade Agreement (Nafta) has affected the farming sector, with the US dominating trade. In the five years prior to the implementation of Nafta in January 1994, farm output grew by 3.85 million tonnes, compared to an increase of just 2.1 million tonnes in the five years after the agreement came into effect. Between 1995 and 2001, the value of farm imports from the US increased from US$3.3 billion to US$7.4 billion, while Mexico's farm exports to the US grew from US$3.8 billion to US$5.3 billion. Mexico has become increasingly dependent on US food imports and by 2002 imported 95 per cent of the soya beans, 59 per cent of the rice and 40 per cent of the beef consumed domestically.

President Fox's pro-Nafta approach has come under increasing criticism from the Mexican public. Farmers fear that the subsidies to US's farmers will put them out of business. In January 2003, tariffs on 80 agricultural imports from the US and Canada were lifted as part of Nafta's provisions. Farmers' unions called on the government to renegotiate the trading rules, but the government refused and offered to negotiate a package of compensatory policies instead.

Crop production in 2004 included: 30,250,884 tonnes (t) cereals in total, 20,000,000t maize, 3,500,000t wheat, 1,109,420t barley, 6,300,000t sorghum, 1,734,810t potatoes, 2,026,610t bananas, 959,000t coconuts, 45,126,500t sugar cane, 310,861t green coffee, 48,405t cocoa beans, 2,148,130t tomatoes, 1,040,390t avocados, 21,895t tobacco, 6,475,411t citrus fruit, 146,636t fibre crops, 333,201t oilcrops, 1,751,506t pulses, 1,503,010t mangoes, 1,853,610t chillies & peppers, 456,638t grapes, 14,758,654t fruit in total, 10,013,516t vegetables in total. Livestock production included: 5,040,237t meat in total, 1,543,090t beef, 1,058,205t pig meat, 42,140t lamb, 41,626t goat meat, 2,272,080t poultry, 1,906,476t eggs, 10,028,233t milk, 56,808t honey, 5,661t sheepskins, 4,282t greasy wool, 176,230t cattle hides.

Fishing

Mexico's level of fish production is relatively high, with demand being met almost entirely by domestic production. Imports represent only 8.2 per cent of total seafood consumption.

Shrimps, tuna, mackerel, bass, perch, bonito, shark, oysters have risen in importance in the Mexican fishing sector. The leading fish producing states – Sinaloa, Sonora, Baja California, Veracruz and Baja California Sur – contribute to approximately 65.2 per cent of the country's total catch. Annually 70 per cent of the total catch comes from the Pacific Ocean compared to 30 per cent from the Gulf of Mexico, Caribbean and non-coastal states.

Forestry

Approximately 55.2 million hectares of Mexico's total landmass is covered by forests and the country is endowed with vast resources of soft and hard woods. However, deforestation is becoming a problem in certain areas and total forest cover decreased by about one per cent during the 1990–2000 period. Around 4 per cent of the country's total forested area is protected.

Most forestry products are produced for domestic consumption, mainly softwood sawnwood and wood-based panels. In a typical year imports of forest products amount to US$2.4 billion and exports amount to US$197 million.

Industry and manufacturing

The industrial sector is an important economic activity in Mexico, accounting for a significant proportion (29 per cent) of total GDP. About one fifth of total employment is accounted for by the sector.

The *maquiladoras* (in-bond assembly lines) make, assemble or process components and raw materials bought 'in-bond' from the US which are then re-exported duty-free. The growing importance of *maquiladora* exports to the US has made the Mexican economy more exposed to US demand. The US economic slowdown in 2001 and 2002 led to a contraction in the *maquiladora* sector.

Tourism

Mexico's tourism industry continues to grow strongly and the country remains Latin America's premier tourist destination. Travel and tourism now accounts for 14.5 per cent of total GDP and 14.2 per cent of total employment. Capital investment in the industry has also increased significantly in recent years and now accounts for 10.4 per cent of total capital investment in the economy.

Mexico rode out the effects of events such as the 11 September 2001 terrorist attacks in the US, suffering only a slight fall in visitor numbers to 19.8 million in 2002, while revenues increased. The sector was in recovery by 2004 and the prospects for considerable expansion are encouraging, with 20,237,400 people visiting the country in 2004 alone. This stability has been partly due to more Americans, wishing to avoid overseas travel and to holiday closer to home, visiting Mexico, many by cruise ships.

Mining
Mining is an important industry in Mexico and the country is a major producer of gold, silver and base metals. Mexico accounts for approximately 17 per cent of total world production of silver, 38 per cent of celestite production and 29 per cent of bismuth production. The mining sector continues to attract significant foreign investment, the vast majority of which comes from the US and Canada.
There are four major domestic producers: Industrias Peñoles, Grupo Industrial Menera Mexico, Empresas Frisco and Luismin. The main mining states are Sonora, Coahuila, Zacatecas, Chihuahua, Baja California Sur, San Luis Potosí, Durango and Guanajuato.

Hydrocarbons
Mexico is a significant producer of oil, with large proven reserves of 14.8 billion barrels. The country has the fourth largest proven reserves in the Western Hemisphere and produces some 3.8 million barrels per day (bpd). Net exports of oil amount to approximately 1.7 million bpd, the vast majority of which (79 per cent) is exported to the US.
Oil revenues account for one-third of total government income. Although Mexico is not a member of the Organisation of the Petroleum Exporting Countries (OPEC), government policy has often been to cut production in line with OPEC targets in an effort to increase world prices.
Most oil fields lie in or near the Gulf of Mexico. The largest producing field is within the Gulf of Campeche, which produces, on average, 65 per cent of total oil output. Mexico has the eleventh-largest refining capacity in the world which has improved the country's export potential. Mexico has six refineries with a total capacity of 1.5 million bpd. The government plans to increase refinery capacity by 350,000bpd in 2006.
Mexico has proven gas reserves of 420 billion cubic metres with production of 37.1 billion cubic metres. Most gas production is associated with oil extraction. Gas production is increasingly unable to fulfil domestic demand and Mexico is likely to import an increasing amount of gas from the US. However, Petróleos Mexicanos (Pemex), the state oil corporation, believes that by 2008, gas production will have increased by 50 per cent over 1999 levels. Although Pemex dominates the upstream gas industry, the downstream sector has undergone liberalisation since the passing of the 1995 Natural Gas Law, which allows private companies to participate in gas transportation, storage and distribution. Mexico has proven coal reserves of 1.2 billion tonnes, mostly located in Coahuila in the north-east. Most is used for steel production and electricity generation. Coal-fired generators supply 10 per cent of Mexico's electricity output.

Energy
Mexico's capacity for electricity generation is approximately 45.9GW, an increase on recent years. Approximately 83 per cent of total electricity generated comes from conventional thermal sources, 9 per cent from hydroelectricity and 5 per cent from nuclear power, while 3 per cent is derived from other renewables. Mexico's energy minister has stated that the country will need to spend about US$51 billion over the next 10 years in order to meet demand for electricity in the country. This would mean the construction of an extra 28GW of electricity generation capacity. Plans to construct three nuclear plants have been delayed, although the Laguna Verde plant has already been charged with radioactive materials. Hydroelectricity consumption is constant; nuclear energy consumption is declining marginally.
There has been considerable congressional opposition to President Fox's moves to privatise the electricity sector, including his moves to decrease subsidies for electricity charges to consumers. However, independent power producers (IPPs) have become a major source of investment in the Mexican electricity sector.

Banking and insurance
Mexico's banking and financial services sector is now well established, following privatisation in 1990. The sector had previously been nationalised in 1982. There are three main types of account held in Mexican banks; peso denominated checking accounts, US dollar checking accounts and certificates of deposit
Banco de México issues currency, controls monetary policy and is responsible for exchange rates and national reserves. Participation of the private sector is encouraged in a capital market involving leasing, mutual funds, insurance and brokerage. The banking crisis of 1995 caused by the turmoil of peso devaluation, resulted in the closure of several banks. The government was forced to inject huge amounts of emergency capital into the system. Mexico had 44 banks, 13 of which were government-owned.
Banamex is the country's largest bank, and comprises the operations of Citigroup and Banacci, which merged in August 2001.

Central bank
Banco de México

Main financial centre
Mexico City

Time
Generally GMT minus six hours (Baja California Sur, Nayarit, Sinaloa, Sonora: GMT minus seven hours; Baja California Norte: GMT minus eight hours). (Clocks are put forward one hour in summer).

Geography
Mexico is the largest country in Central America. To the north it is bordered by the US and to the south by Guatemala and Belize. The Gulf of Mexico and the Caribbean Sea lie to the east, and the Pacific Ocean and Gulf of California to the west. Mexico comprises a great variety of terrain, ranging from swamp to desert, from tropical lowland jungle to high alpine vegetation and from thin, arid soils to others so rich that they can support three crops a year. More than half the country is at an altitude of over 1,000 metres and much is over 2,000 metres.
Mexico has a northern frontier of 2,400km with the US and a southern frontier of 885km with Guatemala and Belize. It has a coastline of 2,780km on the Gulf of Mexico and the Caribbean and of 7,360km on the Pacific and the Gulf of California.
The central land mass is complex but may be simplified as a plateau flanked by an eastern and a western range of mountains running roughly parallel to the coasts. The northern part of the plateau is low, arid and thinly populated. The southern section of the central plateau is crossed by a volcanic range of mountains in which the intermont basins are high and separated. The mountainous southern end of the plateau, the heart of Mexico, has ample rainfall and although comprising only 14 per cent of the land, it holds nearly half the country's population. Mexico City lies in a small high intermont basin measuring 50 square km.

Climate
Varies with altitude. Tropical southern region and coastlands are hot and wet, while the highlands of the central plateau are temperate. Temperature in Mexico City ranges from 5–25 degrees Celsius (C) with occasional sharp frosts in winter (December–February).
Climate and vegetation depend on altitude. The *tierra caliente* (hot area) takes in the coastal and plateau lands below 750 metres. The *tierra fria* (cold zone) is from 2,000 metres upwards. The climate of the inland highlands is mostly mild, but with sharp changes of temperature between day and night, sunshine and shade. Generally, winter is the dry season and summer the wet season. There are only two areas where sufficient rain falls all

Mexico

year round. The first lies south of Tampico, the capital of Tamaulipas state, along the lower slopes of the Sierra Madre Oriental and across the isthmus of Tehuantepec into Tabasco state, and the second along the Pacific coast state of Chiapas. The two areas represent about 12 per cent of the total surface area. Apart from these favoured regions, the rest of Mexico is arid.

Dress codes
People generally dress smartly in Mexico City. Shorts are worn only at holiday resorts. Dress codes for business and leisure are usually the same as those of Europe. There is little central heating and moderately warm clothing is needed in the winter, particularly at night. The capital, Mexico City, is 2,240 metres above sea level. At lower altitudes temperatures can be very high and lightweight clothing is essential.

Entry requirements
Requirements for Mexico are complex and comprehensive guidance should be obtained from consular sections of local embassies before departure, any infringement of regulations can result in fines and expulsion.

Passports
Required for all, except citizens of Canada and the US with acceptable proof of identity.
A tourist card is essential, as visitors cannot leave the country without one, they are available free from some travel agencies, at the airport, in-flight, or issued at immigration, and should be carried at all times.

Visa
The regulations for entry into Mexico are complex and visitors are advised to confirm all aspects of visa requirements before travelling. Visas are not required by those using a tourist card, which are issued only to tourists and are valid for 30 days. All other visitors require visas. Business visas are divided into two, 'lucrative' and 'non-lucrative', and applications must be accompanied by a business letter of accreditation stating the nature of business, proof of sufficient funds for length of stay and a full itinerary, plus an invitation from a local company. See www.mexonline.com/visa.htm for more information.

Currency advice/regulations
There are no restrictions on import/export of foreign or Mexican currency. US dollars are the easiest currency to exchange. Unofficial money-changers offer substantially better rates than banks or hotels. Many establishments in cities or tourist areas accept payment in US dollars.

Customs
There are sometimes rigorous searches for drugs, firearms or large sums of currency, and expensive jewellery or electronic equipment may attract attention and demands for customs duty. There are restrictions on the import of motor vehicles.

Prohibited imports
Firearms are prohibited, although it is possible to obtain an import licence for a hunting rifle from Mexican consulates.

Health (for visitors)
Mandatory precautions
A yellow fever vaccination certificate is required if arriving from an infected area.
Advisable precautions
Diphtheria, tuberculosis, hepatitis A and B, typhoid, tetanus and polio vaccinations. Malaria risk exists in some rural areas – prophylaxis recommended. There is a rabies risk. Dengue fever is endemic in northern regions.
Bottled water and water supplied from taps marked 'drinking/sterilised water' in hotels can be drunk without precautions. All other water should be regarded as potentially contaminated.
Mexico City is at a high altitude, visitors may take some time to acclimatise to the atmosphere. The levels of pollution in Mexico City are extremely high and are considered a health threat, so precautions should be taken.
Health insurance is advised. Medical facilities are good and pharmacies are permitted to diagnose and treat minor ailments.

Hotels
Six classified types of hotels, with maximum rates set by government.
Mexico City is one of the biggest cities in the world, so location is very important. The main hotels are in the business, financial and commercial area along Reforma Avenue.
Advisable to book in advance. Fifteen per cent value-added tax, and service, are added to bills. 10 per cent tip usual.

Public holidays
Fixed dates
1 Jan (New Year's Day), 5 Feb (Constitution Day), 21 Mar (Birthday of Benito Juárez), 1 May (Labour Day), 5 May (Battle of Puebla Day), 16 Sep (Independence Day), 12 Oct (Columbus Day), 2 Nov (All Souls' Day), 20 Nov (Revolution Day), 12 Dec (Virgin of Guadalupe Day), 25 Dec (Christmas Day).
Variable dates
Easter Holiday

Working hours
Hours of business in Mexico City are variable and hours in other parts of the country vary considerably according to the climate and local custom.

Banking
Mon–Fri: 0900–1330; some banks are open on Saturday afternoon.
Business
Mon–Fri: 0800–1500.
Government
Mon–Fri: 0800–1500.
Shops
Mon–Sat: 1000–1800/1900.

Electricity supply
110–117V AC, 60 cycles. Two-pin flat plugs (as in USA) are used.

Social customs/useful tips
During the working day moderate punctuality is appreciated although some lateness is tolerated. It is acceptable to arrive late for evening social occasions which often continue well into the night.
Mexicans are patient, courteous and hospitable and will often treat visiting foreigners with polite reserve. An effort to speak Spanish is much appreciated. Otherwise it is advisable not to presume too much until you know the people concerned fairly well.
Tipping in hotels, restaurants and bars is expected since service charges are not added to the bill. A normal tip is 15 per cent. If service has been very good, 20 per cent should be given.
The law is seldom a problem for foreigners, although the police can be difficult with motorists. There is no perfect way of dealing with this but it is a good rule never to offer a bribe. A better defence is to have available the name of a good Mexican contact.
Car owners in Mexico City are required to leave their vehicles at home one day a week. This is an attempt to deal with the chronic pollution problem which can cause headaches and eye irritation to visitors.

Security
It is unwise to carry large sums of money or valuables in Mexico City, where the number of assaults is rising.
Visitors should be wary of walking through neighbourhood streets during festivities. Many Mexicans own guns and they tend to fire them in the air to celebrate, especially towards evening. Visitors should give a wide berth to any local dispute on the street since these can rapidly flare into fights.
Armed robbery in urban areas is a risk. Short-term opportunistic kidnapping is common. Visitors should dress down, and exercise care when using cashpoints.

Getting there
Air
National airline: Aeroméxico (AM) and Mexicana (MX)
International airport/s: Mexico City-Benito Juárez (MEX), 13km south of city; duty-free (0600–2400), restaurants

(0700–2400), bank/bureau de change, 24-hour refreshments, chemist (0500–2200), tourist information (0900–2000), 24-hour left luggage, post office (0900–1900), first aid (with vaccinations for cholera and yellow fever available) car hire.
A taxi to the city takes about 45 minutes. Prepaid taxi tickets are available from the 'Authorised Taxi Service' booth in baggage reclaim; authorized taxis are white and mustard yellow with an aeroplane logo. Travellers are strongly advised to take an authorised, prepaid taxi and to always lock taxi doors when inside.
Major hotels run shuttle minibuses from the airport. There is also a regular airport bus to the city centre.
Other airport/s: Acapulco (ACA) 26km from city; Guadalajara (GDL) 20km from city; Monterrey (MTY) 24km from city. All include restaurant, bank and car hire facilities; and access by taxi and bus.
Airport tax: Approximately US$18, sometimes included in the ticket price, transit passengers are exempt.

Surface
Road: There are roads into Mexico from the US, Belize and Guatemala. Drivers should note that permission is required to bring a car into Mexico for longer than 72 hours.
Rail: Connections with Mexico can be made from any city in the US or Canada. All trains are provided with pullman sleepers, restaurant cars and club cars and most are air conditioned.
Water: Regular passenger ships run from the US and South America. There are also riverboat services from Flores and Tikal (Guatemala) to Palenque, Chiapas in Mexico. Enquire locally for further details.
Main port/s: Gulf of Mexico coast: Altamira, Cd del Carmen, Coatzacoalcos, Pto Madero, Tampico, Veracruz; Pacific coast: Acapulco, Ensenada, La Paz, Lázaro Cardenas, Mazatlán, Manzanillo, Puerto Vallarta, Salina Cruz, Santa Rosalia.

Getting about
National transport
Air: There is a comprehensive network of daily scheduled services between main commercial centres. Departure tax: approximately US$20.
Road: There are 95,000km of paved roads, about half of which are operated by the federal government, and the other half by the state governments. There are also more than 5,600km of toll roads, which are operated by private companies. Mexico's roads carry more than 85 per cent of the nation's overland freight and almost all intercity passengers.
Detailed advice is readily available on driving hazards (e.g. animals at night) and procedures (e.g. on narrow bridges).
Buses: Three kinds, first- and second-class and local. Advisable to book seats in advance in Baja California. Buses with odd numbers run north-south, even east-west. Peribus service circulates Mexico City.
Rail: Rail services include special first-class, regular first-class and second-class. Routes include Guadalajara to Mexico City; Monterrey to Mexico City; Mexico City to Veracruz to Tapachula; Cuidad Juárez to Chihuahua. Services are slower than buses but electrification is in progress. There are sleeper services between Mexico City and Guadalajara, Monterrey, Veracruz, Ciudad Juárez, Chihuahua, Mérida. It is advisable to book well in advance.
Water: There are regular ferries from the mainland to the Caribbean Islands of Isla Mujeres and Cozumel.

City transport
Taxis: Taxis are usually fitted with meters, but these are often not used. Agree fare in advance. No tip is necessary.
Fixed route taxis can be identified by lime-green colour, rank taxis by coral and those with no fixed route by yellow. There are around 17 fixed routes. The number of fingers held out of a taxi window indicates the number of seats left.
Special tourist taxis, *turismo*, have English-speaking drivers.
Flagging the green 'beetle' taxis in the city is not recommended due to the rising number of reported hijackings and robberies by taxi drivers. The safest means of transport is a *taxi de sitio* – dial-a-cab services which charge about double the metered street taxi rates, but which are still cheap by international standards. These can be found outside every hotel.
It is best to carry a map of Mexico City (Guia Roji is recommended) as taxi drivers cannot be relied on to know their way around the huge city.
Buses, trams & metro: Mexico City Metro, with eight lines, is excellent, but often crowded. Runs 0500–0000 Mon–Sat; opens 0700 (Sun). Maps not displayed at all stations, but can be obtained at Insurgentes station on pink line.
There is also a small tramway network, and extensive bus and trolley bus services. The latter system has recently been modernised, and also has a flat fare. There is a state-run bus and trolley bus service in Guadalajara, with trolley buses running in tunnels, and also extensive private bus services.
Car hire
Car hire is widely available, with or without a driver, but often expensive. A foreign licence is acceptable. Car hire is not recommended for business travellers or tourists because of excessive traffic, aggressive drivers, and counter-pollution measures which mean that on certain days of the week, driving is off limits.

BUSINESS DIRECTORY
The addresses listed below are a selection only. While World of Information makes every endeavour to check these addresses, we cannot guarantee that changes have not been made, especially to telephone numbers and area codes. We would welcome any corrections.

Telephone area codes
The international direct dialling (IDD) code for Mexico is +52, followed by area code and subscriber's number:

Acapulco	744	Mexico City	55
Chihuahua	614	Monterrey	81
Ciudad Juárez	656	Oaxaca	951
Durango	618	Puebla	222
Guadalajara	33	Tampico	833
León	477	Torreón	817
Mérida	999	Veracruz	229

Useful telephone numbers
Locatel (government-operated service to locate missing persons: 658-1111.
Sectur (24-hour help to tourists in trouble): 250-8359 or 250-0150.

Chambers of Commerce
American Chamber of Commerce Mexico, Lucerna 78, Colonia Juarez, 06600 México, DF (tel: 5141-3800; fax: 5703-3908; e-mail: amchammx@amcham.com.mx).

British Chamber of Commerce in Mexico, 30 Río de la Plata, 6500 México, DF (tel: 5256-0901; fax: 5211-5451; e-mail: britchamexico@britchamexico.com).

Chihuahua Cámara Nacional de Comercio, Servicios y Turismo, 1800 Avenida Cuauhtemoc, 31020 Chihuahua (tel: 416-0000; fax: 415-1928; e-mail: cfn@infosel.net.mx).

Confederación de Cámaras Nacionales de Comercio, Servicios y Turismo, 144 Balderas, Colonia Centro, 06079 México, DF (tel/fax: 5722-9300; e-mail: sistemas@concanacored.com).

Guadalajara Cámara Nacional de Comercio, Servicios y Turismo, 4095 Avenida Vallarta, Fraccionamiento Camino Real, 45000 Guadalajara (tel: 3880-9090; fax: 3880-9097; e-mail: direccion@canacogdl.com.mx).

Juarez Cámara Nacional de Comercio, Servicios y Turismo, 4505 Avenida Henry Dunant y Avenida M Diaz, 32315 Ciudad Juarez (tel: 113-707; fax: 112-674; e-mail: canacojr@hotmail.com).

Mexico City Cámara Nacional de Comercio, 42 Paseo de la Reforma, Colonia Centro, 06048 México, DF (tel: 535-2502; fax: 703-2958; e-mail: presidencia1@ccmexico.com.mx).

Mexico

Puebla Cámara Nacional de Comercio, Servicios y Turismo, 2704 Avenida Reforma, 72160 Puebla (tel: 480-705; fax: 480-800; e-mail: canacopu@axtel.net.mx).

Banking

Banamex, Actuario Robero Medellin 800, Colonia Santa Fé, 01219 México, DF (tel: 1226-2639; tel: 5999-2888).

Bancomer, Montes Urales 620,Colonia Lomas de Chapultepec, 11000 México, DF (tel: 5201-2264; fax: 5238-7790).

Banorte, Periférico Sur 4355, Colonia Jardines en la Montaña, 14210 México, DF (tel: 5169-9300; fax: 5169-9460).

Bital, Paseo de la Reforma 156, Juarez, 06600 México DF (tel: 5721-5715; fax: 5721-3846).

Santander Mexicano, Prolongación Paseo de la Reforma 500, Colonia Lomas de Santa Fé, 01210 México, D F (tel: 5257-8000; fax: 5629-4742).

Scotiabank Inverlat, Manuel Avila Camacho 1, 11009 México, DF (tel: 5229-2053; fax: 5395-9050).

Central bank

Banco de México, Avenida 5 de Mayo 1, Colonia Centro, Delegación Cuauhtémoc, 06059 (tel: 5237-2000; fax: 5237-2070; e-mail: sidaoui@banxico.org.mx).

Travel information

Benito Juárez International Airport, Av. Capitán Carlos León s/n Col. Peñón de los Baños Del. Venustiano Carranza, México, D.F. CP 15620 (tel: 571-3600; fax: 726-0107).

Fondo Nacional de Fomento al Turismo (FONATUR) 22nd Floor, Insurgentes Sur 800, Colonia del Valle, 03100 México DF (tel: 5687-0567/8; fax: 5687-5058, 5682-5058; email: ibotas@fonatur.gob.mx; internet: www.fonatur.gob.mx).

Infotour, Zona Rosa, Amberes 54, Mexico City (tel: 525-9380).

Ministry of tourism

Secretaría de Turismo (SECTUR) Presidente Mazaryck 172, Colonia Polanco, 11570 México DF (tel: 250-8555; fax: 250-4406 (general enquiries), 254-0942 (marketing), email: correspondencia@mexico-travel.com; internet: www.mexico-travel.com).

National tourist organisation offices

Consejo de Promoción Turística de México, Mariano Escobedo 550, 11580 México DF (tel: 258-1090/2; email: cptmex@infosel.net.mx; internet: www.visitmexico.com).

Ministries

Ministry of Agrarian Reform (SRA), Tepozteco 36, 1er Piso, Col Vertiz Narvarte, 03020 Mexico (tel: 579-6094; fax: 579-3767).

Ministry of Agriculture, Rural Development and Livestock (SAGAR), Av Insurgentes Sur 476, 50. piso, Col Roma Sur, 06700 Mexico (tel: 584-0808; fax: 584-1177).

Ministry of Communication and Transport (SCT), Xola y Av Universidad, Cuerpo C, PB, Col Narvarte, 03028 Mexico (tel: 538-5148; fax: 519-9748).

Ministry of Defence (SEDENA), Blvd Manuel Avila Camacho y Av Industria Militar, Col Lomas de Sotelo, 11600 Mexico (tel: 395-6766; fax: 557-1370).

Ministry of Education (SEP), Brasil 31, PB oficina 115, Col Centro, 06029 Mexico (tel: 329-6827; fax: 329-6822).

Ministry of Energy (SE), Av Insurgentes Sur 552, 1er. Piso, Col Roma Sur, 06769 Mexico (tel: 584-4304; fax: 564-9782).

Ministry of Finance and Public Credit (SHCP), República de El Salvador 47, PA, Col Centro, 06080 Mexico (tel: 709-6675; fax: 709-3272).

Ministry of Fishing, Environment and Natural Resources (SEMARNAP), Anillo Periférico Sur 4209, 3er Piso, Col Jardines en la Montaña, 14210 Mexico (tel: 628-0891; fax: 628-0780).

Ministry of Foreign Affairs (SRE), Eje Central Lázaro Cardenas 257, ala 'A', 1er Nivel, Col Guerrero, 09600 Mexico (tel: 782-3660; fax: 327-3025).

Ministry of Health (SSA), Lieja 8, 50. piso, Col Juárez, 06600 Mexico (tel: 553-7670; fax: 286-5497).

Ministry of the Interior (SG), Abraham Gonzalez 48, PB, Col Juárez, 06699, Mexico (tel: 535-2718; fax: 535-9952).

Ministry of Labour and Social Welfare (STPS), Periférico Sur 4271, Edificio A, 1er Nivel, Col Fuentes del Pedregal, 14149, Mixico (tel/fax: 645-3715).

Ministry of Naval Affairs (SM), Eje 2 Oriente 861, Tramo Heroica Escuela Naval Militar, Col Los Cipreses, Coyoacan, 04830 Mexico (tel: 684-8188; fax: 679-6411).

Ministry of Social Development (SEDESOL), Av Constituyentes 947-B, PB, Col Belén de las Flores, 01110 Mexico (tel: 515-4508; fax: 272-0118).

Ministry of Trade and Industry (SECOFI), Av Alfonso Reyes 30, 20 piso, Col Condesa, 06140 Mexico (tel: 729-9193; fax: 729-9314).

Other useful addresses

Asociación Nacional de importadores y Exportadores de la República Mexicana, Monterrey 130, Col Roma Sur, 06700, México, DF (tel: 564-9379; fax: 584-5317).

Asociación Nacional para el Fomento de las Exportaciones Mexicanas, Ed de las Instituciones 702, Ocampo 250 Poncente Apartado 64100, Monterrey NL (tel: 428-010, 422-143, 422-154; fax: 28-207).

Asociación de Personal Técnico para Conferencias Internacionales AC, Universidad 1855-502, México 20, DF (tel: 550-0170).

British Embassy, Lerma 71, Col. Cuauhtemoc, 06500 Mexico City (207-2569, 207-2089/2149; fax: 207-2593, 207-7672).

Comptroller General (SECOGEF), Av Insurgentes Sur 1735, PB Ala Norte, Oficina 39, Col Guadalupe Inn, 01020 México (tel: 662-2762; fax: 662-4511).

Confederación de Cámaras Industriales de los Estados Unidos Mexicanos, Manuel Maria Contreras 133, 8, Cuauhtemoc, 06597, México DF (tel: 546-9053; fax: 535-6871).

Consejo Nacional de Comercio Exterior, Tiaxcala 177 Desp 803, Apartado 06100, México DF (tel: 286-8744, 286-8798; fax: 211-8465).

Dirección General de Telecommunicaciones, Lázaro Cárdenas 567 11 Piso Ala Norte, Col Navarate, 03020 México, DF (tel: 519-4049, 530-3492, 519-0908; fax: 559-9812).

Instituto de Intérpretes y Traductores SA, Rio Rhin 40, 06500 México 5, DF (tel: 566-7722, 566-8312).

Instituto Mexicano del Petróleo, Avenida Eje Central Lázaro Cardenas 152, 07730 Apartado 14-805, México 14, DF (tel: 567-6600).

International Telegraph Office, Balderas 14-18 Colon, México DF.

Mexican Embassy (USA), 1911 Pennsylvania Avenue, NW, Washington DC 20006 (tel: 202-728-1600; fax: 202-728-1698; e-mail: mexembusa@aol.com).

Mexican Investment Board MIB, Paseo de la Reforma No. 915, Lomas de Chapultepec, 11000 México (tel: 202-7804; fax: 328-9930).

Mexican Stock Exchange, Paseo de la Reforma 255, Colonia Cuauhtemoc, 06500 México (tel: 726-6600; fax: 726-6805).

Pemex (Petróleos Mexicanos), Avenida Marina Nacional 329, México 17, DF (tel: 250-2611, 254-2044).

Public Telex Office, Vallejo y Norte 45, México 2, DF/San Bartolo Naucaplan, México 16, DF.

Secretariat of State for Commerce and Industrial Development, Alfonso Reyes 30, México, DF (tel: 286-1823, 211- 0036; fax: 286-0804).

Secretariat of State for Energy, Mines and Federal Industry, Insurgentes Sur 552, 3, 06769 México, DF (tel: 564-9790; fax: 574-3396).

Secretariat of State for Finance and Public Credit, Palacio Nacional, 1 Patio Mariano, 06066 Piso ofna 3045, México, DF (tel: 518-5420; fax: 542-2821).

US Embassy, PO Box 3087, Paseo de la Reforma 305, Colonia Cuauhtemoc, 06500 Mexico City, DF (tel: 211-0042; fax: 207-8938).

Internet sites

Communicación Mass Media de Mexico (Spanish): http://www.mexnews.com

Comprehensive information site: http://www.mexonline.com

Central bank http://www.banxico.org.mx

El Heraldo newspaper http://www.heraldo.com.mx

General directory http://www.mexicoweb.com.mx

General guide http://www.mexconnect.com

Mexicana: airline http://www.mexicana.com

Mexican government agencies, chambers of commerce and other trade institutions (English) http://www.mexicosi.com

Statistics: http://www.inegi.gob.mx

Stock exchange http://www.bmv.com.mx

Travel & tourism information http://www.go2mexico.org.mx

Travel & tourism information http://www.visitmexico.com

Federated States of Micronesia

COUNTRY PROFILE

Historical profile
The Federated States of Micronesia (FSM) comprises four island states – the capital state of Pohnpei (formerly Ponape), Chuuk (known until 1990 as Truk), Yap and Kosrae. These were formerly Japanese League of Nations mandated islands.
1947 The islands became part of the UN's Trust Territory of the Pacific Islands (TTPI), administered by the US under a UN mandate.
1978 the FSM gained sovereignty following a constitutional convention and referendum.
1979 On implementing the FSM constitution, former districts became States of the Federation.
1982 FSM signed a Compact of Free Association (CFA) with the US, which would maintain defence responsibility.
1986 The Compact came into force for a 15-year period.
1990 The Trusteeship was ended by the UN Security Council.
1991 The islands joined the UN.
1999 Congressional elections were held and Leo Amy Falcam was elected president.
2001 US funds under the CFA were extended for a further two years to allow for negotiation over the terms of a new Compact.
2002 Typhoon Mitag devastated the island of Yap, which needed US federal funds to recover and rebuild.
2003 In congressional elections, Joseph J Urusemal was elected apresident. The second CFA was signed with the US.
2004 In April, damage from typhoon Sudal left 1,500 people homeless in the state of Yap.
2005 In the 8 March parliamentary elections, 10 non-partisan congressional candidates were elected.

Political structure
Constitution
The Federated States of Micronesia is a federation of four states – Pohnpei, Chuuk, Kosrae and Yap – bound to the US by a Compact of Free Association. The US is responsible for defence and security issues.
Each state has a constitutional government with an elected governor and lieutenant governor.
The government consists of Congress and the executive branch.

Form of state
Self-governing territory in free association with the US.
The executive
The president and vice president, who must come from different states, are elected from congressional members for four-year terms. The president nominates members of the Cabinet with the advice and consent of Congress.
National legislature
Congress consists of fourteen members. Ten members (five from Chuuk, three from Pohnpei, one from Yap and one from Kosrae) are elected for two years; the remaining four (one from each state) are elected for four years.
Congress is a unicameral body comprising 10 senators elected for a two-year term in single-seat constituencies and four senators elected for a four-year term by proportional representation.
Only Chuuk's legislative body is bicameral; other states have a unicameral legislature.
Last elections
8 March 2005 (parliamentary); 11 May 2003 (presidential).
Results: Parliamentary: nonpartisan candidates were elected to the 10 available two-year seats.
Presidential: Joseph J Urusemal was elected.
Next elections
2007 (presidential and parliamentary)

Political parties
There are no political parties.

Political situation
Now that the second Compact of Free Association (CFA) with the US, signed on 14 May 2003, is in operation some of its hard realities are being felt. At the first meeting of the Joint Economic Management Committee (JEMCO), in August 2004, the representatives of both the federal and state governments of FSM were told in clear terms, by US representatives, that the terms of the Compact would be adhered to strictly. The first Compact was seen by the US as the unfettered spending of funds by island legislators, with the added taint of corruption, and it was keen that this was not repeated with the new Compact.
So FSM federal and state governments will have to look to local sources of income to overcome their financial shortfalls as Compact monies can no longer be spent on leasing land and paying government wages. These two areas of expenditure are

KEY FACTS

Official name: Federated States of Micronesia

Head of State: President Joseph J Urusemal (elected and sworn in 11 May 2003)

Head of government: President Joseph J Urusemal

Area: 607 volcanic islands and coral atolls with land area of just over 700 square km

Population: 124,141 (2004)

Capital: Palikir (in Pohnpei state)

Official language: English

Currency: US dollar (US$) = 100 cents

GDP per capita: US$2,090 (2004)*

GDP real growth: -3.30% (2004)

Unemployment: 16.00% (2004)

Inflation: 1.50% (2004)

Balance of trade: -US$127.00 million (2003)

* estimated figure

going to pose the biggest headaches for federal and state governments. Land is in short supply and owners will not willingly sell their assets, while at the same time public facilities already exist on leased land and have to be serviced. The Public sector is the largest source of employment on the islands and it will be a painful necessity to have to reduce its size to accommodate reduced US funding. The hard decisions that will have to be taken are likely to have a political backlash and there are few politicians anywhere willing to risk the electorates' rejection, so FSM policies may vacillate for a while longer until someone can state clearly to all the new realities of FSM living within its means.

Population
124,141 (2004)
Ethnic make-up
The population is composed of nine Micronesian and Polynesian groups.
Religions
Roman Catholic (50 per cent), Protestant (47 per cent).

Education
The education system is modelled after the US educational system. Over 30 per cent of the population attend secondary schools. Private elementary and secondary schools also exist, sponsored by religious groups. Although the College of Micronesia-FSM provides two- and three-year programmes, most students prefer to enrol in US tertiary educational institutions. The Micronesia Maritime and Fisheries Academy in the State of Yap was set up to provide effective training in maritime and fisheries technologies, to cater for the growing demand for trained personnel in the expanding fishing industry.
Compulsory years: 6 to 14.
Enrolment rate: 142 per cent gross primary enrolment, of relevant age groups (including repeaters) (World Bank 2003).

Health
There are inadequate primary health care facilities, with little secondary and tertiary-level treatment facilities. In some states there are shortages of essential medical supplies including contraceptives. As a result patients have little choice but to travel to health facilities overseas. Government funds are channelled towards curative services rather than preventative and primary health care. The Asian Development Bank has granted loans for training health workers, improving medical supplies and extending a limited health insurance scheme to provide broader and universal coverage.
Total expenditure on health is 7–8 per cent of GDP, of which 72 per cent is government spending. Total per capita health expenditure typically amounts to US$319 per annum.
Life expectancy: 68.9 years (World Bank)
Fertility rate/Maternal mortality rate: 3.25 births per woman (2005)
Birth rate/Death rate: 25.1 births per 1,000 population; 4.9 deaths per 1,000 population (2005).
Infant mortality rate: 30.2 per 1,000 live births (2005)

Welfare
Although the FSM does not produce a poverty profile as such, recent household income and expenditure surveys suggest that around 40 per cent of households could be considered as low income. Despite some remittances from overseas migrants, the number of low income households is still high. The lowest income households are on the outer islands where opportunities for formal sector employment and commercial activities are few.

Main cities
Palikir (capital, in Pohnpei State, estimated population in 2003) 11,600, Weno, (Chuuk) 25,900, Tol (Chuuk) 11,000, Kolonia Town (Pohnpei) 6,400.

Languages spoken
English is the common language. Yap has four languages – Yapese, Ulithian, Woleaian, and Satawalese; Pohnpei languages are Pohnpeian, Nukuoroan and Kapingamarangian, Chuukese in Chuuk and Kosraean in Kosrae.
Official language/s
English

Media
Press
There are two private newspapers, *JK Report* and *Micronesia Focus*, first published in 1994. The FSM Public Information Office publishes *National Union*, a bi-weekly newsletter. State governments operate their own newsletters such as *Office of the Governor Pohnpei State Weekly Digest*, also available at http://www.fm/PohnpeiGov/. *The Island Tribune* is Micronesia's bi-weekly publication.
Broadcasting
Radio: There are radio stations in each state. Radio broadcasts are transmitted at least 18 hrs/day in English and the main local dialects.
Television: TV coverage is fairly widespread, with some cable relay. There is a state television station in Yap and two private television stations in Pohnpei.

Economy
Fishing and tourism are the main sectors of economic activity in FSM. Marine products generate almost all export revenues. The most important issue regarding the Micronesian economy is the future of US funding arrangements. The Compact of Free Association (CFA) between the US and FSM has seen a substantial flow of money to the Pacific nation.
Public expenditure varies between islands, representing 29 per cent of Pohnpei's GDP and 78 per cent of Kosrae's GDP. In May 2003, the US and the FSM agreed a new CFA, which guarantees grant assistance until 2023 and provides for a trust fund, expected to generate enough income to enable the FSM to offset the loss of CFA revenue from 2024. The US government has control over the administration of the trust fund until 2023. FSM is required to provide US$30 million to set up its trust fund. Initial contributions will be augmented annually by gradually increasing contributions from the US. All earnings from the trust fund will remain untouched until 2023 and will be reinvested. At an assumed annual rate of return of 6 per cent, the trust fund is expected to generate earnings from 2023 onward that would be enough to replace the annual US contributions to the budget. The planned reduction in CFA grant assistance was reflected in the territory's 2004 budget, which allowed for expenditure cuts to produce an overall budget surplus estimated at 1.9 per cent of GDP. A constitutional amendment to enable simultaneous national and state jurisdiction of a

KEY INDICATORS — Federated States of Micronesia

	Unit	2000	2001	2002	2003	2004
Population	m	0.12	0.12	0.12	0.12	0.12
Gross domestic product (GDP)	US$bn	0.23	–	–	0.28	*0.23
GDP per capita	US$	1,925	1,783	1,978	2,000	*2,090
GDP real growth	%	2.5	1.1	0.3	2.4	-3.3
Inflation	%	3.2	2.0	0.5	1.5	1.5
Total reserves minus gold	US$m	113.0	98.3	117.4	89.6	54.8
Foreign exchange	US$m	111.6	96.9	115.8	87.8	52.9

* estimated figure

Federated States of Micronesia

value added tax (VAT) failed to gain the required level of voter support and no progress was made in establishing an autonomous tax administration.
In April 2004, the US government declared Yap island state a major disaster area and announced it would pay 75 per cent of the cost of damage caused by typhoon Sudal.

External trade
Imports
Principal imports are food, manufactured goods, machinery, equipment and beverages. Imports are approximately three times exports. Imports totalled US$149 million in 2003.
Main sources: US, Australia, Japan
Exports
Principal exports are fish, garments, bananas and black pepper. Some beef, fruit and vegetables are also exported.
Copra was formerly Yap's principal export, but this has been overtaken by betel nut. During the period of March 2003 to February 2004, Yap exported to other Pacific islands about US$3 million worth of its betel nut and pepper leaf, traditionally, used in chewing. A 'chew' consists of a betel nut wrapped in pepper leaf with a touch of lime powder made from burned coral. The combination stains teeth red. Betel nut is described as mildly narcotic.
Main destinations: Japan, US, Guam

Agriculture
Farming
The agricultural sector contributes approximately 17 per cent to GDP. Subsistence farming is the main occupation and provides most of the food consumed in the territory.
Crop production in 2004 included: 11,800 tonnes (t) cassava, 140,000t coconuts, 3,000t sweet potatoes, 2,000t bananas, 3,100t vegetables, 300t plantains, 295t fresh fruit, 90t rice and 33t cocoa beans. Livestock production included: 245t beef, 13t goat meat, 873t pig meat and 135t poultry meat.
Fishing
Fishing is the mainstay of the economy and generates most of the country's export revenues. International fishing fleets pay to fish in FSM's rich territorial waters, including one of the world's best tuna grounds. However, the sector is dominated by foreign owned companies operating offshore and so employs few local people.
The Pohnpei State government expanded its local fishing industry in 2003, using vessels which had been donated by the government of the Republic of Korea. Fishing provides a primary source of protein for the local population.
FSM also typically harvests 150,000 pearls annually.

Industry and manufacturing
Small-scale industries include handicrafts, fish processing, bottling, copra processing, bakeries and boat building. The Pohnpei Agricultural and Trade School runs a small coconut products plant, which makes 'Oil of Ponape' toiletries. Most private sector activity is in retail and wholesale trade which are dependent on demand generated by government spending.

Tourism
Tourism accounts for only 6 per cent of GDP, but is a significant foreign exchange earner. The Asian Development Bank has identified tourism as one of FSM's highest potential growth industries, although the cost of airfares is seen as a hiderance to expansion. Tourist numbers have been down, a trend that began in 2000 and although there was a recovery with 14,038 tourist arrivals in 2002 by 2004 numbers were as low as 10,000 people.
FSM is particularly attractive to divers and in 2004 tourist hotels related to the activity had an 80 per cent occupancy rate while general resorts reported typical occupancy rates of around 40 per cent. The region's most spectacular scenery is underwater. The island of Chuuk has an underwater-wreck-museum where more than 60 Japanese ships, as well as planes, that were sunk during the Second World War are open to divers to view.

Mining
Small mineral deposits exist, but there are doubts about the economic viability of commercial exploitation, which would be hampered by a shortage of land to accommodate any displaced population.

Banking and insurance
There are three commercial banks which serve the four states: Bank of the Federated States of Micronesia, Bank of Guam and the Bank of Hawaii. A government chartered FSM Development Bank is the main financial institution used to foster the growth of new business ventures and private sector development.

Time
GMT plus 12 hours

Geography
The Federated States of Micronesia (FSM), together with Palau, form the archipelago of the Caroline Islands, about 800km east of the Philippines.

Climate
Warm and humid, temperatures 23–30 degrees Celsius with humidity around 80 per cent. Rainfall is variable, but the minimum is generally 250mm per annum. Hurricanes are possible.

Entry requirements
Passports
Required by all except US citizens with proof of citizenship. Passports must be valid for 120 days beyond date of entry.
Visa
Not required by US citizens with proof of adequate funds. Entry permits granted to all others with proof of return/onward passage and adequate funds for stays up to 30 days. Business visits need an entry permit, (see www.visit-fsm.org/visitors/permit.pdf).
Currency advice/regulations
No restrictions on import and export of local currency.
Foreign currency: amounts over US$5,000 must be declared.

Health (for visitors)
Mandatory precautions
Vaccination certificates required for yellow fever if travelling from infected area.
Advisable precautions
Vaccinations for diphtheria, tuberculosis, hepatitis 'A' and 'B', polio, TB, tetanus, typhoid and paratyphoid are advisable.
Leprosy has been endemic for generations.
Water precautions are necessary. There is a cholera risk due to lack of access to safe water.
There is a rabies risk.

Hotels
There are 362 hotel rooms within the FSM, including 168 in Kolonia Town, Pohnpei; 105 on Weno, Chuuk; 45 in Colonia, Yap and 44 in Lelu Kosrae.

Credit cards
Limited to certain businesses and hotels in the state centres.

Public holidays
Fixed dates
1 Jan (New Year's Day), 11 Jan (Kosrae Constitution Day), 1 Mar (Yap Day), 31 Mar (Pohnpei Culture Day), 10 May (FSM Constitution Day), 8 Sep (Kosrae Liberation Day), 11 Sep (Pohnpei Liberation Day), 24 Oct (United Nations Day), 3 Nov (National Day), 8 Nov (Pohnpei Constitution Day), 24 Dec (Yap Constitution Day), 25 Dec (Christmas Day).
Variable dates
Good Friday, Kosrae Thanksgiving Day (fourth Thu in Nov).

Working hours
Banking
Mon–Thurs: 0930–1430; Fri: 0930–1600.
Business
Mon–Fri: 0800–1700.
Government
Mon–Fri: 0800–1700.
Shops
Mon–Sat: 0800–2000; Sun 0900–1030.

Nations of the World: A Political, Economic and Business Handbook

Telecommunications
Postal services
US postal rates apply. Post offices, which are located in each of the state centres, are opened daily, except weekends.
Mobile phones
Cellular telephone services are available on Yap, Pohnpei and Kosrae, with plans to expand the service to Chuuk by 2006.
Internet/e-mail
FSM Telecom provides internet access to Pohnpei, Kosrae, Chuuk and Yap.

Electricity supply
110 volt and US type outlets are used.

Social customs/useful tips
Tips are neither expected nor encouraged.

Getting there
Air
National airline: Air Micronesia.
International airport/s: Pohnpei (PNI), 5km south of Kolonia Town.
Other airport/s: Chuuk (TKK), Yap (YAP), Kosrae (KSA).
Airport tax: Departure tax: Pohnpei US$10, Chuuk US$15, Kosrae US$10, Yap none.

Getting about
National transport
A trip to the outer islands can be complicated and arrangements should be made at least several months in advance.
Air: Pacific Missionary Aviation (PMA) in Yap State and in Pohnpei State provide domestic air service. There are airstrips in the outer islands of Ulul and Ta in Chuuk State.
Road: The road network has been upgraded in many areas through a resurfacing programme begun in the late 1990s.
Taxis: Cheap and readily available in most centres.
Water: Passenger and freight services between the islands and atolls are provided by state-owned vessels. The frequency of inter-island services is governed by weather conditions, but trips to inhabited islands take place at least every 30–45 days.

BUSINESS DIRECTORY
The addresses listed below are a selection only. While World of Information makes every endeavour to check these addresses, we cannot guarantee that changes have not been made, especially to telephone numbers and area codes. We would welcome any corrections.

Telephone area codes
The international direct dialling (IDD) code for the FSM is +691, followed by area code and subscriber's number:
Chuuk 330 Pohnpei 320
Kosrae 370 Yap 350

Useful telephone numbers
Pohnpei
Police: 320-2221
Fire: 320-2223
Ambulance: 320-2213
Chuuk
Police: 330-2223
Fire: 330-2222
Ambulance: 330-2444
Kosrae
Police: 911
Fire: 370-3333
Ambulance: 370-3012
Yap
Police: 911
Fire: 350-2415
Ambulance: 350-3446

Chambers of Commerce
Chuuk Chamber of Commerce, PO Box 700, Weno, Chuuk 96942 (tel: 330-2318; fax: 330-2314).

Kosrae Chamber of Commerce, PO Box 1075, Tofol, Kosrae 96944 (tel: 370-2044; fax: 370-2066; e-mail: kosraecci@mail.fm).

Pohnpei Chamber of Commerce, PO Box 405, Kolonia, Pohnpei 96941 (tel: 320-2452; fax: 320-5277).

Banking
Bank of the Federated States of Micronesia, Corporate Headquarters (tel: 320-2850; fax: 370-3568; email: bofsmhq@mail.fm).

Bank of Guam, Chuuk Office (tel: 330-2567; fax: 330-2640).

Bank of Hawaii, Kosrae Office (tel: 370-3230; fax: 370-2027).
Central bank

Travel information
Chief of Immigration, Office of the Attorney General, Palikir, Pohnpei 96941 (tel: 320-5844; fax: 320-2234).

Pohnpei International Airport, PO Box 1150, Kolonia Town, Pohnpei 96941 (tel: 320-2682/2793/3999; fax: 320-2798).

Ministries
Department of Foreign Affairs and Trade, Pacific Islands Branch, R G Casey Building, John McEwan Crescent, Barton ACT 0221, Australia (fax: +62(2)6261-2332).

Secretary for Foreign Affairs, Pohnpei (tel: 320-2641; fax: 320-2933).

Secretary for Economic Affairs, Pohnpei (tel: 320-2646; fax: 320-5854).

Other useful addresses
British Embassy, PO Box No 61, Bairiki Tarawa (tel: 21-327; fax: 21-488).

Chuuk State Government, Weno, Chuuk State, 96942.

FS of Micronesia Public Information Office, FSM Government, Box P.S. 34, Palikir, Pohnpei, 96941.

Kosrae State Government, Tofol, Kosrae, 96944.

Office of the Governor, Yap State Government, PO Box 39, Colonia, Yap, 96943.

Pohnpei State Government, Kolonia, Pohnpei, 96941.

The Secretary of Finance, PO Box P.S. 158, Palikir, Pohnpei, 96941 (tel: 320-2640; fax: 320-2380).

Internet sites
FSM Telecom: http://www.telecom.fm

Government website: http://www.fm.org

Tourist information: http://www.visit.micronesia.fm

US Office of Insular affairs: http://www.doi.gov/oia

Moldova

Formerly ruled by Romania, with which its citizens have close linguistic, cultural and historic ties, Moldova became part of the Soviet Union at the close of the Second World War and Russian troops were stationed in the country. At the time of the break-up of the USSR and the creation of the Russian Federation in 1991, Moldova, along with the other Russian satellite states became independent. Moldova's Slavic population seized the opportunity to declare the territory east of the Dniestr River the 'Republic of Transdniestr'. Although Russian troops pulled out of Moldova, they remain in the breakaway territory, which is now under the *de facto* rule of an elected pro-Russian 'president', Igor Smirnov. Transdniestr remains internationally unrecognised except by Russia. The election and continued re-election of Smirnov has been criticised by both Moldovan President Vladimir Voronin and his supporter in the dispute, Romanian President Traian Basescu.

Politics

While Transdniestr continues to look to Russia, the ethnic Moldovans in the western territory, although under a pro-Russian Communist government from 2001 to 2005, now favour ties with the West – as does their neighbour Romania, which also aspires to join the European Union (EU). Although Moldova was the first of the former Soviet satellite states to elect a Communist government after the break-up of the USSR, the same government has in four years done a complete U-turn. Voronin's Partidul Comunistilor Moldova (PCM) (Communist Party of Moldova), elected in 2001, changed its politics but not its name, campaigned in the 2005 election on a pro-Western platform and was re-elected.

At the heart of the change was a rapidly deteriorating relationship with Russia over the issue of Transdniestr. The Russian Federation tried to influence the 2005 Moldovan elections by intensively favourable coverage of pro-Russian candidates in the Russian mass media and through meetings and agitation campaigns using the CIS-EMO, a Russian elections monitoring organisation, which is not internationally recognised as independent.

The Moldovans denied the CIS-EMO entry, but some members of the organisation entered illegally, distributed leaflets and actively participated in the election campaign. They were arrested and deported back to Russia.

On the other hand, Romania continues to support Moldova not only over the Transdniestr issue, but in its overall anti-Russia stance. Both criticise the EU. They expected the 2005 meeting of its Organisation for Security and Co-operation in Europe (OSCE) to make progress in convincing Russia to withdraw its troops from Moldova's separatist region. This was the third time the OSCE had failed to call for the withdrawal of the Russians. Basescu reiterated Romania's total support for Moldova which, it said, must obtain political control over its whole territory. Voronin has since expressed disappointment with the result of a newly launched EU monitoring mission along Transdniestr's border with Ukraine aimed at quelling the smuggling of arms, drugs and people.

Basescu has also assured Voronin that he will not allow Moldova to suffer from Russia's move to phase out the supply of subsidised gas for ex-Soviet states.

KEY FACTS

Official name: Republica Moldoveneasca (Republic of Moldova)

Head of State: President Vladimir Voronin (leader of PCM) (since 2001; re-elected 4 Apr 2005)

Head of government: Prime Minister Vasile Tarlev (PCM) (since 2001; re-appointed by the President 8 Apr 2005)

Ruling party: Partidul Comunistilor din Moldova (PCM) (Communist Party of Moldova) (since 2001; re-elected 6 Mar 2005)

Area: 33,700 square km

Population: 4.21 million (2004)

Capital: Chisinau (Kishinev)

Official language: Moldovan (in latin script)

Currency: Leu (L) = 100 bani

Exchange rate: L12.58 per US$ (Oct 2005)

GDP per capita: US$716 (2004)

GDP real growth: 7.00% (2004)

Labour force: 2.21 million (2004)

Unemployment: 8.00% (2003)

Inflation: 12.30% (2004)

Balance of trade: -US$800.00 million 2004

Foreign debt: US$1.30 billion (2003)

Announced by Russia's state gas supplier Gazprom, it is seen as a means to pressure the countries such as Moldova, who are seeking closer relations with the West.

Basescu said that the Romanian government is ready to offer Moldova gas and electricity 'if the prices charged by Russia rise excessively'. He would always be ready to support Moldova, no matter how big the difficulties.

The EU has urged Russia and Moldova to resume talks about future gas supplies. Austria, current president of the EU, called on both parties to resume bilateral talks to achieve a fair and mutually acceptable solution. And a spokesman for Gazprom said the company expected to sign a contract with Moldova 'shortly'. A contract covering gas supplies over 2006 had been prepared. The Moldovans had said all related issues would be co-ordinated soon and the contract signed. The proposed price was US$160 per 1,000 cu m.

However, in January 2006, Voronin discussed the issue with his Ukrainian counterpart, Viktor Yushchenko, who reportedly promised he would help Moldova with gas from Ukrainian reserves. Voronin was quoted as saying Gazprom's price was not a fair market price, 'but the Moldovan government should continue negotiations with the Russians'.

In an unrelated statement, defence minister Valeriu Plesca said that Moldova had earmarked US$10 million for military purposes in 2006, 8.8 per cent more than in 2005. The extra money would be used to modernise the country's air defence system.

Economy

The Moldovan authorities established a considerable degree of macroeconomic stability over 2005, despite the challenge of managing significant inflows of remittances from Moldovans working abroad. Economic growth continued to be robust and inflation abated somewhat. At the same time, the main sources of growth – household consumption and construction – remained heavily dependent on inflows of remittances which now equal 30 per cent of gross domestic product (GDP). Real GDP growth had been around 7 per cent over the past decade. After peaking at over 14 per cent in April 2005, year on year inflation was projected at around 10 per cent.

Fiscal policy continued to support the effort to bring inflation down. The government was expected to post a cash surplus of 0.5 per cent of GDP in 2005. The National Bank of Moldova tightened monetary policy in 2005. Growth in reserve money slowed from 48 per cent year-on-year at end-January to 20 per cent in the fourth quarter, though credit growth remained robust.

Higher energy prices have had a significant impact on the balance of payments. The current account was expected to have worsened significantly during 2005 to a deficit of about five per cent of GDP, from less than three per cent in 2004.

The International Monetary Fund (IMF) said in December 2005 that growth was likely to slow marginally in 2006 and over the next several years, given the impact of higher energy prices and emerging tightness in adjacent labour markets. Avoiding a more pronounced slowdown would depend on a continued recovery in investment, particularly of the private sector. The IMF has suggested that fiscal policy in 2006 should remain cautious both to support lower inflation and to avoid crowding out private sector investment. As general government expenditure had risen from around 33 per cent of GDP in 2003 to about 37 per cent in 2005, it was now time to examine carefully the quality and composition of government spending.

The 2006 budget contained several positive structural features. A number of tax exemptions had been eliminated; the government had begun to repay outstanding credits to the central bank and transfers of central bank profits would now take place only once per year on the basis of audited accounts. The budget had also begun to accumulate resources needed to help settle outstanding arrears to external creditors.

The IMF said the reform of public administration was exceptionally important to improve the business environment. Moldova could count on the support of its international development partners in this effort, which should begin with reviews of all levels of the central public administration.

The recently concluded inventory of the government's asset holdings in the economy, and its intention to reinvigorate the privatisation process were very welcome.

Creation of a national agency to promote competition seemed long overdue. Judicial reform seemed to be needed, given complaints by the business community about the ability of the courts to enforce private property rights.

Risk assessment

Economy	Poor
Political situation	Poor
Regional stability	Fair

COUNTRY PROFILE

Historical profile
Moldova is a remnant of the medieval principality of Moldavia (later called Bessarabia). Once part of Romania, Moldova maintains close ties with Romania and a majority of Moldovans consider themselves to be ethnic Romanians.
1940 The Moldovan Soviet Socialist Republic (SSR) was established within the Soviet Union. The Moldovan SSR included land annexed from Romania and the Ukraine, providing much of the basis for the inter-communal strife.
1989 Achieved *de facto* independence from the former Soviet Union.

KEY INDICATORS — Moldova

	Unit	2000	2001	2002	2003	2004
Population	m	4.28	4.28	4.25	4.23	4.21
Gross domestic product (GDP)	US$bn	1.30	1.40	1.50	2.09	*2.60
GDP per capita	US$	296	399	420	493	716
GDP real growth	%	2.1	6.1	7.2	6.0	7.0
Inflation	%	31.3	9.8	5.3	18.0	12.3
Exports (fob) (goods)	US$m	476.6	569.4	611.0	790.0	1,030.0
Imports (fob) (goods)	US$m	783.2	882.4	972.0	1,403.0	1,830.0
Balance of trade	US$m	-306.6	-312.9	-360.0	-613.0	-800.0
Current account	US$m	-131.0	-118.3	-103.1	-181.0	-180.0
Foreign debt	US$bn	1.3	1.2	1.4	1.3	–
Total reserves minus gold	US$m	230.2	229.0	268.9	302.3	470.3
Foreign exchange	US$m	229.8	228.3	268.6	302.2	470.2
Exchange rate	per US$	12.43	12.87	13.51	13.50	12.33

* estimated figure

Moldova

1990 Moldova's attempts to become an independent republic were hindered by the country's economic weaknesses and its strained relations with Russia. Ethnic Russians proclaimed the 'Transdniestr Republic' on the left bank of the Dniestr River.

1991 Civil war erupted between the Transdniestr separatists and Moldova. Russian troops were deployed in Moldova to oversee a cease-fire agreed between the warring factions. Moldova formally declared its independence, with Mercea Snegur as the country's first president, and joined the Commonwealth of Independent States (CIS).

1992 Moldova was recognised by the UN. The Partidul Popular Crestin-Democrat (PPCD) (Christian-Democrat People's Party) resigned from government. A new coalition government took office.

1994 Moldova pursued a pro-Western policy and entered into NATO's Partnership for Peace (PfP) programme. The extreme left Partidul Democrat Agrar din Moldova (PDAM) (Agrarian-Democratic Party of Moldova) won the elections. A new consitution was introduced.

1996 Petru Lucinschi won the presidential elections.

1998 The Partidul Comunistilor din Moldova (PCM) (Communist Party of Moldova) won the biggest share of the vote in the parliamentary elections, but was unable to form a government as it was short of an absolute majority in the Parlamentul (Parliament). Right-wing parties, which had finished behind the PCM in the elections, joined together and formed a coalition government, led by Ion Ciubuc.

1999 The government collapsed. Its successor, an alliance of several centrist and centre-right parties also collapsed, following defections and a no-confidence vote. A non-affiliated government emerged, led by Dumitru Braghis.

2000 Against President Lucinschi's wishes, Moldova was transformed into a parliamentary republic – giving the parliament the opportunity to elect the president instead of election by popular vote. Parliament failed to elect a new president when neither candidate received the 61 votes required for outright victory.

2001 The PCM won the parliamentary elections and Vasile Tarlev was appointed prime minister. Vladimir Voronin, leader of the PCM, was elected president by parliament. Russia committed itself to removing troops from Moldova by 2002 as drawn up by the Organisation for Security and Co-operation in Europe (OSCE). Moldova joined the World Trade Organisation (WTO). Igor Smirnov was re-elected as self-styled president of the breakaway Transdniestr region.

2002 The announcement of plans to make Russian an official language and compulsory in schools sparked months of mass protests which ended only when the scheme was shelved. The OSCE deadline for the withdrawal of Russian troops from Transdniestr was extended until the end of 2003.

2003 Moldova was told it must meet at least three conditions in order to restore relations with the World Bank: to elaborate a poverty reduction strategy, resume relations with the IMF and solve a dispute between the government and Unión Fenosa (a Spanish company which owns three Moldovan energy distribution networks).

2004 In July, the Russian and Ukrainian-speaking Transdniestr republic closed several schools which use Romanian, Moldova's official language. Transdniestr also blocked the railway traffic, and terminated the power service, to Moldova. President Voronin requested the establishment of an international monitoring of the Transdniestr section of the Moldova-Ukrainian border.

2005 The ruling PCM and President Vladimir Voronin were re-elected on 6 March and 4 April, respectively. On 8 April, the President reappointed Vasile Tarlev as prime minister.

Political structure
Constitution
The 1977 constitution was replaced in August 1994, establishing the country as a 'presidential, parliamentary republic' based on political pluralism and 'the preservation, development and expression of ethnic and linguistic identity'. The constitution enforces the separation of judicial, legislative and executive powers. Moldova's independence and neutrality are enshrined in the constitution, as are the rights of all ethnic minorities.

For administrative purposes Moldova is divided into 40 districts (*raioane*) and 10 cities. Gagauz-Yeri and Transdniestr are guarenteed autonomous status, although the unrecognised separatist government of Transdniestr also claims outright independence.

Form of state
Parliamentary democratic republic

The executive
Executive power is held by the president of the republic, who must approve legislation and may also propose it. The president nominates the prime minister and government.

Candidates for the presidency must be over 35 years of age, resident in the country for at least 10 years and speakers of the national language. The president is elected for a term of four years by the parliament. The president is limited to two consecutive terms of office.

National legislature
The 101-member Parlamentul (parliament) is the legislative body with the power to appoint the president. It can also approve or reject presidential nominations for the prime minister and government. The government must be appointed within 30 days of parliamentary elections or fresh elections must be called.

The term of parliament is four years, with elections by direct universal suffrage for all those aged over 18 years, with a proportional representation electoral system. There are two parliamentary sessions per year (February–July and September–December), although an extraordinary session may be called at the request of the president of the republic or by the chair of parliament.

Legal system
The legal system is based on civil law. The Constitutional Court is the highest legal authority. It reviews the legality of legislative acts and must validate the election of the president and all members of parliament. Its independence is guaranteed by the constitution and judges, once selected, cannot be removed without their consent. The Constitutional Court consists of six judges, two each appointed by the president, parliament and Higher Council of Magistrates, all for a six-year term.

The rest of the justice system is administered by the Supreme Court, Appeals Court and lesser courts. Following recommendation by the Higher Council of Justice, the judges of the Supreme Court are appointed by parliament, and those of all lesser courts by the president of the republic, all for a renewable term of five years. The Higher Council of Magistrates consists of 11 members, of which five (the minister of justice, the president of the Supreme Court, the president of the Court of Appeal, the president of the Court of Business Audit and the prosecutor general) are automatic members, a further three are judges appointed by the Supreme Court and three are academic lawyers appointed by parliament.

Last elections
4 April 2005 (presidential); 6 March 2005 (parliamentary).

Results: Presidential: Vladimir Voronin, leader of the PCM, was re-elected by parliament, winning 75 votes against one for Gheorghe Duca.

Parliamentary: the ruling Partidul Comunistilor din Moldova (PCM) (Communist Party of Moldova) was re-elected with 46.1 per cent of the vote (about 56 seats out of 101), the Democratic Moldova bloc 28.4 per cent (about 34) and the Partidul Popular Crestin Democrat (PPCD) (Christian Democrat People's

Party) 9.1 per cent (about 11). Turnout was 63.7 per cent.
Next elections
2009 (parliamentary and presidential)

Political parties
Ruling party
Partidul Comunistilor din Moldova (PCM) (Communist Party of Moldova) (since 2001; re-elected 6 Mar 2005)
Main opposition party
Partidul Popular Crestin Democrat (PPCD) (Christian Democrat People's Party)

Population
4.21 million (2004)
Ethnic make-up
The high number of ethnic Ukrainians and Russians in Moldova stems from the former Soviet Union's forced emigration policies in an attempt to dilute the ethnic Moldovan population. There are internal disputes with ethnic Russians and Ukrainians in the separatist Transdniestr region and with Gagauz Turks in the south. Ethnic groups in Moldova include: Moldovan/Romanian (64.5 per cent); Ukrainian (13.8 per cent); Russian (13 per cent); Gagauz (3.5 per cent); Bulgarian (2 per cent); and others (3.2 per cent).
Religions
Christianity is the majority religion in Moldova, the principal denomination being the Eastern Orthodox Church (98.5 per cent). The Gagauz also adhere to Orthodox Christianity despite their Turkic roots. There are Romanian and Turkish liturgies in Moldova, but the Russian Orthodox Church (Moscow Patriarchy) has jurisdiction.
Although there are an estimated 20,000 Roman Catholics in Moldova, the Moldovan branch of the Roman Catholic Church, founded in 1848, has few active congregations. Approximately 1.5 per cent of the population is Jewish.

Education
Primary education lasts for four years, at aged 10 students move on to secondary school for seven or eight years. This is divided into five years of lower secondary school and may be followed by two or three years of upper secondary school, following either technical or academic programmes, leading to either higher education or further training. Lessons may be given in either Romanian or Russian. There are several private higher education institutions.
Before the collapse of the Soviet Union, Moldova's education system was completely integrated into the Soviet system. This meant that most teaching was in the Russian language. Since independence, the curriculum has become much more focussed on Moldovan history and culture. The Moldovan government has restored the Romanian language in schools and added courses in Romanian literature and history to the curriculum. The governments of Romania and Moldova established strong ties between their education systems. Several thousand Moldovan students have attended school in Romania, and the Romanian government has donated textbooks to replace Soviet-era books.
The government's decision to introduce Russian in primary schools as a mandatory subject in January 2002 was a cause of much controversy. In February 2002, the government announced that the Russian language lessons would be optional.
Literacy rate: 99 per cent male; 98.6 per cent female, adult rates in 2002 (World Bank).
Compulsory years: 6 to 15.
Enrolment rate: 97 per cent total primary enrolment of the relevant age group (including repetition rates); 81 per cent secondary enrolment (World Bank).
Pupils per teacher: 23 in primary schools.

Health
By 2002, 94 per cent of infants aged less than one year had been immunised against measles.
HIV prevalence: 0.2 per cent aged 15–49 in 2003 (World Bank)
Life expectancy: 65.18 years (2005)
Fertility rate/Maternal mortality rate: 1.81 births per woman (2004)
Birth rate/Death rate: 15.27 births and 12.79 deaths per 1,000 people (2005 estimates)
Infant mortality rate: 40.42 per 1,000 live births (2005)
Head of population per physician/bed: 3.6 physicians and 12.1 hospital beds per 1,000 people (World Bank estimates)

Welfare
A social insurance system covers old age pensions, worker's disability, survivors, sickness and maternity benefit and family allowance, plus unemployment payments. Contributions are obtained from workers at 1 per cent of earnings (23 per cent for self-employed); 29–30 per cent employer's payroll, dependent on industry or enterprise; central government pays *ad hoc* flat-rate payments; regional (Republics), local authorities and employers can also provide supplementary benefits, from their own budgets, for specific needs. Moldova remains one of the poorest countries in the region and pensioners remain particularly disadvantaged, accounting for 20 per cent of the population. The government intends to introduce private pensions to supplement the current state pension system. In 1999, legislation on private pensions allowed for the establishment of both open and closed pension funds based on voluntary contributions.
Pensions
The minimum retirement age is 62 years with a full pension dependent on 32 years of insurance cover.

Main cities
Chisinau (Kishinev) (capital, estimated population 709,900 in 2003), Tiraspol (209,800), Balti (175,400), Tighina (144,900).

Languages spoken
The 1994 constitution states that Moldovan is the country's official language, although it allows for the use of other languages in the country's ethnic minority areas. Officially known as 'limba moldoveneasca' (language of Moldova), Moldovan is a dialect of Romanian. Russian is the first language of about one-third of the population, and is more universally spoken than Moldovan. Most people are bilingual.
The government attempted to introduce a language law in 1989 which would force government officials to speak both Moldovan and Russian. Since many Russian-speakers could not speak Moldovan and needed time to learn the language, the parliament decided in 1994 to postpone the law indefinitely. The law was a major factor in accelerating the separatist movements of the Russian-speaking Transdniestr region and of the Gagauz-Yeri minority who speak Gagauz (a Turkish dialect). Other minority languages include Ukrainian and Bulgarian. The government's decision, although later annulled, to introduce Russian in primary schools as a mandatory subject in 2002 was the cause of much controversy.
Official language/s
Moldovan (in latin script)

Media
Despite the guarantees of free expression enshrined in the constitution, following the election of the Communist Party to power in 2001 the media sector has been subjected to growing administrative and legal pressures designed to exercise control over it. There is, in reality, little real independence within the media, particularly the state-owned media. Whether privately or publicly owned, editorial interference by political and business interests is commonplace. Employees of the state-owned TeleRadio-Moldova went on strike in 2002 to protest against censorship at the company.
Press
In 2002, 180 newspapers and magazines were in publication, of which some 100 had national circulation, and 80 local circulation. Around 20 per cent of those with

national circulation were partly funded by the state. Political parties published some 15 per cent and the rest were under private or corporate ownership.

A poll commissioned by the Independent Journalism Centre showed that 44 per cent of Moldovans do not read a newspapaer at all, and a further 20 per cent read one less than once a week.

Dailies: *Nezavisimaia Moldova* is a Russian-language daily of the Government of the Republic of Moldova. *Chisinau News* is one of the most widely read dailies. Other general interest newspapers include the Romanian-language *Jurnal de Chisinau* and the Russian-language *Kommersant Moldoviy*, *Kishinyovskie Novosti*, *Komsomolskaya Pravda*, *Moldavskie Vedomosti* and *Novaya Gazeta*.

Business: Business publications include the Russian-language *Delovaya Gazeta* and *Ekonomicheskoe Obozrenie* and the Romanian-language business magazine *Observator Economic*.

Periodicals: The *East-West Observer* is an English-language monthly newspaper.

Broadcasting

Radio and televison broadcast licences are issued by the Broadcast Co-ordinating Council (BCC). Licences are issued on the basis of a number of criteria encompassing the plurality of options, equality in the treatment of participants, the quality and diversity of programming, free competition, domestic broadcast productions and the impartiality and independence of broadcast programmes.

There are some 115 private local radio and television stations; a number of these cover about 70 per cent of the country including Chisinau Municipality's 'Antena C' and the private stations HitFM and Russkoe Radio.In addition to the public televison station Moldova 1, Russia's public broadcaster ORT and Romania's TVR also have national coverage in Moldova. No radio or television stations are owned by political parties.

Economy

Immediately after independence in 1991, Moldova experienced a catastrophic economic collapse and became one of Europe's poorest economies. Between 1991 and 2000, the economy recorded positive growth only once, expanding by 1.3 per cent in 1997. Official estimates showed a 66 per cent fall in GDP. Since 2000, when GDP growth was 2.1 per cent, there has been a general upward trend, with GDP registering seven per cent growth by 2004. Growth has not returned the economy to pre-independence levels and per capita incomes remain among the lowest in Europe.

Although Moldova has reasonable social indicators, including a low level of illiteracy and long life expectancy, poverty is a huge problem with around 80 per cent of the population living below the poverty line.

External trade

A large percentage of Moldova's external trade is undertaken with other CIS countries. A 10-year partnership and co-operation agreement between the EU and Moldova was in force until 2005.

Imports

Mineral products and fuel, machinery and equipment, chemicals and textiles.

Main sources: Ukraine (16.8 per cent total, 2004), Russia (14.7 per cent), Germany (12.5 per cent), France (9.9 per cent), Italy (8.0 per cent), Romania (5.3 per cent)

Exports

Exports include foodstuffs, textiles and machinery.

Main destinations: Russia (31.4 per cent total, 2004), Italy (10.7 per cent), Germany (9.5 per cent), Romania (9.4 per cent), France (6.9 per cent), Ukraine (5.8 per cent), Belarus (4.3 per cent)

Agriculture

Farming

Agriculture remains a key sector of the national economy. The sector contributes around a fifth of GDP and is a considerable source of export revenue. It employs over 40 per cent of the working population. Moldova's main resources are its climate and the rich black *chernozem* soil covering 75 per cent of the land, making it ideal for growing wine grapes, tobacco, sugar beet and for raising dairy cattle. Grains, vegetables and fruits are also important. The animal husbandry sector specialises in the breeding of livestock, pigs and poultry.

The majority of production continues to be from state farms and co-operatives, although as the land reform programme progresses this is expected to change. Agro-industrial complexes are dominant in meat and dairy production. Pork is the main domestic protein source. A quarter of total meat production is exported. There are around 150 wineries in Moldova and 170,000 hectares (ha) of vineyards. The wine making industry has attracted foreign investment and is dependent upon markets in the CIS. The majority of annual sugar exports go to former Soviet republics. Moldova is also a major tobacco producer.

Crop production in 2004 included: 2,830,300 tonnes (t) cereals in total, 1,840,000t maize, 690,000 t wheat, 318,000t potatoes, 260,000t barley, 907,000t sugar beets, 600,000t grapes, 138,410t oilcrops, 150,000t pulses, 21,100t treenuts, 338,000t apples, 95,000t tomatoes, 18,000t chillies & peppers, 10,200t tobacco, 1,024,710t fruit in total, 380,800t vegetables in total. Livestock production included: 86,300t meat in total, 23,000t beef, 38,000t pig meat, 2,500t lamb, 22,200t poultry, 37,426t eggs, 628,000t milk, 2,200t honey, 960t sheepskins, 3,230t cattle hides.

Fishing

Only 20 fish species, including crucian carp, perch, bream and soodak, are of any commercial importance. Most of the fish resources are concentrated in natural and artificial lakes devoted to fish breeding.

Forestry

Forest and wooded land account for about one-tenth of the land area, with forest cover estimated at 325,000 hectares (ha). All forests in Moldova are state-owned. About two-thirds of the forest is available for wood supply, while the rest is protected and conserved. Timber includes oak, beech and ash.

Production is mostly for domestic consumption. More than half of all wood consumed is used as fuel or processed into charcoal. The forestry industry faces a shortage of raw materials and is not sufficient to meet the domestic markets. Moldova imports sawnwood and paper. Wood and wood products account for around four per cent of annual GDP. Moldova typically produces approximately 500,000 cubic metres of timber per annum.

Exports of forest material in 2004 amounted to US$3.7 million, while imports amounted to US$29.2 million

Industry and manufacturing

Industry accounts for around 25 per cent of GDP. A large proportion of industrial production is concentrated in the breakaway Transdniestr region, where most of Moldova's electricity, metallurgy and metallurgical equipment are produced.

The agro-industrial complex is at the heart of the economy, carrying out the production, transportation, processing, storage and sale of agricultural products. Other industries include electronics, machine tools, tractors, agricultural engineering, building materials, chemicals and furniture manufacture.

Tourism

Tourism is at an early stage of development. The economic value of tourism is recognised and efforts are being made to entice visitors from outside the traditional east European market. Visitor numbers have fallen in recent years: here were around 17,000 arrivals in 2004 compared with 19,000 in 2000. Moldova lacks obvious tourist attractions, so the country's rural charms are being exploited with village holidays, hunting and vineyard tours. The small size of the country is presented as an advantage, allowing all of it to be toured in a short time. Conference and other business tourism is also being encouraged. New infrastructure is being constructed and old stock renovated.

Hydrocarbons
Total domestic oil reserves are minimal with limited production capacity. The Valenskoye field has commercial reserves of around 73 million barrels, which Moldova is planning to exploit in partnership with foreign investors. Potential production is estimated at 732,000 barrels per year. Moldova imports some 22–29 million barrels of oil annually to meet its consumption requirements, which were projected to reach an estimated 25,000 barrels per day (bpd) in 2005. Although Moldova had traditionally imported most of its oil products from Russia, estimates show that supplies from Romania and Ukraine meet nearly 99 per cent of current oil demand.

Gas reserves are estimated at 25 billion cubic metres. Moldova imports three million cubic metres of natural gas annually from Russia, 40 per cent of which goes to the industrialised Transdniestr region. The monopoly domestic gas distributor Moldova-Gaz is heavily indebted to Gazprom, the Russian gas monopoly, with supplies being suspended on occasion to force payment.

Moldova has substantial reserves of coal (10 million tonnes), which should last for the foreseeable future at recent low rates of production. Most production is low-grade bituminous (tar) coal, used in construction rather than power generation. For energy purposes, Moldova imports approximately 420,000 tonnes of hard coal per annum.

Energy
Moldova has limited electricity generating capacity. Although it has three power stations with a total capacity of 301MW, part of the equipment is worn out and must be replaced. Much capacity is in the disputed province of Transdniestr.

Moldova is trying to conserve energy and to develop alternative power sources – solar, wind and geothermal.

Financial markets
Stock exchange
Moldova's embryo economy has yet to develop recognisable financial markets. With founding capital of US$60,000 the Moldova Stock Exchange (MSE) was established in 1993 and began activity in 1995. There are over 1,000 companies listed on the MSE, of which 500 are traded regularly, although most of these are small- or medium-sized.

Banking and insurance
Central bank
Banca Nationala a Moldovei (BNM) (National Bank of Moldova)

Time
GMT plus two hours (GMT plus three hours late Mar to late Sep)

Geography
Moldova is a landlocked country in south-eastern Europe, bordered to the north, east and south by Ukraine and to the west by Romania. Most of the country consists of flat plains with low hills. Approximately 11 per cent of Moldova is forested.

Moldova is a fertile plain with small areas of hill country in the centre and north. The main rivers are the Dniestr, which flows through the eastern regions into the Black Sea in the south-west, and the Prut, which marks the western border with Romania and which joins the Danube at the southern tip of Moldova.

The separatist Republic of Transdniestr (not officially recognised) lies between the eastern Ukrainian border and the Dniestr River.

Climate
With a temperate, continental climate Moldova has long hot summers and chilly winters. Average temperatures vary between -2 degrees Celsius (C) and 22 degrees C. Extremes of temperature can reach 35 degrees C during summer and -25 degrees C (with a good deal of ice and snow) in the winter. Average annual rainfall is 500–550mm in the northern and central areas and 450mm in the south.

Dress codes
Business dress is usually quite conservative, but not excessively formal.

Entry requirements
Passports
Required by all. Passports must be valid for at least six months after the date of departure.

Visa
Required by all except CIS nationals. Visit www.consularassistance.com/visa_us.html for the requirements and a visa application form; to be submitted to the nearest consulate for processing. Limited stay visas can be obtained at Chisinau airport and some major road crossings from Romania however these cost more than those organised in advance. Arrival by train requires a visa before travelling.

Currency advice/regulations
Import of local currency is prohibited; foreign currency must be declared on arrival. Export of local currency is prohibited; foreign currency can be exported up to the amount declared on arrival. Travellers cheques are not in general use. The Russian rouble is in use in Transdniestr.

Customs
A small amount of personal goods are allowed in duty-free. On arrival declare all foreign currency and valuable items such as jewellery, cameras, computers and musical instruments.

Health (for visitors)
Mandatory precautions
Vaccination certificates for cholera and yellow fever are mandatory if travelling from an infected area. Any person applying for a visa for a stay of more than three months must present a certificate showing that the individual is HIV negative. Only tests performed at clinics approved by the Moldovan government are accepted.

Advisable precautions
It is advisable to be 'in date' for the following immunisations: diphtheria, polio and tetanus (within 10 years), typhoid fever, hepatitis 'A' (moderate risk only), hepatitis 'B', tuberculosis and tick-borne encephalitis. Healthcare is free in Moldova (although medicines must be purchased). There are chemists where you can buy basic drugs (aspirin, etc), but it is wise to take a supply of frequently used medicines with you, including precautionary antibiotics if travelling outside main urban areas. A travel kit including disposable syringes is a reasonable precaution. There is a rabies risk. Water precautions recommended (water purification tablets may be useful).

Credit cards
Credit cards are not in general use.

Public holidays
Fixed dates
1 Jan (New Year's Day), 7–8 Jan (Orthodox Christmas), 14 Jan (Orthodox New Year's Day), 8 Mar (Women's Day), 1 May (Labour Day), 9 May (Victory Day), 27 Aug (Independence Day), 31 Aug (Limba Noastra/National Language Day).

Variable dates
Orthodox Easter

Working hours
Banking
Mon–Sat: 0900–1500 for banking facilities; 0900–1800 for bureau de change facilities.

Business
Mon–Fri: 0900–1800 (appointments best between 0900–1000).

Government
Mon–Fri: 0900–1800.

Shops
Mon: 0800–1700, Tue–Sat: 0800–2100.

Electricity supply
220V AC 50 Hz.

Moldova

Weights and measures
Metric system

Social customs/useful tips
Business appointments are essential and punctuality appreciated. Business cards are usually exchanged. There are many customs and traditions to be understood. Gratuities are becoming more customary, particularly in international hotels.
Take flowers if invited to someone's home and leave shoes at the door.

Security
Although safer than many Western cities, the streets of Chisinau have become more dangerous since independence, particularly after dark. Care should be taken to avoid unlit areas, even in the city centre. There are few embassies in Chisinau (no British Embassy, for instance). Before departure to Moldova, visitors are advised to check with their own ministry of foreign affairs for information on who to contact in the case of an emergency. The British Foreign & Commonwealth Office (FCO), for example, advises its nationals to contact the British Embassy in Bucharest in Romania.
Avoid all travel in the eastern region of Transdniestr.

Getting there
Air
The majority of air travellers fly to Moldova via Moscow, Kiev or Bucharest, but there are direct services from some major European centres. Air Moldova services are not extensive.
National airline: Air Moldova; Moldavian Airlines.
International airport/s: Chisinau International (KIV), 13km south-east of Chisinau.
Surface
Road: The principal route runs from Odessa in the Crimea into Moldova through Tiraspol, north to Chisinau, Bel'tsy and then back into Ukraine. Buses run to Chisinau from Bucharest, Romania.
Rail: The Moldovan rail network is connected to that of Ukraine, Romania and Russia. The principal rail routes connect Chisinau with Tiraspol and Ukraine to the east, and Lasi in Romania to the west. The journey time to Bucharest is approximately 11.5 hours, to Moscow 22 hours and Sofia 23 hours. First-class sleeping carriages, booked in advance from Chisinau station, are recommended.
Water: The Dniestr River flows into the Black Sea in Ukraine, near the port of Odessa. It is used more for industrial transportation than for passengers.

Getting about
National transport
Road: The road network, although extensive, is in need of significant investment and repair. The main routes run from Kagul to Chisinau via Komrat and from Chisinau to Lipkany via Bel'tsy. Roads from Tiraspol in Transdniestr to Chisinau and other destinations in the rest of Moldova may be subject to closure due to conflict in the breakaway region.
Buses: There are buses between the larger towns.
Rail: Most larger towns are connected by rail. Lines run north-south from Kagul and the southern border with Ukraine to Lipkany and the northern border with Ukraine. Owing to the Transdniestr conflict, routes from Chisinau and Kagul to Tiraspol and Bendery are liable to disruption.
Water: The Dniestr River runs parallel to Moldova's eastern border, and is extensively used, although mostly for industrial rather than passenger transport.
City transport
The names of streets are in both Moldovan and Russian.
Taxis: Taxis are widely available and can be picked up at stands or hailed anywhere in the city.
Car hire
A national licence with authorised translation or international driving licence is required.

BUSINESS DIRECTORY

The addresses listed below are a selection only. While World of Information makes every endeavour to check these addresses, we cannot guarantee that changes have not been made, especially to telephone numbers and area codes. We would welcome any corrections.

Telephone area codes
The international direct dialling (IDD) code for Moldova is +373, followed by the area code and subscriber's number:

Chisinau	2	Bendery	32
Bel'tsy	31	Tiraspol	33

Useful telephone numbers
Ambulance: 903
Fire: 901
Police: 902
Operator assistance for international telephone calls: 071

Chambers of Commerce
American Chamber of Commerce in Moldova, Joly Alon Hotel, 37 Maria Cebotari Street, Chisinau 2012 (tel: 238-122; fax: 238-120).

Moldova Chamber of Commerce and Industry, 151 Stefan cel Mare Street, Chisinau 2004 (tel: 221-552; fax: 234-425; e-mail: president@chamber.md).

Banking
Banca Comerciala Romana SA Sucursala, 32A Tricolorului Street, Chisinau 2012 (tel:. 220-549; fax: 223-509; e-mail: bcr@cni.md).

Banca Sociala, 61 Banulescu-Bodoni Street, Chisinau 2006. (tel: 221-481; fax: 224-230).

BTR Moldova. 18 Renasterii Street, Chisinau 2005. (tel: 201-100; fax: 201-101; e-mail: office@btr.md).

Businessbanca, 9 Alexandru cel Bun Street, Chisinau 2012. (tel: 223-338; fax: 222-370).

Chisinau Municipal Bank, 83 Stefan cel Mare Avenue, Chisinau 2012 (tel/fax: 228-090).

Comertbank, 63 Columna Street, Chisinau 2001. (tel: 541-356; fax: 543-151; e-mail: combank@chmoldpac.md).

Energbank, 78 Vasile Alexandri Street, Chisinau 2012. (tel: 544-377; fax: 253-409).

Export - Import, 6 Stefan cel Mare Avenue, Chisinau 2001. (tel: 272-583; fax: 546-234; e-mail: exim@eximbank.com).

Finance and Trade Bank, 26 Pushkin Street, Chisinau 2012. (tel: 227-435; fax: 228-253; e-mail: fincom@fcb.mldnet.com).

International Commercial Bank (Moldova), 108 Mitropolit Dosoftei Street, Chisnau 2012. (tel: 226-025; fax: 225-053; e-mail: info@icbsb.md).

Investprivatbank, 34 Sciusev Street, Chisinau 2001. (tel: 274-386; fax: 540-510; e-mail: bnc@ipb.mldnet.com).

Mobiasbanca, 65 Tighina Street, Chisinau 2001. (tel/fax: 541-974; e-mail: info@bcmobias.moldova.su).

Moldindconbank, 38 Armeneasca Street, Chisinau 2012. (tel: 225-521; fax: 279-195; e-mail: computer@micb.net.md).

Moldova - Agroindbank, 9 Cosmonautilor Street, Chisinau 2006. (tel: 222-770; fax: 242-454).

PetrolBANK, 33 Ismail Street, Chisinau 2001. (tel: 500-101; fax: 548-827; e-mail: juri@petrolbank.com).

Savings Bank, 115 Columna Street, Chisinau 2012. (tel: 244-722; fax: 244-731; e-mail: bem@cni.md).

Unibank, 26 Pushkin Street, Chisinau 2012. (tel: 225-586; fax: 220-530).

Universalbank, 180 Stefan cel Mare Avenue, Chisinau 2004. (tel: 246-406; fax: 246-489; e-mail:stabil@mail.universalbank.md).

Victoriabank, 141 August 31 Street, Chisinau 2004. (tel: 233-065; fax: 233-933; e-mail: mail@victoriabank.md).

Central bank
Banca Nationala a Moldovei, 7 Renasterii Avenue, Chisinau 2006 (tel: 221-679; fax: 220-591; e-mail: webmaster@bnm.org).

Ministries
Ministry of Agriculture and Food Industry, 162 Stefan cel Mare Boulevard, Chisinau (tel: 233-427; fax: 232-368).

Ministry of Culture, 1 Piata Marii Adunari Nationale, Chisinau (tel: 227-620; fax: 232-388).

Ministry of Defence, 84 Vasile Alexandri Street, Chisinau (tel: 781-156; fax: 233-507).

Ministry of Economy and Reforms, Piata Marii Adunari Nationale 1, 277033 Chisinau (tel: 221-133; fax: 234-064).

Ministry of Education, 1 Piata Marii Adunari Nationale (tel: 233-151; fax: 233-474).

Ministry of Finance, Cosmonautilor Street, 277012 Chisinau (tel: 233-575; fax: 228-610).

Ministry of Foreign Affairs, 1 Piata Marii Adunari Nationale, Chisinau (tel: 233-940; fax: 232-302).

Ministry of Foreign Economic Relations, Piata Marii Adunari Nationale 1, Chisinau 277033 (tel/fax: 234-628).

Ministry of Health, 1 Vasile Alexandri Street, Chisinau (tel: 721-010; fax: 738-781).

Ministry of Industry and Trade, 69 Stefan cel Mare Boulevard, Chisinau (tel: 233-556; fax: 227-346).

Ministry of Internal Affairs, 75 Stefan cel Mare Boulevard, Chisinau (tel: 221-201; fax: 222-723).

Ministry of Justice, 82, 31 August Street, Chisinau (tel: 233-340; fax: 234-797).

Ministry of Labour, Social Protection and Family, 1 Vasile Alexandri Street, Chisinau (tel: 737-572; fax: 723-000).

Ministry of National Security, 166 Stefan cel Mare Boulevard, Chisinau (tel: 239-454; fax: 242-018).

Ministry of Privatisation and State Property Administration, 26 Puskin Street, Chisinau (tel: 234-350; fax: 234-336; internet site: http://privatization.md).

Ministry of Territorial Development, Public Utilities and Construction, 3 Gheorghe Tudor Street, Chisinau (tel: 259-111; fax: 259-499).

Ministry of Telecommunications and Informatics, 134 Stefan cel Mare Boulevard, Chisinau (tel: 221-001; fax: 241-553).

Ministry of Transport and Road Construction, 12/A Bucuriei Street, Chisinau (tel: 629-450; fax: 624-875).

Other useful addresses
British Embassy (there is no British representative in Moldova but the British Embassy in Moscow has some responsibility), Commercial Department, Kutuzovsky Prospeckt 7/4, Moscow 121248 (tel: 956-7477; fax: 956-7480).

Business Centre of Moldova Ltd., Stefan cel Mare 180, Room 303, 277004 Chisinau (tel: 247-914; fax: 247-915).

Department of Civil Protection and Exceptional Situations, 69 Cheorghe Asachi Street, Chisinau (tel: 233-430; fax: 233-430).

Department of Customs Control, 65 Columna Street, Chisinau (tel: 549-460; fax: 263-061).

Department of Energy Resources and Fuel, 50 Eminescu Street, Chisinau (tel: 221-010; fax: 222-264).

Department of Environmental Protection, 73 Stefan cel Mare Boulevard, Chisinau (tel: 226-161; fax: 233-806).

Department of National Relations, 109/1, Alexei Mateevici Street, Chisinau (tel: 240-292; fax: 243-610).

Department of Publishing, Polygraphy and Trade of Books, 180 Stefan cel Mare Boulevard, Chisinau (tel: 246-525).

Department of Standards, Metrology and Technical Control, 48 Serghei Lazo Street, Chisinau (tel: 247-991; fax: 222-321).

Department of Statistics, 124 Stefan cel Mare Avenue, Chisinau 227001 (tel: 233-549; fax: 545-162).

MoldEnergo, 78 Vasile Alexandri Str, 277012 Chisinau (tel: 221-065; fax: 253-142).

Moldexpo International Exhibition Centre, 1 Ghioceilor, 277008 Chisinau (tel: 627-416; fax: 627-420).

Moldovan Foreign Trade Organisation, ul Sadovaya 65, 277018 Chisinau (tel: 244-436; fax: 223-226).

Moldova-Gaz, 38 Albisoara Str, 277005 Chisinau (tel: 256-778; fax: 240-014).

Moldova Stock Exchange, 73 Stefan cel Mare, 277001 Chisinau (tel: 265-554; fax: 228-969).

Moldovan Embassy (USA), 2101 S Street, NW, Washington DC 20008 (tel: 202-667-1130; fax: 202-667-120-4; e-mail: moldova@dgs.dgsys.com).

Moldsilva (Forestry Association), 124 Stefan cel Mare Blvd, 277012 Chisinau (tel: 262-256; fax: 223-251).

National Association of Banks, 7 Renasterii Str, 277006 Chisinau (tel: 225-177; fax: 229-382).

National Foreign Trade Company (Moldova-EXIM), 65 Mateevici Str, 277012 Chisinau (tel: 223-226; fax: 244-436).

National Fuel Association, 90 Columna Str, 277001 Chisinau (tel: 223-078; fax: 240-509).

State Company Teleradio Moldova National TV and Radio, 64 Hincesti Highway, 277028 Chisinau (tel: 721-077, 721-863).

Internet sites
Business information: http://www.infomarket.md

Business network: http://www.mbinet.md

Chamber of Commerce: http://www:chamber.md

Freezone and export processing: http://www:moldova-freezone.com

General information (in Moldovan - Romanian): http://www.moldova.md

General government and economy: http://www.moldova.org

IMF Moldova office: http://www.imf.md

Internet resources directory: http://www.ournet.md

Ministry of Economy - Trade department: http://www.trade.moldova

Moldovan parliament: http://www.parliament.md

National Bank rates: http://www.mldnet.com

Monaco

COUNTRY PROFILE

Historical profile
In the late thirteenth century, internal strife within the Holy Roman empire forced the Grimaldi family to take refuge in Provence.
1297 Francois Grimaldi led a group of partisans into Monaco, which has been ruled by the family ever since.
Honore II signed a treaty of friendship with France, guaranteeing the independence of the principality.
1814 The principality was re-established after abolition during the French Revolution.
1861 Independence under French protection. The first constitution was introduced.
1918 Louis, the heir to the throne, was a bachelor and the next male in line to succeed if Louis died without an heir was a German prince, the Duke of Urach. France would not countenance a German monarch and therefore imposed a constitutional provision that only the monarch's own children could inherit the throne.
1949 Prince Rainier III, embodying divine right, succeeded to the throne.
1956 Prince Rainier married the US actress, Grace Kelly.
1962 A constitution was enacted allowing for sharing of legislative powers between the monarch and elected national council; principle of divine right was abolished.
1982 Princess Grace was killed in a car accident.
1988 The Union Nationale et Démocratique (UND) (National and Democratic Union) won the elections.
1993 The UND was defeated by two lists of candidates, known as Liste Campora and Liste Medecin.
1993 Monaco was admitted to the UN.
1998 UND won the elections.
2000 France threatened to take legislative measures against Monaco unless it clamped down on money laundering activities.
2001 France and Monaco reached an agreement on money laundering. As part of the co-operative, Monaco agreed to work more closely with the Financial Oversight Commission (FOC) to revise rules governing investment management companies.
2002 Monaco adopted the euro as its official currency. Due to Prince Rainier's failing health and the bachelor status of his son, Prince Albert, parliament passed a change to the 1918 law of succession, allowing one of Prince Rainier's daughters, Caroline or Stephanie, to succeed Albert if he became sovereign and died childless; the daughters' children would also be in line of succession. Liechtenstein concluded an agreement with Monaco over the prevention of money laundering and terrorist financing.
2003 The Union pour Monaco (UPM) (Union for Monaco) alliance, led by Stephané Valeri, won a landslide majority in the parliamentary elections, ending the 40-year rule of the UND.
2004 Prince Rainier was diagnosed with heart problems, which had developed over several years.
2005 Prince Rainier III died on 6 April. He came to the throne in 1949 and was the longest serving monarch in Europe. He was succeeded by his son, Prince Albert II.

Political structure
Constitution
Under the 1962 constitution, Monaco is governed under the authority of the monarch, a minister of state and a unicameral National Council.
Only Monégasques may vote.
In April 2002, parliament passed a change to the 1918 law of succession, allowing one of Prince Rainier's daughters – Caroline or Stephanie – to inherit the throne from Prince Rainier's son, Albert, if he became sovereign and died childless. In such circumstances, the daughters' children would be in line of succession. The 1918 law had allowed only the monarch's own children to inherit the throne. Without a change in the law, there was a danger that the state would be without a successor and sovereignty would automatically be transferred to France.
Form of state
Parliamentary democratic monarchy
The executive
The monarch is the head of state. The monarch nominates the minister of state from a list of three French diplomats submitted by the French government. As head of the Council of Government (three members appointed by the monarch), the minister of state exercises executive power under the monarch.
The laws are initiated by the monarch; the Council of Government prepares draft legislation in his name; the National Council passes laws and the national budget (in public session); the monarch alone promulgates laws which are then published in the *Journal de Monaco*.

KEY FACTS

Official name: Principauté de Monaco (The Principality of Monaco)

Head of State: Prince Albert II (acceded to the throne 6 Apr 2005)

Head of government: Minister of State Patrick Leclercq

Ruling party: Union pour Monaco (UPM) (Union for Monaco) coalition, comprising: Union Nationale pour l'Avenir de Monaco (UNAM) (National Union for the Future of Monaco), Rassemblement pour la Famille Monégasque (RFM) (Rally for the Monegasque Family) and non-partisans

Area: 2 square km

Population: 32,000 (2004)

Capital: Monaco-Ville

Official language: French and Monégasque

Currency: Euro (eur) = 100 cents

Exchange rate: eur0.83 per US$ (Oct 2005)

GDP per capita: US$22,500 (2003)

Labour force: 30,540 (2003)

Unemployment: 3.10% (2003)

The government is assisted by two consultative bodies: the Council of State and the Economic Council.
National legislature
Legislative authority resides with the 18-member National Council elected every five years by universal adult suffrage. The National Council has no power to topple the government.
Legal system
Although judicial authority is vested in the monarch, it is delegated to the courts and tribunals, which dispense justice in the monarch's name, but completely independently (there is no minister of justice in the Principality).
Last elections
9 February 2003 (parliamentary)
Results: Parliamentary: The UPM won 21 of the 24 seats.
Next elections
2008 (parliamentary)

Political parties
Ruling party
Union pour Monaco (UPM) (Union for Monaco) coalition, comprising: Union Nationale pour l'Avenir de Monaco (UNAM) (National Union for the Future of Monaco), Rassemblement pour la Famille Monégasque (RFM) (Rally for the Monegasque Family) and non-partisans
Political situation
There was a landslide majority for the UPM alliance, led by Stephané Valeri, in the parliamentary elections that ended the 40-year rule of the UND. The UND, which had held all the seats in the previous parliament, only managed to hold on to three seats. The swing in favour of the UPM was largely due to the increasing unpopularity of the UND leader, Jean-Louis Campora, who had served as parliamentary speaker for 30 years. Campora lost his seat in the election.
Turnout was 80 per cent, but only around 20 per cent of the total population was eligible to vote due to the constitutional nationality requirements.

Population
32,000 (2004)
Ethnic make-up
According to the 2000 census, around 7,000 of the total population are Monégasques, 11,000 French, 7,000 Italian and some 2,000 British.
Religions
The state religion is Catholicism, but religious freedom is guaranteed by the constitution. Other religions practised are Anglicanism, Baha'i, Judaism, Protestantism.

Health
Total expenditure on health was 7.6 per cent of GDP in 2001, of which government spending was 56.1 per cent.
By 2002, 99 per cent of infants aged less than one year had been immunised against measles.
Infant mortality rate: 4.0 per 1,000 live births (World Bank)

Main cities
Monaco-Ville (capital, estimated population 1,400 in 2003), Monte Carlo (15,400), La Condamine (14,600).

Languages spoken
Italian and English are widely spoken and understood. The traditional Monégasque language is spoken by the older generation of Monégasques and is taught in schools. Ligurian and Occitan are also spoken.
Official language/s
French and Monégasque

Media
Press
Dailies: The Centre de Presse is the official distribution channel for information and photographs in the Principality of Monaco. Dailies including Monaco editions of French newspapers *Nice-Matin* and *L'Echo de la Côte d'Azur* are available. Other French dailies are widely read.
Weeklies: The *Journal de Monaco* is an internal government journal published weekly by the ministry of state.
Periodicals: French newspapers are widely available as well as English books and magazines. The *Monaco Hebdo* covers Monaco's current affairs. *The Riviera Reporter* is an English-language magazine for residents in the French Riviera, published every two months.
Broadcasting
Radio: Radio Monte Carlo (RMC) is part-owned by the French government. Broadcasts are in French and Italian as well as overseas broadcasts in 12 languages. Riviera Radio, based in RMC studio complex, broadcasts in English 24 hours per day. Evangelical programmes are broadcast in numerous foreign languages by Trans World Radio.
Television: Tele Monte Carlo broadcasts 24hrs/day, mainly pop videos.

Economy
Monaco enjoys a small, open and diversified economy based on tourism, the convention business, banking and insurance, but with a significant industrial sector. State income is derived from taxes (55 per cent from VAT), postage stamps and public monopolies. Gambling revenue accounts for 4.35 per cent of total income. The standard of living is high, with per capita income of US$22,500.
Although Monaco is not a member of the EU, France's membership gives it access to the European marketplace. In 2002, along with France, Monaco adopted the euro as its official currency.
The late Prince Rainier endeavoured to broaden the base of the local economy, notably with the Fontvieille development of 22ha of reclaimed land to the west of the old town, which is now a centre for light industry and low-cost housing. Monaco's total area has been increased by one-tenth by this project.
The Organisation for Economic Co-operation and Development (OECD) named Monaco as one of five countries as unco-operative tax havens, the others being Andorra, Liberia, Liechtenstein and the Marshall Islands.
Monaco is diversifying into the knowledge-based industry, aiming to become a European leader in multimedia, the Internet and telecommunications.

External trade
Monaco imports and exports products and services from all over the world and is heavily dependent upon imports from France. EU rules of free circulation of goods apply.
Exports
There is full customs integration with France, which collects and rebates Monegasque trade duties. Monaco also participates in EU market system through customs union with France
Farming
There is no commercial agriculture in Monaco.

Industry and manufacturing
Around 200 firms employing 4,000 people typically account for about 33 per cent of GDP. Main products are cosmetics, healthcare, pharmaceuticals, precision instruments, glass, plastics, electrical goods, electronics, textiles and food processing. Also important are construction and public works.

Tourism
Tourism contributes around 25 per cent of GDP. Monaco attracts around 260,000 tourists annually. Most visitors are day trippers. The casino and the annual Grand Prix motor race are major attractionons. The oceanographic museum, formerly directed by Jacques Cousteau, is one of the most renowned institutions of its kind in the world. Monaco is expanding its conference and exhibition activities to enhance its appeal to the business travel market.

Energy
Monaco is entirely reliant on imports from France to meet its energy requirements. The Société Monégasque de l'Electricité et du Gaz is responsible for distribution.

Banking and insurance
There are nearly 50 banks and around 20 other financial institutions catering to 130,000 clients worth US$78 billion. In

addition to commercial and retail services, Monaco has in recent decades increasingly provided private banking and wealth management services. Monaco's banking system operates under French banking law and is subject to regulation by the Banque de France.

Monaco's reputation as a tax haven with a secretive banking system has made enemies in other jurisdictions, which accuse Monaco of abetting money-laundering and tax evasion. Monaco has been resistant to pressure to be more be more rigorous and transparent in its dealings, but does take action against money-laundering under existing legislation. In addition, mutual assistance agreements to exchange information on money-laundering have been concluded since 2001 with several countries, including France, Spain, Belgium, and Switzerland .

Monaco was obliged to accede to the EU Savings Tax Directive, which took effect in July 2005. Under the withholding tax option, Monaco's banks and financial institutions will automatically deduct tax, initially 15 per cent rising to 35 per cent by 2011, from income earned on interest and other savings of EU citizens and transfer it to the national tax departments. Monaco will be able to retain its banking secrecy by being allowed to withhold information on non-residents' savings. Monaco has also agreed to supply information on tax fraud, for criminal or civil trials, and notify EU member states about additional malpractices.

Central bank
European Central Bank
Monaco does not have a central bank, but monetary links to France have included acceptance of French currency and subsequently the euro as legal tender, while financial institutions located in Monaco have access to the Banque de France on the similar terms to French banks.

Main financial centre
Monaco-Ville

Time
GMT plus one hour (GMT plus two hours from late March to late September).

Geography
Monaco is a small enclave in south-eastern France, about 15km east of Nice, on the Mediterranean coast.

Climate
The climate is Mediterranean with mild winters and warm summers. The hottest months are July and August, with average temperatures of 25 degrees Celsius.

Entry requirements
Passports
Passports are not required by nationals of countries which are signatories of the Schengen Accords, which includes most EU member states. Passports must be valid for three months beyond the length of stay.

Visa
Not required for visits up to three months provided visitors arrive from France and adhere to French entry requirements. See www.monaco-consulate.com/links.htm then FAQs for further information. French visas are required by all, except citizens of EU, North America, Australasia and Japan, for stays up to three months; this includes business trips by representatives of foreign entities with an invitation from a local company or organisation. Proof of adequate funds for stay, an itinerary, a guarantee of repatriation if necessary and return/onward ticket are also required. For further exceptions and full details visit www.diplomatie.gouv.fr/thema/dossier.gb.asp and follow the path (entering France) to the database, a copy of the application form can be found there. A Schengen visa application (offered in several languages) can be also downloaded on www.eurovisa.info/ApplicationForm.htm.

Currency advice/regulations
There are no restrictions on imports of foreign exchange.

Health (for visitors)
Mandatory precautions
None
Advisable precautions
Up-to-date tetanus and polio immunisations.

Hotels
Classified into one- to four-star and predominantly four-star/luxury categories. Monaco has around 2,500 hotel rooms, most of which are four-star. The occupancy rate is around 50 per cent.

Credit cards
All credit cards are accepted.

Public holidays
Fixed dates
1 Jan (New Year's Day), 26–27 Jan (Feast of St Dévote), 23 Mar (Mi-Carême, half-day), 1 May (Labour Day), 15 Aug (Assumption Day), 1 Nov (All Saints' Day), 19 Nov (National Day/ Fête du Prince), 8 Dec (Immaculate Conception), 25 Dec (Christmas Day).
Variable dates
Easter Monday, Ascension Day, Whit Monday, Corpus Christ (May/Jun).

Working hours
Banking
Mon–Sat: 0900–1200 and 1400–1630 (except Saturday afternoons preceding Bank Holidays). Banque Franco-Portugaise, Monte Carlo, is open on Saturdays.
Business
Mon–Fri: 0900–1200 and 1400–1700.
Shops
Mon–Sat: 0900–1830.

Security
Monaco has relatively low rates of crime. Pickpockets operate in train stations and subways.

Getting there
Air
The nearest international airport is at Nice (NCE), Côte d'Azur, France, 22km from Monaco. Heliport facilities in Monte Carlo (MCM) are operated by Heli-Air Monaco and Monacair.
Airport tax: There is no airport departure tax.
Surface
Road: Cannes and Nice are 50km and 18km from Monaco. No formalities are required to cross the frontier between France and Monaco.
Rail: An extensive network links the Principality to neighbouring towns. TGV connection to Paris is available from Marseilles. Daily and overnight through trains are also available.
Water: The major harbours are situated at Condamine (Hercule port) and at Fontvielle, which can handle yachts. Intercontinental liners can anchor in the bay of Monaco.

Getting about
National transport
There are around 50km of roads and 1.6km of railways (operated by Société Nationale des Chemins de Fer Français).
Buses: Good bus connections are available to Nice and other towns. A direct service is available from Nice Airport to Monaco, stopping at a number of hotels.
Taxis: Available from Casino Square, Monaco Monte Carlo Railway station, Metropole and the Post Office of Monte Carlo.
A surcharge is added after 2200hrs.
City transport
Taxis: Taxis are available from Casino Square, Monaco Monte Carlo Railway Station, Fontvielle, Place des Moulins and the Post Office of Monte Carlo.
Buses, trams & metro: Buses operate every five minutes from Monaco-Ville to the casino and every 10 minutes to the railway station and the beaches.

BUSINESS DIRECTORY
The addresses listed below are a selection only. While World of Information makes every endeavour to check these addresses, we cannot guarantee that changes have not been made, especially to telephone numbers and area codes. We would welcome any corrections.

Nations of the World: A Political, Economic and Business Handbook

Telephone area codes
The international direct dialling (IDD) code for Monaco is +377, followed by an eight-digit number.

Useful telephone numbers
Police (emergencies):17 (switchboard): 9315-3015
Ambulance/Fire services (emergencies): 18 (switchboard):9330-1945
Medical/paramedic team/ambulance: 9375-2525
Doctor or chemist on duty:9325-3325
Princess Grace General Hospital, Av Pasteur (emergencies): 9325-9869; (switchboard): 9325-9900.
Main Post Office, Palais de la Scala: 9325-1111.
Car pound (Parking des Ecoles car park), Av des Guelfes, Monte Carlo: 9315-3084.

Chambers of Commerce
Monaco Economic Development Chamber, 11 Rue du Gabian, BP 653, MC 98013 Monaco (tel: 9798-6868; fax: 9798-6869; e-mail: info@cde.mc).

Banking
Banque Franco Portugaise (BFP), 5 Av Princesse Alice, MC 98000 (tel: 9350-1115; fax: 9350-1921).
Banque Générale du Commerce, 2 Av des Spélugues, Monte Carlo (tel: 9350-1762).
Banque Internationale de Monaco, Sporting d'Hiver, 2 Av Princesse Alice, Monte Carlo (tel: 9216-5757; fax: 9216-5750).
Barclays Bank plc, 31 Av de la Costa, Monte Carlo (tel: 9315-3535; fax: 9325-1568).
Crédit Foncier de Monaco, 11 Bd Albert 1er, MC98000 (tel: 9310-2000; fax: 9310-2350).
Société Générale, 16 Ave de la Costa (tel: 9315-5700); also at 17 Bd Albert 1er (tel: 9350-8692).
Société Monégasque de Banque Privée, 9 Boulevard d'Italie, MC 98000 (tel: 9315-2323).

Central bank
European Central Bank (ECB), Kaiserstrasse 29, D-60311 Frankfurt am Main, Germany (tel: +49(69)13-440; fax: +49(69)1344-6000).

Travel information
Automobile Club of Monaco, 23 Boulevard Albert 1er, Monte Carlo (tel: 9315-2600).
Heli-Air Monaco, Av des Ligures, Monaco (tel: 9205-0050).
Monaco Bus Company, 3 Av Pdt J F Kennedy (tel: 9350-6241).
Station Master, Monaco/Monte Carlo station, Avenue Prince Pierre (rail passenger information) (tel: 9310-6015); (timetable information) (tel: 9310-6003).
Service de la Marine, Direction des Ports (information regarding yacht harbours), 7 Av du Pdt J F Kennedy, BP 468, MC 98012 Monaco Cedex (tel: 9315-8678).

National tourist organisation offices
Direction du Tourisme et des Congrès, 2a Boulevard des Moulins, MC-98000 Monte Carlo (administration) (tel: 9216-6116; fax: 9216-6000); (information) (tel: 9216-6166).

Other useful addresses
Centre de Congrès, Bd Louis II, Monaco (tel: 9310-8400).
Centre d'Informations Administratives, 23 Av Prince Héréditaire Albert, Monaco (tel: 9315-4026).
Centre de Presse, 4 Rue des Iris, Monte Carlo (tel: 9330-4227).
Centre de Rencontres Internationales, Ave d'Ostende, Monaco (tel: 9310-8600).
Comité des Fêtes, Monaco-ville (tel: 9330-8004).
Direction de l'Expansion Economique (Directorate of Economic Expansion), 'Le Concorde', 11 Rue du Gabian, BP 665, MC98000 Monaco Cedex (tel: 9798-6868; fax: 9798-6869; e-mail: info@cde.mc; internet site: http://www.cde-monaco.com).
Directorate of Fiscal Services, 57 Rue Grimaldi, MC98000 (tel: 9315-8122; fax: 9205-8155).
Douanes, 7 Av Président JF Kennedy, Monaco (tel: 9330-2600).
Mairie de Monaco, Monaco-ville (tel: 9315-2863).
Ministère d'Etat, Monaco-ville (tel: 9315-8000).
Monte Carlo Main Post, Square Beaumarchais (Palais de la Scala) (tel: 9350-6987).
Radio Monte Carlo (RMC), 16 Bd Princesse Charlotte, Monte Carlo (tel: 9315-1617).
Service du Contrôle Technique et de la Circulation (traffic control service), 23 Av Prince Héréditaire Albert, Monaco (tel: 9315-8000).
Service de l'Urbanisme et de la Construction, 23 Av Prince Héréditaire Albert, Monaco (tel: 9315-8000).
Télé Monte Carlo, 16 Bd Princesse Charlotte, Monaco (tel: 9315-1415).

Internet sites
Banking and investment advice: http://www.cmb.mc
Monaco online: http://www.monaco.mc/
Monte Carlo web directory: http://monte-carlo.mc/

Mongolia

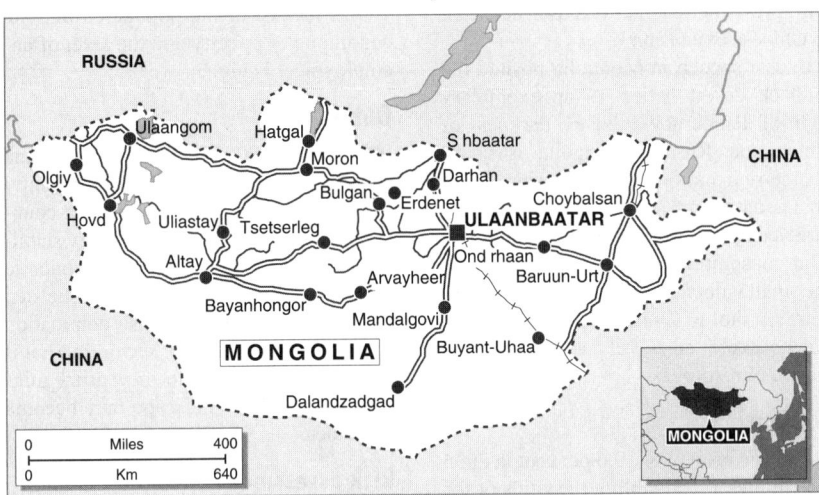

KEY FACTS

Official name: Mongol Uls (The State of Mongolia)

Head of State: President Nambaryn Enkhbayar (MPRP) (elected 22 May 2005, inaugurated 24 Jun 2005)

Head of government: Prime Minister Miyeegombo Enkhbold (MDC) (appointed by parliament Jan 2006)

Ruling party: Coalition government: Mongolian People's Revolutionary Party (MPRP) and Motherland Democratic Coalition (MDC) (from Aug 2004).

Area: 1,565,000 square km

Population: 2.61 million (2004)

Capital: Ulaanbaatar (Ulan Bator) (formerly Urga)

Official language: Khalkha Mongolian

Currency: Tugrik (Tug)

Exchange rate: Tug1,215.00 per US$ (Oct 2005)

GDP per capita: US$512 (2004)

GDP real growth: 6.00% (2004)

Labour force: 1.35 million (2004)

Unemployment: 3.80% (2003) (official); 20.00% (2003) (unofficial)

Inflation: 5.00% (2004)

Balance of trade: -US$147.00 million 2004

Foreign debt: US$1.10 billion (2003)

Annual FDI: US$113.00 million (2003)

Mongolia is famed for its legendary thirteenth century conqueror Ghengis Khan, who created the largest empire in history. However, since the break-up of this huge alliance, the country has been ruled for 200 years by China and for 70 years by the Soviets. Having experienced years of glorious empire, foreign rule and communism, in 1990 the country adopted democracy. The political process has been dynamic of late with the election of a new president, popular demonstrations, and the arrival of a new prime minister after mass cabinet resignations. In 2005, the country was catapulted into the world media, albeit briefly, by the visit of US President W George Bush.

Domestic politics

Mass protests in Kyrgyzstan in March 2005 which precipitated the fall of that government inspired reformists in Mongolia to also turn out and line the streets of the capital Ulaanbaatar. Protesters toasted the Kyrgyzstan rebels as allies, and demanded another set of government elections and a crackdown on corrupt practices. Elections held in June 2004 were mired in allegations of fraud and embezzlement. The prime ministerial response to the public outcry was a call for silence and calm.

In May 2005 the former communist party, Mongolian People's Revolutionary Party (MPRP), candidate and one-time prime minister Nambaryn Enkhbayar was elected as president, winning 53 per cent of the vote. Turnout was a healthy 75 per cent. As prime minister, Enkhbayar had courted the youth vote by performing on stage alongside platform-heeled Mongolian pop group Lipstick. He was a self-confessed fan of UK prime minister Tony Blair, duly hiring a British spin-doctor and describing the MPRP as 'communist monsters'. The Buddhist Enkhbayar is a talented and bilingual scholar, having translated novels by British authors such as Charles Dickens and Virginia Woolf. The Mongolian presidential role is more figurehead than ruler, but Enkhbayar's importance may be heightened by the current of popular dissatisfaction and the fact that the government is formed of a coalition.

At January 2006, 10 MPRP ministers – more than half of the cabinet – resigned, thus forcing the coalition government to disband and the prime minister, Tsakhia Elbegdorj, to resign. The MPRP criticised Elbegdorj for high inflationary rates and inadequate economic growth. Popular protests were held in the freezing cold streets of Ulaanbaatar, some in support of and some against the prime minister. All, however, called for an end to corruption and for the country's endemic poverty to be addressed. There is a feeling in the country that the poor have been forgotten since the fall of the communist regime, and that divisions of wealth have widened.

On 11 January, two weeks after the mass resignations Miyeegombo Enkhbold, chairman of the MPRP, was named as the new prime minister, ending the interval of political turmoil. A party official was quoted as saying of the new leader: 'He's known as someone who doesn't talk much, but does the work'.

Foreign affairs

In October 2005 the US secretary of defense, Donald Rumsfeld, visited Mongolia and expressed American gratitude for the work of 146 Mongolian troops serving in Afghanistan and Iraq. In return, Rumsfeld was given a horse, which he named Montana, then left it in the capable hands of a Mongolian farmer. The US is investing US$18 million in the development of a Mongolian peace-keeping force and in the building up of arms. US troops are also participating in peace-keeping operations in the country. However, Rumsfeld denied that the US had any plans to set up a permanent military base there.

George Bush's four-hour visit a month later was the first ever visit of a US President to the region. He echoed Rumfeld's expressions of gratitude and praised the country for its embrace of democracy and rejection of communism. Although it is the first presidential visit, the two countries have had ties for some time. The global superpower had an input in the drafting of the 1992 Mongolian constitution and has invested substantially in Mongolian aid programmes. The US has given US$100 million in recent years in efforts to phase out communism and introduce free and fair government.

However, observers suggested that Bush's primary motive was in fact not to say thank you in person for Mongolian military contributions. Rather, the worldwide strategic alliances being built by the US are part of a ploy to surround China with pro-American nations as a deterrent to Chinese expansion.

Bush's speech in Mongolia posited the outback desert nation as an exemplary light of democracy amid the darkness of China and Russia. Mongolia is a resource-rich nation, with deposits of oil, coal and uranium, which could be heavily targeted by a China looking to fuel its rampant consumption. The US's embrace of the small vulnerable nation sounds a small warning shot to China that Mongolia cannot be exploited merely as a pawn and source of resources.

Economy

Economic growth of 10.6 per cent in 2004 was impressive, doubling the gains of the previous year. FDI in the mining sector was a primary driver of growth, helped by opening of a new gold mine. The 18 per cent growth in the agricultural industry also contributed to budgetary success. The deficit was reduced to an all-time low, thanks to increased taxation revenues mostly garnered from growing businesses. Tourism also helped pour money into the country after a poor year in 2003 due to the Sars crisis.

GDP growth was predicted to continue, but at a slower pace in 2005 and 2006 with rates forecast at 7.0 and 6.3 per cent respectively. The Mongolian economy can be volatile as it is so heavily reliant on agriculture. Extreme weather conditions have been known to wipe out annual crops. For this reason the IMF have recommended that Mongolia diversify its economy and switch to more reliable bases of income.

Over a third of the population exist in conditions of poverty and the level of unemployment is high.

Outlook

In November 2005, Mongolia and China announced that they were to start jointly developing coal fields in the desert country. This should bring better energy stability to China and substantial economic benefits to Mongolia. It could be one step on the path towards Chinese domination of the Mongolian energy sector, but not if Bush can help it. With the new prime minister the political landscape may become smoother.

Risk assessment

Economic	Good
Political	Fair
Regional Stability	Good
Stock Market	Small

COUNTRY PROFILE

Historical profile
The Mongolian People's Republic (MPR) was formerly known as the Manchu Province of Outer Mongolia.
1911 Following the republican revolution, Mongolian princes declared the province's independence.
1921 The Mongolian People's Party was founded and a Provisional People's government was established.
1924 The Mongolian People's Republic was proclaimed.
1961 Mongolia became a member of the UN, and was accorded diplomatic recognition by West European states.
1987 Mongolia was finally granted diplomatic recognition by the US.
1991 Mongolia's main backer, the USSR, disintegrated, ending decades of economic and political support for the country.
1992 A new constitution was introduced, establishing Mongolia as a democratic parliamentary state. Mongolia's official title became the State of Mongolia.
1997 Natsagiin Bagabandi of the Mongolian People's Revolutionary Party (MPRP) (formerly the Mongolian People's Party), was elected president.
1999 Rinchinnyamiyn Amarjargal became prime minister.

KEY INDICATORS — Mongolia

	Unit	2000	2001	2002	2003	2004
Population	m	2.50	2.53	2.56	2.58	2.61
Gross domestic product (GDP)	US$bn	0.97	1.02	1.30	1.13	*1.52
GDP per capita	US$	388	421	431	438	512
GDP real growth	%	1.1	1.1	3.9	5.5	10.6
Inflation	%	11.6	11.2	1.6	4.7	5.0
Exports (fob) (goods)	US$m	529.0	653.0	524.0	501.0	853.0
Imports (fob) (goods)	US$m	679.0	815.0	680.2	659.0	1,000.0
Balance of trade	US$m	-149.0	-162.0	-156.2	-158.0	-147.0
Current account	US$m	-166.0	-171.0	-158.0	-70.0	-40.0
Foreign debt	US$bn	0.9	0.9	1.0	1.1	1.3
Total reserves minus gold	US$m	178.8	205.7	349.6	236.1	236.3
Foreign exchange	US$m	178.7	205.6	349.5	235.9	236.1
Exchange rate	per US$	1,076.67	1,097.70	1,110.31	1,125.50	1,185.30

* estimated figure

Mongolia

2000 The MPRP won the parliamentary elections. Nambariin Enkhbayar, leader of the MPRP, was elected prime minister by the Great Hural.

2001 The incumbent president, Natsagiin Bagabandi of the MPRP, was re-elected.

2002 Prime Minister Mikhail Kayanov of Russia visited Mongolia to boost economic co-operation between the two countries.

2003 Two Mongolians, who visited northern China, became the country's first confirmed Severe Acute Respiratory Syndrome (Sars) cases.

2004 In April, the World Bank endorsed a new Country Assistance Strategy (CAS) and US$18 million urban water credit. On 20 August, parliament appointed Tsakhiagiyn Elbegdorj (MDC) as prime minister and on 28 September, parliament approved his cabinet.

2005 Nambaryn Enkhbayar (MPRP) won the 22 May presidential elections.

2006 Ten ministers, members of the MPRP, tendered their resignations on 10 January, triggering a crisis which led to a vote in parliament in favour of dissolving the coalition government. The MPRP nominated Miyeegombo Enkhbold as the new prime minister. With 38 of parliament's 76 seats the MPRP is the largest party, but will still need the support of minor parties in order to form a majority. The MDC has 34 seats.

Political structure

Constitution
The constitution entered into force on 12 February 1992. A January 1998 constitutional amendment stated that legislators were eligible to serve concurrently as prime minister or as other ministers. The January amendment was later effectively nullified by the Constitutional Court ruling of 24 November 1998 that prohibited members of the People's Great Hural from holding cabinet posts. On 15 March 2000, the Constitutional Court cancelled amendments to the 1992 constitution, which had been approved by the People's Great Hural, and later vetoed by the president.

Form of state
Parliamentary republic

The executive
The head of state is the president, nominated by parties in the People's Great Hural, and elected by popular vote for a four-year term.

National legislature
The legislature, the 75-member unicameral People's Great Hural, is directly elected every four years by all citizens over 25-years-old. The People's Great Hural elects a prime minister and appoints a cabinet, in consultation with the president.

Legal system
A mixture of Russian, German and US law.

Last elections
22 May 2005 (presidential); 27 June 2004 (parliamentary).

Results: Presidential: Nambaryn Enkhbayar (MPRP) won 53.4 per cent of the vote and Mendsaikhany Enkhsaikhan (MDC) 20 per cent; turnout was 74.9 per cent.

Parliamentary: the Mongolian People's Revolutionary Party (MPRP) won 36 seats and the Motherland Democratic Coalition (MDC) 34 seats.

Next elections
2008 (parliamentary); 2009 (presidential).

Political parties

Ruling party
Coalition government: Mongolian People's Revolutionary Party (MPRP) and Motherland Democratic Coalition (MDC) (from Aug 2004).

Main opposition party
Civil Courage Republican Party (CCRP)

Population
2.61 million (2004)

Religions
Tibetan Buddhist Lamaism and Shamanism, Islam (4 per cent).

Education
Primary schooling lasts for four years until aged 12. Secondary education is divided into four years compulsory lower secondary schooling for students aged 12–16 years and two years upper secondary for those aged 16–18 years. Only students of upper secondary schools progress to higher education. Technical and vocational schools admit graduates of both lower and upper secondary schools. Government and private institutions provide higher education and offer BA, MA and PhD degrees.

Public expenditure on education typically amounts to 5.7 per cent of annual gross national income.

Literacy rate: 98.5 per cent total, 98.4 per cent female, adult rates (World Bank).

Compulsory years: Eight to 16.

Enrolment rate: 88 per cent gross primary enrolment, of relevant age group (including repeaters); 56 per cent gross secondary enrolment (World Bank).

Pupils per teacher: 31 in primary schools.

Health
Annual government spending is around 72 per cent, and foreign spending 15 per cent, of the total expenditure on health, which is approximately 6 per cent of GDP. About 98 per cent of infants aged less than one year are immunised against measles.

HIV prevalence: 0.1 per cent aged 15–49 in 2003 (World Bank).

Life expectancy: 65.9 years (World Bank).

Fertility rate/Maternal mortality rate: 2.4 births per woman; maternal mortality 150 per 100,000 live births (World Bank).

Infant mortality rate: 56 per 1,000 live births; 12.5 per cent children under aged five were malnourished (World Bank).

Head of population per physician/bed: 2.6 physicians and 11.5 hospital beds per 1,000 people (World Bank).

Welfare
Growing unemployment and a weak social safety net remain the country's prime concern. About 36 per cent of Mongolia's population still live below the official poverty line. Many poor are unable to work and rely on social security to meet their basic needs. In 2001, the Asian Development Bank (ADB) granted two loans totalling US$12 million to strengthen Mongolia's social security services. The first loan of US$8 million will be used to support policy and legal reforms to enhance the delivery of social welfare services and strengthen social insurance schemes. A second ADB loan of US$4 million will invest in projects such as nursing homes, services for the disabled and day care centers. The government aims to replace the large centralised institutions with smaller community-based nursing homes and day care centers. The Government is providing co-financing of US$2 million. The Ministry of Social Welfare and Labour as the executing agency will implement the project over five years, until end October 2006. ADB has also provided a US$600,000 technical assistance grant financed by the Japanese Government. More than 100,000 people are registered as disabled by Mongolia's Ministry of Social Welfare and Labour. About 40,000 disabled people, who are capable of working, remain jobless.

Main cities
Ulaanbaatar (which translates as 'Red Hero') (Ulan Bator) (formerly Urga) (capital, estimated population 804,200 in 2003), Erdènèt (72,300), Darhan (69,600).

Languages spoken
Russian is the principal foreign language, although English is being encouraged. Kazak is also spoken in western Mongolia.

Official language/s
Khalkha Mongolian

Media

Press
The newspapers with the largest circulations are the government *Odriyn Sonin*, successor to the state-owned *Ardyn Erh* (established in 1990) and *Zasgiyn Gazryn*

Medee (weekly), *Nügel Buyan* (police) and *Ulaanbaatar* (local government). The party newspapers *Ardchilal* (MNDP), *Ug* (MSDP) and *Unen* (MPRP) appear less frequently. English-language weekly newspapers include the *Mongol Messenger* and the on-line publication *Mongolia This Week* (http://www.mongoliathisweek.mn).

Broadcasting
Radio: Services are broadcast in Mongolian and also Russian, Chinese, English, French, Japanese and Kazakh.

Television: Thanks to satellite relays 100 per cent of the population can receive Mongolian programmes. Russian television is received by satellite ground stations all over the country and US television in Ulaanbaatar for a few hours daily. Kazakhstan Television is available in the predominantly Kazakh Bayan-Olgiy aimak of western Mongolia.

Economy
Increasing foreign investment is a priority for the government, which is undertaking political and economic reform simultaneously in order to attract foreign capital. A central aspect of this policy is the privatisation of state companies. It is hoped that stronger, more viable companies will help foster economic growth.

At the beginning of 2004, Russia wrote off Mongolia's long-standing US$10 billion debt for loans received during the Soviet era. In exchange, Mongolia had to pay around US$300 million and conduct the final transfer of former Soviet shares in its biggest enterprises to Russia. Mongolia would have found it impossible to repay the debt, which was about 10 times the country's GDP.

In April 2004, the World Bank endorsed a new Country Assistance Strategy (CAS) and US$18 million urban water credit for Mongolia; the CAS outlines a programme of support of about US$88 million over four years.

Economic growth doubled in 2004 to 10.6 per cent of GDP, exceeding expectations, as a consequence of rising world commodity prices and a mild winter. Macroeconomic stability remains a priority for the government and efforts are needed to reduce poverty and to deliver public services to rural areas.

External trade
Imports
Main imports are machinery and equipment, fuel, vehicles, food products, industrial consumer goods, chemicals, building materials, sugar and tea.

Machinery, chemicals and energy typically account for more than 90 per cent of imports.

Main sources: Russia (31 per cent total, 2004), China (23.1 per cent), Japan (8.4 per cent), South Korea (6.7 per cent)

Exports
The main export products are copper, apparel, livestock, animal products, cashmere, wool, hides, fluorspar and other non-ferrous metals.

Main destinations: China (50.7 per cent total, 2004), US (26.3 per cent), Canada (5.3 per cent), UK (4.3 per cent), Russia (4.2 per cent)

Agriculture
Farming
Agriculture accounted for around 21 per cent of GDP in 2004 and employed 40 per cent of the workforce.

Major crops include barley, potatoes and wheat. Primary meat products include beef and veal, chicken, horse, camel, lamb and pork. The major agricultural exports are carded hair, wool sheepskins, beef and fine animal hair.

In 2004, there was an improvement in animal husbandry following a milder than usual winter, although crop production fell.

Crop production in 2004 included: 154,400 tonnes (t) cereals in total, 150,000t wheat, 67,000t potatoes, *2,500t barley, *1,100t pulses, *3,700t treenuts, *1,900t oats, *125t fruit in total, 44,075t vegetables in total. Livestock production included: 261,231t meat in total, 80,000t beef, *600t pig meat, 99,800t lamb, 35,000t goat meat, 35,200t horsemeat, *10,000t camel meat, 425t eggs, 325,000t milk, *10t honey, 17,780t cattle hides, 28,800t sheepskins, 19,200t greasy wool.
* estimate

Industry and manufacturing
The industrial sector contributes around 28 per cent to GDP and employs 12 per cent of the workforce. Industrial activity is centred on Ulaanbaatar and other main cities and is based mainly on agricultural products and mining. Products include bricks, cement, lime, sawn timber, scoured wool, felt, felt boots, woollen fabric, leather footwear, soap, flour, garments, matches, bakery goods, confectionery, meat products, beer and vodka.

In 2004, industrial expansion increased by around five per cent compared with less than two per cent the previous year, due to an expansion of gold mining output.

Tourism
The tourist sector has recovered from the disappointing results of 2003, occasioned by the Sars outbreak. Visitor arrivals increased by 67 per cent in 2004. The improvement is expected to continue.

Mining
The mining sector's contribution to GDP increased from 10 per cent to 20 per cent by 2004.

Mongolia boasts one of the richest reserves of mineral resources in the world, but economic mismanagement and a shortage of infrastructure have hindered exploitation.

The Erdenet copper-molybdenum complex, an open-pit mining and concentrating development 340km from Ulaanbaatar, accounts for a large proportion of exports by value. Copper reserves are large enough for another 60 years. Other mines include fluorspar at Bor-Ondör and gold at Ih-altat. Gold mining has increased significantly since 1990. Mongolia has approximately 2,000 tonnes of gold reserves. Major gold-producing areas are Naran, Tolgoi and Zamar.

Other minerals present include iron, zinc, silver, tungsten, tin, lead and graphite, but production levels are limited by inefficient extraction methods.

Mineral products account for around 40 per cent of the country's total exports. Almost all of Mongolia's copper concentrates are exported to Russia and China. A law passed in 1995 permits full foreign ownership of mining ventures in Mongolia, including those involving precious metals. Gold producers are no longer forced to sell to the Mongolian central bank at prices below the prevailing international price.

The first foreign investment gold mine, Boroo Gold, opened in 2004 and immediately pushed up Mongolia's output by 40 per cent.

Hydrocarbons
Mongolia does not produce oil or natural gas. Mongolia has no oil refineries and imports refined oil to supply its domestic demand, mainly from Russia; over half of these imports are gasoline. Over 550,000 tonnes of oil products are consumed annually. Exploration is taking place and small reserves of oil have been identified. Mongolia has sizeable deposits of coal and produces around 5.6 million tonnes a year, most of which is lignite. Coal accounts for around 80 per cent of primary energy consumption. Mongolia exports around 11,000 tonnes of coal a year.

Energy
Mongolia has an electricity capacity of 788MW, derived mainly from coal-fuelled thermal power stations. Intermittent shortage of fuels for dump trucks and railway locomotives and station maintenance difficulties result in frequent power cuts and low generation totals.

Mongolia

Financial markets
Stock exchange
The Mongolian Stock Exchange in Ulaanbaatar was founded in 1991.

Banking and insurance
There is a two-tier banking system. Mongolia's first private commercial bank, the Central Asia Bank (CAB), established in 1992, collapsed in June 1996 due to bad debt and poor management. The Reconstruction Bank of Mongolia was established as a universal commercial bank in January 1997.

In March 2003, AG Bank was sold to Japanese-based H S Securities for US$6.9 million, following a three-year restructuring programme. The Trade and Development Bank of Mongolia was sold for US$12.23 million to Swiss-based Banca Commerciale Lugano and US-based Gerald Metals in May 2003.

Central bank
Bank of Mongolia
Main financial centre
Ulaanbaatar

Time
GMT plus eight hours

Geography
Mongolia is a landlocked country in central Asia, with Russia to the north and the People's Republic of China to the south, east and west.

Climate
Summers are warm and wet, and winters extremely cold. In Ulaanbaatar, winter temperatures range from -4 degrees Celsius (C) to -50 degrees C, with an average of -26 degrees C in January; in summer from 0–40 degrees C, with an average of 17 degrees C in July. Relative humidity ranges from 65 per cent (July–August) to 75 per cent (November–February). Rainfall is low, with an average of 233mm per year in Ulaanbaatar (two-thirds of which falls June–August) and 116–344mm per year elsewhere. On average, there are 250 cloudless days a year.

Entry requirements
Passports
Required by all.
Visa
Required by all, except those exempt: visit www.embassyofmongolia.co.uk/visas.htm for a full list. Business and tourist visitors staying for more than 30 days are referred to as temporary residents and apply with a non-tourist visa; a local contact or business partner will increase the chance of visa approval. When granted, visitors must register with the Foreign Citizens Bureau in Ulaanbaatar within seven days of arrival. Visitors who need to register must de-register before leaving Mongolia, at the Office of Immigration, Naturalization and Foreign Citizens. After de-registering, an 'exit visa' from the consular department of the Mongolian Ministry of Foreign Affairs will be issued.

Contact the nearest consulate for further advice and to confirm all aspects of visa requirements before travelling.

Currency advice/regulations
The import of local currency is limited to Tug815. The import of foreign currency is limited to US$2,000.
The export of Mongolian currency is forbidden, although foreign currency export is permitted up to the amount imported.

Customs
Importation of pornography and export of valuable antiques is strictly prohibited. Customs regulations are enforced by strict examinations. Firearms for sporting purposes require a licence. Import allowances included 200 cigarettes and two litres of alcohol.

Health (for visitors)
Rabies is a health risk.
Mandatory precautions
No vaccination certificates are required.
Advisable precautions
Immunisations for diphtheria, polio, TB, hepatitis 'A', hepatitis 'B', meningitis, tetanus and typhoid are recommended.

Hotels
There are six suitable hotels for foreign visitors in Ulaanbaatar, but in the countryside facilities are basic.

Credit cards
Visa and American Express.

Public holidays
Fixed dates
1 Jan (New Year's Day), 1 Jun (Mothers' and Children's Day), 11–13 Jul (Naadam), 26 Nov (Independence Day).
Variable dates
Tsagaan Sar (Lunar New Year) (Jan/Feb)

Working hours
Banking
Mon–Fri: 0930–1230; 1400–1500.
Business
Mon–Fri: 0900–1800.
Government
Mon–Fri: 0900–1800.
Shops
Mon–Sat: 1000–1800 (some food shops stay open later). Some open Sunday.

Telecommunications
Telephone/fax
In order to subscribe to International Direct Dial, it is necessary to have a valid contract permitting private phone usage and a request must be submitted to the Mongolian Telecommunications Authority (MTA).
Many ministries and major hotels provide access to fax machines.

Weights and measures
Metric system.

Social customs/useful tips
It is conventional to shake hands on meeting and leaving.

Getting there
Air
National airline: MIAT-Air Mongol (Mongolyn Irgeniy Agaaryn Teever Mongol); routes to Almaty (Kazakhstan), Beijing and Höhhot (China), Irkutsk and Moscow (Russian Federation), Sofia (Bulgaria).
International airport/s: Ulaanbaatar Buyant-Ukhaa (ULN), 15km from city.
Airport tax: International departure tax of US$12 for non-nationals.
Surface
Rail: Ulaanbaatar is served by the Trans-Mongolian Railway connecting Moscow and Beijing. Trains leave daily for Irkutsk and Moscow, and twice weekly for Beijing. There are frequent delays on the routes to Beijing and Siberia. Trains operate on summer and winter schedules, alternating in May and October.

Getting about
National transport
Travel for foreigners is normally arranged in advance, and outlying places are often reached by plane. Some towns (e.g. Darhan) and industrial/mining areas are also served by rail routes (two classes); trains on international routes have sleeping and restaurant cars.
Air: MIAT-Air Mongol operates an extensive domestic network. Regular air services provide the best means of long-distance internal travel, although delays and cancellations are frequent. There are officially 21 airports, but only eight have paved runways.
Road: There are 46,700km of roads and tracks. Only 3 per cent of roads are paved (mainly around the cities). Many of the unpaved roads and cross-country tracks are impassable during the summer, because of flooding or waterlogging. The poor railway network dictates that roads provide the only access routes to 16 of Mongolia's 21 provinces.
Buses: Inter-urban bus services are available. There are many long-distance bus routes.
Rail: In addition to the cities served by the Trans-Mongolian Railway (Sühbaatar, Darhan, Ulaanbaatar, Dzamyn-Uüd and Saynshand), there are branch lines to various industrial centres and mining towns, including Erdenet, Baganuur and Bor-Ondör. Total network 1,815km.
City transport
Taxis: Taxis are available for journeys from the airport to the city centre, with a journey time of 15 minutes.

Buses, trams & metro: There are trolley-buses and buses. Service 11 operates 0600–2200 from airport to city centre, journey time 30 minutes.

Car hire

A private car and driver can be arranged in most hotels in Ulaanbaatar. Rates vary from around US$0.50 per kilometre to fixed rates for daily, weekly or monthly hire.

Local licence required. This can be obtained on production of a valid national licence (fee US$30).

BUSINESS DIRECTORY

The addresses listed below are a selection only. While World of Information makes every endeavour to check these addresses, we cannot guarantee that changes have not been made, especially to telephone numbers and area codes. We would welcome any corrections.

Telephone area codes

The international direct dialling code (IDD) for Mongolia is +976, followed by area code and subscriber's number:
Ulaanbataar   11

Useful telephone numbers

Police: 102
Fire: 101
Ambulance: 103
Car hire
Ulaanbaatar
Car Base: (tel: 379-965).

Chambers of Commerce

Mongolian National Chamber of Commerce & Industry, 11 J Sambuu Street, Ulaanbaatar 38 (tel: 312-501; fax: 324-620; e-mail: info@mongolchamber.mn).

Ulaanbaatar Chamber of Commerce, Box 254, Ulaanbaatar 210136 (tel: 329-912; fax: 311-385; e-mail: ubcc@magicnet.mn).

Banking

Agricultural Bank, PO Box 185, Peace Avenue, Ulaanbaatar (tel: 457-880; fax: 458-670); e-mail: haab@magicnet.mn).

Anod Bank of Mongolia, PO Box 361, 18 Commerce Street, Chingeltei, Ulaanbaatar (tel: 327-566; fax: 313-070); e-mail: anod@magicnet.mn).

The Bank of Mongolia, Baga Toiruu-9, Ulaanbaatar (tel: 322-166; fax: 311-471).

Credit Bank, Suknbaatar Square, 20A, Ulaanbaatar (tel: 321-897; fax: 321-897).

Erelbank Ltd, Chingis Avenue, Khan-uul District, Ulaanbaatar (tel: 343-387; fax: 343-567).

Golomt Bank of Mongolia, PO Box 22, 4th Floor, Sukhbaatar Square 3, Central Place of Culture, Ulaanbaatar (tel: 311-530; fax: 312-307).

Mongol Post Bank, PO Box 874, Kholboochdiin Street 4, Ulaanbaatar (tel: 310-301; fax: 328-501).

Savings Bank, 6 Commerce Street, Ulaanbaatar (tel: 327-467; fax: 327-467).

Trade & Development Bank of Mongolia, 7 Commerce Street, Ulaanbaatar (tel: 327-020; fax: 312-418).

Ulaanbaater City Bank, PO Box 370, Baga toiruu 15, Ulaanbaatar (tel: 312-155; fax: 311-067).

Zoos Bank, 6 Choimbalin, Chingeltei, Ulaanbaatar (tel: 329-537; fax: 329-537).

Central bank

Bank of Mongolia, Baga Toiruu 9, Ulaanbaatar 46 (tel: 310-392; fax: 311-417; e-mail: feprmd@mongolbank.mn).

Travel information

Flight information (0800-2200 hours) (tel: 119).

Juulchin, Ulaanbaatar (tel: 320-246, 328-428).

MIAT-Air Mongol (Mongolyn Irgeniy Agaaryn Teever Mongol), Buyant-Ukhaa 43, Ulaanbaatar 210734 (tel: 323-858).

Ulaanbaatar Buyant-Ukhaa Airport, Ulaanbaatar 34 (tel: 379-986; fax: 379-744).

Ministries

Ministry of Finance, Ulaanbaatar 46.

Ministry of Foreign Relations, Ulaanbaatar 11.

Ministry of Trade and Industry, 11 Sambuu St, Ulaanbaatar 46 (tel: 706-146; fax: 326-325).

Other useful addresses

British Embassy, 30 Enkh Taivry Gudamzh, PO Box 703, Ulaanbaatar 13 (tel: 458-133; fax: 458-036).

Mongol An Corporation, Baigal Ordon, Ulaanbaatar 38 (tel/fax: 360-067).

Mongolian Business Development Agency (MBDA), U Barsbold (fax: 311-092; e-mail: mbda@magicnet.mn).

Mongolian Embassy (US), 2833 M Street, NW, Washington DC 20007 (tel: 202-333-7117; fax: 202-298-9227; e-mail: monemb@aol.com).

Mongolian Stock Exchange, Sukhbaatar Square 14, Ulaanbaatar (tel: 310-501; fax: 325-170; e-mail: msebatj@magicnet.mn).

School of Economic Studies (Economic Institute), National University of Mongolia (fax: 325-349; e-mail: suvd@magicnet.mn).

State Statistical Board, Ulaanbaatar 11 (fax: 324-518).

Internet sites

Guide to Mongolia (with links): http://www.mongoliaonline.com

Mongolian Stock Exchange: http://mse.com.mn

Parliament of Mongolia: http://www.parl.gov.mn/english.htm

School of Economic Studies: http://www.ses.edu.mn

State Property Committee: http://www.spc.gov.mn

Montserrat

COUNTRY PROFILE

Historical profile
1493 Montserrat was first sighted by Columbus.
1632 Britain gained possession of the island and English and Irish Catholic settlers from the Protestant island of St Kitts and Nevis colonised Montserrat.
1648 There were some 1,000 Irish families on the island.
1651 The first slaves were brought to the island and the economy became based on sugar.
1871–1956 Montserrat was part of the Leeward Islands, and then became a British Dependent Territory.
1958–62 Montserrat was part of the Federation of the West Indies. From 1960 the island had its own administrator (the title was changed to governor in 1971).
1995 The Soufriere Hills volcano began to erupt.
1997 A massive volcanic eruption destroyed the capital Plymouth, the airport and the port, and left the southern half of the island uninhabitable. Nineteen people were killed, thousands were left homeless and the population fell to around 4,000 as many fled to Britain and nearby Caribbean islands. David Brandt replaced Bertrand Osborne as chief minister.
1998 Reconstruction work began under the UK's Sustainable Development Plan.
1999 The UK government announced volcanic activity had dropped to safe levels. Evacuees began to return.
2000 The growth of a new lava dome at the Soufriere Hills volcano once again threatened the island.
2001 The New People's Liberation Movement (NPLM) won the legislative elections.
2002 A constitutional review was begun.
2003 On 12 July, there was another major eruption at the Soufriere Hills volcano.
2004 In March, there was an increase in volcanic activity and people in the evacuation zone were told to leave the area immediately. On 10 May, Deborah Barnes-Jones was sworn in as governor. In August temporary protected status, granted in 1995, was removed from US-based Montserratians by the US Department of Homeland Security.
2005 The new airport was opened on 11 July allowing access for international visitors.

Political structure
Constitution
Montserrat's governor is appointed by the British monarch. The governor is responsible for defence, internal security (including the police force), external affairs, the public service and international financial services.
Other aspects are dealt with by the executive council.
Form of state
British Caribbean dependency
The executive
The executive council consists of the governor, attorney general, financial secretary, chief minister and three other ministers.
National legislature
The legislative council has 11 members, seven elected for a five-year term in single-seat constituencies, two ex-officio members, two nominated members and a speaker chosen from outside the council.
Last elections
April 2001
Next elections
By 2006

Political parties
Ruling party
New People's Liberation Movement (NPLM) (elected 2 Apr 2001)
Main opposition party
People's Progressive Alliance (PPA)
Political situation
There has been considerable dissatisfaction with the slowness of reconstruction since the volcanic eruptions in 1997. The British government has been blamed for not providing sufficient funds and the repatriation of residents has been slow.
In 2003 over 200 people signed a letter accusing the governor of undermining the island's economy by refusing to allow residents with homes in the exclusion zone to return. It is hoped that the new governor will be more effective.

Population
9,341 * (2005)
Ethnic make-up
Afro-Caribbean (95 per cent), white (5 per cent).
Religions
Anglican, Methodist, Roman Catholic, Pentecostal, Seventh-Day Adventist.

Education
Montserrat has a high level of literacy. Primary education formally begins at the age of five and continues until the age of 11. The state provides for a full five-year secondary education. Secondary schools offer programmes for academic entry courses to higher education and technical, vocational skills training. The

KEY FACTS

Official name: Montserrat

Head of State: Queen Elizabeth II; represented by Governor Deborah E V Barnes-Jones (sworn in 10 May 2004)

Head of government: Chief Minister John Osborne (since Apr 2001)

Ruling party: New People's Liberation Movement (NPLM) (elected 2 Apr 2001)

Area: 102 square km

Population: 9,341 * (2005)

Capital: Plymouth – destroyed by volcano in 1997; temporary headquarters at Blades

Official language: English

Currency: East Caribbean dollar (EC$) = 100 cents

Exchange rate: EC$2.70 per US$ (fixed)

GDP per capita: US$3,400 (2003)

GDP real growth: -1.00% (2003)

Labour force: 4,520 (2003)

Unemployment: 6.00% (2003)

Inflation: 2.60% (2003)

Balance of trade: -US$20.60 million (2004)

Foreign debt: US$8.90 million (2003)

Visitor numbers: 15,700 (2003)

* estimated figure

University of the West Indies School of Continuing Studies offers university level courses.

The Montserrat Community College project, which is jointly funded by the EU and the UK-based Department for International Development (DfID), will cost EC$6 million (US$1.8 million). The new college will include classrooms, laboratories, library and offices.

Compulsory years: 2 to 16.

Health
Periodic volcanic eruption has wreaked havoc with health service maintenance, record keeping, and the overall collection of information. The immunisation programme continued to operate well throughout the volcanic emergency.

Life expectancy: 78 years: male 76 years; female 80 years (2003).

Fertility rate/Maternal mortality rate: 1.8 births per woman (2003)

Birth rate/Death rate: 17.6 births per 1,000 population; 7.3 deaths per 1,000 population (2003).

Infant mortality rate: 7.8 per 1,000 live births (2003)

Head of population per physician/bed: The number of health staff that remained after the volcanic crisis began was less than 50 per cent.

Welfare
Montserrat remains dependent on the British government for budgetary aid and to finance its capital programmes. Previous Public Sector Investment Programmes were aimed at developing critical infrastructure in the habitable North. The emphasis was on accommodating the displaced population on the island and providing housing for a number of migrant workers from neighbouring Caribbean islands. The British Government has approved £10 million (US$ 14 million) for housing over a period of five years (2001–06).

The Social Welfare System in Montserrat has developed a comprehensive Poverty Protection Programme providing various forms of assistance to its people.

Main cities
Plymouth (estimated population 3,500 before being evacuated in 1996 (due to volcanic activity); by the end of 1997, the city had been destroyed by volcanic eruptions).

Interim government buildings have been built at Brades Estate, in the Carr's Bay/Little Bay vicinity at the north-west end of Montserrat.

Languages spoken
Official language/s
English

Media
Press
The *Montserrat News* and the *Montserrat Reporter* (www.montserratreporter.org/) are both weeklies.

Broadcasting
Radio: Radio services are transmitted by Radio Montserrat (government-owned); and ZGEM FM (privately owned).
Television: There is one cable television service. External broadcasts are received from Antigua, Puerto Rico, St Kitts and USA.

Economy
Volcanic activity between 1995–97 left around half of the island uninhabitable and two-thirds of the population fled as the economy fell into ruin. The milling of imported rice for the European market was a major source of revenue prior to 1997, but ended with the closure of the sole factory, likewise the country's electronic components assembly plant was also forced to close. As a result, manufacturing has gone into recession and Montserrat has fallen into a period of de-industrialisation. All manufacture is small-scale and production is for the local market only.

Intensive reconstruction efforts have helped pull the island out of a deep and prolonged recession, aided by US$33 million in funds from the UK Department for International Development (DfID). By 2004 Montserrat had recorded three years of sustained growth as real GDP grew by 4.3 per cent, compared with 1.2 per cent in 2003. The growth was registered in construction of hotels and restaurants, wholesale and retail trade and transport and government sectors, all indicating a rise in tourist sector activity. Tourism has slowly begun to recover with visitor stay-overs increasing. The government has the tourist industry at the centre of Montserrat's recovery and has allocated US$2.6 million to fund projects in its Tourism Repositioning Strategy, 2004–06.

Discussions on the Country Policy Plan (CPP) in February 2004 were productive. Priority areas for assistance over 2004–07 from the DfID were completion of the new airport, support for private sector development, tourism, housing, improvement of the road network and the Little Bay development as the new capital.

Agricultural production was affected by ash from the Soufriere Hills volcano, which damaged 95 per cent of the crops in the ground at the end of July 2004. The budget, which was presented in March 2004, estimated that the revenue collection would be increased by 10 per cent on that of 2003, as a result of the late billing of the 2003 property tax and a general arrears collection drive in 2004. The government anticipates an expansion of the tourism sector resulting from the re-occupation of Old Towne and Isles Bay, and the offshore educational institutions.

In August 2004, the European Commission (EC) allocated US$13.2 million to Montserrat to develop essential infrastructure and to promote private sector development.

External trade
A large trade deficit, caused by the need to import most basic commodities and a very narrow export base, is traditionally offset by earnings from tourism, remittances from Montserratians living abroad and some British aid.

Imports
Main imports include machinery and transportation equipment, foodstuffs, manufactured goods, fuels, lubricants, and related materials. Imports totalled US$25.4 million in 2004.

Main sources: US, UK, Trinidad and Tobago, Japan, Canada

KEY INDICATORS — Montserrat

	Unit	2000	2001	2002	2003	2004
Population	m	*0.00	0.00	*0.01	*0.01	*0.01
GDP per capita	US$	5,898	5,000	5,000	3,400	–
GDP real growth	%	-3.0	-2.8	4.6	1.2	4.3
Inflation	%	0.5	4.9	3.5	2.6	–
Exports (fob) (goods)	US$m	1.1	0.7	1.5	0.7	4.8
Imports (fob) (goods)	US$m	-19.0	-17.1	-22.4	17.0	25.4
Balance of trade	US$m	-17.9	-16.3	-20.9	-17.0	-20.6
Current account	US$m	-6.5	-5.6	-8.2	–	–
Total reserves minus gold	US$m	10.4	12.5	14.4	15.2	14.1
Foreign exchange	US$m	10.4	12.5	14.4	15.2	14.1
Exchange rate	per US$	2.70	2.70	2.70	2.70	2.70

* estimated figure

Exports
The export base is in effective convalescence following the volcanic eruptions. The closure of the rice mill and the electronic assembly plant, which together accounted for 90 per cent of exports before the volcanic eruption, dealt a severe blow to the island's exports. Exports were US$4.8 million in 2004.

Main destinations: US, Antigua and Barbuda

Agriculture
Farming
The agricultural sector was declining prior to the volcanic eruptions (1995–97), when approximately 25 per cent of land area was cultivated. There was a further setback when the Soufriere Hills volcano erupted in April 2004, covering 95 per cent of planted crops with ash. Agriculture used to contributed around 4 per cent to GDP, employing 5 per cent of the labour force.

The main crops have traditionally been potatoes, tomatoes, carrots, cabbages, cucumbers, sweet potatoes and string beans.

The evacuation order issued in 1996 forced farmers to abandon fields in the danger zone, which was still in place in 2005; those entering the area face legal action.

Output in the agricultural sector has been reduced to merely producing goods for domestic consumption. With the south of the island destroyed by the volcano, land has become a precious commodity. Much of the land in the north is unsuitable for farming. Development efforts now focus on high-yield crops and restoring self-sufficiency in vegetables and livestock.

Crop production in 2004 included: 140 tonnes (t) potatoes, 20t sweet potatoes, 140t mangoes, 100t tomatoes, 150t bananas, 80t citrus, 15t chillies & peppers, 710t fruit in total, 160t roots & tubers, 475t vegetables in total. Livestock production included: 900t meat in total, 720t beef, 60t pig meat, 48t lamb & goat meat, 72t poultry, 63t eggs, 2,250t milk.

Fishing
The typical total annual fish catch is only 50t.

Industry and manufacturing
The industrial sector used to account for around 19 per cent of GDP and 10 per cent of employment and included rum, textiles and electronic appliances. After the electronic component assembly plant and the rice milling factory were forced to close due to the volcanic eruptions, the manufacturing sector's share of GDP fell from 5.9 per cent to less than 1 per cent. Manufacturing output is concentrated on two small furniture businesses.

Construction is the largest sector of the economy – mainly due to the demand for housing and basic infrastructure. This has been bolstered by substantial grants from the British government.

Discussions are being held with an Irish company with a view to establishing a factory to utilise volcanic ash in manufacturing roofing slates and other building construction materials for export.

Tourism
The tourism sector used to contribute around a fifth of GDP and was a major foreign exchange earner. After the volcanic eruptions began in 1995, the sector virtually disappeared, mainly due to the destruction of Plymouth, the island's capital, and the main airport. Despite continued volcanic activity, reconstruction of the infrastructure and marketing of the island's attractions have been a priority. A new airport opened in Gerald, the new capital, on 11 July 2005. Scheduled, daily flights to Antigua and St Maarten connect with international flights from North America and Europe. The airport will be open to charter flights from other Caribbean islands.

Growing numbers of tourists are attracted to Montserrat by the live volcano. The main viewing point is the Montserrat Volcanic Observatory where the pyroclastic flows of lava can be observed. Total visitor arrivals are increasing, albeit from a low start base. Visitors from the English-speaking Caribbean make up around 40 per cent of stay-over tourist arrivals.

Hydrocarbons
Montserrat does not produce any hydrocarbons and imports and consumes around 400 barrels per day (bpd) of refined oil products. Supplies come from the US and Trinidad and Tobago.

Montserrat does not import either natural gas or coal.

Banking and insurance
The banking sector was severely effected by the volcano eruption, which destroyed the buildings of the country's main banks. Barclays Bank pulled out of the island while the Royal Bank of Canada reduced its range of services. The locally-owned Bank of Montserrat continues to operate. The seven members of the Organisation of Eastern Caribbean States (OECS), Antigua and Barbuda, Dominica, Grenada, Montserrat, St Kitts and Nevis, St Lucia and St Vincent and the Grenadines, share a common currency and central bank. The British Virgin Islands and Anguilla are associate members.

Montserrat has implemented the new EU tax directive, introduced in July 2005, as a British Caribbean Dependency. Details of all EU nationals' deposits will be forwarded to the tax department of the relevant EU country, allowing tax to be levied in their home country.

Montserrat has also agreed to supply information on tax fraud, for criminal or civil trials, and notify EU member states about additional malpractices.

Central bank
The Eastern Caribbean Central Bank, St Kitts & Nevis

Offshore facilities
The government is trying to promote offshore banking on the island. In 2005 Montserrat had 11 offshore banks, and only the Oxford Bank and Trust Company Ltd of Brazil is a shell bank and does not have a physical presence on the island. There are likely to be more offshore banks with offices operating in Montserrat in the future due to the United States Patriot Act, which came into effect in December 2001. The Act prohibits US banks from doing business with foreign shell banks.

Time
GMT minus four hours

Geography
Montserrat is one of the Leeward Islands in the West Indies. It is a mountainous, volcanic island, which lies about 55km (35 miles) north of Basse Terre, Guadeloupe, and about 43km (27 miles) south-west of Antigua.

Climate
The island has tropical weather with a mean temperature of 30 degrees Celsius and low humidity due to tradewinds. There is little variation throughout the year. The wettest months are from September–November, and the driest from February–June.

Dress codes
Casual lightweight clothing, and during the winter months a light jacket or sweater for the late evening is advisable.

Entry requirements
Passports
Required by all except nationals of Canada, US and UK with proof of identity. Caricom citizens may travel on an official ID card, which must bear a photograph of the individual.

Visa
As an overseas territory of the UK, visas are required by all with few exceptions; however some visitors may be eligible, a full list is posted on www.britainincanada.org/Visa/overseas.htm.

For visa-free visitors, including those arriving on business and staying for up to three months, an onward/return ticket and sufficient funds for the stay are necessary.

Currency advice/regulations
No restrictions on import and export of foreign currency, but declaration is required on arrival.

Health (for visitors)
Mandatory precautions
Yellow fever vaccination certificate if arriving within six months from an infected area.
Those arriving from areas of known epidemics, including cholera must have vaccination certificates.

Advisable precautions
Typhoid and polio vaccinations are recommended. Tap water is considered safe.

Credit cards
Few shops, hotels or restaurants accept credit cards.

Public holidays
Fixed dates
1 Jan (New Year's Day), 17 Mar (St Patrick's Day), 25–26 Dec (Christmas Holiday), 31 Dec (Festival Day).

Variable dates
Good Friday, Easter Monday, Labour Day (first Mon in May), Whit Monday, August Monday (first Mon in Aug).

Working hours
Banking
Bank of Montserrat: Mon, Tue, Thurs: 0800–1400; Wed 0800–1300; Fri: 0800–1500.
Royal Bank of Canada: Mon–Thurs: 0800–1400; Fri 0800–1500.

Business
Mon–Fri: 0800–1200, 1300–1600. Some businesses close early Wed: 0800–1200, and some open Sat: 0800–1230.

Government
Mon–Fri: 0800–1600.

Shops
0800–1600. Most shops close early in the afternoon on Wednesday and Saturday.

Electricity supply
220V AC, 60 cycles; also 400V, three-phase.

Getting there
Air
International airport/s: The new airport at Gerald was officially opened in July 2005. Facilities include duty-free and refreshments. Daily, scheduled flights, operated by Winair, from Antigua and St Maarten connect with international carriers from North America and Europe. The airport will be opened to chartered services from surrounding island.

Airport tax: Departure tax US$16; Caricom nationals US$9.

Surface
Water: Bermuth Line and West Indies Shipping Service provide ferry services from Miami (USA). A high-speed ferry link operates from Deep Water Harbour, near St John's, Antigua. There are twice daily ferry sailings; the journey time is about one hour.

Getting about
National transport
It is illegal and dangerous to enter the Exclusion Zone the south of the island, from Plymouth and southward to St Patrick's through Windy Hill and Harris and down to the east coast to the site of the old Bramble airport.

Air: A helicopter service that used to fly to surrounding islands now fly tourists over volcanic areas.

Road: Over 85 per cent of the remaining roads are all-weather, linking main centres.

Buses: Buses are privately owned and readily available. Occasional minibus services operate throughout island.

City transport
Taxis: Readily available. Legal fixed-rate system.

Car hire
Temporary licences can be obtained on production of national licence. Traffic drives on the left.

BUSINESS DIRECTORY
The addresses listed below are a selection only. While World of Information makes every endeavour to check these addresses, we cannot guarantee that changes have not been made, especially to telephone numbers and area codes. We would welcome any corrections.

Telephone area codes
The international direct dialling code (IDD) for Montserrat is +1 664, followed by subscriber's number.

Chambers of Commerce
Montserrat Chamber of Commerce and Industry, PO Box 384, Brades (tel: 491-3640; fax: 491-3639; e-mail: chamber@candw.ag).

Banking
Bank of Montserrat, PO Box 10, St Peters (tel: 491-3843; fax: 491-3163; e-mail: bom@candw.ag).

Royal Bank of Canada, PO Box 222, Olveston (tel: 491-2426/7/8; fax: 491-3391; e-mail: rbcmont@candw.ag).

Central bank
Eastern Caribbean Central Bank, Agency Office, PO Box 484, St Peter's Rectory, St Peter's, Montserrat (tel: 491-6877; fax: 491-6878).

Travel information
Carib Aviation, Antigua (tel: +462-3147; fax: 462-3125).

Carib World Travel, Antigua (tel: +460-6101; fax: 480-2995).

Montserrat Aviation Services, PO Box 257, Nixons, Geralds (tel: 491-2533/2362; fax: 491-7186; e-mail: monair@candw.ag; internet: www.fly-winair.com).

National tourist organisation offices
Montserrat Tourist Board, 7 Farara Plaza, Bld B&C: PO Box 7, Brades (tel: 491-2230/8730; fax: 491-7430; e-mail: info@montserrattourism.ms; internet site: http://www.visitmontserrat.com).

Ministries
Governor's Office Lancaster House, Olveston (tel: 491-2688/9; fax: 491-8867; e-mail: govoff@cnadw.ag).

Ministry of Finance, Government Headquarters, Brades (tel: 491-2356/2777/3057; fax: 491-2367; e-mail: minfin@candw.ag).

Other useful addresses
British High Commission, 11 Old Parham Road, Box 483, St John's, Antigua (tel: 00-1-268-462-0008; fax: 00-1-268-462-2806).

Development Unit, Government Headquarters, Brades (tel: 491-2066/2557; fax: 491-4632; e-mail: devunit@candw.ag).

Financial Services Commission, Phoenix House, PO Box 188, Brades (tel: 491-6887/8; fax: 491-9888; e-mail: fscmrat@candw.ag).

Montserrat government in UK, 7 Portland Place, London W1B 1PP. (tel: +020-7031-0317; internet: www.montserratfirst.co.uk).

National Development Foundation Montserrat Ltd, PO Box 337, Davy Hill (tel: 491-3070; fax: 491-6566; e-mail: mon;ndf@candw.ag).

Internet sites
Montserrat info: http://www.volcano-island.com.

Montserrat Volcano Observatory (MVO): http://www.mvo.ms

Morocco

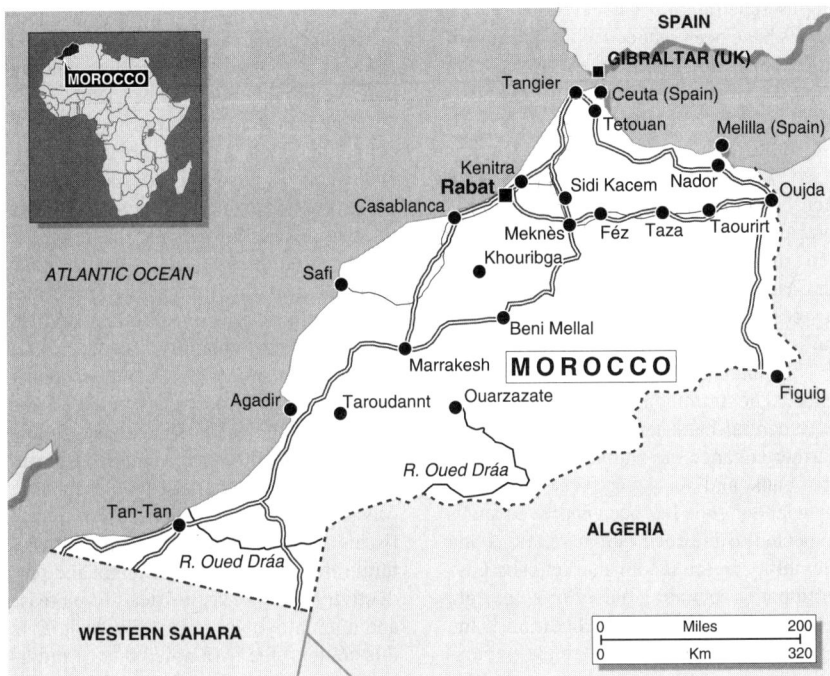

The Kingdom of Morocco is the most westerly of the North African countries known as the Maghreb. Strategically situated with both Atlantic and Mediterranean coastlines, but with a rugged mountainous interior, the country remained independent for centuries while developing a rich culture blended from Arab, Berber, European and African influences.

The king has said the fight against poverty is a priority, earning him the name 'guardian of the poor'. Officials cite improved access to basic services in shanty towns and among the rural poor. But some non-government organisations say little has changed beyond the statistics, with poverty still widespread and unemployment remaining high.

One of the King's key reforms has been the *Mudawana*, a family law which grants more rights to women. The king maintains it is in line with Koranic principles but it has been opposed by religious conservatives.

Morocco has enjoyed macroeconomic stability since the early 1990s. Inflation has remained low. The external current account has been in surplus since 2001 and external reserves have increased to a comfortable level. However, fiscal deficits have remained large and the authorities have used part of the privatisation receipts to finance increased expenditures.

Economy

Morocco faces problems typical for developing countries: restraining government spending, reducing constraints on private activity and foreign trade, and achieving sustainable growth. Long-term challenges include preparing the economy for freer trade with the US and European Union (EU), improving education and job prospects for Morocco's youth, and raising living standards.

Growth has been insufficient to significantly reduce poverty and unemployment. It averaged three per cent annum over the last decade. Recurrent droughts contribute to increasing poverty in rural areas. The unemployment rate remains high, particularly in urban areas. Although the growth of the non-agricultural sector has become more resilient to agricultural output

KEY FACTS

Official name: Al Mamlaka al Maghrebia (The Kingdom of Morocco)

Head of State: King Mohammed VI (since Jul 1999)

Head of government: Prime Minister Driss Jettou (appointed by the King 9 Oct 2002)

Ruling party: Coalition government from Nov 2002: Union Socialiste des Forces Populaires (USFP) (Socialist Union of Popular Forces); Parti de l'Istiqlal (Istiqlal) (Independence Party)

Area: 711,000 square km

Population: 29.89 million (2004 census)

Capital: Rabat

Official language: Arabic

Currency: Dirham (Dh) = 100 centimes

Exchange rate: Dh9.08 per US$ (Oct 2005); (roughly pegged at Dh10 per euro, which circulates widely)

GDP per capita: US$1,629 (2004)

GDP real growth: 3.50% (2004)

Labour force: 12.46 million (2004)

Unemployment: 12.10% (2004)

Inflation: 2.00% (2004)

Balance of trade: -US$6.49 billion (2004)

Foreign debt: US$17.07 billion (2004)

KEY FACTS

Official name: Western Sahara (The legal status of the territory and the issue of sovereignty are unresolved; they are contested by Morocco and Polisario, which in Feb 1976, formally proclaimed a government-in-exile of the Sahrawi Arab Democratic Republic (SADR)).

Head of State: President Mohammed Abdelazziz (Polisario) (since 1982)

Head of government: Prime Minister Abdelkader Taleb Oumar (from 29 Oct 2004)

Ruling party: Independence movement – Frente para la Liberación de Saguia al Hamra y Río de Oro (Polisario) (Popular Front for the Liberation of Saguia al Hamra and Río de Oro)

Area: 266,000 square km

Population: 300,900 (2004)

Capital: Laayoune (El Aaiún)

Official language: Arabic and Spanish

Currency: Moroccan dirham (Dh) = 100 centimes; the currency used in the Occupied Zone

Exchange rate: Dh9.08 per US$ (Oct 2005); (roughly pegged at Dh10 per euro, which circulates widely)

Labour force: 12,000 (2003)

Aid flow: US$10.00 million (annually)*

* estimated figure

---

shocks, it is insufficient to significantly reduce unemployment.

Large state-owned enterprises have been privatised and remaining public enterprises are being restructured or prepared for privatisation. In the area of trade liberalisation, the implementation of the association agreement with the EU, Morocco's main trading partner, is proceeding as scheduled. Most Favoured Nation tariffs have been reduced to a maximum of 10 per cent for goods freely traded with the EU. Morocco is bidding for membership of the EU, but there appears to be little enthusiasm for the idea within Europe itself. It has been accorded the status of non-Nato ally by Washington, which has praised its support for the US-led war on terrorism. After deadly suicide bombings in Casablanca in 2003, Morocco launched a crackdown on suspected Islamic militants

The financial sector is being strengthened. The imminent promulgation of a new central bank and banking laws will further enhance the autonomy of the central bank and its supervisory power. A new labour code has been approved and is expected to improve labour relations and flexibility in the labour market. The government is pursuing its efforts to fight poverty, improve social conditions, and enhance the rights of the female population. The impact of these reforms on Morocco's growth rates should be observed in the medium-term.

The unfavourable agricultural situation will continue to affect macroeconomic conditions. Overall growth is projected at about one per cent. The current account is likely to register a small deficit partly because of a high level of imports of food products and higher oil bill. Nonetheless, the overall balance of payments is expected to remain in surplus. The fiscal deficit is expected to increase to about 5.5 per cent of GDP despite continued favourable revenue performance. Expenditures will increase, reflecting the repercussions on civil service wage payments after awards in 2004. Privatisation receipts will help contain the debt to GDP ratio at about 70 per cent, despite the issuance of debt to cover old pension fund arrears (2.4 per cent of GDP).

Morocco needs to achieve sustained high rates of growth in non-agricultural output. In the context of its increasing integration into the world economy, accelerated structural reforms and fiscal consolidation are essential elements.

Morocco's political situation remains stable. The current coalition government took power after the September 2002 parliamentary elections and the next parliamentary elections are scheduled for September 2007. The authorities believe that poverty, unemployment, and social exclusion are the root causes of Islamic extremism, which is a major political concern. Achieving social development is therefore at the top of the government's agenda. Poverty, which is particularly pervasive in rural areas, is estimated at 15 per cent of the population, while the economically vulnerable reach 40 per cent.

A medium-term framework aimed at achieving high growth objectives, assumes that, in the context of moderate export growth in an increasingly competitive international environment, the domestic market would continue to be the main source of growth. Structural reforms, public investment in infrastructure, and reduced output volatility would foster private investment. As the economy grows and tax burdens are reduced and shared among a widened tax base, a more stable and steadily increasing private consumption growth pattern would enhance private investor confidence. Also tied to fiscal consolidation and ongoing structural reforms, private investment and productivity are forecast to steadily increase and unemployment to steadily decline. In this context, the IMF noted that a gradual transition to a flexible exchange rate would ensure a proper balance between all sources of growth. Growth is expected to significantly rebound in 2006 following the negative agriculture shock in 2005, with a gradual increase in non-agricultural growth thereafter. The increase in non-agricultural growth is expected to come from higher private investment and increased productivity.

Politics

Morocco was a French protectorate from 1912 to 1956, when Sultan Mohammed became king. He was succeeded in 1961 by his son, Hassan II, who ruled for 38 years. He played a prominent role in the search for peace in the Middle East, given the large number of Israelis of Moroccan origin, but was criticised for his suppression of opposition at home.

A truth commission set up to investigate human rights violations during Hassan's reign has confirmed nearly 10,000 cases, ranging from death in detention to forced exile.

After his death in 1999 Hassan was succeeded by his son, who became King Mohammed VI and is seen as a moderniser who would press on towards establishing a constitutional monarchy. He has allowed moderate Islamist parties to operate legally. Political prisoners were released and notorious and officially non-existent prisons were closed. Restrictions on the press have been eased and a programme of economic liberalisation has attracted foreign investment. Bomb attacks in Casablanca in 2003 prompted the government to enact new anti-terrorism laws and to step up its campaign against extremist groups. But some rights groups say the measures have eroded human rights. The King has wide powers: under the constitution he can dissolve parliament and dismiss or appoint the prime minister.

Risk assessment

Politics	Improving
Economy	Improving
Regional stability	Poor

COUNTRY PROFILE

Historical profile

In Morocco's early history, the country was ruled by Idris (788–985), a descendant of the Prophet Mohammed, and by two religious movements, the Almoravids and the Almohads. The Almohads were succeeded by the Merinids and there followed a period in which there were alternating periods of anarchy and prosperity, as Berber tribes clashed with intruding Arab tribes and with Spanish and Portuguese colonists on the Mediterranean and Atlantic coasts. The Alawi Sultans ruled Morocco until 1912, when the French established a protectorate, leaving Spain to annex the Rif and Ifni. In 1953, the highly respected Sultan Mohammed V was deposed, leading to a guerrilla war, which eventually forced the French to reinstate the Sultan and grant independence in 1956.

A dispute with Spain in 2002 over the tiny island of Perejil revived the issue of the sovereignty of Melilla and Ceuta, small enclaves on Morocco's Mediterranean coast, administered by Madrid for centuries. The issue of Morocco's occupation of Western Sahara also remains unresolved; in 2004, it was reported that Morocco would not contemplate holding a referendum that would include the possibility of independence, but it might consider granting wider autonomy. In foreign policy, Morocco has always leaned towards the West, to the extent of expressing its intention to join the EU.

1777 Morocco was the first country to recognise the newly sovereign USA. The Treaty of Peace and Friendship between the two countries (negotiated in 1787) is the longest unbroken US treaty relationship.

1860 Spain declared war in a dispute over the Ceuta enclave and won a further enclave and an enlarged Ceuta.
1884 Spain created a protectorate in coastal areas of Morocco.
1904 France and Spain agreed on respective zones of influence in the country.
1912 Morocco became a French protectorate under the Treaty of Fez. Spain continued to operate its coastal protectorate.
1923 France, Spain and Britain set up the international zone of Tangier.
1921–26 A rebellion in the Rif mountains, led by Abdel Krim, was eventually quelled by French and Spanish troops.
1943 The Istiqlal (Parti de l'Istiqlal) (Independence Party) was founded and an independence struggle began.
1956–57 Independence was granted by France and Spain. Tangier became Moroccan once more. Spain kept its two coastal enclaves. Sultan Sidi Mohammed ben Youssef adopted the title of King Mohammed V and established an hereditary monarchy.
1961 Mohammed V died and was succeeded by King Hassan II. He introduced political liberalisation.
1963 The first general elections were held.
1965 Following student riots and civil unrest, the King declared a state of emergency and suspended parliament.
1971 There was a failed attempt to depose the King and to establish a republic.
1972 A constitution was adopted.
1973–76 The Frente Popular para la Liberación de Saguia el Hamra y Río de Oro (Polisario) (Popular Front for the Liberation of Saguia el Hamra y Río de Oro), formed with Algerian support, aimed at an independent state in Spanish Sahara, a territory south of Morocco, controlled by Spain. King Hassan ordered a 350,000-strong Green March into the territory, attempting to annex it for Morocco. Spain agreed to withdraw from the region (later to become Western Sahara) and to transfer it to joint Moroccan-Mauritanian control. Polisario announced the formation of the Saharawi Arab Democratic Republic (SADR) and formed a government-in-exile. Western Sahara was divided betweem Morocco and Mauritania. Fighting continued between Moroccan military and Polisario forces.
1977 Morocco left the Organisation of African Unity (OAU) in protest at the SADR's admission to the body.
1983 Relations between Morocco and Algeria improve.
1988 Full diplomatic relations with Algeria were resumed.
1991 A UN-monitored cease-fire began in Western Sahara.
1998 The moderate socialist Union Socialiste des Forces Populaires (USFP) (Socialist Union of Popular Forces) won the elections and formed a government.
1999 King Hassan II died suddenly and his son, Mohammed VI, acceded him.
2000 King Mohammed VI began a process of modest political liberalisation.
2002 King Mohammed married Salma Bennani, a 24-year-old computer engineer; the marriage to a commoner was a break with Royal Moroccan tradition. Morocco occupied the tiny, uninhabited island of Leila or Isla del Perejil (Parsley Island) off its coast and owned by Spain, and prompted an international spat. After the general election, the two main parties – the USFP and Istiqlal – formed a coalition government. Driss Jettou was appointed prime minister.

KEY INDICATORS — Morocco

	Unit	2000	2001	2002	2003	2004
Population	m	29.00	29.20	29.61	30.36	29.89
Gross domestic product (GDP)	US$bn	33.50	32.80	37.30	44.50	*50.06
GDP per capita	US$	1,155	1,123	1,217	1,527	1,629
GDP real growth	%	2.4	5.7	4.5	5.5	3.5
Inflation	%	1.9	0.6	4.1	1.2	2.0
Exports (fob) (goods)	US$m	7,419.0	7,100.0	7,660.0	8,172.0	9,744.0
Imports (fob) (goods)	US$m	10,665.0	10,200.0	12,080.0	13,263.0	16,238.0
Balance of trade	US$m	-3,235.0	-4,100.0	-4,300.0	-5,091.0	-6,494.0
Current account	US$m	-501.0	-263.0	-218.0	303.0	610.0
Foreign debt	US$bn	19.9	17.8	18.0	16.4	—
Total reserves minus gold	US$m	4,823.0	8,474.0	10,133.0	13,851.0	16,337.0
Foreign exchange	US$m	4,612.0	8,262.0	9,915.0	13,634.0	16,107.0
Exchange rate	per US$	10.63	11.30	10.86	9.50	8.87

* estimated figure

2003 Senegal and Morocco signed agreements on closer co-operation. There were suicide bombings in Casablanca killing 41 and injuring many more.
2004 An earthquake in the north killed over 500 people. In July a free trade agreement was signed with the US after Morocco had been designated a major non-NATO ally.
2005 Prime Minister Jettou announced that Morocco wanted to establish a TGV (French high-speed train service) by 2015, between Casablanca, Marrakech and Agadir.

Political structure
Constitution
Adopted 10 March 1972; amended 1992 and 1996.
The constitution prohibits a one-party political system.
The King is *Amir al Moumineen* (Commander of the Faithful), hereditary head of state and supreme commander of the armed forces. He appoints the cabinet on the recommendation of the prime minister.
The King is empowered to declare a state of emergency and dissolve parliament if necessary.
Form of state
Constitutional monarchy
The executive
Executive power rests with the prime minister and cabinet, who serve a five-year term.
National legislature
Legislative powers are exercised by the bicameral Barlaman (parliament).
The 325-member Majlis an Nuwab (Assembly of Representatives, lower house) is directly elected for a five-year term in multi-seat constituencies. It debates legislation presented to it by the government. Approved legislation is automatically promulgated a month later.
Local councils elect 60 per cent of the 270 representatives to the Majlis al Mustasharin (Assembly of Councillors, upper house); the remainder are elected indirectly from unions and chambers of commerce. The upper house has the power to overrule the government with a no-confidence vote.
Legal system
The legal system is based on Islamic law and a combination of French and Spanish civil law codes. The Supreme Court is responsible for reviewing government legislation.
Last elections
27 September 2002 (parliamentary)
Results: Parliamentary: the USFP won 50 seats, Istiqlal 48 seats, the PJD 42 seats, the RNI 41 seats. Turnout was 51.2 per cent.

Next elections
2007 (parliamentary)
Political parties
Ruling party
Coalition government from Nov 2002: Union Socialiste des Forces Populaires (USFP) (Socialist Union of Popular Forces); Parti de l'Istiqlal (Istiqlal) (Independence Party)
Main opposition party
Parti de la Justice et du Développement (PJD) (Justice and Development Party) (Islamists), Rassemblement National des Indépendents (RNI) National Rally of Independents.

Population
29.89 million (2004 census)
Ethnic make-up
Mostly Berbers and Arabs. There is a small Jewish minority and an estimated 60,000 foreign residents, mainly of French, Spanish and Italian origin.
Religions
Islam is the state religion. Sunni Muslim (98 per cent). There are small minority Jewish and Roman Catholic communities.

Education
The illiteracy rate is as high as 83 per cent among women in rural areas. The government aims to increase the literacy to 76 per cent by 2010. Public expenditure on education is about 5 per cent of annual Gross National Income (GNI) and includes subsidies to private education at all levels.
Primary, or first stage education lasts until the age of 12, then students move onto second stage until aged 15, when they choose between an academic general secondary school or a technical secondary school for three years. At aged 18 the academic students undertake the Baccalauréat for progression to higher education. Technical students may undertake a further two years study in their specialised skill.
Higher education is provided by 13 universities, specialised schools and institutes under the supervision of the National Ministry of Education. Besides a traditional system of higher education, there are 28 executive training institutes (Etablissements de Formation des Cadres), which provide specialised training under the direct control of ministerial departments. There are also eight Grandes Ecoles d'Ingénieurs (engineering schools). A private university opened in September 1994. Universities are mainly public institutions with budgetary autonomy.
In 2003, schools began to teach Tamazight, the Berber language which predates Arabic in north Africa; children will have to learn using Arabic, Latin and Berber scripts.
Literacy rate: 50.7 per cent total, 38.3 per cent female, adult rates in 2002 (World Bank).
Compulsory years: 7 to 14.
Enrolment rate: 86 per cent gross primary enrolment of relevant age group (including repeaters); 39 per cent gross secondary enrolment (World Bank).
Pupils per teacher: 28 in primary schools.

Health
It is estimated that less than 20 per cent of Moroccans have access to healthcare. Approximately 5 per cent of the government budget is allocated to the health sector each year, less than 1 per cent of GDP. Public hospitals are free, but patients must buy medicine and pay for certain services, such as X-rays. Medical fees are reimbursed only for children. There are basic health services in rural areas, including local dispensaries, rural hospitals and provincial hospitals. Government policy specifically targets the reduction of infant deaths, the provision of family planning services, nutrition awareness programmes and campaigns against malaria and tuberculosis.
HIV prevalence: 0.1 per cent aged 15–49 in 2003 (World Bank)
Life expectancy: 68.7 years (World Bank).
Fertility rate/Maternal mortality rate: 2.7 births per woman (2003); maternal mortality 230 per 100,000 live births (World Bank).
Birth rate/Death rate: Seven deaths and 25 births per 1,000 head of population (World Bank).
Infant mortality rate: 36 per 1,000 live births (World Bank)

Welfare
There is a stark contrast between the living standards of the rural and urban population. In 2004, 19 per cent of the population lived below the poverty line. In rural areas over a third of the population are classified as poor.
Morocco's social security system is based on the Caisse Nationale de la Sécurité Sociale (CNSS) (National Social Security Fund), which is funded by subscribers' contributions and interest on investments. All salaried workers in industry, commerce and services must belong to the CNSS. Civil servants belong to a similar scheme, run by the Caisse Nationale des Organismes de Prévoyance Sociale (CNOPS).
In cases of illness or accident, an employee can receive 50 per cent of salary after the eighth day. The employee can claim this benefit for up to 52 weeks every two years. Maternity benefit, equal to 50

per cent of salary, is paid for up to 10 weeks. The invalidity pension is equal to 50 per cent of salary for someone who has worked between five and 15 years. If a worker dies, the family is entitled to a payment equal to two months' salary. Old age pensions, equal to 50 per cent of salary, are payable to employees who have contributed for at least 15 years. The retirement age is 60. A pension is paid to the family of a deceased retired worker, provided they had worked for more than 15 years.

Main cities
Casablanca (commercial centre, estimated population 2.95 million in 2004, Greater Casablance 3.6 million), Rabat (capital, 1.6 million), Fez (1.0 million), Marrakesh (755,200), Agadir (622,100), Tangier (604,000), Meknès (578,700), Oujda (341,600).

Languages spoken
Business literature and correspondence should be in French or Arabic.
Arabic is spoken in general. French is taught in school and is more commonly spoken in government, business and among the Moroccans elite.
There are three main dialects of Tamazight (the Berber language) spoken all over the country. Tamazight belongs to the Afro-Asiatic family and is related to ancient Egyptian and Ethiopian.
Berber groups and their dialects: Shleuh (Ishalhiyan), in the High Atlas, Tashalhit dialect; Imazighen (Imazighen), Middle Atlas/Eastern High Atlas, Tamazight dialect; Rifans (Irifiyan), Northern Morocco, Tarifit dialect.
In the north, Spanish is widely spoken, while in the bigger cities like Casablanca, English is very common.

Official language/s
Arabic

Media
The government uses the media to strengthen national unity and aid cultural, economic and social development. This has meant extending the state media network to remote areas, improving training and modernising technical equipment. The government owns the official newsagency, Maghreb Arab Presse. While print media is predominantly independent, electronic media remains largely under government control.

Press
Dailies: Principal newspapers in Arabic, French and English include the government owned *Al Anbaa, Le Matin du Sahara et du Maghreb, Maroc Hebdo, La Nouvelle Tribune, La Gazette du Maroc, Al Annbaa, Al Jarida Al Maghribia, Al Bayane, Morocco Today* and *News Express*. On-line news services include the daily French *(www.)marocnews.com*.
Business: Numerous periodicals are available in French and Arabic, including the business weekly *La Vie Economique*. *l'Economiste* carries financial news.

Broadcasting
Radio: Extensive national and external services are available in Arabic, French, English, Spanish and Berber. The government controls Radio-Television Marocaine (RTM). The French language Medi-1 is a private radio station. The government has been encouraging more private radio stations to operate in Morocco since 2001.
Television: Local television stations broadcast for over 60 hours per week, with advertising in Arabic and French. The nationwide network is basically state-controlled, but a private cable channel is also in operation.

Advertising
There are several local advertising agencies operating on a relatively small scale in Morocco. Television advertising has a 70 per cent share of the total market, followed by print media and billboard advertising. Advertising on the Internet is increasingly popular with companies that seek to target selected consumer groups.

Economy
The economy has much to commend it with a well managed monetary policy that has achieved macroeconomic stability for over a decade. It has a current account surplus, low inflation at 2.0 per cent in 2004 and foreign exchange reserves which are strong. Therefore, the weakness in the economy, from its slow growth of 3.5 per cent GDP, over-reliance on the agriculture sector and high unemployment and underemployment, mars what could be the economy of an industrialised state. Agricultural production is extremely vulnerable to climatic shocks and droughts have a direct affect on the 50 per cent of the population that depend on the sector for their livelihood and correlates to rural poverty. To achieve long-term stability the economy has to be diversified with increased secondary and tertiary industries. State owned entities have been, or are in the process of being sold off, while trade liberalisation is ongoing. These measures will enhance Morocco's competitiveness, and maintain exports to its primary market, the EU, while reforms are being completed.
In June 2004, the World Bank approved a US$37 million loan for the development of Morocco's rural roads, with a view to increasing road access to 80 per cent of the rural population by 2015. Another World Bank loan, of US$100 million, was approved in July to support the Moroccan government's efforts to improve public resource management, a key step for accelerated growth and poverty reduction.

Investment in social development will be included in medium-term budget objectives to improved access to education, healthcare, housing, basic infrastructure and rural development.
Morocco has implemented the regime the IMF has consistently argued should be adopted by developing countries with strong fiscal controls and a liberalised economy, it remains to be seen as to when Morocco reaps the benefits of its efforts.

External trade
Morocco belongs to the Arab Maghreb Union (AMU) with Algeria, Libya, Mauritania and Tunisia. It also has a European Free Trade Association (EFTA) agreement, implemented in 2000 which will eventually remove all tariffs between the two by 2012.
In March 2004, Morocco and the US concluded a free trade agreement.

Imports
Principal imports are crude oil, textile fabric, telecommunications equipment, wheat, gas and electricity, transistors and plastics.
Main sources: France (21.2 per cent total, 2004), Spain (14.9 per cent), Germany (7.3 per cent), Italy (6.9 per cent), Saudi Arabia (4.8 per cent), China (4.8 per cent)

Exports
Principal exports are clothing, fish, inorganic chemicals, transistors, crude minerals, fertilisers (including phosphates), petroleum products, fruits and vegetables.
Main destinations: France (25.3 per cent total, 2004), Spain (18.4 per cent), UK (8.0 per cent), Italy (4.9 per cent), Germany (4.6 per cent), US (4.6 per cent)

Agriculture
Farming
The agricultural sector contributed 16.7 per cent to GDP on 2004, it typically employs 40 per cent of the workforce which can rise to 50 per cent during the harvest. Around 70 per cent of the 7.9 million hectares (ha) of arable land is cultivated, mainly by subsistent farmers.
Principal crops are wheat, barley, maize (grown in the rain-fed areas), citrus fruits, beans, chick peas and other pulses, tomatoes (mainly for export), potatoes, olives and oilseeds. Important agri-export crops are sugar cane, sugar beet (the production of which is being developed to cut down on sugar imports) and cotton.
Livestock productivity and crop yields have remained low and regular food imports of grain are necessary to meet domestic cereal requirements. Agricultural development has also been hampered by the

small size of the majority of holdings and restricted access to EU markets. Many long-term government projects are under way, including irrigation schemes, development of new techniques and financial incentives to farmers.

As the increasing population puts pressure on available resources, access to water will become more difficult. The World Bank has estimated that Morocco will become a water deficit country by 2020.

Some 32,500 tonnes of cannabis is grown annually in the deprived north of Morocco for the European market. King Mohammed has made developing the north a priority in government policy in order to combat illicit crop cultivation.

Crop production in 2004 included: 8,590,610 tonnes (t) cereals in total, 5,539,840t wheat, 2,760,340t barley, 16,900t rice, 24,130t maize, 1,440,000t potatoes, *1,269,600t citrus fruit, 1,201,230t tomatoes, 269,410t pulses, 4,560,000t sugar beet, 142,217t oilcrops, 992,000t sugar cane, 267,000t grapes, 69,400t dates, 4,000t tobacco, 470,000t olives, 393,140t apples, 2,703,335t fruit in total, 5,192,570t vegetables in total. Livestock production included: 599,500t meat in total, 148,000t beef, 33,000t game meat, 10,000t edible snails, 124,000t lamb and goat meat, *280,000t poultry, *230,000t eggs, 3,000t honey, 1,364,700t milk, 20,250t cattle hides, 12,800t sheepskins, 40,000t greasy wool.
* estimate

Fishing
The fishing sector offers considerable potential, although export markets for the main catch, sardines, are restricted by strong competition from Spain, Portugal and France. The total catch is estimated at around one million tonnes a year, of which 150,00 tonnes is shellfish and 930,000 tonnes is marine fish.

Morocco's fleet fishes in both Atlantic and Mediterranean waters and has an agreement to fish in the Gulf of Guinea. As well as its own ports, some of Morocco's catch is landed in Portugal. Fish frozen at sea is landed at Agadir and Tan-Tan.

The government is modernising the fishing fleet and ports to exploit the rich potential of local fishing grounds. The EU donated US$22.2 million to build four new fishing villages on Morocco's Mediterranean coast. A US$13 million expansion programme at Sidi Ifni fishing port, enabled catches in excess of 50,000 tonnes per annum.

After pursuing a policy of leasing fishing rights to foreign countries such as South Korea, Japan, the former Soviet Union, Spain and Portugal, the government is now encouraging national private enterprises in the sector.

Morocco has an agreement with Norway concerning co-operation on fishery issues, exchange of expertise and data and bilateral investment promotion.

Forestry
Only 9 per cent of land area is forested and most of Morocco's wood needs are imported.

Industry and manufacturing
The industrial sector accounts for 30–35 per cent of GDP and employs 37 per cent of the workforce. Most activity is concentrated in the Casablanca area.

The main industry is the processing of phosphates into phosphoric acid and fertilisers. Food processing is another major industry. Other significant industries include oil refining, steel, cement, chemicals, pharmaceuticals, toiletries, metallurgy, textiles, leather, paper and timber, metals, rubber, plastics and vehicle assembly. The textile and leather industries employ one quarter of the industrial workforce, and export successfully.

Industrial development has switched in recent years away from import substitution and towards encouraging the manufacture of goods for export, support for small- and medium-sized producers, devolution of spending powers to local authorities and investment in other areas of the country away from Casablanca. Industrial production increased by 0.5 per cent in 2003.

Tourism
The tourism sector is active as a competitive destination for European tourists and is expected to contribute 9.5 per cent of GDP and 14.7 per cent of total employment in 2005. To further encourage tourism, the prices of accommodation, restaurants and service charges have been reduced. Police checks on tourists have also been relaxed.

The private sector has pooled resources to set up a National Tourism Federation to plan renovation of hotels, development of infrastructure and coastal resorts. The continuing privatisation of state-owned hotels should contribute to the growth of the sector. Around 13 per cent of all capital investment in 2005 are planned to be in travel and tourism.

The government's tourist strategy is to attract 10 million visitors by 2010. Tenders were invited, in June 2005, for a new beach resort at Taghazout, this will be the fifth resort in a string of six, as contained in The Azur Plan.

The civil unrest that resulted in the 2003 Casablanca bombings appears to have been moderated and improved Morocco's international image. The government has launched a campaign to triple the number of Arab tourists visiting, at a time when Western destinations have been less welcoming to them.

Mining
Government policy has been to open up the mining sector to investments by both minor and major mining companies. There are more than 90 mining companies producing 20 different mineral products. The sector contributes approximately 15 per cent to GDP and employs 4 per cent of the workforce.

Although phosphates account for 92 per cent of mineral production, smaller quantities of other minerals are produced, including 500,000 tonnes of anthracite. Morocco has large deposits of lead, zinc, copper, iron, fluorine, silver, manganese, cobalt, antimony, barytine, salt and other minerals.

Phosphate mining and the production of phosphoric acid are of vital importance to the Moroccan economy, although a large proportion of reserves is located in the disputed Western Sahara area occupied by Morocco since 1975. The sector is controlled by the state through the country's largest company, Office Chérifien des Phosphates (OCP). OCP is the world's largest exporter of phosphate rock. With reserves of approximately 110 billion tonnes, Morocco is estimated to contain three-quarters of the world's phosphate reserves.

Iron ore deposits in the northern Rif region, 25km from the port of Beni Eznar, include 18.2 million tonnes of magnetite ore, which could bring in 700,000–800,000 tonnes of ore per year. Silver, copper, zinc and lead are also mined.

Hydrocarbons
In 2004, Morocco had proven oil reserves of two million barrels producing 200 barrels per day (bpd) from its Sidi Rhelem oil field. With total consumption of around 150,000bpd, Morocco is heavily reliant on imported oil. Oil accounts for over 80 per cent of total energy requirements, mainly imported from Saudi Arabia. Exploration projects are under way onshore, mainly in the south-west and north-east, and offshore. By mid-2005 there were 15 foreign companies actively engaged in exploration.

Morocco has two oil refineries: Samir and Sidi Kacem with a combined capacity of 155 billion bpd. Samir was partly destroyed by fire in 2002; in June 2005 a US$628 million contract to modernise was let to Snamprogetti SpA (Italy) and Tekefen Company (Turkey). The upgrade is expected to by completed by 2008. Morocco signed two controversial oil deals with TotalFinaElf of France and Kerr-McGee (US-based) to explore in the disputed Western Sahara in 2001. The

Morocco

Polisario Front, Western Sahara's independence movement, protested against the deals and invited companies to bid for 12 of its own offshore exploration rights. International protest campaigns have limited the involvement of all but Kerr-McGee in Western Sahara. The legality of these contracts can only be settled after the status of Western Sahara is internationally recognised.

Although Morocco contains only limited natural gas reserves at 1.2 billion cubic metres in 2004, the country is a major transit centre for Algerian gas exports to Europe. The Maghreb-Europe pipeline transports Algerian gas to Spain via Morocco and the Straits of Gibraltar. Ultimately it is planned to carry 20 billion cubic metres of gas per year to Europe, via Spain.

There is only one coal mine, at Jerada, with 91 million tonnes of reserves but with declining production most coal is imported from South Africa and Poland.

Energy

Morocco has a total installed electricity generating capacity of over 4GW, with plans to increase capacity to cater for its rapidly growing demand for electricity. To avoid blackouts and government expenditure the private sector is increasing its market share of electricity generation. The Office National de l'Electicité (One) is solely responsible for electricity transmission and distribution.

Morocco has completed 40 per cent of the construction of a nuclear reactor and is looking to other non-fossil fuel energy sources to provide 10 per cent its energy needs by 2011, including wind turbines and hydro- and solar power.

The country's goal is to supply 80 per cent of rural areas by 2008, and by 2005, 55 per cent of outlying villages had access to electricity.

The entire energy sector is expected to be liberalised by 2007.

Financial markets
Stock exchange

The Bourse de Casablanca (Casablanca Stock Exchange) (CSE) is a private company with stock held by brokers.

Despite an increase in foreign interest in the CSE, major foreign participation has yet to materialise. The limited size of the CSE is a disincentive to foreign investment. The daily volume of trade averages little more than US$10 million, too small for many international investors. Another obstacle to growth of the CSE is government regulation. In an attempt to curb the outflow of foreign exchange the government has legislated against Moroccans investing their funds abroad. As a consequence, insurance companies and mutual funds are competing intensively for the relatively few stocks available, inflating prices and making them comparatively unattractive to other investors.

Banking and insurance

The Banque Marocaine du Commerce Extérieur (BMCE) was the first Moroccan bank and has grown steadily since 1995. It has broadened its international shareholder base and opened new branches throughout Morocco and abroad. At 8 per cent it has the largest capitalisations on the stock exchange, and around 25 per cent of that of the banking sector. The Banque Commerciale du Maroc (BCM) holds the sector's best return on equity. It has a bad debt reduction strategy, and lower levels of bad debts than its competitors.

The Banque Centrale Populaire (BCP), the Banque Nationale pour le Développement Economique (BNDE) and the Crédit Immobilier et Hôtelier (CIH) are scheduled for privatisation. They are criticised for being burdened with high levels of bad debt and may need radical restructuring if they are to survive and compete in an adverse economic climate.

Central bank
Bank al Maghrib

Main financial centre
Casablanca

Time
GMT

Geography
Morocco is situated in the extreme north-west of Africa. It has a long coastline on the shores of the Atlantic Ocean and, east of the Strait of Gibraltar, on the Mediterranean Sea, facing southern Spain. Morocco's eastern frontier is with Algeria, while to the south lies the disputed territory of Western Sahara.

Climate
Varies widely with area; while Mediterranean on the coast, it is hotter and drier inland and Alpine in the High Atlas, yet Saharan in the south. Summer is from May–October. It is dry and hot, with temperatures between 23–28 degrees Celsius (C) on the coast, 30–45 degrees C inland. Winter runs from November–April, with light rain on the coast, average temperature 15–21 degrees C, and a dry inland with temperatures between 20–30 degrees C.

Dress codes
Lightweight suits are best for formal wear. Women should dress modestly. Some visitors adopt the traditional *jellaba*, which is more comfortable in both hot and cool weather and is usually worn by men. It can get cool quickly after dark, so a light overcoat or wrap is advised.

Entry requirements
Passports
Required by all. Passports must be valid for at least six months from the date of entry.
Visa
Required by all, except citizens of EU, North America and Australasia, for visits including business trips up to three months, for further exceptions contact the nearest consulate.
Currency advice/regulations
The import and export of local currency is prohibited, except for repatriation of salaries.
Unlimited import of foreign currency, although amounts over the equivalent of Dh15,000 should be declared. Export is allowed of foreign currency up to amount declared on arrival. Up to half of the Moroccan currency purchased by a visitor during his stay may generally be re-exchanged for foreign currency on the production of relevant receipts.
Prohibited imports
Import restrictions apply to firearms, explosives, used clothes and used tyres.

Health (for visitors)
Mandatory precautions
Vaccinations against yellow fever are required if arriving from an infected area.
Advisable precautions
Typhoid, tetanus and polio vaccinations are recommended. Anti-malaria precautions should be taken. Water may be contaminated. Milk is unpasteurised and should be boiled.

Hotels
Inexpensive and widely available. Two main types: graded hotels (which are given a one- to five-star rating by the Tourist Board) and small (and usually old) unlisted hotels. A service charge and local tax is normally added to bill.

Credit cards
Major credit cards widely accepted.

Public holidays
Fixed dates
1 Jan (New Year's Day), 11 Jan (Independence Day), 1 May (Labour Day), 30 Jul (Feast of the Throne), 14 Aug (Oued Eddahab Allegiance Day), 20 Aug (The King and the People's Revolution Day), 21 Aug (King Mohammed's Birthday), 6 Nov (Anniversary of the Green March), 18 Nov (Independence Day).
Variable dates
Eid al Adha (two days), Islamic New Year, Birth of the Prophet (two days), Eid al Fitr (two days).

The Islamic year contains 354 or 355 days, with the result that Muslim feasts advance by 10–12 days against the Gregorian calendar. Dates of feasts vary according to the sighting of the new moon, so cannot be forecast exactly.

Working hours
Banking
Winter: Mon–Fri: 0800–1130 and 1400–1830. Summer: Mon–Fri: 0800–1600. Ramadan: Mon–Fri: 0900–1530.
Business
Winter: Mon–Fri: 0800–1200 and 1400–1800/2000. Summer hours vary, some work Mon–Fri: 0800–1500/1600, others revert to winter hours. Ramadan: Mon–Fri: 0900–1500/1600.
Government
Winter: Mon–Fri: 0800–1200 and 1430–1800. Summer: Mon–Sat: 0800–1600. Ramadan: Mon–Sat: 0900–1500.
Shops
Shops are usually open between 0800 and 1800, often closing for a few hours in the middle of the day.

Telecommunications
Mobile phones
Network coverage is mainly available in the cities in the west.

Electricity supply
110–127V or 220V AC, 50 cycles.

Social customs/useful tips
Business visits during the Muslim month of Ramadan are best avoided, as many businesses close during part or all of this period. During Ramadan, visitors should respect Muslim traditions and avoid drinking, eating and smoking in public during daylight hours.
Pork and alcohol are forbidden to Muslims at all times, so these should not be offered, although in practice alcohol is widely available and its consumption not considered an insult to Islam.
Business practices in most respects are similar to those in France and Spain. Tipping is common for most services, including hotel porters, cinema usherettes, cloakroom attendants, railway porters, and so on. In hotels and restaurants a service charge is normally added to the bill. Taxi drivers (in *grand* taxis only) will expect a 10 per cent tip.

Security
Street crime is a problem, especially in the larger cities where petty theft is rife. Women may also encounter sexual harassment on the streets at any time, especially when walking alone.

Getting there
Air
National airline: Royal Air Maroc
International airport/s: Casablanca-Mohammed V (CMN), 30km south of city, bar, buffet, restaurant, bank, post office, car hire; Rabat-Salé (RBA), 10km from city, buffet, restaurant, bank, post office, shops, car hire.

Other airport/s: Agadir-Inezgane (AGA), 6.5km south of city, bar, buffet, bank, car hire; Fez-Sais (FEZ), 10km from city; Tangier-Boukhalef Souahel (TNG), 15km from city, restaurant, bank, car hire; Marrakesh (RAK), 6km from city.
Airport tax: None
Surface
Road: Road access is possible from Algeria via Oujda.
Rail: There are good rail connections to Tunisia, France and Spain (via rail-ferry link). The international rail link is via Oujda. In 2002, rail links to Algeria were suspended.
Water: Regular car ferry and hydrofoil services connect Spain, France and Gibraltar with Tangier and the Spanish administered ports of Ceuta and Melilla.
Main port/s: Agadir, Casablanca (major freight port), Jorf Lasfar, Kenitra, Mohammedia, Nador, Safi, Tangier (main passenger port).

Getting about
National transport
Air: Royal Air Maroc operates domestic services to main centres. Regional Airlines is another domestic carrrier.
Road: Morocco has approximately 30,000km of surfaced roads. The links between main centres are generally good. Some of the 30,000km country roads need care and/or local knowledge. The Atlas Mountains may be impassable in winter.
Buses: There are frequent, cheap services between towns. Long-distance services include: Tangier-Oujda, Fez-Marrakesh; Agadir-Casablanca and Tangier-Casablanca. It is advisable to book in advance.
Rail: A limited (1,893km) but efficient network is operated by Office National des Chemins de Fer (ONCF). Fares are cheap. Three classes are available. Air-conditioning, air-conditioned sleeping cars – couchettes and restaurant cars are available; supplements may be payable. Routes include: Oujda-Fez-Rabat-Casablanca, Marrakesh-Casablanca-Rabat and Casablanca-Rabat-Tangier.
City transport
Taxis: The *grand* taxis (Moroccan bus-taxis), seating up to six persons, operate along specific routes and can be arranged at hotel receptions, or can be found outside bus and train stations and the airport. They are cheaper than a conventional taxi for long journeys and more comfortable and convenient than a bus. The *Petit* taxis are metered and operate within cities. Fares vary considerably; drivers prefer to set fares in advance, rather than use the meter, so each journey is preceded by a negotiation. A 10 per cent tip is usual.

Buses, trams & metro: Agadir, Casablanca, Tangier and other main towns have good bus services. Tickets can be bought in advance of journeys. There is a shuttle bus service from the Casablanca rail station to the CTM Gare Routière (bus station) which takes at least 45 minutes, depending on traffic.
Trains: Train service every 30 minutes connects Casablanca's Mohammed V Airport with the city's main railway stations, Voyageurs and Port.
Car hire
Car hire is widely available but expensive. Major hire companies operate from Agadir, Casablanca and Tangier. National or international driving licences are accepted. Driving is on the right.

BUSINESS DIRECTORY

The addresses listed below are a selection only. While World of Information makes every endeavour to check these addresses, we cannot guarantee that changes have not been made, especially to telephone numbers and area codes. We would welcome any corrections.

Telephone area codes
The international dialling code (IDD) for Morocco is +212, followed by area code and subscriber's number:

Agadir	48	Mohammedia	232
Casablanca	22	Rabat	37
Fes	55	Tangier	39
Marrakech	44		

Chambers of Commerce
American Chamber of Commerce in Morocco, Hyatt Regency Casablanca, Place des Nations Unies, Casablanca (tel: 293-028; fax: 481-597; e-mail: amcham@amcham-morocco.com).

British Chamber of Commerce for Morocco, 65 Avenue Hassan Seghir, Casablanca (tel: 448-860; fax: 448-868; e-mail: britcham@casanet.net.ma).

Casablanca Chambre de Commerce, d'Industrie et des Services, 98 Boulevard Mohammed V, PO Box 423, Casablanca (tel: 264-327; fax: 268-436; e-mail: ccisc@cciscx.gov.ma).

Chambre de Commerce Internationale, Boulevard de Bordeaux, Casablanca (tel: 225-111; fax: 225-119; e-mail: icc@casanet.net.ma).

French Chambre de Commerce et d'Industrie du Maroc, 15 Avenue Mers Sultan, PO Box 15810, Casablanca (tel: 209-090; fax: 200-130; e-mail: cfcim@cfcim.org).

Marrakech Chambre de Commerce, d'Industrie et de Services, Djnan El Harti Gueliz, Marrakech (tel: 431-951; fax: 430-950; e-mail: ccismar@iam.net.ma).

Morocco Fédération des Chambres de Commerce et d'Industrie, 6 Rue Erfoud, Rabat (tel: 766-108; fax: 767-076; e-mail: fccjsm@maghrebnet.net.ma).

Rabat Chambre de Commerce, d'Industrie et de Services, 6 Rue Ghandi, PO Box 131, Rabat (tel: 703-185; fax: 703-166; e-mail: ccisrs@ccisrs.org.ma).

Tangiers Chambre de Commerce, d'Industrie et de Services, Angle Rue Ibn Taymia et Rue El Hariri, Tanger (tel: 946-026; fax: 942-954; e-mail: cciswtg@iam.net.ma).

Banking
ABN Amro Bank (Maroc) SA, PO Box 13478, 47 Rue Allal Ben Abellah, Casablanca 20000 (tel: 266-027; fax: 222-514).

Banque Centrale Populaire, 101 Boulevard Mohamed Zerktouni, Casablanca (tel: 222-589; fax: 222-699; e-mail: aslamti@cpm.co.ma).

Banque Commerciale du Maroc, 2 Boulevard Moulay Youssef, Casablanca (tel: 224-169; fax: 469-916).

Banque Marocaine du Commerce Extérieur SA, PO Box 13.425, 140 Avenue Hassan II, Casablanca 01 (tel: 220-0325, 220-0467; fax: 220-0005, 220-0060).

Crédit du Maroc SA, PO Box 13579, 48-58 Boulevard Mohammed V, Casablanca 20000 (tel: 477-000; fax: 277-127, 206-076/77).

Crédit Immobilier et Hôtelier, 187 Avenue Hassan II, Casablanca 20000 (tel: 222-7863; fax: 248-7537, 227-8631).

Groupement Professionel des Banques du Maroc (Moroccan Banking Association), 71 Avenue des Forces Armées Royales, Casablanca (tel: 311-624; fax: 311-911).

Société Marocaine de Dépôt et de Crédit, 79 Avenue Hassan II, Casablanca (tel: 224-114; fax: 271-590).

Wafabank, 163 Avenue Hassan II, Casablanca (tel: 220-0200, 227-1091, 226-5151, 222-4105; fax: 226-3621).

Central bank
Bank al Maghrib, PO Box 445, 277 Avenue Mohammed V, Rabat (tel: 702-626; fax:706-677).

Travel information
Office National des Chemins de Fer (ONCF) Tourist Office, 98 Boulevard Mohammed V, Casablanca (tel: 221-524).

Royal Air Maroc, 44 Avenue des Forces Armées Royales, Casablanca (tel: 311-122; fax: 442-409).

Ministry of tourism
Ministry of Economy, Finance and Tourism, Quartier Administratif, Chellah, Rabat (tel: 760-147; 760-509; fax: 761-575; e-mail: ministre@mfie.gov.ma; internet site: http://www.tourisme-marocain.com/frame/infos.htm).

National tourist organisation offices
Morocco National Tourist Board (ONMT), Rue Oued Fes, Angle Avenue Al Abtal, Agdal, Rabat (tel: 681-531; fax: 777-437; e-mail: visitemorocco@mbox.azure.net).

Ministries
Prime Minister's Office, Palais Royal, Le Méchouar, Rabat (tel: 762-709; fax: 769-995).

Ministry of Agriculture and Rural Development, Place Abdallah Chefchaouni, Quartier Administratif, Rabat (tel: 760-933; fax: 763-378).

Ministry of Communication, 10 Rue de Béni Mellal, Place de la Grande Poste, Avenue Mohammed V, Rabat (tel: 766-016; fax: 766-908; internet site: http://www.mincom.gov.ma).

Ministry of Economic Forecasts and Planning, Avenue Al Haj Cherkaoui, Agdal, Rabat (tel: 761-415; fax: 760-771).

Ministry of Economy, Finance and Tourism, Quartier Administratif, Chellah, Rabat (tel: 760-147; 760-509; fax: 761-575; e-mail: ministre@mfie.gov.ma; internet site: http://www.finances.gov.ma).

Ministry of Education, Bab Rouah, Rabat (tel: 771-822; fax: 772-042).

Minister of Employment, Vocational Training, Social Development and Solidarity (tel: 760-695; fax: 766-633).

Ministry of Equipment, Quartier Adminisatratif, Chellah, Rabat (tel: 762-811; fax: 765-505).

Ministry of Foreign Affairs and Co-operation, Avenue Roosevelt, Rabat (tel: 762-841; fax: 764-679; e-mail: mail@maec.gov.ma; internet site: http://www.maec.gov.ma).

Minister of Habous and Islamic Affairs, Le Méchouar, Rabat (tel: 766-801; fax: 765-257; e-mail: webmaster@habous.gov.ma).

Ministry of Health, 335 Boulevard Mohammed V, Rabat (tel: 761-121; fax: 768-401; e-mail: webmaster@sante.gov.ma).

Ministry of Higher Education and Scientific Research, Charia Bouregreg, Rabat (tel: 707-496; fax: 737-236).

Ministry of Human Rights (tel: 673-131; fax: 671-967).

Ministry of Industry, Commerce, Energy, and Mines, Quartier Administratif, Chellah, Rabat (tel: 761-868; fax: 766-265; e-mail: ministre@mcinet).

Ministry of Interior, Quartier Administratif, Rabat (tel: 761-861; fax: 762-056).

Ministry of Justice, Place Mamounia, Rabat (tel: 732-941; fax: 730-772).

Minister of Land Management, Urban Affairs, Housing and the Environment (tel: 763-539; fax: 763-510).

Ministry of Parliamentary Relations, Quartier Admistratif, Agdal, Rabat (tel: 775-170; fax: 775-468).

Ministry of Public Service and Administrative Reform (770-894; fax: 775-690).

Ministry of Public Sector and Privatisation (internet site: http://www.minpriv.gov.ma).

Ministry of Sea Fisheries, Quartier Administratif, Rabat (tel: 770-154; fax: 778-540).

Ministry of Transport and Merchant Marine (tel: 774-266; fax: 779-525).

Ministry of Youth and Sport, Boulevard Ibn Sina, Agdal, Rabat, (tel: 680-045; fax: 680-916).

Other useful addresses
Bourse de Casablanca (Stock Exchange), Avenue de l'Armée Royale, Casablanca (tel: 452-626; fax: 452-625; e-mail: contact@casablanca-bourse.com).

British Consulate-General, 43 Boulevard d'Anfa, Casablanca (tel: 221-653; fax: 265-779; e-mail: british.consulate@casanet.net.ma).

British Embassy, 17 Boulevard de la Tour Hassan, Rabat (tel: 729-696; fax: 704-531; e-mail: britemb@mtds.com).

Confédération Générale des Enterprises du Maroc (CGEM), Angle Avenue des Forces Armées Royales et Rue Mohamed Errachid, Casablanca (tel: 252-696; fax: 253-839).

Fédération des Industries Chimiques et Parachimiques (FICP), 36 Rue Chaouia, Casablanca (tel: 229-215; fax:225-613).

Fédération des Industries de la Conserve des Produits Agricoles du Maroc (FICOPAM), 77 Rue Mohamed Smiha, Casablanca (tel: 303-953; fax: 303-534).

Fédération des Industries Métallurgiques, Mécaniques, Electriques et Electroniques (FIMME), 147 Rue Mohamed Smiha, Casablanca (tel: 301-683; fax: 940-587).

Moroccan Centre for Export Promotion, 23 Rue Bnou Majed El Bahar, Casablanca (tel: 302-210; fax: 301-793).

Moroccan Embassy (USA), 1601 21st Street, NW, Washington DC 20009 (tel: 202-462-7979; fax: 202-265-0161; e-mail: sifarausa@erols.com).

National Telecommunications Regulatory Agency (ANRT), Boulevard Ennakhil, Rabat (tel: 717-312; e-mail: webmaster@anrt.net.ma).

Office pour le Développement Industriel (ODI), 10 Rue Ghandi, Rabat (tel: 708-460; fax: 707-695).

ONAREP (national oil company), 34 Avenue Al Fadila, Rabat (tel: 281-616; fax: 281-634; e-mail: benkhadr@onarep.com).

United States Embassy, 2 Avenue de Mohamed El Fassi, Rabat (tel: 762-265; fax: 765-661).

Internet sites
Africa Business Network: http://www.ifc.org/abn

AllAfrica.com: http://allafrica.com

African Development Bank: http://www.afdb.org

Information on Morocco – historical events, cities, economy, culture and media: http://www.dsg.ki.se/maroc/

Mbendi AfroPaedia (information on companies, countries, industries and stock exchanges in Africa): http://mbendi.co.za

Menara Yellow Pages (in French): http://www.menara.co.ma/pagejauneHome.asp

Mozambique

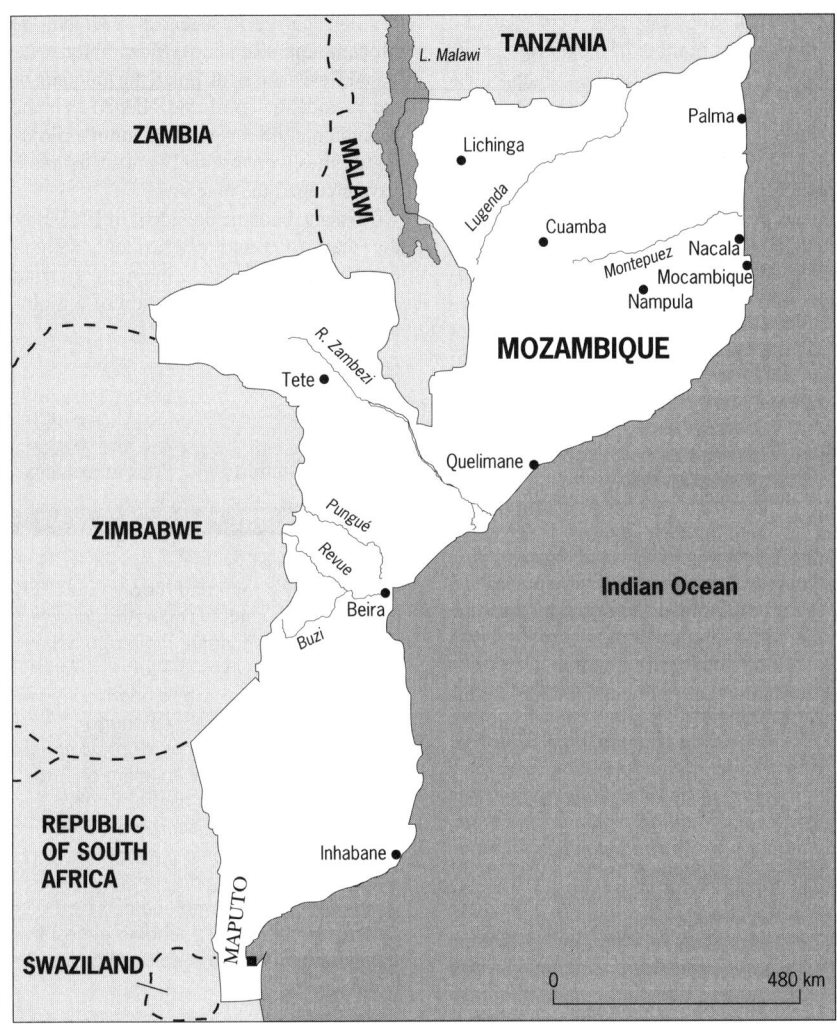

KEY FACTS

Official name: República de Moçambique (Republic of Mozambique)

Head of State: President Armando Guebuza (Frelimo) (sworn in 2 Feb 2005)

Head of government: Prime Minister Luisa Diogo (from 17 Feb 2004)

Ruling party: Frente de Libertação de Moçambique (Frelimo) (Front for the Liberation of Mozambique) (re-elected 1–2 Dec 2004)

Area: 799,380 square km

Population: 18.58 million (2004)

Capital: Maputo

Official language: Portuguese

Currency: Metical (MT) = 100 centavos

Exchange rate: MT24,636.00 per US$ (Oct 2005)

GDP per capita: US$292 (2004)

GDP real growth: 7.80% (2004)

Labour force: 10.01 million (2004)

Unemployment: 21.00% (2003)

Inflation: 12.60% (2004)

Balance of trade: -US$283.50 million 2004

Foreign debt: US$966.00 million (2003)

The Mozambique economy continued to perform well in 2005 despite the spike in petroleum prices, although a severe drought has left about 800,000 people in need of food aid until the next crop season starting in March 2006. Looking ahead, the main challenge will be to maintain high and broad-based economic growth and make further progress in alleviating poverty.

Economy

Under the 2006 fiscal framework, recurrent spending is to be contained in order to ensure that priority spending, especially in the social sector and on infrastructure, can be maintained. Inflows of foreign aid will be allocated to the most economically and socially productive purposes. The agreement transferring majority ownership of the Cahora Bassa dam operating company to Mozambique provides the authorities with the opportunity to pursue infrastructure development of the country.

After Mozambique's impressive performance over the past decade – average growth rate of eight per cent – the country needs a second wave of reforms to deepen and accelerate structural changes to sustain high and broadbased growth.

Increased tax revenues, stronger public sector operations, reducing the costs of doing business, promotion of labour-intensive sectors, and the implementation of a rural development strategy are the key areas. The government is preparing a new Plano de Acção para Redução da Pobreza Absoluta (PARPA) for 2006–10, which is expected to be finalised during the first half of 2006.

The predominant role of the government in the economy has been diminished through an important privatisation programme, a sharp reduction in subsidies and military spending, and the elimination of the central bank financing of the government deficit. The main economic distortions were removed through the liberalisation of most administrative prices, the trade and exchange systems, and interest rate regime.

Private sector development, especially in the agriculture sector, is, however, still constrained by a lack of infrastructure, access to credit due to wide interest rate spreads, high and volatile lending rates and a poor lending environment that partly reflects inefficient judicial procedures for loan recovery and difficulties in obtaining land titles to serve as collateral. The financial system remains small, bank-based, concentrated in urban areas and highly dollarised. The central bank's capacity to supervise the banking system effectively needs strengthening. The cumbersome administrative procedures and rigid labour regulations impose heavy costs on business.

The relatively small and undiversified traditional export sector still cannot fully exploit market access opportunities in developed countries despite preferential agreements. This is due mainly to weak transportation infrastructure and inability to meet quality standards in developed countries.

Export-oriented megaprojects have so far been highly capital-intensive, geared to natural resource exploitation or both. In addition, although the government's investment strategy has been very effective in attracting a number of megaprojects, its granting of privileges to the megaprojects has limited their contribution to government revenue and foreign reserves.

Mozambique's medium-term prospects depend critically on its pursuit of prudent macroeconomic policies and an accelerated pace of structural reforms. The main macroeconomic objectives over the medium term are to maintain a rate of real annual growth between six and eight per cent and to gradually reduce annual inflation to six per cent.

External account developments will continue to be dominated by megaprojects. In particular, total exports will slow down, reflecting mostly a projected decrease in aluminum prices. The current account deficit, before grants, is expected to remain in the range of 13–15 per cent of GDP. It should continue to be covered by foreign aid and higher private capital inflows, mainly related to the two new titanium ore projects. Official international reserves should be kept at more than four months of imports of goods and services.

External and public debt appears sustainable, with the external debt-to-GDP ratio projected at 20 per cent in the next 10 years before declining gradually to 15 per cent in 2025, and the public debt-to-GDP ratio to decline to 37 per cent by 2020.

Politics

President Armando Guebuza, from the ruling Frelimo party, succeeded Mozambique's long-time leader Joaquim Chissano, who stepped down after 18 years in power, in February 2005. The main opposition party, Resistencia Nacional de Moçambique (Renamo) (Mozambique National Resistance), disputed the outcome of the presidential poll and alleged that the election had been rigged. Monitors said irregularities were probably not sufficient to have changed the outcome.

Chissano became president in 1986 after the death of founding president, Samora Machel, and oversaw a move away from Marxism and the introduction of a multi-party constitution.

Risk assessment

Economic	Good
Political	Stable
Regional stability	Poor/improving

COUNTRY PROFILE

Historical profile

Mozambique's recorded history dates from the tenth century when Arab and Indian traders were visiting Sofala to buy gold brought down to the coast by Africans from the Manica hills and the goldfields inland. In 1497 Portugal's Vasco da Gama called at Mozambican ports en route to India. A system of European trade from a few centres on the coast was developed: Mozambique town and island had become the most important of them by the middle of the seventeenth century. Mozambique achieved independence in 1975, ending almost five centuries of Portuguese colonial presence in the country.

In the third century, Bantu tribes settled the area. The Shona empire was established by the eleventh century between the Limpopo and Zambezi rivers.

1498 Portuguese explorer Vasco da Gama landed on the shores of what is now Mozambique.

Portuguese settlements were quickly established, but full-scale colonisation did not begin until the seventeenth century. In the eighteenth and nineteenth centuries, Mozambique served as a major slave-trading centre.

1842 Portugal abolished the slave trade, although the practice continued.

1891 Mozambique's southern and western borders were defined by the British and Portuguese.

1932 Portugal broke up the companies which owned the land and controlled

KEY INDICATORS — Mozambique

	Unit	2000	2001	2002	2003	2004
Population	m	17.69	17.99	18.31	18.44	*18.58
Gross domestic product (GDP)	US$bn	4.80	3.60	3.60	4.30	*5.55
GDP per capita	US$	282	204	197	239	292
GDP real growth	%	1.6	13.9	9.9	7.0	7.8
Inflation	%	12.7	21.9	16.8	10.8	12.6
Exports (fob) (goods)	US$m	364.0	704.0	682.0	880.0	689.4
Imports (fob) (goods)	US$m	1,046.0	1,117.0	1,260.0	1,445.0	972.9
Balance of trade	US$m	-682.0	-413.0	-580.0	-565.0	-283.5
Current account	US$m	-763.6	-850.0	-1,120.0	-527.0	-690.0
Total reserves minus gold	US$m	725.1	715.6	819.2	998.5	1,130.3
Foreign exchange	US$m	725.0	715.5	819.1	998.4	1,130.3
Exchange rate	per US$	15,447	20,704	23,114	23,348	22,581

* estimated figure

Mozambique

trade and imposed direct rule over Mozambique.
1962 The Frente de Libertação de Moçambique (Frelimo) (Front for the Liberation of Mozambique) was established and launched a military campaign for independence.
1975 Mozambique gained independence. A one-party system was implemented with Frelimo as the sole legal party. Mozambican support for the independence war in Rhodesia (Zimbabwe) and the African National Congress (ANC) in South Africa led to frequent reprisals from the governments of those countries. Independence was followed by 16 years of civil war against the rebels of the Resistencia Nacional de Moçambique (Renamo) (Mozambique National Resistance), a guerrilla army supported first by Rhodesia and later by South Africa and the US.
1977 Frelimo adopted Marxism-Leninism as its official doctrine.
1984 Frelimo reached a deal with South Africa in which it would halt its support for the ANC in return for an end to South Africa's aid to Renamo.
1986 President Machel was killed in an airplane crash; Joaquim Chissano became president.
1989 Frelimo formally abandoned Marxism-Leninism in favour of democratic socialism and a market economy. Renamo's support faltered as the civil war was already turning in the government's favour.
1990 A new consititution was promulgated to allow for a multi-party electoral system.
1992 A cease-fire was agreed, followed by a full peace agreement.
1994 In the first multi-party elections, Frelimo won an absolute parliamentary majority. Joaquim Chissano was re-elected president.
1995 Mozambique joined the Commonwealth, the only member not to have been a British colony.
1998 Low turnout for local elections, which were boycotted by the opposition, Renamo, due to flaws in voter registration prompted the government to overhaul the voting procedures for the national elections.
1999 In the second general elections, Joaquim Chissano was re-elected president and Frelimo increased its parliamentary majority.
2000/01 Mozambique was devastated by a tropical cyclone and severe flooding. There was rioting over Renamo allegations that the 1999 elections were rigged; international observers claimed the elections were free and fair.
2003 In the first three months, Cyclone Delfina and Cyclone Japhet caused extensive damage. On 10 July, President Chissano became chairman of the African Union (AU) for one year.
2004 Armando Guebuza (Frelimo) won the 1–2 December presidential elections and Frelimo was re-elected in parliamentary elections.
2005 On 2 February, Armando Guebuza (Frelimo) was sworn in as president. In December a new bridge spanning the Zambezi between Sofala and Zambezia provinces was begun. It is scheduled for completion in 2008.

Political structure
Constitution
The 1975 independence constitution was replaced by the 1990 constitution, which provides for a multi-party system, direct elections and a free market economy.
Form of state
Unitary republic
The executive
The head of state is the president, directly elected for a five-year term, who can be re-elected on only two consecutive occasions, and who governs with his appointed prime minister and Council of Ministers.
National legislature
Legislative power is vested in the 250-seat unicameral Assembleia de la República (Assembly of the Republic), elected by direct universal adult suffrage every five years.
Legal system
Based on Portuguese/Roman law and the 1990 constitution. Since 1996, there has been a Law Reform Commission which has the responsibility for revising legislation.
Last elections
1–2 December 2004 (presidential and parliamentary)
Results: Presidential: Armando Guebuza of the ruling Frelimo won 63.7 per cent of the vote and Afonso Dhlakama of Renamo 31.7 per cent.
Parliamentary: Frelimo won 62 per cent of the vote (160 seats out of 250) and Renamo 29.7 per cent (90). Turnout was 36.3 per cent.
Next elections
2009 (presidential and parliamentary)

Political parties
Ruling party
Frente de Libertação de Moçambique (Frelimo) (Front for the Liberation of Mozambique) (re-elected 1–2 Dec 2004)
Main opposition party
Resistencia Nacional de Moçambique (Renamo) (Mozambique National Resistance)

Population
18.58 million (2004)
Ethnic make-up
Indigenous tribal groups, including Ronga, Shangaan, Chokwe, Manyika, Sena and Makua (99 per cent); European (1 per cent).
Religions
Some 300 registered religions, including traditional beliefs (50 per cent), Christianity (majority Roman Catholic) (30 per cent), Muslim (20 per cent).

Education
Primary education lasts until the aged 13. At this point students attend either a general or technical secondary school. The general school lasts for five years when students graduate for progression into higher education. Technical secondary school lasts for three years with a further two years for advanced courses.
The war devastated the education sector. However, by the end of the 1990s, the primary school network had recovered to levels seen in 1983. In 1999, there were 6,600 first-level primary schools (first to fifth years) attended by 2.1 million children. A third of primary school children attend schools that are so crowded that classes are oversubscribed by over 300 per cent. Educational provision is far worse in the second-level primary schools (sixth and seventh years), with only 440 operating in the entire country. The secondary school sector consists of 81 schools, with fewer than 64,000 students receiving basic secondary education.
There are around 7,000 students enrolled in Mozambique's six university-level institutions and 15,000 in vocational colleges.
Literacy rate: 46.5 per cent total; 31.4 per cent female, adult rates (World Bank).
Compulsory years: 6 to 13
Enrolment rate: 60 per cent gross primary enrolment, 7 per cent gross secondary enrolment; of relevant age group (including repeaters) (World Bank).
Pupils per teacher: 58 in primary schools

Health
With resources targetted at the growing problem of HIV/Aids, other healthcare needs are increasingly neglected. Moreover, the IMF forced the government to abandon its commitment to free healthcare provision and it is estimated that rural Mozambicans must walk an average of 46km to reach the nearest doctor. While modern health services reach around 40 per cent of the population the maternal mortality rate is high, and cholera has been rampant due to poor sanitation. However, mobile medical brigades have formed the backbone of the government's inoculation campaign, with polio virtually eradicated.
HIV/Aids
Mozambique has been one of the countries worst affected by the Aids pandemic which is sweeping Africa. Central

provinces are more affected than southern and northern provinces with infection trends following the major transport routes and areas bordering Zimbabwe, Malawi and Zambia. In the cities of Chimoio and Tete, HIV seroprevalence in pregnant women is over 20 per cent.
HIV prevalence: 12.2 per cent aged 15–49 in 2003 (World Bank)
Life expectancy: 40.7 years (2002) fallen from 45 years 1994–2000 (World Bank).
Fertility rate/Maternal mortality rate: 5.0 births per woman (2003); maternal mortality 1,100 per 100,000 live births (World Bank).
Birth rate/Death rate: 20 deaths and 40 births per 1,000 head of population (World Bank 2002).
Infant mortality rate: 101 per 1,000 live births (World Bank)
Head of population per physician/bed: 0.9 hospital beds per 1,000 people.

Welfare
World Bank figures show 69 per cent of the population live in poverty.
Economic liberalisation, hailed as the driving force behind Mozambique's high growth levels, has also removed the safety nets that existed under the command economy. The minimum wage of US$30 per month is paltry and in many companies even the minimum is not paid and workers often receive their wages weeks or months late. There is no longer a basic ration of subsidised food, leaving many in the growing informal economy with little to eat.

Main cities
Maputo (capital, estimated population 1.1 million in 2004), Matola (489,700), Beira (458,200), Nampula (349,800), Chimoio (197,300), Nacala (182,500), Quelimane (173,100).

Languages spoken
Portuguese is spoken by less than 30 per cent of the population. English is widely spoken in business circles.
There are three main African language groups: Tsonga, Sena-Nyanja, Makua-Lomwe.
Official language/s
Portuguese

Media
Press
The 1990 constitution provides for press freedom. With the opening up of independent newspapers, the share of the civil war-era government newspapers has fallen. The most important media company to arise is the co-operative Mediacoop, which owns the successful *Media Fax*, faxed to hundreds of direct subscribers but read very widely, the periodical *Mozambique Inview* and the weekly *Savana*. Agencia de Informação de Moçambique (AIM) provides a daily bulletin in Portuguese and English and a monthly bulletin in French and English.
Dailies: The main privately owned publications are *Media Fax*, *Imparcial* and *Demos*. The government publishes *Noticias de Moçambique*.
Weeklies: *Tempo* (government), *Savana* (independent) and *Domingo* (government) are the main weeklies in circulation.
Business: Other fax newsletters targetted at businesses include *Metical* and *Correio de Manha*.
Periodicals: *Mozambique Inview* is an independent bi-monthly publication.
Broadcasting
Radio: Each province has its own broadcasting station which transmits programmes in Portuguese and local languages.
Radio Moçambique provides programmes in Portuguese, English and local languages. The programmes consist mainly of light entertainment, interspersed with news and political broadcasts. The only radio broadcaster with national coverage, it is owned by the government but operates independently of the information ministry.
Television: Maputo enjoys several local television stations. These are Radiotelevisão Klint, Radio Televisão de Portugal and the São Paulo, Brazil-based Miramar. Transmission coverage outside the region surrounding Maputo is poor, but there are moves to improve the situation. The national television broadcaster is Televisão de Moçambique (TVM).
Advertising
Television is probably the most effective way of reaching Mozambique's middle classes. Prime time slots are inexpensive and may sell for a few hundred US dollars. Other target groups are avid radio listeners.

Economy
Mozambique has become one of Africa's largest growing destinations for foreign investment, which, supported by donor aid, has spurred a remarkable economic growth since the end of the war. Annual GDP growth is currently around seven per cent.
The economy is primarily agricultural, with farming employing 80 per cent of the working population. The sector provides a large part of export revenues. The main cash crops include sugar and cotton, although these products face problems competing on the international market. Cashew nut production has been hard hit by the closure of the country's cashew nut processing industry due to trade liberalisation and has declined as a cash crop. The sector's contribution to GDP is declining, accounting for around 25 per cent of GDP in 2005, compared with 30 per cent in 1994.
The service sector employs around 10 per cent of the population and consists mainly of the tourist industry, transport, communications and clerical work.
Industry's share of the economy is increasing, contributing 35 per cent of GDP in 2004. The sector employs up to 10 per cent of the population, mainly in food processing (maize and wheat flour, sugar and salt), beverages, aluminium smelting and light industry, such as textiles, soap, batteries, radios and bicycles. It is largely responsible for the continuing expansion of the economy. Mozambique's development is expected to be dominated by mega-projects, such as the Mozal aluminium smelter, the 900km Sasol pipeline from Beira, the Maputo Corridor (project to develop infrastructure between southern Mozambique and South Africa), the Chibuto heavy sand project and others. The economy is diversifying rapidly and transport, metallurgy, manufacturing, energy, tourism, timber and fishing are all growth areas.

External trade
The large visible trade deficit has fallen since 2001 due to an increase in aluminium production and exports.
On 31 December 2002, the US approved Mozambique as being eligible for tariff preferences under the Africa Growth and Opportunities Act (AGOA). The legislation requires that countries are only eligible for greater access to US markets provided they have made continued progress toward a market-based economy, the rule of law, free trade, poverty reduction and the protection of workers' rights. This process is reviewed annually.
Imports
Principal imports are machinery and equipment, vehicles, fuel, chemicals, metal products, foodstuffs and textiles.
Main sources: South Africa (35.7 per cent total, 2004), Australia (10.9 per cent), US (3.7 per cent)
Exports
Principal exports are aluminium, prawns, cashews, cotton, sugar, citrus, timber and bulk electricity.
Main destinations: Belgium (32 per cent total, 2004), Italy (13.9 per cent), Spain (12.6 per cent), Germany (9.8 per cent), Zimbabwe (4.7 per cent)

Agriculture
Farming
The agricultural sector is the mainstay of the economy, employing 80 per cent of the workforce, mainly engaged in subsistence farming, and accounting for around a quarter of GDP. The main cash crops are cashew nuts, tea, sugar, sisal, cotton, copra, tobacco, oil seeds and some citrus

fruits. Maize is the main subsistence crop, but cassava, millet, sorghum, groundnuts, beans and rice are also grown.

Some 45 per cent of the land area is considered suitable for agriculture, but only 4 per cent of that is under cultivation. Most production is carried out through rain-fed farming and much continues to be done by hand, with only 7 per cent of farmers using traction (animal or mechanical) and only 2 per cent using fertilisers and pesticides. The agricultural sector is dominated by peasant family smallholdings, which occupy 90 per cent of the total cultivated area. Only 5 per cent of cultivated land is used by commercial operations, which grow cash or export crops. There is significant large potential for foreign investment in the agriculture sector due to the fertility and availability of unused cultivatable land.

Peace, good rains and an increase in the area under cultivation have resolved the chronic food deficit seen in the 1980s. However, food stocks are low and most families do not produce enough to build up a reserve of food and money that would see them through a bad harvest. Floods and drought in 2000–03 have revealed the level of the country's dependence on international food aid in times of crisis. In 2002, the UN's World Food Programme (WFP) estimated that over 500,000 people in the south and central districts were facing severe food insecurity. The ongoing structural adjustment programme has exacerbated problems associated with fragile marketing systems and poor infrastructure. The state marketing body intervenes in the market in order to pay farmers for crops they have been unable to sell, either due to low prices on the open market or because the transport infrastructure is too poor. However, with bank credit scarce and with a reluctance of international financial institutions to support marketing boards, the state has been unable to fulfil its role completely. This has encouraged the growth of unscrupulous middlemen who demand lower farm gate prices.

The estimated crop production for 2004 included: 1,812,100 tonnes (t) cereals in total, 1,248,000t maize, 6,150,000t cassava, 48,000t millet, 80,000t potatoes, 66,000t sweet potatoes, 314,000t sorghum, 201,000t rice, 90,000t bananas, 205,000t pulses, 265,000t coconuts, 30,500t citrus fruit, 28,900t fibre crops, 58,000t treenuts, 87,500t oilcrops, 12,000t tobacco, 600t green coffee, 24,000t mangoes, 400,000t sugar cane, 10,500t tea, 43,000t papayas, 334,500t fruit in total, 116,700t vegetables in total. Estimated livestock production included: meat in total, 90,000t meat in total, 38,100t beef, 12,840t pig meat, 2,712t lamb and goat meat, 40,398t poultry, 14,000t eggs, 68,765t milk, 390t honey, 5,080t cattle hides.

Fishing
Fishing is of increasing importance. Prawns have become one of the sector's main exports. Mozambique's sustainable fish catch is estimated at 500,000 tonnes, including 300,000 tonnes of anchovy. The sustainable catch of prawns is estimated at 14,000 tonnes. Inland fish farming, especially of prawns, has been developed and is expected to contribute substantially to a 7.7 per cent rise in production in 2005.

Forestry
There is an important forestry sector, based on the exploitation of hardwoods from Zambezia, Sofala, Nampula, Manica and Niassa provinces. Almost 50 per cent of land is categorised as other wooded land. Wood fuel comprises almost 80 per cent of the country's energy needs. A wide variety of non-wood forest products includes grass, bamboo, medicinal plants and other wild edible plants. Forestry resources are exploited on a more systematic basis than previously and the government compels timber concerns to initiate reforestation programmes. Overall, Mozambique has an estimated one million hectares (ha) of productive woodland. The government-owned Industrias Florestais de Manica (Ifloma), which manages 20,000ha of forest, has established a sawmill and particle-board factory with Swedish government and Arab fund assistance.

Industry and manufacturing
During the 1980s and 1990s, government policy emphasised the production of consumer goods, especially food, beverages and textiles, where supplies can be locally sourced, in an attempt to reduce import dependency and strengthen the market for peasant farmers producing cash crops. However, industry suffered from capital shortages, poor infrastructure and the high cost of credit. Manufacturers rely largely on internal funding from operating profits or owner savings. Recent metallurgical investments promise a dramatic departure from Mozambique's import substituting industrialisation strategy. The greatest problems have occurred in the food processing industry, with cashew nut and sugar production particularly hit. Cashew nut prices have plummeted due to increased output in India, where production is more cost-effective and tree-planting has increased. India intends to become self-sufficient in cashew nuts, dealing a big blow to this important sector in Mozambique. The situation has been exacerbated by the damaging policy of trade liberalisation demanded by the World Bank, which had originally advised Mozambique to stop processing cashew nuts domestically, close down the processing factories and export unshelled nuts to India.

Sugar refining is another industry which was in the doldrums. Mozambican sugar mills were severely affected by the civil war, which virtually wiped out the industry. Foreign investment, mostly from South African companies such as Illovo, has been the driving force behind the rehabilitation of the sector.

By far the most important industrial project in Mozambique is the Mozal aluminium smelter. The plant is owned by BHP-Billiton (the leading shareholder), Mitsubishi, South Africa's Industrial Development Corporation (IDC) and the Mozambican government. The US$1.2 billion smelter is one of the largest industrial projects in sub-Saharan Africa and began production in June 2000, six months ahead of schedule. Mozal is already the world's cheapest producer of aluminium, and costs will fall as capacity is increased. The completion of the project will lead to around US$800 million in aluminium exports per year, increasing total exports by over 300 per cent of 2000 levels and adding up to 20 per cent to GDP. However, most of the profits from the smelter will be repatriated by its foreign investors and since it is highly capital intensive, it will not have a significant impact on employment. Although Mozal appears as a success story for Mozambique's development, it will have a limited long-term role in alleviating poverty and generating growth in other sectors.

Tourism
The sector has not played a significant role in the economy, due to the impact of the war. There is potential for the development of tourism in the south-eastern coastal region, where the beaches are attracting visitors as well as investment, especially from South Africa. The government is interested in developing high-value, low volume tourism and is rehabilitating the national parks. The first to reopen, the Maputo Elephant Park, is intended to with nature reserves and parks in neighbouring countries to form a transfrontier conservation and tourism zone.

Mining
Mining is limited to gold in Manica province, pegmatites, ilmenite, zircon, rutile, monazite, tantalum, copper, marble and semi-precious stones. The sector is small and typically contributes to 1.4 per cent of exports and less than 0.25 per cent of GDP.

There are around 50,000 artisan miners who concentrate their operations on gold and gemstone extraction. Kenmare Resources has two gold licences in Niassa, with reserves of 200,000 ounces. Kenmare also has a licence for the titanium reserves at Congolone, which is considered one of the most valuable undeveloped titanium mines in the world. In mid-2003, the company announced it was investing US$200 million in developing the reserves to produce ilmenite, rutile and zircon by 2005. The titanium reserves near Xai-Xai, about 250km north of Maputo, have the potential to develop a second large mineral smelter project in the region. There are considerable secondary mineral resources, including iron, graphite, fluorites, mica, lime clays, tin, nickel and bauxite. There has been little foreign interest in developing these resources.

Hydrocarbons
There are no known reserves of oil in Mozambique. The government believes that there is oil in the Rovuma basin and elsewhere and in 2005 appealed to major petroleum companies to engage in exploration. Mozambique relies entirely on refined oil imports, mainly from South Africa, and consumes 8,200 barrels of oil per day.

There are substantial reserves of gas. There are three onshore gas fields: Pande, Temane and Buzi-Divinhe. Pande has reserves of 59 billion cubic metres (CUM); Temane has 28 billion cum; and Buzi-Divinhe has 281 million cum. Mozambique is likely to become a major gas producer in the region. An 865km pipeline to export gas to South Africa was opened in 2004.

Coal is mined at Moatize in Tete province. Proven coal reserves are approximately six billion tonnes.

Energy
Mozambique is one of the largest energy producers in the Southern African Development Community (SADC). A large proportion of the country's electricity supply is produced by one coal-fired power station. The Cahora Bassa dam produces electricity for export to South Africa. With considerable potential in hydroelectric power and gas-fired power stations, there is a distinct possibility that Mozambique will become an electricity exporter in years to come. However, with only 5 per cent of households connected to the electricity supply, there is room for improving domestic supply.

New generating plants are scheduled to begin operations by 2006. These include the Moatize thermal power station (1,000MW), the expansion of the Cahora Bassa hydroelectric plant (550MW) and the Mepanda Uncuna hydroelectric station (2,500MW). The construction of new dams is facing mounting domestic and international opposition. With flooding becoming a regular occurrence, many ecologists believe dams pose a significant threat to farming communities, particularly when dams release flood waters.

Financial markets
The listing of enterprises has seen slow and modest growth, although the privatisation programme will provide potential for growth.

Stock exchange
The Bolsa de Valores de Moçambique (BVM) (Mozambique Stock Exchange) opened in October 1999.

Banking and insurance
All banks in Mozambique are privately owned, with more foreign competition entering the sector with the completion of the bank privatisation process in January 2002 when Banco Austral was sold to Absa.

Central bank
Banco de Moçambique, with branches throughout the country.

Main financial centre
Maputo

Time
GMT plus two hours

Geography
Mozambique lies on the east coast of Africa, south of the equator. It is bordered by Tanzania to the north; Malawi, Zambia and Zimbabwe to the west; South Africa and Swaziland to the south and south-west; and by the Indian Ocean to the east (2,470km of coastline).

The country is divided into the coastal lowlands and plateaux (200–600 metres over most of the central region and north, reaching 1,000 metres in the north-west). The country is crossed by a large number of rivers, including the Zambezi (navigable for 460km), the Limpopo and the Save.

Climate
Mozambique has two main seasons: a hot, normally wet season from October to March and a cooler, mostly dry season from April to September.

In the extreme south the mean annual temperature is around 23 degrees Celsius (C), with a difference of about 8 degrees C between the hottest and coldest months. In the north the mean annual temperature is about 25 degrees C. The temperature in Maputo is influenced by the direction of the wind and wide variations are experienced, especially during the cool season. Temperatures in Maputo can reach as high as 45 degrees C. Most rain falls in the second half of the hot season. Northern regions receive 640–1,280mm and southern regions may receive 260–1,540mm. The average is 770mm.

Dress codes
During the hot wet season (October–March) light cotton clothes are advisable. During the temperate dry season (April–September) light or medium weight clothing should suffice. Warmer clothing is required for frequent cold spells.

Entry requirements
Passports
Required by all. Passports must be valid for a minimum of six months beyond the intended date of departure.
Visa
Required by all. UK tourists may obtain visas at the Ressano Garcia (South Africa) and Namaacha (Swaziland) borders, as well as Maputo airport. Business visas, valid for a 30-days stay, must be obtained well in advance of arrival. Application forms should include a business letter from the visitor's company and include an itinerary.
Prohibited entry
Foreign nationals who had the status of 'National of Mozambique' before 25 Jun 1975, except those with documentation proving renunciation of this status within 90 days of that date.
Currency advice/regulations
Import/export of local currency prohibited. Unlimited import of foreign currency is allowed but amounts must be declared on arrival. Export of foreign currency is limited to the amount declared on arrival. It is advisable to take travellers cheques or currency in US dollars or South African rand. Travellers entering Mozambique have to fill out a statement detailing the amount of currency in bank notes, cheques and travellers cheques being brought into the country. The declaration is passed over to the Exchange Control Office at the point of entry.
Prohibited imports
Narcotics. A permit is required for firearms.

Health (for visitors)
Mandatory precautions
Yellow fever certificate if arriving from an infected area.
Advisable precautions
Cholera is a serious risk in the country and vaccination is advisable. Typhoid, polio, tetanus and hepatitis 'A' vaccinations are also advised. Hepatitis 'B' and 'E' are present in Mozambique. Malaria prophylaxis is essential as risk exists throughout the country, and cerebral malaria occurs in some places. There is a risk of rabies. Water precautions are advisable, especially in the rural areas where bilharzia is present. Some milk is unpasteurised and should be boiled. Avoid dairy products

and only eat well-cooked hot meat and fish. Vegetables must be cooked and fruit peeled.

Medical facilities are minimal and many medicines are not available. Carry basic medical supplies, medicines and sterile syringes. Full medical insurance is essential. Insurance cover which provides for medical evacuation by air to South Africa is extremely advisable.

Hotels
Reasonable accommodation is available in Maputo. Bills must be paid in hard currency or by American Express credit card. Tipping is permitted.

Public holidays
Fixed dates
1 Jan (New Year's Day), 3 Feb (Heroes' Day), 7 Apr (Day of the Mozambican Woman), 1 May (Workers' Day), 25 Jun (Independence Day), 7 Sep (Lusaka Agreement Day), 25 Sep (Armed Forces' Day), 25 Dec (National Family/Christmas Day).

Working hours
Banking
Mon–Fri: 0745–1130.
Business
Mon–Thu: 0730–1230, 1400–1730; Fri: 0730–1230, 1400–1700.
Government
Mon–Thu: 0730–1230, 1400–1730; Fri: 0730–1230, 1400–1700.
Shops
Mon–Fri: 0800–1230; 1400–1800; Sat: 0800–1330.

Electricity supply
220 V AC, 50 cycles.

Social customs/useful tips
The courtesies and modes of address customary in Portugal and other Latin countries are still observed. Visitors are normally addressed as O Senhor. Occasionally *camarada* (comrade) is used, but this is not correct outside the circles of the ruling party, Frente de Libertaçao de Moçambique (Frelimo), and is discouraged.

Security
Street crime is an increasingly serious problem, with armed robbery prevalent in Maputo. Visitors should not carry or display cash or jewellery, and are advised not to venture outside well-lit, busy streets. Unfamiliar areas and downtown Maputo at night are certainly to be avoided. Female visitors should not walk unaccompanied along any beaches in Mozambique. Visitors should check conditions with the local authorities before travelling outside major urban areas and should be aware that Mozambique has a severe problem with landmines left over from the conflict between Frelimo and Renamo. Travel by convoy is advisable, as in addition to mines, there is the risk of theft of vehicles at gunpoint.

Identity documents should be carried at all times.

Getting there
Air
National airline: Linhas Aéreas de Moçambique (LAM) (Mozambique Airlines)
International airport/s: Maputo International (MPM), 3km north of Maputo. Airport facilities include bank, restaurant, bar, snack bar, car hire and post. Beira (BEW), 13km from the city, receives flights from Europe, other African countries and the US. Airport facilities include restaurant, shops and a post office.
Visitors should arrange to be met at the airport on arrival.
Airport tax: Departures: US$20 (intercontinental flights only), US$10 (intracontinental flights only); not applicable for transit passengers.
Surface
Road: Road access is possible from all neighbouring countries except Tanzania; good paved roads from South Africa and Zimbabwe. The condition of roads in Mozambique is poor and banditry along major highways threatens the safety of road travellers. Travel outside Maputo often requires four-wheel drive vehicles.
Rail: Rail services can be sporadic and unreliable. Six times a week there is a train from Johannesburg to the Mozambique border at Komatipoort where there is a connection to Maputo (journey time 15 hours). There is an overnight train from Durban to Maputo. A service runs from Harare to Beira. There are connections from Malawi to Beira but the border has to be crossed on foot.
Water: There are no regular passenger services.
Main port/s: Beira, Maputo, Nacala and Quelimane.

Getting about
National transport
Be aware of the situation in the area you are visiting, and remember that landmines are still present.
Air: Travel between major cities within Mozambique is best by air, although flights are heavily booked. LAM operates domestic service to main towns. Local and charter flights can also be obtained from TTA and other companies with offices at Maputo Airport. Metavia has light planes operating a shuttle service between Maputo and Nelspruit. There is little night-time flying.
Road: There are an estimated 29,810km of roads in Mozambique. Good roads connect Maputo to Xai-Xai, Maputo to Juchoke, Maputo to Beira, Maxixe to Vilanchulo, Nampula to Nacala, Beira to Chimoio and Beira to Tete. The surface of other roads varies.
Buses: There are services covering most parts of the country but are restricted by the state of the roads.
Rail: There is no single rail network. Instead there are three networks: one in the south (Maputo to Swaziland, South Africa and Zimbabwe), one in the centre (Beira to Zimbabwe and Malawi) and one in the north (Nacala to Malawi and to Lichinga). These systems are not connected since the Portuguese did not build any trunk lines north-south. There are also some isolated branch lines (Xai-Xai to Manjacase; Inhambane to Inharrime; and Quelimane to Mocuba)
City transport
Taxis: Available in almost every city, taxis are metered but for long journeys fares should be negotiated. A 10 per cent tip is usual. Taxis are rarely available at the airport.
Car hire
Car rental is available from airports or hotels. A car and driver can be hired by the hour or day. Only hard currency will be accepted. International licence required. Traffic drives on the left. Driving after dark can be hazardous due to other vehicles travelling without headlights.

BUSINESS DIRECTORY
The addresses listed below are a selection only. While World of Information makes every endeavour to check these addresses, we cannot guarantee that changes have not been made, especially to telephone numbers and area codes. We would welcome any corrections.

Telephone area codes
The international dialling code (IDD) for Mozambique is +258 followed by the area code and subscriber's number:

Beira	3	Maputo	1
Chokwe	21	Nampula	6

Chambers of Commerce
American-Mozambique Chamber of Commerce, Rua Mateus Sansão Muthemba 452, Maputo (tel: 492-904; fax: 492-779; e-mail: mail@mail.ccmusa.co.mz).

Mozambique Camara de Comercio, Rua Mateus Sansão Muthemba 452, Maputo (tel: 491-970; fax: 492-211).

Portugal-Mozambique Chamber of Commerce, Hotel Rovuma Centro de Escritórios, Rua da Sé 114, Maputo (tel: 300-229; fax: 300-232; e-mail: ccpmoc@teledata.mz).

South Africa-Mozambique Chamber of Commerce, FACIM, Avenida 10 de Novembro, Maputo (tel/fax: 431-621).

Nations of the World: A Political, Economic and Business Handbook

Banking
Banco Comercial do Moçambique, PO Box 865, Av 25 de Setembro 1800, Maputo (tel: 307-533, 307-471, 307-532; fax: 307-564/557/543).

Banco Internacional de Moçambique SARL, Av Zedequias Manganhela 478, Maputo (tel: 429-390/3; fax: 429-389).

Banco Standard Totta de Moçambique SARL, PO Box 2086, Praça 25 de Junho Nr 1, Maputo (tel: 423-041/5, 424-405, 301-616; fax: 426-967, 423-029).

Banco de Fomento SARL; Av. Julius Nyerere 1016, Maputo (tel. 494-010/1; fax: 494-401).

Banco de Moçambique, PO Box 423, Av 25 de Setembro 1679, Maputo (tel: 428-150/9; fax: 429-721).

BIM Investimento SARL, Av Kim III Sung 961, Maputo (tel: 490-085/7; fax: 490-212; e-mail: bimi@vircom.com).

BNP Nedbank (Mocambique) SARL, PO Box 1445, Prédio 33 Andares; Av 25 de Setembro 1230, Maputo (tel: 306-700; fax: 306-305; e-mail: bnpnebank@bnpnedbank.co.mz).

Novo Banco SARL, Av.do Trabalho, 750-Sede, Maputo (tel: 407-755/6, 408-209; fax: 407-755/6, 408-210; e-mail: novobanco@teledata.mz).

Uniao Comercial de Bancos (Moçambique) SARL, Av. Fredrich Engels 400, Maputo (tel: 499-900, 495-221-5 fax: 498-675; e-mail: banque_fc@teledata.mz).

Central bank
Banco de Moçambique, Avenida 25 de Setembro 1695, PO Box 423, Maputo, Mozambique (tel: 428-150 fax: 429-721; e-mail: cdi@bancomoc.mz).

Travel information
Aeroporto de Maputo (Linhas Aéreas de Moçambique), CP 2060, Maputo (tel: 465-026, 465-137, fax: 735-601, 465-564).

Empresa Nacional de Turismo (ENT) (Mozambique National Tourism Company), CP 417, Praca dos Trabalhadores 9, Maputo (tel: 421-305, 427-191; fax: 430-181).

Hotel and Tourism Business Association, Maputo (tel: 425-562).

Linhas Aereas de Moçambique, Aeroporto de Mavalane, CP 965, Maputo (tel: 465-561/9).

Transportes e Trabalhos Aéreos (TTA) (air taxi services, etc), PO Box 2054, Aeroporto de Mavalane, Maputo (tel: 465-292, 465-028).

Ministries
Ministry of Commerce, Industry and Tourism, Praça do 25 Junho 37, Maputo (tel: 426-091/7).

Ministry of Finance and Planning, Praça da Marinha Popular, CP 272, Maputo (tel: 420-648; fax: 425-240).

Ministry of Industry and Energy, Avenida 25 de Setembro, PO Box 2904, 1502 Maputo (tel: 420-963, 492-011).

Ministry of Trade, PO Box 1831, Maputo (tel: 426-091/7; fax: 421-305).

Other useful addresses
Agência de Informação de Moçambique (AIM), CP 896, Maputo (tel: 430-795).

Agência Nacional de Frete e Navegação (ANFRENA) (main national shipping agency), Rua Consiglieri Pedroson 366, CP 1430, Maputo (tel: 427-064, 428-111).

BP Mozambique, PO Box 854, Maputo (tel: 425-021/5; fax: 426-042).

British Council, Travessa da Catembe 21 (corner of Av Martires de Inhaminga 1421), CP 4178, Maputo (tel: 421-571; fax: 421-577).

British Embassy, Av Vladimir I Lenine 310, CP 55, Maputo (tel: 420-111/2/5/6/7; fax: 421-666).

Commonwealth Development Corporation, Maputo (tel: 421-325; fax: 422-150).

Direcção Nacional Portos e Caminhos de Ferro (railways), PO Box 276, Maputo (tel: 420-748, 424-133, 430-151).

Empresa Nacional de Minas, PO Box 1152, Maputo (tel: 423-933).

Empresa Nacional de Portos e Caminhos de Ferro de Moçambique, Maputo (tel: 427-173).

Empresa Nacional Petroleos de Moçambique (Petromoc), PO Box 417, Maputo (tel: 427-191/7).

FACIM, PO Box 1761, Maputo (tel: 423-713, 427-151/2; fax: 427-129) (annual international trade fair).

Hidroelectrica de Cabora Bassa (HCB) (operators of Cabora Bassa power complex), Head Office, CP 263, Songo, Tete (tel: 82-221/4; fax: 82-364); PO Box 4120, Maputo (tel: 400-551, 400-647, 491-346, 492-976).

Imprensa Nacional de Moçambique (publishes statistical bulletins, census information etc), PO Box 275, Maputo.

Maputo Development Corridor, Maputo (tel: 426-359; fax: 430-159).

Mozambique Embassy (USA), Suite 570, 1990 M Street, NW, Washington DC 20036 (tel: 202-293-7146; fax: 202-835-0245; e-mail: embamoc@aol.com).

Mozambique Institute of Export Promotion (IPEX) (Government agency for export promotion), Av 25 de Setembro 1008, PO Box 4487, Maputo (tel: 423-343).

Office for Foreign Investment Promotion (GPIE), Av 25 de Setembro 2049, 2 andar, PO Box 2049, Maputo (tel: 422-456/7; fax: 422-459).

Radio Moçambique, PO Box 2000, Maputo (tel: 434-041/5, 432-591; fax: 421-816).

Technical Unit for Enterprise Restructuring (UTRE) (information on company tenders for privatisation and investment opportunities), Ministry of Planning and Finance, Rua da Imprensa No 256, 7th Floor, Suites 704-708, PO Box 4350, Maputo (tel: 426-514/6; fax: 421-541).

Televisão de Moçambique, Av Julius Nyerere 942, PO Box 2675, Maputo (tel: 491-198).

World Bank, Maputo (tel: 492-841; fax: 492-893).

Internet sites
Africa Business Network: http://www.ifc.org/abn

AllAfrica.com: http://allafrica.com

African Development Bank: http://www.afdb.org

Africa Online: http://www.africaonline.com

Harambee Afrika (UK business club for traders with east, central and southern Africa; includes annotated web resource list): http://www.harambee.co.uk

Mbendi AfroPaedia (information on companies, countries, industries and stock exchanges in Africa): http://mbendi.co.za

Myanmar

For forty years Myanmar has been a military dictatorship, guilty of some of the most prolific human rights abuses, and ostracised by most of the international community. The US, which still uses the country's former name of Burma, named it as an 'outpost of tyranny' at the beginning of 2005.

A human rights disaster

Myanmar's list of human rights abuses is one of the longest in the world. Aung San Suu Kyi, winner of the 1991 Nobel Prize for Peace, is undergoing her third stint of house arrest. She has now been detained for a total of 10 years. Theoretically, she leads the National League for Democracy (NLD), which won an overwhelming 80 per cent majority in the 1990 elections. However, Suu Kyi is incommunicado and her party was prevented from taking office after their victory in the polls. The *junta* forcibly prevents democratic practices such as the right to assemble and freedom of expression, and seeks to destroy the NLD.

The *junta* is intent upon what has been called 'Burmanisation': it is purging ethnic groups, displacing them from the land, as armed groups attack civilians, and carry out rapes and executions.

Ethnic groups are used as slave labour and even child slave labour is rife. In 10 years 2,700 villages, home to ethnic Karen groups, have been bulldozed. Fleeing residents have ended up in temporary camps in dire conditions.

In May 2005 the Western press carried allegations that the Myanmar army has been using chemical warfare in their latest attacks on ethnic rebel groups. Eyewitnesses reported how yellowish smoke emerged from fired shells and those attacked suffered a variety of medical symptoms such as burning and itching eyes, skin lesions and chest pains. Myanmar is strongly suspected of having chemical and biological capabilities.

The July 2005 meeting of Association of Southeast Asian Nations (Asean) was dominated by calls for Suu Kyi's release. In June 2005 neighbouring nations applied pressure on the Myanmar authorities to force them to renounce floating leadership of Asean in mid-2006 on the grounds of the *junta*'s human rights abuses – which would prevent EU leaders from participating in negotiations with Asean. The US and Japan declined to send their top-ranking representatives to the Asean security conference. Myanmar eventually conceded to pressure and ceded its proposed chairmanship, saying that the country needed to concentrate on internal law and order. By giving a platform to Myanmar the regional association would have risked its credibility. However the intervention does contradict the Asean agreement to not meddle in each other's domestic affairs.

The former prime minister, Khin Nyunt, was arrested on corruption charges in July 2005. Nyunt is thought to have been forced out of the ruling *junta* the previous year. The official word on his departure, in October 2004, was that he was retiring for 'health reasons'. This excuse was universally seen as a smokescreen: the real cause for Nyunt's ejection was understood to be the conflict between him and the hard-line military chief Than Shwe. Nyunt was, in strictly relative terms, a more progressive figure, willing to discuss the fate of Suu Kyi, and plans for democratic change, and more informed about international affairs.

In November 2005 the Geneva-based organisation, Global Fund, decided to withdraw US$98 million of funding for health projects in the military dictatorship. The Myanmar government strongly condemned the decision, which will affect thousands of HIV/Aids, TB and malaria sufferers. Over half a million people are thought to have the HIV virus in Myanmar. Global Fund contended that with new travel restrictions on heath workers, it would become difficult to track their own funding and evaluate the projects satisfactorily. It is likely that US pressure was also behind the Fund's dissociation with the controversial state. The UK's Department for International Development (DfID), however, took a different line. It condemned the Global Fund's retreat and issued a statement saying that disease was so serious that 'we can't wait for a change in the political context'.

KEY FACTS

Official name: Myanmar Naingngandaw (The Union of Myanmar)

Head of State: Chairman of the SPDC Senior General Than Shwe

Head of government: Prime Minister Lt General Soe Win (appointed 19 Oct 2004)

Ruling party: State Peace and Development Council (SPDC) (19-member military *junta* since Nov 1997)

Area: 676,552 square km

Population: 52.81 million (2004)

Capital: Pyinmana (from November 2005)

Official language: Myanmar

Currency: Kyat (Kt) = 100 pyas

Exchange rate: Kt6.42 per US$ (Oct 2005)

GDP per capita: US$167 (2004)

GDP real growth: 5.00% (2004); *4.5% (2005)

Labour force: 27.46 million (2004)

Unemployment: 5.20% (2004)

Inflation: 9.00% (2004)

Balance of trade: US$383.00 million (2004)

Foreign debt: US$6.10 billion (2003)

Annual FDI: US$95.30 million (2003)

* estimated figure

Nations of the World: A Political, Economic and Business Handbook

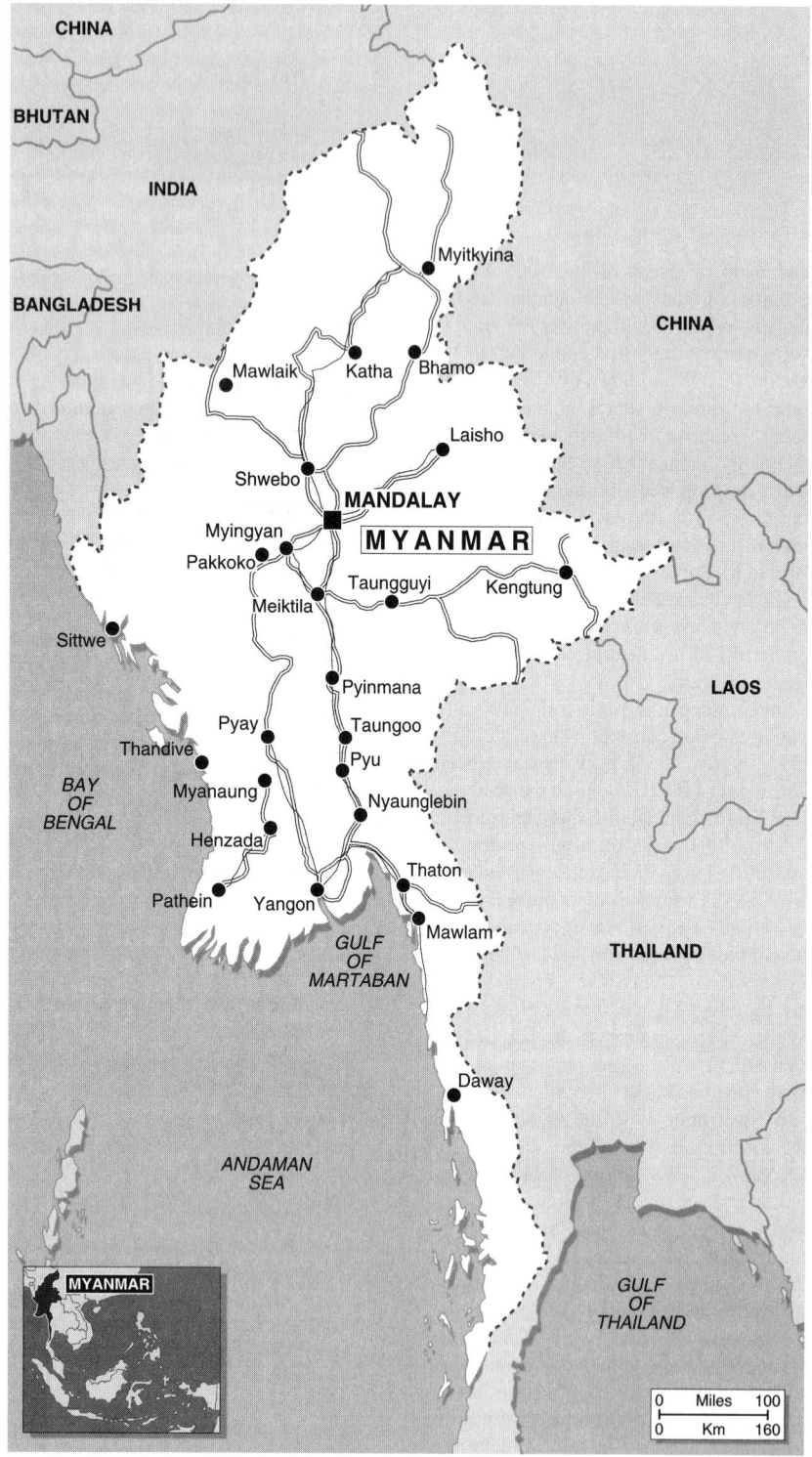

on neighbouring South-east Asian countries to help press the need for peace and democracy. While America has tried to freeze Myanmar out of the international community and has imposed economic sanctions, Thailand has co-operated in the hope of facilitating an eventual adoption of democracy.

The EU have introduced some limits on investment in Myanmar but the NLD and other pro-democracy activists advocate the levying of more serious economic sanctions.

The *junta* has held the reins of power for over 40 years and is clinging to them tightly for fear of the imprisonment of its generals once it loosens its grip. The former prime minister of Malaysia has suggested that these commanders be granted judicial immunity to encourage them to allow the introduction of democracy.

Escalation of tensions

In May 2005 multiple bombs ripped through crowded shopping malls and conference centres in what was then the capital, Yangon (Pyinmana was named the capital in 2005). Over twenty people were killed in the explosions, which, the *junta* said were carried out by foreign-trained ethnic groups belonging to the All Burma Students Democratic Front. After the attacks the information minister Kyaw Hsan issued a statement claiming that behind the bombs was 'a world famous organisation of a certain superpower nation'. Hsan was widely believed to mean the CIA and the United States.

The ruling *junta* is comprised of ethnic Burmese and ethnic minorities, who are engaged in a power struggle and semi-permanent in-fighting. The expulsion of the former prime minister, Khin Nyunt, fanned the flames of internal unrest. He was arrested alongside two of his sons and many of his officials. Nyunt was relatively sympathetic to the claims of ethnic rebels. His demise has angered ethnic groups and has seriously ruptured the cease-fire agreed with the *junta*. There has been a growing realisation that 'none of the things the cease-fire groups asked for were accepted', as Harn Yaung Hwe, of the Europe-Burma Centre, said. The Karen National Union and the Shan State Army North have both stepped up hostilities. Shan politicians as well as those from the NLD were arrested and there were reports of four deaths in custody in the first half of 2005.

Economy

GDP growth was expected to be 4.5 per cent in 2005. While this is a respectable

In December 2005 international frustration and criticism intensified. Asean urged military leaders to relinquish authoritarian control, respect human rights and allow democratic change. The foreign minister of Malaysia announced plans to inspect the political situation for himself. There has been talk of expelling Myanmar from Asean if they continue to defy foreign demands, although there is no framework for dismissing a member from the association.

America is one of the most vocal critics of the military regime. US secretary of state Condoleezza Rice lamented in July 2005 that 'there seems never to be progress' in the country's human rights arena and called

figure, future prospects are not good. Many countries are retreating from economic ties and investment with the country because of its poor human rights reputation. As a result many garment factories have closed.

China, however, has no such scruples and is likely to be a large investor in coming years. Already 100 Chinese timber companies are involved in logging activities in Myanmar. There are estimates that 95 per cent of Myanmar timber shipments to China were illegal, meaning that the much-needed sum of US$250 million is sidelining the Myanmar fiscal system.

Half the budget is spent on the military, with very low rates of investment in social welfare.

In June 2005 the ruling *junta* repossessed the commercial Myanmar Universal Bank and surrounded all branches with soldiers to prevent people withdrawing their savings. It was a sudden and unexplained takeover which will seriously undermine the country's financial sector.

A new capital

In November 2005 the Myanmar military suddenly decided to relocate the national capital from Yangon to an isolated compound near Pyinmana, a town in the centre of the country. Brigadier General Kyaw Hsan promoted the new capital as a place with better transportation links. Mountains enclose and tower over the new capital, a strategic location for a reclusive military regime fearful of US attacks. Civil servants were threatened with treason charges if they opposed the relocation. At the time of the move, Pyinmana was not much more than a building site.

Outlook

Amnesty International claimed that human rights were 'deteriorating' in November 2005. The military seem to be stepping up its intimidation and authoritarian tactics.

GDP growth is expected to fall to 3.5 per cent in 2006 although China will prove to be an important economic ally.

Risk assessment

Economy	Poor
Politics	Poor
Regional stability	Poor

COUNTRY PROFILE

Historical profile
Burma (Myanmar) was annexed to British India in the nineteenth century.
1937 Burma became a separate British dependency, with limited self government.
1942 Japan invaded and occupied the country.
1945 Burmese nationalists helped Allied forces to re-occupy the country.
1948 The Union of Burma became independent outside the Commonwealth, with U Nu as the first prime minister.
1962 U Nu was overthrown in a coup led by Ne Win. The Revolutionary Council suspended the constitution and instituted authoritarian control through the Burma Socialist Programme Party (BSPP).
1964 Political parties were outlawed.
1973 A new constitution was approved. BSPP became the only authorised political party and the country's name was changed to the Socialist Republic of the Union of Burma.
1974 The revolutionary council was dissolved and Ne Win was elected president by the state council.
1978 An election gave Ne Win the mandate for four more years in power.
1988 A military government, the State Law and Order Restoration Council (SLORC), took power in September, ending months of unrest. It took over the function of the former ruling party, the BSPP, and the parliament, or Pyithu Hluttaw.
1989 The change of name from Burma to Myanmar was claimed to be for the benefit of the minority, non-Burmese sections of the population.
1990 The government fulfilled its promise to hold multi-party elections, but said a new constitution must be brought into effect before power could be transferred to the victorious National League for Democracy (NLD), led by Aung Sang Suu Kyi.
1996 The law and order situation deteriorated and open conflict erupted. SLORC closed the universities and detained protesters.
1997 Bomb attacks were aimed at leading SLORC figures. Several thousand Karen National Union (KNU) ethnic minority refugees were forced across the Thai border leading to international protests when refugees were killed by SLORC forces. The US imposed economic sanctions, banning investments by US companies. The Association of Southeast Asian Nations (Asean) admitted Myanmar as a full member of the Association. A governing military junta, formed by the top four SLORC leaders, was named the State Peace and Development Council (SPDC).
1998 The SPDC detained some 110 leading members of the NLD.
1999 Madame Aung Sang Suu Kyi was physically isolated from her supporters by the authorities, who, early in the year, refused her dying husband a visa to come and visit her for the last time. The International Labour Organisation (ILO) banned Myanmar from its activities until it ceases using forced labour.
2001 The military junta approached Aung San Suu Kyi to arrange talks – the first contact in five years. President Jiang Zemin of China visited Myanmar – the first Chinese head of state to visit the country since the military junta seized power in 1988.
2002 Aung San Suu Kyi (NLD) was released from house arrest.
2003 In April, the military junta introduced a new rice trading policy, totally removing the government's control of rice, which it had held for the previous 40

KEY INDICATORS — Myanmar

	Unit	2000	2001	2002	2003	2004
Population	m	47.75	48.30	48.97	50.89	*52.81
Gross domestic product (GDP)	US$bn	6.00	4.70	4.41	6.72	–
GDP per capita	US$	122	97	90	132	167
GDP real growth	%	6.2	5.4	5.5	5.1	5.0
Inflation	%	10.3	21.1	46.9	40.0	9.0
Unemployment	%	5.8	5.1	5.1	5.1	5.2
Natural gas output	bn cum	4.4	6.2	6.5	6.9	7.4
Exports (fob) (goods)	US$m	1,618.8	2,544.0	2,900.0	2,600.0	2,137.0
Imports (fob) (goods)	US$m	2,134.9	2,736.0	2,200.0	1,900.0	1,754.0
Balance of trade	US$m	-516.1	-192.0	700.0	700.0	383.0
Current account	US$m	410.0	290.0	150.0	20.0	-40.0
Total reserves minus gold	US$m	223.0	400.5	470.0	550.2	672.1
Foreign exchange	US$m	222.8	399.9	469.9	550.1	672.1
Exchange rate	per US$	6.52	6.75	6.57	6.35	5.75

* estimated figure

years. In June, Japan suspended aid to Myanmar in protest at the detention of Aung San Suu Kyi, who was re-arrested in May. On 25 August, General Khin Nyunt was appointed prime minister.
2004 In January, the government and the Karen National Union, the most significant ethnic group fighting the government, agreed to end hostilities. In May, the constitutional convention began, despite a boycott by the NLD, whose leader, Aung San Suu Kyi, remains under house arrest. On 19 October, General Khin Nyunt resigned and was replaced as prime minister by Lt General Soe Win. On 26 December, an earthquake off the island of Sumatra caused a *tsunami* that devastated coastal areas in the region. The final estimate for Myanmar was 61 dead or missing, 5,000 displaced, where the area worst affected was the Irrawaddy Delta.
2005 In November, a decision to transfer the seat of government from Yangon to Pyinmana was announced.

Political structure
Constitution
From November 1997, the principal organs of power are the State Peace and Development Council (SPDC), headed by a chairman, and the 40-strong military-dominated cabinet.
Politically, Myanmar is spread over seven divisions where the ethnic Burmans are in the majority, and seven states where the non-Burmans, the ethnic minority groups, are in the majority.
On 17 May 2004, the government said it would reconvene the country's National Convention, in order to reopen negotiations on a constitution; this should result in a referendum on a new constitution and fresh elections. The National Convention was established in 1993, but it was adjourned in March 1996 following the withdrawal of the National League for Democracy (NLD), protesting against the undemocratic proceedings.
Last elections
27 May 1990 (parliamentary)
Results: Parliamentary: a Pyithu Hluttaw (People's Assembly) with 489 members elected on 27 May 1990 was not allowed to constitute itself.

Political parties
Ruling party
State Peace and Development Council (SPDC) (19-member military junta since Nov 1997)
Main opposition party
National League for Democracy (NLD)

Population
52.81 million (2004)

Ethnic make-up
The indigenous population is Mongoloid. More than two-thirds are Burmans, racially akin to the Tibetans and the Chinese. There are also several indigenous minorities with their own language and culture – the Karen, Shan, Mon, Chin and Kachin; each group has its own state. The population includes immigrant minorities from India and China.
Religions
Theravada Buddhism (88 per cent), Christianity (7 per cent), Islam (3 per cent), Hinduism (0.5 per cent).

Education
Schooling begins in kindergarten for one year, then on to junior school for four years.
Secondary education is not compulsory and is divided into two phases: middle school, for four years, where all students undertake a general programme of learning; then upper secondary school where they elect to undertake either an academic course leading to higher education, or technical school, each lasting for two years. Technical education prepares students for admission to the government technical institutes or trade schools, or advancement on to university engineering courses.
All universities and colleges are financed by the state, although a nominal fee is charged for studies.
Literacy rate: 85.3 per cent total; 81.6 per cent female, adult rates (World Bank).
Compulsory years: Five to 10.
Enrolment rate: 121 per cent gross primary enrolment of the relevant age group (including repetition rates); 30 per cent gross secondary enrolment (World Bank).
Pupils per teacher: 46 in primary schools.

Health
Government spending on health and education combined is less than 1 per cent of GDP – among the lowest in the world. Annual total expenditure on health is about 2 per cent of GDP, of which government spending is approximately 18 per cent. Access to clean drinking water is available to over 68 per cent of the population.
In August 2005 the Global Fund to Fight Aids, Tuberculosis and Malaria announced that is was withdrawing from its US$98 million health programme due to government restrictions on health workers in the country. Malaria and TB are widespread.
HIV/Aids
Stories of emigrant Burmese labour in Thailand uniformly infected with hepatitis and/or HIV/Aids are commonplace. Foreign estimates place some 2 per cent of the population as HIV positive. The proportion is many times higher in the army and areas crossed by the 'needle trail' of heroin exports into Manipur, India, and Yunnan, China, among others. This is a clear legacy of neglect of basic human development under the *junta*, in favour of internal and external security expenditures, and will be a dangerous and pressing cost to the Burmese economy over the long term, possibly on a sub-Saharan African level.
Without official statistics published, it can only be an estimated by aid workers that there are over 610,000 people with HIV/Aids, making Myanmar the centre of one of south-east Asia's worst epidemics. UN endorsed initiative have been suspended in the face of government restrictions introduced following a change in *junta* leadership.
HIV prevalence: 1.2 per cent aged 15–49 in 2003 (World Bank)
Life expectancy: 57.3 years (World Bank)
Fertility rate/Maternal mortality rate: 2.8 births per woman; maternal mortality 230 per 100,000 live births (World Bank).
Birth rate/Death rate: 10 deaths to 26 births per 1,000 people (World Bank).
Infant mortality rate: 76 per 1,000 live births (World Bank)
Head of population per physician/bed: 0.3 physicians and 0.6 hospital beds available per 1,000 people.

Welfare
The department of social welfare (DSW) under the ministry of social welfare, relief and resettlement implements social welfare services in eight different areas of social needs by both direct and indirect means covering the aged, children, youths and women welfare services. There is provision for the rehabilitation of ex-drug addicts and the disabled. It provides grants-in-aids to voluntary organisations.
In Myanmar, all government servants retire at the age of 60, and are entitled to gratuity and pension.
There are approximately 45 homes for the aged throughout the country, which provide food, clothing, shelter and healthcare services to the aged. The traditional family structures also provide ample care for the aged. Several religious organisations donate large sums of money towards social welfare.

Main cities
Yangon (formerly Rangoon) (capital, estimated population 4.5 million in 2004), Mandalay (1.2 million), Mawla Myaing (formerly Moulmein, 395,900), Pathein (formerly Bassein, 212,600), Bago (198,000), Monywa (161,000), Sittwe (formerly Akyab, 159,200), Meiktila (157,900), Taung-gyi (149,600).

Languages spoken
English is used in business circles.
Official language/s
Myanmar

Media
Press
Dailies: In Yangon, *The New Light of Myanmar*, the multi-language official daily newspaper of the military junta was previously called *The Working People's Daily*. Other newspapers in Myanmar include *Burma Daily*, *Loktha Pyithu Nesin*, *Kyemon* (The Mirror), *Myotaw* (evening tabloid) and *Yadanabon* (Mandalay).
Periodicals: *Burma Focus* is a bi-monthly newsletter.

Broadcasting
Radio: Radio Myanmar broadcasts in English. Myanmar Broadcasting Service also broadcasts in Myanmar and other local languages. The Democratic Voice of Burma radio station (www.communique.no/dvb/) based in Oslo promotes free speech, democracy and human rights in Burma by non-violent means. Radio Free Burma is a weekly Burmese-Language radio programme from 2NBC Sydney, Australia.
Television: The first station opened in 1980.

Advertising
Advertising is available in the press, in cinemas and on poster sites, which are subject to government control. Direct mail advertising is available.

Economy
The economy is centralised and based mainly on agriculture and forestry, with an important black market sector.

In addition to state-owned enterprises, there is a thriving co-operative sector. The private sector, which includes traders, farmers, small-scale industries and transport enterprises, is growing.

The target is to transform the economic structure into an agro-based industrial economy.

Economic policy is guided by the five-year economic plan, which runs from 2001–06. There are severe structural constraints, including shortages of power and foreign exchange and a widening budget deficit. Tourism has slumped due to international sanctions and boycotts called by Myanmar's opposition. Foreign debt is equal to around three-quarters of GDP. Tax evasion is widespread and the government is limited in raising tax revenue by the size of the grey economy. Defence expenditure is high, yet education and health expenditures have been cut to curb public sector deficits.

A financial crisis at the beginning of 2003 depressed domestic demand and the garments and textile sectors were hit by sanctions introduced by the US in July 2003 in response to the detention of Aung San Suu Kyi.

Although the long-term prospects for sustained growth are good, the banking system needs to be strengthened and more investment is needed in basic infrastructure, education, health and reduction of poverty.

No multilateral or bilateral aid agency will openly help to ease Myanmar's financial problems until there is some evidence of progress on democracy, human rights and narcotic eradication. Myanmar is still a large producer of the opium poppy, and will therefore continue to face US sanctions. Myanmar has vowed to eradicate opium production by 2014, a date regarded as too late by many in the international community.

External trade
Most import demands and exports originate with trade corporations and state boards. Trade is handled by the Myanmar Export Import Services using the Myanmar Five Star Line for shipping. The picture of external trade presented by official statistics does not reflect the considerable amount of smuggling and black market trading.

Imports
Principal imports fabric, crude oil, petroleum products, plastics, machinery, transport equipment, construction materials and foodstuffs.
Main sources: China (28.3 per cent total, 2004), Singapore (20.6 per cent), Thailand (19.1 per cent), South Korea (6.2 per cent), Malaysia (4.7 per cent)

Exports
Principal exports are clothing, gas, wood products, pulses, beans, fish and rice.
Main destinations: Thailand (37 per cent total, 2004), India (14 per cent), China (6.2 per cent), Japan (5.1 per cent), UK (4.0 per cent)

Agriculture
Farming
Agriculture accounts for around 60 per cent of GDP and provides around 56 per cent of employment. About 15 per cent of the total land area is cultivated.

Myanmar is usually self-sufficient in rice, although adverse weather conditions and an uninvested farming sector can cause shortages. Other main crops are sugar cane, wheat, maize, jute, cotton, beans, wheat and vegetables. Cattle, pigs, buffaloes, sheep, goats and poultry are raised for domestic consumption. Oil palm and rubber plantations are replacing forest in some areas.

Crop production in 2004 included: 22,892,000 tonnes (t) cereals in total, 22,000,000t rice, 6,368,000t sugar cane, 600,000t maize, 130,000t cassava, 400,000t potatoes, 530,000t plantains, 2,447,800t pulses, 100,000t garlic, 350,000t coconuts, 86,190t fibre crops, 697,000t oilcrops, *49,000t tobacco, 3,000t green coffee, 70,000t pimento, *36,000t natural rubber, 715,000t groundnuts in shells, 24,700t tea, *56,000t cotton lint, 150,000t millet, 1,670,000t fruit in total, 3,838,000t vegetables in total. Livestock production included: 536,644t meat in total, 114,000t beef, 22,950t buffalo meat, *132,000t pig meat, *2,450t lamb, 11,120t goat meat, 256,574t poultry, 110,995t eggs, 667,000t milk, 240t honey, 23,997t cattle hides, 415t sheepskins, 450t greasy wool.
* estimate

Forestry
Around 50 per cent of the land area is forest, containing about 75 per cent of world teak resources. Heavy logging is carried out, mostly of export hardwoods, bamboo and fuel, leading to fears of rapid deforestation.

Annual exports in 2004 amounted to US$401 million and imports to US$21 million.

Annual production in 2004 was: 39.8 million cubic metres (mcum) roundwood, 2.8mcum sawlogs and veneers, 1.0 mcum sawnwood, 34,100 cubic metres (cum) wood-based panels, 3,000cum veneer sheets, 35.7mcum woodfuel, 35,000 tonnes charcoal.

Industry and manufacturing
The industrial sector accounts for around 7 per cent of GDP and employs around 9 per cent of the workforce.

Small enterprises predominate. Manufacturing industries include food processing (sugar, tobacco, palm oil, rice), cement, textiles, beverages, cigarettes, aluminium products, paper and nails, steel, cotton yarn, soap, pharmaceuticals and fertilisers. Textile and jute production is being expanded.

There are 20 industrial zones. Foreign direct investment (FDI) is weak.

Tourism
Some liberalisation of the tourist industry has occurred. Tourists may now stay in licensed private hotels and travel on specially licensed buses from which they were previously prohibited. Tourism revenue is the second largest legal source of foreign exchange.

Mining
Mining accounts for around 4 per cent of GDP and employs around 3 per cent of the workforce.

Minerals mined include ores of zinc, lead, tin and copper, silver, gypsum, limestone and gems such as rubies, sapphires and jade.

Nations of the World: A Political, Economic and Business Handbook

Hydrocarbons
Myanmar has proven oil reserves of around 50 million barrels and produces four million barrels of oil a year. Oil production does not meet demand and Myanmar relies on oil imports.
Myanmar has proven gas reserves of 353 billion cubic metres and produces eight billion cubic metres of gas a year. Around five billion cubic metres of gas is exported annually.
Myanmar produces a small quantity of coal for domestic consumption.

Energy
Myanmar is seeking to develop its considerable hydroelectric generating potential, but is constrained by the cost factor.
In many parts of the country severe shortages are the norm.

Financial markets
Stock exchange
The Myanmar Securities Exchange Centre opened in 1996.

Banking and insurance
Since 1995, the government has allowed foreign banks to operate in Myanmar which have opened representative offices, to set up joint ventures with private local banks.
Myanmar is on the Organisation for Economic Co-operation and Development (OECD) Financial Action Task Force (FATF) list of non-co-operative countries on money laundering.
In early 2003, there was trouble in the financial sector with the collapse of some private finance companies, which had taken deposits from the public. The problem spread to some private banks and large amounts of cash were withdrawn by depositors. A stronger regulatory framework for the banking system and a strategy to identify and resolve the problem banks are necessary to restore confidence in the sector.
Central bank
Central Bank of Myanmar

Time
GMT plus six and a half hours

Geography
Myanmar lies in the north-west region of South-east Asia between the Tibetan plateau and the Malay peninsula. It is bordered by Bangladesh and India to the north-west, the People's Republic of China and Laos to the north-east and by Thailand to the south-east.

Climate
There are three seasons: the rainy season May/June–October with high humidity and monsoon rains; the hot season February/March–May with likely temperatures of 37 degrees Celsius (C) (coastal and delta areas) to 40 degrees C (central region); and the cool, dry season November–February with temperatures of 16 degrees C (central region) to 21 degrees C (coastal and delta areas). Average rainfall varies from 5,000mm (northern hills and coastal areas) to 2,500mm (delta areas) to 750mm (central region).

Dress codes
Revealing or sloppy clothing is not advisable on any occasion. There are no strict rules regarding business attire.

Entry requirements
Passports
Required by all. Must be valid for six months.
Visa
Required by all. Tourist and business visas, applied for well in advance of arrival, are valid for 28 days; business visas may be extended for a further 28 days. An application form can be downloaded from www.myanmartravelagent.com/. When completed, it can be submitted to the consulate section of the nearest Myanmar Embassy. For a business visa a letter of introduction should also be included, with a full itinerary.
Currency advice/regulations
There is no limit on the amount of foreign currency which may be imported, but any amount over US$2,000 must be declared on entry, including American Express cards. Myanmar currency may not be exported or imported. Exchange controls are strictly enforced, and it is best to retain all foreign exchange receipts. The Myanmar Foreign Trade Bank handles all foreign exchange transactions.
Customs
Personal effects are allowed duty-free, but customs regulations are restrictive and it is best to travel light. All jewellery must be declared on entry.

Health (for visitors)
Mandatory precautions
Yellow fever certificate if arriving from infected area.
Advisable precautions
It is advisable to be 'in date' for polio (within 10 years), tetanus (within 10 years), hepatitis A and B, rabies (within one to three years, depending on exposure to risk), Japanese B encephalitis (within three years if travelling June to September), tuberculosis (children should be immunised at any age; less important for adults; skin test available if in doubt about immune status), diphtheria (within 10 years). Dengue fever occurs intermittently, especially in the northern Mandalay division. The most recent outbreak was in 2002.
If travelling through the country it is advisable to be vaccinated against cholera.
Only Yangon (Rangoon) city and areas above 1,000m are malaria free; if in doubt, take malaria prophylaxis.
It is advisable to carry a pack of sterilised needles or 'Aids' kit, and to take any medicines required – they are in short supply.
Water should be boiled and filtered before drinking. It is advisable to drink bottled water.
There is a rabies risk.

Hotels
Accommodation has been described as 'decrepit almost to the extent of charm'. There is no official rating system. Main Yangon (Rangoon) hotels can arrange an interpreter or translation services if necessary. Some Yangon hotels require payment in foreign currency. A 10 per cent service charge is usually added to the bill, and a 5–10 per cent tip is usual.

Credit cards
American Express, Diners Club, Master, Visa, JCB are accepted at airlines, major hotels and supermarkets.

Public holidays
Fixed dates
4 Jan (Independence Day), 12 Feb (Union Day), 2 Mar (Peasants' Day), 27 Mar (Armed Forces Day), 13–16 Apr (Maha Thingyan/Water Festival), 17 Apr (Myanmar New Year), 1 May (May Day), 19 Jul (Martyrs' Day), 6 Dec (National Day), 25 Dec (Christmas Day).
Variable dates
Eid al Adha, Full Moon of Tabaung (Feb/Mar), Full Moon of Kasone (Apr/May), Full Moon of Waso/Beginning of Buddhist Lent (Jul/Aug), Full Moon of Thadingyut/End of Buddhist Lent (Oct), Diwali/Deepavali (Oct/Nov), Tazaungmon Full Moon Day (Nov), Kayin New Year (Dec).
In general, Hindu and Buddhist festivals are declared according to local astronomical observations.

Working hours
Banking
Mon–Fri: 1000–1400.
Business
Mon–Fri: 0930–1630.
Government
Mon–Fri: 0930–1630.
Shops
Mon–Sun: 0600–2200.

Electricity supply
230V AC, 50 cycles single-phase; five or 15 amp plugs with three round pins for power.

Weights and measures
Imperial system (the metric system and local units are also in use).

Social customs/useful tips
Shoes and socks must be removed before entering any religious building, and visitors should not wear shorts.

The title 'U' (pronounced 'oo') is the equivalent of 'Mr' in English. When addressing people always use the appropriate prefix and family name. Many people do not have a first name.

The head is considered the temple of the body and should not be touched by other people. It is also considered the ultimate in bad manners to put one's feet on the table or cross one's legs so that the sole of the shoe points at someone. This is because the feet are considered to be the least clean part of the body.

The code of standard behaviour is referred to as 'bamahsan chin'. According to this mode of conduct, people are expected to respect elders, exhibit discretion in dealing with the opposite sex, be aware of Buddhist sayings and have an ability to recite some Buddhist verses. Additionally, one should maintain a reserved and indirect approach to another person and not be direct at all. This can lead to misunderstandings, especially in business dealings.

Getting there
Air
National airline: Myanmar Airways.
International airport/s: Yangon (RGN), 19km from city centre, with duty-free shop, bar, restaurant, buffet, bank, post office and hotel reservations. From airport to city centre the journey time is by taxi is 45 minutes, by bus 30 minutes.
Airport tax: A US$10 international departure tax on tickets purchased in Myanmar only.
Surface
Road: There are some overland entry points on the borders with China.

Getting about
Not all parts of the country are open to visitors, and some are subject to guerrilla or bandit activity.
National transport
Tourists are required to keep to officially designated tourist areas and all arrangements for internal travel must be made well in advance via Myanmar Travel and Tours. Travel outside Yangon (Rangoon) is difficult to arrange. No attempt should be made to travel to restricted areas.
Air: Flying to the numourous internal destinations is the only efficient method of traversing the country. However, the carriers have a less than perfect safety record. Charter flights are available. For tickets contact Myanmar Travel and Tours.
Road: There is a large network of roads all over the country, which are being upgraded, and new roads are being built.
Buses: Owing to an ongoing privatisation programme, there is a fleet of privately-operated air-conditioned buses which accept payment in Kyat and US dollars. The main routes are from Yangon (Rangoon) to Meiktila, Pyay, Mandalay and Taunggyi.
Rail: Myanmar Railways operates services to main centres, with sleeping accommodation available on the recommended Yangon (Rangoon)-Mandalay express service. The Mandalay-Lashio-Myitkyina service is also rated 'good'. Restaurant or buffet car facilities are generally not available, and second-class travel is not recommended.
Water: There is extensive river and coastal traffic. Trips can only be made as part of an organised tour.
City transport
Taxis: Within Yangon (Rangoon) the government operates blue taxis with standard fares; otherwise, fares are by negotiation. Taxis can be shared or hired on a time basis.
Buses, trams & metro: There are antiquated and overcrowded bus services in all cities; they are not recommended for visitors. Yangon has a circular rail system.
Car hire
Tourists are not permitted to drive. Cars are hired with driver.

BUSINESS DIRECTORY

Telephone area codes
The international direct dialling (IDD) code for Myanmar is +95 followed by area code:

Bassein	42	Moulmein	32
Mandalay	2	Prome	53
Monywa	71	Yangon	1

Useful telephone numbers
Ambulance: 192, 71-111
Red Cross: 295-133
Police (emergency): 199
(headquarters): 282-541, 284-764
Telephone enquiries: 100
Booking (inland): 101
Booking (overseas): 130, 131, 667-444, 667-555, 667-601/2
Airport Security: 662-677
Customs: 284-533
Immigration: 286-434

Chambers of Commerce
Myanmar Federation of Chambers of Commerce & Industry, 504 Merchant Street, Kyauktada Township, Yangon (tel: 243-150; fax: 248-177; e-mail: ird@umfcci.com.mm).

Banking
Asia Wealth Bank, Ahlone, River View Housing Project, Olympic Tower II, Yangon (tel: 212-701; fax: 212-704).

First Private Bank Ltd, 619-621 Merchant Street, Pabedan T/S, Yangon (tel: 251-748; fax: 242-320).

Innwa Bank Ltd; 554-556 Corner of Merchant Street & 35th Street, Yangon (tel: 254-641, 254-647; fax: 254-431).

Kanbawza Bank Ltd; 1st Floor, Lanmadaw Condo Centre, No. 02/06, 02/07 Lanmadaw Street, Latha T/S, Yangon (tel: 212-780; fax: 212-778).

Myanmar Agricultural Development Bank, No. 1/7 Corner of Latha St & Kanna Rd, Latha T/S, Yangon (tel: 253-180, 250-569; fax: 245-119).

Myanmar Economic Bank, 1-19 Sule Pagoda Rd, Pabedan T/S, Yangon (tel: 289-329; fax: 283-679).

Myanmar Foreign Trade Bank, PO Box 203, 80-86 Maha Bandoola Garden Street, Kyauktada T/S, Yangon (tel: 284-911; fax: 289-585, 254-585).

Myanmar Industrial Development Bank Ltd, 26/42 Pansodan Street, Kyauktada T/S, Yangon (tel: 249-536; fax: 249-529).

Myanmar Investment and Commercial Bank, 170/176 Bo Aung Kyaw Street, Botataung Township, Yangon (tel: 250-509; fax: 281-775).

Myanmar Livestock & Fisheries Development Bank Ltd, 654-666 Corner of Merchant Street & Shwe Bon Tha Street, Pabedan T/S, Yangon (tel: 249-620; fax: 243-240).

Myanmar Citizens Bank Ltd, 383 Maha Bandoola St, Kyauktada T/S, Yangon (tel: 283-209, 283-719; fax: 245-932).

Myanmar May Flower Bank Ltd, Yadana Housing Project, 9 Mile, Pyay Rd, Mayangon T/S, Yangon (tel: 661-261; fax: 661-262).

Myanmar Oriental Bank Ltd, 166-168 Pansodan Street, Yangon (tel: 246-596; fax: 251-831).

Myanmar Universal Bank Ltd, 81 Theinbyu Rd, Botataung T/S, Yangon (tel: 297-337; fax: 245-449).

Yoma Bank Ltd, 1 Kun Gyan Road, Mingalar Taung Nyunt Township, Yangon (tel: 703-493; fax: 246-548).

Central bank
Central Bank of Myanmar, PO Box 184, 24/26 Sule Pagoda Road, KTDA, Yangon (tel: 83-665).

Travel information
Eva Air, 345 Bo Aung Kyaw Road, Kyauktada Township, Yangon (tel: 240-399, 240-997; fax: 278-701).

Flight information (2300-1100 hours) (tel: 62-712).

Hotel reservations (24 hours) (tel: 62-701).

Myanmar Airways, 104 Strand Road, Kyamaryut Tsp., Yangon (tel: 273-505, 267-800(Airport); fax: 289-583).

Myanmar Hotels and Tourism (enquiries) (tel: 577-328, 282-013, 278-386).

Myanmar Railways (enquiries) (tel: 274-027).

Myanmar Travels and Tours, 77-91 Sule Pagoda Road, PO Box 559, Yangon (tel: 275-328, 282-013, 280-321; fax: 282-535).

Yangon Airport (information) (tel: 662-692).

Ministries

Ministry of Agriculture and Irrigation, Thiri Mingala Lane, Kaba Aye Pagoda Road, Yankin Tsp, Yangon (tel: 665-587; fax: 664-493).

Ministry of Commerce, 228-240 Strand Road, Pabedan Tsp, Yangon (tel: 289-660; fax: 289-578).

Ministry of Communications, Post and Telecommunications, 80 Corner of Merchant St & Theinbyu Street, Botahtaung Tsp, Yangon (tel: 292-019).

Ministry of Construction, 39 Nawaday Street, Botahtaung Tsp, Yangon (tel: 283-938).

Ministry of Co-operatives, 259-263 Bogyoke Aung San Street, Kyauktada Tsp, Yangon (tel: 277-096, 280-280; fax: 287-919).

Ministry of Defence, Ahlanpya Phaya Street, Yangon (tel: 281-611).

Ministry of Education, Theinbyu Street, Botahtaung Tsp, Yangon (tel: 285-588).

Ministry of Energy, 23 Pyay Road, Yangon (tel: 221-060; fax: 222-964).

Ministry of Finance and Revenue, 26 Setmu Road, Kyauktada Tsp, Yangon (tel: 284-763).

Ministry of Foreign Affairs, Pyay Road, Dagon Tsp, Yangon (tel: 222-844; fax: 222-950).

Ministry of Forestry, Thirimingala Lane, Kabe Aye Pagoda Road, Mayangon Tsp, Yangon (tel: 289-184; fax: 664-459).

Ministry of Health, Theinbyu Street, Botahtaung Tsp, Yangon (tel: 277-334; fax: 282-834).

Ministry of Hotels and Tourism, 77-91 Sule Pagoda Road, Kyauktada Tsp, Yangon (tel: 282-075; fax: 287-871).

Ministry of Immigration & Population, Theinbyu Street, Botahtaung Tsp, Yangon (tel: 249-215).

Ministry of Industry (I), 192 Kaba Aye Pagoda Road Yangon (tel: 566-066).

Ministry of Industry (II), 56 Kaba Aye Pagoda Road, Yangon (tel: 661-140; fax: 667-156).

Ministry of Information, 365-367 Bo Aung Kyaw Street, Kyauktada Tsp, Yangon (tel: 245-631; fax: 289-274).

Ministry of Labour, Theinbyu Street, Botahtaung Tsp, Yangon (tel: 278-320; fax: 256-185).

Ministry of Livestock Breeding and Fisheries, Theinbyu Street, Botahtaung Tsp, Yangon (tel: 280-398; fax: 289-711).

Ministry of Mines, 90 Kanbe Road, Yankin Tsp, Yangon (tel: 577-316).

Ministry of National Planning and Economic Development, Theinbyu Street, Botahtaung Tsp, Yangon (tel: 280-816; fax: 282-101).

Ministry of Development of Border Areas and National Races and Development Affairs, Theinbyu Street, Botahtaung Tsp, Yangon (tel: 280-032; fax: 285-257).

Ministry of Rail Transport, 88 Theinbyu Street, Botahtaung Tsp, Yangon (tel: 292-769).

Ministry of Science and Technology, 6 Kaba Aye Pagoda Road, Yangon (tel: 665-686).

Ministry of Social Welfare, Relief & Resettlement, Theinbyu Street, Botahtaung Tsp, Yangon (tel: 282-610).

Ministry of Transport, 363/421 Merchant Street, Yangon (tel: 296-815; fax: 296-824).

Other useful addresses

ASEAN Investment Promotion Agency, Myanmar Investment Commission Office, Directorate of National Planning and Economic Development, Ministry of National Planning and Economic Development, No 653/691 Merchant Street, Pabedan, Yangon (tel: 272-219, 272-009).

British Embassy, Commercial Section, 80 Strand Road, Box No 638, Rangoon (tel: 281-700; fax: 289-566).

Central Statistical Organisation, New Secretariat, Yangon (tel: 270-578).

Department of Health, 36 Theinbyu Street, Botahtaung Tsp, Yangon (tel: 290-038, 290-578; fax: 290-581).

Information & Public Relations Department, 22-24 Pansodan Street, Kyauktada Tsp, Yangon (tel: 282-289, 280-753; fax: 289-274).

Livestock Foodstuff & Milk Products Enterprise, Pyay Road, 10th Mile, Mayangon Tsp, Yangon (tel: 664-244; fax: 240-109).

Myanmar Embassy (US), 2300 S Street, NW, Washington DC 20008 (tel: 202-332-9044; fax: 202-332-9046; e-mail: thuriya@aol.com).

Myanmar Export and Import Services, 622-624 Merchant Street, Yangon (tel: 280-260, 271-737; fax: 289-587).

Myanmar Fisheries Enterprise, 654 Merchant Street, Latha Tsp, Yangon (tel: 20-710, 95-211; fax: 222-951, 289-576).

Myanmar Gems Enterprise, 66 Kaba Aye Pagoda Road, Mayangon Tsp, Yangon (tel: 660-140, 552-714; fax: 660-904).

Myanmar General Industries, 192 Kaba Aye Pagoda Road, Yankin Tsp, Yangon (tel: 660-521, 273-246; fax: 56-066).

Myanmar Investment Commisssion, 653/691 Merchant Road, Yangon (tel: 272-912, 272-219; fax: 282-101).

Myanmar Oil and Gas Enterprise, 604 Merchant Street, Pabedan Tsp, Yangon (tel: 282-121, 282-153; fax: 222-964, 222-965).

Myanmar Petrochemical Enterprise, 23 Pyay Road, Lanmadaw Tsp, Yangon (tel: 222-816, 222-822; fax: 222-960).

Myanmar Ports Authority, 10 Pansodan Street, Yangon (tel: 283-122).

Myanmar Post & Telecommunications, 43 Bo Aung Gyaw Street, Kyauktada Tsp, Yangon (tel: 285-840, 285-842; fax: 290-429).

Myanmar Railways, Bogyoke Aung San Street, Pabedan Tsp, Yangon (tel: 274-027, 284-220; fax: 282-267).

Myanmar Television & Radio Broadcasting Department, Pyay Road, Kamaryut Tsp, Yangon (tel: 531-014, 531-316; fax: 530-211).

Myanmar Textile Industries, 192 Kaba Aye Pagoda Road, Yankin Tsp, Yangon (tel: 566-320, 550-448; fax: 566-053).

Post & Telecommunications Department, 125 Pansodan Street, Kyauktada Tsp, Yangon (tel: 283-737; fax: 286-365).

Road Transport, 375 Bogyoke Aung San Street, Pabedan Tsp, Yangon (tel: 278-087, 278-235; fax: 289-716).

US Embassy, 581 Merchant Street, Yangon (tel: 282-055; fax: 280-409).

Water Resources Utilisation Department, Aung Thaiddi Kone, Bahan Tsp, Yangon (tel: 549-917, 549-960).

Internet sites

Myanmar Resources: http://www.myanmars.net

Official Website of Myanmar: http://www.myanmar.com

Myanmar Business Information: http://www.myanmarpyi.com

Radio Free Myanmar: http://users.imagiware.com/wtongue/dvb2.html

Namibia

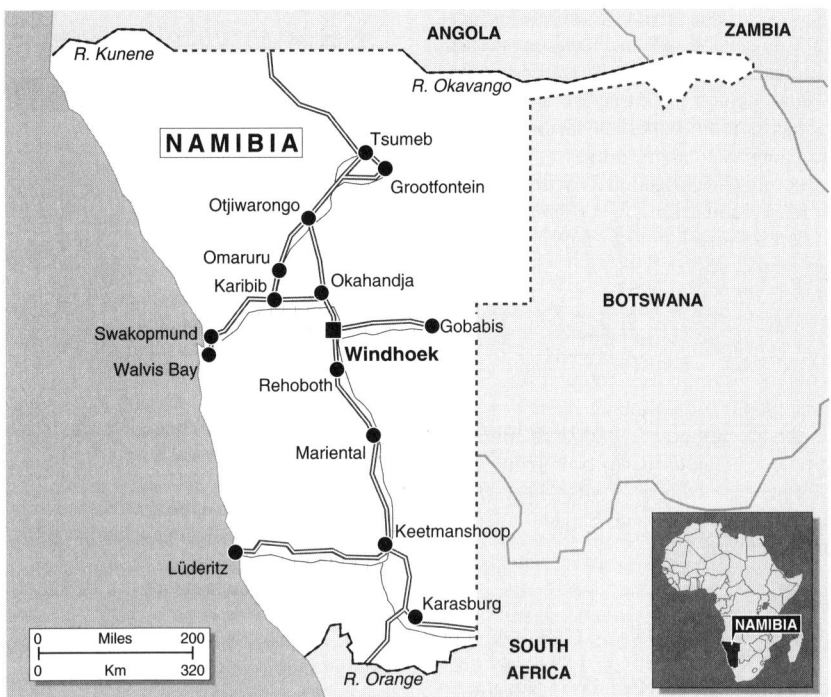

KEY FACTS

Official name: Republic of Namibia

Head of State: President Hifikepunye Pohamba (Swapo) (sworn in 21 Mar 2005)

Head of government: Prime Minister Nahas Angula (appointed by the President 21 Mar 2005)

Ruling party: South West African People's Organisation (Swapo)

Area: 824,269 square km

Population: 1.97 million (2004)

Capital: Windhoek

Official language: English

Currency: Namibian dollar (N$) = 100 cents; at par with the South African commercial Rand

Exchange rate: N$6.36 per US$ (Oct 2005)

GDP per capita: US$2,261 (2004)

GDP real growth: 4.40% (2004)

Labour force: 809,000 (2004)

Unemployment: 35.00% (2003)

Inflation: 5.50% (2004)

Balance of trade: -US$117.00 million 2004

Foreign debt: US$517.00 million (2003)

South Africa occupied the German colony of South-West Africa during First World War and administered it as a mandate until after the Second World War, when it annexed the territory. In 1966 the Marxist South West Africa People's Organisation (Swapo) launched a war of independence for the area that was soon named Namibia, but it was not until 1988 that South Africa agreed to end its administration in accordance with a United Nations' peace plan for the entire region. Namibia won its independence in 1990 and has been governed by Swapo since.

Namibia is heavily dependent on the extraction and processing of minerals for export. Mining accounts for 20 per cent of GDP. It is a primary source for gem-quality diamonds, which are mined and marketed in partnership with De Beers. The capital intensive, highly mechanised mining sector employs only three per cent of the workforce. A high per capita GDP hides a great inequality of income distribution.

Growth prospects

The country's long-term growth prospects are promising, provided that the government implements structural reforms. To strengthen private sector activity, these should include measures to privatise parastatals, raise labour skills, improve access to finance and capital, and strengthen the flexibility of the economy. Under these assumptions, annual growth could reach 4 per cent over the medium term.

The government remains committed to reduce the public debt ratio over the medium term to bring it close to the target of 25 per cent of gross domestic product (GDP), but this is a daunting task in light of the sharp decline of Southern African Customs Union (Sacu) receipts projected for the second half of the decade with the restructure of the union to more fairly reflect the financial situations and interests of its members. The receipts will drop to 7.5 per cent of GDP by 2009/10 from 11.5 per cent in 2004/05.

A decline in international reserves reflects the continued capital outflows by Namibian pension funds and insurance companies seeking the broader investment opportunities in South Africa's financial markets. The authorities are trying to strengthen domestic financial markets to contain such outflows and are also considering a tightening of domestic asset requirements.

Namibia's *Vision 2030* is a long-term development planning framework to guide the policies and implementation strategies. It was developed through a participatory process, with technical advice by the United Nations' Development Programme. Its overarching economic objective is to transform Namibia into a diversified and industrialised country. Real annual growth is targeted to accelerate steadily to 9.5 per cent by 2030, unemployment to markedly decline.

In discussion with the International Monetary Fund (IMF) the government expects growth to accelerate to four per cent over the medium-term, based on strong world growth, increased trade integration, and buoyant domestic demand in light of stable macroeconomic conditions and low interest rates.

There are concerns that with the decline in Sacu revenues, a need to curtail and re-allocate spending and consider revenue enhancing measures may put pressures on the generous tax incentives given to operations within export processing zones and under other regimes. However, most fiscal adjustment over the medium-term will need to come from the expenditure side. This will involve reductions in the wage bill, subsidies to parastatals, and spending for goods and services.

The costs and benefits of tax incentives have been actively debated. While some counterparts stressed the importance of export processing zones in attracting foreign direct investment and generating employment, others pointed to the hitherto limited benefits and the associated revenue loss and said that international experience suggested that investors considered political and economic stability and the availability of infrastructure and skilled labour as more important factors in their decisions than tax incentives.

Namibia's obligations to the World Trade Organisation (WTO) commit it to trade liberalisation. It is engaged in bilateral trade negotiations with the United States, the EU and Mercosur (in South America). Jointly with its Southern African Development Community (SADC) partners, Namibia is creating a free trade area encompassing the 14 member states of the community by 2008. Namibia's simple average tariff has been reduced to 11.4 per cent, compared with 24 per cent a decade ago and the sub-Saharan average of 20 per cent.

Politics

Hifikepunye Pohamba, representing the ruling Swapo party, won a landslide victory in presidential elections in November 2004 and was inaugurated in March 2005. He was Sam Nujoma's chosen successor. He is a founder member of the ruling Swapo. He said he would pursue his mentor's policies, including proposed land reforms. He has warned of a possible 'revolution' should white farmers not agree to sell land to the government.

Born in 1935, Pohamba went into exile in the 1960s and later studied in the Soviet Union. Sam Nujoma remains as the leader of Swapo.

Risk assessment

Economic	Fair
Political	Fair
Regional stability	Poor

COUNTRY PROFILE

Historical profile

German missionaries first arrived in Namibia in the 1840s. The Cape Colony (in modern South Africa) controlled the port at Walvis Bay from 1878. The Germans penetrated the interior after 1884 when a Dr Nachtigal established German rule. The Germans exploited the conflicts between the indigenous tribes to subjugate the territory, finally defeating the Hereros in 1904 and reducing the people further under an extermination order from 80,000 to 8,000 people.

1884 Declared a German territory (except Walvis Bay, which was occupied in 1878 by the British).
1920 Mandated to South Africa by the League of Nations.
1958 The South West African People's Organisation (Swapo) formed from the anti-contract labour movement.
1966 South Africa introduced apartheid laws, the UN terminated its mandate and Swapo launched an armed struggle for independence.
1973 The UN withdrew its mandate and recognised Swapo as the 'sole authentic representative of Namibian people'.
1985 South Africa established the Transitional Government (TG), an un-elected black majority government consisting of members of six different tribal parties, instructing it to draw up a constitution.
1988 South Africa turned down the TG's constitutional draft; independence was agreed by South Africa, Angola, Cuba, (the then) USSR and USA.
1989 Free and fair elections were held under the auspices of the UN. South Africa withdrew its forces. The Swapo leader, Sam Nujoma, formed a transitional ministerial team.
1990 Independence was granted and Nujoma became Namibia's first president.
1994 Walvis Bay and 12 offshore Penguin Islands were formally transferred from South African to Namibian sovereignty. In Namibia's first post independence presidential and National Assembly elections in December, Swapo and Nujoma defeated the Democratic

KEY INDICATORS — Namibia

	Unit	2000	2001	2002	2003	2004
Population	m	1.74	1.78	1.79	1.88	*1.97
Gross domestic product (GDP)	US$bn	3.50	3.00	2.90	3.00	*5.46
GDP per capita	US$	2,011	1,647	1,379	1,594	2,261
GDP real growth	%	3.9	2.0	2.7	4.0	4.4
Inflation	%	9.2	9.5	11.3	9.0	5.5
Exports (fob) (goods)	US$m	1,480.0	1,367.0	1,210.0	1,210.0	1,356.0
Imports (fob) (goods)	US$m	1,621.0	1,610.0	1,370.0	1,380.0	1,473.0
Balance of trade	US$m	-141.0	-243.0	-140.0	-170.0	-117.0
Current account	US$m	320.0	60.0	110.0	170.0	260.0
Foreign debt	US$bn	0.2	0.3	0.2	0.5	–
Total reserves minus gold	US$m	260.0	234.3	323.1	325.2	345.1
Foreign exchange	US$m	259.9	234.2	323.1	325.1	344.9
Exchange rate	per US$	6.94	8.61	10.02	7.56	6.46

* estimated figure

Namibia

Turnhalle Alliance party of Mishake Muyongo.
1999 President Sam Nujoma and the ruling Swapo won the presidential and legislative elections.
2002 President Sam Nujoma dismissed his prime minister, Hage Geingob and replaced him with Theo-Ben Gurirab, the former foreign minister
2003 Flood waters from the Zambezi River affected 10,000 villagers in the eastern Caprivi.
2004 In January, Germany expressed regret for the colonial-era killing of tens of thousands of ethnic Hereros.
2005 Hifikepunye Pohamba (Swapo) was sworn in as president on 21 March, taking over from Sam Nujoma who had led the country to independence from South Africa; Nahas Angula was appointed prime minister.

Political structure
Constitution
In 1999 the constitution was altered to allow President Nujoma to serve a third term.
Form of state
Multi-party republic
The executive
Executive power rests with the president, who is head of state, elected by universal suffrage for a five-year term, with the assistance of a cabinet headed by a prime minister appointed by the president.
National legislature
Legislative power is vested in a bicameral parliament comprising a directly elected, 72-member National Assembly with a five-year term, and an indirectly elected National Council (26 members, two members from each of Namibia's 13 regions), with a six-year term.
Last elections
1999 (presidential and parliamentary)
Results: Presidential: Samuel Daniel Shafiishuna Nujoma (Swapo) won 76.8 per cent of the vote.
Parliamentary: the South West African People's Organisation (Swapo) won 76.1 per cent of the vote (55 seats).
Next elections
15 November 2004 (presidential); 16 November 2004 (parliamentary).

Political parties
Ruling party
South West African People's Organisation (Swapo)
Main opposition party
Congress of Democrats (CoD)

Population
1.97 million (2004)
Ethnic make-up
87.5 per cent black, 6.5 per cent mixed race (coloured) and 6.0 per cent white.

Religions
Christianity (approximately 80 per cent), traditional beliefs (20 per cent).

Education
Primary schooling is compulsory and lasts for seven years. Secondary education is divided into two stages, junior secondary between the ages of 12 and 15 and senior secondary level lasting for another two years. A final two-year school course may be undertaken for the pre-university certificate, until aged 19.
The country has a serious lack of secondary school teachers and because of the remoteness of villages many older children are unable to complete high school. Public expenditure on education amounts to approximately 4 per cent of annual GDP.
Literacy rate: 83.3 per cent total; 82.8 per cent female, adult rates (World Bank).
Compulsory years: Five to 21
Enrolment rate: 131 per cent gross primary enrolment, 62 per cent gross secondary enrolment; of relevant age group (including repeaters) (World Bank).

Health
As a result of HIV/Aids, the annual cost of public healthcare has risen steadily. Total expenditure on health is 7 per cent of GDP, of which government spending is 67–68 per cent.
Over 68 per cent of infants aged less than one year are immunised against measles. Access to clean drinking water is available to over 77 per cent of the population.
HIV/Aids
Namibia has one of the highest rates of HIV infection in the world. If the trend continues, the number of individuals living with the disease will rise to 400,000 by 2006. Aids is the main single cause of death for all age groups. UNAIDS estimates that the annual loss to GDP per capita growth will be 1.5 per cent by 2010.
HIV prevalence: 21.3 per cent aged 15–49 in 2003 (World Bank)
Life expectancy: 40.3 years (World Bank)
Fertility rate/Maternal mortality rate: 4.8 births per woman; maternal mortality 230 per 100,000 live births (World Bank).
Infant mortality rate: 48 per 1,000 live births (World Bank)
Head of population per physician/bed: One physician per 5,000 people.

Welfare
The social pension scheme (from 1949) has massive anti-poverty objectives. Surveys in Namibia have shown that pension-dependent households are better off than small farmers. The scheme offers a non-contributory social pension for its elderly citizens. Namibia's 85,000 social pensioners receive a much lower amount each month compared to South Africa and Botswana. The social pension also supports unemployed adults, young grandchildren and other relatives. Increasingly, the pension is providing vital support to relatives of those suffering from HIV/Aids, with many elderly people fostering Aids orphans. The social pension costs the Namibian government an average of 4.8 per cent of total government expenditure.
Rape constitutes a massive problem in society. It is estimated that as many as 15,000 people a year could be victims of rape or attempted rape with only one in every 20 rapes being reported to the police.

Main cities
Windhoek (capital, estimated population 221,000 in 2003), Rehoboth (36,000), Rundu (30,500), Oshakati (29,300), Swakopmund (26,200).

Languages spoken
English is the first language of only 7 per cent of the population. All documents, notices and directional signs are in English. German and Afrikaans are widely used throughout the country.
There are six main African languages: Oshiwambo, Herero, Nama-Damara, Kwangali (Okavango region), Lozi (Caprivi region) and Tswana.
Official language/s
English

Media
Press
Dailies: Include *Allgemeine Zeitung*, *Die Republikein*, *Namibian*, *Namibia News*, *National Mirror* and *Windhoek Advertiser*.
Weeklies: Include *New Era* (published by the government since 1991), *Tempo* and *Sunday Republikein*. *Namib Times* (Walvis Bay) is a bi-weekly newspaper.
Business: *Namibia Economist* is a weekly publication covering financial and economic news.
Periodicals: *Monitor* is a monthly published from Windhoek.
Broadcasting
Radio: Local services in English, the principal African languages, Afrikaans, broadcast by state owned Namibian Broadcasting Corporation (NBC).
Television: The NBC broadcasts on one channel in English only; South Africa's M-net pay TV company also broadcasts. In October 2002, President Sam Nujoma (also information minister) ordered state television to stop showing western programmes.

Economy
South Africa remains Namibia's most important trading partner and occupies a position of major importance in Namibia's economic future. The

Namibian economy is dependent on the production and export of primary products, the most important of which are diamonds, uranium, fish and beef.

The government is attempting to diversify economic activities. Namibia offers relatively low labour costs, and, at Walvis Bay, a strategic location for sea exports to the southern African region. The government is targeting manufacturing, tourism, transshipment and energy as the prime sectors for new business.

The second five year national development plan (NDP2), which runs from 2001/02 to 2005/06, aims to diversify the economy through the promotion of private investment in the processing of locally produced raw materials and tourism. Spending always exceeds the outlays outlined in the budget due to unauthorised expenditure by government ministries. The Namibian dollar is on a fixed peg with the South African rand at a rate of one-to-one, so consequently monetary policy is mostly dictated by the decisions of the South African Reserve Bank (SARB). The rand's volatility and SARB's corrective measures, for instance, helped undermine Namibia's macroeconomic stability in 2002 and the first half of 2003.

Unemployment continues to be a major problem at a rate in excess of 30 per cent, together with under-employment at 15 per cent. The government's land re-allocation programme might be a means of addressing this issue. If the programme is successful, unemployment rates may decrease, but much will depend on the training opportunities for native farmers who turn to subsistance farming for a living. Namibia saw good economic growth in 2003 and 2004 with GDP rising by over 4 per cent, but this trend is not expected to be maintained in 2005. Some sectors, particularly the important fishing industry, affected by rising oil prices, have contracted in 2005.

External trade
Namibia, at independence, opted for full membership of the Common (Rand) Monetary Area and Southern African Customs Union (Sacu) with all tariffs, trade and exchange controls conforming to those applied in South Africa. On 31 December 2002, the US approved Namibia as being eligible for tariff preferences under the African Growth and Opportunities Act (AGOA). The legislation requires that countries are only eligible for greater access to US markets provided they have made continued progress toward a market-based economy, the rule of law, free trade, poverty reduction and the protection of workers' rights. This process is reviewed annually.

Regional trade is expected to improve with the opening in May 2004 of a road bridge across the River Zambezi, between Namibia and Zambia.

Imports
Principal imports are foodstuffs; petroleum products and fuel, machinery and equipment, and chemicals.
Main sources: US (50 per cent total, 2004), EU (31 per cent)

Exports
Principal exports are diamonds (typically 35 per cent), copper, gold, zinc, lead, uranium, cattle, processed fish and karakul skins.
Main destinations: EU (79 per cent total, 2004), US (4 per cent)

Agriculture
Farming
The agricultural sector contributes around 11 per cent to GDP and employs 39 per cent of the workforce. Only half the country is suitable for farming. In the north, yields remain low on average, due to overgrazing.

Farming supports directly or indirectly some 70 per cent of the population. There is wide disparity in land access between the 12,000, mainly white-owned, commercial farms and subsistence farmers, who number some 60 per cent of the population.

Commercial farming is dominated by livestock ranching – cattle in the north-central districts, sheep (karakul and mutton) and ostriches in the south – and accounts for 80 per cent of total agricultural output. Namibia normally produces some 40 per cent of its maize requirements from commercial farms and is generally self-sufficient in millet, the main food crop grown in the north by communal farmers. Beef is the most high-value product and exports go to the EU with an annual quota of 60,000 tonnes.

The government is pursuing a land reform programme to redistribute lands owned by white farmers. While initially the policy was to be implemented on a voluntary basis, expropriation orders began to be issued in 2005 against reluctant farmers. Crop production in 2004 included: 98,000 tonnes (t) cereals in total, *8,000t wheat, *33,000t maize, 6,000t sorghum, 9,000t pulses, 295,000t roots and tubers, 8,500t grapes, *621t oilcrops, 500t dates, 5,100t seed cotton, *1,683t cotton lint, *51,000t millet, 4,000t tomatoes, 23,000t fruit in total, 18,000t vegetables in total. Livestock production included: 107,640t meat in total, 77,253t beef, 577t pig meat, 14,040t lamb, 5,040t goat meat, 4,400t game meat, 6,330t poultry, 2,518t eggs, 109,000t milk, 8,250t cattle hides, 1,560t sheepskins, 2,200t greasy wool.
*estimates

Fishing
The south-east Atlantic is a rich fishing ground, with sardines, hake and mackerel being the main species.

The government declared a 370km exclusive economic zone and banned unlicensed foreign trawlers after independence. A new fishing policy designed to maximise shore-based processing, and long-term concessions to 159 operators (including 54 new ones) were granted. Namibia has a 300-strong fishing fleet and foreign trawlers operate under charter. 60,000 tonnes of fish are caught annually, 90 per cent of which is exported. The industry employs 40,000 people and accounts for eight per cent of GDP.

Industry and manufacturing
The industrial sector contributes around 25 per cent of GDP and employs 8 per cent of the workforce.

There is a small and highly specialised manufacturing sector, concentrated in Windhoek and Walvis Bay, with food processing (meat, agronomic products, fish) and beverages (beer and soft drinks) predominant. Other activities include structural metal products, non-metal mineral products, wood furniture, leather goods. An export processing zone (EPZ) regime was established in 1995; it provides incentives to investors in manufacturing plants producing goods mainly for export, including a zero income tax liability for an unlimited period.

Tourism
Tourism is expected to contribute 5.6 per cent to GDP in 2005.

Mining
The mining sector is the traditional backbone of the economy, contributing around 20 per cent to GDP.

Around 7 per cent of government revenues and a third of the country's foreign exchange earnings come from diamonds. Namdeb Diamond Corporation (50 per cent owned by De Beers and 50 per cent owned by the Namibian government) mines the world's richest source of high quality gem diamonds onshore north of Oranjemund, while offshore diamond recoveries by De Beers Marine have expanded significantly since commercial mining began in 1991.

Namibia Minerals Corporation (Namco) was listed on the Namibian and Toronto stock exchanges and held the country's largest marine diamond mining concession, but went into liquidation in December 2002.

The Skorpion zinc mining complex is one of the largest zinc producers in the world. Costs of extraction at Skorpion are low at around US$0.40 per kg, compared to the industry average of around US$0.70 per kg. This puts it in a good position to compete in tough markets.

Primary gold production started in 1989 and significant quantities of copper, lead, pyrite, salt and zinc are also produced while there are large unexploited deposits of base, precious and industrial minerals. Marble, granite and semi-precious stones such as rose quartz, tourmaline, amethyst and blue-lace agate are also mined; the government is seeking to promote local value by adding processing. Larger mines are mainly owned by foreign multinationals from South Africa and the UK.

Namibia is also a major uranium producer.

Hydrocarbons
Some exploration has taken place in Namibia with seven onshore wells and eleven offshore wells having been built. There is potential for oil production, however this would be a high risk venture for any companies interested. There is no refinery capacity and Namibia relies on refined oil imports. Dependence on South Africa for oil products has been reduced with supplies procured from Angola and overseas refineries.

Natural gas reserves total around 80 billion cubic metres. The Kudu offshore gas field in the south contains 36.8 billion cubic metres of natural gas. In September 2002, Royal Dutch/Shell pulled out of the Kudu field claiming reserves were not sufficient to support a liquefied natural gas (LNG) offshore export facility. The company claimed it needed at least 140 billion cubic metres to make the proposed US$2.5 billion facility commercially viable. In 2004 the Namibian government announced the acquisition of a 10 per cent share in the Kudu fields.

Namibia does not produce coal. A small amount is imported from neighbouring countries to meet energy demands.

Financial markets
Stock exchange
The Namibian Stock Exchange (NSE) was launched in October 1992.

Banking and insurance
The banking sector is small, with four private commercial banks. The ratio of non-performing loans is relatively low, making the sector stable and financially sound.
Central bank
Bank of Namibia
Main financial centre
Windhoek

Time
GMT plus two hours

Geography
Namibia lies in south-western Africa, with South Africa to the south and south-east, Botswana to the east and Angola to the north. The country has a long coastline on the Atlantic Ocean. The narrow Caprivi Strip, between Angola and Botswana in the north-east, extends Namibia to the Zambezi river, giving it a border with Zambia. The arid Namib Desert stretches along the west coast, while the easternmost area is part of the Kalahari Desert.

Climate
Namibia has one of the driest climates in the world. Sub-tropical; hottest months January–February (20–29 degrees Celsius (C)); coldest June–July (6–18 degrees C).

Entry requirements
Passports
Required by all; must be valid for six months after intended departure date.
Visa
Required by all, except tourist visitors from North America, Australasia, most of Europe, and some Asian countries, (for a full list of exceptions visit: www.embassyofnamibia.se/Welcome.htm). Business visas require a letter of invitation or a full list and addresses of business contacts to be visited in Namibia. A certified copy of the return ticket should also be submitted. For a multiple entry visa, application should be made to the Ministry of Home Affairs on arrival in Windhoek.
Currency advice/regulations
Import and export of local currency is limited to N$500. Foreign currency is unrestricted but must be declared on arrival, and export is allowed up to declared amount.

Health (for visitors)
Mandatory precautions
Yellow fever vaccination certificate required if arriving from an infected area.
Advisable precautions
Hepatitis 'A' and 'B', tetanus, typhoid and polio vaccinations. Malaria risk exists in most areas in the north. Water in all main towns is purified and safe to drink. There is a risk of rabies. To avoid the risk of bilharzia, only use well maintained, chlorinated swimming pools.

Hotels
Classified from one to four stars. Accommodation in towns outside Windhoek is limited apart from Swakopmund so should always be booked well in advance. Luxury lodges or bungalow accommodation is available at Etosha and other national parks; there is also an expanding range of desert lodges and guest farms.

Credit cards
International cards are widely accepted throughout the country.

Public holidays
Fixed dates
1 Jan (New Year's Day), 21 Mar (Independence Day), 1 May (Workers' Day), 4 May (Cassinga Day), 25 May (Africa Day), 26 Aug (Heroes' Day), 10 Dec (International Human Rights Day), 25 Dec (Christmas Day), 26 Dec (Family Day).
Variable dates
Easter Holiday, Ascension Day.

Working hours
Banking
Mon–Fri: 0900–1530; Sat: 0830–1100.
Business
Mon–Fri: 0800–1700.
Government
Mon–Fri: 0800–1700.

Telecommunications
Mobile phones
MTC provides a GSM900 network.

Electricity supply
220 V AC

Getting there
Air
National airline: Air Namibia
International airport/s: Windhoek Airport (WDH), 40km from city. Facilities include restaurant, bars, duty-free, post office, bureau de change and car hire. Buses return to the airport from the Kalahari Sands Hotel in Windhoek.
Airport tax: None
Surface
Road: Tarred highways link the South African border via Keetmanshoop to Windhoek then Oshakati and the northern border with Angola, and between Windhoek and Swakopmund-Walvis Bay. The new Trans-Kalahari highway from Botswana via Ghanzi, along with the Trans-Caprivi tarred highway, provide direct road links between Walvis Bay and central Africa.

A road bridge across the River Zambezi, between Namibia and Zambia, opened in May 2004.

Rail: Main line runs from South African border via Keetmanshoop and Windhoek to Swakopmund, Walvis Bay, and via Otavi to Tsumeb and Grootfontein, the northern railheads.
Main port/s: Walvis Bay is a modern, deep-water harbour, Lüderitz is older and smaller.

Getting about
National transport
Air: Flying is the most efficient way of connecting with all main towns, either using the extensive scheduled services or charter flights.
Road: Roads are generally well maintained. There are 64,799km of road, of which 7841km are tarred, while the rest are gravel and earth. The former

Owambo region in the north of the country is inhabited by about 44 per cent of the population, yet is served by only 5 per cent of the total road network.

The Trans-Kalahari and Trans-Caprivi highway provide the backbone of a network serving rural areas as well as connecting landlocked countries with the coast.

Buses: A luxury bus service exists between Windhoek and all major towns.

Rail: The main rail routes in Namibia are Windhoek-Keetmanshoop-De Aar, Walvis Bay-Swakopmund-Windhoek-Tsumeb and Lüderitz-Keetmanshoop. First- and second-class carriages are available on these routes. Light refreshments are offered on some services. On overnight services, seats in first-class compartments convert to four couchettes and those in second-class to six couchettes.

City transport

Taxis: Available in main towns; 10 per cent tip is usual.

Buses, trams & metro: Bus services are not well developed and there is generally no transport except taxis.

Car hire

Available in Windhoek city centre, international airport, Walvis Bay.

Although roads between major towns are generally of a good standard, the distances involved can be prohibitive; four-wheel drive is advisable if going off the main routes.

International driving licence is required. Traffic drives on the left. The general speed limit is 60kph in built-up areas and 120kph on open roads. Safety belts must be used at all times.

BUSINESS DIRECTORY

The addresses listed below are a selection only. While World of Information makes every endeavour to check these addresses, we cannot guarantee that changes have not been made, especially to telephone numbers and area codes. We would welcome any corrections.

Telephone area codes

The international dialling code (IDD) for Namibia is +264 followed by the area code and subscriber's number:

Keetmanshoop 631   Swakopmund 641
Luderitz   6331 Tsumeb   671
Mariental   661   Windhoek   61

Chambers of Commerce

Namibia Chamber of Commerce and Industry, 2 Jenner Street, PO Box 9355, Windhoek (tel/fax: 228-009; e-mail: ncciqh@iwwn.com.na).

Windhoek Chamber of Commerce and Industries, 315 Swa Building, 7 Post Street Mall, PO Box 191, Windhoek (tel: 222-000; fax: 233-690; e-mail: whkchamber@namib.com).

Banking

Bank of Windhoek, 262 Independence Avenue, PO Box 15, Windhoek (tel: 299-1229; fax: 299-1285).

City Savings and Investment Bank, PO Box 63, FGI Building, Post St Mall, Windhoek (tel: 221-262; fax: 221-555).

Commercial Bank of Namibia, 12-20 Bulow Street, PO Box 1, Windhoek (tel: 295-9111, 295-2014; fax: 295-2046; e-mail: cbon@iwwn.com.na).

First National Bank Namibia, 209 Independence Avenue, PO Box 195, Windhoek (tel: 229-610; fax: 225-994).

Standard Bank Namibia, Mutual Platz Building, Post Street Mall, PO Box 3327, Windhoek (tel: 294-2283; fax: 294-2583).

Central bank

Bank of Namibia, PO Box 2882, 71 Robert Mugabe Avenue, Windhoek (tel: 283-5111; fax: 283-5067; e-mail: general.inquiries@bon.com.na).

Travel information

Air Namibia, PO Box 731, Transnamib Building, Eros Airport, Windhoek 9000; (tel: 38-220; fax: 36-460); Town Office (tel: 229-630; fax: 236-460); Central Reservations (tel: 298-2552; fax: 221-382).

Automobile Association, PO Box 61, Windhoek (tel: 224-201).

Etosha Northern Tourism and Publicity Association, PO Box 779, Tsumeb (tel: 220-728; fax: 220-916).

Lodge and Guest Farm Reservations, PO Box 21783, Windhoek (tel: 226-979; fax: 226-999).

Namibia Resorts International, PO Box 2862, Windhoek (tel: 233-145; fax: 234-512).

Southern Tourism Forum, Private Bag 2125, Keetmanshoop (tel: 2095; fax: 3818).

Tour and Safari Association of Namibia, PO Box 5144, Windhoek (tel: 232-748; fax: 228-461).

National tourist organisation offices

Namibia Tourism Board, Independence Avenue, Private Bag 13346, Windhoek (tel/fax: 284-2360, 284-2364; e-mail: tourism@mweb.com.na; internet site: http://www.tourism.com.na).

Ministries

Ministry of Agriculture, Water and Rural Development, Private Bag 13184, Windhoek (tel: 202-9111; fax: 229-961).

Ministry of Basic Education and Culture, Private Bag 13186, Windhoek (tel: 293-9411; fax: 224-277).

Ministry of the Environment and Tourism, Private Bag 13346, Swabour Building, Independence Avenue, Windhoek (tel: 284-2111; fax: 229-936).

Ministry of Finance, Private Bag 13295, Windhoek (tel: 209-9111; fax: 236-454).

Ministry of Fisheries and Marine Resources, Private Bag 13355, Windhoek (tel: 205-3911; fax: 233-286).

Ministry of Foreign Affairs, Private Bag 13347, Windhoek (tel: 282-9111; fax: 223-937).

Ministry of Higher Education, Vocational Training, Science & Technology, Private Bag 13391, Windhoek (tel: 253-670; fax: 253-671).

Ministry of Information and Broadcasting, Private Bag 13344, Windhoek (tel: 283-911; fax: 222-343).

Ministry of Mines and Energy, Private Bag 13297, Windhoek (tel: 284-8111; fax: 283-643).

Ministry of Trade and Industry, Private Bag 13340, Windhoek (tel: 283-7111; fax: 220-148).

Ministry of Works Transport and Communication, Private Bag 13341, Windhoek (tel: 208-9111; fax: 228-560).

President's Office, State House, Private Bag 13339, Windhoek (tel: 220-010; fax: 221-770).

Prime Minister's Office, Private Bag 13338, Windhoek (tel: 287-9111; fax: 226-189).

Other useful addresses

British High Commission, PO Box 22202, 116 Robert Mugabe Avenue, Windhoek (tel: 223-022; fax: 228-895; e-mail: bhc@iwwn.com.na).

Investment Centre, Private Bag 13340, Windhoek (tel: 283-7335; fax: 22-0278).

Meat Board of Namibia, PO Box 38, Windhoek (tel: 233-280; fax: 228-310).

Namibia Crafts Centre, 40 Talstreet, Windhoek (tel: 222-236).

Namibia Development Corporation, Private Bag 13252, Windhoek (tel: 206-9111; fax: 23-3943).

Namibia Power Corporation, PO Box 2864, Windhoek (tel: 205-4111; fax: 23-2805).

Namibian Embassy (USA), 1605 New Hampshire Avenue, NW, Washington DC 2009 (tel: 202-986-0540; fax: 202-986-0443; e-mail: embnamibia@aol.com).

Namibian Ports Authority, PO Box 361, Walvis Bay (tel: 20-8201; fax: 20-8242).

Namibia

National Planning Commission (NPC), Office of the President, Private Bag 13356, Windhoek (tel: 222-549; fax: 226-501).

Offshore Development Company, Private Bag 13397, Windhoek (tel: 239-032; fax: 231-001).

Ombudsman's Office, Private Bag 13211, Windhoek (tel: 225-998; fax: 226-838).

Telecom Namibia, PO Box 297, Windhoek (tel: 201-2221; fax: 223-323).

TransNamib Ltd, Private Bag 13204, Windhoek (tel: 298-1111; fax: 298-2053).

UK High Commission, 116A Leutwein Street, PO Box 22202, Windhoek (tel: 223-022; fax: 228-895).

US Embassy, Private Bag 12029, 14 Lossen Street, Ausspannplatz, Windhoek (tel: 221-601; fax: 229-792).

Windhoek Show Society, PO Box 1733, Windhoek (tel: 224-748; fax: 227-707).

Internet sites

Africa Business Network: http://www.ifc.org/abn

AllAfrica.com: http://allafrica.com

African Development Bank: http://www.afdb.org

Africa Online: http://www.africaonline.com

Harambee Afrika (UK business club for traders with east, central and southern Africa; includes annotated web resource list): http://www.harambee.co.uk

Mbendi AfroPaedia (information on companies, countries, industries and stock exchanges in Africa): http://mbendi.co.za

Office of Prime Minister: http://opm.gov.na

Nauru

KEY FACTS

Official name: Republic of Nauru

Head of State: President Ludwig Scotty (elected 22 Jun 2004)

Head of government: President Ludwig Scotty

Ruling party: There is no formal party system. The only party represented in parliament is Naoero Amo (Nauru First), which supported the election of President Scotty. Parliament is traditionally dominated by independents. (Supporters of President Ludwig Scotty won a majority in 23 Oct 2004 parliamentary elections.)

Area: 21 square km

Population: 11,700 (2004)

Capital: Owing to its small size and absence of urban development, Nauru has no capital. Yaren is the main town.

Official language: Nauruan

Currency: Australian dollar (A$) = 100 cents

Exchange rate: A$1.31 per US$ (Oct 2005)

GDP per capita: US$5,000 (2003)

Unemployment: 90.00% (2004)*

Inflation: 2.80% (2003)

Balance of trade: -US$19.10 million 2004

Foreign debt: US$33.30 million (2003)

* estimated figure

COUNTRY PROFILE

Historical profile
1798 Sighted by the British and named Pleasant Island.
1887 Nauru became a German protectorate.
1888 Became part of the (German) Marshall Islands.
1900 Phosphate was discovered.
1906 Mining began under an agreement signed by the Australian Pacific Phosphate Company and the German government.
1914 Nauru was captured by Australian forces.
1919 After Germany's defeat, the island was placed under the joint administration of the UK, Australia and New Zealand. The three countries formed the British Phosphate Commission in order to share phosphate-mining revenues.
1942 Nauru was invaded by the Japanese.
1945 At the end of the Second World War, Nauru was made a UN Trust Territory under Australian Administration.
1968 The adoption of the Nauru constitution established it as an independent republic with a parliamentary system of government. Hammer DeRoburt was Nauru's first head of state.
1970 Nauru took control of its phosphate industry.
1976 Parliament unseated DeRoburt after objections to his autocratic style.
1978 DeRoburt was re-elected.
1989 Bernard Dowiyogo was elected president, defeating DeRoburt by 10 votes.
1995 Lagumot Harris defeated Dowiyogo.
1996 Harris resigned and Dowiyogo returned to power. Dowiyogo was ousted in parliament and Kennan Adeang became president; he in turn was replaced by Reuben Kun.
1997 Kinza Clodumar won the presidential election, backed by Bernard Dowiyogo.
1998 Dowiyogo replaced Clodumar as president.
1999 Dowiyogo was defeated in parliament and René Harris, a former president of the Nauru Phosphate Corporation, was elected president.
2000 René Harris resigned and Dowiyogo was re-elected president.
2001 Nauru accepted Australian aid for taking asylum-seekers wishing to settle in Australia. Parliament ousted Dowiyogo and re-elected former President Harris.
2002 More than 400 asylum-seekers were sent to Nauru after being rescued from a sinking ferry bound for Australia.
2003 On 8 January, Harris was ousted in a parliament motion by Bernard Dowiyogo but this was challenged in the Supreme Court of Nauru. Harris gave up the presidency on 18 January. Dowiyogo was elected with nine votes against eight for Kinza Clodumar. Dowiyogo died of a heart attack on 9 March. Derog Gioura was appointed acting president and then replaced by Ludwig Scotty in May elections. René Harris replaced him in August after Scotty lost a no-confidence vote.
2004 A constitutional crisis arose when Ludwig Scotty resigned as speaker of parliament and parliament was unable to pass any legislation, particularly finance bills. On 22 June, René Harris' government collapsed and Ludwig Scotty was re-elected president. On 1 October, Scotty dissolved parliament and declared a state of emergency. On 23 October, supporters of Scotty won a majority in parliamentary elections.
2005 1 June, Nauru severed ties with China and re-established links with Taiwan.

Political structure
Constitution
Republic
Voting is compulsory for all over the age of 20.

The executive
The president is head of state and head of government. The president, elected by parliament, governs for a three-year term, with the assistance of a cabinet of four or five ministers appointed from within parliament.

National legislature
Legislative power is vested in a 98-member unicameral parliament, elected for a three-year term in multi-seat constituencies.

Last elections
23 October 2004 (parliamentary); 28 June 2004 (presidential).
Results: Parliamentary: supporters of President Ludwig Scotty won a majority in parliamentary elections.

Next elections
2007 (presidential and parliamentary).

Political parties
Ruling party
There is no formal party system. The only party represented in parliament is Naoero Amo (Nauru First), which supported the election of President Scotty. Parliament is

traditionally dominated by independents. (Supporters of President Ludwig Scotty won a majority in 23 Oct 2004 parliamentary elections.)

Political situation
Frequent changes of presidents has been the norm, with the post changing hands three times in 2003. The country's debt of over US$165 million led to a stalled 2004 budget and the threat of bankruptcy. Just after René Harris organised a restructured loan in Australia, he was ousted from office by parliament in June 2004 as a result of a vote of no confidence. Former president Ludwig Scotty was re-elected to the presidency.

Population
11,700 (2004)
Ethnic make-up
Nauruan (58 per cent), other Pacific islanders (26 per cent), Chinese (8 per cent), European (8 per cent). The indigenous population is of Micronesian descent.
Religions
Protestant (66 per cent), Roman Catholic (33 per cent).

Labour market and unemployment
The Nauru Phosphate Company (NPC) is pressured into retaining high staffing levels, despite declining output, and is unable to meet salary expenses. Youth unemployment stood at an estimated 35 per cent in 2003.

Education
Schooling is provided free and is compulsory from aged 4–16. 10 per cent of schoolchildren are expected to complete secondary education.
Scholarships are available for higher education overseas.

Health
Total expenditure on health is about 7.5 per cent of GDP, of which government spending is 88–89 per cent.
The population's general health is not good; Nauru has a high rate of type two diabetes, with one-third of adults suffering from the disease due to the consumption of large amounts of processed food. In May 2004, a report ranked Nauruans as the most obese people in the world. A new diabetes centre has been set up as a focal point to provide multi-faceted treatment and education.
Life expectancy: 62 years: male 58 years; female 66 years (2003).
Fertility rate/Maternal mortality rate: 3.4 births per woman (2003)
Birth rate/Death rate: 26 births per 1,000 population; seven deaths per 1,000 population (2003).
Infant mortality rate: 10.3 per 1,000 live births (2003)

Main cities
Owing to its small size and absence of urban development, Nauru has no capital. Yaren is the main town (estimated population 4,900 in 2003).

Languages spoken
Nauruan and English, which is widely spoken and used for most government and commercial purposes.
Official language/s
Nauruan

Media
Press
The Department of Island Development and Industry publishes the main weekly newspaper *Nauru Bulletin* in Nauruan and English. Other newspapers include the fortnightly *Central Star News* published on Saturdays and *Nauru Chronicle*.
Broadcasting
Government radio service broadcasts local and world news. Nauru Television (NTV), commissioned in 1991, is government-owned.

Economy
Nauru's economy has relied almost solely on phosphate mining, but falling prices and a lack of demand have left the nation dependent on aid and the income from Australia for a refugee processing centre. By 2003/04, reserves of Nauru's chief natural resource, phosphate, were nearly exhausted and revenues from phosphate production nolonger covered operating costs.
In April 2004, all the Australian assets of the Nauru Phosphate Royalties Trust were placed into receivership after the Trust failed to renegotiate a loan that was due to the US General Electric Capital Corporation on 5 January 2004. The government's total debt to the US firm was US$165 million.
Nauru signed up to a re-financing agreement in Australia in June 2004.
Because the cost of living has increased, more people have resorted to subsistence farming and fishing in order to survive. Australia's assistance is essential in maintaining water and power supplies, as well as education services and health, which is also assisted by the International Organisation for Migration, in return for services in refugee camps.
In August 2004, Papua New Guinea said it would contribute about US$15,575 to help Nauru.

External trade
Nauru does not publish trade statistics.
Imports
Imports include food, fuel, manufactures, building materials and machinery.
Main sources: Australia (59.1 per cent total, 2004), Indonesia (16.7 per cent), UK (4.3 per cent), Germany (4.1 per cent)

Exports
Phosphates, besides financial services, are the sole export. Exports totalled US$27 million in 2003.
Main destinations: South Africa (37.6 per cent total, 2004), India (19.7 per cent), Germany (17.9 per cent), South Korea (10.2 per cent), Japan (6.3 per cent)

Agriculture
Farming
Arable land is confined to a strip 150–300 metres between the beach and the cliff, surrounding a vast crater caused by the phosphate mine.
Artisanal vessels (canoes and aluminium dinghies) supply fish for local consumption. Most food is imported.
There are long-term plans to rehabilitate former mining land into agricultural land with funds from the Australian government.
Crop production in 2004 included: 1,600 tonnes (t) coconuts, 208t oilcrops, 450t vegetables in total and 275t fruit in total. Livestock production: 73t meat in total, 69t pig meat, 4t poultry, 16t eggs.
Fishing
The total fish catch is typically 400 tonnes per annum.

Industry and manufacturing
Phosphate processing is the only industry.

Tourism
Nauru is not a tourist destination, but with the decline of phosphate reserves attempts have been made to develop it. There is a national tourism office. As well as being remote, the island's attractions are limited, diving and fishing being the main attractions. Infrastructure is weak. There are at present two hotels, both relatively expensive. The island is linked to Australia by Air Nauru.

Environment
Rehabilitation of the island is necessary after decades of phosphate mining. Nauru was one of the first countries to sign the Framework Convention on Climate Change. Rising sea levels related to global warming mean that in the future habitable low-lying land areas will be at risk from tidal surges and flooding.

Mining
Nauru's phosphate reserves, the legacy of millennia of fossilised bird excreta, represented the highest-grade phosphate ore in the world. It is estimated that reserves will be exhausted by around 2008. There are plans to reach deeper sources via boring coral, in a more involved secondary mining process.

Hydrocarbons
Nauru does not produce any hydrocarbons and depends entirely on imports.

Banking and insurance
There are no reliable commercial banking services in Nauru. Setting up a viable domestic banking system will be a major task to be addressed in the government's economic reform programme.
Central bank
The Bank of Nauru is insolvent and operates on a very limited basis.
Offshore facilities
Nauru is in the process of closing down its offshore banking sector, and thereby closing off access of criminal monies to money laundering. The 2004/05 budget set aside funds for the establishment of a financial investigations unit to support the implementation process. The OECD's Financial Action Task Force on Money Laundering (FATF), proposed to withdrew counter-measures from Nauru in October 2004, but did not remove it immediately from the list of non-co-operative countries on money laundering.

Time
GMT plus 12 hours

Geography
Nauru is a small island in the central Pacific Ocean, lying about 40km (25 miles) south of the Equator and about 4,000km (2,500 miles) north-east of Sydney, Australia. Banaba (Ocean Island), in Kiribati, is about 300km (185 miles) to the east.

Climate
Tropical, tempered by sea breezes, but humid (80 per cent) with variable rainfall. Temperatures range from 24–34 degrees Celsius in the shade. Monsoon season from November–February; average annual rainfall is 2,060mm. Between May–October is the best time to visit.

Entry requirements
Passports
Required by all.
Visa
Required for visits up to 30 days, with proof of sufficient funds, accommodation and return/onward passage.
Currency advice/regulations
No limit to the amount of currency, either Australian or foreign, which may be taken into Nauru.
Prohibited imports
Importation of firearms and ammunition is prohibited.

Health (for visitors)
Mandatory precautions
Cholera vaccination certificate if arriving from or via an infected area within five days. Yellow fever vaccination certificate if arriving from an infected area.
Advisable precautions
Vaccination for diphtheria, tuberculosis, hepatitis 'A' and 'B', polio, tetanus, typhoid. There is a rabies risk. Main water is chlorinated but may cause mild stomach upset. Local water may be contaminated. There are no medical specialists, and serious cases are sent to Australia by Air Nauru.

Credit cards
American Express, Diners Club and Visa are accepted.

Public holidays
Fixed dates
1 Jan (New Year's Day), 31 Jan (Independence Day), 17 May (Constitution Day), 26 Oct (Angam Day), 25–26 Dec (Christmas Holiday).
Variable dates
Good Friday, Easter Monday.

Working hours
Banking
Mon–Thu: 0900–1600; Fri: 0900–1630.
Business
Mon–Fri: 0800–1200, 1330–1630.

Telecommunications
Nauru's telecommunications services are regulated and provided by the Nauru Department of Telecommunications. An intra-island and international radio communications system is provided by Australian facilities.
Telephone/fax
Telephone service is automatic.
Postal services
Airmail to Europe takes up to a week.

Electricity supply
110/240V AC, 50Hz

Weights and measures
Metric system

Social customs/useful tips
In business an informal attitude prevails, shirts and smart trousers or skirts are acceptable and only on very special occasions is more formal wear advisable. It is customary to shake hands on meeting and taking leave.
Gratuities are not customary. The minimum drinking age is 21 years.

Getting there
Air
National airline: Air Nauru.
International airport/s: Nauru Island International (INU); buses run to Yaren after each arriving plane.
Airport tax: International departures include an airport service fee of A$25.
Surface
Water: The main sealinks are with Australia, New Zealand and Japan. Without a natural harbour most commercial vessels moor offshore, in what are reputedly some of the world's deepest permanent anchorages.

Getting about
National transport
Road: A main road (19.3km) circles the island, and all residential areas are linked by surfaced roads. A regular local bus service operates around the island. Buada and the phosphate areas are linked by an inland road.
Rail: Approximately 5km of railway serve the phosphate mining area.
Car hire
Car hire can be arranged locally. Traffic drives on the left. A national driving licence should suffice.

BUSINESS DIRECTORY
The addresses listed below are a selection only. While World of Information makes every endeavour to check these addresses, we cannot guarantee that changes have not been made, especially to telephone numbers and area codes. We would welcome any corrections.

Telephone area codes
The international direct dialling (IDD) code for Nauru is +674 followed by subscriber's number.

Useful telephone numbers
Police: 110
Fire: 119
Ambulance: 118 or 117

Banking
Central bank
Bank of Nauru, PO Box 289, Civic Centre, Aiwo District (tel: 444-3267; fax: 444-3203; e-mail:bon@cenpac.net.nr).

Travel information
Air Nauru, Government Building, Yaren District (tel: 444-3141, 444-3418; fax: 444-3170).

Nauru International Airport, PO Box 40, Nauru Air Corporation (tel: 444-3754/3141; fax: 444-3282-3705).

National tourist organisation offices
National Tourist Office, c/o Special Project Officer (Culture and Tourism), Department of Island Development and Industry, Government Offices, Aiwo District (tel: 444-3191; fax: 444-3791).

Ministries
Address for all Government Offices: Government Offices, Yaren District.

Chief Secretary, Secretary to Cabinet, Public Service Commissioner and Registrar of Births, Deaths and Marriages (tel: 444-3133; fax: 444-3110).

Secretary for Education (tel: 444-3130; fax: 444-3718).

Secretary for External Affairs (tel: 444-3191, 444-3701; fax: 444-3105).

Secretary for Finance (tel: 444-3285, 444-3287; fax: 444-3125).

Nauru

Secretary for Health (tel: 444-3702; fax: 444-3106).

Secretary for Island Development and Industry (tel: 444-3281; fax: 444-3705) (economic development and privatisation and foreign investment).

Secretary for Justice (tel: 444-3747, 444-3160; fax: 444-3108).

Secretary for Works and Community Services (tel: 444-3703; fax: 444-3718).

Other useful addresses

Directorate of Telecommunications, Private Bag, Yaren (tel: 444-3132; fax: 444-3111).

Nauru Finance Corporation, PO Box 306, Yaren (tel: 3390; fax: 3345) (responsible for promoting economic diversification, including offshore banking).

Internet sites

Nauru International Airport: http://www.airnauru.com.au

Nauru website: http://www.nauruwire.org

Nepal

KEY FACTS

Official name: Nepal Adhirajya (Kingdom of Nepal)

Head of State: King Gyanendra Bir Bikram Shah Dev (crowned by the State Council 4 Jun 2001)

Head of government: King Gyanendra Bir Bikram Shah Dev (assumed power 1 Feb 2005)

Ruling party: Transition government (from 9 Jul 2004)

Area: 147,181 square km

Population: 26.41 million (2004)

Capital: Kathmandu

Official language: Nepali

Currency: Rupee (NRs) = 100 paisa

Exchange rate: NRs70.34 per US$ (Oct 2005)

GDP per capita: US$239 (2004)

GDP real growth: 3.50% (2004); 2.5% (2005)*

Labour force: 11.92 million (2003)

Unemployment: 47.00% (2003)

Inflation: 4.00% (2004); 4.00% (2005)*

Balance of trade: -US$1.15 billion (2004)

Foreign debt: US$2.55 billion (2003)

* estimated figure

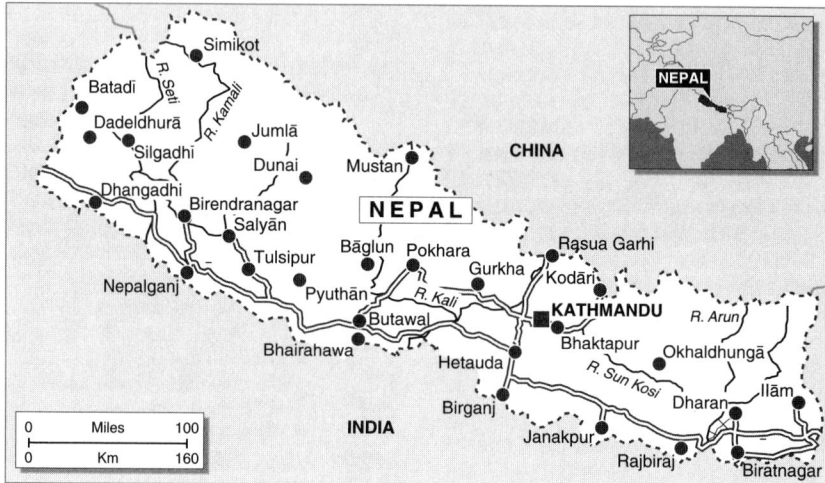

The people of Nepal no longer believe in the living god, King Gyanendra. He is trying to hold the country together while it is being torn in several directions: Maoist rebels are launching bombs attacks in the hope of securing communist rule, while politicians and human rights activists are campaigning for democracy and refusing to co-operate in the King's sham elections. For now the army are co-operating with royal decree, putting down protests and arresting the opposition – but even their sympathy might run out if asked to become more heavy-handed with an angry and oppressed populace.

Politics

Governance of Nepal has been especially tumultuous since the Crown Prince, 29-year old Eton-educated Dipendra, drunkenly massacred nine members of the royal family including his parents, the King and Queen, in 2001. It took just 90 seconds for all the corpses to mount in a revenge-tragedy-like tableau. Strangely, the comatose Dipendra was King for the three days he spent in hospital before dying of self-inflicted injuries.

King Gyanendra succeeded the murdered monarchs and the next year, in 2002, dismissed parliament as a response to the growing Maoist insurgency. He chose a new prime minister, Lokendra Bahadur Chand, instructing him to prioritise the creation of peace. In 2003 came the welcome news that a new cease-fire had been agreed with the Maoists. However, efforts to address the Maoist demands and reconcile them with political party interests proved too much for Chand and he resigned prematurely in the same year.

Undaunted, the King appointed another prime minister, Surya Bahadur Thapa, and urged him to embark on new peace negotiations. These proved to be insufficient as in 2003 the rebel insurgents took up their weapons again, precipitating Thapa's resignation in May 2004. The King seemed to have little option but to bring back Sher Bahadur Deuba, who had been prime minister between 2001–02. Except this did not last long either.

The King assumed all control himself in February 2005, declaring a state of emergency to address the problems of the rebel uprising and the corruption of political parties. King Gyanendra elected royalist officials but professed his intention of restoring the democratic process in 2008. The state of emergency involved censorship of the press and suspension of telephone lines, including mobile telephones. The state of emergency expired in May 2005.

The Maoist insurgency was initially sparked in 1996. Since then rebels and counter-forces have killed 12,000 in the struggle to establish communist rule. Both

Nepal

sides have been accused of torture and brutal violence. However the Maoists may be changing tack, realising that the world would not allow a rebel coup to upset regional stability in between two of the leading global economies, China and India. But it is not just the Maoists who are dissatisfied.

In February and March 2005 large-scale protests were carried out in efforts to restore the country's suspended democracy. As demonstrating was banned, hundreds were placed under arrest. The King's authoritarianism has united the multi-faceted domestic opposition, as well as outsiders such as the US, UK and India. It has fomented a real appetite for republicanism and an end to the 250-year old monarchy. The Indian embassy in the Nepalese capital, Kathmandu, said that they were 're-evaluating aspects of the relationship'. The Indian prime minister, Manmohan Singh, issued a last-minute refusal to attend a regional summit in February 2005, to ensure there was no legitimising hand-shaking photo-opportunity available. The head of the Human Rights Organisation of Nepal said in February 2005 that 'the whole country is like a prison', referring to the fact that many human rights activists and politicians were under house arrest. Nepal has the highest number of unexplained disappearances anywhere in the world.

The US, UK, France and the EU temporarily removed their diplomats from embassies in Nepal and the UK withdrew plans to give over US$2 million of military assistance to Nepal – restoration of funds could come with democratic strings attached. The UN called the situation a 'very serious' crisis, in July 2005.

However, foreign governments do not want to risk playing into the hands of the Maoists by imposing sanctions on the king's rule. India itself has a communist rebel movement which would be reinvigorated by Maoist success next door.

In May 2005 King Gyanendra terminated the state of emergency but did not restore media freedoms or communications. In December 2005 the King announced his third cabinet reshuffle of the year and declared that that local elections, the first in eight years, would be held on 8 February 2006. The King was given a cynical reception by politicians and the public alike. Maoists, along with seven political parties, have promised to protest against the voting and refuse to put themselves forward as candidates: they have no faith in ballots they say are only intended to falsely legitimise the King's autocratic ruling circle.

The drama continued into 2006. In early January thousands formed a mass protest in Janakpur, demanding the restoration of democracy. In response King Gyanendra arrested politicians and human rights activists in a series of early morning raids and cut off all domestic and international communications. Pro-democracy activists called the country out into the streets. However, a curfew was imposed in the capital and protests were banned in two of the country's main towns. The secretary of the country's Communist Party declared 'this government has gone insane', while India announced its 'grave concern'. While the streets were teeming with angry citizens and their battles with the police, the King had retreated to the countryside. In January the Maoists abandoned the cease-fire they declared in September 2005 after little acknowledgement from the government. The military had been prepared to give up their arms in response but the King would not allow such a move. Before the end of January Maoists had launched 10 attacks, killing several people, although they did make a statement to say that future violence would only be directed against the autocratic government. By the end of January the ideological gap between the Maoists and the country's main political parties was closing. All sides were edging towards the idea of a ceremonial monarchy whereas previously politicians had supported an active role for the King in politics.

At the forefront of the protestors' minds must be the events of 1990, when a series of bloody confrontations prompted the then King Birendra to bring democracy to the Himalayan region.

Economy

In January 2005 the WTO Multi-fibre Agreement (MFA) production quotas, which had in effect guaranteed Nepal a role in the global market, were removed. This legislation had been introduced in the 1970s and its removal is one of the most significant recent events in the global economy. Retailers are now free to find the cheapest markets without restrictions. This deregulation puts great pressure on prices and China is predicted to dominate the market initially. The Nepalese garment market was worth half the total national exports market but it will struggle to maintain this level in the face of increased competition. In the year after the industry shake-up, sales to the US plummeted 42 per cent.

GDP growth was a projected 2.5 per cent in 2005 and inflation a reasonable 4 per cent. However, there is little optimism for future growth with the near collapse of one of the country's biggest industries and with such a stormy political landscape.

Outlook

The King is becoming increasingly cornered: by a solidifying domestic opposition and almost universal condemnation from the international community. Only China is still happily exporting arms to the autocracy. The King will either have to compromise with activists, or step up the violence and repression. The February ballot will clearly inflame tensions and the

KEY INDICATORS — Nepal

	Unit	2000	2001	2002	2003	2004
Population	m	23.21	23.21	23.70	25.05	*26.41
Gross domestic product (GDP)	US$bn	5.50	5.60	5.70	6.29	*6.71
GDP per capita	US$	239	241	240	251	239
GDP real growth	%	6.1	5.0	-0.6	2.6	3.5
Inflation	%	3.5	2.8	2.9	4.8	4.0
Exports (fob) (goods)	US$m	785.7	942.0	782.0	720.0	740.0
Imports (fob) (goods)	US$m	1,578.3	1,774.0	1,707.0	1,600.0	1,890.0
Balance of trade	US$m	-792.7	-832.0	-773.0	-880.0	-1,150.0
Current account	US$m	-277.4	158.0	-53.0	130.0	160.0
Foreign debt	US$bn	2.8	2.7	3.0	2.5	–
Total reserves minus gold	US$m	946.9	1,037.7	1,017.6	1,222.5	1,462.2
Foreign exchange	US$m	939.4	1,030.4	1,009.8	1,213.1	1,452.5
Exchange rate	per US$	71.09	74.95	77.88	74.75	73.67

* estimated figure

King cannot necessarily count on the army's loyalty.

Future potential for economic development could come in the shape of hydroelectric power – exported to India – or tourism. However with such a turbulent domestic situation neither tourists nor investors are willing to take the risk of involvement. Not only this, but increased violence could prompt some form of economic sanctions.

Risk assessment

Economic	Poor
Political	Poor
Regional Stability	Poor

COUNTRY PROFILE

Historical profile

Modern Nepal began its formation in the second half of the eighteenth century, when the kingdom of Gorkha, led by Prithivi Narayan Shah, began to expand.
1768 Shah conquered Kathmandu and completed unification of what is today's Nepal.
1792 Nepal's expansion was halted by Chinese armies in Tibet.
1816 Nepal became a British protectorate after the Anglo-Nepalese war.
1846 Jang Bahadur Rana extracted a decree from the monarch that transferred sovereign powers to the family of Ranas, who ruled as hereditary prime ministers for 104 years.
1923 Nepal's independence was recognised by Britain, although it retained control of the country's foreign affairs.
1950–59 King Tribhuvan fled to India, intensifying the revolt led by the Nepali Congress Party (NCP) against the Ranas oligarchy. It ended with an agreement brokered by India which recognised the role of the monarch, legalised political parties and established a constitutional monarchy. In the eight years that followed, the King ruled the country while political parties took shape.
1959 The first election under a new constitution was won by the NCP.
1960 King Mahendra seized control and suspended parliament and politics.
1962 He introduced a new constitution establishing a 'party-less Panchayat' system which banned political competition and parties. The King retained absolute powers.
1972 King Mahendra died in 1972 and was succeeded by his son, King Birendra, who continued his father's policies.
1979 After a series of protests against the Panchayat system, the King ordered a national referendum: the choice was between a 'reformed' panchayat or a multi-party democracy. A narrow majority voted in favour of the Panchayat, with reforms allowing direct elections – but still on a non-party basis.
1985 The NCP began a campaign of civil disobedience for the restoration of the multi-party system.
1986 Elections were boycotted by the NCP.
1990 Pro-democracy protests were staged by the NCP and leftist groups which resulted in killings and mass arrests by the police. The King bowed to pressure and agreed a new democratic constitution.
1991 The NCP won the elections and Girija Prasad Koirala became prime minister.
1994 Koirala's government was toppled due to party infighting. The Communist Party of Nepal-United Marxist-Leninist (CPN-UML) emerged as the largest single party in the elections and formed a minority government.
1995 The CPN-UML government was toppled, making way for a number of coalition and minority governments, until another round of elections was held in 1999.
1996 While the mainstream parties jostled for power in the centre, the Maoists launched their 'people's war'.
1998 The CPN-UML suffered a major blow when a faction of the party broke away.
1999 The NCP won the general elections; Krishna Prasad Bhattarai became prime minister.
2000 Bhattarai was forced him to step down due to party infighting. Koirala became prime minister again. The NCP remained effectively divided between the supporters of Koirala and Bhattarai.
2001 Crown Prince Dipendra killed his closest family members, including King Birendra and Queen Aishwarya, in a drunken shooting spree, before committing suicide. Gyanendra Bir Bikram Shah Deva became king. The Maoists increased their violent campaign of opposition. Koirala resigned and Sher Bahadur Deuba (NCP) became prime minister. In July a truce was agreed between the rebels and the government. In November the peace talks failed and the insurgency resumed as violence escalated
2002 Over 500 people were killed in two separate attacks and the Maoists successfully staged a five-day general strike. The prime minister proposed that the state of emergency be extended but this was opposed by the ruling NCP, and opposition. King Gyanendra dissolved parliament and called for fresh general elections; the ruling NCP suspended Deuba from the party for advising the King to do so. King Gyanendra dismissed Deuba, abolished the Council of Ministers and assumed executive powers. The King appointed Lokendra Bahadur Chand as prime minister.
2003 On 1 February, Maoist rebels and the government agreed to a cease-fire. Prime Minister Chand resigned on 30 May. King Gyanendra appointed his own nominee, Surya Bahadur Thapa of the Rastriya Prajatantra Party (RPP) as prime minister. In August the Maoists ended the truce. Violence and political stalemate marked the end of the year.
2004 On 23 April, Nepal became the 147th member of the World Trade Organisation (WTO). Prime Minister Thapa resigned after weeks of civil protest. Former prime minister, Sher Bahadur Deuba, was re-appointed. In August, a blockade of Kathmandu by the Maoist rebels ended after one week.
2005 On 1 February, King Gyanendra dismissed Deuba and assumed absolute power for himself, siting the imperative of defeating the Maoists. A royal anti-graft commission sentenced former prime minister Deuba to two years imprisonment for corruption. In September the rebels declared a unilateral cease-fire. Maoists and opposition parties agreed a strategy to restore democracy. Nepal, Bhutan, Bangladesh, India, Maldives, Pakistan and Sri Lanka signed the South Asia Free Trade Agreement (SAFTA), to come into effect on 1 January 2006.
2006 Maoists rebels threatened to disrupt the municipal polls scheduled for 8 February.

Political structure

In 2002, parliament was dissolved by the King on the grounds that it was incapable of handling the Maoists rebels and the King assumed executive powers, running the country with the help of the army. The country's five main political parties staged protests, saying that the King must either call fresh elections or reinstate the elected legislature. In 2004, the King announced that parliamentary elections would be held within 12 months, but were postponed until 2006.

Constitution

The powers of the monarch were considerably reduced by the 1990 constitution.

Form of state

Constitutional monarchy

The executive

Executive authority is held by the King, under emergency powers (2002).
A 31-member advisory Council of Ministers was formed, by the King, in July 2004.

National legislature

The Sansad (parliament) has two chambers – the popularly and fully elected 205-member Pratinidhi Sabha (House of Representatives) elected for a five-year term in single-seat constituencies, and the

Nepal

60-member Rashtriya Sabha (National Assembly), of which 35 members are elected by the the Pratinidhi Sabha, 15 members are representatives of Regional Development Areas and 10 are appointed members.

Legal system
Independent judiciary

Last elections
3/17 May 1999 (parliamentary)
Results: Parliamentary: the Nepali Congress Party (NCP) won with 36.3 per cent of the vote (110 seats).

Next elections
8 February 2006 (municipal)

Political parties
Ruling party
Transition government (from 9 Jul 2004)
Main opposition party
The Nepali Congress Party (NCP) refused to join the transition government.

Population
26.41 million (2004)
Ethnic make-up
Nepal has a mixture of Indo-Caucasian and Tibeto-Mongoloid people and a number of Tibetan refugees. There are 61 different ethnic and caste groups and many have their own language and dialect.

Religions
Hinduism (90 per cent), Tibetan Buddhism (5.3 per cent), Islam (2.7 per cent). Nepal is a Hindu kingdom, but it allows other religions to practise their faiths. It is illegal to proselytise. The Kumari Devi is revered by both Hindus and Buddhists in Nepal as a 'living Goddess'.

Education
The education system is based on the Chinese model. A non-compulsory pre-school education can begin at aged three. Primary schooling lasts for five years at the end of which students are separated into academic and technical programmes. The academic programme is divided into lower secondary, upper secondary and higher secondary schooling in a cycle of three, two and two years until the age of 18 when, if they have been successful, students may access higher education courses at university or other institutions. The three-year lower secondary schools are of two types: general and Sanskrit. Upon completing the second stage, exams undertaken by students allows advancement to the higher secondary school or graduation with a school leaving certificate.

The Tribhuvan University, Mahendra Sanskrit University, Kathmandu University and Purbanchal University and B P Korala Institute of Health Science mainly provide higher education.

The technical programme is divided into cycles of either four and two, or four and four, years and students graduate with either a craftsman's certificate at age 16 or a technical certificate at aged 18.

Literacy rate: 44 per cent total; 26.4 per cent female, adult rates (World Bank).
Compulsory years: Six to 16.
Enrolment rate: 113 per cent gross primary enrolment of the relevant age group (including repeaters); 42 per cent gross secondary enrolment (World Bank).
Pupils per teacher: 39 in primary schools.

Health
National morbidity patterns show ailments related to inadequate water and sanitation account for more than 70 per cent of all sickness reported. Furthermore, around 10,000 people die from cancer after a long-term exposure of arsenic compounds in drinking water. Annual total expenditure on health is about 5 per cent, of which government spending is approximately 30 per cent.

HIV/Aids
The UN estimated 60,000 people are living with HIV/Aids in 2003, which represents 0.25 per cent of the total population.
HIV prevalence: 0.5 per cent aged 15–49 in 2003 (World Bank)
Life expectancy: 60.2 years (World Bank estimate)
Fertility rate/Maternal mortality rate: 4.1 births per woman (World Bank)
Infant mortality rate: 61.0 deaths per 1,000 live births; 48 per cent of children aged under five are malnourished (World Bank).
Head of population per physician/bed: 0.05 physicians and 0.2 hospitals available per 1,000 people.

Welfare
The government of Nepal and the Asian Development Bank (ADB) signed a partnership agreement aiming to reduce the incidence of poverty from over 40 per cent of the population to less than 10 per cent by 2017. The problems related to rural poverty are being tackled by improving access to impoverished areas. Several non-government organisations have stepped up their aid to tackle poverty and disease in the country.

It is estimated that more than 10 out of 100 people in Nepal suffer from one or the other form of disability. The government does not have concrete programmes to address the problems facing the disabled.

Main cities
Kathmandu (capital, estimated population 729,000 in 2003); in the entire Kathmandu Valley, including three cities and surrounding villages, there are over 1.2 million people; Biratnagar (174,600); Lalitpur (169,100); Pokhara (166,400); Birgunj (117,200); Dharan (100,800).

Languages spoken
Maithili, Bhojpuri, Hindi, Bengali and Newari are some other languages spoken. English is spoken, mainly in urban centres.

Official language/s
Nepalese

Media
Press
Dailies: There are approximately 185 regular newspapers and magazines. The internet news portal, www.nepalnews.com, has its own breaking news as well as news from almost all major newspapers. *Himal South Asian* is a newsmagazine aimed at a South Asian readership.

Nepal has 10 broadsheet, daily newspapers published in Kathmandu. The state-run Gorkhapatra Corporation publishes two dailies. English-language dailies include *Kathmandu Post* and *The Rising Nepal*. Nepali dailies include *Gorakhpatra*, *Kantipur*, *Mahanagar*, *Samacharpatra* and *Sandhya Times*.

Weeklies: Most weeklies are published in the Nepali language. Local Nepali-language weeklies include *Deshanter*, *Chalphal*, *Dristi*, *Budhabar*, *Jana Aastha* and *Sapthahik Bimarsha*. English-language weeklies are *Spotlight*, *Sunday Despatch*, *Sunday Post*, *Telegraph*, *Independent*, *People's Review* and *Nepali Times*, which is the most widely read.

Business: Business publications include *Business Age* and *New Business Age*.

Periodicals: Monthly publications include *Apsara*, *Kamana* and *On Time*. There are many specialised publications catering for the tourism industry. These include *Nepal Traveller* and *Nepal Travel Trade Reporter* (both published monthly).

Himal Khabarpatrika and *Nepal* are the market leaders in fortnightly publications. *Explore Nepal* (local English newspaper) and *Cyber Post* are also published fortnightly.

Broadcasting
Radio: State-run Radio Nepal broadcasts on medium and short waves and has the largest coverage and reach. It leases FM time slots to private broadcasters. Nepal has licensed over 25 local, private FM stations, of which about 20 are operational. Kathmandu alone has eight private stations, which are largely commercial. Nepal also has a new genre of FM radio run by community groups, co-operatives and non-governmental organisations.
Television: State-run Nepal Television (NTV) dominates the airwaves with signals reaching about 55 per cent of the

population. NTV began broadcasting via satellite in 2001. Nepal also has private cable operators. One of these runs Channel Nepal broadcasting via satellite from Thailand because unresolved licensing disputes have held up its permission to up-link from Nepal.

Economy
Nepal is a poor country, plagued with insurgency. It has a largely agrarian economy – over 80 per cent of Nepalis are engaged in agriculture, which contributes 40 per cent of GDP. Because of Nepal's dependence on agriculture, the annual monsoon rain, or lack of it, strongly influences economic growth. Industry accounts for around 22 per cent of GDP, and travel, hotels and restaurants together make up the rest.

Remittances from Nepalis working abroad have grown into a major source of hard currency. Nepal also receives substantial amounts of external assistance from India, the UK, the US, Japan, Germany, the Scandinavian countries and several multilateral organisations.

Nepal began planned development in the early 1950s. Because Nepal's population has grown steadily, there has been only a marginal growth in average per capita income. Reforms have included current account convertibility, de-licensing imports, liberalising entry, restructuring taxes and lowering tariffs and privatising public enterprises.

Insurgency, the massacre of the royal family in June 2001 and the global slowdown have affected the important tourism sector, which has experienced a sharp decline. Higher spending on security in the government's war with the rebels, as well as wage rises for the civil service, have contributed to increased budget deficits in recent years. Nepal launched its 10th (five-year) economic development plan in 2002; the Medium-Term Expenditure Framework links projects prioritised in the plan with annual spending.

In November 2003, the IMF approved a three-year US$72 million Poverty Reduction and Growth Facility (PRGF) arrangement.

Negative growth of 0.6 per cent in 2002 was largely due to the Maoist insurgency. In 2003, GDP grew 2.6 per cent and 3.5 per cent in 2004.

Nepal became a member of the World Trade Organisation in April 2004.

External trade
Imports
The principal imports gold, machinery and equipment, petroleum products and fertiliser.

Main sources: India (43 per cent total, 2004), UAE (10.0 per cent), China (10.0 per cent), Saudi Arabia (4.4 per cent), Singapore (4.0 per cent)

Exports
The principal exports have been garments, woollen carpets and Pashmina (together accounting for almost 50 per cent of total export earnings), handicrafts, leather goods, grain and jute goods. The ending of the Multi-fibre Agreement in 2005 has slashed textile exports.

Main destinations: India (48.8 per cent total, 2004), US (22.3 per cent), Germany (8.5 per cent)

Agriculture
Farming
Agriculture accounts for around 40 per cent of GDP, providing most foreign exchange earnings and 80 per cent of employment. Only about 25 per cent of the total land area is cultivable; another 33 per cent is forested and most of the rest is mountainous. The lowland Terai region produces an agricultural surplus, part of which supplies the food-deficient hill areas.

Major food crops are rice, maize, wheat, barley and millet. The principal cash crops are sugar cane, soya beans, oilseeds, tobacco, potato and jute. Cattle, buffaloes, goats, sheep, pigs, yaks and poultry are also raised. River fish are an important source of protein.

Much of the agriculture is rain-fed and is carried out in the narrow strip of plains in the south along the border with India. Agricultural land is highly fragmented. Production is extremely vulnerable to adverse weather conditions, with little irrigation. Deforested plains and lower hilltops are terraced for rice production. Severe soil erosion is becoming a problem.

Nepal has removed all subsidies on fertilisers, which makes it difficult for Nepali produce to compete with highly subsidised Indian agro-products. There are some transport subsidies for taking fertilisers to remote districts.

Crop production in 2004 included: 7,590,630 tonnes (t) cereals in total, 4,300,000t rice, 1,387,191t wheat, 1,590,097t maize, 1,643,357t potatoes, 283,378t millet, 260,785t pulses, 91,094t citrus fruit, 53,626t oilcrops, 3,310t tobacco, 17,290t fibre crops, 16,890t jute, *90,000t ginger, *36,000 various herbs and spice, 2,305,326t sugar cane, 11,651t tea, 34,036t apples, 645,130t fruit in total, 3,877,000t vegetables in total. Livestock production included: 256,862t meat in total, *48,450t beef, 133,600t buffalo meat, 15,389t pig meat, 2,779t lamb, 40,540t goat meat, 16,104t poultry, *27,300t eggs, 1,310,053t milk, 4,640t cattle hides, 618t sheepskins, *33,462t buffalo hides.
* estimate

Forestry
Forests occupy around 33 per cent of Nepal's land area. The canopy cover in the mid-hills is growing thicker as a result of the government's successful policy of handing over forests to local communities. Deforestation is still high in the government-managed forests of the plains. Export of forest products in 2004 amounted to US$3.9 million and imports to US$13.6 million. Timber is mainly smuggled into India.

Production in 2004 included 14.0 million cubic metres (mcum) roundwood, 1.3mcum sawlogs and veneers, 630,000 cubic metres (cum) sawnwood, 30,000cum wood-based panels, 12,7mcum woodfuel, 68,939mt charcoal.

Industry and manufacturing
Industry accounts for around 21.7 per cent of GDP. The sector consists mainly of manufacturing low-end consumer goods – principally carpets, garments and handicrafts. The development of this sector is constrained by poor infrastructure, a small local market, high industrial factor costs and lack of access to the sea.

Nepal offers duty concessions on raw material imports and start-up tax holidays for new industry, but foreign direct investment flows have remained slow.

The end of the Multi-fibre Agreement in 2005 has had a devastating effect on the textile industry.

Tourism
Tourism is an important element in the economy, but has been badly affected in recent years by the global economic downturn, international terrorism, continuing civil war, the Sars outbreak and the *tsunami* of December 2004 (although Nepal was not directly affected, visitors to the whole region fell). In periods of calm, visitor numbers pick up, as shown in 2003 when arrivals increased by 23 per cent during a truce in the civil war and fell again after it ceased. The *tsunami* and continuing instability resulted in lower annual arrivals in 2005: 277,129 compared with 288,356 the previous year. Numbers were down in the earlier part of 2005, improving as the year wore on. Whereas there was a decline in tourists from the West, the number of Asian visitors increased.

Mount Everest is Nepal's greatest attraction.

Environment
The Sagarmatha (Mount Everest) Pollution Control Committee (SPCC), set up in 1991, spends US$15,000 cleaning up the Sagarmatha National Park every year. The government charges a minimum of US$50,000 for each expedition to Mount Everest, and ploughs back 30–40 per

Nepal

cent of this and other tourist fees to support the SPCC's work. Since the old trekking routes pose serious problems to the indigenous communities already, there are many opposing voices among the environmentalists in Kathmandu.

Mining
Mining and quarrying accounts for around 0.5 per cent of GDP.
Among the major known mineral reserves only limestone has been extracted for commercial use in considerable volumes. Nepal also has deposits of lead, zinc, marble, iron ore and magnesite.

Hydrocarbons
No economically extractable hydrocarbon reserves have been discovered in Nepal. The government has invited foreign companies to explore for oil. About 15,250 barrels per day of refined oil are imported.
Nepal does not import natural gas. Nepal has a small coal industry with reserves of around two million tonnes. Annual output meets less than 5 per cent of domestic demand and about 531,000 tonnes of coal are imported

Energy
Nepal has an electricity generating capacity of 610MW, mostly supplied by hydropower, but around 10 per cent from thermal plants. Only one per cent of Nepal's energy needs is met by electricity. The hydropower potential is considerable, with estimated economically viable capacity of 43,000MW, which could supply a majority of the population, mostly rural, who lack access to lectricity. Annual demand for electricity continues to rise. Wood fuel accounts for around 75 per cent of energy used, with agricultural waste providing most of the rest.

Banking and insurance
Central bank
Nepal Rastra Bank
Main financial centre
Kathmandu

Time
GMT plus five hours and forty-five minutes

Geography
Nepal is a landlocked, roughly rectangular country located south of the Himalayan mountain range. It is about 885km long (east to west) and an average non-uniform, north-south width of 193km. The country is divided into five development regions and 75 districts. Ecologically, Nepal is divided into three regions—mountain, hill and terai (plains). India borders Nepal in the east, south and west. China borders Nepal in the north. The topography is rugged and harsh and with a vertical distance of less than 200km, the altitude changes from sea level to the highest point on earth – the 8,848m Mount Everest.

Climate
The climate is generally temperate but harsh and cold at high altitudes. The low-lying plains are hot in summer and warm during the winters. The high mountains are permanently covered with snow (above 4,800 metres). High temperatures range between 17–30 degrees Celsius (C) and lows are in the range of 0–17 C. May–September is the monsoon season; July is the wettest month and also the hottest.

Dress codes
If travelling outside Kathmandu, it is respectable and practical to wear casual trousers and full-sleeved shirts and jackets. Shorts may be acceptable only in urban centres.

Entry requirements
Passports
Required by all except nationals of India. Entry may be refused, and airlines may not carry passengers holding passports with less than six months validity.
Visa
Required by all except nationals of India. Tourist visas are issued on arrival. Overnight visas are issued free of cost.
The Nepal Tourism Board website (www.welcomenepal.com) provides updated information on changes in related policies and rules.
Business visa are only issued to those who have been officially recognised as either a) the official representative (of a commercial entity that has obtained a licence to invest in the Kingdom of Nepal in a business or industrial enterprise) or b) an individual, who has obtained a licence to invest in Nepal in export trade. Applications for multiple-entry business visas (one or five years) need to be made in advance. Application should be made to the Director General, Department of Immigration, Kathmandu (www.immi.gov.np). An authorisation from the relevant Nepalese ministry is needed, as are photocopies of the relevant pages of the visitor's passport. The applicant will be sent application forms which must be returned fully completed. If accepted, the visa will be stamped on the visitor's passport at Kathmandu airport.
Currency advice/regulations
Tourists carrying more than US$2,000, or equivalent foreign currency, should declared this on the Custom Declaration Form on arrival. The export of currency above US$2,000, or equivalent, is illegal. Retain currency exchange receipts to exchange Nepali currency when departing. Currency can be exchanged at banks or authorised foreign exchange dealers and at major hotels. All daily papers publish the day's exchange rates.
Only Indian and Nepali nationals may carry Indian currency; possession of Indian Rs500 bills is illegal in Nepal.
Customs
Personal effects are imported duty-free. Import of certain goods, such as beef, weapons, explosives and wireless radio transmitters, may be prohibited. Cameras and a reasonable amount of film are permitted.
Exporting goods which are 100 years or older is illegal. Exports of antiques and religious artefacts must be certified and cleared by the Department of Archaeology.

Health (for visitors)
Mandatory precautions
Vaccination certificate for yellow fever if travelling from an infected area.
Advisable precautions
Vaccinations for diphtheria, tuberculosis, hepatitis 'A' and 'B', Japanese 'B' encephalitis, meningitis, polio, tetanus, typhoid. Anti-malarial precautions are advisable. Rabies is a risk.

Hotels
Nepal has about 100 tourist-class hotels, ranging from up-market five-star deluxe to those with one-star ratings. Other accommodation includes over 750 non-star-rated, but affordable and safe, speciality establishments.
Hotels may be full during the tourist season and it is advisable to book in advance.

Credit cards
All major credit cards are accepted by large tourist hotels and shops. Most used are American Express, Mastercard and Visa.

Public holidays
Fixed dates
11 Jan (National Unity Day), 29 Jan (Martyrs' Day), 19 Feb (National Democracy Day), 8 Mar (Women's Day), 14 Apr (Nepali New Year), 9 Nov (Constitution Day), 29 Dec (King Birendra's Birthday).
Variable dates
Vasant Panchami (Jan/Feb), Shivaratri (Feb/Mar), Ghode Jatra (Festival of Horses) (Mar), Holi (Mar), Chaite Dashain (Mar/Apr), Ram Nawami (Birthday of Lord Ram) (Mar/Apr), Lord Buddha's Birthday (Apr/May), Rakshya Bandhan (Janai Purnima) (Aug), Gai Jatra/Procession of Cows (Aug/Sep), Krishna Asthami (Birthday of Lord Krishna) (Aug/Sep), Teej (Festival of Women) (Sep), Dasain (Durga Puja Festival) (Oct), Diwali/Deepawali (Oct/Nov), Indra Jatra/Festival of Rain God (Oct/Nov).

In general, Hindu and Buddhist festivals are declared according to local astronomical observations.

Working hours
Banking
Mon–Fri: In Kathmandu Valley 0930–1500. Major city banks have automatic teller machines (ATMs). Some banks open at weekends.
Business
Sun–Fri: 1000–1700.
Government
Mon–Fri: 0900–1700.
Shops
Sun–Fri: 1000–1900 (some shops also open on Saturdays).

Weights and measures
Metric system (local measures are also used).

Social customs/useful tips
The traditional form of greeting is called *namaste* – performed by placing the palms together at chest height and bowing slightly; it means 'I celebrate the divinity in you'. Some Nepali women may prefer not to shake hands with people of the opposite sex. Always use your right hand to eat or pass anything on. Remove shoes before entering temples and homes. Sons are expected to care for their mothers in old age; there is a high respect for elders.

Security
Internal terrorist activities have seen indiscriminate attacks in and around the capital as well as tourist areas, visitors are advised to exercise extra vigilance and also take care to respect any local curfews.

Getting there
Air
National airline: Royal Nepal Airlines (mainly flies regional routes and Japan).
International airport/s: Kathmandu Tribhuwan International (KTM), 6km from Kathmandu.
Airport tax: International departures NRs1,000; departure to SAARC countries NRs770. There is also a domestic departures tax. The rates change almost every year and it is advisable to check with travel agents. (SAARC countries are Bangladesh, Bhutan, India, Maldives, Pakistan and Sri lanka).
Surface
Road: There are many access routes from India and Tibet.

Getting about
National transport
Air: The only way to reach many parts of Nepal is by air. Nepal has 44 domestic airports and 120 helicopter landing strips. Royal Nepal Airlines and private airline companies have flights to and from these airports. Special helicopter charters can also be arranged. Flights may be delayed during the rainy months; otherwise, they are an efficient means of getting around.
Road: There is a road network of over 13,000km. The roads are not well maintained. Kathmandu, Pokhara and Biratnagar are linked by surfaced road. Transport is difficult outside main centres. The Mahendra Highway makes west Nepal accessible throughout the year. The mountainous nature of the country means that many of its roads are unusable, especially during the winter and the monsoon.
Buses: Long distance day or night bus services operate from Kathmandu to all cities of Nepal.
Rail: The only line serves Jaynagar to Janakpur and Bizalpura.
City transport
Taxis: Metered taxis can be hailed in Kathmandu. Private taxis are also available at the hotels, but they may cost more.
Buses, trams & metro: The airport bus to the city centre takes 35 minutes.
Car hire
Driving is on the left. An international driving permit is required. Local authorities also issue a local permit upon presentation of a national licence. Chauffeur-driven car hire is available.

BUSINESS DIRECTORY
The addresses listed below are a selection only. While World of Information makes every endeavour to check these addresses, we cannot guarantee that changes have not been made, especially to telephone numbers and area codes. We would welcome any corrections.

Telephone area codes
The international direct dialling (IDD) code for Nepal is +977, followed by area code and subscriber's number:

Bhairawa	71	Janakpur	41
Bhaktapur	1	Kathmandu	1
Birgunj	51	Nepalgunj	81
Biratnagar	21	Patan	1
Dhangadhi	91	Pokhara	61

Useful telephone numbers
Police: 100
Directory enquiries: 197

Chambers of Commerce
Federation of Nepalese Chambers of Commerce and Industry, Shahid Shukra FNCCI Milan Marg, Teku, Kathmandu (tel: 426-2061; fax: 426-2007; e-mail: fncci@mos.com.np).

Nepal Britain Chamber of Commerce and Industry, British Embassy Premises, Lainchaur, PO Box 106, Kathmandu (tel: 441-0583; fax: 441-8137; e-mail: info@nbcci.org).

Nepal Chamber of Commerce, Chamber Bhawan, Kantipath, PO Box 198, Kathmandu (tel: 422-2890; fax: 422-9998; e-mail: chamber@wlink.com.np).

Nepal-US Chamber of Commerce and Industry, TNT Building, Tinkune, Koteshwor, PO Box 2769, Kathmandu (tel: 447-8020; fax: 447-4508; e-mail: nusacci@vishnu.ccsl.com.np).

Banking
Agricultural Development Bank, Ramshahpath, Kathmandu (tel: 211-744, 211-802/3; fax: 225-329).

Himalayan Bank Ltd, PO Box 20590, Karmachari Sanchaya Kosh Building, Tridevi Marg, Thamel, Kathmandu (tel: 227-749, 250-201; fax: 222-800).

Nepal Arab Bank Ltd (Nabil Bank), PO Box 3729, Kantipath, Kathmandu (tel: 211-784/6; fax: 226-905).

Nepal Bangladesh Bank Ltd, PO Box 9062, Bijuli Bazar, Naya Baneshwor, Kathmandu (tel: 490-767/70; fax: 490-824, 493-259) .

Nepal Bank Ltd, Dharmapath, Kathmandu (tel: 221-185, 224-337; fax: 226-905).

Nepal Grindlays Bank Ltd, PO Box 3990, Naya Baneswor, Kathmandu (tel: 212-683/6; fax: 226-762).

Nepal Indosuez Bank Ltd, PO BOx 3412, Durbar Marg, Kathmandu (tel: 228-229/232; fax: 226-349).

Rastriya Banijya Bank, Singha Durbar Plaza, Kathmandu (tel: 252-595, 268-409, 251-982; fax: 252-931).

Citibank, PO Box 2826, c/o Hotel Yak & Yeti, Durbar Marg, Kathmandu (tel: 228-884; fax: 227-884).

Standard Chartered Bank, PO Box 1526, Durbar, PO Box 1526, Durbar, Marg, Kathmandu (tel and fax: 220-129).

Central bank
Nepal Rastra Bank, PO Box 73, Baluwatar, Kathmandu (tel: 422-1763; fax: 425-4170; e-mail: nrb@mos.com.np).

Travel information
Automobile Association of Nepal, c/o Traffic Police Office, Kathmandu (tel: 211-093).

Everest Air, Durbar Marg, Kathmandu (tel: 224-188; fax: 226-795).

Himalayan Helicopters PVT Ltd, Durbar Marg, Kathmandu (tel: 217-236; fax: 225-150).

Kathmandu Tribhuvan International Airport, Air Traffic Controller, Gauchar (tel: 472-258 or 473-985, ext 486; fax: 474-180; e-mail: tiao@mod.com.mp).

Nepal

Nepal Mountaineering Association, 16/53 Ramshah Path, PO Box 1435, Kathmandu (tel: 211-596).

Royal Nepal Airlines, PO Box 401, RNAC Building, Kantipath, Kathmandu 711000 (tel: 214-511; fax: 225-348).

Tourist Information Centre, Basantpur, Kathmandu; Tribhuwan International Airport, Kathmandu (tel: 470-537).

Ministry of tourism
Ministry of Tourism and Civil Aviation, Tripureshwor, Kathmandu (tel: 225-870, 214-836; fax: 227-758).

National tourist organisation offices
Nepal Tourism Board, Tourist Service Centre, Bhrikuti Mandap, Kathmandu (tel: 256-909, 256-229; fax: 256-910; e-mail: info@ntb.wlink.com.np; internet site: http://www.welcomenepal.com).

Ministries
Ministry of Commerce, Babar Mahal, Kathmandu (tel: 223-489, 224-805; fax: 225-594).

Ministry of Finance, Hari Bhawan, Kathmandu (tel: 224-527, 227-367; fax: 227-529).

Ministry of Industry, Tripureshwor, Kathmandu (tel: 213-880, 213-838; fax: 226-112).

Other useful addresses
Asian Development Bank (ADB), Nepal Resident Mission, Srikunj Kamaladi Ward No 31, Block 2597, Ka.Na.Pa. Kathmandu; Postal address: PO Box 5017 K.D.P.O., Kathmandu (tel: 227-779; fax: 225-063; e-mail: adbnrm@mail.asiandevbank.org; internet site: http://www.adb.org/).

British Embassy, Laimchaur, PO Box 106, Kathmandu (tel: 414-588, 410-583, 411-590, 411-281; fax: 411-789).

Department of Commerce, Kathmandu (tel: 227-364, 227-404).

Director General, Department of Immigration, Kathmandu (tel: 223-681).

National Planning Commission, PO Box 1284, Singha Dubar, Kathmandu (tel: 215-000).

Nepal Economic and Commerce Research Centre, PO Box 285, 7/358 Kohity Bahal, Kathmandu (tel: 215-336).

Nepal Industrial Development Corporation (NIDC), NIDC Building, PO Box 10, Durba Marg, Kathmandu (tel: 411-211, 411-225).

Royal Nepalese Embassy (USA), 2131 Leroy Place, NW, Washington DC 20008 (tel: (1)202-667-4550; fax: (1)202-667-5534; e-mail: info@nepalembassyusa.org).

Trade Promotion Centre, Kathmandu (tel: 524-771, 524-772; fax: 521-637).

United Nations Development Programme, United Nations Building, Pulchowk, PO Box 7, Kathmandu (tel: 523-200; fax: 523-991).

Internet sites
Asian Sources Online: http://asiansources.com

Market information: http://www.feer.com

News portal: http://www.nepalnews.com

The Netherlands

KEY FACTS

Official name: Koninkrijk der Nederlanden (The Kingdom of The Netherlands)

Head of State: Queen Beatrix (crowned 30 April 1980)

Head of government: Prime Minister Jan Peter Balkenende (CDA) (prime minister from Jul 2002 until 16 Oct 2002; reappointed to lead coalition 27 May 2003)

Ruling party: Coalition government from 27 May 2003: Christen Democratisch Appèl (CDA) (Christian Democratic Appeal); Volkspartij voor Vrijheid en Democratie (VVD) (People's Party for Freedom and Democracy); Democraten 66 (D66) (Democrats 66)

Area: 41,473 square km

Population: 16.36 million (2004)

Capital: The Hague (seat of government); Amsterdam (legal and cultural)

Official language: Dutch and Frisian

Currency: Euro (eur) = 100 cents (from 1 Jan 2002; previous currency guilder, locked at f2.20 per euro)

Exchange rate: eur0.83 per US$ (Oct 2005)

GDP per capita: US$35,416 (2004)

GDP real growth: 1.30% (2004)

Labour force: 8.33 million (2004)

Unemployment: 4.70% (OECD, 2004)

Inflation: 1.40% (2004)

Balance of trade: US$40.40 billion (2004)

Foreign debt: US$1,699.39 billion (2004)

Annual FDI: US$273.80 billion (cumulative, 1995–2004, OECD)

A traditionally open and tolerant society – The Netherlands is known for its 'coffee houses' selling hash and other recreational drugs – the country is becoming increasingly illiberal. With the assassination of anti-immigration politician Pym Fortuyn in May 2002, and the murder of film-maker Theo van Gogh in late 2004, controversial political figures have started to watch their backs. The government is cracking down on immigration and the people are becoming more eurosceptic – they threw out the EU constitution in a referendum in June 2005.

Post WWII

The Netherlands in 1945 was long removed from its golden age of greatness in the seventeenth century. For most of the years that separated the old and the post-war eras, The Netherlands had become something of a European backwater, of little influence and less power. True it had an empire, centred on Indonesia. Even this, though, was a legacy and situated largely outside what was then seen as the mainstream of world history,

Religion was the key element in the ordering of society. Calvinism and Catholicism in old Holland were profoundly, almost rigidly, conservative. The entrepreneurial spirit which had so animated the golden age, even in the midst of religious conviction, had worn thin. What remained were agricultural pursuits, the sleepy administration of the empire and recollections of better days. When Hitler's armies crossed the frontier in 1940, all this was brought to an end. The five-year-long occupation was a nightmare, but it also caused The Netherlands to wake up. After the Second World War, everything changed. By the advent of the twenty-first century, Holland had a flourishing economy; Dutch multinationals like Shell, Unilever and Philips were among the largest corporations in the world and many other enterprises, from banks to construction firms, had left their mark on the global scene.

Social democracy

It has been said that after the war, social democracy replaced religion as The Netherlands' national creed. The welfare state, which began in the early 1950s, came to occupy a place at the heart of Dutch society. From the cradle to the grave, Dutch citizens were coddled and comforted, so that poverty became rare and pretty relative and good health became the national norm. Paradoxically, despite the cushion provided by the state, The Netherlands' work rate and industrial productivity have always been among the highest in Europe. Of increasing concern is the fact that many people in Holland, especially young people and immigrants, no longer possess the work ethic that once characterised the country. Whole sections of Dutch society – not to be confused with the genuinely unemployed – appear to see little value in regular work, preferring to spend their time in an economically adjusted form of café society. Many are 'professional' students in their sixth or seventh year of study.

Economy

The Netherlands is a well-developed economy increasingly based on high technology industries and services, especially in international transport and shipping. It has long been one of Europe's most open economies, with the value of its trade equivalent to 106 per cent of GDP.

While many continental European countries are still trying to restructure rigid labour markets and over-regulated economies, The Netherlands economy is based on the, until recently, successful so-called Polder consensus model combining low unemployment with low inflation. With its skilled and multilingual workforce, The Netherlands looks well placed to remain as important a business, financial and trading centre in the 'new' global economy as it was for the 'old'. However, there are concerns that it is losing international competitiveness and tightness in the labour market means that the government's most urgent task must be to draw displaced workers back into the workforce. Inflationary pressures are rising and though Amsterdam remains cheap by comparison to London, Frankfurt or Paris, the government has used fiscal policies as a brake on the economy.

In 2003 after decades of steady growth and rising prosperity, the Dutch economy found itself, alongside Germany, at the bottom of the European growth league a situation that continued in the first half of 2004, lagging well behind Europe as a whole, not to mention the US. Having shrunk by an estimated 0.9 per cent in 2003, the first contraction sine the 1980s, GDP growth was predicted to be 0.7 per cent for 2005. According to The Netherlands' Bureau for Economic Policy Analysis, this means that the average growth figure for the period 2001–04 will be less than 0.5 per cent annually.

Over 10 per cent of the Dutch workforce has retired early, on often generous disability benefits, creating concealed unemployment without which the OECD calculates that the real rate of unemployment could be as high as 20 per cent.

The wave of privatisations during the 1990s was motivated by government efforts to reduce state debt in preparation for the introduction of the euro. Successive Dutch governments have used budget surpluses to reduce public debt. At the end of 2005 The Netherlands' debt was projected at 58.7 per cent of GDP (the European Union's target is 60 per cent).

The budget deficit for 2005, 1.8 per cent of GDP, was well within the 3 per cent required by the EU's Pact for Stability and Growth. The OECD estimates that The Netherlands needs to run a budget surplus of 1.25–1.75 per cent until 2012, thereby reducing government debt, if it is to be able to afford future social benefits. The government's stated goal is to bring the deficit down to 0.7 per cent of GDP in 2007.

In presenting his 2006 budget, finance minister Gerrit Zalm proposed US$3.1 billion worth of tax breaks in efforts to revive domestic consumption, which has been very low since 2000. He also expanded last year's policy of cutting corporate taxes: from 34.5 per cent in 2004 to 29.6 per cent in 2006. Another cut is in the pipeline for 2007. On the other hand he also tightened up rules on disability and unemployment benefits, and the rules on early retirement. The prime minister predicted growth for 2006 at 2.5 per cent, a clear end to five years of near-zero growth. Unemployment is also expected to fall, down to 475,000, a reduction of 25,000 people. This announcement of good news has done little, however, for the prime minister's waning popularity.

Immigration

Tolerance, rather than toleration has long been a part of the Dutch make-up. Since the Second World War The Netherlands has justifiably prided itself on its liberal, non-racist culture. However, as the economy flagged and jobs became harder to get, things changed. In February 2004 the Dutch parliament approved legislation providing for the expulsion of some

KEY INDICATORS — The Netherlands

	Unit	2000	2001	2002	2003	2004
Population	m	15.86	16.00	16.03	16.20	*16.36
Gross domestic product (GDP)	US$bn	368.90	380.50	413.70	413.70	*577.26
GDP per capita	US$	23,100	23,810	26,510	31,883	35,416
GDP real growth	%	3.5	1.4	0.6	-0.9	1.3
Inflation	%	2.5	4.5	3.9	2.3	1.4
Unemployment	%	2.7	2.0	2.3	3.7	–
Natural gas output	bn cum	57.3	61.4	59.9	58.3	68.8
Exports (fob) (goods)	US$m	205,653.0	207,102.0	243,360.0	243,300.0	293,100.0
Imports (fob) (goods)	US$m	187,107.0	183,514.0	217,710.0	201,100.0	252,700.0
Balance of trade	US$m	18,545.0	23,588.0	29,000.0	42,200.0	40,400.0
Current account	US$m	13,764.0	12,405.0	9,870.0	15,000.0	19,400.0
Total reserves minus gold	US$m	9,643.0	9,034.0	9,563.0	11.0	10,102.0
Foreign exchange	US$m	7,004.0	5,930.0	6,017.0	7,180.0	6,657.0
Exchange rate	per US$	2.39	2.41	1.04	0.88	0.80

* estimated figure

26,000 asylum seekers resident in The Netherlands. The move attracted a lot of popular support and just as much opposition from the asylum seekers – many of whom had been resident in The Netherlands for more than 5 years and in some cases for 10 years, while applying for residence. Under the legislation, all those asylum seekers who arrived before April 2001 were offered air tickets to their country of origin and given eight weeks in which to leave. Those who refused to leave risked facing a six-month jail sentence. By March 2005 nearly 5,000 refugees left without being forced while 519 people had been deported. Opinion polls indicated more than 60 per cent support for an amnesty to be granted to all those asylum-seekers who have been living in The Netherlands for more than 5 years. Somewhat ironically, Dutch asylum applications have dropped by around 75 per cent since 2000. The anti-asylum legislation was something of a setback to The Netherlands' reputation for tolerance on social matters and risked establishing a pattern for the treatment of asylum seekers in other European countries.

Terrorism

In November 2004 Theo van Gogh, whose film *Submission* had been critical of Islamic treatment of women, was murdered for being an 'enemy of Islam'. His killer, Mohammed Bouyeri, a Dutch Muslim, was jailed for life in July 2005, the first person to be found guilty under the country's recently revised anti-terror laws. Bouyeri said he 'acted out of conviction', and was alleged to have had terrorist intent. Muslims make up 13.2 per cent of Amsterdam's population and the case is thought to have widened social divisions. The Dutch MP, Aayan Hirsi Ali, wrote the screenplay for van Gogh's film and has been in hiding ever since his murder.

External relations

On 1 June 2005, the EU constitution was put to the vote in The Netherlands. A defeat was widely predicted and the government spent an extra last-minute US$4.2 million to try to stem the tide of euroscepticism, surprising in a founder country, formerly at the heart of the EU. The referendum, the first in the country for 200 years, was widely seen as a vote of confidence in the national government. The complacency of the government, for trying to manipulate the vote, was roundly condemned. The UK *Financial Times* has called the prime minister, Jan Peter Balkenende, 'more of a crisis-manager than a governor'. Reasons cited by 'no' voters included the fear of an influx of economic migrants from Eastern Europe, and the knowledge that the euro was to blame for the country's spiralling inflation and the resultant crash in the value of pensions and savings accounts. Recent religious tension in The Netherlands has fuelled many voters' hostility towards Turkish accession to EU member status – the influence of its overwhelmingly Muslim population is feared by Dutch conservatives.

Three days after the French threw out the EU constitution, 62 per cent of Dutch voters followed suit. This threw the whole document into an uncertain future, with the UK government quietly resolving not to go to the polls any time soon. The rejection of the constitution was not planned for.

Many Dutch citizens – especially young people – have an ambiguous attitude towards the US. Like it or not, its culture is increasingly their culture, its influence unavoidable. None the less, The Netherlands provided political support to the 2003 Iraq War and deployed 1,100 troops after the end of hostilities alongside British troops in the Al Muthanna province in southern Iraq. Although the government supported the US-led invasion, it was particularly keen not to alienate France and Germany, which opposed the war. During the war, foreign minister Jaap de Hoop Scheffer expressed his desire for The Netherlands to play a mediating role between the US's European supporters and those European states opposed to the war. His diplomatic skills had not gone unnoticed and he was chosen in September 2003 to replace the UK's Lord Robertson as NATO secretary general.

Outlook

Having emerged from economic stagnation, things are improving for The Netherlands. The economy is highly dependent on a continued recovery in global trade. Any sustained rise in the oil price will be bad news for The Netherlands.

Unemployment and the contentious immigration legislation both risk generating social unrest. Increasing participation in the workplace and increasing productivity and competitiveness are crucial tasks if economic growth is to be strong. If the Balkenende government can see through its modest economic reform programme and enable the economy to consolidate around an acceptable budget deficit, it will have achieved a lot.

Risk assessment

Economic	Improving
Political	Good
Regional Stability	Good
Stock Market	Good

COUNTRY PROFILE

Historical profile

1579 The Protestant majority in the Netherlands rebelled against the Catholic Habsburg Empire and declared independence, with William of Orange crowned Prince William I of Holland and Zeeland. In the seventeenth century, the Netherlands became a powerful trading nation with an empire in the East Indies (modern day Indonesia) and the Caribbean. In the 1650s, the Dutch fought several wars against the English, mainly due to colonial rivalry.
1688 William of Orange (the grandson of William I) acceded to the English throne as William III, ending conflict between the two countries.
1704–06 The English army under John Churchill helped to defeat attempts by the combined armies of Austria and France to invade the Netherlands.
1804 The Netherlands was occupied by the French under Napoleon.
1812 The Netherlands was liberated by British and Prussian armies.
1815 A renewed invasion attempt by Napoleon was defeated at the Battle of Waterloo. Attempts to unify Catholic Belgium with the Netherlands at the Vienna Conference failed, and the two countries remained separate.
1914–18 The country remained neutral in the First World War.
1940–45 During the Second World War, the Netherlands was occupied by Germany despite its neutrality.
1949 The policy of neutrality was abandoned and the Netherlands became a founder member of NATO.
1958 The Netherlands was a founding member of the European Economic Community (EEC).
1980 Queen Juliana abdicated in favour of her eldest daughter Princess Beatrix.
1989 The Christen Democratisch Appèl (CDA) (Christian Democratic Appeal) and Volkspartij voor Vrijheid en Democratie (VVD) (People's Party for Freedom and Democracy) government fell in its second term when VVD refused to support Prime Minister Ruud Lubbers' proposal for a 20-year environmental protection programme. A centre-left cabinet was formed by CDA and the Partij van de Arbeid (PvdA) (Labour Party), with Lubbers still as leader.
1992–93 The government of Ruud Lubbers was discredited by a serious economic recession.

The Netherlands

1994 Elections resulted in a three-party coalition, headed by Wim Kok (PvdA), and including VVD and Democraten 66 (D66) (Democrats 66). The CDA was frozen out of power for the first time since the First World War.
1998 The coalition government of PvdA, D66 and VVD, headed by Prime Minister Wim Kok, continued after winning an increased majority in elections.
1999 The Netherlands was a founder member of European Economic and Monetary Union (Emu). D66 threatened to leave the coalition after its proposals for constitutional reform were defeated in parliament, but a compromise was reached.
2000 Ruud Lubbers was chosen to head the UN High Commission on Refugees (UNHCR). After 25 years of debating, a bill to legalise euthanasia was approved.
2001 Prime Minister Wim Kok announced he would not seek re-election for a third term.
2002 Euro currency replaced the guilder. For a country that had not experienced any major political upheavals since the Second World War, this turned out to be a year to remember. Pim Fortuyn, leader of the Lijst Pim Fortuyn (LPF) (List Pim Fortuyn), was shot dead. The CDA won the parliamentary elections. The LPF emerged as the second largest party. The vote ended eight years of Labour-led centre-left domination in government. Jan Peter Balkenende was appointed prime minister, leading a fragile coalition government of CDA, LPF and VVD members. After the resignation of two LPF ministers, the cabinet collapsed and Balkenende resigned. A caretaker government was put in to run the country until the formation of a new cabinet. In October, Prince Claus von Amsberg, the husband of Queen Beatrix of the Netherlands, died.
2003 After parliamentary elections, Prime Minister Balkenende was reinstated to head a coalition government, led by the CDA, and including the VVD and the D66.
2004 Former Queen Juliana (1948–80), died in March. In November, prominent film-maker Theo van Gogh was murdered by an Islamist radical. Tit-for-tat attacks on Dutch mosques and churches ensued.
2005 In a referendum on 1 June, The Netherlands became the second country to reject a proposed constitution for the EU, three days after the French turned the proposal down. In December, the Dutch parliament legislated to introduce a test on Dutch language and culture for would-be migrants. Also in December, the Dutch immigration minister pledged to examine the issue of banning the wearing of the burqa in public.

Political structure
Constitution
Under the constitution of 1983, The Netherlands is divided into 12 administrative provinces. Each province is run by a royal commissioner and an elected Provinciale Staten (regional parliamentary assembly). Each regional assembly elects its own governing executive (Gedeputeerde Staten) from among its members. Both council and executive are presided over by a royal commissioner, who is appointed by the crown.
The 672 municipalities, including the major cities, each have an elected council which in turn elects aldermen to sit on the municipal executive along with a mayor, who is appointed by the crown.
The constitution guarantees equality and freedom from discrimination on the grounds of religion, political opinion, race, or sex. The constitution is unique in placing upon the government a duty to promote environmental protection both domestically and internationally.
Where there is no adult successor to the throne or the serving monarch is unable to exercise royal prerogative, the national legislature has the power to appoint a temporary regent.
The Kingdom of the Netherlands also includes overseas territories in the Caribbean – Aruba (which has been a separate entity since 1986) and the Netherlands Antilles (Bonaire and Curaçao). Aruba is unlikely to proceed to independence in the foreseeable future and will therefore remain a member of the Dutch Commonwealth.
Form of state
Parliamentary democratic monarchy
The executive
The monarch is the head of state but has few executive powers. However it does become actively involved in resolving political crises (for example, at times when no agreement could be reached on the formation of a cabinet). The monarch has the power to appoint the prime minister (on the recommendation of the national assembly), to dissolve the national assembly and call new elections.
The principle executive functions are carried out by the prime minister, who is selected by the national assembly and appoints a council of ministers from both inside and outside the assembly. State ministers are not allowed to continue to sit as members of the national assembly.
National legislature
Legislative power is vested in the Staten Generaal (States General), a bicameral national assembly.
The lower house is the 150-member Tweede Kamer (Second Chamber), which is directly elected by the d'Hondt system of proportional representation (a system invented in The Netherlands which takes account of the country's provincial units) for a four-year term. It is empowered to debate bills and pass approved measures to the upper house, the Eerste Kamer (First Chamber), for enactment.
The First Chamber has 75 members who are indirectly elected by the 12 provincial assemblies for a period of four years. The First Chamber does not initiate legislation, but is responsible for approving or rejecting bills presented by the Second Chamber. The First Chamber cannot amend legislation directly, but acts which it rejects are likely to be amended in the Second Chamber and represented for approval.
Legal system
The Supreme Court is the highest legal body in the country and it hears appeals arising from cases previously heard in the lower courts. It also has the power of cassation over legislation deemed to conflict with the constitution.
There are five Appeal Courts at lower levels. Most cases are heard either at the 19 Provincial Courts of Justice or at the 62 Municipal Courts. Judges are nominated by the crown and serve for life.
Last elections
10 June 2004 (European Parliament); 22 January 2003 (parliamentary).
Results: European Parliament: CDA won 24.4 per cent of the vote (seven seats out of 27), PvdA 23.6 per cent (seven), VVD 13.2 per cent (four), GroenLinks (Green Left) 7.4 per cent (two), Europe Transparent 7.3 per cent (two), Socialistische Partij (SP) (Socialist Party) 7 per cent (two), Christen Unie/Staatkundig Gereformeerde Partij (CU/SGP) (Christian Union/Politically Reformed Party) 5.9 per cent (two) and Democraten 66 (D66) (Democrats 66) 4.2 per cent (one); turnout 39.1 per cent.
Parliamentary (Second Chamber): the ruling Christen Democratisch Appèl (CDA) (Christian Democratic Appeal) won a narrow victory (44 seats) over the opposition Partij van de Arbeid (PvdA) (Labour Party) (42 seats); Volkspartij voor Vrijheid en Democratie (VVD) (People's Party for Freedom and Democracy) (28 seats); Socialistische Partij (SP) (Socialist Party) (nine seats); Lijst Pim Fortuyn (LPF) (List Pym Fortuyn) (eight seats); Groen Links (GL) (Green Left) (eight seats); Democraten 66 (D66) (Democrats 66) (six seats); ChristenUnie (CU) (Christian Union) (three seats); Staatkundig Gereformeerde Partij (SGP) (Political Reformed Party) (two seats). Turnout was 80.4 per cent.
Parliamentary (First Chamber): CDA (23 seats); PvdA (19 seats); VVD (15 seats); SP (four seats); LPF (one seat); GL (five seats); D66 (three seats); CU (two seats); SGP (two seats); Onafhankelijke

Senaatsfractie-Fryske Nasjonale Partij (FNP) (Frisian National Party) (one seat).
Next elections
2007 (parliamentary)

Political parties
Ruling party
Coalition government from 27 May 2003: Christen Democratisch Appèl (CDA) (Christian Democratic Appeal); Volkspartij voor Vrijheid en Democratie (VVD) (People's Party for Freedom and Democracy); Democraten 66 (D66) (Democrats 66)
Main opposition party
Partij van de Arbeid (PvdA) (Labour Party)

Population
16.36 million (2004)
Ethnic make-up
Dutch (96 per cent); others, predominantly Afro-Caribbean (Surinamese), Indonesian, Moroccan and Turkish (4 per cent).
Religions
Catholic (34 per cent), Protestant (28 per cent), Muslim (3 per cent), Jewish (1 per cent).

Education
Primary schooling may begin at aged four, and continue until aged 12. At aged 12, pupils are channelled into secondary schools with courses designed for their aptitude. The length of time in these schools varies dependent on the courses undertaken; mixed general and vocational courses last for four years and pre-university courses last six years.
Schools are either publicly maintained by government, state or municipal authorities, (attended by 28 per cent of children), or private schools, mostly denominational (attended by 72 per cent of children). Total public expenditure on education is equivalent to approximately 5 per cent of annual GNP.
Compulsory years: 5 to 16.
Enrolment rate: 109 per cent and 106 per cent, male and female gross enrolment rates respectively, of relevant age groups for primary schools, (including repeaters); 126 per cent and 122 per cent, male and female gross enrolment rates respectively, of relevant age groups for secondary schools, (including repeaters), 1997–2000 (Unicef 2004).
Pupils per teacher: 14 in primary schools.

Health
The private sector is important in the supply of healthcare in the Netherlands and private health insurance is compulsory for most wage earners. Total expenditure on health is some 8–9 per cent of GDP, of which government spending is 63–64 per cent; private expenditure is about 37 per cent, of which some 42–43 per cent is pre-paid health insurance plans.

HIV prevalence: 0.2 per cent aged 15–49 in 2003 (World Bank)
Life expectancy: 78.5 years (World Bank)
Fertility rate/Maternal mortality rate: 1.8 births per woman; maternal mortality 7 per 100,000 live births (World Bank).
Infant mortality rate: 4.8 deaths per 1,000 live births (World Bank)
Head of population per physician/bed: 2.6 doctors and 11.3 hospital beds per 1,000 people. Although, at 64 per million people, the number of specialist surgeons is the lowest in the EU.

Welfare
The Netherlands provides generous income support linked to the minimum wage. However, following a government drive to limit the growth of social security spending, the criteria for eligibility for benefits has been narrowed and earnings-related benefits have been reduced from 80 to 70 per cent of previous income.
As in many EU countries, the ageing population is threatening to make the funding of state pensions an unsustainable burden on public finances over the next 30 years. In 2000, expenditure on pensions was some 5.7 per cent of GDP, but this is projected to rise to the equivalent of 8.4 per cent by 2020 and 11.2 per cent by 2030.

Main cities
Amsterdam (legal capital, estimated population 737,900 in 2003), Rotterdam (600,700), The Hague (seat of government, 465,900), Utrecht (263,900), Eindhoven (206,900), Tilburg (200,000), Groningen (176,600), Almere (168,300), Breda (165,300), Nijmegen (156,300).

Languages spoken
English, German and French are widely spoken. About 2.9 per cent of the population speak Frisian, mostly in the province of Friesland in the north-east. Turkish and Arabic are also spoken.
Official language/s
Dutch and Frisian

Media
Press
Dailies: There are almost 50 daily newspapers. Leading national dailies include *De Telegraaf*, *AD Magazine*, *Metro* (tabloid), *Nederlands Dagblad*, *Trouw*, *Algemeen Dagblad*, *De Volkskrant* and *NRC Handelsblad*.
Weeklies: There are several magazines, most of which are published by United Dutch Publishers (VNU). Weeklies include *De Telegraaf Weekeinde*, *Flair*, *NRC Handelsblad* and *De Volkskrant*.
Business: Major publications include *Elseviers Weekblad* (weekly), *Management Team* (fortnightly), *Elsevier Financial Planning*, *ABN AMRO Zaken Bulletin* and *Aaneen* (trade union magazine). The Dutch Business Association (DBA) publishes *Dutch Business Magazine* 10 times a year.
Periodicals: Foreign (especially European) newspapers and magazines are available at kiosks, bookstalls and hotels. The *Nederlandse Staatscourant* is the government information gazette, published by the state-owned press. Others of general interest include *M*, *Het Beste*, *CJP Magazine* and *ECI*.
Broadcasting
There are eight major public broadcasting associations which are allocated airtime and a share both of advertising revenues on public TV channels and radio stations and the TV and radio licence revenue, according to their public support through subscriptions. They were joined in late 1989 by the commercial Luxembourg channel RTL Véronique (RTL4) which also broadcasts programmes in Dutch.
The former Netherlands broadcasting service, Nederlandse Omroep Stichting, which parcels out airtime on the three public television channels, is now split into two organisations, the Nederlandse Omroepprogramma Stichting (NOS), which transmits general interest programmes, and the Nederlandse Omroepproductie Bedrijf (NOB), which provides services to the other broadcasters (although they are no longer compelled to use it).
Radio: Radio is more extensively deregulated than television. In addition to the five national channels there are 10 regional stations and approximately 180 local channels. Overseas broadcasting in Dutch is undertaken by Radio Nederland Wereldomroep (RNW).
Television: Television programmes are broadcast on three main channels. Transmission time is allotted according to the number of subscribers. TV programmes are broadcast in their original languages – often English – with Dutch subtitles. About 90 per cent of homes can receive cable TV services and the take-up rate for satellite TV is very high.
Advertising
Advertising is accepted in all forms of media, although TV and radio advertising is restricted to 30 and 40 minutes per day respectively for each station or channel. Most advertising is direct, in newspapers and magazines. Advertisements for TV and radio are accepted by Stichting Ether Reclame (STER), the company responsible for commercial airtime on the broadcasting network. Advice on agents can be obtained from the Dutch advertising association, Nederlandse Vereniging van Erkende Reclame Adviesbureaus (VEA).

The Netherlands

Economy
The Netherlands has a well-developed economy increasingly based on high technology industries and services, especially in international transport and shipping. However, membership of the EU and the European monetary union (EMU) has cost the country much in the four years since The Netherlands converted to the euro in 2001. The Dutch economy was overheating in the late 1990s leading to a property boom and spiralling wage costs. It has since been recognised that the guilder was undervalued when it was converted to the euro in 2001, which with its low exchange rate – set elsewhere and without regard for Dutch needs to curb spending – fuelled further speculation and inflation. The economy began a cycle of boom and bust as unemployment jumped from 3.3 per cent in 2001 to 6.7 per cent by 2005 and the government was forced to introduce austerity measures to bring the economy back into solvency. The economy contracted by 0.9 per cent in 2003. The economy was slowly beginning to recover by 2004, but as the euro began to appreciate Dutch net exports and domestic demand fell. Although high oil prices placed further pressure on the economy, GDP grew by 1.3 per cent in 2004.

GDP contracted by 0.5 per cent in the first quarter of 2005 but expanded by 1.5 per cent in the following two quarters. The OECD forecasts growth of 2.4 per cent in 2006. Unemployment remains high but fell to 6.1 per cent in early 2006. Core inflation is expected to edge down slowly. The OECD recommends that the government stimulate labour supply with measures to reduce poverty traps in order to enhance employment prospects for low-skilled workers.

The OECD 2005 *Economic Policy Reforms* makes a number of employment related recommendations including:
- reforming disability benefit schemes to shorten the duration of access to benefit
- simplifying administrative procedures, especially by linking government agencies with each other
- remove barriers to product market competition
- ease residential zoning restrictions to stimulate supply of housing.

External trade
There has been a regular trade surplus since 1981 owing to increased competitiveness and relatively low levels of imports. Dutch trade is equivalent to 3.7 per cent of the world total. Approximately 77 per cent of foreign trade is conducted with EU countries, particularly Germany, Belgium and France, but the early weakness of the euro helped its exports to other parts of the globe. Amsterdam is a major centre for trade in tobacco, diamonds and precious metals.

The effects of a tightening labour market in the late 1990s were offset by high levels of deregulation, allowing the Netherlands to maintain export competitiveness in many sectors.

Imports
Main imports include machinery and transport equipment, chemicals, fuels, foodstuffs and clothing.

Main sources: Germany (17.7 per cent total, 2004), Belgium (10.2 per cent), US (7.8 per cent), China (7.1 per cent), UK (6.6 per cent), France (4.9 per cent)

Exports
Major exports include gas, organic chemicals, agricultural products and foodstuffs, machinery and electronics.

Main destinations: Germany (25 per cent total, 2004), Belgium (12.6 per cent), UK (10.1 per cent), France (9.8 per cent), Italy (6.0 per cent), US (4.2 per cent)

Agriculture
Farming
The agricultural sector employs 4 per cent of the workforce and contributes 3 per cent to annual GDP, accounting for 25 per cent of total exports.

Despite high population density in the Netherlands, approximately 70 per cent of all land area is under cultivation. Population growth and wider commercial land use, combined with rising water levels, are placing considerable pressure on land resources.

Overall, Dutch farms tend to be larger than those in other EU member states, with only 25 per cent of farms smaller than five hectares, compared to an EU norm of 50 per cent. Productivity rates are consequently higher than the EU average, and the Netherlands is a net contributor to the EU's Common Agricultural Policy (CAP) budget.

Fundamental reform to the CAP was introduced throughout most of the EU on 1 January 2005. The subsidies paid on farm output, which tended to benefit large farms and encourage overproduction, were replaced by single farm payments not conditional on production. This is expected to reward farms that provide and maintain a healthy environment, food safety and animal welfare standards. The changes are also intended to encourage market conscious production and cut the cost of CAP to the EU taxpayer. The Netherlands is due to introduce this measure on 1 January 2006.

Dutch farmers are the world's most prolific consumers of pesticides, using 19,000 tonnes of active chemical ingredients per annum (an average 10 kilograms per hectare), with potatoes and flower bulbs the most intensively sprayed crops. Environmental legislation, which came into force in 2000, is designed to halve the level of chemical usage and some particularly damaging pesticides have been banned altogether.

Given the Netherlands' small surface area and high population density, farming is generally highly concentrated, specialised and efficient. Dairy farming is the most substantial activity, involving over a third of the country's farmers.

Traditional Dutch horticulture, in particular the production of flowers and bulbs, is the highest value-added sector. The Netherlands typically has over 24,000 hectares (ha) of land dedicated to open floriculture, and a further 7,000ha of floriculture under glass.

The crop production in 2003 included: 1.8 million metric tonnes (mmt) cereals in total, 1.2mmt wheat, 6.4mmt potatoes, 371,700 metric tonnes (mt) barley, 196,000mt maize, *15,500mt pulses, 595,000mt tomatoes, 6.4mmt sugar beets, 385,000mt apples, 612,000mt fruit in total, 3.6mmt vegetables in total. Livestock production included: 2.4mmt meat in total, *464,000mt beef, *1.4mmt pig-meat, 20,000mt lamb, 518,000mt poultry, 653,000mt eggs, *10.8mmt milk, 47,500mt cattle hides, 3,950mt sheepskins, 2,700mt greasy wool.
* estimate

Fishing
The typical Dutch fish catch is over 500,000 tonnes per annum, of which approximately 450,000mt is seafood. Around 20 per cent of the fish catch is exported, generating annual revenues of approximately US$250 million.

Forestry
Total forest area is 339,000 hectares (ha) or approximately 10 per cent of total land area. Almost all wood needs are imported, but The Netherlands is a major re-exporter of forest products. Total imports of forest material in 2004 amounted to US$5.1 billion, while exports amounted to US$3.3 billion.

Production in 2004 included 1,026,000 cubic metres (cum) roundwood, 736,000cum industrial roundwood, 273,000cum sawnwood, 393,000cum sawlogs and veneers, 290,000cum woodfuel.

Industry and manufacturing
The Netherlands has a broad industrial base. In 2004, manufacturing contributed 36 per cent to GDP and employ over 20 per cent of the labour force. Due to the small home market, Dutch industry is heavily dependent on foreign trade. It is also reliant upon imports of raw materials as industrial inputs.

As in most Western European countries, the industrial sector is increasingly focussed on high value-added manufacturing, where technological and skills advantages counteract the lower labour and production costs in emerging industrial economies. The Netherlands' lack of natural resources has increased its dependency on its manufacturing sector and imported materials.

Owing to rapid growth and the need for efficient land use, the construction industry is also significant and often pioneering in the field of space-saving design work. Manufacturing accounts for 15.1 per cent of GDP and construction for a further 5.2 per cent.

Industrial production growth for the Netherlands was estimated at 0.8 per cent for 2004.

Tourism

The growing tourism sector was affected in 2001 by foot-and-mouth disease, which restricted movements to some extent, followed by the 11 September terrorist attacks in the US, as a result of which tourist arrivals began to decline. In 2002 and 2003, large areas were closed due to an outbreak of fowl pest, while the introduction of the euro led to increased prices. The Iraq war and the flu-like Sars outbreak added to the sector's woes. In addition to falling arrival numbers from the US and Japan, tourism from Germany, the largest market, also declined. In June 2004, the Dutch Tourism Board began an aggressive marketing campaign to revitalise the country's tourism sector.

Hydrocarbons

The hydrocarbons sector accounts for approximately 9 per cent of GDP and employs 4 per cent of the workforce.

Onshore deposits of oil were first discovered in the late 1930s near The Hague, but attention shifted in the 1940s to better deposits in the Schoonebeek region. It was in the nearby port of Rotterdam that the Dutch oil industry came to be based. Offshore oil, by comparison, is a relatively recent discovery. The Netherlands produces around 28 per cent of its oil needs domestically, with almost 70 per cent of production coming from offshore deposits. However, average oil production in the Netherlands has fallen over recent years as a result of diminishing reserves in a number of oil fields in the Dutch sector of the North Sea. In 2003, total reserves stood at around 106 million barrels; consumption was 951,000 barrels per day (bpd) in 2002.

The largest onshore gas field is at Groningen, first discovered in the 1960s. This was the main source of gas until the discovery of offshore deposits. Natural gas reserves are around 1.77 trillion cubic metres (62.5 trillion cubic feet). Although it is expected that gas reserves will be depleted by 2030, the rate of new discoveries is sufficiently high that Dutch gas production is expected to continue beyond that time. Reserves were estimated to have dropped by 18 trillion cubic feet in 2002. Total natural gas production decreased by 2.9 per cent in 2002, with offshore production falling by 7.8 per cent. The Netherlands is a substantial net exporter of gas, importing only 8 per cent of total supplies and exporting approximately 48 per cent of domestic production.

The Netherlands has estimated coal reserves of 500 million tonnes, but poor deposit quality, high labour costs and falling demand made extraction unprofitable and the last coal pit was closed in 1970. Approximately 25 million short tonnes of coal are imported annually, of which over 90 per cent is consumed by Dutch thermal power stations.

Energy

The Netherlands has an electricity capacity of 20 million kilowatts (KW). Natural gas provides over 50 per cent of electric power needs and oil around 20 per cent. Nuclear power supplies around 4.5 per cent and the remainder by other material such as coal. The long-term emphases is on developing sustainable energy sources such as solar and wind power.

There is one nuclear power station in operation however development of nuclear power has been slow owing to popular opposition. Attempts to force the reactor to close early have been abandoned but the reactor is still anticipated to close at the end of its licensed period. There has been discussion about building a new reactor but without any determination in the near future.

Financial markets
Stock exchange

The Amsterdam Exchanges (AEX) are part of Euronext, an integrated cross-border single currency stock, derivatives and commodities market composed of the Brussels, Paris and Amsterdam exchanges. The merged exchange has four indices, Euronext 100 and Next 150, blue chip indices of the top 250 stocks, Next Economy, which lists high technology stocks, and M Prime, the largest index, which is for the remaining stocks in traditional sectors. These indices will not initially supplant Amsterdam's own AEX-25 blue-chip, Estar (high technology), Midkap (other stocks) and AAX (all-share) indices. Euronext is the largest European exchange in terms of cash trading volume and is the second-largest exchange in Europe in terms of the number and total market capitalisation.

Banking and insurance

Banking supervision remains the responsibility of De Nederlandsche Bank (DNB). The oversight of currency transactions was in the hands of DNB until 2002, when it was assumed by the European Central Bank (ECB). Foreign banks operating in the Netherlands face no special restrictions.

The Dutch banking sector is dominated by three banking conglomerates, ABN Amro, ING Bank and Rabobank Nederland, which together control approximately 75 per cent of total domestic lending. Including Bank Nederlandse Gemeeten and the joint Belgian/Dutch banking group Fortis, these banks are estimated to hold almost 90 per cent of domestic banking assets, loans and deposits.

In 1995, ING bought Britain's Baring Bank for £1 when Baring was on the verge of collapse after the activities of employee and 'rogue trader' Nick Leeson. ING sold at a profit its remaining Baring division in November 2004.

Central bank
De Nederlandsche Bank (DNB); European Central Bank (ECB).

Main financial centre
Amsterdam

Time
GMT plus one hour (GMT plus two hours from late March to late September).

Geography
The Netherlands is situated in Western Europe, bordered to the east by Germany and to the south by Belgium. The North Sea lies to the north and west, giving the country a coastline of over 450km. Except for small areas in the east of the country, the Netherlands' topography is dominated by river plains and flatlands which provide excellent growing conditions for agriculture and which facilitate the construction of a transport infrastructure. The major rivers are the Nederrijn, which flows from the north coast to Rotterdam on the west coast, and the Maas, which enters the country on the border with Belgium at Maastricht and flows into the North Sea on the west coast.

More than a third of the country is below sea level and made up of the *polder*, land reclaimed from the sea by the construction of successive sea-walls over the years, but especially since the 1930s.

In the south-west of the country, the major cities of Amsterdam, Rotterdam, The Hague and Utrecht form a heavily urbanised area known as the Randstad or ring city. The flat character of the land, population density and intensive land use have heightened awareness of environmental issues such as air, soil and water pollution and the threat of rising sea levels caused by global warming.

The Netherlands

Climate
The country has an equitable north European climate, with warm though often damp summers and occasionally severe winters. Average temperatures peak in July and August at around 17 degrees Celsius (C), but manage barely 2 degrees C in January and February before picking up sharply in April and May. Rainfall is heaviest in March and April, when on average 76mm and 81mm respectively are recorded. July and August, by comparison, are the driest months with 41mm and 43mm of rainfall respectively. A raincoat is recommended in any season.

Dress codes
Formal dress is usual for business; otherwise, no special restrictions apply. Warm clothing is recommended in winter, especially in coastal regions.

Entry requirements
Passports
The Netherlands is a signatory of the Schengen Accord and passports are not required by the holders of national identity cards issued in other Accord countries in Europe, plus Liechtenstein, Malta, Monaco, and Switzerland, although passports may be useful for identification in banking and other business transactions. Passports are required by all other nationals, and all visitors should note that operation of the Schengen Accords has been occasionally suspended as a precaution against illegal immigration.

Visa
Required by all, except nationals of EU and Schengen Accord signatory countries; North America, Australasia, or Japan. For further exceptions contact the nearest consulate. Schengen visas cover all entry needs; for business trips, an original invitation from a business contact in The Netherlands is necessary when applying. A Schengen visa application (offered in several languages) can be downloaded on www.eurovisa.info/ApplicationForm.htm.

Currency advice/regulations
There are no restrictions on the import or export of currency. Travellers' cheques are widely accepted. Commission charges vary considerably in Amsterdam.

Customs
Personal effects are duty-free. There are few customs formalities for visitors entering from other EU countries.

Prohibited imports
There are no special prohibitions aside from products banned in the Netherlands such as narcotics and firearms.

Health (for visitors)
EU nationals are covered for medical treatment. There are no mandatory health precautions, and no advisable precautions are necessary beyond standard travel insurance. Certain medications may be taken to the Netherlands provided a doctor's prescription accompanies.

Hotels
Classified from one- to five-star by Netherlands Board of Tourism, the Royal Dutch Touring Club and the Royal Netherlands Automobile Club. Accommodation may be booked through the Netherlands Reservation Centre in Leidschendam (tel: (070)202-500). Advisable to book well in advance during spring and summer. Foreign nationals must present passports before booking in, and are automatically registered with local police.

Credit cards
All major credit cards are accepted.

Public holidays
Fixed dates
1 Jan (New Year's Day), 30 Apr* (Queen's Day), 5 May ^ ^ (Liberation Day), 25 Dec (Christmas Day), 26 Dec (Boxing Day).
* Shops may be open.
^ ^ Public holiday for the civil service only.

Variable dates
Good Friday, Easter Monday, Ascension Day, Whit Monday.

Working hours
Banking
Mon–Fri: 0900–1600, some open Sat and on late shopping evenings.
Business
Mon–Fri: 0830–1730.
Government
Mon–Fri: 0830–1700.
Shops
0830/0900–1730/1800 (half-day closing usually Mon or Wed). Main shops open Sat and Thu/Fri evening.

Telecommunications
Mobile phones
There is comprehensive GSM coverage throughout the country

Electricity supply
220V AC.

Social customs/useful tips
Appointments are necessary and business cards are exchanged, although the business climate is less formal than in some Western European countries and cordiality and consensus at business meetings are highly valued. The best months for business visits are considered to be March to May and September to November. When invited to a meal in a Dutch home it is usual to bring flowers or a small gift.

Security
There are no special problems with security in the Netherlands, although increased caution against petty theft is advised in the heavily populated areas of Rotterdam and Amsterdam.

Getting there
Air
National airline: Koninklijke Luchtvaart Maatschappij (KLM) (Royal Dutch Airlines) Air France and KLM merged in May 2004.
International airport/s: Amsterdam Schiphol (AMS), 15km south-west of city; facilities include restaurants, duty-free, banks, showers, a business centre, conference rooms and car hire. There are regular, scheduled train and bus routes into the city, travel time 15–30 minutes. Taxis are numerous.
A direct, express train connects Schiphol with main cities in Holland, and some cities in Belgium.
A limited range of international flight destinations also originate from Eindhoven (EIN), 8km north of city; Maastricht (MST), 7km from city; Rotterdam (RTM), 8km north-west of city.
Airport tax: None
Surface
Road: Major routes from the rest of Europe are by a superb network of motorways, well signposted with green 'E' symbols, indicating international highways.
Water: There are good connections between all major European ports. Boat trains operate to the Hook of Holland from many European countries.
The Netherlands is a leading international maritime shipper with extensive port facilities.
Main port/s: Ferries berth at Vlissingen, Rotterdam and Hook of Holland (Hoek van Holland).

Getting about
National transport
Air: Groningen (GRQ) in the north has connecting flights to the international airports. Den Helder (DHR), in the west is one of the largest heliports in Europe providing access to offshore oil and gas fields; charter planes are also available. Other internal services link Amsterdam, Eindhoven, Rotterdam and Maastricht.
Road: The Dutch road system is easily accessible and very well maintained. Roadways include high speed expressways, limited access motorways, dual highways and secondary roads. All roads are well signposted with red 'A's indicating national highways, and smaller routes indicated by yellow 'N's.
Buses: Most bus services run between 0600–2330. The Interliner is a service used for longer distances and has very few stops. The Connexxion serves the major part of Holland including the provinces of

Noord and Zuid Holland, Gelderland, Overijssel and Zeeland.
Rail: There is an hourly service, running 24 hours, between Utrecht, Amsterdam, Schiphol, The Hague and Rotterdam. The Netherlands Railways operate an Intercity (IC) network connecting the big cities. IC trains only stop at the major stations. Local trains provide transportation to smaller cities. Tickets can be purchased from railway stations, but do not need to be bought in advance.
Water: There is an extensive network of inland waterways. Scheduled boat services operate from Enkhuizen to Urk and Staveren and between the mainland and the islands in the north.
City transport
The Netherlands has been divided into zones with set tariffs. A strippenkaart, containing 15 strip tickets, is valid throughout the country for travel on buses, trams and subways, including trips within cities. To travel within one zone costs two strips. An extra strip is charged for each subsequent zone. A time limit, mentioned on the back of the card, allows for an interchange with other transport systems within the same zone.
Taxis: Taxis have blue licence plates with black letters and figures. You can book a taxi in advance or, in some larger cities, hail them on the street. Prices may vary between regions and are sometimes open to negotiation.
A *treintaxi* (train-taxi) is a publicly shared taxi, offering shared costs.
Buses, trams & metro: Amsterdam has an intergrated public transport service that runs between 06.00 to 00.30 daily throughout the city; night buses run between 00.30– 07.30. Tickets (strippenkaart) can be purchased from a tobacconist, post office or railway station. They should be franked when boarding, for each trip.
Elsewhere, city buses run within the boundaries of larger towns. A metro runs in Rotterdam, as well as trams, which also run in The Hague. They typically run between 0600–0000. The metro and trams are usually faster than city buses.
Trains: The train to the city centre from Schiphol is an efficient mode of transport. Inter-city train tickets are not interchangeable with local passenger services.
Ferry: There are ferries running on the canals of Amsterdam and Rotterdam, although these services are more for tourist purposes than for convenience.
Car hire
Car hire is widely available, the minimum age is dependent on insurance usually 21 years. An international driving license is necessary for all non-EU drivers. Traffic drives on the right. Speed limits: urban areas 50kph, normal roads 80kph, motorways 120kph. The wearing of seat belts is compulsory. It is illegal to use a handheld mobile phone while driving (including times when vehicle is stationary in traffic). Do not ignore parking fees as failure can result in a fine and if not paid within 24 hours, the car will be towed away when the cost of retrieval becomes very high.

BUSINESS DIRECTORY

The addresses listed below are a selection only. While World of Information makes every endeavour to check these addresses, we cannot guarantee that changes have not been made, especially to telephone numbers and area codes. We would welcome any corrections.

Telephone area codes
The international direct dialling (IDD) code for The Netherlands is +31, followed by area code and subscriber's number:

Amersfoort	33	The Hague	70
Amsterdam	20	Leiden	71
Breda	76	Rotterdam	10
Eindhoven	40	Tiel	344
Haarlem	23	Utrecht	30

Useful telephone numbers
Directory enquiries: 068-008 (national), 060-418 (international)
Operator: 060-410
Police/fire: 0611
National public transport information service: 0900-9292

Chambers of Commerce
American Chamber of Commerce in The Netherlands, 58 Scheveningseweg, 2517 KW The Hague (tel: 365-9808; fax: 364-6992; e-mail: office@amcham.nl).

Amsterdam Chamber of Commerce, 5 De Ruyterkade, 1013AA Amsterdam (tel: 531-4000; fax: 531-4799; e-mail: post@amsterdam.kvk.nl).

Arnhem Chamber of Commerce, 525 Kronenburginsel, 6800 KZ Arnhem (tel: 353-8888; fax: 353-8999; e-mail: info@arnhem.kvk.nl).

British-Netherlands Chamber of Commerce, Oxford House, 328L Nieuwezijds Voorburgwal, 1012 RW Amsterdam (tel: 421-7040; fax: 421-7003; e-mail: info@nbcc.co.uk).

Maastricht Chamber of Commerce, 5 Pierre de Coubertinweg, 6225 XT Maastricht (tel: 350-6666; fax; 350-6660; e-mail: info@maastricht.kvk.nl).

Netherlands Federation of Chambers of Commerce, 1 Watermolenlaan, 3440 AG Woerden (tel: 426-911; fax: 426-216; e-mail: site@vvk.kvk.nl).

Rotterdam Chamber of Commerce, 40 Blaak, 3000 AL Rotterdam (tel: 402-7777; fax: 414-5754; e-mail: dvergeer@rotterdam.kvk.nl).

The Hague Chamber of Commerce, 30 Koningskade, 2502 LS The Hague (tel: 328-7100; fax: 326-2010; e-mail: info@denhaag.kvk.nl).

Tilburg Chamber of Commerce, 1 Reitseplein, 5000 LG Tilburg, (tel: 594-4122; fax: 468-6215; e-mail: info@tilburg.kvk.nl).

Utrecht Chamber of Commerce, 50 Kroonstraat, 3500 AA Utrecht (tel: 326-3211; fax: 231-2804; e-mail: servicecenter@utrecht.kvk.nl).

Zwolle Chamber of Commerce, 1 Govert Flinckstrasse, 8021 ET Zwolle (tel: 455-3800; fax: 453-7424; e-mail: info@zwolle.kvk.nl).

Banking
ABN Amro Bank, 10 Gustav Mahlerlaan, 1082 PP Amsterdam (tel: 628-9393; fax: 628-7637; e-mail: postbox@abnamro.com).

ASN Bank, 28 Alexanderstraat, 2514 JM The Hague (tel: 0800-0380; fax: 361-7948; e-mail: informatie@asnbank.nl).

NIB Capital Bank, 4 Carnegieplein, 2517 KJ The Hague (tel: 342-5425; fax: 363-5425).

ING Bank, De Amsterdamse Poort, 1102 MG Amsterdam (tel: 563-9111; fax: 563-5700; e-mail: info@ingbank.com).

Postbank NV, 506 Haarlemmerweg, 1014 BL Amsterdam (tel: 584-9111; fax: 584-6600; e-mail: postbank@postbank.nl).

Rabobank Nederland, 18 Croeselaan, 3521 CB Utrecht (tel: 216-0000; fax: 216-2672; e-mail: info@rabobank.nl).

Central bank
De Nederlandsche Bank, 1 Westeinde, 1017 ZN Amsterdam (tel.: 524-9111; fax: 524-2500; e-mail: info@dnb.nl).

European Central Bank (ECB), Kaiserstrasse 29, D-60311 Frankfurt am Main, Germany (tel: +49(69)13-440; fax: +49(69)1344-6000; e-mail: info@ecb.int).

Travel information
Algemene Nederlandse Vereniging van VVVs (ANVV) (association of tourist information offices), 25 Hogeweg, 3814 CC Amersfoort (tel: 33-756-060; fax: 33-723-146; e-mail: anvv@euronet.nl).

Amsterdam Schiphol Airport, 202 Evert van der Beekstraat, Schiphol-Centrum, Haarlemmermeer (tel: 601-9111; fax: 604-1475; e-mail: info@schiphol.nl).

The Netherlands

Amsterdam Tourist Office (VVV), 10 Stationplein, 1012 AB Amsterdam (tel: 551-2512; fax: 625-2869; e-mail: info@amsterdamtourist.nl).

KLM Royal Dutch Airlines, 55 Amsterdamseweg, Schiphol Airport, 1182 GP Amstelveen (tel: 20-649-9123; fax: 20-649-300; e-mail: info@klm.nl).

Netherlands Reservation Centre, 1 Nieuwe Gouw, 1442 LE Purmerend (tel: 299-689-144; fax: 299-689-154; e-mail: info@hotelres.nl).

National tourist organisation offices
Toerisme Recreatie Nederland, Vlietweg 15, 2266 KA Leidschendam (tel: 370-5705; fax: 320-1654; e-mail: info@nbt.nl; internet: www.holland.com).

Ministries

Ministry of Agriculture, Nature Management and Fisheries, 73 Bezuidenhoutseweg, 2594 AC The Hague (tel: 378-6868; fax: 378-6100; e-mail: info@minlnv.nl).

Ministry of Defence, 38 Kalvermarkt, 2511 CB The Hague (tel: 318-8802; fax: 318-8320; fax: defensie.voorlichting@co.dnet.mindef.nl).

Ministry of Economic Affairs, 30 Bezuidenhoutseweg, 2594 AV The Hague (tel: 308-1986; fax: 347-4081; e-mail: ezinfo@postbus51.nl).

Ministry of Education, Culture and Science, 4 Europaweg, 2711 AH Zoetermeer (tel: 323-2323; fax: 323-2320; e-mail: info@minocw.nl).

Ministry of Finance, 7 Korte Voorhout, 2511 CW The Hague (tel: 342-7540; fax: 342-7900; internet site: http://www.minfin.nl).

Ministry of Foreign Affairs, 67 Bezuidenhoutseweg, 2594 AC The Hague (tel: 348-6486; fax: 348-4848; e-mail: dvl-info@minbuza.nl).

Ministry of General Affairs, 20 Binnenhof, 2513 AA The Hague (tel: 356-4100; fax: 356-4683).

Ministry of Health, Welfare and Sport, 5 Parnassusplein, 2511 VX The Hague (tel: 340-7911; fax: 340-7890; e-mail: info@minvws.nl).

Ministry of Housing, Spatial Planning and the Environment, Rijnstraat 8, 2515 XP The Hague (tel: 339-3939; fax: 339-1352; e-mail: info@minvrom.nl).

Ministry of the Interior and Kingdom Relations, Schedeldoekshaven 200, 2511 EZ The Hague (tel: 426-6426; fax: 363-9153; e-mail: info@minbzk.nl).

Ministry of Justice, Schedeldoekshaven 100, 2511 EX The Hague 9 (tel: 370-6850; fax: 370-7594; e-mail: voorlichting@minjus.nl).

Ministry of Social Affairs and Employment, 4 Anna van Hannoverstraat, 2595 BJ The Hague (tel: 333-4444; fax: 333-4033; e-mail: info@minszw.nl).

Ministry of Transport, Public Works and Water Management, 1-6 Plesmanweg, 2597 JG The Hague (tel: 351-6171; fax: 351-7895; e-mail: info@minvenw.nl).

Other useful addresses

Algemeen Nederlands Persbureau (national news agency), 49 Handelskade, 2288 BA Rijswick (tel: 70-414-1414; fax: 70-414-1401; e-mail: nieuwsdienst@anp.nl).

American Embassy, 102 Lange Voorhout, 2514 EJ The Hague (tel: 310-9209; fax: 361-4688; e-mail: usemb@usemb.nl).

British Embassy, 10 Lange Voorhout, 2514 ED The Hague (tel: 427-0427; fax: 427-0345).

Congrestolken (conference interpreters), 11 Jan van Goyenkade, 1075 HP Amsterdam (tel: 625-2535; fax: 626-5642; e-mail: interpreters@conferenceinterpreters.com).

Euronext Amsterdam (stock exchange), Beursplein 5, 1012 JW Amsterdam (tel: 550-4444; fax: 550-4900; e-mail: info@euronext.nl).

Federation for Dutch Export (Fenedex), 14 Raamweg 2596 HL The Hague (tel: 330-5600; fax: 330-5656; e-mail: info@fenedex.nl).

Netherlands Convention Bureau, 166 Amsteldijk, 1079 LH Amsterdam (tel: 646-2580; fax: 644-5935; e-mail: info@nlcongress.nl).

Netherlands Council for Trade Promotions (NCH), 181 Bezuidenhoutseweg, 2594 AH The Hague (tel: 344-1544; fax: 385-3531; e-mail: info@nchnl.nl).

Netherlands Embassy (USA), 4200 Linnean Avenue, NW, Washington DC (tel: 202-244-5300; fax: 202-362-3430; e-mail: webmaster@netherlands-embassy.org).

Netherlands Foreign Investment Agency (CBIN), 2 Bezuidenhoutseweg, 2594 AV The Hague (tel: 379-8818; fax: 379-6322; e-mail: info@nfia.nl; internet site: http://www.nfia.com).

Netherlands Foreign Trade Agency (EVD), 181 Bezuidenhoutseweg, 2594 AG The Hague (tel: 778-8888; fax: 778-8889; e-mail: eic@info.evd.nl; internet site: http://www2.holland.com/trade/).

Statistics Netherlands (CBS), 428 Prinses Beatrixlaan, 2273 XZ Voorburg (tel: 70-337-3800; fax: 70-387-7429; e-mail: infoserve@cbs.nl; internet site: (in Dutch): http://www.cbs.nl/enindex.htm).

Internet sites

Dutch Tourist Board:
http://www.visitholland.com

Dutch yellow pages
http://www.markt.nl./dyp/index-en.html

Netherlands web directory:
http://www-nl-menu.nl

Tourist information:
http://www:holland.com

Tourist information: http://www: nbt.nl

Hotel information:
http://www:hotelsinholland.com

Statistics: http://www: cbs.nl:

Netherlands Embassy in the USA:
http://www: netherlands-embassy.org

Dutch Rrailways: http://www: ns.nl

Ministry of Foreign Affairs:
http://www: minbuza.nl

Dutch Parliament:
http://www:parlement.nl

Ministry of Finance: http://www:minfin.nl

The Netherlands Antilles

KEY FACTS

Official name: Nederlandse Antillen (The Netherlands Antilles)

Head of State: Queen Beatrix of the Kingdom of The Netherlands (since 1980); represented by Governor General Frits Goedgedrag (from 1 Jul 2002)

Head of government: Prime Minister Etienne Ys (sworn in 3 Jun 2004)

Ruling party: Coalition government

Area: 800 square km

Population: 222,960 (2004)

Capital: Willemstad (on Curaçao)

Official language: Dutch, English and Papiamento

Currency: Netherlands Antilles guilder (Naf) = 100 cents

Exchange rate: Naf1.79 per US$ (Oct 2005); (official rate pegged to US$ since Jan 2000)

GDP per capita: US$11,400 (2003)

GDP real growth: 1.00% (2004)

Labour force: 101,000 (2004)

Unemployment: 15.00% (2003)

Inflation: 2.50% (2004)

Balance of trade: -US$877.00 million (2003)

Foreign debt: US$1.35 billion (2003)

COUNTRY PROFILE

Historical profile
The islands of the Netherlands Antilles were first inhabited by Carib and Arawak Indians.
1493 Christopher Columbus was the first European to sight the islands.
1499 The Spanish explorer, Alonso de Ojedo, visited Curaçao but left without establishing a settlement.
1527 The islands were settled, mainly by Spanish and Portuguese Jews escaping persecution.
1634 The Dutch East India Company took over the islands, 'persuading' the settlers to depart.
1642–46 Peter Stuyvesant was governor.
1816 After a number of changes in possession, the islands – Curaçao and Bonaire (known as the Leeward islands), St Eustatius, Saba and St Maarten (half of which is the French territory of St Martin) (which are known as the Windward Islands) – were confirmed as Dutch territory.
1863 Slavery was abolished.
1916 The first oil refinery was opened in Curaçao.
1954 Internal autonomy was granted.
1986 Aruba separated from the other islands (Curaçao, Bonaire, St Maarten, St Eustatius and Saba), which became the Antilles of Five; both entities are part of the Kingdom of The Netherlands, which is responsible for defence and foreign policy.
1998 The general election resulted in a six-party coalition government under Prime Minister Suzanne Camelia-Römer.
1999 The Partido Laboral Krusado Popular (PLKP) (Labour Party People's Crusade) left the coalition, to be replaced by the Partido Antiá Restrukturá (PAR) (Party for the Restructured Antilles), with Miguel Pourier becoming prime minister.
2000 In a referendum, St Maarten voted in favour of separate status within the Kingdom of The Netherlands.
2002 The ruling coalition was returned to power in the elections in January. Etienne Ys became prime minister.
2003 In February, US-based Polar Cove, an enterprise information security consultant, established a security monitoring centre in Curaçao, providing security protection to on-line gaming companies. On 22 July, Ben Komproe succeeded Etienne Ys as prime minister. On 11 August, Mirna Louisa-Godett took office as prime minister.
2004 In January, the cabinet recovered from a coalition split due to a corruption crisis, but remained in power following an official offer of support from the Democratische Partij (DP) (Democratic Party) of Bonaire. On 4 April, the coalition government collapsed when the National People's Party (PNP) left, because it was no longer willing to work with Justice Minister Ben Komproe. On 6 April, Prime Minister Mirna Louisa-Godett resigned. Etienne Ys was sworn in as prime minister on 3 June.
2005 In April the islanders of Curacao voted to become an autonomouns state within the Kingdom of The Netherlands and break with The Netherlands Antilles. The tiny neighbouring island, Sint Eustatius, decided to remain within the Antilles.

Political structure
Each island has a local administration, part of which is elected.
Constitution
29 December 1954
Form of state
Overseas territory of The Netherlands
The executive
Executive power for external affairs and defence is exercised by the governor general (as the representative of the sovereign of The Netherlands), assisted by an advisory council of at least five members. The governor general is appointed by the monarch for a six-year term.
National legislature
Internal affairs are handled by the governor general and the council of ministers. The council of ministers is elected by, and responsible to, the legislature, the Staten (Estates), which has 22 members – Curaçao (14), Bonaire (three), St Maarten (three), Saba (one), St Eustatius (one) – elected for a four-year term, by universal adult suffrage and proportional representation.
Following legislative elections, the leader of the majority party is usually elected prime minister by the Staten.
Legal system
The legal system is based on Dutch civil law, with some English common law. Judges are appointed by the monarch. Rights of appeal exist from The Netherlands Antilles Court of Appeals to the Supreme Court of The Netherlands, in The Hague.
Last elections
18 January 2002 (parliamentary)

The Netherlands Antilles

Results: Parliamentary: the ruling coalition of six parties, led by the Frente Obrero Liberashon 30 Di Mei (FOL) (Workers' Liberation Front 30th of May) (23 per cent of the vote, five seats) and Partido Antiá Restrukturá (PAR) (Party for the Restructured Antilles) (21 per cent of the vote, four seats) was returned to power in the elections to the Staten.

Next elections
2006 (parliamentary)

Political parties
Ruling party
Coalition government
Main opposition party
National Alliance of Sint Maarten; Democratische Partij Sint Maarten.

Population
222,960 (2004)
Ethnic make-up
African and mixed race (85 per cent), Carib Amerindian, white, East Asian.
Religions
Roman Catholic, Protestant, Jewish, Seventh-Day Adventist.

Education
Primary schooling lasts for six years (from age six to 12) and junior secondary school lasts four years (age 12 to 16). Following primary education, students have a choice of attending technical or vocational colleges in place of secondary school.

Higher education is provided by the Universiteit van de Nederlandse Antillen (University of the Netherlands Antilles). There is also a nursing school and a teacher training college in Curaçao.
Literacy rate: 97 per cent, adult rate (2003)

Health
Curaçao has two general hospitals and one surgical hospital and receives patients from the other islands of The Netherlands Antilles. Most health professionals receive training in The Netherlands.

It is estimated that around 30 per cent of the population of the Netherlands Antilles suffer from hypertension; psychological problems are also highly prevalent among adults. The general standard of health among the Antilleans is poor, with poor nutrition and little or no exercise undertaken by the adult population. The Dutch government has assigned priority to encouraging the population to develop healthier lifestyles.

HIV/Aids
In 2003 there were 432 confirmed cases of HIV infection. There is a national strategic action plan to halt the rapid spread of the disease. The drugs problem on the islands could prove to be a potent source of transmission.
Life expectancy: 76.3 years (World Bank)

Fertility rate/Maternal mortality rate: 2.1 births per woman (World Bank)
Birth rate/Death rate: 16 births per 1,000 population; 6.4 deaths per 1,000 population (2003).
Infant mortality rate: 11 per 1,000 live births (2003)

Welfare
A public insurance programme covers 100 per cent of health care costs for blue-collar workers. There is also an insurance fund for retired workers. Private companies also provide insurance plans for their employees. A social security fund covers employees of small private establishments.

Main cities
Willemstad (capital, on Curaçao, estimated population 60,100 in 2003). Kralendijk (Bonaire) and Philipsburg (St Maarten).

Languages spoken
English in St Maarten, St Eustatius and Saba.
Papiamento (a local patois mixture of Portuguese, Spanish, Dutch, English and French) in Curaçao and Bonaire.
Spanish is widely understood and spoken.
Official language/s
Dutch, English and Papiamento

Media
Press
Dailies: Daily newspapers include *Amigoe* (Curaçao) and *Daily Herald* (St Maarten).
Weeklies: *The Bonaire Reporter* is the island's English language weekly.
Business: Business publications include *Business Curaçao* (English) and the quarterly *Curaçao Inc Reporter*.

Broadcasting
Two commercial channels operated by Netherlands Antilles Television Co Ltd and Leeward Broadcasting Co. Numerous radio stations include Radio Hoyer (Curaçao) operating on solar energy. Cable system with six US channels operated by Television Distribution System (TDS) for Curaçao.

Economy
The Netherlands Antilles economy, virtually devoid of natural resources, is heavily service-oriented, and based largely on oil-refining and transshipment, tourism, offshore financial services and harbour and ship repair facilities. Dutch aid remains important to the economy.

The unemployment rate remains high at 15 per cent in 2003. The islands enjoy a high per capita income and a well-developed infrastructure, compared with other countries in the region.

External trade
Trade in the Netherlands Antilles is dominated by Curaçao's crude oil imports and the export of refined oil products.
Imports
Include crude petroleum, food and manufactures.
Main sources: Venezuela (53.5 per cent total, 2004), US (23.2 per cent), The Netherlands (5.2 per cent)
Exports
Main exports include petroleum products.
Main destinations: US (27.3 per cent total, 2004), Venezuela (13.5 per cent), Bahamas (7 per cent), Singapore (4.5 per cent), Honduras (4.5 per cent), The Netherlands (4.3 per cent), Guatemala (4.1 per cent)
Re-exports
Curaçao re-exports petroleum and derived products.

Agriculture
Farming
The agricultural sector contributes 1 per cent to GDP and employs 5 per cent of the workforce.

KEY INDICATORS — The Netherlands Antilles

	Unit	2000	2001	2002	2003	2004
Population	m	0.21	0.18	0.22	0.22	0.22
Gross domestic product (GDP)	US$bn	2.48	2.49	2.40	2.40	–
GDP per capita	US$	11,400	11,400	10,911	11,400	–
GDP real growth	%	-2.3	-3.5	0.7	0.5	–
Inflation	%	4.7	1.8	1.4	2.0	–
Exports (fob) (goods)	US$m	1,290.0	1,280.0	589.3	553.0	–
Imports (fob) (goods)	US$m	2,880.0	2,785.0	1,602.7	1,430.0	–
Balance of trade	US$m	-1,590.0	-1,505.0	-1,013.4	-877.0	–
Total reserves minus gold	US$m	261.0	301.0	406.0	373.0	415.0
Foreign exchange	US$m	261.0	301.0	406.0	373.0	415.0
Exchange rate	per US$	1.73	1.78	1.79	1.79	1.79

About 8 per cent of total area is cultivated arable land. Soil is generally poor and rainfall inadequate for most crops. Small amounts of fruit and vegetables are grown for local consumption.
Livestock production in 2004 included: 579 tonnes (t) meat in total, 18t beef, 188t pig meat, 74t lamb and goat meat, 300t poultry, 510t eggs, 410t milk.

Fishing
There is little commercial fishing except on St Maarten. The typical total annual fish catch is over 900t; shellfish, molluscs and cephalopods account for another 10t per annum.

Industry and manufacturing
The industrial sector contributes about 19 per cent to GDP and employs 20 per cent of the workforce. It is dominated by petroleum refining and transshipment. Manufacturing is concentrated on food processing and import substitution (paints, paper, soap, beer, chemicals).
The emphasis is on diversification into light export-based industries such as electronics and pharmaceuticals.

Tourism
Tourism is the major industry on the islands of Curaçao and St Maarten, while there is increasing tourist activity in Bonaire. The majority of visitors are from the US (around 40 per cent of stay-over arrivals), followed by South America, the Netherlands, Canada and the Caribbean.

Mining
There are known deposits of pumice on St Eustatius. Salt production has decreased in recent years.

Hydrocarbons
The Netherlands Antilles has no hydrocarbon resources. The 1914 discovery of oil in Venezuela was the impetus for the island of Curaçao's choice as the location for one of the largest oil refineries in the world. Crude oil is imported mainly from Venezuela and Mexico under the San Jose Pact. Some of this is consumed domestically but the majority is refined and exported.
The Netherlands Antilles do not import natural gas or coal.

Banking and insurance
Under an EU tax directive introduced in July 2005 in a number of associate and dependent EU countries, the Netherlands Antilles will impose a withholding tax to be passed to the relevant EU country but retain the anonymity of the saver.
Withholding taxes will begin at 15 per cent and rise to 35 per cent by 2011.
The Netherlands Antilles has also agreed to supply information on tax fraud, for criminal or civil trials, and notify EU member states about additional malpractices.

Central bank
Bank van de Nederlandse Antillen
Offshore facilities

Time
GMT minus four hours

Geography
The Netherlands Antilles (the Antilles of Five), located in the Caribbean Sea, comprises two island groups, the Netherlands Leeward and the Netherlands Windward islands, about 800km (500 miles) apart. The former group (Curaçao and Bonaire) lies about 80km north of Venezuela; the latter group (St Eustatius, Saba and the southern half of St Maarten – the northern half of St Maarten is a dependency of Guadeloupe) lies about 260km east of Puerto Rico.
Curaçao and Bonaire have an average annual termperature of 27 degrees Celsius (C), with regular trade winds; average rainfall is 560mm. St Eustatius, Saba and St Maarten also average 27 degrees C, but have more rainfall, about 1,100mm per year. Temperatures are cooler and precipitation heavier at higher elevations. Curaçao consists of low hills. The southern part of Bonaire is flat and arid, while the northern end is hilly; the land is arid. Saba is a rugged island of volcanic origin; the highest point, Mount Scenery, rises to 887 metres. St Eustatius is hilly with a central flat plain; it is of volcanic origin. St Maarten is hilly, except for the western region, which forms a large lagoon.

Climate
Low levels of humidity and rainfall on Curaçao and Bonaire where temperatures average 29 degrees Celsus. Average annual rainfall on Curaçao is 550mm. Temperatures are cooler on St Maarten, Saba and St Eustatius due to the north-east trade winds averaging 26 degrees Celsius and higher levels of rainfall from May–December.

Entry requirements
Passports
Required by all, except nationals of Belgium, France, Germany, Luxembourg and The Netherlands, who only need national identity cards. US and Canadian nationals do not need passports.
Visa
Visas are not required by all; the length of stay varies for different nationals, from 14 days up to three months. For further detail visit www.oranda.or.jp/index/english and click on ' Consular Info'.
Diplomatic missions of The Netherlands issue visitors visas for the Netherlands Antilles.
All visitors must provide evidence of sufficient funds for their stay and a return/onward ticket.

Currency advice/regulations
There are no restrictions regarding the import and export of local currency.

Health (for visitors)
Mandatory precautions
Yellow fever vaccination certificate required if arriving from an infected area.
Advisable precautions
Typhoid and polio vaccinations are recommended.

Hotels
There are numerous tourist hotels on St Maarten, Curaçao and Bonaire. Accommodation is very limited on Saba and St Eustatius. Government tax of 5 per cent and 10–15 per cent service charge is added to the bill.

Public holidays
Fixed dates
1 Jan (New Year's Day), 30 Apr (Queen's Birthday), 1 May (Labour Day), 2 Jul (Curaçao Flag Day), 6 Sep (Bonaire Day), 11 Nov (St Maarten Day), 16 Nov (St Eustatius Day), 6 Dec (Saba Day), 25 Dec (Christmas Day), 26 Dec (St Stephen's Day).
Variable dates
Carnival (Feb), Good Friday, Easter Monday, Ascension Day.
Jewish establishments closed at the Jewish New Year and Yom Kippur.

Working hours
Banking
Mon–Fri: 0830–1200, 1330–1630.
Business
Mon–Fri: 0800–1200, 1330–1630.
Government
Mon–Fri: 0800–1200, 1330–1630.
Shops
Mon–Sat: 0800–1200, 1400–1800. Gift shops open on Sundays and public holidays when cruise ships call.

Electricity supply
Variable: 120/127/220V AC at 50 cycles or 60 cycles.

Getting there
Air
National airline: ALM Antillean Airlines (Antilliaanse Luchtvaart Maatschappij) and Windward Islands Airways.
International airport/s: Curaçao (CUR), 12km north of Willemstad, duty-free shop, bar, restaurant, buffet, bank, post office, shops, hotel reservations, car hire; St Maarten-Queen Juliana (SXM), 15km from Philipsburg, duty-free shop, bar, restaurant, shops, hotel reservations, car hire; Bonaire-Flamingo (BON), 3.5km south of Kralendlijk.
Airport tax: US$10 for domestic departures and US$20 for international departures.

The Netherlands Antilles

Surface
Water: There is a weekly ferry to Curaçao from Venezuela.

Main port/s: Willemstad (Curaçao). A new pier at Otrabanda in the western part of Willemstad will be able to handle liners too large for the previous harbour facilities.

Getting about
National transport
Air: ALM operates services between the islands, and between Netherlands Antilles and Aruba. Services also provided by ABC Commuter, Windward Islands Airways and Air Aruba.

Road: The network on all islands is all-weather, though less extensive on Saba and St Eustatius.

Buses: Regular services operate in and around main centres. Car/jitney services and sightseeing tours are also available. There are no regular services on smaller islands.

City transport
Taxis: Taxis are usually identified by 'TX' before the licence plate or by 'Bus' for collective taxis on Curaçao. It is advisable to negotiate fares for tours in advance. Tipping is discretionary.

Car hire
Car hire is widely available at reasonable prices. An international licence is required.

BUSINESS DIRECTORY

The addresses listed below are a selection only. While World of Information makes every endeavour to check these addresses, we cannot guarantee that changes have not been made, especially to telephone numbers and area codes. We would welcome any corrections.

Telephone area codes
The international dialling code (IDD) for The Netherlands Antilles is +599, followed by subscriber's number (preceded exceptionally by 9 for Curaçao).

Chambers of Commerce
Bonaire Chamber of Commerce and Industry, 53 Kaya Grandi, Kralendijk (tel: 717-5595; fax: 717-8995; e-mail: boncommerce@bonairelive.com).

Curaçao Chamber of Commerce and Industry, 1 Kaya Junior Salas, PO Box 10, Willemstad (tel: 9461-3918; fax: 9461-5652; e-mail: businessinfo@curacao-chamber.an).

St Maarten Chamber of Commerce & Industry, 11 CA Cannegieter Street, Philipsburg (tel: 542-3595; fax: 542-3512; e-mail: info@sintmaartenchamber.org).

Banking
ABN–AMRO Bank, Pietermaai 17, PO Box 469, Willemstad, Curaçao (tel: 638-111).

Algemene Bank Nederland, Frontstraat, PO Box 295, Philipsburg, St Maarten (tel: 23-505).

Banco di Caribe, Schottegatweg Oost 205, PO Box 3785, Willemstad, Curaçao (tel: 616-588; fax: 615-220).

Banco Industrial de Venezuela C A, Handelskade 12, PO Box 701, Willemstad, Curaçao (tel: 611-621; fax: 616-534).

Banco Mercantil, Abraham de Veerstraat I, PO Box 565, Curaçao (tel: 611-566).

Bank of Nova Scotia (Scotiabank), Backstreet 61, Philipsburg, PO Box 303, St Maarten (tel: 22-262; fax: 22-435).

Barclays Bank plc, Front Street 19, PO Box 141, Philipsburg, St Maarten (tel: 3511; fax: 24-531).

The Chase Manhattan Bank, Soualiga Building, Cannegieter Road (Pondfill) and Mullet Bay Hotel, PO Box 221, St Maarten (tel: 23-726 (Soualiga Bldg), 42-110 (Mullet Bay); fax: 23-629).

Citco Bank Antilles N V, Schottegatweg Oost 44, PO Box 707, Willemstad, Curaçao (tel: 370-388; fax: 77-902).

Maduro & Curiel's Bank N V, Plaza Jojo Correa 2-4, PO Box 305, Willemstad, Curaçao (tel: 611-100).

Maduro & Cureil's Bank (Bonaire) N V, Kralendijk, PO Box 66, Bonaire (tel: 8414).

McLaughlin Bank N V, Wilhelminaplein 14–16, PO Box 763, Willemstad, Curaçao (tel: 612-820).

Orco Bank N V, Dr H Fergusonweg 10, PO Box 3987, Curaçao (tel: 372-000; fax: 376-741).

Windward Islands Bank Ltd, Pondfill, Philipsburg, PO Box 220, St Maarten (tel: 22-335).

Central bank
Bank van de Nederlandse Antillen, 1 Simon Bolivar Plein, Willemstad, Curaçao (tel: 9434-5500; fax: 9461-5004; e-mail: info@centralbank.an).

Travel information
National tourist organisation offices
Bonaire Government Tourist Bureau, Kaya Simon Bolivar 12, Bonaire (fax: 8408).

Curaçao Tourist Development Foundation, PO Box 3266, Pietermaai 19, Curaçao (tel: 616-000; fax: 612-305).

St Maarten Tourist Board, Ruyterplein, Philipsburg (tel: 22-337).

Ministries
Ministry of Finance, Pietermaai 4–4A, Willemstad, Curaçao (tel: 612-052).

Office of the Minister Plenipotentiary of the Netherlands Antilles, Badhuisweg 175, 2597 JP The Hague, The Netherlands (tel: (3170)351-2811; fax: (3170)351-2722).

Other useful addresses
British Consulate, PO Box 3803, Brombadiersweg z/n, Willemstad, Curaçao (tel: 369-366; fax: 369-533).

Curaçao Inc (for business information), International Trade Centre Bldg, Piscaderabay, PO Box 6112, Curaçao (tel: 636-250; fax: 636-485).

Curaçao Industry and International Trade Development Co (CURINDE), Emancipatie Boulevard 7, Curaçao (tel: 376-000; fax: 371-336).

Foreign Investment Agency Curaçao, Scharlooweg 174 Willemstad, Curaçao (tel: 657-044; fax: 615-788).

International Trade Centre (promotion of investment opportunities, exhibition hall and conference facilities), PO Box 6005, International Trade Centre Building, Piscadera Bay, Curaçao (tel: 624-433, 636-250; fax: 624-408, 636-485).

Island Government of Curaçao, Department of Economic Affairs, Hoogstraat 18, Curaçao (tel: 624-066; fax: 626-596).

New Caledonia

KEY FACTS

Official name: Nouvelle Calédonie (New Caledonia)

Head of State: President of France (Jacques Chirac), represented by High Commissioner Michel Mathieu (from Sep 2005)

Head of government: President of the Government Marie-Noëlle Thémereau (AE) (elected 29 Jun 2004)

Ruling party: Four-party coalition government led by Avénir Ensemble (AE) (Future Together) with four cabinet seats, equalling Rassemblement pour la Calédonie dans la République (RPCR) (Rally for Caledonia in the Republic), and including Union Nationale pour l'Indépendance-Front de Libération Nationale Kanak et Socialiste (UNI-FLNKS) (National Union for Independence-Kanak and Socialist National Liberation Front) and Union Calédonien (UC) (Caledonian Union).

Area: 18,575 square km – Grande Terre island: 16,600 square km

Population: 226,800 (2004)

Capital: Nouméa (on Grande Terre)

Official language: French

Currency: Comptoirs Français du Pacifique franc (CFPf) = 100 centimes

Exchange rate: CFPf98.91 per US$ (Aug 2005); (pegged CFPf119.25 per euro)*

GDP per capita: US$14,000 (2003)*

Labour force: 79,400 (2003)*

Unemployment: 19.00% (2003)*

Inflation: 1.10% (2004)*

Balance of trade: -US$600.00 million (2003)*

Foreign debt: US$79.00 million (2003)*

Visitor numbers: 99,203 (2004)*

* estimated figure

COUNTRY PROFILE

Historical profile
1766 Sighted by Europeans.
1774 Captain James Cook named the island after the Latin name for Scotland.
1853 New Caledonia became a French colony.
1863 Nickel deposits were discovered. The displacement of villages which stood on new mine sites and the encroachment of settlers' cattle on Kanak land provoked several rebellions, all of which were suppressed by the French authorities.
1864–97 The island became a penal colony.
1942 New Caledonia was transformed into a US military base during the Second World War.
1946 The colony became a French territory.
1988 Jean-Marie Tijbaou, leader of the Front de Libération Nationale Kanak et Socialiste (FLNKS) (Kanak and Socialist National Liberation Front), signed the Martignon Accord which divided New Caledonia into three distinct regions.
1989 Tijbaou was assassinated.
1998 A national referendum voted overwhelmingly in favour of the Nouméa Accord, giving increased autonomy and a referendum on independence in 15–20 years.
1999 A three-party coalition government was formed, dominated by Rassemblement pour la Calédonie dans la République (RPCR) (Rally for Caledonia in the Republic).
2001 The territory's president, Jean Lèques, (RPCR), resigned. Pierre Frogier (RPCR) replaced him.
2002 Negotiations started on the future adoption of the euro. Ethnic clashes between native Kanaks and Wallisian immigrants were caused by land disputes. President Pierre Frogier's government was dissolved automatically after the resignation of a minister; he was re-elected president on 28 November.
2004 The parliamentary elections held on 9 May resulted in a four-party coalition, led by the Avénir Ensemble (AE) (Future Together). Marie-Noëlle Thémereau was elected president.
2005 Michel Mathieu was appointed High Commissioner, taking up the post in September.

Political structure
Constitution
Under the Nouméa Accord of 1998, New Caledonia has a special status within the French constitution. The local government, elected by universal suffrage, has wider degrees of autonomy regarding legislative issues. Up until 2010, France will retain power only over justice, public order, currency, defence and foreign affairs outside the South Pacific region.
France is also obliged to conduct up to three referenda between 2013–18 on independence. Until then, the High Commissioner has overall responsibility for the territory while the president of the Territorial Congress is the head of local government.
New Caledonia is represented in the French parliament by two deputies and one senator; it is due to get an extra senator following the 2007 elections.
The territory is divided into three provinces, each with its own assembly and local executive. There is an economic and social committee, which has an advisory role, and a Custom Senate, which advises the government on matters affecting the indigenous Kanak community.

Form of state
Self-governing territory of France

The executive
The Territorial Congress elects the 11-member executive that elects the president of the government, for which an absolute majority of votes is required.

National legislature
A 54-member Territorial Congress, comprised of the members of the four regional councils, is elected for a six-year term by proportional representation, which ensures that no party gets a majority and that parties participate in coalition governments.

Last elections
9 May 2004 (parliamentary)
Results: Parliamentary: RPCR won 24.5 per cent of the vote (16 seats); Future Together 22.8 per cent (16 seats); UNI-FLNKS 13.7 per cent (eight seats); UC 11.9 per cent (seven seats); four other parties shared the remaining seven seats.

Next elections
2010 (parliamentary)

Political parties
Ruling party
Four-party coalition government led by Avénir Ensemble (AE) (Future Together) with four cabinet seats, equalling Rassemblement pour la Calédonie dans la République (RPCR) (Rally for Caledonia in the Republic), and including Union Nationale pour l'Indépendance-Front de Libération Nationale Kanak et Socialiste

New Caledonia

(UNI-FLNKS) (National Union for Independence-Kanak and Socialist National Liberation Front) and Union Calédonien (UC) (Caledonian Union).

Political situation
The conflicts of the 1980s were centred round whether or not the country should become independent. The majority (44 per cent) Melanesian population were in favour of a free association with France, while the European population (34 per cent) and other minorities mostly wanted to retain closer ties with France. The Noumea Accord of 1998 (which ended the conflicts) stated that a government should be elected by the Congress on a basis of proportional representation, which under the Interior Rules of the Congress provides for all parties with more than six seats in Congress to have at least one member in the cabinet.

The first elections after the Noumea Accord saw the (European supported) Rassemblement pour la Calédonie dans la Republique (RPCR) (Rally for Caledonia in the Republic) win with 24 of the 54 seats. The Front de Libération Nationale Kanak et Socialiste (FLNKS) (Kanak National and Socialist Liberation Front) won 12 seats and the Parti de Libération Kanak (PALIKA) (Party of Kanak Liberation) six seats. There followed several years of controversy, concerning the position of vice president, until the 2001 elections when Déwé Gorodney of PALIKA was chosen as vice president by then President Pierre Frogier.

In the 2004 elections the RPCR's share of the vote dropped to 24.4 per cent (16 seats) while the newly formed Avenir Ensemble (AE) (Future Together), together with a number of RPCR disident and other settler-backed groupings, won 16 seats, as did the pro-independence groups. With such an even distribution of parties in the Congress the allocation of ministerial portfolios was four each to the RPCR and AE and the pro-independence parties three. The election, by the Congress, of the president was a compromise on behalf of the RPCR, who agreed that Marie-Noëlle Thémereau of the AE should become president; Déwé Gorodney remained vice president.

Population
226,800 (2004)

Ethnic make-up
Of the total population, 45 per cent are Melanesian Kanaks, 34 per cent Europeans (mainly French), 20 per cent are Wallisians and the remainder are mainly Tahitian, Indonesian and Vietnamese. The wealthy southern province is mainly inhabited by Europeans and the remainder of the country is mostly populated by the poorer ethnic Kanak community.

Education
Education is provided free for the compulsory years. Primary education covers ages six to 11 years and secondary education from aged 12 to a maximum of 18 years. There is a major shortage in the supply of trained secondary school teachers.

Public expenditure on education is typically 7 per cent of GNP. Nearly US$30 million was allocated, up to 2005, to implement the government's policy of equity funding for the early childhood education sector. The government also doubled funding for adult literacy, setting aside US$18 million to fund the Adult Literacy Strategy. More emphasis has been given to Māori and Pacific children with special educational needs.

In October 2005 the government introduced a new primary school curriculum which places more emphasis on local culture and history and allows lessons to by taught in Kanak. The changes will come into force in early 2006.

Compulsory years: Six to 15
Enrolment rate: 101 per cent gross primary enrolment of the relevant age group (including repeaters) (World Bank 2003).
Pupils per teacher: 18 in primary schools.

Health
Life expectancy: 73.7 years (World Bank)
Fertility rate/Maternal mortality rate: 2.5 births per woman (World Bank)
Infant mortality rate: Seven deaths per 1,000 live births.

Main cities
Nouméa (capital, on Grande Terre, estimated population 86,400 in 2003).

Languages spoken
Thirty Canaque languages are spoken. English is often understood.

Official language/s
French

Media
Press
Dailies: Les Nouvelles Calédoniennes is the only daily newspaper in New Caledonia.

Weeklies: Weeklies include Télé 7 Jours, Les Nouvelles Hebdo, L'Echo Calédonien and Dimanche Patinane.

Broadcasting
Radio: Radio France Outre Mer (RFO). Private local radio services operate 24 hours a day; stations include NRJ 2000, Radio Djiido and RRB.
Television: Metropolitan and international TV programmes are broadcast by the state broadcasting authorities. There are two channels.

Advertising
Advertising is available in the local press, on radio and TV and in cinemas.

Economy
There is a lack of economic diversity. The economy is almost entirely dependent on transfers from France, nickel extraction and processing and foreign aid. Infrastructure development has enjoyed a limited boost with the development of new mining and smelting enterprises, such as the development of the Koniambo deposit.

The territory's nickel production contributes around 12 per cent of global output and up to 10 per cent of GDP.

Although the French military presence in New Caledonia has been a source of internal tensions, it also makes a significant contribution to the local economy. France contributes around 25 per cent of GDP, 80 per cent of which covers healthcare, education and public sector wages. GDP per capita is one of the highest in the region.

New Caledonia uses the euro-pegged Comptoirs Français du Pacifique franc (CFPf) as its currency. The government began negotiations in 2002 over the adoption of the euro, which would boost the territory's chances of attracting investment and tourism. However, the move would have to overcome the objections of pro-independence groups.

World nickel prices have enjoyed high prices since 2003, benefiting New Caledonia's exports.

The world's largest nickel development operation is underway in the southern Goro provinces. The consortium, headed

KEY INDICATORS — New Caledonia

	Unit	2000	2001	2002	2003	2004
Population	m	0.21	0.21	0.22	0.22	0.23
Gross domestic product (GDP)	US$bn	3.10	3.15	3.03	3.16	–
GDP per capita	US$	14,833	15,000	14,616	14,000	–
Inflation	%	0.6	2.3	-0.6	-0.6	1.1
Tourist numbers	'000	–	–	–	–	*99.2
Exchange rate	per US$	117.54	128.58	125.11	107.01	96.04

* estimated figure

by Inco Ltd (Canada) and including Sumitomo Metal Mining Co and Mitsui & Co of Japan, will be spending some US$1.88 billion in the Goro Nickel Development Project. Annual production is expected to be 60,000 tons of nickel oxide and up to 5,000 tons of cobalt carbonate. The project is scheduled to become operational in 2007.

The new and improved infrastructure made necessary by building the nickel plants will also benefit other sectors of the economy, such as tourism, education and health.

About US$26 million aid, spread over five years, was granted to New Caledonia by the EU in September 2004; the aid is to be used to train local professionals in skills necessary to meet the economy's needs in the territory's three northern provinces.

External trade
Imports
Main imports are machinery and equipment, fuels, chemicals and foodstuffs.
Main sources: France (47.3 per cent total, 2004), Singapore (12.3 per cent), Australia (9.6 per cent), New Zealand (4.8 per cent)
Exports
Main exports are processed ferro-nickels, nickel ore and fish
Main destinations: Japan (23.1 per cent total, 2004), France (17.5 per cent), Taiwan (14.3 per cent), Spain (8.4 per cent), South Korea (8.4 per cent), South Africa (5.3 per cent), Australia (4.5 per cent)

Agriculture
Farming
The agricultural sector typically accounts for as little as 2 per cent of GDP. Although the soil is fertile, only 10 per cent of the land area is cultivated. There is a ratio of around 50-50 for locally grown to imported foods. The number of farmers has fallen by almost 50 per cent since the early 1990s, with the greatest percentage loss in the northern province.

About one-third of the main island's land area is devoted to cattle raising, chiefly on the central and north-west coasts. Exports of coffee and copra crops have increased since the 1990s.

Crop production in 2004 included: 16,000 tonnes (t) coconuts, 3,910 cereals in total, 3,800t maize, 2,000t potatoes, 3,000t sweet potatoes, 2,800t cassava, 2,300t taro, 11,000t yams, 2,080t oilcrops, 4,000t vegetables in total, 4,200t fruit in total, 40t coffee. Livestock production included: 6,282t meat in total, 1,400t pig meat, 4,000t beef, 840t poultry, 42t sheep and goat meat, 1,600t eggs, 3,600t milk, 60t honey.

Fishing
Tropical shrimp farming has been developed, although the farms are fragile as there is always the risk of disease. Fishing is both for local consumption and for export, mainly to Japan.
Annual fish production typically includes 2,800t marine fish, 1,900t other seafood and 343,000 units of pearls and shells.
Forestry
Domestic forests supply about 35 per cent of timber demand, with some reforestation undertaken.

Industry and manufacturing
The industrial sector typically contributes 20 per cent to GDP. Main industries include nickel processing, domestic equipment, clothing, foodstuffs and beer.

There are three major nickel processing projects in the pipeline. New Caledonia's only existing nickel processing plant, owned by the Société le Nickel (SLN), is undergoing renovations to increase production from 60,000 tonnes to 75,000 tonnes annually. SLN will increase activity at one of its mines to supply enough ore for the plant's increased capacity. The project is expected to be completed in 2006.

Construction of a US$1.50 billion Koniambo nickel processing plant in the north, with production starting in 2008 is projected to output 60,000 tonnes of nickel a year.

Construction of a plant in the south, at Goro, is due to be completed by 2007. At an estimated capital cost of US$1.88 billion it is expected to produce 60,000 tonnes of nickel and 4,300–5,100 tonnes of cobalt annually, beginning in 2007.

Tourism
Tourism has been struggling since 2001 following the 11 September attacks in the US, the ongoing decline of the Japanese economy, French nuclear testing and the SARS epidemic. The high point in visitor numbers was 2000, when 109,587 arrivals were recorded.

Since then numbers have not shown any particular trend with arrivals at 99,203 in 2004, slightly down on the 101,983 in 2003. Cruise ship visits in early 2004 showed a healthy improvement, but still only account for 20,000 arrivals.

Stay-overs have not kept pace with hotel occupancies staying at around 55 per cent. A number of major tourist-related projects are currently under construction. Japan and France are the main markets, followed by Australia and New Zealand.

Mining
New Caledonia holds between 25–40 per cent of known world nickel deposits and is one of the world's largest producers.
There are several mines in New Caledonia, the principal ones are located at Koniambo, Tiebaghi, Thio, Kouaoua, Nepoui-Kopeto and Etoile du Nord.

The potential production capacity of the seven main nickel mining operators making up Société Le Nickel (SLN) has been estimated at 830,000 tonnes a year, with reserves expected to last until 2012. SLN is 60 per cent owned by France's Eramet and 30 per cent by the Société Minière de Sud Pacific (SMSP), which is owned by ethnic Kanak groups.

Nickel and ferronickel production accounts for up to 10 per cent of GDP and contributes 80 per cent of foreign earnings.

Chrome extraction is undertaken. There are also deposits of iron ore, copper, manganese, lead and zinc.

SLN is expanding its smelting plant in Nouméa, and in order to supply enough ore for the plant's increased capacity, it is increasing production at one of its mines from 250,000 tonnes to one million tonnes a year, creating around 200 new jobs. The project is to be completed in 2006.

In August 2004, a public enquiry on the future of the US$1.8 billion Goro nickel mining project in the Southern Province recommended the project go ahead, but precautions should be taken against environmental pollution.

Hydrocarbons
No significant oil, gas or coal reserves have been identified in New Caledonia. It relies on imports of hydrocarbons to meet domestic demand.

Energy
Around 80 per cent of electricity generation is produced by thermal generators. Renewable sources of energy, including hydroelectricity and wind generation, are growing in importance. The nickel extraction of smelting sectors consume around 75 per cent of electricity output.

Banking and insurance
Central bank
The Paris-based Institut d'Emission d'Outre-Mer (IEOM) provides all central banking services except foreign exchange reserves.
Main financial centre
Nouméa

Time
GMT plus 10 hours

Geography
New Caledonia comprises one large island and several smaller ones, situated in the south Pacific Ocean, about 1,500km (930 miles) east of Queensland, Australia. The main island is New Caledonia (la Grand-Terre). It is long and narrow. Rugged mountains divide the west of the

New Caledonia

island from the east, and there is little flat land. The nearby Loyalty Islands and a third group of islands, the uninhabited Chesterfield Islands, lie about 400km north-west of the main island.

Climate
Hot (average temperature 26 degrees Celsius (C)), with occasional tropical depressions and cyclones, from mid-November to mid-April; and cool (average temperature 23 degrees C), with moderate rains, from mid-May to mid-September. Rainfall is quite irregular and can be extremely heavy. The east coast (at about 2,000mm/pa) has twice the rainfall of the west; the wettest months are January, February and March.

Entry requirements
Passports
Required by all except certain French nationals.
Visa
Required by all, except citizens of EU, North America, Australasia and Japan, for stays up to one month; this includes business trips by representatives of foreign entities with an invitation from a local company or organisation. Proof of adequate funds for stay, an itinerary, a guarantee of repatriation if necessary and return/onward ticket are also required. For further exceptions, full details and a copy of the application form visit www.diplomatie.gouv.fr/thema/dossier.gb.asp and follow the path (entering France) to the database.
Customs
Personal effects are allowed entry duty-free. Duty is not payable on goods of EU origin, although all imported goods are subject to a general tax, and an increasing number of goods require import licences. Importation of parrots, parakeets, pigeons, turtle-doves and non-domestic mammals is prohibited; plants and seeds require a health certificate. Export of Cagous and objects of ethnographic interest are prohibited.

Health (for visitors)
Mandatory precautions
Vaccination certificate required for yellow fever if travelling from infected area.
Advisable precautions
Vaccination for diphtheria, tuberculosis, hepatitis 'A' and 'B', polio, TB, tetanus, typhoid. There is a rabies risk.
There has been an increased risk of dengue fever, visitors are advised to use mosquito repellent, a mosquito net at night, and wear protective clothing at dawn and dusk, to reduce the risk.

Hotels
Tourist hotels are classified by category and size on the five-star system. Hotel tax is levied, the amount varying according to classification. Details of rural or tribal lodgings in some Melanesian villages and areas are available from tourist information offices. Upper-end bungalow accommodation is growing.

Credit cards
Most major credit cards are accepted.

Public holidays
Fixed dates
1 Jan (New Year's Day), 1 May (Labour Day), 8 May (1945 Victory Day), 14 Jul (Bastille Day), 15 Aug (Assumption Day), 24 Sep (New Caledonia Day), 1 Nov (All Saints' Day), 11 Nov (Armistice Day), 25 Dec (Christmas Day), 31 Dec (New Year's Eve).
Variable dates
Easter Monday, Ascension Day, Whit Monday.

Working hours
Some shops and offices open half day on Sat and Sun.
Banking
Mon–Fri: 0715–1545.
Business
Mon–Fri: 0730–1130, 1330–1730. Sat: 0730–1130.
Government
Mon–Fri: 0730–1130, 1215–1600.
Shops
Mon–Fri: 0730–1100, 1400–1800. Half-day Sat and Sun.

Telecommunications
Telephone/fax
International communications are via the Intelsat satellite system, which is 99 per cent automatic.

Electricity supply
220V AC, with two-pin plug fittings.

Weights and measures
Metric system

Social customs/useful tips
Tipping is not customary. Islanders find it offensive when women sunbathe topless.

Getting there
Air
National airline: Air Calédonie International (Aircalin).
International airport/s: Nouméa La Tontouta International (NOU), 48km from Nouméa; duty-free shop, bar, restaurant, bank, shops, car hire.
Airport tax: There is no airport departure tax.
Surface
There are regular shipping services from Australia, Europe, Japan, New Zealand and South East Asia. The main port at Nouméa can handle containers.

Getting about
National transport
Air: Air Calédonie operates regular flights from Nouméa's domestic airport, Magenta, to the east and west coasts of New Caledonia island and daily flights to the Ile des Pins, Maré, Tiga, Lifou and Ouvea. Charter and tour airplanes and helicopters available.
Road: Grand Terre, the main island, has a total road network of approximately 5,000km, about 71 per cent sealed in municipal areas and a considerable length of track suitable for four-wheel drive and similar vehicles. Exercise care driving along the west or east coast, as some roads are not sealed. The Canala-Thio main road is one-way only, with direction of traffic changing at scheduled times.
Buses: Regular bus services operate on Grand Terre.
Water: Small trading vessels sail to nearby islands. There are more regular links between Grande Terre and Ile des Pins, and Loyalty Islands.
City transport
Taxis: Taxis are available in the central square (Place des Cocotiers), with some operating 24hrs. Charges are for time and distance. There is a surcharge after 1900 and on Sundays.
Buses, trams & metro: Buses from the airport to city centre usually take about 60 minutes.
Car hire
Self-drive car hire is available in Nouméa. A current valid driving licence is required. Driving is on the right-hand side of the road.

BUSINESS DIRECTORY

The addresses listed below are a selection only. While World of Information makes every endeavour to check these addresses, we cannot guarantee that changes have not been made, especially to telephone numbers and area codes. We would welcome any corrections.

Telephone area codes
The international dialling code (IDD) for New Caledonia is +687 followed by subscriber's number.

Useful telephone numbers
Fire station: 18
Police: 17
Ambulance (Nouméa): 252-100

Banking
Bank of Hawaii-Nouvelle Calédonie, BP L3, 25 Avenue de la Victoire, Avenue Henri Lafleur, 98849 Nouméa Cedex (tel: 257-400; fax: 274-147).

Banque Calédonienne d'Investissement, BP K5, 50 Avenue de la Victore, 98849 Nouméa (tel: 256-565; fax: 274-035).

Banque Nationale de Paris Nouvelle Calédonie, BP K3, 37 Ave Henri Lafleur, 98800 Nouméa (tel: 258-400; fax: 258-459).

Société Générale Calédonienne de Banque; 44 rue de l'Alma, Siége et Agence Principale, 98848 Nouméa (tel: 256-300; fax: 276-245).

Central bank
Institut d'Emission d'Outre-Mer (IEOM), 5 rue Roland Barthes, 75598 Paris Cedex 12, France (tel : +33 1 5344-4141; fax : +33 1 4347-5134; e-mail: contact@ieom.fr).

Travel information
Air Calédonie, 39 rue de Verdun, Nouméa (tel: 286-564; fax: 281-340).

Groupement Interprofessionnel 'Destination Nouvelle Calédonie', 39-41 rue de Verdun, PO Box 688, Nouméa (tel: 272-632; fax: 274-623).

Nouméa La Tontouta International Airport, BP2, Tontouta 98840 (tel: 352-500; fax: 352-535; e-mail: ccita@cci.nc).

Nouméa Tourist Office, 24 rue Anotole France, BP 2828, Nouméa 98.800 (tel: 287-580; fax: 287-585).

National tourist organisation offices
New Caledonian Tourism Promotion Board (internet site: http://www.nouvelle-caledonie-tourisme.nc).

Other useful addresses
Institut Territorial de la Statistique et des Etudes Economiques, PO Box 823, 5 rue Gallieni, Nouméa (tel: 275-481, 283-156; fax: 288-148).

South Pacific Commission, PO Box D5 Cedex, Nouméa (tel: 262-000; fax: 261-844).

Internet sites
South Pacific Tourism Organisation: http://www.tcsp.com/new_caledonia/index.html

New Caledonia website (in French): http://www.yahoue.com/

Travel information: http://perso.wanadoo.fr/caledonie/indexe.htm

New Zealand

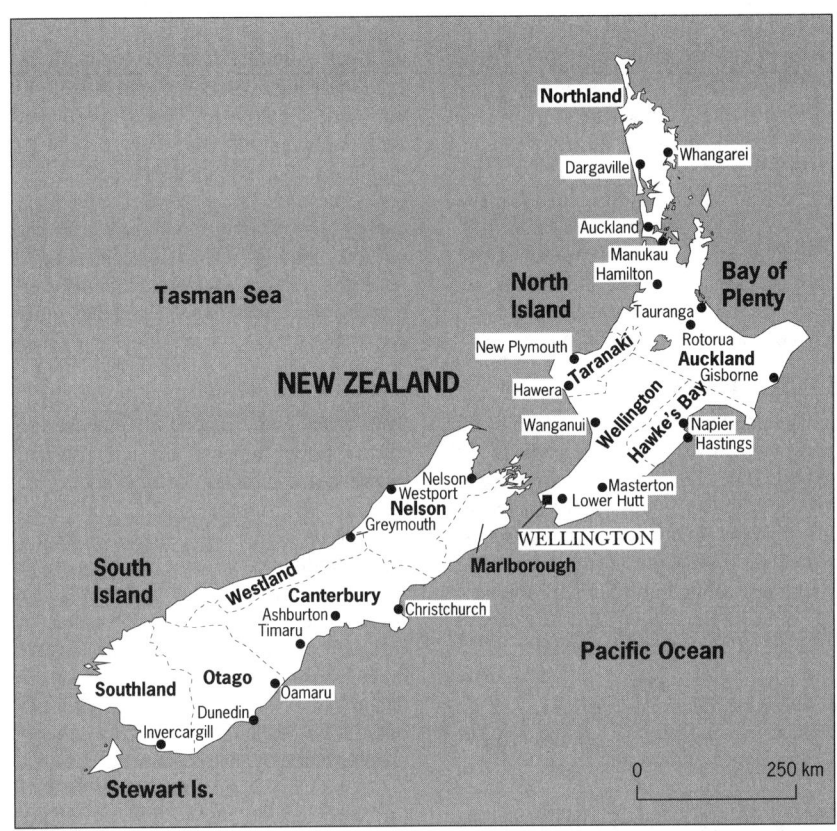

KEY FACTS

Official name: The Dominion of New Zealand

Head of State: Queen Elizabeth II, represented by Governor General Dame Silvia Cartwright (appointed 4 Apr 2001)

Head of government: Prime Minister Helen Clark (NZLP) (elected 27 Nov 1999; re-elected 17 September 2005)

Ruling party: The New Zealand Labour Party (NZLP) in coalition with the New Zealand Progressive Party

Area: 268,676 square km: North Island (115,690 square km); South Island (152,356 square km)

Population: 4.04 million (2004)

Capital: Wellington

Official language: English, Māori

Currency: New Zealand dollar (NZ$) = 100 cents

Exchange rate: NZ$1.44 per US$ (Oct 2005)

GDP per capita: US$23,899 (2004)

GDP real growth: 5.00% (2004)

Labour force: 1.94 million (2003)

Unemployment: 3.90% (OECD, 2004)

Inflation: 2.30% (2004)

Balance of trade: -US$1.43 billion (2004)

Foreign debt: US$33.00 billion (2003)

Annual FDI: US$19.70 billion (cumulative, 1995–2004, OECD); US$2.60 billion (OECD, 2004)*

* estimated figure

Excitement is not normally associated with life in New Zealand, where mowing the lawn on the 'section' (house plot) constitutes an important Sunday activity. For much of the population, the vicarious satisfaction of a victory, or even the collective sorrow of a defeat, by the national rugby team – the All Blacks – provides a conversational topic for weeks to come.

Elections – again

Elections come round pretty quickly in New Zealand, every three years. The September 2005 elections almost rivalled the rugby in excitement. Although incumbent prime minister Helen Clark became the first Labour prime minister to win three straight terms, she did so with a majority of only one seat, over the second placed National Party. Labour had lost one seat, down to 50, but the National Party, headed by former central bank governor Jim Brash, had gained 27. This gave the National Party an unprecedented 48 seats with a 39.6 per cent share of the vote, almost double its share in the 2002 elections. The National Party's gains, however, were largely at the expense of the smaller parties. The nail-biting result meant that neither of the two major parties held an outright majority. This left Labour leader Helen Clark seeking a deal to form a coalition government with one or more of the six minor parties represented in parliament.

After several weeks of horse trading, Mrs Clark announced the formation of a coalition government with the one seat Jim Anderton's Progressive Party, which was to be the only other party in the government. The coalition depended on the support of both the United Future New Zealand Party (seven seats) and the New

Zealand First Party (three seats) in votes of confidence. In an unexpected and controversial move, Mrs Clark appointed the maverick New Zealand First Party leader, Winston Peters, as foreign minister. Although holding this important ministerial position, Mr Peters would not be a member of the cabinet.

In the pre-election period, National Party leader Don Brash had sought to highlight New Zealand's increasingly sensitive race issue. In the election, the Māori Party had polled 2.1 per cent, winning four seats in parliament. Seven seats in New Zealand's parliament are reserved for Māori MPs. These seats, which originally only numbered four under an allocation introduced in the nineteenth century, have traditionally been held by the New Zealand Labour Party. The National Party had threatened to do away with the seats if elected. Foreign minister Peters is well-known for his anti-immigration views, particularly in respect of Asian and Muslim immigrants. Mr Brash's National Party had also promised an end to privileges and concessions for the indigenous Māori community.

The debate over Māori land rights had focussed on Māori claims to coastal lands, which include New Zealand's beaches. In 2004, in what was seen by many Māori as the thin end of the wedge, the government had passed a law securing ownership of the foreshore and the sea bed for the crown (which under New Zealand's English legal system means the state). An outright election victory by the National Party would certainly have introduced a period of tension between the communities. In some of New Zealand's larger towns and cities, tensions can already run high. Some sections of the Māori community have failed to integrate into New Zealand society. The same is the case with much of the immigrant community from the Pacific islands, notably Samoa, Tonga and the Cook Islands. This disaffection was disturbingly portrayed in Lee Tamahori's 1994 film, *Once Were Warriors*. The Māori are the Polynesian warrior-race which settled, or more accurately, conquered New Zealand some 1,000 years ago. As depicted in this film, sexual equality is not a basic tenant of the Māori lifestyle. However, in the urbanised area of south Auckland where the film takes place, alcoholism, violence and unemployment are portrayed as common.

Economic hiccough

New Zealand's economy has grown by 25 per cent over a six-year period, well above the OECD average of 16 per cent. Ironically, the very strength of the economy, operating at close to capacity levels on the back of sustained domestic demand growth has created problems for the central bank. In December 2005 the central bank raised annual interest rates to 7.25 per cent, by a long chalk the highest in the developed world.

A number of factors lie at the heart of the imbalance within the New Zealand economy. House price inflation and consumer credit growth have both rocketed up at a rate of some 15 per cent annually. At one stage, in the last quarter of 2003, house price inflation had soared to an annual rate of 25 per cent. A tight labour market and increased public spending have fuelled the rise. In New Zealand's three year election cycle election promises play an exaggeratedly important role as an election is never far off. In the run-up to the 2005 elections, both the major political parties had included a commitment to increased government spending in their election proposals; the Labour Party's manifesto foresaw an increase of 5 per cent. The tight labour market, created in part by above average levels of youth emigration, has also meant increased inflationary pressures, with the annual rate topping the central bank's targeted 3 per cent mark.

Over-valued dollar

The central bank's use of the interest rate to cool down the economy has also had negative side-effects. The most noticeable of these has been the steady appreciation of the New Zealand dollar against all the major trading currencies. In a five-year period the currency has appreciated by some 70 per cent against the US dollar. In early December 2005 it reached 20-year highs, causing economists to warn of the dangers of over-valuation. The high value of the New Zealand dollar has not only fuelled inflation by making imports cheaper, it has also made it increasingly difficult for New Zealand's exporters to compete in world markets. Of critical importance to the New Zealand economy are exports of meat, dairy products and timber, all of which have suffered. In consequence, New Zealand's current account deficit has reached record levels, roughly corresponding to 8 per cent of GDP.

In December 2005 international capital markets seemed to be awakening to the possibility that the New Zealand dollar might have peaked, and be riding for a fall. Large scale selling saw the currency drop by around 1.5 per cent against major currencies, to NZ$1.42 to the US dollar. Some analysts are expecting the rate to fall as low as NZ$1.67 to the US dollar by the end of 2006, with New Zealand's interest rates dipping to an annual 6.5 per cent, down from the 7.25 per cent reached at the end 2005.

In its Budget Policy Statement for 2006, the New Zealand treasury was at pains to point out that considerable progress had been made in building towards a robust

KEY INDICATORS — New Zealand

	Unit	2000	2001	2002	2003	2004
Population	m	3.83	3.93	3.95	3.99	*4.04
Gross domestic product (GDP)	US$bn	50.20	49.60	58.20	76.30	*99.69
GDP per capita	US$	13,091	12,892	14,274	18,497	23,899
GDP real growth	%	3.6	2.7	4.5	3.2	5.0
Inflation	%	2.7	2.6	2.7	1.7	2.3
Unemployment	%	6.0	5.3	5.2	4.8	–
Natural gas output	bn cum	5.5	5.8	5.5	4.1	3.6
Coal output	mtoe	2.4	2.5	2.6	3.2	3.0
Exports (fob) (goods)	US$m	13,484.0	13,918.0	14,340.0	16,505.0	20,456.0
Imports (fob) (goods)	US$m	12,848.0	12,447.0	15,010.0	18,559.0	21,889.0
Balance of trade	US$m	636.0	1,471.0	-659.0	2,054.0	-1,433.0
Current account	US$m	-2,734.0	-1,587.0	-1,950.0	-3,530.0	-6,040.0
Total reserves minus gold	US$m	3,116.0	3,008.0	3,739.0	4,907.0	5,294.0
Foreign exchange	US$m	2,783.0	3,418.0	3,258.0	4,235.0	4,786.0
Exchange rate	per US$	2.10	2.26	2.14	1.72	1.51

* estimated figure

New Zealand

long-term fiscal position by reducing debt to prudent levels (in the 1980s New Zealand had been one of the world's most heavily indebted countries) and building up financial assets in the New Zealand Superannuation Fund. Providing for New Zealand's ageing population has for some time been a major government preoccupation. New Zealand's external debt as a percentage of GDP stood at 23.2 per cent in mid-2005, and is expected to drop below 20 per cent by 2010. Central to New Zealand fiscal strategy has been the policy of meeting the cost of capital spending from operating surpluses rather than from borrowing.

The 2006 budget followed up on a number of the Labour Party's election pledges. Student loans were to cease bearing interest from April 2006 and the so-called Working for Families package was to be extended to cover 350,000 families. In line with an agreement reached with the New Zealand First Party before the election, old-age pensions are to be linked to the average national wage. The budget provided for NZ$1.9 billion (US$1.32 billion) of new capital expenditure over a two year period – NZ$780 million (US$542 million) in 2006/07, and NZ$540 million (US$375 million) in 2007/08.

Economic outlook

Economic growth in the first three months of 2005 had proved disappointing, reflecting the problems created by the over-valued dollar and following the trend set in the three preceding quarters. Growth, at 0.6 per cent for the quarter, represented an annual rate just less than 2.5 per cent, well down on central bank expectations. The government expects the economy to slow down until early 2007, regaining some momentum in the period up to March 2008. The uncertainty in the equation is the extent and depth of both slowdown and recovery. The New Zealand government has outlined two scenarios – one in which a relatively rapid depreciation in the exchange rate produces a higher than expected rate of economic growth. A second scenario envisages a period of generalised weakness where not only domestic demand remains depressed, but where exports also remain weak. Despite the sustained consumer confidence and expenditure seen in late 2005, New Zealand's business community remains faced with increased purchase and capital costs, as well as higher labour costs in the tight employment market. This has been reflected in reduced margins and weaker business confidence. Were this state of affairs to persist, margins would be further reduced, resulting in lower levels of investment and a more hesitant labour market. Private consumption would be likely to slow down alongside a less buoyant labour market, persistently high mortgage rates and slower house price growth. Were the economy to slow down at a slower rate than expected, and inflation to remain unchecked, New Zealand's interest rates would have to remain high.

Risk assessment

Economy	Good
Politics	Good
Regional stability	Good

COUNTRY PROFILE

Historical profile
Perched on the edge of the world in the South Pacific, New Zealand is both at the centre of the world stage and at its geographic periphery. The country's 4 million people enjoy a high standard of living. Auckland, the country's largest city, tied for fourth place in a recent survey of quality of life in the world's main cities. The country has a strong awareness of its indigenous heritage. Maoris settled the islands some 1,000 years ago, long before the first Europeans sighted land in 1642. Relations between the indigenous population and the descendants of Europeans were cemented in the Treaty of Waitangi in 1840, in what is generally considered the founding document of the nation. New Zealand is a member of the Commonwealth and uses the British parliamentary system. However, links with Britain are tenuous at best and developing relations with Australia and South-East Asia are of more pressing priority.
Migrants from Polynesia arrived in New Zealand and colonised it between 800–1000AD.
1642 Dutch explorer Abel Tasman was the first European to sight New Zealand.
1769 and 1779 British explorer James Cook charted the islands of New Zealand. After his second voyage, British and other European settlers began to arrive.
1815 The first British missionaries arrived in New Zealand.
1840 European settlers and the Māori tribes signed the Treaty of Waitangi, under which European settlers agreed to respect Māori land rights in return for recognition of British rule.
1845–47 Māoris revolted against land loss.
1852 New Zealand became a self-governing British colony.
1858 A series of major Māori revolts began in response to encroachments by Europeans on to Māori land.
1860–72 Māoris revolted again. The conflict was resolved after the Europeans promised to abide by the Treaty of Waitangi.
1893 New Zealand became the first country to give women the right to vote.
1898 The government introduced old age pensions.
1907 New Zealand became an independent dominion within the British Empire.
1914–18 New Zealand fought alongside the UK during the First World War and suffered heavy casualties in the Gallipoli campaign in Turkey in 1915.
1931 The Westminster Declaration established the concept of a Commonwealth between the UK, New Zealand and several other former British colonies.
1939–45 New Zealand fought alongside the UK during the Second World War.
1947 Dominion status began to be phased out and replaced by the Commonwealth.
1951 New Zealand formed the ANZUS military pact with Australia and the US.
1963 New Zealand agreed to provide a military presence in Vietnam – initially with a military advisors.
1965 Under increasing US pressure for the commitment of troops in Vietnam, a non-combative engineering force was augmented by a field artillery battery of around 120 men.
1972 The last New Zealand troops were withdrawn from Vietnam.
1975 A legal tribunal ruled that there should be an investigation into whether Māori land rights under the Treaty of Waitangi had been systematically ignored. This led to a vast number of lawsuits under which Maori tribes demanded financial reparations for the illegal confiscation of their lands.
1984 Prime Minister David Lange declared New Zealand a 'nuclear free zone' and forbade nuclear-powered vessels to dock at New Zealand ports.
1985 French secret agents bombed and destroyed the Greenpeace ship Rainbow Warrior in Auckland Harbour, killing one person.
1986 US suspended ANZUS obligations towards New Zealand.
1989 Lange resigned and was replaced by Geoffrey Palmer.
1990 The National Party (NP) won its first election victory for 10 years, with Jim Bolger becoming prime minister.
1993 The NP won elections. A referendum on electoral reform showed a majority in favour of proportional representation.

Nations of the World: A Political, Economic and Business Handbook

1996 New Zealand adopted a new parliamentary electoral system called Mixed Member Proportional (MMP), which was designed to give better representation for smaller parties and the Māori community.
1997 Bolger resigned rather than face a leadership challenge from cabinet minister Jenny Shipley, who went on to become New Zealand's first woman prime minister.
1998 The NP-led coalition collapsed, leaving the NP as a minority government reliant on support from independent MPs.
1999 New Zealand sent troops to join UN peace-keeping forces in East Timor. In the November general elections, the NP was defeated by the New Zealand Labour Party (NZLP) and its leader Helen Clark became prime minister of a coalition government.
2001 The government re-nationalised Air New Zealand 12 years after it was privatised.
2002 A coalition governmen, led by NZLP, took office.
2004 In July, official contact with Israel was suspended after two Israelis were jailed for attempting to obtain New Zealand passports for Mossad agents. The convicted men were deported in September. In November a law was passed making all of the coastline public property. Māori opposition claim the law infringes the *Treaty of Waitangi*.
2005 The general election held on 17 September resulted in no clear winner. Prime Minister Helen Clark formed a coalition government on 17 October.

Political structure
Constitution
New Zealand has no written constitution. Its constitutional history dates back to the signing of the *Treaty of Waitangi* in 1840, when the indigenous Māori people ceded sovereignty over New Zealand to the British monarch. The Constitution Act 1986 brought together the most important constitutional provisions.
New Zealand is an independent parliamentary democracy and member of the Commonwealth. Government is based on the Westminster (United Kingdom) model.

Form of state
Constitutional monarchy

The executive
The head of state is the British sovereign, represented by a governor general who acts on the advice of the cabinet. The governor general is appointed by the sovereign on the advice of the New Zealand government.
The prime minister and cabinet are responsible to the legislature and are appointed by the governor general acting upon its advice. The prime minister and cabinet must be chosen from among elected members of parliament.
The Executive Council is a formal body made up of the cabinet and the governor general, who acts on the cabinet's advice. The cabinet consists of the prime minister and ministers, who must be chosen from among elected members of parliament.

National legislature
Legislative power is vested in a unicameral parliament (the House of Representatives). It has 120 members, elected for three-year terms through general elections at which all residents over 18 years of age are entitled to vote. Four seats are reserved for Māori representatives.
Mixed Member Proportional (MMP) voting was introduced for the first time in the 1996 elections, replacing the first-past-the-post system. Under MMP, the single-chamber parliament was enlarged from 99 to 120 seats, with half representing specific electorates. The remainder are chosen from party lists. Parties must gain a minimum of 5 per cent of the vote before they can be represented in parliament.
Authority for raising revenue by taxation and for public expenditure must be granted by parliament. It also controls the government through its power to pass a resolution of no confidence.

Legal system
The law consists of common law, New Zealand statutes and some British statutes. The judiciary is independent from the executive. High Court judges, who also sit on the Court of Appeal, are appointed by the governor general and cannot be removed from office except by the sovereign or the governor general.

Last elections
17 September 2005 (parliamentary)
Results: Prime Minister Helen Clark's New Zealand Labour Party (NZLP) won 41.1 per cent of the vote (50 seats out of 120); New Zealand National Party (NP) (39.1 per cent, 48 seats); New Zealand First Party (NZFP) (5.7 per cent, seven seats); Green Party of Aotearoa (GPA) (5.3 per cent, six seats); Maori Party (2.1 per cent, four seats); United Future New Zealand (UFNZ) (2.7 per cent, three seats); ACT New Zealand (ACT NZ) (1.5 per cent, two seats); New Zealand Progressive Party (NZPP) (1.2 per cent, 1 seat) .

Next elections
2008 (parliamentary)

Political parties
Ruling party
The New Zealand Labour Party (NZLP) in coalition with the New Zealand Progressive Party
Main opposition party
National Party (NP) (50 seats)

Population
4.04 million (2004)
Ethnic make-up
Approximately 77.3 per cent of the population is of European origin, with Māoris representing another 14.5 per cent, Pacific Islanders 5.6 per cent and others 2.6 per cent. Pacific Islanders are attracted by job opportunities and a higher standard of living. However, socio-economic problems plague the Māoris and Pacific Islanders.
Religions
Anglican (25 per cent), Presbyterian (18 per cent), Roman Catholic (15 per cent), Methodist (5 per cent), Baptist (2 per cent) and other Christian religions (34 per cent).

Education
Education is free and secondary admission is non-selective. Primary education covers ages five to 12 years and secondary education ages 13 to 16 years. A one-year sixth form follows and leads to a one-year pre-university course.
Public expenditure on education is typically 7 per cent of GNP. Nearly NZ$30 million (US$14.5 million) was allocated to implement the government's policy of equity funding for the early childhood education sector and funding for adult literacy was doubled, to NZ$18 million (US$8.7 million) as part of the Adult Literacy Strategy.
A campaign was launched that targets the Māori community called *Te Mana*, with a specific objective of providing education from a Māori perspective to youths, parents, life-long learners and teachers. It uses television, IT and a magazine, which has expanded to include study guides and a website, with relevent, current and contemporary tutoring.
Literacy rate: 99 per cent, adult rate
Compulsory years: Six to 17
Enrolment rate: 101 per cent gross primary enrolment of the relevant age group (including repeaters); 113 per cent gross secondary enrolment (World Bank).
Pupils per teacher: 18 in primary schools

Health
The health system is made up of the public, private and voluntary sectors. The public sector provides free treatment at hospitals for immediate and major medical problems as well as chronic complaints, some continuing care and maternity and geriatric care. It also provides health benefits and subsidises pharmaceutical benefits and laboratory tests. The provision of mental health services is largely the responsibility of the public sector (with a small voluntary sector contribution) caring for both acute and chronic cases. It also provides free dental health

New Zealand

treatment for school-age children. The public sector meets more than three-quarters of the total cost of healthcare and subsidises healthcare provided by general practitioners and specialists in private practice.

Private healthcare includes services provided by general practitioners, dentists, pharmacists and therapists in both public and private hospitals. The state subsidises many of these services although the main feature of this sector is the steady and rapid growth of private health and medical insurance.

Annual total expenditure on health is about 8 per cent, of which government spending is approximately 77 per cent; private expenditure is around 23 per cent, of which spending on pre-paid plans is estimated at 27 per cent.

HIV prevalence: 0.1 per cent aged 15–49 in 2003 (World Bank)
Life expectancy: 79.1 years (World Bank)
Fertility rate/Maternal mortality rate: 1.9 births per woman; maternal mortality 15 per 100,000 live births (World Bank)
Birth rate/Death rate: 15 births and Seven deaths per 1,000 people (World Bank)
Infant mortality rate: 5.0 per 1,000 live births (World Bank)
Head of population per physician/bed: 2.3 physicians and 6.2 hospital beds per 1,000 people

Welfare

New Zealand Superannuation (NZS), which is a universal, publicly provided pension, is at the core of its retirement income system provided to everyone over the age of 64 years and who meet certain residential qualifications. It is estimated that more than 92 per cent of older people receive NZS.

The government has tried to develop the welfare system, which actively works with beneficiaries to boost their skills. In 2002/03, a NZ$3 million (US$1.4 million) pilot programme was initiated to encourage sickness and invalids benefit recipients to participate in paid work and community-based activities.

Main cities

Wellington (capital, North Island, estimated population 178,000 in 2004); Auckland, North Island (406,000); Manukau, North Island (358,000); Christchurch (358,000); North Shore, North Island (244,200); Waitakere, North Island (191,000); Hamilton (150,400); Dunedin (113,600); Tauranga (103,600).

Languages spoken

Some Polynesian dialects are spoken and a variety of other languages, reflecting the diverse origins of New Zealand's immigrant population.

Official language/s
English, Māori

Media

The media in New Zealand is independent and free from official restraint and censorship, operating within the constraints of libel laws and other statutes. Key players in the sector are merging with Internet service providers and telecommunications companies as part of the general convergence in the creation and distribution of information and entertainment.

Press
Dailies: There are several dailies in circulation. *New Zealand Herald* has the largest daily circulation and is published in Auckland. There are approximately nine morning and 23 evening papers which are published daily in the main towns. A few of the dailies published in main centres are distributed throughout the surrounding provinces. Other major dailies including the regional ones are *Herald*, *Dominion*, *Evening Post*, *Waikato Times*, *Press* and *Otago Daily Times*. On-line daily news service can be obtained from *New Zealand News.net* (www.newzealandnews.net/) and *Aucklandlive News* (www.aucklandlive.co.nz/news) that delivers up to date news covering local issues.

Weeklies: The two Sunday papers published in English from Auckland and Wellington are *Sunday Star Times* and *Sunday News*. Other major English-language weekly publications are *Listener*, *TV Guide*, *Truth*, *New Zealand Women's Weekly* and *Women's Day New Zealand*. Other regional language weeklies include *Samoa Post* and *Samoana* (Samoan), *Taimi o Tonga* and *Lao & Hia* (Tongan).

Business: The leading business journal is the weekly *National Business Review*. On-line business news is carried by *National Business Review* (www.nbr.co.nz/). *Nieu Economic Review* is an English-language monthly publication.

Periodicals: The majority of local magazines and community newsletters are published monthly. Some of these periodicals are *The Lakesider* (Upper Clutha), *Aroha Nui Otara Community Newspaper* and *Fangufangumana* in Tongan. Several local Maori-language monthly and quarterly publications in circulation are *Te Karaka* and *Toi te Kupu* (full colour tabloid). Bi-lingual publications in Māori and English are *Pu Kaea*, *Kia Hiwa Ra*, *Pipiwharauroa* and *Mana*. *Cook Islands Sun* is a bi-annual English-language publication. *Pacific Network Newspaper* published in English, Niuean, Tongan and Samoan provides news of the wider Pacific community.

Broadcasting
Radio: Radio New Zealand, a former service of the Broadcasting Corporation of New Zealand, was established as a fully commercial state-owned enterprise in 1988. With 35 commercial radio stations, three non-commercial radio networks (National Radio, Concert Programme and AM Network) and a shortwave service (Radio New Zealand International), it is one of the largest single radio operators in the world.

Television: There are three television stations, with about one-third of the programming produced in New Zealand. In addition, there are two pay-per-view vendors, Sky Television, offering a further five channels, and Telstra Saturn, with services in Wellington, Auckland and Christchurch. Television New Zealand (TVNZ) operates two of the three free channels, and claims to have 100 per cent coverage. The other channel, operated by TV3 Network Limited, has approximately 96 per cent coverage. Cable TV is a common means of accessing programmes. There are, in addition, local community stations.

Advertising
Advertising is available on commercial radio and TV, in the press, in cinemas and outdoors on buses and inside telephone booths. Direct mail advertising services are available. Various laws regulate the advertising of certain products, including drugs, cosmetics and medical instruments. Self-regulation is the responsibility of the Advertising Standards Authority and the Advertising Standards Complaint Board. The Broadcasting Standards Authority is responsible for radio and television advertising regulations.

Economy

New Zealand has been transformed from an agrarian society to an industrialised nation by the economic restructuring that took place after 1984. The economy was opened up to world markets and the government eliminated all domestic and export subsidies and most tariffs. New Zealand is reputed to be among the most open economies in the world, while inflation has consistently stayed under the government's 3 per cent target since the mid-1990s. Manufacturing has led growth while traditional sectors have stagnated or shown only modest growth levels. In the period 1992–2002 New Zealand recorded an average annual growth rate of 3.6 per cent, easily outperforming many other developed economies. To have maintained this during the global downturn of 2000–02 was a considerable achievement.

In opening itself up to international trade and investment, New Zealand became highly exposed to events in Asia. This was evident during the Asian Crisis of 1998, which precipitated a collapse in the value of the New Zealand dollar. Even so, the country fared better than most in Asia and the Pacific due to its flexibility and its robust corporate and financial sectors and made a quick recovery.

Favourable terms of trade and a rise in farming output combined with a competitive exchange rate have boosted the economy. Although committed to monetary stability, both the IMF and the OECD have cautioned the government to maintain its track record on fiscal management as pressures to spend more on health and education grow.

In the long term, New Zealand will need to reduce its large current account deficit (its share of world trade is declining) and sustain the growth in productivity, particularly its quality of human capital. The perception of New Zealand as a safe haven, coupled with low levels of unemployment, have contributed to a relatively high level of net immigration. This development has eased skills shortages which were threatening to restrict economic growth. Even so, the key challenge is New Zealand's relatively low levels of labour productivity, underlying which are low levels of private sector research and development, skills shortages at management and employee level and relatively low investment in new technologies.

The OECD, in its 2005 *Economic Policy Reforms*, recommended:

- strengthening incentives to move from welfare to work
- expanding early childhood education and improving teacher quality
- removing restrictions on foreign investment in businesss activities, while protecting sensitive land by imposing land-use constraints
- enhancing the business environment by improving the regulatory framework to enable infrastructure bottlenecks such as transport and energy to be addressed
- ensuring that employment relations legislation supports efficient labour market outcomes.

External trade

New Zealand's policy is to substitute tariffs for import licensing as a main form of industry protection. Its reliance on imports of raw materials and capital equipment for industry and supply of output relative to domestic demand has made the country strongly trade-oriented and overall tariff levels are low.

Imports
Main imports include machinery and equipment, vehicles and aircraft, petroleum, electronics, textiles and plastics.
Main sources: Australia (28.6 per cent total, 2004), Japan (10.7 per cent), US (10 per cent), China (6.6 per cent), Germany (4.2 per cent), Singapore (4.1 per cent)

Exports
Main exports include dairy products, meat, timber and timber products, fish and machinery.
Main destinations: Australia (19.6 per cent total, 2004), US (14.3 per cent), Japan (11.4 per cent), China (6.3 per cent), UK (5.1 per cent)

Agriculture
Farming
The New Zealand (NZ) agricultural sector is almost unique among its developed nation competitors in being virtually free of subsidies, with farming produce being forced to compete against that produced in countries that do provide subsidies and incentives to their farmers. With a level of producer support estimate of 1 per cent (the OECD average is around 31 per cent) the agricultural industry still provides around 70 per cent of export earnings. The removal of subsidies was both a burden and a boon to the NZ industry. Farmers contended with a fluctuating international market, which was dependent on the state of the general economy and specifically the value of the NZ dollar, while reorganising and diversifying. To compete, the industry shed obsolete equipment and old practices in favour of reinvestment and embracing market economies. The industry also adopted the latest research and development findings, applying biotechnology and information technology to improve productivity.

Beef and sheep farming have been the mainstay of the country's agricultural sector for over a century. Since subsidies were withdrawn in 1982, these sectors have been rationalised and have seen a fall in the number of farms and animals. Productivity in meat and wool has increased since 1994 with 14 per cent more lambs born to 32 per cent fewer ewes. Weight gain of the average lamb at slaughter and lamb meat production have increased.

Dairy farming, particularly in the South Island, has increased with the addition of 1,650 new farms since 1994; the number of dairy cows rose by 52 per cent to 5.24 million.

Exports of flowers and wines have steadily increased, with horticulture exports amounting to NZ$2.20 billion (US$1.46 billion) by 2004.

The agriculture, fishing and forestry sectors together account for approximately 7–8 per cent of GDP and provide employment for over 11 per cent of the workforce. Of the total land area, grazing accounts for almost 12 million hectares (ha), horticulture over 100,000ha and planted forests 1.9 million ha.

Deer farming has led to a rapid growth in venison exports, and goats are reared for mohair. Wheat production is sufficient to meet national demand, as do crops including barley, maize and fresh vegetables. Other products include apples, pears, stone and berry fruits, citrus and sub-tropical fruits.

Crop production in 2004 included: 881,700 tonnes (t) cereals in total, 287,000t wheat, 170,000t maize, *500,000t potatoes, 380,000t barley, 32,200t pulses, *29,650t citrus fruit, 166,000t grapes, *87,000t tomatoes, 320,000t kiwi fruit, *1,870t oilcrops, *885t hops, 500,000t apples, 34,500t oats, 3,100t fibre crops, 1,130,620t fruit in total, 999,814t vegetables in total. Livestock production included: 1,466,240t meat in total, 720,000t beef, 53,400t pig meat, 509,000t lamb, 1,330t goat meat, 31,000t game meat, 149,065t poultry, 49,200t eggs, 14,780,000t milk, *12,252t honey, 59,000t cattle hides, 102,000t sheepskins, *229,600t greasy wool.
* estimate

Fishing
The seafood industry is one of New Zealand's top five export earners. The total fish catch is typically around 700,000 tonnes per annum, of which 80 per cent is produced through marine fishing. Annual export revenues from fishing amount to around US$150 million.

Forestry
Forests cover about 27 per cent (eight million ha) of New Zealand's land area. Of this, around 6.2 million ha are indigenous forest and 1.9 million ha are plantations. The majority of plantations, cultivating exotic species, are in the central region of North Island. Some 95 per cent of plantations grow exotic softwoods, of which 80 per cent are *Pinus Radiata*, 10 per cent Douglas Fir and 10 per cent other species. The state owns 55 per cent of the exotic resource, with forestry companies, Māori incorporates, local authorities and individuals owning the remainder. Chile is New Zealand's major competitor in the market for *Pinus Radiata*. The planting of exotic species began on a large scale in 1923; there was a second major planting in the 1960s and these trees are now reaching maturity, which will boost the supply of mature trees over the medium-term.

In 2004 New Zealand produced over one million cubic metres (cum) of panel products and over 500,000cum of paper products. The total value of forest products in 2004 was NZ$3.22 billion (US$2.13 billion). In the long term a vibrant log processing industry, comparable to that of the southern US, could be developed.

Timber production in 2003 included 21,399,000 cubic metres (cum) roundwood, 21,399,000cum industrial roundwood, 70,000cum sawnwood, 9,146,000cum sawlogs & veneer logs, 79,000cum wood-based panels.

Industry and manufacturing

The industrial sector typically accounts for under a fifth of GDP, employs just over a fifth of the workforce, and accounts for a similar proportion of export earnings. The industrialisation that took place from the mid-1980s helped increase the added value of New Zealand's traditional sectors. Meat, dairy and fruit produce are processed in New Zealand for markets in Asia and Europe. Biotechnology, communications and information technology are also sectors growing in importance.

Tourism

Tourism is the principal earner of foreign exchange. The sector, which provides employment for around 10 per cent of the workforce, is expected to contribute 7.1 per cent to GDP in 2005. Visitor numbers continue to rise, having weathered the impact of recent external crises, including the Sars outbreak of 2003, which damaged many other countries' tourism industries, and demonstrating the strength of the sector. 2.1 million visitors were recorded in 2004, compared with 1.9 million in 2003.

Mining

The mining sector typically accounts for 2 per cent of GDP and employs 1.5 per cent of the workforce. Gold, silver, ironsand, clays, sand and aggregates are the main minerals mined. Ironsand is used to produce steel and is exported to Japan. Other metals include tungsten, manganese, copper, lead, zinc, tin, mercury (as cinnabar), platinum, titanium and aluminium (as bauxite). Non-metallic minerals include aggregates for roads; clays for ceramics and fillers; bentonite for bonding and drilling; limestone for agriculture and cement; and dolomite, serpentine, silica sand, sulphur, diatomite, mica, pumice and feldspar.

Hydrocarbons

New Zealand has around 190 million barrels of proven oil reserves and, in 2004, produced 7.6 million barrels per annum. Production has declined by around 50 per cent in recent years. Domestic consumption is rising. Without further investment, New Zealand's oil and gas reserves are expected to decline from about 2005.

New Zealand has around 84.9 billion cubic metres (cum) of natural gas reserves. Most of the gas is produced from the large offshore Taranaki Maui field, which is expected to be depleted by 2008. Small discoveries by Westech Energy and Orion Exploration were made in the largely unexplored East Coast Basin in 1998. Fletcher Challenge's March 2000 discovery at its Pohokura well is expected to start producing gas in 2006; estimated reserves are 21 million cum.

New Zealand has 8.6 billion tonnes of recoverable coal reserves and produces 3.2 million tonnes oil equivalent. Coal is New Zealand's largest energy resource. Coal production is increasing to meet domestic demand as oil and gas production falls, especially to supply steelworks and thermal power stations. Lignite makes up 82 per cent of recoverable coal resources, with sub-bituminous coal comprising 14 per cent and bituminous coal comprising less than 4 per cent. A substantial proportion of coal is exported to markets in Japan, India, South Africa, South America, Europe and China.

Energy

New Zealand has installed electricity generating capacity of around 8.5GW. Hydro-power generated on numerous rivers and lakes provides around 70 per cent of all electricity generated, with another 5 per cent coming from geothermal sources. Most of the rest has been supplied by natural gas, but with the depletion of reserves and the need to expand capacity to meet the growing demand for electricity, coal, of which New Zealand has abundant reserves, is becoming increasingly important.

Financial markets
Stock exchange

New Zealand's stock exchanges are in Auckland, Christchurch, Dunedin and Wellington. The largest of the four is the New Zealand Stock Exchange (NZSE) in Auckland. On 30 May 2003, the NZSE re-named itself the NZX.

Banking and insurance

Banking has been opened up to international competition, but domestic demand for credit remains weak. All but one of New Zealand's 18 banks are foreign-owned.

Central bank

The Reserve Bank of New Zealand (RBNZ) formulates and implements monetary policy and is the supervisory authority for New Zealand's registered banks.

New Zealand

Main financial centre
Wellington

Time
GMT plus 13 hours October–March; GMT plus 12 hours March–October.

Geography
New Zealand consists of two main islands (North Island and South Island) and other outlying islands, the biggest of which is Stewart Island off the southern tip of South Island.

New Zealand is in the south-west Pacific, 1,600km south-east of Australia, separated from it by the Tasman Sea, and has no continental neighbours to the east before South America. Its combined length is over 1,600km and it is about 450km across at its widest point. Mount Cook in the Southern Alps is its highest point at 3,764 metres – one of more than 230 named peaks above 2,300 metres.

Climate
New Zealand is a temperate country with a variable and unpredictable climate, generally drier and warmer on North Island than on South Island, particularly in winter. Rainfall averages 600–1,500mm annually and strong winds are common. On North Island, January temperatures average 18 degrees Celsius (C) and in winter 4 degrees C. It is 3 to 5 degrees C colder on South Island.

Dress codes
Visitors should take warm clothing during the winter months, from May to October. Even in the summer, from December to early March, a light sweater is an essential travelling item. Suits are worn for business meetings. For leisure, smart casual clothes are acceptable.

Entry requirements
Passports
Passports are required by all and must be valid for three months beyond the intended length of stay.

Visa
Required by all. Business visas may not be required for company representatives, a visitors visa is sufficient for stays up to three months. However proof of onward/return tickets and sufficient funds are required.

Visit www.immigration.govt.nz/ for further information.

Currency advice/regulations
There are no restrictions on the import and export of local and foreign currencies. Cash amounts over NZ$10,000 (or equivalent) must be declared.

Customs
Equipment used with animals, camping equipment, golf clubs and used bicycles must be declared. Firearms and weapons

are strictly controlled and require a police permit.
Personal effects are allowed duty-free: 200 cigarettes, 4.5 litres of wine/beer, or goods up to the value of NZ$700 (or equivalent) are permitted.
Visitors arriving from countries suffering from certain diseases affecting livestock and plants may have items of clothing and produce disinfected.

Prohibited imports
Narcotics, weapons such as flick knives, plants or plant material, animals or their by-products (these include any fruit, vegetables or meat – cooked or raw), and biological specimens.

Health (for visitors)
A reciprocal health agreement for urgent medical treatment exists with the United Kingdom. Some proof of UK residence will be required.

Mandatory precautions
There are no compulsory vaccinations.

Advisable precautions
Travellers are advised to have up-to-date tetanus and polio immunisations.

Hotels
Motel, serviced-unit accommodation is widespread. Neither a service charge nor tipping is customary. Advance booking is advisable for major hotels in urban centres.

Credit cards
All major credit cards are accepted.

Public holidays
Fixed dates
1–2 Jan (New Year), 29 Jan (Anniversary Day Auckland/Northland), 6 Feb (Waitangi Day), 25 Apr (Anzac Day), 25 Dec (Christmas Day), 26 Dec (Boxing Day).

Variable dates
Easter Holiday, Queen's Official Birthday (first Mon in Jun), Labour Day (Oct).

Working hours
Mid-December to mid-February is the summer holiday season during which the majority of New Zealanders take most of their annual leave.

Banking
Mon–Fri: 0900–1630.

Business
Mon–Fri: 0900–1700.

Government
Mon–Fri: 0800–1630.

Shops
Mon–Thu: 0900–1730; Fri: 0900–2100; Sat: 0900–1230. Some shops open on Sundays.

Electricity supply
230/240V AC, 50 hertz, with three-pin flat plug fittings and bayonet-type light sockets, although most hotels supply 110V AC sockets for razors.

Weights and measures
Metric system

Social customs/useful tips
In general, be polite and patient. New Zealanders appreciate frankness and like prompt timekeeping for business meetings. Business can also be discussed over lunch and dinner. Late night life can be sparse. People tend to go to bed early and start work early.
Should a visitor be invited to a formal Māori occasion the *hongi* (pressing of noses) is common.
Tipping is acceptable but is not particularly sought after and there is sometimes a built-in service charge at hotels and restaurants.

Security
The cities are safe, even at night.

Getting there
Air
National airline: Air New Zealand
International airport/s: Auckland International, Mangere (AKL), 22km south of Auckland, with duty-free shop, bar, restaurant, bank, hotel reservations, post office, shops, car hire; Christchurch International (CHC), 10km from Christchurch, with duty-free shop, bar, restaurant, buffet, bank, hotel reservations, post office, shops, car hire; Wellington International (WLG), 8km south-east of Wellington, with duty-free shop, bar, restaurant, buffet, bank, hotel reservations, post office, shops, car hire.
Airport tax: International departures, up to NZ$25, transit passengers exempt for up to 24 hours.

Surface
Water: Apart from cruise ships there are no regular passenger ships sailing to New Zealand.
Main port/s: Auckland (containers), Dunedin, Lyttelton (containers), Tauranga, Wellington (containers), Port Chalmers (containers), Picton, Opua.

Getting about
National transport
Air: There are good regular air services between the four major cities (Wellington, Auckland, Christchurch and Dunedin) with links to smaller, regional towns and tourist centres. Internal air services serve some 30 airports. Air New Zealand and Ansett New Zealand operate the majority of regular domestic services, and other operators include Mount Cook Airlines, Eagle Airways, Wairarapa Airlines and Bell-Air. Charter services are also available. There is a departure tax from Palmerston North Airport.
Road: The road network includes over 11,000km of state highways. The main routes are surfaced, and roads are generally well-maintained.

Buses: Luxury coach services link the main centres. Advance booking for these is advisable, especially during the main holiday periods (December–February and Easter).
Rail: New Zealand's rail network was re-nationalised in July 2004. It operates over 4,300km of track. Express services link the main centres on both islands.
Water: Interisland Lines operates a regular service between Wellington and Picton several times a day. Advance booking is advisable, especially during the main holiday periods December–February and Easter.

City transport
Taxis: Taxis may be hired from ranks or by telephone 24 hours a day, although there is an extra charge for telephone booking. Fares are generally charged per km, but rates vary throughout the country and are generally higher at night and on weekends. Tipping is not customary.
The taxi journey from Auckland International Airport to the city centre takes 35 minutes; from Christchurch Airport to city centre 15 minutes; from Wellington Airport to city centre 20 minutes.
Buses, trams & metro: Shuttle buses run from the international airports to the city centres.

Car hire
Self-drive car hire is available in main centres. It is advisable to book ahead at motels when touring. Visitors may drive using Australian, British, Canadian, US or international driving licences. Driving is on the left-hand side of the road. Parking can be a problem in larger cities. Outside the major centres there is little traffic, country areas being sparsely populated.

BUSINESS DIRECTORY
The addresses listed below are a selection only. While World of Information makes every endeavour to check these addresses, we cannot guarantee that changes have not been made, especially to telephone numbers and area codes. We would welcome any corrections.

Telephone area codes
The international direct dialling code (IDD) for New Zealand is +64, followed by area code and subscriber's number:

Auckland	9	Nelson	3
Bay of Plenty	7	New Plymouth	6
Christchurch	3	Palmerston North	6
Dunedin	3	Rotorua	7
Gisborne	6	Tauranga	7
Hamilton	7	The South Island	3
Hastings	6	Timaru	3
Invercargil	3	Wanganui	6
Manawatu	6	Wellington	4
Napier	6	Whangarei	9

Useful telephone numbers
Emergency (all services): 111

New Zealand

Chambers of Commerce

American Chamber of Commerce in New Zealand, Affco House, 12-26 Swanson Street, PO Box 106002, Auckland Central 1001 (tel: 309-9140; fax: 309-1090; e-mail: amcham@amcham.co.nz).

Auckland Chamber of Commerce, 100 Mayoral Drive, PO Box 47, Auckland (tel: 309-6100; fax: 309-0081; e-mail: akl@chamber.co.nz).

British New Zealand Trade Council, PO Box 37162, Parnell, Auckland (tel/fax: 522-0526; e-mail: info@bnztc.co.nz).

Canterbury Employers Chamber of Commerce, 57 Kilmore Street, PO Box 359, Christchurch (tel: 366-5096; fax: 379-5454; e-mail: info@cecc.org.nz).

New Zealand Chambers of Commerce & Industry, 109 Featherston Street, PO Box 11043, Wellington (tel: 472-3376; fax: 471-1767).

Otago Chamber of Commerce & Industry, WestpacTrust Building, 106 George Street, Dunedin (tel: 479-0181; fax: 477-0341; e-mail: office@otagochamber.co.nz).

Wellington Regional Chamber of Commerce, 109 Featherston Street, PO Box 1590, Wellington 6015 (tel: 914-6500; fax: 914-6524; e-mail: info@wgtn-chamber.co.nz).

Banking

ANZ Banking Group (New Zealand) Limited, PO Box 1492, ANZ Tower, Level 9, 215-229 Lambton Quay, Wellington (tel: 496-6938; fax: 496-6934).

ASB Bank Ltd, 198-204 Lambton Quay, Wellington (tel: 499-0864; fax: 495-2102).

Bank of New Zealand, PO Box 2392, State Insurance Centre, 1 Willis Street, Wellington (tel: 474-6999; fax: 474-6861).

BNZ Finance Ltd; PO Box 401, Level 24, BNZ Centre, 1 Willis Street, Wellington (tel: 495-3630; fax: 495-3632).

National Bank of New Zealand Ltd, PO Box 1791, 1 Victoria Street, Wellington 6000 (tel: 498-6020; fax: 494-4023).

Reserve Bank of New Zealand, PO Box 2498, 2 The Terrace, Wellington (tel: 472-2029; fax: 473-8554).

Westpac Banking Corporation, PO Box 691, 157 Lambton Quay, Wellington (tel: 381-1430; fax: 470-8202).

Central bank

Reserve Bank of New Zealand, 2 The Terrace, PO Box 2498, Wellington (tel: 472-2029; fax: 473-8554; e-mail: rbnz-info@rbnz.govt.nz).

Travel information

Air New Zealand, Customer Support, Private Bag 92007, Auckland 1020 (tel: 255-8758; fax: 256-3531; internet site: http://www.airnz.co.nz/).

Intercity Coachlines (InterCity Group (NZ)), PO Box 26 601, Epsom, Auckland (tel: 623-1503; email: info@intercitygroup.co.nz; internet site: http://www.intercitycoach.co.nz).

Interislander (ferry service) (Ticket Office) PO Box 2085, Wellington (tel: 498-3302; fax: 498-3090; email: info@interislander.co.nz; internet site: http://www.interislander.co.nz).

National tourist organisation offices

New Zealand Tourism Board, PO Box 95, Wellington (tel: 472-8860; fax: 478-1736; internet site: http://www.purenz.com).

Ministries

Ministry of Agriculture and Fisheries, PO Box 2526, Wellington (tel: 474-4100; fax: 474-4111).

Ministry of Civil Defence, PO Box 5010, Wellington (tel: 473-7363; fax: 473-7369).

Ministry of Commerce, PO Box 1473, Wellington (tel: 472-0030; fax: 473-4638).

Ministry of Consumer Affairs, PO Box 1473, Wellington (tel: 474-2750; fax: 473-9400).

Ministry of Defence, PO Box 5347, Wellington (tel: 496-0999; fax: 496-0859).

Ministry of Education, Private Bag 1666, Wellington (tel: 473-5544; fax: 499-1327).

Ministry for the Environment, PO Box 10362, Wellington (tel: 473-4090; fax: 471-0195).

Ministry of Foreign Affairs and Trade, Private Bag 18-901, Parliament Bldgs, Wellington (tel: 472-8877; fax: 472-9596).

Ministry of Forestry, PO Box 1610, Wellington (tel: 472-1569; fax: 472-2314).

Ministry of Health, PO Box 5013, Wellington (tel: 496-2000; fax: 496-2340).

Ministry of Mäori Development, PO Box 3943, Wellington (tel: 494-7100; fax: 494-7010).

Ministry of Pacific Island Affairs, PO Box 833, Wellington (tel: 473-4493; fax: 473-4301).

Ministry of Research, Science and Technology, PO Box 5336, Wellington (tel: 472-6400; fax: 471-1284).

Ministry of Transport, PO Box 3175, Wellington (tel: 472-1253; fax: 473-3697).

Ministry of Women's Affairs, PO Box 10049, Wellington (tel: 473-4112; fax: 472-0961).

Ministry of Youth Affairs, PO Box 10300, Wellington (tel: 471-2158; fax: 471-2233).

Prime Minister and Cabinet Department, Executive Wing, Parliament Bldgs, Wellington (tel: 471-9700; fax: 473-2508).

Other useful addresses

Airways Corporation of New Zealand, 44-48 Willis Street, PO Box 294, Wellington (tel: 471-1888; fax: 471-0395; internet site: http://www.airways.co.nz/).

British High Commission, PO Box 1812, 44 Hill Street, Wellington 1 (tel: 472-6049; fax: 471-1974).

British/New Zealand Trade Council Inc, 22 Newton Road, Newton, Auckland (tel: 378-9066; fax: 378-0539).

Central Region Health Authority, PO Box 10097, 155 The Terrace, Wellington (tel: 472-7633; fax: 472-7639).

Coal Corporation of New Zealand Ltd, PO Box 439, Wellington (tel: 474-3600; fax: 474-3601).

Commerce Commission, PO Box 2351, Wellington (tel: 471-0180; fax: 471-0771).

Conservation Department, PO Box 10420, Wellington (tel: 471-0726; fax: 471-1082).

Customs Department, PO Box 2218, Whitmore Street, Wellington (tel: 473-6099; fax: 473-7370).

Earthquake Commission, PO Box 311, Wellington (tel: 499-0045; fax: 499-0046).

Electricity Corporation of New Zealand, PO Box 930, Wellington (tel: 472-3550; fax: 473-7091).

Hillary Commission for Sport, Fitness and Leisure, PO Box 2251, Wellington (tel: 472-8058; fax: 471-0813).

Housing Corporation of New Zealand, PO Box 5009, Wellington (tel: 495-1045; fax: 472-3152).

Human Rights Commission, PO Box 6751, Wellesley Street, Auckland (tel: 309-0874; fax: 377-3593).

Inland Revenue Department, PO Box 2198, Wellington (tel: 472-1032; fax: 499-0806).

Internal Affairs Department, PO Box 805, Wellington (tel: 495-7200; fax: 495-7222).

Justice Department, PO Box 180, Wellington (tel: 472-5980; fax: 499-2295).

Labour Department, PO Box 3705, Wellington (tel: 473-7800; fax: 495-4009).

Land Corporation Ltd, PO Box 5349, Wellington (tel: 471-0400; fax: 473-4966).

New Zealand Embassy (USA), 37 Observatory Circle, NW, Washington DC 20008 (tel: 202-328-4800; fax: 202-667-5227; e-mail: nz@nzemb.org).

New Zealand Manufacturers' Federation, 3–9 Church Street, PO Box 11543, Wellington (tel: 473-3000; fax: 473-3004).

New Zealand Minerals Industry Association, Druids Building, 188 Lambton Quay, PO Box 5039, Wellington (tel: 499-9871; fax: 499-9873; e-mail: nzmia@xtra.co.nz).

New Zealand Stock Exchange, Caltex Tower, 286-292 Lambton Quay, PO Box 2959, Wellington (tel: 472-7599; fax: 473-1470).

New Zealand Trade Development Board (TRADENZ), Pastoral House, 25 The Terrace, PO Box 10341, Wellington (tel: 499-2244; fax: 473-3193).

Overseas Investment Commission, 2 The Terrace, PO Box 2498, Wellington (tel: 471-3838; fax: 471-3655).

Race Relations Office, PO Box 12411, Thorndon, Wellington (tel: 499-5885; fax: 499-5998).

Radio New Zealand, PO Box 2092, Wellington (tel: 474-1555; fax: 474-1712).

Statistics Department, 85 Molesworth Street, PO Box 2922, Wellington (tel: 495-4600; fax: 472-9135).

Survey and Land Information Department, Private Box 170, Charles Ferguson Building, Wellington (tel: 473-5022; fax: 472-2244).

Telecom New Zealand, PO Box 1473, Christchurch (tel: 374-0253; internet site: http://www.telecom.co.nz).

Television New Zealand Ltd, PO Box 3819, Auckland (tel: 377-0630; fax: 375-0828).

Tranz Rail Ltd, Private Bag, Wellington (tel: 498-3095; fax: 498-3322).

Treasury Department, PO Box 3724, Wellington (tel: 472-2733; fax: 473-0982).

Works and Development Services Corporation Ltd, PO Box 12041, Wellington (tel: 496-1300; fax: 471-0224).

Internet sites

AA Travel: http://www.aatravel.co.nz/main/index.shtml

Air New Zealand: http://www:airnz.com

Asia Pacific Economic Co-operation (APEC): http://www.apecsec.org.sg

Auckland Airport: http://www.auckland-airport.co.nz

Destination New Zealand (gateway site): http://www.destinationnz.co.nz

Economic & Trade Development Agency: http://www.nzte.govt.nz

General Information: http://www:nz.com

Immigration: http://www:immigration.govt.nz

Ministry of Foreign Affairs and Trade: http://www:mft.govt.nz

New Zealand Government: http://www.govt.nz/

New Zealand Herald newspaper: http://www:nzherald.co.nz

Parliament: http://www:parliament.govt.nz

Reserve Bank: http://www:rbnz.govt.nz

Statistics: http://www:stats.govt.nz

Stock exchange: http://www:nzse.co.nz

Treasury: http://www:treasury.govt.nz

Tourism: http://www:purenz.com

WebNZ Platinum Business Directory: http://nz.com/webnz/YellowPages

White Pages: http://www:whitepages.co.nz

Yellowpages: http://www.yellowpages.co.nz

Nicaragua

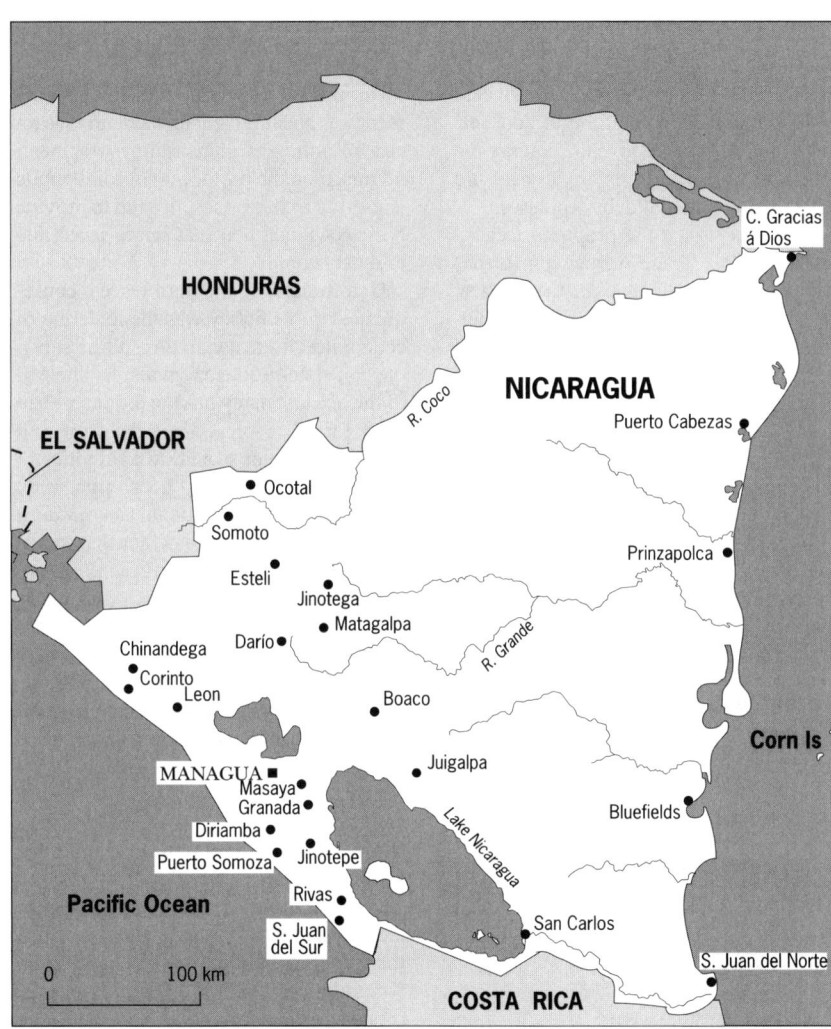

KEY FACTS

Official name: República de Nicaragua (Republic of Nicaragua)

Head of State: President Enrique Bolaños Geyer (PLC) (since Jan 2002)

Head of government: President Enrique Bolaños Geyer

Ruling party: Partido Liberal Constitucionalista (PLC) (Constitutionalist Liberal Party) (since 2001)

Area: 147,950 square km

Population: 5.98 million (2004)

Capital: Managua

Official language: Spanish

Currency: Córdoba de oro (gold córdoba) (C) = 100 centavos

Exchange rate: C16.37 per US$ (Oct 2005)

GDP per capita: US$788 (2004)

GDP real growth: 4.00% (2004)

Labour force: 2.23 million (2004)

Unemployment: 24.00% (2003)

Inflation: 8.20% (2004)

Balance of trade: -US$1.27 billion 2004

Foreign debt: US$5.80 billion (2003)

The presidency of Enrique José Bolaños Geyer has typified the self-indulgent brand of politics that has become inextricably linked with Nicaragua over the years. Political ambushes by the opposition and infighting within the president's own party have both been a feature of his administration, since it came to power in 2001.

Bolaños, of mixed Spanish and Germanic ancestry, successfully opposed the governing Frente Sandinista de Liberación Nacional (FSLN) (Sandinista National Liberation Front) throughout the 1980s and was imprisoned for his efforts. He also saw his business interests shut down and eventually confiscated by the authorities as the Sandinistas attempted to remove him from the country's political arena.

The ultimate political streetfighter, Bolaños fought back and eventually climbed his way up the greasiest of greasy polls that is the Nicaraguan political system, to become former president Arnoldo Alemán's vice president. In 2001, Bolaños, running on the Partido Liberal Constitucionalista (PLC) (Constitutional Liberal Party) ticket, successfully saw off former president Daniel Ortega's FSLN challenge for the presidency.

After being sworn in, Bolaños launched an anti corruption drive that eventually led to the sentencing of his former boss, Alemán, to twenty years imprisonment on charges of money laundering and fraud, among other offences. However, his decision to go after Alemán by making him a symbolic figure of his clampdown on political practice, and his decision to break away from the PLC (to form the Alliance for the Republic, (APRE)), has left him exposed to attacks from both ends of the political spectrum. In September and October both the PLC and the FSLN threatened to team up together in order to impeach the president. Though this initiative later tailed off, a reinvigoration of the impeachment drive remains a distinct future possibility.

Steady growth

The Nicaraguan economy has grown steadily since 2003 and the IMF forecasts growth of 3.5 per cent for 2005 with an increase of half a per cent to 4 per cent in 2006. Inflation continues to decrease, having hit 8.2 per cent per annum in 2004. The rate of inflation now stands at around 6.5 per cent and the IMF expects it to fall to 4–6 per cent in 2006.

Although the figures look promising, Nicaragua remains plagued by poverty; it is the second-poorest country in the Western Hemisphere after Haiti. Spending on education and health has taken a backseat to debt servicing. In terms of GDP, the country has one of the highest external debts in the world and was one of the first countries to qualify for the IMF's Enhanced Heavily Indebted Poor Countries (HIPC) initiative.

Although some of the government's failure to meet budgetary targets stem from its own corruption and incompetence, many of the problems are rooted in the ailing health of the economy, which has been blighted by a series of natural disasters and poor prices for its main commodity exports, particularly coffee. In January 2004, the country received some good news as the World Bank and the IMF wiped out 80 per cent of Nicaragua's debt by supporting US$4.5 billion of debt service relief. This could give the country the opportunity to address poverty as pressure from a rising national debt decreases.

Nicaragua signed the proposed Central American Free Trade Agreement (Cafta) in August 2004, along with Costa Rica, the Dominican Republic, El Salvador, Guatemala and Honduras. Cafta was ratified by Congress in 2005 and is predicted by many to safeguard Nicaragua's economic progress in years to come, though various economic analysts offer a different prognosis regarding the potential effects of Cafta. Nicaragua's relationship with the US is very important to the economy. The US remains the country's largest trading partner, accounting for a quarter of the country's imports and receiving some 60 per cent of its exports.

Industry and agriculture

Agriculture plays a very significant role in the economy of Nicaragua, contributing about a quarter of the country's total GDP. The sector also employs up to 30 per cent of the total workforce. The principal export crop is coffee, which represents approximately a fifth of total export earnings. The Nicaraguan government is actively engaged in the agricultural sector although it is estimated that upwards of 60 per cent of cultivated land is in the hands of private smallholders. Despite continuous agrarian reform, food production has not kept up with demand owing mainly to poor weather, war damage and shortages of vital inputs.

During the 1980s, the national government of Nicaragua launched an unsuccessful policy of industrial development, premised on the promotion of joint public and-private enterprises, in a bid to provide basic consumer goods at prices accessible to most people.

Unfortunately, one unforeseen consequence of this policy was the lowering of economic efficiency as a result of subsidies on state-produced goods. By the end of the decade, many private producers had been forced to close their factories, sell out to the state or scale down activities.

However, there has been significant growth in the non-traditional *maquiladora* (assembly line) sector, which has made use of the Free Trade Zones (FTZs). Concentrated mainly on textiles, particularly clothing, for the US market, the *maquiladora* sector has rapidly become a major sub-sector in Nicaraguan industry. Low labour costs and minimal labour regulation have made it both an attractive opportunity for foreign investors and a target for trade unions and labour rights activists.

Arrears to the World Bank and Inter-American Development Bank (IDB), totalling US$320 million, were cleared at the start of the 1990s. Since then the government has been successful in winning international backing for its policies, in particular trade and financial sector reforms, such as the elimination of state monopolies in foreign trade, the liberalisation of the marketing system for basic grains and assistance with liberalising the foreign exchange system.

The most important projects undertaken in recent years have reflected a renewed priority placed on large-scale agri-industrial production, which had been neglected by the government in the early 1990s. The two biggest have been the Timal sugar refinery and the Sebaco food-processing complex. The Timal sugar refinery, located north of Managua in the Tipitapa-Malacatoya lowlands, cost US$200 million and was financed through loans and donations from a consortium of

KEY INDICATORS — Nicaragua

	Unit	2000	2001	2002	2003	2004
Population	m	5.07	5.22	5.36	5.67	*5.98
Gross domestic product (GDP)	US$bn	2.40	2.60	2.20	4.10	*4.35
GDP per capita	US$	430	430	474	495	788
GDP real growth	%	4.3	3.0	1.0	2.3	4.0
Inflation	%	11.6	4.8	4.5	5.2	8.2
Unemployment	%	9.8	23.0	23.0	24.0	–
Exports (fob) (goods)	US$m	652.8	592.0	641.0	596.0	750.0
Imports (fob) (goods)	US$m	1,647.3	1,789.0	1,580.0	1,624.0	2,020.0
Balance of trade	US$m	-994.5	-1,040.0	-939.0	-1,028.0	1,270.0
Current account	US$m	-505.0	-972.0	-724.0	-723.0	-950.0
Foreign debt	US$bn	7.5	7.1	6.5	5.8	–
Total reserves minus gold	US$m	488.5	379.9	448.1	502.1	668.2
Foreign exchange	US$m	488.4	379.6	448.1	502.0	667.7
Exchange rate	per US$	12.69	13.37	14.21	15.00	15.94

* estimated figure

14 countries, including Cuba, France, Spain and Canada, as well as from the Central American Bank for Economic Integration (CABEI). The refinery was designed by Cuban engineers and is capable of producing 7.55 tonnes of refined sugar daily. It also produces energy from the sugar cane refuse. The Sebaco food-processing complex is engaged in canning, dehydration and frozen food processing for export markets. A new industrial free zone law was approved by Congress in the mid-1990s, with a total area of 48,000 square km (30,000 square miles).

Outlook

President Bolaños appears to have isolated himself politically having made too many enemies in too short a period of time. The president's clampdown on corruption in public life is very much welcomed, as Nicaragua has been plagued by administrative malpractice for years. However, by targeting former president Arnoldo Alemán he has alienated many in his own party. This in turn, has opened up the door for the FSLN, who are desperate to get back into power, to form an unofficial anti-Bolaños pact, which resulted in the attempt to impeach him in mid-2005. Though Bolaños has succeeded in producing positive economic growth for his fellow citizens, his brave choice of political tactics may yet come back to haunt him in 2006, if a further attempt to impeach his office is successful.

Risk assessment

Politics	Poor
Economy	Improving
Regional stability	Stable

COUNTRY PROFILE

Historical profile

1821 The Central American provinces (Costa Rica, Guatemala, Honduras, Nicaragua and El Salvador) declared independence from Spain.
1822 Central American confederation annexed itself to the Mexican Empire, under General Agustín de Iturbde, later Emporer Agustín I.
1823 Agustín I was overthrown and Mexico became a republic. The Central American states formed the United Provinces of Central America.
1825 Costa Rica, Guatemala, Honduras, Nicaragua and El Salvador formed the Central American Federation (CAF).
1838 The CAF was dissolved and Nicaragua became a fully independent republic.
1855–57 Nicaragua was ruled by a US buccaneer, William Walker, who proclaimed himself president after being invited by the Liberals. He was overthrown in 1857 following intervention by other Central American states. He attempted to take over Nicaragua for a second time, but was repelled by the British navy. He made another attempt to seize the country in 1860, but was captured by the British and executed.
1860 British ceded control over the Caribbean coast to Nicaragua.
1893 General José Santos Zelaya, a Liberal, seized power and established a dictatorship.
1909 Zelaya was driven from office following a US-backed coup. Nicaragua allowed the US to run its customs and excise (raising money to pay the foreign debt), the national bank and the railway.
1912–25 The US established a number of military bases.
1929–33 Guerrillas led by Augusto César Sandino campaigned against US military presence.
1934 Sandino was assassinated on the orders of the National Guard commander, General Anastasio 'Tacho' Somoza García. The US marines left with Somoza ruling as a puppet dicatator.
1956 General Somoza was assassinated and was succeeded as president by his son, Luis Somoza Debayle.
1961 The Frente Sandinista de Liberación Nacional (FSLN) (Sandinista National Liberation Front) was founded. The Central American Common Market (CACM) was formed, comprising Nicaragua, Costa Rica, El Salvador, Honduras and Guatemala.
1967 Anastasio Somoza Debayle was officially elected president, succeeding his brother Luis.
1969 CACM collapsed following the 'soccer war' between El Salvador and Honduras.
1978 Prominent opposition leader and editor of La Prensa newspaper, Pedro Joaquín Chamorro, was assassinated, leading to a general strike and consolidation within the opposition.
1979 The Somoza dynasty was overthrown by a cross-party junta led by the FSLN. The new government seized land and private businesses owned by Somoza and his allies who had fled the country.
1981 The US broke off diplomatic links with Nicaragua claiming it was part of the communist 'evil empire'. A number of opposition leaders fled to Costa Rica and Honduras where they established guerrilla groups known as 'counter-revolutionaries' or Contras.
1982 The US began the Contra war against Nicaragua, arming counter-revolutionaries allied to supporters of the former Somoza regime and using bases in Honduras.
1984 Daniel Ortega, leader of the nine ruling comandantes, was elected president (the only opposition candidate withdrew). The US mined Nicaragua's harbours. Nicaragua began legal action against the US in the World Court for violating international law.
1986 The Nicaraguan government closed La Prensa after it began receiving funds from the CIA. The US was found to have given aid to the Contras, funded with arms sales from the US to Iran in what became known as the Iran-Contra Affair. The World Court found the US guilty of violating international law and ordered reparations. The US ignored the judgement.
1988 The government and the Contras agreed a cease-fire.
1990 The US-backed Unión Nacional Opositora (UNO) assumed office after elections in which it defeated the FSLN. The presidential opposition candidate, Violeta Chamorro, publisher of La Prensa, won the presidential election.
1994 Following defections from the UNO coalition, the de facto ruling coalition became a centrist block in alliance with the FSLN.
1996 Arnoldo Alemán won the elections.
1997 President Alemán was inaugurated. His right-wing Alianza Liberal (AL) (Liberal Alliance), dominated by the Partido Liberal Constitucionalista (PLC) (Constitutionalist Liberal Party), was the largest single group in the National Assembly.
1998 Hurricane Mitch devastated large parts of Nicaragua.
1999 The FSLN and the AL entered into a pact in order to force through controversial laws that worked against the emergence of a 'third force' in Nicaraguan politics.
2000 The FSLN made significant gains in the municipal elections, winning the major cities including the capital, Managua.
2001 PLC and Enrique Bolaños (PLC) were the winners of the elections.
2002 President Bolaños took office.
2003 In March, the FSLN re-elected Ortega as party leader.
2004 In January, 80 per cent of Nicaragua's debt to the World Bank was wiped out. An agreement was reached in July with Russia to cancel Nicaragua's huge debt incurred with the former Soviet Union.
2005 In April violent street protests were carried out following fuel price rises. The government and an alliance of opposition parties entered into a power struggle. By October, the political impasse had declined after Congress agreed to delay constitutional reforms until 2007.

Political structure

In addition to their unicameral national parliaments, El Salvador, Guatemala,

Honduras, Nicaragua, Panama and Dominican Republic, which acceded to the Central American Parliament in February 2004, also return directly elected deputies to the supranational Central American Parliament.

Constitution
The National Assembly approved constitutional reforms in January 2000 which provide outgoing presidents and vice presidents with a lifelong seat in the legislature. Other constitutional reforms included a reduction of the percentage of votes required to elect a president without the need for a run-off election, from 45 per cent to 35 per cent of the total, and the restructuring of the judiciary, the electoral authorities and the comptroller general's office, giving the two main parties a bigger share of the posts.

The country comprises 16 departments which are divided into two zones: the Pacific zone and the Atlantic zone.

The minimum voting age is 16 years.

Form of state
Presidential democratic republic

The executive
Power is vested in the president who is head of state and commander-in-chief of the armed forces, elected for a period of five years by universal adult suffrage. The president appoints a cabinet of ministers.

National legislature
Legislative power is vested in the unicameral National Assembly, consisting of 90 members elected by adult suffrage by proportional representation every five years. In addition, former presidents and vice presidents hold seats for life and occupied three seats following the 2001 elections.

Legal system
The Nicaraguan legal system comprises civil and military courts. The highest court is the Supreme Court, which administers the judicial system and nominates all appellate and lower court judges. The Supreme Court consists of 12 magistrates elected for seven-year terms by the National Assembly.

Last elections
4 November 2001 (presidential and parliamentary)

Results: Presidential: Enrique Bolaños Geyer (PLC) won 56.3 per cent of the vote against José Daniel Ortega Saavedra (FSLN) with 42.3 per cent.
Parliamentary: Partido Liberal Constitucionalista (PLC) (Constitutional Liberal Party) won 53.2 per cent of the vote, 47 seats; Frente Sandinista de Liberación Nacional (FSLN) (Sandinista National Liberation Front) 42.1 per cent, 43 seats.

Next elections
2006 (presidential and parliamentary)

Political parties
Ruling party
Partido Liberal Constitucionalista (PLC) (Constitutionalist Liberal Party) (since 2001)

Main opposition party
Frente Sandinista de Liberación Nacional (FSLN) (Sandinista National Liberation Front)

Population
5.98 million (2004)

Ethnic make-up
Mestizo (mixed indigenous-European) (69 per cent), European (17 per cent), black (9 per cent) and indigenous people (5 per cent).

Creole and Indian peoples live in the eastern region of the country on the Atlantic coast. The Creoles number some 26,000, the Miskitos 182,000 and the Sumus 9,000. There are also two very small indigenous groups – the Ramas and the Garifunos.

Religions
The majority of the population is Catholic, although mainstream Protestant and evangelical groups make up 20 per cent of the population. The majority of the Atlantic coast population is Moravian. There is no official religion.

Education
Nicaragua has been slowly moving towards universal primary enrolment despite severe setbacks resulting from Hurricane Mitch in 1998.

Primary education is free for six years although a report issued by the Nicaraguan Office of the Advocate for Children and Youth revealed that 80 per cent of children in primary and secondary state schools were required to pay a minimum fee per month, including voluntary contributions to teachers' salaries and payments for examinations, in violation of the constitutional right to free education for children.

Secondary education runs in two cycles of three and two years and leads to higher education, or in a cycle of two and three years leading to a technical qualification. There are both state universities and private universities. The Consejo Nacional de Universidades is responsible for all higher education planning. Nicaragua's major institutions of higher education are the Jesuit-run Central American University, Managua (UCA), the public National Autonomous Universities in Managua and León (Unan) and the private, Harvard-affiliated Central American Institute of Business Administration (Incae) outside Managua.

Spending on primary education amounts to less than US$10 per capita.

Literacy rate: 67.1 per cent total; 67.4 per cent female, adult rates in 2002 (World Bank).
Compulsory years: 6 to 12.
Enrolment rate: 102 per cent gross primary enrolment of the relevant age group (including repeaters); 55 per cent gross secondary enrolment (World Bank).
Pupils per teacher: 36 in primary schools.

Health
Although public health improved during the 1990s, access to medical facilities continues to be uneven and many of the country's poor, particularly in rural areas and on the Atlantic coast, are experiencing inadequate healthcare due to government cutbacks in 2002/03. A growing market of private services exists, but the ministry of health continues to be the main provider of services for the Nicaraguan population as a whole.

Government spending emphasises primary healthcare with priority given to improving local healthcare systems, through national, departmental, regional and municipal co-ordination. The World Bank's International Development Association (IDA) funded the rehabilitation of healthcare centres, nutrition centres for children, and schools for training nurses and other healthcare workers, and the provision of social services.

HIV prevalence: 0.2 per cent aged 15–49 in 2003 (World Bank)
Life expectancy: 68.8 years (World Bank)
Fertility rate/Maternal mortality rate: 3.4 births per woman (2003); maternal mortality 150 per 100,000 live births (World Bank).
Infant mortality rate: 30 per 1,000 live births; 12.2 per cent of children under aged five are malnourished (World Bank).

Welfare
Under the presidency of Arnoldo Alemán (1997–2001), welfare expenditure was squeezed as a result of the government's IMF-dictated austerity measures and high levels of debt servicing. Funds for social protection remain decentralised and the responsibility for resource management lies with local authorities. There are no clear regulations about the amount of money that can be allocated or is necessary for the municipalities. An increasing number of self-employed people do not have access to social protection mechanisms.

Nicaragua's welfare programme combines a traditional cash transfer programme with financial incentives for families to obtain preventive healthcare and education and to participate in other government-sponsored welfare-related programmes.

Nicaragua

In 2001, the government initiated a welfare reform programme under the auspices of a three-year Poverty Reduction and Growth Facility (PRGF) arrangement with the IMF. Pension reform is central to the structural adjustment programme. A pension system of privately managed individual accounts was introduced in the last quarter of 2001. Under the pension reform, the country changed from a pay-as-you-go pension system to a defined contribution system in which contributions are safeguarded. The reform was designed to contain the fiscal deficit created by the previous system, broaden the base of contributors and contribute to the development of domestic financial markets.

The Nicaraguan Institute for Social Security and Welfare (INSSBI) operates nursing homes for the elderly and rehabilitation centres for the physically and mentally handicapped, for prostitutes, drug addicts and alcoholics.

Main cities
Managua (capital, estimated population 1.2 million in 2004), León (164,200), Chinandega (129,100), Masaya (118,000).

Languages spoken
Some business people speak English. In the Bluefields (Atlantic) region, English is particularly widely spoken.

Many names of towns, medicines, foods, flora and fauna are in the Nahuate language.

On the Atlantic Coast, Indian towns and ethnic communities still preserve their language and cultural traditions. Autonomous law guarantees bilingual education in the Miskito, Creole, English, Sumus, Ramas and Garifuna dialects.

Official language/s
Spanish

Media
There has been no censorship since 1988, the Interior Ministry is legally responsible for supervision of the media, including the imposition of fines and suspensions from publishing of up to four days for infractions.

Press
Dailies: The main daily newspapers are *La Prensa*, *Bolsa de Noticias*, *Ciberdiario de Nicaragua*, *El Nuevo Diario*, *La Tribuna*, *Barricada*, all based in Managua. Other dailies include *El Centroamericano*, *Novedades*, *El Pueblo*, *Confidencial*, *Notifax*, and *Tiempos del Mundo*.

Weeklies: An influential weekly paper is *La Crónica*.

Periodicals: *Boletina La* is a popular women's magazine.

Broadcasting
Radio: There are approximately 60 public and private radio stations. Among the most prominent are Radio Corporación and Radio Impacto.

Television: At the end of the 1980s the media law was repealed, making private TV stations possible. There are two TV stations, both of which are state-run and broadcast throughout the country, although Channel 6 carries a stronger signal than Channel 2.

Economy
The Nicaraguan economy has grown steadily since 2003 and the outlook for the economy in 2006 appears to be good. The IMF forecasts growth of 3.5 per cent for 2005 with an increase of half a per cent to 4 per cent in 2006. Inflation continues to decrease, having hit 8.2 per cent per annum in 2004. The rate of inflation now stands at around 6.5 per cent and the IMF expects it to fall to 4 per cent in 2006.

Under the Sandinista government of the 1980s, the Nicaraguan economy went into reverse. A US trade embargo, the flight of many businessmen into exile, the civil war and the demise of the Soviet Union seriously undermined this predominantly agricultural economy. By the time the Sandinistas were defeated in the 1990 elections, Nicaragua was battling hyperinflation with interest rates soaring. Since the early 1990s, the government has won international backing for trade and financial sector reforms.

Despite the election in 1989 of a US-backed coalition government led by President Violeta Chamorro, it was years before the economy stabilised and recovered from war and diplomatic isolation. Under President Arnoldo Alemán (1997–2001), GDP growth rose to record levels and inflation fell to single-digit figures, while non-traditional sectors boomed with high levels of investment in the new export processing zones (EPZs). The impressive improvement in macroeconomic fundamentals was spurred on by a process of free-market liberalisation. Although the figures look promising, Nicaragua remains plagued by poverty; it is the second-poorest country in the Western Hemisphere after Haiti. Spending on education and health has taken a backseat to debt servicing. In terms of GDP, the country has one of the highest external debts in the world and was one of the first countries to qualify for the IMF's Enhanced Heavily Indebted Poor Countries (HIPC) initiative.

Strict fiscal targets are a requirement under the country's three-year US$129 million Poverty Reduction and Growth Facility (PRGF), agreed with the IMF in December 2002. Failure to meet them in the past meant that Nicaragua was automatically ineligible for debt relief under HIPC. However, the IMF expressed its approval of the policies of the Bolaños administration and in December 2002 agreed US$2.5 million in assistance. Although some of the government's failure to meet budgetary targets stem from its own corruption and incompetence, many of the problems are rooted in the ailing health of the economy, which has been blighted by a series of natural disasters and poor prices for its main commodity exports, particularly coffee.

In January 2004, the country received some good news as the World Bank and the IMF wiped out 80 per cent of Nicaragua's debt by supporting US$4.5 billion of debt service relief. This could give the country the opportunity to address poverty as pressure from a rising national debt decreases.

External trade
Nicaragua signed the proposed Central American Free Trade Agreement (Cafta) in August 2004, along with Costa Rica, the Dominican Republic, El Salvador, Guatemala and Honduras.

The US is Nicaragua's largest trading partner, accounting for a quarter of the country's imports and receiving some 60 per cent of its exports.

Imports
As Nicaragua has developed its manufacturing base, imports of services, intermediate goods and capital goods have all risen while imports of consumer goods have slowed.

Principal imports include consumer goods, machinery and equipment, raw materials and petroleum products.

Main sources: US (26.3 per cent total, 2004), Venezuela (9.6 per cent), Costa Rica (7.5 per cent), Mexico (7.1 per cent), Guatemala (6.1 per cent), El Salvador (4.1 per cent)

Exports
Principal exports include coffee, beef, shrimp and lobster, tobacco, gold, sugar and peanuts.

Main destinations: US (63.5 per cent total, 2004), El Salvador (9.0 per cent), Costa Rica (4.2 per cent)

Agriculture
Farming
Agriculture plays a very significant role in the economy of Nicaragua, contributing about a quarter of the country's total GDP. The sector also employs up to 30 per cent of the total workforce.

The principal export crop is coffee which represents around a fifth of total export earnings. Meat, cotton, bananas and sugar are the other main agricultural exports. Maize, rice, beans and sorghum are also grown. Timber, tobacco, sugar cane and rubber are geared towards Nicaragua's agro-industrial sector.

The Nicaraguan government is actively engaged in the agricultural sector although it is estimated that upwards of 60 per cent of cultivated land is in the hands of private smallholders. Despite continuous agrarian reform, food production has not kept up with demand owing mainly to poor weather, war damage and shortages of vital inputs.

Crop production in 2004 included: 881,700 tonnes (t) cereals in total, 4,090,910t sugar cane, 241,701t rice, 521,943t maize, 30,000t potatoes, 113,954t sorghum, 61,091t bananas, 41,000t plantains, 75,000t citrus fruit, 117,300t cassava, 99,545t groundnuts in shell, 223,679t pulses, 54,000t oil palm fruit, 43,521t oilcrops, 5,375t fibre crops, 2,182t tobacco, 70,909t green coffee, 240,091t fruit in total, 33,300t vegetables in total. Livestock production included: 141,281t meat in total, 70,455t beef, 6,500t pig meat, 2,000t horsemeat, 53t lamb and goat meat, 62,273t poultry, 23,184t eggs, 641,091t milk, *390t honey.

* estimate

Fishing
Nicaragua's typical annual fish catch is over 28,000mt, 16,500mt of which is shellfish. The main seafood exports are shellfish, particularly shrimp and lobster. Offshore fishing consists mainly of tuna, bass and mackerel. The government follows an export subsidy policy, providing tax rebates on every kilogramme of trawled shrimp and farmed shrimp exported.

Forestry
Some 3.2 million hectares (ha) of Nicaragua is covered by forests and woodlands, amounting to 60 per cent of the country's total landmass. Nicaragua has some of the largest humid tropical rainforests concentrated in the north and east, in the Caribbean lowlands. Forest lands lie principally in the southern Atlantic coastal region. Species include pine, cedar and other hardwoods covering four million hectares. The government is keen to develop plans for self-sustaining exploitation of the forests. The Food and Agriculture Organisation (FAO) has estimated timber reserves at 33 million cubic metres. In the period 1990–2000, deforestation caused an average annual loss of 3 per cent of forest cover, the equivalent of 117,000ha.

The forestry industry thrives on sawnwood production, most of which is exported. Nicaragua imports moderate quantities of paper and wood-based panels. Most of the forest wood is used for fuel consumption.

In a typical year production constitutes 6 million cubic metres (cum) roundwood, 45,000cum sawnwood, 124,000cum sawlogs and veneers, 6 million cum woodfuel and 22,000t charcoal.

Industry and manufacturing
Since the 1990s, there has been significant growth in the non-traditional *maquiladora* (in bond) sector, which has made use of the country's free trade zones (FTZs). Concentrated mainly on textiles, particularly clothing, for the US market, the *maquiladora* sector has rapidly become a major sub-sector in Nicaraguan industry. Low labour costs and minimal labour regulation have made it both an attractive opportunity for foreign investors and a target for trade unions and labour rights activists.

The most important projects undertaken since the mid-1990s have reflected a renewed priority placed on large-scale agro-industrial production, which had been neglected by the government in the early 1990s. The two biggest have been the Timal sugar refinery and the Sebaco food processing complex.

Investment in Nicaragua's fledgling manufacturing sector is crucial and reliant on structural reforms to make the sector more competitive and efficient. In the past, investment resources were often diverted to the defence sector, while factories closed as a result of non-availability of replacement parts and basic inputs.

Tourism
Nicaragua's tourism sector expanded significantly throughout 2005. The sector now accounts for 6.9 per cent of total GDP and 5.6 per cent of total employment. Visitor numbers grew until 2001, when the 11 September terrorist attacks in the US damaged the sector. 483,000 arrivals were recorded in 2001, a decline of 0.6 per cent on the previous year. A further fall to 472,000 visitors occurred in 2002, but 2003 showed a recovery of 7.65 per cent. Visitor numbers, as at end 2004, were 521,800. Capital investment in the sector has increased accordingly and now constitutes 7.1 per cent of total capital investment in the economy.

The development of Nicaragua's tourism sector, which has considerable potential, especially ecotourism, has been obstructed by residual negative perceptions about its stability and inadequate infrastructure. These difficulties are gradually being overcome. A generous incentive law was introduced in 1999 to encourage tourist-related investment, but, while improving, infrastructure is still patchy. Despite the disadvantages under which it has operated, tourism has become Nicaragua's main source of foreign exchange, earning around US$110 million per annum. The majority of visitors come from the other Central American countries, but about a fifth are from the USA.

Environment
The deforestation and cultivation of marginal lands in Nicaragua contributed to the mudslides after Hurricane Mitch hit the country in late 1998, while flooding was made worse due to a lack of watershed management.

Mining
Nicaragua is endowed with deposits of both gold and silver. The country also has mineral deposits, including copper, zinc, platinum, iron, magnesium, chrome, titanium, tungsten, lead, cadmium, bismuth, bentonite, marble, clay, masonry stone, limestone and gypsum.

Gold and silver are mined intensively in Siuna and Bonanza, inland from the northern Atlantic coast region. More modest mining activity takes place in Chontales and Nueva Segovia. Geological studies of the region identify the existence of a reserve of gold in the area of La Libertad, which could have a productive lifetime of 70 years. The reserves are estimated at 3.8 million ounces of gold and 4.9 million ounces of silver.

All natural resources are state property and exploitation rights are leased on a long-term basis. Since huge portions of the central areas of Nicaragua's mineral reserves have already been leased, the scope for investment remains limited. The decline in global gold prices has affected the fortunes of foreign companies and the value of exports diminished.

The Toronto-based Black Hawk international mining and exploration company owns the El Limon mine through its 95 per cent-owned subsidiary Triton Minera SA. The mine, located 140km north of Managua, has been in continuous production for more than 50 years, gaining from both open pit and underground operations. Mill capacity is 1,000 tonnes per day and gold recoveries exceed 80 per cent.

Hydrocarbons
Nicaragua relies heavily on imports of fossil fuels to meet demand for energy consumption, as it has little known deposits of its own. The country imports approximately 84 per cent of its energy requirements, primarily from Mexico and Venezuela under the San José pact. Legislation in July 2002 marked the opening of the country's hydrocarbon resources to foreign investors. Foreign companies are allowed oil exploration, which includes onshore concessions, as well as offshore blocks in the Atlantic and

Pacific Oceans. One of the main problems for development is that both Colombia and Honduras claim the available 44,000 square miles of the Caribbean on offer as belonging to them.

There are no proven natural gas reserves and use of gas is negligible. A gas pipeline from Mexico to Guatemala, completed in 2004, could be extended to Nicaragua as part of a wider Central American gas pipeline network. There is also the possibility of pipeline construction from Colombia's northern offshore fields to Panama with connections to Nicaragua, but no plans have been formally agreed upon.

Coal is not imported or consumed in Nicaragua.

Energy

Nicaragua's demand for electricity is growing, driven by the country's recent economic growth and development. A major objective of the national government remains the electrification of rural areas. In 2003 the World Bank agreed terms on a US$12 million loan to finance off-grid rural areas. The loan is part of Nicaragua's National Rural Electrification Program, which aimed to bring electric power to 70 per cent of rural areas by 2005 and 90 per cent by 2012.

The government estimates that demand for electricity will grow by 6 per cent annually between 2000–20, requiring nearly US$2 billion in investment. Nicaragua currently has two 50MW hydroelectric plants, one 33MW geothermal plant, two diesel plants with combined output of 91MW and five thermoelectric plants which together generate a total of 220MW. The country will need up to 1,200MW of extra generating power by 2020 if it is to satisfy demand growth. The government has attempted to attract foreign capital to the electricity sector through the privatisation of the Empresa Nicaragüense de Electricidad (Enel) (Nicaraguan Electricity Company).

Nicaragua is involved in plans for the Sistema de Interconexion Electrica para America Central (SIEPAC), an electricity grid that would connect Nicaragua to the national transmission grids of Guatemala, Honduras, El Salvador, Costa Rica and Panama. It is envisaged that SIEPAC will be completed by 2006.

Financial markets
Stock exchange

The Bolsa de Valores de Nicaragua was opened in January 1994. Government bonds dominate transactions on the stock market.

Banking and insurance

In recent years the banking and financial services sector of Nicaragua has undergone a degree of stabilisation, which in turn has resulted in increasing deposit levels. However, the sector still remains fragile and vocal critics have accused the regulatory authorities of failing to tackle the state banking system's overdue debt which has contributed to a feeling of pessimism in some quarters. Moreover, the government's bail-out of the country's third largest bank – Interbank – in 2000 amid reports of widespread corruption did nothing to reassure foreign investors and donors of the legitimacy of the country's banking system. The failure of the Banco Nicaraguense de Industria y Comercio (Banic) to resolve its debt led to another government intervention in the banking sector in August 2001. Banic's assets and liabilities were subsequently auctioned off to Banpro, which had already absorbed Interbank in October 2000.

The chaos in the banking sector led to a shake-up of the regulatory system. In 2003, the government introduced a new, rigorous framework to bring the legal framework in line with the Basel Core Principles.

Although foreign banks were permitted to remain in Nicaragua when the banking system was nationalised in 1979, they were no longer permitted to accept local deposits. The branches of US, British and Canadian commercial banks continue to operate non-deposit business.

Central bank
Banco Central de Nicaragua (BCN)

Main financial centre
Managua

Time
GMT minus six hours

Geography

Nicaragua is in the Central American isthmus, with the Pacific Ocean to the west and the Caribbean Sea to the east. Honduras is to the north and Costa Rica to the south. The Pacific plateau is noted for its rich lands, and is where the larger farms which grow crops for export are to be found, particularly in the northern area of Chinandega. The Atlantic plateau, occupying fully half of the national territory, is largely pasture savannah; small gold and silver mines are also found in this area. The lands along the Rio Coco (forming the border with Honduras) are a rich banana-growing area, and are worked largely by the Miskito Indians. Tropical rainforest predominates in the southern Atlantic coast adjacent to Costa Rica. Corn Island, in the Caribbean Sea, is home to a fishing community.

Climate

Tropical with high humidity; cooler and drier at higher altitudes. Average temperature 27.5 degrees Celsius (C). Dry season from December–May; temperatures reach 30–35 degrees C in Managua. Rainy season from May–November; temperatures up to 27–30 degrees C in Managua. Nicaragua has a semi-tropical climate; the hottest month is May (27–32 degrees C in Managua) and the coldest is January (23–30 degrees C in Managua). Temperatures may be up to 10 degrees C lower in the mountain range that runs the length of the country. The rainy season (May–December) is referred to as 'winter'; and the dry season (December–April) as 'summer'.

Dress codes

On the most formal of occasions Nicaraguan men traditionally wear the Caribbean-style *guayabera,* in white, although an increasing number of men today prefer to wear a suit and tie. Nicaraguan women seldom wear trousers and usually dress rather formally.

Entry requirements
Passports

Required by all. Passport must be valid for at least another six months from the date of entry. Passport and entry card must be carried all the time.

Visa

Required only by those listed at http://nicaragua.embassyhomepage.com/ and follow link to visas. All other visitors may visit for whatever purpose for up to 30 days. On arrival a tourist card must be obtained and the fee paid in US dollars, an extension can be obtained locally, failure to do so will result in a fine.

Currency advice/regulations

There is no limit to the import or export of local and foreign currency. Tourists have to exchange US$60 at the official rate at airport or border entry points and are required to show that they have at least US$200 to cover their stay.

Health (for visitors)
Mandatory precautions
None.

Advisable precautions

Dengue fever is present in Nicaragua. Inoculations against tetanus, hepatitis 'A', typhoid and polio are advisable. Malaria prophylaxis if travelling outside urban areas. Tap water, especially outside Managua, should be considered unsafe for consumption by visitors. Most over-the-counter remedies are available in generic form at local pharmacies in urban areas.

Hotels

Availability is limited but there are good hotels in Managua, the main coastal towns and along the Pan-American Highway. Bills are subject to 10 per cent sales tax, and must usually be paid in dollars. A 10 per cent tip is usual.

Public holidays
Fixed dates
1 Jan (New Year's Day), 1 May (Labour Day), 30 May (Mothers' Day), 19 Jul (Liberation Day), 1 Aug (Santo Domingo Day), 14 Sep (Battle of Jacinto), 15 Sep (Independence Day), 2 Nov (All Souls' Day), 8 Dec (Immaculate Conception), 25 Dec (Christmas Day).
Variable dates
Maundy Thursday, Good Friday.

Working hours
Banking
Mon–Fri: 0800–1600; Sat: 0800–1200.
Business
Mon–Fri: 0800–1700; Sat: 0800–1300.
Government
Mon–Fri: 0800–1700.

Electricity supply
110V AC, 60 cycles

Social customs/useful tips
It is helpful to know something of the political background and affiliations of those you are meeting.
Men and women shake hands in Nicaragua and social kisses on one cheek are also exchanged. The use of titles, such as Doctor, Arquitecto, Licenciado, Profesora, is widespread and it is courteous to learn and use the correct titles for both men and women.
Do not immediately launch into a business conversation. It is considered polite to first get to know the person to whom you are talking.
At a large social gathering do not expect your host or hostess to introduce you to every individual. Feel free to circulate and introduce yourself.
A small gift for the host or hostess is always appreciated.
Late-night parties, with dinner served at 2200 or 2300, are common. Guests should not plan to arrive on time for a large social gathering and to be up to two hours late is acceptable. For smaller gatherings, arrival about 30 minutes later than the specified time is considered appropriate.

Security
Nicaragua has a low rate of violent crime compared to other Central American countries and armed groups involved in the civil war have been demobilised. With the persistent decline of the economy, however, cases of robbery – usually not violent – have increased sharply.

Getting there
Air
International airport/s: Managua-Augusto César Sandino (MGA), 9km from city; duty-free shop, bar, restaurant, buffet, post office, shops (restricted hours in some instances), banks.
Airport tax: International departures US$32 and domestic departures US$3; excluding transit passengers.
Surface
Road: The Pan-American Highway is well maintained and runs from Honduras, through Managua, to Costa Rica.
Main port/s: Bluefields, Corinto, Puerto Cabezas, Puerto Sandino, San Juan de Sur, Puerto Arlen Siu.

Getting about
National transport
Air: Nicaragüenses de Aviación (Nica Airlines) runs regional, passenger and cargo services.
Road: The western region is provided with most sealed roads connecting the more populated areas of the country. There is only one major road to the Caribbean side and this stops, before the coast, at Rama.
Buses: Services are regular and connect main towns served by the road system (e.g. Managua-Rama, Managua-León, Chinandega, Corinto).
Rail: Several services a day link Managua to the port of Corinto, via León; and Managua to Granada on Lake Nicaragua.
Water: A boat service links Rama and Bluefields port on the Caribbean coast.
City transport
Taxis: Taxis are in short supply; fares should be negotiated in advance of journeys and tipping is not necessary.
Buses, trams & metro: City buses are cheap and crowded.
Car hire
Foreign licence are acceptable for short stays (up to 30 days). Due to poor public transport, hired cars may often be the best way to get around in Managua. However roads are often in poor repair and needs a skilled driver to avoid mishap. Drivers in accidents are always arrested even if they are insured and appear to be blameless. Licensed drivers can be hired, through local car rentals, they are familiar with local roads and conditions and, in the case of a traffic accident, will be taken into custody, in accordance with the law.

BUSINESS DIRECTORY
The addresses listed below are a selection only. While World of Information makes every endeavour to check these addresses, we cannot guarantee that changes have not been made, especially to telephone numbers and area codes. We would welcome any corrections.

Telephone area codes
The international dialling code (IDD) for Nicaragua is +505 followed by subscriber's number.

Chambers of Commerce
American Chamber of Commerce of Nicaragua, Centro Finarca, PO Box 2720, Managua (tel: 267-3098; fax: 267-3099; e-mail: amcham@amchamnic.org.ni).

Nicaraguan Cámara de Comercio, Rotonda Gueguense, PO Box 135, Managua (tel: 268-3505; fax: 268-3600; e-mail: comercio@ibw.com.ni).

Banking
Banco de América Central (BAC), Apdo 2304 Managua (tel: 670-220; fax: 670-224).

Banco de Crédito Centroamericano (Bancentro), Edificio Bancentro, KM. 4-1/2 Carretera Masaya (tel: 782-777; fax: 786-001).

Banco de Exportación (Banexpo), Centro Comercial Metrocentro, Managua (tel: 73-087/73-094/73-103; fax: 73-154).

Banco de la Producción (Banpro), Plaza Libertad, Contiguo a Metrocentro, Apdo 2309, Managua (tel: 782-508/783-278/784-188; fax: 784-113).

Banco de Préstamos (Banpres), Esquina Opuesta Hotel Intercontinental, Managua (tel: 223-046/223-048; fax: 223-057).

Banco Europeo de Centro América SA (BECA), Apdo 188, Managua (tel: 224-791; fax: 783-827).

Banco Mercantil, Gerente General Oscar Martín Aguado A., Plaza Banco Mercantil, Managua (tel 668-228/668-231; fax: 668-024).

Banco Nacional de Desarrollo (Banades), Apdo 328-1447, Managua (tel: 671-334; fax: 670-869).

Central bank
Banco Central de Nicaragua, Km 7 carretera sur, PO Box 2252, Managua (tel: 265-0500; fax: 265-0561; e-mail: bcn@bcn.gob.ni).

Travel information
Aerolíneas Nicaragüenses (AERONICA), Contiguo Aeropuerto Internacional August C Sandino, Apdo 3688, Managua, JR (tel: 31-801).

Instituto Nicaragüense de Turismo, Avenida Bolivar Sur, Apdo 122, Managua (tel: 25-436; fax: 25-314).

Ministry of tourism
Ministry of Tourism, Residencial Bolonia, Hotel Intercontinental, 1c. al Oeste 1c. al Sur, Managua (tel: 222-6610, 222-6617; fax: 222-6618).

Ministries
Ministry of Agriculture and Livestock, Km 8 1/2, Carretera a Masaya, Managua (tel: 276-0200; fax: 276-0256).

Nicaragua

Ministry of Construction and Transport, Frente Al Estadio Nacional, Managua (tel: 222-5111; fax: 222-6429).

Ministry of Economy and Development, Carretera a Masaya, Km 6 1/2 Frente a Centro Comercial Camino de Oriente, Managua (tel: 267-0161; fax: 278-4590).

Ministry of Education, Centro Cívico Camilo Ortega, Managua (tel: 265-0046; fax: 265-0715).

Ministry of the Environment and Natural Resources, Carretera Norte, Km 12 1/2, Managua (tel: 263-1343; fax: 263-2833).

Ministry of External Co-operation, Casa Ricardo Morales Aviles, Managua (tel: 228-5002; fax: 228-2026).

Ministry of Finance, Frente a la Asamblea Nacional, Managua (tel: 222-7231; fax: 278-5984).

Ministry of Foreign Affairs, Barrío Altagracia, Frente a Restaurante Los Ranchos, Managua (tel: 266-6222; fax: 266-2572).

Ministry of Health, Complejo Concepción Palacios, Managua (tel: 289-7554; fax: 289-7997).

Ministry of Industry and Commerce, Km 6, Carretera Masaya, Apdo 2412, Managua (tel: 70-116).

Ministry of the Interior, Barrio 19 de Julio, Edif Silvio Mayorga, Managua (tel: 285-005; fax: 627-910).

Ministry of Labour, Estadio Nacional, 300 vs. al Norte, Managua (tel: 228-1168; fax: 228-2028).

Ministry of the Presidency, Avenida Bolivar, Detrás de la Asamblea Nacional, Managua (tel: 278-5299; fax: 222-3448).

Ministry of Social Action, Pista de Resistencia ENEL Central, 150vs. al Sur, Managua (tel: 267-2907; fax: 267-0768).

Ministry of Tourism, Residencial Bolonia, Hotel Intercontinental, 1c. al Oeste 1c. al Sur, Managua (tel: 222-6610, 222-6617; fax: 222-6618).

Ministry of Transport and Construction, Frente al Estadio Nacional, Managua (tel: 283-698, 282-061, 225-954; fax: 282-161).

Ministry of Works, Estadio Nacional, 400 Metros Al Norte, Managua (tel: 226-002, 222-115, 226-677; fax: 22-208, 622-103).

Other useful addresses

Association of Nicaraguan Producers and Exporters of Non-Traditional Products (APENN), Del Restaurante Terraza 1/2 C Al Norte (tel: 668-276, 668-279).

Bank of Central American Economic Intergration (BCIE), Edificio BCIE, 2do, piso, Plaza España, Managua (tel: 266-4120; fax: 266-4125).

British Embassy, El Reparto Los Robles 1, entrada principal de la Primera Etapa, Los Robles, Managua (tel: 780-014, 780-887, 674-050; fax: 784-085).

Central American Institute of Business Administration (INCAE), Carretera Sur Km 15 1/2, Managua (tel: 58-403, 58-404).

Centre of Export and Investments, Hotel Intercontinental, 1c, abajo 3 1/2c al Sur, Managua (tel: 268-1063; fax: 266-4476; e-mail: cei@cei.lbw.com.ni).

Development Bank (BID), Carretera a Masaya, Km 4 1/2, Managua (tel: 267-0831; fax: 267-3469).

Dirección General de Promoción de Exportaciones, Km 6, Carretera a Masaya, Apdo 2412, Managua, JR (tel: 70-154).

Empresa Nicaragüense de Promoción de Exportaciones, Apdo 1449, Managua.

Exports of the Handicraft Industry, S.A., Centro de Feria la Pinata (tel: 670-358; fax: 670-192).

Institute of Local Governments, Los Arcos, Entrada principal, 20 varas al Sur, Managua (tel: 266-6050; fax: 244-4567).

Institute of National Technology, Centro Cívico, Managua (tel: 265-0049; fax: 265-1976).

Institute of Nicaraguan Insurance and Re-insurance, Carretera Sur, Km 4 1/2, Managua (tel: 268-0239; fax: 268-0265).

Institute of Nicaraguan Social Security (NSS), Semáforos del Hotel Intercontinental, 2c abajo, 1c al lago, Contiguo a Policlínica Central, Managua (tel: 222-7445; fax: 222-7454).

Institute of Statistics and Censors, Frente Hospital Lenin Fonséca, Managua (tel: 266-7663; fax: 266-7872).

International Development Agency (AID), Semáforos Centroamérica, 400 mts al Oeste, Managua (tel: 267-3909; fax: 277-0210).

Nicaraguan Electricity, Frente Entrada a Colegio Rigoberto López, Pérez, Managua (tel: 277-4159; fax: 267-1700).

Nicaraguan Centre of Technological Information (CENIT), Sandy's 11/2 C. Arriba (tel: 75-812, 675-325).

Nicaraguan Canals and Irrigation Authority, Carretera Sur Km 5, Managua (tel: 266-7863; fax: 266-7872).

Nicaraguan Development Fund, AP 2598, Managua (tel: 666-077, 666-066).

Nicaraguan Embassy (USA), 1627 New Hampshire Avenue, NW, Washington DC 20009 (tel: 202-939-6531; fax: 202-939-6532; ofemb@embanic.org).

Nicaraguan Institute for Economic and Social Investigations (INIES), del Hospital Alejandro Davila Bolanas, 3 c. al Lago, Managua (tel: 23-418, 24-932).

Nicaraguan Investment Fund (of Central Bank), Shell de Colonia Centroamericana, Media al Lago, Managua (tel: 71-043, 71-044).

Nicaraguan Telephone Company, Residencial Villa Fontana, Edificio Ville Fontana, Managua (tel: 228-5280; fax: 228-4628).

Port Authority, Residencial Bolonia, Optica Nicaragüense, 1c al Lago, 1c abajo, Managua (tel: 266-3274; fax: 266-4622).

Superior Council of Private Enterprise (COSEP), del Restaurante Terraza, Media cuadra al lago, Managua (tel: 23-510, 27-130).

UN High Commission for Relief (ACNUR), Residencial Bolonia, Contiguo a Viajes Atlantida, Managua (tel/fax: 268-0476).

US Embassy, Km e44 1/2, Carretera Sur, Apdo 327, Managua (tel: 666-010).

World Bank, Plaza España, Edificio Málaga, Modulos No A 1/A 22, Managua (tel: 226-0562; fax: 266-1000).

Internet sites

Banco Central de Nicaragua: http://www.bcn.gob.ni/

Nicaraguan Centre for Exports and Investments (CEI): http://www.cei.org.ni

Organisation of American States: http://www.oas.org

Ministry of Foreign Affairs: http://www.cancilleria.gob.ni/

Nicaraguan stock exchange: http://bolsanic.com/

Nicaraguan Solidarity Campaign: http://www.nicaraguasc.org.uk/

Nicaragua Network: http://www.nicanet.org/

La Prensa: http://www.laprensa.com.ni/

El Nuevo Diario: http://www.elnuevodiario.com.ni/

La Noticia: http://www.lanoticia.com.ni/

Niger

KEY FACTS

Official name: République du Niger (Republic of Niger)

Head of State: President Mamadou Tandja (MNSD) (since 1999; re-elected 4 Dec 2004)

Head of government: Prime Minister Hama Amadou (MNSD) (appointed 3 Jan 2000)

Ruling party: Mouvement National de la Société de Développement (MNSD) (National Movement for a Developing Society) (since 1999; re-elected 4 Dec 2004)

Area: 1,267,000 square km

Population: 12.67 million (2004)

Capital: Niamey

Official language: French

Currency: CFA franc (CFAf) = 100 centimes (Communauté Financière Africaine (African Financial Community) franc). New notes have been issued; old notes cease to be legal tender from Jan 2005.

Exchange rate: CFAf544.07 per US$ (Oct 2005); CFAf655.95 per euro (pegged from Jan 1999)

GDP per capita: US$258 (2004)

GDP real growth: 0.90% (2004)

Labour force: 5.53 million (2003)

Inflation: 0.40% (2004)

Balance of trade: -US$75.00 million (2003)

Foreign debt: US$1.60 billion (2003)

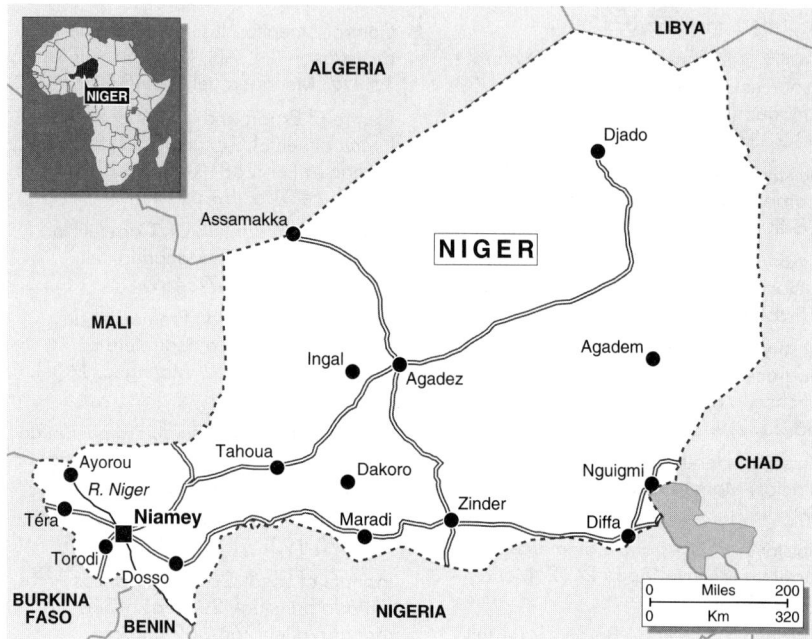

The drought and intense locust attacks in Niger over 2004 affected a quarter of the population and caused acute malnutrition and starvation in the course of 2005. The drought and a significant deterioration in the terms of trade in 2005 due to higher oil prices reduced economic growth and triggered steep price increases.

Economy

Niger is one of the poorest countries in the world with minimal government services and insufficient funds to develop its resource base, which includes the world's largest deposits of uranium. The largely agrarian and subsistence-based economy is frequently disrupted by extended droughts common to the Sahel region of Africa. Drought cycles, desertification, a 3.3 per cent population growth rate, and the drop in world demand for uranium have undercut the economy.

Niger's external position weakened in 2005, but the balance of payments situation is expected to improve over the medium-term. The external current account deficit is expected to widen, mainly reflecting higher food and energy imports. Medium-term prospects in the external sector will be affected by government plans to invest in export-supporting activities, such as irrigation, that would facilitate the emergence of marketable new and higher-volume agricultural products. Further emphasis is being placed on minerals and oil exploration, as well as on developing tourism. On this basis, the external current account deficit would narrow to six per cent of GDP by 2008.

Niger's main challenge is to strengthen economic growth and reduce its vulnerabilities. Priorities include the implementation of a rural sector strategy, with emphasis on developing irrigation infrastructure and diversifying the economy including through the development of tourism. The government plans to organise a donor conference in early 2006 to mobilise much-needed development finance.

The medium-term fiscal framework has been revised to take into account the effects of the drought. However, for 2006, revenues are projected to turn out lower than budgeted because of the need to continue duty free imports of food, given the continuing concerns about food security. The government has also to undertake additional capital spending on projects aimed at enhancing food security so as to prevent a recurrence of 2004 and 2005 situations. Revenue-enhancing measures should reverse the fall in government income by 2007/08.

Budget 2006

In the 2006 budget, revenue is targeted at 10.8 per cent of GDP, expenditure at 21.7 per cent, but expenditure equivalent to 1.3 per cent of GDP is contingent on obtaining additional donor assistance. The basic fiscal deficit will be respectively, 1.5 per cent of GDP or 2.8 per cent.

After taking into account a slower reduction of domestic payments arrears (0.5 per cent of GDP), the remaining financing gap for 2006, estimated at 3.9 per cent of GDP, is expected to be mainly covered by identified financing assurances from development partners.

To ensure that revenue objectives for 2007–08 are met, the government plans to implement key revenue measures to expand the tax base and strengthen collection efforts. Accordingly, the government will put in place a presumptive tax of 0.25 per cent on transit/re-export of tobacco products and a property tax on land. Most importantly, it will focus on strengthening tax and customs administration. Key actions are in the areas of streamlining customs clearance procedures, strengthening customs valuations, enhancing audits for major taxes and duties and closely monitoring the use of exemptions.

Politics

Niger became independent from France in 1960 and experienced single-party and military rule until 1991, when Colonel Ali Saibou was forced by public pressure to allow multi-party elections, which resulted in a democratic government in 1993. Political infighting brought the government to a standstill and in 1996 led to a coup by Colonel Ibrahim Baré. In 1999 Baré was killed in a coup by military officers who restored democratic rule and held elections that brought Mamadou Tandja to power in December of that year.

Tandja won a second and final term in the second round of presidential elections in December 2004. He heads the ruling Mouvement National de la Société de Développement (MNSD) (National Movement for a Developing Society). Born in 1938, he took part in a coup which overthrew Diori Hamani, Niger's first elected president, in 1974, and subsequently served as interior minister. He stood in the presidential election of 1993, but was beaten by Mahamane Ousmane. In 1996 he again ran for president, but lost to the incumbent ruler, Ibrahim Mainassara. He has won praise for overseeing a return to relative stability in Niger.

Risk assessment

Economic	Poor
Political	Stable
Regional stability	Deteriorating

COUNTRY PROFILE

Historical profile
France created the 'Territories of the Middle Niger' in 1898 as an autonomous military territory. In 1906 the colony was incorporated into French West Africa and lingering opposition was finally crushed in 1914. Niger became a separate colony in 1922 and the capital was transferred from Zinder to Niamey in 1926. Nationalism first awoke after the Second World War, but Niger did not become independent until 1960.
Present-day Niger was at one time occupied and ruled by, among others, the Songhai empire in the west, the Hausa kingdoms in the centre and the Kanam-Bournu empire around Lake Chad in the east.
1800s The British were the first Europeans to explore the area.
1891–1911 France colonised the region, although it did not gain full control until much later and even then resistance movements continued.
1960 Niger gained independence from France under the presidency of Hamani Diori.
1974 Diori was overthrown and replaced by Lieutenant Colonel Seyni Kountche.
1987 Kountche's died and was replaced by Brigadier Ali Saibou.
1989 Civilian rule was re-introduced with a new constitution, under a one-party system. Ali Saibou was re-elected president.
1990 The Tuareg people in the north began a rebellion.
1991 Seibou lost power to a transitional government led by Andre Salifou.
1992 A referendum overwhelming approved a new multi-party constitution
1993 Multi-party elections resulted in the Mahamane Ousmane being elected president; his coalition, the Alliance of the Forces of Change (AFC), won most seats in parliament.
1995 A peace accord was signed between the government and the Tuareg.
1996 Ousmane was toppled in a coup and replaced by Ibrahim Maïnassara Baré. A military-backed civilian government was formed. Maïnassara won the presidential election.
1997 A peace accord with the last Tuareg rebel group was signed.
1999 President Maïnassara was assassinated and Major Daouda Mallam Wanké assumed power. A new constitution was approved, which balanced the power between the president, prime minister and the National Assembly. Mamadou Tandja won the presidential election.
2000 Droughts caused widespread food shortages.
2001 After another poor harvest, food prices escalated and famine ensued.
2002 The EU granted US$319.5 million for Niger's poverty reduction effort.
2003 The US claimed Iraq had attempted to purchase uranium from Niger. A claim rejected by the government.

KEY INDICATORS — Niger

	Unit	2000	2001	2002	2003	2004
Population	m	10.83	11.20	11.58	12.13	*12.67
Gross domestic product (GDP)	US$bn	1.80	1.90	2.20	2.55	*3.08
GDP per capita	US$	167	170	190	210	258
GDP real growth	%	-1.4	7.6	3.0	4.0	0.9
Inflation	%	2.9	4.0	2.7	-1.8	0.4
Exports (fob) (goods)	US$m	253.0	283.0	288.0	293.0	–
Imports (fob) (goods)	US$m	298.0	347.0	469.0	368.0	–
Balance of trade	US$m	-45.0	-64.0	-181.0	-75.0	–
Current account	US$m	-110.0	-90.0	-140.0	-160.0	-190.0
Total reserves minus gold	US$m	80.3	106.9	133.9	114.1	67.6
Foreign exchange	US$m	69.1	95.8	121.6	98.7	53.4
Exchange rate	per US$	711.98	733.04	696.99	574.89	528.29

* estimated figure

2004 In April, the World Bank and the IMF supported a US$1.20 billion debt relief programme. Incumbent Tandja was re-elected president in December and the ruling MNSD won the parliamentary elections.
2005 Taxes were increased by 20 per cent and sparked widespread protests. In July the UN warned that three million faced starvation due to a severe drought after locusts had damaged crops.

Political structure
Constitution
The 1989 constitution has been amended twice to introduce multiparty democracy and balanced power between the president, prime minister and National Assembly.
Voting: universal suffrage over 18 years. There are eight administrative regions, divided into 36 districts.

Form of state
Presidential, unitary, multiparty republic.

The executive
The directly elected president is the Head of State, elected for a five-year term, renewable only once.
The president, shares power with the prime minister but has final responsibility for co-ordinating the actions of the executive branch of government. The president names the prime minister, from a list of three candidates, who become head of government and is accountable to parliament.

National legislature
An elected 113-member Assemblée Nationale (National Assembly) with a maximum five-year term.

Legal system
Based on French civil law system and customary law.

Last elections
16 November 2004 (presidential); 4 December 2004 (parliamentary).
Results: Presidential: Mamadou Tandja won 65.5 per cent of the vote and Mahamadou Issoufou 34.5 per cent. Turnout was 45 per cent.
Parliamentary: MNSD won 47 seats out of 113, the PNDS 25 seats, CDS 22 seats, the Social Democratic Rally seven, the Rally for Democracy and Progress six, the Alliance for Democracy and Progress five and the Party for Socialism and Democracy in Niger one. Turnout was 44.7 per cent.

Next elections
2009 (presidential and parliamentary)

Political parties
Ruling party
Mouvement National de la Société de Développement (MNSD) (National Movement for a Developing Society) (since 1999; re-elected 4 Dec 2004)

Main opposition party
Parti Nigerien pour la Démocratie et le Socialisme (PNDS) (Niger Party for Democracy and Socialism), Convention démocratique et sociale (CDS) (Democratic and Social Convention).

Population
12.67 million (2004)
Ethnic make-up
Hausa (56 per cent), Djerma (22 per cent), Tuareg (8 per cent).
Religions
Islam (85 per cent), traditional beliefs (14.5 per cent), Christianity (0.5 per cent).

Education
Public expenditure on education is around 2 per cent of GDP.
Primary education is free and compulsory and lasts until aged 12. Secondary schooling is divided, beginning with the first cycle secondary school from aged 12 to 16, then second cycle secondary school from aged 16 to 19, when students are expected to graduate with a Baccalauréat. Alternatively, at aged 16 students may elect to undertake a three year technical course. All education is conducted in French.
Literacy rate: 17.1 per cent total; 9.3 per cent female, adult rates (World Bank).
Compulsory years: 6 to 12
Enrolment rate: 29 per cent gross primary enrolment, 7 per cent gross secondary enrolment; of relevant age groups (including repeaters) (World Bank).
Pupils per teacher: 41 in primary schools

Health
Total expenditure on health is 3-4 per cent of GDP, of which government spending is 39-40 per cent and foreign spending was about 17 per cent.
Improved water sources are available to 59 per cent of the population.
A recurring drought and a devastating locust invation destroyed the 2004 harvest and in July 2005 the UN estimated a third of the population were short of food and that 150,000 children were 'severely malnourished'. The UN world food programme increased the number of people being fed by over one million through the Niger emergency operation.

HIV/Aids
There are an estimated 64,000 people living with HIV/Aids, of which 36,000 are women. In addition there are 5,900 children (0-17) HIV positive and 24,000 orphans. In 2003 there were 4,800 deaths due to Aids, although Niger has so far escaped much of the African pandemic. However, with 25-35 per cent of sex workers testing positive, there is a chance that increased population mobility and a lack of condom use could make Niger vulnerable.
HIV prevalence: 1.2 per cent aged 15-49 in 2003 (World Bank)
Life expectancy: 46.4 years (World Bank)
Fertility rate/Maternal mortality rate: 7.1 births per woman; maternal mortality 590 per 100,000 live births (World Bank).
Infant mortality rate: 154 per 1,000 live births; 40 per cent of children aged under five are malnourished (World Bank).
Head of population per physician/bed: 2.4 physicians and 1.5 hospital beds available per 1,000 people.

Welfare
Around 61.4 per cent of the population live on less than US$1 per day and 85.3 per cent live on less than US$2 per day. The distribution of wealth is highly unequal with a Gini index of 50.5 and the richest 20 per cent of the population owning 53.3 per cent of the total wealth.

Main cities
Niamey (capital, estimated population 748,600 in 2003), Zinder (202,300), Maradi (189,000), Agadez (122,000), Tahoua (95,900), Arlit (84,100) (built for the uranium industry).

Languages spoken
Tamazight (the Berber language) is recognised as a national language. Tamazight belongs to the Afro-Asiatic family and is related to ancient Egyptian and Ethiopian. Others languages in daily use include Hausa, Djerma, Tamacheq, Fulani, Arabic, Kanauri, Courmantché and Toubou.
Official language/s
French

Media
Press
News bulletins include *Le Sahel* (daily), *Sahel Hebdo* (weekly) both in French, *Anfani* and *Le Republicain* covering issues of general interest. *Alternative* is a semi-monthly publication from Niamey.
Weeklies: *Sahel Dimanche* is a privately owned Sunday newspaper and is renowned for its objective reporting.
Broadcasting
Radio: The government operates La Voix du Sahel radio service in French and several Niger languages.
Television: Télé-Sahel broadcasts every day.

Economy
As one of the least developed countries in the world, Niger is heavily dependent on foreign aid and loans. Agriculture is the main source of income for most Nigerien households and subsistence farming predominates.

Uranium exports provide the largest amount of the country's foreign exchange, although mining only employs a small percentage of the workforce and exports have declined since a worldwide slump in 1980. In the long-term, Niger hopes to move away from dependence on uranium with the exploitation of other mineral resources, such as gold and oil. The Samira gold mine opened in 2004 with expectations of foreign exchange earnings of US$28 billion by 2010.

In April 2004, the World Bank and the IMF supported US$1.20 billion in debt relief under the enhanced Heavily Indebted Poor Countries (HIPC) initiative.

The IMF is also pushing, as part of Niger's three-year Poverty Reduction and Growth Facility (PRGF), programme to reduce budget deficits, strengthen revenue, keep wages down and reallocate government expenditure to increase measures for privatisation. However, problems with food security, negative trade growth and continued dependency on foreign aid restricts Niger's ability to meet IMF targets.

External trade
There are regular trade and current account deficits, partly financed by aid flows and foreign borrowing.

In 2002, the US approved Niger as being eligible for tariff preferences under the African Growth and Opportunities Act (AGOA).

Imports
Principal imports are foodstuffs, machinery, vehicles and parts, petroleum and cereals.

Main sources: France (17.4 per cent total, 2004), Côte d'Ivoire (11.3 per cent), Italy (8.4 per cent), Nigeria (7.3 per cent), Germany (6.5 per cent), US (5.5 per cent), China (4.8 per cent)

Exports
Principal exports are uranium ore, livestock, cow-peas and onions.

Main destinations: France (47.1 per cent total, 2004), Nigeria (22.7 per cent), Japan (8.6 per cent), US (5.4 per cent)

Agriculture
Farming
Subsistence farming and stock rearing contribute around 40 per cent to GDP and employ 70 per cent of the workforce. Less than 3 per cent of the total land area is cultivated.

Hides and skins and cotton account for around 20 per cent of export earnings. The government is encouraging market gardening – galmi onions are an important cash crop.

Production of the two principal food crops, millet and sorghum, is generally insufficient to satisfy domestic needs, even in times of good rains, and is supplemented by food aid. Other food crops include rice, cowpeas and green beans.

Recurrent drought and desertification have had a serious impact on livestock rearing and have led to significant food shortages with disastrous consequences. The government is investing heavily in anti-desertification schemes and is encouraging animal husbandry.

In 2004 locust plagues attacked crops and damaged much of the harvest and exposed around 3.5 millions to food shortages. By October 2005 the UN World Food Programme had completed distributing food aid to 3 million people. Rains in mid-2005 were enough to bring about a good harvest but the country has inadequate food reserves.

Crop production for 2004 included: 3,168,800 tonnes (t) cereals in total, 2,500,000t millet, 100,000t cassava, *4,200t potatoes, *30,000t sweet potatoes, 780,000t sorghum, *76,500t rice, 571,305t pulses, *100,000t tomatoes, 72,751t oilcrops, 7,800t dates, 5,400t various spices, *220,000t sugar cane, *17,000t chillies & peppers, 1,500t pepper spice, 50,800t fruit in total, 644,900t vegetables in total. Livestock production included: 133,027t meat in total, 37,000t beef, 1,418t pig meat, 15,200t lamb, *25,200t goat meat, 15,000t game meat, 28,960t poultry, *10,540t eggs, *315,400t milk, 5,600t cattle hides, 1,900t sheepskins, *7,800t camel meat.

* estimate

Industry and manufacturing
The industrial sector is small-scale, contributing around 7 per cent to GDP and employing 5 per cent of the workforce. Manufacturing is concentrated on the processing of agricultural commodities such as sugar refining, brewing, cotton ginning, tanning and flour/rice milling.

Other activities include small-scale production of cement and metals, textiles, plastics, soft drinks and construction materials.

Industrial development is handicapped by the shortage of capital and skilled labour and by the country's weak infrastructure.

Tourism
The tourist sector is expected to contribute 1.7 per cent of GDP and provide employment for 3.5 per cent of the workforce. There is much room for expansion and travel and tourism is estimated to attract 9.1 per cent of all capital investment.

Mining
The mining sector accounts for around 11 per cent of GDP and employs 5 per cent of the workforce.

Niger is the third-largest exporter of uranium and has been the country's principal export since early 1970s. Proven reserves total 280,000 tonnes with extraction undertaken mainly at two opencast mines, at Arlit and Akouta. Production stagnated at 3,000–3,200 tonnes due to a world slump in the demand for uranium. Production has increased in recent years, but depressed prices on the world market have seen the value of uranium exports fall. The major export markets are France, Japan, Spain, Germany and Egypt.

Other minerals exploited are the tin-bearing ore cassiterite, phosphates, molybdenum, salt and coal. There are also known reserves of iron ore.

The Samira mine in Niamey, in the Koma Bangou concession in west Niger, produced its first, 15kg, gold bar in October 2004. The mine will produce 5,000 ounces of gold annually and, over its six-and-half-year life, is expected to produce three tonnes and earn US$28 billion. The government owns 20 per cent and two Canadian mining companies the other 80 per cent of the mine. Gold prospecting agreements have been reached with three other Canadian companies for further research in the region.

Imperial Metals is drilling for diamonds on the M'Banga concession.

Hydrocarbons
Oil was discovered in the Termit Basin, east of Niamey, in January 2005. The test drill achieved 2,540 barrels per day (bpd). Exploration remains sporadic. Niger is entirely dependent on the import of refined oil products, typically it imports around 5,000 bpd.

There are small coal reserves at Tchirozerine (1,000 km north of the capital). These reserves stand at around 780,000 tonnes. There is negligible domestic demand, although this is set to rise. There has been a further discovery of coal reserves in Takanamat, in central Niger. Natural gas is neither produced nor consumed.

Energy
Domestic generation (mainly thermal) meets about 50 per cent of local needs, the deficit being imported from Nigeria. Niger and Nigeria signed a power supply agreement which guaranteed Niger 45MW of electricity in return for the uninterrupted flow of water along the Niger river. This means that Niger is unable to dam the river in its territory. Niger had an estimated hydroelectric potential of 250MW.

Banking and insurance
Central bank
Banque Centrale des Etats de l'Afrique de l'Ouest

Main financial centre
Niamey

Time
GMT plus one hour

Geography
Niger is a landlocked country in western Africa, with Algeria and Libya to the north, Nigeria and Benin to the south, Mali and Burkina Faso to the west and Chad to the east.

Climate
Niger is very hot with temperatures ranging from 28–44 degrees Celsius. There is rain mainly in the south from June–September. Frequent Sahara dust storms occur from November–January. The dry season is from October–May.

Entry requirements
Passports
Required by all and must have at least six month validity left; nationals of certain African countries may visit with national ID cards.
At each overnight stay passports must be presented to the police. As passports will be stamped each time, they will require enough blank pages for the visit. There is a prohibition for any travel by a route other than that stamped in the passport by the police.
Visa
Required by all, except citizens of some African countries close to Niger. Contact the nearest Niger embassy for further details and an application form. Visitors are required to supply proof of return/onward passage and funds, for living expenses of US$500. All documents require a French translation.
An exit permit will be required, from the Immigration Department in Niamey, before departure (except for citizens who do not require an entry visa).
Currency advice/regulations
No restriction on import of foreign currency subject to declaration. Declaration forms must be retained and all transactions recorded. Local currency import is unlimited. There are limits on the export of local currency.

Health (for visitors)
Mandatory precautions
An international yellow fever vaccination certificate; a cholera vaccination certificate if arriving from an infected area.
Advisable precautions
Typhoid, hepatitis A, tetanus and vaccinations. Malaria prophylaxis should be taken as risk exists throughout the country. There is a rabies risk. Water precautions should be taken. Polio is endemic.
Personal medicines can be difficult to obtain.

Hotels
There are good hotels in Niamey. A 5 per cent service charge is usually added to bills.

Public holidays
Fixed dates
1 Jan (New Year's Day), 24 Apr (National Concord Day), 1 May (Labour Day), 3 Aug (Independence Day), 18 Dec (Republic Day), 25 Dec (Christmas Day).
Variable dates
Easter Monday, Eid al Adha, Birth of the Prophet, Eid al Fitr.
The Islamic year contains 354 or 355 days, with the result that Muslim feasts advance by 10–12 days against the Gregorian calendar. Dates of feasts vary according to the sighting of the new moon, so cannot be forecast exactly.

Working hours
Banking
Mon–Fri: 0800–1100 and 1600–1700.
Business
Winter: Mon–Fri: 0730–1230, 1500–1800; Sat: 0730–1230.
Summer: Mon–Fri: 0730–1230, 1530–1830; Sat: 0730–1230.
Government
Oct–Feb: Mon–Fri: 0730–1230 and 1500–1800; Mar–Sep: Mon–Fri: 0730–1230 and 1530–1830.
Shops
Mon–Fri: 0800–1200, 1600–1900; Sat: 0800–1200.

Electricity supply
220/380V AC, 50 cycles

Getting there
Air
National airline: Air Afrique (Niger is a shareholder).
International airport/s: Niamey International (NIM), 12km south-east of city; bar, currency exchange, post office, shops, car hire, hotel courtesy coaches.
Airport tax: None.
Surface
Road: The Nigerian and Burkina Faso borders have been re-opened and road access is possible. Access from Algeria and Mali is difficult, but a surfaced road connects Benin with Niamey. Access from Chad is restricted.
Water: Ferries on the Niger River coming from Mali are dependent on the water level.

Getting about
National transport
Air: Charter flights are available in Niamey.
Road: Main highways link Tillabery with N'guigmi, Tahoua and Arlit. Petrol is not always available. Best months for road travel December–March. Visitors must report to police on arrival at main centres.
Buses: Services operate from Niamey to Zinder, Agadez, and other towns.
City transport
Taxis: Fixed rates apply for long-distance and urban services. Taxis in Niamey are cheap and widely available. Tipping is optional.
Journey time from airport to city centre 10 minutes.
Car hire
Self-drive or chauffeur-driven cars are available in Niamey. Drivers compulsory outside the capital. International driving licence required. Petrol and spares in short supply.

BUSINESS DIRECTORY
The addresses listed below are a selection only. While World of Information makes every endeavour to check these addresses, we cannot guarantee that changes have not been made, especially to telephone numbers and area codes. We would welcome any corrections.

Telephone area codes
The international direct dialling code (IDD) for Niger is +227, followed by subscriber's number.

Useful telephone numbers
Police: 17
Fire: 18

Chambers of Commerce
Maradi Chamber of Commerce and Agriculture, PO Box 79, Maradi (tel: 410-366; fax: 410-451).

Niger Chamber of Commerce, Agriculture, Industriy and Handicrafts, Place de la Concertation, PO Box 209, Niamey (tel: 732-210; fax:: 734-668; e-mail: cham209n@intnet.ne).

Zinder Chambre of Commerce and Agriculture, PO Box 83, Zinder (tel: 510-087; fax: 510-217).

Banking
Bank of Africa (Niger, Head Office); BP 10 973, Immeuble Sonara II, Niamey (tel: 733-620, 733-621; fax: 733-818).

Banque Centrale des Etats de l'Afrique de l'Ouest (Agency); BP 487, Rond Point de la Poste, Niamey (tel: 722-491/92; fax: 734-743).

Banque Commerciale du Niger (Head Office); BP 11 363, Rond Point Maourey, Niamey (tel: 733-915, 733-331; fax: 732-163).

Banque Internationale pour l'Afrique au Niger (Head Office); BP 10350, Avenue de la Mairie, Niamey (tel: 733-101; fax: 733-595; e-mail: bia@intnet.ne).

Banque Islamique du Niger pour le Commerce et l'industrie (BINCI), BP 12754, Immeuble El-Nasr, Niamey (tel: 732-730, 732-740; fax: 734-735).

Caisse de Prêts aux Collectivités Territoriale, BP 730, Route Torodi, Rive droite, Niamey (tel: 723-412, 723-080).

Caisse Nationale d'Epargne, Avenue du Niger, BP 11778 Niamey (tel: 732-498, 732-499; fax: 735-812)

Crédit du Niger, BP 213, Blvd de la République, Niamey (tel: 722-701, 722-702; fax: 722-390).

Ecobank-Niger, BP 13804, Niamey (tel: 737-181, 901-052; fax: 737-204, 737-203).

Société Nigérienne de Banque, BP 891, Ave de la Mairie, Niamey (tel: 734-569, 734-643; fax: 734-693).

Central bank
Banque Centrale des Etats de l'Afrique de l'Ouest, Direction Nationale, Rue de l'Uranium, PO Box 487, Niamey (tel: 722-491; fax: 734-743).

Travel information
Niamey International Airport, ASECNA, BP 1096, Niamey (tel: 732-517/518/519, 732-381/382; fax: 735-512).

Ministry of tourism
Ministère du Tourisme et d'Artisanat BP 12710, Niamey, Niger (tel: 736 522; fax: 732 387).

National tourist organisation offices
Office du Tourisme du Niger, BP 612, Niamey.

Other useful addresses
Centre for Investment Promotion, BP 12129, Niamey (tel: 736-836; fax: 736-772).

Conseil National de Développement, c/o Ministry of Planning, Niamey (tel: 722-233).

Direction des Statistiques, c/o Ministry of Planning, Niamey (tel: 722-799).

Embassy of the Republic of Niger, 154 rue du Longchamp, 75116 Paris, France (tel: (+33-1) 4504 8060; fax: (+33-1) 4504 7973).

Niger Embassy (US), 2204 R Street, NW, Washington DC 20008 (tel: 202-483-4224; fax: 202-483-3169; e-mail: ambassadeniger@hotmail.com).

Office Nationale des Ressources Minières (Onarem), BP 210, Niamey (tel: 723-935).

Société Nationale de Commerce et de Production du Niger, BP 615, Niamey.

Société Nigérienne de Produits Pétroliers (Sonidep), BP 2735, Niamey (tel: 733-335).

SONHOTEL (Société Nigerienne de Gestion des Hôtels de l'Etat) (tel: 732-387).

Syndicat des Commerçants, Importateurs et Exportateurs du Niger, BP 535, Niamey.

Internet sites
Africa Business Network: http://www.ifc.org/abn

AllAfrica.com: http://allafrica.com

African Development Bank: http://www.afdb.org

Africa Online: http://www.africaonline.com

Mbendi AfroPaedia (information on companies, countries, industries and stock exchanges in Africa): http://mbendi.co.za

Nigeria

KEY FACTS

Official name: Federal Republic of Nigeria

Head of State: President General Olusegun Obasanjo (PDP) (since May 1999; inaugurated for second term 29 May 2003)

Head of government: President General Olusegun Obasanjo

Ruling party: People's Democratic Party (PDP)

Area: 923,768 square km

Population: 141.59 million (2004)

Capital: Abuja – federal capital since 1991; Lagos – commercial capital.

Official language: English

Currency: Naira (N) = 100 kobo

Exchange rate: N130.75 per US$ (Oct 2005)

GDP per capita: US$500 (2004)

GDP real growth: 3.50% (2004)

Labour force: 55.93 million (2004)

Unemployment: 2.60% (2004)

Inflation: 15.00% (2004)

Oil production: 2.51 million bpd (2004)

Balance of trade: US$16.85 billion 2004

Foreign debt: US$29.70 billion (2003)

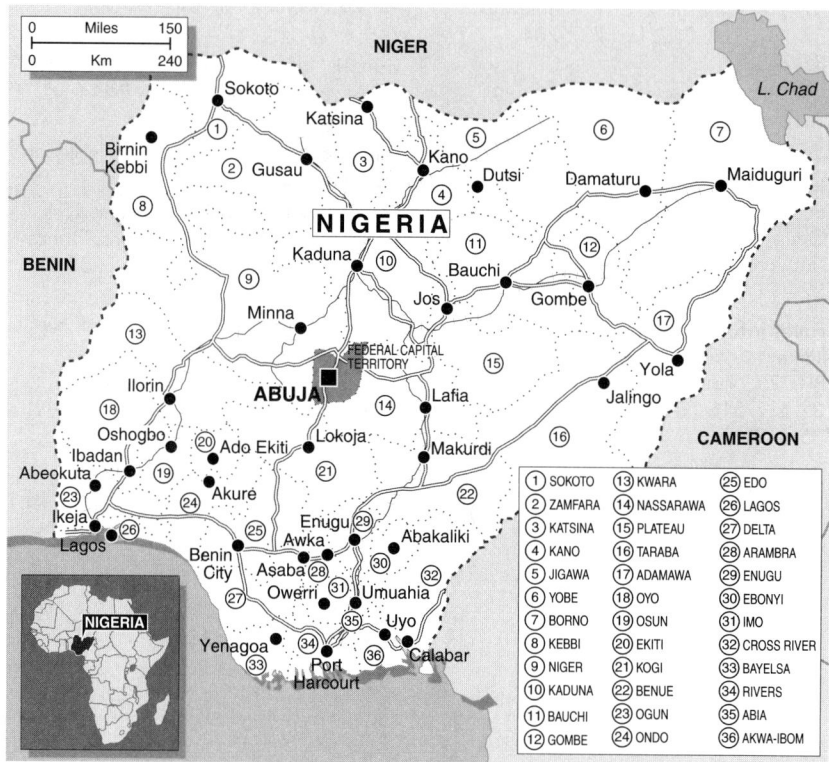

In October 2005, the International Monetary Fund (IMF) approved an initial two years of support for Nigeria's national economic empowerment and development strategy. The new Policy Support Instrument (PSI) is designed for countries that may not need, or want, IMF financial assistance, but still seek IMF advice. The IMF said that Nigeria had made commendable progress in implementing its 'homegrown' economic reform programme and the approval of a PSI programme signified IMF endorsement of Nigeria's plans. They were ambitious but realistic. Clear, measurable assessment criteria and benchmarks had been developed. Importantly the programme had been submitted to the National Assembly. This would greatly facilitate macroeconomic management by strengthening the co-ordination of fiscal policies in all tiers of government.

The medium-term outlook for Nigeria is broadly positive. Formulation of the 2006 budget began with the aim of reducing the non-oil fiscal deficit, thus making the budget more supportive of the deflationary policy. The federal budget, for the first time, is being prepared in the context of a medium-term expenditure framework; state budgets should strengthen macroeconomic performance and encourage economic growth and diversification. The government has also initiated a broad and ambitious structural reform programme aimed at improving public service delivery and the business environment. This includes measures to strengthen budgetary procedures, advance civil service reforms, restructure the banking system, unify the foreign exchange markets, rationalise the external tariff system, and improve governance and transparency.

Debt restructuring

There can now be further discussions about a debt-restructuring agreement with Paris Club creditors. There is already agreement in principle on a phased approach whereby Nigeria would clear its arrears in full, receive a debt write-off of up to Naples terms, and buy back the remainder of its debt. The creditors expressed their readiness to invite Nigeria to negotiate the elements left open as soon as Nigeria had concluded the PSI.

Nigeria will continue to require IMF technical assistance to strengthen its institutional capacity to implement sound economic policies. The authorities have identified key priority areas such as exchange rate unification, bank restructuring, tax policy and administration, and public expenditure management. They have agreed that improving the quality and timeliness of economic and social statistics are critical to support the formulation and monitoring of macroeconomic policies.

No more boom–bust

This all adds up to Nigeria breaking from its boom-bust policies of the past. Many analysts believe Nigeria should aim to build on the success of its economic policies in 2004. Expansionary monetary and fiscal policies that were pursued in 2005 threatened to undermine the gains achieved in that year. The build-up of liquidity in the banking system, in particular, risks undoing the recent gains in reducing inflation.

Serious challenges remain, however. President Olusegun Obasanjo's government faces the daunting task of reforming a petroleum-based economy, the revenues of which have been squandered through corruption and mismanagement. It must also defuse longstanding ethnic and religious tensions, if it is to build a sound foundation for economic growth and political stability.

The push to meet the objectives of the programme cannot be made without significant investment in infrastructure, education and health. Poor infrastructure has been identified as the single most important constraint to development in Nigeria. The private sector cannot be expected to play the role of engine of growth without an improvement in infrastructure. It is estimated that an annual real GDP growth of eight per cent is needed and current estimates indicate a financing gap of about US$4 billion per annum

Yet, Nigeria has the lowest aid per capita among sub-Saharan countries, at about US$2 per capita, compared to the region's average of US$28.2. Nigeria has remained current on its debt service obligations to its multilateral and other creditors while maintaining dialogue with its Paris Club creditors; the Government is paying only the interest obligations of its bilateral debt. This, in itself, has put enormous pressure on the nation's resources. It would be impossible to implement the programme and achieve the UN's Millennium Development Goals if the external debt of about US$35 billion (of which Paris Club is US$30 billion) is to be fully serviced.

A key challenge going forward will be to maintain an appropriate stance and mix of fiscal and monetary policies, in view of the importance of reversing the upsurge in inflation that was associated with the expansionary monetary and fiscal policies in early 2005. While the government is committed to containing spending the projected increase in spending is still large, and the resulting fiscal expansion will place more of the burden of controlling inflation on the central bank. The bank has taken stronger measures to reduce money growth-including increased sales of foreign exchange, more aggressive open market operations, and a further increase in cash reserve requirements.

Implementation of the agreement in principle that Nigeria has reached with its creditor in the Paris Club of international sovereign lenders should improve investor confidence and free up resources for poverty reduction. The programme, supported by the PSI, provides an important opportunity for Nigeria to consolidate the gains achieved so far and address the significant remaining challenges stemming from past economic mismanagement and resistance to reform from vested interests.

Politics

Nigeria was ruled by the military for nearly 16 years under the present president Olusegun Obasanjo. In 1979 he earned the distinction of becoming Africa's first modern military leader to hand over power to civilian rule. Renouncing politics, he then returned to his home state to set up a pig farm.

In 1995 he was jailed for his part in an alleged coup plot against military dictator Sani Abacha, but was set free three years later by new military leader General Abubakar. He became a civilian head of state in 1999 in elections that followed a transition programme started by Abubakar.

Nigeria adopted a new constitution in 1999, and a peaceful transition to civilian government was completed. Obasanjo won a second term in April 2003, gaining more than 60 per cent of the vote in Nigeria's first civilian-run presidential poll for 20 years. Although the elections were marred by some irregularities, Nigeria is currently experiencing its longest period of civilian rule since independence.

With South African President Thabo Mbeki, Obasanjo is an architect of the New Partnership for African Development (Nepad). A key player in the Commonwealth, he reluctantly supported Zimbabwe's suspension over political violence in 2002.

Born in 1937, he is an ethnic Yoruba from the south-west of Nigeria. He joined

KEY INDICATORS — Nigeria

	Unit	2000	2001	2002	2003	2004
Population	m	111.50	118.20	121.50	138.00	141.59
Gross domestic product (GDP)	US$bn	41.10	39.20	43.00	58.40	*72.11
GDP per capita	US$	319	331	316	370	500
GDP real growth	%	3.8	2.9	0.5	3.2	3.5
Inflation	%	6.9	18.0	13.7	14.0	15.0
Oil output	'000 bpd	2,103.0	2,148.0	2,013.0	2,185.0	2,508.0
Natural gas output	bn cum	11.0	13.4	17.7	19.2	20.6
Exports (fob) (goods)	US$m	20,441.0	18,700.0	14,910.0	27,416.0	33,990.0
Imports (fob) (goods)	US$m	13,696.0	15,544.0	14,750.0	18,692.0	17,140.0
Balance of trade	US$m	6,745.0	3,156.0	3,700.0	8,724.0	16,850.0
Current account	US$m	4,810.0	1,430.0	-5,050.0	-2,208.0	2,020.0
Foreign debt	US$bn	31.9	32.1	31.0	32.9	35.0
Total reserves minus gold	US$m	9,911.0	10,457.0	7,233.0	7,128.0	16,956.0
Foreign exchange	US$m	9,910.0	10,456.0	7,331.0	7,128.0	16,955.0
Exchange rate	per US$	101.70	111.23	122.48	134.98	132.89

* estimated figure

the army in 1958 and came to prominence in 1970 as the officer who accepted the surrender of Biafran forces in the 1967–70 civil war.

Risk assessment

Economy	Improving
Politics	Fair – improving
Regional stability	Fair

COUNTRY PROFILE

Historical profile
Throughout its recent history, Nigeria has been run by a northern political elite drawn from the country's majority Muslim population. Military dictatorship managed to suppress underlying religious and ethnic tensions, which have simmered since the outbreak of the Biafran civil war in the 1970s. The election in 1999 of President Obasanjo, a former military dictator who voluntarily handed over power to a civilian government in 1979, was seen by members of the northern elite as concentrating economic and political power in the predominantly Christian south, even though he is a Muslim and is supported by many northerners. Obasanjo's election as a civilian president ended more than 15 years of unbroken military rule; the military has ruled for 29 years out of a total of four decades since Nigeria's independence. Yet, underlying regional resentments have intensified the growing ethnic and religious divisions within the country, threatening to tear the federal state apart. By 2002, Obasanjo was presiding over a country in turmoil, with his leadership undermined by a wave of violence and the move towards sharia (Islamic law) in many northern states. Massacres carried out by vigilante groups and the army became commonplace and Nigeria has confirmed its position as one of the world's most violent and corrupt countries.

The violent divisions within Nigerian society are exacerbated by deepening and widespread poverty, which has not been alleviated by the exploitation of the country's enormous natural resources. Oil has gone hand-in-hand with corruption, which has sapped the economy of its strength and inhibited the growth of non-oil sectors. Economic stagnation and poor governance have led to the collapse of IMF programmes, preventing Nigeria's chances of securing relief on its high level of foreign debt.

Democracy has brought little economic relief or encouraged greater respect for Nigeria's governing institutions. The opportunity Nigeria had to reform its institutions and rejuvenate the private sector appears to have been squandered by the short-term and parochial attitudes of the country's politicians. Additionally, widespread human rights violations are continuing unabated.

Between the eleventh and fourteenth centuries, a number of Islamic Hausa kingdoms flourished in the area of modern-day Nigeria, while in the fourteenth and fifteenth centuries the Yoruba empire developed into a regional power, and the Ibo (Igbo), with a diffuse political structure, lived in the east. The Yoruba first made contact with Europeans (Portuguese) in the fifteenth century, who, along with other European nations, began trading in slaves from West Africa.
1914 The territory that is now Nigeria was taken over by the British.
1922 A legislative council was set up. Much local power was left in the hands of traditional chiefs.
1947 A constitution established a federal system of government which attempted to take into account the interests of the three main regions of the colony – the northern and mainly Muslim Hausa and Fulanis, the predominantly Catholic Ibo in the east and the mixed Anglican and Muslim Yoruba in the west.
1960 Nigeria became independent.
1963 The Federal Republic of Nigeria was proclaimed.
1967–70 Three eastern states attempted to secede, as the Ibo people claimed their independence, resulting in the Biafran Civil War. Estimates for the death toll during the war range between 500,000 and two million.
1970s The Opec-led doubling of the price of oil in October 1973 and again in 1974, led to Nigeria becoming one of Africa's wealthiest states. Nigeria experienced a construction and consumer boom until the price of oil plummeted in the early 1980s.
1985 After 25 years of political turbulence, General Ibrahim Babangida seized power, he was widely supported by intellectuals, the press, some former politicians and the business community. The General pledged to return Nigeria to civilian rule, but the hand-over date was repeatedly postponed.
1993 Elections were held, but were later annulled. Babangida stepped down from office. General Sani Abacha seized power in a coup d'état. He began to suppress all opposition.
1995 Ken Saro-Wiwa, Nigerian writer and advocate of the Ogoni people in eastern Nigeria, and eight other minority rights activists were executed. There was international outrage against both the government and Shell Oil Company, which had allegedly polluted Ogoni land. Nigeria was suspended from the Commonwealth and the EU imposed sanctions.
1998 Abacha died and General Abdulsalam Abubaker became Head of State. A full electoral timetable was announced for the first time.
1999 State legislative, National Assembly and presidential elections were held. Olusegun Obasanjo was declared the winner in the presidential elections.
2000 Sharia (Islamic law) was adopted in several northern states and opposed by the Christian minority. Religious and ethnic tensions grew and hundreds of deaths resulted from clashes between Muslims and Christians. Equatorial Guinea and Nigeria signed a treaty agreement about demarcation of their maritime border.
2001 The heads of Nigeria's army, navy and air force were all encouraged to retire. President Obasanjo set up a National Security Commission in an attempt to halt the communal violence, sparked mainly by religious opposition, which had resulted in thousands of deaths.
2002 The parliament unanimously rejected legislation that would have banned new political parties from contesting presidential and legislative elections in 2003. Nigeria rejected the International Court of Justice ruling that gave sovereignty of the oil-rich Bakassi peninsula, to Cameroon.
2003 President Obasanjo of the People's Democratic Party (PDP) was re-elected and the PDP won large majorities in the Lower House and the Senate. EU observers said the elections were marred by 'serious irregularities'.
2004 In January, the UN brokered talks between Nigeria and Cameroon about their disputed border and both countries agreed to start joint security patrols. After religious clashes in the central Plateau State, a state of emergency was declared there in May. On 18 August, Swiss authorities said that they would unfreeze most of the US$500 million deposited in Switzerland by the dictator Sani Abacha.
2005 The opposition boycotted the national political reform conference (NPRC), called to discuss constitutional reform, claiming it had too few powers; it was inaugurated on 21 February.
2006 On 1 January the Central Bank of Nigeria (CBN) announced that 13 banks faced liquidation for failing to meet the N25 billion capitalisation target.

Political structure
Constitution
The 1979 constitution was amended in 1999, when significant powers were devolved to the 36 states.
The political system is divided into three tiers: the federal or central level, the state level and local government.
Under a presidential system, the president, who is also the commander-in-chief of the armed forces, is vested with executive

Nigeria

powers under the constitution of the federal republic. The president and his ministers form the federal executive council with the president as the chairman.

A similar structure exists in the states where the governor and his commissioners form the state executive councils. Each state has a legislature, executive and judiciary, although their legislative arm is unicameral.

Form of state
Federal republic comprising 36 states and the Federal Capital Territory (FCT, Abuja).

The executive
The Federal Executive Council is headed by an elected president who serves no more than two four-year terms.

The president is both Head of State and head of government, initiating the policies and programmes of the government and ensuring that they are implemented after they have been passed into law by the legislature. The success or failure of any government depends largely on the incumbent president who combines the roles of the chief executive with those of the ceremonial Head of State.

Despite his wide-ranging power, the president has restrictions, which include ratification of all his major appointments by the National Assembly. The president is excluded from membership of both houses of the National Assembly. Although he is empowered to conduct foreign affairs, all treaties require the ratification of the Senate. Only the National Assembly can declare war and peace. While he appoints members of the judiciary, he cannot remove them.

National legislature
The legislative powers of federal government are vested in a bicameral National Assembly. The Senate has 109 seats, three from each state and one from the FCT; members elected by popular vote to serve four-year terms and the House of Representatives 360 seats, with members elected by popular vote to serve four-year terms.

Each of the states of the federation has a unicameral legislature.

Legal system
Nigeria's legal system is based on English common law, Nigerian customs and tradition, and *Sharia* (Islamic law). *Sharia* predominates in the northern Islamic states.

Last elections
19 April 2003 (presidential); 12 April 2003 (parliamentary).

Results: Presidential: President Obasanjo (PDP) was re-elected for a second term with 61.9 per cent of the vote; Muhammadu Buhari (ANPP) 32.2 per cent. Turnout was 69.1 per cent.
Parliamentary: the PDP won both the House of Representatives and the Senate. PDP 53.7 per cent of the vote, (76 seats), ANPP 27.9 per cent of the vote, (27 seats), AD 9.7 per cent of the vote, (6 seats). Turnout was 50 per cent.

Next elections
2007 (presidential and parliamentary)

Political parties
Ruling party
People's Democratic Party (PDP)
Main opposition party
All Nigerian People's Party (ANPP); Alliance for Democracy (AD)

Population
141.59 million (2004)
Ethnic make-up
Hausas (21 per cent), Yorubas (20 per cent), Ibos (17 per cent) and Fulani (9 per cent) comprise the four major tribes.
Religions
Islam (about 50 per cent), Christianity (about 40 per cent), traditional beliefs (about 10 per cent).

Education
Primary schooling lasts for six years. Admittance to secondary schooling is through examination. Junior secondary school lasts for three years until age 15 with progress on to senior secondary school until age 18. Some students may undertake technical, vocational schooling from age 12 and can undertake academic and specialised subjects and graduate at age 18.

Around 7 per cent of the government's budget is allocated to education.

Literacy rate: 66.8 per cent total; 59.4 per cent female, adult rates (World Bank).
Compulsory years: Six to 15
Enrolment rate: 98 per cent gross primary enrolment of relevant age group (including repeaters); 33 per cent gross secondary enrolment (World Bank).
Pupils per teacher: 34 in primary schools

Health
The Federal Ministry of Health (FMOH) provides policy and technical guidance to the 36 states and the federal capital territory (Abuja), co-ordinating state efforts towards the goals set by the national health policy. Annual health expenditure stands at around 3–4 per cent of GDP, of which government spending is approximately 23 per cent and foreign spending about 7 per cent.

The primary healthcare network has seriously declined with low level coverage of services such as immunisation and supply of essential drugs. The Health System Fund is a major project implemented by the state and federal ministries of health aimed at institutional development, training and an essential drug programme. Nigeria has a growing problem of HIV/Aids as well as a significant rise of other non-communicable diseases, however, with 65 per cent of the population living below the poverty line, health measures can provide only short-term solutions to systemic problems.

In early March 2004 the Islamic northern state of Kano was the site of the worst outbreak of polio in the world and Unicef, which was overseeing the immunisation programme, was in difficulty trying to persuade local administrators that the vaccine did not contain high levels of female hormones, suspected as 'part of a Western plot to make Muslims infertile'. This outbreak followed a six-month vaccine boycott. Nigeria had almost half the number of worldwide cases of polio in 2003; the fear of aid agencies was that without a thorough vaccination programme the disease, which by 2004, was already spreading into neighbouring countries, would undermine the international eradication programme. In May 2004, the northern states abandoned their eight months ban on the polio vaccine. In October–November 2004 a mass immunisation campaign began in 22 countries spanning the Sahel region of Africa, from Senegal in the west, to Mali in the north and the Central African Republic in the east. For a population to be at only a minor risk to polio outbreaks 85 per cent must be vaccinated; it is estimated that, in many of the at risk countries, only 50 per cent were immunised.

Improved water sources are available to 39 per cent of the population.

HIV/Aids
An estimated 3.5 million adults and children are living with HIV/Aids and there are over one million orphans due to Aids. In March 2004 it was disclosed, by Dr Chindo Bissala, the co-ordinator of the State Action Committee against Aids (SACA), that 254,000 persons living in Niger State were confirmed as HIV positive. Dr Bissala was not optimistic that much was being done to check the spread of the disease and that generally people failed to recognise the problem.

In 2003, the government allocated US$157 million for prevention and control activities.

HIV prevalence: 5.4 per cent aged 15–49 in 2003 (World Bank)
Life expectancy: 44.9 years (World Bank)
Fertility rate/Maternal mortality rate: 5.6 births per woman; maternal mortality 800 per 100,000 live births (World Bank).
Birth rate/Death rate: 39.6 births and 13.9 deaths per 1,000 people
Infant mortality rate: 98 per 1,000 live births; 28.7 per cent of children aged under five-years suffer malnutrition (World Bank).

Nations of the World: A Political, Economic and Business Handbook

Head of population per physician/bed: 0.2 physicians and 1.7 hospital beds typically available per 1,000 people

Welfare
The Nigerian public service schemes, the private sector self-administered and insured scheme, the National Provident Fund (NPF) and the Nigeria Social Insurance Trust Fund (NSITF) schemes, provide for old age, survivorship, invalidity and industrial injury benefits, gratuity and pension. The Workmen's Compensation Act provides for industrial injury benefits. Despite the existence of these bodies, the social security system is virtually non-existent in Nigeria.

The pensions fund management is divided into two categories: government schemes and occupational schemes. The government scheme provides basic social benefits that are not earnings-related, and earnings-related pension provisions. Such schemes are funded mainly through contributions from the government, with minimal contributions from the scheme members. The government policy allows individuals in self-employment to claim premiums paid to any insurance company, provided such premiums do not exceed 10 per cent of the individuals total income. This is in addition to any relief claimed in respect of life assurance policies. The occupational pension schemes consists of private companies' schemes, which are employment related and financed jointly by the employers and employees.

Main cities
The seat of government is Abuja, Federal Capital Territory, in central Nigeria (estimated population 165,700 in 2004). Lagos is the former capital and main port (Apapa) (estimated population 8.7 million).

Capitals of the 36 states are: Kaduna (state of Kaduna) (1.6 million), Kano (Kano) (3.4 million), Jos (Plateau) (761,800), Sokoto (Sokoto), Maiduguri (Borno) (1.0 million), Ilorin (Kogi – formerly Kwara) (780,700), Ibadan (Oyo) (3.2 million), Port Harcourt (Rivers) (1.1 million), Calabar (Cross River), Bauchi (Bauchi), Minna (Niger), Makurdi (Benue), Abeokuta (Ogun) (542,900), Akure (Ondo), Ikeja (Lagos), Owerri (Imo), Katsina (Katsina), Uyo (Akwa Ibom), Benin City (Edo) (1.1 million), Enugu (Enugu), Yola (Adamawa), Umuahia (Abia), Awka (Anambra), Asaba (Delta), Birnin Kebbi (Kebbi), Lokoja (Kogi), Yenogou (Bayelsa) (609,000), Abakaliki (Ebonyi), Ado-Ekiti (Ekiti), Gombe (Gombe), Lafia (Nassarawa), Gusau (Zamfara), Osogbo (Osun), Jalingo (Taraba), Dutse (Jigawa), Damaturu (Yobe).

Languages spoken
English is used in business and public life. Hausa, Yoruba and Ibo are widely spoken.
Official language/s
English

Media
Press
The government controls the media through a media council, which has the power to discipline journalists and bar them from working. There are also strict laws of libel and an Official Secrets Act. However, the press is officially free and is often critical of the government. The News Agency of Nigeria (NAN), the country's only news agency, is government-owned but not official.

Dailies: At least 20 dailies circulate nationally. Three evening papers are published in Lagos and one in Ibadan. Principal dailies include *Daily Times*, *National Concord*, *New Nigerian*, *The Guardian*, *Daily Sketch*, *The Punch*, *Vanguard*, *Daily Champion*, *Comet News*, *Post Express* and *The Tribune*. *Al Mizanr* is published in the local language Hausa.

Weeklies: There are several weekly news magazines, notably *Newswatch*, *African Concord*, *Abuja Mirror*, *Today* and *African Guardian*.

Business: *Policy* is a business and investment magazine.

Broadcasting
Radio: The government-controlled Federal Radio Corporation of Nigeria (FRCN) operates Nigeria's radio network. It operates an external service but reception outside Lagos is poor. Four regional zonal services broadcast in English and appropriate local languages from stations based in Lagos, Ibadan, Kaduna and Enugu. External services broadcast in English, French, Hausa, Arabic, German, Swahili. In addition to the national service, each state runs its own commercial radio station. FRCN is divided into five zones:
Lagos (English speaking);
Enugu (English, Ibo, Izon, Efik and Tiv);
Ibadan (English, Yoruba, Edo, Urhobo and Igala);
Kaduna (English, Hausa, Kanuri, Fulfulde, and Nupe);
External Services (English, French, Hausa, Arabic, German and Swahili).

Television: The Nigerian Television Authority (NTA) has 25 stations nationwide and claims an audience of 30 million people for its main network news bulletin at 2100. Several states also run their own stations. There are 14 companies operating private television stations.

Economy
Nigeria's economic decline since the 1980s has been one of the most spectacular in Africa, considering its size and potential. Following the corrupt dictatorship of General Sani Abacha (1993–98), who along with his cronies effectively looted the country of wealth from it huge oil revenue, Nigeria has had to contend with large debt repayments.

At the beginning of 2005, and into President Olusegun Obsanjo's second term in office, foreign debt was US$36 billion, and annual repayments were US$6 billion, the drain on the economy was crippling. Nigeria paid more in debt repayment each year than total public spending on healthcare; foreign aid per capita was the lowest in Africa – apart from Libya, which had been ostracised for political reasons – and had left Nigerians among the poorest in the world.

As one of the worlds leading oil exporters Nigeria was ineligible for debt relief under the Heavily Indebted Poor Countries (HIPC) initiative and it was only through negotiations with the Paris Club of international sovereign lenders – who hold around 80 per cent of all Nigeria's debt – that debt relief was secured. The record high prices for oil in 2004–05 had given Nigeria a windfall that allowed it to negotiate seriously. In October 2005 an agreement was secured whereby Nigeria would pay back an initial US$6 billion, then the Paris Club members will write off US$18 billion and Nigeria will buy back the rest of the debt at a 25 per cent discount. The agreement should be completed by April 2006, and it has been estimated that Nigeria will save US$1 billion per year in debt servicing.

The agreement was predicated on the IMF giving Nigerian efforts in economic reforms an endorsement and providing ongoing appraisal. Nigeria is in partnership with the UK's Department of International Development, to set up a monitoring system to track debt funds released for health, education, agriculture and utilities. This is intended to allay concerns regarding mismanagement and corruption, while the government will put forward legislation for improved standards of governance, increased deregulation and tighter control of public finances.

Growth in GDP was 3.5 in 2004, little changed from the 3.2 in 2003, while inflation was high at 15 per cent. Oil and gas production maintains growth and dominates the economy; the government has yet to succeed in diversification. Nevertheless, the IMF concluded that macroeconomic performance had improved in 2004 and that government had achieved fiscal discipline. A degree of stability in the exchange rate was reached and international reserves grew to US$23 billion by the end of May 2005.

The government has moved to tackle public sector corruption and improve

transparency of public policies as well as civil service reforms to strengthen budgetary procedures.
Nigeria has much to gain by these reforms and much to lose if it fails to bring its economy into compliance with accepted international standards for financial management. It has shown a willingness to begin the task and the IMF will be monitoring the situation closely.

External trade
In 2002, the US approved Nigeria as being eligible for tariff preferences under the African Growth and Opportunities Act (AGOA).

Imports
Principal imports include fuel (because of the inefficiency of Nigeria's oil refineries), raw materials, machinery, chemicals, transport equipment, manufactured goods, food and live animals.
Main sources: US (9.1 per cent total, 2004), China (8.8 per cent), UK (8.7 per cent), Netherlands (6.3 per cent), France (6.1 per cent), Germany (5.7 per cent), Italy (4.7 per cent)

Exports
Principal exports are crude oil and petroleum products (typically 95 per cent of total), cocoa, rubber, timber and manufactured goods.
Main destinations: US (48.2 per cent total, 2004), India (8.1 per cent), Spain (7.4 per cent), Brazil (5.5 per cent), Japan (4.1 per cent)

Agriculture
Farming
Contribution to GDP by the agriculture sector fell to 16.6 per cent in 2004, down from the 26.4 per cent in 2003, even though annual growth has remained steady at 6.5 per cent. It contributes just 3 per cent to exports and receives much official encouragement.
The sector has suffered a relative decline because of the dominance of oil in the economy, but it is still the main area of employment, employing around half the workforce.
Land suitable for arable production has been put at 25 per cent of the total area, of which about 12 per cent is currently cultivated. The country suffers from soil degradation, deforestation and water pollution.
Key government policies include food self-sufficiency and boosting non-food crops to meet demand from the agri-processing sector. The sector is still dominated by unproductive smallholders raising subsistence crops such as sorghum, maize, cassava, yams, millet, rice and increasing quantities of wheat – up to 70 per cent of which is for private consumption. Nigeria is a leading world producer of cassava and the second largest producer of ginger.
Plantations, sometimes owned by, or in partnership with, multinational corporations, are gaining ground in producing raw materials for commercial use, for example grain for breweries. Irrigation schemes, higher producer prices, the expansion of credit and improvements in the rural infrastructure are beginning to show positive results.
Cash crops include cocoa, rubber (nearly all exported), coffee, cotton and palm kernels. Cocoa is Nigeria's largest foreign exchange earner after oil. The palm oil sector is being redeveloped. Livestock farming is important, while poultry farming is rapidly increasing.
Crop production in 2004 included: 22,783,000 tonnes (t) cereals in total, 3,542,000t rice, 4,779,000t maize, 4,027,000t taro, 26,587,000t yams, 6,282,000t millet, 8,028,000t sorghum, 2,516,000t sweet potatoes, 38,4179,000t cassava, 8,700,000t oil palm fruit, 657,000t potatoes, 2103,000t plantains, 2,367,000t pulses, 140,900t fibre crops, *3250,000t citrus fruit, 2,470,790t oilcrops, 2,937,000t groundnuts in shell, 366,000t cocoa beans, 3,520t green coffee, 142,000t natural rubber, 776,000t sugar cane, 9,127,000t fruit in total, 8,270,000t vegetables in total. Livestock production included: 1,066,947t meat in total, 280,000t beef, 208,231t pig meat, 100,650t lamb, 147,066t goat meat, 211,000t poultry, 476,000t eggs, *432,000t milk, 59,000t cattle hides, 18,300t sheepskins
*estimate

Fishing
Over N30 billion (US$238 million) is spent annually on fish imports despite the country's large fishing potential.
There is extensive fishing in the Niger River network and along the south coast.

Forestry
Nigeria has 15 per cent forest cover and an additional 54 per cent of other wooded land comprising mainly savannah. There are growing forestry operations in the tropical zones in southern Nigeria and north of Port Harcourt. The extensive network of national parks and reserves protect around 5 per cent of its forests. The average annual deforestation is around 2.5 per cent, or the equivalent of 400,000ha of forest cover.
Nigeria is one of the largest wood producers in Africa showing an annual harvest of more than 100 million cubic metres, most of which is used for fuel consumption. The large-scale industrial forestry sector produces sawn timber, plywood, particleboard and paper mostly to meet local demands.
Northern Nigeria is most threatened by deforestation and government concerns over desertification hav led to urgent action plans including a US$44.5 million National Tree Nursery Programme.

Industry and manufacturing
Production costs in industry are considerably increased by a lack of basic infrastructure, which compels every factory to have its own standby electricity plant and sometimes a water borehole. Companies also find it difficult to source vital components from abroad with uncertain supplies of foreign exchange, although this situation is gradually improving thanks to the liberalisation of the economy.
The textile industry used to be one of Nigeria's more productive sectors. However, the Kano Textile Traders Association claims that imports of finished textile materials from China, Pakistan and India have resulted in the collapse of the textile industry. WTO agreements blocking advantageous exports to the US, and Ecowas tariff reductions allowing cheaper imports from neighbouring countries, have reduced the number of textile firms from a high of 250,000 to a current 50,000 with only 65 textile mills remaining. The number of job loses amounts to around 200,000.
Industrial production increased by 4.6 per cent in 2004.

Tourism
The tourism sector is expected to account for 1.5 per cent of GDP, or US$1 billion in 2005 and employ around 6.4 per cent of the working population. While travel and tourism is only expected to attract around US$340 million or 2.4 per cent of total capital investment in 2005, overall it should generate about US$4.7 billion in total tourist exports.
Nigeria has many diverse environments and attractions to offer the intrepid traveller, as well as marketing the country as a destination for eco-tourists it also emphasises it peoples and local customs.

Environment
Drilling operations in the Niger Delta region have created huge pollution problems from oil spills and explosions. Oil exploitation has been a fact of life for many people living in the Delta, particularly the Ogoni people.
Nigeria's pollution problems are exacerbated by the fact that the country does not have a pollution control policy. Analysts have reported that during oil production, Nigeria flares more natural gas than any other country in the world, contributing to global warming. The government hopes to end gas flaring by 2008.

Mining

Nigeria used to be one of the world's largest producers of tin, with production based around the highland district of Jos. It is now the smallest of the Association of Tin Producing Countries (ATPC). The country's only tin smelter is at Makeri. Tin reserves are estimated at 16,000 tonnes. Independent estimates place iron ore reserves at 800 million tonnes, averaging 37 per cent metal content.

Deposits of uranium, lead, zinc, tungsten and gold have not yet been exploited. There are 65 sites in Nigeria where gold has been located. The Iperindo gold project in Oshun State has a resource of some 400,000 ounces of gold.

Nigeria Mining Corp has taken up a number of projects including gold, tantalum and tin with the aim of attracting more capital in anticipation of increased private sector involvement.

Hydrocarbons

The petroleum sector is the mainstay of the economy, contributing 20 per cent to annual GDP and 75 per cent to government revenues. In 2004, Nigeria's proven oil reserves stood at 35.3 billion barrels, most of which is located in the Niger River Delta; production averaged 2.5 million barrels per day (bpd). Oil production dominates the Nigerian economy, accounting over 80 per cent of foreign earnings. At current production levels, reserves should last for approximately another 30 years. Nigeria hopes to increase production to four million bpd by 2010.

The Dutch/UK oil company Shell announced that the Bonga deepwater oil field had gone into production in November 2005. It is expected to produce 225,000bpd and add 10 per cent to Nigeria's total production.

Multinational oil companies are in partnership with the Nigerian government for oil exploration and production. While the oil located is premium light and easily extractable, domestic political and managerial problems have led to Nigeria being discribled as 'one of the most difficult operating environments' in the world. Corruption has been blamed for much of the squandering of US$340 billion in oil revenue earned since 1965. So much so that of the 20 million people, in 3,000 communities living in the Niger River Delta, 70 per cent live on less than US$1 per day. Oil companies claim that government investment has not been forthcoming – down by US$1 billion in 2005 – so that key environmental plans, such as ending flaring of waste gas by 1 January 2008 will probably be missed.

Oil installations are frequently vandalised and company staff taken hostage, resulting in major disruptions to oil production. Some of the attacks are motivated by those who resent the development of the oil industry, the destruction of their environment and the uneven distribution of oil wealth to the federal rather than state governments. Illegal siphoning of fuel to supply the black market has resulted in a number of major explosions with hundreds of deaths each year. The government estimates that around 300,000bpd of oil is sold illegally on to the black market each year.

Nigeria has only four refineries producing 445,000bpd, about half their full capacity. All new exploration contracts require international oil companies to make a commitment to investing in new refining capacity.

Proven gas reserves stood at five trillion cubic metres in 2003, making Nigeria the second-largest African source of natural gas after Algeria. However there has been relatively little investment in projects to gather gas for commercial use, and Nigeria is considered to be the biggest burner of waste gas globally.

Production was 20.6 billion cubic metres in 2004. At this production rate, reserves could last for several hundred years. Nigeria would like to provide gas as its principle source of domestic energy however capital investment in the necessary infrastructure is unavailable.

Nigeria, Ghana, Togo and Benin signed a deal for a US$500 million pipeline project to pump Nigerian natural gas across the region. Construction began in 2005 and will be ongoing for several years. Chevron Texaco will build and manage the pipeline.

Nigeria has plentiful coal reserves, although production supplies only a tiny percentage of domestic energy requirements. Coal exports are negligible, due to obsolete equipment and a lack of investment following years when the coal sector was a government monopoly.

Energy

Three hydroelectric stations and five thermal stations should provide around 5,900MW of installed electric generating capacity, although neglect and a lack of funding mean that actual capacity is only 2,000MW. The government's long-term objective is to increase capacity to 25,000MW.

It is estimated that only 10 per cent of rural households and 40 per cent of the total population have access to electricity. The government aims to increase total electricity coverage to 85 per cent by 2010 by building 16 new power plants and 15,000km of transmission lines. The development of hydroelectric power stations is hampered by persistent droughts and funding difficulties. As a result the government is turning to developing a solar energy system to serve rural communities not served by the national grid.

Financial markets

Stock exchange

The Nigerian Stock Exchange (NSE) was established in 1960 as the Lagos Stock Exchange and became the NSE in 1977. The NSE conducts its business on six trading floors spread across the country. It has branches in Lagos, Kaduna and Port Harcourt, with the bulk of business conducted in Lagos. Most transactions are concentrated in the banking, conglomerates, breweries and food and drink sub-sectors. The banking sector, which offers high yields, is the most active sub-sector in the NSE, representing around 46 per cent of all transactions. On 3 January 2006, 22 banks were suspended from the trading floor following the withdrawal of their licences by the regulatory authorities.

Banking and insurance

Nigeria's banking sector is the second-largest in Africa behind South Africa, but it has experienced difficulties in recent years. Since the late 1990s, the Central Bank of Nigeria (CBN) has worked towards cleaning up the banking sector. The end of military rule in 1999 saw international banks return to Nigeria, although they concentrate their operations in Lagos and Abuja supplying services for big businesses and Nigerian expatriates. The CBN does not differentiate between licensing of commercial and merchant banks, which enables merchant banks to issue cheques and allows them to access the CBN's clearing house.

In 2005 the CBN began restructuring the banking sector by setting a minimum capital requirement that has forced banks into consolidation. The IMF is advising the CBN on the banking reform programme. A persistent obstacle to the banking sector's development is Nigeria's culture of fraud; the CBN has been keen to address, the advance fee fraud scams, run by criminal gangs. A Financial Intelligence Unit monitors the banking environment to strengthen the anti-money laundering framework that is under way.

Other problems include the federal and state governments' borrowing from domestic banks, which has severely restricted liquidity in the banking sector.

It was announced in March 2005 that the introduction of the shared currency, the Eco, in Nigeria, Ghana, Guinea, Sierra Leone and The Gambia, which was due in July 2005, would be postponed. The currency was proposed to facilitate trade and growth with an ultimate plan to merge it with the CFA franc.

On 1 January 2006 the CBN announced that 13 banks faced liquidation for failing

Nigeria

to meet its N25 billion capitalisation target.
Central bank
Central Bank of Nigeria (CBN)
Main financial centre
Lagos
Offshore facilities
Nigeria is on the Organisation for Economic Co-operation and Development (OECD) Financial Action Task Force (FATF) list of non-co-operative countries on money laundering.

Time
GMT plus one hour

Geography
Nigeria is bordered to the west by Benin, to the north by Niger, to the north-east by Chad, to the east by Cameroon and to the south by the Bight of Benin (Atlantic Ocean). The main rivers, the Niger and Benue, merge in the centre of the country, dividing it into three main regions of north, south and east. The north consists of dry savannah, the south of dense jungle, with mangrove swamps nearer the coast, and the east of a plateau leading into the country's only major mountain range along the Cameroon border.

Climate
The climate varies from tropical on the coast to sub-tropical in the north. There are two main seasons, the rainy season from April to October and the dry season from November to March, which is characterised by a cool dust haze from the Sahara known as the harmattan.
Average temperatures remain fairly constant throughout the year at 29 degrees Celsius (C) in the south. The average daytime temperature in the north is 42 degrees C, but the temperature can drop to as low as 6 degrees C at night.
Humidity is high in the south, with a maximum varying from 100 per cent to 80 per cent. Rainfall is heavy on the coast, ranging from about 180cm a year in the south-west to 430cm in the south-east. Near-temperate conditions are common on the central plateau and along the hilly north-eastern border with Cameroon.

Dress codes
Suits or traditional dress are worn for business meetings, but otherwise dress is informal. Pure cotton, linen or feather-light wool are the best materials for the year-round hot and humid climate.
Women are advised to dress modestly, especially in the Islamic north.
For social occasions, dress as for a business meeting.

Entry requirements
Passports
Required by all and must be valid for six months.
Visa
Required by all; some exception are made for citizens of countries located close to Nigeria. Visas should be obtained before arrival, contact the nearest consular office, or visit the relevant website to obtain or download an application form.
Business visitors will require a letter of invitation, from an organisation or individual, addressed to the Visa Section of the High Commission or Embassy. A declaration of full compliance of all entry requirements or proof of sufficient funds for expenses (such as traveller's cheques to be cashed in Nigeria), must be lodged. Any individual inviting a visitor must attach photocopies of the first five pages of his/her own passport, while a resident must enclose a copy of his/her residence permit.
Customs
Laws against exporting Nigerian antiquities are strictly enforced.
Prohibited imports
Sparkling wines and beer, fruits and vegetables, eggs and cereals, precious metals and textiles including mosquito netting.

Health (for visitors)
Mandatory precautions
Yellow fever vaccination certificate required if coming from an infected area.
Advisable precautions
The risk of contracting yellow fever is highest in Lagos and Kaduna states, and cholera is a serious risk throughout the country; visitors are strongly recommended to have vaccinations for these diseases.
Other diseases that require preventative measures are HIV, polio, typhoid, hepatitis 'A, B, C' and 'E', TB, dengue fever and malaria. To avoid bilharzia, only use well-maintained and chlorinated swimming pools. Polio is endemic.
Water is unsafe outside urban areas and precautions are essential. Bottled water is recommended for use, even when cleaning teeth. Food should be thoroughly washed before consumption, and only well-cooked meat, preferably hot, should be eaten. Dairy products made from local milk are to be avoided.
Walking in bare feet, or even open sandals, can attract parasites, notably jikkers. Visitors should seek advice before accepting treatment involving hypodermic needles or blood transfusions. Medical insurance is essential and an adequate supply of personal medicines is necessary.

Hotels
There is a wide range of hotels available, though rooms difficult to obtain and expensive in Lagos. Bills must be paid in foreign currency and a high deposit in advance is required to cover estimated length of stay. Most main hotels are air-conditioned.

Credit cards
Credit cards are not widely used.

Public holidays
Fixed dates
1 Jan (New Year's Day), 1 May (Workers' Day), 1 Oct (National Day), 25–26 Dec (Christmas Holiday).
Variable dates
Easter Holiday, Eid al Adha, Eid al Fitr, Birth of the Prophet.
The Islamic year contains 354 or 355 days, with the result that Muslim feasts advance by 10–12 days against the Gregorian calendar. Dates of feasts vary according to the sighting of the new moon, so cannot be forecast exactly.

Working hours
Banking
Mon: 0800–1500; Tue–Fri: 0800–1300 (some banks work until 1600 or 1700); Sat, some banks only: 1000–1500.
Business
Mon–Fri: 0800–1230 and 1400–1630. Some offices also Sat: 0800–1200.
Government
Mon–Fri: 0730–1530, some states also Sat: 0800–1300.
Shops
Mon–Fri: 0800–1200 and 1430–1800; Sat: 0800–1300.

Telecommunications
Mobile phones
There are GSM roaming facilities available, with coverage throughout most of the country.

Electricity supply
230V AC, 50 cycles

Social customs/useful tips
Because of the prodigious traffic jams, called 'go-slows', which often grip Lagos, it is hard to be punctual, so both Nigerians and expatriates are generally tolerant of latecomers.
Appointments with government officials should be made in advance. With business executives, a more informal attitude prevails. Business cards are exchanged after introduction and business is mostly conducted in English. Meetings can be long and they are less formal than in Europe. It is customary to shake hands on meeting and taking leave.
Confirm the business organisation's status with the Chamber of Commerce, Corporate Affairs Commission, Abuja and the Federal Ministry of Commerce and Tourism, Abuja, before entering into a firm contract.
Local customs and conventions should be adhered to, particularly in Muslim areas in the northern states. Women should not wear trousers.

Gifts are welcomed but not essential, unless hospitality extends to accommodation and/or meals, in which case gifts are expected on departure.

Gratuities are around 10 per cent. A service charge is usually added to restaurant and hotel bills. Tips are not expected by taxi drivers. Giving 'dash' or gratuities for other commercial services is widespread, although officially discouraged.

Security

Security remains a serious problem in several Nigerian cities, but chiefly in Lagos. The biggest threat comes from armed robbers. They either attack houses at night or, more frequently, stop cars at gunpoint on urban or country expressways and order the driver to hand over the keys. Petty theft is also common; moneybelts are advisable.

The government says that the incidence of armed robbery is declining, although no reliable statistics have been published to establish the claim.

During outbreaks of violence, the capital is likely to be dotted with checkpoints manned by armed police, where visitors should remain calm and courteous. It is not necessary to offer a bribe at these roadblocks.

Getting there
Air

National airline: Virgin Nigeria; Nigeria Airways was liquidated in 2003.

International airport/s: Abuja Nnamdi Azikiwe (ABV), 35km from city; Kano-Mallam-Aminu Kano (KAN), 8km from city, duty-free shop, restaurant, bank, post office, shops, car hire; Lagos-Murtala Muhammed (LOS), 22km from city, duty-free shop, restaurant, bar, buffet, bank, post office, car hire; Port Harcourt (PHC), 24km from city.

It is advisable to be met at Lagos airport by someone you know, or someone who can prove their identity. Also make sure you do not give your passport to anyone but the immigration officer. Check in early for return flight, because overbooking is common; British Airways allows passengers with luggage to check in at the airport from mid-day; those with hand luggage may check in early at its office in Victoria Island or at the Sheraton Hotel in Ikeja.

Airport tax: Departure tax: US$35, except transit passengers.

Surface

Road: There are good roads linking Niger (Maradi, Zinder, Agadez, Niamey) to Kano, and from Benin; all-weather roads from Cameroon (Maroua, Mokolo) and Chad (N'Djamna). The southern road from Cameroon (Mamfe) to Enugu is not generally recommended.

Water: Nigeria has the biggest port facilities and international sailings in the region.

Main port/s: Apapa (Lagos), Port Harcourt, Calabar and the Delta Port complex including Warri, Sapele and Koko.

Getting about
National transport

Air: There is a number of local airlines providing intercity services. Routes and airlines frequently change.

If flying from Lagos, it is advisable to go to the airport and confirm that the aircraft is actually going to fly and that you have a definite confirmed seat before buying ticket. Beware of touts.

Road: A national road network system of 113,000km links all main centres. Principal main roads connect Lagos and Port Harcourt in the south with Kano and Katsina in the north. The motorway running from Lagos-Ibadan is often congested. There are often long delays in major towns.

Some secondary roads can become impassable during rainy season.

Buses: Scheduled coach services include: Kaduna-Jos; Lagos-Umuahia.

Rail: There are some 3,500km of railway, mostly single track.

Rail travel is cheap, but slow. There are two classes. Some trains have restaurant cars and buffet facilities and some have air-conditioning.

There are two main rail lines: Lagos-Kano Express (via Ibadan and Minna) with branches to Baro, Kaura Namoda and Nguru, Plateau Express (Lagos-Jos); and Port Harcourt-Kano with branch to Jos and Maiduguri.

Water: There are over 8,575 km of waterways including the Niger and Benue rivers, with ferry services on these and along the southern coast.

City transport

Taxis: Taxis are widely available in Lagos and other main towns. The traditional taxis are usually yellow Peugeots in Lagos (these charge by distance), other colours elsewhere. Also numerous cars belonging to car hire companies. Taxi ranks are mainly found at the big hotels. Fare and tip should be agreed before starting journey. All drivers should have an Identity Card.

Journey time from Lagos Murtala Mohammed Airport to city centre is around 40 minutes.

Car hire

Available in most of the large towns through the main hotels. International driving licence and two passport-sized photographs required; chauffeur-driven services generally recommended.

Be aware that in Lagos the Lagos State Traffic Management Authority (Lastma) has wide powers and frequently stops and seizes vehicles for minor, alleged, offences. On the spot 'fines' are frequently suggested. Owners of vehicles that are impounded have to pay a daily charge to recover them.

BUSINESS DIRECTORY

The addresses listed below are a selection only. While World of Information makes every endeavour to check these addresses, we cannot guarantee that changes have not been made, especially to telephone numbers and area codes. We would welcome any corrections.

Telephone area codes

The international direct dialling code (IDD) for Nigeria is +234, followed by area code and subscriber's number:

Abuja	9	Katsina	65
Akure	34	Lagos	1
Bauchi	77	Maiduguri	76
Calabar	87	Makurdi	44
Enugu	42	Minna	66
Ibadan	22	Owerri	83
Ikeja	1	Oyo	38
Ilorin	31	Port Harcourt	84
Jos	73	Sokoto	60
Kaduna	62	Yola	75
Kano	64	Zaria	69

Useful telephone numbers

Police	199
Fire and ambulance	999

Chambers of Commerce

Abuja Chamber of Commerce and Industry, International Trade Fair Centre, Airport Road, PO Box 86, Abuja (tel: 523-0453; fax: 523-6231; e-mail: anmgbemere@hotmail.com).

British-Nigerian Chamber of Commerce, Ebani House, 149 Broad Street, Lagos (tel: 264-1266; fax: 266-0298; e-mail: hq@n-bcc.org).

Enugu Chamber of Commerce, Industry, Mines and Agriculture, International Trade Fair Complex, Abakaliki Road, PO Box 734, Enugu (tel: 250-575; fax: 252-186; e-mail: eccima@infoweb.abs.net).

Ibadan Chamber of Commerce and Industry, Commerce House, Ring Road, PO Box 5168, Ibadan (tel: 317-223; fax: 311-647; e-mail: icci@infoweb.abs.net).

Kaduna Chamber of Commerce, Industry, Mines and Agriculture, Kaduna-Zaria Road, Rigachikun, PO Box 728, Kaduna (tel: 318-794; fax: 318-795; e-mail: kadccima@inet-global.com).

Kano Chamber of Commerce and Industry, Trade Fair Complex, Zoo Road, PO Box 10, Kano (tel: 666-936; fax: 667-138; e-mail: kaccima@hotmail.com).

Nigeria

Lagos Chamber of Commerce and Industry, 1 Idowu Taylor Street, Victoria Island, PO Box 109, Lagos (tel: 774-6617; fax: 262-3665; e-mail: inform@lagoschamber.com).

National Association of Chambers of Commerce, Industry and Agriculture, 15A Ikorodu Road, Maryland, PO Box 12816, Lagos (tel: 496-4727, 496-4737; e-mail: naccima@pinet.com.ng).

Port Harcourt Chamber of Commerce, Industry, Mines and Agriculture, 169 Aba Road, PO Box 71, Port Harcourt (tel: 330-394; fax: 243-307; e-mail: phccima@hotmail.com).

Banking

Nigerian Industrial Development Bank Ltd (NIMB), PMB 205, 1st Floor, NIMB Building, 4th Avenue, Plot 207, Cadastral Zone AO, Off Herbert Macaulay Way, Central Business District, Abuja (tel: 234-6579; fax: 234-6578).

Commercial Bank (Crédit Lyonnais Nigeria) Ltd, PMB 12829, Plot 146B Ligali Ayorinde, Victoria Island Annex, Lagos (tel: 262-5700; fax: 262-5699).

Ecobank Nigeria plc, 2 Ajose Adeogun St, Victoria Island, Lagos (tel: 262-0910/4; fax: 261-6568, 262-0920).

Investment Banking & Trust Co Ltd (IBTC), PMB 71707, IBTC Place, Walter Carrington Crescent, Victoria Island, Lagos (tel: 262-6520/40; fax: 262-6541/2; e-mail: IBTC@IBTCLagos.com; internet site: http://www.IBTCLagos.com).

Lion Bank of Nigeria plc, PMB 12852, 121/125 Broad St, Lagos (tel: 266-914, 266-7735).

Nigerian Industrial Development Bank Ltd (NIDB), PMB 2357, NIDB House, 63/71 Broad St, Lagos (tel: 266-3495, 266-1545; fax: 266-7074, 266-6733).

Central bank

Central Bank of Nigeria, PO Box 0187, Zaria Street, Garki, Abuja (tel: 234-3191; fax: 234-3137; e-mail: info@cenbank.org).

Travel information

ADC Airlines (tel: 496-5750; reservations: 496-1942).

Nigeria Airways, PO Box 136, Murtala Muhammed Airport, Lagos (tel: 190-0470).

Ministry of tourism

Federal Ministry of Culture and Tourism, Area 1 Secretariat Complex, Garki, Abuja (tel: 234-2727).

National tourist organisation offices

Nigerian Tourism Developemnt Corporation, Old Secretariat, Area 1, Garki, PMB 167, Abuja (tel: 234-2764; fax: 234-2775; e-mail: information@nigeriatourism.net).

Ministries

Federal Ministry of Agriculture and Rural Development, Area 1 Secretariat Complex, Garki, Abuja (tel: 314-1185).

Federal Ministry of Aviation, New Federal Secretariat Complex, Shehu Shagari Way, Abuja (tel: 523-2112).

Federal Ministry of Commerce, Area 1 Secretariat Complex, Garki, Abuja (tel: 234-1884).

Federal Ministry of Communications, New Federal Secretariat Complex, Shehu Shagari Way, Abuja (tel: 523-7183).

Federal Ministry of Culture and Tourism, Area 1 Secretariat Complex, Garki, Abuja (tel: 234-2727).

Federal Ministry of Defence, Ship House, Central Area, Abuja (tel: 234-0534).

Federal Ministry of Education, New Federal Secretariat Complex, Shehu Shagari Way, Abuja (tel: 523-2800).

Federal Ministry for Federal Capital Territory, Area 11, Garki, Abuja (tel: 523-4014).

Federal Ministry of Finance, Garki, Abuja (tel: 234-4686).

Federal Ministry of Foreign Affairs, Maputo Street, Zone 3 Wuse District, Abuja (tel: 523-0576).

Federal Ministry of Health, New Federal Secretariat Complex, Shehu Shagari Way, Abuja, (tel: 523-0576).

Federal Ministry of Industries, Area 1 Secretariat Complex, Garki, Abuja (tel: 523-0576).

Federal Ministry of Information, Radio House, Herbert Macaulay Way, Garki, Abuja (tel: 234-6350).

Federal Ministry of Internal Affairs, Area 1 Secretariat Complex, Garki, Abuja (tel: 234-6884).

Federal Ministry of Justice, New Federal Secretariat Complex, Shehu Shagari Way, Abuja (tel: 523-5194).

Federal Ministry of Labour and Productivity, New Federal Secretariat Complex, Shehu Shagari Way, Abuja (tel: 523-5980).

Federal Ministry of Police Affairs, New Federal Secretariat Complex, Shehu Shagari Way, Abuja (tel: 523-0549).

Federal Ministry of Power and Steel, New Federal Secretariat Complex, Shehu Shagari Way, Abuja (tel: 523-7064).

Federal Ministry of Science and Technology, New Federal Secretariat Complex, Shehu Shagari Way, Abuja (tel: 523-3397).

Federal Ministry of Solid Minerals Development, New Federal Secretariat Complex, Shehu Shagari Way, Abuja (tel: 523-5830; fax: 523,6518; e-mail: minsolmindev@linkserve.com).

Federal Ministry of Sports and Social Development, New Federal Secretariat Complex, Shehu Shagari Way, Abuja (tel: 523-5905).

Federal Ministry of Transport, National Maritime Agency Building, Central Area, Abuja (tel: 523-7053).

Federal Ministry of Water Resources, Area 1 Secretariat Complex, Garki, Abuja (tel: 234-2376).

Federal Ministry of Women's Affairs and Youth Development, New Federal Secretariat Complex, Shehu Shegari Way, Abuja (tel: 523-7051).

Federal Ministry of Works and Housing, Mabushi Districti, Abuja (tel: 521-1622).

Other useful addresses

African Petroleum plc, AP House, 54-56 Broad Street, PO Box 512, Lagos (tel: 260-0050/9, 260-0145/9; fax: 263-5290).

Bureau of Public Enterprises, 1 Osun Crescent, Off Ibrahim Babangida Way, Maitama, Abuja (tel: 413-4673; fax: 413-4674; internet site: http://www.bpeng.org).

British High Commission, 11 Eleke Crescent, Victoria Island, PO Box 12136, Lagos (tel: 261-9531/7; fax: 261-4021).

Chevron Nigeria Ltd, 2 Chevron Drive, Lekki Peninsular, PMB 12825, Lagos.

Economic Community of West African States (ECOWAS), 6 King George V Road, Lagos (tel: 260-0720/5).

Manufacturers' Association of Nigeria, 12th Floor, Unity House, 37 Marina, PO Box 3835, Lagos.

National Council on Privatisation, Secretariat, Bureau of Public Enterprises, 1 Osun Crescent, Off Ibrahim Babangida Way, Maitama District, PMB 442, Garki, Abuja (tel: 413-4660/4670/4673; fax: 413-4671/4672/4674; e-mail: bpegen@micro.com.ng).

National Maritime Authority, 4 Burma Road, Apapa, Lagos.

National Planning Commission, Federal Secretariat, Shehu Shagari Way, Abuja (tel: 523-6628; fax: 523-6625).

National Science & Technology Development Agency, PO Box 12695, Lagos.

Nigerian Communications Commission, 72 Ahmadu Bello Way, Benue Plaza, Abuja (tel: 234-2327, 234-4590/2; fax: 234-4593; e-mail: ncc@cyberspace.net.ng; internet site: http://www.ncc.gov.ng).

Nigeria Export Processing Zone Authority, 4th Floor, Radio House, Herbert Macauley Way (South), PMB 037, Garki-Abuja (tel: 234-3060; fax: 234-3061).

Nigerian Embassy (USA), 1333 16th Street, NW, Washington DC 20036 (tel:202-986-8400; fax: 202-462-7124).

Nigeria-São Tomé and Príncipe Joint Development Authority, Plot 1101 Aminu Kano Crescent, Wuse II, Abuja (tel: 524-1069; fax: 524-1052; e-mail: enquiries@nigeriasaotomejda.com; internet site: http://www.nigeriasaotomejda.com).

Ports Sector Reforms, Bureau of Public Enterprises, 1 Osun Crescent, Off Ibrahim Babangida Way, Maitama, PMB 442, Garki, Abuja (tel: 413-4634/46; fax: 413-4671/2/4; e-mail: husmanbpeng.org).

Internet sites

Portal site: www.nigerianation.com

Africa Business Network: http://www.ifc.org/abn

AllAfrica.com: http://allafrica.com

African Development Bank: http://www.afdb.org

Africa News Online: http://www.allafrica.com

Africa Online: http://www.africaonline.com

Mbendi AfroPaedia (information on companies, countries, industries and stock exchanges in Africa): http://mbendi.co.za

Movement for the Survival of the Ogoni People (MOSOP): www.mosopcanada.org/index1.html

Niue

COUNTRY PROFILE

Historical profile
The first inhabitants arrived from Tonga, Samoa and Fiji between AD600 and AD1000.
1774 Visited by Captain James Cook and given the name, Savage Island
1846 Conversion to Christianity commenced by the London Missionary Society.
1900 Niue became a British protectorate.
1901 Niue was formally annexed to New Zealand, as part of the Cook Islands.
1960 The first Niue Assembly was established.
1974 Niue was granted 'self-government in free association with New Zealand'. It became the smallest self-governing state with that status.
1982 Robert Rex was elected prime minister.
1992 Robert Rex died. He was succeeded by Young Vivian.
1993 Frank Lui won the election and became prime minister.
1996 Lui was re-elected.
1999 Sani Elia Lakatani of the Niue People's Party (NPP) was elected prime minister.
2001 The US imposed trading sanctions on Niue due its tax haven status. Niue announced plans to launch a satellite communications system by the year 2006.
2002 All 20 members of the Legislative Assembly were re-elected and Young Vivian of the NPP was elected prime minister.
2003 The NPP was dissolved in July, despite which the coalition government continued.
2004 In January, a 300km per hour cyclone, Heta, devastated Niue. Many Niueans living in New Zealand returned to help with the clean-up operation.
2005 In the 30 April parliamentary elections, Prime Minister Young Vivian retained his seat unopposed. He was re-elected prime minister by the Legislative Assembly by 17 votes to three for the independents' candidate, Mrs O'Love Jacobsen. In June the prime minister proposed constitutional changes, whereby the parliamentary term would be extended from three years to five and the cabinet increased from four ministers to six.

Political structure
Constitution
Under the 1974 constitution, New Zealand remains responsible for defence and foreign affairs and is ready to provide necessary economic and administrative assistance. Niueans are New Zealand citizens.
The head of state, the British monarch, is represented in Niue by the Governor General of New Zealand.
Village affairs are handled by 14 village councils of three to five members, elected to three-year terms in conjunction with the Community Affairs Office.
Form of state
Self-governing state, in free association with New Zealand.
The executive
The four-member executive cabinet is headed by a prime minister elected by the Legislative Assembly, who in turn appoints three ministers.
National legislature
The island is governed by a 20-member Legislative Assembly – 14 elected from village constituencies and six from the common roll – elected by popular vote for a three-year term.
Last elections
30 April 2005 (parliamentary)
Results: Parliamentary: 16 of the sitting MPs were elected to continue for another term, plus four new ones. Young Vivian was re-elected prime minister by the Legislative Assembly by 17 votes to three for the independents' candidate, Mrs O'Love Jacobsen.
Next elections
2008 (parliamentary)

Political parties
The Niue political system is not based on formal political organisations. Until 2003, two loose groupings existed: the Niue People's Party (NPP) and the Alliance of Independents. The NPP was dissolved in July 2003 and all candidates in the 2005 elections ran as independents.
Ruling party
There are no political parties
Main opposition party

Political situation
Niue, unlike a number of other Pacific Islands, remains relatively stable. The 2002 elections, in which almost 100 per cent of those eligible to vote did so, returned all 20 incumbent representatives to the Assembly. Constituencies are small and eight of the 14 village candidates were unopposed. The Niue People's Party (NPP) won

KEY FACTS

Official name: Republic of Niue

Head of State: Queen Elizabeth II, represented by the Governor General of New Zealand

Head of government: Prime Minister Young Vivian (elected by the Legislative Assembly May 2002; re-elected May 2005)

Ruling party: There are no political parties

Area: 256 square km

Population: 1,700 (2004); over 20,000 Niueans reside in New Zealand.

Capital: Alofi is the main town.

Official language: English, Niuean

Currency: New Zealand dollar (NZ$) = 100 cents

Exchange rate: NZ$1.44 per US$ (Oct 2005)

GDP per capita: US$3,600 (2003)

GDP real growth: -0.30% (2003)

Inflation: 1.00% (2003)

Balance of trade: -US$2.24 million (2003)

Foreign debt: US$418,000 (2003)

Visitor numbers: 2,558 (2004)

six of the 20 seats and with the support of independents was able to form a coalition government with a majority of 14.
There were disagreements over the 2002/03 budget in mid-2002 which led Prime Minister Young to sack Sani Lakatani (NPP founder) from the cabinet. The NPP was disolved in 2003, but nevertheless the coalition government continued unchanged.
In 2004 the government turned down a potentially lucrative (and probably questionable) scheme to issue Niue passports to South Koreans. As Niue has no rights to issue its own passports (all Niue residents are citizens of New Zealand and hold New Zealand passports) this would have involved special legislation, which would have been unlikely to become law. Niue's High Commissioner to New Zealand, Hima Takelesi, was quoted as saying 'Niue does not want to be associated with anything that is a bit dodgy... It took us long enough to get off the OECD blacklist for offshore banking'.
In May 2004 Mrs O'Love Jacobsen, a former cabinet minister, raised the issue of the allocation of 40 free homes which had been donated by French Polynesia after Cyclone Heta had devasted the island in January. Gaston Flosse, who was president of French Polynesia at the time, had said the homes were to be given to those displaced families who had lost everything; but Mrs Jacobsen accused the government of allocating some of the houses to people who didn't live on the island, or were in villages that had not been in the danger zone. She said that the government appeared to be trying to make money out of the people's misfortunes.

Population
1,700 (2004); over 10,000 Niueans are resident in New Zealand.
Ethnic make-up

Population
1,700 (2004); over 20,000 Niueans reside in New Zealand.
Ethnic make-up
The population is mainly of Polynesian (Tongan) descent, with some New Zealand elements.
Religions
Predominantly Christian.

Education
The education system is modelled on New Zealand's with services provided free until aged 14. For the first four years teaching may be in either Niuean or English.
In 2004, the schools increased the content of Niuean language in the curriculum.
Compulsory years: Five to 14

Health
Total expenditure on health was 7.7 per cent of GDP, in 2001, of which government spending was 97 per cent.

Main cities
Alofi (estimated population 404 in 2004).

Languages spoken
English is widely understood. The people who live in the north speak a Polynesian dialect which differs from the dialect of the people living on the rest of the island who speak a language closer to Tongan.
Official language/s
English, Niuean

Media
Press
The *Niue Star* is a private publication that is published weekly in English and Niue. New Zealand-registered Company Administrative Services' *Niue News* (www.cas.nu/niue_news.htm) has a daily on-line English news service that is provided free by the publishers of the monthly independent *Niue Economic Review* and is maintained by Savage Island Technologies and RockET Systems.
Broadcasting
Controlled by the Broadcasting Corporation of Niue.
Radio: Radio Sunshine broadcasts are transmitted on AM594/FM91 six days/week during limited hours.
Television: Television Niue broadcasts in English and Niue in the evenings only, usually 1730–2200.

Economy
Niue is dependent on New Zealand financial assistance (approximately 25 per cent of total government revenue) for its economic survival.
The economy is mainly agricultural, with the people earning wages on government work and raising vegetables, fruit, pigs and poultry for their own consumption. Industry is limited to agricultural production, although some small building and joinery operations have been started.
Sales of postage stamps and remittances from Niuean workers overseas are important sources of revenue.
Under the Niue Concerted Action Plan, New Zealand aid at around US$3.2 million per annum is designed to make the economy become self-sufficient. Niue has been hit in recent years by reductions of budgetary aid from New Zealand, as the aid programme has come under review. Many investors have left as the future looks uncertain.
In order to boost Niue's meagre income, the government leases international telephone codes for use by foreign companies and has built a quarantine station for alpaca – a wool-bearing llama-like South American mammal – *en route* to Australia. Marketing of the '.nu' Internet domain name has been a controversial income source.
The Niue government has been criticised for allowing the public sector to grow faster than the economy. However, privatisation of the telecommunications, forestry, power and water supplies are planned if buyers could be found for such assets.
The government is also hoping to gain revenue from investment partnerships in fishing and organic products and is seeking interest in developing tourism.
In August 2004, Niue passed a record budget amounting to NZ$24.3 million (US$15.9 million) – US$11,786 per capita. Special project funding was included in the budget to help reconstruction after Cyclone Heta in January 2004.

External trade
There is free trade between Niue and New Zealand.
Imports
Main imports are food, live animals, manufactured goods, machinery, fuels, lubricants, chemicals and medicines.
Main sources: Principally from New Zealand, Fiji, Japan, Samoa, Australia, US.
Exports
Copra, footballs, stamps, handicrafts and agricultural products – coconut cream, honey, vanilla, passion fruit, paw paws, root crops and limes.
Main destinations: Principally to New Zealand, Fiji, Cook Islands, Australia

Agriculture
Farming
Development of agriculture has been hindered by the limited amount of fertile or cultivable land, lack of surface water and susceptibility to drought conditions. Only 20 per cent of land can be used for agriculture. Cyclones are a major problem. Alienation of land is forbidden, but leases may be granted for a maximum term of 66 years.
In March 2004, the UN provided US$700,000, together with four technical advisers, to help set up an irrigation system.
Limes and passion fruit are grown for export. Goats have been introduced on a trial basis.
Production in 2004 included: 2,500 tonnes (t) coconuts, 3,200t taro, 250t sweet potatoes, 120t yams, 110t citrus fruit, 580t fruit in total, 325t oilcrops, 100t vegetables in total, 110t citrus. Livestock production included: 75t meat in total, 55t pig meat, 2t beef, 18t poultry, 12t eggs, 50t milk, 6t honey.
Fishing
Annual fishing production typically includes 200t marine fish. A new fish plant opened in 2004 employing 30 people.

Niue

Forestry
About 20 per cent of the land area is forest with millable timber, and logging serves local demand.
Malaysian logging companies have approached the government to harvest timber from the small hardwood forests. Not everyone is in agreement with such production that could leave the island deforested and the terrain at more risk from cyclones.

Industry and manufacturing
The Office of Economic Affairs is responsible for planning and financing productive ventures relating to agriculture, tourism and industry. Niue Handicrafts handles production and marketing of objects plaited from pandanus and coconut palm leaves.
Small-scale industries include honey extraction and bottling, saw milling, joinery, furniture and handicrafts.
Investment has been made in the vanilla and forestry industries.

Tourism
Development of tourism is a priority, with emphasis on eco-tourism, but has been impeded by poor planning, uncertain air connections with New Zealand and nature in the form of seasonal cyclones. Visitor numbers have been small but rising; 2,758 arrivals were recorded in 2003. Additional Polynesian Airlines flights were announced in November 2002. The devastating Cyclone Heta in January 2004 damaged infrastructure and many of the island's scenic attractions. By June 2004 tourist services were back to normal and arrivals for the year totalled 2,558.

Hydrocarbons
Niue does not produce any hydrocarbons and relies on imports to meet domestic energy needs. Niue imports refined oil and imports around 20 barrels per day. Niue does not import gas or coal.

Banking and insurance
Central bank
Reserve Bank of New Zealand
Offshore facilities
In 2002, the introduction of US sanctions on banking activities was a major blow to Niue. The US accused Niue of having connections to Latin American tax haven operations.
Niue licensed six offshore banks operating in Australia, which the Organisation for Economic Co-operation and Development (OECD) wanted to close down. In June 2002, the Niue Legislative Assembly repealed the legislation which authorised the issuing of banking licences and Niue was removed from the OECD Financial Action Task Force (FATF) blacklist of places associated with money laundering.

Following the government's decision in 2004 not to renew four offshore banking licences, the international business company registry of Mossack Fonseca of Panama was informed that its operations would be shut down by the end of 2006.

Time
GMT minus eleven hours

Geography
Niue is a coral island in the Pacific Ocean about 480km (300 miles) east of Tonga and 930km (580 miles) west of the southern Cook Islands.

Climate
Subtropical and humid, with temperature 25–30 degrees Celsius and average rainfall of nearly 200cm per annum.

Entry requirements
Passports
Required by all.
Visa
Not required by tourist visitors staying less than 30 days. Visitors are required to have return/onward tickets and sufficient funds for length of stay and suitable accommodation. Visitors may extend their stay by applying to the Immigration officials upon arrival, an extension permit of three months (cost of NZD$30) is usually granted.
Further information may be obtained from the Immigration Department, PO Box 69, Alofi, Niue Island (email: immigrationniue@mail.gov.nu).
Prohibited imports
Firearms and ammunition.

Health (for visitors)
Mandatory precautions
Vaccination certificates for yellow fever are required if travelling from infected area.
Advisable precautions
Vaccinations for diphtheria, TB, hepatitis 'A' and 'B', polio, tetanus and typhoid are all recommended. There is a rabies risk. It is advisable to take water precautions.

Public holidays
Fixed dates
1 Jan (New Year's Day), 4 Jan (Takai Commission Holiday), 6 Feb (Waitangi Day), 25 Apr (Anzac Day), 16–19 Oct (Constitution Celebrations), 17 Oct (Peniamina's Day), 25 Dec (Christmas Day), 26 Dec (Boxing Day).
Variable dates
Good Friday, Easter Monday, Queen's Official Birthday (first Mon in Jun).

Working hours
Banking
Mon–Thur: 0900–1500; Fri: 0830–1500.
Business
Mon–Fri: 0730–1530.

Shops
Mon–Fri: 0830–1600; Sat: 0830–1500.

Telecommunications
Telecom Niue is the island's largest generator of revenue. Media reports claimed that Nuie was a centre of internet pornography and this brought controversy to the island as officials claimed the island was not responsible for the material; Niue leases its internet domain suffix .nu to a US company.
Telephone/fax
Fully automatic service is available to Niue on a 24-hour basis.
Mobile phones
The Harris Cellular Network provides fixed and mobile coverage for Niue.
Internet/e-mail
Internet User's Society Niue (IUS-N) provides free non-commercial e-mail and Internet on-line connections to permanent residents of Niue and approved governmental departmental users.
In 2003, IUS-N launched free broadband Internet services for locals at its island Internet café and the world's first free nationwide WiFi Internet access service.

Social customs/useful tips
It is customary to shake hands on meeting and taking leave. Gratuities are not encouraged.

Getting there
Air
There are connections from Auckland, New Zealand; Sydney, Australia; Samoa; Fiji and Los Angeles, US.
International airport/s: Hanan (IUE), 7km north of Alofi.
Airport tax: International departures NZ$25.
Surface
There are no port facilities. Ships anchor off Alofi and barges transfer cargo.

Getting about
National transport
Road: There are approximately 130km of all-weather road and 96km bush track negotiable by heavy trucks and four-wheel drive vehicles. A 60km road circles the island and roads link main centres.
Car hire
Visitors with an overseas driver's licence must obtain a local licence from the Niue police department before driving a hired vehicle. It is advisable to reserve hire vehicles before arrival.
Driving is on the left.

BUSINESS DIRECTORY
The addresses listed below are a selection only. While World of Information makes every endeavour to check these addresses, we cannot guarantee that changes have not been made, especially

to telephone numbers and area codes. We would welcome any corrections.

Telephone area codes
The international direct dialling code (IDD) for Niue is +683 followed by subscriber's number.

Useful telephone numbers
Police, fire and ambulance:999/4000
Hospital:998.

Chambers of Commerce
Niue Chamber of Commerce and Industry, PO Box 160, Alofi (tel: 43-99; fax: 40-17; e-mail: chamber@sin.net.nu).

Banking
Westpac Banking Corporation, PO Box 76, Alofi (tel: 4221; fax: 4043).

Central bank
The Reserve Bank of New Zealand, PO Box 2498, Wellington, New Zealand (tel: 0064-4-472-2029; fax: 0064-4-4738554).

Travel information
Air Nauru, Government Building, Yaren District, Republic of Nauru (tel: (674)3141, 3418; fax: (674)3170).

Niue Immigration Office, PO Box 67, Alofi.

Niue International Airport (Hanan), PO Box 83, Alofi (tel: 4020, 4133, 4096; fax: 4010).

National tourist organisation offices
Niue Tourism Office, PO Box 42, Alofi (tel: 4224; fax: 4225; internet site: http://www.niueisland.com).

Other useful addresses
Broadcasting Corporation of Niue, PO Box 26, Alofi (tel: 4026; fax: 4217).

Business Advisory Service, Alofi (tel: 4228).

Office of Economic Affairs, PO Box 42, Alofi (tel: 4126).

Office of the Prime Minister. PO Box 40, Alofi (tel: 4200; fax: 4206, 4232).

Office of the Secretary to Government, PO Box 67, Alofi (tel: 4017; fax: 4232).

Internet sites
Niue government website: http://www.gov.nu

Niue website: http://www.niueisland.nu

South Pacific Tourism Organisation: http://www.tcsp.com/niue/index.html

Norfolk Island

COUNTRY PROFILE

Historical profile
1774 First European sighting of Norfolk Island by Captain James Cook. He named the island in honour of the Ninth Duchess of Norfolk.
1788 Norfolk Island was occupied by the British.
1790 A settlement was established to supply the New South Wales penal colony.
1814 The settlement was abandoned.
1825 The island was re-settled as a penal colony.
1856 The British authorities moved the 193 descendants of the *Bounty* mutineers from Pitcairn Island to Norfolk Island.
1858 16 Pitcairners returned to Pitcairn Island after a dispute with the British about land ownership. Other Pitcairners followed.
1897 Norfolk Island became a dependency of New South Wales.
1914 Norfolk Island became a Territory under the authority of the Commonwealth of Australia.
1979 The Norfolk Island Act conferred a measure of self-government.
1992 Norfolk Islanders became entitled to vote in elections for the Australian parliament.
2000 Norfolk Islanders signed a deal with researchers to study the population for genes that predispose people to high blood pressure or migraines.

Political structure
Constitution
The Norfolk Island Act of 1979 provides for an administrator appointed by the governor general of Australia and responsible to the Australian government, a Legislative Assembly and Executive Council. The Act provides that proposed laws passed by the Legislative Assembly must be presented to the administrator for assent.
Both the Legislative Assembly and Executive Council are presided over by the president of the Legislative Assembly.
Since 1992, Norfolk Islanders are entitled to vote in elections for the Australian parliament.
Form of state
Self-governing Territory of Australia
The executive
The Executive Council is made up of four of the members of the Legislative Assembly. Each member of the Executive Council holds the position of Minister and has one or more portfolios. The Executive Council devises governmental policy and advises the administrator on all matters relating to the government of the island.
National legislature
There is a nine-member Legislative Assembly elected for a three-year term.
Legal system
The judicial system consists of a Supreme Court and a Court of Petty Sessions.
Last elections
20 October 2004 (parliamentary)
Results: Parliamentary: Chief Minister Geoffrey Robert Gardner won with 17.2 per cent of the vote. Turnout was 91.2 per cent.
Next elections
2007 (parliamentary)

Political parties
There are no political parties.
Ruling party

Population
2,828 (2005)*
Ethnic make-up
Approximately 37 per cent of the permanent population were born on Norfolk Island (of which 47 per cent are of Pitcairn descent), 31 per cent were born on the Australian mainland and 23 per cent were born in New Zealand.
Religions
Anglicans (40 per cent), Roman Catholics (12 per cent), Uniting Church of Australia (16 per cent) and Seventh-Day Adventist (5 per cent).

Education
Infant, primary and secondary schooling is provided by the Norfolk Island Government. Education is free until the age of 15.
Compulsory years: six to 15

Main cities
Burnt Pine, Kingston.

Languages spoken
English is spoken in business circles. Norfolk, a dialect derived from the language evolved by the *Bounty* mutineers and their Tahitian wives (a mixture of mainly English and Tahitian) and brought by settlers from Pitcairn Island in the nineteenth century, is also in use.
Official language/s
English.

Media
Press
The local weekly newspaper *The Norfolk Islander* is published every Saturday. National newspapers from Australia and New Zealand are available depending on mainland flights.

KEY FACTS

Official name: Norfolk Island

Head of State: Queen Elizabeth II and Australia are represented by Administrator Grant Tambling (since 1 Nov 2003).

Head of government: Assembly President and Chief Minister Geoffrey Robert Gardner (since 2001; re-elected 20 Oct 2004)

Area: 35 square km

Population: 2,828 (2005)*

Capital: Kingston

Official language: English.

Currency: Australian dollar (A$) = 100 cents

Exchange rate: A$1.31 per US$ (Oct 2005)

Labour force: 1,345 (2005)*

Visitor numbers: 40,000 (annually)

* estimated figure

Nations of the World: A Political, Economic and Business Handbook

Broadcasting
Radio: Radio VL2NI is government-owned and locally-run.
Television: TVN is a privately-owned station. Australian Broadcasting Corporation programmes are relayed by satellite.

Economy
Norfolk Island's economy is based largely on its tourist industry, catering mainly to visitors from Australia and New Zealand. It receives no direct grants or aid from Australia.
Australian income tax and other federal taxes, such as property tax or stamp duty, do not apply in Norfolk Island.
Australia has restored a number of historic buildings and provides certain technical services for public works on the island.
In addition to importing most of its requirements, Norfolk Island has developed a re-export industry geared to its tourist industry. Sales of re-export goods to tourists have, however, been inhibited by the imposition of an A$400 (US$250) duty-free limit by the Australian government.
Sales of Norfolk Island postage stamps contribute to the island's revenue.

External trade
Imports
Main imports are fuel, food, consumer goods, alcohol, building materials, jewellery, footwear and clothing.
Imports totalled US$17.90 million in 2003.
Main sources: Australia, neighbouring Pacific islands, NZ and EU
Exports
Main exports are Norfolk Island pine, kentia palm and gerbera seeds, avocados and some wood and ceramics local crafts and postage stamps.
Exports totalled US$1.50 million in 2003.
Main destinations: Australia, neighbouring Pacific islands, NZ and EU

Agriculture
Farming
Only 12 per cent of land is cultivatable so production is constrained by poor terrain, porous soil, a low water table and fragmented holdings. Many farms are run on a part-time basis. Crops tend to be seasonal, and provide cereals, vegetables and fruit. There is a successful commercial hydroponic vegetable garden. Livestock is limited to cattle and poultry and the island is self-sufficient in beef, poultry and eggs.
Fishing
The lack of a harbour restricts fisheries development, and catches serve local consumption only.
Forestry
The Norfolk Island pine and kentia palm seeds are an important export and some hardwood afforestation is being undertaken.

Industry and manufacturing
The island produces its own handicrafts, chocolates, beers, liqueurs (including an 'aromatised whiskey' called *Convict's Curse*) and arabica coffee. Grapes are being planted for a wine industry.

Tourism
Since the mid-1960s, tourism has been the mainstay of the island's economy. The Norfolk Island Government Tourist Bureau promotes Norfolk Island in Australia and New Zealand, the island's primary markets. Approximately 40,000 tourists visit Norfolk Island each year.
It is a sub-tropical island with world-class scuba diving and fishing. There are areas of sub-tropical rainforest, much of it protected in national parks, with a network of tracks which is ideal for walking, birdwatching, cycling or horse riding.

Hydrocarbons
There are unexploited offshore oil and gas fields.

Energy
Norfolk Island Administration is the electricity supply authority. Electricity is expensive and in limited supply.

Banking and insurance
There are branches of the Commonwealth Bank of Australia (which has an ATM) and Westpac Banking Corporation on the island.

Time
GMT plus eleven and a half hours.

Geography
Norfolk Island lies off the eastern coast of Australia about 1,400km east of Brisbane, to the south of New Caledonia and 640km north of New Zealand. Norfolk Island is hilly and fertile, with a coastline of cliffs. It is about 8km long and 4.8km wide. The territory also includes uninhabited Phillip Island 7km south of the main island.

Climate
The island has a sub-tropical climate. Temperatures can range from 11–27 degrees Celsius, with an average rainfall of 1,346mm per year. November tends to be the driest month and the wetter months are May to August. Most rain falls at night. Average morning humidity is around 80 per cent.

Dress codes
Clothing should be comfortable and casual to suit the subtropical climate. A sweater is advisable on winter nights. A hat and sunscreen are necessary in summer.

Entry requirements
Passports
Required for all, except for a stay of up to three months by holders of a Document of Identity issued to citizens of Australia.
Visa
Required by all, except Australian and New Zealand citizens. Norfolk Island is a self-governing Australian Territory and visas must be obtained in advance from Australian consulates.
Most citizens of EU and North America can apply for an Electronic Travel Authority (ETA), issued by a travel agent or airline, or can be applied for online. Visit www.eta.immi.gov.au for details of those eligible, and follow links to the application site. ETA-eligible business visitors may stay for up to three months without additional documentation.
Those not eligible for an ETA must apply using form 456, through the nearest embassy or mission. Business visas will require: a letter of invitation from a local company or organisation, a business letter from an employer stating purpose of trip and details of employee's function, proof of sufficient funds, and a full itinerary. Further details and application form can be obtained at www.immi.gov.au/allforms. Confirmed accommodation must be obtained prior to arrival.
Currency advice/regulations
There are no restrictions on import and export of local and foreign currency.
Prohibited imports
Imports of fruit, vegetables, flowers and seeds; pork and poultry from New Zealand are also prohibited.

Health (for visitors)
Mandatory precautions
Vaccination certificates required for yellow fever if travelling from infected area.
Advisable precautions
Vaccination for diphtheria, TB, hepatitis 'A' and 'B', polio, tetanus, typhoid. Rabies is a risk.

Public holidays
Fixed dates
1 Jan (New Year's Day), 26 Jan (Australia Day), 6 Mar (Foundation Day), 25 Apr (Anzac Day), 8 Jun (Bounty Day), 25 Dec (Christmas Day), 26 Dec (Boxing Day). If Christmas Day or New Year's Day falls on a Saturday, the next Monday is given as a holiday.
Variable dates
Good Friday, Easter Monday, Queen's Official Birthday (second Mon in Jun), Thanksgiving Day (last Wed in Nov).

Working hours
Banking
Mon–Thu: 0930–1600; Fri: 0930–1700.

Norfolk Island

Business
Mon, Tue and Thu, Fri: 0900–1700; Wed and Sat: 0900–1200.

Shops
Traditionally trading hours are from 0900–1700. Some shops close for lunch between 1230 and 1400. Most shops close on Wed and Sat afternoon, and all day Sunday. Supermarkets and newsagents are open seven days a week.

Telecommunications
Telephone/fax
International Direct Dialling telephones, telegrams and facsimile services are available on the island. Public IDD coin operated telephone booths are open 24 hours. Local calls are free of charge.

Postal services
Norfolk Island has its own postal service and produces its own postage stamps.

Mobile phones
In 2002, the Norfolk Island residents voted against allowing a mobile phone service on the Island.

Electricity supply
Diesel generated 240V 50 cycles.

Social customs/useful tips
Tipping is not expected. It is customary to shake hands on meeting and taking leave. Punctuality on social occasions is appreciated.

Getting there
Air
The Norfolk Jet Express flies from Sydney and Brisbane (Australia) and Auckland (New Zealand).
International airport/s: Norfolk (NLK).
Airport tax: A$30 for international departures, payable at the airport when leaving or at the Visitor Information Centre prior to departure.
Surface
Water: Ships anchor offshore.

Getting about
National transport
Road: The entire road network amounts to 200km.
Buses: There is no public transport system on the island, but tour buses are available for tourists.
City transport
Taxis: There is a limited taxi service.
Car hire
Arrangements may be made locally for hiring cars, motorcycles and bicycles.

BUSINESS DIRECTORY
The addresses listed below are a selection only. While World of Information makes every endeavour to check these addresses, we cannot guarantee that changes have not been made, especially to telephone numbers and area codes. We would welcome any corrections.

Telephone area codes
The international direct dialling (IDD) code for Norfolk Island is +672, followed by area code 3 and subscriber's number.

Useful telephone numbers
Police: 922
Fire: 955
Ambulance: 911

Banking
Commonwealth Bank of Australia, Burnt Pine (tel: 2144).

Westpac Banking Corporation, Burnt Pine (tel: 2120).

Travel information
Norfolk Island Government Tourist Bureau, PO Box 211, Norfolk Island 2899 (tel: 22-147; fax: 23-109; e-mail: info@norfolkisland.com.au).

Internet sites
Norfolk Island website:
　http://www.norfolk.gov.nf
　http://www.pitcairners.org

Northern Marianas

KEY FACTS

Official name: Commonwealth of the Northern Mariana Islands

Head of State: President George W Bush

Head of government: Governor Benigno R Fital (Covenent) (took office Jan 2006)

Ruling party: Covenant Party (since 1 Nov 2003)

Area: 471 square km (14 islands) – Saipan (122 square km); Tinian (101 square km)

Population: 78,800 (2004)

Capital: Garapan (Saipan)

Official language: English

Currency: US dollar (US$) = 100 cents

GDP per capita: US$12,500 (2003)

Labour force: 6,010 (2003)

Inflation: 1.20% (2003)

COUNTRY PROFILE

Historical profile
Ancestors of the native Chamorros settled on the islands in about 2000 BC.
1521 Magellan claimed the islands for Spain.
1698 The native population was transferred to Guam.
1899 The Germans bought the islands from the Spaniards.
1914 The Japanese seized the islands from the Germans.
1947 Northern Marianas was the first Japanese territory in the Western Pacific to be invaded by the US; it became a part of the Trust Territory of the Pacific Islands (TTPI), administered by the US, under a mandate granted by the UN.
1975 The islands became self-governing with a bicameral legislature after a referendum.
1984 American civil and political rights were made available to the islands' residents.
1986 Following the end of the UN mandate, the islands acquired US Commonwealth status. Residents were granted US citizenship.
1990 The UN Security Council formally terminated the Trusteeship in December. Under the covenant, the US has responsibility for foreign affairs and defence.
1997 Pedro Tenorio was elected governor, having been out of office for eight years.
2001 The Republican Party was re-elected and Juan Babauta (Republican) was elected governor.
2003 The Covenant Party won the 1 November parliamentary elections.
2004 On 31 March, Anatahan's active volcano had a small eruption. On 29 June, Governor Juan N Babauta declared a state of emergency due to the extensive damage caused by Typhoon Tingting. Northern Marianas and Guam were struck by Supertyphoon Chaba in August and a second 30-day state of emergency was declared.
2005 Numerous (over 500) small earthquakes were recorded in three uninhabited islands. Anatahan volcano also continued erupting, with a big eruption in April sending ashfall up to 15,000 metres, reaching as far as Palau and the Philippines.

Political structure
Constitution
The 1986 constitution provides for an executive governor and a bicameral legislature. Northern Marianan citizens have US citizenship while having control over internal affairs. They do not vote in US elections.
Form of state
Self-governing commonwealth in political union with the US
The executive
An executive governor and lieutenant governor are elected every four years by universal suffrage.
National legislature
A bicameral legislature consisting of an 18-member House of Representatives (elected every two years) and a nine-member Senate (with staggered terms), all elected in single-seat constituencies for two-year terms.
Legal system
Most US laws apply except in taxation, customs, immigration and minimum wages.
Last elections
5 November 2005 (parliamentary and gubernatorial).
Results: Parliamentary: the Covenant Party won seven seats out of 18 in the House of Representatives, the Republicans seven, the Democrats two and independents two. In the Senate, the Covenant Party won three seats out of nine, the Republicans three, the Democrats two and independents one.
Gubernatorial: Benigno R Fitial (Covenant Party) won with 28.1 per cent of the vote, Heinz S Hofschneider (independent) 27.3 per cent, Juan Babauta (Republican) 26.6 per cent, Froilan C Tenorio (Democrat) 18 per cent.
Next elections
November 2007 (parliamentary), November 2009 (gubernatorial).

Political parties
Ruling party
Covenant Party (since 1 Nov 2003)
Main opposition party
Democratic Party (DEM)

Political situation
The Commonwealth of the Northern Mariana Islands (CNMI) has no direct representation in the US Congress – its interests are looked after by the delegate from Guam. A bill to rectify this and create a delegate seat for the CNMI in the US House of Representatives failed to pass the 108th Congress in 2004. However, a second bill instruduced in early 2005 is expected to pass, in which case the election for the CNMI's first elected congressional delegate will be in 2006.

Northern Marianas

Corruption and illegal activities, although not necessarily by politicians, have bruised the reputation of Northern Marianas. Two senators were convicted for fraud while a number of members of the legislature were accused of legal impropriety and four people were convicted following the collapse of the Bank of Saipan, where several government agencies held multi-million dollar accounts.

Population
78,800 (2004)
Ethnic make-up
There are tensions between the resident population and people from other countries – Philippines, Republic of Korea, Thailand and China. Approximately 75 per cent of the native population is Chamorro, the rest are Carolinian.
Religions
Roman Catholic and indigenous beliefs.

Education
Education is based on the US system. There are several private schools available to cater for the international community.
Literacy rate: 97 per cent, adult rate.
Compulsory years: Six to 16

Health
The major medical needs of the population are met by the Commonwealth Health Centre (CHC). The CHC operates inpatient and outpatient services. There is 24-hour emergency care available provided by a team of emergency nurses, emergency physicians and support staff. In addition to the CHC, there are several private health clinics. All medical services are required to meet US standards, although the cost of medical care is much cheaper than in the US.

Main cities
Garapan (Saipan) (capital, population 4,105), San Antonio and Koblerville.

Main islands
Six islands, including the three largest (Saipan, Tinian and Rota) are inhabited.

Languages spoken
Chamorro and Carolinian are the native tongues and are widely spoken. Japanese and Korean are also spoken.
Official language/s
English

Media
Press
The English language dailies include *Saipan Tribune* and *Marianas Variety* with local and international news. Other publications are *Marianas Review* and *Marianas Focus*. Several regional daily and weekly publications in circulation include *Pacific Chronicle* carrying local news from Phillippines, *Saipan Shinbun* in Japanese and *Pacific Daily News*.
Broadcasting
Radio: Broadcasts by KSAI Radio (religious station), KYOI Radio and KCNM-AM/KZMI-FM (both commercial).
Television: TV transmission by cable and satellite.

Economy
The economy of the islands is small and has few natural resources. Bilateral aid from the US remains an important source of income, particularly aid directed towards improving the inadequate infrastructure. Tourism and textiles, the mainstays of the economy, both suffered set backs in 2005.
By July 2005 four major garment factories had closed with over 2,000, most non-residents, left without work. The factory closures are caused by the ending of the Multi-Fibre Agreement (MFA) whereby the Commonwealth of the Northern Mariana Islands (CNMI) and other developing countries had been allowed to export garments, which in the case of the CNMI was principally to the US.
Tourism is the leading foreign exchange earner, with Japanese tourists making up some 70–75 per cent of visitors. However, Japanese airline, JAL, announced that it would be stopping its two flights a day in October 2005. A report commissioned by the CNMI Strategic Economic Development Council estimated that the islands stood to lose over US$200 million in tourism revenue annually, and over 2,500 jobs. There were more than 535,000 tourists to CNMI in 2004, with an average spend of US$685 per visitor. In August there was hope that Japan's second airline, All Nippon Airways (ANA), would be able to replace some of JAL's flights.
It was reported in August 2005 that a Seattle-based fishing company had secured the necessary permissions to begin long-line fishing, for swordfish, tuna and other species, from the islands.
Typhoon damage had been extensive in 2004, when the islands were struck by typhoon Tingting in June and by supertyphoon Chaba in August. Estimates put the damage caused by Chaba at around US$18 million.

External trade
Main trading partners: US and Japan.
Imports
Principal imports are food, construction equipment and materials and petroleum products.
Main sources: US, Japan
Exports
The principal export is garments; minor exports include livestock, tuna fish, fruit and vegetables.
Main destinations: Mainly to US

Agriculture
Farming
The agricultural sector contributes approximately 14 per cent to annual GDP. Cultivable land is rich and volcanic. Vegetables such as coconuts, breadfruit, tomatoes, melons and cucumbers are widely grown on smallholdings. Livestock is reared for export. The copra industry is also important.
Fishing
The fishing sector has revived following a blanket ban in some areas, introduced in 2000, due to over-fishing. Stocks include black-tip sharks, tuna, emperor ship and bonito. Tuna is transshipped en route to the US via the canneries at Pago Pago (Fagatogo) in American Samoa.

Industry and manufacturing
The industrial sector contributed approximately 19 per cent to annual GDP while the garment industry flourished under the Multi-Fibre Agreement (MFA). However, when this ended in 2004 exports to the US were threatened by even cheaper exports from China and a number of factories closed, putting some 2,000 workers out of their jobs.
Other industrial activity consists of construction, small-scale fish processing and handicrafts manufacture.

Tourism
Tourism is an important sector of the economy, though not as dominant as it was during the 1990s. Japan continues to provide the vast majority of visitors, followed by Korea and, to a lesser extent, the US. The industry's fortunes changed in response to Japan's 1997 economic recession. There had been 736,117 arrivals in 1996, which fell to 490,165 in 1998, although numbers rose thereafter they fell back to below 500,000 as a consequence of the 11 September 2001 terrorist attacks in the US. In 2004 visitor numbers were back over the half million mark, but the cancellation of JAL's twice weekly flights from Tokyo from October 2005 is expected to have a devasting affect unless Japan's second airline, ANA, can replace the flights. Japanese make up 70–75 per cent of visitors.
Direct tourism revenue in 2004 was US$367 million, with indirect revenue estimated at US$733 million. Without JAL's flights direct revenue could fall to as low as US$216 million.

Banking and insurance
Central bank
Federal Reserve

Time
GMT plus 10 hours

Nations of the World: A Political, Economic and Business Handbook

Geography
The Northern Marianas comprises 16 islands (all the Marianas excluding Guam) in the western Pacific Ocean, about 5,300km (3,300 miles) west of Honolulu, Hawaii.

Climate
The climate is tropical marine.

Entry requirements
Passports
Passports required by all except US citizens with proof of citizenship.
Visa
Visas are required by all. Visitors from the Americas, EU, Australisia and Japan may visit visa-free for up to 30 days. Other visitors should contact the Division of Immigration – see www.mymarianas.com for details. Such applications must be made four weeks before intended departure.
Currency advice/regulations
The US dollar is the official currency. There are no restrictions on import and export of local and foreign currency.

Health (for visitors)
Mandatory precautions
Vaccination certificate required for yellow fever if travelling from an infected area.
Advisable precautions
Vaccination for diphtheria, TB, hepatitis 'A' and 'B', polio, tetanus, typhoid. Rabies risk.
Water from the mains is usually chlorinated and although safe to drink, may cause mild abdominal upsets. Drinking water outside the main cities and towns may be contaminated. Sterilisation by boiling is thus advisable.
Full medical facilities are available, although they are not free of charge. Health insurance is advisable.

Hotels
There is a 10 per cent hotel tax. A tip of 10–15 per cent is usual.

Credit cards
Major credit cards are accepted on Saipan and at car rental agencies on Rota.

Working hours
Banking
Mon–Thu: 0900–1500, Fri: 1000–1800.
Business
Mon–Fri: 0800–1200, 1300–1700.
Government
Mon–Fri: 0730–1130, 1230–1630.
Shops
Mon–Sat: 0800–2000, Sun: 0800–1800.

Electricity supply
220/240V, 50Hz

Weights and measures
Imperial

Getting there
Air
International airport/s: Saipan International (SPN), 5km south-east of Chalan Kanoa, duty-free shops, bar, restaurant, currency exchange, handicraft shop and car hire.
Airport tax: There is no departure tax.
Surface
Main port/s: Saipan, Tinian, Rota.

Getting about
National transport
Air: There are several daily flights between Saipan and Tinian and between Rota and Saipan.
Road: Roads are good on the main islands, particularly around the main centres. Driving is on the right-hand side.
Buses: There is no public bus system on Saipan, although shuttle buses run between the major towns.
Water: There are sea links between the islands.
City transport
Taxis: A taxi service is available on Saipan. Taxis are metered and privately owned.
Buses, trams & metro: Tour bus from airport to city centre, journey time is about 15 minutes.

BUSINESS DIRECTORY
The addresses listed below are a selection only. While World of Information makes every endeavour to check these addresses, we cannot guarantee that changes have not been made, especially to telephone numbers and area codes. We would welcome any corrections.

Telephone area codes
The international direct dialling (IDD) code for Northern Marianas is +1 670, followed by area code:

Rota	532	Tinian	433
Susupe City	234		

Useful telephone numbers
Police: 911

Chambers of Commerce
Saipan Chamber of Commerce, PO Box 500806, Saipan MP 96950 (tel: 233-7150; fax: 233-7151; e-mail: saipanchamber@saipan.com).

Banking
Central bank
Bank of Saipan, PO Box 500690, Saipan MP 96950 (tel: 235-6260; fax: 235-1802; email: bankofsaipan@saipan.com).

Travel information
Continental Micronesia (formerly Air Micronesia), PO Box 138CK, Saipan MP 96950 (tel: 234-8223; fax: 234-8358).

Marianas Visitors Bureau, PO Box 861, Saipan MP 96950 (tel: 234-8325/8327; fax: 234-3596).

Office of Immigration, Saipan 96950.

Saipan International Airport, PO Box 1055, Saipan 96950 (tel: 664-3500/01; fax: 234-5962; e-mail: cpa.admin@saipan.com).

Travel Bureau, PO Box 503 Rota (tel: 532-3561; fax: 532-3562).

Internet sites
Commonwealth of the Northern Marianas General Information: http://www.cnmi.net/

Government of Northern Marianas Homepage http://www.marianas-islands.gov.mp/

Newspapers and Media http://www.kidon.com/media-link/northernmarianas.html

US Office of Insular affairs: http://www.doi.gov/oia

Norway

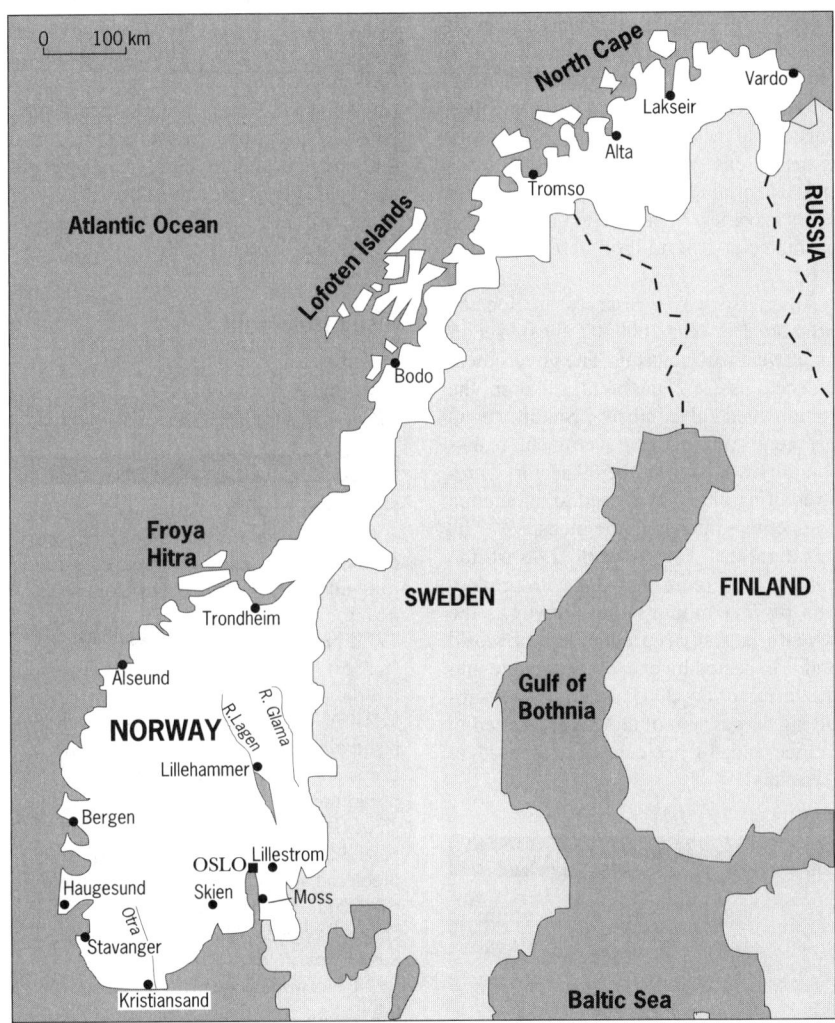

KEY FACTS

Official name: Kongeriket Norge (Kingdom of Norway)

Head of State: King Harald V

Head of government: Prime Minister Jens Stoltenberg (DNA) (since 2000, re-elected September 2005)

Ruling party: Coalition: Det Norske Arbeiderparti (DNA) (Norwegian Labour Party), Sosialistisk Venstreparti (SV) (Socialist Left Party), Senterparti (SP) (Centre Party) (since September 2005)

Area: 323,985 square km

Population: 4.58 million (2004)

Capital: Oslo

Official language: Norwegian

Currency: Norwegian krone (Nkr) = 100 ore

Exchange rate: Nkr6.59 per US$ (Jul 2005)

GDP per capita: US$54,521 (2004)

GDP real growth: 2.90% (OECD, 2004)(2004)

Labour force: 2.36 million (2004)

Unemployment: 4.40% (OECD, 2004)

Inflation: 0.40% (2004)

Oil production: 3.19 million bpd (2004)

Balance of trade: US$33.58 billion (2004)

Foreign debt: US$292.43 billion (2004)

Annual FDI: US$36.50 billion (cumulative, 1995–2004, OECD); US$2.20 billion (OECD, 2004)*

* estimated figure

The archetypal stable European state, Norway is a constitutional monarchy complete with a parliamentary system of government. The King of Norway's power is almost exclusively ceremonial, with the majority of power being in the hands of the office of the prime minister. The current prime minister is Jens Stoltenberg of the Det norske Arbeiderparti/Arbeiderpartiet (DNA /AP) (Norwegian Labour Party). Stoltenberg is considered by most Norwegian and external political commentators to be on the right wing of the DNA, which is a broadly centre-left political party.

The telegenic 46-year old Stoltenberg has been leader of the DNA since 2002. On 12 September 2005 Stoltenberg led his party to electoral triumph and went on to form a broad coalition with the Sosialistisk Venstreparti (SV) Socialist Left Party and the Senterpartiet (SP) (Centre Party). The forming of the coalition government marked a historic moment in the country's political history, as DNA joined a coalition government for the first time.

Stoltenberg's victory in the 2005 election meant that he assumed the premiership for the second time in his political career. The DNA leader had previously assumed the country's political leadership back in 2001 following a power struggle within the governing party. In the 2005 election the DNA won 61 of a total of 87 seats won by the broad coalition, out of a grand total of 169, on a turn out of over 77 per cent.

Economy

In terms of GDP per capita, Norway is one of the wealthiest countries in the world. The economy is unique among Western European countries for its large and dominant offshore sector. Oil and gas extraction accounts for about 19 per cent of the country's GDP. Since the 1980s the economy has experienced a major structural change, becoming increasingly focussed on service industries, which account for about 37 per cent of GDP. Traditional primary sectors, like agriculture, forestry and fishing, have declined in terms of their contribution to GDP.

The buoyant energy sector has provided the country with strong fundamentals with which to ride out global shocks, most recently the global economic slowdown in 2001 and 2002, and which presented no long-term threat to growth. Income from oil exports is invested in the Petroleum Fund, some of which is used for the fiscal budget, but the main longer-term purpose is to prime the economy once oil reserves decline. In 2005, the value of Norway's Petroleum Fund stood at US$179 billion.

A key challenge for the government is the tight nature of its labour market, especially in the construction and health sectors. Norwegian firms have had to look abroad to fill vacancies as the unemployment rate is relatively low at around 4 per cent. Shortages in the labour market have caused high wage growth, leading to a loss of competitiveness in Norwegian exports.

Natural resources

Norway is the world's third largest net oil exporter after Saudi Arabia and Russia. Oil production doubled in the 1990s as improved recovery techniques were introduced and new wells came on stream. Reserves of 8.5 billion barrels (2005) ensure that production can carry on for many years to come. Oil production in 2004 was estimated at 3.31 million barrels per day (bpd).

All of Norway's reserves are located offshore. Between 2000–02, the oil sector underwent restructuring. The government reduced its 78.2 per cent stake in the state-owned oil company, Statoil, to 60 per cent. While the government resists foreign ownership of the oil sector, its restructuring plan is designed to maintain a competitive interest in the industry.

Natural gas reserves were 2.46 trillion cubic metres (cum) in 2004 with production of 73.4 billion cum. Norway is the seventh-largest gas producer in the world and is expected by end-2005 to move into the top five. By 2005, Norway was supplying 30 per cent of the gas consumed in France and 40 per cent of that used in Germany.

Outlook

Prime Minister Jens Stoltenberg's victory in the 2005 parliamentary elections means that his DNA party will govern as part of a coalition government for the first time. The broad based nature of the coalition may cause some problems somewhere down the road, as competing interest groups battle for prominence within the governing élite. For the time being at least Stoltenberg should be able to govern successfully as a unifying, centrist figure. Norway's economy remains strong and the country should continue to record steady levels of growth in 2005 (3.1 per cent) and 2006 (3.2 per cent), respectively, in accordance with the IMF's latest forecast.

Risk assessment

Politics	Good
Economy	Good
Regional stability	Excellent

COUNTRY PROFILE

Historical profile
1397 Under the Kalmar Union, the Kingdom of Norway ceased to exist as a separate nation and was ruled by Danish governors.
1720 Norway, a dominion of Denmark, was lost to Sweden following the Great Nordic War.
1814 An *Act of Union* with Sweden recognised Norway as an independent Kingdom with its own constitution and parliament.
1905 The Norwegian parliament dissolved the *Act of Union* with Sweden. A plebiscite voted for full independence and a return to a monarchy. Denmark's Prince Frederick VIII became Norway's King Haakon VII.
1911 Norwegian Roald Amundsen was the first person to reach the South Pole, 35 days before Englishman Robert Scott.
1914–18 Norway adopted a policy of neutrality in the First World War.
1920 An international agreement on the Svalbard Arctic archipelago gave full sovereignty to Norway.
1940 Despite neutrality, Norway was invaded and occupied by the Germans in the Second World War. There was active resistance to the Nazi puppet government of Vidkun Quisling.
1945 Norway abandoned its policy of neutrality and lent troops to take part in the Allied war effort.
1949 Norway became a member of NATO.
1935–65 With the exception of the years of German occupation Det Norske

KEY INDICATORS — Norway

	Unit	2000	2001	2002	2003	2004
Population	m	4.48	4.50	4.51	4.54	*4.58
Gross domestic product (GDP)	US$bn	161.80	163.70	189.40	221.60	*250.17
GDP per capita	US$	36,030	36,360	42,123	48,672	54,521
GDP real growth	%	2.8	2.7	1.4	0.4	2.9
Inflation	%	3.1	3.0	1.3	2.5	0.4
Unemployment	%	3.4	3.5	4.2	4.5	–
Oil output	'000 bpd	3,347.0	3,414.0	3,330.0	3,260.0	3,188.0
Natural gas output	bn cum	52.4	57.5	65.4	73.4	78.5
Exports (fob) (goods)	US$m	60,062.0	58,610.0	60,310.0	68,138.0	82,993.0
Imports (fob) (goods)	US$m	34,562.0	33,637.0	34,570.0	39,895.0	49,418.0
Balance of trade	US$m	25,500.0	24,973.0	26,000.0	28,243.0	33,576.0
Current account	US$m	22,986.0	24,078.0	26,470.0	26,643.0	34,360.0
Total reserves minus gold	US$m	27,597.4	23,277.5	31,999.8	37,220.0	44,307.5
Foreign exchange	US$m	26,706.9	22,197.5	30,692.1	35,890.2	43,078.2
Exchange rate	per US$	8.80	8.99	7.95	6.85	6.74

* estimated figure

Norway

Arbeiderparti (DNA) (Labour Party) held continuous office.
1952 Norway joined the Nordic Council, set up to promote co-operation between Nordic parliaments.
1959 Norway was a founding member of the European Free Trade Association (EFTA).
1957 King Olav V came to the throne.
1965 Centre-right coalition unseated the DNA government.
1960–80s From the late 1960s to early 1980s oil and gas were discovered in the Norwegian sector of the North Sea and within a decade their exploitation accounted for one-third of Norway's GDP.
1972 Norwegians rejected a proposal for membership of the European Community (EC).
1973–1981 Minority DNA government held power.
1981–86 The first majority conservative government since 1928 came to power. Following labour disputes, the government was defeated on its austerity programme.
1986 Minority DNA government was elected with Harlem Brundtland as Norway's first female prime minister.
1989 The election was won by a coalition of conservative, Christian democrat and centre parties.
1991 King Olav V died; he was succeeded by his son Harald V.
1992 Norway withdrew from the International Whaling Treaty, provoking international controversy.
1994 In a referendum, Norway rejects membership of the EU by 52.2 per cent (turnout 88.6 per cent).
1993 Norway brokered secret negotiations for a peace deal between Israel and the Palestinian Liberation Organisation that led to the *Oslo Accords*.
1997 The DNA failed to equal its 1993 performance in the general election. Kjell Magne Bondevik of the Kristelig Folkeparti (KrF) (Christian People's Party) set up a minority centrist coalition government.
2000 The government fell after Bondevik was defeated in a vote of no-confidence over controversial plans to build gas-fired power plants. A DNA-led government came to power under Jens Stoltenberg.
2001 In August, Norway and Australia became embroiled in a diplomatic row when a Norwegian-registered cargo ship attempted to set ashore, in Australia, Afghan refugees it had rescued at sea. In parliamentary elections in September, no party emerged with a majority. Stoltenberg and the DNA government resigned and Bondevik returned as prime minister, leading a centre-right coalition.
2003 Norway took the lead in trying to broker a peace deal in Sri Lanka.
2004 In June, the government intervened to end a strike by oil workers seeking better pension rights and job security.
2005 In January, a law came into effect making it mandatory for all public companies to allocate 40 per cent of all board of director positions to women. Parliamentary elections held on 12 September were won by a coalition of socialist parties led by DNA with the Sosialistisk Venstreparti (SV) and Senterpartiet (SP), winning between them 87 out of 169 parliament seats. Stoltenberg became prime minister for the second time. In Novermber, Norway became embroiled in two diplomatic rows, one with Russia, the other with Spain, over fishing rights off the Norwegian island of Svalbard.
2006 In January, a law came into effect making it mandatory for all private companies to allocate 40 per cent of all board of director positions to women.

Political structure
Constitution
The constitution dates from 1814. Norway is divided into 19 counties. There is universal direct suffrage for those aged 18 years and over.
Form of state
Parliamentary democratic monarchy
The executive
Executive power (nominally held by the monarch) is exercised by the Statsråd (Council of State), which is led by the prime minister, who is responsible to the Storting (parliament).
The Council of State is appointed by the monarch, with the approval of parliament. Following parliamentary elections, the leader of the majority party or the leader of the majority coalition is usually appointed prime minister by the monarch, with the approval of the parliament.
National legislature
Legislative power is vested in a unicameral Storting (parliament) comprising 165 members elected by a system of proportional representation (modified Sainte-Lague system) for four-year terms. The Storting is divided into a Lagtinget (upper house) and a Odelstinget (lower house) by internal election, although it sits as a single body except when discussing new legislation. There is no right of dissolution between elections.
Legal system
The legal system is a mixture of customary law, civil law, and common law traditions. The Hoyesterett (Supreme Court) renders advisory opinions to the legislature, when asked. Justices are appointed by the monarch. Norway accepts compulsory International Court of Justice (ICJ) jurisdiction, although with reservations.
Last elections
12 September 2005 (parliamentary)

Results: Parliamentary: No party emerged from the elections with a majority in parliament.
The DNA won 61 seats (32.8 per cent of the vote), the FrP 38 seats (22.1 per cent), Hoyre 23 seats (14.1 per cent), the SV 15 seats (8.8 per cent), KrF 11 seats (6.8 per cent), SP 11 seats (6.5 per cent), Librals 10 seats (5.9 per cent), RV 1,2 per cent, KYST 0,8 per cent and others 1,9 per cent. Turnout was 76.6 per cent.
Next elections
2009 (parliamentary)
Political parties
Ruling party
Coalition: Det Norske Arbeiderparti (DNA) (Norwegian Labour Party), Sosialistisk Venstreparti (SV) (Socialist Left Party), Senterparti (SP) (Centre Party) (since Sep 2005)
Main opposition party
Fremskrittspartiet (FrP) (Progress Party)

Population
4.58 million (2004)
Ethnic make-up
Predominantly Norwegian. In addition, there are about 60,000 Sami (Lapps), mainly in the north of the country, although there are substantial Sami communities in larger cities.
Religions
More than 90 per cent of all Norwegians belong to the Church of Norway, an Evangelical Lutheran denomination. There are also small Roman Catholic, Jewish and Muslim communities.

Education
All public education in Norway is free. Primary education lasts for seven years; lower secondary education and upper secondary education, which is not compulsory, last for three years, from 13 to 16 and 16 to 19 respectively. On completion of a three-year course at an upper secondary school, students can apply to university. Alternatively, students may, at aged 16, undertake either technical training at vocational schools or practical training at apprenticeship schools; for three years.
Primary and lower secondary education is founded on the principle of every individual having a statutory right to primary, lower secondary and upper secondary education in a unified school system that provides equal education for all on the basis of a single national curriculum.
The right to upper secondary education has been in force since 2000, while the right to primary and lower secondary education was implemented from August 2002.
Higher education in Norway is mainly offered at state institutions, notably four universities, six university colleges, 26 state

colleges and two art colleges. A degree candidate may combine studies from universities and colleges, as the courses offered are at the same academic level. The 26 colleges primarily offer shorter courses of a more vocational nature than those offered by the universities.
Compulsory years: Six to 16
Enrolment rate: 100 per cent gross primary enrolment of the relevant age group (including repeaters); 119 gross secondary enrolment (World Bank).
Pupils per teacher: Seven in primary schools

Health
Total expenditure on health is 8 per cent of GDP, of which government spending is 85–86 per cent.
A national health insurance scheme covers medical treatment in hospitals and the reimbursement of costs for medical attention and medicines for certain chronic diseases. Sickness benefit is paid for short-term illness, while chronic or long-term illness is covered by a disability allowance. A small sum is charged for medicine and primary care. The majority of hospitals are state-run.
HIV prevalence: 0.1 per cent aged 15–49 in 2003 (World Bank)
Life expectancy: 79.0 years (World Bank)
Fertility rate/Maternal mortality rate: 1.8 births per woman; maternal mortality 6 per 100,000 live births (World Bank).
Birth rate/Death rate: 13 births and 10 deaths per 1,000 population (World Bank).
Infant mortality rate: 3.4 per 1,000 live births (World Bank)

Welfare
The extensive welfare system has greatly reduced the gap between rich and poor. Social security legislation stipulates that everyone has the right to employment, housing, education, welfare and healthcare. The main general social insurance schemes are the National Insurance Scheme (NIS) and the Family Allowance Scheme. The NIS is a compulsory insurance and pension system and covers pensions, unemployment pay and healthcare for all Norwegians.
A basic retirement pension, adjusted annually, is guaranteed for all Norwegians of 67 years and older regardless of assets or previous income.
Non-pensioners whose income falls below a certain minimum qualify for supplementary benefits. These may include loans or other financial assistance from the local municipality. All families with children under 16 receive a family allowance according to the number of children.
The government subsidises low-cost housing through loans with low rates of interest and easy repayment terms. Families living in housing financed by a state bank can receive an allowance for housing costs should they have difficulties meeting their living expenses.

Main cities
Oslo (capital, estimated population 791,500 in 2003), Bergen (211,200), Stavanger (168,600), Trondheim (144,000), Fredrikstad-Sarpsborg (96,000), Drammen (89,100), Porsgrunn-Skien (84,300), Kristiansand (63,400), Tromsø (51,200).

Languages spoken
Norwegian has two main dialects: Bokmål and Nynorsk. Finnish and Sámi are also spoken. English is widely understood and spoken, especially in urban areas.

Official language/s
Norwegian

Media
Press
There are over 210 newspapers, which reach almost 90 per cent of the adult population, and 1,100 magazines. Activity is concentrated in south-eastern Norway, especially around Oslo where the majority of papers are published. Local papers tend to dominate each particular region. Newspapers receive extensive support from the state.
Dailies: Major national and popular dailies include *Verdens Gang* (www.vg.no), *Oppland Arbeiderblad*, *Nationen* (mainly on agricultural and environmental issues), *Aftenposten AM*, *Dagbladet*, *Adresseavisen*, *Bergens Tidende*, *Bergensavisen* and *Aftenposten PM*. *Stavanger Aftenblad* provides daily news from one of Norway's regional newspapers. *Norway Post* is a online English edition (www.norwaypost.no).
Weeklies: These include *Verdens Gang Sunday*, *Aftenposten Sunday*, *Dagbladet Sunday*, *Innherreds Folkeblad-Verdalingen*, *Klar Tale* and *Ranaposten*. *NorNewsNet* (www.nornews.net) is a bi-weekly newsletter in English for Norwegians worldwide.
Business: A large number of business publications cover various aspects of Norwegian trade and industry, but most tend to have comparatively small and specialised readerships. The main publication is *Dagens Naeringsliv*. Others include *Upstream*, *Finansavisen* and two fortnightly publications *Økonomisk Rapport* and *Kapital*.
Periodicals: A large number of general and special interest magazines exist. Those aimed at women and the teens/twenties market have the largest circulations.

Broadcasting
The Norwegian Broadcasting Corporation's (NRK) monopoly was abolished in the mid-1980s. There are two national radio networks. Fifty-four per cent of national television programme time is devoted to Norwegian productions.
Radio: There are 383 radio stations, 158 commercial. Radio is divided into three groups: non-commercial national radio, commercial national radio and local radio stations. There are three main broadcasters: NRK, P4 and Radio 1. A growing number of local FM stations operate.
Television: There are seven TV stations, six commercial. Channel Scansat TV-3 broadcasts Scandinavian language programmes via cable. A commercially funded second channel, TV-2, broadcasts seven hours each evening.
More than a dozen different European channels are broadcast via satellite-cable, including several pan-Scandinavian channels.

Advertising
All usual media are available. The largest expenditure is on advertising cars, office equipment and travel. There is a ban on advertising for tobacco and all types of alcohol (except the very weakest kind of beer).

Economy
In terms of GDP per capita, Norway is one of the wealthiest countries in the world. The economy is unique among Western European countries for its large and dominant offshore sector. Oil and gas extraction accounts for about 19 per cent of the country's GDP. Since the 1980s the economy has experienced a major structural change, becoming increasingly focussed on service industries, which account for about 37 per cent of GDP. Traditional primary sectors, like agriculture, forestry and fishing, have declined in terms of their contribution to GDP.
The buoyant energy sector has provided the country with strong fundamentals with which to ride out global shocks, most recently the global economic slowdown in 2001 and 2002, and which presented no long-term threat to growth. Income from oil exports is invested in the Petroleum Fund, some of which is used for the fiscal budget, but the main longer-term purpose is to prime the economy once oil reserves decline. In 2005, the value of Norway's Petroleum Fund stood at US$179 billion.
A key challenge for the government is the tight nature of its labour market, especially in the construction and health sectors. Norwegian firms have had to look abroad to fill vacancies as the unemployment rate is relatively low at around 4 per cent. Shortages in the labour market have

Norway

caused high wage growth, leading to a loss of competitiveness in Norwegian exports.

Domestic activity increased in 2004 and, against the background of an anticipated upswing in exports, GDP for the year grew by 3.3 per cent.

External trade
Although Norway has consistently rejected EU membership, it is a member of the European Economic Area (EEA), which gives Norway access into the EU's single market.

Imports
Main imports include machinery and equipment, chemicals, metals and foodstuffs.

Main sources: Sweden (15.7 per cent total, 2004), Germany (13.6 per cent), Denmark (7.3 per cent), UK (6.5 per cent), China (5.0 per cent), US (4.9 per cent), Netherlands (4.4 per cent), France (4.3 per cent), Finland (4.1 per cent).

Exports
Principal exports are crude oil and petroleum products, natural gas, machinery and equipment, metals, chemicals, ships and fish.

Main destinations: UK (22.4 per cent total, 2004), Germany (12.9 per cent), Netherlands (9.9 per cent), France (9.6 per cent), US (8.4 per cent), Sweden (6.7 per cent)

Agriculture
Farming
The agricultural sector typically accounts for 2 per cent of GDP and employs around 6 per cent of the workforce. Grain and fodder are main lowland crops; mountain farms mainly raise livestock and grow fodder. Grain production is increasing, especially barley and oats, although wheat and rye are increasing in importance. The main grain-growing districts are in southern and central Norway. Coarse fodder, mostly hay and silage, can be cultivated at high altitudes and in the far north. Other crops include potatoes, other roots, berries and fruits. Crop yields per hectare have risen consistently over the last three decades. Some dairy produce is exported and there is self-sufficiency in meat, milk, cheese, butter, fish and potatoes.

Norway's agricultural policy has two main aims. The first is to promote a high degree of self-sufficiency in animal products and secondly to ensure an adequate livelihood for the country's 120,000 farmers and smallholders. In many regions, agriculture and related activities are the main source of income. Farm prices are set annually by agreement between the government and agricultural organisations. Almost all farmland is privately owned and farms tend to be small. Produce is bought and distributed by large co-operative purchasing and sales organisations.

The total cultivated area is just over 868,500 hectares (ha), only 3 per cent of the mainland area. Agricultural production is hampered by difficult topographical conditions and an unfavourable climate. However, Norwegian agriculture is generally efficient, with a high degree of mechanisation and emphasis on training and research.

Crop production in 2004 included: 1,426,500 tonnes (t) cereals in total, 419,800t wheat, 368,500t oats, 340,000t potatoes, 646,200t barley, 3,800t oilcrops, 9,000t tomatoes, 10,500t apples, 23,120t fruit in total, 128,900t vegetables in total. Livestock production included: 269,060t meat in total, 83,000t beef, 105,000t pig meat, 24,000t lamb, 3,000t game meat, 47,000t poultry, 48,000t eggs, 1,720,000mt milk, 1,500t honey, 8,325t cattle hides, 7,320t sheepskins, 4,900t greasy wool.

Fishing
Fishing is a significant industry in the northern and western regions. Fish, including farmed fish, is Norway's second largest export group, accounting for 20 per cent of all exports. Mackerel, cod and capelin are the main species caught, but catches have been falling because of overfishing. The typical annual export value of fish is between Nkr 25–30 billion (US$3.3– 4 billion) and as a whole the fishing industry provides work for 23,000 people.

Whale hunting in 2004 produced 809 tonnes of meat, which was mainly sold in Norway as steaks. In 2003 Norway advised pregnant women and mothers who were breast-feeding infants to avoid whale meat due to the contamination, in wild caught whales, of traces of toxic mercury. Stocks of whale blubber, amounting to 363 tonnes, were turned into animal fodder, in 2004 when no other use could be found for them. Around 270 tonnes remain and Norway would like to sell it to Japan where the fat is considered a delicacy.

Fish farms produce mainly salmon and trout, although some are experimenting with other fish, such as halibut. Norway has the world's largest farmed salmon industry, producing about half the total supplies of Atlantic salmon. Demand for farmed salmon has increased by 20–30 per cent annually, but production normally exceeds demand. The emerging new markets in southern Europe are seen as a useful outlet for the surplus, even though salmon exports are in competition with EU production and the EU sets a minimum price requirement for sales from Norway. Salmon comprises 31 per cent of Norway's fish exports.

In February 2005 Norway challenged the EU imposed trade restrictions and import ceiling before the WTO. Norway's salmon sales account for 60 per cent of the EU market with exports valued at US1.29 billion. The UK and Ireland claimed salmon was being sold below production cost and that this was unfair competition. In April the EU imposed a 16 per cent duty on salmon while it investigated whether Norwegian exporters were 'dumping' salmon stocks on EU markets. This duty was replaced in June 2005 with a less punitive levy and a decision on whether or not the EU continues to penalise this sector is due by the end of January 2006.

Norway's relationship with Russia is complicated by a number of fishing-related disputes. In November 2005, Norway detained several Russian trawlers operating inside Norway's Svalbard protected zone. In December 2005, Russia announced a ban on the import of Norwegian salmon, effective from 1 January 2006, on health grounds.

Also in November 2005, Norwegian authorities arrested Spanish trawlers operating off Svalbard and confiscated illegal halibut catches. In response, the Spanish government lodged an official protest with the EU.

Forestry
Forest cover is estimated at 8.8 million hectares (ha). In 1990–2000, forest cover increased by an annual average of 31,000ha. Some 22 per cent of the total land area is productive woodland. Most forests are situated in southern and central Norway. Spruce, used for making pulp and paper, makes up about 50 per cent of the forest. Pines account for about 30 per cent and broad-leafed trees for around 15 per cent. Mechanisation and automation have allowed logging in previously inaccessible forest land.

About 85 per cent of forest land is privately owned by farmers. The forestry sector has a well-developed co-operative sales apparatus. Forest-owner organisations have become more active in processing.

The forestry and the forest-products industry, contributes heavily to local economies. Norway exports nearly 90 per cent of the paper and paperboard production and nearly a quarter of the pulp production. Imports of roundwood and sawnwood, mainly from Sweden, have increased considerably. Per capita consumption of forest products is among the highest in Europe.

Export of forest materials in 2004 amounted to US$1.8 billion, while imports amounted to US$1.2 billion.

Production in 2004 included 8,780,000 cubic metres (cum) roundwood, 7,551,000cum industrial roundwood, 2,230,000cum sawnwood, 4,160,000cum sawlogs and veneers, 3,360,000cum pulpwood, 493,000cum wood-based panels, 1,229,000cum wood fuel.

Industry and manufacturing
The industrial sector typically accounts for around 32 per cent of GDP and employs 19 per cent of the workforce. Manufacturing accounts for barely 13 per cent of both GDP and employment (compared with around 22 per cent in 1970) and has developed more slowly than in most other industrial countries. The main industries include chemicals, fish processing, metals, timber and pulp and paper production. The goals of industrial policy have traditionally been to maximise employment and the quality of production, maintain the rural population, promote a just and equitable distribution of wealth and income, and keep control over natural resources. Secondary goals have been to control inflation, protect the environment and achieve a balance between imports and exports.

The state channels financial resources to industry on concessionary terms through its Industry Fund and via state banks. Enterprises in depressed or uncompetitive markets are also given soft loans through the state-run District Development Fund. The government aims for around 2 per cent of GDP to be invested in research and development (R&D). Priorities for R&D spending are biotechnology, communications, electronics, metallurgical technology and aquaculture.

Industrial production increased by an estimated 5.2 per cent in 2004.

Tourism
Over 3.5 million tourists visited Norway in 2004, a 7 per cent increase on the 2003 numbers. Discount airlines and direct flights were credited with providing the strong growth. Booking for cruise liners visiting Norway in 2005 passed 300,000 by the beginning of the year; the growth in cruising has risen fourfold in 20 years.

Environment
With the highest environmental standards in the world, sulphur emissions have plummeted by over 80 per cent since 1980. Pollution is kept low by the country's extensive hydroelectric production, although per capita nitrogen oxide emissions are among the highest in the world. In December 2001, environmentalists accused Norway December 2001 of undermining the spirit of the Kyoto Protocol for announcing plans to triple coal production in Svalbard.

Mining
Norway has a highly skilled workforce, experienced in mining, quarrying and processing.

Activity is confined to small-scale mining of iron ore, copper, titanium, coal (on Spitsbergen), zinc, lead and pyrites. Most of these ores and concentrates are exported.

Mining continues to contract, causing many problems in areas where there is no alternative employment. However, the country's mining potential has yet to be fully explored and it is believed that Norway has the capacity to develop super-quarries.

On the south coast, near Lillesand, feldspars and quartz are found. Graphite, with differing carbon content and quality, is produced on the island of Senja and research is being carried out to upgrade the quality. Large dimension stones like granite, marbles and quartzites, are available in large quantities. Larvikite is one of the most predominant stones, there are also exclusive marbles, including Norwegian Rose, to be found in the north. From the quarries in northern and central Norway high quality quartzite and phullite-slate are processed. Rock aggregate is found along the coast, in both large sizes and quantities, making transportation very easy.

Hydrocarbons
Norway is the world's third largest net oil exporter after Saudi Arabia and Russia. Oil production doubled in the 1990s as improved recovery techniques were introduced and new wells came on stream. Reserves of 8.5 billion barrels (2005) ensure that production can carry on for many years to come. Oil production in 2004 was estimated at 3.31 million barrels per day (bpd). All of Norway's reserves are located offshore.

Between 2000–02, the oil sector underwent restructuring. The government reduced its 78.2 per cent stake in the state-owned oil company, Statoil, to 60 per cent. While the government resists foreign ownership of the oil sector, its restructuring plan is designed to maintain a competitive interest in the industry.

Natural gas reserves were 2.46 trillion cubic metres (cum) in 2003 with production of 73.4 billion cum. Norway is the seventh-largest gas producer in the world and is expected by 2005 to move into the top five. By 2005, Norway is expected to supply 30 per cent of the gas consumed in France and 40 per cent of that used in Germany.

Norway's coal comes from Spitsbergen, on the Svalbard Islands, off the country's northern coast, which also has the country's only coal-fired power plant. In 2002, 1.73 million tonnes of coal was produced 1.32 million tonnes and imported to meet domestic demand.

Energy
Norwegian electricity output exceeds demand, with some of the surplus being exported to Sweden and Denmark. Hydro-electric plants supply 99 per cent of output. Plans for new gas-fired power plants in Kollsnes and Karst have failed in the face of strong opposition by environmentalists. Statoil, the forestry group Norske Skog and Elkem industrial group have extended the time scale on plans to build a 800MW gas-fired power station in Skogn, to be fully operational by late 2006.

Financial markets
Stock exchange
In 1993, the Norwegian Stock Exchange, known as the Oslo Børs, joined Norex, an alliance that includes Sweden's Stockholmsbörsen, the Copenhagen Stock Exchange and the Icelandic Stock Exchange. The four members use the same trading system and follow similar rules and regulations.

Banking and insurance
Central bank
Norges Bank (Bank of Norway)
Main financial centre
Oslo

Time
GMT plus one hour (GMT plus two hours from late March to late September)

Geography
Norway lies on the west side of the Scandinavian peninsula, in north-west Europe. Its extended coastline faces the North Sea and the North Atlantic Ocean. It is the fifth-largest country in Europe and it has the third-lowest population density in Europe after Greenland and Iceland. The coastline measures 28,000km if fjords and inlets are included, 2,650km if they are not.

The capital, Oslo, in the south, lies on the same latitude as Greenland and Alaska, while Hammerfest on the northern tip of the Norwegian mainland, is the most northerly town in the world. The Svalbard Arctic archipelago is part of Norway, and sovereignty is also exercised over Jan Mayen island and the uninhabited island dependencies of Bouvet and Peter I. In Antartica, Queen Maud Land is a Norwegian dependency.

Norway shares a 1,619km land border with Sweden, and within the Arctic Circle, a 716km frontier with Finland and a 196km border with Russia.

The terrain mostly consists of high plateaux, deep fjords and mountains. More than 70 per cent of the mainland consists

Norway

of mountains, glaciers, lakes, forest and moorland. The highest peak is Galdhoepiggen in the south which reaches 2,469 metres above sea level. Only 2.8 per cent of the land area is cultivable soil, while another 20 per cent is productive forest.

Climate
Influenced by the Atlantic Gulf Stream and westerly winds, the climate is much warmer than that of other countries on the same latitude. The temperature varies little from north to south, but there is a big contrast between the inland and coastal regions. In winter, while the interior freezes hard, most fjords and harbours remain ice-free. The average annual temperature is 8 degrees Celsius (C) along the west coast, and -2 degrees C in the northernmost county, Finnmark. January and February are the coldest months, while July and August are the warmest. The average annual rainfall is 1,960mm in Bergen and 740mm in Oslo. Northern Norway is popularly known as the 'Land of the Midnight Sun'. In Finnmark the midnight sun is visible from mid-May to late-July, and the period of darkness lasts from mid-November to late-January.

Dress codes
Clothing to suit the climate is vital because of the extremes in weather; heavy coats, warm boots, gloves and ear protection are required in winter and light clothing in summer. Normal European business attire, otherwise dress is generally casual.

Entry requirements
Passports
Passports are required by all and must be valid for three months beyond the date of stay. Nationals of countries which are signatories of the Schengen Agreement, may visit on national IDs.
Visa
Visas are not required by nationals of most European countries, US, Canada, Australasia, Japan or transit passengers. For further exceptions, contact the nearest embassy. A Schengen visa application (offered in several languages) can be downloaded from www.eurovisa.info/ApplicationForm.htm.
Currency advice/regulations
The export of local currency is limited to Nkr5,000. The export of foreign currency is unlimited if proof of import or conversion from another currency can be produced.
Customs
Personal effects duty-free, plus duty-free allowance. Imported products from certain countries such as Japan, South Korea and some East European countries require a licence. Imported cars are heavily taxed.

Prohibited imports
Illegal narcotics, firearms.

Health (for visitors)
Mandatory precautions
None.
Advisable precautions
There are reciprocal health agreements with most other west European countries that cover hospital treatment. The cost of other treatment may be partially reimbursed under the Norwegian National Insurance Scheme (NIS) but, receipts must be presented to the national insurance office of the district where treatment was given, before visitors departs.

Hotels
There are a wide range of hotels available in most towns, most of which are family-run, but no official rating system is in operation. Private accommodation can be obtained through local tourist offices or accommodation offices in central railway stations. There is a service charge of 15 per cent, included in the bill, but tipping is also expected.

Credit cards
Major credit cards are accepted.

Public holidays
Fixed dates
1 Jan (New Year's Day), 1 May (Labour Day), 17 May (Constitution Day), 24 Dec (Christmas Eve, afternoon only), 25 Dec (Christmas Day), 26 Dec (Boxing Day), 31 Dec (New Year's Eve, afternoon only).
Variable dates
Maundy Thursday, Good Friday, Easter Monday, Ascension Day, Whit Monday.

Working hours
Banking
0815–1530 (Mon–Fri), 0815–1700 (Thur).
Business
0900–1600 (Mon–Fri).
Government
0830–1600 (Mon–Fri).
Shops
0900–1700 (Mon–Wed), 0900–1900 (Thursday), 0830–1300 (Saturday). Many shops are increasingly introducing longer opening hours, and some are open on Sundays.

Electricity supply
220V AC

Social customs/useful tips
Punctuality is expected. Shake hands on meeting. Business lunches are rare. The main meal of the day is generally taken at home at 1700 hours, though people will expect to eat later if invited out.

Security
Serious crime is not a big problem. It is usually safe to walk at night in major cities, such as Oslo and Bergen, although some neighbourhoods are less safe than others. Car theft, on the other hand, is fairly common and one should never leave a car unlocked, especially in the major cities.

Getting there
Air
National airline: SAS Braathens
International airport/s: Oslo International Airport (OSL) (Gardermoen) 47km north of city. Facilities include duty-free, banks/bureaux de change, restaurants and cafes, car hire, laundry/dry cleaning, shoe repair and key-cutting. Photocopying and fax services are available from the information desk in Departures; there are also Internet facilities.
Other airport/s: Bergen (BGO), 19km from city; Stavanger (SVG), 14.5km south-west of city.
There are 52 airports with regular intercontinental flights to Europe and the US.
Airport tax: None
Surface
Road: The only routes are from Sweden or Finland in the north.
Rail: There are daily train connections from Stockholm to Oslo and Trondheim. There are also train connections between Oslo and Gothenburg, Copenhagen and Helsingborg.
Water: There are frequent ferry services to Denmark, UK and Germany.
Main port/s: Oslo, Kristiansand, Bergen and Larvik.

Getting about
National transport
Air: Efficient services, operated by various carriers, link all major and many smaller towns. Charter sea and land planes are widely available.
Road: The road network is extensive, certain roads in the mountainous areas could be closed in winter and spring. It is necessary to check with the authorities prior to departure. Main highways between Oslo and other major cities are kept open all year around.
Buses: Norway has an extensive bus network and long distance buses are comfortable. Tickets are sold on the buses. The main bus company is the Nor-Way Bussekspress (see: www.nbe.no) with routes connecting every main city.
Rail: Norway has a good, though somewhat limited, national rail system. All railway lines are operated by the Norwegian State Railways (Norges Statsbaner or NSB). From Oslo, the main lines go to Stavanger, Bergen, Åndalsnes, Bodø and Sweden. Rail services are comfortable.
Water: There are regular and efficient motor ship services visiting all the major ports. There are also numerous local ferry, hydrofoil and catamaran services.

Nations of the World: A Political, Economic and Business Handbook

City transport

Taxis: Taxis are available in most cities. They can be obtained at ranks or by telephone (Oslo 388-090, Bergen 900-990, Stavanger 526-040). Telephone numbers of taxi stands are listed in the directory under 'Drosjer'. Meters are compulsory. It is not expected that the tip will be more than small change.

In addition to regular taxis, there are airport taxis, cheaper taxis which must be ordered in advance by groups of up to three people, and wheelchair taxis.

Buses, trams & metro: There are eight tram lines and five metro lines in Oslo, plus numerous bus services. Public transport runs from 0530–2400 everyday. Tickets are best pre-purchased and self-cancelled, there is one hour's free transfer between any of the modes. (www.trafikanten.no can offer more information). Buses serving the airport take about 45 minutes and there is also a new regional bus station for services further afield.

Trains: A high-speed airport express train leaves every 10 minutes to and from Oslo's central station (20 minutes).

Ferry: Ferries from Oslo to Bygdøy leave from Rådhusbrygge, while ferries to the island in Oslofjord leave from Vippetangen.

Car hire

Available from airports and major towns. For travel between towns public transport tends to be quicker and much cheaper. Studded or winter tyres are recommended during winter. There are strict laws against drinking and driving and wearing seatbelts is compulsory. The speed limit in built-up areas is 50kph and 80kph on highways.

BUSINESS DIRECTORY

The addresses listed below are a selection only. While World of Information makes every endeavour to check these addresses, we cannot guarantee that changes have not been made, especially to telephone numbers and area codes. We would welcome any corrections.

Telephone area codes

The international direct dialling (IDD) code for Norway is +47, followed by subscriber's number.

Chambers of Commerce

Bergen Chamber of Commerce and Industry, 11 Olav Kyrresgt, 5014 Bergen (tel: 5555-3900; fax: 5555-3901; e-mail: firmapost@bergen-chamber.no).

British-Norwegian Chamber of Commerce, 1 Dronning Maudsgate, 0250 Oslo (tel: 2311-1790; fax: 2283-4120; e-mail: bncc@c21.net).

Kristiansand Chamber of Commerce, PO Box 269, 4663 Kristiansand (tel: 3812-3970; fax: 3812-3979; e-mail: post@kristiansand-chamber.no).

Oslo Chamber of Commerce, 30 Drammensveien, PO Box 2874 Solli, 0230 Oslo (tel: 2212-9400; fax: 2212-9401; e-mail: mail@chamber.no).

Stavanger Chamber of Commerce, 1 Rosenkildetorget, PO Box 182, 4001 Stavanger (tel: 5151-0880; fax: 5151-0881; e-mail: post@stavanger-chamber.no).

Trondheim Chamber of Commerce, PO Box 778 Sentrum, 7408 Trondheim (tel: 7388-3110; fax: 7388-3111; e-mail: firmapost@trondheim-chamber.no).

Tromsø Chamber of Commerce and Industry, 83 Grønnegata, PO Box 464, 9255 Tromsø (tel: 7766-5230; fax: 7766-5253; e-mail: firmapost@tromso-chamber.no).

Banking

Christiania Bank og Kreditkasse, PO Box 1166, N-0107 Oslo (tel: 2248-5000; fax: 2248-4749).

Den norske Bank, Stranden 21, Aker Brygge, N-0021 Oslo (tel.: 2248-1050; fax: 2248-1870; internet site: http://www.dnb.no; e-mail: dnb@dnb.no).

Fokus Bank A/S, Vestre Rosten 77, PO Box 6090, N-7466 Trondheim (tel: 7288-2011; fax: 7288-2061).

Postbanken, Akersgata 68, N-0180 Oslo (tel: 2297-6000; fax: 2297-7665; internet site: http://www.postbanken.no).

Central bank

Norges Bank, Bankplassen 2, PO Box 1179, Sentrum, 0107 Oslo (tel: 2231-6000; fax: 2241-3105; e-mail: central.bank@norges-bank.no).

Travel information

National bus company: http://www.nbe.no

National railway company: http://www.nsb.no/internet/en/index.jhtml

SAS Braathens (tel: +49 054000; internet site: www.sasbraathens.no/Pages/EN/WebRes/braathens.html)

National tourist organisation offices

Norwegian Tourist Board, Stortorvet 10, N-0155 Oslo; PO Box 722 Sentrum, N-0105 Oslo (tel: 2414-4600; fax: 2414-4601; e-mail: norway@ntr.no; internet site: http://www.visitnorway.com).

Ministries

Department of Transport and Communications, Akersgaten 59, PO Box 8010 Dep, N-0030 Oslo (tel: 2224-9090; fax: 2224-9571).

Ministry of Agriculture, PO Box 8007 Dep, N-0032 Oslo (tel: 2224-9090; fax: 2224-9555).

Ministry of Finance (Finansdepartementet), Akersgaten 40 (Blokk G), PO Box 8008 Dep, N-0030 Oslo (tel: 2224-9090; fax: 2224-9510; internet site: http://www.finans.dep.no).

Ministry of Foreign Affairs, 7 Juni-Plassen/Victoria Terrasse, PO Box 8114 Dep, N-0032 Oslo (tel: 2224-3600; fax: 2224-9580/81).

Ministry of Industry and Trade, Grubbegt 8, PO Box 8148 Dep, N-0033 Oslo (tel: 2224-9090; fax: 2224-9565).

Ministry of Petroleum and Energy, Einar Gerhardsens Plass 1, PO Box 8148 Dep, N-0033 Oslo (tel: 2224-6107; fax: 2224-9525).

Other useful addresses

Directorate of Immigration, PO Box 8108 Dep, N-0032 Oslo (tel: 2335-1500; fax: 2335-1504).

Næringslivets Hovedorganisasjon (Confederation of Norwegian Business and Industry), Middelthuns Gate 27, Pb 5250 Majorstua, N-0303 Oslo (tel: 2296-5000; fax: 2296-5593).

Norges Eksportrad (Export Council of Norway), Drammensveien 40, N-0243 Oslo (tel: 2292-6300: fax: 2292-6400).

Norges Varemesse (the Norwegian Trade Fair Foundation), PO Box 75, NO-2001 Lillestrøm (tel: 6693-9100: fax: 6693-9101; internet site: http://www.messe.no/).

Norinform, Norwegian Information Service, PO Box 241 Sentrum, N-0103 Oslo (tel: 2211-4685; fax: 2242-4887).

Norwegian Trade Council, N-0243 Oslo (tel: 2292-6300; fax: 2292-6400).

Oslo Bors (stock exchange), Tollbugaten 2, Box 460, Sentrum, 0105 Oslo (tel: 2234-1700; fax: 2234-1925; e-mail: info@ose.no; internet website: http://www.oslobors.no).

Royal Norwegian Embassy (US), 2729 34th Street, NW, Washington DC 20008 (tel: 202-333-6000; fax: 202-337-0870; e-mail: emb.washington@mfa.no).

Statistics Norway, PO Box 8131 Dep, N-0033 Oslo 1 (tel: 2109-0000; fax: 2109-4973; internet site: (English section) http://www.ssb.no//www-open/english/).

Internet sites

Nordic Pages: http://www.markovits.com/nordic/

Yellow Pages: http://www.gulesider.no

Oman

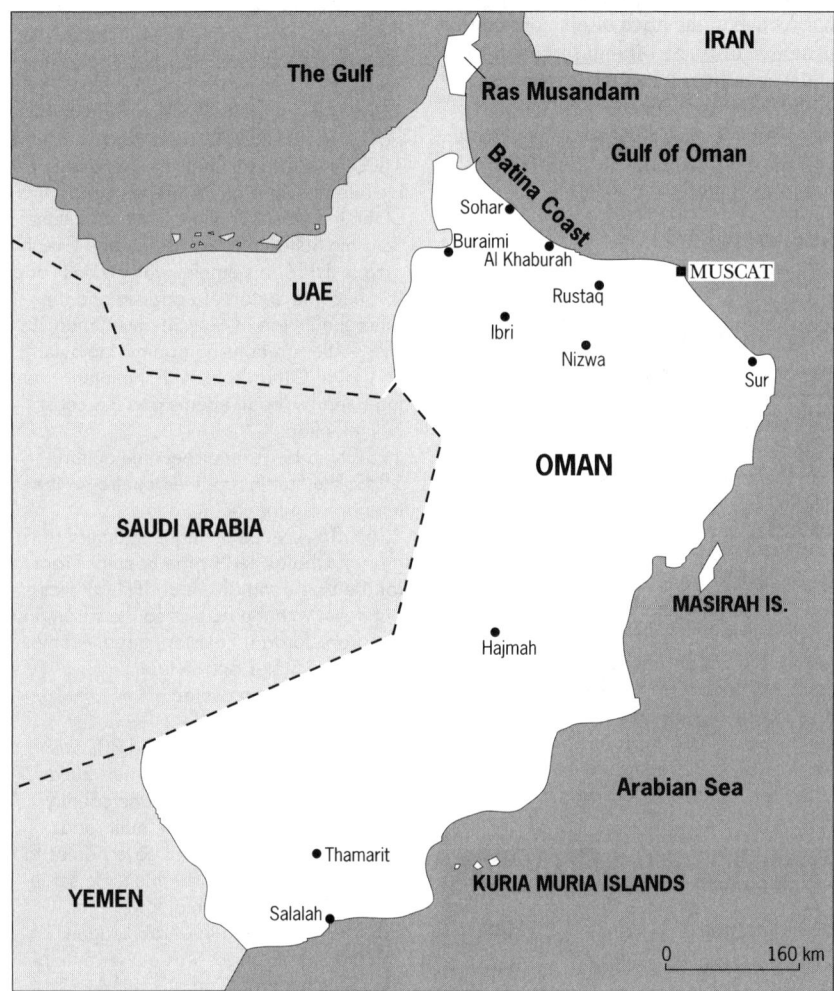

KEY FACTS

Official name: Sultanatu Oman (Saltanat Uman) (Sultanate of Oman)

Head of State: Sultan Qaboos bin Said

Head of government: Sultan Qaboos bin Said

Ruling party: Political parties are not permitted.

Area: 320,000 square km (including Kuria Muria Islands)

Population: 3.23 million (2004)

Capital: Muscat (Masqat)

Official language: Arabic

Currency: Omani rial (RO) = 1,000 baiza

Exchange rate: RO0.39 per US$ (pegged to US$)

GDP per capita: US$10,339 (2004)

GDP real growth: 2.50% (2004)

Labour force: 782,000 (2004)

Unemployment: 15.00% (2004)

Inflation: 1.60% (2004)

Oil production: 785,000 bpd (2004)

Balance of trade: US$6.77 billion (2004)

Foreign debt: US$4.81 billion (2004)

It was a year without major incident for Oman in 2005. Unlike other Arab dynastic states in the region, such as Saudi Arabia, the United Arab Emirates (UAE) and Kuwait, there was no changing of the guard or any other succession-related upheaval. The sultan and prime minister Qaboos bin Said continued his long reign, dating back to 1970.

Economic diversification needed

Currently, Oman derives 40 per cent of its GDP from oil revenues. In recent years it has been working hard to develop non-oil sectors, with tourism receiving particular government investment. Moreover, in 2005, foreign investors were invited to boost the country's oil reserves through renewed exploration. Despite declines in crude oil production of around 5 per cent in 2005, recent high oil prices have meant continued high revenues from the hydrocarbon sector. Omani oil production has declined slowly every year since 2001.

GDP growth is forecast to be around 1.9 per cent in 2005. During the year, the government took steps to co-ordinate the introduction of a value added tax with Oman's Gulf Co-operation Council (GCC) partners – Saudi Arabia, the UAE, Kuwait, Qatar and Bahrain – and the

Anti-Islamist crackdown

Oman experienced a rare crackdown in January 2005, when nearly 100 suspected Islamists were arrested and charged with plotting to overthrow the government. Of these, 31 were jailed but subsequently received pardons from the Sultan in June. The jailed men included academics, civil servants and Islamic scholars. All denied the charges. The last major crackdown, in 1994, also ended with the granting of royal pardons.

Relative to other Arab monarchic states, dissent has been generally well managed in Oman. The sultanate was the first Arabian Gulf state to introduce a consultative assembly (in 1981) and this has since been split into two chambers, one elected (the Majlis ash Shura), the other appointed (the Majlis al Dawla) by the Sultan. Political parties are banned. Women have been granted the right to vote and in March 2004, the Sultan appointed the first woman minister with a portfolio.

Expulsions continue

In 2005, the government continued its policy of deporting migrants seeking work without permits. Between 2004 and 2005, the government deported 42,000 Pakistanis.

A threat from Iraq

Although Oman has thus far avoided the outbreaks of Islamic militancy that have plagued Saudi Arabia, Kuwait, Jordan and Iraq in recent times, an attack in November suggests that insurgents in Iraq have included the Omani embassy in their list of targets. Al Qaeda's leader in Iraq, Abu Musab al Zarqawi, has long insisted that Arab states break off relations with Iraq's various post-Ba'athist governments.

Outlook

Although economists have warned that Oman's GDP growth in 2006 is exposed to a decline in the price of oil, continuing disruption of Iraq's oil industry and a potential crisis over Iran's nuclear ambitions will probably keep prices high. In January 2006, Oman signed a free trade agreement with the US. Elections to the Majlis ash Shura are due in 2007.

Risk assessment

Politics	Stable
Economy	Improving
Regional stability	Fragile

COUNTRY PROFILE

Historical profile

Oman's history differs in many respects from that of its neighbours. It is, for example, the only non-European state to have held colonial possessions in Africa, ruling Zanzibar (now a part of Tanzania) and other East African enclaves for long periods. Omani navigators were acquainted not only with the coasts of India and the east Indies, but also reached as far as southern China. Oman's location also gave it strategic importance for European powers bent on eastward expansion and discovery. The Portuguese quickly appreciated this, occupying strategic locations in the sixteenth century and building numerous coastal forts, some of which can still be seen. For the British, Oman's principal importance was its location on the route to India, which led to a quasi-colonial relationship with the UK.

1507–1650 The Portuguese occupied Muscat and established a garrison there until they were expelled by Imam Sultan bin Saif.
1737–49 The Persians invaded and after they were driven out, the Al bin Said dynasty came to power, which still rules the country.
1798 The first treaty of friendship was signed between Oman and Britain.
1800s The Omani empire expanded to include Zanzibar and Mombasa and parts of the Indian subcontinent. When Sultan Said bin Sultan (known as Said the Great) died in 1856, his empire was divided: one son became Sultan of Zanzibar and the other the Sultan of Muscat and Oman.
1913 After an uprising against the Sultan, control of Oman split, with the interior being ruled by Ibadit imams and the coast by the Sultan.
1932 Said bin Taimur became Sultan.
1959 The Sultan regained control of the interior from the Ibadit imams.
1965–75 A rebellion in the southern region of Dhofar, led by the Popular Front for the Liberation of Oman (PFLO), was put down with the help of soldiers from India, Iran, Jordan, Pakistan, Saudi Arabia, the Trucial States and Britain.
1964 Oil was discovered.
1967 Extraction began.
1970 Qaboos bin Said, aged 30, overthrew his father, Said bin Taimur. Sultan Qaboos started to open up the country and, using money from oil, built roads, schools and hospitals and gave homes to people and boats to fishermen. He set in place strict environmental laws.
1971 Oman joined the Arab League.
1978 Sultan Qaboos was active in helping implement the Camp David Accords, signed by Israel and Egypt.
1981 Oman helped found the Gulf Co-operation Council (GCC).
1985 Oman established full diplomatic relations with the Soviet Union for the first time.
1991 During the Gulf War, Oman was used as a base for forces fighting Iraq. Sultan Qaboos established the Majlis Ash Shura (Consultative Council).
1996 Sultan Qaboos promulgated the 'Basic Statute of the State', or Basic Law, the Gulf's first written constitution.
1997 The Sultan issued a decree allowing women to stand for election to, and vote for, the Majlis Ash Shura, and two women were elected.

KEY INDICATORS — Oman

	Unit	2000	2001	2002	2003	2004
Population	m	2.52	2.60	2.70	2.97	*3.23
Gross domestic product (GDP)	US$bn	19.70	20.10	20.30	21.70	0.00
GDP per capita	US$	8,336	8,158	7,854	7,876	10,339
GDP real growth	%	4.9	5.9	1.9	6.3	2.5
Inflation	%	-1.0	-1.1	-0.7	0.3	1.6
Oil output	'000 bpd	961.0	959.0	898.0	823.0	785.0
Natural gas output	bn cum	8.5	13.4	14.8	16.5	17.6
Exports (fob) (goods)	US$m	11,319.0	11,079.0	11,170.0	12,055.0	13,140.0
Imports (fob) (goods)	US$m	4,593.0	5,933.0	6,000.0	7,653.0	6,373.0
Balance of trade	US$m	6,726.0	5,146.0	5,170.0	4,402.0	6,767.0
Current account	US$m	3,347.0	2,297.0	2,280.0	2,285.0	2,700.0
Total reserves minus gold	US$m	2,379.9	2,364.9	3,173.5	3,593.5	3,597.3
Foreign exchange	US$m	2,310.9	2,277.0	3,064.8	3,466.6	3,484.5
Exchange rate	per US$	0.39	0.39	0.39	0.39	0.38

* estimated figure

Oman

1999 Oman and the UAE signed a border agreement, which defined their disputed common frontier.
2000 Majlis Ash Shura elections involving just 25 per cent of the adult population and no parties were allowed, with candidates hand-picked by the Sultan. Oman joined the World Trade Organisation (WTO).
2001 Oman became an important base for international military operations against the Taliban government in Afghanistan.
2002 Voting rights were extended to all citizens over the age of 21.
2003 The 83-seat Majlis Ash Shura was freely elected for the first time.
2004 Sultan Qaboos appointed Oman's first female minister with portfolio.
2005 In May, a state security court convicted 31 people of plotting to overthrow the Sultan and install an Islamist government.

Political structure
Constitution
In November 1996, Sultan Qaboos bin Said promulgated the 'Basic Statute of the State', or Basic Law, the Gulf's first written constitution, that clarified the royal succession, provided for a legislature and guaranteed basic civil liberties for Omani citizens within a framework of Islamic and traditional law.

The country is divided into 59 *wilayat* (regions), each under the authority of a *wali* (governor). There are special governates for the cities of Muscat and Salalah, with Muscat consisting of six separate *wilayat*.

Form of state
Absolute monarchy

The executive
Executive and legislative power lies with Sultan Qaboos bin Said, who appoints the Council of Ministers and other officials and promulgates laws by decree.

National legislature
In 1991, Sultan Qaboos established a Majlis Ash Shura (Consultative Council), in which each of the 59 *wilayat* were represented.

In 1996, a draft law set up a bicameral parliament (Council of State), consisting of an upper chamber or Majlis Addawla (41 members appointed by the monarch) and a transformed lower chamber (Majlis Ash Shura), with 83 members elected by limited suffrage. The assembly meets with the Council of Ministers once a year at which Cabinet members present their departments' plans. Majlis power is limited to proposing and reviewing legislation and, although it can affect policy on minor issues, it remains relatively powerless.

In the September 2000 elections Sultan Qaboos had ultimate control over both the choice of candidate for each council seat and the eligibility to be a member of what is a very limited electorate. The elections involved just 25 per cent of the adult population with voters over 30 and vetted by the ministry of interior. The electorate included sheikhs, wise men, dignitaries, graduates and intellectuals; women can both vote and stand for election to the Majlis Ash Shura. Term of office is three years.

In November 2002, the Sultan announced the introduction of universal suffrage, with everyone over the age of 21 years eligible to vote for the 83-member Majlis Ash Shura.

Legal system
The legal system is mainly the preserve of Sharia courts, which apply Islamic law. The local courts are administered by *qadis* (Islamic judges) appointed by the minister of justice. Appeals from local courts are heard at the Court of Appeal in Muscat.

Last elections
4 October 2003 (Majlis Ash Shura (Consultative Council), freely elected for the first time)

Next elections
2006 (Majlis Ash Shura)

Political parties
Ruling party
Political parties are not permitted.
Main opposition party
There is no legal opposition.

Population
3.23 million (2004)

Ethnic make-up
Predominantly Arab, with non-Arab pockets in long-established Baluchi, Iranian and Gujarati communities. Many Omanis are of Zanzibari descendancy (prior to 1964, Zanzibar had been part of the Sultanate of Oman).

Religions
Islam is the official religion. The majority are Ibadi Muslims with about one-quarter being Sunnis. There is a small concentration of Shi'ite Muslims in Muscat.

Education
The government sponsors literacy centres in an attempt to improve the literacy rate. Primary education lasts from aged six to 12. Secondary education consists of two stages: first the preparatory school for three years then the secondary school for a further three years. Islamic Institute secondary schools accept students who have completed their preparatory study in a mosque. It teaches the same subjects as secondary schools but with an emphasis on Islam and the Arabic language.

Literacy rate: 74.4 per cent total; 65.4 per cent female, adult rates in 2002 (World Bank).
Compulsory years: None.
Enrolment rate: 76 per cent gross primary enrolment of relevant age group (including repeaters); 67 per cent gross secondary enrolment (World Bank).
Pupils per teacher: 26 in primary schools.

Health
Free medical care is available throughout the Sultanate for all Omani citizens. In 2000, the WHO rated the Oman healthcare service in the top 10 worldwide, with first place in delivery efficiency and the utilisation of financial resources. Since 2001 the health development plan has been concentrating on the expansion of improved primary healthcare in villages and towns and providing additional specialist treatment centres.

Total expenditure on health is around 3 per cent of GDP, of which government spending is 85 per cent; private spending (such as insurance) is 18 per cent.

HIV prevalence: 0.1 per cent aged 15–49 in 2003 (World Bank)
Life expectancy: 74.2 years (World Bank)
Fertility rate/Maternal mortality rate: 4.0 births per woman (2003); maternal mortality 19 per 100,000 live births (World Bank).
Birth rate/Death rate: 28 births and 3 deaths per 1,000 people respectively (World Bank).
Infant mortality rate: 10 per 1,000 live births (World Bank)

Welfare
Most Omanis depend on the extended family for financial support. Since 1984 the Ministry of Social Affairs has run a scheme of monthly welfare payments for eight categories of Omani citizens, provided that they can prove indigence. The categories are: orphans, divorcees, people unable to work, refugees, widows, spinsters, people over 60 years of age and the families of prisoners.

The Sultanate of Oman has extended social security benefits for workers in the private sector. Since the issue of the Social Insurance law in 1992, the Public Authority for Social Insurance (PASI) has registered companies and establishments in the private sector including workers and their families, who are entitled to receive sickness, injury and disability benefits, pension and death compensation.

The Association for the Welfare of Handicapped Children, a charitable organisation, supplements the work of the ministry of social affairs, labour and vocational training with centres at Al-Khoudh, Quriyat and Bilad Banu Bu Hassan. The government has made donations towards women's training centres and nurseries for childcare. Special attention is given to the needs of the disabled, particularly young

needs of the disabled, particularly young people who are encouraged to join the training centre at Al-Khoudh. The centre also cares for severely disabled children between 3–14 years of age. The ministry has developed sport facilities as part of the disabled welfare programme. The Oman Charitable Organisation (OCO), a non-governmental body, has co-operated with the ministry to build 45 shelters at a cost of RO58,500 (US$152,161) for the Bedu living in remote areas of the country and assisted with programmes for the disabled.

Main cities
Muscat (Masqat) (capital, estimated population 54,800; including suburbs 797,000 in 2003), Salalah (178,100), Sohar (129,300), Ibri (116,600).

Languages spoken
English is spoken in business circles. KiSwahili is often spoken among the older generation and those of Zanzibari descent. Given the size of the immigrant population, Farsi, Urdu and Baluchi are common languages.

Official language/s
Arabic

Media
Press
The government abolished censorship of independent newspapers in 1985. A law requires that all publications and journalists be licensed by the Ministry of Information. The maximum penalty for publishing material deemed unacceptable is three years' imprisonment. The national news agency is the Oman News Agency (ONA).
Dailies: Those in Arabic include the *Oman Daily*, *Alquds Newspaper* and the independent daily *Al-Watan*. English language dailies that are government-owned include *Oman Daily Observer* and *Independent Times of Oman*.
Periodicals: *Oman Today* is published every two months.

Broadcasting
Radio: Both of Oman's radio stations are government-run and the presentation of programmes alternates between studios in Muscat and Salalah. There are broadcasts in both English and Arabic.
Television: Oman has two government-run television channels. In 1992 the government lifted a ban on the private purchase of satellite dishes. In urban areas, virtually every household has a television.

Advertising
With the rise of English-language media, in particular through cable television, western advertisers are rapidly developing the industry in Oman.

Economy
Since Sultan Qaboos came to power in 1970, Oman has been seen as one of the developing world's fastest growing economies. With a population of 3.23 million and a per capita income of over US$10,339 in 2004, Oman is a middle-income developing country. The country relies heavily on oil revenues, which account for around 40 per cent of GDP. Oman has only limited resources and although oil has been used as the motor for economic development, the government continues to diversify so as not to be too dependent on a single resource. The stated aim of economic diversification is to reduce oil's domination of the economy until it accounts for less than 20 per cent of GDP and to encourage private sector investment.

Oman has developed liquefied natural gas (LNG) production, a manufacturing sector, ports and telecommunications. Since the early 1990s, each of these sectors has registered major gains. While since the late 1990s, the economy has benefited from relatively high oil prices, diversification remains the top development priority. A US$2.4 billion aluminum smelter, to begin operations in 2007, could spearhead further diversification in the economy.

The government has set an economic development target, Vision 2020, to achieve a level of growth on a par with the Asian Tiger economies by 2020. The seventh five-year plan will commence in 2006. Membership of the World Trade Organisation since 2000 has reduced barriers to entry in Oman and opened the country to foreign investment.

Although standards of living are improving, illiteracy remains a significant problem and could hinder economic growth. Unemployment levels are high at around 15 per cent in 2004, while around a quarter of the population live below the poverty line.

External trade
Imports
Principal imports are machinery and transport equipment, manufactured goods, food, livestock and lubricants.
Main sources: UAE (17.5 per cent total, 2004), Japan (16.6 per cent), UK (8.5 per cent), Italy (6.4 per cent), Germany (5.2 per cent), US (4.7 per cent), India (4.3 per cent)

Exports
Crude oil (typically 70 per cent of total exports), liquefied natural gas (LNG), fish, processed copper, textiles and dates.
Main destinations: China (27.6 per cent total, 2004), South Korea (17.8 per cent), Japan (12.7 per cent), Thailand (11.7 per cent), UAE (6.6 per cent)

Agriculture
Farming
Agriculture accounts for around 3 per cent of GDP and employs around 200,000 people. Agriculture and fisheries account for an average 35 per cent per annum of Oman's main non-oil exports. Main crops include dates, alfalfa, lucerne, wheat, mangoes, limes and bananas, with market gardening of tomatoes, cabbages, aubergines, okra and cucumbers.

The shortage of water and pasture and the salinity of the soil are the main constraints on agricultural development. The emphasis of government investment in this sector has been on digging wells, repairing old irrigation systems and building dams to trap rainwater which previously ran off into the sea. Irrigation studies show potential arable land to be twice that under cultivation, but agriculture already uses over 90 per cent of the available water. Apart from a narrow coastal strip (the Batinah coastline), most of Oman is either mountain or desert.

A network of collection and distribution centres is run by the Public Authority for Marketing Agricultural Produce (Pamap). Pamap exports fruit and vegetables, particularly bananas, and operates a banana ripening and packing factory at Salalah and a handling centre at Al Suwaiq. Estimated crop production in 2004 included: 5,775 tonnes (t) cereals in total, 1,425t wheat, 2,515t papayas, 238,000t dates, 15,500t potatoes, 33,000t bananas, 2,950t sorghum, 7,500t citrus fruit, 11,000t mangoes, 43,000t tomatoes, 1,270t tobacco, 293,315t fruit in total, 186,500t vegetables in total. Estimated livestock production in 2004 included: 43,412t meat in total, 4,160t beef, 13,110t lamb, 13,750t goat meat, 5,840t poultry, 8,600t eggs, 104,020t milk, 480t cattle hides, 6,552t camel meat.

Fishing
The fishing industry is well developed and has helped to diversify the economy. Stocks include between 15,000 and 27,000 tonnes of kingfish, 50,000 tonnes of tuna and 2,000 tonnes of shellfish. The total fish catch typically varies between 118,000 to 160,000 tonnes per annum. Oman Fisheries Co SAOG is the largest fishing company in the country. It undertakes processing and marketing of fish and fishery products, which are approved for export to European countries. Exports include fresh fish, frozen fish and seafood (prawns, crabs and lobsters). The Gulf Co-operation Council (GCC) states are the destination for almost half of Omani fish exports.

Forestry
There is very little forest or woodland in Oman with forest cover estimated at

1,000 hectares, mainly composed of scattered areas of Juniperus forest in the Hajar Mountains. About 10 million date palms are grown along the northern Batinah coastal strip. Although some wood is used for domestic consumption, there is no significant commercial exploitation. Much of the demand for wood and paper products is met through imports.

Industry and manufacturing
The government is acutely aware that oil reserves are low and the population is growing significantly with a high proportion of young people. As a result, government policy aims to promote growth and employment through encouraging private sector investment in industry. This has been done by offering incentives such as tax exemptions, customs protection, soft or interest-free loans and by providing infrastructure, usually in the form of industrial estates. It favours small- to medium-sized industries which are import-substituting, use local raw materials, have a relative advantage in export markets or employ a high ratio of Omanis. A series of five-year development plans, started in 1976, outline the government's main objectives of self-sufficiency, import substitution and the diversification of the economy to reduce reliance on oil. The five-year plans call for the manufacturing, trade and financial services sectors to contribute 80 per cent to annual GDP by 2020.
Industrial production increased by 4 per cent in 2003.

Tourism
As part of its programme of diversification, the government has introduced measures designed to promote private sector participation in the tourist industry. Tourism is believed to be capable of generating more foreign earnings and employment opportunities than heavy industry. The sector is expected to contribute 1.8 per cent to GDP in 2005. The government wants tourism to account for 5 per cent of GDP by 2020.
The sector, following World Trade Organisation advice, has targeted upmarket visitors, but more recently the example of Dubai has stimulated interest in the mass market. In June 2005, the construction of a huge, privately-financed resort called 'Blue City', costing US$15 billion, was announced. The project, covering 35 square kilometres along the al-Sawardi sea-front, will take 15 years to complete.

Mining
Mining typically contributes around 1 per cent to annual GDP and employs around 3 per cent of the workforce.
Oman has large resources of industrial rocks and minerals, some of which are already being exploited. They include silica sand, dolomite, limestone, gypsum, ornamental stone, clays, rockwool, iron oxides, heavy sands, wollastonite, celestite, asbestos, aggregate, laterite and barite. Mineral deposits of copper, manganese, lead, iron, zinc, chrome, phosphates, gold, silver and nickel exist, many of them in inaccessible areas. Government policy is to exploit raw materials wherever commercially feasible and diversify the development of its mineral resources. As in other sectors of the economy, the government aims for self-sufficiency and the mineral-based industry is expected to contribute significantly to the growth of GDP in coming years. The indigenous mineral-based industries include cement, limestone, ceramics and construction and the production of processed marble, gold ore, chromite, industrial and edible salt and clays. The government has encouraged the processing of ores within Oman rather than exporting them untreated.
In the late 1990s, the Japan International Corporation discovered new gold and copper deposits at Ghuzayn and Daris, which led to the development of potential areas for copper and gold mineralisation. Copper and chromite are mined near Sohar by thegovernment-owned Oman Mining Company (OMCO). Saudi Arabia is the main market for cathode copper production. There are probable copper ore reserves of 15.2 million tonnes at Rakah and Hayl al Safil in the Willayat of Yanqul, about 275km from the smelter. Chromite reserves are put at two million tonnes and annual production is around 6,000 tonnes. Chromite is exported to Japan and China. Gold and silver are produced from the copper oxide deposits by the OMCO processing plant.

Hydrocarbons
Oil is the major sector of the economy, providing nearly 80 per cent of the country's export earnings and contributing 40 per cent to GDP. In 2004, proven oil reserves stood at 5.6 billion barrels. Production stood at 785,000 barrels per day (bpd), 4.4 per cent down on 2003. The reserves are located in the northern and central regions. Yibal, which produces around 180,000 bpd, is the largest oil field. Production has risen as new fields have been exploited – the Mukhaizina field (25,000bpd), the Burhaan field (24,000bpd) and the al-Noor field (9,400bpd). 263.6 million barrels were exported in 2004, compared with 278.5 million barrels in 2003. The decline in both production and exports of oil in recent years is offset by rising prices.
Proven natural gas reserves were one trillion cubic metres in 2004, but potential reserves are thought to be double that figure. Gas production stood at 17.6 billion cubic metres in 2004, an increase of 6.7 per cent on 2003 output. Oman is concentrating its efforts on developing liquefied natural gas (LNG) production. The existing natural gas pipeline network is being extended with the aid of foreign construction companies. The natural gas deposits in central Oman were linked by US$124 million and US$180 million pipelines to the coastal cities of Sohar and Salalah respectively in August 2002. Coal deposits with reserves of over 22 million tonnes have been discovered in the Wadi Muswa and Wadi Fisaw areas of the Sharqiya near Sur. Coal from the Al Kamil field is of good quality, and could be used to provide the energy for a 300MW generator over a period of some 40 years, using 600,000 tonnes annually.

Energy
Installed electricity generating capacity is around 2.5 GW. Demand is growing rapidly at 5 per cent per annum. Natural gas is used to reduce domestic demand for oil, mainly by power plants, copper smelters and cement plants. Electricity reaches all populated areas except for some remote mountain villages. About 86 per cent of the country is fully supplied.
The 280MW Al Kamil power plant, built by International Power plc, the 430MW Barka power plant, owned by AES, the 240MW integrated power plant, owned by PSEG, to supply the Dhofar region, and the 140MW plant at Qarn Alam, owned by Bharat Heavy Electricals, all run on natural gas.

Financial markets
Stock exchange
The Muscat Securities Market (MSM) opened in 1989 with the purpose of attracting local savings and international capital. Modelled on the Amman (Jordan) exchange, the MSM has acquired a reputation for good management.

Banking and insurance
Oman has a robust banking sector both foreign and domestic with two specialised banks subsidised by the government – the Oman Housing Bank and the Oman Bank for Industrial Development. However, experts believe the sector is over-banked and have called for mergers to consolidate the sector.
Central bank
Central Bank of Oman
Main financial centre
Muttrah Business District

Time
GMT plus four hours

Nations of the World: A Political, Economic and Business Handbook

Geography
Oman lies at the south-eastern tip of the Arabian peninsula, bordering Yemen, Saudi Arabia and the United Arab Emirates (UAE). The Musandam Peninsula in the far north is separated from the rest of Oman by UAE territory. The coastline is 1,700km long.

There are two distinct areas of population, centred on the Hajar mountains in the north and the Batina plain and its hinterland in the south. Between them lies 800km of virtually uninhabited gravel plain.

Climate
Most of the country is hot and arid, with noon temperatures in summer exceeding 40 degrees Celsius (C) and annual rainfall of around 100mm. There is a higher rainfall over the mountains. The southern region, however, has a tropical climate, with noon temperatures between 27 and 33 degrees C all year round and a rainy season from June to August.

Dress codes
Formal clothing is recommended for public places and in general the body should be fully covered. Businessmen should wear suits and ties to appointments, but the jacket can be carried. Shorts are not allowed, except for sports. Women are advised to dress modestly. Swimwear should be worn only at hotel pools and on the beach.

Entry requirements
Passports
Required by all.
Visa
Required by all. As from July 2003 citizens of most of the Americas, Europe, Australasia and many Asian countries may visit on a combined tourist, business and short visit visa which can be obtained at the port of entry. Visitors no longer require sponsorship from a local resident or organisation
Further details can be found at http://www.rop.gov.om/services_passport2.asp including the full list of those visitors who may use this facility. Those who do not appear on the list of eligibility should contact the nearest Omani Embassy and apply for a visa as required.
Oman has a joint visa agreement with the Emirate of Dubai, visitors with a visa for either country may cross to the other without a further visa, however the term of visit is a maximum of three weeks.
Prohibited entry
Holders of Israeli passports are not allowed entry.
Currency advice/regulations
There are no currency control regulations, although capital transfers abroad exceeding RO20,000 (US$52,000) require approval from the Central Bank of Oman. There are numerous Omani and foreign bank branches in the cities, as well as licensed money-changers.
Customs
Personal effects, most goods from Gulf Co-operation Council (GCC) countries and imports for Petroleum Development Oman (PDO) or the government are duty free. Video cassettes are temporarily impounded for police examination.
Prohibited imports
Although goods of Israeli origin and imports from Israel are no longer supposed to be illegal in Oman, goods produced by companies boycotted by the Arab League are prohibited. At a meeting in Damascus, Syria, in 2001, recommendations were approved calling for a revival of the boycott of all exports from Israel to Arab states. There are restrictions on the import of arms, ammunition, certain motor vehicles, and dangerous drugs. Alcohol is prohibited. The importation of clothing bearing Koranic inscriptions are banned.

Health (for visitors)
Mandatory precautions
Vaccination certificate against yellow fever if travelling from infected area.
Advisable precautions
Health facilities are good but expensive for foreigners. Health insurance is therefore recommended for visitors.
It is advisable to be vaccinated against typhoid, hepatitis, polio and tetanus. Anti-malaria precautions should also be taken.
Milk is unpasteurised and should be boiled or avoided. Vegetables should be cooked and fruit peeled before consumption.

Hotels
There are several five-star hotels in Muscat. Prices are steep compared with Dubai and Abu Dhabi.
A tax of 17 per cent is included in all bills. Dhofar coast beaches are the main tourist area.

Credit cards
Major credit cards and traveller's cheques are accepted. Local banks do not cash personal cheques.

Public holidays
Fixed dates
1 Jan (New Year's Day), 18 Nov (National Day), 19 Nov (Sultan's Birthday), 31 Dec (Bank Holiday).
Variable dates
Eid al Adha (four days), Eid al Fitr (four days), Islamic New Year, Birth of the Prophet (two days).
The Islamic year has 354 or 355 days, with the result that Muslim feasts advance by 10–12 days against the Gregorian calendar each year. Dates of the Muslim feasts vary according to sightings of the new moon, so cannot be forecast exactly.

Working hours
Business starts early, particularly in high summer. Oil companies, government-run ports and industries start at 0700; many other companies at 0800.
Work hours are affected by Ramadan, the Muslim holy month of fasting during daylight hours, with most people working only a six-hour day or a 36-hour week. Most officials work 0900–1300, but many useful contacts can be made and renewed during and after the evening Iftar meal.
Banking
Sat–Wed: 0800–1200; Thu: 0800–1130.
Business
Sat–Thu: 0830–1300, 1530–1830.
Government
Sat–Wed: 0730–1430.
Shops
Sat–Wed: 0800–1300, 1600–1800; Thu: 0800–1300. Shops in the souk are often open beyond 1800.

Telecommunications
Mobile phones
A GSM service that covers the Capital Area, Batinah coast, Salalah and parts of the interior.

Electricity supply
220/240V AC, plug fittings two or three-pin round or three-pin flat types.

Weights and measures
Metric.

Social customs/useful tips
Handshaking is the normal form of greeting and business cards are exchanged at business meetings. Appointments are required for business meetings and there is an increasing trend towards punctuality. However, visitors should also be prepared to wait and to make several visits to the same office before formalities are completed.
It is discourteous to eat, drink or smoke in front of Muslims in daylight hours during Ramadan. It is polite to accept the refreshments customarily offered to visitors. Alcohol is available in hotel bars and restaurants. Non-Muslims with liquor permits from the Omani police can buy alcoholic drinks at special stores for consumption at home.
The government regularly issues strong-worded ordinances designed to keep the country clean and tidy. It is an offence, for example, to drive a dirty car or hang out washing in view of main roads. Foreigners should take care to observe these regulations, although the police rarely enforce them.

Oman

Security
Oman is the most stable country in the Arabian peninsula. Even levels of petty crime are minimal.

Getting there
Air
There are flights from UK, USA, Australia, India and many Middle Eastern States. Oman Air services are predominantly internal or short-haul to other Gulf states, although it also has routes to the Indian subcontinent.
National airline: Oman Air.
International airport/s: Seeb International Airport (MCT), 40km from Muscat, with duty-free shops and a restaurant; Salalah International Airport, near the southern city of Salalah.
Airport tax: None
Surface
Road: The Yemen border is not open to travellers, but there are road links with the United Arab Emirates, including regular bus services between Muscat and Dubai.
Water: There are some ferry services into Muscat from other Gulf States.

Getting about
National transport
Air: There are six civil airports. Oman Air is the national domestic carrier. It operates daily scheduled flights to Salalah Airport and daily flights to Fahud and Marmul. There are also flights to the Musandam Peninsula, Buraimi, Sur and the island of Masirah. All flights should be booked well in advance and confirmed on the day before travelling.
Road: An excellent asphalt road system links all the main centres. A 780km highway links Dhofar with the north.
There are over 9,000km of paved roads (550km of dual carriageway) and over 22,000km of unpaved track roads. Improvements and the widening of existing highways is being carried out, and linking roads between towns and villages of the interior are being constructed.
It is possible to drive along the coast from Quriyat to Sur in a four-wheel drive vehicle.
Buses: National bus services run twice daily to Salalah by luxury coach from the bus stations at Ruwi and the Muttrah Corniche. Local services in the capital area. Contact the Oman National Transport Company (ONTC), PO Box 620, Muscat (tel: 590-046, 590-603).
Taxis: There is an excellent network of minibuses which operate as 'service' taxis linking up the major centres of population.
Water: There are regular ferry services from Muscat to Khasab on the Musandam Peninsular.

City transport
Taxis: Taxis are expensive by Gulf standards; they should have a scale of charges, but it is advised to negotiate fares in advance (there are no meters). Tipping is not usual. Some hotels offer a courtesy pick-up service; others offer the service but charge.
Buses, trams & metro: An urban bus service operates in Muscat, but is not recommended for visitors.
Car hire
It is necessary to hold an international driving licence when hiring a car in Oman. Check licence rules in advance. Speed limits are 120kph and driving is on the right-hand side of the road. Most hotels have self-drive car hire facilities.

BUSINESS DIRECTORY

The addresses listed below are a selection only. While World of Information makes every endeavour to check these addresses, we cannot guarantee that changes have not been made, especially to telephone numbers and area codes. We would welcome any corrections.

Telephone area codes
The international direct dialling (IDD) code for Oman is +968, followed by subscriber's number.

Useful telephone numbers
Capital area
Police: 560-099
Fire: 999
International operator: 195
International enquiries: 197
Directory enquiries: 198
Operator: 190

Chambers of Commerce
Oman Chamber of Commerce and Industry, PO Box 1400, Ruwi 112 (tel: 707-674; fax: 708-497; e-mail: occi@chamberoman.com).

Banking
Bank Dhofar, PO Box 1507, Ruwi 112 (tel: 790-466; fax: 797-246; e-mail: info@bankdhofar.com).

BankMuscat, PO Box 1708, 112 Ruwi (tel: 456-365; fax: 456-077; e-mail: info@bankmuscat.com).

Industrial Bank of Oman, PO Box 2613, Ruwi 112 (tel: 706-786; fax: 706-986; e-mail: indlbank@omantel.net.om).

Majan International Bank, PO Box 2717, Ruwi 112 (tel: 780-388; fax: 780-643; e-mail: majanbk@omantel.net.om).

National Bank of Oman, PO Box 2613, 112 Ruwi (tel: 706-786 fax: 706-986; e-mail: ask@nbo.om).

Oman Arab Bank, PO Box 2010, Ruwi 112 (tel: 706-265; fax: 797-736; e-mail: mktoab@omantel.net.om).

Oman Development Bank, PO Box 309, Muscat 113 (tel: 738-021; fax: 738-026; e-mail: odebe@omantel.net.om).

Oman Housing Bank, PO Box 2555, Muscat 112 (tel: 704-444; e-mail: i-ohb@i-ohb.com.om).

Oman International Bank, PO Box 1216, P C 112 Ruwi (tel: 576-039, 576-618; fax: 576-040; e-mail: omintbnk@omantel.net.om).

Central bank
Central Bank of Oman, PO Box 1161, Ruwi 112 (tel: 702-222; fax: 702-253).

Travel information
Seeb International Airport, PO Box 58, Muscat 111 (tel: 519-285; fax: 510-805).

Gulf Air, PO Box 1444, Ruwi 112 (tel: 703-222; fax:793-381).

Oman Air, PO Box 58, Seeb International Airport, Muscat 111 (tel: 519-953; fax: 521-075).

Oman Automobile Association, PO Box 2874, Muscat 111 (tel: 510-239;fax: 510-276; e-mail: omanauto@omantel.net.om).

Oman Aviation Services, PO Box 58, Muscat 111 (tel: 519-237; fax: 510-805).

Oman National Transport Company, PO Box 620, Muscat 113 (tel: 590-046; fax: 590-152; e-mail: ontc01@omantel.net.om).

Ministry of tourism
Directorate General of Tourism, Ministry of Commerce and Industry, PO Box 550, Muscat 113 (tel: 771-6527; fax: 771-4213; e-mail: dgt@mocioman.org; internet: omantourism.gov.om).

Ministries
Ministry of Agriculture and Fisheries, PO Box 467, Muscat 113 (tel: 696-300; fax: 605-304).

Ministry of Awqaf and Religious Affairs, PO Box 3232, Ruwi 112 (tel: 696-870; fax: 601-109).

Ministry of Civil Service, PO Box 3994, Ruwi 112 (tel: 696-000; fax: 601-771).

Ministry of Commerce and Industry, PO Box 550, Muscat 113 (tel: 771-3500; fax: 771-7239).

Ministry of Defence, PO Box 113, Muscat 113 (tel: 312-605; fax: 702-521).

Ministry of Education, PO Box 3, Muscat 113 (tel: 775-209; fax: 708-485).

Ministry of Foreign Affairs, PO Box 252, Muscat 113 (tel: 699-500; fax: 696-641).

Ministry of Health, PO Box 393, Muscat 113 (tel: 602-177; fax: 602-647).

Ministry of Higher Education, PO Box 82, Ruwi 112 (tel: 695-330; fax: 694-481)

Ministry of Housing, Electricity & Water, PO Box 1491, Ruwi 112 (tel: 603-800; fax: 699-180).

Ministry of Information, PO Box 600, Muscat 113 (tel: 603-222; fax: 601-638; internet: www.omanet.com).

Ministry of Interior, PO Box 127, Ruwi 112 (tel: 602-244; fax: 660-644).

Ministry of Justice, PO Box 354, Ruwi 112 (tel: 697-699; fax: 602-725).

Ministry of Legal Affairs, PO Box 578, Ruwi 112 (tel: 605-802; fax: 605-697).

Ministry of National Economy, PO Box 506, Muscat 113 (tel: 738-201; fax: 737-068).

Ministry of National Heritage & Culture, PO Box 668, Muscat 113 (tel: 602-555; fax: 697-060).

Ministry of Oil and Gas, PO Box 551, Muscat 113 (tel: 603-333; fax: 696-972).

Ministry of Regional Municipalities, Environment and Water Resources, PO Box 323, Muscat 113 (tel: 692-550; fax: 693-995).

Ministry of Social Development, [PO Box 560, Muscat 113 (tel: 602-444; fax: 699-357).

Ministry of Transport and Telecommunications, PO Box 338, Ruwi 112 (tel: 697-888; fax: 696-817).

Other useful addresses
British Embassy, PO Box 300, 185 Mina al Fahral, Muscat 113 (tel: 693-086; fax: 693-088; e-mail: becomu@omantel.net).

Capital Market Authority, PO Box 3265, Ruwi 112 (tel: 771-7609; fax: 771-6691.

Development Council, PO Box 881, Muscat 113 (tel: 698-900; fax: 696-285).

High Commitee for Conferences, PO Box 891, Muscat 113 (tel: 698-221; fax: 607-497).

Muscat Securities Market, PO Box 3265, Ruwi 112 (tel: 771-2607; fax: 777-6353).

Oman International Trade and Exhibitions (OITE), PO Box 112, Ruwi 112 (tel: 564-303; fax: 565-165; e-mail: oitex@omantel.net.om).

Oman Oil Company, PO Box 261, Qurm 118 (tel: 567-392; fax: 567-386; e-mail: oman-oil@omantel.net.om).

Omani Centre for Investment Promotion and Export Development, PO Box 25, Wadi Kabir 117 (tel: 771-2344; fax: 771-0890; e-mail: info@ociped.com).

Omani Embassy (USA), 2535 Belmont Road NW, Washington DC 20008 (tel: 202-387-1980; fax: 202-745-4933; e-mail: emboman@erols.com).

Petroleum Development Oman (PDO), PO Box 81, Muscat 113 (tel: 678-111; fax: 677-106).

Public Establishment for Industrial Estates, PO Box 2, Rusayl 124 (tel: 626-080; fax: 626-349; e-mail: info@pete.com).

Salalah Port Services Company, PO Box 105, Muscat 118 (tel: 567-188; fax: 567-166).

US Embassy, PO Box 202, Medinat Al Sultan Qaboos 115 (tel: 698-989; fax: 699-189; e-mail: aemctcns@gto.net).

Internet sites
Arab net: http://www.arab.net/welcome.html

Arabia on-line: http://www.arabia.com

Gulf business explorer: http://www.igulf.com/main.htm

Oman online archives of political, economic and business news: http://www.newsbriefsoman.info

Times of Oman: http://omantimes.com/

Pakistan

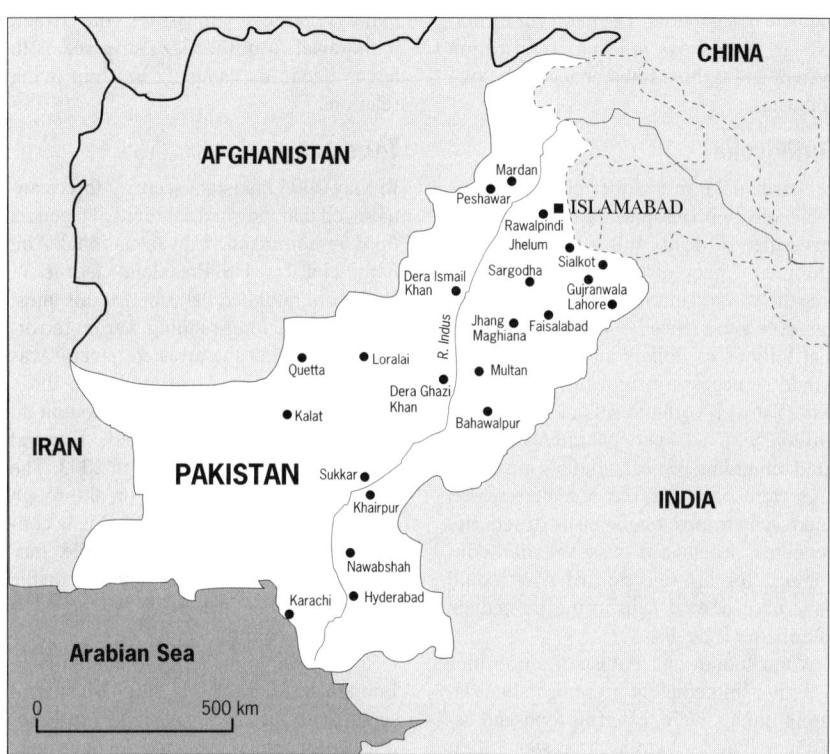

KEY FACTS

Official name: Islami Jamhuriya e Pakistan (Islamic Republic of Pakistan)

Head of State: President Pervez Musharraf (sworn in 20 Jun 2001)

Head of government: Prime Minister Shaukat Aziz (sworn in 28 Aug 2004)

Ruling party: Pakistan Muslim League-Qaid e Azam (PML-QA)

Area: 803,943 square km

Population: 157.06 million (2004)

Capital: Islamabad

Official language: Urdu (national language) and English

Currency: Rupee (Rp) = 100 paisa

Exchange rate: Rp59.67 per US$ (Oct 2005)

GDP per capita: US$550 (2004)

GDP real growth: 6.50% (2004)

Labour force: 57,415 (2004)

Unemployment: 8.30% (2004) (additional underemployment)

Inflation: 6.70% (2004)

Balance of trade: -US$3.38 billion (2004)

Foreign debt: US$33.97 billion (2004)

Pakistani ruler General Pervez Musharraf can claim successes in the economy and in being seen to crack down on terrorist activity. There was progress in confidence building and peace measures with India following the peace agreement of 2004. Japanese sanctions on Pakistan were finally ended in 2005, after seven years. Japan had taken the action in response to Pakistan's carrying out of nuclear tests in 1998. It was a record year in the cotton harvest thanks to an industry expansion and perfect weather conditions.

India-Pakistan relations

The two countries have gone to war three times since partition and independence in 1947, twice over the border area of Kashmir. The disputed region of Kashmir has been the site of a 15-year violent uprising in which over 40,000 people have been killed. In early 2005 an election was held for the first time in nearly 30 years. Turnout was high despite widespread intimidation and five deaths. Pakistan has said that it wants a referendum to be held on the position of Kashmir, but India has resisted these calls.

India wants the line of control to have the status of an international border whereas Pakistan will concede only to it being a 'soft border'. Previously Musharraf has demanded that a deal on Kashmir be a prerequiste to normalising relations with India; in 2005, however, to the pleasure of US diplomats, he seems to have allowed the dispute to be put on the back burner while progress is made in other areas.

A peace progress was initiated in 2004 and saw progress in February 2005 when officials announced the future opening of a new civilian bus service to ferry passengers across the line of control (LoC) that divides the Kashmir region. Those using the service need to attain entry permits, rather than passports, which India initially sought. It is the first bus service to travel this route since before the partition and has mostly symbolic weight. The announcement was significant in generating confidence among locals, who finally would be able to travel to meet separated family members. The ceasefire also agreed at this time has survived, reflecting popular fatigue with continued violence.

Shortly after the bus service was announced General Musharraf agreed to attend a cricket tour in India, for the first time for years. This was not all plain sailing as Pakistan diplomats objected to the official match itinerary, requesting that the Ahmedabad match be re-located outside of Gujarat, for fears about the security of the Muslim side. This state was the scene of a massacre in 2002 which left almost 2,000 Muslims dead. Muslim girls were subject to a huge wave of sexual violence and rape. The Indian authorities claim that the massacre was a spontaneous response to the Muslim torching of a train carrying Hindu worshippers. However, observers have noted that the events bore the hallmarks of careful planning – by nationalists who seek to create an official Hindu state.

New Delhi suffered multiple bomb attacks in October 2005 which were blamed on Muslim terrorists from Pakistan. Despite the bombing however, India and Pakistan made further diplomatic progress with a relaxation of travel rules, allowing relatives to travel over five crossing points to see family affected by the earthquake.

A subsequent bombing, this time in November 2005 in Indian-controlled Kashmir, did not help relations. Five people died in a car bomb attack, which was carried out by suicide bombers from Jaish-e-Mohammed, a large Islamic group in the region which India claims is sponsored by the Pakistani government.

In August 2005 India and Pakistan reached a nuclear accord promising to give notice to the other before launching ballistic missile tests. The pact will formalise an up-to-now informal notification system and tighten links between the two countries.

Earthquake

An earthquake in October 2005 hit Pakistan badly, with a force of 7.6 on the Richter scale, a death toll of 73,000 and millions of people rendered homeless. It was the worst natural disaster the country has ever experienced. The UN estimated that billions of dollars and several years would be necessary for a full reconstruction. The IMF offered a loan of US$375 million, with a 0.5 per cent interest rate, to fund rebuilding projects. India's aid offerings were accepted, but not their search and rescue troops, on the basis of security concerns. Musharraf was roundly condemned for his rejection of what could have been crucial help in the immediate aftermath of the disaster.

When Indian and Pakistani authorities were not immediately present, radical Islamic groups were, offering food and assistance and helping bolster their reputations among the Kashmiri population. Musharraf admitted that some extremist groups under official surveillance, Jamaat-ud-Dawa and Al-Rasheed Trust, were among the most active in relief efforts.

Musharraf accepted humanitarian aid offered by Israel for the first time ever. Although Pakistan refuses to accept diplomatic relations with Israel, the Israeli withdrawal from the Gaza strip seems to have been a catalyst in improving relations.

Terrorism

In May 2005 Pakistani security forces announced that they had captured al Qaeda's third in command, Libyan national Abu Faraj al Liby. US President George W Bush congratulated Pakistan for this latest victory in the long-running war on terrorism, saying that the arrested general was 'a direct threat to America and to those who love freedom'. Liby is thought to have tried to assassinated General Musharraf on two occasions in 2003. The Pakistani leader said that the breakthrough arrest has helped cripple the al Qaeda control network. The capture, while morale-boosting, did not shed any light on the whereabouts of the reclusive terrorist chief Osama bin Laden.

In response to the terrorist bombings in London on 7 and 21 July 2005, Musharraf said that al Qaeda was not significantly active in his country and could not have masterminded the UK attacks. The UK and Pakistan indignantly blamed the other for the London bombings. Three of the four bombers were of Pakistani origin, but Musharraf pointed to the fact these extremists were homegrown, 'born, educated and bred in England'.

The issue of *madrassas*, Islamic schools, surfaced after the London attacks, with some commentators blaming the perceived zealous, anti-West teaching carried out in these institutions for fostering extremist violence. Estimates put the number of *madrassas* in Pakistan at around 10,000. Traditionally these schools have sent students to Afghanistan to perform military training but in the wake of the 9/11 attack in the US Musharraf has distanced himself from the Taliban. Pakistan feels that the negative publicity surrounding Pakistan's record on terrorism is impacting on its tourism and business sectors.

Nevertheless, the Pakistani authorities did carry out a crackdown on suspected terrorists and 300 people were arrested. They also sent a message to the *madrassas*

KEY INDICATORS — Pakistan

	Unit	2000	2001	2002	2003	2004
Population	m	137.50	140.50	143.73	150.40	*157.06
Gross domestic product (GDP)	US$bn	61.30	59.70	61.20	68.60	*96.11
GDP per capita	US$	446	425	426	470	550
GDP real growth	%	3.9	2.7	4.5	5.1	6.5
Inflation	%	4.4	3.1	3.6	3.2	6.7
Unemployment	%	7.8	6.3	9.0	7.3	7.0
Natural gas output	bn cum	19.0	19.9	20.9	21.1	23.2
Coal output	mtoe	1.5	1.5	1.6	1.4	1.3
Exports (fob) (goods)	US$m	8,739.0	8,934.0	9,140.0	10,889.0	13,352.0
Imports (fob) (goods)	US$m	9,898.0	10,202.0	9,430.0	11,333.0	16,735.0
Balance of trade	US$m	-1,159.0	-1,268.0	-290.0	-444.0	-3,382.0
Current account	US$m	-96.0	-1,951.0	1,590.0	4,204.0	280.0
Foreign debt	US$bn	32.1	32.0	35.1	32.3	–
Total reserves minus gold	US$m	1,513.0	3,640.0	8,078.0	10,941.0	9,799.0
Foreign exchange	US$m	1,499.0	3,636.0	8,076.0	10,693.0	9,554.0
Exchange rate	per US$	53.65	61.93	59.20	57.82	58.33

* estimated figure

notifying them of a requirement to register officially with the government by the end of 2005, which will led to the possibility of official inspections.

In December 2005 Abu Hamza Rabia, a high ranking al Qaeda operative was killed in the northern borderlands near Afghanistan.

Polls

The holding of the first local elections for three years were held in August 2005. There were accusations of corruption and vote rigging and the dismissal of female candidates. The elections are a precursor to a possible resumption of democracy in 2007. The strength of the ruling Pakistan Muslim League will be put to an important test. If Musharraf is to have confidence in tackling Islamic extremism, his party needed a strong approval rating in these polls. A weak performance would have been a sign he needs to consult more with the opposition. The General claimed victory, taking two out of a possible four provinces. However, opposition parties denounced the polls as fraudulent.

Economy

The economy is in the best shape it has been in for twenty years, with success largely underpinned by high levels of investment and a busy large-scale manufacturing sector. FDI has doubled since 2000 to a current level of US$1 billion. The textiles sector was the star performer, with growth of 24 per cent. Economic growth was 6.5 per cent in 2004 and a projected 7.4 per cent in 2005. The demand for credit was very high partly due to a rise in imports of industrial machinery, and also due to activity in the textiles sector. Pakistan's credit bureau and the recent introduction of new safeguards are to be praised for this upturn.

The budget deficit is under control at 4 per cent of GDP, compared to figures of 7.5 per cent in the 1980s and 1990s. However, the earthquake is thought to have put pressure on deficit figures, which are expected to rise to 4.1–4.3 per cent. The long-term reconstruction works will dent public finances despite foreign aid. However, Kashmir generated little national income, with most business activity taking place 1,000km away in the capital Karachi. Investor confidence was largely unaffected by the earthquake. The stock market passed 9,000 points in the aftermath of the earthquake, demonstrating a general business confidence. March 2005 was the first time the stock market had reached the 10,000 barrier. At this point, the Pakistani stock market was the best performer in the world.

The United Bank, one of Pakistan's largest, took on an extra 2,000 staff within a year and saw its profits perform very well, with returns of US$47 million in the early half of 2005. Commercial banks saw profit rises of over 90 per cent in the same period.

Increased loans have paid for the motorbikes and car boom, which has seen sales double from 2004 to 2005. Privatisation deals were prolific in 2005. Pak Arab Fertilizer, Pakistan Telecom, Pakistan State Oil and the National Refinery were up for sale, either in their entirety or in part. These deals constitute the largest privatisation programme the country has seen.

Outlook

General elections are due to be held in 2007 and will represent a make or break chance for Pakistan to embrace democracy. More than half of Pakistan's 58-year history has been one of military government. The poll will also be crucial in indicating the path the country takes in terms of its Islamic movement – radical or moderate. The extremists have a much better chance of victory if the economy crashes or the country suffers more disaster. As the country borders Afghanistan and Iran, a triumph for Islamic extremists would have global repercussions.

Musharraf has promised to discard his military robing and quit as chief of the military, but so far has failed to do ; 2007 is his next deadline for change. He has claimed to want re-election as a citizen candidate. However if he is to succeed he will need to build stronger cross-party alliances. To continue to isolate figures like former prime ministers Benazir Bhutto and Nawaz Sharif is likely to be to his eventual disadvantage.

The economic fundamentals are robust and healthy – it is political events which threaten to upset the country's economy. Unrest, uprisings and extremism will all undermine performance. Rising global oil prices could hit GDP growth and the credit sector. Pakistan wants to send a signal to world markets, publicising the country and its recent strong economic performance – and will do this by issuing US$500 million in bond issues in 2006.

A gas pipeline is in the offing, between Pakistan, Iran and India, although collaboration with Iran is frowned upon by most of the international community. The pipeline will be worth US$3 billion and could seriously cut Pakistan's dependence on oil imports. This is no small thing when an energy crisis has been predicted.

Risk assessment

Economic	Good
Political	Fair
Regional Stability	Fair
Stock Market	Good

COUNTRY PROFILE

Historical profile

The Muslim League, founded in 1906 in British India to safeguard the interests of Muslims, supported Britain in the Second World War while the Indian National Congress was banned. Consequently the Muslim League flourished and won nearly all the Muslim votes in the 1946 election and in 1947 with the division of the continent into India and West and East Pakistan, became Pakistan's major political party, under Muhammed Ali Jinnah.

The failure of the British to ensure a smooth transition to independence for Pakistan and India led to one of the bloodiest events of the twentieth century as a massive shift in the population took place. Over five million Hindus fled from the Punjab and Sindh provinces, while nearly six million Muslims fled from India into West Pakistan and over three million Muslims fled to East Pakistan. There were over half a million deaths.

The origins of the Kashmir conflict stem from this division. British policy was for the more than 550 Indian princely states to accede to either Pakistan or India, based on demographics and geographical location. For most states it was simple enough to decide but predominately-Muslim Kashmir had a minority Hindu administration and the Maharaja, Hari Singh Bahadur, wanted Kashmir to remain independent. This was unacceptable to both India and Pakistan and Bahadur eventually opted to accede to India. India deployed troops after Muslim rebels in western Kashmir set up an Azad (free) government and Pakistan, in support of what it saw as its subject people and territory under threat, went to war. A UN mediated cease-fire was concluded, including a cease-fire line (the Line of Control – LoC) and a referendum to determine popular support for the province's future. In 1953 Kashmir was integrated into India as a State and the plebiscite was never held.

There have been intermittent skirmishes, battles and wars between Pakistan and India ever since. The latest cease-fire, in 2003, allowed for a Test series of cricket matches in 2005 (won by Pakistan), the first bus-link for 57 years across the LoC, and an exchange of visits by the then Prime Minister of India, Atal Bihari

Vajpayee in 2004, and by President Musharraf to India in 2005.
1906 The Muslim League was founded to promote Indian Muslim separatism.
1940 The Muslim League endorsed the idea of a separate nation for Indian Muslims.
1947 Pakistan, (including East Pakistan or what is now Bangladesh), was granted independence as a British Dominion following the partition of the British Indian Empire. The ruler of the Muslim-majority states of Jammu and Kashmir joined secular India rather than Islamic Pakistan. India and Pakistan have disputed Kashmir ever since.
1948 Muhammed Ali Jinnah, the first governor general of Pakistan, died. Pakistan and India fought over the disputed territory of Kashmir.
1951 Liaquat Ali Khan, Jinnah's successor, was assassinated.
1956 The Islamic Republic of Pakistan was proclaimed.
1958 Martial law was declared and General Ayub Khan took power.
1960 Ayub Khan became president.
1965 Pakistan and India fought over Kashmir.
1969 General Yahya Khan took control when Ayub Khan resigned.
1970 Tensions between East and West Pakistan escalated following the separatist Awami League's success in the general elections.
1971 A civil war broke out when East Pakistan attempted to secede. India intervened in support of East Pakistan, which broke away to become Bangladesh.
1972 The Simla peace agreement set a new LoC in Kashmir; India and Pakistan agreed to settle the dispute through peaceful and mutual means.
1973 Zulfiqar Ali Bhutto became prime minister.
1977 Allegations that Bhutto's party, Pakistan People's Party (PPP) won the general elections due to vote-rigging sparked widespread civil disturbances. General Zia ul Haq led a military *coup d'état* and deposed Bhutto.
1978 General Zia became president.
1979 The deposed prime minister Zulfiqar Ali Bhutto was hanged, having been convicted of murdering a political rival, (in a trial that was widely condemned as unfair).
1980 The US pledged military assistance to Pakistan in order to strengthen the Islamist opposition to the Soviet occupation in Afghanistan.
1985 After nearly eight years of martial law, parliamentary democracy with a civilian prime minister was reintroduced.
1986 Benazir Bhutto, (the daughter of former prime minister Bhutto), returned from exile to lead the PPP.

1988 Former military dictator and president, Zia ul Haq, remained pre-eminent until he died with the US ambassador and top Pakistani army officers in a mysterious air crash. General elections on a party basis were finally allowed and were won by the PPP and Benazir Bhutto became prime minister.
1990 Bhutto was dismissed on charges of incompetence and corruption, and Nawaz Sharif was elected prime minister.
1991 Sharif began a programme of economic liberalisation and incorporated *Sharia* (Islamic law) into the legal code.
1993 The military pressured President Khan and Prime Minister Sharif into resigning. Benazir Bhutto returned to power after winning the general elections.
1996 President Leghari dismissed Bhutto's government for corruption.
1997 The Pakistan Muslim League (PML) won the elections and Sharif returned to power as prime minister.
1998 India and Pakistan each conducted underground nuclear tests, leading to widespread international condemnation and US sanctions.
1999 Bhutto and her husband were convicted of corruption and given jail sentences *in absentia*; they remained in exile. Over 1,000 people died in clashes between Pakistani and Indian forces around Kargil in Kashmir. General Pervez Musharraf led a military coup that deposed Sharif. Pakistan was expelled from the Commonwealth.
2000 US President Bill Clinton visited to urged a return to democracy. Sharif was sentenced to life imprisonment on hijacking and terrorism charges, but was later pardoned and sent into exile in Saudi Arabia.
2001 General Musharraf assumed the presidency (dismissing the incumbent President Tarar) and dissolved parliament. Musharraf backed the US war on terrorism in Afghanistan, which led to the US lifting some of the sanctions imposed after the 1998 nuclear testing. Two Pakistan-backed Kashmir militant groups attacked India's parliament; India imposed sanctions.
2002 Musharraf took steps to curb religious extremism and banned two militant groups. He consolidated his power after a referendum, which was criticised as unconstitutional, approved his presidency for a further five years. Following the October general election, Mir Zafarullah Khan Jamali was elected prime minister. Tension between India and Pakistan increased and only intense diplomatic efforts prevented war.
2003 A cease-fire began across the LoC, dividing the disputed state of Kashmir and the Himalayan glacier Siachen – the first formal cease-fire since the insurgency began in 1989. After a two-year ban, Pakistan and India agreed to resume direct air links and allow over-flights. President Musharraf survived an assassination attempt.
2004 The Prime Minister of India, Atal Bihari Vajpayee, visited Pakistan for a meeting with President Musharraf. Pakistan was re-admitted to the Commonwealth. On 26 June, Prime Minister Jamali resigned; Shaukat Aziz was elected by the National Assembly and sworn in as prime minister on 28 August.
2005 The first bus-link for 57 years between divided India- and Pakistan-held Kashmir commenced on 8 April. Not only did the Pakistani cricket team return victorious in May from its first tour of India in six years, but diplomatic relations were also boosted. Pakistan, Bhutan, Bangladesh, India, Maldives, Nepal and Sri Lanka signed the South Asia Free Trade Agreement (Safta), to come into effect on 1 January 2006.
2006 The third bus link between Pakistan and India was launched in January – the service (Lahore-Amritsar) is the first direct link across divided Punjab since partition in 1947. 'Bus diplomacy' is proving popular and successful and will include a rail link between Sindh province and Rajastan state when it is relaunched in February; it was last run in 1965.

Political structure
Constitution
The federal constitution comprises four semi-autonomous provinces – Punjab, Sindh, North West Frontier Province (NWFP) and Baluchistan – as well as federally administered tribal areas (FATAs) and the federal capital area (FCA) of Islamabad. The constitution is an amended version of one promulgated in 1973.
In October 2002, parliament and regional assemblies were elected for the first time since they were suspended following the military take-over led by General Pervez Musharraf in October 1999. Everyone over the age of 18 years and who is not deemed insane is allowed to vote.

Form of state
Federal Islamic republic

The executive
Prior to the October 1999 military coup, executive power rested with the cabinet, responsible to parliament and headed by the prime minister.
On 15 October 1999, executive power was vested in General Pervez Musharraf, who took the title of chief executive, and replaced the cabinet with a National Security Council (NSC), composed of military officers. He subsequently made himself president on 20 June 2001. His

Pakistan

rule was extended by five years after a referendum in April 2002 and he granted himself sweeping new powers, including the right to dismiss an elected parliament. A bill to allow President Pervez Musharraf to remain as army chief as well as president was signed into law in December 2004.

National legislature
The Majlis-i-Shura (parliament) has two chambers: the National Assembly and the Senate. The National Assembly has 342 members and is elected every five years, with 272 members elected in single-seat constituencies on a first-past-the-post basis, 60 female members chosen by the parties in accordance with their share of seats and 10 seats for minority groups, including religious minorities and the Quadiani and Lahori tribes. The National Assembly elects the prime minister from among its members.

The Senate has 100 members elected by the provincial assemblies. The four provinces are allocated 14 seats each, while the federally administered tribal areas (FATA) are assigned eight directly elected seats. The Federal Capital Area (FCA) is awarded two seats, distributed to parties on the basis of their support in the national assembly elections. Each province is also allocated four seats for technocrats and the Islamic clergy and four seats for women. A further two seats, one for technocrats and another for women, are allocated to the FCA.

Legal system
The Supreme Court is the highest court of justice. Each of the four provinces has a High Court. The Federal *Sharia* (Islamic) Court hears appeals against the decisions of lower courts under Islamic laws in force concurrently with ordinary laws, and its decisions can be appealed before a *Sharia* Appellate Bench of the Supreme Court.

Each province is divided into a number of districts, each of which is under the judicial jurisdiction, both civil and criminal, of a principal court presided over by a district or sessions judge. Subordinate civil judges and magistrates dispense justice at lower levels of the judicial hierarchy. Following the coup of 12 October 1999, the army declined to adopt martial law. Therefore, the judicial system continues to operate.

Last elections
February 2003 (Senate); October 2002 (National Assembly); 2002 referendum; 31 December 1997 (presidential).
Results: Senate: the ruling party, PML-QA, won most seats in the upper house.
National Assembly: the Pakistan Muslim League-Qaid e Azam (PML-QA) obtained 76 seats (28 per cent of the vote), the Pakistan People's Party Parliamentarians (PPPP) 62 seats (23 per cent) and the Muttahida Majlis e Amal (MMA) 53 seats (19 per cent).
Mir Zafarullah Khan Jamali (PML-QA) was elected prime minister by the National Assembly; he received 172 votes against 86 for Fazlur Rahman and 70 for Shah Mahmood Qureshi.
Presidential referendum: self-appointed President Musharraf won 97.7 per cent of the vote to extend his rule by five years.

Next elections
2007 (presidential and legislative)

Political parties
Ruling party
Pakistan Muslim League-Qaid e Azam (PML-QA)
Main opposition party
The Pakistan People's Party Parliamentarians (PPPP) is the largest opposition party in the National Assembly. The Muttahida Majlis e Amal (MMA) is the largest opposition party in the Senate, the second largest opposition party in the National Assembly and is the largest party in two of the country's four provinces: North West Frontier Provice (NWFP) and Baluchistan.

Population
157.06 million (2004)
Ethnic make-up
Punjabi, Sindhi, Pashtun, Baluchi and others including Mohajirs (Muslim emigrés from India). The populations are relatively homogeneous in Punjab, Baluchistan and North Western Frontier Province (NWFP) (predominantly Pashtun), but Sindh is more diverse, with many non-Sindhi communities in the cities of Karachi and Hyderbad. Precise ethnicity statistics are unobtainable, but a regional population breakdown can be used as an approximate estimate of ethnic proportions in the country as a whole. The most recent figures are as follows: Punjab (56 per cent), Sindh (23 per cent), NWFP (13 per cent) and Baluchistan (5 per cent).
Pakistan is home to millions of Afghan refugees and to one million illegal immigrants from Bangladesh, Sri Lanka, Iran, Iraq and India.

Religions
Islam 97 per cent, Christianity 1.5 per cent, Hinduism 1.5 per cent.

Education
More than 200,000 extra teachers have been recruited since 2001, most under US donor funding estimated at US$10 million.
The government proposes to establish an international centre of computer science in collaboration with the European Centre of Nuclear Physics. Free internet connections have been extended to public sector universities. A nationwide network of schools called the National Centres for the Rehabilitation of Child Labour (NCRCL) has been set up with 33 schools in areas where child labour is rampant.
Literacy rate: 45.7 per cent total; 30.6 per cent female, adult rates in 2003.
Compulsory years: Five to 15
Enrolment rate: 40 per cent in secondary schools.
Pupils per teacher: 40 in primary schools.

Health
Annual government spending is about 24 per cent, and foreign spending around 2 per cent, of the total expenditure on health, which is approximately 4 per cent of GDP.
Many in poorer rural areas have limited access to healthcare facilities. Although there have been improvements in provision, facilities remain relatively poor, and there are still fewer than 800 hospitals for the entire country, providing less than one hospital bed for every 1,000 people. Pakistani authorities have made some efforts to provide increased preventive health care. Particular attention has been given to the provision of safe drinking water supplies, and the government claims that about 88 per cent of the Pakistani population have access to safe drinking water. The World Bank estimates that this is accurate for urban areas only, and the figure among the rural population is thought to be lower, with only about 50 per cent having access to proper sanitation.
The main objectives for the Ninth Five-Year Plan (1998–2003) were to increase the Contraceptive Prevalence Rate (CPR) from 24.4 per cent to 40.3 per cent by the end of 2003 and reduce the population growth from 2.4 per cent to 1.9 per cent for the same period. Latest estimates for 2003 puts the population growth at 2.1 per cent.
Some areas of the country's health services improved over the previous decade, including better access to immunisation and family planning services. Low government expenditure and the poor quality of private health care continue to be a problem. One quarter of the national budget is spent on the military, compared with less than 7 per cent on health.
HIV prevalence: 0.1 per cent aged 15–49 in 2003 (World Bank)
Life expectancy: 64.1 years (World Bank)
Fertility rate/Maternal mortality rate: 4.5 births per woman (World Bank)
Birth rate/Death rate: 9.51 deaths to 32.11 births per 1,000 people (World Bank).
Infant mortality rate: 74 per 1,000 live births (2003); 38 per cent of children

aged under five are malnourished (World Bank).

Head of population per physician/bed: 2,700 people per physician; 1,500 people per hospital bed.

Welfare

A Poverty Alleviation Programme includes pension, death and marriage grants, and a policy formulated for the elimination of bonded and child labour. An estimated 40 per cent of the urban population lives in slums or other poor housing areas.

Main cities

Islamabad (capital, estimated population 800,000 in 2004), Karachi (10.8 million), Lahore (5.9 million), Faisalabad (2.3 million), Rawalpindi (1.6 million), Gujranwala (1.4 million), Multan (1.4 million), Hyderabad (1.3 million), Peshawar (1.2 million)..

Languages spoken

There are 69 other languages, including Punjabi, Sindhi, Pashtu, Baluchi, Seraiki.

Official language/s

Urdu (national language) and English

Media

Press

Under General Musharraf, some newspapers are openly critical of the government, although the government has the power to close down publications. Foreign correspondents are allowed to move freely in Pakistan, but are barred from some border areas.

Dailies: There are over 100 Urdu daily newspapers, most published on a semi-national or local basis. Pakistan's leading newspaper is the Urdu *Daily Jang*, an independent newspaper published simultaneously from Karachi, Lahore, Rawalpindi and Quetta. Other prominent Urdu and Sindhi language newspapers include *Urooj*, *Nawa-i-Waqt* (independent, published in Karachi, Lahore, Multan and Rawalpindi), *Imroze* (circulated principally in Lahore and Multan), *Jasarat* (Karachi), *Mashriq* (Lahore), *Millat* (English and Urdu), *Daily Kawish* and *Daily Ibrat Hyderabad*.

There are around 14 English-language papers, including *Pakistan Times*, *Dawn*, *The Muslim*, *The Nation*, *Hi Pakistan*, *Pakistan Today*, *The Frontier Post* and *Pakistan Observer*, which provide local, national and international news.

Weeklies: *Friday Times* is the independent weekly paper.

Business: *Business Recorder* is Pakistan's national financial daily.

Periodicals: Almost all major foreign magazines are available in Pakistan, although specific issues may be banned from time to time if they carry material deemed offensive to Islam or critical of Pakistan.

Broadcasting

Radio and television are controlled by the state-run Pakistan Broadcasting Corporation (PBC) and the Pakistan Television Corporation (PTC) respectively, which follow government policy instructions. Films shown on television are censored to meet conservative Islamic standards of morality. Both radio and television also give considerable air time to religious programmes.

Radio: The PBC operates a nationwide home service as well as regional and local services, broadcasting for a total 240 hours daily in 21 local languages from 22 transmitters, principally on medium-wave frequencies. It also operates a range of external services for a total 30 hours daily in 15 languages on short-wave frequencies.

Television: Television was introduced to Pakistan in the late 1960s, and can now be received throughout the country, with the PTC providing national as well as regional services.

Advertising

Advertising is available in the press, in cinemas and on commercial radio and television.

Economy

The state of the economy is determined by the strength of the agricultural sector, which is vulnerable to climatic conditions. Record cotton and wheat crops contributed to stronger than forecast growth in 2004/05. In the same period, large-scale manufacturing, telecoms and financial services showed strong growth.

The functioning of the economy in the provinces can be beyond the control of central government, especially in the North West Frontier Province (NWFP) and Baluchistan. In the former, the distance from the capital and intense poverty along with its proximity to Afghanistan have combined to create an area dominated by heroin processing and arms smuggling. In Baluchistan, an area rich in gas reserves (which the country needs, given declining reserves elsewhere), local tribesmen resent the arrival of foreign oil and gas exploration teams to the extent that the kidnapping and ransom of foreign workers is not uncommon.

The country has benefited from the lifting of international sanctions. The government's commitment to the US-led war on terrorism helped secure a number of bilateral grant packages, amounting to US$1.16 billion.

Progress is being made towards reducing debt. A Debt Policy Co-ordination Office, established by the government, is preparing a 10-year debt reduction path, and a Fiscal Responsibility and Debt Limitation Bill commits the government to eliminating the revenue deficit by 2007 and to reducing the outstanding public debt to 60 per cent of GDP by 2012.

The 2004 budget included various measures for continuing tax reform: a number of units were set up in cities, where taxpayers are able to pay all their taxes (corporate income tax, sales tax, excise duty) at one place; self-assessment is to be introduced; by 2007, there is to be one corporate tax rate, and as a step towards this, the budget reduced tax rates for banks and private limited companies.

External trade

Imports

Main imports include petroleum, petroleum products, machinery, plastics, transport equipment, edible oils, paper and paperboard, iron and steel and tea.

Main sources: China (10.8 per cent total, 2004), US (10.2 per cent), UAE (9.3 per cent), Saudi Arabia (9.0 per cent), Japan (7.0 per cent), Kuwait (5.3 per cent), Germany (4.2 per cent)

Exports

Main exports include textiles (garments, bed linen, cotton cloth, and yarn), rice, leather goods, sports goods, chemicals, manufactures, carpets and rugs.

Main destinations: US (21.3 per cent total, 2004), UAE (9.8 per cent), UK (7.1 per cent), Germany (5.2 per cent), Hong Kong (4.2 per cent), Saudi Arabia (4.1 per cent)

Agriculture

Farming

Agriculture represents around a quarter of GDP and is the driver of the economy, supplying food and raw materials for the manufacturing sector. Sustainable economic development requires long-term growth in agriculture. Main food crops include wheat, rice, maize, barley, millet, sorghum, sugar cane, tobacco, groundnuts, pulses, potatoes, onions, mangoes and citrus fruit. Cotton is the main cash crop and the largest foreign exchange earner, with productivity rising as greater use is made of insecticides. Rice is also an important export. Livestock production includes goats, sheep, cattle, buffaloes, pigs, donkeys, horses, mules, camels and poultry, and accounts for around 7.5 per cent of GDP, providing meat, eggs, dairy products, leather and wool, as well as draught power and fertiliser for cultivation. There are around 27 million hectares available for agriculture. Typically 26 per cent of agricultural land is given over to arable crops, while 6.25 per cent is permanent pasture. There are grazing difficulties in border regions, where Afghan refugees have brought about three million head of cattle with them.

The agricultural policies pursued by successive governments have traditionally been geared towards attaining self-sufficiency in the production of foodstuffs, increasing cash crop production and maximising foreign exchange earnings from the export of agricultural commodities such as cotton and rice. There was a record cotton crop harvested in 2004, which was attributed to an increase in area cultivated and productivity through the use of fertilisers.

In 2005, the government removed the 25 per cent import duty on imported raw and refined sugar. The removal was prompted by an expected shortfall of about a half a million tonnes in sugar. The sugar cane harvest was lower than expected as some farmers switched some land use over to cotton growing in expectation of higher profits, which resulted in local sugar prices rising sharply. Cane growers are critical of the poor condition of canals that provide an inadequate irrigation system, which currently hampers production. They are pressing for long-term investment to provide new dams and improve the canal network.

Owing to a shortage of unused cultivatable land, planners have concentratied on increased yields per hectare rather than an expansion of planted acreage. The government announced support for procurement prices for all major crops before sowing, and has encouraged farmers to adopt modern cultivation practices by providing them with subsidised inputs such as chemical fertilisers, pesticides and improved seed varieties. As the use of these inputs has become more popular and the government's budgetary constraints have become more pressing, these subsidies are gradually being phased out, but farmers are being compensated through rising crop prices.

The extended use of pesticides and fertilisers has been accompanied by a selective mechanisation of farm operations, facilitated by a liberal import policy for farm machinery and an expansion of domestic manufacturing capacity for the production of agricultural equipment. Mechanisation has become a routine operation for small farmers, who hire harvester's from richer farmers, and gain a higher yield in return. Farmers have called on the government to address the problems constraining the agricultural sector by allowing them a three-year remission period on their debts, deregulation, improving irrigation and water use and waiving tax and loan recovery in the areas worst hit by drought. Special attention is being given to the problems of small farmers who suffer mainly from a lack of finance. To alleviate this problem, the government has traditionally adopted a liberal stance towards the provision of rural credit, which is disbursed by the state-run Agricultural Development Bank of Pakistan (ADBP), commercial banks and co-operatives.

In July 2004 the rupee was devalued and rice exports became more competitively priced at US$10 a tonne cheaper than regional competitors.

Crop production in 2004 included: 30,508,500 tonnes (t) cereals in total, 19,767,000t wheat, 7,486,500t rice, 2,775,000t maize, 1,854,700t potatoes, 53,419,000t sugar cane, 953,000t pulses, 1,089,000t mangoes, 1,657,900t dry onions, 1,670,000t citrus fruit, 171,936t various spices, 2.40t roots and tubers, 7,350,000t seed cotton, 2,450,000t cotton lint, 294,000t tomatoes, 93,700t tobacco, 50,400t treenuts in total, 1,169,984t oilcrops, 650,000t dates, 5,302,140t fruits in total, 5,107,600t vegetables in total. Livestock production included: 1,952,580t meat in total, 598,000t buffalo meat, 395,000t beef, 182,000t lamb, 355,000t goat meat, 406,680t poultry, 378,200t eggs, 28,624,000t milk, 1,500t honey, 96,000t cattle hides, 41,580t sheepskins, 39,700t greasy wool.

Fishing
Pakistan is largely self-sufficient in freshwater fish and seafood, with an active fishing fleet operating out of Karachi and on the Indus river. The typical annual fish catch is around 600,000 tonnes, of which 380,000 tonnes is through marine fishing. Around 87,000 tonnes of fish is exported, almost all of which is freshwater fish.

Forestry
Forests cover only 17,000 square kilometres, equivalent to 3 per cent of the country. A higher level of forestation is needed to improve the quality of the environment, reducing the severity of flooding and the impact of strong winds and sandstorms. The authorities have encouraged a growth in forests, with forest cover increasing by an average of 1.84 per cent per annum.

Around 90 per cent of Pakistan's wood production is used for fuel. Wood and wood-based products contribute little to external trade, while Pakistan imports around US$130 million worth of forest products annually.

Industry and manufacturing
Industry contributes around 25 per cent to annual GDP, employing an estimated 17 per cent of the labour force.

Manufactured and semi-manufactured goods, mainly cotton textiles and garments, account for around 60 per cent of Pakistan's exports. The manufacturing sector depends on the agricultural sector for most of its raw materials: cotton for weaving, spinning and processing industries, leather and wool for handicrafts and carpet weaving. There is a growing emphasis on private sector development, with around 85 per cent of manufacturing output in private hands.

Tourism
Tourism has been slow to develop, hampered by lack of facilities and infrastructure as well as fears of terrorist attacks, hijackings and kidnappings which are endemic in some areas of the country. A large proportion of visitors tend to be overseas Pakistanis and their families. The sector collapsed in 2003, in the wake of the September 2001 terrorist attacks in the US and two major earthquakes in November 2002, but has seen a recovery in the following years. There were 648,000 arrivals in 2004, a 29.4 per cent increase on the previous year. The improvement of relations with India resulted in the opening of borders and easing of movement between the two countries and there was an increase in the number of visitors from other Asian countries.

Environment
In its efforts to improve living standards for its citizens Pakistan has compromised environmental standards in favour of economic development. Hazardous chemicals, including agricultural run-off, industrial activity and vehicle emissions all add to pollution in general and water contamination in particular.

Mining
Pakistan has deposits of a wide range of minerals, including uranium, rock phosphate, gypsum, iron ore, copper, gold, silver, magnesium, chromite, antimony, barite, rock salt, sulphur, porcelain, china clays and gemstones.

The government is seeking to enhance the role of the mining sector, which has historically played a negligible role in the Pakistan economy. In the past, priority has been given to the further development of rock phosphate mining at Kakul in the North West Frontier Province and the establishment of copper and iron ore mines at Saindak and Nokundi in Baluchistan. These projects have been delayed by insufficient investment, economic inviability and the poor quality of reserves.

Pakistan typically produces nine million tonnes of limestone, 800,000 tonnes of rock salt, 300,000 tonnes of argonite and marble, 30,000 tonnes of barytes, 30,000 tonnes of soap stone, 15,000 tonnes of sulphur, 2–3,000 tonnes of bauxite and 23 tonnes of uranium per annum.

Hydrocarbons
Pakistan had proven reserves of around 49 million cubic metres (cum) in 2004 and produced 60,000 barrels per day (bpd). There is no prospect of Pakistan becoming self-sufficient in oil. Domestic

consumption stands at around 350,000 bpd. Pakistan is reliant on imports, which amount to around 18 million cum. Punjab and Sindh provinces produce all of Pakistan's oil output. The government wants to reduce dependency on imports and has encouraged foreign investment to boost production and raise domestic capacity. Exploration is taking place both onshore and offshore.

The state-owned Pakistan Petroleum is the largest exploration and production company as well as the largest gas production company; the government has plans to sell off 15 per cent of it to private investors.

Pakistan has a proven reserve of 75.8 billion cum of natural gas and produces 22.6 million cum per year, all of which is consumed domestically. Gas supplies around half of Pakistan's energy requirements. Consumption is growing and additional sources, including new fields in Pakistan and pipelines from Iran and Oman, are being explored. The most productive gas field is in Sui, producing 18.3 million cum per day.

Pakistan has estimated coal reserves of around 3,300 tonnes. Coal does not have a significant role in Pakistan's energy usage, but substantial new deposits of higher quality coal in the vicinity of Tharparkar should change its profile.

The government has set up the Gas Regulatory Authority (GRA) and Petroleum Regulatory Board (PRB) to separate out government functions from state-owned entities that are in the process of being privatised.

Energy
Pakistan has 18GW of electric generating capacity, with thermal plants making up 68 per cent, hydroelectricity making up 28 per cent and nuclear power contributing 2.6 per cent. Less than half the population is connected to the national grid and significant growth in demand is expected in the long-term.

Foreign investment has spurred rapid growth in the sector, helping to reduce the number of power cuts. Poor distribution infrastructure and electricity theft means that about 30 per cent of transmission is lost. Frequent droughts can also hamper electricity production.

Much of the energy sector is owned by the state and dominated by two parastatal utility companies: the Water and Power Development Authority (Wapda) and the Karachi Electricity Supply Company (KESC). Plans to privatise the two utility groups have made slow progress.

A number of independent power producers operate in Pakistan.

Financial markets
Stock exchange
Pakistan has three stock exchanges, located in Karachi, Lahore and Islamabad, of which the Karachi Stock Exchange (KSE) is the most important. Since the lifting of exchange controls in 1994, progress on the KSE has been disrupted by domestic and international upheaval.

Banking and insurance
The banking sector is dominated by state-owned banks: the United Bank Ltd (UBL), Habib Bank Ltd (HBL) and the National Bank of Pakistan (NBP).

In June 2002, the Islamic bench of Pakistan's Supreme Court reversed a decision made in 1999 to outlaw charging interest on bank transactions as un-Islamic. The move came less than a week ahead of a deadline by which all financial institutions had to conform to an Islamic system of banking, which prohibits fixed rates of interest. If the measures had gone ahead, Pakistan would have become the first country to adopt a pure Islamic system. Banks had argued that full Islamicisation of the banking system would create chaos, leading to a possible collapse of the financial sector. Foreign banks were prepared to quit Pakistan if interest charging was abolished. International lenders were also wary of the changes, jeopardising Pakistan's ability to secure foreign loans.

Instead of converting to a fully Islamic financial system, Pakistan has effectively had to accept, at least in the medium-term, a dual system which allows Islamic and conventional banks to coexist. The problem facing Pakistan is the high level of non-performing loans (NPLs) in the banking system caused mainly by economic mismanagement in the past.

The governor of the central bank, Ishrat Hussein, has indicated his desire to allow clients freedom of choice between Islamic and conventional banking.

Central bank
State Bank of Pakistan

Main financial centre
Karachi

Time
GMT plus five hours

Geography
Pakistan is a wedge-shaped country bordering India to the east, China to the north-east, Afghanistan to the north and Iran to the west. Its southern boundary is the shore of the Arabian Sea.

Pakistan has some of the hottest deserts and highest mountains in the world. The areas north of the capital Islamabad are mountainous, with a temperate climate. The world's second-highest mountain, K-2 (8,611 metres), also known as Mount Godwin Austen, is located in the Karakoram Range, where the Himalayas meet the Hindu Kush.

The plains of the Punjab and Sindh, irrigated by the Indus river and its tributaries, are the main agricultural areas. Apart from its temperate Makran coast on the Arabian Sea, Baluchistan is a vast and mostly empty area of deserts and low bare hills.

Climate
The terrain ranges from mountainous to desert, and the climate varies accordingly. It is cool in the mountains and foothills, with rain in summer and snow in winter, and hot in summer and cool in winter in plateau regions, with some rain in winter. The Indus valley experiences year-round heat, with extreme heat and dry winds in summer. Temperatures vary from an average of 15 degrees Celsius (C) in January to an average of 37 degrees C in May–July. Summer temperatures can rise as high as 50 degrees C in northern Sindh and eastern Baluchistan. The monsoon season lasts from mid-July–September when the average monthly rainfall amounts to 16cm. The best time for tourists to visit is between October and April.

Dress codes
Pakistan is an Islamic country where modesty in dress is the rule. The widely worn national dress is the *salwaar kameez*, a unisex combination of baggy shirt and trousers completely covering the arms and legs. Western-style suits are seen only in big cities. Tourists are advised to dress modestly, especially when outside cities like Karachi, Lahore and Islamabad. Women are expected to dress soberly and act discreetly and a headscarf is essential when visiting holy places.

Entry requirements
Passports
Required by all.

Visa
Required by all. Business travellers must provide, with their application form, an invitation or sponsorship from a local company or organisation; a business letter of intention from an employer; a full itinerary; proof of financial guarantee of maintenance and emergency repatriation; return/onward passage. See www.pakistan.embassyhomepage.com for details of requirements and embassy locations worldwide.

Visitors staying over 30 days must register with the District Foreigners Registration Office within 30 days of arrival; over-staying the visa allowance can be treated as a criminal offence. Indian and Afghan visitors must register within 24 hours of arrival.

Pakistan

Prohibited entry
Israeli passport holders.

Currency advice/regulations
The amount of domestic currency which may be imported or exported is limited to Rp100 (US$2) per person. Sterling and US dollars are generally the easiest foreign currencies to convert. Facilities for currency exchange outside the main cities tend to be limited. Foreign exchange receipts should be retained.

Customs
Personal effects are allowed duty-free. Visitors are not permitted to import alcohol. Motor vehicles may be imported duty-free for a period of up to three months. Export of certain antiques may require a permit.

Prohibited imports
Alcohol and matches are not permitted. Fruit and plants may be destroyed to prevent agricultural diseases entering the country.

Health (for visitors)
Mandatory precautions
A vaccination certificate is required for yellow fever and cholera, if travelling from an infected area.

Advisable precautions
Vaccinations recommended for dengue fever, cholera, diphtheria, tuberculosis, hepatitis A and B, Japanese B encephalitis, polio, tetanus, typhoid. Malaria precautions should be taken. Rabies risk. Water should be boiled before drinking. Polio is endemic.
Medical facilities outside Islamabad and Karachi are limited, insurance and adequate supplies of prescription medicine are essential.

Hotels
There are modern hotels in major centres; price and quality can vary substantially and advanced booking is advised.
A 10 per cent service charge is usually added to bill; further tipping optional.

Public holidays
Fixed dates
23 Mar (Pakistan Day), 1 May (May Day), 14 Aug (Independence Day), 6 Sep (Defence Day), 11 Sep (Death of Quaid-i-Azam), 9 Nov (Allama Mohammad Iqbal's Birthday), 25 Dec (Birthday of Qaid-i-Azam).

Variable dates
Eid al Adha (two days), Eid al Fitr (three days), Islamic New Year, Ashura (two days), Birth of the Prophet.
The Islamic year contains 354 or 355 days, with the result that Muslim feasts advance by 10–12 days against the Gregorian calendar. Dates of feasts vary according to the sighting of the new moon, so cannot be forecast exactly.

Working hours
Banking
Mon–Thu and Sat: 0900–1330; Fri: 0900–1130.

Business
Mon–Thu and Sat: 0900–1700; Fri: 0900–1230, 1430–1700.

Government
Mon–Thu and Sat: 0900–1700; Fri: 0900–1230.

Shops
Sat–Thu: 0800/0900–1800/1900.

Electricity supply
220–240V AC, with two or three-pin round plug fittings.

Weights and measures
Metric system (local units are also in use).

Social customs/useful tips
It is customary to shake hands on meeting and taking leave. Business appointments should be made in advance. Business cards are exchanged after introduction. The attitude to punctuality is variable. Visits during Ramadan should be avoided. Visitors should make themselves familiar with local customs and care should be taken to respect Muslim conventions. For instance, use the right and not the left hand when shaking hands and passing or receiving anything. In the northern areas of Baltistan (Skardu, etc), Gilgit, Hunza and the Chitral Valley, do not photograph airports, military installations, bridges or women. In the Kalash Valleys, women may be photographed with their permission, and will usually pose, for payment.

Security
Those planning to travel to Pakistan should take care and be confident of their personal security arrangements throughout their visit.
There is a risk to everyone from indiscriminate attacks and sectarian violence, including tribal killings, armed car-jacking, robbery, kidnap, murder and bombings in public places such as markets, offices and public transport. Although these may not be aimed at foreigners, there is always a risk of being caught up in such attacks. Large-scale demonstrations that become violent can occur, throughout Pakistan, at short notice. Visitors should monitor local media and avoid any demonstrations announced or gatherings encountered.
There is also a serious threat of criminal violence. Theft, burglary and the kidnapping of businessmen is becoming endemic, especially in Karachi. Visitors of visibly western origin should not linger in public places. In major towns, especially Karachi, travellers should confine themselves to business areas, and avoid the back streets and bazaars.
Avoid long road journeys (except between major cities), cross-country journeys, and non-essential travel to the border areas of Afghanistan and India (Kashmir province). If visitors must travel to these regions, contact with Pakistani authorities should be made in advance. Police protection may be arranged, as necessary; advice about a No Objection Certificate (issued by the Pakistani Ministry of Foreign Affairs) can also be obtained.

Getting there
Air
There are flights into Karachi from most major airports in Europe, Asia and the Middle East.
In January 2004, the airline service between Pakistan and India was restored.
National airline: Pakistan International Airlines (PIA)
International airport/s: Quaid-e-Azam International, Karachi Civil (KHI), 12km north-east of Karachi; duty-free and tax-free shops, bar, restaurant, buffet, bank, hotel reservations, post office, shops.
Other airport/s: Lahore (LHE), 3km south-east of Lahore; restaurant, bank, post office, shops, car hire; Peshawar (PEW), 4km from Peshawar; Islamabad International (ISB), 8km from Islamabad; restaurant, car hire, banks, post office.
Airport tax: None

Surface
Road: Generally in poor condition. Access via India (Amritsar-Lahore) and China (the 805km Karakoram Highway serving Sinkiang Province-Islamabad and Rawalpindi via the Khunjerab Pass), plus road connections to Iran. India and Pakistan agreed in February 1999 to run a bus service four times weekly between Delhi and Lahore, the first since independence from the UK in 1947. The route from China is open to foreigners, but not to most Pakistanis.
Routes from Afghanistan (via Qandhar-Chaman-Quetta or Kabul-Peshawar), are closed following the fighting in that country.
Rail: A line runs from Iran (Zahedan-Naukundi-Quetta).
The train service between Pakistan and India was restored in January 2004 – one train a week between Lahore in Pakistan and Attari in India.
Water: There are some ferry services from Bombay, although these are not widely used.
Main port/s: Karachi and Bin Qasim (southeast of Karachi).

Getting about
National transport
Air: Four carriers operate daily flights to 37 cities, providing better access than other forms of travel. Two-hour flight times compared to 24-hour road trips.

Road: The 800km Karakoram Highway permits entry to northern areas. The only multi-lane road is a two-lane highway linking Karachi and Peshawar. Although a new network of highways has greatly facilitated inter-city road travel, it can still be long, hot and harrowing. Avoid travelling at night on mountain roads in northern areas.

Buses: The air-conditioned 'Flying Coach' national buses available between main centres (hourly between Lahore and Rawalpindi) are recommended over the local buses, which are colourful but not very reliable. Seats should be booked in advance. The minibuses operating on various routes are generally recommended.

Rail: There is an extensive rail network with over 8,775km of track, but it is slow and somewhat dilapidated. It is not suited to the business traveller working to a tight timetable. The main route runs Karachi-Lahore-Rawalpindi-Peshawar, with three classes. Certain services include air-conditioning, restaurant cars, sleeping cars, ice containers and 'women only' accommodation. Advance booking is generally advisable, and is essential for some services.

Water: Although the Indus is unnavigable in many places, there are some passenger boats operating on certain stretches, which are recommended more for tourism than commercial travel.

City transport
Business travellers are advised to avoid arriving in Karachi at night and to ensure they are met at the airport.

Taxis: Taxis can be hired at all big hotels, and provide the most practical way for visitors to travel in cities. It is advisable to keep the taxi for the return trip as taxis do not usually cruise looking for passengers and there are not many taxi stands. Waiting costs are low, especially when compared to the time and trouble the traveller would face in looking for another taxi. Hotel taxi drivers are more likely to speak at least some English than those from taxi stands. Metered taxis are painted black and yellow, although the meter may not be used. Tipping normally 10 per cent.

Car hire
Self-drive and chauffeur-driven car hire is available, and minibuses may be hired. Driving is on the left-hand side of the road. National licence and international driving permit required.

BUSINESS DIRECTORY

The addresses listed below are a selection only. While World of Information makes every endeavour to check these addresses, we cannot guarantee that changes have not been made, especially to telephone numbers and area codes. We would welcome any corrections.

Telephone area codes
The international direct dialling (IDD) code for Pakistan is +92 followed by area code and subscriber's number:

Faisalabad	41	Multan	61
Gujranwala	431	Peshawar	91
Hyderabad	221	Quetta	81
Islamabad	51	Rawalpindi	51
Karachi	21	Sialkot	432
Lahore	42	Sukkur	71

Useful telephone numbers
Karachi
Police: 222-222/224-400
Fire: 74-891
Ambulance: 73-259/70-600
International calls: 0102
Calls to India, Bangladesh, China: 102
To check on booked call: 0104
Islamabad
Police: 23-333
Fire: 27-222
International call: 109
To check on booked call: 103
All places
Directory enquiries: 17

Chambers of Commerce
American Business Council of Pakistan, NIC Building, PO Box 1322, Abbasi Shaheed Road, Karachi 74400 (tel: 567-6436; fax: 566-0135; e-mail: abcpak@cyber.net.pk).

Federation of Pakistan Chambers of Commerce and Industries, Federation House, Sharea Firdousi, Main Clifton Road, Karachi 75600 (tel: 587-3691; fax: 587-4332; e-mail: info@fpcci.com.pk).

Hyderabad Chamber of Commerce and Industry, PO Box 99, Aiwan-e-Tijarat, Saddar, Hyderabad (tel: 2784-973; fax: 784-972; e-mail: hcci@paknet3.ptc.pk).

Islamabad Chamber of Commerce and Industry, Aiwan-e-Sanat-o-Tijarat, Islamabad (tel: 225-0526; fax: 225-2950; e-mail: icci@brain.net.pk).

Karachi Chamber of Commerce and Industry, PO Box 4158, Aiwan-e-Tijarat, Karachi 74000 (tel: 241-6091; fax: 241-6095; e-mail: info@karachichamber.com).

Lahore Chamber of Commerce and Industry, 11 Sharah-e-Aiwan-eTijarat, Lahore (tel: 630-5538; fax: 636-8854; e-mail: sect@lcci.org.pk).

Quetta Chamber of Commerce and Industry, PO Box 117, Zarghoon Road, Quetta (tel: 824-857; fax: 821-948; e-mail: qcci@hotmail.com).

Rawalpindi Chamber of Commerce and Industry, Chamber House, 108 Adamjee Road, Rawalpindi (tel: 556-6238; fax: 558-6849; e-mail: chamber@rcci.org.pk).

Overseas Investors Chamber of Commerce and Industry, Chamber of Commerce Building, Talpur Rd, Karachi (tel: 241-0814; fax: 242-7313; e-mail: oicci@global.net.pk).

Banking
Allied Bank of Pakistan Ltd., Khayaban-e-Iqbal, Main Clifton Road, Bath Island, Karachi (tel: 567-8155; fax: 568-3312, 568-0134).

Federal Bank for Co-operative, 85-W, Rizwan Centre, Blue Area, PO Box 1218, Islamabad (tel: 81-2469).

Faysal Bank Limited, PO Box 472, 11/13 Trade Centre, I. I. Chundrigar Road, Karachi (tel: 263-8011-20; fax: 263-7975).

Habib Bank Ltd, Habib Bank Plaza, 1.1 Chundrigar Road, Karachi (tel: 241-8000/8034; fax: 241-4191).

Industrial Development Bank of Pakistan, State Life Building 2, Off 1.1. Chundrigar Road, Wallace Road, Karachi (tel: 241-9160/9168; fax: 241-1990).

Metropolitan Bank Limited, PO Box 1289, Spencer's Building, I.I. Chundrigar Road, Karachi (tel: 263-6740; fax: 263-0404/5).

Muslim Commercial Bank ltd, Adamjee House, 1.1 Chundrigar Road, Karachi 74000 (tel: 241-4090/9, 241-4110/9; fax: 241-3116).

National Bank of Pakistan, 1.1 Chundrigar Rd, Karachi (tel: 241-6789; fax: 241-6769).

United Bank Limited, 1.1 Chundrigar Road, PO Box 4306, Karachi (tel: 2417100; fax: 243-7068).

Central bank
State Bank of Pakistan, PO Box 4456, 1.1 Chundrigar Road, Karachi 74000 (tel: 921-2400 fax: 921-2433; e-mail: info@sbp.org.pk).

Travel information
Aero Asia, Karachi (tel: 778-3476, 778-3033).

Automobile Association of West Pakistan, 8 Multan Rd, PO Box 76, Lahore.

Karachi Automobile Association (KAA), Standard Insurance House, 1 Chundrigar Rd, Karachi 0226 (tel: 232-173).

Pakistan International Airlines (PIA), PIA Bldg, Quaid-e-Azam International Airport, Karachi 75200 (tel: 412-011; fax: 772-7727, 457-0419).

Ministry of tourism
Ministry of Culture and Tourism, 13-T/U, Comm Area, F-7/2, Islamabad (tel: 27-023).

Pakistan

National tourist organisation offices
Pakistan Tourism Development Corporation, House 2, St 61, F-7/4, PO Box 1465, Islamabad 44000 (tel: 811-001/2/3/4; fax: 824-173).

Ministries

Ministry of Commerce, Industry and Production, Block A, Pakistan Secretariat, Islamabad (tel: 921-0277; fax: 920-5241; e-mail: mincom@meganet.com.pk).

Ministry of Communications and Railways, Block D, Pakistan Secretariat, Islamabad (tel: 920-1252; fax: 920-6171).

Ministry of Culture, Sports, Minority Affairs and Youth, College Road, Shalimar 7/2, Islamabad (tel: 921-3121; fax: 922-1863).

Ministry of Defence, Pakistan Secretariat No II, Rawalpindi 46000 (tel: 927-1114; fax: 927-1115).

Ministry of Education, Block D, Pakistan Secretariat, Islamabad (tel: 920-1401; fax: 920-2851; e-mail: pak@yahoo.com).

Ministry of the Environment, Local Government, Rural Development, Labour, Manpower and Overseas Pakistanis, Islamabad (tel: 922-4579; fax: 920-2211; e-mail: envir@isb.compol.com).

Ministry of Finance, Revenues, Economic Affairs, Planning and Development, and Statistics,Block Q, Pakistan Secretariat, Islamabad (tel:920-3687; fax: 921-3780; e-mail: finance@isb.paknet.com.pk).

Ministry of Food, Agriculture & Livestock, Block B, Pakistan Secretariat, Islamabad (tel: 920-3307; fax: 922-1246).

Ministry of Foreign Affairs, Constitution Avenue, Islamabad (tel: 921-0335; fax: 920-4205; e-mail: pak.fm@usa.net).

Ministry of Health, Block C, Pakistan Secretariat, Islamabad (tel: 921-1622; fax: 920-5481; e-mail: sehat@apollo.net.pk).

Ministry of Information and Ministry Development, Cabinet Block, Pakistan Secretariat, Islamabad (tel: 920-7314; fax: 920-2448; e-mail: dgep@isb.comsats.net.pk)

Ministry of the Interior, Block R, Pakistan Secretariat, Islamabad (tel: 921-0086; fax: 920-1472).

Ministry of Kashmir Affairs, Northern Affairs, States and Frontier Region, Housing and Works, Block R, Pakistan Secretariat, Islamabad (tel: 920-3032; fax: 920-2494; e-mail: safron@isb.perd.net.pk).

Ministry of Law, Justice, Human Rights and Parliamentary Affairs, Islamabad (tel: 921-0062; fax: 920-2628; e-mail: molaw@comsats.net.pk).

Ministry of Petroleum and Natural Resources, Block A, Pakistan Secretariat, Islamabad (tel: 921-1220; fax: 920-1770; e-mail: info@mpnr.gov.pk).

Ministry of Religious Affairs, Zakat and Usher, Plot 20, Ramna-6, Islamabad (tel: 920-1909; fax: 920-1646; e-mail: mara@paknet.ptc.pk).

Ministry of Science and Technology, Shaheed-e-Millat Secretariat, Islamabad (tel: 920-8026; fax: 920-2603; e-mail: minister@most.gov.pk).

Office of the President, Constitution Avenue, Islamabad (tel: 922-0136; fax: 920-3938; e-mail: psecyp@isb.paknet.com.pk).

Office of the Chief Executive, Islamabad (tel: 922-2666; fax: 920-4632).

Other useful addresses

All-Pakistan Textile Mills Association, 44-A Lalazar, Off MT Khan Rd, PO Box 5446, Karachi (tel: 552-296).

Asian Development Bank, Pakistan Resident Mission, Overseas Pakistani Foundation (OPF) Building, Sharah-e-Jamhuriyat, G-52, Islamabad (tel: 825-011; fax: 823-324; e-mail: adbpim@mail.asiandevbank.org).

Board of Investment, Saudi Pak Tower, 61-A Jinnah Ave, PO BOx 3100, Islamabad (tel: 817-165/2, 218-267/6; fax: 217-665, 215-554, 263-9580).

British High Commission, Diplomatic Enclave, Ramna 5, PO Box 1122, Islamabad (tel: 822-131/5; fax: 826-217).

British Deputy High Commission, York Place, Clifton, Karachi 6 (tel: 532-041/6; fax: 587-4014).

British Trade Office, 65 Mozang Road, PO Box 1679, Lahore (tel: 631-6589/90; fax: 631-6591).

Export Promotion Bureau, Government of Pakistan, Block A, Finance & Trade Centre, Sharea Faisal, Karachi (tel: 566-0305/9; fax: 566-0300, 568-0422/4010).

Institute of Marketing Management, 68-B Block 2, PECHS, Karachi (tel: 455-8365).

Islamabad Stock Exchange (tel: 215-047/50).

Karachi Cotton Association, Cotton Exchange Bldg, 1.1 Chundrigar Rd, Karachi (tel: 241-0336/2570).

Karachi Stock Exchange (Guarantee) Ltd, Stock Exchange Bldg, Stock Exchange Rd, Karachi 2 (tel: 242-5501/2/3/4/5; fax: 241-0825).

Lahore Stock Exchange (tel: 636-8000, 636-8333).

Oil Companies Advisory Committee, 5th Floor, Karim Chambers, Mereweather Rd, Karachi (tel: 568-2246/8).

Pakistan Art Silk Fabrics & Garments Exporters Association, 204 Amber Estate, Shahrah-e-Faisal, Karachi (tel: 360-919, 368-488).

Pakistan Cotton Association, 5 Amber Court, Shaheed-e-Millat Rd, Karachi (tel: 438-461).

Pakistan Embassy (USA), 2315 Massachusetts Avenue, NW, Washington DC 20008 (tel: 202-939-6200; fax: 202-387-0484; e-mail: parepwashington@erols.com).

Pakistan Fruit & Vegetables Exporters, Importers & Manufacturers Association, 8 New Onion & Potato Market, University Rd, Karachi (tel: 493-7126, 493-125).

Pakistan Handicrafts Manufacturers & Exporters Association, MA Jinnah Rd, Karachi (tel: 772-8121).

Pakistan Shipowners Association, Ralli Brothers Bldg, Talpur Rd, Karachi (tel: 242-7154).

Privatisation Commission, Government of Pakistan, 5A Constitution Avenue, EAC Building, Islamabad (tel: 920-5146; fax: 920-3076, 921-1692; e-mail: info@privatisation.gov.pk).

Sindh Coal Authority, F-158/A-I, Block 5, Clifton, Karachi (tel: 583-3549, 583-3550; fax: 587-4708).

Internet sites

Gateway site for official and media information: http://www.islamabad.net/off

Pakistan argricultural information: http://www.pakissan.com

Pakistan Government Homepage: http://www.pak.gov.pk/govt.html

Pakistan Yellow pages: http://www.jamal.com/

Trade index of Pakistan: http://www.PakistanBiz.com

UK trade export site: http://www.tradepartners.gov.uk

Palau

KEY FACTS

Official name: Belu'u era Belau (Republic of Palau)

Head of State: President Tommy Remengesau (since Nov 2000; re-elected 2 Nov 2004)

Head of government: President Tommy Remengesau

Area: 380 square km

Population: 20,802 (2004)

Capital: Koror

Official language: English, Palauan

Currency: US dollar (US$) = 100 cents

GDP per capita: US$6,135 (2004)

GDP real growth: 2.00% (2004)

Labour force: 9,845 (2003)

Unemployment: 2.30% (2003)

Inflation: 0.20% (2004)

Balance of trade: -US$81.00 million (2003)

Aid flow: US$156 (2004)

Visitor numbers: 83,041 (2004)

COUNTRY PROFILE

Historical profile
1686 Spain claimed the Caroline Islands, including Palau.
1783 A British landing on Palau inaugurated a century of trading links.
1885 The Spanish claim to the Caroline Islands was upheld by the Pope.
1899 Spain sold the islands to Germany.
1914 Japan occupied the islands.
1947 Palau became part of the Trust Territory of the Pacific Islands, administered by the US under an UN trusteeship mandate.
1978 Palau voted against becoming a part of the Federated States of Micronesia.
1980 Palau adopted its own constitution in July.
1981 Palau became the Republic of Palau with Haruo Remeliik as its first president.
1982 A Compact of Free Association with the US (CFA) was signed.
1985 President Remeliik assassinated in June. Lazarus Salii elected president in September.
1987 Palau voted to amend its constitution to allow approval of the CFA by a simple majority.
1988 The Palau Supreme Court ruled the constitutional change invalid on procedural grounds. President Salii committed suicide in August. Ngiratkel Etpiison elected president in November.
1989 Agreements with the US provided aid in paying off foreign debt and funds for new development.
1992 Kuniwo Nakamura elected president in November.
1993 Palau voted in a referendum to adopt the CFA.
1994 Palau became an independent republic under the CFA.
1996 President Kuniwo Nakamura was re-elected.
2000 Tommy Remengesau won the presidential election in November.
2002 President Remengesau vetoed a gambling bill that would have allowed casinos to operate in the country, stating that despite weak economic conditions, he did not wish to encourage gambling.
2003 A new airport terminal was completed.
2004 An outbreak of dengue fever was reported in July/August. Incumbent Tommy Remengesau re-elected president in November.

Political structure
Constitution
The constitution was promulgated in January 1981.
Each state has a governor.
A council of chiefs advises the government on matters of traditional law and custom.
Voting: universal suffrage over 18 years.
Form of state
Republic, in free association with the US.
The executive
The president is head of state and head of government, elected for a four-year term by popular vote.
National legislature
The Olbiil Era Kelulau (OEK) (National Congress) has two chambers – a nine-seat Senate (upper chamber), elected by popular vote on a population basis for a four-year term, and a 16-member House of Delegates (lower chamber), elected by popular vote for a four-year term.
Legal system
The legal system is based on Trust Territory laws, acts of the legislature, municipal, common and customary laws.
Last elections
2 November 2004 (presidential and parliamentary)
Results: Presidential: incumbent Tommy Remengesau was re-elected with 64 per cent of the vote against Polycarp Basilius with 36 per cent.
Parliamentary: non-partisans were elected. No parties exist.
Next elections
November 2008 (presidential and parliamentary)

Political parties
There are no political parties.

Population
20,802 (2004)
Ethnic make-up
Palauan (Micronesian with Malayan and Melanesian mixtures) 70 per cent; Asian (Filipinos, Chinese, Taiwanese and Vietnamese) 28 per cent; white 2 per cent.
Religions
Predominantly Christian, although one third of the population practise an indigenous religion known as Modekngei.

Education
The school system of Palau follows that of the US. Education is compulsory until the age of 14. Palauian and English are taught in schools, but English has gradually become the main instruction medium. There were 22 elementary schools, one

high school, seven private schools and one community college. Around 94 per cent of school-aged children attend school and 97 per cent complete elementary school. The completion rate for high school students is 78 per cent.

Health
Government spending was around 90 per cent, and foreign spending 10 per cent of total expenditure on health, which is 9 per cent of GDP.

Only around 75 per cent of the population have access to medical facilities.

By 2002, immunisation against measles, for children aged up to one year, was universal – a 25 per cent improvement in four years.

Life expectancy: 68.5 years
Infant mortality rate: 23 per 1,000 live births (World Bank)

Welfare
There is no social welfare system.

Main cities
Koror (capital, population 13,300).

Languages spoken
Local languages and Japanese spoken in some states.

Official language/s
English, Palauan

Media
Press
The Government Media Office publishes the *Palau Gazette*. *Tia Belau* is a local publication covering Palauan and US news. Other available newspapers include the *Pacific Daily News* and *Palau Tribune* (weekly) printed in Guam.

Broadcasting
Radio: One government-operated radio station (Voice of Palau). Radio broadcasts are transmitted at least 18 hours per day in English and Palauan.
Television: Island Cable Television and STV-TV are two privately owned TV stations operated in Palau. TV coverage is fairly widespread.

Economy
Palau has one of the highest standards of living in the Pacific and is classified as a middle-income country.

Since the end of Japanese occupation in 1945, the US has retained control over defence and foreign policy matters in return for several hundred million dollars in aid over 15 years (1994–2009). Of the US$630 million guaranteed under the Compact of Free Association with the US, US$70 million was placed in an investment fund, to provide a US$5 million boost to the annual budget.

Palau is a member of the region's two main economic organisations, the South Pacific Forum and the South Pacific Commission.

The economy is based on agriculture, fishing and tourism. The tourism sector remained buoyant through the collapse of the Asian economies in the late 1990s and it is hoped that improved travel infrastructure in the region will bolster visitor numbers in the short term.

Foreign fishing vessels (mainly from Japan and Taiwan) pay royalties to fish in Palau's Exclusive Economic Zone. The government is investigating alleged use of the territory for money laundering activities.

A two-lane highway, the Palau Compact Road, around the main island, Babeldaob, will be an important addition to Palau's infrastructure and basis for economic growth. With the road's completion in 2005–06, all Palau's major public infrastructure projects that started after the signing of the Compact in 1994, will have been constructed.

External trade
Imports
Principal imports are machinery and equipment, fuels, metals and foodstuffs.
Main sources: US, Guam, Japan, Singapore, South Korea

Exports
Main exports include shellfish, tuna, copra and garments, which have become a major export following investment by Chinese firms, eager to take advantage of Palau's access to the US market.
Main destinations: US, Japan, Singapore

Agriculture
Farming
Agriculture accounts for around 1 per cent of GDP, with farming accounting for around 0.5 per cent. Subsistence farming of taro, bananas, sweet potatoes, tapioca and vegetables, with pig and poultry raising, is the main occupation. Commercial farming is practised where climate and soils are favourable. Land is parcelled into an estimated 20,000 holdings; a Land Commission maintains a register to provide security of land tenure for Palauan citizens.

Fishing
Fishing supplies the principal source of protein and export revenues. Fishing revenue is valuable because of the sale of fishing licences to large foreign fleets, permitting them to fish within Palau's Exclusive Economic Zone.

Industry and manufacturing
Small-scale industries include handicrafts, garments, fish processing, bottling, bakeries and boat building. Industry typically represents around 7–9 per cent of GDP, but has been boosted by on-going activity in the construction industry to around 15 per cent.

Tourism
Tourism is Palau's principal economic activity. It caters largely to the Asian market, most visitors coming from Taiwan and Japan. Arrivals, which had shown healthy growth in the mid-1990s, peaking at 73,719 in 1997, fell sharply from 1998 as a result of the economic recession, followed by the depreciation of the Japanese yen against the US dollar in 2000–02 and the 11 September 2001 terrorist attacks in the US. Despite the outbreaks of SARS in 2003 and dengue fever in 2004, the sector has recovered, recording 83,041 tourist arrivals in 2004.

Hydrocarbons
In June 2004 Palau approved oil exploration measures to be set up in the country. This would establish a framework for the possible development of reserves. Fossil fuel makes up for around 85 per cent of Palau's energy requirements. Currently, Palau relies on the import of hydrocarbons from the US to meet its requirements.

Banking and insurance
Palau has a well-developed banking sector with 12 commercial banks in operation and one development bank, several of which are representative offices of US or Asian corporations. US banks are dominant, holding around 80 per cent of deposits. The main banks are the Bank of Guam and the Bank of Hawaii.

KEY INDICATORS — Palau

	Unit	2000	2001	2002	2003	2004
Population	m	0.02	0.02	0.20	0.02	0.02
Gross domestic product (GDP)	US$bn	0.12	0.12	0.11	0.17	*0.13
GDP per capita	US$	6,147	6,416	5,482	9,000	6,135
GDP real growth	%	1.0	1.0	-0.1	2.0	2.0
Inflation	%	–	–	–	–	0.2
Balance of trade	US$m	–	–	–	-81.0	
Tourist numbers	'000	49.7	58.6	50.4	59.9	830.4

* estimated figure

Nations of the World: A Political, Economic and Business Handbook

Time
GMT plus ten hours

Geography
Palau consists of more than 200 islands in a chain about 650km (400 miles) long, lying about 7,150km (4,450 miles) south-west of Hawaii and about 1,160km (720 miles) south of Guam. Together with the Federated States of Micronesia, Palau forms the archipelago of the Caroline Islands.

Climate
Warm and humid, with temperatures between 23–30 degrees Celsius and humidity around 80 per cent. Rainfall (variable, minimum 250 mm/year), can occur in downpours. Typhoons are possible.

Entry requirements
Passports
Required by all; US citizens need only show proof of citizenship.
Visa
Not required. Special regulations may apply to some non-tourist destinations within the islands.
Entry permits, issued on arrival, are granted for stays of less than 30 days with proof of return/onward passage and adequate funds for maintenance. Extended entry permits are issued upon application to Chief of Immigration, Bureau of Legal Affairs, Ministry of Justice, PO Box 100, Koror, Palau 96940, fee US$100.
Currency advice/regulations
No restrictions on import and export of local and foreign currency. Foreign currency over US$5,000 must be declared.
Prohibited imports
Illicit drugs and weapons

Health (for visitors)
Mandatory precautions
Cholera and yellow fever immunisations are required for those arriving from infected areas.
Advisable precautions
Vaccination for diphtheria, TB, hepatitis 'A' and 'B', polio, tetanus and typhoid are recommended. There is a rabies risk. Hospitals often expect immediate cash payment for medical treatment. In July/August 2004, there was an outbreak of dengue fever.

Hotels
There are hotels and guest-houses in Koror, Peleliu and Angaur.

Credit cards
Major credit cards are widely accepted at main visitor facilities.

Public holidays
Fixed dates
1 Jan (New Year's Day), 15 Mar (Youth Day), 5 May (Senior Citizens' Day), 1 Jun (President's Day), 9 Jul (Constitution Day), 1 Oct (Independence Day), 24 Oct (United Nations Day), 25 Dec (Christmas Day).
Variable dates
Labour Day (first Mon in Sep), Thanksgiving Day (fourth Thu in Nov).

Working hours
Banking
Mon–Thu: 0930–1430, Fri: 0930–1700.
Business
Mon–Fri: 0800–1700; Mon–Fri: 0730–1630.
Government
Mon–Fri: 0800–1700; Mon–Fri: 0730–1630.
Shops
Mon–Sat: 0800–2000, (Sun) 0800–1800.

Telecommunications
Telephone/fax
Palau National Communications Corporation provides all modern public and private telecommunications facilities, including phone cards, international calls and mobile phones.
Internet/e-mail
In 2004, Palau signed over rights to its domain – .pw – to a Massachusetts, US, company

Electricity supply
115/230V AC 60Hz

Social customs/useful tips
An informal attitude prevails in business. Business cards are sometimes exchanged. Business is usually conducted in English. Visitors should familiarise themselves with local customs. Permission should be sought before photographing people. Gratuities are optional.

Getting there
Air
National airline: Palau Micronesia Air (PMA)
Launched in August 2004, PMA, Palau's first locally-owned airline, suspended operations in December 2004 subject to restructuring.
International airport/s: Koror Babelthaob (ROR), 19km north-east of Airai. A new airport terminal was completed in 2003.
Airport tax: US$20

Getting about
National transport
Road: Outside administrative areas, the road network may consist of tracks not passable to ordinary vehicles. Ngiwal, Melekeok and Ngaremlengui each have road systems which link up with the main hamlets.
Driving is on the right with 40km per hour as the maximum allowable speed. Passing is prohibited anywhere in Palau.

In July 2005, Japan awarded almost US$20 million in grants to improve Palau's roads.
Water: Peleliu and Anguar each have a regular mode of transport via municipal boats. Other inter-island services rely on privately operated boats.
City transport
Taxis: Journey time from the airport to the city centre is around 30 minutes.

BUSINESS DIRECTORY

The addresses listed below are a selection only. While World of Information makes every endeavour to check these addresses, we cannot guarantee that changes have not been made, especially to telephone numbers and area codes. We would welcome any corrections.

Telephone area codes
The international direct dialling code (IDD) for Palau is +680, followed by subscriber's number.

Useful telephone numbers
Ambulance: 488-1411
Police: 911

Chambers of Commerce
Palau Chamber of Commerce, PO Box 1742, Koror 96940 (tel: 488-3400; fax: 488-3401; e-mail: pcoc@palaunet.com).

Banking
Bank of Guam, PO Box 338, Koror 96940 (tel: 488-1648/2696/2697; fax: 488-1384).

Bank of Hawaii, PO Box 340, Koror 96940 (tel: 488-2602/2428; fax: 488-2427).

Bank Pacific, PO Box 1000, Koror 96940 (tel: 488-5635; fax: 488-4752).

Melekeok Government Bank, PO Box 1711, Koror 96940 (tel: 488-2066 /5342/5343; fax: 488-2065; email: mgbank@palaunet.com).

Pacific Savings Bank, PO Box 399, Koror 96940 (tel: 488-1859/1860; fax: 488-1858; email: bank@palaunet.com).

Palau Central Bank Inc., PO Box 786, Koror 96940 (tel: 488-1891; fax: 488-2065).

Palau Construction Bank, PO Box 1714-S111, Koror 96940 (tel: 488-1946; fax: 488-5753; email: pc-bank@palaunet.com).

Rizal Commercial Banking Corporation, PO Box 37, Koror 96940 (tel: 488-2804; fax: 488-1892; email: pdcgroup@palaunet.com).

Travel information
Continental Micronesia, PO Box 138CK, Saipan MP 96950, Northern Mariana Islands (tel: (670)234-8223; fax: (670)234-8358).

Palau

National tourist organisation offices

Palau Visitors' Authority, PO Box 256, Koror, ROP 96940 (tel: 488-2793/1930; fax: 488-1453; internet site: http://www.visit-palau.com).

Other useful addresses

British Deputy High Commissioner for Fiji (for information on Palau) Suva, Fiji.

Office of the President, PO Box 100, Koror, ROP 96940 (tel: 488-2403/2523/2541/2828).

Palau/Hawaii Liaison Office, 1441 Kapiolani Blvd, Suite 1120, Honolulu, Hawaii 96814 (tel: (808) 941-0988/89; fax: (808) 943-1689).

Palau/Guam Liaison Office, ITC Bldg, Suite 615, PO Box 9457, Tamuning, Guam 96911 (tel: 646-9281/81).

Internet sites

Palau visitors site: http://www.destmic.com/palau.html

US Office of Insular affairs: http://www.doi.gov/oia

Palestine

KEY FACTS

Official name: Palestine

Head of State: President of the Palestinian Council Mahmoud Abbas (Fatah) (sworn in 15 Jan 2005)

Head of government: As of end-Jan 2006, Hamas, which won the 25 Jan election, had not appointed a prime minister

Ruling party: Harakat al Muqawama al Islamia (Hamas) (Islamic Resistance Movement) won the 25 Jan 2006 election

Area: 6,257 square km (West Bank 5,879 square km; Gaza Strip 378 square km)

Population: 3.52 million (2004)

Official language: Arabic

Currency: Israeli new shekel and Jordanian dinar (NIS)

Exchange rate: NIS4.60 per US$ and JD0.71 per US$ (Oct 2005)

GDP per capita: US$700 (2003)

GDP real growth: -18.50% (2003)

Labour force: 774,000 (2004)

Unemployment: 27.20% (2004); 27.0% (2005)*

Inflation: 4.40% (2003)

Balance of trade: -US$1.30 billion (2003)

* estimated figure

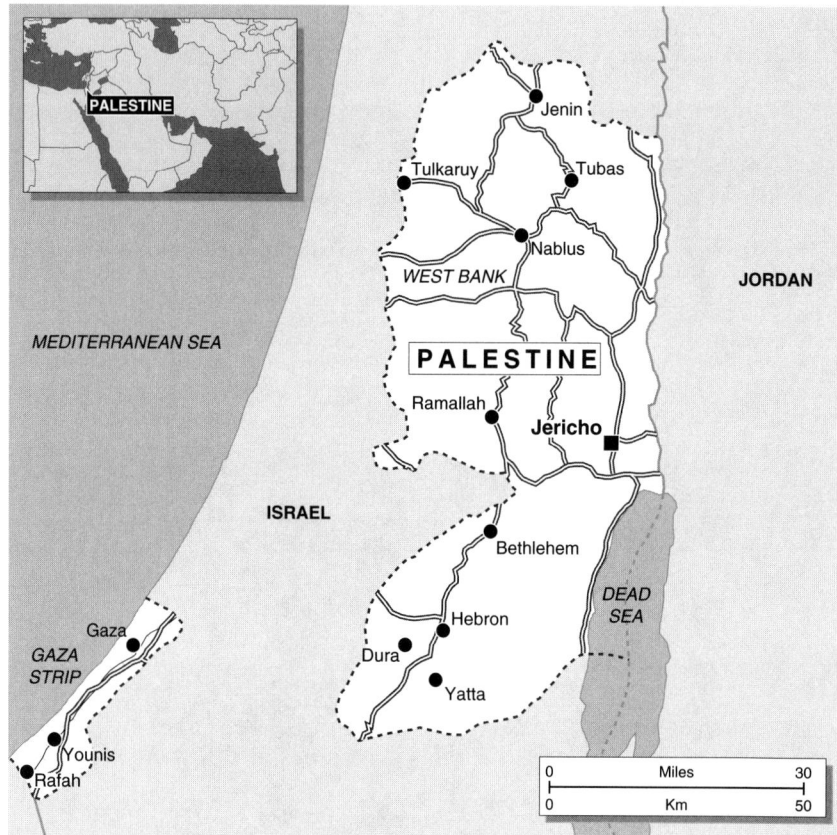

In 2005, the Palestinians experienced, as the saying goes, 'interesting times'. Moreover, much of what was experienced was beyond their control. It was also a year of political change within the Palestinian Occupied Territories. The Harak al Tahir al Falistin (Fatah) (Movement for the Liberation of Palestine), the main representative of the Palestinian people since 1969, suffered several blows at the ballot box in 2005, with worse to come in 2006.

Economic collapse

Choked by a myriad of Israeli checkpoints in both the West Bank and Gaza Strip since the outbreak of the Second *Intifada* in 2000, the Palestinian economy continued to crumble in 2005. Goods and services were barely allowed transit within the Occupied Territories, let alone to the outside world. The Palestinian Authority (PA), the Palestinian government in those parts of the Occupied Territories not under Israeli army or settler control, racked up a budget deficit of over US$800 million in 2005. The World Bank warned, in January 2006, that the Palestinian economy was increasingly 'unsustainable'. Official unemployment ran at 27 per cent in 2005, although it was 35 per cent in the Gaza Strip. The poverty rate was 48 per cent overall and 65 per cent in the Strip.

Some respite was achieved after September, when Gazans were able to take over greenhouses evacuated by Israeli settlers in August. However, the frequent closure by Israel of Gaza's external access points has meant that produce often cannot reach its market.

Palestine

Year of the truce

On 8 February 2005, the PA reached a truce with Israel, aimed at bringing to an end the al Aqsa or Second *Intifada* that had begun in September 2000. The truce was a direct result of the ascension to power of the new PA president, Mahmoud Abbas. Israel had refused to negotiate with his predecessor, Yasser Arafat but Arafat's death in November was seen by the Israeli government as an opportunity for renewed talks. According to the Israeli human rights NGO, B'tselem, at least 3,300 Palestinians had died during the al Aqsa *Intifada*, including more than 600 under the age of 18. Nearly 1,000 Israelis were also killed, including more than 100 under the age of 18.

The truce built upon efforts by the PA and Israel to co-ordinate security provisions in the Gaza Strip, where, from January, Palestinian police were allowed to deploy without threat of attack from the Israeli Defense Force (IDF). The IDF also announced in January that it would refrain from attacks within PA-controlled territory. The truce also included provisions for the transfer of security control of five West Bank cities to the PA and the release of hundreds of Palestinian prisoners from Israeli jails. In return, the PA was expected to rein in militant groups within the Occupied Territories, particularly Harakat al Muqawama al Islamia (Hamas) (Islamic Resistance Movement), Harakat al Jihad al Islami al Filastini (Palestinian Islamic Jihad Movement) (PIJ) and militants aligned to Fatah.

In terms of implementation, both the Palestinians and the Israelis failed on several counts. By the end of 2005, Israel had still only transferred to the PA control of Jericho and Tulkarm. Moreover, the IDF soon reoccupied the latter. Prisoner releases, a key demand by the PA, were repeatedly delayed and staggered by Israel, although eventually nearly 1,000 prisoners were released. In March, after pressure from the PA and Egypt, Hamas and the largest of the Fatah-aligned militant groups, the al Aqsa Martyrs Brigade, agreed to extend an informal truce. There were several breaches during the year, although even the IDF acknowledged that there was a significant reduction in the level of violence. However, the PIJ refused to be party to this arrangement and continued its attacks against Israeli military and civilian targets.

Israel's disengagement

In August and September of 2005, Israel unilaterally withdrew its settlers and soldiers from the Gaza Strip and parts of the northern West Bank. Israeli prime minister Ariel Sharon had been preparing the ground in Israel for this withdrawal since December 2003 but little had been done to co-ordinate the operation with the PA. The PA president, Mahmoud Abbas, urged Israel to co-ordinate the disengagement with his government and lobbied the US government to ensure that Israel would do so. Abbas feared that without such co-ordination, Hamas would simply claim credit for the withdrawal and cite it as the product of its own militancy. With several elections due in 2005 and early 2006, Abbas was concerned that Hamas would threaten his own party, Fatah's, stranglehold on Palestinian politics.

Israel eventually briefed the PA security services as to some of its disengagement plans and, in July, President Abbas moved to the Gaza Strip to personally oversee his forces.

Although President Abbas managed to insert a PA presence into the disengagement process, his bid to ensure that the PA could actually control events on the ground in the wake of the Israeli withdrawal was less successful. The disengagement only underscored the extent to which the Gaza Strip was beyond PA control. Just after the Israeli withdrawal, Hamas took the unusual step of publicly naming its military leaders, all of whom had gone to ground since Israel intensified its bid to assassinate key Hamas personnel in 2004. This publication was seen by analysts as a bid to link Israel's disengagement with Hamas' campaign of violent resistance to the occupation. Moreover, the PA's ruling party, Fatah, publicly acknowledged its weakness by including Hamas and other groups on a committee established to oversee the development of the land formerly occupied by Israeli settlers and soldiers.

In the wake of the disengagement, chaotic scenes erupted at the Rafah border crossing into Egypt. Civilians, assisted by Hamas members, stormed the border. Many Palestinian families had been divided between the Gaza Strip and Egypt since 1967, when Israel conquered the Strip from the Egyptians. Intra-Palestinian violence, between rival branches of the security services and between rival political parties, also wracked the Gaza Strip. The most high profile incident of this nature was the murder of Musa Arafat, former security chief and cousin to the late Yasser Arafat, on 7 September. Kidnappings of foreign aid workers also took place. Although President Abbas pledged to end the 'armed chaos' in the Gaza Strip, there was little sign of this materialising in 2005.

The occupation grinds on

Although Palestinians took control of the Gaza Strip and four small sections of the northern West Bank in 2005, the Israeli occupation continued apace elsewhere. The Israeli government in 2005 approved the building of hundreds of new housing units in Israeli settlements in the West Bank. The Israelis also stepped up efforts to complete its 'separation barrier' in the West Bank. Accordingly, up to 8 per cent of Palestinian land in the West Bank and tens of thousands of Palestinians were included on the Israeli side of the barrier. A confidential EU report, leaked in November, asserted that Israeli efforts to separate, through the building of the barrier, Arab East Jerusalem from the rest of the West Bank were particularly assiduous in 2005.

Checkpoints, both fixed and mobile, continued to choke Palestinian efforts to travel, and trade between their cities and villages. Most Palestinian population centres were effectively enclaves, surrounded

KEY INDICATORS — Palestine

	Unit	2000	2001	2002	2003	2004
Population	m	2.79	3.00	3.45	3.49	*3.52
Gross domestic product (GDP)	US$bn	4.29	4.00	2.90	3.45	–
GDP per capita	US$	1,536	1,500	840	700	–
GDP real growth	%	-5.9	-12.0	-62.0	-18.5	-1.0
Inflation	%	2.7	1.0	–	–	–
Exports (fob) (goods)	US$m	591.0	472.0	–	–	–
Imports (fob) (goods)	US$m	2,837.0	1,724.0	–	–	–
Balance of trade	US$m	-2,250.0	-1,252.0	–	–	–
Exchange rate	per US$	4.08	4.21	4.63	4.60	4.48

* estimated figure

by Israeli troops and settlers. This blockade was maintained, according the Israeli government, in order to prevent the movement of terrorists. The IDF also frequently raided Palestinian towns in search of suspected militants.

Changing of the guard

Palestinian politics entered a new era in 2005, not least because of the death of PA President Yasser Arafat in November 2004. Mahmoud Abbas, Arafat's number two within the Palestine Liberation Organisation (PLO), was anointed by the ruling Fatah as Arafat's natural successor. Abbas had also previously served as PA prime minister in 2003. Abbas duly won presidential elections in January 2005, taking 62 per cent of the vote with a turnout of 66 per cent. For the first time since 1969 the leadership of the Palestinians was not concentrated in the hands of one man – Arafat. While Abbas served as PA president and PLO chairman, the Fatah chair went to Farouk Kaddoumi.

President Abbas made significant changes to the PA government in February, making something of a break from the Arafat era. Although he re-appointed Fatah's Ahmed Qureia as PA prime minister, he also named to the cabinet several figures who had been pushed into the political wilderness by Arafat. These included Mohammed Dahlan, a former security chief respected by many in Israeli and American circles, and Nasser Yousef, also a former security chief.

However, while the Fatah-dominated PA attempted to renew itself in 2005, power was already in reality slipping from its grasp. Local elections, staggered throughout the year, brought far more change to Palestinian politics than the establishment desired. Beginning in December 2004 and continuing in January, May, September and December of 2005, Palestinians voted for new city and village councils in the Gaza Strip and the West Bank. These were the first Palestinian elections contested by Hamas, who had boycotted previous polls. Fatah emerged as the biggest vote-winner in all of these elections bar the December 2005 poll. However, starting from a base of zero, Hamas' gains were startling and only confirmed suspicions that a post-Arafat Fatah was no longer the monolithic entity it once was. In January, Hamas won majorities in 10 local councils in the Gaza Strip and in May, it took control of former Fatah strongholds in Qalqilya, Bethlehem and Rafah. After losing some momentum in September's elections, Hamas crushed Fatah in December elections, winning in three of the West Bank's biggest cities: Jenin, Nablus and al Bireh. Tellingly, after each election, the Fatah-led government attempted to delay future votes, fearing further losses to Hamas.

Fatah's woes were exacerbated on 14 December, when senior members opposed to the party's old guard formed a breakaway party, al Mustaqbal (The Future). Marwan Barghouti, widely considered to be the most popular Palestinian leader and a future president led the split. Barghouti is currently serving multiple life sentences in an Israeli jail but managed to attract several senior Fatah members, including Mohammed Dahlan and Jibril Rajoub. The catalyst for the split was Fatah's refusal to continue with primaries for places on Fatah's list for upcoming national elections. Barghouti had convincingly won the primaries but the Fatah establishment had threatened to ignore the result. The Fatah rift was healed on 28 December when President Abbas conceded to Barghouti.

Hamas' electoral triumphs extended onto the national stage on 25 January 2006, when it won a landslide victory in elections to the Palestinian Legislative Council (PLC). The PLC is the legislature of the PA and its largest party generally makes up the PA government. There had been no elections to the PLC since 1996. Hamas won 76 out of the 132 seats, compared to Fatah's 43.

Outlook

With the Hamas landslide victory in January 2006, Palestinians are entering the unknown. Fatah has dominated Palestinian politics for nearly four decades and few predicted such a dramatic collapse. Israel, the US and many others in the international community have announced that they will refuse to deal with a PA headed by Hamas, unless Hamas renounce violence and recognise Israel. The US, one of the PA's single biggest donors, has threatened to cut off all financial aid to the Palestinians if Hamas enter government without such changes. Hamas has thus far reiterated its position that it has the right to resist occupation through force of arms and that it will not recognise Israel.

As the formation of a new government could take weeks, some states, including Israel, have begun to moderate their position slightly. The World Bank, among others, warned in January that the PA is on the brink of total financial and administrative collapse if new funds are not found. After some debate, the EU has agreed to continue funding the PA for the time being. The Israeli government is said to be mulling the idea of releasing tax revenue owed to the PA, frozen in the wake of Hamas' victory, at least until such time as Hamas actually takes power.

Many analysts predict that moderates within Hamas will move the party away from some of its more hard-line positions regarding Israel. Much like the PLO in the 1980s, the argument goes, Hamas will eventually rehabilitate itself due to the necessity for gaining international recognition for its goal of an independent Palestinian state. Some Hamas leaders have, since 25 January, flagged the possibility of some kind of accommodation with Israel but even these have not declared an end to their ambition to see an Islamic state established in all of Israel and the Palestinian Occupied Territories. Khaled Meshaal, Hamas' most senior leader, has indicated that Hamas will abide by all agreements made by the out-going government 'as long as it is in the interest of our people'. Hamas has also indicated that it wants to form a coalition government with Fatah, although Fatah officials have so far ruled this out.

As for the actual transfer of power itself, this has got off to a rocky start. The government of Prime Minister Qureia resigned immediately after the election and President Abbas has announced that he will invite Hamas to form a government. Members of the PA security services as well as militias aligned to Fatah have been protesting throughout the West Bank, demanding the resignation of President Abbas and other senior Fatah figures. Violent confrontations between Fatah and Hamas supporters also broke out in the days immediately following Hamas' victory. It remains to be seen whether or not the PA security services will take orders from a Hamas-led government and how Hamas' own military wing, the Izz al Din al Qassam Brigade, will fit in with these. Some in Hamas point to the example of Hizbollah (Party of God) in Lebanon, which fields a militia and also holds cabinet seats in government, as a formula for future governance.

Outside Israel, many governments in the region will be watching Hamas carefully. Egypt has already urged Hamas to disarm. The Palestinians are the first Arabs in the modern era to vote for a change of government and have the result actually recognised by the incumbent. De facto one-party states such as Egypt, Syria and Yemen, all with their own religious opposition parties, can be expected to act to minimise any 'knock-on' effect within

Palestine

their own borders. However, with the Arab world press having widely reported, and in many instances welcomed, the Hamas victory, it may be that the tiny PA proves to be a catalyst for wider regional change in 2006.

Risk assessment

Politics	In flux
Economy	Continuing decline
Regional stability	Tense

COUNTRY PROFILE

Historical profile

With the outbreak of the First World War, Britain promised the independence of Arab lands under Ottoman rule in return for Arab support against Turkey, which had entered the war on the side of Germany. The two pacts which sealed Palestine's future were the Sykes-Picot agreement and the Balfour Declaration. The Sykes-Picot agreement divided the Ottoman Arab region into zones assigned to France and Britain and the Balfour Declaration suggested the establishment in Palestine of a national home for the Jewish people, pledging that nothing would be done to prejudice the civil and religious rights of the Arabs. After the War, the Council of the League of Nations assigned to Britain a mandate for the Ottoman Arab territory of Palestine, a region that covered present-day Israel and Jordan, plus the Golan Heights region (claimed by Syria). The British divided the mandate into two parts, designating all lands west of the Jordan River as Palestine and those east of the river as Transjordan. The League of Nations mandate also addressed the goal of restoring a Jewish homeland in Palestine.

1916 The Sykes-Picot agreement.
1917 The Balfour Declaration.
1922 The Ottoman Arab territory of Palestine was mandated to Britain; it was divided into Palestine and Transjordan.
1929 Riots in Jerusalem between Arab Palestinians and Jews were sparked by a dispute over the use of the western wall of the Al Aqsa Mosque (the site is sacred to Muslims, and Jews claim it as part of their temple).
1936–39 The Arab Higher Committee opposed Jewish immigration to Palestine and the Peel Commission concluded that the mandate was unworkable. Legislation limiting the number of Jewish immigrants was introduced by the British government.
1945 Many of the Jews who had survived the Nazi German Holocaust arrived and Jewish extremists began to oppose Britain's immigration legislation.
1946 Transjordan became independent and was later re-named Jordan.
1947 Britain decided to leave. The UN adopted Resolution 181, which called for the establishment of both Jewish and Arab states within Palestine and a partition plan was drawn up, based solely on population, with Jerusalem as an international zone under UN jurisdiction. The Jews agreed to the partition; the Arabs did not.
1948 Conflict ensued between Arabs and Jews. Jewish leaders announced the formation of the State of Israel, open to the immigration of Jews from all countries. Egypt, Iraq, Lebanon, Syria and Jordan joined Palestinian and other Arab guerrillas and invaded Israel. The armistice agreements extended the territory under Israel's control beyond the UN partition boundaries. Many Arabs became refugees in the surrounding Arab countries, ending the Arab majority in the new Jewish state.
1957 Harak al Tahir al Falistin (Al Fatah) (Movement for the Liberation of Palestine) was formed by Arab students, including Yasser Arafat – an Egyptian Palestinian, who grew up in the Gaza Strip.
1964 The Palestine Liberation Organisation (PLO) was founded in Egypt as a Palestinian nationalist umbrella organisation dedicated to the establishment of an independent Palestinian state; later, it operated from Lebanon.
1967 Israel launched and won the Six Day War against Egypt, Jordan and Syria, taking control of the Sinai peninsular and the Gaza Strip, which had been Egyptian territory, together with the Golan Heights, formerly claimed by Syria. Around 300,000 Palestinian Arabs fled to Jordan. After the Six-Day War, control of the PLO devolved to the leadership of the various fedayeen militia groups, the most dominant of which was Yasser Arafat's Al Fatah.
Israel's settlement policy started; it occupied the Sinai peninsular (returned to Egypt in 1982), the Golan Heights, the Gaza Strip and the West Bank, including East Jerusalem; the Jews transferred to these areas became known as settlers.
1969 Arafat was appointed chairman of the PLO's Executive Committee.
1970 Civil war (Black September) between the Jordanian army and Palestinians followed airplane hijackings by a Palestinian resistance group. The PLO was forcefully expelled from its bases in Jordan and moved to Lebanon.
1973 Lebanon was used by the Palestinians as a base for activities against Israel. In retaliation, Israeli commandos raided Beirut, killing three associates of Yasser Arafat. Arab states officially recognised the PLO as the representative of the Palestinians.
1981 Israel annexed East Jerusalem.
1982–85 Israel invaded Lebanon to prevent the PLO from carrying out armed resistance to its rule in the occupied territories of the Gaza Strip and the West Bank. A Western multinational force monitored the evacuation of the PLO; it relocated to Tunis, where it stayed until it moved to the Palestinian autonomous areas (Gaza and Jericho) in 1994.
1987 The Palestinians launched an *intifida* (uprising) against the Israelis. The Harakat al Muqawama al Islamia (Hamas) (Islamic Resistance Movement) was formed in the Gaza Strip. It has two goals: to undertake armed resistance to Israeli rule in the West Bank and the Gaza Strip and to establish a sovereign, independent state located in historic Palestine (present-day Israel, the West Bank, and the Gaza Strip). There was an upsurge in violence as large numbers of Jews from the Soviet Union began to settle in the West Bank and the Gaza Strip.
1988 The State of Palestine was declared, as outlined in the UN partition plan 181, the new state being recognised only by states that did not recognise Israel.
1993–95 The Oslo Peace Accords laid the basis for transfer of authority from the Israeli military administration to the PLO in the Gaza Strip and an undefined area around the town of Jericho in the West Bank. A follow-up treaty, Oslo II, was signed, which envisaged Palestinian autonomy with Israeli troop units withdrawing from the West Bank.
1996 Yasser Arafat was elected president of the Palestinian Legislative Council (PLC), the assembly of the Palestinian Authority (PA).
1998 The Wye peace agreement between the Israelis and the Palestinians, brokered by the US, ended 19 months of deadlock in the peace process.
2000 Israel agreed to allow the PA to control 39.8 per cent of the West Bank. However, after Israel's right-wing opposition leader, Ariel Sharon, visited the Temple Mount in Jerusalem and reiterated Israel's claims to Muslim holy places in the city, a second *intifada* was launched by Palestinians and a total blockade was imposed by Israel on the West Bank and Gaza.
2001 Israel's government, led by Sharon, declared the PA to be a terrorist-supporting organisation and launched Operation 'Defensive Shield', invading the PA-controlled West Bank and Gaza, attacking its institutions and besieging Arafat's headquarters. Deaths in Israel by Palestinian suicide bombers increased.
2002 Saudi Arabia proposed a peace initiative and a UN Security Council resolution endorsed a Palestinian state and called for the cessation of hostilities. Israel besieged Arafat's compound in Ramallah and reoccupied most of the West Bank. The Israeli military carried out many

attacks attempting to destroy militant Hamas and Islamic Jihad targets. For five weeks the Israeli army surrounded militants and civilians taking sanctuary in the Church of the Nativity in Bethlehem; it ended when 13 militants were sent into exile. Israel began building a barrier between it and Gaza claiming it was the only way to control infiltration of militant terrorists.
2003 US President George W Bush unveiled the Road Map to Peace, with a cease-fire and end to Jewish settlements in the occupied territories and the creation of an independent Palestinian state by 2005. Ahmed Qureia became prime minister.
2004 In February, Sharon, declared he would remove all Jewish settlements in Gaza. President Yasser Arafat became ill and died in Paris on 11 November.
2005 On 9 January, Mahmoud Abbas (also known as Abu Mazen) was elected president of the Palestinian Authority, by an overwhelming majority. He persuaded Hamas and Islamic Jihad to agree to an unofficial cease-fire. On 8 February, at the Sharm El Sheikh summit in Egypt, a truce was signed by Sharon and Abbas, ending four years of violence between Israel and Palestine. On 20 February, President Abbas and the Israeli cabinet approved the removal of Jewish settlers from Gaza and part of the West Bank. Having objected to the first proposed cabinet dominated by the 'old guard', a revised cabinet composed largely of professionals and technocrats was appointed.
2006 Mahmoud Abbas said in January that he would not run for president again when his current term ends in 2009. Elections in January were won convincingly by Hama.

Political structure
Constitution
A provisional framework for the Palestinian state was approved by the Palestinian Legislative Council in a 1996 Draft Basic Law. This law will be fully endorsed when a permanent settlement is achieved.
Form of state
Parliamentary Democracy
The executive
Executive power is vested in the head of the Palestinian National Authority (PNA – also known as the Palestinian Authority (PA)), who is president, elected by direct universal suffrage for up to two five-year terms, and Head of State.
The president is head of armed and security forces, is responsible for initiating and proposing laws and foreign policy. The president appoints a prime minister, who forms a cabinet.

National legislature
The unicameral Palestinian Legislative Council (PLC) was established in 1994 and is composed of 132 members plus the president as an *ex officio* member. The PLC's members are elected in 16 multi-seat constituencies for 5-year terms.
Legal system
The Basic Law provides for an independent judiciary.
The High Judicial Council oversees the administration of a hierarchy of courts beginning with the magistrate courts, Courts of first Instance, Courts of Appeal and The Supreme Court.
Last elections
25 January 2006 (parliamentary); 9 January 2005 (presidential).
Results: Presidential: Mahmoud Abbas, also known as Abu Mazen, candidate of the mainstream Harak al Tahir al Falistin (Fatah) (Movement for the Liberation of Palestine), was elected president of the Palestinian council with 62.3 per cent of the vote against independent candidate, Mustafa Barghouti, 19.8 per cent. Turnout was 70 per cent.
Parliamentary: Harakat al Muqawama al Islamia (Hamas) (Islamic Resistance Movement) won 76 seats in the 132-member national legislature. Harak al Tahir al Falistin (Fatah) (Movement for the Liberation of Palestine) won 43 seats. The Popular Front for the Liberation of Palestine (PFLP) won 3 seats. Three groupings (The Alternative, Independent Palestine and Third Way) won 2 seats each. Independents won the 4 remaining seats. Turnout was 74.6%.
Next elections
2010 (presidential).

Political parties
The only legal party is the Harak al Tahir al Falistin (Fatah) (Movement for the Liberation of Palestine), the political wing of the Palestine Liberation Organisation (PLO).
Ruling party
Harakat al Muqawama al Islamia (Hamas) (Islamic Resistance Movement) won the 25 Jan 2006 election

Population
3.52 million (2004)
Ethnic make-up
Gaza: Palestinians and other Arabs (99.4 per cent), Israelis (0.6 per cent).
West Bank: Palestinians and other Arabs (83 per cent), Israelis (17 per cent).
Religions
The majority of the population is Muslim (mainly Sunni); also Jewish and Christian minorities.

Education
Formal basic education is provided to the majority of those who are of primary school age (94.7 per cent), although the quality of education does not correspond to the rising demand.
The education sector has suffered tremendous decline since the Israeli occupation. Most of the schools in the Gaza Strip are overcrowded and run two to three shifts per day. It is estimated that there are 1,175 schools of which 995 are in the West Bank and 180 in the Gaza Strip. The education ministry in its five-year reform project (2000–05) is keen on developing a Palestinian curriculum emphasising studies in Palestinian identity and has invested in providing textbooks and improving the teaching methods in schools. It will also encourage the private sector to invest in vocational training, which otherwise concentrates on building and running cultural centres.
There are six universities in the West Bank and two in the Gaza Strip. West Bank Universities include Birzeit, Al Najah, Bethlehem, Al Quds University, Hebron University and Al Quds Open University.

Health
The Israeli occupation has almost paralysed the provision of healthcare to the civilian population. Most hospitals and clinics are unable to operate and as a result 73 per cent of Palestinians in rural areas are deprived of medical treatment. Vaccinations among children have been largely hindered spreading the fear of epidemics. Moreover, elderly people with chronic diseases suffer from acute shortages of medicine.
A hospital in Gaza, funded by the EU, is largely unworkable as staff, patients and supplies are denied access by Israeli authorities during times of trouble.
Life expectancy: 73 years (2003)
Fertility rate/Maternal mortality rate: 4.9 births per woman (2003)
Birth rate/Death rate: 37.5 births per 1,000 population; 4.1 deaths per 1,000 population (2003).
Infant mortality rate: 22 per 1,000 live births (2003)

Welfare
The UN World Food Programme (WFP) aims to provide basic food support to 500,000 non-refugee Palestinians, in the West Bank and Gaza Strip. It targets those who have been classified as 'social hardship cases' (360,000 people according to latest estimates) and are eligible for welfare assistance from the PNA. In Jerusalem, an Emergency Food Crisis Group, chaired by WFP, has been established with the help of other UN agencies, non-governmental organisations and donors.
The Israeli occupation has forced the poverty level higher than ever before. While unemployment stands at 30 per cent, an

Palestine

estimated 40 per cent of Palestinian households have a monthly income that is less than US$200 per month. The percentage is 45 per cent in Gaza and 37 per cent in the West Bank.

Estimates show that 38 per cent of refugees live in the Palestinian territories; 15.8 per cent in the West Bank and 21.9 per cent in the Gaza Strip. The PNA along with other international non-government organisations have been struggling to rehabilitate the housing conditions of people in the refugee camps such as Jenin and Nablus. The Palestinian Housing Council has been active in providing low cost housing. More than 400,000 Palestinians are deprived of electricity and running water.

Main cities
Gaza Strip: Gaza (also called Gaza City); Deir al Balah became the first town to come under Palestinian self-rule in May 1994.
West Bank: East Jerusalem, Jericho, Ramallah, Nablus, Hebron, Jenin.

Languages spoken
Arabic. Hebrew is spoken by Israeli settlers. English is widely understood.
Official language/s
Arabic

Media
Press
The Palestine News Agency, Wafa, was established in 1995. A number of Palestinian newspapers are based in Nazareth, outside the PNA.
Dailies: There are several Arabic language daily newspapers including *As Sennara, Al Hayat al Jadedah, Al Esteqlal, Al ayyam Daily Newspaper, Arab Gate* and *Al Quds Alarbi*.
Weeklies: Weeklies include *Kul-Alarab, Assabeel Weekly, Filsteen Almoslima* and *Akhbar Alnaqab*.
Periodicals: Monthly publications include the Arabic electronic newspaper *Falasteen Electronic Newspaper* and the English language *Palestine Times*.
Broadcasting
The Palestinian Broadcasting Corporation broadcasts from Ramallah.

Economy
'We are obliged to mix politics with economics in Palestine' said Dr Hassan Adnan Yassin, the general manager of the Palestinian Stock Exchange, and his words encapsulate Palestine's seemingly intractable problems. Analysts, World Bank officials, donor countries' representatives are all agreed that without the free passage for Gazan merchandise no amount of aid can sustain the territory. Israel, it seems, is equally certain that without its security being guaranteed – an assurance no country can claim in the current climate of international terrorism that uses suicide bombings – it will not relinquish its oppressive hold, by abrogating its customs union with Gaza, which threatens to stifle Palestine's prospective economic viability. Aid to Palestine amounts to US$1 billion per annum and this is soaked up, not by investing in people and infrastructure but, by maintaining a community whose economy is shattered. Israel has targetted and destroyed the infrastructure, institutions and private property in the PA-controlled West Bank and Gaza Strip. Since 2000 (when the second *intifada* uprising began) the economy has declined by 15 per cent and per capita gross national income has contracted by 33 per cent. GDP declined further by 1 per cent in 2004. The economy also suffered from suspected corruption and aid is now channelled through a World Bank trust fund rather than given directly to the Palestinian Authority. Unemployment was around 27 per cent in 2005 and over 60 per cent of households lived below the poverty line. The trade deficit – almost two-thirds with Israel – increased more rapidly than domestic production in 2004 and represented 65 per cent of GDP. Palestine has paid Israel the equivalent of all its international aid plus 50 per cent of the remittances of its workers in Israel for this deficit, since 2001. It will be another blow if Israel's proposal to withdraw work permits to Palestinian labourers in 2008 is carried out.

It has been estimated that since 2000 opportunity lost to GDP has been around US$6.4 billion, or 140 per cent of the size of the economy before 2000.

International proposals for US$3 billion in investment is predicated on Israel allowing free passage of people and goods to markets. The EU has proposed that it will back a loan guarantee for investors fund, supply technical aid to Palestine to improve its customs security and US$30.5 million to construct a cargo terminal. However, it still wants to see more progress in the peace negotiations before such measures are implemented.

Israel's obduracy as it slowly constricts Palestine's economy and its ability to provide for its people is likely to produce the conditions that serve terrorist organisations very well, while undermining the authority of legitimate rule. Gaza's 1.5 million population needs to trade with, most particularly, the populous West Bank and the rest of the world.

External trade
All exports have to be shipped through Israel. In 2005 Israel accounced that it would not renew its commitment to the customs union with Gaza. Palestine has no operational ports or airports to ship goods directly to markets other than Israel. The land border at Rafah in southern Gaza is policed by Palestinian and Egyptian military and provides a less than satisfactory means of access.
Imports
Food, consumer goods and construction materials.
Main sources: Israel, Egypt, West Bank
Exports
Citrus fruit, flowers, olives, fruit, vegetables and limestone.
Main destinations: Israel, Egypt, Jordan

Agriculture
Farming
The sector has been badly damaged by the Israeli-Palestinian conflict since 2000 when agriculture contributed 7 per cent to GDP and employed about 25 per cent of the workforce.

Before the second *intifada* and the Israeli invasion of the West Bank and Gaza, about a quarter of the land area was cultivated and smallholdings of five hectares (ha) or less dominated. Crops, including olives, grapes and almonds, took up 60 per cent of cultivated rain-fed areas and field crops (mainly cereals) about 30 per cent. Olive growing accounted for more than 50 per cent of cultivated land.

The Separation Barrier has led to confiscation and levelling of Palestinian lands and by mid-2004 around 260 square kilometres, or 15 per cent of agricultural land had been lost to production.

Crop production in 2004 included: 67,800 tonnes (t) cereals in total, 45,000t wheat, 22,000t barley, 550t sorghum, 55,000t potatoes, 5,000t sweet potatoes, 85,000t olives, 200,000t tomatoes, 41,500t eggplants, 12,700t chillies & peppers, 7,600t bananas, 58,000t grapes, 8,500t figs, 3,700t dates, 6,605t pulses, 72,130t citrus fruit, 4,580t treenuts in total, 19,893t oilcrops, 178,795t fruits in total, 585,750t vegetables in total. Livestock production included: 102,367t meat in total, 9,700t beef, 12,212t lamb, 3,655t goat meat, 76,800t poultry, 41,480t eggs, 181,240t milk, 400t honey, 1,200t cattle hides, 1,290t sheepskins.

Industry and manufacturing
There are proposals by a US-Led syndicate to invest US$500 million in industry and manufacturing after the withdrawal of Israeli troops from Gaza, but only if Israel allows free access of goods through its territory to overseas markets.

Tourism
Foreign investment has been sought to help develop tourism facilities throughout the West Bank; however, the fledging tourism sector has been devastated by the conflict with Israel.

Nations of the World: A Political, Economic and Business Handbook

Financial markets
Stock exchange
The Palestine Securities Exchange (PSE) in the West Bank town of Nablus started operating 1997. It was founded by the Palestinian Development Investment Company (Padco); PalTel – the telecommunications company – is the exchange's largest company trading.

Banking and insurance
Central bank
The Palestine Monetary Authority (PMA), was established in 1995, with responsibilty for licensing, supervising and inspecting banks; determining the liquidity requirements on all deposits held by banks operating in the self-rule areas; managing foreign exchange reserves and foreign currency transactions. The PMA also has the power to regulate and supervise capital activities in the self-rule areas including the licensing of capital market institutions, finance companies and investment funds.
Main financial centre
Ramallah

Time
GMT plus two hours; (GMT plus three hours from April to September).

Geography
Palestine is bordered in the north, west and south by Israel, and by Jordan in the east. The Gaza Strip lies along the Israeli Mediterranean coast to the south-west of Palestine. The Dead Sea is situated in the south-east of Palestine and in Jordan.

Climate
Summer (Apr–Oct): temperatures range from 23 degrees Celsius (C) to 31 degrees C; humidity 70–75 per cent. Winter (Nov–Mar): temperatures range from 15–20 degrees C. Rainfall: Nov–Mar in periodic downpours.

Entry requirements
Passports
There are tight restrictions on entry and passport holders are advised to contact their own foreign affairs ministry to assertain the status of their travel documents.
The Israeli Ministry of the Interior insists that Palestinian citizens holding dual nationality must enter and leave Israel on a Palestinian passport and they are required to obtain travel documents to depart. Israeli exit tax at land borders: US$16.
NB When crossing into Israel from any border other than the West Bank, it is important to note that an Israeli stamp, or exit stamp from any of the neighbouring countries, will mean entry is barred to almost any other Arab country. It is possible to request that the passport should not be stamped and a separate form is stamped instead and attached to the passport; the form can be removed when exiting the country.
Visa
Egypt and Jordan have open borders with Palestine, access was via the Allenby bridge (West Bank/ Jordan) or the border crossing at Rafah (Gaza/Egypt). However, since Israel commands these access points and limits admission, practical entry can only be gained through Israel first. Israel has agreements with 65 countries for visa-free travel, including most citizens from Europe, the Americas, Australasia and some Asian countries (visa applications can be downloaded from: www.mfa.gov.il/mfh/go.asp?MFHJ05eb0). Travel within the West Bank and Gaza is not possible without passing through multiple Israeli military checkpoints. Permission should be obtained from Israeli authorities in advance.
Currency advice/regulations
Most places accept US dollars, Israeli shekels and Jordanian dinars. Trading can be in either US dollars or pounds sterling.

Hotels
There is a lack of good hotels in the West Bank and Gaza.

Public holidays
Fixed dates
14 Nov ('National' Day)
Variable dates
Eid al Adha, Islamic New Year, Birth of the Prophet, Ascent of the Prophet, Eid al Fitr.
The Islamic year contains 354 or 355 days, with the result that Muslim feasts advance by 10–12 days against the Gregorian calendar. Dates of feasts vary according to the sighting of the new moon, so cannot be forecast exactly. Islamic year 1426: 10 February 2005 to 30 January 2006.

Working hours
The working week varies, to accommodate Christian, Jewish or Muslim religious schedules.
Official working hours in the West Bank and Gaza are: Sat–Wed: 0900–1400; Thu: 0800–1200; Fri: closed.
Many private companies operate longer hours and a few work on Fridays.

Telecommunications
Telephone/fax
Palestine Telecommunications Company (Paltel) has a monopoly for providing telephony to the PA areas.

Security
Foreign nationals warned not to travel to the West Bank and Gaza Strip, which are subject to terrorist and military activity.

Getting there
Air
International airport/s: Dahaniya Gaza International Airport is not in operation. It is located south of Gaza City near the Egyptian border.
Surface
Gaza is accessible from the Rafah border, in the south, into Egypt. The Allenby Bridge crossing from the West Bank into Jordan is controlled by Israel.
Road: Private vehicles cannot cross from Israel into the Gaza Strip and may be stopped at checkpoints entering or leaving the West Bank.
Main port/s: An internationally funded port was opened in the late 1990s, with the aim of reducing the need for Palestinian trade to go through Israel before reaching the outside world. However, access to and from the port has become restricted due to the Israeli occupation of the West Bank and Gaza Strip in early 2002. All access to Gaza is via the port of Haifa.

Getting about
National transport
Road: Gaza Strip has a small, poorly developed road network.
West Bank has 4,500km of roads, of which 2,700km are paved; Israel developed many highways to service their settlements.
Buses: Buses run from East Jerusalem to Nablus and between Tel Aviv and Ramallah.
Taxis: Collective taxis regularly commute between Gaza and Ramallah, Jerusalem or Hebron.
Rail: Gaza Strip had one line which has been abandoned due to disrepair.
There are no railways in the West Bank.
Water: There are no waterways.
City transport
Taxis: Taxis operate in the main cities.
Car hire
Palestinian licence plates are either green or blue, whereas Israeli number plates are yellow. Visitors are advised not to drive vehicles with yellow licence plates in the West Bank or Gaza Strip.

BUSINESS DIRECTORY
The addresses listed below are a selection only. While World of Information makes every endeavour to check these addresses, we cannot guarantee that changes have not been made, especially to telephone numbers and area codes. We would welcome any corrections.

Telephone area codes
The international direct dialling code (IDD) for Palestine is +970, followed by area code and subscriber's number:

Bethlehem	2	Jericho	2
Gaza	7	Jerusalem	2
Hebron	2	Nablus	9
Jenin	6	Ramallah	2

Palestine

Chambers of Commerce

Bethlehem Chamber of Commerce and Industry, PO Box 59, Bethlehem (tel: 274-2742; fax: 276-4402; e-mail: bcham@palnet.com).

European Palestinian Chamber of Commerce, 19 Nablus Road, PO Box 20185, Jerusalem (tel: 626-4883; fax: 626-4975; e-mail: epcc@palnet.com).

Federation of Palestinian Chambers of Commerce, Industry and Agriculture, Al-Rashid Street, PO Box 54107, Jerusalem (tel: 628-0727; fax: 628-0644; email: fpccia@palnet.com).

Gaza Palestinian Chamber of Commerce, PO Box 33, Gaza (tel: 282-1172; fax: 286-4588; e-mail: gazacham@palnet.com).

Hebron Chamber of Commerce and Industry, King Faisal Street, PO Box 272, Hebron, West Bank (tel: 222-8218; fax: 222-7490; e-mail: hebcham@hebronet.com).

Jenin Chamber of Commerce, Industry and Agriculture, City Centre, Jenin (tel: 250-1107; fax: 250-3388; e-mail: jencham@hally.net).

Jericho Commercial, Industrial and Agricultural Arab Chamber, PO Box 91, Jericho (tel: 232-3313; fax: 232-2394; e-mail: jercom@palnet.com).

Jerusalem Arab Chamber of Commerce, Al-Rashid Street, PO Box 19151, Jerusalem 91191 (tel: 628-2351; fax: 627-2615; e-mail: chamber@alqudsnet.com).

Nablus Chamber of Commerce and Industry, PO Box 35, Nablus (tel: 238-0335; fax: 237-7605; e-mail: nablus@palnet.com).

Qalqilya Chamber of Commerce, Industry and Agriculture, PO Box 13, Qalqilya (tel: 294-1473; fax: 294-0164; e-mail: chamberq@hally.net).

Ramallah and Albeireh Chamber of Commerce and Industry, PO Box 256, Ramallah (tel: 295-6043; fax: 298-4691; e-mail: ramcom@palnet.com).

Tulkarm Chamber of Commerce and Industry, PO Box 51, Tulkarm (tel: 267-1010; fax: 267-5623; e-mail: tulkarm@palnet.com).

Banking

Al-Ahli Jordan Bank, Al-Quds Street, PO Box 550, Ramallah (tel: 998-6370; fax: 998-6372).

Al-Ittihad Bank for Saving and Investment, Commercial Centre, Al-Barid Street, PO Box 1557, Ramallah (tel: 298-6412/5; fax: 298-6416).

ANZ Grindlays, Al-Shuweitreh Street, PO Box 1, Nablus (tel: 238-4555; fax: 238-4563).

ANZ Grindlays, PO Box 19390, East Jerusalem (tel: 626-3444; fax: 626-3311).

Arab Bank, Al-Harajeh, PO Box 1476, Ramallah (tel: 298-2456; fax: 298-2444).

Arab Land Bank, PO Box 565, Jerusalem/Ramallah Road, Ramallah (tel: 298-5958; fax: 295-8426/5).

Arab Palestinian Investment Bank, Regional Headquarters, Al-Harajeh Building, PO Box 1268, Ramallah (tel: 298-7126; fax: 298-7125).

Bank of Jordan, Al-Quds Street, PO Box 1328, Ramallah (tel: 295-2696; fax: 295-2705).

Bank of Palestine, Al-Rimal Quarter, Omar El-Mukhtar Street, PO Box 50, Gaza (tel: 286-5676; fax: 282-8974).

British Bank of the Middle East, PO Box 2067, Al-Quds Street, Ramallah (tel: 298-7802, 298-1551; fax: 298-7804).

Cairo Amman Bank, Ramallah Branch (tel: 298-3503; fax: 295-2764).

Cairo Amman Bank, Wadi El-Tuffah Street, PO Box 665, Hebron (tel: 993-6768; fax: 993-6770).

Cairo Amman Bank, El-Hussein Circle, Nablus (tel: 238-1301; fax: 238-0188).

Commercial Bank of Palestine, Al-Awdah Street, PO Box 1799, Ramallah (tel: 295-4102; fax: 295-3888).

Jordan Gulf Bank, Al-Sa'ah Circle, Ramallah (tel: 998-7680; fax: 998-7682).

Jordan Housing Bank, Rukab Street, PO Box 1473, Ramallah (tel: 998-6255; fax: 998-6275).

Jordan Kuwait Bank, Commercial Centre, Sufian Street, PO Box 33, Nablus (tel: 237-7223; fax: 237-7181).

Palestinian Construction Bank, Al-Bireh, Al-Silwadi Building, Ramallah (tel: 995-4796; fax: 995-4797).

Palestinian International Bank, Al-Bireh, Al-Ahliyeh College Street, PO Box 3636, Ramallah (tel: 998-7467; fax: 998-7148).

Palestinian International Bank, PO Box 1244, Gaza (tel: 282-7360; fax: 282-5269).

Palestinian Investment Bank, Midan Al-Nahda, Al-Hilal Street, PO Box 3675, Ramallah (tel: 998-7880; fax: 998-7881).

Palestinian Islamic Bank, PO Box 1244, Al-Rimal Quarter, Omar El-Mukhtar Street, Gaza (tel: 282-7360; fax: 282-5269).

Central bank
Palestine Monetary Authority, Nablus Road, Ramallah (tel: 959-921; fax: 295-9922; e-mail: info@pma-ram.pna.net).

Travel information

The Higher Council for the Arab Tourist Industry, PO Box 19850, East Jerusalem (tel: 628-1805; fax: 628-7981).

Ministry of Tourism and Antiquities, Bethlehem (tel: 274-1581/3; fax: 274-3753; e-mail: mota@pl.org; internet site: http://www.visit-palestine.com).

Ministries

Ministry of Agriculture, Abu Khadrah Building, Gaza (tel: 286-5990; fax: 286-3926).

Ministry of Economy and Trade, PO Box 1629, Ramallah, West Bank (tel: 298-1214/5; fax: 298-4011).

Ministry of Finance, Omer El-Mokhtar Street, Government Departments Complex, Gaza (tel: 282-4368; fax: 282-3356).

Ministry of Housing, PO Box 4034, Omer El-Mokhtar Street, Government Departments Complex, Gaza (tel: 282-2233/4; fax: 282-2235).

Ministry of Industry, PO Box 1629, Ramallah, West Bank (tel: 298-7641/2; fax: 298-7440).

Ministry of Planning and International Co-operation, PO Box 4017, Omer El-Mokhtar Street, Government Departments Complex, Gaza (tel: 282-9260; fax: 282-4090).

Ministry of Telecommunications, Gaza (tel: 282-5612; fax: 282-4555).

Ministry of Tourism and Antiquities, Bethlehem (tel: 274-1581/3; fax: 274-3753).

Other useful addresses

Arab Medical Professions College, Al-Bireh (tel: 995-5611).

Birzeit University, Ramallah (tel: 995-7650; fax: 995-7656).

College of Islamic Studies, PO Box 21402, Beit Hanina (tel: 585-3918).

Fine Arts Institute, Ramallah (tel: 995-5974).

Girls' Arts College, PO Box 19377, Jerusalem (tel: 627-3477; fax: 627-3477).

Hebron Polytechnic College, Hebron (tel: 992-8912; fax: 993-8912).

Hebron University, Hebron (tel: 992-0995).

Higher Council for the Arab Tourist Industry, PO Box 19850, East Jerusalem (tel: 628-1805; fax: 628-3981, 628-7981).

Ibrahimieh Community College PO Box 19014, Jerusalem (tel: 626-4216; fax: 628-2925).

Jerusalem Open University, PO Box 51800, Jerusalem (tel: 581-7237; fax: 581-6734).

Khaduri College, PO Box 7, Tulkarem (tel: 671-026; fax: 672-7733).

Palestine Agricultural Relief Committee (PARC), PO Box 25128, Jerusalem (tel: 583-1897, 583-3818; fax: 582-1898).

Palestinian Economic Council for Development and Reconstruction (PECDAR), PO Box 1629, Dahyet El-Bareed, West Bank (tel: 574-7040; fax: 574-9032).

Palestine Securities Exchange, PO Box 128, Nablus, West Bank (tel: 237-5946; fax: 237-5945).

Palestinian Standards Institute, PO Box 1648, Nablus, West Bank (tel: 238-5721; fax: 237-5745).

Palestine Telecommunications Company Ltd (PATEL), PO Box 1570, Al-Adel Street, Nablus (tel: 237-6225; fax: 237-6227; e-mail: paltel@palnet.com).

Internet sites

Palestinian National Authority (links to other sites): http://www.pna.org

Palestinian News Agency: http://www.wafa.pna.net/EngText/IndexE.htm

The Electronic Intifada: http://electronicintifada.net

Panama

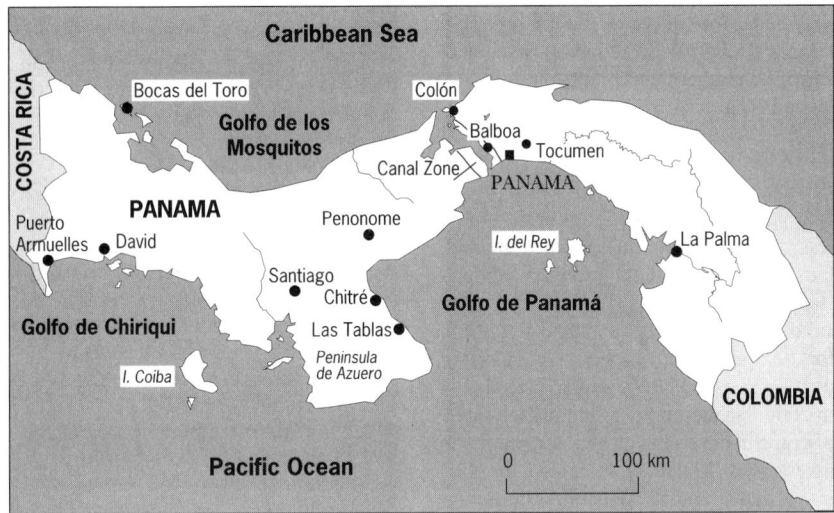

KEY FACTS

Official name: República de Panamá (Republic of Panama)

Head of State: President Martín Erasto Torrijos Espino (PRD) (sworn in 1 Sep 2004)

Head of government: President Martín Erasto Torrijos Espino

Ruling party: Coalition government formed by the Partido Revolucionario Democratico (PRD) (Democratic Revolutionary Party) and the Partido Popular (PP) (People's Party) (from May 2004)

Area: 77,082 square km

Population: 3.04 million (2004)

Capital: Panama City

Official language: Spanish

Currency: Balboa (B and US$) and US dollar = 100 cents

Exchange rate: B and US$1.00 per US$ (fixed peg)

GDP per capita: US$4,524 (2004)

GDP real growth: 6.00% (2004)

Labour force: 1.29 million (2004)

Unemployment: 12.60% (2004)

Inflation: 0.50% (2004)

Balance of trade: -US$1.59 billion 2004

Foreign debt: US$7.00 billion (2003)

A representative democracy with three branches of government – executive, legislative and judiciary – Panama has had its fair share of problems with dictatorial rule as well as poor governance from those democratically elected. The country operates a multi-party system with up to eight parties competing for popularity and votes. Though the two dominant parties have traditionally been the Partido Revolucionario Democrático (PRD) (Democratic Revolutionary Party) and the Partido Panameñista (Panameñista Party) – known as the Arnulfista Party until August 2005 – the electorate is normally split so many ways come election time that a coalition is often necessary to govern effectively.

A family affair

Politics in Panama is something of a family affair. The present incumbent President Martín Erasto Torrijos Espino is the son of former dictator Omar Torrijos Herrera, president of Panama from 1968–78. The younger Torrijos ran for the presidency back in 1999, but lost the race to Mireya Elisa Moscoso Rodríguez de Arias, whose late husband, Arnulfo Arias, a three-time former president of the country, had been unseated by the elder Torrijos during a military coup in 1968.

The younger Torrijos ran again in 2004 and won after Moscoso's Arnulfista-led government sunk to a dire approval rating of just 15 per cent. A series of corruption scandals including the infamous *Durodollar* affair (involving a government secretary allegedly embezzling huge amounts of public funds and stashing them in her freezer) did for Moscoso and her party. The scandals allowed Torrijos, a shrewd political operator, to launch a simple and very successful campaign advocating a triple policy 'shopping list': 'reduce corruption, create more jobs, improve security'. Torrijos proved victorious in the election and has since governed in coalition with the smaller Partido Popular (PP) (People's Party) as part of the Patria Nueva alliance.

Economic progress

The economy of Panama grew steadily during 2001–04. The IMF's projected growth figure for 2005, at 3.5 per cent, is down on the 2004 figure of 6 per cent. However, the overall outlook for the economy looks fairly good with relatively low inflation of approximately 2.4 per cent, forecast to fall to 1 per cent by the end of 2006. The IMF predicts growth of 4 per cent for Panama in 2006. Panama's invisible earnings derived from the Canal, offshore financial services and the trans-isthmian oil pipeline offset its regular trade deficit. Debt rescheduling and World Bank and IMF loans have improved the overall external position.

In stark contrast to other countries in the Central American region, Panama's economy does not rely on primary commodities. As a result of its strategic position, Panama has developed a strong service sector linked to international trade and banking. The services sector contributes approximately 75 per cent to overall GDP in Panama. Agriculture contributes 10 per cent of GDP (low by Latin American standards), industry makes up 12 per cent and construction an estimated 7 per cent.

The leading role of the services sector, particularly shipping and the Cólon Free Zone (CFZ), protects the Panamanian economy from the impact of adverse weather conditions on the agricultural sector and of low global commodity prices, which have adversely affected other Central American economies. CFZ offers duty-free storage and redistribution to over 1,000 foreign companies.

Tourism is now a very important industry in Panama. The sector has been actively developed by the national government as a key economic sector and now accounts for approximately 13.5 per cent of total GDP and 12.9 per cent of total employment in the country. Still at an early stage of development, tourism offers considerable potential for growth. In addition to the Canal, there is a variety of inland and coastal destinations, particularly conducive to eco-tourism, and heritage attractions. Cruise ship visits are being encouraged and account for a growing proportion of arrivals.

Panama has a highly unequal income distribution with 40 per cent of the country living below the poverty line. This is curbing foreign investment in the country and the government understands this situation needs to change. However, President Torrijos took office in September 2004 with plans to improve public finances and takes a strong role in reducing crime and corruption rather than concentrating on alleviating poverty.

Outlook

Panama's growth has been steady in recent years and the economy is generally less susceptible to international market fads than other commodity-dependent states in the region. The IMF forecasts solid growth of 3.5 per cent and 4 per cent for 2005 and 2006 respectively. If President Torrijos is able to govern effectively in 2006 and clampdown on the high level of crime in the country, then foreign direct investment (FDI) will continue to flow into Panama and the economy, traditionally reliant on external capital, will carry on growing.

Risk assessment

Politics	Stable
Economy	Stable
Regional stability	Good

COUNTRY PROFILE

Historical profile
1502 European explorers first visited Panama.
1519 Panama became part of the Vice-royalty of New Andalucia.
1821 Following independence from Spanish rule Panama joined the union of Central American provinces and became part of the confederacy of Gran Colombia. (Gran Colombia collapsed in 1830 and Panama became part of Colombia).
1846 The US signed a treaty with Colombia to build a railway across the isthmus.
1880 A canal, to link the Atlantic and Pacific oceans, was begun by Ferdinand de Lesseps, (who had previously built the Suez Canal), with French backing. Tropical disease killed thousands of workers; financial difficulties halted the project.
1903 After Colombian parliamentarians refused to endorse a treaty with the US to build a canal the US encouraged the Panamanians to rebel and declare independence. The new rulers signed a treaty with the US that gave rights for the building and independent operation of a canal and surrounding area called the Canal Zone. The treaty was granted in perpetuity.
1914 The Panama canal was completed.
1939 Panama ceased to be a US protectorate.
1941–68 Panama was mostly ruled by presidents representing the landowners, traders and building companies. Arnulfo Arias, ousted in 1941, was an unpredictable populist orator, much loved by the crowds. He was in and out of office between 1949–68.
1977 President Omar Torrijos and US president Jimmy Carter signed a treaty under which the US would hand back control of the canal to Panama and withdraw its troops by the end of 1999.
1981 Torrijos, president since 1968, died in a plane crash.
1983 General Manuel Antonio Noriega became commander of the National Guard. He increased his own power and that of the guard, which he renamed the Panama Defence Forces and assumed de facto rule of Panama.
1988 The US accused Noriega of drug trafficking. Noriega declared a state of emergency.
1989 The opposition, Alianza Democrática de Oposición Civilista (Civil Democratic Opposition Alliance) and its presidential candiate Guillermo Endara, won the elections. Noriega declared the results invalid. The US increased diplomatic pressure and threats until Noriega declared a 'state of war'. The US invaded and removed Noriega from power. He was taken to the US to stand trial on charges of drug smuggling. Endara became president.
1991 Constitutional changes adopted included the abolition of a standing army.

KEY INDICATORS — Panama

	Unit	2000	2001	2002	2003	2004
Population	m	2.86	2.91	2.96	3.00	*3.04
Gross domestic product (GDP)	US$bn	10.06	10.20	12.30	12.90	*13.79
GDP per capita	US$	3,517	3,520	4,155	3,870	4,524
GDP real growth	%	2.3	0.3	0.5	4.0	6.0
Inflation	%	1.4	-0.3	1.0	1.7	0.5
Unemployment	%	13.3	14.4	16.0	16.0	–
Exports (fob) (goods)	US$m	5,748.8	5,833.8	1,670.0	1,269.0	5,885.6
Imports (fob) (goods)	US$m	7,039.7	6,709.5	3,050.0	3,383.0	7,470.9
Balance of trade	US$m	-1,290.9	-825.7	-1,380.0	-2,114.0	-1,585.3
Current account	US$m	-926.8	-499.4	-548.0	-491.0	-240.0
Total reserves minus gold	US$m	722.6	1,091.8	1,828.8	1,011.0	630.6
Foreign exchange	US$m	706.8	1,075.5	1,656.6	992.5	611.4
Exchange rate	per US$	1.00	1.00	1.00	1.00	1.00

* estimated figure

1992 Noriega was found guilty of drug offences and sentenced to 40 years in a US prison.

1994 Ernest Pérez Balladares won the presidential election.

1999 Mireya Elisa Moscoso Rodríguez of the Partido Arnulfista (PA) (Arnulfista Party) won the presidential elections, becoming Panama's first female president.

2000 Under the Torrijos-Carter treaty ownership and control of the Panama Zone was handed back to Panama on 1 January. President Moscoso set up a tribunal to investigate crimes and human rights abuses during the military control of 1968–89. The PA lost control of the National Assembly and an alliance led by the Partido Revolucionario Democrático (PRD) (Democratic Revolutionary Party) formed a majority.

2002 Panama signed a framework trade agreement with its five Central American neighbours to boost trade in the region. The PA gained from the defections of three members of the opposition PRD when they voted to approve Moscoso's appointees for the Supreme Court. The three deputies were accused by the PRD of accepting US$1 million in bribes. President Moscoso set up a commission to investigate corruption.

2003 A free trade agreement (FTA) with El Salvador, the first in Panama's history, came into effect in April.

2004 Martín Torrijos won presidential elections on 2 May. The PRD won most seats in the parliamentary elections, however a coalition government was formed by the PA, Movimiento de Renovación Nacional (Morena), Movimiento Liberal Republicano Nacionalista (Molirena) (Nationalist Republican Liberal Movement) and Partido Democrático (PD) (Democratic Party). On 1 September, Martín Torrijos was sworn in as president. In November it was announced that the Panama Canal had made record profits of US$1 billion during the financial year.

2005 From May to June, protesters took to the streets and strikes were called by unions after plans to increase pension contributions and raise the retirement age were announced.

Political structure

In addition to their unicameral national parliaments, El Salvador, Guatemala, Honduras, Nicaragua, Panama and Dominican Republic, which acceded to the Central American Parliament in February 2004, also return directly elected deputies to the supranational Central American Parliament.

Constitution

Panama's constitution dates from 1972 and was reformed in 1983 and 1994.

Form of state

Presidential democratic republic

The executive

The president is both head of state and head of government, elected for a period of five years by universal adult suffrage. The Cabinet is appointed by the president.

National legislature

The unicameral Asamblea Legislativa (National Assembly) has 78 seats. Members are elected by popular vote for a five-year term.

Legal system

The Corte Suprema de Justicia (Supreme Court of Justice) has nine judges appointed for 10-year terms. There are five superior courts and three courts of appeal.

Last elections

2 May 2004 (presidential and parliamentary)

Results: Presidential: Martín Torrijos won 47.5 per cent of the vote, former president Guillermo Endara Galimany 30.6 per cent, José Miguel Alemán 17 per cent and Ricardo Martinelli 4.9 per cent. Parliamentary: the opposition, PRD, won 41 seats out of 78, outgoing president Mireya Moscoso's Arnulfista Party 17 and Solidarity nine.

Next elections

May 2009 (presidential and parliamentary)

Political parties

Ruling party

Coalition government formed by the Partido Revolucionario Democratico (PRD) (Democratic Revolutionary Party) and the Partido Popular (PP) (People's Party) (from May 2004)

Main opposition party

Partido Arnulfista (PA) (Arnulfist Party) (conservative)

Population

3.04 million (2004)

Ethnic make-up

The population is predominantly mestizo, a mingling of indigenous Indian groups, Spanish and African (65 per cent), and Afro-Caribbean (14 per cent). Indians make up approximately 6 per cent of the total population. There are also descendants of North Americans, Chinese, French, Italians, Greeks and Asians (15 per cent).

The most numerous of Panama's indigenous groups are the Guaymi Indians who live primarily in the western provinces of Chiriqui, Bocas del Toro and Veraguas. The next most populous indigenous group is the Cuna, who live mainly in the San Blas Islands and along the nearby coast. The Choco is another indigenous group.

Religions

Traditionally the population is about 90 per cent Roman Catholic, with Protestants, Muslims, Baha'i and Hindus accounting for 5 per cent.

Education

Schooling lasts for 12 years, six years each in an elementary and a secondary school. Education is free up to university level. University education lasts for six years. There are three universities and nearly one in three of the relevant age group attends them.

Higher education is mainly provided by universities, schools and institutes. There are both public and private universities. State universities are autonomous. The University of Panama is responsible for establishing the guidelines relating to the universities in the country.

Literacy rate: 92 per cent male, 91 per cent female; adult rates (World Bank).
Compulsory years: Six to 15
Enrolment rate: 106 per cent gross primary enrolment of relevant age group (including repeaters); 69 per cent gross secondary enrolment (World Bank).

Health

Panama has both a free public health care system and a private system that are generally served by the same professionals. Panama's hospitals, clinics and insurance plans are scrambling to meet the healthcare needs of wealthier Panamanians, many of whom are retired US civil servants. The cost of healthcare in Panama is lower than in the US and is often of better quality. This is fuelling 'healthcare tourism', with US citizens visiting Panama for medical and surgical treatment.

HIV prevalence: 0.9 per cent aged 15–49 in 2003 (World Bank)
Life expectancy: 75 years (World Bank)
Fertility rate/Maternal mortality rate: 2.4 births per woman (World Bank)
Infant mortality rate: 18 per 1,000 live births (World Bank)

Welfare

There is a large difference between welfare levels in the cities and in the countryside in Panama. While the percentage of the population below the poverty line is 15 per cent in urban areas, it rises to 65 per cent in rural areas. The national average is 37 per cent.

Panama's social security system is financed through a 6.75 per cent contribution from individual incomes and a 2.75 per cent contribution from company payrolls. Retirement ages are 62 for men and 57 for women. Medical services are provided through the Social Insurance Fund. Sick workers can claim 70 per cent of their average earnings from the last two months for a maximum period of 52 weeks.

Nations of the World: A Political, Economic and Business Handbook

Main cities
Panama City (capital, estimated population 438,200 in 2003), Colón (44,400).

Languages spoken
English is widely used, so much so that Panama should be considered bilingual. English is particularly spoken along the Caribbean coast and in the capital. Three distinct indigenous groups, the Cuna, Guaymi and Choco, also speak either Cuna, Movere or Embera.

Official language/s
Spanish

Media
Press
Dailies: The leading daily newspaper is *La Prensa*. A right-wing opposition daily, *Primera Plana,* was launched in 1990. There are two English language daily papers, *The Star* and *The Herald*. Other dailies include *La República* (evening), *Crítica Libre, Diario el Siglo, La Estrella de Panamá* and *El Panamá América*. Some of the major US dailies and a few European newspapers can be found in Panama City. *El Siglo* (http://www.elsiglo.com) carries digital news with interesting links.
Weeklies: *El Heraldo* (Panamá) is published in Spanish every week.
Business: Business publications include *Enlace*, a Spanish language monthly on local and international trade, *Revista Centro Financiero, FOB Zona Libre De Colón* (trade directory) and *Revista Análisis*.
Periodicals: There are some periodicals featuring travel and holiday news.
Broadcasting
The vast majority of television and radio broadcasting is in Spanish. There are 82 AM and 31 FM radio stations and six television stations.

Economy
The economy of Panama grew steadily during the 2001–04 period. Projected growth for 2005, at 3.5 per cent, is down on the 2004 figure of 6 per cent. However, the overall outlook for the economy looks fairly good with relatively low inflation of approximately 2.4 per cent, forecast to fall to 1 per cent in 2006. The IMF predicts growth of 4 per cent for Panama in 2006.
Unlike other countries in the Central American region, Panama's economy does not rely on primary commodities. As a result of its strategic position, Panama has developed a strong service sector linked to international trade and banking. The services sector contributes approximately 75 per cent to overall GDP in Panama. Agriculture contributes 10 per cent of GDP (low by Latin American standards), industry makes up 12 per cent and construction an estimated 7 per cent

The leading role of the services sector, particularly shipping and the Cólon Free Zone (CFZ), protects the Panamanian economy from the impact of adverse weather conditions on the agricultural sector and of low global commodity prices, which have adversely affected other Central American economies. CFZ offers duty-free storage and redistribution to over 1,000 foreign companies.
Panama has a highly unequal income distribution with 40 per cent of the country living below the poverty line. This is curbing foreign investment in the country and the government understands this situation needs to change. However, President Martín Torrijos took office in September 2004 with plans to improve public finances and to take a strong role in reducing crime and corruption rather than concentrating on alleviating poverty.

External trade
Panama's invisible earnings derived from the CFZ, the Canal, offshore financial services and the trans-isthmian oil pipeline offset its regular trade deficit. Debt rescheduling and World Bank and IMF loans have improved the overall external position.
Panama's exports are sold onto markets in the US, Nigeria, Germany, South Korea, Peru, Costa Rica, Belgium and Japan.
Imports
Principal imports are capital goods, foodstuffs, consumer goods and chemicals.
Main sources: Japan (32.9 per cent total, 2004), China (10.6 per cent), US (9.8 per cent), South Korea (7.2 per cent), Singapore (7.1 per cent), Italy (4.5 per cent) Main suppliers to the Colón Free Zone are Japan, (typically 20 per cent of total value), US (15 per cent), Taiwan (10 per cent) and Hong Kong (10 per cent). The principal items traded in the duty-free zone are electronics, watches, pharmaceuticals, toiletries, clothing and jewellery.
Exports
Principal exports are bananas, shrimp, sugar, coffee and clothing.
Main destinations: US (12.2 per cent total, 2004), Nigeria (9.4 per cent), Germany (8.4 per cent), South Korea (8.2 per cent), El Salvador (5.7 per cent), Peru (5.1 per cent), Costa Rica (5.1 per cent), Japan (4.1 per cent)

Agriculture
Farming
Panama's principal cash crops include bananas, sugar cane and coffee. Approximately 60 per cent of the country's total landmass is in agricultural use. About 16 per cent is cultivated while the remainder is natural pasture and forest. Food production does not meet domestic demand and consequently food imports are supplied by the US in order to meet the shortfall.
As a result of its accession to the World Trade Organisation (WTO) in 1997, Panama's trading regime has been liberalised to reduce the average tariff level to 15 per cent for agricultural goods, regarded as one of the lowest in Latin America.
The agricultural sector is ailing and has experienced difficulties resulting both from metereological factors and poor demand for products. The strengthening of the agricultural sector is a government priority and includes upgrading irrigation systems and equipment. Problems include the decline in the price of coffee on international markets, which threatens to deepen rural poverty.
Crop production in 2004 included: 381,000t tonnes cereals in total, 1,650,000t sugar cane, 80,000t maize, 525,000t bananas, 129,000t plantains, 296,000t rice, 29,000t yams, 30,000t cassava, 25,000t potatoes, 2,750t chillies & peppers, 2,300t tobacco, 15,883t oilcrops, 15,000t coconuts, 65,000t oil palm fruit, 23,000t tomatoes, 40,000t citrus fruit, 8,700t green coffee, 450t cocoa beans, 125t tea, 9,000t pulses, 766,000t fruit in total, 168,850t vegetables in total. Livestock production included: 159,018t meat in total, 53,500t beef, 20,518t pig meat, 85,000t poultry, 20,000t eggs, 181,000t milk, 6,960t cattle hides.
Fishing
The vast majority of Panama's annual fish catch is exported to the US- approximately 80 per cent- with the EU being the second biggest buyer of Panamanian fish.
Deep-sea shrimp fishing is the major activity in the sector and this type of fishing increased in increased in importance after the improvement to the port and fishing terminal at Vacamonte was completed in 1994.
Freshwater fishing and marine products have increased in production steadily since the 1990s. Lobster exports rose by 39 per cent and there were also increases in the sales of fresh and frozen fish. The exception was shrimp exports, which dropped by 50 per cent.
Forestry
The majority of Panama's forested area has semi-deciduous tropical moist vegetation, while plantation forest comprises mainly pine. Approximately 40 per cent of the country's total landmass is covered by forests.
Panama has a large network of protected forest areas. However, large-scale deforestation has led to an annual average loss of 1.65 per cent, the equivalent of 52,000ha of forest cover.
The forest industry produces modest quantity of industrial roundwood, which is

used for manufacturing sawnwood and panels. Some amount of forest products particularly paper is imported. Between 1998–2002 exports doubled; in a typical year imports of forest products amount to approximately US$69 million and exports total US$12 million.

Production in 2003 included 1,386,521 cubic metres (cum) roundwood, 153,000cum industrial roundwood, 26,000cum sawnwood, 63,000cum sawlogs & veneer logs, 8,000cum wood-based panels, 1,233,521cum wood fuel, 4,793t charcoal.

Industry and manufacturing
Panama's industrial sector remains relatively small scale, contributing around 12 per cent to total GDP and employing 16 per cent of the total workforce. The sector is predominantly geared toward domestic consumption.

The main industrial centres are Panama City and Colón, inclusive of food processing (about a third of the gross value of manufacturing output), textiles and clothing, footwear and leather goods, chemicals, plastics, paper, beverages, cigarettes, construction materials and petroleum products from the Las Minas refinery near Colón (capacity 100,000bpd). The emphasis is on encouraging foreign investment in labour-intensive, light assembly, export-based industries.

Tourism
Tourism is now a very important industry in Panama. The sector has been actively developed by the national government as a key economic sector and now accounts for approximately 13.5 per cent of total GDP and 12.9 per cent of total employment in the country.

Still at an early stage of development, tourism offers considerable potential for growth. In addition to the Canal, there is a variety of inland and coastal destinations, particularly conducive to ecotourism, and heritage attractions. There were 592,200 arrivals in 2004. Cruise ship visits are being encouraged and account for a growing proportion of arrivals.

Environment
Deforestation continues at an alarming rate, even in National parks and the Canal watershed. About 80 per cent of Panama's coral reefs have been destroyed. Soil erosion is becoming a serious problem in many areas, and Panama's desert in the province of Los Santos (the legacy of slash and burn ranching activities) is expanding.

Illegal gold mining by Colombian immigrants is also contaminating rivers and local water supplies in the Darien and Portobello National parks.

There is serious pollution in the Bay of Panama.

Mining
At present, the mining sector of the Panamanian economy contributes very little to GDP and accounts for a small section of the total labour force. Approximately 0.1 per cent of GDP is generated by the sector and 0.2 per cent of total employment is accounted for by it. However, the mining sector in Panama is, at present, severely underdeveloped. It is estimated that, if properly developed, the sector could grow to contribute as much as 15 per cent of total GDP and directly employ up to 4,000 people.

The government is keen on promoting exploration of gold and copper deposits. Tax concessions and other benefits are available to foreign companies interested in developing the resources. However, proposals for new mines often face strong local opposition.

Copper reserves in Panama are considered to be relatively large with significant deposits in Cerro Colorado and Petaquilla, although the development of the mines has been slow. It is estimated that copper reserves at Cerro Colorado are one billion tonnes, making it one of the world's largest deposits. The Petaquilla studies show copper reserves of 1.1 billion tonnes and significant quantities of gold and molybdenum. The Cerro Quema mine has estimated gold reserves in the region of 300,000 ounces of microscopic gold.

There are also known reserves of manganese, and limited extraction of limestone, clays, gravel and sea salt. Cement is produced by Empresa Estatal de Cemento Bayano at a plant with a capacity of 300,000 tonnes per year (tpy).

Hydrocarbons
Owing to the fact that it does not possess substantial hydrocarbon reserves, Nicaragua is forced to export the vast majority of its energy needs, approximately 70 per cent. Some discoveries of oil and gas deposits have been made but not in commercially viable quantities. Therefore Panama continues to import all of the oil and coal it consumes.

There are coal deposits in provinces of Colón and Chiriquí. Panama has a refining capacity of around 60,000 barrels per day (bpd) and imports around 57,000bpd. Production of oil is very limited with production levels of around 1,000bpd.

The Panama Canal is a major transit centre, because of this Panama is very important to the hydrocarbon industry.

Petroleum products account for 14 per cent of total Canal shipments and is the largest commodity that passes through the canal. Around two-thirds of these petroleum products travel from the Atlantic to the Pacific. There are also plans to link North and South American gas and electricity grids, Panama would be essential to this idea.

Panama does not produce or import natural gas. However, it does import coal to meet consumption levels, around 69,000 tonnes.

Energy
The Plan Plan Puebla-Panama was signed in 2001. The document, which calls for an integration of electricity markets in the Central American region, includes Panama, Costa Rica, Honduras, Nicaragua, and El Salvador among its signatories. There has been a rapid development of hydroelectric energy production in Nicaragua in recent years in, with the total potential estimated at 2,500MW. La Estrella, Los Valles and La Fortuna plants supply around 70 per cent of the country's electricity requirements.

Financial markets
Stock exchange
There has been a stock exchange in Panama since 1960.

La Central Latinoamericana de Valores S.A. (LATIN CLEAR) began operations in May 1997, under the auspices of the Inter-American Development Bank (IDB) and the Asociación de Bolsas de Comercio de Centroamérica y Panamá (BOLCEN) (Stock Exchange Association for Central America and Panama). It serves as a regional central securities depository.

Banking and insurance
The banking and financial services sector is regulated by the Comisión Bancaria Nacional. The central bank carries out retail and commercial transactions and development banking, it is government-owned and operates as a depository of public funds. Only coins are minted locally, the notes in circulation being US dollars. Interest rates follow US dollar rates.

Panama banking was rated as top for tier one capital, among banks in Central America, as recently as 2004. The Panamanian banking sector is expected to benefit from growth in Central America rather than trying to compete against Brazil, Mexico or Argentina. Before the overall liberalisation of the banking sector in Latin America, banks had used Panama as a base to target markets in the rest of the region; those same banks can now target other Latin American markets directly.

Although it does not have the same size of assets in its banking sector, Panama has always seen its main competitors as the

Nations of the World: A Political, Economic and Business Handbook

Cayman Islands and the Bahamas. Panama requests all banks to have a physical presence in the country.

Central bank
Banco Nacional de Panamá

Main financial centre
Panama City

Time
GMT minus five hours

Geography
Panama is a narrow country situated at the southern end of the isthmus separating North and South America. To the west is Costa Rica and to the east is Colombia in South America. The Caribbean Sea lies to the north and the Pacific Ocean to the south.

The eastern section of the country, adjoining Colombia, is thinly populated. The western section of the country, near the Costa Rican border, is the richest agricultural area.

Climate
For its relatively small area, the geography of Panama's 'S'-shaped isthmus is quite varied and consists of three distinct areas. The largest, which accounts for approximately 85 per cent of the land area, is lowland coastal areas, with a tropical rainy climate. Here the temperature ranges from 21 degrees Centigrade (C) to 31 degrees C. The rainy season is approximately April–December, with the heaviest rains falling in November (about 570 mm). Rainfall is significantly heavier on the Pacific coast than on the Caribbean. The driest season is January–April. About 10 per cent of the land area lies between 700 metres and 1,490 metres and has a temperate climate.

The remaining 5 per cent of the land is at an altitude of about 1,520 metres and is cold.

Dress codes
Like most of Central America, Panama remains fairly conservative and formal in respect of dress. Although Panama City is cosmopolitan, it is not considered proper for adults to wear shorts in the city, regardless of the heat. It is also considered inappropriate for women to wear trousers or shorts in public, either in the city or countryside. A certain amount of leniency is allowed to foreigners, who are thought not to know any better.

For business appointments, men should wear suits and women should wear dresses. A man may wear a *panabrisa*, a loose fitting, short sleeved shirt, which is not tucked into the trousers. However, these are not generally worn by top officials or businessmen during formal business meetings.

Entry requirements
Passports
Required by all.

Visa
May be required. The list that sets out which nationalities require which visas, or tourist cards, can be found at: www.consuladogeneraldepanama.com/visas.htm (follow link to 'Foreign Countries requirements'), also what necessary information may be required for either. Business visitors arriving on a tourist card may proceed without further authorisation. All visits are restricted to 30 days and proof of return/onward passage must be provided. Contact local authorities if duration of stay is expected to be longer than 30 days.

Currency advice/regulations
There are no restrictions on import or export of foreign exchange or Panamanian currency. Visitors must have a minimum of US$300. Local currency exists only as coins and is interchangeable with US currency of the same denomination.

Health (for visitors)
Mandatory precautions
Cholera vaccination certificate if arriving from an infected area. Yellow fever vaccination certificate may be required for visits to certain regions.

Advisable precautions
A yellow fever vaccination certificate is required only for those who are going to visit the provinces of Bocas del Toro and Darien. Typhoid and polio vaccinations are advisable. Malaria risk exists in rural areas – prophylaxis recommended (in some places malaria is reported to be resistant to chloroquine). Water precautions should be taken, especially outside cities. Rabies is endemic.

Medical insurance is necessary as medical charges are high.

Hotels
There is a wide variety of hotels available. It is advisable to book in advance, particularly between December and May. There is a 10 per cent government surcharge on bills. Tipping 10 per cent (not compulsory).

Credit cards
Major credit cards are accepted.

Public holidays
Fixed dates
1 Jan (New Year's Day), 9 Jan (Martyrs' Day), 1 May (Labour Day), 15 Aug (Panama City Day/Assumption Day), 3 Nov (Independence Day, from Colombia), 4 Nov (Flag Day), 5 Nov (Colón City Independence Day, Colón City only), 10 Nov (First Call for Independence from Spain), 28 Nov (Independence Day, from Spain), 24 Dec (Christmas Eve, half-day), 25 Dec (Christmas Day), 31 Dec (New Year's Eve).

For public holidays falling on a Sunday, the following Monday is observed as a holiday.

Variable dates
Carnival (two days, Feb), Ash Wednesday, Maundy Thursday, Good Friday.

Working hours
Banking
Mon–Sat: 0800–1300.

Business
Mon–Fri: 0800–1200, 1400–1700; Sat: 0800–1200.

Government
Mon–Fri: 0900–1700.

Shops
Mon–Sat: 0800–1200, 1400–1800/1900.

Electricity supply
110V AC, 60 cycles (domestic), 220V AC (industrial).

Social customs/useful tips
The use of titles, such as Doctor, Arquitecto, Licenciado, Profesora, is widespread, and it is courteous to learn and use the correct titles for both men and women. Do not immediately launch into a business conversation. It is considered polite to first get to know the person to whom you are talking.

Men and women shake hands in Panama and social kisses on one cheek are also exchanged. At a large social gathering do not expect your host or hostess to introduce you to every individual. Feel free to circulate and introduce yourself. A small gift for the host or hostess is always appreciated.

Late night parties with dinner served at 2200 or 2300 are common. It is accepted to be up to two hours late for a large social gathering, 30 minutes for smaller gatherings.

Panama is an eclectic country, with a ready acceptance of immigrants from all over the world. Public celebrations therefore express the hybrid nature of its diverse cultures. Although once part of Colombia, Panamanian culture and traditions are uniquely its own and show Caribbean rather than South American influence. However, there is little interchange between different social and ethnic groups.

Domestic servants are common in middle and upper class Panamanian households. They generally serve the meals. House guests should tip domestic servants after extended visits.

Do not take photos without permission, especially of Indians. Be prepared to pay for them if permission is given.

Panama

Security
Common street crime has always been prevalent in Panama City and Colón, but poverty as a result of the disrupted economy has worsened the situation. Visitors are warned specifically to avoid the San Miguelito squatter section of Panama City. The US Department of Justice International Criminal Investigation Training Assistance Program (ICITAP) provides training for Panama's new Public Force police in forensics, management and investigative techniques, and the handling of urban disorder. The intention is to eventually transform the former soldiers into a civilian police force.

The Judicial Technical Police (PTJ) is responsible for the struggle against the still prevalent narcotics traffic. The PTJ, which is supposed to work jointly with the Customs Service, is composed of former Panamanian Defence Force members and is widely reported to be corrupt.

Getting there
Air
National airline: Copa (Compañía Panameña de Aviación)
International airport/s: Panama City-Tucumen (PTY), 27km from city; duty-free shop, bar, restaurant, buffet, bank (restricted hours), post office, shops, hotel reservations, car hire.
Airport tax: International departures include an airport service charge of B20 levied on all passengers, except those in transit connecting within nine hours and infants under two years.

Surface
Road: The Pan-American Highway links Panama with Costa Rica. Routes to Colombia are not generally recommended.
Rail: A rail link runs between Puerto Armuelles and David.
Main port/s: Balboa (Pacific), Cristóbal (Atlantic).

Getting about
National transport
Air: Frequent internal flights by Copa and others link main centres, eg Panama City with David (generally Mon–Sat only) and Colón (Mon–Fri).
Road: Main means of transportation. Panama section of Pan-American Highway connects Chepo and Panama City with Costa Rican border. The Trans-Isthmian Highway links Panama City and Colón.
Buses: Regional buses link most towns. Ticabus run modern air-conditioned service to main centres; it is advisable to book in advance.
Rail: Ferrocarril de Panamá run trains daily between Panama City and Colón (it takes around 1.5 hrs, is single class, with air-conditioning extra) and between Puerto Armuelles and David.

City transport
Taxis: Large (*grandes*) and small (*chicos*) taxis available. Can be ordered by telephone; fixed fare system varies by size of taxi and number of zones traversed. Negotiate fares beforehand. Tipping 10 per cent.
Car hire
Available in main towns and at the airport. International licence required. After 90 days a local permit is required.

BUSINESS DIRECTORY
The addresses listed below are a selection only. While World of Information makes every endeavour to check these addresses, we cannot guarantee that changes have not been made, especially to telephone numbers and area codes. We would welcome any corrections.

Telephone area codes
The international direct dialling (IDD) code for Panama is +507, followed by the customer's number.

Chambers of Commerce
American Chamber of Commerce and Industry of Panama, PO Box 168, Balboa Ancon, Panama (tel: 269-3881; fax: 223-3508; e-mail: amcham@panamcham.com).

Colón Cámara de Comercio, Agricutura e Industrias, Calle 6, Avenida Amador Guerrero 322, Colón (tel: 441-7223; fax: 441-7281; e-mail: camcolon@pananet.com).

Panama Cámara de Comercio, Industria y Agricultura, Avenidas Cuba y Ecuador 33A, PO Box 74, Zona 1, Panama (tel: 225-1233; fax: 227-4186; e-mail: infocciap@panacamara.com).

Panama Federacion de Cámaras de Comercio e Industria, Avenida Cuba, Zona 1, Panama (tel: 225-4615; fax: 227-4186).

Banking
Asociación Bancaria de Panamá, Apartado 4554, zona 5, Panama (tel: 263-7044).

Banco Comercial de Panamá SA (BANCOMER), PO Box 7659, Panama (tel: 263-6800; fax: 263-8033).

Banco Continental de Panamá SA, PO Box 135, Via España, Panama 9A (tel: 263-5955; fax: 263-7646).

Banco Disa, PO Box 7201, Panama 5 (tel: 263-5933; fax: 264-1084).

Banco de Latinoamérica SA (BANCOLAT), PO Box 4401, Panama 5 (tel: 264-0466; fax: 263-7368).

Banco del Istmo SA, PO Box 6-3823, El Dorado, Panama (tel: 269-5555; fax: 269-5168).

Banco del Pacífico SA, PO Box 6-3100, El Dorado, Panama (tel: 263-5833; fax: 263-7481).

Banco General SA, PO Box 4592, Panama 5 (tel: 227-3200; fax: 227-3427).

Banco Internacional de Costa Rica SA (BICSA), PO Box 600, Panama 1 (tel: 263-6822; fax: 263-6393).

Banco Internacional de Panamá SA (BIPAN), PO Box 11181, Panama 6 (tel: 263-9000; fax: 263-9514).

Banco Latinoamericano de Exportaciones SA (BLADEX), PO Box 6-1497, El Dorado, Panama (tel: 263-6766; fax: 269-6333).

Banco Nacional de Panamá, International Operations Department, PO Box 5220, Panama 5 (tel: 263-8292).

Banco Panamericano SA (PANABANK), PO Box 1828, Panama 1 (tel: 262-0881; fax: 269-1537).

Comisión Bancaria Nacional, Piso 12, Edificio de Boston, Viá Espana, Panama (tel: 223-2855; fax: 223-2864).

Central bank
Banco Nacional de Panamá, Via Espana 120, Torre Banco Nacional, PO Box 5220, Panama 5 (tel: 263-5151; fax: 269-0091).

Travel information
Air Panamá, Avenida Justo Arosemena y Calle 39, Apartado 8612, Panama City.

COPA Airways, Avenida Justo Arosemena y Calle 39, Apartado 8612, Panama City.

National tourist organisation offices
Panama Tourism Bureau, Atlapa Convention Centre, PO Box 4421, Zone No. 5, Panama City (tel: 226-7000; fax: 226-4002; internet site: http://www.panamatours.com; www.panamainfo.com; www.ipat.gob.pa).

Ministries
Ministry of the Canal (tel: 263-4545; fax: 263-4355).

Ministry of Commerce and Industry, Edificio de la Loteria, Piso 21, Ave Cuba, Apartado 9658, Zona 4, Panama (tel: 227-4177; fax: 227-3927).

Ministry of Development and Agriculture, Edificio 576, Altos de Curundu, Avenida Frangipany, Panama (tel: 232-5041; fax: 232-5044).

Ministry of Education, Apartado 2440, Zona 3, Panama (tel: 262-2000; fax: 262-9087).

Ministry of Employment and Social Welfare, Apartado 2441, Zona 3, Panama (tel: 225-7503; fax: 225-4529).

Ministry of Finance and Treasury, Calle 35 y 36 entre Ave, Perú y Cuba, Apdo 5245, Zona 5, Panama (tel: 227-4879; fax: 227-2357).

Ministry of Foreign Affairs, Amador, Edificio, Panama 4 (tel: 228-2815; fax: 227-2716).

Ministry of Government and Justice, Calle 1 a, San Felipe, Apartado 1628, Zona 1, Panama (tel: 212-0287; fax: 212-0372).

Ministry of Health, Calle 36 y Ave Cuba, Apartado 2048, Zona 1, Panama (tel: 225-6080; fax: 227-5276).

Ministry of Housing, Ave Mexico y calle 12 de octubre, Apartado 5228, Zona 5, Panama (tel: 262-4358; fax: 262-9250).

Ministry of Labour and Social Welfare, Avenida Balboa, Edif de Diego, 7 Piso, Apdo 2441, Zona 3 (tel: 225-7503; fax: 225-4529).

Ministry of Planning and Economic Policy, Via Espana, Edif OGAWA, Apartado 2694, Zona 3, Panama (tel: 269-2810; fax: 264-7755).

Ministry of the President, Palacio Presidencial, San Felipe, Panama (tel: 227-9662; fax: 227-4119).

Ministry of Property and Finance, Calle 35 y 36, entre Ave Perú Ave Cuba, Pamana (tel: 227-3992; fax: 227-2357).

Ministry of Public Works, Curundu Edif 1019, Apartado 1632, Zona 1, Panama (tel: 232-5333; fax: 232-5776).

Other useful addresses

ARI Promotion and Marketing Department, PO Box 2097, Balboa Ancón, Panama (tel: 228-8037/5668; fax: 228-1698/7488; e-mail: ari@sinfo.net).

Asociación Panameña de Radiodifusión SA, Avenida 11 y Calle 28, Apdo 1795, Panama City (tel: 225-0160).

British Embassy, Commercial Section, Torre Swiss Bank, 4, Urb Marbella, Calle 53, Apdo 889, Panama 1 (tel: 269-0866; fax: 223-0730).

Central Post Office, Plaza Catedral, Calle 6, Panama City.

Colón Free Zone, Avenida Roosevelt, Apdo 1118, Colón (tel: 441-5794, 441-5114, 445-1033, 445-1559; fax: 445-2165).

Consejo Nacional de Inversiones (CNI), Edif Banco Nacional de Panamá, Apdo 2350, Panama (tel: 647-211).

Consular and Maritime Affairs, PO Box 5245, 50th Street and 69th Street, Plaza Guadalupe, San Francisco, Panama 5 (tel: 270-0166, 277-0326; fax: 270-0716).

Corporación Azucarera La Victoria, Apartado 1228,, zona 1, Panama (tel: 229-4797; fax: 229-4806).

Dirección Nacional de Medios de Comunicación Social (Panamanian Media Authority), Ministerio de Gobierno y Justicia, Apartado 1628, zona 1, Panama (tel: 262-3197/3166; fax: 262-1490).

Empleos y Servicios de Oficina SA (translator Service), Avenida 4, Panama City (tel: 225-0527).

Instituto de Recursos Hidráulicos y Electrificación (IRHE), Edif Poli, Avenida Justo Arosemanay 26 Este, Apdo 5285, Panama 5 (tel: 262-6272).

Instituto Panameño de Comercio Exterior, Avenida Manuel Icaza, Apdo 1897, El Dorado 6, Panama.

Panama Stock Exchange, Calle Elvira Mendez y Calle 52, Edificio Vallarino, Panama (tel: 269-1966; fax: 269-2457).

Panamanian Embassy (USA), 2862 McGill Terrace, NW, Washington DC 20008 (tel: 202-483-1407; fax: 202-483-8413: e-mail: panaemb@erols.com).

ProPrivat, Ave Perú y Calle 35, Apartado Postal 1464-Paitilla, Panama (tel: 225-0123/6172/4387/0630; fax: 227-4620).

Sindicato de Industriales de Panamá, Apdo 952, Panama City (tel: 230-0619).

Universal Congress of the Panama Canal, 31 Bedford Square, London WC1B 3SG, UK (tel: +44(0)171-314-1662; fax: +44(0)171-314-1683; e-mail: congreso@pananet.com).

US Embassy, Avenida Balboa entre Calle 37 y 38, Apdo 6959, Panama 5 (tel: 227-1777; fax: 203-9470).

Internet sites

Daily internet newspaper: *El Siglo*: http://www.elsiglo.com

General information on doing business in Panama:
http://www.infonetsa.com/infonetsa/incorp/buss1.htm

Papua New Guinea

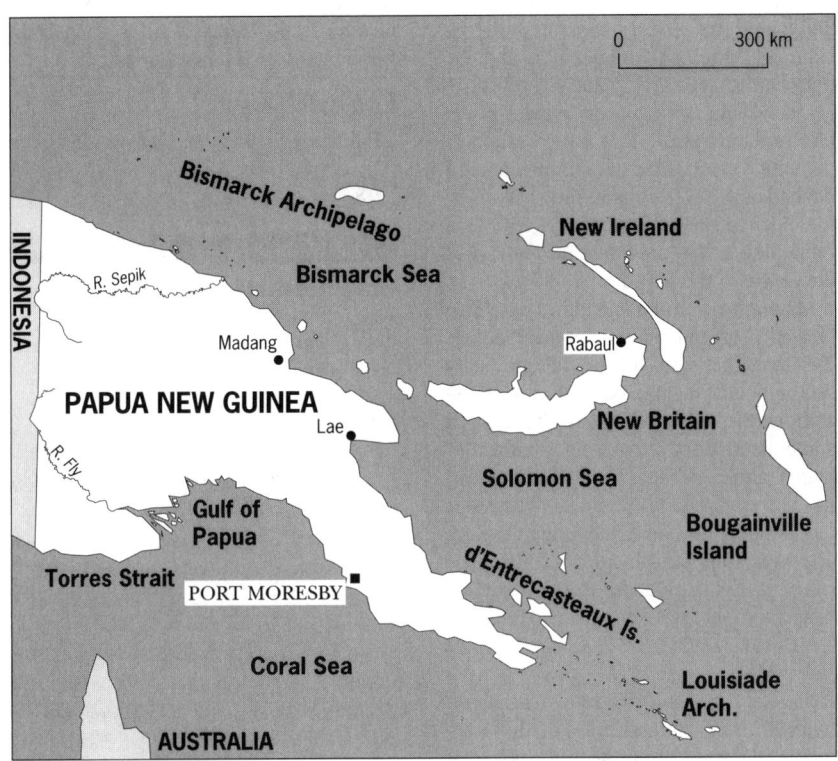

KEY FACTS

Official name: The Independent State of Papua New Guinea (PNG)

Head of State: Queen Elizabeth II; represented by Governor General Sir Paulias Matane (sworn in 29 Jun 2004)

Head of government: Prime Minister Sir Michael Somare (NAP) (elected by parliament 5 Aug 2002)

Ruling party: Coalition government of 13 parties and 20 independent MPs, led by the National Alliance Party (NAP) (from Aug 2002)

Area: 462,840 square km

Population: 5.50 million (2004)

Capital: Port Moresby

Official language: English, Tok Pisin, Motu

Currency: Kina (K) = 100 toea

Exchange rate: K3.02 per US$ (Oct 2005)

GDP per capita: US$686 (2004)

GDP real growth: 2.50% (2004)

Labour force: 2.73 million (2004)

Inflation: 7.40% (2004)

Balance of trade: US$1.08 billion 2004

Foreign debt: US$2.80 billion (2003)

Visitor numbers: 56,185 (2003)

International donors and Papua New Guineans alike had hoped that the country's spiralling social, economic and political problems would begin to stabilise in 2005. However, progress was mixed.

Economic growth, just

In 2003, Papua New Guinea (PNG) managed to achieve economic growth for the first time in three years. Since 2003, there has been both progress and setbacks. After a relatively good year in 2004, GDP growth slowed to an estimated 1.7 per cent in 2005. Inflation also rose to 9.6 per cent.

The politics of aid (and shoes)

In 2003, PNG signed an aid deal with its traditional financial supporter, Australia. The US$600 million Enhanced Co-operation Package (ECP) provided for support in a variety sectors including law and order, justice, economic management, public sector reform, border control and transport security and safety.

However, relations between the two country's have long been complicated by the fact that PNG was once ruled as a colony by Australia. Accusations, from Port Moresby, of neo-colonialism and patronising behaviour are not uncommon. The ECP proved to be no exception. In December 2004, the PNG government was incensed by an Australian think-tank's report, which suggested that PNG was heading for social and economic meltdown. In May 2005, the PNG Supreme Court ruled that the deployment of 210 Australian police in PNG under the provisions of the ECP broke local laws. The Australian police were initially deployed to assist with law and order issues in the country and it had been stipulated in the ECP that they would be immune from local prosecution. Despite the ensuing chill in PNG-Australian relations, the Australian police units were allowed to return to PNG in August, although with a restricted mandate.

In April, relations between PNG and Australia took another one of its period nosedives when PNG prime minister Sir Michael Somare was forced to remove his shoes during a brush with Australian airport security. Somare expressed his outrage and accused the Australian authorities of treating him like a suspected terrorist.

Local policing condemned

Policing issues again took centre state in August, when the US-based non-governmental organisation Human Rights Watch (HRW) published an investigation into police behaviour in PNG. Local police were condemned as perpetrators of extreme violence, particularly against women and children. Responding to the report, the PNG police minister, Bire Kimisopa, admitted that women were regularly raped while in police custody. As if on cue, in November police gunned down 2 pupils at a high school in Enga, in the PNG highlands. The students had been throwing rocks at the police during an attempt to arrest the school principal.

Landmark elections

On 20 May 2005, the people of Bougainville began voting in landmark elections, for a president and parliament. According to the terms of a 2001 peace agreement, which formally brought to an end nearly 14 years of separatist conflict, the island of Bougainville was to have its own autonomous president and parliament – the Bougainville Autonomous Government (BAG). This set it apart from PNG's 18 other provinces. Bougainville is also permitted to hold a referendum from 2011 on full independence from PNG.

A former separatist leader, Sam Kabui, won the presidency in a landslide – taking more than 55 per cent of the vote in the first round. Kabui's party, the Peoples' Congress Party (PCP) emerged as the largest faction in the 40-seat parliament and proceeded to form a coalition government.

During the election campaign, observers had feared that Francis Ona, the self-proclaimed 'king' of Bougainville and the only senior separatist leader to refuse to lay down his arms and participate in the electoral process, might try to sabotage the vote. Ona insisted upon immediate independence for Bougainville. However, the election passed peacefully, with Ona remaining in his mountain stronghold in the centre of the island.

Matters were complicated in July, when Ona died of malaria. Many analysts predict that Ona's followers will gradually accommodate themselves to the new BAG authorities. However, there have been some disturbances involving members of Ona's anti-peace agreement movement, the Mekamui Defense Force (Mekamui is the indigenous name for Bougainville). The Mekamui hard-liners still control territory in the highlands of Bougainville, particularly around Panguna.

Outlook

Relations between PNG and Australia remain bruised from a series of disagreements stemming from the ECP, not least over the issue of policing. However, PNG's relations with Australia have experienced numerous peaks and troughs since PNG achieved independence from Australia in 1975. The fact remains that Australia is PNG's largest aid donor and trading partner.

With rises in world oil prices, PNG can expect a windfall from the export of its own domestic fields. Moreover, if relations between Port Moresby, the BAG and Mekamui hard-liners can continue to be regulated peaceably, PNG can expect big profits from Bougainville's long-interrupted gold and copper mines.

Risk assessment

Politics	Stable
Economy	Fragile
Regional stability	Stable

COUNTRY PROFILE

Historical profile
Papua New Guinea (PNG) was formed by the merger of the Territory of Papua, under Australian rule from 1906, with the Trust Territory of New Guinea, a former German possession which Australia administered from 1914, first under a military government, then under a League of Nations mandate, established in 1921, and later under a trusteeship agreement with the UN.
1942–45 Parts of both territories were occupied by Japanese forces during the Second World War.
1949 A joint administration for the two territories was established by Australia. The union was named the Territory of Papua and New Guinea.
1971 The territory was renamed Papua and New Guinea.
1975 Became independent as Papua New Guinea.
1988 Conflict on Bougainville Island began when a number of locals, unhappy with the level of royalties they were receiving from the Panguna copper mine and concerned about its environmental impact, began to protest. The islanders' opposition organised itself into the Bougainville Revolutionary Army (BRA) and full-scale war began.
1989 Panguna mine was closed down by protesters.
1997 Prime Minister Julius Chan attempted to hire UK-based mercenaries to quell the nine-year Bougainville uprising, prompting intervention by the Australian navy and the resignation of Chan. Bill Skate, a reformist, was elected prime minister in July. The government that took power with Skate was dominated by politicians from the previously ousted government.
1998 The government signed a truce with the secessionist group, the BRA, seeking to end the nine-year rebellion on the island of Bougainville, in which up to 20,000 are believed to have been killed.

KEY INDICATORS — Papua New Guinea

	Unit	2000	2001	2002	2003	2004
Population	m	4.81	5.30	5.39	5.45	*5.50
Gross domestic product (GDP)	US$bn	3.50	3.10	2.80	3.40	*3.09
GDP per capita	US$	682	569	519	569	686
GDP real growth	%	-1.3	-3.4	-3.1	2.0	2.5
Inflation	%	15.6	9.3	11.8	11.8	7.4
Oil output	'000 bpd	69.0	57.0	46.0	–	–
Exports (fob) (goods)	US$m	2,214.0	2,105.0	2,210.0	1,800.0	2,437.0
Imports (fob) (goods)	US$m	1,502.0	1,299.0	1,420.0	1,423.0	1,353.0
Balance of trade	US$m	712.0	806.0	780.0	377.0	1,084.0
Current account	US$m	41.0	-277.0	286.0	243.0	640.0
Total reserves minus gold	US$m	286.9	422.6	321.5	494.2	632.6
Foreign exchange	US$m	274.5	413.6	315.0	489.9	631.2
Exchange rate	per US$	2.88	3.48	3.81	3.61	3.22

* estimated figure

Papua New Guinea

The People's Progress Party (PPP) left the ruling coalition, joining opposition parties and groups in an attempt to oust Skate's government. The prime minister announced the suspension of parliament.
1999 The interim Bougainville Reconciliation Government (BRG) held its first sitting. Skate resigned from the PNG premiership and was replaced by Sir Mekere Morauta of the People's Democratic Movement (PDM).
2000 Morauta was forced to adjourn parliament after a bid to limit inter-party defections threatened to trigger a vote of no confidence in his government. Local landowners brought a suit against Rio Tinto in the US courts, for environmental and social damage at Panguna.
2001 The Bougainville Peace Agreement was signed between the government of Papua New Guinea and leaders of Bougainville. Papua New Guinea accepted Australian aid for taking asylum-seekers who sought to settle in Australia.
2002 Elections were won by Sir Michael Somare's National Alliance Party (NAP); parliament elected Somare as prime minister and he formed a coalition government of 13 parties and 20 independent MPs, led by the NAP.
2003 A new heads of agreement was signed in July for the proposed US$6 billion PNG gas pipeline to Queensland, Australia. On 23 November, the Supreme Court ruled that the election of Sir Albert Kipalan as governor general was invalid. Parliament Speaker Bill Skate became acting governor general following the expiration of the term of Sir Silas Atopare. In December, Sir Pato Kakaraya was elected governor general, defeating Sir Albert Kipalan by 52 votes to 39.
In December, an agreement signed by Papua New Guinea and Australia introduced more Australian involvement in PNG in areas of law and order and public administration.
2004 On 31 March, the Supreme Court ruled the election of Sir Pato Kakaraya as governor general null and void and ordered a new election. On 18 May, Prime Minister Sir Michael Somare dismissed the People's National Congress (PNC) ministers from the cabinet.
In May, talks got under way to finalise the constitution for the autonomous government of Bougainville province.
Sir Paulias Matane was sworn in as governor general of PNG on 29 June.
2005 In elections held from 20 May to 2 June, Joseph Kabui of the Bougainville People's Congress was elected president of the Bougainville Autonomous Government. Rebel leader of the Bougainville secessionists, Francis Ona, died in July.

Political structure
Constitution
The political structure is that of a unicameral parliamentary democracy. The present constitution came into effect in 1975 when the country became independent within the Commonwealth.
The 1975 constitution provided for the decentralisation of power to 20 provincial governments. Since then, Papua New Guinea (PNG) has been developing a system of local government.
An amendment to the constitution in 1977 led to the formation of 20 elected provincial governments which enjoy limited legislative and administrative powers and are funded mainly by central government.
Administrative divisions:

Bougainville	Milne Bay
Central	Morobe
Chimbu	National Capital
Eastern Highlands	New Ireland
East New Britain	Northern
East Sepik	Sandaun
Enga	Sth Highlands
Gulf	Western
Madang	Western Highlands
Manus	West New Britain

In May/June 2005, Bougainville elected an autonomous government to run the island, with PNG's federal government retaining control over defence and the economy.
Form of state
Sovereign independent state; it is a member of the Commonwealth.
The executive
The British monarch is the head of state and is represented by the governor general whose normal term of office is six years. Effective power resides with the prime minister and his cabinet, the National Executive Council. The governor general is appointed on the recommendation of the National Executive Council and on the basis of a simple majority vote in parliament. The prime minister is appointed by the head of state on the proposal of parliament.
National legislature
The National Parliament is a unicameral legislature, with 109 members, elected by universal adult suffrage. The normal term of office is five years. Eighty-nine of the parliamentary seats represent open constituencies and the remaining 20 seats represent the provincial constituencies. The speaker and deputy speaker, who may not hold ministerial posts, are elected by parliament.
The National Parliament was reconvened on 24 July 2001, having been adjourned in November 2000 by Prime Minister Sir Mekere Morauta to avoid a motion of no confidence.

Legal system
The legal system is based on English common law. The national judicial system comprises the Supreme Court, the national court and subsidiary courts. The Supreme Court is responsible for all matters concerning the interpretation of the constitution and is the final court of appeal. The Chief Justice is appointed by the head of state and the judiciary is formally independent of other branches of government.
Last elections
15–29 June 2002 (parliamentary)
Results: Parliamentary: the National Alliance Party (NAP) obtained 19 seats; the People's Democratic Movement (PDM) 13 seats.
Next elections
2007 (parliamentary)

Political parties
Papua New Guinea has no real party system and most members of parliament function as independents, although they have various party labels.
Ruling party
Coalition government of 13 parties and 20 independent MPs, led by the National Alliance Party (NAP) (from Aug 2002)
Main opposition party
People's Democratic Movement (PDM)

Population
5.50 million (2004)
Ethnic make-up
Most of the population is Melanesian. There are numerous other ethnic groups in Papua New Guinea's 20 provinces, including those of Papuan, Polynesian and Micronesian descent. There is a sizeable minority of Australians, some Europeans and a small Chinese community in the country's limited commercial centre.
Religions
The indigenous population is mainly pantheistic, although a significant proportion has adopted Christianity. There are more than 10 different Christian religious groups in the country, including a substantial Roman Catholic congregation (22 per cent of the population) and various Protestant congregations (44 per cent). Indigenous beliefs account for 34 per cent of the population.

Education
Education standards before independence were poor, reflected in low literacy levels in the workforce. School fees have to be paid although these are subsidised by the government. Staff shortages remain an acute problem at secondary level. Lack of materials and up to date curricula are further burdens for the education system. Despite these disadvantages, there has been some development, made possible by help from the Australian government, through AusAid. AusAid has improved the

condition of student housing and provided science laboratories in several schools. In April 2004, Japan made a grant of US$2.6 million to the University of Goroka.
Literacy rate: 66 per cent, adult rates (2003).
Enrolment rate: 80 per cent gross primary enrolment of relevant age group (including repeaters); 47 per cent gross secondary enrolment (World Bank).
Pupils per teacher: 38 in primary schools.

Health
The population suffers from poor health. The government provides hospitals and other health care facilities, and while hospital treatment is available in all major centres, they have varying levels of service and efficiency. A charge on the basis of ability to pay is levied for health services, although most people are treated free or make only a small contribution.
Spending on health is about 4.5 per cent of GDP, of which government spending is around 90 per cent (including foreign expenditure on aid projects of around 20 per cent of the total), private expenditure is 10 per cent, with pre-paid health insurance plans providing about 9 per cent of spending.
In May 2004, health authorities stated that the maternal death rate in PNG was greater than in any other Pacific island; over 1,000 women per annum, die of complications. A survey in late 2004 found that 1 per cent of expectant mothers were testing possitive for HIV and fears are that PNG has reached the trigger point for a widespread epidemic of Aids. PNG is to receive US$20 million to fight malaria from the Global Fund, set up to fight malaria, Aids and tuberculosis; the money was allocated for a five-year period, with the first US$6 million forwarded in May 2004. Insecticide impregnated anti-malaria nets have been provided by the World Health Organisation and Australian aid, to increased numbers of children and reduced the incidence of the desease, acknowledged as the number one killer of children in PNG.
A measles inoculation programme to vaccinate over 120,000 children, mostly in the East Sepik Province, was undertaken in 2004.

HIV/Aids
There is a serious AIDS epidemic in PNG, which has the largest number of HIV positive citizens in the Pacific region. While the prevalence rate is only 2 per cent, for those at most risk the rate is 16 per cent. In 2002, 15,000 people had the disease, by August 2005 the reported number was over 40,000, however screening of 3000 A&E patients at the Port Moresby General Hospital found 18 per cent were HIV positive; other evidence indicates the current prevalence rate is doubling each year. The World Health Organisation advised local health authorities in 2004 that the HIV/Aids strategies in place were ineffectual. With the rates of infection at an alarming rate one critic described the government sponsored awareness campaign methods as 'too lenient' predicting that without change, by 2014 the infection rate would be 20 per cent of the population.
In August 2005 220 new HIV/Aids cases were being reported each month.
HIV prevalence: 2 per cent aged 15–49 in 2005
Life expectancy: 57.2 years (World Bank). Men outlive women in PNG, mainly due to women having less access to food, healthcare and education, and having a heavier workload and multiple pregnancies.
Fertility rate/Maternal mortality rate: 4.3 births per woman (2003)
Birth rate/Death rate: 31 births per 1,000 population; 7.6 deaths per 1,000 population (2003).
Infant mortality rate: 69 per 1,000 live births (2003)
Head of population per physician/bed: 11,700 people per doctor, and 247 people per hospital bed.

Welfare
A number of defined-contribution provident funds provide limited social benefits. A National Provident Fund (NPF) provides social benefits for employees of private-sector companies with 20 or more personnel, while the Public Officers' Superannuation Fund (POSF) provides a similar facility for public servants.

Main cities
Port Moresby (capital, estimated population 324,900 in 2003), Lae (107,400), Madang (35,300), Goroka (17,900), Rabaul (15,900).

Languages spoken
Tok Pisin or Pidgin is the lingua franca of the islands. It is derived from Melanesian Pidgin and includes German and English words. English is spoken by only 1–2 per cent of the population but is the language of government and business, however in parliamentary sessions, Pidgin is used. Motu is spoken by Motuan villagers and has been modified into Police Motu which is spoken widely in the southern region. There are 715 indigenous languages.

Official language/s
English, Tok Pisin, Motu

Media
Press
There are numerous newspapers and magazines published in English, Pidgin and vernacular languages.
Dailies: The two main daily newspapers are *The National* (www.thenational.com.pg) and *Papua New Guinea Post-Courier* (www.postcourier.com.pg) published Monday to Friday. Both are English-language newspapers and foreign-owned.
Weeklies: *Times of Papua New Guinea* is a well-regarded weekly publication in English.
Broadcasting
Radio: The National Broadcasting Commission radio station broadcasts in English, Pidgin and various other local languages. Three commercial radio stations are in operation. Services from Australia are received.
Television: Fiji Television Limited acquired 100 per cent of PNG's only television station EMTV, in late 2004. EMTV has an estimated 2.5 million audience and about 38 per cent of the advertising market. The previous owner, Media Niugini, had held the licence to broadcast for 17 years before selling it for A$2.1 million (US$2.72 million). The Media council has stated that ownership was not an issue but maintaining local content and community initiatives in broadcasting were.

Economy
Economic development has been hampered by PNG's rugged geography, making resources difficult and expensive to extract, impeding communications and limiting agricultural activity to coastal areas and upland plateaux. The majority of the population live outside organised economic activity and only a small, well-connected minority benefit from the country's riches – mainly in the mining sector. Agriculture provides a subsistence livelihood for around 80 per cent of the population, although it contributes around 27 per cent of GDP.
The economy is largely dependent on the export of commodities that are vulnerable to widely fluctuating global prices, such as coffee, copper, copra, cocoa and gold. Mineral deposits (including hydrocarbons) account for nearly three-quarters of exports.
Although the PNG economy has been improving, the high population growth rate is causing social indicators to decline and the government needs to attend to the basic education and health service needs of the growing population.

Papua New Guinea

External trade

Imports
Principal imports are machinery and transport equipment, manufactured goods, food, fuels and chemicals.
Main sources: Australia (45.2 per cent total, 2004), Singapore (21.1 per cent), New Zealand (7.5 per cent), Japan (4.2 per cent), China (4.2 per cent)

Exports
Principal exports are oil, gold, copper ore, timber, palm oil, coffee, cocoa, crayfish and prawns.
Main destinations: Australia (27.7 per cent total, 2004), China (5.8 per cent), Japan (5.7 per cent), Germany (5.0 per cent)

Agriculture

Farming
Agriculture accounts for around 27 per cent of GDP. More than 80 per cent of the population depend on agriculture for their livelihoods. Approximately 5 per cent of land area is cultivated arable, which is restricted by dense rain forests and mountainous terrain.

Coconuts, coffee, cocoa, palm oil, rubber and tea are grown as cash crops on plantations, emloying around one-third of those engaged in agriculture.

Processing, quality control and pricing for main crops are the concern of the Coffee Marketing Board and the Copra Marketing Board, which operate stabilisation funds for these products and for cocoa. Smallholdings produce 70 per cent of all coffee for export, in addition to subsistence crops of yams, sago, cassava, bananas, pineapples, vegetables, sweet potatoes, tea, natural rubber, groundnuts, sorghum and rice, with some raising of pigs, goats and poultry.

A 2004 study showed that the population of PNG was eating less imported meat and rice. With the devaluation of the kina since the 1990s, it is thought that fewer people can afford the imported food and are returning to their native diets, which PNG farmers have been quick to provide. Food production has kept pace with the population growth.

The estimated crop production for 2004 included: 10,600 tonnes (t) cereals in total, 1,250,000t oil palm fruit, 256,000t taro, 520,000t sweet potatoes, 280,000t yams, 235,000t green corn, 120,000t cassava, 3,800t sorghum, 5,600t treenuts, 870,000t bananas, 2,750t pulses, 1,482,800t roots & tubers, 650,000t coconuts, 475,740t oilcrops, 42,500t cocoa beans, 60,000t green coffee, 442,000t sugar cane, 4,000t natural rubber, 9,000t tea, 1,792,200t fruit in total, 499,660t vegetables in total. Estimated livestock production included: 392,947t meat in total, 3,225t beef, 64,000t pig meat, 320,000t game meat, 5,606t poultry, 5,607t eggs, 150t honey.

Fishing
One considerable resource Papua New Guinea has yet to exploit is its fishing grounds, probably the world's richest. The total annual fish catch is over 300,000 tonnes, but the country's waters have been estimated to be capable of supplying up to one million tonnes of fish a year. Papua New Guinea's waters are home to more than 1,800 different species of fish. Activity in the sector is largely centred on domestic fleets tapping the country's 2.3 million square kilometres exclusive fishing zone. Foreign fleets have been excluded from the zone. Papua New Guinea has become one of the biggest players in the Western tuna fish industry. The growth of the industry has been encouraged by favourable government policies such as the removal of export duties on fisheries products.

Forestry
The economy benefits from huge exports of tropical logs, while the sawn timber industry caters to domestic demands. Forests and woodlands cover around 93 per cent of land area, but are subject to deforestation for tropical timber exports and to pollution from mining projects. The government is seeking to regain control of an industry which seems to have operated outside existing regulations and in which political corruption has played an important part. There has been little monitoring of commercial operations and reforestation is inadequate. PNG has a relatively small plantation estate.

PNG has an established presence in the Asian log market and exports around one million cubic metres of logs annually to South Korea, as well as around 400,000 cubic metres to Japan.

In 2004, forest exports amounted to US$224.2 million and imports amounted to US$8.7 million.

Timber production in 2004 included: 7.2 million cubic metres (mcum) roundwood, 1.7mcum industrial roundwood, 97,000 cubic metres (cum) pulpwood, round & split, 1.6mcum sawlogs & veneer logs, 70,000cum sawnwood, 79,000cum wood based panels, 5.5mcum wood fuel.

Industry and manufacturing
The industrial sector, including mining, accounts for around 40 per cent of GDP and employs 10 per cent of the workforce. Manufacturing accounts for around 9 per cent of GDP.

Industry is focussed on mining (gold, silver, copper), crude oil and processing agricultural products. Copra crushing, palm and coconut oil processing, sugar processing, brewing, meat production, plywood production and wood chip production are prominent. Government policy, through the Industrial Centres Development Corporation, aims to promote non-mining sectors, particularly import substitution and export-oriented industries such as manufacturing and downstream processing. Main activities include boat-building, steel fabrication and manufacture of cement, paper products, soap, matches, chemicals, paint, sawn timber, furniture, plywood, bottles and cigarettes.

Tourism
Tourism is at an early stage of development, but, with over 90 per cent of the land area still forested, there is enormous potential especially for adventure and eco-tourism. The sector is expected to contribute 5.8 per cent of GDP in 2005. The authorities recognise the economic value of tourism and have stepped up promotion and infrastructure development. A problem which was identified as a cause of a decline in visitor numbers in recent years was a perception of lawlessness in PNG. The decline was reversed by 2003, assisted by improved air connections, and continued into 2004, when 60,715 arrivals were recorded. Australia is the largest market, followed by Japan and other Asian countries. Around two-thirds of visits are for business purposes, but leisure tourism is an increasing proportion of the total, enhanced by cruise ship visits.

Environment
Papua New Guinea, Philippines, Indonesia, Australia and Solomon Islands are the countries with the most coral reef fish species.

Mining
Mining contributes around 8 per cent of GDP. Copper and gold are the most important export minerals. Most mineral resources are difficult and costly to extract.

Hydrocarbons
PNG has proven oil reserves of around 200 million barrels. Annual production, destined mostly for Asian and Australian markets, has declined significantly from its high of 140,000 barrels per day (bpd) in the 1990s to around 46,000 bpd. There is active exploration for oil both onshore and offshore. The challenge facing Papua New Guinea is to bring other discoveries online as older fields are depleted. PNG may have substantial untapped reserves of oil and gas, although the rugged terrain and the problems of inaccessibility are major obstacles to exploration and recovery costs are very high. There can also be problems in gaining permission to use land because of the land ownership system. InterOil Corporation completed the construction of Papua New Guinea's first oil refinery at Napa Napa in 2004. The

refinery can process 32,500bpd at full capacity and supply the PNG domestic market, leaving 35 per cent of its output for foreign export.

PNG has natural gas reserves totalled 431 billion cubic metres, but as yet there is no extraction industry. A gas pipeline linking PNG to Queensland, Australia, is under construction. Although this pipeline remains a government priority, there is increasing emphasis on developing downstream gas processing facilities.

There are no known coal reserves or production in PNG. Negligible quantities of coal are imported.

Energy
Around 80 per cent of electricity supply is generated by hydro-power, most of the remainder by oil-fired thermal stations. The major hydroelectric schemes are located at Port Moresby, Ramu River and the Gazelle Peninsula.

Financial markets
Stock exchange
The Port Moresby Stock Exchange (POMsox) was established in 1999. It is one of the world's smallest exchanges, with only 13 listed companies in 2004. These include Credit Corporation (PNG) Limited and foreign companies: Durban Roodepoort Deep (DRD), Cue Energy Resources, Highlands Pacific, InterOil Corporation, Lihir Gold and Mosaic Oil. Total turnover for week ending 20 August 2004 was K131,673.10.

Banking and insurance
Central bank
Bank of Papua New Guinea
Main financial centre
Port Moresby

Time
GMT plus 10 hours

Geography
PNG lies east of Indonesia and north of the north-eastern extremity of Australia. It extends over 1,300km from north to south, from the equator to Cape Baganowa in the Louisiade Archipelago at latitude 11 degrees south and for 1,200km from the border with Irian Jaya to longitude 160 degrees east. Although the bulk of the country's land area is formed by the mainland, PNG includes many smaller islands, principally the Bismark Archipelago, which largely comprises New Britain, New Ireland and Manus, and the North Solomon Islands of which Bougainville and Buka are the largest. PNG has coastlines extending for a total of 5,152km. Its highest point is Mount Wilhelm, at 4,509 metres.

The country is a land of great geographic diversity. The central core of the mainland has a massive system of mountain ranges but there is also an extensive range of foothills as well as volcanoes (the Pacific 'Rim of Fire') and low-lying coastal swamps. The country is endowed with substantial mineral wealth and has good agricultural potential with fertile soil and abundant rainfall. There are large expanses of tropical forest and good fishery stocks.

Climate
PNG has a tropical climate with an average maximum temperature of 33 degrees Celsius (C) and an average minimum of 22 degrees C. Temperature and humidity are fairly constant throughout the year. The Highlands region has a more temperate climate than the rest of the country. Papua New Guinea also has seasonal monsoons, varying considerably between regions. Rainfall totals up to 4,600mm per year in some areas.

Dress codes
As PNG is in the tropics, light clothes are worn at all times, although travellers to the Highlands may require sweaters for the evening. Business wear is usually lightweight trousers and a short sleeved shirt. The Australian sartorial influence can be seen in the wearing of shorts and long socks by males even in administrative positions. Jackets are not normally required but safari suits are often worn. Formal evening wear is seldom required but sometimes tropical formal wear is stipulated on invitations and this would mean a long sleeved shirt and tie for men and a cocktail dress for women.

Entry requirements
Passports
Required by all. Passports must be valid for 12 months from the date of entry.
Visa
Required by all.
All travellers should be in possession of sufficient funds for onward or return flight before the expiry date of their visa.
Visa conditions are liable to change and should be checked before travelling.
Currency advice/regulations
There are no restrictions on importing local and foreign currency. Non-residents can export foreign currency up to the amount imported. However, foreign exchange remains controlled, and is only available through authorised dealers.
Customs
The export of items of ethnographic interest is banned.

Health (for visitors)
Mandatory precautions
Vaccination certificates are required for yellow fever if travelling from an infected area.

Advisable precautions
Foreign visitors to PNG should take precautions against malaria, and those visiting the remote areas of the country should also be inoculated against typhoid and hepatitis 'A' and 'B'. Tuberculosis is prevalent in the country as is Aids. A vacination for Japanese encephalitis is available and recommended for visitors planning an extended stay or onward travel to other pacific islands.

Hotels
In addition to Western-style hotels, the Tourist Board operates a scheme of village-style guest-houses run by nationals. Tipping is not usual.

Public holidays
Fixed dates
1 Jan (New Year's Day), 13 Jun (Queen's Birthday), 21 Jul (Remembrance Day), 16 Sep (Independence/Constitution Day), 25–26 Dec (Christmas Holiday).
Variable dates
Good Friday, Easter Monday.

Working hours
Banking
Mon–Thu: 0800–1500; Fri: 0800–1600.
Business
Mon–Fri: 0800–1630.
Government
Mon–Fri: 0800–1600.
Shops
Mon–Fri: 0900–1630/1700; Sat: 0900–1200. Markets open all daylight hours.

Electricity supply
240/415V AC, 50 cycles; plugs are three-pin Australian type.

Weights and measures
Metric system

Social customs/useful tips
The use of first names is common in business, reflecting the tendency (of Australian origin) towards informality. The Papua New Guineans have a relaxed attitude to punctuality and this can make it difficult for the foreign visitor to keep to a schedule of appointments or to make business arrangements.

The belief in magic and sorcery is still widespread. There is little interest in national issues but local group and tribal sympathies are strong. Pressure from the provinces has resulted in the formation of a separate and tribal level of provincial government.

The traditional (custom) land tenure system promotes social stability and equal access to land within clans. Land disputes are endemic. Tipping is not practised or encouraged.

Papua New Guinea

Security
It has been advised that visitors to PNG should take care and ensure their personal safety at all times. PNG is characterised by regionalism and tribalism, with widespread corruption and prevalent violent crime bordering on anarchy. Law and order remain very weak in Port Moresby and Lae, reflecting the rising level of unemployment in the urban areas and a breakdown in the customary lines of authority. Criminal gangs of so-called 'rascals' have become a serious problem, and particularly worrying is a growing tendency in some areas for firearms to be used. Robbery, vehicle hijacks, assaults and random shootings are all common. Violent incidents can occur without warning and while foreigners are not necessarily the target they are visible and can be engulfed by them. Outside urban areas the situation is better, although sporadic tribal fighting is common and areas where it is reported, such as the Southern Highlands Province, is a particularly dangerous area and should be avoided.

Getting there
Air
National airline: Air Niugini (US$15.8 million profit in 2003).
International airport/s: Port Moresby Jacksons International (POM), 11km south of Port Moresby; duty-free shop, bar, buffet, bank, post office, hotel reservations, shops and car hire.
Airport tax: There is a departure tax of K30.

Surface
Cruise ships call, and passenger accommodation is sometimes available on cargo ships.
Main port/s: Services operate from Australia, the Far East, Europe and the west coast of the US to Alotau, Anewa Bay, Kavieng, Kieta, Kimbe, Lae, Lorengau, Madang, Oro Bay, Port Moresby, Rabaul, Samarai, Wewak and Vanimo.

Getting about
National transport
The government at times declares a state of emergency in Port Moresby because of the increasing problem of violent crime, and travellers should make enquiries about curfew provisions. Much domestic travel is by air.
Air: Air Niugini, Air Link, Islands Aviation, Talair, Bougair and Douglas Airways operate flights to the hundreds of smaller air strips in remote locations. Helicopter and light aircraft charter is available from some 20 small companies.
Road: The 4,900km road system is being extended. Few road networks connect the various provinces because of the mountainous terrain. Only about 7 per cent of the road network is paved.

Buses: PMVs (public motor vehicles), usually light buses or covered trucks, operate within and between main centres from bus shelters in towns (or they can be hailed elsewhere).
Rail: There is no railway network in Papua New Guinea.
Water: Sea and river transport are available. Inland waterways total 10,940km.

City transport
Taxis: Metered taxi service is available in main centres, but scarce and expensive. Negotiate fares wherever possible.
Buses, trams & metro: Journey time from airport to city centre is 20–60 minutes.

Car hire
A number of international car hire companies operate. An international driving licence is required.

BUSINESS DIRECTORY
The addresses listed below are a selection only. While World of Information makes every endeavour to check these addresses, we cannot guarantee that changes have not been made, especially to telephone numbers and area codes. We would welcome any corrections.

Telephone area codes
The international direct dialling (IDD) code for Papua New Guinea is +675 followed by subscriber's number.

Useful telephone numbers
Police, fire and ambulance: 000

Chambers of Commerce
Lae Chamber of Commerce and Industry, PO Box 265, Lae, Morobe Province (tel: 472-2340; fax: 472-6038; e-mail: lcci@global.net.pg.

Papua New Guinea Chamber of Commerce and Industry, PO Box 1621, Trukai Building, Lawes Road, Konebadu, Port Moresby, NCD (tel: 321-3057; fax: 321-0566; e-mail: pngcci@global.net.pg).

Port Moresby Chamber of Commerce and Industry, PO Box 1764, Monian Tower, Douglas Street, Port Moresby (tel: 321-3077; fax: 321-4203; e-mail: info@pomcci.org.pg).

Banking
ANZ Banking Group (PNG), 3rd Floor, Defens Haus, Cnr Champion Parade and Hunter St, Port Moresby (tel: 322-3333; fax: 322-3306).

Bank South Pacific Limited (BSP), PO Box 173, Douglas Street, Port Moresby 121 NCD (tel: 321-2444; fax: 321-7302).

Indosuez Niugini Bank Limited, PO Box 1390, Burns Haus, Champion Parade, Port Moresby (tel: 321-3533; fax: 321-3115).

Maybank (PNG) Limited, PO box 882, Waigani Drive, Waigani (tel: 325-0101; fax: 325-6128).

Central bank
Bank of Papua New Guinea, PO Box 121, ToRobert Haus, Douglas Street, PO Box 121, Port Moresby 111 (tel: 322-7200; fax: 321-1617; e-mail: webmaster@bankpng.gov.pg).

Travel information
Air Niugini, PO Box 7186, Boroko (tel: 273-200; fax: 273-482).

Flight information (24 hours) (tel: 273-321).

Melanesian Tourist Services, PO Box 707, Madang (tel: 822-766; fax: 823-543).

Port Moresby Jacksons International Airport, Air Niugini, PO Box 7186, Boroko, Port Moresby (tel: 372-3209, 327-3647; fax: 273-663).

National tourist organisation offices
PNG Tourism Promotion Authority, PO Box 1291, Port Moresby, Boroka, NCD (tel: 320-0211; fax: 320-0223).

Ministries
Ministry of Agriculture and Livestock, PO Box 417, Konedobu NCD (tel: 325-9544; fax: 325-9722).

Ministry of Bougainville Affairs, House Tisa (2nd Floor), PO Box 343, Waigani NCD (tel: 325-2977; fax: 325-8038).

Ministry of Churches, Family Affairs, & NGO's, National Parliament, PO Parliament, Port Moresby NCD (tel: 327-7350; fax: 320-0903).

Ministry of Civil Aviation, PO Box 684, Boroko NCD (tel: 323-6185; fax: 325-1919).

Ministry of Commerce and Industry, PO Box 375, Waigani NCD (tel: 327-6621; fax: 323-3050).

Ministry of Defence, Murray Barracks, Free Mail Bag Service, Boroko NCD (tel: 327-346; fax: 327-7480).

Ministry of Education, Culture and Science, PSA Haus, PO Box 446, Waigani NCD (tel: 323-3944; fax: 327-7480).

Ministry of Employment and Youth, PO Box 5644, Boroko NCD (tel: 327-7578; fax: 327-7480).

Ministry of Environment, PO Box 6601, Boroko NCD (tel: 325-0174; fax: 325-0182).

Ministry of Finance and Internal Revenue, PO Box 777, Port Moresby NCD (tel: 322-6613; fax: 322-6856).

Ministry of Fisheries, Investment Haus (8th Floor), PO Box 2016, Port Moresby NCD (tel: 321-3443; fax: 320-3024).

Ministry of Foreign Affairs and Trade, PO Box 422, Waigani NCD (tel: 327-7545; fax: 325-4467).

Ministry of Forests, PO Box 1550, Boroko NCD (tel: 327-7591; fax: 327-7589).

Ministry of Health, Aopi Centre (5th Floor), PO Box 807, Boroko NCD (tel: 301-3605; fax: 301-3604).

Ministry of Justice, Po Box 591, Waigani NCD (tel: 323-0138; fax: 323-0241).

Ministry of Lands, Aopi Centre (4th Floor), PO Box 5665, Boroko NCD (tel: 301-3102; fax: 301-3205).

Ministry of Mining and Energy, NIC Building (1st Floor), Private Mail Bag, Port Moresby NCD (tel: 327-7350; fax: 320-0903).

Ministry of Petroleum and Gas, Parliament House, Waigani NCD (tel: 327-7752; fax: 327-7753).

Ministry of Police and Correctional Institution Services, PO Box 5097, Boroko NCD (tel: 327-7519; fax: 327-7528).

Ministry of Provincial and Local level Government Affairs, PO Box 1287, Boroko NCD (tel: 301-1000; fax: 325-0553).

Ministry of Public Enterprises, Communications and Assisting Prime Minister on Infrastructure and Public Investment Program Matters, PO Parliament, Waigani NCD (tel: 327-7366; fax: 327-7387).

Ministry of Public Service, Morauta House, (2nd Floor, PO Box 519, Waigani NCD (tel: 327-6440; fax: 323-3050).

Ministry of Rural Development, PO Box 639, Waigani NCD (tel: 327-6767; fax: 327-6349).

Ministry of Transport, PO Box 1489, Port moresby NCD (tel: 321-1866; fax: 320-0556).

Ministry of Treasury and Corporate Affairs, Vulupindi Haus (4th Floor), PO Box 710, Waigani NCD (tel: 328-8460; fax: 328-8433).

Office of the Prime Minister, Parliament House (4th Floor), National Parliament, Waigan NCD (tel: 327-7489; fax: 327-7497).

Other useful addresses

British High Commission, Kiroki Street, Waigani, PO Box 4778, Boroko, Port Moresby (tel: 211-677, 251-643; fax: 253-547).

Bureau of Customs, PO Box 932, Port Moresby NCD (tel: 321-2488; fax: 321-3004).

Department of Industrial Development, PO Box 5644, Goroko (tel: 272-286).

Electricity Commission of PNG, PO Box 1105, Boroko NCD (tel: 324-3200; fax: 325-0072).

Forest Research Institute, PO Box 314, LAE, Morobe Province (tel: 342-4188; fax: 432-4357).

Investment Promotion Authority, PO Box 5053, Boroko NCD (tel: 321-7311; fax: 321-2819).

National Curltural Commission, PO Box 7144, Boroko NCD (tel: 325-3288; fax: 325-9119).

National Housing Corporation, PO Box 1550, Boroko NCD (tel: 324-7200; fax: 325-9918).

National Institute of Standards and Industrial Technology, PO Box 3042, Boroko NCD (tel: 327-2102; fax: 325-2403).

National Statistical Office, PO Wardstrip, Waigani NCD (tel: 327-1499; fax: 325-1869).

Papua New Guinea Embassy (US), Suite 805, 1779 Massachusetts Avenue, NW, Washington DC 20036 (tel: 202-745-3680; fax: 202-745-3679; e-mail: kunduwash@aol.com).

Papua New Guinea Investment Corporation, PO Box 155, Port Moresby (tel: 212-855; fax: 211-240).

Post and Telecommunication Corporation, PO Box 1349, Boroko NCD (tel: 300-4000; fax: 300-4098).

Small Business Development Corporation, PO Box 481, Port Moresby NCD (tel: 325-0100; fax: 325-3725).

US Embassy, PO Box 1492, Port Moresby (tel: 211-455; fax: 213-423).

Internet sites

Asian Development Bank: http://www.adb.org

Government departments: http://www.niugini.com/govdepts.html

Investment promotion authority: http://www.ipa.gov.pg

Tourism Council of the South Pacific: http://www.tcsp.com

Paraguay

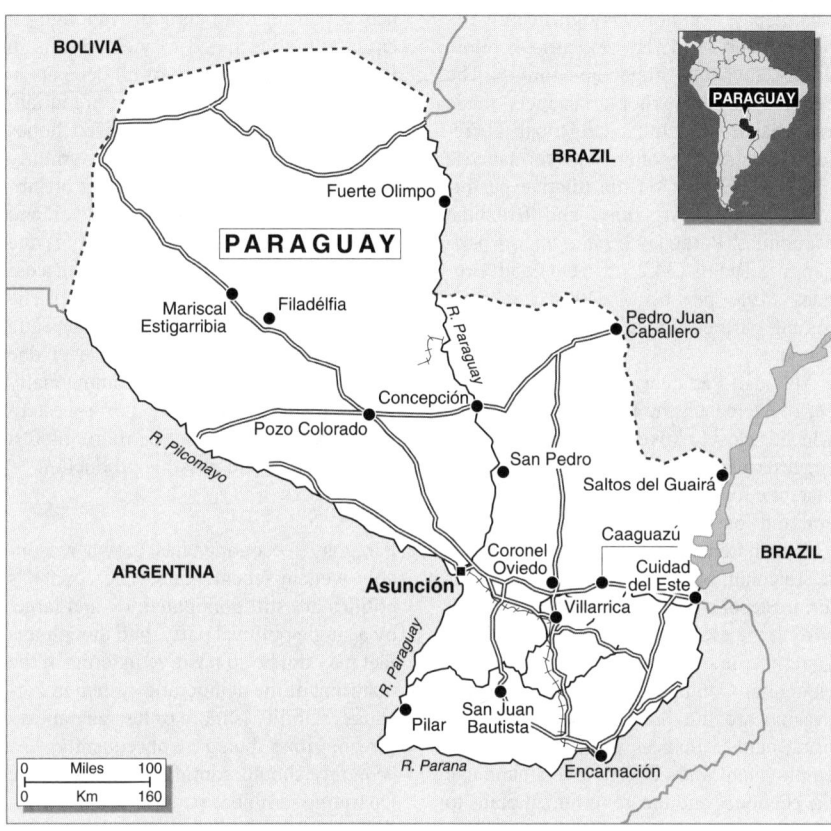

KEY FACTS

Official name: República del Paraguay (Republic of Paraguay)

Head of State: President Nicanor Duarte Frutos (ANR) (sworn in 15 Aug 2003)

Head of government: President Nicanor Duarte Frutos

Ruling party: Asociación Nacional Republicana/Partido Colorado (ANR) (National Republican Alliance/Red Party) (elected 27 Apr 2003)

Area: 406,752 square km

Population: 5.85 million (2004)

Capital: Asunción

Official language: Spanish and Guaraní

Currency: Guaraní (G)

Exchange rate: G6,130.00 per US$ (Oct 2005)

GDP per capita: US$1,155 (2004)

GDP real growth: 2.10% (2004)

Labour force: 2.24 million (2004)

Unemployment: 15.10% (2004)

Inflation: 5.20% (2004)

Balance of trade: -US$394.00 million 2004

Foreign debt: US$3.20 billion (2003)

Until the drafting of the 1992 constitution, Paraguay operated a highly centralised system of governance. The major legacy of the 1992 constitution is the division of constitutional powers that was successfully institutionalised as a result of its creation. The presidency is decided by the entire electorate every five years, while the country's Congress is made up of an 80-member Chamber of Deputies and a 45-strong Senate.

Partido Colorado still dominant

The current incumbent President is Nicanor Duarte Frutos of the Asociación Nacional Republicana/Partido Colorado (National Republican Association/Colorado Party) (ANR-PC), traditionally the most powerful political organisation in the country. Though other parties are explicitly permitted to compete in elections, they are generally thought to stand little chance of achieving electoral success against the might of the conservative ANR-PC. Other political parties include the major opposition force Partido Liberal Radical Auténtico (PLRA) (Authentic Radical Liberal Party) of the liberal left and the Movimiento Patria Querida (Movement Fatherland of the Best).

In common with several other past and present political leaders in the South and Central American region Duarte has a background as a sports journalist. In the mid-1980s he began to branch out into political journalism and wrote social and economic commentaries in the national press. After joining ANR-PC in the late 1980s he became a prominent member of the Asunción political elite, rising to become minister of education and culture by the mid-1990s. Following a political bust up in 1997 Duarte took the bold step of resigning his ministerial portfolio to join a political splinter group.

Despite having resigned his government post, Duarte was able to retain his political power base and in 2001 he prepared his candidacy for the presidency of ANR-PC. Having gained the presidency of the party Duarte ran for president of the country in 2003. In the April 2003 election Frutos led the ANR-PC to a widely anticipated victory at the polls, beating the opposition PLRA, or the *liberales* as they are popularly known, into second place.

Positive growth

Paraguay's economy has grown positively in every year since 2003 having recorded a contraction of 3.9 per cent in 2002. Inflation is now much lower than the 2003 level of 15.6 per cent and currently stands at approximately 5 per cent. The IMF predicts growth 3 per cent for 2005 and the economy is expected to grow by 3.5 per cent in 2006. The introduction of a strict IMF structural adjustment programme, the *El Niño* climatic changes and a series of banking crises were among the factors responsible for the economy's poor performance over the past decade, despite political and economic liberalisation.

Paraguay is heavily reliant on trade with the other three members of the Mercado Común del Sur (Mercosur) (Common Market of the South): Brazil, Argentina and Uruguay. The rapid depreciation of the Brazilian real has created setbacks for Paraguayan trade since 1999 by increasing the value of its exports on the Brazilian market, which is the lynchpin of the country's economy. The recession and economic crisis in Argentina has also damaged the Paraguayan economy, with Argentine producers breaking quota agreements and dumping agricultural produce. The large fall in the value of the guaraní in 2002 was of comfort to many of the country's economic sectors, particularly agriculture, which benefited from becoming more competitive.

Paraguay's economy is significantly dependent on exports of cattle, cotton, grains, soybeans, sugar and timber. The country also re-exports products made elsewhere to Argentina and Brazil. Therefore, Paraguay's economic performance is highly dependent on the relative performance of the Argentine and Brazilian economies. Paraguay's main export partners are Brazil (34.2 per cent) and Uruguay (19.6 per cent). Other important trading partners include Switzerland and China.

Although Paraguay is the poorest member of Mercosur, the large informal sector which is closely linked to contraband trade suggests that official statistics underestimate the real size of the economy in general and foreign trade flows in particular. The main items of this illicit trade are coffee, alcohol, perfume, consumer electronics, tobacco, cars, drugs and soya beans.

With the election of Duarte in 2003 the government's priorities are radically changing. Combating corruption and tax evasion are the President's priorities to bring public finances in order. High unemployment and poverty levels handicap the economy and the government plans to tackle these issues, although tackling national debt is likely to be prioritised. The continued growth of the economy remains heavily dependent on sustained growth in Argentina and Brazil.

Reliance on energy imports

Paraguay has no proven reserves of crude oil, though the country uses oil for approximately 46 per cent of its total energy consumption. Therefore, Paraguay relies heavily on oil from abroad. Although oil exploration has failed to yield results in Paraguay, the discovery of oil deposits in the border regions of Formosa (Argentina) and Chaco (Bolivia) have raised hopes that Paraguay may also have oil. Currently however Paraguay relies entirely on imports to meet demand for its crude oil and petroleum products. A new refinery is due to come on stream at Villa Elisa with a capacity of 40,000 barrels per day (bpd). The country does not produce natural gas and consumption is negligible. However due to a possible discovery of commercially viable natural gas in the north-western Chaco region there may be more interest in exploration and possible production.

Outlook

Paraguay's economy has grown reasonably well in recent years. The country's politics are still dominated, by and large, by a single political party, and though this fact may not be so positive in terms of the maturing of the democratic system in Paraguay, stability is more or less guaranteed for the time being. Consequently, the economy should continue to grow as the Duarte government persists in its clampdown on corruption and other vices damaging to economic competitiveness.

Risk assessment

Politics	Stable
Economy	Improving
Regional stability	Stable

COUNTRY PROFILE

Historical profile
1537 The Spanish began colonising the plains of Paraguay.
1811 Paraguay gained independence from Spain.
1864–70 A disastrous war against Argentina, Brazil and Uruguay was lost. It halved Paraguay's population and stripped it of 155,400 square km of land.
1870 Occupation forces set up a provisional government with a liberal-democratic constitution, although the constitution was never put into practice.
1874 The Partido Colorado (PC) (Colorado Party) (also known as the Red Party),

KEY INDICATORS — Paraguay

	Unit	2000	2001	2002	2003	2004
Population	m	5.52	5.57	5.70	5.78	*5.85
Gross domestic product (GDP)	US$bn	7.50	7.10	5.40	5.80	*7.13
GDP per capita	US$	1,362	1,254	959	921	1,155
GDP real growth	%	-0.4	-0.1	-3.9	1.0	2.1
Inflation	%	9.0	7.3	10.5	15.6	5.2
Exports (fob) (goods)	US$m	2,373.3	2,463.0	2,240.0	2,451.0	2,936.0
Imports (fob) (goods)	US$m	2,905.6	2,959.0	2,520.0	2,666.0	3,330.0
Balance of trade	US$m	-532.3	-530.0	-270.0	-215.0	-394.0
Current account	US$m	-137.3	-236.0	-50.0	17.0	90.0
Foreign debt	US$bn	2.7	3.3	3.4	3.2	–
Total reserves minus gold	US$m	760.6	713.5	629.2	968.9	1,168.1
Foreign exchange	US$m	630.4	584.3	486.8	811.2	1,001.1
Exchange rate	per US$	3,486.40	4,105.90	5,985.00	6,695.00	5,974.60

* estimated figure

Paraguay

representing the land-owning elite, was formed.
1887 The Liberal party, who advocated a minimal state and representative government, was formed.
1883 A Colorado government began driving peasants off the land and selling it to foreign investors.
1904 After a revolution the Liberal party seized power and introduced political and economic changes.
1932–35 The Chaco War with Bolivia over disputed territory.
1936 The army, which held the government responsible for loosing the Chaco War, overthrew the government of President Eusobio Ayala (Liberal) in February and installed war hero Rafael Franco as president, an act that virtually destroyed the Liberals as a political force. The Partido Revolucionario Febrerista (PRF) (*Febrerista* Revolutionary Party) government was a mix of political ideologies, including Communists and Fascists. It implemented land re-distribution and workers rights. Franco's government had popular support but its policies were hastily devised and led to protests when Decree Law 152, promising a 'totalitarian transformation', was announced. The divergent political opinions within the government finally pulled it apart, although Franco continued to hold power with a new party, the Unión Nacional Revolucionaria (Revolutionary National Union). He was unable to provide more land to his peasant supporters and was undermined by Liberal party supporters in the army.
1937 Franco lost support of the army when he withdrew troops from the territories won in Chaco in 1935. The army revolted and returned the Liberal party to power.
1938 A treaty was signed between Bolivia and Paraguay following an international peace conference. It returned most of the disputed land to Bolivia.
1940 The military regime installed Higinio Morínigo, a follower of Nazi Germany's Adolf Hitler, as president.
1946 Following the defeat of Germany and Japan, Paraguay's chief trading partners, Morínigo legalised liberal, communist and *Febrerista* parties.
1947 Paraguay descended into civil war, following the emergence of political divisions within the army.
1948 The PC deposed Morínigo, leading to a series of coups and short-lived regimes.
1949 Federico Chaves became president.
1954 General Alfredo Stroessner led a *coup d'état* that deposed Chaves. Stroessner was re-elected seven times under the constitutional 'state-of-siege'

provision. His dictatorship was ruthless against all opposition.
1967 A new constitution endorsed Stroessner's dictatorship. Paraguay was isolated within the world community.
1989 Stroessner was deposed in a bloodless coup by General Antonio Rodríguez who later won the presidential election. However the military-backed National Republican Association-PC won the parliamentary elections.
1993 Juan Carlos Wasmosy was elected president and the PC won a majority of parliamentary seats in the first free presidential and multi-party elections.
1998 Raúl Cubas Grau (PC) won the presidential election, despite allegations of fraud.
1999 Cubas resigned, following the assassination of his vice president, Luís Argaña. Luis González Macchi was appointed as interim president.
2000 Supporters of dissident Colorado leader, General Lino Oviedo, staged an unsuccessful coup. Oviedo fled and was found by Brazilian police at a Brazilian border hideout.
2001 Paraguay asked for, but was denied, Oviedo's extradition.
2002 President Macchi was accused of corruption. Violent street protestors demanded his resignation. He was impeached by congress in December.
2003 In February, President Macchi survived his impeachment trial; the Senate voted 25–18 against him, short of the two-thirds majority (30 votes) necessary to remove him from power. Nicanor Duarte Frutos won the April presidential elections. Macchi was again charged with corruption and put on trial.
2004 In June, former military commander, General Oviedo, was arrested after returning from exile in Brazil. An estimated 464 shoppers were killed in a three storey supermarket fire, it was the worst fire in Latin American history. In September the daughter of former president, Raúl Cubas, was kidnapped.
2005 On 16 February, the body of Cecilia Cubas was found in a shallow grave. President Nicanor ordered a crackdown on organised crime, blamed for widespread kidnapping and murder. The government's plans to privatise the public utilities sector was voted down by the lower house of the Paraguayan legislature in June. In August Paraguay hosted the world's first ever conference of landlocked nations, which was attended by some 30 states.

Political structure
Constitution
Paraguay became an independent republic in 1811. Under the dictatorship of Alfredo Stroessner (1954–89) a new constitution was introduced in 1967 which granted strong powers to the executive, entrenching political control in the hands of the ruling Partido Colorado (PC) (Colorado Party). In 1992, a new constitution was enacted.
There are 19 departments and 213 municipalities each with their own directly elected administration.
In 1990, a new electoral law was passed. Among its provisions were the introduction of proportional representation, provision for a second round in the event that no candidate secures an absolute majority in presidential elections, the prohibition of compulsory deductions from salaries of public-sector workers for political parties, the selection of party authorities by the direct vote of all members, a ban on party affiliation by members of the armed forces and the police and the lifting of a previous ban on electoral alliances by political parties.

Form of state
Presidential democratic republic

The executive
Under the constitution executive power is exercised by the president of the republic, who must be a Roman Catholic. The president is elected directly by popular vote for five years and formulates and enacts legislation. Executive power rests with the president who appoints a council of 11 ministers. The president has powers to rule by decree when congress is in recess. The president cannot be re-elected.

National legislature
The legislature is the bicameral National Congress, made up of the Senate (45 members) and the Chamber of Deputies (80 members). The term of both chambers is normally five years, coinciding with that of the presidency, and representation is decided by the vote in the presidential elections.

Legal system
At the apex of the judiciary is the Supreme Court which has the power to declare legislation unconstitutional. The five members of the Supreme Court are appointed by the president and their tenure of office coincides with that of the presidency.
There are appeal courts and lower level criminal and civil courts.

Last elections
27 April 2003 (presidential and congressional)
Results: Presidential: Nicanor Duarte Frutos won 37 per cent of the vote, Julio César Franco 24 per cent and Pedro Fadul 23 per cent.
Congressional: Asociación Nacional Republicana/Partido Colorado (ANR) (National Republican Alliance/Red Party) 32.9 per cent of the vote, 16 seats; Partido Liberal Radical Auténtico (PLRA)

(Authentic Radical Liberal Party) 24.3 per cent, 12 seats.
Next elections
2008 (presidential and congressional)

Political parties
Ruling party
Asociación Nacional Republicana/Partido Colorado (ANR) (National Republican Alliance/Red Party) (elected 27 Apr 2003)
Main opposition party
Partido Liberal Radical Auténtico (PLRA) (Authentic Radical Liberal Party)

Population
5.85 million (2004)
Ethnic make-up
Over 95 per cent of the population is of Spanish-Guaraní origin. There are approximately 40,000 indigenous people in the country, most of whom live in the Chaco region.
In addition, there are large Korean, German and Japanese immigrant communities, along with small Italian and Polish communities, and some communities of people originating from Lebanon, Taiwan and Hong Kong.
Religions
Roman Catholicism is the state religion and is practised by 90 per cent of the population, the remainder are mostly Protestants.

Education
There are just over 4,300 primary schools and an estimated 92 per cent of the relevant age group attends primary school. Secondary education begins aged 13 years and comprises two cycles of three years each.
Paraguay has two universities – the National and the Catholic. The state-run Universidad Nacional de Asunción has a student enrolment of around 20,000. It comprises 11 faculties, law and social sciences, medicine, economics, chemistry, dentistry, philosophy, agriculture, veterinary science, fine arts, architecture and engineering. It also has six Institutes and six Higher Schools.
Literacy rate: 94 per cent male, 92 per cent female; adult rates (World Bank).
Compulsory years: Seven to 13
Enrolment rate: 111 per cent gross primary enrolment of relevant age group (including repeaters); 47 per cent gross secondary enrolment (World Bank).
Pupils per teacher: 21 in primary schools

Health
Total expenditure on health is about 8 per cent of GDP, of which government spending is around 38–39 per cent. Private expenditure is between 61–62 per cent of which some 28–20 per cent is pre-paid health insurance plans.

HIV prevalence: 0.5 per cent aged 15–49 in 2003 (World Bank)
Life expectancy: 71.0 years (World Bank)
Fertility rate/Maternal mortality rate: 3.8 births per woman; maternal mortality 190 per 100,000 live births (World Bank).
Infant mortality rate: 25 per 1,000 live births (World Bank)
Head of population per physician/bed: 1.1 physicians and 1.3 hospital beds available per 1,000 people.

Welfare
The Social Security Institute was formed by Decree Law 17071 in 1948, and is regulated by Decree Law 1860 of 1950. The laws refer to health, medical care and sickness benefits. Workers, their wives and children up to 16 have the right to receive medical, surgical and dental attention, medicine and hospitalisation, as well as cash subsidies for temporary illnesses, maternity and death. Old age pensions are paid to those who have made the necessary contributions. The social security system is in disarray and in 2001 the IMF urged the government to stop lending money to the system.
Women must not work for three weeks before or six weeks after childbirth. During these periods a woman receives a cash subsidy from the Social Security Institute. The worker has the right to receive an allowance equal to 5 per cent of the legal minimum wage for each child under 17 for whose maintenance and education he is responsible. This allowance is wholly the employer's expense and is discontinued once the worker's wage reaches 200 per cent more than the legal minimum.

Main cities
Asunción (capital, estimated population 525,100 in 2003), Cuidad del Este (239,500) (on the Brazilian border), Encarnación (72,300) (on the Argentine border), Pedro Juan Caballero (66,400).

Languages spoken
Guaraní, the aboriginal Indian tongue is widely spoken. In some rural districts, the less educated speak little or no Spanish.
Official language/s
Spanish and Guaraní

Media
Press
There is freedom of the press.
Dailies: The main national dailies and Sunday newspapers are *ABC Color*, *Diario El Dia*, *Diario Popular*, *Ultima Hora*, *El Diario Noticias* and *La Nacion* all published in Spanish and based in Asunción.
Broadcasting
Radio: There is one government radio station, Radio Nacional del Paraguay, and 11 private radio stations in Asunción.

Television: There are two television channels, both privately owned – Televisión Cerro Cora (Canal 9) and Red Privada de Televisión (Canal 13). Cable TV is available. All broadcasts are in Spanish.

Economy
Paraguay's economy has grown in every year since 2003 having recorded a contraction of 2.3 per cent in 2002. Inflation is now much lower than the 2003 level of 14.2 per cent and currently stands at approximately 5 per cent. The IMF's projected growth for 2005 is 3 per cent and the economy is expected to grow by 3.5 per cent in 2006.
The introduction of a strict IMF structural adjustment programme, the *El Niño* climatic changes and a series of banking crises were among the factors responsible for the economy's poor performance over the past decade, despite political and economic liberalisation.
Paraguay is heavily reliant on trade with the other three members of the Mercado Común del Sur (Mercosur) (Common Market of the South): Brazil, Argentina and Uruguay. The rapid depreciation of the Brazilian real has created setbacks for Paraguayan trade since 1999 by increasing the value of its exports on the Brazilian market, which is the lynchpin of the country's economy. The recession and economic crisis in Argentina has also damaged the Paraguayan economy, with Argentine producers breaking quota agreements and dumping agricultural produce. The large fall in the value of the guaraní in 2002 was of comfort to many of the country's economic sectors, particularly agriculture, which benefited from becoming more competitive.
Although Paraguay is the poorest member of Mercosur, the large informal sector which is closely linked to contraband trade suggests that official statistics underestimate the real size of the economy in general and foreign trade flows in particular. The main items of this illicit trade are coffee, alcohol, perfume, consumer electronics, tobacco, cars, drugs and soya beans.
With the election of Nicanor Duarte Frutos in 2003 the government's priorities are radically changing. Combating corruption and tax evasion are the President's priorities to bring public finances in order. High unemployment and poverty levels handicap the economy and the government plans to tackle these issues, although tackling national debt is likely to be prioritised. The continued growth of the economy remains heavily dependent on sustained growth in Argentina and Brazil.

Paraguay

External trade
Paraguay's economy is significantly dependent on exports of cattle, cotton, grains, soybeans, sugar and timber. The country also re-exports products made elsewhere to Argentina and Brazil. Therefore, Paraguay's economic performance is highly dependent on the relative performance of the Argentine and Brazilian economies.

Paraguay's main export partners are Brazil (34.2 per cent), Uruguay (19.6 per cent), Switzerland (7.8 per cent) and Argentina (5.3%). The majority of Paraguay's imports come from Brazil (32.5 per cent), Argentina (21.6 per cent) and China (12.7 per cent). Paraguay is a full member of Mercosur, the Common Market of the South.

Imports
Main imports include road vehicles, consumer goods, tobacco, petroleum products and electrical machinery.

Main sources: Brazil (24.3 per cent total, 2004), US (22.3 per cent), Argentina (16.2 per cent), China (9.9 per cent), Hong Kong (5.0 per cent)

Exports
Main exports include soybeans, animal feed, cotton, meat, edible oils, electricity, timber and leather.

Main destinations: Brazil (27.8 per cent total, 2004), Uruguay (15.9 per cent), Italy (7.1 per cent), Switzerland (5.6 per cent), Argentina (4.3 per cent), Netherlands (4.2 per cent)

Re-exports
Paraguay trades in a high level of re-exports, mainly through informal channels such as smuggling.

Agriculture
Farming
Paraguay's agricultural sector remains important to the country's economy. The sector employs approximately 40 per cent of the labour force and contributes 29 per cent to total GDP.

Agricultural products account for more than 90 per cent of exports. Approximately 5 per cent of total land area is arable land or under permanent crops, pasture constitutes 35 per cent of the land and 50 per cent is woodland/forest.

While the fertile eastern region is ideal for arable farming and cattle grazing the rich soil has been subject to erosion since the 1970s. There are extensive forests with a variety of timbers. The potential of the Chaco region to the west is still to be realised, dependent as it is upon the exploitation of its known groundwater resources for irrigated farming.

Principal export crops are cotton and soya beans, which together account for more than two-thirds of export earnings. Sawn timber, meat products and, to a lesser extent, fruit, vegetables and hides are also exported. Sugar cane, wheat, tobacco and various new specialist crops for industrial use are expanding as more land comes under cultivation. Paraguay has nearly achieved self-sufficiency in basic foodstuffs (rice, maize, wheat, beans). Agricultural production fluctuates from year to year owing to climatic conditions (both flooding and drought) and widespread smuggling (particularly livestock and soya beans).

Crop production in 2004 included: 2,002,106 tonnes (t) cereals in total, 715,000t wheat, 5,500,000t cassava, 3,583,680t soya beans, 3,637,000t sugar cane, 125,000t rice, 1,120,000t maize, 166,932t sweet potatoes, 42,160t sorghum, 16,535t tobacco, 3,353t green coffee, 736,326t oilcrops, 44,031t bananas, 285,120t citrus fruit, 67,508t pulses, 10,910t chillies & peppers, 52,392t pineapples, 28,680t mangoes, 109,000t cotton lint, 330,000t seed cotton, 467,300t fruit in total, 5,668,022t vegetables in total. Livestock production included: 492,947t meat in total, 215,000t beef, 156,000t pig meat, 2,273t lamb, 38,774t poultry, 100,810t eggs, 362,040t milk, 1,710t honey, 34,412t cattle hides.

Fishing
Despite its landlocked geographical status, Paraguay's annual fish catch amounts to approximately 10,000 tonnes. The illegal trade of fishery products remains a problem despite attempts by the authorities to bring it under control.

Forestry
Paraguay has a significant area of forested land, accounting for approximately 30 per cent of the country's total landmass. The majority of the forested areas are to the east of the Paraguay river. Historically, deforestation has been a problem in Paraguay. The country lost, on average 0.51 per cent of forest cover each year during the 1990-2000 period. This amounted to a decrease of 123,000 hectares year on year.

Local forest resources produce moderate volumes of sawn timber and panels, most of which is usually exported. Domestic demand for paper is usually met by imports. Consumption of wood fuel is significant. In a typical year, the export of forest products amounts to US$37.4 million while imports total US$44.1 million.

Production in 2003 included 9,886,503 cubic metres (cum) roundwood, 4,044,000cum industrial roundwood, 3,515,000cum sawlogs and veneers, 550,000cum sawnwood, 161,000cum wood-based panels, 5,842,503cum wood fuel, 181,642mt charcoal.

Industry and manufacturing
In a typical year for the economy of Paraguay the industrial sector accounts for approximately a quarter of total GDP. Though Paraguay is South America's least industrialised country, the sector does account for just under 20 per cent of the total workforce.

Manufacturing is small-scale and geared to the processing of primary products with agro-industry representing about 70 per cent of total industrial production. Construction contributes approximately 6 per cent of GDP. Manufacturing is centred on the processing of agricultural products, particularly textiles, cotton yarn, wood products, beef products, and industrial and edible oils. The country is self-sufficient in cement and there is an oil refinery (capacity 10,000 barrels per day (bpd)) and steel works (150,000 tonnes per year).

Contrasting with other Latin American countries, which have undergone a process of industrialisation based on import-substitution, development strategy in Paraguay has emphasised export-led growth. This involved minimal protection for domestic industry, whose growth problems have been compounded by the small size of the home market, high freight costs for imported products and the effects of extensive smuggling of a wide range of consumer goods from neighbouring countries.

Tourism
The tourism industry of Paraguay remains underdeveloped, with potential for greater economic productivity. The sector's contribution to total GDP has increased to 7.3 per cent and now accounts for 6.4 per cent of total employment.

In a typical year 211,400 people visit the country, with most arriving from Argentina and Brazil, often on day trips in search of bargains and duty-free goods.

Environment
In 2004, USAID reported that indiscriminate exploitation threatened the country's natural resources. In the eastern border region, which had been largely uncultivated until the 1970s, the rich topsoil was severely eroded and unmanaged use of land was jeopardising the largest underground water aquifer on the continent.

Mining
Paraguay's mining sector is negligible, contributing just 0.5 per cent to GDP in a typical year. The national government has attempted to introduce a programme of financial incentives in order to promote exploration for petroleum, lead and uranium. It has also encouraged mineral prospecting by granting tax concessions. However, few commercial reserves have

been discovered and the sector employs just 0.3 per cent of the country's total workforce.

Studies commissioned by the Dirección General de Recursos Minerales (DGRM), with the support of the United Nations Development Programme (UNDP), have revealed that opportunities exist for the commercial extraction of marble, pyrophyllite, granite, slate, talc, gypsum and lignite.

Paraguay has limited proven mineral reserves and at present mining is concentrated on the extraction of salt, gypsum, limestone, kaolin and other clays. Prospecting has revealed the existence of uranium and bauxite, manganese, iron ore and copper. From the 1990s, none have been found in large enough quantities to overcome the high extraction costs involved.

Hydrocarbons

Paraguay has no proven reserves of crude oil, though the country uses oil for approximately 46 per cent of its total energy consumption. Therefore, Paraguay relies heavily on oil from abroad, importing 25,400 barrels per day (bpd) in 2005. Although oil exploration has failed to yield results in Paraguay, the discovery of oil deposits in the border regions of Formosa (Argentina) and Chaco (Bolivia) have raised hopes that Paraguay may also have oil. Currently however Paraguay relies entirely on imports to meet demand for its crude oil and petroleum products. A new refinery is due to come on stream at Villa Elisa with a capacity of 40,000 barrels per day (bpd). The refining capacity in 2003 was 7,500bpd. In early 2002, Paraguay's state oil company Petropar awarded six companies a one-year concession to transport oil and oil derivatives from Argentina to Paraguayan ports on the Paraguay River. Petropar expects to import some 800,000 cubic metres of petroleum products under this concession. The country does not produce natural gas and consumption is negligible. However due to a possible discovery of commercially viable natural gas in the north-western Chaco region there may be more interest in exploration and possible production. There are discussions about building a 850km pipeline from south Bolivia to Asunción, Paraguay's capital. This would mean that demand for natural gas in Paraguay may increase along with the country becoming an important transit centre for Bolivian natural gas. It is predicted that this pipeline will be operational by late 2004.

Paraguay does not produce or import coal.

Energy

In a typical year Paraguay generates approximately 51.3 billion kilowatthours (kwh) of electricity and consumes just 3.5 billion kwh. Paraguay is the second largest net exporter of electricity in the world, trailing only France.

Paraguay's electricity supplies come mainly from the massive 12.6GW Itaipú hydroelectric plant on the River Paraná, the largest hydroelectric power plant in the world with Brazil as the co-owner, and the 3.2GW Yacyretá plant, with is co-owned by Argentina. Fifty per cent of the energy generated belongs to Paraguay, much of which is exported to Brazil.

Banking and insurance

Paraguay's banking and financial services sector has suffered from numerous crises and bad loans. The sector has undergone slow reform and the government has persisted in its policy of propping up ailing banking houses over recent years.

In 2002, the already weakened financial system was hit by a run on deposits at Banco Alemán, the country's third largest bank, prompting the central bank to place the troubled institution in trusteeship. The monetary authority's swift action prevented the collapse of other institutions, but the financial system remains fragile. Deposits fell by 20 per cent in 2002 and lending activity ground to a virtual halt. Non-performing loans at the end of 2002 stood at 22 per cent for the system as a whole.

The institution with the most problems was the state-owned Banco Nacional de Fomento (BNF) (National Development Bank), where non-performing loans surpass 50 per cent. According to a February 2003 study by the Superintendent of Banks, on a scale of 100 to 400, with 100 being the maximum, BNF scored 400 in the categories 'profitability' and 'liquidity' and 369 in the category 'assets'. In the first half of 2003 discussions were under way in Congress to have the state bail out the bank, an undertaking that is expected to cost at least US$70 million.

Central bank
Banco Central del Paraguay.

Time

GMT minus four hours (GMT minus three hours from October to March)

Geography

Paraguay is a landlocked country in central South America. Bolivia lies to the north, Brazil to the east, and Argentina to the south and west. The River Paraguay effectively splits the country in two, with an area known as the Chaco to the west, which comprises 61 per cent (246,950 square km) of the country's land area. The Chaco is a tract of flat and infertile scrub forest country, inhabited by only 3 per cent of the national population.

In contrast, the eastern region is a much richer area in which most of the population is concentrated.

This region is divided into two by a high ridge of hills. East of the hills lies the Paraná Plateau and west of it lies a fertile plain which stretches to the River Paraguay. This treeless plain is flooded once a year and is covered by coarse grass. In this area rice, sugar, tobacco, grains and cotton are grown.

The Paraná Plateau is 300–600 metres in height. This area was originally forest and has high rainfall. Much of the plateau is located in Argentina and Brazil and the River Paraná runs across it.

The Chaco lying to the west of the River Paraguay is scrub forest used mostly for cattle. Along the river there are grassy plains and clumps of palms, but the land becomes drier towards the west and it is almost desert in the north-west. The Chaco region is divided into the Low Chaco with open palm forest and marshes used for extensive cattle ranching; the Middle Chaco scrubland with a mix of hardwood, including the quebracho tree, bottle tree, and cactus (since 1930 this area has been settled by Mennonites who have formed three colonies with populations of 10,000); and the High Chaco, with low thorn forest cover and very hot summer temperatures. Much of this area is a national park, with jaguars, tapirs, puma and wild hog found here.

Climate

The climate is subtropical with an average annual temperature of 22.5 degrees Celsius (C). The hot season is October–March and the average temperature rises to 31.5 degrees C. The temperate season is from April to September when the average temperature is 14.5 degrees C. The heaviest rains take place during this period, and the average annual rainfall is 150cm. In spring and autumn the arrival of cold fronts from the south can cause temperatures to fall suddenly by 10–20 degrees C within a few hours.

Dress codes

In the cities, businessmen wear European-style clothing; shorts are normally worn only for recreation.

Entry requirements

Passports
Required by all, except tourists from the Mercado Común del Sur (Mercosur) (Common Market of the South).

Visa
Required by all; except citizens from countries included on the list found at www.paraguayembassy.co.uk/exemptlist.h

Paraguay

tm. All visits must commence within 90 days of visa issue. Business travellers should either contact the nearest consular section to request, or download, an application form. An invitation from a local company or organisation, provision of adequate funds for stay and proof of return/onward passage are necessary.

Currency advice/regulations
There are no restrictions on the import/export of foreign or local currency.

Health (for visitors)
Mandatory precautions
Yellow fever vaccination certificates are required if arriving from an infected area.
Advisable precautions
It is advisable to be inoculated against hepititis 'B, D' and 'A', tetanus, typhoid and TB. Dengue fever and rabies are also present. Malaria prophylaxis is an advantage.

Mains water is usually safe to drink in Asunción and other major towns. Elsewhere precautions should be taken. Bottled water is advisable for the first few weeks of any stay. Milk is unpasteurised and should be boiled. Dairy products likely to have been made from local milk should be avoided, and meat and fish should be well cooked.

Public holidays
Fixed dates
1 Jan (New Year's Day), 1 Mar (Heroes' Day), 1 May (Labour Day), 15 May (Independence Day), 12 Jun (Peace of Chaco), 15 Aug (Foundation of Asunción), 29 Sep (Battle of Boquerón), 8 Dec (Immaculate Conception), 25 Dec (Christmas Day).
Variable dates
Maundy Thursday, Good Friday.

Working hours
Banking
Mon–Fri: 0900–1215.
Business
Mon–Fri: 0800–1200 and 14.30–1900; Sat: 0800–1200.
Government
Mon–Fri: 0700–1300.
Shops
Mon–Sat: 0900–2100. Some shops open 0730–2000.

Electricity supply
220V AC, 50 cycles

Social customs/useful tips
Business people are punctual and expect appointments to be kept. Business cards are exchanged on visits and it is usual to shake hands when arriving or leaving an office or home. The best time to visit is between May and September

While most businessmen may speak English, it would be advantageous to have some knowledge of Spanish. It is important to use the correct mode of address in writing or in speech.

Most do not wear a jacket and tie during office hours, but visitors, including businesswomen, are advised to wear lightweight business suits.

A 10–15 per cent tip is usually included on hotel and bar bills.

Security
Normal precautions apply. The level of street crime is much lower than other countries in Latin America.

Getting there
Air
National airline: Transportes Aéreo del Mercosur (TAM Mercusor).
International airport/s: Asunción-Silvio Pettirossi International Airport (ASU), 16km from city; bureau de change, duty-free, restaurants and car hire. Travel time to city centre by taxi or bus is 20 minutes.
Airport tax: International departures US$18; domestic departures US$3, except 24-hour transit passengers.
Surface
Road: There are paved roads from Brazil (Rio de Janeiro-Asunción; length 1,700km) and from Argentina (Buenos Aires-Asunción, length 1,450km) and are considered good, less so the access from Bolivia.
Rail: A regular service by means of a train-ferry runs to Posadas (Argentina), where a connection can be made to Buenos Aires. Services are slow.
Water: There are ferry links with Argentina, Bolivia and Brazil. For journeys to Buenos Aires check the route chosen is the most direct. From Brazil, boats connect Corumba with Asunción.
Main port/s: Asunción (on River Paraguay), approximately 1,500km from the sea; in suitable conditions ships can reach Concepción, 290km upstream; smaller vessels travel another 950km after that.

Getting about
National transport
Air: There are six carriers operating scheduled services to most parts of the country. Planes can be chartered and seats booked on air taxis for many destinations. Flights are frequently affected by weather.
Road: Around 10 per cent of the total network is surfaced, those serving main centres are in good condition. The main route is triangular, linking Asunción, Encarnación and Ciudad del Este. The Trans-Chaco Highway runs to the Bolivian border, but is paved only halfway. Some unsurfaced roads are closed in bad weather conditions; service stations etc may be widely spaced.

Buses: There are frequent express (usually comfortable) services linking major towns; for longer distances it is advisable to make advance bookings (eg Asunción-Encarnación; Asunción-Ciudad del Este).
Rail: The main route is Asunción-Villarrica-Encarnación but the service is slow.
Water: The river Paraná is a major access route from the Atlantic coast. Asunción-Concepción service is not frequent and takes 24 hours, Asunción-Pilar 20 hours, and Asunción-Encarnación nine hours.

City transport
Taxis: In Asunción metered taxis operate with a minimum fare system; they can be hired on time basis; a 10 per cent tip is optional.
Buses, trams & metro: Private companies operate bus and minibus services in the capital. Two tram routes also operate.
Car hire
Foreign or international licences are acceptable. Chauffeur and self-drive cars are available at reasonable rates.

BUSINESS DIRECTORY

The addresses listed below are a selection only. While World of Information makes every endeavour to check these addresses, we cannot guarantee that changes have not been made, especially to telephone numbers and area codes. We would welcome any corrections.

Telephone area codes
The internatioanl direct dialling (IDD) code for Paraguay is +595, followed by area code:

Asunción	21	Encarnación	71
Ciudad Del Este	61	Pilar	86
Concepción	31	Villarrica	541
Coronel Oviedo	521		

Chambers of Commerce
American-Paraguayan Chamber of Commerce, General Diaz 521, Edificio El Faro Internacional, Piso 4, Asunción (tel: 442-136; fax: 442-135; e-mail: pamchamb@conexion.com.py).

British–Paraguayan Chamber of Commerce, Gral Diaz 521, Edificio Internacional Faro, Piso 2, Asunción (tel/fax: 498-274; e-mail:britcham@infonet.com.py).

Paraguay Cámara Nacional de Comercio y Servicios, Estrella 540-550, Asunción (tel: 493-321; fax: 440-817; e-mail: info@ccparaguay.com.py).

Banking
Private Banking Association (ABP), Juan O'Leary y Estrella, 30 Piso Asunción (tel: 491-450; fax: 491-450).

Nations of the World: A Political, Economic and Business Handbook

Banco Alemán Paraguayo, Estrella No 505 y 14 de mayo, Zona Postal 1428, Asunción (tel: 490-166/9, 444-714/6; fax: 447-645).

Banco Comercial Paraguayo, Av Mariscal López 780, Zona Postal 2350, Asunción (tel: 207-251/7, 440-504; fax: 207-259).

Banco Continental, Estrella No 621, Apartado postal 2260, Asunción (tel: 446-915/18; fax: 442-001, 441-377).

Banco de Asunción, Palma Esquina 14 de mayo, Asunción Central (tel: 493-191/8; fax: 493-190).

Banco de Inversiones del Paraguay, Palma No 202, Esquina Nuestra Señora de la Asunción, Apartado postal 702, Asunción (tel: 449-550, 498-593/94; fax: 443-749).

Banco de la Nación Argentina, Chile y Palma, Apartado postal 064, Asunción (tel: 447-433, 449-463; fax: 444-365).

Banco del Paraná, Yegros y 25 de mayo, Apartado postal 2298, Asunción (tel: 446-827, 446-691/5; fax: 498-909).

Banco do Brasil, Oliva y Nuestra Señora de la Asunción, Apartado postal 667, Asunción (tel: 90-121, 90-126; fax: 448-761).

Banco do Estado de São Paulo, Ind Nacional, Esquina Fulgencio R Moreno, Apartado postal 2211, Asunción (tel: 494-981/3; fax: 494-985).

Banco Exterior, Yegros y 25 de mayo, Apartado postal 824, Asunción (tel: 492-072/9; fax: 448-103).

Banco Finamerica, Chile y Oliva, Apartado postal 824, Asunción (tel: 491-021/025; fax: 445-159, 445-604).

Banco General, Chile y Haedo, Apartado postal 3202, Asunción (tel: 496-815/9; fax: 496-822).

Banco Holandés Unido, E V Haedo 103, Esquina Independencia Nacional, Apartado postal 1180, Asunción (tel: 490-001; fax: 491-734).

Banco Nacional de Fomento, Independencia Nacional y Cerro Cora, Asunción (tel: 444-440/1/2/3; fax: 446-053).

Banco Paraguayo Oriental de Inversión y Fomento, Azara 197 Esquina Yegros, Apartado postal 1496, Asunción (tel: 444-212 al 16; fax: 446-820).

Banco Real del Paraguay, Calle Estrella y Alberdi, Apartado postal 1442, Asunción (tel: 493-171/80; fax: 443-664).

Banco Sudameris Paraguay, Independencia Nacional y Cerro Cora, Apartado postal 1433, Asunción (tel: 494-542/8, 444-172/3).

Citibank, Chile, Esquina Estrella, Apartado postal 1174, Asunción (tel: 494-951/9; fax: 444-820).

Interamerican Development Bank (BID), Edif. Aurora 1-3 pisos, Caballero esq. Eligio Ayala, Casilla 1209, Asunción (tel: 492-061; fax: 446-537).

Interbanco, 14 de mayo 339, Apartado postal 392, Asunción (tel: 494-992/5; fax: 448-587).

ING Bank (Internationale Nederlanden Bank), Av España y San Rafael, Apartado postal, 10007 Asunción (tel: 606-423; fax: 606-437).

Lloyds Bank, Palma Esq. Juan E O'Leary, Casilla Postal 696, Asunción (tel: 443-580; fax: 443-569).

Central bank
Banco Central del Paraguay, Federación Rusa y Sargento Marecos, Asunción (tel/fax: 610-088; e-mail: ccs@bcp.gov.py).

Travel information
Dirección Nacional de Turismo, Palma 468, Alberdi/Oliva, Asunción (tel: 441-530; fax: 491-230).

Transportes Aéreo Marilia (TAM), Oliva 467, Asunción (tel: 91-041; fax: 96-484).

Ministries
Ministry of Agriculture and Livestock, Presidente Franco 479, Asunción (tel: 443-791, 449-614; fax: 441-036).

Ministry of Defence, Avenids Mcal López y Vice Pte Sánchez, Asunción (tel: 204-771; fax: 211-583).

Ministry of Education and Culture, Chile 898 c/ Humaitá, Asunción (tel: 443-078; fax: 443-919).

Ministry of Exterior Relations, Presidente Franco c/ O'Leary, Asunción (tel: 493-872; fax: 493-910).

Ministry of Finance, Chile 128 esq Palmas, Asunción (tel: 440-010; fax: 448-283).

Ministry of Foreign Affairs, Juan E O'Leary y Pte, Franco, Asunción (tel: 494-593, 493-872; fax: 493-910).

Ministry of Health and Public Welfare, Av Petirrossi y Brasil, Asunción (tel: 207-328; fax: 206-700).

Ministry of Housing, Chile 128 c/ Palma, Asunción (tel: 440-010; fax: 448-283).

Ministry of Industry and Commerce, Avenida España 323, Asunción (tel: 204-638; fax: 213-529; internet site: http://www.mic.gov.py).

Ministry of the Interior, Chile c/ Manduvirá, Asunción (tel: 493-661; fax: 448-446).

Ministry of Justice and Labour, Avda. Dr. Gaspar Rodriguez de Francia c/ EE.UU., Asunción (tel: 447-196, 491-555; fax: 440-066).

Ministry of Public Health and Social Welfare, Av. Pettirossi c/Brasil, Asunción (tel: 207-328; fax: 206-700).

Ministry of Public Works and Communications, Olivia c/ Alberdi, Asunción (tel: 444-411, 496-666; fax: 443-625).

Other useful addresses
Administración Nacional de Electricidad (ANDE) (National Electricity Board), España el Padre Caroloto 360, Asunción (tel: 22-713/719).

Administración Nacional de Telecom (Antelco – Telecommunications Authority), Alberdi, esq General Diaz, Asunción (tel: 44-001).

Agencia Publicitaria Visión, 25 de Mayo, 966, Asunción (tel: 24-796).

Asociación Paraguaya de Cias de Seguros, 15 de Agosto esq Lugano, Casilla 1435, Asunción (tel: 446-474; fax: 444-343).

British Airways, Azara 192, Asunción (tel: 490-020).

British Embassy, Av. Boggiani 5848, C/R16 Boquerón, Casilla 404, Asunción (tel: 595-21 612 611; fax: 595-21 605 007).

Association of Cotton Ginners, CADELPA, Av. Boggiani 4744, Asunción (tel: 595 21 609-272; fax: 595 21 600-739).

Customs Office, Colón c/ Plaza Isabel La Católica, Asunción (tel: 492-202, 495-086; fax: 445-085).

Dirección General de Estadísticas y Censos (National Statistics Office), Dr Miguel Torres, Asunción (tel: 610-331, 663-489).

Federation of Agroindustrial Exporters (FEDEXA), Brasilia 840 c/Sgto. Gauto, Asunción (tel: 208-855, 205-749; fax: 213-971).

Federation of Industrial and Commercial Production (FEPRINCO), Palma 751 c/ Ayolas, Edif. Unión Club, Piso 3, Asunción (tel: 444-963; fax: 446-638).

Importens Association (Centro de Importadores), Montevideo 671, Montevideo 671 c/ E.V. Haedo, Asunción (tel: 441-295, 490-291; fax: 441-295).

Industrial Union of Paraguay (UIP), Cerro Corá 1038 Casilla 782, Asunción (tel: 212-556; fax: 312-260).

Municipality of Asunción, Mariscal López y Cap. Villamayor Bloque A, 1er Piso Asunción (tel: 610-576, 610-577; fax: 610-578).

Paraguayan Embassy (USA), 2400 Massachusetts Avenue, NW, Washington DC 20008 (tel: 202-483-6960; fax:

202-234-4508; e-mail: embapar@erols.com).

Petróleos Paraguayos (Petropar), Oliva 299, 4er piso, Casilla 571, Asunción (tel: 95-117).

Planning Office, Pdte. Franco c/ Ayolas, Edif. Ayfra, Piso 3, Asunción (tel: 491-159, 448-366; fax: 496-510).

Private Construction Association (CAPACO), Victor Hugo casi Cervantes, Asunción (tel: 295-424).

Pro Paraguay (Promotion of Exporters and Importers), Padre Cardozo 469 c/ España, Asunción (tel: 208-276, 208-641; fax: 200-425).

Rural Association of Paraguay (ARP), Ruta Transchaco Km 14, Mariano Roque Alonso (tel: 291-036, 291-061; fax: 291-061).

Siderurgia Paraguaya (Sidepar), Azara 197, 6er piso, esq Yegros, Casilla 2441, Asunción (tel: 95-963).

Soybean Exporters Association (CAPECO), Av. Brasilia 840, Asunción (tel: 208-855; fax: 595 21 213 971).

US Embassy, Avenida Mcal Lopez 1776, casilla 402, Asunción (tel: 213-715; fax: 213-728).

Water Authority (Corporación de Obras Sanitarias Corposana), JoséBerges: e/Brasil y San José, Asunción (tel: 25-001/003).

Internet sites

ABC Color (newspaper): http://www.diarioabc.com.py

Noticias (newspaper) http://www.diarionoticias.com.py

Office of the President: http://www.presidencia.gov.py

The Congress of Paraguay: http://www.camdip.gov.py

Peru

KEY FACTS

Official name: República Peruana (Peruvian Republic)

Head of State: President Alejandro Toledo Manrique (PP) (since Jul 2001)

Head of government: Prime Minister Pedro Pablo Kuczynski (sworn in 16 Aug 2005)

Ruling party: Coalition led by Perú Posible (PP) (Possible Peru)

Area: 1,285,216 square km

Population: 27.55 million (2004)

Capital: Lima

Official language: Spanish, Quechua and Aymara

Currency: Nuevo sol (S/) = 100 centimos

Exchange rate: S/3.35 per US$ (Oct 2005)

GDP per capita: US$2,349 (2004)

GDP real growth: 5.10% (2004)

Labour force: 10.94 million (2004)

Unemployment: 8.80% (2004) (additional underemployment)

Inflation: 3.70% (2004)

Balance of trade: US$2.73 billion 2004

Foreign debt: US$29.20 billion (2003)

Annual FDI: US$1.39 billion (2004)

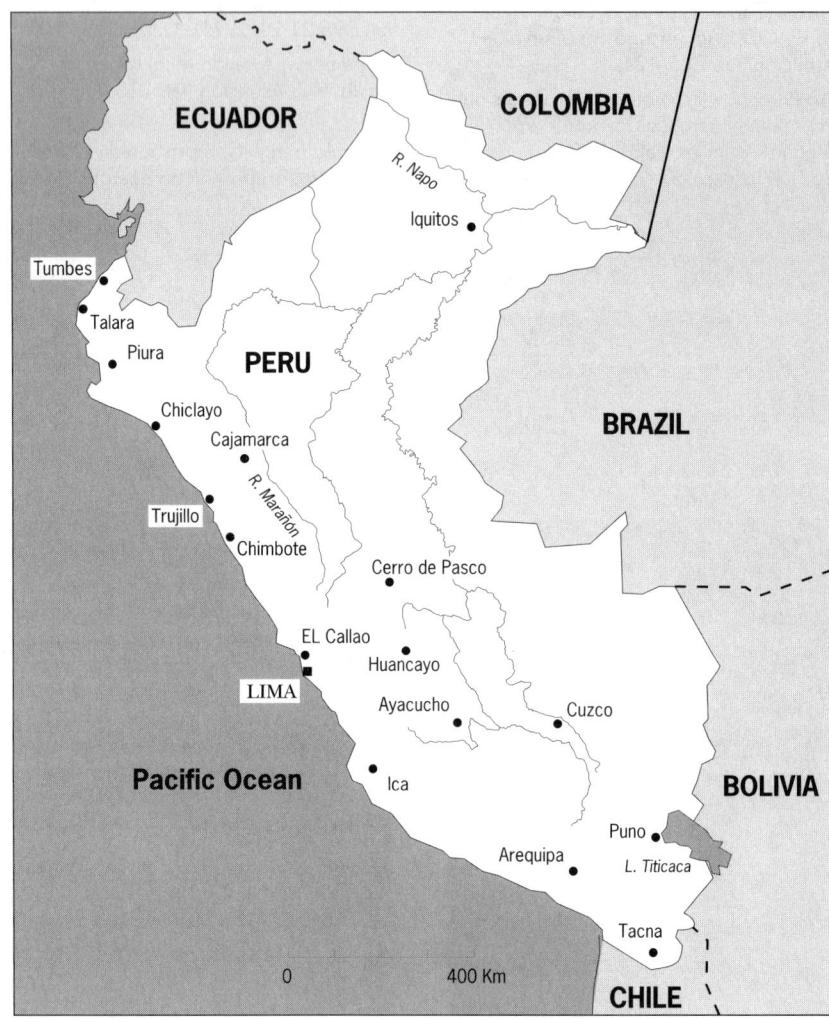

Peruvians will choose from a total of 24 presidential candidates, the highest number in two decades, when they go to the polls on 9 April 2006. In many ways the political cycle in 2005 has been a prelude to the election, with various high profile public figures positioning themselves in anticipation of polling day. Among the candidates are conservative Lourdes Flores, former president Alan Garcia and former army officer and arch nationalist Ollanta Humala. On the economic front, Peru's transformation from a politico-economic loose cannon in previous years, to macroeconomic stability is virtually complete.

Chile: old habits die hard

Peru and Chile have traditionally endured frosty relations, a legacy of the former's defeat during the 1879–84 War of the Pacific. The present generation of political leaders, particularly the hugely unpopular President Alejandro Celestino Toledo Manrique, have used the ongoing dispute with its neighbour as a useful distraction from domestic political malpractice. In November the Peruvian congress approved a proposal by Toledo to redraw the country's southern border to include 38,000sq km of fertile fishing territory presently controlled by Chile. December saw the foreign ministry claim that it was willing to take Chile to international arbitration over a maritime border dispute.

Both consensus and unity are guaranteed by a rhetorical war with Chile and this line of thinking may have been inherent in Peru's newly appointed Prime Minister Pedro Pablo Kuczynski's likening of Chilean political tactics to a 'pincer movement'. Oxford and Princeton educated Kuczynski, who has made no secret of his desire to become president, has also completed something of a political rehabilitation in recent years. The former IMF economist was sacked as finance minister in 2002 but has since regained the post before being appointed prime minister during the summer. In his new position he has attempted to re-position himself as a politically neutral technocrat in the hope of distancing himself from the negative persona of Toledo.

However, Kuczynski suffers from an important political ailment in Latin America, that of association with Washington. His retention of dual US-Peruvian citizenship has left him exposed to accusations of split loyalties from opposition parties. Relations with neighbouring Venezuela have also been strained, Peru having recently recalled its ambassador to the country for 'consultations'. The ire of the Peruvian government was stirred when Venezuelan President Hugo Chávez rolled out the red carpet for the Peruvian nationalist presidential candidate Ollanta Humala to Caracas, thereby interfering in Peruvian internal affairs.

Peru's Chávez?

Following his warm embrace by Chávez, in Caracas, Humala, a retired lieutenant colonel and staunch nationalist, has surged in the polls. The man who led a failed coup in 2000 has drawn obvious comparisons with his leftist Venezuelan sponsor and the recent victory of fellow firebrand Evo Morales in Bolivia has only added to his campaign's momentum. Furthermore, Peru's electoral history has traditionally thrown up victories for outsider 'insurgent' candidates, Alberto Ken'ya Fujimori's victory in 1990 and Toledo's in 2001 being cases in point. Humala's recent rise in the polls and his unique brand of leftist rhetoric has alarmed many within the governing Perú Posible (PP) (Peru Possible) party. He has claimed, in a similar manner to Morales in Bolivia, that the coca trade would be legalised under his watch, and has categorically stated his desire to nationalise several industries. Ominously for foreign business interests in the country, he has talked of the 'colonisation' of natural resources by international companies: 'nationalism is about defending national markets and national interests' is a mantra he has repeated on several occasions.

Fujimori returns… in disgrace

Former president Alberto Ken'ya Fujimori (1990–2000) was arrested in Chile on 7 November 2005. Fujimori's arrest means that three of Peru's most prominent political leaders now live their lives behind bars, an unhappy legacy of the country's political past. The former president, who retains considerable popularity in certain areas following his success in combatting the Shining Path insurgency during the 1990s, was charged with 21 separate offences. The worst of these was the alleged sanctioning of the massacre of 15 people in the impoverished Lima neighbourhood of Barrios Altos, yet his supporters still championed the strongman and placed his name on the provisional ballot for 2006. (This followed previous talk of a 'virtual' campaign for the presidency while in exile in Japan!) Fujimori will not be standing after all, however, as the national electoral agency has ruled that the ex-president cannot run in 2006 and will in fact be ineligible for public office until 2011.

Export-led mining sector fuels growth

Over recent years the economy has been successfully run by a tightly knit group of technocrats that has helped turn the country into a successful story of macroeconomic stabilisation, following years of branding as the politico-economic 'basket-case' of South America. Growth in real GDP has been consistent and looks set to remain within the 4.5–5.5 per cent range, according to the IMF's latest forecast. The rate of inflation has also remained firmly in check, currently standing at approximately 2 per cent. In July a doubling of export revenues since the Toledo government came to power in 2001 was recorded. Total export revenues now stand at US$14 billion. The export boom has been predominantly driven by the high price of minerals courtesy of growing China-led global demand. As a producer of gold, silver, zinc, and molybenum, Peru is uniquely placed to stake advantage of such a boom.

Despite the success of the mining industry in generating large export revenues, the sector remains endangered by a problem of violence simmering under the surface. Attacks by environmental protestors on foreign companies have risen throughout 2005, the latest victim being British mining company Monterrico Metals, though Canadian and American firms have also been targeted. The government has been cricitised by prominent figures in the mining industry for not providing adequate protection in mining zones. Security for foreign mining interests will continue to be paramount in coming years as the industry needs to secure foreign capital investment if it is to develop to full capacity. The debate as to the suitability of the

KEY INDICATORS — Peru

	Unit	2000	2001	2002	2003	2004
Population	m	25.66	25.80	25.90	26.73	*27.55
Gross domestic product (GDP)	US$bn	53.50	54.10	56.90	60.60	*68.39
GDP per capita	US$	2,083	2,052	2,065	2,154	2,349
GDP real growth	%	3.1	0.2	5.2	4.0	5.1
Inflation	%	3.8	2.0	0.2	2.5	3.7
Unemployment	%	6.5	8.2	8.4	9.0	–
Oil output	'000 bpd	100.0	102.0	98.0	92.0	93.0
Exports (fob) (goods)	US$m	7,026.0	7,700.0	–	8,986.0	12,546.0
Imports (fob) (goods)	US$m	7,349.0	7,454.0	7,370.0	8,255.0	9,818.0
Balance of trade	US$m	-323.0	246.0	370.0	731.0	2,728.0
Current account	US$m	-1,628.0	-1,094.0	-862.0	-1,061.0	-70.0
Foreign debt	US$bn	28.4	27.7	27.9	29.2	–
Total reserves minus gold	US$m	8,374.0	8,671.8	9,339.0	9,776.8	12,176.4
Foreign exchange	US$m	8,372.5	8,670.1	9,338.3	9,776.4	12,176.1
Exchange rate	per US$	3.49	3.51	3.49	3.48	3.41

* estimated figure

ministry of mining to set environmental and security regulations is ongoing, with many suggesting the establishment of an independent body similar to the Environmental Protection Agency in the United States.

The Paris Club, some GE executives, and a potential trade deal with the US
In June, then finance minister Kuczynski announced that Peru would pay back up to US$2 billion of its bilateral debt to the Paris Club group of creditor governments – including France, Italy, Spain, Germany and the US – by August 2005. The news came after Peru agreed pre-payment deals with both Russia and Poland. The payment was heralded as the first step in the 'implementation of a cautious and balanced debt management strategy' by the Paris Club. Kuczynski went on to claim that the early repayment would facilitate Peruvian savings of as much as US$400 million per year over the next few years.

In August 2005 Jeffrey Immelt and Jack Welch, current and former directors of US giant General Electric (GE), along with some 24 other GE employees, were arrested on charges of breach of contract. A local businessman, Guilermo Gonzales, claimed that the individuals concerned guzumped him after he invested US$10 million in a joint project. However, biased rulings against foreign operators has been a feature of the Peruvian judicial system over the years and many appeals have been launched. The high-profile nature of the GE case provided the government with a diplomatic problem in that it has been in the midst of bargaining for a trade deal with the United States. Any such further cases and more rumours of judicial unfairness will only add grist to the mill for those intent on taking their capital elsewhere. Significantly, after months of negotiations, Peru and the United States struck a wide-ranging trade agreement in early December.

Outlook

Though his government is by far the most unpopular in South America, Toledo and his team of fellow technocrats have so far executed a tidy economic plan for Peru. Growth is not spectacular but it remains strong and the continuation of sensible macroeconomic policy initiatives will result in continued expansion. However, judicial problems within the country need to be solved and the spectre of violence continues to haunt the largely foreign owned mining industry. Moreover, Peru's hard won economic stability may well be jeopardised by the nascent rise of the dynamic Humala. Victory for the ex-military nationalist, as some polls currently suggest, would undoubtedly mark a leftward shift, though both Peruvians and external observers alike will have to wait until April 2006 for the answer to this most burning of questions.

Risk assessment

Economy	Stable
Politics	Stable
Regional stability	Poor
Stock Market	Stable

COUNTRY PROFILE

Historical profile
1500s The Inca empire stretched from the Pacific Ocean east to the sources of the Paraguay and Amazon rivers and from the region of modern Quito in Ecuador south to the Maule River in Chile.
1532 Francisco Pizarro of Spain led an armed expedition into the region. Weakened by a civil war over succession to the throne, the Inca empire was easily overturned by the Spanish.
1542 The vice-royalty of Peru was established with Lima as its capital.
1569 Francisco de Toledo was appointed by the Spanish crown to administer the colony. He established a harsh, repressive system of government that ensured political stability by co-opting indigenous people as low-level officials. The system of government lasted for almost 200 years.
1820 José de San Martín led an invasion army into Peru with the support of rebel Chilean troops in a regional war against Spanish imperial rule.
1821 Peru became independent from Spain after San Martín's forces captured Lima.
1824 Simón Bolívar (who later led Bolivia to independence) became head of state of a centralised state, which included a unicameral legislature.
1826 Bolívar left Peru, which was subsequently ruled by a series of military commanders.
1845 Ramón Castilla became president, ensuring a period of stability and economic development.
1860 Peru adopted a liberal constitution for the first time.
1864 Peru went to war with Spain over control of the guano-rich Chincha Islands. Aided by Ecuador, Bolivia and Chile, Peru defeated the Spanish.
1879–84 Peru backed Bolivia in the War of the Pacific with Chile, but Chile invaded Peru and occupied Lima.
1884 The Treaty of Ancón was signed with Chile. Peru's nitrate-rich province of Tarapacá was handed over to Chile, which also occupied the provinces of Tacna and Arica. The poor state of the nation's economy, weakened by war and the loss of resource-rich regions, undermined governments for the next 30 years.
1895 Civilian rule began, although it was tainted by corruption and economic mismanagement.
1919 President Augusto Leguía launched an *autogolpe* (self-coup), against his own government in order to abolish democratic rule and establish a dictatorship.
1924 The Alianza Popular Revolucionaria Americana (APRA) (American Revolutionary People's Alliance), the country's first mass-based political party, was formed and led by Haya de la Torre.
1930 Leguía was overthrown by a group, including the military, the ruling oligarchy and APRA. A tripartite system of government was formed between the three groups; APRA soon left the alliance to lead a series of popular uprisings. In the early 1930s, APRA was banned.
1933 Luis Miguel Sánchez Cerro, president since 1931 was assasinated. The Congress appointed General Benavides as president.
1939 Manuel Prado y Ugarteche (a moderate) was elected president; he relaxed the government's attitude to APRA.
1945 Free elections took place and José Luís Bustamente y Rivero won the presidency.
1948 General Manuel Odría, staged a *coup d'état*. His military *junta* banned the APRA.
1962 The APRA became the largest party in congress, but fell short of the one-third required to form a government, and entered a coalition with former military leader Manuel Odría, and his supporters. The military seized power and called new elections.
1963 The election of Fernando Belaúnde Terry as president marked the beginning of genuine democracy in Peru.
1968 Belaúnde nationalised Standard Oil's Peruvian subsidiary, the International Petroleum Company (IPC). General Juan Velasco Alvarado led a palace coup that removed Belaúnde from office. The military *docenio* (12-year rule) began.
1970s The Maoist *Sendero Luminoso* (Shining Path) terrorist group was formed by Abimael Guzman.
1975 Velasco was removed from office by General Franscisco Morales Bermúdez.
1978 A Constituent Assembly was elected, with leftist parties winning an unprecedented 36 per cent of the vote, although APRA won most of the seats.
1979 A new constitution was promulgated, which provided for free elections to be held every five years.
1981 Belaúnde returned to power under fresh elections enabled by the new

constitution. The Peruvian economy was in a weak state, aggravated by the guerrilla group, Shining Path, which attacked rural areas and imposed its rule on villages. Military efforts to eliminate Shining Path were ineffectual. It is estimated that over 70,000 people were killed during the insurgency led by Shining Path. Debt repayment was suspended and Peru was denied further international loans.

1990 Alberto Fujimori won the presidential election. Under international pressure was he introduced a programme of sweeping economic reforms by removing state subsidies, privatising state-owned assets and reducing state involvement in virtually all aspects of the economy. These measures reduced inflation and increased growth.

1992 Guzman, the leader of the Shining Path, was captured. Fujimori instigated an *autogolpe*. He suspended the constitution, dismissed the National Assembly and assumed wide emergency powers, appointing ministers to a new, smaller, unicameral chamber. The economy had begun to recover but regional disparity had increased.

1993 The constitution was reinstated with some amendments.

1995 President Fujimori was elected for a second term. Several setbacks undermined his position including the collapse of foreign direct investment due to the worldwide effects of the Asian financial crisis, and the damage to agriculture from *El Niño*.

2000 Fujimori was sworn in for a third presidential term – after much-criticised elections – without a controlling majority in the National Congress. Fraud tainted his presidency and a bribery scandal prompted him to flee to Japan, from where he resigned. Valentin Paniagua became caretaker president.

2001 Alejandro Toledo won the presidential election and his party, Perú Posible (PP), won the congressional elections.

2002 Power was devolved when 25 regional presidents were elected. The centre-left APRA, led by former president Alan García, took 12 of the 25 regional presidencies.

2003 Toledo's presidency lost its popular support. He dismissed Beatriz Merino as prime minister and appointed Carlos Ferrero Costa.

2004 In February, President Toledo reshuffled his cabinet for the fifth time since coming to power. Prime Minister Ferrero survived a no-confidence vote in November.

2005 Prime Minister Carlos Ferrero resigned after the president appointed his close friend Fernando Olivera Vega as foreign minister. Pedro Pablo Kuczynski became prime minister on 16 August. In November, former President Fujimori was arrested in Chile. Peru and the US signed a trade agreement in December. Also in December, the national government declared a state of emergency in six provinces following the suspected killing of eight police officers by Shining Path guerrillas.

Political structure
Constitution
Peru's constitution dates from 29 December 1993. The country is divided into 25 regions which each elect a president once every five years. Regions are divided into provinces, which in turn are divided into districts governed by mayors elected by direct popular vote every three years. The voting age is 18 years.

Form of state
Presidential democratic republic

The executive
Executive power is vested in the president, who is elected for a five-year term by universal adult suffrage. The president governs with the assistance of a prime minister and an appointed Council of Ministers. The prime minister is president of the Council of Ministers.

National legislature
Legislative authority is vested in a unicameral 120-member National Congress elected for a five-year term from a single national list.

Legal system
The judiciary consists of a 16-member Supreme Court, the ministry of justice and the nine-member Constitutional Court. By constitutional right the judiciary is entitled to at least 2 per cent of the central government budget. Members of the Supreme Court are appointed by the president. The posts are permanent, but members of the court must be aged over 50 and retire at 70.

Last elections
April/June 2001 (presidential); April 2001 (congressional).
Results: Presidential run-off: Alejandro Toledo Manrique (PP) won 53.1 per cent of the vote against Alan Gabriel Ludwig García Pérez 46.9 per cent.
Parliamentary: Perú Posible (PP) (Possible Peru) 26.3 per cent of the vote, 45 seats; Alianza Popular Revolucionaria americana (APRA) (American Revolutionary People's Alliance 19.7 per cent, 26 seats; Unidad Nacional (UN) National Unity) 13.8 per cent, 17 seats; Frente Independiente Moralizador (FIM) (Moralising Independent Front) 11 per cent, 11 seats.

Next elections
April 2006 (presidential and congressional)

Political parties
Ruling party
Coalition led by Perú Posible (PP) (Possible Peru)
Main opposition party
Alianza Popular Revolucionaria Americana (APRA) (American Revolutionary People's Alliance)

Population
27.55 million (2004)
Ethnic make-up
45 per cent indigenous, 37 per cent *mestizo*, 15 per cent white, 3 per cent black, Asian or other.
Religions
Catholic (95 per cent), others (5 per cent).

Education
Adult literacy is relatively high in Peru. The 9 per cent difference in male and female literacy reflects the gender division in education provision.
The government provides free education for children up to the age of 15. Primary education lasts for six years, with secondary education divided into two stages of three and two years each. In rural areas, 40 per cent of the children traditionally help in the fields, with all but a few abandoning their schooling.
Literacy rate: 94 per cent male, 85 per cent female; adult rates (World Bank).
Compulsory years: Six to 15
Enrolment rate: 123 per cent gross primary enrolment of the relevant age group (including repeaters); 73 per cent gross secondary enrolment (World Bank).
Pupils per teacher: 27 in primary schools

Health
About three million people are in the pension and health schemes administered by the state-owned Peruvian Institute of Social Security (IPSS). Salaried workers are obliged to contribute to the scheme, which provides free health care.
The health ministry budget covers health care for those outside the IPSS system. A small charge is made for treatment under this service.
Total expenditure on health is around 5 per cent of GDP, of which government spending is about 55 per cent. Private expenditure is 45 per cent of which some 17 per cent is pre-paid health insurance plans.
HIV prevalence: 0.5 per cent aged 15–49 in 2003 (World Bank)
Life expectancy: 70 years (World Bank)
Fertility rate/Maternal mortality rate: 2.7 births per woman (World Bank)
Infant mortality rate: 26 per 1,000 live births; 8 per cent of children aged under five are malnourished (World Bank).

Head of population per physician/bed: 1 physician and 1.4 hospital beds per thousand people.

Welfare

Peru reformed its pension system in 1993, allowing the investment of individual accounts in real assets and introducing private pension funds to replace state pensions. In addition, the system provides disability and survivors' benefits administered by insurance companies, and old-age pensions.

Employees are required to pay social security taxes equivalent to 13 per cent of their gross income into the public Oficina de Normalización Provisional (ONP) pension fund. Alternatively, employees may opt to pay 11.4 per cent of their salary into a private pension scheme. Workers are allowed to continue joining the old pay-as-you-go system, although the new system urges employers to pay more per worker into the private system than they were paying under the old system. One major challenge for the pension system in Peru is that as much as 51 per cent of the workforce is in the informal economy, covered by neither the old nor the new system.

Main cities

Lima (capital, estimated population 8.3 million in 2004), Arequipa (837,300), Trujillo (725,200), Chiclayo (598,400), Iquitos (401,400), Piura (363,600).

Languages spoken

English is spoken in the main tourist regions.

Official language/s

Spanish, Quechua and Aymara

Media

Press

Press freedom is guaranteed under the 1993 constitution. The biggest selling newspaper is *Ojo*, a tabloid. It has a centrist editorial line. *El Comercio* (Peru's oldest newspaper founded in 1839) is staunchly anti-communist but has become less strident in recent years. It has extensive business and foreign news sections. *Expreso* is the third largest in sales. *El Peruano* is the official State Gazette.

The state owns two tabloid newspapers, *La Crónica* and *La Tercera*. There is also a state-owned domestic news agency, *Andina*, which aims to provide an alternative to the major international news agencies.

Dailies: National dailies and Sunday newspapers are *El Comercio, El Mundo, La Nación, Ojo* and *La República*.

Weeklies: Includes *Revista Caretas*, covering politics, and *Gente (Perú)*.

Business: Publications include the daily *Gestión*, the weekly *Oiga* and *The Andean Report*.

Broadcasting

Radio: There are some 550 (mainly commercial) radio stations and 15 TV channels in Peru. Of the 15 channels, nine are found in Lima and only three transmit nationally.

Television: Major television channels are Panamericana Television and America Television.

Economy

Growth in the Peruvian economy has picked up since a poor performance in 2001. Growth in 2004 was 5.1 per cent while the IMF forecasts growth of 5.5 per cent for 2005 and 4.5 per cent in 2006. Inflation was 3.7 per cent in 2004 and is set to decrease to around 2 per cent by 2006.

The economy had been badly hit by the combined effects of the Asian crisis and the El Niño weather phenomenon in the late 1990s. The maintenance of tight monetary and fiscal policies introduced by Alberto Fujimori when president, to stabilise the economy and reduce public debt merely exacerbated these external shocks. The inauguration of Alejandro Toledo as president in 2001 eased fears over Peru's long-term political and economic stability. Although the economy had been in recession, the flexible exchange rate system and strong financial structure established by the Fujimori administration gave the Toledo administration a strong base with which to pursue economic recovery.

The rise in metal prices and improved market access helped spur GDP growth in 2002 to 5.2 per cent. A surge in growth in the fisheries and manufacturing sectors was accompanied by strong private sector domestic demand, which offset the negative effects of the global slowdown. Private consumption growth was the result of increases in disposable incomes and higher levels of employment. Growth could have been higher had the Toledo administration not cut public expenditure to meet the fiscal deficit target agreed with the IMF. GDP growth slowed in 2003 to 4 per cent, largely due to the decline of investor confidence. Social problems including an increasing unemployment level, poverty and corruption have affected political stability, resulting in a poor investment climate.

External trade

Peru is a full member of the Andean Community free trade area. Other members include Colombia, Ecuador and Venezuela. Peru is also a member of the South American Community of Nations, which aims to integrate the Andean Community and Mercosur by 2007.

As a member of the Andean Community, Peru has bilateral trade agreements with Argentina, Brazil and Chile. In 2002, the US Congress voted to allow Peru duty-free access for a range of Peruvian products, including textiles and apparel, under the Andean Trade Promotion and Drug Eradication Act.

Imports

Principal imports are petroleum and petroleum products, plastics, machinery, vehicles, iron and steel, wheat and paper.

Main sources: US (29.2 per cent total, 2004), Spain (8.5 per cent), Chile (6.9 per cent), Brazil (5.6 per cent), Colombia (5.2 per cent), China (4.0 per cent)

Exports

Main exports include mining – copper, gold, zinc (typically 40 per cent of total), crude petroleum and petroleum products, and coffee.

Main destinations: US (29.5 per cent total, 2004), China 9.8 per cent), UK (8.0 per cent), Chile (5.3 per cent), Japan (4.7 per cent), Switzerland (4.4 per cent)

Agriculture

Farming

The agricultural sector employs approximately 33 per cent of the population and contributes 9 per cent to GDP. Less than 3 per cent of Peru's land area is devoted to arable production and permanent crops. Subsistence farming predominates and productivity is low due to drainage and salinity problems, although productivity increased during the 1990s.

The government has given priority to farming as part of its programme to channel resources to the poorer regions and increase self-sufficiency. The highest priority sectors include rice, corn and wheat. By reviving traditional irrigation and terracing methods the government hopes to extend cultivation through the use of marginal land, while also promoting modern farming techniques.

Production has increasingly begun to focus on the winter export markets of the EU and the US. It is along the northern coast of Peru where export crops such as oranges, mangos, asparagus, passion fruit and limes are grown, together with cotton, rice and sugar for the domestic market. Animal husbandry (sheep, poultry and cattle) is important in southern regions.

Coffee production is receiving considerable support from the US Agency for International Development (USAID), the United Nations Development Programme (UNDP) and GTZ, the German technical co-operation agency. Attempts to improve the production and marketing of Peruvian coffee, which has suffered since the left-wing military government of Juan Velasco effectively nationalised coffee marketing in the 1970s, have proved fruitful.

Crop production in 2004 included: 3,388,800 tonnes (t) cereals in total,

2,996,090t potatoes, 1,816,621t rice, 1,180,769t maize, 168,744t wheat, 176,901t barley, 961,362t cassava, 185,830t sweet potatoes, 185,275t pulses, 7,950,000t sugar cane, 208,538t oil palm fruit, 42,198t olives, 160,460t seed cotton, 181,198t tomatoes, 176,137t green coffee, 28,096t cocoa beans, 1,548t tea, 18,300t various spices, 1,660,310t plantains, 764,846t citrus fruit, 273,159t mangoes, 194,714t papayas, 12,200t tobacco, 3,781,717t fruit in total, 1,974,781t vegetables in total. Livestock production included: 957,907t meat in total, 151,916t beef, 87,721t pig meat, 33,504t lamb, 6,680t goat meat, 32,155t various indigenous meats, 643,171t poultry, 172,753t eggs, 1,285,491t milk, 1,200t honey, 20,600t cattle hides, 9,328t sheepskins, 11,614t greasy wool.

Fishing
The *El Niño* weather phenomenon of the late 1990s severely damaged the Peruvian fishing industry. The sector has now fully recovered and is performing well. One of the world's largest suppliers of fishmeal, Peru is also a major producer of canned, frozen and salted fish.

The shrimp industry has traditionally been a source of local employment, mainly in the northern coastal departments of Tumbes and Piura. Large quantities of shrimp are exported to the US, Canada, Spain and Taiwan. The shrimp industry is investing in improving the water quality of ponds and is also importing genetically treated baby shrimps to prevent white spot virus attacks in the future, which had caused production to decline.

Forestry
In a typical year Peru's exports of forestry products amount to US$94 million while its imports over US$234 million. A little over half of the country's total landmass is covered by forests, most of which are located in the montaña region.

The northern Pacific coast has areas of dry forests and savannas. The state owns all natural forests. There are significant numbers of privately-owned plantations, primarily consisting of eucalyptus. In 1990–2000 deforestation accounted for an annual average loss of 0.40 per cent, the equivalent of 269,000 hectares (ha) of forest cover. Estimates in 2002 showed that forest cover was about 65 million ha. Peru produces a variety of woods including cedar, mahogany, dyewoods and other products, such as rubber and raw quinine from the Amazon Basin. Most production is geared towards sawn timber and panels with some quantities of bagasse pulp and solid wood products. Production in 2003 included 10,265,473 cubic metres (cum) roundwood, 1,192,000cum industrial roundwood, 1,069,000cum sawlogs and veneers, 557,000cum sawnwood, 56,000cum wood-based panels, 9,073,000cum wood fuel, 488,557t charcoal.

Industry and manufacturing
The industrial sector of the Peruvian economy makes a significant contribution of approximately 37 per cent to total GDP. About 15 per cent of the country's total workforce is employed in industry. Manufacturing activity, centred in Lima and Callao, includes food processing, beverages, fishmeal, chemicals, petrochemicals, rubber, plastics, basic metallurgy, metal products, cement, textiles, footwear, paper products, machinery and motor vehicle assembly. Large firms dominate the sector.

Traditionally, Peruvian governments have taken an interventionist and protectionist approach in order to support local industries and promote employment. By 2003, the Toledo administration had overseen the privatisation of all but a few of the state-owned industries not already sold by the previous Fujimori administration.

Tourism
The development of the tourist industry continued throughout 2005. Travel and tourism now accounts for 8.2 per cent of total GDP and employs 7.6 per cent of the country's workforce.

With its rich variety of environments and archaeological sites, Peru has much to offer and tourism is becoming an important contributor to the country's economic revival. More then a million visitors were recorded in 2000. Although numbers fell in late 2001, as a consequence of the earthquake in June and the 11 September terrorist attacks in the US, they picked up again during 2002, a trend which continued in 2003. An important agreement was reached with the US in 2002, allowing unlimited air traffic between the two countries. Some 927,400 people visited Peru in 2004.

Mining
Peru's mining sector contributes approximately 15 per cent to total GDP. The country remains one of the world's largest producers of silver, copper, zinc and lead. The mining sector as a whole accounts for around 8 per cent of total employment in Peru.

Copper dominates the economy, not only as the main export earner, but also as a major source of employment. Export revenue is set to rise as new investments come on stream. Southern Peru Copper Corporation, controlled by US-based Asarco, remains the largest copper producer with an annual output of around 340,000 tonnes of fine copper content from its mining operations at Toquepala and the open pit Cuajone mine. Minera Yanacocha gold mine is the largest private gold producer in Peru, producing 40 per cent of the country's gold production. Other important minerals include tin, iron and steel. By 2002, the state's role in the sector was limited to supervising the commitments made by companies and administering new concessions. International companies such as Asarco, Avocet Ventures, Barrick Gold, BHP, Cyprus and Arequipa Resources generate much of Peru's mineral production.

Barrick Gold's Lagunas Norte gold deposit exploration during 2002 resulted in an increase in its estimated resource from 3.5 million to 7.3 million ounces of gold. In 2004, after the President had promulgated a law to levy royalties of 1–3 per cent of sales on some mining companies, Anglo American pulled out of an auction to develop a large copper deposit. Violence directed against foreign mining interests in Peru has led the national government to attempt to clamp down on activists.

Hydrocarbons
Peru's proven oil reserves stand at approximately 253 million barrels. Production of oil in Peru has slowed considerably over the past two decades as no new deposits have been unearthed and oil fields have matured.

With oil consumption at nearly 163,000bpd, Peru needs to import oil, mainly from Colombia, Ecuador and Venezuela.

The government hoped for more interest in exploration in 2003 and 2004 after it reduced royalties on oil and gas exploration and production in 2002.

Peru's natural gas reserves totalled 246.21 billion cubic metres (cum) in 2004. Annual production is estimated at 438 million cum, all of which is consumed domestically. The largest gas reserves are located in the Amazon region. Peru's main natural gas field is located at Camisea, with proven gas reserves the equivalent of 2.2 million barrels of oil. Peru produces a small amount of coal, however it is almost entirely reliant on imports to meet domestic consumption levels. In a typical year, Peru produces 20,350 tons, and imports 1,210,000 tons, of coal.

Energy
Approximately half of Peru's 6,100MW of instilled generating capacity is powered by hydroelectric power. The remainder is generated using traditional thermal sources.

Much of Peru's electric sector remains in the hands of the government, including the electric tariff commission (CTE). Many utilities are fully or partly state-owned, including ElectroPeru (the largest generator), Edegel, Egenor, Egasa and Egesur. The privatisation of Egasa and Egesur was abandoned in 2002 following large-scale protests.

Three Colombian companies, Interconexion Electrica (ISA), Trascelca and Empresa de Energia de Bogatá (EEB), took control of Peru's electricity network and set up Red de Energia del Peru to manage the system.

Financial markets
Stock exchange
The Lima Stock Exchange (LSE) opened in 1971.

Banking and insurance
Peru's banking and financial services sector has suffered a series of external shocks in recent years, with the Asian crisis, *El Niño* and turmoil in Brazil and Russia affecting confidence in emerging markets. Restoring confidence in Peru is widely considered to be just a matter of time, with the country's regulatory system among the most effective in the region. Moreover, the presence of foreign competition (foreign banks account for four of the country's top five banks), a tough provisioning system and a federal programme to facilitate commercial debt restructuring, meant that in 2002 the Peruvian banking sector was less affected by external crises than many in the region. Peru's banking sector includes over 25 commercial banks and a number of local savings banks, with the four largest groups accounting for over 60 per cent of the systems assets, loans and deposits.
Central bank
Banco Central de Reserva del Perú
Main financial centre
Lima

Time
GMT minus five hours (except from January to April, GMT minus four hours); Iquitos and Cuzco GMT minus five hours all year.

Geography
The geography of Peru, the third-largest country in South America, ranges from Andean peaks almost 7,000 metres high to tropical Amazonian rain forests and burning coastal deserts.

Peru is bordered by Ecuador and Colombia to the north, Brazil and Bolivia to the east, Chile to the south and the Pacific Ocean to the west.

Almost half the population lives in a narrow coastal strip which covers about 10 per cent of the country's total area. The coastal zone, running 3,079km from Ecuador to Chile, is a desert cut by rivers and oases which are fed by melting snow from the Andes.

The Andes cover around 30 per cent of Peru and form a plateau averaging 3,000 metres high studded with towering peaks. The highest summit is Huascaran at 6,768 metres. In the Andes there are many fertile valleys, such as those of Cuzco and Cajamarca. Lake Titicaca in the south, at an altitude of 3,815 metres, is the highest navigable lake in the world.

East of the Andes, around 60 per cent of Peru's area is covered by the jungle of the Amazon basin. Ecuador claims a large section of the northern Amazonian territory. The area is flat and very low. Iquitos, the main town in the area, is about 4,000km from the mouth of the Amazon but only 106 metres above sea level.

Climate
Although Peru lies between the equator and the tropic of Capricorn, only the Amazonian jungle has a typically tropical climate, with high rainfall and humidity and little seasonal change in temperatures. The effects of altitude in the Andes and the cold Humboldt current flowing up from the south moderates the climate in the central and coastal sections. Temperatures in the capital, Lima, vary only slightly throughout the year due to the cold Humboldt current. They rarely rise above 28 degrees Celsius (C) in summer or dip below 12C in winter. Although Lima is set in a coastal desert, with annual rainfall around 48mm, the sky is overcast with a thick sea mist from June to September. This can be so dense as to resemble light drizzle and requires the use of a raincoat. In the Andes, the rainy season lasts from December to March and makes some road travel hazardous. About three-quarters of Cuzco's average annual rainfall of 80cm falls in this period.

Dress codes
Peruvians dress relatively informally, especially in the summer months from January to March when many government officials and other professionals go to work in casual loose-fitting clothes. In winter, jackets and ties for men and skirts for women are more common.

Entry requirements
Passports
Required by all.
Visa
Required by all business travellers. Applications must include an employer's letter of introduction, or if self-employed, the same from the local chamber of commerce, detailing purpose of visit and length of stay; proof of adequate funds and return/onward passage.

Most tourist visitors from Europe, the Americas, Australasia and Asia do not need visas. For confirmation see http://www.peruembassy-uk.com/ and follow link to visa. Visits, for both business and tourist purposes, are valid for up to 90 days.
Currency advice/regulations
There are no controls on the amount of currency imported. The export of foreign exchange is limited to the amount imported. An official two-tier exchange rate has existed since 1988.

Health (for visitors)
Mandatory precautions
A yellow fever vaccination certificate is required if arriving from an infected area.
Advisable precautions
Yellow fever vaccination is recommended (essential for visits to some rural areas). Diphtheria, TB, typhoid, polio, tetanus and hepatitis A and B vaccinations are also advisable.

Malaria risk exists in some rural areas – prophylaxis is recommended.

Water precautions should be taken – it is advisable to drink only bottled water.

Hotels
In main centres hotels are classified by stars (maximum five) according to available facilities. In smaller towns, the best accommodation is often the government-run *Hoteles Turistas*. All hotel bills include 15–21 per cent service charge and tourism tax. An additional 5 per cent tip is usual.

Visitors arriving in Lima are well advised to inform their hotel of their arrival flight number and time. Most major hotels operate a free courtesy coach service to Jorge Chávez airport and will meet arriving guests.

Public holidays
Fixed dates
1 Jan (New Year's Day), 1 May (Labour Day), 29 Jun (St Peter and St Paul's Day), 28–29 Jul (Independence Day Celebrations), 30 Aug (St Rose of Lima Day), 1 Nov (All Saints' Day), 8 Dec (Immaculate Conception), 24 Dec (Christmas Eve, half-day), 25 Dec (Christmas Day).
Variable dates
Maundy Thursday (half-day), Good Friday.

Working hours
Banking
Mon–Fri, Jan–Mar: 0815–1130.
Mon–Fri, Apr–Dec: 0915–1245. Some banks may open afternooons.
Business
Mon–Fri: 0900–1300 and 1430–1630.
Government
Mon–Fri: 0900–1300 and 1430–1630.
Shops
Mon–Sat: 1000–1300 and 1600–1900.

Peru

Telecommunications
Mobile phones
GSM 1900 service available around the largest cities and towns.

Electricity supply
Generally 220V AC, 60 cycles. Exceptions include Arequipa (220V AC, 50 cycles) and Iquitos (110V AC, 60 cycles).

Social customs/useful tips
It is customary to shake hands on meeting and taking leave. Professional titles should be used and although most people have two family names, only the first is used. The style of business is generally relaxed and the informal *tu* form is commonly used with younger Spanish-speaking business visitors. Meetings should be arranged in advance and reconfirmed. Visiting cards are used. While Peruvians are sometimes inclined to be late for appointments, visitors are expected to be punctual.

Never point the soles of your feet at anyone; it is considered highly insulting.

Security
Internal terrorist groups no longer pose a threat to security in most regions, however *Sendero Luminoso* (Shining Path) terrorists are still active in the Apurimac, Ene and Lower Huallaga Valleys. Travellers on the road between Lima and Cuzco should be aware of the risk of armed robbery and hijacks of buses and cars.

It is not considered safe to walk around the centre of Lima at night. There is a high level of street crime particularly in the city centre. Extreme caution should be taken on all streets, especially in pedestrian precincts. Visitors should be careful not to display valuables – especially at bus stations, railways and airports. Travellers should never journey outside the principal cities after dark and as a general rule are advised to use air travel wherever possible.

If you are robbed, report immediately to the nearest police station and ensure you receive a certified copy of the official statement.

Getting there
Peru's dominant carrier, AeroContinente, collapsed in July 2004 after the US government designated its owner as a 'drug kingpin' and its regular flights across Latin America were halted.

Air
National airline: There has been no national airline since the collapse of Aeroperú in 1999. Plans to expand the small, state-owned Tans were put on hold after a crash in 2005 killed 39 passengers.

International airport/s: Lima, Jorge Chávez International (LIM), 16km west of city; duty-free shop, bar, restaurant, bank, post office, shops, hotel reservations, baggage storage, car hire.

Airport tax: The international airport tax, excepting Lima, is US$10. The international airport tax to be paid in Lima is US$25 and for domestic flights is US$4.

Surface
Road: Road access is possible from Ecuador, Chile and Bolivia via the Pan-American Highway.

Main port/s: Callao, Pacasmayo, Paita, Salaverry, San Juan, Matarani, Chimbote.

Getting about
National transport
Visitors are advised to contact the tourist police or the South American Explorers' Club in Lima for up-to-date information on travel to the interior of the country.

Air: AeroCondor operates regular services between Lima and all main towns. In early 2005 a number of airlines were planning flights in Peru, including Magenta Air, Peru Airlines and Wayra Peru. Spain's Marsans Group, which owns Aerolineas Argentinas and Chile's start-up Aerolineas del Sur, says it hopes to start a Peruvian domestic carrier, or for Aerolineas del Sur to fly within Peru.

Due to weather conditions flights are sometimes delayed or cancelled. It is essential to reconfirm bookings as flights are often overbooked.

Road: Major links include: Pan-American Highway, paved over most of the distance, running north to south along the coast from the Ecuador border to Lima (with a north-east arm into the Sierra, through Arequipa and on to the Bolivian frontier). The Trans-Andean Highway runs from Lima to Pucallpa, via La Oroya and Huanuco. The Central Highway connects Lima with La Oroya, Huancayo, Huancavelica, Ayacucho, Cuzco and Puno (linking with the Pan-American Highway spur from Arequipa). Highways between the coast and mountain regions are often blocked by landslides in the rainy season (Dec–Apr).

Buses: Cheap but fairly uncomfortable services are available on the Pan-American Highway north to Ecuador, south to Chile and on the highway to Callejon de Huaylas in northern Andes. Yellow city buses and mini-buses connect Lima with Callao and the residential suburbs.

Rail: There are regular rail services between Lima and La Oroya with branches to Cerro de Pasco, Huancayo and Huancavelica. The Southern Railway of Peru operates between Arequipa and Puno (on Lake Titicaca) with one weekly connection (Wed) by steamer across the lake to Bolivia. Also regular rail connections from Puno to Cuzco. A short line runs from Tacna to Arica in Chile.

Railways have separate summer and winter schedules.

City transport
Taxis: Taxis are the quickest means of travel in main cities. They can be hailed in the street or found on ranks. The use of private, radio-controlled taxis is recommended over cruising taxis. If you must travel alone, never enter a taxi containing anyone other than the driver and always lock the rear doors and roll up the rear windows if possible.

Taxis from *estaciones* (recognised ranks), for example in front of hotels and at airport, usually charge 50 per cent more. *Colectivos* (communal taxis) carrying up to six persons follow set routes into the city suburbs. In Lima they leave from La Colmena on both sides of the Plaza San Martín and charge officially-set fares. It is advisable to agree the fare in advance as they do not have meters.

There is a 50 per cent surcharge after midnight and on public holidays.

Car hire
Major international companies operate in Lima and other main centres. Chauffeur and self-drive cars available. International licence preferred and credit cards essential. Cost includes basic insurance cover. Traffic is congested in Lima.

BUSINESS DIRECTORY
The addresses listed below are a selection only. While World of Information makes every endeavour to check these addresses, we cannot guarantee that changes have not been made, especially to telephone numbers and area codes. We would welcome any corrections.

Telephone area codes
The international dialling code (IDD) for Peru is +51 followed by the area code:

Ayacucho	64	Huancayo	64
Callao	14	Iquitos	94
Cajamarca	44	Lima	14
Cuzco	84	Trujillo	44

Useful telephone numbers
Police: 313-040
Fire: 723-333
Ambulance: 400-200

Chambers of Commerce
American Chamber of Commerce of Peru, Avenida Ricardo Palma 836, Lima 18 (tel: 241-0708; fax: 241-0709; e-mail: amcham@amcham.org.pe).

British-Peruvian Chamber of Commerce, Avenida José Larco 1301, Lima 18 (tel: 617-3090; fax: 617-3095; e-mail: bpcc@bpcc.org.pe).

Lima Cámara de Comercio, Avenida Gregorio Escobedo 398, Lima 11 (tel: 463-8080; fax: 463-2837; e-mail: presidencia@camaralima.org.pe).

Trujillo Cámara de Comercio y Producción de la Libertad, Jirón Junín 454, PO Box 729m Trujillo (tel: 231-114; fax 242-888; e-mail: camara@camaratru.org.pe).

Banking

Banco Banex, Av República de Panamá 3680, San Isidro, Lima 27 (tel: 210-0071; fax: 440-3298).

Banco do Brasil SA, Avenue Camino Real 348, Torre el Pilar Piso 9, San Isidro, Lima 27 (tel: 221-2258; fax: 442-4208).

Banco Continental, Av República de Panamá 3073, 27 Lima (tel: 421-7272; fax: 441-8922).

Banco de Comercio, Jr Lampa 560, Piso 2, Lima 1 (tel: 428-9400; fax: 426-8454).

Banco de Crédito del Perú, Av Huarochiri y Calle Centenario, 156 URB Las Ladera de Melgarejo, Lima 12 (tel: 349-0304; fax: 349-0548).

Banco de Desarrollo, Jr Camaná 700, Lima 1 (tel: 428-6360; fax: 427-7665).

Banco Exterior de Los Andes y de España, Extebandes, Av Canaval Y Moreyra 454, Lima 27 (tel: 442-2121; fax: 440-4572).

Banco Financiero Del Perú, Avenue Ricardo Palma 229, Lima 18 (tel: 241-0324; fax: 447-8766).

Banco Interamericano de Desarrollo, Paseo de la República 3245, 14th Floor, PO Box 270154, San Isidro, Lima 27 (tel: 442-3400).

Banco Interamericano de Finanzas (BIF), Ricardo Rivera Navarrete 543, Lima 27 (tel: 221-2888; fax: 221-2489).

Banco Interandino Saema, Augusto Tamayo 120, Lima 27 (tel: 471-7777; fax: 441-1404).

Banco Internacional Del Perú (Interbanc), Jr De La Unión 600, Lima 1 (tel: 427-2000; fax: 426-2630).

Banco Latino, Av Paseo de la República 3505, Lima 27 (tel: 422-1290; fax: 442-6200).

Banco del Libertador, Av P De la República 3245, San Isidro, Lima 27 (tel: 442-1661; fax: 441-4908).

Banco de Lima, Esquina Puno y Carabaya 698, Lima 1 (tel: 426-8676; fax: 426-2356).

Banco Mercantil del Peru SA, Av Rivera Navarrete 641, Lima 27 (tel: 442-1290; fax: 442-5277).

Banco de la Nación (national bank), Av Nicolas de Piérola, Lima 1 (tel: 426-2000; fax: 426-1133).

Banco del Nuevo Mundo, Av Paseo de la República 3033, 27 Lima (tel: 472-5121; fax: 440-2940).

Banco del Progreso - Probank, Av Javier Prado Este 595, 27 Lima (tel: 421-2800; fax: 441-1058).

Banco Regional del Norte (Norbank), Av Emancipación 199, Lima 1 (tel: 422-3589; fax: 442-2703).

Banco República, Jr Camaná 700, Lima 1 (tel: 444-3214; fax: 444-3774).

Banco Santander, A Tamayo 120, San Isidro, Lima 27 (tel: 221-5000; fax: 221-5001).

Banco Solventa, Av Aviación 2401, Piso 11, San Borja (tel: 225-0505; fax: 225-0505).

Banco Sudamericano SA, Av Camino Real 815, Lima 27 (tel: 221-1111; fax: 442-3392).

Banco del Sur del Perú (Bancosur), Chinchón 986, San Isidro, Lima 27 (tel: 442-1170; fax: 442-1178).

Banco del Trabajo, Av Paseo de La República 3587, San Isidro, Lima 27 (tel: 421-9000; fax: 421-2521).

Banco Wiese Ltdo, Jr Cuzco 245, Lima 1 (tel: 428-6000; fax: 426-3977).

Citibank NA, Av Camino Real 456, Torre Real, Piso 5TO, Lima 27 (tel: 421-400; fax: 440-9044).

Central bank
Banco Central de Reserva del Perú, Jr Miróquesada 441, Lima 1 (tel: 427-6250; fax: 427-5880; internet site: http://www.bcrp.gob.pe).

Travel information
FOPTUR (tourist promotion), Jirón de la Unión 1066, Belen, Lima (tel: 323-559; fax: 429-280).

South American Explorers' Club, Avenida Portugal 146, Lima 00 (tel: 431-4480).

Tourist Bureau of Complaints (INDECOPI), Lima (tel: 224-8600, 224-7888).

Tourist Police (speak several languages; wear white belts over their green dress uniforms), Lima (tel: 471-2994, 471-2809); toll-free number for tourists who are outside of Lima (tel: 0800-422-579).

Ministry of tourism
Ministry of Industry, Tourism, Integration and International Trade Negotiations, Calle Uno Oeste, Corpac, San Isidro, Lima 27 (tel: 224-3347; fax: 224-3264).

Ministries
Ministry of Agriculture, Avenida Salaverry s/n, Jesús María, Lima (tel: 433-3034; fax: 432-9098).

Ministry of Defence, Avenida Arequipa 291, Lince, Lima (tel: 435-9567; fax: 433-5150).

Ministry of Economy and Finance, Jr Junín 339, Lima (tel: 427-3930; fax: 431-7836).

Ministry of Education, Avenida San Develde 160, San Borja, Lima (tel: 436-1240; fax: 433-0230).

Ministry of Energy and Mines, Avenida Las Artes s/n, San Borja, Lima (tel: 475-0206; fax: 475-0689).

Ministry of Fisheries, Calle Uno Oeste s/n, Urbanización Corpac, San Isidro, Lima (tel: 224-3336; fax: 224-3233).

Ministry of Foreign Affairs, Palacio de Torre Tagle, Jr. Ucayali 363, Lima (tel: 427-3860; fax: 426-3266).

Ministry of Health, Avenida Salaverry Cdra 8, Jesús María, Lima (tel: 432-3535; fax: 431-3671).

Ministry of the Interior, Plaza 30 de Agosto 150, San Isidro, Lima (tel: 475-2995; fax: 441-5128).

Ministry of Justice, Scipión e Llona 350, Miraflores, Lima (tel: 441-7320; fax: 440-4407).

Ministry of Labour and Social Promotion, Avenida Salaverry 655, Jesús Maria, Lima (tel: 433-2512; fax: 433-8126).

Ministry of the Presidency, Avenida Paseo de la República 4297, Lima (tel: 446-5886; fax: 447-0379).

Ministry of Transport, Communications, Housing and Construction, Avenida 28 de Julio 800, Lima 1 (tel: 433-1212; fax: 433-9378).

Ministry for Women's Promotion and Human Development, Avenida Emancipación 235 o Esquina Jr Camaná 616, Lima 1 (tel: 426-4336).

Other useful addresses
Adex (export association), Javier Prado Este No 2875, San Borja, Lima (tel: 346-2530; fax: 346-1879; e-mail: postmast@adex.org.pe).

Andean Group, Avda Paseo de la República, Casilla Postal 3237, Lima.

Asociación de Bancos del Perú (Bank Association), Av Antonio Miro Quesada 247 of 409, Lima 1 (tel: 428-8850, 427-6378, 428-5136).

British Embassy, Edif El Pacífico Washington, Piso 12, Plaza Washington, Esq Avda Arequipa, Casilla 854, Lima 100 (tel: 334-738, 839, 334-932; fax: 334-735); for genuine emergency outside hours, leave message on answerphone (tel: 433-4738, 433-4839, 433-4932).

Centromin (Empresa Minera del Centro del Perú SA), Avda Javier Prado Este 2175, San Borja, Apdo 2412, Lima 34 (tel: 365-924; fax: 358-782).

Peru

Cepri (Electroperú Privatisation), Avda Pedro Miotta s/n, Lima 29 (tel: 661-844; fax: 661-899).

Cofide (Corporación Financiera de Desarrollo), Camino Real 390, San Isidro, Lima 27 (tel: 422-550; fax: 423-384).

Conaco (Confederación Nacional de Comerciantes) (National Federation of Commerce), Avenida Abancay 210, Lima (tel: 273-528, 286-026).

Conite (National Commission for Investments and Foreign Technology), Avenida Abancay 500, Piso 6 (MEF), Lima 1.

Copri (Private Investment Promotion Committee), Comité Especial de Minero Perú SA, Bernardo Monteagudo No 222, Piso 12, Lima 17 (tel: 461-4300; fax: 462-7049).

Corpac (Corporación Peruana de Aeropuertos y Aviación Comercial), Aeropuerto Internacional Jorge Chávez, Avenida Faucett s/n, Callao (tel: 529-570).

DHL Worldwide Courier, Avenida La Marina 2469, San Miguel (tel: 525-559).

Electroperú, Centro Cívico, Paseo de la República 144, Lima 1 (tel: 310-664).

Empresa Nacional de Ferrocarriles del Perú, Ancash 207, Apdo 1379, Lima (tel: 289-440).

Enapu SA (National Port Company), Avenida Guardia Chalaca s/n, Callao (tel: 299-210).

Hierroperú (State Iron Company of Peru), Avenida Paseo de la República 3587, Lima (tel: 410-636).

International Translation Service, Avenida Arequipa 3200, San Isidro, PO Box 6046, Lima (tel: 411-396).

Lima Stock Exchange, Pasaje Acuna 191, Lima (tel: 286-280; fax: 337-650).

Mineroperú (State Mining Company of Peru), Avenida Bernardo Monteagudo Orrantia 222, Magdalena del Mar, Lima (tel: 620-740; fax: 627-049).

Peruvian Embassy (USA), 1700 Massachusetts Avenue, NW, Washington DC (tel: 202-833-9860; fax: 202-659-8124; e-mail: peru@peruemb.org).

PetroPerú (State Petroleum Company), Paseo de la República 3361, San Isidro, Lima 27 (tel: 411-919).

PromPerú, Comisión de Promoción del Perú (investment promotion), Edificio Mitinci, Piso 13, calle 1 Oeste S/N, Lima 27 (tel: 224-3125/3271/3279; fax: 224-3323; e-mail: perunet@promperu.gob.pe).

Skyway SA (international courier), Centro Com. Camino Real, 1103, PO Box 2552, Lima 100 (tel: 402-353, 229-225, 416-725).

Sociedad de Industrias (Society of Industries), Los Laureles 365, San Isidro, Lima 27 (tel: 408-700).

US Embassy, Avda Garcilaso de la Vega 1400, Apdo 1995, Lima 100 (tel: 338-000; fax: 316-682).

Internet sites

PromPerú, Comisión de Promoción del Perú (for general information on Peru and daily updates):
http://www.rcp.net.pe/perunet

ADEX, Asociacion de Exportadores:
http://www.adexperu.org.pe

Philippines

KEY FACTS

Official name: Republika ng Pilipinas (Republic of the Philippines)

Head of State: President Gloria Macapagal Arroyo (since Jan 2001; elected 10 May 2004 for a six-year term)

Head of government: President Gloria Macapagal Arroyo

Ruling party: Coalition led by Laban ng Makabayang Masang Pilipino (LaMMP) (Struggle of the Nationalist Filipino Masses) (since May 1998)

Area: 300,439 square km (7,107 islands)

Population: 83.41 million (2004)

Capital: Manila (on Luzon)

Official language: Filipino (based on Tagalog)

Currency: Peso (P) = 100 centavos

Exchange rate: P56.04 per US$ (Oct 2005)

GDP per capita: US$1,014 (2004)

GDP real growth: 6.10% (2004)

Labour force: 33.70 million (2003)

Unemployment: 11.80% (2004)

Inflation: 5.50% (2004)

Balance of trade: -US$6.38 billion 2004

Foreign debt: US$60.30 billion (2003)

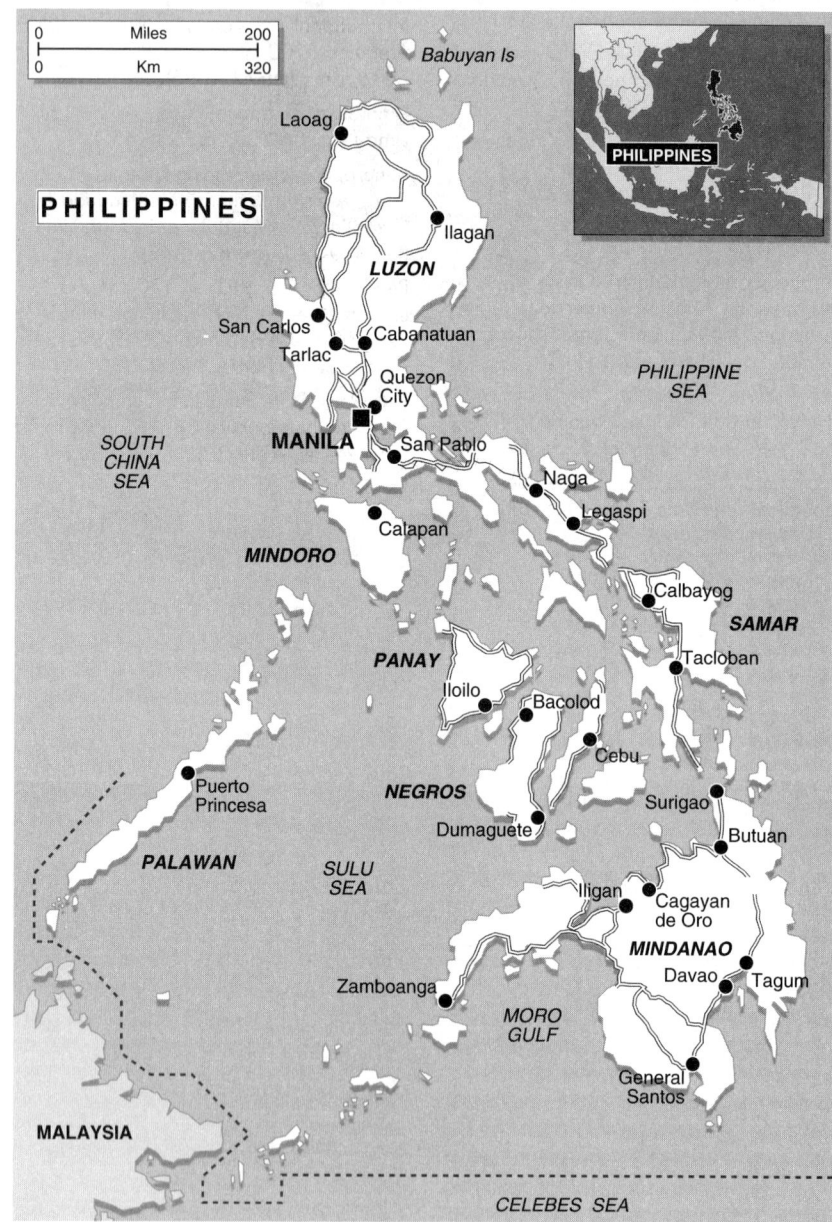

The Philippine Islands became a Spanish colony during the 16th century; they were ceded to the US in 1898 following the Spanish-American War. In 1935 the Philippines became a self-governing commonwealth. Manuel Quezon was elected President and tasked with preparing the country for independence after a 10-year transition. In 1942, during the Second World War, the islands fell under Japanese occupation and US and Filipino soldiers fought together during 1944–45 to retake them.

On 4 July 1946 the Philippines attained independence under Ferdinand Marcos. His 21-year rule ended in 1986, when a

Philippines

widespread popular rebellion forced him into exile and installed Corazon Aquino as president. Her presidency was hampered by several coup attempts, which prevented a return to full political stability and economic development.

Fidel Ramos was elected president in 1992 and his administration was marked by greater stability and progress on economic reforms. In 1992, the US closed its last military bases on the islands. Joseph Estrada was elected president in 1998, but in January 2001 after his stormy trial on corruption charges broke down, was succeeded by his vice president, Gloria Macapagal Arroyo. Arroyo was elected to a six-year term in May 2004, but in 2005 allegations against her led to calls for her impeachment. Key cabinet members resigned. On September 6, the impeachment charges were dismissed by the House of Representatives.

Economy

The Philippines was less severely affected by the Asian financial crisis of 1998 than its neighbours, aided in part by its high level of annual remittances from those of its citizens working overseas and also because it had no sustained run-up in asset prices or foreign borrowing prior to the crisis. From a 0.6 per cent decline in 1998, GDP expanded by 2.4 per cent in 1999 and 4.4 per cent in 2000, but in 2001, in the context of the global economic slowdown, an export slump, and political and security concerns, slowed to 3.2 per cent. As Asia continued to recover, growth in the Philippines accelerated to nearly five per cent from 2002, reflecting the continued resilience of the services sector, improved exports and agricultural output. While final results have not yet been announced, it appears that the economy performed better over 2005 than many expected given the level of political turbulence after the election of President Gloria Macapagal Arroyo in May 2004.

Under her presidency economic reforms advanced at a significant pace. In the power sector, average generation tariffs were raised by half, substantially cutting losses of the state-owned National Power Corporation. In the financial sector, the sale of non-performing assets began to gain traction. In the fiscal area, several tax measures were taken, culminating in Congress passing a landmark expanded value added tax (VAT) law in May 2005 that had the potential to sharply reduce the fiscal deficit. Then, allegations against President Arroyo led to calls for impeachment. The authorities took steps to calm financial markets, but not before reform measures had been compromised and the VAT law put on hold. On 1 September1, the Supreme Court declared the VAT law to be constitutional, and five days later the charges against Arroyo were dismissed. However, a subsequent appeal to the Supreme Court seeking to scrap the VAT law has put it on hold again. Should it eventually be scrapped, it is unlikely the authorities will be able to achieve their goal of balancing the budget by 2010.

But the primary risk to the near-term outlook for the Filipino economy is that the prevailing state of uncertainty proves to be protracted and sidelines economic reforms. If reforms were to stall, investment would likely remain subdued.

Targets missed

The government had predicted an eight per cent growth in exports, but three per cent is the maximum that can now be expected. The main constraints to a better performance came not from domestic concerns, but rather from changes in the global environment. Higher oil prices resulted directly in higher energy and transport costs and indirectly slowed global consumer demand that in turn impacted on the Philippine's export performance.

Largely because of the oil shock, over 2005 the Philippines experienced annual inflation of between seven and eight per cent. This discouraged both consumer as well as business spending and pushed up the cost of doing business in the country. This was exacerbated by the government ignoring the advice of many businessmen and pushing through measures to increase government revenue that included higher taxation. This was in part to alleviate fiscal constraints that limit the country's ability to finance infrastructure and social spending. The Philippines' consistently large budget deficit has produced a high debt level. This has forced Manila to spend a large portion of the national government budget on debt service. Large unprofitable public enterprises, especially in the energy sector, contribute to government debt because of slow progress on privatisation. Credit rating agencies have expressed concern about the Philippines' ability to service its debt which will further influence the imposition of more new revenue measures.

Aided by continued compression of capital spending, the 2005 budget appears to be on course to achieving the deficit target of 3.5 per cent of gross domestic product (GDP). Estimates are that growth over 2005 will have been respectable, but unexciting. GDP is expected to have grown by around 4.7 per cent over 2004. It averaged 4.6 per cent over the first nine months, slower than the 6.1 per cent recorded in 2004, but indications are that it picked up in the fourth quarter. Gross national product (GNP) grew faster than GDP, because of a huge surge in remittance income – up by more than 20 per cent on 2004 to an estimated US$13 billion. The latest estimates of GNP growth over 2005 are 5.5 per cent, with official figures showing average growth of 5.4 per cent in the first nine months.

KEY INDICATORS — Philippines

	Unit	2000	2001	2002	2003	2004
Population	m	76.40	77.00	79.90	81.65	*83.41
Gross domestic product (GDP)	US$bn	74.70	71.00	71.40	80.60	*86.43
GDP per capita	US$	990	860	893	1,010	1,014
GDP real growth	%	4.4	3.2	4.6	4.0	6.1
Inflation	%	5.0	6.1	3.1	3.0	5.5
Unemployment	%	10.1	11.0	15.4	10.7	11.8
Exports (fob) (goods)	US$m	37,298.0	31,242.0	34,380.0	35,414.0	38,728.0
Imports (fob) (goods)	US$m	30,381.0	28,496.0	33,980.0	36,972.0	45,109.0
Balance of trade	US$m	6,917.0	2,746.0	1,600.0	-1,558.0	-6,381.0
Current account	US$m	9,081.0	4,503.0	4,200.0	2,050.0	3,890.0
Foreign debt	US$bn	51.9	52.4	59.9	60.3	–
Total reserves minus gold	US$m	13,052.0	13,476.0	13,329.0	13,655.0	13,116.0
Foreign exchange	US$m	12,936.0	13,353.0	13,200.0	13,523.0	12,980.0
Exchange rate	per US$	44.19	50.99	52.36	54.50	56.05

* estimated figure

Although welcome as a boost to consumer spending, this higher remittance income may have been a reflection of an unwelcome brain drain as professionals increasingly seek employment overseas – a trend that will most likely continue for a while as the economy fails to supply the jobs necessary for a rapidly growing population.

Foreign investment over the year to September/October 2005 is already up on 2004. According to the central bank, net foreign portfolio investments amounted to US$2.1 billion in 2005, or more than four times the US$486.8 million recorded in 2004. Inflows (US$5.5 billion), of which 70 per cent were invested in Manila stocks, exceeded outflows (US$3.4 billion). Philippine equities were up 21.6 per cent in dollar terms, making it one of the best emerging markets in East Asia. Net foreign direct investment (FDI) also surged by 64 per cent to US$863 million in the first 10 months of 2005 from US$525 million a year ago.

It is estimated that US$2.5 billion was generated from the influx of 2.6 million foreign tourists in 2005, up from US$2 billion and 2.3 million tourists in 2004. The growth of revenue from tourism is expected to accelerate in the coming year. Exports of information technology-enabled services, particularly business process outsourcing (BPO) and call/contact centres, doubled to US$2 billion in 2005. Total merchandise exports, however, grew by just 2.7 per cent to US$37.39 billion in the 11 months ending November 2005, way below the government's target of eight to 10 per cent.

Filipinos were net savers over 2005. Official data shows that financial services grew 13.2 per cent year-on-year in the nine months ending September. This partly explains the slowdown in personal consumption expenditure (PCE) growth to 4.8 per cent in the first nine months of 2005, from an average of five to six per cent in previous years.

The slowdown in PCE growth can also be attributed to the poor performance of the agriculture and fishery sectors, which employ a fifth of the population. This sector grew by just two 2.0 per cent in 2005, because of a prolonged dry spell and a string of typhoons. The industry sector grew at a faster rate of 4.6 per cent in the first nine months of 2005 mainly because of a 5.4 per cent increase in manufacturing output, while services grew by 6.1 per cent on the back of a strong performance of the BPO sector.

The improving economic fundamentals are expected to have pushed the value of the peso up by six per cent over 2005, making it the fifth best performing currency in the world and the best in Asia. Gross international reserves rose to US$18.41 billlion as of December 2005, up 13.5 per cent on December 2004.

Risk assessment

Economic	Satisfactory
Political	Satisfactory
Regional stability	Fragile
Stock market	Improving

COUNTRY PROFILE

Historical profile
The Philippines became a Spanish colony in the sixteenth century.
1898 During the Spanish-American War, the independence of the Philippines was declared by General Emilio Aguinaldo, leader of the revolutionary movement, with the support of the US. By the Treaty of Paris, Spain ceded the islands to the US.
1935 A constitution was ratified by plebiscite, giving the Philippines internal self-government and providing independence after 10 years.
1946 The islands were occupied by Japanese forces from 1942–45. US rule was restored at the end of the Second World War, and the Philippines became an independent republic with Manuel Roxas as its first president.
1965 After a succession of presidents, under the control of US economic interests and the Filipino land-owning class, Ferdinand Marcos won elections.
1972 Martial law was imposed by the President, in order to deal with subversive activity and to introduce drastic reforms.
1973 A new constitution was ratified by President Marcos. Transitional provisions gave the president the combined authority of the presidency and the premiership without any fixed term of office.
1981 Martial law was lifted.
1986 Ferdinand Marcos claimed to have defeated his challenger, Corazon Aquino, in the general election. However, it was so blatantly rigged that the result triggered a popular revolt. Marcos and associates fled the country and Aquino took over.
1987 A plebiscite ratified a new constitution with Aquino as president. Congressional elections confirmed her popular support.
1992 In the presidential and legislative elections, Aquino's chosen successor, Fidel Ramos, succeeded her as president, although his supporters failed to achieve an overall majority in the legislature.

1994 President Ramos' Lakas ng Edsa (Lakas-NUCD) (National Union of Christian Democrats) party formed an electoral pact with the Laban ng Makabayang Masang Pilipino (LaMMP) (Struggle of the Nationalist Filipino Masses).
1995 Candidates representing the Lakas-NUCD/LDP alliance secured the bulk of the seats contested in the mid-term elections.
1996 A peace agreement was reached with Mindanao's Muslim rebels, the Moro Islamic Liberation Front (MILF).
1998 Joseph Estrada easily won the presidential elections. Estrada replaced Ramos, who during his six years in power had built up a reputation for ensuring the political stability and economic growth urgently required after the Marcos era.
2000 President Estrada was impeached by the lower house of the legislature after allegations that he had accepted bribes and diverted taxes for personal use.
2001 Estrada was stripped of his powers by a Supreme Court ruling, paving the way for the inauguration of Vice President Gloria Macapagal Arroyo as president. Supporters of President Arroyo won control of the Senate in the legislative elections. The government's offer of enhanced autonomy to Mindanao, instead of independence, was turned down by the MILF.
2002 Filipino and US military forces launched joint exercises near to the stronghold of Abu Sayyaf, the high-profile Muslim rebel whose group was believed to have links with al Qaeda. Tensions in southern Philippines increased following a declaration made by exiled Filipino Muslim leader Nur Misuari for an independent Muslim state. Indonesia, Malaysia and the Philippines signed a pact to counter terrorism and to stop a network that is believed to be bent on turning all three into a single Islamic state.
2003 The army intelligence chief, Brigadier General Victor Corpus, resigned in August after a mutiny led by young army officers calling for the resignation of the government was quelled without bloodshed.
2004 On 10 May, Gloria Arroyo was elected president for a six-year term, defeating her nearest rival, actor Fernando Poe, by more than a million votes. The opposition claimed that there were irregularities in the poll.
2005 In September, the opposition failed in an attempt to impeach President Arroyo for election fraud in 2004.

Political structure
Constitution
Between January 1987 and February 1988, the Philippines adopted a new constitution, elected a newly created two-tier congress, and voted in provincial

Philippines

governors, and town and city councils around the country. The written constitution provides for a presidential system of government with separation of powers and was ratified by national referendum in February 1987. The drafting of the constitution was designed to prevent the emergence of another dictator.

Its principal provisions are that sovereignty resides in the people, and all government authority emanates from them; war is renounced as an instrument of national policy; and civilian authority is supreme over military authority. It has wide powers to check the presidency, including presidential impeachment, the right to lift any imposition of martial law, veto of presidential appointments and human rights protection. These steps completed the rebuilding of democratic structures after two decades of martial law and dictatorial rule by Ferdinand Marcos, whose presidency was ended in the near-bloodless revolution of February 1986.

Suffrage is granted to all citizens over 18 years of age who have resided for at least one year previously in the Philippines, and for at least six months in their voting district. Voting is by secret ballot.

Local government is vested in 13 regions, with provincial, city and municipal councils.

Form of state
Republic

The executive
Executive power is vested in the directly elected president and an appointed cabinet.

The constitution allows the president a single six-year term and prevents any vice president from serving for more than two successive terms.

The president is head of state, chief executive of the republic and commander-in-chief of the armed forces. The vice president is elected on a separate ticket and may represent a different political party.

National legislature
The 1987–88 constitution established a bicameral legislature. It has wide powers to check the presidency, including presidential impeachment, the right to lift any imposition of martial law, veto of presidential appointments and human rights protection.

The Senado (Senate) (upper chamber) has 24 members elected by proportional representation; the 12 senators receiving the largest share of the popular vote serve six-year terms, while the rest serve three-year terms.

The Kapulungan Mga Kinatawan (House of Representatives) (lower chamber) has 260 members, 52 allocated via proportional representation from party lists and 208 elected in single-seat constituencies. House of Representatives members serve terms of three years.

Legal system
Based on Spanish and Anglo-American law.

There is a formal separation of powers between legislative, executive and judiciary. There are also the following courts: the Supreme Court, the court of appeals (formerly the intermediate apellate court), regional trial courts, metropolitan trial courts, municipal trial courts and municipal circuit trial courts. Other laws have created special courts such as the Sandiganbayan (with an anti-corruption brief), and the Sharia courts (for matters involving Muslims). The Supreme Court comprises a chief justice and 14 associate judges, 10 of whom are required to declare on constitutional matters.

Last elections
10 May 2004 (presidential and congressional)
Results: Presidential: Gloria Arroyo was elected for a six-year term, defeating her nearest rival, actor Fernando Poe, by more than a million votes.
Congressional: supporters of President Arroyo won control of the Senate.

Next elections
2007 (congressional); 2010 (presidential).

Political parties
Ruling party
Coalition led by Laban ng Makabayang Masang Pilipino (LaMMP) (Struggle of the Nationalist Filipino Masses) (since May 1998)

Main opposition party
Partido Demokratikong Pilipino-Laban (PDP-Laban)

Population
83.41 million (2004)

Ethnic make-up
Filipinos are of Malayan descent with Chinese and Spanish ancestries. There are around six million tribal Filipinos – 60 ethnological groups – comprising approximately 8 per cent of the total population, mainly around North Luzon, central Luzon and western Mindanao and the Sulu Islands.

Religions
The Philippines is the only country in Asia with a Christian majority. About 85 per cent of the population are baptised Roman Catholics; a sect, the Philippine Independent Church which, since 1902, has not recognised the authority of the Holy See, (4 per cent). There is a strong Muslim presence (5 per cent) especially on Mindanao and a Protestant minority (4 per cent). Buddhism and other beliefs (2 per cent) account for the remainder.

Education
Primary education lasts for four years followed by two years of intermediate and four years of secondary education. Instruction is in both English and Filipino at elementary level, while English is the usual language at secondary level and beyond. However, a curriculum for secondary schools, introduced in 1989, made Filipino (Tagalog) the language of instruction for all subjects except mathematics and the sciences.

Both public and private universities offer higher education. Estimates in 2001 showed that 72 per cent of all students were enrolled in private higher education institutions. Public expenditure on education typically amounted to 3.4 per cent of annual gross national income between 1994–1997.

Literacy rate: 95 per cent male and female; adult rates (World Bank).
Compulsory years: 6 to 12
Enrolment rate: 117 per cent gross primary enrolment of relevant age group (including repeaters); 78 per cent gross secondary enrolment (World Bank).
Pupils per teacher: 35 in primary schools

Health
Total expenditure on health is 3–4 per cent of GDP, of which government spending is 45–46 per cent, and foreign spending 3–4 per cent. Private expenditure is 55–56 per cent of which 19–20 per cent is pre-paid health insurance plans.
HIV prevalence: 0.1 per cent aged 15–49 in 2003 (World Bank)
Life expectancy: 69.9 years (World Bank)
Fertility rate/Maternal mortality rate: 3.2 births per woman; maternal mortality 170 per 100,000 live births (World Bank).
Infant mortality rate: 27 per 1,000 live births; 32 per cent of children aged under five are malnourished (World Bank).
Head of population per physician/bed: 0.1 physicians and 1.1 hospital beds typically available per 1,000 people.

Welfare
The government runs a comprehensive social security scheme, providing a retirement fund, hospital coverage, funeral grants, sickness and disability leave and maternity benefits. Three separate and complementary social security programmes are operated by the state. The first is the basic scheme, providing a pension plan and illness, disability and maternity leave. The second is employee compensation covering disability or work related death and the third is medical care, providing for hospital coverage. Despite government intentions, only a small proportion of the population benefit from these schemes. Income disparities

Nations of the World: A Political, Economic and Business Handbook

are extreme, with approximately one out of every four residents in Manila a squatter. Two-thirds of the population live below the national poverty line, with the richest 20 per cent typically receiving more than half of the country's income. At least five million families are estimated to be in extreme poverty or severely malnourished.

Main cities
Metropolitan Manila (on Luzon) (capital, estimated population 10.3 million in 2004). Cebu, on Visayas (761,900), is competing with Manila as the country's business capital; Davao, on Mindanao (911,600); Iloilo, on Panay (384,600).

Languages spoken
English is widely understood and generally used in government and commerce. There are altogether 11 long-established cultural and racial groups, each with their own language. The major linguistic groups are Tagalog, Ilocano, Cebuano, Hiligaynon, Bicolana, Waray, Pampanago and Pangasinense. Other languages include Leytenhon-Samarnon, Maranao, Tausog and highland ethnic languages. Based on a survey by the national census and statistics office, a representative population of 8.6 million Filipinos showed that 2.5 million speak Tagalog as a mother language and 2.1 million speak Cebuano. The rest of the surveyed population speak one of the more than 80 other dialects in the country. Arabic and Chinese dialects are spoken by a minority of the population.

Official language/s
Filipino (based on Tagalog)

Media
Press
Dailies: The major daily and Sunday newspapers include *Abante*, *Ang Pilipino Star Ngayon*, *Sunday Punch* and *Manila Standard*. Others are *The Daily Tribune* (independent), *The Phillippine Post*, *The Manila Times* and the *Manila Bulletin* with a large circulation. Other community dailies include the *Sunstar Daily*, *Mindanao Gold Star Daily* and the *Mindanao Daily Mirror*. English language newspapers with on-line editions updated regularly include the *Philippine Star* (www.philstar.com) and *Philippine Daily Inquirer* (www.inq7.net).
Weeklies: Most dailies have Sunday editions. Other weeklies include *The Leyte Forum*, *The Phillippine Star Week* on Sundays and the *Women's Journal*.
Business: *Agriscope* covers issues on agribusiness. *Channelworld Phillippines* is a monthly business publication.
Periodicals: Periodicals include the women's quarterly *Attitude*.

Broadcasting
Radio: There are approximately 320 radio stations in the Philippines. About 10 per cent are government-owned and there are a handful of non-commercial religious and educational stations. The vast majority, however, are commercial.
Television: There are over 50 originating television stations around the country, five of them in Manila, and about 30 relay stations. All are commercial stations, including the government-owned Channel Four.

Advertising
Advertising is available in the press, radio, television, cinemas and via direct mail.

Economy
Under Ferdinand Marcos' 20-year tenure, the Philippine economy suffered serious stagnation, when compared to its regional neighbours (annual GDP growth 1976–86 was a meagre 1.8 per cent). His economic policy of granting monopoly privileges to cronies while systematically robbing the country, eliminated domestic and foreign investment and increased the trade gap as export competitiveness declined precipitously. During this period income inequality also widened considerably as wealth became concentrated in the hands of the operators of large conglomerates, which still wield considerable influence over the economy. Consequently, the key problem in the post-Marcos era has been how to open up the economy without creating a backlash from big business.

The liberalisation process began in earnest when Fidel Ramos replaced Corazon Aquino as president in 1992. The government subsequently adopted an IMF structural adjustment plan, and legislative and institutional reforms combined with fiscal and monetary stability became key tenets of the government's economic policy. Despite these positive developments under the programme, the Philippine economy continues to be beset by several deep-rooted structural flaws. Concentration of ownership in the hands of a few large companies has slowed the pace of economic liberalisation in the past and will continue to do so. Inadequate and poorly maintained infrastructure, particularly transport, water and sewage services, will hamper economic growth for many years and the state remains unable to provide improved health and education for the country's massive underclass. Further, despite the concentration of agriculture in Mindanao, the inability of recent governments to achieve peaceful co-existence with the Muslim rebels there, discourages much-needed investment on the island. As a result, the Arroyo administration has found it difficult to maintain momentum of the economic reform.

The Philippine economy grew by 6.1 per cent in 2004. In 2003, the Philippines suffered from drought and the service sector declined after an outbreak of Severe Acute Respiratory Syndrome (Sars). Falling interest rates and higher farm output pushed up consumer spending, which offset the effects of global economic slowdown. The Philippines are highly dependent on the economic state of America and Japan, its two major export destinations. In 2004, better weather and improvement in the world economic situation worked to the Philippines' advantage, increasing output in agriculture and manufacturing, and growth exceeded expectaions.

The upward growth rate was not sustained in 2005, when a decline in the global electronics market affected exports and bad weather hit agriculture. Growth for 2005 was forecast at less than five per cent.

External trade
The Philippines has maintained its export-led recovery despite regional slowdowns.

A major contributing factor to the export performance was until 2005 the country's largely unheralded success in electronics. In the long run, however, the country must diversify its export products and markets.

Imports
Principal imports are raw materials, machinery and equipment, fuels, vehicles and vehicle parts, plastic, chemicals and grains.

Quantitative restrictions on all agricultural imports, except rice, are being removed as part of government's reforms. By 2004 a uniform tariff of 4 per cent applied to all goods.
Main sources: Japan (20.6 per cent total, 2004), US (16 per cent), Singapore (8.4 per cent), China (7.4 per cent), Hong Kong (5.3 per cent), South Korea (5.2 per cent), Taiwan (4.5 per cent), Malaysia (4.4 per cent)

Exports
Principal exports are electrical equipment, and transport equipment, garments, optical instruments, coconut products, fruits and nuts, copper products and chemicals.
Main destinations: US (17.5 per cent total, 2004), Japan (15.8 per cent), China (11.4 per cent), Hong Kong (8.3 per cent), Singapore (7.7 per cent), Taiwan (6.4 per cent), The Netherlands (6.0 per cent), Malaysia (5.5 per cent), Germany (4.2 per cent)

Agriculture
Farming
Agriculture, once the main contributor to GDP, has lost its position to the services

Philippines

sector. It accounts for around 14 per cent of GDP and employs about 41 per cent of the labour force.

Some 35 per cent of the total land area is used to cultivate food crops, mostly on smallholdings.

About one-third of the population depends on coconuts, the major export crop. Other commercial crops include sugar cane, hemp, bananas, coffee, tobacco, peanuts and various fruits. Rice and maize production is sufficient to meet domestic demand and other crops include sweet potatoes, cassava, plantains, pineapples, mangoes and cocoa.

The Asian Development Bank has highlighted the need for further reforms to stimulate rural development, to improve irrigation systems, which cover only 42 per cent of irrigatable areas, and to improve the yield and production of paddy rice.

Livestock reared for local consumption include cattle, goats, pigs and poultry.

Crop production in 2004 included: 19,910,190 tonnes (t) cereals in total, 14,496,800t rice, 5,413,390t maize, 1,641,240t cassava, 544,245t sweet potatoes, 69,456t potatoes, 2,800,000t sugar cane, 14,344,920t coconuts, 225,000t oil palm fruit, 170,779t tomatoes, 100,911t green coffee, 5,650t cocoa beans, 4,587t pepper spice, 22,675t ginger, 5,638,060t bananas, 967,535t mangoes, 1,759,290t pineapples, 69,650t Manila hemp, 47,800t tobacco, 179,200t citrus fruit, 1,945,008t oilcrops, 96,000t natural rubber, 12,171,864t fruit in total, 5,134,452t vegetables in total. Livestock production included: 2,363,873t meat in total, 79,720t buffalo meat, 179,229t beef, 1,376,129t pig meat, 33,600t goat meat, 681,385t poultry, 549,000t eggs, 11,550t milk, 15,290t cattle hides.

Fishing
The fishing industry is a big export earner for the Philippines. During the mid-1990s, the annual net trade surplus in fish products amounted to almost US$100 million. In recent years, thousands of hectares, estimated at 40 per cent of former sugar lands, have been converted into shrimp aquaculture ponds. The southern Philippines have traditionally been bountiful for tuna fishermen, but the tuna catch decreased during the 1990s. There is massive overcapacity at Philippine canneries and fishing companies blame years of unrestrained plunder, rising imports and the destruction of the habitat for the slump in the annual catch.

Since the government initiated a reef development plan to create artificial fish spawning grounds, production of fish has increased dramatically, and the Philippines now boasts the largest area of developed estuarine fishponds in southeast Asia.

Forestry
Woodland and forests cover 51 per cent of the land area and contain an estimated 1.45 billion cubic metres of hardwood. Exports of logs were phased out to assist the local timber processing industries. The reafforestation programme is markedly behind schedule, but is being accelerated. Production in 2004 included 15.8 million cubic metres (cum) roundwood, 246,000cum sawnwood, 346,000cum sawlogs and veneers, 151,000cum pulpwood, 13.1 million cum woodfuel, 45,581 tonnes charcoal.

Industry and manufacturing
The industrial sector accounts for around a third of GDP and employs 16 per cent of the workforce.

Food and beverage processing is the main manufacturing activity, including sugar, meat, fruit and vegetables, fish and shrimp processing, soft drinks and alcoholic beverages. Electronics (semiconductors, circuit boards etc) has been the fastest growing sector of the economy. Production of computers and computer parts is principally carried out by Japanese, US, South Korean and Taiwanese companies. Other major industries include petroleum and coal products, chemicals and chemical products. Main light industrial products, which are often produced from imported materials or components, are cotton and textiles, vehicles, chemicals, machine tools and electrical and consumer goods such as refrigerators, radios, TVs, freezers, air-conditioning equipment, sewing machines and watches.

Tourism
Tourism is under-developed, despite recognition of its economic potential and the attractiveness of the Philpines as a destination. Although visitor numbers are rising, at around two million visitors a year, the Philippines compares badly with its regional rivals. The sector contributes less than three per cent to GDP, being expected to account for 2.7 per cent in 2005. The Philippines lacks adequate tourist infrastructure and accommodation away from the resort areas. There are few international airports outside Manila to allow growth in tourism from North America and Europe and terrorism fears are a deterrent. The Philippines did not even benefit much from the impact of the December 2004 *tsunami* on rival destinations. 2004 saw an increase in the number of arrivals from Asian countries, who made up around 50 per cent of the total of 2.29 million visitors. The US remains the largest market with around 21 per cent of visitors in 2004. The government is seeking to promote the Philippines as a tourist destination, although not with the vigour of even its smallestr rivals. The government's aim is to attract five million visitors by 2010.

Environment
Tree felling in the 1980s caused erosion and soil degradation, and in 1989 deforestation was prohibited by law.

New mining regulations introduced after copper leakages into river systems in the mid-1990s, stipulate that companies must allocate 10 per cent of initial costs for environmental improvements, and set aside a further 3–5 per cent of mining and milling costs for an environmental protection programme, to be audited annually.

Fishing methods using dynamite and cyanide to stun tropical fish in the coral reefs have poisoned the reef and killed other sea creatures living there.

Philippines, Indonesia, Australia, Papua New Guinea and Solomon Islands are the countries with the most coral reef fish species.

Mining
The mining sector accounts for 2 per cent of GDP and a similar proportion of the workforce.

The Philippines is the second largest gold producer in Asia (after Indonesia) and one of the top 20 producers in the world. It also produces large quantities of silver. There are copper reserves estimated at 3.6 billion tonnes.

Nickel (fourth-largest reserves in the world after Cuba, New Caledonia and Indonesia), chromium, manganese, zinc, mercury, sand, gravel and rock asphalt are also mined. Other metal and mineral resources include iron ore (reserves, mainly laterite, 1.3 billion tonnes), molybdenum, lead, platinum, palladium, cadmium, cobalt, uranium, phosphate, guano, sulphur, pyrites, limestone, shale, gypsum, clay, kaolin, feldspar and silica sand. Large mineral resources, scattered throughout the archipelago, remain unmeasured and untouched.

Hydrocarbons
The Philippines has proven oil reserves of 152 million barrels and produces around 25,000 barrels per day (bpd). With consumption at 333,000 bpd in 2004, the Philippines is still heavily reliant on imports of crude oil and petroleum products, which amounted to 307,000 bpd in 2004.

The Philippines has natural gas reserves of 133 billion cubic metres (cum). Natural gas is being used to replace oil for electricity generation. The US$4.5 billion development of the Malampaya offshore field, containing up to 73.2 billion cum of gas, is one of the largest investments the

Philippines has ever seen. The field is being developed by an international consortium, including operator Shell Philippines Exploration (SPEX) (45 per cent), Texaco (45 per cent) and the Philippine National Oil Company (PNOC) (10 per cent). The Philippines has around 300 million tonnes of recoverable coal reserves and produces around two million tonnes per year (tpy), which satisfies around 25 per cent of annual domestic consumption. The remaining 75 per cent is imported, primarily from Indonesia, China and Australia. The sector has been affected by the increasing use of natural gas since 2001.

Energy
The Philippines has installed electricity generation of 12GW, 65 per cent of which is thermal, 19 per cent hydroelectric and 16 per cent geothermal.

The country is spearheading the development of environmentally friendly electricity generation. The Philippines is the largest user of geothermal power in the world. The government estimates that geothermal energy has saved the country US$2.5 billion in oil imports since the industry was launched in 1971 and has prevented the emission of thousands of tonnes of hydrocarbon gases – although the coal sector continues to expand. By 2020, almost 50 per cent of the country's power generation, currently dependent on imported oil, will come from gas-driven plants fed from the country's gas fields.

The government also plans to complete the restructuring process that involves full electrification of the archipelago. Private investment in the energy sector will also be encouraged.

Financial markets
Stock exchange
The Philippine Stock Exchange (PSE) was created in 2000 after the merger of the Manila and the Makati Stock Exchanges.

Banking and insurance
The government made its first step to liberalise the banking sector in 2000 when it introduced a general banking law, allowing foreign banks to gradually take over domestic banks. However, the government continues to intervene in the sector, bailing out banks that experience difficulties.

Philippines was removed from the OECD Financial Action Task Force (FATF) list of non-co-operative countries on money laundering in 2005.

Central bank
Bangko Sentral ngPilipinas (Central Bank of the Philippines).
Main financial centre
Manila, Makati

Time
GMT plus eight hours

Geography
The Philippines is an archipelago of 7,107 islands, some large and some only islets, stretching more than 1,700km north to south. Fewer than 5,000 of the islands have names, and less than 2,000 are inhabited.

The nearest neighbours are Indonesia and parts of Malaysia to the south and Taiwan to the north. To the west, across the South China Sea, are Vietnam and peninsular Malaysia. The Pacific Ocean is to the east. The Philippines is situated in the centre of the Asia Pacific region – Japan, South Korea, Hong Kong, Thailand, Malaysia, Singapore and Indonesia can all be reached within two to four hours flying time.

Nearly 95 per cent of the population live on the 11 largest islands. These are mostly mountainous, except for coastal areas and the central plain on Luzon, the largest island (104,683 square km). The second largest island is Mindanao (94,596 square km) in the south, followed by Palawan (14,896 square km), Panay (12,327 square km) and Mindoro (10,245 square km).

There are some 40 active volcanoes scattered across the country and 21 less active ones. The most recent serious volcanic activity was in 1991, when Mount Pinatubo erupted, 90km north-west of Manila.

Climate
The climate is tropical, with an average temperature of 27 degrees Celsius. Tropical storms and typhoons are common between July–October and they can hit any part of the country. The Philippines is vulnerable to the *El Niño* phenomenon, which has severely affected agricultural output. The climate is drier and more comfortable between October–February, and can be very pleasant at the higher elevations.

Dress codes
National dress, often worn by men in the office or at any formal occasion, is the *barong* or embroidered native shirt worn outside the trousers. Reflecting US influence, business suits are almost as prevalent. National dress for women, a scoop-necked dress with ballooning short sleeves, is worn at formal social occasions, not for work. Leisure wear tends to be 'smart casual'.

Entry requirements
Passports
Required by all and must be valid for six months beyond the intended length of stay.
Visa
Required by only a few nationals; all others, including business travellers, may visit for up to 21 days, with proof of return/onward passage. See www.dfa.gov.ph/consular/visa.htm to confirm exemption.

A visa for an extension to the permitted 21 days, particularly for business trips requires a company letter of introduction outlining purpose of visit and itinerary. Contact the nearest consular section to obtain a visa application form.
Currency advice/regulations
Physical import and export of local currency up to P5,000 is allowed. Amounts exceeding this amount require authorisation from the Central Bank of the Philippines.

No restrictions on foreign currency, but amounts over US$25,000 must be declared on arrival and only up to the declared amount can be exported.

Outside the capital, there is a shortage of facilities for changing foreign currency. It is therefore advisable to carry a sufficient amount of local currency when travelling to provinces.

Travellers cheques and major foreign currency may be cashed in large commercial banks and central bank dealers in Metro Manila, and they are also accepted in most hotels, restaurants and shops. Always use authorised money changers or banks.
Customs
Personal effects are allowed duty-free. Visitors may import motorcycles and boats duty-free for stays of up to one month; longer stays require a bond guaranteeing re-export.

Health (for visitors)
Mandatory precautions
Vaccination certificate required for yellow fever if travelling from an infected area.
Advisable precautions
Vaccinations for diphtheria, tuberculosis, hepatitis 'A' and 'B', Japanese B encephalitis, polio, tetanus and typhoid are advisable. Anti-malaria precautions should be taken if travelling outside urban areas. There is a rabies risk. Tap water is generally clean and safe to drink in the towns.

Hotels
A service charge of 13 per cent and a government tax of 10 per cent are usually added to hotel bills, and gratuities are not necessary, but it is customary to leave small change.

Credit cards
International credit cards are widely accepted in major establishments throughout big cities.

Public holidays
Fixed dates
1 Jan (New Year's Day), 9 Apr (Bataan and Corregidor Heroes' Day), 1 May (Labour Day), 12 Jun (Independence Day), 1

Philippines

Nov (All Saints' Day), 30 Nov (Bonifacio Day), 25 Dec (Christmas Day), 30 Dec (Rizal Day), 31 Dec (New Year's Eve).

Variable dates
Maundy Thursday, Good Friday, Easter Monday, National Heroes' Day (last Sun in Aug), Eid al Fitr.
Easter is a major holiday in the Philippines and travel may be disrupted.

Working hours
Working hours vary. Some banks and offices open for a half day on Saturday and, in the Manila area, many shops open for a half day on Sunday.

Banking
Mon–Fri: 0900–1600. Automated banking systems exist (24 hours).

Business
Mon–Fri: 0800–1200/1300, 1300/1400–1700; Sat: 0830–1200.

Government
Mon–Fri: 0730–1130, 1230–1630 or 0800–1200, 1300–1700.

Shops
Mon–Sat: 0930–2030. Most tourist shops open on Sundays.

Electricity supply
220 or 110V AC, 60 cycles with flat and round two-pin plug fittings.

Weights and measures
Metric system, with some local units still in use.

Social customs/useful tips
It is customary to shake hands on meeting and taking leave. If people have an academic or professional title (e.g. doctor, director) they should be addressed by their title. Senior citizens should be treated with particular respect. Shoes should be removed before entering someone's home. Central to Filipino values is the concept of maintaining 'face'. Anything which appears to constitute a slight to a Filipino can have serious consequences. Criticism, however mild, of anyone present is to be avoided. New ideas need to be carefully introduced. A strong personal element to relationships, including those of business and state, makes refusal of frequently proffered hospitality offensive. It can be common to receive a positive answer to a question when the appropriate answer is negative. Reciprocity of hospitality is also required. Despite the appearance of extensive westernisation, conservative values usually apply.

Religious matters are taken seriously, but so is superstition to the extent that no building displays a thirteenth floor. Belief in witches happily co-exists alongside more mainstream religions.

Punctuality is aimed at, but not always achieved. Tips of about 10 per cent for most services are considered standard.
Gift-giving, on the smallest pretext, is widely practised, although the gift itself may be inexpensive.

Old-style chivalry towards women reigns supreme, disguising the extent to which women's dominance at home translates into effective control of the Filipino male. Male visitors will be offered companions as a matter of course, but should not extend this apparent availability into loose behaviour with women outside the bounds of the sex industry.

The most important tradition is that of *utang na loob*, or a lifelong debt of gratitude. This is not just a matter of mutual back-scratching. It is a deeply felt belief that even small favours can never be fully repaid, so that complex networks of loyalties develop, providing a hidden structure to relationships.

Another important tradition is that of *pakikisama*, or co-operating with the team view. Group identification is all-important, reaching back to one's class at school, or to one's village of origin. Approval of the group is often needed before any serious decision is reached. In this context, the supreme importance of family links can be seen, and the paramount significance of family honour understood.

Security
Widespread poverty makes robbery the most common crime. Changing money at a black-market operator will probably deliver you into the hands of pickpockets outside. Foreigners are rarely targetted for more violent crimes.

Getting there
Air
National airline: Philippine Airlines (PAL)
International airport/s: Ninoy Aquino Airport (MNL) is 12km south of Manila; facilities include bank, duty-free, post office and car hire. There are bus and taxi services to the city (by bus 60–90 minutes and 25 minutes by taxi).
Other airport/s: Mactan International Airport (CEB) is on Cebu Island, 45km from the city centre. Hotels provide their own transport and taxis can be hired.
Airport tax: P550 for international departures.

Surface
Water: It may be possible to find a passenger-carrying freight ship from Hong Kong or Singapore. Between Borneo and Mindanao there is the danger of smugglers and pirates operating.
Main port/s: Manila, Batangas City, General Santos, Cebu, Davao, Iloilo, Zamboanga, Cagayan de Oro.
The former US naval base at Subic, a free zone, has port facilities.

Getting about
National transport
Air: Philippine Airlines (PAL), Cebu Air, Air Philippines and AAI-Island Hopper are the main operators of relatively inexpensive domestic flights. Proof of identity may be requested at the check-in.
Road: The network of 164,000km of roads (44 per cent surfaced) is mainly confined to coastal areas, with 68,600km of highways, 60 per cent of which are surfaced. The Maharlika Highway runs from Luzon to Mindanao, with connecting ferry services. Roads can be winding and bumpy.
Buses: There are bus services between the towns and also jeepneys, which are shared taxis equipped to carry up to 14 passengers on bench seats. Fares are similar to buses.
Rail: The only railway line runs from Manila to Ragay in south Luzon. Train services are slow; some have restaurant cars and air-conditioning.
Water: Inter-island services are operated by several companies, some with air-conditioned cabins and dining rooms. There are numerous public and private ports, many serving coastal shipping traffic.

City transport
If travelling by road, allow extra travel time between appointments – there are many traffic jams. Tricycles (motorbikes with sidecars) and trishaws are a cheap alternative for shorter distances around towns.
Taxis: Metered taxis are available. Ensure the driver puts on the meter.
Taxis are plentiful and cheap, but not easy to hail. Because traffic is heavy, drivers frequently will refuse to take you beyond the local district. For this reason it may be worthwhile retaining one driver for the course of a day.
Tipping taxi drivers is not customary.
The Philippines' famous jeepneys are shared taxis which ply regular routes and are cheap.
A taxi from Ninoy Aquino International Airport to the city centre takes about 20–30 minutes.
Buses, trams & metro: Numerous inexpensive bus services operate in and around main centres, but they can be crowded, and knowledge of the area is recommended before travelling by bus. The journey time from Ninoy Aquino International Airport to the city centre is about 60–90 minutes.
Philippine Airlines offers connecting passengers a shuttle service between the city's international and domestic airports (a 20–30 minute ride). The service operates every 15 minutes.
The Metrorail Light Rail Transit (LRT) is an overhead railway which runs from north to south Manila.

1195

Nations of the World: A Political, Economic and Business Handbook

Car hire
Self-drive and chauffeur-driven car hire is available. It is advisable to hire a car and driver. Local driving habits make traffic conditions extremely difficult. International driving licences are acceptable. Driving is on the right-hand side of the road.

BUSINESS DIRECTORY

The addresses listed below are a selection only. While World of Information makes every endeavour to check these addresses, we cannot guarantee that changes have not been made, especially to telephone numbers and area codes. We would welcome any corrections.

Telephone area codes
The international dialling code (IDD) for the Philippines is +63, followed by the area code and subscriber's number:

Bacolod	34	Iloilo	33
Cebu	32	Manila	2
Dagupan	75	San Pablo	49
Davao	82		

Useful telephone numbers
Manila
Police: 599-011
Fire: 581-176

Chambers of Commerce
American Chamber of Commerce of the Philippines, Corinthian Plaza, Paseo de Roxas, Legazpi Village, PO Box 2562, Makati, Manila (tel: 818-7911; fax: 811-3081; e-mail: info@amchamphilippines.com).

British Chamber of Commerce of the Philippines, c/o British Embassy, 6752 Ayala Avenue corner Makati Avenue, Makati, Manila (tel: 580-8359; fax: 893-9073; e-mail: administrator@bccphil.com).

Cebu Chamber of Commerce and Industry, CCCI Center, Corner 11th and 13th Avenues, North Reclamation Area, Cebu City (tel: 232-1421; fax: 232-1422; e-mail: ccci@gsilink.com).

Davao City Chamber of Commerce and Industry, DCCII Building, JP Laurel Avenue, Davao City (tel: 221-4148; fax: 226-4433; e-mail: dccii@skynet.net).

European Chamber of Commerce of the Philippines, Axa Life Center, Sen Gil Puyat Avenue corner Tindalo Street, Makati, Manila (tel: 845-1324; fax: 845-1395; e-mail: info@eccp.com).

Philippine Chamber of Commerce and Industry, Salcedo Towers, 169 HV dela Costa Street, Salcedo Village, Makati, Manila (tel: 844-5713; fax: 843-4102; e-mail: pcci@philcham.com).

Banking
Allied Banking Corp, Allied Bank Centre, 6754 Ayala Avenue corner Legaspi Street, Makati, Manila (tel: 816-331; fax: 816-0921).

Bank of the Philippine Islands, PO Box 1827 MCC, BPI Bldg, Ayala Avenue, corner Paseo de Roxas, Makati City (tel: 818-5541; fax: 815-9434).

Development Bank of the Philippines, DBP Building, Makati Avenue corner Sen Gil Puyat Avenue, Makati, Manila (tel: 818-9511; fax: 818-6699).

Equitable PCI Bank, Equitable PCI Bank Tower 1, Makati Avenue corner HV Dela Costa Street, Makati, Manila (tel: 817-7330; fax: 817-6984).

Land Bank of the Philippines, 319 Sen Gil Puyat Avenue, Makati, Manila (tel/fax: 814-0179).

Metrobank, Metrobank Plaza Building, Sen Gil Puyat Avenue, Makati, Manila (tel: 810-3311; fax: 817-6248; e-mail: metrobank@metrobank.com.ph).

Philippine National Bank, Cacho-Gonzales Bldg, cor Aguirre & Transierra Sts, Legaspi Village, Makati City 1229 (tel: 892-8780; fax: 840-3039).

Rizal Commercial Banking Corporation, RCBC Building, 333 Sen Gil Puyat Avenue, Makati, Manila (tel: 819-3061; fax: 891-0775).

Security Bank Corporation, SBTC Building, 6776 Ayala Avenue, Makati, Manila (tel: 888-7340; fax: 893-2563; e-mail: inquiry@securitybank.com.ph).

Union Bank of the Philippines, SSS (Makati) Building, Ayala Avenue corner Herrera Street, Makati, Manila (tel: 892-0011; fax: 840-0168).

Central bank
Bangko Sentral ng Pilipinas, A Mabini Street, Corner Pablo Ocampo Street, Malate, Manila 1004 (tel: 524-7011; fax: 523-1252; e-mail: bspmail@bsp.gov.ph).

Travel information
Cebu Pacific Air, 30 Pioneer Street corner EDSA, Mandaluyong, Manila (tel: 636-4938; fax: 637-9165; e-mail: feedback@cebupacificair.com).

Hotel and Restaurant Association of the Philippines, Suite 200, Hotel Intramuros de Manila, Plaza San Luis Complex, Cabildo Street corner Ordante Street, Intramuros, Manila (tel: 527-5113; fax: 527-99273; e-mail: hrap@info.com.ph).

Manila Ninoy Aquino International Airport, Pascay City, Manila (tel: 832-2938; fax: 833-1180).

Philippine Airlines (PAL), Philippine Airlines Centre, Legazpi Street, Legazpi Village, Makati, Manila (tel: 815-6481; fax: 813-6715; e-mail: philair@pal.com.ph).

Philippine Motor Association, 683 Aurora Boulevard, Quezon City, Manila (tel: 723-0808; fax: 726-5878; e-mail: pmanet@I-next.net).

Philippine Tourism Authority, Room 522, DOT Building, TM Kalaw Street, Ermita, Manila (tel: 524-2809; fax: 521-2532; e-mail: info@philtourism.com).

Philippine Travel Agencies Association, EGI-Rufino Plaza Taft Avenue corner Sen Gil Puyat Avenue, Pasay City, Manila (tel: 552-0026; fax: 552-0030; e-mail: ptaa@ptaa.org.ph).

Ministry of tourism
Department of Tourism, Kalaw Street, Rizal Park, Manila (tel:524-1751; fax: 521-7374; e-mail: deptour@info.com.ph).

National tourist organisation offices
Tourism Council of the Philippines, Suite 326, PICC Building CCP Complex, Roxas Blvd, Metro Manila (tel: 831-2404, 833-1462).

Ministries
Office of the President, Malacanang Palace, JP Laurel Street, San Miguel, Manila (tel: 564-1451; fax: 742-1641).

Department of Agrarian Reform, Elliptical Road, Diliman, Quezon City (tel: 928-3979; fax: 929-3088).

Department of Agriculture, Elliptical Road, Diliman, Quezon City (tel: 920-4358; fax: 920-3986).

Department of Budget and Mangement, General Solano Street, San Miguel, Manila (tel: 735-4929; fax: 735-4927).

Department of Defence, Camp Aguinaldo, Quezon City (tel: 911-6193; fax: 911-6213).

Department of Education, Culture and Sports, Meralco Avenue, Pasig, Manila (tel: 634-2925; fax: 636-4876).

Department of Energy, PNCP Complex, Meritt Road, Fort Bonifacio, Makati, Manila (tel: 844-2850; fax: 817-8603).

Department of Environment and Natural Resources, Visayas Avenue, Diliman, Quezon City (tel: 929-6633; fax: 920-4352).

Department of Finance, Vito Cruz corner Mabini Street, Malate, Manila (tel: 523-4255; fax: 521-9495).

Department of Foreign Affairs, 2330 Roxas Boulevard, Pasay City, Manila (tel: 831-8955; fax: 832-1597).

Department of Health, Rizal Avenue, Santa Cruz, Manila (tel: 743-8301; fax: 711-6055).

Department of the Interior and Local Government, EDSA corner Reliance Street, Mandaluyong, Manila (tel: 631-8777; fax: 631-8831).

Philippines

Department of Justice, Padre Faura Street, Ermita, Manila (tel: 521-8344; fax: 521-1614).

Department of Labour & Employment, San Jose Street, Intramuros, Manila (tel: 527-2118; fax: 527-3499).

Department of Public Works and Highways, Bonifacio Drive, Port Area, Manila (tel: 527-4111; fax: 527-5635).

Department of Science and Technology, General Santos Avenue, Bicutan, Taguig, Manila (tel: 837-2939; fax: 837-2937).

Department of Social Welfare and Development, Constitution Hills, Quezon City, Manila (tel: 931-8101; fax: 931-8191).

Department of Tourism, Kalaw Street, Rizal Park, Manila (tel:524-1751; fax: 521-7374).

Department of Trade and Industry, 385 Sen Gil Puyat Avenue, Makati, Manila (tel: 895-3515; fax: 896-1166).

Department of Transportation and Communications, Ortigas Avenue, Pasig, Manila (tel: 726-7106; fax: 632-9985).

National Economic and Development Authority, Amber Avenue, Pasig, Manila (tel: 631-3716; fax: 631-3747).

Other useful addresses

ASEAN Investment Promotion Agency, Board of Investments (BOI), Industry and Investments Building, 385 Sen Gil J Puyat Avenue, Makati, Manila (tel: 890-1332; fax: 895-3512).

ASEAN Secretariat, 70 Jl Sisingamangaraja, Jakarta 12110, Indonesia (tel: 62 (21) 726-2991; fax: 739-8234; e-mail: termsak@asean.or.id).

Asian Development Bank, 6 ADB Avenue, Mandaluyong, Manila (tel: 632-4444; fax: 636-2444; e-mail: information@adb.org).

Board of Investments, Industry and Investments Building, 385 Sen Gil Puyat Avenue, Makati, Manila (tel: 897-6682; fax: 895-3521; e-mail: mis@boi.gov.ph).

British Embassy, L V Locsin Building, 6752 Ayala Avenue corner Makati Avenue, Makati, Manila (tel: 816-7116; fax: 819-7206).

Bureau of Export Trade Promotion, New Solid Building, 357 Sen Gil Puyat Avenue, Makati, Manila (tel: 899-0133; fax: 890-4707; e-mail: betpod@dti.gov.ph).

National Economic Development Authority, NEDA Building, Blessed Joseph Maria Escriva Drive, Pasig, Manila (tel: 631-0945; fax: 633-6011; internet site: http://www.neda.gov.ph).

Petroleum Association of the Philippines, c/o 7/F Basic Petroleum Building, C. Palanca Jr Street, Legaspi Village, Makati, Manila (tel: 817-3329; fax: 817-0191).

Philippine Convention and Visitors Corporation, Legazpi Towers, 300 Roxas Boulevard, Pasay City, Manila (tel: 525-9318; fax: 521-6165; e-mail: pcvcnet@info.com.ph).

Philippine Electronics & Telecommunications Federation, 7/F PS Bank Building, Tindalo Street corner Sen.Gil Puyat Avenue, Makati, Manila (tel/fax: 813-6397).

Philippine Exporters Confederation, Roxas Boulevard corner Sen Gil Puyat Avenue, Pasay City, Manila (tel: 833-2531; fax: 831-2132; e-mail: philxprt@I-next.net; internet site: http://www.philexport.org/launch/index.htm).

Philippines Embassy (US), 1600 Massachusetts Avenue, NW, Washington DC 20036 (tel: 202-467-9300; fax: 202-467-9417; e-mail: uswashpe@aol.com).

Philippines Food Processors and Exporters Organisation, Suite 304, JS Contractor Building, 423 Magallanes Street, Intramuros, Manila (tel: 527-5540; fax: 527-5539).

Philippine Information Agency, PIA Building, 1100 Visayas Avenue, Quezon City, Manila (tel: 921-7941; fax: 920-4394; e-mail: odg@pia.gov.ph).

Philippine Iron and Steel Traders Association, 700 Aurora Boulevard, Quezon City, Manila (tel: 722-0536; fax: 721-3599).

Philippine International Trading Corporation, Philippines International Centre, 46 Sen Gil Puyat Avenue, Makati, Manila (tel: 845-4376; fax: 845-4363; e-mail: pitc@info.com.ph).

Philippine Stock Exchange, Exchange Road, Ortigas Centre, Pasig, Manila (tel: 636-0122; fax: 634-5920; e-mail: write@pse.org.ph).

Subic Bay Metropolitan Authority, Building 229, Waterfront Road, Subic Bay Freeport Zone, Olongapo City (tel: 252-4365; fax: 252-3014; e-mail: bgroup@sbma.com).

Textile Producers Association of the Philippines, Room 513, Downtown Center Building, 516 Quintin Paredes Street, Binondo, Manila (tel: 241-1144; fax: 241-1162).

US Embassy, 1201 Roxas Boulevard, Ermita, Manila (tel: 523-1001; fax: 522-4361).

Internet sites

Philippine Consulate General Toronto (gateway site): http://www.philcongen-toronto.com/links.htm

Philippine National Statistics Offices: http://www.census.gov.ph/

Tanikalang Ginto (small gateway site): http://www.filipinolinks.com/business/businformation.html

Pitcairn Island

KEY FACTS

Official name: Pitcairn, Henderson, Ducie and Oeno Islands (Pitcairn Island)

Head of State: Queen Elizabeth II, represented by UK High Commissioner to New Zealand and Governor (non-resident) of the Pitcairn Islands Richard Fell

Head of government: Commissioner of Pitcairn (based in New Zealand), Leslie Jaques

Area: 27 square km (four islands)

Population: 47 (2004) (all on Pitcairn Island)

Capital: Adamstown

Official language: English

Currency: Pound sterling (£) (£=100 pence); New Zealand dollar (NZ$=100 cents)

Exchange rate: £0.57 per US$; NZ$1.45 per US$ (Nov 2004)

COUNTRY PROFILE

Historical profile

1767 Pitcairn's island (as it was originally called, after the young seaman on the *Swallow* who first spotted it) was sighted and its position recorded, although the longitude was incorrect. The island was uninhabited.

1790 Pitcairn's inaccessibility made it a perfect hideaway for the survivors of the mutinous crew of the British HMS *Bounty*, led by the Master's Mate, Fletcher Christian, and their Tahitian consorts when they arrived in January. Because the island's longitude had been misrecorded in 1767 (it was in fact some 200 miles from its recorded position), it was 18 years before an American whaler, the *Topaz* next found the island.

1808 The community of descendants of Christian's original 27-strong group of settlers was discovered by a group of American whalers.

1838 Pitcairn Island was constituted a British colony when Captain R Elliot of HMS *Fly* gave the Pitcairners formal authority to elect 'a magistrate or elder to be periodically chosen among themselves and answerable for their proceedings to Her Majesty's government'.

1855 The prison on Norfolk Island was decreed to be shut down, but because of increased whaling activity and other traffic in the South Pacific it was considered by the British government to be prudent to colonise the island on a permanent basis. As the resources of Pitcairn Island were by now deemed to be insufficient for the islanders it was suggested that the Pitcainers might relocate to Norfolk Island, a similarly isolated island.

1856 The British offer of Norfolk Island was accepted and all 193 islanders were moved on the *Morayshire*, with their material possessions, including animals, tools, relics and documents, arriving on 8 June.

1858 16 of the original Pitcairners left Norfolk Island and returned to Pitcairn Island after a land ownership dispute; the second Pitcairn settlement was established. They were followed by other disenchanted groups over the next decade.

1999 British economic aid to the island was withdrawn.

2000 British police began investigating allegations of child molestation by islanders.

2003 A scientific diving expedition began studying marine life surrounding the islands. In April 13 men went on trial accused of sex crimes. Islanders warned that if the men were jailed their society would collapse through lack of manpower. The UK dismissed the Pitcairn Island commissioner, Leon Salt, amid claims that he had obstructed the pursuit of the alleged child rapists.

2004 The Supreme Court of Pitcairn Island (sitting in New Zealand) dismissed a defence motion, on behalf of the men put on trial for sex offences, which claimed Pitcairn was not British as the islanders had never surrendered their independence and therefore Britain did not have jurisdiction over them. The Court also ruled that the defendants' trial without a jury would not breach their civil rights. Six men were found guilty, including the mayor Steve Christian; four were sentenced to between two and six years in prison and two to community service. Chief Justice Charles Blackie said that harsher sentences could have an adverse effect on life on the island, when, for instance, they are needed as crew on the longboat which brings supplies ashore. On 15 December, Jay Warren, who was cleared of indecent assault, was elected mayor for three years. Leslie Jaques was appointed Commissioner of Pitcairn by the British government. He is charged with developing the island and giving it a future.

2005 Commissioner Leslie Jaques visited the island in March. He wants to encourage new business ventures and eco-tourism and believes that a population of around 155 (compared to the current just under 50) would be a sustainable level. On 24 May the Supreme Court rejected the appeal of the men convicted of sexual assault, and confirmed Britain's sovereignty and jurisdiction over the islands.

Political structure
Constitution
The Pitcairn Order of 1970 and the Pitcairn Royal Instructions provide for the constitution. It established the office of governor, who is appointed by the British monarch. The governor is also the UK High Commissioner to New Zealand. The governor has full legislative authority and has the power to create laws, subject to approval by the monarch. The UK government has the power to legislate directly for Pitcairn Island.
Form of state
British dependent territory
The executive
The UK High Commissioner to New Zealand is also the governor of Pitcairn Island.

The non-resident commissioner of Pitcairn serves as liaison between the governor and the Island Council. He is represented on the island by the governr's representative, who, in 2005 was Richard Dewell.

National legislature
Internal matters are dealt with by the unicameral 10-member Island Council (part nominated and part elected: six elected by popular vote, one appointed by the six elected members, two appointed by the governor and one seat for the Island Secretary; members serve one-year terms and are elected on 24 December every year). Decisions made are implemented by an Internal Committee.

Legal system
The Island Court is presided over by the Island Magistrate elected every three years.

Last elections
December 2004.
Results: Jay Warren was elected mayor for a three-year term. Mike Warren was elected to the Chairmanship of the Council. The chairman and councillors are elected in December each year.

Next elections
24 December 2006 (parliamentary)

Political parties
There are no political parties.
Political situation
The isolation of Pitcairn Islanders was highlighted by the trial in 2003 and 2004 of a group of 13 men for alleged sex crimes. As a result the British government began funding much needed infrastructural projects to provide the community with a worthwhile future. Funds have been made available to upgrade the island's roads, jetty and slipway to improve access for tourists and to make the life easier for the islanders. Communications both physical and long-distance are being increased.

Population
47 (2004) (all on Pitcairn Island)
Ethnic make-up
The inhabitants are mostly descendants of mutineers from the *Bounty*, and Tahitian women, who settled in Pitcairn in 1790.
Religions
Christian (Seventh-day Adventist).

Education
Island children go to school in New Zealand when they are 16 and few return.

Languages spoken
Pitkern (Pitcairn dialect – a mixture of English and Polynesian) uses many eighteenth century expressions.
Official language/s
English

Media
Press
The Pitcairn Islands Study Centre (PISG) publishes *Pitcairn Log* and the on-line *Pitcairn News Page* (http://library.puc.edu/pitcairn/news-summary.html), covering key news stories. The PISG in the UK publishes *UK Log*. *Mare Magazine* publishes a regular column about Pitcairn, in German.
Periodicals: The *Pitcairn Miscellany*, started in 1959, publishes monthly, with a circulation of over 3,000 sent to subscribers worldwide. In May 2004, its on-line version was launched; it is produced by the island's schoolteacher and students; see www.miscellany.pn.
The *Pitcairn Postcard Magazine* is an occasional publication illustrating Pitcairn Island postcards, for collectors and people interested in Pitcairn.

Economy
The major sources of public revenue are the sale of postage stamps, which were first introduced in 1940, to collectors, the sale of handicrafts to passing ships and interest on some investments. There is no retail trading except from a small co-operative store which was established on the island in 1967. Bartering is an important part of the economy.
Except for minor licences, there is no formal taxation – every person between the age of 15–65 is required to perform public work each month, in lieu of taxation. Allowances and wages are paid to members of the community who participate in local government activities and who perform communal services. Local expenditure is estimated and controlled by the Island Council. The financial administration for Pitcairn Island is vested in the governor.
There is no price index maintained on the island and there are no statistics relating to external trade, GDP, trade balance etc. Pitcairn Island licensed its internet suffix '.pn', which generated around US$100,000 in 2000, however revenue has since fallen.
The internet provides the islanders with a small international market. A limited amount of honey is exported, generating around US$15,000 per annum. Pitcairn's isolation means that the honey produced is pure and disease free. The islanders have set up the Pitcairn Island Producer's Co-operative (PIPCO) to promote honey production. In 2003, PIPCO temporarily suspended the sale of honey after supply failed to keep up with demand and a backlog of orders developed.
The Pitcairn Investment Fund (PIF) provides financial subsidies for transportation and costs of island living. To extend the life of the Investment Fund, the islanders modified the subsidy plan to allow the PIF to remain solvent until 2010, extending it at least five years beyond earlier projections.
Modest and simple banking facilities are proposed to allow islanders access to funds through the treasurer's office and made available for purchases in New Zealand.
The island costs around US$1 million a year to run, but brings in just half that in revenue. In August 2004, the Pitcairn Island economy received US$6.5 million from the UK government and the EU to save it from bankruptcy.
A US$6 million upgrade of the island's infrastructure began in February 2005, with the start of upgrades for roads and slipway, and construction of the new jetty. By improving facilities and offering jobs in tourism, agriculture and fisheries, the British government is hoping that the population can be doubled to a more sustainable level.

External trade
Imports
The principal imports are fuel oil, machinery, building materials, textiles, flour, sugar and other foodstuffs.
Exports
The main exports are fruits, vegetables, wood carvings, basketry and stamps.

Agriculture
Farming
The island has highly fertile volcanic soil and rainfall is adequate. Main crops include a wide variety of fruits and vegetables, including citrus, sugar cane, watermelons, bananas, yams, beans and honey. Taro and coconuts are also grown. There is some goat and poultry rearing.
In 2005 the development of a new, US$14,000, nursery began. The potential for exporting Pitcairn plants will be investigated.
Fishing
Fish is caught for the islanders' own consumption.

Industry and manufacturing
Production is limited to handcrafted miro-wood carvings, basketry, Pitcairn Island flags and postage stamps.

Tourism
There are no beaches on Pitcairn and landing on Pitcairn is tricky. The construction of a new jetty began in February 2005.
The UK government has made US$6.6 million available to improve roads, a slipway and the jetty, in anticipartion of attracting tourists.
There will be no more than 30 visitors at any one time and the emphasis will be on

ecotourism. The improvements began in February 2005.

Environment
Deforestation is a problem, caused by historic slash-and-burn agriculture and settlement.

Mining
Manganese, iron, copper, gold, silver, and zinc have been discovered offshore.

Hydrocarbons
There are no known hydrocarbon resources, all fuels are imported.

Energy
Electricity is produced by diesel generators. Two small windmills will be build to gauge the viability of supplying electricity through windpower.

Time
GMT minus nine hours

Geography
The islands consist of Pitcairn Island and three uninhabited islands, Henderson, Ducie and Oeno. Pitcairn is situated about midway between Peru and New Zealand. The island is volcanic in formation and has a rocky coastline with cliffs. Pawala Valley Ridge, 347 metres, is the highest point.

Climate
Subtropical and humid, with temperatures ranging from 13–30 degrees Celsius (C), averaging 18 degrees C in August and 24 degrees C in February. There are south-east trade winds. The rainy season runs from November to March with a possibility of typhoons. Rainfall varies, but can exceed 2,000mm per year.

Entry requirements
Passports
Must be valid for six months beyond the intended length of stay.
Visa
Required by all; referred to as a Licence to Land and Reside. This should be applied for, from the governor (Pitcairn Island Administration Office in Auckland), for visits up to six months. The application must include a certificate of good health, proof of return/onward passage, US$300 per week for maintenance and health insurance (including emergency repatriation). See http://www.government.pn/noticapp.htm for the full list of requirements.

Health (for visitors)
Mandatory precautions
Vaccination certificates are required for yellow fever if travelling from an infected area.
Advisable precautions
Vaccination is recommended for diphtheria, tuberculosis, hepatitis 'A' and 'B', polio, tetanus and typhoid. There is a risk of rabies.

Public holidays
Variable dates
Queen's Official Birthday (second Sat in Jun)

Telecommunications
External contacts are by SSB, wireless telegraphy, radio telephone and one satellite phone. Some islanders are amateur radio enthusiasts.
Internet/e-mail
Satellite connection give Pitcairn residents access to the Internet.

Getting there
Air
There is no airfield on Pitcairn Island. Mangareva, in French Polynesia, is the nearest airstrip.
Surface
Water: There are very few scheduled shipping services, with three regular supply and mail ships per annum from New Zealand. There are no port facilities yet. Vessels anchor or heave to off the island. Longboats go out from the island to the ships to pick up mail, passengers, etc, but bad weather can prevent contact. Ocean Voyages Incorporated organises occasional yacht charters from Tahiti to Pitcairn.

Getting about
National transport
Road: Road are in the process of being upgraded.
Water: In Bounty Bay, on the north side of the island, there is a slip for launching the islanders' longboats.

BUSINESS DIRECTORY
The addresses listed below are a selection only. While World of Information makes every endeavour to check these addresses, we cannot guarantee that changes have not been made, especially to telephone numbers and area codes. We would welcome any corrections.

Telephone area codes
The international direct dialling (IDD) code for Pitcairn Island is +124 followed by the customer's number.

Ministries
Commissioner's and Governor's Office (non-resident), Pitcairn Islands Administration, Private Box 105696, Auckland, New Zealand (tel: 00-9-64-366-0186; e-mail: pitcairn@iconz.co.nz; internet site; http://www.government.pn).

Other useful addresses
Friends of Pitcairn (e-mail: Bkuchau@aol.com).

Pitcairn Island Administration (stamps and flags enquiries) (e-mail: stamps@pitcairn.gov.pn).

Pitcairn Island Study Group, Secretary, David Sleep, 6 Palace Gardens, 100 Court Road, Eltham, London SE9 5NS, UK (tel: (00-44) 020-8859-5033; e-mail: david.sleep@virgin.net).

Pitcairn Log, Editor, Dr Everett L Parker, 719 Moosehead Lake Road, Greenville, ME, USA (tel: (00-1) 0441-9727; e-mail: eparker@midmaine.com).

Pitcairn Postcard Magazine (e-mail: david.ransom@appleonline.net).

Internet sites
Friends of Pitcairn: http://groups.yahoo.com/group/FRIENDSofPITCAIRN/

Official government website: http://www.government.pn/

Pitcairn Island: http://www.lareau.org/pitc.html

Pitcairn Island Study Group: http://www.PISG.org

Pitcairn Miscellany (monthly): http://www.miscellany.pn/

Pitcairn News Page: http://www.library.puc.edu/pitcairn/news-summary.html

Pitcairn Postcard Magazine: http://www.appleonline.net/David.Ransom/Pages/ppm1.html

Poland

KEY FACTS

Official name: Rzeczpospolita Polska (Republic of Poland)

Head of State: President Lech Kaczynski (PiS) (elected Oct 2005)

Head of government: Kazimierz Marcinkiewicz (PiS) (elected 25 Sep 2005)

Ruling party: Prawo i Sprawiedliwosc (PiS) (Law and Justice) leads a minority government with eight non-partisan members of parliament

Area: 312,683 square km

Population: 38.19 million (2004)

Capital: Warsaw

Official language: Polish

Currency: Zloty (Zl) = 100 groszy

Exchange rate: Zl3.25 per US$ (Oct 2005); (currency allowed to float from 11 Apr 2000)

GDP per capita: US$6,227 (2004)

GDP real growth: 5.30% (2004); 4.5% (2005)

Labour force: 16.95 million (2004)

Unemployment: 18.80% (OECD, 2004)

Inflation: 3.50% (2004)

Balance of trade: -US$5.58 billion (2004)

Foreign debt: US$126.69 billion (2004)

Annual FDI: US$56.20 billion (cumulative, 1995–2004, OECD); US$6.20 billion (OECD, 2004)*

* estimated figure

Poland is an ancient nation conceived around the middle of the tenth century. Its fortunes peaked over the next 600 years, but during the following century, the strengthening of the gentry and internal disorders weakened the nation. In a series of agreements between 1772 and 1795, Russia, Prussia and Austria partitioned Poland among themselves. Poland did not regain its independence until 1918, but was then overrun by Germany and the Soviet Union in the second World War. It became a Soviet satellite state following the war, but its government was comparatively tolerant and progressive. Labour turmoil in 1980 led to the formation of the independent trade union *Solidarnosc* (Solidarity) that over time became a political force and by 1990 had won parliamentary elections and the presidency. During the early 1990s the country was able to transform its economy into one of the most robust in Central Europe. Poland steadfastly pursued a policy of economic liberalisation throughout the 1990s and today stands out as a success story among transition economies. Even so, much remains to be done, especially in bringing down the unemployment rate – currently the highest in the European Union (EU).

World Bank assistance

Poland was one of the founding members of the World Bank, participating in the United Nations Monetary Conference in Bretton Woods. After resigning from its membership in the 1950s, it rejoined in June 1986. The World Bank's office in Poland was

1201

opened in 1990 and its first loan to the country was provided in that year. Since then, the World Bank has supported the country's economic transformation through lending, advice and technical assistance.

The bank is currently assisting Poland make the most of its EU membership. It is helping enhance the country's transport infrastructure and the government's capacity to use EU Structural Funds. These are intended to bring improvements to economically depressed and socially deprived areas and to narrow the differences in income between the 'new' and 'old' EU members as fast as possible.

World Bank commitments to the country have totalled US$5719.2 million for 40 operations. Thirteen ongoing projects are mainly focussed on upgrading the infrastructure and energy sectors, protecting the environment, and promoting rural development. Most of the World Bank's policy advice to Poland has been in the form of informal technical notes and papers and through workshops and seminars. The bank has a strong programme to assist Poland in combating corruption. It has also provided advice and analysis on promoting corporate social responsibility and improving the education system.

Privatisation

The privatisation of small- and medium-sized state-owned companies and a liberal law on establishing new firms has encouraged the development of the private business sector in Poland, but legal and bureaucratic obstacles alongside persistent corruption are hampering its further development. The Vodafone group is among companies and investors negotiating to buy a major stake in Polish mobile phone operator, Polkomtel. Over 2006, Telekomunikacja Polska (TP) will be introducing Voice over Internet (VoIP) services in co-operation with Italtel and Cisco and lease WiFi technology to its customers.

The largest operator of fuel depots in Poland, Naftobazy says it will announce profits of 40.8 million zloty for 2005, double those of 2004. Naftobazy says 2006 will be a year of development in which the company will boost profits to more than 54 million zloty and increase revenues by 10 per cent to 233 million zloty.

But, in 2005, progress stalled. The restructuring and privatisation of 'sensitive sectors' (coal, steel, railroads, and energy) is largely on hold. Reforms in health care, education, the pension system, and state administration have resulted in larger-than-expected fiscal pressures. Further progress in public finance depends mainly on reducing losses in state enterprises and overhauling the tax code to incorporate the growing grey economy and farmers, most of whom pay no tax.

Poland in Europe

Poland joined NATO in 1999. With its transformation to a democratic, market-oriented country largely completed, Poland is an increasingly active member of European organisations. It joined the EU in May 2004, and a subsequent surge in exports to the EU contributed to strong growth over that year. Poland stands to benefit from US$23.2 billion in EU funds, available through 2006. Farmers have already begun to reap the rewards of membership via booming exports, higher food prices, and EU agricultural subsidies.

The previous Socialist-led government introduced a package of social and administrative spending cuts to reduce public spending by US$17 billion by 2007, but full implementation of the plan was trumped by election-year politics in 2005. *Solidarnosc* had suffered a major defeat in the 2001 parliamentary elections when it failed to elect a single deputy to the lower house of Parliament. The new leaders of the trade union subsequently pledged to reduce its political role.

Poland now woos Russia. Its new President Lech Kaczynski – elected in December 2005 – has described Russia as a country of exceptional importance to Poland and 'a state with which we would like to have the best relationship possible'. He hoped 2006 would be the year when this would happen – and he will work to see it does. Kaczynski has expressed his intention to work directly with Prime Minister Kazimierz Marcinkiewicz – who took office in October 2005 – in shaping the country's foreign policy.

Russia has subsequently invited Polish companies to invest, modernise old factories and move their assembly lines to Russia, where, it says, companies are unable to satisfy their domestic markets, forcing Russia to import almost 50 per cent of its food. The government would create a special industrial zone to offer better investment conditions. Over the first six months of 2005, Polish companies invested US$111.3 million (357 million zloty) in Russia.

Pipeline politics

However, Kaczynski's words were before Russia's interruption during December of deliveries of natural gas to Poland, when Marcinkiewicz moved fast to open talks with Norway and other potential gas suppliers to boost energy security. He promised to build a new sea port capable of receiving shipments of liquefied natural gas and increase domestic natural gas extraction.

KEY INDICATORS — Poland

	Unit	2000	2001	2002	2003	2004
Population	m	38.65	38.25	38.23	38.20	*38.19
Gross domestic product (GDP)	US$bn	158.50	176.00	183.10	209.60	*241.83
GDP per capita	US$	4,110	4,560	4,730	5,507	6,227
GDP real growth	%	4.0	1.0	1.3	3.3	5.3
Inflation	%	10.1	5.5	1.9	0.8	3.5
Unemployment	%	16.1	16.2	17.8	19.3	19.5
Natural gas output	bn cum	3.7	3.9	4.0	4.0	4.4
Coal output	mtoe	68.1	72.5	70.8	70.8	69.8
Exports (fob) (goods)	US$m	28,255.0	30,275.0	32,950.0	61,000.0	81,596.0
Imports (fob) (goods)	US$m	41,423.0	41,950.0	43,300.0	66,700.0	87,180.0
Balance of trade	US$m	-13,168.0	-11,675.0	-10,352.0	-21,372.0	-5,584.0
Current account	US$m	-9,952.0	-7,166.0	-6,700.0	-277.0	-3,640.0
Foreign debt	US$bn	68.2	70.8	81.9	64.0	–
Total reserves minus gold	US$m	25,656.9	25,648.4	28,649.7	32,579.1	35,323.9
Foreign exchange	US$m	25,414.8	25,161.6	27,959.2	31,724.9	34,552.8
Foreign direct investment (FDI)	US$bn	10.6	6.9	6.1	6.6	7.9
Exchange rate	per US$	4.35	4.09	4.08	3.79	3.65

* estimated figure

Marcinkiewicz has also voiced concerns about the negative impact on Poland of a Russian-German plan to build an undersea gas pipeline across the floor of the Baltic Sea, bypassing Poland.

He says the project means it is unlikely that a second pipeline will be built alongside Russia's Yamal pipeline, which carries natural gas from the Russian far east across Poland to Western Europe. He wants the so-called Yamal II project to go ahead so Poland can become more secure in its energy supplies and earn more income from transit fees.

The International Monetary Fund (IMF) commented in December 2005 that the markets were watching the actions of the new Polish government closely for early signs of decisive policies to address fiscal and structural weaknesses essential to sustaining, and indeed strengthening, investor and market confidence. The ambitiousness of any reform programmes would be pivotal to economic outcomes in the next several years.

Outlook

In 2006, growth was likely to increase, though by how much would largely depend on investment. Private consumption should accelerate while exports continue to benefit from good export market growth and improvements in competitiveness over the past few years. The current account deficit has remained within safe limits. Investment was the major uncertainty. With indecisive signals on policies, it could remain sluggish, or if investor concerns about future policies and the business environment were addressed, it could pick up strongly.

From about three per cent in 2005, growth in GDP could rise in 2006, but it was too early to say whether this would be modest at 3.5 to four per cent, or, with faster investment growth, substantially stronger. Inflation should remain subdued during the next two years, interest rates should be held steady.

The revenue estimates in the 2006 budget, which assumed continuation of the high tax buoyancies of 2005, were optimistic. Not only would any tax cuts or new tax incentives in 2006 be a mistake, but also greater-than-planned spending restraint would be needed. Even more important is fiscal strategy beyond 2006. State deficits would need to be reduced, a strategy to selectively restrain spending growth would be essential. Expenditure restraint should be designed to support investment and employment. A priority in the medium-term fiscal strategy was to better target social support – the highest in the region relative to GDP – and reduce the share of government resources it absorbs. Other initiatives, including plans under consideration to merge and close government agencies, could be welcome sources of savings and efficiency gains. To sharpen the focus on spending restraint, such a growth-enhancing fiscal strategy should be guided by a ceiling on the medium-term spending path, grounded in objectives for debt reduction.

Risk assessment

Politics	Unstable
Economy	Fair to good
Regional stability	Good

COUNTRY PROFILE

Historical profile

Poland's geographical position between east and west Europe has put it at the mercy of the great European powers.
1918 An independent republic was declared at the end of the First World War.
1919–21 The Polish-Russian War broke out in February 1919. After the Poles defeated the Russians during the Battle of Warsaw in August 1920, a peace treaty was eventually signed in April 1921.
1939 The Second World War began as Germany, with military assistance from the Soviet Union, invaded Poland. German forces occupied Poland until 1945, when the Soviet Union, now on the side of the Allies, liberated the country.
1945 After the end of the Second World War, Poland came under the Soviet Union's sphere of influence and it annexed Poland's eastern provinces. The Soviet Union established a puppet government in Poland, comprised mostly of communists of the Polskiej Partii Robotniczej (PPR) (Polish Workers' Party) and Polskiej Partii Socjalistycznej (PPS) (Polish Socialist Party). Communist rule did not end until 1989.
1948 The PPR and PPS merged to form the Polska Zjednoczona Partia Robotnicza (PZPR) (Polish United Workers' Party) to cement Poland's one-party political system.
1956 Riots due to food shortages resulted in the reinstatement of Wladyslaw Gomulka as the first secretary of the PZRP. Gomulka had been distrusted as too liberal in 1948. Liberalisation and some economic reform ensued.
1970 Food price strikes brought about the resignation of Gomulka, who was succeeded by Edward Gierek.
1980–82 The rise of the trade union, *Solidarnosc* (Solidarity), under Lech Walesa, followed strikes at the Gdansk, Gdynia and Szczecin shipyards. The right to form independent unions was recognised by the government. General Wojcieck Jaruzelski succeeded Gierek as PZPR leader.
Serious unrest continued during the 1980s, including a period of martial law, the imprisonment of *Solidarnosc* leaders and the abolition of independent unions.
1987 Government plans for rapid economic reform necessitating further hardship were rejected in a referendum, but political reform was approved.
1989 *Solidarnosc* was granted legal recognition in time for the partially free elections, after which it helped to form a coalition government.
1990 Lech Walesa became Poland's first democratically-elected president.
1991 The first completely free parliamentary elections were held, resulting in the election of a new centre-right government under Prime Minister Jan Olszewski. He was succeeded by Waldemar Pawlak, who was unable to form a government.
1992 Hanna Suchocka became prime minister (Poland's fifth prime minister since the end of communist rule in 1989).
1993 Suchocka resigned in March and in September, elections under the new 5 per cent threshold rule (parties not reaching this level are not eligible for parliamentary representation) reduced the number of parties in parliament. Voters opted for a slowdown in the pace of market-led economic reforms by bringing back the former communists – the Sojusz Lewicy Demokratycznej (SLD) (Democratic Left Alliance). A coalition government of the SLD and the Polskie Stronnictwo Ludowe (PSL) (Polish People's Party) was formed. Waldemar Pawlak of the PSL became prime minister.
1995 Aleksander Kwasniewski (SLD) was elected president.
1996 Poland became a member of the Organisation for Economic Co-operation and Development (OECD).
1997 A new constitution strengthened the powers of parliament. The Akcja Wyborcza Solidarnosc (AWS) (Solidarity Electoral Action) formed a centre-right coalition government with Unia Wolnosci (UW) (Freedom Union) after the election.
1999 Poland joined NATO.
2000 UW withdrew from the coalition government in order to slow pace of reform. Kwasniewski was re-elected president.
2001 After parliamentary elections, Leszek Miller, leader of the centre-left SLD, formed a left-wing coalition government with the Unia Pracy (UP) (Labour Union) and the PSL.
2002 Poland's 2004 entry to the EU was confirmed by the EU Council.
2003 The coalition split when the PSL was ejected from government after it refused

to vote in favour of government legalisation. The SLD and UP carried on as a minority government.
2004 Poland entered the EU on 1 May. Leszek Miller resigned on 2 May; Marek Belka (SLD) was sworn in as prime minister. Belka lost a confidence vote on 14 May. He was re-nominated prime minister on 11 June, and parliament endorsed his government on 24 June.
2005 The referendum on the EU constitution, expected in 2005, was postponed indefinitely. There was a swing to the right in the 26 September general elections. Lech Kaczynski was elected president on 23 October and a new government was formed on 2 November with Kazimierz Marcinkiewicz as prime miinister.

Political structure
Constitution
The 1952 constitution was amended in 1989 and 1990. Poland is divided into 49 regional *vovoids* (administrations).
Form of state
Parliamentary democratic republic
The executive
The president is head of state, directly elected by universal suffrage for a five-year term. The president has the power to dissolve parliament and nominates the prime minister. Supreme executive power is vested in the Council of Ministers, headed by the prime minister, responsible to the Sejm.
National legislature
The legislative is the bicameral parliament, which has 460 members in the lower house, the Sejm, and 100 members in the upper house, the Senat (Senate), who are directly elected for four years.
Legal system
The apex of the legal structure is the Supreme Court, whose judges are elected by the State Council for five years. The Council also appoints a prosecutor general. Below the Supreme Court are district and special courts. Family courts deal with cases involving divorce and domestic relations.
Last elections
13 June 2004 (European Parliament); 25 September 2005 (parliamentary); 8 October 2000 (presidential)
Results: European Parliament: PO won 24.1 per cent of the vote (15 seats out of 54), LPR 15.9 per cent (10), PiS 12.7 per cent (seven), S 10.8 per cent (six), UP 9.3 per cent (five), UW 7.3 per cent (four), PSL 6.3 per cent (four) and SDPL 5.3 per cent (three); turnout 20.4 per cent.
Parliamentary: The PiS gained 28 per cent of the vote, the PO 24 per cent, the SLD 11 per cent the S 10 per cent, LPR 9 per cent and PSL 6 per cent. Turnout was less than 40 per cent.

Presidential: Aleksandr Kwasniewski won with 53.9 per cent of the vote.
Next elections
25 September 2005 (parliamentary); October 2005 (presidential).

Political parties
Ruling party
Prawo i Sprawiedliwosc (PiS) (Law and Justice) leads a minority government with eight non-partisan members of parliament
Main opposition party
The left-wing Sojusz Lewicy Demokratycznej (SLD) (Alliance of Democratic Left) gained third place in the elections but has to be confirmed as the main opposition party.

Population
38.19 million (2004)
Ethnic make-up
Poland is one of the most ethnically uniform countries in Europe. The non-Polish population, including Ukrainians, Germans and Russians, accounts for only 1.3 per cent of the total population.
Religions
The population is predominantly Roman Catholic. There are small communities of Protestants, Orthodox Christians and Jews.

Education
Public expenditure on education is typically equivalent to 7.5 per cent of annual GNP, including subsidies to private education at the primary, secondary and tertiary levels.
Education is provided free of charge; primary schooling lasts for eight years followed by secondary, academic and technical or vocational qualifications. Under the former communist state, technical education was biased towards heavy industries and the decline of these industries has left large sections of the mature workforce in need of retraining. Current government aims are to improve education and information technology skills as part of its long-term growth programme. Students attending Poland's most prestigious universities must pass a tough entrance exam. Since 1990, over 280 private universities have opened, providing an extra 50,000 graduates for the employment market. Typical fees for private universities can vary from US$530 (the average monthly wage), up to US$1,855 per annum, for high cost subjects like medicine.
Compulsory years: 7 to 14
Enrolment rate: 96 per cent gross primary enrolment, 98 per cent gross secondary enrolment, of relevant age groups (including repeaters) (World Bank).
Pupils per teacher: 15 in primary schools.

Health
Primary healthcare is provided by a network of healthcare centres and specialist physicians. Initial reforms during the 1990s started with the decentralisation of healthcare (mostly primary care) and the introduction of new payment mechanisms to doctors. This led to a range of publicly subsidised private providers.
The concept of primary healthcare is now based on family medicine. Clinics are run by family practitioners who provide a wide range of healthcare services, or make referals to contracted specialists. Development according to this model has signalled movement towards the privatisation of state-owned primary healthcare. Private healthcare services are provided to eligible individuals via contracts with sickness funds.
A common form of mobile healthcare delivery is the non-public clinic (npzoz), which typically employs two or more doctors. The high investment cost has limited the number of private hospitals to gynaecological and surgical clinics.
HIV prevalence: 0.1 per cent aged 15–49 in 2003 (World Bank)
Life expectancy: 74.6 years (World Bank)
Fertility rate/Maternal mortality rate: 1.2 births per woman; maternal mortality 8 per 100,000 live births (World Bank).
Infant mortality rate: 6.0 per 1,000 live births (World Bank)
Head of population per physician/bed: 2.3 physicians and 5.3 hospital beds per 1,000 people.

Welfare
Poland has operated a dual state-run social insurance system and a mandatory private insurance system since 1999. The system, for those under the age of 30, who are obliged to join, consists of a modified social insurance and individual accounts.
Social insurance covers employees, members of co-operatives, self-employed artisans, homeworkers, lawyers and clergy. Special systems exist for independent farmers.
Poland is unique among the former Soviet bloc countries in creating Kasa Rolniczego Ubezpiecznia Spolecznego (KRUS) (Office of Rural Social Insurance), a farmers' social security system, distinct and separate from the workers' system.

Main cities
Warsaw (capital, estimated population 1.7 million in 2004), Lodz (778,200), Krakow (733,100), Wroclaw (632,200), Poznan (581,200), Gdansk (456,700), Szczecin (415,700), Bydgoszcz (384,700).

Poland

Languages spoken
There is a small German-speaking community and German is widely understood and spoken. Kashubian, Ukrainian and Belarusian are also spoken. English and French are used in business circles.

Official language/s
Polish

Media

Press
English-language newspapers and magazines are widely available in Warsaw and in other major towns and cities.

Dailies: In 1989 Solidarity launched *Gazetta Wyborcza*, the first daily opposition newspaper in Communist Europe for over 40 years. It is Poland's largest daily newspaper. *Trybuna Slaska* is the successor of the former party organ *Trybuna Ludu*. The government has a 51 per cent share in the popular daily *Rzeczpospolita*. Other dailies include *Super Express*, *Dziennik Polski*, *Gazeta w Krakowie* and *Zycie Warszawy* (Life).

Weeklies: One of the most influential weeklies is *Polityka*. Others include *Nie* (satirical), *Przyjaciolka* (womens' magazine), *Wprost* (news) and *Poradnik Domowy* (home ideas). Sports magazines, TV/radio guides and youth magazines are also widely available. *Gazeta Polska* (www.gazetapolska.pl) is a Polish weekly newspaper with online archive and offers discussions on current Polish politics.

Business: There are several trade newspapers published by the Polish Chamber of Foreign Trade and the Foreign Trade Publicity and Publishing Enterprise (Agpol). *Wydawnictwa Komunikacyji* and *Lacznosci* are technical papers published by Naczelna Organizacja Techniczna (NOT). The most influential periodicals are *Gazeta Bankowa* (bankers' weekly), *Zycie Gospodarcze* (economic weekly), *Rynki Zagraniczne* (three per week; foreign trade) and *Handel Zagraniczny* (monthly; foreign trade).

Broadcasting
Radio: There were 250 public and commercial radio stations in 2002. Four programmes are transmitted nationally and there is a foreign service which broadcasts in most European languages.

Television: There were 70 television stations in 2002. The most popular television channels are TVP 1 and TVP 2 run by state-owned Telewizja Polska (TVP) (Polish Television). Polsat is the only terrestrial private channel.

Advertising
Print advertising is on the increase, due mainly to many new titles plus improved availability of raw materials. A number of privately owned or co-operative advertising and business consultancies have appeared. TV and radio are popular advertising media. Poland's advertising market is estimated to be worth US$430 million.

Almost 50 per cent of advertising expenditure by foreign firms is in the form of exhibitions (organised by Agpol), a further 30 per cent on advertising in the press, and the remainder mostly on posters.

Economy

After a decade of high import-led growth in the 1970s, economic performance was undermined in the 1980s by high levels of inflation, a heavy debt burden, labour unrest and contraction in export demand. The first democratically elected government in 1991 instituted a shock restructuring policy, allowing prices to be set by the market and leaving firms to sink or swim in a climate dictated by market forces. Although heavy industry bore the brunt of economic changes, the early 1990s were also difficult for other sectors, such as light industry.

Economic reforms were continued by the SLD government (1993–95), although difficult reforms in sectors such as agriculture and social welfare were ignored or delayed. The coalition government that took power in 1997 began to tackle some of these more difficult reforms. By 2003, the Polish population had endured high levels of unemployment and rising inequality for nearly a decade and there were indications that many wanted a return to the command economy of Poland's Communist past.

The Polish economy is regarded as one of the success stories of post-communist transitional Europe. Economic reforms and liberalisation have attracted investment, and EU accession negotiations were characterised by the government's commitment to maintaining economic progress and reform. Poland was admitted to the EU on 1 May 2004.

GDP growth in 2004 was 5.3 per cent, higher than forecast, and is estimated at 4.5 per cent for 2005. Inflation jumped from 0.8 per cent in 2003 to 3.5 per cent in 2004. However, Poland still has a number of fiscal problems, the public debt has been increasing by 4 per cent of GDP per annum and the general government deficit was almost 6.0 per cent of GDP in 2004, with the rate of debt accumulation likely to accelerate further in 2005. It is therefore essential that the government begins significant fiscal consolidation.

In line with other Central European currencies, the zloty has appreciated steadily since the beginning of 2004 – by 15 per cent against the euro, and nearly 25 per cent against the US dollar. Exports to the EU surged after Poland became a member in 2004, but will become less competitive if the zloty continues to appreciate.

Unemployment is high by EU and OECD standards – 18.8 per cent in 2004 – and the government has made job creation a priority. The privatisation of sensitive sectors such as steel, energy and coal have been put on hold, despite pressure from the EU for reform.

Between 2004 and 2006, the 10 EU accession countries will receive funding of up to eur25.1 billion (US$28.2 billion), which will include money for agriculture, infrastructure modernisation and regional aid. Poland will receive the largest amount of approximately eur11.2 billion (US$12.5 billion) or 45 per cent.

External trade
Since 1989, Poland has successfully reoriented its external trade away from Russia and towards Western Europe, with the EU accounting for over 60 per cent of Polish trade by 2001. The downside to the country's economic revival has been increasing trade and current account deficits. Poland has a significant level of unrecorded cross-border trade, mainly due to German and East European visitors buying relatively cheap goods and services in Poland.

Imports
Main imports include machinery and transport equipment (38 per cent), intermediate manufactured goods, chemicals, minerals, fuels, lubricants, and related materials.

Main sources: Germany (29.8 per cent total, 2004), Italy (8.0 per cent), France (7.0 per cent), Russia (6.9 per cent), Netherlands (5.3 per cent), Belgium (4.2 per cent)

Exports
Principal exports are machinery and transport equipment (37.8 per cent), intermediate manufactured goods, miscellaneous manufactured goods, food and live animals.

Main destinations: Germany (29.8 per cent total, 2004), Italy (6.3 per cent), France (5.4 per cent), UK (4.7 per cent), Czech Republic (4.4 per cent)

Agriculture
Farming
Poland's large agricultural sector remains handicapped by structural problems, surplus labour, small farms and a lack of investment. There are about 2 million small private farms averaging eight hectares in size. Production is concentrated in livestock farming (dairy and pigs), cereals, potatoes, sugar beet and oilseed. Pork and poultry output have increased considerably. The agricultural sector contributes around 3 per cent to GDP and employs around a quarter of the workforce.

The government's agricultural policy is largely dictated by the need to join the EU Common Agricultural Policy (CAP) over a 10-year transition period. Poland is a net importer of food and its membership of the CAP is likely to have a positive impact on EU finances.

Between 2004 and 2006, the EU will spend eur7.6 billion (US$8 billion) on Polish agriculture in the form of direct subsidies, export subsidies and funds to allow intervention in the market. In the period 2004–06, the government has the opportunity to top-up EU funding, up to 55 per cent in 2004, 60 per cent in 2005, and 65 per cent in 2006, of the levels enjoyed by other member states. During its transitional entry stage Poland has decided to implement the reform of the CAP on 1 January 2009. The reform was introduced throughout most of the EU on 1 January 2005, when subsidies on farm output, which tended to benefit large farms and encourage overproduction, were replaced by single farm payments, not conditional on production. The change is expected to reward farms that provide and maintain a healthy environment, food safety and animal welfare standards. The changes are also intended to encourage market conscious production and cut the cost of CAP to the EU taxpayer.

Crop production in 2004 included: 28,173,879 tonnes (t) cereals in total, 9,450,486t wheat, 2,201,956t maize, 4,129,078t rye, 1,461,813t oats, 13,746,000t potatoes, 3,476,514t barley, 274,549t pulses, 1,292,329t rapeseed (canola), 212,700t tomatoes, 495,845t oilcrops, 1,300,000t cabbages, 22,000t tobacco, 11,471,800t sugar beet, 2,500,000t apples, 3,000t hops, 3,438,100t fruit in total, 5,192,900t vegetables in total. Livestock production included: 3,283,400t meat in total, 317,000t beef, 2,100,000t pig meat, 1,400t lamb, 843,200t poultry, 510,000t eggs, 12,400,850t milk, 11,000t honey, 39,000t cattle hides, 430t sheepskins, 1,250t greasy wool.

Fishing
Poland has no immediate access to oceanic fishing grounds, but it has its own deep-sea fleet, which has been granted an EU export licence. It has about 44 fish processing plants regulated by EU requirements.

While annual fish consumption has remained stable – at around 215,000 tonnes – Poland's fishing industry is in decline, with the local catch representing an estimated 41.7 per cent of domestic consumption.

Forestry
Forests account for less than 33 per cent of Poland's land area. Over 90 per cent of forested land is available for wood supply and the most common species are coniferous, mostly Scots pine. Pollution and insect infestation have degraded much of the forestry resources, although the government has attempted to repair the damage by placing most of the forests under protection. Only the Bialowieza primeval forest is excluded from harvesting. Export of forest products in 2004 amounted to US$1.7 billion, while imports amounted to US$1.9 billion. Production in 2004 included 32,634,000 cubic metres (mcum) roundwood, 29,234,000cum industrial roundwood, 3,850,000cum sawnwood, 12,992,000cum sawlogs and veneers, 13,960,000cum pulpwood, 6,364,000cum wood-based panels, 3,400,000cum woodfuel.

Industry and manufacturing
The industrial and manufacturing sectors form the mainstay of the economy, accounting for around a third of GDP. Heavy export-based industries, such as shipbuilding, metallurgy (particularly steel), chemicals, motor vehicles and cement, dominate. The 1990s saw growth in sectors such as electronics and light industries, while food processing, glass, beverages, textile and forestry industries are also significant. The Polish car market is the sixth largest in Europe behind Germany, Italy, France, UK and Spain. The best investment opportunities are considered to be in food, textiles, timber, paper, mechanical engineering and furniture. The steel sector was the focus of early restructuring plans in preparation for entry into the EU. Progress has been slow due to opposition from trade unions.

Tourism
Poland is a popular destination, which is recovering from the effects of the general slump in world tourism from 2000. Whereas there were around 20 million tourist arrivals in 1995, by 2003 numbers had fallen to 13.7 million. In 2004, there was an improvement, when 14.3 million arrivals were recorded. The expansion of budget airlines is seen as an important component in the enhanced tourist figures. The sector, which employs 7.9 per cent of the workforce, is expected to account for 1.6 per cent of GDP in 2005. Most visitors are from neighbouring countries, in particular Germany.

The sector is dominated by the formerly state-owned Orbis SA company, a holding company for Orbis Travel, Orbis Transport and Orbis Hotels.

Poland is seen as having the potential for much greater development since accession to the EU. It is thought that Poland could have over US$23 billion in tourism receipts and 1.5 million jobs if the focus on travel and tourism were fully met.

Environment
Cutting pollution was a condition for Poland's entry into the EU.

While industry has tackled its pollution domestic consumers burn coal in boilers and fires, and more people are buying cars to add to the growing traffic jams on Poland's roads (motor vehicle population is expanding at 30 per cent a year).

Mining
Rich mineral resources include the largest deposits of copper ore in Europe and substantial deposits of coal, zinc-lead ores, sulphur and salt. Lesser deposits include nickel and precious metals such as silver.

Hydrocarbons
Poland has oil reserves of around 96 million barrels. Oil production of around 16,800 barrels per day (bpd) is well below the national oil demand. Poland relies on crude oil imports for some 98 per cent of domestic demand, mostly from Russia. Domestic refining does not meet demand; around 20 per cent of refined liquid fuels are imported. The oil industry contributes 8.5 per cent to GDP.

Poland has gas reserves of 170 billion cubic metres (cum). Gas production meets around 50 per cent of local needs. Polskie Górnictwo Naftowe i Gazownictwo (PGNiG), the Polish oil and gas company, plans to increase its gas distribution network by 2010.

Poland has coal reserves of 22.2 billion tonnes. Coal makes a significant contribution to Poland's energy needs, meeting 95 per cent of the country's primary energy production and 65 per cent of electricity generation. Polish coal exports, mostly to Europe, are a major source of foreign exchange. Coal accounts for two per cent of GDP.

Energy
Poland has installed electricity capacity of around 35 GW, most of which is generated by coal-fired power plants. Polskie Sieci Elektroenergetyczne runs the electricity network. Poland has one of the largest power generation sectors in central and eastern Europe.

Financial markets
Stock exchange
The Gielda Papierow Wartosciowych (GPW) (Warsaw Stock Exchange) was re-established in 1991. A relatively small number of listings dominate, with banks and the copper company KGHM Polska Miedz accounting for a quarter of the market capitalisation. There are over 200 companies listed on the GPW.

Banking and insurance
Banks are moving into new areas, such as investment banking, retail banking and asset management. Foreign banks have

Poland

increased their involvement in the sector – over 70 per cent of Polish banking assets are administered by foreign companies. In the period 2000–05 the banking sector expanded by 14 per cent per annum as foreign competition increased and banking services attracted more customers.

Central bank
Narodowy Bank Polski (NBP) (National Bank of Poland)

Main financial centre
Warsaw

Time
GMT plus one hour

Geography
Poland is situated to the north of Central Europe, with Germany to the west, the Czech Republic to the south-west, Slovakia to the south and the Russian Federation enclave around Kaliningrad on the Baltic coast to the north. There is a short border with Lithuania to the north-east and Belarus lies beyond the northern part of the eastern border and Ukraine the southern. Poland has a 520km coastline along the Baltic Sea to the north-west. The country's borders are marked by the Odra and Neisse rivers in the west, the River Bug in the east, the Sudetic Mountains in the south-west and the Carpathian range of mountains in the south-east.

The highest point in the country is 2,499 metres at Rysy on the border with Slovakia. The two major rivers are the Odra and the Vistula which rise in the Sudetic and Carpathian mountains respectively, along the southern borders, and flow into the Baltic Sea.

Climate
Poland has a continental climate with cold winters and warm summers. The mountainous regions of the south have a long, cold winter and a relatively short summer. Areas around the Baltic are warmer, with an average temperature of minus one degree Celsius (C) in January and 18 degrees C in July. Southern Poland has annual rainfall of more than 1,500mm, while the rest of the country experiences moderate rainfall of 500–650mm per year. The Vistula and Odra rivers are usually frozen for about two months each year.

Dress codes
Dress codes are generally similar to western European. Lightweight clothing is required from June to August, medium to heavyweight for the rest of year, plus a heavy topcoat in winter.

Entry requirements
Passports
Required by all. Passport must be valid for at least three months after arrival.

Visa
Required by all. For business trips, a formal invitation from a local company or organisation giving specific details regarding the purpose and duration of the intended trip is necessary. Also required are: a company letter from the applicant's employer regarding his/her status, proof of financial means and receipt of payment for full board accommodation, and return/onward passage.
Contact the nearest consular section or embassy for further information and application form.

Currency advice/regulations
The import or export of local currency is prohibited. The import and export of foreign currency is unlimited, however all monies must be declared. Refunds of local currancy are possible against exchange receipts.

Customs
A customs and currency declaration must be completed and presented at border on entry.

Health (for visitors)
Mandatory precautions
None.

Advisable precautions
Hepatitis 'A', tetanus and polio immunisations. Rabies is a health risk.

Hotels
Most locally run belong to the Orbis hotel chain and are classified one- to four-star, and Lux are internationally run chains, Intercontinental, Holiday Inn, Novotel, etc. Accommodation can be scarce in all main towns, so it is advisable to book at least six weeks in advance. In an emergency a large travel agency or airline may be able to provide a hotel room. Bills include 10–15 per cent service charge; tipping around 10 per cent is customary.

Credit cards
Are readily accepted where displayed signs are shown.

Public holidays
Fixed dates
1 Jan (New Year's Day), 1 May (Labour Day), 3 May (National Day), 15 Aug (Assumption Day), 1 Nov (All Saints' Day), 11 Nov (Independence Day), 25–26 Dec (Christmas Holiday).

Variable dates
Easter Monday, Corpus Christi (May/Jun).

Working hours
Banking
Mon–Fri: 0800–1800.
Polski Bank Kredytowy, Warsaw Okecie airport Mon–Fri: 0730–1700, Sat: 0730–1130. Banks at Katowice Pyrzowice airport Mon–Fri: 0830–1500.

Business
Mon–Fri: 0800–1600.

Government
Mon–Fri: 0800/0900–1500/1600.

Shops
Mon–Sat: usually 1100–1900, but food shops often 0600/0700–1800/1900. Companies and shops, other than food shops, close on 'Free Saturdays' which vary from business to business, but usually three per month (one for shops).

Electricity supply
Domestic 220V AC, 50 cycles; adaptor need for continental-type, round two-pin sockets.
Industrial 380V AC.

Weights and measures
Metric system

Social customs/useful tips
Organisations do not stop for lunch in the middle of the day. The main meal *obiad* is taken from 1500. Formal address in the Polish language is expected. Polite small talk is appreciated as a prelude to talking business. Persistance and patience is required for successful conclusions to business.

Security
Poland has no particular problem with security and street crime, although since the collapse of communism, street crime has increased. Normal precautions should be followed.

Getting there
Air
National airline: Polskie Linie Lotnicze LOT (Polish Airlines LOT).
International airport/s: Warsaw-Okecie (WAW), 10km southwest of the city (20–40 minutes by bus; 20–30 minutes by taxi); duty-free, post office, banks and bureaux de change, bars and restaurants, left-luggage, tourist information and car hire.
Other airport/s: Kraków-Balice (John Paul II International) (KRK), 11km from the city. Wroclaw-Strachowice (WRO), 10 km from the city. Katowice International (KTW), 34km from the city. Gdansk-Trojmaaaiasto (GDN), 10km from the city.
Airport tax: None

Surface
Road: Access is best through Germany. All vehicle documentation should include car registration, driver's national driving licence and valid Green Card motor insurance. An International Driving Permit is also required.
Rail: EuroCity rail services from Western Europe pass through Germany (from Berlin, travelling time is approximately 80 minutes), the Czech Republic or the Slovia Republic. Main lines also link Warsaw with Cologne, Vienna, Budapest and Prague. There are car-sleeper services

from the Hook of Holland to Poznan/Warsaw.
Water: Pol Ferries operates between Poland and Sweden, Denmark and Finland.

Getting about
National transport
Air: LOT operates regular services connecting all major cities.
Road: Approximately 154,000km surfaced roads, of which 80 per cent are main roads.
The motorways include a north-south expressway, the Polish section of the Helsinki-Warsaw highway, known as the Via Baltica, and an expressway from Golonice to Opole.
Buses: Extensive bus and coach services are operated by Polish Motor Communications (PKS) and Polski Express.
Rail: There are approximately 30,000km of track. Some lines are narrow-gauge, and some are steam-hauled. Diesel is typical with only 33 per cent of the lines electrified. Regular services are operated by Polskie Koleje Panstwowe (PKP) (Polish State Railways), connecting major towns. Intercity express trains are inexpensive and reliable.
Polrailpass tickets valid for between 8–30 days are available from travel agents and railway offices, both locally and internationally. For an additional sum tickets for sleeping berths are available.
Water: About 4,000km of navigable inland waterways, including about 400km of canals. Ferries and hydrofoils link Baltic resorts in summer.

City transport
Taxis: Metered taxis are available in all main towns; they can be hired from ranks or ordered by phone. Payment in hard currency may be required; tipping is usual. A surcharge is imposed for journeys between 2300–0500, out of town, and at weekends.
Buses, trams & metro: Regular public transport operates 0530–2300. Good bus services in all towns, also trams in some. Tickets can be bought at RUCH kiosks and used indiscriminately. In Warsaw seven-day tram tourist tickets can be bought at 37 Senatorska Street (entrance E) (Mon–Wed) 0730–1700, (Thu–Fri) 0730–1400.
A metro is in operation in Warsaw.
Larger hotels have an airport shuttle service. There is a free Lufthansa shuttle bus upon arrival at Katowice airport; reservation 24 hours in advance necessary (by travel agent or Lufthansa).

Car hire
A hirer must be over 21 years and have held a full licence for a year. Rental firms are available in all main towns through ORBIS. International driving licence and insurance cover recommended. Minimum renting period is 24 hours. Payment is by cash or credit card. Speed limits: built-up areas 60kph, normal roads 90kph, motorways 100kph.

BUSINESS DIRECTORY
The addresses listed below are a selection only. While World of Information makes every endeavour to check these addresses, we cannot guarantee that changes have not been made, especially to telephone numbers and area codes. We would welcome any corrections.

Telephone area codes
The international direct dialling code (IDD) for Poland is +48, followed by area code and subscriber's number:

Bialystok	85	Lódz	42
Bydgoszcz	52	Lublin	81
Gdansk	58	Poznan	61
Katowice	32	Szczecin	91
Kraków	12	Warsaw	22
Leszno	65	Wroclaw	71

Useful telephone numbers
Ambulance: 999
Customs information: 694-5596
Central Tourist Information Office: 270-000
Fire Brigade: 998
Intercity directory assistance: 912
Local directory assistance: 911/913
Police emergency service: 997
Radiotaxi: 919 (complaints 224-444)
Tow-truck service: 981, 954

Chambers of Commerce
American Chamber of Commerce in Poland, Warsaw Financial Centre, 53 ulica Emilii Plater, 00-113 Warsaw (tel: 520-5999; fax: 520-5998; e-mail: office@amcham.com.pl).

British-Polish Chamber of Commerce, 2 ulica Zimna, 100-138 Warsaw (tel: 654-5971; fax: 654-1675; e-mail: bpcc@bpcc.org.pl).

Banking
ABN Amro Bank, ul. Foksal 19, 00-950 Warsaw (tel: 695-4900).

AmerBank, Marszalkowska 115, 00-102 Warsaw (tel: 248-505; fax: 249-981).

American Express Bank, ul Krakowskie Przedmiescie 11, 00-068 Warsaw (tel: 625-4144).

Bank Gospodarki Zywnosciowej (commercial bank), ul Grzybowska 4, 00-131 Warsaw (tel: 206-606, 200-251; fax: 206-112).

Bank Handlowy w Warszawie SA, (foreign exchange bank), PO Box 129, ul Chalubinskiego 8, 00-950 Warsaw (tel: 303-000, 300-100; fax: 300-113).

Bank Polska Kasa Opieki SA (Grupa Pekao), Grzybowska 53/57, PO Box 1008, 00-950 Warsaw (tel: 656-0000; fax: 656-0004; e-mail: info@pekao.com.pl).

Bank Przemyslowo-Handlowy (Bank BPH), ul Na Zjezdzie 11, 30-527 Krakow (tel: 422-3333, 618-7888; fax: 618-7843, 618-7803).

Bank Rozwoju Eksportu SA (export development bank), PO Box 728, Bankowy 2, 00-950 Warsaw (tel: 829-0000; fax: 829-0081).

Bank Zachodni we Wroclawiu (Western Bank in Wroclaw), 41–43 Ofiar Oswiecimskich St, 50-850 Wroclaw (tel: 446-621, 444-333; fax: 34-917).

Bre Bank SA, ul Senatorska 18, PO Box 728, PL 00-950 Warsaw (tel: 829-0000; fax: 829-0033).

Citibank, ul. Senatorska 12, 00-082 Warsaw (tel: 657-7200).

Creditanstalt, ul Prosta 69, 00-838 Warsaw (tel: 637-9000; fax: 637-9099).

ING Bank, ul. Emilii Plater 28 pietro 7, 00-950 Warsaw (tel: 630-5695).

Lodzi Bank Rozwoju SA, PO Box 465, ul Piotrkowska 173, 90-950 Lodz (tel: 361-716; fax: 375-893).

National Credit Bank, Nowy Swiat 6–12, 00-950 Warsaw (tel: 210-321; fax: 296-988).

Polski Bank Rozwoju SA (Polish development bank), ul Zurawia 47–49, 00-680 Warsaw (tel: 628-0490, 628-0790; fax: 628-6164; (Saturday 2120-828); satellite phone and fax: (39) 120-828, 120-844).

Powszechny Bank Gospodarczy w Lodzi, Pilsudskieo 12, 90-950 Lodz (tel: 361-470, 362-886; fax: 362-870).

Powszechna Kasa Oszczednosci Bank Panstwowy (state savings bank), ul Swietokrzyska 11–21, 00-950 Warsaw (tel: 220-0321, 226-3839; fax: 226-3863).

WBK (Wielkopolski Bank Kredytowy SA), 60-967 Posnan Place, Wolnosci 16 (tel: 56-4900; fax: 52-1113).

Central bank
Narodowy Bank Polski, ul Swietokrzyska 11/21, 00-919 Warsaw (tel: 653-1000; fax: 620-8518; e-mail: nbp@nbp.pl).

Travel information
Central Bus Station, Warszawa Zachodnia Aleje Jerozolimskie 144 (tel: 236-394/6).

Central Railway Station, Warszawa Centralna 54 Aleje Jerozolimskie (tel: 255-001, 255-000).

Foundation for Tourism Development, Ul Mazowiecka 7, 00059 Warsaw (tel: 269-238; fax: 269-695).

Poland

International train connections – information (tel: 204512); local train connections – information (tel: 200-361).

LOT (reservations office of the Polish Airlines), Aleje Jerozolmskie 6579, 00-697 Warsaw (tel: 306-306); airport information in Warsaw (tel: 628-1009).

Lufthansa Warsaw Airport Office (tel: 650-4510); town office, Al Jerozolimskie 56c, Warsaw (tel: 630-2555; fax: 630-2535); Katowice Airport Office (tel: 184-5045); town office Al Korfantego 51, Katowice (tel: 106-2443; fax: 106-2444).

State Sports and Tourism Administration, Swietokrzyska 12, 00916 Warsaw (tel: 263-787; fax: 694-5176).

Warsavawfie Centrum Informacji Gurwstycznej (Warsaw Tourist Information Centre), Zankowy Square 1/13, 00-262 Warsaw (tel: 635-1881; fax: 310-464).

Ministry of tourism
National Administration of Tourism and Physical Culture, ul. Swietokrzyska 12, 00-916 Warsaw (tel: 694-5555; fax: 826-2172).

National tourist organisation offices
ORBIS (tourist board), 16 Bracka Street, 00-028 Warsaw (tel: 260-271); tourist centre ul Krucza 16, Warsaw.

Ministries
Ministry of Agriculture and Rural Development, ul. Wspólna 30, 00-930 Warsaw (tel: 623-1000; fax: 623-2750; e-mail: kancelaria@minrol.gov.pl).

Ministry of Culture and National Heritage, Ul Krakowskie Przedmiescie 15/17, 00-071 Warsaw (tel: 620-0231; fax: 826-7533).

Ministry of Defence, ul. Klonowa 1, 00-909 Warsaw (tel: 845-0441; fax: 455-378; e-mail: bpimon@wp.mil.pl).

Ministry of Education, Al. Szucha 25, 00-918 Warsaw (tel: 628-0461; fax: 628-0461; e-mail: minister@men.waw.pl).

Ministry of the Environment, ul. Wawelska 52/54, 02-922 Warsaw (tel: 825-0001; fax: 253-332; e-mail: info@mos.gov.pl).

Ministry of Foreign Affairs, Al. Szucha 23, 00-580 Warsaw (tel: 523-9000; fax: 629-0287; e-mail: poland@mfa.gov.pl; internet: www.msz.gov.pl).

Ministry of Health, ul. Miodowa 15, 00-923 Warsaw (tel: 831-3441; fax: 831-1553; e-mail: rzecznik@mzios.gov.pl).

Ministry of Internal Affairs and Administration, ul. Batorego 5, 02-514 Warsaw (tel: 621-0251; fax: 628-9983; e-mail: wp@mswia.gov.pl).

Ministry of Justice, Al. Ujazdowskie 11, 00-950 Warsaw (tel: 521-2808; fax: 628-1692; nagorska@ms.gov.pl).

Ministry of Labour and Social Policy, ul. Nowogrodzka 1/3/5, 00-513 Warsaw (tel: 661-0100; fax: 628-4048; e-mail: bip@mpips.gov.pl).

Ministry of Post and Telecommunications, pl. Malachowskiego 2, 00-940 Warsaw (tel: 656-5000; fax: 826-4840; e-mail: rzecznik@ml.gov.pl).

Ministry of Transport and Maritime Economy, ul. Chalubinskiego 4/6, 00-928 Warsaw (tel: 624-4000; fax: 628-5365).

Ministry of the Treasury, ul. Krucza 36, 00-522 Warsaw (tel: 695-9000; fax: 625-1114; e-mail: minister@mst.gov.pl).

President's Office, ul. Wiejska 10, 00-902 Warsaw (tel: 695-2900; fax: 695-3819; e-mail: listy@prezydent.pl).

Prime Minister's Office, Al Ujazdowskie 1/3, 00-583 Warsaw (tel: 694-66983; fax: 625-2637; e-mail: cirinfo@kprm.gov.pol).

Other useful addresses
Amex, Orbis Travel, 22 Hewelluska Ul, Gdansk (tel: 31405); Orbis Travel, 1 F Focha Ave, 30111 Krakow (tel: 224-632); Krakowskie Przedmiescie, 0069 Warsaw (tel: 635-3061).

Association of Polish Craft, Miodowa 14, 00-950 Warsaw (tel: 311-461; tel/fax: 635-7981).

British Consul (Szczecin), Ul Starego Wiarusa 32, 71-206 Szczecin (tel: 487-0302; fax: 487-3697).

British Embassy, Corporate Centre, 2nd Floor, Emilii Plater 28, Warsaw 00-688 (tel: 625-3030; fax: 625-3472); Aleja Roz 1, 00-556 Warsaw (tel: 628-1001/5; fax: 621-7161).

Central Board of Customs, Swietokrzyska 12, 00-916 Warsaw (tel: 694-5555). Press Office (tel: 694-5882; fax: 827-3427).

Central Statistical Office, International Co-operation Division, Al Niepodleglosci 208, 00-925 Warsaw (tel: 608-3113; fax: 608-3870; e-mail: j.szczerbinska@gus.stsp.gov.pl).

Co-operation Fund, Ul Zurawia 4a, 00-503 Warsaw (tel: 693-5165/827/868; fax: 693-5815/365).

DRT Poland (accounting and management consulting), Aleje Ujazdowskie 6A, 1st Floor, 00-461 Warsaw (tel: 293-285; fax: 290-107).

Energy Restructuring Group, Ministry of Industry and Trade, 2 Mysia Street, 00926 Warsaw 63 (tel: 625-6280; fax: 625-6305, 628-0970).

Euro Information Centre Network/Correspondence Centre, Ul Zurawia 6/12, 00-503 Warsaw (tel: 625-1319; fax: 625-1290).

European Integration Committee, Aleje Ujazdowskie 9, 00-583 Warsaw (tel: 694-7354; fax: 629-4888).

Foreign Exchange & International Operations Office, Wielkopolski Bank Kredytowy, Pl Wolnosci 15, 60-967 Poznan (tel: 514-553; fax: 521-113).

Foreign Trade Research Institute Market Information Center of Foreign Trade, Krucza 38/42, 00-512 Warsaw (tel: 629-1222; fax: 628-8680).

Foundation for Privatisation, 36 Ul Krucza, 00525 Warsaw (tel: 628-2198/99; fax: 625-1114); external department (tel: 693-5419, 693-5818; fax: 693-5300).

Government Centre for Strategic Studies, Wspolna 4, 00-926 Warsaw (tel: 661-8111); Press Office (tel: 661-8664; fax: 629-1619).

Government Information Department, Ul. Wiejska 4/6, 00-902 Warsaw (tel: 694-2500; fax: 694-1911).

Housing and Urban Development Office, ul. Wspolna 2, 00-926 Warsaw (tel: 661-8111; fax: 628-5887).

Industrial Development Agency, ul Wspolna 4, 00-930 Warsaw (tel: 628-7954, 628-0934; fax: 628-2363).

Institute of Tourism, Ul Merliniego 9A, 02-511 Warsaw (tel: 488-560; fax: 488-561).

Main Post Office (open 24 hours), 31–33 Swietokrzyska Street, Warsaw.

National Administration of Tourism and Physical Culture, ul. Swietokrzyska 12, 00-916 Warsaw (tel: 694-5555; fax: 826-2172).

NOT (technical interpreter service), Czackiego 3–5, Warsaw (tel: 267-461).

Parliament, Sajm RP, ul. Wiejska 4/6/8, 00-902 Warsaw (tel: 694-2500; fax: 694-2215).

Polcargo (cargo experts and supervisors), Zeromskiego 32, Box 223, 81963 Gdynia (tel: 213-921/957).

Polcomex, Marszalkowska 140, Box 478, 00-061 Warsaw (tel: 266-810).

Polish Agency for Foreign Investment (PAIZ), Al Roz 2, 00-556 Warsaw (tel: 621-6261; fax: 621-8427).

Polish Chartering Agents (Polfracht), Ul Pulaskiego 8, Box 206, 81368 Gdynia (tel: 214-991).

Polish Corporation of Trade Fairs and Economic Exhibition Organisers, Ul Glogowska 26, 60-734 Poznan (tel:

661-532, 692-245; fax: 661-053; e-mail: korptarg@soho-online.com).

Polish Embassy (USA), 2640 16th Street, NW, Washington DC 20009 (tel: 202-234-3800; fax: 202-328-6271; e-mail: information@ioip.com).

Polish Foundation for Promotion and Development of SMEs, Ul Zurawia 4a, 00-503 Warsaw (tel: 693-5868/18/27; fax: 693-5815/365).

Polish Public Roads, Ul Wspolna 1/3, Warsaw (tel: 300-885, 244-572; fax: 628-1345).

Polish State Railways (PKP), Ul Chalubinskiego 4/6, 00-928 Warsaw (tel: 628-4909, 293-596; fax: 244-039, 621-9557, 244-870).

Polservice Foreign Trade Enterprise, 8 Chalubinskiego Street, 00-613 Warsaw (tel: 300-522; fax: 300-076).

Polska Agencja Interpress (Polish information agency), Ul Bagatela 12, 00-585 Warsaw (tel: 628-2221; fax: 628-4651).

Polska Agencja Prasowa (Polish press agency), Ul Jerozolimskie 7, 00-950 Warsaw (tel: 628-0001; fax: 213-439).

Polskie Linie Oceaniczne (Polish Ocean Lines), Ul 10 Lutego 24, 81-364 Gdynia (tel: 201-901).

Poznan International Fair Co Ltd, Ul Glogowska 14, 60-734 Poznan (tel: 869-2000; fax: 866-5827; e-mail: info@mtp.com.pl); Department of Services (tel: 668-320, 692-547; fax: 660-642); Department of Employment (contracts out exhibition stall personnel) (tel: 666-721, 692-250; fax: 665-827).

State Committee of Science and Technology, ul, Wspolna 1/3, 00-529 Warsaw (tel: 628-4071; fax: 628-0922).

Technology Agency, Krucza 38/42, 00-512 Warsaw (tel: 661-8610; fax: 628-3611).

Telekomunikacja Polska SA, Special Projects Department, Ul Obrzezna 7, 02-691 Warsaw (tel: 275-037; fax: 276-789); External Department, Telephony Polskie Fundacja (Polish Telephone Foundation), Al Stanow Zjednoczonych 24, 03-964 Warsaw (tel/fax: 136-833; fax: 120-544).

Telephony Polskie Fundacja (Polish Telephone Foundation), Ul Waszyngtona, 53 A m 19, 04074 Warsaw (tel: 102-292; fax: 102-292, 120-554).

Universal SA (foreign trading company), Al Jerozolimskie 44, 00-950 Warsaw (tel: 8144-3135, 693-6091/92; fax: 278-312).

Internet sites

Official Website of Poland: http://poland.pl

Business Directory: http://www.polish-bus.com/anghome.html

Business Polska: http://www.polska.net

Polish company directory: http://www.teleadreson.com.pl

Polish Embassy, London: http://home.btclick.com/polishembassy

Warsaw Business Journal: http://www.wbj.pl

Portugal

KEY FACTS

Official name: República Portuguesa (Portuguese Republic)

Head of State: President Jorge Sampaio (PS) (since 1996; re-elected Jan 2001); Aníbal Cavaco Silva (PSD) won the 22 Jan 2005 election and takes office 9 March.

Head of government: Prime Minister José Sócrates (PS) (from 12 Mar 2005)

Ruling party: Partido Socialista (PS) (Socialist Party) (elected 20 Feb 2005)

Area: 92,072 square km

Population: 10.50 million (2004)

Capital: Lisbon

Official language: Portuguese

Currency: Euro (eur) = 100 cents (from 1 Jan 2002; previous currency escudo, locked at esc200.48 per euro)

Exchange rate: eur0.83 per US$ (Oct 2005)

GDP per capita: US$16,375 (2004)

GDP real growth: 1.00% (2004)

Labour force: 5.43 million (2004)

Unemployment: 6.70% (OECD, 2004)

Inflation: 2.50% (2004)

Balance of trade: -US$17.89 billion (2004)

Foreign debt: US$309.68 billion (2004)

Annual FDI: US$30.90 billion (cumulative, 1995–2004, OECD); US$1.10 billion (OECD, 2004)*

* estimated figure

It was an eventful year in Portuguese politics with prime ministerial and presidential elections, both of which resulted in a change of party – from right to left, and left to right respectively. The focus of both campaigns was entirely economic: with a recent recession and a staggering budget deficit, Portuguese wealth per head is falling behind that of some of its formerly Communist eastern European neighbours.

General election

Portugal's weak economic status – it is the poorest country in Western Europe – must in some part be due to the political upheaval the country experiences on an almost annual basis. The country re-adopted democracy in 1974 after a right-wing dictatorship and since then has had 16 different governments. José Manuel Barroso, the president of the European Commission, resigned as prime minister and leader of the right-leaning Partido Social Democrata (PSD) (Social Democratic Party) in July 2004, to be replaced briefly by the former Lisbon mayor and night club enthusiast Pedro Santana Lopes. He was decisively thrown out in the 2005 general election, called one year prematurely as a result of lack of confidence in his leadership.

In February 2005 José Sócrates, the leader of the Partido Socialista (PS) (Socialist Party), was elected as prime minister, replacing the previous centre-right coalition. It was the first time that the party had won an outright majority in parliament – with 45 per cent of votes – in the history of Portuguese elections.

Sócrates, who claims his inspiration is UK Prime Minister Tony Blair, has announced ambitious reform plans to put an end to the country's economic woes. In 2003 Portugal entered a recession, the worst in the EU. Unemployment reached 7.1 per cent. Growth in 2004 was about 1 per cent, which Socrates aims to treble in coming years. His proposals include a huge boost to state investment in research and development and the creation of 150,000 jobs.

Sócrates proceeded to select two former Communists as part of his government, and a vocal critic of the US war in Iraq as his foreign minister.

Presidential election

Two former prime ministers went head to head in the presidential polls of January 2006. The president has the power of veto over national legislation and can call snap elections although is otherwise ceremonial. The octogenarian socialist Mário Soares, a key player in overthrowing Portugal's right-wing dictatorship in the 1970s, lost out to the conservative, and younger, Aníbal Cavaco Silva. Soares had said his standing was 'an encouragement to all elderly people who refuse to die before their time has come'. However, the electorate showed that their priorities were economic, in voting for Silva (with 50 per cent of the vote), who had promised to curb the budget deficit – in contrast to Soares (14 per cent) who admits himself to be more interested in ideology than in macroeconomics. Even the septuagenarian poet, Manuel Alegre, polled more of the vote (20 per cent) than Soares. Silva and Prime Minister Sócrates are not dissimilar in their outlook on economic reform.

Economy

The economy took a downward turn in 2002, and has stayed down ever since, dropping the country into recession by 2003 when the economy shrank by 1.2 per cent. The government drew up a *Portugal 2010* document to speed up productivity growth. The plan identified six barriers to increased productivity: informality, regulation and competition, land planning red tape, public services, labour market legislation and Portugal's industrial inheritance.

Measured in purchasing power parity, Portugal's gross domestic product (GDP) per capita is 71 per cent of the European Union (EU) average. Portugal has consistently registered GDP per capita figures above the EU average, but has slipped behind its EU partners since 1999. The IMF predicted in 2005 that it would take Portugal 35 years to reach the average euro-zone GDP figures. The beginning of 2006 brought the disheartening news that the Czech Republic and Slovenia both enjoy higher per capita wealth than Portugal.

Portugal's worst sin in EU eyes is its budget deficit – at 6.2 per cent it is the highest in the euro-zone. Sócrates believes it will take Portugal three years to contain the deficit within the EU's limit of 3 per cent. This flouting of financial regulations means that Portugal has been the focus of punitive measures and the credit rating bureau Standard and Poor's have lowered Portugal's debt rating from AA to AA-. Fitch Ratings maintained Portugal's AA rating in June 2005 but reversed its outlook from 'stable' to 'negative', along with Italy.

Of some concern is the fact that the labour productivity gap between Portugal and the EU as a whole appears to have widened. This represents a reversal of the trend in the period 1995–99 when productivity growth in Portugal exceeded that of the EU average. Lower levels of productivity growth, combined with excessive wage increases have resulted in the erosion of Portugal's cost competitiveness and a cumulative loss of export market share. The government decided to halt all civil service promotions and the recruiting of new staff until the close of 2006. Pension schemes are being reformed and career and wage scales are being re-addressed. The retirement age will be pushed up five years, to 65.

A significant contributory factor to the budget deficit is Portugal's traditionally low ratio of tax revenues. Tax breaks will be phased out, tax evasion and fraud tackled, and the upper level of income tax will be lifted up to 42 per cent. The VAT rate will be raised from 19 to 21 per cent and tax margins on cigarettes and petrol will be increased, in efforts to boost taxation revenues. The austerity measures and tax increases were greeted with a series of protests from public workers and trade unions.

Having announced all these measures, the finance minister Luís Campos e Cunha resigned unexpectedly in July 2005, for personal reasons. The new finance minister, Fernando Teixeira dos Santos, is the fourth in a year but promised that the changeover would not adversely affect the stability of the finance policy and that 'there is no change in direction'.

In October 2005, Santos predicted that the sale of energy companies will raise US$2.4 billion pounds in the immediate term. In 2005 the equivalent of 0.3 per cent of GDP was gained from privatisation sales, which is due to rise to 1.1 per cent in 2006. The scale of the sell-offs is huge. Galp Energia and Rede Eléctricia Nacional, will be sold in 2006

KEY INDICATORS — Portugal

	Unit	2000	2001	2002	2003	2004
Population	m	10.23	10.31	10.38	10.45	*10.50
Gross domestic product (GDP)	US$bn	105.30	109.90	121.30	149.30	*168.28
GDP per capita	US$	10,600	10,940	11,920	14,799	16,375
GDP real growth	%	3.4	1.6	0.4	-1.2	1.0
Inflation	%	2.9	4.4	3.7	3.3	2.5
Unemployment	%	3.9	4.0	5.1	6.4	–
Exports (fob) (goods)	US$m	24,750.0	25,795.0	25,140.0	31,172.0	38,110.0
Imports (fob) (goods)	US$m	38,891.0	38,774.0	37,690.0	44,821.0	55,999.0
Balance of trade	US$m	-14,141.0	-12,979.0	-13,100.0	-13,649.0	-17,888.0
Current account	US$m	-11,012.0	-9,959.0	-9,120.0	-7,549.0	-13,270.0
Total reserves minus gold	US$m	8,908.0	9,666.0	11,179.0	5,174.0	6,582.0
Foreign exchange	US$m	8,539.0	9,228.0	10,656.0	4,631.0	5,993.0
Exchange rate	per US$	217.10	219.01	1.04	0.88	0.80

* estimated figure

Portugal

with sales of Inapa, TAP-Air Portugal and Portucel Soporcel also in the pipeline.

Foreign affairs

Portugal's main foreign policy concern is its relations with the EU. Unlike France or Germany, which also have high budget deficits, Portugal was forced to respond to EU pressure to reduce or balance its budget deficit when the EU threatened to stop providing Portugal with cohesion funding. Between 2000–06, Portugal will receive US$25 billion from the EU to fund the development and modernisation of the transport network. As more of the cohesion funds are now going to the EU accession countries, Portugal could be faced with either receiving a reduced amount of funding or none at all. It is also feared that the EU's reform of the Common Agricultural Policy (CAP) will adversely affect Portugal. The main aim of CAP reform is to reduce EU spending on agricultural subsidies (approximately eur40 billion (US$43.4 billion) per year) due to the extra costs of EU enlargement from 2004. Portugal currently receives eur2 billion (US$2.1 billion) annually in farming subsidies, but this is expected to fall if the CAP reforms are implemented in 2006.

The country's new foreign minister, Diogo Freitas do Amaral, has formerly been the vice prime minister and minister for foreign affairs, and minister of defence, as well as a one month stint as interim prime minister. He has declared himself openly 'anti-Bush', and has been a keen presence in anti-Iraq invasion marches. Portugal sent a small contingent of military police to Iraq but pulled out in February 2005. The country has continued to contribute funds to reconstruction.

Outlook

The government's recent sweeping cuts on public spending and workplace reforms should begin to bear fruit in 2006. GDP growth of 1.2 per cent is predicted, which would bring an eventual end to the negative and zero figures of late. 2006 will go down as the year of privatisation.

Risk assessment

Economic	Improving
Political	Good
Regional Stability	Good
Stock Market	Fair

COUNTRY PROFILE

Historical profile

Until the twelfth century, the Atlantic coastal regions of the Iberian peninsula were occupied by the Phoenicians, Greeks, Romans, Visigoths and the Moors. Following internal struggles and an end to the Moors' rule, Afonso Henriques declared himself king and founded an independent Portugal in the late 1100s.

1383 The seventh Portuguese King, Fernando I, died. The Spanish Castillians invaded Portugal in an attempt to claim the country's throne.
1385 João I of Avis defeated the Castillians and became King.
1400s Portugal expanded its trading routes by colonising parts of Africa, Asia and the Americas.
1558 Portugal tried to colonise Morocco. After Portugal was defeated, the country went into economic and imperial decline.
1580 King Phillip II of Spain invaded Portugal. It remained under Spanish rule until a revolt in 1640.
1600s Portugal colonised Brazil and became a major gold exporter. Portugal became a major trading partner to Britain.
1793–1801 Portuguese and Spanish troops invaded France, but were defeated. Portugal was forced to temporarily break relations with Britain as part of a peace settlement with France.
1807–10 Portugal re-established relations with Britain and declared its neutrality. France and Spain invaded Portugal three times after it had refused to break relations with Britain. A joint Anglo-Portuguese Army eventually expelled the occupation forces.
1822–24 Brazil declared its independence in 1822. An attempt to introduce a new constitution in Portugal failed. Royalists refused to accept the constitution, which would have separated the powers of the monarchy, government and judiciary, and launched uprisings against the government. Power remained in the hands of the monarchy.
1828–51 Liberals rebelled against the Royalist government. Despite splitting into moderate and radical elements, the Liberals eventually gained control of the government.
1907–08 The Republicans, who were gaining support among the population, failed in an attempt to overthrow the government of João Franco.
1908, Republican extremists assassinated King Carlos I. His son, Manuel II succeeded him as Portugal's last king.
1910 The army overthrew the monarchy forcing the King to abdicated. A Republican government was installed and Portugal was declared a republic. Teófilo Braga was appointed as Portugal's first president.
1911 A new constitution was introduced confirming Portugal's republican status and introducing a bicameral legislature.
1914–18 Portugal fought alongside Britain and France in the First World War.
1926 A military coup d'état overthrew the government and replaced it with a junta. The coup leader, General Gomes da Costa, was temporarily appointed head of the junta before General Oscar Fragoso Carmona replaced him.
1928 General Carmona was appointed president and Colonel José Vicente de Freitas became prime minister.
1932 A civilian academic, António de Oliveira Salazar, was appointed prime minister. Salazar introduced a new constitution consolidating authoritarian government.
1939–45 Portugal was neutral during the Second World War, but allowed the Allies to establish military bases in the Azores.
1955 After initially being blocked by the Soviet Union, Portugal was allowed to join the UN.
1968 Marcello José das Neves Caetano succeeded Salazar who had suffered a stroke and coma.
1970 Salazar died.
1974 A group of army officers of the Movimento das Forças Armadasa (MFA) (Armed Forces Movement), and led by General António de Spínola staged a coup d'état and overthrew Caetano's government. A provisionary coalition government restored civil liberties and freedom of the press, abolished the secret police and freed political prisoners.
1975 Portugal granted independence to its African territories, where wars against nationalist forces had long been a drain on the economy; military spending had absorbed about 40 per cent of GDP per annum. Portugal also withdrew from East Timor. Many expatriates return from former colonies. The first free parliamentary elections were held, with victory for the Partido Socialista (PS) (Socialist Party). Mário Lopes Soares becomes prime minister and General Antonio Ramalho Eanes won the presidency. Banks and many industries were nationalised.
1976 A new constitution was introduced, officially establishing Portugal as a parliamentary democracy. The constitution was later amended in 1982, 1989, 1992 and 1997.
1977–86 A period of political instability with 17 left-wing coalition governments in power.
1986 Portugal joined the forerunner of the EU, the European Community (EC). Former prime minister Mário Soares became the first civilian president for 60 years.
1987 In the general election, Partido Social Democrata (PSD) (Social Democratic Party) became the first majority party in parliament since the 1974 revolution.

Anibal Cavaco Silva was elected prime minister.
1991 Mário Soares was re-elected president in January and PSD won re-election. In February, Portugal, on behalf of its former colony East Timor, took Australia to the International Court of Justice (ICJ). Portugal alleged that Australia, by offering recognition of Indonesia's occupation of East Timor in 1975, had failed to observe the right of the East Timorese to national self-determination. The ICJ ruled in 1995 that it could not exercise jurisdiction in the matter.
1995 PSD lost to the PS in the general election. António Guterres became prime minister.
1996 The presidential election was won by the PS's Jorge Sampaio.
1998 Portuguese voters narrowly rejected in a referendum a proposal to legalise abortion.
1999 António Guterres and the PS were re-elected. Macau, Portugal's last colonial territory, was returned to China. Portugal joined the EU single currency unit.
2001 Jorge Sampaio was re-elected as president for a second five-year term. Guterres resigned as prime minister after the PS was defeated in local elections.
2002 Euro currency replaced the escudos. After parliamentary elections in which the PS government was unseated, the PSD leader, José Manuel Durão Barroso, formed a coalition government, comprising PSD and Partido Popular (PP) (Popular Party).
2003 The last extension on the Via Infante motorway Lisbon-Algarve-Spain (known as the A22) was opened.
2004 Prime Minister Barroso resigned on 5 July; he assumed the presidency of the European Commission.
2005 The opposition PS won the 20 February parliamentary elections and José Sócrates (PS) became prime minister. In October, Portugal's constitutional court ruled against the government's decision to hold a referendum on relaxing the country's abortion laws.
2006 Aníbal Cavaco Silva won the presidential election on 22 January. He will take office on 9 March.

Political structure
Constitution
The constitution was promulgated in 1976 and amended in 1982, 1989, 1992 and 1997. Voting is by direct universal suffrage. Voting age: 18 years.
Form of state
Parliamentary democratic republic
The executive
The president, who is directly elected for a maximum of two consecutive terms of five years, appoints a prime minister, and, on his recommendation, the rest of the government.
The principal organ of executive power within the government is the Council of Ministers which is responsible to parliament.
National legislature
Legislative power is vested in the president, the unicameral Assembléia da República (parliament) and the government.
The Assembléia da República comprises 230 members elected for four-year terms by proportional representation in 20 multi-seat constituencies.
The president can dissolve parliament, call elections and is supreme commander of the armed forces.
Legal system
The legal system is based on the 1976 constitution.
Last elections
20 February 2005 (parliamentary); 13 June 2004 (European Parliament); 22 January 2006 (presidential).
Results: Parliamentary: Partido Socialista (PS) (Socialist Party) won 45.1 per cent of the vote (121 seats out of 230), Partido Social Democrata (PSD) (Social Democratic Party) 28.7 per cent (75), the Coligação Democrática Unitária (CDU) (United Democratic Coalition), comprising Partido Comunista Português and Partido Ecologista Os Verdes (PCP and OV) (Portuguese Communist Party and Ecologist Party The Greens) 7.6 per cent (14), the rightist Partido Popular (PP) (Popular Party) 7.3 per cent (12) and the Bloco de Esquerda (BE) (Left Bloc) 6.4 per cent (eight). Turnout was 65 per cent.
European Parliament: the PS won 45 per cent of the vote (12 seats out of 24), Partido Social Democrata (PSD) (Social Democratic Party)-Centro Democratico Social/Partido Popular (CDS/PP) (Social Democratic Centre/Popular Party) 34 per cent (nine), Coligação Democrática Unitária (CDU) (United Democratic Coalition), comprising Partido Comunista Português and Partido Ecologista Os Verdes (PCP and OV) (Portuguese Communist Party and Ecologist Party The Greens) 9 per cent (two), BE 5 per cent (one); turnout 38.7 per cent.
Presidential: Anibal Cavaco Silva won in the first round with 50.7 per cent of the vote.
Next elections
2011 (presidential); 2009 (parliamentary).

Political parties
Ruling party
Partido Socialista (PS) (Socialist Party) (elected 20 Feb 2005)
Main opposition party
Partido Social Democrata (PSD) (Social Democratic Party)

Population
10.50 million (2004)
Ethnic make-up
Predominantly Portuguese. There are immigrant groups from former African colonies – Cape Verde, Mozambique, Angola, Guinea-Bissau and São Tomé. Also from East Timor and Chinese from Macao. There were 200,000 members of ethnic minorities in Portugal in 2000 (1.8 per cent of the total population).
Religions
Roman Catholic (97 per cent), Protestant denominations (1 per cent).

Education
Basic education is undertaken between the ages of six and 15. Secondary education is optional and is undertaken over three years. Higher education is divided into two sub-systems: university education and non-university higher education and it is provided in autonomous public universities, private universities, polytechnic institutions and private higher education institutions of other types. The two systems of higher education are linked and it is possible to transfer from one to the other. It is also possible to transfer from a public institution to a private one and vice versa.
Literacy rate: 94 per cent male, 89 per cent female; adult rates (World Bank).
Enrolment rate: 128 per cent gross primary enrolment of the relevant age group (including repeaters); 98 per cent gross secondary enrolment (World Bank).
Pupils per teacher: 12 in primary schools.

Health
Health care is delivered under a national health service, which is accessible to all Portuguese citizens and to citizens of member states of the EU.
Annual total expenditure on health is about 9 per cent of GDP, of which government spending is approximately 69 per cent. Private expenditure is around 31 per cent, of which 4 per cent is pre-paid health insurance plans.
HIV prevalence: 0.4 per cent aged 15–49 in 2003 (World Bank)
Life expectancy: 76.2 years (World Bank).
Fertility rate/Maternal mortality rate: 1.4 births per woman; maternal mortality 8.0 per 100,000 live births (World Bank).
Birth rate/Death rate: 11 deaths to 12 births per 1,000 people (World Bank).
Infant mortality rate: 4.0 per 1,000 live births (World Bank).
Head of population per physician/bed: 3.1 physicians and four hospital beds available per 1,000 people.

Welfare
Portugal's social security system is characterised by a general contributory scheme

Portugal

covering all workers and their families, with special arrangements for self-employed persons and a non-contributory protection scheme for people facing social or economic problems. Benefits available under the general scheme include sickness (cash benefits), birth/adoption, accidents at work and occupational diseases, invalidity, old age and death, unemployment and dependants.

Self-employed persons are entitled to a compulsory insurance scheme and there is an opt-in extended benefits scheme relating to sickness, occupational diseases and dependants. Membership of the general scheme is compulsory. In addition, there is a voluntary social security scheme for those not in work or who are in work but are not covered by the general scheme. As a rule, the employer pays the contributions and deducts the employee's social security contribution from his or her pay. Employers are also responsible for full financing of the protection of employees against accidents at work and occupational diseases.

Main cities
Lisbon (capital, estimated population 559,400 in 2003), Oporto (264,200).

Languages spoken
Business languages include English, Spanish and French.

Official language/s
Portuguese

Media
Press
Dailies: *Jornal de Noticias* especially read in the north of the country, is the largest Portuguese daily. *Diario de Noticias* is a national daily based in Lisbon. Other dailies include *Record*, *Correio da Manha* and *O Público*.

Weeklies: Major weeklies are published in Lisbon. The most widely circulated weekly is *Expresso*, followed by *O Independente*. Women's magazines such as *Máxima*, *Mulher Moderna*, *Guia*, *Maria* and *Marie Claire* are also popular. *Sojornal* is a weekly of general interest. *The News* is Portugal's national weekend newspaper.

Business: The most influential business newspapers are *Diário Económico* (daily) and *Vida Económica* (weekly). The economic sections of weekly newspapers are also informative. Leading business magazines include *Journal de Negócios*, *Valor*, *Expansão* and *Fortuna*. *Anglo-Portuguese News* (APN), the leading British expatriate paper, covers money matters and has an economics section.

Broadcasting
Radio: There are over 280 radio stations, including 278 commercial stations. Portugal has one private national radio station, Radio Renascença, founded in 1936, which is owned by the Roman Catholic Church and has the widest audience in the country. The state-owned Radiofusão Portuguesea EP (RDP) runs three nationwide stations, Antena 1, Antena 2 (classical music) and Rádio Comercial.

Television: There are three commercial TV stations. A nationalised company, Radiotelevisão Portuguesa (RTP), runs the two national TV channels – RTP 1 (vhf) and RTP 2 (uhf) (non-commercial from 1997) – and the regional stations in Madeira and the Azores. SIC and TVI, with close ties with the Roman Catholic church in Portugal, are private stations.

Advertising
Television is the most popular medium, taking about 45 per cent of total advertising, followed by radio, newspaper and magazine advertisements. Other methods used are cinema shorts, posters, direct mail and door-to-door canvassing. There are about 50 advertising agencies, mainly specialising in radio and TV work and newspapers

Economy
Portugal has a small mixed economy with heavy dependence on foreign trade and few natural resources. Tourism and an export-oriented manufacturing sector are of growing importance.

Portugal, which has the lowest per capita income in the euro-zone, is also one of the EU's poorer members. Following accession to the EU in 1986, it achieved economic stability and higher than average growth, mainly due to a high inflow of EU funding and structural reforms. The years of robust growth gave way in 2001 to stagnation, exacerbated by preparations for adoption of the euro, and by 2003 the economy was in recession. After receiving an official reprimand in 2001 for the high country budget deficit, the government made an austerity programme a priority. The situation began to improve in 2004, with GDP growth showing a modest but fitful recovery at 1 per cent. In 2005, however, the public finances were found to be in a worse state even than reported, necessitating further emergency measures. Portugal received another official EU reprimand and despite a government austerity plan, Portugal is still expected to run a budget deficit of six per cent of GDP for 2005, twice the permitted EU level.

The European Commission forecasts GDP growth of less than 1.0 per cent in 2006 and around 1.25 per cent in 2007.

External trade
Portugal's trade is highly integrated with EU markets.

Imports
Main imports are machinery and transport equipment, chemicals, petroleum, textiles and agricultural products.

Main sources: Spain (29.3 per cent total, 2004), Germany (14.4 per cent), France (9.7 per cent), Italy (6.1 per cent), The Netherlands (4.6 per cent), UK (4.5 per cent)

Exports
Main exports include clothing and footwear, machinery, chemicals, cork and paper products and hides.

Main destinations: Spain (24.8 per cent total, 2004), France (14 per cent), Germany (13.5 per cent), UK (9.6 per cent), US (6.0 per cent), Italy (4.3 per cent), Belgium (4.1 per cent)

Agriculture
Farming
About 34 per cent of the land area is arable, 9 per cent is under pasture and 32 per cent is used for forestry or is woodland. Farming is the most backward sector of the economy and crop yields and animal productivity are well below the EU average due to a legacy of low agricultural investment, minimal machinery, little use of fertiliser, poor soil quality and a fragmented land tenure system.

The EU's Common Agricultural Policy (CAP) is the basis for agricultural development in Portugal. Investment and productivity have risen under the CAP, but Portuguese agriculture remains backward by EU standards. The CAP is based on three broad principles:
- the EU is treated as a single market for agricultural produce
- EU farmers are given preference over outside suppliers
- the cost of the CAP is met by EU member governments.

Fundamental reform to the CAP was introduced on 1 January 2005 in Portugal. Portugal was the only EU member state to vote against the reform package when it was finalised in June 2003. As of January 2005, the subsidies paid on farm output, which tended to benefit large farms and encourage overproduction, were replaced by single farm payments not conditional on production. This is expected to reward farms that provide and maintain a healthy environment, food safety and animal welfare standards. The changes are also intended to encourage market conscious production and cut the cost of CAP to the EU taxpayer.

Portugal is the world's largest exporter of tomato paste and a leading exporter of wine. Its principal agricultural imports are wheat and meat.

The main crops grown in Portugal are cereals (wheat, barley, corn and rice), potatoes, grapes, olives and tomatoes.

Crop production in 2004 included: 1,287,000 tonnes (t) cereals in total, 1,250,000t potatoes, 251,000t wheat, 148,000t rice, 798,000t maize, 287,000t apples, 13,400t cherries, 14,000t figs, 21,210t pulses, 69,100t treenuts, 321,200t citrus fruit, 1,000,000t grapes, 1,100,000t tomatoes, 73,577t oilcrops, 270,000t olives, 484,000t sugar beet, 1,935,000t fruit in total, 2,328,700t vegetables in total. Livestock production included: 689,000t meat in total, 105,000t beef, *330,000t pig-meat, 22,500t lamb, 225,000t poultry, 125,450t eggs, 2,060,800t milk, *4,600t honey, 11,354t cattle hides, *4,200t sheepskins, 7,800t greasy wool.
* estimate

Fishing
The waters around Portugal are rich fishing grounds. Sardines, anchovies and tuna are caught near the coast and species such as cod are caught by deep sea trawlers in the North Atlantic.
Portugal's territorial waters were ceded to the EU on its accession. This stimulated investment of the fishing sector and helped modernise the industry.

Forestry
Portugal's forests are a major natural resource. More than one-third of the country's total continental territory (3.1 million hectares out of a total of 8.9 million hectares) is forested, notably with pine, cork oak and eucalyptus. More than 90 per cent of forested land is privately owned, the highest proportion in the EU.
Portugal's cork production supplies around 52 per cent of the world market. Cork forests are declining and being replaced by eucalyptus plantations as plastic corks become more popular in wine bottles. Eucalyptus trees are contributing to desertification as they require large amounts of water to grow.
Exports of forest material in 2004 amounted to US$1.7 billion, while imports amounted to US$1.1 billion.
The summers of 2003 and 2005 saw large-scale devastation of Portugal's forests through fire, particularly in the north and centre of the country. In 2003 alone, 215,000 hectares, an area approximately the size of Luxembourg, were destroyed.
Production in 2004 included 9,672,000 cubic metres (mcum) roundwood, 9,072,000cum industrial roundwood, 1,383,000cum sawnwood, 2,553,000cum sawlogs and veneers, 6,339,000cum pulpwood, 1,215,000cum wood-based panels, 600,000cum woodfuel.

Industry and manufacturing
Although it contributes around 38 per cent to GDP and employs 32 per cent of the workforce, industry remains relatively underdeveloped and dependent on imported energy and materials.
Portugal faces a difficult transition from traditional industries – clothing, textiles and footwear – afflicted by low value-added products, inefficient management and outmoded technology, to a diversified industrial base.
Important industries include processed cork, paper, cement, fertilisers, steel and glassware. High-growth sectors include vehicle manufacture, semiconductors, electronics, plastics, food processing and franchising.
Industrial production increased by 1.5 per cent in 2003 and an estimated 1.1 per cent in 2004.

Tourism
The sector earns as much as a quarter of total export earnings, and employs 8 per cent of the labour force.
The tourism ministry has encouraged investors to modernise and re-equip existing units, construct additional facilities such as golf courses and conference centres and diversify from beach holidays into sports and cultural tourism.
The Algarve is estimated to account for 50 to 60 per cent of the Portuguese tourist business. New destinations, such as the Douro valley, are being developed.
The UK, Germany, Spain and France account for 75 per cent of all tourism to Portugal, although efforts have been made to tap new tourist sources, such as Japan. Recovering from the slump of 2002–03 when tourist numbers fell due to the Sars outbreak and the Iraq War, tourist receipts for 2003–04 were boosted by the Euro 2004 football competition
Portugal has invested in major infrastructure, aiding the tourism industry, with the addition of several new motorways and airport extensions. Cultural sites also received government investment as they attacted more visitors.
Tourist arrivals increased by 4.20 per cent in 2003, compared to 2002.

Mining
The mining sector contributes around 1 per cent of GDP and employs a similar fraction of the workforce. Although there is considerable mineral wealth, deposits are scattered and not easily exploitable on a large scale. The most important mineral resources include non-metallic ores such as rock salt, pyrites (the reserves in the Alentejo region make up nearly 23 per cent of total worldwide reserves) and excellent quality marble. Large reserves of uranium are also available. Small-scale mining of tin, copper, tungsten concentrates, marble, stone and iron pyrites takes place.

Hydrocarbons
Portugal imports around 90 per cent of its total energy demands and all of its oil demands. Over 25 per cent of the oil is used for electricity generation. Petrogal operates two oil refineries in Portugal with a joint refining capacity of 304,174 bpd, accounting for around two-thirds of the country's oil product sales. Despite exploration efforts Portugal has no proven commercially viable oil reserves. In September 2005, Portugal agreed to lend 2 per cent of its oil stockpile to the US in order to alleviate the damage inflicted by Hurricane Katrina.
In the past few years natural gas consumption has increased considerably. A liquid natural gas (LNG) terminal has been built at the port of Setubal, south of Lisbon, connected by a pipeline extended along the Atlantic coast to the northern town of Braga. The pipeline is linked to the European natural gas network via Spain, providing an alternative source of supply for Europe.
Coal is scarce and of poor quality and production ceased when the last coal mine closed in 1994. Portugal imports small quantities of coal, which is used entirely for electricity production. Demand is declining due to the development of other means of producing electricity.

Energy
Portugal is heavily dependent on imported fuels, particularly oil (70 per cent). Hydroelectricity contributes around 50 per cent of electricity generated.
Portugal and Spain's electricity grids are connected. Electricidade de Portugal (EdP) is the national power utility.

Financial markets
Stock exchange
In January 2002, shareholders of the Bolsa de Valores de Lisboa e Porto (BVLP) (Lisbon and Oporto Stock Exchange), which was formed by the union of the two cities' exchanges in 1999, agreed to the acquisition of BVLP by Euronext, the pan-European exchange created in September 2000. The bourse was renamed Euronext Lisbon.

Banking and insurance
The booming economy has benefited banks. Although there has been some political resistance, the arrival of the euro will continue to bring about takeovers in the banking sector as Portugal's leading banks are far behind the size of those in other euro-zone countries. Banco Santander Central Hispanico, Spain's largest bank, has been attracted to the sector.
In October 2005, a number of Portugal's major banks were the subject of police investigations centred on allegations of

money-laundering and tax evasion. Those involved include the Banco Espirito Santo and Millenium-bcp.
Central bank
Banco de Portugal (Bank of Portugal); European Central Bank (ECB).
Main financial centre
Lisbon

Time
GMT (GMT plus one hour from late Mar to late Sep)

Geography
Mainland Portugal lies in western Europe on the Atlantic side of the Iberian peninsula, bordered by Spain to the north and east, and there are two archipelagos in the Atlantic Ocean – the Azores and the Madeira Islands.

Climate
Situated in the middle of the northern hemisphere, Portugal has a mild welcoming climate. However, the difference between the north/south and coast/inland weather is marked. Inland areas have more variable weather than coastal regions. To the south of the Tagus river the Mediterranean influences are clear. Long, hot, humid summers and dry, short, relatively mild winters. May–October dry and warm, November–April cool with rain in north, mild in south (though often wet and windy January–March). Temperatures vary between 8–28 Celsius.

Dress codes
Business people dress conservatively in dark blue or grey suits and ties.

Entry requirements
Visa
Visas are not required by nationals of European countries. The nearest Portuguese consulate or a travel agent should be consulted prior to departure. A Schengen visa application (offered in several languages) can be downloaded on www.eurovisa.info/ApplicationForm.htm.
Currency advice/regulations
There is no limit on the import of local and foreign currency, but amounts should be declared on entry.
Customs
Personal effects duty-free, plus small duty-free allowance for those travelling from outside EU.

Health (for visitors)
Mandatory precautions
Yellow fever vaccination certificate required for Azores and Madeira only if arriving from infected areas.
Advisable precautions
Up-to-date tetanus and polio immunisations are recommended. Long-term visitors should consider hepatitis 'A' immunisation. In main towns water is drinkable, but visitors are advised to drink bottled water.
The health system is underdeveloped in comparison with northern Europe.

Hotels
Various hotel standards are available throughout the country, and are classified from one- to five-star. There is a 10 per cent service charge. A tip is also expected, usually 10 per cent. Accommodation should be booked well in advance, especially during the holiday season, when all hotels become very busy.

Credit cards
All usual credit cards are widely accepted.

Public holidays
Fixed dates
1 Jan (New Year's Day), 25 Apr (Liberty Day), 1 May (Labour Day), 10 Jun (Portugal Day), 15 Aug (Assumption Day), 5 Oct (Republic Day), 1 Nov (All Saints' Day), 1 Dec (Restoration of Independence Day), 8 Dec (Immaculate Conception), 25 Dec (Christmas Day).
Variable dates
Carnival (Feb), Good Friday, Corpus Christi (May/Jun).

Working hours
Banking
Mon–Fri: 0830–1500. A few banks in Lisbon open on Sat morning. Large network of automatic telling machines.
Business
Mon–Fri: 0900–1300 and 1500–1900.
Government
Mon–Fri: 0930–1200 and 1430–1800, closed 1730 on Mon and Tue.
Shops
Mon–Sun: 1000–2300/2359; Sat: 0900–1300.

Electricity supply
220V AC

Social customs/useful tips
Important business should be dealt with in person. Business negotiations may be conducted in English or French, but it is advisable to check whether an interpreter is required. The Portuguese like to entertain. Lunch usually takes place between 1200 and 1400, dinner between 1900 and 2200.
The Portuguese are extremely courteous, helpful and open to foreigners. Men always shake hands when they meet strangers or male friends. Women often kiss each other or their male friends once on each cheek.
It is impolite to refuse an offer of coffee. Tips should be given to anyone who carries out a service for you. There is no set rule on how much to tip.

Getting there
Air
National airline: TAP-Air Portugal.
International airport/s: Lisbon (LIS), 7km north of capital. Facilities include 24-hour *bureau de change*, banks, tourist information (0600–0200), post office, duty-free shops (0700–0130) and car hire.
A special 'airbus' departs for the city centre every 20 minutes. Greenline Buses: 44, 45 and 83 run, every 15 minutes, from 0530–0100, to the city centre and main railway station. Taxis are available, with a surcharge after 2200hrs.
Other airport/s: Oporto (OPO), 11km from city, Faro (FAO), 4km from city; Funchal (FNC) on Maderia; and Santa Maria (SMA) in the Azores, 3.2km from Vila do Porto.
Lisbon, Oporto and Faro airports serve the Portuguese mainland. Funchal and Oporto Santo serve Madeira. San Miguel, Santa Maria and Lajes serve the Azores.
Airport tax: There is no airport departure tax.
Surface
Car and passenger ferry services are available from various Spanish crossover points. There are several road and rail routes through Spain, mostly via Madrid.
Main port/s: The three most important ports are Lisbon, Leixes (Oporto) and Sines (south of Lisbon). Others (from north to south) are Viana do Castelo, Aveiro, Figueira da Foz, Setúbal, Portimao and Faro. There are container terminals at Lisbon and Leixes. Sines is the main oil importing terminal.

Getting about
National transport
Air: TAP and domestic charter airlines operate scheduled flights between most major cities, Madeira and the Azores.
Road: Over 52,000km of roads, including about 22,000km of main or national roads. Local roads are often narrow and of poor quality, linking rural communities with the provincial roads. Lisbon-Oporto and Lisbon-Algarve roads are very good.
Buses: Regular coach services link major towns. There is a large variety of services between Lisbon and the southern coast.
Rail: The nationalised railway company – Caminhos de Ferro Portugueses, EP (CP) – owns about 3,600km of track, of which 500km are electrified.
Services between main centres – Oporto and Lisbon, Lisbon and Faro – are good, and include express trains with restaurant cars; seats on these should be booked in advance. Rail services on other lines are poor.
Water: The 800km of inland waterways are only rarely used. Some coastal

shipping operates, including services to Madeira and the Azores.
City transport
Taxis: Lisbon taxis are green and black. They are relatively cheap and offer an efficient service. A tip of 15 per cent is expected. Taxis may be scarce during rush-hours.

Buses, trams & metro: Good services in main centres, such as Lisbon and Oporto.

Car hire
Self-drive and chauffeur-driven cars are available throughout the country.
An international driving licence or full national licence is required, as well as an international insurance Green Card.
Motoring information is available from 'Automovel Clube de Portugal' in Lisbon. The wearing of seat belts is compulsory outside city areas.
Driving in Portugal can be hazardous. In proportion to the number of vehicles, the country has one of the highest death and accident rates in Europe.

BUSINESS DIRECTORY

The addresses listed below are a selection only. While World of Information makes every endeavour to check these addresses, we cannot guarantee that changes have not been made, especially to telephone numbers and area codes. We would welcome any corrections.

Telephone area codes
The international dialling code (IDD) for Portugal is +351, followed by area code and subscriber's number:

Beja	284	Faro	289
Braga	253	Lisbon	21
Braganca	273	Madeira	291
Coimbra	239	Oporto	22
Covilha	275	Ponta Delgado	296

Chambers of Commerce
American Chamber of Commerce in Portugal, 155 Rua D Estefânia, 1000-154 Lisbon (tel: 357-2561; fax: 357-2580; e-mail: nop37676@mail.telepac.pt).

British-Portuguese Chamber of Commerce, 8 Rua da Estrela, 1200-669 Lisbon (tel: 394-2020; fax: 394-2029; e-mail: info@bpcc.pt).

Coimbra Chamber of Commerce and Industry, Rua Coronel Júlio Veiga Simão, Edificio Novotecna, 3020-260 Coimbra (tel: 497-160; fax: 494-066; e-mail: geral@cec.org.pt).

Madeira Chamber of Commerce and Industry, 41 Avenida Arriaga, 9004-507 Funchal (tel: 206-800; fax: 206-868; e-mail: geral@acif-ccim.pt).

Ponta Delgada Chamber of Commerce and Industry, 13 Rua Ernsto do Canto, 9504-531 Ponta Delgada, Azores (tel: 305-000; fax: 305-050; e-mail: ccipd@ccipd.pt).

Porto Chamber of Commerce and Industry, Rua Ferreira Borges, Palácio da Bolsa, 4050-253 Porto (tel: 399-000; fax: 399-090; e-mail: cciporto@mail.telepac.pt).

Portuguese Chamber of Commerce and Industry, 89 Rua das Portas de Santo Antão, 1169-022 Lisbon (tel: 322-4050; fax: 322-4051; e-mail: geral@port-chambers.com).

Banking
ABN AMRO Bank NV, Av da Liberdade 131, 5, Lisbon (tel: 321-1800; fax: 321-1900).

Associação Portuguesa de Bancos (Portuguese Bankers' Association), 35 Avenida da República, Lisbon (tel: 357-9804; fax: 357-9533, 352-9682).

Banco BPI SA, Rua do Comércio 132, Lisbon (tel: 887-4801, 887-3161, 311-1000; fax: 346-7308).

Banco Comercial Português SA, International Division, Rua Augusta 62–74, Lisbon (tel: 321-1780, 312-5936; fax: 321-1789; e-mail: dint@bcp.pt); Investor Relations Division (tel: 321-1080; e-mail: investors@bcp.pt).

Banco Espírito Santo e Com de Lisbon, Avenida da Liberdade 195, Lisbon (tel: 315-8331; fax: 353-2931, 350-8977).

Banco Internacional de Crédito, Avenida Fontes Pereira de Melo 27, Lisbon (tel/fax: 315-7135).

Banco Mello, Av José Malhoa, Lote 1682, Lisbon (tel: 720-1500; fax: 720-1766, 720-1599; e-mail: investor@bancomello.pt).

Banco Nacional Ultramarino (commercial bank), Av 5 de Outubro 175, Lisbon (tel: 793-3223, 793-0112; fax: (International Department) 793-8952).

Banco Pinto e Sotto Mayor (commercial bank), Rua do Ouro 28, Lisbon (tel: 340-3000, 347-6261; fax: (International Department) 357-3973).

Banco Português do Atlântico SA, Tagus Park, Edif Serv 1, Piso 2, Oeiras (tel: 422-4000; fax: 422-4489).

Banco Santander Portugal SA, Praça Marquês de Pombal 2, Lisbon (tel: 310-7000; fax: 315-4963).

Banco Totta & Açores SA (commercial bank), Rua do Ouro 88, Lisbon (tel: 321-3000; fax: 321-1582).

Caixa Geral de Depósitos (savings bank), International Department, Largo do Calhariz, Lisbon (tel: 790-5018; fax: 790-5068).

Central Banco de Investimento SA, Rua Castilho 233-4, Lisbon (tel: 386-4097; fax: 387-3208).

Credito Predial Português, Rua Augusta 237, Lisbon (tel: 321-4200; fax: (International Department) 313-7438).

Finibanco, Av de Berna, 10-1064, Lisbon (tel: 790-2800; fax: 790-2801).

Central bank
Banco de Portugal, Rua Francisco Ribeiro 2, 1150-165 Lisbon (tel: 313-0000; fax: 314-3938; e-mail: info@bportugal.pt).

European Central Bank (ECB), Kaiserstrasse 29, D-60311 Frankfurt am Main, Germany (tel: +49(69)13-440; fax: +49(69)1344-6000; e-mail: info@ecb.int).

Travel information
Comissão Municipal de Turismo de Lisboa, Pavilhao Carlos Lopes, Parque Eduardo VII, 1000 Lisbon (tel: 315-1736, 315-1915/6/7/8; fax: 352-1472).

Comissão Municipal de Turismo do Oporto, Rua Clube dos Fenianos 25, 4000 Oporto (tel: 323-303, 312-543; fax: 208-4548).

Dr Francisco Sá Carneiro Airport, 4470 Maia/Oporto (tel: 941-2534, 948-2141).

Faro Airport, 8000 Faro (tel: 81-8582).

Lisbon Airport, 1700 Lisbon (tel: 849-4323, 849-4248; fax: 848-5974).

Palácio Foz, Praça dos Restauradores, 1200 Lisbon (tel: 346-3643, 342-5231).

Praça D Joao I 43, 4000 Oporto (tel: 317-514).

Tourist Office, Palacio Foz, Praca dos Restauradores, 1200 Lisbon (tel: 346-6307; fax: 346-8772).

Vilar Formoso (Fronteira), 6355 Vilar Formoso (tel: 52-202).

Ministry of tourism
Ministry of Trade and Tourism, Av da República 79, 1000 Lisbon (tel: 793-0412).

National tourist organisation offices
Direcção Geral do Turismo (tourist board), Av. António Augusto Aguiar 86, 1099 Lisbon (tel: 575-162).

Ministries
Ministry of Agriculture, Food and Fisheries, Praça do Comércio, 1149-010 Lisbon (tel: 346-3151; fax: 347-7890).

Ministry of Culture, Palácio Nacional da Ajuda, 1349-003 Lisbon (tel: 361-4500; fax: 364-9999).

Ministry of Defence, Avenida Ilha da Madeira, 1400-204 Lisbon (tel: 303-4500; fax: 303-4525).

Portugal

Ministry of Economy, Rua da Horta Seca 15, 1200-221 Lisbon (tel: 322-8600; fax: 322-8741).

Ministry of Education, Avenida 5 de Outubro 107-13, 1069-018 Lisbon (tel: 795-0330; fax: 793-3618).

Ministry for Employment, Praça de Londres 2-14, 1049-056 Lisbon (tel: 844-1700; fax: 847-0027).

Ministry of the Environment, Rua do Século 51-2, 1200-433 Lisbon (tel: 3223-2500; fax: 323-2531).

Ministry of Finance, Avenida Infante D Henriques 5, 1149-009 Lisbon (tel: 888-4675; fax: 886-0032).

Ministry of Foreign Affairs, Largo do Rilvas, 11399-030 Lisbon (tel: 394-6000; fax: 390-9708).

Ministry of Health, Avenida João Crisóstomo 9-6, 1049-062 Lisbon (tel: 354-4560; fax: 354-0302).

Ministry of Home Affairs, Praça do Comércio, 1149-015 Lisbon (tel: 323-3000; fax: 342-7372).

Ministry of Industry and Energy, Rua da Horta Seca 15, 1200 Lisbon (tel: 346-3091/6091; fax: 347-5901).

Ministry of Justice, Praça do Comércio, 1149-019 Lisbon (322-2300; fax: 347-9208).

Ministry of Planning, Public Works and Territorial Administration, Palacio Penafiel, Rua de S Mamede ao Caldas 21, 1149-050 Lisbon (tel: 886-1119; fax: 886-3827).

Ministry of Science and Technology, Praça do Comércio - Ala Oriental, 1149-003 Lisbon (tel: 881-2000; fax: 888-2434).

Ministry of Social Security, Rua Rosa Araújo 43, 1250-194 Lisbon (tel: 353-0049; fax: 353-0074).

Prime Minister's Office, Rua da Imprensa a Estrela 2, 1200 Lisbon (tel: 397-4091; fax: 395-1616).

Other useful addresses

Agencia de Informação LUSA (news agency), Rua Dr João Couto, Lote C, Lisbon (tel: 714-4099).

Associação Industrial Portuguesa, Praça das Indústrias, Lisbon (tel: 639-044).

Associação Industrial Portuense, Avenida da Boavista 2611, Oporto (tel: 672-257).

Bolsa de Valores de Lisboa (Lisbon Stock Exchange), Edificio da Bolsa, Rua Soeiro Pereira Gomes, Lisbon (tel: 790-0000; fax: 795-2021; e-mail: Infomktg@bvl.pt; internet site: http://www.bvl.pt/).

Confederação da Indústria Portuguesa (represents employers), Avenida 5 de Outubro 35, Lisbon (tel: 547-454).

Comissão Co-ordenação Regiao (CCR) Norte, Rua Rainha D Estefania 251, Oporto (tel: 695-236/7/8/9/0; fax: 600-2040).

CCR Algarve, Praça da Liberdade 2, Faro (tel: 802-401; fax: 803-591).

CCR Lisboa e Vale do Tejo, Rua Artilharia Um 33, Lisbon (tel: 387-5541; fax: 691-292).

Instituto de Apoio às Pequenas e Médias Empresas Industriais (IAPMEI), Rua Rodrigo da Fonseca 73, Lisbon (tel: 562-211).

Instituto Nacional de Estatistica (INE), Av António José de Almeida 2, Lisbon (tel: 847-0050; fax: 848-9480; internet site: http://www.ine.pt).

Investimentos Comércio e Turismo de Portugal (ICEP), Av 5 de Outuburo 101, Lisbon (tel: 793-0103; fax: 355-6897; e-mail: icepdiesnar@mail.telepac.pt).

Madeira Development Company, Rua da Mouraria, No 9-1, PO Box 4164, Funchal, Codex-Madeira-Portugal (tel: (351-91)201-333; fax: (351-91)201-399).

Portugal Telecom (PT), Investor Relations, Lisbon (tel: 500-1701, 500-8739; e-mail: manuel.j.castela@telecom.pt).

Portuguese Embassy (USA), 2125 Kalorama Road, NW, Washington DC 20008 (tel: 202-328-8610; fax: 202-462-3726; e-mail: embportwash@mindspring.com).

Privatisation Office, c/o Ministério das Finanças – Commissão de Acompanhamento das Privatizacöes (c/o Ministry of Finance – Commission for the Accompaniment of Privatisations), Av Infante D Henrique 5, Lisbon (tel: 618-0057).

Radiotelevisão Portuguesa – RTP (Portugal's radio/television broadcaster), 197 Avenida 5 de Outubro, Lisbon (tel: 793-1774; fax: 796-6227).

Sociedade de Desenvolvimento da Madeira SA (SDM), Rua da Mouraria, No 9-1, PO Box 4164, Funchale Codex Madeira (tel: (351-91)201-333; fax: (351-91)201-399; e-mail: sdm@sdm.pt; internet site: http://www.sdmadeira.pt/).

Sociedade Independente de Comunicação – SIC (independent broadcasting company), 119 Estrada da Outurela, Carnaxide, Linda a Velha (tel: 417-3138; fax: 417-3118).

Televisão Independente – TVI (independent television broadcasting), Pt16-s 603-B Rua 3, Matinha, Lisbon (tel: 858-7968; fax: 858-2319).

Internet sites

Guide to business:
http://www.portugaloffer.pt/

Guide to investing in Portugal:
http://www.portugal.org/investing/index.html

Lisbon Airport:
http://www.ana-aeroportos.pt

Yellow Pages:
http://www.paginasamarelas.pt/

Puerto Rico

KEY FACTS

Official name: Estado Libre Asociado de Puerto Rico (Commonwealth of Puerto Rico)

Head of State: President of the US George W Bush

Head of government: Governor Aníbal Acevedo Vilá (from 2 Jan 2005)

Ruling party: Partido Popular Democrático (PPD) (Popular Democratic Party)

Area: 8,897 square km (Puerto Rico comprises the main island plus two smaller islands (Vieques and Culebra) and numerous smaller islets.)

Population: 3.91 million (2004)

Capital: San Juan

Official language: Spanish, English

Currency: US dollar (US$) = 100 cents

GDP per capita: US$12,659 (2004)

GDP real growth: 2.70% (2004)

Labour force: 1.52 million (2004)

Unemployment: 12.00% (2003)

Inflation: 8.90% (2004)

Balance of trade: US$17.80 billion (2003)

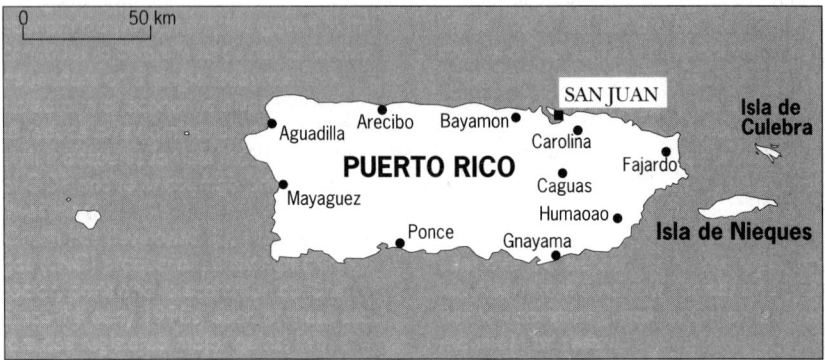

The spotlight was once again turned on Puerto Rico's constitutional status in 2005. At first glance victory for the ruling Partido Popular Democrático (PPD) (Popular Democratic Party) in gubernatorial elections in December 2004 suggested the onset of a lull in such talk. The PPD and its gubernatorial candidate, Aníbal Acevedo Vilá, were proponents of keeping Puerto Rico as a commonwealth dependency of the USA. However, the tiny margin of the victory, 0.2 per cent, and events in 2005 were to ensure that the issue remained a live one.

Big fish, little pond

Puerto Rico continued to outshine most of its Caribbean neighbours in 2005, in terms of main economic indicators. In August, fDi magazine (a foreign direct investment magazine, published by the *Financial Times* group in London), awarded Puerto Rico the title of 'Caribbean Country of the Future'. Puerto Rico was ranked in the top three of 13 out of 26 economic categories assessed by the magazine.

Part of Puerto Rico's economic success, relative to the rest of the region, has been its company taxation policy. Firms from the US mainland have flocked to Puerto Rico in recent years to set up office in the island's tax free environment. Towns like Barceloneta, population 20,000, now host dozens of pharmaceutical companies. Called 'Viagra town' by some due to the amount of the drug produced there, Barceloneta is almost totally dependent upon pharmaceutical companies for its employment and revenue needs. Some analysts argue that this arrangement is unsustainable and dangerously exposes the population to shifts in global taxation regimes.

GDP growth for 2005 is forecast at 2.5 per cent.

Constitutional status

In July, Puerto Ricans voted in a referendum to abolish the Commonwealth's bicameral parliamentary system. A unicameral system was subsequently adopted.

In September, the issue of Puerto Rico's constitutional status was again thrust into the spotlight when FBI agents killed the fugitive Filiberto Ojeda Rios in a shoot-out near the Puerto Rican town of Hormigueros. Ojeda Rios was wanted on the US mainland for a bank robbery committed in 1983. He was also the leader of the Macheteros (the Cane Cutters), the main Puerto Rican independence movement. Hundreds protested as the news of Ojeda Rios' death broke. Although support for independence in Puerto Rico rarely tracks above 3 per cent in opinion polls, many Puerto Ricans regarded Rios as an eccentric hero, fighting against overwhelming odds. His death at the hands of the FBI also sparked accusations that US mainland officials operate in Puerto Rico as if they have impunity.

In December 2005, a special US presidential taskforce handed down its findings

Puerto Rico

on the future status of Puerto Rico. The report advocated holding a referendum on whether or not Puerto Ricans wanted a change in status. In the case of a 'yes' vote, a second referendum on whether the island's people wanted outright independence or to become the 51st state of the USA would be held. US president George W Bush has yet to give a preference.

Outlook

Despite Puerto Rico's privileged economic position relative to its insular neighbours, its own economy remains dangerously exposed to downward swings in the US economy. Moreover, as it is almost totally dependent upon imports, continued high oil prices may trigger high inflation.

In 2006, the US government is expected to state its position on whether or not Puerto Ricans will be given the opportunity to vote on their future relationship with the US.

Risk assessment

Politics	Stable
Economy	Fragile
Regional stability	Stable

COUNTRY PROFILE

Historical profile
1493 The island was inhabited by some 100,000 Taíno Indians (an Arawak culture that also occupied most of Hispaniola and part of Cuba) at the time of the first European sighting by Columbus.
1508 Juan Ponce de Léon landed from Hispaniola and took control of the island. He named it San Juan.
1898 The island was ceded to the US by Spain at the end of the Spanish-American war. The US ruled it as an unincorporated territory.
1917 The inhabitants became citizens of the US.
1948 Puerto Rico elected Luis Muñoz Marín as its first governor.
1952 A new constitution designated Puerto Rico a self-governing commonwealth within the US.
1967 A plebiscite rejected the option of becoming a state of the US.
1993 The statehood option was rejected for a second time in a national referendum.
1998 Puerto Ricans again narrowly rejected the option of statehood in favour of maintaining the constitutional *status quo*.
2000 Sila Maria Calderón Serra became the first female governor. Partido Popular Democrático (PPD) (Popular Democratic Party) won the parliamentary elections.
2001 The Blue Riband Commission was empanelled to review large transactions made by the previous (Rosselló) administration.
2002 Puerto Rico failed to get an injunction stopping US naval training on the island of Vieques.
2003 The closure of the US navy base on Vieques will lose Puerto Rico an estimated US$300 million per year in revenues.
2004 In 2 November gubernatorial elections, Aníbal Acevedo Vilá and former governor Pedro Rosselló won about 48 per cent each. In December the close-run election was given to Acevedo Vilá.
2005 On 2 January, Aníbal Acevedo Vilá became governor. A referendum agreed that the Senate and House of Representatives should be replaced by a unicameral legislature. In December a US presidential task force recommended that a referendum should be called to decide whether the islanders wanted a change in status. A 'yes' vote would trigger a further referendum on whether Puerto Rico should become independent or the 51st state of the US.

Political structure
Constitution
The local government consists of executive, legislative and judicial branches. Puerto Rico has 78 municipal governments.
Detailed laws governing the status and relationship of the Commonwealth of Puerto Rico with the US cover, among other aspects: military conscription, tax and trade, social security, citizenship, constitutional changes and internal autonomy.
There is universal suffrage from aged 18 years.
Form of state
Puerto Rico is an overseas commonwealth territory and freely associated state of the US.
Both the constitution of Puerto Rico and the US constitution are applicable. Puerto Rican nationals are US citizens but do not vote in US presidential elections.
The executive
The Head of State is the president of the US.

Executive power is exercised by the governor, elected by popular vote every four years, who leads a cabinet of 15 ministers.
National legislature
The Asamblea Legislativa (Legislative Assembly) has two chambers.
The Cámara de Representantes (Chamber of Representatives) has 51 members, elected for a four-year term, 40 elected in single-seat constituencies – 11 at large by proportional representation. Up to an additional three seats can be allocated to allow the opposition to have one-third of the seats.
The Senado (Senate) has 28 members, elected for a four-year term – 16 members elected in two-seat constituencies and 11 at large by proportional representation and one additional seat to allow the opposition to have one-third of the seats.
In 2005 the vote in a national referendum favoured replacing the Senate and House of Representatives with a unicameral legislature.
Legal system
The civil and commercial codes; penal, procedural, public (including constitutional) laws are fashioned after US models.
Last elections
2 November 2004 (gubernatorial); November 2000 (parliamentary).
Results: Gubernatorial: Aníbal Acevedo Vilá and former governor Pedro Rosselló won about 48 per cent each.
Parliamentary: the Partido Popular Democrático (PPD) (Popular Democratic Party) won with 30 seats in the Chamber of Representatives and 18 seats in the Senate.
Next elections
2008 (gubernatorial);
Political parties
Ruling party
Partido Popular Democrático (PPD) (Popular Democratic Party)
Main opposition party
Partido Nuevo Progresista (PNP) (New Progressive Party)

KEY INDICATORS — Puerto Rico

	Unit	2000	2001	2002	2003	2004
Population	m	3.88	3.92	3.96	3.97	3.98
Gross domestic product (GDP)	US$bn	26.00	44.20	46.10	45.66	68.95
GDP per capita	US$	6,842	11,513	11,653	11,500	12,659
GDP real growth	%	3.6	1.7	-0.2	0.5	2.7
Inflation	%	5.7	8.3	4.5	5.0	8.9
Unemployment	%	11.0	12.3	12.3	12.0	12.0
Balance of trade	US$m	11,500.0	17,800.0	18,190.0	17,800.0	–

Population
3.91 million (2004)

Ethnic make-up
There is a fusion of three main cultures: native Indian, European and African. The Spanish *conquistadores* initially came to the New World without wives or family and married into the native population, producing the *mestizo* (Spanish and Taío) and the *mulatto* (Spanish and African) groups.

The Spanish settlers brought in African slaves to work in the sugar cane plantations. When migration restrictions were relaxed, more Spanish came, together with a large contingent of Corsicans and a small number of Irish.

Thousands of mainland Americans have established themselves in Puerto Rico and migrants have also come from the Dominican Republic, Canada, Europe, Asia, Cuba and South and Central America.

Religions
99 per cent of the population are Christians (85 per cent Roman Catholic). Religion has traditionally played an important role in the island's history. The religious groups have been instrumental in fostering community co-operation and providing health and educational services.

Education
Six years of elementary (primary) school are followed by three years of junior high school and three years of senior high school. All teaching is conducted in Spanish, although English is a compulsory subject at all levels. There are 34 post-school educational institutions, both government and private. The State University has three main campuses and six colleges. Special training programmes are provided in technical and vocational schools, as well as on-the-job training for labour skills for which a workforce does not exist.

Literacy rate: 93.7 per cent male, 94 per cent female; adult rates (World Bank).
Compulsory years: Six to 16

Health
HIV/Aids
It is estimated that there are 7,397 people living with HIV/Aids.
Life expectancy: 78.29 years (2005)
Fertility rate/Maternal mortality rate: 1.75 per woman (2005)
Birth rate/Death rate: 12.88 births and 7.54 deaths per 1,000 population (2005)
Infant mortality rate: 9.28 per 1,000 live births (2005)

Welfare
The US social security system is in operation, together with Puerto Rico's own health, unemployment, and workers' compensation schemes. Employer contributions to the unemployment and social security funds are compulsory. Despite a high per capita national income, about 60 per cent of the population were recorded as living below the official US poverty line, and 45 per cent of the population received federal food stamps. Federal medical aid is also provided. These provide an important cushion against the effects of unemployment, to which a further safety valve is supplied by emigration. There are more Puerto Ricans living in New York than in San Juan.

Main cities
San Juan (capital, population estimated at 433,900 in 2003), Bayamón (209,300), Ponce (159,400), Carolina (172,900).

Languages spoken
Spanish is the primary language of the vast majority of Puerto Ricans. English as an important second language is taught in public and private schools from first grade through to tertiary institutions. Government affairs are conducted in Spanish while English is the language of commerce.

Official language/s
Spanish, English

Media
Press
Dailies: The three main dailies widely circulated include *El Vocero de Puerto Rico*, *Nuevo Día Interactivo* and *San Juan Star* (English). Other regional dailies and those published from San Juan are *Apuntenlo*, *El Cronista*, *La Esquina*, *La Estrella de Puerto Rico*, *El Expresso*, *El Impacto*, *Impresiones*, *El Periódico*, *Primera Hora*, *Puerto Rico Herald* and *Vieques Times*.
Weeklies: *Caribbean Business*.
Periodicals: *Que Pasa* is an Official Visitor's Guide published bi-monthly.

Broadcasting
Around 115 national commercial radio stations and nine television stations broadcast.

Economy
By international standards, the economy is in a parlous state. Puerto Rico has few natural resources and is heavily dependent on federal aid from the US government. Real improvements to Puerto Rico's economic status will come only with an upswing in the US economy. The Calderón government (2000–04) brought about major improvements to Puerto Rico's business environment. Calderón's primary economic aim was to diversify the economy from the tourist sector to the high-tech and manufacturing industries. Changes include the slashing of capital gains taxes and lowering operating costs for manufacturing plants. There still exists a high degree of red tape and Puerto Rico has yet to adopt a private sector mentality. The weaknesses in Puerto Rico's manufacturing sector, accounting for 42 per cent of GDP, are being addressed, essential if exports are to remain steady and economic growth sustained. Regional agreements such as the North American Free Trade Agreement (Nafta) have made countries such as Mexico attractive low wage, tariff free alternatives to Puerto Rico. However, Puerto Rico is hoping to gain from the implementation of the Free Trade Area of the Americas (FTAA). Governor Calderón lobbied for permanent tax exemption status, saying this would be the best way to secure the Commonwealth's fiscal autonomy from federal government. With approximately 50 per cent of the economy supported by special exemptions for foreign firms, the repeal of tax incentives will severely undermine Puerto Rico's ability to compete with its Caribbean neighbours, prompting concern that the economy could collapse. Susceptible to external shocks due to the reliance on imports, the recent high prices of oil have had a detrimental effect on the economy, raising inflation.

The exit of the US Navy in 2003 will have had some impact on the economy. The Navy injected around US$300 million into the economy each year and was one of the nation's largest employers. Their exit increased unemployment and reduced government revenues.

External trade
There was a regular trade surplus from 1985 due to increased exports of manufactured goods. Since Nafta was signed however, the level of exported manufactured goods has dropped as Mexico, with its lower wages, has become a major supplier to the US and Canada. The balance of payments is still reliant on US federal aid flows.

The US accounts for over 75 per cent of the island's imports and exports, much of which are intra-company shipments of parts from US companies and exports of finished goods in return. This flow of materials and products creates profits for private companies and jobs for workers in Puerto Rico and the US.

Puerto Rico is hoping to transform itself into a 'trade bridge' between North and South America, and between the Americas and Europe.

Imports
Principal imports include chemicals, machinery and equipment, clothing, food, fish and petroleum products.
Main sources: US (55.0 per cent), Ireland (23.7 per cent), Japan (5.4 per cent)

Exports
Principal exports include chemicals, electronics, apparel, canned tuna, rum, beverage concentrates and medical equipment.

Puerto Rico

Main destinations: US (90.3 per cent), UK (1.6 per cent), The Netherlands (1.4 per cent), Dominican Republic (1.4 per cent)

Agriculture

Farming

The agricultural sector is small-scale and only contributes 0.3 per cent to GDP while employing 2 per cent of the workforce. Only 10 per cent of land is suitable for agriculture. An additional 25 per cent of the island is composed of uplands, partially suited for agricultural purposes. Dairy and livestock farming is of increasing importance.

Farming on the island has changed considerably since the 1940s and 1950s, when traditional small-scale farming methods prevailed and sugar cane, coffee and tobacco were the dominant crops. Of these, only coffee has survived, but it lags behind milk and poultry production. Milk production accounts for 34 per cent of total gross farm income. Changes in consumer preferences are slowly taking place as the population ages.

Around 90 per cent of food requirements are met by imports. Almost all of Puerto Rico's farm output is consumed locally, although small quantities of coffee are exported to Europe and Japan. Some fruit and vegetables, mangoes, tomatoes and onions also go to Europe.

Agriculture has been traditionally based on sugar, coffee, pineapples, plantains, bananas, livestock products and poultry. Sugar production declined during the 1980s, partly due to the closure of the Central Cambalache sugar mill in 1982. Coffee production meets only three-quarters of local demand but half of production is exported. Livestock production has not displayed the same rate of decline as arable agriculture, but is still insufficient to meet local demand. The cost of imported feed represents a major constraint on development.

The estimated crop production for 2004 included: 450 tonnes (t) cereals in total, 450t maize, 1,900t sweet potatoes, 450t cassava, 2,450t yams, 1,088t pulses, 10,390t roots and tubers, 27,600t citrus fruit, 50,000t bananas, 82,000t plantains, 17,400t mangoes, 5,000t tomatoes, 3,200t coconuts, 416t oilcrops, 320,000t sugar cane, 12,800t green coffee, 6,500t chillies and peppers, 15,000t pineapples, 201,800t fruit in total, 25,050t vegetables in total. Estimated livestock production included: 89,690t meat in total, 15,000t beef, 14,500t pig meat, 190t lamb and goat meat 60,000t poultry, 15,150t eggs, 377,000t milk, 40t honey, 1,496t cattle hides.

Fishing

Although fishing is conducted on a relatively small scale, it is nevertheless important. Puerto Rico used to be a major tuna supplier to the USA but in recent times has faced a number of problems such as increased competition from south-east Asia. The annual production of processed fish is around 4,000 tonnes.

Industry and manufacturing

The industrial sector forms the mainstay of the economy, contributing approximately 42 per cent to GDP and employing 11 per cent of the workforce. Financial services produce 17 per cent of GDP and trade accounts for 11.6 per cent, other industries produce less than 10 per cent of GDP. Most of the island's manufacturing output is shipped to mainland US. Industrialisation has been the focus of government economic policy since the late 1940s when a programme known as 'Operation Bootstrap' was launched. In 1950, there were 82 industrial plants in Puerto Rico, but by 1965 there were around 1,000. Since then industrial development has tended to be more capital intensive and dependent upon highly skilled labour.

Production is centred on food processing, textiles, petrochemicals, rum distilling, pharmaceuticals, metal fabrication and assembly of electrical/electronic components.

Most of the assembly industries are US-owned and are heavily dependent on the US market. Manufacturers exporting goods to the US benefit from being within the US Customs zone, with the US dollar as the local currency, and US legal protection of intellectual property – particularly useful for IT industries.

The US Commerce Department's Foreign Trade Zones Board has approved the conversion of all the island's industrial parks into free trade zones (FTZs). This, together with Puerto Rico's generous incentives package and skilled workforce has in the past made the island a prime destination for companies looking to expand or relocate. However, competition, from Mexico in particular, has had an adverse effect.

The island's agricultural industry makes an important contribution to the economy through the food industry services of prepared food and retail sales.

The pharmaceutical industry is crucial to Puerto Rico; 16 of the top 20 pharmaceutical drugs in the US are manufactured in Puerto Rico and all the leading US manufacturers are represented, some with major investments. There is heavy investment by US computer and electronics companies, footwear and rubber goods manufacturers. The K-Mart Corporation, the US retailing group, is well represented in Puerto Rico.

Tourism

Tourism is an important source of revenue and Puerto Rico benefits from its connection with the US, from where 80 per cent of visitors come. Although it is a major player in the region, the sector accounts for only around 7 per cent of GDP, a much lower share than other major destinations in the Caribbean. Over five million arrivals were recorded in 2003, a quarter of them being cruise passengers. In January 2004 Disney Cruise Line announced that San Juan would be included in it scheduled ports of call; passenger arrivals recorded between January–October 2004 reached 1,065,215 an increased of 13.5 per cent over 2003.

To meet the growing pressure of competition from its neighbours, Puerto Rico has embarked on a vigorous programme of promotion and infrastructure development, with particular attention on the US and European markets. A new self-contained, all-inclusive resort – Paradisus Puerto Rico, owned by Spain's Sol-Melia – was opened in 2004. It comprises a 500 room hotel and individual accommodation, with sports, entertainment and convention centre. In 113 acres of the Puerto Rico Convention District, on the peninsula of Isla Grande, the US$415 million Convention Centre opened in mid-2005; with over 175,000 square metres, it will be the largest such facility in the Caribbean. Previously unexploited parts of the island are being marketed.

Mining

Activity in this area is extremely small – production is centred on non-metals such as stone, sand, salt and clay.

There are small unquantified reserves of copper, nickel, cobalt, iron, chromium, lead, gold and silver.

Hydrocarbons

Puerto Rico has no hydrocarbon reserves and relies entirely on imports of fuels. Imported oil accounts for just over 90 per cent of Puerto Rico's total primary energy consumption. Puerto Rico typically consumes over 225,000 barrels per day (bpd), all of which is imported. There are two refineries, one located at the Bayamon refinery owned by the Caribbean Petroleum Corporation and the other owned by Royal Dutch/Shell and located at Yabucoa.

Puerto Rico started importing liquid natural gas (LNG) in 2000, to supply the new gas fuelled power plant EcoEléctrica. Most LNG is imported, mainly from Trinidad and Tobago.

All coal products are imported, and since the completion in 2002 of a coal-fired plant in Guayama, demand for coal is slowly increasing.

Energy
Puerto Rico depends on imported energy fuels, mainly from Trinidad and Tobago, Venezuela and the Netherlands Antilles. The Puerto Rico Electric Power Authority (Prepa) is the second-largest municipally-owned US utility. Demand for power is growing at 3.5 per cent a year; in 2003 electicity consumption was 23.7 billion kWh. Additional capacity is also being provided through the refurbishing of some Prepa power stations and the opening of new plants. This will add significantly to Prepa's capacity. Prepa spent US$1.9 billion during the period 2000–03 to improve generating, transmission and distribution infrastructure. Many companies still maintain their own generators as essential back-up.

Banking and insurance
The Puerto Rican commercial banking system comprises about 17 banks with around 300 branches. Financial deregulation and consolidation in the industry have improved operating conditions. Major US banks include Citibank, Chase Manhattan and First National Bank of Boston. Foreign banks include Royal Bank of Canada, Bank of Nova Scotia, Banco Central de Madrid, Banco Bilbao Vizcaya and Banco de Santander.
Banco Popular de Puerto Rico, Puerto Rico's largest bank, continues to expand into US Hispanic markets.

Central bank
There is no central bank.
Such functions as fiscal agent for the Commonwealth of Puerto Rico and its public entities, and the provision of development loans to the public as well as the private sector, are undertaken by the Government Development Bank for Puerto Rico (GDB).

Time
GMT minus four hours

Geography
Puerto Rico comprises the main island, together with the small offshore islands of Vieques and Culebra and many other smaller islets, lying about 80km (50 miles) east of Hispaniola (Haiti and the Dominican Republic) in the Caribbean Sea. Roughly 160km long by 48km wide, Puerto Rico is the smallest and most westerly of the Greater Antilles. The centre of the island is composed of dead volcanoes, the highest of which, the Cordillera Central, has an elevation of 1,325 metres. To the north of the mountains lies a belt of broken limestone country, and then a fertile coastal plain. The whole island is well supplied with rivers. Only about 1 per cent of the country remains forested and is largely reserved.

Climate
Tropical with extremes of heat tempered by constant sea winds. Temperatures are 28–30 degrees Celsius (C) in summer, and 21–26 degrees C in winter. Rainfall is heaviest in the second half of the year, especially June–October. Puerto Rico lies in the 'hurricane belt'.

Dress codes
Suits and ties are customary for businessmen since almost all offices are air conditioned. A jacket and tie may be required in first class restaurants. The Hispanic Caribbean *guayabera*, a long decorated shirt, is worn increasingly commonly.

Entry requirements
Passports
Required by all except nationals of US and Canada.
Visa
US entry requirements apply. Visas required by all, except US and Canadian citizens with proof of identity, and foreign nationals from countries that have visa free entry to the US and are in possession of machine readable passports under 'Visa Waiver Program' (VWP) due to be introduced in October 2005. All other visitors and passport holders must apply for a visa. Visits, for both tourism and business, and visas are valid for up to 90 days. A return/onward ticket is also required.
Further information can be found at http://travel.state.gov/ including information on temporary business visas. More detailed information can be found at http://uscis.gov/graphics/services/visa_info.htm.
Currency advice/regulations
No restrictions on import/export of any currency to the value of US$10,000. Higher amounts must be declared.

Health (for visitors)
The standard of health care in both government and private hospitals is high, but expensive.
Mandatory precautions
None
Advisable precautions
Hepatitis A occurs in the northern Caribbean. There is also a risk of rabies. Travellers should consider vaccination before travelling. Dengue fever, transmitted by mosquitoes, is endemic in rural areas. Its initial symptoms may be similar to influenza. Bilharzia parasites may be present in rivers.
No special precautions are necessary for food and drink.

Hotels
There are several modern business hotels in San Juan. There are also *paradores*, government-owned inns, that are of a reasonable standard. Fifteen per cent tip usual.

Public holidays
Fixed dates
1 Jan (New Year's Day), 6 Jan (Epiphany), 10 Jan (Eugenio Maria De Hostos' Birthday), 22 Mar (Emancipation Day), 4 Jul (US Independence Day), 15 Jul (Luis Muñoz Rivera's Birthday), 25 Jul (Constitution Day), 26 Jul (José Celso Barbosa's Birthday), 11 Nov (Veterans' Day), 19 Nov (Discovery of Puerty Rico Day), 25 Dec (Christmas Day).
Each town celebrates a festival or fiesta in honour of a local patron saint. These can last up to 10 days.
Variable dates
Eugenio Maria de Hostos' Birthday (second Mon in Jan), Martin Luther King's Birthday (third Mon in Jan), Washington's Birthday (third Mon in Feb), Good Friday, José de Diego Day (Apr), Memorial Day (last Mon in May), Labour Day (first Mon in Sep), Columbus Day (second Mon in Oct), Thanksgiving Day (fourth Thu in Nov).

Working hours
Banking
Mon–Fri: 0830–1430. (Some banks 0830–1700; some banks open Sat.)
Business
Mon–Fri: 0800–1700.
Government
Mon–Fri: 0800–1630.

Electricity supply
120V AC

Social customs/useful tips
Despite links with the US and the almost universal ability in the business community to understand English, the use of Spanish by the visitor is appreciated.
Hotel and restaurant staff, and taxi drivers, may expect tips of 15–20 per cent. Service charges are rarely included in restaurant bills.
Puerto Rico combines the lifestyle and social customs of the modern US and the traditional Spanish-speaking Caribbean.

Security
Poverty and unemployment have helped to contribute to a growing crime rate, particularly in San Juan. As in all cities, it is unwise to leave articles unattended in parked cars or hotel rooms.

Getting there
Air
There are direct flights from Europe. Latin American countries are connected via Miami. There are also numerous other

connections via New York. Other US cities are also well connected to Puerto Rico.

International airport/s: Luis Muñoz Marín (SJU), 14.5km east of San Juan; duty-free shop, bar, restaurant, bank, post office, shops, hotel reservations, car hire.

Airport tax: None

Surface

Main port/s: Ponce, Mayagüez and San Juan (major Caribbean hub for maritime shipping).

Getting about
National transport

Air: American Eagle links San Juan, Ponce and Mayagüez.

Road: Modern highways link all main centres. The island's roads are being extended.

Buses: Regular bus (*guagua*) services operates in San Juan from central terminal at Plaza Colón.

Buses are scarce after 2100.

Taxis: Officially regulated, independently owned *públicos* (publicly shared) taxis have 'P' or 'PD' at the end a licence plate and run regular routes from established points, picking up and dropping off passengers along the way. They are an inexpensive way of reaching urban areas and provincial towns less accessible by public transport.

Water: There is a ferry service linking the islands of Culebra and Vieques to the port of Fajardo, on the east coast of Puerto Rico.

City transport

Taxis: Official *Taxi Turístico*, are white only cabs providing services that charge set rates between the airport or pier to major tourist destinations. Commercial, metered taxis can be hailed in the street or, for a small charge, ordered by telephone. Chartered trips outside usual taxi zones should be negotiated at the beginning of a journey. A fifteen per cent tip is usual.

Buses, trams & metro: A new transit system *Tren Urbano* (Urban Train) was opened in December 2004; regular serivices running through the San Juan metropolitan area have yet to be fully implemented. A trial service runs from Río Piedras to Universidad. The completed route includes 16 new stations running 17.2km from Sagrado Corazón to Bayamón Centro. The metro is integrated into the bus system.

There are local bus services (*guaguas*). Routes begin from Bayamón, Catano, Río Piedras and the city centre.

Car hire

It is advisable to book through the airline well in advance. Foreign licences are acceptable.

BUSINESS DIRECTORY
The addresses listed below are a selection only. While World of Information makes every endeavour to check these addresses, we cannot guarantee that changes have not been made, especially to telephone numbers and area codes. We would welcome any corrections.

Telephone area codes
The international dialling code (IDD) for Puerto Rico is +1, followed by area code (787) and subscriber's number.

Chambers of Commerce
Puerto Rico Chamber of Commerce, PO Box 9024033, San Juan 00902 (tel: 721-6060; fax: 723-1891; e-mail: camarapr@camarapr.net).

West of Puerto Rico Chamber of Commerce, PO Box 9, Mayagüez 00681 (tel: 832-3749; fax: 832-4287).

Banking
Banco Central Corp, 221 Ponce de León Avenue, Hato Rey, San Juan (tel: 250-2510; fax: 250-3393).

Banco Comercial de Mayagüez, Mayagüez 00708 (tel: 834-3717).

Banco de Ponce, Plaza Degetau, Ponce 00731 (tel: 842-8000).

Banco Popular, M. Rivera Avenue and Bolivia Street, Hato Rey, San Juan (tel: 765-9800; fax: 764-1706).

Banco Santander de Puerto Rico, 207 Ponce de León Avenue, Hato Rey, San Juan (tel: 759-7070; fax: 751-3639).

Government Development Bank for Puerto Rico, PO Box 42001, San Juan 00940-2001 (tel: 726-2525).

Central bank

Government Development Bank for Puerto Rico, PO Box 42001, San Juan 00940-2001 (tel: 722-2525; fax: 721-1443; e-mail: gdbcomm@bgf.gobierno.pr).

Travel information
National tourist organisation offices

Puerto Rico Tourism Company, 301 San Justo Street, PO Box 4435, Old San Juan Station 00905 (tel: 721-2400; fax: 725-4417; internet site: http://www.gotopuertorico.com).

Ministries
Department of Agriculture, PO Box 10163, San Juan (tel: 721-2120; fax: 723-9747).

Department of Economic Development and Commerce, F.D. Roosevelt Ave 355, 4th Floor, Hato Rey, 00918 (tel: 764-1175 fax: 765-7709).

Department of Education, PO Box 190759, 00919 (tel: 758-4949; fax: 250-0275).

Department of Justice, PO Box 191, 00912 (tel: 721-2900; fax: 724-4770).

Department of Labour and Human Resources, 505 Munoz Rivera Avenue, 00918 (tel: 754-5353; fax: 753-9550).

Department of Natural and Environmental Resources, PO Box 5887, 00906 (tel: 724-8774; fax: 723-4255).

Department of the State, PO Box 3271, 00902 (tel: 722-2121; fax: 725-7303).

Department of the Treasury, PO Box 4515, 00902 (tel: 721-2020; fax: 723-6213).

Department of Transportation and Public works, PO Box 41269, 00940 (tel: 722-2929; fax: 728-8963).

Government of Puerto Rico Economic Development Administration, PO Box 362350, San Juan 00936 (tel: 758-4747; fax: 764-1415).

Office of the Governor, La Fortaleza, 00901 (tel: 721-7000; fax: 721-7483).

Other useful addresses
Caribbean Development Programme, Puerto Rico Department of State, PO Box 3271, San Juan, 00912 (tel: 721-1751; fax: 723-3304).

Legislative Assembly, Capitol Building, 00901 (tel: 724-5200; fax: 724-2428).

Puerto Rico Bankers' Association, 820 Banco Popular Center, San Juan, 00918 (tel: 753-8630; fax: 754-6077).

Puerto Rico Industrial Development Company (FOMENTO), FD Roosevelt Ave, Hato Rey, San Juan, 00918; PO Box 362350, San Juan, PR 00936-2350 (tel: 758-4747; fax: 754-9640; internet site: http://www.pridco.com).

Puerto Rico Manufacturers' Association, PO Box 192410, San Juan, 00919 (tel: 759-9445; fax: 756-7670).

Puerto Rico Ports Authority, PO Box 362829, San Juan (tel: 723-2260; fax: 724-6444).

San Juan Convention Bureau, Ashford Avenue 1110, San Turce, 00907 (tel: 725-2110).

Supreme Court, Supreme Court Building, 00901 (tel: 723-6033; fax: 725-4910).

Internet sites
Urban transit: http://www.urbanrail.net

Welcome to Puerto Rico: http://www.welcometopuertorico.com

Yellow and White Pages: http://www.escapetopuertorico.com/ypages

Qatar

KEY FACTS

Official name: Dawlat Qatar (State of Qatar)

Head of State: Emir Sheikh Hamad bin Khalifa al Thani

Head of government: Prime Minister Sheikh Abdullah bin Khalifa al Thani

Area: 11,437 square km

Population: 649,600 (2004)

Capital: Doha

Official language: Arabic

Currency: Rial (QR) = 100 dirhams

Exchange rate: QR3.64 per US$ (fixed)

GDP per capita: US$37,610 (2004)

GDP real growth: 9.90% (2004)

Labour force: 350,000 (2004)

Inflation: 7.50% (2004)

Oil production: 990,000 bpd (2004)

Balance of trade: US$8.85 billion (2004)

Foreign debt: US$18.62 billion (2004)

In 2005, Qatar joined the list of Arab states hosting terrorist attacks on ex-patriot populations in the name of Islam. It also looked set to become one of the biggest exporters of natural gas in the world.

A gas-fired economy

In 2005, Qatar signed several multi-billion dollar (US) deals aimed at exploiting the country's liquid natural gas (LNG) reserves. In February, ExxonMobil and Royal Dutch-Shell signed extraction and export agreements worth US$12.8 and US$6 billion respectively. In November, Qatar launched a US$14 billion project with the US government that will build the world's largest LNG plant.

Qatar's proven gas reserves are the third largest in the world, accounting for about 5 per cent of the world's total.

Qatari GDP growth is forecast to be around 6.7 per cent in 2005, fuelled mainly by high oil prices. Hydrocarbon exports make up more than 60 per cent of GDP and 70 per cent of government revenues.

Doha bombing

Qatar had remained free of terrorist attacks since the US-led invasion of Iraq in March 2003 – despite hosting the American Central Command forward base. However, in March 2005, a suspected suicide bombing near a British school in the Qatari capital of Doha killed one British citizen and injured twelve others. It was the first such attack against Westerners in the emirate. Around 1,000 people later marched through the city to express solidarity with the victims.

Local politics

In April, the Emir, Sheikh Hamad bin Khalifa al Thani, sacked two cabinet ministers and his chief of staff for their involvement in a share-dealing scandal. The dismissals were noted as unusual by analysts as one of those sacked was a member of the Emir's own family, Abdullah bin Mohammed bin Saud al Thani.

In June, Qatar's first written constitution came into force. The constitution had been approved at a referendum in April 2003 and provides for a partially elected legislative body. The devolution of legislative powers was unprecedented in the emirate's history. The constitution also guarantees expression, assembly and religious freedom. The first election to the new parliament will be in 2007.

Al Jazeera in the news

In November, the Qatari-based Arab satellite TV station *al Jazeera* learnt of allegations that US president George W Bush had suggested bombing its headquarters. The British newspaper, the *Daily Mail*, published the allegations. The paper also asserted that British prime minister Tony Blair had dissuaded the US president. The US government denied the claims. *Al Jazeera* protested and renewed its call for an investigation into the US bombings of its offices in Kabul and Baghdad – attacks the US insists were accidents.

Qatar and Israel

Although Qatar does not maintain diplomatic relations with Israel, in October it took the unprecedented step of funding a sports infrastructure in an Israeli Arab town. Previously, Gulf States had funded projects in areas under the Palestinian

Authority's control but never within Israel itself.

Qatar and Russia

A murky affair involving two Russian agents convicted in Qatar of assassinating a Chechen government-in-exile representative in February 2004 came to a suitably murky end in 2005. Qatar had released the pair into Russian custody in December 2004 on the proviso that they serve out their sentences. In February 2005, Russian authorities admitted that they did not know the whereabouts of the agents. The Chechen in question, the former vice president and acting president of the self-declared Chechen Republic of Icheria, Zelimkhan Yanderbiyev, was in Qatar to raise funds for the separatists. Qatar and other Gulf States have been very profitable fundraising grounds for the Chechens in recent years.

Outlook

It is now likely that Qatar will be targeted again by Islamic extremists seeking to attack Western interests and populations in the Gulf area. As more hydrocarbon, and in particular LNG, fields come online in 2006, Qatar can expect further multi-billion dollar budget surpluses.

Risk assessment

Politics	Stable
Economy	Booming
Regional stability	Fragile

COUNTRY PROFILE

Historical profile
The Al Khalifa family of Bahrain occupied the northern part of Qatar until 1868. That year, at the request of Qatari nobles, the British negotiated the termination of the Khalifa claim to Qatar, except for the payment of tribute. The tribute ended with the occupation of Qatar by the Ottoman Turks in 1872, when the Khalifa family moved to Bahrain.
The Al Thani family gained control of Doha in the middle of the nineteenth century. After being part of the Turkish Ottoman empire, the country became a British protectorate from 1916 until 1971, when it declared its independence. Originally one of the poorest of the Gulf states with its income based on pearling, fishing and trading, Qatar has developed, with the exploitation of large oil and gas fields, into one of the richest Gulf states, with one of the highest per capita incomes in the world.
632 Advent of Islam.
1700s Mining and pearl fishing settlements were established along the coast.
1868 Qatar's first Al Thani Emir, Sheikh Mohammed bin Thani, signed a treaty with Britain.
1871–1916 A treaty with the Turks allowed them to place a garrison in Doha. After Turkey entered the First World War on the side of Germany, the Turkish forces were expelled by the British.
1916 Qatar became a British protectorate with Sheikh Abdullah bin Jassim al Thani as ruler.
1930 The collapse of the pearl trade devastated the economy.
1939 Oil was discovered, but the Second World War delayed exploitation.
1949 Qatar began exporting oil.
1950s Qatar's infrastructure was modernised and extended, using oil revenues.
1968 Britain announced its intention to withdraw from the Gulf by 1971.
1971 Qatar became independent. Land disputes with Bahrain ensued.
1972 Sheikh Khalifa bin Hamad al Thani became Emir after deposing his uncle.
1980s and 1990s Qatar had territorial disputes with Bahrain and Saudi Arabia.
1990 After Iraq invaded Kuwait, Qatar allowed foreign forces into the country and Qatari troops took part in the liberation of Kuwait.
1995 In a bloodless coup, Sheikh Hamad bin Khalifa al Thani, replaced his father Sheikh Khalifa.
1996 Qatar began exporting liquefied natural gas. Based in Qatar and funded by the Emir, the pan-Arab Al Jazeera satellite TV station was launched.
1999 A democratisation programme began when male citizens over the age of 18 were allowed to vote in municipal council elections. Only half the 40,000 eligible to vote actually registered.
2000 The Emir's cousin and 32 others were jailed for life for planning a coup, in 1996, which was foiled.
2001 In the land dispute, the International Court of Justice (ICJ) awarded sovereignty of The Hawar Islands including the Dibal and Jarada shoals to Bahrain. Qatar was awarded the Zubarah town and the shallows surrounding the islet of Fasht el Dibal. A border dispute with Saudi Arabia was also settled. In WTO trade talks, held in Doha, called for the US, EU and Japan to open their markets and remove agricultural export subsidies.
2002 The Al Udeid air base was redeveloped in preparation for the Iraq War when it became the HQ for the US Central Command.
2003 A referendum approved a new constitution, which guarantees equal rights and a 45-member parliament. The Emir named his younger son, Prince Tamim, as crown prince, replacing his elder son Prince Jassim.
2004 Exiled, former Chechen president, Zelimkhan Yanderbiyev, was assassinated in Doha. Russia had accused him of terrorism and links to al Qaeda. Two Russian agents were convicted of the murder. Around six thousand members of the Al Ghfran clan, a sub-set of one of Qatar's largest tribes, had their citizenship revoked on the grounds that they held dual nationality with Saudi Arabia.
2005 On 19 March, a suicide bombing in Doha injured 12 and killed one Briton. It was the first major terrorist attack in Qatar. The new constitution was implemented in June.

KEY INDICATORS — Qatar

	Unit	2000	2001	2002	2003	2004
Population	m	0.58	0.59	0.60	0.62	*0.65
Gross domestic product (GDP)	US$bn	16.40	16.20	16.30	20.43	*28.50
GDP per capita	US$	27,415	27,866	29,091	30,438	37,610
GDP real growth	%	11.6	5.2	3.0	8.5	9.9
Inflation	%	1.7	1.4	1.7	2.0	7.5
Oil output	'000 bpd	796.0	783.0	755.0	917.0	990.0
Natural gas output	bn cum	28.5	32.5	29.3	30.8	39.2
Exports (fob) (goods)	US$m	11,094.0	10,858.0	11,030.0	10,900.0	15,000.0
Imports (fob) (goods)	US$m	2,500.0	3,252.0	4,830.0	3,900.0	6,150.0
Balance of trade	US$m	8,594.0	7,606.0	6,200.0	7,000.0	8,850.0
Current account	US$m	3,200.0	3,530.0	3,260.0	6,840.0	11,960.0
Total reserves minus gold	US$m	1,158.0	1,312.7	1,566.8	2,944.2	3,395.9
Foreign exchange	US$m	1,079.1	1,190.8	1,404.2	2,758.1	3,225.4
Exchange rate	per US$	3.64	3.64	3.64	3.64	3.64

* estimated figure

Nations of the World: A Political, Economic and Business Handbook

Political structure

Constitution
A new, written constitution came into effect on 8 June 2005. It provides for the hereditary rule of the al Thani family. A new unicamal, legislative authority was inaugurated.

Form of state
Constitutional Emirate

The executive
Executive power is vested in the Emir, who is the Head of State. He appoints a prime minister and ministers. He also appoints 15 members of the Majlis al Shura. The Emir is the supreme commander of the armed and security forces.

National legislature
The unicameral Majlis al Shura (Advisory Council) has 45 seats – 30 directly elected and 15 appointed by the Emir. The council has legislative authority, approves the budget and monitors the executive authority. Its 45 members serve four-year terms. Sessions of the council are public, although they may be held *in camera* by request of a third of its members or by a request from the cabinet. No law can be issued unless endorsed by the Emir, who has the right to dissolve the council by decree.

Legal system
Two former court systems – civil and *Sharia* (Islamic law) – were merged under a higher court, the Court of Cassation, established for appeals, under a new judiciary law issued in 2003.

Last elections
None. Members of the *Majlis al Shura* have been appointed until the first elections are held.

Next elections
2006 or 2007

Political parties
Political parties are not permitted.

Population
649,600 (2004)

Ethnic make-up
Arab (40 per cent), Pakistani (18 per cent), Indian (18 per cent), Iranian (10 per cent), others (14 per cent).
Expatriates comprise about 80 per cent of the total population. Some foreign nationals have been resident in Qatar for many years and come largely from the Indian sub-continent, other Arab countries and south-east Asia. The number of non-national children is high, indicating a trend among non-nationals to settle in the country.

Religions
Islam is the state religion. Most Qataris (95 per cent) are Sunni Muslims of the strict Wahhabi sect, known as *muwahhidun* (unitarians); they shun the veneration of saints and shrines. The small Hindu and Christian communities do not have formal places of worship.

Education
Primary education begins at aged six and lasts until aged 12. From aged 12 to 15 students attend a preparatory school and if they pass their promotional examination go forward to secondary school. There are three different types of secondary schools: academic, commercial and technical, and each offer three-year courses. However, girls are only allowed to attend the academic secondary schools.
In 2004, Qatar announced that it would spend US$900 million on a huge new medical teaching hospital to be built on the outskirts of Doha; it is expected to be completed by 2008. An endowment of US$8 billion will also be provided to carry out research. The hospital's teaching programme will be run in partnership with the US Cornell University, and have US$200 million per annum to spend on research, initially concentrating on women's health and paediatric medicine. The emphasis on research is a new direction for medical facilities in the region.

Literacy rate: 83 per cent, adult rate (2003)
Compulsory years: None.

Health
All residents have access to free medical services.
Life expectancy: 75 years (World Bank 2003)
Fertility rate/Maternal mortality rate: 2.5 births per woman (2003)
Birth rate/Death rate: 16 births per 1,000 population; 4.4 deaths per 1,000 population (2003).
Infant mortality rate: 11 per 1,000 live births (2003)

Welfare
The state provides generous welfare services for indigenous Qataris.

Main cities
Doha (capital, estimated population 318,500 in 2003), ar Rayyan (194,800), al Wakrah (244,000).

Languages spoken
English is widely spoken in business circles. Correspondence with government organisations is normally conducted in Arabic.

Official language/s
Arabic

Media

Press
The government formally lifted censorship of the media in 1995 and since then government interference has remained limited.
Dailies: The main daily newspapers are *al Sharq*, *al Raya*, and *al Arab* (mainly political), *al Watan*. The *Qatar Post* and *The Peninsula* are published in English.
Weeklies: The *Gulf Times* is published in English.
Periodicals: Include the monthly *al Sehah Magazine* and the quarterly publication *This is Qatar*. *Qatar Info Quarterly* (http://www.qatar-info.com) is a web site magazine, aimed at expatriates and visitors, covering issues of general interest.

Broadcasting
Local reception of some services from neighbouring states is quite good.
Radio: Radio broadcasts are in Arabic and in English. Urdu and French programmes are also available. The Qatar Broadcasting Service is the only domestic radio station.
Television: The launch of Al Jazeera TV Channel in 1997 raised the profile of Qatari television internationally as a media channel that aimed to cover sensitive political issues without any overt criticism of the State of Qatar and some of its close Gulf allies, specifically Saudi Arabia. Qatar state television runs three channels, one main Arabic service, one Koran channel, one English channel and one satellite channel. Cable satellite TV is also available throughout Qatar and offers some 20 channels.

Advertising
Advertising is available in the press, on commercial TV and in cinemas. Publicity material for general distribution should be in Arabic. Newspapers account for approximately 89 per cent of total advertising expenditure.

Economy
Since the discovery of oil in 1939, Qatar's economic development has been largely based on the hydrocarbons sector and has resulted in its citizens having the world's highest per capita income. As a relatively small oil producer, the country is vulnerable to shifts in the international oil market, however record prices gave it large windfall payments in 2004–05. The country's oil earnings contribute over 55 per cent of GDP, making the country's economy reliant on the continuation of the oil and gas industry.
Record gas exports and oil prices have driven export revenue and the economy grew in 2004 with a GDP of 9.9 per cent, up from the 8.5 per cent in 2003. However, inflation also jumped, from 2.0 per cent in 2003 to 7.5 per cent in 2004. Industrial production accounted for 77.3 per cent of GDP, of which manufacturing was only 7.6 per cent in 2004, and services contributed 22.5 per cent. The foreign debt of US$17billion, in 2004, was due largely to the investment in hydrocarbons processing projects.

Contracts to build a US$5 billion airport were signed in January 2004 and phase one of the airport construction is due for completion in 2009. This large investment will be an impetus for growth and possibly assist the country's diversification strategy by encouraging tourism.

A US$6 billion project to build a liquefied natural gas plant in Qatar will boost the country's gas earnings even further. Further investment in refining and petrochemical development has been agreed between Qatar Petroleum and US ExxonMobil. An agreement was signed in May 2005 to build the world's largest petrochemical plant. The US$2 billion plant is expected to produce around 1.6 million tonnes of ethylene per annum. The project is due to begin in 2006 and completed in 2010.

To improve the country's long-term prospects, the government has introduced incentives to encourage diversification towards the non-oil sector, in particular light industry. It has also relaxed its restrictive policies on foreign investment and encouraged stronger private investment. Although key personnel involved in all projects must be Qatari, the foreign investment law implemented in 2000 allows 100 per cent foreign equity in most commercial sectors, including agriculture, manufacturing, healthcare, education, tourism, power and water plants and mining.

External trade
Imports
Principal imports are machinery and transport equipment, food, chemicals. Virtually everything (except concrete and steel bars) has to be imported.

Main sources: France (24.4 per cent total, 2004), UK (8.9 per cent), Germany (8.8 per cent), Japan (8.7 per cent), US (6.2 per cent), Italy (5.5 per cent), UAE (4.1 per cent)

Exports
Exports are dominated by liquefied natural gas (LNG), crude oil, petroleum products, fertilisers and steel.

Main destinations: Japan (43.8 per cent total, 2004), South Korea (16.1 per cent), Singapore (10.8 per cent)

Agriculture
Farming
The agricultural sector in 2004 only contributed 0.2 per cent to GDP; it employs 1 per cent of the workforce. The country is 70 per cent self-sufficient in summer vegetables and 40 per cent in winter vegetables; 25 per cent in dairy produce and 10 per cent in cereals. Other crops include fruit, dates, fodder crops and cereals.

All agricultural land in Qatar is owned by the government, which is keen to support and encourage agricultural production. However, this is limited by the scarcity of water and the unfavourable terrain. In 2005 a new industrial project was begun in Ras Laffan, it will provide a desalination plant as part of the plan and may be used in irrigation. Only about 8,000 hectares of the estimated 65,000 hectares of cultivable land (5.7 per cent of the total land area) is farmed.

Major emphasis is placed on educating the population in agricultural techniques, experimenting with new methods of cultivation and developing better marketing structures.

One project considered vital to long-term productivity is experimental cultivation of crops on sand using solar energy and sea water. In April 2003, the Islamic Development Bank approved a US$24 million loan to Qatar to finance a soya bean scheme.

The estimated crop production for 2004 included: 6,358 tonnes (t) cereals in total, 4,650t barley, 35t wheat, 1,700t maize, 45t potatoes, 800t citrus fruit, 140t grapes, 3,500t eggplants, 850t chillies & peppers, 7,000t tomatoes, 16,500t dates, 2,250t cabbages, 200t figs, 17,990t fruit in total, 45,880t vegetables in total. Estimated livestock production included: 14,519t meat in total, 1,120t camel meat, 324t beef, 8,175t lamb, 700t goat meat, 4,200t poultry, 5,000t eggs, 35,250t milk, 49t cattle hides, 1,090t sheepskins.

Fishing
Fish catches meet 70 per cent of demand. Fish stocks have declined as a result of water pollution.

Industry and manufacturing
The industrial sector contributes 7.6 per cent of GDP; it employs around 25 per cent of the working population.

Non-oil, heavy industry, often developed as state-owned joint ventures, received the bulk of government investment in industry and now contributes about 9 per cent of national revenues. The government offers incentives to encourage private sector development of light industry. Industries include the production of intermediate building materials (cement, concrete, moulded aluminium, marble tiles and paving stone), food processing, freezing and packaging, paper products, batteries, paint, plastics, detergents, lubricants, household utensils and furniture. The government has pledged to spend US$110 million in industrial plant development, most of which is concentrated in the industrial city of Messaieed.

Tourism
Tourism is being developed as part of the government's programme of economic diversification. Qatar is promoted as an up-market destination, with the emphasis on resorts, festivals, shopping, conferencing, culture and sport. A master plan, announced in May 2004, will channel massive investment into the creation of the facilities and infrastructure, with the aim of increasing visitor numbers from around 400,000 to 1 million by 2010. Several luxury hotels have been opened since 2000. Construction work in connection with the Asian Games, which Qatar will host in 2006 has already boosted the sector. A new international airport at Doha, scheduled for completion by 2015, is envisaged as a regional gateway.

Travel and tourism is expected to contribute US$1 billion in 2005, or 4.2 per cent, to GDP and employ 21.8 per cent of all workers. The sector is estimated to have attracted 11.1 per cent of total capital investment in 2005, of US$633 million. Tourism generates around 18 per cent of total export revenue and is a growth industry.

Hydrocarbons
The hydrocarbons sector contributes around 55 per cent to GDP. Oil reserves stood at 15.2 billion barrels in 2004 and are expected to last until 2030 at the latest. The largest reserves of crude oil are found onshore, particularly at the Dukhan oil field, which produces around half of Qatar's total oil output. Production stood at 785,000 barrels per day (bpd) in 2004. All oil operations are nationalised under the Qatar General Petroleum Company (QGPC). About 80 per cent of crude output is exported under contract to Japan.

The government entered into a number of production sharing agreements (PSAs) with companies such as Chevron and BP Amoco after the oil sector was opened up to foreign investment in 1995.

Proven natural gas reserves stood at around 25.8 trillion cubic metres in 2004, with annual natural gas production at 39.2 billion cubic metres. Qatar possesses nearly 6 per cent of the world's proven gas reserves, concentrated largely in the massive North Field, off the north-east coast, which is the largest known non-associated gas field in the world.

In 2003, Qatar Petroleum opened its fourth liquid natural gas (LNG) plant, which has a capacity of 2,900 tonnes per day (tpd) of ethane, 2,700tpd of propane, 1,900tpd of butane and 708tpd of natural gas liquid condensates. According to the government, the opening of the plant doubled the output of its gas-related products. Two other LNG plants are run by Qatar LNG Company (QatarGas) and Ras Laffan LNG Company with long-term contracts supplying LNG to Japan, South

Korea, and Spain. Contracts for other destinations are in negotiation.
Qatar does not produce or import coal.

Energy
Qatar has an electricity generation capacity of 1,880MW. As a result of rapidly rising demand, the government has embarked on a process of restructuring the electricity sector with an emphasis on attracting foreign investment. It has also sought to prevent rampant electricity demand by limiting free residential electricity and charging for electricity consumption exceeding a certain predetermined level. The Ras Abu Fontas power station has been re-furbished with increased generating capacity of 1,030MW. A new power plant in the Ras Laffan industrial complex began operations in May 2004 with a generating capacity of 750MW. Independent power projects (IPPs) are likely to increase in number as the government seeks to inject foreign investment into the electricity sector.
The Qatar General Electricity and Water Company (QEWC) is part-privatised and is 43 per cent owned by the state with the rest owned by Qatari investors.
Solar energy is being developed in conjunction with desalination.

Financial markets
In 2005 government plans to develop a regional financial services centre were agreed. Initially the centre will provide Qatar-based project financing, bond insurance and asset management to financial institutions and allow them to enter the liquefied natural gas markets. A regulator was appointed to the post of head of the financial services centre in March 2005.

Stock exchange
The Doha Securities Market became operational in 1996 and the stock exchange was opened in 1997; foreigners were allowed to trade in 2000. The market is dominated by banks, which account for around 50 per cent of trading activity. Services account for around 40 per cent of trading.

Banking and insurance
The banking sector consists of 15 commercial banks, including seven locally owned banks. There are 12 insurance companies, the majority of which are foreign-owned; the largest is the locally-owned Qatar Insurance Company.

Central bank
The Qatar Central Bank (QCB)

Main financial centre
Doha

Time
GMT plus three hours

Geography
Qatar occupies a peninsula, projecting northwards from the Arabian mainland, on the west coast of the Gulf. It is bordered, to the south, by Saudi Arabia and the United Arab Emirates. The archipelago of Bahrain lies to the north-west. On the opposite side of the Gulf lies Iran.

Climate
Desert climate with extremely hot and humid summers, when temperatures can reach 44 degrees Celsius from July–September, and mild winters with occasional rainfall.
Among the proposals to meet the water shortage are the construction of a 700km pipeline from the Karun River in northern Iran to Qatar, as well as the development of more desalination plants.

Entry requirements
Passports
Required by all except certain seamen.
Visa
Required by all; except nationals of neighbouring countries.
For all others, requirements are subject to change and it is advisable to contact an embassy of Qatar for up-to-date information. Business and tourist visas (valid for 21 days) may be obtained on arrival. However, obtaining a visa in advance will save time.
Prohibited entry
Holders of passports issued by Israel.
Currency advice/regulations
There are no exchange restrictions. Israeli currency is prohibited.
Customs
Personal effects are duty-free. Certain goods (firearms, ammunition, drugs and alcohol) may only be imported under licence.
Import of pork and pork products, cultured pearls, and obscene or seditious literature is forbidden.
Importers must register with the Controller of Companies and appear on the Chamber of Commerce's register of importers. All foodstuffs must be labelled in Arabic.
Prohibited imports
Alcohol, even for personal consumption.

Health (for visitors)
Mandatory precautions
Vaccination certificate against yellow fever if travelling from infected area.
Advisable precautions
Typhoid, tetanus and polio vaccinations. An AIDS test is required in order to obtain a residence permit.

Hotels
There is a selection of first-class hotels. Tax of 17 per cent is added to the bill.

Credit cards
Major credit cards are accepted.

Public holidays
Fixed dates
27 Jun (Accession of the Emir), 3 Sep (Independence Day), 31 Dec (banks only).
Variable dates
Eid al Adha (five days), Eid al Fitr (four days), Islamic New Year.
The Islamic year has 354 or 355 days, with the result that Muslim feasts advance by 10–12 days against the Gregorian calendar each year. Dates of the Muslim feasts vary according to sightings of the new moon, so cannot be forecast exactly.

Working hours
Friday is the weekly holiday, and oil company offices are also closed on Thursday afternoons.
Start your business as early as possible, particularly in high summer. Oil companies, government-run ports and industries start at 0700; many other companies at 0800.
During Ramadan, the Muslim holy month of fasting during daylight hours, most officials work 0900–1300 but many useful contacts can be made and renewed during and after the evening *Iftar* meal.
Banking
Sat–Wed: 0730–1130; Thu: 0730–1100; Fri: closed.
Business
Sat–Thu: 0800–1200, 1600–1800; Thu: oil companies work half day only; Fri: closed.
Government
Sat–Thu: 0700–1300; Fri: closed.
Shops
Sat–Thu: 0830–1230, 1630–2030; Fri: most shops are closed, although some supermarkets are open.

Telecommunications
Mobile phones
GSM coverage is available

Electricity supply
220/240V AC, with three-pin flat plug fittings most common.

Weights and measures
Metric system; other weights are still in use, however.

Social customs/useful tips
Correspondence and technical literature is acceptable in English.
At business meetings it is not uncommon for several people to be present. While in negotiations be careful about committing yourself orally. In a traditional Muslim Sharia Court, oral evidence carries far more weight than written. You should also be aware that you will be held to the letter of any agreement.
Keep contracts as simple as possible; the main part should be couched in easily translated terms with detailed ramifications of the deal relegated to annexes.

Amendments should be avoided as they are considered dishonourable. Increasingly, be prepared to consider contracts under local law – with the provision of neutral (ie Swiss, Dutch) arbitration.

In public places, women should dress modestly.

Refrain from taking photographs without permission.

Pork should not be eaten in the presence of Muslims. It is polite to avoid eating, drinking or smoking in front of Muslims, during daylight hours in the month of Ramadan (when such consumption in public is illegal).

The purchase of alcohol is restricted to expatriate residents with a special liquor permit (not available to Muslims) and its consumption is confined to their private homes. Alcohol is a particularly sensitive subject in Qatar and the utmost discretion must be shown at all times by those permitted to consume it.

Getting there
Air
National airline: Qatar Airways
International airport/s: Doha International (DOH), 8km from city, with restaurant, bank, hotel reservations, shops, car hire.

A taxi from the airport to the city centre takes about 15 minutes. The larger hotels will send transport to the airport to collect their guests.

Airport tax: International departures QR20; not applicable to transit passengers.

Surface
Road: Tarmac roads link all towns and villages in Qatar with Saudi Arabia. It is also possible to enter by good roads from the UAE.

Main port/s: Passenger services through Mina Salman, Mina Manama and Mina Muharroq, with ferries to Iran and Bahrain.

Getting about
National transport
Road: High priority is given to the construction of Qatar's road network, which includes more than 1,000km of good roads (some dual carriageway). There is a ring road system around Doha.

The Trans-Arabian Highway which links Doha with Saudi Arabia provides a continuous land connection between Qatar and Europe. Another highway which was build in conjunction with the UAE, links Qatar with the Gulf countries' network.

Buses: Doha's public bus service provides transport to and from the neighbouring towns. There is no public transport within the city.

City transport
Taxis: Taxis are orange and white and have black-on-yellow number plates, with metered fares.

Two-tier (day and night) fare system applies within the Doha city limits. They can be hired on a time basis, with a set hourly rate.

Some hotels offer a courtesy pick-up service; others offer the service but charge. A limousine can be booked through the hotel.

Car hire
If hiring for more than seven days, it is necessary to obtain a 30-day local licence – international or foreign licences are not acceptable. For this, a foreign or international licence, a letter from a local sponsor and passport must be produced within a week of arrival, and a test on road signs may be required. Third-party insurance is compulsory.

Speed limits are 60kph in cities and 100kph on highways. Traffic drives on the right.

Air-conditioned cars are available for hire, with a driver, and can be delivered to the airport or hotel.

BUSINESS DIRECTORY

The addresses listed below are a selection only. While World of Information makes every endeavour to check these addresses, we cannot guarantee that changes have not been made, especially to telephone numbers and area codes. We would welcome any corrections.

Telephone area codes
The international dialling code (IDD) for Qatar is +974, followed by subscriber's number.

Useful telephone numbers
Emergency (all services):	999
International operator:	150
Directory enquiries:	180
International enquiries:	190
Speaking clock (English):	140

Banking
Al Ahli Bank of Qatar, PO Box 2309, Doha (tel: 4326-611; fax: 4444-652).

Al Mashriq, PO Box 173, Doha (tel: 4413-213; fax: 4413-880).

Arab Bank Ltd., PO Box 173, Doha (tel: 4437-979; fax: 4410-774).

Bank Saderat Iran, PO Box 2256, Doha (tel: 4414-646; fax: 4428-077).

Banque Paribas, PO Box 2636, Doha (tel: 4433-844; fax: 4410-861).

British Bank of the Middle East (BBME), PO Box 57, 810 Abdulla bin Jassim Street, Doha (tel: 4423-124; fax: 4416-353).

Bank Saderat Iran, PO Box 2256, Doha (tel: 4414-646; fax: 4430-121).

Bank of Oman Ltd., PO Box 173, Doha (tel: 4413-213; fax: 4413-800).

Commercial Bank of Qatar Ltd, PO Box 3232, Doha (tel: 4490-222; fax: 4438-182).

Doha Bank, PO Box 3818, Doha (tel: 4446-660; fax: 4416-631).

Grindlays Bank Plc, PO Box 2001, Doha (tel: 4425-466; fax: 4428-077).

Qatar Industrial Development Bank, PO Box 22789, Doha (tel: 4421-600; fax: 4416-631).

Qatar International Islamic Bank, PO Box 664, Doha (tel: 4409-409; fax: 4444-101).

Qatar Islamic Bank, PO Box 559, Doha (tel: 4438-000; fax: 4412-700).

Qatar National Bank, PO Box 1000, Doha (tel: 4407-407; fax: 4413-753; e-mail: webmaster@qatarbank.com).

Standard Chartered Bank, PO Box 29, Doha (tel: 4414-252; fax: 4413-739).

The Arab Bank Ltd, PO Box 172, Doha (tel: 4437-979; fax: 4410-774).

United Bank Ltd, PO Box 242, Doha (tel: 4438-666; fax: 4424-600).

Central bank
Qatar Central Bank, PO Box 1234, Doha (tel: 456-456; fax: 413-650; e-mail: elzainys@acb.gov.qa).

Travel information
Doha International Airport information (tel: 4438-111).

Gulf Air, PO Box 138, Manama, Bahrain (tel: (973)322-200; fax: (973)440-466).

Qatar Airways, Almana Tower, PO Box 22550, Doha (tel: 4430-707; fax: 4352-433).

Qatar National Hotels Co, PO Box 2977, Doha (tel: 4426-414; fax: 4431-223).

Ministry of tourism
Ministry of Information, PO Box 1836, Doha (tel: 831-333; fax: 831-518).

Ministries
Ministry of Amiri Diwan Affairs, PO Box 923, Doha (tel: 4468-333; fax: 4412-617).

Ministry of Communications and Transport, PO Box 3416, Doha (tel: 4464-000; fax: 4413-886).

Ministry of Defence, PO Box 37, Doha (tel: 4604-111; fax: 4608-366).

Ministry of Education, PO Box 80, Doha (tel: 4333-444; fax: 4413-954).

Ministry of Electricity and Water, Department of Electricity, PO Box 41, Doha (tel: 4326-622; fax: 4426-608).

Ministry of Endowments and Islamic Affairs, PO Box 232, Doha (tel: 4452-222).

Ministry of Foreign Affairs, PO Box 250, Doha (tel: 4334-334; fax: 4442-777).

Ministry of Information and Culture, PO Box 1836, Doha (tel: 4831-333; fax: 4831-518).

Ministry of Interior, PO Box 920, Doha (tel: 4430-000; fax: 44330-168); Passport and Immigration Division, PO Box 122, Doha (tel: 4443-300); Police Headquarters, PO Box 920, Doha (tel: 4330-000); Police Traffic Division, PO Box 8989, Doha (tel: 4868-000; fax: 4872-624); Residence Permits, PO Box 122, Doha (tel: 4325-588); Visa Section, PO Box 122, Doha (tel: 4328-129).

Ministry of Justice, PO Box 2377, Doha (tel: 4435-777; fax: 4832-868).

Ministry of Labour, Social Affairs and Housing, PO Box 201, Doha (tel: 4321-955; fax: 4432-929).

Ministry of Municipal and Agricultural Affairs, PO Box 2727, Doha (tel: 4336-336; fax: 4430-239).

Ministry of Public Health, PO Box 42, Doha (tel: 4441-555; fax: 4429-565).

National Oil Distribution Company (NODCO), PO Box 50033, Mesaieed (tel: 4776-555; fax: 4771-232).

Other useful addresses

Broadcasting and Television Corporation, PO Box 1836, Doha (tel: 4831-333; fax: 4831-518).

Central Tenders Committee, PO Box 1968, Doha (tel: 4413-089; fax: 4439-360).

Department of Civil Aviation, PO Box 3000, Doha (tel: 4426-262; fax: 4429-070).

Department of Commercial Affairs, PO Box 22355, Doha (tel: 4432-103; fax: 4431-412).

Department of Customs, PO Box 81, Doha (tel: 4457-457; fax: 4414-959).

Department of Economic Affairs, PO Box 1968, Doha (tel: 4416-234; fax: 4415-731).

Department of Environmental Affairs, PO Box 7634, Doha (tel: 4320-825; fax: 4415-246).

Department of Financial Affairs, PO Box 83, Doha (tel: 4461-444; fax: 4413-617).

Department of Income Tax, PO Box 83, /diga (tel: 4461-444; fax: 4413-617).

Department of Industrial Development, PO Box 2599, Doha (tel: 4832-121; fax: 4832-024).

Department of Museum and Antiquities, PO Box 2777, Doha (tel: 4438-123).

Department of Post, PO Box 713, Doha (tel: 4835-555; fax: 4837-777).

Department of Safety, Quality and Environment, PO Box 47, Doha (tel: 4402-538; fax: 4402-207).

Department of Water, PO Box 162, Doha (tel: 4494-444).

Doha Securities Market, PO Box 22114, Doha (tel: 4328-025; fax: 4326-497).

Exhibitions Department, PO Box 1968, Doha (tel: 4834-450; fax: 4834-480).

Exploration and Development of New Ventures Department, PO Box 3212, Doha (tel: 4491-288; fax: 4831-850).

Government House, ¡PO Box 83, Doha (tel: 4461-444).

HH the Emir's Doha Palace, PO Box 923 (tel: 4415-888).

Information and Computer Services Department, PO Box 47, Doha (tel: 4402-240; fax: 4413-629).

Al Jazeera Satellite Channel, PO Box 23123, Doha (tel: 4890-890; fax: 4885-333).

Legal Affairs and Contracts Department, PO Box 3212, Doha (tel: 4491-467; fax: 4831-752).

Materials Department, PO Box 47, Doha (tel: 4332-222; fax: 4343-458).

Petroleum Engineering Department, PO Box 47, Doha (tel: 4402-440; fax: 4402-215).

Pharmaceuticals and Medicines Control Department, PO Box 1919, Doha (tel: 4447-828; fax: 4425-399).

Qatar Broadcasting Services, PO Box 3939, Doha (tel: 4894-4444; fax: 4894-202).

Qatar Clean Energy Company (QACENCO), PO Box 22074, Doha (tel: 4415-556; fax: 4415-640).

Qatar Embassy (USA), 4200 Wisconsin Avenue, NW, Washington DC 20016 (tel: 202-274-1603; fax: 202-237-0061; e-mail: washington@mofa.gov.qa).

Qatar Fertiliser Company (QAFCO), PO Box 50001, Doha (tel: 4770-252; fax: 4771-655).

Qatar Fuel Additives Company (QAFAC), PO Box 22700, Doha (tel: 4433-700; fax: 4433-766).

Qatar General Petroleum Corporation, Headquarters: PO Box 3212, Doha (tel: 4491-491; fax: 4836-999; internet site: http://www.qgpc.com.qa); Oil and Gas Operations: PO Box 47, Doha (tel: 4402-000).

Qatar Liquefied Gas Company (QATARGAS), PO Box 22666, Doha (tel: 4739-400; fax: 4739-423).

Qatar National Cement Company, PO Box 1333, Doha (tel: 4350-800).

Qatar Petrochemical Company (QAPCO), PO Box 756, Doha (tel: 4321-105; fax: 4324-700).

Qatar Public Telecommunications Corp, PO Box 217, Doha (tel: 4400-333; fax: 4413-904).

Qatar Steel Company Ltd, PO Box 50090, Doha (tel: 4770-011; fax: 4771-424).

Qatar Television, PO Box 1944, Doha (tel: 4894-444; fax: 4438-316).

Ras Laffan Liquefied Natural Gas Company, PO Box 2400, Doha (tel: 4859-400; fax: 4833-855).

State Audit Bureau, PO Box 2466, Doha (tel: 4441-000; fax: 4412-101).

Internet sites

Arab net: http://www.arab.net/welcome.html

Arab world on line: http://www.awo.net/business/bestopps/home.htm

Arabia on line: http://www.arabia.com

Gulf business explorer: http://www.igulf.com/main.htm

Réunion

COUNTRY PROFILE

Historical profile
The island was uninhabited until the beginning of the seventeenth century when Arab explorers called it Diva Margabin. The Portuguese renamed it Ilha Santa Apolonia and the French settlers called it l'Île Bourbon. After the French Revolution it was given its current name, La Réunion.
1642 The island was first occupied by France and was ruled as a colony.
1946 La Réunion became a French Département d'Outre-Mer (DOM) (Overseas Department).
1973 The headquarters of French military forces in the Indian Ocean was established on the island.
1974 La Réunion was further incorporated into the French political system and granted the status of region of France.
1983 France granted autonomy in the administration of La Réunion through devolution, establishing a Regional Council.
1992 A contentious newcomer to local politics, Camille Sudre, the owner of a pirate television station, created the Free-DOM party, which won the largest block of seats in the Regional Council. The result was annulled when Sudre's TV broadcasts for his party were deemed political propaganda.
1993 The Free-DOM party led by Camille Sudre's wife, Marguerite, won the elections with a reduced majority.
1996 Unemployment reached 40 per cent.
1998 Paul Vergés was elected head of the Regional Council.
2001 Gonthier Friederici became *préfet*.
2002 La Réunion adopted the euro as its official currency.
2004 There was volcanic activity at Piton de la Fournaise on 9 January. On 16 August, Dominique Vian took office as *préfet*.
2005 Laurent Cayrel was appointed *préfet* on 29 June.

Political structure
Constitution
28 September 1958 (French Fifth Republic)
Under the 1946 constitution of the French Fourth Republic, La Réunion became a Département d'Outre-Mer (DOM) (Overseas Department) of France. In 1974, it was granted additional status as a region of France.
La Réunion is represented in the French National Assembly in Paris by five directly elected deputies and in the Senate by three indirectly elected senators.
Since 1983, following the French government's policy of decentralisation, regional councils have been elected with powers similar to those of the regions.
Administration is by a préfét appointed by the government in Paris.
The local government comprises a Conseil Général (General Council) of 44 members and a 45-member Conseil Régional (Regional Council), both directly elected for six-year terms.
There are five *arrondisements*.
Form of state
Département d'Outre-Mer (DOM) (Overseas Department) of France, with additional status as a région (region) of France.
Legal system
French legal system

Political parties
Free-DOM (right-wing group); Parti Communiste de Réunion (PCR) (Réunion Communist Party); Rassemblement pour la République (RPR) (Gaullist Rally for the Republic); two factions of the Parti Socialiste (PS) (Socialist Party); Union pour la France (UPF) (Union for France); Union pour la Démocratie Française-Centre Démocratique Sociale (UDF-CDS) (Union for French Democracy-Social Democratic Centre).

Population
778,400 (2004)
Ethnic make-up
African (64 per cent), Indian (28 per cent), European (2.2 per cent) and Chinese (2.2 per cent) descent.
Religions
The majority of the population is Roman Catholic (86 per cent); there are also groups of Hindus, Muslims and Buddhists.

Education
Literacy rate: 89 per cent, adult rate (2003)

Health
Health services comply with French standards.
Life expectancy: 73.4 years; male 70 years; female 77 years (2003).
Fertility rate/Maternal mortality rate: 2.5 births per woman (2003)
Birth rate/Death rate: 20 births per 1,000 population; 5.5 deaths per 1,000 population (2003).
Infant mortality rate: Eight per 1,000 live births (2003)

KEY FACTS

Official name: La Réunion

Head of State: President Jacques Chirac (president of France)

Head of government: Prime Minister Jean-Pierre Raffarin, represented by *Préfet* Laurent Cayrel (appointed 29 Jun 2005)

Area: 2,512 square km

Population: 778,400 (2004)

Capital: Saint Denis

Official language: French

Currency: Euro (eur) = 100 cents

Exchange rate: eur0.83 per US$ (Oct 2005)

GDP per capita: US$4,800 (2003)

GDP real growth: 2.50% (2004)

Labour force: 309,900 (2003)

Unemployment: 36.00% (2003)

Balance of trade: -US$2.29 billion (2003)

Nations of the World: A Political, Economic and Business Handbook

Head of population per physician/bed: There are some 1,270 doctors, 275 pharmacies and 17 hospitals, including clinics.

Main cities
Saint Denis (capital, population 131,557, March 1999 census), Saint Paul (87,712), Saint Pierre (68,915), Le Tampon (60,323), Saint Louis, Le Port, Saint André.

Languages spoken
As well as French, Creole is commonly spoken.
Official language/s
French

Media
Press
Le Journal de L'Ile is a French daily published from St Denis.
Broadcasting
The television service Antenne Réunion broadcasts on the island; Canal Réunion is a subscription television channel. Société Nationale de Radiodiffusion et de Télévision pour l'Outre-Mer (RFO) relays radio and television services in French.

Economy
La Réunion is dependent on France for 75 per cent of its GNP.
Sugar cane used to dominate the economy, accounting for up to 85 per cent of export earnings, but the dependence on agriculture made the country vulnerable to external price fluctuations, and adverse climatic conditions. The government has been looking at ways to diversify the economy, focussing on tourism.
The service sector has grown considerably and provides around three quarters of GDP, with agriculture shrinking and providing only 8 per cent of total GDP.
In December 2003, the EU approved French air transport subsidies for Réunion, which should help boost tourist numbers. GDP growth was 2.5 per cent in 2004, less than the 3.8 per cent in 2003. Although social indicators are good, unemployment is a pressing problem affecting almost 40 per cent of the labour force. There is a great income and social divide between the majority of the population, which is impoverished and black, and the rich minority, which is white or Indian.

External trade
Imports
The main imports are manufactured goods, food, beverages, tobacco, machinery and transportation equipment, raw materials, and petroleum products.
Main sources: France (64 per cent), Bahrain (3.0 per cent), Germany (3.0 per cent), Italy (3.0 per cent).

Exports
The main export is sugar (63 per cent), rum and molasses, perfume essences and lobster.
Main destinations: France (74 per cent), Japan (6.0 per cent), Comoros (4.0 per cent)

Agriculture
Farming
Sugar cane, the main crop, is grown on 30,900 hectares. Cash crops include tea and tobacco. Ylang-ylang, vetiver and geraniums are used as components of aromatic essences.
The agriculture sector contributes about 8 per cent to GDP and employs approximately 13 per cent of the workforce. Around 22 per cent of the land is cultivated. Much of the island's food supply is imported.
Crop production in 2004 included: 17,000 tonnes (t) maize, 3,700t potatoes, 1,800t cassava, 1,800t bananas, 2,000,000t sugar cane, 5,350t citrus fruit, 1,100t pulses, 4,000t tomatoes, 6,150t roots and tubers, 10,000t pineapples, 1,035t various spices, 42,460t fruit in total, 51,020t vegetables in total. Livestock production included: 35,100t meat in total, 1,750t beef, 94t lamb and goat meat, 12,000t pig meat, 2,016t rabbit meat, 19,227t poultry, 5,700t eggs, 23,300t milk, 100t honey.
Fishing
Typical annual fish catches are over 4,000mt and crustacea catches are over 15mt.

Industry and manufacturing
The industrial sector contributes about 19 per cent to GDP and employs some 12 per cent of the workforce.
The production of processed sugar and rum accounts for most industrial activity. The Ecopipe steel pipe mill (funded by the French government and South African private capital) started operations in 1997 at Le Port, on the west coast of Réunion. It has the capacity to produce 15,000 tonnes a year and employs 80 people.

Tourism
Tourism is now the principal economic activity. As a *département* of France, the majority of visitors tend to be French. Numbers fell as a consequence of the 11 September 2001 terrorist attacks in the US, when worldwide travel dropped. In 2003 recovery was under way with 432,000 tourist arrivals recorded. La Réunion's link with France gives its tourism sector an edge, in the European market, over its local rivals.
Air Austral is able to offer the cheapest flights from Europe to the region, while the island's currency is the euro.

Mining
There are no significant mineral resources.

Hydrocarbons
There are no hydrocarbon reserves and Réunion relies entirely on the import of refined oil, including gasoline, jet fuel and distillate. Import costs are generally high as they come from France.
Distribution and marketing of fuel products is carried out by Esso, Total, Caltex, SRPP, Shell and Elf.

Energy
Approximately 60 per cent of the power is hydroelectric. Réunion has one thermal power plant that runs on imported coal. This produces around 39 per cent of Réunion's electricity needs. Réunion does not import or consume natural gas.

Banking and insurance
Central bank
Banque de France; European Central Bank (ECB).

Time
GMT plus four hours (winter); GMT plus three hours (summer).

Geography
Réunion is an island in the Indian Ocean, lying about 800km (500 miles) east of Madagascar. It is a volcanic, mountainous island.

Climate
The climate varies greatly according to altitude: at sea-level, it is tropical, with average temperatures between 20 and 28 degrees Celsius (C); in the uplands, it is much cooler, with average temperatures between 8 and 19 degrees C. From July to November, the temperature in high altitude places can drop to 10 degrees C during the day and to 6 degrees C at night.
Rainfall is abundant; the cyclone season lasts from December to April.
Summer runs from November to April with an average temperature of 27 degrees C. Winter stretches from May to October with an average temperature of 23 degrees C.

Dress codes
Generally light summer clothes are required, with some woollen garments for chilly evenings.

Entry requirements
Passports
Citizens of the EU can use a valid identity card; all other citizens require a valid passport.
Visa
Required by all, except citizens of EU, North America, Australasia and Japan, for stays up to one month; this includes business trips by representatives of foreign entities with an invitation from a local

Réunion

company or organisation. Proof of adequate funds for stay, an itinerary, a guarantee of repatriation if necessary and return/onward ticket are also required. For further exceptions, full details and a copy of the application form visit www.diplomatie.gouv.fr/thema/dossier.gb.asp and follow the path (entering France) to the database.

Health (for visitors)
There are no compulsory vaccinations. Passengers from endemic countries should be inoculated against yellow fever.

Advisable precautions
Vaccinations for diphtheria, tetanus, typhoid fever, hepatitis A and tuberculosis are advisable, and precautions should be taken against malaria.

Credit cards
Major credit cards are accepted.

Public holidays
Fixed dates
1 Jan (New Year's Day), 1 May (Labour Day), 8 May (1945 Victory Day), 14 Jul (Bastille Day), 15 Aug (Assumption Day), 1 Nov (All Saints' Day), 11 Nov (Armistice Day), 20 Dec (Abolition of Slavery Day), 25 Dec (Christmas Day).

Variable dates
Easter Monday, Ascension Day, Whit Monday.

Working hours
Banking
Mon–Fri: 0800–1600.
Business
Mon–Fri: 0800–1200; 1400–1800.
Shops
Mon–Sat: 0830–1200; 1430–1800.
Some food stores are open on Sunday.

Telecommunications
Telephone/fax
The telephone network is entirely automatic and is linked to metropolitan France and the rest of the world via satellite.

Mobile phones
There is a cell phone network (SFR) and partnership agreements between cell phone companies. Most subscribers from outside countries can use their cell phones in Réunion (it is, however, advisable to check with the phone company).

Electricity supply
220V

Weights and measures
The metric system is in use.

Getting there
Air
National airline: Air Austral (Air France is a shareholder) operates scheduled services to Madagascar and the Comoros. In December 2003, Air Austral was awarded subsidies from France, which will enable it to reduce its operating costs on the Paris-Réunion route.

International airport/s: Roland-Garros airport, near Saint Denis (in the north), 5km from town.

Other airport/s: Pierrefonds airfield near Saint Pierre (in the south).

Airport tax: There is no airport departure tax.

Surface
Water: There are limited passenger services to the island. Cruise liners are more likely to call at Mauritius or the Seychelles.

Main port/s: Port de la Pointe des Galets (two ports: port Ouest and port Est).

Getting about
National transport
Road: A *route nationale* circles the island, following the coast and linking all the main towns, and another crosses the island from south-west to north-east linking Saint Pierre and Saint Benoît. There are 370km of main roads, 754km of secondary roads and nearly 1,600km of smaller secondary roads, all in good condition. A French or international driver's licence is required. The highway code is the same as for France. Driving is on the right.

Buses: The island's bus service, called *Cars jaunes*, links most towns.

BUSINESS DIRECTORY
The addresses listed below are a selection only. While World of Information makes every endeavour to check these addresses, we cannot guarantee that changes have not been made, especially to telephone numbers and area codes. We would welcome any corrections.

Telephone area codes
The international dialling code (IDD) for Réunion is +262; this is followed by another 262 and then the subscriber's number.

Useful telephone numbers
Available services for visiting cell phone users:
Emergency calls: (free) 112
Telephone enquiries:
(call SFR for information) 222
Suberscriber services: (local rate) 900

Chambers of Commerce
Réunion Chamber of Commerce Industry, 13 Rue Pasteur, PO Box 120, 97463 Saint-Denis cedex (tel: 942-100; fax: 942-290; e-mail: sg.dir@reunion.cci.fr).

Banking
Banque de la Réunion, 27 rue Jean-Chatel, 97711 Saint Denis, Cedex 9 (tel: 400-123; fax: 400-061).

Banque Nationale de Paris Intercontinentale (BNPI), 67 rue Juliette-Dodu, Saint Denis (tel: 403-030).

Banque Régionale d'Escompte et de Depot (BRED), 33 rue Victor-Mac-Auliffe, Saint Denis (tel: 901-560).

Caisse d'Epargne Ecureuil, 55 rue de Paris, Saint Denis (tel: 948-000).

Crédit Agricole, 18 rue Félix-Guyon, Saint Denis (tel: 909-100).

Banque Française Commerciale (BFC'OI'), 60 rue Alexis-de-Villeneuve, Saint Denis (tel: 405-555).

Central bank

Banque de France, 1 rue la Vrillière, 75001 Paris, Dept 75, France (tel: +33(1)4292-4292 fax: +33(1)4292-4500); European Central Bank (ECB), Kaiserstrasse 29, D-60311 Frankfurt am Main, Germany (tel: +49(69)13-440; fax: +49(69)1344-6000).

Travel information
Air Austral, 4 Rue de Nice, PO Box 611, 97473 Saint Denis Cedex (tel: 909-090, 488-020 (airport); fax: 909-091).

Air France Océan Indien, 7 Avenue de la Victoire, PO Box 845, 97477 Saint Denis Cedex (tel: 403-838, 488-086 (airport); fax: 403-840).

Air Liberté, 83 Rue Labourdonnais, Roland Garros Airport, 97400 Saint Denis (tel: 947-200, 488-384 (airport); fax: 416-800, 488-386).

AOM French Airlines, 7 Rue Jean Chatel, 97400 Saint Denis (tel: 947-777, 488-099 (airport); fax: 200-716).

Comité du Tourisme de la Réunion, Place du 20 Décembre 1848, PO Box 615, 97472 Saint Denis (tel: 210-041; fax: 202-593); representative in France: 90 Rue la Boétie, 75008 Paris, France (tel: +33 (1) 4075-0279; fax: +33 (1) 4075-0273).

La Maison de la Montagne, 10 Place Sarda Garriga, 97405 Saint Denis Cedex (tel: 907-878).

Office du Tourisme Syndicat d'Initiative de Saint Denis, 48 Rue Sainte Marie, 97400 Saint Denis (tel: 418-300; fax: 213-776; e-mail: ctr@la-reunion-tourisme.com; internet site: http://www.la-reunion-tourisme.com, http://www.la-reunion.web-france.com/).

Ministries
Direction Départementale des Affaires Sanitaires et Sociales, Rue Georges Brassens, BP 199, 97490 Sainte-Clothilde (tel: 486-060; fax: 486-008).

Direction Départementale du Travail et de l'Emploi, 24 Rue Maréchal Leclerc, 97488 Saint Denis Cedex (tel: 486-600; fax: 486-666).

Direction Régionale des Affaires Culturelles, 31 Rue Amiral Lacaze 97400 Saint Denis (tel: 219-171; fax: 416-193).

Direction Régionale de la Jeunesse et des Sports, 14 Allée des Saphirs, BP 297, 97487 Saint Denis Cedex (tel: 901-616; fax: 213-864).

Other useful addresses

Agence Nationale pour l'Emploi 10 Rue Champ Fleury, 97490 Sainte Clothilde (tel: 219-236; fax: 417-383).

Association of the Hotel Industry, Centhor – PO Box 6, 1 Route du Théatre, 97435 Saint Gilles les Hauts (tel: 553-730; fax: 553-729).

Association pour le Développement Industriel de la Réunion, 18 Rue Milius, 97468 Saint Denis Cedex (tel: 214-269; fax: 203-757).

British Consul, 94b Avenue Leconte Delisle, 97490 Sainte Clotilde (tel: 291-491; fax: 293-991).

Civil Aviation Management, 11 Avenue de la Victoire, 97489 Saint Denis Cedex (tel: 930-000; fax: 211-331).

Compagnie Générale Maritime (CGM), 2 Rue de l'Est, BP 2010, 97822 Le Port Cedex (tel: 420-088; fax: 432-304).

Conseil Général, Hôtel du Département, 2 Rue Source, 97400 Saint Denis (tel: 903-030; fax: 903-999).

Conseil Régional, Hôtel de la Région, Avenue René Cassin, Le Moufia, 97494 Sainte Clothilde Cedex (tel: 487-000; fax: 487-071).

Federation of Tourist Offices of Réunion Island (FROTSI), Résidence Saint Anne, 97400 Saint Denis Cedex (tel: 217-376; fax: 218-447).

Institut National de la Statistique et des Etudes Economiques, Service Régional de la Réunion, 15 Rue de l'Ecole, 97490 Sainte Clotilde (tel: 295-157).

Palais du Justice, 166 Rue Juliette Dodu, 97488 Saint Denis (tel: 405-858; fax: 219-532).

Préfecture de la Réunion, Délégation Régionale au Commerce, á l'Artisanat et au Tourisme, 2 Avenue de la Victoire, 97400 Saint Denis Cedex (tel: 407-758; fax: 407-701, 417-374).

Rectorat de la Réunion, 24 Avenue Georges, Brassens, 97702 Saint Denis, Messagerie Cedex 9 (tel: 481-010; fax: 481-366).

Société de Développement Economique de la Réunion (SODERE), 26 Rue Labourdonnais, 97469 Saint Denis (tel: 200-168; fax: 200-507).

Syndicat des Exportateurs d'Huiles Essentielles, Plantes Aromatiques et Medicinales de Bourbon, 38 bis Rue Labourdonnais, 97400 Saint Denis (tel: 201-023).

Syndicat des Fabricants de Sucre de la Réunion, BP 57, 97462 Saint Denis (tel: 216-700; fax: 412-413).

Syndicat des Producteurs de Rhum de la Réunion, BP 57, 97462 Saint Denis (tel: 216-700; fax: 412-413).

Syndicat Patronal du Bâtiment de la Réunion, BP 108, 97463 Saint Denis (tel: 210-381; fax: 215-507).

Internet sites

Africa Business Network: http://www.ifc.org/abn

African Development Bank: http://www.afdb.org

Mbendi AfroPaedia (information on companies, countries, industries and stock exchanges in Africa): http://mbendi.co.za

Romania

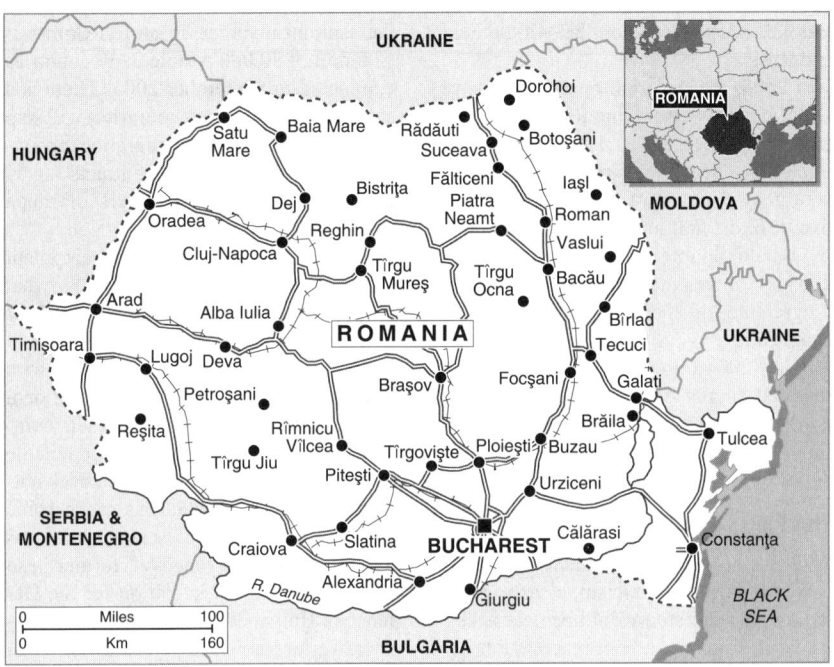

In April 2005 Romania signed the European Union (EU) accession treaty. This long-awaited document heralds a future of economic and social modernisation, development, security and integration for the once-communist, still impoverished country. January 2007 was named as the all-important date of Romanian entry into the EU. Romania also had the dubious honour of being the first European nation to discover outbreaks of avian flu in 2005. The prolonged and multiple flooding in the spring and summer was equally troublesome. The floods were the worst for 40 years, prompting the evacuation of over 3,500 people and power cuts in 17 villages. Infrastructure and transport was seriously affected. By August several dozen had died.

Politics

Governmental and popular aspirations to join the EU defined political and economic policy in 2005.

In July, Prime Minister Tariceanu resigned, with the announcement 'this is an irrevocable decision'. Less than two weeks later he revoked it. Tariceanu claimed to be re-instating himself in response to the country's heavy flooding. He declared that the country needed stable leadership at this time and promised to rebuild damaged infrastructure.

In August Tariceanu reshuffled his coalition government. Four major players were replaced, in the hope that fresh faces could accelerate reforms needed for EU accession. The reshuffled ministers are those responsible for European integration, finance and health, along with the deputy prime minister.

Economy

With eyes on the eventual adoption of the single currency, the government re-launched the national currency in July. The system was streamlined with the removal of four digits. This move should preclude any repeat of the 300 per cent hyperinflation of 1993, after the disintegration of the Soviet Union. In 2005 the projected rate was a much healthier 7.5 per cent. The old and new currencies will be concurrent until 31 December 2006.

The second major financial reform carried out in 2005 was the slashing of taxes.

KEY FACTS

Official name: Romania

Head of State: President Traian Basescu (PD) (elected 12 Dec 2004)

Head of government: Prime Minister Calin Popescu Tariceanu (PNL) (from 13 Dec 2004)

Ruling party: Coalition government: Partidul National Liberal (PNL) (National Liberal Party), Partidul Democrat (PD) (Democratic Party), Uniunea Democratica Maghiara din Romania (UDMR) (Hungarian Democratic Alliance of Romania), Partidul Umanist din România (PUR) (Humanist Party of Romania)

Area: 237,500 square km

Population: 21.48 million (2004)

Capital: Bucharest

Official language: Romanian

Currency: New leu (plural lei) (Nleu) The new leu was introduced 1 Jul 2005; four zeroes were removed from the old leu; Nleu1 = 10,000 old lei; euro1 = Nleu3.6.

Exchange rate: Nleu2.95 per US$ (Oct 2005)

GDP per capita: US$3,207 (2004)

GDP real growth: 8.30% (2004)

Labour force: 10.48 million (2004)

Unemployment: 6.80% (2004)

Inflation: 11.90% (2004)

Oil production: 119,000 bpd (2004)

Balance of trade: -US$4.39 billion 2004

Foreign debt: US$13.70 billion (2003)

Paradoxically, this move is hoped to generate greater revenue from taxation, as it will lessen the incentive for fraud. The black market in Romania is currently estimated to account for almost half of GDP. In January the government instituted a new uniform income tax rate of 16 per cent, down from 20–40 per cent. No Western country has standardised taxation rates in this way but it is becoming a common practice in ex-communist countries. Estonia, Russia, Georgia, Latvia and Serbia all have a homogenous tax rate. Although the tax generates better rates of compliance, it does also severely restrict opportunities for wealth redistribution.

Business

The Romanian bank, Casa de Economii si Consemnatiuni (CEC), invited bids for a privatisation takeover in October 2005. Offers were submitted by seven European banks, including those of Austria, Greece, Hungary and Italy. The CEC accounts for 5.6 per cent of the market and consists of 1,400 branches. It will be a lucrative takeover although the institution needs to be restructured and modernised. The Banca Comerciala Romana (BCR), the country's biggest bank, with 25 per cent of market share, is also being privatised. It has an estimated value of eur5.6 billion and 300 branches. Commercial banking is developing quickly in Romania, in terms of size and competitiveness. The sale of these two banks will be influential: after privatisation, 90 per cent of banking assets will be under foreign control.

In 2005 Italy announced the construction of a new oil pipeline between Romania and Trieste. The 1,500km, eur2 billion pipe will traverse Romania, Serbia, Croatia, Slovenia and Italy and will lessen European dependence on the Middle East and Russia.

In 2004, the Austrian energy company OMV bought Petrom, the Romanian state energy provider, for eur1.5 billion. Share prices have been very strong this year and Wolfgang Ruttenstorfer, the chief executive, forecast that investment in the country would double to eur3 billion from 2005–10. Investment will accompany a programme of modernisation and staff cutbacks.

In late 2004 Europa, a British company, reported having discovered gas in Bilca, northern Romania. When this source is fully exploited, gas production could double.

The European Union

The EU accession document was conceived with some cynicism, clearly stipulating that accession would be delayed by a year if Romania did not reach tough EU standards, particularly in judicial matters. While demands that Romania tackle prolific domestic corruption and introduce more transparency in its judiciary are fair, the strictness with which Romania is being treated is perhaps disproportionate.

EU citizens are generally not favourably disposed towards Romanian accession: only 17 per cent of Austrians and 28 per cent of Germans proclaimed support for the aspirant member, in an EU Commission poll of 30,000 people in 30 countries conducted in September 2005. There is a suspicion that poorer countries will sap EU funds, prompt mass migration, and attract lucrative foreign contracts away from western states by offers of much cheaper labour.

The prospect of regional development aid and expanded markets is exactly what attracts Romania to the EU. In 2005 17 new reforming laws were conceived to harmonise anti-corruption measures with EU standards. However, the constitutional court disallowed the laws in their complete form, deeming them irreconcilable with existing legislation. This setback notwithstanding, Tariceanu has made some progress. Perhaps his wisest decision was to appoint Monica Macovei, former head of the Romanian Association for the Defence of Human Rights, as his justice minister. Tariceanu has appealed to the West to lend their expertise in tackling fraud. In January 2005, the managers of the Rafo Onesti oil company were investigated for large-scale tax evasion, and former politicians were stripped of their immunity from prosecution. The culture of inveterate corruption is beginning to change.

Romania should be able to meet EU standards on fraud, but possibly not by 2007 as required. The country missed out on EU accession in 2004 because it could not reform quickly enough. In October 2005, the European Commission released a not wholly positive interim report on Romania's reforming progress. Criticism was focussed on administrative capabilities and food safety as well as corruption. Another task Romania has yet to complete is the termination, or at least the reduction, of state subsidies, especially to the steel industry.

More daunting is the prospect of cementing territorial borders. Existing EU countries are urging new members to construct Europe like a fortress to thwart illegal immigration and contraband trading. Romania will control 1,500km of the EU's perimeter. From 2004–06 the EU is pledging eur125 million to Romania to tighten its border controls. This money is

KEY INDICATORS — Romania

	Unit	2000	2001	2002	2003	2004
Population	m	22.40	22.30	21.65	21.57	*21.48
Gross domestic product (GDP)	US$bn	37.00	40.00	43.74	57.37	*73.17
GDP per capita	US$	1,640	1,770	2,020	2,660	3,207
GDP real growth	%	1.8	5.3	4.9	4.5	8.3
Inflation	%	45.7	30.0	22.5	15.0	11.9
Unemployment	%	11.5	8.6	9.2	8.9	–
Oil output	'000 bpd	131.0	130.0	127.0	123.0	119.0
Natural gas output	bn cum	13.8	12.6	10.8	12.6	13.2
Coal output	mtoe	6.4	7.3	6.7	7.1	6.9
Exports (fob) (goods)	US$m	10,366.0	11,385.0	13,880.0	17,618.0	23,540.0
Imports (fob) (goods)	US$m	12,050.0	15,552.0	17,860.0	23,983.0	28,430.0
Balance of trade	US$m	-1,684.0	-4,167.0	-3,980.0	-6,365.0	-4,890.0
Current account	US$m	-1,359.0	-2,317.0	-1,530.0	-3,311.0	-5,370.0
Foreign debt	US$bn	10.7	11.1	13.3	13.7	–
Total reserves minus gold	US$m	3,922.0	3,923.0	6,125.0	8,040.0	14,616.0
Foreign exchange	US$m	3,921.0	3,916.0	6,123.0	8,040.0	14,616.0
Foreign direct investment (FDI)	US$bn	1.1	1.2	1.1	–	–
Exchange rate	per US$	21,708.7	29,060.8	32,763.0	33,952.0	32,527.0

* estimated figure

being invested in thermal imaging equipment as well as speedboats. Already this has made an impact: in 2004, 700 illegal immigrants and 73 guides were seized. Corruption among border police remains problematic.

Foreign affairs

The highlight of the foreign affairs calendar was the visit made by US Secretary of State, Condoleezza Rice, in December. After a deal was signed between the two countries, giving America three military bases on Romanian soil, Rice flattered her hosts by calling them one of US's 'best allies'. This marks a shift in US policy: they have been moving their bases eastwards across Europe to be nearer the more turbulent regions of the Middle East and North Africa. Romania sees the US presence as protection against the spectre of Russia and neighbouring countries such as Moldova and Georgia. Romanians still feel gratitude to America for its help in facilitating Romania's transition from a communist state to a market economy. This latest alliance also raises the profile of Romania, with the prime minister hoping it will lead to greater influence with the UK and US. Another incentive is the chance that the military agreement could open doors to US investment in the region.

The friendship with the US is not without its complications, however. Romania has been one of the US's least critical supporters in the Iraq invasion and still has over 800 troops stationed in the territory. There has been no significant domestic opposition to the sending of troops. However, in March 2005 three Romanian journalists were captured in Iraq and held hostage for two months. They were threatened with execution and video footage was broadcast on *al Jazeera* television showing the group at gunpoint. Though the journalists were eventually released alive, the episode did invest a more questioning attitude of the war in the Romanian public.

Furthermore, when Rice visited Europe in late 2005, she was hit with serious allegations about CIA involvement in torture and secret jails. Romania was one of the main countries suspected of complicity, of allowing secret prisons on its territory. This problem could resurface in the next round of EU talks, with key European states notably hostile towards George Bush and suspicious of co-operation.

In July a new ferry route was opened, funded by the EU. The ferry will traverse the Danube river to link Romania to Bulgaria.

Bird flu

Almost worse than the catastrophic flooding in spring and summer was the discovery in October of the first outbreak of H5N1 avian flu in Europe. The illness struck ducks in the delta region and is thought to have come from migrating birds. Seventeen thousand birds were culled in the Danube Delta villages, an area placed under quarantine. Another 30,000 killings of poultry were carried out in other villages. Though not proven to prevent the H5N1 strain, 20,000 people were given flu vaccinations. This has serious economic as well as health repercussions, given that poultry finances the local economy and now the EU has banned imports of birds from Romania.

Risk assessment

Economic	Stable
Political	Stable
Regional Stability	Stable
Stock Market	Stable

COUNTRY PROFILE

Historical profile

1881 After surviving numerous invasions and regional upheavals, Romania became an independent country headed by a monarchy.
1918 Romania supported the Allies during the First World War and gained territory close to its borders.
1919 Hungary attacked Romania in retaliation for lost territory. The Romanians quickly defeated Hungary and briefly occupied parts of the country.
1920 Romania gained further parts of Hungarian territory through the Treaty of Trianon.
1929–34 Romania's agricultural sector was severely affected by a collapse in international grain prices. With the country in recession, the fascist and German-funded Iron Guard movement increased in popularity. In 1933, the organisation assassinated the prime minister, Ion Duca.
1938 King Carol, the head of state, declared Romania a royalist dictatorship and appointed a right-wing government. Carol ordered the arrest and execution of members of the Iron Guard.
1940 Military officers, helped by the Iron Guard, seized power. General Ion Antonescu forced Carol to abdicate. Carol's son, Michel V, replaced him as King. German troops were deployed in Romania and the country joined the Axis powers.
1941 The Iron Guard attempted to rebel against the Romanian government after they were ordered to disarm. A joint Romanian and German operation crushed the Iron Guard's rebellion.
1943 The Soviet Union invaded Romania.
1944 Antonescu's government was overthrown and replaced by a Communist coalition government.
1947–48 The monarchy was deposed and the Communist government declared the Romanian People's Republic.
1965 Nicolae Ceausescu took the position of first secretary of the Partidul Comunist Roman (RCP) (Romanian Communist Party).
1974 Ceausescu became president.
1989 Riots in the city of Timisoara ignited a nationwide revolt. Parts of the army joined the revolutionaries, forming the Frontul Salvarii Nationale (FSN) (National Salvation Front). Ceausescu and his wife, Elena, were summarily executed by a military tribunal and nearly 45 years of Communist dictatorship came to an abrupt and bloody end.
1990 Ion Iliescu was elected president, winning 85 per cent of the vote as the FSN candidate. Petre Roman formed a new government.
1991 Roman resigned as prime minister and was replaced by Teodro Stolojan after his reform programme led to civil unrest. Stolojan successfully guided Romania's new constitution through a referendum and a parliamentary vote.
1992 Presidential elections were again won by Iliescu, who had formed his own political party, the Frontul Democrat al Salvarii Nationale (FDSN) (Democratic National Salvation Front), following a split within the FSN.
1996 Iliescu stood again for the presidency and was defeated by Emil Constantinescu of the Conventia Democrata Romana (CDR) (Romanian Democratic Convention) coalition. The FSN re-named itself the Partidul Democratiei Sociale din Romania (PDSR) (Democratic Social Party of Romania).
1998 After becoming prime minister in 1996, Victor Ciorbea (of the ruling CDR coalition) resigned and was replaced by Radu Vasile.
1999 After relations with his cabinet collapsed, Vasile was replaced as prime minister by Mugur Isarescu.
2000 Cyanide leaked from a mine in northern Romania and polluted rivers in Hungary and Yugoslavia. Ion Iliescu won the presidency in the second round of voting. After parliamentary elections Adrian Nastase became prime minister, heading a coalition government, comprising the PDSR, Partidul Social Democrat Roman (PSDR) (Romanian Social Democratic Party) and the Partidul Umanist din Romania (PUR) (Humanist Party of Romania).

2001 Iliescu's PDSR merged with the PSDR to become the Partidul Social Democrat (PSD) (Social Democratic Party).
2002 Nato invited Romania to join the alliance.
2003 A 5 per cent reduction in payroll taxes was implemented in January to cut labour costs, improve the business environment and reduce the rate of unemployment. In an October referendum, 90 per cent of voters approved constitutional amendments to bring Romania closer to EU law.
2004 Romania joined NATO on 2 April. Bucharest mayor, Traian Basescu, of the opposition won the run-off presidential elections in December, ending the long reign of Ion Iliescu. On 13 December, Calin Popescu Tariceanu was asked by President Basescu to form a government.
2005 In May Romania approved the EU accession treaty. Romania introduced the new leu on 1 July; four zeroes were removed from the old leu. In July, Prime Minister Calin Popescu Tariceanu and his cabinet resigned. However, after severe floods killed 20 people, he retracted his resignation in order to focus on the reconstruction of the country.

Political structure
Constitution
The 1991 constitution proclaimed a democratic, pluralist system of government in which citizens' freedom and rights are guaranteed, although there are no specific measures protecting minority rights. It also stipulated the separation of the three public authorities – legislative, executive and judicial.

Both parliament and the president are elected by universal vote every four years. The president may not remain a member of any political party, and is limited to a maximum two terms in office.
Members of the Chamber of Deputies are required to be of a minimum age of 23 years while members of the Senate and the president are required to be over 35 years of age.
Romania is divided into 40 administrative counties, with Bucharest divided into administrative sectors. Each county, town and village has its own local authority headed by an elected, executive mayor and an elected council. Local government is based on the principle of local autonomy and decentralisation of public services, with locally elected mayors, city and county councils. A prefect for each county is appointed by central government as the ultimate authority for that region.
The minimum voting age is 18 years.
On 19 October 2003, 90 per cent of voters approved changing the constitution to bring it closer to EU law. Under the constitutional changes, private property is guaranteed, the police is demilitarised and the justice system is independent; ethnic minorities may use their mother tongue when dealing with the state and foreigners are permitted to buy land in Romania.

Form of state
Parliamentary democratic republic

The executive
The president nominates the prime minister and the government on the basis of a vote of confidence from parliament and is the commander-in-chief of the armed forces. The president's term of office is four years, renewable once only.

National legislature
The two-chamber Parlamentul Romaniei (Romanian Parliament) consists of Camera Deputatilor (Chamber of Deputies) (327seats) and a Senatul (Senate) (143 seats) and is the supreme representative body and sole law-making authority. The parliament is elected for a four-year term.

Legal system
The legal system is based on the Napolenic Code and the 1991 constitution. There is an independent judiciary, although judges are appointed by the president and parliament. The Supreme Court comprises judges appointed by the president for a term of six years. It administers law, but cannot undertake judicial review. This is undertaken by the Constitutional Court, which comprises nine judges appointed by the president and parliament for a period of nine years.

Last elections
28 November 2004 (first round presidential, and parliamentary); 12 December 2004 (second round presidential); 19 October 2003 (constitutional referendum).
Results: Constitutional referendum: 90 per cent of voters approved a constitution which brought Romania closer to EU law. Presidential (first round): Prime Minister Adrian Nastase of the Social Democratic Party (PSD) won 40.9 per cent of the vote, Traian Basescu of the Democratic Party (PD) 33.9 per cent and Corneliu Vadim Tudor of the Greater Romania Party (PRM) about 13 per cent.
Presidential (second round): Bucharest mayor, Traian Basescu (PD), beat Prime Minister Adrian Nastase (PSD) with 51.2 per cent of the vote to Nastase's 48.8 per cent.
Parliamentary: the PSD won 36.6 per cent of the vote for the lower house and 37.1 per cent for the Senate, the Justice and Truth, the main opposition alliance of the Democratic Party (PD) and the National Liberal Party, won 31.3 per cent and 31.8 per cent, the PRM 12.9 per cent and 13.6 per cent and the Hungarian Democratic Union 6.2 per cent.

Next elections
2008 (presidential and parliamentary)

Political parties
Ruling party
Coalition government: Partidul National Liberal (PNL) (National Liberal Party), Partidul Democrat (PD) (Democratic Party), Uniunea Democratica Maghiara din Romania (UDMR) (Hungarian Democratic Alliance of Romania), Partidul Umanist din România (PUR) (Humanist Party of Romania)

Main opposition party
Alianta Dreptate si Adevar (DA) (Justice and Truth Alliance)

Population
21.48 million (2004)
Ethnic make-up
Romanian (89 per cent), Hungarian (9 per cent), German (0.4 per cent), Ukrainian, Serb, Croat, Russian Turk and Gypsy (1.6 per cent). The Hungarian minority live principally in the Transylvania region. Around half of the then resident ethnic Germans returned to Germany in 1990 and many of the remainder have followed in recent years. Other small ethnic groups include Jews and a number of Greeks and Armenians.

Religions
Romanian Orthodox (70 per cent), Roman Catholic (6 per cent, of which 3 per cent are Uniate), Protestant (6 per cent), and unaffiliated (18 per cent). Since the revolution of 1989 there has been complete religious freedom. The dominant religion is Romanian Orthodox, with over 18 million believers, headed by a Patriarch based in Bucharest. The Roman Catholic Church has approximately 1.35 million members, and includes adherents of the Armenian, Latin and Romanian (Byzantine) rites. The Hungarian and German minorities are predominantly Protestant, and there are communities of the Old-Rite Christian Church (an Orthodox sect) and the Armenian-Gregorian Church. Despite emigration there is still a small Jewish community.

Education
Romania's transition to a market economy made a comprehensive reform of the education sector necessary. The World Bank has supported three reform projects with loan contributions amounting to US$170 million. The centralised education system, with a standard curriculum and ineffective student evaluation system, has been replaced by a flexible curriculum framework, alternative textbooks and a modern evaluation system. Improvements in teacher training, financing and management are under way.
Primary education begins at age seven and lasts until age 11. Lower secondary education lasts for four years until age 15. Upper secondary courses take another four years to complete. Romania's five

types of secondary schools specialise in different areas of education, including general secondary schools, vocational and art schools, those specialising in physical education and teacher training. Minority language schooling is available, mainly in Hungarian and German. Higher education is offered in both public and private institutions.

Public expenditure on education typically amounts to 3.6 per cent of annual gross national income.

Literacy rate: 98.4 per cent, adult rate (2003)

Compulsory years: Seven to 15.

Enrolment rate: 104 per cent gross primary enrolment of relevant age group (including repeaters); 78 per cent gross secondary enrolment (World Bank).

Pupils per teacher: 20 in primary schools.

Health

As primary healthcare units suffer due to financial shortage, there is over-concentration of already scarce resources on hospitals. Outbreaks of infectious diseases, often contracted in hospitals, are common.

Annual total expenditure on health is 6–7 per cent of GDP, of which government spending is about 79 per cent. Private expenditure is approximately 21 per cent, of which 8 per cent is pre-paid health insurance plans.

HIV prevalence: 0.1 per cent aged 15–49 in 2003 (World Bank)

Life expectancy: 70.1 years (2003)

Fertility rate/Maternal mortality rate: 1.3 births per woman (World Bank)

Birth rate/Death rate: 10.8 births per 1,000 population; 12.3 deaths per 1,000 population (2003).

Infant mortality rate: 18 per 1,000 live births (2003)

Head of population per physician/ bed: 1.8 physicians and 7.6 hospital beds per 1,000 people.

Welfare

The comprehensive state insurance scheme, with premiums paid by enterprises and institutions on behalf of employees, provides free health care and benefits for all Romanian citizens. An unemployment allowance was created in 1991 and there are also funds allocated to sickness benefits, children's allowance and pensions. Employers make social security contributions of 28–38 per cent, unemployment fund contributions of 5 per cent and disabled fund contributions of 1 per cent on gross salaries. Employees pay 3 per cent of gross salaries to the supplementary pension fund and 1 per cent to the unemployment insurance fund.

There is high unemployment in Romania and there has been a 40 per cent fall in real wages since 1989. Survival is partly due to the fact that most Romanians do not pay rent or have a mortgage, since over 90 per cent were able to buy their homes for the equivalent of a few months rent after the revolution. Many also have small plots of farm land for subsistence farming. It is expected that there will be a housing crisis for future generations, with many houses too small to be occupied by more than one family. Mortgages to buy houses are very expensive and are almost impossible to obtain. The government's housing programme aims to complete the tower blocks and apartments that were left unfinished after the revolution, and then allocate funds to social housing.

There is wide variation between urban and rural infrastructure, with less than 10 per cent of country dwellers living in houses with running water and sewerage.

Main cities

Bucharest (capital, estimated population 1.9 million in 2004), Iasi (321,600), Constanta (320,000), Cluj-Napoca (316,400), Timisoara (316,100).

Languages spoken

The most significant minority language is Hungarian. German and English are spoken in tourist regions. Romanian, although a Romance language developed from Latin, has influences from Slavic languages as well as Hungarian, French and Turkish.

Official language/s

Romanian

Media

Press

Following the 1989 revolution, there was an explosion of publications from across the political spectrum. The press is highly regionalised and includes publications in minority languages such as Hungarian, German and Serbian. Over 60 per cent of the population read one or more newspapers a day. There are around 10 national dailies, as well as dailies and weeklies published in the main cities. Newspapers tend to be independent, governmental or published by a political party.

Dailies: The most important independent national dailies are *Evenimental Zitei* (a mass-market newspaper), *Adevarul*, *Cronica Romana*, *Curierul National*, *Nine O'Clock*, *Azi*, *Tineretul Liber*, *Libertatea* (Ringier), and *Romania Libera* (the opposition newspaper). *Allgemeine Zeitung für Rumanien* is the German regional newspaper, published five times per week. Others are *Buna Ziua Brasov*, *Cronica Romana*, *Dimineata* and *Nord Est*.

Weeklies: The Sunday newspapers include *Adevarul*, *Cronica Romana*, *Curierul National*, *Nine O'Clock* (English) and *Azi*.

Business: The most widely known business publications in English are *Capital* (weekly), *Romanian Investment Review*, *Romanian Law Digest*, *Quarterly Bulletin*, *Romanian Insight*, *Bucharest Business Week*, *In Review* monthly, *The Business Review*, *Economistul*, *Mesagerful Economic*, and *Tribuna Economica*.

Periodicals: Many special interest and business publications are published, mostly by independent companies.

Broadcasting

Radio: There are three domestic channels operated by Radiodifuziunea Romana, plus foreign broadcasts in 13 languages.

Television: The two state-owned channels are operated by Televiziunea Romana (TVR) (Romanian Television), broadcasting on TVR1, with 100 per cent coverage, and TVR2, with 40 per cent coverage. Service is centred in Bucharest. There are a large number of state operated local services and several commercial networks, including Channel 2, Pro TV, Tele 7 ABC, Antena 1 and Canal 38.

Advertising

An increasing number of advertising agencies is being established in Romania, many as joint ventures with Western firms (Saatchi & Saatchi and Lintas Worldwide are two of the main investors). As well as advertising through television and radio, cinema advertising is increasingly popular. Billboard locations are growing and advertising on public transport vehicles is common. Advertisements can also be placed through State Public Relations Agency (Publicom), in Bucharest, on TV or radio.

Economy

The 1993 refusal by the IMF to grant Romania further credits unless it followed strict fiscal and monetary policies proved the turning point for the country. The government's 1994 austerity budget was a success, lowering inflation and boosting the economy. By 1996, the government had introduced 80 economic reform laws and tried to liberalise prices, reduce industrial and agricultural subsidies, introduce large-scale privatisations, exchange rate flotation, tackle corruption and sanction tight monetary control by the central bank.

After negative growth in the period 1997–99, the economy has grown steadily from the year 2000. GDP growth in 2004 was 8.3 per cent, up from 5.2 per cent in 2003. Disinflation in 2004 was 11.9 per cent and an estimated 8.2 per cent in 2005. The average inflationary rate from 2000–04 was 22.4 per cent. The IMF attributes Romania's strong credit growth to macroeconomic stabilisation and capital inflows. Exports are thriving, with annual growth of over ten per cent.

Productivity has been strengthened significantly and contributions to social security have been cut. These measures have benefited competitiveness. The drawback of rapid credit growth is its threat to macroeconomic stability. The trade balance could suffer as consumer demand climbs. Another problem with the Romanian economy is the current account deficit, which almost doubled to 7.5 per cent of GDP in 2004.

The EU has urged Romania to fight corruption, speed up economic reforms and tackle judicial reforms as well as public administration reforms. Romania has carried out the majority of necessary structural reform but needs now to concentrate on corporate governance.

The prospect of Romania's accession to the EU in 2007 is proving a significant factor in attracting foreign direct investment (FDI). The largest amounts of foreign investment derive from The Netherlands, Germany and France.

External trade

Romania's markets and external trade have been developing since 1989 and the fall of Nicolae Ceausescu. In 1994 the EU recognised the country as a functioning market economy.

Romania is an associate member of the EU and the European Free Trade Association (EFTA), and government policy is aimed at integrating the country into Western markets.

Romania is also party to the Central European Free Trade Agreement (CEFTA), which also includes Bulgaria, Czech Republic, Hungary, Poland, Slovakia and Slovenia. Continued differences over agriculture and the fact that CEFTA members have tended to trade far more heavily with the EU than with each other have limited the significance of the agreement. Romania joined many neighbouring states in signing the Stability Pact's Memorandum of Understanding (MoU) on Trade Liberalisation and Facilitation in June 2001. The MoU should eventually introduce free trade in Central and Eastern European states conincidng with their accession to the EU and adoption of the single currency in 2007.

Imports

Main imports include machinery and equipment, fuels and minerals, chemicals, textile and products, basic metals and agricultural products
Main sources: Italy (18.3 per cent), Germany (17.9 per cent), France (7.2 per cent), Hungary (6.1 per cent), Russia (5.7 per cent), Austria (5.5 per cent), Turkey (4.3 per cent)

Exports

Main exports include textiles and footwear, metals and metal products, machinery and equipment, minerals and fuels, chemicals and agricultural products
Main destinations: Italy (20.9 per cent), Germany (15.4 per cent), France (7.3 per cent), Turkey (7.0 per cent), UK (6.1 per cent), Austria (5.0 per cent)

Agriculture
Farming

The agricultural sector accounts for 12.8 per cent of GDP and employs 25 per cent of the workforce.

The total agricultural area is 147,900 sq km, of which 94,100 sq km is arable. Arable land, pastures and hayfields cover 59.5 per cent of Romania, forests 26.7 per cent and vineyards 2.5 per cent. Romania is Central Europe's most important agricultural producer after Poland. Important agricultural produce includes grapes (the leading European producer), corn, wheat, maize, rye, sugar beet, oilseed, potatoes, plums, apples and meat. Although there has been progress in restructuring the sector, it has been slower than international financial institutions would like. Moreover, concerns have also been expressed at the re-introduction of import barriers and subsidies to protect the sector from Hungarian wheat and flour exports.

The restitution and privatisation of land has – in comparison with enterprise privatisation – advanced at a rapid pace, with over 85 per cent of agricultural land in private ownership by 2002. Land restitution was highly politicised, with arguments surrounding the amount of land that was returned to claimants. Claims exceeded by a third the amount of land held in state hands, and delays in the process held up investment in the sector. Although land restitution was a major step forward, problems facing the sector include the small size of farms, no functioning land market, very few rural credit and investment schemes, and an extremely limited distribution and marketing infrastructure. There may be a trend towards protectionism in Romanian agricultural policy as the government considers shielding the domestic sector from competitive producers within the EU, which Romania is theoretically in line to join in 2007.

In October 2005 Romanian officials discovered bird flu in three ducks near the Danube. Thousands of birds were killed and quarantine imposed on others. The authorities began testing humans for the disease.

Crop production for 2004 included: 24,231,556 tonnes (t) cereals in total, 7,734,980t wheat, 14,541,564t maize, 4,220,210t potatoes, 1,405,996t barley, 4,963t rice, 1,230,398 grapes, 1,330,085t tomatoes, 736,464t oilcrops, 672,723t sugar beets, 237,240t chillies and peppers, 298,506t soya beans, 1,097,837t apples, 3,041,498t fruit in total, 4,572,883t vegetables in total. Livestock production included: 775,800t meat in total, 162,800t beef, 376,000t pig meat, 67,547t lamb, 6,300t goat meat, 146,568t poultry, 395,042t eggs, 5,413,703t milk, 14,500t honey, 22,499t cattle hides, 13,686t sheepskins, 17,613t greasy wool, 1,000t cocoons, silk.

Fishing

Romania's fishing sector has declined in the past decade, making little contribution to GDP. National consumption is falling too. Fisheries in the Black Sea have been spoilt by eutrophication and overfishing. Carp, mackerel and sardines are the principal catches. European spratt and anchovy are also plentiful. There are an estimated 10,000 persons working in the fishing industry.

Fish farming, including primary processing, packaging and trade will be improved through major investment projects.

Forestry

Forest and other wooded land accounts for less than one-third of the land area, with forest cover estimated at 6.4 million hectares (ha). Most of the forest area is located in the Carpathian mountainous region in the centre and west of the country. About nine-tenths of the forest is available for wood supply and is largely semi-natural. The growing stock consists of Norway spruce as the principal coniferous species, with beech and oak the main deciduous varieties. Although most of the forest is owned by the state, claims for restitution have increased private ownership.

Forests provide sufficient raw materials for the domestic industry to meet internal demands and also product for exports. Romania has a well developed timber and wood processing industry, concentrated in the northern regions of Moldavia and Transylvania. Substantial investments have been made to modernise older mills so as to improve its existing export base. Over half of the sawnwood production is exported, while more value-added products such as parquet, solid wood panels and furniture are obtained from hardwoods. Most of the paper demand is met by imports.

Export of forest material in 2004 amounted to US$898.4 million, while imports amounted to US$525.0 million. Production in 2004 included 15,777,000 cubic metres (mcum) roundwood, 12,762,000cum industrial roundwood, 4,588,000cum sawnwood, 8,166,000cum sawlogs and veneers, 2,500,000cum pulpwood, 951,000cum wood-based panels, 3,015,000cum woodfuel.

Romania

Industry and manufacturing
The industrial sector accounts for 36.3 per cent of GDP with manufacturing accounting for 27 per cent of GDP.
Industrial production increased by an estimated 4 per cent in 2004.
The main industries are textiles and footwear, light machinery and auto assembly. Mining, timber, construction materials, chemicals, food processing and petroleum refining are all also significant sectors.

Tourism
The tourism sector declined following the collapse of Communism, despite the wealth of attractions. Poor infrastructure, including existing but deteriorating facilities, and inadequate marketing, as well as competition from neighbouring destinations, have contributed to the malaise. The sector contributes only 1.3 per cent to GDP. The industry supplies 115,000 jobs, which amounts to 1.2 per cent of the workforce.
3.4 million arrivals were recorded in 2004, an improvement on previous years. State-owned tourist resources have been privatised and the Ministry of European Integration is allocating financial assistance to the sector.

Mining
Taken together, the mining and hydrocarbons sectors account for around 13 per cent of GDP and employ 8 per cent of the workforce. Output dramatically declined in the 1990s, reflecting prolonged restructuring. Romania's mining industry is well developed, although it suffers from outdated technology and a lack of investment.
Mineral deposits include salt, lignite, iron ore, bauxite, manganese and small quantities of gold, zinc, uranium, tin and copper. Romania aims to exploit domestic resources instead of relying on imports, even if the initial cost is high. Annual zinc output is around 28,000 tonnes, aluminium output around 150,000 tonnes and copper output around 30,000 tonnes. Minvest, privatised in 1999, accounts for 60 per cent of Romania's copper production.
The government opened the gold mining sector to foreign exploration in 1999. Gabriel Resources, a Canadian company, are behind a US $400 million project to create Europe's largest open-pit gold mine in the Rosia Montana valley. The International Finance Corporation (IFC) have refused financial backing to the proposal, which would displace 2,000 residents and produce high levels of hazardous cyanide.

Hydrocarbons
Oil reserves stood at 0.5 billion barrels in 2004. Production has fallen from 294,000 barrels per day (bpd) in 1976 to 119,000bpd in 2004, while consumption is 212,000bpd. Although production covers under half of total consumption, Romania has the potential to become self-sufficient in oil and could become an important oil producer. Idle oil wells are being re-opened following the liberalisation of state prices and rising world prices. Foreign investors began to show an interest in Romania in the late 1990s, including TotalFinaElf and Sterling Resources (Canada), who were given a five-year licence to explore around 700,000 hectares near Craiova, southern Romania.
Russia's LUKOIL is a major player in the downstream sector, with a majority stake in the third-largest refinery in Romania, the Petrotel refinery. It has an annual capacity of 4.2 million tonnes, three million tonnes of which comes from LUKOIL's own fields and the rest from Romanian fields. Other refineries have also sought external links, although the Romanian government is in general wary of Russian interests expanding into the domestic industry.
Natural gas reserves stood at 0.3 trillion cubic metres in 2004. Even though Romania is central and eastern Europe's largest natural gas producer, in 2004, production has fallen. In 1994 production stood at 18.7 billion cubic metres and in 2004 this figure was 13.2 billion. Gas is imported by pipeline through Ukraine. Russia is Romania's sole gas provider, although the Romanian government is seeking to diversify its foreign sources of gas. Ukraine, Moldova, Italy and Norway have been identified as potential sources. Romgaz operates the national gas distribution system and is entirely owned by the state.
Coal reserves stood at 494 million tonnes at end-2004. Production totalled 6.9 million tonnes oil equivalent (toe) in 2004, down slightly from the previous year.

Energy
There is significant domestic production of oil, gas and coal. Although dependent on Russian imports to satisfy domestic oil needs, Romania houses ten of south-eastern Europe's eleven oil refineries. The Petrotel refinery was upgraded in October 2004 to conform to EU standards. The company was privatised together with Petromidia.
In 2005 construction began on a new oil refinery near Bucharest. The project is a joint venture between South Korean LG International and Petrom, the national oil company. At the end of 2005 construction of a crude oil pipeline, the South East European Line (SEEL), commenced. It will connect Romania to Italy, via Serbia and Bosnia. By 2007 inflows through this line are projected to reach 480,000 bpd.
Gas is the most important domestic fuel resource, and Romania is the region's biggest producer. However, output is declining significantly. In 2004 two more gas companies were privatised, taking the total percentage of private gas providers to 40 per cent. By 2007 the government intends to have opened up the gas market in its entirety to conform to EU regulations. Seventy per cent of electricity production in Romania is produced in thermal power plants, 20 per cent in hydroelectric power plants and 10 per cent in the Cernavoda Unit I nuclear reactor. In December 2002, Canada announced that it would guarantee up to US$207 million in loans towards the construction of a new nuclear reactor, the 'Cernavoda II'. The project is being managed by the Atomic Energy of Canada and is expected to be completed by the end of 2006. There is a lot of public opposition to the reactor, not least because the country already has a surplus of generational capacity.

Financial markets
Stock exchange
After a 50-year gap, the Bucharest Stock Exchange (BSE) was re-opened in 1995.

Banking and insurance
Since the early 1990s, the banking sector has undergone major restructuring and privatisation, although some areas of the banking, insurance, legal and financial sectors require upgrading. About 55 per cent of the banking system is foreign owned. Privatisation of Romania's largest bank, Banca Comerciala Romana (BCR), is scheduled for completion in 2006. When both BCR and Casa de Economii si Consemnatiuni (CEC) are privatised, the banking sector will be 90 per cent foreign owned and highly competitive.
Central bank
Banca Nationala a Romaniei (BNR) (National Bank of Romania)
Main financial centre
Bucharest

Time
GMT plus two hours (GMT plus three hours between the last Sunday in March and the last Saturday in September).

Geography
Romania is situated in south-eastern Europe in the lower Danube basin bordering the Black Sea to the south-west (250km of coastline). Much of the country forms part of the Balkan Peninsula. Romania is the largest of the Balkan states. Ukraine is to the north, Moldova to the north-east, Hungary to the north-west, Serbia and Montenegro and Macedonia to the south-west and Bulgaria to the south.

Nations of the World: A Political, Economic and Business Handbook

Romania is divided into four geographical areas. Moldavia and Transylvania (forest and mountains) make up the northern half, which is divided by the Carpathian Mountains. South of the Carpathians is the Danube plain of Walachia (including Bucharest), with the lower Danube marking the border with Bulgaria. Romania's Black Sea coastline incorporates the Danube delta and the port of Constanta.

Climate
Romania has a moderate, continental temperate climate with long hot summers and cold winters. Snow falls throughout the country, although winters are coldest in the Carpathian mountains with snow between December and April, and mildest on the Black Sea coast. Mean temperatures in Bucharest are minus 2.4 degrees Celsius (C) in January and 22.8 degrees C in July. The coldest month is January with a mean temperature of minus 7 degrees C, rising to a peak of 30 degrees C in July. Temperatures can differ by 5–10 degrees C from the plains to the mountains. The wettest month is June with approximately 85mm of rain; the driest September with 30mm. The Black Sea water temperature is approximately 26 degrees C in July and August.

Dress codes
The business dress code is usually informal, with ties, sports jackets or blazers acceptable for meetings.
Clothing should be medium-weight, plus a heavy topcoat and overshoes for winter. Lightweight clothing and a light raincoat are advisable for summer.

Entry requirements
Passports
Passports are required by all visitors.
Visa
Required by all; except those listed at http://www.roembus.org/ (see consular section). An application form can also be downloaded. Business visitors, when required to apply for visas, should provide a letter of invitation from a local company certifying purpose of visit; proof of sufficient funds for maintenance (US$100 per day); medical and accident insurance and return/onward passage.

Currency advice/regulations
Foreign currency up to the equivalent of US$10,000 in cash can be brought into Romania. It must be declared and no more than the amount declared can be taken out of the country. Sums larger than US$10,000 must be transferred through banks.
No more than Lei1 million can be imported or exported.
Changing money at private exchange offices is often better than at banks. Kiosks are required to advertise an official rate, but ask if they can offer a better deal. Romania is largely a cash only economy. Traveller's cheques can be changed at banks and hotels, but they charge huge commissions. US dollars are the preferred hard currency.

Customs
Strict inspection of luggage on arrival and departure is likely. Personal effects, 200 cigarettes and two litres of alcoholic beverages, are permitted duty-free. There are strict regulations concerning the temporary import or export of firearms, antiquities and medications.

Health (for visitors)
Hospital emergency rooms provide free first aid, but charge for all other medical services.
Mandatory precautions
There are no special requirements.
Advisable precautions
Typhoid, diphtheria and both hepatitis 'A' and 'B' inoculations are recommended, as well as inoculation against tick-borne encephalitis. It is advisable to boil water or drink mineral water where possible, although water in mountainous regions is supplied from local springs and is safe. Rabies is a health risk.
Basic medical supplies are limited, especially outside major cities, so always travel with sufficient medication.

Hotels
Classified as de luxe, A and B. Accommodation outside Bucharest is generally cheaper. Advisable to purchase pre-paid vouchers for accommodation through travel agents, as a confirmed reservation, if not pre-paid, is not a guarantee of accommodation.

Credit cards
Credit cards are not widely used but are accepted in most major hotels. American Express, Visa and Eurocard are preferred. Credit card transactions are charged at a worse rate than that offered by exchange bureaux

Public holidays
Fixed dates
1–2 Jan (New Year), 1 May (Labour Day), 1 Dec (National Day), 25–26 Dec (Christmas Holiday).
Variable dates
Orthodox Easter Monday

Working hours
Banking
Mon–Fri: 0900–1200 and 1300–1500. Creditbank, Bucharest Otopeni airport, open 1000–1800 daily.
Business
Mon–Fri: 0800–1700, lunch usually 1230–1300. Business hours can be haphazard with many offices closing on Friday afternoons.
Government
Mon–Fri: 0800–1700, lunch usually 1230–1300.

Telecommunications
Mobile phones
There is widespread coverage, particularly in the major cities.

Social customs/useful tips
Traditional Central European courtesies with a measure of Latin informality are expected. Punctuality is observed to a degree. Shaking hands is the traditional form of greeting. Accepting hospitality from and giving social invitations to officials is normal, usually taking place in restaurants or hotels.
Smoking is prohibited on public transport and in cinemas and theatres, although many Romanians smoke and Western cigarettes are greatly appreciated.
Tips are expected by porters, chambermaids and taxi drivers.
Anyone photographing demonstrations risks arrest.
It is advisable to avoid the many stray dogs in and around Bucharest.

Security
Crimes against tourists are a growing problem in Romania. Money exchange schemes targetting travellers are becoming increasingly common. Bogus policemen are an increasing hazard for the unwary business traveller. Their technique is to demand to see proof of identification, and then make off with a visitor's wallet. Keep passports separate from other valuables.
Extreme caution must be taken with unofficial change vendors: they are illegal and often fraudulent.

Getting there
Air
National airline: Transporturi Aeriene Romane (Tarom) (Romanian Air Transport)
International airport/s: Otopeni (OTP), 16km north of capital; Baneasa (BBU), 9km north of the capital.
Transport from Otopeni to the city centre includes bus service 783, which operates 0530–2359 every 15 minutes, with a journey time of 40 minutes. Taxis are available, with a journey time of 25 minutes. Limousines and minibuses are also available.
Airport tax: None
Surface
Road: International roads connect Romania with Hungary. The E64 from Budapest goes through Arad, Brasov, Campina and Ploiesti to Bucharest. From Germany, the E60 goes via northern Hungary before going through Oradea. The route from

Romania

Bucharest to Ukraine goes north through Bacau and to Chernovtsy in southern Ukraine. From Moldova, take the road from the border to the town of Husi. The better road links are via Germany, Austria and Hungary.

The best route from Hungary is the E64 from Budapest to Szeged, although the E60 is a more frequently used route from Hungary to Germany.

Rail: There are good rail connections with all neighbouring countries. The main international train from Western Europe to Romania is the Wiener Waltzer, from Basel to Bucharest (it only operates between June–September). Other rail routes run from Berlin-Lichtenberg through Hungary (the Baltic Express). There is a less well-maintained rail link from Bulgaria.

Water: Ships provide regular passenger services and cruises on the Danube, starting at Passau in Germany, through Austria, Slovakia, Hungary, Serbia, to Giurgiu (48km from Bucharest), and finally Constanta on the Black Sea.

Main port/s: Black Sea ports: Constanta, Mangalia and Sulina.

Danube ports: Orsova, Drobeta-Turnu Severin, Turnu Magurele, Giurgiu, Oltenita, Calaras, Cernavoda. Braila, Galati and Tulcea, are both river and sea ports. The Danube is used heavily for freight transport since the opening of the 62.4km canal link with the Black Sea.

Getting about

National transport

Air: Tarom operates relatively cheap internal flights from Baneasa airport to Constanta, Arad, Bacau, Craiova, Iasi, Deva, Caransebes, Baia Mare, Cluj-Napoca, Iasi, Satu Mare, Timisoara, Oradea, Tirgu Mures, Sibiu, Suceava and Tulcea.

Road: Romania has almost 73,000km of roads, of which 14,700km are national roads – 4,680km of the national roads are included within the European Road Network ('E' roads).

Buses: There are local services to most towns and villages.

Taxis: Inter-city travel by taxi is much more expensive than by bus.

Rail: Efficient and cheap services are operated by the state railway company, Caile Ferate Romane (CFR) (Romanian State Railways), between all main cities and towns. All long-distance trains have sleeping compartments. Seats must be reserved in advance on the *rapide* and express trains running from Bucharest to Timisoara, Cluj-Napoca, Iasi, Constanta and Brasov, for which supplements must also be paid. Bucharest's principal station is the *Gara de Nord*.

Water: The principal navigable waterway is the Danube. Information on Danube cruises is available from the National Tourist Office (ONT).

City transport

Taxis: Take a metered taxi or negotiate a price before setting off. A 10 per cent tip is normal. To call for a taxi, dial 953 or 941. Beware the informal operators who ply the routes between the main hotels and the airport, often offering unofficial currency exchange services.

Buses, trams & metro: With a relatively efficient public transport network it is easy to get around Bucharest. Bus/tram tickets can be purchased from the yellow painted booths or in some hotels; they should be punched immediately upon entering the vehicle.

Car hire

Self–drive and chauffeur-driven cars are available through the National Tourist Office (ONT). Petrol coupons can be obtained from the ONT, hotels or the Romanian Automobile Club. International or national driving licences are required. Traffic drives on the right, although Romanian driving can be very unpredictable. Nevertheless, Romanian traffic laws are very strict. Speed limits are 120km per hour on highways, 90km per hour on other roads and 50km per hour in built-up areas Driving under the influence of alcohol is illegal.

BUSINESS DIRECTORY

The addresses listed below are a selection only. While World of Information makes every endeavour to check these addresses, we cannot guarantee that changes have not been made, especially to telephone numbers and area codes. We would welcome any corrections.

Telephone area codes

The international dialling code (IDD) for Romania is +40, followed by area code and subscriber's number:

Braila	239	Gaesti	245
Brasov	268	Oradea	259
Bucharest	21	Ploiesti	244
Cluj-Napoca	264	Sibiu	269
Constanta	241	Timisoara	256

Useful telephone numbers

Fire brigade: 981
Police: 955
Ambulance: 961
Special ambulance service (pregnant women or women with small children): 969
Emergency hospital: 679-4310
Special information: 951
Time: 958
Railway information: 952
Weather report: 959
Enquiries: 930, 931, 932

Chambers of Commerce

American Chamber of Commerce in Romania, Union International Centre, 11 Ion Cimpineanu Street, Sector 1, 78664 Bucharest (tel: 315-8694; fax: 312-4851; e-mail: amcham@amcham.ro).

Brasov Chamber of Commerce and Industry, 18-20 M Kogalniceanu Street, 2200 Brasov (tel: 412-357; fax: 477-333; e-mail: ccibv@ccibv.ro).

Constanta Chamber of Commerce, Industry, Shipping and Agriculture, 84 Mircea cel Batran Street, bl MF1, Constanta tel: 619-854; fax: 619-454; e-mail: office@ccina.ro)

Prahova Chamber of Commerce and Industry, 8 Cuza Voda Street, Ploiesti (tel: 513-122; fax: 516-666; e-mail: office@cciph.ro).

Romania and Bucharest Chamber of Commerce and Industry, 2 Octavian Goga Boulevard, Sector 3, Bucharest (tel: 322-9535; fax: 322-9542; e-mail: ccir@ccir.ro).

Sibiu Chamber of Commerce, Industry and Agriculture, 1 Telefoanelor Street, 2400 Sibliu (tel: 210-503; fax: 211-831; e-mail: cciasb@cciasb.ro).

Timisoara Chamber of Commerce, Industry and Agriculture, 3 Piata Victoriei, 300030 Timisoara (tel: 490-766; fax: 490-311; e-mail: cciat@cciat.ro).

Banking

Banca Agricola, B-dul Voda, Sector 3, Bucharest (tel/fax: 323-6027).

Banco Comerciala Romana, B-dul Regina Elisabeta 5, Sector 3, Bucharest (tel: 312-6185; fax: 312-0056).

Bankco-op, 13 Ion Ghica St, Bucharest (614-3900; fax: 312-0037).

Romanian Bank for Development, 4 Doamnei St, Bucharest (tel: 613-3200, 615-9600; fax: 615-7603).

Romanian Commercial Bank, 14 Republicii Ave, Bucharest (tel: 614-5680, 615-7560; fax: 614-3213).

Central bank
National Bank of Romania (NBR), 25 LipscaniStreet, Bucharest 70421 (tel: 615-2750; fax: 312-3831; e-mail: bnr@bnro.ro).

Travel information

East Railway Station, 1 Garii Obor Ave, Bucharest (tel: 635-0702).

Domestic Railway Agencies, Str Brezoianu 10, Bucharest (tel: 613-2644/43; Calea Grivitei 139, Bucharest (tel: 650-7247).

International Railway Agency, Bd I.C. Bratianu 44 bis, Bucharest (tel: 613-4008).

Lar-Romanian Airlines, 3-4 Stirbei-Voda Ave, Bucharest (tel: 615-3276, 615-3206; fax: 312-0148).

Lufthansa Airport Office (tel and fax: 312-7670); town office, Boulevard Magheru 18, Bucharest (tel: 650-6766; fax: 312-0211).

North Railway Station, 6 Garii St, Bucharest.

Otopeni Airport (tel: 633-6602).

Romavia SA (Charter Flights), 1 Dimitrie Cantemir Ave, Bucharest (tel: 311-1055; fax: 311-1051).

Tarom - Head Office, 16,5 km, Bucuresti-Ploiesti Ave, Bucharest (tel: 663-3137, 212-0122 information; fax: 312-9767).

Tarom Agency (Domestic Flights), 59-61 Buzesti St, Bucharest (tel: 659-4125 information, 659-2855 booking).

Tarom Agency (International Flights), 10-14 Domnita Anastasia St, Bucharest (tel: 615-0499 information, 615-2747, 613-4295 booking; fax: 614-6524).

Ministry of tourism
Ministry of Tourism, Str Apolodor 17, 5th Floor, Room 16, Sect 5, 70663 Bucharest 5 (tel: 410-7287; fax: 312-6767; internet site: http://www.turism.ro).

National tourist organisation offices
National Tourist Office (ONT Carpati), Blvd Magheru 7, Bucharest 1 (tel: 614-1922, 312-2598; fax: 312-2954).

Ministries
Ministry of Agriculture, Blvd Carol I 24, 70312 Bucharest (tel: 614-4020; fax: 312-4410).

Ministry of Communications and Information Technology, 14 Libertatii Blvd, 76106 Bucharest 5 (tel: 400-1100, 312-0017; fax: 400-1329; internet site: http://www.mcti.ro).

Ministry of Culture, Piata Presei 1, Bucharest 71341 (tel: 223-1516; fax: 223-4951).

Ministry of Defence, Str Izvor 1-3, 70642 Bucharest (tel: 410-4040; fax: 312-0863).

Ministry of Foreign Affairs, Aleea Modrogan 14, 71274 Bucharest (tel: 212-2160; fax: 230-7489).

Ministry of Health, Str Ministerului 1-3, 70109 Bucharest (tel: 222-3850; fax: 312-4916).

Ministry of the Interior, Str Mihai Voda 3-5, 070622 Bucharest (tel: 311-2021; fax: 614-0909).

Ministry of Justice, Bd Mihail Kogalniceanu 33, 70602 Bucharest (tel: 614-4400; fax: 323-6179).

Ministry of Labour and Social Protection, Str Dem I Dobrescu 2, 70119 Bucharest (tel: 222-3850; fax: 312-2768).

Ministry of National Education, Str Gen Berthelot 28-30, 70749 Bucharest (tel: 614-4588; fax: 312-4719).

Ministry of Privatisation, Str Ministerului 2-4, 70109 Bucharest (tel: 222-3850; fax: 312-0809).

Ministry of Public Finance, Str Apolodor 17, 70663 Bucharest (tel: 410-3400; fax: 312-2077).

Ministry of Public Works and Land Use Planning, Str Apollodor 15-17, Sector 6, 70663 Bucharest (tel: 410-1933; fax: 411-1138).

Ministry of Youth and Sports, Str Vasile Conta 16, 70139 Bucharest (tel: 211-5550; fax: 211-1710).

Office of the Prime Minister, Piata Victoriei 1, 71201 Bucharest (tel: 212-1660; fax: 222-5814).

Presidency of Republic, Building Geniului 1 Cotroceni Palace, Bucharest 76238 (tel: 410-0581; fax: 312-1247).

Other useful addresses
Administration of Sulina Free Trade Zone, Dr Marcovici Str 2, Ground Floor, Bucharest (tel: 613-8733).

Agency for Restructuring, 152 Calea Victoriei, Sector 1, Bucharest (tel: 212-2424; fax: 212-1176).

Asigurara Romaneasca SA (Asirom), Str Smirdan 5, 70406 Bucharest (tel: 312-5020; fax: 312-4819).

British Embassy, Str Jules Michelot 24, 70154 Bucharest (tel: 312-0303; fax: 312-9741).

Centrul Roman pentru Dezvoltarea Intreprinderilor Mici si Mijlocii (Crimm)-PMU, 20 Ion Campineanu Str, Sector 1, 70709 Bucharest (tel: 311-1995/6/7; fax: 312-6966).

Chamber of Deputies, 1 Parlamentului Str, Bucharest (tel: 335-0111; fax: 312-0827).

Constanta South Free Zone Administration, Ferry Boat Terminal Building Agigea, code 8711, Jud Constanta (tel: 741-378, 618-718, 619-100 (ext 2118, 2162); fax: 639-000, 619-729, 693-913).

Council for Reform, Piata Victoriei 1, 71201 Bucharest (tel: 222-3687; fax: 222-4686).

Council for Economic Co-ordination, Strategy and Reform, Piaja Victoriei 1, 71201 Bucharest (tel: 222-3687, 312-4767; fax: 222-4686).

Department for European Integration (tel: 312-6928; fax: 312-6929).

Department of Public Information (tel: 222-3619; fax: 222-6088).

Department for Selective Restructuring of the State Ownership Fund, 6-10, Callea Grivitei, Sector 1, Bucharest (tel: 650-4822; 659-7693).

Economic Reform and Strategy and Co-ordination Council, 1 Victoriei Sq, Bucharest (tel: 617-7977; fax: 312-4686).

Fiman Fund PMU, 6-8 Povernei Str, Bucharest (tel: 212-2912; fax: 211-1937).

Insurance and Reinsurance Company SA (Aatra), Str Smirdan 5, 79118 Bucharest (tel: 150-986; fax: 139-306).

Land Reclamation Agriculture Department, Sos Oltenitei 35-37, 75501 Bucharest (tel: 634-5020; fax: 312-3712).

Lignite Public Authority, Str Tudor Vladimirescu 2, 1400 Târgu-Jiu (tel: 321-2513; fax: 321-664).

National Administration of Roads, Blvd Dinicu Golescu 38, 77113 Bucharest (tel: 312-8496).

National Agency for Privatisation, Str Ministerulei 2-4, 4th Floor, Bucharest sector 1 (tel: 615-8558, 614-9495, 312-3030, 614-7854; fax: 312-0809/3030, 613-6136).

National Committee for Statistics, 16 Libertatii Str, Sector 5, Bucharest (tel: 312-4875; fax: 312-4873).

National Council for Environmental Protection, Piata Victoriei 1, Bucharest (tel: 143-400).

Navrom (Romanian Shipping Company), 8700 Constanta (tel: 615-821; fax: 618-413).

Nord-Est Press (Independent news agency), Str Smirdan 5, 6600 Iasi (tel/fax: 144-776).

Petrotel SA, Str Mihai Bravu 235, Jud Prahova, 2000 Ploiesti (tel: 146-671; fax: 142-408).

Project Implementation Unit within the Authority for Privatisation and Management of the State Ownership, Bucharest (tel: 303-6417; fax: 303-6416).

Radiodifuziuna Romana, Str Gral Berthelot 61-62, PO Box 63-1200, Bucharest (tel: 633-4710; fax: 312-3640).

Radioteleviziuna Romana (Romanian Radio and Television), Calea Dorobantilor 191, PO Box 63-1200, Bucharest (tel: 334-710; fax: 337-544).

Radio Nord-Est, Str Smirdan 5, 6600 Iasi (tel: 145-530; fax: 146-363).

Rafo SA, Str Cauciucului 2, Jud Bacau, Onesti (tel: 324-786; fax: 323-267).

Research Institute for Foreign Trade, Str Apollodor 17, 5 Bucharest (tel: 312-3652, 631-1293; fax: 312-5652).

Romania

Romanian Agency for Energy Conservation, Splaiul Independentei 202A, 77208 Bucharest (tel: 650-6470; fax: 312-3197).

Romanian Commodity Exchange, 71341 Bucharest 1, Presei Libere Sq, Bucharest (tel: 01-617-2231; fax: 01-312-2167).

Romanian Development Agency (RDA), Boulevard Magheru 7, Bucharest 1 (tel: 615-6686, 312-3311; fax: 613-2415).

Romanian Embassy (USA), 1607 23rd Street, Washington DC 20008 (tel: 202-332-4846; fax: 202-232-4748; e-mail: info@roembus.org).

Romanian Government, 1 Victoriei Sq, Bucharest (tel: 222-3677; fax: 222-6088).

Romanian National Commission for Unesco, Str Anton Cehov 8, 71292 Bucharest (tel: 633-3223; fax: 312-763).

Romanian Parliament, Calea 13, Septembrie 1, 76117 Bucharest (tel: 335-0111).

Romanian Post Office, 14 Libertatii Avenue, 70106 Bucharest 5 (tel: 400-1102; fax: 400-1515).

Romanian State Railways (SNCFR), Blvd 38 Dinicu Golescu, Sector 1-Cod 78123 Bucharest (tel: 617-0148).

Romexpo SA (Trade fairs and exhibitions). Bd Marasti 65-67, 71331 Bucharest (tel: 618-1160; fax: 618 3725).

Rompres (Romanian News Agency), Piata Presei Libere I, 71341 Bucharest (tel: 618-2878; fax: 617-0487).

Secretariat for the Privatisation and Restructuring Programmes within the Council for Co-ordination, Strategy and Economic Reform, 1 Piata Victoriei, Sector 1, Bucharest (tel: 312-8445, 222-8335; fax: 312-6932).

Senate of Romania, 1 Revolutiei Sq, Bucharest (tel: 615-0200, 617-0160; fax: 312-1752).

Societatea Nationala a Cailor Ferate, State Ownership Fund, CA Rosetti Str 21, Bucharest (tel: 611-4943).

State Ownership Fund, RDA Business Centre, World Trade Plaza, 2 Expozitiei Avenue, Ground Floor, Bucharest (tel: 230-0760).

Supreme Court of Justice, 4 Rahovei Str, Bucharest (312-0920; fax: 613-0882).

Prosecutor General's under the Supreme Court of Justice, 2-4 Unirii Ave, Bucharest (tel: 631-1750, 781-3065; fax: 781-6210).

Televiziuna Romana – Telecentrul Bucuresti, Calea Dorobantilor 191, PO Box 63-1200, Bucharest (tel: 633-4710; fax: 633-7544).

USA Embassy, Str Tudor Arghezi 7-9, Bucharest (tel: 312-4042; fax: 312-0395).

Internet sites

Romanian Embassy:
http://www.roembus.org

Yellow Pages:
http://www.romanianyellowpages.com/~mozaic/

Romanian Home Page:
http://www.ici.ro/romania

Russia

KEY FACTS

Official name: Rossiiskaya Federatsiya (Russian Federation)

Head of State: President Vladimir Putin (since May 2000; re-elected 14 Mar 2004)

Head of government: Prime Minister Mikhail Fradkov (appointed 1 Mar 2004)

Ruling party: Yedinaya Rossiya (United Russia) (re-elected 7 Dec 2003) is the largest party in the State Duma (it was formed in Dec 2001 by the merger of the Mezhregional'noye Dvishenie Yedinstvo (Medved) (Inter-Regional Movement Unity) and the Otechestvo-Vsya Rossiya (OVR) (Fatherland-All Russia))

Area: 17,075,000 square km

Population: 146.74 million (2004)

Capital: Moscow

Official language: Russian

Currency: Rouble (R) = 100 kopeks

Exchange rate: R28.46 per US$ (Oct 2005)

GDP per capita: US$4,093 (2004)

GDP real growth: 7.10% (2004)

Labour force: 78.52 million (2004)

Unemployment: 8.30% (2004) (additional underemployment)

Inflation: 10.90% (2004)

Oil production: 9.29 million bpd (2004)

Balance of trade: US$87.14 billion 2004

Foreign debt: US$153.50 billion (2003)

Annual FDI: US$4.43 billion (Jan–Jun 2004)

Since 1991 when the superpower of the Soviet Union was broken up into 15 different and separate republics, Russia has been moving towards an open economy and democracy. However, not moving very convincingly or quickly. The legacy of communism – one-party rule, nationalisation of industry, centralisation and repression – has proved irrepressible. President Vladimir Putin has clawed back most of the state control that had been relaxed since the early 1990s. He is, however, more liberal economically than socially.

Economy

Russia began its comprehensive transition towards a market economy in the early 1990s, under the stewardship of President Boris Yeltsin and his then acting prime minister for the period June–December 1992, Yegor Gaidar. Gaidar also served as economics minister from September 1993 to January 1994. The initial period of liberalisation, often referred to as economic 'shock therapy', saw extreme economic instability coupled with recession and hyperinflation. The privatisation programme created a new rich oligarchy that replaced the old Soviet bosses – many high-level technocrats became powerful businessmen.

Many of Russia's problems stem from the pace and shape of the liberalisation programme, which was largely directed by a caucus of foreign free marketers, particularly in the International Financial Insitutions (IFIs), whose ideas were already going out of fashion in the West.

The liquidation of the Soviet Union led to a disintegration of its constituent parts. The oil-rich regions in Kazakhstan and Tajikistan were given independence, while the food basket economies in Eastern Europe moved away from Russian domination. The privatisation programme pushed by the IFIs in return for their support involved selling valuable state assets at rock-bottom prices. Without subsidies, the country's main employers shed their labour force by the millions, generating widespread poverty which was coupled with spiralling prices as shortages of food and other basic goods began to bite. Output sank while the black market grew exponentially, causing the rouble to become almost worthless. Added to this was the major financial crisis of 1998 which was brought on by unsustainable levels of debt, exacerbating the country's problems. Inflation hit 150 per cent in that year.

The Putin era is seen as an attempt to redress many of the worst excesses of Russian neo-liberalism, which led to extreme macroeconomic instability. The tail end of the Yeltsin era, in which Putin was prime minister, saw parts of the economy gradually improve. A devaluation of the rouble and the rise in oil prices largely saved the country from complete collapse in 1999 and 2000. This generated a broad industrial recovery and a healthy trade surplus by 2002, although this was largely consumed by debt servicing costs. In 1998, foreign debt was around 90 per cent of GDP, since reduced to around 28 per cent by 2004.

High energy prices have earned Russia considerable amounts of foreign exchange on its hydrocarbons resources, while keeping domestic energy prices low and allowing GDP growth to increase. The global slowdown slowed Russia's GDP growth in 2002, but 2005 saw GDP growth of 5.5 per cent. Inflation was down to 14 per cent in 2004.

Foreign direct investment (FDI) was US$3.43 billion in the period January–June 2004, up 35.3 per cent compared to January–June 2003. In June 2004, the World Bank agreed investment of US$1.0–US$1.5 billion in Russia over the next three years.

G8 presidency

Already by early 2006, Russia had put its cards on the table, showing not only a strong economic and political hand, but demonstrating the traditional 'Russian Bear' willingness to implement policies that might not find favour with everybody. In January 2006 Putin took the chair of the G8 group of nations (United States, Canada, Britain, France, Germany, Italy, Japan and Russia) – this is the first time Russia has ever held the rotating presidency. His close Kremlin aide Andrei

Russia

Illarionov, the man credited with politically manoeuvring Russia into the G8, immediately resigned in protest at what he called Putin's increasing authoritarianism. Although he had seen his influence diminish over the past two years, Illarionov had sought to hold his position for as long as possible, condemning Putin's rejection of economic liberalisation. Economists had hoped Illarionov could steer Russia to economic success.

Gas prices

Illarionov's resignation was triggered by a sudden increase in Russia's Gazprom price for gas pumped to the Ukraine. Kiev refused to accept a more than fourfold jump in prices 'for purely commercial reasons'. Russia retaliated by turning off the taps for two days. Illarionov pointed out that the price hike was in breach of a contact made in the summer of 2004 to peg the price for five years until 2009.

European Union (EU) diplomats at the G8 meeting were surprised by the Gazprom announcement. They had been expecting Russia to strike a more accommodating attitude regarding relations with its neighbours and the West, particularly with regards to its energy strategy.

The business rationale Gazprom cited for its decision was a thin disguise for political action against the Ukraine and to make clear Russia's potential to use its immense energy resources to its political and economic advantage. The new Ukrainian government was being punished for its policy of pursuing membership of the EU and NATO, the rest of the world was being shown that Russia is well placed to dominate the Eurasian energy industry for the rest of the century. It has 38 per cent of the world's gas reserves, slightly greater than the 35 per cent held by the Middle East. Russia is second only to Saudi Arabia in oil reserves; although BP surmises that they could be so large as to make Russia the number one in reserves world-wide.

Russia has seen a rapid energy-led boom, with real growth in GDP at five per cent per annum. If this is to continue, new markets must be found and old ones expanded. Gazprom is looking further afield than Ukraine to export its gas. A Baltic Sea pipeline, to be ready by 2020, could serve an energy-hungry northern Europe. The UK, which currently buys negligible amounts of Russian gas, is by 2020 going to have to import 90 per cent of its supplies, when its North Sea reserves are depleted. A pipeline extension to the UK is under consideration.

But it is in the central and southern countries of Europe, such as France, Italy and the various Balkan states, that Russia's oil-led expansion should be the greatest. In the vast easternmost reaches of Eurasia Russia has a huge competitive edge over any other supplier. The Chinese colossus is the obvious market, but Japan is in fierce contention to secure its vital energy resources from Siberia, both Sakhalin Island and the mainland.

The Japanese would like a US$5 billion 2,200-mile pipeline from Angarsk to Nakhodka, from which oil could be exported at up to 1 million barrels per day to Japan, Korea, China and the US. The Japanese have invested US$1 billion in exploring for Russian oil and gas, and are ready to follow it with US$8 billion in more exploration and the pipeline to Nakhodka. Hi-tech Japanese exploration could make for a better estimate of the size of Russia's reserves.

The ill-fated Yukos was behind a potential private deal with the Chinese. It is now on the back-burner, but China is far too big to ignore. The deal was for an estimated US$3 billion 1,400-mile pipeline from Angarsk to Daqing, shipping 600,000 barrels per day (bpd) to China's Mao-era industrial complex there. Russia produced about 8 million bpd in 2003, which could be doubled by 2015 – in order to supply both the Chinese and the Japanese markets.

Stern Merkel

After a stern statement from Berlin criticising his actions, Putin and Gazprom had to back down. A compromise deal was agreed on 5 January, whereby Ukraine agreed to pay US$95 per 1,000 cubic metres, up from the US$50 previously, but well short of the US$220–230 demanded by the Russians. Chancellor Angela Merkel proved a very different opponent from her predecessor, Gerhard Schröder. Putin hardly wanted his G8 presidency to be dominated by him being berated by Germany's 'Iron Lady' for allowing Russia to break faith with Ukraine.

Nations of the World: A Political, Economic and Business Handbook

Germany was too important as a customer and investor to alienate.

Merkel has radically altered the course of her country's foreign policy towards Russia. A fluent Russian speaker, as a result of an upbringing in Communist East Germany, she was uniquely qualified out of the Western leaders to take a tough line with Putin. She tackled him on the sensitive subject of Moscow's nuclear co-operation with Iran, on the state of Russian democracy, and on the behaviour of Russian forces in Chechnya, as well as on the reliability of Russia's enormous energy supplies. She did not shy away from criticing a new law that would strictly regulate the activities of foreign human rights organisations in Russia. She called it an 'irritation' and promised she would monitor the law's effects, prompting Putin to assure her in public that the lawful activities of foreign human rights groups would be unaffected.

Merkel's predecessor, Gerhard Schröder, had taken a softer line and had been accused of allowing Berlin's foreign policy to be dominated by Russia at the expense of Eastern Europe and Washington. Klaus Mangold, chairman of Germany's East-West Industry Committee, said Merkel's visit was likely to bring about a key shift in Russian-German relations.

'Freedom is at the centre of her political beliefs', he said. 'Coming from the East, she has a different view of Russia.'

Chechnya

A determined separatist movement still rages in Chechnya. In November 2005 elections were held in the region, the first since 1999. Putin hailed the result as a triumph, as the pro-Kremlin United Russia party won over half the seats. However voting was carried out in less than free conditions and human rights activists paid little heed to the results, denouncing the entire operation as a farce.

Outlook

Real GDP is expected to rise 5.2 per cent in 2006, much the same as the 2005 figure. Putin will be looking to capitalise on his time in the world spotlight, as president of the G8, and reminding even more powerful countries that Russia will be crucial in keeping their factories, cars and power well fuelled in the future. Russian dealings with Iran look set to generate many newspaper column inches in 2006. Iran has stopped letting UN inspectors into its nuclear research bases and a deal is on the cards which would allow Iran to use Russian-produced fuel for its nuclear power programme.

Risk assessment

Economy	Fair
Politics	Fair
Regional stability	Poor

COUNTRY PROFILE

Historical profile

The first monarchic dynasty ruled from the ninth century and built Kiev as its capital. It was overthrown by the Mongol invasion in the thirteenth century.

In the fifteenth century, the Grand Prince of Moscow, Ivan III, annexed the rival principalities of Russia and became its first national sovereign.

Ivan IV (Ivan the Terrible) further expanded Russia's frontiers and became the first holder of the title of Tsar.

Peter the Great (1682–1725) and Catherine the Great (1762–96) consolidated the regime.

1812 The French invasion of Russia ended when France was driven out.

In the mid-nineteenth century, most of Siberia was annexed and expansion to the south and east continued until 1905.

1917 The Russian leader, Tsar Nicholas II, abdicated. The Bolshevik coup, under the leadership of Lenin, forced out the liberal government.

1918–20 Civil war between the communist Bolsheviks and anti-Bolsheviks, the right-wing white army. The civil war ended in defeat for the white army, despite assistance from the UK, France, Japan and the US.

1922 The Union of Soviet Socialist Republics (USSR) was formed by Russia, Ukraine, Belarus and the Transcaucasus region.

1924 Following Lenin's death, Josef Stalin took over the leadership of the USSR as the general secretary of the Communist Party of the Soviet Union (CPSU) and a period of industrialisation, collectivisation of agriculture and purges of Stalin's opponents began. Key leadership rival Leon Trotsky was exiled in 1927 and assassinated in 1940.

1939 The USSR signed a non-aggression pact, the Molotov-Ribbentrop Treaty, with Nazi Germany. Soviet forces assisted the German invasion of Poland. The USSR also invaded Finland but was forced to respect Finnish independence in a 1940 peace agreement.

1941 After the USSR was invaded by Germany, it joined the Allies and declared war on the Axis powers.

1944–45 The USSR liberated parts of Eastern Europe and Eastern Germany, these being pulled into its sphere of influence after the Second World War. Western Europe, meanwhile, fell under the

KEY INDICATORS — Russia

	Unit	2000	2001	2002	2003	2004
Population	m	145.49	144.70	144.27	145.51	146.74
Gross domestic product (GDP)	US$bn	247.00	310.00	346.50	435.35	*582.39
GDP per capita	US$	1,697	2,140	2,400	2,992	4,093
GDP real growth	%	8.3	5.0	4.0	6.3	7.1
Inflation	%	20.8	21.5	16.2	13.0	10.9
Unemployment	%	11.0	8.7	8.3	7.6	–
Oil output	'000 bpd	6,536.0	7,056.0	7,698.0	8,543.0	9,285.0
Natural gas output	bn cum	545.0	542.4	554.9	578.6	589.1
Coal output	mtoe	115.8	120.8	113.8	124.9	127.6
Exports (fob) (goods)	US$m	105,565.0	103,194.0	107,250.0	135,929.0	183,452.0
Imports (fob) (goods)	US$m	44,862.0	53,764.0	63,830.0	78,539.0	96,307.0
Balance of trade	US$m	60,703.0	49,430.0	46,200.0	57,390.0	87,145.0
Current account	US$m	46,317.0	35,092.0	32,810.0	35,866.0	59,610.0
Foreign debt	US$bn	162.0	154.4	159.5	153.5	–
Total reserves minus gold	US$m	24,264.3	32,542.4	44,052.0	73,174.9	120,808.8
Foreign exchange	US$m	24,262.6	32,538.1	44,050.0	73,172.1	120,805.1
Foreign direct investment (FDI)	US$bn	-0.3	4.0	2.4	–	–
Exchange rate	per US$	28.13	29.17	31.28	30.56	28.81

* estimated figure

sphere of influence of the US, marking the start of the Cold War.

1949 The USSR became the world's second nuclear power (after the US), when it exploded its first atomic bomb.

1953 Following Stalin's death, Nikita Krushchev took over the leadership of the USSR.

1955 The Warsaw Pact was established by the USSR and its satellite eastern European states as a security apparatus to defend the region against NATO.

1962 The USSR's deployment of nuclear missiles in Cuba, within striking distance of the US, led to the 14-day missile crisis between the US and the USSR.

1964 After Krushchev's fall from power, the USSR was led by Leonid Brezhnev.

1979 Soviet forces invaded Afghanistan to prop up the communist Afghan government.

1982 After Brezhnev's death, Yuri Andropov became leader of the USSR.

1984 Konstantin Chernenko replaced Andropov, following his death.

1985 Chernenko died. His successor, Mikhail Gorbachev, instigated a programme of social, political and economic reforms, centred on two slogan concepts: perestroika (restructuring) and glasnost (openness).

1989 The USSR withdrew from Afghanistan. Communist rule ended in most of eastern and central Europe.

1991 Boris Yeltsin was elected as Russia's president. An attempted coup against Gorbachev, still officially the USSR president, by communist hardliners resulted in the CPSU being banned. Gorbachev resigned as USSR president, the USSR ceased to exist and the Commonwealth of Independent States (CIS) was formed by 11 of the former USSR republics, including Russia. In December, Dzhokhar Dudayev won presidential elections in Chechnya and proclaimed independence from Russia.

1992 In June, Yeltsin appointed Yegor Gaidar acting prime minister. In December, Yeltsin appointed Viktor Chernomyrdin prime minister.

1993 An anti-government uprising in Moscow in October was crushed by the Russian Army. President Yeltsin dissolved the Supreme Soviet and replaced it with the Federal Assembly, comprising the State Duma and the Federation Council. A new consitution was introduced.

1994 In December, Russian troops invaded Chechnya, which is *de facto* independent, but *de jure* part of Russia. Uzbekistan and Russia signed an economic integration treaty.

1995 In the parliamentary elections, the reformed Kommunisticheskaya Partiya Rossiiskoi Federatsii (KPRF) (Communist Party of the Russian Federation) won the largest vote. In June, Chechen rebels seized hundreds of hostages during a raid on the southern Russian town of Budenovsk. More than 100 are killed in the ensuing violence.

1996 In January, Chechen rebels seize thousands of hostages in the Russian town of Kizlyar. In April, President Dudayev of Chechnya is killed by the Russian airforce; he is succeeded by Zelimkhan Yandarbiyev. Boris Yeltsin was re-elected president. In May, a peace treaty was signed between Russia and Chechen separatists, temporarily ending the conflict. In August, Chechen forces drove the Russian army out of Grozny.

1997 Yeltsin and the Belarussian president, Aleksander Lukashenko, signed the Treaty on the Union of Belarus and Russia. The treaty aimed to increase political and economic co-operation between the two states from January 2000. In May, Yeltsin and new Chechen president Aslan Maskhadov signed a formal peace agreement.

1998 The Russian rouble collapsed, sending Russia into temporary economic crisis. The rouble was revalued (one new rouble = 1,000 old roubles). In March, Yeltsin appointed Sergei Kiriyenko prime minister. In August, Yeltsin appointed Chernomyrdin prime minister for the second time but failed to get parliamentary approval. In September, Yeltsin appointed Yevgeny Primakov prime minister.

1999 In May, Yeltsin appointed Sergei Stepashin prime minister . July-August, an Islamist separatist group declared the Russian republic of Dagestan to be independent. Chechen fighters under the command of the former prime minister of Chechnya, Shamil Basayev, invaded Dagestan in support of the separatists. In August, Yeltsin appointed Vladimir Putin as prime minister. In September, a series of bomb explosions in Russian cities are blamed on Chechen separaatists. In October, Russia launches a second invasion of Chechnya. On 31 December, just before midnight, Yeltsin resigned. Putin became acting president.

2000 In January, Putin appointed Mikhail Kasyanov prime minister. In March, Putin was elected president. The presidents of Belarus, Kazakhstan, Kyrgyzstan, Russia and Tajikistan (formerly the Customs Five) established the Eurasian Economic Community (EEC). In November, two prominent critics of the Putin administration, media tycoons Boris Berezovsky and Vladimir Gusinsky, are summoned for questioning by state prosecutors. Both men go into self-imposed exile.

2001 The Russian army started a gradual withdrawal of troops from Chechnya. The Federation Council approved the introduction of the new rouble in Belarus as of 1 January 2005, in preparation for introducing a new single currency in Russia and Belarus by 2008. The main pro-Putin parties created the Yedinaya Rossiya (YR) (United Russia) party. Tajikistan, China, Russia, Kazakhstan, Kyrgyzstan and Uzbekistan formed the Shanghai Co-operation Organisation (SCO) and agreed to fight ethnic and religious militancy, while promoting investment and trade.

2002 The US and Russia agreed to cut 70 per cent of their nuclear arsenals. Flash floods hit Black Sea tourist resorts. Chechen Prime Minister Stanislav Ilyasov resigned and was appointed by President Vladimir Putin as federal minister of Chechnya affairs. The head of the administration, Akhmed Kadyrov, appointed Mikhail Babich as prime minister of Chechnya. Chechnya's leading rebel warlord, Shamil Basayev, claimed responsibility for the Moscow theatre siege in which 119 hostages died.

2003 On 5 February, Akhmed Kadyrov dismissed Chechen Prime Minister Mikhail Babich and on 10 February, Anatoly Popov was appointed in his place. In September, Russia, Ukraine, Kazakhstan and Belarus signed an economic union treaty. Yedinaya Rossiya (United Russia) won the 7 December parliamentary elections.

2004 President Putin dismissed Prime Minister Kasyanov's government on 24 February and Deputy Prime Minister Viktor Khristenko was named acting prime minister. On 1 March, President Putin named EU envoy, Mikhail Fradkov, as his new prime minister; the appointment was confirmed by the Duma on 5 March. Incumbent Vladimir Putin won the 14 March presidential elections.

On 17 March, Sergei Abramov was confirmed as prime minister of Chechnya (pro-Moscow government). Chechen president, Akhmad Kadyrov, was killed in an explosion on 9 May; Prime Minister Sergei Abramov became acting president; on 29 August, Alu Alkhanov won the presidential elections. In September, at least 330 people died in the Beslan school massacre when Chechen terrorists held Russian schoolchildren and teachers hostage. On 5 October, Alu Alkhanov was sworn in as president of Chechnya.

In November, Putin openly backed Viktor Yanukovych in Ukraine's presidential election. In December, the Russian foreign ministry criticised Organisation for Security and Co-operation in Europe (OSCE) observers, who had declared the supplementary presidential election in Ukraine to be free and fair.

2005 On 9 February, Prime Minister Mikhail Fradkov's government survived a vote of no confidence. In Chechnya in

March, Russian special forces killed the Chechen rebel leader, Maskhadov. In March, Russia gave asylum to President Askar Akayev of Tajikistan, who was facing widespread demonstrations against his government.

In May, the former 'oligarch' and head of the oil company Yukos, Mikhail Khodorkovsky, was jailed for tax evasion and fraud.

On 13 November a blast at a chemical factory in Jilin, north-east China, resulted in a spillage of highly toxic benzene and nitrobenzene into the Songhua river, which is a tributary of the Amur river which runs through south-east Russia where cities draw their water supplies from the Amur. President Putin restricted the operations of NGOs in December. He also tightened state control over the media and tightened electoral laws.

2006 In January, Russia's state-owned gas company Gazprom turned off gas supplies to Ukraine, temporarily affecting supplies in Central and Western Europe. Gazprom had demanded from Ukraine a higher price for its gas and the dispute escalated into a diplomatic row between the Russian and Ukrainian governments. Also in January, Russia clashed with Bulgaria over similar gas supply issues; Russia negotiated with Iran over the transfer of Iran's uranium enrichment programme to Russia, in an effort to prevent Iran from developing nuclear weapons.

Political structure
Constitution
The constitution was adopted in December 1993. The Russian Federation consists of 89 republics and regions, including the federal cities of Moscow and St Petersburg.
Electoral system: universal direct suffrage over the age of 18.

Form of state
Federal state with a republican form of government

The executive
Executive power is held by the president, who has the right to veto parliamentary legislation, while issuing decrees on which the Federal Assembly may advise but not veto. The president is elected for a four-year term.

The cabinet is appointed by the prime minister, who is appointed by the president.

On 1 September 2000, President Putin decreed the formation of the State Council of the Russian Federation, which has consultative functions only, advising the president on issues concerning the relationship between the central administration and the regions.

National legislature
The 1993 constitution created a bicameral Federalnoe Sobranie (Federal Assembly), comprising a lower house, the 450 seat Gosudarstvennaya Duma (State Duma) and an upper house, the 178-seat Sovet Federatsii (Federation Council), with two deputies from each of Russia's 89 republics and regions (representatives of regional executives and legislative bodies). Half of the State Duma members are elected from party lists and half in a simple majority contest from territorial constituencies. A party failing to gain at least 5 per cent of the total vote cannot win parliamentary seats. Four-year terms are served.

Legal system
The legal system is based on civil law. There is judicial review of legislative acts. The top levels of the judicial branch consist of: the Constitutional Court, which reviews the constitutionality of federal legislation; the Supreme Court, which is the highest civil and criminal judiciary body; and the Supreme Arbitration Court, which resolves economic disputes between subjects of the Federation. The Supreme Court and Supreme Arbitration Court preside over a federal system of lower criminal and civil courts.

Last elections
14 March 2004 (presidential); 7 December 2003 (parliamentary).
Results: Presidential: incumbent Vladimir Putin won with 71.2 per cent of the vote, against 13.7 per cent for opposition Communist Party candidate, Nikolai Kharitonov, Sergey Glazyev 4.1 per cent, Irina Khakamada 3.9 per cent and Oleg Malyshkin (Liberal Democratic Party) 2.0 per cent; turnout was 64.3 per cent.. Parliamentary: Yedinaya Rossiya (United Russia) won 37 per cent of the vote, the Kommunisticheskaya Partiya Rossiiskoi Federatsii (KPRF) (Communist Party of the Russian Federation) 12.7 per cent, the Liberal-Democratic Party 11.8 per cent, the Rodina Bloc 9.1 per cent and Yabloko 4.3 per cent.

Next elections
2007 (parliamentary); 2008 (presidential).

Political parties
Ruling party
Yedinaya Rossiya (United Russia) (re-elected 7 Dec 2003) is the largest party in the State Duma (it was formed in Dec 2001 by the merger of the Mezhregional'noye Dvishenie Yedinstvo (Medved) (Inter-Regional Movement Unity) and the Otechestvo-Vsya Rossiya (OVR) (Fatherland-All Russia))

Main opposition party
Kommunisticheskaya Partiya Rossiiskoi Federatsii (KPRF) (Communist Party of the Russian Federation)

Population
146.74 million (2004)
Ethnic make-up
Russian (82 per cent), Tatars (4 per cent) and Ukrainians (3 per cent).
Religions
The majority of the population is Christian, mainly Russian Orthodox. Religion, while not actually forbidden under communism, was officially discouraged. Religious observance and interest is growing steeply with the relaxation of state restrictions. Russian Orthodox Christmas was made an official holiday for the first time in 1991.

Russia also has sizeable Muslim (12 million) and Jewish (700,000) minorities.

Education
After compulsory education at age 15, secondary (complete) general education begins. Students may also enter vocational schools or non-university level higher education institutions. Initial vocational schools offer one-and-a-half to two years of vocational education. Secondary (complete) general education continues for two years and ends when students are aged 17–18 years.

Higher education is provided by 553 public and 260 non-public accredited higher education institutions. Education in public higher education is free of charge. There are three levels of higher educational institutions including those lasting between two to four years and an advanced level lasting between five and six years. The government aims to diversify higher education courses and boost the private sector. In addition to universities in the public and private sector, there are 3,000 non-university institutions in Russia. Public expenditure on education was equivalent to approximately 3.5 per cent of annual gross national income in 1997 and included subsidies to private education at the primary, secondary and tertiary levels. In March 2001, it was estimated that the government owed the education sector US$197 million. The salaries of teachers amount to R1.126 (US$39) per month.

Literacy rate: 99.6 per cent, adult rate (2003)
Compulsory years: Six to 15 years.
Enrolment rate: 107 per cent total primary enrolment of the relevant age group (including repeaters) (World Bank).
Pupils per teacher: 20 in primary schools.

Health
UN reports indicate a growing concern over Russia's falling birth rate, low life expectancy and unusually high male mortality rate, with the possibility that population in the greater part of Russian regions could halve every 35–40 years. This

Russia

alarming trend comes amid reports of the reappearance on Russia's borders of diseases such as anthrax and bubonic plague, causing deaths in Siberia and southern Russia. HIV/Aids, TB, syphilis, drug addiction and alcoholism are also contributing to the crisis in the health sector.

Russia has long worried about its declining male population, but overall statistics are just as bleak. Russia has one of the highest rates of abortion in the world, with 66 for every 100 pregnancies.

Annual total expenditure on health is around 5 per cent of GDP, of which government spending is about 68 per cent. Private expenditure is approximately 32 per cent, of which 4–5 per cent is pre-paid health insurance plans.

HIV/Aids
HIV/Aids has spread in Russia at a time when infection rates have been steady and declining for a number of years in Europe and North America. Few Russians can afford the expensive new treatments that have been discovered in the past few years. HIV/Aids cases have more than trebled since 2000. Russian health officials blame the high number of HIV/Aids cases on intravenous drug use rather than sexual activity.

HIV prevalence: 1.1 per cent aged 15–49 in 2003 (World Bank)
Life expectancy: 65.7 years (2003)
Fertility rate/Maternal mortality rate: 1.3 births per woman (World Bank)
Birth rate/Death rate: 10 births per 1,000 population; 14 deaths per 1,000 population (2003).
Infant mortality rate: 16 per 1,000 live births (World Bank)
Head of population per physician/bed: 1.3 physicians and 3.1 hospital beds per 1,000 people.

Welfare
In January 2005, widespread demonstrations forced Vladimir Putin to amend newly instigated reforms to the benefits system after they were introduced. The plan to offer cash payments in exchange for what had been free services such as medicines, transport and subsidised housing continued but the amounts were increased and pension payments brought by a month. About 34 million pensioners, infirm and war veterans are estimated to be affected by the changes, with the lowest payments at just US$7.5 per month. Critics said that the implimentation of the change was mishandled and the calculations sloppy, whereas the government believes that 'monetising' benefits was the only option to streamline social benefits and generate considerable cost savings. This set-back is thought, by some, to risk Putin's reform agenda.

Given budgetary constraints, reforms are targetted at increasing the transparency and efficiency of Russia's main social funds and eliminating unproductive social programmes. There have been massive increases in health service funding, especially to reduce infant mortality rates and bring healthcare up to world standards. Maternity benefits are being enhanced in order to induce women to stay at home for two or three years.

The tax code has been used to unify and reduce the different social security contributions but, despite recent tax cuts, average real incomes remain low.

Unemployment benefits based on past earnings remain very low due to high inflation. Income inequality levels have consequently been increasing and it is estimated that about 20.4 per cent of the population live below the minimum subsistence level laid down by the state.

Main cities
Moscow (capital of the Russian Federation, estimated population 11.3 million in 2004); St Petersburg (formerly Leningrad) (4.6 million); Novosibirsk (1.4 million); Nizhny Novgorod (formerly Gorki, 1.3 million); Yekaterinburg (formerly Sverdlovsk) (1.3 million); Samara (formerly Kuybyshev) (1.2 million); Rostov-on-Don (1.1 million); Omsk (1.1 million); Kazan (capital of the sovereign republic Tatarstan) (1.1 million); Cheljabinsk (1.1 million); Volgograd (1.0 million), Ufa (1.0 million); Vladivostok (592,100); Irkutsk (594,400); Krasnodar (644,900).

Languages spoken
There are as many as 100 local ethnic languages, some of the larger groupings include Baskin, Chuvash Tatar and Yakut. Russian is spoken throughout the country. Russian and most local languages are written in variants of the Cyrillic alphabet, which was devised by the ninth century saints, Cyril and Methodius. In September 2000, the Tatarstan republic (population four million, a large minority of whom are Russian) began a 10-year transition period for the switch in schools from Cyrillic to the Latin alphabet for the local Turkic language. Russian is the second language spoken in Tatarstan. However, Russian MPs voted in June 2002 to make the use of the Cyrillic alphabet mandatory throughout the country.

On 5 Feb 2003, the State Duma passed a law making Russian the official state language, prohibiting the use in public documents of foreign words or expressions that have Russian-language equivalents).

Ukrainian, Mordvin and Chechen are also spoken.

Official language/s
Russian

Media
Press
Dailies: The official news agency is the Information Telegraph Agency (ITAR–TASS). *Strana.Ru* is a nationwide Russian-language information service, incorporating the functions of a daily newspaper, an analytical magazine and an information news agency with regional branches across the country. Strana runs an English-language on-line magazine, the *Russian Observer* (http://www.russianobserver.com). Major newspapers are *Izvestia, Moskovskii Komsomolets, Kommersant Daily, Nezavisimaya Gazeta/Independent Newspaper, Novosti, Pravda* (in both Russian and English), *Trud, Spid-info, Ekstra M, Centre, Sovershenno Sekretno, Megapolis Express* and *Iz Ruk v Ruky*. *Russia Today* is an English-language daily.

Weeklies: *Argumenty i Facty (Arguments & Facts)* is a Russian language weekly newspaper that contains in-depth analysis of the latest Russian political and economic events. *The Russia Journal* and *Russia News Journal* contain weekly news, analysis, and political opinion. *Moskovskie Novosti* is a weekly international socio-political newspaper. *St Petersburg Times* is an English-language weekly. *Delovoj Petersburg* (Russian, English and German) is published three times in the week.

Business: *Moscow Times* is an English-language business publication.

Periodicals: *Vladivostok News* is an English-language periodical covering political, business information in the Primorie.

Broadcasting
Radio: There are 26 radio stations broadcasting from Moscow, 21 of which are commercial.

Television: There are 10 television stations broadcasting from Moscow, of which five are commercial. Satellite communications are used for national and international transmission of Central Television programmes.

In April 2001, NTV, the only independent TV station, which was owned by the Media-Most group, was taken over by Gazprom, Russia's monopoly gas company.

In July 2001, the government banned majority foreign ownership of national television stations.

Russia's only independent national television station, TV6, was liquidated in January 2002. However, the station was relaunched by a group of journalists and Kremlin-backed businessmen in March 2002.

In June 2003, the last of the independent current affairs television channels, TVS, closed and a sports channel replaced it.

Advertising
Commercial advertising is widely available. Limited television and radio advertising is available to Western companies; billboards and illuminated signs can be bought in most major cities.

Economy
Russia began its comprehensive transition towards a market economy in the early 1990s, under the stewardship of President Boris Yeltsin and his then acting prime minister for the period June–December 1992, Yegor Gaidar. Gaidar also served as economics minister from September 1993 to January 1994. The initial period of liberalisation, often referred to as economic 'shock therapy', saw extreme economic instability coupled with recession and hyperinflation. The privatisation programme created a new rich oligarchy that replaced the old Soviet bosses – many high-level technocrats became powerful businessmen.

Many of Russia's problems stem from the pace and shape of the liberalisation programme, which was largely directed by a caucus of foreign free marketers, particularly in the International Financial Insitutions (IFIs), whose ideas were already going out of fashion in the West.

The liquidation of the Soviet Union led to a disintegration of its constituent parts. The oil-rich regions in Kazakhstan and Tajikistan were given independence, while the food basket economies in Eastern Europe moved away from Russian domination. The privatisation programme pushed by the IFIs in return for their support involved selling valuable state assets at rock-bottom prices. Without subsidies, the country's main employers shed their labour force by the millions, generating widespread poverty which was coupled with spiralling prices as shortages of food and other basic goods began to bite. Output sank while the black market grew exponentially, causing the rouble to become almost worthless. Added to this was the major financial crisis of 1998 which was brought on by unsustainable levels of debt, exacerbating the country's problems. Inflation hit 150 per cent in that year.

The Putin era is seen as an attempt to redress many of the worst excesses of Russian neo-liberalism, which led to extreme macroeconomic instability. The tail end of the Yeltsin era, in which Putin was prime minister, saw parts of the economy gradually ease. A devaluation of the rouble and the rise in oil prices largely saved the country from complete collapse in 1999 and 2000. This generated a broad industrial recovery and a healthy trade surplus by 2002, although this was largely consumed by debt servicing costs. In 1998, foreign debt was around 90 per cent of GDP, since reduced to around 28 per cent by 2004. The country's foreign debt stood at US$153.5 billion in 2003. There have been extraordinary levels of capital flight (amounting to around US$200 billion per annum) and many workers went unpaid. Wage arrears amounted to R31.14 billion (about US$1.04 billion) as of 1 October 2003. High energy prices have earned Russia considerable amounts of foreign exchange on its hydrocarbons resources, while keeping domestic energy prices low and allowing GDP growth to increase. The global slowdown slowed Russia's GDP growth to 4 per cent in 2002, but it reached 6.3 per cent in 2003. Inflation was down to 10.9 per cent in 2004. Foreign direct investment (FDI) was US$3.43 billion in the period January–June 2004, up 35.3 per cent compared to January–June 2003. In June 2004, the World Bank agreed investment of US$1.0–US$1.5 billion in Russia over the next three years,

The IMF estimates that real GDP grew 7.1 per cent in 2004, slowing to 6.5 per cent in 2005. The government needs to accelerate reforms (especially a reform plan for Gazprom) and in the medium term, the cost of structural reforms makes further growth doubtful.

According to the draft submitted in August 2004, the 2005 budget surplus will be R278.11 billion (about US$9.50 billion), the budget revenues are projected to be R3.33 trillion (about US$113.86 billion), with budget expenditures planned to be R3.05 trillion (about US$104.30 billion).

External trade
Imports
The principal imports include machinery and equipment, consumer goods, medicines, meat, sugar and semi-finished metal products.

Main sources: Germany (16.7 per cent total, 2004), China (7.1 per cent), Ukraine (6.7 per cent), Italy (5.9 per cent), Finland (5.0 per cent), France (4.5 per cent), Japan (4.5 per cent)

Exports
The principal exports include petroleum and petroleum products, natural gas, timber and timber products, metals, chemicals, and a wide variety of civilian and military manufactures.

Main destinations: Germany (8.4 per cent total, 2004), The Netherlands (6.7 per cent), China (6.4 per cent), US (5.8 per cent), Ukraine (5.7 per cent), Italy (5.4 per cent), Turkey (4.5 per cent)

Agriculture
Farming
Production in the agricultural sector in Russia has fallen since reforms began in 1992, following the substantial reduction in large state subsidies. The livestock sector contracted by about half. Progress has been particularly slow in land reform, and Russia still lacks a free market in agricultural land. Agricultural production contributes only 7 per cent of GDP, with 133 million hectares (ha) of arable land, and a large agrarian workforce constituting nearly 14 per cent of the total.

The sector has suffered due to incomplete agriculture-specific and economy-wide institutional reform, such as price and trade reform, as well as privatisation. Russia has the potential to increase grain exports significantly if such reforms are implemented and the situation seems to be improving. Wheat and barley are the most significant crops produced in Russia that are widely traded on world markets.

Crop production ('000) in 2004 included: 76,231 tonnes (t) cereals in total, 45,413t wheat, 17,180t barley, 3,546t maize, 2,872t rye, 4,955t oats, 35,073t potatoes, 4,068t cabbages, 1,117t millet, 1,684t pulses, 2,018t tomatoes, 318t grapes, 4,801t sunflower seed, 112t fibre crops, 2,217t oilcrops, 21,848t sugar beets, 555t soya beans, 2,030t apples, 215t strawberries, 178t plums, 3,941t fruit in total, 15,504t vegetables in total. Livestock production included: 4,822t meat in total, 1,907t beef, 1,656t pig meat, 141t lamb and goat meat, 1,030t poultry, 2,006t eggs, 32,156t milk, 52t honey, 220t cattle hides, 12t sheepskins, 45t greasy wool.

Fishing
There has been a very noticeable drop in recorded fisheries production in Russia, since the end of the Soviet Union. Production shortfalls have resulted in rising prices and steadily increasing imports of fish and fishery products.

Russia's lucrative caviar industry, based on the Caspian Sea and long stymied by dwindling stocks, was effectively shut down from June 2001 to March 2002 by an international ban on the export of caviar products, imposed by the Convention on International Trade in Endangered Species (CITES). The US government unilaterally introduced its own ban in November 2002 and CITES reimposed an international ban in January 2006.

In addition to the consequences of major economic and political changes, aquaculture and inland capture fisheries continue to face problems resulting from environmental impacts on water quality and quantity affecting living aquatic resources. The environmental degradation of inland waters through industrial, urban and agrochemical pollution, and the damming of major rivers has had significant local impacts on fish stocks. As a result of the large-scale uptake of water for irrigation, the original fish fauna of Russia has been significantly modified.

Production from subsistence and recreational fisheries is seldom accurately reflected in the official statistics, and it is likely that production from these sectors plays an important role for food supply in the country. However, capture fisheries in many inland waters of the region, including, in particular, reservoirs and lakes, continue to depend heavily on stocking of fry and fingerlings produced in hatcheries, lake farms and artificial spawning grounds, or by other types of enhancement measures.

Improved stocking and fisheries management measures provide the potential for significant increases in fish production from reservoirs and lakes in Russia. It is estimated that fisheries production from reservoirs could be increased between four and six-fold by improved stocking; inland fish production could realistically be doubled by 2010. It is expected that recreational fisheries, often contributing significantly to household food supply, will gain increasing importance.

The annual total fish catch is approximately five million tonnes. Russia imports some 6,000 tonnes of sea products while it exports around 117,000 tonnes annually.

Forestry

Russia has by far the largest forested area of any country in the world with forest and other wooded land constituting more than half of its land area estimated at 851.3 million hectares (ha) or almost 55 per cent of the total land area. Russia accounts for more than 20 per cent of global forest resources, more than 35 per cent of temperate/boreal forests in terms of area and 45 per cent in terms of growing stock. The area of forest is fairly stable, showing a marginal average annual increase of 0.02 per cent, or the equivalent of 135,000ha of forest cover. The importance of Russia's forests as a regulator of the global carbon balance, and mitigation of climate change, is difficult to overestimate.

The predominant coniferous species are larch and spruce. The deciduous species are represented mainly by birch, aspen and oaks (either European or Mongolian), and hornbeam, ash, maple and elm to a lesser degree. Mature and over-mature stands, situated mainly in the Asian part of Russia, prevail and about two-thirds of the forest is available for wood supply.

Russia is one of the largest producers and exporters of industrial roundwood in the world market. Significant volumes of sawn wood, plywood and pulp and paper are exported. The forest industry is almost completely privatised, although the forests and the roundwood production remain under state control.

Export of forest material in 2004 amounted to US$6.4 billion, while imports amounted to US$1.1 billion. Production in 2004 included 182,000,000 cubic metres (cum) roundwood, 134,000,000cum industrial roundwood, 21,500,000cum sawnwood, 58,758,000cum sawlogs and veneers, 54,171,000cum pulpwood, 7,159,000cum wood-based panels, 48,000,000cum woodfuel; 1,900,000 tonnes (t) recovered paper, 1,979,000t newsprint, 601,000 printing and writing paper.

Industry and manufacturing

The industrial sector accounts for 30 per cent of GDP and provides employment for a third of the working population. Factors that continue to dog efficiency include wasteful consumption of fuel and raw materials, antiquated machinery, poor technology and management and overstaffing. Early on in the reform process emphasis was placed on individual enterprise and factory production decisions, resulting in anarchic management practices.

Major production bottlenecks in the 1990s included steel, construction inputs (such as cement) and consumer and light industry products (such as television sets, robots and computers).

Emphasis during the 1990s was on light industry, modernisation and computerisation. Towards the end of the 1990s, there were attempts by major industrial and manufacturing companies to consolidate their activities, with many mergers. The sector remains reliant on large- and medium-sized firms to increase production and stimulate growth, particularly in engineering and metallurgy working.

Industrial production increased by 3.7 per cent in 2003 and an estimated 6.4 per cent in 2004.

Tourism

Russia is an increasingly important tourist destination with considerable potential, but it only accounts for 1.7 per cent of GDP. It attracts around 8 million holiday visitors. However, foreign exchange earnings are offset by the larger outflow of Russian tourists. The sector remains relatively undeveloped. Infrastructure is inadequate. Expansion is hindered by a shortage of tourist-oriented accommodation, not only in the provinces, but also in Moscow and other major cities, where luxury hotels have been the norm. Investment is being directed towards increasing the availability of two- and three-star hotels.

Other problems include visa regulations and the lack of a structured national tourism organisation. In July 2004, the St Petersburg region secured EU funding support for an initiative to develop its tourism industry.

Mining

Russia is the world's largest producer of iron ore, asbestos, manganese ore, nickel, chromite, platinum group metals and potassium salts, and the second-largest producer of gold, lead and phosphate ores. There are vast reserves, but extraction has been held back due to rising production costs, labour shortages and a shortage of technology.

Major foreign exchange earners include gold and diamonds. Estimated annual production of diamonds is 12,000 tonnes. Russia is estimated to have 30 per cent of world iron ore reserves and 20 per cent of many other minerals. Significant quantities of iron ore, chromium, nickel, asbestos and fertiliser materials are exported.

There are large deposits of antimony, beryllium, cadmium, mercury, molybdenum, tin and vanadium plus workable deposits of all rare earth metals.

Large-scale investment in the sector is improving extraction and processing techniques, while reducing wastage and controlling production costs. Gold production in 2005 totalled 157.6 tonnes, much of which originates in Russia's Sakha Republic (formerly Yakutia). This represents a decline in production of nearly 7 per cent since 2004.

Hydrocarbons

Russia had 69.1 billion barrels of proven oil reserves in 2003. Crude oil production increased by 11 per cent in 2003 to 8.54 million barrels per day (bpd) and increased again in 2004 to 9.27 million bpd, making it the second largest producer in the world after Saudia Arabia. Russia is also the second largest oil exporter in the world, again after Saudia Arabia, exporting 6.67 million bpd. Its production increases have been far higher than any other non-member of the Organisation of the Petroleum Exporting Countries (OPEC). Russia has 42 refineries with a total capacity of 5.51 million bpd, which require further development and investment due to their inefficiency and ageing. Recovery of the estimated 139 million tonnes of crude oil from western Siberia began in 1998 and production is expected to reach six million tonnes per annum by the end of 2004. The government is at present promoting extensive oil exploration and extraction in eastern Siberia, particularly in the Sakha Republic (formerly Yakutia). In 2004, based on proven oil reserves, the International Energy Agency estimated that production in

Russia would continue to expand for another two to three years before entering a period of decline.

Proven gas reserves of 47 trillion cubic metres (2003) account for around 26.7 per cent of world reserves. Russia has the world's largest reserves and is the world's largest producer of natural gas, with production totalling 578.6 billion cubic metres in 2003. Gas meets nearly 55 per cent of the country's energy needs, a ratio forecast to reach 60 per cent by 2010, with production anticipated to double from the current level. Construction of the 1,213 km Blue Stream pipeline was completed in October 2002 and transit began in 2003. It will supply Turkey with 15.9 billion cubic metres of natural gas, more than 60 per cent of its domestic needs. Gazprom has proposed a new pipeline to bypass Ukraine because of a continuing dispute between Russia and the Ukraine over gas transit. To this effect, in December 2005, work began on a trans-Baltic Sea gas pipeline linking the Russian town of Vyborg with the German town of Greifswald. Gazprom hold a 51 per cent stake in the venture and has recruited former German chancellor Gerhard Schröder to chair the project. New gas and fields off the coast of Sakhalin Island, in Russia's far east, have been in development since 2003 but these face criticism from environmentalists concerned with the impact on local marine life.

Coal reserves totalled 157.0 billion tonnes oil equivalent (toe) in 2003. Russia produced 124.9 million toe, an increase of 8.8 per cent on 2002 production levels. The government had hoped to expand coal production to 335 million tonnes in 2010 and 430 million tonnes by 2020.

Russia's hydrocarbon sector is dominated by state-owned enterprises, foremost of which are Gazprom (gas) and Rosneft (oil). This is the product of a government policy, particularly since 2004, to regain control of key resources in the wake of chaotic liberalisation in the early 1990s and has at times involved questionable methods. In December 2004, President Putin backed a move to strip the privately owned Yukos oil company of its main production arm, Yuganskneftegas, and subsequently permitted its purchase by the state-owned oil company Rosneft. This left Rosneft in control of some 16 per cent of Russia's total crude oil output. In the process, Yukos chairman Mikhail Khodorkovsky, who resisted the takeover, was jailed for fraud. In June 2005, the government increased its stake in Gazprom from 38 to 51 per cent. Gazprom currently controls 20 per cent of the world's natural gas reserves. In October 2005, Gazprom bought the Sibneft oil company from Roman Abramovich, giving the Kremlin (via Gazprom and Rosneft) control of over one third of Russia's total oil output. In December 2005, the Russian parliament voted to lift the ceiling on foreign ownership of Gazprom shares above 20 per cent but the government's 51 per cent stake remains in place.

Energy

Russia is the second-largest generator of electricity in the world with installed capacity of 206GW and an output of about 860 billion kWh (2004 estimate), of which about 63 per cent is produced thermally, 21 per cent by hydroelectricity and 16 per cent nuclear. The sector is in a poor state and requires investment of up to US$11 billion annually between 2002–05 to expand and maintain existing electricity generation. The Russian government has only allocated US$1 billion per annum and it is unlikely that the sector will attract significant foreign capital. As a result, the country faces an energy crisis that could dampen industrial development and therefore hinder economic growth.

Russia's 31 nuclear power plants are being assessed. By 2001, four plants had come to the end of their 30-year prescribed service life and 16 of its reactors are of the same design as the one in Chernobyl, Ukraine. By 2010, another 10 reactors will be due for closure.

The government has prioritised the need to extend the working life of these plants. In January 2001, Russia announced it will build 40 nuclear reactors by 2020 to prevent an energy crisis. The 1,000MW Rostov-1 reactor began operating in March 2001. Russia commissioned five new nuclear power plants in 2001, increasing the country's generating capacity by a further 3,000MW by 2005.

In March 2004, the Putin government began to reform the electricity sector, with the intent of introducing greater competition and partial privatisation. Gazprom, the state-controlled gas company, has begun to buy into electricity sector.

Russia exports electricity to most countries of the former USSR and also to China, Poland, Turkey and Finland. In October 2003, Russia and the EU agreed to fully integrate their respective power grids by 2007.

Financial markets
Stock exchange
The main exchange markets are the Russian Exchange and the St Petersburg Stock Exchange.

Enthusiasm for Moscow stocks diminished following the collapse of the rouble in 1998. The fall partly reflected continued uncertainty about investing in the country, as well as international downward pressure driven by scepticism about the fast-growing 'new economy'. Stability of the rouble's exchange rate in 2002 encouraged financial market participants to invest in government securities.

Banking and insurance

Most major banks are located in Moscow. The majority of Russian banks suffer from being undercapitalised and the high rate of inflation has constantly eroded their reserves. This is not surprising given the high degree of fragmentation in the sector. The system has been criticised for having too many owner-operators; this is a situation with potential for abuse. The retail banking sector is still in its infancy and branch networking is not particularly common. Foreign banks are not permitted to open their own branches in Russia and instead must rely upon subsidiaries, which drives up their costs. President Putin reiterated his opposition to direct foreign entry in December 2005. The US has protested this decision and has pointed out that Russia's desire to join the WTO will require banking liberalisation.

In June 2003, Russia was removed from the Organisation for Economic Co-operation and Development (OECD) black list of havens for money laundering.

Beginning 29 July 2004, the Central Bank revoked the licences for operations of three Moscow banks: the Commercial Bank of Savings, the Industrial Export-Import Bank and the Investment and Commercial Moscow Housing Construction Bank.

Central bank
Central Bank of the Russian Federation
Main financial centre
Moscow

Time

The Russian Federation covers nine time zones, from GMT plus three hours (for example Moscow and St Petersburg) to GMT plus 12 hours (for example Petropavlovsk-Kamchatsky).

Geography

The Russian Federation is the largest country in the world at 17.07 million square km. Even European Russia (west of the Ural Mountains), which is only a quarter of the total landmass, dwarfs all other European countries. Major cities and towns are concentrated in western Russia, with the population thinning out to the far north and east.

Norway lies to the far north-west of Russia, with Finland, Estonia, and Latvia to the north. Belarus and Ukraine lie to the south-west of European Russia, the southern borders of which are with the Trans-Caucasian states of Georgia and Azerbaijan, and with Kazakhstan. In the north-west, near St Petersburg, there is a short coastline where there is access to the Baltic Sea via the gulf of Finland. Towards

Russia

the south, European Russia has a coastline on the Black Sea in the south-west, with the Caspian Sea to the east. Beyond the Ural Mountains, the Siberian and Far Eastern regions have southern frontiers with the People's Republic of China, Mongolia, and in the south-east, North Korea. The eastern coastline is on the Sea of Japan, the Sea of Okhotsk, the Pacific Ocean and the Barents Sea. The northern coastline is on the Artic Ocean. The region around Kaliningrad on the Baltic Sea is separated from the rest of the Russian Federation by Lithuania to the north and east, and has a coastline on the Baltic Sea.

The territory includes a wide variety of physical features. European Russia and western Siberia form a vast plain. Between the Black and Caspian Seas in the south, the land is more undulating, until it reaches the foothills of the Caucasus mountain range in the far south. The northern regions of both Asian and European Russia are inhospitable areas, much of the territory being covered by permafrost.

Europe's highest mountain, Elbrus (at 5,642 metres), is just on the Russian side of the Georgian border. Russia has Europe's longest river, the 3,690km Volga which rises north-west of Moscow and flows east before turning south to the Caspian Sea. The two largest lakes in Europe are also in Russia. Lake Ladoga (18,390 square km) and Lake Onega (9,600 square km) are both north-east of St Petersburg.

Climate

The climate in Russia is extremely varied. The north is arctic, with an extensive zone of permafrost, but there are a few subtropical zones in the southern region of the country. The majority of the land mass is continental or moderate continental. The Russian winter is deservedly famous: winter snow cover lasts as long as 160 days in St Petersburg.

Moscow has a warm spring with an average temperature of 18 degrees Celsius (C) in the period April to May. It is often hot in summer (June to August 20–30 degrees C), mild in autumn (September to October 10–15 degrees C) and freezing (down to minus 30 degrees C) for the rest of the year. Average annual rainfall is 575mm.

Average temperatures in the southern Siberian town of Irkutsk range from minus 20.8 degrees C in January to 17.9 degrees C in July. Average annual rainfall is 458mm, most of which falls in the summer. In the far north of Siberia, the average January temperature is minus 46.8 degrees C.

The Far Eastern region combines the extreme temperatures of Siberia with monsoon-type conditions common elsewhere in Asia. The mean temperature in January in the eastern port of Vladivostok is minus 14 degrees C; in August the average is 21 degrees C.

In the more moderate western portion of Russia, the average January temperature is slightly below zero. Summer is very hot in some areas. The snow in European Russia begins to melt in March and the muddy transition period demands waterproof footwear.

Dress codes

Dress well as business people are judged by their attire. Warm outer clothes, hats, gloves and footwear are essential in winter, although interiors are well heated. The most important factor is neatness. Shoes should be polished and clothes pressed. Russians themselves do not always wear a suit and tie at business meetings, but it is wise to err on the safe side. Dark suits, white shirts and conservative ties are the norm, with business suits for women. Formal evening wear is not normally necessary. Summer dress is modest.

Entry requirements

Passports
Required by all.

Visa
Required by all. See www.rusemblon.org/ and follow link to application forms to download a visa form. US citizens should also download the supplementary questionnaire. All travellers should assess the general information link to see if the additional requirements affect them.

Visitors must register their visas within three working days of arrival in Russia with the local branch of the Ministry of the Interior. Most major hotels will do this for their guests automatically. All visas are issued with an exit visas included.

Business travellers must include, with their application, a letter of invitation from the Russian Foreign Ministry or its regional representatives or Ministry of the Interior or its local offices. The letter must contain the official seal and legal address of the agency, a document registration number, date of registration, the signature and name of official authorized to issue invitations, and a travel itinerary with dates of stay and names of persons involved. Also to be included is a letter from a foreign employer (or own letter if self-employed) giving personal details, a full itinerary, purpose of visit and a guarantee accepting full responsibility for any expenses incurred. The right to request the submission of all original documents is reserved by the embassy, and multiple entry visas require original letters of invitation in all cases.

Currency advice/regulations
Import of local currency is prohibited. There is no limit on the amount of foreign currency taken in, but a declaration is required. Export of local currency is permitted up to the equivalent of US$1,500. Amounts exceeding US$1,500 require authorisation from a bank or completion of customs declaration form TC-28, confirming that the specified amount was imported.

It is possible to withdraw money from automated teller machines in Moscow and St Petersburg using cards belonging to the leading Western networks. Bring unmarked US dollar bills (printed after 1991), preferably in mint condition, for travel to more obscure regions.

Shops, hotels and restaurants may advertise dollar prices, but you must still pay in roubles.

Customs
Small amount of personal goods are allowed in duty-free. On arrival declare all foreign currency and valuable items such as jewellery, cameras, computers and musical instruments. You will be required to fill out a customs declaration and it is vital that this be stamped and kept in a safe place; leaving the country without it can sometimes be difficult.

Health (for visitors)

Mandatory precautions
Visitors from Asia, South America and Africa require a certificate for yellow fever inoculation; an HIV/Aids certificate is required for long-stay visitors only. If arriving at Moscow, this is not usually demanded.

Advisable precautions
It is advisable to be 'in date' for the following immunisations: polio (within 10 years), tetanus (within 10 years), typhoid fever, hepatitis 'A', hepatitis 'B', tuberculosis, tick-borne encephalitis.

Water precautions are recommended (water purification tablets may be useful, especially in St Petersburg, where the water supply is infected by giardia).

There is a risk of rabies.

Russian medical care is not up to Western standards. A travel kit including a disposable syringe is a reasonable precaution. Any medicines known to be required should be taken by the visitor, and it could be wise to have precautionary antibiotics if going outside major urban centres.

Hotels

Moscow has an increasing number of Western-run hotels. Accommodation is difficult to obtain in Moscow at short notice. It is crucial to make bookings in advance as hotels refuse to check in a guest without a reservation. First-class and tourist class are available, with all prices fixed by Intourist. Main hotels have foreign currency restaurants and bars. Tipping is increasingly common, typically 10 per cent.

Credit cards
Credit cards are not widely accepted outside Moscow and St Petersburg, where, through automated teller machines (ATMs), you can make cash withdrawals, even in US dollars.

Public holidays
Fixed dates
Incorporating changes made by the Duma in December 2004.
1–10 Jan (New Year Holiday), 7 Jan (Russian Orthodox Christmas), 14 Jan (Russian Orthodox New Year), 23 Feb (Defender of Fatherland Day), 8 Mar (Women's Day), 1 May (Labour Day), 9 May (Victory Day), 12 Jun (Russia Day), 4 Nov (Day of National Unity).
Variable dates
Russian Orthodox Good Friday and Easter Monday.

Working hours
Banking
Mon–Fri: 0930–1730. In major cities banks open again between 1300–1800. Moscow Sheremetyevo 2 airport 0800–2030 daily. Open 24 hours at St Petersburg Pulkovo airport.
Business
Mon–Fri: 0900–1800 (appointments best between 0900–1000).
Shops
Mon–Sat: 0900–1900.

Telecommunications
Telephone/fax
The telephone network remains underdeveloped.
Internet/e-mail
Electronic mail is the cheapest form of communication in Russia.

Electricity supply
220V AC

Social customs/useful tips
A firm handshake is important as is negotiating an agenda at the beginning of the meeting. Smoking in meetings is very common. Ask permission before lighting a cigarette and offer cigarettes generously. Written communications are particularly important with large bureaucracies. Address the recipient formally and keep a copy of everything.
It is customary to take a small gift on a business or social visit. Offering basic food is considered insulting. Offer little luxuries.
It is impolite to take along people who are not invited to a social function. If you are offered a second helping of caviar, resist the temptation and refuse. The offer will be made again, but it is polite to refuse the first time.

Many Russians take certain superstitions somewhat seriously. Do not give an even number of flowers, for example, as this is for funerals only; do not greet people in a doorway – it is considered unlucky. Strict punctuality is of no great importance. On the other hand, a certain amount of attention is paid to niceties, such as seeing someone off at a train station. Carry some form of identity at all times.

Security
The normal precautions should be taken when visiting Russia – avoid showing large amounts of cash or expensive personal belongings. Avoid travelling alone at night in Moscow and St Petersburg, particularly on the metro.

Getting there
Air
National airline: Aeroflot-Russian International Airlines (ARIA)
International airport/s: Moscow-Sheremyetevo International (SVO), 29km north-west of city centre, two terminals, duty-free, bureau de change, information desks; Moscow-Vnukovo (VKO), 29km south-west of city; Moscow-Domodedovo (DME), 40km south-east of city; St Petersburg-Pulkovo (LED), 17km from city; Irkutsk (IRK), 7km from city.
Airport tax: None
Surface
Road: Major highways connect Moscow to Kiev (Ukraine) and Moscow to Minsk (Belarus), Riga (Latvia) and Warsaw (Poland).
Rail: The Russian/CIS rail network (around 87,079km) extends to all the former USSR countries. The sleeper coach from London-Brussels-Berlin-Warsaw-Moscow takes around 53 hours. Through-trains are also available from major Western and Eastern European cities and from Turkey, Iran, Mongolia and China.
Water: There are sea links from Finland, Norway, Sweden and Germany and from the Ukraine in the west. In the east, a weekly ferry runs between Vladivostok and Niigata-Fushiki in Japan.
Main port/s: There are ports at Vladivostok, Magadan, Nakhodka and Petropavlovsk (Pacific Ocean), Sochi (Black Sea) and Makhachkala (Caspian Sea). The major Western ports are St Petersburg (Baltic Sea) and Kaliningrad. Links to the Atlantic are provided by the Murmansk (Arctic Ocean) and Archangelisk ports.

Getting about
National transport
Air: There is an extensive internal air service operated by Aeroflot and Transaero

(due to a small fleet, flights are more often delayed than those of Aeroflot).
The internal network centres around Moscow's four airports. Domestic airports include Vnukovo (VKO), Domodedovo (DME) and Bykovo (BKA), located in Moscow.
Road: In general the few roads connecting with Siberia are impassable during winter. Secondary roads are often untarred.
Distances between major cities are extensive: Moscow to St Petersburg 692km (432 miles); Moscow to Odessa 1,347km (837 miles). Approximately 60 per cent of the road network needs to be rehabilitated or upgraded. The Russian government built 65,000km of new roads between 1995–2000.
Buses: Long-distance coach services operate.
Rail: Rail is the major means of transport. There is a cheap and efficient service to all major towns. There is an extensive network of commuter and inter-city services, most offering first and second class seats or accommodation.
The rolling stock needs modernising and trains are typically over-crowded and over-booked. Food is often available on inter-city services but, because of the generally poor quality, most passengers bring their own. Many carriages have a samovar which produces hot water for drinks. Security can be a problem, especially on overnight services. The famous Trans-Siberian railway stretches from Moscow to Vladivostok; this seven-day journey is recommended only for hearty train lovers and adventurers.
The railways are wide gauge. Almost all the rail network is electrified. Sleepers should be booked well in advance. Reform of the railways is being carried out in three stages. The first stage was completed in early 2003 with the creation of a joint stock company, Russian Railways, and the restructure of the railways ministry.
Water: Rivers play an important role in transport; in summer it is possible to travel great distances either by cruises or river passenger boats. Routes include: St Petersberg-Astrakhan on the Caspian sea, and St Petersberg-Rostov-on-Don on the Black Sea. These routes may include detours via Moscow.
The largest inland waterway is the River Volga. There are a number of inland ports and canals.
City transport
Taxis: Use only officially marked taxis and do not share them with strangers. They may be identified by a checkerboard on the side of the car. A green light at the top right hand corner of the windscreen

indicates availability. They can be hired at taxi ranks or by telephoning.
Tariffs for foreigners are often subject to negotiation and may be charged in hard currency.
It is possible to find a reliable taxi firm in the airport arrivals section at Moscow airport. Payment is by credit card though fares may have to be negotiated with the driver as the fare shown on the meter may not correspond with the fare asked. Arrangements to be met at the airport in advance can be made by contacting Intourist, or telephoning Moscow Taxi (tel: 238-1001). The journey time by taxi from Moscow airport to the city centre is around 30 minutes.
Beware of illegal taxi touts operating both in the airport area and in the city centre.
Buses, trams & metro: Cheap and reliable, though often crowded, available from 0600–0100. Bus services 5817 and 551 from Moscow airport to the city centre operate between 0500–2359 every 10 minutes, with a journey time of 30–45 minutes. Long distance coach services operate.
Trains: An express train service from Moscow airport to the city centre operates every 30 minutes.

Car hire
Available in major towns. International driving licence required with Russian translation of details. Notification of route to be taken should be given if travelling outside main cities.
Visitors travelling in private cars should be in possession of their passport and visa, and an itinerary card complete with visitor's name and citizenship and car registration number.
Traffic drives on the right. Speeds are limited to 60kph (37mph) in built-up areas and 90kph (55mph) elsewhere. Cars are required to display registration plates and stickers denoting the country of registration.

BUSINESS DIRECTORY

The addresses listed below are a selection only. While World of Information makes every endeavour to check these addresses, we cannot guarantee that changes have not been made, especially to telephone numbers and area codes. We would welcome any corrections.

Telephone area codes
The international direct dialling code (IDD) for Russia is +7, followed by the area code and subscriber's number:

Chelyabinsk	3512	St. Petersburg	812
Ekaterinberg	3432	Smolensk	0812
Kaliningrad	0112	Tula	0872
Moscow	095	Vladivostok	4232
Nizhny Novgorod	8312	Yakutsk	41122

Useful telephone numbers
International operator: (English-speaking operator): 8196
General enquiries (Moscow area): 09
Police: 02
Fire: 01
Ambulance: 03

Chambers of Commerce
American Chamber of Commerce in Russia, 7 Dolgorukovskaya Street, Moscow 127006 (tel: 961-2141; fax: 961-2142; e-mail: info@amcham.ru).

Moscow Chamber of Commerce and Industry, 22 Akademika Pilyugina Street, Moscow 117393 (tel: 132-7510; fax: 132-0547; e-mail: mtpp@mtpp.org).

Nizhny Novgorod Region Chamber of Commerce and Industry, 1 Oktyabrskaya Square, Nizhny Novgorod 603005 (tel: 194-210; fax:194-009; e-mail: tpp@rda.nnov.ru).

Russian Federation Chamber of Commerce and Industry, 6 Ilyinka Street, Moscow 109012 (tel: 929-0009; fax: 929-0360; e-mail: tpprf@tpprf.ru).

St Petersburg Chamber of Commerce and Industry, 46-48 Chaikovsky Street, St Petersburg 191194 (tel: 279-2833; fax: 272-6406; e-mail: spbcci@spbcci.ru).

South Ural Chamber of Commerce and Industrym 63 Vasenko Street, Chelyabinsk 454080 (tel: 661-816; fax: 665-223; e-mail: mail@tpp.chelreg.ru).

Smolensk Chamber of Commerce and Industry, 12 Karl Marx Street, Smolensk 214000 (tel: 554-142; fax: 237-450; e-mail: smolcci@keytown.com).

Tula Chamber of Commerce and Industry, 25 Krasnoarmeisky Prospekt, Tula 300600 (tel: 364-517; fax: 360-216; e-mail: tulacci@tula.net).

Banking
Agropromstraybank, Krasina Per, 123056 Moscow (tel: 254-4263; fax: 254-7081).

Gazprombank, Nametkina Str 16B, 117420 Moscow (tel: 719-1697/17; fax: 719-1763).

ING Bank Eurasia, ul Krasnaya Presnya 31, 125178 Moscow (tel: 755-5400; fax: 755-5459; fax: 755-5499).

Sberbank (savings bank), Vavilova Str 18, 117817 Moscow (tel: 971-4981, 957-5690, 957-5862; fax: 957-5731; internet site: http://www.sbrf.ru).

SDM Bank, 73 Volokolamskoe Shosse, 123424 Moscow (tel: 490-1545, 491-7572, 490-0703; fax: 490-6509).

United Export Import Bank (UNEXIM), 11 Masha Paryvaeva Street, PO Box 207, 107078 Moscow (tel: 232-3727; fax: 975-2205; e-mail: mailbox@mail.unexim.ru).

Vnesheconombank (Bank for Foreign Economic Affairs), Akademika Sakharova Prospekt 9, 107996 Moscow (tel: 207-1037).

Vneshtorgbank (Bank for Foreign Trade), Kuznetskiy Most Str 16, 103031 Moscow (tel: 929-8900; fax: 956-3727).

Central bank
Central Bank of the Russian Federation, 12 Neglinnaya Sreet, 107016 Moscow (tel: 771-9100; fax: 921-6465; e-mail: webmaster@www.cbr.ru).

Travel information
Aeroflot, 37/9 Leningradsky Prospect, Moscow 125836 (tel: 155-5737; fax: 155-5556; enquiries: tel: 156-8002 [international]; 155-0922 [domestic]; St Petersburg (tel: 327-3873).

British Airways, Moscow (tel: 578-2736); St Petersburg (325-2565).

Central Hotels Information Centre, Kompositorskaya ul 25-5, Moscow.

Committee for Tourism, St Petersburg Administration, 41 Nevsky Prospekt, St Petersburg 191025 (tel: 312-2541; fax: 315-9796; e-mail: travel@mail.wplus.net).

Intourservice (trade and travel association), ul Mokhovaya 16, 103009 Moscow (tel: 203-3191/6780).

Russian Railways, ul Novobasmannaya 2, 107174 Moscow (tel: 262-1628; fax: 262-6561).

Railway Enquiries (Moscow) (tel: 266-9000/333).

Thomas Cook Russia (tel: 244-2754).

Ministries
Ministry of Agriculture and Food, 1-11 Orlikov Lane, Moscow 107139 (tel: 207-8000; fax: 207-8362, 288-9580).

Ministry of Atomic Energy, 24-26 Bolshaya Ordynka Str, Moscow 101100 (tel: 239-4753; fax: 233-4679).

Ministry for Civil Defence, Emergencies and Disaster Resources, 3 Teatralniy Pr-D, Moscow 103012 (tel: 926-3901; fax: 924-5683).

Ministry for Communications, 7 Tverskaya Str, Moscow 119332 (tel: 229-6966, 292-7070; fax: 292-7128).

Ministry of Construction, Comp 2, 8 Stroitelei Str, Moscow 117987 (tel: 930-1755; fax: 938-2202).

Ministry for Co-operation Between CIS Member Countries, 7 Varvarka Str, Moscow 103073 (tel: 206-1365; fax: 206-1084).

Ministry of Culture, 7 Kitaiskiy Pr-D, Moscow 103693 (tel: 925-1195; fax: 928-1791).

Ministry of Economics, 19 Noviy Arbat Str, Moscow 103025 (tel: 203-7534; fax: 203-7482).

Ministry of Education, 6 Chistoprudniy B-R, Moscow 101856 (tel: 927-0568; fax: 924-6989).

Ministry for Environmental Protection and Natural Resources, 4-6 B Gruzinskaya Str, Moscow 123812 (tel: 254-7683; fax: 254-8283).

Ministry of Finance, 9 Ilyinka str, Moscow 103097 (tel: 298-9101, 923-0967; fax: 925-0889).

Ministry of Foreign Affairs, 32-34 Smolenskaya-Sennaya Sq, Moscow 121200 (tel: 244-1606; fax: 230-2130).

Ministry for Foreign Economic Relations, 32-34 Smolenskaya-Sennaya Sq, Moscow 121200 (tel: 244-2450; fax: 244-3068/3981).

Ministry for Fuel and Power Development, 7 Kitaiskiy Pr, Moscow 103074 (tel: 220-5500; fax: 220-4818).

Ministry of the Interior, 16 Zhitnaya Str, Moscow 117049 (tel: 237-7585, 924-6572, 222-6669; fax: 925-2098).

Ministry of Justice, 4 Vorontsovo Pole Str, Moscow 109830 (tel: 209-6009/98; fax: 916-2903).

Ministry of Labour, 1 Birzhevaya Sq, Moscow 103706 (tel: 261-2030, 928-8208; fax: 230-2407).

Ministry for Nationalities and Regional Policy, 19 Trubnikovskiy Lane, Moscow 121819 (tel: 248-8635; fax: 202-4490).

Ministry of Public Health, 3 Rakhmanovskiy Lane, Moscow 103051 (tel: 928-4478; fax: 921-0128).

Ministry for Railways, 2 Novo-Basmannaya Str, Moscow 107174 (tel: 262-9901; fax: 262-9095).

Ministry for Science and Technology, 11 Tverskaya Str, Moscow 103905 (tel: 229-1192; fax: 230-2823).

Ministry for Social Protection, Bld 1, 4 Slavianskaya Sq, Moscow 103715 (tel: 220-9511/9384; fax: 924-3690).

Ministry of Transport, 10 Sadovo-Samotyochnaya Str, Moscow 101433 (tel: 200-0809; fax: 200-3356).

Other useful addresses

British Consulate, Sfoskaya Nberezhnaya 14, Moscow (tel: 956-7420; fax: 956-7420).

British Consulate, St Petersburg, Pl Proletarsky, Dikatury 5, 193124 St Petersburg (tel: 325-6036; fax: 325-6037; e-mail: uk.stpet@vmail.sprint.com).

British Consulate for Southern Russia, Petrak, 3a Fabrichnaya Street, Novorossisk (tel: 93-319; fax: 34-959).

British Embassy, Kutuzovsky Prospekt 7/4, Moscow 121248 (tel: 956-7200, 956-7477; fax: 956-7480, 956-7420; e-mail: uk.moscw@vmail.sprint.com).

British Trade Office, 4th Floor, 15a Gogol Street, Ekaterinburg 620151 (tel: 564-931; fax: 592-901; e-mail: uk.ekate@vmail.sprint.com).

BSCC British-Russian Business Centre, 42 Southwark Street, London SE1 1UN (tel: (0)171-403-1706; fax: (0)171-403-1245); 22/25 Bolshoi Strochenovskiy Pereulok, Moscow 113054 (tel: 230-6120; fax: 230-6124).

Delegation of the European Union (Office of), 2/10 Astakhovsky Pereulok, Moscow 109208 (tel: 956-3600; fax: 956-3615).

Expocentr, 1a Sokolnicheskiy val, Moscow 107113 (tel: 268-7083) (responsibility for organising, on a commercial basis, international and foreign exhibitions and symposia).

Foreign Investment Promotion Centre (FIPC), Ul Novy Arbat 19, 119898 Moscow (tel: 203-4863; internet site: http://www.fipc.ru/fipc/).

Foreign Trade Arbitration Commission, Moscow (tel: 205-6855).

Interstate Statistical Committee of the Commonwealth of Independent States, 39 Myasnitskaya Str, Moscow 103450 (tel: 207-4237/4802/4567; fax: 207-4592; e-mail: Statpro@Sovam.com).

Russian Federation Embassy (USA), 2650 Wisconsin Avenue, NW, Washington DC 2007 (tel: 202-298-5700; fax: 202-298-5735; e-mail: russ-amb@cerfnet.com).

Russian Federation Foreign Trade Organisation, Barrikabnaya Str Bld 8-5, 123242 Moscow (tel: 254-8090; fax: 253-9675).

Russian Information Telegraph Agency (ITAR-TASS) (news agency), Tverskoy bul 10, Moscow (tel: 3229-8053).

Russian Television and Radio, Corolov St 12, Moscow (tel: 217-7898; fax: 288-9508).

State Committee for Statistics, 39 Myasnitskaya Street, Moscow 103450 (tel: 207-4902; fax: 207-4640).

TACIS Technical Assistance Centre, 165 Nemirovicha-Danchenko, Novosibirsk 630087 (tel: 465-395, 464-836; fax: 464-426; e-mail: centre@tac.sib.ru).

US Consulate, St Petersburg (tel: 275-1701).

Internet sites

Moscow business telephone list: http://www.mbtg.net/art_eng.html

Moscow business telephone guide (in Russian and English, updated 10 times annually): http://www.mbtg.net

Rusline (government information, company directories): http://www.rusline.com

Moscow Guide: http://www.moscow-guide.ru

Russian web directory: http://www.ru/

Useful telephone numbers: http://www.moscow-guide.ru/general/TelephoneNum.htm

Rwanda

Tensions in the Great Lakes region continue to impact on Rwanda and are being closely monitored. While a main Hutu rebel group announced its voluntary disarmament in April 2005, little progress has been made toward its implementation. The United Nations mission (MONUC) in the Democratic Republic of Congo has stepped up efforts to accelerate the demobilisation of militias. Separately, the African Union (AU) has announced that it will send a large contingent of peacekeepers. In June, the international community expressed concern over the repatriation of 6,500 Rwandese asylum seekers from Burundi, following a decision by the two governments to reclassify refugees from each other's country as illegal immigrants.

Rwanda is a poor country with about 90 per cent of the population engaged in mainly subsistence agriculture. The country is striving to rebuild its economy, with coffee and tea production being among its main sources of foreign exchange, after the 1994 genocide decimated this fragile economic base. Nearly two thirds of the population lives below the poverty line. Rwanda has made substantial progress in rehabilitating its economy to pre-1994 levels. It continues to receive substantial aid money and received IMF-World Bank Heavily Indebted Poor Country (HIPC) debt relief in 2005. However, its high defence expenditures cause tension between the government and international donors and lending agencies. An energy shortage and instability in neighboring states may slow growth in 2006, while the lack of adequate transportation linkages to other countries continues to handicap export growth.

Economy

With economic policy implementation broadly on track, indications are that at the end of 2005, growth is at the upper end of the 4–5 per cent range, reflecting mostly an expected recovery in agricultural production due to good weather conditions. The result of a poor first harvest and rising energy prices, headline inflation rose to 13 per cent in March, but declined to 11 per cent in June; inflation excluding these items remained subdued at around five per cent. A tighter-than-programmed fiscal policy helped to contain reserve money growth while international reserves increased to almost six months of imports at end-June.

Nevertheless, the conduct of monetary policy has been weak. The National Bank of Rwanda allowed a doubling of banks' excess reserves which led to a substantial decline in interest rates. An unexpected substantial increase in private sector credit in April–May could partly reflect a delayed effect of this looser monetary stance. The current account deficit widened in the first quarter, reflecting a surge in externally financed imports. The exceptionally high imports stemmed mostly from NGO-related activities. While they were financed from abroad, the tighter fiscal stance together with higher-than-programmed project disbursements resulted in a temporary increase in international reserves.

The 2005 programme sought to lay the foundations for stronger medium-term growth. The authorities have embarked on a number of new initiatives with medium term implications: an excessive government car fleet and car allowances to civil servants has been cut, the civil service wage bill is being slimmed down, and given the acute electricity shortages and high energy costs the power station being built on Lake Kivu is being accelerated and tariffs restructured.

KEY FACTS

Official name: Republika y'u Rwanda (Republic of Rwanda)

Head of State: President Paul Kagame (FPR) (the first Tutsi to hold presidential office since Rwanda became independent in 1961; officially elected president 17 Apr 2000; re-elected 25 Aug 2003)

Ruling party: Front Patriotique Rwandais (FPR) (Rwanda Patriotic Front) (Tutsi-dominated) (elected 29–30 Sep 2003)

Area: 26,338 square km

Population: 8.59 million (2004)

Capital: Kigali

Official language: Kinyarwanda, French and English.

Currency: Rwanda franc (Rwf)

Exchange rate: Rwf540.75 per US$ (Oct 2005)

GDP per capita: US$215 (2004)

GDP real growth: 4.00% (2004)

Labour force: 4.57 million (2003)

Inflation: 12.00% (2004)

Balance of trade: -US$190.22 million 2004

Foreign debt: US$1.30 billion (2003)

There is broad agreement with the International Monetary Fund (IMF) that, in the case of a real exchange rate appreciation from a scaling up of donor assistance, the best policy would be to allow the nominal exchange rate to appreciate as this would have a less adverse impact on the poor than a rise in inflation.

The structural reform agenda will remain focussed on the delivery of public services and the development of the private sector. With various initiatives for export promotion under way, there is a need to co-ordinate and focus efforts. There have been delays in the privatisation of the tea estates (which are largely outside the authorities' control), and where productivity needs a significant boost.

Rwanda's financial system is shallow and dominated by the commercial banking system. Banking services are basic, while credit to the private sector is concentrated in few sectors and mostly short term. Banks compete for deposits and loans of a group of only about 50 corporate customers. While about one-third of households have an account in financial institutions, insurance penetration is low, pensions are largely restricted to a public system, and the capital market is limited to treasury bills. Parts of the legal and regulatory frameworks governing the financial and commercial sectors are dated, including in accounting, auditing, insolvency, leasing, and anti-money laundering. As financial institutions are too small to achieve economies of scale and adequate risk diversification, Rwanda will need to strive for greater harmonisation of policies and establishment of a more open market in financial services.

Politics

In August 2003 Paul Kagame – who had been selected as candidate by MPs in 2000 – claimed a landslide victory in the first presidential elections since the 1994 genocide. Born a Tutsi in western Rwanda in 1957, Kagame grew up in Uganda, where his parents fled to escape Hutu violence. He joined Yoweri Museveni – now Uganda's president – and became his intelligence chief. He established the Rwandan Patriotic Front (RPF), which ended the 1994 genocide.

Rwanda has experienced relative stability under Kagame, who reportedly tolerates no criticism or challenge to his authority. He is an incorruptible teetotaler who downplays any ethnic agenda in Rwanda, presenting himself as a Rwandan and not a Tutsi. The genocide in Rwanda was the worst in modern times and the country remains influenced by the ethnic tension associated with the traditionally unequal relationship between the dominant Tutsi minority and the majority Hutus. Although in 1959 the ethnic relationship was reversed and 200,000 Tutsis fled to Burundi, lingering resentment led to periodic massacres of Tutsis.

In 1994 the shooting down of a plane carrying President Juvenal Habyarimana, and his Burundian counterpart triggered major fighting. The Tutsi-led Rwandan Patriotic Front (RPF) launched a campaign to control the country. After the brutal massacre of at least 800,000 Tutsis and Hutus had been brutally massacred the Tutsis took control.

Two million Hutus fled to Zaïre (now the Democratic Republic of Congo (DRC)). They joined Zaïrean forces to attack local Tutsis. Rwanda responded by invading refugee camps dominated by Hutus.

Zaïrean leader Laurent Kabila could not banish the Hutu extremists, prompting Rwanda to support the rebels trying to overthrow him. Although Rwanda withdrew its forces from DRC after a peace deal with Kinshasa, tensions still simmer, with Rwanda now accusing the DRC army of aiding Hutu rebels in the east.

Rwanda has used traditional community courts to try those suspected of taking part in the 1994 genocide. But those accused of orchestrating the slaughter appear before an International Criminal Tribunal in northern Tanzania.

Risk assessment

Economic	Improving
Political	Improving
Regional stability	Poor

COUNTRY PROFILE

Historical profile

Once known as the land of a thousand hills, Rwanda became synonymous with genocide and massacre in the 1990s as members of the Hutu tribe went on the rampage. Their target consisted primarily of members of the minority Tutsi tribe, but also included moderate Hutus and critics of the government. In contrast to its neighbour, Burundi, where the majority Hutu population was long subjected to minority Tutsi overlordship, Rwanda had experienced its 'peasants revolt' in the early sixties and political power was firmly in Hutu hands. But the Tutsi still formed a sizeable proportion of the educated élite and Hutu resentment was never far below the surface. In 1994 it exploded with shattering consequences that took the world by surprise.
1899 Rwanda, which for a long time had been an independent monarchy, was absorbed into German East Africa.
1916 It was taken over by Belgium, along with what is now Burundi.
1918 After the First World War ended, the two became Ruanda-Urundi, a Belgian-administered trust territory of the League of Nations (and later, the UN).
1950s Belgian missionaries encouraged the formation of a modern Hutu identity.
1961 Rwanda's monarchy was abolished and a republic was proclaimed.
1962 Independence was granted.
1963 A massacre killed about 20,000 people, mostly Tutsis, causing many to flee to Uganda.

KEY INDICATORS — Rwanda

	Unit	2000	2001	2002	2003	2004
Population	m	7.62	7.95	8.04	8.32	8.59
Gross domestic product (GDP)	US$bn	1.79	1.70	1.73	*1.68	*1.85
GDP per capita	US$	231	206	213	242	215
GDP real growth	%	6.0	6.7	7.3	3.2	4.0
Inflation	%	3.9	3.4	2.0	7.4	12.0
Exports (fob) (goods)	US$m	69.1	93.0	78.0	68.0	69.8
Imports (fob) (goods)	US$m	222.3	340.0	342.0	253.0	260.0
Balance of trade	US$m	-153.2	-247.0	-260.0	-185.0	-190.2
Current account	US$m	-90.0	-100.0	-120.0	-130.0	-50.0
Foreign debt	US$bn	1.4	1.3	1.2	1.3	–
Total reserves minus gold	US$m	190.6	212.1	243.7	214.7	314.6
Foreign exchange	US$m	189.5	199.7	233.6	184.9	284.4
Exchange rate	per US$	389.70	442.99	477.50	528.28	574.62

* estimated figure

Rwanda

1973 President Gregoire Kayibanda, was overthrown by Major General Juvenal Habyarimana.

1990 Some 10,000 rebel Tutsi guerrillas invaded Rwanda from Uganda and occupied several towns.

1993 President Habyarimana signed a power-sharing agreement with the Tutsis. A UN mission was sent to monitor the agreement.

1994 The death of Habyarimana in a plane crash in April (which also killed the president of Burundi), triggered the breakdown of civil society. Extremist Hutu militia began the systematic murder of Tutsis. Within four months an estimated 800,000 Tutsis and moderate Hutus were killed. The Tutsis Front Patriotique Rwandais (Rwandan Patriotic Forces) (RPF) forced the militia to flee, taking with them around two million Hutu refugees, who fled in fear of reprisal for the genocide, into neighbouring Democratic Republic of Congo (DRC), Tanzania and Burundi.

1995 The militia responsible for the genocide were able to take control of the refugee camps and deter people from returning to Rwanda on pain of death. Mass repatriation efforts were complicated by screening operations, which were needed to identify genocide rebels from genuine refugees.

President Pasteur Bizimungu and a transitional coalition government were sworn in.

1998 The United Nations Human Rights Field Office in Rwanda (HRFOR) was withdrawn when its mandate was not renewed.

1999 An extension of the transitional government's term of office was approved.

2000 Pasteur Bizimungu resigned and Paul Kagame was officially elected president in a joint vote of the Rwandan legislature and cabinet.

2001 A peace agreement was signed between Rwanda and Uganda. A new national flag, emblem and anthem were unveiled.

2002 Rwanda and the Democratic Republic of Congo (DRC) signed a peace agreement.

2003 In a May referendum, voters approved a new, more democratic constitution; critics said it would be hard to unseat the ruling party under the new constitution. Incumbent Paul Kagame won the August presidential elections and the ruling party, FPR, won the parliamentary elections.

2004 In March, Kagame denied he ordered the attack on the president's plane in 1994, sparking the genocide. Former president Bizimungu was sentenced to 15 years imprisonment for embezzlement, inciting violence and associating with criminals.

2005 The Forces Democratiques De Liberation Du Rwanda (FDLR) Democratic Liberation Forces Of Rwanda declared they were ending hostilities. A mass release of 36,000 prisoners took place as part of the process of reconciliation; many had confessed to acts of genocide.

Political structure

Constitution
A new 2003 constitution prevents a one-party dominance of the political system and bans incitement to racial hatred. It stipulates that no party can hold more than 50 per cent of the seats in cabinet, even if it secures an absolute majority in parliamentary elections.
The president, prime minister and president of the lower house cannot belong to the same party.

Form of state
Republic

The executive
The president is eligible for election for two seven-year terms.

National legislature
Under the new constitution, there is a two-tier parliament, with members serving five-year terms.
The Chamber of Deputies is composed of 80 members, including 53 members from political organisations and independent members, 24 women representatives (at least two from each province), two representing the youth and one representing the disabled groups.
The Senate is composed of 26 members elected as follows: 12 members (at least two from each province), eight appointed by the president, four from the forum of political parties and two each from the universities.

Last elections
29–30 September and 2 October 2003 (parliamentary); 25 August 2003 (presidential).
Results: Parliamentary: the first legislative elections since the 1994 genocide were won by the ruling party, the FPR, with 73.8 per cent of the vote, followed by the SDP with 12.3 per cent and the Liberal Party with 10.6 per cent; turnout was 99.5 per cent.
Presidential: President Paul Kagame won with 95.1 per cent of the vote. The scale of the victory indicated he had the support of a majority of both Tutsis and Hutus.

Next elections
2008 (parliamentary); 2010 (presidential).

Political parties

Ruling party
Front Patriotique Rwandais (FPR) (Rwanda Patriotic Front) (Tutsi-dominated) (elected 29–30 Sep 2003)

Main opposition party
Social Democratic Party (SDP)

Population
8.59 million (2004)

Ethnic make-up
There are three ethnic groups: the Hutu (90 per cent), the Tutsi (9 per cent) and the Twa (1 per cent).

Religions
Roman Catholic (56 per cent), Protestant (26 per cent), Adventist (11.1 per cent), Islam (4.6 per cent), indigenous beliefs (0.1 per cent).

Education
On completion of primary education, a competitive entrance examination allows students to progress to the first cycle secondary school for general education, from age 13 to 16. The second cycle secondary school covers either modern or classical humanities, from age 16 to 19. Technical education is provided for students who have completed two to three years general secondary education, although some may begin straight from primary education joining four-year courses. Education suffered badly as communities and the social infrastructure were devastated by the internal conflict of the early 1990s. This included the destruction of schools and educational institutions, as well as the loss of trained teachers. By 1998 it was estimated that approximately one-third of school-age children were not in school (having died or become refugees) and two-thirds of teachers were secondary school graduates with no teacher training (VSO 2003).

Literacy rate: 70.4 per cent, adult rate (2003)
Compulsory years: Seven to 13.
Enrolment rate: 95.5 per cent net primary (World Bank).

Health

HIV/Aids
The average life expectancy of Rwandan citizens has reduced to under 40 due to the Aids epidemic. In 2003 there were 230,000 people HIV positive, of which 130,000 were women. There were also 22,000 children (0–17 years) with HIV/Aids and 160,000 orphans created by Aids. There has been evidence that national adult prevalence has fallen in Rwanda since reaching a peak in the mid-1990s (UNAID 2003).

HIV prevalence: 5.1 per cent aged 15–49 in 2003 (World Bank)
Life expectancy: 39.8 years (World Bank)
Fertility rate/Maternal mortality rate: 5.7 births per woman (World Bank)
Birth rate/Death rate: 40 births per 1,000 population; 21.7 deaths per 1000 population (2003).
Infant mortality rate: 118.0 per 1,000 live births (World Bank)

Welfare
More than half the population live below the national poverty line. According to the 2002 UN Development Report, 84.6 per cent of the population exist on less than US$2 per day and 35.7 per cent on less than US$1 per day.

Main cities
Kigali (capital, estimated population 298,100 in 2003), Ruhengeri (39,900), Butare (38,700), Gisenyi (29,600), Cyangugu (19,500).

Languages spoken
KiSwahili is also used among traders.
Official language/s
Kinyarwanda, French and English.

Media
Press
The government publishes the *Daily Bulletin (ARP)*, and weekly newspapers *La Relève* in French and *Imvaho* in Kinyarwanda. The church publishes the newspaper *Kinyamateka* and the children's newspaper *Hobe* in Kinyarwanda.
Broadcasting
Radio: Two SW and eight FM radio stations broadcast daily from 0500 to 0800 and from 1100 to 2300 in various languages including Kinyarwanda, French, KiSwahili and English.
Television: Rwanda Television is the only major broadcasting company in the country.

Economy
The country has had to contend with much damaged caused during the civil war, not only to its infrastructure but also to its economy. The IMF and World Bank have been closely involved Rwanda's recovery. The domestic saving ratio is the lowest in Africa and the economy is still fragile and vulnerable to external shocks, so that it relies on external aid; any reduction in funds can have an adverse impact. Aid also has an inflationary effect as large sums are channelled through the few available banks. About 30 per cent of bank deposits are in US dollars. Inflation was 12 per cent while GDP growth was 4.0 per cent in 2004.

The government has set an increase in agricultural productivity as a priority. Growth was at only 0.5 per cent in 2004. Industrial production, at 21 per cent did not increase its share of GDP either, although it grew by 4.3 in 2004.

The government's medium-term strategy has been to reduce the country's high current account deficits, tackle the burgeoning level of debt and integrate the Rwandan economy in regional and international markets. In the long run, there is a need for diversification in a country where about 90 per cent of the population is engaged in mostly subsistence farming. Rwanda will continue to be the centre of international aid efforts for many years to come.

External trade
On the advice of international financial institutions, the government is looking to restructure its economy to diversify exports while preventing excessive damage caused by fluctuating international commodity prices.

In 2002, the US approved Rwanda as being eligible for tariff preferences under the African Growth and Opportunities Act (AGOA).

Imports
Principal imports include foodstuffs, machinery and equipment, steel, petroleum products, cement and construction material.
Main sources: Kenya (21.9 per cent total, 2004), Germany (7.8 per cent), Belgium (7.7 per cent), Uganda (5.9 per cent), France (5.9 per cent)

Exports
Principal exports include coffee, tea, hides and tin ore.
Main destinations: Indonesia (35.4 per cent total, 2004), China (7.1 per cent), Germany (3.4 per cent)

Agriculture
Farming
The agricultural sector contributes about 40 per cent to GDP and employs 90 per cent of the labour force. Approximately 30 per cent of the land area is cultivated arable land, 31 per cent pasture and 9 per cent forest; tree planting programmes are under way to combat deforestation.

The main food crops are beans (17 per cent of cultivated land), sweet potatoes (14 per cent), sorghum (7 per cent), plantains, bananas, potatoes, cassava and maize. Crop yields fluctuate due to drought, soil erosion and underinvestment.

The coffee industry is scheduled for privatisation although little progress has been made. Coffee production fell so the government is encouraging the growth of speciality coffees that receive higher prices on the international market. If this move is successful, export revenues could be boosted, but if not, it is unlikely the failing coffee industry will recover swiftly.

Tea overtook coffee as the country's main export.

Crop production for 2004 included: 318,944 tonnes (t) cereals in total, 136,359t taro, 912,108t cassava, 1,072,772t potatoes, 908,306t sweet potatoes, 3,033,545t roots and tubers, 2,469,741t plantains, 16,772t wheat, 88,209t maize, 163,772t sorghum, 46,191t rice, 214,983t pulses, 6,521t oilcrops, 3,800t tobacco, 20,017t green coffee, 14,493t tea, 70,000t sugar cane, 18,251t soya beans, 2,546,096t fruit in total, 267,000t vegetables in total. Livestock production included: 46,673t meat in total, 22,965t beef, 11,000t game meat, 3,318t pig meat, 2,673t goat meat, 1,449t poultry, 2,300t eggs, 137,097t milk, 30t honey, 3,312t cattle hides, 182t sheepskins.

Industry and manufacturing
The industrial sector contributed 21.5 per cent to GDP in 2004 and typically employs 6 per cent of the workforce. Industries include brewing, food processing, cigarette production, soaps, plastics, tin smelting and textiles. Growth of the sector is limited by the small domestic market, transport difficulties and irregular supply of imported fuels and raw materials which comprise 77 per cent of inputs. Industrial production increased by 4–5 per cent in 2004.

Tourism
Rwanda receives around 16,000 tourists annually and is aiming to become Africa's newest eco-tourism destination. It plans to raise the number of visitors to 70,000 by 2010 and boost tourism income to US$99 million a year.

Mining
The mining sector contributes 7 per cent to GDP and employs 1 per cent of the workforce.

Extraction of cassiterite (known reserves 90,000 tonnes) has been carried out since 1985, on an artisanal scale only.

Hydrocarbons
Rwanda has no upstream oil industry or refining plants and imports all its refined petroleum products from Kenya and Tanzania. The proposed Kenya-Uganda 320 km oil pipeline will benefit Rwanda through the lower costs of transportation of imported oil.

There are around 70 billion cubic metres of methane gas in Lake Kivu, with a regenerative capacity of around 250 million cubic metres per annum. Rwanda has been looking to exploit this resource since 1998. In 2005, an agreement was signed with a private operator to develop and gather commercial quantities of gas for use in electricity production.

Rwanda does not import or consume natural gas nor does it have significant coal reserves.

Energy
The subsistence farming sector currently relies on wood and charcoal.

Electrogaz, Rwanda's privatised national electricity generating company, has a power generating capacity of 10MW. In March 2005 an agreement was signed with the UK company Dane Associates to build a 35MW power station at Kibuye by

March 2007, with all electricity supplied to Electrogaz.

Urban areas and industry energy requirements are met by hydroelectricity generated by the Ntaruka, Mukungwa and Sebeya stations. The Rusizi power station has been developed with Burundi and DRC and generates more than 40 per cent of the energy used in Rwanda.

In mid-2002, the Israeli Electric Company announced that it was conducting a preliminary study on the construction of a 25MW power station, using gas from Lake Kivu. The Gisenyi Electric and Gas Company also hopes to construct a plant that would have an initial capacity of 2.5MW, eventually expanding to 10MW. Analysts believe that Lake Kivu has enough natural gas to produce 200MW of electricity.

Banking and insurance
Central bank
Banque Nationale du Rwanda
Main financial centre
Kigali

Time
GMT plus two hours

Geography
Rwanda is a landlocked country in central Africa, just south of the Equator, bounded by the Democratic Republic of Congo to the west, by Uganda to the north, by Tanzania to the east and by Burundi to the south.

Climate
Warm, tempered by altitude. Rainfall is low and is concentrated in two seasons from mid-January to mid-May, and mid-October to mid-December. Average temperatures in Kigali range from 12–14 degrees Celsius (C) at night to 28–32 degrees C during the day. Cooler in the highland areas.

Entry requirements
Passports
Required by all. Passports must be valid for three months.
Visa
Are not required for visits up to 90 days; entry permits are issued on arrival, when visitor must provide evidence of sufficient funds for stay and return/onward passage. Business travellers or tourist staying for longer must apply for a visa. A business visa requires a letter of introduction by an employer stating purpose of visit.
Currency advice/regulations
Import and export of local currency is limited to a maximum Rwf5,000. Import of foreign currency is unlimited, but amounts should be declared on arrival; export is only allowed up to the amount declared.

Health (for visitors)
Mandatory precautions
Yellow fever vaccination certificate is required by all.
Advisable precautions
Hepatitis A, tetanus, typhoid and polio vaccinations. Malaria prophylaxis is recommended. Water precautions should be taken. Aids is prevalent. There is a rabies risk.

Hotels
Tend to be expensive in Kigali; cheaper in Butare, Gisenyi and Ruhengeri. Advisable to book in advance.

Public holidays
Fixed dates
1 Jan (New Year's Day), 28 Jan (Democracy Day), 7 Apr (Genocide Memorial Day), 1 May (Labour Day), 1 Jul (Independence Day), 4 Jul (Liberation Day), 1 Aug (Harvest Festival), 15 Aug (Assumption Day), 8 Sep (Culture Day), 25 Sep (Republic Day), 25 Dec (Christmas Day), 26 Dec (Boxing Day).

Working hours
Banking
Mon–Fri: 0800–1200, 1400–1700; Sat: 0700–1300.
Business
Mon–Fri: 0800–1230, 1330–1700.
Government
Mon–Fri: 0800–1230, 1330–1700.
Shops
Dawn to dusk.

Telecommunications
Mobile phones
A GSM900 coverage exists.

Electricity supply
220V AC

Security
The threat of attack from rebel groups continues and despite the cease-fire in neighbouring DRC, the border regions are volatile. Local advice should be sought by those proposing to visit such areas; a military escort may be necessary. The Virunga national park and surrounding areas in the north-west should be avoided as the risk of visitors being kidnapped remains very real.

Kigali and major towns in the east, such as Butare and Gitarma, can be visited, but precautions need to be taken. Cars should not be left unattended in the centre of town and walking after dark or carrying large amounts of money or valuables is ill-advised.

Getting there
Air
National airline: Air Rwanda
International airport/s: Kigali-Kanombe (KGL), 12km east of city; duty-free shop, bar, currency exchange, post office, shops, coach, taxi service.
Airport tax: None
Surface
Road: Roads from Uganda, Tanzania and Burundi are well-surfaced.
Water: Although landlocked there is a link on Lake Kivu, between the north and south.
Main port/s: Gisenyi, Cyangugu.

Getting about
National transport
Air: Air Rwanda operates internal services between Kigali, Gisenyi and Kamembe. It also operates to Entebbe (Uganda) and Bujumbura (Burundi).
Road: All cities are linked to Kigali by paved roads, and the roads Ruhengeri-Cyanika and Kayonza-Kagitumba are paved. Other roads are poor with many being impassable in bad weather.
Buses: Reliable regular bus services are available from Kigali to the main cities and between some cities themselves. Private minibuses (belonging to an association called ATRACO) also operate between Kigali and other cities.
Water: Services run between Gisenyi and Cyangugu, on Lake Kivu.
City transport
Taxis: They can be found in large towns; fares should be agreed at the start of journey and tipping is not necessary.
Car hire
Limited service is available in Kigali. International driving licence is required. All-weather roads are sparse and in poor condition.

BUSINESS DIRECTORY

The addresses listed below are a selection only. While World of Information makes every endeavour to check these addresses, we cannot guarantee that changes have not been made, especially to telephone numbers and area codes. We would welcome any corrections.

Telephone area codes
The international dialling code (IDD) for Rwanda is +250, followed by subscriber's number.

Chambers of Commerce
Fédération Rwandaise du Secteur Privé, PO Box 319, Kigali (tel: 83-538; fax: 83-532; e-mail: frsp@rwanda1.com).

Banking
Banque à la Confiance d'Or, BP 2059, Kigali (tel: 75-780, 75-763; fax: 75-761).

Banque Commerciale du Rwanda, BP 354, Boulevard de la Revolution, Kigali (tel: 75-591, 76-117; fax: 73-395).

Banque Continentale Africaine (Rwanda) SA, BP 331, 20 Kigali, Boulevard de la Revolution, Kigali (tel: 74-456/7/8; fax: 73-486).

Banque de Commerce, de Developpement et d'Industrie, BP 3268, Kigali (tel: 74-143, 74-132, 74-427; fax: 73-790, 74-479).

Banque de Kigali, BP 175, 63 Avenue du Commerce, Kigali (tel: 76-931/2/3/4; fax: 73-461, 75-504).

Banque Nationale du Rwanda, BP 531, Kigali (tel: 74-282, 75-249; fax: 72-551).

Banque Rwandaise de Developpment, BP 1341, Kigali (tel: 75-079, 75-080; fax: 73-569).

Campagne Generale de Banque, BP 5230, Kigali (tel: 86-875; fax: 86-876).

Union des Banques Populaires du Rwanda, BP 1348, Kigali (tel: 73-564; fax: 73-579).

Central bank
Banque Nationale du Rwanda, Avenue Paul VI, BP 531, Kigali (tel: 574-282; fax: 572-551; e-mail: webmaster@bnr.rw).

Travel information
Air France, BP 411, Kigali (tel: 75-566).

Air Rwanda, 28 Boulevard de la Révolution, BP 808, Kigali (tel: 75-492, 85-997; fax: 72-462).

Office Rwandais du Tourisme et des Parcs Nationaux, BP 905, Kigali (tel: 76-514/5, 73-396; fax: 76-512; e-mail: Ortpn@rwandatel1.rwanda1.com).

Rwanda Travel Service, BP 140, Kigali (tel: 72-210).

Rwanda Explorations, BP 1514, Kigali (tel: 73-284).

Other useful addresses
Agence Rwandaise de Presse (ARP), 27 avenue du Commerce, BP 83, Kigali (tel: 75-665).

Economat Général (tobacco exports), BP 45, Ruhengeri.

L'Institut des Sciences Agronomiques du Rwanda, BP 138, Butare.

Office des Cafés, BP 104, Kigali (tel: 75-277).

Office du Pyrèthre au Rwanda, BP 79, Ruhengeri.

Office du Thé, BP 1344, Kigali (tel: 72-416).

Rwandan Embassy (USA), 1714 New Hampshire Avenue, NW, Washington DC 20009 (tel: 202-232-2882; fax: 202-232-4544; e-mail: rwandemb@rwandemb.org).

Internet sites
General information: www.rwanda.net

Africa Business Network: http://www.ifc.org/abn

African Development Bank: http://www.afdb.org

Africa Online: http://www.africaonline.com

AllAfrica.com: http://allafrica.com

Harambee Afrika (UK business club for traders with east, central and southern Africa; includes annotated web resource list): http://www.harambee.co.uk

Mbendi AfroPaedia (information on companies, countries, industries and stock exchanges in Africa): http://mbendi.co.za

St Helena

COUNTRY PROFILE

Historical profile
1502 St Helena was sighted by Portuguese mariners on 21 May (St Helena's Day).
1513 The island was first settled.
1633 The Dutch claimed possession.
1659 The East India Company took possession of the uninhabited island.
1673 The island was briefly captured by the Dutch, before being regained by the East India Company.
1815 Napoleon Bonaparte was exiled to the island, where he died in 1821, his body being returned to France in 1840.
1834 The island passed under British control in April.
1981 The 1981 Nationality Act ended the islanders' British citizenship and right of abode, which they had held since 1673.
1992 The islanders established a Citizenship Commission, which began its case for full British citizenship in 1997.
1999 The 'Partnership for Progress and Prosperity' White Paper re-confirmed the UK government's long-term financial support for St Helena. The paper also proposed to restore the right of abode in the UK for St Helenians.
2001 Only non-partisans were elected to the Legislative Council in June.
2002 In January, the islanders voted in a referendum in favour of air access. In May, full British citizenship was restored to the islanders.
2004 In January, the St Helena government announced trial changes to the mail ship schedule, which commenced in September.
2005 Elections were held 31 August. An environmental team from the UK conducted the first stage of investigations required to carry out an Environmental Impact Assessment (EIA) for the proposed new airport on Prosperous Bay Plain in October and November..

Political structure
St Helena has an appointed governor assisted by an Executive Council (the chief secretary, the financial secretary, attorney general and committee chairmen) and also by a Legislative Council (made up of the same ex-officio members and 12 elected members). Restoration for the islanders of full British citizenship was granted in May 2002.
The creation of a new overseas territories minister within the Foreign and Commonwealth Office (FCO) and the establishment of an Overseas Territories Consultative Council were both implemented in 1999, but responsibility for the British Overseas Territories, including St Helena, remains divided between the FCO and the Department for International Development.

Constitution
The St Helena Constitution Order came into force in February 1989. It sets out the separation of powers and the responsibilities of the executive, legislature and judiciary.

Form of state
British overseas territory

Last elections
31 August 2005 (parliamentary)
Results: Parliamentary: only non-partisans were elected; turnout was 47 per cent.

Next elections
2009 (parliamentary)

Political parties
No parties exist.

Population
7,400 (2004)

Ethnic make-up
Black African (50 per cent), white (25 per cent), Chinese (25 per cent).

Religions
Anglican (majority), Baptist, Seventh-Day Adventist, Roman Catholic.

Health
Life expectancy: 74.5 years male; female 80.4 years (2003).
Fertility rate/Maternal mortality rate: 1.5 births per woman (2003)
Birth rate/Death rate: 13 births per 1,000 population; 6.3 deaths per 1,000 population (2003).
Infant mortality rate: 21 per 1,000 live births (2003)

Main cities
Jamestown (capital, estimated population 1,500 in 2003).

Languages spoken
Official language/s
English

Media
Press
Weeklies: The *St Helena Herald* has an on-line version (www.news.co.sh).
Business: There are some interesting business publications following the latest projects on the island. The RMS *St Helena* (Andrew Weir Shipping Ltd), which has regular services to the island from UK and Cape Town, publishes the *RMS Shipping News*. The Island of St Helena Coffee Company, Jamestown, provides on-line

KEY FACTS

Official name: St Helena Colony with Dependencies

Head of State: Queen Elizabeth II

Head of government: Governor and Commander-in-Chief David J Hollamby (since 1999)

Area: 122 square km

Population: 7,400 (2004)

Capital: Jamestown

Official language: English

Currency: St Helena pound (StH£) = 100 pence

Exchange rate: StH£0.57 per US$ (Oct 2005); (pegged to pound sterling)

GDP per capita: US$2,500 (2003)

Labour force: 3,500 (2003)

Unemployment: 14.00% (2003)

Inflation: 3.20% (2003)

Balance of trade: -US$14.43 million (2003)

information on business matters (www.st-helena-coffee.sh).

Periodicals: The St Helena News Bureau publishes the periodical *St Helena and South Atlantic News Review* and the monthly *The St Helena Catalogue*.

Broadcasting
Radio: The government radio service operates daily from 0900–2200 Mon–Fri, and 1900–2200 Sat–Sun, and relays a number of BBC World Service programmes.

Radio St Helena provides a daily news service from Monday to Friday, featuring local events and information.

Television: Cable & Wireless provides a two channel television service for 24 hours a day relaying selected programmes from BBC World, CNN, Supersport, Discovery Channel and MNET, a South African commercial service.

Economy
St Helena was developed as a re-victualling post for East India Company ships returning from the East. With the decline of sail from the 1870s, the island has struggled to find a basis for its economy. The production of New Zealand flax was started in 1874 and had some success during times of high world prices. However, St Helena's terrain is not suited to plantation cropping and the industry, heavily subsidised for most of its history, finally collapsed in 1966.

St Helena depends on aid from the UK for between 20–25 per cent of its recurrent public sector budget of approximately StH£10 million (US$14.2 million). Fishing licence sales earn StH£0.75 million (US$1 million) in revenue per annum. Local catches, philatelic sales, livestock and timber additionally provide the main sources of revenue, together with remittances from offshore workers which are estimated to be worth StH£2–3 million (US$2.8–4.2 million) per year.

Andrew Weir Shipping Ltd took over the management of the *RMS St Helena* from Curnow Shipping in 2001. Plans to build an airstrip were approved by a referendum held in 2002. There is also a privately funded proposal by Shelco for an airport/golf course/airline scheme.

A new mail ship schedule, which started a one-year trial in September 2004, will provide a more regular service, which it is hoped will also benefit the tourism sector.

External trade
Coffee exports have received much publicity but total production is only three tonnes per year (tpy). The coffee is the world's most expensive. It is sold as an exclusive product in the UK, but is also exported to Japan and Switzerland. There are ambitious plans to increase production to 30tpy by 2005, but quality control and marketing are likely to become increasing problems. Canned tuna is exported through Windmill Foods of Crediton, Devon.

Imports
Principal imports are food, beverages, tobacco, fuel oils, animal feed, building materials, motor vehicles and parts, machinery and parts.

Main sources: UK (35.1 per cent total, 2004), US (18.5 per cent), South Africa (18.4 per cent), Tanzania (8.5 per cent), Australia (5.7 per cent), Spain (4.3 per cent)

Exports
Principal exports are fish (frozen, canned, and salt-dried skipjack, tuna), coffee and handicrafts.

Main destinations: US (27.1 per cent total, 2004), Tanzania (24.5 per cent), Indonesia (9.6 per cent), Japan (8.8 per cent), UK (6.2 per cent), Spain (5.1 per cent)

Agriculture
Farming
With volcanic origins, hills and deep valleys dominate the landscape. Semi-desert gives way to upland grasslands and lush valleys over a very short distance. Arable and garden land is about 3 per cent of the total area, forest and woodland 5 per cent, pasture 11 per cent, barren and badland 53 per cent. New Zealand flax (hemp) was grown until the 1960s, but much of this land is now planted with trees. Principal crops include potatoes, coffee, bananas, vegetables, sweet potatoes.

Livestock raising is a main activity but there is no dairy production and all dairy products are imported.

Agricultural production does not meet demand. Seed potatoes, onions and eggs are all imported in quantity.

Fishing
In the past, the government of St Helena earned StH£1.0 million (US$1.4 million) per annum from fishing licence revenue, but fish stocks have declined.

There is a local fishery run by the St Helena Fisheries Corporation, which buys the fish from the local fishermen. The Fisheries Corporation reported that in 2002, 223.5 tonnes of fish were landed. Tuna represented 43 per cent of the catch, with the rest comprising mostly swordfish, shark, mackerel, conger and filefish. In the period January–April 2003, fish landings amounted to 150 tonnes, almost all of which was tuna.

The boats range from eight to 13 metres in size and fish on a daily basis. They meet EU standards and carry ice with them. All of the catch is landed within 12 hours.

St Helena has satellite surveillance, but no patrol boat to stop unlicensed boats fishing the waters.

Industry and manufacturing
Local fishermen sell their catch to the St Helena Fisheries Corporation (a government parastatal). St Helena Fisheries Corporation sells its product in frozen and smoked form primarily to the UK and South Africa and supplies the domestic market.

Working in partnership with the St Helena Fisheries Corporation, Argos Helena Ltd, a joint UK-Spanish owned company, runs a blast freezer and fish processing/canning facility. Locally caught high-quality tuna is processed for export to the European Union and the Far East. The Corporation's fish products have organic certification from the Soil Association in the UK.

Tourism
St Helena has few resources and a declining population. Tourism is seen as a means of rescuing the island's economy and future. However, until the new airport is ready, access is restricted. Heavy seas make yachting anchorage unsafe.

The only means of reaching the island at the moment is by the RMS *St Helena*, which carries only 128 passengers on a round trip from UK to South Africa six or seven times a year. From September 2004, the vessel will operate year-round in the South Atlantic, providing more frequent trips from Cape Town to Walvis Bay, St Helena and Ascension Island. Although the rugged nature of the island has precluded air access, the possibility of constructing an airstrip is being investigated.

Tourism is currently worth about StH£250,000 per annum and employs around 50 people. Projections suggest that it could support 200 jobs and generate a value of StH£1 million (US$1.4 million) if transport links are improved.

Hydrocarbons
St Helena does not have any hydrocarbon reserves and relies entirely on the import of refined oil products to meet energy needs. St Helena does not import natural gas or coal.

Time
GMT

Geography
St Helena is situated in the South Atlantic Ocean and is 1,950km (1,200 miles) due west from the south-west coast of Africa and 2,900km (1,800 miles) east of South America. The nearest land is one of its dependencies, Ascension Island, 1,130km (700 miles) to the north-west.

St Helena

The island is of volcanic origin. It is mountainous, presenting an almost continuous line of high, sheer cliffs, cut only by a few narrow and steep-sided valleys around its coastline. It is criss-crossed by deep valleys and slopes steeply from the central ridges to the sea. The highest point is Diana's Peak (820 metres above sea-level).

Climate
Summer temperatures range from 21–29 degrees Celsius (C); winter 18–24 degrees C on coasts; inland temperatures may be five degrees lower; annual average rainfall in Jamestown around 200mm, inland up to 950mm.

Entry requirements
Passports
Required by all.
Visa
All visitors must have the Administrator's written permission to land, before travelling. An 'Ascension Island Entry Permit' form (valid for St Helena), to be completed, can be downloaded from www.ascension-island.gov.ac/visitors.htm. Entry is only granted with evidence of visitors full medical insurance policy, covering medical evacuation by air, when necessary.

Health (for visitors)
There is one general hospital based in Jamestown and six health clinics on the island. The health service is not free and all St Helenians have to pay fees for medical treatment. UK Passport holders visiting the island pay local rates for medical treatment, while non-UK residents have to pay higher fees.
Mandatory precautions
None.

Working hours
Business
Mon–Fri: 0830–1230 and 1300–1600.
Government
Mon–Fri: 0830–1230, 1300–1600.
Shops
Mon–Sat: generally 0900–1700.

Getting there
Air
St Helena has no airport and can only be reached by sea. The possibility of constructing an airstrip is being investigated. Wideawake Airfield on Ascension Island, a US military base, provides regular flights to and from the UK. Negotiations with the US authorities concluded in October 2003 with the signing of an agreement, allowing air-charter access to the airfield.
Surface
Water: The RMS *St Helena* calls at St Helena on an irregular, but time-tabled basis. From September 2004, the vessel is to operate year-round in the South Atlantic, providing more frequent trips from Cape Town to Walvis Bay, St Helena and Ascension Island. The ship is operated under contract by Andrew Weir Shipping Ltd on behalf of the owners, St Helena Line Ltd.
Bookings can be made through Passenger Services Department, Andrew Weir Shipping Ltd, Dexter House, 2 Royal Mint Court, London EC3 N4XX, UK (tel: +44 (0)207-575-6480; fax: +44 (0)207-575-6200; e-mail: reservations@aws.co.uk).
Air connections can be made with the ship either through Cape Town, via commercial flights, or via military flights from Royal Air Force Brize Norton in Oxfordshire, UK to Ascension Island.
Main port/s: Jamestown

Getting about
National transport
Road: Road network of 80–85km classified as all-weather; at least further 60km surfaced and 25–30km suitable for dry-weather travel only. Roads are best described as steep and tortuous. Because most roads are single lane, motoring etiquette requires the driver coming down to make way for upcoming traffic.

BUSINESS DIRECTORY
The addresses listed below are a selection only. While World of Information makes every endeavour to check these addresses, we cannot guarantee that changes have not been made, especially to telephone numbers and area codes. We would welcome any corrections.

Telephone area codes
The international dialling code (IDD) for St Helena is +290 followed by subscriber's number.

Chambers of Commerce
St Helena Chamber of Commerce, c/o The Castle, Jamestown. (fax: tel: 22-58; fax: 25-98).

Travel information
For air travel and bookings on the RMS St Helena:
Passenger Services Department, Andrew Weir Shipping Ltd, Dexter House, 2 Royal Mint Court, London EC N4XX, UK (tel: +44 (0)207-575-6480; fax: +44 (0)207-575-6200; e-mail: reservations@aws.co.uk).
St Helena Line, Andrew Weir Shipping (SA) Pty Ltd, 3rd Floor, BP Centre, Thibault Square, Cape Town, South Africa (tel: +27-21-425-1165; fax: +27-21-421-7485; e-mail: sthelenaline@mweb.co.za; internet site: http://www.aws.co.uk).
Miss Kerry Yon, Solomon and Co plc, Jamestown (tel: 2523; fax: 2423; e-mail: solco.shipping@helanta.sh).

National tourist organisation offices
St Helena Tourism, Jamestown (tel: 2158; fax: 2159; e-mail: StHelena.Tourism@helanta.sh; internet site: http://www.sthelenatourism.com).

Ministries
Governor's Office, The Castle, Jamestown (tel: 2555; fax: 2598; e-mail: OCS@helanta.sh).
St Helena Government Representative, Ms Kedell Warboys, Suite 5, 30b Wimpole St, London W1G 8YB, UK (tel: +44 (0)207-224-5025; fax: +44 (0)207-224-5035).

Other useful addresses
Argos Atlantic Cold Stores, PO Box 151, Jamestown (tel: 2333; fax: 2334; e-mail: argos@argonaut.co.sh).
Cable & Wireless Fax Bureau, The Briars, Jamestown.
Director of Inward Investment, Office of the Chief Secretary, Government of St Helena, Jamestown (tel: 2470; fax: 2598; e-mail: DEPD@atlantis.co.ac).
Information Office, Broadway House, Jamestown (Information Officer Johnny Drummond) (tel: 2612; fax: 2802; e-mail: info.office@atlantis.co.ac).
Miles Apart (books, maps, videos on South Atlantic Islands), 5 Harraton House, Exning, Newmarket, Suffolk CB8 7HF, UK (tel: +44 (0)1638-577-627: fax: +44 (0)1638-577-874); 5929 Avon Drive, Bethesda, Maryland 20814, USA (tel/fax: +1301-571-8942; e-mail: familycarter@msn.com).
The Postmistress, The Philatelic Bureau, The Post Office, Jamestown (fax: 2242).
St Helena Commercial Representative, Mr Wes Huxtable, 1 The Stables, Great Hyde Hall, Sawbridgeworth, Herts CM21 9JA, UK. (tel: +44 (0)1279-725-833; fax: +44 (0)1279-724-894; e-mail: weston@huxtable.freeserve.co.uk).
St Helena Desk Officer, Foreign and Commonwealth Office, Room, King Charles Street, London SW1A 2AH, UK (tel: +44 (0)207-270-2695).
St Helena Development Agency, No 2 Main St, Jamestown (tel: 2920, fax: 2166, e-mail: shda@atlantis.co.uk).
The St Helena Link (cultural information), Trevor Hearl, 49 Noverton Lane, Prestbury, Cheltenham, Glos GL52 5DD, UK (tel/fax: +44 (0)1242-244-430).

Internet sites
East India Company (coffee): http://www.theeastindiacompany.com
St Helena Development Agency: http://www.shda.helanta.sh/
St Helena government: http://www.sainthelena.gov.sh
St Helena News: http://www.news.co.sh
St Helena web portal: http://www.sthelenaonline.com

St Kitts and Nevis

KEY FACTS

Official name: Federation of St Christopher and Nevis

Head of State: Queen Elizabeth II; represented by Governor General Sir Cuthbert Montroville-Sebastian (since 1996)

Head of government: Prime Minister Denzil Douglas (SKNLP) (since Jul 1995)

Ruling party: St Kitts and Nevis Labour Party (SKNLP) (since Jul 1995; last re-elected Oct 2004)

Area: 269 square km

Population: 47,951 (2004)

Capital: Basseterre (St Kitts)

Official language: English

Currency: East Caribbean dollar (EC$) = 100 cents

Exchange rate: EC$2.70 per US$ (fixed)

GDP per capita: US$10,351 (2004)

GDP real growth: 5.10% (2004)

Labour force: 18,172 (2003)

Unemployment: 4.50% (2003)

Inflation: 2.40% (2004)

Balance of trade: -US$123.20 million (2004)

Foreign debt: US$314.20 million (2004)

COUNTRY PROFILE

Historical profile
1623 Britain settled St Christopher (known as St Kitts), which became the first British colony in the West Indies.
1628 Nevis was settled by the British.
1816 Anguilla was joined to the territory.
1932 The St Kitts and Nevis Labour Party (SKNLP) was formed and campaigned for independence for the islands.
1958 St Christopher-Nevis-Anguilla became a member of the attempted West Indies Federation.
1960 A new constitution was granted to each of the British territories in the Leeward Islands. It provided for government through an administrator and an enlarged Legislative Council.
1962 The West Indies Federation was dissolved after the departure of Jamaica.
1967 St Christopher-Nevis-Anguilla, led by the pro-independence SKNLP, attained Associated Statehood, giving them full internal autonomy, while the UK retained responsibility for defence and foreign relations. The Legislative Council was replaced by a House of Assembly, the administrator became governor and the chief minister became the state's first premier.
1971 Anguilla reverted to being a *de facto* British dependency after rebelling against rule from St Kitts.
1980 Anguilla was formally separated from St Kitts and Nevis. The SKNLP lost power for the first time in 30 years to a coalition of the People's Action Movement (PAM) and the Nevis Reformation Party (NRP).
1983 Independence from Britain.
1995 The SKNLP won the election.
1997 The Nevis Island Assembly elections were won by the Concerned Citizens' Movement (CCM) with three seats. The opposition Nevis Reformation Party (NRP) secured the remaining two seats.
1998 A referendum on independence for Nevis failed to achieve the two-thirds majority required for approval.
2000 The ruling SKNLP was re-elected and Denzil Douglas began a second term as prime minister.
2001 The Nevis ruling party, the CCM, won four seats in the elections to the five-seat Nevis Island Assembly (NIA).
2002 US Airways began flying a direct service from the US mainland to St Kitts.
2003 In March, the largest hotel complex in the eastern Caribbean region opened at Frigate Bay.
2004 A US$90 million private sector investment plan was approved in March, whereby NaturalSweet Corporation agreed to proceed with the cultivation and commercial development of stevia, a natural herbal plant. The ruling SKNLP won the parliamentary elections in October.
2005 In July the last harvest of sugar cane was delivered to the last refinery, which ceased operations after the last run was made, and ended a centuries old industry. International competition and a lack of cane cutters oversaw the demise of the sugar manufacturing corporation with debts of over US$150 million.

Political structure
Constitution
The constitution of 1983 gives the island of Nevis considerable autonomy within a federal framework.
Form of state
Independent parliamentary democratic state; it is a member of the Commonwealth with the British monarch as head of state, represented by a governor general, who exercises executive power.
Nevis has limited self-government.
National legislature
The legislature is the National Assembly comprising 11 members elected for a five-year term (eight from St Kitts, three from Nevis) plus three appointed members.
The cabinet headed by a prime minister is collectively responsible to the National Assembly.
Legal system
The legal system is based upon English common law. Appeals go to the Eastern Caribbean Supreme Court based on Saint Lucia. The final court of appeal is the Privy Council in the UK.
Last elections
25 October 2004 (National Assembly); 2001 (Nevis Island Assembly (NIA).
Results: Parliamentary: the ruling Labour Party won seven seats out of 11, the Concerned Citizens' Movement two, the People's Action Movement one and the Nevis Reformation Party one.
Nevis parliamentary: the Nevis ruling party, the Concerned Citizens' Movement (CCM), won four seats in the five-seat NIA.
Next elections
2009 (National Assembly)

Political parties
Ruling party
St Kitts and Nevis Labour Party (SKNLP) (since Jul 1995; last re-elected Oct 2004)

St Kitts and Nevis

Political situation
Electoral reform has been a topic of discussion for a while. The government confirmed that it would be willing to introduce legislation when the debate concluded. In June 2004, the prime minister rebutted opposition claims that he was reluctant to bring forward legislation, on the grounds that it could not be implemented in the short time before the next general election. Since the election in October 2004, the issue has remained in discussion and a Commonwealth assessment mission visited St Kitts and Nevis in August 2005 to advise on proposals for reform.

Population
47,951 (2004)
Ethnic make-up
Black African (91 per cent), mixed race (5 per cent), Asian (3 per cent), British, Portuguese and Lebanese descent (1 per cent).
Religions
Anglican (25 per cent), Methodist (25 per cent), Pentecostal (8 per cent), Moravian (7 per cent), other Protestant (12 per cent), Roman Catholic (7 per cent), Hindu (1 per cent).

Education
Compulsory years: Five to 17
Enrolment rate: 101 per cent boys, 94 per cent girls gross primary enrolment of relevant age group (including repeaters) (Unicef 2004).

Health
Life expectancy: 71.5 years (World Bank)
Fertility rate/Maternal mortality rate: 2.1 births per woman (World Bank)
Birth rate/Death rate: 18.5 births per 1,000 population; nine deaths per 1,000 population (2003).
Infant mortality rate: 19 per 1,000 live births (World Bank)

Main cities
Basseterre (capital of St Kitts, estimated population 11,500 in 2003), Charlestown (capital of Nevis, 1,300).

Languages spoken
Official language/s
English

Media
Press
There are no daily newspapers. Weekly publications include *The Democrat*, *The Observer* and the bi-weekly *Labour Spokesman*.
Broadcasting
The government-owned commercial radio and television station is ZIZ.
Radio: There are four radio stations: Choice and ZIZ in St Kitts; Voice of Nevis (VON) and Radio Paradise in Nevis.
Television: There is ZIZ Television and two cable television systems.

Economy
After several years of poor performance, falling to as low as 0.8 per cent growth in 2002, the economy bounced back in 2004, under the influence of an improving international economy. All sectors, led by the crucial tourist industry, showed improvement over previous years. The overall economy grew by around five per cent in 2004. Inflation, which had kept low for several years under a tight fiscal regime along with the exchange rate peg to the dollar, remained stable in 2004 at 2.4 per cent.
The health of the economy remains contingent on developments in the outside world, such as recession in the US, but also natural disasters.

External trade
Imports
Main imports are machinery, manufactures, food and fuels.
Main sources: US (33.1 per cent total, 2004), Italy (19.4 per cent), Trinidad and Tobago (10.5 per cent), UK (9.8 per cent), Denmark (6 per cent)
Exports
Main exports are machinery, food, electronics, beverages and tobacco.
Main destinations: US (58 per cent total, 2004), Canada (9 per cent), Portugal (8.3 per cent), UK (6.9 per cent)

Agriculture
Farming
The agricultural sector contributes around 3 per cent to GDP.
Historically, the most important crop has been sugar. About 80 per cent of available arable land on St Kitts has been given over to sugar growing, with around 30 per cent of the labour force being employed in the industry. Production has been declining in recent years for a variety of reasons and the industry has been running at a loss for many years. It was decided to stop producing sugar for export after the 2005 harvest, following the change of policy by the EU to reduce guaranteed prices for sugar.
Diversification into food crops has been encouraged to reduce dependence on imports and has become more pressing with the decline in importance of the sugar industry. Owing to poor pasturage and other problems, the livestock sector remains underdeveloped; it is, however, being encouraged by the government and production increased by 15.2 per cent in 2004, compared with 2.7 per cent in 2003.
Crop production in 2004 included: 160 tonnes (t) potatoes, 150t sweet potatoes, 193,000t sugar cane, 1,000t coconuts, 1,300t fruit in total, 210t pulses, 100t tomatoes, 139t oilcrops, 685t vegetables in total. Livestock production included: 700t meat in total, 125t beef, 294t pig meat, 137t lamb and goat meat, 144t poultry, 210t eggs.
Fishing
Inshore fishing is a traditional occupation and a significant source of protein.
The fisheries management unit introduced new fishing methods resulting in a fish catch that increased over 40 per cent during the first year. Other improvements include a new fisheries complex, opened in 2003, housing commercial storage and a fish market, constructed in Basseterre on St Kitts, while on Nevis the largest fishing facility includes a fish processing plant, walk-in freezers and market, is sited in Charlestown.

KEY INDICATORS — St Kitts and Nevis

	Unit	2000	2001	2002	2003	2004
Population	m	0.04	0.04	0.05	0.05	0.05
Gross domestic product (GDP)	US$bn	0.33	0.34	0.34	0.34	*0.40
GDP per capita	US$	8,211	8,570	7,727	8,800	10,351
GDP real growth	%	7.5	1.8	0.8	1.2	5.1
Inflation	%	2.1	2.6	2.1	2.0	2.4
Exports (fob) (goods)	US$m	54.6	47.0	61.3	47.0	60.1
Imports (fob) (goods)	US$m	172.6	152.0	171.7	152.0	183.3
Balance of trade	US$m	-118.0	-105.0	-114.3	-105.0	-123.2
Current account	US$m	-70.0	-100.0	-130.0	-110.0	-100.0
Total reserves minus gold	US$m	45.2	56.4	65.8	64.8	78.5
Foreign exchange	US$m	45.1	56.3	65.6	64.7	78.3
Exchange rate	per US$	2.70	2.70	2.70	2.70	2.70

* estimated figure

Industry and manufacturing
The industrial sector contributes around 24 per cent to GDP, with manufacturing contributing around 10 per cent. Manufacturing activities have declined, with contraction in electrical and electronic components, due to poor US demand. The recession also led to a decline in domestic demand for locally produced manufactured goods.
In March 2004, the government approved a US$90 million investment plan by NaturalSweet Corporation to proceed with the cultivation and commercial development of stevia, a natural herbal plant, and construction of a plant to produce a dietary supplement.

Tourism
The tourism sector was badly affected by hurricane damage to the islands' tourism infrastructure in 1999 and 2000 and the terrorist attack in the US in 2001. The sector has recovered with improved marketing, government investment in port facilities at Basseterre, the construction of new hotels and improved air connections with other Caribbean islands and the US. The completion of a cruise ship pier at Porte Zante in late 2002 helped the tourist industry to eclipse sugar as the prime source of foreign exchange earnings. The improved international economic climate, especially in the US, has consolidated the sector's strong growth since 2002. Tourism is forecast to contribute 7.8 per cent to GDP in 2005.
There were 389,867 visitors in 2004, compared with 246,789 in 2003, with both air and cruise arrivals showing a marked increase of 32.6 per cent and 78 per cent respctively. Tourism provides work for 8.9 per cent of the labour force.

Hydrocarbons
St Kitts and Nevis does not have any hydrocarbon reserves and relies on imports of refined oil products. In 2001 it imported 710 barrels per day (bpd) to meet domestic demand. Gas and coal are not imported. The planned natural gas pipeline from Trinidad and Tobago linking the Caribbean islands could mean St Kitts and Nevis will import natural gas in the future.

Energy
St. Kitts and Nevis is planning the commercial development of geothermally-fuelled electric power plants.

Financial markets
Stock exchange
The St Kitts-based Eastern Caribbean Securities Exchange (ECSE) was launched by the Eastern Caribbean Central Bank (ECCB) in October 2001. The Bank of Nevis Ltd, based in St Kitts and Nevis, was one of only two securities listed on the ECSE at the start of trading activity.

Banking and insurance
The state-owned Development Bank provides credit to finance agriculture, industry, education and mortgages.
The seven members of the Organisation of Eastern Caribbean States (OECS), Antigua and Barbuda, Dominica, Grenada, Montserrat, St Kitts and Nevis, St Lucia and St Vincent and the Grenadines, share a common currency and central bank. The British Virgin Islands and Anguilla are associate members.
Central bank
East Caribbean Central Bank (ECCB)
Offshore facilities
After St Kitts and Nevis was listed by the OECD as a tax haven which was unco-operative in fighting money laundering, the government passed the Money Laundering (Prevention) Bill, the Financial Services Intelligence Unit Bill and the Financial Services Commission Bill. The latter Bill established the Financial Services Commission as the main regulatory body for the offshore sector.
In 2002, St Kitts and Nevis was removed from the blacklist drawn up by the OECD.

Time
GMT minus four hours

Geography
St Kitts and Nevis is situated at the northern end of the Leeward Islands chain of the West Indies, with Saba and St Eustatius (both in the Netherlands Antilles) to the north-west, Barbuda to the north-east and Antigua to the south-east. Nevis lies about 3km (2 miles) to the south-east of St Kitts, separated by a narrow strait.

Climate
Tropical, tempered by trade winds, with an annual mean temperature of 27 degrees Celsius. December–April are the driest months. Rain can occur throughout the year, although generally wetter from May–October.

Entry requirements
Passports
Not required by citizens of Canada, UK and US subject to proof of identity, maximum length of stay six months, onward tickets required.
Visa
Required by all except nationals of Commonwealth, Scandinavian and most EU countries, US, Switzerland and certain other countries.
Currency advice/regulations
No restriction on import and export of foreign currency. Local currency imports should be declared; export allowed up to the declared amount.

Health (for visitors)
Mandatory precautions
Vaccination certificates for yellow fever and cholera required when travelling from infected areas.
Advisable precautions
Typhoid, polio vaccinations. Water precautions.

Hotels
Advisable to book in advance. A 9 per cent room tax is added to bills and 10 per cent service charge usual.

Public holidays
Fixed dates
1 Jan (New Year's Day), 2 Jan (Carnival Day), 19 Sep (Independence Day), 25 Dec (Christmas Day), 26 Dec (Boxing Day).
Variable dates
Good Friday, Easter Monday, May Day (first Mon in May), Whit Monday, Queen's Official Birthday (second Sat in Jun), August Monday (first Mon in Aug).

Working hours
Banking
Mon–Fri: 0800–1200/1300. Also Fri: 1500–1700.
Business
Mon–Fri: 0800–1200, 1300–1600/1630. Businesses generally close Thu: afternoons and open Sat: 0800–1600.
Government
Mon–Fri: 0800–1200, 1300–1600/1630.

Electricity supply
220V AC, 60 cycles. (Some hotel supplies are at 110V AC.)
Electricity is supplied from diesel engine generators and is available island-wide.

Getting there
Air
National airline: Atlantic Caribbean International Airlines (ACIA).
International airport/s: Robert L Bradshaw Golden Rock International Airport (SKB), 3.2km from Basseterre, duty-free shop, restaurant, hotel reservations.
Airport tax: US$17 international departures; not applicable to 24 hour transit passengers.
Surface
Main port/s: Basseterre (St Kitts) has a deep-water harbour, Charlestown (Nevis).

Getting about
National transport
Air: Scheduled daily flights between the two islands. Newcastle Airport (NEV) is on Nevis.
Road: There is a 300km road network. Main routes cover perimeters of both islands.

St Kitts and Nevis

In January 2004, the Caribbean Development Bank (CDB) approved a loan of US$7.56 million to finance the construction of a new by-pass to reduce traffic congestion in Basseterre.

Buses: Regular but unscheduled bus services are operated.

Water: The government operates daily commercial boat service between St Kitts and Nevis, except on Thu and Sun.

City transport

Taxis: Serve both islands; standard fare system applies, 10 per cent tip usual.

Car hire

National licence required in order to obtain visitor's temporary licence. Traffic drives on the left.

BUSINESS DIRECTORY

The addresses listed below are a selection only. While World of Information makes every endeavour to check these addresses, we cannot guarantee that changes have not been made, especially to telephone numbers and area codes. We would welcome any corrections.

Telephone area codes

The international direct dialling code (IDD) for St Kitts and Nevis is +1 869, followed by subscriber's number.

Chambers of Commerce

St Kitts/Nevis Chamber of Industry and Commerce, South Independence Square, PO Box 332, Basseterre (tel: 465-2980; fax: 465-4490; e-mail: skchamber@caribsurf.com).

Banking

Bank of Nevis, The Main Street, Box 450, Charlestown, Nevis (tel: 469-5564/5796; fax: 469-5798).

Bank of Nova Scotia, Fort Street, Box 433, Basseterre, St Kitts (tel: 465-4141; fax: 465-8600).

Barclays Bank, The Circus, Box 42, Basseterre, St Kitts (tel: 465-2519/10/2449/1081/2264; fax: 465-1041).

Development Bank of St. Kitts & Nevis, Church Street, Box 249, Basseterre, St. Kitts (tel: 465-2288/2964/4041; fax: 465-4016).

National Bank, Central Street, Box 343, Basseterre, St Kitts (tel: 465-2204; fax: 465-1050).

Nevis Co-Op Banking Company, Chapel Street, Box 60, Charlestown, Nevis (tel: 469-5277/0113/4; fax: 469-1493).

Royal Bank of Canada, Cnr Bay Road & Fort Street, Box 91, Basseterre, St Kitts (tel: 465-2259/2409/2389/4374; fax: 465-1040).

Central bank

Eastern Caribbean Central Bank, Bird Rock Road, PO Box 89, Basseterre (tel: 465-2537; fax: 465-5615; e-mail: eccbrei@caribsurf.com).

Travel information

Nevis Tourism Bureau, Charlestown, Nevis (tel: 469-1042; fax: 469-1066).

St Kitts-Nevis Hotel and Tourism Association, PO Box 438, Basseterre, St Kitts (tel: 465-5304; fax: 465-7746).

Ministry of tourism

Ministry of Trade, Industry and Tourism (National Development Corporation), Government Headquarters, Basseterre (tel: 465-2521, 465-4106; fax: 465-5202, 465-1778).

National tourist organisation offices

St Kitts-Nevis Department of Tourism, Pelican Mall, PO Box 132, Basseterre, St Kitts (tel: 465-2620; fax: 465-4040).

Ministries

Ministry of Agriculture, Lands, Housing and Development, Education, Youth and Community Affairs, Government Headquarters, PO Box 186, Basseterre (tel: 465-2521; fax: 465-9069).

Ministry of Health, Labour and Women's Affairs, Government Headquarters, Basseterre (tel: 465-2521; fax: 456-1316).

Office of The Prime Minister, Government Headquarters, PO Box 186, Basseterre (tel: 465-2103; fax: 465-1001).

Other useful addresses

Attorney General's Office, Government Headquarters, Basseterre (tel: 465-2521; fax: 465-5202).

Eastern Caribbean Securities Exchange, PO Box 94, Bird Rock, Basseterre (tel: 466-7192; fax: 465-3798; e-mail: Info@ECSEonline.com).

Financial Services Department, PO Box 186, Basseterre (tel: 466-5048; fax: 466-5317; internet site: http://www.fsd.gov.kn/).

Government Offices, Administration Building, Charlestown (465-5521; fax: 465-5202).

Investment Promotion Agency, Bay Road, Basseterre (tel: 465-4106).

St Kitts-Nevis Information Service, Government Headquarters, Church Street, Basseterre (tel: 465-2521; fax: 466-4504; e-mail: skninfo@caribsurf.com; internet site: http://www.stkittsnevis.net).

St Kitts-Nevis Manufacturers' Association, PO Box 392, Basseterre (tel: 465-6226).

Internet sites

Caribbean Export Development Agency: http://www.cartis.com/

Government press releases: http://www.stkittsnevis.net

Organisation of American States: http://www.oas.org

St Lucia

KEY FACTS

Official name: St Lucia

Head of State: Queen Elizabeth II; Governor General Dr Calliopa Pearlette Louisy (since Sep 1997)

Head of government: Prime Minister Kenny Anthony (SLP) (since May 1997; re-elected Dec 2001)

Ruling party: St Lucia Labour Party (SLP) (since May 1997; re-elected Dec 2001)

Area: 616 square km

Population: 160,500 (2004)

Capital: Castries

Official language: English

Currency: East Caribbean dollar (EC$) = 100 cents

Exchange rate: EC$2.70 per US$ (fixed)

GDP per capita: US$4,021 (2004)

GDP real growth: 2.00% (2004)

Labour force: 43,800 (2003)

Unemployment: 21.00% (2004)

Inflation: 0.70% (2004)

Balance of trade: -US$303.80 million (2004)

Foreign debt: US$339.80 million (2004)

Visitor numbers: 813,681 (2004)

COUNTRY PROFILE

Historical profile
1605 Britain made an unsuccessful attempt to colonise the islands which were populated by a Carib people.
1642 France claimed sovereignty.
1814 After changing hands 14 times during the seventeenth and eighteenth centuries, St Lucia became a British colony. It formed part of the Windward Islands.
1924 A representative government was introduced.
1951 The first elections under universal adult suffrage were won by the St Lucia Labour Party (SLP).
1958 St Lucia joined the attempted West Indies Federation.
1962 The West Indies Federation was dissolved.
1967 St Lucia became an Associated State of the UK with full autonomy over internal affairs.
1979 St Lucia gained independence.
1992 The United Workers' Party (UWP) won the elections.
1997 The SLP won the elections.
2002 Hurricane Lili destroyed around half of the banana crop.
2003 An amended constitution replaced an oath of allegiance to the British monarch with a pledge of loyalty to St Lucia. Julian Hunte, St Lucia's foreign minister, was elected president of the UN General Assembly June session, the smallest country ever to lead the 191-member world body.
2004 In March, the Caribbean Development Bank (CDB) approved a loan to help St Lucia build infrastructure against flooding in coastal cities. Radio Caricom, the Voice of the Caribbean Community was officially launched on 4 July 2004. St Lucia is a 'pilot state' in the project.
2005 In December, Air Jamaica announced the introduction of non-stop flights from New York to St Lucia from February 2006.

Political structure
Form of state
Domocratic, independent state and member of the Commonwealth.
The executive
The British monarch is Head of State; the governor general (exercises executive power) and appoints the prime minister, who is the person likely to command majority support in the House of Assembly.
National legislature
Bicameral: an appointed Senate (six members appointed on the prime minister's advice, three on that of the leader of the opposition and two chosen by the governor general, acting after external consultation); and House of Assembly (17 members elected by popular vote to single-member constituencies for a five-year term).
Legal system
The legal system is a hybrid of English common law with a strong influence of French civil law.
Appeals are heard by the Eastern Caribbean Supreme Court. The final court of appeal is the Judicial Council of the Privy Council in the UK.
Last elections
December 2001 (parliamentary)
Results: Parliamentary: the ruling St Lucia Labour Party (SLP) won 14 of the 17 seats.
Next elections
December 2006 (parliamentary)

Political parties
Ruling party
St Lucia Labour Party (SLP) (since May 1997; re-elected Dec 2001)
Main opposition party
United Workers' Party (UWP) (three seats)
Political situation
Since August 2005 when St Lucia was chosen as one of the countries to host Cricket World Cup 2007, and in particular the England team's matches, the atmosphere in the country has been buoyant. The prime minister has referred to the opportunity this will afford the country on several occasions, stating that direct investment for tourism and infrastructure have already been secured. A US$380 million tourist resort (a sum 25 per cent greater than St Lucia's entire budget for one year), a new water supply improvement project and coastal protection measures are all seen as necessary to enhance, not only the lives of native St Lucians but also, the much needed income from tourism. With tourism bringing in over US$121.8 million in 2004 the government is using its foreign earnings to bolster the economy as less well performing sectors, such as industry and manufacturing force workers to concentrate in fewer sectors.

St Lucia

Population
160,500 (2004)
Ethnic make-up
Black African (90 per cent), mixed race (6 per cent), East Indian (3 per cent).
Religions
Roman Catholic (90 per cent), Anglican (3 per cent) other Protestant (7 per cent).

Education
The education system is in great need of reform. Hampering the development of the island's education is the instructor-led method of learning but there has been little attempt to progress to a more learner-orientated approach.
The secondary education system will benefit from the construction of two new schools, with allocated funds of US$23 million, in 2005/06. The new facilities, one geared to the arts and the other towards agriculture and science will provide places for over 700 students. The government is aiming to achieve universal secondary education and has been aided by the World Bank Education Development Plan.
Compulsory years: 4 to 16.
Enrolment rate: 101 per cent primary and 85 per cent secondary enrolment; 111 per cent and 104 per cent enrolment respectively of boys and girls of relevant age group (including repeaters) (Unicef 2004).

Health
The provision of healthcare will be changed within 2005/06 when the environment levy will be replaced with a fixed tax on consumer goods of between 3.5–4 per cent and will be called the health and environment levy. It is expected to raise US$11 million to fund services for most of the population.
The government is concerned about the loss of medical personnel. Nurse migration, due to low pay, lack of opportunities and poor working conditions, has left Victoria Hospital the principal hospital facility chronically understaffed.
The European Commission has granted US$23 million in 2005 for a new hospital to replace Victoria Hospital, to be built on a new site. Construction is scheduled to begin in early 2006.

HIV/Aids
The Caribbean has the second highest rate of HIV/aids infection, after sub-Saharan Africa and the impact on the economy is already being felt with St Lucia losing around US$74 million since the mid-1980s. In February 2005 the Global Fund to Fight Aids approved a grant of US$10.1 million, over 2005–10, to help St Lucia fight the epidemic. The programme is targeting a 50 per cent reduction in HIV patients and HIV/Aids deaths as well as mother-to-infant transmission reduced from 30 per cent to less than 10 per cent.
Life expectancy: 74 years (World Bank)
Fertility rate/Maternal mortality rate: 2.1 births per woman (World Bank)
Birth rate/Death rate: 21 births per 1,000 population; five deaths per 1,000 population (2003).
Infant mortality rate: 16 per 1,000 live births (World Bank)
Head of population per physician/bed: 47.3 physicians per 100,000 people (WHO).

Welfare
The social welfare system in St Lucia has been described as unfair, partial and out of touch with social realities and legislation is out of date. The Catholic Church run homes for the elderly and assistance is provided to the needy. There is no law protecting children born outside of marriage with regard to their property rights and no laws against sexual harassment.

Main cities
Castries (capital, estimated population 60,300 in 2003).

Languages spoken
English and French patois.
Official language/s
English

Media
Press
The Voice and *The Star* (www.stluciastar.com), are published three times a week. *Saint Lucia One Stop* (www.sluonestop.com) is a local news service covering local news and business. Weekly papers include *The Crusader*, *The Vanguard*, *St. Lucia Mirror* (www.stluciamirroronline.com) and *One Caribbean*.

Broadcasting
Two private and one government-owned radio services operate.
There are two television stations. There are also several American channels available.
Broadcasts are in Creole, English, French and German.
Radio: A new radio service – Radio Caricom, the Voice of the Caribbean Community – was officially launched at the 25th Meeting of the Conference of the Heads of Government in Grenada on 4 July 2004. Barbados, Belize, Grenada and St Lucia are 'pilot states' in the project, which will eventually be available to all member states.

Economy
The economy has made a good recovery since hurricane Lili devastated the island in late 2002, with infrastructure repaired and crop production back to pre-hurricane levels. However, the economy is always vulnerable to natural disasters. Manmade problems range from rising international oil prices to the threat to exports of St Lucia's principal crop, bananas. There has been an international wrangle between several Central and South American banana producers and the European Union since 1999 over import duties. In 2005 the World Trade Organisation (WTO) ruled that the EU's preferential import duties for Caribbean countries contravened the WTO agreement for free trade and that the EU would have to accept Latin American bananas on the same terms as Caribbean bananas. The ramifications for St Lucia's balance of trade can only be estimated, although the industry acknowledges that, with the overwhelming competition, exports will fall. Nevertheless, GDP growth

KEY INDICATORS — St Lucia

	Unit	2000	2001	2002	2003	2004
Population	m	0.15	0.16	0.16	0.16	0.16
Gross domestic product (GDP)	US$bn	0.71	0.66	0.66	0.87	*0.73
GDP per capita	US$	4,733	4,125	4,125	5,400	4,021
GDP real growth	%	0.7	-3.7	-4.0	1.5	2.0
Inflation	%	3.6	2.1	-0.2	1.0	0.7
Exports (fob) (goods)	US$m	54.8	45.0	66.0	68.3	77.5
Imports (fob) (goods)	US$m	308.0	311.0	267.0	319.4	381.4
Balance of trade	US$m	-253.2	-266.0	-201.0	-251.1	-303.8
Current account	US$m	-82.4	-60.0	-90.0	-13.0	-70.0
Total reserves minus gold	US$m	78.8	88.9	93.9	106.9	132.5
Foreign exchange	US$m	77.0	87.1	91.9	104.7	130.2
Exchange rate	per US$	2.70	2.70	2.70	2.70	2.70

* estimated figure

in 2004 was 2.0 per cent, driven by a buoyant tourism sector. GDP growth is expected to exceed 5 per cent due to the capital investment ahead of the cricket world cup in 2007.

Tourism has overtaken all other sectors, producing the lion's share of GDP. The government struggles to maintain fiscal discipline to reduce public debt. Visitor numbers in 2004 were high at 298,431, up 7.8 per cent on 2003 figures, due in the main to strong European currencies against a weak US dollar. US visitors switched from higher priced European to Caribbean destinations. Cruise ship passenger numbers were also up, by 22.4 per cent to 481,279.

To minimise the effect of adverse external forces economic diversification is a priority for the government, with farmers encouraged to grow various cash crops such as mangoes and avocados; a lucrative deal was signed in 2005 to supply over 25 tonnes of cocoa beans to a leading US chocolate manufacturer. Other development projects focus on computer-driven information technology.

External trade
Regular trade deficits are offset by invisible earnings from tourism, workers' remittances and aid flows. St Lucia has a Goods Distribution Free Zone (GDFZ) at Vieux Fort in the south.
Imports
Main imports are food, manufactured goods, machinery and transportation equipment, chemicals and fuels.
Main sources: US (30 per cent total, 2004), Trinidad and Tobago (17.5 per cent), UK (8.5 per cent), Venezuela (8.4 per cent)
Exports
Main exports bananas (41 per cent of total), clothing, cocoa, vegetables, fruits and coconut oil.
Main destinations: UK (49.3 per cent total, 2004), US (19.9 per cent), Antigua and Barbuda (5.4 per cent), Dominica (5.2 per cent), Trinidad and Tobago (4.4 per cent)

Agriculture
Farming
The agricultural sector used to be the mainstay of the economy, but has been overtaken by tourism. It contributed 5.4 per cent of GDP in 2004. Over 50 per cent of the total area is cultivated arable land.

The main export crop is bananas and St Lucia continues to be the leading Windward Island banana producer. Although it suffered a number of setbacks, in 2004 production rose by 22.2 per cent to 41,512 tonnes. However, under a 2005 ruling by the WTO, exports to the EU no longer receive preferential treatment and it is unlikely that previous export levels will be maintained in the face of stiff competition from larger Central and South American plantations.

Diversification into other cash crops has been encouraged. In August 2005, a multi-million dollar deal was signed between St Lucia and the World's Finest Chocolate Inc to supply 256,800 kilogrammes of cocoa beans a year. There has been an increase in non-banana agriculture production, in particular in copra cultivation, which has resulted in increased exports of coconut oil to Jamaica. Also grown are traditional fruits and vegetables for the domestic and regional markets, and tree crops, such as mangoes and avocados.

Crop production in 2004 included: 800 tonnes (t) sweet potatoes, 1,000t cassava, 300t taro, 4,500t yams, 14,000t coconuts, 41,500t bananas, 1,300t plantains, 3,878t citrus, 28,000t mangoes, 30t cocoa beans, 250t pepper spice, 215t other spices, 1,820t oilcrops, 157,923t fruit in total, 11,120t roots and tubers, 1,000t vegetables in total. Livestock production included: 2,102t meat in total, 528t beef, 713t pig meat, 142t lamb and goat meat, 720t poultry meat, 482t eggs, 800t milk.
Fishing
The typical total annual fish catch is over 2,000t, shellfish, molluscs and cephalopods account for another 77t per annum.

Industry and manufacturing
The manufacturing sector is negligible and manufacturing activity is dominated by food and drinks production, electrical products and corrigated paper production.

Tourism
Tourism has become the most important sector generating most activity in St Lucia's economy. Travel and tourism represented 42.8 per cent of the country's economy in 2004, generating US$348.6 million in business transactions. The tourist industry earned US$121.8 million in 2004 or 15 per cent of total GDP. Capital investment in tourism amounted to 40.2 per cent overall or US$72.2 million. The tourist industry employed 11,000 people or 15.9 per cent of total employment. Visitor numbers in 2004 were 7.8 per cent up on the 2003 numbers and arrivals for the first quarter of 2005 were 19.8 compared to the same period in 2004. Over 122,000 visitors arrived in the first six months of 2005 and it was recognised that differentials between high and low seasons have disappeared with numbers remaining steady through the year.

The cricket world cup will be held on the island in 2007, and several projects are designed to be completed to accommodate sports fans. Three new developments will add greatly to St Lucia's capacity for tourism. A multi-use resort was begun in May 2005, with plans for 3,000 rooms with multiple amenities. The development is located on 130 acres and estimated at US$380 million with partial completion by 2007.

A major hotel with 124 apartments overlooking the bay of Marigot is expected to be completed by February 2006.

Eco-tourism will benefit from a new aerial tram project that will provide a raised, suspended ride through the rain-forest canopy in the Babonneau forest.

In 2005 the International Bank for Reconstruction and Development agreed a loan of US$3.7 million, while the International Development Association granted US$3.8 million to go towards the cost of coastal and flood protection works protecting the town of Dennery. These amounts are in addition to the US$80 million loan approved by the Caribbean Development Bank (CDB) in March 2004, also to help St Lucia protect itself against flooding in coastal regions.

Hydrocarbons
Saint Lucia does not have any hydrocarbon reserves, it relies entirely on imported refined oil products.

Energy
Attempts to reduce dependence on imported fuel include the construction of a dam in Roseau and a geothermal project in Soufrière. The main power station is Cul de Sac, south of Castries.

In 2004, St Kitts and Nevis, along with Dominica and St Lucia, one planning the commercial development of geothermal electric power plants.

Banking and insurance
The seven members of the Organisation of Eastern Caribbean States (OECS), Antigua and Barbuda, Dominica, Grenada, Montserrat, St Kitts and Nevis, St Lucia and St Vincent and the Grenadines, share a common currency and central bank. The British Virgin Islands and Anguilla are associate members.
Central bank
Eastern Caribbean Central Bank, St Kitts and Nevis
Offshore facilities
St Lucia is a relatively new entrant to the offshore financial sector. The Organisation for Economic Co-operation and Development (OECD) removed St Lucia from its blacklist of non-complainant government implementing anti-money laundering legislation after St Lucia introduced measures consistent with the OECD's call for transparency in the banking sector.

Time
GMT minus four hours

St Lucia

Geography
St Lucia is in the Windward Islands group of the West Indies, 40km (25 miles) to the south of Martinique and 32km (20 miles) to the north-east of St Vincent, in the Caribbean Sea. The island is volcanic, with spectacular mountain scenery.

Climate
The mean annual temperature is 26 degrees Celsius. The island is cooled by the north-east trade winds. The weather is driest from January–April. The rainy season is from July–October.

Entry requirements
Passports
Required by all, except citizens of US, Canadian and the Commonwealth who possess valid identification, return tickets and are staying for less than six months.
Visa
Requirements vary for citizens, country by country. See www.stluciacg.com/consulate/services_entry.htm for a full list and procedures, plus an application form to be downloaded.
Currency advice/regulations
No restrictions on local currency provided export does not exceed import. There are no restrictions on the import and export of foreign currency. Visitors must satisfy immigration that they have sufficient funds for their length of stay.

Health (for visitors)
Mandatory precautions
Yellow fever vaccination certificate required if arriving from an infected area.
Advisable precautions
Typhoid, polio vaccination. Medical services are limited. Travel insurance is essential, including cover for repatriation. Hospitalisation is costly and doctors often expect immediate cash payment befor treatment begins.

Hotels
Bills include 8 per cent tax and usually a 10 per cent service charge.

Public holidays
Fixed dates
1–2 Jan (New Year), 22 Feb (Independence Day), 1 May (Labour Day), 1 Aug (Emancipation Day), 13 Dec (Festival of Lights and Renewal), 25–26 Dec (Christmas Holiday).
Variable dates
Good Friday, Easter Monday, Whit Monday, Corpus Christi (May/Jun), Thanksgiving Day (first Mon in Oct).

Working hours
Banking
Mon–Thu: 0800–1300; Fri: 0800–1200, 1500–1700.
Business
Mon–Fri: 0800–1230, 1330–1630.
Government
Mon–Fri: 0800–1230, 1330–1630.
Shops
Mon–Fri: 0830–1230, 1330–1600; Sat: 0800–1200. Gablewoods shopping mall Mon–Sat: 0900–2100.

Electricity supply
220V AC, 50 cycles; UK standard 3-pin plugs.

Weights and measures
The imperial system will be converted to the metric systems during 2005.

Getting there
Air
National airline: St Lucia is a shareholder in the regional airline LIAT.
International airport/s: Hewanorra (UVF), 67km south of Castries, duty-free shop, bar, restaurant, shops, car hire, tourist information outlet; Vigie (SLU), 3km from Castries, bar, restaurant, car hire.
Airport tax: EC$54 departure tax
Surface
Main port/s: Castries, Vieux Fort, Soufrière.

Getting about
National transport
Road: All centres are served by a well maintained road network. Main roads constitute over half of 800km network.
Buses: Unscheduled local basic services are offered by independent drivers.
Water: Boats ply to various destinations.
City transport
Taxis: Taxis are relatively cheap and widely available. A fixed rate system operates but it is advisable to negotiate fares in advance, especially for long journeys. Tips are not expected.
Car hire
Available in Castries, Vieux Fort and Soufrière and through hotels. A national or international licence is acceptable. Traffic drives on the left.

BUSINESS DIRECTORY
The addresses listed below are a selection only. While World of Information makes every endeavour to check these addresses, we cannot guarantee that changes have not been made, especially to telephone numbers and area codes. We would welcome any corrections.

Telephone area codes
The international direct dialling code (IDD) for St Lucia is +1 758, followed by subscriber's number.

Useful telephone numbers
Emergencies	911
Tourist Board	452-5968
	453-0053

Chambers of Commerce
St Lucia Chamber of Commerce, Industry and Agriculture, Vide Bouteille, PO Box 482, Castries (tel: 452-3165; fax: 453-6907; e-mail: info@stluciachamber.org).

Banking
Bank of Nova Scotia, 6 Wm Peter Blvd, Box 301, Castries (tel: 452-2292, fax: 453-1051; e-mail: bns@candw.lc).

Barclays Bank, Bridge Street, Box 335, Castries (tel: 452-3306; fax: 452-6860).

CIBC Caribbean, Wm Peter Blvd, Box 350, Castries (tel: 452-3751; fax: 452-3735).

Caribbean Banking Corporation, Micoud Street, Box 1531, Castries (tel: 452-2265; fax: 452-1668, 451-7484).

First National Bank of St Lucia Ltd, 21 Bridge Street, Box 168, Castries (tel: 450-7000; fax: 453-1630).

National Commercial Bank of St. Lucia, Waterfront Branch, Box 1031, Castries (tel: 452-2103/3562; fax: 453-1604, 451-7106; e-mail: ncbslu@candw.lc).

Royal Bank of Canada, Wm Peter Blvd, Box 280, Castries (tel: 452-2245, 451-6537; fax: 452-7855).

St Lucia Development Bank, National Insurance Bldg Block A, Waterfront, Box 368, Castries (tel: 452-3561/1493, 453-0236; fax: 453-6720).

Central bank
Eastern Caribbean Central Bank, Agency Office, Financial Centre, Bridge Street, Castries (tel: 452-7449; fax: 453-6022).

Travel information
St Lucia Hotel and Tourism Association, Pointe Seraphine, PO Box 545, Castries (tel: 452-5978).

Ministry of tourism
Ministry of Trade, Industry and Tourism, Government buildings, Block B, John Compton Highway, Castries (tel: 452-2611, 452-1706; fax: 453-4787, 453-7347).

National tourist organisation offices
St Lucia Tourist Board, PO Box 221, Castries (tel: 452-4094; fax: 453-1121; internet: www.stlucia.org).

Ministries
Ministry of Agriculture, Lands, Fisheries and Forestry, Mongiraud Street, Castries (tel: 452-2526; fax: 453-6314).

Ministry of Commerce, International Financial Services and Consumer Affairs, 4th Floor, Block B, Waterfront, Castries (tel: 468-4219, 453-7055; internet site: http://commerce.gov.lc/).

Ministry of Community Development, Social Affairs, Youth, Sports, Co-operatives and Local Government, Government Building, The Waterfront, Castries (tel: 453-1487; fax: 453-7921).

Ministry of Education, Culture and Labour, Micoud Street, Castries (tel: 452-2476; fax: 453-2109).

Ministry of Finance, Statistics, Development and Negotiations, Old Government Buildings, Laborie Street, Castries (tel: 452-5315; fax: 453-1648).

Ministry of Foreign Affairs, Home Affairs, Trade and Industry, New Government Buildings, John Compton Highway, Castries (tel: 452-1178; fax: 452-7427, 453-7347).

Ministry of Health, Information and Broadcasting, Chausee Road, Castries (tel: 452-6730; fax: 453-1614).

Ministry of Legal Affairs and Women's Affairs, Paynier Street, Castries (tel: 452-3622; fax: 453-6315).

Ministry of Planning, Establishment and Training, PO Box 709, Government Buildings, Castries (tel: 452-2611; fax: 453-1648).

Office of the Prime Minister, New Government Buildings, Block C, The Waterfront, Castries (tel: 452-6519; fax: 453-7352).

Other useful addresses

British High Commission, 24 Micoud St, Castries (tel: 452-2484; email: britishhc@candw.lc).

Cable & Wireless Public Telex Booth, Bridge Street, Castries (tel: 452-3301; fax: 452-2363).

Embassy of St Lucia 3216 New Mexico Avenue, NW, Washington, DC 20016, USA (tel: (202) 364-6792, fax: (202) 364-6723; email: eofsaintlu@aol.com; internet: www.sluonestop.com).

Financial Centre Corporation, NIS Building, Ground Floor, The Waterfront, Castries (tel: 455-7700; fax: 455-7701; e-mail: fcc@stluciaoffshore.com; internet site: http://www.pinnaclestlucia.com/).

National Development Corporation (NDC), PO Box 495, Monplaisir Building, Brazil Street, Castries (tel: 452-3614; fax: 452-1814; e-mail: devcorp@candw.lc; internet site: http://www.stluciandc.com/).

National Research & Development Foundation (NTDF), PO Box 3067, La Clergy, Castries (tel: 452-4253; fax: 453-6389; e-mail: ntdf@candw.lc).

Organisation of Eastern Caribbean States Natural Resources Management Unit (OECS NRMU), PO Box 1383, Morne Fortune, Castries.

Police Headquarters, Bridge Street, Castries (tel: 452-3854/5).

St Lucia Air and Sea Ports Authority, Micoud St, PO Box 651, Castries (tel: 452-2893; fax: 452-2062).

St Lucia Yacht Services Ltd, PO Box 188, Castries (tel: 452-5057).

Windward Islands Banana Growers' Association (WINBAN), Box 115, Compton Building, William Peter Boulevard, Castries (tel: 452-3975).

Internet sites

Government of St Lucia: http://www.stlucia.gov.lc/

The Star Newspaper: http://www.stluciaStar.com/

St Lucia Search Engine: http://www.stlucia.com/

St Vincent and the Grenadines

COUNTRY PROFILE

Historical profile
The country's first known inhabitants were Arawak Indians, who were later driven out by Carib Indians.
1498 The principal island was sighted by Colombus. No immediate European immigration followed this discovery.
1779 France occupied the island.
1783 Possession of the islands was passed from France to Britain under the Treaty of Versailles, as part of the Windward Islands.
1812 The volcano, La Soufrière, erupted and destroyed most of the island of St Vincent.
1834 After the emancipation of slaves by Britain, indentured labour from the East Indies and Portugal was brought in to remedy the labour shortage.
1958 St Vincent and the Grenadines became part of the attempted West Indies Federation.
1962 Dissolution of the West Indies Federation.
1970 St Vincent and the Grenadines gained independence.
1998 The New Democratic Party (NDP), led by Prime Minister James Mitchell, was re-elected for a fourth term in office.
2000 Anti-government demonstrations forced the government to agree to an election by March 2001. Prime Minister Sir James Mitchell stepped down and Arnhim Eustace became prime minister and leader of the NDP.
2001 The Unity Labour Party (ULP) won the elections and Ralph Gonsalves became prime minister.
2002 Death of Sir Charles James Antrobus, governor general since 1996. He was replaced by his deputy, Monica Dacon, until Frederick Ballantyne was sworn in.
2003 The leaders of the Organisation of the Eastern Caribbean States (OECS) agreed to set up an economic union and introduce a common passport for nationals of the member countries.
2004 In March 2004, the first interim report on the constitution was made by the Constitutional Review Commission (CRC).
2005 A further interim report on the constitution was published by the CRC in February. The 4 December parliamentary elections were won by the ULP.

Political structure
Constitution
The 1979 constitution is being reviewed by the Constitutional Review Commission (CRC); the first interim report was made in March 2004.
Form of state
Independent state; it is a member of the Commonwealth.
The executive
The British monarch is the head of state, represented by a governor general who exercises executive authority and is appointed on the prime minister's advice.
National legislature
The governor general appoints six senators to the legislature, the House of Assembly (four on the prime minister's advice and two on the advice of the leader of the opposition); the other 15 representatives in the House are elected for five years by universal adult suffrage.
Legal system
The legal system is based on English common law with variations. Magisterial district courts exercise both civil and criminal jurisdiction up to a certain limit. The primary court of first instance is the High Court of Justice, from which appeal is made to the Eastern Caribbean Court of Appeal. Final appeals go to the Privy Council in the UK.
Last elections
4 December 2005 (parliamentary)
Results: Parliamentary: Unity Labour Party (ULP) 55.3 per cent (12 out of 15 elected seats), New Democratic Party (NDP) 44.7 per cent (3 seats). Turnout was 63.7 per cent.
Next elections
2010.

Political parties
Ruling party
Unity Labour Party (ULP) (since 2001; re-elected Dec 2005)
Main opposition party
New Democratic Party (NDP)

Population
119,400 (2004)
Ethnic make-up
Most of the population are the descendants of African slaves brought to the island to work on plantations. There are also a few white descendants of English colonists, as well as some East Indians, Carib Indians and a minority of mixed race.
Religions
Anglican (32 per cent), Methodist (18 per cent), Roman Catholic (10 per cent), Seventh-Day Adventist, Hindu, other Protestant (40 per cent).

KEY FACTS

Official name: Commonwealth of St Vincent and the Grenadines

Head of State: Queen Elizabeth II; Governor General Frederick Ballantyne (from Sep 2002)

Head of government: Prime Minister Ralph Gonsalves (ULP) (since Mar 2001; re-elected Dec 2005)

Ruling party: Unity Labour Party (ULP) (since 2001; re-elected Dec 2005)

Area: 388 square km

Population: 119,400 (2004)

Capital: Kingstown

Official language: English

Currency: East Caribbean dollar (EC$) = 100 cents

Exchange rate: EC$2.70 per US$ (fixed)

GDP per capita: US$3,512 (2004)

GDP real growth: 2.80% (2004)

Labour force: 67,000 (2003)

Unemployment: 22.00% (2003)

Inflation: 2.00% (2004)

Balance of trade: -US$131.90 million (2003)

Foreign debt: US$167.20 million (2003)

Education
Education is not compulsory, but children are expected to attend school between the ages of five and 15. Public schooling is provided free of charge up to age 15, although books and equipment have to be supplied by parents. An estimated 95 per cent of the population attend school, but attendance may drop when family needs are pressing. There are 65 primary schools and 23 secondary schools. Around 10 per cent of the population have no formal education and are illiterate.

The emphasis on academic subjects in secondary schools has shifted to include more practical courses like carpentry and agricultural studies.

Health
Health care is free until the age of 17. There are six public hospitals in Kingstown and five other hospitals in rural areas. There is also a mental health institution and an old people's residence.

A national family planning policy has been in place since 1974 and as a result the fertility rate has dropped considerably.
Life expectancy: 72.9 years (World Bank)
Fertility rate/Maternal mortality rate: 2.1 per woman (World Bank)
Birth rate/Death rate: 17 births per 1,000 population; six deaths per 1,000 population (2003).
Infant mortality rate: 23 per 1,000 live births (World Bank)
Head of population per physician/bed: 1 doctor for every 2,960 people.

Welfare
The social welfare system is weak. There is no national health insurance, nor any pension allowance for the elderly. The infant mortality rate is high.

There is a limited framework for the protection of children and the number of child abuse cases that are reported is high.

The situation is generally difficult for disabled people, who seldom leave their homes. There is one institution that offers care and support to the elderly.

Main cities
Kingstown (capital, estimated population 17,600 in 2003).

Languages spoken
English, Vincentian Creole
Official language/s
English

Media
Press
Dailies: *The Daily Herald* was the first international daily newspaper published from Kingstown.
Weeklies: Weeklies include *Searchlight*.
Broadcasting
Government-owned radio station and two private cable television services, using US satellite programmes.

Economy
Tourism and agriculture are the principal sectors of the economy. St Vincent and the Grenadines traditionally relied on banana exports for its economic survival, but, following the 1999 decision by the EU to end its preferential treatment of bananas imported from former colonies, sought to diversify, primarily through expanding tourism. Diversification continues to be an imperative and the government is looking to the revitalisation of the financial services sector to contribute to this process.

After a period of decline, growth began returning to the economy in 2002 and has continued to rise gradually. In 2004, tourism and banana output recovered from a disappointing 2003 to boost the economy. The construction industry was stimulated further by increased demand for residential and commercial accommodation.

External trade
There is a heavy dependence on banana exports and aid flows.
Imports
Main imports are foodstuffs, machinery and equipment, chemicals and fertilisers, minerals and fuels.
Main sources: France (21 per cent total, 2004), Italy (12.4 per cent), Singapore (11.2 per cent), US (10.9 per cent), Trinidad and Tobago (9.9 per cent), Japan (7.3 per cent), Spain (4.9 per cent)
Exports
Main exports are bananas (39 per cent of total), taro, arrowroot starch and tennis racquets.
Main destinations: France (30.5 per cent total, 2004), Spain (19.6 per cent), Italy (17.7 per cent), Greece (11.7 per cent), UK (7.8 per cent)

Agriculture
Farming
The agricultural sector is traditionally the mainstay of the economy, but its contribution to GDP, which stood at 40 per cent in 1960, has fallen to around nine per cent. Half of the total land area is arable with only a small proportion unused. St Vincent is the world's leading producer of arrowroot and an exporter of coconut oil. Carrots and plantains are also cash crops. The main food crops are sweet potatoes, tannias, yams, vegetables, and various fruits.

Bananas (grown mainly on small farms under the auspices of St Vincent Banana Growers Association) are the main export crop. The production of bananas, and earnings from their export, have declined in recent years. Unfavourable weather conditions, a sharp fall in the average domestic currency price received for fruit, and a reduction in the average green wholesale price of fruit have weakened the industry. An estimated 25 per cent of the 2004 crop was lost as a result of Hurricane Ivan in September

The EU will to phase out preferential treatment for banana producers from former colonies by 2006, to create a level playing field with Latin American banana growers (mostly US firms). The liberalisation of the banana trade has made it difficult for family-run businesses in St Vincent to compete.

Crop production in 2004 included: 1,225 tonnes (t) sweet potatoes, 2,200t yams,

KEY INDICATORS — St Vincent and the Grenadines

	Unit	2000	2001	2002	2003	2004
Population	m	0.11	0.12	0.12	0.12	0.12
Gross domestic product (GDP)	US$bn	0.33	0.34	0.36	0.34	*0.40
GDP per capita	US$	2,973	3,070	3,005	2,900	3,512
GDP real growth	%	1.8	-0.6	1.1	2.2	2.8
Inflation	%	0.2	0.8	1.0	0.3	2.0
Consumer prices	1995=100	108.4	109.3	110.2	–	–
Exports (fob) (goods)	US$m	51.8	43.0	68.4	53.7	–
Imports (fob) (goods)	US$m	142.9	186.0	185.6	185.6	–
Balance of trade	US$m	-91.2	-143.0	-117.2	-131.9	–
Current account	US$m	-26.3	-60.0	-40.0	-50.0	-50.0
Total reserves minus gold	US$m	55.2	61.4	53.2	51.2	75.0
Foreign exchange	US$m	54.5	60.8	52.5	50.4	74.2
Exchange rate	per US$	2.70	2.70	2.70	2.70	2.70

* estimated figure

St Vincent and the Grenadines

45,000t bananas, 1,500t plantains, 650t maize, 3,225t citrus fruit, 720t cassava, 20,000t sugar cane, 2,550t coconuts, 445t chillies & peppers, 1,150t apples, 1,464t mangoes, 170t coffee beans, 175t cocoa beans, 150t nutmeg, 500t other spices, 85t tobacco leaves, 424t oilcrops, 340t pulses, 52,680t fruit in total, 9,800t roots and tubers, 4,315t vegetables in total. Livestock production included: 1,058t meat in total, 182t beef, 550t pig meat, 76t lamb and goat meat, 250t poultry, 625t eggs, 1,200t milk.

Fishing
The typical total annual fish catch is over 45,800t. Shellfish, molluscs and cephalopods account for another 1,800t per annum.

Industry and manufacturing
The industrial sector employs around 8 per cent of the workforce and contributes 10 per cent to GDP.

Activity is primarily based on agricultural processing. Units in operation include those producing cigarettes, tobacco products, coconut oil, textiles and clothing, soft drinks, fruit juices, milk, beer, rum, furniture, arrowroot starch, tyre retreading, concrete blocks and quarry products. A flour mill, serving all the Windward Islands, a box factory and a yacht building yard are the main export industries.

The sector has continued to contract since 1999, although in 2004 the brewery, the second largest manufacturer, reported its best year since then.

Tourism
Tourism is a vital part of the islands' economy. The percentage of GDP in 2005 is forecast to be 10.3 per cent (and 10 per cent of GDP growth for the year) while the sector employs 9.6 per cent of the work force.

St Vincent is a volcanic island and has only one white sand beach; the industry is thus limited, and there is only minimal scope for further expansion. The Grenadines have more white sand beaches, and the government has stepped up promotional work in the sector's main markets of the US, the UK, Canada and the Caribbean. Infrastructure is being gradually upgraded. Particular attention has been paid to encouraging the cruise ship market. Visitor numbers increased in 2004 to 261,475, compared to 241,748 in 2003. Arrivals by air rose by 10.4 per cent and 20.1 per cent by sea.

Hydrocarbons
St Vincent and the Grenadines has no hydrocarbon resources. It relies entirely on imports of refined oil. Natural gas and coal are not imported.

Energy
Hydroelectric power generates 44 per cent of energy requirements. The government is exploring ways to tap the active volcano, La Sourière, for geothermal energy. Many people have private generators.

Banking and insurance
The banking sector contributes around 6 per cent of GDP.

The seven members of the Organisation of Eastern Caribbean States (OECS) (Antigua and Barbuda, Dominica, Grenada, Montserrat, St Kitts and Nevis, St Lucia and St Vincent and the Grenadines), share a common currency and central bank. The British Virgin Islands and Anguilla are associate members.

Central bank
Eastern Caribbean Central Bank, St Kitts and Nevis.

Offshore facilities
The offshore financial centre is an important element of the economy. The Exchange of Information Act, passed in 2002, attempts to increase financial transparency and accountability. An International Banks Act was also passed in 2002 that aims to strengthen the supervision of banking activities.

St Vincent and the Grenadines was removed from the OECD Financial Action Task Force (FATF) list of non-co-operative countries on money laundering in June 2003, after reforms had been implemented. The government, recognising the sector's importance to its diversification policy, responded by strengthening the regulatory and supervisory framework in line with international best practice. At end-2003, the former Offshore Finance Authority (OFA) was renamed the International Financial Services Authority of St Vincent and the Grenadines (IFSA).

In April 2004, the IFSA reported that in real terms 2004 had seen a growth in the registration of international business companies of 84 per cent over the same period in 2003.

Time
GMT minus four hours

Geography
St Vincent and the Grenadines is situated in the Windward Islands group, approximately 160km (100 miles) west of Barbados in the West Indies. St Lucia is 34km (21 miles) to the north-east and Grenada is to the south. St Vincent is the main island. It is volcanic. There are also 32 smaller islands and cays known as the St Vincent Grenadines, the northerly part of an island chain stretching between St Vincent and Grenada. The principal islands of the group are Bequia, Canouan, Mustique, Mayreau, Isle D'Quatre and Union Island.

Climate
Tropical, tempered by trade winds, with temperature range 18–32 degrees Celsius. High levels of rainfall from May–November, especially in the north.

Entry requirements
Passports
Required by all except nationals of Canada and US for visits not exceeding six months.
Visa
Not required as length of stay established by immigration authority on arrival.
Currency advice/regulations
Declaration usually required on arrival. Export must not exceed import.

Health (for visitors)
Mandatory precautions
Yellow fever vaccination certificate required if arriving from an infected area.
Advisable precautions
Typhoid, polio vaccination.

Hotels
Wide range of good hotels available at reasonable prices, except on the privately owned islands of Palm, Mustique and Petit St Vincent, where rates are higher. Seven per cent tax is added to room rates; 10 per cent tip is usual if service charge not included on bill.

Public holidays
Fixed dates
1 Jan (New Year's Day), 14 Mar (National Heroes' Day), 1 May (Labour Day), 1 Aug (Emancipation Day), 27 Oct (Independence Day), 25 Dec (Christmas Day), 26 Dec (Boxing Day).
If a holiday falls on a Sunday, the following Monday is taken as a public holiday.
Variable dates
Good Friday, Easter Monday, Whit Monday, Carnival Monday (first Mon in Jul), Carnival Tuesday (first Tue in Jul).

Working hours
Banking
Mon–Fri: 0800–1300; also Fri: 1500–1700.
Business
Mon–Fri: 0800–1200, 1300–1600; Sat: 0800–1200.
Government
Mon–Fri: 0800–1200, 1300–1600; Sat: 0800–1200.

Electricity supply
220/240V AC, 50 cycles

Getting there
Air
National airline: St Vincent is a shareholder in LIAT.
International airport/s: St Vincent-ET Joshua Airport (SVD), 3km from

Kingstown. Flights arrive from surrounding Caribbean islands.
Airport tax: EC$40 on international departure, excluding 24 hour transit passengers.
Surface
Main port/s: Kingstown

Getting about
National transport
Air: There are landing strips (suitable for light planes) on Mustique and Union islands and an airport at Canouan. LIAT and Air Martinique provide scheduled services to many other islands in the Caribbean. Mustique Airways, St Vincent Airways and St Vincent and the Grenadines Air are available for charter. Regional airline Carib Express based at Barbados.
Road: The total network is over 1,000km, about 450km of which is paved.
Buses: Buses are fairly widespread. Stopping is on demand rather than at pre-specified points.
Water: Regular ferry boats ply between the islands.
City transport
Taxis: Taxis are usually ordered by telephone. A fixed-rate system applies; a 15 per cent tip is usual.
Car hire
An international or temporary Vincentian licence is required. Traffic drives on the left.

BUSINESS DIRECTORY

The addresses listed below are a selection only. While World of Information makes every endeavour to check these addresses, we cannot guarantee that changes have not been made, especially to telephone numbers and area codes. We would welcome any corrections.

Telephone area codes
The international direct dialling code (IDD) for St Vincent is +809, followed by subscriber's number.

Useful telephone numbers
Local information: 118.
International information: 115.
Police: 457-1211.
Kingstown General Hospital: 456-1185.

Chambers of Commerce
St Vincent Chamber of Commerce and Industry, Corea's Building, Halifax Street, PO Box 134, Kingstown (tel: 457-1464; fax: 456-2994; e-mail: svgcic@caribsurf.com).

Banking
Bank of Nova Scotia, 76 Halifax Street, Box 237, Kingstown (tel: 457-1601; fax: 457-2623).

Barclays Bank, Halifax Street, PO Box 604, Kingstown (tel: 456-1706; fax: 457-2985).

CIBC Caribbean, Halifax Street, Box 212, Kingstown (tel: 457-1587; fax: 457-2873).

Canadian Imperial Bank of Commerce, Halifax Street, Box 212, Kingstown (tel: 457-1587/2873; fax: 457-2873).

Caribbean Banking Corporation, 81 South River Road, Box 118, Kingstown (tel: 456-1501; fax: 456-2141).

Development Corporation, Sharpe Street, Box 841, Kingstown (tel: 457-1358; 457-2838).

First St. Vincent Bank, Lot 112 Granby Street, Box 154, Kingstown (tel: 456-1873; fax: 457-2675).

National Commercial Bank, Bedford Street, Box 880, Kingstown (tel: 457-1844; fax: 457-2612).

New Bank, Blue Caribbean Bldg Bay Street, Box 1628, Kingstown (tel: 457-1411, 456-2453; fax: 457-1357).

Owens Bank, Box 1045, Kingstown (tel: 457-1230; fax: 457-2610).

St. Vincent Co-operative Bank, Corner Long Lane Upper & South River Road, Box 886, Kingstown (tel: 456-1894).

Central bank
Eastern Caribbean Central Bank, Agency Office, PO Box 839, Granby Street, Kingstown (tel: 456-1413; fax: 456-1412).

Travel information
Air Martinique (tel: 458-4528; fax: 458-4187).

Mustique Airways, PO Box 1232, Arnos Vale (tel: 458-4380; fax: 456-4586).

St Vincent Airways, Arnos Vale (tel: 456-4176).

National tourist organisation offices
Department of Tourism, Bay Street, PO Box 834, Kingstown (tel: 457-1502; fax: 451-2425; e-mail: tourism@caribsurf.com; internet site: www.svgtourism.com).

Ministries
Ministry of Agriculture and Labour, Administrative Building, Kingstown (tel: 456-1410; fax: 457-1688).

Ministry of Communications and Works, Administrative Building, Kingstown (tel: 456-1111; fax: 456-2168).

Ministry of Education, Youth and Women's Affairs, Administrative Building, Kingstown (tel: 457-2282; fax: 457-1114).

Ministry of Foreign Affairs and Tourism, Administrative Building, Kingstown (tel: 456-1111; fax: 456-2610).

Ministry of Health and the Environment, Administrative Building, Kingstown (tel: 457-1729; fax: 456-2610).

Ministry of Housing, Local Government and Community Development and Sports, Administrative Building, Kingstown (tel: 456-1111; fax: 456-2610).

Ministry of Legal Affairs and Information, Administrative Building, Kingstown (tel: 456-1111; fax: 457-2898).

Ministry of Trade, Industry and Consumer Affairs, Administrative Building, Kingstown (tel: 457-1223; fax: 457-2880).

Office of The Prime Minister, Administrative Building, Kingstown (tel: 456-1703; fax: 457-2152).

Other useful addresses
British High Commission PO Box 132, Granby Street, Kingstown (tel: 457 1701; fax: 456 2750; email: bhcsvg@caribsurf.com).

National Broadcasting Corporation, PO Box 705, Kingstown (tel: 457-1111).

Offshore Finance Authority, Kingstown (tel: 456-2577; fax: 457-2568; e-mail: info@stvincentoffshore.com; internet site: http://www.stvincentoffshore.com).

Radio St Vincent and the Grenadines, PO Box 705, Kingstown (tel: 456-1516).

Statistical Office, Central Planning Division, Ministry of Finance and Planning, Kingstown (fax: 457-2943).

St Vincent and the Grenadines Embassy (US), Suite 102, 1717 Massachusetts Avenue, Washington DC 20036 (tel: 462-7806).

St Vincent Development Corporation (DEVCO), PO Box 841, Granby Street, Kingstown (tel: 457-1358; fax: 457-2838).

Internet sites
Caribbean newspaper online: http://caribbeannetnews.com

Samoa

COUNTRY PROFILE

Historical profile
The first Polynesians settled in the islands around 600BC. A former German protectorate, Samoa was governed by New Zealand from 1914 until its citizens voted for independence in 1961. The Independent State of Samoa was known as Western Samoa until 1997.
1722 The Dutch navigator, Jacob Roggeveen, was the first European to sight the islands.
1831 The London Missionary Society arrived in Samoa to convert native Samoans, establishing a British presence.
1889 The *Treaty of Berlin* between Britain, the US and Germany promised an independent Samoan government.
1899 The Berlin treaty was annulled by the *Tripartite Treaty*, which granted the US rights to all eastern islands of the Samoan group and giving Germany the remainder. In exchange for withdrawing its claim to Samoa, Britain gained control of Germany's rights in Tonga, Niue, and the Solomon Islands (excluding Bougainville).
1914 New Zealand occupied Western Samoa during the First World War and continued to administer it after the War under a League of Nations' mandate.
1929 Eleven members of the passive Mau independence movement were killed by New Zealand authorities.
1946 After the Second World War, Western Samoa was administered as a UN Trust Territory by New Zealand.
1961 In a UN-supervised plebiscite the majority voted for independence.
1962 Western Samoa became the first Pacific island to declare independence.
1970 Western Samoa became a member of the Commonwealth.
1990 Voters approved universal suffrage and increased the legislature's term from three to five years.
1991 The general election employed universal suffrage for all those over 21.
1997 The constitution was amended and Western Samoa was re-named Samoa.
1998 The government imposed restrictions on media freedom.
2000 Samoa was one of the first to sign the Pacific Island Countries (free) Trade Agreement. Two former cabinet ministers, sentenced to death for a murder attempt on a fellow politician who could have exposed them for corruption, had their death sentences commuted to life imprisonment.
2001 In parliamentary elections incumbent prime minister, Tuiaepa Sailele Malielegaoi, Human Rights' Protection Party (HRPP) won a closely run election and retained control of the legislative assembly (*Fono*) with the support of independent members.
2002 New Zealand formally apologised for its poor treatment of Samoan citizens in colonial times.
2004 The death penalty was abolished – the punishment had not been used since the 1930s.
2005 Samoa was awarded the 2007 South Pacific Games.

Political structure
Constitution
The O le Ao O le Malo (Head of State) acts as a constitutional monarch with the power to dissolve the Fono (legislative assembly) and to appoint a prime minister with its recommendation.
The executive
Executive power rests with the prime minister who selects the 12-member cabinet. The Head of State does not play an active role in government. He appoints the prime minister on the Fono's recommendation and approves the laws passed by the Fono. The Head of State is appointed for a life term although after the death of the current Chief Malietoa Tanumafili II, the Head of State will be elected for a five-year term only.
National legislature
The unicameral 49-member Fono is elected, by universal suffrage, for a period of up to five years. Only those members of the Matai (elected clan leaders), are eligible to stand for election to the assembly.
Last elections
2001 (parliamentary)
Results: Parliamentary: HRPP was re-elected with 23 seats (45.1 per cent of the vote); SNDP 13 seats (23.5 per cent), Samoan United Peoples Party one seat; independents 12 seats.
Next elections
2006 (parliamentary)

Political parties
Ruling party
Human Rights Protection Party (HRPP) (re-elected Mar 2001)
Main opposition party
Samoan National Development Party (SNDP)

Population
171,800 (2004)

KEY FACTS

Official name: Malotuto'atasi o Samoa (Independent State of Samoa) (dropped 'Western' Jul 1997)

Head of State: Malietoa Tanumafili II (since 1963)

Head of government: Prime Minister Tuilaepa Sailele Malielegaoi (HRPP) (since Nov 1998)

Ruling party: Human Rights Protection Party (HRPP) (re-elected Mar 2001)

Area: 2,840 square km (nine islands): Savai'i (1,708); Upolu (1,118)

Population: 171,800 (2004)

Capital: Apia (on Upolu)

Official language: Samoan

Currency: Tala or Samoan dollar (S$) = 100 senes, or cents

Exchange rate: S$2.72 per US$ (Oct 2005)

GDP per capita: US$1,750 (2004)

GDP real growth: 3.20% (2004)

Labour force: 90,000 (2003)

Inflation: 2.40% (2004)

Balance of trade: -US$114.60 million (2003)

Foreign debt: US$197.00 million (2003)

Visitor numbers: 29,388 (2003) (holiday visitors)

Nations of the World: A Political, Economic and Business Handbook

Ethnic make-up
Samoan (92.6 per cent); European and Polynesian mixed race (7 per cent); Europeans (0.4 per cent).

Religions
Christian

Education
The introduction of the bilingual, single curriculum in primary and secondary schools has increased the number of students successfully completing schooling. Teaching methods and teacher's tools, including dictionaries, grammars and workbooks for teachers, were re-oriented so that the focus became localised and seen as more relevant to the student's lives. The dual streaming of academic and non-academic students in secondary schools was discontinued and has improved the educational outcome of more students.

Literacy rate: 98.9 per cent, adult male rate; 98.4 per cent adult female rate (World Bank).
Compulsory years: Five to 13
Enrolment rate: 91.9 per cent net primary enrolment; 67.4 per cent net seconday enrolment (World Bank).

Health
Life expectancy: 69.5 years (World Bank)
Fertility rate/Maternal mortality rate: 4.0 births per woman (World Bank)
Birth rate/Death rate: 15 births per 1,000 population; six deaths per 1,000 population (2003).
Infant mortality rate: 19 per 1,000 live births (World Bank)

Main cities
Apia, on Upolu (capital, estimated population 40,000).

Languages spoken
English is widely spoken. The Samoan language has an equal status with English in schools.

Official language/s
Samoan

Media
Press
Dailies: The *Samoa Observer* is a leading daily. *Samoa Live* (www.samoalive.com/samoanews.htm) is the leading local on-line network with regional Asia Pacific and international news links. Other regular publications include the *Samoa Times* and *South Seas Star*.
Weeklies: Local weekly publications include *Newsline*, *Le Samoa*, *Samoa Post* and *Samoa Weekly*.
Business: *Talanei News* (www.samoana.org/talanei) covers business news.
Periodicals: Periodicals include *Savali* and *Samoa Sports Monthly*.

Broadcasting
One private radio station operates, in addition to two government radio stations. Some foreign services are available. It is possible to pick up television broadcasts from American Samoa.

Advertising
Most weekly newspapers accept advertising; facilities available on Radio 2AP and Radio 98FM. Cinemas do not offer advertising facilities.

Economy
The economy is based on agriculture, tourism, manufacturing, overseas remittances and foreign aid.

In 2004 the economy was hit by damage caused by Cyclone Heta. Economic growth dropped from 3.5 per cent in 2003 to 2.3 per cent in 2004. Improved tourist visits, up from 93,000 to 97,000 over 2003–04, were offset by increased food and energy prices (26.8 per cent increase in the price of local goods and services and a 2.7 per cent increase in the price of imported goods) which pushed up inflation rates from 4.2 per cent in 2003 to as high as 16.4 per cent by the end of 2004. However, the underlying inflation rate remains low and the central bank forecasts inflation by the end of 2005 will be 2.1 per cent.

The service sector, and tourism in particular, employs about 30 per cent of workers and generates over 50 per cent of GDP. To be the host of the 2007 South Pacific Games will give a boost to both tourism and construction in Samoa. The government has begun improvements in tourist infrastructures by upgrading roads and bridges and there are four new hotels and two resorts in various states of production. One resort planned will include a 5 star hotel, built for the growing ecotourism market.

Construction has led growth in the industry sector, which accounts for just over 25 per cent of GDP although it only employs around 6 per cent of workers. The largest manufacturing entity is a Japanese-owned automotive components factory that exports parts to Australia under a market-access concession arrangement. Agriculture (including fishing) accounts for around 17 per cent of GDP and employs about 64 per cent of the workforce.

Samoa is a stable democratic country that has taken measures to liberalise its economy in an attempt to attract foreign direct investment; however it may overcome this only when it is no longer designated a less developed country (LDC). In the meantime construction is expected to maintain economic growth as most major projects are not due for completion until 2007.

External trade
Imports
Principal imports are machinery and equipment, industrial supplies and foodstuffs.
Main sources: New Zealand (23.1 per cent total, 2004), Fiji (17.9 per cent), Taiwan (10.7 per cent), Australia (9.6 per cent), Singapore (9.1 per cent), Japan (8.1 per cent), US (5.3 per cent)

Exports
Samoa exports about 50 different products. However, the export base remains

KEY INDICATORS — Samoa

	Unit	2000	2001	2002	2003	2004
Population	m	0.17	0.17	0.17	0.17	0.17
Gross domestic product (GDP)	US$bn	0.25	0.25	0.26	0.28	*0.36
GDP per capita	US$	1,387	1,407	1,509	1,672	1,750
GDP real growth	%	6.9	6.2	1.8	3.5	2.3
Inflation	%	1.0	3.8	8.1	4.2	*16.0
Consumer prices	1995=100	116.5	121.2	130.8	–	–
Exports (fob) (goods)	US$m	14.6	17.5	13.7	15.5	–
Imports (fob) (goods)	US$m	108.6	130.3	112.9	130.1	–
Balance of trade	US$m	-94.0	-112.8	-99.2	-114.6	–
Current account	US$m	-10.0	-30.0	-20.0	-10.0	*1.0
Foreign debt	US$bn	0.2	0.2	0.2	0.2	–
Total reserves minus gold	US$m	63.6	56.6	62.5	83.9	95.5
Foreign exchange	US$m	59.7	52.8	58.3	79.3	90.7
Exchange rate	per US$	3.21	4.41	3.39	2.99	2.78

* estimated figure

Samoa

narrow, with processed coconut products such as coconut oil and cream providing 44 per cent of export earnings. Principal exports are fish, coconut oil and cream, copra, taro, automotive parts, garments and beer.

Main destinations: Australia (60.7 per cent total, 2004), Indonesia (17.1 per cent), US (4.9 per cent)

Agriculture
Farming
Agriculture, including fishing, typically accounts for 17 per cent of GDP and employs over 60 per cent of the workforce with smallholdings producing surpluses in Samoa's fertile volcanic soil, enough for healthy export sales.

A devastating blight of the taro in 1994, which almost wiped out the entire stock, led to a diversification that is benifitting the economy in 2005. Export of nonu juice in 2004 earned US$632,000 and replaced fresh fish as Samoa's principle foreign exchange earner. Other produce under development include macadamia nuts, annatto (dye), timber and cattle.

In August 2004 a shipment of sheep arrived from Fiji where they had been specially bread to have a high meat content and to be suitable for tropical climates. Production of subsistence crops include cassava, breadfruit maize and taro.

Agriculture was hit hard by Cyclone Heta in early 2004, disrupting the food supply and pushing up prices.

Production in 2004 included: 17,000 tonnes (t) taro, 2,600t yams, 140,000t coconuts, 21,500t bananas, 44,350t fruit in total, 18,230t oilcrops, 4,000t mangoes, 3,600t papayas, 3,000t plantains, 1,020t vegetables in total, 650t citrus fruit, 500t cocoa beans, 450t tomatoes, 300t cassava, 140t tobacco, 100t spices, 2,600t yams, 18,230t oilcrops, 130t vanilla. Livestock production included: 5,140t meat in total, 1,000t beef, 3,800t pig meat, 340t poultry, 260t eggs, 1,500t milk, 400t honey.

Fishing
Fishing is one of Samoa's major export earners. The typical annual fish catch is around 11,000t (an increase from 7,500t in 1998); there are concerns that overfishing is depleting fish stocks.

Forestry
In 2003 forest exports amounted to US$972,000 and imports amounted to US$5.6 million. Production in 2003 included 131,000 cubic metres (cum) roundwood, 61,000cum industrial roundwood, 21,000cum sawnwood, 58,000cum sawlogs & veneer logs, 70,000cum wood fuel.

Industry and manufacturing
The industrial sector typically accounts for over 25 per cent of GDP and employs approximately 6 per cent of the workforce. Small-scale manufacturing and industry has expanded. The government's industrial area of Vaitele (on Upolu) houses a brewery, a cigarette factory and a match factory.

Other industries include copra processing, food processing, light engineering, woodworking and manufacture of coconut oil, paint, concrete and construction materials, bottled gases, plastic bags, corned beef and garments. US food processors have expressed interest in investing in fish-processing capacity.

Output of automotive wiring harnesses for export increased following the extension of the Yazaki Samoa plant, the largest employer. However production fell in 2004. Garment exports also declined when production was interupted by a move to new premises.

Industrial production grew in 2004 by 2.6 per cent, led by construction both private and public. The construction sector, following the damage from Cyclone Heta in January 2004, sparked a boom and coupled with major building projects in offices, schools, the National University of Samoa and the facilities for the South pacific Games, have more than bolstered the declines seen in other areas of the economy.

Tourism
Tourism is the main economic activity and the largest foreign exchange earner. The number of visitors continues to rise by about 20 per cent. Visitor numbers in 2003 totalled 93,000, and increased to 97,000 in 2004 – partly due to Samoa hosting the Pacific Forum meetings. The main markets are American Samoa and New Zealand.

There is still competition between tourists and business travellers for limited accommodation; however this should ease when the new hotels and resorts are finally completed by 2007.

Hydrocarbons
As there are no hydrocarbon reserves, Samoa relies entirely on the import of refined oil that makes up around 58 per cent of Samoa's energy consumption. Imports come from New Zealand, Australia, Fiji and the US. Samoa does not import natural gas or coal.

Energy
The Electric Power Corporation operates a wood-fuel power station. There are four hydroelectric plants. Growth in demand is running at about 7 per cent per year.

Banking and insurance
The government has increased its deposits in the banking system over the last few years, enabling commercial banks to lend and boosting private sector credit growth. Banks are strongly capitalised and earn good profits.

Central bank
Central Bank of Samoa

Time
GMT minus 11 hours

Geography
Samoa lies in the southern Pacific Ocean about 2,400km (1,500 miles) north of New Zealand. American Samoa is to the east of the country. Samoa comprises two large and seven small islands, of which five are uninhabited.

Climate
Temperatures 24–30 degrees Celsius (hottest in March) and high humidity. Rainy season November–April, rainfall at least 5,000 mm/year, heaviest in January.

Entry requirements
Passports
Passport or certificate of identity with photograph required by all.
Visa
Required by all for a period not exceeding 30 days. Application forms can be obtained from Samoan missions in Australia, New Zealand, US (New York), and Belgium (Brussels), or Immigration Office, Prime Minister's Department in Samoa. From 1 May 2005, travellers from American Samoa must obtain entry permits to enter Samoa.
Currency advice/regulations
Import and export of local currency is prohibited. No limits on foreign currency.
Customs
Personal effects allowed duty-free.
Prohibited imports
Firearms, ammunition, explosives, drugs and pornography are prohibited. Plants and animals may enter subject to approval from the Department of Agriculture and Forestry.

Health (for visitors)
Mandatory precautions
Vaccination certificate for yellow fever if travelling from an infected area.
Advisable precautions
Vaccinations for diphtheria, tuberculosis, hepatitis 'A' and 'B', polio, tetanus, typhoid. There is a rabies risk.

Credit cards
Major credit cards are accepted.

Public holidays
Fixed dates
1–2 Jan (New Year), 25 Apr (Anzac Day), 10 May (Mothers-of-Samoa Day), 1 Jun (Independence Day), 3 Nov (Arbor Day),

25 Dec (Christmas Day), 26 Dec (Boxing Day).
Variable dates
Good Friday, Easter Monday, Labour Day (first Mon in Aug), *Lotu-a-Tamaiti* (second Mon in Oct, the day after White Sunday).

Working hours
Banking
Mon–Fri: 0830–1500.
Business
Mon–Fri: 0800–1200, 1300–1630.
Government
Mon–Fri: 0800–1200, 1300–1630.
Shops
Mon–Fri: 0800–1200, 1330–1630; Sat: 0800–1230.

Telecommunications
Mobile phones
Telecom Samoa Cellular operates a D-AMPS cellular network.

Electricity supply
230V AC

Weights and measures
Imperial system, with metric systems in use.

Social customs/useful tips
Appointments should be made in advance. Ties need only be worn for formal meetings. English is used for business and commerce. Care should be taken to respect local customs and practices. Samoans do not like to disagree with someone in authority, or not give the anticipated reply, which can lead to misunderstandings by foreign visitors (a 'yes' can mean 'no'). Gratuities are optional and gifts for excellent service are appreciated. The minimum drinking age is 18 years.

Getting there
Air
National airline: Polynesian Airlines
International airport/s: Faleolo International (APW), 34km west of Apia.
Airport tax: International departures S$20; not applicable to 24-hour transit passengers.
Surface
Ferry services operate to American Samoa; shipping services to New Zealand, Australia, Japan and other Pacific islands, as well as Europe and US. Apia and Asau are the main ports.
Travellers between Samoa and Tokelau must have either a visa or a valid, machine readable passport or face a S$20,000 fine.

Getting about
National transport
Air: Polynesian Airlines operates regular services between Maota (near Salelolga), and Asau in Savai'i, and a service to Fagali'i Airport (on Upolu) (NB Fagali'i airport is closing in January 2005).
Buses: Scheduled bus services operate in and around Apia and Salelolaga (Savai'i).
Water: Ferry services operate between Apia and Savai'i.
City transport
Taxis: Taxi service is available in Apia.
Car hire
International or national driving licences required. Traffic drives on the left.

BUSINESS DIRECTORY
The addresses listed below are a selection only. While World of Information makes every endeavour to check these addresses, we cannot guarantee that changes have not been made, especially to telephone numbers and area codes. We would welcome any corrections.

Telephone area codes
The international direct dialling (IDD) code for Samoa is +685 followed by subscriber's number.

Useful telephone numbers
Police, fire and ambulance: 999.

Chambers of Commerce
Samoa Chamber of Commerce and Industry, PO Box 2014, Lotemau Centre, Vaea Street, Apia (tel: 21-237; fax: 21-578; e-mail: info@samoachamber.com).

Banking
ANZ Bank (Samoa) Ltd, PO Box L1855, Beach Road, Apia (tel: 22-422; fax: 24-595, 23-807).

Australia and New Zealand Banking Group Ltd, PO Box L1855, Apia (tel: 22-422; fax: 24-595).

Development Bank of Samoa, PO Box 1232, Apia (tel: 22-861; fax: 23-888).

International Business Bank Corp Ltd; Level 2, Chandra Hse, Convent St, Apia (tel: 22-393; fax: 23-253).

National Bank of Samoa Limited; PO Box L3047, Apia (tel: 23-077; fax: 23-085).

Pacific Commercial Bank Ltd, PO Box 1860, Beach Road, Apia (tel: 20-000; fax: 22-848).
Central bank
Central Bank of Samoa, Central Bank Building, Private Bag, Apia (tel: 34-100; fax: 20-293; e-mail: cbs@samoa.net; internet: www.cbs.gov.ws).

Travel information
Faleolo International Airport, Private Bag, Apia (tel: 23-201, 23-202, 42-050; fax; 24-281; e-mail: etuale@samoa.net).

Polynesian Airlines, PO Box 599, Beech Road, Apia (tel: 21-261; fax: 20-023).
National tourist organisation offices
Samoa Visitors' Bureau, PO Box 862, Apia (tel: 20-878; fax: 20-886; e-mail: samoawsvb@pactok.peg.apc.org; internet site: http://www.visitsamoa.ws).

Other useful addresses
Asian Development Bank (ADB), South Pacific Regional Mission, La Casa di Andrea, Fr. Dr. W. H. Lini Highway; PO Box 127, Port Vila (tel: +678 2 23-300; fax: +678 2 23-183; email: adbsprm@adb.org; internet: www.adb.org/SPRM).

Department of Statistics, PO Box 1151, Apia.

Department of Trade, Commerce and Industry, Chandra House, Trade Information Centre, PO Box 862, Apia (tel: 20-471; fax: 21-504; e-mail: IPU@tci.gov.ws; internet: www.tradeinvestsamoa.ws).

Government of Samoa P.O. Box L 1864 Apia (tel: 24-799, 63-115; fax: 21-742, 26-396; e-mail: contact@govt.ws).

Immigration Office, Prime Minister's Department P.O. Box L1861 Apia, (tel: 20-291, 20-292; e-mail: pmdept@ipasifika.net).

Samoan Embassy (USA), Suite 800D, 820 Second Avenue, New York, NY 10017 (tel: 202-599-6196; fax: 202-599-0797; e-mail: samoa@un.int).

Internet sites
Samoan Government site:
http://www.govt.ws

South Pacific Tourism Organisation:
http://www.tcsp.com

San Marino

COUNTRY PROFILE

Historical profile
San Marino is completely surrounded by Italy. It is the oldest surviving republic in the world, having been an independent republic since the year 301 AD.
1600 The constitution was ratified on 8 October.
1926 An additional electoral law was passed, which serves some of the functions of a constitution.
1988 San Marino joined the Council of Europe.
1990–92 Governed by a coalition of Partito Democratico Progressista (PDP) (Progressive Democratic Party), (ex-communists) and Partito Democratico Cristiano Sammarinese (PDCS) (San Marino Christian Democratic Party).
1992 In March PDCS formed a coalition with the Partito Socialista Sammarinese (PSS) (San Marino Socialist Party). San Marino became a member of the UN.
1993 In the general election, the PDCS won 26 seats and the PSS, 14 seats; the coalition continued.
1998 After the elections, the coalition continued.
2001 Differences within the PDCS/PSS coalition government led to early parliamentary elections (they were originally scheduled for May 2003). The elections resulted in a continuation of the coalition government.
2002 San Marino replaced the lira with the euro currency. Antonio Lazzaro Volpinari and Giovanni Francesco Ugolini took office as captains-regent for six months from April. Giuseppe Maria Morganti and Mauro Chiaruzzi took over on 1 October.
2003 Pier Marino Menicucci and Giovanni Giannoni were installed as captains-regent on 1 April and on 1 October, Giovanni Lonfernini and Valeria Ciavatta took over.
2004 On 1 April, Paolo Bollini (Socialist) and Marino Riccardi (Democrat) were installed as captains-regent. Giuseppe Arzilli (Christian Democrat) and Roberto Raschi (Socialist) took office as captains-regent on 1 October.
2005 Fausta Simona Morganti (Democrat) and Cesare Antonio Gasperoni (Christian Democrat) took office as captains-regent on 1 April. In August San Marino and the Kingdom of Nepal established diplomatic relations. Claudio Muccioli (Christian Democrat) and Antonello Bacciocchi (Socialist) took office as captains-regent on 1 September.

Political structure
Constitution
The constitution was ratified on 8 October 1600. An additional electoral law was passed in 1926, which serves some of the functions of a constitution.
The country is divided into nine *castelli* (municipalities), each governed by a Captain.
The executive
The Consiglio Grande e Generale (CGeG) (the Great and General Council) elects two members every six months to act as captains-regent, who function jointly as heads of state and, together with a 10-member Congress of State (cabinet), exercise executive power. The secretary of state for foreign affairs has come to assume many of the prerogatives of a prime minister.
The Congress of State is elected by the CGeG for a five-year term.
National legislature
Legislative power is vested in the unicameral Consiglio Grande e Generale (CGeG) (Great and General Council), with 60 members elected by universal adult suffrage for five-year terms.
Last elections
June 2001 (parliamentary)
Results: Parliamentary: PDCS won 25 seats, PSS 15 and the PPDS 12.
The PDCS/PSS coalition government continued.
Next elections
June 2006 (parliamentary)

Political parties
Ruling party
Coalition: Partito Democratico Cristiano Sammarinese (PDCS) (San Marino Christian Democratic Party) and Partito Socialista Sammarinese (PSS) (San Marino Socialist Party) (since 1992; re-elected Jun 2001; new government appointed 25 Jun 2002)
Main opposition party
Partito Progressista Democratico Sammarinese (PPDS) (Progressive Democratic Party)

Population
28,900 (2004)

KEY FACTS

Official name: Repubblica di San Marino (The Republic of San Marino)

Head of State: Two Captaini-Reggenti (Captains-Regent), elected for six months at a time Claudio Muccioli (Christian Democrat), and Antonello Bacciocchi (Socialist), installed 1 Oct 2005)

Ruling party: Coalition: Partito Democratico Cristiano Sammarinese (PDCS) (San Marino Christian Democratic Party) and Partito Socialista Sammarinese (PSS) (San Marino Socialist Party) (since 1992; re-elected Jun 2001; new government appointed 25 Jun 2002)

Area: 61 square km

Population: 28,900 (2004)

Capital: San Marino

Official language: Italian

Currency: Euro (eur) = 100 cents

Exchange rate: eur0.83 per US$ (Oct 2005)

GDP per capita: US$34,600 (2003)

GDP real growth: 7.50% (2003)

Labour force: 18,500 (2003)

Unemployment: 2.60% (2003)

Inflation: 3.30% (2003)

Visitor numbers: 3.00 million (2003)*

* estimated figure

Ethnic make-up
The population includes Sammarinese and Italians.
Religions
Roman Catholic

Education
Schooling is free of charge and until aged 16. Primary schooling lasts until aged 11, then on to lower secondary education for three years, from ages 11 to 14, of general education, then the last two years of either technical or specialised academic study. Higher secondary schools, from aged 16 to 19, provide two-year courses in preparation for higher education.
Higher education is provided by the Università degli Studi della Repùbblica di San Marino, and its Istituto di Cibernetica.
Compulsory years: 6 to 15.

Health
The age of the population has risen, reflecting a general trend in Western Europe; those aged over 60 increased from 21.5 per cent of the population in 1991 to 24.3 per cent, in 2001. Total health expenditure, per capita, is around US$2,800 per annum.
Life expectancy: 81.4 years: male 77.9 years; female 85.3 years (2003).
Fertility rate/Maternal mortality rate: 1.3 births per woman (2003)
Birth rate/Death rate: 10.5 births per 1,000 population; eight deaths per 1,000 population (2003).
Infant mortality rate: 4.0 per 1,000 live births (World Bank)
Head of population per physician/bed: 252 doctors per 100,000 (WHO 2003)

Main cities
San Marino (capital, estimated population 4,400 in 2003); Serravalle (8,900); Borgo Maggiore (6,400).

Languages spoken
Italian

Official language/s
Italian

Media
Press
The two dailies published in Italian from San Marino are *Il Quotidiano* and *Corriere di San Marino*. Italian and foreign newspapers are also widely available. These include *La Repubblica*, *La Stampa*, *Il Corriere della Sera*, *L'Unità*, *Il Sole 24 Ore* and *Il Manifesto*.
Broadcasting
Radio: Radio stations include RTV, which is government-controlled, and the private broadcaster Radio Titano. Certain Italian stations can also be received.
Television: The state television channel is called RTV. Channels from Italy can also be received.

Economy
San Marino's economy is closely linked with that of Italy, which surrounds it geographically. The Sammarinese budgetary position has generally been healthier than the Italian one. Enjoying good economic health, thanks to the banking sector, to (mainly Italian) foreign investment and to trade with Italy and some further-flung economies, San Marino registers a year-on-year surplus on its balance of payments.
The economy of San Marino is impressive in its diversity, a characteristic which has contributed to economic stability. The main source of revenue is tourism. The traditional industry of quarrying for building stone is also important. Emphasis is being placed on light manufacturing industries. Sales of postage stamps and coins to collectors provide 10 per cent of the government's income.
San Marino adopted the euro in 2002, which should enhance the republic's economic prospects by reducing costs and risks associated with exchange rates. However, given that the majority of San Marino's trade is conducted with neighbouring Italy, a weak euro does not benefit San Marino as much as other exporting countries.

External trade
There is a customs and currency union with Italy, and a customs union with the EU.
Italy accounts for 87 per cent of all external trade.
Imports
Imports predominantly consist of food and manufactured goods.
Exports
Important exports include building stone, lime, wood, chestnuts, wheat, wine, baked goods, hides and ceramics.

Agriculture
Farming
The republic was formerly dependent on agriculture and forestry. The agricultural sector employs around 1 per cent of the workforce. Approximately 17 per cent of the land is arable. Principal crops include olives, grapes, wheat and corn.

Industry and manufacturing
Quarrying for building stone is a traditional industry.
Manufacturing employs 41 per cent of the workforce, construction 11 per cent, and services, transport and communications 19 per cent.

Tourism
Tourist numbers in 2004 amounted to 2.6 million, down from the 2.8 million in 2003, this was the second year of negative growth. Only in 2002 was growth possitive at 2.2 per cent. Tourism has been depressed by the downturn in the Italian economy, and less Italian visitors arrive.

Banking and insurance
The banking sector is of strategic importance to San Marino's economy, making a sizeable contribution to the state revenue; its banks are profitable, well-provisioned and cost efficient. The Istituto di Credito Sammarinese (ICS) operates as a central bank, although it does not have an independent monetary policy. San Marino is a signatory of a new EU tax agreement with non-EU countries. San Marino will impose a withholding tax, up to 35 per cent, to be passed to the tax department of an EU citizen's country, but retaining the anonymity of the saver.
San Marino has also agreed to supply information on tax fraud, for criminal or civil trials, and notify EU member states about additional malpractices.
Central bank
The Instituto di Credito Sammarinese (ICS); European Central Bank (ECB).

KEY INDICATORS — San Marino

	Unit	2000	2001	2002	2003	2004
Population	m	0.03	0.03	0.03	0.03	0.03
Gross domestic product (GDP)	US$bn	–	–	–	0.88	–
GDP real growth	%	2.2	5.5	0.3	–	*2.0
Inflation	%	2.6	2.8	2.3	2.5	2.1
Unemployment	%	3.0	2.4	3.9	4.5	2.9
Total reserves minus gold	US$m	135.2	133.5	183.4	252.7	355.6
Foreign exchange	US$m	129.6	127.9	177.3	245.9	348.3
Tourist numbers	'000	3,100.0	3,000.0	3,100.0	2,800.0	2,600.0
Exchange rate	per US$	1,972.14	2,115.24	1.04	0.88	0.80

* estimated figure

San Marino

Time
GMT plus one hour (GMT plus two hours from late March to late September).

Geography
San Marino is a landlocked country of 61.2 square kilometres, entirely surrounded by and located in central Italy. The Italian region of Emilia-Romagna borders to the north and east and the Marche to the south and west. The capital, also called San Marino has eight satellite villages. The geography is mountainous dominated by Mount Titano, the highest peak.

Climate
San Marino enjoys a Mediterranean climate with warm summers and dry, cold winters. Temperatures can range between 0–30 degrees Celsius.

Dress codes
Lightweight clothing for summer, medium-weight and topcoat for winter.

Entry requirements
As per Italy

Visa
No visa requirements for citizens of most of Europe, the Americas, Australasia and some Asian countries, visiting for up to 90 days. For a full list, and further information for those citizens not included on the list of visa-free travel, visit www.italyemb.org/Visti.htm. A Schengen visa application (offered in several languages) can be downloaded from www.eurovisa.info/ApplicationForm.htm.

Business travellers who do not have visa-free arrangements must provide a letter from their employer guaranteeing travel expenses, including full itinerary and purpose of the trip. Letters of invitation from all Italian companies to be visited, and a current (not over 90 days) *Visura Camerale* issued by the Italian Chamber of Commerce should be attached; a return/onward ticket must be produced before collection of the passport and visa from the issuing Consular Office; who may request any additional documents at its discretion.

Within eight days of arrival in Italy the visa traveller must appear before local police authorities to receive a 'Residency Permit' and will also need to show proof of health insurance.

Prohibited entry
Visitors may be refused entry for public security or health reasons, or if not holding visible means of support and onward/return tickets and documents for their next destination.

Currency advice/regulations
The import and export of local or foreign currency up to eur10,300 is allowed. Any amount over this must be declared on Form V2 at customs on arrival.

Health (for visitors)
Mandatory precautions
None

Advisable precautions
Up-to-date tetanus and polio immunisations are recommended. Long-term visitors should consider hepatitis 'A' immunisation.

Hotels
There are approximately 30 hotels of various standards.

Credit cards
Credit cards are widely accepted.

Public holidays
Fixed dates
1 Jan (New Year's Day), 6 Jan (Epiphany), 5 Feb (Liberation Day), 25 Mar (Arengo Day), 1 Apr (Investiture of the new Captains Regent), 1 May (Labour Day), 28 Jul (Fall of Fascism Anniversary), 15 Aug (Assumption Day), 3 Sep (Republic Day), 1 Oct (Investiture of the new Captains Regent), 1 Nov (All Saints' Day), 2 Nov (All Souls' Day), 8 Dec (Immaculate Conception), 24–26 Dec (Christmas Holiday), 31 Dec (New Year's Eve).
If a holiday falls on a Sunday, the following Monday will be observed as a public holiday.

Variable dates
Good Friday, Easter Monday, Corpus Christi (May/Jun).

Working hours
Banking
Mon–Fri: 0830–1330, 1530–1630.
Shops
Mon–Sat: 0830–1300, 1530–1930.

Telecommunications
Mobile phones
Networks 900/1800 GSM are in operation.

Electricity supply
220V AC 50Hz

Getting there
Air
Main international airports: Rimini (RMI) (Italy), 27km from San Marino, or Bologna (BLQ) (Italy), 135km from San Marino.

Surface
A regular bus service runs along the highway between Rimini, Italy, and the capital. The nearest railhead is at Rimini.

Getting about
National transport
The roads are good. A funicular (cable car) operates between Borgo Maggiore and the capital.

BUSINESS DIRECTORY

The addresses listed below are a selection only. While World of Information makes every endeavour to check these addresses, we cannot guarantee that changes have not been made, especially to telephone numbers and area codes. We would welcome any corrections.

Telephone area codes
The international direct dialling (IDD) code for San Marino is +378 followed by 0549 and subscriber's number.

Chambers of Commerce
Agency for Promotion and Development of the Economy, 33 Via G Giacomini, 47890 San Marino (tel: 914-001; fax: 913-473; e-mail: info@apse.sm).

Banking
Central bank
Istituto di Credito Sammarinese (ICS), 120 Via del Voltone, 47890 San Marino (tel: 882-325; fax: 882-328; e-mail: icsrel@omniway.sm); European Central Bank (ECB), Kaiserstrasse 29, D-60311 Frankfurt am Main, Germany (tel: +49(69)13-440; fax: +49(69)1344-6000).

Travel information
National tourist organisation offices
Ufficio di Stato per il Turismo (state tourist office), Contrada Omagnano 20, 47031, San Marino (tel: 882-998).

Other useful addresses
Azienda Autonoma di Stato Filatelica e Numismatica (AASFN) (stamps and coins), 5 Piazza Garibaldi, 47031 San Marino (tel: 882-370; fax: 882-363; e-mail: aasfn@omniway.sm).

British Consulate, 2 Lungarno Corsini, 1-50123 Florence (tel: 212-594; fax: 219-112).

Direzione Generale PPTT (post and telecommunications),17 Contrada Omerelli (tel: 882-555; fax: 992-760).

Notizie de San Marino, Radiotelevisione Italiana, 14 Viale Mazzini, 1-00195 Rome (fax: 372-5680).

Office for Industry, Handicrafts and Trade, Palazzo Mercuri (tel: 992-745, 991-385).

Secretariat of State for Finance and the Budget, Palazzo Begni (tel: 992-345).

Internet sites
Web portal for trade: http://www.tradecenter.sm/index_e.htm

São Tomé and Príncipe

KEY FACTS

Official name: República Democrática de São Tomé e Príncipe (Democratic Republic of São Tomé and Príncipe)

Head of State: President Fradique Banderia Melo de Menezes (ADI) (inaugurated 3 Sep 2001)

Head of government: Prime Minister Maria do Carmo Silveira (from 8 Jun 2005)

Ruling party: Coalition government led by the Movimiento de Libertaçao de São Tomé e Príncipe (MLSTP) (Movement for the Liberation of São Tomé and Príncipe), including Movimento Democrático das Forças da Mudança (MDFM) (Forces of Change Democratic Movement) and Acção Democrática Independente (ADI) (Independent Democratic Action)

Area: 964 square km

Population: 162,000 (2004)

Capital: São Tomé

Official language: Portuguese

Currency: Dobra (Db) = 100 centavos

Exchange rate: Db7,755.00 per US$ (Oct 2005)

GDP per capita: US$402 (2004)

GDP real growth: 6.00% (2004)

Unemployment: 50.00% (2003)*

Inflation: 12.80% (2004)

Balance of trade: -US$34.30 million 2004

Foreign debt: US$253.80 million (2003)

* estimated figure

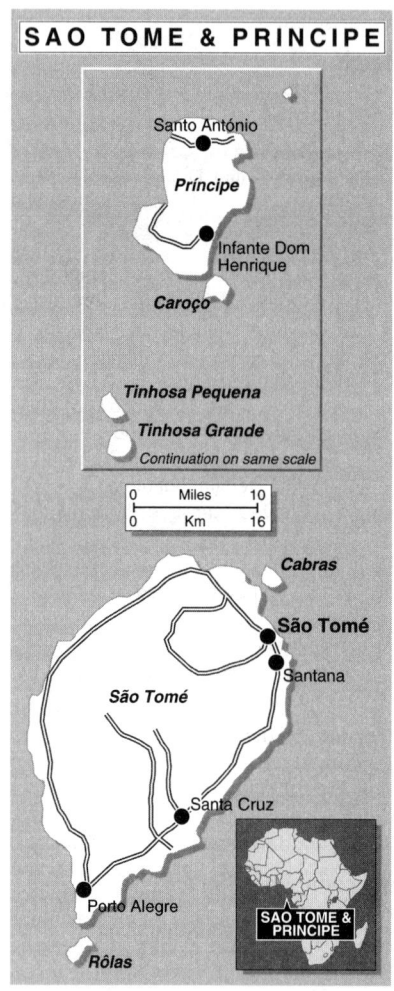

After a previous Poverty Reduction and Growth Facility (PRGF) fell off the rails, and subsequent unwillingness on the International Monetary Fund (IMF)'s part to re-engage during a time of a 'difficult political environment', the IMF in August 2005, approved a three year SDR2.96 million (US$4.3 million) programme for São Tomé and Príncipe. There is a limit to disbursements before 31 July 2006 of SDR1.269 million (US$1.9 million). The country benefited from US$200 million in debt relief in December 2000 under the Highly Indebted Poor Countries (HIPC) programme, and is expected to benefit from an additional round of relief in early 2006, which will help bring down the country's (at end 2005) US$370 million estimated debt.

The medium-term programme for 2005–07 has an ambitious reform agenda. The attainment of its objectives would bolster efforts to address the country's macroeconomic imbalances, while substantially reducing poverty. The timely execution of a broad range of institutional and structural reforms supported by technical and financial support from development partners, would mobilise concessional financing from donors, and strengthen policy credibility.

Oil to the rescue

São Tomé and Príncipe is trying to shake off its dependence on agriculture, primarily the export of cocoa. Falls in production and prices have left the island state heavily reliant on foreign aid. The government has been searching for a new economic backbone and in 2004, found it. São Tomé is optimistic about the development of petroleum resources in its territorial waters in the oil-rich Gulf of Guinea that are being jointly developed in a 60–40 split with Nigeria. The first production licences were sold in 2004, though a dispute over licensing with Nigeria delayed São Tomé's receipt of more than US$20 million in signing bonuses for almost a year. Oil production is expected to start no earlier than 2012.

Tourism too?

There is also potential for a more developed tourist industry. Promoters say the islands have plenty for visitors to see, but hurdles include ignorance about the country and the difficulties of getting there. Exports of tourism and cocoa are equivalent to a third of GDP of US$60 million. Since 1998, there has been no investment in hotel infrastructure.

Fiscal consolidation, which will require reining in expectations fueled by the prospect of oil riches, while protecting pro-poor spending, remains an essential element of macroeconomic stabilisation. The continuous large increases in the civil service wage bill are a matter of concern.

São Tomé and Príncipe

Managing the oil revenue

An Oil Revenue Management Law is to allow for a comprehensive structural reform programme in the areas of agriculture, basic education and health services, public expenditure management, and the privatisation of state enterprises.

The mindful management of oil resources is at the center of the citizens' concerns considering the possibilities that could emerge for the improvement of their lives. It is not known with certainty the potential of the existing hydro-carbonates and of their commercial viability, but first the marine borders with neighbouring countries Gabon and Equatorial Guinea have to be delimitated.

Politics

A wealthy cocoa exporter, President Fradique de Menezes was elected in July 2001 with 65 per cent of the vote. A week-long military coup in July 2003 toppled his government, while he was on a private visit to Nigeria. De Menezes returned to São Tomé after an agreement to restore democratic rule was reached with the coup leaders.

He wants revenues expected to be generated from new offshore oil fields to be used to improve public services. He is keen to reduce São Tomé's isolation and favours stronger ties with West Africa.

De Menezes is the country's third president, after Miguel Trovoada, who served two five-year terms, the maximum permitted by the constitution (1990–2001) and Pinto da Costa (1975–91).

Risk assessment

Economic	Improving
Political	Good
Regional stability	Excellent

COUNTRY PROFILE

Historical profile

Sao Tomé and Príncipe became independent in July 1975, ending five centuries of Portuguese colonial rule. At the helm of the first independent government was the Movimiento da Liberacao do Sao Tomé e Príncipe (MLSTP) (Movement for the Liberation of Sao Tomé and Príncipe) and its Secretary General Dr Manuel Pinto da Costa, the country's first president.
Self- rule had not been an automatic consequence of the April 1974 coup d'état in Portugal. The new Portuguese government's first inclination was to keep the archipelago, along with Portugal's other colonies, in a confederation of Lusitanian states. The MLSTP's exiled leaders, head-quartered in Gabon, had established a perfectly legal Civic Association on the islands to organise the mobilisation of the population and to force Lisbon's hand. It was only after a wave of strikes and demonstrations that Portugal's military rulers finally agreed to negotiate with the MLSTP and, in November 1974, to sign an agreement (the Algiers Accords) promising the country independence the following July.
The MLSTP had been a heterogeneous movement, containing a wide spectrum of political views within its ranks. Its exiled leaders were generally conservative in outlook, for some years based in Gabon under the protection of its pro-Western (these were the times of the Cold War, which was also waged in Africa) President Omar Bongo. But a new breed of young militants had emerged within the ranks of the Civic Association during the unrest of 1974. Both sides were accommodated in the composition of the transitional government set up to run the country in the run-up to independence. Not surprisingly, the government was split from the day of its formation, a political tradition that has sadly endured.
1469–72 The islands were first sighted by Portuguese sailors.
1485 The town of São Tomé was founded; Príncipe was not settled until 15 years later. The islands quickly became the largest sugar producing area in the world and used slave labour.
1700–1800 Coffee and cocoa plantations were also set up using slave labour.
1875 Slavery was abolished, only to be replaced by a system of forced labour. The labour force consisted mainly of workers brought by the Portuguese from Angola, Mozambique and Cape Verde. On several occasions they launched rebellions against their colonial rulers which were brutally suppressed.
1951 The islands became an overseas province of Portugal.
1974 The end of fascist rule in Portugal marked the beginning of independence for its overseas colonies. A transitional government was established.
1975 The Democratic Republic of São Tomé and Príncipe gained independence from Portugal. Manuel Pinto da Costa, the leader of the Movimiento de Libertação de São Tomé e Príncipe (MLSTP) (Movement for the Liberation of São Tomé), made a clean sweep in the general elections and became the first president and the Marxist MLSTP was the only legal party allowed. The economy was hard-hit when Portugal withdrew support, then when most plantations were quickly nationalised foreign investors and workers left; the islands developed strong links with Cuba.
Under colonial administration there had been little investment in education or healthcare systems for the local population; at independence the literacy rate was 10 per cent and there was only one doctor in the entire country.
1980s A severe drought and a drop in world prices for cocoa crippled the economy. Pinto da Costa began a process of releasing economic ties with the Eastern Bloc in favour of a capitalist, market economy.
1989 Changes within MLSTP began; multi-party democracy was introduce as an objective.
1990 The MLSTP changed its name and adopted MLSTP-PSD (Social Democratic Party) to fight the next election. A multi-party constitution was approved by

KEY INDICATORS — São Tomé and Príncipe

	Unit	2000	2001	2002	2003	2004
Population	m	0.15	0.16	0.16	0.16	0.16
Gross domestic product (GDP)	US$bn	0.05	0.05	0.05	0.05	*0.06
GDP per capita	US$	350	313	306	300	402
GDP real growth	%	3.0	4.0	5.0	5.0	6.0
Inflation	%	11.0	9.8	9.2	9.0	12.8
Exports (fob) (goods)	US$m	4.0	5.0	5.1	5.5	6.7
Imports (fob) (goods)	US$m	29.0	23.0	28.0	24.8	41.0
Balance of trade	US$m	-25.0	-18.0	-22.9	-19.3	-34.3
Current account	US$m	-10.0	-10.0	-10.0	-10.0	-20.0
Foreign debt	US$bn	0.3	0.3	0.4	0.3	–
Total reserves minus gold	US$m	11.6	15.5	17.4	25.5	19.8
Foreign exchange	US$m	11.6	15.5	17.3	25.4	19.8
Exchange rate	per US$	7,978.20	8,842.10	9,088.30	8,859.85	9,900.40

* estimated figure

referendum, allowing direct and free elections for the presidency and legislature.
1991 The ruling MLSTP-PSD lost the country's first election, defeated by the Partido da Convergencia Democrática-Grupo de Reflexão (PCD-GR) (Democratic Convergence Party-Reflection Group). Miguel Trovoada, an independent candidate supported by the PDC-GR, was elected president. The currency was devalued by 40 per cent as part of stringent austerity measures, imposed by the IMF and the World Bank in exchange for economic assistance.
1994 The MLSTP-PSD won most seats, but fell short of an overall majority, in the National Assembly.
1995 In April, Príncipe was granted autonomy; the MLSTP-PSD won most seats in its assembly.
Continuous strikes by public employees for promised pay rises destabilised the president and government. An abortive coup resulted in the formation of a coalition government which included members of the Ação Democrática Independente (ADI) (Independent Democratic Action), the Coligação Democrático da Oposição (CDO) (Democratic Opposition Coalition) and the Frente Democrática Crista (FDC) (Christian Democratic Front).
1996 Trovoada was re-elected president. Prime Minister Armindo Vaz d'Almeida was removed from office his position was taken by Raw Wagner da Conceiçao Bragança Neto (MLSTP-PSD).
1998 Election to the National Assembly resulted in a victory for the centre-left MLSTP-PSD.
2001 Fradique de Menezes won the presidential election.
2002 National Assembly elections were misread until the Supreme Court ruled that the MLSTP had won 24 of the 55 seats. After Gabriel Costa dismissed, Maria das Neves was appointed as the country's first female prime minister.
2003 The constitution was revised in January. On 16 July, a military coup staged by Major Fernando Pereira toppled the government while President Menezes was out of the country. President Menezes signed an accord with the coup leaders, which restored democratic rule and included an amnesty for the insurgents. On 1 August, Prime Minister das Neves resigned but was reappointed several days later. In October, bidding began for offshore oil blocs controlled by São Tomé and Príncipe and Nigeria.
2004 In March, the president and prime minister clashed over control of oil deals. Maria das Neves was dismissed as prime minister on 15 September, after a series of corruption scandals. Damião Vaz d'Almeida became prime minister.
2005 Maria do Carmo Silveira was nominated prime minister after Damião Vaz d'Almeida's resignation on 2 June; her government was approved on 8 June.

Political structure
Constitution
The 5 November 1975 constitution was revised in September 1990, following a national referendum, which approved a multi-party constitution, allowing direct and free elections for the presidency and legislature. The constitution was revised again in January 2003.
The island of Príncipe was granted political and administrative autonomy in April 1995.
Form of state
Sovereign, unitary and democratic state.
The executive
The president is elected for a maximum of two five-year terms of office.
National legislature
Legislative power is vested in the Assembleia Popular Nacional (National People's Assembly), which has 55 members serving a four-year term and holds two sessions a year. The members are elected by party list vote from 12 multi-seat constituencies.
There are six district assemblies on Sao Tomé.
The island of Príncipe has a seven-member Regional Assembly.
Legal system
Portuguese legal system. The Supreme Court is appointed by the National Assembly.
Last elections
3 March 2002 (parliamentary); July 2001 (presidential).
Results: Parliamentary: the Movimiento de Libertaçao de São Tomé e Príncipe (MLSTP) (Movement for the Liberation of São Tomé and Príncipe) and the Movimento Democrático das Forças para a Mudança-Partido de Convergência Democrática (MDFM-PCD) (Democratic Movement of Forces for Change-Party of Democratic Convergence) of President Fradique de Menezes, 23 seats each; Uê Kédadji (UK) won nine seats. After a re-run, the Supreme Court ruled that the MLSTP had won an extra seat.
Presidential: Fradique De Menezes was elected.
Next elections
2006 (parliamentary and presidential)

Political parties
Ruling party
Coalition government led by the Movimiento de Libertaçao de São Tomé e Príncipe (MLSTP) (Movement for the Liberation of São Tomé and Príncipe), including Movimento Democrático das Forças da Mudança (MDFM) (Forces of Change Democratic Movement) and Acção Democrática Independente (ADI) (Independent Democratic Action)

Population
162,000 (2004)
Ethnic make-up
There are five groups among the islands' inhabitants: the Filhos da Terra are the descendants of imported slaves and Europeans (mostly Portuguese); the Angolares are descendants of former castaway slaves from Angola, now primarily fishermen; the Forros are descendants of slaves freed when slavery was abolished in 1875; the Servicais are migrant labourers from Angola, Mozambique and Cape Verde, and the Tongas are their children, born on the islands.
Religions
Eighty per cent of the population are Roman Catholic, Evangelical Protestant or Seventh-Day Adventist.

Education
The literacy rate for the period 1995–2001 was estimated at 63 per cent.

Health
Total government expenditure on health was 2.3 per cent of GDP in 2000.
Life expectancy: 66 years (World Bank)
Fertility rate/Maternal mortality rate: 4.3 births per woman (World Bank)
Birth rate/Death rate: 42 births per 1,000 population; seven deaths per 1,000 population (2003).
Infant mortality rate: 75 per 1,000 live births (World Bank)
Head of population per physician/bed: 46.7 doctors per 100,000 people (WHO 2003).

Main cities
São Tomé (capital, estimated population 52,300 in 2002) Trinidad (14,200), Santo Amaro (7,200).

Languages spoken
Portuguese is spoken by 95 per cent of the population; Lungwa Santomé is the main national dialect and Fôrro and Crioulo are also spoken.
Official language/s
Portuguese

Media
Press
There are two weekly newspapers, *Revolução* (official organ of Ministry of Information) and *Diário da República*. The weekend newspaper and magazine available is *Povo*. The sole independent newpaper is *O Parvo*.
Broadcasting
Radio: Approximately 25,000 receivers in use. Home service broadcast in Portuguese by Radio Nacional de São Tomé e Príncipe.

São Tomé and Príncipe

Television: The state-run television service is Televisao Saotomense (TVS).

Economy

São Tomé and Príncipe, which has one of the lowest per capita incomes and one of the highest debt ratios in the world, is primarily dependent on foreign aid and cocoa exports. The economy has suffered from dependence on cocoa, the country's principal commodity export, which is susceptible to fluctuations in world prices and other factors.

Construction activity related to the development of the oil, shipping and tourism sectors and a rise in cocoa prices have boosted GDP growth from 2001. The country experienced a positive turnaround in 2000 and growth rates rose from 4 per cent in 2002, 5 per cent in 2003 and to 6.0 per cent in 2004.

In the 1990s, São Tomé and Príncipe experienced high levels of inflation, reaching 81 per cent in 1997. Under the IMF staff-monitored programme (SMP), inflation is targetted to fall to 7 per cent. By the end of 2003 inflation had dropped to 9 per cent, but it risen again to 12.8 per cent by 2004.

The net value of total outstanding external debt has fallen in recent years, largely due to the efforts made at debt reduction under the IMF and World Bank's enhanced Heavily Indebted Poor Countries (HIPC) initiative. Debt relief under HIPC is projected at 9 per cent of GDP between 2001–07. The IMF projects that debt service as a percentage of government revenue will be reduced to an average of 12 per cent during 1999–2009 from 44 per cent in 1999.

The discovery of oil reserves in the Gulf of Guinea offers the prospect of future growth and prosperity. Development of the oil sector in the region of the islands is being undertaken in conjunction with Nigeria. Exploration commenced in 2005. If successful, it will be several years before production and export of oil starts. There are already some benefits as construction and other activities increase to cater to the industry.

External trade

On 31 December 2002, the US approved São Tomé and Príncipe as being eligible for tariff preferences under the Africa Growth and Opportunities Act (AGOA). The legislation requires that countries are only eligible for greater access to US markets provided they have made continued progress toward a market-based economy, the rule of law, free trade, poverty reduction and the protection of workers' rights. This process is reviewed annually.

Imports

Principal imports are machinery and electrical equipment, food products and petroleum products.

Main sources: Portugal (50.5 per cent total, 2004), Germany (10.0 per cent), US (5.1 per cent), The Netherlands (4.5 per cent), South Africa (4.2 per cent)

Exports

Principal exports are cocoa (80 per cent), copra, coffee, palm oil.

Main destinations: The Netherlands (39.1 per cent total, 2004), China (11.8 per cent), Germany (8.6 per cent), Belgium (6.9 per cent), Philippines (6.7 per cent), France (4.5 per cent)

Agriculture

Farming

Plantation agriculture forms the basis of the economy, but growth is slowing. It accounted for 17 per cent of GDP in 2004, which represents a decline in the sector's contribution. Cocoa is the main crop, accounting for around 90 per cent of exports. Cocoa production, once the biggest in the world, has fallen over the years and now totals about 4,000 tonnes a year.

The plantations were nationalised after independence to their detriment, but have since been privatised.

The second-largest export crop is coffee; other cash crops are copra, palm kernels, cinnamon, pepper and breadfruit. Priority is being given to the diversification of food crops in an effort to reduce the large food import bill.

The estimated crop production for 2004 included: 2,500 tonnes (t) maize, 5,800t cassava, 28,000t taro, 1,500t yams, 27,900t bananas, 37,500t roots and tubers, 28,500t coconuts, 40,000t oil palm fruit, 7,775t oilcrops, 3,500t cocoa beans, 30t cinnamon, 30,800t fruit in total, 6,500t vegetables in total. Estimated livestock production included: 875t meat in total, 1223t beef, 92t pig meat, 25t lamb and goat meat, 636t poultry, 385t eggs, 145t milk, 21t cattle hides.

Fishing

Fishing remains small-scale, but is being encouraged for local consumption and possible future export.

Industry and manufacturing

The industrial sector is limited to small-scale manufacturing concerns such as soap, soft drinks, timber processing, palm oil, bricks and textiles. The development of oil fields in the Gulf of Guinea is likely to increase industrial activity associated with the sector, particularly construction. In 2002, the government announced it was developing a number of export processing zones (EPZs) in order to exploit the country's position as a regional trading platform. These will give incentives to investors, with tax breaks and free movement of goods.

Tourism

Tourism is under-developed. It has tended towards the luxury market, catering mainly to Portuguese and French visitors. The sector has potential and infrastructure is being expanded. Tourism is expected to contribute 14.4 per cent to GDP in 2005.

Mining

São Tomé and Príncipe has no mineral resources.

Hydrocarbons

São Tomé and Príncipe is dependent on imported refined oil products. Oil-derived products supply 96 per cent of commercial energy requirements. Distribution and marketing of fuels is carried out by the state-owned oil company, Empresa Nacional de Combustiveis e Oleos (Enco).

São Tomé and Príncipe has established with Nigeria a joint authority to manage offshore oil exploration in the oil-rich Gulf of Guinea. Under the accord, Nigeria will receive 60 per cent of revenues and São Tomé and Príncipe 40 per cent. Several blocks in the joint development zone were awarded in 2004 and 2005. The first exploration and production contract was signed in February 2005. Preliminary indications suggest that there may be substantial commercial reserves of oil in the area. If confirmed, production is expected to commence some time after 2010.

São Tomé and Príncipe does not produce or import gas or coal.

Energy

Installed electricity generating capacity is around 9MW. Blackouts are frequent.

Banking and insurance

Main financial centre
São Tomé.

Time

GMT.

Geography

São Tomé and Príncipe lies in the Gulf of Guinea, off the west coast of Africa. There are two main islands, São Tomé and Príncipe, and the country also includes the rocky islets of Caroço, Pedras and Tinhosas, off Príncipe, and Rôlas, off São Tomé.

Climate

Equatorial with high temperatures and humidity. Average temperatures remain fairly constant throughout the year with a daily range from 20–32 degrees Celsius (C). Driest month July, wettest March.

Entry requirements

Passports
Required by all.

Visa
Required by all and apply for well in advance.
European visitors should contact the São Tomé e Príncipe embassy consulate in Brussels; US visitors should contact the consulate in either New York or Atlanta; visitors from Canada and Australia should contact the Canadian embassy in Libreville in Gabon (See: Other useful addresses, for further information).

Currency advice/regulations
There are no restrictions on the import of currency. Export is allowed up to the amount declared on entry.

Health (for visitors)
Mandatory precautions
Yellow fever vaccination certificate is required by all.

Advisable precautions
Yellow fever, typhoid, tetanus, hepatitis A and polio vaccinations. Malaria prophylaxis should be taken. Water precautions are recommended. There is a rabies risk.

Hotels
There is a limited number of reasonable hotels.

Public holidays
Fixed dates
1 Jan (New Year's Day), 3 Feb (Heroes' Day), 1 May (Labour Day), 12 Jul (Independence Day), 6 Sep (Armed Forces Day), 30 Sep (Agricultural Reform Day), 26 Nov (Argel Accord Day), 21 Dec (São Tomé Day, Catholic), 25 Dec (Christmas Day).

Variable dates
Ash Wednesday, Good Friday.

Working hours
Banking
Mon–Fri: 0730–1130, 1430–1630.
Business
Mon–Fri: 0730–1200, 1430–1800.
Government
Mon–Fri: 0800–1200, 1500–1800; Sat: 0800–1300.
Shops
Mon–Sat: 0800–1200, 1500–1900.

Telecommunications
Unwittingly São Tomé, with its suffix .st, provides over 75 per cent of all porn pages located on African websites, after a Swedish and local company (granted management by the US Internet Assigned Numbers Authority) sold the government rights without approval while handing this small nation an image problem. As the government cannot rescind contracts it is demanding a share of the income generated, which when domain names can command large fees from users, and .st 'the street domain' charges an annual US$46 could provide a welcome bonus to the São Tomé national coffers.

Telephone/fax
Local telephone telegraph service described as good but international facilities are poor. Forty-five per cent automatic service.

Electricity supply
220V AC

Weights and measures
Metric

Social customs/useful tips
Business is conducted in Portuguese. Many executives speak French, and some speak English.

Getting there
Air
A new airline service, by TAAG of Angola, flies weekly from Cape Verde.
International airport/s: São Tomé (TMS), 5.5km from town.
Airport tax: Adult international departures US$20.
Surface
Main port/s: São Tomé (not deep water).

Getting about
National transport
Air: Restricted services link the two islands. Travellers should book their seats well in advance, to avoid being stranded.
Road: There are only about 300km of roads, of which about two-thirds are asphalted, but the network is being improved.
Buses: Frequent, efficient service on São Tomé. Limited bus service on Príncipe.
City transport
Taxis: On São Tomé a minivan or collectivo shared taxi can be taken to anywhere on the island. There are no fixed schedules and they leave only when they are full; this is no other public transport available.

BUSINESS DIRECTORY
The addresses listed below are a selection only. While World of Information makes every endeavour to check these addresses, we cannot guarantee that changes have not been made, especially to telephone numbers and area codes. We would welcome any corrections.

Telephone area codes
The international dialling code (IDD) for São Tomé and Príncipe is +239, followed by subscriber's number.

Chambers of Commerce
Camara de Comircio, Industria, Agricultura e Servicios, Avenida Marginal 12 de Julho, PO Box 527, Saõ Tomé (tel: 122-2723; fax: 122-1409; e-mail: ccias@cstome.net).

Banking
Banco Comercial do Equador, CP 361, Rua de Moçambique, São Tomé (tel: 21-898; fax: 21-989).

Banco Internacional de S Tomé e Príncipe, CP 536, Praça da Independência 3, São Tomé (tel: 22-991; fax: 22-427, 23-462).

Central bank
Banco Central de São Tomé e Príncipe, CP 13, Praça da Independencia, São Tomé (tel: 21-966, 21-300; fax: 22-501, 22-777).

Travel information
TAP–Air Portugal, Rua Patrice Lumumba, near Praça Indepêndencia (tel: 22-307, 21-432).

National tourist organisation offices
Tourism Office, CP40, Avenue Marginal, 12 de Julho, São Tomé (tel: 221-542).

Other useful addresses
Canadian embassy, PO Box 4037 Libreville, Gabon (tel: (+241) 737-354; fax: 737-388; email: ibrve@dfait-maeci.gc.ca).

Nigeria-São Tomé and Príncipe Joint Development Authority, Plot 1101 Aminu Kano Crescent, Wuse II, Abuja, Nigeria (tel: (+234-9) 524-1069; fax: (234-9) 524-1052; e-mail: enquiries@nigeriasaotomejda.com; internet: http://www.nigeriasaotomejda.com).

São Tomé and Príncipe Embassy (USA), 7th Floor, 400 Park Avenue, New York 10044 (tel: (+1-212) 317-0533; fax 317-0580; email: stp1@attglobal.net).

São Tomé and Príncipe Consulate (USA), Suite 305, 512 Means Street, Atlanta GA 30318, USA (tel: (+1-404) 221-0203; fax: 221-1006; e-mail: consul@saotome.org).

São Tomé and Príncipe Embassy, Square Montgomery, 175 Avenue de Tervuren, 1150 Brussels, Belgium (tel: (+32) 734-9966; fax: 734-8815).

STP-Press, c/o Rádio Nacional de São Tomé e Príncipe, Avenida Marginal de 12 de Julho, CP 44, São Tomé (tel: 22-217).

Internet sites
AllAfrica information:
http://allafrica.com/saotomeandprincipe/

National Assembly (in Portuguese):
http://212.54.130.162/

São Toméand Príncipe tourist site:
http://www.saotome.st/

São Tomé and Príncipe website:
http://www.sao-tome.com

Saudi Arabia

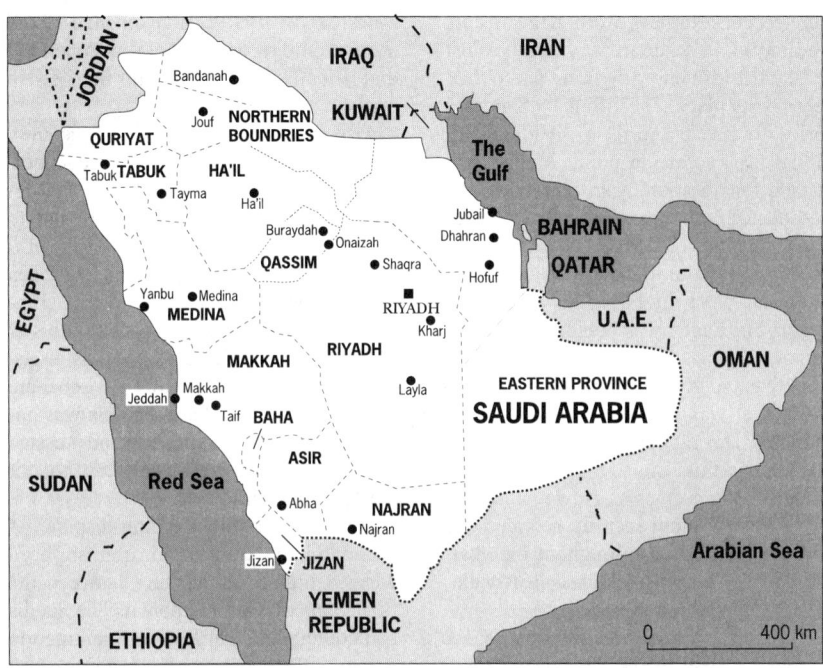

Saudi Arabia entered into a new era in 2005, with the passing on of its long-reigning King, Fahd bin Abdul Aziz al Sa'ud. Crown Prince Abdullah bin Abdul Aziz al Sa'ud, the late King's half-brother, succeeded him. Saudi Arabia also held its first, by Saudi standards, democratic elections in 2005. Unfortunately for Saudi Arabia, anti-government and anti-Western Islamist militants continued to launch attacks across the country.

Oil surge

According to the IMF, Saudi Arabia experienced a 34 per cent jump in oil revenues in 2005, as the price of oil reached record levels. The government channelled some of this wealth into reducing its debt burden to 45.5 per cent of GDP. Public sector employees were also granted a 15 per cent pay rise. The current account surplus expanded to 30 per cent of GDP. The IMF also praised the government for its investment in the non-oil sector. Also in June, BP signed a US$2 billion deal with the Saudis to develop the country's petrochemical industry.

In November, Saudi Arabia was accepted as a member of the WTO.

The death of King Fahd

On 1 August 2005, King Fahd passed away. He had been Saudi Arabia's monarch since 1982, although since suffering a stroke in 1995 his half-brother Crown Prince Abdullah had run the day-to-day affairs of the kingdom. The King had been hospitalised in May and had not been expected to recover. As King, Fahd had been a key backer of anti-Soviet forces in Afghanistan and later extended his support to the Taleban – Saudi Arabia was one of only three countries ever to recognise the Taleban government. Fahd also invested heavily in Pakistan, particularly in its *madrasas* (religious schools). The late King is also remembered for allowing the stationing of US troops on Saudi soil, from the time of the Iraqi invasion of Kuwait.

The new King, Abdullah, is Fahd's 81-year old half-brother. Having been crown prince since 1982 and having effectively ruled the kingdom since 1995, Abdullah was the natural successor. Upon ascending to the throne on 3 August, King Abdullah pledged to rule in the name of justice. Abdullah's half-brother and full

KEY FACTS

Official name: Mamlaka al Arabiya as Sa'udiya (The Kingdom of Saudi Arabia)

Head of State: The Custodian of the Two Holy Mosques, King Abdullah bin Abdul Aziz al Sa'ud (from 1 Aug 2005)

Head of government: King Abdullah bin Abdul Aziz al Sa'ud (from 1 Aug 2005)

Ruling party: No political parties – absolute monarchy.

Area: 2,149,690 square km (approximately)

Population: 23.34 million (2004)

Capital: Riyadh

Official language: Arabic

Currency: Saudi riyal (SR) = 100 halalas

Exchange rate: SR3.75 per US$ (fixed)

GDP per capita: US$9,972 (2004)

GDP real growth: 5.30% (2004)

Labour force: 7.17 million (2004)

Unemployment: 25.00% (unofficial, 2004)

Inflation: 0.20% (2004)

Oil production: 10.58 million bpd (2004)

Balance of trade: US$85.22 billion (2004)

Foreign debt: US$25.90 billion (2003)

brother to Fahd, Sultan bin Abdul Aziz was named Crown Prince.

Democracy, of sorts

Saudi Arabia began to flirt with democracy in 2005, the first such experience in the history of the kingdom. In January, the government announced plans to expand the Majlis al Shura (Consultative Council), a consultative body appointed by the King. The government also stated that it would increase the powers of the Majlis, which at present can challenge but not propose or amend legislation.

The democratic experiment gathered pace February–April, when Saudi men over the age of 21 were allowed to vote in elections for newly formed local councils. Conservative Islamist candidates won in the Riyadh area and candidates identifying themselves as political and religious moderates won the most seats in councils in Jeddah, Mecca and Medina. Turnout was particularly high in Ash Sharqiyah (Eastern Province), home to most of Saudi Arabia's traditionally oppressed Shi'a population. Council members will only be allowed to advise on local affairs. The councils were formally constituted in December 2005.

In November, Saudi women were allowed to vote and stand in elections for the first time. The election was to the Jeddah Chamber of Commerce and Industry. Two women won seats.

Saudi militancy

Since May 2003, more than 200 people, both Saudis and foreigners, have been killed in Saudi Arabia in attacks by Islamist militants identifying themselves as al Qaeda followers. There was no respite for the Saudi government in 2005. The extent of the violence was underscored in August, when King Abdullah pledged to crush al Qaeda. Saudi Arabia was, for all intents and purposes, fighting an insurgency. Some of the insurgents were recent returnees from Afghanistan, Chechnya and other areas where Islamist or Islamist-influenced fighting was or had been taking place. The killing by Saudi security forces in April, of Abdullah al Mejjati was a case in point. Mejjati was wanted for questioning in relation to the Casablanca bombing of 2003 and the Madrid bombing of 2004. The incoming Saudi ambassador to the US, Prince Turki al Faisal, went so far as to assert that Osama bin Laden was behind the attacks in Saudi Arabia.

In June, the government published a list of 36 most-wanted men, linked to the insurgency. During the course of 2005, several men on this list were killed, captured or handed themselves in. However, shoot-outs between Saudi security services and militants carried on throughout the year. Most of the clashes occurred in Riyadh, Jeddah and Qassim province.

Regional diplomacy

As one of the largest and wealthiest states in the Middle East, Saudi Arabia was an active player in the region in 2005. Its key foreign policy interests were the Israel-Palestinian conflict and the emergence of a Shi'a-dominated government in Iraq.

In March, Saudi Arabia again pushed its peace plan for the Israel-Palestinian conflict, first mooted by then Crown Prince Abdullah in 2002. The plan proposes accepting the 1967 cease-fire line between Israel and its Arab neighbours as the basis of a future Palestinian state (approximately 22 per cent of the area of the original British mandate established in Palestine in 1919). In exchange, Arab states would recognise Israel and open full and friendly relations with the Jewish State.

Also in March, Saudi Arabia reluctantly withdrew its hitherto relatively unconditional support for Syria. Syria had requested Saudi backing in its attempt to face down international calls for its withdrawal from Lebanon, which had been precipitated by the assassination in February of former Lebanese prime minister Rafik Hariri. Instead, the Saudis urged Syria to pull its troops out of Lebanon. This suggested that Saudi Arabia was unwilling to go against US, EU and Russian demands for withdrawal, at least not for the sake of Syria.

In October, a long-running dispute between Saudi Arabia and Iran surfaced when a high-level meeting between the two countries was postponed. The Saudis had complained that Iran was gaining too much influence in neighbouring Iraq through its connections with the new Shi'a-dominated government. Saudi Arabia has harboured suspicions against its own Shi'a population and fears any extension of Shi'a influence in the region and in particular the emergence of a new Shi'a-run state on its northern borders. Shi'a are estimated to make up between 5 and 8 per cent of Saudi Arabia's population – around one million people, mainly in the Ash Sharqiyah province.

Another tragedy at the Haj

It was another tragic year for many Muslim pilgrims visiting the holy sites of Mekkah and Medina, in Saudi Arabia's west, to perform a Haj (pilgrimage). More than 350 people were killed during a stampede in Mekkah and scores more were killed when a hotel housing pilgrims collapsed. Thousands have been killed in recent decades during the Haj, mainly due to inadequate safety standards and lack of adequate facilities.

Outlook

Although many key militants were killed, captured or handed themselves in in 2005, Saudi Arabia will almost certainly experience more attacks.

KEY INDICATORS — Saudi Arabia

	Unit	2000	2001	2002	2003	2004
Population	m	20.35	21.40	21.98	22.66	*23.34
Gross domestic product (GDP)	US$bn	173.30	186.50	188.70	214.70	*250.56
GDP per capita	US$	8,469	8,881	8,584	8,879	9,972
GDP real growth	%	4.5	1.8	2.1	2.9	5.3
Inflation	%	-0.9	-0.4	-0.4	0.7	0.2
Oil output	'000 bpd	9,115.0	8,768.0	8,680.0	9,817.0	10,584.0
Natural gas output	bn cum	47.0	53.7	56.4	61.0	64.0
Exports (fob) (goods)	US$m	77,584.0	73,032.0	67,270.0	84,076.0	126,063.0
Imports (fob) (goods)	US$m	27,741.0	28,645.0	30,950.0	33,928.0	40,841.0
Balance of trade	US$m	49,843.0	44,387.0	38,700.0	50,148.0	85,222.0
Current account	US$m	14,336.0	14,502.0	11,680.0	29,702.0	49,280.0
Total reserves minus gold	US$m	19,585.0	17,596.0	20,610.0	22,620.0	27,291.0
Foreign exchange	US$m	18,036.0	14,796.0	16,715.0	17,662.0	23,273.0
Exchange rate	per US$	3.75	3.75	3.75	3.75	3.75

* estimated figure

The new King, Abdullah, is widely regarded, both inside the country and outside, as an experienced operator. He will no doubt continue to prosecute the war against al Qaeda in his country and continue implementing the gradual democratic reforms that he has championed for so long. His release of three leading dissidents in August 2005 bodes well, although the limits of Abdullah's tolerance for calls for reform from outside the government should not be overestimated. Although Abdullah is regarded as being in good health, he turns 82 in 2006. Abdullah's heir apparent, Prince Sultan is also in his 80s, is in relatively poor health and has in the past criticised the democratic reform process.

With oil prices likely to remain high for at least part of 2006, Saudi Arabia can expect further massive increases in oil export-derived profits.

Risk assessment

Politics	Stable
Economy	Booming
Regional stability	Fragile

COUNTRY PROFILE

Historical profile
The Arabian peninsula, including modern-day Saudi Arabia, became part of the Turkish Ottoman empire in the sixteenth century. Although under the overall rule of the Ottoman Sultan, local leaders developed varying degrees of autonomy.
The espousal of a strict interpretation of Sunni Islam, known as Wahhabism, by the al Sa'ud ruling family led the country to develop a strongly religious self-identity. Al Sa'ud dynasty's monopoly of power meant that during the twentieth century, successive kings were able to concentrate on modernisation and developing the country's role as a regional power, and due to its vast oil resources, Saudi Arabia has become one of the wealthiest nations in the Middle East. The ruling family has tried to preserve stability by clamping down on extremist elements, but it is possible that its refusal to tolerate any kind of opposition may have encouraged the growth of various terrorist groups, including Osama bin Laden's al Qaeda, supported by those who resent the US's role in the Middle East.
1871 The Ottomans took the province of Al Ahsa.
1891 The Rashidi family seized control of Riyadh from the Sa'ud family, which was exiled to Kuwait.
1902 Abd al Aziz and other members of the deposed Sa'ud family regained control of Riyadh, expelling the Rashidis.
1913 Al Ahsa was taken back from the Ottomans by Abd al Aziz. The Anglo-Ottoman Convention established the 'Blue Line' as the eastern Arabian boundary between the Ottoman and British empires.
1914 Abd al Aziz signed a treaty with the Ottomans.
1915 The first Anglo-Saudi treaty provided recognition of Abd al Aziz.
1919–26 Between 1919 and 1925, Abd al Aziz defeated the four Arabian states of Hejaz, Asir, Ha'il and Jauf and incorporated them. Abd al Aziz took Makkah (Mecca) from King Ali of al Hejaz. In 1925, Medina, Yanbu and Jeddah surrendered to Abd al Aziz, and in 1926, Abd al Aziz was proclaimed King of Al Hejaz and Sultan of Najd and its dependencies.
1927 In the second Anglo-Saudi treaty, the British recognised the full independence of Abd al Aziz, while the Saudi leader acknowledged the British treaty relationships with the sheikhdoms of the Gulf.
1932 The Kingdom of Saudi Arabia was established when the two monarchies of Najd and Al Hejaz merged, with Abd al Aziz as King.
1933 His eldest son, Sa'ud, was named crown prince.
1938 Oil was discovered and production started under California Arabian Standard Oil Company (CASOC).
1944 CASOC changed its name to Arabian American Oil Company (Aramco).
1945 Oil exploration and exploitation increased after the Second World War and the country's infrastructure was modernised and developed with the growing oil revenues.
1953 King Abd al Aziz died and was succeeded by Crown Prince Sa'ud ibn Abdul Aziz al Sa'ud.
1960 Saudi Arabia was a founding member of OPEC (Organisation of Petroleum Exporting Countries).
1964 King Sa'ud was deposedby his brother, Faisal ibn Abdul Aziz al Sa'ud, previously the crown prince and prime minister.
1972 Saudi Arabia gained controlled of 20 per cent of Aramco.
1973 An oil boycott was led by Saudi Arabia against Western countries that supported Israel in the 6 October War against Egypt and Syria. Oil prices subsequently quadrupled and world economy went into depression.
1975 King Faisal was assassinated by one of his nephews and was succeeded by Khalid ibn Abdul Aziz al Sa'ud.
1979 Saudi Arabia cut off diplomatic relations with Egypt after the Egyptian-Israeli Peace Treaty was signed. The Grand Mosque of Makkah was seized by extremists; the government regained control and executed those captured.
1980 Saudi Arabia took over full control of Aramco.
1981 Saudi Arabia was a founder member of the GCC (Gulf Co-operation Council).
1982 King Khalid died and Fahd ibn Abdul Aziz al Sa'ud, his brother, became King.
1986 The King Fahd Causeway between Bahrain and Saudi Arabia opened.
1987 Diplomatic relations with Egypt were resumed.
1991 Saudi Arabia was the launch pad for a US-led military operation, which ejected Iraqi forces occupying Kuwait.
1992 King Fahd announced the country's Basic Law, which declares that the Quran is the country's constitution, and he proposed setting up a Majlis al Shura (Consultative Council).
1993 The Majlis al Shura was inaugurated.
1994 Osama bin Laden, who was later to become notorious as the leader of al Qaeda, a terrorist organisation, reportedly responsible for flying two aircraft into the World Trade Centre in New York in September 2001, was stripped of his Saudi nationality.
1995 King Fahd suffered a debilitating stroke and handed over de facto power to Crown Prince Abdullah.
1996 A bomb exploded at the US military complex near Dhahran.
1997 The Majlis al Shura membership was increased from 60 to 90.
1999 Women were allowed to attend a session of the Majlis al Shura for the first time.
2000 Yemen and Saudi Arabia signed a treaty resolving 65 years of dispute over land and sea boundaries.
2001 Saudi Arabia and Iran signed a security accord to combat terrorism, drug trafficking and organised crime. Out of 19 hijackers involved in the 11 September attacks in the US, 15 were Saudi nationals. King Fahd said that terrorism should be eradicated and that it is prohibited by Islam. Identity cards were issued to women for the first time.
2002 New criminal rights came into force banning torture and giving suspects legal representation. Crown Prince Abdullah proposed a peace initiative for Israel and Palestine, at the Beirut Summit of the Arab League. He suggested a settlement between Israel and the whole Arab world if Israel withdrew from all Palestinian territories it had occupied since 1967.
2003 Saudi Arabia denied US air bases and troops access to Iraq through its territory during the second invasion of Iraq. More than 300 Saudi intellectuals, including women, signed a petition calling for

far-reaching political reforms and around 270 people were arrested when attending a rally in Riyadh, also calling for political reform. King Fahd granted wider powers to the Majlis al Shura, enabling it to initiate legislation without first seeking his permission.
2004 There was a stampede at the Haj pilgrimage in February, in which 251 people died. Security forces killed local al Qaeda leader, Abdul Aziz al Muqrin.
2005 In February, Saudis (men only) voted in the first-ever nationwide municipal elections. Security forces killed 14 Islamist militants in April, including Abdulkarim al Mejjati, accused of masterminding the bombings in Casablanca, Morocco, in 2003, and whose role in the 2004 bombing in Madrid, Spain, was being investigated. King Fahd died on 1 August and was succeeded by his half-brother Crown Prince Abdullah bin Abdul Aziz. Saudi Arabia became a member of the World Trade Organisation on 11 December.

Political structure
Constitution
Saudi Arabia is an absolute monarchy. The country's 1992 Basic Law declares that the Quran is the country's constitution.
A system of provincial government was introduced in 1993. Thirteen regional authorities, subdivided into 103 governorates, provide provincial services alongside district councils and tribal and village councils. The 13 provinces are governed by princes or close relatives of the royal family and governors are appointed by the King.
Form of state
Absolute monarchy
The executive
The Custodian of the Two Holy Mosques, King Fahd ibn Abdul Aziz al Sa'ud, heads the government as prime minister and general commander of the armed forces. Crown Prince Abdullah ibn Abdul Aziz al Sa'ud is first deputy prime minister and commander of the National Guard.
The 25-member Council of Ministers, an executive body appointed for a four-year term by the King, serves as an instrument of royal authority, passing legislation that becomes law once ratified by royal decree. The majority of the Council is comprised of members of the royal family, with the King as Council leader.
National legislature
There is no elected legislature. A Majlis al Shura (Consultative Council) was formed in 1993; it provides a forum for debate. Membership was increased from 60 to 90 in 1997, serving a four-year term. Members are appointed by the King. On 30 November 2003, King Fahd granted wider powers to the Majlis al Shura, enabling it to initiate legislation without first seeking his permission.
Legal system
Saudi Arabia has judicial-Islamic courts of first instance and appeals based on *Sharia* (Islamic law) and the *Sunna* (practices or mode of life) of the Prophet Mohammed. Judges are appointed by the King on the recommendation of the Supreme Judicial Council, comprised of 12 senior jurists. Royal decrees and ministerial resolutions have been used to complement *Sharia* in modern Saudi Arabia and a dual system has developed. *Sharia* judgements generally override the judgements of non-*Sharia* tribunals. The King is the final court of appeal and has the power of sentencing or pardoning those found guilty of breaking the law.
In 2002, a new criminal justice system came into force, which included a ban on torture and the right of suspects to legal representation.
Last elections
None
Next elections
Legislative elections are not held. February 2005 (local elections; women are barred from voting)

Political parties
Ruling party
No political parties – absolute monarchy.

Population
23.34 million (2004)
Ethnic make-up
The majority of Saudis originate in the peninsula and are of Arab extraction, but there is a sizeable minority of the population which has migrated mainly from central Asia and China. One-third of the population is non-Saudi. Most of these are from Yemen, Pakistan, Thailand and the Philippines as well as a significant number from Western Europe and North America.
Religions
The majority of the population is Sunni (Wahhabi) Muslim, with around 8 per cent Shi'a Muslim, the latter being mainly located in the Hasa (Eastern) Province. Sufism is practised throughout the Hejaz, and there is a Sunni Salafi opposition movement which, in particular, opposes the authoritarian rule of the clergy.
Islam's two holiest cities of Makkah (Mecca) and Medina are both in Saudi Arabia.
Despite Islam's recognition of Christians and Jews as People of the Book, public adherence to other faiths is forbidden in the Kingdom.

Education
Although education at all levels is free, it is not compulsory. Both primary and secondary education last for six years and begin at the ages of six and 12 years respectively. On average, boys receive an extra year of schooling (nine years) compared to girls and their education is completely segregated.
The educational system is geared to a future of high technology with computer science taught as a basic subject in secondary schools. However, the education system is widely recognised as being outdated and inefficient. There are over 22,700 schools and colleges, which are attended by about five million students.
Literacy rate: 79 per cent, adult rate (2003)
Enrolment rate: 77 per cent boys; 75 per cent girls, total primary enrolment (including repetition rates) of the relevant age group between 1994–2000 (World Bank).
Pupils per teacher: 13 in primary schools.

Health
All medical care, including the cost of medicines, is provided free for Saudi citizens.
Saudi Arabia provides a two-tier health service plan. The first tier comprises a network of over 3,500 primary healthcare centres and clinics established throughout the country. These centres are supplemented by a fleet of mobile clinics that routinely visit the more remote villages and provide basic medical services. A network of over 300 advanced hospitals and specialised clinics spanning the urban areas constitute the second tier of health services with a capacity of almost 45,000 beds. The King Fahd Medical City in Riyadh is probably the largest medical facility in the Middle East.
Life expectancy: 73.3 years (World Bank)
Fertility rate/Maternal mortality rate: Six births per woman (2003)
Birth rate/Death rate: 37 births per 1,000 population; six deaths per 1,000 population (2003).
Infant mortality rate: 46 deaths per 1,000 live births (2004)
Head of population per physician/bed: There are 1.7 physicians and 2.3 hospital beds typically available for 1,000 people.

Welfare
The General Organisation for Social Insurance (GOSI) administers programmes that support workers or their families in cases of disability, retirement and death and also covers occupational hazards for employees. Another major programme provides social security pensions, benefits and relief assistance to the disabled, the elderly, orphans and widows without income. The seventh Development Plan

(2000–04) aims to expand national programmes for the rehabilitation and welfare of the handicapped, and immunisation of all children against infectious diseases.

Out of the 60 centres around the country that care for those with social, economic and physical problems, six specialise in rehabilitation of juvenile delinquents, nine in assisting the elderly and 14 in caring for orphans. A particularly important government policy has been to provide interest-free, easy-term loans towards low cost home construction for students and low-income employees.

Main cities
Riyadh (capital, estimated population 3.8 million in 2004), Jeddah (2.8 million), Makkah (Mecca) (1.7 million), Dammam (697,700).

Languages spoken
Mainly Arabic, with English widely spoken in business and diplomatic circles.
Official language/s
Arabic

Media
Press
In principle, the press is not subject to any legal restriction affecting freedom of expression. Most newspaper publishing firms are private sector groups, owned by individuals with broad experience of newspaper and magazine publishing. However, in practice, censorship is strict and criticism of the government is automatically censored. The Kingdom's press code, in force since 1964, gives the government considerable powers to intervene in the media as it judges necessary.

All newspapers and journals are pro-government. The official news agencies are the Islamic Press Agency (Jeddah) and the Saudi Press Agency (operated by the Ministry of Information, Riyadh).

Dailies: Leading Arabic dailies include *Asharq al Awsat, al Watan, al Yaum Newspaper, Okaz, al Jazirah, Naseej News, al Bilad, al Massaiah, al Madinah al Rayath Newspaper* and *al Nadwa*. English language dailies are *Arab News Riyadh Daily* and *Saudi Gazette*.

Weeklies: There are a number of magazines and periodicals, including *al Yamama* and *Igraa*. *Um al Qura* is the official weekly newspaper issued by the Saudi government.

Business: The leading business journal is the *Saudi Economic Survey* (weekly in English).

Periodicals: *Alnafetha*

Broadcasting
Radio: The Saudi Arabian Broadcasting Service (SABS) is run by the Information Ministry and has 30 radio stations including those in Riyadh, Jeddah, Dammam and Abha. It broadcasts programmes in Arabic and English and runs overseas services in Urdu, Indonesian, Persian, French, Somali and Swahili. Aramco Radio station at Dhahran broadcasts in English.

Television: Saudi Arabian Government Television (SAGT) has 97 stations including six main stations at Riyadh, Jeddah, Medina, Dammam, Qassim and Abha. It has two channels and broadcasts for eight hours a day. It operates under the auspices of the Information Ministry in Riyadh. A number of Arabic-language satellite channels also broadcast in Saudi Arabia.

Advertising
Saudi Arabia is the largest advertising market in the Gulf, with total advertising expenditure typically reaching US$300 million. Newspaper advertising is the most popular form, representing over 60 per cent of total spending.

Economy
Oil was discovered in Saudi Arabia in the 1930s, although large-scale production did not begin until after the Second World War. Since a rapid expansion in the country's economic development in the 1960s, Saudi Arabia's economic fortunes have depended largely on the international oil price. Nowadays oil accounts for around 90 per cent of the country's exports and 70 per cent of the government's revenues, this means Saudi Arabia is vulnerable to external shock.

Pressure for economic reform intensified during the 1990s, as oil prices remained weak for much of the decade, but it was not until 1994 that the government took action to cut government spending and permit the private sector to take a more active role in the economy. Higher oil prices immediately following this initiative eased budgetary and foreign payments constraints, also lessening the government's resolve to carry out necessary structural economic reforms. Ultimately, the economy is underpinned by its vast oil reserves, which will last another century at current rates of production. Diversification is needed to strengthen the economy, but reliance on oil continues.

The slow pace of economic reforms and the lack of accountability in government is being questioned by the public who want an explanation as to how the oil money is spent, particularly with unexplained persistent budget deficits and a lack of transparency.

A closer partnership with the EU was agreed in August 2003 with Saudi Arabia reducing import tariffs on EU goods by 12 per cent. There are plans to open up the service sector further, to attract EU investment. This was one of the first steps towards joining the World Trade Organisation (WTO), which was achieved in December 2005. As a member of the WTO, Saudi Arabia has undertaken to liberalise its trade regime and accelerate its integration into the world economy.

External trade
Saudi Arabia has been advised to open its domestic market to foreign goods and services, in order to speed up talks on its application to join the World Trade Organisation (WTO).

Imports
Main imports are machinery and equipment, foodstuffs, chemicals, vehicles and textiles. US goods to be imported during 2006 will be US$10.7 billion.

Main sources: US (9.3 per cent total, 2004), Germany (6.8 per cent), Japan (6.7 per cent), UK (5.4 per cent), China (5.0 per cent)

Exports
The major export is petroleum (typically over 90 per cent of total); minor exports include chemical products, construction material, agricultural, animal and food products.

Main destinations: US (19.3 per cent total, 2004), Japan (16.4 per cent), South Korea (8.7 per cent), China (5.8 per cent), Singapore (4.5 per cent)

Agriculture
Farming
The sector contributes around 5 per cent to GDP and employs 4 per cent of the labour force. Agricultural produce accounts for only around 5 per cent of non-oil exports.

Agricultural development projects have helped Saudi Arabia achieve self-sufficiency in wheat, eggs, some dairy products and vegetables. The development of water desalination plants is crucial to future development.

The role of agriculture in the overall economy is being re-evaluated. Subsidies have created large surpluses of wheat, while agricultural production has depleted scarce water supplies.

The agricultural sector is heavily subsidised and accounts for 90 per cent of Saudi Arabia's 14–16 billion cubic metres of annual water consumption. The policy of agricultural expansion has come under heavy criticism, as some 3,000 tonnes of water is required to produce one tonne of wheat, most of which is then exported. At present rates of depletion, fossil water sources are not expected to last more than 20 years. The importance of conservation and subsidy reduction to slow water demand is clear, but this needs to be balanced against the need to expand Saudi Arabia's agricultural output.

Most agricultural activity is north of Riyadh in Qasim, Hail and Al-Jauf areas and on a smaller scale in Wadi Dawasir and Abha. Despite significant growth in agricultural production, Saudi Arabia increasingly relies on imports to meet the demands of a rapidly growing population. Crop production in 2004 included: 2,792,199 tonnes (t) cereals in total, 2,358,000t wheat, 138,432t barley, 43,697t maize, 243,746t sorghum, 320,897t potatoes, 8,200t pulses, 2,151t oilcrops, 900,540t dates, 440,033t tomatoes, 101,653t grapes, 73,204t eggplants, 140,000t citrus fruit, 1,322,193t fruit in total, 1,949,897t vegetables in total. Livestock production included: 643,300t meat in total, 22,800t beef, 76,000t lamb, 22,500t goat meat, 480,700t poultry, 140,000t eggs, 1,149,000t milk, 153t honey, 41,300t camel meat, 32,000t sheepskins.

Fishing
Saudi Arabia has a small and developing fishing industry. The Saudi Fisheries Company (SFC) operates the fishing fleet, comprising 49 vessels. SFC operates four processing plants in Dammam, Jazan, Jeddah and Riyadh. Annual catch includes bream, barracuda, mackerel, sardine and tuna.

Forestry
Forest and wooded land accounts only for 1 per cent of Saudi Arabia's total land area. Most wood products are imported.

Industry and manufacturing
Saudi Arabia's economy is dominated by the oil industry, with the majority of manufactured goods imported and the services sector largely supporting the hydrocarbon sector. The industrial sector accounts for around 55 per cent of GDP, while manufacturing accounts for only 10 per cent. The government has played a major role in the economy since an industrialisation programme was launched in the 1960s. Despite attempts to develop the private sector and withdraw the state from the economy, such attempts have not progressed very far. The main sector, oil, is dominated by the largest domestic oil company – the 100 per cent state-owned Saudi Arabian Oil Company (Saudi Aramco). Upstream oil exploration and development, the country's most lucrative industry, is closed to foreign investment, with all activities undertaken by Saudi Aramco.

The state also intervenes in the price of domestic goods, with significant subsidies provided on a wide range of agricultural, utility and industrial products. As a result, the domestic economy rarely reflects international market prices.

Tourism
Little effort has been made to attract non-Arab tourists. The annual pilgrimage (haj) brings some two million Muslim visitors each year to the holy cities, Makkah and Medina. Other principal destinations are the capital, Riyadh, and the commercial centre, Jeddah.

The government has established a commission for tourism to develop the sector as part of its diversification policy. Facilities are being expanded to encourage the domestic population to spend their holidays in the country (an estimated US$6 billion is spent on overseas vacations each year) and pilgrims on haj to extend their visits. With the basic infrastructure already developed, resources are going into accommodation and recreational facilities, including resort cities and amusement parks.

The commission has also been charged with developing plans to promote the country to non-Muslim visitors. Around 6,000 such tourists visit each year, mainly in groups organised by Saudi Arabian Airlines. The development of Saudi holiday destinations for western tourists may prove to be difficult to achieve, as local conditions clash with tourist expectations. Not all historic sites are open to non-Muslims, while hotel resorts must conform to Islamic traditions of modest dress, temperance and the social separation of men and single women.

Tourism is expected to contribute around two per cent to GDP in 2005.

Mining
The exploitation of mineral resources other than oil is the responsibility of the petroleum and minerals resources ministry.

The principal minerals are gold, silver, copper, zinc, lead, iron, magnesite, bauxite, phosphates, beryl, fluorite, magnesium, salt and sulphur and certain radioactive minerals. Other sought-after minerals are those used for making cement and plaster such as granite, sandstone, coral stone and marble. Saudi Arabia is self-sufficient in these materials. Industrial minerals produced include limestone, gypsum, sulphur, marble, clay and salt. Much of the mineral deposits can be extracted by surface mining or quarrying. A new mining code passed in January 2005 seeks to attract more foreign companies, mainly by giving them greater freedom to invest as they see fit. Gold exploration has been opened up to foreign companies for the first time.

Hydrocarbons
Saudi Arabia is the world's largest producer and exporter of oil, with proven reserves of 262.7 billion barrels. Output stood at 10.6 million barrels per day (bpd) in 2004. Oil exports make up over 90 per cent of total export revenues and around 40 per cent of GDP. The United States is one of Saudi Arabia's largest customers, but following the war in Iraq more emphasis is placed on exporting to Europe, China and Russia.

Saudi Arabia has eight refineries with a total capacity of 2.06 million bpd in 2004, an increase of 7.8 per cent over 2003. While there are approximately 80 oil and gas fields in Saudi Arabia, over half of the country's reserves are located in eight fields. Of these, the most significant is Ghawar (the world's largest onshore oil field), Abqaiq, Safaniya (the world's largest offshore field), and Berri. Natural gas reserves amounted to 6.75 trillion cubic metres in 2004. Total gas production in 2004 was 64 billion cubic metres, an increase of 6.6 per cent over the previous year. This is all consumed domestically. Future exploration by Saudi Aramco is to be focussed on pure natural gas in order to meet domestic demand, which is growing at about 8 per cent a year. Previously, all the gas produced was a by-product of oil production. A number of new gas fields have been discovered in recent years.

Energy
Generating capacity is estimated at 25GW. Power demand is growing at a rate of 4.5 per cent per annum; Saudi Arabia has the world's highest per capita consumption. It is estimated that 66GW will be needed by 2020, calling for investment of US$2 billion per annum, mainly from the private sector and most of which will be spent on gas-fired power stations. The sector is monopoly-conytrolled by the Saudi Electricity Company (SEC), which was established in April 2000 as a joint-stock company, 50 per cent owned by the Saudi government.

Financial markets
Stock exchange
The Saudi stock exchange was opened to foreign investment in 1997. Saudi Arabia's stock market is around twice the size of the Egyptian stock market, the second largest in the Middle East and North Africa region. The market is led by the banking sector. In October 2001, the Saudi Arabian Monetary Agency (SAMA) created a new stock market, Tadawul, which offers high-tech trading and real-time transactions. It is envisaged that Tadawul will become part of a regional market network.

Banking and insurance
Islamic banking rules are in force. The sector comprises 10 domestically-owned banks. Foreigners cannot own more than 49 per cent of domestic banks and foreign participation is mostly in the form of joint-ventures.

Central bank
Saudi Arabian Monetary Agency (SAMA)

Saudi Arabia

Main financial centre
Riyadh

Time
GMT plus three hours. No seasonal variations.

Geography
Saudi Arabia is a mainly barren land covering an area of 2.24 million square km. On the western coast is the Tihama plain, a hot region almost devoid of rainfall but with a humid coast. Inland from the Tihama rises a steep escarpment. In the centre of the Kingdom lies the Najd region and the Rub al-Khali (Empty Quarter) lies in the south-east. The eastern province, containing the oil fields, has an undulating topography with rocky outcrops.

Climate
Average maximum temperatures are 38 degrees Celsius (C) in summer and the winter minimum is 13 degrees C. The summers are generally hot and dry (although humidity in some areas may reach 90 per cent) and the winters are cold. The coastal towns tend to be hot and humid all year. Rainfall in the Kingdom rarely exceeds 250mm a year, except in the extreme south-west.

Dress codes
A lightweight suit or jacket and trousers are advised. A tie and a long sleeved shirt should be worn at business meetings, but a jacket is not essential. Women should dress modestly, covering their arms and knees. Expatriate women often find it convenient to wear an *abaya*, a wrap-around shoulder cloak.

Entry requirements
Passports
Required by all except certain seamen and pilgrims (with passes). The passport must be valid for at least six months beyond the proposed stay.
Visa
Required by all (including pilgrims). All applicants should apply for visas through a visa agency accredited to an embassy of Saudi Arabia. Contact the nearest consulate for an appropriate agency list. During Haj and Umrah, pilgrims and visitors must have a valid certificate of vaccination against the ACWY strains of meningitis. For business visas a letter of invitation from a Saudi company, endorsed by the Saudi Chamber of Commerce in Saudi Arabia, must be faxed directly to the Consulate to which the application is submitted. The original or copy of this invitation, including an introduction letter from the employee's company addressed to the Embassy, should be submitted with the application form.
Women visitors are required to be met by their sponsor upon arrival. Women travelling alone, who are not met by sponsors, may experience delays before being allowed to enter or, if in transit, to continue their journey.
Further information can be found at www.mofa.gov.sa/ooo/visa/business_visas.htm
Prohibited entry
Travellers who arrive obviously inebriated are liable to arrest or deportation. Israeli nationals are barred from entering the Kingdom. An Israeli visa or stamp in a visitor's passport is likely to result in a ban on entry. Consultation with Saudi officials prior to departure is strongly recommended.
Currency advice/regulations
No currency restrictions.
Customs
Duty is chargeable on many imported items, starting at 12 per cent but rising to 20 per cent for goods normally manufactured in the Kingdom; no duty on samples of low value though.
Prohibited imports
The penalty for smuggling, promoting or circulating illegal drugs is capital punishment.
Other prohibitions include anything with an alcoholic content, certain foodstuffs (such as pork), pornography and censored literature. Prescription drugs should be carried only in small quantities in original containers. Dogs are banned, with the exception of guard dogs, hunting dogs and guide dogs.

Health (for visitors)
Mandatory precautions
A certificate of vaccination against yellow fever is required if travelling from an infected area.
During Haj and Umrah, pilgrims and visitors must have a valid certificate of vaccination against the ACWY strains of meningitis.
Advisable precautions
Vaccinations against cholera, typhoid and polio are recommended. Medical facilities in the Kingdom are excellent and there are few obvious health hazards.

Hotels
There are many good hotels in the Kingdom. Alcoholic drinks are strictly prohibited.

Credit cards
All major credit cards are accepted.

Public holidays
Fixed dates
23 Sep (Saudi National Day)
For civil purposes, Saudi Arabia uses the Umm-ul-Qura calendar.
Variable dates
Eid al Adha (five days), Eid al Fitr (three days).

During the Hajj (when pilgrims visit Mecca), which immediately precedes Eid al Adha, government offices and some businesses will be closed for 10 days. Work schedules may be seriously disrupted during the month of Ramadan, and businesses may take time off for other Islamic holidays.
The Islamic year contains 354 or 355 days, with the result that Muslim feasts advance by 10–12 days against the Gregorian calendar. Dates of feasts vary according to the sighting of the new moon, so cannot be forecast exactly.

Working hours
Banking
Sat–Wed: 0830–1200 and 1700–1900; Thu: 0830–1130; 1000–1330 during Ramadan.
Business
Sat–Wed: 0800–1200, 1630–2000 in Riyadh; 0900–1330, 1630–2000 in Jeddah; 0730–1200, 1430–1730 in Eastern Province (closed Thu afternoon and Fri).
Private business offices in other areas: 0800–1200; 1500–1800.
Government
0730–1430 (Sat–Wed); 1000–1430 during Ramadan.
Shops
0800/0830–1200 and 1600–2100/2200; closed Thursday and Friday and four times a day for prayer for up to half an hour.

Telecommunications
Mobile phones
A GSM network is available.

Electricity supply
127V or 220V AC, 60 cycles, with two-pin European-type plugs and both bayonet and screw light fittings in use. 380V AC, 60 cycles is used by industry.

Social customs/useful tips
Punctuality is not always a Saudi virtue. While the foreign businessman will be expected to arrive at a meeting punctually, his Saudi counterpart may think nothing of being late or even of not showing up at all. Always shake hands (with your right hand) on meeting and leaving.
Much time is spent in exchanging small talk at business meetings, and embarking on business matters before the atmosphere is favourable may cause offence. Creating trust is as important as proving competence. Decision-making is often based on the bedouin tradition of consensus, rather than merely on the basis of the pros and cons of the case submitted. The opinions of family and community are revered, though the younger generation is increasingly adopting western business habits. Hospitality to the stranger lies at the heart of Arabian life. It is polite to

accept at least one cup of tea or coffee when it is offered: oscillate the coffee cup when you do not want any more, otherwise the server will continue to fill it. Do not eat or drink with the left hand, as it is considered unclean; do not point the sole of your shoe at a Saudi at any time. You may ask after a man's children but not after his wife.

Saudi women are generally barred from public life. They do not drive and schools and universities are segregated.

Murder, apostasy (by Muslims) and adultery are capital crimes. However, adultery must have been witnessed by four adult males who have seen the whole act. Execution for adultery is stoning to death for the woman and public beheading for the man, although the sentence is rarely carried out these days. Another rarely enforced law states that a thief convicted for a third time shall have his hand cut off. Any form of killing, whether premeditated or not, technically provides the victim's family with the choice of blood revenge or 'blood money', although the former is never exacted against a foreigner in, say, a traffic accident.

The possession of alcohol is illegal. Although it is discreetly available it should not, in general, be offered to Saudis.

Security

The level of street crime has traditionally been far lower than in the west because of the severity of the penalties imposed. The influx of immigrant workers since the early 1970s has encouraged incidents of theft, although murder and violent crimes such as mugging and rape remain relatively rare.

Getting there

Air
National airline: Saudia (Saudi Arabian Airlines); largest carrier in the Middle East.
International airport/s: Dhahran International (DHA), 13km south-east of Dhahran, with hotel, buffet, bank, post office, shops and car hire; Jeddah, King Abdul Aziz International (JED), 18km north of city, with hotel, restaurant, bank, post office, shops, car hire and special pilgrimage facilities (during the annual pilgimages, the number of passengers using Jeddah airport can swell by 1.5m adding considerable delays to passport and visa controls); and Riyadh King Khaled International (RUH), 35km from the city, with ultra-modern facilities including mosque and air cargo terminal.
Airport tax: International departures: SR50 from Jeddah and Riyadh International airports; not applicable to 24 hour transit passengers.

Surface
Road: There are links to all countries sharing a common border with Saudi Arabia, as well as Bahrain via the causeway (of which a toll is charged).
Main port/s: Dammam, Jeddah, Jizan, Jubail Ras Tanura and Yanbu.

Getting about

National transport
Non-Muslims may not travel to the holy cities of Medina and Makkah (Mecca).
Air: There are 23 domestic airports including Al Julaidan, 12km from Medina. Saudia operates a comprehensive schedule of domestic flights between Jeddah, Riyadh and Dhahran and other major centres. Always confirm flight bookings 24-hours before take-off, especially during the annual pilgrimage (Haj).
Road: The total length of the Saudi road network is over 144,000km, of which 45,522km is asphalted and the remainder earth-surfaced. The network is being constantly upgraded and expanded and much of it, particularly on the main routes, is of the highest standard.
Buses: Saudi Arabian Public Transport Company (SAPTCO) operates bus services within three major urban areas, airport bus services and inter-city bus services between major centres.
Rail: Daily rail service links Riyadh and Damman, with refreshments and air-conditioning available.

City transport
Taxis: All taxis are orange and should have visible meter and taxi number in addition to normal registration. Although drivers are supposed to use the meters, it is best to agree the fare in advance. Taxi drivers do not expect a tip.
White American air-conditioned saloons and white London taxis with clearly identifiable 'limousine' logos are operated by a number of companies within the cities and especially to and from airports. These limousines have virtually replaced ordinary taxis. Fixed fares for specific journeys are prominently displayed at airports and available from drivers.

Car hire
Available at airports and main hotels. Driving licence required. Valid licences from most countries will be accepted by car hire companies. Women are not allowed to drive. Driving on the right-hand side of road at maximum 110kph on motorways and 40kph in cities. Insurance claims are not legally enforceable unless a police certification of the damage is obtained. Chauffeur-driven service is usually recommended.

BUSINESS DIRECTORY

The addresses listed below are a selection only. While World of Information makes every endeavour to check these addresses, we cannot guarantee that changes have not been made, especially to telephone numbers and area codes. We would welcome any corrections.

Telephone area codes

The international direct dialling (IDD) code for Saudi Arabia is +966, followed by area code and subscriber's number:

Jeddah	2	Medina	4
Hofuf	3	Qatif	3
Makkah	2	Riyadh	1

Useful telephone numbers

Emergency police: 999
Ambulance: 997
Traffic accidents: 993
Fire: 998
Directory enquiries: 905

Chambers of Commerce

Abha Chamber of Commerce & Industry, PO Box 722, Abha (tel: 227-1818; fax: 227-1919).

Al-Baha Chamber of Commerce & Industry, PO Box 311, Al-Baha (tel: 725-0476; fax: 727-0146).

American Business Association - Eastern Province, PO Box 1868, Al-Khobar 31952 (tel: 882-5288 ext 1253; fax: 882-5288 ext 1497; e-mail: abaep@al-bustinet.com).

American Businessmen's Group of Riyadh, PO Box 8273, 11482 Riyadh (tel: 478-2738; fax: 476-4363).

British Businessmen's Group - Jeddah, PO Box 393, Jeddah (tel: 622-5550; fax: 622-6249; e-mail: bbj@tri.net,sa).

Eastern Province Chamber of Commerce and Industry, PO Box 719, Dammam 31421 (tel: 857-1111; fax: 857-0607).

Jeddah Chamber of Commerce and Industry, PO Box 1264, Jeddah 21431 (tel: 651-5111; fax: 651-7373; e-mail: info@jcci.org.sa; website: www.jcci.org.sa).

Jizan Chamber of Commerce & Industry, PO Box 201, Jizan (tel: 322-5155; fax: 322-3635).

Makkah Chamber of Commerce and Industry, PO Box 1086, Makkah (tel: 534-3838; fax: 534-2904).

Medina Chamber of Commerce and Industry, PO Box 443, Medina (tel: 826-8961; fax: 826-8965).

Najran Chamber of Commerce & Industry, PO Box 1138, Najran (tel: 522-2216; fax: 522-3926).

Riyadh Chamber of Commerce and Industry, PO Box 596, Riyadh 11421 (tel: 404-0044; fax: 402-1103; website: www.riyadhchamber.com).

Tabuk Chamber of Commerce & Industry, PO Box 567, Tabuk (tel: 422-0464; fax: 422-7387).

Saudi Arabia

Taif Chamber of Commerce and Industry, PO Box 1005, Taif (tel: 736-6800; Fax: 738-0040).

Yanbu Chamber of Commerce & Industry, PO Box 58, Yanbu (tel: 322-7722; fax: 322-6800).

Banking

Arab National Bank, PO Box 56921, Riyadh 11411 (tel: 402-9000; fax: 403-0052).

Al Bank al Saudi al Fransi, PO Box 56006, Riyadh 11421 (tel: 477-4770; fax: 404-2311).

Al Rajhi Banking & Investment Corporation, PO Box 28, Riyadh 11411 (tel: 405-4244; fax: 403-2969).

Bank al Jazira, PO Box 6277, Jeddah 21442 (tel: 660-8820; fax: 661-3044).

National Commercial Bank, PO Box 3555, Jeddah 21421 (tel: 644-6644; fax: 643-7670; internet site: http://www.alahli.com/islamic_banking).

Riyad Bank, PO Box 22622, Riyadh 11411 (tel: 401-0908; fax: 404-0090).

Saudi American Bank, PO Box 833, Riyadh 11421 (tel: 477-4770).

Saudi British Bank, PO Box 9084, Riyadh 11413 (tel: 405-0677; fax: 405-0660).

Saudi Hollandi Bank, PO Box 1467, Riyadh (tel: 406-7888; fax: 401-0968).

Saudi Investment Bank, PO Box 3533, Riyadh (tel: 477-8433; fax: 478-1557).

Central bank

Saudi Arabian Monetary Agency, PO Box 2992, Riyadh 11169 (tel: 463-3000; fax: 466-2936; e-mail: info@sama.gov.sa).

Travel information

Saudia, PO Box 620, 21421 Jeddah (tel: 684-2000; fax: 686-4552; internet: www.saudiarabian-airlines.com).

Ministries

Ministry of Agriculture & Water, PO Box 2639, Airport Road, Riyadh 11195 (tel: 401-6666; fax: 403-1415).

Ministry of Communication, PO Box 3813, Airport Road, Riyadh 11178 (tel: 404-3000; fax: 403-1401).

Ministry of Defence and Aviation, Airport Road, Riyadh 11165 (tel: 478-5900; fax: 401-1336).

Ministry of Education, Airport Road, Riyadh 11148 (tel: 404-2888; fax: 401-2365).

Ministry of Foreign Affairs, Nesseriya St. Riyadh 11124 (tel: 406-7777; fax: 403-0159; internet site: http://www.mofa.gov.sa).

Ministry of Health, PO Box 21217, Airport Road, Riyadh 11176 (tel: 401-2220; fax 402-9876).

Ministry of Higher Education, PO Box 1683, Riyadh 11153 (tel: 464-4444; fax: 441-9004).

Ministry of Information, PO Box 843, Nasseriya Street, Riyadh 11161 (tel: 401-4440; fax: 402-3570).

Ministry of Interior, PO Box 2933, Airport Road, Riyadh 11134 (tel: 401-1944; fax: 403-1185).

Ministry of Islamic Affairs, Endowments, Call and Guidance, Riyadh 11232 (tel: 473-0401).

Ministry of Labour & Social Affairs, PO Box 1182, Omar Ibn Al-Khatab Street, Riyadh 11157 (tel: 477-1480; fax: 477-7336).

Ministry of Justice, University Street, Riyadh 11137 (tel: 405-7777).

Ministry of Municipal and Rural Affairs, PO Box 5736, Nasseriya Street, Riyadh 11136 (tel: 441-5434; fax: 456-3196).

Ministry of Petroleum/Mineral Resources, PO Box 757, Airport Road, Riyadh 11189 (tel: 478-1661; fax: 479-3596).

Ministry of Pilgrimage, Omar Ibn Al-Khatab Street, Riyadh 11183 (tel:402-2200; fax: 402-2555).

Ministry of Post, Telegraphs & Telephones, Intercontinental Road, Riyadh 11112 (tel: 463-7225; fax: 405-2310).

Ministry of Public Works & Housing, Weshem Street, PO Box 56059, Riyadh 11151 (tel: 402-2268; fax: 402-2723 (public works), 406-7376 (housing)).

Other useful addresses

Arabian Oil Company, PO Box 256, Khafji 31971 (tel: 766-0555; fax: 766-2001).

Arab Petroleum Investments Corporation, PO Box 448, Dhahran Airport 31932 (tel: 864-7400; fax: 894-5076).

Arab Satellite Communiction Organisation, PO Box 1038, Riyadh 11431 (tel: 464-6666; fax: 465-6983).

Central Department of Statistics, PO Box 3735, Off Airport Road, Riyadh 11187 (tel:405-9638; fax: 405-9493).

Central Planning Organisation, Ministry of Planning, Riyadh.

Civil Defence, Airport Road, Riyadh 11174 (tel: 479-2828; fax: 478-0846).

Civil Service Commission, Washem Street, PO Box 18367, Riyadh 11114 (tel: 402-6900; fax: 403-4998).

Customs Department, PO Box 3483, Riyadh 11471 (tel: 401-3334; fax: 404-3412).

Dammam Seaport (King Abdul Aziz Sea Port) PO Box 28062, Dammam 31188 (tel: 833-2500; fax: 857-9223).

Dhahran International Expo, PO Box 7519, Dammam 31742 (tel: 833-7900; fax: 833-8010).

Director-General of Mineral Resources, PO Box 2880, Jeddah 21461 (tel: 631-0355; fax: 631-0357).

Directorate General of Zakat and Income Tax, Off Airport Road, Riyadh 11187 (tel: 404-1537; fax: 404-1495).

Federation of GCC Chambers, PO Box 2198, Dammam 31451 (tel: 826-5943; fax: 826-6794).

General Electricity Corp. (ELECTRICO), PO Box 1185, Riyadh 11431 (tel: 477-2772; fax: 477-5322).

General Organisation for Petroleum & Minerals (PETROMIN), PO Box 757, Riyadh 11189 (tel: 498-0995).

General Organisation for Social Insurance (GOSI), PO Box 2963, Riyadh 11461 (tel: 477-7735; fax: 477-9958).

General Organistion for Technical Education and Vocational Training, PO Box 7823, Riyadh 11472 (tel: 405-2770; fax: 406-5876).

General Ports Authority, PO Box 5162, Riyadh 11422 (tel: 476-0600).

General Presidency for Girls' Education, Television Street, Riyadh 11192 (tel: 402-9877; fax: 403-9570).

Grievances Court (Diwan-Al-Mazalem) Morabba-Nasseria Street, Riyadh 11138 (tel: 402-1724; fax: 403-4296).

Institute of Public Administration (IPA), PO Box 205, Riyadh 11411 (tel: 476-1600; fax: 479-2136).

International Airports Projects, PO Box 6326, Jeddah 21174 (tel: 685-4200).

Irish Embassy, Diplomatic Quarter, PO Box 94349, Riyadh 11693 (tel: 488-2300; fax: 488-0927; e-mail: irishembassy@awalnet,net.sa).

Jeddah Broadcasting Service, Broadcasting Station, Jeddah.

Jeddah Seaport, (Jeddah Islamic Port) PO Box 9285, Jeddah 21188 (tel: 643-2552).

King Abdul Aziz City for Science and Technology, PO Box 6068, Riyadh 11442 (tel: 478-8000; fax: 488-13756).

Meteorology and Environment Protection Agency, PO Box 1358, Jeddah 21431 (tel: 651-8887).

National Guard, PO Box 9799, Riyadh 11423 (tel: 491-2400; fax: 491-2824).

Presidency of Civil Aviation, Off Palestine Road East, PO Box 887, Jeddah 21421 (tel: 667-9000).

Real Estate Development Fund, PO Box 5591, Riyadh 11433 (tel: 477-5120; fax: 479-0148).

Royal Commission for Jubail and Yanbu, PO Box 5864, Riyadh 11432 (tel: 479-4444; fax: 477-5404).

Saline Water Conversion Corporation (SWCC), PO Box 5968, Riyadh 11432 (tel: 463-0501; fax: 463-1952).

Saudi Arabian Airlines Corporation, PO Box 620, Jeddah 21421 (tel: 684-2000; fax: 686-4552).

Saudi Arabian Embassy (USA), 601 New Hampshire Avenue, NW, Washington DC 20037 (tel: 202-342-3800; fax: 202-944-3140; e-mail: info@saudiembessy.net).

Saudi Arabian Oil Company (Saudi Aramco), PO Box 5000, Dhahran Airport 31311 (tel: 875-5229; fax: 876-6520).

Saudi Arabian Standards Organisation, PO Box 3437, Riyadh 11471 (tel: 479-3332; fax: 479-3063).

Saudi Aramco (Saudi Arabian Oil Company), PO Box 5000, Dhahran 31311 (tel: 875-4915; fax: 873-8490).

Saudi Basic Industries Corporation (SABIC), PO Box 5105, Riyadh 11422 (tel: 401-2033; fax: 401-2045).

Saudi Export Development Centre, PO Box 16683, Riyadh 11474 (tel: 405-3200; fax: 402-4747).

Saudi Fund for Development, PO Box 50483, Riyadh 11523 (tel: 464-0292; fax: 464-7450; e-mail: info@sfd.gov.sa; website: www.sfd.gov.sa).

Saudi National Shipping Company, Po Box 8931, Riyadh 11492 (tel: 478-5454; fax: 477-8036).

Saudi Ports Authority, Riyadh 11188 (tel: 405-0005; fax: 405-9974).

Saudi Public Transport Co, PO box 10667, Riyadh 11443 (tel: 454-5000; fax: 454-2100).

Saudi Railroad Organisation, PO Box 92, Dammam 31411 (tel: 871-2222; fax: 827-1130).

Saudi Red Crescent Association, al Dhabab Road, Riyadh 11129 (tel: 406-9072; fax: 405-1566).

Youth Welfare Organisation, PO Box 965, Riyadh 11421 (tel: 401-4576; fax: 401-0376).

Internet sites

Arab net: http://www.arab.net/welcome.html

Arabia on line: http://www.arabia.com

Saudi Arabia Information Resourse (in London): http://wwwsaudinf.com

Saudi Embassy, London, with web links to other Saudi enterprises: http://www.saudiembassy.org.uk/index2.htm

Saudi Times: http://www.sauditimes.com

Senegal

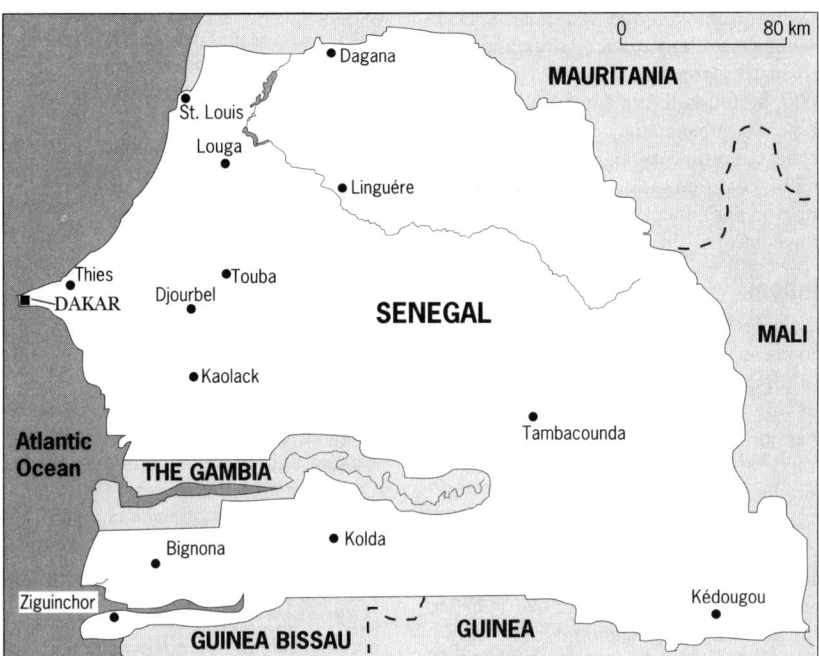

KEY FACTS

Official name: République du Sénégal (Republic of Senegal)

Head of State: President Abdoulayé Wade (sworn in Apr 2000)

Head of government: Prime Minister Macky Sall (appointed 21 Apr 2004)

Ruling party: Re-shuffled government (from 22 Apr 2004; President Abdoulayé Wade's coalition, Sopi (Change), an alliance of 40 parties dominated by the Parti Démocratique Sénégalais (PDS) (Senegalese Democratic Party).

Area: 196,192 square km

Population: 10.63 million (2004)

Capital: Dakar

Official language: French

Currency: CFA franc (CFAf) = 100 centimes (Communauté Financière Africaine (African Financial Community) franc). New notes have been issued; old notes cease to be legal tender from Jan 2005.

Exchange rate: CFAf544.07 per US$ (Oct 2005); CFAf655.95 per euro (pegged from Jan 1999)

GDP per capita: US$733 (2004)

GDP real growth: 6.00% (2004)

Labour force: 4.67 million (2004)

Unemployment: 48.00% (2003)

Inflation: 0.50% (2004)

Balance of trade: -US$754.00 million 2004

Foreign debt: US$3.10 billion (2003)

Senegal's economic targets seek to seek to raise the country's real annual growth rate in the medium- to long-term to an annual average of seven per cent. It has the track record to achieve such a target – after seeing its economy contract by 2.1 per cent in 1993, Senegal made an impressive turnaround, and over 1995–2004 recorded real annual growth of more than five per cent.

Key components of Senegal's economic and financial plan for the years ahead are that the government will seek to improve quality and expand availability of basic social services; but will continue its infrastructure investment programme and strategy to promote the growth of private investment. The government will pay special attention to the type of risk assumed in public/private partnership (PPP) operations, especially in the context of financing major infrastructure projects. The World Bank will be asked to prepare feasibility assessments. An investment code and the new corporate tax legislation will be simplified.

The improvement in access to credit for the establishment and growth of enterprises, in particular small and medium- sized enterprises, is a priority. The government wants the central bank, banks and financial institutions, microfinance institutions, and the regional stock market to foster the contribution of the financial sector to the development of economic activity.

Initiatives at regional level will be to increase bank financing to the economy, promote the regional financial market, and enhance the soundness of the financial sector. The government has already hired 60 magistrates trained in economic and financial matters to build the capacity of the courts to improve the enforcement of financial contracts and reduce the cost of financial intermediation.

The authorities will continue to pay special attention to the exposure of banks to large enterprises, to which they remain vulnerable.

Real growth in 2005 reflected a sustained expansion of all sectors. Primary sector growth was a result of recovery of grain production after the decline in 2004, growth of the secondary sector led mainly by construction and public works.

The basic fiscal balance stood at 0.7 per cent of gross domestic product in 2005 compared with 1.4 per cent in 2004. The overall deficit, including grants, moved to 2.9 per cent of GDP from 2.7 per cent.

Starting with the 2006 budget, the government will ensure the consistency of the capital expenditure budget with actual expenditure. In preparing the public investment programme, the government will take account of capacity constraints, recurrent expenditures, and the level of domestic and external debt that is compatible with public debt sustainability.

The ongoing tax reform should support a lasting and sustainable level of fiscal revenue collection and foster a flexible and attractive environment for private enterprise. Efforts have been stepped up to fight tax fraud and tax evasion.

To cut back on the awarding of contracts by officials, the government will reduce the per centage of such 'single bids' to 20 per cent of the total contracts granted by government.

To implement all this, 15,000 new employees have been recruited into the civil service. They are being paid on a performance related basis. The International Monetary Fund (IMF) has endorsed the programme but criticised some areas. It suggests more resources for the health and social service sectors, taking advantage of a US$149 million Heavily Indebted Poor Countries (HIPC) debt write-off by the IMF effective January 2006. A strengthening of public expenditure management and the enhancement of fiscal transparency and governance is crucial, it says, and adds that more needs to be done to improve investment planning and evaluation.

Politics

President Abdoulayé Wade is a lawyer and a veteran politician He has been exiled and imprisoned several times. He founded the Parti Démocratique Sénégalais (PDS) (Senegalese Democratic Party) and has run in five presidential races. In March 2000, he found himself in a political impasse. The presidential polls were not held at the same time as legislative elections, and his coalition government was in a minority in parliament. A year later his party won control of the national assembly.

Outlook

Senegal remains one of the most stable democracies in Africa. It has an established multi-party system and a tradition of civilian rule and peaceful transfers of power over its 45 years of independence from France. It has a long history of participation in international peacekeeping. Although poverty is widespread and unemployment is high, the country has one of the region's more stable economies. Wade supports stronger ties with the United States and greater regional integration with a unified external tariff and a more stable monetary policy.

Risk assessment

Economy	Fair/good
Politics	Fair/good
Regional stability	Satisfactory

COUNTRY PROFILE

Historical profile

Senegal has always enjoyed a prominence out of proportion to its relatively small population and modest economic importance. The site of France's earliest settlements in Black Africa, which appeared on its coastline in the mid-17th century, it subsequently became the main communications, industrial and administrative centre for the whole of French West Africa. As a result, Senegal had better internal communications and a more developed industrial sector than the surrounding territories.

The long association with France was also a close one. While other more prosperous francophone countries may display the external trappings of European society – traffic jams, concrete high-rises etc – the towns of Senegal also reflected a thorough familiarity with French culture. The relationship was symbolised by the fact the country's first president, Léopold Senghor, was a député in the French parliament and a distinguished French poet before Senegal became independent in 1960.

As a consequence of the gradual collapse of the Empire of Ghana, which encompassed a large part of Senegal, many kingdoms developed and flourished between the thirteenth–fourteenth centuries in Senegal's current territory, including Djolof, Fouta, Cayor, Baol, Sine and Saloum. Portuguese traders made contact with these kingdoms in the fifteenth century. They were followed by the British, French and Dutch in the sixteenth century who all attempted to gain control of strategic points on the slave trade routes to the Americas. By the end of the nineteenth century, France controlled the whole of Senegal.

1960 Senegal gained independence from France as part of the Federation of Mali, which almost immediately collapsed due to conflicts between the political leaders of the two territories (former French Soudan and Senegal). An independent Senegal was proclaimed under President Leopold Senghor.

1978 The first multi-party elections were held.

1980 President Senghor resigned.

1981 Abdou Diouf became president.

1982 Fighting began in Casamance between the Movement des Forces Démocratiques de Casamance (MFDC) (Democratic Forces of Casamance Movement), a separatist movement, and Senegalese government troops.

1983 The ruling Parti Socialiste Sénégalais (PS) (Senegal Socialist Party) returned to power with an overwhelming majority.

1993 Diouf was re-elected.

KEY INDICATORS — Senegal

	Unit	2000	2001	2002	2003	2004
Population	m	9.52	9.80	10.07	10.35	*10.63
Gross domestic product (GDP)	US$bn	4.40	4.60	4.90	6.50	*7.67
GDP per capita	US$	462	469	485	530	733
GDP real growth	%	5.6	5.7	4.8	6.3	6.0
Inflation	%	0.7	3.1	2.2	0.2	0.5
Exports (fob) (goods)	US$m	997.0	992.0	1,050.0	1,332.0	1,374.0
Imports (fob) (goods)	US$m	1,500.0	1,678.0	1,850.0	2,247.0	2,128.0
Balance of trade	US$m	-503.0	-686.0	-800.0	-91.5	-754.0
Current account	US$m	-230.0	-210.0	-300.0	-420.0	-470.0
Foreign debt	US$bn	3.4	3.5	3.9	3.1	–
Total reserves minus gold	US$m	383.5	447.3	637.4	794.5	998.8
Foreign exchange	US$m	380.8	438.0	626.3	781.8	989.1
Exchange rate	per US$	711.98	733.04	683.75	574.89	528.29

* estimated figure

Senegal

1994 The CFA Franc was devalued in January.

1998 Parliamentary elections were won by the PS. The constitution was amended to include a second legislative chamber, the Senate, with the president appointing 20 per cent of the delgates and most of the rest chosen by an electoral college. The opposition boycotted the Senate elections and the PS won all the seats, later winning a majority in the elections for the expanded National Assembly.

1999 The government entered into a peace initiative with the secessionist MFDC, which resulted in a cease-fire later in the year.

2000 Presidential elections were won by Abdoulayé Wade, of the Parti Démocratique Sénégalais (PDS) (Democratic Party of Senegal).

2001 A 90 per cent vote favoured the proposed new constitution that limited presidential power. President Wade's coalition won the parliamentary elections.

2002 The EU paid Senegal US$63 million for fishing rights to exploit Senegalese waters until 2006. When the Senegalese ferry, Joola, sank off the Gambian coast 1,863 passengers were killed.

2003 The MFDC declared the Casamance secessionist war was over. President Wade and King Mohammed VI of Morocco agreed a mutual political and economic accord.

2004 In November, the president and Father Diamacoune Senghore, leader of the MFDC, signed a peace deal. Disarmament and regional reconstruction was programmed to begin within weeks.

2005 Transport between Senegal and The Gambia was blockaded in a dispute which broke out in October over border ferry tariffs.

Political structure
Constitution
The 2001 constitution allows for the formation of opposition parties, gives enhanced status to the prime minister and sets the length of the president's term of office at five years. It also gives the president power to dissolve the National Assembly after it has served for two years and call fresh parliamentary elections.

Form of state
Unitary republic

The executive
Executive power is vested in the president who is head of state and commander-in-chief of the armed forces. The president is directly elected by universal adult suffrage, for a five-year term (reduced from seven years in the 2001 constitution).

In the event of the presidency falling vacant, the president of the National Assembly automatically becomes head of state.

National legislature
Legislative power is held by the 120-member National Assembly, under the 2001 constitution. The prime minister is appointed by the president and the Council of Ministers is appointed by the prime minister in consultation with the president.

Legal system
The members of the Supreme Court of Justice are appointed by the president, on the advice of the Superior Court of Magistrates, which determines the constitutionality of laws. The High Court of Justice is appointed by the National Assembly from its members; it has the power to impeach the president or members of the government.

Last elections
29 April 2001 (parliamentary); 27 February/19 March 2000 (presidential).
Results: Parliamentary: President Wade's coalition, Sopi (Change), an alliance of 40 parties dominated by the Parti Démocratique Sénégalais (PDS) (Senegalese Democratic Party), won 90 of the 120 seats; the PS, which had dominated parliament since 1960, came third, with 10 seats.
Presidential: Abdoulaye Wade won 58.49 per cent of the vote, Abdou Diouf 41.51 per cent.

Next elections
2005 (presidential); 2006 (parliamentary).

Political parties
Ruling party
Re-shuffled government (from 22 Apr 2004; President Abdoulayé Wade's coalition, Sopi (Change), an alliance of 40 parties dominated by the Parti Démocratique Sénégalais (PDS) (Senegalese Democratic Party).

Main opposition party
Parti Socialiste Sénégalais (PS) (Socialist Party)

Population
10.63 million (2004)

Ethnic make-up
Wolof (43 per cent), Pular (24 per cent), Serer (15 per cent), Jola (4 per cent), Mandinka (3 per cent), Soninke 1 per cent), European and Lebanese (1 per cent).

Religions
Islam (94 per cent), Christian (mainly Roman Catholic) (5 per cent), indigenous beliefs (1 per cent).

Education
The investment in education amounts to 3.2 per cent of GDP. The government is pursuing a broad based programme to eliminate illiteracy by 2010.

Primary education is provided free of charge and is officially compulsory. However, attendance is low and on average approximately half the relevant age groups do not attend. School attendance rates in urban areas can be as high as 80 per cent, while those of rural areas can be as low as 30 per cent.

Secondary school lasts for seven years and is divided into two cycles of four- and three-years. The first cycle is middle school when all students undertake general education. At the age of 16, all those that pass an exam can choose between a general; short or long term technical; vocational or professional, upper secondary school. Only the general and professional schools culminate in a baccalauréat (at age 18) and students can continue to Dakar University or the smaller university at Sanar near Saint Louis. Vocational and technical secondary schools concentrate on applied subjects, particularly agriculture.

Literacy rate: 40 per cent, adult rate (2003).
Compulsory years: Six to 12.
Enrolment rate: 71 per cent gross primary enrolment of relevant age group (including repeaters); 16 per cent gross secondary enrolment (World Bank).
Pupils per teacher: 58 in primary schools.

Health
In August 2002, the UN Population Fund released US$11 million for implementing a reproductive health programme in the Kolda and Tambacouanda regions of southern Senegal.

Annual government spending is around 59 per cent, and foreign spending 20 per cent, of the total expenditure on health, which is approximately 5 per cent of GDP. Private expenditure is 41 per cent, of which 8 per cent is pre-paid health insurance plans.

HIV prevalence: 0.8 per cent aged 15–49 in 2003 (World Bank)
Life expectancy: 52.3 years (World Bank)
Fertility rate/Maternal mortality rate: 4.9 births per woman (World Bank)
Birth rate/Death rate: 36 births per 1,000 population; 11 deaths per 1,000 population (2003).
Infant mortality rate: 78 per 1,000 live births (World Bank)
Head of population per physician/bed: 0.1 physicians and 0.4 hospital beds per 1,000 people.

Welfare
Most Senegalese are heavily indebted and poverty stricken. According to the World Bank, around 26 per cent of the population live below US$1 a day and around 68 per cent live on less than US$2 a day. There is a state medical service and workers receive some maternity and family benefits, but the welfare system is unable

1307

to provide sufficient economic security for Senegal's poor.

Main cities
Dakar (capital, estimated population 2.6 million in 2004), Thiès (269,900), Kaolack (233,300), Ziguinchor (211,500), St Louis (150,200).

Languages spoken
The main national languages are Jola-Fogny, Malinke, Mandinka, Pulaar, Serere-Sine, Soninke and Wolof. There are 36 spoken living languages. In business, it is essential to speak French. Very few executives speak English.

Official language/s
French

Media
Press
The press is subject to a Code de la Presse, adopted in March 1979, which stipulates that owners of national newspapers and magazines must be Senegalese. The same Code de la Presse provides for regulation and authorisation of journalists working in the national press, although there are no restrictions on the publication and distribution of the papers and magazines themselves.
Dailies: The daily national newspaper *Le Soleil* is controlled by the government. Other important dailies are *Sud quotidien*, *Le Dasasa*, *Politicien*, *L'Info* (published by Groupe Com 7), *L'Aurore (Wal Fadjri)* and *Le Matin*.
Weeklies: *Cafard Libéré* is a weekly publication.
Periodicals: Various political parties and independent owners publish journals, mostly available in French. There are two satirical journals *Le Cafard Libéré* (weekly) and *Le Politicien* (fortnightly). Other monthly publications include *Monde Islamique*, *Promotion* and *Thies tribune*.
Broadcasting
The broadcast media is state-owned. The state broadcasting company is Office de Radiodiffusion-Télévision du Sénégal (ORTS). The official (government-controlled) news agency is Agence de Presse Sénégalaise.
Radio: Two state-run radio networks broadcasting in French, Portuguese, Arabic, English and six African languages, from Rufisque, St Louis, Ziguinchor, Kaolack and Tambacounda.
Television: Television broadcasts began in 1973 but are restricted to Dakar and the surrounding area. ORTS has one television channel.

Economy
Although Senegal's macroeconomic fundamentals were strong, President Wade, on his election in 2000, inherited a legacy of financial mismanagement and uneven developmen. Despite relatively high levels of economic growth, averaging around 5 per cent throughout the 1990s, much of the wealth was siphoned off by the political elite. Since 1979, Senegal has been the guinea-pig for IMF-inspired structural adjustment policies, yet the country remains dominated by a peasant economy, with high levels of urban unemployment, despite being the most industrially advanced of the countries which once formed French West Africa.
Although a supporter of free market policies, President Wade is evidently not happy with programmes advocated by the World Bank. His agenda is to appeal to private investors for infrastructure projects and capital improvements. To attract sufficient private capital into his ambitious development programme, Wade plans to exploit the country's relative proximity to Europe, as well as its political and economic stability.
Several factors have limited investment. The country's economy is beset by a drought cycle which has, in the past, diminished export growth. Liberalisation of the economy has not helped matters. Groundnuts, which once represented the country's main source of export income, have declined after the country reduced trade barriers, exposing the sector to a world commodity market that was drifting into depression.
In terms of economic diversification, Senegal is better placed than other West African countries. It has a relatively advanced industrial sector that accounts for 21 per cent of GDP and employs over 17 per cent of the population. The likelihood that Senegal can forge an independent development programme without significant development aid is doubtful over the medium-term.
Civil unrest resulted in a decline of tourist revenues in early 2003, but the economy recovered and showed GDP growth of around 6 per cent. Unemployment remains one of Senegal's most prominent problems with just under half the population jobless, the majority being urban youth. High unemployment rates hinder the reduction of poverty with around 54 per cent of the population living below the poverty line.

External trade
Senegal is part of the Union Economique et Monetaire Ouest Africaine (UEMOA) (West African Economic and Monetary Union).
On 31 December 2002, the US approved Senegal as being eligible for tariff preferences under the Africa Growth and Opportunities Act (AGOA). The legislation requires that countries are only eligible for greater access to US markets provided they have made continued progress toward a market-based economy, the rule of law, free trade, poverty reduction and the protection of workers' rights. This process is reviewed annually.
Imports
Principal imports are food and beverages, capital goods and fuels.
Main sources: France (26.2 per cent total, 2004), Nigeria (12.1 per cent), Thailand (5.3 per cent), Belgium (5.0 per cent), Spain (4.2 per cent)
Exports
Principal exports are fish, groundnuts (peanuts), petroleum products, phosphates and cotton.
Main destinations: India (13.8 per cent total, 2004), France (10.6 per cent), Mali (10.0 per cent), Italy (6.0 per cent), Côte d'Ivoire (5.7 per cent), Spain (4 per cent)

Agriculture
Farming
Agriculture contributes around 17 per cent to GDP and employs 70 per cent of the working population. Farming is carried out almost exclusively on smallholdings and is relatively inefficient. Agricultural development has been hindered by poor transport infrastructure. Since 1984, Senegal has liberalised the sector by reducing state intervention. As a result, the distribution of fertilisers has ceased to be a state monopoly and is now handled by the private sector. The government phased out subsidised credit for agricultural supplies but also established an agricultural development bank, the Caisse Nationale de Crédit Agricole. Marketing co-operatives were replaced by village co-operatives which enjoyed greater autonomy. In 2002, the UN Food and Agricultural Organisation (FAO) initiated a six-year small-scale agricultural project in several villages, introducing simple technologies useful for raising yields in rice and vegetables.
The main subsistence crops are sorghum and millet, although production of rice is increasing. Horticultural output is also rising, supplying the domestic market and providing exports of out-of-season fruit and vegetables to European markets. Cash crops include groundnuts, cotton and sugar. Groundnut farming is crucial to the economy and employs a large percentage of the rural population. The Société National de Commercialisation des Oléagineux de Sénégal (Sonacos), the national groundnut company, was privatised in December 2004.
Sugar cane is the only sector with large plantations, which are operated by Compagnie Sucrière du Sénégal (CSS). Both groundnut and cotton output have been affected by the lack of farm credit and high levels of debt.

Cattle, sheep and goats are widely kept for domestic use. Poultry numbers are showing a long-term increase and there has been a marked increase in the sheep population since the mid-1980s.

In 2004, the worst locust plague for 15 years attacked crops across much of west Africa and the Sahel region of southern Sahara. Crops in Senegal were severely admaged. The UN organised a nine-country response group with Morocco and Algeria sending aid of vehicles and pesticide, but a year after the warning was first given, it was estimated that only 3 per cent of the 4.3 million hectares that require spraying had been treated. Mauritania is the hatching ground for the largest swarms although the insects are breeding elsewhere in the region.

Crop production in 2004 included: 1,200,119 tonnes (t) cereals in total, 422,623t maize, 180,000t cassava, 379,166t millet, 132,400t sorghum, 264,500t rice, 40,300t pulses, 188,250t roots and tubers, *35,000t citrus fruit, 161,007t oilcrops, 465,000t groundnuts in shell, 850,000t sugar cane, 54,946t seed cotton, 22,000t cotton lint, *139,500t fruit in total, 567,049t vegetables in total. Livestock production included: 168,644t meat in total, 47,750t beef, 10,000t pig meat, 15,500t lamb, 16,620t goat meat, 65,400t poultry, 34,000t eggs, 129,068t milk, 550t honey, 9,550t cattle hides, 3,211t sheepskins, 6,938t horsemeat.

* estimate

Fishing
Fishing is important for the export revenues from the fish processing and canning industries, as well as licence revenues from foreign ships operating in Senegalese waters. Fish and fish products are typically the largest single item in export earnings. The fisheries sector is targetted for expansion, with assistance being given to artisan fishermen, and the development of producer groups. Finance for this programme is partly derived from the foreign fishing licence revenues. The Senegalese government is supporting the development of marine fish farming (tuna, oysters, prawns and lobsters).

In January 2002, Senegal refused to extend a fishing rights accord which had allowed EU vessels to fish in Senegalese waters since 1997. The EU and Senegal clashed over which areas should be fished and the length of the rest periods, which are essential for fish stock recovery. The Senegalese authorities raised the problem of overfishing and illegal methods employed by EU trawlers, which is causing fish stocks to plummet and has put Senegalese fishermen's livelihoods at risk; around 500,000 people in Senegal depend on the fishing industry for an income. In June 2002, the EU agreed to pay Senegal eur64 million (US$62 million) for the right to exploit its fishing grounds until 2006. The deal bans pelagic fishing, in which a net is dragged by two trawlers which results in significant wastage, and imposes a two-month rest period. Conservationists dismissed the deal, claiming it would continue to seriously undermine fish stocks and local livelihoods.

Forestry
Forest resources in Senegal are modest, although the country is well forested with 38 per cent forest cover estimated at 6.2 million hectares (ha) and an additional 30 per cent of other wooded land. Deforestation occurs at an average rate of 0.7 per cent per year. Desertification continues to be a major environmental problem in northern Senegal. The country has established significant areas of plantation forest to meet fuel and fodder needs. A programme of reforestation now under way aims to include the revival of gum arabic production.

Wood is mostly used for fuel consumption, while production of sawn timber and industrial roundwood caters to the domestic market. Some amount of wood and paper is also imported. In 2004, total imports of forest products amounted to US$52.5 million, while exports amounted to US$2.0 million.

Production in 2004 included 6.0 million cubic metres (cum) roundwood, 23,000cum sawnwood, 40,000cum sawlogs and veneers, 5.2 million cum woodfuel, 110,208mt charcoal.

Industry and manufacturing
The industrial sector contributes around 25 per cent to GDP, with the manufacturing sector contributing 17 per cent of GDP. Most industry is located inside the Dakar area of the Cap Vert peninsula. The only heavy export industries are an oil refinery at Dakar-Mbao, a sulphuric/phosphoric acid plant at Darou Khoudou and a fertiliser complex at Mbao.

The main industrial activity is light industry, processing locally-produced primary commodities for export and manufacturing import substitution goods to meet local demand. The government's industrial policy aims to make the economy more market-responsive and less centrally controlled. This entails a reduction in government participation in industry, price liberalisation and the encouragement of foreign investment (through a more favourable tax regime) and small businesses (through special incentives). It gives priority to high-value and export industries, especially chemicals, textiles, food processing and leather goods. The food-processing sector and, to a lesser extent, textile manufacturing, are influenced heavily by agricultural performance, as they rely mainly on locally produced inputs. Therefore, industrial performance is affected by climatic conditions in a similar way to the agricultural sector. Light industry is mostly privately-owned and relies heavily on foreign capital and management skills. Lack of adequate infrastructure has curtailed industrial development outside the capital.

Tourism
The state tourism agency is involved both in promoting the country in Europe (particularly in Italy and the UK), and in encouraging foreign investment in the development of further tourist facilities. The government sees tourism as a key foreign currency earner. Tourism is expected to contribute 3.5 per cent to GDP in 2005.

Mining
The mining sector contributes around 7 per cent to GDP and employs 3 per cent of the workforce.

Extraction of calcium and phosphates from open mines near Thiès are the most important mining activities. Workable deposits are estimated at around 130 million tonnes. Production (around 1.5 million tonnes per annum) is mainly for export, although it is also an important source of supply for the fertiliser complex at Mbao. Phosphates represent around 17 per cent of export earnings, although production declined by 30 per cent over the 1990s. The phosphate mine in the Matam area holds deposits of around 40.5 million tonnes.

Titanium, zircon and rutile are mined along the south coast of Cap Vert. The total available iron ore reserves at the Faleme iron ore project near the Mali border are estimated at 391 million tonnes, enough to sustain mining activities for over 30 years at the planned production rate of 12 million tonnes of marketable products per year. The Farangalia and Goto deposits hold estimated reserves of 250 million tonnes.

Hydrocarbons
Senegal's oil requirements are met by imports. Downstream, the Société Africaine de Raffinage (SAR) refinery has a nominal capacity of 17,000 barrels per day (bpd). The government is actively promoting increased offshore petroleum exploration along with its neighbouring countries. Gas reserves are estimated at three billion cubic metres and are primarily located offshore. Annual gas production is around 1.4 billion cubic metres. Gas currently produced on the Diam Niadio East concession is supplied to Société Nationale d'Electricité (Senelec). All of this is

consumed domestically. No natural gas is imported. There is a small natural gas field at Diam-Niadio, which has been used to fire a generator. The market for butane has increased more than 15-fold since 1974, and further expansion is forecast. The government has been encouraging its use, as an alternative to firewood. Senegal does not produce or import coal.

Energy
Electric power is supplied from six thermal stations, with a total installed capacity of 422MW. Virtually all commercial energy requirements are imported.

Only one in three people in Senegal has access to electricity. In rural areas, wood provides most fuel requirements, with consequent serious deforestation. A programme of reforestation is under way. The government's 10-year energy plan aims to substitute 50 per cent of imported oil by local products, including oil/gas from the Dome Flore offshore field, peat deposits from Niayés and the expansion of hydropower from the Senegal and Gambia Rivers.

The government has failed to divest the Société Nationale d'Electricité (Senelec), the state-owned electricity company, despite two attempts at privatisation.

Banking and insurance
Eight commercial banks operate in Senegal, with the three largest banks holding approximately two-thirds of total deposits. The largest bank in Senegal is the Société Générale de Banques au Sénégal (SGBS). The SGBS faces strong competition from its main rival, the Banque International pour le Commerce et l'Industrie du Sénégal (BICIS).

The banking sector is overseen by the Banque Centrale des Etas de l'Afrique de l'Ouest (BCEAO), which sets policy throughout the Union Economique et Monetaire Ouest Africaine (UEMOA) (West African Economic and Monetary Union).

Central bank
Banque Centrale des Etats de l'Afrique de l'Ouest (BCEAO)
Main financial centre
Dakar

Time
GMT

Geography
Senegal lies on the west coast of Africa, bordered to the north by Mauritania, to the east by Mali, and to the south by Guinea and Guinea-Bissau. Senegal surrounds the small state of The Gambia, which straddles the River Gambia in the south-west of Senegal, and forms a narrow enclave extending some 320 kilometres (200 miles) inland.

The country is low-lying and flat, and is situated in the savannah grasslands. Apart from the River Gambia and the Senegal River, which forms the northern boundary, most rivers are seasonal and dry up in the arid winter months.

Climate
The climate is tropical in the south (Casamance) and more temperate in the north.

The best time to visit is October–June, when it is cool and dry. The safest time to avoid the rain is mid November–April, but it is hot and humid during the day (cooler at night). During the rainy season, July–September, the humidity gets very high and the days very hot. In the southern part of the country, the rainy season can extend through October.

Dress codes
There is no restriction on clothing, although women are advised to dress modestly. In the dry season lightweight European clothing is suitable, and many government ministers wear lounge suits. Businessmen and other officials wear local dress – the *boubou*. Tropical clothing (not white) is necessary in the wet season.

Entry requirements
Passports
Required by all.
Visa
Required by all; except nationals of the EU, North America, Japan and many countries in the region for visits up to 90 days (for a full list of exceptions see www.senegalembassy.co.uk). Visitors should contact the nearest consulate to obtain an application form. Proof of return/onward passage is necessary. Business travellers should include a letter of invitation, from a local company or organisation, and a business letter of intent, with their application form.
Currency advice/regulations
Local currency import is unlimited but export to countries outside the CFA franc zone is prohibited. Within the French Monetary Area, up to CFAf20,000 can be exported.

All foreign currency must be declared on arrival and departure. The amount taken out must not exceed the amount brought in. Travellers cheques should be French francs or US dollars, as sterling is not widely accepted.

Health (for visitors)
There is no national health service, and medical assistance outside Dakar is minimal.
Mandatory precautions
A yellow fever certificate is required if arriving from an endemic area.

Advisable precautions
It is advisable to have immunisations for typhoid, polio, hepatitis 'A', tetanus and yellow fever. Malaria prophylaxis should be taken as risk exists throughout the country. Rabies and bilharzia are present. Visitors should avoid swimming or paddling in fresh water. Unboiled water and milk, raw fruit and vegetables should be avoided.

Hotels
Air-conditioned hotels are available in Dakar, although they can be expensive. Hotel bills usually include service charges and local tax. Tipping is therefore optional.

Credit cards
Major credit cards are accepted in hotels, by airlines and some shops. (Not American Express.)

Public holidays
Fixed dates
1 Jan (New Year's Day), 4 Apr (Independence Day), 1 May (Labour Day), 15 Aug (Assumption Day), 1 Nov (All Saints' Day), 25 Dec (Christmas Day).
Variable dates
Easter Monday, Ascension Day, Whit Monday, Eid al Adha, Eid al Fitr, Islamic New Year, Birth of the Prophet,
The Islamic year contains 354 or 355 days, with the result that Muslim feasts advance by 10–12 days against the Gregorian calendar. Dates of feasts vary according to the sighting of the new moon, so cannot be forecast exactly. Islamic year 1426: 10 February 2005 to 30 January 2006.

Working hours
Banking
Mon–Fri: 0800–1115, 1430–1630.
Business
Mon–Fri: 0800–1230, 1300–1600.
Government
Mon–Fri: 0800/ 0900–1200, 1500–1800; Sat: 0800/0900–1200.
Shops
Mon–Sat: 0800–1200, 1430–1800.

Electricity supply
127/220V AC, 50 cycles. Plugs and sockets are mainly two-pin (round), and lampholders are mainly screw-type, but bayonet is also found.

Social customs/useful tips
Visitors should be punctual for appointments and visiting cards should be presented at business meetings. French-style formalities are observed. These include shaking hands when greeting and before departing.

When arriving at a village, the traveller should first visit the headman or schoolteacher, who will often act as an

Senegal

interpreter and provide introductions to the local people and customs.
Use the right hand when shaking hands and passing or receiving anything. Visits should be avoided during the Islamic month of Ramadan.
A service charge is normally added to the bill. Gratuities are not customary for taxis. The minimum drinking age is 20 years. Smoking is banned in some public places, including mosques.

Security
Purse snatching and pickpocketing is on the increase, particularly in the downtown area of Dakar. Avoid political gatherings and street demonstrations and maintain security awareness at all times.
The permission of the Senegalese authorities is required for travel to certain areas of the Casamance region where attacks from armed separatist rebels and bandits occur.

Getting there
Air
National airline: Air Sénégal
International airport/s: Dakar-Leopold Sedar Senghor (Code: DKR), 17km north west of city; duty-free shop, bar, restaurant, buffet, bank, post office, shops, car hire, taxis.
Airport tax: There is no airport departure tax.
Surface
Road: Principal road routes are from the Gambia, Mali, Mauritania – those from Guinea are not generally recommended. A 720 metre bridge over the Mansoa river has improved the traffic flow on the trans-African coastal road between Bissau, Guinea-Bissau, and Senegal.
Rail: Twice weekly rail services operate between Dakar and Bamako (Mali) via Kaolack and Tambacounda.
Main port/s: Dakar is the second-largest port in West Africa and serves Senegal, Mauritania and the Gambia. The port has extensive facilities for fishing vessels and fish processing.

Getting about
National transport
Air: Air Sénégal links Dakar with all the main towns.
Small aircraft can be chartered from Africair Service.
Gambia Air Shuttle operates a twice-daily service between Dakar and Banjul in the Gambia.
Road: Tarred roads are mainly near the coast; inland areas are served by roads of variable quality. Main highways: Dakar to St. Louis, Rosso, Djourbel, Joal, Koalack and Ziguinchor.
Buses: Coach services Dakar-Ziguinchor; Tambacounda-Ziguinchor; Tambacounda-Gaoual are operated subject to demand.
Rail: The railway links Dakar with Tambacounda to the east, and with St. Louis and Linguère to the north-east.
Water: There was a ferry service from Dakar to Ziguinchor, which is currently suspended. The Senegal river in the north is only navigable for parts of the year: for three months as far as Kayes (Mali); for six months as far as Kaedi (Mauritania); and all year as far as Rosso and Podor. Other rivers include the Saloun and the Casamance.
City transport
Taxis: Taxis are plentiful in Dakar. Most vehicles are licensed and fitted with meters. Tipping is not customary.
Buses, trams & metro: Large green and yellow public buses operate a regular flat-fare service.
Car hire
An international or national driving licence, insurance and car registration document (Carte Grise) are required. Vehicles coming from the right always have right of way.

BUSINESS DIRECTORY
The addresses listed below are a selection only. While World of Information makes every endeavour to check these addresses, we cannot guarantee that changes have not been made, especially to telephone numbers and area codes. We would welcome any corrections.

Telephone area codes
The international dialling code (IDD) for Senegal is +221, followed by subscriber's number.

Useful telephone numbers
Police: 823-7149, 823-2529, 823-8383.

Chambers of Commerce
Union des Chambres de Commerce, d'Industrie et d'Agriculture de Senegal, 1 Place de l'Independence, PO Box 118, Dakar (tel: 823-7189; fax: 823-9363; e-mail: cciad@telecomplus-sn).

Dakar Chambre de Commerce, d'Industrie et d'Agriculture, 1 Place de l'Indépendance, PO Box 118, Dakar (tel: 823-7189; fax: 823-9363; e-mail: ccaid@telecomplus.sn).

Diourbel Chambre de Commerce, d'Industrie et d'Agriculture, PO Box 7, Diourbel (tel/fax: 971-1203; e-mail: ccdiour@cyg.sn).

Fatick Chambre de Commerce, d'Industrie et d'Agriculture, PO Box 66, Fatick (tel/fax: 949-1425).

Kaolack Chambre de Commerce, d'Industrie et d'Agriculture, Rue Noirot, PO Box 203, Kaolack (tel: 941-2050; fax: 941-2291; e-mail: cciak@visto.com).

Kolda Chambre de Commerce, d'Industrie et d'Agriculture, Quartier Escale, PO Box 23, Kolda (tel: 996-1230; fax: 996-1068; e-mail:cciakd@sentoo.sn).

Louga Chambre de Commerce, d'Industrie et d'Agriculture, 2 Rue Glozel, Quartier Thiokhma, PO Box 26 Louga (tel: 967-1114; fax: 967-4658; e-mail: ccial@sentoo.sn).

Saint Louis Chambre de Commerce, d'Industrie et d'Agriculture, 10 Rue Blanchot, PO Box 19, Saint Louis (tel: 961-1088; fax: 961-2980; e-mail: cciasl@tpsnet.sn).

Tambacounda Chambre de Commerce, d'Industrie et d'Agriculture, PO Box 27, Tambacounda (tel: 981-1014; fax: 981-2995).

Thies Chambre de Commerce, d'Industrie et d'Agriculture, 96 Avenue Lamine Gueye, PO Box 3020 Thies (tel: 951-1002; fax: 951-1397; e-mail: cciath@tpsnet.sn).

Ziguinchor Chambre de Commerce, d'Industrie et d'Agriculture, Rue de Général de Gaulle, PO Box 26, Ziguinchor (tel: 991-1310; fax: 991-2163).

Banking
Banque de l'Habitat du Sénégal, PO Box 229, 69 Boulevard Général de Gaulle, Dakar (tel: 8231-004; fax: 8238-043).

Banque Internationale pour le Commerce et l'Industrie du Sénégal SA, PO Box 392, 2 Avenue du Président L Senghor, Dakar (tel: 8390-390; fax: 8233-707).

Banque Islamique du Sénégal, PO Box 3381, Immeuble Abdallah Fayçal, Dakar (tel: 8496-262; fax: 8224-948).

Banque Senegalo-Tunisienne (BST), PO Box 4111, Immeuble Kebe, 97 Avenue André Peytavin, Dakar (tel: 8237-576; fax: 8238-238).

Caisse Nationale de Crédit Agricole du Sénégal, PO Box 3890, 45 Avenue Albert Sarraut, Dakar (tel: 8222-300; fax: 8212-606).

Compagnie Bancaire de l'Afrique Occidentale, PO Box 129, 2 Place de l'Indépendance, Dakar (tel: 8231-000; fax: 8232-005).

Crédit Lyonnais Sénégal, PO Box 56, Boulevard El Hadji Djily Mbaye, Angle Rue Huart, Dakar (tel: 8231-008; fax: 8238-430).

Société Générale de Banques au Sénégal SA, PO Box 323, 19 Avenue du Président L Senghor, Dakar (tel: 8395-500; fax: 8219-119).

Central bank
Banque Centrale des Etats de l'Afrique de l'Ouest, Boulevard du Général de Gaulle, PO Box 3159, Dakar (tel: 823-1330; fax: 823-5757).

Travel information

Ministry of tourism
Ministry of Tourism and Environment, 23 Rue Calmette, BP 4049, Dakar (tel: 8211-126; fax: 8229-413).

National tourist organisation offices
National Tourist Office, Ministry of Tourism and Air Transport, 23 Rue Calmette, PO Box 4049, Dakar (tel: 236-502).

Ministries

Ministry of Armed Forces, Batîment Administratif, Avenue Roume, Dakar (tel: 8231-216; fax: 8236-338).

Ministry of Commerce, Batîment Administratif, Avenue Roume, Dakar (tel: 8229-542; fax: 8219-132).

Ministry of the Habitat, Ex-Camp Lat-Dior, Dakar (tel: 8233-278; fax: 8236-245).

Ministry of the Interior, Place Washington, Dakar (tel: 8234-151; fax: 8210-542).

Ministry of Justice, Batîment Administratif, Avenue Roume, Dakar (tel: 8238-042; fax: 8232-727).

Ministry of Modernisation of the State, Rue Emile Zola, Dakar (tel: 8232-922; fax: 8229-764).

Ministry of National Education, Rue Calmette, Dakar (tel: 8224-123; fax: 8218-930).

Ministry of Tourism and Environment, 23 Rue Calmette, BP 4049, Dakar (tel: 8211-126; fax: 8229-413).

Ministry of Women, Children and the Family, Rue Beranger Ferraud, Dakar (tel: 8236-919; fax: 8236-673).

Prime Minister's Office, Batîment Administratif, Avenue Roume, Dakar (tel: 8224-917; fax: 8225-578).

Other useful addresses

British Embassy, 20 rue du Docteur Guillet, PO Box 6025, Dakar (tel: 8237-392, 8239-971; fax: 8232-766).

Direction de la Statistique, BP 116, Dakar (tel: 8230-881).

Foire Internationale de Dakar (SOFIDAK), route de l'Aéroport, BP 3329, Dakar (tel: 8231-011).

Port Autonome de Dakar, 35 boulevard de la Libération, Dakar (tel: 8224-545, 8227-421).

Senegalese Embassy (UK) 39 Marloes Road, London W8 6LA (tel: (020) 7937-7237, 7938-4048; fax: (020) 7938-2546; internet: www.senegalembassy.co.uk).

Senegalese Embassy (US), 2112 Wyoming Avenue, NW, Washington DC 20008 (tel: 202-234-0540; fax: 202-352-6315).

Société de Développement Agricole et Industriel du Sénégal, 23 avenue Roume, PO Box 222, Dakar (tel: 8251-818).

Société Nationale d'Etudes et de Promotion Industrielle, BP 100, derrière Residence Seydou Nourou Tall, Dakar (tel: 8252-130).

Société Nationale des Télécommunications du Sénégal (SONATEL), 6 rue Wagane Diouf, BP 62, Dakar (tel: 8231-023, 8214-242).

Société Nouvelle des Etudes de Développement en Afrique, 36 rue Calmette, PO Box 2084, Dakar (tel: 8234-231).

Syndicat des Commerçants, Importateurs et Exportateurs de l'Ouest Africaine (Scimpex), angle rue Parent et avenue Abdoulaye Fadiga, PO Box 806, Dakar (tel: 8213-662).

US Embassy, avenue Jean XXIII, PO Box 49, Dakar (tel: 8234-296; fax: 8222-991).

Internet sites

Africa Business Network: http://www.ifc.org/abn

AllAfrica.com: http://allafrica.com

African Development Bank: http://www.afdb.org

Press agency (in French) http://www.aps.sn/

Web portal: http://www.au-senegal.com/

Serbia and Montenegro

In 2005, the story of the Državna zajednica Srbija i Crna Gora (hereafter SiCG) (State Union of Serbia and Montenegro) was one of multiple parts. While SiCG secured coveted Stabilisation and Association Agreement (SAA) accession talks with the EU on 10 October, more news was generated by events in the state's various constituents. Montenegro intensified its bid to secede, as did the Serbian province of Kosovo, populated overwhelmingly by ethnic Albanians. Rumblings in favour of greater autonomy were also heard in Serbia's Vojvodina province.

Economies apart

Although the economies of Serbia, on the one hand, and Montenegro, on the other, are not divorced from each other, the main economic indicators for 2005 confirm a decade-long pattern of separation. Serbia's GDP grew by 6.1 per cent in the first half of 2005, and recorded an average inflation rate of 18 per cent. Its more industrially-based economy suffered from a decline in industrial production compared to 2004 levels of output. In May, the IMF extended a loan to Serbia in exchange for the implementation of an austerity

KEY FACTS

Official name: Serbia and Montenegro (on 4 Feb 2003, the Federal Republic of Yugoslavia was abolished and replaced with a looser federation of its two member states, Serbia and Montenegro)

Head of State: President Svetozar Marovic (from 7 Mar 2003)

Head of government: President Svetozar Marovic (from 12 Mar 2003)

Ruling party: 18-party Demokratska Opozicija Srbije (DOS) (Democratic Opposition of Serbia) coalition

Area: 102,173 square km

Population: 11.03 million (2004)

Capital: Belgrade

Official language: Serbian

Currency: Serbia: dinar (D) ; Montenegro: euro (eur) (from 1 Jan 2002; previous currency Deutshe mark, locked at DM1.96 per euro); Kosovo: euro (eur) (from 1 Jan 2002; previous currencies Deutsche mark and dinar)

Exchange rate: D70.73 per US$ (Oct 2005); Montenegro and Kosovo: eur0.83 per US$ (Oct 2005)

GDP per capita: US$2,893 (2004)

GDP real growth: 7.20% (2004)

Labour force: 3.93 million (2004)

Unemployment: 30.00% (2004); 50.00% (Kosovo, 2004)*

Inflation: 9.50% (2004)

Balance of trade: -US$6.28 billion 2004

Foreign debt: US$9.20 billion (2003)

* estimated figure

KEY FACTS

Official name: Republika Crna Gora (Republic of Montenegro) (ROM)

Head of State: President Filip Vujanovic (since Nov 2002; elected 11 May 2003)

Head of government: Prime Minister Milo Đukanovic (DPS) (resigned from presidency to lead government from 26 Nov 2002; confirmed 8 Jan 2003)

Ruling party: Coalition government (from 8 Jan 2003) comprising Demokratska Partija Socijalista Crna Gore (Democratic Party of Montenegrin Socialists); Social-Demokratska Partija (SDP) (Social-Democratic Party); Gradanska Partija Crne Gore (GPCG) (Citizens' Party of Montenegro)

Area: 13,800 square km

Population: 660,000 (2004)

Capital: Podgorica

Official language: Serbian, Albanian

Currency: Euro (eur) = 100 cents (from 1 Jan 2002; previous currency Deutsche mark, locked at DM1.96 per euro)

Exchange rate: eur0.77 per US$ (Nov 2004)

GDP real growth: 3.10% (2004)

Unemployment: 22.30% (2004)

Inflation: 2.40% (2004)

Annual FDI: US$18.00 million (12 months to May 2004)

---

programme, designed to cut a spiralling budget deficit, privatise key industries and tackle Serbia's high inflation levels. Compliance was also sweetened by an offer from the Paris Club of creditors to write off US$700 millions of Serbia's debts. However, Serbia was reprimanded in August by the IMF for failing to adhere to the terms of the aid package. By November, the Serbian government managed to pass a budget for 2006 that complied with most of the IMF's demands.

Montenegro's economy grew by a more modest 4.1 per cent but inflation was only 2.3 per cent. Since 2000, Montenegro has used a separate currency to that of Serbia, firstly the German mark and, from 2002, the euro. Although relatively poor, Montenegro showed signs of significant upward development in 2005. The tourism industry boomed, with a 16.8 per cent increase on 2004 figures. The budget deficit was reduced, as was domestic debt, and investment rose.

End of the union in sight?

Since its formal inception in February 2003, the SiCG has experienced considerable centrifugal pressure. Montenegro, having only reluctantly signed up to the agreement in the first place, ensured the inclusion of a clause that would effectively enable it to secede after three years. With the deadline for exercising this opt-out clause looming, Montenegro's President Filip Vujanović and Prime Minister Milo Đukanovic spent 2005 preparing the ground for a referendum widely predicted to take place in April 2006.

Complicating this drive to independence were negotiations between the EU and SiCG over the SAA, generally regarded as a first step on the road to EU membership. From 2001, the EU had invested great effort in ensuring that SiCG remain united. Janvier Solana, the EU's High Representative for Common Foreign and Security Policy, was personally involved in the 2003 union and by all accounts was keen to use the SAA talks in 2005 as a carrot for future SiCG unity. Moreover, in November, an EU delegation to Montenegro made it clear that the EU preferred the continued existence of SiCG. However, if this was his intent, Solana was to be disappointed many times over in 2005. Đukanovic repeatedly stated that he would rather forgo EU membership if it meant no independence for Montenegro. From August, a dispute over the position of the union defence minister drove a further wedge between Serbia and Montenegro. Having lost out, Montenegro announced its intention to examine setting up its own defence ministry – in breach of the SiCG constitution. Persistent disunity among anti-independence parties in Montenegro in 2005 also gave little hope to those outside Montenegro championing the union's cause.

In recognition of this centrifugal pressure, the Council of Europe, in May, asked its Venice Commission to advise on how best to conduct a referendum on independence in Montenegro that was free, fair and recognised as legitimate by all stakeholders. Both pro- and anti-independence supporters in Montenegro agreed to abide by the Commission's findings.

Kosovo: decision time approaching

Administered by the United Nations Mission in Kosovo (UNMIK) since 1999, Kosovo had been in a state of limbo for years – technically under Serbian sovereignty but effectively a UN protectorate. The UN Security Council approved the opening of talks on Kosovo's final status in October 2005. Interested parties immediately went into overdrive to make their cases heard. In November, the parliaments of Kosovo and Serbia traded tit-for-tat resolutions for and against independence respectively. Serbia continued to offer 'more than autonomy, less than independence'. Unfortunately for Serbia, a number of officials from a variety of countries (Slovenia, Switzerland, France and the Czech Republic) made it known, both privately and publicly, that independence for Kosovo was inevitable. In November, Montenegro's President Đukanovic also urged Serbia to be 'realistic' over the issue of Kosovo's status, suggesting that the Montenegrin government was prepared to accept Kosovan independence. On the other hand, Serbia managed, in 2005, to garner support for its position from Russia and Romania. Some within Serbia itself, including President Boris Tadić, floated other proposals for Kosovo's future during the year, including a partition of the province, into Serb and Albanian zones. Both the EU and UNMIK officials flatly rejected this proposition. Moreover, talk of partition stirred up latent tension in Serbia's Preševo valley, adjacent to Kosovo. In November, ethnic Albanians in the area reiterated their demand that they be included in any land-swap between Serbia and Kosovo.

In Kosovo itself, the local political scene remained remarkably calm, despite three potentially destabilising developments in March. The Albanian Kosovar prime minister, Ramush Haradinaj, was

Serbia and Montenegro

indicted by the International Criminal Tribunal for the former Yugoslavia (ICTY) and surrendered voluntarily to The Hague. President Ibrahim Rugova, the prime mover behind the ethnic Albanian drive to win independence from Serbia, survived an attempt on his life in March; but then in January 2006 succumbed to lung cancer. Also, March brought the first anniversary of major inter-ethnic rioting in Kosovo, in which 19 people died and 900 were injured.

The Serb minority continued to boycott the province's institutions, including the parliament. The boycott was supported by Serbia's prime minister, Vojislav Kostunica. Unfortunately for the Serb minority, this meant that they had little influence over negotiations, finalised in July 2005, between Albanian Kosovars and UNMIK on the subject of administrative decentralisation.

Vojvodina: new autonomy desires

The European Parliament adopted, in September and after heavy lobbying during the year by Hungary, a resolution criticising Serbia's treatment of minorities in Vojvodina. Serbs in Vojvodina, a semi-autonomous province in northern Serbia, constitute a plurality of the population but there are also significant Hungarian and Croatian minorities. The NGO Human Rights Watch (HRW) echoed the European Parliament's sentiments in a report published in October, and also drew attention to abuses against Serbia's Bošniak minority in the southern Sandžak region. The Hungarian, Croat and Bošniak minorities all pressed the Serbian government for greater self-determination in 2005.

Serbian politics: deep divisions

Although Serbia's political elite broadly agreed on the matter of Kosovo, this was where consensus ended. Confirmed in office in March 2004, the 18-party governing coalition had a rough ride in 2005. In August, the Socijaldemokratska Partija (SDS) (Social Democratic Party) left the coalition to join the opposition. President Tadić, a member of the opposition Demokratska Stranka (DS) (Democratic Party), frequently clashed with Prime Minister Kostunica's government over both domestic and foreign policy. Tadić, for instance, adopted a more flexible position on independence for Kosovo and Montenegro than the government. In May and December, President Tadić delayed signing into law several government bills, and in December openly called for fresh elections. Opinion polls in 2005 consistently named Tadić the most popular politician in Serbia and reported that his DS and the ultra-nationalist Srpska Radikalna Stranka (SRS) (Serbian Radical Party) would win the most seats in the event of an election. Kostunica, once lionised by the public for his role in the overthrow of former Serbian strongman Slobodan Milošević, was polled as being less popular than Milošević himself.

The dark past reaches out

In 2005, Serbia came under intense international pressure to arrest the two most prominent figures in the Bosnia and Hercegovina civil war still wanted for alleged war crimes: Radovan Karadžic and Ratko Mladić. Both are widely believed to be hiding in Serbia and Montenegro. In January, the US suspended a multi-million dollar aid package to Serbia on the grounds that the Serbian authorities had not done enough to capture Karadžic and Mladic. The EU Enlargement Commissioner, Olli Rehn, also made it clear that progress on SAA talks would be dependent upon progress on tracking down alleged war criminals. In a victory for robust diplomacy and a sign that the Serbian government rated the conclusion of a SAA highly, five high-ranking military figures were transferred to the ICTY in The Hague between February and April. The US released the aid package to Serbia in June and the EU began SAA entry talks in October. However, in a report to the UN Security Council in December, the Chief Prosecutor for ICTY, Carla Del Ponte, submitted a report critical of Serbia's compliance over war crimes suspects. The pressure mounted again on Serbia when, on 8 December, Croatia's last major war crimes suspect was arrested in Spain. At year's end, both Karadžic and Mladić were still at large.

Outlook

It is highly likely that the SiCG will cease to exist in its current form in 2006. An independence referendum in Montenegro appears unstoppable and will probably take place by the end of April, as planned by the Ðukanovic government. Opinion polls in 2005 consistently reported 41–44 per cent support for independence, with around 38 per cent against. This breakdown approximately reflects the ethnic make-up of Montenegro, with people identifying themselves as Montenegrin generally more independence minded than those identifying themselves as Serbian. It is possible that the 16 per cent of

KEY FACTS

Official name: Republika Srbije (Republic of Serbia) (ROS)

Head of State: President Boris Tadić (sworn in 11 Jul 2004)

Head of government: Prime Minister Vojislav Kostunica (appointed 20 Feb 2004)

Ruling party: Coalition government: the Democratic Party of Serbia, G17 Plus, the Serbian Renewal Movement and New Serbia, with support from the Socialist Party (confirmed by parliament 4 Mar 2004)

Population: 10.00 million (2004)

Capital: Belgrade

Official language: Serbian

Currency: Serbian dinar (D) = 100 paras

Exchange rate: D59.82 per US$ (Nov 2004)

the population who identify themselves as Bošniak or Albanian will have the casting vote. The recommendation of the Venice Commission's advisory report, published in December 2005, that Montenegrin citizens living in Serbia not be allowed to vote in the referendum is predicted to favour the independence camp. Such Montenegrins are considered more likely to vote against independence.

The SiCG will also face the very real possibility of the secession of Kosovo in 2006. With some analysts predicting the end of final status talks in June, the Balkans could witness the emergence of three new independent states, Serbia, Montenegro and Kosovo. Of the three, Kosovo will face the most profound economic challenges and will no doubt remain under some form of EU supervision for years to come. The death of President Rugova on 21 January, from lung cancer, has caused status talks to be delayed until February and raised fears of a violent power struggle. Serbia will again face pressure to apprehend war crimes suspects, possibly to the detriment of its EU membership hopes, and Montenegro will have to convince a sceptical EU of its economic viability.

Risk assessment

Economic	Poor
Political	Poor
Regional stability	Poor

COUNTRY PROFILE

Historical profile
Far-reaching political and economic changes began in what was then the Socialist Federal Republic of Yugoslavia in 1989 and 1990. The old political system based on a centrally directed communist party, or League of Communists of Yugoslavia (LCY), disintegrated, fatefully weakening the federal structures. Individual republics and regions, no longer held together by the force of former president, Josip Broz Tito, who had died in 1980, were now dominated by their respective nationalist movements. First Slovenia and Croatia (in June 1991), then Macedonia (December 1991) and Bosnia and Hercegovinia (1992), declared their independence from the federation. By 2003, all that was left of Tito's Federation of nearly 24 million people were two member states, Serbia and Montenegro, with a population of some 11 million. These two re-formed themselves into a looser federation. The union – comprising the republics of Serbia and Montenegro and the autonomous provinces of Vojvodina and Kosovo – established a 126-member unicameral parliament, the Skupstina Srbije i Crne Gore (Assembly of Serbia and Montenegro).

The Serbs are believed to be an ethnic Slavic clan that settled in the Balkans by the eleventh century. A Serbian state was established in the twelfth century.

1389 The Turks defeated the Serbs at the Battle of Kosovo, and Serbia become an Ottoman subject state.
1860 Turkish troops left. Serbia signed a series of alliances with Montenegro, Romania and Greece. The Serbia-Greece pact assigned ownership of Bosnia and Hercegovina (BiH) to Serbia, with Thessaly and Epirus going to the Greeks.
1876 Serbia was again defeated by Turkey, although Austrian protection prevented the Serbs from falling under Turkish rule.
1878 Austria invaded Serbia. The Treaty of Berlin settled Serbian independence. Montenegro was also recognised as an independent state and doubled in size.
1913 The London Conference reduced the territory claimed by Albania after recognising its independence. Kosovo was granted to Serbia and Cameria (Chamouria) to Greece.
1914 Growing hostility in relations between the Serbs and the Habsburgs of Austro-Hungary came to a head with the assassination of the Austrian Archduke Frans Ferdinand by a Serbian nationalist, Gavrilo Princip. Austria and Germany declared war on Serbia, resulting in the First World War.
1918 After being occupied by enemy forces for three years, the Kingdom of Serbs, Croats and Slovenes was formed.
1929 The Kingdom was renamed Yugoslavia.
1941 Parts of Yugoslavia were occupied by the Germans, Italians, Hungarians and Bulgarians. An independent Croatian state was formed, encompassing parts of BiH.
1945–46 Following the end of the Second World War, Serbia and Montenegro became two of the constituent republics of a federated Yugoslavia. As the leader of the Yugoslav Communist Party (YCP), Josip Broz Tito became head of state and a Soviet-style constitution was adopted. The other republics were BiH, Croatia, Macedonia, Slovenia and the two autonomous regions of Vojvodina and Kosovo.
1948 Yugoslavia was expelled from the Communist Information Bureau (Cominform), responsible for co-ordinating Communist activities throughout the world.
1953 Tito was elected president in January.
Constitutions adopted in 1953, 1963 and 1974 increased the autonomy extended to the country's constituent republics.
1955 After building a relationship with the West, Yugoslavia restored relations with the Soviet Union.
1960–70s To keep Yugoslavia out of the Cold War, President Tito pursued a policy of non-alignment and the country became one of the founder members of the Non-Alignment Movement (NAM).
1980 Tito's death led to a rotating collective presidency.
1989 Differences and friction between the wealthier republics, Slovenia and Croatia, and the different ethnic groups intensified. Serbian and Montenegrin constitutions were inaugurated.
1990 Multi-party elections brought into power a government in Croatia which supported outright independence.
1991–92 The secession of Croatia, Slovenia and BiH led to invasions of these republics by the Jugoslovenska Narodna Armija (JNA) (Yugoslav National Army). In Slovenia, the JNA was promptly defeated. JNA units were eventually incorporated into the ethnic Serb armies in BiH and the Krajina region in Croatia. The reduced

KEY INDICATORS — Serbia and Montenegro

	Unit	2000	2001	2002	2003	2004
Population	m	10.71	11.00	11.00	11.02	11.03
Gross domestic product (GDP)	US$bn	7.50	10.40	14.00	18.08	*24.00
GDP per capita	US$	701	979	1,268	1,641	2,893
GDP real growth	%	5.0	8.1	3.5	2.5	7.2
Inflation	%	113.5	91.1	27.5	11.4	9.5
Unemployment	%	26.8	27.5	28.4	29.9	30.0
Exports (fob) (goods)	US$m	1,923.0	2,003.0	2,050.0	2,300.0	3,254.0
Imports (fob) (goods)	US$m	3,772.0	4,838.0	5,470.0	6,300.0	9,538.0
Balance of trade	US$m	-1,849.0	-2,835.0	-3,400.0	-4,000.0	-6,284.0
Current account	US$m	-340.0	-530.0	-1,380.0	-1,550.0	-3,160.0
Exchange rate	per US$	12.48	40.07	62.73	56.90	0.80

* estimated figure

Serbia and Montenegro

Yugoslav state, comprising Serbia, Montenegro, Vojvodina and Kosovo, was not internationally recognised and deprived of its UN seat.
1993 Zoran Lilic was elected Yugoslav president, replacing Dobrica Cosic, who had criticised the president of Serbia, Slobodan Milosevic.
1995 Milosevic was one of the signatories of the Dayton Peace Agreement, which ended the civil war in BiH.
1996 Yugoslavia and Croatia signed an agreement of mutual recognition, formally ending five years of hostility.
1997 Milosevic, for 10 years the president of Serbia, took over as the Yugoslav president. A coalition government, led by Milosevic's Socialisticka Partija Srbije (SPS) (Socialist Party of Serbia), remained in power in Serbia, despite losing its parliamentary majority in elections. The first election for the presidency of Serbia was invalidated because less than half the electorate voted; Milan Milutinovic was elected president of Serbia at the end of the year.
1998 Since the 1980s, the Milosevic regime had been gradually reducing the civil rights of the ethnic Albanians in Kosovo. Opposition to this gathered momentum during the 1990s as the Ushtria Çlirimtare e Kosovës (UÇK) (Kosovo Liberation Army) began to carry out armed offensives and bombings against the Yugoslav authorities. By the beginning of the year, the UÇK controlled approximately half of the province of Kosovo. Yugoslav security forces launched a counter-offensive against the UÇK, destroying villages and displacing many thousands of Kosovans.
Mirko Marjanovic (Montenegrin prime minister since 1994) was re-appointed to form a government in Montenegro.
1999 Vuk Draskovic resigned from the Yugoslav government and took his party out of the coalition. After unsuccessful mediation, NATO launched air strikes in March against Yugoslav targets. In June, Yugoslav forces withdrew entirely from Kosovo. NATO deployed peace-keeping troops in Kosovo, which became an international protectorate under UN control.
2000 After the Demokratska Opozicija Srbije (DOS) (Democratic Opposition of Serbia) leader, Vojislav Kostunica, won the Yugoslav presidential election, the Constitutional Court annulled the election and ruled Milosevic should serve until the end of his mandate. Milosevic was subsequently overthrown and Kostunica took over. Yugoslavia was allowed back into the UN after eight years. A coalition government for Yugoslavia was agreed, composed of members from the 18-party DOS alliance.

Local elections held in Kosovo were won by the Lidhja Demokratike e Kosovës (LDK) (Democratic League of Kosovo), led by Ibrahim Rugova.
The DOS won the parliamentary elections in Serbia.
2001 Milo Djukanovic's Pobjeda je Crne Goru (PjCG) (Victory for Montenegro) coalition won the Montenegrin parliamentary elections.
Slobodan Milosevic was extradited to stand trial at the International Criminal Tribunal for the former Yugoslavia (ICTY) in The Hague.
The LDK won 46 per cent of the vote in the Kosovan parliamentary elections, but failed to get a majority. A Kosovan assembly composed of 120 members was established.
2002 The Kosovan assembly elected Ibrahim Rugova as president; Bajram Rexhapi of the Partia Demokratike e Kosovës (PDK) (Democratic Party of Kosovo) was elected as prime minister of a power-sharing 10-member cabinet.
Montenegrin President Milo Djukanovic's Demokratska Lista za Evropsku Crnu Goru (DLECG) (Democratic List for a European Montenegro) alliance won the parliamentary elections.
Parliamentary Speaker Natasa Micic was appointed Serbia's acting president after the results of three separate presidential elections were declared invalid due to insufficient voter turnout.
2003 Yugoslavia was renamed Serbia and Montenegro on 4 February. Yugoslav President Kostunica stepped down and was replaced as head of state of Serbia and Montenegro by Svetozar Marovic, a Montenegrin. The Serbian prime minister, Zoran Djindjic, was assassinated on 12 March. Filip Vujanovic won the Montenegrin presidential election on 11 May.
2004 Boris Tadic, a pro-West liberal, was elected president of Serbia on 27 June. The Democratic League of Kosovo won the parliamentary elections and Ramush Haradinaj was nominated prime minister by President Ibrahim Rugova, who had been re-elected.
2005 The prime minister of Kosovo, Ramush Haradinaj, resigned on 8 March and Adem Salihaj became acting prime minister. On 10 June, the US resumed aid to Serbia as a reward for improved co-operation with the International War Crimes Tribunal in The Hague. On 29 September, the EU agreed to open talks with Serbia and Montenegro on a stabilisation and association agreement that could lead to EU membership. Five former Serbian policemen accused of taking part in the 1995 Srebrenica massacre went on trial in Belgrade on 20 December.

Political structure
Constitution
The constitution was put into place on 4 February 2003, when the Federal Republic of Yugoslavia was abolished and replaced with a looser federation of its two member states, Serbia and Montenegro.
Form of state
Confederal parliamentary democratic republic, with two constituent states, the Republic of Serbia (Republika Srbije) and the Republic of Montenegro (Republika Crna Gora), and the autonomous provinces of Kosovo and Vojvodina. Kosovo has been governed by the UN Interim Administration Mission in Kosovo (UNMIK) since 1999, under the authority of UN Security Council Resolution 1244 and has self-government.
The executive
The federal president is appointed by the Serbia and Montenegro parliament for a term of four years. The federal president oversees the work of a five-member cabinet or Council of Ministers, which is responsible for foreign affairs, defence, economic policy and human rights.
Each of the two republics' presidents is elected by universal adult suffrage for a five-year term.
Kosovo has its own president and interim government which are responsible for the economy, education, health, agriculture and tourism, but requires UN approval to introduce or change any new legislation in these areas. The UN, represented by the head of the UN Interim Administration in Kosovo (UNMIK), also has the power to dissolve the assembly and call new elections. The president is appointed by the Kosovan assembly for a period of three years.
National legislature
In March 2003, 126 deputies of the unicameral Skupstina Srbije i Crne Gore (Assembly of Serbia and Montenegro) were elected by the respective assemblies of the two member states – 91 from Serbia and 35 from Montenegro.
Since 1999, the UN has adopted administrative control of the autonomous region of Kosovo. In December 2001, Kosovo introduced its own Kuvendi/Skupstina (assembly), composed of 120 members. Seats in the assembly are divided along ethnic lines (100 seats for ethnic Albanians and 20 for the minorities) and is elected every three years.
Legal system
The legal system is based on the constitutional charter of Serbia and Montenegro, which was ratified February 2003. The Serbia and Montenegro Court is the highest court. It comprises judges elected for a period of six years by the Serbia and Montenegro Assembly upon the recommendation of the Council of Ministers.

Last elections
Serbia and Montenegro: March 2003 (parliamentary).
Serbia: 27 June 2004 (second round presidential, new legislation does not require a minimum 50 per cent turnout); 13 June 2004 (first round presidential); 28 December 2003 (parliamentary); 16 November 2003 (re-run presidential, invalid). Montenegro: 11 May 2003 (presidential run-off); 20 October 2002 (parliamentary).
Kosovo: 23 October 2004 (parliamentary); 3 December 2004 (presidential).
Results: Serbia second presidential: Boris Tadic defeated Tomislav Nikolic.
Serbia parliamentary: the Srpska Radikalna Stranka (SRS) (Serb Radical Party) won 27.7 per cent of the vote (82 of 250 seats), the Demokratska Stranka Srbije (DSS) (Democratic Party of Serbia) 18 per cent (53), the Demokratska Stranka (DS) (Democratic Party) 12.6 per cent (37), G17 Plus 11.4 per cent (34), the Srpski Pokret Obnove-Nova Srbija (SPO-NS) (Serbian Renewal Movement-New Serbia) 7.7 per cent (23) and the Socijalisticka Partija Srbije (SPS) (Socialist Party of Serbia) 7.7 per cent (21); turnout was 58.7 per cent.
Serbia first presidential: Tomislav Nikolic won 30.4 per cent, Boris Tadic 27.6 per cent, Bogoljub Karic 18.2 per cent and Dragan Marsicanin 13.3 per cent.
Montenegro presidential run-off: Filip Vujanovic won 63 per cent of the vote, Miodrag Zivkovic 31 per cent and Dragan Hajdukovic 4 per cent; turnout was 48 per cent (parliament has abolished the minimum 50 per cent turnout rule).
Montenegro parliamentary: the Demokratska Lista za Evropsku Crnu Goru (DLECG) (Democratic List for a European Montenegro) alliance won 44.8 per cent of the vote (39 seats out of 75), the Zajedno za Promjene (ZzP) (Together for Changes) alliance 35.9 per cent (30 seats), the Liberalni Savez Crne Gore (LSCG) (Liberal Alliance of Montenegro) 5.4 per cent (four) and the Albanci Zajedno (Albanians Together) alliance 2.3 per cent (two); turnout was 77.5 per cent.
Serbia and Montenegro parliamentary: Demokratska Opozicija Srbije (DOS) (Democratic Opposition of Serbia) 37 seats, DLECG 19.
Serbia and Montenegro presidential: Svetozar Marovic was elected president by parliament.
Kosovo parliamentary: the Democratic League of Kosovo (LDK) won 45.3 per cent of the vote, 49 seats in parliament; the Democratic Party of Kosovo (PDK) 28.7 per cent, 31 seats; the Alliance for the Future of Kosovo (AAK) 8.3 per cent, nine seats; the Hour Party 6.3 per cent (nine), the Albanian Christian Democratic Party of Kosovo 1.8 per cent (two), the Turkish Democratic Party of Kosovo 1.4 per cent (two) and the Justice Party 1 per cent (two). Turnout was 51 per cent.
Kosovo presidential: parliament re-elected Ibrahim Rugova as president (64–32).

Next elections
Serbia and Montenegro: 2007 (parliamentary).
Serbia: 2009 (presidential).
Montenegro: 2007 (presidential).
Kosovo: 2007 (presidential and parliamentary).

Political parties
Ruling party
18-party Demokratska Opozicija Srbije (DOS) (Democratic Opposition of Serbia) coalition
Main opposition party
Serbia and Montenegro: Demokratska Lista za Evropsku Crnu Goru (DLECG) (Democratic List for European Montenegro).
Serbia: Socijalisticka Partija Srbije (SPS) (Serb Socialist Party).
Montenegro: Zajedno za Promjene (ZzP) (Together for Changes) alliance.

Population
11.03 million (2004)
Ethnic make-up
Serbian (63 per cent), Albanian (14 per cent), Montenegrin (6 per cent) and Hungarian (4 per cent).
Religions
Serbian Orthodox (65 per cent), Islam, Roman Catholic and Protestant.

Education
With less developed education systems than Slovenia and Croatia during the Tito period, Serbia and Montenegro had an adult illiteracy rate of 10 per cent in 1990 (in Kosovo, the figure was then 17 per cent).
Primary education lasts for eight years from aged seven. Secondary education is provided in grammar, vocational and art schools with courses lasting up to four years. Higher education in Serbia is provided in universities and colleges. Higher education in Montenegro is only provided at university level.
There are five universities in Serbia and Montenegro (Belgrade, Novi Sad, Nis, Kragujevac and Podgorica) and one in Kosovo (Pristina). However, graduate unemployment is high.
During the build-up to the conflict in Kosovo, education became a very controversial issue, with the majority Albanian population refusing to be taught in the Serbian language. Alternative or Albanian language education thus emerged in Kosovo. There was a major exodus of younger and more educated people abroad during the 1990s. In 1994 alone, around 100,000 people, or around 1 per cent of the population, may have emigrated. If this trend is not reversed, the country's future socio-economic development could be seriously threatened.
Literacy rate: 99 per cent total; 97 per cent female; adult rates (Unicef 2004).
Compulsory years: 7 to 15
Enrolment rate: 66 per cent gross primary enrolment, 59 per cent gross secondary enrolment; of relevant age group (including repeaters) (Unesco).
Pupils per teacher: 20 primary; 14 secondary, (Unesco 2002)

Health
Since 1992, the extent and quality of healthcare provision has sharply deteriorated in Serbia and Montenegro. However, a well-developed private healthcare system has emerged for the better-off. Formerly largely free at the point of delivery and funded by a universal social insurance tax levied on all employees and employers, public healthcare provision now requires all kinds of charges, most notably for imported medications.
Total expenditure on health is 3–4 per cent of GDP, of which government spending is about 45–46 per cent.
HIV prevalence: 0.2 per cent aged 15–49 in 2003 (World Bank)
Life expectancy: 72.8 years (World Bank)
Fertility rate/Maternal mortality rate: 1.7 births per woman (World Bank)
Birth rate/Death rate: 12.7 births and 10.6 deaths per 1,000 population (2003).
Infant mortality rate: 12 per 1,000 live births (World Bank)
Head of population per physician/bed: 2 doctors and 5.3 hospital beds typically available per 1,000 people

Welfare
Welfare provision in Serbia and Montenegro was relatively generous during the Tito period, when retirement pensions were around 80 per cent of average monthly incomes. Some indexation of pensions and other welfare benefits also existed at this time.

Main cities
Belgrade (capital of Serbia and Montenegro; also capital of Serbia, estimated population 1.3 million in 2004); Podgorica (179,000), capital of Montenegro; Pristina (capital of Kosovo) (204,500); Novi Sad (capital of Vojvodina) (191,300).

Languages spoken
Serbian, Croatian, Bosnian, Hungarian, Slovak, Albanian (principally in Kosovo), Macedonian and Slovenian are all spoken. English is the most commonly used foreign business language. Other

Serbia and Montenegro

languages include German, English, Russian and Italian.
Official language/s
Serbian

Media
Press
Dailies: Major Serbian dailies include *Danas, Dnevnik, Vecernje Novosti Politika* and *Vijesti*. Bi-lingual publications in Serbian and English are *Blic* and *Borba*. *Monitor* is published in Montenegro.
Weeklies: *Nedeljni Telegraf* is Serbia and Montenegro's largest weekly newspaper. *Vojvodina Weekly* is an independent, open weekly newspaper about cultural, political, economic, agriculture and sport issues in Vojvodina. Other significant weeklies are *Nin* (Belgrade) and *International Weekly* (Belgrade, published in English).
Business: Main business papers include *Privredni pregled* (Belgrade/daily) and *Ekonomska politika* (Belgrade/weekly).
Broadcasting
There are two main radio and television networks, one in Serbia (based in Belgrade and Novi Sad) and one in Montenegro (based in Podgorica). Radio Srbija i Crna Gora (RSCG) (Radio Serbia and Montenegro) broadcasts daily in six foreign languages on short wave. B92 is a very popular independent radio, satellite and Internet station.
The Organisation for Security and Co-operation in Europe (OSCE) has been assisting in restructuring and reforming Serbia and Montenegro's broadcasting since 2001. Its main work has been to help Radio Televizije Srbije (RTS) (Radio Television Serbia) to modernise. RTS is Serbia and Montenegro's largest state broadcaster. It has become the main source for the population to confront the country's past of the 1990s, broadcasting Slobodan Milosevic's war crimes trial at The Hague live and documentaries on Serbia's involvement in the 1992–95 Bosnian civil war.
Advertising
All principal media are available through advertising agencies or directly. There are still Western agencies operating in Belgrade. Tobacco and alcohol advertising is banned on television, but the authorities are now turning a blind eye as television stations need advertising revenue for repairs.

Economy
By 1990, the last year of comparative economic normality, the republics of Serbia and Montenegro together accounted for around 35 per cent of the combined GDP of the former Yugoslav state. Relative to population (around 40 per cent of the Yugoslav total in 1990), Serbia's share of all Yugoslav GDP, foreign exchange-denominated exports and service income was below that of Slovenia and Croatia. On the other hand, Serbia's share of imports payable in foreign exchange was then relatively large, with the resultant trade deficit (US$1.3 billion in 1990) financed by foreign exchange and other transfers from elsewhere in Yugoslavia. These transfers were also central to the servicing of Serbia's large foreign debt.
Serbia's orientation towards non-foreign exchange denominated markets elsewhere in Yugoslavia and beyond was far greater than that of Slovenia and, to a lesser extent, Croatia. Structurally, Serbia's economy in the 1990s had many of the characteristics of relative underdevelopment, including an emphasis on the domestic export of low value raw materials and semi-processed goods and a barter-based form of foreign trade in predominantly non-Western markets. At the federal level of government, Serbia then also benefited from internal economic transfers, although these were mainly directed to Kosovo during the post-war period.
Montenegro is pursuing its own policy of reconstruction, assisted by international investment and trade. Serbia is breaking out of its state-controlled siege economy following the fall of Slobodan Milosevic. The economy of Kosovo is being rebuilt with substantial international assistance. Serbia and Montenegro is also being provided with financial assistance, including World Bank and IMF loans. Foreign investment is deterred by the country's bad track record of corruption and crime. The uncertain political climate following the assassination of Serbia's Prime Minister Zoran Djindjic further destabilised economic policies and discouraged investment.
Steady growth in GDP has been occurring since 2000, largely due to successes in structural reform. Serbia and Montenegro needs steady growth to address its low standard of living with around a third of the population living close to the poverty line. Unemployment is a rising problem with rates of 30 per cent.

External trade
Serbia and Montenegro is working towards signing agreements with other Balkan states via the Stability Pact for South Eastern Europe. In June 2001, the country was one of the signatories of the Stability Pact's Memorandum of Understanding (MoU) on Trade Liberalisation and Facilitation. The MoU and the Stability Pact could eventually create a free trade area in the Balkans, with a potential market of over 55 million people.

Imports
Main imports include machinery and transport equipment, fuels and lubricants, manufactured goods, chemicals, food and live animals and raw materials.
Main sources: Germany (20.2 per cent total, 2004), Italy (18.1 per cent), Austria (9.0 per cent), Slovenia (6.1 per cent), France (5.1 per cent), The Netherlands (4.4 per cent), Bulgaria (4.3 per cent), Greece (4.2 per cent)
Exports
Principal exports include manufactured goods, food and live animals and raw materials.
Main destinations: Italy (30.1 per cent total, 2004), Germany (16.6 per cent), Austria (7.4 per cent), Greece (7.1 per cent), France (5.3 per cent), Slovenia (4.2 per cent), US (4.1 per cent)

Agriculture
Farming
Agriculture is the mainstay of the economy, accounting for up to 70 per cent of GDP. The main crops are wheat, maize, sugar beet and tobacco. There are extensive orchards and livestock is reared. Agricultural exports and imports have a high importance for the whole economy. Animal husbandry is still developing and is of minor importance.
About 80 per cent of the total agricultural area, which is the equivalent of 4.96 million hectares, are under mixed farming systems with elements of ecological farming. Most of the highly productive soil, located in the lowlands, receives small quantities of rainfall.
The agricultural sector in Serbia and Montenegro is hampered by shortages of industrial goods such as fertiliser, with an estimated US$44 million investment needed to ensure sufficient supplies of agro-chemicals annually. The country also suffers periodically from droughts which reduce agriculture production and economic growth.
Crop production in 2004 included: 9,584,640 tonnes (t) cereals in total, 2,746,000t wheat, 6,287,000t maize, 410,000t barley, 119,390t oats, 1,098,000t potatoes, 2,643,034t sugar beets, 119,600t pulses, 3,750t citrus fruit, 490,000t grapes, 185,000t tomatoes, 4,300t figs, 237,123t oilcrops, 10,000t tobacco, 183,571t apples, 561,000t plums, 160,000t chillies & peppers, 25,000t garlic, 332,000t soya beans, 1,676,896t fruit in total, 1,185,200t vegetables in total. Livestock production included: 860,530 meat in total, 170,000t beef, 582,000t pig meat, 20,000t lamb, 85,600t poultry, 76,000t eggs, 1,825,000t milk, 2,900t honey, 12,500t cattle hides, 4,200t sheepskins, 2,500t greasy wool.

Forestry

Forestry has experienced only slight falls in output, mainly because at times shortages of other fuels increase the demand for firewood locally.

Exports of forest material in 2004 amounted to US$139.1 million, while imports amounted to US$352.8 million. Production in 2004 included 3,520,000 cubic metres (cum) roundwood, 1,423,000cum industrial roundwood, 575,000cum sawnwood, 1,138,000cum sawlogs and veneers, 196,000cum pulpwood, 59,000cum wood-based panels, 2,097,000cum woodfuel.

Industry and manufacturing

Prior to the 1999 Kosovo War, Serbia and Montenegro had a diversified industrial base with major industries including metal processing, food production, textile and other manufacturing. The industrial sector accounted for almost US$1 billion of former Yugoslavia's exports. Much of the energy-dependent industry, including chemicals and iron and steel, collapsed because of shortages of energy and raw materials following the imposition of sanctions in 1999.

The damage done by the Nato bombing campaign to manufacturing was second only to the destruction to hydrocarbons and energy production. Total industrial production is thought to have fallen by 60 per cent, with whole sectors being wiped out. The sector's share of GDP dropped from 45 per cent to 15–20 per cent. Previously, over 40 per cent of the labour force were employed in industry, but more than 100,000 jobs were lost immediately as a result of industrial destruction. Financial aid and FDI have been crucial to rebuilding Serbia and Montenegro's industrial base.

Tourism

The revival of the tourist sector is seen as central to the reconstruction of the economy of Serbia and Montenegro after the upheavals of recent years. It was seriously damaged, but is gradually recovering. Montenegro, in particular, has been successful in attracting European visitors and reducing dependence on Serbians. Considerable investment in renovation and expansion of infrastructure is required to sustain continued growth. Tourism is expected to contribute 1.2 per cent to GDP in 2005.

Mining

Serbia and Montenegro has a significant mining sector. Lead and zinc are produced in substantial quantities. There is a large gold and silver mine at Bor in eastern Serbia. The fact that many of the most valuable non-ferrous metal mineral deposits are in Kosovo makes the area of great economic importance. In the longer-term, there is likely to be considerable foreign investor interest in Serbia and Montenegro's non-ferrous metal mineral ore resources, particularly copper and gold.

Hydrocarbons

Serbia and Montenegro has oil reserves of around 78 million barrels. Most of oil production is undertaken in the autonomous province of Vojvodina. Production is not sufficient to meet domestic consumption and 53,000 bpd are imported. Serbia and Montenegro has natural gas reserves of 48 billion cubic metres, about 60 per cent of the Balkan region's total reserves. Russia supplies over 60 per cent of Serbia and Montenegro's gas needs. A small amount of natural gas is produced domestically in Vojvodina.

The province of Kosovo has extensive coal reserves, comprising a large proportion of the estimated total of 18.2 billion tonnes for Serbia and Montenegro. Coal is also extracted in the Kolubara and Kostolac basins in central Serbia, and in Pljevlja, Montenegro.

Energy

Serbia and Montenegro depends on imports of oil and gas for about 40 per cent of its energy despite increased utilisation of local resources of coal and water power. Hydroelectric power accounts for nearly 60 per cent of electricity generation and thermal for 40 per cent.

Much of Serbia and Montenegro's energy sector has been damaged by neglect, lack of investment and NATO bombing in 1999.

Financial markets
Stock exchange

Opened in 1990, the Beogradska Berza (BB) (Belgrade Stock Exchange) is not an important financial intermediary in Serbia and Montenegro. With more privatisation being undertaken and improved relations with the West, the prospects for Serbia and Montenegro's financial markets look good in the long-term.

Banking and insurance

Begradska Banka, Jugobanka, Investbanka and Beobanka, four of the country's old banking giants, were closed down in January 2002.

Central bank

Narodna Banka Srbije (NBS) (National Bank of Serbia).
Centralna Banka Crne Gore (CBCG) (Central Bank of Montenegro); European Central Bank (ECB).

Main financial centre

Belgrade

Time

GMT plus one hour (GMT plus two hours from late March to late September).

Geography

Situated in the central Balkan Peninsula in south-eastern Europe, Serbia and Montenegro consists of three parts: the Great Danubian Plains of Vojvodina to the north, where the two main rivers are the Sava and the Danube, which meet at Belgrade; the hilly and forested areas of inner (central) and southern Serbia, where the main rivers are the Drina, Morava and Vardar; and the Dinaric Alps and Adriatic coastline of Montenegro to the south-west.

Serbia and Montenegro is bordered by Hungary to the north, Croatia and Bosnia to the west, Albania and Macedonia to the south and south-east, and Bulgaria and Romania to the east. Along the River Danube, Serbia and Montenegro has borders with Croatia and Romania. The River Drina marks the border between Serbia and Bosnia. In the Adriatic Sea, there are maritime boundaries with Italy, Croatia and Albania.

Climate

The climate in Serbia and Montenegro is largely continental, with Mediterranean influences on the Montenegrin coast. Inland, the summers are very hot and the winters bitterly cold. The average summer temperature in Belgrade is 22 degrees Celsius (C) and in winter the average temperature is zero degrees C. In Montenegro, summer temperatures can exceed 30 degrees C, but the winters are warmer than in inland areas. Precipitation is generally constant, with average annual rainfall in Belgrade of around 635mm. Snowfall is extensive in winter. In most of Montenegro, changeable mountainous weather conditions predominate.

Entry requirements
Passports

Passports are required by all and must be valid for at least six months after the intended departure date.

Visa

Required by all, with the exception of most European, North American and Australasian visitors for both business and tourist reasons. Visit www.yuembusa.org/english/services/services_visas.htm for a full list of exceptions and lengths of stay permitted.

Those visitors that require visas should contact the nearest embassy for an application form. Business travellers in this category will require a letter of invitation from a local company giving the nature of business, duration of visit and a full itinerary, plus a letter from the employing company confirming details; and proof of sufficient

Serbia and Montenegro

funds for living expenses and medical insurance.

Currency advice/regulations
Exchange bureaux may offer better exchange rates than hotels, banks and travel agencies. Euros have attracted better rates than US dollars. There is no limit on the amount of foreign currency brought into the country, although it must be declared. Foreign currency is extremely scarce in Serbia and visitors are unlikely to be allowed to take any out of the country.

Customs
Various personal articles and goods are allowed duty-free. There are customs barriers between Serbia, Montenegro and Kosovo. Serbia and Montenegro plan to eventually introduce a customs union.

Health (for visitors)
Mandatory precautions
Vaccination certificates are not required.
Advisable precautions
Hepatitis 'A', hepatitis 'B', diphtheria, polio, TB, typhoid, tetanus vaccinations are recommended. There is a rabies risk.

Hotels
Hotels are classified into five categories: L (extra), A, B, C and D; boarding houses into three, I, II and III. There is a 10–20 per cent service charge. Visitors must also pay a residential tax, which varies between regions.

Credit cards
International credit cards are accepted in large hotels and businesses in Serbia, and since 2001, Montenegro has accepted major credit cards.

Public holidays
Fixed dates
1 Jan (New Year's Day), 7 Jan (Orthodox Christmas Day), 27 Apr (Statehood Day), 1–2 May (Labour Days), 9 May (Victory Day), 29 Nov (Republic Day).
Variable dates
Orthodox Good Friday, Orthodox Easter Monday.

Working hours
Banking
Mon–Fri: 0700–1500; Sat: 0800–1400. Belgrade airport 0800–2000.
Business
Mon–Fri: 0800–1500.
Government
Mon–Fri: 0730–1530.
Shops
Mon–Fri: generally in larger towns: 0800–2000 (some shops closing between 1200 and 1700); Sat: 0800–1500.

Telecommunications
Mobile phones
GSM 900/1800 services available throughout most of the country.

Electricity supply
220V AC

Social customs/useful tips
It is traditional for the chairman of negotiations to welcome guests formally with drinks before commencing a meeting. Punctuality depends on the ethnic region: it is important in some, more casual in others. As elsewhere, it is customary to shake hands on meeting and taking leave.

Security
Despite high levels of poverty, crime rates remain low in Serbia and Montenegro. The security situation in Serbia improved after the fall of Slobodan Milosevic in 2000 and Western visitors are unlikely to face police or military interference in ordinary activities. However, armed conflict continues in the Presevo Valley area of southern Serbia and in parts of Kosovo itself, and the crime rate (including violent crime) is high in Kosovo. Visitors are advised to avoid these areas unless absolutely necessary. Any travel into these areas should only take place in organised groups after seeking advice from the local authorities before the journey is made.

Getting there
Air
National airline: JAT Airways. Montenegro has its own airline – Oki Airways.
International airport/s: Surcin Belgrade Airport (BEG), 19km west of Belgrade; Tivat (TIV), 4km from city; Podgorica (TGD) and Pristina (PRN).
Airport tax: International departures attract tax (not-applicable to transit passengers). The amount varies between airports and carriers, travellers should expect to pay about eur15.

Surface
Road: There are border crossings from Hungary, Romania, Bulgaria, and Albania, as well as from the former Yugoslav republics of Bosnia and Hercegovina, Croatia and Macedonia.
Serbia and Montenegro is participating in the pan-European 'Corridor 10' project, which proposes a highway connecting Bulgaria, Greece, Macedonia and Serbia and Montenegro. It is planned that Serbia and Montenegro's section of the highway will be completed by 2004. However, a 120km section from Belgrade to the Macedonian border has not been built due to a lack of funding.
Rail: It is possible to travel to Belgrade via the Hungarian border crossing.
Water: Ships provide regular passenger service and cruises on the Danube, starting at Passau in Germany, to Vienna, passing through Slovakia and Hungary. There are also links with the rivers Rhine and Main and the Black Sea.

Passenger ferries operate between Bar (in Montenegro) and Italy.
Main port/s: Bar, Kotor and Zelenika.

Getting about
National transport
Air: There are regular air services by JAT Airways to Podgorica.
Road: There are some 48,423km of roads, including 374km of motorways. The main route links Belgrade with Subotica (via Novi Sad), Kragujevac and Nis. According to official estimates, 40 per cent of main roads and 60 per cent of local roads are operating at less than full capacity. About US$5 billion is required to fund the complete restoration of Serbia and Montenegro's road network. A number of highway construction projects are being undertaken, but will require around US$1.7 billion to be completed.
Buses: An extensive network of express buses links all of Serbia and Montenegro's towns, although fuel shortages can often restrict services. Multi-journey tickets are available and sold through tobacconists. In general, fares paid to the driver are usually double the price of pre-purchase tickets.
Rail: Internal rail services are often overbooked, unreliable and unsafe. There are some 4,000km of track, of which over a quarter is electrified. Using the international express, fast trains link Belgrade with Subotica, Novi Sad, Kragujevac, Nis, Pristina and Podgorica, as well as the port of Bar.
Water: There is a well established inland waterways system, based on the Danube, Sava, Tizsa and Begej rivers.

City transport
Taxis: Good services operate in most large cities and towns. All taxis are metered, with an extra charge for baggage. Taxis from Belgrade airport to city centre have a journey time 20–25 minutes.
Buses, trams & metro: All cities/towns are served by buses; trams only in the centre of Belgrade and in Subotica. The service is generally regular.

Car hire
Cars can be hired in most main towns through travel agencies. There is a speed limit of 120kph on motorways and 60kph in built-up areas. Drive on the right and give way to traffic from the right unless clearly marked otherwise. Seat belts are compulsory in front seats.
To be on the safe side, carry an international driver's licence as well as a national licence.

BUSINESS DIRECTORY
The addresses listed below are a selection only. While World of Information makes every endeavour to check these addresses, we cannot guarantee that

Nations of the World: A Political, Economic and Business Handbook

changes have not been made, especially to telephone numbers and area codes. We would welcome any corrections.

Telephone area codes
The international direct dialling (IDD) code is +381, followed by area code and subscriber's number:

Belgrade	11	Pec	39
Kragujevac	34	Podgorica	81
Krusevac	37	Pristina	38
Leskovac	16	Uzice	31
Novi Sad	21		

Useful telephone numbers
Police: 92
Fire: 93
Ambulance: 94

Chambers of Commerce
American Chamber of Commerce in Serbia and Montenegro, 30 Vlajkoviceva, 11000 Belgrade (tel: 334-5961; fax: 324-7771; e-mail: info@amcham.yu).

Belgrade Chamber of Economy, 12 Kneza Milosa, 11001 Belgrade (tel: 264-1355; fax: 264-2029; e-mail: mmj@komberg.org.yu).

Kragujevac Chamber of Commerce and Industry, 10 Mose Pijade, 34000 Kragujevac (tel: 335-805; fax: 334-049; e-mail: rpkkg@eunet.yu).

Montenegro Chamber of Economy, 29 Novaka Miloseva, 81000 Podgorica (tel: 230-545; fax: 230-943; e-mail: pkcg@cg.yu).

Serbian Chamber of Commerce and Industry, 13-15 Resavska, 11000 Belgrade (tel: 324-0611; fax: 323-0949; e-mail: centar@pks.co.yu).

Uzice Regional Chamber of Commerce, 52 Dimirija Tucovica, 31000 Uzice (tel: 513-483; fax: 514-184; e-mail: office@rpk-uzice.co.yu).

Banking
Association of Serbian Banks (Udruzenje Banaka Srbije), Bulevar Kralja Aleksandra 86, 11000 Belgrade (tel: 302-0760; fax: 337-0179).

Atlas Banka, 4 Stanka Dragojevica St, Podgorica, Montenegro (tel: 248-830; fax: 248-930; e-mail: atlasmont@cg.yu).

Euromarket Banka, Ulica Slobode 4, Podgorica 81000, Montenegro (tel: 2250933; fax: 225-410; e-mail: euromarket@cg.yu).

JIK Banka, Belgrade, Knez Mihailova 42 (tel: 632-822; fax: 183-198).

Kreditna Banka Beograd, Belgrade, Lenjinov Bulevar 111 (tel: 222-4428; fax: 144-923).

Montenegrobanka, 81000 Podgorica, Bulevar Revolucije 1 (tel: 0814-4344; fax: 0815-1199).

Panonska Banka, 21000 Novi Sad, Bulevar 23 Oktobra 76 (tel: 021-612-444; fax: 021-613-939).

PKB Banka, Belgrade, 29 Novembra 68/a (tel: 753-366; fax: 750-932).

Privredna Banka, Belgrade, Brace Jugovica 17 (tel: 623-272; fax: 627-247).

Privredna Banka, 21000 Novi Sad, Grckoskolska 2 (tel: 0212-6333; fax: 021-623-025).

Vojvodjanska Banka, 21000 Novi Sad, Trg Slobode 7 (tel: 021-621-277; fax: 021-624-940).

Yugoslav Bank for International Economic Co-operation (Jubmes), 11070 Belgrade, Bulevar Avnoj-a 121, PO Box 219 (tel: 215-7222; fax: 131-457).

Central bank
Narodna Banka Srbije (NBS) (National Bank of Serbia), 12 Kralja Petra Street, 11000 Belgrade, (tel: 302-7100; fax: 324-8814; e-mail: gen.sec@nbs.8814).

Centralna Banka Crne Gore (CBCG) (Central Bank of Montenegro), Nemanjina obala 7, Podgorica 81400 (tel: 224-786, 225-966; fax: 224-298; e-mail: info@cb-cg.org; internet site: http://www.cb-cg.org).

European Central Bank (ECB), Kaiserstrasse 29, D-60311 Frankfurt am Main, Germany (tel: +49(69)13-440; fax: +49(69)1344-6000).

Travel information
Automotive Association of Serbia and Montenegro (AMS SCG), Information Centre, Belgrade, Ruzveltova 18 (tel: 980-419-555; fax: 419-888).

Tourist Association of Montenegro, 81000 Podgorica, Bulevar Lenjina 2 (tel: 0814-1591).

Tourist Association of Serbia, Belgrade, Dobrinjska 11 (tel: 645-166).

JAT Airways, Belgrade, Ho Si Minova 16 (tel: 224-222).

Association of Serbian and Montenegrian Travel Agencies (YUTA), Belgrade, Kondina 14 (tel: 328-686).

Ministry of tourism
Federal Ministry of Tourism, Nemanjina 22, 11000 Belgrade (tel/fax: 643-068).

Ministries
Federal Ministry of Agriculture, Bulevar AVNOJ-a 104, Belgrade (tel: 602-774; fax: 604-028).

Federal Ministry of Defence, Kneza Milosa 37, Belgrade (tel: 645-254; fax: 656-975).

Federal Ministry of Development, Science and Environment, Bulevar Lenjina 2, Belgrade (tel: 635-910).

Federal Ministry of The Economy, Bulevar Lenjina 2, Belgrade (tel: 695-734; fax: 636-775).

Federal Ministry of Finance, Bulevar Lenjina 2, Belgrade (tel: 604-579; fax: 222-4120).

Federal Ministry of Foreign Affairs, Kneza Milosa 24, Belgrade (tel: 684-582; fax: 681-572).

Federal Ministry of Foreign Trade, Bulevar Lenjina 2, Belgrade (tel: 696-453; fax: 222-2363).

Federal Ministry of the Interior, Bulevar Lenjina 2, Belgrade (tel: 636-074; fax: 685-073).

Federal Ministry of Internal Trade, Bulevar Lenjina 2, Belgrade (tel: 696-037).

Federal Ministry of Justice, Bulevar Lenjina 2, Belgrade (tel: 141-997).

Federal Ministry of Labour, Health and Social Policy, Bulevar AVNOJ-a 104, Belgrade (tel: 198-083; fax: 602-929).

Federal Ministry of Sports, Bulevar Lenjina 2, Belgrade (tel: 222-4879).

Federal Ministry of Telecommunications, Kneza Milosa 20, Belgrade (tel: 198-864; fax: 3233-480).

Federal Ministry of Tourism, Nemanjina 22, 11000 Belgrade (tel/fax: 643-068).

Federal Ministry of Transport, Bulevar AVNOJ-a 104, Belgrade (tel: 604-576; fax: 636-775).

Ministry of Finance, Belgrade, Palata Federacije (tel: 222-4240; fax: 646-775).

Ministry for Foreign Affairs, 11000 Belgrade, Kneza Milosa 24 (tel: 682-555).

Ministries for Information, International Economic Relations, Economy, Trade, Agriculture, Transport and Communications, Belgrade, Omladinskih Brigada 1 (tel: 602-555; fax: 195-244).

Government of Serbia and Montenegro, Bulevar Lenjina 2, Belgrade (tel: 602-683; fax: 636-775).

Prime Minister of Montenegro's Office, Jovana Tomasevica bb, Podgorica, Yugoslavia (tel: 42-530; fax: 42-329).

Prime Minister of Serbia's Office, Nemanjina 11, Belgrade (tel: 684-882; fax: 659-682).

Other useful addresses
Agency of Montenegro for Economic Restructuring and Foreign Investment, Jovana Tomasevica bb, 81000 Podgorica, Montenegro (tel: 242-640; fax: 245-756; e-mail: anaz@mn.yu).

Aluminium Industry of Montenegro (tel: 620-616; fax: 620-955; e-mail: kap.board@cg.yu).

Serbia and Montenegro

British Embassy, Generala Zdanova 46, 11000 Belgrade (tel: 645-055/34/87; fax: 659-651; e-mail: britmb@eunet.yu).

Directorate for Construction of Highways in Montenegro, Podgorica, Montenegro (tel: 625-110, 625-102; fax: 624-353).

Embassy of the United States of America, Kneza Milosa 50, 11000 Belgrade (tel: 645-655, 646-481; fax: 645-221).

Canadian Embassy, Kneza Milosa 75, 11000 Belgrade (tel: 644-666/644-5474; fax: 641-480; e-mail: bgrad01.x400.gc.ca).

Federal Secretary of Information, Bulevar Lenjina 2, Belgrade (tel: 222-4350; fax: 637-188).

Jugoslovenska Radio-Televizija, Generala Zdanova 28, 11000 Belgrade (tel: 330-194; fax: 434-023).

Kosovo Trust Avency, Privatisation Department, Green Building (Duhani), Rruga Vellusha II, Pristina, Kosovo (tel: 500-400-255; fax: 248-076; e-mail: soetenders@eumik.org; internet site: http://www.kta-kosovo.org).

Medjunarodni Pres Centar, Trg Republike 5, 11000 Belgrade (tel: 637-722; fax: 184-576).

Novinska Agencija Tanjug (news agency), Obilicev Venac 2, Box 439, Belgrade 11001 (tel: 332-221).

Roads Directorate of the Republic of Serbia, Ljube Cupe 5, 11000 Belgrade (tel: 454-779; fax: 444-5557; e-mail: dzpnapl@eunet.yu).

Serbia and Montenegro Statistical Office, Kneza Milosa 20, Box 203, 11000 Belgrade (tel: 685-572; fax: 681-995; internet: http://www.statserb.sr.gov.yu).

Internet sites

Belgrade News: http://www.belgradenews.com

B92 independent broadcasting station: http://www.b92.net

European Commission/World Bank, Balkans reconstruction web site: http://www.seerecon.org

Montenegro tourism: http://www.visit-montenegro.com

Official web site of Serbia and Montenegro: http://www.gov.yu

Serbia and Montenegro Secretariat of Information: http://www.ssinf.sv.gov.yu

Serbian Ministry of Information: http://www.serbia-info.com

Seychelles

KEY FACTS

Official name: Republic of Seychelles

Head of State: President James Michel (appointed 14 Apr 2004)

Head of government: President James Michel

Ruling party: Front Progressiste du Peuple Seychellois (FPPS) (Seychelles People's Progressive Front) (since 1993; last re-elected Dec 2002)

Area: 453 square km

Population: 82,800 (2004)

Capital: Victoria

Official language: Creole, French and English

Currency: Seychelle rupee (SR) = 100 cents

Exchange rate: SR5.52 per US$ (Oct 2005)

GDP per capita: US$8,499 (2004)

GDP real growth: -2.00% (2004)

Labour force: 30,900 (2003)

Inflation: 4.00% (2004)

Balance of trade: -US$137.20 million 2004

Foreign debt: US$170.00 million (2003)

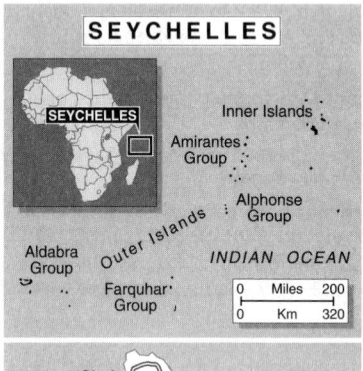

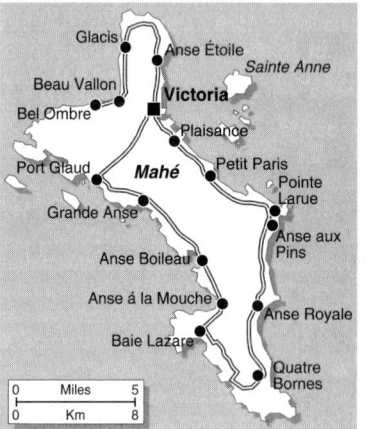

The Seychelles, which declared independence from Britain in 1976, is a republic and member of the Commonwealth. The country is comprised of approximately 115 islands spread over a large area of the western Indian Ocean. The largest of the islands, Mahe, on which is the country's capital, Victoria, is 153 sq km in area.

A good life

Citizens of the Indian Ocean archipelago enjoy a high per capita income, good health care and education. Although the economy is based largely on tourism, tuna canning and fishing make significant contributions.

There are no active International Monetary Fund programmes, or World Bank projects in Seychelles, although the bank has approved two loans in a total amount of US$10.7 million. Previous World Bank assisted projects in the Seychelles have included agriculture, fishing, and forestry; health and other social services; industry and trade; law, justice and public administration; transportation; water, sanitation and flood protection.

Since independence, per capita output in Seychelles has expanded to roughly seven times the old near-subsistence level. Seychelles' tourist sector employs 30 per cent of the labour force and provides more than 70 per cent of hard currency earnings. Fine beaches and turquoise seas are among the main draws for visitors. The archipelago is home to giant tortoises and sea turtles.

The government encourages foreign investment in the industry, and also tries to reduce dependence on tourism by promoting the development of farming, fishing, and small-scale manufacturing. The international terror attacks of recent years have adversely affected the islands' tourism. A persistent budget deficit, tight controls on exchange rates and the scarcity of foreign exchange have impaired short-term economic prospects.

Problem

A lengthy struggle between France and Great Britain for the islands ended in 1814, when they were ceded to the latter. Independence came in 1976. A year later, prime minister Albert René overthrew the president, James Mancham, and embarked on a programme to give the poorer people a greater share of the country's wealth. Four years later, with the help of Tanzanian troops, René thwarted an attempt by South African mercenaries to restore Mancham. An army mutiny in 1982, followed by several attempted coups, suffered a similar fate.

In 1991, possibly in response to pressure from foreign creditors and aid donors, René restored multi-party democracy. He stepped down in 2004 and was succeeded by James Michel, who had served alongside him since 1977.

Michel pledged to more economic reform. He is a member of the ruling Seychelles People's Progressive Front of which René remains head.

Risk assessment

Economic	Poor
Political	Fair
Regional stability	Good

Seychelles

COUNTRY PROFILE

Historical profile
The Seychelles, a cluster of 89 granite and coral islands in the Indian ocean some 1,000 miles from the African coast, won independence from the United Kingdom in 1976, after two centuries of colonial rule. The islands had been uninhabited until they were occupied in the 18th century by the French, who explored the islands in the 1740s and later settled there with their African slaves, in the 1770s. During the Napoleonic wars, the British blockaded the islands and the Seychelles changed hands several times between 1796 and 1810. British sovereignty was finally confirmed in the Treaty of Paris in 1814. Administered as a dependency of Mauritius for nearly a century, the Seychelles became a Crown Colony in 1903.

The uninhabited islands were sighted by the Portuguese explorer Vasco da Gama in the early sixteenth century, but it was not until the 1770s that any attempt to settle them was made when French farmers landed and introduced cinnamon, clove and nutmeg plantations (worked by slaves).

1794 The islands were taken over by the British and administered from Mauritius.
1903 Seychelles became a separate colony.
1948 The first elections to the legislative assembly took place.
1964 The Seychelles' first political organisations were established – the Seychelles Democratic Party (SDP) led by James Mancham and the Front Progressiste du Peuple Seychellois (FPPS) (Seychelles People's Progressive Front) (formerly the SPUP) of France-Albert René.
1975 The Seychelles was granted internal self-government; the SDP and the FPPS formed a coalition government under the premiership of Mancham.
1976 Became an independent republic. James Mancham became president and René became prime minister.
1977 René seized power in an armed coup and established a one-party state with the FPPS as the sole legal party.
1982 A mutiny in the army was put down by pro-government troops.
1991 René re-established a multi-party democracy.
1993 Multi-party presidential and legislative elections resulted in a landslide victory for both President René and the FPPS.
1998 Presidential and legislative elections were won by President René and the FPPS.
2001 Presidential elections resulted in a victory for President René (54.2 per cent of the vote).
2002 The FPPS won the parliamentary elections.
2004 On 14 April, President René, who came to power in a bloodless coup in 1977, retired and Vice President James Michel was sworn in as president. On 26 December, the Indian Ocean tsunami caused structural damage, but little loss of life.

Political structure
Constitution
In a June 1993 referendum, a new constitution was approved, institutionalising multi-party politics and providing for the establishment of a National Assembly.
Form of state
Republic
The executive
Executive power rests with the president, elected for a five-year term; renewable three times.
National legislature
The Assemblée Nationale (National Assembly) of 34 members, with 25 members directly elected on a constituency basis and the remaining nine allocated on a proportional basis. The term of the National Assembly is five years.
Last elections
4–6 December 2002 (parliamentary); 31 August/2 September 2001 (presidential) (two years before the scheduled date and the first time that presidential elections were held separately from legislative elections)
Results: Parliamentary: the ruling Front Progressiste du Peuple Seychellois (FPPS) (Seychelles People's Progressive Front) was re-elected with 54.3 per cent of the vote (23 seats out of 34) and the Seychelles National Party (SNP) 42.6 per cent (11); turnout was 87 per cent.
Presidential: France-Albert René was re-elected with 54.19 per cent of the vote, Wavel Ramkalawan 44.95 per cent and Philippe Boulle 0.86 per cent; this was the first time that presidential elections have been held separately from legislative elections
Next elections
2006 (presidential); 2007 (parliamentary).

Political parties
Ruling party
Front Progressiste du Peuple Seychellois (FPPS) (Seychelles People's Progressive Front) (since 1993; last re-elected Dec 2002)
Main opposition party
Seychelles National Party (SNP)

Population
82,800 (2004)
Ethnic make-up
The islanders have a variety of ethnic origins – African, French, Indian, Chinese and Arab.
Religions
Practically the whole population is Christian, with 87 per cent belonging to the Roman Catholic faith.

Education
The government provides free education. The school-going age population is largely concentrated on Mahe, the main island where most of the economic activities are concentrated. There are only two private schools as well as public schools. Total expenditure in public education has grown in real terms. The pupil per capita cost in (public) primary schools is typically US$910.
Literacy rate: 90 per cent (plus)
Compulsory years: 6 to 15
Pupils per teacher: 15 in primary schools (Unesco)

Health
The total expenditure on health in 2000 was 6.2 per cent of GDP, of which government expenditure was 66.9 per cent of total.
The Victoria Hospital has about 445 beds and there are 56 in-patient admissions

KEY INDICATORS — Seychelles

	Unit	2000	2001	2002	2003	2004
Population	m	0.08	0.08	0.08	0.08	0.08
Gross domestic product (GDP)	US$bn	0.60	0.63	0.63	0.63	*0.70
GDP per capita	US$	7,453	7,725	7,777	7,625	8,499
GDP real growth	%	1.2	1.0	-2.4	-5.1	-2.0
Inflation	%	7.6	6.0	6.0	7.0	4.0
Exports (fob) (goods)	US$m	128.0	215.3	236.7	235.0	256.2
Imports (fob) (goods)	US$m	351.0	386.9	376.3	380.0	393.4
Balance of trade	US$m	-223.0	-171.7	-139.6	-145.0	-137.2
Current account	US$m	-40.0	-140.0	-110.0	-10.0	-30.0
Total reserves minus gold	US$m	43.8	37.1	69.8	67.4	34.6
Foreign exchange	US$m	43.7	37.1	69.8	67.4	34.6

per bed per year. Health care is provided free of charge.
Life expectancy: 73.2 years (World Bank)
Fertility rate/Maternal mortality rate: 2.0 births per woman (World Bank)
Birth rate/Death rate: 17 births per 1,000 population; 6.5 deaths per 1,000 population (2003).
Infant mortality rate: 11 per 1,000 live births (World Bank)

Welfare

The social security law requires employers and employees to contribute to a national pension programme that gives retirees a modest pension. Self-employed persons contribute by paying 15 per cent of gross earnings. The government also provides low-cost housing and housing loans. There is welfare provision for children and the disabled.

Main cities

Victoria, on Mahé island (capital, estimated population 23,000 in 2003), Anse Royal (3,700).

Languages spoken

Creole is the local language, but English is used in business and government circles. French is also widely spoken.
Official language/s
Creole, French and English

Media

Press
Dailies: *Seychelles Nation* (www.seychelles-online.com.sc) is the online version of the daily government newspaper published from Monday to Saturday. There is one daily newspaper, *Nation*, which is government-owned.
Weeklies: *Seychelles Weekend Nation* is published on Saturdays.
Periodicals: *The People* is a monthly publication. A few periodicals are also published in English, French and Creole.
Broadcasting
Radio Television Seychelles (RTS) runs radio and television services in Creole, English and French. Reception is good on Mahé and the other main islands.

Economy

The Seychelles has the highest standard of living in Africa, but economic diversification is necessary. The economy is reliant on tourism and fishing and suffers a foreign exchange shortage, partly due to government spending and high imports of food and equipment. The fishing industry is a major foreign currency earner, which the government is seeking to develop further.
Beyond fishing and tourism, the country is looking to develop in areas such as telecommunications, financial services, light industry and international conferencing.

This will require considerable foreign investment and the government will need to institute policies and adopt attitudes more compliant to investors.
External shock, high government spending and lower revenues caused GDP to decline by 5.1 per cent in 2003 and by 2 per cent in 2004. Inflation also peaked in 2003 at 7 per cent, from 0.2 per cent in 2002. In December 2004, the *tsunami* caused by an earthquake off the coast of Sumatra, Indonesia, reached the Seychelles, causing widespread damage to infrastructure and adding to concerns about the longer-term stability of the economy, dependent as it is on fishing and tourism.

External trade

The visible trade deficit is partially offset by earnings from tourism which is the main foreign exchange earner, plus foreign aid and investment, rental from a US satellite tracking station and a BBC relay station.
The Seychelles International Trade Zone (ITZ) is a business park for export-orientated activities. As an African, Caribbean and Pacific (ACP) country, it enjoys quota-free, duty free access to the EU under the Conotou convention; as a member of the Common Market for Eastern and Southern Africa (Comesa), it enjoys the same trade benefits in Eastern and Southern Africa.
Preferential import tariffs are granted to goods from Indian Ocean Commission (IOC) member countries – Mauritius, Comoros, Madagascar, Réunion. In return, Seychelles receives preferential import tariffs from IOC countries.
On 31 December 2002, the US approved Seychelles as being eligible for tariff preferences under the African Growth and Opportunities Act (AGOA). The legislation requires that countries are only eligible for greater access to US markets provided they have made continued progress toward a market-based economy, the rule of law, free trade, poverty reduction and the protection of workers' rights. This process is reviewed annually.
Imports
Principal imports are machinery and equipment, foodstuffs, petroleum products and chemicals.
Main sources: Saudi Arabia (15.6 per cent total, 2004), Spain (14.1 per cent), France (11.0 per cent), Singapore (7.5 per cent), Italy (7.3 per cent), South Africa (7.3 per cent), UK (5.0 per cent)
Exports
Principal exports are processed tuna, frozen fish, mace and copra.
Main destinations: UK (29.1 per cent total, 2004), France (17.1 per cent), Spain (11.8 per cent), Japan (9.2 per cent), Italy (8.1 per cent), Germany (6.2 per cent), The Netherlands (4.3 per cent)
Re-exports
Petroleum products.

Agriculture

Farming
With the expansion of the tourist industry, the overall importance of agriculture to the economy has declined, although it is still important as a source of foreign exchange and employment. In 2004, the sector accounted for 2.6 per cent of GDP. There is a shortage of cultivable land and fertile soil. Approximately 4 per cent of the total land area is agricultural, much of which is given over to copra and cinnamon, which are the major export crops. Farming is traditionally organic and eco-friendly.
Small quantities of coconuts, vanilla, tea and limes are exported. Crops grown for local consumption include tropical fruits, cassava, sweet potatoes, yams, sugar cane, bananas, tea and vegetables; rice, the staple food crop, has to be imported. Seychelles is self-sufficient in pork, chicken, fish and some vegetables.
There are a number of large farms, 650 small farms and thousands of smallholdings, which the government hopes will reduce dependence on imported foods.
Government reforms include privatisation of state farms, while setting up smaller co-operatives, new marketing structures, upgrading infrastructure and irrigation facilities for farms. An animal feed factory has been established by the Seychelles Marketing Board (SMB) to support production of meat and eggs. About 98 per cent of milk is imported. The government is encouraging the production of bananas and mangoes.
The estimated crop production for 2004 included: 150 tonnes (t) cassava, 1,970t bananas, 3,200t coconuts, 60t citrus fruit, 190t tomatoes, 160t pineapples, 416t oilcrops, 30t mangoes, 200t cinnamon, 225t tea, 2,475t fruit in total, 1,940t vegetables in total. Estimated livestock production included: 1,742t meat in total, 30t beef, 1,105t pig meat, 20t goat meat, 587t poultry, 2,182t eggs, 310t milk.
Fishing
The fishing industry is an important source of income and foreign exchange, accounting for around 85 per cent of domestically-produces exports. It is being expanded as part of the government policy of economic diversification, with foreign companies being encouraged to become involved. HJ Heinz acquired a 60 per cent majority stake in the government-owned Indian Ocean Tuna processing factory. Heinz has invested nearly

Seychelles

US$8 million in the plant, which operates in the country's International Trade Zone. France and Italy are the main importers of Seychelles tuna.

The fishing infrastructure sustained damage from the *tsunami* in December 2004. The Seychelles sells fishing licences in its exclusive 1.3 million square km economic zone. Despite the desire for a growth in capacity and productivity through the development of commercial fishing operations, small-scale artisanal fishing still represents about one-third of fishing exports.

Industry and manufacturing
The industrial sector, including mining, manufacturing, construction and power, accounted for 27.5 per cent of GDP in 2004.

There is a small-scale manufacturing sector. The main activities include the production of canned tuna, soft drinks, juices, jams, beer, cigarettes, paints, assembling of television sets and processing of cinnamon and coconuts.

Emphasis is on private-sector investment. The government aims to expand light industry in other areas such as artisanal products, packaging, assembly and services.

Tourism
Tourism is the country's main economic sector, accounting for 70 per cent of foreign exchange earnings and around 40 per cent of employment. Tourism is expected to contribute 33 per cent of GDP in 2005. Seychelles is marketed as an exclusive destination. There are tight building controls limiting accommodation and favouring luxury hotels. The high cost of holidaying in Seychelles had resulted in a slight decline in visitor numbers in 2003, while at the same increasing receipts. Most visitors come from European and African countries. The Indian Ocean tsunami in December 2004 caused some damage to infrastructure.

Mining
Some granite is quarried. Offshore surveys have indicated the presence of certain metals on the seabed.

Hydrocarbons
The downstream oil industry is highly important, accounting for 25 per cent of imports and supplying 95 per cent of energy needs. There are no refineries in the Seychelles. Downstream activities are directed by the state-run Seychelles Petroleum Company.

The Seychelles does not produce oil, but there are indications of exploitable offshore reserves. The Seychelles National Oil Company co-ordinates the search for hydrocarbons, but there has been no activity in recent years. The government has revised legal and fiscal regimes to encourage exploration. An agreement was concluded in January 2005 with PetroQuest International to explore the southern shelf

The Seychelles do not produce or import natural gas. Some gas reserves have been found offshore, but they have not been exploited.

The Seychelles does not produce or import coal.

Energy
Electricity is provided from petroleum and gas turbines. Annual generation of electricity amounts to around 83GW.

Banking and insurance
Central bank
Central Bank of Seychelles

Time
GMT plus four hours

Geography
The Republic of Seychelles comprises more than 100 islands, widely scattered over the western Indian Ocean. Apart from the Seychelles archipelago, the country contains several other island groups, the southernmost being about 210km (130 miles) north of Madagascar.

Climate
Tropical and humid. Average temperature 24–32 degrees Celsius throughout the year. Hottest months December–May; wettest from December–March; cooler from June–November. The islands lie outside cyclone belt.

Entry requirements
Passports
Required by all. Passports must be valid for duration of stay.
Visa
A Visitor's Permit is issued on arrival, valid for one month (extensions are possible for three-month periods, fee SR200). All persons must hold onward or return tickets or pay a deposit equivalent to the value of a return ticket to the country of origin, and have confirmed accommodation and sufficient funds for the intended length of stay (March 1999).
Currency advice/regulations
Unlimited import/export of foreign currency is permitted. Only legal to exchange foreign exchange for Seychelles Rupees through a bank.
Travellers may take or send out of Seychelles up to SR100 of domestic currency.

Health (for visitors)
Mandatory precautions
Yellow fever certificate if arriving from infected area.
Advisable precautions
Hepatitis A, tetanus, typhoid and polio vaccinations. There is a rabies risk.

Hotels
Good standard and widely available. All the large hotels in Mahé are on the beach. Advisable to book and confirm reservation in advance, particularly at Christmas and during August. Government trades tax of 5 per cent is added to bill, and usually also a service charge. Tipping optional.

Credit cards
Major credit cards widely accepted.

Public holidays
Fixed dates
1–2 Jan (New Year), 1 May (Labour Day), 5 Jun (Liberation Day), 18 Jun (National Day), 15 Aug (Assumption Day/La Digue Festival), 1 Nov (All Saints' Day), 8 Dec (Immaculate Conception), 25 Dec (Christmas Day).
Variable dates
Good Friday, Easter Saturday, Corpus Christi (May/Jun).

Working hours
Banking
Mon–Fri: 0830–1300; Sat: 0800–1200.
Business
Mon–Fri: 0800–1200, 1300–1600.
Government
Mon–Fri: 0800–1200, 1300–1600.
Shops
Mon–Fri: 0800–1200, 1330–1700; Sat: 0800–1200; some open Sun morning.

Electricity supply
240V AC, 50 cycles. Plugs are three-pin bayonet.

Getting there
Air
National airline: Air Seychelles.
International airport/s: Seychelles-Pointe Larue International (Code: SEZ), Mahé Island, 10km from Victoria; duty-free shop, bar, restaurant, buffet, bank, shops, car hire.
Airport tax: Departure tax: US$40 (payable in foreign currency only), US$10 (transit passengers – less than 24 hours).
Surface
Main port/s: Victoria, on Mahé island, has a deep harbour. The Government plans to make Victoria a major regional transshipment centre.
Privatisation of stevedoring operations has increased the productivity of the port. Lane Marine won stevedoring contract in 1995 but administration of port remains with Port & Marine Services Division of Ministry of Tourism & Transport.

Getting about
National transport
Air: Air Seychelles operates regular services from Mahé to Praslin, Desroches, Fregate, Bird and Dennis islands.
Aircraft charters are available to Assumption, Farquhar and Poivre.

Nations of the World: A Political, Economic and Business Handbook

Helicopter Seychelles provides services and charters from Mahé.

There are plans to expand the outer island airport at Praslin with World Bank funds. Airstrips exist on most of the outlying islands.

Road: The islands have 323km of roads, of which 231km are surfaced.

Mahé and Praslin are the only islands with appreciable surfaced roads. There are gravel roads elsewhere.

Buses: A cheap, regular bus service (provided by Seychelles Public Transport Corporation) operates to most areas of Mahé from Victoria. Services also operate on Praslin and La Digue.

Water: Regular ferry services connect Mahé and the islands of Praslin and La Digue. The Marine Charter Association in Victoria assists with boat charters to other islands.

City transport

Taxis: Available on Mahé and Praslin. Fixed charges, tipping is optional.

Car hire

Available on Mahé and Praslin. Victoria and certain villages impose a speed limit of 40kph, elsewhere it is 65kph. Advance reservation advisable. Foreign or international driving licence required.

BUSINESS DIRECTORY

The addresses listed below are a selection only. While World of Information makes every endeavour to check these addresses, we cannot guarantee that changes have not been made, especially to telephone numbers and area codes. We would welcome any corrections.

Telephone area codes

The international dialling code (IDD) for Seychelles is +248, followed by subscriber's number.

Chambers of Commerce

Seychelles Chamber of Commerce & Industry, Ebrahim Building, PO Box 1399, Victoria, Mahé (tel: 323-812; fax: 321-422; e-mail: scci@seychelles.net).

Banking

Development Bank of Seychelles, PO Box 217, Independence Ave, Victoria (tel: 224-471; fax: 224-274).

Seychelles International Mercantile Banking Corporation Ltd, PO Box 241, Ground Floor, Victoria House, State House Avenue, Victoria (tel: 225-011; fax: 224-670).

Seychelles Savings Bank Limited; PO Box 531, Independence Ave, Victoria (tel: 225-251; fax: 224-713).

Central bank

Central Bank of Seychelles, Independence Avenue, PO Box 701, Victoria, Mahé (tel: 225-200; fax: 224-958; e-mail: cbs@seychelles.sc).

Travel information

Air Seychelles, Victoria House, PO Box 386, Victoria (tel: 225-300; fax: 225-159).

National Travel Agency, Kingsgate House, PO Box 611, Victoria (tel: 224-900; fax: 225-111).

Seychelles Tourism Marketing Authority, PO Box 1262, Victoria, Mahé (tel: 620-000; fax: 620-620).

Travel Services (Seychelles) Ltd., Victoria House, PO Box 356, Victoria (tel: 322-414; fax: 325-010).

Ministry of tourism

Ministry of Tourism and Transport, Independence House, PO Box 92, Victoria (tel: 225-313; fax: 225-131).

National tourist organisation offices

Seychelles Tourist Office, PO Box 92, Victoria, Mahé (tel: 25-315, fax: 25-333).

Ministries

Investment Development Advisory Services (IDEAS), c/o Ministry of Finance and Communication, 3rd Floor, Central Bank Building, Box 313, Victoria (tel: 225-252; fax: 225-265).

Ministry of Administration and Manpower, National House, PO Box 56, Victoria (tel: 383-000; fax: 224-936).

Ministry of Agriculture and Marine Resources, Independence House, PO Box 166, Victoria (tel: 224-030; fax: 225-245).

Ministry of Community Development, Independence House, PO Box 199, Victoria (tel: 224-030; fax: 225-287).

Ministry of Education and Culture, Mont Fleuri (tel: 224-777; fax: 224-859).

Ministry of Finance and Communication, 3rd Floor, Central Bank Building, PO Box 313, Victoria (tel: 225-252; fax: 225-265).

Ministry of Foreign Affairs, Planning and Environment, Mont Fleuri (tel: 224-688; fax: 224-845).

Ministry of Health, PO Box 52, Mont Fleuri (tel: 388-000; fax: 224-792).

Ministry of Industry, Maison du People, Victoria (tel: 224-030; fax: 225-086).

Ministry of Local Government Youth and Sports, Oceangate House, Victoria (tel: 225-477; fax: 225-262).

Other useful addresses

Island Development Company (IDC), PO Box 638, New Port, Victoria (tel: 224-640; fax: 224-467).

Public Utilities Corporation (PUC):

Electricity: PO Box 174, Victoria (tel: 322-444; fax: 321-020).

Water: Unity House, PO Box 34, Victoria (tel: 322-444; fax: 322-127).

RTS Radio, PO Box 321, Union Vale, Victoria (tel: 224-161).

RTS TV, PO Box 321, Hermitage, Mahé (tel: 224-161).

Seychelles Agricultural Development Company Ltd., PO Box 172, Victoria (tel: 276-618).

Seychelles Broadcasting Corporation, Hermitage, PO Box 321, Victoria (tel: 224-161; fax: 224-641).

Seychelles Embassy (USA), Suite 400, 820 Second Avenue, New York, NW, 10017 (tel: 202-972-1785; fax: 202-972-1786; e-mail: seychelles@un.int).

Seychelles Fishing Authority (SFA), PO Box 449, Victoria (tel: 224-521; fax: 224-508).

Seychelles Industrial Development Corporation (SIDEC), PO Box 537, Victoria (tel: 224-941; fax: 225-121).

Seychelles International Business Authority (SIBA), PO Box 991, Central Bank Building, Victoria (tel: 225-402; fax: 225-851).

Seychelles Licensing Authority, PO Box 3, Francis Rachel Street, Victoria (tel: 224-314; fax: 224-256).

Seychelles Marketing Board, PO Box 516, Victoria (tel: 224-444).

Seychelles Timber Company, Grand Anse, Mahe (tel: 278-343).

State Assurance Corporation ofSeychelles, Pirate's Arms Building, PO Box 636, Victoria (tel: 225-000; fax: 224-495).

Internet sites

Africa Business Network: http://www.ifc.org/abn

AllAfrica.com: http://allafrica.com

African Development Bank: http://www.afdb.org

Africa Online: http://www.africaonline.com

Harambee Afrika (UK business club for traders with east, central and southern Africa; includes annotated web resource list): http://www.harambee.co.uk

Mbendi AfroPaedia (information on companies, countries, industries and stock exchanges in Africa): http://mbendi.co.za

Sierra Leone

The West African state of Sierra Leone emerged from a decade of civil war only four years ago. It had the support of Britain, the former colonial power, and 17,000 United Nations' peacekeepers who disarmed tens of thousands of rebels and militia fighters whose trademark was to hack off the hands of their victims. A UN-backed war crimes court has been set up to try those who bear the 'greatest responsibility' for the wartime brutalities.

Sierra Leone is rich in diamonds. Illicit trade in them funded the war and gave rise to the term 'blood diamonds'. NGO posters showed dying children and glittering diamonds and urged consumers to stop buying the gems. The international diamond industry, including several African countries, managed to avoid a consumer boycott by banding together and against stringent international checks, certifying their diamonds as Diamonds for Development. Diamond marketing organisations would buy only such certified stones. Cross-border diamond trafficking still exists.

Economy

Sierra Leone is an extremely poor country with tremendous inequality in income distribution. While it possesses substantial mineral wealth (as well as diamonds there is titanium ore, bauxite, iron ore, gold and chromite), agricultural and fishery resources, its economic and social infrastructure is not well developed, and serious social disorders continue to hamper economic development. About two-thirds of the working-age population engages in subsistence agriculture. Manufacturing consists mainly of the processing of raw materials and of light manufacturing for the domestic market. Alluvial diamond mining remains the major source of hard currency earnings, accounting for nearly half of Sierra Leone's exports. Donors and international financial institutions say that the economic and structural reforms sought by Sierra Leone will require a longer period to implement than the government would have them believe.

They say monetary policy needs to be more proactive, and the central bank more vigilant in ensuring that commercial banks remain sound and well capitalised. Should, as is forecast, public sector management strengthen, a shift in the balance of reforms in favour of the private sector would promote much needed private investment. In this regard, an aggressive privatisation agenda would assist in raising revenue as well as enhancing efficiency and require the support of the banks.

Both the government and the aid agencies are looking to the current International Monetary Fund-supported arrangement to play a catalytic role in mobilising external assistance. Sierra Leone has implemented an economic reform programme supported by the IMF since 2001 and has expressed an interest in a longer-term arrangement.

Identified support from donors was projected to fall from US$143 million in 2004 to US$94 million in 2005. External reserves remain low, in comparison to Sierra Leone's vulnerability to external shocks, and the reserves were projected to decline to 2.8 months of imports by end-2005.

With strong output gains expected in 2005 and beyond, Sierra Leone's main challenge is to keep inflation under control while supporting an expansion in real activity. Domestic resource mobilisation and assistance from donors will be critical not

KEY FACTS

Official name: Republic of Sierra Leone

Head of State: President Ahmad Tejan Kabbah (SLPP) (elected 1996; re-elected 14 May 2002)

Head of government: President Ahmad Tejan Kabbah

Ruling party: Sierra Leone People's Party (SLPP) (elected 14 May 2002)

Area: 72,325 square km

Population: 4.85 million (2004)

Capital: Freetown

Official language: English

Currency: Leone (Le) = 100 cents

Exchange rate: Le2,910.74 per US$ (Oct 2005)

GDP per capita: US$201 (2004)

GDP real growth: 7.40% (2004)

Labour force: 2.00 million (2003)

Inflation: 13.70% (2004)

Balance of trade: -US$155.00 million (2003)

Foreign debt: US$1.50 billion (2003)

Nations of the World: A Political, Economic and Business Handbook

only for successfully implementing medium-term poverty-reduction programmes but also for enabling Sierra Leone to advance toward longer-term goals.

Politics

President Ahmad Tejan Kabbah won a new five-year term in elections in May 2002 and is credited with bringing in foreign assistance to rescue his country from itself. He first took office in March 1996 following war-time elections that formally ended four years of army rule. However, disgruntled soldiers toppled him in May 1997. A West African intervention force reinstated him within a year.

Kabbah spent 21 years working for the UN Development Programme, based in New York, Lesotho and Tanzania. He returned to Sierra Leone in 1992.

Outlook

The short- to medium-term fate of the economy depends upon the maintenance of domestic peace and the continued receipt of substantial aid. The government is slowly re-establishing its authority after the 1991–2002 civil war that resulted in tens of thousands of deaths and the displacement of more than two million people (about one-third of the population). The last UN peacekeepers withdrew in December 2005, leaving full responsibility for security with domestic forces. A new civilian UN office remains to support the government. Mounting tensions relate to planned 2007 elections. Deteriorating political and economic conditions in Guinea and the tenuous security situation in neighbouring Liberia may present challenges to continuing stability in Sierra Leone.

Risk assessment

Economic	Improving
Political	Improving
Regional stability	Improving

COUNTRY PROFILE

Historical profile

The English translation of Sierra Leone means Lion Mountains. In fact, its educated élite would jokingly refer to it as the Athens of Africa, when the country became known – in West Africa at least, as a centre of education. It was in Freetown, the settlement established by the British in 1787 to provide a home for freed slaves (later mainly captives freed from slave ships who had never left African waters) that, in 1827, established the institution that was to become Fourah Bay College. There, in the late 19th century, University education began in West Africa. Many future African leaders and politicians attended the college.

By 1876 Freetown was already well-endowed with educational establishments. But it was not until 1896 that the greater part of modern Sierra Leone, called until independence the Protectorate was added to the original British colony.

Emerging from a lengthy civil war, Sierra Leone is an extremely poor African country with a highly unequal distribution of wealth. Surviving on its substantial mineral, agricultural and fishery resources, the country's economic and social infrastructures are gravely under-developed.

1787 The state was founded by the British as a homeland for freed slaves.
1808 Freetown became a British colony. Over the following 60 years around 70,000 ex-slaves arrived in the country, mainly in the Freetown area. The colonial authorities appointed non-indigenous Africans to the civil service and senior administrative positions, thus laying the foundation for future civil strife.
1954 Sierra Leone was allowed some degree of self-rule through a new local administration. Sir Milton Margai of the Sierra Leone People's Party (SLPP) was appointed the head of the newly-established administration.
1961 Sierra Leone gained independence from Britain in April, but remained part of the Commonwealth. Sir Milton Margai became the country's first prime minister.
1964 Following Sir Milton's death, his half-brother, Sir Albert Margai, was appointed prime minister.
1967 The All Peoples Congress (APC) won the parliamentary election, its leader, Siaka Stevens, was appointed prime minister. Sierra Leonean military officers staged a coup.
1968 After an army revolt, Stevens and the APC returned to government.
1971 Sierra Leone became a republic. Stevens was appointed as the country's first president.
1978 A new constitution established one-party rule with the APC as the only legal party.
1985 Stevens retired, Major General Joseph Momoh became president.
1991 Rebels opposed to the Momoh government – principally the Revolutionary United Front (RUF) led by Foday Sankoh – launched a series of attacks, which took much of the eastern part of the country. They were backed by Liberia.
1992 A coup brought Captain Valentine Strasser to power. He presided over a military government, which suspended the constitution and ruled by decree.
1996 Strasser was deposed by Brigadier Julius Bio. Multi-party elections ended four years of military rule. Ahmed Tejan Kabbah of the SLPP became president.
1997 Major Johnny-Paul Koroma led a coup and ousted Kabbah, who went into exile. The Armed Forces Revolutionary Council (ARFC) was installed, backed by the RUF. International sanctions were imposed. The Economic Community of West African States (Ecowas) dispatched a peace-keeping force, the Ecowas Monitoring Group (Ecomog) in order to reinstate the government of President Kabbah. A peace accord was reached in October.
1998 Ecomog launched a military offensive against the AFRC after Koroma showed no sign of implementing the 1997 agreement and steppin down from power.

KEY INDICATORS — Sierra Leone

	Unit	2000	2001	2002	2003	2004
Population	m	4.41	4.57	4.76	4.80	*4.85
Gross domestic product (GDP)	US$bn	0.64	0.68	0.79	0.81	*1.08
GDP per capita	US$	133	133	151	169	201
GDP real growth	%	3.8	5.4	6.6	6.5	7.4
Inflation	%	-0.9	2.6	-3.7	8.2	13.7
Exports (fob) (goods)	US$m	75.0	78.0	103.0	35.0	–
Imports (fob) (goods)	US$m	161.0	303.0	290.0	190.0	–
Balance of trade	US$m	-86.0	-225.0	-187.0	-155.0	–
Current account	US$m	-100.0	-130.0	-50.0	-80.0	-100.0
Foreign debt	US$bn	1.3	1.2	–	–	–
Total reserves minus gold	US$m	50.9	51.6	84.7	66.6	125.1
Foreign exchange	US$m	45.6	51.2	60.6	32.1	74.1
Exchange rate	per US$	2,092.13	1,986.15	2,099.03	2,230.00	2,701.30

* estimated figure

Sierra Leone

Ecomog ejected the AFRC from Freetown and Kabbah returned to Sierra Leone. The RUF remained in control of large areas outside the capital. The civilian population in rebel held territories were subjected to brutal treatment, with limb amputations meted out to victims of all ages.

1999 RUF rebels counter-attacked the capital and were finally driven off after weeks of fierce fighting. Liberia was accused of supporting the rebels and trading weapons for diamonds, mined in rebel territories. The government and the FUC signed a peace agreement, allowing for the deployment of UN peace-keeping forces.

2000 Foday Sankoh condemned the presence of UN forces in the country. The UN reported that civilians continued to be mutilated, raped and abducted in rebel held areas. RUF rebels clashed with UN troops when they were required to disarm. Over 13,000 UN troops held a limited peace in the south while British paratroopers trained government forces. Under a UK plan, thousands of British troops arrived to stabilise President Kabbah's regime. Sankoh was captured in Freetown where he had been hiding for weeks. Within two months, Britain withdrew most of its forces leaving a contingent to continue training local government forces.

2001 Military operations continued to push into lawless regions of the country and restore civil society. Legislative and presidential elections were postponed because of the unstable security situation in the country.

2002 In January the 11-year civil war was officially declared ended and state of emergency measures were lifted. Ahmad Tejan Kabbah (SLPP) won a landslide victory as president. The SLPP won the parliamentary elections.

2003 Agriculture production recovered to pre-war levels, as many people displaced during the civil war returned to their homes. In July, rebel leader Foday Sankoh died of natural causes while awaiting trial for war crimes.

2004 The first local elections in more than three decades were held in May. A war crimes court, staffed by senior US legal personnel, began taking evidence in June. The court is mandated for three years and empowered to 'arrest, try and convict' those accused of war crimes.

2005 In November the UN agreed that former Liberian leader Charles Taylor should be handed over to Sierra Leone to stand trial for war crimes perpetrated by Sierre Leone insurgents he had supported while he was Liberian president. The last UN-troops withdrew in December.

Political structure

Constitution
The 1991 referendum, adopting a multi-party parliamentary system, based on the US model, was amended in 2002, and introduced the District Block System (DBS) for voting.

Form of state
Unitary republic

The executive
Executive power is vested in the president, who is both Head of State and head of government. The president is directly elected for up to two, five-year terms. The president appoints ministers, approved by parliament. The cabinet is composed of ministers who are answerable to the president.

National legislature
The national legislature is the 112-member House of Representatives. Under the District Block System (DBS), eight representatives from each of Sierra Leone's 14 districts are elected by proportional representation. In addition, 12 paramount chiefs, each representing a district, also sit in parliament.

Legal system
It is based on English law and is composed of a Supreme Court, Appeals Court and a High Court.
A special war crimes court, operating under Sierra Leonean law, was set up in 2004 to try those accused of heinous war crimes.

Last elections
14 May 2002 (presidential and parliamentary)
Results: Presidential: Ahmad Tejan Kabbah won 70.6 per cent of the vote, Ernest Koroma 22.4 per cent.
Parliamentary: the SLPP won 83 of 112 seats, the APC 27 and the Peace and Liberation Party two. The former rebels, the RUF, failed to win a single seat.

Next elections
2006 (legislative); 2007 (presidential).

Political parties

Ruling party
Sierra Leone People's Party (SLPP) (elected 14 May 2002)

Main opposition party
All People's Congress (APC)

Population
4.85 million (2004)

Ethnic make-up
African groups: Temne (30 per cent), Mende (30 per cent), others (20 per cent)); Creole (Krio) (descendants of freed Jamaican slaves settled in the Freetown area in the late-18th century) (10 per cent); refugees from Liberia's civil war and small numbers of Europeans, Lebanese, Pakistanis and Indians.

Religions
Islam (60 per cent), indigenous beliefs (30 per cent), Christian (10 per cent).

Education
Government plans to increase primary school enrolment and to reduce the gender gap in education has only been under way since 2001 and while enrolment levels are rising the gender gap has also widened. The civil conflict has left about 50 per cent of primary schools functioning in inadequate accommodation. Unicef is assisting in the provision of teaching and learning materials and teacher training, it is also funding the Complementary Rapid Education for Primary Schools (CREPS) programme, designed to enable over-aged children to complete the primary school programme.
Primary education begins at aged six and lasts for six years. Junior secondary school lasts for three years. Students who are successfully may progress to the senior secondary school for a further three years and then onto university.
The University of Sierra Leone is the only institute of higher learning.
Literacy rate: 36 per cent (2004)
Compulsory years: Six to 12.
Enrolment rate: 39 per cent, boys; 34 per cent, girls; primary enrolment (Unicef).

Health
UN programmes aid the healthcare system to improve the country's ranking in the Human Development Index which is only one higher than Niger which, in 2005, is the lowest ranking. Around 70 per cent of the population lives below the poverty line.
Technical aid, rehabilitation and funding will be provided through a four-year programme (2004–07), including measures to improve water sources and sanitation and HIV/Aids education and prevention.
Donor support will have to be sustained over the long-term to cope with the ongoing rehabilitating of civil war amputees.

HIV/Aids
Aids has killed between two to three times more people than during the civil war, yet has received relatively little attention. Around 68,000 people are infected with HIV/Aids, 3,300 of them are under 15-years-old. Since the beginning of the epidemic, over 56,000 children have lost their mother or both parents. The spread of the disease is due to a low prevelance of condom use.
HIV prevalence: 0.9 per cent adult population (government statistic)
The Global Fund to Fight HIV/Aids, Tuberculosis and Malaria states government statistic significantly underestimates the prevalence rate and puts the figure closer to 3.4 per cent generally, and 5 per cent

in Freetown. An international medical charity that undertook a study in Freetown in 2004 found a prevalence rate of 4.6 per cent among prenatal women, a typically non-risk group, which suggests the prevalence rate could be higher even than the Global Funds' estimation.

In February 2005 the government announced that it would undertake a nationwide survey to provide 'baseline information' about HIV/Aids in Sierra Leone.

Life expectancy: 34 years (Unicef, 2004)
Fertility rate/Maternal mortality rate: 5.6 births per woman (World Bank). Maternal mortality, 1,800 per 100,000 live births (Unicef 2004).
Birth rate/Death rate: 44 births per 1,000 population; 20.7 deaths per 1,000 population (2003).
Infant mortality rate: 166 per 1,000 live births (World Bank)

Main cities
Freetown (capital, estimated population 1.1 million in 2004), Koidu (113,700), Makeni (110,700), Bo (82,400).

Languages spoken
English is the main medium for business. Mende is spoken principally in the south, Temne in the north and Krio (English-based Creole) is spoken by 10 per cent of the population and understood by 95 per cent.
Official language/s
English

Media
Press
Dailies: Main daily newspapers are *The Pool Newspaper*, *Concord Times*, *Awoko*, *Independent Observer*, *Standard Times* and *Daily Mail*.
Weeklies: Weeklies include *New Sierra Leonean*, *Vision* and *Weekend Spark*.
Business: The Ministry of Information and Broadcasting publishes the quarterly *Sierra Leone Trade Journal*.
Broadcasting
Two commercial radio and one commercial TV stations (mainly received in Freetown area). Broadcasts in English, French and local languages.

Economy
Despite its extensive mineral resources, that include large quantities of alluvial diamonds, Sierra Leone is an impoverished country. The brutal 11-year civil war that ended in 2002 was largely funded by diamonds mined by itinerant diggers attached to rebel forces.

Sierra Leone was granted, by the World Bank and IMF, a debt reduction package under the Heavily Indebted Poor Countries (HIPC) initiate, in 2002. This package was estimated to be worth US$950 million in debt servicing obligations. For its part the Sierra Leonean government has introduced ride-ranging structural reforms and pursued practical macroeconomic policies to enhance the country's potential recovery.

To promote growth and reduce poverty the government has focussed on six key targets: state security, a sustainable fiscal position, raising domestic savings and investment, increasing infrastructure, agricultural and rural development and promoting the private sector.

While agriculture provides one of the largest elements of GDP at around 40 per cent, diamonds provide the most foreign revenue. Since diamond certification was introduced in 2000, revenues have almost doubled year-on-year and earned US$126 million in 2004. A quarter of diamond taxes are reinvested in mining communities to provide social assets such as schools and roads, as well as co-operatives to help miners market their finds.

The economy is beginning to recover with improved business confidence. GDP was estimated at 1.08 in 2004, showing a modest rise from the 0.81 in 2003. However, inflation was high at 13.7 per cent due to high fuel costs, the expansionary monetary policy and a depreciating currency.

The economy is broadly open and the government is attempting to attract direct foreign investment through the sale of state-owned financial, utilities, commercial and transport entities. The government is also aware that, politically, outright sale of national assets may be unpalatable to the majority of Sierra Leoneans so it has proposed incremental privatisation, with management contracts offered along with public/private partnerships.

Bureaucratic barriers to business start-ups and one-stop shops have reduced delays and it is hoped these will encourage foreign and domestic investment. Sierra Leone has one of the worst rates of gross domestic savings in Africa and much needs to be achieved to encourage a reversal in this pattern. Nevertheless, in 2004, 21.4 per cent of GDP was gross domestic investment; private investment was 12.5 per cent and government investment was 8.9 pre cent.

External trade
In 2002, the US approved Sierra Leone as being eligible for tariff preferences under the African Growth and Opportunities Act (AGOA).
Imports
Principal imports are foodstuffs (typically over 30 per cent of total value), machinery and transport equipment, manufactured goods, fuels and lubricants, and chemicals.

Main sources: Germany (17.3 per cent total, 2004), UK (9.2 per cent), Côte d'Ivoire (8.0 per cent), US (8.0 per cent), Ukraine (4.9 per cent), The Netherlands (4.7 per cent), China (4.5 per cent), Denmark (4.2 per cent)
Exports
Principal exports following the civil war are diamonds, rutile, cocoa, coffee and fish.
Main destinations: Belgium (63.1 per cent total, 2004), Germany (11.9 per cent), US (5.8 per cent)

Agriculture
Farming
The civil war seriously disrupted agricultural activity, destroying the homes and livelihood of many farming families. This will impact on food security for a number of years to come.

The agricultural sector contributes around 50 per cent to GDP and employs 65–75 per cent of labour force. Many young people have left rural areas since 2002 to find work in the cities.

Area under cultivation is approximately 25 per cent of the total land area. It is limited by a traditional land tenure system and is mostly in the hands of smallholders engaged in subsistence farming.

Major cash export crops are cocoa, coffee, palm kernels and ginger. Despite government efforts towards self-sufficiency, rice imports have risen. Other food crops include maize, cassava, sweet potatoes and sorghum.

Production has been hampered by poor infrastructure, a lack of incentives and a poor marketing and distribution system. The estimated crop production for 2004 included: 309,300 tonnes (t) cereals in total, 10,000t maize, 390,000t cassava, 25,500t sweet potatoes, 21,000t sorghum, 265,000t rice, 30,000t plantains, 58,700t pulses, 418,100t roots and tubers, 16,000t groundnuts in shell, 195,000t oil palm fruit, 85,000t citrus fruit, 15,000t tomatoes, 56,168t oilcrops, 11,000t cocoa beans, 18,000t green coffee, 28,000t sugar cane, 181,500t fruit in total, 235,000t vegetables in total. Estimated livestock production included: 23,259t meat in total, 5,400t beef, 2,320t pig meat, 1,210t lamb, 11,334t poultry, 8,290t eggs, 21,250t milk, 500t honey, 1,290t cattle hides, 220t sheepskins.

Fishing
The fishing sector has two distinct patterns. Coastal fishing, undertaken by men, is commercially driven with catches either sold fresh or preserved for transport inland. Inland fishing is performed by women and largely for private consumption.

Sierra Leone

Coastal fishing fleets have contracted since 2001, however production has risen.

The majority of vessels harvest shrimps.

Industry and manufacturing

The industrial sector accounts for around 30 per cent of GDP and employs 5 per cent of the workforce.

The sector is mainly limited to food processing and light manufacturing of consumer goods such as cigarettes, alcoholic beverages, plastic footwear, nails, paint and confectionery. Emphasis is placed on import substitution industries, but attempts to establish heavy industry have met with only limited success and have been undermined by political instability.

Expansion is limited by weak local demand, power shortages, foreign exchange shortages and low investment.

Tourism

The tourist sector is expected to contribute US$27 million or 2.9 per cent of GDP, while employing over 47 thousand people and should attract 3.4 per cent of all capital investment in 2005.

The country has much to offer with a diverse landscape and friendly people although continued peace is paramount. The main foreign investors in Sierra Leone's tourist sector are Chinese companies who see the opportunities for refurbished and new tourist attractions as sound investments. A US$266 million ocean-front tourism complex with holiday homes, golf course and five-star hotel, was signed in 2004 and is due to be opened in 2006. Another US$270 million invested in various hotels developments is expected to help set off a tourism boom.

Mining

The mining sector contributes around 35 per cent to GDP and employs 10 per cent of the workforce.

Diamonds play an essential part in the economy. In 2004, US$126.7 million gem-quality diamonds were exported and revenue earned was US$4.2 million. The government, in an effort to bring artisanal mining into legal and regulated operation and minimise smuggling, has introduced a certification system for exporting diamonds and created a mining community development fund to return a percentage of the taxes back to the local population. Sierra Leone has one of the world's largest deposits of rutile (a titanium ore). The Sierra Rutile mining operation was closed and damaged during the civil war. In March 2005 a re-start operation was undertaken and the facility is expected to begin production in early 2006.

Bauxite mining is also an important sector with large reserves at Sieromco and Port Loko. Production was suspended due to the civil war. Foreign investment is necessary to begin a re-start operation.

Hydrocarbons

Sierra Leone imports all its oil requirements.

There are large deposits offshore within the West African region, which it is not economically viable to extract currently. Sierra Leone does not produce or import natural gas or coal.

Energy

The Sierra Leone Electricity Company (SLEC) oversees electricity generation and supply.

Installed generating capacity is approximately 100MW (mostly oil-fired thermal power stations). However, the supply is is insufficient and undependable.

A US$300 million hydroelectric project under construction on the Seli River at Bumbuna with a capacity of 53MW, will supply power to Freetown and northern provinces by mid-2006.

The serious energy shortage has forced many citizens to buy personal diesel generators; more than 86 per cent of the population uses bio-mass (wood fuel, kerosene charcoal) for energy.

Banking and insurance

The banking sector has been weakened by war. However, the government has given the central bank power to tighten fiscal controls and prepare some for sale. The IMF is wary of donor funds that are distributed through local banks, bypassing the close scutiny and anti-corruption measures instituted by the central bank.

It was announced in March 2005 that the introduction of the shared currency, the eco, in Sierra Leone, Ghana, Guinea, Nigeria and The Gambia, which was due in July 2005, would be postponed. The currency was proposed to facilitate trade and growth with an ultimate plan to merge it with the CFA franc.

Central bank
Bank of Sierra Leone

Main financial centre
Freetown

Time
GMT

Geography

Sierra Leone lies on the west coast of Africa, with Guinea to the north and east and Liberia to the south.

Climate

Tropical, with high humidity and rainfall. Dry season November–April, wet season rest of year. Average temperature range of 21–32 degrees Celsius remains fairly constant throughout the year.

Entry requirements

Passports
Required by all and must be valid for six months.

Requirements may be subject to change at short notice; contact the Embassy before departure.

Visa
Required by all, and must be obtained in advance. Citizens of Ecowas countries are exempt. Contact the nearest embassy for an application form. All visas require evidence of return/onward passage; tourists must provide evidence of hotel reservations.

Business visitors should include a letter of invitation from a local contact and a letter of introductory from their employer outlining the purpose of the trip, the nature of business and contacts in Sierra Leone. For new business, an applicant must provide evidence of commercial veracity and financial standing.

Currency advice/regulations
Local currency up to Le50,000 and unlimited foreign currency can be imported, but it must be declared. Export of local currency up to Le50,000 and foreign currency up to the amount imported and declared. Travellers cheques in sterling or US dollars are preferred, but opportunities to cash them are limited. All foreign exchange transactions must be handled through the banks and official exchange offices.

Customs
All visitors must complete a customs declaration form for presentation on entering country.

All gem stones require an export licence.

Prohibited imports
Narcotics

Health (for visitors)

Mandatory precautions
Yellow fever, malaria and cholera vaccination certificates are required.

Advisable precautions
Hepatitis A, tetanus, polio, and typhoid vaccinations. Malaria prophylaxis should be taken. HIV/Aids is prevalent. Water precautions should be taken. There is a rabies risk. Use only well maintained, chlorinated swimming pools to avoid bilharzia. Lassa fever can be contracted in Kenema and the east; seek urgent medical advice for any fever not positively identified as malaria.

Visitors should carry basic medical supplies and any prescription medication necessary. Medical and emergency insurance (to include repatriation) is strongly recommended.

Hotels

Available in Freetown, especially at Lumley Beach, within easy taxi access of the centre of Freetown. Limited availability outside capital. Credit cards accepted only in major hotels and payment required in US dollars. A service charge is usually included in bill.

Credit cards
Not accepted.

Public holidays
Fixed dates
1 Jan (New Year's Day), 27 Apr (Independence Day), 25 Dec (Christmas Day), 26 Dec (Boxing Day).
Variable dates
Good Friday, Easter Monday, Eid al Adha, Birth of the Prophet, Eid al Fitr. The Islamic year contains 354 or 355 days, with the result that Muslim feasts advance by 10–12 days against the Gregorian calendar. Dates of feasts vary according to the sighting of the new moon, so cannot be forecast exactly. Islamic year 1426: 10 February 2005 to 30 January 2006.

Working hours
Banking
Mon–Thu: 0800–1330; Fri: 0800–1400.
Business
Mon–Fri: 0800–1200, 1400–1630.
Government
Mon–Fri: 0800–1230, 1330–1645; close 1500 on Fri.
Shops
Mon–Fri: 0800–1200, 1400–1630; shops open Sat.

Electricity supply
230/240V AC, 50 cycles. Voltage fluctuation and power cuts occur.

Social customs/useful tips
Carry some form of identification at all times.

Security
Sierra Leone is emerging from its brutal civil war and, as UN troops are maintaining the peace, the security situation is improving. Visitors should take care and avoid the border region with Liberia. Travelling outside the capital at night is not recommended, as much for the poor state of the roads as any armed conflict.

Getting there
Air
National airline: Sierra National Airlines
International airport/s: Freetown-Lungi International (FNA), 20km north of city; bar, currency exchange, post office, shops.
Airport tax: International departures US$20, payable in hard currency. Transit passengers are exempt.
Surface
Road: There are routes from Guinea Republic and Liberia, but access depends on the prevailing political situation.

Water: From Guinea Republic and Liberia.
Main port/s: Freetown

Getting about
National transport
Public transport is neither reliable nor safe. The heavy rainy season, which lasts for several months between May and November makes travel to outlying areas both difficult and hazardous.
Road: Most main roads in Freetown are paved but have potholes; unpaved side streets are generally navigable. A major road resurfacing and repair programme in Freetown is slowly improving the quality of roads in the city. Most roads outside Freetown are unpaved. All roads are unlit and potholes are common.
Buses: Buses in Freetown tend to be overcrowded and unreliable. Regular service Freetown-Kambia, Freetown-Pendembu, Freetown-Makeni-Kabala.
Rail: There are no passenger services.
City transport
Public transport, when it exists, is neither reliable nor always safe.
Taxis: Available at the airport and in main towns; fares by negotiation; tipping is not usual. It is considered safer to use taxis that work in conjunction with an hotel.
Buses, trams & metro: There are buses from the airport to the city centre, but the services can be erratic.
Helicopter: Services operate between Freetown and Lungi airport – flight time five minutes.
Ferry: Links Lungi Airport with central Freetown and Lumley Beach area.
Car hire
Car hire is available at relatively high rates. International driving licence required.

BUSINESS DIRECTORY
The addresses listed below are a selection only. While World of Information makes every endeavour to check these addresses, we cannot guarantee that changes have not been made, especially to telephone numbers and area codes. We would welcome any corrections.

Telephone area codes
The international direct dialling code (IDD) for Sierra Leone is +232, followed by area code and subscriber's number:
Freetown   22

Chambers of Commerce
Sierra Leone Chamber of Commerce, Guma Building, Lamina Sankoh Street, PO Box 502, Freetown (tel: 226-305; fax: 228-005; e-mail: cocsl@sierratel.sl).

Banking
Bank of Sierra Leone, PO Box 30, Siaka Stevens Street, Freetown (tel: 226-501; fax: 224-764).

First Merchant Bank of Sierra Leone Ltd, Sparta Building, 12 Wilberforce Street, Freetown (tel: 228-493; fax: 228-318).

National Development Bank Ltd, 21/23 Siaka Stevens Street, Freetown (tel: 226-791/2; fax: 224-468).

Rokel Commercial Bank (Sierra Leone) Ltd, PO Box 12, 25-27 Stevens Street, Freetown (tel: 222-501; fax: 222-563).

Sierra Leone Commerical Bank Ltd, 29-31 Siaka Stevens Street, Freetown (tel: 225-264; fax: 225-292).

Standard Chartered Bank Sierra Leone Ltd, PO Box 1155, 9 -11 Lightfoot Boston Street, Freetown (tel: 226-220, 225-021; fax: 225-760).

Union Trust Bank Ltd, 2 Howe Street, Freetown (tel: 222-792, 226-954; fax: 226-214).

Central bank
Bank of Sierra Leone, Siaka Stevens Street, Freetown (tel: 226-501; fax: 224-764; e-mail: info@bankofsierraleone.org).

Travel information
Sierra National Airlines, Leone House, PO Box 285, 25 Pultney Street, Freetown (tel: 2075, 6297; fax: 2026).

Ministry of tourism
Ministry of Tourism and Culture, Stadium Hostel, Syke Street, Freetown (tel: 241-256).

National tourist organisation offices
National Tourist Board of Sierra Leone, International Conference Centre, Aberdeen Hill PO Box 1435, Freetown (tel: 272-520, 272-396; fax: 272-197; e-mail: ntbinfo@sierratel.sl).

Ministries
Department of Finance, Secretariat Building, George Street, Freetown (tel: 26-911, 22-211; fax: 28-355).

Ministry of Information and Broadcasting, Youyi Building, Brookfields, Freetown.

Ministry of Tourism and Culture, Wallace Johnson Street, Freetown (tel: 26-345, 24-776).

Ministry of Trade and Industry, Ministerial Building, George Street, Freetown (tel: 26-045, 22-755, 22-706; fax: 28-373).

Other useful addresses
Central Statistics Office, Tower Hill, Freetown (tel: 23-897, 24-267).

National Trading Co, Howe Street, Freetown (tel: 23-986, 26-179).

Sierra Leone Embassy (USA), 1701 19th Street, NW, Washington DC 20009 (tel: 202-939-9261; fax: 202-483-1793; e-mail: saloneweb@starpower.net; internet: www.sierra-leone.org).

Sierra Leone External Telecommunications (SLET) Office, Wallace Johnson Street, Freetown (tel: 22-801, 24-591).

Sierra Leone High Commission (UK), 245 Oxford Street, London W1D 2LX (tel: 020-7287-9884; fax: 020-7734-3822; e-mail: info@slhc-uk.org.uk; internet: www.slhc-uk.org.uk).

Sierra Leone Ports Authority, PO Box 386, Freetown.

Internet sites

Africa Business Network: http://www.ifc.org/abn

African Development Bank: http://www.afdb.org

AllAfrica.com: http://allafrica.com

Africa Online: http://www.africaonline.com

Mbendi AfroPaedia (information on companies, countries, industries and stock exchanges in Africa): http://mbendi.co.za

Sierra Leone: http://www.sierra-leone.org

Sierre Leone government: http://www.sierraleone.gov.sl

Singapore

KEY FACTS

Official name: Repablik Singapura, Xinjiapo Gongheguo, Singapur Kutiyarasu, Republic of Singapore

Head of State: President Sellapan Ramanathan (S R Nathan) (since Sep 1999, re-elected 17 Aug 2005)

Head of government: Prime Minister Lee Hsien Loong (sworn in 12 Aug 2004)

Ruling party: People's Action Party (PAP) (since 1965; re-elected Nov 2001)

Area: 636 square km

Population: 4.22 million (2004)

Official language: English, Mandarin Chinese, Malay, Tamil.

Currency: Singapore dollar (S$) = 100 cents

Exchange rate: S$1.69 per US$ (Oct 2005); the S$ is pegged to US dollar by the Monetary Authority of Singapore (MAS)

GDP per capita: US$24,740 (2004)

GDP real growth: 8.40% (2004)

Labour force: 2.15 million (2004)

Unemployment: 3.40% (2004)

Inflation: 1.70% (2004)

Balance of trade: US$18.80 billion 2004

Foreign debt: US$8.20 billion (2003)

Visitor numbers: 6.13 million (2003)

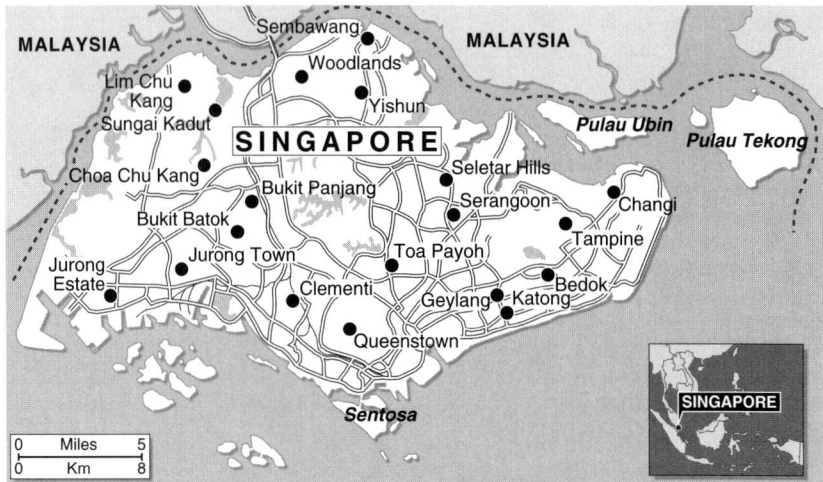

The Asian city-state of Singapore has greater GDP wealth per capita than the European average, a developed concrete island nation tucked away between Malaysia and Indonesia. It has one of the highest densities worldwide of shopping malls and restaurants, which reflects the favoured pastimes of the mainly Chinese, but also Malay, Muslim and ethnic Indian population. The trafficking of chewing gum into this country incurs a 12 month jail sentence and a hefty cash fine.

Leadership

Most countries have their founding fathers. Many countries in Asia also have ruling dynasties. Singapore's founding father is the country's first prime minister and leader of the independence movement, Lee Kwan Yew, who became senior minister and 'power behind the throne' in 1990, a position he held until July 2004, when he assumed the title of 'Minister Mentor'. His decision to step down from day-to-day management had been a masterstroke, since it averted the succession problem that has bedevilled strong post-independence leaders all over Asia.

Lee passed the baton to his relatively colourless deputy Goh Chok Tong. Goh performed well as the head of a meritocratic government and his interregnum had extended to 13 years when he announced on 17 August 2003, at a National Day celebration, that he was stepping down before 2005 and allowing Lee's son, BG (short for Brigadier General) Lee Hsien Loong, to fill the position of prime minister. BG Lee is Harvard and Cambridge educated and is following a noticeably more authoritarian agenda than his predecessor.

Civil liberties

Singapore Prime Minister Lee Hsien Loong said in October 2005 that he did not believe an 'idealised form' of democracy was the right framework for Singapore. Neither, he said, were gay pride marches appropriate in a country where homosexuality is still viewed by some as sinful and taboo.

On his departure from the post in October 2005, US ambassador, Frank Lavin condemned Singapore's record on free speech, forecasting that the government 'will pay an increasing price for not allowing full participation of its citizens'. Lavin conceded to the strengths of an essentially one party state but also criticised the resultant lack of debate and discussion.

In May 2005, the execution of a convicted marijuana smuggler prompted an outcry against the country's severe drug laws. Drug smuggling in the city state automatically incurs the death penalty, which many feel is too harsh. In November 2005 an Australian citizen, Guyen

Tuong Van was also sentenced to death by hanging for drugs offences, to the anger and frustration of Australian Prime Minister John Howard.

In May 2005, a student at a Singapore science agency, was forced to apologise after making critical remarks online about the institution's scholarship system. Observers felt the case had worrying implications for the future of internet and press freedom in the country. Not long afterwards, two men in their twenties were imprisoned in October 2005 under the 1948 Sedition Act after publishing material on the web offensive to Singapore's Islamic community. While China uses search filters to control freedom of information on the internet, Singapore clamps down on offenders in the law courts. Singapore has strict defamation laws and is ranked bottom of a Reporters Without Borders league of developed countries in the area of media freedom.

In October 2005, the UK's Warwick University pulled out of plans to set up a campus in Singapore, citing likely restrictions on academic freedom and reservations about the limitations on freedom of speech and assembly. Singapore probably was not too worried: already established are the campuses of many US universities – the University of Chicago, the Johns Hopkins University, the University of California and the Cornell and Stanford universities to name a few. In 2005 the prestigious Indian Institute of Management-Bangalore (IIM-B) opened a campus in the country and will initially offer a part-time course taught online.

A study by the US NGO Human Rights Watch (HRW) in December 2005 condemned the fact that foreign maids and domestic workers, largely Filipino and Indonesian, are not legally protected from exploitation and abuse. They work excessively long hours for little money, are often physically and sexually assaulted, subject to poor living conditions and often lack food. HRW said that Singapore was breaking international legislation by excluding maids from its protective labour laws.

International organisations are unanimous in praise for Singapore's legal and political progress – and unanimous in condemnation of its civil liberties laws. The Singaporean authorities claim that such a tight control on expression is necessary to ensure order in a country with a potentially volatile mix and ethnicities and religions.

International relations

Like many Asian countries, Singapore has a love-hate relationship with the United States. South-East Asia is of prime importance to American national interests and Singapore has a strategic position, not only for its economic importance but also for its influence in Asean – which is seen by the US as an occasionally useful and effective political organisation in approaching political problems of global or regional importance. This has ensured US tolerance of some of Singapore's less democratic aspects. But Singapore, and other South-East Asian states, are often criticised by governmental and non-governmental organisations in the West for being authoritarian in character and for violating human rights. Despite its manifest economic success, Singapore has been unable to gain admission to the prestigious Organisation for Economic Co-operation and Development (OECD) which does not consider it to be a democracy.

Singapore nevertheless puts great emphasis on its close association with the US and has been vocal in its support for the war against terrorism. Singapore is today the biggest US customer in South-East Asia and more than 1,300 American companies operate in the city state.

Singapore, despite its strong internal security arrangements, feels uncomfortably close to Indonesia in the wake of Islamic unrest there and is a potential target of international terrorists.

The economy

Singapore has been one of Asia's fastest growing economies in recent years although not on a Chinese scale. In 2005 growth was projected at 3.9 per cent by the IMF although Prime Minister Lee announced in a New Year address that growth had reached 5.7 per cent. External demand continued to be the major driving force, with domestic consumption showing an improvement over previous years. Manufacturing is an important source of Singaporean wealth and is the hard disk drive capital of the world, responsible for one-third of the world's output. In 2005, Singapore surged ahead to be a global leader in the IT market, with a computer literate workforce and cutting-edge technological infrastructure.

Six of the top ten world pharmaceutical firms manufacture in Singapore although the first quarter of 2005 saw a substantial decline in output in this unpredictable sector.

Tourism also helped boost revenues in 2005 with an historic nine million tourist arrivals. In order to encourage even more foreign arrivals, the Lee government passed a bill to legalise gambling in April 2005, paving the way for the proposed construction of two large casinos.

In February 2005, Singapore announced plans to reduce income tax from 22 to 20 per cent as an incentive to foreign investment and small businesses. The move is a reaction to the threat of China and is designed to heighten the state's competitiveness.

In June 2005, the Singaporean port company PSA International bought a 20 per cent share in the Hong Kong International Terminal in a US$800 million arrangement. The two port operators are some of the world's biggest players and will be in a position to determine pricing of port fees in the region, although they will face

KEY INDICATORS — Singapore

	Unit	2000	2001	2002	2003	2004
Population	m	4.02	4.10	4.15	4.19	*4.22
Gross domestic product (GDP)	US$bn	102.68	85.60	87.00	91.34	*106.82
GDP per capita	US$	25,864	20,890	20,920	21,821	24,740
GDP real growth	%	10.3	-2.0	2.2	0.5	8.4
Inflation	%	1.4	1.0	-0.4	0.6	1.7
Unemployment	%	4.4	3.3	4.7	4.9	3.7
Exports (fob) (goods)	US$m	138,931.0	121,731.0	125,590.0	144,134.0	174,000.0
Imports (fob) (goods)	US$m	127,531.0	115,961.0	116,230.0	127,898.0	155,200.0
Balance of trade	US$m	11,400.0	5,770.0	8,700.0	16,236.0	18,800.0
Current account	US$m	21,797.0	23,288.0	23,300.0	28,550.2	27,880.0
Total reserves minus gold	US$m	80,132.0	75,375.0	82,021.0	95,746.0	112,232.0
Foreign exchange	US$m	79,685.0	74,851.0	81,367.0	81,367.0	111,498.0
Exchange rate	per US$	1.72	1.79	1.79	1.72	1.69

* estimated figure

pressure from cheaper ports seeking to undercut bigger names.

Singapore is one of the major petroleum refining centres of Asia, and the third biggest in the world, with total crude oil refining capacity of nearly 1.3 million barrels per day (bpd). ExxonMobil said in early 2005 that it would be expanding its petrochemical complex, developing a new ethylene cracker. The extension will be finished during 2006, and will increase output from 75,000 tonnes per year to more than 900,000. Royal Dutch/Shell will also invest in a new naphtha cracker in its Jurong Island plant.

Policy issues

After physical security, the Singapore government's overriding concern remains the maintenance of the economy's competitiveness. The old capital-intensive oil- and chemical-based heavy industries will not provide long-term economic security for Singapore when wages in neighbouring Indonesia and Malaysia are a fraction of those in Singapore. The government sees the economy's future being tied to developing value-added services and developing its impressive human resources further with the aim of making Singapore a globally competitive, knowledge-intensive city, especially in financial services, telecommunications and energy.

Productivity must be increased substantially in the services sector for Singapore to be globally competitive. This requires an accelerated attack on over-regulation as well as privatisation of public sector service suppliers. Further financial liberalisation is required to internationalise the economy's capital markets.

The government continues to encourage the development of a more competitive and sophisticated labour force as well as biotechnology and the information and communications technology industries.

The IMF recommended in April 2004 that Singapore should disclose the performance details of the Government of Singapore Investment Corp (GIC), the state-managed investment fund, in order to boost investor confidence in government finances. GIC is one of the region's biggest institutional investors and controls funds of US$100 billion. The finance ministry declined to take the IMF up on its suggestion.

Financial markets

Financial markets tend to run in cycles since they are driven by a combination of the fluctuations of the underlying economic realities and investors' perceptions of these realities, especially their emotional and psychological reactions. Some commentators refer to this as the fear and greed symptoms. The last time investors became enthusiastic about emerging markets was in 1993/94 when some of the great and good in Wall Street briefly discovered that there were stock markets outside North America. Asia received the full blast of those walls of money and markets were driven to peaks from which they first declined gently and then crashed after the Asian crisis of 1997/98. They have been recuperating since then.

The Singapore market is well regulated and corporate governance standards are the highest in the region, according to the regional stockbroker Credit Lyonnais Securities Asia (CLSA). Singapore is uniquely exposed to the global trading environment and like the rest of the region is tied to US economic developments. However, beyond its own attractions, Singapore is seen as especially attractive for US companies to invest in in order to give them an additional leg up into Asean and even EU markets.

Outlook

Economic growth for the first half of 2006 was set to be robust due to high world demand in the electronics sector. High global oil prices have benefited Singapore's petroleum refinery sector, and the profits could continue into the coming months. Domestic spending was set to rise and the property sector was expected to increase in value too, thanks to measures pushed through in 2005 to revive the sector.

There were predictions that, with the economy in good shape, the government might be tempted to call a premature general election.

Risk assessment

Economic	Good
Political	Fair
Regional Stability	Good
Stock Market	Good

COUNTRY PROFILE

Historical profile

The Republic of Singapore consists of Singapore Island, where Singapore City is located, and 57 smaller islands. One of these, Pedra Branca (Batu Putih), is claimed by Malaysia.

1819 Sir Stamford Raffles established a trading station in Singapore for the British East India Company. Singapore's free trade policy with no taxation attracted merchants from the entire region. The port captured much of the entrepôt trade of the East Indies. During the nineteenth century thousands of immigrant Chinese, Indians, Indonesians and Malays emigrated there.
1824 The Sultan of Johore allowed the British East India Company full control of the territory.
1826 Singapore, Malacca and Penang were incorporated into the Straits Settlements, part of the British East India Company.
1867 The Straits Settlements became a crown colony.
1942 During the Second World War, the island was captured and controlled by the Japanese.
1945 The British regained control of Singapore.
1946 The Straits Settlement dissolved. Penang and Malacca became part of Malaya while Singapore was made into a British Crown Colony.
1954 Lee Kuan Yew founded the People's Action Party (PAP). It attracted a strong following among the poor and the non-English speaking population.
1959 Singapore achieved internal self-government. The PAP won the election and Lee Kuan Yew became the first prime minister. Under Lee Kuan Yew, government opposition was suppressed. Lee's government attracted much international critisism for its authoritarian approach. Under Lee's leadership however, Singapore became a financial and industrial powerhouse.
1963 Singapore became a state of the Federation of Malaysia.
1965 The Republic of Singapore was legally declared an independent, sovereign state.
1967 Singapore was a founder member of the Association of Southeast Asian nations (Asean).
1971 The last British troops were withdrawn from Singapore.
1984 For the first time in Singapore's political history, two opposition MPs were elected to parliament.
1990 Goh Chok Tong took over from Lee Kuan Yew as prime minister.
1993 In the first direct presidential election, the PAP candidate, Ong Teng Cheong, secured the post.
1997 The PAP was re-elected.
1999 Sellapan Ramanathan (S R Nathan) was declared president.
2001 A political rally by parliamentarian J B Jeyaretnam of the Workers' Party of Singapore (WPS) was allowed by the government to take place – the first permitted outside an election period. The PAP was re-elected.
2003 The Sars virus affected Singapore early in the year, infecting 206 people and killing 31. By the end of May, the

World Health Organisation (WHO) declared that Singapore was free of Sars. A free trade agreement between Singapore and the US came into effect.
2004 After 14 years, Prime Minister Goh Chok Tong stood down and Lee Hsien Loong was sworn in as prime minister on 12 August.
2005 President S R Nathan was appointed to a second term on 17 August after rivals were disqualified.

Political structure
Constitution
The 1959 constitution was amended in 1965, 1988, 1991 and 1996. Consequently, there are now 15 Group Representation Constituencies (GRCs) which elect teams of up to six members of parliament. At least one member of each team has to be of minority (non-Chinese) ethnic origin. The number of single member constituencies has been reduced from 21 to eight.
In the 1991 amendment, the position of president was modified to become a directly elected post with a six-year term. The responsibilities of the office were extended to include the safeguarding of Singapore's financial reserves, and the right to veto senior civil service and judicial appointments. Only those who have served as cabinet ministers, chief justice, senior civil servants or have headed a large company are eligible as presidential candidates.
Elections must be held within three months of the dissolution of parliament.
There is full adult suffrage; voting is compulsory for all citizens aged 21 years and over.

Form of state
Republic

The executive
Executive power is vested in the cabinet, which is presided over by the prime minister and responsible to the unicameral parliament. The political hegemony of the People's Action Party (PAP) is absolute and parliamentary oversight of executive power is virtually non-existent. In 1995, a three-judge tribunal ruled that the president had no power to veto any bill that sought to restrict his existing powers.

National legislature
The unicameral parliament has 90 members. Seven are appointed by the president and 83 are elected for a five-year term in single and multi-seat constituencies.
Parliament can include in its membership up to nine nominated members of parliament (NMPs).

Legal system
Singaporean law is based on English common law.

The independence of the judiciary is safeguarded by the constitution. Judicial power is vested in Singapore's Supreme Court and in the Subordinate Courts. The Supreme Court consists of the High Court, the Court of Appeal and the Court of Criminal Appeal. The chief justice is appointed by the president, acting on the advice of the prime minister.
The Subordinate Courts consist of District Courts, Magistrates' Courts, Juvenile Courts, Coroners' Courts and Small Claims Tribunals. District judges, magistrates and coroners are appointed on the recommendation of the chief justice. Although the constitution stipulates that the judiciary should act independently of government, it rarely does so in practice. Judges and judicial officials are appointed and dismissed by the president and judicial redress against abuses of executive power is therefore limited.
Sharia is the religious court with jurisdiction over Muslim law and domestic proceedings between Muslim parties.

Last elections
3 November 2001 (parliamentary); 27 August 2005 (presidential) (cancelled as imcumbent President Ramnathan was the only candidate to meet the Presidential Select Committee requirements).
Results: Parliamentary: the ruling party, PAP, was re-elected with 75.3 per cent of the vote, obtaining 82 seats.
Presidential: the 27 August 2005 election was cancelled as Sellapan Ramanathan (S R Nathan) was the only candidate declared eligible.

Next elections
2006 (parliamentary).

Political parties
Ruling party
People's Action Party (PAP) (since 1965; re-elected Nov 2001)
Main opposition party
Singapore Democratic Party (SDP)

Population
4.22 million (2004)
Ethnic make-up
Singapore is a multi-racial society. There are approximately 950,000 non-nationals. Chinese make up the majority of the population (77 per cent), and Malays (14 per cent), Indians (8 per cent), and other ethnic groups (1 per cent) make up the remainder.
Religions
Buddhism (32 per cent), Taoism (22 per cent), Islam (Sunni) (15 per cent), Christianity (13 per cent) and Hinduism (3 per cent) are the main religions. Other religions include Zoroastrianism (0.6 per cent) and Judaism. The constitution provides for freedom of worship.

Education
Primary school lasts for six years between the ages six and 12. Lower secondary education last for four years and students must attain good exam results to progress on to higher secondary school for a further three years, before advancing to higher education. There are three kinds of tertiary institutions: universities, polytechnics, and other centres of public and private training. The government almost wholly finances the National University of Singapore and the Nanyang Technological University. Many Singaporean students go abroad for their university education, increasingly to the US. However, institutions, such as the University of Chicago and Insead, are opening campuses in Singapore to meet local demand.
Public expenditure on education typically amounts to 3 per cent of annual gross national income. In 2001 S$6,577 million was spent on education (Asian Development Bank 2004).
Literacy rate: 93.2 per cent, adult rate (2003)
Compulsory years: 6 to 12
Enrolment rate: 94 per cent gross primary enrolment of relevant age group (including repeaters); 74 per cent gross secondary enrolment (World Bank).
Pupils per teacher: 25 in primary schools

Health
Singapore has managed to create a developed country healthcare system at relatively little cost. The health care system has a mixture of private and public provision and shows radically improved healthcare indices.
The private sector provides over 60 per cent of primary healthcare through doctors in private practice. Hospital healthcare is mostly public sector, with only 20 per cent of beds in the private sector. The government provides public subsidies through a ward system in public hospitals. Basic healthcare is financed through Central Provident Fund (CPF) Medisave accounts. Between 6 and 8 per cent of a worker's monthly contribution to the CPF, depending on age, is set aside for Medisave, a mandatory national health programme which encourages individuals to pay for their own healthcare. An additional endowment fund, Medifund, is targetted at poor and indigent Singaporeans.
Government officials have warned that if Singapore's predominantly Chinese population age too quickly, this could lead to expensive healthcare problems. Official statistics show that the number of Singaporeans aged 64 and above will rise fourfold to make up 20 per cent of the

total population by the year 2030, when the population is projected to decline after it has reached a 7.9 million peak.

HIV prevalence: 0.2 per cent aged 15–49 in 2003 (World Bank)

Life expectancy: 80.4 years: male 77.5 years; female 83.6 years (2003)

Fertility rate/Maternal mortality rate: 1.4 births per woman (World Bank)

Birth rate/Death rate: 12.8 births per 1,000 population; 4.3 deaths per 1,000 population (2003).

Infant mortality rate: 3.6 per 1,000 live births (2003)

Head of population per physician/bed: 1.6 physicians and 3.6 hospital beds per 1,000 people

Welfare

The government discourages dependence on the state for social security; rather, all workers and employers contribute to the compulsory savings scheme, the CPF. The CPF has developed into a wide-ranging social security scheme covering retirement, home ownership and health needs. Members can withdraw their savings upon reaching 55 but must set aside a minimum amount to ensure they have enough money for their retirement. The minimum amount to be saved every year was capped at S$80,000 (US$43,618) in 2003. Employment assistance is provided free of charge by the Ministry of Manpower.

Some 85 per cent of the population is housed in accommodation built and developed by the Housing and Development Board (HDB), set up in 1960 as a statutory board of the Ministry of National Development to provide low-cost public housing.

Main cities

Singapore is a city-state (estimated population 4.2 million in 2004).

Languages spoken

English is the main administrative language and is almost universally understood. In parliamentary debates, members may speak in English, Malay, Mandarin Chinese or Tamil, and simultaneous translations are provided. Other dialects of Chinese, mostly Hokkien (Fukienese) and Cantonese, are also spoken.

Most Singaporeans are bi- or tri-lingual.

Official language/s

English, Mandarin Chinese, Malay, Tamil.

Media

Press

Newspapers and magazines are published only under government licence. Singapore Press Holdings (SPH) is one of the largest companies listed on the Singapore Exchange, controlling six daily newspapers, a regional magazine and a book distribution network.

Dailies: The two main Chinese-language dailies are *Lian He Zao Bao* (United Morning News) and *Lian He Wan Bao* (United Evening News). The major English-language dailes are *The Straits Times* and *Business Times*. *Berita Harian* (in Malay) and *Tamil Murasu* (in Tamil) have smaller circulations. International editions of foreign newspapers are also available.

Business: There are numerous trade publications, including *Singapore Business*, *Building Materials and Equipment SE Asia*, *The Manufacturer*, *Cargo News Asia* and *Petroleum News*.

The leading business magazine is *Singapore Business*. *The Straits Times* and *Business Times* have domestic and international business news. *The Economic Bulletin* is published by the Singapore International Chamber of Commerce. *The Asia Times* is a regional daily business newspaper.

Broadcasting

Radio: The Singapore Broadcasting Corporation (SBC) broadcasts radio programmes in English, Mandarin, Malay and Tamil. SBC operates nine radio stations. Foreign broadcasters operate around 10 stations.

Rediffusion (Singapore) Ltd operates a wired broadcasting service, with advertising facilities in each of the four languages.

Television: The SBC broadcasts television programmes daily in English, Mandarin, Malay and Tamil. Many hotel TVs are linked to SBC Tem, a teletext system, which operates 0600–2400.

Singapore CableVision (SCV), a government-linked company, transmits multi-channel cable television. All channels are monitored to prevent programmes being broadcast that the government might deem to be undesirable.

Advertising

Advertising is available in the press, on commercial radio, television, cinemas and via direct mail and house-to-house distribution of samples. Outdoor advertising, especially posters used for short-term advertising campaigns are widely used. Expenditure on advertising as a percentage of GDP is typically 1 per cent or just over. There are also numerous trade magazines and trade fairs for business-to-business marketing.

Economy

The Singaporean economy has perhaps been the best managed in the Asia-Pacific region. Despite unorthodox economic policies, such as artificially increasing wages in order to move the economy towards greater capital intensity, sustained economic growth and low inflation have transformed Singapore into one of the richest countries in the world, with a GDP per capita which is the envy of many industrialised nations. Lacking in any natural resources, it has capitalised upon its human capital and fortunate location on the Straits of Malacca, closure of which would affect half of the world's shipping. Strong economic growth for the past few decades has been achieved by a combination of economic liberalism, government investment in selected sectors and an efficient bureaucracy.

Singapore's traditional strengths are first in trade and subsequently in its substantial value-added high-technology electronics manufacturing sector. Life sciences and petrochemicals are also significant. However, its economic planners are realising that Singapore's future lies in its historically more sluggish service sectors, if it is to maintain its competitive edge. Manufacturing now makes up only a quarter of GDP, and the small size of the economy is putting upward pressure on land and labour costs. Singapore has accordingly become keen to promote itself not just as Asia's premier banking centre, but as a world-class provider of financial services. The goal is clearly to limit dependence on less mature regional economies and vulnerability to their financial and political difficulties.

The outbreak of Severe Acute Respiratory Syndrome (Sars) in March 2003 adversely affected the economy with the service sector declining rapidly, with an estimated 20 per cent decline in the tourist industry. This, combined with the global economic slowdown, meant that Singapore suffered from its worst quarterly contraction on record in the second quarter of 2003. Despite this, a swift recovery from Sars, resulting in a tourist sector revival along with noticeable global recovery, allowed Singapore to rebound dramatically in 2004 with GDP growth of 8.4 per cent. Wage reforms, in 2003, were instituted to increase Singapore's competitiveness against emerging economies, such as China. These reforms are designed to produce wages linked to performance as opposed to seniority, thus increasing efficiency.

External trade

Few imported goods are subject to quota restrictions or licences and in most instances are duty-free. Out of 2,200 items in the trading classification, only 8 per cent are subject to import duties. Singapore's entrepôt function has shifted from exporting goods from the South-East Asian region to becoming a gateway for goods into the region. While all exports are technically subject to control, there are restrictions only on a few categories.

Singapore

Imports
Principal imports are machinery and equipment, mineral fuels, chemicals and foodstuffs.
Main sources: Malaysia (15.3 per cent total, 2004), US (12.7 per cent), Japan (11.7 per cent), China (9.9 per cent), Taiwan (5.7 per cent), South Korea (4.3 per cent), Thailand (4.1 per cent)

Exports
Principal exports are machinery and equipment (including electronics), consumer goods, chemicals and fuels.
Main destinations: Malaysia (15.2 per cent total, 2004), US (13 per cent), Hong Kong (9.8 per cent), China (8.6 per cent), Japan (6.4 per cent), Taiwan (4.6 per cent), Thailand (4.3 per cent), South Korea (4.1 per cent)

Agriculture

Farming
Only 3 per cent of Singapore's land area is used for agriculture. Singapore has some 2,000 licensed farms producing poultry, eggs, vegetables, fruit, orchids (both for domestic demand and export) and ornamental plants. Less than 6 per cent of fresh vegetables is produced locally, with the rest imported from Malaysia, Indonesia, China and Australia. Although agriculture plays only a minor role in Singapore's economy, the Primary Production Department promotes intensive farming methods. Agrotechnology parks have been developed on 554 hectares of land in Murai, Sungai Tengah, Nee Soon and Loyang.

Crop production in 2004 included: 130 tonnes (t) coconuts, 17t oilcrops, 10t roots and tubers, 10t fruit in total, 5,001t vegetables in total. Livestock production included: 115,510t meat in total, 35t beef, 19,500t pig meat, 27t lamb, 8t goat meat, 95,948t poultry, 17,200t eggs.

Fishing
With limited agricultural and water resources, there is little scope for the development of Singapore's fisheries, although fish is an important component of the Singaporean diet. Singapore relies mainly on imports for domestic consumption. The government's priority is to increase imports through trade relations. The quality of Singapore's own catch is often decsribed as poor. Rapid urbanisation and development have damaged natural habitats and caused the quality of inshore fish to deteriorate.

Forestry
Forests constitute only 7 per cent of the total land area of Singapore. There are three major forest reserves – Bukit Timah, Palau Ubin and Sungei Buloh. Singapore produces plywood and veneer and imports pulp and paper.

Industry and manufacturing

The industrial sector accounts for around 35 per cent of GDP. Manufacturing employs around 19 per cent of the workforce and construction employs a further seven per cent. Electronics is the largest industry and typically contributes about 14 per cent to GDP, accounting for 70 per cent of non-oil exports. The second largest industry group encompasses life sciences, chemicals and petroleum refining. Other major industries include transport equipment, especially shipbuilding, and related repair and conversion activities.

Tourism

Tourism contributes around three per cent of GDP. Government policy is to build on the sector's success and increase its role in the economy as a means of diversification. To this end, two huge casino resorts are being planned.

8.94 million arrivals were recorded in 2005, a seven per cent increase on 2004. Singapore's major markets are Indonesia, China, Malaysia, Japan, Australia, UK, India, US, South Korea and Thailand.

Environment

The Singapore Green Plan (SGP), released in 1992, called for 5 per cent of the country's land to be classified as protected areas. Around S$3 billion (US$1.7 billion) was allocated towards the upgrade of sewage treatment, a refuse incineration plant and improvements to water sources in 2002.

Hydrocarbons

Singapore does not have any oil or natural gas reserves and is entirely reliant on imports. Singapore is one of Asia's principal oil refining centres, with 11 refineries and total oil refining capacity of around 1.3 million barrels per day (bpd). The refining industry was hit hard by the Asian Economic Crisis of 1997/98. The establishment of refineries in Singapore's major export markets has also had a negative effect. New refineries in India significantly reduced Indian demand for oil from Singapore, while a new plant in Melaka, Malaysia, has increased competition. With Singapore's large refining industry there has been rapid growth of the petrochemical industry.

Demand for natural gas in Singapore is rising, due to the government's policy on cutting carbon emissions in power generation and the growing petrochemical industry. Singapore depends on Malaysia and Indonesia for a steady supply of natural gas for power generation. This includes the 155 million cubic feet provided by Malaysia through a transnational pipeline, the first of its kind in Asia. Singapore's policy is to avoid over-dependence on one country for its gas supply. A gas pipeline connecting Singapore to Indonesia was inaugurated in 2003.

Singapore does not produce or import coal.

Energy

Singapore has an electricity-generating capacity of around 9.0GW. The electricity is supplied by four thermal power stations, fuelled mainly by natural gas.

Banking and insurance

Full liberalisation is expected by 2007, including the freeing up of retail banking. The government is also looking at plans to privatise the central provident fund (CPF), a compulsory savings mechanism which forces employers and employees to contribute. Access to CPF funds would allow banks to hold more of the country's savings.

Central bank
Monetary Authority of Singapore

Main financial centre
Singapore

Time

GMT plus eight hours

Geography

Singapore consists of the main island of Singapore and 58 smaller islands, more than 20 of them inhabited. Lying 137km north of the equator, it is linked to peninsular Malaysia to the north by a causeway carrying a road, railway and water pipeline across the narrow Straits of Johor, and separated from Indonesia to the south by the Straits of Singapore. In 2001, the Malaysian government was actively trying to promote increased use of a second link between the two countries, an expressway between Johor Baru and Singapore, as an alternative to the traditional causeway.

The island of Singapore itself is 42km long and 23km wide, with a coastline measuring 138km. It can be divided into three broad regions: a central hilly region, an area of hills and valleys in the west, and a relatively flat eastern region.

Climate

The climate is equatorial, with uniformly high temperatures, high humidity and mean annual rainfall of 2,463mm with no defined wet or dry season. Mean daily temperatures range from a minimum 24 degrees Celsius (C) to a maximum 31 degrees C. The hottest month is May. The driest month is July, with an average rainfall of 70mm. November to January are generally the cooler and wetter months. Sometimes it rains for several days continuously and there may be serious flooding. Between monsoons, from April to November, there are regular pre-dawn thunderstorms, known as Sumatras. Singapore has an average of 180 lightning days a year.

Dress codes
Dress is generally informal, with light summer clothing the norm. A shirt and tie, or a safari suit, is the usual office dress for men, although jackets may be required in some restaurants for dinner; women should also dress smartly for business. Singapore's predominantly Chinese population follows Western fashion, although a small section among the minority Indian and Malay communities wear traditional dress.

Entry requirements
Passports
Passports are required by all, with a few exceptions. Passports must be valid for six months from day of departure.
Visa
Are not required by most nationals. See http://app.ica.gov.sg/travellers/entry/visa_requirements.asp for a list of travellers who must make an application. An Immigration Officer will determine the length of visit and grant a social visit pass on the basis of sufficient funds for maintenance during the expected stay and confirmed return/onwards passage, (including relevant visas for further destinations). Women who are pregnant by six months or more, should make prior application for entry through the nearest Singapore overseas mission.
Retain the Disembarkation/Embarkation card for submission to the immigration officer when departing.
Prohibited entry
Entry may be refused to male visitors whose hair reaches below the collar or extends over the ears or eyebrows. Despite its informal atmosphere, Singapore has tough laws against drug trafficking. People convicted of trafficking more than 15 grammes of heroin can face the death penalty.
Currency advice/regulations
There are no restrictions on the import or export of currency. Credit cards and travellers cheques are widely accepted.
Customs
Personal effects are duty-free.
Prohibited imports
Include: chewing gum, chewing tobacco and imitation tobacco products, cigarette lighters of pistol or revolver shape, controlled drugs and psychotropic substances, endangered species and by-products, firecrackers, obscene articles, publications, video tapes and software, reproduction of copyright publications, video tapes or disks, records or cassettes, or seditious and treasonable materials.

Health (for visitors)
Mandatory precautions
Yellow fever vaccination certificates for anyone who, within the preceding six days, has been to an infected area.
Advisable precautions
Vaccinations for diphtheria, tuberculosis, hepatitis 'A' and 'B', polio, tetanus and typhoid are advisable. Tap water is safe. All necessary medicines (especially sleeping pills, depressants, stimulants, etc.) must have a physician's certification declaring their prescribed use.
The Singapore Medical Centre, on the sixth floor of Tanglin shopping centre, houses a large community of specialist doctors.

Hotels
Most international-class hotels have shopping arcades, bars and swimming pools. Tipping is discouraged. A 3 per cent tax and a 10 per cent service charge are generally added to the hotel bill.

Credit cards
All major credit cards are widely accepted.

Public holidays
Fixed dates
1 Jan (New Year's Day), 1 May (Labour Day), 9 Aug (National Day), 25 Dec (Christmas Day).
Variable dates
Chinese New Year (Jan/Feb), Good Friday, Vesak Day, Diwali (Hindu, Oct/Nov), Eid al Adha, Eid al Fitr.
Owing to its multi-ethnic composition, Singapore celebrates a wide range of religious festivals and holidays in addition to those listed. Many festivals are based on a lunar calendar, while the dates of some are only finalised at the last minute. Check with the Singapore Tourist Promotion Board for exact dates and locations affected.

Working hours
During the Lunar New Year, many Chinese firms close for the whole week.
Banking
Mon–Fri: 1930–1500; Sat: 0930–1200; 0900–1500 (selected banks only).
Business
Mon–Fri: 0900–1300, 1400–1700.
Government
Mon–Fri: 0800–1300, 1400–1700.
Shops
Mon–Sat: 1930–2100. Some shops, particularly in tourist areas, open on Sundays.

Electricity supply
220–240V, 50 Hz, with three-pin (square) plug fittings.

Weights and measures
Metric system, with local variations.

Social customs/useful tips
Singaporeans are highly 'face' conscious and try to avoid self-embarrassment at all time.
Observe local etiquette – suit jackets remain off only as a concession to the climate, otherwise Western-style business formalities are in place.
Visiting cards are essential (although government officials do not use them). The cards should be presented with both hands. As a courtesy, it is a good idea to have cards printed in both Chinese and English. Cards should never be written on, put away before the meeting is over, or left behind.
When addressing Chinese persons, family or surname is mentioned first. When addressing Malay persons, the first of their two family names is used. Singaporean Indians use many different conventions. Men and women should not touch each other. The heads of children should not be patted.
Tipping is not customary; it is not illegal, but is officially discouraged. In hotels and restaurants a 10 per cent service charge is included in the bill.
On-the-spot fines can be imposed for some offences. Smoking is not permitted in public buildings and restaurants, and is restricted in other public places.
Singapore celebrates the religious and cultural festivals of its four major communities, and therefore the year is punctuated by a series of colourful festivals. Celebration of the Chinese New Year, the main event in the Chinese calendar, centres on traditional reunion dinners and visits to friends and relations. Business people should avoid visiting at Christmas, Easter, Chinese New Year, Islamic and Hindu religious holiday periods.

Security
Tourists can walk the streets without fear of being robbed or attacked.

Getting there
Air
National airline: Singapore Airlines (SIA).
International airport/s: Changi International Airport (SIN), 20km north-east of Singapore City, two terminals with Skytrain transportation between terminals, free-of-charge, transit hotel complexes in both terminals with business facilities, disabled facilities, medical centre, banks/bureaux de change, bars, pharmacy, duty-free shops, car rental, child facilities, post office, restaurants, shops, tourist information.
Work on Terminal 3 began in 2002. On completion in early 2006, the third terminal will add a capacity of 20 million passengers a year, bringing the airport's total annual capacity to 64 million passengers.

Singapore

Airport tax: The departure tax of S$15 is usually included in the price of the air ticket.

Surface
Road: Road transport arrives via two causeways from Malaysia, with express bus services from Kuala Lumpur and Johore Bahru.

Rail: There are rail services to Kuala Lumpur and Bangkok.

Water: There are excellent sea links with other countries.

Getting about
National transport
Road: The road network comprises some 2,900km of roads, including about 100km of expressways. Vehicular access to the Central Business District (CBD) is restricted and there are charges for vehicles entering the area at certain times. A causeway links the Singapore road system with that of Malaysia across the Straits of Johor. There is a second link expressway between Johor and Singapore.

Buses: Timetables for the extensive and inexpensive bus network are widely available at news-stands. Fares to various destinations are displayed on a signboard on the front of the bus stop.

Rail: The Mass Rapid Transit System (MRTS) includes a light overland railway network which reaches all districts of Singapore Island.

Water: Regular ferry services from the World Trade Centre operate to some of the islands; others may be reached by charter boats.

City transport
A Tourist Day Ticket can be purchased for use on the MRTS and buses. It can be obtained up to seven days in advance, at MRTS stations.

The Transit Link Farecard can be purchased at MRTS stations and bus interchanges. Visitors can get the remaining card value refunded before they leave Singapore, at any sales counters.

Bicycles with sidecars (trishaws) are less common than they were, but can be hired for tours. There is no standard fare structure.

Taxis: Metered taxis are widely available from taxi pick-up points (they cannot be flagged down in the street). Before undertaking a journey, make sure the driver knows the destination; check that the meter is running. Taxi companies are allowed to set their own fares. The basic meter fare is displayed on the window of the rear door and details of other surcharges are displayed on the fare card in all taxis. There is a 50 per cent surcharge of the metered fare from 2400–0600, a surcharge for taxis travelling from (but not to) Changi Airport and a surcharge for each adult in excess of two passengers. Taxis can also be hired by the hour. The six-seater Maxicab shuttle service plies between the Singapore Changi Airport and most hotels.

Buses, trams & metro: The easy-to-use bus service is extensive.

The 67km Mass Rapid Transit System (MRTS) consists of two lines running north/south and east/west, with 42 stations (15 of them underground, 26 elevated, one ground level) which is fast, clean and efficient.

Car hire
An international driving licence is required for car hire. Driving is on the left. Coupons for use of the public car parks managed by the Urban Redevelopment Authority (URA) or Housing & Development Board (HBD) can be purchased at post offices, URA parking kiosks and some gas/petrol stations. Car hire companies are listed in the Yellow Pages of the telephone directory.

BUSINESS DIRECTORY
The addresses listed below are a selection only. While World of Information makes every endeavour to check these addresses, we cannot guarantee that changes have not been made, especially to telephone numbers and area codes. We would welcome any corrections.

Telephone area codes
The international direct dialling (IDD) code for Singapore is +65, followed by subscriber's number.

Useful telephone numbers
Police: 999
Fire/ambulance: 995
Directory enquiries: 103
International calls: 104
International enquiries: 162
Trunk calls to Malaysia: 109
Time of Day: 1711
Flight information: 6542-1234
Bus information: 6287-2727
AA road service (24 hrs): 6748-9911
Post Office information: 6533-0234, 6532-4536
Immigration Department: 6532-2877
Telecoms Customer Services Centres: 6734-3344, 6534-3111

Chambers of Commerce
American Chamber of Commerce in Singapore, Shaw Centre, 1 Scotts Road, Singapore 228208 (tel: 6235-0077; fax: 6732-5917; e-mail: info@amcham.org.sg).

British Chamber of Commerce Singapore, Cecil Court, 138 Cecil Street, Singapore 069538 (tel: 6222-3552; fax: 6222-3556; e-mail: info@britcham.org.sg).

Singapore Chinese Chamber of Commerce & Industry, SCCCI Building, 47 Hill Street, Singapore 179365 (tel: 6337-8381; fax: 6339-0605; e-mail: corporate@sccci.org.sg).

Singapore Indian Chamber of Commerce and Industry, Tong Eng Building, 101 Cecil Street, Singapore 069533 (tel: 6222-2855; fax: 6223-1707; e-mail: sicci@sicci.com).

Singapore International Chamber of Commerce, John Hancock Tower, 6 Raffles Quay, Singapore 048580 (tel: 6224-1255; fax: 6224-2785; e-mail: general@sicc.com.sg).

Singapore Malay Chamber of Commerce, 72A Bussorah Street, Singapore 199485 (tel: 6297-9296; fax: 6392-4527; e-mail: smcci@singnet.com.sg).

Banking
ABN Amro Bank NV, 63 Chulia Street (tel: 6231-8888; fax: 6532-3108).

ABSA Bank Ltd, 7 Temasek Boulevard, Suntec Tower One (tel: 6333-1033; fax: 6333-1066).

Agricultural Bank of China, 80 Raffles Place, UOB Plaza 2 (tel: 6535-5255; fax: 6538-7960).

American Express Bank Ltd, 16 Collyer Quay, Hitachi Tower (tel: 6538-4833; fax: 6534-3022).

Arab Bank plc, 80 Raffles Place, UOB Plaza 2 (tel: 6533-0055; fax: 6532-2150).

Arab Banking Corporation (BSC), 35-01 Republic Plaza Singapore, 9 Raffles Place, 048619 (tel: 6535-9339; fax: 6532-6288).

Asahi Bank Ltd, 1 Temasek Avenue, Millenia Tower (tel: 6333-0378; fax: 6333-0797).

Bangkok Bank plc, 180 Cecil Street (tel: 6221-9400; fax: 6225-5852).

Bank of America, National Association, 9 Raffles Place, Republic Plaza Tower 1 (tel: 6239-3888; fax: 6239-3068).

Bank of China, 4 Battery Road, Bank of China Building (tel: 6535-2411; fax: 6534-3401).

Bank of East Asia Ltd, 137 Market Street, Bank of East Asia Building (tel: 6224-1334; fax: 6225-1805).

Bank of India, 138 Robinson Road, Hong Leong Centre (tel: 6222-0011; fax: 6225-4407/225-2976).

Bank of Montreal, 150 Beach Road, Gateway West (tel: 6296-3233; fax: 6296-5044).

Bank of New York, 1 Temasek Avenue, Millenia Tower (tel: 6432-0222; fax: 6337-4302).

Bank of Nova Scotia, 10 Collyer Quay, Ocean Building (tel: 6535-8688; fax: 6532-2440).

Bank of Singapore, Tong Eng Building, 101 Cecil Street 01-02, 0106 (tel: 6223-9266).

Bank of Tokyo-Mitsubishi Ltd, 9 Raffles Place, Republic Plaza (tel: 6538-3388; fax: 6538-8083).

Chase Manhattan Bank, Shell Tower, 50 Raffles Place, 048623 (tel: 6530-4135, 6224-2888; fax: 6530-4331).

Far Eastern Bank, 156 Cecil Street, Far Eastern Bank Building, PO Box 2950, 0106 (tel: 6221-9055).

Hongkong & Shanghai Banking Corp Ltd, 21 Collyer Quay, 19-00 Hongkong Bank Building (tel: 6530-5412; fax: 6225-0663).

Indian Overseas Bank, 64 Cecil Street, IOB Building (tel: 6225-1100; fax: 6224-4490).

Industrial and Commercial Bank, ICB Building, 2 Shenton Way, 0106 (tel: 6221-1711).

Overseas Chinese Banking Corporation, OCBC Centre, 65 Chulia Street, 0104 (tel: 6535-7222; fax: 6533-7891).

Overseas Union Bank, OUB Centre, 1 Raffles Place, 0104 (tel: 6533-8686; fax: 6533-2293).

Standard Chartered Bank, 6 Battery Road (tel: 6225-8888; fax: 6225-9136).

United Overseas Bank, UOB Plaza, 80 Raffles Place, 048624 (tel: 6533-9898; fax: 6534-2334).

Central bank
Monetary Authority of Singapore, MAS Building, 10 Shenton Way, Singapore 079117 (tel: 6225-5577; fax: 6229-9491; e-mail: webmaster@mas.gov.sg).

Travel information
Automobile Association (AA) of Singapore, 336 River Valley Road (tel: 6737-2444).

Singapore Airlines (SIA), Airline House, 25 Airline Road, Singapore 1781 (tel: 6542-3333; fax: 6545-5034; internet site: http://www.singaporeair.com).

Tourist Promotion Board, Tourism Court, 1 Orchard Spring Lane, Singapore 247729 (tel: 6736-9423; fax: 6736-6622).

Ministries
Ministry of Communications, 39th Storey PSA Building, 460 Alexandra Road, Singapore 119963 (tel: 6270-7988; fax: 6279-9734).

Ministry of Defence, Gombak Drive (off Upper Bukit Timah Road), Mindef Building, Singapore 2366 (tel: 6760-8188; fax: 6762-0112).

Ministry of Development, c/o Meeting Planners Pte Ltd, 2nd Floor, Pico Centre, 20 Kallang Avenue, Singapore 1233 (tel: 6297-2822; fax: 6296-2670, 6292-7577).

Ministry of Environment, Sewerage Department, 14-00 Environmental Building, 40 Scotts Road, Singapore 228231 (tel: 6732-7733; fax: 6731-9699 (sewerage dept), 6731-9456 (general).

Ministry of Finance, 8 Shenton Way, 43rd, 45th, 46th and 50th Storey, Treasury Building, Singapore 0106 (tel: 6225-9911; fax: 6320-9435 (budget), 6320-9932 (PSD), 6224-6847 (revenue)).

Ministry of Foreign Affairs, 250 North Bridge Road, 07-00 Raffles City Tower, Singapore 0617 (tel: 6336-1177, 6330-5795 (after hours); fax: 6339-4330).

Ministry of Information, Communications and the Arts, Public Relations Department, 460 Alexandra Road 36-00, PSA Building, Singapore 0511 (tel: 6270-7988; fax: 6279-9765); Media Division, MITA Building, 140 Hill Street, 2nd Storey, Singapore 179369 (tel: 6837-9666).

Ministry of Manpower, 18 Havelock Road, Singapore 059764 (tel: 6438-5122; fax: 6534-4840; internet: www.mom.gov.sg).

Ministry of National Development, National Development Building, Maxwell Road, Singapore 0106 (tel: 6222-1211; fax: 6322-6254).

Ministry of Trade & Industry, 48-01 Treasury Building, 8 Shenton Way, Singapore 06811 (tel: 6225-9911; fax: 6323-9260).

Other useful addresses
American Business Council, 10-12 Shaw House, 354 Orchard Road, Singapore 0923 (tel: 6235-00770).

ASEAN Investment Promotion Agency, Economic Development Board, 250 North Bridge Road, 24-00 Raffles City Tower, Singapore 0617 (tel: 6336-2288; 6338-8265).

ASEAN Secretariat, 70 A J1 Sisingamangaraja, Jakarta 12110, Indonesia (tel: 62(21)726-2991, 724-3372; fax: 724-3504, 739-8234; e-mail: asean.or.id).

The Association of Banks in Singapore, 12-08 MAS Building, 10 Shenton Way, Singapore 0207 (tel: 6224-4300; fax: 6224-1785).

The Association of Small & Medium Enterprises, Blk 139 Kim Tain Road, Singapore 0316 (tel: 6271-2566; fax: 6271-1257).

British Business Association, 41 Duxton Road, Singapore 0208 (tel: 6227-7861; fax: 6227-7021).

British Businessmen's Association, 3rd Floor, Inchcape House, 450-452 Alexandra Road, Singapore 0511 (tel: 6475-4192).

British Council, 30 Napier Road, Singapore 1025 (tel: 6473-1111; fax: 6472-1010).

British High Commission, Tanglin Road, Singapore 912401 (tel: 6474-0461; fax; 6475-2320).

Civil Aviation Authority of Singapore, Singapore Airtropolis, Changi Airport (tel: 6542-1122; fax: 6545-6222).

Construction Industry Development Board, Annexe A, 3rd Storey, National Development Building, 9 Maxwell Road, Singapore 0106 (tel: 6225-6711; fax: 6225-7307).

Controller of Immigration, 95 South Bridge Road, Pidemco Centre, Singapore (tel: 6532-2877; fax: 6530-1840).

Customs & Excise Department, 03-01 & 10-01 World Trade Centre, 1 Maritime Square, Singapore 099253 (tel: 6272-8222; fax: 6375-2090).

Economic Development Board, 24-00 Raffles City Tower, 250 North Bridge Road, Singapore 0617 (tel: 6336-2288; fax: 6339-6077).

Export Credit Insurance Corporation of Singapore Ltd, 10 Shenton Way, 17-03 MAS Building, Singapore 0207 (tel: 6220-8344; fax: 6224-2887).

Housing and Development Board, 3451 Jalan Bukit Merah, HDB Centre, Singapore 0315 (tel: 6273-9090).

Immigration Department, 7th & 8th Storey, 08-26 Pidemco Centre, 95 South Bridge Road, Singapore 0105 (tel: 6532-2877; fax: 6530-1840).

Inland Revenue Authority of Singapore, Fullerton Building, B1-00 Fullerton Square, Singapore 049178 (tel: 6535-4244; fax: 6535-5393).

International Merchandise Mart PTE Ltd (IMM), Unit 04-01, 2 Jurong East Street 21, Singapore 609601 (tel: 6568-2000; fax: 6568-2500).

Jurong Town Corporation, Jurong Town Hall, 301 Jurong Town Hall Road, Singapore 609431 (tel: 6560-0056; fax: 6565-5301).

National Arts Council, Arts Division, MCD Building, 512 Thomson Road, Singapore 1129 (tel: 6258-9595; fax: 6350-6118).

National Productivity Board, 2 Bukit Merah, Central NPB Building, Singapore 0315 (tel: 6734-5534).

Port of Singapore Authority (PSA), PSA Building, 460 Alexandra Road, Singapore 119963 (tel: 6274-7111; fax: 6274-4677).

Public Utilities Board, PUB Building, 111 Somerset Way, Singapore 0207 (tel: 6235-8888; fax: 6731-3020).

Registry of Trade and Businesses, 05-01/15 International Plaza, 10 Anson Road, Singapore 0207 (tel: 6227-8551; fax: 6225-1676).

Singapore Confederation of Industries (formerly Singapore Manufacturers' Association), SMA House, 20 Orchard Road, Singapore 238830 (tel: 6338-8787; fax: 6339-3340).

Singapore Embassy (US), 3501 International Place, NW, Washington DC 20008 (tel: 202-537-3100; fax: 202-537-0876; e-mail: singemb.dc@verizon.net).

SIMEX, Singapore International Monetary Exchange, Square, 07-00 OUB Centre, Singapore 0104 (tel: 6535-7282; fax: 6535-7382).

Singapore Hotel Association, 11 Mount Sophia, Singapore 228461 (tel: 6339-9918; fax: 6339-3795).

Singapore Importers and Exporters Association, 2nd Floor, 76-C Robinson Road, Singapore 0106 (tel: 6222-3451).

Singapore Institute of Standards and Industrial Research (SISIR), 1 Science Park Drive, Singapore 0511 (tel: 6778-7777; fax: 6778-0086).

Stock Exchange of Singapore, 26-01/08 The Exchange, 20 Cecil Street, Singapore 049705 (tel: 6535-3788; fax: 6535-0775).

Telecommunication Authority of Singapore, TAS Building, 35 Robinson Road, Singapore 068876 (tel: 6738-7788; fax: 6733-0073).

Trade Development Board, 07-00 Bugis Junction Office Tower, 230 Victoria Street, Singapore 188024 (tel: 6271-9388; fax: 6274-0770).

US Embassy, 30 Hill Street, Singapore 0617 (tel: 6338-0251; fax: 6338-8472).

Work Permit and Employment Department, Ministry of Labour, 18 Havelock Road, Singapore 059764 (tel: 6534-1511; fax: 6539-5344/5).

Internet sites

Singapore Connect:
http://sgconnect.asia1.com.sg

Singapore Government:
http://www.gov.sg

Singapore Statistical Office:
http://www.singstat.gov.sg

Singapore Yellow Pages:
http://www.yellowpages.com.sg

Slovakia

KEY FACTS

Official name: Slovenská Republika (Slovak Republic)

Head of State: President Ivan Gasparovic (formerly HZD) (from 15 Jun 2004)

Head of government: Prime Minister Mikulas Dzurinda (leader of SDKU) (since Nov 1998)

Ruling party: Coalition government led by Slovenská Demokratická a Krestanská Únia (SDKÚ) (Slovak Democratic and Christian Union) and including Strana Madarskej Koalície-Magyar Koalíció Pártja (SMK) (Hungarian Coalition Party), Krest'ansko-Demokratické Hnutie (KDH) (Christian Democratic Movement) and Aliancia Nového Obcana (ANO) (New Citizen Alliance) (from 2002)

Area: 49,035 square km

Population: 5.42 million (2004)

Capital: Bratislava

Official language: Slovak

Currency: Slovak koruna (Sk) = 100 haléru

Exchange rate: Sk32.26 per US$ (Oct 2005); Slovakia entered ERMII in Nov 2005 when the rate was set at SK38.4550 to the euro.

GDP per capita: US$7,603 (2004)

GDP real growth: 5.50% (2004)

Labour force: 2.62 million (2004)

Unemployment: 18.00% (OECD, 2004)

Inflation: 7.50% (2004)

Balance of trade: -US$430.00 million (2004)*; -US$600.00 million (OECD, 2003)

Foreign debt: US$18.71 billion (end 2nd qtr 2004)

Annual FDI: US$11.80 billion (cumulative, 1995–2004, OECD); US$1.10 billion (OECD, 2004)*

* estimated figure

Having been part of Greater Hungary, then ruled by the Soviet Empire, then half of Czechoslovakia, this mostly Roman Catholic mountainous landlocked republic is now standing on its own two feet. It has been independent since 1993 when it broke away from the Czech republic. Slovakia joined NATO and the EU in the spring of 2004 and entered the Exchange Rate Mechanism in 2005. Things are looking good.

Politics

Since October 1998, the Slovenská Demokratická a Krestanská Únia (SDKÚ) (Slovak Democratic and Christian Union) has led a coalition government that includes the Krest'ansko-Demokratické Hnutie (KDH) (Christian Democratic Movement), the Strana Madarskej Koalície-Magyar Koalíció Pártja (SMK) (Hungarian Coalition Party) and the Aliancia Nového Obcana (ANO) (New Citizen Alliance). However, there is a parliamentary election pencilled in for September 2006. If opinion polls are anything to go by, a third of people will vote for the opposition Strana Smer-Tretia Cesta (Smer) (Direction Party). All other parties are expected to poll under 13 per cent of the vote each. Among the smaller players is the party the president came from, the Hnutie za Demokraciu (HZD) (Movement for Democracy).

Prime Minister Mikulas Dzurinda, of the SDKU, won a second term in September 2002. He has become a major figure on the world stage, despite being domestically unpopular. The US and the EU have hailed his reforming drives as an example to other emerging nations.

Economy

Dzurinda has steered the way towards economic success. Slovakia's central position in Central Europe, low taxes, political stability and low labour costs have all caught the eyes of many foreign investors, particularly French and German motor manufacturers such as Peugeot-Citroen. Foreign investment doubled from 2004–05, to a current level of US$2.6 billion.

The Statistics Bureau announced that in the third quarter of 2005 GDP grew by 6.2 per cent – this makes Slovakia one of the fastest growing economies in eastern Europe. Growth is being driven by exports and galloping household consumption. Economists have warned, however, that these growth rates and the economic structure make the economy liable to overheating. In particular, rising domestic consumption could bump prices up.

Slovakia

Investment and economic growth have created high numbers of new jobs. In the third quarter of the year, 2.24 million people in Slovakia were in employment, a rise of 36,000 on the previous year. The unemployment rate decreased 1.9 per cent to 15.6 per cent. The average wage in the national economy increased by 7.6 per cent in real terms to eur441.7 a month.

Euro

In November 2005 Slovakia entered the Exchange Rate Mechanism, the 'waiting room' for adoption of the euro, seven months before expectations. The country will remain in the ERM for a minimum of two years but currently entry into the euro-zone is set for January 2009. The ahead of schedule development will only encourage further investment and business confidence. The other key Maastricht condition for joining the euro is to keep the budget deficit below 3 per cent. Slovakia was expecting to end 2005 with a deficit of 3.34 per cent. The International Monetary Fund (IMF) says the government must now prioritise the creation of the right conditions to transfer smoothly to the euro. The IMF acknowledged that Slovakia was meeting the Maastricht criteria for long-term interest rates and public debt, but said several risks and challenges remained. It was of paramount importance to decrease inflation and the fiscal deficit. It recommended a cautious approach to additional pressures on incomes that could emerge with the predicted higher economic growth. Budgeted expenditures should be adhered to, which included public spending.

Privatisation

Although the IMF says growth is being primarily driven by the private sector, one potential privatisation deal is dividing politicians. Coalition leaders have voiced doubts about the proposed sale of the country's Bratislava and Kosice airports – the enormously lucrative deal could collapse. Parliament's chairman, Pavol Hrusovsky, also questioned the airport sell-off. The opposition leader Robert Fico (Smer) said he would reverse the sale if he were to be elected in the September polls.

However, the Slovakian transport minister, Pavol Prokopovic, is in favour of the deal. The recommended bidder at US$222 million is TwoOne which runs Vienna airport and whose investment partners include Austrian Raiffeisen Zentralbank (RZB) and Slovak finance group Penta. Opponents of the deal express fears that the smaller Slovakia airport will suffer if it is run by the operator of Vienna International Airport, which is just across the border in Austria.

Outlook

Looking ahead, the IMF believes a strengthening of economic growth and the external current account position can be expected. The composition of growth is likely to shift toward net exports, with the commencement of production at new plants in the automobile industry – Kia and PSA Peugeot-Citroen launch production in 2006. The IMF predicts real growth of 5.75 per cent in 2006 and 6.5 per cent in 2007.

Private consumption growth is projected to moderate somewhat, on the assumption that real wage growth will slow and the propensity of households to save will remain stable. Some easing of investment growth is likely with the completion of several large foreign-financed projects.

The inflation targets for end-2006 and end-2007 are ambitious. Though, it may be feasible to achieve headline CPI inflation of 2.5 per cent by end-2006, there are uncertainties about lowering it further to the end-2007 target of two per cent. The risk of inflationary pressures from declining economic slack cannot be discounted. A pick up in growth driven by the tradable sector is likely to result in higher unit labour costs in the non-tradable sector and could feed through to inflation. The effect could, however, be tempered if retail competition continues to intensify as it has in the recent past. The IMF forecasts headline CPI inflation remaining about 2.5 per cent over 2007.

Addressing the high unemployment problem is a continuing challenge. The introduction and incentive package that seeks to promote foreign investment in high unemployment regions, and the creation of a venture capital scheme for small and medium-sized enterprises should help increase employment opportunities. More attention should be given to reducing the bureaucracy surrounding construction permits, and to further speeding up the enforcement of contracts in courts. In these areas, Slovakia is trailing behind other EU countries.

Risk assessment

Economic	Good
Political	Satisfactory
Regional stability	Good

COUNTRY PROFILE

Historical profile
Slovakia, called Oberungarn (Upper Hungary) in some older maps, had politically been a part of the Hungarian kingdom for centuries, ever since the Moravian Kingdom had been destroyed in 902.
1536–1783 Bratislava, formerly Pressburg, was the capital of Hungary.
1867–1917 The Habsburg domains in central Europe were reconstituted as the dual monarchy of Austria-Hungary. Slovakia's struggle for independence

KEY INDICATORS — Slovakia

	Unit	2000	2001	2002	2003	2004
Population	m	5.39	5.40	5.40	5.41	5.42
Gross domestic product (GDP)	US$bn	19.20	20.50	23.70	32.50	*41.09
GDP per capita	US$	3,557	3,783	4,370	6,010	7,603
GDP real growth	%	2.0	3.8	4.4	4.2	5.5
Inflation	%	12.0	7.1	3.4	8.6	7.5
Unemployment	%	17.8	18.6	18.2	17.6	14.3
Exports (fob) (goods)	US$m	11,896.0	12,691.0	14,400.0	21,838.0	29,240.0
Imports (fob) (goods)	US$m	12,791.0	14,685.0	16,500.0	22,479.0	29,670.0
Balance of trade	US$m	-895.0	-1,994.0	-2,100.0	-641.0	-430.0
Current account	US$m	-694.0	-1,755.0	-1,900.0	-277.0	-1,390.0
Foreign debt	US$bn	9.4	12.5	13.2	9.6	–
Total reserves minus gold	US$m	4,022.0	4,141.0	8,809.0	11,678.0	14,417.0
Foreign exchange	US$m	4,022.0	4,140.0	8,808.0	11,677.0	14,416.0
Foreign direct investment (FDI)	US$bn	2.1	1.5	4.0	0.6	1.1
Exchange rate	per US$	46.04	48.36	43.62	36.14	32.22

* estimated figure

suffered a setback when Hungary's parliament gained a large degree of political autonomy from the Austrian administration in Vienna. The policy of Magyarisation that the Hungarian administration strove to achieve – Hungarian was to be the exclusive language of administration, jurisdiction and education – was most disturbing to Slovakia.

1918 At the end of the First World War, Slovakia announced its independence from the Austro-Hungarian empire and incorporation into the new Republic of Czechoslovakia with Thomas Masaryk as the country's first president.

1938 Czechoslovakia ceded its German-speaking areas of Sudetenland to Germany.

1939–45 The country fell under German control until the end of the Second World War.

1946 The Czechoslovak Communist Party (CPCz) formed a power-sharing government following national elections.

1948 After mass protests and strikes orchestrated by the Communists, a government crisis left the CPCz with a majority in government.

1949–67 Stalinist-style rule, complete with party purges.

1968 Alexander Dubcek, the CPCz leader, introduced the policy of 'socialism with a human face', which ended with the crushing of the reformist movement by the Soviet army.

1969–88 There were on-going protests at occupation by the Soviet troops. Václav Havel and a group of dissidents called for the restoration of civil and political rights. Mass demonstrations in 1988 marked the anniversary of the 1968 invasion.

1989 The new spirit of *glasnost* was met with scepticism as the government initially resisted political and economic change. However, large public demonstrations in the major cities, the 'Velvet Revolution', led to the resignation of the Communist Party leadership. Václav Havel was elected president and a pluralistic political system and market economy were introduced.

1990 The country was renamed the Czech and Slovak Federative Republic. The first free elections since 1946 led to the establishment of a coalition government involving all major parties, with the exception of the CPCz, and Havel was re-elected president.

1991 The Soviet forces completed their withdrawal.

1992 In elections, the Czech voters backed the centre-right, while the Slovaks supported Slovak separatists and left-wing parties. Vladimir Meciar (a supporter of Slovak separatism) became Slovak prime minister. He opposed the rapid privatisation of the public sector proposed by the Czech prime minister, Václav Klaus. Neither was prepared to compromise and agreed to the separation of Slovakia, despite President Havel's objections.

1993 Czechoslovakia divided into two independent countries, the Czech Republic (comprising the regions of Bohemia and Moravia) and the Slovak Republic (Slovakia). Michal Kovac became president of the Slovak Republic, with Vladimir Meciar continuing as prime minister.

1994 Meciar was voted out of office in March and was replaced by Jozef Moravcik. Moravcik lasted until the National Council elections in December when Meciar was returned to power with a new coalition government.

1997 A referendum to debate electoral change became a farce when the central question was withdrawn and the majority of voters stayed away.

1998 Kovac's presidential term expired and Prime Minister Meciar assumed some presidential powers. The refusal of opposition parties to co-operate with Meciar, despite his party, Hnutie Za Demokratické Slovensko (HZDS) (Movement for Democratic Slovakia), gaining the most seats in the elections, led to Mikulas Dzurinda becoming prime minister.

1999 Rudolf Schuster elected president.

2000 Dzurinda, the leader of the main coalition partner, the Slovenská Demokratiká Koalícia (SDK) (Slovak Democratic Coalition), registered a new political party, the Slovenská Demokratická a Krestanská Únia (SDKÚ) (Social Democratic Christian Union), as the successor to the SDK, in order to give himself an electoral platform to contest the 2002 elections.

2002 The parliamentary elections were won by the SDKÚ, led by Dzurinda; he formed a centre-right coalition government with the Hungarian Coalition Party (SMK), the Christian Democratic Movement (KDH) and the New Citizen Alliance (ANO). NATO invited Slovakia to join the alliance by 2004.

2003 Voters in the May referendum approved of EU membership in 2004.

2004 Ivan Gasparovic won the presidential election on 17 April with 59.9 per cent of the vote. Slovakia entered the EU on 1 May. Ivan Gasparovic took office on 15 June.

2005 Slovakia entered the European Exchange Rate Mechanism (ERMII) in November.

Political structure
Constitution
The constitution was ratified in 1992. No new government can be formed until the president has accepted the resignation of the former one. Further amendments in January and February 2001 created an independent council, increasing the powers of the constitutional court, and paved the way for reform of the public administration.

With reference to accession to EU and NATO, an amendment to the constitution was approved on 1 July 2001, which reclassified the relationship between national and international law, introduced judicial regulations and allowed for the creation of a second tier of self-administrative government in the regions.

Electoral system: Universal direct suffrage for party lists. All electoral coalitions have to win 5 per cent of the vote for every party they contain.

Form of state
Parliamentary democratic republic

The executive
Executive power lies with the prime minister and ministers, the former being appointed by the president.

The head of state is the president, elected by the National Council of the Slovak Republic by secret ballot for a period of five years. A majority of three-fifths of all deputies' votes is required for the president to be elected.

National legislature
Legislative authority is vested in the 150-member Národná Rada Slovenskej Republiky (National Council of the Slovak Republic) which is directly elected for a four-year term.

Legal system
Slovakia's legal system is partly based on the Czechslovakian system introduced before independence in 1993. The judiciary is independent of the government, although the president appoints judges to both the Constitutional Court and Supreme Court. The Constitutional Court is responsible for ensuring that legislation adheres to the constitution and 13 judges are appointed for a period of 12 years. Judges of the Supreme Court are appointed for an unlimited time period.

As part of the process toward accession to the EU, Slovakia has been attempting to harmonise its existing and new legislation with that of the organisation.

Last elections
13 June 2004 (European Parliament); 3/17 April 2004 (presidential); 20/21 September 2002 (parliamentary).

Results: European Parliament: SDKÚ won 17.1 per cent of the vote (three seats out of 14), LS-HZDS 17.1 per cent (three), Strana Smer-Tretia Cesta (Smer) (Direction Party) 16.9 per cent (three), KDH 16.2 per cent (three) and SMK 13.2 per cent (two); turnout 17 per cent.

Presidential run-off: Ivan Gasparovic (Hnutie za Demokraciu (HZD) (Movement for Democracy)) won with 59.9 per cent of the vote against Vladimír Meciar

Slovakia

(Ludová Strana-Hnutie Za Demokratické Slovensko (LS-HZDS) (People's Party-Movement for a Democratic Slovakia)) 40.1 per cent; turnout was 43.5 per cent.

Parliamentary: Prime Minister Dzurinda's Slovenská Demokratická a Krestanská Únia (SDKÚ) (Slovak Democratic and Christian Union), the Strana Madarskej Koalície-Magyar Koalíció Pártja (SMK) (Hungarian Coalition Party), Krest'ansko-Demokratické Hnutie (KDH) (Christian Democratic Movement) and Aliancia Nového Obcana (ANO) (New Citizen Alliance) together held 78 of parliament's 150 seats; turnout was 70 per cent.

Next elections
2006 (parliamentary); 2009 (presidential).

Political parties
Ruling party
Coalition government led by Slovenská Demokratická a Krestanská Únia (SDKÚ) (Slovak Democratic and Christian Union) and including Strana Madarskej Koalície-Magyar Koalíció Pártja (SMK) (Hungarian Coalition Party), Krest'ansko-Demokratické Hnutie (KDH) (Christian Democratic Movement) and Aliancia Nového Obcana (ANO) (New Citizen Alliance) (from 2002)

Main opposition party
Ludová Strana-Hnutie Za Demokratické Slovensko (LS-HZDS) (People's Party-Movement for a Democratic Slovakia)

Population
5.42 million (2004); 5.38 million (OECD, 2003)

Ethnic make-up
The chief non-Roma minorities are Hungarians (10.8 per cent of the population), Czechs (3 per cent), Ruthenians, Ukrainians, Germans and Poles. Roma, although making up only 1.5 per cent of the overall population, make up a significant minority in some areas, and are growing faster than the national average.

Religions
Roman Catholic (60.3 per cent), Protestant (8.4 per cent), Orthodox (4.1 per cent).

Education
Slovakia has universal literacy and offers free education to all. Enrolment at all levels is high and there is no noticeable gender disparity. Languages of instruction are English and Slovak, although Hungarians may be taught in their own language.
In June 2004 the government failed, in a vote in parliament, to introduce student loans for teriary education.

Compulsory years: 6 to 15
Enrolment rate: 102 per cent total primary enrolment, 94 per cent gross secondary enrolment; of the relevant age groups (including repeaters); (World Bank).
Pupils per teacher: 20 in primary schools

Health
There is a significant disparity between male and female life expectancy (9 years), partly due to the unbalanced diet and high cigarette and beer consumption by men, which the government is attempting to reduce.

HIV prevalence: 0.1 per cent aged 15–49 in 2003 (World Bank)
Life expectancy: 73.4 years (World Bank)
Fertility rate/Maternal mortality rate: 1.2 births per woman (World Bank)
Birth rate/Death rate: 10 births per and nine deaths per 1,000 population (2003).
Infant mortality rate: 7.0 per 1,000 live births (World Bank)
Head of population per physician/bed: 3 physicians and 7.5 hospital beds per 1,000 people.

Welfare
Slovakia has a 42.5 hour working week with a minimum wage set by the government. It has a well-developed social security system, including health, unemployment and pension benefits. Employees contribute 12 per cent of their wages to social security schemes and employers an additional 38 per cent.

Main cities
Bratislava (capital, estimated population 428,800 in 2003), Kosice (233,600), Presov (92,300), Nitra (87,200).

Languages spoken
The Czech and Slovak languages are mutually comprehensible. Hungarian is widely spoken, especially in the south and east.
A large proportion of the population, particularly those engaged in industry and foreign trade, speaks German. Russian is also spoken by some executives. English is increasing, especially among the younger generation.

Official language/s
Slovak

Media
Press
Dailies: There are some 20 dailies. The main daily newspapers include *Novy CAS, Pravda, Praca, Sport Nike, Slovenska Republika, SME/Smena, Národná Obroda, Slovak Spectator, Korzo, Hospodarske Noviny* and *Nové Mesto*.
Weeklies: The main weekly newspaper is *Nedelna Pravda*. Other weekly magazines include *Eurotelevizia, Zivot, Slovenka* and *Express*.

Business: *Slovakia Daily Surveyor* is the most complete Internet guide to Slovakia with daily news, top stories, background information, business related issues, essays, reviews, polls, and links to other web sites. Other business and financial publications include *Riki Multimedia Magazine* and *Kompass Slovakia*.
Periodicals: *Slovak Spectator*, an English-language newspaper, is published every second Wednesday.

Broadcasting
Radio: There are 22 commercial radio stations. Slovenska Radio broadcasts nationally. Foreign radio stations are allowed to broadcast – Europe 2 (French) and BBC World Service (English, Czech and Slovak).
Television: There are several commercial TV stations, of which two have extensive coverage. State-owned Slovenska Televizia (STV), broadcasts nationally on channels STV1 and STV2.
VTV, a private channel, broadcasts by cable and satellite, with about 10 per cent share of viewing. A second channel (OK3) broadcasts a mixture of CNN, BBC, Sky and other international stations. TV Nova has gained an impressive increase in audience in the western part of Slovakia. TV Markiza, a private terrestrial station, began broadcasting in 1996. Due to its proximity to Austria, television broadcasts from there can easily be picked up in the western part of Slovakia.

Advertising
There are a number of foreign and domestic advertising agencies. The most commonly used media include newspapers, radio and television. Urban areas in Bratislava, Dubnica, Nitra, Poprad, Zvolen and Kosice can be reached by private radio advertising. Posters have been widely used, and are to be found in post offices, telephone booths, public transport, outdoor pillars and public routes.

Economy
Although Slovakia was politically isolated during the 1990s, its economy has shown signs of vibrancy, particularly under the previous governments of Prime Minister Mikulás Dzurinda. Growth has been strongly positive since the mid-1990s and inflation has remained at a respectable level. However, despite the appearance of growing prosperity, structural change is badly needed. The experience of Slovakia since the end of the Cold War reflects its use within Czechoslovakia as a command military-industrial economy which had built up very rapidly over a relatively fragile base – until Czechoslovakia was formed out of the ashes of the Austro-Hungarian Empire in 1918, Slovakia was considered to be a backward agricultural society.

Since 2002, the government has been committed to curbing fiscal deficits on a sustained basis, thereby alleviating the burden of economic stabilisation on monetary policy. Unemployment remains high, but the government is reforming the over-generous welfare system and stimulating labour supply and demand. Welfare benefits are being reduced, the retirement age increased and pension benefits made dependent on work and contribution history. Labour code reforms make both permanent and temporary job creation less costly and targetted employment subsidies are being introduced for the long-term unemployed. Incentives for small businesses and the self-employed have been increased.

The favourable operating environment has attracted more foreign direct investment (FDI) and the Slovak economy is growing. With labour costs remaining the second lowest in Organisation for Economic Co-operation and Development (OECD) countries, Slovakia is set to become the top OECD manufacturer of cars per capita in 2005.

Between 2004 and 2006, the 10 EU accession countries will receive funding of up to eur25.1 billion (US$28.2 billion), which will include money for agriculture, infrastructure modernisation and regional aid. Slovakia will receive eur1.4 billion (US$1.6 billion).

Domestic demand, which began to expand in the first half of 2004, has remained strong and GDP growth is expected to remain at between 4.75–6.0 per cent for the foreseeable future. Employment rates have not maintained such a healthy level and are not expected for fall below 17 per cent much before late 2006. Unemployment is regionally based, however, and Bratislava and Trenciansky have unemployment rates of less than 10 per cent.

GDP growth of 4.8 per cent is forecast for 2005, a slight fall from the 5.3 per cent in 2004.

Fiscal policy outcomes have been good but, to remain on target to join the European Monetary Union (EMU) in 2009, strict adherence to planned expenditure cuts is needed. Tighter fiscal policies will have to be implemented if there are any signs of economic overheating or renewed exchange rate appreciation. GDP is expected to rise to 5.7 per cent in 2006.

OECD recommendations for continued growth include:

reducing the tax wedge for low-income workers to stimulate low-skilled job creation in the formal sector

reforming the education system to improve human capital so that teaching outcomes are improved, and access to tertiary education is opened up while competition between universities is encouraged

reducing state control of business operations in network industries and limiting special voting rights by the state in entities in certain sectors

monitoring price development in network services and responding to anti-competition behaviour with full enforcement of new regulatory framework.

External trade
Slovakia's foreign trade is increasingly orientated towards the West. Slovak steel exports to the EU are no longer subject to quotas.

Imports
Principal imports include machinery and transport equipment (41 per cent), intermediate and other manufactured goods, fuels and chemicals.
Main sources: Germany (29.6 per cent total, 2004), Czech Republic (17.1 per cent), Russia (9.5 per cent), Austria (7.1 per cent), Italy (5.4 per cent), Hungary (4.3 per cent)

Exports
Principal exports include vehicles (26 per cent), machinery and electrical equipment, base metals, chemicals and minerals, and plastics.
Main destinations: Germany (35.7 per cent total, 2004), Czech Republic (13.4 per cent), Austria (8.6 per cent), Italy (5.6 per cent), US (4.8 per cent), Poland (4.8 per cent), Hungary (4.3 per cent)

Agriculture
Farming
The agricultural sector suffered from under-investment during the communist era. In an attempt to increase productivity, a land restitution act was adopted in 1990, under which all agricultural land taken by the state between 1948–55 was returned to its original owners.

Agriculture contributes around 3.5 per cent to GDP.

Wheat, maize and barley are exported. Only 10 per cent of potato requirements are imported, and about 20 per cent of raw sugar requirements. Slovakia is a net importer of oil crops, although the margin is very small, with equal amounts of rape and mustard seed imported and exported. Slovakia is mostly self sufficient in meat, eggs and milk.

During its EU transitional entry stage, Slovakia has decided to implement the reform of the Common Agricultural Policy (CAP) on 1 January 2009. The reform was introduced throughout most of the EU on 1 January 2005, when subsidies on farm output, which tended to benefit large farms and encourage overproduction, were replaced by single farm payments, not conditional on production. The change is expected to reward farms that provide and maintain a healthy environment, food safety and animal welfare standards. The changes are also intended to encourage market conscious production and cut the cost of CAP to the EU taxpayer.

Crop production in 2004 included: 3,792,971 tonnes (t) cereals in total, 1,764,846t wheat, 862,435t maize, 124,340t rye, 381,891t potatoes, 915,903t barley, 54,469t pulses, 56,537t grapes, 61,469t tomatoes, 184,954t oilcrops, 1,298t tobacco, 1,598,773t sugar beets, 262,660t rapeseed (canola), 192,278t fruit in total, 328,144t vegetables in total. Livestock production included: 311,870t meat in total, 41,217t beef, 136,454t pig meat, 2,227t lamb, 127,300t poultry, 67,589t eggs, 1,098,445t milk, 2,500t honey.

Fishing
The fishing sector, based on inland fisheries and imported sea-fish, is not significant, producing around 2,500 tonnes a year.

Forestry
Forest and other wooded land accounts for over two-fifths of the land area, with forest cover estimated at 2.1 million hectares (ha). More than 80 per cent of the forest is available for wood supply and the rest is preserved. The ownership structure of forest areas has changed considerably since 1990 as a result of privatisation and restitution. Half of the forested area is state-owned.

Consumption of forest products per capita is below the European average. Nearly all of the roundwood is processed in the country, using much of the hardwood and softwood species. Slovakia is a net exporter of forestry products and although the industry is in need of modernisation, it is a significant earner of foreign exchange. Over three-quarters of sawnwood produced is exported, mostly to Hungary. The pulp industry utilises half of the hardwood production, recovered paper and some non-wood fibre pulp. The bulk of exports also constitute paper and pulpboard.

Exports of forest material in 2004 amounted to US$872.2 million, while imports amounted to US$540.4 million. Production in 2004 included 7,240,000 cubic metres (cum) roundwood, 6,936,000cum industrial roundwood, 1,837,000cum sawnwood, 3,119,000cum sawlogs and veneers, 3,397,000cum pulpwood, 508,000cum wood-based panels, 304,000cum woodfuel.

Industry and manufacturing
Industry accounts for around 30 per cent of GDP and 30 per cent of employment. Industrial production fell by approximately

20 per cent after the end of the Communist regime and privatisation has been unable to inject the necessary cash required for investment. Compared to neighbouring Hungary and Czech Republic, Slovak industry is marked by inefficiency, hidden bankruptcies and government subsidies. The principal industries are the manufacture of machinery, chemicals and rubber, food and beverages, and iron metallurgy. Slovakian industry remains more vulnerable to the instability of Eastern European markets than its Czech neighbour. The long-term prospects for the sector depend on how successfully the country can recover from the dislocation of its traditional markets and find new ones for such key industries as steel. Half of all foreign direct investment (FDI) in Slovakia goes to the manufacturing sector.

Tourism
Tourism has been slow to develop, the government providing little incentive. EU accession boosted the number of visitors to Slovakia in 2004 to over a million, but many were for short periods of a few days. The government is seeking to encourage more domestic tourism. The sector is expected to contribute 1.9 per cent in 2005.

Mining
Slovakia has workable deposits of antimony ore, mercury, iron ore, copper, lead, zinc, precious metals, limestone, dolomite, gravel, brick loam, ceramic materials and stone salt. In each case, except iron ores, only small quantities are actually mined.

Hydrocarbons
Slovakia has oil reserves of nine million barrels and produces about 1,000 barrels per day (bpd) of oil. Production does not meet consumption levels, over 98 per cent of all oil consumed having to be imported. Oil imports come from Russia through two pipelines, which transports around 187,000bpd, 57 per cent going to the Slovnaft refinery in Bratislava and the rest to the Czech Republic.
Slovakia has natural gas reserves of 530 billion cubic feet. Slovakia relies on the import of natural gas to meet demand. Around 7 billion cubic metres are consumed annually, nearly all of this was imported from Russia. Slovakia is as an important transit route for gas and around a quarter of gas consumed in Western Europe and 70 per cent of Russia's total gas exports to the west transits through Slovakia.
Coal is mined on a large scale. Reserves could last more than 40 years. Most is low quality brown coal (lignite) and looks likely to diminish as a key energy source due to the amount of pollution it causes. Coal consumption has fallen since 1993 due to the decreasing domestic output, largely through the closing of inefficient mines, restructuring and the need to cut greenhouse gas emissions in compliance with EU standards.

Energy
Slovakia has installed electricity generating capacity of 7.8 million kW. Most of the electrical capacity is from thermal sources, the rest coming from hydroelectric and nuclear stations. Emphasis is placed on the commissioning of new nuclear power stations and the upgrading of Chernobyl-style reactors. Slovakia is a net exporter of electricity.

Financial markets
Stock exchange
The Bratislava Stock Exchange (BSE) is the country's main bourse. The equity-based SAX is the main index and its base of 100 was set in the third quarter of 1998. There is also a bond-based SDX index.
Until recently, foreign interest in the bourse was low due to poor perceptions of Slovakia engendered by the Meciar government. However, as Slovakia geared up for accession to the EU, investor attitudes experienced something of a turnaround. International financial investors made a series of purchases of koruna-denominated debt.
The growth of the local bourse continues to face foreign investor wariness due to low levels of capitalisation, illiquidity and a lack of transparency as well as few exciting rich pickings. This has been compounded by the lack of initial public offerings (IPOs) and the government's failure to float shares in its privatisation programme.

Banking and insurance
Slovakia's banking system has been reformed, although the sector has been plagued by bad debts coupled with massive losses affecting a third of banks. As a result, economic structuring has been essential to both macroeconomic stability and the integrity of the banking sector. Many of the country's larger banks have been privatised. In early 2002, a 66.7 stake in Slovenska Poistovna (Slovak Insurance Bank) was sold to Germany's Allianz AG for US$142 million. Smaller banks have closed as the central bank has imposed a tough regulatory framework on commerce, with greater power given to creditors.
Central bank
Narodna Banka Slovenska (NBS) (National Bank of Slovakia)
Main financial centre
Bratislava

Time
GMT plus one hour (GMT plus two hours from late March to late September)

Geography
Slovakia is a landlocked, hilly country in the heart of Europe. Around 80 per cent of the country has an altitude of over 750 metres above sea level. The High Tatra Mountains in the north give way to large lowlands, broad valleys and meadows in the south.
Slovakia is bordered by the Czech Republic to the west (the border is 215km long), by Poland to the north (444km), Ukraine to the east (90km), Hungary to the south (515km) and Austria to the south-west (the border with Austria is only 15km from the capital, Bratislava).
The High Tatra Mountains are on the northern Polish border and the Low Tatras are in the centre and east of the country. The highest peak is Gerlach in the High Tatras (2,655 metres), with the lowest point the Bodrog river near Streda and Bodrogom (95 metres).
There are numerous rivers flowing south to the lowland areas, including the Váh, Nitra, Hron and Hornád. The River Danube marks part of the southern border. The lowland areas are in the south-west and south-east of the country.

Climate
Slovakia has a continental climate (warm summers and cold winters). Maximum temperatures are 32 degrees Celsius (C) to 35 degrees C; July is the hottest month (average 29.9 degrees C). Minimum temperatures are -12 degrees C to -20 degrees C. January is the coldest month (average -8 degrees C). Long-term average rainfall is approximately 490mm.

Dress codes
Most people dress in standard casual wear. For winter, mediumweight clothing is required with a heavy coat. For summer, lightweight clothing is suitable. For business meetings, men should wear a suit and tie.

Entry requirements
Passports
Required by all. Passport must be valid for eight months from the date of issue of the visa.
Visa
Required by all, except citizens of North America and EU; for a full list of exceptions and variable lengths of stay see www.foreign.gov.sk (or www.slovakia.org and follow link through tourism to visa information).
Visitors are required to have onward/return passage.
Currency advice/regulations
Import of local currency is prohibited. There are no restrictions on import of foreign currency, but it must be declared on arrival.

Local currency up to Sk100 can be exported, and foreign currency up to the amount declared on entry.

Customs
Items of value, such as cameras, must be disclosed on entry.

Health (for visitors)
Mandatory precautions
Full medical insurance, covering the whole territory of the Slovak Republic, is required. Random checks at Slovak points of entry are carried out and entry can be refused if no medical insurance for the whole country can be produced.

Credit cards
Credit cards are generally accepted by major hotels and restaurants.

Public holidays
Fixed dates
1 Jan (New Year's Day/Independence of the Slovak Republic), 6 Jan (Epiphany), 1 May (Labour Day), 8 May (Liberation of the Republic), 5 Jul (St Cyril and St Methodius Day), 29 Aug (Anniversary of the Slovak National Uprising), 1 Sep (Constitution Day), 15 Sep (Our Lady of the Seven Sorrows Day), 1 Nov (All Saints' Day), 17 Nov (Day of Freedom and Democracy), 24–26 Dec (Christmas Holiday).
Variable dates
Good Friday, Easter Monday.

Working hours
Banking
Mon–Fri: 0800–1700. There are also exchange offices in the main city centres, which operate seven days a week until 1900.
Business
Mon–Fri: 0800–1600.
Government
Mon–Fri: 0900–1700.
Shops
Mon–Fri: 0900–1800; Sat: 0900–1200; some shops remain open late on Thursday evenings.

Electricity supply
Domestic: 220V, 50 cycles AC. Industrial: 360V, 50 cycles.

Weights and measures
Metric system. In addition, the following measures are used: quintal or metric hundredweight = 100 kg. Food is usually purchased by the decagramme and kilogram.

Social customs/useful tips
Appointments should be made in advance and punctuality is important. Shaking hands is customary when meeting people and on parting. Business is conducted in Slovak; many executives speak a second language – German, Russian or English. When drinks are served, it is considered polite to wait for everyone to be served and then wish each person *Nazdravi* ('to your health'). At meals it is usual to wait for everyone to be served before starting and to wish everyone *bon appetit* or *dobrou chut* just before eating. The terms *Pan* (Mr), *Pani* (Mrs) and *Slecna* (Miss) are used. *Slecna* is used for single women under 30 only; single women over 30 will usually be addressed as *Pani*.
Gratuities are between 5 and 10 per cent. The minimum drinking age is 18 years. When visiting private homes it is customary to take flowers for the hosts. Visitors also generally leave their shoes in the hallway, partly as a mark of respect and partly because of pollution in the streets. Men always take off their hats indoors. Illegally parked cars tend to be towed away by the police and it is advisable to park at attended car parks where the cost is relatively low.

Security
Street crime, especially in the towns, has become a problem since the 1989 revolution because the police tend to keep a low profile. Although the situation has improved, it is still advisable to carry as little in the way of valuables and cash as possible. Car vandalism and theft are also problems.

Getting there
Air
National airline: Air Slovakia
International airport/s: MR Stefanik Airport (BTS), 9km from Bratislava; post office, bank, bureau de change, restaurant, duty free shop.
Airport tax: There is no airport departure tax.
Surface
Road: Access routes include Czech Republic, Poland, Ukraine, Hungary and Austria. There is a motorway from Bratislava to Prague.
Rail: Slovakia also has rail connections with Vienna, Hamburg, Berlin, Warsaw, Budapest, Moscow and St Petersburg.
Water: Ships provide regular passenger service and cruises on the Danube, from Passau and Regensburg (Germany) via Vienna (Austria). There are also links with the Rhine and Main rivers and the Black Sea.

Getting about
National transport
Air: Internal connections are provided by Slovak Airlines (9S), Sky Europe Airlines and Air Slovakia (GM).
Road: The road network is extensive and in good condition. The major route is from Bratislava to Presov and Kosice.
Buses: There is an extensive coach network. **Rail:** The internal rail network is operated by Railways of the Slovak Republic (ZSR). Express trains linking Bratislava and the main cities and resorts operate daily. Reservations should be made in advance. Fares are low although supplements are included for travel on express trains.
Water: There are 279km (173 miles) of navigable waterways with the Danube providing the main linkage route.
City transport
Taxis: There is a good service operating in all main towns – cheap and plentiful. Most taxi drivers produce a receipt on request. There are surcharges for journeys between 2200 and 0600.
For visits to companies on the outskirts of town, the Yellow Taxis are the most efficient, friendly and reliable.
Buses, trams & metro: The journey from Prague to Bratislava takes about four hours by bus. Bratislava is well served by trams and buses.
Blue badges on tram and bus stops indicate an all-night service.
Car hire
Car hire is available in major towns. Traffic drives on the right. There is an extensive network of roadside restaurants and petrol stations. Emergency telephones are located at half mile intervals on motorways and the emergency system is generally quick and reliable.
The speed limit in towns is 60kph (37mph), outside towns 90kph (56mph) and 130kph (81mph) on motorways. Seat belts are compulsory and drink driving is strictly prohibited.

BUSINESS DIRECTORY

The addresses listed below are a selection only. While World of Information makes every endeavour to check these addresses, we cannot guarantee that changes have not been made, especially to telephone numbers and area codes. We would welcome any corrections.

Telephone area codes
The international direct dialling code (IDD) for Slovakia is +421, followed by area code and subscriber's number:

Banska Bystricá	48	Nitra	37
Bratislava	2	Presov	51
Kosice	55	Zilina	41

Useful telephone numbers
Police: 158
Ambulance: 155
Fire: 150
Directory enquiries: 154

Chambers of Commerce
American Chamber of Commerce in the Slovak Republic, Hotel Danube, 1 Rybne namestie, 81338 Bratislava (tel: 5934-0508; fax: 5934-0556; e-mail: director@amcham.sk).

Slovakia

Banska Bystrica Regional Chamber of Commerce and Industry, 4 namestie S Moysesa, 97401 Banska Bystrica (tel: 412-5643; fax: 412-5636; e-mail: sopkrkbb@sopk.sk).

Bratislava Regional Chamber of Commerce and Industry, 6 Jasikova, 82673 Bratislava (tel: 4829-1257; fax: 4829-1260; e-mail: sopkrkbl@scci.sk).

British Chamber of Commerce in the Slovak Republic, 14 Cukrova, 81339 Bratislava (tel/fax: 5292-0371; e-mail: director@britcham.sk).

Kosice Regional Chamber of Commerce and Industry, 48/A Trieda SNP, 04011 Kosice (tel: 641-9477; fax: 641-9470; e-mail: sopkrkke@scci.sk).

Lucenec Regional Chamber of Commerce and Industry, 2 Vajanskeho, 98401 Lucenec (tel: 433-3939; fax: 433-3937; e-mail: sopkrklc@scci.sk).

Nitra Regional Chamber of Commerce and Industry, 4 Akademicka, 94901 Nitra (tel: 653-5466; fax: 733-6739; e-mail: sopkrknr@scci.sk).

Presov Regional Chamber of Commerce and Industry, 22 Masarykova, 08001 Presov (tel: 773-2818; fax: 773-2413; e-mail: sopkrkpo@scci.sk).

Slovak Chamber of Commerce and Industry, 9 Gorkeho, 81603 Bratislava (tel: 5443-3291; fax: 5413-1159; e-mail: sopkurad@sopk.sk).

Trencin Regional Chamber of Commerce and Industry, 2 Jilemnickeho, 91101 Trencin (tel: 652-3834; fax: 652-1023; e-mail: sopkrktn@scci.sk).

Trnava Regional Chamber of Commerce and Industry, 2 Trhova, 91701 Trnava (tel: 551-2588; fax: 551-2603; e-mail: sopkrktt@sopk.sk).

Zilina Regional Chamber of Commerce and Industry, 31 Halkova, 01001 Zilina (tel: 723-5101; fax: 723-5102; e-mail: sekrza@za.scci.sk).

Banking
Bank Austria, Mostava 6, 811 02 Bratislava (tel: 539-9111; fax: 539-9406).

Citibank (Slovakia), Viedenska cesta 5, 851 01, Bratislava (tel: 894-223; fax: 802-689).

Consolidation Bank SFI, Cintorisíka 21, 81499 Bratislava (tel: 368-011; fax: 321-353).

Crédit Lyonnais Bank Slovakia, Medena 22, 811 02 Bratislava (tel: 325-320).

Czechoslovak Commercial Bank, Michalská 18, 81563 Bratislava (tel: 534-5230; fax: 533-2775).

Deíln Banka as, Frantiskánske nám 8, 81310 Bratislava (tel: 333-376; fax: 330-376).

General Credit Bank, Námestie SNP 19, 81856 Bratislava (tel: 531-7283; fax: 531-7020/05).

ING Bank, Kolarska 6, 811 06 Bratislava PO Box 123 (tel: 5346-111).

Investment and Development Bank, Stúrova 5, 81855 Bratislava (tel: 326-121; fax: 321-433).

Istrobanka as, Laurinská 1, 81101 Bratislava (tel: 539-7524; fax: 533-1744).

Konsolidacna Banka Bratislava, Cintorinska 21, 814 99 Bratislava (tel: 321-387; fax: 321-353).

Polnobanka as, Vajnorská 21, 83265 Bratislava (tel: 273-964; fax: 259-024).

Post Bank, PO Box 149, Gorkého 3, 81499 Bratislava (tel: 329-253; fax: 211-204).

Slovak Credit Bank, Námestie SNP 13, 81499 Bratislava (tel: 306-5409; fax: 362-691).

Slovak Savings Bank, Námestie SNP 18, 81607 Bratislava (tel: 560-6580; fax: 560-6220).

TATRA Bank, Vajanského nábrezie 5, 81006 Bratislava (tel: 210-3519; fax: 324-760).

Volksbank, Námestie SNP 15, 81000 Bratislava (tel: 381-1140; fax: 364-847).

Central bank
Narodna banka Slovenska (National Bank of Slovakia), Imricha Karvasa 1, 81325 Bratislava (tel: 5787-1111; fax: 5787-1100; e-mail: webmaster@nbs.sk).

Travel information
Slovak Airlines (domestic flights), Ivanka Airport, Bratislava, (tel: 4857-5170/1; internet: www.slovakairlines.sk).

Slovak Association of Travel Agents, Bajkalská 25, 821 01 Bratislava 2, (tel: 5341-9058; fax: 5823-3385; email:sack@ba.sknet.sk; internet: www.sack.sk).

Slovak Tourist Board (Bratislava office), PO Box 76, Bajkalská 27, 850 05 Bratislava 55, (tel: 5342-1023-5; fax: 5342-1021; email: sacrba@sacr.sk; internet: www.slovakiatourism.sk).

Ministry of tourism
Ministry of Economy (Tourism Section) Mierováá 19, 827 15 Bratislava (tel: 4333-0066; fax: 4854-3321; email: icom@economy.gov.sk; internet: www.economy.gov.sk).

National tourist organisation offices
Slovak Tourist Board. Nám. L Štúra 1, PO Box 35, 974 05 Banská Bystrica 5, (tel: (48) 413-6146-8; fax: (48) 413-6149; email: sacr@sacr.sk; internet: www.slovakiatourism.sk).

Ministries
Ministry of Administration and Privatisation of National Property, Drienova 24, 82009 Bratislava (tel: 230-678; fax: 233-335).

Ministry of Agriculture, Dobrovicova 12, 81266 Bratislava (tel: 368-561, 456-111; fax: 3066-294).

Ministry of Construction and Public Works, Spitalska 8, 81644 Bratislava (tel: 536-1111; fax; 536-1203).

Ministry of Culture of the Slovak Republic, Dobrovicova 12, 81331 Bratislava (tel: 323-295; fax: 368-140).

Ministry of Defence, Kutuzovova 7, 83247 Bratislava (tel: 250-320; fax: 258-907).

Ministry of Economy of the Slovak Republic, Mierová 19, 82715 Bratislava (tel: 574-1407; fax: 237-827).

Ministry of Education and Sciences, Stromova 1, 81330 Bratislava (tel: 370-4111; fax: 370-4333).

Ministry of the Environment of the Slovak Republic, Namestie L Stura 1,, 81235 Bratislava (tel: 516-2458; fax: 516-2457).

Ministry of Finance of the Slovak Republic, Stefanovicova 5, 81308 Bratislava (tel: 518-2562; fax: 396-146).

Ministry of Foreign Affairs, Hlboka Cesta 3, 83336 Bratislava (tel: 438-1111; fax: 438-2005; internet: http://www.foreign.gov.sk).

Ministry of Heal, Limbova 2, 83105 Bratislava (tel: 377-940; fax: 377-659).

Ministry of the Interior, Pribinova 2, 81272 Bratislava (tel: 546-1111; fax: 368-835).

Ministry of Justice, Zupné námestie 13, 81311 Bratislava (tel: 535-3111; fax: 531-5952).

Ministry of Labour, Social Welfare and Family of the Slovak Republic, Spitálska 4, 81643 Bratislava (tel: 338-2414; fax: 362-150).

Ministry of Transport and Communications, Nam Slobody 6, 81005 Bratislava (tel: 395-251; fax: 256-414).

Office of the Government, Nam Slobody 1, 84218 Bratislava (tel: 359-5111; fax: 397-595).

Office of the President, Stefanikova ul 1, 81104 Bratislava (tel: 531-7567; fax: 531-7065).

Other useful addresses
Bratislava International Commodity Exchange, Ruzinovská 1, 82102 Bratislava (tel: 522-6311; fax: 522-6318).

Bratislava Stock Exchange, Vysoká 17, 81499 Bratislava (tel: 386-121; fax: 386-103).

British Embassy, Panskà 16, 81101 Bratislava (tel: 5441-9632; fax: 5441-0002; e-mail: bebra@internet.sk).

Federation of Employers' Unions and Associations of Slovak Republic, Information and Consulting Centre, Drienová 24, 82603 Bratislava (tel: 235-024; fax: 233-542).

National Agency for Development of Small and Medium Enterprises, Nevädzová 5, 82101 Bratislava (tel: 237-472/563, 231-873; fax: 522-2434); External Advisors (tel: 237-472; fax: 522-2434); BIC (Business Innovation Centre) (tel: 290-7417; fax: 522-2434, 290-7217).

National Property Fund PARP PMU, Drienova 27, 82656 Bratislava (tel: 561-1258, 561-1230, 561-1447, 235-280, 231-300, 231-531; fax: 561-1446, 235-280); external department (tel: 250-248; fax: 259-208).

Slovak National Agency for Foreign Investment and Development (SNAFID), Sládkovicova 7, 81106 Bratislava (tel: 533-5175; fax: 533-5022); Slovenska polnohospodarska a potravinarska komora, Krizna 52, 82108 Bratislava (tel: 566-2657, 526-1778; fax: 526-7336, 211-251).

Slovak Republic Embassy (USA), 3523 International Court, NW, Washington DC 20008 (tel: 202-237-1054; fax: 202-237-6438; e-mail: info@slovakembassy-us.org).

Statistical Office of the Slovak Republic, Mileticova 3, 82467 Bratislava (tel: 215-802; fax: 214-587).

Transport Department, Dept of European Integration, Namestie Slobody 6, 81370 Bratislava (tel: 499-766, 498-156 Ext. 331, 498-841, 495-251; fax: 499-761).

Internet sites

Slovakia Daily Surveyor:
http://www.slovensko.com

Slovaks and Slovakia:
http://www.slovak.com

Slovak Republic Government:
http://www.government.gov.sk

Slovak tourist organisation:
http://www.slovakia.org

Slovenia

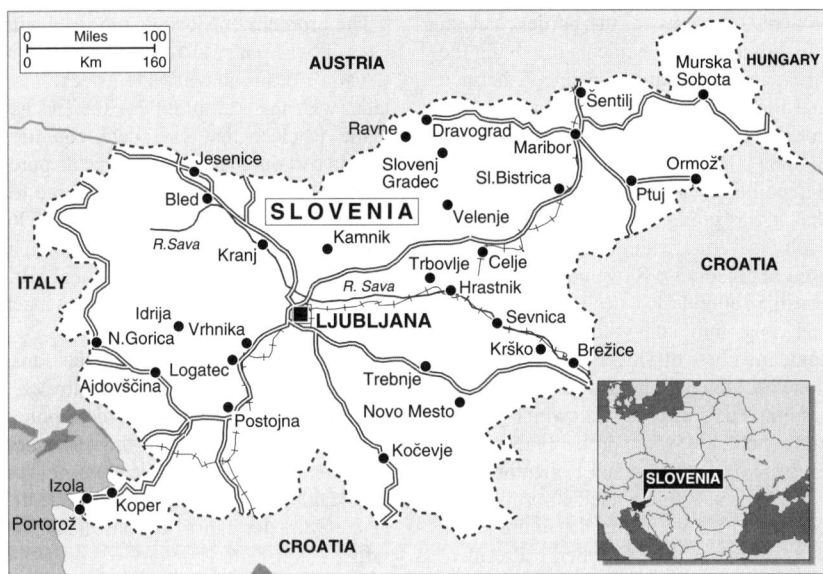

In 2005, Slovenia experienced its first full year as a member of the EU. However, despite having traded for years on its image as a Central European as opposed to a Balkan state, ironically it was the Balkans that set Slovenia's regional agenda.

High praise for the economy

The IMF issued high praise for Slovenia in a report published in March 2005 and in September, the World Economic Forum ranked Slovenia the world's 32nd most competitive economy – up from 33rd in 2004. Slovenia's GDP grew by an estimated 3.9 per cent in 2005 and recorded inflation of 2.7 per cent.

Slovenia and the EU

Unlike in some new member-states, the EU retained popular affection in Slovenia in 2005. In February, the Slovene parliament comfortably ratified the EU Constitution. A poll in September also revealed that the vast majority of Slovenes believed that entry into the EU had benefited the country and that future enlargement was a good thing. Slovenia also ended the year well placed to accomplish its plan to adopt the euro in 2007. However, during negotiations in Brussels for the 2007–13 EU budget, the government of Prime Minister Janez Jansa insisted that Slovenia would not be a net contributor.

New government growing pains

For the centre-right coalition government of Prime Minister Jansa, 2005 was its first full year in office. The government, and in particular foreign minister Dimitrij Rupel, found itself increasingly in conflict with the Slovene president, Janez Drnovšek. President Drnovšek is a former leader of the opposition Liberalna Demokracija Slovenije (LDS) (Liberal Democracy of Slovenia) – one of the parties ousted by Jansa in 2004. On several occasions in 2005, Drnovšek expressed foreign policy positions at odds with government policy. This was most vividly illustrated in October, when the president stated that he believed Kosovo should be an independent state, contrary to the government's more cautious position.

In December, thousands of people rallied in the capital Ljubljana to protest against the government's decision to cut social security benefits and introduce a

KEY FACTS

Official name: Republika Slovenija (Republic of Slovenia)

Head of State: President Janez Drnovšek (inaugurated 23 Dec 2002)

Head of government: Prime Minister Janez Jansa (leader of SDS) (elected in parliament 9 Nov 2004)

Ruling party: Coalition government led by Slovenská Demokratska Stranka (SDS) (Slovenian Democratic Party), and including Nova Slovenija Krsanski Ljudska Stranka (Nsi) (New Slovenia Christian People's Party) and Slovenska Ljudska Stranka (SLS) (Slovenian People's Party) (from Nov 2004)

Area: 20,251 square km

Population: 2.00 million (2004)

Capital: Ljubljana

Official language: Slovene

Currency: Tolar (T) =100 stotin (replaced Yugoslav dinar 8 Oct 1991)

Exchange rate: T198.40 per US$ (Oct 2005)

GDP per capita: US$16,447 (2004)

GDP real growth: 4.40% (2004); *3.9% (2005)

Labour force: 857,400 (2003)

Unemployment: 10.60% (2004)

Inflation: 3.60% (2004); *2.7% (2005)

Balance of trade: -US$1.04 billion 2004

Foreign debt: US$7.90 billion (2003)

* estimated figure

flat tax. Opinion polls in that month revealed a marked drop in nation-wide support for the government.

Nasty image

In April, NGOs and the ombudsman warned the government that Slovenia was in danger of becoming an intolerant society, with regards to ethnic minorities, gays and lesbians. Also in April, in the town of Novo Mesto, the Roma community threatened a boycott of a local school, alleging that the school authorities were segregating Roma children from Slovene children. Driving home the point that Slovenia had some work to do on minority rights, the European Monitoring Centre on Racism and Xenophobia accused Slovenia of having done nothing to reverse a 1992 government decision to 'erase' 18,000 people from its population register. These 18,000 had originated from other Yugoslav republics but had been living in Slovenia as citizens since independence in 1991.

Slovenia and the Balkans

Slovenia's relations with its former co-Yugoslav republics dominated much of its foreign policy agenda in 2005. During first half of the year, much work was done to repair relations with Croatia. Even though sections of Slovenia's terrestrial and maritime border with Croatia had been contested since 1991, Slovenia was a strong supporter of Croatia's bid to join the EU. However, an incident on the disputed border during the October 2004 election campaign, in which a Slovene politician was arrested by Croatian police for illegal entry, dramatically heightened tensions between the two countries. Slovenia's then prime minister, Anton Rop, even threatened to withdraw support for Croatia's EU membership talks. In a bid to dampen tension, in June, Slovenia and Croatia held a joint government sitting in Croatia. An accord was signed, to the effect that every effort would be made to avoid incidents on the border. Yet, in July, almost daily incidents involving the Croatian coastguard, Slovene fishermen and Slovene tourist operators in the disputed Bay of Piran were reported. Much of June's good work was also undone in September, when Slovenia announced that it was going to declare an exclusive ecological zone in the Adriatic. As Croatia does not recognise Slovenia's proclaimed maritime boundary, it declared the ecological zone null and void. In December, some members of Slovenia's ruling coalition threatened to hold a referendum on Croatia's EU aspirations, which in the current climate would probably result in a Slovene veto of Croatian EU membership.

Slovenia also found itself embroiled in a dispute with Serbia over the future status of Kosovo. In October, President Drnovšek suggested that Kosovo be allowed independence, prompting Serbia to cancel Drnovšek's planned state visit to Belgrade. Compounding this problem was the suspicion in Belgrade that Ljubljana also favoured independence for Serbia's sister republic, Montenegro.

Outlook

Slovenia should continue to experience economic growth in 2006. The IMF forecasts GDP growth of 4.0 per cent and inflation of 2.4 per cent. Both figures suggest that Slovenia will be well placed to fulfil the economic criteria for the adoption of the euro by 2007.

The problem of Slovenia's border with Croatia was not resolved in 2005. Given Croatia's desire to complete its accession talks with the EU in 2007 – the EU has made it clear that candidate countries should sort out their international disputes before joining – it will be imperative for both sides to reach a compromise in 2006. Slovenia rejected an offer from Croatia, in October 2005, to seek international arbitration and the two sides have yet to reach a resolution framework.

The declining popularity of the Jansa government and President Drnovšek's tendency to pre-empt government policy may cause some jitters in the governing coalition. However, with elections not due until 2008, there is plenty of scope for Prime Minister Jansa to consolidate his grip.

Risk assessment

Economic	Good
Political	Stable
Regional stability	Satisfactory

COUNTRY PROFILE

Historical profile
In the thirteenth century, Slovenia became a hereditary possession of the House of Habsburg.
1867 The Slovenes fell under the jurisdiction of the Austrian Crown.
1918 After the downfall of the Austro-Hungarian Empire, Slovenia became a part of the new 'Kingdom of Serbs, Croats and Slovenes' (re-named Yugoslavia in 1929).
1941 Yugoslavia was divided between Germany, Italy, Hungary and Bulgaria.
1945 Following the end of the Second World War, Slovenia became a constituent republic of the Yugoslav Federation. Josip Broz Tito assumed power, and a Soviet-style constitution was adopted. The other republics were:
Bosnia-Hercegovina, Croatia, Macedonia, Montenegro and Serbia, and the two autonomous regions of Vojvodina and Kosovo.
1950-80s Constitutions adopted in 1953, 1963 and 1974 increased autonomy extended to the constituent republics.

KEY INDICATORS — Slovenia

	Unit	2000	2001	2002	2003	2004
Population	m	1.99	2.00	2.00	2.00	2.00
Gross domestic product (GDP)	US$bn	18.26	18.70	20.00	26.30	*32.18
GDP per capita	US$	9,128	9,390	10,005	14,084	16,447
GDP real growth	%	4.6	3.0	3.0	3.1	4.4
Inflation	%	8.9	9.4	7.1	5.6	3.6
Unemployment	%	12.2	11.8	11.7	11.3	–
Exports (fob) (goods)	US$m	8,807.9	9,341.9	10,380.0	12,738.0	15,817.8
Imports (fob) (goods)	US$m	9,946.9	9,963.9	10,850.0	13,812.0	16,862.1
Balance of trade	US$m	-1,138.9	-622.0	-572.0	-1,074.0	-1,044.3
Current account	US$m	-611.7	-66.4	-375.0	15.0	-200.0
Foreign debt	US$bn	6.2	6.7	9.2	7.9	
Total reserves minus gold	US$m	3,196.1	4,330.0	6,980.2	8,496.9	8,793.4
Foreign exchange	US$m	3,110.0	4,244.3	6,852.6	8,343.1	8,662.3
Foreign direct investment (FDI)	US$bn	0.1	0.3	1.9	–	–
Exchange rate	per US$	222.66	242.75	234.55	204.43	192.36

* estimated figure

Slovenia

The ruling Slovene Communists supported the Croats' demand for a confederal Yugoslavia during the 1960s and 1970s, although never to the point of provoking repression.
1986 Milan Kucan became the leader of the Slovene Communists.
1990 Kucan guided Slovenia towards independence following multi-party general elections, resulting in a six-party centre-right coalition, the Demokratska Opozicija Slovenije (DeMOS) (Democratic Opposition of Slovenia), under the leadership of Lozle Peterle.
1991 After a 10-day war against the Yugoslav army, Slovenia won independence.
1992 Slovenia was admitted to the UN. Following the collapse of the DeMOS government, Janez Drnovšek took over as interim prime minister.
In the elections, the Liberal Democrats emerged as the largest party and Janez Drnovšek became prime minister at the head of a five-party coalition. Milan Kucan was elected president.
1994 The Liberal Democrats merged with the Democratic Party and the Ecologists to create the Liberalna Demokracija Slovenije (LDS) (Liberal Democrats of Slovenia).
1996 After the general elections, the LDS and its former opponent, Slovenska Ljudska Stranka (SLS) (Slovenian People's Party) formed a coalition with the Demokratièna Stranka Upokojencev Slovenije (DeSUS) (Democratic Party of Slovenian Pensioners). Drnovšek was re-elected prime minister.
1997 Kucan was re-elected president for a second and last consecutive five-year term.
2000 Withdrawal of the SLS from the government coalition prompted its collapse. A centre-right government, composed of the SLS and Slovenski Krsèanski Demokrati (SKD) (Slovenian Christian Democratic Party), together with the Socialdemokratska Stranka Slovenije (SDSS) (Social Democratic Party of Slovenia) was formed. The general election was won by the LDS, led by the former prime minister, Janez Drnovšek, who formed a coalition government.
2001 Slovenia was named as one of eight countries likely to gain EU membership in 2004 at the European Council's Laeken summit.
2002 In November, NATO invited Slovenia to join the alliance by 2004 and in December, the EU confirmed Slovenia's accession also in 2004.
Prime Minister Janez Drnovšek won the presidential run-off. Anton Rop of the LDS, the senior coalition party, was elected prime minister with 63 votes for and 24 votes against (to be elected, Rop needed 46 votes from the members of parliament).
2003 In a March referendum, 89.6 per cent of Slovenes voted to join the EU and 66 per cent voted to join NATO.
2004 Slovenia joined NATO in March and entered the EU on 1 May. Slovenska Demokratska Stranka (SDS) (Slovenian Democratic Party) won the 3 October parliamentary elections and Janez Jansa was elected prime minister by parliament.
2005 Parliament ratified the EU constitution in February. A poll in September showed that a majority of Slovenes felt they had benefited from EU membership.

Political structure
Constitution
The Slovenian constitution was adopted in December 1991 and amended in 1997 and 2000.
Form of state
Parliamentary democratic republic
The executive
The president, who is elected by universal adult suffrage for a term of five years, is head of state and commander-in-chief of the armed forces. The president proposes a candidate for prime minister to the Skupšcina Slovenije (Assembly of Slovenia) after consultation with parliamentary groups. The assembly has the final power of appointment of the prime minister and the government.
National legislature
The Assembly of Slovenia is a bicameral legislature and consists of the Drzavni Zbor (National Assembly) and the Drzavni Svet (National Council).
The National Assembly is the principal legislative body and consists of 90 members elected for a four-year term. Through proportional representation, 88 members are elected, with two non-elected representatives of the country's Hungarian and Italian minorities.
The government is made up of members of the National Assembly, and it is answerable to that body.
The 40 members of the National Council sit for a five-year term. Twenty-two are directly elected and 18 appointed by an electoral college to represent various groups. The Council fulfils a mainly advisory role, but may veto decisions of the National Assembly and must approve the composition of any government.
Legal system
The legal system is based on the 1991 constitution.
The judiciary is structurally independent from the government, with the Constitutional Court empowered to determine the conformity of national legislation with the constitution. All civil and criminal cases are dealt with by eight basic and four higher courts, and the Supreme Court is the final court of appeal. Prosecutions are the responsibility of the Public Prosecutor and to safeguard defendants rights there is also a Public Attorney. The Justice Ministry is the administrative authority of the Slovenian judiciary.

Last elections
3 October 2004 (parliamentary); 13 June 2004 (European Parliament); 1 December 2002 (run-off presidential); November 2002 (presidential).
Results: Parliamentary: Slovenska Demokratska Stranka (SDS) (Slovenian Democratic Party) 29.1 per cent of the vote (29 seats out of 70); Liberalna Demokracija Slovenije (LDS) (Liberal Democracy of Slovenia) 22.8 per cent (23 seats); Zdruena Lista Socialnih Demokratov (ZLSD) (United List of Social Democrats) 10.2 per cent (10 seats); Nova Slovenija Krsanski Ljudska Stranka (Nsi) (New Slovenia Christian People's Party) (9.0 per cent) (nine seats); Slovenska Ljudska Stranka (SLS) (Slovenian People's Party) (6.8 per cent (seven seats); Slovenska Nacionalna Stranka (SNS) (Slovenian National Party) (6.3 per cent) (six seats); Demokratina Stranka Upokojencev Slovenije (DeSUS) (Democratic Party of Retired People of Slovenia) (4.0 per cent) (four seats).
European Parliament: Nova Slovenija Krščanski Ljudska Stranka (Nsi) (New Slovenia Christian People's Party) won 23.5 per cent of the vote (two seats out of seven), LDS 21.9 per cent (two), Demokratska Stranka Slovenije (DSS) (Democratic Party of Slovenia) 17.7 per cent (two) and Zdruzena Lista Socialnih Demokratov (ZLSD) (United List of Social-Democrats) 14.2 per cent (one); turnout 28.3 per cent.
Presidential run-off: the prime minister, Janez Drnovsek, won 56 per cent of the vote against 44 per cent for Barbara Brezigar; turnout was 64.4 per cent.
Next elections
2007 (presidential); 2008 (parliamentary).

Political parties
Ruling party
Coalition government led by Slovenská Demokratska Stranka (SDS) (Slovenian Democratic Party), and including Nova Slovenija Krsanski Ljudska Stranka (Nsi) (New Slovenia Christian People's Party) and Slovenska Ljudska Stranka (SLS) (Slovenian People's Party) (from Nov 2004)
Main opposition party
Socialdemokratska Stranka Slovenije (SDSS) (Social Democratic Party of Slovenia)

Population
2.00 million (2004)

Nations of the World: A Political, Economic and Business Handbook

Ethnic make-up
Around 88 per cent of the population are Slovenes, with small numbers of ethnic Serbs, Croats, Muslims, Albanians, Hungarians, Italians and Germans. Only the Italian and Hungarian communities are officially recognised minorities.

Religions
Roman Catholic (71 per cent), Lutheran (1 per cent), Islam (1 per cent).

Education
Unlike other parts of the former Yugoslavia, where adult illiteracy remains a major socioeconomic problem, Slovenia has always had a relatively highly educated society. Adult illiteracy is therefore virtually non-existent.

Primary and initial secondary schooling are combined in one school for nine-years. At aged 15 students are channelled onto one of three paths, general, technical or vocational. General and technical education lasts for four years, while vocational courses last for either two or three years.

As a critical determinant of future socioeconomic development, higher education experienced significant growth during the 1990s. Unesco estimates total gross enrolment rates for tertiary education at over 60 per cent. Law, business and economics remain popular courses, while further education institutions find it difficult to attract students to technical courses, resulting in a lack of skills in certain sectors of the workforce.

Literacy rate: 99.7 per cent, adult rate (2003)
Compulsory years: 6 to 15
Enrolment rate: 98 per cent gross primary enrolment, 92 per cent gross secondary enrolment; of relevant age groups (including repeaters) (World Bank).
Pupils per teacher: 12 in primary schools.

Health
Formerly entirely state controlled and funded, healthcare is now a growing private sector activity so that Slovenia is comparable with the EU for healthcare provision. In the long-term though, more funds will have to be directed towards it due to its ageing population. Healthcare provisions also includes a well-developed network of medicinal spas for all types of ailments. Lower healthcare charges attract paying customers from neighbouring countries.

Private health insurance is increasing rapidly and the government has encouraged additional forms of health insurance, and the preparation of national preventative programmes, that should reduce dependency on the state and bolster private sector provision.

HIV prevalence: 0.1 per cent aged 15–49 in 2003 (World Bank)
Life expectancy: 76.1 years (World Bank)
Fertility rate/Maternal mortality rate: 1.2 births per woman (World Bank)
Birth rate/Death rate: Nine births per 1,000 population; 10 deaths per 1,000 population (2003).
Infant mortality rate: 4.0 per 1,000 live births (World Bank)

Welfare
The Pension and Disability Act, which significantly reformed the pension system, became effective from 2000 and consists of a reformed pay-as-you-go scheme, with a supplementary fund as part of waged contracts. The minimum age of retirement for women has gradually risen and the amount of full pensions reduced relative to the wage rate.

The government ensured better legal protection for workers by defining their rights at the minimum level, and strengthened investment in the area of labour, family and social welfare.

Main cities
Ljubljana (capital, estimated population 258,000 in 2003), Maribor (92,400), Celje (37,300), Kranj (35,200).

Languages spoken
The main minority languages are Albanian, Hungarian and Italian, but Hungarian and Italian are officially recognised. Serbian, Croatian, German, English and French are also spoken.

Regional identities and dialects remain very strong.

Official language/s
Slovene

Media
Press
Slovenia has a well-developed print sector. Almost uniquely in former Yugoslavia, the Slovene print media is now officially uncensored . More recently, a number of émigré-financed newspapers, such as *Republika*, have become strongly critical of the government. Mainstream publishing has experienced major economic difficulties, mainly because of a small domestic market and the high unit price of books published locally.

Dailies: The main publications include*Delo* (attracting 48 per cent newspaper adspend) and *Slovenske Novice*, the only national daily tabloid. Some youth publications, such as *Mladina*, have played an important political role in recent years. Other dailies include *Dnevnik*, *Vecer*, *Vestnik*, *Primorske Novice* and *Slovenec*.

Weeklies: The variety includes *Druzina* on religious topics, *Antena* mainly targetting young people, *Dolenjski* provides general information and local news. Other weeklies providing general information include *Gorenjski Glas*, *Jana*, *Kmecki Glas*, *Mladina*, *Nedeliski Dnevnik*, *Primorske Novice*, *7dni* and *Vestnik Murska Sobota*. *Stop* caters specifically to media information. The Ljubljana International Press Centre publishes *In* every Friday in Slovenian and English.

Business: There are several English-language business publications, including *Slovenian Business Report*, *Flaneur* (bi-monthly politics and economy) and *MM Slovenia* (marketing).

Periodicals: The free monthly newspaper, *Delnicar*, has the highest circulation.

Broadcasting
During the tourist season, there are broadcasts in German, English and Italian each day covering: news, traffic news, weather and tourist directions.

Radio: There are 55 commercial radio stations. The state-owned national radio station remains the market leader with its second channel (VAL 202).

Television: Formerly a state-controlled monopoly, Radio Televizija Slovenija (RTV) (Radio Television Slovenia), is the main broadcaster, operating two channels, Slovenia 1 and 2.

Austrian, Italian and Hungarian broadcasts are easily available in Slovenia. VCR ownership and use is well developed, and imports of foreign TV, film and video material is also growing rapidly.

Altogether there are seven commercial TV stations, but RTV is the only national TV station, besides Pop TV.

Advertising
Advertising has grown rapidly since the 1990s in both the broadcasting and print media which has enabled the print media to grow, despite a slight fall in circulation.

Economy
Slovenia was by far the most economically advanced and developed of the six Yugoslav republics and has continued to experience economic growth since 1993. Privatisation of the economy and structural reforms have improved the business environment and allowed for greater foreign participation in Slovenia's economy, which is helping to lower unemployment. In March 2004, Slovenia became the first EU transition country to graduate from borrower status to donor partner at the World Bank.

Between 2004 and 2006, the 10 EU accession countries will receive funding of up to eur25.1 billion (US$28.2 billion), which will include money for agriculture, infrastructure modernisation and regional aid. Slovenia will receive eur892.8 million (US$1.0 billion). With the accession countries altogether expected to pay into the EU budget approximately eur14.8 billion

(US$16.6 billion) during the first three years of membership, the total net cost of EU enlargement will be eur10.3 billion (US$11.5 billion). If enlargement proves to be more costly during 2004 and 2006, the EU could spend an extra eur15.7 billion (US$17.6 billion).

External trade
Slovenia has shifted emphasis to EU markets.
Imports
Main Imports are machinery and transport equipment, manufactured goods, chemicals, fuels and lubricants and food.
Main sources: Germany (20.1 per cent total, 2004), Italy (17 per cent), Austria (14.1 per cent), France (10.4 per cent)
Exports
The principal exports are manufactured goods, machinery and transport equipment, chemicals and food.
Main destinations: Germany (18.4 per cent total, 2004), Austria (11.4 per cent), Italy (11.1 per cent), Croatia (7.6 per cent), France (7.5 per cent), Bosnia and Herzegovina (4.6 per cent)

Agriculture
Farming
Agriculture accounts for around 2.5 per cent of GDP and employs six per cent of the workforce.

Farming is generally carried out on smallholdings of less than 25 hectares (ha). There are also a number of large farms and co-operatives which produce most food exports as well as food consumed domestically. Agricultural production fell substantially after independence, but recovered quickly and is above pre-independence levels.

The restoration of farming land and forests to claimants continues, although agricultural development is still being held up. Several issues pertaining to rural development, including aid to underdeveloped regions and environmental programmes, are on the political agenda. When Slovenia joined the EU in 2004, it became eligible for EU subsidies and rural development funds through the Common Agricultural Policy (CAP), but, like the other new accession countries, Slovenia will only get the full amount by 2013. This follows the EU decision to introduce CAP support funds gradually over a 10-year period.

During its transitional entry stage, Slovenia has decided to implement the reform of the CAP on 1 January 2007. The reform was introduced throughout most of the EU on 1 January 2005, when subsidies on farm output, which tended to benefit large farms and encourage overproduction, were replaced by single farm payments, not conditional on production. The change is expected to reward farmers that provide and maintain a healthy environment, food safety and animal welfare standards. The changes are also intended to encourage market conscious production and cut the cost of CAP to the EU taxpayer. Slovenia's introduction of the new CAP before its fellow accession countries will align it with most of Europe and lessen disruption during the transition period imposed as part of the EU entry requirements.

Crop production in 2004 included: 586,278 tonnes (t) cereals in total, 146,829t wheat, 357,6210t maize, 171,475t potatoes, 59,729t barley, 1,500t hops, 1,984t pulses, 3,694t treenuts, 134,792t grapes, 5,431t tomatoes, 545t oilcrops, 213,092t sugar beets, 230,000t apples, 2,145t olives, 6,140t chillies & peppers, 410,640t fruit in total, 63,6820t vegetables in total. Livestock production included: 182,028t meat in total, 46,900t beef, 71,300t pig meat, 950t lamb, 62,400t poultry, 20,000t eggs, 651,000t milk, 2,350t honey, 5,789t cattle hides.

Fishing
The annual commercial catch of fish amounts to between 1,815 and 2,270 tonnes. This excludes the catches of private fishermen estimated between 182 and 272 tonnes. Another 136 tonnes of fish is obtained by mariculture. About 454 tonnes of freshwater fish is bred on fish farms. Slovenia imports about 7,258 tonnes of fish annually.

Slovenia's legislation on fisheries is largely oriented towards Europe, although more resources will be necessary to meet the requirements of the EU's Common Fisheries Policy (CFP). Slovenia has a fisheries agreement with Croatia and is also a member of the General Fisheries Commission for the Mediterranean.

Forestry
Slovenia has a significant forestry sector. Forest cover is estimated at 1.1 million hectares (ha). The sector has a long tradition of sustainable management and less than a third of the forest area is publicly owned. Only a small area of forest is available for wood supply. Forestry forms the basis of a number of key industrial sectors, notably furniture making, paper, pulp and construction materials. The industry includes both large and small saw mills, which rely on the domestic supply of raw materials. Paper is mainly exported to European countries. Per capita consumption of forest products remains around the European average.

Exports of forest material in 2004 amounted to US$624.0 million, while imports amounted to US$540.0 million. Production in 2004 included 2,551,000 cubic metres (cum) roundwood, 1,826,000cum industrial roundwood, 461,000cum sawnwood, 1,372,000cum sawlogs and veneers, 283,000cum pulpwood, 474,000cum wood-based panels, 725,000cum woodfuel.

Industry and manufacturing
Manufacturing accounts for 24 per cent of GDP and industry overall for 32 per cent. The manufacture of capital goods has traditionally been the mainstay of Slovenia's industry, with iron and steel, metal working and machine-building accounting for a third of total manufactured added value. With intermediate goods accounting for 15 per cent and consumer goods for 55 per cent of manufactured added value, Slovenia has all the characteristics of an advanced industrial economy. Slovenia is anxious to boost its exports to the EU. This strategic redirection of its industrial exports will require a complete restructuring of its entire industrial sector. The major structural problems are low levels of new investment, over-manning, technological backwardness and too many industrial enterprises for what is now a small domestic market with limited export potential. The newer and rising consumer goods industries, such as electrical products, are expected to become more capital intensive in order to compete internationally. High-technology industries based on computing and high added-value have yet to make a significant appearance.

Tourism
Tourism is a major industry, offering coastal holidays, skiing, golf and other sports, spa treatment and river trips. It employs some 16,000 people. Slovenia can provide around 80,000 beds in various accommodation facilities (hotels, motels, tourist villages, health-resorts, boarding-houses) all over the country. In 2004, the sector recorded its best year since before independence in 1991. There were 2,341,281 arrivals, an increase of 4.28 per cent over 2003, and an increasing number of overnight stays. Tourism is expected to contribute 2.9 per cent to GDP in 2005.

Hydrocarbons
Slovenia has oil reserves of less than 50 million barrels, with production being less than 500 barrels per day (bpd). Slovenia relies almost entirely on imports of refined oil to meet consumption levels. The sole refinery was closed in 1999 as it became uneconomical to operate. Downstream operations dominate the sector.

Slovenia has negligible reserves of natural gas and relies entirely on imports of around 1 billion cubic metres annually. Algeria and Russia are the sole suppliers of natural gas to Slovenia. Gazprom, the Russian gas company, provides 60 per

cent of Slovenia's imports. The state-owned natural gas company, Geoplin, is responsible for the sale of gas within the country as well as transit to Croatia. Natural gas provides for around 12 per cent of the country's total energy needs.
Slovenia has proven coal reserves, mainly lignite found in the Saleška Valley near Velenje, and sub-bituminous coal in several other parts of the country. Exploitable reserves at Velenje amount to 227 million tonnes, and production could be sustained for 60 years. The sub-bituminous reserves are of low quality with high ash and sulphur content. Coal provides for one-quarter of the country's energy needs.

Energy
Slovenia has installed electricity capacity of 2.65GW, generated by thermal, hydropower and nuclear stations. The sole nuclear plant, sited at Krško, is jointly-owned with Croatia. Slovenia is a net exporter of electricity.

Financial markets
Stock exchange
The Ljubljanska Borza (LJSE) (Ljubljana Stock Exchange) opened in 1989.
The main LJSE index, the SB120, is dominated by Krka and Lek, the country's two large pharmaceutical firms.

Banking and insurance
Slovenia has a well-developed banking sector. The central bank and the finance ministry are responsible for implementing EU banking directives.
Nova Ljubljanska Banka (NLB) and Nova Kreditna Banka Maribor, both state-owned, dominate the sector, together holding some 40 per cent of banking assets. The merger of the Abanka and Banka Vipa in December 2002 created a new bank, Abanka Vipa, which now has a major slice of the Slovenian banking sector.
Foreign banks own around 30 per cent of the banking sector. Approximately 96 per cent of SKB Banka was sold to France's Société Générale and a 34 per cent stake in NLB was sold to Belgium's KBC Bank.
Central bank
Banka Slovenije (BSI) (Bank of Slovenia)
Main financial centre
Ljubljana

Time
GMT plus one hour (GMT plus two hours from late March to late September)

Geography
An Alpine country dominated by the Julian Alps in the north-west, Slovenia has an area of 20,251 square km. It is bordered by Italy to the west, Austria to the north, Hungary to the east and Croatia to the south. There is a 46km coastal strip on the Adriatic Sea, around the Istrian port of Koper. Slovenia has half of its territory covered in forests, including some remnants of primeval forests, particularly around Kocevje in the south.
The country is divided into four main geographic regions: Gorenjska (Julian Alps), Zagorska (Danubian Plain), Primorska (Adriatic coastline and Littoral) and Dorenjska (Ljubljana Basin and Dinaric Mountains).

Climate
Slovenia has an Alpine climate in the main, with continental and Mediterranean influences to the north-east and south-west respectively. The annual median temperature at Ljubljana is 9.5 degrees Celsius (C). The warmest month is July, with an average temperature of 22.5 degrees C; the coldest is January, with an average temperature of -3.4 degrees C. Summer and winter temperature averages are 21 and 0 degrees C respectively. Precipitation is heavy, with an annual average rainfall of 1,407mm at Ljubljana. The lower lying areas subject to non-Alpine climatic influences are drier and warmer than the rest of the country.
The dominance of Alpine climatic conditions means that changes in local weather can be very sudden. In the Julian Alps, violent storms and floods are often a major problem. Winter snowfall has been limited in recent years, thereby adversely affecting tourism. Air pollution has also changed the weather in a number of places, notably in the Ljubljana Basin.

Dress codes
Formal dress is the norm for business and social meetings in Slovenia. Business visitors should be smartly dressed.

Entry requirements
Passports
Passport valid for duration of stay is required by all except nationals of EU countries with a valid national ID card and nationals of Croatia and Hungary with a valid national ID card.
Visa
Required by all, with some exceptions. See www.sigov.si/mzz/eng/index.html and follow path to locate visitor's country of origin, for notification of need for visa. If required, see www.gov.si/mzz/ang/useful_info/ visa_info.html for full details.
Currency advice/regulations
The import and export of local currency is limited to the equivalent of T500,000. The import and export of foreign currency is unrestricted, although amounts in excess to the equivalent of T3,000,000 should be declared, with a bank certificate.
Travellers cheques are widely accepted. To avoid additional exchange rate charges, visitors are advised to take travellers cheques in euros, US dollars or pounds sterling.

Health (for visitors)
There are no special requirements.

Credit cards
American Express, Mastercard, Eurocard and Visa are accepted. Credit cards can be used to get cash advances from banks.

Public holidays
Fixed dates
1–2 Jan (New Year), 8 Feb (Preseren/Culture Day), 27 Apr (Resistance Day), 1–2 May (Labour Day), 25 Jun (National Day), 15 Aug (Assumption Day), 31 Oct (Reformation Day), 1 Nov (All Saints' Day), 25 Dec (Christmas Day), 26 Dec (Independence Day).
Variable dates
Easter Monday, Pentecost.

Working hours
A legacy of the Yugoslav period, service in the state sector can be slow, notably in shops and banks. The Slovene government bureaucracy is cumbersome and slow.
Banking
Mon–Fri: 0730–1800; Sat: 0730–1200.
Business
Mon–Fri: 0800–1600.
Government
Mon–Fri: 0800–1600.
Shops
Mon–Fri: 0700–1900 or 0800–2000; some shops also open Sat: 0800–1300/1500, Sun: 0800–1200.

Telecommunications
Mobile phones
GSM 900 and 1800 services available throughout most of the country.

Electricity supply
220V AC. Round two-pin plugs are used.

Weights and measures
Metric system

Social customs/useful tips
For business meetings, when appointments are made, visitors should be punctual. Business cards are essential. Slovenia has a reputation for being efficient and reliable. Executives will generally have a good knowledge of German, English and sometimes Italian. There is a well-developed network of local agents, advisers, consultants and lawyers willing to act for foreign companies.
Slovenians are a rather reserved people with a tendency towards formality. As in Austria and Germany, titles are widely used. Informality on the part of a foreigner is not considered acceptable. It is not unusual for Slovenians to prefer to hold business discussions over lunch. Athough smoking is generally accepted, it

Slovenia

is restricted in many public places and buildings.
Visitors should carry some form of identity at all times.

Security
Slovenia has a low crime rate. Sometimes tourists are the targets of pickpockets and purse-snatchers, especially on the trains.

Getting there
Air
National airline: Adria Airways
International airport/s: Ljubljana (LJU), 27km from city centre; Maribor (MX), 12km from city.
Airport tax: None
Surface
Road: Most frontier posts are open for road traffic from Italy, Austria, Hungary and Croatia.
Rail: Connections are available from major Western and Eastern European cities. Eurocity Mimara train connects Zagreb, Ljubljana, Munich and Leipzig. Direct trains to Slovenia are available from Italy (Rome, Milan, Venice and Trieste), Austria (Vienna and Villach) and Hungary (Budapest). Transport for cars may be available on some routes.
Water: The Prince of Venice catamaran runs regular scheduled trips between Venice and Izola.
Main port/s: Koper, Izola, Piran and Portoroz.

Getting about
National transport
Air: Domestic airports are situated at Maribor (MBX) in eastern Slovenia, with Potoroz (POW) on the Adriatic coast. There are regular services from the capital, Ljubljana.
Road: There is a good network of roads in Slovenia, many of which are in good condition. The main arterial road goes south-west to north-east from Sezana/Koper, near Italy, to Ljubljana, Celje and Maribor, near the border with Austria and Hungary. It can be congested. The roads are clearly signposted, with rest and food facilities. The following are toll motorways: Ljubljana-Razdrto, Arja vas-Hoce and Ljubljana-Kranj.
Buses: Good nationwide services operated by a number of companies.
Rail: There are good rail connections and rail travel is inexpensive.
City transport
Taxis: Taxis are metered. Available in Ljubljana and other major cities, but are relatively expensive. A tip is not expected. Foreigners are likely to be overcharged, especially from Ljubljana airport to the centre of Ljubljana; the airport bus service is therefore a good alternative.
Buses, trams & metro: Most city centres are served by trams, and the suburbs by buses. The service is generally cheap and regular. Fares can be paid in cash, but tokens are cheaper. Tokens for buses can be purchased on newspaper stands, at post offices and in supermarkets.
Car hire
The major car hire companies operate in Slovenia, although rates can be very high. The AMZS provides good quality emergency roadside service (call 987).
Speed limits are 130kph (81mph) on motorways, 90kph (56mph) on roads outside residential areas and 50kph (31mph) in cities and residential areas. Safety belts are compulsory and school buses must not be overtaken.
Full national driving licences are required. Traffic in Ljubljana is now very congested. Finding parking spaces in the centre of the city is thus very difficult. Use of a car in the city on weekdays is not advisable. Third party insurance for foreigners is compulsory.

BUSINESS DIRECTORY
The addresses listed below are a selection only. While World of Information makes every endeavour to check these addresses, we cannot guarantee that changes have not been made, especially to telephone numbers and area codes. We would welcome any corrections.

Telephone area codes
The international direct dialling code (IDD) for Slovenia is +386, followed by area code and subscriber's number:

Celje	3	Murska Sobota	02
Koper	5	Nova Gorica	5
Kranj	4	Novo Mesto	7
Krsko	7	Postojna	5
Ljubljana	1	Ravne	2
Maribor	2	Trbovlje	3

Useful telephone numbers
Police	92
Fire brigade	93
First aid, ambulance	94
Road assistance (AMZS automobile association)	987
General information	981
Telephone information	988

Chambers of Commerce
American Chamber of Commerce in Slovenia, 55 Pod Hribom, 1000 Ljubljana (tel: 581-6285; fax: 581-6111; e-mail: office@am-cham.si).

Koper Chamber of Commerce and Industry, 2 Ferrarska, 6000 Koper (tel: 639-5311; fax: 639-5316; e-mail: kozlovic@hg.gzs.si).

Ljubljana Chamber of Commerce and Industry, 9 Dimiceva, 1504 Ljubljana (tel: 230-1133; fax: 431-3040; e-mail: samardzija@hg.gzs.si).

Maribor Chamber of Commerce and Industry, 24 Talcev, 2000 Maribor (tel: 220-8700; fax: 252-2283; e-mail: breznik@hg.gzs.si).

Northern Primorska Chamber of Commerce and Industry, 3 Trg Edvarda Kardelja, 5000 Nova Gorica (tel: 330-6030; fax: 330-6031; e-mail: velikonja@hg.gzs.si).

Novo Mesto Chamber of Commerce and Industry, 5 Novi Trg, 8000 Novo Mesto (tel: 332-2182; fax: 332-2187; e-mail: goles@hg.gzs.si).

Postojna Chamber of Commerce and Industry, Cankarjeva 6, 6230 Postojna (tel: 720-0111; fax: 726-5344; e-mail: tiselj@hg.gzs.si).

Slovenia Chamber of Commerce and Industry, 13 Dimiceva, 1504 Ljubljana (tel: 589-8000; fax: 589-8100; e-mail: infolink@gzs.si).

Banking
Abanka Vipa dd, Slovenska 58, 1517 Ljubljana (tel: 471-8100; fax: 432-5165; e-mail: info@abanka.si; internet site: http://www.abanka.si/).

Bank Austria dd, Smartinska 140, 1000 Ljubljana (tel: 587-6600; fax: 587-6684; e-mail: info@si.bacai.com).

Banka Celje dd, Vodnikova 2, 3000 Celje (tel: 543-1000 fax: 548-3511; e-mail: info@banka-celje.si).

Banka Koper, Pristaniska 14, 6502 Koper (tel: 665-1100; fax: 639-7842; e-mail: infor@banka-koper.si; internet site: http://www.banka-koper.si).

Factor Banka dd, Tivolska 48, 1000 Ljubljana (tel: 230-6600; fax: 230-7760; e-mail: info@factorb.si).

Gorenjska Banka dd, Bleiweisova 1, 4000 Kranj (tel: 208-4000; fax: 202-1503; e-mail: info@gbkr.si)..

Hypo-Alpe-Adria Bank dd, Trv Osvobodine fronte 12, 1000 Ljubljana (tel: 300-4400; fax: 300-4401; e-mail: hypo-banka@hypo.si).

Koroska Banka dd, Glavni trg 30, 2380 Slovenj Gradec (tel: 884-9111; fax: 884-2382).

Krekova Banka, Slomskov trg 18, 2000 Maribor (tel: 229-3100; fax: 252-2261; e-mail: info@krekova-banka.si).

Nova Kreditna Banka Maribor, Vita Kraigherja 4, 2505 Maribor (tel: 229-2290; fax: 252-4333, 252-4371; e-mail: info@nkbm.si).

Nova Ljubljanska Banka dd, Trg Republike 2, 1520 Ljubljana (tel: 425-0155; fax: 252-2422; e-mail: info@nlb.si).

Postna Banka Slovenije dd, Vita Kraigherja 5, 2000 Maribor (tel:

228-8200; fax: 228-8210; e-mail: info@pbs.si).

Probanka dd, Gosposka ulica 23, 2000 Maribor (tel: 252-0500; fax: 252-5882; e-mail: info@probanka.si).

SKB Banka dd, Ajdovscina 4, 1513 Ljubljana (tel: 433-213; fax: 231-4549: e-mail: info@skb.si).

Slovenska Investicijska Banka dd, Copova 38, 1000 Ljubljana (tel: 242-0300; fax: 242-0521; e-mail: sib@si-banka.si).

Slovenska Zadruzna Kmetijska Banka dd, Kolodvorska 9, 1000 Ljubljani (tel: 472-7100; fax: 472-7405); e-mail: info@szkbanka.si).

Volksbank-Ljudska Banka dd, Dunajska 128 a, 1101 Ljubljana (tel: 530-7400; fax: 520-7555; e-mail: banka@volksbank.si).

Central bank
Banka Slovenije, Slovenska 35, 1505 Ljubljana (tel: 471-9000; fax: 251-5516; e-mail: bsl@bsi.si).

Travel information
National tourist organisation offices
Slovenska Turisticna Organizacija (Slovenian Tourist Organisation), WTC, Dunajska 156, 1001 Ljubljana (tel: 589-1840; fax: 589-1841; e-mail: info@slovenia-tourism.si; internet: http://www.slovenia-tourism.si).

Ministries
Ministry of Agriculture, Forestry and Food, Dunajska 52, 1000 Ljubljana (tel: 478-9000; fax: 478-9021; e-mail: janez.vertacnik@gov.si).

Ministry of Culture, Cankarjeva 5, 1000 Ljubljana (tel: 478-5900; fax: 478-5901; e-mail: mkinfo@gov.si).

Ministry of Defence, Kardeljeva ploscad 25, 1000 Ljubljana (tel:471-2211; fax: 131-8164; e-mail: darko.lubi@pub.mo-rs.si).

Ministry of the Economy, Kotnikova 5, 1000 Ljubljana (tel: 478-3600; fax: 478-3522; e-mail: tatjana.zabasu@gov.si).

Ministry of Education, Science and Sport, Zupanèièeva 6, 1000 Ljubljana (tel: 478-5437; fax: 478-5669; e-mail: info@mss.edus.si).

Ministry of Environment and Spatial Planning, Dunajska 48, 1000 Ljubljana (tel: 478-7400; fax: 478-7422; e-mail: info.mop@gov.si).

Ministry of Finance, Zupanèièeva 3, 1502 Ljubljana (tel: 478-5211; fax: 478-5655; e-mail: tilen.majnardi@mf-rs.si).

Ministry of Foreign Affairs, Presernova 25, 1000 Ljubljana (tel: 478-2000; fax: 478-2340; e-mail: info.mzz@gov.si).

Ministry of Health, Stefanova 5, 1000 Ljubljana (tel: 478-6001; fax: 478-6058; e-mail: ministrstvo.zdravsto@gov.si).

Ministry of the Information Society, Langusova 4, 1000 Ljubljana (tel: 478-8223; fax: 478-8142; e-mail: mid@gov.si).

Ministry of the Interior, Stefanova 2, 1000 Ljubljana (tel: 472-5111; fax: 251-4330;e-mail: jelka.smreka@mnz.si).

Ministry of Justice, Zupanèièeva 3, 1000 Ljubljana (tel: 478-5211; fax: 251-0200; e-mail: stojan.klancar@gov.si).

Ministry of Labour, Family and Social Affairs, Kotnikova 5, 1000 Ljubljana (tel: 478-3450; fax: 478-3456; e-mail: zmaga.grah@gov.si).

Ministry of Transport, Langusova 4, 1000 Ljubljana (tel: 478-8000; fax: 478-8139; e-mail: mpz.info@gov.si).

Office for European Affairs, Subièeva 11, 1000 Ljubljana (tel: 478-24-47; fax: 478-2310; e-mail: svez@gov.si).

President's Office, Erjavceva 17, 1000 Ljubljana (tel: 478-1205; fax: 478-1357).

Prime Minister's Office, Gregorèièeva 20, 1000 Ljubljana (tel: 478-1000; fax: 478-1607).

Other useful addresses
Agency of the Republic of Slovenia for Restructuring and Privatisation, Kotnikova Ulica 28, 1000 Ljubljana (tel: 131-2122; fax: 131-6011).

British Embassy, Fourth Floor, Trg Republike 3, 1000 Ljubljana (tel: 200-3910; fax: 425-0174; e-mail: info@british-embassy.si).

Government Office for European Affairs, Subiceva 11, 1000 Ljubljana (tel: 478-2228; fax: 478-2310).

Government of the Republic of Slovenia, Gregorciceva 20, 1000 Ljubljana (tel: 478-1100; fax: 478-1607).

Government PR and Media Office, Slovenska 29, 1000 Ljubljana (tel: 478-2629; fax: 251-2312).

Institute for Macroeconomic Analysis and Development, Gregorciceva 25, 1000 Ljubljana (tel: 478-2112; fax: 478-2070).

Ljubljana Stock Exchange, Trg Republike 3, 1000 Ljubljana (tel: 477-5500; fax: 477-5507, 477-5508).

Slovenian Embassy (USA), 1525 New Hampshire Avenue, NW, Washington DC 20036 (202-667-5363; fax: 202-667-4563; e-mail: slovenia@embassy.org).

Small Business Development Centre, Dunajska 156, 1001 Ljubljana (tel: 189-1870; fax: 188-1178).

Statistical Office of the Republic of Slovenia, Vozarski Pot 12, 1000 Ljubljana (tel: 241-5300; fax: 241-5344).

Trade and Investment Promotion Office (TIPO), Kotnikova 28, 1000 Ljubljana (tel: 478-3557; fax: 478-3599; e-mail: tipo@gov.si; internet site: http://www.investslovenia.org).

Internet sites
Government PR and Media Office: http://www.uvi.si/eng/service/addresses/index.html

The Republic of Slovenia website: http://www.sigov.si

Solomon Islands

COUNTRY PROFILE

Historical profile
The Solomon Islands were settled between 2,000–3,000 BC by Austronesians, Neolithic people from south-east Asia.
1568 The Spanish explorer, Álvaro de Mendaña, first visited the islands. The islands were named after King Solomon as Mendana hoped that the islands were rich with gold.
The islands were left alone until the mid-nineteenth century when whaling ships stopped off for supplies.
1893 The central islands became a British protectorate.
1899 In the Tripartite Treaty; Britain gained control of the whole of the Solomon Islands in exchange for withdrawing its claim to Samoa.
1942–45 During the Second World War, Japanese occupied the islands and US troops fought one of the fiercest battles on Guadalcanal.
1945 Britain resumed the administration of the islands.
1946 An independence movement was founded to resist British rule.
1976 Self-government was granted.
1978 The Solomon Islands became fully independent.
1997 In the general election Bartholomew Ulufa'alu (a Mataita) won.
1999 Ethnic violence broke out on Guadalcanal as a native's militia, the Isatabu Freedom Movement (IFM), tried to evict thousands of immigrant Mataitan. The Malaita Eagles Force (MEF) militia seized control of the capital, Honiara, claiming it was protecting Malaitan interests.
2000 Fighting broke out between the IFM and MEF, which seized the parliament. Prime Minister Ulufa'alu was forced to resign. The violence resulted in the breakdown in civil order with security and police forces often siding with one faction or another. In October, the IFM and MEF signed *The Townsville Peace Agreement* in Australia.
2001 The murder of the IFM rebel leader threatened the peace agreement. In parliamentary elections no party achieved overall majority. Sir Allan Kemakeza, of the People's Alliance Party (PAP), was elected prime minister by the new 50-member parliament.
2002 Law and order worsened and the economy began to collapse.
2003 Faced with continuing violence, the Governer General formally requested international assistance. The government endorsed the request for an international peace-keeping force. The force – Regional Assistance Mission of the Solomon Islands (RAMSI) – led by Australia, arrived in July. In response Harold Keke announced a cease-fire of his IFM forces in the west of the island of Guadalcanal; many viewed him as a bandit warlord, particularly after he ordered the razing of two villages. As part of RAMSI, 300 police officers were deployed. Keke surrendered to RAMSI forces. With peace restored RAMSI was scaled down.
2004 On 7 July, Nathaniel Waena was sworn in as governor general. A constitution for a new federal system of government was drafted.
2005 In July, the EU signed an agreement to provide US$13 million in aid. Keke was sentenced to life imprisonment for murder.

Political structure
Constitution
The Crown is represented by a governor general appointed by the British monarch on the recommendation of parliament. There are nine administrative areas each administered by elected provincial assemblies, and the tenth, Honiara, is administered by a town council.
A draft constitution for a new federal system of government will be considered in 2005.
Form of state
Independent democracy, with British monarch as Head of State
The executive
Executive power rests with the prime minister and the cabinet of ministers he appoints.
National legislature
The unicameral National Parliament consists of 50 members, including the prime minister and his cabinet of 18 ministers. Parliament elects the prime minister from its membership.
Last elections
December 2001 (parliamentary)
Results: Parliamentary: PAP 20 seats; Association of Independent Members (AIM) 13 seats; SIAC (includes Solomon Islands Liberal Party) 12 seats.
Next elections
By December 2005 (parliamentary)

Political parties
Ruling party
People's Alliance Party (PAP)
Main opposition party
Association of Independent Members (AIM)

KEY FACTS

Official name: Solomon Islands

Head of State: Queen Elizabeth II, represented by Governor General Nathaniel Waena (took office 7 Jul 2004)

Head of government: Prime Minister Sir Allan Kemakeza (PAP) (elected by parliament 2001)

Ruling party: People's Alliance Party (PAP)

Area: 27,556 square km – Guadalcanal: 5,302 square km

Population: 524,000 (2004)

Capital: Honiara (on Guadalcanal)

Official language: English

Currency: Solomon Islands dollar (SI$) = 100 cents

Exchange rate: SI$7.30 per US$ (Oct 2005)

GDP per capita: US$464 (2004)

GDP real growth: 6.00% (2004)

Labour force: 233,000 (2004)

Inflation: 6.80% (2004)

Balance of trade: -US$35.00 million (2003)

Foreign debt: US$137.00 million (2003)

Visitor numbers: 4,000 (Jan–Aug 2003)

Nations of the World: A Political, Economic and Business Handbook

Political situation
It was a year of picking up the pieces and trying to restore a degree of normality to the people of the Solomon Islands in 2004, as foreign troops, as requested by the government, had imposed peace allowing the state to take up their responsibilities again. Overseas donors, Australia and New Zealand in particular, provided some urgently needed funds to kick-start the economy; they also provided personnel to fill the voids left after the civil inrest. The roots of the troubles lay in the migration of some 20,000 poor workers from the Malaita island to urban areas and tribal lands on the neighbouring island of Guadalcanal thereby setting up ethnic tensions with the local Gwale people. It took four years before the violence was suppressed and the rule of law returned. However, academics have warned that sustained long-term progress cannot work without the underlying problems of land reform being addressed. The poverty and unemployment has to be overcome before a settled peace can be guaranteed in the Solomon Islands.

The improved political stability allowed the economy to grow by 6 per cent in 2004 and could be sustained at 3 per cent in the short-term as palm oil production and gold mining activities start up again.

The government has also made political changes to mitigate ethnic tensions, although the most far-reaching legislation, for a federal government has, by mid-2005, yet to be ratified. General elections are scheduled for the end of 2005 when the implications of federalism may form the chief topic of debate as the country assesses its recent history.

Population
524,000 (2004)

Ethnic make-up
About 93 per cent Melanesian, 4 per cent Polynesian, 1.5 per cent Micronesian, European, Chinese and others. Many of the inhabitants of Western and Choiseul Provinces in Malaita are from Papua New Guinea. Ethnic disputes have simmered since the end of the Second World War, as Malaitans have migrated to Guadalcanal for work.

Religions
Anglican (45 per cent), Roman Catholic (18 per cent), other Protestants (33 per cent). There are some native religions, especially on Malaita.

Education
Primary education last for six years. Lower secondary schooling lasts for three years and finishes at aged 15. Upper secondary school lasts for two years and is completed in a one-year sixth form. Students who have completed these years may attend a one-year's foundation programme to enter the University of the South Pacific; or enrol in a college of higher education. The Solomon Islands has one of the lowest literacy rates in the world and the government intends to tackle this with the aid that has been forthcoming since 2003 so that by January 2005 free education was offered to all primary school aged children.

Literacy rate: 64 per cent, adult rate (2003).
Compulsory years: Six to 15
Enrolment rate: 104 per cent boys, 90 per cent girls: gross primary enrolment (including repeaters); 21 per cent boys, 1 per cent girls: gross secondary enrolment (Unicef 2004).

Health
The Solomon Islands suffer from one of the highest malaria incidence rates in the world. It varies across the country with Honiara, Western Province and Choiseul Province the worst affected. Population growth and the mortality of mothers and children are one of the highest in the South Pacific due to endemic infectious diseases and low quality of rural health care.

Hospitals and pharmacies are limited, there are eight hospitals, the largest is the Central Hospital in Honiara. Church missions provide medical facilities on outlying islands. Serious health conditions usually require immediate medical evacuation to the nearest reliable medical facilities which are in Australia or New Zealand.

Life expectancy: 69.5 years (World Bank)
Fertility rate/Maternal mortality rate: 5.3 births per woman (World Bank)
Birth rate/Death rate: 32.5 births per 1,000 population; four deaths per 1,000 population (2003).
Infant mortality rate: 19 per 1,000 live births (World Bank)
Head of population per physician/bed: One doctor per 3,600 patients.

Welfare
Political instability and fighting have caused extensive damage requiring emergency rehabilitation of critical infrastructure. The Post-Conflict Emergency Rehabilitation Project entails restoration of government offices, roads, bridges, water supply and sanitation facilities, schools, and health facilities. The cost of restoration work on Guadalcanal and nearby provinces has been estimated at between US$30–35 million.

Main cities
Honiara, on Guadalcanal (capital, estimated population 54,600 in 2003), Gizo (on Gizo Island) (8,300), Auki (on Malaita) (5,000).

Languages spoken
There is no main native language although nearly all the languages are distantly related to the Oceanic Austronesian language group. There are at least 12 different language groups containing 87 various languages and dialects. Melanesian pidgin is the *lingua franca*. It has evolved since the time of the first traders, whalers, missionaries and labour recruiters. The vocabulary is derived from English with Melanesian syntax and uses different intonations. English, as a first language, is spoken by 1–2 per cent of the population.

Official language/s
English

KEY INDICATORS — Solomon Islands

	Unit	2000	2001	2002	2003	2004
Population	m	0.44	0.45	0.46	0.47	0.52
Gross domestic product (GDP)	US$bn	0.28	0.26	0.24	0.23	*0.24
GDP per capita	US$	714	637	514	497	554
GDP real growth	%	-14.3	-9.0	-1.6	5.0	6.0
Inflation	%	6.9	7.6	9.4	10.1	6.8
Exports (fob) (goods)	US$m	43.0	50.6	54.9	74.2	*83.0
Imports (fob) (goods)	US$m	66.0	80.8	63.9	82.0	*-102.0
Balance of trade	US$m	-23.0	-30.1	-9.0	-7.8	-19.0
Current account	US$m	-30.0	-30.0	-10.0	*0.1	20.0
Total reserves minus gold	US$m	32.0	19.3	18.3	37.2	80.6
Foreign exchange	US$m	31.3	18.7	17.5	36.4	79.7
Exchange rate	per US$	5.09	5.40	6.75	7.49	7.48

* estimated figure

Media

Press

Dailies: The English-language newspapers include *Solomon Star*, *Solomon Voice*, (bi-weekly) and *Solomon Times*.

Periodicals: There are a number of periodicals covering issues of development, regional, international news and religious issues. The *Solomon Nius*, a monthly government publication, is available free and details official activities. There is also *LINK*, a bi-monthly magazine published by the non-government organisation, Solomon Islands Development Trust. Other periodicals are *Mere Save* (bi-annual), *Provincial Newsletter* (church news), *Taem Bifo*, *Voice Katolika* and *Wespac News*.

Broadcasting

Radio: The Solomon Islands Broadcasting Corporation produces radio programmes in English and Pidgin, transmitting local and overseas programmes 118 hours per week from Honiara, Gizo (in Western Province), Santa Cruz and Malaita.

Television: Terrestrial television services are not available, although satellite transmissions can be received.

Advertising

Newspapers, radio and cinemas accept advertising.

Economy

The economy is based on agriculture, with 90 per cent of the population living in rural areas. Much real national income is derived from non-market, subsistence production of food crops, fish, meat, fuel and services. Primary products, mainly timber and fish, led to a 6 per cent growth rate in 2004, with inflation down to 6.8 per cent. Foreign investment is leading to a slow recovery. A memorandum of understanding has been signed with a Papua New Guinea-based palm oil company that proposes to reconstruct the palm oil operation on Guadalcanal. Some interest is being shown in mineral exploration although the Gold Ridge gold mine is yet to reopen. Logging remains a high foreign income earner, although it is being operated at an unsustainable level and government plans to curb production is expected to reduce revenue from the industry by 2007.

Overall, the economy suffers from the high cost of imported fuel and low worldwide prices for its agricultural products. The government's National Economic Recovery, Reform and Development Plan, 2003–06, includes public sector reform. Services contributed 24 per cent to the 2004 growth rate. The payment of wage arrears to public service workers also fuelled consumption and helped government accounts as funds came back in better than expected revenue collection.

The 2004 budget followed the settlement of Solomon Island arrears to the Asian Development Bank (ADB) and World Bank, and tightened expenditure controls as its central plank. International aid also targetted comprehensive reforms and good governance.

The budget provided for a balanced cash position, with budget support from Australia and New Zealand amounting to almost 25 per cent of total revenues. New Zealand's contribution was set aside for education.

In an effort to stamp out corruption, Solomon Islands is in the process of revising its foreign investment laws, which are time-consuming and costly. The system under discussion aims to create a single registration process, after which foreign companies will be treated in the same way as local companies.

The medium-term outlook is for faster economic growth, led by exports and externally funded government spending. In September 2004, the ADB announced grants worth US$3 million for transport and for the development of private businesses, and in July 2005, the Solomon Islands signed agreements to US$13 million in EU funding for development programmes.

External trade

Imports

Principal imports are food, plant and equipment, manufactured goods, fuels and chemicals.

Main sources: Australia (25.3 per cent total, 2004), Singapore (23.8 per cent), New Zealand (5.3 per cent), India (4.8 per cent)

Exports

Principal exports are timber (around 50 per cent of total), fish, copra, palm oil and cocoa.

Main destinations: China (28.2 per cent total, 2004), Thailand (15.7 per cent), South Korea (15.7 per cent), Japan (9.7 per cent), Philippines (5.1 per cent)

Agriculture

Farming

Agriculture typically accounts for over 60 per cent of GDP and almost three-quarters of the workforce. About 25–30 per cent of total land area is suitable for intensive, non-traditional agriculture, mainly on Guadalcanal. Over 85 per cent of land is communally owned, which deters investment.

The islands are self-sufficient in beef and vegetables. Copra and cocoa are produced for market on smallholdings and private plantations.

The Government Shareholding Agency, in association with major plantations, has been encouraging new coconut and cocoa planting and extension of the palm oil plantations.

Production in 2004 included: 5,500 tonnes (t) cereals in total, 330,000t coconuts, 155,000t oil palm fruit, 5,500t rice, 1,800t melons, 83,000t sweet potatoes, 40,000t taro, 80,580t oilcrops, 2,500t cassava, 4,000t cocoa beans, 19,330t fruit in total, 7,800t vegetables in total, 200t peppers and spice, 29,000t yams. Livestock production included: 748t beef, 2,280t pig meat, 280t poultry, 480t eggs, 1,365t milk.

Fishing

Commercial fishing and fish processing around the islands is mainly of skipjack tuna. Fish exports account for about one-third of total export earnings. Domestic seafood demand is served by small, local operations.

Production, in general, has fallen since a high in 1997 when the typical annual marine fish catch was 63,000t, to around 30,000t by 2004. Likewise there were 182,000 units of pearls and shells harvested in 1997 and only 54,000 by 2004.

The first black cultured pearls, produced over a seven-year period at a demonstration farm near Gizo, were auctioned in Australia in June 2004.

Forestry

Logging is one of the country's main economic lifelines, contributing around 18 per cent of GDP. The forests contain some 170,000 hectares of exploitable land having 13 million cubic metres of commercial timber. However, instead of the 250,000cum recommended by environmentalists as sustainable felling, felling described as 'unsustainable' by the Asian Development Bank, accelerated in 2004 as logging companies increased production ahead of new legislation aimed at curbing exploitation of the natural forests. Production in 2003 included 692,000 cubic metres (cum) roundwood, 554,000cum sawlogs and veneer logs, 12,000cum sawnwood, 138,000cum wood fuel.

Industry and manufacturing

The industrial sector accounts for around 5 per cent of GDP and employs some 5 per cent of the workforce.

Manufacturing activities include palm oil, rice milling, fish smoking, canning and freezing, saw milling, copra drying, food processing, tobacco, soft drinks, production of nails, detergents and soaps, wood and rattan furniture, fibreglass articles, boats, clothing, handicrafts, shell jewellery, buttons.

Most timber is exported as logs, but an increasing proportion is being sawn; the government hopes to develop wood processing to enable profitable marketing of sawn timber and veneers.

Tourism
Tourism in normal circumstances constitutes an important element of the economy, with diving and fishing being popular attractions. Prior to 2000, tourist arrivals were in excess of 15,000, but ethnic violence during 2000–03 precipitated an almost total collapse in numbers with only 1,245 arrivals in 2001, the lowest on record. The situation had sufficiently stabilised to see numbers begin to rise in 2004, especially from Australia and New Zealand, although poor air services remain an impediment. There has also been a revival of hotel construction and refurbishment.

Environment
The Solomon Islands was ranked second, after Indonesia, for coral reef fish species and the range and variety of its corals. The main environmental problems are deforestation, soil erosion and major, possibly irreversible, destruction to coral reefs There is a lack of resources to control the activities of the logging companies.

Mining
The mining sector typically accounts for 1 per cent of GDP, and employs 1 per cent of the workforce.
Panning of alluvial gold produces some 50–100kg per annum.
Undeveloped mineral resources include small deposits of copper, lead, zinc, silver, nickel, cobalt, bauxite, phosphates and asbestos.
Bugotu Nickel Ltd is working on a feasibility study of the lateritic nickel deposits on Takata and San Jorge, Isabel Province. The nickel resource is estimated at 45 million tonnes.
Ross Mining of Australia opened the Gold Ridge gold mine, 45km from Majuro, with reserves of about three million ounces which will last over 10 years. The violence of the civil unrest caused the operations at the mine to be suspended; by early 2006 it had still not reopened.

Hydrocarbons
There are no hydrocarbon reserves and the Solomon Islands relies entirely on imported refined oil to meet domestic demand.

Energy
New Zealand contributed NZ$1 million towards restoring a regular power supply to the capital, after the civil unrest in 2003.

Banking and insurance
The ADB considers the banking sector to employ limited competition with strong participation by Australian financial institutions.

Central bank
Central Bank of Solomon Islands
Main financial centre
Honiara, on Guadalcanal Island

Time
GMT plus 11 hours

Geography
The Solomon Islands is a scattered Melanesian archipelago in the south-western Pacific Ocean, east of Papua New Guinea. The country includes most of the Solomon Islands – those to the north-west belong to Papua New Guinea, Ontong Java Islands (Lord Howe Atoll), Rennell Island and the Santa Cruz Islands about 500km (300 miles) to the east.

Climate
Warm and humid, equatorial with average temperatures from 22 degrees Celsius (C) (mountainous areas inland) to 28 degrees C (coastal areas). Rainfall averages about 3,500mm per annum, but varies greatly according to location and mostly falls Nov–Apr, when cyclones may occur as well.

Entry requirements
Passports
Required by all.
Visa
Visas required by all except citizens of UK, Commonwealth countries, US and some European countries. Travellers with onward passage and adequate funds may obtain a visitor's permit, for up to two months, on arrival.
Currency advice/regulations
There is no restriction on the importation of currency, but travellers are advised to declare any foreign currency on arrival and may only export up to the same amount of that currency.
Customs
Personal effects (including an allowance of alcoholic beverages and tobacco) are allowed duty-free. Import licences are required for spirits, wines, tobacco, cigars, cigarettes, firearms, ammunition, animals, seeds, soil and plant material.

Health (for visitors)
Mandatory precautions
Vaccination certificate required for yellow fever if travelling from an infected zone.
Advisable precautions
Vaccination for diphtheria, tuberculosis, hepatitis 'A' and 'B', polio, tetanus, typhoid. Malaria is a problem, especially in Honiara, and prophylaxis should be taken. Hookworm is endemic and any itchy rash should be checked by a physician. There is a rabies risk.

Hotels
There are over 60 hotels. Visitors are advised to book well in advance. Hotel tax of 10 per cent is added to bill. In addition to Honiara's three hotels, there are resorts, guesthouses and government resthouses of varying standards and quality scattered throughout the islands. Tipping is not customary or encouraged.

Public holidays
As well as the listed public holidays, each province has its own public holiday.
Fixed dates
1 Jan (New Year's Day), 7 Jul (Independence Day), 25 Dec (Christmas Day), 26 Dec (National Day of Thanksgiving). Each part of the Solomon Islands has its own Province Day: 25 Feb (Choiseul), 2 Jun (Isable), 8 Jun (Temotu), 29 Jun (Central Island), 20 Jul (Rennell), 1 Aug (Guadalcanal), 3 Aug (Makira/Ulawa), 15 Aug (Malaita), 7 Dec (Western Province).
If a Province Day falls on a Sunday, the following Monday is observed as a public holiday.
Variable dates
Good Friday, Easter Monday, Queen's Official Birthday (second Fri in Jun).

Working hours
Banking
Mon–Fri: 0830–1500.
Business
Mon–Fri: 0730/0800–1200, 1300–1630/1700; Sat: 0730/0800–1200.
Government
Mon–Fri: 0800–1200, 1300–1630.
Shops
Mon–Fri: 0800–1700; 0800–1200; Sat: 0800–1200. Many shops open Sat afternoon and Sun; Chinese stores often open at other times. There are several 24-hour stores in Honiara.

Electricity supply
240/220V AC with flat three-pin plug fittings and bayonet-type sockets, typical of Australia.

Weights and measures
Officially, the metric system is in use.

Social customs/useful tips
Tipping is not customary, and visitors are strongly advised to refrain from the practice. Women should avoid wearing shorts and make sure their legs are adequately covered to avoid giving offence. The social structure of the Solomon Islands is extremely complex, with traditions, culture and even language varying from island to island and among villages on the same island.

Security
The security situation has improved since 2003, however resources are still limited and response times to calls for assistance may be slow. Attacks on foreign nationals are rare however personal security

Solomon Islands

precausions should be taken if visiting the island of Malaita and rural Guadalcanal. Swearing is a crime and can lead to large civil fines and even jail.

Getting there
Air
National airline: Solomon Airlines.
International airport/s: Honiara Henderson International (HIR), 13km from Honiara; buffet and car hire. Taxis from the airport to the city centre take about 15 minutes.
Airport tax: International departure tax of SI$40; not applicable to infants and transit passengers who do not leave the transit area.
Surface
Water: Regular shipping links with Australia, New Zealand, Hong Kong, Japan, UK and Europe.

Getting about
National transport
Air: Solomon Airlines and Western Pacific Airline provide inter-island transport from Henderson Airport to most main islands and towns. Charter services are available.
Road: There are about 100km of bitumen roads in the urban areas of Honiara, Auki, Malaita and Gizo, Western Province. Other roads are coral or gravel surfaced, and are mostly in the rural areas. Terrain can be difficult.
Buses: Bus services operate in and around Honiara.
Water: Inter-island shipping services are operated by private companies and missions. The government provides the main means of transport. Boats are used to transport cargo and also carry passengers in varying degrees of comfort; some trading centres have wharves suitable for small vessels and some are being enlarged.
City transport
Taxis: Taxis available in Honiara. Advisable to check the fare before hiring a taxi. Journey time from airport to city centre 15 minutes.
Tipping not customary or encouraged.
Buses, trams & metro: There is a shuttle bus to and from the airport 0600–1800 hours, journey time 25 minutes.
Car hire
Car hire is available; driving licences with four months' unexpired duration are acceptable. Driving is on the left.

BUSINESS DIRECTORY
The addresses listed below are a selection only. While World of Information makes every endeavour to check these addresses, we cannot guarantee that changes have not been made, especially to telephone numbers and area codes. We would welcome any corrections.

Telephone area codes
Dialling code for Solomon Islands, IDD access code +677 followed by subscriber's number.

Useful telephone numbers
Police and fire: 23-666
Fire: 999
Ambulance: 25-566
Marine emergency: 21-535
Emergencies outside Honiara: 111
Directory enquiries: 101
Overseas operator: 102
Shipping and time: 107
Operator assistance: 100
Customs: 22-301
Immigration: 22-243

Chambers of Commerce
Solomon Islands Chamber of Commerce and Employers, PO Box 650, Honiara (tel/fax: 229-70; e-mail: chamberc@welkam.solomon.com.sb).

Banking
Australia and New Zealand Banking Group Ltd (ANZ), PO Box 10, Honiara (21-835; fax: 22-957, 24-463).
Development Bank of Solomon Islands, PO Box 911, Honiara (tel: 21-595, 21-596 fax: 23-715).
National Bank of Solomon Islands, PO Box 37, Honiara (tel: 21-874; fax: 24-358, 23-478).
Westpac Banking Corporation, PO Box 466, Mendana Avenue, Honiara (tel: 21-222; fax: 23-419).

Central bank
Central Bank of Solomon Islands, PO Box 634, Honiara (tel: 21-791 fax: 23-513; e-mail: info@cbsi.com.sb).

Travel information
Flight information (24 hours) (tel: 36-106, 36-326).
Guadalcanal Travel Service, PO Box 114, Honiara (tel: 22-586/7; fax: 26-184).
Honiara Henderson International Airport, PO Box G20, Honiara (tel: 36-561, 36-720/1; fax: 36-775, 36-743, 36-028).
Solomon Islands Airlines, PO Box 23, Mendana Avenue, Honiara (tel: 20-031; fax: 23-992).
Western Pacific Airline, PO Box 411, Honiara (tel: 36-533; fax: 36-476).

Ministry of tourism
Ministry of Culture, Tourism and Aviation, PO Box G20, Honiara (tel: 21-540; fax: 21-689).

National tourist organisation offices
Solomon Islands Tourist Authority, PO Box 321, Honiara, Guadalcanal (tel: 22-442; fax: 23-986).

Ministries
Ministry of Agriculture and Fisheries, PO Box G13, Honiara (tel: 21-327; fax: 21-955).
Ministry of Commerce, Industries and Employment, PO Box G26, Honiara (tel: 21-849; fax: 25-084).
Ministry of Education and Human Resources Development, PO Box G28, Honiara (tel: 23-900; fax: 20-485).
Ministry of Finance, PO Box 26, Honiara (tel: 23-700; fax: 20-392).
Ministry of Foreign Affairs, PO Box G10, Honiara (tel: 21-250; fax: 20-351).
Ministry of Forest Environment and Conservation, PO Box G24, Honiara (tel: 25-848; fax: 21-245).
Ministry of Health and Medical Services, PO Box 349, Honiara (tel: 20-830; fax: 20-085).
Ministry of Home Affairs, PO Box G11, Honiara (tel: 21-621; fax: 22-606).
Ministry of Justice and Legal Affairs, PO Box 404, Honiara (tel: 21-181; fax: 25-610).
Ministry of Lands and Housing, PO Box G38, Honiara (tel: 21-430; fax: 20-094).
Ministry of Mines and Energy, PO Box G37, Honiara (tel: 21-521; fax: 25-811).
Ministry of National Planning and Development, PO Box G30, Honiara (tel: 25-063; fax: 25-138).
Ministry of Police and National Security, PO Box G4, Honiara (tel: 22-208; fax: 25-949).
Ministry of Post and Telecommunication, PO Box G25, Honiara (tel: 21-821; fax: 21-472).
Ministry of Provincial Government and Rural Development, PO Box G35, Honiara (tel: 21-140; fax: 21-289).
Ministry of Transport, Works and Utilities, PO Box G8, Honara (tel: 26-560; fax: 26-458; e-mail: sidapp@pipolfastaem.gov.sb).
Ministry of Youth, Women, Sports and Recreation, PO Box G39, Honiara (tel: 25-490; fax: 25-686).
Office of the Prime Minister, PO Box G1, Honiara (tel: 22-202, 21-863; fax: 21-608, 25-470).

Other useful addresses
Asian Development Bank (ADB), South Pacific Regional Mission, La Casa di Andrea, Fr. Dr. W. H. Lini Highway; PO Box 127, Port Vila (tel: +678 2 23-300; fax: +678 2 23-183; adbsprm@adb.org; internet: http://www.adb.org/SPRM).
Controller of Customs and Excise, Customs and Excise Division, Ministry of

National Planning and Development, PO Box G30, Honiara.

Foreign Investment Board, Ministry of Commerce, Industries and Employment, PO Box G26, Honiara (tel: 21-849, 23-015, 21-928; fax: 25-084, 21-651).

Governor General, PO Box 252, Honiara (tel: 22-222, 21-777; fax: 23-335).

Investment Corporation of Solomon Islands Ltd, PO Box 570, Honiara (tel: 22-511; fax: 21-263).

Solomon Islands Ports Authority, PO Box 307, Honiara (tel: 22-646; fax: 23-994).

Solomon Islands Statistics Office, PO Box G6, Honiara (tel: 23-700).

Telekom Office, Mendana Avenue, Honiara (tel: 21-576; fax: 23-110).

Trading Co (Solomons) Ltd, Mendana Avenue, PO Box 114, Honiara, Guadalcanal (tel: 22-588).

Internet sites

Asia Business Connection (gateway site): http://asiabiz.com

Solomon Islands Department of Commerce, Employment and Trade: http://www.commerce.gov.sb

Somalia

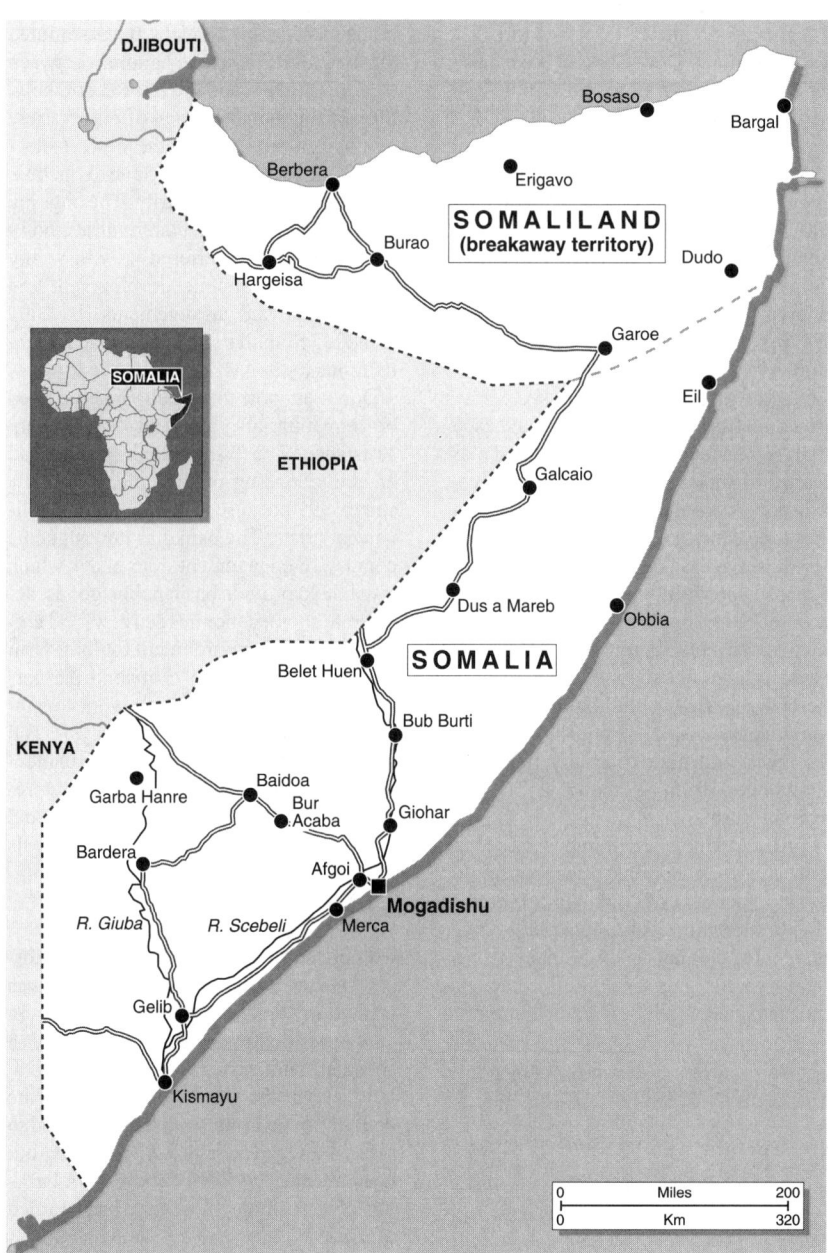

KEY FACTS

Official name: Jamhuriyadda ee Soomaaliya (Republic of Somalia)

Head of State: President Abdullahi Yusuf Ahmed (elected by the Transitional National Assembly sitting in Nairobi, Kenya, 10 Oct 2004)

Head of government: Prime Minister Mohammed Ali Ghedi (appointed by the President 3 Nov 2004)

Ruling party: Government (from 1 Dec 2004, based in Nairobi, Kenya)

Area: 738,000 square km

Population: 11.56 million (2004)

Capital: Mogadishu

Official language: Somali

Currency: Somali shilling (SoSh) = 100 centesimi

Exchange rate: SoSh2,070.00 per US$ (Oct 2005)

GDP per capita: US$120 (2003)

GDP real growth: 2.80% (2004)

Labour force: 4.20 million (2004)

Inflation: 100.00% (2003)

Balance of trade: -US$217.00 million (2003)

Foreign debt: US$2.60 billion (2003)

NOTA

Somalia is experiencing profound political crisis and instability. Travel to the country should be avoided unless absolutely necessary. Visitors should seek advice prior to departure, and register their presence with the diplomatic representatives of their own country on arrival.

Somalia has been without an effective central government since President Siad Barre was overthrown in 1991. Years of fighting between rival warlords and an inability to deal with famine and disease have led to the deaths of up to one million people.

A two-year United Nations' humanitarian effort primarily in the south was able to alleviate famine conditions, but having suffered significant casualties, the UN withdrew in 1995. Order had not then been restored. The mandate of the transitional government created in August 2000 in Arta, Djibouti, had expired.

A government at last?

In 2004, after protracted talks in Kenya, the main warlords and politicians signed a deal to set up a new parliament, which later appointed Abdullahi Yusuf president. His election took place in Kenya because the Somali capital Mogadishu was regarded as being too dangerous. Yusuf's administration is the fourteenth attempt to establish a government since 1991; it has no civil service or government buildings. In the north, the self-proclaimed state of Somaliland and the region of Puntland run their own affairs. Somaliland, which is not recognised internationally, has enjoyed relative stability. Puntland, which Yusuf declared autonomous and later ruled, is his home.

The Somali government officially relocated from Kenya 13 June 2005, but now Yusuf is at loggerheads with some warlords and government members over where the administration should be based. He and prime minister Mohammed Ali Ghedi oppose a move to Mogadishu, citing security reasons, and are based in Giohar, north of the capital. However, in January 2006 the government agreed to hold its first meeting in Somalia at the town of Baidoa in the first quarter of the year.

Yusuf pledged to promote reconciliation and to set about rebuilding the country. But his government, plagued by internal disagreements, has failed to end the country's anarchy. In 2005, he requested the UN and the World Bank to lead an assessment of what must be done in the country to prepare for a reconstruction and development programme prior to a donor's conference to be held in Rome and co-hosted by Sweden and Italy. This is proceeding against a background of continued conflict as numerous warlords and factions fight for control of Mogadishu and the south. Lawlessness is rife; the capital is in ruins and under factional control. Suspicion of Somali links with global terrorism further complicates the situation.

The World Bank rates Somalia one of the poorest countries in the world. The United Nations' Development Index has it at 161 out of 163 countries. Extreme poverty (living on less than one dollar a day) is estimated to the lot of between 45 and 55 per cent of the population. Gross primary school enrolment was 17 per cent in 2002, one in five Somalis is illiterate. Health indicators place Somalia among the worst countries in Africa. Life expectancy is 47 years; under-five mortality is 224 per 1,000 live births and maternal mortality 16 per 1,000 live births.

Despite this, the private sector has grown impressively in recent years, especially in service activities – trade and marketing, financial (including remittances), transport, communications, other infrastructure services, and educational and health services. The Somaliland secessionists provide port facilities to land-locked Ethiopia and have established commercial ties with regional states. There is significant investment in commercial ventures, including airlines, telecommunications, hotels, fishery resources, and trade, partially funded by remittances from Somalis living and working abroad.

Agriculture is the most important sector, with livestock normally accounting for about 40 per cent of GDP and 65 per cent of export earnings. Livestock, hides, fish, charcoal and bananas are Somalia's principal exports; sugar, sorghum, corn, qat and machined goods the principal imports. Somalia's small industrial sector, based on the processing of agricultural products, has largely been looted and sold as scrap metal.

Despite the seeming anarchy, Somalia's service sector has managed to survive and grow. Telecommunication firms provide wireless services in most major cities. In the absence of a formal banking sector, money exchange services have sprouted throughout the country, handling between US$500 million and one billion annually. Mogadishu's main market offers a variety of goods from food to the newest electronic gadgets. Hotels continue to operate, and militias provide security. The ongoing civil disturbances and clan rivalries, however, have interfered with any broad-based economic development and international aid arrangements. In 2004 and 2005 Somalia's overdue financial obligations to the IMF continued to grow.

Donor support to Somalia has focussed on humanitarian relief and development assistance. The World Bank has not had an active lending programme in Somalia since 1991 because of the political and financial crisis. The bank has now signed a country re-engagement note under which it will help provide basic public goods, accelerate socioeconomic recovery, and create an enabling environment for long-term institutional and policy change. In partnership with the UNDP, it will work to support macroeconomic data analysis and dialogue, create an enabling environment for the livestock and meat industry, prepare a plan to address HIV/Aids issues and promote capacity building for skills development.

Politics

Comprised of a former British protectorate and an Italian colony, Somalia was created in 1960 when the two merged. In 1970 President Siad Barre proclaimed a socialist state, paving the way for close relations with the USSR. In 1977, with the help of Soviet arms, Somalia attempted to seize the Ogaden region of Ethiopia, but was defeated by Soviet and Cuban backing for Ethiopia, which had turned Marxist.

Barre was overthrown in 1991 by opposing clans, but they could not agree on a replacement and the country plunged into lawlessness and clan warfare. After the collapse of Barre's regime, the north-west part of Somalia unilaterally declared itself the independent Republic of Somaliland.

Clan leaders elected Abdulkassim Salat Hassan president in 2000, but his

KEY INDICATORS — Somalia

	Unit	2000	2001	2002	2003	2004
Population	m	9.28	10.40	10.76	11.16	11.56
Gross domestic product (GDP)	US$bn	1.30	1.46	1.30	1.34	–
GDP per capita	US$	140	140	122	120	–
GDP real growth	%	–	–	–	3.5	–
Inflation	%	–	100.0	100.0	100.0	–
Exports (fob) (goods)	US$m	120.0	126.0	–	126.0	–
Imports (fob) (goods)	US$m	–	–	–	343.0	–
Balance of trade	US$m	–	–	–	-217.0	–
Foreign debt	US$bn	2.6	2.5	2.7	2.6	–
Exchange rate	per US$	2,587.58	2,620.00	2,620.00	2,620.00	2,620.00

government achieved very little and in 2004 he was replaced by Abdullahi Yusuf Ahmed.

Yusuf Ahmed had led a guerrilla movement in the 1970s aimed at ousting the Somali dictator Siad Barre. In the 1990s he emerged as the pre-eminent leader of his native Puntland region and declared the territory autonomous in 1998.

His prime minister Mohamed Ali Ghedi aims to reconcile the clan fiefdoms. An official of the African Union, Ghedi was relatively unknown in political circles when he was appointed in November 2004. He promised to form an inclusive government, and to strive for reconciliation among Mogadishu's warlords.

Risk assessment

Economic	Poor
Political	Poor
Regional stability	Poor

COUNTRY PROFILE

Historical profile

Somalia was part of the Arab-controlled Indian Ocean trading network until the early sixteenth century. As external Arab influence waned prominent clans rose and assumed control of their regions. The country was divided into protectorates established by the British and Italians. In the nineteenth century much of the Ogaden Desert – ethnically part of Somalia – was annexed by the Ethiopian empire of Menelik I; the area has remained part of Ethiopia ever since.
1900 Somalia was controlled by the British in the north (British Somaliland Protectorate), and Italy in the south (Italian Somaliland).
1950–60 Italian Somaliland was a UN Trust Territory, under Italian administration.
1960 The northern and southern regions were united when granted independence from the UK and Italy. Aden Abdullah Osman Daar was elected president.
1967 Abdi Rashid Ali Shermarke won the presidential election.
1969 President Shermarke was assassinated in a *coup d'état* and the military leader, Mohammed Siad Barre, became president. The country was renamed the Somali Democratic Republic, political parties were banned and the National Assembly dissolved.
1970 Barre declared Somalia a socialist and one-party state under the Somali Revolutionary Socialist Party.
1974–75 A major drought effected thousands and caused widespread starvation.
1977 Ethnic Somalis in the Ogaden rebelled against Ethiopian control and war began when Somali troops invaded the territory.
1978 Abdullahi Yusuf Ahmed led a failed military coup against Barre.
1980s There were devastating droughts which caused widespread starvation throughout most of the decade.
1981 The president appointed members of his own Marehan clan to government posts, at the expense of other, Mijertyn and Isaq, clans.
1982 Disaffected clans, with Ethiopian military support, attacked government positions. Although the government repulsed the rebels, clashes continued throughout the 1980s.
1988 A peace agreement with Ethiopia ended the Ogaden war but civil tensions increased.
1989 As the security situation worsened, Barre offered to resign and hold free elections in 1990.
1991 President Barre fled after rebels entered Mogadishu and the state of Somalia collapsed. Numerous international efforts were made to resolve the situation but effective central government was lacking for almost a decade. War-lords controlled territories through violence and clan allegiances as civil society degenerate into fiefdoms of factional fighting. The self-styled Somaliland Republic (in the north), headed by Mohammed Ibrahim Egal, broke away from war-torn Somalia.
1992 After a period of intense conflict between the numerous clans, the US sent a force to protect the UN humanitarian aid effort and help restore order.
1993 The Addis Ababa Accords were signed. The UN began peace-keeping operations, taking over from US Marines. US Task Force Rangers launched a military offensive (later known as the Battle of Mogadishu) against General Aideed and the Somali National Alliance (SNA). Eighteen US troops, and up to 1,000 Somalis, were killed.
1994 The US withdrew all of its forces from Somalia.
1995 The remainder of the UN peacekeeping force withdrew.
1996 General Aideed died from gunshot wounds. His son, Hussein Aideed, replaced him as head of the clan-based gang.
1997 Twenty-six of Somalia's 28 factions signed the Cairo Declaration peace accord.
1998 The leaders of the north-eastern region of Puntland, including Abdullahi Yusuf Ahmed, declared the region autonomous.
1999 Inter-clan violence continued in central and southern Somalia. President Guelleh of Djibouti announced an international peace plan based on the participation of Islamic and civil groups rather than warlords.
2000 A four-month reconciliation conference in Djibouti ended when the transitional national government (TNG) elected a civilian as the country's first president since 1990 – Abd al Qasim Salad Hassan. Hussein Aideed, and other war lords, in Somalia, and Abdullahi Yusuf, president of Puntland, opposed the TNG.
2001 Militia loyal to Aideed attacked TNG forces. Jama Ali Jama deposed Abdullahi Yusuf as president of Puntland but was later overthrown by Abdullahi Yusuf who recaptured the presidency, with the help of Ethiopian forces. The president of Somaliland, Muhammad Haji Ibrahim Egal, died and was succeeded by Dahir Riyale Kahin.
2002 A cease-fire was agreed between 21 warring factions and the TNG.
2003 Dahir Riyale Kahin of the ruling United People's Party (UDUB) (Somaliland), won presidential and parliamentary elections. A peace conference, the Somali National Reconciliation Conference, was set up in Kenya
2004 In January, at peace talks, warlords and politicians signed a deal to set up a new parliament; the Transitional National Assembly (TNA) was inaugurated and for security reasons continued to be held in Kenya. Abdullahi Yusuf, (president of Puntland), won the TNA presidential elections held on 10 October. Abdullahi appointed Mohammed Ali Ghedi as prime minister. On the 26 December the south-Asian *tsunami* hit the region of Puntland, resulting in hundreds of deaths.
2005 A cabinet was formed in January. In December the UN Food and Agricultural Organisation warned that the worst harvests in 10 years in southern Somalia meant that up to two million people would need food aid. Poor rains were the main cause, the FAO predicting that the harvest would be as low as 25 per cent of the average. This meant that livestock too were dying from a lack of food and water.

Political structure
The self-styled republics of Somaliland and Puntland have their own elected governments (but are unrecognised internationally). In April 2002, a new state was declared in south-western Somalia.
Constitution
The Somali National Reconciliation Conference, held in Mbagathi, Nairobi, Kenya, began on 27 June 2003. On 5 July 2003, the Leaders Committee agreed that Somalia should adopt a federal system of government, with selection of the MPs being carried out by the signatories (political leaders) to the Declaration of Cessation of Hostilities signed in Eldoret,

Kenya, on 27 October 2002, and by certain politicians, who were officially invited. If the government fails to complete the process of federalism throughout Somalia within a period of two-and-a-half years, parliament should withdraw its vote of confidence, necessitating the formation of a new transitional government to complete the process of federalism within one year.

Form of state
Federal republic

The executive
The president is elected by parliament. The prime minister is appointed by the president.

National legislature
In August 2004, a 275-seat transitional parliament was inaugurated in Nairobi, Kenya. Parliament serves a four-year term.

Legal system
At independence in 1960, Somalia had four legal systems: English common law, Italian law, Islamic Sharia and Somali customary law. In 1973, the Siad Barre regime introduced a unified civil code. There is no national judicial system.

Last elections
10 October 2004 (presidential elections by the Transitional National Assembly in Kenya); 14 April 2003 (Somaliland presidential/parliamentary elections).
Results: Third round presidential elections: Abdullahi Yusuf Ahmed won 189 against 79 for Abdullahi Ahmed Addou. Second round: Ahmed won 147 votes, Addou 83, and Mohammed Qanyare Afrah 38.
First round: Ahmed, the president of the breakaway region of Puntland, won 80 votes, followed by former finance minister Addou with 35 and Afrah with 33.
Somaliland presidential: the president of Somaliland, Dahir Riyale Kahin of the ruling United People's Party (UDUB), was re-elected with 42.08 per cent of the vote against 42.07 per cent for Ahmed Mohammed Silanyo of the Kulmiye party (Bringing People Together).

Next elections
2008

Political parties
There are no formal political parties – warlords and their supporters wield most of the power. Political organisation largely reflects membership of clans and sub-clans. There are 28 main factions. The main groups include the Somali Reconstruction and Restoration Council (SRRC), United Somali Congress-Somali National Alliance (USC-SNA) and the Rahanwein Resistance Army (RRA).

Ruling party
Government (from 1 Dec 2004, based in Nairobi, Kenya)

Population
11.56 million (2004)

Ethnic make-up
Somali (85 per cent), Bantu, Arabs and others (15 per cent).

Religions
Islam is the state religion (majority Sunni Muslims) (98 per cent), Christian minority (2 per cent).

Education
The UN Children's Fund (Unicef) supports 352 primary schools in central and southern Somalia, out of 418 that are operational. Additionally, Unicef has rehabilitated 35 schools, trained 2,300 teachers and initiated a school improvement programme. Several non-government organisations have concentrated on adult literacy programmes and civic education. Private education has recently been re-established in Somali, although school fees are proving to be out of reach of the ordinary Somali family.
Somaliland expatriates residing in the United Arab Emirates (UAE) have initiated efforts to raise funds for the Amoud University. The University, established in 1997 in Boroma, is essentially a community project. In June 2003, Somalia opened its first medical college, the Benadir University Medical College (BUMC), since 1991. BUMC will be funded by donations from Somali physicians and by tuition fees.
The education sector received only 12 per cent funding in the Consolidated Appeals Process (CAP), 2003. About 40 per cent of all teachers are unqualified and many have not completed their primary school education.
Literacy rate: 17.1 per cent, adult rate: 35 per cent, adult rate for the urban population; 10 per cent for rural and nomadic populations (2003).
Female adult literacy is estimated to be 52 per cent of the male rate.
Compulsory years: Six to 14.
Enrolment rate: Primary school enrolment increased by 29 per cent in 2002, compared to 2001, and there were 30 per cent more teachers. In 2003, one out of six children received formal primary education. Female primary school enrolment was 53 per cent of the male rate.

Health
The country's health services collapsed during the war and access to healthcare depends mostly on external assistance. Unicef remains the key provider of essential medical services and supplies to 123 maternal and child health centres, 174 health posts, and 16 hospitals.
Surveys in areas with high concentrations of displaced families show malnutrition rates as high as 40 per cent. Only 1.5 per cent of one to two years old are vaccinated. In addition, Somalia has the highest incidence of tuberculosis in the world, while cholera is endemic in most areas. In March 2004, Somalia was removed from the UN list of countries with endemic polio, as no new cases had been reported in two years.
It is estimated that 31 per cent of the population have access to improved water facilities.
In 2003, 50 per cent of the urban population and 15 per cent of the rural population had access to health services.
Life expectancy: 47.4 years (World Bank)
Fertility rate/Maternal mortality rate: 6.9 births per woman (World Bank)
Birth rate/Death rate: 46.4 births per 1,000 population; 17.6 deaths per 1,000 population (2003).
Infant mortality rate: 133 per 1,000 live births (World Bank)
Head of population per physician/bed: 0.4 physicians and two nurses per 100,000 people.

Welfare
Insecurity continues to be the greatest threat to the lives and welfare of the population, who are highly dependent on external assistance. International aid is jeopardised by widespread factional fighting, the kidnapping of aid workers and also by the mining of all major roads in Northern Gedo, the area most in need of food aid. An estimated 400,000 Somalis are internally displaced.
Although the World Food Programme (WFP) supports the repatriation of refugees with a nine-month food supply or cash equivalent, more than 10 per cent of the population require emergency food assistance. In May 2003, the WFP distributed 1,355 tonnes of food around Somalia.

Main cities
Somalia: Mogadishu (capital, estimated population 1.2 million in 2004), Kismayu (209,300), Merca (179,700).
Somaliland: Hargeisa (241,200), Berbera (222,700), Burao (55,900), Erigavo (19,100).
Puntland: Bosaso (33,200), Garowe (22,800), Galkayo (20,100), Lasanod (16,000).

Languages spoken
Somali is one of the major languages of Africa and belongs to a set of languages called lowland Eastern Cushitic. It did not have a written form until the Latin script was adopted in 1972. Arabic, Italian and English (mainly for business) are also in use.
Arabic and English are to be the second official languages of the Transitional Federal Government of Somalia, as agreed

on 5 July 2003 at the Somali National Reconciliation Conference.

Official language/s
Somali

Media
Press
Dailies: Daily publications from Mogadishu include *Mogadishu Times*, *Quran* and *Xog-Ogaal*. *Jamhuurriya* is published from Hargeisa. There are Internet daily news services from *Somali Press Online* (http://home.ica.net/~somalipress/) and *Dhambaal*.
Weeklies: Weeklies include *Dadka*, *Panorama*, *Republican* (Hargeisa), *Sanca* and *Xurmo*.
Periodicals: Periodicals are mainly monthly publications including *Ayaamaha* and *Himilo*.

Economy
Somalia is a predominantly agricultural country. Agriculture provides around 40 per cent of GDP, with the result the economy is particularly susceptible to adverse climatic conditions. With periodic floods and droughts, harvests are frequently insufficient to sustain the population. This makes Somalia dependent on foreign food aid to avert famine.

The permanent economic gloom has been aggravated by civil strife, which has wrecked the economy. Since hostilities began, the economy has broken down under the jurisdiction of several regional or clan leaders. The situation is complicated by the break-away Republic of Somaliland, which has become an autonomous zone with its own currency and government. Another autonomous region, the Puntland State of Somalia, has its own chaotic economic policy.

Somaliland represents the strongest local economy and has undergone something of a boom since it declared independence in 1991. The autonomous region has undergone a modest transformation with infrastructural improvements and an emergent business elite. Without international recognition, however, Somaliland cannot access funds from the IMF or World Bank or develop trade relations. The Puntland State, where many Somalis wish to remain part of Somalia, faces many of the problems faced by Somalia proper, including factional fighting and almost complete economic collapse.

A Coca-Cola bottling plant opened in July 2004, becoming the largest investment the country has received since 1991. This is a much-needed investment that could spur growth in the business climate.

In October 2004, the UN estimated that at least US$5 billion would be needed to rebuild Somalia.

External trade
The poor balance of trade reflects the continuing need for the large-scale import of fuels and food.

Imports
Principal imports are manufactures, petroleum products, foodstuffs, construction materials and qhat.
Main sources: Djibouti (28.8 per cent total, 2004), Kenya (13.1 per cent), India (9.3 per cent), Brazil (5.4 per cent), Oman (5.2 per cent), UAE (5.1 per cent)

Exports
Principal exports are livestock, bananas, hides, fish, charcoal and scrap metal.
Main destinations: Thailand (31.3 per cent total, 2004), UAE (22.8 per cent), Yemen (14.9 per cent), India (8.5 per cent), Oman (5.4 per cent), China (4.1 per cent)

Agriculture
Farming
Agriculture is the most important sector in the economy. It contributes about 65 per cent to GDP and employs 65 per cent of the working population. It is often badly affected by drought, as well as by the chaos of recent years.

Livestock, particularly camels, is the principal foreign exchange earner, accounting for 40 per cent of GDP. Exports are mainly to Arabian Gulf states and formerly to Saudi Arabia. A Saudi ban on the import of allegedly diseased Somali livestock has damaged the trade.

Much of the land is desert or semi-desert and only 13 per cent is cultivated, making food security a constant concern. Some crops are grown on the fertile land in the Juba and Scebali valleys, but the farmers have been displaced by nomads. Subsistence farmers grow maize and sorghum. Wheat and rice are imported. The most important cash crops are bananas, cotton and frankincense.

Industry and manufacturing
The industrial sector is small, contributing about 5 per cent to GDP and employing 8 per cent of the working population. The principal industries are meat and fish processing, sugar refining, fruit and vegetable canning, textiles and leather goods. Many factories are idle, because foreign exchange shortages have cut off foreign inputs.

Tourism
There are no tourism facilities.

Mining
There are significant mineral resources, but they have not yet been commercially exploited. The most important regions include an area extending from the Ethiopian border to beyond Berbera in Somaliland and west of the River Scebali near Mogadishu. The former contains reserves of copper, gold, molybdenum and bismuth, while the latter contains iron, gold and apatite.

The country also contains reserves of uranium, marble, manganese, tin, beryl and columbite. Salt and gypsum were extracted commercially before the civil war began.

Hydrocarbons
There are no proven oil reserves, but there are indications of oil and gas potential. Exploration was conducted by oil majors until 1991, when they withdrew after the outbreak of the civil war. The Republic of Somaliland has invited international companies with exploration rights within its self-declared territories to return, but despite some interest, international investors appear to be waiting until legal issues arising from the existence of pre-1991 contracts can be settled. In August 2005, the new government announced that it would welcome approaches by foreign firms to, but warned against concluding exploration contracts with local administrations, which would not be recognised. Somalia relies on imports for its fuel needs.

Downstream, Somalia has a single oil refinery with a capacity of 10,000 barrels per day (bpd), although it has not been in use for some years and is probably in a state of disrepair.

Somalia has one natural gas field with reserves of around 7 billion cubic metres, although political and economic chaos have prevented exploitation. Currently, there are no production or imports of natural gas.

Somalia does not produce or import coal.

Energy
Electricity generation amounts to under 100MW and is fuelled by diesel, which has to be imported. A monopoly of electricity generation and supply is owned by the Ente Nazionale Energia Elettrica (ENEE).

Banking and insurance
The first commercial bank to be established since 1990, the Universal Bank of Somalia (UBSOM), was launched on 22 January 2002. The bank is 51 per cent owned by Somalis and 49 per cent by overseas investors. UBSOM has links with 62 overseas banks in 72 countries.

Central bank
Central Bank of Somalia

Main financial centre
Mogadishu

Time
GMT plus three hours

Geography
Somalia lies on the east coast of Africa, with Ethiopia to the north-west and Kenya

to the west. There is a short frontier with Djibouti. Somalia has a long coastline on the Indian Ocean and the Gulf of Aden, forming the Horn of Africa.

Climate
Tropical. Humid on coast, drier in north. Average temperatures 27–32 degrees Celsius (C) throughout year, but can reach 42 degrees C on coast. Dry seasons from January–February and August–September. Rainy seasons from March–June and October–December.

Dress codes
Lightweight clothes are required. Women should dress modestly.

Entry requirements
Passports
Required by all.
Visa
The civil war has disrupted typical consular services worldwide. Visas are required by the break-away territories of Somiland and Puntland and can be obtained at the port of entry. Travellers should contact their own ministry of foreign affairs for advice about local conditions and travelling to Somalia.
Currency advice/regulations
Import/export of only small amounts of local currency is allowed. Import of foreign currency is unlimited, but it must be declared on a form for which a small charge may be made. Currency transactions should be recorded at each exchange. Export of foreign currency is limited to the amount declared on arrival.
The Somali shilling is the unit of currency, except in Somaliland, which uses the Somaliland shilling. US dollars are accepted everywhere.

Health (for visitors)
Mandatory precautions
Yellow fever and cholera certificates if arriving from an infected area.
Advisable precautions
Hepatitis 'A' and 'E' are widespread and hepatitis 'B' is hyperendemic.
Meningococcal meningitis may occur; yellow fever, cholera, typhoid and polio vaccinations are advisable. Malaria prophylaxis should be taken as risk exists throughout the country (two types of prophylaxis are recommended). The water system is poor so precautions are essential.
A comprehensive medical pack and all medication is essential for the traveller as there is little to be found in the country. Medical emergency insurance (including repatriation) is a minimal requirement.

Hotels
Available in principal towns. Service charge of 10 per cent added to bills.

Credit cards
Credit cards are not accepted in Somalia.

Public holidays
Fixed dates
1 Jan (New Year's Day), 1 May (Labour Day), 26 Jun (Independence Day), 1 Jul (Foundation of the Republic).
Variable dates
Eid al Adha, Eid al Fitr (three days), Ashura, Birth of the Prophet.
The Islamic year contains 354 or 355 days, with the result that Muslim feasts advance by 10–12 days against the Gregorian calendar. Dates of feasts vary according to the sighting of the new moon, so cannot be forecast exactly. Islamic year 1426: 10 February 2005 to 30 January 2006.

Working hours
Banking
Sat–Thu: 0800–1130.
Business
Sat–Thu: 0800–1230, 1630–1900.
Government
Sat–Thu: 0800–1400.
Shops
Sat–Thu: 0900–1300, 1600–2000.

Telecommunications
Surprisingly, an effective telecommunications system exists in major towns in Somalia.

Electricity supply
220V AC, 50 cycles. The electricity system is poor.

Social customs/useful tips
Islamic customs should be respected. It is the convention to use the right hand when shaking hands and passing or receiving anything. Muslims are not permitted to drink alcohol or eat pork. Do not smoke or drink in public during Ramadan. Refusal of offered refreshment is considered discourteous. Shoes should be removed on entry to mosques.

Security
Any visit to Somalia should be undertaken only after a risk assessment has been carefully weighed; terrorism is a constant threat and the consideration of personal safety should be kept fully focussed. Armed robbery and kidnapping by numerous bands of militia is endemic. Hargeisa, capital of the self-declared Republic of Somaliland is the only place that may offer a relatively secure environment in the country. Foreign nationals should register their presence with their respective diplomatic representatives.

Getting there
Air
Air Somalia, a privately owned Somali airline, launched in February 2001, flies to and from surrounding countries. The Kenyan government lifted its ban on flights to Somalia from 8 July 2003.
International airport/s: Mogadishu International (MGQ), 6.4km from city.
Surface
Road: There are road links with Kenya in the south and Djibouti in the north. Four-wheel drive vehicles are recommended.
Rail: There is no railway system in Somalia.
Main port/s: El Ma'an, Bassasso, Kismayu, Merca, Mogadishu.
Berbera is the economic lifeline for the self-declared Somaliland Republic.

Getting about
National transport
Air: Air Somalia flies between Mogadishu and 10 towns throughout the country.
Road: Travel may be restricted outside Mogadishu. Local enquiries should be made. Good roads from Mogadishu to Kismayu (via Merca) and Baidoa in the southern part of the country, and to Hargeisa and Berbera in the north. Most other routes are mainly tracks and gravel roads. Driving is on the right. Travel to Hargeisa and Berbera is restricted because of insecurity.
Buses: The network outside Mogadishu is restricted, with few and irregular bus services.
Water: Coastal shipping of both freight and passengers is extensive. The number of incidents of piracy off the Somali coast has increased sharply in the last few years.
City transport
Taxis: Fares by negotiation; tipping is not usual. Can be hired on a time basis.
Car hire
Car hire is available in Mogadishu, with four-wheel drive vehicles obtainable from Marill (Somalia) Limited. There are no traffic lights in the country except in Hargeisa in Somaliland. The condition of the roads makes driving difficult and night driving is dangerous due to the absence of lighting.

BUSINESS DIRECTORY

The addresses listed below are a selection only. While World of Information makes every endeavour to check these addresses, we cannot guarantee that changes have not been made, especially to telephone numbers and area codes. We would welcome any corrections.

Telephone area codes
The international direct dialling (IDD) code for Somalia is +252, followed by area code and subscriber's number:
Mogadishu   1

Somalia

Chambers of Commerce
Somalia Chamber of Commerce, Industry and Agriculture, PO Box 27, Via Asha, Mogadishu (tel: 80-726).

Banking
Commercial and Savings Bank of Somalia, PO Box 203, Juley Street 1st, Mogadishu (tel: 22-861, 22-959).

Central bank
Central Bank of Somalia, PO Box 11, Corso Somalia 55, Mogadishu, Somalia (tel: 215-241; fax: 215-026).

Travel information
Daallo Airlines, PO Box 1954, Djibouti-ville, Djibouti (tel: (+253) 353-401, 351-765; fax: (+253) 356-660).

Somali Airlines (operations suspended since 1991), PO Box 726, Via Medina, Mogadishu (tel: 81-533; fax: 80-489).

Other useful addresses
Agricultural Development Corporation, PO Box 930, Mogadishu.

Livestock Development Agency of Somalia, PO Box 1759, Mogadishu.

National Petroleum Agency of Somalia, PO Box 573, Mogadishu.

Somali Broadcasting Service, Ministry of Information and National Guidance, Private Bag, Mogadishu (tel: 2455).

Statistical Department, PO Box 1742, Mogadishu (tel: 80-385).

Internet sites
Africa Business Network: http://www.ifc.org/abn

African Development Bank: http://www.afdb.org

Africa Online: http://www.africaonline.com

AllAfrica.com: http://allafrica.com

Puntland State of Somalia: http://members.tripod.com/~Puntland/

Somalia News: http://www.somalianews.com

Somaliland official website: http://www.somalilandgov.com

United Nations Somalia: http://www.unsomalia.org

Universal Bank of Somalia: http://www.univbank.org

South Africa

KEY FACTS

Official name: Republic of South Africa

Head of State: President Thabo Mbeki (ANC) (since Jun 1999; re-elected 23 Apr 2004)

Head of government: President Thabo Mbeki

Ruling party: African National Congress (ANC) (re-elected 14 Apr 2004)

Area: 1,127,200 square km

Population: 47.56 million (2004)

Capital: Cape Town (legislative); Johannesburg (financial); Pretoria (administrative); Bloemfontein (judicial)

Official language: Afrikaans, English, Ndebele, Sesotho, Northern Sotho, SiSwati, Tsonga, Tswana, Venda, Xhosa, Zulu.

Currency: Rand (R) = 100 cents

Exchange rate: R6.36 per US$ (Oct 2005)

GDP per capita: US$4,500 (2004)

GDP real growth: 3.70% (2004)

Labour force: 19.14 million (2004)

Unemployment: 26.20% (2004) (including workers no longer looking for employment)

Inflation: 1.40% (2004)

Balance of trade: US$115.00 million 2004

Foreign debt: US$24.70 billion (2003)

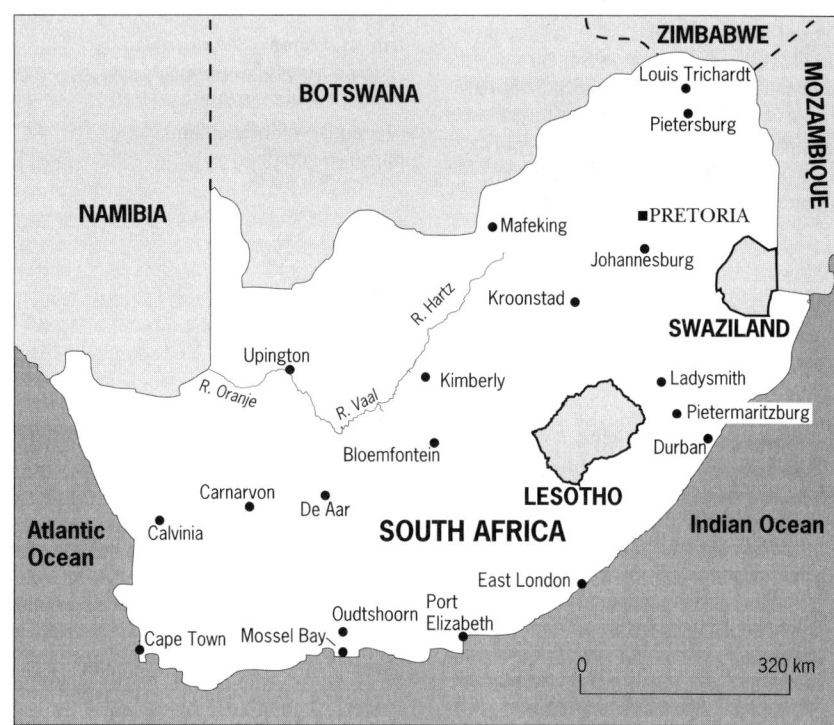

South Africa – dubbed by Archbishop Desmond Tutu Africa's 'Rainbow Nation' because of its diverse ethnic and cultural mix – is the major economic driving force within the 14-nation southern African region. It absorbs a substantial share of their exports through the Southern African Customs Union (Sacu) – a long standing association of South Africa, Botswana, Namibia, Swaziland, and Lesotho.

Operations of South African companies are to be found not only in the southern African countries, but also in Zambia, Tanzania, Nigeria, Ghana, Mozambique and further north. The stock of South Africa's foreign direct investment in the rest of Africa almost doubled to 9 per cent of its total stock in 2003 from 5 per cent in 2000. The peg of the currencies of Lesotho, Namibia and Swaziland to the rand within the Common Monetary Area contributes to the maintenance of low inflation across the region.

Good growth, high unemployment

Sacu members' fiscal policies are also linked to some extent. Shared customs and excise duties constitute a major part of the revenues of Lesotho, Namibia and Swaziland.

The short-term outlook for South Africa is broadly favorable, with the main risk potential a worsening of the external environment. South Africa faces important challenges in the form of high unemployment and widespread poverty, and high prevalence of HIV/Aids. The banking system is sound. Various initiatives are underway to facilitate access to banking services by the poor: there are already some positive results. It is estimated that one third to one half of the adult population has no access to banking services.

Stubborn unemployment is of concern and the easing of labour legislation – including to allow centralised collective bargaining and streamlined dismissal procedures – is critical to any significant impact on the figures. Further liberalisation and simplification of the trade regime as ways of enhancing competitiveness and raising productivity would also positively impact on unemployment.

Economic performance is good. Real growth was up to 4.8 per cent in the second quarter of 2005 against 3.5 per cent in the first quarter. It was driven primarily by strong final domestic demand, but with support from a strong performance by the manufacturing sector which grew by 7.3 per cent after having contracted in the first quarter.

Over the first half of 2005, import growth slowed while exports remained steady and as a result the current account deficit declined to 3.3 per cent of GDP. Inflation has stayed within the official 3–6 per cent target band since September 2003, and is expected to remain so during 2005–06.

Gross international reserves increased to an estimated 178 per cent of short-term external debt as of end-June 2005, from the equivalent of 70 per cent at end-2003. Fitch upgraded South Africa one notch to BBB+ to bring its ratings in line with Moodys and Standard and Poor's.

The fiscal deficit fell to 1.5 per cent of GDP in 2004/05, from 2.3 per cent a year earlier, reflecting strong tax revenues. Low domestic interest rates, favourable growth prospects, and improved business confidence pushed the Johannesburg Stock Exchange all-share index up by 10 per cent in real terms in the first half of 2005 after a gain of 18 per cent in 2004. Boosted by falling interest rates and new demand by an emerging black middle class residential property prices rose by 28 per cent in real terms in 2004; growth persists, but at a lower rate.

The International Monetary Fund (IMF) projects real growth of 4 per cent in 2005 and 3.6 per cent in 2006. Inflation is expected to increase from current levels, but to remain within the target band; and the external current account deficit to widen to 3.8 per cent of GDP before narrowing moderately over 2006.

The fund says the main short-term risks arise from the possibility of deterioration in the external environment. A pronounced slowdown in global growth would reduce demand for South African exports, erode consumer and business confidence and dampen growth. Also, a weakening of global appetite for emerging market assets could put downward pressure on the rand with a potential adverse impact on growth.

On the monetary policy stance, some upside risks to the inflation outlook may be emerging. The prediction is for a period of increasing inflation with the CPIX inflation rate rising above five per cent in early 2006 before slowing down gradually.

Despite concerns over the appreciation of the rand, South Africa's flexible exchange rate has continued to serve the country well. The government plans to continue with the policy of building up international reserves when market conditions are favorable but otherwise not intervening in the foreign exchange market.

South Africa's share of world export markets has remained broadly constant since the mid-to late 1990s, but exports have declined in volume. Metals and commodities have benefited from higher world prices; manufacturing has performed more modestly and textiles very poorly. Indicators as to areas the government should look at point to the cost of investing and doing business in South Africa, education standards, availability of skilled labour, and the quality of infrastructure.

One thing business is happy with is the government's relaxing of capital controls which included over the year the removal of limits on outward foreign direct investment. The main remaining restrictions comprise limits on overseas investments by institutional investors and the prohibition of portfolio investment abroad by non-financial firms.

South Africa's trade regime has been liberalised substantially over the last decade. However, some sectors are still highly protected. While average tariff rates are similar to the average in other emerging markets, the number of tariff peaks above 15 per cent and the share of non ad valorem duties tend to be higher.

Not too much privatisation yet

State-owned enterprises (SoEs) continue to play a significant role in the economy, and the authorities see them as a key vehicle for strengthening infrastructure and public service delivery. Privatisation does not at the moment seem a popular option. They account for 1.2 per cent of total employment, with combined assets the equivalent of 12.8 per cent of GDP and a turnover of 6.1 per cent of GDP. The major entities are Eskom (energy), Transnet (transportation), and Denel (defense). Over the next few years they and other SoEs will be major players in the further development of electricity, ports, the railways, roads and water resources. South Africa has de-emphasised the role of privatisation as a way of enhancing efficiency and will instead focus on the operational restructuring of the large,

KEY INDICATORS — South Africa

	Unit	2000	2001	2002	2003	2004
Population	m	43.69	44.40	44.62	46.09	*47.56
Gross domestic product (GDP)	US$bn	125.50	113.30	110.70	165.60	*212.78
GDP per capita	US$	2,863	2,549	2,461	3,624	4,500
GDP real growth	%	3.4	2.2	2.6	2.6	3.7
Inflation	%	5.4	5.7	9.2	5.8	1.4
Unemployment	%	*40.0	*40.0	30.0	31.0	*26.2
Coal output	mtoe	118.8	126.7	126.8	134.6	136.9
Exports (fob) (goods)	US$m	31,434.0	30,642.0	32,040.0	32,179.0	48,430.0
Imports (fob) (goods)	US$m	27,202.0	25,677.0	27,560.0	26,021.0	48,545.0
Balance of trade	US$m	4,231.0	4,966.0	3,800.0	6,158.0	115.0
Current account	US$m	-170.0	-40.0	690.0	-1,490.0	-5,330.0
Foreign debt	US$bn	24.9	24.1	25.0	24.7	–
Total reserves minus gold	US$m	6,083.0	6,045.0	5,904.0	6,496.0	13,141.0
Foreign exchange	US$m	5,793.0	5,765.0	5,601.0	6,164.0	12,794.0
Exchange rate	per US$	6.94	8.61	10.02	7.56	6.45

* estimated figure

together with the sale of their non-core assets.

Medium-term, South Africa says it can generate annual growth of 4 per cent, the IMF forecast between 3.25 to 3.5 per cent, with a baseline scenario of average annual real growth of 3.5 per cent over 2005–10 and says reducing unemployment under this baseline would be difficult.

Significant progress has been made with Broad Based Black Economic Empowerment. This initiative uses several tools to achieve empowerment of the black population, including voluntary sector-specific 'charters' that set targets for a range of empowerment indicators, including percentage of black ownership, black participation in management, and skills development. Several sectors, significantly the mining industry, have made significant progress. Progress on land reform remains mixed. Against a target of 30 per cent of agricultural land under black ownership by 2015, to date only four per cent has been achieved. The programme includes land restitution (return of land lost due to racially discriminatory laws) and land redistribution (purchase of land by black individuals facilitated by government grants and loans).

Politics

After the British seized the Cape of Good Hope area in 1806, many of the Dutch settlers (Boers) trekked north to found their own republics. The discovery of diamonds (1867) and gold (1886) spurred wealth and immigration and intensified the subjugation of the native inhabitants. The Boers resisted British encroachments, and were militarily defeated although their culture persists to this day. The resulting Union of South Africa operated under a policy of apartheid – the segregated development of the races. The 1990s brought an official end to racial segregation and separate development although it had already changed out of all recognition, and ushered in black majority rule.

The apartheid government eventually negotiated itself out of power, and the new leadership under Nelson Mandela, who worked in a limestone quarry while he served 26 years on Robben Island, South Africa's high security political jail, for his part in the struggle for independence, encouraged reconciliation, himself welcoming even his former jailers to his home. Now, diversity is a key feature of South Africa, where, as the British Broadcasting Corporation (BBC) reported, community leaders include rabbis and chieftains, rugby players and returned exiles, where traditional healers ply their trade around the corner from stockbrokers and where housing ranges from mud huts to palatial homes with swimming pools.

President Thabo Mbeki was elected by parliament to a second five-year term in April 2004 following the landslide general election victory of the ruling African National Congress (ANC). He took over as president when Nelson Mandela stepped down in mid-1999. He was born in 1942 into one of the leading families active in black politics. His father was a leading thinker in the South African Communist Party. He has said that he will not stand again in the elections due in 2009.

Mbeki played a central role both in planning the armed insurrection that caused the first cracks in white rule and the talks that led to its end. He has mediated in African conflicts, including those in Ivory Coast, Burundi and Democratic Republic of Congo.

Risk assessment

Economic	Satisfactory and improving
Political	Satisfactory
Regional stability	Poor
Stock market	Good but deteriorating

COUNTRY PROFILE

Historical profile
The sudden, in political terms, change from white, minority ruled South Africa to black, majority ruled South Africa that happened in the early 1990s astonished and delighted the international community. The world had watched as Nelson Mandela walked to freedom on 11 February 1990; it watched again as long, snaking lines of South Africans patiently queued to vote in their first ever free election in April 1994, and it cheered when Nelson Mandela became president of sub-Saharan Africa's most developed nation on 10 May 1994. The anti-apartheid campaign had been one of the most successful campaigns ever – the economic sanctions, the boycott of wine and oranges, the sport's boycott (which perhaps hurt the white South Africans most of all), the 'Free Mandela' t-shirts, marches in London's Trafalgar Square, isolation at the United Nations, all contributed.

When F W de Klerk became prime minister in 1989, just three weeks before the September elections (in which the Nationalist Party (NP) lost 30 seats), few would have predicted that in five years there would be black majority rule. De Klerk pushed for 'talks about talks' between his ruling NP and Nelson Mandela's African National Congress (ANC); de Klerk wanted sanctions lifted immediately, Mandela wanted them kept in place until the ANC were certain change in South Africa had become irreversible. Whatever the differences then, the road to a negotiated settlement had begun.

The change of presidents from Nelson Mandela to Thabo Mbeki in June 1999 served to convince South Africans that they had made it as a democratic nation.

1652 The Dutch East India Company set up a supply station which became Cape Town, supplying sailing ships to and from the Dutch East Indies (Indonesia).
1795 Britain took control of the Cape.
1806 The Cape Colony became British and settlement began in 1820.
1835 Mass treks by Afrikaners (Boers) moved inland, fighting the Ndebele and Zulus.
1899–1902 After many battles, the Boer War was eventually won by the British. With the signing of the Treaty of Vereeniging on 31 May 1902, all Boers became British subjects.
1910 The Union of South Africa was established from the former British colonies of Cape and Natal and the Boer republics of Transvaal and Orange Free State. South Africa became a self-governing dominion led by former Boer generals.
1912 The Native National Congress, the precursor to the African National Congress (ANC), was founded.
1913 The Land Act was introduced to prevent blacks, except those in Cape province, from buying land outside reserves.
1914 The National Party was founded.
1919 South West Africa (Namibia), formerly a German colony, came under South African administration.
1948 Apartheid (separateness) laws excluding non-whites from political and economic influence were applied by successive National Party governments.
1950 The population was classified by race. The Group Areas Act was passed to segregate blacks and whites. The South African Communist Party (SACP) was banned. The ANC responded with a campaign of civil disobedience led by Nelson Mandela.
1960 Apartheid laws were brutally enforced; the most notorious incident was the Sharpeville massacre. The ANC became the main black political organisation opposing the government and consequently was banned.
1961 South Africa was declared a republic and left the Commonwealth. Mandela launched the ANC's military wing which began a campaign of disruption and sabotage.
1964 Nelson Mandela, leader of the ANC, was jailed for life. The UN imposed sanctions against South Africa.
1976 More than 600 people were killed in the Soweto uprising.

South Africa

1983 An interim constitution established power-sharing of three population groups (whites, Asians and mixed race (coloured)), effectively excluding participation of blacks.
1989 P W Botha (prime minister from 1978–83 and president from 1983–89) was replaced by F W de Klerk; he began a reform programme that started the dismantling of apartheid.
1990 Nelson Mandela was released from prison. The ban on the ANC was lifted. Namibia was granted independent.
1991 The last apartheid laws were repealed. Fighting broke out between the ANC and the Zulu Inkatha movement.
1993 A non-racial constitution was formulated through a multi-racial negotiating forum. A transitional Government of National Unity (GNU) was established replacing the three-chamber, racially-based parliament.
1994 In the first non-racial, fully democratic elections, the ANC won a majority of seats in parliament and Nelson Mandela became president. South Africa successfully reapplied for Commonwealth membership and took up its seat in the UN General Assembly for the first time in 20 years.
1996 The new constitution was adopted. A Truth and Reconciliation Commission (TRC) was set up. Those that perpetrated and suffered human rights abuse were allowed to record their experiences for mutual recognition.
1998 The TRC branded apartheid a crime against humanity and held the ANC accountable for numerous human rights abuses. South Africa intervened militarily in Lesotho to prevent civil war breaking out in the kingdom.
1999 Thabo Mbeki was elected president by the National Assembly. The ANC increased its share of the election vote and formed a coalition government with the mainly Zulu Inkatha Freedom Party (IFP).
2000 Despite President Mbeki's controversial views on Aids, South Africa played host to the 13th World Aids Conference in July. The Democratic Party, the New National Party (NNP) and the Federal Alliance merged to form the Democratic Alliance (DA), which won a quarter of the vote in local elections.
2001 It was proposed that the name of Pretoria be changed to the City of Tshwane and the Port Elizabeth to the Nelson Mandela Metropolitan Municipality. Legal action against the South African government by 39 multi-national pharmaceutical companies over the production of generic Aids drugs was dropped. This enabled South Africa, and many other poor countries, to import cheaper drugs to combat the epidemic. The DA collapsed after the NNP pulled out of the coalition.
The government was cleared of unlawful conduct over allegations of corruption in arms deal with European firms. The High Court ruled that pregnant women must be given anti-retroviral drugs to prevent HIV transmission to their infants.
2002 The name of Northern Province was changed to Limpopo Province. The Organisation of African Unity (OAU) became the African Union (AU) with President Mbeki as the first chairman. Right-wing extremists were accused of bombing atrocities in Soweto; 17 were arrested.
2003 Walter Sisulu, a key veteran figure in the anti-apartheid struggle, died.
2004 The ruling ANC won a landslide victory in the general elections. On 23 April, Thabo Mbeki was elected unopposed for a second term as president.
2005 Mbeki sacked his deputy, Jacob Zuma, who was charged with corruption. Phumzile Mlambo-Ngcuka was named as his successor on 21 June. She holds the highest office for a woman in South Africa. Nelson Mandela retired from public life.

Political structure
Constitution
The constitution was implemented in February 1997.
South Africa consists of a central government and nine provincial governments. The head of a province is called a premier.
The right to regional autonomy is enshrined in the constitution, subject to the principles of the national constitution.
Electoral system: list-system proportional representation based on universal adult suffrage, aged over 18.
Form of state
Federal republic
The executive
Executive powers are vested in the president, who is both Head of State and head of government, and is elected by the National Assembly for no more than two, five-year terms.
The president, must appoint all but two cabinet members from National Assembly members.
National legislature
The bicameral legislature consists of the National Assembly with between 350–400-members, elected by popular vote. Seats are apportioned to political parties dependent on their share of the vote.
The National Council of Provinces (NCOP) aligns national legislation that affects the provinces. The NCOP has 54 permanent members and 36 special delegates.
Both institutions serve for five year terms.

Legal system
Based on Roman-Dutch law and the constitution.
An anti-prejudice law was passed in 2000.
Last elections
23 April 2004 (presidential); 14 April 2004 (parliamentary).
Results: Presidential: Thabo Mbeki (ANC) was elected by the National Assembly unopposed for a second term as president. Parliamentary: the ANC won 69.7 per cent of the vote (279), the DA 12.4 per cent (50) and the Inkatha Freedom Party 7 per cent (28). Turnout was 76.7 per cent.
Next elections
2009 (presidential and parliamentary)

Political parties
Ruling party
African National Congress (ANC) (re-elected 14 Apr 2004)
Main opposition party
Democratic Alliance (DA)
In 2000, the New National Party (NNP), which ruled South Africa from 1948 to 1994, merged with the Democratic Party (DP) and the Federal Alliance (FA) to form the DA. The NNP suspended its participation in the DA in 2001.

Population
47.56 million (2004)
Ethnic make-up
Black (75 per cent), white (13 per cent), coloured (9 per cent), Asian (3 per cent).
Religions
Christian (68 per cent), Islam (2 per cent), Hindu 1.5 per cent, indigenous beliefs and animist 28.5 per cent.

Education
Public expenditure on education amounts to 5.5 per cent of GDP.
Primary education begins at age six and lasts for six years. Junior secondary school lasts until age 15 when students may choose between an academic programme lasting a further three years at a senior secondary school or a vocational, technical course lasting two years in technical schools.
Government strategy for national schooling includes higher qualified teachers appointed to poorer schools and equalising school expenditure for all racial groups.
Literacy rate: 86.4 per cent, adult rate
Compulsory years: Six to 15
Enrolment rate: 133 per cent gross primary enrolment of relevant age group (including repeaters); 95 per cent gross secondary enrolment (World Bank).
Pupils per teacher: 45 in primary schools.

Health
There are major national programmes in operation including the Integrated Nutrition Programme, the Polio and Measles

Immunisation Campaign and Telemedicine (an interactive medical exchange based on information technology).

A R40 million (US$4.6 million) protocol signed between South Africa, Swaziland and Mozambique to control the spread of malaria lays the basis for a common programme of action in these countries.

HIV/Aids

South Africa has one of the highest HIV/Aids infection rates in the world and by January 2005 1.25 million sufferers had died of Aids, with over 1,000 Aids-related deaths recorded each day. An estimated 5.6 million people are HIV positive in South Africa which has the largest number of individuals living with the virus in a single country.

Aids has become a political issue with President Mbeki initially refusing to acknowledge the extent of the problem. Current programmes are now attempting to catch up on earlier inadequate measures while the government focussed on preventative measures.

In 2003, an international agreement allowed costly anti-retroviral (ARV) drugs to be bought at lower prices (this measure was partly prompted by the emergence of generic drugs), and the government agreed to distribution programmes. The nationwide use of ARVs is seen by Aids groups as a significant weapon in the fight to limit the damage the disease inflicts on sufferers, their families and the community at large.

Former president Nelson Mandela publicly announced that his son had died of Aids in January 2005, saying, 'Let us give publicity to HIV/Aids and not hide it, because the only way of making it appear to be a normal illness, just like TB, like cancer, is always to come out and say somebody has died because of HIV.' In April 2004, Inkatha opposition leader, Mangosuthu Buthelezi, had announced that his son had also died of Aids.

During the 2004 election campaign ARV programmes were promised, with medication to be offered to the most vulnerable for free. However since then the ruling ANC party's standpoint appears ambivalent towards these Western pharmaceutical measures.

South Africa is still in the process of addressing the deprivation wrought on black communities during the apartheid era including, poverty, poor primary healthcare, minimal education and families fractured by migratory work. This legacy has left women more vulnerable to the disease, and, by transmission, their children (20 per cent of children infected with HIV die of Aids before aged 5); in the age range 15–24 there is a 2:1 ratio of female to male HIV infection (UNAids 2004). The number of orphans is growing, from 2.2 million in 2003, to an expected 3.1 million or 18 per cent of all children by 2010. A local study reported in 2003 that life expectancy for women is expected to fall to 37 years by 2010, a drop of 17 years from 54 in 1999, male life expectancy will fall to 38 years at the same time. If this trend does not alter there will be noticeably fewer mid-adult women than men in the next two decades. By 2009 deaths by Aids-related illness is expected to exceed all other causes of death.

The South African pharmaceutical company, Aspen, was granted approval by US regulators to manufacture and supply antiretroviral drugs for local patients.

HIV prevalence: 21.5 per cent, aged 15–49 years
5.3 million adults and children living with HIV
27.9 per cent pregnant women (attending antenatal services) HIV positive
2.9 million women living with HIV
370,000 Aids deaths (adults and children) in 2003
(UNAids estimates, end 2003)

Life expectancy: 44 years (WHO 2005)

Fertility rate/Maternal mortality rate: 2.8 births per woman (World Bank)

Birth rate/Death rate: 18.9 births per 1,000 population; 18.4 deaths per 1,000 population (2003).

Population data issued by South Africa's Medical Research Council in March 2004 recorded a 44 per cent increase in adult deaths between 1998–2003, after population growth and improved registration had been factored in; deaths of women 20–49 increased by 168 per cent. It was concluded that this growth was due to Aids.

Infant mortality rate: 53 per 1,000 live births (World Bank)

Head of population per physician/ bed: 0.6 physicians per 1,000 people.

Welfare

The social assistance programme of the Department of Social Development provides benefits to approximately three million people comprising the elderly, persons with disabilities and children under the age of seven years. The government has emphasised the need to transform expensive institutional services into a more self-reliant approach towards individual and community care. Access to welfare grants is, however, limited. The State Maintenance Grants have been phased out and the availability of services for victims of violence across the country remains equally limited. Lack of an integrated approach towards allocations, capacity to spend and monitor the funds are some of the key problems relating to the distribution of poverty relief funds.

Main cities

Cape Town (legislative capital, estimated population 3.0 million in 2004), Durban (2.5 million), Johannesburg (financial capital 2.0 million), Pretoria (administrative capital, 1.5 million), Soweto (1.5 million), Port Elizabeth (848,400), East London (463,200), Msunduzi (433,300), Benoni (413,500), Vereeniging (392,500), Bloemfontein (judicial capital, 378,000).

The metropolitan region of Bloemfontein is the Mangaung Local Municipality.

Cape Town has three official names, the other two being Kaapstad (in Afrikaans) and iKapa (in Xhosa); its metropolitan region is the City of Cape Town.

Durban municipality is known by its Zulu name, eThekwini Municipal Area.

The metropolitan region of East London is Buffalo City.

Port Elizabeth is also known by English speakers as P E and the Friendly City, as *Die Baai* (The Bay) by local Afrikaans speakers and *iBhayi* by Xhosa speakers; its metropolitan region is the Nelson Mandela Metropolitan Municipality.

Pretoria is known as Tshwane among the Sotho-speaking population; its metropolitan region is the City of Tshwane Metropolitan Municipality.

Languages spoken
Official language/s
Afrikaans, English, Ndebele, Sesotho, Northern Sotho, SiSwati, Tsonga, Tswana, Venda, Xhosa, Zulu.

Media
Press
Press freedom is guaranteed by the constitution. The Freedom of Commercial Speech Trust plays an important role in industry self-regulation, forestalling government intervention.

Dailies: Major dailies include: *The Sowetan* (South Africa's largest selling daily with a circulation of over two million), *Beeld* (Afrikaans), *The Star*, *Daily News*, *Ilanga*, *Argus*, *The Citizen* and *Cape Times*. *Die Burger* is a regional Afrikaans newspaper translated daily to English. WOZA (www.woza.co.za) is South Africa's daily online newspaper geared to covering the news and views of the business and policy-making community.

Weeklies: *Daily Mail & Guardian* is South Africa's leading independent newspaper published weekly. The largest Sunday papers are *Sunday Times* (English), *The Sunday Star* (English), *Sunday Independent*, *Sunday Nation*, *City Press* (English) and *Rapport* (Afrikaans). Other weeklies mainly published from Johannesburg and Cape Town include *New Nation*, *Die*

Afrikaner, *Partriot*, *Post*, *The Southern Cross* and *Sowetan Sunday World*.
Business: Business publications include *Business Times*, *Business Day* and *Financial Mail*. *Personal Finance* covering business issues is a South African Independent Newspapers publication.

Broadcasting
Radio: Commercial radio services broadcast throughout the country in various languages. The South African Broadcasting Corporation (SABC) is the national public service broadcaster. It also operates an external radio service in four languages – English, French, Portuguese and kiSwahili.
Television: With the exception of the M-Net, television is state-influenced (SABC) comprising four networks. During the election period the media are monitored by the Independent Media Commission.

Advertising
South Africa's sophisticated advertising industry boasts full-range services, and the presence of subsidaries of prominent international agencies. Specialist media buying companies, as well as fee (non-commision) arrangements, have appeared. Television, radio, newspapers, magazines, outdoor advertisements, cinema and the Internet provide direct marketing opportunities.

Deregulation has brought further independent television channels and radio stations.

Anti-smoking legislation has affected agencies with tobacco accounts, and further regulation of comparable goods, including alcohol, is expected.

Economy
South Africa has a highly diversified and open economy. It has highly developed sectors in mining, agriculture, manufacturing and services providing an economy characteristic of a modern industrialised state. The alternative economy has the character of an emerging economy with poor infrastructure and a tendency to the informal, with high unemployment and low wages producing an uneven distribution of wealth. There has been a concerted effort to produce a more equitable structure but the economy is still split largely between the affluent white minority and the poorer black majority. Whites still own large tracts of fertile land and direct most of the industry and service sectors, while many blacks remain poor, landless and languishing in the country's shanty towns. There is the beginnings of a black middle class which is growing more and more afluent and demanding of the government.

As a primary component of its economic strategy, the government introduced black economic empowerment (BEE) codes, in 2005. To conform, companies have to demonstrate the principles of BEE by favouring black employment, and fostering their promotion within their organisations. Government contracts are awarded following a scrutiny of businesses to establish compliance. The lack of training during the apartheid period has led to the lack of a pool of black managers and executives. Many major employers have now begun courses or backed scholarships to address the situation.

The economy is largely based on the country's abundant mineral and energy resources. Manufacturing is underpinned by the mining sector while gold and diamonds dominate exports. Foreign investors are attracted to the country's robust infrastructure, with developed transport, water and electricity networks. Dams have been built on the rivers and provide water for irrigation, industrial and household use. There are also developed professional services while the stock exchange is ranked seventeenth in the world.

The government has many social problems to tackle that hinder economic growth. Around half the population lives in poverty with limited access to health and education facilities and utilities. The Aids prevalence rate has risen to over 20 per cent and has put a strain on, and will continue to hamper, future development. Diversification away from the mining sector continues to show progress although an alarming exodus of young qualified whites is creating serious skilled manpower shortages. South Africa's tourism sector has expanded considerably since the end of the apartheid era but it still has a very long way to go before reaching its full potential.

The economy in 2004 was strong with GDP growth at 3.7 per cent, based largely on strong domestic demand due to growing disposable income, a large reduction in interest rates, and rising house and stock prices. Consequently, unemployment fell to 26.2 per cent in September 2004. Employment rose but at a rate less than the growing labour force so that unemployment rose slightly to 26.5 per cent by March 2005.

The South African Reserve Bank (SARB) has a flexible exchange rate policy and has built up an impressive international reserve and has improved South Africa's debt risk.

The rand strengthened in 2004 and commodity prices rose in line. The trade deficit widened to 3.2 per cent of GDP – up from 1.5 per cent in 2003 – as imports grew robustly to surpass exports. Foreign investment in emerging assets weakened in 2005 and the currency dropped slightly accordingly.

In the short term, the economic outlook is expected to remain buoyant due to low interest rates and the government's moderately expansionist fiscal policy, and the helpful growth in the global economy. Nevertheless the warnings from the IMF include a need to tackle the problem of high unemployment, widespread poverty and the large wealth disparity, which it felt could be eased through labour market reforms and further trade liberalisation. Crime is still unacceptably high and social deprivation and HIV/Aids can only be ameliorated by social and economic progress through clearly defined and targetted programmes.

External trade
South Africa is a member of the Southern African Customs Union (Sacu) and the Southern African Development Community (SADC). With its SADC partners, South Africa intends to allow duty-free status to 85 per cent of trade between members by 2008, and 100 per cent by 2012. South Africa has bilateral trade agreements with the EU and Thailand.
South Africa is eligible for tariff preferences under the African Growth and Opportunities Act (AGOA); most of its products enter the US tax-free.
In November 2005 the government warned its cotton textile manufacturers that no import quotas would be imposed on Chinese textiles and that they would have to compete and find new markets. The 1 January 2005 WTO ruling stopping preferential import tariffs has curbed South African garment exports to the US.

Imports
Principal imports are machinery and equipment, chemicals, petroleum products, scientific instruments and foodstuffs.
Main sources: Germany (14.2 per cent total, 2004), US (8.5 per cent), China (7.5 per cent), Japan (6.9 per cent), UK (6.9 per cent), France (6.0 per cent), Saudi Arabia (5.6 per cent), Iran (5.0 per cent)

Exports
Principal exports are gold (around 20 per cent of total), diamonds, metals and metal products, minerals, machinery and equipment. South Africa is also a major exporter of granite, asbestos, iron, manganese, chrome and titanium ore.
Main destinations: US (10.2 per cent total, 2004), UK (9.2 per cent), Japan (9.0 per cent), Germany (7.1 per cent), The Netherlands (4.0 per cent)

Agriculture
Farming
South African agricultural is open to market forces and farmers take responsibility for production decisions, and pricing and distribution. The country has achieved self-sufficiency in staple grains, such as

maize and wheat, and basic foodstuffs such as fresh milk and other dairy products, meat, vegetables and fruit. The agricultural sector accounted for 3.4 per cent of GDP in 2004, with a growth rate of 1.2 per cent. The sector employs around 13 per cent of the workforce.

LandCare is a key community support programme in the National Department of Agriculture which aims to promote sustainable land management practices and prevent land degradation in rural areas. The government policy of forging partnerships to stimulate black empowerment is growing within the agricultural sector. Nevertheless land reforms to enable black farmers access to quality land has been slow with only 3 per cent redistributed by 2005 – of the 30 per cent planned for by 2014 – prompting a series of 'symbolic' property invasions, similar to those carried out in Zimbabwe.

South Africa has about 33 per cent of the southern hemisphere's deciduous fruit market in Europe. After minerals and metals, deciduous fruit is the country's largest export industry. The wine industry yields significant indirect benefits for the economy as a major employer and exporter. However, growth and competitiveness in the wine and tobacco industries is likely to be hampered by higher excise duty.

Oilseed production for bio-diesel offers a unique opportunity to facilitate such partnerships.

Crop production ('000 tonnes) for 2004 included: 12,225 tonnes (t) cereals in total, 1,761t wheat, 9,737t maize, 1,574t potatoes, 205t barley, 449t sorghum, 220t bananas, 103t pulses, 677t sunflower seed, 763t apples, 374t pears, 1,624t roots and tubers, 1,717t citrus fruit, 1,683t grapes, 417t tomatoes, 157t pineapples, 13t tea, 369t oilcrops, 32t tobacco, 19,094t sugar cane, 128t groundnuts in shell, 220t soya beans, 5,486t fruit in total, 2,349t vegetables in total.

Livestock production (in tonnes) included: 1,821,401t meat in total, 625,000t beef, 134,420t pig meat, 108,000t lamb, 17,000t game meat, 36,380t goat meat, 899,101t poultry, 340,000t eggs, 2,552,000t milk, 900t honey, 76,830t cattle hides, 18,420t sheepskins, 44,156t greasy wool.

Fishing

The general policy towards fisheries has been the protection of marine ecology and the promotion and sustained utilisation of the sea and its resources.

South Africa is largely self-sufficient in white fish and has a substantial export surplus and is self-sufficient in canned fish. Some 10 per cent of the abalone yield and 25 per cent of rock lobster is marketed locally and the rest is exported, mainly to the Far East. Cultivation of oysters and mussels is growing steadily and the possibility of cultivating abalone is being researched.

Of domestic fishmeal demand of 260,000 tonnes per year (tpy), 60,000tpy is locally produced and the rest is imported.

Fishing quotas for foreign vessels are issued in terms of formal bilateral fisheries agreements. Of all the quota fish caught in South Africa's exclusive fishing zone (200 nautical miles offshore), foreign catches make up only 2.4 per cent. The figure does not include non-quota species such as tuna. Foreign boats are allocated quotas for hake, hose mackerel and squid.

Forestry

About 7 per cent of the total land area is forested, with forest cover estimated at 8.9 million hectares (ha). About 27 per cent of the total land area is wooded. The country has extensive forest plantations and a large network of more than 200 protected areas covering nearly 5 per cent of the forest areas, including around 20 national parks. Deforestation accounts for around 1 per cent per annum or the equivalent of 8,000ha of forest cover. Government policy has focussed on making South Africa self-sufficient in wood and wood products, taking into account the country's limited water supply and scarcity of suitable habitats. Industrial roundwood is produced in large quantities. The forestry industry is dependent on resources available from plantations and produces a wide range of wood and paper products. Although it produces and exports pulp and paper, significant volumes of paper are also imported.

Exports of forest materials amount to US$1.3 billion while imports amounted to US$577.7 million in 2004.

Timber production in 2004 included 33,159,400 cubic metre (cum) roundwood, 21,159,400cum industrial roundwood, 2,171,300cum sawnwood, 14,833,300cum pulpwood, 5,235,900cum sawlogs and veneer logs, 1,021,600cum wood-based panels, 12,000,000cum wood fuel, 200,600t charcoal, 1,188,000t chemical wood pulp, 336,000t newsprint.

Industry and manufacturing

South Africa is one of Africa's most industrialised countries and enjoys a strong resource base. Most of the raw materials and semi-manufactured goods required by industry are available from local sources. Only clothing and textiles, furniture (hardwoods), chemicals and transport equipment (components) still rely to a lesser extent on imports of raw materials or intermediate goods. Output is dominated by engineering and metal products, especially steel, and it has become a world leader in manufacturing railway rolling stock, mining equipment and other machinery. Major steel companies include Iscor and Highveld Steel.

Other major growth areas are automobile production and the chemical industry. Although food and tobacco processing remain of great importance, their share of total output has fallen significantly. Food products, iron and steel and transport equipment together account for about a third of total gross manufacturing output. Other manufactures include paper and paper products, fabricated metal products, electrical and non-electrical machinery.

Industrial production accounted for 31.8 per cent of GDP, in 2004, of which 20 per cent was manufacturing; overall, services accounted for 64.9 per cent. All showed a growth increase of 3.2 per cent, 2.6 per cent and 4.1 per cent respectively.

Tourism

The tourism sector typically contributes up to 5 per cent of GDP and is an important source of foreign exchange. While visitor numbers increased in 2004, tourist spending fell by 7.4 per cent on the previous year, which led to a slight drop in employment. Estimates for 2005 show tourism contributing 3.9 per cent to GDP. The sector is expected to attract US$5.7 million or 14.1 per cent of total capital investment.

Europe constitutes the greater part of the overseas market (typically 65 per cent), followed by Asia (15 per cent), North America (12 per cent), Australasia (5 per cent), the Middle East (2 per cent) and the Indian Ocean Islands (1 per cent).

South Africa's tourism sector has expanded considerably since the end of the apartheid era but it still has a very long way to go before reaching its full potential. The country, which receives 52 per cent of the 13.4 million visitors to southern Africa each year, is positioning itself as the hub of a region-wide 'tourism park' wherein visitors will be able to move from one southern African country to another without going through formal borders. By pooling their resources and attractions together, southern African countries hope to emulate the islands of the Caribbean and increase tourist numbers. In the meantime, South Africa is steadily moving towards becoming the most popular conference destination in Africa.

Mining

South Africa is the world's foremost producer and exporter of gold and platinum, and a significant exporter of diamonds, iron ore, asbestos, manganese ore, vanadium, ferro-chromium, chrome ore and granite.

South Africa

International commodities traded in US dollars have all been affected by the rise in the rand since 2003 and most mining companies have experienced a drop in profits due to the disparity of expenses incurred in other currencies

A leading aluminium manufacturer, Alcan, has plans to build a smelter at Coega, near Port Elizabeth. Originally production would have reached 600,000 tonnes annually, however, in September 2005 plans were halted while a feasibility study was undertaken to facilitate a 900,000 tonnes processing plant. A smelter is expected to be operational by 2008.

The government has begun plans to introduce a state diamond trader company and producers such as UK-based, diamond company De Beers (founded in South Africa and the world's leading diamond trading company) would be required to forward a percentage of rough diamonds intended for export to the new Diamond Exchange and Export Centre (DEEC) for cutting and polishing by local craftsmen.

Diamonds, which had been exempt, are expected to be subject to a new export tax of 15 per cent following legislation due in 2006.

At least 40 per cent of the world's total recoverable gold reserves are in South Africa. Precious metals' producers will also be required to refine more of their output locally to provide more metals for South African design and manufacturing.

The mining sector only accounts for 6 per cent of GDP and South Africa sees value added diamond and gold processing as a source of added revenue and employment. The mining sector employs 6 per cent of the country's labour force and contributes up to one-third of the export revenue.

Hydrocarbons

South Africa's primary fuel is coal. It has over 49.5 billion tonnes of recoverable reserves – around 5 per cent of the world's total – and is the third largest net exporter globally.

It also had small reserves of oil but these were never enough to match its consumption. The majority of its oil is imported from the Middle East, with Iran and Saudi Arabia as the chief suppliers, however to reduce its dependency on this region South Africa has entered into agreement with Angola, Equatorial Guinea and Nigeria (the largest supplier of the African sources).

There has been much investment in synthetic fuels and South Africa is the world's largest producer of oil from coal and produces motor petroleum, distillates, kerosene and alcohols.

The country's oil refining capacity is over 468,500bpd, while oil consumption amounts to around 525,000bpd (2004). Refined products are sold in the local market and exported to East Africa and the Indian sub-continent. A 2002 joint venture by Sasol/Total for a US$123 million extension to its Natref refinery, increasing capacity by nearly 17,000bpd. According to estimates, South Africa has 22.1 billion cubic metres of natural gas reserves. Production is estimated at around 1.4 billion cubic metres per annum, all of which is consumed locally. US-based Forest Oil Corporation estimated the recoverable reserves at the Ibhubezi Prospect at 84.9 billion cubic metres, the production of which would be geared towards regional electrification. This has sparked further exploration around the western coast of South Africa. There is huge potential for South Africa to increase natural gas production.

Coal provides a significant source of foreign exchange. Most of South Africa's reserves are bituminous, with 45 per cent in ash content and only one per cent in sulphur content. Around 70 per cent of the recoverable reserves are located in three fields – Waterberg, Witbank and Highveld. Production levels were around 134.6 million tonnes of oil equivalent (toe) and 88.9 million toe is consumed domestically.

Energy

The bulk supply electricity company, Eskom, a self-financing, parastatal utility company, has an installed generating capacity of about 36,000MW. Largely through Eskom, South Africa supplies almost 60 per cent of the total electricity generated on the continent of Africa. Nevertheless, a third of South Africa's population does not have access to the national grid. Eskom is the fourth-largest power company in the world by capacity and is being restructured with a view to eventual privatisation.

The government is hoping to expand private sector involvement in the electrification drive, in the generation, transmission and distribution sectors. In October 2004 the government announced investment of US$26 billion until 2009, to improve the electricity infrastructure.

Eskom produces about 97 per cent of South Africa's electricity needs, with the balance made up by mines, industries and municipalities with their own small stations. It operates 17 coal-fired power stations, two hydroelectric, two pumped storage schemes, two gas turbine stations and the country's only nuclear power plant at Koeberg. Three inactive power stations will be re-commissioned at a cost of US$1.96 billion, with assistance from a foreign company skilled in such work to increase capacity. The 2,000MW nuclear power station, operated by Eskom and supervised by the Council for Nuclear Safety, is likely to remain the only nuclear facility for some time.

The extension of the electricity grid to less privileged, mainly rural, areas is a major priority of the government's energy policy. The emphasis is toward renewable energy resources such as solar energy and hydropower. The National Energy Council is investigating possibilities in this area. Renewable energy sources account for around 5 per cent of primary energy needs.

South Africa exports electricity to Botswana, Lesotho, Mozambique, Namibia, Swaziland and Zimbabwe. It also imports a small amount of electricity from neighbouring countries, mostly from Namibia, although the amount varies widely in accordance with the capacity of other countries to supply.

Financial markets
Stock exchange

After years of isolation, South Africa's financial markets have changed rapidly to adopt international standards and operate in a competitive global market. Since 1994, the Johannesburg Stock Exchange (JSE) has deregulated the market allowing the ownership of local brokers by foreign companies and banks. Anglo American dominates the JSE, with price changes in its stocks substantially affecting the market's indices. As such, the JSE is influenced to a significant extent by world gold prices. The South African Futures Exchange (Safex) was taken over by the JSE in 2001, following the approval of the country's competition regulators.

Among projects to continue improving efficiency and competitiveness is the creation of a paperless financial exchange, known as Strate (share transactions totally electronic). Strate is 50 per cent owned by the JSE, but is open to all electronic settlements including those not listed as JSE securities. Such improvements are vital if South Africa's financial markets are to cope with rapidly rising volumes and with competition from other emerging markets. The market response to Strate began as strong and positive.

The JSE broke through the 19,000 level for the first time in January 2006.

Banking and insurance

The financial services sector has changed rapidly since South Africa re-entered the global economy in the 1990s. Domestic banks have restructured and foreign banks compete fiercely in the commercial sector.

The South African Reserve Bank (SARB) (central bank) supervises the domestic and international activities of banks, discount houses and building societies. It issues the country's currency and is the custodian of South Africa's gold and foreign exchange reserves. It is responsible for the implementation of monetary policy which it formulates in conjunction with the finance ministry.

In May 2005, the UK's third largest bank, Barclays, purchased a 60 per cent share in South Africa's third largest, Absa. Bought for R33 billion (US$5.2 billion) it was the single largest foreign investment deal since apartheid ended.

Central bank
South African Reserve Bank (SARB)
Main financial centre
Pretoria (renamed Tswane)

Time
GMT plus two hours

Geography
South Africa occupies the southern extremity of the African continent. It is bordered by Namibia to the north-west, by Botswana and Zimbabwe to the north, by Mozambique to the north-east, and by Swaziland to the east.

Climate
Sub-tropical, with regional variations. In Cape coastal area, summers, October–March, are warm with temperature averaging 25–28 degrees Celsius (C); average wet winter temperature 17–20 degrees C. In Pretoria and other high veld areas, winters are warm and dry, while most rain falls during the hot summer. On the Natal coast humidity can be high during the summer, while the winter is drier with temperatures around 22–24 degrees C. Most rain falls during the summer months.

Entry requirements
Passports
Required by all.
Visa
Required by all and not issued on arrival. Some nationals from the EU, North America and Australasia are allowed to visit visa-free and will be granted a temporary visitors permit for up to three months. All visitors must have proof of return/onward passage, and may have to show evidence of sufficient funds for the intended stay. For further information and exceptions, contact the nearest embassy.
Currency advice/regulations
Import and of local currency is limited to R5,000 and export to R500 per person. Unlimited amount of foreign currency may be imported although amount must be declared.
Customs
Licences required for certain imports, including consumer goods; all items need certificates of origin and value.

Health (for visitors)
Mandatory precautions
Yellow fever vaccination certificate required if travelling from infected areas, (certificates are not valid until 10 days after immunisation).
Advisable precautions
Vaccinations are necessary for typhoid and hepatitis 'B' and a vaccination for hepatitis 'A' is advisable. To avoid the risk of bilharzia, only use well-maintained, chlorinated swimming pools. Malaria exists throughout the year in certain areas of northern Transvaal, eastern Lowveld and northern Natal; prophylaxis should be taken for visits to these areas. Water precautions should be taken in rural areas. Aids is prevalent.

Hotels
A wide choice is available in main commercial centres. It is advisable to make reservations well in advance, especially during December and January, March and April.

Public holidays
Fixed dates
1 Jan (New Year's Day), 21 Mar (Human Rights Day), 27 Apr (Liberty Day), 1 May (Labour Day), 31 May (National Women's Day), 16 Jun (Youth Day), 10 Oct (Heritage Day), 16 Dec (Reconciliation Day), 25 Dec (Christmas Day), 26 Dec (Day of Goodwill).
Variable dates
Good Friday, Easter Monday/Family Day.

Working hours
Banking
Mon–Fri: 0830–1530; Sat: 0830–1100. Some banks have extended hours.
Business
Mon–Fri: 0730/0830–1600/1700. Some businesses have extended hours.
Government
Mon–Fri: 0730/0830–1600/1700.
Shops
Mon–Fri: 0830–1700; Sat: 0830–1300. Certain shops are open on Sundays.

Telecommunications
Mobile phones
There are GSM roaming facilities available, with coverage throughout most of the country.

Electricity supply
Usually 220/230V AC, but 220/250V in Port Elizabeth and 250V in Pretoria.

Social customs/useful tips
There are no particular taboos, but visitors should be mindful that in certain parts of the country strong racist attitudes still prevail. It is best not to get involved in political discussions.

Visitors should not photograph security institutions.

Security
Visitors should avoid visiting black townships without guidance from reliable local residents and without a trustworthy companion. Certain townships in the Pretoria-Witwatersrand-Vereeniging region and around the Cape Town, Durban and Pietermaritzburg regions should be avoided unless a visit is absolutely necessary – notably Thokoza, Sebokeng, Alexandra, Boipatong, Katlehong, Langa, Mitchell's Plain, Gugulethu, Khayelitsha, Crossroads, KwaMashu and Mpumulanga.

Periodic attacks on visitors to townships have occurred and the crime rate has soared as unemployment and politically-related violence have increased. Street crime is less of a problem in major urban areas, though care must be taken in central Johannesburg at night. Care must also be taken when visiting extreme right-wing strongholds such as Ventersdorp in the Western Transvaal. It is advisable not to carry unnecessary valuables, expensive jewellery and large amounts of money.

Crime in Johannesburg continues to escalate. Do not resist if confronted. Avoid walking in the streets alone after shopping. Use taxis at night and only those booked through a reputable hotel or among those listed in the official Johannesburg guide. Keep car doors locked while you are in the vehicle or when it is parked. If you are driving after dark, keep car doors locked and avoid slowing down.

Getting there
Air
National airline: South African Airways
International airport/s: Johannesburg Intenational (JNB), serves as a hub for flights to other countries in the region. It is 24km from city, duty-free shop, bar, restaurant, buffet, bank, post office, shops, car hire, airport bus; Cape Town International (CPT), 22km east of city, duty-free shop, car hire, bank, bar and restaurant; Durban International (DUR), 16km from city, duty-free shop, car hire, bank, bar and restaurant.
Other airport/s: Bloemfontein (BFN), 10km east of the city; Port Elizabeth (PLZ), 25km from the city.
Airport tax: None
Surface
Road: Possible from Botswana, Lesotho, Namibia, Swaziland, Zimbabwe and Mozambique. Ttravellers are generally advised to check regulations and conditions regarding entry by road with the Automobile Association of South Africa.

The Maputo Corridor project includes a link from the Atlantic coast at Namibia's Walvis Bay across the Kalahari desert to

join the South African road network, linking the western side of southern Africa with the Indian Ocean at Maputo, Mozambique. There is a toll road between Witbank in South Africa and Maputo.
Rail: There are services from Mozambique, Botswana and through Zimbabwe from Namibia.
Main port/s: Cape Town, Durban, Port Elizabeth and East London.

Getting about
National transport
Air: All major cities and towns are linked with regular, scheduled services. South African Airways, Inter Air and Sun Air fly domestic routes.
Road: Extensive network of tarred roads, including 51,000km linking main centres. Also, 128,777km of untarred roads – some of the remoter sections can become impassable in wet weather.
Buses: Inter-city services are operated by Greyhound, Citiliner and other private companies. Vehicles are a good standard.
Rail: Network of some 24,000km with good services throughout the country. Reservations for express trains should be made well in advance. Two classes available, but visitors are advised to travel first class. Most long distance mainline trains have restaurant cars and all have sleeping accommodation (couchettes operated in both first- and second-class; there is a fee for bedding).
Named services include: Blue Train, a luxury service, running three times a week (Pretoria-Johannesburg-Cape Town; with sleeping accommodation, restaurant cars, air-conditioning, suites, staterooms available); Trans Orange, once a week (Durban-Cape Town); Trans Natal, daily (Durban-Johannesburg).

City transport
Taxis: Widely available in all towns. Cannot be hailed in the street; must be called from a rank. Fares within the city areas depend on distance and time, while longer distance fares are lower and are obtained on a quotation basis. 10 per cent tip is usual.
Buses, trams & metro: There are bus and metro networks in all main towns. Fares in Cape Town and Johannesburg are zonal, with payment in cash or with ten-ride pre-purchase 'clipcards' from kiosks. In Pretoria, there are various pre-purchase ticket systems. In Durban, conventional buses vie for passengers with minibuses and combi-taxis (both legal and illegal); also found in other South African towns. Although cheap and very fast, they should be used with care.
Trains: There are frequent local trains in the Cape Town and Pretoria and Johannesburg urban areas. All trains have first- and second-class accommodation.

Car hire
Self-drive and chauffeur-driven cars are widely available. An international driving licence is required unless visitor's national licence carries the photograph and signature of the holder.
Driving is on the left. Speed limits: built-up areas 60kph; country roads 100kph; declared freeways and some main roads 120kph. Heavy fines for speeding.

BUSINESS DIRECTORY
The addresses listed below are a selection only. While World of Information makes every endeavour to check these addresses, we cannot guarantee that changes have not been made, especially to telephone numbers and area codes. We would welcome any corrections.

Telephone area codes
The international dialling code (IDD) for South Africa is +27, followed by area code and subscriber's number:

Bloemfontein	51	Ladysmith	361
Cape Town	21	Pietermaritzburg	331
Durban	31	Port Elizabeth	41
Johannesburg	11	Pretoria	12

Chambers of Commerce
American Chamber of Commerce, 60 Fifth Street, PO Box 1132, Houghton 2041, Johannesburg (tel: 788-0265; fax: 880-1632; e-mail: administrator@amcham.co.za).

Bloemfontein Chamber of Business, 37 Kellner Street, PO Box 87, Bloemfontein 9300 (tel: 447-3368; fax: 447-5064; e-mail:bcci@intekom.co.za).

Cape Town Regional Chamber of Commerce and Industry, 19 Louis Gradner Street, PO Box 204, Cape Town 8000 (tel: 402-4300; fax: 402-4302; e-mail: info@capechamber.co.za).

Durban Chamber of Commerce & Industry, 190 Stanger Street, PO Box 1506, Durban 4000 (tel: 335-1000; fax: 332-1288; e-mail: chamber@durbanchamber.co.za).

Johannesburg Chamber of Commerce and Industry, Private Bag 34, Corner Empire Road and Owl Street, Auckland Park 2006, Johannesburg (tel: 726-5300; fax: 782-2000; e-mail: info@jcci.co.za).

Ladysmith Chamber of Commerce and Industry, PO Box 7, Ladysmith 3370 (tel: 631-0541; fax: 637-4407; e-mail: lcci@futurenet.co.za).

Pietermaritzburg Chamber of Business, Royal Show Grounds, Commercial Road, PO Box 11734, Dorpspruit 3206, Pietermaritzburg (tel: 345-2747; fax: 394-4151; e-mail: pcb@futurenet.co.za).

Port Elizabeth Regional Chamber of Commerce and Industry, 22 Grahamstown Road, PO Box 2221, North End 6056, Port Elizabeth (tel: 484-4430; fax: 487-1851; e-mail: info@pechamber.org.za).

Pretoria Chamber of Commerce and Industry, 852 Park Street, PO Box 40653, Arcadia 0007, Pretoria (tel: 342-3236; fax: 342-1486; e-mail: pcci@mweb.co.za).

South African Chamber of Business, 24 Sturdee Avenue, PO Box 213, Saxonwold 2132, Johannesburg (tel: 446-3800; fax: 446-3847; e-mail: info@sacob.co.za).

Banking
Absa Bank Ltd, 2nd Floor, ABSA Towers North, 180 Commissioner Street, Johannesburg 2001 (tel: 350-4000; fax: 350-3768).

International Bank of Southern Africa Ltd, 3rd Floor, Sunnyside Ridge Bldg, 32 Princess of Wales Terrace, Parktown, Johannesburg 2193 (tel: 644-3300, 643-6740, 643-6743; fax: 643-1122).

Nedcor Bank Ltd, 135 Rivonia Rd, Sandown, Sandton, Johannesburg 2001 (tel: 294-4444; fax: 295-5555).

South African Bank of Athens Ltd, Bank of Athens Building, 116 Marshall Street, Johannesburg 2001 (tel: 832-1211; fax: 838-1001, 833-7976).

Standard Bank of South Africa Ltd, 5 Simmonds Street, Johannesburg 2001 (tel: 636-9111; fax: 636-3544).

Central bank
South African Reserve Bank, 370 Church Street, PO Box 427, Pretoria 0001 (tel: 313-3911; fax: 313-3197; e-mail: info@.resbank.co.za).

Travel information
Automobile Association of South Africa, Denis Paxton House, Alladale Road, Kyalami Midrand 1685; PO Box 596, Johannesburg 2000 (tel: 799-1000; fax: 799-1960; e-mail: aasa@aasa.co.za).

Blue Train Reservations, PO Box 2671, Joubert Park 2044 (tel: 334-8459; fax: 334-8464; e-mail: bluetrain@transnet.co.za).

Coach Services: Translux Express, PO Box 2383, Johannesburg 2000 (tel: 774-3333; fax: 774-3318); Greyhound Coach Lines, PO Box11229, Johannesburg 2000 (tel: 830-1301; fax: 830-1528); Intercape Mainliner, PO Box 618, Bellville 7535 (tel: 386-4400; fax: 386-2488).

Eastern Cape Tourism Board, PO Box 186, Bisho 5605 (tel: 635-2115; fax: 636-4019; e-mail: info@ectourism.co.za).

Free State Department of Environmental Affairs and Tourism, PO Box 264,

Bloemfontein 9300 (tel: 403-3435; fax: 448-8361).

Gauteng Tourism Authority, The Rosebank Mall, Rosebank 2196 (tel: 327-2000; fax: 327-7000; e-mail: tourism@gauteng.net).

KwaZulu-Natal Tourism Authority, PO Box 2516, Durban 4000 (tel: 304-7144; fax: 305-6693; e-mail: info@tourism-kzn.org).

Mpumalanga TourismAuthority, PO Box 679, Nelspruit 1200 (tel: 752-7001; fax: 759-5441; e-mail: mtanlpsa@cis.co.za).

Northern Cape Tourism Board, Private Bag X5017, Kimberley 8300 (tel: 832-2657; fax: 831-2937; e-mail: tourism@northerncape.org.za).

Northern Province Tourism Board, PO Box 1309, Pietersburg 0700 (tel: 288-0099; fax: 288-0094; e-mail: ceo@greatnorth.co.za).

North-West Parks and Tourism Council, PO Box 4488, Mmabatho 2735 (tel: 386-1225; fax: 386-1158; e-mail: nwptb@iafrica.com).

Rovos Rail Reservations, Victoria Hotel, PO Box 2837, Pretoria 0001 (tel: 323-6052; fax: 323-0843).

South African Airways, Airways Towers, 39 Wolmarans Street, Bloemfontein; PO Box 7778, Johannesburg 2000 (tel: 356-2059; fax: 356-1795; e-mail: help@flysaa.com; internet site: http://www.saap.vwv.com/).

South African National Parks, 643 Leyds Street, Muckleneuk, Pretoria; PO Box 787, Pretoria 0001 (tel: 343-1991; fax: 343-0905; e-mail: reservations@parks-sa.co.za).

Western Cape Tourism Board, Private Bag X9108, Cape Town 8000 (tel: 426-5639; fax: 426-5640; e-mail: info@capetourism.org).

Ministry of tourism
Ministry of Environmental Affairs and Tourism, Fedsure Forum Building, 315 Pretorius Street, Pretoria; Private Bag X447, Pretoria 0001 (tel: 310-3611; fax: 322-0082).

National tourist organisation offices
South African Tourism, Bojanala House, 12 Rivonia Road, Illovo 2196 (tel: 778-8000; fax: 778-8001; e-mail: info@southafrica.net; internet site: http://www.southafrica.net).

Ministries
N.B. For the following Ministry addresses: Pretoria (administrative), Cape Town (legislative).

Ministry of Agriculture and Land Affairs, Private Bag X250, Pretoria 0001 (tel: 319-6886; fax: 321-8558); Private Bag X9087, Cape Town 8000 (tel: 465-7690; fax: 465-6550).

Ministry of Arts, Culture, Science and Technology, Private Bag X727, Pretoria 0001 (tel: 337-8378; fax: 324-2687); Private Bag X9156, Cape Town 8000; (tel: 465-4850; fax: 461-1425).

Ministry of Communications, Private Bag X882, Pretoria 0001 (tel: 427-8111; fax: 362-6915); Private Bag X9151, Cape Town 8000 (tel: 462-1632; fax: 462-1646).

Ministry of Correctional Services, Private Bag X853, Pretoria 0001 (tel: 323-8803; fax: 323-4111); Private Bag X9131, Cape Town 8000 (tel: 462-2314; fax: 465-4375).

Ministry of Defence, Private Bag X427, Pretoria 0001 (tel: 355-6119; fax: 347-0118); PO Box 47, Cape Town 8000 (tel: 469-6070; fax: 465-5870).

Ministry of Education, Private Bag X603, Pretoria 0001 (tel: 312-5501; fax: 323-5989); Private Bag X9034, Cape Town 8000 (tel: 465-7350; fax: 461-4788).

Ministry of Environmental Affairs and Tourism, Private Bag X447, Pretoria 0001 (tel: 310-3611; fax: 322-0082); Private Bag X9154, Capetown 8000 (tel: 465-7240; fax: 465-3216).

Ministry of Finance, Private Bag X115, Pretoria 0001 (tel: 323-8911; fax: 323-3262); PO Box 29, Cape Town 8000 (tel: 464-6100; fax: 461-2934).

Ministry of Foreign Affairs, Private Bag X152, Pretoria 0001 (tel: 351-0005; fax: 351-0253); 120 Plein St, Cape Town 8001 (tel: 464-3700; fax: 465-6548).

Ministry of Health, Private Bag X399, Pretoria 0001 (tel: 328-4773; fax: 325-5526); Private Bag X9070, Cape Town 8000 (tel: 465-7407; fax: 465-1575).

Ministry of Home Affairs, Private Bag X741, Pretoria 0001 (tel: 326-8081; fax: 321-6491); Private Bag X9102, Cape Town 8000 (tel: 461-5818; fax: 461-2359).

Ministry of Housing, Private Bag X645, Pretoria 0001 (tel: 421-1311; fax: 341-8513); Private Bag X9029, Cape Town 8000 (tel: 465-7295; fax: 465-3610).

Ministry of Intelligence Services, PO Box 56450, Arcadia 0007(tel: 338-1800; fax: 323-0718); PO Box 51278, Waterfront 8002 (tel: 401-1800; fax: 461-4644).

Ministry of Justice and Constitutional Development, Private Bag X276, Pretoria 0001 (tel: 323-8581; fax: 321-1708); Private Bag X256, Cape Town 8000 (tel: 465-7506; fax: 465-2783).

Ministry of Labour, Private Bag X499, Pretoria 0001 (tel: 322-6523; fax: 320-1942); Private Bag X9090, Cape Town 8000 (tel: 461-6030; fax: 462-2832).

Ministry of Minerals and Energy, Private Bag X646, Pretoria 0001 (tel: 322-8695; fax: 322-8699); Private Bag X9111, Cape Town 8000 (tel: 462-2310; fax: 461-0859).

Ministry of Provincial and Local Government, Private Bag X802, Pretoria 0001 (tel: 334-0705; fax: 326-4478); Private Bag X9123, Cape Town 8000 (tel: 462-1441; fax: 461-0851).

Ministry of Public Enterprises, Private Bag X15, Hatfield 0028 (tel: 431-1000; fax: 342-7224); Private Bag X9079, Cape Town 8000 (tel: 461-6376; fax: 465-2381).

Ministry of Public Service and Administration, Private Bag X884, Pretoria 0001 (tel: 314-7911; fax: 328-6529); Private Bag X9148, Cape Town 8000 (tel: 465-5491; fax: 465-5484).

Ministry of Public Works, Private Bag X890, Pretoria 0001 (tel: 324-1510; fax: 325-6380); Private Bag X9155, Cape Town 8000 (tel: 462-4184; fax: 461-6962).

Ministry of Safety and Security, Private Bag X463, Pretoria 0001 (tel: 339-2800; fax: 339-2819); Private Bag X9080, Cape Town 8000 (tel: 465-7400; fax: 461-2073).

Ministry of Social Development, Private Bag X885, Pretoria 0001 (tel: 312-7637; fax: 321-2658); Private Bag X9153, Cape Town 8000 (tel: 465-4011; fax: 465-4469).

Ministry of Sport and Recreation, Private Bag X869, Pretoria 0001 (tel: 334-3100; fax: 321-8493); Private Bag X9149, Cape Town 8000 (tel: 465-5506; fax: 465-4402).

Ministry of Trade and Industry, Private Bag X274, Pretoria 0001 (tel: 322-7677; fax: 322-7851); Private Bag X9047, Cape Town 8000 (tel: 461-7191; fax: 465-1291).

Ministry of Transport, Private Bag X193, Pretoria 0001 (tel: 309-3131; fax: 328-3194); Private Bag X9129, Cape Town 8000 (tel: 465-7260; fax: 461-6845).

Ministry of Water Affairs and Forestry, Private Bag X313, Pretoria 0001 (tel: 36-8733; fax: 328-4254); Private Bag X9052, Cape Town 8000 (tel: 464-1500; fax: 465-3362).

Office of the President, Private Bag X1000, Pretoria 0001 (tel: 337-5100; fax: 321-8870); Private Bag X1000,

South Africa

Cape Town 8000 (tel: 464-2100; fax: 464-2123).

Other useful addresses

Association of Advertising Agencies (AAA), PO Box 2289, Parklands 2121 (tel: 781-2772; fax: 781-2796; e-mail: aaa@gem.co.za).

Afrikaanse Handelsinstituut (AHI) (Afrikaans Trade Institute), Lynnwood Galleries, 354 Rosemary Street, Lynnwood 0081; PO Box 35100, Menlopark 00101 (tel: 348-5440; fax: 348-8771; e-mail: pta@ahi.co.za).

Association of Marketers (ASOM), 8 Sloane Street, Bryanston, Sandton; PO Box 98859, Sloane Park 2152, Bryanston (tel: 706-1633; fax: 706-4151; e-mail: asom@pixie.co.za).

Board on Tariffs and Trade, Fedlife Forum, Cnr Van der Walt and Pretorius Streets, Private Bag X753, Pretoria 0001 (tel: 322-8244; fax: 322-0149).

British High Commission, 255 Hill Street, Arcadia, Pretoria 0002 (tel: 483-1200; fax: 483-1302); 91 Parliament Street, Cape Town 8001 (tel: 461-7220; fax: 461-0017).

Chamber of Mines of South Africa, PO Box 61809, Marshalltown 2107 (tel: 498-7100; fax: 834-4251).

Chemical & Allied Industries Association, 15th Floor, Metal Box Centre, 25 Owl Street, Auckland Park 2006 (tel: 482-1671; fax: 726-8310).

Clothing Federation of South Africa, 42 van der Linde Street, Bedfordview 2008 (tel: 622-8125; fax: 622-8316).

COEGA Development Corporation, Libra Chambers, Cnr Oakworth Road and Carnarvon Place, Humerail, Port Elizabeth; Private Bag X13130, Humewood, Port Elizabeth 6013 (tel: 507-9111; fax: 585-5445; e-mail: info@coega.co.zu).

Government Communications and Information System (GCIS), 356 Vermeulen Street, Pretoria; Private Bag X745, Pretoria 0001 (tel: 314-2127; 325-2030; e-mail: govcom@gcis.pwv.gov.za; internet site: http://www.gcis.gov.za).

ICC Durban (international convention centre), 45 Ordnance Road, Durban 4001; PO Box 155, Durban 4000 (tel: 360-1000; fax: 360-1005; e-mail: mktg@icc.co.za).

Industrial Development Corporation of South Africa, 19 Fredman Drive, Sandton 2146; PO Box 784055, Sandton 2146 (tel: 269-3000; fax: 269-3116; e-mail: callcentre@idc.co.za).

Iscor Limited, Roger Dyason Road, Pretoria West; PO Box 450, Pretoria 0001 (tel: 307-3000; fax: 307-4721; e-mail: webmaster@iscor.com).

JSE Securities Exchange (stock exchange), 1 Exchange Square, 2 Gwen Lane, Sandown, Sandton 2196; Private Bag X991174, Sandton 2146 (tel: 520-7000; fax: 520-8584; e-mail: miscellaneous@jse.co.za).

South African Association for the Conference Industry (SAACI), PO Box, Kloof 3640 (tel 764-6977; fax: 764-6974; e-mail: sec@saaci.co.za).

South African Business Initiative for Reconstruction and Development, 17th Floor, Metal Box Centre, 25 Owl Street, Auckland Park 2092 (tel: 482-5100; fax: 482-5507).

South African Diamond Board, 5th Floor, SA Diamond Centre, 240 Commissioner Street, Johannesburg 2001 (tel: 334-8980/6; fax: 334-8898; e-mail: mabombol@sadb.co.za).

South African Embassy (USA), 3051 Massachusetts Avenue, NW Washington, DC (tel: 202-232-4400; fax: 202-265-1607; e-mail: safrica@southafrica.net).

South African Foreign Trade Organisation (SAFTO), Export House, 71 Maud Street, Sandton; PO Box 782706, Sandton 2146 (tel: 883-3737; fax: 883-6569; e-mail: safto@apollo.is.co.za).

South African Petroleum Industry Association, Trust Bank Centre, Adderley Street, Cape Town 8001; PO Box 7082, Roggebaai 8012 (tel: 419-8054; fax: 419-8058).

Statistics South Africa, Steyn's Building, 274 Schoeman Street, Pretoria 0002; Private Bag X44, Pretoria 0001 (tel: 310-8911; fax: 322-3374; e-mail: info@statssa.pwv.gov.za; internet site: http://www.statssa.gov.za/).

Trade and Investment South Africa, Rex Welsh House, Maud Street, Sandown, Sandton 2196; PO Box 782084, Sandton 2146 (tel: 884-2206; fax: 884-3236; e-mail: isa@isa.org.za).

US Embassy, 877 Pretorius Street, Pretoria; PO Box 9536, Pretoria 0001(tel: 342-1048; fax: 342-2244).

Internet sites

African Development Bank: http://www.afdb.org

Africa Online: http://www.africaonline.com

AllAfrica.com: http://allafrica.com

Harambee Afrika (UK business club for traders with east, central and southern Africa; includes annotated web resource list): http://www.harambee.co.uk

Johannesburg Stock Exchange: http://www.jse.co.za/

Maputo development corridor: http://www.dbsa.org/Development_Corridors/Corridors/Maputo

Mbendi AfroPaedia (information on companies, countries, industries and stock exchanges in Africa): http://mbendi.co.za

Province of the North West Tourist Board: http://www.tourismnorthwest.co.za/

South African Development Community (SADC): http://www.sadcreview.com

South African Futures Exchange: http://www.safex.co.za/

South African yellow pages: http://www.ipages.co.za/

Trade Web: http://www.trade.co.za/Africa Business Network: http://www.ifc.org/abn

South Georgia

KEY FACTS

Official name: South Georgia and the South Sandwich Islands (SGSSI)

Head of State: Queen Elizabeth II

Head of government: Commissioner Howard J S Pearce (resides in Falkland Islands)

Area: 3,755 square km

Population: 20 (2004) (British Antarctic Survey (BAS) scientists)

Capital: King Edward Point (administrative centre)

Official language: English

Currency: Falkland Islands pound or pound sterling (FI£ or £) = 100 pence

Exchange rate: FI£ or £0.57 per US$ (Oct 2005); (pegged to pound sterling)

COUNTRY PROFILE

Historical profile
1775 Captain Cook landed and took formal possession of South Georgia and the South Sandwich Islands (SGSSI).
1904 A whaling station was established by the Norwegian C A Larsen.
1908 The UK government annexed SGSSI by Letters Patent as part of the Falkland Islands Dependencies and the islands came under UK administration.
1965 Leith Harbour, the last shore-based whaling station in South Georgia, was closed.
1982 Argentine military forces occupied South Georgia for 22 days. South Georgia and the South Sandwich Islands became overseas territories of the UK.
2001 The UK military garrison closed and was replaced by a British Antarctic Survey (BAS) base at King Edward Point. There is a biological station on Bird Island.
2003 Three ships ran aground during bad weather in May; the crews were rescued by the residents.
2005 July Alan Huckle named next Commissioner, taking up appointment in 2006. A revised version of the 2000 environment management plan has been drafted and published on the British Antarctic Survey's website. The new plan will be publushedin 2006 and will set out environmental policies for the next five years.

Political structure
South Georgia and the South Sandwich Islands (SGSSI) are overseas territories of the UK, legally distinct from the Falkland Islands but, for convenience, they are administered from the Falkland Islands. With no indigenous or permanent inhabitants, there is no need for representative government, but a separate constitution for the territory was promulgated in 1985. The governor of the Falkland Islands is also the commissioner for the SGSSI; in this capacity he consults the Falklands Executive Council on those matters relating to the territory which might affect the Falkland Islands.
Other administrative posts based in Stanley, Falkland Islands, include the assistant commissioner who is also director of the SGSSI Fisheries, a financial secretary and attorney general. The marine officer, based at King Edward Point, is responsible for customs, immigration, posts and fisheries liaison.

Population
20 (2004) (British Antarctic Survey (BAS) scientists)

Main cities
King Edward Point (administrative centre); Grytviken, formerly a whaling station on South Georgia, was the garrison town.

Languages spoken
Official language/s
English

Economy
The South Georgia Environmental Management Plan was set out in 2000 and was revised in 2005, covering the period from 2006 to 2010. The British government is committed to providing a sustainable policy framework which conserves, manages and protects the rich natural environment, at the same time allowing for human activities and the generation of revenue.
Income is derived from fishing licences, fees for transshipping fish catches, tourist landing charges and the sale of postage stamps. A fishing licence costs US$110,000 per year, regardless of which country the boats come from.

Agriculture
Fishing
Large-scale fishing began in 1969/70 by Soviet bloc countries. In 1993, the UK extended its territorial waters around the SGSSI from 19.3km (12 miles) to 321.8km (200 miles) and created the SGSSI Maritime Zone. In 1996, new laws opened fishing grounds with a licensing scheme. Approximately 100–200,000 tonnes of krill are caught around South Georgia each year. The SGSSI government applies conservation measures to the maritime zone, but has the right to impose additional measures if appropriate. There is satellite imagery surveillance of the fishing zone.
The toothfish total allowable catch (TAC) for the 2006/07 season was increased by 15 per cent by the SGSSI and approved by the Convention for the Conservation of Antarctic Marine Resources

Tourism
Visitors arrive mainly by tour ships, although an international airport is planned. Passenger numbers increased slightly in 2004 to 3,765, carried by 40 vessels. The largest number came from the US (32 per cent), followed by the UK (25 per cent) and Germany (15 per cent). There were also 18 visits by by private as well as

South Georgia

commercial yachts. Extended walks, ie more than one kilometre from the landing site, are growing in popularity, as are visits to the nesting sites of the wandering albatross, especially Prion Island, which is carefully managed.

Environment
A draft of the South Georgia Environmental Pan 2005 (for the period 2006–10) was published on the British Antarctic website in January 2006. The final Plan will be published later in the year.

South Georgia is the breeding ground for some 85 per cent of the world's southern fur seal population, as well as significant populations of elephant seals, albatrosses, petrels and penguins. In 1910, reindeer were introduced by Norwegian whaling companies.

The South Sandwich Islands represent a maritime ecosystem.

Time
GMT minus two hours

Geography
South Georgia is an isolated, mountainous sub-Antarctic island, which lies in the South Atlantic Ocean, 2,150km east of Tierra del Fuego and about 1,390km east-south-east of the Falkland Islands. Surrounded by cold waters originating from the Antarctic, South Georgia has a harsher climate than expected from its latitude. More than 50 per cent of the island is covered by permanent ice with many large glaciers reaching the sea at the head of fjords. The main mountain range is the Allardyce Range, which has its highest point at Mount Paget (2,960m).

The South Sandwich Islands, which comprise a chain of active volcanic islands around 240km long, lie about 750km south-east of South Georgia. The climate is wholly Antarctic and in the late winter, the islands may be surrounded by pack ice.

Climate
South Georgia and the South Sandwich Islands are prone to very sudden and unexpected changes of weather.

Entry requirements
All visitors must apply to the Office of the Commissioner, South Georgia and South Sandwich Islands, Government House, Stanley, Falkland Islands (tel: +500-27-433, fax: +500-27-434; e-mail:gov.house@horizon.co.fk) at least 60 days in advance of their journey for permission to land. Application forms can be obtained from the Commissioner's office or on-line from the official South Georgia government website (www.sgisland.org). Details of all places to be visited must be provided and there is a landing fee of £55 per visitor. There are no search-and-rescue facilities.

Passports
Passports must be valid for a minimum of six months.

Visa
Not required, but visitors must report to the Marine Officer at King Edward Point, Cumberland Bay East.

Health (for visitors)
Advisable precautions
There are no medical facilities available. Comprehensive medical emergency insurance is necessary as well as sufficient stocks of prescribed medication. Sunburn is a problem in this sub-polar region, sunblock should be applied regularly.

All of the historic buildings in the territory present a safety risk; they are storm damaged and flimsy, causing wind blown asbestos particles. Visitors should not approach within 200 metres of them without permission of the Marine Officer at King Edward Point.

Credit cards
The museum shop accepts VISA and Mastercard, but not American Express.

Working hours
Government
Mon–Fri: (winter) 1100–1515, 1630–1930; (summer) 1200–1615, 1730–2030.

Telecommunications
Postal services
A new post code for the islands has been issued through the Universal Postal Union: SIQQ 1ZZ.

Getting there
Air
There is currently no normal air access, but there are plans for an international airport.
Surface
The only access is by navy or cruise ships.

Getting about
National transport
Road: There are no road links on the islands.

BUSINESS DIRECTORY
The addresses listed below are a selection only. While World of Information makes every endeavour to check these addresses, we cannot guarantee that changes have not been made, especially to telephone numbers and area codes. We would welcome any corrections.

Other useful addresses
British Antarctic Survey, High Cross, Madingley Rd, Cambridge CB3 OET, UK (tel: +44(0)1223-221-400; fax: +44(0)1223-362-616; e-mail: information@bas.ac.uk).

Licensing Officer SGSSI, Fisheries Department, Stanley, Falkland Islands (tel: +500-27-260; fax: +500-27-265; e-mail: fish.fig@horizon.co.fk).

Office of the Commissioner, South Georgia and South Sandwich Islands, Government House, Stanley, Falkland Islands (tel: +500-27-433; fax: +500-27-434; e-mail:gov.house@horizon.co.fk).

Internet sites
British Antarctic survey: http://www.antartic.ac.uk

Government website: http://www.sgisland.org

South Atlantic Remote Territories Media Association: http://www.sartma.com

Spain

KEY FACTS

Official name: Reino de España (Kingdom of Spain)

Head of State: King Juan Carlos I (since 1975)

Head of government: Prime Minister José Luis Rodríguez Zapatero (PSOE) (sworn in 17 Apr 2004)

Ruling party: Partido Socialista Obrero Español (PSOE) (Spanish Socialist Workers' Party) (elected 14 Mar 2004)

Area: 504,782 square km, including the Balearic and Canary Islands, and the Ceuta and Melilla enclaves in North Africa

Population: 41.90 million (2004)

Capital: Madrid

Official language: Castilian Spanish, Catalan (in Catalonia including the Balearics), Basque (in the Basque provinces), Valencian (Province of Valencia), Galician (Galicia).

Currency: Euro (eur) = 100 cents

Exchange rate: eur0.83 per US$ (Oct 2005)

GDP per capita: US$24,144 (2004)

GDP real growth: 2.70% (2004); 3.5% (3rd quarter 2005)

Labour force: 18.82 million (2003)

Unemployment: 10.80% (2004), 9.4% (Aug 2005)

Inflation: 3.10% (2004); 3.7% (Dec 2005 – monthly figure)

Balance of trade: -US$64.52 billion (2004)

Foreign debt: US$1,217.77 billion (2004)

Annual FDI: US$184.00 billion (cumulative, 1995–2004, OECD); US$9.90 billion (OECD, 2004)*

*estimated figure

If 2004 was a year of political turbulence and personal tragedies for Spain, 2005 turned out to be the year of the constitutions, an altogether calmer prospect. In contrast to the furore that accompanied France, and later Holland's, rejection of the much vaunted European constitution, Spain's approval of the same constitution in February 2005 went almost unnoticed. Not that the result – a massive *Sí* to the constitution – surprised anyone. Since joining the European Union (EU), Spain has been one of its most unquestioning advocates.

Estatut

By the second half of 2005, Spain's own constitution had become an issue, following moves by the autonomous Catalan region in the north-east of the country to move towards greater independence. The Catalan moves placed the minority socialist government of prime minister José Luis Rodriguez Zapatero in a difficult position. Dependent upon Catalan support to retain a working majority, Zapatero also found himself facing considerable opposition to the proposed new Catalan constitution from many elected representatives from the rest of Spain, who felt that any further concessions to Catalan independence threatened Spanish national identity and territorial integrity. The statute, the *Estatut* was finally approved by parliament in November 2005 following a record-breaking 11-hour debate. Opposition to the *Estatut*, manifested itself in the period preceding Christmas with sporadic boycotts of Catalan products, notably the region's cava, the Spanish equivalent of France's champagne.

Spain's autonomous regions, of which Catalonia and the Basque Country offer the highest profiles, already enjoy widespread autonomy. They are able to run their own educational system (important to both regions, where cultural and linguistic differences are important), health service, and – in the case of the Basque country – their own tax affairs. Opposition to the perceived concessions granted to Catalonia is widespread in Madrid.

Finance minister Pedro Solbes has registered his concern, accusing the autonomous regions of having too many layers of government and inefficiently deploying their financial resources. The regions, notably Catalonia, countered that they are, in fact, net contributors to central government.

Basque plans for greater independence were set back in the April regional elections when the Eusko Alberdi Jeltzalea-Partido Nacionalista Vasco (EAJ-PNV) (Basque Nationalist Party) not only lost four seats, but also lost its majority in the regional parliament. Batasuna, the banned political wing of the outlawed ETA had outmanoeuvred Madrid by getting its supporters to vote for the little known Communist Party. This allowed ETA to maintain a political presence and exert political pressure on Madrid. Basque demands are in some ways more extreme than those of Catalonia, summed up as 'the recognition of the Basque nation and our right to self determination'. Unlike in Catalonia, where the Catalan language is very much the lingua franca, a visitor to either of the region's major cities, Bilbao and San Sebastian could be forgiven for remaining unaware that he was in a culturally different region.

2006 got off to a tenuous start with the arrest of army lieutenant general José Mena Aguado for allegedly proposing armed opposition to the Catalan moves. General Mena had expressed the view that the Catalan *Estatut* had serious consequences for the Spanish armed forces as an institution. Referring to the status of Catalan as an official language, General Mena claimed that the obligatory knowledge and teaching of Catalan in the region 'verged on the insolent' and that there would be 'serious consequences for the armed forces as an institution, and its members, if the Catalan charter is approved in its current terms'. Mena's remarks were viewed by many as a less than oblique reference to the failed military insurrection of 1981.

Economy

In comparison to those of its European neighbours, the Spanish economy continued to perform well in 2005. GDP grew by 0.8 per cent in the third quarter, reaching an annual growth rate of 3.5 per cent. Growth was largely dependent on construction and services. The manufacturing sector continued to post very modest growth, barely reaching one per cent in mid-2005. Activity in the agricultural and fisheries sectors was adversely affected throughout the first half of 2005 by the continuing drought. As with many things Spanish, however, a number of the fundamentals remained to be addressed by the Zapatero administration. 2004 had seen a record eur40 billion current account deficit; imports had grown sharply, but traditional economic mainsprings such as tourism and direct foreign investment (FDI) had languished. Inflation had remained stuck at 3.1 per cent in 2004, the continuing high rate popularly attributed to the introduction of the euro. By September 2005, the inflation rate had peaked at 3.7 per cent, reflecting the impact of dearer energy prices. By October 2005, however, the 12 month inflation rate looked to have dropped back to 3.5 per cent.

House price increases remained buoyant, holding at double digit rates. The Madrid stock exchange has also remained strong, with significant rises over the year. The growth rate in credit for house purchases remained at the high level of 24 per cent, while household debt ratio reached an all time high of almost 110 per cent of disposable income.

Employment

Spanish industrial and agricultural productivity continued to lag behind its competitors. In its October 2005 bulletin, the Bank of Spain saw fit to underline the importance of the country's loss in competitiveness. The government's National Reforms Programme (NRP) sets out ambitious targets for medium and long term policies to promote employment and productivity growth. An overall employment rate of 66 per cent is forecast for 2010 (the figure for mid-2005 was 57.4 per cent, up from the 56.7 per cent recorded for the same period in 2004) and per capita GDP is targeted to reach the EU average by 2010. These ambitions may turn out to be insufficiently ambitious as an increasing number of manufacturing jobs and facilities are moved to more competitive Asian centres. Spanish industry has been slow to wake up to the uncomfortable reality that it is no longer an obviously attractive manufacturing centre for more developed economies. Within the EU, Spain now has to compete not only with the low wages of Poland or Slovakia, but also with their more highly trained workforces. And competition from within the EU is no longer what it's about – jobs are also being lost to China, India and Vietnam. An estimated 40 multinationals have shut up shop or sold their Spanish facilities since 2002. These shortcomings in productivity, (which actually declined between April and June 2005) combined with Zapatero's failure to address the reform of Spain's complex and outdated tax and labour legislation have meant that although to date job creation has remained strong, much of the economy continues to rely on labour-intensive, low wage jobs. Spain in 2005 risked reverting to its pre-EU role, where jobs were largely created in the tourism and agricultural sectors, or by state subsidised industries. Patent applications are low, as are the levels of exports classified as 'hi-tech.'

KEY INDICATORS — Spain

	Unit	2000	2001	2002	2003	2004
Population	m	39.47	39.50	39.42	40.66	41.90
Gross domestic product (GDP)	US$bn	562.60	582.30	638.90	836.10	*991.44
GDP per capita	US$	14,100	14,460	16,210	20,335	24,144
GDP real growth	%	4.4	2.8	2.2	2.5	2.7
Inflation	%	3.4	3.6	3.6	3.2	3.1
Unemployment	%	14.1	13.0	11.4	11.4	–
Coal output	mtoe	10.9	8.0	7.4	7.0	6.7
Exports (fob) (goods)	US$m	115,081.0	117,561.0	118,920.0	151,876.0	184,255.0
Imports (fob) (goods)	US$m	147,836.0	149,061.0	153,680.0	200,088.0	248,779.0
Balance of trade	US$m	-32,755.0	-31,500.0	-40,000.0	-38,212.0	-64,524.0
Current account	US$m	-17,257.0	15,082.0	-14,500.0	-23,676.0	-49,160.0
Total reserves minus gold	US$m	30,989.0	29,582.0	34,535.0	19,788.0	12,389.0
Foreign exchange	US$m	29,516.0	27,905.0	32,590.0	17,513.0	10,481.0
Exchange rate	per US$	180.18	181.77	1.04	0.88	0.80

* estimated figure

Activity in the services sector grew by 4 per cent in the second quarter of 2005, with the numbers employed in the sector growing by 4.3 per cent. The Labour Force Survey for the third quarter of 2005 showed a 5.1 per cent increase in the number employed in services.

The fact that, even in areas of relatively high unemployment, much of the low cost labour force was made up of immigrants, did little to improve social cohesion. The increase in employment in the agricultural sector represented a turnaround at least in the number of jobs, although it too was accompanied by a drop in productivity. Employment in the economy as a whole continued to rise in the second quarter of 2005, by 3.2 per cent over the previous year. Spain's working population grew by 2.9 per cent in the third quarter of 2005, down slightly from the 3.4 per cent recorded in the second quarter.

Domestic consumption remained strong, although much of this was fuelled by persistently high levels of domestic credit. According to the Bank of Spain, domestic demand grew by 5 per cent in the third quarter of 2005, compared to 5.6 per cent in the previous quarter. This represented a slowdown in real disposable income over 2004; a factor in the levelling off of domestic demand in mid-year (which also led to a drop in imports) was the effect of the personal income tax reforms introduced in 2003.

Exports and tourism

Trade in exported goods seemed to shake off the uncertainty of the earlier part of the year, although overall uncertainty in global trade meant that the upturn in exports was less strong than originally forecast. In the second quarter of 2005 goods exported were up by 2.6 per cent over the preceding year, following the contraction of 2 per cent registered in the first quarter of 2005. However, foreign trade figures issued by the Customs Department for July and August (when much of Spanish industry closes for its summer vacation) showed a drop in exports of 1.4 per cent. The hardest hit region was the EU, where Spanish exports showed an alarming drop of 3.8 per cent. Exports to the rest of the world – albeit much smaller in volume – grew by 4.3 per cent. Imports of goods rose by 8.5 per cent in mid-2005. Figures for July and August represented the general slowdown in commercial activity, with imports growing by only 4.3 per cent in real terms.

Tourism, which is a key component of the Spanish economy, showed a distinct recovery over 2004, with visitor levels – if not expenditure per head – well up. In July and August 2005 total real spending by tourists increased by 6.3 per cent and overnight stays rose by 4.6 per cent. Actual tourist numbers rose by 7 per cent. Overall revenue increases are held back by a worryingly progressive decline in expenditure per tourist. Investments in up-market golf and tennis resorts have been called into question as Spain's finite water resources showed signs of diminishing. A further factor is the growth in low cost airlines, opening up a market in high volume, but low cost, tourism.

Fiscal policy has been less of a headache for the Spanish government than has been the case elsewhere in Europe. Provisional figures put forward for the 2005 national expenditure exercise suggested that the government had achieved a surplus of 0.1 per cent of GDP. In September 2005 the government submitted the draft state budget for 2006 to parliament. Buoyant tax revenues are expected to offset other factors, enabling the government to posit a surplus of 0.2 per cent of GDP for 2006, up on the 0.1 per cent for 2005 and the deficit of 0.1 per cent posted in 2004. The relatively healthy state of its finances enabled the government to provide for a reduction in public debt to a level of around 45 per cent of GDP.

Convivencia

Following the 2004 Madrid bombings, the Zapatero government has found itself in something of a muddle as to what to do about its Muslim population, which is estimated to number around one million. Since the *reconquista* of 1492 when Spain's Muslim and Jewish populations were summarily deported, Spaniards have not had to worry much about co-habiting with 'foreign' religious groupings. Although Spain's Muslim community is small in comparison to those of some other west European countries, the proximity of Morocco and other predominantly Muslim countries makes it a very real issue. The realisation that Spain's Muslims constitute a real religious grouping is not easy for all Spaniards to accept. Least of all in those areas where unemployment is high. Under the aegis of the 1992 Foundation for Co-existence, which brought together Islamic, Jewish and Protestant groupings, the Zapatero administration has struggled to find a way of reconciling the ambitions and aspirations of its Muslim population with the distrust and religious opposition felt by a large part of the population. Mr Zapatero has referred to Spain's 'alliance of civilisations', but many suspect that this is part of a growing desire among the Socialist government to be all things to all men.

In May 2005 Spain attracted criticism from its European neighbours by granting a three-month amnesty to 700,000 of its illegal immigrants. Under the scheme, immigrants who could prove that they had been resident in Spain for six months were granted annually renewable resident and work permits. The largest single group of illegal immigrants were the Ecuadoreans (21 per cent) followed by Romanians, Moroccans and Colombians. Fears were expressed that Spain would become the EU's immigration back-door for countries that imposed stricter conditions.

Risk assessment

Politics	Good
Economy	Good
Regional Stability	Good

COUNTRY PROFILE

Historical profile

The Spanish are descended from the Iberians, Celts, Romans and Arabs that conquered the peninsula up to the eighth century.

From around the eleventh century a Christian Reconquista (Reconquest) of territories lost to the Moors began in earnest. In the thirteenth century, Castilla and Aragón emerged as the two main kingdoms in the peninsula. In the fifteenth century, the kingdoms united, following the marriage of the princess of Castilla and the heir to the throne of Aragón, Isabella I and Ferdinand V. The Catholic Monarchs completed the Reconquista, united all of Spain and launched the Spanish Inquisition, which forced Catholicism on all of the population.

1492 Spain began colonising much of the Americas, beginning with Hispaniola (Haiti and the Dominican Republic), following Christopher Columbus' landings in the region.

1556 Spain took control of Melilla in Morocco.

1560s Spain colonised the Philippines.

1668 Spain took control of Ceuta in Morocco.

1702–14 The major European powers fought to install a new monarchy in Spain in the War of the Spanish Succession, following the death of Charles II in 1700. France eventually installed the grandson of Louis XIV, Philip of Anjou, as the King of Spain.

1778 Spain took control of Fernando Pó (Bioko, now part of Equatorial Guinea).

Spain

1808–13 The Spanish population, with help from Britain, fought against French rule in the War of Independence.

1868 The army revolted against the Spanish monarchy. A military government, led by General Juan Prim, took over the country. Prim offered the Spanish crown to the son of Italian king Victor Emmanuel II, Amadeo of Savoy.

1873 Prim was assassinated. Amadeo of Savoy left Spain after failing to get installed as the new king. The remnants of the government announced the creation of the First Spanish Republic.

1874 Attempts to introduce constitutional and political reforms to the Republic failed and the monarchy was restored.

1884 Spain took control of the Spanish Sahara (now Western Sahara). It became a province of Spain in 1934.

1885 Spain established the colony of Spanish Guinea in Central Africa, comprising Río Muni and Fernando Pó.

1898 Spain lost control of Cuba, Guam, the Philippines and Puerto Rico, after being defeated in Cuba by the US.

1912 Spain and France partitioned Morocco into protectorates. Spain established the Spanish Morocco protectorate.

1923 The war in Morocco and an economic recession resulted in an authoritarian government led by General Miguel Primo de Rivera, taking over Spain.

1926 The Spanish and French defeated the Moroccans, bringing the war to an end.

1930 After failing with economic and political reforms, Primo de Rivera resigned from government

1931 Republican parties won the municipal elections, which led the Spanish King, Alfonso XIII, to abdicate. The Second Republic was declared.

1936–39 Civil war broke out when the democratically elected Republican government was attacked in an attempted *coup d'état*. The Nationalist alliance composed of monarchists, right-wing parties and the army, led by Francisco Franco y Bahamonde, fought to take control of Spain. Fascist Germany and Italy, ignoring arms embargoes, supported Franco's forces with men and materials. The government, denied legitimate arms from other European sources, gained the backing of the Soviet Union and welcomed over 56,000 overseas volunteers to fight in the International Brigades.

1939 Nationalist forces won the Civil War. General Franco became Head of State, established a dictatorship, restricted individual liberties and severely repressed all challenges to his power.

1955 An isolated Spain was allowed to join the UN.

1956 Spain granted Morocco independence, but retained control of the Ceuta and Melilla enclaves in northern Morocco.

1958 Spain handed the Tarfaya enclave in West Africa over to Morocco.

1959 The Euskadi ta Azkatasuna (ETA) (Homeland and Freedom) group was formed with the aim of creating an independent Basque region. ETA is blamed for more than 800 deaths from 1968 to present.

1968 Spanish Guinea in West Africa gained independence and was renamed Equatorial Guinea.

1969 Spain withdraws from the Sidi Ifni enclave in West Africa, handing it over to Morocco.

1973 Prime Minister Admiral Luis Carrero Blanco was assassinated by ETA after the government had executed a number of Basque militants.

1975 General Franco died in November. Juan Carlos, grandson of the last King, Alfonso XIII, was crowned King Juan Carlos I and became Head of State. Also in November, Spain withdraws from Western Sahara.

1977 Restrictions on political activity were lifted and free parliamentary elections were held. The Union de Centro Democrático (UCD) (Union of the Democratic Centre) coalition, led by Adolfo Sáurez González, won.

1978 A new constitution was endorsed. It confirmed Spain as a parliamentary monarchy with freedom for political parties and enshrined the 'indissoluble unity of the Spanish nation'. It also recognised the right to autonomy of its 'nationalities and regions'. ETA was responsible for a terrorist bomb in a Madrid supermarket that killed 21 people and injured 40 others.

1980s Referenda on regional autonomy in the Basque region and Catalonia began the process of devolution. Spain was divided into 17 regions, each with a president and parliament, plus the two self-governing enclaves on the north African coast (Moroccan) – Ceuta and Melilla.

1981 The paramilitary *Guardia Civil* (Civil Guard) attempted a *coup d'état*, holding members of the cabinet and parliament hostage. The coup was aborted when King Carlos demanded that the military must remain loyal to the crown and the constitution.

1982 The Partido Socialista Obrero Español (PSOE) (Spanish Socialist Workers' Party), under Felipe González, won the general election. Morocco laid claim to Ceuta, Melilla and the Canary Islands.

1983 A secret death squad known as the Grupo Antiterrorista de Liberacion (GAL) (Anti-Terrorist Group) was set up funded by the Interior Ministry in order to combat ETA. Between 1983 and 1987, 28 people are murdered by the GAL in what became known as Spain's 'dirty war'. Several of those killed later turned out to have no connection with ETA and revelations surrounding the death squads' activities later contributed to the downfall of the PSOE government.

1986 Spain joined the EU in January.

1986–96 The PSOE won the 1986, 1990 and 1993 parliamentary elections and Felipe González served four terms as prime minister.

1995 José María Aznar, leader of the opposition Partido Popular (PP) (Popular Party) survived an assassination attempt by ETA.

1996 Aznar became prime minister of a PP minority government.

1998 In September, ETA announced a unilateral ceasefire.

2000 In January, ETA called off its ceasefire. In March, the PP won a majority in parliamentary elections.

2001 A new round of talks began between Britain and Spain on the future of Gibraltar.

2002 Euro currency replaced the peseta. In July, 12 Moroccan soldiers landed on the tiny uninhabited, but disputed, *Isla del Perejil* (Parsley Island), close to the Spanish-controlled Ceuta enclave in Morocco. Spain re-occupied the island, to which Morocco lays claim and calls *Leila*. Both countries recalled their respective ambassadors.

Some 400km of Atlantic coastline in northern Spain was severely polluted by oil from the wrecked tanker, *Prestige*. The perceived failure of the PP government to deal with the disaster caused internal divisions, opposition protests and a sharp drop in the PP's poll ratings. The cost of the clean up was estimated at over eur1 billion.

2003 In January, Spain and Morocco agreed to a mutual exchange of ambassadors for the first time since the Perejil/Leila incident. The Herri Batasuna (People Unity) party, believed to be the political wing of ETA, was banned. A Spanish court upheld the ban in August 2005. Government support for the US-lead coalition invasion of Iraq was opposed by an estimated 85 per cent of the population, causing a further deterioration in support for the PP. Prime Minister Aznar declared he would step down at the March 2004 elections. He designated the less charismatic Mariano Rajoy, as his replacement.

2004 In February, ETA announced that it had entered a pact with the autonomous government of Catalonia whereby no terrorist actions would be taken by it in Catalonia. On 11 March, 10 co-ordinated bombs planted in four commuter trains in Madrid exploded during the morning rush hour killing 191 people and injuring over 1,800. ETA denied responsibility and a gang of extremist Islamists, who later committed suicide in a bomb blast during a police raid, were identified as the culprits. The bombings had an immediate effect on the people of Spain who voted the opposition party, PSOE, into power in the 14 March parliamentary elections. José Luis Rodríguez Zapatero (PSOE) was sworn in as prime minister on 7 April.

2005 In February, Spain voted in favour of the EU constitution, but the turnout was low at 42.3 per cent. In June, a delegation of Spanish MPs was barred from conducting a human rights investigation in the former Spanish colony of Western Sahara. In the Basque country's regional elections in April, the moderate nationalist ruling party lost ground to the Socialists but retained office.

In June, at least 250,000 people marched in Madrid to protest against the government's intention to negotiate with ETA.

In August, 17 Spanish troops serving with NATO forces in Afghanistan were killed in a helicopter crash.

In September, Spain reinforced fences protecting its enclaves in North Africa, Ceuta and Melilla, after hundreds of would-be immigrants attempted to storm the territories.

In November, Spain concluded an arms deal with Venezuela, despite protests from the US; Spain hosted the European-Mediterranean Partnership conference, which brought together the 25 EU member states and Turkey, Israel, Algeria, Morocco, Tunisia, Egypt, the Palestinian Authority, Jordan, Syria and Lebanon; Spain launched an investigation into allegations that CIA planes made secret stopovers in Spanish territory in order to transfer terror suspects; Spain's parliament granted Catalonia greater autonomy.

2006 In January, Spain agreed to write off most of the debt owed by Bolivia.

Political structure
Constitution
The constitution dates from the advent of democracy in 1978. Most laws are debated and passed in Congress first, and then in the Senate, the upper house, which can send back amended bills. In case of emergency, the government may issue decrees. They are called Decree Laws if they require ratification by parliament. All laws require the king's ratification and come into force when published in the Official Bulletin.

There are 17 comunidades autónomas (autonomous regions): Andalucia, Aragón, Asturias, Baleares (Balearic Islands), Canarias (Canary Islands), Cantabria, Castilla-La Mancha, Castilla y León, Cataluñya, Comunidad Valencian, Extremadura, Galicia, La Rioja, Madrid, Murcia, Navarra, País Vasco (Basque country). Spain also has sovereignty of five communities on and off the coast of Morocco: the coastal ports of Ceuta and Melilla are administered as autonomous regions; the islands of Chafarinas, Peñon de Alhucemas and Peñon de Velez de la Gomera are under direct Spanish administration.

Autonomous regions have regional parliaments and governments with varying degrees of powers on local affairs. Three regions with a tradition of autonomy and their own language – the Basque country (Euskadi), Cataluñya and Galicia – have these wider powers. The Basque government, for example, raises its own taxes. There is universal suffrage from age 18.

Form of state
Federal parliamentary democratic monarchy

The executive
The president of the government (prime minister) appoints the cabinet and has executive power. He is appointed by the head of state and his appointment must be ratified by the national legislature.

National legislature
The bicameral Las Cortes Generales (The General Courts) is the national legislature.

The Congreso de los Diputados (Congress of Deputies) is the lower house and has 350 members, directly elected every four years under proportional representation.

In the 248-member Senado (Senate) the upper house is composed of 208 senators who are chosen in direct elections in the 51 provinces. An additional 40 senators are appointed as regional representatives. Senators serve a four-year term.

Parties need to gain at least 3 per cent of the vote to gain representation in either house.

Legal system
The Spanish legal system is based on civil law. The Supreme Court is at the summit of the judiciary. There are also 16 Division High Courts, 50 Provincial High Courts and, below these, Courts of First Instance, District Courts, Municipal and Peace Courts. Spain does not accept compulsory jurisdiction by the International Court of Justice (ICJ).

Last elections
20 February 2005 (EU constitutional referendum); 13 June 2004 (European Parliament); 14 March 2004 (parliamentary).
Results: EU constitutional referendum: 77 per cent voted in favour, 17 per cent against; turnout was low at 42.3 per cent.
European Parliament: PSOE won 43.3 per cent of the vote (25 seats out of 54), PP 41.3 per cent (23), Galeuzca 5.2 per cent (three), United Left 4.2 per cent (two) and Europa de los Pueblos (EP) (Europe of the Peoples) 2.5 per cent (one); turnout 45.9 per cent.

Parliamentary: PSOE won 42.6 per cent of the vote (164 seats out of 350); PP, 37.6 per cent (148); UL (United Left) 5 per cent (five), Convergència i Unió (CiU) (Convergence and Union) (coalition of two Catalán parties) 2 per cent (10), Esquerra Republicana de Cataluyna (ERC) (Catalan Republican Left) 2.5 per cent (eight), Eusko Alberdi Jeltzalea-Partido Nacionalista Vasco (EAJ-PNV) (Basque Nationalist Party) 1.6 per cent (seven) and the Coalición Canaria (CC) (Canary Island Coalition) 0.9 per cent (three); Bloque Nacionalista Galego (BNG) 0.8 per cent (two); Chunta Aragonesista (CHA) 0.4 per cent (one); Eusko Alkartasuna (EA) 0.3 per cent (one); Nafarroa Bai (NaBai) 0.2 per cent (one). Turnout was 77.2 per cent.

Next elections
2008 (parliamentary)

Political parties
Ruling party
Partido Socialista Obrero Español (PSOE) (Spanish Socialist Workers' Party) (elected 14 Mar 2004)
Main opposition party
Partido Popular (PP) (People's Party)

Population
41.90 million (2004)
Ethnic make-up
In addition to Spaniards, there are several minor groups, including Gypsies, Portuguese, Latin Americans and North Africans.
Religions
Roman Catholic (94 per cent), Islam, Protestant and Jewish.

Education
Primary schooling begins at the age of six and lasts for six years. Secondary schooling lasts until aged 16 (both of which are provided free). Final exams allow progression to higher secondary schools which teach either academic or vocational programmes. Teaching may be carried out in Spanish, Catalan, Basque, or Galician.

Private schools are responsible for the education of more than 30 per cent of children.

Higher education is only possible after successfully sitting an entrance exam. There are some 20 state universities, four polytechnics, two independent universities and eight technical universities. The development of alternative forms of higher education have made access to established universities more selective. It has also been proposed that the present five-year

university degree courses be reduced to three years.
Public expenditure on education typically amounts to 5 per cent of annual gross national income.
Literacy rate: 97.9 per cent, adult rates (2003)
Compulsory years: Six to 16
Enrolment rate: 109 per cent, gross primary enrolment of relevant age group (including repeaters); 120 per cent, gross secondary enrolment (World Bank).
Pupils per teacher: 15 in primary schools

Health
As Spain's economy has grown, spending on healthcare has risen, reaching 7.5 per cent of GDP, spending just below the Organisation for Economic Co-operation and Development (OECD) average of 7.7 per cent on medical goods and services. Most of this expenditure is in the form of state funding at 71.4 per cent. Efforts are under way to cut the state's pharmaceutical bill, representing 20 per cent of total public health spending. Pre-paid healthcare plans amount to 14.1 per cent of the 28.6 per cent of GDP spent privately on health costs.
The health sector, under the authority of INSALUD, the National Institute of Health, includes hospitals, community health centres and emergency services. The social security health scheme covers all insured persons and their dependants.
HIV prevalence: 0.7 per cent aged 15–49 in 2003 (World Bank)
Life expectancy: 79.6 years (World Bank)
Fertility rate/Maternal mortality rate: 1.3 births per woman (World Bank)
Birth rate/Death rate: 10 births per 1,000 population; 9.5 deaths per 1,000 population (2003).
Infant mortality rate: 4.0 per 1,000 live births (World Bank)

Welfare
The National Institute of Social Security oversees a national insurance scheme, which is compulsory for all employed and self-employed workers. It provides a range of benefits including those for sickness, maternity, accident insurance, retirement pensions and unemployment benefits. Contributions are paid by employees, employers and the state. The employed are classified in a series of professional and labour categories for the purpose of determining social security taxes. Each category has maximum and minimum contribution bases which are revised annually. The state pays retirement pensions from the age of 65 for men and women. Spain offers a special system of unemployment protection for casual workers in agriculture. The Rural Employment Plan combines employment policy measures and social welfare benefits. The benefit is granted to workers who have paid contributions under the Agricultural Social Security Scheme and is equivalent to 75 per cent of the national minimum wage payable for a maximum period of 180 days.

Main cities
Madrid (capital, estimated population 3.3 million in 2004), Barcelona (1.5 million), Valencia (741,100), Seville (679,100), Zaragoza (635,600), Málaga (517,900), Bilbao (342,800).

Languages spoken
Castilian Spanish is the principal language; Catalán, Galician, Euskera (Basque), Aragonese and Asturian are also spoken. English and French are spoken in most business circles.

Official language/s
Castilian Spanish, Catalan (in Catalonia including the Balearics), Basque (in the Basque provinces), Valencian (Province of Valencia), Galician (Galicia).

Media
The constitution enshrines the right to free expression of thoughts, ideas and opinions.

Press
The Spanish printed media market is very mature with a wide variety of respected titles backed up by a plethora of specialist publications. The media is largely free, although in 1998 the government closed down *Egin*, a Basque newspaper, accusing it of being linked with the terrorist organisation ETA. In February 2003, the government also closed down the remaining Basque language newspaper, *Euskaldunon Egunkari*.
Dailies: Most dailies are published from Madrid but these also have a regional circulation, in addition to other regional dailies. These include *El País*, *ABC*, *Diario El Mundo*, *Diario 16*, *Avui*, *Diario Maritimas*, *El Mundo del Siglo XXI*, *Marca* (sports paper), *La Vanguardia*, *El Dia del Mundo de Baleares*, *El Periódico de Cataluña* and *El Correo Español*. *Gara* is a Basque newspaper.
Weeklies: There are several general and special interest magazines and news magazines such as *Cambio 16* and *Tiempo*.
Business: Daily business publications include *Cinco Días*, *El Boletín de la Tarde* and *Expansión*. Other business magazines are *Actualidad Económica*, *Dinero* and *Mercado*.
Periodicals: National and international periodicals of general interest include *Itola!* and *Interviu*.

Broadcasting
Co-ordinated by Radiotelevisión Española (RTVE).
Radio: Radio programmes are broadcast by Radio Nacional de España (RNE) and several commercial and independent stations. Some FM stations broadcast BBC programmes in English. In general the standard of Spanish radio broadcasting is not high – tending towards the down-market, 'phone-in' sectors, rather than programmes reflecting serious broadcasting standards.
Television: Televisión Española (TVE) broadcasts on two nationwide state channels. There are also three private channels, six regional public broadcasters with 10 channels between them, some in Catalan and Basque, and two satellite digital TV networks.
Imported programmes are generally dubbed rather than sub-titled.

Advertising
All usual media are available. TV and hoardings tend to be most popular method, although radio, newspaper and cinema advertising is also widespread. Information, including current rates, appears in a quarterly magazine *Guía de los Medios*.

Economy
Spain has a mixed economy with large agricultural and industrial sectors, and important tourism and banking industries. In the 1990s, emphasis was increasingly placed on regional development, with assistance from the EU. In addition, a key objective of industrial strategy was to improve the efficiency of public enterprises and stem losses, often involving the privatisation of companies.
Since the Maastricht Treaty of 1992, economic policies have been primarily dictated by the financial guidelines laid down in the EU's Stability and Growth Pact (SGP). Spain has been a major net recipient of EU transfers. It received approximately US$10 billion in 2004, or about 1 per cent of Spain's GDP.
Despite its growing economy, Spain has not fully recovered from the economic transition that was necessary for EU membership. The unemployment rate in Spain was still high at 9.4 per cent in August 2005 but down from 10.8 per cent in 2004. While the rate is declining overall, such high rates carry social and economic costs. With the government committed to labour market reforms, including a reduction in union powers and changes to the social security system, more social disquiet cannot be ruled out.
Spain has benefited much more than other countries from low eurozone interest rates: mortgage lending rates ranged between 3.0 and 3.5 per cent in the first half of 2005; at the end of the 1980s they stood at around 16 per cent. The low rates, together with jobs creation (over

500,000 in 2004), led to an unprecedented demand for property, with construction becoming the motor of economic growth. Structural reforms and a sound fiscal policy have also helped boost the economy's health. A change in government in March 2004 has not resulted in any major change in economic policy, with the incoming centre-left government (Partido Socialista Obrero Español) (PSOE) having promised to stick to the outgoing centre-right government's (Partido Popular) (PP) economic reform agenda.

In the first quarter of 2005, Spain received a record 13.6 million foreign tourists, representing a 5 per cent increase in international tourism, compared to the same period in 2004. In December 2005, the Spanish government forecast GDP growth overall of 3.4 per cent for 2005 and 3.3 per cent for 2006.

External trade
Imports
Main imports include machinery and equipment, fuels, chemicals, semi-finished goods, foodstuffs, consumer goods, and medical control instruments.
Main sources: Germany (16.5 per cent total, 2004), France (15.7 per cent), Italy (8.8 per cent), UK (6.3 per cent), The Netherlands (4.8 per cent)
Exports
Major exports include machinery, motor vehicles; foodstuffs, pharmaceuticals, medicines and other consumer goods.
Main destinations: France (19.3 per cent total, 2004), Germany (11.7 per cent), Portugal (9.6 per cent), UK (9.1 per cent), Italy (9.1 per cent)

Agriculture
Farming
Fundamental reform to the Common Agricultural Policy (CAP) was introduced throughout most of the EU on 1 January 2005. The subsidies paid on farm output, which tended to benefit large farms and encourage overproduction, were replaced by single farm payments not conditional on production. This is expected to reward farms that maintain a healthy environment, food safety and animal welfare standards. The changes are also intended to encourage market conscious production and cut the cost of CAP to the EU taxpayer. Spain introduced this measure on 1 January 2006.
Spain is the world's largest producer of olive oil: the industry has been modernising, although olive groves, mainly located in Andalucia, typically suffer periodic drought and work is usually undertaken by low paid migrant workers. The revised CAP should benefit the region by limiting unsustainable growth.

Spain is now the third-largest wine producer in Europe after France and Italy, with a growing tendency towards the quality end of the wine market. EU restrictions limit the amount of land available for vineyards and, with domestic consumers developing a taste for wines of increased quality, the price of grapes and available vineyards has increased enormously. Newer regions are producing quality wines to rival those of the long established Rioja and *Penedes denominaciones*. Cava, the Spanish wine made using the champagne method, is gaining a global reputation for quality and value. Notable among these are Ribera de Duero in Castilla y Leon, where the legendary Vega Sicilia wines are produced, and the *Priorat denominaciones* in Catalonia.

Crop production for 2005 included: 13,791,520 tonnes (t) cereals in total, 3,788,200t wheat, 3,950,700t maize, 2,591,700t potatoes, 4,448,400t barley, 263,000t treenuts, 4,867,300 citrus fruit, 5,879,800t grapes, 4,473,573t tomatoes, 1,007,045t oilcrops, 40,192t tobacco, 3,712,700t olives, 1,130,800 peaches and nectarines, 6,676,900t sugar beet, 953,200t chillies and peppers, 797,700t apples, 328,900t seed cotton, 95,731t cotton lint, 14,805,000t fruit in total, 12,348,273t vegetables in total. Livestock production included: 5,735,735t meat in total, 715,215t beef, 3,310,243t pig meat, 248,027t lamb and goat meat, 1,341,000t poultry, 725,500t eggs, 6.9t milk, 37,000t honey, 80,000t cattle hides, 120t cocoons, silk.

Fishing
As the owner of the largest fishing fleet in the EU, Spain is also the largest consumer of seafood and seafood products in the EU. Spain's total fish catch continues to decline as a result of depleted stocks and lower limits on catches in both EU and non-EU waters. Spain's seafood trade is mainly conducted with other EU countries, Argentina, Morocco and Namibia.

Forestry
Forest and other wooded land accounts for about half the land area, with forest cover estimated at 14.3 million hectares (ha). Most of the forest is available for wood supply. The area of forest has been expanding strongly, at an annual average increase of 0.62 per cent per year. About 80 per cent of forest is privately owned, while the remaining area is mostly owned by municipalities. Forest and other wooded land accounts for 50 per cent of total land area. About 45 per cent of the forest is available for wood supply. The main species are Scots and Aleppo pine, oak, beech, chestnut, poplars and eucalyptus.
Imported raw materials including eucalyptus pulpwood and hardwood logs are used for all primary forest products. Spain is a net importer of paper and sawnwood, although part of the pulp production is exported.
Exports of forest material in 2004 amounted to US$2.6 billion, while imports amounted to US$5.0 billion. Production in 2004 included 16,290,000 cubic metres (cum) roundwood, 14,235,000cum industrial roundwood, 3,730,000cum sawnwood, 7,795,000cum sawlogs and veneers, 5,520,000cum pulpwood, 4,754,000cum wood-based panels, 2,055,000cum wood fuel; 3,650,000 tonnes (t) recovered paper, 310,000t newsprint, 1,205,000t printing and writing paper.

Industry and manufacturing
The industrial sector contributes approximately 34 per cent to GDP and employs over 29 per cent of the labour force. Since joining the EU, Spain's industry and manufacturing sectors have undergone modernisation and restructuring, assisted by large levels of foreign direct investment (FDI). The automotive, telecommunications and chemical industries dominate the sector.
Industrial production grew by 3.3 per cent year-on-year in August 2005 but fell to 0.5 per cent growth in September.

Tourism
Since 1996, Spain has been ranked second, behind the US, for tourist earnings globally, and second, behind France, for tourist numbers. The tourism industry accounts for around 12 per cent of Spain's GDP and accounts for around 8 per cent of total employment.
Spain's reputation for economic sea-and-sand holidays is under seige from eastern Mediterranian resorts, so that the long-term emphasis is now on diversification with quality and variety, year-round tourism and short-break city holidays. The tourism sector contracted by 13 per cent in the wake of the US-led invasion of Iraq in March 2003. Bomb attacks carried out by al-Qaeda against commuter trains in Madrid on 11 March 2004 were expected to have a negative impact on Spain's tourism industry. However, tourism sector growth was between 3 and 4 per cent in the first quarter of 2004.
Visitors from Germany and UK make up over 48 per cent of all tourists. Total tourist receipts for 2005 are expected to amount to eur184.3 million (US$245.6 million).

Mining
The mining sector contributes 1 per cent to GDP. Spain is the world's second-largest producer of natural stone, which accounts for 15 per cent of the total value of

Spanish mining. Marble has become a particularly important source of foreign exchange earnings. Gold, silver and copper mining take place on a small scale. Spain also extracts lignite, iron ore, mercury, pyrites, zinc, lead, copper and tungsten. The traditional production of uranium ore in Spain ceased with the closure of Mina Fé in Salamanca.

Hydrocarbons
Spain is heavily dependent on imported oil, with Mexico and Russia as its largest suppliers. In 2005, Spain had only 158 million barrels of proven domestic oil reserves. Some 99 per cent of the 1.6 million barrels per day (bpd) consumed by Spain in 2004 were imported. Spain's largest domestic production comes from the Casablanca complex in the Mediterranean, which provides 6,500bpd. Spain's total crude oil refining capacity stood at 1.4 million bpd in 2004. Oil consumption relative to that of gas has fallen steadily in Spain over the past two decades. Spain is currently exploring the Atlantic Ocean and the Bay of Cadiz for oil deposits but results have so far been disappointing. Natural gas production is limited and much of Spain's domestic demand is supplied by imports. Consumption levels in 2004 were at 27.3 billion cubic metres. At current rates of production, reserves should last another 25 years. Spain imports gas from Norway, via pipelines through France, and Algeria, via pipelines running through Morocco. In July 2001, Spain and Algeria agreed to build a second trans-Moroccan pipeline, the Medgaz pipeline, which is expected to be complete by 2008.

Environmental restrictions mean that coal, Spain's largest indigenous energy source, is being gradually phased out. Coal reserves totalled 728 million tonnes in 2005. Government coal subsidies are expected to decrease by some 4 per cent per year, which will make the price of Spanish coal uncompetititve in the open market. Production levels in 2004 were at 6.7 million tonnes of oil equivalent (toe), a decrease of 2 per cent on 2003 output. Consumption totalled 21.1 million toe in 2004, up 3 per cent on 2003. In July 2002, the EU ordered Spain to lower its coal production by 65 per cent by 2010. Production subsidies will last until 2008 if coal mines do not improve their economic viability.

Energy
Most of Spain's electricity is generated by conventional thermal power plants (52.3 per cent), followed by hydroelectricity (25.2 per cent), nuclear (14.9 per cent) and other renewables (7.6 per cent). Spain's electricity generation and consumption has increased in recent years at more than double the rate recorded in Western Europe as a whole. Rising consumption has stretched Spain's capacity and has resulted in a number of major blackouts.

Since January 2003, consumers have been able to choose their own electricity supplier.

In January 2004, Spain signed an agreement with Portugal to work towards integrating their respective electricity markets.

Financial markets
Stock exchange
The Bolsa de Madrid is the fourth-largest stock exchange in the eurozone.

Banking and insurance
Central bank
Banco de España; European Central Bank (ECB).
Main financial centre
Madrid

Time
GMT plus one hour (GMT plus two hours from late Mar to late Sep); Canaries GMT (GMT plus one hour during summer).

Geography
Spain is situated in south-western Europe. It occupies most of the Iberian peninsula, sharing it with Portugal to the west. The country includes the Balearic Islands in the Mediterranean Sea (200km south-east of Barcelona), the Canary Islands in the Atlantic Ocean and a few small enclaves in Morocco. Mainland Spain is bounded to the north by the Cantabrian Sea, the Pyrenees and France, to the east by the Mediterranean, and to the south by the Straits of Gibraltar and Morocco.

Climate
Most of Spain has a Mediterranean climate with mild winters and hot summers, although the mountainous north is colder and wetter. Temperatures range from 40 degrees centigrade Celsius (C) to minus 15 degrees C.

Dress codes
Particular attention is paid to dress, although dress codes are not rigid. Most businessmen and male officials wear suits and ties during business hours.

Entry requirements
Passports
Are required by all non-EU visitors and must be valid for at least six months beyond the planned stay. EU visitors and nationals of Andorra, Liechtenstein, Malta, Monaco and Switzerland may use valid national ID cards.
Visa
Required by all; except nationals of EU and Schengen Accord signatory countries. Tourists from North America and Australasia may visit, visa-free, for up to 90 days. All other nationals, visiting for business purposes, should contact the nearest Spanish embassy for a visa application form. Tourists travelling to further Schengen agreement countries may download a visa application (offered in several languages) from www.eurovisa.info/ApplicationForm.htm and submit it to the nearest Spanish embassy.
Currency advice/regulations
No restrictions on import of foreign and local currency, but if amount exceeds equivalent of eur6,009 (US$6,325), it should be declared upon arrival to avoid difficulties on leaving Spain.
Export of currency is unlimited provided the amount does not exceed that declared on arrival.

Health (for visitors)
Mandatory precautions
None
Advisable precautions
Up-to-date tetanus and polio immunisations are recommended. Long-term visitors should consider hepatitis 'A' immunisation. Tap water may not be safe to drink outside the major cities and visitors are advised to drink bottled mineral water. For those travellers from other EU member states possession of a form E111 will provide access to emergency treatment for unexpected illness.

Hotels
Hotels are classified from one- to five-star, plus a 'Grand De Luxe' category (pensions/hostels classified from one- to three-star). *Paradores* (national tourist inns) are also increasingly popular. Accommodation should be booked well in advance, especially during holiday season. NB: Term Residencia denotes establishments without dining-room facilities.

Credit cards
All major credit cards are accepted.

Public holidays
Fixed dates
1 Jan (New Year's Day), 6 Jan (Epiphany), 1 May (Labour Day), 2 May (Fiesta de la Communidad, Madrid only), 15 May (San Isidro, Madrid only), 25 Jul (Patron Saint of Spain, Madrid only), 15 Aug (Assumption Day), 12 Oct (National Day), 1 Nov (All Saints' Day), 9 Nov (Almudena, Madrid only), 6 Dec (Constitution Day), 8 Dec (Immaculate Conception), 25 Dec (Christmas Day).
Variable dates
Maundy Thursday (Madrid and some other towns), Good Friday.

Working hours
Executives rarely arrive in their offices before 0900. Many then go out for coffee, and again for a snack at 1200 to keep them going until a late lunch. Lunches, no

earlier than 1400, and often preceded by a visit to a bar for an aperitivo, are abundant and lengthy. A business lunch, always accompanied by wine, coffee, brandy and cigars, can last from three to five hours. It is considered impolite to get down to business until after dessert. Although many go home for lunch and a brief siesta, an increasing number of companies in big cities are abolishing the long lunch break. In December 2005 the government officially abolished the *siesta* when an law was published decreeing that lunch breaks would be one hour only, thereby allowing civil servants to finish work at 6pm.

In the hot summer months, most ministries and many companies close down for the day at 1400 or 1500. In August, many businesses close down completely.

Banking
Mon–Fri: 0900–1400, Sat: 0900–1300.

Business
Usually open Mon–Fri: 0900–1400 and 1630–1930.

Government
Vary considerably from region to region and according to time of year. In Madrid: Mon–Fri: generally 0900–1330 and 1500–1800; except Jul and Aug, 0830–1430 (1400 on Fri) with only skeleton staff remaining during afternoon.

Shops
Mon–Sat: 0900–1300, 1500–1930.

Electricity supply
220V AC (occasionally 110–125V AC in older buildings).

Social customs/useful tips
Meals are taken later in Spain than in other European countries which means that people go to bed later and also generally go to work later. Dinner is after 2200 and people rarely go to bed before 2400. Leaving someone's home before 0100 can be taken as a sign of boredom. It is acceptable to telephone someone at home until 2400.

Entry into the EU in 1986 has slowly changed customs as Spaniards are keen to be seen as Europeans. However, they remain very attached to an informal and relaxed way of life and enjoyment is an important part of life. Each city and village has its annual festival which would not be complete without dance, songs, wine and a bullfight. Bullfighting remains popular despite a budding animal protection movement, and soccer remains by far the most popular sport. Family and friendship ties are of major importance and often a source of mutual favours. Regional origins also command loyalties. Spaniards, even children of migrants to big cities, constantly refer to their home province. In Catalonia Catalan is very much, and very proudly, the lingua franca, and it helps at least to be able to greet people in Catalan. This is less the case in the Basque country, where fewer people speak Basque, and is not an issue either in Valencia or in Galicia, both of which have their own languages, but where Castilain is the lingua franca for day to day purposes.

Spaniards generally use two surnames, the last being their mother's surname. When addressing someone, either personally or in correspondence, only the first of the surnames is used. *Don* is a widely used title of respect, and is used in conversation with the christian name only. The *tu* (more intimate second person singular) form is today used widely, even on first acquaintance.

Handshaking is the customary form of greeting. Although English is widely spoken, an effort to speak Spanish is appreciated. Business cards are frequently exchanged as a matter of courtesy.

Security
A chronic drug problem, coupled with persistent unemployment and frequent amnesties for petty criminals, has caused an increase in petty crime in big cities. Mugging has become frequent, and often violent, in tourist areas. Many insurance companies no longer cover the theft of car radios.

Getting there
Air
All the major airports can be very busy during the holiday season. A number of so-called 'budget' airlines now serve Spain from other European destinations. Major carriers in this category are Ryanair (Murcia, Sevilla, Reus, Valladolid, and Gerona) from Italy, the UK, and Germanyand Easyjet (Barcelona, Majorca, Madrid, Malaga) from the UK, France and Switzerland.

National airline: Iberia.

International airport/s: Alicante (ALC), 12km south-west of city; Barcelona (BCN) 10km south-west of city; Bilbao (BIO), 9km from city; Madrid Barajas (MAD), 16km north-east of Madrid; Málaga (AGP) 8km south-west of city; Santiago de Compostela (SCQ), 10km north-east of city; Seville (SVQ), 10km east of city, Valencia (VLC), 10km west of city. Also on Balearic Islands: Palma de Mallorca (PMI), 9km south-east of Palma; and on Canary Islands: Gran Canaria (LPA), 19km south of Las Palmas; Tenerife TCI Sur Reina Sofia (TFS), 61km south-west of Santa Cruz de Tenerife.

Airport tax: None

Surface
Good road and rail access from France.
Water: The are regular ferry and shipping services from several countries, UK (Plymouth-Santander), France (Marseilles-Alicante) and Algeria (Algiers-Alicante).

Main port/s: Barcelona, Valencia, Alicante, Málaga, Algeciras, Cádiz, La Coruña, Bilbao, Vigo.

Getting about
National transport
Air: Frequent services from Madrid to all major urban centres are operated by Iberia and Aviación y Comercio (Aviaco).
Road: Roads are based on radial routes centred on Madrid. They are often very busy during the holiday season. Good roads connect all main towns. There is a network of over 150,000km, including 2,000km of motorways (usually toll) mostly confined to coastal regions.
Buses: There are regular bus and coach services between main towns.
Rail: There are approximately 14,410km of track, of which about 11,500km is operated by Red Nacional de Ferrocarriles Españoles (RENFE) (National Network of Spanish Railroads) and the rest (narrow gauge) by Ferrocarriles Españoles de Via Estrecha (FEVE).
Water: Regular steamer and hydrofoil services operated by Compañia Transmediterránea connect Balearic Islands with Barcelona, Valencia and Alicante. Also weekly ferry service to Las Palmas (Canary Islands) from Barcelona.

City transport
Taxis: Available in most major cities; all metered. Tend to have a distinct colour in each city. Tipping between 5–10 per cent.

Car hire
Available at competitive rates in most large towns. A national driving licence is normally all that is required. Drive on the right. Speed limits are 60kph in towns, 100kph on national highways, 120 kph on motorways and 90kph on other roads. Traffic coming from right generally has priority. Seat belts must be worn in front seats. Spanish drivers tend to drive faster than their northern counterparts.

BUSINESS DIRECTORY
The addresses listed below are a selection only. While World of Information makes every endeavour to check these addresses, we cannot guarantee that changes have not been made, especially to telephone numbers and area codes. We would welcome any corrections.

Telephone area codes
The international direct dialling (IDD) code for Spain is +34 followed by area code and subscriber's number:

Alicante	96	León	987
Avilés	98	Madrid	91
Barcelona	93	Málaga	95
Bilbao	94	Salamanca	923
Cádiz	956	Santander	942
Cartagena	968	Seville	95

Spain

Castellón de la Plana	964	Tarragona	977
Ceuta	952	Valencia	96
Granada	958	Valladolid	983
Huelva	959	Vigo	986
La Coruña	981	Zaragoza	976

Chambers of Commerce

American Chamber of Commerce in Spain, 8 Tuset, 08006 Barcelona (tel: 415-9963; fax: 415-1198; e-mail: info@amchamspain.com).

Barcelona Cámara de Comercio, 452 Avenguda Diagonal, 08006 Barcelona (tel: 416-9300; fax: 416-9301).

Bilbao Cámara Oficial de Comercio, Industria y Navegación, 50 Almeda Recalde, 48008 Bilbao (tel: 470-6500; fax: 443-6171; e-mail: info@camarabilbao.com).

British Chamber of Commerce in Spain, 21 Calle Bruc, 08010 Barcelona (tel: 317-3220; fax: 302-4896; e-mail: britchamber@britchamber.com).

Cádiz Cámara Oficial de Comercio, Industria y Navegación, 4 Antonio López, 11004 Cádiz (tel: 010-000; fax: 250-710; e-mail: ccincadiz@camerdata.es).

Consejo Superior de Cámaras de Comercio, Industria y Navegación de España, Calle Velazquez 157, 28002 Madrid (tel: 590-6900; fax: 590-6908; e-mail: csc@cscamaras.es).

Córdoba Cámara Oficial de Comercio e Industria, Pérez de Castro 1, 14003 Córdoba (tel: 296-199; fax: 202-106; e-mail: info@camaracordoba.com).

Franco-Spanish Chamber of Commerce and Industry, Calle Ruiz de Alarcon 7, 28014 Madrid (tel: 522-6742; fax: 523-3642; e-mail: lachambre@lachambre.es).

French Chamber of Commerce and Industry in Barcelona, Passeig de Gràcia 2, 08007 Barcelona (tel: 270-2450;fax: 270-2451; e-mail: ccfbcn@ccfbcn,es).

Granada Cámara Oficial de Comercio, Industria y Navegación, Paz 18, 18002 Granada (tel: 536-276; fax: 536-292; e-mail: ccigranada@camaras.org).

Las Palmas de Gran Canaria Cámara Oficial de Comercio, Industria y Navegación , León y Castillo 24, 35003 Las Palmas de Gran Canaria (tel: 391-045; fax: 362-350; e-mail: webmaster@cameraalp.es).

Madrid Cámara Oficial de Comercio e Industria, Calle Huertas 13, 28012 Madrid (tel: 538-3500; fax: 538-3677; e-mail: camaramadrid@camaramadrid.es).

Málaga Cámara Oficial de Comercio, Industria y Navegación, Cortina del Muelle 23, 29015 Málaga (tel: 221-1673; fax: 222-9894; e-mail: info@camaramalaga.com).

Mallorca, Ibiza y Formentera Cámara de Comercio, Estudio General 7, 07001 Palma de Mallorca (tel: 710-188; fax: 726-302; e-mail: ccinmallorca@camaras.org).

Sevilla Cámara Oficial de Comercio, Industria y Navegación, Plaza de la Contratación 8, 41004 Sevilla (tel: 211-005; fax: 225-619; e-mail: ccinsevilla@camaradesevilla.com).

Valencia Cámara de Comercio, Industria y Navegación, Poeta Querol 15, 46002 Valencia (tel: 103-900; fax: 531-742; e-mail: info@camaravalencia.com).

Zaragoza Cámara Oficial de Comercio e Industria, Calle Isabel La Catolica 2, 50071 Zaragoza (tel: 306-161; fax: 357-945; e-mail: cci@camarazaragoza.com).

Banking

Banco Atlántico SA, Diagonal 407 bis, Barcelona (tel: 237-1240).

Banco Bilbao Vizcaya Argentaria, Plaza de San Nicolás 4, 48005 Bilbao (tel: 424-4620).

Banco de la Exportación SA, Barcas 10, Valencia 2 (tel: 351-7862).

Banco de Sabadell, Plaza Sant Roc 20, 08201 Sabadell (tel: 726-2100).

Banco Español de Crédito (Banesto), Paseo de la Castellana 7, Madrid (tel: 338-1000).

Banco Internacional de Comercio, José Ortega y Gasset 56, 28006 Madrid (tel: 402-8362).

Banco Popular Español, Velázquez 34, 28001 Madrid (tel: 435-3620).

Banco Santander Central Hispano (BSCH) (established April 1999), Apartado de Correos 00045, Santander (tel: 221-200).

La Caixa de Catalunya, Avinguda Diagonal 621, Barcelona 08028 (tel 934-045000).

Confederación Española de Cajas de Ahorros (confederation of Spanish savings banks), Alcalá 27 Madrid 14 (tel: 232-7810).

Consejo Superior Bancario (central committee of Spanish banking), José Abascal 57, Madrid 9 (tel: 441-0611).

La Caixa de Barcelona (savings bank), Avinguda Diagonal 530, 08006 Barcelona (tel: 201-6666).

Central bank

Banco de España, Alcalá 50, 28014 Madrid (tel: 385-000).

European Central Bank (ECB), Kaiserstrasse 29, D-60311 Frankfurt am Main, Germany (tel: +49(69)13-440; fax: +49(69)1344-6000; e-mail: info@ecb.int).

Travel information

Federación Española de Hoteles, Orense 32, 28020 Madrid (tel: 556-7112; fax: 556-7361; e-mail: federahoteles@ipf.es).

Turespaña, Secretaria Gral de Turismo, Castello 115–117 Maria de Molina 50, 28001 Madrid (tel: 411-4014, 411-6011).

Ministries

Ministry for Development, P de la Castellana 67, 28071 Madrid (tel: 597-7000; fax: 597-8502).

Ministry of Economy, Finance and Trade, Alcalá 9, Madrid 28071 (tel: 595-8000).

Ministry of Education and Culture, Alcalá 34, 28071 Madrid (tel: 532-5089; fax: 532-5873).

Ministry of the Environment, Pza San Juan de la Cruz, 28071 Madrid (tel: 597-7000; fax: 597-6349).

Ministry of Foreign Affairs, Pza de la Provincia 1, 28071 Madrid (tel: 379-9549).

Ministry of Health and Consumer Affairs, P del Prado 18-20, 28071 Madrid (tel: 596-1000; fax: 429-3525).

Ministry of Industry and Energy, Paseo de la Castellana 160, Madrid 16 (tel: 349-4806).

Ministry of the Interior, P de la Castellana 5, 28071 Madrid (tel: 537-1000; fax: 537-1177).

Ministry of Justice, San Bernardo 45, 28071 Madrid (tel: 930-2000).

Ministry of Labour and Social Affairs, Agustín de Bethencourt 4, 28071 Madrid (tel: 553-6000; fax: 554-7528).

Ministry of Public Administrations, P de la Castellana 3, 28071 Madrid (tel: 586-1000; fax: 319-2448).

President's Office, Complejo de la Moncloa, 28071 Madrid (tel: 335-3535).

Other useful addresses

Agencia EFE, SA (news agency), Espronceda 32, Apartado 1112, 28003 Madrid (tel: 441-5599).

Agencia para el Desarrollo, Consejeria de Economia e Innocacion Tecnologica, Comunidad de Madrid (fax: 420-6456, 399-7451; e-mail: agencia.desarrollo@madrid.org).

Bolsa de Comercio de Valencia (stock exchange), Pascual y Genis 19, 46001 Valencia (tel: 352-1487).

Bolsa de Madrid (stock exchange), Palacio de la Bolsa, Plaza de la Lealtad 1 (tel: 232-8484).

Central de Reservas de los Paradores de España, Calle Velázquez 25, 28001 Madrid (tel: 435-9700/9744/9768/9814).

Confederación Española de Organizaciones Empresariales (Spanish confederation of employers' organisations), Diego de León 50, 28006 Madrid (tel: 262-4410).

Fira de Barcelona, Avenida Reina Maria Cristina s/n, 08004 Barcelona (tel: 423-3101; fax: 423-8651).

IFEMA (Feria de Madrid), Parque Ferial Juan Carlos 1, 28042 Madrid (tel: 722-5180/5000; fax: 722-5801; e-mail: infoifema@ifema.es).

Instituto Nacional de Estadística (INE), Paseo de la Castellana 183, E-28071 Madrid (tel: 583-9100; fax: 573-2713).

Instituto Nacional de la Seguridad Social, Subdirección General de Relaciones Internacionales, Padre Damián 4, 28036 Madrid (tel: 450-1900).

Spanish Embassy (USA), 2375 Pennsylvania Avenue, NW, Washington DC 20037 (tel: 202-452-0100; fax: 202-833-5670; e-mail: spain@spainemb.org).

Internet sites
Ministry of Tourism: http://www.tourspain.es
Paradores: http://www.parador.es
Iberia: http://www.iberia.com
Spain statistics: http://www.ine.es/welcoing.htm
Spanish yellow pages (in Spanish): http://www.paginasamarillas.es
Current affairs: http://www.sispain.com
Hotel reservations: http://www.red2000.com
Government spokesman: http://www.la-moncloa.es
El Pais newspaper: http://www.elpais.es
Train information: http://www.renfe.es
Bank of Spain: http://www.bde.es
Stock Exchange: http://www.bolsamadrid.es
Andalucia: http://www.andalucia.com
Balearics: http://www.caib.es
Barcelona: http://www.bcn.es
Basque Country: http://www.euskadi.net
Bilbao: http://www.bilbao.net
Canaries: http://www.gobcan.es
Galicia: http://wwwxunta.es
Madrid: http://www.munimadrid.es
Valencia: http://www.gva.es

Sri Lanka

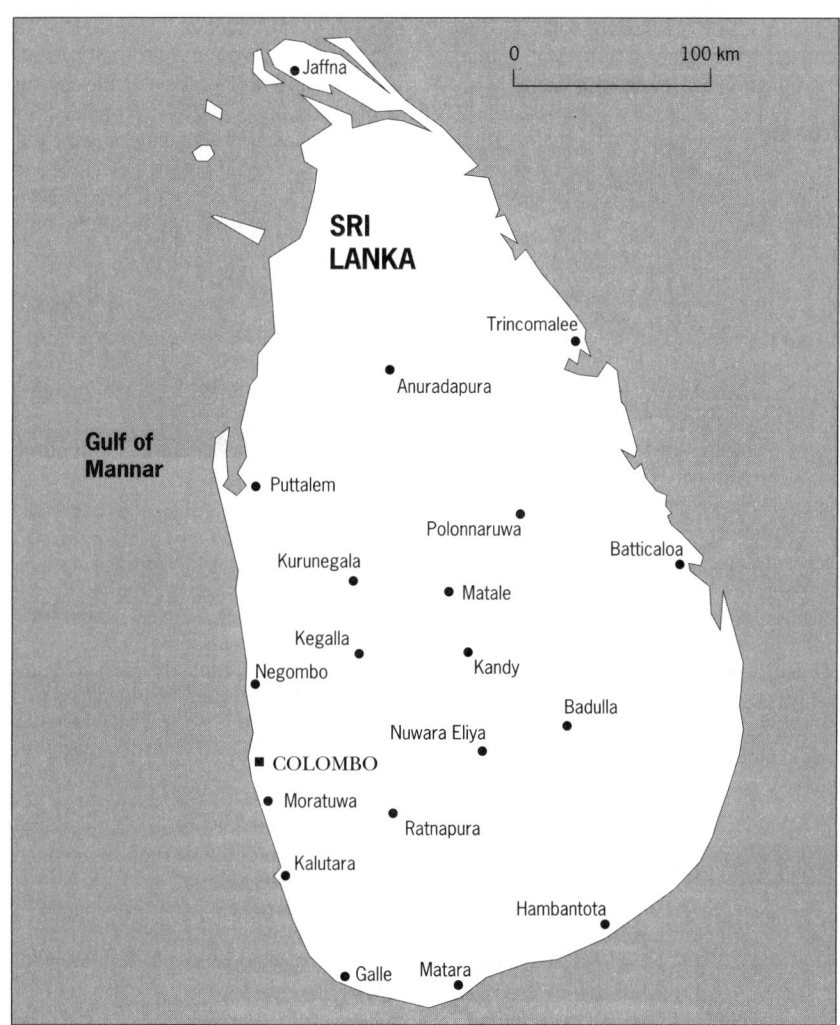

KEY FACTS

Official name: Sri Lanka Prajathanthrika Samajavadi Janarajaya / Llankais Sananayaka socialisak kutiyarasa / Democratic Socialist Republic of Sri Lanka

Head of State: President Mahinda Rajapakse (UPFA) (elected 17 November 2005),

Head of government: Ratnasiri Wickremanayake, appointed by the president, took office on 21 November 2005

Ruling party: Coalition government led by United People's Freedom Alliance (UPFA) (elected 2 Apr 2004)

Area: 65,610 square km

Population: 20.48 million (2004)

Capital: Colombo (official capital); many governmental functions are centred in Sri Jayawardenepura, a suburb of Colombo.

Official language: Sinhala, Tamil, English

Currency: Rupee (Rs) = 100 cents

Exchange rate: Rs101.33 per US$ (Oct 2005)

GDP per capita: US$989 (2004)

GDP real growth: 5.20% (2004)

Labour force: 8.95 million (2004)

Unemployment: 7.80% (2004)

Inflation: 7.60% (2004)

Balance of trade: -US$1.96 billion 2004

Foreign debt: US$9.80 billion (2003)

Ceylon, that 'teardrop' at the foot of India, became independent in 1948 and changed its name to Sri Lanka in 1972. In 2005, Sri Lanka suffered several highs and lows. It began the year in a state of chaos after it had been one of the countries worst hit by the *tsunami* (giant wave) that swept across from Indonesia after an earthquake off the coast of Sumatra island. The final estimate was 35,322 dead or missing, and a further 516,00 displaced – almost 3 per cent of the total population had either died or lost their home. For a small island (65,610 square km), this was a devastating start to the year.

Although the *tsunami* gave rise to an extraordinary out-pouring of giving from around the world, the government of Sri Lanka was ill-placed to manage the great amounts of aid that came, in the form of cash and people. The island's tradition of red tape and tight government planning control meant that vital supplies were caught up in customs delays for weeks, families who wanted to rebuild were they had previously lived were often told they couldn't because a new law, to 'protect' them also forbade them building within 50 metres of the coastline. The aid agencies that came by the dozen seldom spoke or planned with each other, or the government, so valuable time was lost while disputes were settled, or not, and people carried on living in tents, if they were lucky enough to have been given one, or other temporary accommodation. Camps became unnecessarily overcrowded and unsanitary.

The railway line that had been washed away by the wave, and where over 1,000 persons had died, was functioning again in less than two months – a minor triumph amid the general devastation.

However, by the middle of 2005, the business of politics and the economy once more came to the fore.

Politics

The *tsunami* initially brought unprecedented co-operation between the northern rebel Liberation Tigers of Tamil Eelam (LTTE), the Tamil Tigers, and the government in Colombo. The Tamil region of Sri Lanka had been one of the areas hardest hit and needed the most help. But by August this semi-truce was broken when the foreign minister, Lakshman Kadirgamar (a Tamil), was killed and attacks on Sri Lankan soldiers increased. An agreement to give the Tamil Tigers a part in distributing aid failed to be signed in mid-year, despite the efforts of the Norwegian deputy foreign minister, who was mediating between the two sides.

Mahinda Rajapakse of the United People's Freedom Alliance (UPFA) won the presidential elections in November 2005 and he appointed Ratnasiri Wickremanayake as prime minister. Mr Wickremanayake had previously served under former president Chandrika Kumaratunga and is a known hardliner who has advocated a military solution to the conflict with the Tamil Tigers. Although the new president said he was dedicated to upholding the delicate cease-fire with the LTTE, neither he nor his prime minister were received with much enthusiasm by the business community.

Economy

Sri Lanka has largely sustained its growth momentum since 2004, according to the IMF in its annual review. A key challenge in 2005 and 2006 is the management of the reconstruction activity after the *tsunami*. Key to this will be the government's ability or otherwise to perform efficiently and in a transparent manner, while maintaining economic stability.

GDP growth of 5.2 per cent in 2004 was led by domestic demand, especially strong private investment, which contributed to a rapid increase in imports. Exports of goods and services also expanded, aided by textiles and tourism arrivals. However, the rising price of oil was a dampener. The reconstruction activity and a strong agricultural sector is expected to off-set the *tsunami's* adverse impact on the fishing industry, and to a lesser extent, tourism.

The large fiscal deficits and high level of public debt are a potential source of macroeconomic instability and the IMF has called for stronger efforts at fiscal consolidation. It also encouraged the authorities to improve debt management, curtail central bank financing of the budget, initiate a comprehensive tax reform and shift expenditure to priority infrastructure and poverty reduction projects.

Outlook

President Rajapakse is conservative on the economy, and potentially tough on the guerrillas. The Colombo Stock Exchange had reacted adversely to his election, closing down by over 7 per cent on the day the results were announced. Nevertheless, Sri Lanka has a sound economy on which to build in 2006, and if progress can be made towards peace in the north, then 2006 should be an improvement on 2005.

Risk assessment

Economic	Poor
Political	Improving
Regional stability	Poor
Stock market	Improving

COUNTRY PROFILE

Historical profile
Sri Lanka became an outpost of Buddhism after the religion had mostly disappeared in the rest of South Asia. Historic kingdoms included that centred around the central city of Kandy, which resisted Western encroachment until 1815.
1815 The British became the first colonial power to win control of the island, which became known as Ceylon. Tamils from India were brought over to work on the plantations.
1931 The right to vote was introduced by the colonial authorities, who also established a system of power-sharing with the people of Ceylon.
1948 Ceylon gained full independence from British rule.
1949 The right to vote was taken away from Indian Tamils.
1951 Solomon Bandaranaike left the ruling Ekshat Jathika Pakshaya (EJP) (United National Party) to form the Sri Lanka Nidahas Pakshaya (Sri Lanka Freedom Party) (SLFP).
1953 A decision by the EJP government to cut the rice ration in the slump following the Korean War saw riots assume insurrectionary proportions.
1956 Bandaranaike became prime minister. Sinhala was made the state language by Bandaranaike's SLFP government, sparking anti-Tamil pogroms.
1959–60 Bandaranaike was assassinated by a Buddhist monk in 1959. His widow, Sirimavo, was elected SLFP leader and prime minister the following year. She stepped up the nationalisation programme.

KEY INDICATORS — Sri Lanka

	Unit	2000	2001	2002	2003	2004
Population	m	19.40	19.60	19.82	20.15	*20.48
Gross domestic product (GDP)	US$bn	16.30	15.60	16.30	18.20	*20.06
GDP per capita	US$	879	795	822	925	989
GDP real growth	%	6.0	-1.4	3.7	5.9	5.2
Inflation	%	1.2	14.2	8.8	9.0	7.6
Unemployment	%	7.7	7.8	9.0	7.5	–
Exports (fob) (goods)	US$m	5,439.6	4,817.0	4,700.0	5,133.0	5,306.0
Imports (fob) (goods)	US$m	6,483.6	6,705.0	6,110.0	6,672.0	7,265.0
Balance of trade	US$m	-1,044.0	-1,100.0	-1,406.0	-1,539.0	-1,959.0
Current account	US$m	-1,042.4	-370.0	-264.0	-101.0	-640.0
Foreign debt	US$bn	9.0	8.5	9.6	9.8	–
Total reserves minus gold	US$m	1,039.0	1,287.0	1,631.0	2,265.0	2,132.0
Foreign exchange	US$m	976.0	1,226.0	1,564.0	2,193.0	2,058.0
Exchange rate	per US$	77.01	89.38	95.11	96.86	101.19

* estimated figure

Sri Lanka

1964 A pact with India forced half a million Indian Tamil plantation workers to return to India.

1965 The EJP won elections and began attempts to reverse the nationalisation programme.

1970 Sirimavo Bandaranaike began what would be her second term as prime minister, which would last until 1977.

1971 A rural uprising led by the Marxist Janatha Vimukthi Peramuna (JVP) (People's United Liberation Front) was crushed.

1972 The country changed its name from Ceylon to Sri Lanka and Buddhism became the country's official religion.

1976 The main Tamil party, the Federal Party, and other Tamil groups, formed the Tamil United Liberation Front (TULF), calling for a separate Tamil state in the northern and eastern parts of the country. The Liberation Tigers of Tamil Eelam (LTTE) was formed.

1977 A constitutional amendment was passed which established a presidential system of government from the end of the year. In elections, the TULF won all the seats in Tamil areas.

1978 J R Jayewardene became the country's first executive president. Continued violence and pressure from the Tamils led the government to recognise the Tamil language in the new constitution.

1983–84 Tamil terrorist activity and anti-Tamil pogroms broke out. The latter constituted the worst outbreak of violence for many years, sparking a state of emergency. India began training Tamil guerrillas. Conflicts developed in the north of the island between the army and the LTTE.

1985 The first attempts at peace talks with the LTTE failed.

1986 Violence continued to convulse the northern and eastern provinces. Sri Lanka's relations with India were severely strained by the violence. India mediated informally between TULF legislators, Tamil leaders and the Sri Lankan government.

1987 Following an accord with India, more than 7,000 Indian troops were sent to Sri Lanka to try to implement a peace accord. The government signed accords created new councils for Tamil areas in the north and east.

1989 Ranasinghe Premadasa was sworn in as president. The state of emergency which had been in force since May 1983 was repealed.

1990 Indian troops went home after losing more than 1,000 soldiers and failing to achieve their objectives. The LTTE controlled large parts of northern Sri Lanka.

1991 The LTTE was implicated in the assassination of Indian prime minister Rajiv Gandhi.

1993 President Premadasa was killed in an LTTE bomb attack.

1994 The Bahejana Nidasa Pakhsaya (People's Alliance) (PA), a left-wing nine-party coalition centred on the SLFP, won the legislative elections. The prime minister, Chandrika Bandaranaike Kumaratunga (SLFP), was elected president. She appointed her mother, Sirimavo Bandaranaike, as prime minister, for the third time.

1995 Peace talks with the LTTE collapsed and the LTTE resumed its bombing campaign. The government launched a major offensive, driving the LTTE out of its Jaffna stronghold.

1996 The LTTE bombed the capital, Colombo, leading to a nationwide state of emergency.

1998 Sri Lanka's fiftieth anniversary celebrations were marred by renewed fighting between the army and separatist LTTE in the north of the country. The LTTE bombed Sri Lanka's holiest Buddhist site and captured key northern towns in a large offensive.

1999 President Kumaratunga won her second and final term in office. Kumaratunga was partially blinded in one eye during bombing at an election rally.

2000 A state of war was declared. Norway began a mediating role, putting a peace package before the LTTE. The elections resulted in a hung parliament, with the PA dependent on two moderate Tamil-linked parties for support. Sirimavo Bandaranaike, the world's first female prime minister, died soon after casting her vote. An LTTE cease-fire was rejected by the government.

2001 The LTTE was declared a terrorist organisation by Britain and Canada. The LTTE destroyed half of Sri Lankan Airlines fleet at Colombo's airport. Kumaratunga announced a snap election, which was won by the opposition EJP. Ranil Wickremesinghe was appointed prime minister.

2002 A cease-fire negotiated by Norway came into effect, ending the civil war between the government and the LTTE. The ruling party won local elections, which were also billed as a referendum on peace plans. The ban on the LTTE was lifted as a prelude to peace talks in Thailand, where they dropped their demand for independence in favour of regional autonomy with self-government.

2003 In April, the LTTE withdrew from peace talks. In November, the LTTE asked for interim powers over the north and east, where the Tamil population is concentrated. Fearing the break-up of Sri Lanka, the president suspended parliament, assumed the portfolios of three ministers and deployed troops in Colombo as a state of emergency was declared.

2004 The president called a snap election on 2 April, which was won by the his party, the United People's Freedom Alliance (UPFA). Mahinda Rajapakse became prime minister in April. On 26 December, an earthquake off the island of Sumatra caused a *tsunami* that devastated coastal areas of Sri Lanka. The final estimate was 35,322 dead or missing, 516,150 displaced.

2005 The foreign minister, Lakshman Kadirgaamar was assassinated on 13 August. On 17 November, the presidential election was won by Prime Minister Rajapakse (UPFA). Ratnasiri Wickremanayake was appointed prime minister on 21 November. Sri Lanka, Bhutan, Bangladesh, India, Maldives, Nepal and Pakistan signed the South Asia Free Trade Agreement (SAFTA), to come into effect on 1 January 2006.

Political structure
Constitution

The constitution dates from 1978, when a presidential system of government was established. Local authority is represented by 24 district councils in nine provinces and the Pradesiya Sabas (councils based on local administrative divisions). The devolution of power is limited, partly due to non-implementation, and partly due to the fact that Article 2 of the constitution stipulates a unitary state. Also politically significant is Article 9, which guarantees the 'foremost place' to Buddhism among faiths and stipulates the duty of the state to protect and sustain the religion. Both are obstacles to any scheme for devolution. Article 76 further stipulates that parliament may not 'abdicate or in any manner alienate its legislative power', complicating the creation of an autonomous Tamil entity.

The constitutional situation reflects events in 1987, when a peace accord was signed with India, which had intervened to protect the Tamil population. The Indo-Sri Lankan accord introduced a tier of government at provincial level, with elected provincial councils and certain powers delegated from the central government. Traditionally there are nine provinces, but the accord provided for the temporary merger of the Northern and Eastern Provinces (those regarded by Sri Lankan Tamils as their traditional homelands), pending a referendum for which the political conditions have not yet materialised. The constitution provides the executive and security forces with sweeping powers on the declaration of a state of war. The Public Security Ordinance grants the armed forces wide powers of arrest and confiscation and allows home entry without a warrant once a war footing is declared. A two-thirds parliamentary majority is required for the removal of the

president or amendment of the constitution.
Form of state
Socialist democratic republic
The executive
The president is directly elected for a six-year term and is head of state, head of the executive, head of government and head of the armed forces. No presidential incumbent may serve more than two terms. The president has the power to appoint or dismiss the prime minister (whose powers are relatively limited) and the cabinet and to dissolve parliament. After the election victory of the EJP in December 2001, President Kumaratunga agreed to delegate some of her extensive powers to the cabinet.
National legislature
There is a unicameral National State Assembly with a six-year term of office. Of the 225 members, 196 represent the 22 electoral districts and are elected by proportional representation. A further 29 seats are allocated on a proportional representation basis according to the overall national party results.
Legal system
The judiciary is formally independent of the executive. The Supreme Court has sole jurisdiction over interpretation of the constitution. It is also the final arbiter in settling charges against the president. The legal code reflects the system of English law inherited in 1948, with subsequent amendments in line with legal changes in the UK.
Last elections
2 April 2004 (parliamentary); 17 November 2005 (presidential).
Results: Parliamentary: President Chandrika Kumaratunga's United People's Freedom Alliance (UPFA) won 45.8 per cent of the vote (105 seats out of 225), Ekshat Jathika Pakshaya (EJP) (United National Party) 37.9 per cent (82), the Tamil National Alliance (TNA) 6.6 per cent (22) and the Jathika Hela Urumaya Party (National Heritage Party), led by Buddhist Monks, 6.1 per cent (nine).
Presidential: Prime Minister Mahinda Rajapakse of the United People's Freedom Alliance (UPFA) 50.3 per cent of the vote, former prime minister Ranil Wickremesinghe of the United National Party (UNP) 48.4 per cent. Turnout was 73.7 per cent. Rajapakse ws sworn in as president on November 19.
Next elections
2011 (presidential); 2010 (parliamentary).
Political parties
Ruling party
Coalition government led by United People's Freedom Alliance (UPFA) (elected 2 Apr 2004)

Population
20.48 million (2004)
Ethnic make-up
Sinhalese (74 per cent), Tamils (18 per cent), Moors (7 per cent), others (1 per cent).
Sri Lankan Tamils form the overwhelming majority in the Northern Province. The Eastern Province is ethnically mixed with three groups in sizeable numbers – Sri Lankan Tamils, mainly Tamil-speaking Moors (Muslims) and Sinhalese. Indian Tamils, descendants of those brought over by the British to work the tea plantations, are concentrated in the plantation districts of the Central Highlands. Elsewhere the Sinhalese are in the majority and make up about three-quarters of the total population.
Religions
Buddhism (69 per cent), Hinduism (16 per cent), Christian (8 per cent), Muslim (7 per cent). Sinhalese are predominantly Theravada Buddhists and Tamils are Hindus, while Arab and Malay descendants are mainly Muslims.

Education
Public investment in education amounts to 1.3 per cent of GDP. Universal primary education and gender parity, at this level, have been achieved.
Primary and junior secondary school are compulsory, lasting until aged 14. Senior secondary and collegiate schools are discretional and last until aged 18. All schooling until this age is provided free. Teaching is provided in English, Sinhala, Tamil and GCE exams at aged 16 must include a language subject in the student's mother tongue of Sinhalese or Tamil.
The education sector faces problems such as declining efficiency and quality of educational institutions and a shortage of teachers, nevertheless, standards are high and the importance allocated to education is evident in the high literacy rates. Sri Lanka has received assistance from the World Bank, via the International Development Association (IDA). The ongoing Second General Education Project contributed a US$70.3 million for programmes based on improving enrolment, curriculum development and textbook provision. The Asian Development Bank has provided concessional loans to aid the North and East Community Restoration Development project to fund, among other programmes, educational facilities damaged during the internal conflict.
Literacy rate: 92.1 per cent total; 89.6 per cent female; adult rates (World Bank).
Compulsory years: Five to 14
Enrolment rate: 110 per cent, gross primary enrolment of relevant age group (including repeaters); 74 per cent, gross secondary enrolment (World Bank).
Pupils per teacher: 28 in primary schools.

Health
World Bank estimates show that the average life expectancy is higher than in most developing countries and the infant mortality rate is relatively low. Sri Lanka's social indicators showed steady improvement during the 1990s including a decline in the maternal mortality rate. There is increased access by the rural population to safe water (from 29 per cent to over 83 per cent) and sanitation (from 39 per cent to over 60 per cent). However, relevant sources indicate increased incidences of malaria and a high malnutrition rate for children under the age of five. The government's *Samurdhi* (Prosperity) Programme is assisting, particularly the most vulnerable groups, to reduce child malnutrition. Adolescent health services, nutrition and geriatric services and institutions are under strain. The use of traditional medicine (*ayurveda*) to supplement public healthcare is widespread.
HIV prevalence: 0.1 per cent aged 15–49 in 2003 (World Bank)
Life expectancy: 74 years (World Bank)
Fertility rate/Maternal mortality rate: 2.0 births per woman; maternal mortality 30 per 100,000 live births (World Bank).
Birth rate/Death rate: 16 births and 6.5 deaths per 1,000 population (2003)
Infant mortality rate: 13 per 1,000 live births (World Bank)
Head of population per physician/bed: 0.2 physicians and 2.7 hospital beds per 1,000 people.

Welfare
Despite sustained government efforts to introduce various poverty reduction programmes such as direct income transfers and subsidies, about 21 per cent of the country's population are poor. However, estimates on the poverty level exclude the conflict-centered north-east, which has about 2.8 million people, 15 per cent of the total population.
For a number of years poor families have been able to benefit from a food stamps project which provides vouchers for food. A much more ambitious poverty alleviation scheme, the *Janasaviya* programme, begun in the mid-1990s, entitled families to a monthly payment for the purchase of specific consumer goods. The Prosperity Programme is another government sponsored poverty reduction scheme, introduced in 1994, which aims to provide social services and a social safety net to very poor households. Two projects, funded by the Asian Development Bank, are the Emergency Assistance for the Rehabilitation of North and East Sri Lanka,

Sri Lanka

and the Eastern Province Coastal Community Development Project.

Old age, disability and death have been covered since 1958 by a social insurance programme funded from the Employees' Provident Fund (EPF). Employers pay 12 per cent of salaries to the EPF, the country's main social insurance fund, with a further 8 per cent taken from employees. A social assistance programme for the unemployed – arguably the hallmark of a comprehensive welfare system – saw legislation introduced in 1995 in advance of a three-stage phasing in of the programme, aimed at families earning less than Rs1,000 (US$10.41) per month.

Main cities
Colombo (official capital, estimated population 656,100 in 2003); many of the governmental functions are centered in Sri Jayawardenepura, a suburb of Colombo, 118,300), Dehiwala-Mount Lavinia (214,300), Moratuwa (181,000).

Languages spoken
The national languages, Sinhala and Tamil, are widely spoken. English is commonly used in government and is spoken by about 10 per cent of the population.

Official language/s
Sinhala, Tamil, English

Media

Press
The government assumed wide powers to censor the press under the Public Security Ordinance from May 2000.

Dailies: The main English-language dailies are the *Daily News*, *Island* and the *Mirror*. There are at least eight daily newspapers published in Sinhalese and Tamil. These include the Sinhala-language *Dinamina*, *Silamina*, *Divayina* and *Lankadeepa*, and the Tamil-language *Thinakaran* and *Virakesari*. *Spotlight on Sri Lanka* (http://web3.is.lk/spot/) gives daily compilation of online newspaper articles about the country. Official press releases from the government can be obtained from the newslink http://www.news.lk/

Weeklies: The *Sunday Observer*, *The Sunday Leader*, *Sunday Island* and *Sunday Times* are published weekly, together with Sinhalese and Tamil weeklies such as *Virakesari Illustrated Weekly*.

Business: The Ceylon Chamber of Commerce issues the monthly *Ceylon Commerce*, the Ceylon National Chamber of Industries publishes the quarterly *Industrial Ceylon* and the Trade and Shipping Information Service of the Ministry of Trade and Shipping publishes the quarterly *Business Lanka* and *Expo News* fortnightly. The Sri Lanka Ports Authority publishes a quarterly *Sri Lanka Ports News* newsletter, while the Clothing Industry Training Institute publishes *Clothing* magazine and the Greater Colombo Economic Commission brings out the *Sri Lanka Investment News*. *Business Today* is also widely read.

Periodicals: Some of the popular and useful periodicals include *Explore Srilanka*, *Lanka Monthly Digest* and the fashion magazine *Satyn*.

Broadcasting
Radio: The Sri Lanka Broadcasting Corporation transmits three national radio services, in English, Sinhalese and Tamil. Overseas Radio Ceylon has services in five languages including Japanese. There are five radio services with widespread coverage.

Television: There are six television stations operating eight channels. Broadcasts in English are aired every evening on the state-owned Rupavahini and on ITN.

Advertising
Advertising is increasingly important in the Sri Lankan market as new private sector broadcasters in radio and television enter the market. Press, cinema, commercial television and radio all accept advertising. Outdoor advertising is widespread; direct mail advertising must conform to a code of practice.

Economy
Sri Lanka has suffered large loss of life and considerable economic problems due to the civil war between government forces and the separatist Liberation Tigers of Tamil Eelan (LTTE), known as the Tamil Tigers, which broke out in 1983. The conflict has held back GDP growth by up to 2 per cent per annum. Inefficient infrastructure has been one of the main factors dragging down the competitiveness of Sri Lankan products and limiting the country's economic growth potential. Conflict in the north and east has limited the possibility of infrastructural development, while it has been a specific policy of the LTTE to sabotage infrastructural projects.

The sectoral mix reflects an agriculture-based economy that has made considerable progress in diversification. Industry in Sri Lanka accounts for around a quarter of GDP. Tea, textiles, garments and precious gems number among the most prominent exports. The southern and western parts of the country, where most of the country's agriculture and industry are located, have not been directly affected by the war. Tourism is also an important contributor to the economy in these regions.

The economy has recovered since the disastrous year of 2001, when it shrank by 1.4 per cent. Growth, which returned in 2003, has exceeded five per cent in the following years, mainly fuelled by the services sector with strong growth in telecommunications, tourism and financial services. The services sector is the largest component of GDP, contributing around 55 per cent to GDP annually. There is a small but growing information technology sector.

External trade
Imports
Major imports are textile fabrics, mineral products, petroleum, foodstuffs, machinery and transportation equipment.

Main sources: India (14 per cent total, 2004), Singapore (8.0 per cent), China (7.6 per cent), Hong Kong (5.9 per cent), Malaysia (4.6 per cent), Japan (4.6 per cent)

Exports
Major exports are textiles and apparel, tea and spices, diamonds, emeralds, rubies, coconut products, rubber manufactures and fish.

Main destinations: US (31 per cent total, 2004), UK (12.9 per cent), India (5.1 per cent), Belgium (4.9 per cent), Germany (4.9 per cent)

Agriculture
Farming
Sri Lanka's economy is becoming more service-oriented and less dependent on agriculture. By 2004, agriculture accounted for around 18 per cent of GDP (down from 30 per cent in 1980) and employed a third of the labour force. About 44 per cent of the land area is cultivated arable land.

The sector includes mostly large state-owned tea, rubber and coconut plantations and smaller holdings where rice, sugar cane, cassava, sweet potatoes, soya beans, other vegetables, cashew nuts, cocoa, castor, spices, chillies, onions and other crops are produced, sometimes at virtually subsistence level. Other agricultural products include spices, mainly cinnamon, and coffee. Sri Lanka is self-sufficient in rice, the main food crop. Livestock raised include buffaloes, goats, pigs, sheep and poultry.

Agricultural productivity on the small farms is low. The sector as a whole is struggling against declining terms of trade, with a general decline in the price of commodities like coconut and rubber coupled with rising costs, particularly transport.

Plantation crops provide export earnings, although output has declined in recent years. Sri Lanka exports 44 per cent of its rubber output, with production increasingly shifting to crepe rubber and latex. Tea is the most important agricultural export, although there is a lot of room for productivity gains. Smallholdings account for around 58 per cent of total output. The sector is showing signs of improvement. Private tea plantations owned by foreign investors are increasingly common and a number of new tea-blending units have become operational, helping to increase the added value of tea.

Production has matched the steady increase in world demand for spices. Sri Lanka produces over 85 per cent of the world's demand for cinnamon. Spice production accounted for 95.521 hectares of land in 2004.

Crop production in 2004 included: 2.7 million tonnes (mt) cereals in total, 2.6mt rice, 35,200 tonnes (t) maize, 220,780t cassava, 81,270t potatoes, 39,720t sweet potatoes, 600,000t plantains, 23,600t pulses, 341,770t roots and tubers, 1.9mt coconuts, 27,450t citrus fruit, 53,770t tomatoes, 40,480t chillies and peppers, 57,680t pineapples, 258,158t oilcrops, 4,390t tobacco, 2,890t cocoa beans, 8,690t green coffee, 94,700t natural rubber, 17,800t pepper spice, 20,500t various herbs and spices, 4,800t ginger, 990,430t sugar cane, 308,090t tea, 6,130t treenuts, 91,910t mangoes, 1,890t soya beans, 4,770t millet, 834,040t fruit in total, 547,690t vegetables in total. Livestock production included: 130,122t meat in total, 28,200t beef, 3,503t buffalo meat, 2,120t pig-meat, 1,578t lamb and goat meat, 94,721t poultry, 49,643t eggs, 165,580t milk, 5,225t cattle and buffalo hides.

Fishing
Around 90 per cent of the country's fishermen lost their livelihoods in the December 2004 tsunami. The government undertook to re-invest in boats and harbour infrastructure. Those unwilling to go back to sea will be retrained for onshore work, particularly in the building trade.

Fishing typically accounts for 2 per cent of GDP. Production includes prawns, shrimps, lobsters, crabs and sea cucumbers, for export and local consumption. The fisheries produce in the region of 200,000 tonnes of marine fish per year, 30,000 tonnes of freshwater fish and 10,000 tonnes of crustaceans.

New companies engaged in marine fishing qualify for a five-year tax holiday. Fishing activity has been affected both by higher petroleum prices and by the poor security situation.

Forestry
About 38 per cent of the land area (1.94 million hectares) is forested, and forestry accounts for 2 per cent of GDP, providing timber for local demand. Around 15 per cent of land area is subject to national protection. Forests of broadleaved, deciduous and evergreen are adapted to dry and monsoon seasons. Savannah and thorn woodland are found beside coastal areas populated by mangroves. Plantations account for around 316,000 hectares (ha) of forest cover and are established at a rate of 3,100ha per year. In 1990–2000, Sri Lanka lost almost 20 per cent of its natural forest at an average of 35,000ha per annum so that only small fragments of tropical rainforest remain, each less than 10,000 hectares in area. Illegal logging has removed timber from unprotected forests, adding to the reduction. Some tropical timber plantations provide teak, eucalyptus, pine and mahogany, which are commercially farmed, with exports of timber and forestry products totalling US$14.3 million in 2004. Most paper is imported. Non-wood forest products harvested include bamboo, rattan, gums, resins and medicinal plants, cinnamon, cloves, nutmeg and cardamom.

The estimated production for 2004 included: 6.3 million cubic metres (cum) roundwood, 61,000cum sawnwood, 117,000cum sawlogs and veneers, 21,500cum wood-based panels, 5,000cum veneer sheets, 5.6 million cum woodfuel, 1,453 tonnes charcoal.

Industry and manufacturing
Industry contributes around 27 per cent of GDP. One-third of manufacturing output, which accounts for around 15 per cent of GDP, is based on raw materials from the agricultural sector. There are 10 dedicated Export Processing Zones, mainly employing female labour.

A master plan for industrial development, co-ordinated with the Japanese International Co-operation Agency (JICA) and the United Nations Industrial Development Organisation (Unido), identifies electronics, information technology, rubber and plastics, machinery, footwear, textiles and apparel and agro-based industries as target sectors, with policy development responsibilities for these sectors shared between JICA and Unido.

Tourism
Since 2003, benefiting from the truce with the Tamil Tigers, the tourism sector has staged a recovery with visitor numbers passing the half million mark, and continuing to grow. There were 566,202 arrivals in 2004 and, despite the December 2004 tsunami, there was no fall-off in visitor numbers in the immediate aftermath and the sector held steady through the year. The main markets are Europe and the US, but since 2004 there has been a growth in the numbers of arrivals from other Asian countries and Australia. Tourism is expected to contribute 3.8 per cent to GDP in 2005.

Mining
Mining and quarrying account for around 2 per cent of GDP and employ 1 per cent of the workforce. Sri Lanka is rich in minerals such as ilmenite, plumbago, graphite, dolomite, kaolin, rutile, feldspar, quartz, mica, monazite, apatite, industrial clays and limestone. Precious and semi-precious stones, such as sapphires, rubies, catseyes, alexandrites, aquamarines, garnets, tourmalines, zircons, topaz, spinels, amethysts and moonstones provide increasing export income.

Hydrocarbons
Sri Lanka does not have any proven hydrocarbon reserves, but indications of possible deposits off the north and west have been detected and further explration is continuing. Sri Lanka consumes in excess of 75,000 barrels per day (bpd) of oil, all of which is imported. It is used for power generation and transport.

Sri Lanka does not produce or import gas and only imports a small amount of coal.

Energy
Sri Lanka has installed generating capacity of 2.1GW. Hydro-power is the principal source, but its contribution has declined in recent years from over 80 per cent to around 40 per cent in 2005. To overcome the unreliability of weather-dependent hydro-power and to extend coverage and meet the rising demand for electricity, generation is converting increasingly to fossil fuels, particularly coal, which have to be imported. Electricity demand is increasing by around 9 per cent per annum.

The government is planning seven new power generating projects, only two of which are hydro-electric.

Financial markets
Stock exchange
The Colombo Stock Exchange (CSE) is plagued by problems associated with the country's political instability. Poor political risk perceptions caused by the civil war, the much-anticipated general elections and the weakened coalition that finally resulted were thought responsible for much of the decline in the All Share Price Index (ASPI).

Banking and insurance
There are 26 commercial banks, but the sector is dominated by two state banks – Bank of Ceylon and People's Bank – which hold 55 per cent of market share. The government's deficit financing crowds out the private sector, meaning that banks have traditionally focussed on the public sector and reap high spreads from soaring interest rates. Meanwhile, deposit rates are low thanks to Sri Lanka's closed capital account and lack of competition among banks. This has created a perverse situation, where, although government security yields are higher than those from risky bank deposits, money keeps flowing into the banks.

The dominance of the two state banks is holding back development of the sector. Government-mandated lending policies mean that the two are effectively the industry's interest rate setters. Monopoly yields insulate the public banks from competitive problems that would otherwise be caused by managerial slack, poor asset bases and high costs. Organised resistance from unions and a desire to keep the banks' huge funds within the public sector have so far ruled out privatisation, although there are signs the government is amenable to gradual privatisation and an eventual stock market listing.

Central bank
Central Bank of Sri Lanka

Main financial centre
Colombo

Time
GMT plus 5.5 hours

Geography
Sri Lanka lies on the same continental shelf as India, from which it is separated by the shallow Palk Strait. The relief is dominated by the central highland massif, with an average elevation of over 1,500 metres, situated in the south central part of the island. This is surrounded by upland ridges and valleys which in the south-west of the island continue to the coast. The eastern region is an undulating plain with isolated hills and the north has flat, low and fertile plains intersected by ridges.

Climate
Colombo and the south-west experience monsoon rains May–September; the likely temperature range is 22–31 degrees Celsius (C) with average annual rainfall of 2,240mm. The north-east experiences monsoon rains November–February; lower temperatures (down to 10 degrees C) occur inland at higher altitudes, with average rainfall of 1,000–1,500mm a year.

Dress codes
Men usually wear a lightweight or tropical suit and tie for business meetings, and women mostly dress conventionally. On social occasions, dress as for business meetings unless stipulated otherwise. Rainwear is needed, as are warmer clothes for the hilly areas, especially between November and February. Discreet dress in public places is appreciated.

Entry requirements
Passports
Passports are required by all, and must be valid for at least three months from the date of issue of visa.

Visa
Required by all; some exceptions exist, see http://www.slembassyusa.org/consular/visas.html for the full list of nationals who can enter, for one month without a visa, for tourist purposes, and who have return/onward passage. Free-of-charge visas are issued on arrival, at the port of entry.

Business visas must be obtained before arrival and are only issued for 30 days stay (business travellers from SAARC countries may apply for a visa on arrival). All applications should be submitted with a letter from a sponsoring agency in Sri Lanka, plus a letter from the representative's company with their accreditation, a travel itinerary and a copy of onward/return passage. Visa applications may be referred to the relevant authorities in Sri Lanka, therefore adequate time should be included for processing.

Currency advice/regulations
All foreign currency, valuable equipment, jewellery and gems must be declared on arrival; only these and others, purchased locally, may be exported. The import of local currency is limited to Rs1000, and unused currency over Rs 250 has to be reconverted into foreign currency on departure. Exchange Control D form, issued on arrival, is returned at departure. Indian and Pakistani currencies are prohibited. Foreign currency may be exchanged only at banks or authorised dealers. It is advisable to retain foreign exchange, hotel and shopping receipts for proof of purchase.

Customs
Personal effects are allowed duty-free, but must be re-exported on departure. Export of antiques, rare books, palm leaf manuscripts, rare anthropological material and any wild animal, bird or reptile or part thereof is restricted, if not prohibited. Importation of firearms, ammunition, explosives, dangerous weapons, drugs and pornography is strictly prohibited.

Health (for visitors)
Medical facilities are adequate if limited. Immediate cash payment is often required by doctors and hospitals. Singapore and Thailand are typical evacuation destinations for those with severe medical problems.

Mandatory precautions
A vaccination certificate for yellow fever is required if travelling from an infected area. Infants under one year are exempt.

Advisable precautions
Vaccination for diphtheria, tuberculosis, hepatitis 'A' and 'B', Japanese B encephalitis, polio, tetanus and typhoid is recommended. Anti-malaria precautions should be taken. There is a rabies risk. Water should be boiled and filtered before drinking. Fruit must be washed in such water and peeled.
An outbreak of dengue fever throughout the island, in 2004, has led to over 4,000 incidents of the disease and 44 deaths. Although there is no preventive medication, visitors are advised to use mosquito repellent, a mosquito net at night, and wear clothing covering as much skin as possible during dawn and dusk, to reduce the risk. Symptoms match those of severe flu with high fever and muscle aches.

Hotels
A 10 per cent service charge is added to hotel bills.

Credit cards
International credit cards such as American Express, Visa and Mastercard are widely accepted by hotels and shops. Traveller's cheques are accepted.

Public holidays
Fixed dates
1 Jan (New Year's Day), 4 Feb (Independence Day), 13–14 Apr (Sinhala and Tamil New Year), 1 May (Labour Day), 17 Dec (Ramazan), 25 Dec (Christmas Day).

Variable dates
Good Friday, Tamil Thai Pongal Day (Jan), Mahasivarathri (Feb), Vesak (Buddha Purnima) (May), Diwali (Hindu, Oct/Nov), Eid al Adha, Birth of the Prophet Mohammed, Eid al Fitr.
Although not official public holidays, Poya holidays are observed on the day of each full moon.
Hindu, Muslim and Buddhist festivals are timed according to local sightings of various phases of the moon.

Working hours
Banking
Mon–Fri: 0900–1500.
Business
Mon–Fri: 0900–1700.
Government
Mon–Fri: 0830–1615.
Shops
Mon–Fri: 0900–1730; Sat: 0900–1300.

Electricity supply
230–240V AC, 50 cycles

Weights and measures
Metric system (local units also in use)

Social customs/useful tips
Alcoholic drinks are not served in hotels or restaurants on Poya (full moon) days. Footwear and headgear should be removed before entering Buddhist shrines; photographing statues of the Buddha is acceptable but not posing beside them; a yellow-robed Buddhist bhikku should not be asked to pose for photographs nor should visitors attempt to shake hands with him.
Filming with a video camera and other photography near military and government installations is prohibited.
Appointments should be made in advance. Punctuality is appreciated. Men shake hands on meeting and taking leave. Some people may prefer not to shake hands with those of the opposite sex.

The form of address is Mr or Mrs followed by family or surname, and people with an academic or professional title should be addressed by their full title.

Visitors should take note of local customs and take care to respect religious conventions. It is the convention to use the right and not the left hand when shaking hands and passing or receiving anything. Restaurants usually add a service charge but further gratuities are optional.

Security

A cease-fire, signed by rebels in early 2002, has meant the security situation has eased, however visitors should continue to avoid areas north of Puttalam, Anuradhapura and Nilaveli as well as the eastern side of the island south of Trincomalee including Batticaloa.

The areas once under conflict were heavily mined and travelling off main roads can be hazardous; warning notices are posted. Visitors must comply with any instruction issues at all road blocks and security checks.

Registration with the relevant national embassy on arrival is highly advisable.

Getting there

Air

National airline: Sri Lankan Airlines (formerly Air Lanka)

International airport/s: Colombo Bandaranayake International (CMB), 32 km north of Colombo, with duty-free shop, bar, restaurant, buffet, bank, hotel reservations, post office, car hire and rail link to Colombo (journey time 1.25 hrs).

Airport tax: International departures include an embarkation tax of Rs500, excluding infants under two years and 24 hour transit passengers who do not leave the airport.

Surface

Rail: Rail-ferry-rail tickets incorporating the Rameswarum (India) to Talaimannar ferry, can be obtained from Madras (India) to Colombo.

Water: There are ferry services between Rameswaram (India) and Talaimannar. Ferry services may be suspended during bad weather and shipping has been attacked by the LTTE in the past.

Main port/s: Colombo (containers, LASH, ro-ro), Trincomalee, Galle, Kandasanturai.

Getting about

National transport

Air: Upali Travel and Air Travel operate domestic services to several destinations; charter planes and helicopters are also available.

Road: The extensive road network has 27,000km of road, 19,000km of which is surfaced.

Buses: Express services are available to all main destinations and should be booked in advance. Some services have air-conditioning.

Rail: Regular services link Colombo to other main centres. Some services offer air-conditioning, dining cars and first-class accommodation. The service to Jaffna has been discontinued.

City transport

The Ceylon Government Railway runs trains twice per day, journey time 60 minutes, from the international airport to city centre.

Taxis: Metered taxis usually have yellow tops and red numbers on a white plate. Although mini-cabs are generally accurately metered, inaccurate meters or excessive charging should be reported to the police. Air-conditioned taxis cost 10 per cent more. A 10 per cent tip is usual. Journey time from the international airport to city centre is 45–60 minutes.

Buses, trams & metro: From airport to city centre, PTB service 187, every 30 minutes, journey time 60 minutes; Intercity Service 187, every 30 minutes, journey time 30 minutes.

Trains: From airport to city centre, Ceylon Government Railway, twice per day, journey time 60 minutes.

Car hire

Self-drive and chauffeur-driven car hire are available. Avoid driving yourself. If driving, do not ignore 'no parking' signs (in Colombo vehicles parked illegally are destroyed by security forces suspecting a terrorist bomb). It is highly advisable to be aware of all traffic laws and parking restrictions.

Chauffeur-driven cars are generally recommended and are cheaper. Mini-buses and coaches are also available to hire. Traffic is generally congested and the average rate of progress on roads nationwide is 30kph. Many roads are one-way only. Driving is on the left.

A national or international driving licence must be presented for local endorsement (on weekdays only) at the Automobile Association (AA) office in Colombo.

BUSINESS DIRECTORY

Telephone area codes

The international direct dialling code (IDD) for Sri Lanka is +94, followed by area code and subscriber's number:

Colombo Central	1	Moratuwa	1
Dehiwela	1	Negombo	31
Galle	9	Nuwara Eliya	52
Jaffna	21	Panadura	34
Kandy	8	Trincomalee	26
Kurunegala	37		

Useful telephone numbers

Emergency: 433-333
Police, fire and ambulance: 90
Accident service: 693-184/185
Directory enquiries: 161
International calls: 100
Trunk calls: 101
Speaking clock: 104
Phonograms: 133
Flight information Air Sri Lanka: 452-281 (24 hrs)
Other airlines: 452-861 (24 hrs)

Chambers of Commerce

American Chamber of Commerce in Sri Lanka, Colombo Hilton Hotel, Lotus Road, Colombo 1 (tel: 233-6073; fax: 233-6072; e-mail: amcham@itmin.com).

Ceylon Chamber of Commerce, 50 Navam Mawatha, PO Box 274, Colombo 2 (tel: 245-2183; fax: 243-7477; e-mail: info@chamberlk).

Federation of Chambers of Commerce and Industry of Sri Lanka, 29 Gregory's Road, PO Box 2015, Colombo 7 (tel: 698-225; fax: 699-530; e-mail: info@fccisl.org).

National Chamber of Commerce of Sri Lanka, 450 DR Wijewardene Mawatha Street, PO Box 1375, Colombo 10 (tel: 268-9600; fax: 268-9596; e-mail: sg@nccsl.lk).

Banking

Bank of Ceylon, 4 Bank of Ceylon Mawatha, Colombo 1 (tel: 448-348; fax: 448-606).

Commercial Bank of Ceylon, 21 Bristol St, Colombo 1 (tel: 445-010; fax: 449-889; e-mail: email@combank.net).

DFCC Bank, 73/5 Galle Road, Colombo 3 (tel: 440-366; fax: 440-376; e-mail: dfcc@sri.lanka.net).

Hatton National Bank, 10 RA de Mel Mawatha, Colombo 3 (tel: 343-473; fax: 440-658).

National Development Bank, 40 Navam Mawatha, Colombo 2 (tel: 437-701; fax: 440-262).

Pan Asia Bank, 450 Galle Road, Colombo 3 (tel: 565-564; fax: 565-576; e-mail: panasia@pabnk.lk).

People's Bank, 110 Sir James Peiris Mawatha, Colombo 2 (tel: 324-188; fax: 447-671).

Sampath Bank, PO Box 997, Sampath Centre Building, 110 Sir James Peiris Mawatha, Colombo 2 (tel: 300-260; fax: 300-143).

Seylan Bank, Ceylinco Seylan Towers, 90 Galle Road, Colombo 3 (tel: 437-901; fax: 433-072).

Union Bank of Colombo, World Trade Centre, Echelon Square, Colombo 1 (tel: 346-346; fax: 346-356).

Sri Lanka

Central bank
Central Bank of Sri Lanka, PO Box 590, 30 Janadhipathi Mawatha, Colombo 1 (tel: 247-7000; fax: 247-7712; e-mail: cbslgen@sri.lanka.net).

Travel information
Automobile Association of Ceylon, 40 Sir Macan Markar Mawatha, Galle Face, Colombo 3 (tel: 421-528; fax: 446-074).

Bandaranayake International Airport, Katunayake (tel: 252-861; fax: 253-187).

Sri Lankan Airlines, 37 York Street, Colombo 1 (tel: 735-555; fax: 735-122; e-mail: ulweb@srilankan.lk; internet site: http://www.airlanka.com).

Ministry of tourism
Ministry of Tourism and Sports, 64 Galle Road, Colombo 3 (tel: 441-577; fax: 441-500).

National tourist organisation offices
Sri Lanka Tourist Board, 78 Steuart Place, Colombo 3 (tel: 437-059; fax: 437-953; e-mail: ctb_dm@sri.lanka.net).

Ministries
Ministry of Agriculture, 'Sampathapaya', 82 Rajamalwatte Road, Battaramulla (tel: 886-623).

Ministry of Aviation and Airports Developments, 64 Galle Road, Colombo 3.

Ministry of Buddha Sasana and Religious Affairs, 135 Anagarika Dharmapala Mawatha, Colombo 7 (tel: 329-064; fax: 437-992).

Ministry of Constitutional Affairs and Industrial Development, 73/1 Galle Road, Colombo 3 (tel: 327-553; fax: 449-402).

Ministry of Co-operative Development, 349 Galle Road, Colombo 3.

Ministry of Cultural Affairs, 'Sethsiripaya', Battaramulla.

Ministry of Defence, 155 Baladaksha Mawatha, Colombo 3 (tel: 430-860; fax: 541-529).

Ministry of Development, Rehabilitation & Reconstruction of the East and Rural Housing Development, 43/89 Bristol Building, York Street, Colombo 1.

Ministry of Development, Rehabilitation & Reconstruction of the North and Tamil Affairs, North and East: 121 Park Road, Colombo 5.

Ministry of Education, 'Isurupaya', Sri Jayewardenepura Kotte, Battaramulla (tel: 865-141; fax: 865-162).

Ministry of Ethnic Affairs and National Integration, 152 Galle Road, Colombo 3.

Ministry of Finance and Planning, Secretariat Building, Colombo 1 (tel: 433-937; fax: 449-823; e-mail: minfi@boisrilanka.org).

Ministry of Fisheries and Aquatic Resources Development, Maligawatte, Colombo 10 (tel: 446-183; fax: 541-184).

Ministry of Foreign Affairs, Republic Building, Colombo 1 (tel: 325-371; fax: 446-091; e-mail: for_min@sri.lanka.net).

Ministry of Forestry and Environment, Unity Plaza Building, Colombo 4 (tel: 588-274; fax: 583-290).

Ministry of Health, 'Suwasiripaya, 385 Wimalawasa Mawatha, Colombo 10 (tel/fax: 692-694).

Ministry of Higher Education and IT Development, 18 Ward Place, Colombo 8.

Ministry of Highways, 'Sethsiripaya', Battaramulla.

Ministry of Information and Media, World Trade Centre, Echelon Square, Colombo 1.

Ministry of Internal & International Commerce, Muslim Religious Affairs, and Shipping Development, Insurance Building, Vauxhall Street, Colombo 2.

Ministry of Irrigation and Water Resources Management, 500 TB Jayah Mawatha, Colombo 10 (tel: 687-491; fax: 694-968).

Ministry of Justice, Superior Courts Complex Colombo 12 (tel: 329-044; fax: 320-785).

Ministry of Labour, Labour Secretariat, Kirula Road, Colombo 5 (tel: 588-078; fax: 582-938).

Ministry of Land Development and Minor Export Agriculture, 'Govijana Mandiraya', Rajamalwatte Road, Battaramulla.

Ministry of Estate Infrastructure and Livestock Developemnt, 45 St Michael's Road, Colombo 3.

Ministry of Mahaweli Development, 500 TB Jayah Mawatha, Colombo 10 (tel: 687-491; fax: 687-386).

Ministry of Plan Implementation, 'Sethsiripaya', Battaramulla (tel: 862-721; fax: 862-478).

Ministry of Ports Development and Development of the South, 45 Laden Bastian Road, Colombo 1 (tel: 421-231; fax: 423-485).

Ministry of Post and Telecommunications, 'Sethsiripaya', Battaramulla.

Ministry of Power and Energy, 80 Flower Road, Colombo 7.

Ministry of Provincial Councils and Local Government, 330 Union Place, Colombo 2 (tel: 421-211; fax: 347-529).

Ministry of Public Administration, Home Affairs and Plantation Industries, Independence Square, Colombo 7 (tel: 696-211; fax: 695-279).

Ministry of Rural Industrial Development, Janakala Kendraya, Pelawatte, Battaramulla.

Ministry of Samurdhi, Rural Development, Parliamentary Affairs and Up-Country Development, 7A Reed Avenue, Colombo 7 (tel: 689-589; fax: 688-945).

Ministry of Science and Technology, 320 TB Jaya Mawatha, Colombo 10.

Ministry of Social Services and Housing Development for Fishing Community, 'Sethsiripaya', Battaramulla.

Ministry of Transport, 1 DR Wijewardana Mawatha, Colombo 10 (tel: 687-105; fax: 694-547).

Ministry of Urban Development, Construction and Public Utilities, 'Sethsiripaya', Battaramulla (tel: 862-721; fax: 864-765).

Ministry of Vocational Training, 475/32 Kotta Ropad, Rajagiriya.

Ministry of Women's Affairs, 177 Nawala Road, Colombo 5.

Ministry of Youth Affairs, 7A Reed Avenue, Colombo 7.

Other useful addresses
Board of Investment of Sri Lanka (BOI), World Trade Centre, Echelon Square, Colombo 1 (tel: 436-639; fax: 447-994; internet site: http://www.boisrilanka.com/boihome/boi.htm).

British High Commission, 190 Galle Road, Colombo 3 (tel: 437-336; fax: 430-308; e-mail: bhc@eureka.lk).

Colombo Plan, 28 St Michael's Road, Colombo 3 (tel: 564-448; fax: 564-531; e-mail: cplan@slt.lk).

Colombo Stock Exchange, World Trade Centre, Echelon Square, Colombo 1 (tel: 446-581; fax: 445-279; inernet site: http://www.lanka.net/cse).

Sri Lanka Embassy (USA), 2148 Wyoming Avenue, NW, Washington DC 20008 (tel: 202-483-4025; fax: 202-232-7181; e-mail: slembassy@starpower.net).

Sri Lanka Export Credit Insurance Corporation, Export Guarantee House, Colombo 2 (tel: 719-410; fax: 719-400; e-mail: slecic@tradenetsl.lk).

Sri Lanka Export Development Board, 42 Navam Mawatha, Colombo 2 (tel: 300-675; fax: 300-715; e-mail: serve@edbtradenetsl.lk).

Sri Lanka Importers', Exporters' and Manufacturers' Association, PO Box 12, Colombo 10 (tel: 696-321; fax: 522-524; e-mail: sliema@isplanka).

Sri Lanka Tea Board, 574 Galle Road, Colombo 3 (tel: 582-236; fax: 589-132; e-mail: tboard@sri.lanka.net).

Sudan

KEY FACTS

Official name: Jamhuryat es Sudan (Republic of Sudan)

Head of State: President Omar Hassan Ahmad al Bashir (re-elected Mar 1996 and Dec 2000)

Head of government: President Omar Hassan Ahmad al Bashir

Ruling party: National Congress Party (NCP) (elected Dec 2000) (in coalition with the Democratic Salvation Front and, from May 2001, the Democratic Unionist Party (DUP) and the Muslim Brotherhood)

Area: 2,505,813 square km

Population: 37.99 million (2004)

Capital: Khartoum

Official language: Arabic

Currency: Sudanese dinar (SD) (worth 10 Sudanese pounds (S£)), introduced 31 Jul 1999

Exchange rate: SD238.20 per US$ (Oct 2005)

GDP per capita: US$617 (2004)

GDP real growth: 7.30% (2004)

Labour force: 13.80 million (2004)

Unemployment: 18.70% (2003)

Inflation: 8.40% (2004)

Oil production: 301,000 (2004)

Balance of trade: -US$191.60 million 2004

Foreign debt: US$21.10 billion (2003)

Even with peace, chronic instability resulting from the long-standing civil war between the Muslim north and the Christian south, adverse weather, and weak world agricultural prices ensure that much of the population of Sudan will remain at or below the poverty line for years. Decades of fighting have left the infrastructure of the entire country in tatters. The ongoing conflict in Darfur region has been described by the United Nations (UN) as the world's worst humanitarian crisis. While the north and south inched closer to peace, in 2003 rebels in the Darfur region seeking greater autonomy began an insurrection. Pro-government Arab militias are accused of using the situation to carry out a campaign of ethnic cleansing against non-Arab groups in the region. The Muslim government of the north did seek to impose *Sharia* (Islamic law) on the whole country, but the large non-Muslim southern population managed to block the move.

Peace at last

After two years of bargaining the government and rebels signed a comprehensive peace deal in January 2005. The country has a new constitution, and a new government of national unity was formed after more than 20 years of civil war with the south. The deal provides for a high degree of autonomy for the Christian south, where rebels say they have been marginalised. The region will also share oil revenue equally with the Muslim north, but southern leaders say the north has given only a fraction. Northern officials blame delays on bureaucracy. This has led to fears the southern conflict, in which two million people died, could rekindle if nothing is done to share growing oil income equitably. President Omar al Bashir announced in November that he expected production to double to one million barrels a day.

The potential economic dividends of peace could be great. Sudan has large areas of cultivatable land, as well as gold and cotton. Its oil reserves are ripe for even further exploitation.

The south will remain largely autonomous until 2010 and will then stage a referendum on complete secession.

Trouble in Darfur

The situation in Darfur has been precarious and pressure is mounting for a political solution to the conflict. Much more delay could see the Khartoum government face charges of genocide on an alarming scale. More than 1.5 million people have fled their homes and tens of thousands have been killed. The UN has reported attacks by bandits on civilians and humanitarian workers, clashes among rebel factions, kidnappings and the killing of peacekeepers.

The United Nations said in January it wanted the United States and European countries to help form a tough mobile force in Darfur. An immediate response from new African Union (AU) chairman President Denis Sassou-Nguesso of the Republic of Congo, was that only African forces can lead peacekeeping missions in Darfur. Africa would only accept help from elsewhere on condition that a 7,000-strong, African peacekeeping team led the operation. Foreign troops must support the AU forces. The AU has admitted it is struggling to find the US$17 million needed each month to maintain its present operation.

Economy

Economically, the Sudanese government has sound policies. It has been implementing International Monetary Fund (IMF) macroeconomic reforms and in 1999 began exporting crude oil and recorded its first trade surplus, Increased oil production, revived light industry, and expanded export processing zones helped sustain growth at 8.6 per cent in 2004. These achievements are at serious risk if the killing continues.

At this critical juncture, the government has the opportunity to bring about a number of important economic and political reforms to foster peace and economic development in the whole country.

The prospects are that in 2006, higher oil production will help finance additional expenditures, but resources should be allocated to priority sectors and high-return projects within a macroeconomic framework conducive to low inflation. A large increase in oil output next year will come at an opportune time given Sudan's infrastructure and pro-poor spending needs and will permit a commensurate increase in transfers of oil revenues to the south and other states to foster national unity.. At the same time, self-insuring against an oil price shock through building up savings in the oil savings account will be critical, as well as donor support to finance reconstruction projects. Capacity constraints in several areas call for cautious and prioritised increases in spending. Equally important will be to effect an increase in fuel prices that will reduce the burden of the subsidy on the budget while at the same time minimising the impact of the price increase on the poor.

In addition to priority fiscal reforms, the authorities are planning to conduct an investment climate assessment in collaboration with the World Bank within the context of a broader review of the environment for private sector growth.

Sudan's external debt remains unsustainable. The end-2004 stock of external public debt was estimated at US$26 billion (nine times exports of goods and services in net present value terms), of which about 86 per cent is in arrears. Restoring Sudan's external viability will require exceptional debt relief.

Lastly, the national unity government is expected to increase its interaction with donors and prepare an interim poverty reduction strategy. The UN is leading efforts to co-ordinate donor activity in Sudan, and the World Bank has established two multi-donor trust funds to finance projects of both the national government and the government of the south. Following up on the road map provided recently and prepared jointly with the World Bank and the UN, the authorities are planning to finalise an interim poverty reduction strategy by mid-2006.

Further actions will be needed in 2006 to safeguard macroeconomic stability. Oil production and revenues are expected to increase rapidly, and the authorities will have the opportunity to devote additional resources for pro-poor spending and infrastructure projects. At the same time, the 2006 budget will need to be carefully designed to balance the need to preserve macroeconomic stability, avoid excessive crowding out of the private sector, meet expenditure priorities, and carry out an appropriate reduction in fuel subsidies. A prudent monetary policy will be required to ensure that inflation objectives are achieved. Sudan's structural reform efforts

KEY INDICATORS — Sudan

	Unit	2000	2001	2002	2003	2004
Population	m	31.10	31.70	32.56	35.86	37.99
Gross domestic product (GDP)	US$bn	11.90	14.10	15.90	17.68	*19.56
GDP per capita	US$	450	442	487	493	617
GDP real growth	%	9.7	5.7	5.0	5.9	7.3
Inflation	%	8.0	6.0	6.0	10.3	8.4
Oil output	'000 bpd	174.0	211.0	233.0	255.0	301.0
Exports (fob) (goods)	US$m	1,806.7	1,698.7	1,840.0	2,095.0	3,777.8
Imports (fob) (goods)	US$m	1,200.0	1,395.1	1,500.0	1,476.0	3,586.2
Balance of trade	US$m	606.7	303.6	336.0	619.0	-191.6
Current account	US$m	-556.8	-618.3	-954.0	-1,015.0	-1,450.0
Total reserves minus gold	US$m	247.3	117.9	440.9	847.5	1,626.1
Foreign exchange	US$m	247.3	117.8	440.7	847.2	1,626.1
Exchange rate	per US$	257.12	258.70	257.70	259.25	257.91

* estimated figure

Politics

President Omar Hassan Ahmad al Bashir entered into a power-sharing administration in July 2005 alongside his former enemy, the southern ex-rebel leader John Garang, who has since died. The event marked an important step in the implementation of the January 2005 peace deal. Bashir remains the overall leader of Sudan, but Garang's successor, Salve Kiir, leads an interim administration in southern Sudan.

Omar al Bashir took power in a June 1989 military coup against the elected government of Prime Minister Sadiq al Mahdi. He dissolved parliament, banned political parties and set up and chaired the Revolutionary Command Council for National Salvation, which ruled through a civilian government. He formed an alliance with Hassan al Turabi, the leader of the National Islamic Front, who became the regime's ideologue and is thought to be behind the introduction of *Sharia* in the north in 1991. In 1993 Bashir dissolved the Revolutionary Command, concentrating power in his own hands.

He was elected president in 1996, and Hassan al Turabi became speaker of parliament. A new constitution was drawn up and in 1999 opposition groups were allowed to operate on a limited basis.

But in late 1999 Bashir dissolved parliament and declared a state of emergency. The move followed attempts by al Turabi to give parliament the power to remove the president and to re-establish the post of prime minister. He was imprisoned and later accused of treason after signing a deal with separatist rebels in the south.

Bashir was elected for a second term in 2000. Supporters of the National Congress Party filled the parliament. The opposition boycotted the poll, accusing Bashir of vote-rigging. In January 2006, in response to criticisms of his country's human rights record, he withdrew his candidacy for the presidency of the African Union in favour of President Sassou-Nguesso of the Republic of Congo.

Risk assessment

Politics	Poor
Economy	Improving
Regional stability	Poor

COUNTRY PROFILE

Historical profile
Sudan is the largest country in Africa, covering a massive 2.5 million square kilometres. In the twentieth and twenty-first centuries, its very size and the difficulty of creating a homogenous body politic hindered its political and economic development. Since the Pharaohs of 2000 BC, through the Arabs, the Ottomans in the nineteenth century to the rather one-sided Anglo-Egyptian condominium established in 1899, Sudan was governed from Egypt. Following the 1952 Egyptian *coup d'état* that overthrew King Farouk, Sudanisation increased, finally leading to independence on 1 January 1956.

Ominously, just before independence there had been a mutiny of troops in the southern town of Juba, which eventually developed into a full-blown civil war between Sudan's Arab, Muslim north and the non-Muslim, black African south. In 1972, with the signature of the Addis Ababa agreement, the Khartoum government thought the civil war was over, but it was only the end of its first bloody phase. After two years of bargaining, the government and rebels signed a comprehensive peace deal in January 2005. The civil war is said to have cost the lives of 1.5 million people.

1821 The swamps of southern Sudan were unaffected by the Arab-controlled northern regions until the Turks defeated Egypt, conquered northern Sudan and opened the south to trade.
1869 After the opening of the Suez Canal, the British became involved in Sudan.
1881–85 Mohammed Ahmed, who proclaimed himself the long-looked-for Mahdi (the guided one), led his followers, the Muslim Sudanese, in a rebellion against Egyptian mis-rule; General Gordon was sent by Britain to quash the rebellion. In 1885, Gordon and the British army were massacred by the Mahdi's army at Khartoum. Sudan was ruled by the Mahdi for the next 17 years. The Mahdi united the tribes in a modern Islamic state.
1898 The Mahdi was defeated by the British and Anglo-Egyptian army.
1899 Sudan was ruled as an Anglo-Egyptian condominium until it achieved independence as a parliamentary republic in 1956.
1945 At the end of the Second World War, political parties emerged: the Umma Party was created by supporters of the Mahdi while the Ashiqqa Party was established by rivals of the Mahdi and eventually became the National Union Party (NUP).
1956 Sudan gained independence. With southern calls for a federation or even secession rejected, a civil war broke out between the largely Muslim north and the largely Christian/Animist south.
1958 A military coup led by General Ibrahim Abboud overthrew the civilian government of Prime Minister Abd Allah Khalil. Martial law was declared and Abboud proclaimed himself prime minister.
1962 Civil war began in the south, led by the Anya Nya movement.
1964 The 'October Revolution' overthrew Abboud and a national government was established.
1969 Colonel Jaafar Mohammed al Nimieri led the 'May Revolution' military coup, installing a revolutionary council.
1972 Nimieri became the country's first elected president and gave the southern provinces a degree of autonomy under the Addis Ababa agreement between the government and the Anya Nya, reducing the level of fighting.
1978 Oil was discovered in southern Sudan.
1983 The President increased the Islamisation campaign when the autonomy agreement was revoked and *Sharia* (Islamic law) was introduced.
The Sudan People's Liberation Movement (SPLM) was established; its armed wing, the Sudan People's Liberation Army (SPLA) gained control of much of the south.
1985–86 Nimieri was ousted in a bloodless coup and after a brief period of military rule, Sadiq al Mahdi, the great-grandson of the Great Mahdi, became prime minister after elections in 1986.
1989 Sadiq al Mahdi was replaced following another bloodless coup by the National Salvation Revolution; Omar Hassan Ahmad al Bashir became chairman of the Revolutionary Command Council for National Salvation (RCCNS).
1993 The RCCNS was abolished after Omar al Bashir was appointed president; Sudan returned to civilian rule, although the country was not strictly a democracy.
1995 Egyptian President Mubarak accused Sudan of being involved in an attempt to assassinate him in Addis Ababa.
1996 The first presidential and legislative elections since 1989 were held; Omar al Bashir was elected president with a five-year term. Sanctions were imposed against Sudan by the UN for the country's failure to extradite three men suspected of involvement in the 1995 Mubarak assassination attempt.
1997 The Khartoum Peace Agreement was ratified by the National Assembly. Peace talks between the SPLA and the government resumed in Nairobi.
1998–99 Voters in a referendum endorsed a new constitution, which was promulgated at the beginning of 1999. Sudan began to export oil. After a power struggle within the ruling National Congress Party (NCP), between Bashir and Hassan al Turabi, the President imposed a

state of emergency and dissolved the National Assembly.

2000 Omar al Bashir and the ruling National Congress Party (NCP) were re-elected. Most opposition parties boycotted the elections.

2001 Hassan al Turabi, was arrested after his party, the Islamist Popular National Congress (PNC), a splinter from the NCP, signed a memorandum of understanding with the SPLA; more arrests were made and the PNC was banned. The UN Security Council approved the lifting of sanctions imposed in 1996. The UN's World Food Programme estimated that three million people were facing famine.

2002 After peace talks in Kenya, the government and the SPLA signed the Machakos Protocol: the government accepted the right of the south to seek self-determination after a six-year interim period; the southern rebels accepted application of *shariah* law in the north.

2003 Rebels in the western region of Darfur rose up against the government, claiming the region was being neglected by Khartoum. The PNC leader, al Turabi, was released and the ban on his party lifted.

2004 Army officers and opposition politicians, including al Turabi, were arrested over an alleged coup plot. Bashir agreed to grant autonomy to the south for six years, split the country's oil revenues with the southern provinces and allow the southerners to vote in a referendum of independence at the end of the six-year period.

The conflict in the western region of Darfur between nomad Arab militia and black African villagers gained world attention. The government denied that it supported the *Janjaweed* militias, accused of systematic killings of African villagers, and said that there was no evidence of any atrocities.

2005 The government and the Sudan People's Liberation Army (SPLA) signed a peace agreement in January which ended a 22-year civil war. SPLA leader, John Garang, was appointed vice president for the six-year period of reconciliation, and a new constitution gave a large degree of autonomy to the insurgent south. The peace agreement ended most hostilities in Darfur, where the two-year conflict had torn apart the lives of over 2.5 million people. In April, security forces arrested many members and top officials of the main opposition Umma Party (UP), because of planned celebrations marking an anti-government uprising in 1986. Sudan said it had found quantities of oil in its western region of Darfur. On 1 August John Garang was killed in a helicopter crash; riots broke out in Khartoum, when the news was announced, between black southern Sudanese and northern Arabs. Garang's deputy, Salva Kiir, was named as his successor as vice president and president of Southern Sudan. More violence broke out in Darfur in September when Arab militia attacked a refugee camp. Many thousands of southern Sudanese have returned from the north and neighbouring countries and are adding to the burden of an already stretched aid and feeding programme. In late December, Chad declared 'a state of belligerence' with Sudan. In an effort to ease tensions between the two countries, President Obasanjo of Nigeria, in his capacity as head of the African Union, held separate meetings, on his farm outside Lagos, with a Sudanese envoy and Chad's President Deby.

2006 In January the AU extended the mandate for its peace-keeping force by a further 10 months, although unless further funding becomes available after March the extension will in effect be for two months only.

Political structure
Constitution
A multi-party parliamentary system was introduced in 1986, comprising a five-member Supreme Council and a 360-member Majlis Watani (National Assembly).

In 1994, the government increased the number of states to 26. Each state has a wali (governor), legislative council and council of ministers. In March 2002, the government indicated that it would replace elections for the wali with a system of electoral colleges which would submit six possible candidates, giving the president the final decision on appointments. A new constitution was promulgated on 1 January 1999, allowing opposition political associations to register prior to the elections. Eligibility for voting was reduced from 18 to 17 years on 3 January 1999.

Form of state
Federal republic

The executive
The president has inherited most of the powers of the now disbanded Revolutionary Command Council of National Salvation (RCCNS), which assumed unified powers in the 1989 military coup. These include the right to override constitutional elections to the 26 state governorships. Executive power at the operational level resides with the cabinet, which includes both civilian and military representatives. In 2002, the government scrapped the two-term limitation to the presidency. The president is directly elected by universal suffrage.

National legislature
The Majlis Watani (National Assembly) was elected in December 2000, a year after it was suspended by presidential decree. Out of a total of 360 seats, 270 are directly elected for a four-year term in single-seat constituencies, 35 members represent women, 26 members represent university graduates and 29 are representatives of trade unions.

Legal system
Sharia (Islamic law) with an admixture of English common law operates officially at the federal level, although individual states choose whether or not it should apply at state level. In practice the legal system is split along political lines, with *Sharia* imposed universally in the north, but ineffective in the rebel-held south. The judiciary is in theory politically independent under the constitution introduced at the beginning of 1999. However, military or paramilitary elements influence the judiciary or operate direct extra-judicial military rule throughout the country.

Last elections
December 2000 (parliamentary and presidential)

Results: Presidential: Omar al Bashir was re-elected with 86.5 per cent of the vote. Parliamentary: the ruling National Congress Party (NCP) won 355 seats in the elections to the National Assembly.

Next elections
December 2004 (parliamentary); 2005 (presidential).

Political parties
Ruling party
National Congress Party (NCP) (elected Dec 2000) (in coalition with the Democratic Salvation Front and, from May 2001, the Democratic Unionist Party (DUP) and the Muslim Brotherhood)

Main opposition party
Umma Party (UP)

Population
37.99 million (2004)

Ethnic make-up
Black (52 per cent), Arab (39 per cent), Beja (6 per cent). In the north and central regions the population consists mainly of Muslim Arabs and Nubians. In the south the people are socially, culturally and historically related to the peoples of east Africa.

Religions
Islam (Sunni Muslim) in the north (70 per cent); in the south traditional beliefs (25 per cent) and Christianity (5 per cent).

Education
Elementary education for those aged six to 12 years is free. Intermediate education starts at the age of 13 and lasts three years. Secondary education starts at 16 years and also lasts for three years. Students completing secondary education are eligible for university. There are five universities, two in Khartoum (one is a

branch of Cairo University), an Islamic university at Omdurman and universities at Juba and Wad Medani.

Public expenditure on education typically amounts to 1 per cent of annual gross national income.

Unicef has voiced concerns at the low-level of public spending on education and at low enrolment and high dropout rates, calling for, among other things, significantly increased public spending, stronger teacher training and in particular the attention given to girls' education. Interventions to promote girls' education have resulted in an increase in the enrolment of girls by 5.7 per cent. The percentage of total girls' enrolment increased marginally from 45.3 per cent in 2000–01 to 45.6 per cent in 2001–02. Nationally, enrolment in primary schools increased by 5.8 per cent.

In 2002 Unicef undertook, with BRAC (an international NGO educational organisation specialising in providing schooling in poor rural areas), to provide 100 primary schools under the Village Girls Schools Project, in southern Sudan, within three years.

Literacy rate: 61 per cent, adult rate (2003)
Compulsory years: Six to 14.
Enrolment rate: 51 per cent gross primary enrolment of relevant age group (including repeaters); 21 per cent gross secondary enrolment (World Bank).
Pupils per teacher: 29 in primary schools.

Health
Public health services are organised by the ministry of health. Some health care is provided free of charge. Total expenditure on health is about 3.5 per cent of GDP, of which government spending is about 19 per cent.

In August 2004 epidemiologists of the Global Polio Eradication Initiative announced that new cases of polio had been confirmed in the Darfur region of Sudan. The infection is believed to have spread from Northern Nigeria.

HIV/Aids
The conflict in southern Sudan has left many destitute; UN peacekeepers are expected to provide a buffer between the warring sides and when this happens UNAids will send in teams to ensure HIV/Aids is not an inevitable consequence of the peace-keepers' arrival and the sex-industry that usually develops in conflict zones.

HIV prevalence: 2.3 per cent aged 15–49 in 2003 (World Bank)
Life expectancy: 58.6 years (World Bank)
Fertility rate/Maternal mortality rate: 4.4 births per woman (World Bank)

Birth rate/Death rate: 36.5 births per 1,000 population; 9.6 deaths per 1,000 population (2003).
Infant mortality rate: 63 per 1,000 live births (World Bank)
Head of population per physician/bed: 0.1 physicians and 1.1 hospital beds per 1,000 people.

Welfare
Social insurance in Sudan is not provided through the government. There is no social security budget.

Main cities
Khartoum (capital, estimated population 1.5 million in 2004), Omburman (2.2 million), Khartoum North (1.3 million), Port Sudan (450,400), Nyala (376,200), El Obeid (343,000), Kassala (336,500), Wad Medani (286,700), Juba (162,400), Atbara (105,500).

Languages spoken
Arabic and English are used in business. African languages include Nilotic and Nilo-Hamitic. The government is considering eliminating the official teaching and use of English as part of its Islamisation programme.

Official language/s
Arabic

Media
The media are tightly constrained by censorship laws, statutory government ownership, harrasment by the security forces, and an unsurprising amount of corresponding self-censorship.

Press
Following the 1989 military coup, all press publications were banned except for the newspaper of the armed forces. Since 1997, press restrictions have eased with increasing discussion of some domestic and foreign policy issues. Ownership of publications by individuals or political groups is banned. The board and chairman of a publication must be government-appointed, and 26 per cent of the publisher's equity go to the government. The National Press and Publications Council (NPPC) has the power to suspend any publication. A wide variety of English and Arabic-language publications operate in the shadow of the government's information policy.

Dailies: There are nine daily newspapers published from Khartoum. Arabic language dailies include *Akhir Khabai* and *Al-Waan. Al-Rayaam* is a political newspaper. The main national dailies (state-controlled) are *Al Sudan al Hadith, Al-Ingaz Al-Wakari* and *Al-Quwait Al-Musalaha*. The Sudan News Agency (www.sunanews.net/) carries the latest news on Sudan from different English language sources. *Sudan Globe* (www.sudanglobe.com/) provides daily on-line news service. *Sudan.Net* (www.sudan.net/) provides daily news in both Arabic and English languages from various government and non-government organisations.

Weeklies: Weekly publications include *Akhbar Al Mujtama, Azzizati* (bi-weekly) and *Al Aliha* covering sports.

Periodicals: Periodicals include the Arabic political monthly magazine *Addaraweesh* and the political newspaper *Mehairah* covering current issues. The Sudanese Communist party publishes the monthly newspaper *Al-Midan*. There is a monthly English-language magazine, *Sudan Now*.

Broadcasting
Directly controlled by government, radio and television come under the purview of a special military censor. All broadcasting is controlled by the state-owned National Radio and Television Corporation based in Omdurman.

Radio: The Sudan Broadcasting Corporation broadcasts daily radio programmes in Amharic, Arabic, English, French, Somali and Tigrinya.

Television: The Sudan National Broadcasting Corporation is responsible for television programmes, which are broadcast for about 40 hours a week.

In February 2000, the government signed a contract to import a 25MW transmitter, to broadcast over Unity state, including the areas of Bentiu and Rubkona.

There are restrictions on satellite dish ownership, but satellite services are offered in tandem with domestic. A six-channel cable network offers CNN, Saudi Middle East Broadcasting Corporation (MEBC), Kuwait-TV and Dubai-TV.

Economy
Sudan's economy is predominantly agricultural. Subsistence farming is combined with cash crops such as gum arabic, sesame and cotton. Economic growth is being fuelled by oil production, but has resulted in little improvement to living standards which in the oil-producing south have deteriorated due to the effects of the prolonged civil war. The conflict has resulted in resources being designated to security rather than to social improvement; as a result, the social indicators are below average for sub-Saharan Africa.

The expanding oil and gas reserves are of great interest to foreign investors and Sudan stands to become one of the world's leading oil producers. The Sudanese economy is undergoing rapid development, although this has been skewed towards the north. Oil production has boosted the trade balance with oil export revenues accounting for around 70 per cent of Sudan's total export earnings. Civil

Sudan

war in the south, continuing US sanctions and poor infrastructure have been obstacles to growth, but the oil industry has attracted growing investment and participation in recent years from the Far East. The development of the oil and gas sectors will inevitably transform the economic profile of Sudan.

An escalating humanitarian crisis is attracting international scrutiny and is likely to put pressure on the government and economy. Hundreds of thousands have been displaced and farms have been left to deteriorate. Despite the social crisis, GDP has continued to grow. However, unemployment remains high at around 20 per cent.

External trade
Imports
Principal imports are foodstuffs, manufactured goods, refinery and transport equipment, medicines and chemicals, textiles and wheat.
Main sources: Saudi Arabia (11.7 per cent total, 2004), China (10.7 per cent), UAE (6.2 per cent), Egypt (5.2 per cent), Germany (4.9 per cent), India (4.6 per cent), Australia (4.1 per cent), UK (4.0 per cent)
Exports
Principal exports are crude oil and petroleum products; cotton, sesame, livestock, groundnuts, gum Arabic and sugar.
Main destinations: China (64.3 per cent total, 2004), Japan (13.8 per cent), Saudi Arabia (3.7 per cent)

Agriculture
Farming
Sudan is a semi-arid country and a large part is desert. Irrigated farmland constitutes about one-fifth of the total cultivated area, but produces about 50 per cent of total crop production. The traditional farming areas are semi-arid and used for livestock rearing, while export crops are grown in the irrigated areas, mostly in the Gezira area between the Blue and White Niles. The country is often racked by drought and famine.

Agriculture accounted for around 30 per cent of GDP in 2004. The majority of the population work on the land.

Principal export crops are cotton, oil seeds (mainly groundnuts and sesame) and gum arabic (used in soft drinks, baking, cosmetics, pharmaceuticals and other industrial applications), of which Sudan is the world's largest producer. Main food crops include sorghum (dura) and millet. Cotton is the main cash crop providing 45 per cent of agricultural export earnings, followed by gum arabic and sesame (21 per cent). Livestock-raising is of considerable importance, employing about 40 per cent of the population. Sudan is aiming to become self-sufficient in rice and tea production.

Sudan has attempted to tackle the problem of land usage. Government policy aims to increase the area of cultivable land (only about 10 per cent of the potential arable land is under cultivation) through the rehabilitation and expansion of existing irrigation schemes. A planting scheme has given precedence to food crops over land devoted to cotton production and export.

Estimated crop production in 2004 included: 3,791,748 tonnes (t) cereals in total, 2,600,000t sorghum, 1,200,000t groundnuts in shell, 332,000t wheat, 60,000t maize, 10,400t cassava, 16,000t potatoes, 8,700t sweet potatoes, 15,748t rice, 74,000t bananas, 172,100t roots and tubers, 72,000t pulses, 330,000t dates, 150,060t citrus fruit, 700,000t tomatoes, 5,200t pineapples, 564,330t oilcrops, 195,000t mangoes, 3,350t jute, 5,500,000t sugar cane, 137,000t yams, 173,000t tea, 87,000t cotton lint, 784,000t millet, 1,100,000t fruit in total, 1,900,000t vegetables in total. Estimated livestock production included: 714,675t meat in total, 325,000t beef, 41,175 camel meat, 144,000t lamb, 126,000t goat meat, 29,500t poultry, 47,000t eggs, 5,106,250t milk, 710t honey, 56,280t cattle hides, 22,500t sheepskins.

Fishing
Sudan possesses vast freshwater and marine fishing potential. The freshwater sources comprise rivers and lakes. The Nile alone has an estimated potential output of 60,000 tonnes of fish a year, but the fisheries are barely exploited. Fishing on the Red Sea coastline is also under-exploited and is being encouraged with government assistance.

Over 95 per cent of the Sudanese catch of fish is obtained from inland fisheries on the Nile, its tributaries and associated swamp lands. Subsistence fishing is widespread, but the commercial sector is under-developed. Marine fishing is mainly carried out by artisanal fishermen in small boats.

Sudan exported around US$1 million of fish per annum before the war, but now exports only a small amount of dried and salted fish.

Forestry
Sudan has 17 per cent forest cover, most of which is located in the mountains and the wooded savannahs. In 1990–2000, forest cover diminished by an average of 1.44 per cent per annum or around 960,000 hectares (ha) per year. Rapid deforestation is a result of demand for fuelwood. Sudan produces a large amount of industrial roundwood, mainly for posts and poles, and also produces sawnwood, although not enough to ensure self-sufficiency. Sudan's most important non-wood forest product is gum arabic. Sudan is also one of the world's main producers of olibanum resin. Imports of forest materials amounted to US$34.4 million, while exports amounted to US$1.1 million in 2004.

Production in 2004 included: 19.7 million cubic metres (cum) roundwood (of which 6.4 million cum industrial roundwood), 50,700cum sawnwood, 123,000cum sawlogs and veneers, 1,500cum wood-based panels, 17.5 million cum woodfuel, 849,878mt charcoal.

Industry and manufacturing
The industrial sector contributed around 28 per cent to GDP in 2004 and employs 10 per cent of the workforce. The main activities are oil refining, agricultural products, textiles and leatherwares.

Tourism
The revival of tourism, which was destroyed by the civil war, is being planned. The sector is expected to contribute around one per cent to GDP in 2005.

Mining
The mining sector has played a relatively insignificant role in the country's economic development. Chromite, gypsum, gold, copper and iron ore are exploited on a commercial basis. Other mineral deposits include zinc, lead, talc, coal, nickel and tin, phosphate and uranium, but not in sufficient quantities to develop. If financial and infrastructural problems can be overcome, the sector could make a significant contribution to the economy.

Hydrocarbons
Sudan possesses proven oil reserves of around 635 barrels. In 2004, oil production was 343,000 barrels per day (bpd). Estimated oil reserves are at least 1.7 billion barrels and range up to 3 billion barrels. With more oil fields scheduled to come on stream, the government's aim has been to increase oil production to 500,000bpd by the end of 2005. Western oil companies have been deterred from investing in the Sudanese oil sector by US sanctions and the continuing instability, but Asian countries, principally China, India and Malaysia, have been very active, seeking to secure Sudanese oil for their own burgeoning reqirements. Sudan exports both crude and refined oil.

Sudan has several oil refineries and is adding to capacity. An agreement to build a new refinery in Port Sudan was signed in August 2005 with the Malaysian company Petronas.

Total gas reserves stand at around 105 billion cubic metres, but gas production is negligible. Sudan does not consume natural gas and none is imported. This could

change if gas fields are developed, but investor interest in this sector is low.
Coal is neither produced nor imported.

Energy
Sudan has installed electricity generation capacity of 728MW. Generation, distribution and transmission are the responsibility of the state-owned National Electricity Corporation. Sixty per cent of electricity generation is produced by thermal power, mostly oil, and 40 per cent by hydroelectricity, although this varies according to rainfall. The Roseires dam on the Blue Nile produces a large proportion of Sudan's electricity, with installed capacity of 274MW. Hydroelectric sources are being expanded. New dams are under construction, including the Merowe dam and the Kajbar dam. The Merowe facility, which will have capacity of 1,000MW, is being built at the Nile's fourth cataract. The Kajbar Dam, which is located at the Nile's second cataract near the Egyptian border, will have a 300MW capacity. Both are highly controversial due to the impact they will have on regional water resources. The Kajbar dam is also facing opposition from Nubian groups, which are resisting the flooding and destruction of ancient Nubian archeological sites as well as forced resettlement.

Financial markets
Stock exchange
The first stock exchange opened in January 1995.

Banking and insurance
Central bank
Bank of Sudan
Main financial centre
Khartoum

Time
GMT plus two hours

Geography
Sudan lies in north-eastern Africa. Sudan is the largest country in Africa and the ninth largest in the world. It lies entirely within the tropics and is bordered by Egypt and Libya in the north, Ethiopia, Eritrea and the Red Sea in the east, Kenya, Uganda and the Democratic Republic of Congo in the south and the Central African Republic and Chad in the west.
The River Nile and its tributaries, the White and Blue Niles, are the country's most important physical features. The Blue Nile, in particular, plays a vital economic role, supporting 40 per cent of the current irrigated area and with the potential to support 70 per cent of future irrigated land. The Blue Nile is prone to serious seasonal flooding.

Climate
Tropical in the south, hot and dry in the north. In Khartoum, the hottest month is May (26–42 degrees Celsius (C)), the coldest is January (16–32 degrees C). The northern zone receives very little rainfall and is mainly desert. The south is mainly tropical while the central zone is semi-arid grassland.
From mid-April to the end of June the climate is extremely hot and dry. Sandstorms (*haboobs*) are frequent in desert areas between April and September. The rainy season extends from July to September. During this period road travel outside the cities is difficult. In Khartoum, the average temperature by day in the summer is 42 degrees C and 32 degrees C in the winter.

Dress codes
Formal clothing should be worn for business and social engagements. Lightweight clothing is essential at all times, although visitors should carry some warmer clothing if travelling to Sudan during the winter months (November to March). A light raincoat is needed during the months of July, August and September. Women should be aware of the fact that the north is predominantly Muslim and are advised to dress modestly.

Entry requirements
Passports
Required by all. Passports must be valid for six months from date of entry.
Visa
Visas are issued for visits from eight days to three months (extensions can be obtained locally). Tourist visas are issued when either authentic documents from a travel agent detailing reservations, and a return ticket; or a bank statement showing financial capability for the visit, is supplied.
Business visas require sponsorship by a Sudanese company or organisation. The sponsor should supply a letter stating the purpose of the trip, duration of stay, financial responsibility and references in the Sudan. Copies of correspondences with contacts in the Sudan will enhance the application.
If the Sudan embassy in the visitor's country has a website, visa application forms may be offered for downloading.
Visitors are required to register with the Aliens Department within three days of their arrival. Once registered, they are not required to obtain an exit visa.
Prohibited entry
Nationals of Israel and evidence of a previous visit to Israel.
Currency advice/regulations
The import and export of local currency is prohibited; there are no restrictions on the import of foreign exchange, and export is only allowed up to amount imported.

Customs
Alcohol is strictly forbidden. Travellers arriving with alcoholic beverages are liable to immediate arrest.

Health (for visitors)
Mandatory precautions
Visitors travelling to the south of the country will need a valid certificate of vaccination against yellow fever. Travellers entering Egypt from the Sudan must produce either a certificate of vaccination against yellow fever or a location certificate showing that they have not been in a yellow fever area. A valid cholera certificate is required of travellers arriving from infected areas.
Advisable precautions
Yellow fever, cholera, hepatitis A, tetanus, malaria, typhoid, rabies and polio are endemic and vaccinations against all are highly recommended. Water precautions are essential; water and milk should be boiled. Local dairy products should be avoided as milk is unpasteurised; vegetables, meat and fish should be well cooked and eaten hot. Fruit should be peeled. Use only well maintained, chlorinated, swimming pools as bilharzia can be contracted from streams and rivers.
Medical facilities are scarce outside Khartoum. Some health care is provided free of charge, but visitors are advised to take out health insurance which includes emergency repatriation in the event of illness.

Hotels
Accommodation can be difficult to obtain outside Khartoum and Port Sudan. Advisable to book in advance. Service charge of 10 per cent is usual. Hotel bills subject to 10 per cent sales tax.

Credit cards
Credit cards may be accepted but visitors should ensure that they have sufficient hard currency (preferably US dollars) to cover their expenses during their stay.

Public holidays
Fixed dates
1 Jan (Independence Day), 3 Mar (National Unity Day), 6 Apr (Uprising Day), 25 May (May Revolution Anniversary), 30 Jun (Revolution Day), 25 Dec (Christmas Day).
Variable dates
Eid al Adha, Eid al Fitr, Islamic New Year, Birth of the Prophet.
The Islamic year contains 354 or 355 days, with the result that Muslim feasts advance by 10–12 days against the Gregorian calendar. Dates of feasts vary according to the sighting of the new moon, so cannot be forecast exactly. Islamic year 1426: 10 February 2005 to 30 January 2006.

Sudan

Working hours
Banking
Sat–Thu: 0830–1200.
Business
Sat–Thu: 0800–1430.
Government
Sat–Thu: 0800/0830–1330/1400.
Shops
Sat–Thu: 0800–1330, 1730–2000.

Telecommunications
Mobile phones
There are GSM roaming facilities available, with coverage throughout most of the country.

Electricity supply
240V AC

Social customs/useful tips
Visitors should address Sudanese males using the form Sayed (meaning Mr) with the first name only. There are a large number of local traditions and most Muslim customs are observed. Politeness and patience are more important than punctuality. Women are often not present at business or social gatherings.
The Islamic legal and moral code, *Sharia*, was introduced in 1983, suspended in 1985 and reintroduced in the north in 1991. Much of the Christian south is controlled by the rebel Sudan People's Liberation Army (SPLA), which applies its own laws.
There is a ban on alcohol and gambling in the north.
Some souvenirs, such as cheetah skins, although available in the souks (markets) are banned by the Government.
Military establishments should not be photographed, nor should bridges, dams, rail and air transport facilities. Visitors should not attempt to photograph Sudanese people without permission or if they appear reluctant. Photography permits issued by the Tourist Information Office in Khartoum are often ignored by the authorities, who may confiscate film and camera.
Most banks in Sudan are heavily fortified and resemble prisons as much as they do commercial institutions.

Security
Southern Sudan, the Nuba mountains, the Ethiopian and Eritrean borders and the Kassala area near the Eritrean border are all zones of military activity, (including the laying of anti-personnel landmines), and are insecure. There is banditry in Darfur state. Travel in these areas should be avoided unless work is absolutely essential. In general, no land borders into or out of Sudan can be crossed safely, with the exception of the Wadi Halfa crossing into Egypt. The political situation in Sudan is not stable and foreign nationals should contact their embassy, and keep in contact throughout their stay. Before embarking, visitors are advised to consult their embassy for an up-to-date appraisal of the situation, as well as brief themselves regarding developments in the wider region. Demonstrations should be avoided and British and US citizens may wish to keep a low profile.

Getting there
Air
National airline: Sudan Airways.
International airport/s: Khartoum (KRT), 4km from city; duty-free shop, bar, buffet and restaurant.
Airport tax: International departures US$20.
Surface
Road: Roads link Sudan to Egypt, Libya, Chad, Uganda and the Central African Republic. Drivers wishing to enter Sudan by road must apply for permission in Khartoum or from overseas representatives. Applicants must list vehicle and passenger details, with supporting documents from a recognised motoring organisation, or a guarantee from a bank or registered business.
Most border crossings remain dangerous, with the exception of the relatively secure border with Egypt via Wadi Halfa.
Rail: A rail link runs from Cairo to the Aswan High Dam in Egypt. Passengers can then take a river boat on to Wadi Halfa.
Water: Sudan's River Transport Corporation operates regular Nile cruises from Aswan in Egypt to Wadi Halfa. Ferry services to Sudan are available from Saudi Arabia and Yemen.
Main port/s: Port Sudan.

Getting about
National transport
Travellers must obtain special permits to travel anywhere outside Khartoum. These are obtainable from the Passport and Immigration Office in Khartoum. Before travelling, it is advisable to check the security situation in the area. Visitors arriving in any town or city in Sudan must register with the police on arrival and show the necessary paperwork.
Permits are required to visit archaeological or historical sites. These can be obtained from the Department of Antiquities in Khartoum.
Air: Sudan Airways operates a regular service between Khartoum, Port Sudan and El Obeid. Small air taxi companies fly from Khartoum to main towns.
Road: Main tarred roads are the 1,186km route from Port Sudan to Khartoum, from Port Sudan to Kassala and on to Shavak, from Khartoum to Sennar and on to Malakal. Another 800km of tarred roads exist, but the rest of the country's 48,000km network is of very variable quality.
Buses: Scheduled coach services include Khartoum-Kosti, Khartoum-Omdurman, Khartoum-El Fasher, Juba-Nimule, Juba-Faradge.
Rail: A network links Khartoum with Port Sudan, Kassala, Wau, Nyala and Wadi Halfa, but not Juba. Services can be very slow.
Three-class service, with sleeping, dining and air-conditioned cars available.
Water: Ferries and steamers ply the Nile between Khartoum and Juba and on the Sobat and Jur Rivers.
City transport
Taxis: Easily available in Khartoum. Can be hailed, or taken from ranks. Official tariffs, but fares still subject to negotiation in advance of journey.
Car hire
Available in main centres but expensive. National or international driving licence required.

BUSINESS DIRECTORY
The addresses listed below are a selection only. While World of Information makes every endeavour to check these addresses, we cannot guarantee that changes have not been made, especially to telephone numbers and area codes. We would welcome any corrections.

Telephone area codes
The international dialling code (IDD) for Sudan is +249, followed by area code and subscriber's number:

El Obeid	81	Khartoum	11
Kassala	41	Port Sudan City	31

Chambers of Commerce
Union of Sudanese Chambers of Commerce, Gamhoria Street, PO Box 81, Khartoum (tel: 772-346; fax: 780-748; e-mail:@ chamber@sudanchamber.org).

Banking
Bank of Khartoum, PO Box 1008, Khartoum (tel: 81-071; fax: 781-120).

Farmers Commercial Bank, PO Box 1116, Kasr Avenue, Khartoum (tel: 774-960; fax: 773-687).

Tadamon Islamic Bank, PO Box 3154, Baladia Avenue, Khartoum (tel: 785-481, 784-960; fax: 773-840).

Al-Baraka Bank, PO Box 3583, Al-Baraka Tower, Khartoum (tel: 782-964, 777-861; fax: 778-948).

El Nilein Industrial Development Bank, PO Box 466, 1722 United Nations Square, Khartoum (tel: 780-087, 771-586; fax: 785-811, 771-984).

Central bank
Bank of Sudan, Al-Gamaa Avenue, PO Box 313, Khartoum, Sudan (tel: 778-064; fax: 780-273; e-mail: sudanbank@sudanmail.net).

Travel information

Sudan Airways, SDC Building, Street 15, New Extension, PO Box 253, Khartoum (tel: 47-953, 452-359; fax: 47-978, 452-377).

Ministries

Ministry of Agriculture and Forests, Khartoum (tel: 780-951, 770-895).

Ministry of Animal Welfare, Khartoum (tel: 770-895).

Ministry of Aviation, Khartoum (tel: 776-894, 775-993).

Ministry of Culture and Information, Khartoum (tel: 771-967, 771-952).

Ministry of Defence, Khartoum (tel: 774-910).

Ministry of Education, Khartoum (tel: 770-016, 770-121).

Ministry of Energy and Mining, Khartoum (tel: 775-595, 781-043).

Ministry of the Environment and Tourism (tel: 462-604).

Ministry of Finance & National Economy, Khartoum (tel: 77-255).

Ministry of Foreign Affairs, Khartoum (tel: 773-101, 780-261, 780-286).

Ministry of Health, Khartoum (tel: 773-000, 771-110).

Ministry of Higher Education and Scientific Research, Khartoum (tel: 789-970).

Ministry of the Interior, Khartoum (tel: 776-554, 777-271).

Ministry of National Industry, Khartoum (tel: 777-770, 780-560).

Ministry of Public Services, Khartoum (tel: 779-892).

Ministry of Social Planning, Khartoum (tel: 779-008, 774-627).

Ministry of Trade, Khartoum (tel: 778-241, 779-157).

Ministry of Transport, Khartoum (tel: 775-290, 775-419).

Other useful addresses

Sudan Development Corporation, PO Box 710, Khartoum (tel: 79-536).

Sudanese Embassy (USA), 2210 Massachusetts Avenue, NW, Washington DC 20008 (tel: 202-338-8565; fax: 202-667-2406; e-mail: info@sudanembassyus.org).

Internet sites

Africa Business Network: http://www.ifc.org/abn

AllAfrica.com: http://allafrica.com

African Development Bank: http://www.afdb.org

Africa Online: http://www.africaonline.com

Mbendi AfroPaedia (information on companies, countries, industries and stock exchanges in Africa): http://mbendi.co.za

The Sudan Page: http://www.sudan.net/main1.html

Suriname

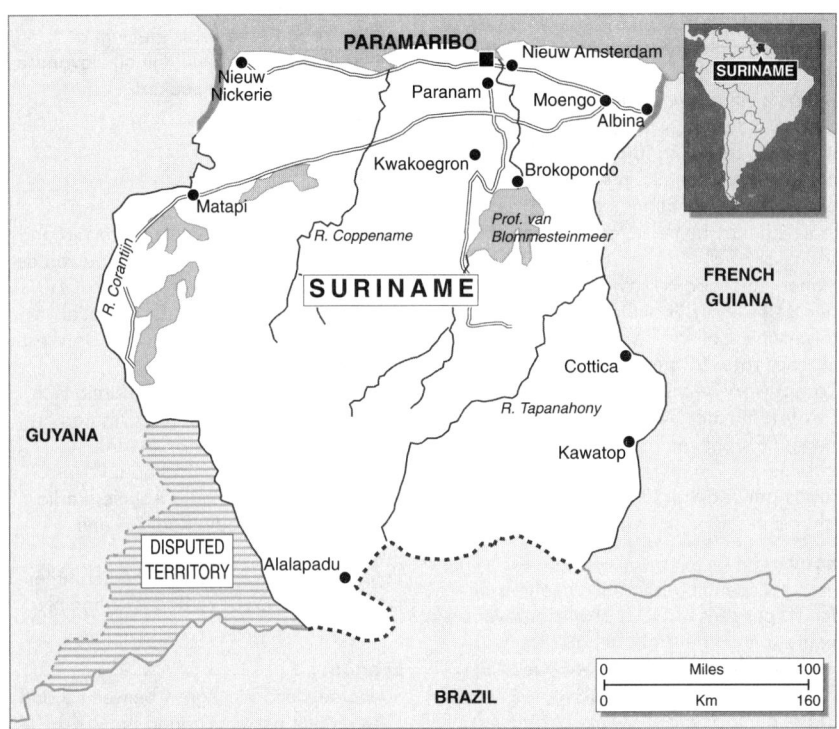

KEY FACTS

Official name: Republiek Suriname (Republic of Suriname)

Head of State: President Ronald Venetiaan (NPS)

Head of government: President Ronald Venetiaan (re-elected by parliamentary vote Aug 2005)

Ruling party: Nieuwe Front voor Democratie (NF) (New Front for Democracy) coalition led by Nationale Partij Suriname (NPS) (National Party of Suriname) (elected May 2000; re-elected 25 May 2005)

Area: 163,265 square km

Population: 460,300 (2004)

Capital: Paramaribo (Parbo)

Official language: Dutch

Currency: Suriname dollar (Su$) = 100 cents

Exchange rate: Su$2.74 per US$ (Oct 2005); (on 1 Jan 2004, guilders were converted to Suriname dollars at Su$1.00 per 1,000 guilders)

GDP per capita: US$2,401 (2004)

GDP real growth: 4.60% (2004); *4.9% (2005)

Labour force: 180,000 (2004)

Unemployment: 17.00% (2003)

Inflation: 9.00% (2004)

Oil production: 10,000 bpd (2003)

Balance of trade: US$145.00 million (2003)

Foreign debt: US$321.00 million (2003)

* estimated figure

COUNTRY PROFILE

Historical profile

1652 The British founded the first settlement but gave it to the Netherlands in a swap for New Amsterdam, the settlement at the mouth of the Hudson river that later became New York. The territory became known as Dutch Guiana.
1973 Henck Arron became prime minister, leading negotiations for independence from the Netherlands, the colonial power.
1975 Dutch Guiana gained independence and was re-named Suriname.
1980 A successful military coup was led by Desi Bouterse.
1980–87 Bouterse ruled with a military government.
1987–88 Parliamentary democracy was returned with the November 1987 general election and the election by the 51-seat National Assembly of the president in January 1988. The National State Council, which has an ill-defined 'advisory' role, included members of the military. Henck Arron became prime minister again, and also vice president.
1990 The military resumed power under Bouterse in December.
1991 A civilian government was elected in May.
1999 The cabinet resigned after there were protests over Suriname's economic problems.
2000 President Jules Albert Wijdenbosch lost the elections, but was to remain in office until the Nieuwe Front voor Democratie (NF) (New Front for Democracy) coalition agreed a candidate. Ronald Venetiaan was chosen by the National Assembly as president.
2002 Hundreds of workers protested after the government decided to close the state-owned banana company, Surland.
2004 On 1 January, Suriname converted its currency – guilders – to Suriname dollars (Su$) at a rate of Su$1.00 per l,000 guilders.
2005 The ruling NF coalition won the 25 May parliamentary elections. In a parliamentary vote for president on 19 July, no candidate won the necessary two-thirds majority. A second round was held on 26

Nations of the World: A Political, Economic and Business Handbook

July, without a winning candidate. On 12 August Ronald Venetiaan took office as president having been re-elected by parliamentary votes 560 out of 879.

Political structure
Form of state
Parliamentary democratic republic
The executive
To win the presidency, a party needs a two-thirds majority in the Assembly. Failing that, the National Assembly, which also contains local and regional councillors, elects the president by simple majority.
National legislature
The unicameral 51-seat National Assembly is elected every five years.
Last elections
25 May 2005 (parliamentary)
Results: Parliamentary: the ruling Nieuwe Front voor Democratie (NF) (New Front for Democracy) coalition won 41.1 per cent of the vote (24 seats out of 51) and the National Democratic Party (NDP) (Nationale Democratische Partij) 23.1 per cent (15 seats); turnout was 65.5 per cent.
Next elections
May 2010 (parliamentary)
Political parties
Ruling party
Nieuwe Front voor Democratie (NF) (New Front for Democracy) coalition led by Nationale Partij Suriname (NPS) (National Party of Suriname) (elected May 2000; re-elected 25 May 2005)
Main opposition party
National Democratic Party (NDP) (Nationale Democratische Partij)
Population
460,300 (2004)

Ethnic make-up
East Indian (37 per cent), Creole (31 per cent), Javanese (15 per cent), Black (10 per cent), Indian (3 per cent), Chinese (2 per cent).
Religions
Hindu (25 per cent), Protestant (25 per cent), Roman Catholic (23 per cent), Islam (20 per cent), traditional beliefs (5 per cent).
Education
Primary schooling begins at age 6 and last until aged 12. An exam deteremines the route either to a general lower secondary, or technical school. Advancement at age 16, following further exams, leads to either an academic, pre-university senior, or upper vocational, school.
Teaching may be delivered in either Dutch or English.
Higher education is provided through either a Univeristy, Institute, Academy, or Polytechnic College.
Literacy rate: 93 per cent adult rate.
Compulsory years: 7 to 12.
Enrolment rate: 92.18 per cent net primary; 2.93 per cent net secondary enrolments.
Pupils per teacher: 17 in primary schools.
Health
The total spending on public health is under 10 per cent of GDP, of which government expenditure is about half.
HIV prevalence: 1.7 per cent aged 15–49 in 2003 (World Bank)
Life expectancy: 70.4 years (World Bank)
Fertility rate/Maternal mortality rate: 2.4 births per woman (World Bank)

Birth rate/Death rate: 19.4 births per 1,000 population; 6.8 deaths per 1,000 population (2003).
Infant mortality rate: 30 per 1,000 live births (World Bank)
Main cities
Paramaribo (Parbo) (capital, estimated population 217,300 in 2003), Lelydorp (17,600), Nieuw Nickerie (13,300).
Languages spoken
Sranan Tongo (Creole) is the *lingua franca*. English, Sarnami (Hindi), Javanese and Chinese are also spoken.
Official language/s
Dutch
Media
Press
Principal dailies include *De Ware Tijd* and periodicals include *Advertentieblad van de Republick Suriname*, *Bulletin C-47*, *CLO Bulletin* and *USB Bulletin*. Other local newspapers are *Parbo Daily* and *De West*.
Broadcasting
Radio: Three government-run stations in Paramaribo: Stichting Radio-Omroep Suriname (SRS), Radio Suriname International (RSI) and Radio Boskopu. Private: Radio Paramaribo, Radio Apintie, Radio Nickerie (RANI), Radio Radhika and Sangeet Mala.
Television: Government-owned commercial TV service by STVS and ATV (mainly Dutch and English).
Economy
Suriname's economy grew between 3 and 5.3 per cent per year during the 2001–04 period. The rate of inflation has been greatly reduced and now stands at 9 per cent, down from a high of 58.6 per cent in 2000. The IMF forecasts growth for 2005 to be 4.9 per cent and predicts continued, though reduced, growth of 3.3 per cent in 2006.
Ronald Venetiaan's government began well. It increased taxes and attempted to control spending, but a large pay rise for civil servants threatened earlier gains in stabilising the economy.
The Netherlands government agreed to restart the aid flow, which will allow Suriname to access international development financing.
Alcoa's US$65 million expansion to its Paranam alumina refinery, which was completed in 2005, will be a boost to Suriname's economy.
Economic prospects for the medium-term depend on renewed commitment to responsible monetary and fiscal policies and to the introduction of structural reforms to liberalise markets and promote competition.

KEY INDICATORS — Suriname

	Unit	2000	2001	2002	2003	2004
Population	m	0.42	0.43	0.43	0.45	0.46
Gross domestic product (GDP)	US$bn	0.51	0.75	0.89	1.50	*1.11
GDP per capita	US$	1,214	1,786	2,104	3,500	2,401
GDP real growth	%	2.9	5.9	2.7	3.8	4.6
Inflation	%	59.1	42.2	28.3	20.0	9.0
Exports (fob) (goods)	US$m	399.1	454.0	369.3	445.0	–
Imports (fob) (goods)	US$m	246.1	457.0	321.9	300.0	–
Balance of trade	US$m	153.0	-3.0	47.4	145.0	–
Current account	US$m	32.3	-190.0	-131.0	–	-150.0
Total reserves minus gold	US$m	63.0	119.3	106.2	105.8	129.4
Foreign exchange	US$m	52.7	109.6	95.9	–	118.0
Exchange rate	per US$	1,322.47	2,178.50	2,346.75	2,346.75	259.28

* estimated figure

Suriname

External trade
Suriname is a full member of the Free Trade Area of the Americas (FTAA) along with 33 other countries. Suriname's main export partners include Norway, Netherlands, US, France, Japan and the United Kingdom.

Imports
Principal imports are capital equipment, petroleum, foodstuffs, cotton, consumer goods
Main sources: US (28.2 per cent total, 2004), The Netherlands (21.1 per cent), Trinidad and Tobago (11.4 per cent), Japan (7.2 per cent), China (4.3 per cent)

Exports
Principal exports are alumina, crude oil, timber, shrimp and fish, rice and bananas.
Main destinations: Norway (31.1 per cent total, 2004), US (16 per cent), Canada (13.2 per cent), Belgium (10.8 per cent), France (8.8 per cent), Iceland (4.6 per cent)

Agriculture
Farming
Just 0.5 per cent of Suriname's total landmass is accounted for by permanent crop and arable land, concentrated predominantly along the coastal plain. Despite the dearth of land devoted to agricultural activities, Suriname is self sufficient in most basic foodstuffs and the sector accounts for up to 10 per cent of total GDP. Some 20 per cent of the country's workforce is employed in the agricultural sector.

The staple food crop and most important agricultural export is rice, the farming of which is highly mechanised. Suriname exports 40,000 tonnes of rice annually to the EU. Other major crops include palm oil, coconuts, bananas, sugar, citrus fruits and coffee. Crop production typically includes: 195,000 metric tonnes (mt) rice, 4,300mt cassava, 9,000mt coconuts, 43,000mt bananas, 11,000mt plantains, 120,000mt sugar cane, 260mt groundnuts, 14,900mt citrus, 1,000mt tomatoes, 3,450mt watermelons, 69,284mt fruit in total, 22,435mt vegetables in total. In a typical year, livestock production includes: 9,179mt meat in total, 2,000mt beef, 1,450mt pig-meat, 60mt lamb and goat meat, 5,670mt poultry, 2,500mt eggs, 8,500mt milk, 86mt honey.

Fishing
The commercial fishing industry accounts for about 7 per cent of Surinam's total export earnings; the sector has grown in importance in recent years. Fishing for shellfish, in particular, has increased. The typical total fish catch is over 19,000mt, plus over 7,700mt of other seafood, per annum.

Forestry
Suriname has vast forestry resources in relation to its size. Approximately 80 per cent of the country's total landmass is covered by forests and woodland, but just 2 per cent is exploited as access is limited. The timber industry is, however, an important sector of the economy. In a typical year for the industry, production includes: 154,000 cubic metres (cum) roundwood, 47,000cum sawnwood and 43,500cum wood fuel.

Industry and manufacturing
Industrial activities in Suriname centre on the processing of agricultural produce (particularly timber), bauxite mining and timber processing. The sector contributes approximately 15 per cent to total GDP and employs one fifth of Suriname's labour force.

In 2003, Alcoa announced a US$65 million, 250,000 tonne expansion to its Paranam alumina refinery, which will increase capacity by approximately 12 per cent. The project was completed midway through 2005.

Tourism
The travel and tourism industry is growing in Suriname. Employment in the sector has risen to 4.9 per cent of the workforce and tourism now represents 5.4 per cent of the country's total GDP.
Ecotourism is growing in importance and has contributed to the permanent protection of 1.62 million ha of tropical forests.

Mining
In a typical year for the economy of Suriname the mining sector contributes approximately 12 per cent of total GDP. The sector also employs some 5 per cent of the country's total workforce.

One of the largest producers of bauxite in the world, Suriname's reserves stand at 600 million tonnes. The US imports 400,000 tonnes of alumina from Suriname each year.

The deposits in the major mining areas, Moengo and Paranam, are maturing and are expected to reach the end of their life in 2006. Other reserves in the east, west and north of Suriname are expected to last until 2025.

Annual gold production is valued at US$25 million per annum, although 80 per cent of this is in the informal sector and much of the country's gold output is smuggled away into French Guiana. In 2004 Cambior, the Canadian mining company, began shipment of gold bars from their Rosebel Gold mine. It is expected that 220,000 ounces of gold will be produced in the first year valued at US$157 per ounce; the government will receive 2.2 per cent royalties from the mine.

Other commercially viable minerals include iron ore, copper, nickel, platinum and kaolin.

Hydrocarbons
Exploration currently underway in the Saramacca oil region is expected to double proven reserves to 350 million barrels. In 2003 total oil reserves stood at 170 million barrels.

The country's only oil refinery produces diesel, heavy vacuum gas oil, fuel oil and bitumen. Staatsolie Maatschappij Suriname is a government-owned company that has exclusive rights to explore and produce hydrocarbons alone or in conjunction with other oil companies. Staatsolie aims to develop the Tambaredjo oil field to produce 20,000 bpd.

Suriname exports oil products mostly to the Caribbean, including Trinidad and Tobago, Curaçao, Guyana, Haiti, Jamaica, Barbados and Antigua. In 2004, a UN tribunal was empowered to settle a dispute over oil-rich territory clamed by both Guyana and Suriname. The disputed maritime area includes an oil-rich concession granted to a Canadian company. This disputed area is predicted to have large hydrocarbon reserves. Investor's are likely to stay away until the dispute is resolved. Suriname does not produce or import natural gas or coal.

Energy
Suriname's total installed electricity generation capacity is approximately 415MW. The Afobakka hydroelectric power station supplies electricity for the country's aluminium industry. Suriname Aluminum Company (Suralco) produces about 75MW of electricity for the Suriname government, roughly 75 per cent of the electricity needs of the capital city of Paramaribo.

In 2004, Suriname's State Energy Company signed a US$23.7 million deal with the Trinidad-based Royal Bank of Trinidad and Tobago to finance part of its local electricity projects estimated to cost US$100 million.

Banking and insurance
Suriname's banking sector has traditionally been highly indebted and needs reform. The government has equity stakes in six of Suriname's eight banks, including a 10 per cent stake in the largest bank, De Surinaamse Bank. Domestic borrowing is mostly undertaken by the government.

Central bank
Centrale Bank van Suriname
Main financial centre
Paramaribo.

Time
GMT minus three hours

Nations of the World: A Political, Economic and Business Handbook

Geography
Suriname is located on the northern part of South America. It borders French Guiana to the east and Guyana to the west. To the west, the Corantijn River forms the border, which is disputed in its most southerly reaches with Guyana. Two other rivers, the Marowijn and Litani form the border with French Guiana. Certain areas of the eastern border are also under dispute.

Climate
Tropical but cooled by trade winds. Rain throughout the year but heaviest from November–January and from April–July. Average daily temperature remains fairly constant throughout the year at 27 degrees Celsius (C); daily range from 22–35 degrees C from May–October; slightly lower temperatures from November–April.

Entry requirements
Passports
Required by all and valid for six months after arrival.
Visa
Required by all and must be obtained before travelling. All visitors must have return/onward passage. Business visas require a letter from the employing company explaining the purpose of visit, and the details of all the contacts in Suriname plus an itinerary. See www.surinameembassy.org for more information and to download an application form.
Currency advice/regulations
Foreign currency over US$10,000 should be declared on arrival. Local currency import and export is limited to Su$1000.

Health (for visitors)
Mandatory precautions
Yellow fever vaccination certificate required if arriving from an infected area.
Advisable precautions
Yellow fever, typhoid and polio vaccinations. Malaria prophylaxis recommended and water precautions should be taken.

Hotels
Paramaribo and Nieuw Nickerie have a number of modern hotels but beds are limited. Service charge of 10 per cent is usual.

Public holidays
Fixed dates
1 Jan (New Year's Day), 1 May (Labour Day), 1 Jul (Abolition of Slavery Day), 25 Nov (Independence Day), 25–26 Dec (Christmas Holiday).
Variable dates
Holi (Hindu, Mar), Good Friday, Easter Monday, Eid al Fitr.
In addition, Chinese, Jewish and Indian businesses will be closed for their own religious holidays.

Working hours
Banking
Mon–Fri: 0800–1500.
Business
Mon–Fri: 0730–1630.
Government
Mon–Fri: 0700–1500.
Shops
Mon–Fri: 0700/0730–1630; Sat: 0730–1300.

Electricity supply
110/127V and/or 220V AC, 60 cycles

Getting there
Air
National airline: Surinam Airways (SLM).
International airport/s:
Paramaribo-Johan Adolf Pengel International Airport (PMB), 45km from city; duty-free, bank, restaurant, post office. A coach meets all arrivals; buses and taxis also available (journey time 45 minutes).
Airport tax: There is an airport facility charge of US$10 for passengers on international flights; not applicable to 24-hour transit passengers.
Surface
Road: Coastal roads link Paramaribo with borders of Guyana (at Nieuw Nickerie) and French Guiana (at Albina). Some bus services operate from Cayenne, French Guiana, to Paramaribo, but they tend to be slow and irregular.
Water: Regular car ferry services run from French Guiana and Guyana.
Main port/s: Paramaribo.

Getting about
National transport
Most infrastructure has been on the country's narrow coastal plain, with links to the interior weak. Much of the sparsely-populated country is accessible only by air or river.
Air: Domestic flights to towns in the interior are operated from Paramaribo (Zorg en Hoop airfield) by Surinam Airways. They also provide services from Paramaribo to the Nieuw Nickerie district, and maintain a charter service.
Road: Coastal towns are linked by road from Nieuw Nickerie, through Paramaribo, to Albina.
Two new bridges over the Coppename and Suriname rivers, opened in 1999 and 2000, link the east and west of the country.
Buses: Paramaribo and most towns have a local bus service. Bus routes link coastal towns but service is irregular and tends to be crowded.
Water: When visiting the interior and some coastal areas, river transport may be the least expensive and often most efficient option. Services are centred on Paramaribo; enquire locally for further details.

City transport
Taxis: Fares by negotiation in advance of journey; tipping is not usual.
Car hire
Available in Paramaribo through main hotels and Tourist Information Office, Waterkant 8, Paramaribo. International driving licences accepted.

BUSINESS DIRECTORY
The addresses listed below are a selection only. While World of Information makes every endeavour to check these addresses, we cannot guarantee that changes have not been made, especially to telephone numbers and area codes. We would welcome any corrections.

Telephone area codes
The international dialling code (IDD) for Suriname is +597 followed by subscriber's number.

Chambers of Commerce
Suriname Chamber of Commerce & Industry, PO Box 139, Mr JC de Miranda Straat, Paramaribo (tel: 473-527; fax: 470-802; e-mail: chamber@sr.net).

Banking
De Surinaamse Bank NV, Henck Arronstraat 26-30, Paramaribo (tel: 471-100; fax: 477-835).

Finabank NV, Dr. S. Redmondstraat 55-61, Paramaribo.

Hakrinbank NV, Dr S. Redmondstraat 11-13, Paramaribo (tel: 477-722; fax: 472-066).

Landbouwbank NV, Lim A Postraat 28-30, Paramaribo (tel: 475-945, 475-101; fax: 410-821).

Nationale Ontwikkelingsbank (NOB), Coppenamelaan 160-162, Paramaribo (tel: 465-000; fax: 497-192).

RBTT Bank (Suriname), Kerkplein 1 Paramaribo (tel: 471-555; fax: 411-325).

Surinaamse Postspaarbank (SPSB), Knuffelsgracht 11-13, Paramaribo (tel: 472-256; fax: 472-952).

Surinaamse Volkscrediet Bank (VCB), Steenbakkerijstraat 2, Paramaribo (tel: 472-616; fax: 472-616).

Central bank
Centrale Bank van Suriname, PO Box 1080, Waterkant 16-20, Paramaribo (tel: 473-741; fax: 476-444; e-mail: info@cbvs.sr).

Travel information
Surinam Airways, PO Box 2029, Coppenamestraat 136, Paramaribo (tel: 465-700; fax: 491-213).

Ministry of tourism
Ministry of Transport, Communication and Tourism, Prins Hendrikstraat 26-28, Paramaribo (tel: 420-422; fax: 420-425).

Suriname

National tourist organisation offices
Surinam Tourism Foundation, Dr JF Nassylaan 2, Paramaribo; PO Box 656, Paramaribo (tel: 410-357; fax: 477-786; email: stsmktg@sr.net (marketing department) or stsur@sr.net (secretary's division); internet: www.sr.net/users/stsur).

Ministries
Ministry of Agriculture, Animal Husbandry and Fisheries, Cultuurtuinlaan, Paramaribo (tel: 474-177; fax: 470-301).

Ministry of Defence, Kwattaweg 29, Paramaribo (tel: 474-244; fax: 420-055).

Ministry of Economic Affairs, Kleine Waterstraat 4, Paramaribo (tel: 75-080).

Ministry of Education, Dr. F. Kaffiludistraat 117-123, Paramaribo (tel: 498-383; fax: 495-083).

Ministry of Finance, Onafhandelijkheidsplein 3, Paramaribo (tel: 472-619; fax: 476-314).

Ministry of Foreign Affairs, Gravenstraat 6-8, Paramaribo (tel: 471-209; fax: 410-851).

Ministry of Justice and Police, Gravenstraat 1, Paramaribo (tel: 473-033; fax: 412-109).

Ministry of Internal Affairs, Onafhankelijkheidsplein 2, Paramaribo (tel: 476-461; fax: 421-170).

Ministry of Labour, Wagenwegstraat 22, Paramaribo (tel: 477-045; fax: 410-465).

Ministry of Natural Resources, Mr. Dr. J.C. de Mirandastraat 13-15, Paramaribo (tel: 473-420; fax: 472-911).

Ministry of Planning and International Co-operation, Dr. S Redmondstraat 118, Paramaribo (tel: 473-628; fax: 421-056).

Ministry of Public Health, Gravenstraat 64, Paramaribo (tel: 474-841; fax: 410-702).

Ministry of Public Works, Verlengde Coppenamestraat 167, Paramaribo (tel: 462-500; fax: 464-901).

Ministry of Regional Development, Van Rooseveltkade 2, Paramaribo (tel: 471-574).

Ministry of Social Affairs and Housing, Waterkant 30-32, Paramaribo (tel: 472-610; fax: 470-516).

Ministry of Trade and Industry, Nieuwe Haven, Paramaribo (tel: 479-886; fax: 477-602).

Ministry of Transportation, Communications and Tourism, Prins Hendrikstraat 26-28, Paramaribo (tel: 420-422; fax: 470-425).

President of the Republic of Suriname, Onafhankelijkheidsplein, Paramaribo (tel: 472-841; fax: 475-266).

Vice President and Council of Ministers, Dr. S. Redmondstraat, 1e Etage, Paramaribo (tel: 474-805; fax: 472-917).

Other useful addresses
Algemene Aannemers Vereniging (AAV), Gravenstraat 73, Paramaribo (tel: 478-419; fax: 474-531).

Associatie van Surinaarns Bedrijfsleven (V.S.B.), Domineestraat 33 boven, Paramaribo (tel: 476-585; fax: 421-160).

Orde van Raadgavende Ingenieursbureaus in Suriname (ORIS), P.O. Box 1864, van Roosmalenstraat no. 30, Paramaribo (tel: 472-275, 474-381; fax: 474-408).

Stichting Planbureau Suriname, PO Box 172, Dr S. Redmondstraat 110, Paramaribo (tel: 473-146).

Suriname Embassy (USA), Suite 108, 4301 Connecticut Avenue, NW, Washington DC 20008 (tel: 202-244-7488; fax: 202-244-5878; e-mail: embsur@erols.com).

Vereniging Surinaams Bedrijfsleven (Suriname Trade and Industry Association), Prins Hendrikstraat 18, PO Box 111, Paramaribo (tel: 475-286/7; fax: 472-287).

Internet sites
De Ware Tijd (English bulletin available): http://www.dwt.net

Economic Commission for Latin America and the Caribbean: http://www.eclac.cl

Inter-American Development Bank: http://www.iadb.org

Organisation of American States: http://www.oas.org

Latin World: http://www.latinworld.com

Latin Trade Online: http://www.latintrade.com

Republic of Suriname homepage: http://www.sr.net.srnet/InfoSurinam

Swaziland

KEY FACTS

Official name: Umbuso weSwatini (Kingdom of Swaziland)

Head of State: King Mswati III

Head of government: Prime Minister Themba Dlamini (from 14 Nov 2003)

Ruling party: Political parties are banned under the 1978 constitution.

Area: 17,363 square km

Population: 1.10 million (2004)

Capital: Mbabane (administrative capital); Lobamba (legislative capital and the seat of the monarchy)

Official language: English and siSwati

Currency: Lilangeni – plural Emalangeni (E) = 100 cents; at par with the South African Rand

Exchange rate: E6.36 per US$ (Oct 2005)

GDP per capita: US$2,172 (2004)

GDP real growth: 2.10% (2004)

Labour force: 416,000 (2004)

Unemployment: 30.20% (2004)

Inflation: 3.50% (2004)

Balance of trade: -US$239.90 million 2004

Foreign debt: US$320.00 million (2003)

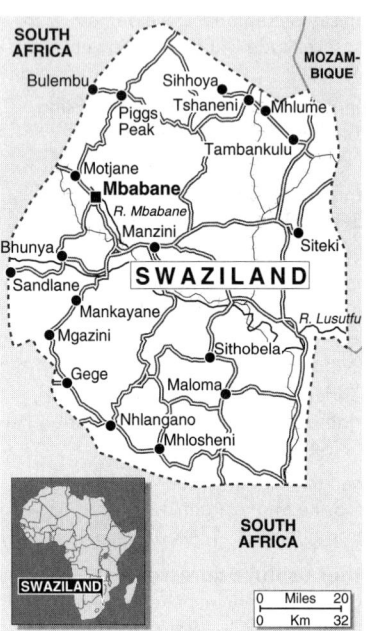

Swaziland faces a serious socioeconomic situation. Although it is classified as a lower-middle-income country, income distribution is highly skewed and 700,000 of the 1.1 million people live on less than US$1 a day. A growing fiscal deficit threatens macroeconomic stability and external viability, and concerns over governance, particularly the rule of law, are threatening to undermine social harmony and investor and donor sentiment. The humanitarian situation is difficult, with persistent high rates of HIV/Aids, unemployment, poverty, and food shortages.

The King rules

Immediate change is unlikely. The mountainous kingdom of Swaziland is one of the world's last remaining absolute monarchies. The 37 year old King Mswati III rules by decrees which have the full force of law. His subjects live mainly in rural areas and maintain traditional ways of life. Mswati upholds the tradition of his father, King Sobhuza II, who reigned for almost 61 years and in 1973 scrapped the constitution and banned political parties. At official meetings, the king's entrance is greeted by heralds who he flies around with him when he travels. Ngweyama – 'the lion' – often appears in public in traditional dress. He has 11 wives and takes a new one at least each year – he has the right to choose any Swazi maiden at the annual Reed Dance as a wife. In 2004 he built a palace for each one at a total cost of US$15 million.

Simmering student and labour unrest continued to pressure the monarchy to grudgingly allow some political reform. In 2003, for the first time, there was a parliamentary election in Swaziland and they are now promised every five years. With political parties banned opposition politicians contest as independents, but against the power of the king, his prime minister and his advisers – many are members of the royal family – the national assembly is largely meaningless. There is an upper house, the Senate – the king appoints 20 of the 30 members.

A long-awaited constitution, signed by the king in 2005, did no more than cement his rule. It maintained the ban on political parties. The king's supporters, and there are many, argue that democracy creates division, and that a monarch is a strong unifying force.

Mswati has shown no enthusiasm for sharing power, but the banned opposition parties and trade unions have been vocal in their demands for greater democracy and limits on the king's power. Their leaders were arrested, further meetings banned. Some of the king's ministers privately concede the king has too much power. Judges, whose rulings he regularly overturns, say he has blatant disregard for the law. His profligate spending has turned international donors away and the country's external debt is now running at 35 per cent of gross domestic product.

The king's national development company – a family enterprise – has an iron grip on all major business and owns one of the two national daily newspapers.

The economy

Economic growth in Swaziland has declined since South Africa's emergence from apartheid. Any advantages it had as an investment location in southern

Swaziland

Africa disappeared within a few months of Nelson Mandela walking to freedom. The country is a landlocked 'island' within South Africa and Mozambique, its currency is pegged to the South African rand. It relies to a large extent on revenues from the Southern African Customs Union (Sacu) and worker remittances from its citizens working in the South African mines substantially supplement domestically earned income. However, the income from Sacu will gradually decline as a new revenue sharing agreement between the member states is implemented.

Sugar and wood pulp remain important foreign exchange earners. Mining has declined in importance with only coal mines and stone quarries active. About nine-tenths of its imports and three-quarters of its exports are trade with South Africa. Manufacturing has been boosted by clothing exports to the US through the Africa Growth and Opportunity Act (AGOA).

The last World Bank project closed in 1994. There are no International Monetary Fund (IMF) loans or arrangements although the IMF believes economic reforms to remove impediments to sustainable economic growth and bring about a broad-based improvement in living standards are urgently required.

Risk assessment

Economic	Poor
Politica	Deteriorating
Regional stability	Poor/improving

COUNTRY PROFILE

Historical profile

Reflecting a similar process among the neighbouring Zulu lands in the early nineteenth century, the Swazi people were unified under a central government by the Nkosi-Diamini clan, which introduced military as well as political reform so that the nation was able to resist both the Zulu onslaught and the Boer treks and so hold its own. But in 1879 gold was found and swarms of fortune-hunters penetrated the country just when a weak heir to the paramountcy had taken over.

King Mbandzeni was just as irresponsible in granting concessions as strangers were reckless in asking for them, so that within a few years the Swazis' land was covered by layers of concessions, many of them in conflict with each other: for the exploitation of minerals, mining of gold, digging for diamonds, building railways, even for running station bars on railways not yet planned; but also for grazing and agriculture. This bonanza created chaos; it handed the soil of the Swazi nation to private white possession and introduced a considerable settled white population. The period of concessions also introduced claims of British over-rule as well as for annexation by the Boer Republic of the Transvaal. Because Britain was as eager to prevent the Boers getting an outlet to the sea as the Transvaal was pressing hard for it, authority over the Swazi nation was divided or in doubt until the Boer War in 1902 ended Boer independence and left Britain in charge of yet another small African territory in Southern Africa.

Before recorded history, an African people of Nguni descent (the ancestral root of the majority of South Africa's indigenous people) migrated southwards from central Africa and eventually, during the mid-eighteenth century, a group settled in the forested, mountainous area which is now Swaziland. These people, the Nkosi Dlamini, became known as the Swazis. Swaziland first emerged as a separate nation in the nineteenth century when King Sobhuza I merged his own people with refugees fleeing from the violent expansion of the Zulus to establish a country capable of resisting the Zulu advance.

1903 After a period of rivalry between the British and the Boers, Swaziland became a British protectorate.
1963 Swaziland's first constitution was introduced.
1964 The first elections resulted in victory for the Imbokodvo National Movement (INM).
1967 Swaziland was granted internal self-government as a protected state. Sobhuza II was recognised as King and head of state; Prince Makhosini Dlamini, leader of the INM, was appointed prime minister.
1968 Independence was granted.
1973 The King revoked the Westminster-based constitution and banned political parties.
1978 The previous constitution was replaced with a system designed to accommodate both western and traditional styles of government. Political parties were banned.
1982 King Sobhuza II died.
1986 After a lengthy selection and training period, Crown Prince Makhosetive was chosen to succeed his father and he was crowned King Mswati III.
1992 Parliament was dissolved and Swaziland was governed by the *Liqoqo* (traditional tribal assembly).
1993 Democratic reforms led to the people directly electing some members of the *Liqoqo*.
1996 The King appointed a Constitutional Review Commission (CRC).
2000 Trade unions demonstrated against the government. The government put five critics of the government under house arrest and banned trade union meetings. The Swaziland Federation of Trade Unions (SFTU) met in South Africa and drew up the Nelspruit Declaration, demanding the formation of an interim government. The government amended the labour laws. Swaziland became eligible for African Growth and Opportunities Act (AGOA) benefits.
2001 A number of political activists were forced into exile in South Africa. Decree 2 was issued by King Mswati, giving the monarch power to overrule court decisions. It was soon repealed after the US

KEY INDICATORS — Swaziland

	Unit	2000	2001	2002	2003	2004
Population	m	1.04	1.06	1.07	1.08	1.10
Gross domestic product (GDP)	US$bn	1.30	1.00	1.20	1.18	*2.41
GDP per capita	US$	1,384	1,087	1,090	1,091	2,172
GDP real growth	%	2.5	1.8	1.6	1.5	2.1
Inflation	%	6.5	7.5	12.5	9.5	3.5
Exports (fob) (goods)	US$m	810.8	794.0	955.2	820.0	900.1
Imports (fob) (goods)	US$m	921.3	890.0	1,034.6	938.0	1,140.0
Balance of trade	US$m	-110.6	-96.0	-79.4	-118.0	-239.9
Current account	US$m	-80.0	-60.0	-70.0	-10.0	-10.0
Foreign debt	US$bn	0.3	0.3	0.3	0.3	–
Total reserves minus gold	US$m	351.8	271.8	275.8	277.5	323.6
Foreign exchange	US$m	340.1	260.5	263.6	264.1	306.5
Exchange rate	per US$	6.81	9.77	10.02	7.56	6.46

* estimated figure

threatened to end the country's benefits under AGOA.

2002 The Internal Security Bill was enacted, which made it illegal to display support for any political party. The Libyan leader, Colonel Muammar al Qadafi, visited Swaziland to give his support to the monarchy.

2003 Parliamentary elections held in October were considered by the opposition to be meaningless since political parties are outlawed. Four in 10 people were estimated to be HIV positive.

2004 King Mswati ordered new palaces to be built for each of his eleven wives, at a cost of US$15 million.

2005 In January a two-day general strike by pro-democracy supporters protested against constitutional changes then before parliament designed to entrench the King's power further.

Political structure

Constitution
The constitution was promulgated in 1978. The country is run on a dual system. The traditional structure of Swaziland is headed by the Ingwenyama (the lion) (King), the Ndlovukazi (the she-elephant) (Queen Mother), and the more than 300 Chiefs who control the largely rural population. The other is the western-style central government, headed by the King, acting together with parliament, cabinet and civil service. Succession to the throne is governed by Swazi law and custom.

The draft of a proposed new constitution was written in 2003. However, it was available only in English and is also to be published in SiSwati during 2004, after which there is to be a further period of national consultation..

The Kingdom is divided into four regions.

Form of state
Absolute monarchy

The executive
Under the 1978 constitution, considerable executive power is vested in the monarch and exercised through a cabinet of ministers (all appointed by the monarch). Royal decrees carry the full force of law.

National legislature
There is a bi-cameral Libandla (legislature) consisting of the Senate (20 members appointed by the King; additional 10 members elected by the House of Assembly from among its own membership), and the Liqoqo (House of Assembly) (55 elective members, directly elected every five years (the first time in 1993), with voters electing one representative from each of the *tinkhundla* (traditional assemblies); 10 further members appointed by the King).

Legal system
The legal system is based on South African Roman-Dutch law in statutory courts and Swazi traditional law and custom in traditional courts. The Court of Appeal is the highest court in Swaziland. Court decisions are often overruled by the King.

Last elections
18 October 2003 (parliamentary)
Results: Parliamentary: the elections were considered by the opposition to be meaningless since political parties are outlawed. Only one of the elected MPs has a political affiliation (former prime minister Obed Dlamini, a member of the Ngwane National Liberation Congress). Several other members of outlawed parties contested seats as independent candidates; turnout was low.

Next elections
2008 (parliamentary)

Political parties
Ruling party
Political parties are banned under the 1978 constitution.

Population
1.10 million (2004)
Ethnic make-up
Africans (97 per cent), Europeans (3 per cent).
Religions
Christianity (60 per cent), traditional beliefs (40 per cent).

Education
Although education is subsidised by government, free public education remains a distant goal. School drop-out rates for children of vulnerable households are increasing, with more than 10 per cent of school drop-outs in the first term due to families forced to use school fees to pay the rising costs of staple foods.

It is estimated that through the loss of parents, due to HIV/Aids, 10 per cent of households are headed by a child.

A survey in 2001 showed there were 728 schools in the country, of which 549 were primary and 179 were secondary/high schools. The University of Swaziland provides higher education. There is scope for vocational training, including nursing, although there are no training institutes for doctors and dentists.

Literacy rate: 82 per cent adult rate (2003)
Compulsory years: None.
Enrolment rate: 128 per cent boys, 121 per cent girls gross primary enrolment (including repeaters); 60 per cent gross secondary enrolment (Unicef 2004).
Pupils per teacher: 37 in primary schools; 20 in secondary schools.

Health
Annual government spending is 68 per cent, and foreign spending 8 per cent, of the total expenditure on health, which is around 3 per cent of GDP.

HIV/Aids
Swaziland has the dire honour of having the highest HIV/Aids rate in the world. Coupled with a regime of ruinous indifference or denial it is allowing so many of its population to suffer and die. In 2005 over US$six million was provided by international donors to help fight the disease but a US$1.5 million anti-retroviral (ARV) drugs programme had to cancel when no government infrastructure was in place to establish an effective way of monitoring patients taking the ARV medication. UNAIDS has said that 'rampant epidemics are under way' in southern Africa. The food crisis Swaziland faces is directly linked to the toll on its young, productive adults, during its longstanding HIV/Aids epidemic. Around 50,000 children have lost their mother or both parents to Aids. UNAIDS estimates that the annual loss to GDP per capita due to Aids will be 1.2 per cent by 2010. Demographically, urban populations have fallen by 5 per cent as HIV sufferers return to their family farms to receive care.

Projections show that by 2010, Swaziland's population with be 25 per cent smaller than it should be on current population growth trends. If left unchecked, HIV/Aids will reduce life expectancy to 27 years with an estimated 36 per cent of the population HIV positive.

HIV prevalence: 38.8 per cent, aged 15–49 total; 56 per cent women in their late twenties.
Life expectancy: 42.5 years (World Bank)
Fertility rate/Maternal mortality rate: 4.2 births per woman (World Bank)
Birth rate/Death rate: 29 births and 21 deaths per 1,000 people (2003)
Infant mortality rate: 105 per 1,000 live births (2003); 10 per cent of children aged under five are malnourished (World Bank).

Welfare
UN estimates show that 66 per cent of Swaziland's population live below the poverty line. The average unemployment rate is about 40 per cent, although this figure is higher in rural areas.

According to the UN World Food Programme in early 2002, some 144,000 people required food aid after a severe drop in agricultural production. The total food aid amounted to 17,720 tonnes.

Main cities
Mbabane (administrative capital, estimated population 69,000 in 2003), Lobamba (legislative capital and the seat of the monarchy, 4,200), Manzini (75,000), Matsapha (20,900).

Swaziland

Languages spoken
Most Swazis are bi-lingual in English and SiSwati. In 2006 concern was expressed that teaching of SiSwati was less than English and that under 25 per cent of students who sat the 2005 Junior Certificate SiSwati examination passed; 92 per cent sitting the English language examination passed.

Official language/s
English and SiSwati

Media
Press
Dailies: National daily and Sunday newspapers are *Times of Swaziland* (www.times.co.sz) and *The Swazi Observer* (www.observer.org.sz).

Weeklies: Weeklies include the *Swazi News* and *Weekend Observer* with on-line news updates.

Periodicals: The *Dzadze Family Magazine* caters to women and consumer interests.

Broadcasting
Radio: Programmes are broadcast by Swaziland Broadcasting and Information Service, Swaziland Commercial Radio Ltd and Trans World Radio. Broadcasts are in SiSwati and English.

Television: Government-owned Swaziland Television Broadcasting Corporation transmits colour services in English. Some programmes are in SiSwati.

Economy
In recent years, Swaziland's GDP has remained strong while inflation has remained in single-digit figures, indicating macroeconomic stability, although growth in GDP per capita is modest. Despite being classified as a middle-income country, the distribution of income is highly unequal and around two thirds of the population lives below the poverty line on less than US$1 per day.

HIV/Aids affects around a third of the population, with prevalence rates rising, resulting in a fall of life expectancy and economic strain. This along with severe drought in 2003–04 has resulted in the cry that the country is suffering a natural disaster.

Swaziland's economic relations with South Africa remain close and the lilangeni is pegged to the rand. Company income taxes are in line with South Africa, although the rate on three-month treasury bills is generally 2 per cent lower.

The government's economic plans include the National Development Strategy which seeks to ensure that by 2022 Swaziland will rank in the top 10 per cent of middle-income developing countries with sustainable economic development and political stability. However, agricultural output has dropped. The King's profligate spending is also hindering social improvements.

External trade
On 31 December 2002, the US approved Swaziland as being eligible for tariff preferences under the African Growth and Opportunities Act (AGOA). The legislation requires that countries are only eligible for greater access to US markets provided they have made continued progress toward a market-based economy, the rule of law, free trade, poverty reduction and the protection of workers' rights. This process is reviewed annually.

Imports
Principal imports are vehicles, machinery, transport equipment, foodstuffs, petroleum products and chemicals.

Main sources: South Africa (95.6 per cent total, 2004), EU (0.9 per cent), (Japan 0.9 per cent), Singapore (0.3 per cent)

Exports
Principal exports are soft drink concentrates, sugar, wood pulp, cotton yarn, refrigerators, citrus and canned fruit.

Main destinations: South Africa (59.7 per cent total, 2004), EU (8.8 per cent), US (8.8 per cent), Mozambique (6.2 per cent)

Agriculture
Farming
The agricultural sector contributes around 13 per cent to GDP and employs half of the working population.

Sugar cane is the principal crop. 38,000 hectares of land are given over to it. With yields of 100 tonnes per hectare, Swaziland is one of the world's most efficient sugar producers. All sugar cane is grown under irrigation. The industry is regulated by the Swaziland Sugar Association (SSA). Sugar is Swaziland's highest export earner and accounts for 51 per cent of total agricultural production, 24 per cent of GDP, 13 per cent of total exports and 57 per cent of foreign exchange earnings. A third of sugar production is exported to the EU at advantageous prices, but a decision by the EU, announced in 2004, to reduce the subsidy bodes ill for continuing prosperity of the sector.

Commercial farming, on the 40 per cent of the land owned by individual (mainly non-Swazi) freeholders, is centred on sugar, citrus, pineapples, tobacco and cotton.

Most maize and cotton is grown by small-scale farmers on Swazi Nation Land (SNL) (60 per cent of the land).

Smallholders own 80 per cent of the livestock. The country's main food crops are maize, beans, groundnuts and sorghum. Food self-sufficiency declined in the 1990s and efforts to expand local fruit and vegetable production by the National Agricultural Marketing Board (Namboard) have had only a limited impact.

In 2002, the country reached crisis point, with a yawning food deficit which required international food assistance to fill. Although the food crisis was related to drought, maize yields were generally low due to poor irrigation and a lack of capital inputs. Farmers have been unable to afford fertiliser and equipment due to the removal of government subsidies. With adequate investment in small-scale SNL farms, Swaziland has the potential to be self-sufficient in maize even during years of drought. In 2003, the UN's World Food Programme reported that food production in Swaziland was 66 per cent of the annual average of the previous five years.

The estimated crop production for 2004 included: 71,070 tonnes (t) cereals in total, 300t wheat, 70,000t maize, 6,000t potatoes, 170t rice, 3,000t pulses, 8,300t roots and tubers, 73,500t citrus fruit, 3,400t tomatoes, 32,000t pineapples, 1,870t oilcrops, 4,000,000t sugar cane, 2,000t cotton lint, 109,600t fruit in total, 10,700t vegetables in total. Estimated livestock production included: 21,642t meat in total, 12,500t beef, 1,133t pig meat, 2,880t goat meat, 5,000t poultry, 1,050t eggs, 37,500t milk, 1,200t cattle hides.

Forestry
Forests cover 8 per cent of total land area.

The value of exports in 2004 amounted to US$62 million.

The estimated production for 2004 included: 890,000 cubic metres (cum) roundwood, 102,000cum sawnwood, 260,000cum sawlogs and veneers, 8,000cum wood-based panels, 560,000cum woodfuel.

Industry and manufacturing
The industrial sector employs over a fifth of the workforce and in 2004 contributed around 46 per cent of GDP. It is traditionally centred on the agro-industries: sugar refining, fruit canning and woodpulp processing. The forest products sector is one of the world's main sources of unbleached pulp.

Starting with textile production, the modern industrial sector has grown rapidly, with the South African market its main outlet. The US's African Growth and Opportunities Act (AGOA) enabled Swazi textile producers to access lucrative US markets, although the US has threatened to withdraw these benefits unless the government undergoes democratic reform. The textile industry was affected in 2005 by increasing competition following the ending of the Agreement on Textiles and

Clothing and by reduction of exports caused by the stronger rand.
Other activities include brick manufacture and shoe production.

Tourism
Tourism is in the early stages of developement. It is a growing sector which is being actively developed by the government. It is expected to contribute 2.4 per cent to GDP in 2005. The main source of visitors in 2004 was South Africa, reflecting the strong rand, followed by other neighbouring countries, Germany, the Netherlands, the UK and France.

Mining
Mining activity has declined due to the depletion of iron ore, diamonds, gold and tin and the closure of the Bulembu asbestos mine. Coal is mined for export to South Africa; around 600,000 tonnes of anthracite were produced in 2004. Mineral production accounts for around 2 per cent of GDP.

Hydrocarbons
There are no known oil or gas reserves. Swaziland is entirely dependent on imports. Swaziland has no refineries. There are substantial reserves of high-quality anthracite coal, which is extracted at the Maloma colliery for export to South Africa. Swaziland's domestic low-quality coal requirements are met by imports from South Africa.

Energy
Swaziland relies on imports of electricity, as well as petroleum and coal, for most of its energy needs. 80 per cent of electricity is supplied by South Africa and twenty per cent by Mozambique. A feeder line connecting South Africa and Mozambique crosses Swaziland.
A hydroelectric station at Maguga Dam on the Komati river, has commenced operations, but has only a maximum output of 19 MW.
Distribution of electricity is unreliable and outages are common. To improve reliability and ease dependence on South Africa, development of power stations using Swaziland's own coal resources is under investigation.

Financial markets
Stock exchange
The Swaziland Stock Exchange (SSE) began operating in 1990, and the Securities Market started in 1998. The SSE is one of the world's smallest bourses.

Banking and insurance
In a report published in December 2002, the IMF praised Swaziland's 'well-developed banking system' and noted that in 2002 'banks' capitalisation, risk management and provisioning appeared to be sound and their non-performing loans were relatively low.' However, the future of the government-owned Swaziland Development and Savings Bank (SDSB) remains in doubt due to its high level of bad loans. The IMF has urged the government to privatise the bank.
Central bank
Central Bank of Swaziland
Main financial centre
Mbabane

Time
GMT plus two hours

Geography
Swaziland lies between the Republic of South Africa and Mozambique. It is the smallest country in the southern hemisphere. It is geographically unique, with ancient rock formations and four distinct areas, each with its own climate and characteristics. Altitudes vary from 400 to 1,800 metres above sea level.

Climate
Mbabane and the rest of the highveld are semi-temperate; drier in Manzini. Temperatures range from about 7–10 Celsius (C) (with occasional frost) during April–September, to 20–30 C during August–January. The wettest months are December and March.
The mountainous Highveld region to the north-west has a temperate climate with hot, wet summers and dry winters when the temperature rises during the day but with cold nights.
The adjacent Middleveld has a warm climate.
Further to the east lies the sub-tropical Lowveld.
The Lubombo region, adjacent to Mozambique, is also sub-tropical.

Entry requirements
Passports
Required by all.
Visa
Required by all; except citizens of UK, North America, Australasia and many African countries. See http://www.gov.sz/ and follow links to tourism and then entry requirements. The length of time visitors may stay visa-free may vary, further information should be obtained form the immigration officer at the point of entry or Swaziland Missions abroad.

Health (for visitors)
Mandatory precautions
A yellow fever certificate is required if arriving from an infected area.
Advisable precautions
Hepatitis 'A', polio, tetanus, typhoid vaccinations are advisable. Anti-malaria prophylaxis is needed in all but the high elevations. There is a very high prevalence of HIV/Aids. Water precautions are essential. Eat only hot, cooked food; avoid dairy, pork and salads; all fruits should be peeled. To avoid bilharzia, use only well maintained, chlorinated swimming pools.

Hotels
There is no official rating system. Accommodation is fairly scarce, especially during national holidays, so rooms should be booked well in advance. Bills generally include the service charge, but a 10 per cent tip is also usual. A 10 per cent government tax is added to the room rates.

Public holidays
Fixed dates
1 Jan (New Year's Day), 19 Apr (Birthday of King Mswati III), 25 Apr (National Flag Day), 1 May (Labour Day), 22 Jul (Birthday of the late King Sobhuza), 6 Sep (Independence Day), 25 Dec (Christmas Day), 26 Dec (Boxing Day).
Variable dates
Good Friday, Easter Monday, Ascension Day, Umhlanga/Reed Dance Day* (Aug/Sep), Incwala Ceremony* (Dec/Jan).
* Dependent on local sightings of the moon.

Working hours
Banking
Mon–Fri: 0830–1300/1430; Sat: 0830–1100.
Business
Mon–Fri: 0800–1300, 1400–1700; Sat: 0815 or 0830–1230.
Government
Mon–Fri: 0800–1300, 1400–1700.

Electricity supply
230V AC, 50 cycles; 15 amp/round pin plugs.

Getting there
Air
National airline: Royal Swazi National Airways
International airport/s: Matsapha (MTS), 9km south-west of Manzini, 40km from Mbabane; refreshments, currency exchange, car hire. No direct intercontinental flights to Swaziland. Regular services via South Africa, Kenya, Tanzania, Mozambique.
Airport tax: International departures include a passenger service charge of E20.
Surface
Road: There are tarred roads from Johannesburg and Durban and from Mozambique (Siteki-Lomahasha road). If you enter Swaziland from South Africa on the N4, via the Oshoek border post, avoid travelling after dark as there is a risk of hijacking. All Swaziland border posts open daily throughout the year; hours of operation vary. Vehicles are subject to searches.

Swaziland

Getting about
National transport
Road: The network is mainly composed of gravel roads, sometimes impassable during the rainy season. The 2003/04 budget allows for road construction and improvements.

Buses: There is a good system.

Taxis: Minibus taxis run shorter routes than the buses, at slightly higher prices.

City transport
Taxis: Scarce. Best to order from hotel. A tip is usual.

Car hire
Self-drive cars are available at airport. A national driving licence is required. Drive on left. General speed limit of 80kph.

BUSINESS DIRECTORY

The addresses listed below are a selection only. While World of Information makes every endeavour to check these addresses, we cannot guarantee that changes have not been made, especially to telephone numbers and area codes. We would welcome any corrections.

Telephone area codes
The international direct dialling code (IDD) for Swaziland is +268, followed by subscriber's number.

Chambers of Commerce
Swaziland Chamber of Commerce and Industry, PO Box 72, Mbabane (tel: 44-408; fax: 45-442; e-mail: chamber@dial.pipex.sz).

Banking
First National Bank of Swaziland Ltd, 2nd Floor, Sales House Building, Mbabane (tel: 45-401/2/3; fax: 44-735).

Nedbank (Swaziland) Limited, PO Box 68, Corner Plaza Mall Street and Bypass Road, Mbabane (tel: 43-351/5; fax: 44-060).

Standard Bank Swaziland Ltd, Standard House, Swazi Plaza, Mbabane (tel: 46-930/1/2, 46-599, 40-830/4; fax: 45-899).

Swazibank, PO Box 336, Gwamile Street (tel: 404-2551; fax: 404-1241; email: vinahnkambule@swazibank.sz).

Central bank
Central Bank of Swaziland, PO Box 546, Warner Street, Mbabane (tel: 404-3221; fax: 404-2683; e-mail: info@centralbank.org.sz).

Travel information
Hotels and Tourism Association of Swaziland, PO Box 462, Mbabane (tel: 42-218; fax: 44-516).

Royal Swazi National Airways, PO Box 839, Matsapa Airport, Manzini (tel: 86-148; fax: 86-756).

Swaziland Government Tourist Office, PO Box 338, Mbabane (tel: 44-556).

Ministry of tourism
Ministry of Tourism & Communications, PO Box 58, Mbabane (tel: 46-420; fax: 46-438); Road Transport Board (tel: 46-420).

Ministries
Cabinet Office, PO Box 395, Mbabane (tel: 42-251; fax: 43-943).

Ministry of Agriculture, PO Box 162, Mbabane (tel: 42-731; fax: 44-700); Rural Development Areas Centre (tel: 23-014).

Ministry of Broadcasting, Information and Tourism, PO Box 338, Mbabane (tel: 42-761/9; fax: 42-774).

Ministry of Defence, PO Box 1928, Mbabane (tel: 42-809; fax: 42-483).

Ministry of Economic Planning and Development, PO Box 602, Mbabane (tel: 43-765; fax: 42-157); Statistics Section (tel: 42-151).

Ministry of Education, PO Box 39, Mbabane (tel: 42-491; fax: 43-880).

Ministry of Enterprise and Employment, PO Box 451, Mbabane (tel: 43-201; fax: 44-711); Trade Promotion Unit (tel: 45-180).

Ministry of Finance, PO Box 443, Mbabane (tel: 48-148; fax: 43-187).

Ministry of Foreign Affairs and Trade, PO Box 451, Mbabane (tel: 42-661; fax: 42-669).

Ministry of Health and Social Welfare, PO Box 5, Mbabane (tel: 42-431; fax: 42-092).

Ministry of Home Affairs, PO Box 432, Mbabane (tel: 42-941; fax: 44-303).

Ministry of Housing and Urban Development, PO Box 1832, Mbabane (tel: 46-035; fax: 44-085).

Ministry of Justice and Constitutional Development, PO Box 924, Mbabane (tel: 43-531; fax: 44-796); Attorney General's Chambers, PO Box 578, Mbabane (tel: 42-807).

Ministry of Natural Resources and Energy, PO Box 57, Mbabane (tel: 46-244; fax: 42-436); Geological Survey & Mines, PO Box 57, Mbabane (tel: 42-411). Rural Water Supply, PO Box 961, Mbabane (tel: 41-231).

Ministry of Public Service and Information, PO Box 338, Mbabane (tel: 42-761; fax: 42-774).

Ministry of Public Works and Transport, PO Box 58, Mbabane (tel: 42-321; fax: 42-364); Civil Aviation (tel: 42-420).

Prime Minister's Office, PO Box 395, Mbabane (tel: 42-251; fax: 43-943).

Deputy Prime Minister's Office, PO Box A33 Swazi Plaza (tel: 42-723; fax: 44-085).

Other useful addresses
Central Co-operative Union, PO Box 551, Manzini (tel: 52-787; fax: 52-964).

Central Statistics Office, PO Box 456, Mbabane (tel: 42-151/4; fax: 42-157).

Central Transport Administration, PO Box 378, Mbabane (tel: 42-871; fax: 43-002).

Civil Service Board, PO Box 158, Mbabane (tel: 42-601).

Cotton Board, PO Box 230, Manzini (tel/fax: 52-775).

Dwaleni Investment Co (Pty) Ltd, PO Box 59, Nhlangano (tel: 78-484; fax: 78-055).

Federation of Swaziland Employers, PO Box 386, Manzini (tel: 22-768).

National Agricultural Marketing Board, PO Box 1713, Matsapha (tel: 85-211; fax: 84-088).

National Maize Corporation, PO Box 158, Manzini (tel: 52-265).

Parliament, King's Office (tel: 61-080). Parliament Offices (tel: 61-286).

Police Headquarters, PO Box 49, Mbabane (tel: 42-051).

Posts and Telecommunications Corporation, PO Box 125, Mbabane (tel: 42-341; fax: 43-130).

Small Enterprise Development Co Ltd, Mbabane Industrial Sites, PO Box A186, Swazi Plaza (tel: 42-811; fax: 40-723).

Statistics Department, PO Box 456, Mbabane (tel: 42-151; fax: 42-157).

Swazi Business Growth Trust, PO Box 78, Eveni (tel: 44-705, 55-116; fax: 44-783).

Swaziland Citrus Board, PO Box 343, Mbabane (tel: 43-547).

Swaziland Commercial Board, PO Box 509, Mbabane (tel: 42-930).

Swaziland Cotton Board, PO Box 230, Manzini (tel: 52-775).

Swaziland Dairy Board, PO Box 1789, Manzini (tel: 84-411; fax: 85-313).

Swaziland Electricity Board, PO Box 258, Mbabane (tel: 46-668; fax: 42-335).

Swaziland Embassy (USA), Suite 3M, 3400 International Drive, NW, Washington DC 20008 (tel: 202-362-6683; fax: 202-244-8059; e-mail: 73451.2752@compuserve.com).

Swaziland Industrial Development Company, PO Box 866, Mbabane (tel: 43-391; fax: 45-619).

Swaziland International Trade Fair, PO Box 877, Manzini (tel: 54-242; fax: 52-314).

Swaziland Meat Industries, PO Box 446, Manzini (tel: 84-165, 84-033; fax: 84-418).

Swaziland National Housing Board, PO Box 798, Mbabane (tel: 45-610; fax: 45-224).

Swaziland Railway, PO Box 475, Mbabane (tel: 42-486; fax: 45-009).

Swaziland Sugar Association, PO Box 445, Mbabane (tel: 42-646).

Swaziland Television Authority, PO Box A146, Swazi Plaza (tel: 43-036; fax: 42-093).

Tinkhundla Headquarters, PO Box A33, Swazi Plaza, Mbabane (tel: 42-723; fax: 44-058).

Water Services Corporation, PO Box 20 Mbabane (tel: 45-584; fax: 45-355).

Internet sites

Africa Business Network: http://www.ifc.org/abn

AllAfrica.com: http://allafrica.com

African Development Bank: http://www.afdb.org

Africa Online: http://www.africaonline.com

Harambee Afrika (UK business club for traders with east, central and southern Africa; includes annotated web resource list): http://www.harambee.co.uk

Mbendi AfroPaedia (information on companies, countries, industries and stock exchanges in Africa): http://mbendi.co.za

Simunye news service: http://www.swazis.org.uk/~news/

Swazi news: http://www.swazinews.co.sz/about.htm

Swazi Observer (closed by the government in 2000, re-opened 2001): http://www.swaziobserver.sz/

Swaziland Solidarity Campaign: http://www.swazis.org

Sweden

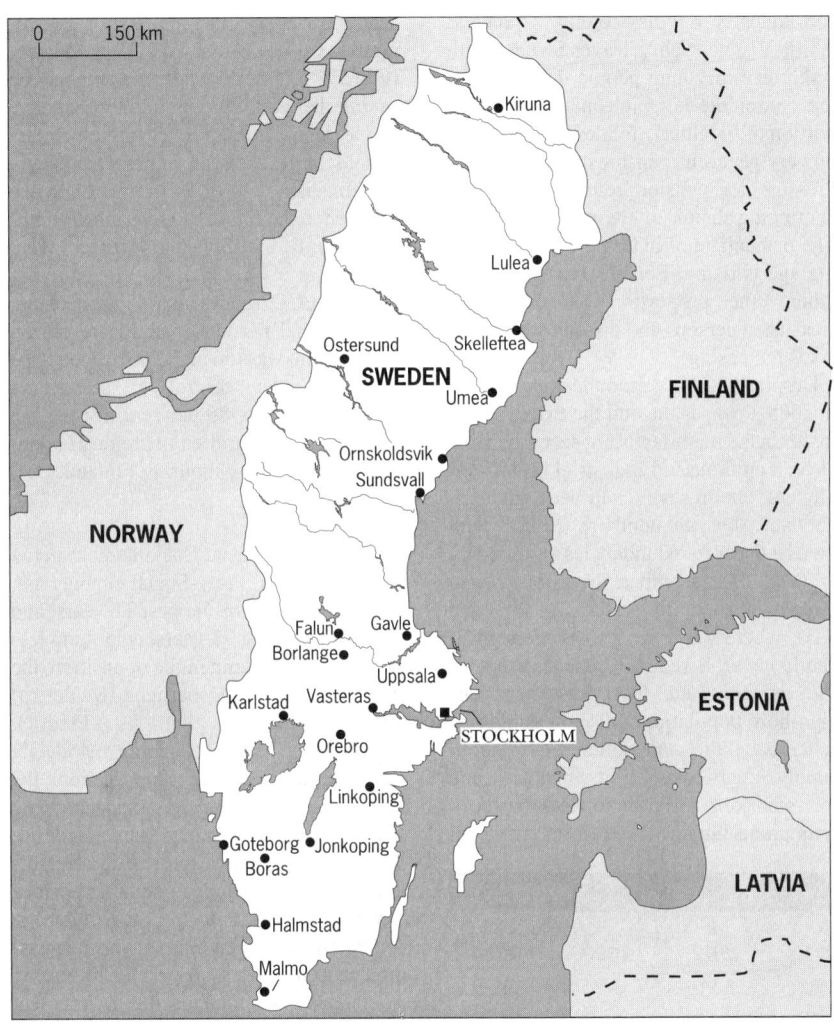

KEY FACTS

Official name: Konungariket Sverige (The Kingdom of Sweden)

Head of State: King Carl XVI Gustaf

Head of government: Prime Minister Göran Persson (S) (since Mar 1996; re-elected 15 Sep 2002)

Ruling party: Arbetarepartiet-Socialdemokraterna (S) (Workers' Party-Social Democrats) (since 1994; re-elected 15 Sep 2002)

Area: 448,964 square km

Population: 8.99 million (2004)

Capital: Stockholm

Official language: Swedish

Currency: Swedish krona (SKr) = 100 öre

Exchange rate: SKr7.73 per US$ (Oct 2005)

GDP per capita: US$38,449 (2004)

GDP real growth: 3.50% (2004)

Labour force: 4.50 million (2003)

Unemployment: 6.40% (OECD, 2004)

Inflation: 1.10% (2004)

Balance of trade: US$23.73 billion (2004)*

Foreign debt: US$513.18 billion (2004)

Annual FDI: US$157.90 billion (cumulative, 1995–2004, OECD)

* estimated figure

This neutral and pacifist kingdom has a great tradition of generous social welfare combined with successful capitalism, with the economy following public-private partnership principles. Sweden ranks sixth out of 177 countries in the UN Human Development Index (HDI), which tracks the quality of countries' education and welfare provisions along with life expectancy. The HDI puts Sweden below Norway, Australia and Iceland but comfortably above the US, UK and Japan. The country has the lowest infant mortality rate, the highest level of female participation in parliament, the highest tax rate and a very high ranking quality of life.

Taxes

The Swedish rate of tax is 51.4 per cent, 10 percentage points above the EU average and the highest in the continent. However, the Swedish population is reconciled to high taxes and recognises their necessity in the provision of high quality social and welfare benefits, to which the prosperous society has become accustomed. The economy does not appear to be unduly hindered, as the economy consistently achieves higher rates of growth than European rivals – Par Nuder, the finance minister commented, 'according to the text books it should not be possible to have such high taxes and such high growth but obviously it is'.

The welfare system is the country's most prized asset. However, the waning momentum for structural reforms is a growing cause for concern. As the European Union (EU) expands and global economic integration gathers pace, it is critical for Sweden to enhance its long-term prospects for growth and welfare.

Economy – good and bad news

In April 2005 the Social Democrats released their spring budget, which noted the strengths of the economy while promising to confront a high unemployment rate, of 5.7 per cent; among young adults, immigrants and older workers, it is considerably higher. The public sector is running a surplus of 0.7 per cent of GDP while public debt has fallen below 50 per cent for the first time for over a decade.

In June 2005 the central bank cut interest rates by half a percentage point, from 2.0 per cent to 1.5 per cent. The move was a reaction to a revised economic outlook – GDP growth of below 2 per cent, when it had been forecast at 3.2 per cent in the spring budget. The IMF figures for 2005 and 2006 are forecast at 2.6 and 2.8 per cent respectively.

Labour

The cost of labour was expected to increase by an annual average of more than 4 per cent in 2005, while Swedish labour costs will remain above the EU average. The economic model, first mooted in Marcus Child's 1931 book *The Middle Way*, was not built to take into account the pressures of globalisation and shifting demographics. A low post-war birth rate, attributed by some to Sweden's famous sexual liberation of the 1960s and a higher than normal percentage of older males, a consequence of the country's Second World War neutrality, leaves Sweden with a shortage of young people willing to do low- to middle-level jobs and a high proportion of fit, elderly folk entitled to retire on very generous pensions at 60 year old. Pressure for pension reforms will be a continuing theme of the next few years. The percentage of older persons of working age is rising. For this reason, among others, the proportion of chronically sick-listed persons and disability pensioners is increasing.

Despite positive announcements early in 2005, towards the end the extent of job losses in the manufacturing sector became clear. Ten thousand industrial sector employees, one in seven, had been made redundant by September 2005, with thousands more redundancies expected by the end of December. Investors began looking abroad, to eastern Europe and Asia, where wages and costs are significantly lower; Swedish FDI is at zero.

It is expected that Sweden's foreign-born population will increasingly be relied on as the main source of its labour supply, particularly in manual and low-paid jobs and a better integration of immigrants into the labour force is crucial.

The immigrant population constitutes 10 per cent of the total, and is set to rise. There is a notable minority Muslim population.

Sweden's car market is predicted to record robust growth, with new passenger-car registrations forecast to rise by 3.8 per cent annually in 2004–08.

Welfare

The Paris-based Organisation for Economic Co-operation and Development (OECD) released a report in June 2005 saying that participation in the workplace had to be increased if Sweden were to sustain its high levels of welfare payments. Absenteeism and long-term sick leave threatened the future of government funding – one fifth of Sweden's workers were off sick on any given day.

The OECD report also suggested that the financial burden of childcare on the government was too high and needed to be brought under control to secure its long-term future; 85 per cent of Swedish youngsters are enrolled in childcare, double the rate in neighbouring Finland.

Politics

The Arbetarepartiet-Socialdemokraterna (AS) (Workers' Party-Social Democrats), the ruling party for the past 11 years, and for 64 of the past 73 years, is looking less solid since a revamp in the opposition, the Moderata Samlingspartiet (Moderata) (Moderate Party) led by Fredrick Reinfeldt. The right-leaning Moderata seeks to attract more support from the working classes, and has stopped being quite so vehement in expressing its desire for tax cuts. The AS, meanwhile, are suffering from a shortage of new ideas, and a series of scandals.

The Swedish handling of the devastation caused by the *tsunami* (tidal wave) in south-east Asia plunged the government into public criticism, with claims they were woefully slow to react; it took a few days for the government to mobilise and send provisions. About 700 Swedes are thought to have been killed in Thailand alone; the foreign affairs minister, Laila Freivalds, earned most criticism as she failed to leave the theatre, in which she was enjoying a play, following the public announcement of the disaster.

In January 2005 an independent commission was established to probe the circumstances of the government's reaction.

Another smaller political spat which impinged upon the ruling AS concerned Lars Ohly, the leader of the coalition partner Vänsterpartiet (Vp) (Left Party). Ohly is

KEY INDICATORS — Sweden

	Unit	2000	2001	2002	2003	2004
Population	m	8.87	8.90	8.90	8.95	*8.99
Gross domestic product (GDP)	US$bn	226.64	209.50	229.80	300.80	*346.40
GDP per capita	US$	25,551	23,590	25,400	34,981	38,449
GDP real growth	%	4.4	1.2	2.0	1.7	3.5
Inflation	%	1.0	2.7	2.0	2.1	1.1
Unemployment	%	4.7	4.0	4.0	4.8	–
Exports (fob) (goods)	US$m	87,431.0	76,200.0	80,750.0	100,939.0	121,700.0
Imports (fob) (goods)	US$m	72,216.0	62,368.0	65,950.0	82,317.0	97,970.0
Balance of trade	US$m	15,215.0	13,832.0	25,000.0	18,622.0	23,730.0
Current account	US$m	6,617.0	6,696.0	11,400.0	11,000.0	28,020.0
Total reserves minus gold	US$m	14,863.0	13,977.0	17,127.0	19,681.0	22,129.0
Foreign exchange	US$m	13,757.0	12,740.0	15,520.0	–	20,611.0
Exchange rate	per US$	9.16	10.33	9.58	7.96	7.35

* estimated figure

accused of having close links with ex-communist figures in Eastern Europe, and indeed proclaimed himself to be a communist – despite the Vp distancing itself from that term in the 1990s. The former leader of the Vp, Gudun Schyman, who quit in 2003, as a result of alcoholism, has voiced her plans for establishing a feminist party to do battle with the Vp.

Outlook

The economy is fundamentally robust but in 2005 negative statistics emerged regarding unemployment, a slowing of growth and a cut in interest rates. Economic and political decisions in 2006 will be dominated by the knowledge that an election is on the horizon. The Moderata has pushed ahead in approval ratings, in spite of its scandal-ridden year. Elections are expected to be held in September 2006. It could be a historic event, with the eventual ousting of long-term incumbents, the AS.

Risk assessment

Economic	Good
Political	Good
Regional Stability	Good
Stock market	Good

COUNTRY PROFILE

Historical profile

1389–1520 Having evolved from a feudal society, Sweden was ruled by Denmark.
1520 The Massacre of Stockhom occurred when the Danish King Kristian II, in an attempt to assert his supremacy, executed resisting Swedish noblemen, which led to a revolt, headed by Gustav Eriksson Vasa.
1523 King Kristian II was defeat by Vasa, who was crowned Gustav I. His victory heralded the start of Sweden's ascendancy in Europe.
1611 Gustav II Adolph (Gustavus Adolphus) became King. He engaged in expansionist policies that attempted to gain control of the Baltic trading routes and which brought him into conflict with neighbouring states.
1629 Sweden fought to possess Prussia and Pomerania (now part of Germany) in the Thirty Years War.
1632 Gustav II was killed at the battle of Lutzen (in Saxony, now part of Germany) and was succeeded by his daughter, Kristina.
1654 Kristina abdicated after converting to Catholicism – an act that was unacceptable in Lutheran Sweden.
1700 Start of the Great Nordic War when Russia, Denmark, Norway and Poland formed an alliance against Sweden and its 15-year old King Karl XII in an attempt to retrieve some of their lost lands.
1700–1720 A succession of battles resulted in the loss of all Swedish lands in Germany, the Baltic provinces of Russia and much of Finland. Success against the Danes in Norway allowed Sweden to consolidate into easily defended borders.
1718 The power of the monarchy diminished and was vested in the Council of Aristocrats who depended on parliament for its authority.
1772 King Gustav III began reforms that strengthened the power of the monarchy. These developments resulted in an almost absolute monarchy.
1792 King Gustav III was assassinated by members of the Swedish nobility. Gustav IV Adolf became King.
1808–09 Sweden was defeated by the Russians. Finland, which was then part of Sweden, was ceded to Russia. King Gustav IV Adolf was replaced by Karl XIII in 1809.
1814 Sweden entered a union with Norway.
1905 The emergence of Norwegian nationalism led Norway to declare independence. A parliamentary form of government emerged in Sweden.
1920s The Arbetarepartiet-Socialdemokraterna (AS) (Workers' Party-Social Democrats) first came to power. Except during 1936, the AS stayed in power from 1932 to 1976.
1939–45 Sweden declared its neutrality during the Second World War, although German troops were transported through its territory to Norway. Sweden also supplied Nazi Germany with iron ore until 1943.
1952 Sweden became a founder member of the Nordic Council.
1959 Sweden became a founder member of the European Free Trade Area (EFTA) with Austria, Denmark, Norway, Portugal, Switzerland and the UK.
1969–71 Olof Palme (prime minister 1969–76 and 1982–86) introduced constitutional reforms. The bicameral legislature was replaced by a unicameral legislature, elected by proportional representation.
1975 A new constitution was promulgated; it reduced the power of the monarchy and limited its role to that of figurehead and ceremonial duties.
1976 A centre-right coalition government, the Centerpartiet (Cp) (Centre Party), and Moderata Samlingspartiet (M) (Moderate Party) won the parliamentary election.
1978 The coalition government collapsed due to disagreement about economic problems and the building of a controversial nuclear power plant. The Folkpartiet Liberalerna (FpL) (Liberal People's Party) formed a new government.
1979 The Cp won the parliamentary elections.
1982 The AS won the parliamentary elections. Olof Palme became prime minister again.
1986 Palme was assassinated in Stockholm by an unknown gunman.
1991 After parliamentary elections, the Moderate Party formed the government with Carl Bildt as prime minister.
1994 The AS won the general election. Sweden joined Nato's Partnership for Peace (PfP) military co-operation programme.
1995 Sweden joined the EU.
1996 Carlsson stepped down as the leader of the AS and prime minister. Göran Persson replaced him.
1998 Following parliamentary elections the AS formed a minority government. AS's reduced vote was believed due to widespread anger at social expenditure cuts.
2002 The AS won the parliamentary elections and continued to lead a minority government that relied on support from the Vänsterpartiet (Vp) (Left Party) and the Miljöpartiet de Gröna (MP) (Environmental Party the Greens).
2003 Foreign Minister Anna Lindh was stabbed to death in a Stockholm department store. In a referendum voters narrowly defeated the proposal to join the single European currency.
2004 The man who confessed to killing Anna Lindh was convicted of her murder and sentenced to life imprisonment, overturning a previous ruling which consigned him to a psychiatric hospital.

Political structure
Constitution
The constitution consists of four separate documents: the *Regeringsformen* (Instrument of Government) passed in 1974, *Successionsordningen* (Act of Succession) dating from 1810, the *Tryckfrihetsförordningen* (Freedom of the Press Act) of 1949 (originating from 1766), and the *Yttrandefrihetsgrundlagen* (Freedom of Expression Act) of 1991. There are 288 municipalities throughout the country, each with a popularly elected council. Immigrants, resident for three years, have the right to vote and run for office in local elections.
Universal suffrage is at aged 18. Voter turnout is traditionally high, between 85–90 per cent.
Under proportional representation 310 parliamentary seats are allocated on a constituency basis, in 28 multi-member constituencies; the remaining seats are divided nationally. To win parliamentary representation, a party must poll either 4

per cent overall – to receive a seat from the national allocation – or 12 per cent in any one constituency for a seat from the national remainder.

Form of state
Parliamentary democratic monarchy

The executive
Executive power is exercised by the Regeringen (cabinet) which is led by the prime minister (elected by parliament) and is responsible to parliament. The prime minister appoints members of the cabinet.

National legislature
Legislative power is vested in the unicameral Riksdag (parliament) (349 members directly elected for a four-year term). In the event of an early dissolution, the new parliament serves only the remainder of the previous parliament's term.

Legal system
The legal system is divided into the general courts and the general administrative courts. The general courts are composed of a Supreme Court (Högsta domstolen), six Courts of Appeal and 95 District Courts which are responsible for criminal cases involving individuals. The Supreme Court is the highest court in the land and is composed of 16 judges appointed by the government. The general administrative courts are responsible for cases involving public authorities and individuals.

Last elections
13 June 2004 (European Parliament); 15 September 2002 (parliamentary).
Results: European Parliament: Arbetarepartiet-Socialdemokraterna (AS) (Workers' Party-Social Democrats) won 24.8 per cent of the vote (five seats out of 19), Moderata Samlingspartiet (Moderata (M)) (Moderate Party) 18.2 per cent (four), Junilistan (June List) 14.4 per cent (three), Vänsterpartiet (Vp) (Left Party) 12.8 per cent (two), Folkpartiet Liberalerna (FpL) (Liberal People's Party) 9.8 per cent (two), Centerpartiet (Cp) (Centre Party) 6.3 per cent (one), Miljöpartiet de Gröna (MP) (Environmental Party the Greens) 5.9 per cent (one) and Kristdemokraterna (KD) (Christian Democrats) 5.7 per cent (one); turnout 37.2 per cent.
Parliamentary:
Arbetarepartiet-Socialdemokraterna (AS) (Workers' Party-Social Democrats) was re-elected with 39.4 per cent of the vote (144 seats out of 349); Moderata Samlingspartiet (M) (Moderate Party) 15.2 per cent (55 seats); Folkpartiet Liberalerna (FpL) (People's Party Liberals) 13.3 per cent (48 seats); Kristdemokraterna (KD) (Christian Democrats) 9.1 per cent (33 seats); Vänsterpartiet (Vp) (Left Party) 8.3 per cent (30 seats); Centerpartiet (Cp) (Centre Party) 6.1 per cent (22 seats); Miljöpartiet de Gröna (MP) (Environmental Party the Greens) 4.6 per cent (17 seats).

Next elections
September 2006 (parliamentary)

Political parties
Ruling party
Arbetarepartiet-Socialdemokraterna (S) (Workers' Party-Social Democrats) (since 1994; re-elected 15 Sep 2002)
Main opposition party
Moderata Samlingspartiet (M) (Moderate Party)

Population
8.99 million (2004)
Ethnic make-up
Native Swedes account for 88 per cent of the population. Around 50 per cent of all foreign nationals are from other Nordic countries (Denmark, Finland, Iceland and Norway).
Sweden has two minority groups of native inhabitants in the north: the Finnish speaking people of the north-east and an estimated 17,000 Sámi (Lapp) people.
Religions
About 90 per cent of the population belong to the Church of Sweden (Lutheran); there are 8 per cent other Protestants and 1 per cent Roman Catholics.

Education
Pre-school classes are offered to any six year old enrolled, the first (and compulsory) school begins at aged seven; both are free of charge and the majority are run by municipalities. In 2001–02 over one million pupils were enrolled (within both); independent schools accounted for 1 per cent of enrolments. The average number of pupils per school was 209, with an average of 108 pupils in independent schools. Many schools are now working with integrated age levels where children of different ages are taught together in the same class. Around three-quarters of all compulsory schools are connected to the Internet. At aged 16 students who have successfully completed their compulsory schooling progress to upper secondary school. Nearly all pupils continue to the upper secondary school. Each municipality has the right to establish its own upper secondary schools and a national curriculum provides a basis for further studies and basic eligibility for higher education.
Higher education is offered in 13 state-run universities and 23 university colleges. There are also three private universities: Chalmers University of Technology, the University College of Jönköping and the Stockholm School of Economics. Further education for adults (aged 20 years and over) is offered within the public adult education system through municipal adult education.
Literacy rate: 99 per cent, adult rate (2003)
Compulsory years: 7 to 16
Enrolment rate: 107 per cent gross primary enrolment, 140 per cent gross secondary enrolment: of relevant age groups (including repeaters and training for unemployed within the age group) (World Bank 2001).
Pupils per teacher: 12 in primary schools

Health
Sweden has for many years actively worked with health promotion in line with the World Health Organisation's (WHO) European 'Health for All' policy. There is a close collaboration between the government and local and regional providers of public medical and healthcare services. A governmental body, the National Public Health Committee, is responsible for providing many recommendations to the government, along with wide-ranging consultation, is being used as a basis for the future development of the healthcare system.
The public sector finances health services, through taxation, for the entire population although the Federation of Health Insurance Societies, (established in 1907), helps to promote a national compulsory system of health insurance.
HIV prevalence: 0.1 per cent aged 15–49 in 2003 (World Bank)
Life expectancy: 80.1 years (World Bank)
Fertility rate/Maternal mortality rate: 1.7 births per woman (World Bank)
Birth rate/Death rate: 9.7 births and 10.6 deaths per 1,000 people (2003)
Infant mortality rate: 2.8 per 1,000 live births (World Bank)
Head of population per physician/bed: 311 per 100,000 people (WHO); 6.3 hospital beds per 1,000 of the population.

Welfare
The Swedish social insurance system is managed by the state and is compulsory for everyone, providing means-tested and general benefits. The main goal of the social insurance is to provide protection against loss of income and is composed of sickness insurance, early retirement pensions, occupational injury insurance and old age pensions. The Social Services Act of 1982 regulates the welfare benefit system while the National Board of Health and Welfare (Socialstyrelsen) supervises the overall quality of social service provision.
A Social Insurance Act was introduced in 2001, dividing social insurance into two categories: a domicile-based insurance scheme, which provides guaranteed benefits, and a work-related insurance scheme, which safeguards against loss of income. These insurance systems are available to

anyone living or working in Sweden. Social insurance is divided into 50 per cent going into pensions, 25 per cent to sickness and disability benefit and 15 per cent to families with children.

The pension system was reformed in 1998 and is composed of various components, including an income-related pension, a premium pension and a guaranteed pension. The premium pension allows a person to invest their own funds into part of the pension scheme. A state pension is guaranteed to all the population on a low income or without any income.

Main cities
Stockholm (capital, estimated population 1.3 million in 2004), Göteborg (506,600), Malmö (245,300), Uppsala (127,300).

Languages spoken
Finnish, Skäine and Sámi are spoken. English, and to a lesser extent German, are also widely spoken.

Official language/s
Swedish

Media
Press
Dailies: The most influential are either owned or run by political parties and trade unions. These include *Aftonbladet* (Social Democratic), *Dagens Nyheter* (Liberal, independent), *Expressen* (Liberal), *Göteborgs-Posten* (Liberal), *Svenska Dagbladet* (Conservative) *Sydsvenska Dagbladet* and *Aktuellt I Politiken, AiP*.

Weeklies: Main Sunday newspapers and weekly publications include *Expressen, Se och Hör, Hemmets Vän, Aftonbladet, Dagens Nyheter* and *Göteborgs-Posten*.

Business: The leading magazine is *Veckans Affärer*. Other publications include the weekly *Affärsvärlden*, the daily *Dagens Industri* and *Finanstidningen*.

Periodicals: These include *Galago* (quarterly), *Grönköpings Veckoblad, Land, Moderna, Tider, Slitz, Sweden International* and *Sweden Today*.

Broadcasting
Radio: There are around 120 radio stations of which 90 are commercial. There are approximately 3.3 million receivers in use. Sveriges Radio broadcasts three national channels. Sveriges Radio broadcasts in six languages, including English.

Television: There are seven TV stations, of which five are commercial. A great variety of satellite channels is available throughout the country. There are two commercial Swedish-language satellite channels, TV3 and TV4, with more than half the nation's households receiving them. Over 1.5 million households receive cable television.

Advertising
Modern and of a high standard, but tends to be expensive. All media are available except state radio and state television. Key categories include automotive, food, financial, fuel and household appliances. The promotion of alcohol consumption is not allowed (except for light beers), while tobacco advertising is restricted to the press only.

Economy
The Swedish economic model, a 'third-way' between capitalism and socialism, was built upon a generous welfare system, a corporatist structure between government, industry and trade unions, and high levels of public sector employment. This was paid for by high rates of marginal income tax, wealth taxes and employer social security contributions. In the 1980s, the weakness of this approach became more apparent, culminating in the recession of 1990–93, when negative economic growth and rapidly increasing unemployment made it unsustainable. The government introduced a number of reforms and an austerity package which stabilised government finances and the economy gradually recovered.

In 2004 a booming export market helped generate a GDP increase of 3.5 per cent. In 2005 trade is levelled off, GDP has settled down to 2.6 per cent growth. 2007 is predicted to bring similar increases of 2.7 per cent. Interest rates meanwhile are at historic lows.

Sweden has largely escaped negative fall-out from the recent global market slump. Business investment climbed in 2004/05 with the telecommunications and car industries performing particularly well. Productivity has strengthened. Domestic consumption, supported by low interest rates, low inflation and higher real wages, remained robust.

These healthy figures have added up to notable current account surpluses. Public finances are in good order, with an estimated surplus of 0.7 per cent.

Nevertheless the warning that tempers the praise is that central government must remain in control of, and limit the negative effects of, long term funding of welfare payments and pension plans for an ageing population.

Another concern is the rise in unemployment although a host of tax incentives and government policies have been recently announced to try to tackle the increase. The OECD has recommended unemployment payment schemes should be overhauled and that tertiary education should be shortened. The IMF urged a streamlining of social security to eliminate disincentives to work, such as relatively high taxes for low earners. Measures such as these are intended to boost employment in general, while increasing the hours worked and overall productivity, which should benefit the economy as a whole.

The central bank has price stability as its overriding monetary policy and limits the consumer price index to 2 per cent plus or minus 1 percentage point. Indeed, consumer prices rose just 0.1 per cent in early 2005. The krona (Sweden is not a member of the eurozone) has risen against the US dollar and continues to be stable against the euro; it was predicted to strengthen further in 2005 as competitiveness remains strong. Public sector consumption is also predicted to rise in 2005–06.

External trade
Germany and other Nordic countries are Sweden's biggest trading partners. During 2005 exports rose 7 per cent in value while the value of imports climbed 12 per cent. The net trade surplus was SEK 135 billion.

Imports
Main imports include machinery, petroleum and petroleum products, chemicals, vehicles, iron and steel, foodstuffs and clothing.

Main sources: Germany (20.2 per cent total, 2004), Denmark (8.2 per cent), UK (7.9 per cent), The Netherlands (7.2 per cent), Finland (7 per cent), France (6.1 per cent), Norway (5.9 per cent), Belgium (4.5 per cent)

Exports
Major exports include engineering products (35 per cent of total), vehicles, paper products, pulp and wood, iron and steel, and chemicals.

Main destinations: US (10.7 per cent total, 2004), Germany (10.3 per cent), UK (7.2 per cent), Denmark (6.6 per cent), Norway (6.2 per cent), Finland (5.9 per cent), Belgium (5.1 per cent), The Netherlands (4.8 per cent), France (4.7 per cent)

Agriculture
Farming
Although Sweden is one of the biggest countries in Europe, its arable land amounts to only 2.8 million hectares (ha) constituting about 7 per cent of the total land area. Grain is harvested on 45 per cent of arable land. Agriculture contributes 2 per cent of GDP and employs less than 2 per cent of the total work force. Dairy products, grains, sugarbeets and potatoes are produced. There are 1.7 million cows in the country. Over the past decade, cattle herd numbers have fallen while yields have risen.

Most farms are family concerns, in which the work is done by members of the family. Part-time farming, with income supplemented by other employment (eg forestry), has become a common feature.

Restructuring and modernisation of equipment have resulted in fewer but larger farms.

Farming is concentrated in the southern regions, where livestock farming predominates.

Sweden's adherence to the EU's Common Agricultural Policy (CAP) has brought some regulation of agriculture. Agricultural support policies have been adjusted to CAP, including production quotas and increased export subsidies. Import licences are required for certain agricultural commodities.

Fundamental reform to the CAP was introduced on 1 January 2005 in Sweden. The subsidies paid on farm output, which tended to benefit large farms and encourage overproduction, were replaced by single farm payments not conditional on production. This is expected to reward farms that provide and maintain a healthy environment, food safety and animal welfare standards. The changes are also intended to encourage market conscious production and cut the cost of CAP to the EU taxpayer.

Crop production in 2003 included: 5.3 million metric tonnes (mmt) cereals in total, 2.3mmt wheat, 1.5mmt barley, 1.1mmt oats, 850,500 metric tonnes (mt) potatoes, 92,670mt pulses, 22,800mt tomatoes, 51,786mt oilcrops, 2.5mmt sugar beet, 18,005mt apples, 32,029mt fruit in total, 277,815mt vegetables in total. Livestock production included: 546,060mt meat in total, 136,300mt beef, 287,500mt pig-meat, 3,700mt lamb and goat meat, 99,850mt poultry, 92,300mt eggs, 3.2mmt milk, 3,400mt honey, 10,200mt cattle hides, 2,160mt sheepskins.

Fishing

The Swedish market for seafood is typically over 150,000 tonnes annually calculated on the basis of product weight. Estimated output from the domestic seafood processing sector amounts to around 85,000 tonnes per year. About 75 per cent of this amount is for the home market with marinated herring being the most important product. Over half of the fishing industry is located in western Sweden. In addition to coastal and deep-sea fishing around the western coast, Sweden has an abundance of natural lakes, which can provide enough fish to meet domestic needs.

Most fish imports are from Norway and Denmark, which together typically account for 75 per cent of total Swedish imports, indicating the importance of the Scandinavian link in its seafood industry.

As the EU presses for radical reform to its Common Fisheries Policy (CFP), Sweden is expected to support its principles based on the ecosystem approach.

Forestry

Forest and other wooded land accounts for nearly 75 per cent of the land area, with forest cover estimated at 27.1 million hectares (ha). Approximately 23 million ha of forest area is available for wood supply.

The forest industry and forestry account for more than 4 per cent of Sweden's GDP, 12 per cent of industrial employment and 15 per cent of Sweden's exports. Sweden's pulp and paper industry is the third-largest in Europe after Germany and Finland. About one-third of Sweden's wood pulp and over half its paper and board are exported. Sweden accounts for more than 13 per cent of paper demand in the EU.

Following large scale divestiture, 52 per cent of forest land is owned privately, 24 per cent is owned by the state (primarily through Sveaskog AB) and 24 per cent through commercial companies.

Exports of forest material in 2004 amounted to US$12.9 billion, while imports amounted to US$2.1 billion. Production in 2004 included 67,300,00 million cubic metres (cum) roundwood, 61,400,000cum industrial roundwood, 16,900,000cum sawnwood, 34,400,000cum sawlogs and veneers, 25,500,000cum pulpwood, 694,400cum wood-based panels, 5,900,000cum wood fuel; 1,500,000 tonnes (t) recovered paper, 2,649,000t newsprint, 3,033,000t printing and writing paper, 5,907,000t other paper and paperboard.

Industry and manufacturing

The powerful industrial sector contributes 29 per cent of GDP and accounts for 75 per cent of all exports. It is a key reason why the Swedish people have one of the highest standards of living in the world. Industrial strength was traditionally based on extensive reserves of iron, timber and the rivers and lakes that provided cheap energy, although in recent years hi-tech production has increased in significance. With such a small domestic market, industry has always had to look overseas for survival and it has profited from the development of a mature export culture.

The state is gradually decreasing its ownership in firms under its control. The government is committed to ending state subsidies for inefficient industries. As a result of this policy, traditional sectors, such as shipyards and the textile industry, have virtually ceased to exist. In other traditional industries, there has been drastic rationalisation and concentration on narrow segments of the market.

The industrial sector is based largely on indigenous resources (iron ore, timber and water-power). Major industries include motor vehicles, food processing, chemicals, iron and steel, transportation equipment, electrical and electronic equipment and forestry products. Sweden's industrial structure tends to be centred on large, capital-intensive companies, due to the nature of tax, social security and labour market regulations, which do not favour smaller firms. Engineering is Sweden's main industrial sector, accounting for around a third of industrial output and for a similar proportion of exports. The country's main engineering companies include Ericsson, Electrolux, Volvo (owned by Ford), SKF, Saab, Scania and Sandvik. Manufacturing employs approximately 30 per cent of the workforce.

The Organisation for Economic Co-operation and Development (OECD) recently named Sweden as one of the leading countries in the Internet and other information technology (IT) markets, along with the US and Finland. In the same month, Sweden topped the International Data Corporation's (IDC) Information Society Index of 55 countries in the IT sector. IT remains an important contributor to the economy. Internet companies in Sweden are managing to survive the burst of the 'dotcom' bubble and the country is at the forefront of the development of mobile telephone Internet technology. Sweden is also beginning to lead the way in the biotechnology sector and has more biotech companies per capita than any other country.

Timber production accounts for just over a fifth of industrial output. Sweden has a large forestry sector supplying raw materials to industry and for export. With 57 per cent of the land area covered in forest, Sweden has the largest timber reserves in Western Europe.

Despite all its strengths, in 2005 a dark cloud formed over Swedish manufacturing. 10,000 workers were victims of redundancies, out of a total of 700,000. Jobs have been lost to countries with lower labour costs such as Asia and Eastern Europe. Another 5,000-8,000 job losses are expected to be announced next year. Business taxes are considered too high and Foreign Direct Investment (FDI) has dropped to zero this year.

Tourism

Tourism is an important part of the growing service sector in Sweden, with the industry accounting for 2.7 per cent of Sweden's GDP. Tourist arrivals numbered 10.4 million in 2004, a significant improvement on the previous year. Norway and Germany are the most frequent visitors. 100,000 people are employed in the industry, comprising 2.4 per cent of the workforce.

Sweden

Mining
The mining sector typically accounts for 9 per cent of GDP and employs 0.5 per cent of the industrial workforce.
Sweden is rich in mineral deposits, the most important of which are iron ore, zinc, lead, copper, silver and pyrites. There are also large deposits of uranium, exploitation of which has been held back by environmental and political objections. Swedish companies focus on making high quality speciality iron and steel.
Sweden's share of total world iron ore output comes to around 2 per cent, making Sweden one of the largest iron ore exporters in Europe. Sweden's shares of the Western world's production of copper, lead and zinc concentrates amount to 1 per cent, 3.7 per cent and 3.3 per cent, respectively.

Hydrocarbons
Sweden is poor in hydrocarbon resources and has limited reserves. As a result, oil represents a large proportion of total Swedish imports. Swedish refineries have an annual capacity of 20 million tonnes. The largest, Scanraff, north of Göteborg on the west coast, has a capacity of over 200,000 barrels per day (bpd). Natural gas is imported in small quantities through a pipeline from Denmark across the Baltic Straits and is used in southern Sweden. In 2004 consumption of natural gas reached 0.8 billion cubic metres. Consumption of coal reached 2.4 million tonnes oil equivalent in the same year.

Energy
The Swedish are among the highest individual electricity consumers in the world. The government began a seven-year programme in 1997 to stimulate energy saving and development of alternative fuels in readiness for the controversial shutdown of the country's nuclear power industry. Currently nuclear power accounts for 50 per cent of electrical energy. In 1999, the Swedish government won legal backing for plans to close the first of the country's 12 nuclear reactors, heralding the dismantling of the nuclear industry. Unit one of the Barseback reactor closed in 1999; the closure of unit two followed in 2005. Sweden's remaining ten plants are expected to be shut down between 2012-2025.
Sweden has abundant renewable resources such as biofuels, water and wind power. There are over 200 major hydropower plants (more than 10 MW) and 2,000 smaller ones. Most hydroelectric plants are sited on the main northern rivers. Hydropower and biofuels combined generate 40 per cent of the nation's energy. Imported oil similarly provides 40 per cent of energy, with nuclear supplying the remaining 20 per cent. Manufacturing and district heating systems are replacing oil use with biofuels and electricity.

Financial markets
Stock exchange
Sweden's stock exchange was restructured in 2001 in an attempt to raise its profile on the international markets. Formally known as the Stockholm Exchange, it rebranded itself as the *Stockholmsbörsen*. In December 2001, the *Stockholmsbörsen*, which handled stocks and stock derivative trading, merged with OM Fixed Income Exchange, which deals in fixed income trading. The exchange is part of Norex, which comprises the stock exchanges of Copenhagen, Oslo, Stockholm and Iceland.
There are over 300 companies listed on the *Stockholmsbörsen*. Ericsson, the major mobile phone manufacturer, has market capitalisation of one-third of the value of all quoted companies and 28 per cent of share trading.

Banking and insurance
Liberalisation and increased openness has boosted the competitiveness of the Swedish financial sector. There have been serveral mergers between banking and insurance firms. There is a predominance of large corporations in the sector. More than 70 per cent of people in this sector are employed by firms with a payroll of more than 200.
Central bank
Sveriges Riksbank
Main financial centre
Stockholm

Time
GMT plus one hour (GMT plus two hours from late March to late September).

Geography
Sweden is situated in north-western Europe. It occupies about 66 per cent of the Scandinavian peninsula and is bordered by Finland to the north-east and Norway to the north-west and west. Approximately 15 per cent of the country lies north of the Arctic Circle. The Baltic Sea and the Gulf of Bothnia are to the east, the Skagerrak and Kattegat to the south-west.

Climate
Because of the Atlantic gulf stream, Sweden has a milder climate than some other regions in the same latitude. The average winter temperature in the north, where there is always snow from December to March, is -12.9 degrees Celsius (C), in central Sweden -3.1 degrees C and in the south -0.7 degrees C. In summer average temperatures are 12.8 degrees C in the north, 17.8 degrees C in central Sweden and 17.2 degrees C in the south.

Dress codes
Clothing to suit the climate is vital because of the extremes. Heavy coats, warm boots, gloves and ear protection are required in winter and light clothing in summer.
Swedes can be informal in business attire, but suits are worn at business meetings and for social events in the evening.

Entry requirements
Passports
Not required by nationals of countries which are signatories of the Schengen Accords, which includes most EU member states.
Visa
Required by all, except citizens of EU, Iceland, Norway, North America, Australasia, Japan or transit passengers, for up to three months. For those that require a visa a Schengen visa covers all entry needs; for business trips, an employment letter giving particulars and travel funds, plus an invitation from a business contact in Sweden and a full itinerary should be included when applying. All visas issued, will adhere to Schengen Agreement requirements throughout signatories region.
Currency advice/regulations
There are no limits on the amounts of Swedish or foreign currency which can be imported or exported.

Health (for visitors)
Mandatory precautions
Vaccination certificates not required unless travelling from an infected area.
Advisable precautions
Up-to-date tetanus and polio immunisations are recommended.

Hotels
There is no official rating system in operation. There is a shortage of accommodation in major cities so reservations should be made well in advance.

Public holidays
Fixed dates
1 Jan (New Year's Day*), 6 Jan (Epiphany*),1 May (Labour Day*), 25 Dec (Christmas Day*), 26 Dec (Boxing Day).
* Shops and offices often close half a day early on the day before an official holiday.
Variable dates
Maundy Thursday, Good Friday, Easter Monday, Ascension Day, Pingst (Whit Monday), Midsummer Holiday (fourth Sat in Jun)*, All Saints' Day (first Sat in Nov)*.
* Shops and offices often close half a day early on the day before an official holiday.

Working hours
Banking
Mon–Fri: 0930–1500 (larger branches open longer).

Business
Mon–Fri: 0830–1700 (often closed one hour earlier in summer).
Government
Mon–Fri 0900–1700.
Shops
Mon–Fri: 0900–1800 (closed 1400 or 1600 on Sat).

Telecommunications
Telephone/fax
Direct dialling throughout country and to most parts of the world. Shops displaying 'TELE' or 'TELEBUTIK' sign offer cheap international phone services (also telex and telefax).
There are some 5.7 million fixed telephone lines in Sweden. More people are switching to ISDN lines (of which there were 270,000), or exclusively using mobile phones.

Postal services
Good service. Stamps are available at most newspaper kiosks and tobacconists. The main post office in Stockholm opens daily from 0800–1800. Approximately 95 per cent of first class letters are delivered overnight. In 1993 Sweden became the first country in the world to completely liberalise the postal market. However, the state-owned postal service, *Posten* still accounts for 95 per cent of the total market for letters. The main competitor is City Mail, which operates mainly in the three largest cities.

Mobile phones
Pay-as-you-go phones are extremely popular, and make up 44 per cent of all subscriptions. Telia accounts for 51 per cent of all mobile phone subscriptions, followed by Tele2 with 33 per cent and Europolitan with 16 per cent.
SweFour was awarded Sweden's fourth GSM licence in May 2002.

Internet/e-mail
The largest ISP's on the Swedish market are Telia, Tele2, Telenordia and Spray/BIP, which together control 77 per cent of the market.

Electricity supply
220V AC

Social customs/useful tips
Swedes appreciate punctuality. A gift of flowers is usual when visiting a business partner's home for the first time. Guests should not start drinking before their hosts have proposed their health.
Think twice before refusing to go to a sauna with a host, since such an invitation is seen as a gesture of confidence and friendship by your host. Business meetings are sometimes conducted in saunas.

Security
Sweden has very low rates of violent crime, but some districts in the major cities should be avoided, particularly at night and particularly by women. Car burglaries and drugs-related crimes are increasing.

Getting there
Air
National airline: Scandinavian Airlines System (SAS).
International airport/s: Stockholm-Arlanda (ARN), 45km north of capital; Stockholm-Västerås (VST), 5km east of Västerås; Göteborg-Landvetter (GOT), 25km east of Göteborg; Malmö-Sturup (MMX), 30km east of Malmö.
Airport tax: None
Surface
Road: The Øresund road and rail link between Copenhagen (Denmark) and Malmö opened in 2000. There are road and rail links with Norway and Finland.
Rail: Statens Jarnvagar (SJ) (State Railways) is the major rail company in Sweden. It runs international highspeed trains between either Stockholm/Göteborg-Copenhagen (Denmark) – journey time five hours/3.30 hours; Stockholm-Oslo – journey time 4.45 hours. These services offer business class accommodation. Overnight trains with sleeping coaches are available between Berlin (Germany) and Malmö.
Water: There are several ferry links with northern Europe.

Getting about
National transport
Infrastructural investments totalling US$13 billion are being made in Sweden between 1993 and 2003, including national trunk roads, railway trunk lines, country roads and road improvements.
Air: There are daily flights connecting all main towns, some by SAS and others by small local airlines.
Road: The road network totals about 420,000km, two-thirds of which are private roads, primarily unpaved forestry roads. Most private roads are open to the public.
Buses: Efficient bus service, mainly controlled by the Statens Jarnvagar (State Railways). Services integrated with rail service.
Rail: There are good, reliable rail links between most major cities and towns. Seats on express services must be booked in advance.
Water: There is an extensive ferry network in and around Sweden.
City transport
Taxis: Available in all major towns. If you order a taxi in advance there is an extra charge. Some taxi companies offer flat rates for travel within urban areas, and others have special fares for women travelling alone at night.
Do not take the first available taxi from Stockholm-Arlanda or Stockholm-Västerås airports to the city. It is advisable to see the cab controller and check that you will only pay the officially approved fixed price for the journey to the city as some drivers will try to leave the meter running, which could result in paying for a roundtrip. Larger taxi companies display driver and car identification in the taxi's front window Gratuities for taxis are around 10 per cent.
Buses, trams & metro: All rail, bus and tram services have a unified ticketing system. Books of 20 travel coupons are available for purchase at Press Agency news-stands.
A city transfer service links Arland and Västerås airports with Stockholm city centre, with a journey time of about 40 minutes. The journey time from Västerås aiport is around 75 minutes.
Trams run in the southern parts of Bromma and Lidingö.
Metro: The *Tunnelbana* serves many districts of Stockholm, with 100 stations marked by a blue T sign. The extended rail service includes outlying suburbs.
Car hire
Available at all airports and stations in main towns. Speed limits: urban areas 50kph, normal roads 70 or 90kph, motorways 90 or 110kph. There is strict enforcement of drink-driving, speeding and other laws. Information and assistance can be sought from a number of organisations, including the Motormännens Riksförbund (Automobile Association) and the Kungl Automobil Klubben (KAK) (Royal Automobile Club).

BUSINESS DIRECTORY
The addresses listed below are a selection only. While World of Information makes every endeavour to check these addresses, we cannot guarantee that changes have not been made, especially to telephone numbers and area codes. We would welcome any corrections.

Telephone area codes
The international direct dialling code (IDD) for Sweden is +46, followed by area code and subscriber's number:

Gävle	26	Malmö	40
Göteborg	31	Norrköping	11
Helsingborg	42	Oxelösund	155
Jönköping	36	Stockholm	8
Karlskrona	455	Sundsvall	60
Karlstad	54	Umeå	90
Luleå	920	Uppsala	18

Useful telephone numbers
Police, fire and ambulance: 112

Chambers of Commerce
American Chamber of Commerce in Sweden, 3 Jakobs Torg, PO Box 16050, 10321 Stockholm (tel: 5061-2610; fax: 5061-2910; e-mail: amcham@chamber.se).

Sweden

British Swedish Chamber of Commerce, 3 Jakobs Torg, PO Box 16050, 10321 Stockholm (tel: 5061-2617; fax: 5061-2915; e-mail: bscc@chamber.se).

Central Sweden Chamber of Commerce, 1 Linnévägen, PO Box 296, 80104 Gävle (tel: 662-080; fax: 662-099; e-mail: chamber@mhk.cci.se).

East Sweden Chamber of Commerce, 3 Nya Rådstugugatan, 60224 Norrköping (tel: 1128-5030; fax: 1113-7719;e-mail: info@east.cci.se).

Jönköping Chamber of Commerce, 11 Elmiavägen, 55454 Jönköping (tel: 301-430; fax: 129-579; e-mail: jncci@jn.wtc.se).

Mid Sweden Chambe of Commerce, 26 Kyrkogatan, 85232 Sundsvall (tel: 171-880; fax: 618-640; e-mail: sdl@mid-chamber.cci.se).

Southern Sweden Chamber of Commerce and Industry, 2 Skeppsbron, 21120 Malmö (tel: 690-2400; fax: 690-2490; e-mail: info@handelskammaaren.com).

Stockholm Chamber of Commerce, 9 Västra Trädgårdsgatan, PO Box 16050, 10321 Stockholm (tel: 5551-0000; fax: 5663-1635; e-mail: info@chamber.se).

Swedish Chambers of Commerce, 9 Västra Trädgårdsgatan, PO Box 16050, 10321 Stockholm (tel: 5551-0036; fax: 5663-1637; e-mail: info@chamber.se).

Uppsala Chamber of Commerce, Uppsala Science Park, 75183 Uppsala (tel: 502-950; fax: 554-458; e-mail: info@uppsala.chamber.se).

Wermland Chamber of Commerce, 6 Södra Kyrkogatan, 65224 Karlstad (tel: 221-480; fax: 221-490; e-mail: info@wermland.cci.se).

Western Sweden Chamber of Commerce and Industry, 18 Mässens Gata, PO Box 5253, 40225 Göteborg (tel: 835-900; fax: 835-936; e-mail: info@handelskammaren.net).

Banking

Götabanken, Sveavägen 14, 10377 Stockholm (tel: 790-4000) and Hamngatan 16, 40509 Gothenburg (tel: 625-000).

Handelsbanken, 20540 Malmö (tel: 245-000; fax: 236-134).

Nordea, Västra Trädgårdsgatan 17, 5 tr, 10571 Stockholm (tel: 614-8558; fax: 614-7530).

Skandinaviska Enskilda Banken, Kungsträdgårdsgatan 8, 10640 Stockholm (tel: 763-5000; fax: 242-394).

Svenska Bankforeningen (Swedish bankers' association), Regeringsgatan 42, Box 7603, 10394 Stockholm (tel: 243-300).

Svenska Handelsbanken, Kungsträdgårdog 2, 10670 Stockholm (tel: 701-1000; fax: 611-5071).

Svenska Sparbanksforeningen (Swedish savings banks' association), Drottninggatan 29, Box 16426, 10327 Stockholm (tel: 572-000).

SwedBank, Brunkebergstorg 8, 10534 Stockholm (tel: 790-1000).

Central bank
Sveriges Riksbank, Brunkebergstorg 11, SE-103 37 Stockholm (tel: 787-0000; fax: 210-531; e-mail: registratorn@riksbank.se).

Travel information
SJ AB, (Swedish railways), SE-105 50 Stockholm (tel: 762-2000; fax: 411-1216: internet site: http://www.sj.se). Booking tickets online: www.swedenbooking.com and email: info@swedenbooking.com

Turistdelgationen (Swedish tourist authority), Vasagatan 44, Box 860, S-10137 Stockholm (tel: 545-15460; fax: 545-15469).

Svenska Turistföreningen (Swedish Tourist Federation) PO Box 25, 101 20 Stockholm, Sweden (tel: 463-2100; fax: 678-1968; internet www.stfturist.se).

National tourist organisation offices
Sveriges Rese-och Turistråd AB (Swedish travel and tourism council), Box 3030, S-10361 Stockholm (tel: 725-5500; fax: 725-5531; internet: www.visit-sweden.com).

Ministries
All ministries in Sweden have the same address: S-10333 Stockholm (tel: 405-1000; fax: 723-1171).

Invest in Sweden Agency, S-10338 Stockholm (tel: 676-8876/0; fax: 676-8888).

Landsorganisationen (LO) (Swedish trades union), 10553 Stockholm (tel: 796-2500).

Handelsdepartementet (Ministry of Trade), 10333 Stockholm (tel: 763-1000).

National Board of Forestry, S-55183 Jönköping (tel: 155-600; fax: 190-740).

National Board of Housing, Building and Planning, Box 534, S-37123 Karlskrona (tel: 53-000; fax: 53-100).

National Board of Trade, Box 1209, S-11182 Stockholm (tel: 791-0500; fax: 200-324).

National Electrical Safety Board, Box 1371, S-11193 Stockholm (tel: 453-9700; fax: 453-9710).

National Maritime Administration, S-60178 Norrköping (tel: 191-000; fax: 101-949).

National Post and Telecom Agency, Box 5398, S-10249 Stockholm (tel: 678-5500; fax: 678-5505).

Statistics Sweden, Karlavägen 100, S-11581 Stockholm (tel: 783-4000; fax: 661-5261).

Stockholm International Fairs, S-12580 Stockholm (tel: 749-4100; fax: 992-044).

Swedish Board of Agriculture, S-55182 Jönköping (tel: 155-000; fax: 190-546).

Swedish Board of Customs, Box 2267, S-10317 Stockholm (tel: 789-7300; fax: 208-012).

Swedish Civil Aviation Administration, S-60179 Norrköping (tel: 192-000; fax: 192-575).

Swedish Board for Investment and Technical Support, BITS, Box 7837, S-10398 Stockholm (tel: 678-5000; fax: 678-5050).

Swedish National Board of Fisheries, Lilla Bommen 6, S-40126 Göteborg (tel: 630-300; fax: 156-577).

Swedish National Board for Industrial and Technical Development (NUTEK), S-11786 Stockholm (tel: 681-9100; fax: 196-826).

Swedish National Road Administration, S-78187 Borlänge (tel: 75-000; fax: 84-640).

Swedish Nuclear Power Inspectorate, S-10658 Stockholm (tel: 698-8400; fax: 661-9086).

Swedish Patent Office, Box 5055, S-10242 Stockholm (tel: 782-2500; fax: 666-0286).

Swedish Standards Institution, Box 3295, S-10366 Stockholm (tel: 613-5200; fax: 411-7035).

Swedish Trade Council, PO Box 5513, S-11485 Stockholm (tel: 783-8500; fax: 662-9093).

Other useful addresses
British Embassy, Skarpögatan 6-8, Box 27819, 11593 Stockholm (tel: 671-9000; fax: 662-9989 (commercial section).

Federation of Commercial Agents of Sweden, Hantverkargatan 46, 11221 Stockholm (tel: 540-975).

Federation of Commercial Agents of Sweden, Western Division, Box 36059, 40013 Göteborg (tel: 192-045).

Federation of Swedish Industries, Storgatan 19, 11485 Stockholm (tel: 783-8000; fax: 662-3595).

Federation of Swedish Wholesalers and Importers, Grevgatan 34, Box 5512, 11485 Stockholm (tel: 635-280).

Handels Arbetsgivareorg (HAO) (commercial employers' confederation), Box 1720, 11187 Stockholm (tel: 762-7700).

Kungl Automobil Klubben (KAK) (Royal Automobile Club), S. Blasieholmshamnen 6, S-11148 Stockholm (tel: 678-0055; fax: 678- 0068).

Motormännens Riksförbund (Automobile Association), Sturegatan 32, PO Box 5855, 10248 Stockholm 5 (tel: 782-3800; fax: 666-0371).

SACO/SR (confederation of professional associations), Box 2206, 10315 Stockholm (tel: 225-200).

Sollentunamassan (organisers of trade fairs), Box 174, 19123 Sollentuna (tel: 925-900; fax: 929-774).

Stockholmsbörsen, SE-10578 Stockholm (tel: 405-6000; fax: 405-6001).

Stockholm Technical Fair (Stockholmsmassan AB), Alvsjo, 12580 Stockholm (tel: 749-4100; fax: 992-044).

Svenska Arbetsgivareforeningen (employers' confederation), Sodra Blasieholmshammen 4A, 10-330 Stockholm (tel: 762-6000; fax: 762-6290).

Sveriges Exportrad (Swedish Trade Council), PO Box 5513, 11485 Stockholm (tel: 783-8500; fax: 663-6706).

Swedish Embassy (USA), Suite 900, 1501 M Street, NW, Washington DC 20005 (tel: 202-467-2600; fax: 202-467-2699; e-mail: ambassaden.washington@foreign.ministry.se).

Swedish Institute, Box 7434, 10391 Stockholm (tel: 789-2000).

Swedish Trade Fair Foundation (Svenska Massan), Skanegatan 26, Box 5222, 40224 Göteborg (tel: 109-100; fax: 160-330).

TCO (central organisation of salaried employees), Box 5252, 10245 Stockholm (tel: 782-9100).

Tidningarnas Telegrambyrå (news agency), Kungsholmstorg 5, 10512 Stockholm (tel: 132-600; fax: 515-377).

Internet sites

Export directory: http://www.swedishtrade.se/sed

Government of Sweden: http://www.sweden.gov.se

Invest in Sweden Agency: http://www.isa.se/

Statistics Sweden: http://www.scb.se/eng/index.asp

Swedish Statistics network: http://www.svenskstatistik.net/eng/index.htm

Virtual Sweden: http://www.sweden.se

Visit Sweden: http://www.visit-sweden.com

Switzerland

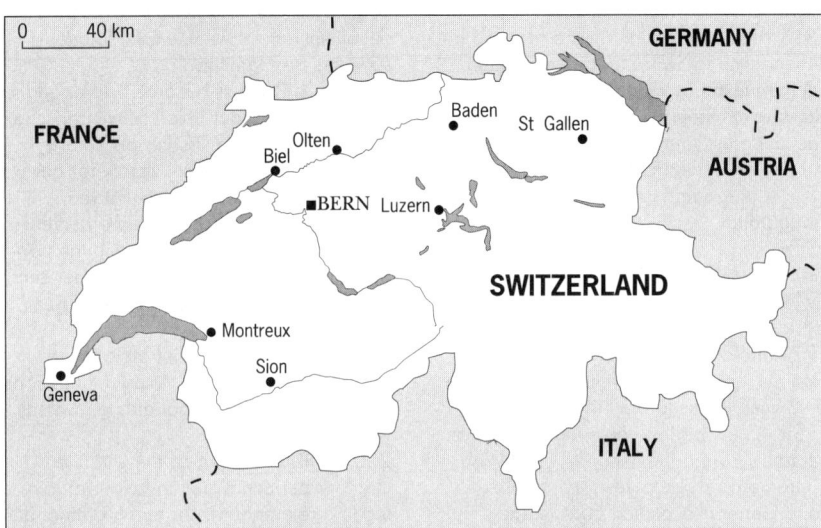

As is often the case in Switzerland, 2005 was a year punctuated by national referenda on controversial issues. Swiss voted in no less than three referenda, on a variety of topics. In two of these, voters backed closer ties with the EU – long a heated point of discussion among the country's politicians and voters.

A fragile recovery

The Swiss economy continued its fragile recovery in 2005, although growth slowed to around 1.25 per cent compared to 1.7 per cent in 2004. With 60 per cent of its exports going to EU member states, any Swiss recovery is ultimately dependent on a recovery in the notoriously sluggish euro-zone.

The referenda

In June and September, Switzerland took another step closer to EU mechanisms, although public opinion remains adamantly against EU membership. In June, 55 per cent of Swiss voters endorsed a government decision to sign up to the EU's Schengen and Dublin agreements. This meant that Switzerland joined a large passport-free zone within the EU and agreed to share information of criminal activity and asylum applications. At the same time, voters also endorsed a proposal to extend rights for same-sex couples. In September, 56 per cent of voters backed a proposal to extend employment rights to citizens from the EU's 10 newest members. The vote had been forced by the senior government coalition party, the far-right Schweizerische Volkspartei (SVP) (Swiss Peoples' Party). The SVP argued that people from the 'EU10' would take jobs away from Switzerland. At around 4 per cent, unemployment is unusually high in Switzerland. A third referendum, held in November, saw Swiss vote 56–44 to extend a 5-year ban on the growing of genetically-modified crops in the country.

Banks come clean(er)

In July, Swiss banks agreed to bring to an end, at least for EU citizens, one of the most famous (or infamous) features of the Swiss banking system – no taxes on accounts held by foreigners. The Swiss agreed that they would in future tax accounts held by EU citizens and repatriate the revenue to the account-holders home countries.

Another, less savoury, chapter in Swiss banking history came to an end in September, when Swiss banks refunded over US$290 million held in accounts linked to the late Nigerian military dictator and

KEY FACTS

Official name: Schweizerische Eidgenossenschaft (German); Confédération Suisse (French); Confederazione Svizzera (Italian) (Swiss Confederation)

Head of State: Federal President Moritz Leuenberger (for 2006) (presidency rotates annually among ministers)

Head of government: Federal President Moritz Leuenberger

Ruling party: Four-party coalition headed by the Schweizerische Volkspartei (SVP) (Swiss People's Party) (since Oct 1999; SVP re-elected 19 Oct 2003); the coalition also includes the Sozialdemokratische Partei der Schweiz (SPS) (Social Democrat Party of Switzerland), the Freisinnig-Demokratische Partei der Schweiz (FDP) (Freethinking-Democratic Party of Switzerland) and the Christlich-Demokratische Volkspartei der Schweiz (CVP) (Christian Democratic People's Party).

Area: 41,293 square km

Population: 7.43 million (2004)

Capital: Bern (German)/Berne (French)

Official language: German, French, Italian and Romansch

Currency: Swiss franc (Swf) = 100 centimes

Exchange rate: Swf1.29 per US$ (Oct 2005)

GDP per capita: US$49,305 (2004)

GDP real growth: 1.70% (2004)

Labour force: 4.26 million (2003)

Unemployment: 4.40% (OECD, 2004)

Inflation: 0.80% (2004)

Balance of trade: US$15.55 billion (2004)

Foreign debt: US$839.55 billion (2004)

Annual FDI: US$88.10 billion (cumulative, 1995–2004, OECD); US$4.50 billion (OECD, 2004)*

* estimated figure

president General Sani Abacha. Another US$170 million is due to be released in 2006. During his reign (1993–98), Abacha and his family are thought to have looted billions from the state, particularly from the oil sector. Nigeria had been seeking the return of stolen monies from Switzerland since 1999. Abacha's son, Abba Sani Abacha, was extradited to Switzerland in April 2005 to face fraud charges.

Oil-for-food scandal

In October, a UN report into the corruption of the UN-administered Iraqi oil-for-food programme implicated a number of Swiss-registered firms. The Swiss government was one of the quickest in the world to fine companies found to have paid kickbacks to then President Saddam Hussein's regime and four Swiss nationals face charges in Switzerland in relation to the international scandal.

Outlook

The OECD forecasts that the Swiss economy will pick up in 2006 and 2007, averaging around 1.75 per cent growth during this period.

As ever, expect more referenda!

Risk assessment

Politics	
Stable	
Economy	Improving
Regional stability	Stable

COUNTRY PROFILE

Historical profile

Switzerland was part of the Holy Roman Empire until 1499 when it gained independence. Switzerland's Roman connection remains strong. The Pope is still guarded by a 105-strong Swiss Guard, drawn largely from the Catholic cantons of central Switzerland.

1515 Switzerland declared its neutrality after nearly being defeated by the French and Venetians.

1648 The Peace of Westphalia concluded the Thirty Years' War in Europe and recognised Swiss independence.

1815 The Congress of Vienna restored independence to Switzerland after it had been annexed by France as part of the Napoleonic Empire during 1798–1803. The Congress laid down the principle of the perpetual neutrality of Switzerland.

1874 The modern constitution was inaugurated.

1914–18 Switzerland was neutral during the First World War.

1919–20 The Treaty of Versailles again recognised Switzerland's neutrality. In 1920, the country joined the League of Nations, but did not join its successor, the UN, when it was formed in 1945.

1939–45 Switzerland pursued a policy of neutrality during the Second World War, but refused refuge to Jews trying to escape German-occupied Europe and traded gold with the Nazis. Swiss banks also provided interest free credits to the Axis powers, which enabled Germany to finance its war effort.

1959 Switzerland was a founder member of the European Free Trade Agreement (EFTA).

1971 Women were granted the right to vote.

1986 The Swiss population rejected UN membership in a referendum.

1988 Switzerland's first female minister, Elisabeth Kopp, resigned from her post following accusations that she had violated official secrecy laws by tipping off her husband about an inquiry into his business affairs.

1992 In the referendum on Swiss membership of the European Economic Area (EEA), a free trade agreement between the EU and EFTA, opponents of the pact won with 50.3 per cent of the vote. Switzerland joined the World Bank and IMF.

1998 Swiss banks agreed to a US$1.25 billion settlement with Jewish Holocaust survivors and families.

1999 Ruth Dreifuss became Switzerland's first female president. The Schweizerische Volkspartei (SVP) (Swiss People's Party) won the largest electoral victory for any party in Switzerland for over 80 years.

2000 A referendum proposed a decrease in the proportion of foreigners in the population to 18 per cent from 19.3 per cent. The proposal was rejected by 63.7 per cent of voters.

2001 Seventy-six per cent of voters rejected a proposal to continue negotiations with the EU. The national airline, Swissair, went bankrupt.

2002 Switzerland joined the UN after fifty-four per cent voted in favour of joining in a referendum. Laurent Moutinot became president of the Council of State of Genève.

2003 In a May referendum, voters rejected proposals to renew a moratorium on building nuclear power plants and phasing out nuclear power. The SVP won the biggest share of the vote in the October parliamentary elections, making it the largest of the four governing parties in the coalition.

2004 On 1 January, Joseph Deiss became federal president for 2004.

2005 Samuel Schmid was elected president for 2005.

2006 Moritz Leuenberger was elected president for 2006.

Political structure

Constitution

Switzerland's constitution dates back to 1874 and has been much amended over the years. It unites more than 3,000 communes and 26 cantons and half-cantons in a confederation which devolves considerable powers to local bodies. Responsibility for determining and administering civil, penal and commercial law, foreign and trade issues, defence, communications, social insurance and energy is reserved for the federal government. The cantons and half-cantons, each of which have their own constitution and government, are responsible for the administration of federal law as well as their own cantonal laws. The communes have local autonomy over roads, local public utilities and the granting of citizenship.

KEY INDICATORS — Switzerland

	Unit	2000	2001	2002	2003	2004
Population	m	7.17	7.20	7.23	7.33	7.43
Gross domestic product (GDP)	US$bn	241.20	247.30	266.80	315.23	*359.46
GDP per capita	US$	33,472	34,100	36,900	43,000	49,305
GDP real growth	%	3.6	1.0	0.3	-0.4	1.7
Inflation	%	1.6	1.0	0.7	0.6	0.8
Unemployment	%	2.0	1.9	2.8	3.9	3.4
Exports (fob) (goods)	US$m	93,294.0	82,064.0	87,590.0	100,000.0	138,164.0
Imports (fob) (goods)	US$m	92,904.0	84,077.0	83,530.0	96,000.0	122,617.0
Balance of trade	US$m	389.0	1,600.0	4,800.0	4,000.0	15,547.0
Current account	US$m	32,542.0	26,100.0	30,800.0	36,400.0	42,870.0
Total reserves minus gold	US$m	32,272.0	32,006.0	40,155.0	47,652.0	55,497.0
Foreign exchange	US$m	30,854.0	30,141.0	38,164.0	45,560.0	53,634.0
Exchange rate	per US$	1.69	1.69	1.52	1.32	1.24

* estimated figure

Switzerland

Major issues are frequently decided by referendum. The constitution, or any of the country's federal laws, may only be amended by the passage of a proposal by national referendum. A national referendum may be called if a petition is signed by 50,000 people (on a legislative matter) or 100,000 people (on a constitutional matter). In some cantons, referenda may be necessary to approve all changes in cantonal legislation. The federal government, or its political opponents, may also initiate a referendum on any issue. Voter turnout averages 40–50 per cent. Since the constitution's inception, voters have been asked to approve over 148 amendments.

Form of state
Federal parliamentary democratic republic

The executive
The chief executive organ in the country is the Federal Council, whose seven members each hold a ministerial portfolio, and whose president and vice president are appointed each calendar year on a rotating basis from among its members.

National legislature
The bicameral Federal Assembly is made up of the National Council, whose 200 members are directly elected for four years by proportional representation, and the Council of States, whose 46 members are elected by the cantons according to the constitution. The Federal Assembly supervises the army, the civil service and the administration of the law as well as electing the Federal Supreme Court, the Federal Tribunal of Insurance and the Federal Council. Members of the Federal Council are elected, usually for a four-year term, from among members of the Federal Assembly.

Legal system
Customary law marginally influences the civil law system. Individual cantons elect and maintain their own magistracy. Each canton has justices of the peace, District Courts, Labour Courts, Courts for Tenancy, an Appeal Court, a Cassation Court and, for more important cases under penal law, a Jury Court. Apart from military courts, there are just two federal judicial authorities: the Federal Supreme Court and the Federal Tribunal of Insurance.

Last elections
16 Sep 2004 (referendum); 19 October 2003 (parliamentary)
Results: Referendum: Moves to relax the country's strict naturalisation laws were rejected. The result was seen as a victory for the right-wing.
Parliamentary: the Schweizerische Volkspartei (SVP) (Swiss People's Party) increased its vote from 22.6 per cent of the overall vote in 1999 to 27.7 per cent, winning 55 seats in the 200-member House of Representatives and an extra seat in the cabinet; the Sozialdemokratische Partei der Schweiz (SPS) (Social Democrat Party of Switzerland) 24.2 per cent (52 seats), the Freisinnig-Demokratische Partei der Schweiz (FDP) (Freethinking-Democratic Party of Switzerland) 16 per cent (36 seats), the Christlich-Demokratische Volkspartei der Schweiz (CVP) (Christian Democratic People's Party) 12.9 per cent (28 seats) and the Grüne Partei der Schweiz (GPS) (Green Party of Switzerland) 7.7 per cent (13 seats); turnout was 42.5 per cent.

Next elections
2007 (parliamentary)

Political parties
Ruling party
Four-party coalition headed by the Schweizerische Volkspartei (SVP) (Swiss People's Party) (since Oct 1999; SVP re-elected 19 Oct 2003); the coalition also includes the Sozialdemokratische Partei der Schweiz (SPS) (Social Democrat Party of Switzerland), the Freisinnig-Demokratische Partei der Schweiz (FDP) (Freethinking-Democratic Party of Switzerland) and the Christlich-Demokratische Volkspartei der Schweiz (CVP) (Christian Democratic People's Party).

Main opposition party
Grüne Partei der Schweiz (GPS) (Green Party of Switzerland)

Population
7.43 million (2004)

Ethnic make-up
Switzerland is dominated by Germans (65 per cent), French (18 per cent) and Italians (10 per cent). Foreigners comprise 19.7 per cent of the population. In a referendum held in September 2000, the Swiss voted against limiting the proportion of foreigners to 18 per cent.

Religions
Roman Catholic (46 per cent), Protestant (40 per cent).

Education
With no central ministry of education, each of the 26 Swiss cantons (semi-autonomous regions) have overall and exclusive responsibility for education. Private schools exist at the level of vocational secondary school but do not attract federate funding or canton control.
Most cantons set the number of compulsory years for primary schooling at six, some others set it at four or five; for lower secondary school most set the minimum years at three, and some at five or four; whichever cycle is used, overall, compulsory schooling lasts for nine years.
Teaching is given in the language of the canton.
At aged 16, students can go into upper level secondary schools (either private or state-run), which offer general or vocational programmes and last for between three and four years. General secondary education (*Matura*), offers academic study, preparing a student for university. Technical high schools provide a range of vocational and training programmes. Typically 85 per cent of students complete upper secondary school.
Switzerland has 12 universities and higher education colleges. There are also a number of science universities and more than 20 polytechnics (*Fachhochschulen*).
In the 1990s, the cantons began a reform of the educational system to ensure that it provided the best means of maintaining a high degree of educated citizens.
Literacy rate: 99 per cent, adult rate (2003)
Compulsory years: Six to 15.
Enrolment rate: 97 per cent gross primary enrolment of relevant age group (including repeaters); 100 per cent gross secondary enrolment (World Bank).
Pupils per teacher: 19 in primary schools.

Health
Healthcare services are entirely private and individuals are expected and, in some areas, obliged, to cover themselves with private health insurance policies. Each canton has responsibility for the provision of healthcare. The type of hospital a patient may be admitted to will depend on the level of health insurance the person holds.
Total expenditure on healthcare is 11–12 per cent of GDP; of which government spending is 57–58 per cent and private expenditure is 41–42 per cent of the total, including about 25 per cent on pre-paid healthcare plans.
HIV prevalence: 0.4 per cent aged 15–49 in 2003 (World Bank)
Life expectancy: 80.5 years (World Bank)
Fertility rate/Maternal mortality rate: 1.4 births per woman (2003); maternal mortality five per 100,000 live births (World Bank).
Birth rate/Death rate: 9.6 births and 8.8 deaths per 1,000 people (2003)
Infant mortality rate: 4.3 per 1,000 live births (World Bank)
Head of population per physician/bed: 3.1 physicians and 3.8 hospital beds available per 1,000 people.

Welfare
Switzerland's comprehensive social welfare system is funded by the state, by employer contributions and by employee national insurance contributions. It is a lagal requirement that all citizens residing for three months or more in Switzerland

must take out minimum healthcare insurance.

Unemployment insurance is compulsory and many employees are also insured against accidents at work. Old age, disability and widow(er)s' pensions are paid out of compulsory contributions. The precise arrangements may differ in each canton.

Over 20 per cent of the federal budget is spent on social welfare. Some social security schemes have their own separate budgets.

Main cities

Bern/Berne (capital, estimated population 122,700 in 2003), Zürich (348,100), Geneva (178,900), Basle (162,800), Lausanne (117,400).

Languages spoken

The national languages are German in central and eastern areas (64 per cent), French in the west (19 per cent) and Italian in the south (8 per cent).

Raeto-Romansch is spoken in the south-east (1 per cent). English is widely spoken.

There are two forms of German spoken. High German, or Hochdeutsch is only spoken in formal situations or used for written work; Swiss-German, or Schwyzertütsch is spoken by all in daily life in German-speaking Switzerland, using different dialects and is incomprehensible to all who speak High German.

Official language/s
German, French, Italian and Romansch

Media

Press
There is a decentralised press owing to regional variations in language and culture, producing a large number of publications with relatively small circulations. There are more than 600 newspapers in total and nearly 2,000 magazines.

Dailies: About 120 regional newspapers (75 per cent printed in German, 20 per cent in French). The most popular are: *Blick* and *Tages Anzeiger*, both published in Zürich. Other dailies include *Berner Zeitung* and *Basler Zeitung*.

Weeklies: Weeklies include *Sonntags Blick*, *Le Matin Dimanche* and *Sonntags Zeitung*. There are also *Finanz und Wirtschaft* (twice weekly) and *Schweizer Handelszeitung* (weekly).

Business: The daily business paper *Neue Zürcher Zeitung* (NZZ) is published in Zürich and is of international repute. Others include *Finanz und Wirtschaft* (twice weekly) and *Schweizer Handelszeitung* (weekly). Two major monthly business magazines are *Bilanz* and *Politik und Wirtschaft*.

Periodicals: Periodicals include *Cigar*, *A-Bulletin*, *Schweizer Demokrat*, *Der Schweizerische Beobachter*, *Nebelspalter*, *Pro* and *Swiss News*.

Broadcasting
Controlled by Swiss Broadcasting Corporation (SBC), under licence from the Federal government. Actual transmission is controlled by Swiss postal and telecommunications service.

Radio: There are three SBC programmes broadcast in French and German, two in Italian and also some broadcasts in Raeto-Romansch as well as some private stations. Swiss Radio International broadcasts in nine languages.

Television: Each linguistic region has its own TV channel and receives broadcasts from other regions. Satellite, cable and teletext are available.

Advertising
Advertising is expensive due to language variations. TV advertising is restricted to specific times and there is no advertising on Swiss state radio. Newspapers, cinemas and direct mail are widely used, but poster advertising is confined to selected sites. Information can be obtained from the Union Suisse d'Agences-Conseils en Publicité in Zürich. The main advertising media are newspapers and magazines.

Economy

Switzerland is one of the wealthiest countries in the world, with a well developed manufacturing sector as well as a highly skilled labour force, an important tourist industry and banking and insurance sectors.

The services sector dominates the economy with 64 per cent of GDP, followed by industry with 34 per cent and agriculture with 2 per cent. Within the services sector, tourism accounts for 6.3 per cent. Despite not being a member of the European Union (EU), the Swiss economy remains heavily dependent on the economic fortunes of the EU, and the euro. Swiss exports are dominated by chemicals (34.9 per cent in 2004) and machinery and electronic goods (23.6 per cent). The EU takes over 65 per cent of Swiss exports (20 per cent to Germany alone) and supplies 76 per cent of imports (over one-third from Germany).

After the wilderness years of the 1990s, the Swiss economy reached a 10-year high in 2000 with a 3 per cent rise in GDP, the result of robust domestic demand coupled with a strong growth in exports. GDP growth slowed from 1.3 per cent in 2001 to 0.1 per cent in 2002 and slowed even further to -0.5 per cent in 2003. This was due to capacity constraints, particularly a labour shortage, coupled with falls in external demand due to the global slowdown and a restrictive fiscal policy. It crept back up to 1.8 per cent in 2004. It is forecast to be 1.0 per cent in 2005. Inflation is traditionally low (0.9 per cent in 2004), although the sharp rise in the price of oil in 2005 is likely to increase it in 2005.

Switzerland's GNP is considerably higher than its GDP. The difference is net property income from abroad (interest, profit and rent), which is large because of the very high level of net external assets. This is the result of years of large current account surpluses.

The unemployment rate was 3.4 per cent in 2004, compared to the OECD's 4.2 per cent for 2003. In June 2005 a referendum on joining the 13 EU countries in the Schengen Agreement on passport-free travel was passed. However, a further referendum in September 2005 on extending a bilateral agreement with the EU, on the free movement of workers, to the ten new EU members may not be so fortunate. This could lead to a crisis in EU-Swiss relations.

Swiss banking is well known for its 'numbered accounts' and secrecy laws. But new, tougher laws on money laundering have led to a drop in foreign money as Switzerland becomes a less attractive destination for unaccounted for monies. In June 2004, Switzerland, along with Andorra, Monaco, San Marino and Liechtenstein agreed, to put in place equivalent measures to those to be applied by the EU's member states as regards the taxation of income from savings. These measures, which came into effect in July 2005, will make Swiss banks even less attractive.
Test

External trade

A trade agreement with the EU was signed in 1998. Germany is by far Switzerland's largest trading partner.

Imports
Main imports are machinery, chemicals, vehicles, metals, agricultural produce and textiles.

Main sources: Germany (29 per cent total, 2004), Italy (11.8 per cent), France (11.1 per cent), US (7.6 per cent), Austria (4.5 per cent), UK (4.5 per cent), The Netherlands (4.3 per cent)

Exports
Principal exports include non- and electrical machinery, chemicals, pharmaceuticals, clocks and watches, textiles and clothing, metals, jewellery and foodstuffs.

Main destinations: Germany (20 per cent total, 2004), France (9.1 per cent), US (9.1 per cent), Italy (8.8 per cent), UK (4.9 per cent)

Agriculture

Farming
The agricultural sector contributes around 2.9 per cent to GDP and employs four per

cent of the workforce, with activity concentrated on dairy farming. Agriculture is a state subsidised sector – approximately 75 per cent of a farmer's income is financed by subsidies. There are around 80,000 peasant farms of less than 20 hectares (ha) remaining, and of these barely half provide full-time occupations for their owners. Holdings of over 20ha number around 13,000. The average farm is less than 16ha in size. Pasture land totals some 8,500 square km, equivalent to a fifth of the total land area. A further 11,700 square km is given over to arable land, orchards and vineyards. Farming is highly mechanised, with one of the highest tractor densities in the world. Farmers have use of large and expensive equipment through machinery syndicates. Government fixing of minimum prices means that meat, sugar, vegetables and fruit are two or three times more expensive than in neighbouring countries, a situation which international agencies such as the World Trade Organisation are anxious to see rectified. There are protective customs barriers and other duties on imported goods as well as actual import restrictions, so that the domestic market remains highly protected, a significant factor in Switzerland's opposition to EU membership.

Crop production in 2004 included: 1.0 million tonnes (t) cereals in total, 456,000t wheat, 220,000t maize, 492,000t potatoes, 230,000t barley, 35,000t oats, 23,500t pulses, 145,0300t grapes, 26,000t tomatoes, 29,070t oilcrops, 1.3 million t sugar beets, 230,000t apples, 502,930t fruit in total, 279,330t vegetables in total.

Livestock production in 2004 included: 441,911t meat in total, 140,000t beef, 234,000t pig-meat, 6,700t lamb, 57,000t poultry, 36,000t eggs, 3.9 million t milk, 4,500t honey.

Fishing
Switzerland's fish industry, based on 123,000 hectares of lakes, is insignificant and declining. Untreated industrial and agricultural effluents are polluting fisheries, while canalisation, underground channelling of watercourses and the absence of suitable spawning grounds have contributed to the reduction of fish habitats.

There are more than 50 fish species found in Swiss waters, but only a few have been used by the fishing industry for food. Catches consist for the most part of lake herring and perch together with various other types of whitefish. Catches of whitefish and perch have steadily declined.

Only around 5 per cent of the fish and fish products consumed within the country are obtained from domestic sources.

Forestry
Forest and other wooded land accounts for nearly a third of the land area, with forest cover estimated at 1.19 million hectares. 90 per cent of the forest area is available for wood supply. 4.5 million cubic metres of wood is produced annually There has been a steady rise in growing stock with afforestation accounting for an annual average increase of 4,000ha of forest covers between 1990 and 2000. More than two-thirds of the forest area is under public ownership.

Domestic consumption is 6.4 million cubic metres. Sensitivity about preserving the scenic environment is high. In light of acid rain damage, particularly in the north-west, as well as increased competition in the sector, the prospects for further growth in production appear limited.

The forest industry has to cope with high labour costs. Although paper production is sufficient to meet domestic demands, the industry is partly dependent on pulp imports. Per capita consumption of forest products remains above the European average.

Exports of forest material in 2004 amounted to US$2.0 billion, while imports amounted to US$2.2 billion. Production in 2004 included 4,713,000 cubic metres (cum) roundwood, 3,713,000cum industrial roundwood, 1,505,000cum sawnwood, 3,200,000cum sawlogs and veneers, 513,000cum pulpwood, 897,000cum wood-based panels, 1,000,000cum woodfuel.

Industry and manufacturing
The industrial sector contributes approximately 30 per cent to GDP and employs about 33 per cent of the labour force. The well-developed export-oriented manufacturing sector is centred on the production of finished goods. Traditional industries include machines, tools, pharmaceuticals, textiles, watchmaking, food processing, chemicals and engineering. Among well-known Swiss companies are Nestlé and Novartis. There is an increasing emphasis on specialisation and the development of high technology products. Swiss companies spend 2.9 per cent of GDP on research and development, one of the highest figures in the world.

Switzerland is home to the world's biggest clock and watch industry, which produces about 8 per cent of annual export revenues.

Tourism
Tourism has traditionally been one of Switzerland's most reliable sources of foreign exchange, especially during the winter when the country becomes a popular destination for skiers. Visitor numbers declined in the wake of the 11 September 2001 terrorist attacks in the US and subsequently by the Iraq war and the Sars outbreak in 2003, which discouraged the important US and Japanese markets, but have improved since 2004. Germany continues to be the main source of visitors, followed by the US and the UK. The sector is expected to contribute 6.2 per cent to GDP in 2005.

China has designated Switzerland as an approved destination for its holidaying citizens. Chinese visitors could swell Switzerland's arrival numbers by millions.

Mining
Switzerland is not richly endowed with mineral deposits. Only rock salt and building materials are mined or quarried in significant quantities.

Hydrocarbons
Switzerland has no fossil energy resources apart from a small deposit of natural gas at Finsterwald and is dependent on imports to meet its energy requirements. Around 1.3 per cent of total energy consumption is of fossil fuels. Oil, gas and coal are all imported. Switzerland consumes around 260,000 barrels per day (bpd) of crude and refined oil. Around three billion cubic metres of natural gas are imported. Coal consumption, which is around 100,000 tonnes of oil equivalent, has declined in recent years, largely for environmental resaons.

Energy
Hydroelectricity is Switzerland'sonly natural energy resource and supplies 12 per cent of total energy requirements. Nuclear energy supplies about 38 per cent. Switzerland is one of Europe's largest per capita users of nuclear fuel and with public support (two referenda in 2003 sanctioned its use) does not intend to decrease its reliance on this form of energy production in the near future.

Switzerland is a net exporter of electricity but a net importer of energy, mainly in the form of petroleum and related products. Dependence on imported oil and gas is declining.

Financial markets
Stock exchange
The SWX Swiss Exchange took steps to internationalise in the late-1990s, with the opening of an overseas office in London in 1999, resulting in 27 per cent of the turnover in Swiss shares being transacted outside the country. In 2000, SWX launched the Virt-X, the first pan-European blue chip bourse, in conjunction with the UK's Tradepoint Financial Services (TFS). The exchange uses the Swiss market's trading platform, trading companies from Europe's leading stock market indices.

Nations of the World: A Political, Economic and Business Handbook

Banking and insurance
Switzerland is the world's biggest offshore private banking centre, but banking secrecy laws and a favourable taxation regime are coming under increasing scrutiny in the light of the dormant accounts scandal and the possibility of EU membership. Switzerland is a signatory of a new EU tax agreement, introduced in July 2005 in a number of non-EU countries. Switzerland will impose a withholding tax, up to 35 per cent, to be passed to the tax department of an EU citizen's country, but retaining the anonymity of the saver, instead of informing the relevant EU country about the amount of money in savings accounts and allowing tax to be levied from the home country.

Switzerland has also agreed to supply information on tax fraud, for criminal or civil trials, and notify EU member states about additional malpractices.

Were Switzerland to join the EU its competitive advantage in financial services would almost certainly be reduced. Banking still remains the largest sector in the canton of Zürich, but the success of these operations lies increasingly with their non-Swiss business.

New banking rules were introduced in January 2003 requiring proof of identity, nationality and date of birth for the ultimate owners of bank accounts opened by financial intermediaries.

Central bank
Swiss National Bank (SNB)

Time
GMT plus one hour (GMT plus two hours from last Sun in Mar to Sat before last Sun in Oct)

Geography
Switzerland is a landlocked country bordered by Germany to the north, Austria to the east, Italy to the south and France to the west.

Located high in the Alpine region of western Europe, most of the country's land area is too mountainous to permit any great density of population, which means that most of the country's population reside in the low-lying urban areas. About half of the country's total land area is covered by rock, water or glaciers, or is forested, and a further quarter is either under grass or cultivation.

Climate
Geographic factors mean, inevitably, that Switzerland experiences particularly marked variations in weather. While winters are generally severe, especially at higher altitudes, summers tend to be warmer than in the countries to the north. Low-lying areas are often wet. Zürich is prone to a heavy atmosphere in certain wind conditions. Temperatures range from about -1 degrees Celsius (C) to 18 degrees C.

Dress codes
Business attire is formal. Warm clothing is essential from September to May, especially in the higher altitudes.

Entry requirements
Passports
Passports should be valid for six months beyond intended stay.
Visa
Visas are required by all. However some exceptions exist and length of stays vary, visit www.swissemb.org/ for detailed list. Business visa for those that need one: i.e. citizens of non visa-free states should have a letter of invitation from a Swiss company and a letter from the visitor's company stating reason for visit and guarantee that all expenses will be covered, to accompany the application.

A visa is not required by EU nationals.
Currency advice/regulations
There are no restrictions on Swiss and other currencies. Importation of coins of gold and platinum are liable to turnover-tax.
Customs
Personal effects and gifts up to value of Swf100 are duty-free.

Health (for visitors)
Mandatory precautions
Vaccination certificates are not usually required.
Advisable precautions
Medical insurance is advisable as treatment is expensive.

Hotels
Hotels keep a high standard throughout the country, and are classified by the Swiss Hotel Association from one- to five-star. A 15 per cent service is included on bill. Reservations should be made well in advance during the (winter) holiday season.

Credit cards
All major credit cards are accepted.

Public holidays
Fixed dates
1 Jan (New Year's Day), 2 Jan (Jan Berchtold's Day), 1 Aug (National Day), 25 Dec (Christmas Day), 26 Dec (St Stephen's Day).
Variable dates
Good Friday, Easter Monday, Ascension Day, Whit Monday.

Working hours
Banking
Regional variations but generally Mon–Fri: 0830–1630. Money exchange at any airport and larger railway stations daily until 2200.
Business
Mon–Fri: 0800–1200, 1330–1700.
Government
Mon–Fri: 0730–1145, 1330–1800, or 0800–1230, 1315–1730.
Shops
Mon–Fri: 0800–1215, 1330–1830 (in larger cities also during lunch hours but Mon morning often closed); Sat: 0830–1600.

Electricity supply
220V AC, 50Hz

Social customs/useful tips
Appointments should always be made before making visits. If the appointment cannot be kept, this should be communicated.

Hand-shaking is frequent. When invited to dinner in a private house, flowers or chocolates for the hosts are the usual gifts. When drinks are served, it is customary to wait until all the party has been attended to, and then to raise the glass with a salute to each.

The Swiss are proud of their often colourful cultural traditions. Traditional costume is still worn daily in a few areas of the country, although in most areas, it is restricted to celebrations and tourist-related events.

Security
There are no special problems with security in Switzerland; normal precautions apply, especially in the cities.

Getting there
Air
There are regular flights by all major international airlines.
National airline: Swiss Air Lines Crossair, the former regional airline, was transformed into the new national carrier, Swiss Air Lines, following the collapse of Swissair in October 2001. The company started operations on 31 March 2002, adopting 'Swiss' as a brand mark on all of its aircraft.
International airport/s: Basle-Mulhouse Euroairport (BSL), 12km from city; Berne Belp (BRN), 9km from city; Geneva International (GVA), 16km north of city; Zürich (ZRH), 13km north of city. Zürich and Geneva airports are directly linked to the national rail system.
Airport tax: There is no airport departure tax.
Surface
Good road and rail links with all surrounding countries. It is advisable to book for rail travel beforehand.
Road: Swiss roads are good, however the terrain makes them awkward to drive, particularly in winter. Major roads and tunnels link Switzerland to all surrounding countries.
Water: There is limited access by water from France, Germany and Italy.

Switzerland

Getting about

National transport

Air: There are several daily flights linking Zürich, Geneva, Basle, Lugano and Berne.

Road: There is a road network of about 100,000km, including 4,318km of motorways. Roads are of good quality but traffic tends to be slow due to terrain and volume of traffic.

Rail: There are over 5,000km of track, practically all electrified. About 58 per cent is operated by Schweizerische Bundesbahnen (SBB) (Swiss Federal Railways) and the rest by about 120 small private companies. Rail journeys between major towns rarely exceed two or three hours.

Water: All the larger lakes are serviced by steamers operated by Swiss Federal Railways (SBB).

City transport

A train from Zürich airport to the city centre takes about 12 minutes, while a taxi can take more than twice as long.

All local city transport is linked together on the same ticketing system. Tickets should be purchased before boarding from ticket dispensers by the stops.

Taxis: Widely available but they do not ply for hire. Zürich taxis have a higher tariff than elsewhere. A 15 per cent service charge is included; no tip required.

Buses, trams & metro: Good services in major towns. Tickets should be bought in advance from vending machines. Multi-journey tickets also available. Flat fare up to five stops.

Helicopter: 'Swift Copters' run a service from Geneva International Airport to the city centre.

Car hire

Self-drive and chauffeur-driven cars available in all main towns. A valid national or international driving licence is required, and insurance is compulsory. Speed limits are 50kph in built-up areas, 80kph on normal roads and 120kph on motorways. Further information can be obtained from the Touring Club Suisse (TCS) or the Automobil Club der Schweiz/Automobile Club Suisse (ACS).

BUSINESS DIRECTORY

The addresses listed below are a selection only. While World of Information makes every endeavour to check these addresses, we cannot guarantee that changes have not been made, especially to telephone numbers and area codes. We would welcome any corrections.

Telephone area codes

The international direct dialling (IDD) code for Switzerland is +41, followed by area code and subscriber's number:

Basel	61	Lucerne	41
Bern	31	Neuchâtel	32
Fribourg	26	St Gallen	71
Genèva	22	Winterthur	52
Lausanne	21	Zürich	1

Useful telephone numbers

Police: 117
Fire brigade: 118
Ambulance: 144
Motor breakdown service: 140
Swiss Air Rescue: 47-47-47
Emergency service of Touring Club of Switzerland: 35-80-00

Chambers of Commerce

American Swiss Chamber of Commerce, 41 Talacker, 8001 Zurich (tel: 211-2454; fax: 211-9572; e-mail: info@amcham.ch).

Basel Chamber of Commerce, 67 Aeschenvorstadt, 4010 Basel (tel: 270-6060; fax: 270-6005; e-mail: hkbb@hkbb.ch).

Bern Chamber of Commerce and Industry, 1 Gutenbergstrasse, PO Box 5464, 3001 Bern (tel: 388-8787; fax: 382-8788; e-mail: info@bern-cci.ch).

British-Swiss Chamber of Commerce, 155 Freiestrasse, 8032 Zürich (tel: 422-3131; fax: 422-3244; e-mail: bscc@bscc.co.uk).

Fribourg Chamber of Commerce, Industry and Services, 37 Route du Jura, 1706 Fribourg (tel: 347-1220; fax: 347-1239; e-mail: cfcis@cci.ch).

Geneva Chamber of Commerce and Industry, 4 Boulevard du Théâtre, PO Box 5039, 1211 Genève 11 (tel: 819-9111; fax: 819-9100; e-mail: ccig@cci.ch).

St Gallen-Appenzell Chamber of Commerce and Industry, 16 Gallusstrasse, 9001 St Gallen (tel: 224-1010; fax: 224-1060; e-mail: sekretariat@ihk.ch).

Swiss Business Federation, 47 Hegibachstrasse, 8032 Zürich (tel: 421-3535; fax: 421-3434; e-mail: info@economiesuisse.ch).

Swiss Chambers of Commerce and Industry, 47 Avenue d'Ouchy, PO Box 315, 1001 Lausanne (tel: 613-3535; fax: 613-3505 e-mail: info@cci.ch).

Vaud Chamber of Commerce and Industry, 47 Avenue d'Ouchy, 1001 Lausanne (tel: 613-3535; fax: 613-3505; e-mail: cvci@cvci.ch).

Winterthur Chamber of Commerce, 15 Neumarkt, 8401 Winterthur (tel: 213-0763; fax: 213-0729; e-mail: info@haw.ch).

Zürich Chamber of Commerce, 5 BleicherwegPO Box 3058, 8022 Zürich (tel: 217-4050; fax: 217-4051; e-mail: direktion@zurichcci.ch).

Banking

Banque Cantonale de Genève, Quai de l'Ile 17, Case postale, 1211 Genève 2 (tel: 317-2727; fax: 793-5960).

Banca della Svizzera Italiana, 2 Via Magatti, 6901 Lugano (tel: 587-111).

Bank Leu, Bahnhofstrasse 32, CH-8001 Zürich (tel: 219-1111).

Crédit Suisse, Paradeplatz 8, CH-8021 Zürich (tel: 215-1111).

Crédit Suisse, Pl Bel-Air 2, Case postale, 1211 Genève 70 (tel: 391-2111; fax: 391-2591).

Sociéte de Banque Suisse, rue de la Confédération 2, Case postale, 1211 Genève 2 (tel: 375-7575; fax: 376-5024).

Swiss Bank Corporation, Aeschenvorstadt 1/Gartenstrasse 9, Basel (tel: 202-020).

Swiss Bankers' Association, Aeschenplatz 4, Postfach 4182, CH-4002 Basel (tel: 235-888).

Swiss Volksbank, Weltpoststrasse 5, 3015 Bern (tel: 328-111).

Union de Banques Suisses, Rue Rhone 8, Case postale, 1211 Genève 2 (tel: 388-1111; fax: 388-9652).

Union Bank of Switzerland, Bahnhofstrasse 45, CH-8000 Zürich (tel: 234-1111).

United European Bank, 11 Quai des Bergues, CP 2280, 1211 Genève (tel: 907-2111; fax: 732-3002).

Zürcher Kantonalbank, Bahnhofstrasse, PO Box 4039, 8022 Zürich (fax: 211-1525).

Central bank

Schweizerische Nationalbank, 15 Börsenstrasse, 8022 Zürich (tel: 631-3111; fax: 631-3911; e-mail: snb@snb.ch).

Travel information

Automobil Club der Schweiz/Automobile Club Suisse (ACS), Case postale 1409, Rue de la Fontenette 21, 1227 Carouge (tel: 342-2233; fax: 301-3711).

Touring Club Suisse (TCS), Bureau principal, Rue Pierre-Fatio 9, 1211 Genève 3 (tel: 737-1212; fax: 786-0992).

National tourist organisation offices

Swiss National Tourist Office, Tödistrasse 7, 8027 Zürich (tel: 288-1111; fax: 288-1205; email: info@switzerland.com; internet: www.myswitzerland.com).

Ministries

Bundesamt für Statistik (BFS) (central statistics office), Schwarzftorstrasse 96, CH-3003 Bern (tel: 323-6011; fax: 323-6061).

Federal Department of Finance, Bundesgasse 3, 3003 Bern (tel: 66-111).

Federal Department of Public Economy, Bundeshaus-Ost, 3003 Bern (tel: 612-111).

Federal Office for Industry, Crafts and Labour, Bundesgasse 8, CH-3003 Bern (tel: 612-944).

Swiss Federal Tax Administration, Eidgenössische Steuerverwaltung, Eigerstrasse 65, CH-3003 Bern (tel: 617-112).

Other useful addresses
British Embassy, Thunstrasse 50, CH-3005 Berne 15 (tel: 352-5021/6; fax: 352-0583).

Embassy of the United States of America, Jubilumstrasse 93, CH-3005 Berne (tel: 357-7011; fax: 357-7344).

Fédération Suisse des Agences de Voyages, Postfach, Hardstrasse 316, CH-8027 Zürich (tel: 426-442).

Swiss Embassy (USA), 2900 Cathedral Avenue, NW, Washington DC 20008 (tel: 202-745-7900; fax: 202-387-2564; e-mail: vertretung@was.rep.admin.ch).

Swiss Federation of Commerce and Industry, Börsenstrasse 26, CH-8022 Zürich (tel: 221-2707).

Swiss Lawyers' Federation, Lavaterstrasse 83, CH-8027 Zürich (tel: 202-5650).

Swiss News Agency, Langgasstrasse 7, CH-3012 Bern (tel: 244-461).

SWX Swiss Exchange, Selnaustrasse 30, Postfach, CH-8021 Zürich (tel: 229-2111).

Union Suisse d'Agences-Conseils en Publicité (advertising), Kurfürstenstr 80, CH-8002 Zürich (tel: 202-6540).

Internet sites
Details of government departments: http://www.admin.ch/ch/e/index.html

Index of Swiss business and tourism: http://www.swissdir.ch

Swiss Federal Statistical office: http://www.admin.ch/bfs/eindex.htm

Yellow pages Switzerland: http://www.pages-jaunes.ch/index.html

Syria

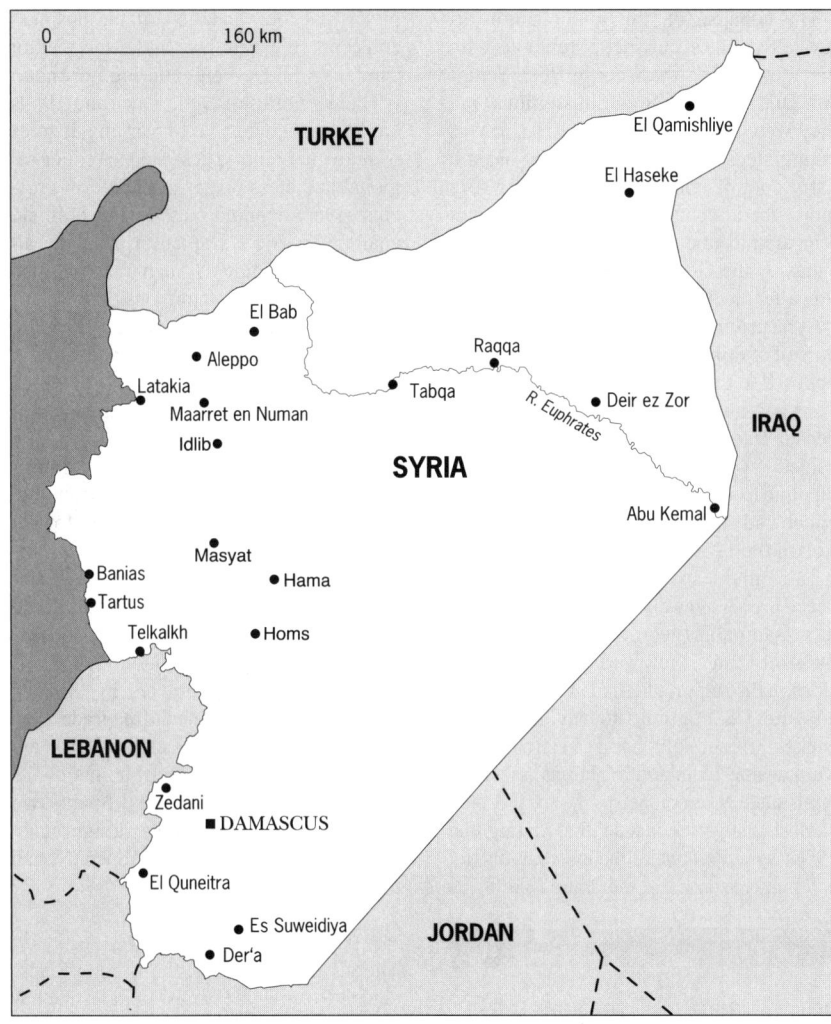

KEY FACTS

Official name: Jumhuriya al Arabya as Suriya (Syrian Arab Republic)

Head of State: President Bashar al Assad (elected Jul 2000)

Head of government: Prime Minister Mohammed Naji al Otari (appointed 10 Sep 2003)

Ruling party: National Progressive Front (NPF) formed by: Hizb al Ba'ath al Arabi al Ishtiraki (Ba'ath Party) (Arab Socialist Rebirth Party), Hizb al Ishtiraki al Arabi (HIA) (Arab Socialist Party), Hizb al Shuyui al Suri (HSS) (Communist Party of Syria), Ittihad al Ishtiraki al Arabi (IIA) (Arab Socialist Unity), Hizb al Dimuqrati al Tawhdidi al Ishtiraki (HDII) (Socialist Unionist Democratic Party), Haraka at Tawhidiyah al Ishtirakiyah (HTI) (Socialist Unity Movement)

Area: 185,180 square km (plus 1,295 square km Israeli-controlled area, Golan Heights)

Population: 19.23 million (2004)

Capital: Damascus

Official language: Arabic

Currency: Syrian pound (Syr£) = 100 piastres

Exchange rate: Syr£52.21 per US$ (Oct 2005)

GDP per capita: US$1,308 (2004)

GDP real growth: 3.40% (2004)

Labour force: 6.02 million (2004)

Unemployment: 20.00% (2003)

Inflation: 3.50% (2004)

Oil production: 536,000 bpd (2004)

Balance of trade: -US$115.00 million 2004

Foreign debt: US$22.00 billion (2003)

In many ways modern Syria has followed the familiar course of 1950s Arab nationalism inspired by the Egypt of Nasser. From 1958 to 1961 it united with Egypt to form the United Arab Republic, but disputes over leadership quickly dissolved that union and Syria formed the Syrian Arab Republic later in 1961.

In 1963 the Ba'ath (renaissance or rebirth) party seized power in Syria. The party professed socialist inclinations – it was conceived in the 1930s as an ideology to fight European colonialism – and the ideology is the same as that of the party that ruled Iraq from the late 1960s until April 2003.

While the Ba'athist leaders described their 1963 seizure of power in Syria as a revolution, it was in fact a coup carried out by a few military officers. It did not result from, neither did it have the support of, a mass uprising.

The resulting regime was a military dictatorship. Salah al Din Bitar became the first president from 1963 to 1966 when a more radical faction seized power. A coup in 1970 brought Hafiz al Assad, a member of the Socialist Ba'ath Party, and the minority Alawite sect, to power and he ruled until his death in 2000, when his son Bashir al Assad was nominated by the People's Council (parliament) and endorsed in a referendum in which he took 97 per cent of the vote. The next presidential and parliamentary elections are in 2007: the constitution guarantees the Ba'ath party 50 per cent of the 250 parliamentary seats.

Regional relations

Syria's internal problems have been compounded by the events of the region. It has engaged in wars against Israel four times. Although it lost the Golan Heights to Israel in the 1967 Arab-Israeli War, more 18,000 Syrians still live there. Syria became militarily involved in Lebanon in 1976 in support of the Christian Maronites. The 1982 Israeli invasion of Lebanon led by Ariel Sharon saw more military clashes between Syria and Israel. In 1989, Syria endorsed the Charter of National Reconciliation, or *Ta'if Accord*, a plan for ending the Lebanese conflict negotiated by Saudi Arabia, Algeria and Morocco. More significantly, in May 1991, Lebanon and Syria signed the Treaty of Brotherhood, Co-operation, and Co-ordination outlined in the *Ta'if Accord*, which intended to establish the basis for Syrian-Lebanese relations. Syria remained in Lebanon.

Israel withdrew its troops from Lebanon in May 2000 and this encouraged Lebanese groups to demand that Syria withdraw its forces as well. The demand was eventually supported by a UN resolution and Syria withdrew in April of 2005.

When dealing with the US, Hafiz often adopted policies more strategic and pragmatic than ideological. His participation on the side of the American coalition during the 1991 Gulf War was a calculated gamble that paid off handsomely financially and in terms of regional politics and international prestige. Syria's support was rewarded by upwards of US$2 billion in aid from the US and the Arab oil producing states of the Gulf.

The collapse of the Soviet Union allowed Syria to secure better relations with the West during the George Bush Senior and Bill Clinton US administrations, but they were shortlived. Even as Bashir was taking steps to relax some of the Ba'ath party control and gradually shifting to a more liberal economic system, Syria was relegated to one step below Axis of Evil status by the George W Bush administration after the 9/11 terror attacks on the US.

Syria provided assistance to the US in its pursuit of militant Islamic groups, but was opposed to the Iraq war. Syrian-Iraqi relations had improved considerably over the decade leading up to the war. Syria had received oil from Iraq after re-opening a pipeline leading to the Mediterranean Sea, which had been shut down in the tense period of the 1980s.

The failure so far of the Arab-Israeli peace process has also relegated Syria to a less favourable geo-political position in the Americans' view and heightened tensions in the region of Bilad al Sham. Israel and the US continue to say that Syria backs Hezbollah and Harakat al Muqawama al Islamia (Hamas) (Islamic Resistance Movement).

Most analysts concede that during the 1950s Syria was one of the most rapidly developing countries in the Third World. Its economic growth was diversified. It boasted one of the healthiest agricultural production systems in the Middle East. It was industrialising at a faster rate than Egypt.

However, the frequent coups and political instability in the early decades of independence, impacted adversely on its development efforts. Ideological concerns led to the nationalisation of most enterprises and the alienation of the business and economic establishment. Many Sunni capitalists fled to neighbouring Lebanon.

The economy of Syria since the 1960s has been characterised by varying degrees of state intervention designed to reduce regional and class disparities. Reform presents severe economic as well as political challenges; Syria's situation is made all the more difficult as such reforms also have a delicate ethnic dimension.

The political risk in Syria is very high. Support from the Gulf States is declining and the unemployment rate, which Bashir's father was so concerned to reduce, is now estimated, unofficially, to be 25 to 30 per cent. The political and military tensions call for increased spending, meaning there will be less money for social welfare support. A solution to this problem could come in the form of greater foreign involvement in the Syrian economy alongside increasing efforts to integrate it into the global economy.

Regional efforts promoted by the EU, such as the Mediterranean free trade zone which has been proposed for 2010, are welcomed by Syria. Bashir maintains good relations with Italy and Spain, two countries that are sure to play a significant role in a more regionally open Syrian economy.

Outlook

The victory of Hamas, the Islamic Resistance Movement (Hamas) in Palestine has been welcomed by Syria, which in the eyes of the West has made it part of their problem. That Syria is considered by the US and Israel a sponsor of terrorism through Hezbollah in Lebanon, and Hamas itself, suggests that Syria will come under increased international pressure.

The Arab nations are eager to moderate Hamas and see it enter government with policies that would avoid a cut-off of international aid to the Palestinians and avert a breakdown in the peace process with Israel. Syria has proposed compensation by the Arabs for any aid to Palestine the Western powers might cut. Damascus has close ties with Hamas, whose politburo leader, Khaled Mashaal, lives there.

KEY INDICATORS — Syria

	Unit	2000	2001	2002	2003	2004
Population	m	16.32	16.60	17.00	18.11	*19.23
Gross domestic product (GDP)	US$bn	16.70	19.80	21.90	21.90	*23.13
GDP per capita	US$	1,001	1,155	1,149	1,226	1,308
GDP real growth	%	2.5	1.7	3.6	0.9	3.4
Inflation	%	-0.4	0.4	0.8	1.5	3.5
Unemployment	%	–	–	–	–	10.8
Oil output	'000 bpd	555.0	551.0	576.0	594.0	536.0
Natural gas output	bn cum	0.0	0.0	0.0	0.0	5.2
Exports (fob) (goods)	US$m	5,146.0	4,900.0	6,300.0	5,593.0	5,685.0
Imports (fob) (goods)	US$m	3,723.0	4,537.0	4,660.0	5,001.0	5,800.0
Balance of trade	US$m	1,423.0	363.0	1,630.0	592.0	-115.0
Current account	US$m	1,062.0	481.0	-68.0	-477.0	-90.0
Exchange rate	per US$	49.60	49.70	46.64	50.21	11.22

* estimated figure

Syria

The ruling Alawite elite could perceive itself as coming under threat from a growing Islamic orthodoxy within Syria, even though the state might benefit from increased investment by Sunni Muslim Syrians. There are already signs that a return of Sunni business is underway. Deputy Prime Minister Abdullah al Dardari said that Islamic banks would open in Syria for the first time in 2006.

Dardari said the banking sector would participate in developing the public monetary sector, to enable it to develop and finance trade and investments in the country. This financial framework should help Syria continue to draw investment interest from Saudi Arabia and the Gulf States. Syria is effectively offsetting the lack of investment from the West by investment from the region.

The political risks that Syria faces now are high as tensions between itself and Israel continue to increase, but there are also internal issues related to Bashir's efforts to liberalise the economy as well as the political system. Bashir cannot move too rapidly. He is a prisoner of the strong minority that relies on the perpetuation of the Assad legacy for its survival. He must also take note of the increasing tensions in the region and continued threats from the US. Reforms will inevitably be gradual.

Risk assessment

Politics	Poor
Economy	Poor
Regional stability	Poor

COUNTRY PROFILE

Historical profile

The history of Syria has been moulded by three historical processes: the movement of tribes from the Arabian Peninsula and the mingling with peoples of earlier settlements to form a rural population whose languages and customs have been Semitic for thousands of years; the movement of armies and goods along the great trade routes and the establishment of alien governments in the towns and valleys; and the resistance of the mountain communities to the incursions of foreign peoples and ideas.

After forming successively part of the Egyptian, Babylonian, Hittite, Greek and Roman empires, Syria fell to the Muslim armies in AD 636. The majority of the people became Muslim and Arabic replaced the older Semitic tongue. After the capital of the Islamic Caliphate moved from Damascus to Baghdad in AD 750, parts of Syria came under external, including Crusader, domination until the whole area became part of the Ottoman Empire in 1516 and remained so until 1918. In the great days of Ottoman rule Syria prospered, but by the nineteenth century it was socially and economically stagnant.

After the defeat and disintegration of the Ottoman Empire in 1918, Syria was occupied by allied (French and British) troops. Prince Faisal, military leader of the Arab revolt against the Ottomans established himself as King of Damascus, but at the same time the allies allocated the mandate for the whole of Syria to France, which had long-standing ties with the Levant states and aimed to control them politically. In 1920, the French ousted Faisal and installed their own administration. In the 20 years of the French mandate there was some economic and social progress, but prolonged political unrest as the Sunni majority rejected French rule. In 1941 Syria was occupied by the British and Free French forces and at the end of the war, with British support, Syria secured independence and the withdrawal of French troops. There followed a period of political instability, a number of *coups d'état* and an abortive union with Egypt until, in 1966, a group of radical members of the Hizb al Ba'ath al Arabi al Ishtiraki (Ba'ath Party) seized power. Army Chief and defence minister General Hafez Assad, the father of the current president, took power in 1970. Sunni Muslims, who had traditionally dominated Syrian political life found themselves replaced by the Ba'athist socialists, comprising Alawites (such as the Assad family) Druzes and other minorities.

1943 Syria achieved independence with Shukri al Kuwatli as its first president.
1948 Syria contributed to a pan-Arab military force that failed to occupy the newly-created state of Israel.
1949 President al Kuwatli was overthrown in a military coup.
1955–59 After a five-year exile in Egypt, Shukri al Kuwatli returned to be president again. Syria moved towards greater economic and political co-operation with Egypt.
1963 The Hizb al Ba'ath al Arabiyah al Ishtiraki (Ba'ath) (Socialist Arab Rebirth Party) (founded in 1947) seized power.
1967 In the Six Day War, Israel seized the Golan Heights from Syria.
1970 Former air force commander and defence minister, Hafez al Assad, seized power in a bloodless coup.
1971 Al Assad was elected president. He was re-elected for four further seven-year terms in 1978, 1985, 1992 and 1999.
1973 In the 6 October War (also known as the Yom Kippur War), Egypt and Syria invaded Israel to reclaim some of the land lost in the Six Day War, but despite some early strategic gains for Egypt and Syria, Israel counter-attacked and repelled the invasion, re-conquering the Golan Heights from Syria.
1976 The Syrian army intervened in the Lebanese civil war to ensure that the Maronites remained in power.
1980 Start of the Iran-Iraq War – Syria backed Iran.
1981 Israel formally annexed the Golan Heights.
1982–87 Israel invaded Lebanon and attacked the Syrian army based there. After hostilities ended, Syrian forces remained in Lebanon.
1990 Syria participated in the US-led allied military operations against Iraq.
1991 Syria attended the Middle East peace conference in Madrid and held bilateral talks with Israel.
2000 Syrian-Israeli talks on the future of the Golan Heights were indefinitely postponed. President Hafez al Assad died and was succeeded by his son Bashar al Assad.
2001 The UN General Assembly voted Syria a two-year seat on the Security Council.
2002 The US declared Syria a state that formed part of the 'axis of evil'.
2003 Muhammed Naji al Otari was appointed prime minister. Syria denied US allegations that it was developing chemical weapons and helping fugitive Iraqis; the US threatened economic and diplomatic sanctions.
2004 The US imposed economic sanctions, saying Syria supported terrorism and failed to stop militants entering Iraq. A UN Security Council resolution called for Syrian forces to leave Lebanon; Syria re-deployed some of its troops stationed around Beirut.
2005 In February, anti-Syrian, former Lebanese prime minister Rafik Hariri was assassinated in a car bomb attack in Beirut. Mass anti-Syrian protests in Beirut ensued. Syria agreed to a partial withdraw of its troops from the Lebanon. The UN and US kept up pressure for the full removal of troops. In April the total withdrawal of forces was achieved. In June the ruling Ba'ath party relaxed a number of laws that allowed some independent political parties, granted more press freedom and relaxed the state of emergency (that has been in place since 1963). In September UN investigators were allowed to question Syrian officials about the assassination of Rafik Hariri. Interior Minister Ghazi Kanaan, accused of being involved in the murder of Hariri, was found dead, apparently of suicide. The UN officially implicated Syria and some of its top officials in the killing of Hariri. Syria rejected the report. Syria, following weeks of pressure, agreed, in November, to allow five senior officials to be interviewed by the UN investigator, Detlev Mehlis.

Political structure

Constitution
The 1973 constitution was amended in 2000, reducing the minimum age of a president from 40 to 34 years.

Form of state
Socialist democratic republic that has been run by a military regime since 1963.

The executive
The president is Head of State, and has almost absolute power as the country is a one-party state with a disproportionate share of power in the hands of the Ba'ath Party and minority Alawite community. The president appoints and dismisses the vice presidents, the prime minister and the Council of Ministers. He holds the posts of commander-in-chief of the armed forces and secretary general of the Ba'ath Party. The Council of Ministers is headed by the prime minister and its members are appointed from the ruling party.
Presidential candidates are nominated by parliament and agreed by referendum for a seven-year term.

National legislature
The 250-member Majlis al Shaab (People's Assembly) is directly elected for a four-year term. The Ba'th Party is guaranteed 167 seats and therefore a majority. The assembly may not initiate laws; it may assess and may occasionally modifies those proposed by the executive branch.

Legal system
The judiciary is guaranteed independence under the constitution, however in practice, the Minister of Justice has the power to appoint, promote and transfer members of the judiciary and has undue influence. The legal system has separate religious and secular courts using *Sharia* (Islamic law) and a civil law code respectively.
Syria has not accepted compulsory International Court of Justice (ICJ) jurisdiction.

Last elections
5 March 2003 (parliamentary)
18 June 2000 Bashar Al-Asad was elected president by referendum, with 97.29 per cent of the vote. He was nominated by the ruling Ba'ath party and ran unopposed.
Results: Parliamentary: the ruling National Progressive Front (led by the Ba'ath Party) won 167 seats out of 250 and independents 83; turnout was 63 per cent.

Next elections
2007 (parliamentary)

Political parties

Ruling party
National Progressive Front (NPF) formed by: Hizb al Ba'ath al Arabi al Ishtiraki (Ba'ath Party) (Arab Socialist Rebirth Party), Hizb al Ishtiraki al Arabi (HIA) (Arab Socialist Party), Hizb al Shuyui al Suri (HSS) (Communist Party of Syria), Ittihad al Ishtiraki al Arabi (IIA) (Arab Socialist Unity), Hizb al Dimuqrati al Tawdhidi al Ishtiraki (HDII) (Socialist Unionist Democratic Party), Haraka at Tawhidiyah al Ishtirakiyah (HTI) (Socialist Unity Movement)

Main opposition party
Most political opposition is severely repressed and leading critics of the government are in exile.

Population
19.23 million (2004)

Ethnic make-up
Arabs (90 per cent); Kurds, Armenians and Assyrians (10 per cent).

Religions
About 90 per cent of the population are Muslim with those of the Sunni denomination outnumbering Alawi (Shi'a) Muslims by about six to one. The remainder are Christian (8 per cent), Druze and Jewish (2 per cent). Religious freedom is provided by the constitution.

Education
Primary schooling lasts for six years. Secondary education, which begins at the age of 12, also lasts for six years and is divided into two three-year cycles. Students may either enter the general or the technical branches, although entry is selective and is based on the Intermediate Level Diploma (*al Kafa'a*) examination. The first cycle is introductory. Technical secondary education is divided into industrial and commercial tracks. There are agricultural and technical schools and four universities, at Damascus, Aleppo, Tishreen and Homs. All higher education institutions are state-controlled and state-financed.

Literacy rate: 77 per cent, adult rate (2003)
Compulsory years: Six to 12.
Enrolment rate: 101 per cent gross primary enrolment, of relevant age group (including repeaters); 43 per cent gross secondary enrolment (World Bank).
Pupils per teacher: 23 in primary schools.

Health
Medical services are relatively well developed in larger towns and cities, but there is considerable variation in rural areas. Annual total expenditure on health is 5–6 per cent of GDP, of which government spending is 43–44 per cent.
HIV prevalence: 0.1 per cent aged 15–49 in 2003 (World Bank)
Life expectancy: 70.5 years (World Bank)
Fertility rate/Maternal mortality rate: 3.4 births per woman (2003); maternal mortality 110 deaths per 100,000 live births (World Bank)
Birth rate/Death rate: 29.5 births and five deaths per 1,000 people (2003).
Infant mortality rate: 16 per 1,000 live births (2003); 13 per cent of children aged under five are malnourished (World Bank).
Head of population per physician/bed: 1.3 physicians and 1.4 hospital beds per 1,000 people.

Welfare
The government maintains a basic range of social welfare provisions, including free healthcare for low-income groups, and is officially committed to improving the quality of state welfare provision as economic conditions allow. The government claims that the expansion of the private sector has led to more young children working. The labour and social affairs minister is responsible for enforcing minimum wage levels in the public and private sectors. The minimum wage (set in late 2000) is Syr£2,664 (US$58) per month in the public sector and Syr£2,425 (US$53) per month in the private sector. The law does not protect temporary workers who are not subject to regulations on minimum wages.

Main cities
Damascus (capital, estimated population 1.7 million in 2004), Aleppo (Halab) (2.0 million), Homs (715,500).

Languages spoken
English is widely spoken and French is spoken predominantly by the older generation.

Official language/s
Arabic

Media

Press
Dailies: The Syrian Arab News Agency (SANA) carries daily news updates, analyses, press reviews, and headlines in English, French and Arabic. The official English-language daily is *Syria Times*. There are a number of Arabic political newspapers, including *Al Baath* (official publication of the Ba'ath Party), *Al Thawra*, *Barq al Shimal*, *Teshreen* and *Al Jamahir*. *Syrie* updates articles from the French newspaper *Le Monde Diplomatique*. *Al Orobo* is published in English, French and Arabic. *Syria Daily* provides the latest headlines in its on-line version (http://www.syriadaily.com).
Weeklies: *Teshreen al Osboi* is a political weekly magazine. *Mawkef al Riyadhi* covers sports news and *al Nass* is a local weekly established in 1953.
Periodicals: Periodical titles are mainly produced by government departments, state organisations, trade unions, political, professional and religious associations. *Al Arabieh* and *Al Nashra al Ektisadyeh* are

women's magazines. *Al Maaloumatieh* is of consumer interest.

Broadcasting
Radio: Broadcasting is run by state bodies supervised by the Directorate General of Broadcasting and Television. The state radio service broadcasts domestic and external programmes in Arabic, French, English, Russian, German, Spanish, Portuguese, Polish, Turkish and Bulgarian.
Television: A satellite channel was launched in 1996.

Advertising
Advertising is available in the press, public cinemas, on commercial TV and outdoors in main centres. Direct mail is available. Advertising is controlled by the Arab Advertising Organisation (AAO). There is no advertising of alcohol or cigarettes and there are restrictions on the use of women in commercials. There are municipal and government taxes on press, TV, cinema and outdoor advertising.

Economy
A strong recovery in exports, particularly in tourism, and a rise in private investment, spurred on by continued reforms had aided the economy in 2004, which showed a growth rate of 3.4 per cent of GDP, recovering from the 0.9 per cent in 2003. Good harvests and a 20 per cent raise in public sector workers' pay also helped the expansion; inflation rose too, up to 3.5 per cent in 2004, from 1.5 in 2003, but did not threaten the recovery. Private investment and exports are expected to stay buoyant in 2005, although the current account will remain weak, in spite of high oil prices, as the volume of oil sales steadily declines. Syria's foreign debt had been addressed by 2005, and loans had been either paid back or re-negotiated. The foreign dept in 2005 was estimated at around US$3 billion, with an annual debt service of about US$650 million.

The main sectors of the Syrian economy are agriculture and hydrocarbons. Syria has begun the process of opening up some of its markets by applying for accession to the WTO in 2001.

Syria will become a net importer of oil by 2012, if no new significant deposits are found in the meantime. Oil has typically provided 20 per cent of GDP, 65 per cent of exports and 50 per cent of government revenue; its unmanaged loss could relegate the economy to that of a low-income country. The government is attempting to diversify and modernise Syria's economy, without upsetting the vested interests, which have controlled the country for the past three decades and been responsible for wide spread corruption, as well as maintaining social stability. Reforms have included the introduction of a consumption tax and liberalisation of many market sectors and foreign capital transactions. However the IMF has warned that oil revenue may be exhausted before the speed and range of reforms have had time to produce new sources of growth and income. The risk then is that Syria would be locked into a 'cycle of financial volatility, fiscal deterioration, low growth and rising unemployment'.

The government acknowledges that the economy is not keeping pace with its growing population. The official unemployment rate is 10.8 per cent but other, independent figures, place it as high as 20 per cent. About 75 per cent of the population is aged below 35 and 40 per cent are aged below 15.

President Bashar's government faces an uphill task, not only are US sanctions in place, impeding US exports to Syria including the much needed technology necessary for industrial modernisation, but also in attempting to open up the heavily centralised structure to competition from private local and foreign investment, dismantling subsidies and streamlining public sector enterprises. It will inevitably encounter resistance at many levels but the consequence if the long-term plans fail to transform the financial system into a modern market orientated economy could be dire for Syria in particular and the region in general.

External trade
Syria is a member of the Greater Arab Free Trade Agreement (GAFTA), from 1 January 2005 customs duties were eliminated between all 10-member countries. It also has agreements with the EU and Turkey.

Imports
Major imports are machinery and transport equipment, electric power machinery, food and livestock, metal and metal products, chemicals and chemical products, plastics, yarn and paper.
Main sources: Italy (7.7 per cent total, 2004), China (7.6 per cent), Germany (7.4 per cent), Turkey (4.5 per cent), France (4.4 per cent)

Exports
Main exports are crude oil, petroleum products, fruits and vegetables, cotton, clothing, meat and live animals, and wheat.
Main destinations: Germany (16.5 per cent total, 2004), Italy (13.5 per cent), UAE (8.6 per cent), Lebanon (7.7 per cent), France (6.3 per cent), Turkey (5.1 per cent)

Agriculture
Farming
Agriculture remains a leading sector of the economy, contributing approximately 25 per cent to GDP and employing around a quarter of the labour force. Agricultural land is mainly privately owned. Approximately 31 per cent of the total land is cultivated. Much of Syria is mountainous and part of the eastern part of the country is desert or semi-desert. The fertile areas include the coastal strip and the Euphrates and Kabur valleys. Intensification of farming in the rain-fed areas is ongoing; these areas account for more than 80 per cent of the total crop area. The al Thaura dam, built with Russian technology, brings irrigation to a vast area.

Main crops are cotton, wheat and barley. Wheat and barley together account for two-thirds of the cultivated area. Extreme fluctuations in grain production from year to year caused by rainfall variability have traditionally caused much hardship for the rural population. Cotton is the main cash crop. Other leading crops include vegetables, citrus fruits, olives, tobacco and sugar beet. Sheep and goats are grazed in many areas. Wool is also an important product.

Population growth in Syria is estimated at 3 per cent, and to ensure food security for its growing population, the government is focussing on a food self-sufficiency strategy, improving crop production technology and crop diversification. Farm production increased in the period 1993–2003 and Syria moved from being a food importer to food exporter.

The estimated crop production for 2004 included: 6,248,803 (t) cereals in total, 4,537,459t wheat, 527,193t barley, 180,000t maize, 500,000t potatoes, 241,113t pulses, 735,000t citrus fruit, 920,000t tomatoes, 26,500t tobacco, 183,000t treenuts, 950,000t olives, 1,250,000t sugar beets, 1,022,769t seed cotton, 331,000t cotton lint, 1,594,282t fruit in total, 2,627,953t vegetables in total. Livestock production included: 391,021t meat in total, 47,350t beef, 450t camel meat, 207,000t lamb, 5,120t goat meat, 130,621t poultry, 167,000t eggs, 1,917,780t milk, 1,920t honey, 7,317t cattle hides, 34,500t sheepskins, 33,600t greasy wool.

Fishing
Syria's small annual fish catch is mostly destined for the domestic market.

Forestry
Syria is lightly forested with less than 3 per cent of forest or woodland cover. In ancient times, Syria had extensive mountain forests but these have largely been cleared or degraded and only remnants of mixed coniferous forest remain. The predominant species include *Abies cilicica*, *Pinus halipensis* and *Pinus brutia*. Syria has established a moderately large area of plantations based on cypress, pine and

eucalyptus species. The country has a modest network of protected areas – State Forest Protection Zones provide the most substantive forest conservation measures. Syria produces very modest volumes of sawn timber, veneer, plywood and particleboard. The majority of demand for wood and paper products is met by imports. Exports in 2004 amounted to US$12.4 million while imports were valued at US$295.7 million.

Industry and manufacturing
The industrial sector contributed 27.1 per cent to GDP in 2004, of which, 24.2 per cent was manufacturing; as a whole it employs around 20 per cent of the labour force. Industrial growth matched the trend in GDP, with a low rate of 0.9 in 2003 that jumped to 2.5 in 2004.

In the mid-1960s the government began a policy of rapid industrialisation, especially in the areas of iron and steel and other heavy industries. Factories turn out a wide range of products, including tractors and television sets.

Many of Syria's industries are agrarian-based, such as food processing and textiles. Sugar processing, an important activity, is mainly conducted by state-owned enterprises. The textile industry is the oldest-established, contributing approximately 15 per cent of export earnings. Other industries include cement, soap, glass, footwear, leather goods and brassware.

Tourism
Tourism is increasingly important, with Syria's magnificent castles and other historical sites attracting over one million tourists a year. Aleppo in the north has been designated a World Heritage Site. A peace agreement between Israel and its Arab neighbours, including Syria, is required for Syria to fully develop its tourist potential which derives from its close proximity to Western Europe, its Mediterranean coastline and its rich history and historical sites.

Tourism is geared to the Middle East market and is heavily concentrated in Damascus. Tourists are mainly Lebanese and Jordanian, although Syria is also popular with the French and citizens from the former Soviet Union. Tourists from other Arab countries account for some 75 per cent of total visitors. Iranian pilgrims are a significant tourist category who visit religious sites around Syria. American- and Canadian-Syrian visitors are also increasing.

In 2003 Syria joined the Euromed Heritage Programme, a computerisation project, sponsored by the EU, which focusses on cultural tourists of archaeology, arts and history, promoting sites through the internet.

The travel and tourism sector is expected to contribute US$5.4 billion or 2.1 per cent of GDP and employ around 6 per cent of the work force in 2005. Tourism is estimated to attract 7 per cent of total capital investment and generate around US$2.7 billion, or 24.1 per cent of in total exports.

Mining
The mining sector contributes up to 10 per cent to GDP and employs around 5 per cent of the working population. Syria has large phosphate deposits which are used in its growing fertiliser industry. Approximately 76 per cent of phosphate mined is exported, with 10 per cent used at the Homs fertiliser factory. Other mineral resources include gypsum.

Hydrocarbons
Proven oil reserves totalled 3.2 billion barrels in 2004 and are only expected to last until 2012.

Oil production was 536,000 barrels per day (bpd) in 2004. Crude oil accounts for up to 65 per cent of total export earnings, 20 per cent of GDP and 50 per cent of government revenue. Further exploration is under way with five blocks allocated to international companies, although in 2005 most Western oil exploration firms had begun to withdraw as no new finds had been made.

Due to Syria's alleged harbouring of terrorists, US sanctions are set to prohibit US investment in Syria's energy sector. This could result in a long-term decrease of production. The UN and Asia are taking a different line to the US on combat of terrorism, they seek to improve relations with the country and perhaps their investment will counter US sanctions.

Total gas reserves are estimated at 370 billion cubic metres (2004), and output in 2004 was 5.2 billion cubic metres. Syria is beginning to convert oil-fired electrical generating plants to gas, as oil stocks decline.

There are several pipelines either in operation, under construction or being planned to transport gas from the Egyptian fields in Sinai to Jordan, Lebanon and Syria – with a possible extension to Turkey and Europe.

The El Arish gas pipeline is, by 2005, in the last stage of completion.

In May 2004, significant gas discoveries were made by a Croatian oil and gas company in the northern central part of Syria. The new gas production will allow Syria to export for the first time. The first oil joint venture between China and Syria was set up in July 2004. The joint venture is between the largest oil producer in China, China National Petroleum Corporation (CNPC) and the state-owned Syrian Petroleum Company (SPC). It is hoped that the establishment of the company – the Sino-Syrian Kawkab Oil Company (SSKOC) – will speed up CNPC's development of the Kbeibe oil field in the north-east of Syria.

In February 2004, Syria and Yemen signed a co-operation agreement in the field of oil, gas and mineral resources. Syria does not produce any coal but imports a small amount, importing around 2,000 short tonnes of coke in 2001.

Energy
The government is promoting the rapid development of gas production for electricity generation. Total installed capacity is scheduled to reach 6,000MW (including hydroelectric capacity of 1,700MW) with an increased capacity of 3,000MW by 2010.

From the 1990s onwards the power industry has been in crisis. Power cuts have been commonplace. The government attempted to address chronic under-capacity in power generation by awarding contracts to build four new power stations and existing power plants underwent modernisation.

A US$300 million electricity line links the grids of three countries – Jordan, Syria and Egypt

All new thermal plants are built to use gas, and existing oil-fired power stations have been converted to gas or combined oil and gas fuel to reduce the overall consumption of oil, freeing up to 150,000 barrels per day (bpd) of oil for export. Factories and oil refineries are gradually expected to convert from fuel oil to natural gas.

Syria's main gas-fired power stations are located in Suwaidiyah (300MW), Deir ez Zor (120MW) and Thayyem (90MW). The General Organisation for Electricity's (GOE) national transmission system supplies all regions via 230kV and 66kV lines.

Financial markets
Stock exchange
In August 2004, Syria became a participant of the Arab Stock Exchange – established in Cairo. Legislation to establish a Syrian Stock Market is, by end-2005, being prepared in co-operation with stock markets in Amman and Istanbul.

Banking and insurance
A series of reforms since 2000 has included official approval of private banking, in joint ventures, with foreign equity limited to 49 per cent, to be sited in 'free zones'. A Monetary and Credit Council (MSC) was establishment to supervise and co-ordinate the activities of private banks. Restrictions on the trading of foreign currency and the need for a majority local

Syria

partner will be a disincentive to a wider pool of potential participants.

Three Lebanese banks – Fransabank, Banque Européenne pour le Moyen Orient and Société Générale Libano-Européenne de Banque – opened branches in the free zones. Five other non-Syrian banks, including the Jordanian Arab Bank and Housing Bank for Trade and Finance (HBTF) were later given approval to begin trading.

The government has eased the ban on domestic nationals opening foreign currency accounts. Nevertheless this reform has been of limited benefit as it is still technically illegal to hold hard currency and most Syrians continue to channel their funds through Lebanese banks. The lack of domestic credit and the poor quality of Syria's banking sector represent a major hindrance to the development of the country's economy.

Central bank
Central Bank of Syria
Main financial centre
Damascus

Time
GMT plus two hours (GMT plus three hours April–September)

Geography
Syria is bordered by Turkey to the north; by the Mediterranean Sea and northern Lebanon to the west; by Israel and Jordan to the south; and by Iraq to the east. Western Syria contains a series of mountain ranges, lying parallel to the Mediterranean. The northern range is separated from Syria's coastline by a narrow plain. The highest peak is Jabal ash Shaykh (Mount Hermon) in the extreme south-west of the country. To the east of the mountains, the Euphrates River crosses partly cultivatable plains in the north, while the central and southern areas consist mainly of desert plains.

Climate
Syria has a moderate Mediterranean climate, four distinct seasons, and cloudless blue skies for the greater part of the year. Temperatures in autumn and spring range between 20 and 25 degrees Celsius (C), 30–35 degrees C in summer (May–September) and 5 to 10 degrees C in winter. Winter is generally moderate but wet in the coastal region and cold inland; summer is hot and dry inland, hot and humid on the coast.

Dress codes
Lightweight clothing is needed during the hottest months (May–September). Both men and women should dress discreetly in public. For business meetings men should wear a suit and tie, women a two-piece suit or equivalent. On social occasions dress as for business meetings unless otherwise indicated.

Entry requirements
Passports
Passports are required by all except Arab League nationals.
NB If a trip to Syria is planned after visiting Jordan, ensure there is no evidence in the luggage that may indicate a visit to Israel.
Visa
Required by all except nationals of certain Middle Eastern countries. All visas should be acquired before travelling. Business visas require a letter of introduction and full itinerary along with the application. Contact the nearest consulate for further details.
Visa extensions are needed for visits over 15 days and can only be obtained from the Syria Immigration and Passport Administration.
Prohibited entry
Nationals of Israel, holders of passports with evidence of travel in Israel.
Currency advice/regulations
Import of local currency is unlimited, however its export is prohibited (except to the Lebanon and limited to Syr£5,000). Foreign currency may be imported and exported to the limit of US$5,000, and must be declared on arrival.
Customs
Gold jewellery must be declared on arrival.
Imports are controlled by licensing, and the import of certain goods, produced domestically, and certain non-essential luxuries is forbidden. Most basic commodities are imported by government agencies only. Trade with Israel is prohibited. Transit visitors (visas valid for up to three days) are not liable for duty.
Prohibited imports
Firearms and ammunition.

Health (for visitors)
Medical services are well developed and many doctors speak English.
Mandatory precautions
A certificate of vaccination against yellow fever is required if travelling from an infected area.
Advisable precautions
Typhoid, tetanus, hepatitis 'A' and polio immunisations are recommended, and anti-malaria precautions should be taken. There is a risk of rabies.

Hotels
Rooms are in short supply, and it is essential to book in advance. At first-class and international hotels, it will be necessary to pay in foreign currency (Arab nationals and resident foreigners exempted).
Hotels in Damascus are located close to most tourist attractions.

Credit cards
Credit cards are accepted in main business areas – contact the card provider for more details. Charge cards are not accepted.
In 2003, the Real Estate Bank (REB) became the first Syrian bank to accept MasterCard and Visa cards issued abroad.

Public holidays
Fixed dates
1 Jan (New Year's Day), 8 Mar (Revolution Day), 21 Mar (Mothers' Day), 17 Apr (Independence Day), 1 May (Labour Day), 6 May (Martyrs' Day), 6 Oct (October Liberation War), 25 Dec (Christmas Day).
Variable dates
Eid al Adha (three days), Islamic New Year, Birth of the Prophet, Eid al Fitr (three days).
The Islamic year contains 354 or 355 days, with the result that Muslim feasts advance by 10–12 days against the Gregorian calendar. Dates of feasts vary according to the sighting of the new moon, so cannot be forecast exactly. Islamic year 1426: 10 February 2005 to 30 January 2006.

Working hours
Friday is the weekend break.
Banking
Sat–Thu: 0800–1400.
Business
Sat–Thu: 0830–1430.
Government
Sat–Thu: 0830/0900–1300/1400, 1600/1700–1900/2000.
Shops
Sat–Thu: (summer) 0930–1400, 1630–2100; (winter) 0930–1400, 1600–2000.

Telecommunications
Mobile phones
Two networks exist: GSM 900 and 1800

Electricity supply
220V, 50Hz AC. The sockets are of the two-pronged European variety.

Weights and measures
Metric system (local units also in use).

Social customs/useful tips
Appointments should be made in advance. Punctuality is appreciated. It is conventional to shake hands on meeting and taking leave. Sometimes a conference visit is a way of doing business. The host may hold several conversations with guests at the same time. It is not customary to start talking business immediately. At meetings it is polite to drink coffee or tea, when offered. It is useful for business cards to have Arabic translations on the reverse side. A few words of Arabic will be appreciated.

Do not smoke or drink in public during Ramadan. Islamic customs should be respected. Shoes should be removed on entry to mosques. Women should dress modestly. It is the convention to use the right and not the left hand when shaking hands and passing or receiving anything. Alcohol is available to visitors.

Do not photograph anything remotely connected with the armed forces, including radio transmission aerials, and remember that some Syrians, particularly in rural areas, may regard cameras with suspicion.

It is considered very impolite for men to sit next to women on buses.

The punishment for possession of drugs is life imprisonment. For drug trafficking, the death penalty applies.

Travellers cheques are generally accepted and it is advisable to take US dollars as well. Accommodation in all hotels must be paid in hard currency, except one-star hotels. Food, beverages, telephone calls etc can be paid in local currency. It is illegal to change money on the streets. Only change money in recognised exchange shops, banks and hotels.

Security
The situation in Syria is calm. Travellers to Syria should keep in touch with developments in the Middle East. Any increase in regional tension might affect travel advice. Visitors are advised to carry identity documents at all times. Avoid driving outside the main cities at night.

Getting there
Air
National airline: Syrian Arab Airlines (Syrianair).
International airport/s: Damascus International (DAM), 29km south-east of city, with banking, refreshments and duty-free shop. A bus service operates every 30 mins from 0600-2300, into the city centre.
Aleppo (ALP) 10km from city, with banking, refreshments and duty-free shop. Taxis are available from both airports, and fares should be negotiated beforehand. Journey time into Damascus city centre is 30 minutes, and 20 minutes into Aleppo.
Airport tax: International departures: Syr£200, excluding transit passengers.
Surface
Road: From Istanbul via Ankara the E5 road runs to Damascus via Aleppo. From the east a road runs from Iran via Iraq, and was considered excellent, however border crossings are currently suspended. From the south the road from Akaba, (the terminus of the E5) runs via Amman (Jordan), and includes stretches of motorway. Other roads include those from the Lebanon and Saudi Arabia.

Service taxis are faster than buses and run between Damascus-Amman or Irbid (Jordan).
Rail: Routes link Syria with Istanbul and Ankarra (Turkey) and Amman (Jordan). Sleepers cars are available and all trains are air-conditioned.
There are rail lines running from northern Iraq to the Syrian coast, however services are currently suspended.
Water: Car ferries sail from Bodrum (Turkey), Rhodes, Heraklion, Santorini and Piraeus (Greece). Cruise ferries are run by Italian, Greek, Cypriot and Turkish companies, with sailings that vary from year to year. Passage may take up to three days. Ferries from Alexandria (Egypt) dock at the Lebanise port of Beirut and the distance to Damascus is shorter than to any Syrian port.
Main port/s: Latakia, Tartus and Banias.

Getting about
National transport
Air: There are internal flights by Syrianair between Damascus, Aleppo, Latakia, Qamishli and Deir Ez Zor.
Road: The 30,208km road network has some 22,500km of relatively good surfaced roads linking main centres.
Buses: Luxury couch services operate between major towns, by Pullman or Karnak. Bus tickets, with assigned seats, should be bought prior to boarding. Qadmous, Al-Ahliah and Al-Ryan are private bus companies.
Minibuses serve smaller locations; they have no schedule and leave when full. Microbuses are modern vans used on short routes between cities and on routes to small towns and villages. They are more comfortable than the minibuses and there is no standing room. Departures are more frequent but they are more expensive than the minibuses. Fares are usually paid on board.
Taxis: May be used to travel between cities as they are affordable; either negotiate a fare with the driver or check that the meter runs correctly. Long-haul 'service' (share) taxis are also available on the more popular routes, they cost more than microbuses but less than a personal taxi hire.
Rail: Two classes of rail service are available, with restaurant cars, sleeping carriages and air-conditioning. The railway links all the major cities and has a regular timetable but, it can be slow so, it may not suit the business traveller.
City transport
Taxis: Yellow cabs in Damascus are expensive; always check the meter has been set. Fares are mostly by negotiation. Drivers do not expect a tip.
In other cities, fares are set by government departments.

Buses, trams & metro: From airport to city centre.
Car hire
Private cars are rarely available, but taxis are reasonably priced.

BUSINESS DIRECTORY
The addresses listed below are a selection only. While World of Information makes every endeavour to check these addresses, we cannot guarantee that changes have not been made, especially to telephone numbers and area codes. We would welcome any corrections.

Telephone area codes
The international direct dialling (IDD) code for Syria is +963, followed by the area code and subscriber's number:

Aleppo	21	Lattakia	41
Damascus	11	Raqqah	22
Hassakah	52	Tartous	43
Homs	31	Zabadani	13

Chambers of Commerce
Federation of Syrian Chambers of Commerce, Mousa bin Nosair Street, PO Box 5909, Damascus (tel: 333-7344; fax: 333-1127; fax: syr-trade@mail.syr).

Aleppo Chamber of Commerce, Amir Palace Hotel Building, Bab Jnein Street, PO Box 1261, Aleppo (tel: 223-8236; fax: 221-3493; e-mail: alepchmb@mail.sy).

Aleppo Chamber of Industry, PO Box 1859, Aleppo (tel: 362-0600; fax: 362-0040; e-mail: alpindus@net.sy).

Damascus Chamber of Commerce, 126 Mouawiah Street, Hariqa, PO Box 1040, Damascus (tel: 221-1339; fax: 222-5874; e-mail: dcc@net.net).

Damascus Chamber of Industry, Mouawiah Street, PO Box 1305, Damascus (tel: 221-5042; fax: 224-5981; e-mail: dci@mail.sy).

Damascus Countryside Chamber of Commerce, Bagdad Street, PO Box 5859, Damascus (tel: 231-5653; fax: 231-3798).

Hasakah Chamber of Commerce and Industry, PO Box 243, Hasakah (tel: 221-645; fax: 313-842).

Homs Chamber of Commerce and Industry, Abulauf Street, PO Box 440, Homs (tel: 469-440; fax: 464-247; e-mail: homschamber@homschamber.org).

Lattakia Chamber of Commerce and Industry, PO Box 124, Lattakia (tel: 479-530; fax: 478-526; e-mail: lattakia@chamberlattakia.com).

Tartous Chamber of Commerce and Industry, PO Box 403, Tartous (tel: 329-852; fax: 329-728; e-mail: info@tarcci.com).

Syria

Banking

Agricultural Co-operative Bank; PO Box 4325, al Naanaa Garden, Damascus (tel: 221-3462, 222-1393; fax: 223-8525).

Commercial Bank of Syria (Banque Commerciale de Syrie) PO Box 933, Yousef Azmeh Square, Damascus (tel: 221-8890, 221-8891; fax: 222-8524).

Industrial Bank; PO Box 7578, Almuhandiseen Building, Maisaloun Street, Damascus (tel: 222-8200; fax: 222-8412).

Popular Credit Bank, PO Box 2841, Maisaloun Street, Damascus (tel: 222-7604, 221-8555; fax: 221-1291).

Real Estate Bank, PO Box 2337, Y al Azme Square, Damascus (tel: 221-8602/3; fax: 223-7938).

Central bank
Central Bank of Syria, PO Box 2254, 29 Ayar Street, Damascus (tel: 221-6802; fax: 224-8329).

Travel information

Middle East Tourism, BP 201, rue Fardoss, Damascus (tel: 211-876).

Silk Road Travel and Tourism, Fardoss Street, PO Box 12958, Damascus (tel: 223-0500/5; fax: 223-1138, 231-5555; e-mail: hanano@silkroad-tours.com).

Syrian Arab Airlines (Syrianair), PO Box 417, Youssef al Azmeh Square, Social Insurance Building, Damascus (tel: 232-159).

Ministry of tourism
Ministry of Tourism, rue Abou Firas al Hamadani, Damascus (tel: 221-0122; fax: 224-2636; internet site: http://www.syriatourism.org).

Ministries

Ministry of Electricity, PO Box 3386, Damascus (tel: 222-3086, 222-9654; fax: 222-9062).

Ministry of Health, Najmeh Suare, Parliament Street, Damascus (tel: 333-9602, 3333-3801, 331-1020; fax: 331-1114).

Other useful addresses

Arab Advertising Organisation (AAO), Moutanabbi Street, PO Box 2842, Damascus (fax: 222-0754).

British Embassy, Kotob Building, 11 Mohd Kurd Ali Street, Malki PO Box 37, Damascus (tel: 371-2561/3; fax: 373-1600).

Cotton Marketing Organisation, BP 729, Rue Bab al araj, Aleppo (tel: 238-486).

Director General of the Damascus International Fair, Kouwatli Street, Damascus (tel: 229-853/840/914).

General Organisation for Cement, PO Box 5265, Damascus (tel: 666-7000/3; fax: 666-1257, 611-7111).

General Organisation for Chemicals and Foodstuffs, PO Box 893, Damascus (tel: 222-8521, 222-5421; fax: 222-6927).

General Organisation for Engineering Industries, PO Box 3120, Damascus (tel: 212-1824/5; fax: 212-3375).

General Organisation for Insurance (The Syrian Insurance Company), PO Box 22679, Damascus (tel: 221-8430/1; fax: 222-0494).

General Organisation for Machinery and Equipment, PO Box 3130, Damascus (tel: 221-8223, 221-8156; fax: 221-1118).

General Organisation for Metals and Building Materials, PO Box 3136, Damascus (tel: 442-0941, 442-0944, 442-0948; fax: 442-4489, 442-0947).

General Organisation for Sugar, PO Box 429, Homs (tel: 467-600/2; fax: 474-780).

General Organisation for the Textile Industries, BP 620, Rue Fardoss, Damascus (tel: 221-6200, 222-7158; fax: 221-6201).

General Organisation for Trading and Distribution, PO Box 15, Damascus (tel: 210-396).

General Organisation of Free Zones, PO Box 2790, Damascus (tel: 219-137).

International Centre for Agricultural Research in the Dry Areas, Box 5466, Aleppo.

Public Establishment for Distribution and Exploitation of Electric Energy (PEDEEE), PO Box 35199, Damascus (tel: 224-5926, 222-3086, 222-9654; fax: 222-3686).

Public Establishment for Electricity Generation and Transmission (PEEGT), PO Box 3386, Damascus (tel: 212-9795, 211-9935; fax: 222-9062).

Syrian Embassy (USA), 2215 Wyoming Avenue, NW, Washington DC 20008 (tel: 202-232-6313; fax: 202-234-9548; e-mail: info@syrianembassy.org).

Internet sites

Al Thawra newspaper: http://www.thawra.com

ArabNet: http://www.arab.net/welcome.html

Arabia Online:http://www.arabia.com

Ministry of Information: http://www.moi-syria.com

Travel Information: http://www.visit-syria.com

Taiwan

KEY FACTS

Official name: Chung-hua Min-kuo (Republic of China)

Head of State: President Chen Shui-bian (MCT) (since 2000; re-elected Mar 2004)

Head of government: Prime Minister Su Tseng-chang (since January 2006)

Ruling party: Min-chu Chin-pu Tang (MCT) (Democratic Progressive Party) (since Dec 2001; re-elected 11 Dec 2004)

Area: 35,961 square km

Population: 23.07 million (2004)

Capital: Taipei

Official language: Mandarin Chinese

Currency: Taiwanese dollar (T$) = 100 cents

Exchange rate: T$33.19 per US$ (Oct 2005)

GDP per capita: US$13,260 (2004)

GDP real growth: 5.70% (2004)

Labour force: 10.00 million (2003)

Unemployment: 4.50% (2004)

Inflation: 1.60% (2004)

Balance of trade: US$5.10 billion 2004

Foreign debt: US$24.70 billion (2003)

Visitor numbers: 2.50 million (annually)*

* estimated figure

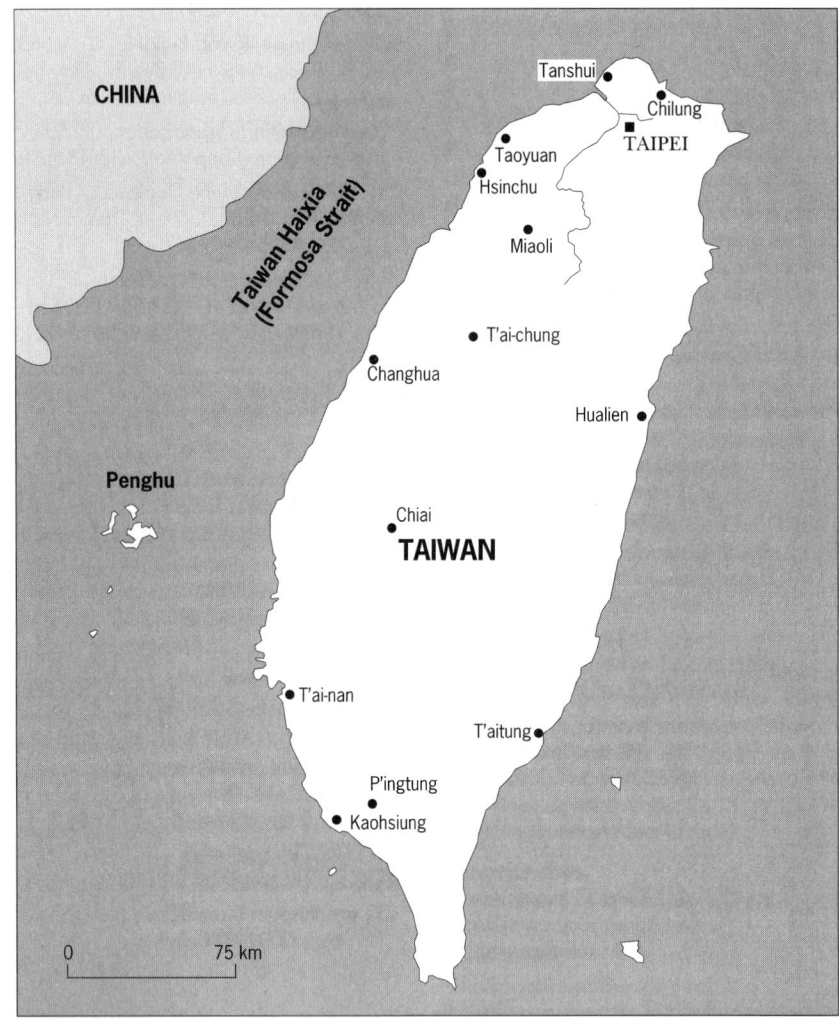

Taiwan is one of Asia's powerhouses and a centre for high-tech exports. The economic crisis that engulfed much of Asia in the late 1990's scarcely caused a ripple in the boardrooms of Taipei. The Taiwanese enjoy one of Asia's highest living standards. Taiwan is a net exporter of capital to the region and Taiwanese companies are themselves seen with increasing frequency on the regional and global business stage. Taiwan's foreign exchange reserves are the third highest of any country in the world.

Economy

The country has made great strides over the past 10 years to open its domestic economy to international competition. For both commercial and strategic reasons, it has sought a role for itself as a regional hub and an alternative centre to Hong Kong and Shanghai from which to develop the Chinese market. Lack of direct transportation links with the mainland continue to hamper its efforts so far in this direction, but there has been rapid progress in other areas that are not dependent on direct links with the mainland.

It has not succeeded as a regional centre, but has become an important market in its own right. Taiwan's industry is becoming increasingly dependent on the export of higher value-added products and is a major purchaser of industrial plant and equipment. Major infrastructure projects underway in the telecommunications, energy and transportation sectors provide opportunities for foreign engineering and technology-based companies. An affluent population of 22 million, fashion conscious and with a high propensity to spend, provides a growing consumer market. Increasingly, the younger generation takes its cue from Japan rather than the US.

The economy is driven by trade and especially exports to the US, Japan and Europe, major markets for Taiwan's rapidly growing high-tech sector. For the past decade, the drivers of growth have been the semiconductor and related electronics industries although there is now a new emphasis on the emerging 'sunrise opportunities' in the biosciences and nanotechnology. Much of the required technology comes from overseas in various ways. Like the Japanese before them, the Taiwanese are good at adapting foreign products, but less efficient at innovation and research. It is increasingly obvious that Taiwan's growth rate needs to be compared to that achieved by the OECD economies and not the norms of the developing world.

Economic growth was better than expected over 2005 and the government is hoping that 2006 will be even better with a forecast of 4.5 per cent.

Unemployment was 4.4 per cent in 2004. Inbound investment was over US$3 billion in 2005, slightly down on 2004. Investments into China are almost 75 per cent of total overseas invesments, demonstrating the island's continuing economic reliance on the mainland.

Politics

The original inhabitants of the former Formosa were of Malay descent. Chinese seafaring merchants established permanent settlements along the Formosan coast and in 1682 the island was formally incorporated into the Chinese Empire. Taiwan became a separate province of China in 1885, but Chinese sovereignty in Taiwan was never absolute. In 1895 Taiwan was ceded by China to Japan.

In the closing days of the Second World War, the allied powers made Taiwan a United Nations' Trust Territory. General Chiang Kai-shek, the mainland China Nationalist leader, accepted Taiwan back from Japan to be administered on behalf of the allies. From 1945 to 1949 he paid little attention to the island as his nationalist armies fighting on the mainland were overwhelmed by the Communist forces. When the Communists triumphed, Chiang, his army and his administration fled to Taiwan.

Taipei became the capital of the 'Republic of China' established by Sun Yat-sen in 1911. To the local Taiwanese, the arrival of the Mandarin-speaking mainlanders and a large army amounted to a new invasion and new colonisation.

However, Chiang's Nationalists might have been inept at fighting a war but they proved highly effective in restoring and transforming Taiwan's economy. Taiwan was the first of the 'Asian Tigers' to develop on the basis of an export led path.

As the economy prospered, the military-backed dictatorship became more benign and by the mid-1980s democracy flourished on Taiwan. A government programme of industrial restructuring and incentives has been largely successful in shifting Taiwan from a low-cost manufacturing centre to a regional centre for high-tech manufactured goods. Divisions between 'mainlanders' and 'Taiwanese' have largely been healed – certainly for the younger generation. As China emerges as a major world power, many among the island's population are looking more to the mainland as the key to their own future.

Taiwan, Republic of China, is a fully independent country. Its population enjoys universal suffrage; it maintains a free press and a democratic electoral system. The President of the country is elected directly by the people. Yet it remains in diplomatic isolation.

This position is a consequence of the Chinese Civil War. Taiwan long ago gave away any claim to the mainland, but China remains steadfast to a policy of reunification. Ominously, China claims the right, if necessary, to use force to 'liberate' Taiwan. In Beijing's eyes, Taiwan's only option is to negotiate the terms of its surrender.

The presidential election of March 2000 saw a shift of power from the Nationalist (Kuomintang) (KMT) party that had ruled Taiwan for almost 50 years to that of the opposition Democratic Progressive Party (DPP). Chen Shui-bian became President although within Taiwan's unicameral legislature, the KMT maintained a majority of seats. Chen's administration was immediately strengthened by a split within the KMT. The 'Taiwan Solidarity Union' (TSU) aligned itself with the DPP while the other faction formed a breakaway right-wing splinter group known as the 'People First Party' (PFP) which joined the KMT in the 'Pan Blue Alliance' against the DPP-TSU in the 'Pan Green Faction'.

Chen was re-elected in 2004, but a year later his power base was shaken, he had not read the signs of a change of heart over the China issue among many of the voters. His DPP-led alliance was defeated in provincial elections and its poor showing was a cause for much soul-searching by Chen. The defeat caused the fracture of the alliance of the DPP and TSU. Chen was continuing to espouse an anti-China sentiment which no longer sat comfortably with the bulk of Taiwan's population. China's emergence as an economic power increasingly meant to them that Taiwan's fate was inextricably bound to that of the

KEY INDICATORS — Taiwan

	Unit	2000	2001	2002	2003	2004
Population	m	22.10	22.50	22.66	22.87	23.07
Gross domestic product (GDP)	US$bn	301.00	282.30	275.70	289.52	305.30
GDP per capita	US$	13,620	12,620	12,228	12,660	13,260
GDP real growth	%	5.9	-1.9	3.5	3.2	5.7
Inflation	%	1.3	–	-0.2	0.1	1.6
Unemployment	%	3.0	4.6	5.2	5.3	4.4
Exports (fob) (goods)	US$m	148,400.0	122,900.0	130,640.0	130,000.0	170,500.0
Imports (fob) (goods)	US$m	133,600.0	107,200.0	112,590.0	113,000.0	165,400.0
Balance of trade	US$m	14,800.0	15,700.0	18,100.0	17,000.0	5,100.0
Current account	US$m	8,900.0	19,028.0	25,000.0	25,700.0	19,010.0
Exchange rate	per US$	33.08	34.00	34.89	34.38	33.35

mainland. Many now openly say it is no longer a matter of 'if' Taiwan reaches a modus vivendi with the mainland, rather 'when'.

Chen refuses to see it that way, much to the chagrin of Washington, Beijing – and the majority of Taiwan's 13 million voters. After a new year speech in which he announced he was anxious to slow down the rate of investment into China by Taiwan's business sector through a new policy of undefined 'active management', the stock market suffered its biggest decline in two months. Business took his remarks to mean the government would start to meddle with companies that were seen to be too actively pro-China.

Differences of opinion between Chen and the-then prime minister Frank Hsieh erupted into the public domain. When the opposition dominated legislature voted down Hsieh's budget – including controversial arms related measures designed to strengthen Taiwan's missile defences against China – it brought down the administration. Hsieh resigned and took the entire cabinet with him. Many politicians and diplomats accused Chen and his advisors of engineering a situation whereby the likeable – but non-compliant – Hsieh would be forced to step aside. Chen immediately appointed his former Chief of Staff, Su Tseng-chang, as premier. A new cabinet was expected after the Lunar New Year holiday, in early February.

Su is a former chairman of the DPP and a frontrunner for the 2008 presidential race. He was handpicked by Chen who clearly believes he will through Su still be able to maintain tight control over policy towards China. This hard-line approach seems destined to alienate the general populace – as well as the business sector – even further.

One small step towards a compromise between Taiwan and the mainland is the annual dispensation for direct flights to and from the mainland over the Lunar New Year festivities. The number of flights allowed in 2006 almost doubled over those of 2005.

Risk assessment

Economy	Improving
Politics	Fair
Regional stability	Fair

COUNTRY PROFILE

Historical profile
Before the arrival of the Europeans, the island was occupied by indigenous people and immigrants from mainland China.

1590 Portuguese navigators discovered Taiwan and called it *Ilha Formosa*, meaning 'beautiful island' in Portuguese. This is the origin of Taiwan's other name, Formosa.
1624 The Dutch arrived in Taiwan.
1629 The Spaniards, alarmed by growing Dutch control of Taiwan, arrived and occupied the northern part of the island.
1630 The Dutch formally settled on the island.
1630–62 The Dutch and Spanish fought for control of the island. The Spanish were defeated and driven off the island. The Dutch strengthened their control after the establishment of the Dutch East India Company. Taiwan became an important trading centre. Chinese resistance eventually grew so strong that the Dutch were driven out.
1700–1800 Chinese mass migration to the island took place with most immigrants fleeing the Japanese-occupied provinces of Guangdong and Fujian.
1885 Taiwan was officially made a province of China.
1895 China ceded control of Taiwan to Japan following the Sino-Japanese war. The Japanese modernised the country, upgrading infrastructure, restoring the communications network and developing agriculture.
1945 After Japan's defeat in the Second World War, Taiwan became a province of the Republic of China, controlled by the Kuomintang (KMT) (Nationalist Party).
1949 The KMT was driven out of the mainland by the communist People's Liberation Army (PLA) led by Mao Zedong. President Chiang Kai-shek withdrew his forces to Taiwan. The KMT asserted that it, rather than the new People's Republic of China, constituted the rightful government of mainland China and that it would eventually resume control of all of China.
1954 The US signed a security agreement with the KMT pledging to protect Taiwan.
1971 The People's Republic of China replaced Taiwan as Chinese representatives at the UN.
1975 Chiang Kai-Shek died. His son, Chiang Ching-kuo, became president.
1987 Martial law and one-party rule were dismantled.
1988 The death of President Chiang Ching-kuo. Taiwan-born Lee Teng-hui became president.
1994 Nationwide local elections were held. The KMT retained its dominance of the political system, although the candidate of the opposition Min-chu Chin-pu Tang (MCT) (Democratic Progressive Party), Chen Shui-bian, was elected mayor of Taipei.
1995 The KMT lost ground to the MCT in the legislative elections.
1996 President Lee Teng-hui comfortably won Taiwan's first direct presidential elections.
1998 The KMT was re-elected, with an increased majority.
1999 Taiwan suffered its worst earthquake for nearly 100 years.
2000 Chen Shui-bian of the MCT won the presidential elections.
2001 President Chen's pro-independence MCT won the parliamentary elections; the KMT lost its majority in parliament for the first time in 50 years.
2002 Taiwan joined the World Trade Organisation. Laws were enacted to put the military under the control of the civilian cabinet. President Chen Shui-bian took over the leadership of the MCT.
2003 The health minister resigned over the Severe Acute Respiratory Syndrome (Sars) crisis.
2004 President Chen Shui-bian (MCT), after surviving an assassination attempt on the eve of the presidential elections, was re-elected on 20 March. In August, parliament voted for constitutional changes, to be confirmed by referendum, and electoral reform. Although President Chen's pro-independence Min-chu Chin-pu Tang (MCT) (Democratic Progressive Party) won the December parliamentary elections, it narrowly failed to take control of parliament.
2005 Yu Shyi-kun's cabinet resigned and on 25 January, the president appointed Frank Hsieh (MCT) as prime minister. In March, China's National People's Congress passed an anti-secession law, enshrining Beijing's claim of sovereignty and its threat of military force in the event of Taiwan's formal independence; more than one million people took to the streets to express opposition to the law. In June, the Supreme Court ruled the 24 March 2004 presidential elections valid.
2006 Prime Minister Hsieh resigned on 16 January. President Chen chose Su Tseng-chang, co-founder of the ruling MCT, as his replacement. A new cabinet was sworn in 24 January.

Political structure
Constitution
The Legislative Yuan, presided over by the prime minister, is the highest government body. It is responsible for passing laws and drafting the budget. It is elected every three years and has the power to dismiss the prime minister.
The 29-member Control Yuan exercises powers of investigation, impeachment and censure over senior officials, including the grand justices of the Judicial Yuan and members of the Examination Yuan, and power of audit over central and local government finances. Its members are

Taiwan

appointed by the president with the approval of the legislature.

The Examination Yuan supervises examinations for entry into public office and deals with personnel questions of the civil service.

The Kuo-min Ta-hui (National Assembly) passed a series of constitutional amendments in April 2000 which reduced itself to an *ad hoc* institution deprived of most of its powers. The powers of initiating constitutional amendments, changing the national boundaries, impeaching the president or vice president and approving the appointment of senior officials, were transferred to the Legislative Yuan. The Kuo-min Ta-hui retains the functions of ratifying constitutional amendments and impeachment proceedings against the president.

The National Assembly is to convene for a month from no later than 31 May 2005 to vote on whether public referenda could be used to change the constitution, which means the abolition of the Assembly itself. Other constitutional amendments slated to go before the Assembly are plans to streamline the Legislative Yuan by halving the number of seats from 225 to 113, beginning from 2007, and the extension of legislators' terms from three to four years and whether it should hand over to grand justices the rights to impeach the president.

Form of state
Representative democracy

The executive
The president is directly elected for a four-year term. The president nominates a prime minister to head the Executive Yuan (cabinet), which is the highest administrative organ of the nation, and is responsible to the Legislative Yuan. The Executive Yuan consists of the ministries and commissions and 19 subordinate administrative organs of state.

National legislature
The Li fa Yuan (Legislative Yuan), with 225 members, is the highest legislative organ of state. Members are elected for a term of three years and are eligible for re-election. Most are elected by universal suffrage, but special representation exists for Taiwan's lowland and aboriginal peoples, as well as overseas Chinese.

Legal system
The Judicial Yuan is the highest judicial organ of state. Justices are appointed by the president with the approval of the Control Yuan. Subordinate organs of the Judicial Yuan include the Supreme Court, the high courts, the district courts, the Administrative Court and the Commission on the Disciplinary Sanctions of Public Functionaries.

Last elections
11 December 2004 (parliamentary); 20 March 2004 (presidential).
Results: Parliamentary: President Chen's pro-independence Min-chu Chin-pu Tang (MCT) (Democratic Progressive Party) won 35.7 per cent of the vote (89 seats out of 225); the Kuomintang (KMT) (Nationalist Party) 32.8 per cent (79), the People First Party 13.9 per cent (34) and the Taiwan Solidarity Union 7.8 per cent (12). Presidential: incumbent Chen Shui-bian (MCT) was re-elected with 50.1 per cent of the vote and Lien Chan (Kuomintang) 49.9 per cent; turnout was 80.3 per cent. There was a dispute over the results and the President promised a recount. In June 2005, the Supreme Court ruled the 24 March 2004 presidential elections valid.

Next elections
2007 (parliamentary); 2008 (presidential).

Political parties
Ruling party
Min-chu Chin-pu Tang (MCT) (Democratic Progressive Party) (since Dec 2001; re-elected 11 Dec 2004)
Main opposition party
Kuomintang (KMT) (Nationalist Party)

Population
23.07 million (2004)
Ethnic make-up
Taiwan's population is mostly ethnic Han Chinese. A majority of these are local Taiwanese, who have language links to Fujian province across the Taiwan Strait. There is a powerful minority of immigrants that came from the mainland during the 1940s, as well as a Hakka minority. Taiwan's non-Han aborigines (yuanchumin) are related to the Polynesian and Malay ethnic groups. They comprise dozens of distinct groups, including the Rukai tribe (about 8,000 strong) and the Clouded Leopard People. They have limited rights and may not sell or develop lands. Indigenous rights groups have campaigned to regain political and economic autonomy in the aboriginal territories that were demarcated during the Japanese occupation.
Religions
The majority of people are Buddhist or Taoist with Confucian influence. Most Chinese make no sharp distinction between Buddhism and Taoism in Taiwan, and most practise a hybrid of these two religions. About 2.5 per cent of the population are Christian.

Education
There are 2,600 primary schools with a total enrolment around two million students. Primary school lasts for six years before entry to junior high school, at aged 12, for three years. Dependent on exam results at aged 15, students may move on to either a senior vocational high school or a senior high school (for more academic courses which lead to entrance exams for higher education). There are 986 secondary schools and 188 vocational institutions.

All education is delivered in Chinese however English is a compulsory subject during the secondary cycles. Higher education is offered at colleges and universities from aged 18. The total number of universities and colleges is 150 and the gross enrolment of graduates aged between 18 and 21 years is nearly 70 per cent per cent.
Compulsory years: Six to 15.
Pupils per teacher: 19 in primary school.

Health
Taiwan's public health sector offers a universal health insurance system, the first in Asia to ensure equal access to care for the entire population. Total expenditure on health per capita is approaching developed country standards.

Taiwan has 700 hospitals and 17,000 clinics and an active pharmaceutical industry.
Life expectancy: 77 years (government statistics, 2004).
Fertility rate/Maternal mortality rate: 1.4 births per woman; maternal mortality 7.86 per 100,000 live births (Government statistics).
Birth rate/Death rate: 3.25 per 1,000 (Government statistics).
Infant mortality rate: 6.7 per 1,000 live births (2003)

Welfare
There is provision for special subsidies and assistance to low-income earners and families, based on variations in regional income distribution for each fiscal year. Some low-income families with children qualify for an additional monthly subsidy. In Taiwan Province, the subsidy is US$52 per child, limited to two children per household.

The elderly comprise a growing proportion of the population. By 2001, 8.6 per cent of the total population was estimated to be over 65. Elderly residents of Taipei City and County, Ilan, Hsinchu, Tainan, Chiayi City, Kaohsiung and Penghu counties benefit from organised pension systems. Residents of these areas who are 65 years or older and are not entitled to other forms of pension or subsidy from the government receive a pension ranging from US$88 to US$176 per month, depending on the county or city of residence. This welfare policy is not universal but is budgeted according to the county or city governments. There is serious shortage of housing for elderly people, despite Taiwan's 350 retirement and nursing homes.

Nations of the World: A Political, Economic and Business Handbook

Main cities
Taipei (capital, estimated population 2.6 million in 2004), Kaohsiung (1.6 million), Taichung (1.0 million), Tainan (755,800), Panchiao (589,700).

Languages spoken
The second language spoken is Fukienese, a dialect of Mandarin, but very different to it, that is spoken in the Fujian province in China. Fukienese is also called Taiwanese. Other Chinese dialects spoken are Shanghaiese, Hakka and Cantonese. English is spoken only by the elite.

Official language/s
Mandarin Chinese

Media
Press
Dailies: The three English-language dailies are *The China Post*, *Taiwan News* (formerly *China News*) and *Taipei Times*. They are all morning papers.
Weeklies: *Free China Journal*, formerly *Free China Weekly*, is published weekly in English.
Business: *Industry of Free China*, a monthly bilingual (English/Chinese) publication of the Executive Yuan's Council for Economic Planning and Development. It publishes extensive economic statistics and articles about current economic performance. Bilingual statistical material is also published by the Department of Statistics, Ministry of Economic Affairs (*Taiwan Industrial Production Statistics Monthly*). The Directorate-General of the Budget, Accounting and Statistics Executive Yuan publishes *Statistical Yearbook* and *Social Indicators of the Republic of China*. Also available is *Monthly Key Economic Indicators of Taiwan the Republic of China*.

Broadcasting
Radio: There are over 200 broadcasting radio stations, two-thirds of them privately owned, with services generally in Chinese.
Television: There are three state-owned TV networks with multiple channels.

Advertising
Advertising is available in the press, in cinemas and via commercial radio and television.

Economy
During the 1980s and 1990s, Taiwan became one of the foremost of the regional 'tiger economies', combining elements of the 'Asian Miracle' of state-guided development with a strong base of competitive, market-oriented small- and medium-sized enterprises. The latter enabled Taiwan to ride out the Asian crisis with relative equanimity as exporters enjoyed a devaluation-led boom.
In the second half of 2001, Taiwan fell into recession. Exports suffered the biggest blow as a result of the global decline in demand for high-tech and electronic produce, a sector that typically accounted for 50 per cent of Taiwan's overall exports. More workers were laid off as operations were shifted to mainland China. The high rate of capital flight to China also damaged the economy.
The foreign investment environment has been good, with joint ventures and direct investment in most sectors enabled since 1995. As part of its commitments as a WTO member, Taiwan, which joined in January 2002, agreed to liberalise its telecommunications market and has opened other sectors of the economy to foreign buyers. Taiwan is concerned that large foreign monopolies will erode the government's influential role and threaten domestic industries. Taiwan is looking to extend its cross-strait links and encourage trade with the mainland.
The economy began to recover in 2002, but was slowed briefly again by the outbreak of Severe Acute Respiratory Syndrome (Sars) in early 2003. Taiwan committed US$1.4 billion to offset the effects of the disease, with a successful outcome – GDP growth reached 3.2 per cent in 2003 and has continued to grow, reaching 5.7 per cent in 2004. Growth was slower in 2005, due to high oil prices, a fall in exports and uncertainty in the high tech sector.
Taiwan is a creditor economy, holding one of the world's largest foreign exchange reserves.

External trade
Taiwan is heavily dependent on foreign trade. Its consistent heavy trade surpluses have amassed an enormous foreign currency reserve (second only to Japan in the 1990s), of which 42 per cent is invested in banks abroad. Taiwan is in the top 15 exporting nations in the world. In 1998, Taiwan announced that it would start cutting tariffs on cars imported from the EU from 30 per cent down to 17.5 per cent by 2008.
Closer economic integration with the mainland may be slowed by fears that political vulnerability could be increased. However, Taiwan's membership of the WTO means that it is compelled to reduce trade barriers. Trade between the Chinese mainland and the Taiwanese islands of Kinmen and Matsu was allowed from January 2001 after Taiwan's 52-year ban on direct trade and communications with China was lifted.

Imports
Imports are dominated by raw materials and capital goods, (over 90 per cent of total), coal, oil and natural gas.
Main sources: China (23 per cent total, 2004), Japan (15 per cent), US (13 per cent)

Exports
Main export are industrial goods (98 per cent of total) including electronics, computers and monitors, and textiles.
Main destinations: China (37 per cent total, 2004), Japan (26 per cent), US (16 per cent)

Agriculture
Farming
The agriculture sector contributes 2 per cent to GDP. Since accession to the WTO in 2002 Taiwan has refocussed its agricultural objectives. The workforce is being reduced by 4 per cent per year until it reaches 633,000 workers and the emphasis will be on quality food rather than quantity. Taiwan's farm plots are generally small, hindering cost-efficient management. Estimates show that 76 per cent of all farming households have less than one hectare (ha) of arable landand 80 per cent have members working part- or full-time in other occupations.
Rice is still the principal and most valuable crop (in quantiy and cultivated land), followed by betel nuts, pineapples, mangoes, sugar cane, watermelons, tea, bamboo shoots, pears, and peanuts. Industrial crops include cotton, hemp and jute.

Fishing
The fishing industry has gradually developed from small-scale coastal fishing to deep-sea commercial fishing. The deep-water fishing industry is large and expanding, supplemented by aquaculture. Eel is an important aquacultural product as are milkfish, tilapia, groupers, tiger prawn and oyster. Intense aqcuaculture has done some damage to the environment by drawing off huge amounts of water. This has caused land to cave in. The government is tackling the problem by encouraging the recycling of freshwater. The government has been actively engaged in international fishery management and has signed official or private fishery agreements with 29 countries.
The annual fish catch in Taiwan is typically 1.4 million metric tonnes.

Forestry
The timber industry is limited by inaccessibility, the poor quality of much of the forestry resources and by an official policy of conserving supplies. Taiwan's forested area covers around 2.1 million hectares, which is about half the land area. Forestry products include sawn timber, plywood, paper and fuel for local use.

Industry and manufacturing
The industrial sector contributes around 35 per cent to GDP, with manufacturing accounting for 95 per cent of industrial

exports. Heavy industries include motor manufacturing, steel production and shipbuilding. Taiwan's main strength is its high-tech industry. In recent years, Taiwan has moved away from manufacturing electronic toys, deemed to be unhealthy for children, and focussed on electronic components. Most production is exported, accounting for an estimated 55 per cent of total exports and 20 per cent of GDP. The government is hoping to develop Taiwan into a green silicon island. In 2002, the Taiwan Industrial Technology Association (TITA) was set up to upgrade industries. TITA will spend US$571 million each year on developing industries such as optoelectronics, aerospace, chemicals, semiconductors, telecommunications and information technology (IT).

Many Taiwanese products have an important share in the global market and the communications industry has been boosted by the liberalisation of the global telecommunications industry.

The main concern for Taiwan's industry is that low-end and mid-range manufacturers are moving to China. To remain competitive, Taiwan needs to focus on developing integrated software design.

Tourism

Tourism contributed 2.78 per cent to GDP in 2004. In 2005, 3,378,000 arrivals were recorded, exceeding the government's target for the year. Of this total, 1,380,000 described themselves as tourists. The government recognises the economic importance of the sector and is actively promoting it and improving facilities. Taiwan is engaging with the mainland government to open the island to Chinese tourists.

Mining

Mining accounts for less than 1 per cent of GDP. Taiwan has few exploitable mineral resources. Due to the depletion of local sources, nearly all of the rare earth and metallic mining products are imported. Over 20 types of minerals are mined in Taiwan, mainly marble, limestone, serpentine and gravel. Marble is Taiwan's most important mineral resource with reserves conservatively estimated at over 300 million tonnes. Marble, salt, sand and gravel constitute the most valuable mineral products. Taiwan also produces iron and steel from imported iron ore and iron scrap and processed products such as aluminium, copper, lead, nickel, tin and zinc from imported raw materials.

Taiwan has four gold-bearing mines with metal content estimated at 100 tonnes. Taiwan utilises its large trade surpluses to import gold.

Hydrocarbons

Taiwan is almost entirely reliant on energy imports. Approximately 99.5 per cent of oil and coal needs and over 80 per cent of natural gas requirements are imported. Taiwan had proven oil reserves of four million barrels in 2004 and produces around 8,000 barrels per day (bpd). Oil consumption is estimated at around one million bpd. Taiwan is dependent on imports from the Middle East ands West Africa. Oil accounts for 46 per cent of total primary energy consumption, mainly by industry. There are four refineries with a total refining capacity of 1.22 million bpd. Taiwan is laying claim to the potentially oil-rich Spratly Islands, an area of contention between Taiwan, Vietnam, China, Brunei, Malaysia and The Philippines. Taiwan has around eight billion cubic metres of gas reserves and produces around 890 million cubic metres per annum. Natural gas consumption amounts to around eight billion cubic metres per annum. Most of Taiwan's imports of liquefied natural gas (LNG) come from Indonesia and Malaysia. The government plans to triple LNG consumption by 2010 as part of its commitment to the environment. Taiwan has coal reserves of 98 million tonnes, but ceased production in 2000. Taiwan consumes 55 million tonnes of coal per annum. Most coal imports come from China, Indonesia and Australia. Coal is used for electricity generation, steel production, cement and petrochemical industries.

Energy

Taiwan has installed electricity generating capacity of around 34.5GW. The state-owned Taiwan Power Company (Taipower) operates 72 power stations. Taipower's output is 68 per cent thermally produced, 17 per cent nuclear and most of the rest by hydro-power. Privatisation of Taipower has been delayed and is expected to take place in 2006.

Independent power producers are allowed to provide up to 20 per cent of Taiwan's electricity under a law passed in 1994. Foreign investors are allowed to participate in the electricity sector.

In June 2004, plans were approved for a 4,000MW LNG-fired complex, the Tatan Power Plant, to be built by Taipower; it is expected to be completed in 2007, before the adjacent LNG terminal becomes operational in 2009, so the plant will run on coal until then. In addition, an 800MW coal-fired power plant at Changhua in central Taiwan will be built by Taipower for around US$1.4 billion and will come online in two stages during 2011.

Financial markets

A computerised over-the-counter (OTC) market, the Taisdaq, was introduced in 1994. Taiwan's financial markets are regulated by the Securities and Futures Commission.

Stock exchange

The Taiwan Stock Exchange (TSE) was opened to indirect foreign investment in 1984. Electronics companies have the largest share of the stock market. The stock exchange's dismal performance in 2001/02 was brought on by the downturn in electronic products that sent the Taiex index spiralling downwards.

Banking and insurance

Foreign banks have been allowed to compete in the Taiwanese market since 1989. In June 2001, the government passed a package of legislation to reform the financial sector. The most important part of this legislation is the financial holding company law, which allows banks, security houses, insurance companies, investment funds, and futures brokerages to be grouped under one entity.

Central bank

Central Bank of China

Main financial centre

Taipei

Offshore facilities

Offshore banking has also been available since 1984. Foreign banks are permitted to set up offshore banking units (OBUs) without first having established a branch in Taiwan.

Time

GMT plus eight hours

Geography

Taiwan is an island, 395km long and 144km across. It has high mountains, rising out of the sea along its eastern shore. The western side is flat and fertile. Taipei is located at the northen end of the island and is the largest city.

Climate

Subtropical with temperatures ranging from 33 degrees Celsius (C) in Jul–Aug to 12 degrees C in Jan–Feb. Average rainfall is 2,500mm per year, with typhoons from May–Oct and occasional snow in the mountains in Jan–Feb.

Entry requirements

Passports

Required by all. Passports must be valid for six months.

Visa

Required by all, except citizens of EU, North America, Australasia and some Asian countries. Visit www.boca.gov.tw/ for a full list of exemptions and application forms. Visa free (tourist) visits are limited to 30 days. All business visits of less than six months may be undertaken on visitors visas. Applications require a business letter of intent and itinerary. All visitors must have return/onward passage.

For details of the closest Taiwanese embassy visit
http://www.eslisland.com/guide/TaiwanEmbassiesabroad.htm.

Currency advice/regulations
Travellers leaving Taiwan may not take out more than US$5,000 cash or the equivalent in any other foreign currency unless it was declared on arrival.

Import and export of local currency is restricted to T$40,000 (US$1,143.51) and 20 coins.

Travellers' cheques in sterling are generally mistrusted, although certain branches of the Bank of Taiwan exchange them for dollars.

International Money Orders are a problem and bank accounts can only be opened by residents.

Customs
Personal effects are duty-free. Gold and silver ornaments must be declared. Import of certain items is controlled, such as military supplies, national defence and communications equipment and poisonous chemicals. Most permitted imports require a licence.

Prohibited imports
Narcotics, gambling aids (including mahjong sets), firearms and explosives are prohibited.

Health (for visitors)
Mandatory precautions
Vaccination certificate for yellow fever if travelling from an infected area.

Advisable precautions
Vaccinations are recommended for diphtheria, tuberculosis, hepatitis 'A' and 'B', polio, tetanus and typhoid. There is a risk of rabies.

Do not drink the tap water – hotels provide boiled water in flasks.

In June 1998, the World Health Organisation (WHO) warned of the unusually high risk of dengue fever. There were 383 suspected cases of Severe Acute Respiratory Syndrome (Sars) in May 2003; 52 people were reported to have died.

Hotels
It is advisable to book hotel rooms in advance. Room facilities usually include TVs and refrigerators. Larger hotels will arrange transport to/from the airport. A 10 per cent service charge is added to the bill. Reasonably priced accommodation is available at Japanese-style hot springs resorts in the mountains.

Credit cards
Not widely used.

Public holidays
Fixed dates
1–3 Jan (Founding of the Republic of China/New Year), 29 Mar (Youth Day), 5 Apr (Tomb-sweeping Day/Anniversary of President Chiang Kai-shek's Passing), 28 Sep (Teachers' Day/Confucius' Birthday), 10 Oct (National Day), 25 Oct (Taiwan Retrocession Day), 31 Oct (Birthday of Chiang Kai-shek), 12 Nov (Birthday of Dr Sun Yat-sen), 25 Dec (Constitution Day).

Variable dates
Chinese New Year (Jan/Feb), Tuen Ng (Dragon Boat) Festival (May/Jun), Mid-Autumn Moon Festival (Sep/Oct).

Working hours
Banking
Mon–Fri: 0900–1530; Sat: 0900–1200.
Business
Mon–Fri: 0830–1230, 1330–1730; Sat: 0830–1230.
Government
Mon–Fri: 0830–1230, 1330–1730; Sat: 0830–1230.
Shops
Sun–Sat: 0900–2200 (department stores 1100–2130).

Telecommunications
Telephone/fax
The telephone system is advanced and has 100 per cent automatic service. On city pay phones the connection will automatically be severed after three minutes, and the caller must redial for local calls. The area code should not be included for calls within the same area. Domestic long-distance calls may be made on private phones or blue-green pay phones. For overseas calls on private phones, the overseas operator may be reached by dialling '100'; overseas calls may also be made on public facilities at International Telecommunications Administration (ITA) offices.

International direct dialling rates are calculated every six seconds.

Electricity supply
110V AC, 60 cycles

Weights and measures
Metric system (some Chinese units in use).

Social customs/useful tips
Shaking hands is the normal form of greeting. When addressing Chinese persons, the family or surname comes first. Business cards are usually exchanged and should be in both Chinese and English. They constitute an important part of the business culture, and Taiwanese expect visitors to carry cards. Cards using mainland (simplified) script are not advisable as this could cause offence.

Visitors should remember that Taiwanese of all backgrounds need to maintain 'face', this means that it is important not to embarrass your Taiwanese counterpart either privately or when in company. Rejection of gifts as small as cigarettes may cause offence, as a sign that the offerer is not considered wealthy. In general, however, the social environment in Taiwan is very liberal and visitors need not fear inadvertently causing offence.

When visiting people's homes, removing shoes is mandatory. The subject of death should be avoided in conversation as it is considered a bad omen.

Getting there
Air
There are no flights between Taiwan and China.

National airline: China Airlines (CAL)
International airport/s: Chiang Kai-Shek International (TPE), 40km south-west of Taipei, with duty-free shop, bar, restaurant, buffet, bank, post office, hotel reservations and shops; Kaohsiung International (KHH).
Airport tax: None
Surface
Water: Regular ferry services run between Keelung and Kaohsiung ports (Taiwan) and Okinawa (Japan). There are also some sea links between Kaohsiung and Macao.
Main port/s: Keelung (including Suao), Hualien, Taichung. Kaohsiung has container facilitiess and an offshore transshipment centre.

Getting about
National transport
Air: Domestic air services operated by China Airlines. Far Eastern Air Transport and seven other carriers connect most of the main cities. Taiwan's second carrier, Eva Air, is a major international carrier.
Road: The road network covers 20,000km, most of it surfaced. A good highway links the main centres between Keelung and Kaohsiung. Bad terrain and one-way systems can make road travel difficult outside urban centres.
Buses: Extensive bus services cover coastal, cross-island and inland areas. Express coach services link Taipei, Kaohsiung and other main centres. Advance booking is recommended. Local bus services are crowded during rush hours. Destinations are clearly marked in English at urban bus stations.
Rail: The railway extends the whole length of Taiwan, mainly along the west coast. Rail services are good, with air-conditioned express trains linking main centres. Urban train stations have destinations marked in English.

A US$17.8 billion high speed 345km rail system linking Taipei with the southern city of Kaohsiung is expected to be operational by October 2005. It is the first build-operate-transfer (BOT) project awarded in Taiwan.
Water: There are ferry services from Kaohsiung and Chiayi to the Pescadores Islands, from Taitung to the Lanyu and Green Islands.

City transport
Rush-hour traffic in Taipei can be chaotic and stressful. Allow plenty of time for getting to and from the airport.
Taxis: Taxis are plentiful but not cheap. Specialist taxis operate (in the manner of buses) on certain routes, but these are not recommended.
Metered taxis are available in Taipei, and fares are metered by kilometres and delay time. Have the destination (and the return address) written in Chinese for the taxi driver's reference.
Tipping is not an established practice, though it is becoming more usual.
From Chiang Kai-Shek airport to city centre the journey time is 45–60 minutes.
Buses, trams & metro: An underground rail system and a Rapid Mass Transit System are under construction in Taipei. Construction is expected to be fully completed by 2009.
Car hire
Self-drive car hire is available, although chauffeur-driven cars are recommended due to traffic conditions. An international driving licence is required. Driving is on the right-hand side of the road.

BUSINESS DIRECTORY

The addresses listed below are a selection only. While World of Information makes every endeavour to check these addresses, we cannot guarantee that changes have not been made, especially to telephone numbers and area codes. We would welcome any corrections.

Telephone area codes
The international direct dialling (IDD) code for Taiwan is +886 followed by the area code and subscriber's number:

Hualien	38	Taichung	4
Kaohsiung	7	Tainan	6
Keelung	32	Taipai	2
Pingtung	8		

Useful telephone numbers
Fire and ambulance: 119.
Police: 110.
English-speaking police: 311-9940, 311-9816 ext 264.
Ambulance: 721-6315.
Women's help-line 581-5469.
International calls: 100.
Directory enquiries: Chinese language 104 (long-distance: 105). English language 311-6796.

Chambers of Commerce
American Chamber of Commerce in Taipei, Chia Hsin Building, 96 Chungshan North Road, Section 2, Taipei 104 (tel: 2581-7089; fax: 2542-3376; e-mail: amcham@amcham.com.tw).

British Chamber of Commerce in Taiwan, Fu Key Building, 99 Ren Ai Road, Section 2, Taipei 106 (tel: 2356-0210; fax: 2356-0211; e-mail: info@bcctaipei.com).

Chinese National Association of Industry and Commerce, 390 Fu Hsing South Road, Taipei 106 (tel: 2707-0111; fax :2 701-7601; e-mail: webmaster@nfict.org).

European Chamber of Commerce Taipei, 285 Zhongxiao East Road, Section 4, Taipei (tel: 2740-0236; fax: 2772-0530; e-mail: ecct@ecct.com.tw).

Taiwan Chamber of Commerce, 158 Sung Chiang Road, Taipei 104 (tel: 2536-5455; fax: 2521-1980; e-mail: tcoc@tcoc.org.tw).

Banking
Bank of Taiwan, 120 Chungking S Road, Sec 2, Taipei (tel: 314-7377; fax: 331-5840).

Chang Hwa Commercial Bank, 23-1 Chang An E Rd, Sec 1, Taipei City (tel: 523-0739; fax: 523-0172).

Chiao Tung Bank, 91 Heng Yang Road, Taipei (tel: 361-3000; fax: 311-3263).

Citibank, PO Box 3343, Citicorp Center, 52 Minsheng E Road, Sec 4, Taipei City 105 (tel: 715-5931; fax: 712-7388).

First Commercial Bank, 30 Chungking S Road, Sec 1, Taipei 10036 (tel: 311-111; fax: 361-0036).

Hua Nan Commercial Bank, 38 Chungking S Road, Sec 1, Taipei (tel: 371-3111; fax: 371-5734).

International Commercial Bank of China, 100 Chi Lin Road, Taipei (tel: 563-3156; fax: 561-1216).

Shanghai Commercial & Savings Bank Ltd, 2 Min Chuan East Road, Section 1, Taipei City (tel: 581-7111; fax: 567-1921).

Standard Chartered Bank, 168 Tun Hwa North Rd, Taipei City 105 (tel: 716-2621, 717-2866; fax: 716-4068).

Taipeibank, 50 Chungshan North Road, Section 2, Taipei City (tel: 542-5656; fax: 542-8870).

Taiwan Co-operative Bank, 77 Kuanchien Road, Taipei (tel: 311-8811; fax: 331-6567).

Central bank
Central Bank of China, 2 Roosevelt Road, Section 1, Taipei 100 (tel: 2393-6161; fax: 2357-1968; e-mail: adminrol@mail.cbc.gov.tw).

Travel information
Chiang Kai Shek International Airport, PO Box 9, Taipei (tel: 398-2001; fax: 383-4801).

China Airlines (CAL), 131 Nanking East Road, Section 3, Taipei 104 (tel: 715-2626; fax: 717-5120).

CKS International Airport Tourist Service Centre (tel: 383-4631/2).

Flight information (24 hours) (tel: 398-2050).

Sungshan Domestic Airport Travel Information Service Centre (tel: 349-1580).

Taiwan Visitors' Association, 5th Floor, 9 Ming Chuan East Road, Sec 2, Taipei (tel: 594-3261; fax: 594-3265).

Tourist Information Hot Line (tel: 717-3737).

National tourist organisation offices
Tourism Bureau, 9F Floor, 280 Chung Hsiao East Road, Section 4, PO Box 1490, Taipei (tel: 721-8541; fax: 773-5487: internet www.taiwantourism.org).

Ministries
Ministry of Economic Affairs, 15 Foochow Street, Taipei (tel: 321-2200; fax: 391-9398).

Ministry of Education (MOE), 5 Chungshan S. Road, Taipei (tel: 356-6051; fax: 397-6920).

Ministry of Finance, 2 Aikuo West Road, Taipei (tel: 322-8000; fax: 321-1205).

Ministry of Foreign Affairs, 2 Chieh Shou Road, Taipei (tel: 311-9292; fax: 314-4972).

Ministry of the Interior (MOI), 5 Hsuchow Road, Taipei (tel: 356-5000; fax: 356-6201).

Ministry of Justice (MOJ), 130 Chungking S. Road, Sec. 1, Taipei (tel: 314-6871; fax: 389-6239).

Ministry of National Defence, Chiehshou Hall, Chungking S. Road, Taipei (tel: 311-6117; fax: 314-4221).

Ministry of Transportation and Communications, 2 Changasha Street, Section 1, Taipei (tel: 349-2900; fax: 389-6009).

Monetary Affairs Dept, Ministry of Finance, 2 Aikuo W Road, Taipei (tel: 321-3836).

President's Office, 122 Chungking South Road, Section 1, Taipei (tel: 311-3731; fax: 314-0746 (the First Bureau); 311-5877 (Protocol Section); 331-1604 (Spokesman's Office).

Other useful addresses
Board of Foreign Trade, 1 Hukou St, Taipei (tel: 351-0271; fax: 351-3603).

British Trade and Cultural Office, 9th floor, Fu Key Building, 99 Jen Ali Road, Section 2, Taipei 10625 (tel: 322-4242; fax: 394-8673).

China External Trade Development Council (CETRA), 4-8th floor, International Trade Building, 333 Keelung Road, Sec 1, Taipei 10548 (tel: 725-5200; fax: 757-6653).

Chinese National Association of Industry & Commerce, 13th floor, 390 Fu Hsing South Rd, Sec 1, Taipei (tel: 707-0111; fax: 701-7601).

Chinese National Export Enterprises Association (CNEEA), 6th floor, 285 Nanking E. Road, Sec. 3, Taipei (tel: 713-8153; fax: 713-0115).

Chinese National Federation of Industries, 12th floor, 390 Fuhsing South Road, Section 1, Taipei (tel: 703-3500; fax: 703-3982).

Chinese Petroleum Corporation, 83 Chung-Hwa Road, Section 1, Taipei 10331 (tel: 361-0221; fax: 371-5944).

Council for Economic Planning and Development, 9/F, 87 Nanking East Road, Section 2, Taipei (tel: 551-3522; fax: 581-8549).

Directorate-General of Budgets, Accounting & Statistics, Executive Yuan, 1 Chung Hsiao East Road, Section 1, Taipei (internet site: http://www.stat.gov.tw/).

Euro-Asia Trade Organisation, 3rd floor, 9 Roosevelt Road, Sec. 2, Taipei (tel: 393-2115; fax: 392-8393).

Government Information Office, Taipei (tel: 322-8888).

Industrial Development Bureau, MOEA, 41-3 Hsinyi Road, Sec. 3, Taipei (tel: 754-1255; fax: 703-0160).

Industrial Development and Investment Centre, MOEA, 4 Chunghsiao W. Road, Sec 1, Taipei (tel: 389-2111; fax: 382-0497).

Industry of Free China, 9th Floor, 87 Nanking East Road, Section 2, Taipei (tel: 543-5988).

International Co-operation Department, MOEA, 15 Foochow St., Taipei (tel: 321-2200; fax: 321-3275).

International Economic Co-operation Development Fund, 7th floor, 51 Chung-Ching S. Road, Sec. 2, Taipei (tel: 396-6316; fax: 396-9147).

International Telecommunications Administration (ITA), 28 Hangchou S. Rd, Sec. 1, Taipei (tel: 344-3781).

International Trade Association of the R.O.C., 8th floor, 148 Chunghsiao E. Road, Sec. 4, Taipei (tel: 772-6252; fax: 752-2411).

Investment Commission, Ministry of Economic Affairs, 8th Floor, 7 Roosevelt Road, Sec 1, Taipei (tel: 351-3151; fax: 396-3970).

Securities and Exchange Commission, 12th Floor, Yangteh Building, 3 Nanhai Road, Taipei (tel: 341-3191; fax: 394-8249).

Taipei Economic and Cultural Representative Office (USA), 4201 Wisconsin Avenue, NW, Washington DC 20016 (tel: 202-895-1800; fax: 202-363-0999; e-mail: contact@tecro-info.org).

Taipei World Trade Centre Exhibition Hall, 5 Hsinyi Road, Section 5, Taipei (tel: 886-2725; fax: 886-1314).

Taiwan Stock Exchange Corp, 85 Yen Ping S Road, Taipei (tel: 311-4020; fax: 311-4004).

Taiwan Textile Federation, 22 Ai-Kuo E. Road, Taipei (tel: 341-7251; fax: 392-3855).

World Trade Center Taichung, 60 Tienpao St, Taichung (tel: 254-2271; fax: 254-2341).

Internet sites

Taiwan business directory: http://www.tbdo.anjes.com.tw/

Taiwan business express: http://www.business.com.tw/

Taiwan News, the Voice of Taiwan: http://www.eTaiwanNews.com

Taiwan Trade Point: http://www.tradepoint.anjes.com.tw/

Tajikistan

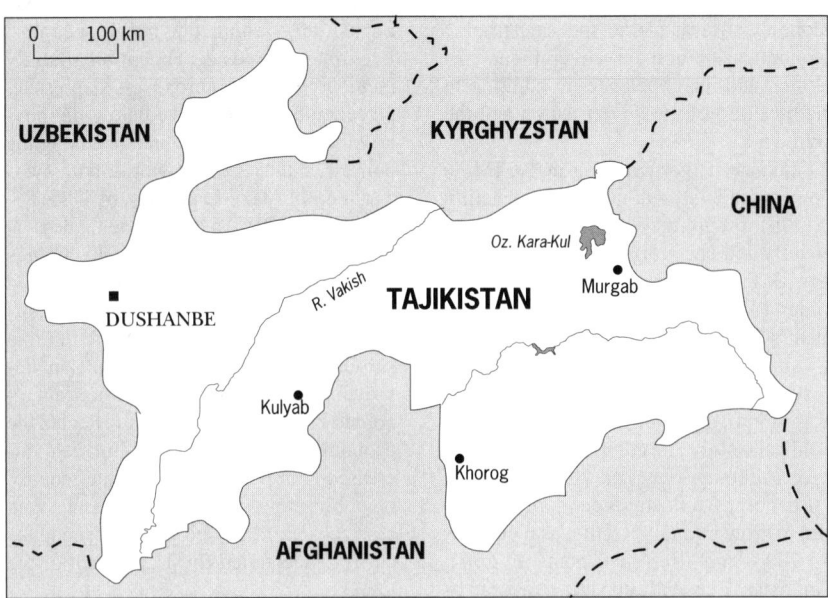

Tajikistan's early years of independence did not go well. The country's five-year civil war had its origins in the tensions between the Moscow-backed government of then president, Rahmon Nabiyev, and a coalition of opposition parties made up of the Democratic Party of Tajikistan (DPT), the Islamic Renaissance Party (IRP) and the smaller Lali Badakhshon, all three combining to form a national, religious, democratic opposition bloc.

Despite government efforts to incorporate the opposition, which had become grouped under the United Tajik Opposition (UTO) banner, the situation deteriorated and civil war eventually broke out in May 1992. By the time the war ended in 1997, it was estimated to have caused some 100,000 deaths. During the civil war, parliament relocated to the town of Chodshand and elected Emomali Rakhmonov as its chairman. Rakhmonov formed a government mainly composed of politicians from the Kulyab region in Tajikistan's south. The end of the war was marked by the signature of a *General Agreement on the Establishment of Peace and National Reconciliation*. At the same time a Commission for National Reconciliation was established, with Abdullo Nuri, the UTO leader, as its chairman.

The peace agreement was consolidated by the presidential and parliamentary elections of 1999 and 2000. Under the agreement, the Islamic Renaissance Party (IRP) a key member of the UTO, was admitted to the Majlis Oli (parliament) following a constitutional amendment on the legalisation of parties based on a religion.

A peaceful stand-off?

After the 2000 elections, Tajikistan entered something of a political stand-off as a general state of war weariness, not to mention the presence of 20,000 Russian troops in the country dampened political ardour. The opposition were granted one third of senior government posts including that of deputy prime minister. A dubious referendum held in June 2003 approved a number of constitutional amendments, including one allowing the president to stand for re-election. Under the reformed constitution, President Rakhmonov will be able to run for a further two consecutive seven year terms after his probable re-election in 2006. In principle, if he lives that long, Rakhmonov if re-elected will

KEY FACTS

Official name: Respublika i Tojikiston (Republic of Tajikistan)

Head of State: President Emomali Rakhmonov (leader since 1992; elected Nov 1994; re-elected 1999)

Head of government: Prime Minister Akil Akilov (since Dec 1999)

Ruling party: Hizbi Demokrati Khalkii Tajikistan (HDKT) (People's Democratic Party of Tajikistan) (re-elected Feb/Mar 2005)

Area: 143,100 square km

Population: 6.54 million (2004)

Capital: Dushanbe

Official language: Tajik (Farsi)

Currency: Somoni (Sm) = 100 dirams (introduced 30 Oct 2000)

Exchange rate: Sm3.18 per US$ (Oct 2005)

GDP per capita: US$329 (2004)

GDP real growth: 10.60% (2004)

Labour force: 2.72 million (2004)

Unemployment: 40.00% (2003) (unofficial)

Inflation: 7.10% (2004)

Oil production: 250 bpd (2003)

Balance of trade: -US$135.50 million 2004

Foreign debt: US$1,000.00 million (2003)

have been Tajikistan's president for 26 years when he finally steps down.

A serious structural weakness in Tajikistan's political make up under the Rakhmonov régime is the exclusion of the Leninabad-based opposition grouping, led by former prime minister Abdumalik Abdullojonov. Leninabad is in the north of Tajikistan, President Rakhmonov comes from the south. Leninabad is the country's most developed and productive region. Tribal allegiances and other considerations apart, the government is thought to fear the possibly divisive influence of the Leninabad opposition. Although quite what their exclusion achieves is debatable.

Economic woes

Tajikistan's GDP per capita is one of the lowest in the former Soviet Union. Agriculture, particularly cotton, dominates the official economy. Industry is largely limited to the Tadaz aluminium smelter, the Nurek hydroelectric power station and small obsolete light industry and food processing factories. Tajikistan, located at the crossroads of Russia, Iran, Pakistan and China, has become a narcotics hub and a major transit route for opium produced in Afghanistan.

Like many transition states, Tajikistan's recent economic history has been one of severe contraction. However, Tajikistan's transition has been more extreme than most. The country was already the poorest of the Soviet republics. The economy was weakened following the collapse of the Soviet Union when Tajikistan lost its subsidies (which accounted for up to 80 per cent of its income) and markets. The five-year civil war effectively destroyed the Tajik economy. The war ravaged the country's limited infrastructure, led to the emigration of some of the country's most qualified and skilled workers and caused state spending to increase. Associated economic and weather problems have forced many to seek survival in the black economy. Many blame the catastrophic economic situation on government corruption and incompetence, in addition to the break-up of the Soviet Union and the civil war.

Tajikistan is participating in the IMF's Poverty and Growth Reduction Facility (PRGF) programme, aiming to reduce poverty and encourage economic growth. The IMF three-year US$65 million loan under PRGF has supported the government's 2002–05 economic programme.

Tajikistan is badly in need of foreign investment. Lack of foreign investor interest is not surprising given the country's recent political history and complex political balance. Although down on 2002 growth of 9.1 per cent, Tajikistan's economy continued to grow strongly. GDP was 6 per cent in 2003 and 10.6 per cent in 2004, Tajikistan's seventh consecutive year of growth following the end of the civil war in 1997. 2004 saw the economy's base broaden according to the Asian Development Bank (ADB). Cotton and aluminium, the two traditional mainstays of the economy accounted for only one third of output. Industrial output increased by 10.2 per cent, services by 14.7 per cent driven by strong retail and transport performances. Agriculture improved, production increasing by 9.6 per cent on the back of a good cotton harvest, although the poor grain crop depressed the overall figure.

Private consumption was the main driving force in GDP growth, combined with a sharp increase in emigrant workers' remittances, that tripled to make up 13 per cent of GDP. An estimated 15 per cent of the population – around one million people – live in households dependent on a family member working abroad. A depressing percentage of Tajiks live below the poverty line in Tajikistan which is among the poorest countries in the world, with average monthly take-home pay of US$15 – less than US$0.50 a day. None the less, at the macroeconomic level, if the figures were to be believed, the government could take heart from a strong fiscal performance. The overall budget moved in to a surplus of 0.9 per cent of GDP, an improvement on the deficit of 0.1 per cent recorded in 2002. This not only reflected the economy's higher growth, but also increased tax revenues and a tighter control on public expenditure. Spending on social services – health, education and social security – accounted for 35 per cent of the total.

Inflation, reflecting strong domestic demand, rose from 8.9 per cent in 2002 to 14.5 per cent, well above the government's target of 9.0 per cent. By 2004, however, it appeared that the inflation rate had dropped to 7.1 per cent.

Despite increased exports, the trade deficit widened as imports grew even more, sucked in by Tajikistan's higher economic growth and the capital goods required by externally financed development programmes. Despite the deterioration in the trade deficit, the current account deficit narrowed to US$21 million, 1.3 per cent of GDP and half the level of 2002. This was largely due to increased remittances from foreign workers, which rose from US$65 million in 2002 to US$202 million in 2003. Total external debt rose by some US$25 million, to US$ 1 billion at the end of 2003; however, as a percentage of an increased GDP figure, it dropped from 82 per cent to 65 per cent. A restructuring arrangement reached with Russia on debts of some US$300 million had allowed for a three year grace period on payments up to 2005 and an extension of maturity from 15 to 17 years. The government's 2004 budget maintained a prudent fiscal stance and reflected World Bank recommendations on the need to maintain increased social welfare budgetary allocations.

KEY INDICATORS — Tajikistan

	Unit	2000	2001	2002	2003	2004
Population	m	6.17	6.29	6.30	6.42	*6.54
Gross domestic product (GDP)	US$bn	1.00	1.16	1.20	1.08	*2.08
GDP per capita	US$	200	184	190	169	329
GDP real growth	%	8.3	10.2	9.1	6.0	10.6
Inflation	%	60.6	38.5	8.9	14.5	7.1
Exports (fob) (goods)	US$m	792.0	652.0	700.0	710.0	1,096.9
Imports (fob) (goods)	US$m	849.0	773.0	800.0	830.0	1,232.4
Balance of trade	US$m	-57.0	-121.0	-100.0	-120.0	-135.5
Current account	US$m	-60.0	-70.0	-30.0	-20.0	-80.0
Foreign debt	US$bn	0.9	0.9	0.9	1.0	–
Total reserves minus gold	US$m	92.9	92.6	89.5	111.9	157.5
Foreign exchange	US$m	85.0	87.7	87.7	111.0	156.2
Exchange rate	per US$	1,823.00	2.37	2.78	2.79	2.97

* estimated figure

Tajikistan

Regional tensions

Russia continues to provide the bulk of the 20,000 strong Commonwealth of Independent States (CIS) peace-keeping force stationed in Tajikistan. The majority of the CIS troops are located on the Tajikistan-Afghanistan border, protecting Central Asia and Russia from the spread of the extremist form of Islam so feared by the region's governments. This perceived threat dominates Central Asian regional relations. The UTO is by no means fundamentalist in the mould of Afghanistan's former rulers, the Taliban, or Osama Bin Laden's al Qaeda, but the prospect of an Islamic-led or influenced UTO government in Tajikistan is not welcomed by Russia or Tajikistan's other northern neighbours.

Russia believes Tajikistan is a convenient refuge and training ground for the Islamic Movement of Uzbekistan (IMU). Additionally, Tajikistan has been a key transit point for drug trafficking originating in Afghanistan. The activities of the IMU, which aims to overthrow Uzbekistan and establish a separate Islamic polity in the Ferghana valley, has made the Tajikistan-Uzbekistan border a zone of continual near-war. The Tajik government has denied the presence of the IMU in Tajikistan.

Tajikistan has been propelled into a series of regional security co-operation initiatives as a result of the concerns of neighbouring states. In April 2000, defence ministers of the then Shanghai Five (China, Russia, Kazakhstan, Kyrgystan and Tajikistan) met to discuss the problem of Islamic insurgency; the meeting was followed by a summit of the country's heads of state, in Dushanbe, in July 2000. Further discussions followed in 2001 with the successor to the Shanghai Five, the Shanghai Co-operation Organisation (SCO).

Tajikistan is a member of the CIS Collective Security Treaty (CST), which includes Armenia, Belarus, Kazakhstan, Kyrgyzstan and Russia. Assistance between CST states is expected in the event of an escalation of the conflict. As part of the CST, a rapid reaction force was established in 2001 to combat the terrorist threat.

When the US launched airstrikes against the Taliban and Bin Laden's al Qaeda in October 2001, Tajikistan immediately offered the use of some of its airbases to the US, although the offer was eventually declined by the US. French troops were reported to have arrived at Dushanbe in early December 2001 en route to Afghanistan. The UK and Germany were among other Western countries to seek permission to establish military bases in Tajikistan. The government hopes that co-operation with the US in its war on terror will assist in its own fight against Islamic militants. The re-appearance of Afghanistan on the international agenda brought the economic plight of the Central Asian republics to the fore. As a result, the Tajikistan government was rewarded for supporting the international effort in Afghanistan by receiving much-needed international aid from the US and the EU.

The government had its knuckles rapped by the IMF in February 2002 for supplying inaccurate data which provided the basis for the release of several tranches of its Poverty Reduction and Growth Facility (PRGF) during 2001. The government was ordered to pay back US$31.6 million by 31 March 2003 as a result of the irregularity, which concerned the undisclosed receipt of loans. The IMF restored aid to Tajikistan in December 2002 as it was satisfied with the overall macroeconomic performance in Tajikistan.

As a result of Tajikistan's support for the US's Afghanistan operation, the country was allowed to join NATO's Partnership for Peace (PfP) in February 2002. PfP allows co-operation between NATO members, Western Europe's neutral states and former Soviet Union states. Tajikistan was the only former Soviet Union country not to have already joined PfP because of its own civil war and poor security.

Relations with Uzbekistan are ambivalent, given evidence of Uzbek support for some Tajik opposition groups and Tajikistan's refusal to allow the Uzbek military onto its territory. The situation is aggravated by the borders drawn up by Stalin's central planners, which purposely divided ethnic groups. The historic centres of the Tajik people, the cities of Bukhara and Samarkand, were allocated to the Soviet Republic of Uzbekistan and they remain a source of tension between the two countries, as do the Uzbek areas of north Tajikistan. Relations with Kyrgyzstan also deteriorated in January 2003 as skirmishes took place along the disputed Tajik – Kyrgyz border. Over 300 Tajiks from the Vorukh enclave destroyed a border post in Kyrgyzstan established in retaliation for alleged harassment of Kyrgyz travellers by Tajik customs and borders officials. Over 100 people from Kyrgyzstan retaliated by destroying a Tajik border post. The tit-for-tat attacks came after both governments had agreed not to establish any border posts in a delimited 1,000km border area.

External pressures are also forcing the neighbours to co-operate in some areas. A joint security headquarters with Uzbekistan and Kyrgyzstan was established in Tajikistan's Soghd *oblast* (region) in August 2000, to support civilian security in areas of IMU operations. Other issues which have raised demand for cross-border co-operation included the flow of narcotics from Afghanistan.

Disagreements still exist between the government and the UTO, which are making the country unattractive to foreign investors. Additionally, factions of the UTO have kidnapped foreign workers to show their dissatisfaction with the progress of the peace process. In June 2001, when the Deputy Interior Minister, Habib Sanguinov, was shot dead in Dushanbe, the UTO was immediately blamed by the government. The following month, a foreign policy advisor to Rakhmonov was also shot dead. In September Minister of Culture Abdurakhim Rakhimov was also killed. There were rumours that the latter's death had been carried out on the orders of al Qaeda leader Bin Laden.

The president himself was involved in a security scare on 9 September 2001, when a man with explosives concealed on his body prematurely blew himself up several hundred metres away. The president had been attending a celebration in the capital marking the tenth anniversary of Tajikistan's independence from the Soviet Union.

Islamic militancy remains the main threat to Tajikistan's progress and Rakhmonov's hold on power. Given that his attempts to develop the economy, which has been damaged by years of neglect and civil war, Rakhmonov does not want any return of the popular support that Islamic political groups have had in the past.

Outlook

To achieve its long-term development and poverty reduction objectives, Tajikistan needs to maintain annual GDP growth above the 6 per cent mark in the medium term. As long as internal and regional stability issues do not intervene and political common sense prevails, then it should be possible for the region's poorest country to continue its slow progress under Russia's watchful eye.

Risk assessment

Economy	Improving
Politics	Fair
Regional stability	Fair

Nations of the World: A Political, Economic and Business Handbook

COUNTRY PROFILE

Historical profile

For much of its history, Tajikistan has come under the control of foreign powers and was introduced to Islam in the eighth century by Arab invaders. From the seventeenth century, it was ruled by the Khan of Bukhara until 1868, when the Russian Empire conquered Central Asia.

Russia continues to provide the bulk of the 20,000 strong Commonwealth of Independent States (CIS) peace-keeping force stationed in Tajikistan. The majority of the CIS troops are located on the Tajikistan-Afghanistan border, protecting Central Asia and Russia from the spread of the extremist form of Islam so feared by the region's governments. Russia believes Tajikistan is a convenient refuge and training ground for the Islamic Movement of Uzbekistan (IMU). Additionally, Tajikistan has been a key transit point for drug trafficking originating in Afghanistan. The activities of the IMU, which aims to overthrow Uzbekistan and establish a separate Islamic polity in the Ferghana valley, has made the Tajikistan-Uzbekistan border a zone of continual near-war. The Tajik government has denied the presence of the IMU in Tajikistan. Russian security forces are scheduled to complete the handover to Tajik forces by the beginning of 2006.

1916–17 The Central Asian republics joined in a violent uprising against Russian rule, which was suppressed. After the October Revolution in Russia, the Russian ruler, Lenin, gave the peoples of Central Asia the right of self-determination.

1920s Southern Tajikistan remained under the control of the Khan of Bukhara while northern Tajikistan was incorporated into Soviet-controlled Turkestan, which also included Uzbekistan, Kyrgyzstan, part of northern Turkmenistan and southern Kazakhstan. Soviet nationalities policy, under the direction of Stalin, saw Soviet rule enforced by Red Army troops who put down fierce Muslim resistance in Central Asia after the Russian civil war.

1924 Tajikistan was granted autonomous status in the Socialist Soviet Republic (SSR) of Uzbekistan.

1929 Tajikistan was detached from Uzbekistan and became a separate SSR.

1930s–80s The country underwent a period of agricultural collectivisation and industrialisation, which was unpopular with the population.

1989 Tajik became the official state language.

1990 Social and ethnic tensions erupted in violence in Dushanbe and along the Tajikistan-Kyrgyzstan border. A state of emergency was declared and Soviet troops were sent to Dushanbe to suppress pro-democracy protests. President Kahar Mahkamov resigned after being accused of supporting an attempted coup against the Soviet leader Mikhail Gorbachev.

1991 The collapse of the Soviet Union resulted in Tajikistan declaring independence. Rahmon Nabiyev was appointed president after winning Tajikistan's first direct presidential elections. Tajikistan joined the Commonwealth of Independent States (CIS), following the collapse of the Soviet Union.

1992 Anti-government demonstrations in Dushanbe turned into civil war between pro-government forces and Islamist and pro-democracy groups. Nabiyev was forced to resign and the CPT government collapsed. Pro-Communists massacred thousands of government supporters in Dushanbe. The CPT regained power and Imamali Rakhmonov became head of state.

1993 The Supreme Court returned the country to one-party rule after banning all political parties other than the ruling CPT. A CIS peace-keeping force was deployed along the Tajikistan-Afghan border to prevent armed incursions by Islamic guerrilla groups.

1994 A cease-fire between the government and the rebels was agreed. A presidential constitution was approved by national referendum. Rakhmonov won the presidential elections, which were deemed by international observers to be neither free nor fair.

1995 Rakhmonov supporters won the legislative elections, which took place without the participation of any of the opposition groups. Fighting erupted on the Afghan border.

1996 A UN-sponsored cease-fire between the government and Islamist rebels came into effect.

1997 Opposition parties were legalised and as part of a peace treaty between the Tajikistan government and the Islamic United Tajik Opposition (UTO), the government agreed to give 30 per cent of its seats to opposition representatives, retaining 50 per cent for itself, and to give the remaining 20 per cent to independents.

1998 The government removed the ban on religious political parties. Rakhmonov pardoned all opposition leaders in exile. Tajikistan joined the CIS Customs Union.

1999 President Rakhmonov was re-elected for a third term. The UTO armed forces were integrated into the state army. Rakhmonov was awarded the order of Hero of Tajikistan..

2000 A new bicameral parliament was set up. The elections were won by the Hizbi Demokrati Khalkii Tajikistan (HDKT) (People's Democratic Party of Tajikistan). A new currency – the somoni – replaced the Tajik rouble. The presidents of Belarus, Kazakhstan, Kyrgyzstan, Russia and Tajikistan (formerly the Customs Five) established the Eurasian Economic Community (EEC).

2001 Tajikistan, China, Russia, Kazakhstan, Kyrgyzstan and Uzbekistan formed the Shanghai Co-operation Organisation (SCO) and agreed to fight ethnic and religious militancy, while promoting investment and trade. Three senior officials were assassinated during the year. Tajikistan offered support to the US-led anti-terror coalition.

2002 Tajikistan became the last Central Asian republic to join NATO's Partnership for Peace (PfP) programme. The number of border guards was doubled to prevent Al Qaeda members from entering the country from Afghanistan to escape US forces.

2003 Russian President Vladimir Putin visited Tajikistan and announced plans to boost Russian military presence. A referendum vote went in favour of allowing President Rakhmonov to run for a further two consecutive seven-year terms after 2006; the opposition said the referendum was a travesty of democracy.

2004 In July, parliament approved a moratorium on the death penalty. Russia formally opened a military base in Dushanbe in October; it also took back control over a former Soviet space monitoring centre at Nurek.

2005 The ruling HDKT won the February/March parliamentary elections.

Political structure

Constitution

A presidential constitution was approved by national referendum in 1994. The constitution granted basic economic and political rights and guaranteed religious freedoms. It gave the president powers to appoint the chairs of regions, districts, cities, including Dushanbe, as well as of the Gorno-Badakshan Autonomous Region and the governor of the National Bank of Tajikistan (central bank), subject to the approval of deputies in parliament. The president also has powers of dismissal over these offices. In addition, the president gained the power to declare a state of martial law and issue decrees, as well as immunity from prosecution. Parliament has the power to impeach the president, subject to the findings of the Constitutional Court. If more than two-thirds of deputies vote in favour of impeachment, parliament may dismiss the president from office.

Form of state

Presidential socialist republic

The executive

The president, elected by universal suffrage every seven years, holds executive power. The government consists of the

Tajikistan

prime minister and cabinet and may present its resignation to the president if it declares it cannot function normally.

In 2003, voters in a referendum were in favour of allowing President Rakhmonov to run for a further two consecutive seven-year terms after 2006.

National legislature
Tajikistan has a two-chamber Majlisi Oli (Parliament).

The Majlisi Mamoyandogan (Assembly of Representatives), the lower house, has 63 members who are elected for a five-year term. Of these, 22 are elected by proportional representation and 41 from single-seat constituencies.

The Majlisi Milliy (National Assembly) forms the second chamber and has 33 members, of whom eight are appointed by the president and the rest elected by deputies in the Majlisi Mamoyandogan. The National Assembly functions only when convened and accordingly meets less frequently than the lower house.

Legal system
The judiciary is constitutionally independent from the legislature and executive. Courts include the Supreme Court, Constitutional Court, Military Court and High Economic Court. In addition there are district and city courts, as well as the Dushanbe City Court. Gorno-Badakshan Autonomous Region has its own court. The president has powers to appoint and dismiss judges of all courts on petition of the minister of justice, except for judges appointed to the Supreme Court, High Economic Court and Constitutional Court. The latter is composed of seven judges elected from the legal profession, one of whom is a representative of Gorno-Badakshan Autonomous Region.

Last elections
13 March 2005 (second round parliamentary); 27 February 2005 (first round parliamentary); November 1999 (presidential).

Results: Parliamentary (second round): the ruling HDKT was re-elected with 74 per cent of the vote (52 seats out of 63); the CPT 13 per cent (four seats); the RPT (8 per cent) (two seats).

Parliamentary (first round): the ruling Hizbi Demokrati Khalkii Tajikistan (HDKT) (People's Democratic Party of Tajikistan) won 49 seats out of 63, the Communist Party of Tajikistan (CPT) three, the Islamic Renaissance Party of Tajikistan (RPT) two and independents six. Turnout was 88 per cent.

Presidential: President Emomali Rakhmonov was re-elected with 97 per cent of the vote.

Next elections
2006 (presidential); 2010 (parliamentary).

Political parties
Ruling party
Hizbi Demokrati Khalkii Tajikistan (HDKT) (People's Democratic Party of Tajikistan) (re-elected Feb/Mar 2005)
Main opposition party
Communist Party of Tajikistan (CPT)

Population
6.54 million (2004)
Ethnic make-up
Tajik (69.1 per cent), Uzbek (25 per cent), Russian (2.7 per cent), with remaining minorities including Tatar and Kyrgyz groups. Tajikistan is the exception among the Central Asian republics in that its population is predominantly Persian rather than Turkic. The Tajiks are made up of a number of closely related ethnic groups which differ both anthropologically (inhabitants of the Pamir mountains in the north are tall, dark complexioned with light-coloured eyes; those from Kuliab are stocky and dark-skinned; northern Tajiks are fair-complexioned, brown- and black-eyed). Customs and rituals also differ.

Religions
The majority (80 per cent) of ethnic Tajiks and Uzbeks are Sunni Muslims; 5 per cent are Shi'a Muslims. Ethnic Badakhshanis belong to the Ismaili Muslim sect and have the Aga Khan as their spiritual leader. There are also Baptists and Bukhara Jews. There is no official religion.

Education
The civil war resulted in disruption to the education system, particularly in rural areas. Public expenditure on education typically amounts to 3 per cent of GDP. Primary education lasts four years, followed by eight years of secondary schooling which is divided into two cycles of five and three years in either general, technical or vocational education. Successful students may progress to either a university or institute of which there are 29 establishments. The Academy of Sciences, established during the Soviet period, is made up of 17 research institutions supporting an academic community of over 3,000.

In December 2003, the Asian Development Bank (ADB) approved a US$7.5 million loan for education reforms to give about 90,000 children better access to quality education. Pilot districts were selected on the basis of poverty levels, infant and maternal mortality rates, girls' enrolment rates, and the proportion of female teachers. About 300 schools in the pilot districts, that were damaged from civil war and lack of maintenance, will receive funding for these measures and to provide textbooks and learning materials, plus pay for enhancing female teacher training.

The total cost of the project is US$9.38 million, 80 per cent of which will be covered by the ADB's loan, while the government will provide the balance of US$1.88 million.

Nationwide, the education system is suffering from an exodus of large numbers of qualified teachers to find better paid work. School attendance levels are also falling, as children are pressed into helping their families cope with the widespread poverty and social vulnerability. Gender imbalance is particularly marked at the upper secondary level, with the proportion of girls declining.

Literacy rate: 99.4 per cent, adult rate (2003).
Compulsory years: Seven to 16.
Enrolment rate: 85 per cent gross primary enrolment (ADB); 76 per cent gross secondary enrolment (Unicef).
Pupils per teacher: 24 in primary schools.

Health
The structure of Tajikistan's health system has evolved from the Soviet model of healthcare with few structural changes. The state funds most of the healthcare services in the country. The health ministry runs national-level healthcare services, while local authorities administer most regional services.

Annual government spending is around 29 per cent, and foreign spending 7 per cent, of the total expenditure on health, which is 3.3 per cent of GDP.

State hospitals have limited supplies of free medicines. People have been increasingly forced to pay for their own healthcare, often buying their own medicines off the street.

The health budget each year has major shortfalls that are partially covered by international aid. The government has introduced more than 11 national and sectoral programmes, including those to combat tuberculosis, prevent HIV/Aids and improve reproductive health. The World Bank began a major rehabilitation project with an estimated expenditure of US$25 million in 2000–03 in the Soghd and Khatlon regions. The project aimed to rehabilitate 300 health posts, rural physician clinics and outpatient facilities.

Tajikistan has the youngest population of any former Soviet states, with 70 per cent aged under 30 years.

Tajikistan has substantial environmental problems that pose risks to human health. There is high risk of communicable disease with the breakdown of public health measures such as mosquito control and immunisation. Less than 50 per cent of the rural population have access to clean water. Tajikistan is one of the primary transfer points for the flow of drugs due to

transparent border controls and poor custom regulations.
HIV prevalence: 0.1 per cent aged 15–49 in 2003 (World Bank)
Life expectancy: 63.6 years (World Bank)
Fertility rate/Maternal mortality rate: 2.9 births per woman (2003); maternal mortality 66.5 per 100,000 live births (World Bank).
Birth rate/Death rate: 32.8 births and 8.5 deaths per 1,000 people (2003).
Infant mortality rate: 76 per 1,000 live births (World Bank)

Welfare
As the poorest of the CIS countries, a significant proportion of Tajikistan's population now faces severe social hardship, especially with most of the country's social welfare budget being spent on pensions. The country relies heavily on overseas assistance, highlighting the failure of the state to create a self-financing welfare system.

Main cities
Dushanbe (capital, estimated population 590,300 in 2003), Khujand (formerly Leninabad) (156,500).

Languages spoken
The Tajik language is very close to Persian, spoken in Iran, and to Dari, spoken in Afghanistan. Although Tajik is spoken locally, in practice, Russian is widely used in government and business. Uzbek is also spoken. The Badakhshanis speak the Pamir languages, but also speak Tajik or Russian. There are three main groups – the Pamir languages, the southern Kulyab and the northern Khodzent dialects.
A State Language law provides for a transition to the Tajik language with Arabic script.
Official language/s
Tajik (Farsi)

Media
Press
Since the end of Tajikistan's five-year civil war in 1997, attacks on the press have fallen, despite the general repressive attitude of the government, which has subjected journalists to harassment, intimidation and censorship.
Some of the 200 newspapers are government-owned and others are linked to political parties and movements. No dailies are published.
Jumhuriyat is government-owned, published in Tajik three times a week.
Broadcasting
The broadcasting law prohibits dissemination of information containing state secrets, inciting of racial discrimination and any form of ethnic or religious hatred.

Radio: A few private radio stations operate alongside state-run Tajik Radio, which operates two national networks.
Television: State-owned channels and stations broadcast in Tajik alongside Russian TV and radio from Moscow. The Voice of the Islamic Republic of Iran (VIRI) is televised from Tehran. There are more than 30 local and regional private TV stations. A private broadcasting company, TV Service, broadcasts 12 channels in Russian, English and Hindi.

Economy
Tajikistan's GDP per capita is one of the lowest in the former Soviet Union. Agriculture, particularly cotton, dominates the official economy. Industry is largely limited to the Tadaz aluminium smelter, the Nurek hydropower station and small obsolete light industry and food processing factories. Tajikistan, located at the crossroads of Russia, Iran, Pakistan and China, has become a narcotics hub and a major transit route for opium produced in Afghanistan.
Like many transition states, Tajikistan's recent economic history has been one of severe contraction, but Tajikistan's transition has been more extreme than most. The country was already the poorest of the Soviet republics. The economy was weakened following the collapse of the Soviet Union when Tajikistan lost its subsidies (which accounted for up to 80 per cent of its income) and markets. The five-year civil war effectively destroyed the Tajik economy. The war ravaged the country's limited infrastructure, led to the emigration of some of the most qualified and skilled workers and caused state spending to increase. Associated economic and weather problems have forced many to seek survival in the black economy. Many blame the catastrophic economic situation on government corruption and incompetence, in addition to the break-up of the Soviet Union and the civil war.
Tajikistan is badly in need of foreign investment, but lack of foreign investor interest is not surprising given the country's recent political history and complex political balance.
Economic growth has become more broad-based in recent years, with about two-thirds of it coming from outside the cotton and aluminum industries. Pprivate consumption has risen and a there has been a large increase in workers' remittances (about 13 per cent of GDP). A rise in global cotton prices helped to finance imports.
Structural reform is continuing.
In the medium term, the economy needs to continue to diversify to develop new sources of economic expansion. Sustaining growth in landlocked Tajikistan is also dependent on promoting mutually beneficial economic co-operation with neighbouring countries.

External trade
Tajikistan continues to trade predominantly with other members of the CIS.
Imports
Main imports are electricity, petroleum products, alumina, machinery and equipment, and foodstuffs.
Main sources: Russia (17.8 per cent total, 2004), Uzbekistan (13.4 per cent), Kazakhstan (9.7 per cent), Ukraine (6.3 per cent), Azerbaijan (6.3 per cent), US (5.8 per cent), Turkey (4.3 per cent)
Exports
The main exports are aluminium, electricity, cotton, fruits, vegetable oil and textiles.
Main destinations: Latvia (13.1 per cent total, 2004), Switzerland (11.5 per cent), Uzbekistan (11.3 per cent), Norway (9.9 per cent), Russia (8.2 per cent), Iran (7.9 per cent), Turkey (7.7 per cent), Italy (6.6 per cent), Hungary (4.4 per cent)

Agriculture
Farming
Agriculture typically accounts for around 23 per cent of GDP and employs 42 per cent of the workforce.
Because of Tajikistan's mountainous nature, only 7 per cent of the land is suitable for farming. Tajikistan is a large net importer of different types of grain. The main agricultural areas are in the lower-lying regions of the south-west and the north-west – part of the Fergana basin. During the Soviet era agriculture was the mainstay of the Tajikistan economy, particularly cotton and wheat. The sector is heavily dependent on irrigation, which covers about 75 per cent of arable land. Irrigation networks have become clogged or are otherwise in need of restoration. Crops constitute about two-thirds, and animal husbandry one-third, of rural production. Cattle, sheep and goats are reared. Important products are cotton, grain, fruits, grapes, vegetables and tobacco leaves. Lack of processing and packing facilities and inefficient distribution mean that large amounts of the vegetable and fruit crops are wasted and that the country often fails even to meet its domestic needs.
Production was devastated by the civil war of 1992–97, and has only slowly recovered with increased production since hostilities ended. Farm machinery has suffered depreciation over the years without replacement, and the quality of seed varieties has fallen.
In a report published in early 2005 – *The Curse of Cotton: Central Asia's destructive monoculture* – the International Crisis Group (ICG) said that while the former

Soviet cotton producing countries of Uzbekistan, Tajikistan and Turkmenistan continued to exploit their cotton growers there was little hope of improving economic development and tackling poverty. The cotton industry is vital to the economy of Tajikistan, yet while the industry continues to rely on cheap labour (including children), land ownership is uncertain, state intervention discourages competition and the rule of law is limited, there is little incentive for the powerful vested interests to reform the system.

In addition to the economic and social costs to the rural populations, the environmental costs of the monoculture have been devastating. The degradation of the Aral Sea in particular has lead to international concern.

Crop production in 2004 included: 631,328 tonnes (t) wheat, 527,000t potatoes, 51,445t rice, 112,951t maize, 93,200t grapes, 1,600t citrus, 28,400t pulses, 225,800t tomatoes, 4,500t treenuts, 556,991t seed cotton, 54,520t oilcrops, 237,600t fruit in total, 831,749t vegetables in total, 2,675 tobacco. Livestock production included: 43,700t meat in total, 23,000t beef, 200t pig-meat, 18,000t lamb, 2,500t poultry, 4,368t eggs, 490,000t milk, 1,000t honey.

Fishing
Fishing remains important for domestic consumption, but pollution and a lack of investment have reduced fish stocks drastically. Tibet stone loach is a common fish in Tajikistan where it is present up to 4,500 metres altitude, but is of no commercial importance. The typical annual fish catch is over 200 tonnes.

Forestry
The state-owned forestry and wooded land accounts for only 5 per cent of land area with forest cover estimated at over 400,000 hectares (ha). Most of the forests located between 1,000 and 3,000 metre altitude are protected. The main stock of the forests include coniferous and juniper species, which are not available for wood supply.

There are no large-scale primary forest industries and the relatively low per capita consumption of forest products is met mainly by imports from the Russian Federation.

Industry and manufacturing
Industry contributes around 24 per cent to GDP.

Industrial production experienced a significant decline throughout the 1990s. The industrial sector is dominated by some 300 large state-owned enterprises in areas such as heavy industry, transport and wholesale trading and is mainly built around inefficient, labour-intensive production.

Aluminium is Tajikistan's key industrial sector. The country has one of the world's largest aluminium smelters, the state-owned Tadaz aluminium smelter, which has a capacity of 517,000 tonnes a year. Located at Tursunzade in western Tajikistan, the plant is a main source of revenue for the government.

Light industry accounts for around 45 per cent of the value of total industrial production. The main sectors are food processing (mainly dairy products, meat, fruit and cooking oil), tobacco, cotton cleaning, silk, textiles, knitted goods, footwear, tanning, carpet weaving and simple electronics.

Tourism
Tourism is undeveloped. The civil war in the nineties wrecked the tourist sector. Infrastructure was backward even before the civil war and has to be developed afresh. The importance of tourism to the economy is recognised and development is being encouraged, with attention to mountaineering, trekking and eco-tourism.

Environment
The Aral Sea is drying up due to the overuse of water from the two main rivers which feed into it and has lost 40 per cent of its water, dropping up to 19 metres. This has resulted in desertification of the surrounding land. A UN study published in 2004 reported that there was no possibility of restoring the water and the need must be on preserving what is left.

The government has endorsed a 2004 joint strategy to resolve the demands of its water requirements with its neighbours.

Mining
Tajikistan has an established history of mineral production. In the Soviet era, the country used to mine and process uranium amounting to around 500,000 tonnes per year of ore, but with demand falling in the post-Soviet era, uranium production ceased in the 1990s. Tajikistan holds around 500,000 tonnes of antimony reserves, 6.2 million tonnes of mercury, 60,000 tonnes of silver and 150 tonnes of gold. Lack of modern equipment and techniques means that some resources are not exploited to full capacity. Antimony, bismuth and mercury have been mined, but most deposits are depleted and the mines closing down. Despite large silver reserves, only around one tonne of silver is produced every year. There are significant deposits of world-class marble; also uranium, radium, arsenic, bismuth, mica and small amounts of potassium salts, molybdenum, sulphur, boron, common salt, carbonates, fluorite, quartz sand, asbestos, lead and zinc. Deposits of semi-precious stones include lapis lazuli, rubies, amethyst and ornamental quartz.

Hydrocarbons
Tajikistan has proven oil reserves of 12 million barrels. The state-owned energy company, Tajikneftegaz, is responsible for all oil exploration, drilling, and production and produces around 3,500 barrels per day of oil. Most of Tajikistan's oil demand needs are met by imports, with Uzbekistan supplying 70 per cent of oil imports. In total, the CIS accounts for over 97 per cent of Tajikistan's oil needs.

Tajikistan has natural gas reserves of 200 billion cubic feet. Tajikistan has a small natural gas extraction industry which meets only a fraction of the annual domestic requirement of 1.1 billion cubic metres. Over 90 per cent of gas consumed in Tajikistan is imported, mainly from Uzbekistan. Gas is supplied via a pipeline running from Uzbekistan to Dushanbe, in exchange for use of a rail corridor and gas pipeline across north Tajikistan.

Tajikistan could have up to six billion tonnes of coal reserves, among of the largest coal deposits in Central Asia, but these have not been proven. There are six large coal fields, with that at Fan Yagnob estimated to contain two billion tonnes of reserves. Mostly brown coal is mined in Yagnob and Myonadu, besides coking coal at Nazarailok in the Karateginsk Valley in the east.

Energy
Tajikistan used to receive energy supplies from Russia in exchange for cotton and minerals. Since independence there have been chronic energy shortages due to a breakdown in communications and infrastructure, especially in the winter period and when water levels are low, given the country's dependence on hydroelectric power.

Tajikistan is a mountainous country with potential to produce hydroelectricity in significant amounts. Energy generation is extremely variable from year to year, depending on the level of rainfall. The electricity monopoly, Barki Tojik (Tajik Electricity), estimates that only 10 per cent of hydroelectric potential is being used. Besides hydroelectric power, oil typically accounts for 23 per cent of energy consumption, natural gas for 17 per cent and coal for 1 per cent. Total generating capacity in Tajikistan is 4.4GW.

The grave investment deficit in power generation is not helped by the fact that production costs of electricity can run higher than market prices. Tajikistan is littered with incomplete power projects, including plans for a chain of nine power stations along the Vaksh river, discontinued because of the civil war.

Nations of the World: A Political, Economic and Business Handbook

Development of the Roghun hydro-power station in eastern Tajikistan has been resumed. Work on the plant began in the 1980s, but construction was never completed due to a lack of funds. The plant will be the largest hydro-power facility in Central Asia, possibly producing enough electricity to meet domestic needs.

Financial markets
Stock exchange
The Tajik commodity exchange was inaugurated in March 1996.

Banking and insurance
The banking sector remains extremely weak, with the five largest banks (which account for 85 per cent of total commercial bank credit and 90 per cent of deposits) handicapped by substantial non-performing loans. A law on Banks and Banking Activity in May 1998 introduced regulations which are close to international standards.
The restructuring of Agroinvestbank, the largest commercial bank, was completed in March 2004.
Central bank
National Bank of Tajikistan

Time
GMT plus five hours

Geography
Tajikistan is situated in the south-east of Central Asia. To the south of Tajikistan lies Afghanistan, Uzbekistan to the north and west, the People's Republic of China to the east and Kyrgyzstan to the north-east.
The terrain is almost entirely mountainous with more than one-half of the country above 3,000 metres. The main mountain ranges are the western Tian Shan in the north, the southern Tian Shan in the central region and the Pamirs in the south-east. The northern Pamirs are the highest mountains of Tajikistan, and of the former Soviet Union – Lenin Peak 7,134 metres and Ismail Samani Peak (formerly Communism Peak) 7,495 metres. There is a dense river network.

Climate
Extreme continental; temperatures range between -20 degrees Celsius (C) and 0 degrees C in January, and from 0 degrees C to 30 degrees C in June, depending on altitude. From -5 degrees C to 35 degrees C in foothills, valleys and Dushanbe; sub-zero temperatures in the Pamir mountains. Rainfall between 150 and 250mm per annum.

Dress codes
Not overly formal but modest, particularly outside Dushanbe.

Entry requirements
Passports
Passports are required by all and must be valid until at least six months after date of planned departure.
Visa
Required by all and preferably obtained in advance, from Russian embassies or consulates who represent Tajikistan abroad. A business visa requires a letter of invitation from a local company or organisation, to be endorsed by the Ministry of Foreign Affairs, and submitted along with a business letter undertaking full financial responsibility for expenses incurred by the representative and a full itinerary.
All visitors must obtain special permission to visit Gorno-Badakhshan autonomous region. Tajikistan and Uzbekistan have mutual visa requirements. Visitors from Russia, Kazhakstan or Uzbekistan should ensure their visas are valid for either re-entry or onward passage.
Currency advice/regulations
Import of local and foreign currency is unlimited provided it is declared on arrival. Export of local currency is prohibited. Foreign currency can be exported, up to the amount declared on arrival.
Traveller's cheques are not generally accepted – Tajikistan is a cash-only economy, although carrying large amounts of cash can be dangerous. US dollars are widely accepted.
Customs
On arrival valuable items such as jewellery, cameras, computers should be declared.

Health (for visitors)
A reciprocal health agreement for urgent medical treatment exists with the United Kingdom. Proof of UK residence will be required. Standards of healthcare are significantly below Western levels, as most trained medical personnel have left the country. Although emergency treatment can be very expensive, doctors and hospitals often expect immediate cash payment. Uninsured visitors requiring urgent medical evacuation may face extreme difficulties. Comprehensive travel and medical insurance, including evacuation by air ambulance, is essential.
Mandatory precautions
Vaccination certificates are required for yellow fever if travelling from an infected area. Visitors staying for longer than 90 days may be submitted to an Aids test, which carries the possibility of infection with HIV or other pathogens, given the lack of medical supplies in Tajikistan.
Advisable precautions
Water precautions are recommended: water purification tablets may be useful, or drink bottled water. The risk of water-borne diseases, including cholera, is high. A typhoid outbreak occurred in October 2003 in Dushanbe.
It is advisable to be 'in date' for the following immunisations: polio (within 10 years), tetanus (within 10 years), typhoid, hepatitis 'A', tuberculosis, tick-borne encephalitis. Anti-malarial precautions are also advisable.
There has been a significant increase in the number of cases of diphtheria. While the low dose, adult booster is unavailable, travellers are advised to be boosted with a reduced dose (0.1ml) of the paediatric single antigen vaccine. If never immunised, use three-dose course of the vaccine.
Any medicines required should be taken by the visitor, and it would be wise to have precautionary antibiotics if going outside major urban centres. A travel kit including a disposable syringe is a reasonable precaution.

Hotels
Visitors are advised to use well-known travel operators with established contacts in Tajikistan. Lack of adequate hotel accommodation. It is advisable to book in advance through Intourist or specialist travel agents. There are no hotels outside the two main towns, Dushanbe and Khodzhent (formerly Leninabad).

Credit cards
Credit cards are not generally accepted.

Public holidays
Fixed dates
1 Jan (New Year's Day), 8 Mar (Mother's Day), 20–22 Mar (Navrus/Persian New Year, three days), 1 May (Labour Day), 9 May (Victory Day), 9 Sep (Independence Day), 6 Nov (Constitution Day).
Tajikistan uses the Persian calendar, which differs from the Gregorian calendar: there are 31 days in each of the first six months of the Persian calendar, 30 days in each of the next five months and 29 days in the last month, except in leap year when it has 30 days.
Persian year 1384: from 21 March 2005 to 20 March 2006.
Variable dates
Eid al Adha, Eid al Fitr (three days).
The Islamic year contains 354 or 355 days, with the result that Muslim feasts advance by 10–12 days against the Gregorian calendar. Dates of feasts vary according to the sighting of the new moon, so cannot be forecast exactly.
Islamic year 1426: 10 February 2005 to 30 January 2006.

Working hours
Banking
Mon–Fri: 0800–1700.

Tajikistan

Business
Mon–Fri: approximately 0900–1800 (appointments are best made in the morning).
Shops
No formal hours, but generally within 0800–2100.

Electricity supply
220V AC

Social customs/useful tips
The increasing influence of Islam is widely evident, particularly in rural areas. The Islamic faith can be traced back to the seventh century in Tajikistan and although religious activity was banned during the Soviet era it has begun to play a more important role in everyday life since the late 1980s. Closer links with Iran (Iranian television is beamed into Tajikistan) have been established since independence, although alcohol (generally vodka) is still freely available and consumed. Gratuities are becoming more customary, particularly in international hotels.
'Dushanbe' – Tajik for Monday – is named after the day when, for centuries, merchants have gathered at Dushanbe's famous oriental bazaar.

Security
The UK Foreign and Commonwealth Office (FCO) and US Department of State continue to advise against all travel to Tajikistan. The country's security problems are the legacy of the civil war and Islamic militants have used Tajikistan territory to stage hostage-taking excursions into Kyrgyzstan and Uzbekistan.
Government measures to deal with the problem have meant the introduction of roadblocks manned by heavily armed security personnel throughout Dushanbe. Armed resistance by those searched has caused casualties among bystanders. Bombings and shootings in public spaces are in any case common as a result of feuding between rival warlord-led factions over control of the narcotics markets. The prevalence of light weapons and local warlords throughout the country mean that care should be taken at all times. Visitors should avoid demonstrations, crowds, or congregations of military personnel.
Visitors may have their movements, hotel rooms and correspondence (including telephone and fax) monitored by security personnel. Taking photographs of military or otherwise strategically significant installations is not advised. There are periodic nightly curfews. Travel alone or on foot after dark is highly inadvisable. Car hire with a driver is advised rather than the use of public transport. Visitors are reminded to be vigilant and to dress down.

Getting there
Air
Flights to and from Tajikistan may be unexpectedly cancelled or subject to substantial delays. Charter flights can be overloaded with merchandise.
National airline: Tajikistan Airlines (state-owned)
International airport/s: Dushanbe (DYU), 2km south of city. Facilities include restaurant, post office, chemist and left luggage. There are bus services, 3 and 12, and train services, 3 and 4, which operate between the airport and city centre, hours 0600–1800, with a journey time of 20 minutes. Taxis operated between 0800–2000, journey time five minutes. Agree a price beforehand.
Other airport/s: Khorog in Gorno-Badakhstan. Flights are subject to bad weather and fuel shortages.
Airport tax: None
Surface
There are border crossings with Afghanistan, Uzbekistan, Kyrgyzstan and China. The country is landlocked.
Road: There are a few primary roads; secondary roads, particularly in mountain areas, are of poor quality. An all-weather road connects the capital Dushanbe to the Samarkand railhead (in Uzbekistan) to the north-west. It is anticipated that a highway will eventually run to China. Vehicles with Tajik licence plates may be refused entry into Uzbekistan.
Rail: Tajikistan is linked to the rail network of the former Soviet republics, with the main line running south from Dushanbe to the Uzbekistan border town of Termez and on to Samarkand, Tashkent and the Black Sea. A line running from Andizhan to Samarkand, both in Uzbekistan, cuts through the northern tip of Tajikistan.
Main port/s: The country is landlocked and the few river ports have no connection to the sea.

Getting about
The country is divided into four oblasts (regions): Gorno-Badakshan autonomous region in the east, Khatlon oblast in the south, Soghd oblast in the north and the Regions of Republican Subordination in the centre.
National transport
Air: Air travel is the only means of transport from Dushanbe to Khujand, or to the Pamirs.
Road: A network of roads connects larger cities and towns, although their condition is generally poor. Approximately 70 per cent of the network was paved during the Soviet era. Road travel, especially in east Tajikistan, can be impeded by checkpoints, from which soldiers or other armed groups may shoot if vehicles do not stop. Travel by road should be undertaken during daylight hours.
Buses: Buses run between towns.
Rail: Excluding industrial lines, Tajikistan has approximately 500km of railway. The north and south of the country are not linked by rail. Visitors should be aware that criminals operate on board international train connections.
City transport
Taxis: Volga taxis with sign on top. Agree a price beforehand.
Car hire
It is advisable to hire a car with a driver.

BUSINESS DIRECTORY
The addresses listed below are a selection only. While World of Information makes every endeavour to check these addresses, we cannot guarantee that changes have not been made, especially to telephone numbers and area codes. We would welcome any corrections.

Telephone area codes
The international direct dialling (IDD) code for Tajikistan is +992, followed by area code and subscriber's number:
Dushanbe 372

Useful telephone numbers
Police: 02
Fire: 01
Ambulance: 03

Chambers of Commerce
Tajikistan Chamber of Commerce and Industry, 21 Mazayeva Street, 734012 Dushanbe (tel: 279-519; fax: 211-480).

Banking
Agroinvestbank, Prospekt S Sherozi 21, Dushanbe (tel: 210-385; fax: 211-206).

Orienbank, 95/1 Rudaki Ave, Dushanbe (tel: 210-920; fax: 211-662).

Tajikbankbusiness (commercial bank), 29 Shotemur Street, 734025 Dushanbe (tel/fax: 210-634).

Tajikvnesheconombank (Tajikistan Bank for Foreign Economic Affairs), Dushanbe (tel: 233-571, 225-952).
Central bank
National Bank of Tajikistan, Prospekt Rudaki 23/2, 734025 Dushanbe (tel: 212-628; fax: 212-502).

Travel information
Dushanbe Airport, 32/1 Titov Street, Dushanbe 734006 (tel: 271-533, 510-041, 212-247; fax: 271-533, 218-685, 510-041).

Flight information (tel: 298-233).
Intourist Tajikistan (travel organisation), Shotemur Str 22, 734001 Dushanbe (tel: 274-973, 275-283; fax: 275-155).

Tajik Air, 31/2 Titov Street, Dushanbe Airport, 734006 Dushanbe (tel: 212-195, 212-297; fax: 510-091, 218-685).

Tourist information (0800-1700 hours) (tel: 298-233, 298-206).

Ministries

Council of Ministers, Prospekt Rudaki 48, 734025 Dushanbe (tel: 232-903; fax: 228-120).

EU Co-ordinating Unit, c/o Ministry of External Economic Relations, Prospekt Rudaki 42, Dushanbe (tel: 222-403, 227-077; fax: 228-120).

Ministry of Agriculture, 46 Rudaki Ave, Dushanbe 734051 (tel: 276-249).

Ministry of Communications, 57 Rudaki Ave, 734025 Dushanbe (tel: 232-284; fax: 212-953; International Relations Department (tel: 216-010; fax: 510-277).

Ministry of Construction, 36 Kirova Street, Dushanbe 734025 (tel: 226-143).

Ministry of Economy and External Economic Affairs, 42 Rudaki Ave, 734025 Dushanbe (tel: 232-944).

Ministry of Finance, Prospekt Kuibysheva 3, 734025 Dushanbe (tel: 273-941; fax: 213-329).

Ministry of Foreign Affairs, 40 Rudaki Ave, 734051 Dushanbe (tel: 221-560, 232-971; fax: 227-051).

Ministry of Foreign Economic Relations, 42 Rudaki Ave, Dushanbe (tel: 232-971; fax: 232-964).

Ministry of Grain Products, 42 Rudaki Ave, Dushanbe 734051 (tel: 276-131).

Ministry of Industrial Afairs, 80 Rudaki Avenue, Dushanbe 734023 (tel: 232-249, 231-845; fax: 232-381).

Ministry of Information, Ulitsa Negmata Karabaeva 17, 734018 Dushanbe (tel: 335-851).

Ministry of Justice, 25 Rudaki Ave, 734025 Dushanbe (tel: 214-405; fax: 218-066).

Ministry of Trade and Material Resources, 37 Bokhtar Street, Dushanbe 734002 (tel: 273-434).

Prime Minister's Office, 80 Rudaki Ave, 734023 Dushanbe (tel: 211-871; fax; 215-110).

Other useful addresses

British Embassy, Ul Gogolya 67, Tashkent 700000, Uzbekistan (accredited also to Tajikistan) (fax: (998 71)120-6549, 120-6430).

Central Asia Research Forum, School of Oriental and African Studies, Thornhaugh Street, London WC1H 0XG, UK (tel: (020) 7323-6300; fax: (020) 7436-3844).

State Statistical Committee (SSC), 17 Bokhtar Street, Dushanbe 734025 (tel: 276-882, 273-638; fax: 275-408).

Tajik Embassy in Uzbekistan, 16 Tarobi Street, Tashkent, Uzbekistan (tel: (998 71) 543-601, 549-966; fax: (998 71) 548-969).

Tajikistan (TDA) Office, c/o Tajik Bank Business, 23/2 Rudaki Avenue, 734620 Dushanbe (tel: 233-512; fax: 224-844).

Tajikvneshtorg (foreign trade organisation), Prospekt Lenina 41, 734051 Dushanbe (tel: 232-903).

Internet sites

Tajikistan Privatisation Agency: http://privatization.tajikistan.com

Tajikistan Resource Page: http://www.eurasianet.org/resource/tajikistan/index.shtml

National Tourism Company: http://www.tajiktour.tajnet.com

Tanzania

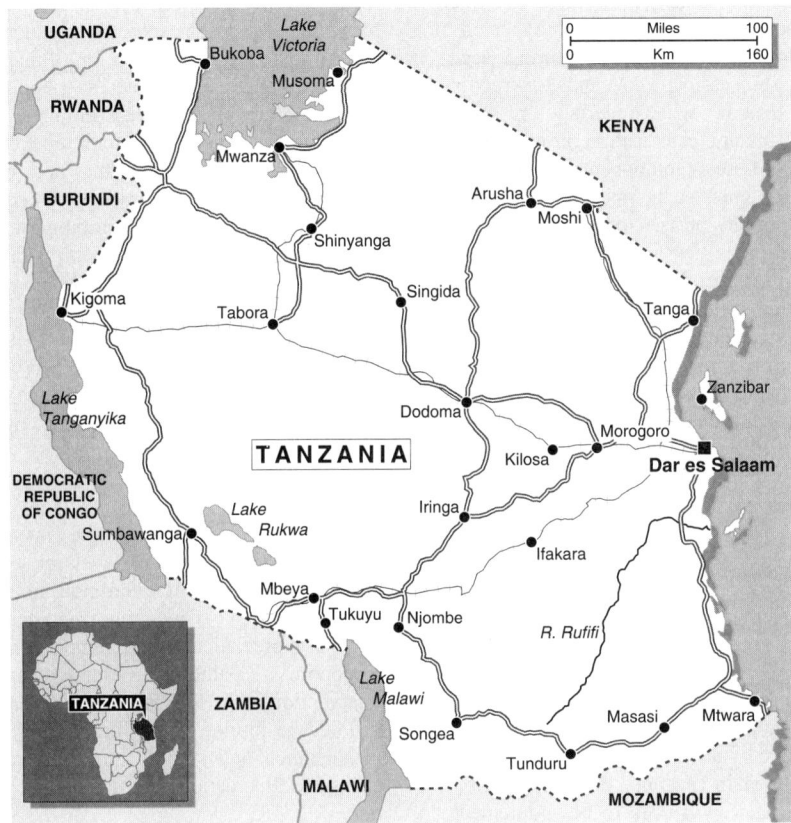

KEY FACTS

Official name: Jamhuri ya Muungano wa Tanzania (United Republic of Tanzania)

Head of State: President Jakaya Kikwete (sworn in 21 Dec 2005)

Head of government: Prime Minister Edward Lowassa (since 29 Dec 2005)

Ruling party: Chama Cha Mapinduzi (CCM) (Party of the Revolution) (since 1977; last re-elected 2005)

Area: 945,087 square km

Population: 36.58 million (2004)

Capital: Dodoma (official capital where the legislature is centred); Dar es Salaam (the former capital is the largest city and *de facto* commercial capital)

Official language: KiSwahili and English

Currency: Tanzania shilling (Tsh) = 100 senti (convertible with currencies of Kenya and Uganda)

Exchange rate: Tsh1,135.50 per US$ (Oct 2005)

GDP per capita: US$295 (2004)

GDP real growth: 6.30% (2004)

Labour force: 18.97 million (2004)

Inflation: 4.60% (2004)

Balance of trade: -US$724.00 million 2004

Foreign debt: US$6.80 billion (2003)

Tanzania is one of the poorest countries in the world, but it has been spared the internal strife that has blighted many African states. Unlike many of them, Tanzania had few exportable minerals. Under its first president, 'Mwalimu' (teacher) Julius Nyerere, it endured many years of socialism which turned out to have been an economic disaster. In 1967 Nyerere issued the *Arusha Declaration*, which called for self-reliance through the creation of co-operative farm villages and the nationalisation of factories, plantations, banks and private companies. A decade later, despite financial and technical aid from the World Bank and sympathetic countries, the programme had completely failed due to inefficiency, corruption, resistance from peasants and the rise in the price of imported petroleum.

After Nyerere's resignation in 1985, his successor, Ali Hassan Mwinyi, attempted to attract foreign investment and loans by dismantling government control of the economy. Benjamin Mkapa, who was elected president in 1995, and current president Jakaya Kikwete have continued the policy.

Economy

The economy depends heavily on agriculture, which accounts for almost half of GDP, provides 85 per cent of exports, and employs 80 per cent of the work force. Topography and climatic conditions, however, limit cultivated crops to only four per cent of the land area. Tourism is an important revenue earner; Tanzania's attractions include Africa's highest mountain, Kilimanjaro, and wildlife-rich national parks such as the Serengeti. Industry traditionally featured the processing of agricultural products and light consumer goods. The World Bank, the International

Monetary Fund (IMF), and bilateral donors have provided funds to rehabilitate Tanzania's out-of-date economic infrastructure and to alleviate poverty.

Sustained IMF-endorsed reforms have generated strong macroeconomic performance in Tanzania. Nevertheless, per capita income remains very low, and Tanzania will need to maintain high growth, low inflation, and a steady pace of structural reforms for many years to achieve inroads against poverty. A new poverty reduction strategy *Mkukuta* provides a roadmap to achieve these objectives.

Tanzania has made major strides over the past decade. Per capita growth has accelerated to nearly 5 per cent per annum, inflation is down to around 4 per cent. Official assistance has increased along with donor confidence, foreign reserves have risen to comfortable levels, the debt burden has fallen, expenditures in priority areas have increased, and poverty is declining.

But trade volume is comparatively low, and the financial sector – although growing rapidly – plays only a limited role in the economy. The cost of doing business remains high, and basic infrastructure remains poor.

The *Mkukuta* strategy

Mkukuta charts Tanzania's direction towards rates of broad-based economic growth of 8–10 per cent per annum. There will be particular attention to stimulating private investment, developing infrastructure, and building the human capacity necessary to develop a competitive economy. Strong growth is expected to continue across all sectors of the economy leading to overall economic growth of 7.5 per cent over the medium-term. Assuming normal rainfall, growth in agriculture is expected to remain strong, at around six per cent a year. In 2004, Tanzania was ranked in the top 10 of global locations for mining investments by the industry's Annual World Risk Survey and growth should remain robust. Strong expansion is expected in 2005–06 in the manufacturing sector, agro-processing, trade, and construction.

Tanzania will undertake rural and peri-urban electrification projects involving different components of the power sector; improve the rail network and rehabilitate the ports. Growth in tourism-related activities is expected to remain buoyant over the forecast period although further rapid expansion of the sector will be constrained by the limited park and accommodation capacity. Inflation is expected to remain at an average of about 4 per cent in 2005–06 and over the medium term.

The budget for 2005/06 envisages an increase in domestic revenue, and higher domestic financing with a concomitant increase in expenditures. Domestic revenue collection is expected to reach at least 14.3 per cent of GDP. Development expenditure is budgeted to increase by 1.2 per cent of GDP to 8 per cent. Despite the significant levels of external support for investment, this will still not be sufficient to meet the substantial demand for public investment in Tanzania. Externally financed assistance will need to be supplemented by domestic financing in order to enhance the productive capacity of the economy. The overall revenue and expenditure estimates should lead to an overall budget deficit of 14 per cent of GDP (6.5 per cent after grants) with domestic financing equivalent to 2.6 per cent of GDP.

The external sector is expected to continue benefiting from increased exports due to solid growth in the mining and manufacturing sectors, and a strong performance of traditional exports. Expanded road infrastructure, the abolition of many local taxes and facilitated access to inputs for production are expected to continue to contribute to high growth in traditional exports volume. Downside is that high oil prices and fast growth of imports of intermediate and capital goods, stemming from the government's initiatives on infrastructure projects, are expected to widen the trade deficit.

An overall international reserves position of around 6.2 months of imports is expected. The central bank will continue to rely more heavily on foreign exchange sales to ease any consequent pressures on liquidity. The Government believes the real exchange rate is broadly in line with fundamentals. While moderate movements around the current level are expected, the government is conscious of the fact that any excessive future depreciations or appreciations could hamper macroeconomic stability. Central bank intervention in the foreign exchange market will be limited to facilitate liquidity management and smooth any short-run excessive fluctuations in the exchange rate.

Monetary policy will be directed towards low inflation and high growth, while maintaining sufficient official foreign reserves. Consistent with the expected increase in money demand, the Bank of Tanzania will target annual M3 growth of 27 per cent which will allow a further increase of credit to the private sector of about 33 per cent. In line with this, the bank will target a reserve money increase of 26.6 per cent.

Politics

Shortly after independence, in 1964 Tanganyika and Zanzibar merged to form the United Republic of Tanzania. One-party rule came to an end in 1995 with the first democratic elections held in the country since the 1970s. Zanzibar's semi-autonomous status and popular opposition have led to two contentious elections since 1995, which the ruling party won despite international observers' claims of voting irregularities.

KEY INDICATORS — Tanzania

	Unit	2000	2001	2002	2003	2004
Population	m	33.64	34.50	35.19	35.89	*36.58
Gross domestic product (GDP)	US$bn	9.00	9.20	9.40	10.10	*10.85
GDP per capita	US$	268	264	253	255	295
GDP real growth	%	4.9	5.6	5.9	5.2	6.3
Inflation	%	5.5	4.9	4.7	4.6	4.6
Exports (fob) (goods)	US$m	665.7	776.4	737.0	1,691.0	1,248.0
Imports (fob) (goods)	US$m	1,339.8	1,492.1	1,890.0	2,682.0	1,972.0
Balance of trade	US$m	-674.1	-716.0	-1,100.0	-911.0	-724.0
Current account	US$m	-480.3	-873.1	-466.0	-1,016.0	-620.0
Foreign debt	US$bn	7.1	6.2	7.2	6.8	–
Total reserves minus gold	US$m	974.2	1,156.6	1,528.8	2,038.4	2,295.7
Foreign exchange	US$m	961.1	1,143.6	1,515.2	2,023.0	2,280.1
Exchange rate	per US$	800.41	876.41	950.50	1,017.70	1,089.33

* estimated figure

Tanzania

The political union between Zanzibar and mainland Tanzania has weathered more than four decades of change. Zanzibar has its own parliament and president.

Jakaya Kikwete, Tanzania's long-serving foreign minister, was declared the winner of presidential elections in December 2005. He vowed to continue the economic reforms set in motion by the outgoing president, Benjamin Mkapa, and to create jobs and tackle poverty. A long-time member of the ruling Chama Cha Mapinduzi (CCM) which has controlled Tanzania since the country's inception and which also governs in semi-autonomous Zanzibar, his presidential aspirations were thwarted in 1995 when he made an unsuccessful bid to represent the party in polls. He was an unswerving supporter of Tanzania's founding president, Julius Nyerere. He is 55, married, and has eight children. His predecessor Benjamin Mkapa retired after 10 years in power.

Risk assessment

Economic	Good
Political	Satisfactory
Regional stability	Poor
Stock market	Limited

COUNTRY PROFILE

Historical profile

In the 1960s, on a continent of newly-independent governments quick to embrace the rhetoric of socialism despite the widespread use of state power to further the vested interests of politicians, Tanzania showed signs of being an exception. Under President Nyerere, whose hobby was translating Shakespeare into Swahili, its official ideology asserted egalitarianism, development based on the communal life and a self-reliant socialism. Government and the leaders of TANU (the Tanganyika African National Union) were exhorted to austerity, not ostentation.

It was all heady stuff. The TANU constitution proclaimed that all citizens together possess the country's natural resources and that the state's responsibility was to intervene actively in the economic life of the country to prevent exploitation. The so-called Arusha Declaration ushered in a period of nationalisation of what President Nyerere called the 'commanding heights' of the economy – banks, insurance companies, breweries and flour mills all ended up being run by civil servants. Nyerere, in tune with much of economic thinking in this pre-Thacherite period, proudly declared that Tanzania had 'firmly rejected the proposition that without foreign investment and aid we cannot develop'.

Self-reliance was seen as an indispensable part of Nyerere's brand of socialism. The basis of Tanzania's new society was to be the traditional African institution of the extended communal family – *ujamaa*. President Nyerere had, with the best intentions, simply got it wrong. Foreign investment, needed for Tanzania's first Five Year Plan was not forthcoming. Investors had taken note of the government's policy statements. They had also noticed the build up of East German 'advisors' in Zanzibar. Investors had a responsibility to their shareholders, which they were not prepared to risk on President Nyerere's woolly idealism.

1832 The increasing importance of Zanzibar as a spice and slave trading centre led the Sultan of Oman to transfer his capital there from Muscat. Around this time, Britain signed a number of agreements with Oman to limit the potential threat to Britain's colonies from France. Meanwhile, Germany signed a number of 'friendship' treaties with local chiefs – treaties which formed the basis of the German East Africa Company which was established to exploit and colonise what became Tanganyika.

1886 The UK and Germany signed an agreement which gave Germany control of mainland Tanzania and the UK control of Zanzibar.

1918 After Germany's defeat in the First World War, the League of Nations mandated the territory to Britain.

1961 Tanganyika gained independence under Julius Nyerere and the Tanganyika Africa National Union (TANU).

1964 The United Republic of Tanzania was formed following the union of Tanganyika and Zanzibar.

1977 The new constitution established a real one-party state for the whole of Tanzania after the Tanganyika African National Union and Zanzibar's Afro-Shirazi Party merged to create Chama Cha Mapinduzi (CCM) (Party of the Revolution).

1979 Tanzania invaded Uganda, forcing its dictator, Idi Amin, to flee to Saudi Arabia.

1985 Nyerere stepped down as president and was replaced by the president of Zanzibar, Ali Hassan Mwinyi.

1992 The constitution was amended to allow multi-party politics.

1995 The first multi-party elections took place. Benjamin William Mkapa (CCM) was elected president and the CCM was re-elected to government. The Zanzibar opposition Civic United Front (CUF) refused to accept the election results in Zanzibar.

1999 A conciliation agreement was signed between the CCM and the CUF, bringing an end to four years of hostility. Julius Nyerere, the former president and founder figure of modern Tanzania, died.

2000 President Benjamin Mkapa was re-elected for a second term. The CCM was re-elected in the parliamentary elections. Because of unfair elections in Zanzibar, a re-run was held in 16 of its 50 constituencies; it was won by the ruling party, the CCM.

2001 There were clashes in Zanzibar between supporters of CUF and the police. The CCM and the opposition CUF signed a further agreement aimed at ending hostilities on Zanzibar.

2002 The African Development Bank (ADB) signed an agreement with the Deputy Minister for Finance, Alhaj Adbisalaam Issa Khatibu, for a loan of approximately US$47 million to partially finance the Dar es Salaam water supply and sanitation project.

2003 In July, the government and the IMF reached agreement over a 2003–06 economic programme, which includes further structural reforms to reduce poverty.

2004 In March, the presidents of Tanzania, Uganda and Kenya signed a protocol in Arusha over a proposed customs union.

2005 Jakaya Kikwete was elected President in the 14 December elections. The CCM retained an outright majority of seats (206) in parliament in the same elections.

Political structure
Constitution

The constitution was introduced in 1965 following the union of Zanzibar and Tanganyika in 1964. Zanzibar is partially autonomous, with 50 political constituencies.

The 1977 constitution established a one-party state for the whole of Tanzania after the two parties merged to create Chama Cha Mapinduzi (CCM) (Party of the Revolution).

Form of state
Republic

The executive

Executive power rests with the president, who is elected by direct popular vote for a five-year term. The president can serve a maximum of two terms.

One vice president is appointed by the president, as is the cabinet (in consultation with the prime minister), and the second vice president is the directly elected president of Zanzibar.

National legislature

The constitution provides for legislative power to be held by a unicameral National Assembly with members serving a term of five years, and for universal adult suffrage. The legislative body, the Bunge, has 274 members with 232 elected for a five-year term in single-seat constituencies. The president allocates 37 special seats to women and five seats are dedicated to members of the Zanzibar House of Representatives.

Legal system
The legal system is based on English common law, the 1977 Union and 1985 Zanzibari constitutions, as amended. The judiciary is relatively independent. A permanent Commission of Enquiry has wide powers to investigate abuses of power. In Zanzibar, *Kadhis* (Islamic courts) have jurisdiction over certain areas of law.

Last elections
December 2005 (presidential and legislative)
Results: Presidential: Jakaya Kikwete (CCM) was elected with 80.2 per cent of the vote, Ibrahim Haruna Lipumba (CUF) 11.7 per cent, Freeman Mbowe (Chadema) 5.9 per cent.
Parliamentary: CCM 206 out of 232 seats in total, CUF 19 seats; Chedema 5 seats. The president appointed 37 women and five members of the Zanzibar House of Representatives to parliament, bring the total of members to 274.

Next elections
14 December 2005 (presidential and legislative) (elections in the mainland were postponed from 30 October until December after the death of an opposition official; the election in Zanzibar went ahead as scheduled).

Political parties
Ruling party
Chama Cha Mapinduzi (CCM) (Party of the Revolution) (since 1977; last re-elected 2005)
Main opposition party
The Civic United Front (CUF) (based in Zanzibar); Chama cha Demokrasia na Maendeleo (Chadema) (Party for Democracy and Progress).

Population
36.58 million (2004)
Ethnic make-up
About 98 per cent of the population is of indigenous African or Arab (Zanzibar) origin, with the remainder mainly from the Indian sub-continent. Those of Indian, Pakistani and Goan descent tend to work in the towns, mainly dominating the trading environment, but also moving into the industrial sector. The small population of Arab descent is mainly engaged in trade. There are about 10,000 Europeans.
Over 120 tribal groups exist in Tanzania, the most important of which are Sukuma (12 per cent of total population), Makonde (4 per cent), Chagga (4 per cent), Haya (3 per cent), Nyamwezi (3 per cent), Ha (3 per cent), Gogo (3 per cent) and Hehe (3 per cent).
Religions
Islam and Christianity are the main organised religions. However, many people adhere to ancient tribal and animist religions. The religious make-up is believed to be Christianity: 33 per cent, Islam: 33 per cent, traditional beliefs: 33 per cent and Hinduism: 1 per cent.

Education
In 2003, three million seven to 13-year-olds were not in school, most enrolled late and intake and transition rates remained very low. This was the a result of the introduction of 'user fees' during the 1990s, when more than two million Tanzanian children were prevented from entering school and the rate of illiteracy began rising at 2 per cent a year. The education system is beset with problems of poor quality and a lack of participation among enrolled students. This reversed the country's early success of the 1960s when the literacy rate was around 91 per cent (the highest in Africa). The root cause of the problem is the government's debt obligations which have forced it to cut back on education. By 2000, the government was spending twice as much per capita on debt repayments than on education.
In 2001, the government announced in 2001 that it would abolish primary school fees, and the World Bank announced US$150 million interest free credit to expand school access and increase school retention at the primary level. During 2001, Tanzania enrolled 1,100,000 pupils in school, a 41 per cent increase over 779,000 in 2000.
The fees for secondary education, however, widened the gap between those participating in primary and secondary education. Parents must pay fees they cannot afford and teachers are under pressure to act as debt collectors to finance their schools. The situation is particularly dire in rural areas where schools are only able to recover around a third of fees. As a result, the education system is beset with problems of poor quality and a lack of participation among enrolled students. Oxfam, the main non-governmental organisation investing in Tanzanian education, estimates that in poorer schools there is only one desk for every 38 pupils and one textbook for every four children. Meanwhile, teachers are trying to cope with crumbling classrooms, falling salaries, worsening conditions and increasing class sizes.
Moreover, gross inequalities have developed between genders and classes, particularly in the fee-paying secondary schools. This has led to a progressive exclusion and marginalisation of adolescents and the most vulnerable children from basic family and community support.
Literacy rate: 78.2 per cent, adult rate (2003)
Compulsory years: Seven to 14.
Enrolment rate: 67 per cent gross primary enrolment; 6 per cent gross secondary enrolment; of relevant age groups (including repeaters) (World Bank).
Pupils per teacher: 37 in primary schools.

Health
The public health sector has been increasingly deprived of funds in recent years due to the government's move towards privatisation of the health service sector. User fees, introduced in the 1990s to ease the government's fiscal problems, have denied pregnant women and the rural poor access to primary healthcare facilities and essential medicines. While the government claims that mothers and children under five years receive free healthcare, in reality it is very different, particularly for those suffering from HIV/Aids, mental health problems and other diseases. Moreover, medicines which are supposed to be free are often in short supply at state-run hospitals and the number of hospital beds per capita has declined since 1990.
HIV/Aids
On top of inadequate health service provision, Aids is a continuing problem with infection rates estimated at over 25 per cent in urban areas. Like many African countries, Tanzania cannot afford the expensive Western drugs needed to treat the effects of Aids and initiatives aimed at the promotion of safe sex are often poorly designed and ineffective.
HIV prevalence: 8.8 per cent aged 15–49 in 2003 (World Bank)
Life expectancy: 42.7 years (World Bank)
Fertility rate/Maternal mortality rate: 5.0 births per woman (2003); maternal mortality 1,100 per 100,000 live births (World Bank)
Birth rate/Death rate: 39.5 births and 17.4 deaths per 1,000 people (2003)
Infant mortality rate: 104 per 1,000 live births (2003); 29.4 per cent of children aged under five were malnourished (World Bank).

Welfare
Between 15 million and 18 million of the total population live below the World Bank poverty line. The state does not have the capacity to function as a welfare provider while its ability to increase poor adult literacy rates, especially among women, remains negligible. Rather than building up the capacity and efficiency of state institutions, multilateral and bilateral donors are contracting out welfare services to non-governmental organisations (NGOs), which have little accountability and whose impact is usually localised and short-term.

Tanzania

Main cities
Dodoma (the official capital where the legislature is centred, estimated population 164,500 in 2003), Dar es Salaam (the former capital is the largest city and the *de facto* commercial capital, estimated population 2.5 million in 2004), Mwanza (302,300), Zanzibar (257,000), Tanga (203,400), Arusha (171,400).

Languages spoken
KiSwahili is the predominant language with English spoken by most people, especially in the main towns. English is the language most used in business.

Official language/s
KiSwahili and English

Media
The government allows private newspapers and private radio and television operators, although these organisations exercise a strong degree of self-censorship.

Press
Dailies: Shihata is the official news agency. Daily newspapers include the government-owned *Daily News* (English) and *Uhuru* (KiSwahili). Both are published in Dar es Salaam. Others are *The African*, *Daily Mail*, *Majira* and *Mtanzania*.
Weeklies: Including Sunday papers, are *Sunday News*, *Mzalendo* (KiSwahili), *Daily News on Saturday*, *East African*, *Express*, *Heko*, *Mfanyakazi*, *Shangwe*, *Sunday Mail*, *Sunday News*, *Sunday Observer*, *Sunday Times* and *Taifa Letu*. The *Government Gazette* is a weekly, which lists official announcements.
Business: Publications include the weekly *Business Times* and *Financial Times*.
Periodicals: A wide range is published. They include *The African Review*, published by the Department of Political Science of the University of Dar es Salaam; *Foreign Trade News Bulletin* published twice a year by the Ministry of Industry. Other popular periodicals are *Tantravel Magazine* (travel trade journal), *Mfanyakazi Magazine*, *Family Mirror*, *Moto Moto*, *Fahari*, *Radi*, *Michapo*, *Watu*, *Klongozi*, *Change*, *Mcheski*, *Mizani* and *Heko*.

Broadcasting
Radio: Radio Tanzania broadcasts internal services in KiSwahili and external services in English. The Voice of Tanzania and Zanzibar broadcasts on three wavelengths in KiSwahili.

Economy
The government's efforts to build an export-oriented economy have been accompanied by a policy of economic stabilisation which entailed the devaluation of the shilling, austerity measures targeting inflation, and moves to cut state bureaucracy and loss-making public enterprises. The IMF and World Bank are keen to promote Tanzania as a success story since the country adopted their liberalising agenda of rolling back the country's corrupt state bureaucracy, breaking protectionist barriers, privatising parastatals and instituting policies to attract foreign investment. Economic fundamentals seem to support this idea. During the years 1997–2002, the country achieved an average growth rate of 4.8 per cent as it developed its infrastructure and engaged in extensive infrastructural projects.

Even with the level of growth at 5.2 per cent in 2003 and 6.3 per cent in 2004, Tanzania's development has not had many noticeable effects on the wider population, particularly the rural poor who make up for around 36 per cent of the population. With the increase of the Aids prevalence rate to around 8 per cent, there will be an increasing strain on the economy – particularly with worsening social indicators. The growth figures, measured in Tanzanian shillings, hide the stagnation of GDP in dollar terms due to currency depreciation; the shilling fell by 20 per cent between 2001 and mid-2003. With a population growth rate of up to 3 per cent, GDP per capita is slowly edging up, albeit from a low level; GDP per capita increased from US$253 in 2002 to US$295 by 2004. The government's ability to commit funds for public services also diminished through trade liberalisation.

In July 2003, the government and the IMF reached agreement over a 2003–06 economic programme, which includes further structural reforms to reduce poverty. There has also been donor support to improve Tanzania's road system to be the best in the region. This could attract investment to a country thought to have poor infrastructure.

Uganda, Kenya and Tanzania signed the Common External Tariff (CET) agreement on 1 January 2005. This will eliminate many barriers to trade and develop common tariffs between the nations.

External trade
On 31 December 2002, the US approved Tanzania as being eligible for tariff preferences under the African Growth and Opportunities Act (AGOA). The legislation requires that countries are only eligible for greater access to US markets provided they have made continued progress toward a market-based economy, the rule of law, free trade, poverty reduction and the protection of workers' rights. This process is reviewed annually.

Imports
Principal imports are consumer goods, machinery and transportation equipment, industrial raw materials and crude oil.
Main sources: South Africa (13.1 per cent total, 2004), China (8.8 per cent), India (6.6 per cent), Zambia (5.4 per cent), UAE (5.4 per cent), UK (4.8 per cent), US (4.8 per cent), Kenya (4.3 per cent)

Exports
Main exports include gold, coffee, cashew nuts, manufactures and cotton.
Main destinations: India (10.2 per cent total, 2004), The Netherlands (6.8 per cent), Japan (6.1 per cent), UK (5.3 per cent), China (5.2 per cent), Kenya (4.8 per cent), Germany (4.4 per cent)

Agriculture
Farming
The agricultural sector is the mainstay of the economy. It contributes around 45 per cent of GDP and over 50 per cent of export earnings. Approximately 70 per cent of the population are peasant farmers. Land laws affecting ownership are complicated and hinder potential investors in agricultural activity. The government has expressed an interest in taking up land reform to attract the private sector.

Tanzania has more than 40 million hectares of arable land, but only six million are cultivated. Only 15 per cent of the country has access to water, and the crops are almost totally dependent on the weather. Coffee, cotton, sisal, tobacco, cashew nuts and tea are the most important crops.

There has been a serious decline in production of most crops. Coffee, cotton and sisal are among the crops which have declined and stagnated, although some export crops are showing signs of growth, including tobacco, tea, cashew nuts and horticulture.

The cashew nut sector has benefited from a return to a system where smallholders deal directly with the buyers. Tanzania supplies more than one-quarter of the global market.

Heavy cotton subsidies in the US have affected cotton production in Tanzania, following the liberalisation of the markets. The effects of subsidies are also felt in traditional industries such as beef, wheat and dairy products and also in non-traditional markets like spices.

The estimated crop production for 2004 included: 4,457,500 tonnes (t) cereals in total, 2,800,000t maize, 6,890,000t cassava, 1,800,000t sugar cane, 71,000t wheat, 260,000t potatoes, 970,000t sweet potatoes, 650,000t sorghum, 647,000t rice, 150,400t bananas, 601,600t plantains, 461,000t pulses, 8,131,000t roots and tubers, 370,000t coconuts, 65,000t oil palm fruit, 39.000t citrus fruit, 14,000t grapes, 145,000t tomatoes, 77,500t pineapples, 155,020t oilcrops, 24,500t tobacco, 3,500t cocoa beans, 57,000t green coffee, 195,000t mangoes, 106,000t treenuts, 12,500t cloves, 7,200t various spices, 25,500t tea, 109,000t cotton lint, 270,000t millet, 1,334,750t fruit in total, 1,192,100t vegetables in total. Estimated livestock production included: 362,207t meat in total, 246,330t beef, 13,000t pig-meat, 10,320t lamb, 30,600t goat meat, 46,957t poultry, 36,745t eggs, 944,000t milk, 27,000t honey, 48,300t cattle hides, 2,580t sheepskins, 3,820t greasy wool.

Fishing
Tanzania has extensive inland as well as marine fisheries, with the freshwater lakes and rivers accounting for over 80 per cent of production. Foreign vessels trawl Tanzania's exclusive economic zones and take their catches elsewhere for processing; the government wishes to attract some of this business to Tanzania. Nile perch and sardines make up over three-quarters of Tanzania's total fish exports. Tanzania exports around US$150 million of Nile perch and related products annually, 80 per cent of which are sold to the EU market. The industry is well-organised and gives employment to over 300,000 people. The government is encouraging domestic fish consumption by developing local fish markets.

Forestry
Tanzania has around 33 million hectares of forests and woodlands. The forests have been under intense pressure from population growth and activities such as harvesting of fuelwood, agricultural demands, fires and illegal logging. The government is seeking to create the conditions for private investment in plantation and sustainable management by local communities.

Industry and manufacturing
The industrial and manufacturing sector accounts for 16.7 per cent of GDP and employs 5 per cent of the workforce. Typically, less than a fifth of industrial production is exported.
Most production is geared towards import substitution and the government has traditionally directed public investment towards the sugar and textile industries, tanneries, pulp and paper mills, the fertiliser industry, cement factories, and sisal and cashew nut processing industries. These are engaged in the processing of local minerals and agricultural raw materials for local consumption. Production also includes paper and pulp, cement, textiles and some light engineering.

Growth has been restricted by a lack of foreign exchange needed for the import of raw materials, spare parts and fuel. Foreign aid is aimed at rehabilitating existing industries, but the government is slowly gearing production towards export markets. The high cost of credit inhibits the development of the private sector which is characterised by small enterprises. Industrial production increased by 8.4 per cent in 2003.
In November 2005, a US$6 billion Mini-Tiger Plan 2020 was launched. Designed to attract foreign direct investment, the scheme aims to expand Tanzania's manufacturing base and increase annual GDP by 2020 to US$40 billion.

Tourism
Tourism is Tanzania's fastest-growing industry. The sector is expected to contribute 4.3 per cent to GDP in 2005. Over 600,000 tourists visited Tanzania in 2004. The government's target is one million visitors by 2010. Tanzania is a comparatively expensive destination, which results in around 50 per cent of visitors entering on short trips from neighbouring countries rather than directly into Tanzania for longer and more lucrative stays. In June 2005, several tourism and travel organisations inaugurated a joint programme to investigate ways of attracting more visitors directly into the country. The government has made tourist visas available at the point of entry into Tanzania. The fact that Tanzania has only a small number of embassies abroad makes it difficult for tourists to obtain the necessary entry visas in advance.

Environment
There is concern about gold mining activities taking place in the Eastern Arc Mountains of Tanzania, which are said to be destroying the Amani nature reserve, a UNESCO-designated biosphere reserve and Balangai forest reserve.

Mining
Tanzania is well-endowed with mineral sources, especially gold, base metals, diamonds and other gemstones. Mining accounts for around 2.3 per cent of GDP and is targeted to increase to 10 per cent by 2025.
Gold mining and production have expanded considerably in recent years. 50 tonnes were produced in 2004. Tanzania is the third largest gold producer in Africa. Gold has become a major export, mainly to the EU.
There is significant interest in the Kagera nickel-copper-cobalt belt, which runs north and east bordering with Burundi. There are considerable reserves of iron, tin, gypsum and kaolin. There is a large phosphate mine at Minjingu, supplying a fertiliser plant at Tanga.
Tanzania is also a significant producer of gems, including a diamond mine in Shinyanga and rubies from Longido. Other gemstones include sapphires and tanzanite, which is unique to Tanzania.

Hydrocarbons
Tanzania imports about 900,000 tonnes per year (tpy) of crude oil. Of this, 55–65 per cent is processed at the country's only refinery. The Tanzanian and Italian Petroleum Refinery (Tiper), based in Dar es Salaam, has a capacity of 750,000 tpy. There is scope for petroleum refining in Dar es Salaam, amounting to 14,900 barrels per day (bpd). More than 50 per cent of imported oil is consumed by vehicles, with industry consuming 25 per cent and the rest used commercially and in homes. Oil continues to account for over 50 per cent of export earnings. Exploration for oil has been taking place since 1980 without success, but exploration is still taking place.
Natural gas reserves were estimated at 28.2 billion cubic metres in 2003. Offshore reserves have been recently discovered at Songo Songo Island in the Indian Ocean, Kimbiji and Mnazi Bay near Mtwara. Ocelot and Trans Canada Pipelines (OTC) are developing the Songo Songo reserves and plan to build a pipeline to deliver gas to Dar es Salaam. The main hydrocarbons development concerns the Songo Songo gas field, which has reserves estimated at 35 billion cubic metres. The Songo Songo project aims to supply gas via pipeline to the Ubungo power plant in Dar es Salaam.
There are proven coal reserves of 200 million tonnes in Mchuchuma in south-west Tanzania near the northern tip of Lake Nyasa, but the only developed colliery is at Songwe-Kiwara with capacity of 100,000 tonnes per year. Studies indicate the Mchuchuma coal deposits could provide fuel for 400MW generating capacity for up to 35–40 years. The coals are bituminous and with low sulphur content.

Energy
Tanzania has a heavy dependence on imports of oil and oil products (900,000 tonnes of crude oil per year), which may account for up to 50 per cent of export earnings, and can be in short supply due to a lack of foreign exchange reserves. Total installed electricity generating capacity is about 577MW, of which about 60 per cent is hydroelectric and the remainder thermal (diesel and coal run). Only about 5 per cent of the country's hydroelectric potential has been developed. Electricity is only available to about 10 per cent of the population of Tanzania,

Tanzania

mainly those who live in towns. Wood fuel is the major energy source in the country, which is having an adverse impact on the environment. Electricity contributes just 0.6 per cent of Tanzania's total energy supply, although it is growing at a rate of 11–13 per cent per annum.

Tanzania has been implementing a rural electrification programme since 1967, but progress has been slow due to the very low population density and the high cost of supplying power to such a dispersed population.

Development plans are concentrated on further utilisation of the country's hydroelectric potential (estimated to be around 3,800MW), which is being developed with the aid of foreign investment. Mainly concentrated in south-west Tanzania and the Rufiji River basin. The Kihansi 180MW hydroelectric project supplements supplies from Mtera hydropower station.

In 2002, Independent Power Tanzania Ltd opened a 100MW plant at Tegeta, outside Dar es Salaam, at a cost of US$162 million. It is supplying state-run electricity company Tanzania Electric Supply Company (Tanesco) with electricity.

The Ubungo power plant is due to be converted from oil to gas, with the addition of a fifth turbine, and will be fed by gas produced from the Songo Songo gasfield when a 200km pipeline to Dar es Salaam is completed in 2007. The plant's capacity at first will be 112MW but this will be increased later. All power generated will be sold to Tanesco through a 20-year purchase agreement.

Financial markets
Stock exchange
Tanzania has a small stock market, the Dar-es-Salaam Stock Exchange (DSE), which operates for three half-sessions per week. In October 2002, the government allowed foreign participation in the DSE The stock exchange is hampered by a lack of participation by foreign investors and the local investor community, which has few surplus funds and remains unconvinced of the value of investing in the stock market. Analysts have suggested that East Africa does not need three exchanges and proposed that Uganda and Tanzania merge their exchanges, especially after the creation of the EAC in late 1999.

Banking and insurance
Central bank
Bank of Tanzania
Main financial centre
Dar es Salaam

Time
GMT plus three hours

Geography
Tanzania consists of Tanganyika, on the African mainland, and the nearby islands of Zanzibar and Pemba. Tanganyika lies on the east coast of Africa, bordered by Uganda and Kenya to the north, by the Democratic Republic of Congo (DRC) to the west, and by Zambia, Malawi and Mozambique to the south. Zanzibar and Pemba are in the Indian Ocean about 40km (25 miles) off the coast of Tanganyika, north of Dar es Salaam. Tanzania is by far the largest country in east Africa. It is divided into three major regions: the coastal plains and river valleys, the central plateau and basin country, and the southern highlands.

The northern coastal area is humid and rainy, with some of the lushest vegetation in Tanzania. Further south the rainfall decreases and the vegetation develops into a drier savanna woodland. Tanzania's major rivers cut across the coastal plains, creating fertile alluvial fans where cotton, sisal and tropical fruits are grown. A few miles inland from the ocean the vegetation switches to tropical savannah woodland.

The central plateau region occupies the major part of the country, wedged between the two rift valleys. The plateau is bordered by Lake Victoria in the north, the Rukwa Valley in the south, Lake Tanganyika and the Ruwenzori Mountains in the west, and the coastal plains in the east. The famous Serengeti Plains and the Masai Steppe are located in the north-east of this central region.

The southern highlands consist of a variety of mountain and hill formations and are sparsely populated.

Climate
Tropical, with variations according to altitude. Rainy seasons April–May and November–December. Warmer on coast, cooler in upland areas. Temperatures range from 23–30 degrees Celsius (C). Climatically, Tanzania can be divided into two major zones, the wet and humid lowlands around Lake Victoria and the Indian Ocean, and the semi-arid plateau region. The coastal area is almost always hot and humid with a rainy season that extends for more than 10 months. The most uncomfortable period is December–April when the temperature sometimes exceeds 32 degrees C, with humidity over 90 per cent. The coolest time of the year, and the best time to visit, is June–September when the temperature drops to 15–21 degrees C with relatively low humidity.

The central plateau has distinct wet and dry seasons with great seasonal variations in temperature. Heavy rains fall in March–May and light rains in November–December.

In Dar es Salaam the rainy seasons are usually March–May and November–December, but these can vary from year to year.

Dress codes
Men should wear a lightweight/tropical suit and tie, and women a lightweight suit or formal dress, for business meetings. Women's dress should be modest. On safari it is considered best to avoid bright colours as they may irritate the animals. Visitors to the highlands are advised to take warm clothing. A light raincoat and umbrella are useful during the rainy season.

Entry requirements
Passports
Required by all.
Visa
Required by all; with a few exception for citizens of some African states. Details can be found on the visa form: see http://www.tanzaniaembassy-us.org. Business travellers should submit an application form with a letter of invitation from a local contact; or introduction by an employing company, detailing nature of business and itinerary.

All visitors must have proof of return/onward passage.
Currency advice/regulations
The import and export of local currency is illegal. The import and export of foreign currency is limited to the amount declared on arrival. A receipt for all money transactions should be obtained and kept until departure.
Customs
Travellers have to go through customs again on arrival in Zanzibar.

Health (for visitors)
Mandatory precautions
A yellow fever vaccination certificate if arriving from areas of known infection, and from those considered infectious by Tanzanian authorities.

Advisable precautions
Cholera and hepatitis 'B' are of most risk, other useful vaccinations include: tetanus, typhoid, hepatitis 'A' and 'E', diphtheria and tuberculosis. Anti-malarial prophylaxis is necessary for visitors, throughout the year. To avoid the risk of bilharzia, only use well-maintained, chlorinated swimming pools. Rabies and sleeping sickness are present.

All water should be regarded as potentially contaminated, use only bottled water (readily available in Dar es Salaam) or boiled and filtered water for drinking, brushing teeth, washing vegetables and reconstituting powdered milk. Other food hygiene precautions should be strictly observed, eat only hot, cooked food.

A reasonable precaution could include a first aid kit with a sterile needle kit and disposable syringes.

Hotels
Accommodation tends to be expensive and can be difficult to obtain, especially in Dar es Salaam, so reservations should be made well in advance and confirmation obtained. Bills must be settled with foreign exchange.

Credit cards
Use restricted to a few shops and hotels, mainly in Dar es Salaam. Hotels mostly accept only American Express and Diners'. Limited use of MasterCard.

Public holidays
Fixed dates
1 Jan (New Year's Day), 12 Jan (Zanzibar Revolution Day), 26 Apr (Union Day), 1 May (Labour Day), 7 Jul (Saba Saba/Industry Day), 8 Aug (Nane Nane/Farmers' Day), 14 Oct (Nyerere Day), 9 Dec (Independence and Republic Day), 25 Dec (Christmas Day), 26 Dec (Boxing Day).
Variable dates
Good Friday, Holy Saturday, Easter Day, Easter Monday, Eid al Fitr, Eid al Adha, Islamic New Year, Prophet's Birthday. The Islamic year contains 354 or 355 days, with the result that Muslim feasts advance by 10–12 days against the Gregorian calendar. Dates of feasts vary according to the sighting of the new moon, so cannot be forecast exactly. Islamic year 1426: 10 February 2005 to 30 January 2006.

Working hours
Banking
Mon–Fri: 0830/0900–1530/1600; Sat: 0830/0900–1100/1130. In Dar es Salaam, the Kariakoo, Temeke and Ubungo branches of the National Bank of Commerce open on Sundays from 0900–1300.
Business
Mon–Fri: 0900–1230, 1500–1700.
Government
Mon–Fri: 0800–1230, 1400–1600.

Telecommunications
Telephone/fax
Telecommunications services are provided by the state-owned Tanzania Posts and Telecommunications Corporation (TPTC). It is responsible to the Ministry of Communications and Public Works.
The main network consists of an east-west microwave system from Dar es Salaam to the Rwanda/Burundi border and a north-south system, with links to Malawi and Zambia in the south and Kenya in the north. Local links are mainly through open wire, although there are some VHF and HF radio links. In Zanzibar there is a Hitachi digital exchange.

There is an Intelsat standard B earth station working to the Indian Ocean satellite, and a standard A earth station working to the Atlantic Ocean satellite.
Tanzania has a GSM network, operated by TRI, which has 3,000 subscribers representing 0.01 per cent of the market.
Postal services
Internal services are slow but fairly reliable. It is advisable to despatch overseas mail by air.
Courier services
Air courier services are available.
Mobile phones
There were around 30,000 mobile phone users in 2003.
Internet/e-mail
There are Internet cafes in Dar es Salaam and Arusha. There were 300,000 Internet users in 2003.

Electricity supply
250V AC, 50 cycles. Usual industrial supply is 400V. Plugs are three square-pin variety.

Weights and measures
The metric system is in use but UK weights and measures are still used in many industries, for example, building.

Social customs/useful tips
Patience is required when doing business in Tanzania. Visitors should use cameras only in private settings and tourist resorts otherwise permission must be sought. Visitors should be aware that bridges, railway stations and public buildings are regarded as security installations and should not be photographed. There are no restrictions on alcohol. Almost all business executives speak English.
Business visitors should address Tanzanians as Mr, Mrs or Ms. The term *Ndugu* is equivalent to comrade in English. The normal greeting when meeting an individual is *Jambo*. Handshaking is normal practice both on meeting and parting. Tanzania has a large number of local traditions, although few will affect the business traveller or tourist. There are no particular taboos, but visitors should be aware of religious customs. Muslims should not be offered pork or ham and many do not drink alcohol. During the Islamic holy month of Ramadan, Muslims do not eat or drink during daylight hours.

Security
Street crime is a serious problem in Tanzania, especially in Dar es Salaam. Be alert at all times. Passports, traveller's cheques, wristwatches and cash are regularly stolen. Use hotel safe deposit boxes and do not carry too much cash.

Getting there
Air
National airline: Air Tanzania.

International airport/s: Dar es Salaam (DAR), 13km from city, duty-free, restaurant, bar, bank, shops, post office; Kilimanjaro International (JRO), 50km from Arusha (between Arusha and Moshi), bar, restaurant, post office, shops. Shuttle bus services run to town centres. Zanzibar (ZNZ), 8km from Kisauni. Taxis are available.
Other airport/s: Dar es Salaam International (DAR), 15km south-west of city centre.
Airport tax: Zanzibar only: international destinations, US$20, national destinations, Tsh 2,000.
Surface
Road: The tarmac road from Tanzania to Zambia is in good condition, as well as the road north to Kenya, but road links from Rwanda Mozambique and Malawi are poor.
Rail: The Tanzania-Zambia Railway Authority (Tazara), jointly owned and administered by the Tanzanian and Zambian governments, operates a 1,860km railway link between Dar es Salaam and New Kapiri Mposhi (copper belt) in Zambia, running twice weekly.
Water: Ferry services connect with ports in Kenya, the Democratic Republic of Congo, Zambia, Uganda, Malawi and Burundi.

Getting about
National transport
Travel by bus and train is possible but can be uncomfortable.
Air: Air Tanzania operates services between Dar es Salaam, Kilimanjaro, Mwanza, several other, small airports, Zanzibar and Pemba. Small private company, Precision Air, also operates scheduled domestic flights to the major cities. Gulf Air and Kenya Airways operate scheduled commercial flights to Zanzibar. Air Zanzibar also operates from mainland Tanzania, Kenya and Uganda using four small aircraft.
Charter companies operate to isolated airfields, national parks and numerous towns.
Road: All-weather roads connect major centres, but minor roads are liable to be impassable in the rainy season except to four-wheel drive vehicles. There are new roads from Songea to Makambako and from Mwanza to Musoma.
The road journey by fast motor vehicle from Dar es Salaam to Arusha (650km) can be completed in about seven hours, and to Mbeya, close to the Zambia border (850km) in under nine hours.
Buses: Inexpensive services link most centres. Routes include: Dar es Salaam-Songea; Dodoma-Moshi; Lindi-Tunduma; Lindi-Mtwara. Services are unreliable.

Rail: The service is to Tanga, Moshi, Morogoro, Dodoma, Tabora, Kigoma and Mwanza, and is slow and crowded.

Water: Several passenger boats run from Dar es Salaam to Zanzibar and Pemba Islands every day. A number of steamer services run during the week on Lake Tanganyika, Victoria and Nyasa, although these may be crowded. Two ferries operate on Lake Malawi on the Tanzanian side between Itungi port and Mbamba bay, passing through various small ports.

City transport
Taxis: It is advisable to use only authorised taxis, available in main towns. Taxis from hotels have fixed rates for journeys within Dar es Salaam. Fares in any other taxis are by negotiation and should be agreed before the journey. Taxi drivers do not expect tips, but 10 per cent would be acceptable.

Buses, trams & metro: Services operate within Dar es Salaam. Flat fare system operates. Generally unreliable and overcrowded and unsuitable for business visitors.

Car hire
Car hire can be arranged via the main hotels, but it is advisable to get a four-wheel-drive if going off the main roads.

BUSINESS DIRECTORY

The addresses listed below are a selection only. While World of Information makes every endeavour to check these addresses, we cannot guarantee that changes have not been made, especially to telephone numbers and area codes. We would welcome any corrections.

Telephone area codes
The international direct dialling (IDD) code for Tanzania is +255, followed by area code and subscriber's number:

Arusha	27	Mwanza	28
Dar es Salaam	22	Zanzibar	24
Kilimanjaro	27		

Chambers of Commerce
Arusha Chamber of Commerce, Industry and Agriculture, PO Box 141, Arusha (tel: 250-8556; fax: 250-4191; e-mail: tccia.arusha@cats-net.com).

Tanzania Chamber of Commerce, Industry and Agriculture, Twiga House, Samora Avenue, PO Box 9713, Dar es Salaam (tel: 212-1421; fax: 211-9437; e-mail: tccia.info@cats-net.com).

Zanzibar National Chamber of Commerce, Industry and Agriculture, Darajani, PO Box 1407, Zanzibar (tel: 223-3083; fax: 223-3349; e-mail: znzchamber@zitec.org).

Banking
Akiba Commercial Bank Limited, PO Box 669, TDFL Bldg (Phase II), Upanga Rd, Dar es Salaam (tel: 118-340-4; fax: 114-173).

Azania Bancorp Ltd, PO Box 9271, Samora Ave, Dar es Salaam (tel: 118-026, 117-998; fax: 36-741).

Bank of Tanzania, PO Box 2939, 10 Mirambo Street, Dar es Salaam (tel: 211-0945/7, 211-0950/2; fax: 212-8151; 211-2671, 211-2573, 211-3325, 211-2537; e-mail: info@bot-tz.org).

Citibank (T) Limited, PO Box 71625, Ali Hassan Mwinyi Road, Dar es Salaam (tel: 117-575, 117-601; fax: 113-910, 117-576).

CRDB Limited, PO Box 268, Maktaba St, Dar es Salaam (tel: 117-442/7).

Diamond Trust Bank (T) Limited, PO Box 115, Jamhuri/Ali Hassan Mwinyi Rd, Dar es Salaam (tel: 114-888/892; fax: 114-210).

Eurafrican Bank (T) Limited, PO Box 3054, NDC Development House, Kivukoni/Ohio Street, Dar es Salaam (tel: 110-928, 111-229, 110-104; fax: 113-740).

Exim Bank (T) Limited, PO Box 6649, 9 Samora Avenue, Dar es Salaam (tel: 119-738; fax: 119-737).

Habib African Bank Limited, PO Box 70086, India St, Dar es Salaam (tel: 111-107/9).

International Bank of Malaysia (T) Limited, PO Box 9362, Haidery Plaza, Upanga/Kisutu St, Dar es Salaam (tel: 110-518, 110-520, 110-571; fax: 110-196).

Kenya Commercial Bank Ltd, PO Box 804, Audit House, 36 Upanga Road, Dar es Salaam (tel: 115-386/7/8; fax: 115-391).

Kenya Commercial Bank (T) Limited, PO Box 804, Peugot Hse, Dar es Salaam (tel: 115-386/7/8; fax: 115-391).

National Micro-Finance Bank Limited, PO Box 9213, Samora Ave, Dar es Salaam (tel: 116-925/9, 116-933, 110-900, 118-785; fax: 114-058).

NBC Limited, PO Box 1863, NBC House, Sokoine Drive, Dar es Salaam (tel: 113-914; fax: 112-887).

Stanbic Bank Tanzania Ltd, PO Box 72647, Sukari House, Ohio Street/Sokoine Drive, Dar es Salaam (tel: 112-195/200; fax: 113-.742)

Standard Chartered Bank Tanzania Ltd, PO Box 9011, Ohio/Sokoine Drive, Dar es Salaam (tel: 1173-50/52, 113-787, 117-377; fax: 113-770, 113-775).

Tanzania Investment Bank, PO Box 9373, Samora Avenue, Dar es Salaam (tel: 111-708/13; fax: 113-438) .

Tanzania Postal Bank, PO Box 9300, Mkwepu Street, Dar es Salaam (tel: 112-358/60, 112-385/9, 116-409, 117-748; fax: 38-212).

Central bank
Bank of Tanzania, 10 Mirambo Street, PO Box 2939, Dar es Salaam (tel: 211-0945; fax: 211-3325; e-mail: info@hq.bot-tz.org).

Travel information
Air Tanzania, Tancot House, City drive, PO Box 543, Dar es Salaam (tel: 211-0245).

Air Zanzibar (tel: 223-1390).

Coastal Aviation (tel: 284-3033).

Dar es Salaam International Airport, PO Box 19043, Dar es Salaam (tel: 284-4610/19; fax: 284-4343, 284-3022, 284-4209).

Kilimanjaro International Airport, PO Box 995, Arusha (tel: 22-941; fax: 28-553).

Precisionair (tel: 211-3036).

Tanzanair, Azikiwe & Samora Ave/Airport International Terminal, PO Box 364, Dar es Salaam (tel: 230-232/4, 246-583; fax: 246-296).

Tanzania National Parks, PO Box 3134, Arusha (tel: 250-1930/1931; fax: 254-8216; e-mail: tanapa@yako.habari.co.tz; internet site: http://www.tanapa.com).

Zanzibar Tourist Corporation, PO Box 216, Zanzibar (tel: 232-344; fax: 233-430).

National tourist organisation offices
Tanzania Tourist Board, IPS Building, 3rd Floor, PO Box 2485, Dar es Salaam (tel: 211-1244/5; fax: 211-6420; e-mail: safari@ud.co.tz).

Ministries
Ministry of Agriculture and Irrigation, PO Box 9192, Dar es Salaam (tel: 286-2480).

Ministry of Energy and Minerals, PO Box 9153, Mkwepu Street, Dar es Salaam (tel: 211-7156).

Ministry of Industries and Commerce, PO Box 9503, Lumumba Street, Dar es Salaam (tel: 218-0049).

President's Office, State House, PO Box 9120, Dar es Salaam (tel: 46-261; fax: 46-913).

President of Zanzibar's Office, PO Box 776, Zanzibar (tel: 30-814; fax: 33-722).

Prime Minister's Office, PO Box 980, Dodoma (tel: 23-320; fax: 46-232; PO Box 3021, Dar es Salaam (tel: 31-081; fax: 46-232).

Other useful addresses
Board of External Trade, PO Box 5402, Dar es Salaam (tel: 33-524).

Board of Internal Trade, PO Box 883, Dar es Salaam (tel: 28-301).

British High Commission, Hifadhi House, Samora Avenue, PO Box 9200, Dar es Salaam (tel: 117-659/665; fax: 112-951).

Cashew Nut Authority of Tanzania, PO Box 533, Mtwara (tel: 2310).

Coffee Authority of Tanzania, PO Box 732, Moshi (tel: 4011).

National Development Corporation, Development House, Kivukoni Front/Ohio Street, PO Box 2669, Dar es Salaam (tel: 211-2893, 211-1460/3; fax: 211-3618; e-mail: ndc@cats-net.com; internet site: http://www.ndctz.com).

National Insurance Corporation of Tanzania Ltd, PO Box 9264, Dar es Salaam (tel: 110-744, 113-052; fax: 113-403).

Presidential Parastatal Sector Reform Commission, 2nd Floor, Sukari House, Sokoine Drive/Ohio Street, PO Box 9252, Dar es Salaam (tel: 211-5482, 211-7988/9; fax: 211-3065/6, 212-2870; e-mail: info@psrctz.com; internet site: http://www.psrctz.com).

Radio Tanzania, PO Box 9191, Dar es Salaam (tel: 38-011/6).

Sea Express Services Ltd, Dar es Salaam (tel: 37-049, 112-508); Zanzibar (tel: 33-002, 33-013).

Southern Paper Mills Co Ltd, (Marketing Dept) Tanzania Elimu Supplies Building, Bandari Road, Dar es Salaam (tel: 111-602, 32-113; fax: 113-233).

State Mining Corporation, PO Box 4958, Dar es Salaam (tel: 28-781).

Tanzania Electric Supply Company Ltd (TANESCO), PO Box 9024, Dar es Salaam (tel: 211-2891; fax: 211-3836; e-mail: mdtan@intafrica.com).

Tanzania Exporters' Association (TANEXA), c/o Sima International, PO Box 1175, Dar es Salaam (tel: 48-948; fax: 73-784).

Tanzania Harbours Authority, PO Box 9184, Dar es Salaam (tel: 21-212; fax: 32-066; internet site: http://www.tanzaniaports.com).

Tanzania National Parks, PO Box 3134, Arusha (tel: 250-1930/1931; fax: 254-8216; e-mail: tanapa@yako.habari.co.tz; internet site: http://www.tanapa.com).

Tanzania Petroleum Development Corporation (TPDC), Managing Director, PO Box 2774, Dar es Salaam (tel: 181-407; fax: 180-047); Director of Exploration and Production, PO Box 5233, Dar es Salaam (tel: 36-086; fax: 29-663; e-mail: tpdcexploration@raha.com); Director of Research & Corporate Services, PO Box 2774, Dar es Salaam (tel: 152-019; fax: 152-017).

Tanzania Railways Corporation, PO Box 468, Dar es Salaam (tel: 26-241).

Tanzania Revenue Authority, PO Bnox 11491, Dar es Salaam (tel: 211-9591/4; fax: 212-8593; e-mail: trais@afsat.com).

Tanzanian Embassy (USA), 2139 R Street, NW, Washington DC 20008 (tel: 202-939-6129; fax: 202-797-7408; e-mail: tanz-us@clark.net).

Television Zanzibar, PO Box 314, Zanzibar (tel: 32-816).

US Embassy, Laibon Road, PO Box 9123, Dar es Salaam (tel: 37-501; fax: 37-408).

Internet sites

Africa Business Network: http://www.ifc.org/abn

AllAfrica.com: http://allafrica.com

African Development Bank: http://www.afdb.org

Africa Online: http://www.africaonline.com

Harambee Afrika (UK business club for traders with east, central and southern Africa; includes annotated web resource list): http://www.harambee.co.uk

Mbendi AfroPaedia (information on companies, countries, industries and stock exchanges in Africa): http://mbendi.co.za

Terres Australes

KEY FACTS

Official name: Le Territoire des Terres Australes et Antarctiques Françaises (French Southern and Antarctic Territories)

Head of State: President of France (Jacques Chirac); *Administrateur Supérieur* Michel Champon (took office 20 Jan 2005)

Head of government: Prime Minister Jean-Pierre Raffarin

Area: 439,797 square km consisting of: Kerguelen Archipelago 7,215 square km, Crozet Archipelago 515 square km, Amsterdam Island 60 square km, Saint Paul Island 7 square km, Adélie and Antarctica 432,000 square km

Population: 90 (2004)

Official language: French

Currency: Euro (eur) = 100 cents

Exchange rate: eur0.83 per US$ (Oct 2005)

COUNTRY PROFILE

Historical profile
The French Southern and Antartic Lands (Territoire des Terres Australes et Antarctiques Francaises) includes the islands of Ile Amsterdam, Ile Saint-Paul, Iles Crozet and Iles Kerguelen in the sounther Indian Ocean. The French also claim a section of Antarctica – Adelie Land – but this claim is not recognised by the US.
1552–59 Saint Paul and Amsterdam Islands were sighted by survivors of a Portuguese expedition led by Ferdinand Magellan.
1772 Captain Marion Dufresne and ship's mate Crozet saw the group of islands, which became known as the Crozet Archipelago.
1772 Yves de Kerguelen sighted another archipelago, later named after him.
1840 Adélie Land, on the Antarctic continent, was sighted and claimed by the French.
1924 A French government decree attached administration for the islands to the government of Madagascar (then a French colony).
1947 France established observation stations.
1955 Terres Australes et Antarctiques were accorded the status of an overseas French territory.
1959 The international community signed the Antarctic Treaty, establishing the legal framework for the management of Antarctica, banning any military activity within the Antarctic continent and guaranteeing the protection of its environment and wildlife.
1961 The Antarctic Treaty came into force.
1993 A co-operation agreement between the national institutes in charge of polar research in France and Italy agreed to construct a permanent scientific base, Concordia, approximately 1,000km from the French scientific base of Dumont d'Urville.
2000–01 The station was built and completed.
2002 Ten countries began working on a glacial project, the European Programme of Glaciology (EPICA), drilling to study the climate in the Antarctic during the last 500,000 years. Drilling reached 2,871 metres and collected ice samples from 520,000 years ago.
2003 The drilling reached the rock base of the Antarctic continent at a depth of 3,300 metres.
2005 On 20 January, Michel Champon took office as *administrateur supérieur*.

Political structure
Le Territoire des Terres Australes et Antarctiques Françaises (French Southern and Antarctic Territories) is a French Térritoire d'Outre Mer (TOM) (Overseas Territory), but is administered under two different international laws. France exercises full sovereignty over the southern islands, unanimously recognised by all nations. However, Adélie Land is administered according to the 1959 Antarctic Treaty, although the US does not recognise France's claim to the Land. The Antarctic Treaty is an international agreement which provides for broad scientific co-operation and demilitarisation of the Antarctic continent and freezes existing territorial claims without prejudicing the solution to the sovereignty problem.
The fully sovereign area is governed by one law and two main decrees. The law of 6 August 1955 confers administrative and financial autonomy on the TOM. The implementation decree of 13 January 1956 defines the TOM's financial system and the decree of 8 September 1956 provides for the TOM's administrative organisation. The TOM is under the authority of a chief administrator, whose official residence is in Paris. The administrator is assisted by an advisory council, which meets twice a year and consists of seven members appointed for five-year terms. The council must be consulted on the TOM's draft budget and it is kept informed and consulted on any proposed new scientific missions or applications for concessions and commercial activities.
The TOM is divided into four districts, each under the authority of a district head appointed by the chief administrator:
Saint Paul and Amsterdam Islands – permanent settlement is Martin de Viviés.
Crozet Islands – settlement is Alfred Faure (Possession Island).
Kerguelen Islands – settlement is Port aux Français.
Adélie Land – settlement is Dumont D'Urville.

Population
90 (2004)

Languages spoken
Official language/s
French

Economy
The Terres Australes have no permanent population but are temporarily habited by

scientific reserch groups. Scientific activities are supported and developed by the Institut Français pour la Récherché et la Technologie Polaires (IFRTP) (French Institute for Polar Research and Technology) and the administration of the TOM is in charge of the logistics. Most of the TOM's economic activities centre around supporting the IFRTP. Fishing is the other main economic activity; others are philately and tourist cruises. Fish catches land on Iles Kerguelen and are then exported to France and Réunion.

External trade
Crayfish and other fish are exported to France and Réunion.

Agriculture
Farming
Research has indicated the viability of large-scale farming of giant brown macrocystis, a type of seaweed.
Fishing
French vessels fish for crayfish off Amsterdam and Saint Paul. There is an agreement between France and Ukraine to fish for icefish and toothfish.
A research programme which has been carried out since 1970, has shown that trout adapt well to a sub-antarctic environment and the result of sea-ranching salmon was also a biological success. There are estimated to be 60 to 120 million tons of krill in the TOM's coastal waters. Around Saint Paul and Amsterdam Islands, there are plentiful supplies of bull head fish, false cod, crayfish and cape lobster.

Tourism
The French research vessel, *Marion Dufresne*, conducts tourist cruises.

Hydrocarbons
A limited amount of oil drilling has been carried out.

Banking and insurance
Central bank
The Paris-based Institut d'Emission d'Outre-Mer (IEOM) provides all central banking services except foreign exchange reserves.

Time
GMT plus five hours

Geography
The territory comprises Adélie Land, a narrow segment of the mainland of Antarctica, and several islands (Kerguelen and Crozet, St Paul and Amsterdam) located in the southern Indian Ocean.

Climate
The climate of Saint Paul and Amsterdam Islands is oceanic, damp and mild. The temperature averages 15 degrees Celsius (C).
The climate is particularly extreme in the Crozet Archipelago – the islands lie at the centre of an area where tropical and antarctic air masses meet, causing deep depressions and cyclone-forming processes. The Kerguelen Islands have a cool, humid climate due to the proximity of the Antarctic continent. The summers last from December to March and are similar to those beyond the Arctic Circle. The winters from May to October are comparatively mild. The climate is unstable with constant winds, sometimes at a speed of 160kph. The temperature of the surrounding sea averages 4 degrees C.
Adélie Land's climate is harsh. The temperature of the coastal area never rises above 4 degrees C in summer and can fall to -37 degrees C in winter.

Entry requirements
Visa
Required by all, except citizens of EU, North America, Australasia and Japan, for stays up to one month; this includes business trips by representatives of overseas companies or organisations. For further exceptions, full details and a copy of the application form visit www.diplomatie.fr/venir/visas/index.html. Proof of adequate funds for stay and return/onward ticket are necessary.

Weights and measures
The metric system is in use.

Getting there
Air
There are no air links with the bases.
Surface
Water: Relief ships bring new personnel and supplies. A charter vessel calls five times a year in the Antarctic islands and another calls twice a year in Adélie Land.

BUSINESS DIRECTORY
The addresses listed below are a selection only. While World of Information makes every endeavour to check these addresses, we cannot guarantee that changes have not been made, especially to telephone numbers and area codes. We would welcome any corrections.

Banking
Central bank
Institut d'Emission d'Outre-Mer (IEOM), 5 rue Roland Barthes, 75598 Paris Cedex 12, France (tel : +33 1 5344-4141; fax : +33 1 4347-5134; e-mail: contact@ieom.fr).

Other useful addresses
Institut Français pour la Recherche et la Technologie Polaires (IFRTP), Technopole Brest Iroise, BP 75, 29280 Plouzane, France (tel: (33-2) 9805-6500; fax: (33-2) 9805-6555).

Terres Australes et Antarctiques Françaises (TAAF), 34 Rue des Renaudes, 75017 Paris (tel: (33-1) 4053-4652; fax: (33-1) 4766-9123).

Thailand

KEY FACTS

Official name: Prathet Thai; Ratcha Anachak Thai (Kingdom of Thailand)

Head of State: King Bhumibol Adulyadej (Rama IX) (since 1946)

Head of government: Prime Minister Thaksin Shinawatra (leader of TRT) (since 2001; re-elected 6 Feb 2005)

Ruling party: Thai Rak Thai (TRT) (Thais Love Thais) party (since Jan 2001; re-elected 6 Feb 2005)

Area: 514,000 square km

Population: 64.34 million (2004)

Capital: Bangkok

Official language: Thai

Currency: Baht (B) = 100 satang

Exchange rate: B41.07 per US$ (Oct 2005)

GDP per capita: US$2,522 (2004)

GDP real growth: 6.10% (2004)

Unemployment: 2.10% (2004)

Inflation: 2.70% (2004)

Oil production: 218,000 bpd (2004)

Balance of trade: US$11.12 billion 2004

Foreign debt: US$49.40 billion (2003)

The February 2005 elections were a landslide victory for the incumbent, telecommunications magnate Thaksin Shinawatra, whose party won 400 out of a possible 500 seats. He is the patriarch of the country's richest family, owners of Shin Corporation, a company whose profits have climbed hugely during Thaksin's leadership. He is also the first leader to last for an entire electoral term – in the 1990s the country had eight different administrations. His success is attributed to his astute judgement, ambitious drive and self-marketing. His party, Thai Rak Thai, meaning Thais love Thais, has focussed on populist policies such as affordable healthcare, a village credit system and forgiveness of farmers' debt. These priorities were reached after extensively canvassing views from millions of poor Thai peasants.

While this is good news, concerns are mounting about Thaksin's authoritarian streak. He is dismissive of inconvenient court judgements and watchdogs and blasé about the human cost of some of his more stringent crime crackdowns. He has used the country's recent Islamic uprisings to consolidate and tighten his grip over the nation.

A cabinet reshuffle in August 2005 rewarded long-standing loyal politicians and was designed to improve the government's tarnished image, hit by a series of corruption scandals. GDP growth has been unimpressive while the budget deficit is widening. The ministry for justice has a shadow cast over it by murder allegations concerning a missing Muslim human rights lawyer, Somchai Neelapachit.

Islamic disquiet

Thailand is a Buddhist country home to a minority Muslim population. In three provinces in the country's southern tip Muslims comprise the majority sector. There are long standing grievances over religious and economic marginalisation. The Muslim population has little acknowledgement at an official level. The southern provinces are consistently the poorest areas of Thai society. They speak a Malay dialect and are akin to neighbouring Malaysians. Recent violence directed against the Muslim world in Iraq and Palestine has resonated in Thailand and government officials suspect al Qaeda involvement in renewed Thai unrest.

This latest violent Islamic uprising has been raging since January 2004. Over 1,000 people have been killed. Bombing victims are often teachers and school workers, targeted for their perceived affiliation to Buddhist officialdom. In July 2005 the government supplied teachers with guns to curb the growing exodus.

The prime minister has labelled the troubled Southern spots 'red zones' and an emergency area. He has pledged to withhold development funds. However, this is likely to exacerbate grievances as the Islamic alienation is a large part economic. Thaksin had previously adopted a 'hearts and mind' tactic, promising to regenerate the area but now it looks like his patience is running out. He has stepped up his powers of arrest, to control the flow of information, tap phones and to crack down on public freedom of expression. He has blacklisted a crowd of suspected, but untried Muslim youth and urged them to attend reconciliation talks. This violation of the 'innocent before proven guilty' principle has ruffled feathers further.

There is widespread suspicion that Thaksin will abuse his increased powers, especially as Thailand does not have a tradition of democracy, and the prime minister does not have a history of tolerating dissent. The Emergency Powers Act, which was rushed through parliament, is subject to no official restriction.

Amnesty International warned at the beginning of 2006 that the government crackdown has been too extreme and heavy handed with reports of torture and unwarranted detention, as well as high levels of unexplained disappearances. The twin violence of the insurgency and the security clampdown has created, the UK human rights group said, a climate of fear.

Tsunami

On 26 December 2004 an earthquake in the Indian ocean off the coast of Sumatra caused a huge *tsunami* (tidal wave), which swept across South-east Asia for seven hours. Over 8,000 people died in Thailand, and 6,000 more lost their homes and livelihoods. As many as half of those who died were foreign tourists. The local economy, largely dependent on agriculture, fishing and tourism, took a battering. The global response was an outpouring of donations, pledges of aid and support – but also criticisms for the lack of any kind of early warning system. Prime Minister Thaksin Shinawatra, told the international donor community that Thailand would not need any financial assistance and could pay fully for reconstruction itself. By 2006 Phuket, one of the islands hardest hit, had benefited from an almost complete reconstruction, with some areas even better off than before – but other devastated regions are likely to remain undeveloped for years to come. The Moken, nomadic people with no official documentation to claim governmental assistance, suffered the most.

Economy

Growth in 2003 and 2004 was over 6 per cent. Bad debt has been curbed and poverty tackled head-on. However, populist strategies have proved expensive and analysts voice doubts about how sustainable Thaksin's spending has been. The economy took a downward turn in 2005. Growth declined to a forecast 3.5 per cent. There were lower outputs in the agricultural sector, particularly rice and sugar cane, as well as fisheries, tourism and airports. Hotels were operating at below 20 per cent occupancy in the first part of the year while domestic consumption was down. Inflation rose, a knock on effect of the *tsunami*, and short term demand for food and transport. Rising global oil prices and poor export growth were also to blame. Construction, unsurprisingly, increased by 13 per cent as the reconstruction of hotels and houses smashed by the

KEY INDICATORS — Thailand

	Unit	2000	2001	2002	2003	2004
Population	m	61.99	62.40	62.96	63.65	*64.34
Gross domestic product (GDP)	US$bn	123.93	114.80	123.60	143.20	*163.49
GDP per capita	US$	1,986	1,857	1,963	2,037	2,521
GDP real growth	%	4.6	1.8	5.2	6.8	6.1
Inflation	%	1.6	1.7	0.6	1.4	2.7
Unemployment	%	3.6	3.3	3.1	0.8	2.0
Oil output	'000 bpd	164.0	178.0	197.0	217.0	218.0
Natural gas output	bn cum	17.8	18.1	18.9	19.6	20.3
Coal output	mtoe	5.1	5.6	5.6	5.4	5.8
Exports (fob) (goods)	US$m	67,949.0	63,202.0	67,400.0	75,430.0	96,107.0
Imports (fob) (goods)	US$m	56,192.0	54,620.0	62,100.0	64,564.0	84,983.0
Balance of trade	US$m	11,757.0	8,582.0	4,200.0	10,866.0	11,124.0
Current account	US$m	9,369.0	6,227.0	6,700.0	8,325.0	7,290.0
Foreign debt	US$bn	80.3	67.1	59.2	51.7	51.0
Total reserves minus gold	US$m	32,016.0	32,355.0	38,046.0	41,077.0	48,664.0
Foreign exchange	US$m	31,933.0	32,350.0	38,042.0	40,965.0	48,498.0
Exchange rate	per US$	40.11	44.43	43.54	41.33	40.26

* estimated figure

tsunami continued apace in 2005 and into 2006.

Outlook

The economy is predicted to recover somewhat to reach GDP growth of 5 per cent in 2006. Oil prices will be a determinant in the fate of the Thai economy but the removal of fuel subsidies has made the country more resilient to the world oil situation. Thaksin however might struggle to maintain high levels of support, with growing disquiet from the Muslim south as well as liberal voters and human rights activists. His heavy-handed approach is unlikely to bring unrest under control although the situation is also dependent on world events in Iraq and the Middle East.

Risk assessment

Economic	Good
Political	Fair
Regional Stability	Good

COUNTRY PROFILE

Historical profile

One of the few Asian countries not to have been colonised, the pattern of modern Thai history has been one of dictatorship with a few slices of democracy. Pibul Songkhram, the strongman from 1938 for almost twenty years, was himself driven into exile by the army chief, Field Marshal Sarit Thanarat. When Sarit died in 1963, he was succeeded by his prime minister, then colonel (and later marshal) Thanom Kittikachorn. For the next ten years Thanom and his military colleagues, Field Marshal Prapas Charusathiara and Thanom's son Colonel Narong – popularly known among Bangkok's diplomatic circle as 'the Father, the Son and the Wholly Gross' dictated, cosyed up to the US and became sucked in to the Indochina conflicts while maintaining an increasingly intolerant régime. In 1972 Thanom promulgated a new constitution that gave him even more powers and allowed him to rule with the support of an assembly in which two thirds of the seats were held by army and police officers.

In the twentieth century Thailand often appeared to be a country on the edge of a revolution; Thanom fell victim to popular protest in the form of student demonstrations, forcing the King to send the hapless trinity into exile. Yet another brief experiment with democracy followed and yet another constitution was promulgated, Thailand's tenth. Periods of intermittent democracy and military rule continued until 2000.

The modern Thai language originates from the Tai-speaking people who migrated south in the first millennium AD from the Chinese province of Yunnan, south of the Yangtze River.

1767 The former capital of Siam, Ayutthaya, fell to Burmese invaders.
1782 King Rama I – first of the Chakri dynasty – was crowned and founded the capital city Bangkok.
1851–68 King Mongkut (Rama IV) began a period of reform and modernisation while adroitly avoiding European colonisation. Treaties were signed with the US, Great Britain, France and Japan, among others. Barriers against traders were eliminated, allowing expansion.
1868–1910 Chulalongkorn, (Rama V) continued his father's programmes by modernising the legal and administrative systems, reforming the political structure and abolishing slavery. He also began construction of a railway network. Some Siam territories in Indochina were ceded to Britain and France.
1910 Vajiravudha (Rama VI) became King. He introduced compulsory education, among other reforms.
1925 Prajadhipok, the brother of Vajiravudha, became King.
1932 A group of students, led by Pibul Songgram and Pridi Phanomyang, in a bloodless *coup d'état* forced King Prajadhipok to replace absolute monarchy with a constitution monarchy and introduce parliamentary government. A new National Assembly was established.
1933 The first general elections were held.
1935 The King abdicated. A council of regency chose his 10-year old brother, Ananda, to be Rama VIII. He was studying in Switzerland at the time.
1938 Pibul Songgram became prime minister
1939 Siam was renamed Thailand.
1941–1946 Under the leadership of Pibul, Thailand allied itself with Japan and allowed Japanese troops to traverse the country. Thailand declared war on the US and Britain but the Thai ambassador in Washington withheld the official declaration and so technically the country remained neutral. Pridi Phanomyang led an American-backed anti-Japanese movement.
1945 Pridi became prime minister and Pibul was jailed briefly for war crimes.
1946 King Ananda returned for the second time from studying in Switzerland but died shortly after in mysterious circumstances. He was succeeded by his brother, Bhumipol Aduldej, the present King Rama IX, although he was not formally crowned until 1950. Inflation and corruption marred the government's reputation.
1947 Pibul led an army *coup d'état* and instituted a military dictatorship. Pibul was staunchly anti-Communist and under his rule the Chinese community, suspected of being Communist sympathisers, was harassed.
1950 Bhumibol Adulyadej became King and was crowned Rama IX. Thailand aligned itself with the US during the Cold War and sent troops to fight in the Korean War.
1957 Pibul was overthrown in a coup led by Field Marshal Sarit Thanarat.
1958 Sarit deposed his own premier, took power himself and imposed martial law and dissolved all political parties.
1973 Student riots destabilised the military government and free elections were held. The King appointed a civilian, Sanya Thammasak, as premier.
1974 A new constitution was introduced, legalising political parties.
1976 The military seized power and Admiral Sa'ngad Chaloryoo, annulled the 1974 constitution and re-introduced martial law. A new constitution was introduced. Thanin Kraivixien became prime minister, he imposed a harsh rule and kept unions under tight control while he carried out anti-Communist purges of the civil service and educational institutions.
1975 With the ending of the Vietnam War Thailand became the temporary home to many refugees from Indochina.
1977 Thanin was overthrown by General Kriangsak Chomanand.
1978 A new constitution was promulgated in which a bicameral National Assembly was established.
1991 Another military coup led by General Suchinda Krapayoon replaced Kriangsak.
1992 General Krapayoon resigned and elections were held. A coalition led by the Pak Prachatipat (PP) (Democratic Party) was victorious.
1995 The Phak Chart Thai (PCT) (Thai Nation Party) won the general election and formed a coalition government.
1997 The constitution was amended to allow the direct election of a prime minister for a four-year term. The baht fell sharply during the Asian financial crisis and led to bankruptcies and unemployment. Chuan Leekpai (PP) was elected prime minister; he worked closely with the IMF to reform the badly damaged economy.
2000 Thailand's first senate election was held. Subsequent rulings against the results by the Election Commission necessitated two further elections.
2001 Elections to the House of Representatives took place. Thaksin Shinawatra became prime minister and the Thai Rak Thai (TRT) (Thais Love Thais) formed a coalition government with the Phak Chart Patthana (PCP) (National Development Party).
2002 The PCT and the Phak Khwam Wang Mai (PKWM) (New Aspiration Party)

joined the ruling coalition. Supachai Panitchpakdi became director general of the World Trade Organisation (WTO).
2003 Although Thailand was not considered a Severe Acute Respiratory Syndrome (Sars) affected area, visitor arrivals had dropped by 20 per cent in April.
2004 January–March a wave of terrorist attacks by separatist Islamic and ethnic Malays from southern provinces killed over 100 people. In April over 100 Islamic insurgents were killed while attacking several police bases in the south. In October, 85 Islamic detainees were killed while in custody following violence at a rally in the south. Many suffocated to death in the back of a police van; an enquiry concluded the tragedy was unforeseen. Avian flu broke out and prompted the slaughter of millions of birds. Six provinces along the west coast of Thailand, including the tourist resorts of Phuket and Khao Lak, were devastated by a *tsunami* which swept the whole region on 26 December after an earthquake off the coast of Sumatra. The final estimate for Thailand was 8,212 dead or missing, 6,000 displaced.
2005 The ruling TRT party won a landslide victory in the 6 February elections; Thaksin Shinawatra is the first Thai prime minister to win a second term in office. Recurrence of avian flu in October.

Political structure
Constitution
Thailand is a constitutional monarchy, with the King as head of state. King Bhumibol Adulyadej, who succeeded to the throne in 1946, is Thailand's longest-reigning monarch.
Thailand's 1997 constitution focussed on improving governance. It established a number of new organisations such as the Election Commission and the National Counter Corruption Commission (NCCC) to combat malpractice.
Local government is vested in 73 provinces, with locally-elected councils operating at all levels. Each province is sub-divided into *amphoe, tambon* and *muban.*

Form of state
Constitutional monarchy

The executive
Executive power lies with the cabinet, headed by a prime minister who must be an elected member of the House of Representatives.

National legislature
The Ratha Sapha (National Assembly) is bicameral. It consists of the 500-member Sapha Poothaen Rassadorn (House of Representatives) and a 200-member Woothi Sapha (Senate).
Members of the House of Representatives are elected for four-year terms in 155 multi-seat constituencies, with 100 seats determined on the basis of proportional representation.
Senate members are elected on a non-partisan platform in single-seat constituencies.
Amendments to the constitution in 1997 introduced direct elections for membership of the Senate. Bills are presented either by the cabinet or by members of the House of Representatives and are enacted into law with the approval of both houses.

Legal system
The constitution provides for an independent judiciary. Courts follow the traditional pattern of courts of first instance, a court of appeal and a Supreme Court.

Last elections
6 February 2005 (House of Representatives)
Results: Parliamentary: the ruling Thai Rak Thai (TRT) (Thais Love Thais) party won 376 seats out of the total 500 seats in the House of Representatives; Pak Prachatipat (PP) (Democratic Party) 97; Chat Thai Party 25; Mahachon Party two.

Next elections
By March 2006 (Senate); 2009 (House of Representatives).

Political parties
Ruling party
Thai Rak Thai (TRT) (Thais Love Thais) party (since Jan 2001; re-elected 6 Feb 2005)
Main opposition party
Pak Prachatipat (PP) (Democratic Party)

Population
64.34 million (2004)
Ethnic make-up
Approximately 80 per cent of the population are Thais, 10 per cent Chinese and 5 per cent Malays. Other ethnic minorities include Laotian, Vietnamese, Kampuchean and a number of hill tribes.
Religions
Buddhist (85 per cent), Muslim (4 per cent), Christian (0.5 per cent), Hindu and Confucian.

Education
Primary schooling lasts for six years until students are aged 13 when they progress to the lower secondary school. At aged 16 students may either follow a general academic or vocational path in an upper secondary school.
There are 16 universities in Thailand, of which 12 are in Bangkok. There are also 21 recognised private colleges of higher education. Culturally, higher education is biased towards the social sciences and humanities, with science and technology accounting for only 22 per cent of total tertiary enrolment.
The education system in Thailand is undergoing major reforms. The main objective is the eventual decentralisation of education in the country as in 2001, policy was implemented through a central office, regional office, provincial office, then a district office. From August 2002 it will be administered through a central office, a local area education office and the school.
The government hopes to transform the learning process from a teacher-oriented system to a learner-oriented method. There are plans to introduce more technology in education.
Literacy rate: 96 per cent, adult rate (2003)
Compulsory years: Six to 16
Enrolment rate: 89 per cent gross primary enrolment; 59 per cent gross secondary enrolment, of relevant age groups (including repeaters), (World Bank).
Pupils per teacher: 21 in primary schools

Health
It is estimated that only 10 per cent of the population have pre-paid health insurance plans. Improve access to healthcare has been promised by the government by implementing a standard B30 (US$0.70) per hospital visit rule across the country. There are fears, however, that the reduced cost will entail a fall in healthcare standards.
The government has as a central objective, the standardisation of healthcare throughout the country. Plans stress the need to reorganise and decentralise public health administration. Private sector healthcare is expanding faster than the public sector, with private healthcare expenditure currently estimated to be running at double the public sector level. Private hospitals (over 370) account for 25 per cent of all hospital beds.
The ministry of health provides free medical services to the poor in all government hospitals. Thailand has well over 1,000 public hospitals, over 13,000 specialised private clinics, over 8,000 health centres and an estimated 0.23 doctors per 1,000 of the population. The health of the Thai population has improved significantly over the last 20–30 years with life expectancy rising by 17 years, the infant mortality rate dropping by about two-thirds and the proportion of the population with access to safe drinking water more than trebling. However, in November 2001, it was reported by the World Bank that 16 per cent of the population were below the poverty line, an increase from 11 per cent in 1996.
In 2004 avian flu broke out, killing nine people and prompting the slaughter of more than 100 million poultry.

HIV/Aids
In a region where conservative leaders have been reluctant to publically endorse

HIV/Aids prevention programmes, Thailand took the initiative in 1994 and introduced a full scale public education and condom distribution programme, so that by 2004 people newly testing HIV positive fell to 21,260, vastly less than the peak of 142,819 in 1991.
HIV prevalence: 1.5 per cent aged 15–49 in 2003 (World Bank)
Life expectancy: 69.3 years (World Bank)
Fertility rate/Maternal mortality rate: 1.8 births per woman (2003); maternal mortality 44 deaths per 100,000 (World Bank).
Birth rate/Death rate: 16.4 births and 6.9 deaths per 1,000 people (2003)
Infant mortality rate: 23 per 1,000 live births (2003); 18 per cent of children aged under five were malnourished (World Bank).

Welfare
The social insurance bill provides for cover during illness or accidents unrelated to work, maternity, disability, funeral expenses, child welfare, pensions and unemployment. The welfare system was radically restructured in 1997 with the introduction of a centralised Government Pension Fund (GPF) worth about B71 billion (US$1.57 billion), replacing the old civil service pension scheme with a privately managed autonomous entity.
The labour department of the Ministry of the Interior manages workers' security and welfare and oversees a compensation fund for workers. In 70 out of 73 provinces, employers with more than 20 workers are required by law to contribute to the compensation fund. This fund provides benefits to employees who suffer injury in the workplace, or who fall ill or die as a result of the performance of their work. On average, 60 per cent of the monthly wages will be paid. This amount should not fall below B2,000 (US$46) and should not exceed B9,000 (US$206). Medical expenses are also paid in the case of an injury and in the case of death, the funeral expenses will be covered by the employer.
The public welfare department (PWD) of the Ministry of the Interior provides welfare services to various groups of people such as children and the young, landless farmers, hill tribe minorities, the destitute, the disabled, the handicapped, the aged and those hit by disaster.
Thaksin Shinawatra has ambitious objectives to deal with social problems in Thailand. These include plans to establish family advisory centres and childcare clinics.
Child prostitution in Thailand has received strong international attention. Eradicating the trade in children and women is likely to be a slow process for Thailand, since anti-trafficking laws have been difficult to implement. Female unemployment in Thailand remains high, so many turn to prostitution to earn their living.

Main cities
Bangkok (local name Krung Thep – City of Angels) (capital, estimated population 6.7 million in 2004).

Languages spoken
Business is conducted in Thai. Chinese (mainly the Zhiu Zhou dialect from southern China) is spoken in major towns. Many senior government officials and businessmen speak some English which, along with French and German, is increasingly being used in tourist areas. Malay and indigenous languages are spoken.
Official language/s
Thai

Media
Press
Dailies: *The Bangkok Post* and *The Nation* are the main English-language newspapers. Other English language newspapers include *Phuket Gazette* and *Pattaya Mail*. Thai-language papers include *ThaiRath*, *Siam Rath*, *Daily News* and *Dao Siam*. Chinese-language papers include *Sing Sian Yit Pao*, *Universal Daily News*, *Sirinakorn* and *Thai Shang Yic Pao*. Matichon Group (www.matichon.co.th/) provides daily newspapers and weekly magazines in Thai. The GNN Media (www.gnnnews.com/) is a daily updated electronic newspaper that provides political, economic, and entertainment news in Thai.
Business: *Asia Times* is a regional daily business newspaper. There are three main English-language business journals: *Investor* (Industrial Finance Corp of Thailand), *Business in Thailand* (Business Information and Research Company) and *Business Review*, a supplement of *Nation*. *Industry*, a bimonthly, is produced for the Association of Thai Industries.
Periodicals: Various international publications such as *New York Times*, *Newsweek*, *The Economist* and *Asiaweek* are sold by newsagents.
Broadcasting
Radio: External services are broadcast in several languages, including English, French, Malay, Lao, Khmer, Chinese, Vietnamese, Japanese and Burmese. There are approximately 360 commercial radio stations and 130 non-commercial.
Television: There are 10 terrestrial (two private) and three cable television stations.
Bangkok has several television channels including Thai Television Company, Army Television, Bangkok Broadcasting Company and Bangkok Entertainment Company and an educational television channel.
Advertising
Advertising is available in the press, on commercial radio and television, in cinemas and outdoors. Static and mobile loudspeakers are widely used. Tobacco advertising is banned, and television advertising of spirits is permitted only after 2200 hours. Annual advertising expenditure is equivalent to 1.4 per cent of GDP.

Economy
While maintaining its position as the world's leading rice exporter, Thailand has steadily diversified its economy. To broaden the traditional agrarian base, the government has long encouraged industrialisation, both generally, through a succession of five-year economic development plans, and specifically, by making incentives available to encourage investment from domestic and foreign sources. Thai governments have acknowledged that the prosperity of Thailand lies in its ability to cope successfully with an increasingly competitive world economy. After a couple of years' growth exceeding six per cent per annum, Thailand suffered a setback in 2005 as a consequence of several unforeseeable occurrences – the *tsunami* of December 2004, which damaged the tourist sector, a recurrence of the avian flu outbreak, a prolonged drought, escalating oil prices and a further escalation of the unrest in the south. Inflation, which had doubled in 2004, continued to rise, while trade and current account balances worsened.
Exports account for around 65 per cent of GDP. Thailand's ability to maintain strong export growth depends on the economic performance of key markets, notably Japan, the USA and the EU. Thailand has a shortage of skilled labour and outdated technology and measures to support productivity and competitiveness will be needed to sustain growth.

External trade
Thailand's economy is heavily dependent on foreign trade, especially with the US and Japan, and it has proved unusually susceptible to fluctuations in the US market.
Australia and Thailand signed a free trade deal on 5 July 2004.
Imports
Principal imports are capital goods, intermediate goods and raw materials, consumer goods and fuels.
Main sources: Japan (23.6 per cent total, 2004), China (8.6 per cent), US (7.6 per cent), Malaysia (5.8 per cent), Singapore (4.4 per cent), Taiwan (4.1 per cent)
Exports
Principal exports are textiles and footwear, fishery products, rice, natural rubber,

jewellery, vehicles and computers and electrical appliances.
Main destinations: US (15.9 per cent total, 2004), Japan (13.9 per cent), China (7.3 per cent), Singapore (7.2 per cent), Malaysia (5.4 per cent), Hong Kong (5.1 per cent)

Agriculture
Farming
Agriculture accounts for around 10 per cent of GDP and employs just over half of the workforce. The rise of the manufacturing industry has meant that agriculture's share of GDP is declining, although farming still provides income for the majority of the population.

About 39 per cent of the total land area is cultivated. Production has generally been increased by expansion of planted acreage, rather than productivity improvements such as irrigation or use of fertilisers. Yield per paddy is one of the lowest in south-east Asia.

Thailand is known as the rice bowl of Asia and is one of the world's leading net exporters of food. The principal rice-growing area is the Chao Phya river basin. Tapioca is mainly produced in the south-east, kenaf in the north-east and maize in the central plain. Thailand is the world's largest exporter of natural rubber. Over 90 per cent of the rubber is produced in the south and most of it is exported through Penang in Malaysia.. Other major crops include sugar, cassava, cotton, jute, tobacco, fruit (especially pineapples), beans, oilseeds and coffee.

Livestock raised includes pigs, cattle, sheep and poultry. Buffaloes, oxen, horses and elephants are used as draught animals.

Crocodiles are farmed for their skins. Agricultural co-operatives are organised by farmers to help co-ordinate joint farming activities and to provide low interest credits to members. The co-operatives are regulated by the ministry of agriculture and co-operatives.

Crop production in 2004 included: 28.2 million tonnes (mt) cereals in total, 23.8mt rice, 21.4mt cassava, 4.2mt maize, 800 tonnes (t) wheat, 94,600t potatoes, 93,000t sorghum, 17,000t barley, 2.0mt bananas, 298,313t pulses, 21.6mt roots and tubers, 1.5mt coconuts, 1.1mt citrus fruit, 43,200t grapes, 266,000t tomatoes, 2.0mt pineapples, 1.0mt oilcrops, 68,000t tobacco, 400t cocoa beans, 61,765t green coffee, 1.7mt mangoes, 3.0t natural rubber, 33,000t ginger, 65.0mt sugar cane, 47,000t treenuts, 125,000t papayas, 25,000t jute-like fibres, 245,000t soya beans, 5,600t tea, 67,200t taro, 5.2mt oil palm fruit, 8.0mt fruit in total, 3.3mt vegetables in total.

Livestock production included: 1.8mt meat in total, 174,845t beef, 60,161t buffalo meat, 677,040t pig-meat, 1200t lamb and goat meat, 964,103t poultry, 698,360t eggs, 842,611t milk, 3,800t honey, 4,500t cocoons, silk.

Fishing
Thailand is the world's main exporter of fish and seafood. Exports typically earn US$4 billion per year. Shrimp products account for over half of the export revenue. Canned tuna is another important export item, typically accounting for 15 per cent of export revenue. The government has focussed on upgrading the fishing industry by cutting production and improving product quality. Shrimp exporters are moving to create more ready-to-eat fish-based products.

In December 2004 Thailand complained to the WTO that the US imposition of import duties was a violation of free-trade agreements. The US imports US$1 billion worth of shrimp and has provisionally set at tariff of 5.56–10.25 per cent on imports it claims are being 'dumped' on US markets.

Forestry
Forests are estimated to cover 17 per cent of total land area, with a further 18 per cent subject of a reafforestation programme following a rapid decrease in the 1980s. There has been a ban on logging in natural forests since 1989 and the government has implemented a number of measures to protect the remaining forests and encourage plantation forest management.

Exports of forest materials amount to US$870.9 million while imports amounted to US$1.0 billion in 2003. Production in 2004 included 27,785,236 cubic metres (cum) roundwood, 7,800,000cum industrial roundwood, 288,000 cum sawnwood, 2,000,000cum pulpwood, 300,000cum sawlogs and veneers, 705,000cum wood-based panels, 19,985,236cum wood fuel, 1,262,465 tonnes charcoal.

Industry and manufacturing
The industrial sector contributed around 44 per cent to GDP in 2004 and employs 15 per cent of the workforce. Manufacturing accounted for around 35 per cent of GDP and 80 per cent of exports.

The majority of industries are in the private sector and most registered factories are small undertakings, but there is a range of medium- and large-concerns. Main industrial products include processed food, precious stones and jewellery, cement, sugar, refined oil, synthetic fibres, textiles, assembled vehicles and parts, paint, steel, paper, pharmaceuticals, galvanised iron sheet, plastics (including artificial flowers), electronics, electrical appliances, glass, tin ingots, condensed milk, tin plate, detergent, hydrochloric acid and caustic soda. The local processing of wood has been encouraged and exports of plywood, veneer, parquet, furniture, household utensils and paper products show significant growth potential.

Tourism
Tourism is Thailand's single most important foreign exchange earner. There were 11.8 million arrivals in 2004, the majority coming from from Malaysia, Japan, the UK, the US and Germany. Despite adverse factors in 2005, notably the December 2004 tsunami, but also avian flu and higher fuel costs, as well as the unrest in the south, visitor numbers did not fall taking the year as a whole. Arrivals numbered around 12 million, an increase of 3 per cent. The projection for the year had been 13 million. There was a rise in tourists from Asian countries and the government intends to pay particular attention to the new Chinese market and to Japan.

Mining
Mining accounts for around 2.5 per cent of GDP and employs three per cent of the workforce.

Mining has been officially designated a priority economic sector eligible for preferential tax and promotional privileges from the Board of Investment. The Bank of Thailand sets guidelines for private commercial banks to extend loans to the sector at prime lending rates.

Although many reserves remain largely unexploited, Thailand has a rich variety of mineral resources, including antimony, fluorite, iron ore, lead, lignite, limestone, manganese, precious stones, tungsten and zinc.

Tin, which is produced in northern, central and southern Thailand, is the most important mining commodity in terms of revenue. It is estimated that only 30 out of 145 tin mines are still active in the country.

Thailand is the world's biggest gem exporter. Low cost labour has helped Thailand remain a leading exporter. China is expected to become a major competitor in gem production and export. While Thailand's gem industry is more developed, China's lower priced stones have already entered the market.

Hydrocarbons
Thailand had proven oil reserves of 580 million barrels in 2004 and produced 218,000 barrels per day (bpd), of which only around 100,000 bpd was crude oil. Consumption was 909,000 bpd, an increase of around nine per cent on 2003. Thailand is dependent on imports, but in the face of a surge in prices in 2005, the government is encouraging refiners to

Thailand

reduce their imports and increasing domestic production. Thailand has four refineries with a joint capacity of around 700,000 barrels per day.
Thailand had natural gas reserves of 430 billion cubic metres in 2004 and produced 20.3 billion cubic metres. Consumption was 28.7 billion cubic metres, an increase of 4.7 per cent on 2003 levels. Most of the output is used for electricity generation. The largest gas field is in Bongkot, in the Gulf of Thailand, and is operated by a subsidiary of the state-owned Petroleum Authority of Thailand (PTT). This field supplies up to 35 per cent of national demand. Domestic demand is increasing at a greater rate than production levels, so to fulfil its requirements Thailand has become a net importer of natural gas from Myanmar.
Thailand had coal reserves of 1.50 billion tonnes in 2004 and produced 5.8 million tonnes oil equivalent (mtce). Consumption was 10.2 mtce, an increase of 10.2 per cent om 2003. Thailand imports coal to meet domestic requirements.

Energy

Thailand had electricity generating capacity of around 26GW in 2005. It is estimated that Thailand will need a further 20GW over ten years to meet future demand. Most of the genration is supplied by natural gas. Electricity is imported from Laos and Malaysia and an interconnector with Cambodia is under construction. Thailand is attempting to reduce its dependence on imported oil by developing use of indigenous natural gas, lignite and hydro-power.
Geothermal resources have been discovered in Chiang Mai, Mae Hong Son, Chiang Rai and Phrae provinces.

Financial markets

Stock exchange

The Stock Exchange of Thailand (SET) handles a daily turnover of B4–8 billion (US$95–191 million). Total capitalisation stood at US$50 billion in 2002, with 383 listed companies.

Banking and insurance

Thailand set up the Thai Asset Management Corporation (TAMC) in 2001 to take over bad loans in the banking sector. The high level of non-performing loans has prevented Thailand's banks from functioning properly. Banks have been reluctant to lend and this has made economic recovery difficult.
Internal reform also continued in 2001–02 as part of the ongoing restructuring drive. The implementation of risk management systems has been high on the agenda. Siam Commercial Bank, Thailand's most profitable bank is concentrating on upgrading technology and attracting more customers to its internet banking system. Thai Farmers Bank underwent major restructuring, splitting its branches into different departments and making them more customer-oriented.

Central bank
Bank of Thailand

Main financial centre
Bangkok

Time
GMT plus seven hours

Geography

Thailand is situated in the Indo-Chinese peninsula, sharing borders with Myanmar to the west and north, Laos to the east and north, Cambodia to the east and Malaysia to the south.
Thailand can be divided into four regions – the central alluvial plain, the semi-arid plateau of the north-east, the mountainous north and the southern peninsula. It covers an area of 513,115 square km, about the size of France, and measures 1,650km from north to south and 800km from west to east. It has a coastline of 2,400km.
Its narrowest part is the Kra Isthmus, which is about 64km wide, with the Gulf of Thailand to the east and the Andaman Sea to the west.

Climate

The climate varies from tropical savannah in the north and tropical monsoon in the south. There are three main seasons: hot (March–May), rainy (June–October) and cool (November–February). In Bangkok temperatures range from 25.3 degrees Celsius (C) in December to 33.6 degrees C in April and May.

Dress codes

Light, loose cotton clothing is advisable, although it should be modest. Sweaters may be needed in the evenings and during the cooler season. Businessmen wear shirts and ties, while jackets are worn for official functions or meetings with government officials; jackets and ties may be required for evening wear at larger hotels. Smart attire is also expected of businesswomen.

Entry requirements

Passports

Required by all. There are additional requirements for holders of passports of Bangladesh, China, Cambodia, India, Laos, Myanmar, Nepal, Nigeria, Pakistan, Sri Lanka and Vietnam, who need to submit personal details to obtain a visa. Passports must be valid six months beyond intended length of stay.

Visa

Required by all, except those tourists visiting for up to 30 days, listed at www.thai-la.net/visa/visa.htm.
A business visitor must complete a non-immigrant visa application and produce a letter of invitation from a Thai company, printed on a company letterhead. The letter must include the host company's registration, stating the 'capital investment' and documentation of the payment of the last two years taxes. Proof of visit for business purposes must also be furnished along with a letter of approval by the Labour Department. Business visas are only valid for up to 90 days.
Extension, for either tourist or business visas, may be granted by the Immigration Bureau in Thailand.

Prohibited entry

Entry is refused to nationals of Afghanistan unless in transit within three hours. Entry may be refused to persons of untidy appearance.

Currency advice/regulations

There is no limit on the amount of foreign currency which may be imported, although it should be declared on arrival. There are no limits on the export of foreign currency, although the amount must be declared. Local currency exports are restricted to B50,000. Foreign currency should be exchanged only by authorised banks and dealers.

Customs

Personal effects are allowed in duty-free. Importation of many goods produced locally may be restricted. Export of images or statues of Buddha, antiques and archaeologically valuable items is only allowed with a certificate from the Department of Fine Arts. Articles exceeding B10,000 in value require a Certificate of Exportation.

Prohibited imports

Narcotic drugs, pornographic material, firearms and certain luxury goods.

Health (for visitors)

Mandatory precautions

A vaccination certificate for yellow fever is required if travelling from an infected area.

Advisable precautions

Vaccination for diphtheria, tuberculosis, hepatitis 'A' and 'B', Japanese 'B' encephalitis, polio, tetanus, typhoid. Malaria precautions should be taken. There is a rabies risk. Water should be boiled and filtered before drinking.

Hotels

Choose a hotel in the district in which you are doing business. Most top hotels have good facilities for meetings and can arrange secretarial services if notified in advance. A 10 per cent service charge and 11 per cent tax are added to hotel bills, and it is customary to give small tips for good service.

Credit cards
Major credit cards, such as Access, American Express, Diners Club, Visa and Mastercard are accepted by main hotels and shops frequented by travellers.

Public holidays
Fixed dates
1 Jan (New Year's Day), 6 Apr (Chakri Day), 13–16 Apr (Songkran/Thai New Year), 1 May (Labour Day), 5 May (Coronation Day), 9 Aug (Sin National Day), 12 Aug (Queen's Birthday), 23 Oct (Chulalongkorn Day), 5 Dec (King's Birthday), 10 Dec (Constitution Day), 25 Dec (Christmas Day), 31 Dec (New Year's Eve).
Holidays falling on a weekend are taken on the following Monday/Tuesday.
Variable dates
Good Friday, Chinese New Year (Jan/Feb), Makha Bucha Day (Feb), Visakha Bucha Day (May), Asanha Bucha Day (Jul), Buddhist Lent Day (Jul), Naga Fire Ball (Oct), Loy Kratong (Nov).

Working hours
Banking
Mon–Fri: 0830–1530.
Business
Mon–Fri: 0830–1700. Sat: 0830–1200.
Government
Mon–Fri: 0830–1630.
Shops
Mon–Sun: 0900–1800/1900. Some shops are open 24 hours.

Electricity supply
220V AC, 50 cycles for domestic use, with plug fittings having two round or flat pins.

Weights and measures
Metric system (local units also in use).

Social customs/useful tips
Always carry business cards and give them to any new acquaintance when introduced. To show respect, offer and accept business cards with both hands, and always read the cards you receive before putting them down.
To the Thais 'face' is very important and losing it can be a disastrous, with little chance of social recovery; all dealings should be controlled, polite and respectful.
Thai business relationships, networks and associations can be extensive and visitors should expect to spend much time cultivating contacts.
Both men and women should dress in smart, light and casually wear. Shorts, bare shoulders, and sandals would be inappropriate in a business setting. Westerners are expected to shake hands and Thais are willing to accommodate this practice. Thai women, however, may still be reluctant to shake hands, and may prefer simply to exchange smiles on being introduced. Thais address each other and foreign visitors by their forename, prefixed by 'khun'.
The head is considered the most esteemed part of the body and the feet the least, so visitors should take care not to touch someone's head (even accidentally) or show the soles of their feet.
Images of Buddha are held sacred and cannot be taken out of Thailand without official permission.
Shoes should be removed when entering a Thai house or Buddhist temple. Women must never touch a Buddhist monk, give things to him, or receive things from him, directly.
Stand up when the royal and national anthems are played on television and radio at 0800 and 1800 every day. It is a criminal offence to make critical or defamatory comments about the King or other members of the Royal family, punishable by a sentence of three to 15 years.

Security
Experienced business visitors should not encounter any problems, particularly in central Bangkok. However, Thailand's position in the world drug trade, puts the gullible traveller at risk.

Getting there
Air
National airline: Thai Airways International.
International airport/s: Don Muang International (BKK), 30km north of Bangkok; duty-free shop, bar, restaurant, buffet, bank, post office, hotel reservations; Chiang Mai International (CNX); Phuket International (HKT), 35km from Phuket; Hat Yai International (HDY), 9km from Hat Yai.
Airport limousines and licensed taxis, with yellow numberplates, can be hired from the official taxi rank at Bangkok airport; there is a reliable bus service to Bangkok city centre. Other international and domestic airports also have taxi and bus services.
Other airport/s: The new Suvarnabhumi airport is expected to be finished during 2005.
Airport tax: When departing, 500 Baht per person, excluding transit passengers. Foreign currency is not accepted.
Surface
Road: The Asian Highway runs from the northern region through Bangkok and on to southern Thailand, crossing the border with Malaysia and ending in Singapore. The Australian-financed US$30 million Friendship Bridge links Thailand and Laos.
Rail: There are three weekly rail services between Singapore and Bangkok via Kuala Lumpur, Ipoh, Butterworth and Haadyai (journey time 48 hours).
Water: Thailand has eight international deep-sea ports operated by the Port Authority of Thailand (PAT), with an additional four private ports permitted to handle container cargo.
Main port/s: Klong Toey is the largest port, handling approximately 14 million tonnes per year (tpy). Laem Chabang is the next largest commercial port, with a capacity of approximately 7.3 million tpy.

Getting about
National transport
Considerable investment is earmarked for improving the country's transport facilities. In remote areas conditions are still uncertain, and banditry occurs in the north-west of the country.
Air: Thai Airways and Bangkok Airways operate domestic services to main centres.
Road: There are over 50,000km of national and provincial roads and highways, with another 135,000km of rural roads. Major roads are generally metalled.
Buses: Long-distance (air-conditioned) express coaches operate between main centres; local services are not generally recommended. In 2001, multi-trip tickets were introduced on Thai buses.
Rail: Thailand's railway network is controlled by the State Railway of Thailand (SRT), which is responsible for building, operating and maintaining Thailand's 4,600km of railway track.
Rail services are generally recommended: the system is equipped with modern rolling stock, including air-conditioned coaches, sleeping accommodation and restaurant cars on main express services. All main lines originate in Bangkok. Four main routes radiate from Bangkok's main station (Hualompong), with the track to the south extending to the Malaysian border.
Water: There are 1,110–1,600km of navigable inland waterways, depending on the season. Various types of ferries and passenger/cargo boats operate on rivers and in coastal areas.
City transport
Avoid rush-hour travel; two-hour traffic jams are routine.
Taxis: Taxis have yellow number plates and, although they are metered, fares should be agreed in advance. Tipping is not customary.
Taxi drivers rarely understand English and it is best to have the name and address of one's destination written in Thai to show to the driver. Air-conditioned limousine services provided by main hotels are more expensive than ordinary taxis. *Tuk tuks* are motorised trishaws. The fastest method of city transport is by motorbike taxi.
Buses, trams & metro: Thai Airways International shuttle bus from Don Muang International Airport to the city centre.

Thailand

Metro: A 20km metro for Bangkok was opened in 1998.
Trains: The Bangkok Mass Transit System opened in 1999. The subway, a new mass transit system, opened on 3 July 2004.
Helicopter: Royal Orchid Sheraton jointly operates a helicopter service between the airport and the River City shopping complex next to the hotel, with a flight time of seven minutes. There is a five-minute walk by connecting bridge to the hotel.

Car hire
Chauffeur-driven car hire is available in Bangkok, Pattaya, Hat Yai, Phuket and Chiang Mai. It is advisable not to drive yourself. An international driving licence is required and driving is on the left. A driving licence is required to ride motorcycles. Executive limousines or private cars are available, for the journey from Don Muang International Airport to the city. It is advisable to book in advance.

BUSINESS DIRECTORY

The addresses listed below are a selection only. While World of Information makes every endeavour to check these addresses, we cannot guarantee that changes have not been made, especially to telephone numbers and area codes. We would welcome any corrections.

Telephone area codes
The international direct dialling code for Thailand is +66, followed by area code and subscriber's number:

Bangkok	2	Nakhon Ratchasima	44
Chiang Mai	53	Nakhon Sawan	56
Khon Kaen	43	Phuket	76
Lampang	54	Udon Thani	42

Useful telephone numbers
Metropolitan Mobile Police: 123, 191, 246-1338/42
Tourist Assistance Centre: 195, 281-5051
Capital Security Police: 123
Fire: 199, 246-0199
Ambulance: 252-2171/75
Directory (Bangkok): 13
Directory (provinces): 183
International calls: 100
Rail travel: 223-1431

Chambers of Commerce
American Chamber of Commerce in Thailand, Kian Gwan Building, 140 Wireless Road, Bangkok 10330 (tel: 251-9266; fax: 651-4472; e-mail: service@amchamthailand.com).

British Chamber of Commerce Thailand, 208 Wireless Road, Bangkok (tel: 651-5350; fax: 651-5354; e-mail: info@bccthai.com).

Chiang Mai Chamber of Commerce, Hillside Plaza and Condotel, Huai-Kaew Road, Chiang Mai 50300 (tel: 223-256; fax: 222-482).

Khon Kaen Chamber of Commerce, 359 Mittaphab Road, Khon Kaen 4000 (tel: 224-521; fax: 225-719; e-mail: info@kkchamber.com).

Nakhon Ratchasima Chamber of Commerce, 1818 Suranarai Road, Nakhon Ratchasima 30000 (tel: 296-120; fax: 296-124).

Phuket Chamber of Commerce, 1 Montree Road, Phuket 83000 (tel: 217-567; fax: 232-038; e-mail: cham,ber@phuket.ksc.co.th).

Thai Chamber of Commerce, 150 Rajabophit Road, Bangkok 10200 (tel: 225-0086; fax: 225-4913; e-mail: tcc@tcc.or.th).

Banking
Bangkok Bank PCL, 333 Silom Road, Bangkok (tel: 231-4333; fax: 236-8281/2).

Bangkok Bank of Commerce Ltd, 99 Surasak Road, Silom, Bangrak, Bangkok 10500 (tel: 234-9230, 235-5040/9; fax: 234-2939).

Bangkok Metropolitan Bank Ltd, 2 Chalermkhet 4 Street, Pomrab, Bangkok (tel: 223-0561; fax: 224-3768).

Bank of Agriculture and Agricultural Co-operatives, 469 Nakhon Sawan Road, Dusit, Bangkok 10300 (tel: 280-0180).

Bank of America NT & SA, 2/2 Wireless Road, Bangkok 10500 (tel: 251-6333; fax: 253-1905).

Bank of Asia PCL, 191 South Sathorn Road, Bangkok 10120 (tel: 287-2211/3; fax: 287-2973/4).

Bank of Ayuthaya Ltd, 1222 Rama III Road, Bangkok 10120 (tel: 296-2000, 683-1000; fax: 683-1304).

Bank of Toyko Ltd, 62 Silom Road, Bangkok (tel: 236-0119/9103; fax: 236-9110).

Chase Manhattan Bank, Siam Shopping Centre, 965 Rama I Road, Bangkok 10330 (tel: 252-1141).

Citibank NA, 127 Sathorn Tai Road, Bangkok (tel: 213-2441; fax: 213-2517).

Deutsche Bank, 21 Sathorn Tai Road, Bangkok (tel: 240-9401; fax: 240-9425).

Export-Import Bank of Thailand, Boon Pong Tower, 1193 Thanon Phahonyothin, Bangkok 10400 (tel: 271-3700, 278-0047; fax: 271-3204).

First Bangkok City Bank Ltd, 20 Yukhon Road 2, Pomrab, Bangkok (tel: 223-0501; fax: 225-3036).

Hongkong & Shanghai Banking Corporation, 64 Silom Road, Bangkok (tel: 267-3000; fax: 236-7687).

Import-Export Bank of Japan, 138 Silom Road, Bangkok 10500 (tel: 235-7373).

Industrial Finance Corp of Thailand, 1770 New Petchburi Road, Bangkapi, Bangkok 10320 (tel: 253-7111; fax: 253-9677).

International Commercial Bank of China, 36/12 PS Tower, Asoke, 21 Sukhumvit, Phrakhanong, Bangkok 10110 (tel: 259-2000; fax: 259-1330) .

Krung Thai Bank Ltd, 35 Sukhumvit Road, Bangkok (tel: 255-2222; fax: 255-9391/6).

Nakornthon Bank Ltd, 90 Sathonthanee Building, Sathorn Nua Road, Bangrak, Bangkok (tel: 233-2111; fax: 236-4226).

Siam Commercial Bank, 9 Rachadapisek Road, Bangkok (tel: 344-1111; fax: 937-7454).

Siam City Bank Public Company Limited, 1101 New Petchburi Road, Bangkok 10400 (tel: 208-5000/5043; fax: 253-1240).

Standard Chartered Bank, 990 Rama IV Road, Bangkok (tel: 636-1000; fax: 636-1198/9).

Thai Danu Bank Ltd, 393 Silom Road, Bangkok (tel: 233-9160/9; fax: 236-7939).

Thai Farmers Bank, 1 Thai farmers Lane, Rat Burana Road, Bangkok (tel: 470-1122; fax: 470-1571).

Thai Military Bank Ltd, 3000 Phahonyothin Rd, Bangkok 10900 (tel: 299-1111, 273-7020; fax: 273-7121/7124).

Central bank
Bank of Thailand, 273 Samsen Road, Bangkok 10200 (tel: 2283-5353; fax: 2280-0449).

Travel information
Police (Tourist) (for reports of theft in order to get a written document for insurance purposes), 29/1 Soi Lang Suan, Ploenchit Road, Lumpini, Bangkok (tel: 255-2964/8).

Royal Automobile Association of Thailand, 151, Soi Aphaisongkram, Phaholyothin, 10900, Bangkok (tel: 511-2230/1).

Thai Airways International Ltd, 6 Thanon Larn Luang, Bangkok (tel: 280-0090, reservations 280-0700) (internal travel).

Thai Airways International Ltd, 89 Vibhavadi Rangsit Road, Bangkok 9 10900 (tel: 513-0121, (reservations) 233-3810; fax: 513-0183) (international travel).

Thai Hotels Association, 203-209/2 Rajdamnoen Klang Avenue, Bangkok 10200 (tel: 281-9496, 281-9579; fax: 281-4188).

National tourist organisation offices
Tourism Authority of Thailand, Le Concorde Building, 202 Rachadapisek Road, Huai Khwang, Bangkok 10320 (tel:

694-1222; fax: 694-1220, 694-1221; e-mail: center@tat.or.th; internet site: http://www.tourismthailand.org).

Ministries

Ministry of Agriculture and Co-operatives, Thanon Ratchadamnoen Nok, Bangkok 10200 (tel: 281-5955, 281-5939; fax: 280-1691).

Ministry of Commerce, Thanon Samamchai, Bangkok 10200 (tel: 282-6171/9; fax: 280-0775).

Ministry of Defence, Thanon Samamchai, Bangkok 10200 (tel: 225-0098, 222-1121; fax: 226-3115).

Ministry of Education, Wang Chan Kasem, Thanon Ratchadamnoen Nok, Bangkok 10300 (tel: 280-0306).

Ministry of Finance, Thanon Rama VI, Bangkok 10400 (tel: 273-9021; fax: 293-9408).

Ministry of Foreign Affairs, Sri Ayutthaya Road, Bangkok 10400 (tel: 643-5000; fax: 643-5180).

Ministry of Industry, Thanon Rama VI, Bangkok 10400 (tel: 202-3000; fax: 202-3048).

Ministry of the Interior, Thanon Atsadang, Bangkok 10200 (tel: 222-1141/55; fax: 223-8851).

Ministry of Justice, Thanon Rachadaphisek, Chatuchak, Bangkok 10900 (tel: 541-2284/91; fax: 541-2307).

Ministry of Labour and Social Welfare, Thanon Mitmaitri, Dindaeng, Bangkok 10400 (tel: 245-4782; fax: 246-1520).

Ministry of Public Health, Thanon Tiwanond, Amphoe Muang, Nonthaburi 11000 (tel: 591-8491; fax: 591-8492).

Ministry of Science, Technology and Environment, Thanon Rama VI, Ratchathewi, Bangkok 10400 (tel: 246-0064; fax: 246-5146).

Ministry of Transport and Communications, 38 Thanon Ratchadanoen Nok, Bangkok 10100 (tel: 283-3000; fax: 281-3959).

Ministry of University Affairs, 328 Thanon Si Ayutthaya, Khet Ratchathewi, Bangkok 10400 (tel: 246-0025, 246-1106/14; fax: 245-8636, 245-8930, 246-8883).

Other useful addresses

Advertising Association of Thailand, 12/14 Prachaniwet 1 Road, Lardyao, Chatuchak, Bangkok 10900 (tel: 591-6461; fax: 589-9470).

ASEAN Investment Promotion Agency, Board of Investment, 555 Vipavadee Rangsit, Chatuchak, Bangkok 10900 (tel: 537-8111; fax: 537-8177; web: www.boi.go.th).

ASEAN Secretariat, 70 A J1 Sisingamangaraja, Jakarta 12110, Indonesia (tel: 62(21)726-2991, 724-3372; fax: 724-3504, 739-8234; web: www.asean.or.id).

Bangkok Mass Transit Authority, 131 Tiumruammitr Road, Huay Kwang, Bangkok 10310 (tel: 246-0339, 246-0741/4, 246-0750/2).

British Embassy, Wireless Road, Bangkok (tel: 253-0191; fax: 255-8619, 255-9278).

Chiangmai Province Commercial Office, Chiangmai City Hall, Chotana Road, Muang District, Chiangmai 50300 (tel: 221-217; fax: 221-121).

Communications Authority of Thailand, 99 Chaeng Watthana Road, Bangkok 10002 (tel: 573-0099).

Customs Department, Atnarong Road, Klongtoey, Bangkok 10110 (tel: 249-0431, 671-7555/7).

Department of Export Promotion, 22/77 Rachadapisek Road, Bangkok 10900 (tel: 513-1909/15, 511-5066/77; fax: 512-1079, 513-1917).

Department of Foreign Trade, Samamchai Road, Bangkok 10110 (tel: 225-1315/29; fax: 224-7269, 225-4763).

Deparetment of Industrial Promotion,Thanon Rama VI, Ratchathewi, Bangkok 10400 (tel: 202-4415/6; fax: 246-0031)

Department of Local Administration, Thanon Asadang, Bangkok 10200 (tel: 222-3852, 222-8847; fax: 222-5858).

Department of Mineral Resources, Rama VI Road, Bangkok 10400 (tel: 246-0034, 246-1161/9).

Eastern Trader's Association for Exporting Fruit-Vegetable, 30/31-32 Trirat Road, Muang District, Chanthaburi 22000 (tel: 325-962; fax: 325-962).

Economic and Social Commission for Asia and the Pacific (ESCAP), United Nations Building, Bangkok (tel: 288-1234; fax: 288-1000).

Election Division, Department of Local Administration, Ministry of Interior, Thanon Asadang, Bangkok 10200 (tel: 221-5871; fax: 222-6886).

Export Promotion Centre-Chanthaburi, 30/31-32 Trirat Road, Chanthaburi 22000 (tel: 325-962/3; fax: 325-962).

Export Promotion Centre-Chiang Mai, 29/19 Singharaj Road, Chiang Mai 50200 (tel: 216-350/1, 221-376; fax: 215-307).

Export Promotion Centre-Hat Yai, 7-15 Jootee-Uthit 1 Road, Hat Yai, Songkla 90110 (tel: 234-349, 231-744; fax: 234-329).

Export Promotion Centre-Khon Kaen, 68/4 Kiang Muang Road, Khon Kaen 40000 (tel: 221-472; fax: 221-476).

Export Promotion Centre-Surat Thani, 148/59 Surat-Nakornsri Road, Bang Kung, Surat Thani , Bangkok 84000 (tel: 286-916; fax: 288-632).

Export Service Centre, Department of Commercial Relations, Ministry of Commerce, 22–77 Thanon Rachadaphisek–Ladprao, Bangkok 10900 (tel: 513-1905).

Federation of Nakhon Ratchasima Industries, 269 Friendship Highway, Tambon Kokgruad Muang District, Nakhon Ratchasima 30280 (tel: 251-028; fax: 251-033).

Federation of Southern Industries, Songkhla Chapter, 165 Southern Industrial Promotion Center Building, 3rd Floor, Karnchanawanitch, Haadyai District, Songkhla 90110 (tel: 211-905).

Federation of Thai Industries, Queen Sirikit National Convention Center, Zone C 4th Floor, 60 New Rachadapisek Road, Klongtoey, Bangkok 10110 (tel: 229-4255; fax: 229-4941).

Federation of Thai Industries, Chiangmai and Nearby Chapter, Northern Industrial Promotion Centre Building, 1st Floor, 158 Tung Hotel Road, Muang District, Chiangmai 50000 (tel: 304-346; fax: 246-353).

Federation of Thai Industries, Khon Kaen Chapter, 359/2 Mittaphab Road, Muang District, Khon Kaen 40000 (tel: 225-679; fax: 225-678).

Federation of Thai Industries, Surathani Chapter, 160/19 Surat-Punpin Road, Makhamtia, Muang District, Surathani 84000 (tel: 285-722).

Federation of Thai Udon Thani Industries and Nearby Chapter, 83/14 Watana Road, Muang District, Udon Thani 41000 (tel: 242-004; fax: 246-498).

Fishery Association of Thailand, 1575 Charoen Nakom Road, Bangkok 10600 (tel: 437-0158/62; fax: 437-1262).

Foreign Bankers Association, 19th Floor, Sathorn Thani Building 2, 92/55 North Sathorn Road, Silom Bangrak, Bangkok 10500 (tel: 236-4730, 236-7224; fax: 236-4731).

General Post Office, 1160 Thanon Jaroenkrung, Bangkok 10501 (tel: 233-1050).

Industrial Estate Authority of Thailand, 618 Nikhom Makkasan Road, Phayathai, Bangkok (tel: 253-0561).

Thailand

Industrial Finance Corporation, 1770 New Petchaburi Road, Bangkok 10500 (tel: 253-7111, 253-9666; fax: 253-9677, 254-8098).

Lawyers Association, 26 Ratchadamnern Avenue, Bangkok 10220 (tel: 224-1873).

National Statistical Office, Lan Luang Road, Bangkok 10100 (tel: 281-3022; fax: 281-3815, 281-3848).

Northern Industrial Promotion Center, 158 Tung Hotel Road, Muang District, Chiangmai 50000 (tel: 245-361; fax: 248-315).

Northern Investment Promotion Office, 369/1 Charoenrat Road, Watgate, Muang District, Chiangmai 50000 (tel: 248-778; fax: 240-919).

Office of the Board of Investment, 555 Vibhavadi-Rangsit Road, (opposite Central Plaza Hotel), Chatuchak, Bangkok 10900 (tel: 537-8111, 537-8155; fax: 537-8177; e-mail: head@boi.go.th).

Office of Foreign Trade, Sanambin Road, Suthep, Muang District, Chiangmai 50200 (tel: 274-672; fax: 277-901).

Office of the National Culture Commission, Thanon Ratchadapisek, Khet Huay Khwang, Bangkok 10310 (tel: 248-5839, 247-0013/19 (ext 201); fax: 248-5841, 248-5851, 248-5845).

Office of the National Economic and Social Development Board, 962 Krung Kasem, Bangkok 10100 (tel: 282-8434; fax: 282-0891).

Port Authority of Thailand, Thanon Sunthornkosa, (tel: 249-0362).

Prime Minister's Office, Government House, Thanon Nakhon Pathom, Bangkok 10300 (tel: 282-6543, 282-6877; fax: 282-8587, 282-8631).

Religious Affairs Department, Thanon Ratchamnoen Nok, Bangkok 10300 (tel: 281-6080 (ext 43, 74 or 40); fax: 281-5415).

Royal Thai Embassy (US), Suite 401, 1024 Wisconsin Avenue, NW, Washington DC 20007 (tel: 202-944-3600; fax: 202-944-3611; e-mail: thai.wsn@thaiembdc.org).

Securities Exchange of Thailand, 32 Sinthon Building, Bangkok 10500 (tel: 250-0001/8).

Southern Industrial Economic Affairs Center, 3rd Floor, Songkhla Industrial Office Building, Karnchanawanitch Road, Muang district, Songkhla 90000 (tel: 321-166; fax: 321-167).

Southern Industrial Promotion Center, Department of Industrial Promotion, 165 Karnchanawanitch, Muang District, Songkhla 90110 (tel: 211-905).

Stock Exchange of Thailand (SET), Sinthon Building, 2nd Floor, 132 Wireless Road, Bangkok 10330 (tel: 254-0960, 254-0969, 256-7100, 256-7109; fax: 254-7120, 256-3040).

Telephone Organisation of Thailand, 89/2 Moo 3 Chaeng Wattana, Bangkok 10002 (tel: 505-1000; fax: 574-9533).

Thai Bankers' Association, 4th Floor, Lake Rachada Office Complex, Building II, Rachadapisek Road, Bangkok 10110 (tel: 264-0883/7; fax: 264-0888).

Thai Mining Association, 79 Prachatipatai Road, Banpanthom, Pranakom, Bangkok 10200 (tel: 282-8947/9; fax: 280-3786, 282-7372).

Thai Petrochemical Industry and Trade Association, 175-177 Surawong Road, Bangkok 10500 (tel: 238-2956/9; fax: 236-3110).

Thai Rice Mill Association, 81 Soi Rong Nam Kheng, Charoenkrung Road, Samphanthawong, Bangkok 10100 (tel: 235-7863, 234-7295; fax: 234-7286).

Trade Statistics Centre, Department of Business Economics, Ratchadamnoen Klang, Bangkok 10200 (tel: 282-6393, 280-1727; fax: 280-0775, 280-0826).

Internet sites

Board of Investment http://www.boi.go.th

Commercial directory: http://www.sino.net.thai/commerce/thaiprod.htm

Thailand government: http://www.thaigov.go.th

Thailand trade directory: http://www.sino.net/index.htm

Timor-Leste

KEY FACTS

Official name: República Democrática de Timor-Leste (Democratic Republic of Timor-Leste) (independence, 20 May 2002)

Head of State: President Xanana Gusmão (Fretilin) (from 20 May 2002)

Head of government: Prime Minister Mari Alkatiri (Fretilin) from 20 May 2002)

Ruling party: Frente Revolucionária do Timor-Leste Independente (Fretilin) (Revolutionary Front for East Timor Independence) (elected 30 Aug 2001)

Area: 19,000 square km

Population: 981,800 (2004)

Capital: Díli

Official language: Portuguese and Tetum (Portuguese is the language of documentation).

Currency: US dollar (US$) = 100 cents (adopted as transitional currency, Jan 2000)

GDP per capita: US$357 (2004)

GDP real growth: 1.00% (2004); *2.5% (2005)

Labour force: 507,000 (2004)

Inflation: 4.10% (2004); *2.5% (2005)

Balance of trade: -US$159.00 million (2004)

* estimated figure

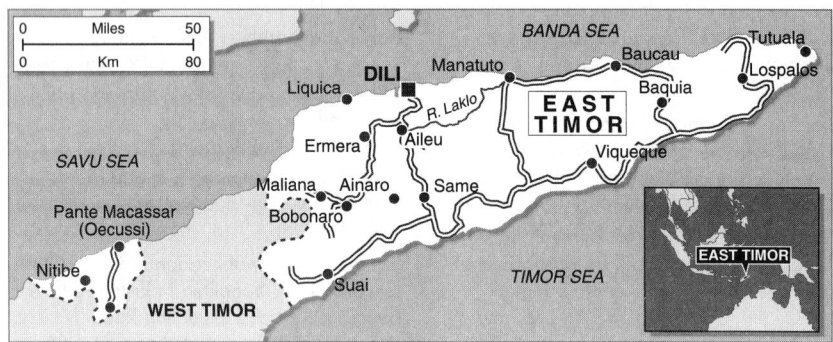

The mainly Catholic, former Portuguese colony of Timor-Leste gained its independence in May 2002, making it the world's youngest country. Independence was hard-won, coming after 25 years of Indonesian rule established by means of an invasion in 1975. In 1999 the UN organised a referendum on the status of the region. Indonesia reacted to the majority vote for Timor-Leste independence with a campaign of violence and brutality. Between 1,000–1,500 were killed in skirmishes. The UN governed the country from 1999 with 10,000 troops and a UN peace-keeping presence remained after independence was won. In May 2005 the UN withdrew from the country.

Post-independence justice?

In 2000 the UN set up a Serious Crimes Unit (SCU) to examine and judge cases of war crimes, murder and rape which occurred during the turmoil of 1999. Although the operation was insufficiently resourced, the panel consisted of one East Timor judge and two foreign judges. The UN convicted 75 people of crimes committed during the election period. More problematic however was the non-compliance of the Indonesians, who would not recognise the authority of the court nor hand over its suspects. Furthermore there was a lack of will for justice among top-level officials in Timor-Leste, who feared long-term damage in their relationship with Indonesia if they took an aggressive or insistent stance towards prosecutions. This reluctance contrasted with the stance of the Timor-Leste Church, which campaigned for justice, and with ordinary people, many of whom became tired of the delays and excuses.

The SCU wound up operations in late 2004. The UN has been highly critical of the impunity enjoyed by criminals. Indonesia itself brought 18 people to court – but no-one to justice. All were either acquitted, or had their sentences quashed. Over 300 people escaped investigation, the most significant being the high-ranking Indonesian General Wiranto.

In July 2005 the UN continued to apply pressure on the fledgling state, recommending international intervention in its justice system and continued efforts in prosecution. If this was not achieved within six months, the UN Commission said, the Security Council should step in to instigate prosecutions instead. There is official resistance to what is seen as international interference. However, in response to UN demands, in December 2004 Indonesia and Timor-Leste agreed to establish a Commission for Reception, Truth and Reconciliation to address and research the events of 1999 and help absorb ex-militia back into society. The Commission is located in Bali and is composed of human rights and legal experts. There is some skepticism about whether this latest organisation will have any teeth.

Foreign affairs

In April 2005 the Indonesian President, Susilo Bambang Yudhoyono, met with the ruler of Timor-Leste, Xanana Gusmao in the capital Dili. Yudhoyono visited cemeteries full of murder victims and discussed

Timor-Leste

the East-West Timor boundary. The resultant successful border accord was an important step towards reconciliation for the two nations.

In 2005 Timor-Leste continued negotiations with Australia about their shared borders, which have implications for hugely lucrative oil and gas fields in the Timor Sea separating the two countries. Timor-Leste sought to divide the waters equidistant between the two shores while Australia wanted it on the continental shelf, nearer to Timor-Leste and, therefore, giving Australia a greater share of the area. An equidistant border would mean four gas fields would fall under the smaller nation's possession: the Bayu-Undan, Corallina, Laminaria and Sunrise fields. The eventual agreement gave Timor-Leste 90 per cent of proceeds from a shared area. Australia surrendered a proportion of its revenues from the Sunrise field.

Economy

The economy suffered hugely from the internal strife of 1999, with GDP falling by 34 per cent in 1999. From 2000, the trend has been upwards although it is most definitely still officially a low-income country. Despite political turmoil Timor-Leste has restored macroeconomic stability by means of prudent fiscal policy. This does not mean the economy is strong. The UN withdrawal in May 2005 and a dwindling of foreign aid had an initially detrimental effect on the economy but recovery is expected in the medium term. GDP growth was forecast at 2.5 per cent for 2005 although this will rise to an expected 4.9 per cent in 2006 when revenue from oil and gas fields in the Timor Sea start to flow in. Income from petroleum has already been rising.

Forty per cent of the population live in poverty and employment is low. Exports are the main drivers of the economy and include coffee, oil and gas. Agriculture employs three-quarters of the workforce. Though large it is not a developed sector, characterised as it is by subsistence farming.

Indonesia and Australia are the country's biggest markets. Investment is key for the country's future financial security. Reform of the insurance, investment and land laws have been carried out in the hope of establishing a competitive business-friendly climate attractive to international enterprise. Remaining obstacles include poor infrastructure and administrative capacity. Timor-Leste wages are higher than in neighbouring countries, which is a disincentive to investment.

Outlook

The IMF has recommended that Timor-Leste concentrate on education and health development. Also, the susistance economy should be modernised and reformed into a market economy. Employment needs to improve and infrastructure needs to be extended.

Risk assessment

Economic	Improving
Political	Improving
Regional stability	Improving
Stock market	Improving

COUNTRY PROFILE

Historical profile
Before the arrival of the Portuguese and Dutch, Timor-Leste was linked by trade to China and India.
1512 Portuguese navigators landed and established Díli as the colonial capital. Sandalwood, honey, wax and slaves were exported.
1749 The eastern half of Timor-Leste became a Portuguese colony and remained so until the mid-1970s, when the Portuguese colonial empire disintegrated. The western half became part of the Dutch East Indies and later Indonesia.
1895 There were several uprisings against Portuguese rule.
1942 The Japanese invaded. Up to 60,000 people were killed during fighting between Australian and Japanese troops.
1945 The end of the Second World War saw the end of Japanese rule.
1974–75 An armed forces coup in Lisbon, Portugal, led to a policy of decolonisation. The Portuguese governor and administration withdrew and the capital, Díli, was occupied by the Marxist Frente Revolucionária do Timor-Leste Independente (Fretilin) (Revolutionary Front for Timor-Leste Independence). Indonesian troops intervened, setting up a provisional government. An estimated 200,000 people died in the military crackdown and famine that followed.
1976 Timor-Leste was integrated into Indonesia, becoming the 27th Indonesian province. This act was never officially recognised by the UN.
1985 The rebels suffered a setback when the Australian government recognised Indonesia's incorporation of Timor-Leste.
1992 Fretilin leader, Xanana Gusmão, was captured by Indonesian troops and convicted of subversion.
1996 Bishop Carlos Belo and foreign minister-in-exile, José Ramos Horta, jointly won the Nobel Peace Prize.
1998 President Suharto of Indonesia was forced to step down. President B J Habibie considered offering Timor-Leste 'special status' and wider autonomy, but Portugal rejected the idea.
1999 The UN Mission organised a referendum, which had a 98.5 per cent turnout, with 78.5 per cent of the population voting for independence. International military intervention halted Indonesian army atrocities and the Indonesian government agreed to grant Timor-Leste extensive autonomy. The first donor conference was held in Tokyo, Japan.
2000 The Lisbon, Portugal, donor conference was held. The UN Transitional Administration for East Timor (UNTAET) established the East Timor Transitional Administration (ETTA). A donor conference was held in Brussels in Belgium.
2001 Gusmão resigned as head of the interim parliament. Timor-Leste voted for an Assembleia Constituinte (Constituent Assembly) in their first democratic election run by the UN. Fretilin won 55 of the 88 seats in the constituent assembly. The ETTA was transformed into the East Timor Public Administration (ETPA) after the elections and Mari Alkatiri was sworn in

KEY INDICATORS — Timor-Leste

	Unit	2000	2001	2002	2003	2004
Population	m	0.00	0.83	0.75	0.87	0.98
Gross domestic product (GDP)	US$bn	0.26	0.39	0.39	0.39	*0.34
GDP per capita	US$	–	478	520	346	357
GDP real growth	%	15.0	18.2	-0.5	-3.0	1.0
Inflation	%	140.0	3.0	-2.0	2.0	4.1
Exports (fob) (goods)	US$m	16.0	4.0	5.0	8.0	8.0
Imports (fob) (goods)	US$m	126.0	237.0	170.0	237.0	167.0
Balance of trade	US$m	-110.0	-233.0	-165.0	-229.0	-159.0
Current account	US$m	–	–	–	–	40.0
Exchange rate	per US$	1.00	1.00	1.00	1.00	1.00

* estimated figure

as chief minister. The gradual reduction of the UNTAET peace-keeping force began.
2002 Xanana Gusmão won the first presidential election. Timor-Leste became independent on 20 May, with Gusmão as president and Mari Alkatiri as prime minister. On 23 July, Timor-Leste became a member of the World Bank group and on 27 September, the country joined the UN.
2003 An Indonesian court sentenced the country's former military chief in Timor-Leste to five years in jail for crimes against humanity, due to his failure to prevent attacks on civilians which followed the 1999 independence vote. The Australian parliament ratified the Timor Sea Treaty, which permits the development of the Bayu-Undan gas field, the royalties from which will fund the country's economic development.
2004 UN Secretary General Annan called for an extension of the UN presence in Timor-Leste, but wanted almost all peacekeepers withdrawn and a shift in focus towards helping fledgling political institutions. In May, a UN-backed tribunal issued a warrant for the arrest of the Indonesian presidential candidate, General Wiranto; the former military chief was accused of human rights abuses in Timor-Leste.
2005 An agreement was signed on 8 April between the leaders of Indonesia and Timor-Leste, recognising the location of their shared land border.
2006 An agreement was signed with Australia in January that will clear the way for the start of oil and gas production in the Greater Sunrise field. Although the companies involved in the Greater Sunrise plan have yet to confirm they will go ahead, the field is estimated to be worth a fortune. The agreement states that Timor-Leste and Australia will share the proceeds equally.

Political structure
Constitution
The constitution, passed in 2001, became valid on 20 May 2002, when Timor-Leste gained independence.
Form of state
Democratic, sovereign, independent and unitary state.
The executive
The president of the republic is the head of state and supreme commander of the defence force, and is elected by universal suffrage. The term of office is five years and no president can serve more than two terms.
The Council of State is the political advisory body of the president, headed by the president. It comprises the speaker of the national parliament, the prime minister, five citizens elected by the national parliament and five citizens designated by the president for the period corresponding to the president's term of office.
National legislature
After independence in May 2002, the 88-seat Constituent Assembly became Timor-Leste's national parliament. Thirteen members are elected in single-seat constituencies and 75 elected by proportional representation.
Legal system
The legal system is under reform, putting in place structures under the new constitution.
Since 2000, the International Development Law Organisation (IDLO) has delivered practical training programmes to Timor-Leste's judges and prosecutors as part of a USAID-funded project for upgrading the system of justice.
Amnesty International issued a report in March 2003 which claimed that Timor-Leste's legal framework was incomplete and that there was 'a lack of clarity among judicial and other relevant officials about existing applicable law'. Some of the main problems include a lack of public defenders, delayed processing of court cases and legislation that was inconsistent with international human rights law and standards. It said that these problems encouraged vigilante violence and a loss of confidence in the legal system among police officers.
Last elections
14 April 2002 (first presidential); 30 August 2001 (parliamentary).
Results: Presidential: Xanana Gusmão won the first presidential elections with 82.7 per cent of the vote against Fancisco Xavier do Amaral with 17.3 per cent. Parliamentary: Frente Revolucionária do Timor-Leste Independente (Fretilin) (Revolutionary Front for East Timor Independence) won 57.4 per cent of the vote (55 seats); Partido Democrático (PD) (Democratic Party) 8.7 per cent (seven seats).
Next elections
August 2006 (parliamentary)
Political parties
Ruling party
Frente Revolucionária do Timor-Leste Independente (Fretilin) (Revolutionary Front for East Timor Independence) (elected 30 Aug 2001)
Main opposition party
Partido Democrático (PD) (Democratic Party)

Population
981,800 (2004)
Ethnic make-up
Before the arrival of the Europeans, peoples of Asia and Insulindia, mainly Malays, Makasare and Papuans, migrated to Timor-Leste.

Religions
Roman Catholic (91.4 per cent), Protestant (2.6 per cent), Muslim (1.7 per cent). There are also Buddhist and Hindu communities.

Education
Around 70 per cent of school age population attend primary school and 44 per cent are enrolled at secondary school. There is a shortage of teachers due to the fact that 80 per cent of Timor-Leste's teachers were Indonesian and the vast majority left following Indonesia's withdrawal. More than half the population is illiterate. The Roman Catholic Church is attempting to implement a literacy programme for the schools as the country needs to educate its people to manage the new nation's bureaucracy.

Health
Life expectancy: 62.2 years (World Bank)
Fertility rate/Maternal mortality rate: 7.6 births per woman (World Bank)
Infant mortality rate: 87 deaths per 1,000 live births; 42.6 children aged under 5 are malnourished (World Bank).

Main cities
Díli (capital, estimated population 50,800 in 2003).
There are 13 districts, each with a capital: Aileu (capital Aileu); Ainaro (Ainaro); Ambeno (Oecussi); Baucau (Baucau); Bobonaro (Maliana); Cova Lima (Suai); Díli (Díli); Ermera (Ermera); Lautem (Lospalos); Liquica (Liquica); Manatuto (Manatuto); Manufahi (Same); Viqueque (Viqueque).

Languages spoken
Tetum and Bahasa Indonesian/Malayu are the local languages. It is estimated that Portuguese is spoken by only 5 per cent of the population, with Tetum spoken by 82 per cent and Indonesian by 43 per cent. Although Tetum is widely spoken, it is an undeveloped language and only recently achieved a standardised grammar and spelling.
Official language/s
Portuguese and Tetum (Portuguese is the language of documentation).

Media
Press
During the UN administered transition period before full independence, international agencies helped to rebuild the Timor-Leste media.
In Timor-Leste's enclave of Oecussi, the only newspaper is *Tolas Weekly Magazine*. Important news sources are, therefore, visitors or returning inhabitants coming by ship, which serves the Díli-Oecussi route only once a week.
Fully paid professional journalists are found in two media organisations, *Timor*

Pos and *Suara Timor Lorosae*. The media is published and broadcast in English, Portuguese, Indonesian and Tetum, while small-scale, local media only use Tetum. *Timor Pos* daily and a few other publications including the daily *Suara Timor Loro Sae* are powered by a single printing machine. *Timor Pos* obtains aid from Newspapers Ltd in Queensland, owned by media giant Rupert Murdoch. Murdoch's aid is seen as the beginning of big capital intrusion into *Timor Pos*, leading to a further divide in the already existing camps of 'professionals' and 'activists' in the press community. Apart from the dilemmas of capital ownership, the question of a neutral press remains important.

Dailies: *Timor Pos* and *Suara Timor Loro Sae*.

Broadcasting

Radio: There are quite a few radio stations, mostly concentrated in Díli, while the outer regions lack communications facilities. The UN and the Catholic Church provide some radio coverage. Radio Timor Kamanek, run by the Catholic Church, has the widest coverage across the largely mountainous terrain, its transmission power being supported by a number of organisations. There is some access to small community radio stations which are mostly run by volunteers. Radio Communidade Maliana (Maliana community radio) is one such example.

Television: Televisaun Timor Lorosa'e (TVTL) began broadcasting an hour a week in Díli in May 2000, and by May 2001, was broadcasting 24 hours a day in Tetum, Indonesian, English and Portuguese. Rural districts show three-hour videotaped summaries of the week's programming on projection screens.

Economy

Timor-Leste is primarily an agricultural economy with coffee as its main export. During the time of the Indonesian occupation (1975–99), it was heavily dependent on external transfers, with approximately 85 per cent of recurrent and capital expenditure coming from Indonesia. The public and private sectors collapsed during the conflicts which broke out in 1999, while GDP fell by 34 per cent and inflation spiralled out of control.

Between 2000–01, the economy made a recovery on the back of UN reconstruction and expatriate consumption, with growth rates of over 15.0 per cent. Large scale rebuilding of infrastructure means that since 1999 investment has accounted for a high level of national GDP – 30 per cent in 2004.

When UN officials left the country in 2002, the country went into recession and GDP contracted. This was not helped by delays in the implementation of development projects. Drought in 2003 and a surge in population pushed down per capita GDP.

The output of important food crops (excluding rice) has returned to pre-1999 levels. The improvement in food supply has helped to reduce inflation from 140 per cent in 2000 to a projected 2.5 per cent in 2005.

Timor-Leste still relies heavily on imports, including rice to feed its population. However, imports did fall by 34 per cent in 2004.

Despite extensive international aid and support, around 42 per cent of the country continues to live below the poverty line and is likely to remain impoverished as growth is unstable. The educated workers pre-1999 were mainly Indonesian and left the country with the onset of violence. The workforce is expanding rapidly due to a high fertility rate, but is largely unskilled. The country's main priorities in the medium-term are setting up a central bank with normal operations and strengthening the revenue base. The latter will be greatly helped by the development of offshore oil and gas fields, which will generate revenue when they come on stream by around 2009. This will help move the government away from dependence on external funding. The exploitation of hydrocarbons is likely to prompt rapid growth of Timor-Leste's economy, with per capita income set to rise from around US$478 in 2001 to US$1,000 or more by 2009. In January 2004, Portugal said it would give Timor-Leste US$63 million in aid over the following three years.

Timor-Leste needs to develop its regulatory framework and administrative capacity more quickly. There are plans for new investment, insurance and export laws which should help create a business climate attractive to investors. The non-oil private sector is underdeveloped: the economy is primarily dependent on subsistence agriculture and government activity. The offshore oil and gas reserves, however, promise to generate good GDP growth.

External trade

Australia and Indonesia are Timor-Leste's main trading partners. In 2004 East Timor's non-oil export reached a value of US$8 million, predominantly coffee. In 2004 Timor-Leste's trade deficit was reduced to US$61 million, or 18 per cent of GDP.

Imports
Principal imports include food, gasoline, kerosene and machinery.
Main sources: Indonesia, Australia, Singapore, Vietnam, Portugal, Malaysia, China

Exports
Vanilla exports are being encouraged. Principal exports are coffee, sandalwood and marble.
Main destinations: Portugal, Taiwan, Germany, US, Indonesia, Australia

Agriculture
Farming
In 2005 agriculture generated 21 per cent of GDP and supplied income for 95 per cent of villages. Prior to 1999, livestock had been a traditional source of income for Timor-Leste. Livestock has a large social and economic function: it is exchanged in marriage, and can be a source of cash income or a savings account. The majority of rural families hold livestock. An IMF vaccination programme in 2004–05 siginificantly reduced the indicidence of disease among farm animals. Investment is required to recommence poultry and livestock farming. Timor-Leste's agriculture has very low productivity due to a lack of technology, modern techniques and money.

The World Bank is encouraging diversification into horticultural products. Vegetables and rice could be grown commercially. The higher elevations in Timor-Leste are ideal for growing pineapples, oranges, mangoes, bananas and papaya.

Coffee is the principal source of foreign exchange for Timor-Leste. It is in the hands of about 45,000 growers with an average of only one hectare each. There are virtually no large scale farms. Wet processed Arabica beans fetch the highest price but the processing facilities were put out of action during the fighting. Arabica beans account for about 80 per cent of the annual harvest. All coffee is produced organically. Renewal and maintenance of the road infrastructure is necessary for the rehabilitation of the coffee industry.

Subsistence farming is giving way to a market economy. The government sees the country's farming future in goods with high margins such as cashew nuts, vanilla and cut flowers. The main priority for now, however, should be food security. Estimate crop production in 2004 included: 135,608 tonnes (t) cereals in total, 70,175t maize, 41,525t cassava, 1,000t potatoes, 26,000t sweet potatoes, 65,433t rice, 4,500t pulses, 111,525t roots and tubers, 14,000t coconuts, 600t citrus fruit, grapes, 3,135t oilcrops, 100t cocoa beans, 14,000t green coffee, 425t various spices, 3,000t mangoes, 7,370t fruit in total, 18,225t vegetables in total. The estimated livestock production included: 28,280t meat in total, 1,000t beef, 540t buffalo meat, 10,000t pig meat, 240t goat meat, 1,360t poultry, 1,600t eggs, 375t milk, 400t honey.

Nations of the World: A Political, Economic and Business Handbook

Fishing
Although there are extensive rich fishing areas in the seas surrounding Timor-Leste, only traditional coastal fishing was practised as there was no established structure for offshore or deep-sea fishing. The government is contemplating establishing an exclusive economic zone for Timor-Leste and administering fishing and other activities in this area. Domestic fish consumption is very low. There are plans to promote the consumption of dried fish which could be more easily distributed from the coast to inner areas.

Forestry
A quarter of Timor-Leste's forested areas are in danger of degradation. Deforestation has caused landslides, and a worsening in soil and water quality. In recent years sandalwood, teak, ebony and redwood have been exploited at an unsustainable rate. The forestry sector, if responsibly managed, has potential for good revenue and significant employment opportunities.

Industry and manufacturing
The coffee industry is large and a service sector is developing in urban areas. The manufacturing industry in Timor-Leste is virtually non-existent. Priority areas for investment are industries processing raw materials from forests and marine and agricultural resources, and industries fabricating agricultural machinery, tools and small- and medium-sized fishing boats. The government is promoting the development of native handicrafts for export.

Tourism
Timor-Leste is looking to tourism to give impetus to the economy and its diversification. The sector is being built from scratch, the pre-independence conflict, during which tourism was not an option, having left the infrastructure in ruins. Attention is being focussed in the initial phase on adventure and eco-tourists, who know what to expect and are prepared to rough it. The longer-term aim is to establish a niche market, exploiting local cultural features as well as the natural attractions, which will distinguish Timor-Leste from its regional competitors. Immediate problems are scarce accommodation, high prices, insufficient and expensive air connections and the perception that the country is still unsafe. Measures to attract foreign investment have been adopted.

Environment
Overfelling of sandalwood trees led to devastating erosion in many areas, and forests and farmland were destroyed in the war.

Mining
At the moment there is no significant mining activity. There are indications however that there could be economically interesting deposits of marble, granite, limestone and gold. The government is in the process of setting up a fiscal policy and regulatory framework, which would enable surveys and exploration to begin.

Hydrocarbons
In March 2003, Australia approved a treaty to allow multi-billion dollar oil and gas developments in the Timor Sea. The deal entitles Timor-Leste to 90 per cent of the production from the Joint Petroleum Development Area (JPDA) of the Timor Sea, which covers the Bayu-Undan, Greater Sunrise, Jahal and Kuda Tasi fields.
ConocoPhillips, the third-largest US oil and gas company received permission in June 2003 to develop the US$1.5 billion Bayu-Undan liquefied natural gas project in the Timor Sea. Production began in February 2004. The Bayu-Undan project is expected to earn US$100 million a year.
An agreement was signed with Australia in January 2006 that will finally clear the way for the start of oil and gas production in the Greater Sunrise field. Although the companies involved in the Greater Sunrise plan have yet to confirm they will go ahead, the field is reckoned to be worth a fortune. The agreement states that Timor-Leste and Australia will share the proceeds equally.

Energy
The national power system was managed by Indonesians who left during the violence of 1999. This left a lack of people technically capable of maintaining power supplies. Generating capacity is around 38.3MW. The government has been investing in electrical infrastructure. Rural areas still have very limited access to electricity and prices are high throughout the country.
Deforestation is a problem: more sustainable energy resources have to be found.

Banking and insurance
By 2005, the banking system consisted of four commercial banks, but most bank deposits are invested abroad. The banking sector requires a stronger regulatory framework and more investment opportunities if it is to grow.
The Banking and Payments Authority (BPA) provides currency – US dollars – to the country's banks. It also supervises commercial banking, strives to ensure monetary stability and moderate inflation. In the future the BPA will develop into a central bank.

Time
GMT plus eight hours

Geography
East Timor lies 1,609km (1,000 miles) south of the Philippines and 644km (400 miles) north-west of Australia. The highest peak is Tatamailau.

Climate
The dry season is between July and October when it becomes very hot and dusty with the monsoon winds blowing off the deserts of Australia. Rainy season: November to June. Temperatures range from 15 degrees Celsius (C) in the mountains to 30 degrees C and above on the north coast. Humidity: 75–85 per cent. There is a risk of tropical cyclones.

Entry requirements
The situation in Timor-Leste is not stable and only essential travel to the region should be undertaken.

Passports
Must be valid for six months beyond the intended date of departure.

Visa
Visas are not required in advance. Entry permits, costing US$25 for visits up to 30 days only, may be obtained on arrival. Foreign business people may apply for a Resident Visa, with proof of the registration of their business.

Currency advice/regulations
The import of some foreign currencies, excluding the US dollar, requires a government-issued licence, it is advisable to seek further information from the authorities.

Customs
Customs duty is 5 per cent and there is a 5 per cent sales tax on commercial imports, with excise taxes on selected imports.

Health (for visitors)
Comprehensive medical and travel insurance is essential as medical services are severely limited. In the event of a medical emergency, evacuation to Australia is probably the only option for treatment, and insurance policies should cover this eventuality. Such treatment carried out locally will require immediate cash payment for doctors' and hospital services.

Advisable precautions
Malaria prophylaxis should be taken. Dengue Fever and Japanese Encephalitis are common throughout the island and tuberculosis is prevalent, while cholera and rabies may also be present. There are no dental or optical services available.

Public holidays
Fixed dates
1 Jan (New Year's Day), 1 May (Labour Day), 15 Aug (Assumption Day), 30 Aug (Constitution Day), 20 Sep (Liberation Day), 1 Nov (All Saints' Day), 8 Dec (

Immaculate Conception), 25 Dec (Christmas Day).
Variable dates
Good Friday

Working hours
Banking
Mon–Fri: 0930–1530.
Business
Mon–Fri: 0800–1700.

Social customs/useful tips
It is advisable to keep an additional copy of one's passport. Visitors should expect to pay all expenses in hard cash.

Security
Travel should not be undertaken during the hours of darkness unless for official purposes. The political situation in Timor-Leste is volatile and visitors are advised to keep away from public demonstrations.

Getting there
Air
International airport/s: Nicolau Lobato International Airport (DIL), serves the capital Dili. It has limited commercial flights and few gound facilities (no money exchanges exist). There are scheduled services to Western and Northern Australia. Baucau Airport (BCH) in Baucau region.
Airport tax: US$10 departure tax.
Surface
The land border crossing between Timor-Leste and the Indonesian province of West Timor opened in Batugadee in May 2000.

Water: Since the Indonesian withdrawal, regular shipping-services have commenced between Díli and Darwin, Australia, and Díli and Singapore.

Getting about
National transport
Outside the capital, infrastructure is extremely limited.

BUSINESS DIRECTORY
The addresses listed below are a selection only. While World of Information makes every endeavour to check these addresses, we cannot guarantee that changes have not been made, especially to telephone numbers and area codes. We would welcome any corrections.

Telephone area codes
The international direct dialling (IDD) code for Timor-Leste is +670, followed by the subscriber's number.

Travel information
Ministry of tourism
Department of Tourism (tel: 333-9173; e-mail: turismo_timorleste@globalpost.org).

Other useful addresses
British Consular enquiries: British Embassy, Deutsche Bank Building, 19th Floor, 80 Jalan Imam Bonjol, Jakarta 10310, Indonesia (tel: (62 21) 390-7484; fax: (62 21) 316-0850).

British Office, The Post Office, PO Box 194, Díli (tel: 101-991; e-mail: dili.fco@gtnet.gov.uk).

Department of Economic Affairs, Industry Division (information on application procedures for investment), 2nd Floor, Fomento Building, Rua Dom Alixio Corte Real, Dili (tel: 333-9172; e-mail: etindpro@hotmail.com).

East Timor Trading (imports/exports, business advice), Rua de Jacinto Candido, Audian, Dili. (tel/fax: 324-621).

Investment Institute, PO Box 371, Dili (tel: 312-210; fax: 325-040).

Trade Division, Department of Economic Affairs and Development (business facilitation services), Dili (tel: 333-9174,/5; e-mail: trade_division@corrieo.org).

US Embassy, Medan Merdeka Selatan 5, Jakarta (tel: (62 21) 344-2211; fax: (62 21) 386-2259; e-mail: jakconsul@state.gov).

Internet sites
East Timor Action Network:
http://www.etan.org/

East Timor Investment Promotion Unit:
http://www.gov.east-timor.org

Timor Leste government:
http://www.gov.east-timor.org

US Embassy:
http://www.usembassyjakarta.org

Togo

KEY FACTS

Official name: République Togolaise (Togolese Republic)

Head of State: President Faure Gnassingbé (RPT) (sworn in 4 May 2005)

Head of government: Prime Minister Edem Kodjo (sworn in 9 Jun 2005)

Ruling party: Rassemblement du Peuple Togolais (RPT) (Rally of the Togolese People) (since 1994; last re-elected Oct 2002)

Area: 56,000 square km

Population: 5.25 million (2004)

Capital: Lomé

Official language: French

Currency: CFA franc (CFAf) = 100 centimes (Communauté Financière Africaine (African Financial Community) franc). New notes have been issued; old notes cease to be legal tender from Jan 2005.

Exchange rate: CFAf544.07 per US$ (Oct 2005); CFAf655.95 per euro (pegged from Jan 1999)

GDP per capita: US$375 (2004)

GDP real growth: 2.90% (2004)

Labour force: 2.12 million (2004)

Inflation: 1.20% (2004)

Balance of trade: -US$161.80 million 2004

Foreign debt: US$1.40 billion (2003)

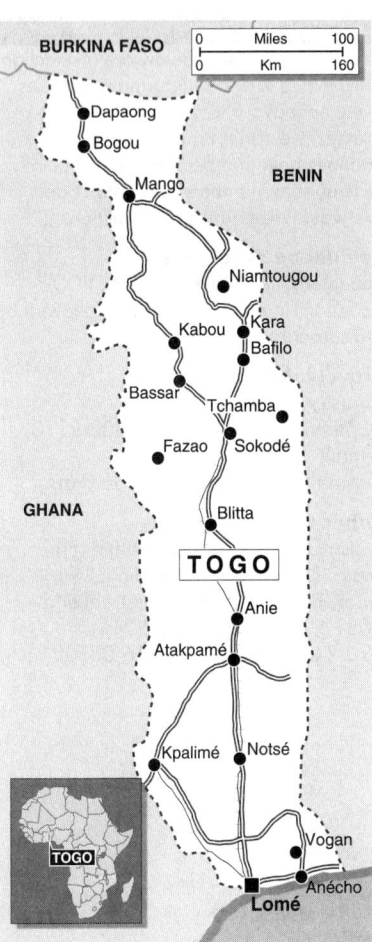

This small sub-Saharan country's economy is heavily dependent on both commercial and subsistence agriculture, which provides employment for 65 per cent of the labour force, although some basic foodstuffs must still be imported. Cocoa, coffee, and cotton generate about 40 per cent of export earnings, with cotton being the most important cash crop. Togo is the world's fourth-largest producer of phosphate.

A decade-long effort, supported by the World Bank and the International Monetary Fund (IMF), to implement economic reform, encourage foreign investment, and bring revenues in line with expenditures has moved slowly. Real progress depends on increased openness in government financial operations, progress toward legislative elections, and continued support from foreign donors. Togo is working with donors to write a poverty reduction paper that could eventually lead to a debt reduction plan.

Togo has come under fire from international organisations for human rights abuses and is plagued by political unrest. While most bilateral and multilateral aid to Togo remains frozen, the European Union, which cut off aid in 1993 over the country's human rights record, initiated a partial resumption of co-operation and development aid in late 2004 based upon commitments by Togo to expand opportunities for political opposition and liberalise portions of the economy.

However, President Gnassingbé Eyadéma died in February 2005 and, supported by the military, was succeeded by his son Faure Gnassingbé. The succession, in contravention of the nation's constitution, was challenged by popular protest and a threat of sanctions from regional and international leaders. Faure Gnassingbé succumbed to pressure and agreed to hold elections in April 2005. He was re-elected and in turn elected Edem Kodjo, the leader of a moderate opposition party, prime minister. Kodjo brought the leaders of two other opposition parties into government.

Economy

The Togolese economy recovered in 2002-03 following two years of decline. The recovery was driven by increased agricultural and phosphate production. Inflationary pressures abated, as food prices declined, following an increase in food production. Notwithstanding this recovery in growth, domestic demand remained weak, as the low level of government spending and the accumulation of domestic payments arrears dampened private sector activities.

The fiscal position was difficult during 2002–03, in view of the low revenue performance and the continued suspension of external aid. Domestic and external payments arrears increased, reaching 18.7 per cent of gross domestic product.

Togo's external position improved in 2004, reflecting mainly favourable developments in the country's main exports and increased private transfers. A bumper cotton crop boosted the volume of cotton exports by more than 40 per cent.

The IMF, whose last engagement with Togo was in 1994, says that Togo's economy continues to face important challenges posed by the country's limited resources and its vulnerability to exogenous shocks, and, in recent years, lapses in policy and reform implementation and by weaknesses in the banking and judicial systems.

The government's financial situation will continue to be difficult without external budgetary support. The IMG has urged the authorities to normalise relations with creditors and donors, including with the European Union, to facilitate the resumption of its aid.

Further progress toward fiscal consolidation and successful implementation of structural reforms would improve Togo's growth prospects, lead to economic diversification, and help maintain competitiveness.

In 2002, the IMF and the government prepared a poverty reduction strategy which the IMF has now suggested should be adopted and the government should seek donors support for its implementation.

Although carrying a heavy debt burden and eligible for assistance under the HIPC initiative of the IMF, Togo has not taken any action to be able to benefit from relief. The IMF has urged action on this.

Politics

French Togoland became Togo in 1960. The first president, Sylvanus Olympio, was assassinated in a military coup three years later. Head of the armed forces Gnassingbé Eyadéma seized power in a 1967 coup and dissolved all political parties. He continued to rule well into 2005. Although political parties were legalised in 1991 and a democratic constitution adopted in 1992, the leadership was accused of suppressing opposition and of cheating in elections.

Togo, a narrow strip of land on Africa's west coast, has for years been the target of criticism over its human rights record and political governance. A joint UN-Organisation of African Unity investigation into claims that hundreds of people were killed after controversial elections in 1998 concluded that there had been systematic human rights violations.

Faure Gnassingbé, the son of Togo's late veteran leader Gnassingbé Eyadéma, was declared the winner of presidential elections in April 2005 with 60 per cent of the votes. The announcement was followed by street violence in the capital involving security forces and opposition supporters, who said the poll had been rigged. The Constitutional Court rejected the claim and a regional delegation said the elections had been broadly free and fair, despite isolated problems. Two months later, the leader of a moderate opposition party, Edem Kodjo, was named as prime minister. Kodjo led the government during the 1990s under Gnassingbé Eyadéma. There had been calls for a government of national unity but talks with the main opposition parties broke down. Kodjo's government includes members of two other opposition parties.

Risk assessment

Economic	Improving
Political	Bad
Regional stability	Improving

COUNTRY PROFILE

Historical profile

Modern Togo is the sector of the once German model colony of Togoland that was mandated to France in 1922. It became an independent republic in 1960. Although not well known outside Africa, Togo has long been able to punch above its weight regionally. It is the only former French colony in West Africa that has actively lobbied for the creation of a regional organisation embracing both anglophone and francophone countries – the West African Economic Community – Ecowas. The groundwork for Ecowas was very much the work of Togo and Nigeria. The name of Togo's capital city, Lomé, also entered the international economic lexicon following the signing of Africa's accords with the (then EEC) European Union, subsequently known as the Lomé Agreement, or the Lomé declaration.

1894 The country, then known as Togoland, became a German colony.
1914 Britain and France invaded and captured Togoland.
1922 Togoland was divided between Britain and France under a League of Nations mandate.
1930–50s The division of Togoland split the indigenous Ewe people, which led to the creation of a nationalist movement which demanded the unification of the two territories.
1956 British-ruled Togoland was incorporated into Ghana.
1960 The French section of Togoland gained independence under the leadership of Sylvanus Olympio and was declared a republic.
1962 A proposed referendum on unification with Ghana was blocked by President Olympio.
1963 Olympio was killed in a coup and replaced by Nicolas Grunitzky.
1967 Grunitzky was in turn ousted by Major General Gnassingbé Eyadéma.
1979 Eyadéma stood and won as the sole candidate in the presidential election.
1985 France intervened militarily to support the Eyadéma regime, following an attempted coup.
1991 President Eyadéma agreed to a national conference to pave the way for multi-party elections. The powers of the president were reduced. Joseph Koffigoh became prime minister and head of a transitional government.
1993 After a series of delays, the country's first multi-party presidential elections

KEY INDICATORS — Togo

	Unit	2000	2001	2002	2003	2004
Population	m	4.63	4.70	4.83	5.04	*5.25
Gross domestic product (GDP)	US$bn	1.30	1.30	1.40	1.34	*2.06
GDP per capita	US$	283	277	290	265	375
GDP real growth	%	-0.7	2.7	2.6	3.0	2.9
Inflation	%	1.9	3.9	3.1	-0.9	1.2
Consumer prices	1995=100	116.5	122.9	124.8	–	–
Exports (fob) (goods)	US$m	346.0	349.0	371.0	449.0	663.1
Imports (fob) (goods)	US$m	406.0	542.0	607.0	561.0	824.9
Balance of trade	US$m	-60.0	-193.0	-236.0	-112.0	-161.8
Current account	US$m	-139.0	-170.0	-140.0	-220.0	-250.0
Foreign debt	US$bn	1.4	1.4	1.6	1.4	–
Total reserves minus gold	US$m	152.3	126.1	205.1	182.5	323.3
Foreign exchange	US$m	151.9	125.5	204.4	181.8	322.7
Exchange rate	per US$	711.98	733.04	696.99	574.89	528.29

* estimated figure

were held. Eyadéma, standing for the Rassemblement du Peuple Togolais (RPT) (Rally of the Togolese People), was the only candidate.

1994 The RPT won the legislative elections, but needed the support of the Union Togolaise pour la Démocratie (UTD) (Togolese Union for Democracy) to form a majority.

1996 After winning three delayed by-elections, the RPT no longer required UTD's support.

1998 Eyadéma won the presidential election; the official results were contested by the opposition parties and criticised by the UN.

1999 The parliamentary elections were boycotted by all opposition parties. An independent electoral commission (CENI), was formed, with equal representation of opposition and government.

2001 The UN and the Organisation of African Unity (OAU) concluded there were hundreds of summary executions and torture in the run-up to the 1998 presidential election.

2002 The ruling RPT won the parliamentary elections; the main opposition parties boycotted the elections. The constitution was amended allowing another term in office for President Eyadéma.

2003 Incumbent Eyadéma won the presidential elections.

2004 The EU resumed partial aid to Togo, suspended since 1993, in recognition of moves towards restoring democracy.

2005 President Gnassingbé Eyadéma died on 5 February. Unconstitutionally, the armed forces conferred power on his son, Faure Gnassingbé. After international pressure he stepped down but later won the presidential elections, on 24 April, against Emmanuel Bob Akitani of the opposition Union des Forces de Changement (UFC) (Union of Forces for Change); the opposition disputed the results and there were violent protests in the streets of the capital, Lomé. A clampdown by security forces provoked thousands of opposition supporters to flee to Benin or Ghana. The Constitutional Court confirmed the election of Faure Gnassingbé as president and he was sworn in on 4 May. Edem Kodjo was sworn in as prime minister on 9 June.

Political structure
Constitution
In 2002 a new, democratic constitution, formally initiating Togo's fourth republic was instituted.
On the death of the president, the chairman of the National Assembly becomes interim president until elections are held. The country is divided into *préfectures*, administered by préfects, and supervised by the interior ministry.

Form of state
Republic

The executive
Executive power is vested in the president, who is elected for a period of five years. The prime minister is the head of government and is selected by the president from the parliamentary majority. A Council of Ministers is appointed by the president and the prime minister.

National legislature
Legislative power is vested in the unicameral, 81-seat, L'Assemblé Nationale (National Assembly). Its members are elected by popular vote to serve five-year terms.

Legal system
Togo has a French-based court system.

Last elections
24 April 2005 (presidential); 27 October 2002 (parliamentary).
Results: Presidential: Faure Gnassingbé (RPT) won 60.2 per cent of the vote, Emmanuel Bob Akitani of the (UFC) 38.2 per cent, Nicolas Lawson of the Renewal and Redemption Party 1 per cent and Harry Olympio of the Rally for Support of Democracy and Development 0.6 per cent; turnout was 63.6 per cent.
Parliamentary: the ruling RPT won 72 seats out of 81; the remaining nine seats were shared by four minor parties; the main opposition parties called for a boycott of the elections and did not present any candidates

Next elections
2007 (parliamentary); 2010 (presidential).

Political parties
Ruling party
Rassemblement du Peuple Togolais (RPT) (Rally of the Togolese People) (since 1994; last re-elected Oct 2002)

Main opposition party
Convergence Patriotique Panafricaine (CPP) (Patriotic Pan-African Convergence), Union des Forces de Changement (UFC) (Union of Forces for Change)

Population
5.25 million (2004)
Ethnic make-up
African (99 per cent), European (1 per cent).
Religions
Traditional beliefs (50 per cent), Christianity (35 per cent) (mostly Roman Catholic), Islam (15 per cent).

Education
Public expenditure on education is 4–5 per cent of GDP, of which per capita expenditure is 16–17 per cent per student.
Literacy rate: 74 per cent male, 45per cent female: adult rates (World Bank)
Compulsory years: Six to 15
Enrolment rate: 124 per cent gross primary enrolment, 36 per cent secondary enrolment; of relevant age groups (including repeaters) (World Bank).
Pupils per teacher: 46 in primary schools

Health
Total expenditure of health is 2–3 per cent of GDP, of which government spending is 48–49 per cent and foreign expenditure is around 10 per cent.
HIV/Aids
The impact of HIV/Aids has yet to peak with deaths, orphans and HIV positive pregnant women all showing an increase. By the end of 2003 there were an estimated 10,000 deaths from Aids, although this number could be as high as 16,000; the difference may be due to underreporting or misdiagnosis.
Of the estimated 110,000 people living with HIV/Aids, 9,300, are children (aged 0–14) and 54,000 are women; and 9 per cent of pregnant women tested were positive for HIV in 2003, which bears out the UNAids message that women and children are typically more vulnerable to HIV/Aids in Africa.
Between 2001–03 the number of orphans (aged 0–17) rose from 8,700 to 9,300.
HIV prevalence: 4.1 per cent aged 15–49 in 2003 (World Bank)
Life expectancy: 49.7 years in 2003 (World Bank). This figure is closer to the 49 years life expectancy in 1980 than the 54.69 years in 2000.
Fertility rate/Maternal mortality rate: 4.9 births per woman (World Bank)
Birth rate/Death rate: 35.2 births and 11.5 deaths per 1,000 people (2003)
Infant mortality rate: 78 per 1,000 live births; 25 per cent of children aged under five are malnourished (World Bank).

Main cities
Lomé (capital, estimated population 676,400 in 2003).

Languages spoken
Ewe and Kabyè are widely spoken.
Official language/s
French

Media
Press
The major news agencies include Afritel and the Agence Togolaise de Presse (ATOP). The main national state-owned newspaper is *Nouvelle Marche*. Other dailies include *La Tribune de Democrate*, *Le Mono*, *Togo Presse* and non-dailies include *Crocodile*, *Kpaka Desenchante* and *Le Temps*.
Broadcasting
Radio: State-operated Radiodiffusion Togolaise runs two radio stations broadcasting in French, English and African languages. There are also three privately-run radio stations.
Television: State-owned TVT Télévision Togolaise broadcasts in French and

Togo

national languages. Major hotels offer satellite TV.

Economy
The economy has been heavily effected by the political instability of Togo. In 1993, the EU – Togo's principal donor source – suspended aid due to the deteriorating state of democracy and human rights violations by the then president, Gnassingbé Eyadéma. By 1994 Togo owed as much in foreign debt as the annual projected government revenue. The economy suffered a general strike in the late 1990s and GDP growth dropped to a negative. The government implemented macroeconomic reforms, tightening expenditure and improving measures to collect taxes and the economy has improved since 2001. Agricultural production has grown since 2002 with good harvests and climate conditions achieving a government goal in food self-sufficiency. In 2004 GDP growth was 2.9, slightly less than the 3.0 per cent in 2003. Inflation was a low 1.2 per cent but this was a rise on the -0.9 per cent in 2003.

There have been no international aid programmes in Togo since 2003, although the EU resumed partial aid, for social welfare projects, in 2004 and The World Bank provides advisory assistance. The IMF suspended its programme to restore macroeconomic reforms until donors recommence their aid.

Subsistence agriculture, which employs three-quarters of the labour force, contributes around 40 per cent of GDP. The main agricultural products – cocoa, coffee and cotton – contribute around 35 per cent of foreign exchange earnings. Phosphate mining was a large revenue earner in the past, but the sector has declined by over 22 per cent, and lack of investment has hindered recovery. The reliance on primary production means that Togo is vulnerable to climatic problems and external economic shock in world commodity prices.

External trade
Imports
Principal imports are fmachinery and equipment, foodstuffs and petroleum products.
Main sources: China (24.7 per cent total, 2004), France (16.1 per cent), Malaysia (5.3 per cent), Italy (4.6 per cent), Germany (4.6 per cent), UK (4.3 per cent), The Netherlands (4.2 per cent), Thailand (4.2 per cent), Belgium (4.2 per cent)
Exports
Principal exports are cotton, phosphates, coffee and cocoa.
Main destinations: Burkina Faso (16 per cent total, 2004), Ghana (14.7 per cent), Benin (9.2 per cent), China (8.1 per cent), Mali (7.5 per cent), The Netherlands (6.6 per cent), Taiwan (4.2 per cent)

Agriculture
Farming
The agricultural sector contributes around 40 per cent to GDP and employs around 75 per cent of the workforce.
Traditional methods of cultivation still prevail despite attempts at rapid modernisation.
Self-sufficiency in basic foodstuffs is generally maintained except during drought years. The majority of farmers are smallholders who raise stock and grow maize, millet, yams, cassava, sorghum and rice.
Cotton, coffee and cocoa are the principal export earners.
Crop production for 2004 included: 787,100 tonnes (t) cereals in total, 485,000t maize, 725,000t cassava, 180,000t sorghum, *115,000t oil palm fruit, 47,024t oilcrops, *1,800t tobacco, 8,500t cocoa beans, *13,500t green coffee, 570,000t yams, 185,000t seed cotton, 76,000t cotton lint, 2,520t various herbs and spices, *50,650t fruit in total, *136,000t vegetables in total. Livestock production included: 34,141t meat in total, *5,713t beef, 4,774t pig meat, 4,070t lamb, 3,731t goat meat, *4,500t game meat, 11,200t poultry, 6,440t eggs, *9,225t milk, 703t sheepskins.
* estimate

Forestry
The value of exports in 2004 amounted to US$4.8 million, while imports amounted to US$8.6 million.
The estimated production for 2004 included: 5,914,769 cubic metres (cum) roundwood, 208,000cum industrial roundwood, 13,000cum sawnwood, 43,000cum sawlogs and veneers, 5,706,769 cum woodfuel, 195,746t charcoal.

Industry and manufacturing
The industrial sector, in 2004, contributed 22.8 per cent to GDP, of which 9.4 per cent was manufacturing, and employed 10 per cent of the workforce.
Activity is centred on the processing of agricultural commodities and the production of phosphoric acid, fertilisers and cement along with beverages, footwear, textiles and plastics.

Tourism
Tourism in 2005 is estimated to earn US$41.7 million or 1.8 per cent of gross GDP, employ 3.8 per cent of the workforce and attract US$50.6 million, or 10.2 per cent of all capital investment. Togo has several distinct environments to offer the tourist, from Atlantic beach resorts to high savannah game parks and tropical forests. Facilities may be basic but should attract eco-tourists wishing to see some unspoiled African landscapes.

Mining
The mining sector contributes around 12 per cent to GDP and employs 5 per cent of the workforce. Mining production is concentrated on phosphates, marble and limestone, although the country has potential for commercial extraction of diamonds, gold and base metals. There are also known reserves of iron ore, bauxite, dolomite and chromite.
Phosphate mining is the second principal export earner after cotton. Reserves are estimated at over 60 million tonnes, mainly located around Lake Togo. There are environmental concerns about the high level of cadmium in Togolese phosphate rock. The possible development of safer but lower-grade carbo-phosphates is being explored. There are 200 identified base metal deposits, including the lead zinc prospect at Pagala which is licensed to Anglo American.

Hydrocarbons
Togo relies entirely on imported oil products, typically over 6,800 barrels per day (bpd) to supply its needs. The government has tried to attract foreign interest in offshore prospecting but the last exploration well was drilled in 1986 and foreign prospectors have not bidded for any offshore blocks, despite oil being found in the regional.
Currently there is no production or import of natural gas. However, with two pipeline projects currently underway so this is set to change. The US$260 million West African Gas Pipeline (WAGP) is currently under construction and will supply natural gas from Nigeria's Escravos field to Togo, Benin and Ghana. The 1,000km pipeline will be managed by Chevron Texaco.
Togo does not produce or import coal.

Energy
Togo is heavily dependent on imported fuel. Electricity is imported from the Akosombo and Nkong hydroelectric dams in Ghana.

Banking and insurance
Central bank
Banque Centrale des Etats de l'Afrique de l'Ouest (Central Bank of West African States).
Main financial centre
Lomé.

Time
GMT.

Geography
Togo lies in West Africa, forming a narrow strip stretching north from a coastline of about 50km (30 miles) on the Gulf of Guinea. It is bordered by Ghana to the

west, by Benin to the east, and by Burkina Faso, to the north.

Climate
Tropical, mean annual temperature 28 degrees Celsius. Drier in the north. Two rainy seasons between April–June and September–October.

Entry requirements
Passports
Required by all except certain African countries. Joint passports are not accepted. Passports must be valid for six months.
Visa
Required by all. Contact the consular section of the nearest Togo embassy for full details and requirements before travelling.
Currency advice/regulations
No restrictions on import of foreign currency. Export of foreign currency must not exceed the amount declared on arrival. No more than CFAf1 million may be taken in and no more than CFAf25,000 exported.

Health (for visitors)
Mandatory precautions
Yellow fever vaccination certificate required by all.
Advisable precautions
Cholera is a serious risk as well as malaria, precautions and prophylactics are essential; seek further medical advice. Hepatitis 'A, B' and 'E', tetanus, typhoid and polio. There is an HIV/Aids risk and a rabies risk.
All water should be regarded as a potential health risk, use only bottled or boiled water for drinking, brushing teeth or making ice. Milk is unpasteurised and should be boiled, avoid dairy products. Eat only hot, cooked food, and peeled fruit.
To avoid the risk of bilharzia, only use well maintained, chlorinated swimming pools.
Medical insurance that includes evacuation is advised.

Hotels
High-standard hotels in Lomé, which should be booked well in advance. Ten per cent tip is usual.

Credit cards
Credit cards accepted.

Public holidays
Fixed dates
1 Jan (New Year's Day), 13 Jan (Liberation Day), 27 Apr (Independence Day), 1 May (Labour Day), 21 Jun (Day of the Martyrs), 15 Aug (Assumption Day), 24 Sep (Anniversary of the Failed Attack on Lomé), 1 Nov (All Saints' Day), 25 Dec (Christmas Day).

Variable dates
Easter Monday, Ascension Day, Whit Monday, Eid al Adha, Birth of the Prophet, Eid al Fitr.
The Islamic year contains 354 or 355 days, with the result that Muslim feasts advance by 10–12 days against the Gregorian calendar. Dates of feasts vary according to the sighting of the new moon, so cannot be forecast exactly. Islamic year 1426: 10 February 2005 to 30 January 2006.

Working hours
Banking
Mon–Fri: 0730–1130, 1430–1600.
Business
Mon–Fri: 0700–1200, 1430–1730.
Government
Mon–Fri: 0700–1200, 1430–1730.
Shops
Mon–Fri: 0800–1200, 1430–1730; Sat: 0730–1230.

Telecommunications
Telephone/fax
International and local phone connections are best in Lomé and more difficult elsewhere.

Electricity supply
220V AC, 50 cycles.

Social customs/useful tips
Business is conducted in French.

Security
Togo is relatively trouble-free, although visitors should be wary of the occasional car hijacking. The coastal area is reported to be dangerous and visitors are advised to travel in groups throughout Togo, rather than alone.

Getting there
Air
International airport/s: Lomé (LFW), 6km from city; duty-free shop, bar, restaurant, buffet, bank, post office, shops, car hire. Taxis operate from 0600 until the last flight (fare CFAfr2000-5000) to the city centre.
Airport tax: US$25 departure tax
Surface
Road: There is a well-surfaced coastal road connecting Accra (Ghana) and Lagos (Nigeria), which runs through Lomé. This route is also connected to Cotonou (Benin) and Ouagadougou (Burkina Faso).
The African Development Bank (ADB) agreed a loan in May 1999 for CFAf10.2 billion to refurbish the main highway (Route Nationale 1) linking Lomé with the northern states.
Main port/s: Lomé. Kpeme handles phosphate shipments. Approximately two million tonnes of cargo are handled annually.

Getting about
National transport
Air: Air Togo flies between Lomé, Sokodé, Mango, Lama-Kara, Niamtougou and Dapaong.
Road: The main surfaced roads run to the borders of neighbouring countries; other roads may not be passable in the rainy season. The main route to the north is called 'Highway of Unity'.
Rail: The main lines run from Lomé to Blitta (midway between Atakpamé and Sokodé), and to Kpalimé.
Water: Coastal ferries operate between the southern ports.
City transport
Taxis: Readily available in Lomé, while shared taxis ply to other main towns; tipping is not usual.
Car hire
International driving licence required.

BUSINESS DIRECTORY

The addresses listed below are a selection only. While World of Information makes every endeavour to check these addresses, we cannot guarantee that changes have not been made, especially to telephone numbers and area codes. We would welcome any corrections.

Telephone area codes
The international direct dialling (IDD) code for Togo is +228, followed by subscriber's number.

Chambers of Commerce
Togo Chamber of Commerce, Agriculture and Industry, Angle Avenues de la Présidence et Georges Pompidou, PO Box 360, Lomé (tel: 221-2065; fax: 221-4730; e-mail: ccit@rdd.tg).

Banking
Banque Internationale pour l'Afrique au Togo SA, BP 346, 13 rue du Commerce, Lomé (tel: 213-286, 212-081; fax: 211-019, 220-238).

Banque Togolaise de Développement, BP 65, Place de L'Independance, Angle Avenue des Nîmes et Avenue Nicolas Grunitzky, Lomé (tel 213-641/2; fax: 214-456).

Banque Togolaise pour le Commerce et l'Industrie, BP 363, 169 Boulevard du 13 Janvier, Lomé (tel: 214-641/42; fax: 213-265).

Ecobank-Togo, BP 3302, 20 Rue du Commerce, Lomé (tel: 217-214 fax: 214-237).

Société Inter Africaine de Banque, BP 4874, 14 rue du commerce, Lomé (tel: 212-830, 211-341; fax: 215-829).

Société Nationale d'Investissement et Fonds Annexes BP 2682, 11 Avenue du 24 Janvier, Lomé (tel: 216-221; fax: 216-225).

Togo

Union Togolaise de Banques, BP 359, Place Van Vollen Hoven, Lomé (tel: 216-411; fax: 212-206).

Central bank
Banque Centrale des Etats de l'Afrique de l'Ouest, Direction Nationale, BP 120, Rue des Nimes, Lomé (tel: 221-2512; fax: 221-7602).

Travel information
National tourist organisation offices
Office National Togolais du Tourisme, BP 1289, Route d'Aného, Lomé, (tel: 214-313, 215-662; fax: 218-927).

Other useful addresses
British Honorary Consul, Lomé (tel: 264-606).

Direction de la Statistique, BP 118, Lomé (tel: 270-662).

Direction des Professions Touristiques, BP 1289, Lomé (tel: 215-662, 214-313).

Kpeme Port Authority, OTP BP 362, Lomé (tel: 213-901; fax: 217-105).

Office des Produits Agricoles du Togo, BP 1334, Lomé (agency dealing with marketing, export, development) (tel: 214-471).

OPTT-Post Office and Telecommunications of Togo, Lomé (tel: 213-737; fax: 210-373).

Togo Embassy (USA), 2208 Massachusetts Avenue, NW, Washington DC 20008 (tel: 202-234-4212; fax: 202-232-3190).

Internet sites
Africa Business Network: http://www.ifc.org/abn

AllAfrica.com: http://allafrica.com

African Development Bank: http://www.afdb.org

Africa Online: http://www.africaonline.com

Mbendi AfroPaedia (information on companies, countries, industries and stock exchanges in Africa): http://mbendi.co.za

Republic of Togolais (in French): http://www.republicoftogo.com

Online Togo news: http://www.togodaily.com

Togo Official website: http://www.afrika.com/togo/html

Tokelau

KEY FACTS

Official name: Tokelau

Head of State: Queen Elizabeth II, represented by Governor General Dame Silvia Cartwright (appointed 4 Apr 2001)

Head of government: Administrator Neil Walter (from 2002); *Ulu-o-Tokelau* Pio Iosefo Tuia 2005

Area: 12 square km (three coral atolls: Nukunonu, Fakaofo, Atafu)

Population: 1,500 (2004). Some 6,000 Tokelauans live in New Zealand.

Capital: Each atoll has its own administrative centre

Official language: Tokelauan (English also spoken)

Currency: New Zealand dollar (NZ$) =100 cents; also Tala or Samoan dollar (S$)

Exchange rate: NZ$1.44 per US$; S$2.73 per US$ (Oct 2005)

GDP per capita: US$1,000 (2003)

Balance of trade: -US$225,000 (2003)

COUNTRY PROFILE

Historical profile
Tokelau's three atolls are believed to have been settled by people from Samoa, Cook Islands and Tuvalu.
1889 The Union Islands became a British protectorate.
1916 At the request of the inhabitants, the United Kingdom annexed the islands and included them within the Gilbert and Ellice Islands Colony (now Kiribati and Tuvalu).
1926 The British government transferred administrative control of the islands to New Zealand.
1946 The islands were renamed Tokelau Islands.
1948 The Tokelau Islands Act made New Zealand the formal administering authority.
1976 The islands were renamed Tokelau.
1994 Executive and administrative functions were delegated by New Zealand to the General *Fono* (or Council of Faipule when the General *Fono* is not in session).
1996 Subordinate legislative power was granted to the General *Fono* by the New Zealand Tokelau Amendment Act.
2001 Tokelau became responsible for its own public service. Dame Silvia Cartwright was appointed governor general.
2002 Neil Walter was appointed administrator.
2003 For the second time, Kolouei O'Brien became the *Ulu o Tokelau* (Head of Tokelau) (the position is rotated annually between the three members of the cabinet) – he last held the post in 2000. In December, a new Principles of Partnership document was signed by New Zealand and Tokelau.
2004 The UN presented a *Special Case Study* on decolonisation and urged colonised countries like Tokelau to become independent. Falani Aukuso, general manager of the government, said that self-determination was preferable but Tokelau could not 'afford to be fully independent'. In August 2004, Prime Minister Helen Clark visited Tokelau, the first visit in more than 20 years from a New Zealand prime minister. While there she witnessed the signing of a new three-year agreement on economic support. The General *Fono* agreed to explore an option of self-government in free association with New Zealand.
2005 The draft constitution was approved in principle by the May General *Fono*, with a further round of talks to be held in all three villages. Agreement was reached on main elements of the Treaty of Free Association, such as the continued right of Tokelauns to New Zealand citizenship and future economic support, including support for the International Trust Fund (ITF). A referendum (the Self Determination Referendum) on the Treaty is set for February 2006.

Political structure
Constitution
Under the 1948 Tokelau Islands Act (through which New Zealand was the formal administering authority), Tokelau is within the territorial boundaries of New Zealand and Tokelauans are New Zealand citizens.
The 1948 Act was amended and subordinate legislative power was granted to the General Fono by the Tokelau Amendment Act in 1996.
Form of state
Self-administering territory of New Zealand.
The executive
All executive and administrative functions are in theory vested in the Wellington-based administrator of Tokelau, who is appointed by New Zealand's ministry of foreign affairs. In 1994, these powers were formally delegated to the General Fono (parliament) or to the Council for Ongoing Government of the three *Faipule* (one from each atoll) when the General Fono is not in session.
National legislature
After electoral reforms in 1999, the General Fono comprises 18 delegates, including the three *Faipule* (one from each atoll) and the *Pulenuka* (village mayor) of each of the three atolls. The delegates are elected by universal suffrage for a term of three years. The General Fono is the paramount decision-making body and approves the national budget. Parliament is chaired by the *Ulu o Tokelau* (Head of Tokelau), a position which is rotated annually among the three *Faipule*, who together form the Council of *Faipule*.
Legal system
The villages have the statutory power to enact their own laws covering village affairs.
Civil and criminal jurisdiction is exercised by commissioners and the New Zealand high court.
There is little crime apart from petty theft and there are no prisons. Punishment generally takes the form of public rebukes, fines or labour.

Tokelau

Last elections
January 2005 (General *Fono*)
Next elections
2008 (General *Fono*)

Political parties
There are no organised political parties.

Political situation
Devolution has come to Tokelau, even if the population isn't completely convinced it wants it. Since the 1970s New Zealand has been attempting to devolve powers to its last colony, this Polynesian territory 30 hours sailing time on the only ferry which visits. The latest initiative, the 'Modern House of Tokelau', begun in 2002, and which has led to the Treaty of Free Association, devolved power to the *Taupulega* (village council) giving it status and a range of responsibilities for local matters. The three villages, on the three atolls, now run all public services and administer political order. The *Taupulegas* each send delegates to the General *Fono*, which deals with international issues, so that individual and communal aspirations are considered together.

To fund the changes and provide for future development the governments of New Zealand and Tokelau contribute to the International Trust Fund (ITF), which at the end of 2004 stood at over US$11 million. The ITF, being built up until 2009, will then be used to generate revenue to maintain and expand Tokelau's prospects and offer a safety net against the frequent natural disasters it experiences, such as cyclones. Tokelauans fear that they will be unable to sustain themselves without the current grants in annual subsidies of over US$15 million supplied by New Zealand, and funds from the UN Development Programme.

Population
1,500 (2004). Some 6,000 Tokelauans live in New Zealand.
Ethnic make-up
The residents are mainly Polynesians, with close links to Samoa.
Religions
Christianity

Education
Each atoll has its own school with classes beginning at pre-school and carrying through to Year 10. The Year 11 class is hosted on a different atoll every five years and is made up of students combined from each atoll. After graduation from school, the top eight or 10 students are given a scholarship for further study overseas. Staff members are qualified teachers, usually from Samoa, Fiji and New Zealand.

Health
Tokelau has two doctors, one dentist, eight nurses and three midwives. Tokelau collaborates with the World Health Organisation (WHO) in health promotion projects. There are hospitals on Atafu, Fakaofo and Nukunono.
Life expectancy: 69 years (2003)

Main cities
Fakaofo (estimated population 540 in 2003), Atafu (140), Nukunonu (90).

Languages spoken
Official language/s
Tokelauan (English also spoken)

Media
Press
There is a bi-monthly publication *Tugaki a Nukunonu* in English and Tokelauan providing local news and features council meetings of elders and other events in the village.
Broadcasting
Radio: Radio broadcasts include one AM and one FM station.
Television: There are no television broadcasts on the islands.

Economy
The economy is based on communal subsistence, agriculture and fishing. The atolls' size, isolation and lack of land-based resources allow little scope for economic development.
Sales of licences to fish for tuna, postage stamps, souvenir coins, handicrafts and remittances from migrant workers are the principal sources of foreign exchange. Grants from New Zealand account for about 80 per cent of expenditure. Funding from the New Zealand bilateral aid programme, the UN Development Programme (UNDP), the South Pacific Commission, the ILO and other international agencies has been the main source of development assistance.
Since 1982, the General Fono has collected a tax on the salaries of public servants unavailable for communal service (called the Community Services Levy) in order to subsidise copra and handicrafts producers, provide honoraria to members of island councils and supplement village projects.
Fees from fishing licences purchased by foreign companies operating within Tokelau's Exclusive Economic Zone raise up to US$700,000 annually.
New Zealand has been devolving powers to Tokelau under the 'Modern House of Tokelau' project, giving each village full responsibility for running all the public services on its atoll. New Zealand's annual subsidies to Tokelau amount to over US$15 million and the UNDP co-ordinates with New Zealand to provide development assistance. The trust fund to which New Zealand and Tokelau have been contributing, stood at over US$11 million at the end of 2004; the fund will be built up until 2009. Tokelauans fear that, without external assistance in future, they will be unable to sustain themselves.
In August 2004, the New Zealand government agreed a grant of nearly US$300,000 towards improving boat access to the islands and a study of improvements to telecommunications. It is estimated that Tokelau's shipping resources will be almost doubled by the funding.

External trade
Imports
Imports are foodstuffs, building materials and fuel.
Exports
Modest exports of stamps, copra and handicrafts.
Main destinations: New Zealand

Agriculture
Farming
The soil is thin and infertile and the land does not rise more than five metres above sea level. Rainfall is erratic and crops are subject to drought and storm damage. The main subsistence crops are coconut and breadfruit, supplemented by pulaka, ta'amu, pandanus, bananas, pawpaw, with experimental crops of cucumbers, tomatoes, beans, cabbage and watermelon. Crop production in 2004 included: 3,000 tonnes (t) coconuts, 61t fruit in total, 300t roots and tubers, 390t oilcrops. Livestock production included: 24t meat in total, 20t pig meat, 5t poultry and 8t eggs.
Fishing
Fishing for tuna, bonito, trevally and mullet supplies the main source of protein for the inhabitants. The clam industry is an area with some potential. The typical annual marine fish catch is 200t.

Industry and manufacturing
Main industries include copra production, woodwork and the manufacture of woven and plaited goods such as hats, mats, bags and fans. The copra industry suffers from volatile world prices.

Tourism
Tokelau is not a tourist destination, but it does attract a small number of visitors. Access is only by cargo vessel from Samoa once a month. The main accommodation is a small hotel. There is opportunity for swimming and snorkelling.

Hydrocarbons
Tokelau has no hydrocarbon reserves and imports all of its fuel needs from New Zealand.

Banking and insurance
The nearest commercial banking services are in Apia, Samoa, although savings

facilities under the control of the administrative officer have been set up on each atoll.

Time
GMT minus 11 hours

Geography
Tokelau comprises three atolls (Atafu, Nukunonu and Fakaofo) lying about 480km (300 miles) north of Samoa in the Pacific Ocean.

Climate
The average mean temperature is 28 degrees Celsius; warmest in May and coolest in July. Rainfall is heavy but irregular. Severe tropical storms are rare, but possible.

Entry requirements
Visa
Tokelau is a dependent territory of New Zealand. Visa requirements are the same as for New Zealand.
A cruising permit must be authorised by the Council of Elders (taupulega) of each island that a yacht wishes to visit. Such permits can be obtained through the Apia Liason Office in Samoa.
Every visitor must pass a simple physical examination to confirm they are free of disease.

Customs
All firearms must be surrendered until departure.

Health (for visitors)
Mandatory precautions
Vaccination certificates required for yellow fever if travelling from infected area.
Advisable precautions
Vaccination for diphtheria, tuberculosis, hepatitis 'A' and 'B', polio, tetanus, typhoid. Rabies is a risk.

Hotels
The Luana Liki Hotel can be found on the atoll of Nukunonu. Prices are approximately NZ$50 per person a day including all meals. There are no hotels on Atafu and Fakaofo, although accommodation can be arranged through local families prior to or upon arrival.

Telecommunications
In August 2004, New Zealand gave a grant of US$300,000 some of which went to fund a study of improvements in telecommunications.
Tokelau has one of the smallest telecommunications networks in the world, and all provided by Telecommunications Tokelau Corporation (TeleTok), a community-owned corporation established in 1996.
Basic local, national and international telecommunications services are provided via a satellite link using the Australian Telstra-designed DAMA-Net.

Social customs/useful tips
Visitors should be considerate of the island's customs, such as paying due respect to all older persons.
Atafu is officially a dry island. Atafu, Fakaofo and Nukunono have only one co-operative store each. Water is scarce everywhere.

Getting there
Air
There are no airfields.
Surface
Only one (public) boat a month visits from Samoa, its nearest neighbour; for the rest of the time this group of isolated atolls, are completely isolated from the rest of the world.
Water: There are no harbour facilities, only small boats may pass through the surrounding reefs, and these passes are too shallow for most yachts. Normally a yacht must anchor on a shelf outside the reef, however conditions are fairly often unsuitable for such anchorage.
There is no limit to the length of stay, however, the Council has the right to ask a yacht to leave if the island's culture, customs, rules or regulations are violated.
Main port/s: Atafu, Fakaofo and Nukunono.

Getting about
National transport
Road: There are no roads and a limited number of vehicles use unpaved tracks.
Water: There is a 50-seat, 19-metre catamaran inter-atoll passenger service, running between Fakaofo, Atafu and Nukunonu atolls.

BUSINESS DIRECTORY
The addresses listed below are a selection only. While World of Information makes every endeavour to check these addresses, we cannot guarantee that changes have not been made, especially to telephone numbers and area codes. We would welcome any corrections.

Telephone area codes
The international direct dialling (IDD) code for Tokelau is +690 followed by subscriber's number.

Other useful addresses
Office for Tokelau Affairs, PO Box 865, Apia, Samoa (tel: (685) 20-822/3).

Tokelau Council of Faipule, PO Box 865, Apia, Samoa (tel: (685) 20-822; fax: 21-761)

Internet sites
General information on Tokelau: www.dot.tk

Government of Tokelau: www.tokelau.org.nz

Tonga

COUNTRY PROFILE

Historical profile
Tonga's dynasty goes back to the tenth century.
1899 Under the Tripartite Treaty, Britain gained control of Germany's rights in Tonga, Niue, and the Solomon Islands in exchange for withdrawing its claim to Samoa.
1965 King Taufa'ahau Tupou IV was crowned.
1992 A Pro-Democracy Movement (PDM) emerged.
1994 The PDM formed the first political party, the People's Party (PP).
1996 In the general election, the PP won a majority of those seats open to popular vote.
1999 The Human Rights and Democracy Movement (HRDM) (formerly the People's Party) won five of the popularly elected nine seats in the Legislative Assembly (HRDM had previously held seven seats).
2000 Prince 'Ulukalala Lavaka Ata was appointed prime minister by the King.
2001 After legislative amendments made by Tonga, the Organisation for Economic Co-operation and Development (OECD) removed Tonga from its blacklist of countries acting as unfair tax havens or associated with money laundering.
2002 In the parliamentary elections, the HRDM won seven of the nine popularly elected seats.
2003 Changes to the constitution were made, giving greater powers to the King and increasing state control of the media.
2004 Royal Tongan Airlines' (RTA) international service collapsed in April after Royal Brunei Airlines repossessed the RTA's sole international passenger jet. In May, a lack of funds forced RTA to halt its inter-island services and liquidators were called in.
2005 In the 16 March parliamentary elections, the HRDM won seven of the nine seats, the same as in 2002, but with the difference that for the first time ever, two of the people's representatives are to become cabinet ministers. Fred Sevele (HRDM) was appointed acting prime minister in April.

Political structure
Constitution
The constitution dates from 1875. Changes to the constitution were made in October 2003, giving greater powers to the King and increasing state control of the media.
Form of state
Hereditary monarchy
The executive
Executive responsibility rests with the king and the prime minister, who is appointed by the king.
National legislature
The Fale Alea (Legislative Assembly) has 30 members, nine members elected for a three-year term in multi-seat constituencies, nine members elected for a three-year term by the nobles, 10 members of the Privy Council and two governors.
Last elections
16 March 2005 (parliamentary)
Results: Parliamentary: the pro-democracy HRDM won seven of the popularly elected nine seats.
Next elections
March 2008 (parliamentary)

Political parties
Ruling party
The pro-democracy Human Rights and Democracy Movement (HRDM)

Political situation
The status of the cabinet and the nobles in parliament has been under attack since the amendments to the constitution restricting freedom of speech was passed in December 2003 and the collapse of the Royal Tongan Airlines in April 2004. Political, public, media and international observers have voiced concerns about the constitutional changes.
Allegations of corruption and mismanagement have been levelled against the government, although respect for the King is almost universal and his reluctance to see more democratic changes means that the role of the royal family in Tongan politics is unlikely to diminish soon.

Population
99,600 (2004)
Ethnic make-up
The population is mainly of Polynesian descent. Only about 300 inhabitants are of European origin.
Religions
The Wesleyan Methodist church is the major denomination.

Education
In June 2005, New Zealand and the World Bank announced their co-operation in a US$10 million project to improve the quality of education in Tonga.
Literacy rate: 98.5 per cent, adult rate (2003)
Compulsory years: 6 to 14.

KEY FACTS

Official name: Kingdom of Tonga

Head of State: King Taufa'ahau Tupou IV (since 1965)

Head of government: Acting Prime Minister Fred Sevele (HRDM) (appointed Apr 2005)

Ruling party: The pro-democracy Human Rights and Democracy Movement (HRDM)

Area: 748 square km (170 islands)

Population: 99,600 (2004)

Capital: Nuku'alofa (on Tongatapu)

Official language: Tongan

Currency: Tongan dollar or Pa'anga (T$) = 100 seniti

Exchange rate: T$1.97 per US$ (Oct 2005)

GDP per capita: US$2,059 (2004)

GDP real growth: 1.00% (2004)

Labour force: 33,908 (2003)

Unemployment: 13.30% (2003)

Inflation: 11.00% (2004)

Balance of trade: -US$61.10 million (2003)

Foreign debt: US$57.50 million (2003)

Visitor numbers: 40,110 (2003)

Nations of the World: A Political, Economic and Business Handbook

Health
In May 2004, a report ranked Tongans the second most obese people in the world. WHO have indicated that this may mask an underlying nutritional deficiency.
Life expectancy: 71.5 years (World Bank)
Fertility rate/Maternal mortality rate: 3.4 births per woman in 2003 (World Bank)
Birth rate/Death rate: 24.5 births and 5.5 deaths per 1,000 people (2003)
Infant mortality rate: 15 per 1,000 live births (World Bank)

Main cities
Nuku'alofa, on Tongatapu (capital, estimated population 24,500 in 2003).

Languages spoken
English is widely spoken. It is used in education and for administrative purposes.
Official language/s
Tongan

Media
Press
In late-2003, the government changed the constitution and brought in two new acts to regulate the media – one dealing with licencing newspapers and the other with who is allowed to own them.
Va'vau Press Limited, the publisher of *Matangi Tonga*, a bi-monthly national news magazine, was refused a licence in February 2004 and *Talaki*, an independent newspaper, was licensed after the appointment of a new editor.
In August 2004, the government approved licences to the *Taimi o Vavau* and to *Dateline News*.
Weeklies: Weeklies are available in both English and Tongan covering local political and economic news. These include *Ko e Kalonikali Tonga/Tonga Chronicle* and *Tonga Times* (bi-weekly) in Tongan and English editions.
Taimi o Tonga is a bi-lingual weekly publication – the government banned *Taimi o Tonga* in 2003, following a March 2002 sedition charge which was later dropped; its licence was re-approved by the government in October 2004.
Periodicals: Periodicals are available in both English and Tongan. *'Eva*, a quarterly tourist magazine, is available free. *Ko e Kele'a* is a bi-monthly bi-lingual publication published by members of the HRDM which provides critical analyses of Tongan economic and political affairs. Others are *Lao & Hia* (fortnightly), *'Ofa ki Tonga*, *Ko e Tohi Fanongonongo* and *Taumu'a Lelei*.

Broadcasting
Radio: Tonga Broadcasting Commission administers radio services heard over a wide geographical area in Tongan and English, with much programming devoted to local interests, culture, etc. There are two radio stations: AM (Tongan) and FM (English).
Television: A private TV station, ASTL-TV3, makes limited broadcasts and A3M-Broadcasting (a religious station) covers Nuku'alofa. The government of Fiji is studying proposals to set up a service serving Fiji, Samoa and Tonga via satellite from a ground station to be built in Fiji. In 2000, the Tonga Broadcasting Commission established an indigenous public television service, Television Tonga.
Advertising
Radio advertising is accepted in Tongan and English.

Economy
Tonga is a small, open economy dependent on the export of agricultural produce (including coconut products), foreign aid and private remittances from abroad to offset its regular trade deficit.
One of the main problems facing Tonga is job creation. There are 2,000 school-leavers per year, but only 500 find jobs and few can emigrate. Unemployment and underemployment are creating social problems.
The collapse of Royal Tongan Airlines (RTA) in April 2004 had an adverse affect on the whole economy, as the only realistic means of arrival is by air. The collateral damage to tourist facilities and local economies of the outlying islands has resulted in recession for them.
Other areas of possible development include offshore oil, fish and vegetable canneries and coconut-based industries. Offshore banking is growing rapidly. Anti-corruption measures are a central part of the economic reform programme.
Agriculture, one of the mainstays of Tonga's economy, picked up in 2003. The economy will remain heavily dependent on foreign remittances from Tongans working abroad and due to the weakness of the Tongan currency, consumer price inflation will remain high.

External trade
The proposed accession of Tonga to the World Trade Organisation (WTO) started in 1995. To this end, Tonga has signed bilateral market access agreements with Australia, the EU, New Zealand and Japan, and in January 2005, signed a bilateral trade agreement with China.
Imports
Main imports are foodstuffs, machinery and transport equipment, fuels and chemicals.
Main sources: New Zealand (46.7 per cent total, 2004), Fiji (21.1 per cent), Australia (10.3 per cent), US (6.7 per cent)
Exports
Main exports are agricultural produce – squash, vanilla beans, root crops and fish.
Main destinations: Japan (51.4 per cent total, 2004), US (24.9 per cent), India (4.1 per cent)

Agriculture
Farming
Agriculture and fishing accounts for around 35 per cent of GDP and employs around half the labour force. The soil is generally fertile, but production can suffer from hurricane damage.
All land is held by the Crown and every adult male Tongan is entitled to a small-holding (alienation of land is forbidden). Two-thirds of the kingdom's families raise their own livestock (pigs and poultry) and subsistence crops of manioc, yams, breadfruit, watermelons, tomatoes, cassava, oranges and capsicum. Coconut, vanilla and bananas are produced for export, as is the tranquiliser ingredient, kava.
Cash crops include squash and vanilla crops and aloe vera, which has become a popular crop among farmers as it has a viable export market and there is a new processing plant in Nuku'alofa.
Crop production in 2004 included: 58,000 tonnes (t) coconuts, 3,500t citrus, 3,700t taro, 130t vanilla, 9,000t cassava, 4,400t yams, 9,800t fruit in total,

KEY INDICATORS — Tonga

	Unit	2000	2001	2002	2003	2004
Population	m	0.10	0.10	0.10	0.10	*0.10
Gross domestic product (GDP)	US$bn	0.12	0.14	0.14	0.24	*0.21
GDP per capita	US$	1,235	1,424	1,320	2,200	2,059
GDP real growth	%	6.2	0.5	1.6	1.9	–
Inflation	%	5.3	6.9	10.4	10.0	11.0
Total reserves minus gold	US$m	27.0	26.1	27.7	42.6	58.3
Foreign exchange	US$m	24.6	23.8	25.1	39.8	55.3
Exchange rate	per US$	1.80	2.12	2.20	1.90	1.97

* estimated figure

Tonga

26,550t vegetables in total, 7,564t oilcrops, 6,000t sweet potatoes, 2,000 roots & tubers, 20,000 squash, 3,000t plantains, 15t coffee, 250t spices, 1,100t melons. Livestock production included: 2,180t meat in total, 342 beef, 1,496t pig meat, 25t goat meat, 317t poultry, 28t eggs, 370t milk, 12t honey.

Fishing
Fishing provides additional food and export revenue. Seaweed is in big demand, particularly from Japanese buyers. The typical annual marine fish catch is over 4,000t, plus over 300t of other seafood.

Forestry
Old coconut tree trunks fulfil up to 25 per cent of timber needs. In 2003 forest exports amounted to US$158,000 and imports amounted to US$2.6 million. Production in 2003 included 2,100 cubic metres (cum) industrial roundwood, 2,009cum sawnwood, 91,000cum wood fuel.

Industry and manufacturing
The industrial sector accounts for 12.7 per cent of GDP and employs approximately 7.0 per cent of the workforce. There is a thriving small-industries centre on a mini-industrial area in Nuku'alofa where most of the more advanced products are made. Annual industrial production is almost US$20 million per annum. Manufacturing accounts for 8 per cent of GDP and employs 5 per cent of the labour force. The wide range of products includes shoes, saddles, footballs, knitwear, wooden toys, corrugated iron, plastic piping, bicycle assembly, wire netting, paper, paint, biscuits and processed milk, pulp and passion fruit processing, dumper truck bodies and mini-excavators.

Tourism
Tourism is an important economic activity and foreign exchange earner, but still relatively underdeveloped. There is potential for expansion and efforts are being made to upgrade the infrastructure. Several hundred yachts visit the harbour annually, boosting the local economy by an estimated US$500,000 per annum. The main market is New Zealand, followed by Australia and the US.
Air visitor arrivals, which include holiday visitors, those visiting friends and relatives as well as those visiting for business or to attend a conference, rose by 10 per cent in 2003 to a record high of 40,110. The sector was dealt a heavy blow in 2004 when Royal Tongan Airlines collapsed. This is particularly serious as the only realistic means of arrival is by air.

Mining
The US Geological Survey has found huge undersea sediment-filled basins that could hold oil deposits near Tonga, the Solomon Islands and Papua New Guinea. German and Russian researchers have discovered copper and zinc deposits off Tonga.

Hydrocarbons
Tonga has no hydrocarbon resources and is entirely dependent on imports from New Zealand. Tonga does not import gas or coal.

Banking and insurance
Main financial centre
Nuku'alofa.

Time
GMT plus 13 hours

Geography
Tonga comprises 172 islands in the south-western Pacific Ocean, about 650km (400 miles) east of Fiji. The Tonga (or Friendly) Islands are divided into three main groups – Vava'u, Ha'apai and Tongatapu. Only 36 of the islands are permanently inhabited.

Climate
From May–November, temperatures are relatively cool and reach between 11–29 degrees Celsius (C). December–April is the wet season, with temperatures reaching 32°C and high humidity. Average rainfall is 1,700mm per year, but varies from place to place.

Entry requirements
Passports
Required by all. Must be valid six months from date of entry. Visitors must hold a valid return ticket to a country that they will be able to enter.
Visa
Tourists and business persons may enter for a period not exceeding 30 days providing that the visitor holds onward/return passage and proof of adequate funds. If visitors wish to extend their stay, permission must be requested locally from the Principal Immigration Officer.
Currency advice/regulations
No restrictions on import and export of local and foreign currency.
Customs
Visitors should not attempt to bring arms or drugs into the kingdom. Otherwise, no restrictions on personal goods. Imports from some countries may require an import licence or be subject to temporary control.
Prohibited imports
Quarantine is required for all imported live animals and plants.

Health (for visitors)
Mandatory precautions
Vaccination certificate for yellow fever if travelling from an infected area.
Advisable precautions
Vaccination for diphtheria, tuberculosis, hepatitis 'A' and 'B', polio, tetanus, typhoid. To avoid Dengue fever insect repellent should be worn at all times, especially during the early morning and evening. There is rabies risk.

Hotels
Information regarding various types of tourist accommodation is available in Nuku'alofa and throughout the islands from the Tonga Visitors' Bureau.

Public holidays
Fixed dates
1 Jan (New Year's Day), 25 Apr (Anzac Day), 4 May (Crown Prince's Birthday), 4 Jun (Independence Day), 4 Jul (King Taufa'ahau Tupou IV's Birthday), 4 Nov (Constitution Day), 4 Dec (Tupou I Day), 25 Dec (Christmas Day), 26 Dec (Boxing Day).
Variable dates
Good Friday, Easter Monday.

Working hours
Sunday is widely observed as a day of rest, with work, sports and transport services forbidden.
Banking
Mon–Fri: 0930–1530; Sat: 0900–1200.
Business
Mon–Fri: 0800–1700; Sat: 0800–1200.
Government
Mon–Fri: 0830–1630.
Shops
Mon–Fri: 0800–1700; Sat: 0800–1200.

Telecommunications
Telephone/fax
Telephone system is fully automatic with 24-hour international communications via Cable and Wireless satellite earth station.

Electricity supply
240V AC.

Weights and measures
Metric system.

Social customs/useful tips
It is customary to shake hands on meeting and taking leave. Those meeting for the first time are addressed by their title and family name. Tongans address each other by their first name. Gratuities are not encouraged or customary.
Appointments should be made in advance. Business cards are exchanged after introduction. Tongans appreciate modesty in dress, casual attire is recommended for most occasions. Beachware is only acceptable at the beach and not in general public places. It is an offence to appear in public without a shirt. Drunkenness is frowned upon; alcohol consumption may be restricted. The minimum drinking age is 18 years.

Nations of the World: A Political, Economic and Business Handbook

Getting there

Air
National airline: Air Fiji provides international access since Royal Tongan Airlines collapsed in 2004.
International airport/s: Fua'amotu International, Tongatapu (TBU), 15km south-east of Nuku'alofa; bank, duty-free shop and car hire. Taxis and buses available to centre.
Airport tax: International departures include a passenger service charge of T$25; not applicable for transit passengers.

Surface
No regular passenger services to the kingdom, but berths may be available on cruise ships visiting Nuku'alofa and Vava'u. Main ports are at Nuku'alofa (on Tongatapu), Neiafu (on Vava'u), Pangai (on Lifuka), Ha'apai.

Getting about

National transport
No public transport, shipping or air services operate into, out of, or on Tonga on Sundays.
Air: Airlines Tonga, a new domestic carrier and Peau 'o Vava'u Airways operate inter-island flights. The Royal Tongan Airlines cancelled its domestic flights in May 2004.
Road: Total road network about 400km, of which 190km are on Tongatapu. Some 80–90 per cent of total bituminised. Horses are often used for transport.
Buses: Buses (or trucks) serve all parts of Tongatapu from Nuku'alofa.
Water: Various shipping lines operate inter-island ferry services. The principal service leaves Nuku'alofa in the afternoon and arrives the following morning in Ha'apia, at Hafeva then Pangia, then goes on to Vava'u; by mid afternoon it retraces its route back to Nuku'alofa. There is no need for advance bookings, schedules may change at short notice due to weather conditions. Charter yachts are available.

City transport
Taxis: Private taxis are for hire. Fares should be agreed before undertaking a journey.

Car hire
Self-drive or chauffeur-driven cars are available. International or national driving licence must be presented to the Police Traffic Department in Nuku'alofa to obtain local driving licence.
Speed limits of 40kph in towns and 65kph in country areas are enforced. Driving is on the left.

BUSINESS DIRECTORY

The addresses listed below are a selection only. While World of Information makes every endeavour to check these addresses, we cannot guarantee that changes have not been made, especially to telephone numbers and area codes. We would welcome any corrections.

Telephone area codes
The international direct dialling (IDD) code for Tonga is +676 followed by subscriber's number.

Useful telephone numbers
Police: 992
Fire: 999
Ambulance: 933

Chambers of Commerce
Tonga Chamber of Commerce, Tungi Arcade, PO Box 1704, Nuku'alofa (tel: 25-168; fax: 26-039; e-mail: chamber@kalianet.to).

Banking
Bank of Tonga; PO Box 924, Nuku'alofa (tel: 23-933; fax: 23-634).
MBf Bank Limited, PO Box 3118, Nuku'alofa, Taufa'ahau Rd, Nuku'alofa (tel: 24-600; fax: 24-662).
National Reserve Bank of Tonga (NRBT); PO Box 25, Nuku'alofa (tel: 24-057; fax: 24-201).
Tonga Development Bank; PO Box 126, Nuku'alofa, Fatafehi Rd, Nuku'alofa (tel: 23-333; fax: 23-775).

Central bank
National Reserve Bank of Tonga, Queen Salote Road, PO Box 25, Nuku'alofa, Tonga (tel: 24-057 fax: 24-201; e-mail: nrbt@reservebank.to).

Travel information
Flight information (0630-1930 hours Mon-Sat) (tel: 32-088).
Fua'amotu International Airport, Ministry of Civil Aviation, PO Box 845, Nuku'alofa (tel: 32-001; fax: 32-003).
Tourist information (tel: 32-060).

National tourist organisation offices
Tonga Visitors' Bureau, PO Box 37, Nuku'alofa (tel: 23-507, 21-733; fax: 22-129; internet: http://www.vacations.tvb.gov.to).

Ministries
Ministry of Civil Aviation, PO Box 845, Nuku'alofa (tel: 32-001; fax: 32-003).
Ministry of Labour, Commerce and Industries, Salote Road, PO Box 110, Nuku'alofa (tel: 23-688; fax: 23-887).
Office of Prime Minister, Ministry of Agriculture, Fisheries and Forestry, Ministry of Marine, Nuku'alofa (tel: 21-300).

Other useful addresses
Asian Development Bank (ADB), South Pacific Regional Mission, La Casa di Andrea, Fr. Dr. W. H. Lini Highway; PO Box 127, Port Vila (tel: +678 2 23-300; fax: +678 2 23-183; adbsprm@adb.org; internet: http://www.adb.org/SPRM).

Internet sites
Government of Tonga: http://pmo.gov.to
Tonga information website: http://www.tongatapu.net.to

Trinidad and Tobago

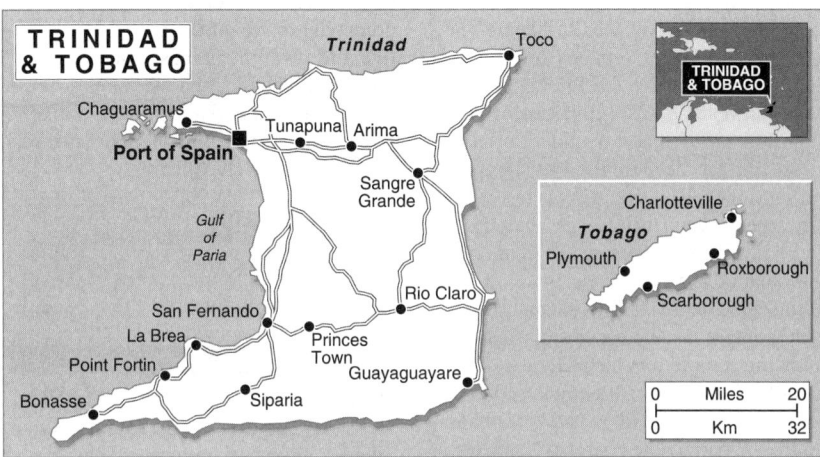

KEY FACTS

Official name: Republic of Trinidad and Tobago

Head of State: President Maxwell Richards (inaugurated 17 Mar 2003)

Head of government: Prime Minister Patrick Manning (PNM) (since Dec 2001)

Ruling party: People's National Movement (PNM)

Area: 5,128 square km

Population: 1.30 million (2004)

Capital: Port-of-Spain

Official language: English

Currency: Trinidad and Tobago dollar (TT$) = 100 cents

Exchange rate: TT$6.28 per US$ (Oct 2005)

GDP per capita: US$9,084 (2004)

GDP real growth: 6.20% (2004)

Labour force: 620,000 (2004)

Unemployment: 10.40% (2004)

Inflation: 3.90% (2004)

Oil production: 155,000 bpd (2004)

Balance of trade: US$2.02 billion 2004

Foreign debt: US$2.80 billion (2003)

Trinidad and Tobago is a democratic republic based on a mixture of the British Westminster model and the French political system. The political machinery of the country includes the positions of president and prime minister. The president's major task is to select the prime minister based purely on election results and to this end the selection is usually an uncontroversial decision based on electoral arithmetic. Though the presidency is normally purely a ceremonial role the present incumbent, Professor George Maxwell Richards, has made several outspoken remarks as to the increasing level of crime being recorded in the country.

Manning's second term

Patrick Augustus Mervyn 'anning is currently serving his second term as Prime Minister of Trinidad and Tobago having won the premiership as leader of the conservative People's National Movement party (PNM) in 2001. Manning's first term commenced in 1991 and he gambled on electoral success one year prior to the constitutional requirement to call elections. Against a backdrop of rising crime, Manning had lost the 1995 election, after which he became Leader of the Opposition.

Five years later, in 2000, Manning contested the election as opposition leader and lost to the governing United National Congress party (UNC). Manning remained as official opposition leader and fought the 2001 general election in which he and his party won 18 seats, tying with the ruling UNC. Former president Arthur Robinson then broke spectacularly with parliamentary procedure when he appointed Manning as prime minister. Manning proceeded to govern without a majority in parliament into 2002, until a state of legislative paralysis ensued. With the necessity of passing the national budget, Manning called a general election in 2002, which the PNM subsequently won.

Ever since, Manning's government has been the subject of allegations of incompetence, occasional corruption and unmasked nepotism. The prime minister came under heavy fire when he appointed his senator wife, Hazal Manning, to the post of minister of education. In addition, five members of his party are currently under investigation on charges of administrative malpractice, while there have been overt suggestions that high profile members of the Manning administration – minister of works Franklin Kahn and minister of energy Eric Williams – received bribes in return for political favours. In November 2005, Kahn, who is also the current president of the ruling PNM, was seperately charged on several counts of misbehaviour in public office. Earlier in the year, in June, it was rumoured that three serving government members were under investigation by the United States Drug Enforcement Administration (USDEA).

On the policy front, the Manning government has been unable to halt the rapidly increasing level of crime in the country, though in fairness this problem has been growing for many years. Manning however, has exacerbated the political crisis surrounding the rise in kidnappings and violent crime by claiming, on the record, that crime is not a problem in present day Trinidad and Tobago. Other policy measures include a reduction in income tax prompted by increasing oil and gas export revenues that have swelled the treasury and thus reduced the government's fiscal burden. Free university education has also been reintroduced. In August 2005, Manning offered his own solution to a pressing socio-economic problem – that of high fertility rates in poor areas of the country. He told his fellow citizens to 'buy a television... and keep looking at the programmes until you fall asleep', so as to occupy themselves and ensure they refrain from any other activities!

Hydrocarbons power growth

Trinidad and Tobago has traditionally been heavily dependent on the production of oil and natural gas, with its economy significantly influenced by the fluctuations of oil and gas prices. The country is the only significant exporter of oil and gas in the Caribbean region, apart from Venezuela on the mainland. The sector accounts for around 40 per cent of GDP. Rising oil prices since 2003 have boosted the nation's economy, while at the same time distorting it, leaving the non-oil sectors lagging behind.

The sustained growth allows for further diversification in the economy, which has centred on information technology and financial services, sectors which have grown in other parts of the Caribbean. The hydrocarbons sector remains one of the most attractive areas for foreign investment however. The government announced in 2004 that it would vigorously pursue further development of Trinidad and Tobago's oil and natural gas reserves.

In recent years, natural gas has overtaken oil in importance to the economy. The country has proven reserves of 740 billion cubic metres. Liquefied natural gas (LNG) output has increased significantly, following completion in 2002 and 2003 of major facilities by the Atlantic LNG Company of Trinidad and Tobago (jointly-owned by the National Gas Company of Trinidad and Tobago, BP-Amoco, British Gas, Suez and Repsol). LNG is exported to the US and Spain for use in electricity, industry and petrochemical production. Trinidad and Tobago is expected to rank as the fifth largest producer of LNG in the world by 2006.

Outlook

The economy of Trinidad and Tobago boomed in 2005 and is set to continue growing quickly throughout 2006. High oil and gas prices on international markets have been the major driver of growth. With geopolitical conditions being shaky in many parts of the oil producing world, the country looks set to benefit from a continuing bull market in energy commodities. The IMF has forecast growth of 6.3 per cent for 2005 and very strong growth of 10.1 per cent for 2006. Though these potential growth rates are extremely positive, the government must continue to implement diversification measures so as to guard against a possible, though unlikely, downturn in international energy markets over the next twelve months.

Risk assessment

Politics	Poor
Economy	Good
Regional stability	Good

COUNTRY PROFILE

Historical profile
1498 Trinidad was sighted by a Spanish expedition led by Christopher Columbus.
1532 The island was colonised by the Spanish.
1595 Spanish colonisers were defeated by an English fleet under Sir Walter Raleigh.
1630s The Dutch settled on Tobago and created sugar plantations.
1763 Trinidad was occupied by France, with Spanish consent.
1781 The French seized Tobago.
1797 Trinidad was seized by the British during the Napoleonic wars.
1802 Trinidad was officially transferred to British sovereignty.
1814 Tobago became a British colony of the Windward Island group.
1834 Slavery was abolished and indentured workers were brought in from India to work on the sugar plantations.
1889 Tobago was amalgamated with Trinidad and together the islands became a unified British colony.
1945 Universal suffrage was granted.
1956 Eric Williams founded the People's National Movement (PNM).
1958 Trinidad and Tobago became part of the British-sponsored West Indies Federation.
1959 Britain gave Trinidad and Tobago internal self-government with Williams as prime minister.
1962 When Jamaica opted to leave the Federation, Trinidad and Tobago followed, becoming independent within the Commonwealth.
1967 Trinidad and Tobago joined the Organisation of American States (OAS).
1968 Anglophone Caribbean states, including Trinidad and Tobago, formed the Caribbean Free Trade Area (Carifta),

KEY INDICATORS — Trinidad and Tobago

	Unit	2000	2001	2002	2003	2004
Population	m	1.29	1.29	1.30	1.30	0.00
Gross domestic product (GDP)	US$bn	7.30	8.90	9.40	10.50	*12.54
GDP per capita	US$	6,186	6,758	7,255	7,355	9,084
GDP real growth	%	4.0	3.5	5.2	6.7	6.2
Inflation	%	3.5	3.2	3.8	3.7	3.9
Unemployment	%	12.1	11.1	11.0	10.2	–
Oil output	'000 bpd	135.0	135.0	162.0	163.0	155.0
Natural gas output	bn cum	12.6	12.9	16.8	24.8	27.7
Exports (fob) (goods)	US$m	4,220.0	4,159.0	4,060.0	5,256.0	6,671.0
Imports (fob) (goods)	US$m	3,557.0	3,552.0	3,110.0	3,922.0	4,650.0
Balance of trade	US$m	663.0	607.0	1,100.0	1,334.0	2,021.0
Current account	US$m	379.0	553.0	350.0	1,351.0	–
Foreign debt	US$bn	2.2	2.1	2.5	2.8	–
Total reserves minus gold	US$m	1,386.3	1,907.1	2,027.0	2,451.1	3,168.2
Foreign exchange	US$m	1,386.2	1,876.0	1,923.5	2,257.8	2,993.0
Exchange rate	per US$	6.30	6.23	6.16	6.15	6.15

* estimated figure

Trinidad and Tobago

which became the Caribbean Community and Common Market (Caricom) in 1973.
1970 A state of emergency was declared after the army mutinied against the minority East Indian population.
1972 The state of emergency was lifted.
1976 On 1 August, Trinidad and Tobago became a republic within the Commonwealth. The PNM won the September parliamentary elections. Ellis Clarke, previously the governor general, was sworn in as the country's first president in December and Eric Williams became prime minister.
1981 Williams died and George Chambers became prime minister.
1986 The PNM lost power – its first defeat since 1957. The Tobago-based National Alliance for Reconstruction (NAR), led by Arthur Robinson, won a decisive victory in the general election.
1987 Noor Hassanali became president.
1990 More than 100 Islamic extremists staged an uprising, blowing up the police headquarters, seizing parliament and holding Prime Minister Robinson and several senior officials hostage. The coup attempt was short-lived.
1991 The NAR lost the December general election to the PNM. Patrick Manning became prime minister.
1995 The Asian-dominated United National Congress (UNC) won most seats in the general election and formed a coalition government with the support of the NAR. Basdeo Panday became prime minister.
1999 Trinidad and Tobago restored the death sentence.
2000 The ruling UNC narrowly won the general election.
2001 The UNC lost its majority and Basdeo Panday's government was brought down. In the December elections the UNC and the PNM each won 18 seats and formed a coalition. Patrick Manning (PNM) was sworn in as prime minister on 24 December. However, Panday abandoned the coalition agreements, paralysing the country.
2002 Prime Minister Patrick Manning's PNM won the general election.
2003 Maxwell Richards was inaugurated as president on 17 March.

Political structure
Constitution
The constitution was adopted in 1976.
Form of state
Republic
The executive
Executive power is divided between the president, who is the head of state, and the prime minister, who is the head of government.

The president is elected every five years by an electoral college made up of members of both houses of parliament.
The prime minister, who has a cabinet composed of members of parliament, is usually the leader of the majority party in the House of Representatives.
National legislature
The parliament is bicameral. The House of Representatives has 36 members elected by universal suffrage for a five-year term. The Senate consists of 31 members appointed by the president: 16 on the prime minister's advice, six on the advice of the leader of the opposition and nine chosen exclusively by the president.
Legal system
An independent judiciary is guaranteed by the constitution. Foreign investors have the same rights as Trinidad and Tobago citizens.
The Supreme Court is the highest legal body. Civil trials are handled by a single judge in the high court without a jury. Decisions made by the high court can be presented for appeal to the three-judge court of appeal. Court of appeal decisions can be appealed to the regional Caribbean Court of Justice (CCJ), which was inaugurated on 16 April 2005, replacing the privy council in London as the highest court of appeal.
Last elections
14 February 2003 (presidential); 10 December 2001 (parliamentary).
Results: Presidential: Maxwell Richards was elected by the Electoral College. Parliamentary: the People's National Movement (PNM) won 20 seats out of 36 and the United National Congress (UNC) 16 seats.
Next elections
2006 (parliamentary); 2008 (presidential).

Political parties
Ruling party
People's National Movement (PNM)
Main opposition party
United National Congress (UNC)

Population
1.30 million (2004)
Ethnic make-up
Black (43 per cent), East Indian (40 per cent), mixed (14 per cent), white (1 per cent), Chinese (1 per cent).
Religions
Roman Catholics (34 per cent), Hindus (30 per cent), Protestants (19 per cent), Muslims (10 per cent).

Education
In 2000, the adult illiteracy rate was estimated at 1.1 per cent and 2.4 per cent respectively for men and women. Primary schooling lasts for seven years followed by secondary, academic and technical or vocational qualifications. World Bank estimates show that the total primary school enrolment of the relevant age group typically stood at 99 per cent for boys and 98 per cent for girls (including repetition rates) between 1994–2000. The number of pupils per primary school teacher is typically 25. Public expenditure on education typically amounted to 3.6 per cent of annual gross national income between 1994–97.
A University of Trinidad and Tobago, costing US$100.00 million, is expected to open in 2006. British Petroleum (BP) donated US$10 million towards construction of the university which will be founded as a charitable trust by the government.
Compulsory years: Five to 11
Pupils per teacher: 25 in primary schools

Health
In 2002, 88 per cent of children were immunised against measles before aged one year; this figure dropped from a high of 91 per cent in 2001. Improved water sources are available to 86 per cent of the population.
Total expenditure on health is around 4 per cent of GDP, of which government spending is 44 per cent.
HIV/Aids
The prevalence rate is relatively high, although the number of deaths due to Aids between 2001–03 did not increase significantly, from an estimated 1,500–1,900. There were 29,000 people living with HIV at the end of 2003, of which 700 were children (aged 0–14). Research among young adults (15-24) showed that 95 per cent knew that a healthy–looking person could be HIV positive, and 33 per cent knew of at least two prevention methods and three myths concerning the disease.
HIV prevalence: 0.1 per cent aged 15–49 in 2003 (World Bank)
Life expectancy: 72 years (World Bank)
Fertility rate/Maternal mortality rate: 1.8 births per woman in 2003 (World Bank). Anaemia is common among 53 per cent of pregnant women.
Birth rate/Death rate: 8 deaths and 13 births per 1,000 people (World Bank)
Infant mortality rate: 17 per 1,000 live births (World Bank)
Head of population per physician/bed: 0.8 physicians and 5.1 hospital beds typically available for 1,000 people.

Welfare
Trinidad and Tobago operates social insurance and social assistance systems that were implemented in 1999. The 1999 law ensures state provision for employees, domestic and agricultural workers, but does not cover self-employed workers. Social assistance covers residents aged 65 or older or aged 40 years for those with special needs, based on a means-test.

Old age pensions are available to men aged 60–65 and above with 750 weeks of contribution and compulsory retirement. The state also operates a welfare system for benefits covering sickness, maternity, medical provision for workers and family allowance, including a food subsidy. Medical care is available in public hospitals and health offices and centres for recipients of means tested pensions. Trinidad and Tobago is experiencing a rise in social problems related to young people, despite the economy's improved performance. Restricted access to the secondary education system and unemployment (which reached 30 per cent for the 15–19 age group in 2001), poverty and reduced family care have contributed to youth involvement in crime and drug abuse.

Main cities
Port of Spain (capital, estimated population 45,300 in 2003) is the commercial centre and main port of entry; San Fernando (60,600) is the chief town in south Trinidad and the centre of the oil industry; Arima (28,900) is east of Port of Spain, increasingly industrialised. Scarborough (estimated population 4,500) is the main town and port of Tobago.

Languages spoken
Hindi is commonly spoken within the East Indian community.
Official language/s
English

Media
Press
There are three daily newspapers, including *Trinidad and Tobago Express* and *Trinidad Guardian*, one bi-weekly and eight weeklies. Two major evening papers are *Evening News* and *The Sun*.
Broadcasting
Radio: There are 10 radio stations.
Television: There are three television stations plus US cable channels. Commercial television operated by state-owned Trinidad and Tobago Television Company (TTT), Channel 6 (CCN) and Channel 4 (AVM).

Economy
Trinidad and Tobago has traditionally been heavily dependent on the production of oil and natural gas, with its economy significantly influenced by the fluctuations of oil and gas prices. The country is the only significant exporter of oil and gas of the Caribbean islands. The sector accounts for around 40 per cent of GDP. Rising oil prices since 2003 have boosted the nation's economy, while at the same time distorting it, leaving the non-oil sectors lagging behind. The sustained growth allows for further diversification in the economy, which has centred on information technology and financial services, sectors which have grown in other parts of the Caribbean.
The hydrocarbons sector remains one of the most attractive areas for foreign investment. The government announced in 2004 that it would vigorously pursue further development of Trinidad and Tobago's oil and natural gas reserves. Trinidad and Tobago has a strong tourism industry, but the agricultural sector is in decline.

External trade
Trinidad and Tobago is a member of the Caribbean Community and Common Market (Caricom) which comprises a common market and customs union.
Imports
Principal imports include machinery, transport equipment, manufactured goods, foodstuffs and live animals
Main sources: US (24.6 per cent total, 2004), Venezuela (12.0 per cent), Germany (10.8 per cent), Spain (7.0 per cent), Italy (5.5 per cent), Brazil (5.0 per cent)
Exports
Principal exports include crude oil and petroleum products, natural gas, chemicals, steel products, fertiliser, sugar, cocoa, coffee, citrus and flowers.
Main destinations: US (66.7 per cent total, 2004), Jamaica (5.7 per cent), France (3.5 per cent)

Agriculture
Farming
About 23 per cent of the total land area is farmed. Although there is abundant rainfall, it is unevenly distributed, some areas becoming waterlogged, thereby curtailing production. Only 3 per cent of arable land is irrigated. About 60 per cent of the country's agriculture is in private hands and 40 per cent is controlled by the government.
The farming of major cash crops (sugar, coffee, cocoa and citrus fruits) has slumped owing to labour shortages, diseases and falling export demand. Output declined by 18 per cent in 2003 and by 20.2 per cent in 2004. Sugar production fell by 25.2 per cent in 2003 and by 42.7 per cent in 2004, due partly to poor quality canes and bad weather, as well as structural problems. Unfavourable weather also adversely affected coffee and cocoa production. Citrus production recovered in 2004 after a bad 2003.
The Agricultural Development Bank (ADB), which is primarily government-owned, provides loans to farmers and finances about 85 per cent of the country's agricultural development.
The Agricultural Development Corporation is charged with developing the agricultural sector. The sector is also the subject of an investment incentive programme, involving tax exemptions for approved projects. Other measures include a US$21 million four-year repair and rehabilitation programme for roads and more funding for water management and flood defence systems.
Crop production in 2004 included: 680,000 tonnes (t) sugar cane, 6,300t cereals in total, 4,800t taro, 3,300t maize, 1,600t yautia, 950t cassava, 3,000t rice, 6,800t bananas, 4,500t plantains, 3,535t pulses, 8,865t roots and tubers, 18,000t coconuts, 13,250t citrus fruit, 4,200t pineapples, 2,340t oilcrops, 1,800t tomatoes, 2,100t eggplants, 180t tobacco, 1,300t cocoa beans, 530t green coffee, 66,730t fruit in total, 23,300t vegetables in total. Livestock production included: 61,470t meat in total, 825t beef, 2,970t pig meat, 75t lamb and goat meat, 57,600t poultry, 3,700t eggs, 10,000t milk, 44t honey.
Fishing
The country does not have a large commercial fishing industry, but relies on small private fishermen whose production does not meet domestic demand. The fishing sector is an important local source of food.
Forestry
Forests cover around one-third of the total land area. Deforestation accounted for an average annual loss of 0.9 per cent, equivalent of 2,000 hectares of forest cover, in 1990–2000. The country has a well-developed commercial forests industry, based primarily on the harvesting of teak and Caribbean pine. Some three-quarters of the wood is used for industrial purposes, and the rest is used for fuel and charcoal. It produces modest quantities of industrial round timber and sawn timber. Much of the domestic demand is met by imports of sawn timber, wood-based panels and paper products. The import of forest materials in 2003 amounted to US$118.6 million, while exports totalled US$1.3 million.
Production in 2003 included: 95,254 cubic metres (cum) roundwood, 60,000cum industrial roundwood, 43,000cum sawnwood, 60,000cum sawlogs and veneers, 35,254cum wood fuel, 1,862t charcoal.

Industry and manufacturing
Trinidad and Tobago is the most industrialised of the Caribbean islands. The industrial sector typically contributes 44 per cent of GDP, of which manufacturing contributes 8 per cent. Development since the 1970s has centred on heavy export-oriented industries, which are geared towards maximising the country's energy resources.

Trinidad and Tobago

The principal manufactured products include refined petroleum, petrochemicals, nitrogenous fertilisers, iron, steel, methanol, plastics, sugar, and various import-substitution products. The growth of the petrochemicals sector has helped offset the effects of a decline in the sugar industry.

Manufacturing output increased by 5 per cent in 2003 and by 6.6 per cent in 2004, partly as a result of more favourable international economic conditions, particularly in other Caricom countries.

Tourism

Trinidad and Tobago is unusual in the Caribbean in not being dependent on tourism. The sector's contribution to GDP for 2005 is forecast at 2.4 per cent. The sector's potential as a means of economic diversification is recognised and the sector is being encouraged and promoted, especially in Tobago, where it is the only industry. Because Trinidad and Tobago is geographically less susceptible to the effects of hurricanes than many of its neighbours, its tourism receives a boost when other Caribbean nations endure harsh weather conditions. The sector provides employment for 34,000 people.

Visitor numbers, which had risen steadily until 2000, fell back for a couple of years due to conditions in the US. Recovery was delayed until 2003, when air arrivals rebounded to a record 409,007 arrivals. Overall figures were nonetheless down, because cruise ship business collapsed from 104,000 passengers to 55,532, a trend which was repeated in 2004.

Whereas the stay-over market has benefited from increased air capacity, the decline in the cruise ship sector follows a reduction in services to the southern Caribbean.

Infrastructure is improving and air routes to Europe and the US are being expanded. The US is the principal market, followed by the Caribbean and the UK.

Mining

Trinidad and Tobago's mining sector revolves around the petroleum industry. Asphalt and pitch sand are extracted. Other minerals quarried include diorite, limestone, argillite clay and porcelainite. The world's largest supply of natural asphalt is found in La Brea on Trinidad.

Hydrocarbons

Trinidad and Tobago is well-endowed with oil and natural gas resources, which make a major contribution to the economy. The sector accounts for 25 per cent of GDP and 75 per cent of the country's export earnings. Rising world prices since 2003 encouraged increased exploration, reversing a decline in oil production. Trinidad and Tobago has proven reserves of 990 million barrels.

Natural gas has overtaken oil in importance to the economy. Trinidad and Tobago has proven reserves of 740 billion cubic metres. Liquefied natural gas (LNG) output has increased significantly, following completion in 2002 and 2003 of major facilities by the Atlantic LNG Company of Trinidad and Tobago (jointly-owned by the National Gas Company of Trinidad and Tobago, BP-Amoco, British Gas, Suez and Repsol). LNG is exported to the US and Spain for use in electricity, industry and petrochemical production. Trinidad and Tobago is expected to rank as the fifth largest producer of LNG in the world by 2006.

A pipeline from Trinidad and Tobago to Martinique and Guadeloupe, connecting several other Caribbean islands, is being planned.

Trinidad and Tobago does not produce or import coal.

Energy

The electricity sector was previously a state monopoly, but since 1994, a joint venture – Powergen – between the government, Amoco, and the Southern Electric Company of Atlanta, operates at a peak of 700MW but has capacity of 1,178MW.

Banking and insurance

The country has a number of international and domestic commercial banks including Citibank, Royal Bank and Scotia Bank.

Central bank
Central Bank of Trinidad and Tobago

Main financial centre
Port of Spain

Time

GMT minus four hours

Geography

Trinidad and Tobago lies in the Caribbean Sea off the eastern coast of Venezuela. Trinidad is the larger of the two islands, Tobago lies 32km north-east of Trinidad. The terrain of Trinidad is principally flat, although three ranges of higher land – peaking at almost 1,000 metres – cross the island from west to east.

Climate

The islands have a humid, tropical climate with a rainy season from June to December, and an annual temperature range between 21 and 32 degrees Celsius.

Dress codes

Dress is generally informal and suited to the hot tropical climate. Men generally wear a shirt and tie for business meetings.

Entry requirements

Passports
Required by all, except nationals of other Caricom countries, for whom other forms of identification such as ID cards and driver's licences are sufficient.

Visa
Required by all who are not exempt; a full list can be found at www3.itu.int/MISSIONS/Trinidad-Tobago/visa_information_final.html. Business travellers should submit an employer's letter stating credentials with the visa application form.

Currency advice/regulations
Travellers must not import or export more than TT$20,000 local currency. Foreign currency up to US$5,000 in value can be imported or exported. Amounts in excess of this limit must be declared on arrival and departure. Traveller's cheques are accepted.

Prohibited imports
Illicit drugs, weapons and explosives, specific animals (including monkeys and mongoose), animals that have died on transit, products used in relation to certain animals (such as used animal blankets and saddles) as well as dung may not be brought into Trinidad and Tobago.

Health (for visitors)

Mandatory precautions
Yellow fever vaccination certificate if arriving from infected area.

Advisable precautions
Yellow fever, hepatitis 'A', polio and tetanus vaccinations are advisable. Water precautions should be taken.

Hotels

A limited range of hotels is available in Trinidad and Tobago. They are generally expensive, although less so in Tobago. A 10 per cent tip is usual. A hotel room tax (in properties of 16 rooms or over) of 10 per cent has replaced value-added tax. Book well in advance if arriving during Carnival time.

Credit cards

Credit cards are accepted.

Public holidays

Fixed dates
1 Jan (New Year's Day), 30 Mar (Spiritual Baptist Shouters' Liberation Day), 30 May (Indian Arrival Day), 19 Jun (Labour Day), 1 Aug (Emancipation Day), 31 Aug (Independence Day), 24 Sep (Republic Day), 25–26 Dec (Christmas Holiday).

Variable dates
Good Friday, Easter Monday, Corpus Christi (May/Jun), Diwali (Hindu, Oct/Nov), Eid al Fitr.

Working hours

Carnival (two-day event immediately preceding Ash Wednesday) is usually taken as an unofficial holiday.

Banking
Mon–Thu: 0800–1400; Fri: 0800–1200, 1500–1700.

Business
Business hours are 0800–1600.
Government
Mon–Fri: 0815–1630.
Shops
Mon–Fri: 0800–1630; Sat: 0800–1200. Supermarkets stay open later in the evenings and are open all day Saturday. Some open on Sunday. Some close on Thursday afternoon.

Telecommunications
Telephone/fax
Although national and international phone access is widely available, the cost of calls is more expensive in Trinidad and Tobago than in most countries in the Caribbean.
Postal services
Airmail to Europe and the US takes one to two weeks.
Courier services
The islands are served by the major international courier companies.
Mobile phones
Telecommunications Service of Trinidad and Tobago (TTST) dominates the cellular phone market.

Electricity supply
Domestic: 115 and 230V AC, 60 cycles. Industrial: 400V, 60 cycles three-phase.

Weights and measures
Metric system legally in use since 1981, but many traders continue to use the imperial system.

Social customs/useful tips
Both the social and business environment in Trinidad and Tobago are friendly and informal, and it is common to be on a first-name basis with people whom you have met before.

Security
The last major instance of political violence was in 1990, and the islands are generally a safe place to visit. The usual precautions against pickpockets should be taken in crowded areas.

Getting there
Air
National airline: BWIA International (Trinidad & Tobago Airways)
International airport/s: Port of Spain-Piarco (POS), 25km east of city; duty-free shop, bar, restaurant, bank, post office, shops, car hire.
Crown Point International, Tobago.
Airport tax: International departure tax and security fee of TT$100; excluding transit passengers.
Surface
Water: Port of Spain, Point Lisas and Point-à-Pierre are the principal ports with cruise ships berthing at Port of Spain.

Main port/s: Trinidad: Chaguaramas, Point Lisas, Port of Spain. Tobago: Scarborough.

Getting about
National transport
Air: There are flights approximately every half-hour operated by BWIA between Port of Spain and Tobago. Regional airline Carib Express (20 per cent owned by British Airways) based at Barbados.
Road: There is an extensive road network of around 8,000km. Major highways run north-south and east-west. Traffic jams are common.
Buses: Cheap and generally crowded.
Water: The two islands are connected by regular ferries and car ferries, from Port of Spain (Trinidad) to Scarborough (Tobago). The journey time is about six hours. The passage can be uncomfortable.
City transport
Taxis: Shared, route taxis are widely used. Routes with standard fares operated by passenger cars bearing 'H' registration plates and two-coloured Maxi Taxis (yellow stripe in Port of Spain). Negotiate fares for regular taxis in advance. Limousine service available at airport. Taxis can be hired by distance, by the hour or by the day.
Car hire
National driving licences of most countries accepted for a period of three months from arrival. Insurance required. Cars drive on left. The maximum speed limit is 80kph on highways.

BUSINESS DIRECTORY
The addresses listed below are a selection only. While World of Information makes every endeavour to check these addresses, we cannot guarantee that changes have not been made, especially to telephone numbers and area codes. We would welcome any corrections.

Telephone area codes
This international direct dialling code for Trinidad and Tobago is +1-868 followed by subscriber's number.

Useful telephone numbers
Police	999
	623-5191
Fire	990
Ambulance	990
	625-3222/3

Chambers of Commerce
American Chamber of Commerce of Trinidad and Tobago, Trinidad Hilton Hotel and Conference Centre, Lady Young Road, Port of Spain (tel: 627-8570; fax: 627-7405; e-mail: inbox@amchamtt.com).

British-Caribbean Chamber of Commerce, Chamber Building, Columbus Circle, West Moorings, PO Box 499, Port of Spain (tel: 637-6966; fax: 637-7427; e-mail: info@britishcaribbean.com).

Caribbean Association of Industry and Commerce, Trinidad Hilton Hotel and Conference Centre, Lady Young Road, PO Box 442, Port of Spain (tel: 623-4830; fax: 623-6116; e-mail: caic@trinidad.net).

Greater Chaguanas Chamber of Industry and Commerce, Kibon House, 1 Endevour Road, Chaguanas (tel/fax: 671-5754; e-mail: admin@chaguanaschamber.com).

South Trinidad Chamber of Industry and Commerce, Cross Crossing Shopping Centre, Lady Hailes Avenue, PO Box 80, San Fernando (tel: 657-9077; fax: 652-5613; e-mail: execoffice@southchamber.com).

Trinidad and Tobago Chamber of Industry and Commerce, Chamber House, Columbus Circle, West Moorings, PO Box 499, Port of Spain (tel: 637-6966; fax: 637-7425; e-mail: chamber@chamber.org.tt).

Banking
Agricultural Development Bank of Trinidad and Tobago, PO Box 154, Port of Spain (tel: 623-6261/5, 625-6539; fax: 624-3087).

Bank of Commerce, PO Box 69, Port of Spain (tel: 627-9325/8; fax: 627-0904).

Bank of Nova Scotia, The Scotia Building, 56–58 Richmond Street, Port of Spain (tel: 625-3566/5222; fax: 623-0256).

Citibank, PO Box 1249, 12 Queen's Park East, Port of Spain (tel: 625-6445/9, 625-1046/9; fax: 624-8131; 625-6820).

Citicorp Merchant Bank, 12 Queen's Park East, Port of Spain (tel: 623-3344; fax: 624-8131).

CLICO Investment Bank, 1 Rust Street, St. Clair, Port of Spain (tel: 628-3628; fax 628-3639).

First Citizens Bank, Park & Henry Streets, Port of Spain (tel: 623-2423, 623-2576/8; fax: 627-5956).

Republic Bank Ltd, PO Box 1153, Port of Spain, Trinidad (tel: 625-3611, 623-0371; fax: 623-0371); Corner Wilson and Castries St, Scarborough, Tobago (tel: 639-2561).

Royal Merchant Bank & Finance Company, 7th Floor, 55 Independence Square, Port of Spain (tel: 625-3511, 624-5212).

The Royal Bank of Trinidad and Tobago, Head Office, Royal Court, 19-21 Park

Trinidad and Tobago

Street, Port of Spain (tel: 623-4291, 625-3764; fax: 624-4866).

Central bank
Central Bank of Trinidad and Tobago, PO Box 1250, Eric Williams Plaza, Independence Square, Port of Spain (tel: 625-4835; fax: 627-4696; e-mail: info@central-bank.org.tt; internet: www.central-bank.org.tt)

Travel information
Cruise Ship Complex, Port of Spain (tel: 627-4477).

Piarco International Airport (tel: 664-5196).

Tourist Information Office, Crown Point Airport (tel: 639-0509).

Tourist Information Office, Piarco Airport (tel: 669-5196).

U.K. Information Office for Trinidad and Tobago, Unit 12 TIDCO Mall, Sangster's Hill, Scarborough (tel: 639-4333; fax: 639-4514).

Ministry of tourism
Ministry of Tourism, Port of Spain (tel: 625-0741).

National tourist organisation offices
Tourism and Industrial Development Company of Trinidad and Tobago Ltd (TIDCO), 10-14 Phillips Street, Port of Spain (tel: 623-1932/4; fax: 623-3848); e-mail: tourism-info@tidco.co.tt.

Ministries
Ministry of Communications and Information Technology, Kent House, Long Circular Road, Maraval (tel: 628-1323; fax: 622-4783).

Ministry of Community Empowerment, Autorama Building, El Socorro Road, San Juan (tel: 675-6728; fax: 674-4021).

Ministry of Consumer Affairs, Agostini Compound, 3 Duncan Street, Port of Spain (tel: 623-7741; fax: 625-4737).

Ministry of Culture, Algico Building, Jerningham Avenue, Queen's Park East, Port of Spain (tel: 625-3012; fax: 625-3278).

Ministry of Education, Hayes Street, St Clair (tel: 622-2181; fax: 628-7818).

Ministry of Energy and Energy Industries, Level 9, Riverside Plaza, Corner Besson & Piccadilly Streets, Port of Spain (tel: 623-6708; fax: 623-2726).

Ministry of Enterprise Development, Level 15, Riverside Plaza, Corner Besson & Piccadilly Streets, Port of Spain (tel: 623-2931; fax: 627-8488).

Ministry of the Environment, Level 16, Eric Williams Finance Building, Independence Square, Port of Spain (tel: 627-9700; fax: 625-1585).

Ministry of Finance, Level 8, Eric Williams Finance Building, Independence Square, Port of Spain (tel: 627-9700; 627-6108).

Ministry of Food Production and Marine Resources, PO Box 389, St Clair Circle, St Clair (tel: 622-1221; 622-8202).

Ministry of Foreign Affairs, Knowsley Building, 1 Queen's Park West, Port of Spain (tel: 623-4116; fax: 627-0571).

Ministry of Health, Corner Duncan Street & Independence Square, Port of Spain (tel: 627-0012; fax: 623-9528).

Ministry of Housing and Settlements, NHA Building, Corner George Street & South Quay, Port of Spain (tel: 624-5058; fax: 625-2793).

Ministry of Human Development, Sacred Heart Building, 16-18 Sackville Street, Port of Spain (tel: 624-2000; fax: 625-7003).

Ministry of Infrastructure Development, Corner Richmond & London Streets, Port of Spain (tel: 625-1225; fax: 625-8070).

Ministry of Integrated Planning and Development, Level 14, Eric Williams Finance Building, Independence Square, Port of Spain (tel: 623-4308; fax: 623-8123).

Ministry of Labour, Manpower Development and Industrial Relations, Level 11, Riverside Plaza, Corner Besson & Piccadilly Streets, Port of Spain (tel: 623-4241; fax: 624-4091).

Ministry of Legal Affairs, 72-74 South Quay, Port of Spain (tel: 625-4586; fax: 625-9803).

Ministry of Local Government, Kent House, Long Circular Road, Maraval (tel: 628-1325; fax: 622-7410).

Ministry of National Security, Temple Court, 31-33 Abercromby Street, Port of Spain (tel: 623-2441; fax: 625-3925).

Ministry of Sport, ISSA Nicholas Building, Corner Frederick & Duke Streets, Port of Spain (tel: 625-5622; fax: 623-4507).

Ministry of Tourism, 45 St Vincent Street, Port of Spain (tel: 627-0002; fax: 625-6404).

Ministry of Transport, Corner Richmond & London Streets, Port of Spain (tel: 625-1225; fax: 627-9886).

Office of The Attorney General, Cabildo Chambers, Corner Sackville & St Vincent Streets, Port of Spain (tel: 623-7010; fax: 625-0470).

Office of The Prime Minister, Whitehall, Maraval Road, Port of Spain (tel: 622-1625; fax: 622-0055).

Other useful addresses
Businessmen's Association of Trinidad and Tobago, PO Box 322, Time Plaza, Room 10, 28 Henry Street, Port of Spain (tel: 623-4568).

Caribbean Employers' Confederation, 43 Dundonald Street, Port of Spain (tel: 625-4723).

Caribbean Industrial Research Institute, O'Meara Industrial Estate, Macoya Road, Trincity, Arima (tel: 662-7161/4; fax: 663-4180).

Export Development Corporation, Export House, 10-14 Phillips Street, PO Box 582, Port of Spain (tel: 623-6022/3; fax: 625-0050).

Industrial Development Corporation, 10-12 Independence Square, PO Box 949, Port of Spain (tel: 623-7291/6, 623-7289).

Management Development Centre, Room 212, Salvatoria Building, PO Box 1301, Port of Spain (tel: 623-4951/3).

National Gas Company of Trinidad and Tobago Limited, Goodrich Bay Road, Point Lisas Industrial Estate, Point Lisas (tel: 636-4662; fax: 679-2384).

Petroleum Company of Trinidad and Tobago Limited (PETROTRIN), Administrative Building, Southern Main Road, Pointe-à-Pierre (tel: 658-4200, 658-4230; fax: 658-1315; e-mail: petroweb@petrotrin.com).

Reinsurance Company of Trinidad and Tobago, Trinre House, 52 Jerningham Avenue, Belmont, PO Box 1087, Port of Spain (tel: 623-6194/6602; fax: 624-4021).

Small Business Association of Trinidad and Tobago, Third Floor, MPU Building, 3 Besson Street, Port of Spain (tel: 624-3666).

Shipping Association of Trinidad and Tobago, Room 12a, 64-66 South Quay, Port of Spain (tel: 623-8570).

Telecommunications Services of Trinidad and Tobago Ltd (TSTT), 54 Frederick Street, PO Box 971, Port of Spain (tel: 624-5756/5703; fax: 625-4585; e-mail: tsttceo@tstt.net.tt).

Tourism & Industrial Development of Trinidad and Tobago Ltd (TIDCO) (foreign investment proposals), 10-14 Phillips Street, Port of Spain (tel: 623-6022/3, 623-3561/3, 623-1932/4; fax: 625-0837; e-mail: trade-info@tidco.co.tt or invest-info@tidco.co.tt).

Tobago House of Assembly, (Foreign Investment Proposals in Tobago), Bacolet Street, Scarborough.

Trinidad and Tobago Development Finance Co Ltd, PO Box 187, 8-10 Cipriani Boulevard, Port of Spain (tel: 623-4665/7, 625-4666/8; fax: 624-3563).

Trinidad and Tobago Embassy (USA), 1708 Massachusetts Avenue, NW, Washington DC (tel: 202-467-6490; fax: 202-785-3130; e-mail: embttgo@erols.com).

Trinidad and Tobago Export Trading Company Limited, Level 4 Long Circular Mall, Long Circular Road, St. James (tel: 622-7968; fax: 628-2349).

Trinidad and Tobago Manufacturers' Association, 8 Stanmore Avenue, Port of Spain (tel: 623-1029/31, fax: 623-1031).

Internet sites

Government website: http://www.gov.tt

Information on economic trends, investment opportunities, infrastructure, news and events: http://www.tidco.co.tt/

Petroleum Company of Trinidad and Tobago Ltd: http://www.petrotrin.com

Prime Minister's Office: http://www.opm.gov.tt

Statistics Office: http://www.cso.gov.tt

Telecommunications Services of Trinidad and Tobago Ltd: http://www.tstt.net.tt

Tourism and Industrial Development Company (TIDCO): http://www.tidco.co.tt

Trinidad and Tobago company database: http://tradepoint.tidco.co.tt/ttcdbase/

Tristan da Cunha

COUNTRY PROFILE

Historical profile
1506 The island was sighted by the Portuguese admiral, Tristão da Cunha, on his way to the East Indies.
1810 The first settlers arrived but failed to establish a permanent community.
1816 The island was annexed by Britain and a garrison established to provide additional security for Napoleon who was incarcerated on St Helena.
1817 The garrison was withdrawn but Corporal Glass elected to stay on the island with his wife to guard the remaining stores and incidentally found the community.
The community gradually developed during the nineteenth century and for a time became relatively prosperous with frequent calls by American whalers in the 1850s. The seven families represented four nations – Britain, Holland, US and Italy. With the decline of sail the island became increasingly isolated and impoverished; sometimes several years passed without a ship calling. The only contact with the outside world was provided by an irregular succession of pastors and a very occasional passing ship.
1938 The island became a dependency of St Helena.
1942 A garrison and radio/meteorological station was established.
1949 The island's extreme isolation ended with the establishment of the crawfish industry.
1950s An official currency, the British sterling, was introduced.
1961 The volcano erupted and the community was evacuated, returning some two years later to re-establish the settlement.
1981 The 1981 Nationality Act ended the islanders' British citizenship and right of abode.
1999 The Nationality Act came under review in the UK government's 'Partnership for Prosperity and Progress' White Paper.
2000 Development of the crawfish industry ended Tristan's dependence on the UK and gave the islanders economic confidence.
2001 The island was hit by a hurricane which inflicted considerable damage.
2003 A report in April said that Tristan's fishing industry had considerable potential for development, providing the necessary infrastructure was put in place by the government.
2004 In January, Tristan da Cunha received a new fire engine paid for by the British government.

Political structure
The Tristan da Cunha archipelago comprises the main island as well as Inaccessible and Nightingale Islands. Gough Island, to the south-east, also comes under Tristan administration. Tristan is the only inhabited island, although there is a meteorological station on Gough Island, maintained by the South African navy. Although technically under St Helena, the island effectively administers itself independently. In May 2002, full British citizenship was granted to the inhabitants of Tristan da Cunha.
Responsibility for Tristan da Cunha, as a British Overseas Territories, is divided between the FCO and the Department for International Development (DfID). The post of Minister for Overseas Territories within the FCO has been created and an Overseas Territories Consultative Council set up. The Council heldd its first annual meeting in 1999.

Constitution
Form of state
As a British Overseas Territory Tristan da Cunha is a dependency of St Helena.
The executive
Executive authority is exercised by an administrator appointed by the FCO, who acts as chairman of the Island Council (three nominated members, eight elected, two ex-officio members; one member must be a woman), which meets six times a year. A chief islander is also elected by the local population to act on a three-yearly basis.
Last elections
November 2003
Next elections
November 2006

Population
300 (2003)
Ethnic make-up
English, Scottish, Irish, Dutch and Italian.

Main cities
Edinburgh of the Seven Seas (capital, estimated population 270 in 2003).

Languages spoken
Official language/s
English

KEY FACTS

Official name: Tristan da Cunha

Head of State: Queen Elizabeth II, represented by Governor David J Hollamby (resides in St Helena)

Head of government: Administrator Mike Hentley (since May 2004)

Area: 98 square km

Population: 300 (2003)

Capital: Edinburgh of the Seven Seas

Official language: English

Currency: Pound sterling (£) = 100 pence

Exchange rate: £0.57 per US$ (Oct 2005)

GDP per capita: US$2,644 (2003)*

* estimated figure

Media
Press
News from Tristan can be obtained from the news websites www.tristantimes.com and www.sartma.com).
The St Helena, Ascension and Tristan da Cunha Philatelic Society publishes the periodical *South Atlantic Chronicle* (formerly *St Helena, Ascension, and Tristan da Cunha Philatelic Society Newsletter*) with news of the latest stamp printing that depicts detailed descriptions of the region's political and economic developments.

Economy
Tristan's economy is based on crawfish (rock lobster), philatelic sales and by sales of handicrafts which are increasingly imported ready-made.

Since the opening of the first crawfish cannery and freezing plant in 1949, the economy has been transformed from subsistence, sometimes near starvation level, to self-sufficiency.

The annual crawfish catch is limited to 340 tonnes, of which 145 tonnes comes from the main island and the balance from the fisheries around Gough, Nightingale and Inaccessible Islands. An agreement was signed with a New Zealand company for catching Patagonian toothfish. Revenue from the industry more than adequately covers the island's running costs and has allowed reserves to be built up. These provided a buffer against the decline in Far Eastern demand.

Other economic activities are hampered by poor access with only about 60 days per year suitable for landing. A new harbour has improved conditions and permits more regular visits particularly by small yachts. Tristan's fresh water is considered to have special properties and there are plans to develop a mineral water export business.

A hurricane in 2001 devastated the only settlement on the island and severely damaged its prosperity. The British government allocated US$106,000 to help the island recover from the disaster.

Plans for a new jetty are going ahead; this is urgently required for the future development of the tourism and fishing industries.

Agriculture
Farming
The cultivated area is estimated at no more than 15 hectares. Potatoes are the main crop. Cattle, sheep and poultry are kept. Each married couple is allowed to graze seven sheep and two cows on settlement land, or any number on the plateau.

Each family grows potatoes on about an acre of ground. Potatoes were first introduced to the island in 1816 when the first settlers arrived and have been grown on the same land each year without rotation; they are easily grown in volcanic soil.

Fishing
Tristan da Cunha's fisheries zone is rich in unique species – rock lobsters, wreckfish, Tristan red scorpion fish, Tristan wrasse and Atlantic amberjack.

The economy is based on crawfish (rock lobster). Fish provide a major source of protein.

Hydrocarbons
Tristan da Cunha does not have any hydrocarbon reserves and relies entirely on imports of refined oil to meet domestic demands.

Time
GMT

Geography
The island of Tristan da Cunha is in the South Atlantic Ocean, 2,400km (1,500 miles) west of Cape Town, South Africa. It comes under the jurisdiction of St Helena 2,100km (1,300 miles) to the north-east. Also in the group are Inaccessible Island 32km (20 miles) west of Tristan; the three Nightingale Islands 3km (20 miles) south; and Gough Island (Diego Alvarez) 350km (220 miles) south.

Climate
Tristan da Cunha has a mild, temperate climate. Temperatures range from 3–25 degrees Celsius. The average annual rainfall is 1,700mm.

Entry requirements
Visa
None required, but visitors must have permission of the Island Council and Administrator to land; this is normally granted. All visitors must have onward/return passage; full medical insurance including emergency evacuation; and sufficient funds for a visit. A small landing fee is charged.

Hotels
There is no hotel accommodation on the island.

Working hours
Government
Mon–Fri: 0830–1230, 1300–1630.

Telecommunications
Telephone/fax
The Administrator's office and the factory in Tristan have satellite communications by telephone and fax.
There is a radio telephone link via Cape Town Radio.

Postal services
In August 2005 Tristan da Cunha was given its own postal code: TDCU 1ZZ. It is expected that this will speed up the time for post deliveries and allow residents to access online shopping services.

Getting there
Air
Surface
Water: The harbour is too small for ships to berth. Passengers are normally ferried to land in small boats and landing is not guaranteed. Improvements to the harbour are vital to the economy.

The RMS *St Helena* makes an annual visit. The ship is operated under contract by Andrew Weir Shipping Ltd on behalf of the owners, St Helena Line Ltd.

Premier Fishing operates two fishing boats, the *Kelso* and the *Edinburgh*, which make irregular connections between Tristan and Cape Town.

The South African Navy operates the *Agulhas* to approximate sailing dates, mainly for official personnel.

Yachts call frequently and offer an alternative means of reaching the island, as does the occasional cruise ship.

BUSINESS DIRECTORY

Telephone area codes
The international direct dialling (IDD) code for Tristan de Cunha is +874 (satellite) followed by subscriber's number.

Travel information
Travel information (for air travel and bookings on the RMS St Helena):

Passenger Services Department, Andrew Weir Shipping Ltd, Dexter House, 2 Royal Mint Court, London EC N4XX, UK (tel: +44 (0)207-575-6480; fax: +44 (0)207-575-6200; e-mail: reservations@aws.co.uk; internet site: http://www.aws.co.uk).

Premier Fishing, PO Box 181, Cape Town 8000, South Africa. (tel +27-21-4190124).

St Helena Line, Andrew Weir Shipping (SA) Pty Ltd, 3rd Floor, BP Centre, Thibault Square, Cape Town, South Africa (tel: +27-21-425-1165; fax: +27-21-421-7485; e-mail: sthelenaline@mweb.co.za).

Miss Kerry Yon, Solomon and Co plc, Jamestown, St Helena, South Atlantic (tel: +290-2523; fax: +290-2423; e-mail: solco.shipping@helanta.sh).

Ministries
Administrator's Office, Edinburgh of the Seven Seas (e-mail: hmg@cunha.demon.co.uk).

Other useful addresses
The Tristan Resource Centre, Michael Swales, Denstone College, Uttoxeter, Staffs, UK (tel: +44 (0)1538-703-322).

St Helena Desk Officer, Foreign and Commonwealth Office, Room, King Charles Street, London SW1A 2AH, UK (tel: (0)207-270-2695).

Tristan da Cunha

Miles Apart (books, maps, videos on South Atlantic Islands), 5 Harraton House, Exning, Newmarket, Suffolk CB8 7HF, UK (tel: +44 (0)1638-577-627; fax: +44 (0)1638-577-874); 5929 Avon Drive, Bethesda, Maryland 20814, US (tel/fax: +1301-571-8942; e-mail: familycarter@msn.com).

Internet sites

Sartma (South Atlantic Remote Territories Media Association): www.sartma.com

Tristan Times: www.tristantimes.com

Tunisia

KEY FACTS

Official name: Jumhuriya at Tunisiya (Republic of Tunisia)

Head of State: President Zine al Abidine Ben Ali (RCD) (since 1987; re-elected to a fourth five-year term 24 Oct 2004)

Head of government: Prime Minister Mohammed Ghannouchi (since Nov 1999)

Ruling party: Rassemblement Constitutionnel Démocratique (RCD) (Democratic Constitutional Rally) (last re-elected 24 Oct 2004)

Area: 164,150 square km

Population: 9.92 million (Government census 2005)

Capital: Tunis

Official language: Arabic

Currency: Dinar (D) = 1,000 millimes

Exchange rate: D1.34 per US$ (Oct 2005)

GDP per capita: US$2,855 (2004)

GDP real growth: 5.80% (2004)

Labour force: 2.69 million (2003)

Unemployment: 13.90% (2004)

Inflation: 3.60% (2004)

Oil production: 69,000 bpd (2004)

Balance of trade: -US$2.43 billion 2004

Foreign debt: US$13.60 billion (2003)

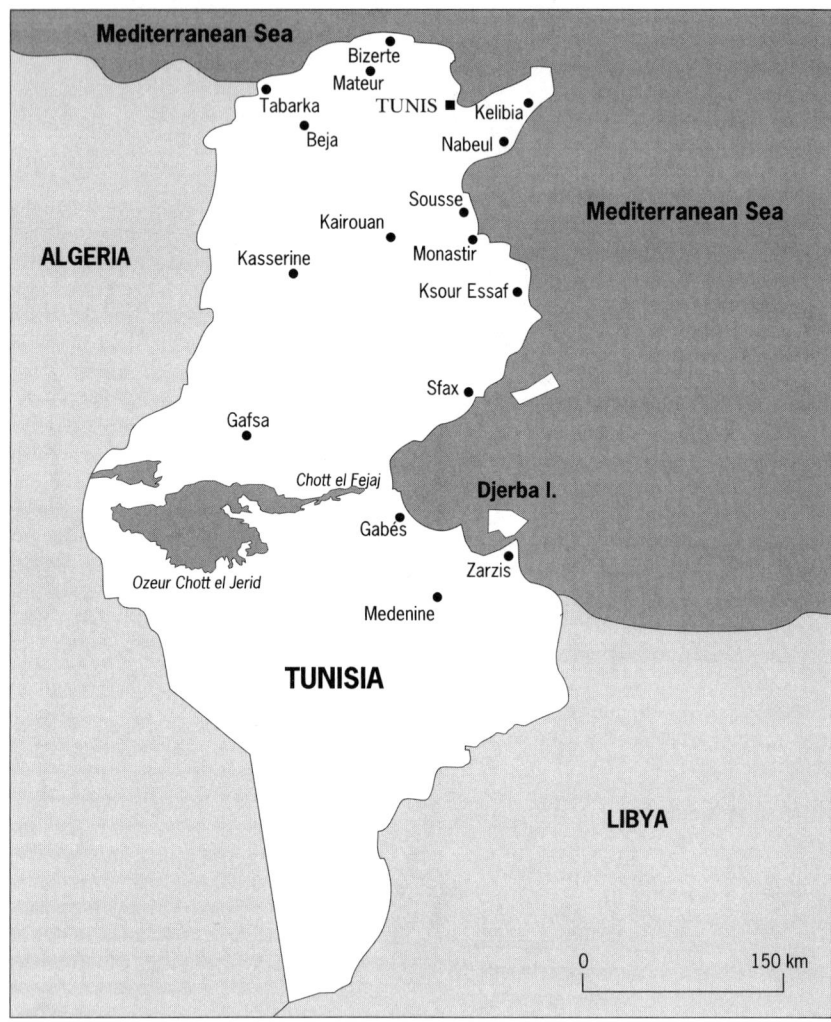

Tunisia has long been important in the Mediterranean. Close to vital shipping lanes, it is of strategic significance. French colonial rule ended in 1956, and Tunisia was led for three decades by Habib Bourguiba, who advanced secular ideas. These included emancipation for women – women's rights in Tunisia are among the most advanced in the Arab world – the abolition of polygamy and compulsory free education. Bourguiba insisted on an anti-Islamic fundamentalist line, but increased his own powers to become a virtual dictator. After 31 years, he was retired on grounds of senility and Zine al Abidine Ben Ali came into office. He will rule at least until 2014, provided he wins the 2009 election.

Although Tunisia has introduced some press freedoms and has freed a number of political prisoners, human rights groups say the authorities tolerate no dissent, although in recent years, it has sought to defuse rising pressure for a more open political society.

Tunisia has a diverse economy, with important agricultural, mining, energy, tourism, and manufacturing sectors. Governmental control of economic affairs, while still heavy has gradually lessened over the past decade with increasing privatisation, simplification of the tax structure, and a prudent approach to debt.

Progressive social policies have helped raise living conditions in Tunisia relative to the region. Tunisia is gradually removing barriers to trade with the European Union. Broader privatisation, further liberalisation of the investment code to increase foreign investment, improvements in government efficiency, and reduction of the trade deficit are among the challenges ahead.

Economy

Tunisia has made significant progress toward its objective of catching up with the economic level of the lower-tier OECD countries. Real per capita income has increased by almost 20 per cent since 2000, the unemployment rate continues to decline, and macroeconomic imbalances remain under control owing to the capacity of the fiscal, monetary, and exchange rate policies to respond rapidly to changing conditions and economic shocks.

Although the growing openness of the economy and market-oriented economic policies have had good results thus far, their benefits could be eroded unless reforms are continued and deepened. An acceleration of reforms is necessary to fully integrate Tunisia into the world market, while maximizing the benefits and controlling the risks of this integration. The main challenge is to accelerate the annual rate of economic growth by at least one to 1.5 per centage points until 2010. Without this additional growth, the authorities' objective of bridging the gap between Tunisia and the OECD countries in terms of per capita income will remain elusive.

The level of private investment, both domestic and foreign, remains low in comparison with more dynamic emerging countries. Weaknesses in the banking and financial sector, particularly the level of nonperforming loans, increases the cost of credit and hampers growth and investment, while at the same time slowing progress toward full convertibility of the dinar and a more dynamic monetary policy.

In the short term, the management of anticipated privatisation receipts and potential balance of payments surpluses are the key macroeconomic challenge.

Real growth should accelerate in 2006 with an upturn in agriculture, an increase in industrial production and activity in the construction sector. Inflation remains under control. The external position is strengthening despite rising oil prices and stagnating demand in Europe. International reserves continue to grow (now more than 3.5 months of imports of goods and services).

External debt remains high, although it should decline considerably in 2006 given the forecast for strong growth and assuming that a portion of privatisation receipts is used to reduce the external debt burden.

The fiscal deficit remains under control despite the impact of higher oil prices. The authorities continued to raise retail petroleum prices in 2005 and further increases are provided for in the 2006 budget. The budget is based on a price of US$60 a barrel and calls for an increase in the fiscal deficit of one-half per centage point to 3.6 per cent of gross domestic product. Financing of the deficit will be through domestic bond issues.

Outlook

The medium term growth target is a 6.2 per cent for the period 2006–10 which the government expects will require an increase in investment of 1.4 per centage points of GDP, an improvement in national savings of 1.8 per centage points of GDP, with a contribution from the government of 1.2 percentage points and a gradual improvement in overall factor productivity. Foreign borrowing should decline in a context of ongoing fiscal consolidation, despite any increased recourse by the private sector to external borrowing to finance its investment.

Risk assessment

Politics	Dictatorial
Economy	Good
Regional stability	Fair

COUNTRY PROFILE

Historical profile

Tunisia was a French protectorate from 1883 until 1955; in 1956 it became independent, ruled by a Bey (the Ottoman term for ruler) and a constituent assembly. In 1957 the assembly abolished the monarchy, proclaimed Tunisia a republic and elected Habib Bourguiba as its first president. The 1959 constitution directed that the presidential and national assembly elections were to take place every five years and that the president may not stand for election for more than three consecutive terms.

Bourguiba, now known as the father of modern Tunisia, stood unopposed for re-election several times, until he was named 'President for Life' in 1974 by a constitutional amendment. The title turned out to be a little optimistic, however, when Bourguiba was ousted by Tunisia's current president and former policeman, Zine al Abidine Ben Ali in 1987. Bourguiba was dismissed on grounds of senility in what became known as the 'doctors' coup'. Tunisia's ruling party, the Rassemblement Constitutionnel Démocratique (RCD) (Constitutional Democratic Assembly) has become accustomed to power, having been the sole legal party for 25 years until 1981. The RCD was originally known as the Partie Destourian Socialiste (PDS) (Socialist Destourian Party).

The strategic significance of Tunisia, situated in the centre of North Africa, close to vital shipping routes, was recognised by the Romans, Arabs, Ottoman Turks and French, making it a hub for control over the region. Tunisia was a French

KEY INDICATORS — Tunisia

	Unit	2000	2001	2002	2003	2004
Population	m	9.56	9.70	9.82	9.90	9.92
Gross domestic product (GDP)	US$bn	19.58	20.00	11.60	25.00	*28.18
GDP per capita	US$	2,046	2,064	1,182	2,186	2,855
GDP real growth	%	4.7	5.0	1.9	4.7	5.8
Inflation	%	2.9	1.9	3.1	2.2	3.6
Unemployment	%	15.3	15.0	15.2	14.7	–
Oil output	'000 bpd	73.0	73.0	78.0	66.0	69.0
Exports (fob) (goods)	US$m	5,840.0	6,606.0	6,860.0	8,027.0	9,679.0
Imports (fob) (goods)	US$m	8,092.0	9,521.0	9,500.0	10,896.0	12,114.0
Balance of trade	US$m	-2,252.0	-2,915.0	-2,640.0	-2,869.0	-2,434.0
Current account	US$m	-821.0	-863.0	-746.0	-738.0	-590.0
Foreign debt	US$bn	10.6	10.4	12.1	13.6	–
Total reserves minus gold	US$m	1,811.0	1,989.2	2,290.3	2,945.4	3,935.7
Foreign exchange	US$m	1,780.9	1,962.2	2,260.2	2,912.9	3,895.0
Exchange rate	per US$	1.37	1.44	1.40	1.28	1.25

* estimated figure

protectorate from 1883 until 1955; in 1956, it became independent, ruled by a monarch (bey – the Ottoman term for ruler) and a constituent assembly. In 1957, the assembly abolished the monarchy, proclaimed Tunisia a republic, and elected Habib Bourguiba as its first president. The 1959 constitution directed that the presidential and national assembly elections were to take place every five years and that the president may not stand for election for more than three consecutive terms. Bourguiba, now known as the father of modern Tunisia, stood unopposed for re-election several times, until he was named 'President for Life' in 1974 by a constitutional amendment. The title turned out to be a little optimistic, however, when Bourguiba was ousted by Tunisia's Zine al Abidine Ben Ali in 1987. Bourguiba was dismissed on grounds of senility in what became known as the 'doctors' coup'.

670 The Arabs conquered Carthage.
1207–1574 After the Arab empire collapsed, Tunisia became part of the Moroccan empire of the Almohads before emerging as the independent Hafsid empire.
1600s The Hafsids were defeated by the Ottomans, who developed a system of rule by a local elite descended from the Turks, the Huseinid beys.
1700s Tunisia became a national monarchy.
1881 France invaded Tunisia from Algeria.
1883 Tunisia was declared a French protectorate.
1930s The Néo-Destour nationalist movement developed under Habib Bourguiba, who was jailed by the French.
1942–43 During the Second World War, German and Italian troops, who came to Tunisia to resist allied forces in Algeria, were driven out by the Allies in 1943.
1956 Tunisia gained independence from France under the leadership of Bourguiba.
1957 The monarchy was abolished and the Republic of Tunisia was declared.
1961–63 The Tunisian government demanded the withdrawal of French troops from Bizerte; fighting broke out between French and Tunisian forces. French forces left Bizerte following an agreement between the French and Tunisian governments in 1963.
1974 A constitutional amendment named Bourguiba 'President for Life'.
1981 The first multi-party parliamentary elections since independence were won by President Bourguiba's party in a landslide victory.
1982–85 The headquarters of the Palestinian Liberation Organisation (PLO) relocated from Beirut to Tunis, where it stayed until it moved to the Palestinian autonomous areas (Gaza and Jericho) in 1994. In 1985, Israel raided the headquarters in revenge for a PLO attack on a yacht in Larnaca, Cyprus.
1987 In conformation with the constitution, Prime Minister Zine al Abidine Ben Ali succeeded President Bourguiba, who was declared by his physicians mentally unfit to rule, due to senility.
1989 President Ben Ali won the presidential election; he was re-elected in 1994; both elections were uncontested.
1999 Ben Ali was re-elected for a third term in the first multi-party presidential elections.
2000 Violence erupted in several towns and cities over increasing levels of poverty and price rises in certain basic commodities.
2002 An al Qaeda terrorist bomb killed 19 people in a synagogue in Djerba. A referendum agreed to abolish the three-term limit for incumbent presidents and to raise the age limit of an incumbent president from 70 to 75.
2004 In May, a two-day summit of Arab leaders was cancelled by the host, Tunisia, for 'differences over political changes'. In October, incumbent Zine al Abidine Ben Ali won 94.5 per cent of the presidential vote, Mohamed Bouchiha won 3.8 per cent. The ruling, Rassemblement Constitutionnel Démocratique (RCD) (Democratic Constitutional Rally), was re-elected with 91.6 per cent of the popular vote.
2005 In July a second parliamentary legislative body, the Chamber of Advisors, was inaugurated with 112 members, drawn from professional bodies, local officials and presidential appointees.

Political structure
Constitution
The constitution was introduced in 1959. Parties must be officially recognised before they can contest elections. Legal opposition parties are guaranteed a minimum of 34 seats in the lower chamber of parliament.
Constitutional amendments in 2002, included unlimited terms of office for the president and a age limit of 75 years and gave the president control over voting procedures and immunity from prosecution for life.
A new second legislative chamber was also agreed.
Form of state
Republic
The executive
Executive power is held by the president, who is also Head of State, elected by universal suffrage for a five-year term. The president sets state policy; he may appoint and dismiss the prime minister. Cabinet members are proposed by the prime minister and endorsed by the president.
The president can serve unlimited terms of office, up to aged 75.
National legislature
The 182-member Chambre des Députés (Chamber of Deputies) is elected for a five-year term by universal adult suffrage. It includes 34 opposition members representing political opposition parties.
The 112-member Chambre des Conseillers (Chamber of Advisors) drawn from professional bodies, local officials and presidential appointees, are appointed for six-year terms.
Legal system
The legal system is based on the French civil law system and Islamic law. There is some judicial review of legislative acts in the Supreme Court.
Last elections
24 October 2004 (presidential and parliamentary)
Results: Presidential: Zine El Abidine Ben Ali was re-elected with 94.5 per cent of the vote, against 3.8 per cent for Mohamed Bouchiha (Popular Unity Party), 1 per cent for Mohamed Ali Halouani (Ettajdid Movement) and 0.8 per cent for Mounir Béji (Social Liberal Party). Turnout was 91.5 per cent.
Parliamentary: ruling RCD, won 152 seats out of 189, the MDS 14, the Popular Unity Party 11, the Unionist Democratic Union seven, the Ettajdid Movement three, and the Social Liberal Party two.
Next elections
2009 (presidential and parliamentary)

Political parties
Ruling party
Rassemblement Constitutionnel Démocratique (RCD) (Democratic Constitutional Rally) (last re-elected 24 Oct 2004)
Main opposition party
Mouvement des Démocrates Socialistes (MDS) (Movement of Democratic Socialists)

Population
9.92 million (Government census 2005)
Ethnic make-up
Arab-Berber (98 per cent), European (1 per cent), other (1 per cent).
Religions
Islam is the state religion – observance is strong (98 per cent); Christianity (1 per cent); Jewish (1 per cent) – there has been a Jewish population on the southern island of Djerba for 2,000 years and there remains a small Jewish population in Tunis which is descended from those who fled Spain in the late fifteenth century.

Education
Education is free up to university level – the government typically spends as much

as 20 per cent of its revenues on an extensive education system. Primary education begins aged six, and lasts for six years. Secondary education begins at 12 and lasts seven years. Registration at primary schools is 95 per cent (100 per cent of boys and 89 per cent of girls) – the highest in north Africa and the Middle East. A compulsory schooling period of nine years has been introduced, although some children still leave school at the age of 12, especially in rural areas. A stronger emphasis has been placed on scientific and technical subjects at secondary level.
Literacy rate: 77.1 per cent in 2004, compared to 68.3 per cent in 1994.
Compulsory years: Six to 16.
Pupils per teacher: 24 in primary schools.

Health
State healthcare is provided free of charge to the families of employees paying social security contributions and at least nominal tax. This covers an estimated 70 per cent of the population. Free state healthcare is also available for those with any kind of disability. The discrepancy between urban and rural access to healthcare diminished during the 1990s, with most rural areas having at least basic health clinics.
There is a well-developed private healthcare sector, with private clinics in towns providing substantially better facilities than state hospitals. Many healthcare professionals have carried out at least part of their training abroad, mostly in France.
HIV prevalence: 0.1 per cent aged 15–49 in 2003 (World Bank)
Life expectancy: 73.2 years (World Bank)
Fertility rate/Maternal mortality rate: 2.0 births per woman (World Bank)
Infant mortality rate: 19 per 1,000 live births; 4 per cent of children under aged five are malnourished (World Bank).

Welfare
The social security system provides pensions for the elderly and disabled, and welfare for orphans and the needy. A total of 945,500 employees, or 47.7 per cent of the workforce, are insured under the social security system. The scheme is financed by compulsory levies from employers and employees. There are no contributions from the state budget. The main social security institution is the Caisse Nationale de la Sécurité Sociale (CNSS) (National Social Security Organisation), which deals with about 45 per cent of outlay.
There is a graded scheme for contributions. The non-agricultural private sector pays most as a proportion of the employee's salary: 11.5 per cent paid by the employer and 6.25 per cent by the employee. In the public sector, where contributions are made to the Caisse Nationale de Retraite et de Prévoyance Sociale (CNRPS) (National Pension Fund), the employer pays 8 per cent and the employee 7 per cent. State pensions are paid to CNSS and CNRPS contributors.

Main cities
Tunis (capital, estimated population 699,700 in 2003), Sfax (270,700), Ariana (217,100), Ettadhamen (188,700), Sousse (155,900), Kairouan (117,700).

Languages spoken
French is the business language. The number of Tunisians speaking English is increasing.
Official language/s
Arabic

Media
Tunis Afrique Press (TAP) is the official news agency and publishes in Arabic, French and English.
Press
The government relies upon direct and indirect methods to restrict press freedom and encourage a high degree of self-censorship. It uses mandatory pre-screening of the print media and controls the advertising revenue to censor 'unacceptable' publications. The constitution guarantees freedom of expression, but the Press Code gives the government wide-ranging powers to ban publications. All opposition party publications have been suspended for varying periods under this code. The Press Code requires that publishers disclose their sources of funding, annual accounts and circulation figures. No group is allowed to control more than 30 per cent of total circulation. In addition, all imported publications must be submitted to government censors.
There are several independent newspapers and magazines, including two opposition party journals.
Dailies: National dailies in French include *Le Renouveau*, *La Presse* and *Le Temps*. Arabic newspapers include *As Sabah*, *Al Nahda*, *Al Horria*, *As-Sahafa* and *Ash-Shourouk*. *Al Horria* is the daily newspaper of the ruling party, Rassemblement Constitutionnel Démocratique (RCD) (Democratic Constitutional Rally), while *As Sabah* is financially independent and supports the opposition Rassemblement Socialiste Progressiste (RSP) (Progressive Socialist Rally). Among the French language newspapers, *Le Temps* is financially independent, unlike the RCD's *Le Renouveau*. International and foreign newspapers are available one day after publication in urban centres, although some issues may be withheld from public sale.

Tunisia

Weeklies: The main French-language weeklies are *Réalités*, *L'Observateur* and *Tunis-Hebdo*. The main Arabic-language weekly is *Ar Rai*. The weekly party publications are the Arabic-language *Al Moustaqbal* and French-language *L'Avenir*, both belonging to the Mouvement des Démocrates Socialistes (MDS) (Movement of Democratic-Socialists). Others are *Dialogue*, *Al Tariq al Jadid* and *Al Mauqif*. *Tunisia News* is an English language weekly in the Maghreb, published on Saturdays.
Business: Economic information is available in *Conjoncture Review*, edited monthly by the Ministry of Economic Affairs, and *L'Economiste Maghrebin*, which is published bi-monthly.
Periodicals: There are also over 140 periodicals and provincial newspapers which are published (91 in Arabic, 45 in French, six in Arabic and French and one in Italian). Another 450 foreign periodicals are also distributed.
Broadcasting
Radio: The national radio station broadcasts in Arabic, while the international station broadcasts mainly in French, with some programmes in Italian, English and German. There are two regional stations, based in Sfax and Monastir.
Television: The government-run Radiodiffusion Télévision Tunisienne, established in 1956, operates two television channels and four radio stations. Channel 1 television broadcasts in Arabic. Channel 2, established in 1983, broadcasts in French. Around 75 per cent of Channel 2's programmes are imported from France. The French network Antenne 2 broadcasts in Tunisia on Channel 2 for several hours per day. 'Hannibal TV', Tunisia's first private satellite television station, started broadcasting on 13 February 2005.
Advertising
Direct mail, outdoor and vehicle advertising, sponsorship of sporting events and print media offer opportunities for advertisers. References to religion are not acceptable. Press advertising tends to be governed by unwritten standards, determined by the publications' editorial policy. Foreign broadcast advertising is even more strictly regulated and advertising rates in the broadcast media are highly discriminatory, standing at three or four times the rate for domestic advertisers. Urban centres in Tunisia are thought to have a marketing profile similar to that of Europe.

Economy
International observers have commended Tunisia on its economic performance in the last few years. It has moved into the middle-income category, one of the few

developing countries in the region to have achieved this, with a sovereign credit rating of BBB.

The economy has been under slow and steady reform since the 1980s, when the state had a greater influence and bearing on its direction. However, prudent economic and fiscal planning, coupled with a move towards a market economy, has produced sustained growth since the 1990s.

In 2004 GDP growth was 5.8 per cent led by a strengthening service sector and bumper harvests in 2003 and 2004. Tourism and increased consumer confidence stimulated domestic demand and inflation rose to 3.6 per cent, from the 2.2 per cent in 2003.

Production in oil and gas has fallen and the government is attempting to diversify the economy further, into industry and manufacturing with a programme to enhance productivity in preparation for global competition.

The agricultural sector, which in official data includes output from fisheries, constituted 12.6 per cent of GDP, compared to 27.8 per cent for industry, of which manufacturing makes up 17.7 per cent and services 59.5 per cent, of which tourism makes up around 10 per cent of GDP. However, agriculture can still have a significant bearing on the economy as it employs just under a quarter of the labour force. Mining makes up approximately 3 per cent of GDP. Remittances from over 600,000 Tunisians living abroad constitute a further important source of foreign exchange.

Tunisia is a country where 55 per cent of the population is aged less than 25 and a growing work force has led to an official unemployment rate of around 14 per cent, however with high underemployment this rate may not reflect the true nature of the jobless market.

The IMF has advised that an early repayment of the external debt would enhance Tunisia's sovereign risk ratings further. The government is expected to consider tax reforms to remove the current complex system that includes too many exemptions and special regimes.

Tunisia has benefitted from proximity to its principal European market and has managed its economy with enough clear objectives to have achived sustained growth and progress.

External trade
Tunisia belongs to the Arab Maghreb Union (AMU) with Algeria, Libya, Morocco and Mauritania. It also has a bilateral trade agreement with the EU, through the Euro-Mediterranean Partnership. Goods are traded between partners with reduced tariffs levied. On 25 February 2004 Tunisia signed a free trade agreement with Jordan, Morocco and Egypt – the Agadir Agreement – between them all tariffs are due to be removed by 1 January 2006.

Exports of goods and services recorded annual growth of 4.0 per cent in 2004, and is projected to grow by 5.3 per cent over 2004–08.

Imports
Main imports are textiles, machinery and equipment, hydrocarbons, chemicals and food.

Main sources: France (27.5 per cent total, 2004), Italy (20.8 per cent), Germany (9.2 per cent), Spain (5.7 per cent)

Exports
Main exports are textiles, mechanical goods, phosphates and chemicals, agricultural products and hydrocarbons.

Main destinations: France (30 per cent total, 2004), Italy (23.3 per cent), Germany (9.3 per cent), Spain (5.3 per cent), Belgium (4.3 per cent), Libya (4.2 per cent)

Agriculture
Farming
The government sees agriculture as a principal growth sector, however it is heavily influenced by the climate and rainfall. The principal area of cultivation is in north, along the Mediterranean coast, where ancient oil groves are still located. Major projects to augment irrigation are underway, with a new dam and reservoir supplying the north-east region and waterways being installed. In the desert south, oasis crops of dates are famous and exported throughout the region and Europe. In the central area rainfall directly affects crop production as a wet year will produce a good harvest; conversely, a dry year risks desertification.

The sector employs around 30 per cent of the population, and contributed 12.6 per cent of GDP in 2004, showing an annual growth of 9 per cent, a drop on the record 21.5 per cent in 2003 when rains produced bumper harvests.

The agricultural investment code offers tax and other financial advantages, while the Agence de Promotion des Investissements Agricoles (APIA) (Agency for the Promotion of Agricultural Investment) channels investment into agriculture. The Banque Nationale Agricole (BNA) provides medium- and long-term credit for agricultural development projects. Since all suitable land is already being farmed, government policy centres on improving yields through new farming techniques and making the most of water resources.

Rural depopulation, an inequitable land tenure system, drought, soil erosion, overgrazing and low producer prices remain the major constraints to development.

The country's 55 million olive trees occupy one-third of all arable land and olive oil, at over 70 per cent of production it is the most important agricultural export. Tunisia is the world's fourth, after Italy, Spain, Greece, largest exporter. In 2003 the harvest was 1.2 million tonnes about four times the typical annual yeald. Other main products from the sector are flour, sugar, tomato paste, milk, wine and animal feed.

The recent growth in organic food has encouraged over 240 operations, which have attracted international certification accredited to the EU, producing among others, olive oil and dates.

Crop production in 2003 included: 2,155,000 tonnes (t) cereals in total, 1,722,000t wheat, 395,000t barley, 375,000t potatoes, 91,174t pulses, *313,000t citrus fruit, *115,000t grapes, 970,000t tomatoes, 83,855t oilcrops, 2,290t tobacco, 350,000t olives, 19,000t various spices, 44,000t almonds, 122,000t dates, 255,000t chillies and peppers, *5,800t garlic, 121,000t apples, 1,044,960t fruit in total, 2,289,130t vegetables in total.
* estimate

The estimated livestock production included: 263,015t meat in total, 63,000t beef, 150t pig meat, 60,000t lamb, 9,500t goat meat, 120,600t poultry, 83,000t eggs, 894,500t milk, 2,500t honey, 5,300t cattle hides, 8,000t sheepskins, 8,800t greasy wool.

Fishing
Most seafood production is for domestic consumption and the sector is relatively undeveloped, with extensive small-scale fishing using more traditional methods. The coastal areas around Sfax and the Kerkennah Islands, where the sea is very shallow, are well-known locally for their fishing industry. Total seafood production is typically around 80,000 tonnes, with some 20 per cent of this exported.

Catches typically include sardines, pilchards, tuna and whitefish. However, tuna fishing is diminishing as Mediterranean stocks decline.

Forestry
An arid climate, a fast-growing population and animal herds have put Tunisia's already limited woodland areas at serious risk. However efforts to reverse the trend have increased forests by 0.2 per cent or 1,000 hectares.

The oak forests of the country's north provide timber and cork.

Exports of forest products in 2004 amounted to US$11.5 million, while imports amounted to US$141 million.

The estimated production for 2004 included: 2,351,308 cubic metres (cum) roundwood, 213,800cum industrial roundwood, 20,400cum sawnwood,

20,800cum sawlogs and veneers, 75,000cum pulpwood, 104,000cum wood-based panels, 2,137,508cum woodfuel, 203,420t charcoal.

Industry and manufacturing
The industrial sector is based primarily on processing domestic raw materials, notably phosphates and agricultural commodities, and textiles, including clothing and leather products. An industrial restructuring programme launched in the mid-1990s has seen high levels of public investment in upgrading businesses' competitiveness in preparation for the liberalisation of markets and European competition. The present strategy is to target specific types of products where relatively cheap labour, proximity to Europe and government incentives can combine to give Tunisia a price and quality advantage over other exporters. The programme has been particularly successful among small- and medium-sized enterprises (SMEs).

Industrial production increased by 4.2 per cent in 2004 and accounted for 27.8 per cent of GDP, of which manufacturing was 17.7, recording growth at 4.6 per cent.

Tourism
The tourism sector accounts for around 10 per cent of GDP. One of the country's highest net earners of foreign exchange, it has been an increasingly important source of employment. Over 80 per cent of visitors come from EU countries; the strong euro resulted in higher than expected number of tourist arrivals, up by 19 per cent, in 2004. Tunisia is a member of the Euromed Heritage Programme, a computerisation project, sponsored by the EU, which focusses on cultural tourists of archaeology, arts and history, promoting sites through the internet.

Travel and tourism is expected to provide 8.8 per cent of GDP, employ 16.5 per cent of total employment and attract US$1.1 billion or 17 per cent of all capital investment in 2005. The industry it estimated to earn overall, US$2.9 billion or, 20 per cent of total exports.

The country has a wealth of archaeological sites, traditional habitats and sandy beaches to provide destinations to cater for the wishes of many different holidaymakers.

Mining
The mining sector contributes 3 per cent of GDP and employs 4 per cent of the working population. Tunisia is the world's fifth-largest source of phosphates although the quality of the rock mined is poor. Extraction (largely in Metlaoui and Gafsa) is geared increasingly towards local phosphate processing rather than exporting it in a raw state. Other important minerals mined include iron ore, salt, fluorspar, barytes, lead, zinc, potash and uranium. Foreign investment is being sought by the government for the mining industry.

Hydrocarbons
Total oil reserves stood at 600 million barrels in 2004; at current production levels, these should last until 2013. Although oil reserves are dwindling, production rose by 2.6 per cent from 66,000 barrels per day (bpd) in 2003 to 69,000bpd in 2003. Growing demand for petroleum has meant that Tunisia became a net importer of oil in 2000. The Tunisian government launched a campaign in 2004, to increase exploration levels for oil and gas. The government is investing US$687 in an attempt to attract further investment. Tunisia has one refinery at Bizerte with a small capacity of 32,000 bpd, therefore the country is reliant on imports of refined products to meet demand.

Tunisia's natural gas reserves amounts to over 97 billion cubic metres. To replace declining oil reserves, the government is promoting the natural gas sector; local production typically meets 80 per cent of domestic demand. However demand for natural gas is increasing at a greater pace than production and the government plans for around half of energy consumption to be natural gas in the long term. Tunisia and Libya began planning pipelines in 2003 to supply natural gas to southern and northern Tunisia; completion is expected in 2006.

Tunisia does not produce coal but imports around 118,000 short tonnes of coke per annum.

Energy
The state-owned electricity and gas company, Société Tunisienne de l'Electricité et du Gaz's (STEG) no longer has a monopoly on power generation, although the company retains its monopoly on distribution.

Emphasis is on expanding electricity production and distribution, and stepping up the oil and gas exploration programme. Demand for electricity is growing by 7 per cent per annum and around 95 per cent of homes have access to electricity. The government intends to add around 300MW of generating capacity every two to three years.

General Electric is to build a US$80 million, 240MW gas power station at Bir M'Cherga, bringing the STEG's capacity to 1,810MW, produced by five power stations (three gas and two thermal power).

Financial markets
Stock exchange
Tunisia's small Bourse des Valeurs Mobilières de Tunis (BVMT) (Tunis Stock Exchange) is state run. Large-scale privatisation could bring more foreign portfolio investment and the government offers significant tax incentives to encourage business to join the exchange but expansion has remain doggedly slow. The privatisation programme, mainly limited to small companies, may not spark the interest to heighten growth on the exchange, in the medium-term.

Despite modest investor interest, the Tunisian capital market is still mainly a retail market, with little activity from local financial institutions. While the number of stocks listed remains relatively few, and in the absence of a secondary market, the stock exchange cannot become a major vehicle for raising capital.

Banking and insurance
Tunisia aims to become the regional financial centre and is keen to build on its status as an economy with investment grade status. However, the banking sector is overcrowded, plagued by bad debts and dominated by the public sector.

The government is determined to rationalise the sector and the government has engaged in a modernisation programme, including privatisation and mergers in a process of consolidation in the sector. The capital base of many banks has improved with the injection of government funds into state-owned banks and the restructuring of non-performing loans.

Central bank
Banque Centrale de Tunisie
Main financial centre
Tunis

Time
GMT plus one hour

Geography
Tunisia is in North Africa, bordered by Algeria to the west and by Libya to the south-east. To the north and east, Tunisia has a coastline on the Mediterranean Sea.

Climate
The northern coastal area has Mediterranean climate with warm, rainy winters (December–March) and hot summers. The southern and inland area is hot and arid. Temperature in Tunis ranges from 6–14 degrees Celsius (C) in January to 21–33 degrees C in August. The wettest month is January and the driest is July.

Dress codes
Formal attire should be worn for business meetings. Women should wear clothes that cover most of the body, including shoulders and legs. In the countryside, western dress and customs are rare and dress should be modest.

Entry requirements
Passports
Required by all

Visa
Required by all; some exceptions, for visits up to three months, include citizens of US, EU, certain Arab, and many Commonwealth countries. A full list of exceptions can be found at http://www.tunisia.or.jp/ (see under visas). Business travellers from these countries may visit as a tourist without further reference. Those visitors, both business and tourist, not included on the list should contact the nearest Tunisian Embassy for information and visa application form at least three weeks before departure.

Currency advice/regulations
Local currency may not be imported or exported; there are no restrictions on the import of foreign currency. However, the re-export of foreign cash is limited to what was imported, and the conversion of dinars into foreign exchange may not exceed 30 per cent of any foreign currency converted during the visit, or D100, whichever is the greater. Therefore all currency forms should be retained.
Traveller's cheques are widely accepted, and preferably made up of sterling or US dollars.

Customs
Visitors may bring in one litre of spirits, two litres of wine, 400 cigarettes (or 100 cigars), a quarter litre of perfume, and one litre of eau de toilette, gifts to the value of D100.

Prohibited imports
Arms (except for hunting), explosives, drugs and all narcotic products, immoral or obscene illustrations and publications, forged books, walkie-talkies.

Health (for visitors)
Mandatory precautions
Yellow fever vaccination certificate required if arriving from an infected area.
Advisable precautions
Immunisation is recommended against diphtheria, hepatitis, polio, tetanus and typhoid. Rabies is present. Water precautions should be taken outside main towns: boil tap water or drink mineral water and wash fresh foods carefully.

Hotels
In general hotels are cheap and easy to find. The state has sold off virtually all its hotels. Classified into five categories. Government hotel tax added to bill. Hotel and restaurant staff expect 10 per cent tip.

Credit cards
Are widely accepted.

Public holidays
Fixed dates
1 Jan (New Year's Day), 20 Mar (Independence Day), 21 Mar (Youth Day), 9 Apr (Martyrs' Day), 1 May (Labour Day), 25 Jul (Republic Day), 13 Aug (Women's Day), 7 Nov (New Era Day/Accession of President Ben Ali).
Many businesses close during July/August.
Variable dates
Eid al Adha, Eid al Fitr, Islamic New Year, Birth of the Prophet.
The Islamic year contains 354 or 355 days, with the result that Muslim feasts advance by 10–12 days against the Gregorian calendar. Dates of feasts vary according to the sighting of the new moon, so cannot be forecast exactly. Islamic year 1426: 10 February 2005 to 30 January 2006.

Working hours
The weekly day of rest is Sunday, not Friday as is usual in the Muslim world. Tunis is virtually closed down during August.
Banking
Mon–Fri: 0730–1130 (summer);
Mon–Thu: 0800–1100 and 1400–1615,
Fri: 0800–1100 and 1300–1600 (winter).
Business
Mon–Sat: 0830–1300 (summer);
Mon–Fri: 0830–1300, 1500–1745 (winter).
Government
Mon–Sat: 0830–1300 (summer);
Mon–Fri: 0830–1300, 1500–1745 (winter). Government offices' opening hours may vary by half an hour.
Shops
Mon–Sat: 0800–1200 and 1600–1900 (summer); Mon–Sat: 0900–1300 and 1500–1900 (winter).

Telecommunications
Telephone/fax
An automatic service is available.
Courier services
No commercial courier firms are allowed to operate.
Mobile phones
There are GSM roaming facilities available, with coverage throughout most of the country.

Electricity supply
220V AC in tourist resorts

Social customs/useful tips
The legacy of French rule is considerable in the towns and a rather formal attitude to courtesy prevails. Senior government or company officials should be addressed as Monsieur and government ministers as Monsieur le Ministre. It is customary to shake hands on meeting and taking leave. Business cards are exchanged after introduction.
Personal relationships are important in business, and time is usually spent in light conversation, over tea or coffee, before embarking on business matters. Regular visits and personal contact are vital in order to establish a relationship of confidence with agents and customers in Tunisia.
Hospitality is important. It is appropriate to present a small gift in appreciation of hospitality.
Islam affects society at every level. A statute passed in the first year of independence enforced equality of the sexes. Nevertheless, gatherings of men and women are usually separate, the sexes are separated in mosques, and only men may enter a cemetery to attend a funeral. Alcohol is freely available in towns, although less common in rural areas. Strict Muslims will not drink alcohol, but many Tunisian men do, and it is acceptable for non-Muslim visitors to do so. The minimum drinking age is 21 years.
Mint tea or fresh lemon or orange juice are typical non-alcoholic drinks. It is polite to accept a drink when offered.
During Ramadan visitors are advised not to eat, drink or smoke in public during daylight hours.

Getting there
Air
All access is via Africa and Europe.
National airline: Tunisair.
International airport/s: Tunis-Carthage (TUN), 8km from the city. Travel time to the city is 15–30 minutes. Djerba-Zarzis (DJE), 9km from Houmek Souk and Monastir (MIR) 9km from the city. All these airports have duty-free shop, bar, buffet, restaurant, currency exchange, post office, car hire. All have buses and taxi service. Sfax-el Maou (SFA), 7km west of city; Tozeur-Nefta (TOE), 10km from city; Tabarka (TBJ), 8km from city. All have duty-free shops and buses and taxi services.
Construction of a new international airport in Enfidha, 75km from Tunis, began in March 2005.
Airport tax: None
Surface
Road: Access is by road from Algeria and Libya.
Rail: Access by rail from Algeria.
Water: Passenger traffic comes mostly to Tunis-La Goulette. Regular passenger ferry services operate between Tunis and France, Italy and Malta.
Main port/s: Tunis-La Goulette, Sfax, Bizerte, Gabes, Sousse and Zarzis; of which Tunis-Goulette and Sfax are the largest.

Getting about
National transport
Air: Tuninter operates regular domestic services linking Tunis with Djerba, Monastir-Skanes, Tozeur-Nefta and Sfax-Tabarka. The air taxi company, Tunisavia, also operates weekly flights to Sfax and some other towns.
Road: The road network extends for around 19,000km, of which main or national roads account for 10,800km. About 57 per cent of the network is

paved. There is a 143km motorway between Tunis and Sousse.

Buses: Extensive services. Long-distance routes include: Tunis-Kelibia; Tunis-Kairouan; Sousse-Sfax; Sousse-Gafsa; Sfax-Gabès-Djerba. Fares are inexpensive. The Société Nationale de Transports operates local buses on 153 routes.

Taxis: Long distance taxis (louages) operate between all main towns; these are considered the fastest method of road transport.

Rail: A 2,200km network links the main towns. There are two classes, some with air-conditioned, first-class accommodation. It is recommended purchasing a ticket in advance; those purchased onboard may be charged at a much higher price. It is an advantage to book in advance especially for air-conditioned trains.

Services include: Tunis-Nabeul/Sfax, Tunis-Bizerte, Tunis-Ghardimaou, Tunis-Gabes, Tunis-Beja, Sfax-Gabes and Sfax-Tozeur.

Water: There are regular ferries from Sfax-Iles Kerkenna and Djerba island.

City transport
In December 2004, work started on a major new bridge linking the Rades and La Goulette suburbs of Tunis, which is anticipated to be finished by 2007. Its traffic capacity, estimated at 3,000 vehicles a day, will greatly facilitate the car flow between northern and southern suburbs of the capital city.

Taxis: Taxis are available in all main towns and are fairly easy to obtain. In louage taxis, the fare is shared by several passengers. Taxis are metered but be aware that some drivers will multiply the fare. Journey time is 15–20 minutes from airport to city centre.

Buses, trams & metro: Extensive services operate in main towns.

Car hire
Cars are easy to hire at principal airports and hotels but are expensive and the condition of the cars vary. Roads are being improved but local driving is erratic. International or national driving licence required. Traffic drives on the right; 100kph speed limit. Permission must be obtained to drive in Saharan areas.

BUSINESS DIRECTORY

The addresses listed below are a selection only. While World of Information makes every endeavour to check these addresses, we cannot guarantee that changes have not been made, especially to telephone numbers and area codes. We would welcome any corrections.

Telephone area codes
The international direct dialling (IDD) code for Tunisia is +216 followed by subscriber's number.

Chambers of Commerce
American-Tunisian Chamber of Commerce and Industry, 10 Avenue Mosbah Jarbou, Rue 7116, El Manar 3, 2092 Tunis (tel: 7188-9780; fax: 7188-9880; e-mail: tacc@tacc.org.tn).

British-Tunisian Chamber of Commerce and Industry, 23 Rue de Jérusalem, 1002 Tunis (tel: 7180-2284; fax: 7180-1535; e-mail: tbcci@gnet.tn).

Cap Bon Chambre de Commerce et d'Industrie, 3 Rue de Fel, Cité Néapolis, PO Box 113, 8000 Nabeul (tel: 7228-7260; fax: 7228-7417; e-mail: cci.capbon@planet.tn).

Central Chambre de Commerce et d'Industrie, Rue Chédly Khaznadar, 4000 Sousse (7322-5044; fax: 7322-4227; e-mail: ccis.sousse@planet.tn).

French-Tunisian Chambre de Commerce et d'Industrie, 39 Rue 8301, 1002 Tunis (tel: 7184-4310; fax: 7184-5962; e-mail: ctfci@planet.tn).

North-Eastern Chambre de Commerce et d'Industrie, 46 Rue Ibn Khaldoun, 7000 Bizerte (tel: 7243-1044; fax: 7243-2379; e-mail: ccine.biz@gnet.tn).

North-Western Chambre de Commerce et d'Industrie, Hedi Chaker Street, 9000 Beja (tel: 7845-6261; fax: 7845-5789; e-mail: ccino.beja@gnet.tn).

Sfar Chambre de Commerce et d'Industrie, 10 Rue Tahar Sfar, PO Box794, 3018 Sfax (tel: 7429-6120; fax: 7429-6121; e-mail:ccis@planet.tn).

South-Eastern Chambre de Commerce et d'Industrie, 202 Avenue Farhat Hached, 6000 Gabes (tel: 7527-4900; fax: 7527-4688; e-mail: csise@gnet.tn).

South-Western Chambre de Commerce et d'Industrie, Rue des Roses, PO Box 46, 2100 Gafsa (tel: 7622-6650; fax: 7622-4150; e-mail: cciso@planet.tn).

Tunis Chambre de Commerce, 1 Rue des Entrepreneurs, 1000 Tunis (tel: 7135-0300; fax:7135-4744; e-mail: ccitunis@planet.tn).

Banking
Alubaf International Bank – Tunis, PO Box 51, Rue 8007 Montplaisir, 1002 Tunis (tel: 783-500 fax: 793-905, 784-343).

Amen Bank, Avenue Mohamed V, 1002 Tunis (tel: 340-511; fax: 349-909).

Banque Arabe Tuniso–Libyenne de Développment et de Commerce Extérieur, PO Box 102, 25 Avenue Kheireddine Pacha, 1002 Tunis (tel: 781-500; fax: 782-818).

Banque du Sud, 95 Avenue de la Liberté, 1002 Tunis (tel: 849-400, 792-400; fax: 782-663).

Banque Internationale Arabe de Tunisie SA, PO Box 520, 70-72 Avenue Habib Bourguiba, 1080 Tunis Cedex (tel: 340-733, 252-655, 340-722; fax: 340-680, 347-648).

Banque Nationale Agricole, Rue Hedi Nouira, 1001 Tunis (tel: 831-000, 831-200; fax: 835-388/950, 832-807).

Société Tunisienne de Banque SA, Rue Hedi Nouira, 1001 Tunis (tel: 340-477, 258-000; fax: 340-009, 348-400, 340-446).

Tunis International Bank, PO Box 81, 18 Avenue des Etats Unis D'Amerique, 1002 Tunis (tel: 782-411; fax: 789-970).

Central bank
Banque Centrale de Tunisie, 25 Rue Hédi Nouira, PO Box 777, 1080 Tunis (tel: 7134-0588; fax: 7134-0615; e-mail: boc@bct.gov.tn).

Central bank
Banque Centrale de Tunisie, 25 Rue Hédi Nouira, PO Box 777, 1080 Tunis (tel: 7134-0588; fax: 7134-0615; e-mail: boc@bct.gov.tn).

Travel information
Tunisair, Boulevard 7 Novembre 1987, 2035 Tunis (tel: 700-100; fax: 700-897).

Tunisian Airports Office, BP 137 et 147, 1080 Tunis Cedex (tel: 754-000).

Tunisian National Railway Company, Gare de Tunis-Ville, Place de Barcelone, Tunis (tel: 244-440).

National tourist organisation offices
Office National du Tourisme Tunisien (ONTT) (Tunisian National Tourist Office), 1 avenue Mohamed V, 1001 Tunis, Tunisia (tel: 341 077; fax: 350 997; email: info@tourism.tunisia.com; internet: www.cometotunisia.co.uk).

Ministries
Foreign Investment Promotion Agency (government), (tel: 792-144; fax: 782-971).

Ministry of Agriculture, 30 rue Alain Savery, 1002 Tunis Belvedere (tel: 287-133).

Ministry of Communication Technologies, Cabinet de Monsieur le Ministre, 3 bis, rue d'Angleterre, 1000 Tunis.

Ministry of Communications, Belvedere du 9 avril 1938, 1030 Tunis (tel: 336-409; fax: 354-628).

Ministry of Economic Development, Direction Générale de la Privatisation, Place Ali Zouaoui, 1000 Tunis (tel: 354-467; fax: 350-975).

Ministry of Defence, 1008 Montfleury, Tunis (tel: 560-244).

Ministry of Education, Boulevard Bab Bnat, Tunis (tel: 263-850; fax: 569-307).

Ministry of Equipment and Housing, Av H Cherita –Cite Jardin, 1002 Tunis (tel: 681-802).

Ministry of Higher Education, 28 rue de Sousse, 1030 Tunis (tel: 782-947).

Ministry of Public Health, Bab Saadoun, Tunis (tel: 260-727).

Ministry of Vocational Training and Employment, 21 rue de Lybie – Lafayette, 1002 Tunis (tel: 782-432).

Other useful addresses

Agence de Promotion de L'Industrie, 63 rue de Syrie, 1002 Tunis-Belvédère (tel: 792-144; fax: 782-482).

Agricultural Investment Promotion Agency, 62 rue Alain Savary, 1003 Tunis Khadra, Tunis (tel: 288-400, 288-091; fax: 782-353).

American Embassy, Zone Nord-Est des Berges du Lac, Nord de Tunis, 2045, La Goulette, Tunisia (tel: 107 000; fax: 962 115; internet: http://usembassy.state.gov/posts/ts1/wwwhemb).

American Express, c/o Carthage Tours, 59 avenue Habib Bourguiba, 1001 Tunis (tel: 254-304; fax: 352-740).

Arab League, avenue Khéreddine Pacha, Tunis.

British Embassy, 5 Place de la Victoire, 1000 Tunis (tel: 245-100, 245-324, 341-444; fax: 354-877; email: britishemb@planet.tn; internet: www.british-emb.intl.tn).

Central Post Office, rue Charles de Gaulle, Tunis.

CEPEX (non-profit government agency for promotion of Tunisian exports), 28 rue v Gandhi, 1001 Tunis (tel: 350-043, 350-801; fax: 353-683; e-mail: cepexedpuc@attmail.com).

Entreprise Tunisienne D'Activités Petrolières, 27 avenue Khéreddine Pacha, 1002 Tunis (tel: 782-288).

Export Promotion Centre, 28 rue Ghandi, 1001 Tunis (tel: 350-344; fax: 353-683).

Industrial Land Agency, 2 rue Badii Ezzamen, Cité Mahrajéne, 1002 Tunis-Belvédère, El Menza I (tel: 797-360, 800-616; fax: 782-303).

Institut National de Statistique, 27 rue de Liban, Tunis (tel: 282-500).

Maghreb Permanent Consultative Committee, 14 rue Yahia ibn Omar, Mutuelleville, Tunis.

National Sanitation Office, 32 rue Hedi Nouira, Tunis (tel: 704-000).

National Water Distribution Company, 67 rue Jawarhel ehru, Montfleury (tel: 493-700; fax: 390-561).

Office du Commerce de Tunisie, avenue Mohammed V, 1002 Tunis (tel: 288-673, 288-864, 682-903; fax: 788-974, 784-974).

Prime Ministry, Privatisation General Directorate, 4 Rue ibn Nadim Montplaisir, 1002 Tunis (tel: 282-467; fax: 281-675).

Tunisian Chemical Group, 5–7 rue Khartoum, 1002 Tunis (tel: 784-488).

Tunisian Electricity and Gas Company, 38 rue Kemal Ataturk, Tunis (tel: 341-311; fax: 349-981).

Tunisian Embassy (USA), 1515 Massachusetts Avenue, NW, Washington DC 20005, USA (tel: +1-202-862-1850; fax: +1-202-862-1858).

Tunisian External Communication Agency, 2 rue d'Algérie, 1001 Tunis (tel: 651-999, 350-202; fax: 341-902).

Union Tunisienne de l'Industrie, du Commerce et de l'Artisanat, 32 rue Charles de Gaulle, Tunis (tel: 243-711).

Internet sites

Information on Tunisia:
http://www.tunisiaonline.com

http://www.investintunisia.tn

http://www.tourismtunisia.com

http://www.tunisie.com

http://www.radiotunis.com

Africa Business Network:
http://www.ifc.org/abn

AllAfrica.com: http://allafrica.com

African Development Bank:
http://www.afdb.org

Mbendi AfroPaedia (information on companies, countries, industries and stock exchanges in Africa): http://mbendi.co.za

Turkey

Turkey was created in 1923 from the remnants of the Ottoman Empire and now stands as one of the largest of the secular Muslim states. Turkey has always been relatively Western-oriented as a nation. Having joined the UN in 1945, the country went on to become an integral member of NATO from 1952 onwards. Traditionally a staunch ally of the United States, Turkey now seeks membership of the European Union (EU) and in this respect 2005 was an historic year, as the country officially began negotiations with the EU regarding future full membership.

The EU and Cyprus

The unresolved issue of Cyprus however, continues to hold the country's EU designs back. Turkey intervened militarily in Cyprus in 1974 to protect Turkish Cypriots and prevent what they thought might be a Greek takeover of the island; the northern 37 per cent of the island remains under Turkish Cypriot control. The Turkish authorities' relationship with its Kurdish citizens has also been fraught over the years. In 1984, the Kurdistan Workers' Party (PKK), a Marxist-Leninist, separatist group, initiated an insurgency in south-east Turkey, often using terrorist tactics to try to attain its goal of an independent Kurdistan. The group, whose leader Abdullah Ocalan was captured in Kenya in February 1999, has largely ceased violent attacks since it declared a unilateral cease-fire in September 1999. Nonetheless, occasional clashes have occurred between Turkish security forces and armed PKK militants, many of whom remain in northern Iraq. In April 2002, the PKK changed its name to the Kurdistan Freedom and Democracy Congress (KADEK) and again in November 2003, changed it to the Kurdistan People's Congress (KHK). Turkey took no part in the invasion of neighbouring Iraq in 2003. The-then Prime Minister Bulent Ecevit refused to allow the US to use Turkish bases to bomb Iraq and was forthrightly against the war in Iraq. Subsequently, Ecevit accused the US of supporting the PKK.

Turkish Prime Minister Recep Tayyip Erdogan made the commencement of EU membership talks a key tenet of his electoral platform. Erdogan has moderated his party over time and his new moderate political organisation has provided him with a perfect vehicle to power. Erdogan's Adalet ve Kalkinma Partisi (AKP) (Justice and Development Party) won a handsome endorsement from the people at the last elections, in 2002, and is keen for Turkey to be taken seriously as a candidate for EU membership during the forthcoming membership talks.

The key state for Turkey to win over to its side is Germany, which could persuade smaller members to its view. Germany's new chancellor, Angela Merkel, was, when in opposition, strongly opposed to Turkish membership of the EU, but has changed her stance. She now says that

KEY FACTS

Official name: Türkiye Cumhuriyeti (Republic of Turkey)

Head of State: President Ahmet Necdet Sezer (since May 2000)

Head of government: Prime Minister Recep Tayyip Erdogan (AKP) (appointed by the President; took office on 14 Mar 2003)

Ruling party: Adalet ve Kalkinma Partisi (AKP) (Justice and Development Party) (since Nov 2002)

Area: 779,452 square km

Population: 71.84 million (2004)

Capital: Ankara

Official language: Turkish

Currency: Yeni Turk Lirasi (New Turkish Lira) (YTL) (The YTL was introduced on 1 Jan 2005, to replace the old Turkish lira (L). YTL1.00 is equal to L1,000,000. The YTL is divided into 100 kurus. Old currency will be withdrawn from circulation, but will still be accepted through 2005.)

Exchange rate: YTL1.35 per US$ (Oct 2005)

GDP per capita: US$4,251 (2004)

GDP real growth: 8.00% (2004)

Labour force: 23.64 million (2004)

Unemployment: 10.20% (OECD, 2004); 4.0% (underemployment 2004)*

Inflation: 10.60% (2004)

Balance of trade: -US$23.83 billion (2004)

Foreign debt: US$161.75 billion (2004)

Annual FDI: US$13.70 billion (cumulative, 1995–2004, OECD); US$2.60 billion (OECD, 2004)*

* estimated figure

'things will develop well' with Turkey, and has acknowledged Erdogan's statement that Berlin and Ankara 'will walk hand in hand as always'. But faced with absorbing 3.5 million Turkish immigrants into German society, many Germans fear Turkey's accession to the EU would bring even more to their doors.

Turkey also has an obstacle to overcome regarding EU membership in the form of its human rights record which, hitherto, has been less than desirable. Take for example the case of novelist Orhan Pamuk often touted as a Nobel Prize candidate, who faces up to three years in jail for 'insulting Turkish identity', by telling a Swiss newspaper that one million Armenians and 30,000 Kurds were killed in the country in the twentieth century. The Istanbul court deliberating the case decided to adjourn the trial until February 2006 to give the justice ministry time to establish whether the case was in line with judicial procedures. Furthermore, the Turkish legal system remains void of an official court of appeal.

EU Enlargement Commissioner Olli Rehn said that 'not just Pamuk but Turkey was on trial'. The trial was a litmus test as to whether Turkey was seriously committed to freedom of expression and reforms that enhanced the rule of law. MEP Camiel Eurlings said it was a black day for Turkey's accession process.

Economy

Turkey has a three-year (from 2005) SDR6.66 billion (US$9.46 billion) Stand-By Arrangement with the International Monetary Fund. In Ankara in December 2005, the fund's first deputy managing director Anne Krueger said Turkey's economy continued to perform well.

Growth had moderated in line with the IMF's assumptions; inflation was in single digits and the public debt burden being reduced steadily. The main challenge to the economic outlook is the widening current account deficit, which had been driven by increasing oil prices and strengthening of the lira.

The authorities' response to the current account developments — a strong 2006 budget, a gradual easing of monetary policy, and stepped-up reserve accumulation — had been appropriate. The authorities should ensure that fiscal policy implementation remained consistent with achieving the public sector primary surplus target of 6.5 per cent of gross national product and that revenue over budget was saved. Should the current account deficit not stabilise, the authorities would need to respond with an appropriate set of policies, including fiscal tightening. Progress on improving both the personal and corporate income tax structures was commendable, but greater efforts were needed to strengthen tax administration.

The central bank's cautious approach to interest rate cuts was appropriate given next year's (2006) more challenging inflation outlook. The bank should also continue to take advantage of favourable market conditions to augment further its international reserves. However, taking into account Turkey's still high public debt and its relatively short maturity, the authorities should continue to take advantage of the current benign global environment to lengthen borrowing maturities further and ensure that policies were consistent with attracting foreign direct investment (FDI).

Several major international companies have invested in Turkey. Ford has stated it aims to increase annual production capacity at its Kocaeli plant from 240,000 to 280,000 units. Ford is investing 225 million Euro in the project. Ford has three plants in Turkey and employs 7,725 people.

Tusas Turkish Aerospace Industries (TAI) has won an award of US$235 million from Alenia Aeronautica SpA, the Rome-based aircraft manufacturing arm of Italian defence giant Finmeccanica. The deal is for offset business as part of a maritime patrol aircraft (MPA) contract last year. Turkey's defence industry executive committee decided in January 2005 to open negotiations with Alenia for the deal. TAI was competing with Spain's Construcciones Aeronauticas SA (CASA), Madrid. In June, Alenia inked a US$219 million deal with Turkey for the sale of a batch of 10 MPAs.

Through Alenia, TAI also manufactures parts for Boeing's B787 aircraft and will soon become the only elevator assembler of B787s in the world. Turkey is becoming an increasingly luring market for Alenia. As part of a broad and aggressive plan to invest in countries where industrial co-operation is possible, Alenia sees TAI as a strategic partner for long-term industrial co-operation for ongoing and future programmes in Turkey and in third countries. In another potential deal that may go up to billions of dollars, Alenia has been promoting TAI to join the European Euro fighter programme.

Outlook

The economic outlook for Turkey is bright. The IMF forecasts growth of 5 per cent during 2005-06. Strong growth will remain a feature of the Turkish economy so long as the country's drive towards full EU membership continues and increased foreign direct investment flows in. However, this eventuality is by no means assured. Though Turkey struck a huge blow when it began the accession talks process in 2005 major European players such as Germany remain stringently opposed to Turkish EU membership. In the Turkish domestic political arena though, EU

KEY INDICATORS — Turkey

	Unit	2000	2001	2002	2003	2004
Population	m	67.42	68.53	69.63	70.71	71.84
Gross domestic product (GDP)	US$bn	203.91	148.00	190.20	242.23	*301.95
GDP per capita	US$	3,120	2,226	2,711	3,313	4,251
GDP real growth	%	7.4	-7.5	7.9	5.8	8.0
Inflation	%	54.9	54.4	45.0	24.5	10.6
Unemployment	%	8.3	8.5	10.3	10.5	9.3
Coal output	mtoe	24.7	–	11.5	–	10.2
Exports (fob) (goods)	US$m	31,214.0	34,379.0	39,830.0	50,000.0	66,896.0
Imports (fob) (goods)	US$m	53,555.0	38,916.0	51,270.0	70,000.0	90,726.0
Balance of trade	US$m	-22,341.0	-4,537.0	-11,440.0	-20,000.0	-23,830.0
Current account	US$m	-9,765.0	3,396.0	-1,540.0	-6,850.0	-15,570.0
Foreign debt	US$bn	114.3	115.3	131.4	147.3	–
Total reserves minus gold	US$m	22,488.0	18,879.0	27,069.0	33,991.0	35,669.0
Foreign exchange	US$m	22,313.0	18,733.0	26,884.0	33,793.0	35,480.0
Exchange rate	per US$	625,219	1,225,588	1,505,500	1,526,225	1,466,813

* estimated figure

Turkey

membership remains the name of the game and President Erdogan will continue to lead his countrymen on the road to Brussels.

Risk assessment

Economic	Satisfactory
Political	Poor
Regional stability	Poor

COUNTRY PROFILE

Historical profile
Founded by Constantine the Great in AD330, Turkey (or Asia Minor as it was known) was for more than 1,000 years the heartland of the Eastern Roman (Byzantine) empire. From the eleventh century, invasions from Central Asia led to the Islamic Turkification of the region, headed by the Ottomans, a name derived from their fourteenth century leader Osman Gazi, who had masterminded the comprehensive defeat of the Byzantines at the Battle of Baphaeon in 1301. The modern republic was established in the 1920s by nationalist leader Kemal Atatürk.

1453 The Ottomans gradually expanded their areas of territorial control, creating the Ottoman empire.
1500s–1800s The Ottoman empire attempted to widen its territorial control into the Mediterranean and Central Europe. This led to conflicts with the major European powers, including the Habsburgs and the Russians. Successive wars eventually undermined the Ottoman empire.
1914–18 Turkey fought in the First World War on the side of the Germans. The majority of Ottoman possessions came under British or French control after the War.
1920–22 Mustafa Kemal, renamed Atatürk (Father of all the Turks) in 1934, led the country in the War of National Liberation, following the dismemberment of the Ottoman empire by the *entente* powers at the end of the First World War.
1923 The Republic of Turkey was established; the independence of the Turkish state was recognised by the Treaty of Lausanne. Atatürk was elected as the Republic's first president. Sweeping changes were made in all areas – legal, political, social and economic. The Islamic legal codes were replaced by Western ones. Turkey is the only Muslim country where the principle of secularism is written into the constitution.
1925 Turkey adopted the Gregorian calendar. The fez (a conical, brimless hat), considered to be a sign of Ottoman backwardness, was prohibited.
1928 Islam ceased to by the State religion. The Arabic script was replaced by the Latin alphabet.
1930 Constantinople was officially renamed Istanbul.
1934 Women were given the vote.
1938 Atatürk died and was succeeded by Ismet Inonu.
1945 President Inonu kept Turkey out of the Second World War, except for the last four months, when it fought on the side of the Allies against Germany. Turkey joined the UN.
1950 The first open multi-party elections were won by the Democratic Party.
1952 Turkey joined NATO.
1960 The government was overthrown by a military coup.
1961 A constitution was approved by referendum, establishing a two-chamber parliament. Elections were held and civilian rule was restored.
1963 An agreement was signed with the European Economic Community (EEC).
1965 Suleyman Demirel became prime minister (he went on to occupy this office seven times).
1971 After a wave of strikes and unrest, there was a period of military supervision of government.
1973 Return to civilian rule.
1974 Turkey invaded northern Cyprus and 37 per cent of the island came under Turkish control, enforcing partition between north and south.
1978 The US lifted the trade embargo it had imposed on Turkey after the 1974 invasion.
1980 A military coup followed civil unrest and martial law was declared throughout the country.
1981 All political parties were disbanded.
1982 A new constitution was approved by referendum. It created a seven-year presidency and reduced parliament to a single house.
1983 New political parties were allowed, subject to strict rules. Turgut Ozal became president.
Northern Cyprus officially declared its independence as the Kuzey Kýbrýs Türk Cumhuriyeti (KKTC) (Turkish Republic of Northern Cyprus) and introduced its own government and legal system. The independence move was rejected by the international community and only Turkey recognised it as a state.
1984 The Kurdistan Workers' Party (PKK) launched a separatist guerrilla war in the south-east.
1987 Martial law ended, enabling Turkey to become a full and active member of the Organisation of Economic Co-operation and Development (OECD), in addition to becoming an associate member of the EEC.
1990 Turkey allowed the use of its bases for the launch of air strikes against Iraq by the US-led coalition in the war to drive Iraqi forces out of Kuwait.
1992 In an anti-PKK operation, Turkish troops entered Kurdish safe havens in Iraq. Turkey joined the Black Sea alliance.
1993 Following the death of Turgut Ozal, Süleyman Demirel became president. Tansu Ciller was appointed as Turkey's first female prime minister. The PKK declared a unilateral cease-fire in March but by July it had broken down.
1995 Turkey launched a major military offensive against the Kurds in northern Iraq. The Ciller coalition collapsed. Although the pro-Islamist Welfare Party (RP) won the elections, it lacked support to form a government. Two major centre-right parties formed an anti-Islamist coalition. Turkey entered the EU customs union.
1996 The centre-right coalition fell and Necmettin Erbakan was appointed prime minister, heading the first pro-Islamic government since 1923.
1997 The Erbakan coalition government collapsed and Mesut Yilmaz was appointed prime minister.
1998 Corruption allegations forced out the Yilmaz government and Bülent Ecevit was appointed prime minister.
1999 The PKK leader, Abdullah Ocalan, captured in Kenya, received a death sentence, later commuted to life imprisonment. Two earthquakes in the Izmit region killed over 17,000 people.
2000 After the failure of a move to change the constitution to allow Süleyman Demirel to stay in office, Ahmet Necdet Sezer was elected president.
2001 Parliament voted to change the constitution to bring it closer to the constitutions in EU countries.
2002 To meet EU conditions on opening membership talks, parliament voted for wide reforms. The Islamist Adalet ve Kalkinma Partisi (AKP) (Justice and Development Party) won a landslide victory in parliamentary elections on 3 November.
2003 Recep Tayyip Erdogan was appointed prime minister on 14 March. Parliament adopted a package of human rights reforms to comply with EU criteria for starting membership talks.
2004 EU leaders agreed to open talks in October 2005 on Turkey's EU accession and Turkey agreed that it would recognise Cyprus as an EU member before accession talks started.
2005 The new Turkish lira, Yeni Turk Lirasi (YTL), was introduced on 1 January. EU accession negotiations commenced in October.

Political structure
Constitution
A 1982 referendum approved a new constitution embodying considerable restrictions on personal liberty.

The constitution was amended in 1999 and 2001. The 1999 amendment was undertaken to ease the path of the privatisation programme while an amendment in October 2001 was aimed at redefining human rights in view of Turkey's aspirations to join the EU. In December 2002, three articles of the constitution were amended, allowing a person with a prison conviction (non-terrorist charge) to stand for parliament. Apart from these additions, the new constitution differs little from the 1926 version, promulgated by Kemal Atatürk, which enshrines Turkey as a secular, democratic and unitary republic.

Only political parties gaining more than 10 per cent of the national vote are entitled to parliamentary seats
Voting eligibility: universal direct suffrage over 18 years.

Form of state
Parliamentary democratic republic

The executive
Executive power rests with the president and council of ministers. The president is the head of state. The president, who serves a seven-year term, is elected by the parliament and appoints the prime minister, who in turn chooses the Council of Ministers. A National Security Council guides government policy in areas of security and law and order. It is chaired by the president and is composed of government ministers and armed forces commanders.

National legislature
Legislative power rests with the unicameral Türkiye Büyük Millet Meclisi (TGNA) (Turkish Grand National Assembly). The TGNA consists of 550 representatives elected directly by adult suffrage for five-year terms. Only political parties gaining over 10 per cent of the vote are eligible to sit in the TGNA.

Legal system
The legal system is based on European models and the 1982 constitution.
The court system is divided into three areas: civil, penal and administrative. The highest courts are the Appeal Court for civil and penal cases and the State Council for tax and administrative cases.

Last elections
3 November 2002 (parliamentary); 5 May 2000 (presidential).
Results: Parliamentary: the reformist Adalet ve Kalkinma Partisi (AKP) (Justice and Development Party), led by Recep Tayyip Erdogan, won 34.3 per cent of the vote (363 seats out of 550), the Cumhuriyet Halk Partisi (CHP) (Republican People's Party) 19.4 per cent (178 seats), Doğru Yol Partisi (DYP) (True Path Party) 9.6 per cent, Milliyetçi Hareket Partisi (MHP) (Nationalist Movement Party) 8.3 per cent, Genç Partisi (GP) (Youth Party) 7.2 per cent, Demokratik Halk Partisi (Dehap) (Democratic People's Party) 6.2 per cent, Anavatan Partisi (AnaP) (Motherland Party) 5.1 per cent, Saadet Partisi (SP) (Felicity Party) 2.5 per cent, Demokratik Sol Partisi (DSP) (Democratic Left Party) 1.2 per cent, Büyük Birlik Partisi (BBP) (Grand Unity Party) 1.1 per cent, Yeni Türkiye Partisi (YTP) (New Turkey Party) 1.0 per cent. The remaining nine seats went to independents.
Presidential: Ahmet Necdet Sezer was elected.

Next elections
May 2007 (presidential); due by November 2007 (parliamentary).

Political parties
Ruling party
Adalet ve Kalkinma Partisi (AKP) (Justice and Development Party) (since Nov 2002)
Main opposition party
Cumhuriyet Halk Partisi (CHP) (Republican People's Party)

Population
71.84 million (2004)
Ethnic make-up
Mainly ethnic Turks, with a large Kurdish minority and small numbers of Armenians, Greeks and Jews.
Religions
Muslim with a small Christian minority. Turkey is a secular state which guarantees complete freedom of worship to non-Muslims.

Education
Although compulsory education is free, facilities are extremely limited, forcing a number of students to attend night school or take private tuition to improve their chances of gaining a place at one of Turkey's 29 universities.
Unicef has highlighted the problem of poor education figures for girls, particularly over the age of 11. In traditional families, it is generally not considered necessary to educate girls beyond primary school, so that less than 40 per cent of girls, aged 11–15, in rural areas are enrolled in secondary school. In 2003, a joint Unicef and government programme aimed at addressing the problem has resulted in new schools opened in areas of most need and transport for students who have to travel long distances. Female enrolment figures have slowly begun to rise. Annual total public expenditure on education is 3–4 per cent of GDP, of which 49 per cent is spent on primary education, 20 per cent on secondary education and 31 per cent on tertiary education (Unicef 2004).
Literacy rate: 86.5 per cent total; 94.3 per cent male; 78.7 per cent female, estimates for 2003.
Compulsory years: Six to 14
Enrolment rate: 105 per cent male, 96 per cent female, gross primary enrolment; 67 per cent male, 48 per cent female, gross secondary enrolment, of relvant age groups (including repeaters), (Unicef 2004).
Pupils per teacher: 23 in primary schools.

Health
Healthcare is provided free of charge. Standards are low, leading many to seek medical services in private hospitals and abroad. Major differences exist in the availability and quality of medical care between major urban centres and eastern parts of the country. Family planning was introduced in the 1960s. Due to opposition from religious groups it did not receive strong support and funding. Nevertheless, population growth has slowed from 2.0 per cent between 1975–2001 to 1.4 per cent 2001–05 (World Bank estimates).
Annual total expenditure on health is around 5 per cent of GDP, of which government spending is approximately 71 per cent. Only 1 per cent of private expenditure on health comes from pre-paid plans.
Life expectancy: 68.6 years (World Bank)
Fertility rate/Maternal mortality rate: 2.4 births per woman (World Bank)
Birth rate/Death rate: 17.95 births per 1,000 population; 5.95 deaths per 1,000 population (World Bank).
Infant mortality rate: 33 per 1,000 live births; 8 per cent of children under aged five are malnourished (World Bank).
Head of population per physician/bed: Approximately 1.2 physicians per 10,000 people

Welfare
The social security system is based on three major organisations, the Social Insurance Institution (SSK), the Emekli Sandigi (government employees' retirement fund) and Bag-Kur for the self-employed.
Mass social security began in 1946 with the SSK giving limited benefits and has been gradually expanded. Membership is compulsory for all salaried employees except civil servants, who join Emekli Sandigi. Social insurance law provides for benefits covering work injury and occupational illness, sickness, maternity, old age, disability and death.

Main cities
Ankara (capital, estimated population 3.5 million in 2004), Istanbul (9.6 million), Izmir (2.5 million), Bursa (1.3 million), Adana (1.3 million), Gaziantep (1.0 million).

Languages spoken
Armenian, Greek and Ladino are used by ethnic minorities. The use of Kurdish was

Turkey

restricted until parliament voted to change the constitution in 2001 and relaxed the restriction. Arabic, Circassian, and Judezmo are also spoken.

Almost all educated Turks have command of a foreign language and English is the dominant language for international business. German and French are also spoken.

Official language/s
Turkish

Media
Press
There are around 250 newspapers and 120 magazines.

Dailies: There are several regional dailies including *Turkish Daily News* as the main English-language publication. Other influential dailies include *Sabah*, *Hürriyet*, *Cumhüriyet*, *Milliyet Basinda Guven*, *Radikal*, *Posta*, *Milliyet Gazetesi*, *Fanatik Gerçek Spor Gazetesi*, *Takvim*, *Aksam Gazetesi*, *Türkiye*, *Yeniyuzyil* and *Zaman Daily Newspaper*.

Weeklies: Several weeklies of general interest include *Pazar Postasi*, *Aksiyon*, *Aktuel*, *Nokta* and *Turkish Probe*.

Business: Publications include *Dünya Ekonomi Politika*, *Capital*, the weekly *Ekonomist*, *Trend*, *Paramatik*, the monthly *Power Ekonomi*, *Borsamatik*, *Marketing Turkiye*, *Market Files*, and *Supermarket Magazine*. The *Finansal Forum* is a daily financial newspaper including detailed economic indicators and reports. *Ticaret* is a regional daily providing important business news.

Periodicals: Periodicals covering general editorial features include *Kibris*, *Kibrisli*, *Kurtulus* and *Soylem*. Other periodicals of consumer interest are the English-language bi-monthly *Istanbul Guide*. *Bizim Anadolu* is a monthly newspaper published in Turkish, English, and French.

Broadcasting
Radio: There are 1,500 commercial radio stations. Radio is the fastest growing medium in Turkey.

Television: Cable and satellite television are rapidly growing. There are 122 TV stations, 13 commercial. In June 2004, programmes in Kurdish and Arabic were broadcast for the first time.

Advertising
Local code of practice/ethics in operation.

Economy
Turkey averaged annual growth of 5.4 per cent in the 1980s and 4.1 per cent in the period 1990–98. By 1998 it had become the world's seventeenth-largest economy and had developed an impressive private sector, although a serious privatisation programme only began in 1997. Russia's financial crisis and domestic political turmoil acted to destabilise the Turkish economy after 1998 and by 2001 the country's economy was close to collapse. A remarkable recovery has since been achieved and Turkey was listed as the OECD's 16th biggest economy in 2004, up from 20th in 2001. Although the economy grew 9.8 per cent in 2004, Turkey has continual debt problems and a current account deficit, which rose to US$15.54 billion in 2004. Both exports and imports rose in 2004, with the country's main foreign currency earners being textiles and tourism, followed by automotive exports, which generated US$10 billion in revenues.

The future prospect of Turkey joining the EU has improved the investor climate, but investors remain wary as membership could be a long way off. It is estimated that when Turkey becomes a member, it could attract US$10–15 billion investment, as opposed to the estimated US$2.6 billion received in 2004.

External trade
Turkey entered a customs union with the EU in 1995. This led to the abolition of customs duties on industrial products imported from the EU and the European Free Trade Association (EFTA) in 1996. Under the terms of the agreement, Turkey has reduced its high tariffs, leading to greater capital flows, but also intense competition from EU states for a share of the lucrative Turkish consumer market. Turkey has also begun trade co-operation with its neighbours on the Black Sea. The Black Sea Trade and Development Bank, the financial arm of the Black Sea Economic Co-operation Organisation (BSECO), aims to promote trade and investment among the 330 million people living within BESCO's 11 member states (Albania, Armenia, Azerbaijan, Bulgaria, Georgia, Greece, Moldova, Romania, Russia, Turkey and Ukraine).

Imports
Principal imports include machinery, chemicals, semi-finished goods, fuels, transport equipment

Main sources: Germany (12.9 per cent total, 2004), Russia (9.3 per cent), Italy (7.1 per cent), France (6.4 per cent), US (4.8 per cent), China (4.6 per cent), UK (4.4 per cent)

Exports
Principal exports are textiles and clothing (typically 37 per cent of total), agricultural products, iron and steel, machinery, fruits, chemical industrial products, vehicles.

Main destinations: Germany (13.9 per cent total, 2004), UK (8.8 per cent), US (7.7 per cent), Italy (7.4 per cent), France (5.8 per cent), Spain (4.2 per cent)

Agriculture
Farming
Agriculture accounts for around 17 per cent of GDP, over 20 per cent of exports and employing about 45 per cent of the labour force. The sector is subsidised, with state support accounting for as much as 7.5 per cent of GDP.

The mainstays of Turkish agriculture are wheat and sheep, although there has been an increase in fruit and vegetable production as well as growth in regional crops such as tea, tobacco, cotton and hazelnuts. Turkey expects to become a leading cotton producer over the next 10 years.

Turkey is the world's largest producer of hazelnuts (70 per cent of the world supply). Production is dominated by Fiskorbirlik, the state-run hazelnut farmers' co-operative.

The GAP south-eastern Anatolian irrigation project, although incomplete, has already raised production and productivity considerably: according to official figures, wheat production nationally has jumped 64 per cent since 1985, barley production by 42 per cent and cotton production by almost 500 per cent. Rice, wheat, soyabeans and potatoes are now produced in more than minimal amounts for the first time. The project will irrigate some 1.8 million hectares (ha), 25 per cent of which will be given over to cotton production.

Turkey remains self-sufficient in food with agricultural exports including tobacco, cotton, dried fruit (hazelnuts, seedless raisins, figs, apricots), pulses (chickpeas and lentils), live sheep, goats, fresh fruits (apples and citrus fruits) and fresh tomatoes. Cereals, especially wheat and barley, are Turkey's most important crops.

Imports, particularly of dairy products and beef, are growing faster than exports. Significant quantities of rice and processed food products are also imported. Liberal trade policies have opened up markets for imports of both cotton and burley tobacco.

Crop production in 2004 included: 33.9 million tonnes (t) cereals in total, 21.0 million t wheat, 3.0 million t maize, 9.0 million t barley, 4.8 million t potatoes, 400,000t rice, 110,000t bananas, 1.6 million t pulses, 2,650t citrus fruit, 3.6 million t grapes, 8.0 million t tomatoes, 1.8 million t cucumbers, 950,347t oilcrops, 160,000t tobacco, 170t vanilla, 1.8 million t olives, 125,000t garlic, 81,000t various spices, 13.1 million t sugar beets, 6.0 million t melons in general, 280,000t figs, 1.8 million t chillies and green peppers, 676,000t treenuts, 25,000t soya beans, 153,800t tea, 2.3 million t apples, 275,000t oats, 277,000t rye, 10.8 million t fruit in total, 24.0

million t vegetables in total. Livestock production included: 1.5 million t meat in total, 391,000t beef, 267,000t lamb, 43,500t goat meat, 954,610t poultry, 791,674t eggs, 10.5 million t milk, 69,540t honey, 28,050t cattle hides, 47,320t sheepskins, 1,950t horsemeat, 46,500t greasy wool.

Fishing
Salt water fishing contributes to 77 per cent of the total fishery production, with 62 per cent of the catches obtained from the Black Sea. Anchovies remain the traditional catch with a potential for further processing. Fishery production also thrives on horse mackerel, whiting and bonito. The main production area for inland fisheries is Lake Van, where gray mullets are mainly caught. The Atatürk Dam and other smaller dams, which were constructed under the Southeast Anatolian Project (GAP), have increased the potential for inland fisheries by over 9,000 tonnes.

Trout constitute more than 60 per cent of the total aquaculture production, 25 per cent of which is obtained from the Aegean Sea. Turkey mainly exports large quantities of canned tuna to the EU and other developed countries.

Forestry
Forest and other wooded land accounts for slightly more than a quarter of the total land area, with forest cover estimated at 10.2 million hectares (ha). Most of the forest is available for wood supply, although it is moderately used for fuel consumption. Only a small area of forest is owned by the state.

Turkey produces a significant quantity of industrial roundwood. Major forest industries rely on local resources for the production of sawnwood, particle board and plywood. The pulp and paper industry is able to meet domestic demand by imports.

Exports of forest material in 2004 amounted to US$203 million, while imports amounted to US$1.1 billion. Production in 2004 included 15,810,00 million cubic metres (cum) roundwood, 10,729,000cum industrial roundwood, 5,615,000cum sawnwood, 5,137,000cum sawlogs and veneers, 3,650,000cum pulpwood, 3,232,000cum wood-based panels, 5,081,000cum wood fuel.

Industry and manufacturing
Industry accounts for 25 per cent of GDP and employs approximately 18 per cent of the labour force.

There have been high levels of industrial growth since the mid-1970s, despite low levels of capital investment and plant utilisation. There has also been rapid development of light industry, general diversification and growth in exports of manufactured goods.

Main areas of specialisation include textiles, ready-to-wear clothes, ceramics and glass, iron and steel, chrome, chemicals and light consumer goods.

The industrial sector is still dominated by large state-owned industries. These State Economic Enterprises are mainly engaged in textiles, food processing, chemicals, metals and motor vehicle production. The food processing sector is growing rapidly and agricultural products continue to provide a large proportion of export revenue. Turkey's non-state industrial sector is dominated by a number of family-run conglomerates. Koc Holding is the largest, with 108 companies operating in 10 core sectors. Koc produces one-third of Turkey's cars, most of its fridges and televisions and owns the biggest supermarket chain. Sabanci Holdings, whic has 50 operating companies, is active in chemicals, textiles, cars, banking, and supermarkets. The third-largest conglomerate, Cukorova, is active in commercial vehicles, paper and mobile telephones, although it is concentrating its efforts on the finance sector. There are also dozens of smaller conglomerates with up to 33 companies.

The textile sector, once one of the engines of Turkish economic growth, is losing the interest of the major conglomerates that dominate Turkey's industrial structure.

Tourism
Tourism has grown rapidly in recent years and is a major contributor to the economy. The sector is the second largest earner of foreign currency after exports. 22 million tourists visited Turkey in 2004, far exceeding forecasts. Tourism is expected to contribute 5.5 per cent to GDP in 2005. Tourist activity is concentrated along the coasts of theAegean and Mediterranean Seas, where the bulk of accommodation is concentrated. Cultural, mountain and winter tourism are being developed.

Mining
Substantial mineral reserves exist, including copper, zinc, lead, iron ore, coal and lignite. Deposits of borax, wolfram and chromite are internationally significant. Turkey is the world's second-largest producer of boron and a leading exporter of chrome. Etibank controls 60 per cent of all mining activity.

Hydrocarbons
Turkey has oil reserves of 300 million barrels. Turkey relies on importing and refining oil, notably from Russia as well as Middle Eastern countries such as Libya and Algeria. Demand is growing by 2–3 per cent per year – slower than overall energy demand, as Turkey moves towards using gas to satisfy its energy needs. The Baku-Tbilisi-Ceyhan oil pipeline opened in May 2005. The 1,760km pipeline carries oil from Azerbaijan's port of Baku through Georgia and then across Turkey to Ceyhan. The pipeline will have a one million barrels per day (bpd) capacity. It is estimated that transit fees will earn the Turkish government revenue of US$300 million a year.

Turkey has natural gas reserves of 8.5 billion cubic metres. Turkey supplies only 2 per cent of its domestic requirements and has to import natural gas for domestic use. Domestic energy demand is projected to grow five-fold by 2020 and gas imports are expected to rise considerably. Turkey's domestic gas consumption has quadrupled since 1992, reflecting government policy of increasing reliance on gas. Gas is cleaner, plentiful in neighbouring countries and allows Turkey to diversify energy sources and increase energy security. Turkey can charge transit fees, as well as bring neighbouring post-Soviet republics into its sphere of influence.

Turkey's coal reserves include 278 million tonnes of anthracite and bituminous coal (hard coal) and 8.3 billion tonnes of sub-bituminous and lignite coal. Despite the huge reserves, production levels have fallen as a result of a lack of investment in the industry. Around 40 per cent of Turkey's lignite is located in the Afsin-Elbistan basin of south-east Anatolia, while hard coal is mined only in one location – the Zonguldak basin of north-west Turkey. Turkish coal, which is used mainly for power generation, is generally of poor quality and highly polluting.

Energy
Turkey is a net energy importer (about 60 per cent of its energy requirements) and is Europe's fastest-growing energy market. Demand is not being met in a country that still experiences frequent blackouts and industrial losses as a result of the energy bottleneck. Total installed generating capacity is around 34,367 MW.

The electricity is generated by coal-fired plants and hydropower. There has been rapid expansion of hydroelectricity capacity with over 100 power plants in operation. There are plans to develop nuclear energy (possibly after 2010) as a source of electricity.

Financial markets
Stock exchange
The Istanbul Stock Exchange (ISE) was established in 1985.

Commodity exchange
The Istanbul Gold Exchange (IGE) expanded its operations to include silver and platinum spot trading from 1999.

Turkey

Banking and insurance
The banking sector was partly responsible for Turkey's financial crisis in 2001, and led the government to reduce the number of state banks from four to three after Emlak Bank was merged into TC Ziraat Bankasi. In October 2001, three private sector banks belonging to the Dogus Group were merged into Garanti while the UK's HSBC purchased Demirbank in November 2001. In June 2002, Pamukbank, the smaller of two banks in Mehmet Emin Karamehmet's Cukurova conglomerate, announced its merger with Turkey's third-largest bank, Yapi Kredi. Rehabilitating the banking sector cost the state (which guaranteed all deposits and previously failed to compensate state banks for issuing subsidised loans at its request) the equivalent of 30 per cent of GDP in 2001/02. The cost of banking reforms was one of the central aims of a US$15.7 billion loan made to Turkey in 2001 by the IMF and the World Bank.

Central bank
Türkiye Cumhuriyet Merkez Bankasi (TCMB) (Central Bank of the Republic of Turkey)

Time
GMT plus two hours (GMT plus three hours from last Sun in Mar to Sat prior to the last Sun in Oct)

Geography
Most of Turkey lies in Asia: the Anatolian peninsula is bordered to the north-east by Georgia and Armenia, to the east by Iran, and to the south by Iraq and Syria. The smaller European part of the country (known as Thrace) is bordered to the west by Greece and Bulgaria. Anatolia and Thrace are separated by the Sea of Marmara, which links the Black Sea and the Aegean Sea. Turkey's coastline is extensive: the Black Sea to the north; the Mediterranean Sea to the south, and the Aegean Sea to the west.

Climate
Coastal regions have a Mediterranean climate, with mild, moist winters and hot, dry summers. The interior plateau has low and irregular rainfall, cold and snowy winters and hot, almost rainless summers. Ankara: 0.3–23 degrees Celsius (C) (Jan–Jul); annual rainfall 367mm. Istanbul: 5–23 degrees C (Jan–Jul); annual rainfall 723mm. Ismir: 8–27 degrees C (Jan–Jul); annual rainfall 700mm.

Dress codes
Although the population is predominantly Muslim, Turkey is a secular state and for the visitor daily life in cities and tourist areas is similar to that in Europe. However, in rural areas, standards are much more conservative and women should be cautious in their dress. They should wear clothing which covers most of the body and probably also a headscarf, or at least be able to cover their hair if the need arises. Topless bathing is illegal but tolerated on southern and Aegean tourist beaches.

Dress for formal occasions is conservative and men normally wear a dark business suit or formal dress. Ties are almost always worn for business meetings. Turkish women dress formally for most social occasions.

Entry requirements
Passports
Required by all. Passports must be valid for at least six months if visa is issued on arrival, and one year if visa is issued at a Turkish consulate.

Visa
Required by all for business purposes; some tourists may visit for up to three months, see www.turkconsulate-london.com/visa.htm#work for a full list of exceptions. Business visas are issued after visitors have requested a visa form from the nearest Turkish Consulate, brief information and the necessary application forms will be forwarded. British tourists may download a visa form from www.turkconsulate-london.com/visaform.htm. US, and non-US citizens residing in the US only, may download a visa from from www.turkishembassy.org/consularservices/forms.

Currency advice/regulations
There are no restrictions on the import of local or foreign currency, although visitors bringing in a large amount of foreign currency should obtain a written declaration from the Turkish authorities. No more than the equivalent of US$5,000 in local currency may be exported. Foreign currency may be exported up to US$5,000, but no more than the amount imported and declared. Currency exchange slips should be retained.

Travellers cheques can be cashed immediately upon proof of identity. To avoid additional exchange rate charges, travellers are advised to take travellers cheques in UK pounds sterling or US dollars.

Customs
Personal effects duty-free and gifts up to the value of US$300 may be brought in duty-free. Purchases over US$50 are subject to value-added tax (VAT) refund. Advisable to produce invoices and foreign currency exchange slips to cover value of purchases. Export of antiquities and some antiques prohibited.

Health (for visitors)
Mandatory precautions
Cholera certificate required if travelling from an infected area.

Advisable precautions
Anti-malaria and anti-cholera precautions are advisable. Hepatitis and rabies are prevalent in all areas, and there have been outbreaks of cholera in eastern Turkey. Malaria tablets should be taken for travel to the Adana area and inoculation against cholera and typhoid for travel to the south-eastern region is advised. A tetanus booster if travelling to central and eastern Anatolia is recommended.

Tap water is unpalatable due to heavy chlorination. Bottled water is easily obtainable in food stores. Medicines are easy to purchase without prescription in local pharmacies (ECZANE). The location of a nearby all-night pharmacy is displayed in any pharmacy window. Medical services are adequate in main city hospitals like Istanbul's American and German hospitals.

Hotels
Classified into five categories – deluxe and first- to fourth-class. Prices vary and many hotels reduce their rates between mid-Oct and mid-Apr. Service charge of 15 per cent usually added and tipping is extra. Twelve per cent VAT is also added. Advance reservations are advisable. Tap water is safe in major hotels.

Credit cards
Access, Diners Club, Visa, American Express and Eurocard are accepted in most hotels, restaurants and shops, and can be used to withdraw money from automatic cash dispensers at banks.

Public holidays
Fixed dates
1 Jan (New Year's Day), 23 Apr (National Independence/Children's Day), 19 May (Youth and Sports Day), 30 Aug (Victory Day), 29 Oct (Republic Day).

Variable dates
Eid al Adha (four days), Eid al Fitr (three days).

The Islamic year contains 354 or 355 days, with the result that Muslim feasts advance by 10–12 days against the Gregorian calendar. Dates of feasts vary according to the sighting of the new moon, so cannot be forecast exactly. Islamic year 1426: 10 February 2005 to 30 January 2006.

Working hours
Banking
Mon–Fri: 0830–1230; 1330–1700.
Business
Mon–Fri: 0830–1200; 1300–1730.
Government
Mon–Fri: 0830–1230; 1330–1730.
Shops
Mon–Sat: 0900–1300; 1400–1900. Large shopping centre (Atakoy Galleria) on the coast road to Istanbul Airport, opens until 2200 every day. Many flower shops open late. Pharmacies display the

location of one opening late. Many food shops open on Sun.

Telecommunications
The telecommunications sector is dominated by state-owned Türk Telekom. The government plans to privatise Türk Telekom and introduced the first phase, the information process, in May 2004. Under its commitments to the World Trade Organisation (WTO), the government is liberalising the telecommunications sector.

Telephone/fax
Public phones operated by discs. Direct dialling available.

Postal services
Main post offices in major cities are usually open 24 hours a day, although only for telephone and post at night.

Electricity supply
220V AC, 50Hz (110V in parts of Istanbul).

Social customs/useful tips
Hospitality is very important. Turkey is a Muslim country and religion plays an important part in Turkish life. Practically all business entertaining is conducted in restaurants and clubs.

Personal contact is the key to doing business. Bureaucracy tends to be the greatest obstacle for foreigners. Information is most easily and efficiently obtained by going directly to the top of any organisation, government or private.

It is polite when visiting the home of a business associate to bring a gift of chocolates, flowers or cake. When entering you may be asked to take off your shoes and put on slippers. Do not be critical of Ataturk, the founder of the Republic, and avoid discussion of Kurds, Armenians and other minorities.

Security
Levels of petty crime in main cities are comparable to those in most Western European cities. Tourists are sometimes invited to visit clubs or bars, and then presented with inflated bills, and coerced to pay them by credit card.

Ultra-leftist and Kurdish terrorists are active in Istanbul and other western cities but do not constitute more than a minor threat. Visitors to south-eastern Turkey are advised to travel only during daylight hours and on major roads. The police monitor checkpoints on roads throughout the south-eastern region. Drivers and all passengers in the vehicle should be prepared to provide identification if stopped at a checkpoint.

Getting there
Air
National airline: Turk Hava Yollari (THY) (Turkish Airlines)

International airport/s: Ankara (ESB) (Esenboga), 35km north-east of the city; facilities include duty-free, banking, restaurants and bars. Buses and taxi services are available into the city.
Istanbul (IST) (Atatüürk, formerly Yesilkoy), 24km west of the city; facilities include 24-hour duty-free, banking, restaurant, bar and car hire. A bus and taxi service is available to the city.
Sabiha Gökçen (SAW) 20km east of the Asian centre, and 45km east of the European centre, of Istanbul. It is Turkey's newest international airport. With banking, duty-free, restaurants and business centre. Taxis are available 24 hours, to destinations in and around Istanbul. A regular shuttle bus service operates into the city centre.

Airport tax: None

Surface
Road: Coach services are available from Austria, France, Germany and Switzerland, as well as a number of countries in the Middle East.
There are connecting routes from the CIS, Greece, Bulgaria and Iran. It is possible to select the northern route via Belgium, Germany, Austria or the southern route through Belgium, Austria and Italy with a car-ferry connection to Turkey.

Rail: Express rail services from Munich, Vienna, Venice, Belgrade, Baghdad and Tehran.
Connections are available from London (Liverpool Street) via the Hook of Holland and Cologne to Istanbul on the Istanbul Express, which also transports cars from other European cities.

Water: Turkish Maritime Lines (TML), the national shipping organisation, and several other cruise lines operate services to Turkey. There are ferry connections with Italy, Cyprus and Greece. For the one-day ferry from the Greek island of Rhodes to Marmaris, a visa is not required.

Getting about
National transport
Air: Turkish Airlines operate regular services between Istanbul, Izmir, Ankara and other major towns. Bodrum regional airport offers internal flights and connections to other nearby Mediterranean destinations. Travelling by air within Turkey is relatively inexpensive.

Road: The Tarsus-Pozanti-Ayrimi-Gaziantep (Tag) motorway connects the southern Antolian region with the rest of Turkey, providing a vital link for the future growth of the region. There has been an extensive road building and maintenance programme in operation since 1999 involving over 1,400km of motorway.

Buses: Many private companies operate day and night services between all cities. Services are generally quicker than trains and prices are competitively low.

Rail: There is 8,542km of rail track. Most major cities and towns are linked by regular rail services.

Water: There are steamship services between Istanbul and most major coastal towns. Car ferries that offer cabins are highly sought-after and should be booked in advance.

City transport
Taxis: Metered taxis available in major towns and cities. Also available are the much cheaper *Dolmus* taxis, which have fixed routes and carry 8–12 passengers. Tipping not customary. For longer journeys the fare should be agreed beforehand. Drivers rarely speak much English and may be new to the city, so advisable to buy a road map.

Buses, trams & metro: Metros run in three of Turkey's main cities – Ankara, Istanbul and Izmir – and are planned for Bursa and Adana.

Car hire
All international companies are represented. Available at main hotels, airports and travel agents but expensive. International driving licence preferred, but most foreign licences accepted. Roads are generally good but local driving erratic. Driving is on the right.

Third party insurance is required. Cars may be imported in Turkey for a maximum of six months in one year. On entry to Turkey, an entry-exit form is filled out.

BUSINESS DIRECTORY
The addresses listed below are a selection only. While World of Information makes every endeavour to check these addresses, we cannot guarantee that changes have not been made, especially to telephone numbers and area codes. We would welcome any corrections.

Telephone area codes
The international direct dialling code (IDD) for Turkey is +90, followed by area code and subscriber's number:

Adana	322	Istanbul (Thrace)	212
Ankara	312	Izmir	232
Bursa	224	Kayseri	352
Dlyarbakir	412	Konya	332
Gaziantep	342	Malatya	422
Istanbul (Anatolia)	216	Samsun	362

Chambers of Commerce
Adana Chamber of Commerce, 52 Abidinpasa Cadessi, Adana (tel: 352-0052; fax: 351-8009; e-mail: basanlik@adan-to.org.tr).

American-Turkish Business Association, Emlak Kredi Bloklari, Levent, 80620

Turkey

Istanbul (tel: 270-6718; fax: 279-0031; e-mail: taba@taba.org.tr).

Ankara Chamber of Commerce, 2 Sogutozu Mahallesi, 06530 Ankara (tel: 285-7950; fax: 2842314; info@atonet.org.tr).

British Chamber of Commerce in Turkey, 18 Mesrutiyet Cadessi, Galatasaray, 34435 Istanbul (tel: 249-0658; fax: 252-5551; e-mail: buscenter@bcct.org.tr).

Istanbul Chamber of Commerce, Resadiye Cadessi, Eminonu, 34378 Istanbul (tel: 455-6000; fax: 513-1565; e-mail: ito@ito.org.tr).

Izmir Chamber of Commerce, 126 Ataturk Cadessi, Pasaport, 35210 Izmir (tel: 441-7777; fax: 446-2251; e-mail: info@izto.org.tr).

Kayseri Chamber of Commerce, 6 Tennuri Sokak, 38040 Kayseri (tel: 222-4528; fax: 232-1069; e-mail: kaytic@kayserito.org.tr).

Konya Chamber of Commerce, 1 Vatan Cadessi, 42040 Konya (tel: 353-4850; fax: 353-0546; e-mail: kto@kto.org.tr).

Samsun Chamber of Commerce and Industry, Hancerli Mahallesi, 8 Abbasasa Sokak, 55020 Samsun (tel: 432-3626; fax: 432-9055; e-mail: samsuntso@samsuntso.org.tr).

Turkey Union of Chambers of Commerce, Industry, Maritime Trade and Commodity Exchanges, 149 Ataturk Bulvari, Bakanlyklar, Ankara (tel: 413-8000; fax: 418-3268; e-mail: info@tobb.org.tr).

Banking

Akbank, Sabanci Center, 80745 4.Levent, Istanbul (tel: 270-2666/0044; fax: 269-7383/8081).

Demirbank, Büyükdere Cadessi 122, 80280 Esentepe, Istanbul (tel: 275-1900; fax: 267-4794/2786).

Esbank, Eskisehir Bankasi, Mesrutiyet Cadessi 141, 80050 Tepebasi, Istanbul (tel: 251-7270; fax: 243-2396).

Garanti Bank, 63 Buyukdere Cadessi, Maslak 80670 Istanbul (tel/fax: 335-3535).

Koçbank, Barbaros Bulvari, Morbasan Sokak, Koza Is Merkezi C Blok, 80692 Besiktas, Istanbul (tel: 274-7777; fax: 267-2987).

Pamukbank, Büyükdere Cadessi 82, 80450 Gayrettepe, Istanbul (tel: 275-2424; fax: 275-8606).

Türkiye Is Bankasi, Atatürk Bulvari 191, 06684 Kavaklidere, Ankara (tel: 428-1140; fax: 425-0750/2).

Yapi ve Kredi Bankasi, Büyükdere Cadessi Yapi Kredi Plaza, A Blok, 80620 Levent, Istanbul (tel: 280-1111; fax: 280-1670/1).

Central bank

Türkiye Cumhuriyet Merkez Bankasy, Ystiklal Cadessi 10 Ulus, 06100 Ankara (tel: 310-3646; fax: 310-7434; e-mail: info@tcmb.gov.tr).

Travel information

Tourism Information Office, Gazi Mustafa Kemal Bul 121, Demirtepe, Ankara (tel: 229-3661, 488-7007).

Turban Travel Avency, Atatürk Bulvari 169, Atayurt Han, Bakanliklar, Ankara (tel: 418-2919).

Turk Hava Yollari (THY Turkish Airlines), General Administration Building, Ataturk Airport Yesilk-y, Istanbul (tel: 574-7402, 663-6300; fax: 574-7444, 663-4744); Cumhuriyet Cad No 199-201, Sisli, Istanbul (tel: 248-2631; fax: 240-2984).

Ministry of tourism

Ministry of Tourism, Inonu Bulvari 5, Ankara (tel: 212-8300; fax: 213-6887; internet site: www.turizm.gov.tr).

Ministries

President's Office, Cankaya, Ankara (tel: 468-5030; fax: 427-1330; internet site: www.cankaya.gov.tr).

Prime Minister's Office, Bakanliklar, Ankara (tel: 419-5896; fax: 417-0476: internet site: www.basbakanlik.gov.tr).

Ministry of Agriculture and Rural Affairs, Ataturk Bulvari 153, Ankara (tel: 417-6000; fax: 417-7168).

Ministry of Culture, Ataturk Bulvari No 29, Ankara (tel: 309-0850; fax: 312-6423).

Ministry of Defence, Ankara (tel: 425-4596; fax: 418-1795).

Ministry of Education, Ataturk Bulvari, Ankara (tel: 419-1410; fax: 417-7027).

Ministry of Energy and Natural Resources, Inonu Bulvari 27, Ankara (tel: 212-6915; fax: 212-3816).

Ministry of the Environment, Eskisehir Yolu, Ankara (tel: 287 9965; fax: 285-2742).

Ministry of Finance, Ankara (tel: 425-0080; fax: 425-0058; internet site: www.maliye.gov.tr).

Ministry of Foreign Affairs, Balgat, Ankara (tel: 287-1665; fax: 287-8811).

Ministry of Forestry, Ataturk Bulvari 153, Ankara (tel: 417-6000; fax: 213-2610).

Ministry of Health, Sihhiye, Ankara (tel: 431-4820; fax: 431-4879).

Ministry of Industry and Trade, Eskisehir Yolu, Ankara (tel: 286-0365; fax: 285-4318).

Ministry of the Interior, Ankara (tel: 418-1368; fax: 418-1795).

Ministry of Justice, Ankara (tel: 419-6050; fax: 417-3954).

Ministry of Labour and Social Security, Inonu Bulvari, Ankara (tel: 212-9700; fax: 215-4962).

Ministry of Public Works and Housing, Vekaletler Cad 1, Ankara (tel: 417-9260; fax: 418-5540).

Ministry of Transport, Ankara (tel: 212-4416; fax: 212-4930).

Other useful addresses

Borsa Komiserligi (stock exchange), Menkul Kiymetler ve Kambiyo Borsasi, Rihtim Caddesi 245, 80030 Karakoy, Istanbul (tel: 298-2100; fax: 298-2500; internet site: http://www.ise.org).

British Consulate General Ankara, Merutiyet Caddesi No 34, Tepebasi, Beyoglu PK33, Ankara (tel: 293-7450; fax: 245-4989).

British Embassy, Sehit Ersan Caddesi 46/A, Cankaya, Ankara (tel: 468-6230/42; fax: 468-3214).

Customs Modernisation Project, Gümrük Müstesarligi, Anafartalar Cad No 6 Kat 14, 06100, Ulus, Ankara (tel: 306-8532, 306-8439; fax: 306-8535).

Director General of Mining, Ankara (tel: 287-9750; fax: 287-9152).

Director General of Press and Publications, Ankara (tel: 468-4967; fax: 468-4966).

Director General of State Water Affairs, Ankara (tel: 418-3415; fax: 418-3409).

Director General of Telecommunications, Ankara (tel: 313-1121; fax: 313-1919).

Embassy of the United States of America, 110 Ataturk Blvd, Ankara (tel: 426-5470, 468-6110; fax: 467-0057/19).

Export Promotion Centre (IGEME), Mithatpasa Cad No 60, Kisilay, Ankara (tel: 418-5351; internet site: http://www.igeme.org.tr).

General Directorate of Foreign Investment, Inönü Bulvari, 06510 Emek, Ankara (tel: 212-8914/5; fax: 212-8916).

Housing Development Administration, Project Implementation Unit, Bilkent Plaza, B1 Blok Kat 1, Bilkent 06530, Ankara (tel: 266-7764, 266-7774; fax: 266-7733).

Modern Tercume Burosu (translation service), Karanfil Sokak 21/4, Yenisehir, Ankara (tel: 417-8122).

Privatisation Administration, Ziya Gokalp Street No 80, Kurtulus 06600 Ankara (tel: 430-0194, 430-4560; fax: 430-6930; e-mail: hascili@oib.gov.tr).

State Institute of Statistics, Necatibey Caddesi 114, Ankara (tel: 417-6440; internet site:

Nations of the World: A Political, Economic and Business Handbook

http://www.die.gov.tr/ENGLISH/index.html).

State Planning Organisation, Necatibey Caddesi 108, Ankara (tel: 417-6440; internet site: http://www.dpt.gov.tr).

Türk Argus Ajansi (translation service), Lamartin Caddesi 32/4 Taksim, Istanbul (tel: 250-5200).

Türk Haberler Ajansi (news agency), Turkocagi Caddesi 1/4, Cagaloglu, Istanbul (tel: 511-4200).

Turkish Embassy (USA), 2525 Massachusetts Avenue, NW, Washington DC 20008 (tel: 202-612-6700; fax: 202-612-6744; e-mail: info@turkey.org).

Turkish International Co-operation Agency, Kizilirmak Cadessi 31, Kocatepe, Ankara (tel: 417-2790).

Türkiye Radyo Televizyon Kurumu, Nevzat Tandogan Caddesi 2, Kavaklidere, Ankara (tel: 428-2230; fax: 414-2767).

Türk Snayicileri ve Isadamlari Dernegi (association of Turkish industrialists and businessmen), Cumhuriyet Caddesi, 233/9-10 Harbiye, Istanbul (tel: 246-2412, 240-1205).

Internet sites

Foreign Trade Secretariat: http://dtm.gov.tr

Republic of Turkey: http://www.turkey.org

State Institute of Statistics: http://www.die.gov.tr

Treasury Secretariat: http://www.treasury.gov.tr

Turkish Foreign Trade and Tourism Centre: http://www.turkex.com

Turkish highways: http://www.kgm.gov.tr/indexe.htm

Turkmenistan

KEY FACTS

Official name: Türkmenistan Jumhuriyati (Republic of Turkmenistan)

Head of State: Turkmenbashi (Leader of all the Turkmen) President Saparmurad Niyazov (since Oct 1990) (President for Life until 2010)

Head of government: President Saparmurad Niyazov

Ruling party: Democratic Party (DP)

Area: 488,100 square km

Population: 5.74 million (2004)

Capital: Ashgabat

Official language: Turkmen

Currency: Manat (M)

Exchange rate: M5,148.00 per US$ (Oct 2005); (official, pegged); M25,000 per US$ (2002) (estimated market rate)

GDP per capita: US$2,469 (2004)

GDP real growth: 7.50% (2004)

Labour force: 2.22 million (2004)

Unemployment: 60.00% (unofficial, 2004)* (no official unemployment)

Inflation: 5.90% (2004)

Oil production: 202,000 bpd (2004)

Balance of trade: US$1.15 billion 2004

Foreign debt: US$2.30 billion (2003)

* estimated figure

Having been annexed by Russia between 1865 and 1885, Turkmenistan became a Soviet Republic in 1925. The country remained part of the Soviet Union until the dissolution of the Communist superpower in 1991. President Niyazov currently occupies the highest office in the land and has retained absolute power over the country since coming to office in 1991. The country has extensive hydrocarbon and natural gas reserves that would provide a welcome fillip to the economy if extraction and delivery projects can be formulated.

Politics

President Niyazov has continued his policy of isolation from the rest of the world. All forms of power – executive, legislative and judicial – remain intensely concentrated in his office. Predictably, given his harsh reign, he has many domestic enemies, a fact that has made his increasingly paranoid. An assassination attempt in November 2003 only added to his obsession with his own personal safety.

Turkmenistan is a vast desert-land, with approximately half of the country's irrigated land planted to cotton; formerly the country was the world's tenth-largest producer, but poor harvests in recent years have led to an almost 50 per cent decline in cotton exports. Niyazov intends to continue using sales of gas and cotton in order to sustain Turkmenistan's erratic economy. Throughout the 1998–2005 period, Turkmenistan suffered from a continued lack of adequate export routes for natural gas and from obligations on extensive short-term external debt. However, total exports rose by 20–30 per cent in 2003–05, largely due to higher international prices for hydrocarbon resources.

Economy

Turkmenistan's economic statistics are virtually unknown and can only really be guessed at. GDP and other statistics that are reported by 'official' sources are subject to wide margins of error. The country joined the IMF on September 22, 1992, but has no outstanding obligations or arrangements with the fund. Overall prospects in the near future are discouraging because of widespread internal poverty, the burden of foreign debt, the government's irrational use of oil and gas revenues, and its unwillingness to adopt market-oriented reforms.

The World Bank has assisted Turkmenistan with three loans and 10 pieces of policy advice over the past 10 years, but says there is little to show in terms of results. The Bank is currently unable to engage more actively with Turkmenistan in light of the country's failure to report its external debt, which is a violation of its agreement with the Bank, and the fact that Turkmenistan has not yet met the Bank's minimum financial resource management standards.

In January 2006, Commissioner for External Relations and European Neighbourhood Policy for the European Union Benita Ferrero-Waldner said the EU had difficulty in working with Turkmenistan. Controls on foreign-funding made implementing projects impossible, even government-approved projects. The question of how to provide assistance in countries where the political will to reform was absent could not easily be answered.

Energy

Over 2005, virtually all of Turkmenistan's limited interactions with the outside world involved exports of natural gas. The aim was to obtain higher payments for the gas from Russia and Ukraine amid continuing uncertainty over what Turkmenistan's reserves and production capacity would be in 2006.

In September, an analyst with the Asian Development Bank stated that production forecasts for Turkmenistan's Daulatabad gas field might not be sufficient to justify the construction of a pipeline through Afghanistan to Pakistan. In June, Russia's Gazprom voiced concerns about Turkmenistan's reserves, Niyazov's government had been slow to provide a promised audit. The issue is particularly important to Gazprom, which has proposed that it boost imports of Turkmenistan gas to 60 to 70 billion cubic metres (cum) a year by 2007. Russian reports have suggested that current production levels do not exceed 45 billion cu m a year.

Turkmenistan attempted in December to impose a price hike from US$44 per 1,000 cum to US$60 on Ukraine and Russia for shipments in 2006, even though there was considerable evidence to suggest it could not deliver. A deal was reached between Kiev and Moscow in early January that would allow Turkmenistan gas to continue to be exported via Russia to Ukraine, at a price yet undecided, but expected to be much more than US$50 per 1,000 cum – one quarter of the world price. Turkmenistan has nowhere else to sell its gas which has put Ukraine in a strong bargaining position.

Turkmenistan has also explored expanded energy exports to China. Deputy Prime Minister Atamurat Berdiev visited China in December and reported that China was interested. Niyazov, who spent much of 2005 shuffling and reshuffling the management of the country's energy sector, is scheduled to take a rare trip abroad to China in April 2006.

Niyazov angered Western energy companies several years ago with his arrogance and conceit that they broke off all negotiations concerning an alternative Caspian Sea gas pipeline to Turkey and beyond.

While natural gas production by Turkmenistan rose only eight per cent over 2005 to 63 billion cum, officials say Niyazov is prepared to massively crank up output in response to any increased demand from Ukraine. Gas exports over 2005 were 45.2 billion cum, or two thirds the amount produced but this year the target is to produce 80 billion cum and export all but two billion. Ukraine is expected to take 40 billion cum, Russia 30 billion and Iran eight billion.

But Niyazov is not satisfied with projected revenues and has said he will start to sell his gas at the global market price by 2007. If Niyazov finds himself unable to get the price he thinks Turkmenistan deserves from Ukraine and Russia, he could cut supplies, but would risk a repetition of the situation that occurred during the first days of 2006, when European customers suffered shortages caused by the Russian Gazprom cut-off.

Outlook

Turkmenistan remains in the iron grip of its all-powerful President Niyazov. Barring assassination, Niyazov will remain in powerful throughout 2006. The dictator's immense power over all decision making in the country has facilitated his ban on opposition groupings and, without any real political infrastructure there is no way that opposition forces, short of violence can remove Niyazov. On the economic front, owing to its vast natural resource base, Turkmenistan continues to grow. The IMF forecasts growth for 2005 to be an exceptional 9.6 per cent, with the 2006 figure predicted to be slightly lower at 6.5 per cent.

Risk assessment

Economy	Good
Politics	Poor
Regional stability	Fair

COUNTRY PROFILE

Historical profile

Turkmenistan, the most ethnically homogenous of the Central Asian republics is largely a desert country, with over 80 per cent of its land mass covered by the Kara Kum desert. The majority of the Turkmen population work in agriculture, principally nomadic cattle raising and intensive agriculture and the hydrocarbons sector. Turkmenistan's economy is based on the production of raw materials, principally gas, oil and cotton, which together generate around 90 per cent of export

KEY INDICATORS — Turkmenistan

	Unit	2000	2001	2002	2003	2004
Population	m	5.30	5.37	5.45	5.59	5.74
Gross domestic product (GDP)	US$bn	4.40	6.00	4.00	4.75	*6.17
GDP per capita	US$	830	1,053	820	850	2,469
GDP real growth	%	17.6	20.5	8.6	10.0	7.5
Inflation	%	7.4	11.6	8.8	5.0	5.9
Oil output	'000 bpd	144.0	162.0	182.0	210.0	202.0
Natural gas output	bn cum	43.8	47.9	49.9	55.1	54.6
Exports (fob) (goods)	US$m	2,508.0	2,526.0	2,860.0	2,970.0	4,000.0
Imports (fob) (goods)	US$m	1,742.0	2,201.0	2,120.0	2,250.0	2,850.0
Balance of trade	US$m	766.0	325.0	735.0	720.0	1,150.0
Current account	US$m	410.0	120.0	580.0	450.0	520.0
Foreign debt	US$bn	2.3	1.9	2.2	2.3	–
Exchange rate	per US$	10,317.00	5,200.00	5,200.00	5,200.00	10.10

* estimated figure

Turkmenistan

revenues. The country is the second-largest gas producer in the Commonwealth of Independent States (CIS), after the Russian Federation and is among the 10 largest cotton exporters in the world.

The Turkmens are a Turkic people divided along tribal lines, the main tribes being the Tekkes of Merv and Attok, the Ersaris, the Yomads and the Goklans. In the seventh century, Arabs conquered Central Asia and introduced Islam. Between the tenth and thirteenth centuries, nomadic Turkmen tribes and Mongols emigrated to what became Turkmenistan. Genghis Khan's Mongol armies then invaded and conquered the region. Between the fifteenth and seventeenth centuries, the southern part of Turkmenistan came under Persian rule, while the northern part was dominated by the states of Khiva and Bukhara, which were predominantly Uzbek.

Present-day Turkmenistan was divided three ways between Tsarist Russia and the Khanates of Bukhara and Khiva until 1881, when Russian troops captured Ashgabat and incorporated the country into Russian Turkestan. The fierce Turkmen tribes south of the Amu Darya River were subdued in 1885.

1917 Central Asian peoples were given the right of self-determination by Lenin after the October Revolution in Russia.

1916–21 Turkmens joined other Central Asians violently opposing a Russian decree conscripting them for non-combatant duties. They fought against the Bolsheviks during the Russian civil war. In 1921, Turkmenistan formed part of the Turkestan Autonomous Soviet Socialist republic (ASSR).

1924 Turkmenistan was given Union Republic status.

1920s–1930s The Soviet programme of agricultural collectivisation and secularisation saw an upsurge in armed resistance and popular uprisings in Turkmenistan.

1960s The completion of the Kara-Kum canal led to a rapid expansion in cotton production. The canal is around 800km long and carries water from the Amu Darya river westwards to Mary and Ashgabat.

1971 Muhammad Gapusov was appointed head of the Turkmenistan Communist Party.

1985 Saparmurad Niyazov replaced Gapusov.

1989 Agzybirlik (Unity), a democratic front led by Turkmenistani intellectuals, was formed, but was banned the following year.

1990 Turkmenistan's Supreme Soviet declared economic and political sovereignty from Moscow and elected Niyazov as its chairman (in effect, state president).

1991 Niyazov supported an attempted military coup against Soviet President Mikhail Gorbachev. Turkmenistan declared independence just before the collapse of the Soviet Union and joined the Commonwealth of Independent States (CIS).

1992 Turkmenistan adopted a new constitution, making the president head of government as well as head of state and giving him the option to appoint a prime minister. Niyazov was re-elected in a direct election in which he was the only candidate allowed to stand.

1993 The manat was introduced as the new national currency. The government began opening up the country to limited foreign investment in the country's oil and gas reserves.

1994 In parliamentary elections, all candidates were returned unopposed. In a referendum, President Niyazov's term of office was extended to 2002 without a new election.

1997 The private ownership of land was legalised.

1998 A natural gas pipeline to Iran was opened.

1999 Parliament made President Niyazov president for life. In parliamentary elections, all the elected officials had been approved by the President.

2001 President Niyazov declared that he wants to retire by 2010, when he will be aged 70.

2002 Turkmenistan became a full member of the Islamic Development Bank (IDB). The President renamed the months of the year after himself, his mother and his spiritual guide, the Ruhnama. He claimed to have escaped an attempt on his life.

2003 In April, President Niyazov signed an agreement with the Russian gas producer, Gazprom, under which Russia will buy 60 billion cubic metres of gas from Turkmenistan annually, starting from 2004. The President cancelled a 1993 dual citizenship agreement with Russia, which sparked a diplomatic row with Moscow.

2004 In March, President Niyazov passed a decree forbidding young men to wear long hair or beards. Listening to car radios and smoking in the street were forbidden and opera and ballet performances were banned. The President ordered construction of a giant ice palace in the Turkmen desert. An agreement on water resources was signed by the Turkmen and Uzbek presidents in November.

In Majlis elections on 19 December, 50 seats were filled, all candidates being supporters of the President.

2005 In May, Amnesty International condemned Turkmenistan's human rights record.

Political structure
Constitution
Turkmenistan was the first Central Asian state to adopt a constitution (on 18 May 1992), which upholds political pluralism, separates legislative, executive and judicial powers and guarantees private ownership of property. However, adherence to the principles of the constitution is rare. Turkmenistan is divided into five administrative regions: Ashkhabat, Turkmenbashi (formerly Krasnovodsk), Mary, Tashauz and Chardzhou.

Form of state
Republic

The executive
The president is head of state, head of government and Supreme Commander of the Armed Forces. The president is directly elected by universal adult suffrage for a maximum of two five-year terms, although in 1999, President Niyazov was nominated president for life by the Khalk Maslakhaty (People's Council). The president must ratify all parliamentary legislation and may legislate by decree; he has the option to appoint a prime minister at any time.

In 2001, President Niyazov announced that he would retire no later than 2010, when he will be 70. Presidential elections are supposed to be held in 2010 and will be open only for younger people who have already held office for five to 10 years and have been approved by the legislature; candidates must have lived in the country for 10 years.

National legislature
The 50-member Majlis (unicameral assembly) is directly elected for a five-year term by universal adult suffrage (over 18 years of age).

The Khalk Maslakhaty (People's Council) is the highest representative body in Turkmenistan. It consists of the president, deputies of the 50-member elected Majlis, cabinet ministers, Khalk Vekillen (who are elected by the citizens of each *entrap* or local authority), the Chairman of the Supreme Court, the Chairman of the Higher Economic Court, the Procurator General, the heads of the administration of *velayats* (regional administrations), mayors of municipal councils and the heads of villages which are administrative centres of *entraps*. The Khalk Maslakhaty meets infrequently.

The president appoints cabinet ministers and chairs sessions of the Khalk Maslakhaty, which is subordinate to the presidency.

Legal system
The legal system is based on civil law. Members of the Supreme Court, the highest judicial body, are appointed by the president. There is no judicial review of legislative acts or presidential decrees.
Last elections
9 January 2005 (parliamentary run-off); 19 December 2004 (parliamentary first round); 1994 (referendum); 21 June 1992 (presidential).
Results: Parliamentary first round: 50 seats were filled. All the candidates were supporters of the President. Turnout was 76.9 per cent.
Presidential referendum: 99.9 per cent of the Turkmenistani people voted to extend President Niyazov's term of office to 2002 without a new election.
In 1999, parliament made President Niyazov president for life.
Next elections
2009 (parliamentary); 2010 (presidential).

Political parties
Ruling party
Democratic Party (DP)
Main opposition party
There are two main opposition parties in Turkmenistan – Agzybirlik (Unity) and the Democratic Progress Party (DPP). They are essentially underground movements and their leaders operate in exile.

Population
5.74 million (2004)
Ethnic make-up
Turkmen (77 per cent), Russian (6.7 per cent), Uzbek (9.2 per cent) and Kazakh (2 per cent).
Religions
The majority of the population are Sunni Muslim (89 per cent). The remainder are predominately Eastern Orthodox Christians (9 per cent).
The government directly controls the hiring, promotion and sacking of Sunni Muslim and Eastern Orthodox clergy.
Turkmenistan has a tradition of Sufism or Islamic mysticism and hosts several important Sufi religious sites.

Education
Secondary specialised education lasts for three to four years. General higher education lasts for four years. The Academy of Sciences in Ashgabat was the Republic's principal college of higher education. However, funding problems meant that by October 2000 the Academy was closed. According to the government, 20 per cent of the relevant age group participate in some form of tertiary education. Those doing so are forced to undergo family checks going back three generations, while overseas education is not sanctioned by the government.

Females constitute 53 per cent of students in secondary education, 38 per cent of students in higher education and 29 per cent of students in professional schools. Although there is equal opportunity for females in education, they are often disadvantaged in employment situations.
A series of reforms have taken place since independence, with the aim of reducing the costs of education in general and vocational education in particular. Vocational training schools provide training to general education graduates, or adults who are required to pay fees. Some schools, especially in the bigger cities, are able to make enough income to maintain or even expand their activities. However, as government spending on vocational training in rural areas was reduced in the late 1990s, a number of vocational schools closed.
The quality of education is widely regarded as poor at all levels, and the sector is likely to come under increasing pressures from budgetary cuts and high population growth in the region. In September 2000, President Niyazov announced the axing of 5,000 jobs in the education sector as part of his drive to control the government's budget. Combined with low wages in the sector, this move is likely to undermine morale and reduce Turkmenistan's relatively high education statistics.
Literacy rate: 98 per cent adult rate (World Bank).
Enrolment rate: 90 per cent gross primary enrolment of relevant age group (including repeaters) (World Bank).

Health
The healthcare system in Turkmenistan has suffered serious under-funding in recent years so that the benefits enjoyed by Turkmenis under the Soviet regime have been lost. Life expectancy has fallen to the lowest of any central Asean state. The president ordered nearly all higher education institutes to be closed and so stopped the training of new doctors and nurses. By the end of 2003, over 15,000 public medical workers had been sacked and free healthcare was abolished. Hospitals outside the capital were closed, leaving 55 per cent of the population, living in rural areas, forced to travel long distances for treatment.
The availability of prescription drugs is severely limited, although the privatisation of pharmacies has led to an increase in the supply of non-prescription drugs. There are no private hospitals or clinics in the region although some practitioners offer basic medical services.
Environmental hazards have contributed to widespread respiratory diseases, which prompted the government to ban smoking in public places. Nevertheless government policy on healthcare has ignored the need for Aids awareness, which is thought, by campaigners, to be an heavily underreported.
HIV prevalence: 0.1 per cent aged 15–49 in 2003 (World Bank)
Life expectancy: 62 years
Fertility rate/Maternal mortality rate: 2.7 births per woman (2003); maternal mortality 65 per 100,000 live births (World Bank).
Infant mortality rate: 79 deaths per 1,000 live births (World Bank).
Head of population per physician/bed: 30 physicians and 11.5 hospital beds per 1,000 people.

Welfare
The government has attempted to deliver social services during the transitional period, but significant fiscal constraints continue to impede the progress of universal social transfers in the long-run. Taxes collected by the state tax service go to the state budget and the social security fund. The social security system is partly financed by payroll taxes set at 30 per cent of wages and voluntary contributions, while the government bears the full cost of social pensions and other subsidies as needed.
The state provides for different types of welfare payments, including pensions and several benefits related to disability, child-care, minimum social allowance, workers compensation, unemployment and family allowances. In 2001, the government decided to double public sector salaries.
Pensions are calculated on the number of years employed and the level of income. In 2001, the minimum monthly pension was set at M100,000 (US$20 at the official rate) and the maximum at M400,000 (US$80). The minimum social allowance benefit is paid to women aged 62 and to men aged 67, amounting to M100,000 per month (US$20) for those who are not entitled to old age retirement benefit. Pensions were doubled in February 2003 following a presidential decree.
Maternity leave benefits are paid according to work experience and income. It is usually paid for 112 days. Workers' compensation benefits are paid at the rate of 6 per cent of salary in cases of unhealthy work conditions and 12 per cent of salary for severely harmful work conditions. Those working in desert areas receive compensation at the rate of 10 per cent of their salary.
The government's human rights record remains extremely poor and it continues to commit serious human rights abuses. Interference with citizens' privacy remains a

Turkmenistan

problem. Domestic violence and discrimination against women are prevalent.

Main cities
Ashgabat (capital, estimated population 727,700 in 2003), Turkmenabat (213,500), Dasoguz (160,400).

Languages spoken
There is a 28 per cent population of Russian or Uzbek speakers. English is also spoken.
Official language/s
Turkmen

Media
The Turkmen government has an absolute monopoly of the media. The authorities monitor media outlets, operate printing presses and lay down editorial policies.
Press
Turkmenistan has the most repressive climate for journalists, according to the US-based Committee to Protect Journalists (CPJ). The state controls all publishing and press freedom is totally absent in Turkmenistan. In 2000, the government adopted a new regulation requiring all publishing houses, along with printers and copying establishments, to obtain a state licence and register their equipment. Foreign correspondents are rarely allowed to visit the country and those who obtain permission have limited access. The aim of the operation was to search for subversive literature.
Some of the newspapers in circulation include *Turkmenistan* and *Watan* (both in Turkmen); *Turkmenskaya Iskra* (Russian) and *Zaman* (Turkish). Almost all the publishers of newspapers and magazines are located in the Ashgabat Press House. *Neutralny Turkmenistan* is owned by the state.
Broadcasting
Turkmen TV, state-owned, operates four channels. Turkmen Radio, state-owned, operates two stations. Russian TV and radio broadcast from Moscow.

Economy
Turkmenistan is largely a desert country, with over 80 per cent of its land mass covered by the Kara Kum desert. The majority of the population work in agriculture, principally nomadic cattle raising and intensive agriculture, and the hydrocarbons sector. Turkmenistan's economy is based on the production of raw materials, principally gas, oil and cotton, which together generate around 90 per cent of export revenues. The country is the second-largest gas producer in the Commonwealth of Independent States (CIS), after the Russian Federation, and is among the 10 largest cotton exporters in the world. Since independence in 1991, the end of state subsidies from Moscow and galloping inflation have caused a huge drop in living standards.
The economy is dominated by the state, which accounts for around 80 per cent of annual output. A control system is prevalent, with the state fixing prices, output targets and controlling the distribution, marketing and trade of most products. Progress on economic reform has been slow and promised wealth generated by massive natural gas reserves remains a distant prospect. Investors remain largely wary of Turkmenistan, whose economy is characterised by an inadequate legal framework, often contradictory laws, corruption and excessive bureaucracy.
Non-payment by neighbouring republics for gas exports has been one of Turkmenistan's biggest problems since independence and, combined with limited export routes, has undermined the ability to take advantage of rising energy prices. Turkmenistan is dependent on a gas pipeline owned by Russia's Gazprom, which has occasionally been closed down in order to maintain high prices for Russian gas exports. The bottleneck in gas exports, which account for around 60 per cent of export revenues, hampers Turkmenistan's access to vital hard currency markets. Economic data are unreliable and policy-making is opaque. The government frequently lies about the state of the economy and public finances, attracting criticism from the IMF and the European Bank for Reconstruction and Development (EBRD) as well as the CIS. While the economy is growing, the increase is at a lower rate than claimed by the government. In real terms, GDP is only around 40 per cent of its level in 1989, two years before independence. Life remains austere for many in Turkmenistan and over half the population lives below the poverty line. Growth is driven by domestic investment – mostly state-led investments in oil and gas extraction, petrochemicals, electricity generation and transmission, textiles, and luxury housing. About 1.5 per cent of GDP is invested by foreign companies developing Turkmen oil fields under production-sharing agreements.
In 2003, the government adopted the Strategy for Turkmenistan's Economic, Political and Cultural Development for the Period up to 2020, which sets production targets for all sectors, to be supported by state-led investments.

External trade
Turkmenistan is highly dependent on trade with Commonwealth of Independent States (CIS) countries, which is quickly drying up. Although export growth has looked impressive in recent years, a large amount of exports are not paid for in cash and many of Turkmenistan's customers are in arrears.
Imports
Principal imports are machinery and equipment, chemicals, and foodstuffs.
Main sources: Russia (14 per cent total, 2004), Ukraine (13.8 per cent), US (11.1 per cent), UAE (8.1 per cent), Turkey (8.0 per cent), Germany (6.8 per cent), France (4.6 per cent)
Exports
Turkmenistan's main exports are natural gas, crude oil, petrochemicals, cotton and textiles.
Main destinations: Ukraine (49.8 per cent total, 2004), Iran (17.2 per cent), Italy (5.3 per cent), Turkey (4.7 per cent)

Agriculture
Farming
Agriculture typically contributes around 20 per cent to GDP. The cultivated land area is around 32 million hectares (ha), with arable land accounting for 19 million ha. Cotton, a major export earner, is cultivated on over 750,000ha of arable land. Turkmenistan was the second largest producer of cotton in the former Soviet Union and the 10th largest producer in the world, with a high annual export earning of US$245 million in 1998 that fell to US$130 million by 2002.
In a report published in early 2005 – *The Curse of Cotton: Central Asia's destructive monoculture* – the International Crisis Group (ICG) said that while the former Soviet cotton producing countries of Uzbekistan, Tajikistan and Turkmenistan continued to exploit their cotton growers there was little hope of improving economic development and tackling poverty. The cotton industry is vital to the economy of Turkmenistan, yet while the industry continues to rely on cheap labour (including children), land ownership is uncertain, state intervention discourages competition and the rule of law is limited, there is little incentive for the powerful vested interests to reform the system.
The government has started to diversify production in the agricultural sector away from the cotton monoculture. This has generated a small export surplus in cereal production and a growth of 18 per cent in wheat production. The 23 per cent rise in agricultural output could possibly signal self-sufficiency in grain production.
Turkmenistan is reliant on an inefficient Soviet irrigation system, which diverts water from the Amu Darya river and has contributed to the drying up of the Aral Sea. The irrigation system suffers from poor management and maintenance, with water losses of about 50 per cent, rising salinity and poor drainage.
An absence of storage and packaging facilities means that up to 30 per cent of the

grain and cotton harvests are lost annually. Livestock accounts for around one-quarter of agricultural production, including the famous Karakul sheep. Crop production in 2004 included: 2.6 million tonnes (mt) wheat, 110,000 tonnes (t) rice, 150,000t potatoes, 180,000t grapes, 10,00t pulses, 250,000t tomatoes, 71,200t oilcrops, 1.0mt seed cotton, 3,000t tobacco, 278,000t fruit in total, 724,400t vegetables in total. Livestock production included: 223,7000t meat in total, 106,000t beef, 95,000mt lamb and goat meat, 14,000t poultry, 35,260t eggs, 1.4mt milk, 8,000mt honey.

Fishing
Turkmenistan has considerable fishing resources, with estimated total reserves at 50,000 tonnes of Caspian Sea fish and 8,000 tonnes of inland water fish. Turkmenbashi, on the Caspian Sea, provides an excellent base for accessing marine resources, being located near the main fishing grounds and remaining ice-free throughout the year. The typical annual fish catch is over 12,000 tonnes; the main fish type is kilka, although herring, shad, mullet and crayfish are also harvested.

Forestry
Less than 10 per cent of Turkmenistan has forest cover. All forested land is owned by the state. There is no large-scale forest industry and most wood products are imported from Russia.

Industry and manufacturing
Industry typically contributes around 45 per cent of GDP and employs 25 per cent of the workforce.
The sector is dominated by the processing of hydrocarbons and other raw materials. The sector is labour intensive and the use of energy and raw materials is wasteful. There is some light engineering industry, which mainly concentrates on the production of cables. US-based Coca-Cola has a plant in Turkmenistan. The GAP-Turkmen joint venture was inaugurated in the mid-1990s and is now a fully vertically integrated jeans producer, using locally produced cotton.

Tourism
The potential for tourism in Turkmenistan, a large part of which is desert, is limited. Attractions include a number of historical and cultural sites. Mountain and coastal resorts are being developed and hotel accommodation is expanding. Visitor numbers are modest at some 8,000 a year, but increasing slowly. Air connections are improving and Ashgabat Airport has been modernised.

Environment
The Aral Sea is drying up due to the overuse of water from the two main rivers which feed into it and has lost 40 per cent of its water, dropping by up to 19 metres. This has resulted in desertification of the surrounding land. A UN study published in 2004 reported that there was no possibility of restoring the water and the need must be on preserving what was is left. The government has endorsed a 2004 joint strategy to resolve the demands of its water requirements with its neighbours. An artificial lake (132 cubic metres deep, 3,460 square km in area) in the Kara Kum Desert is planned to be constructed by 2010 at a cost of US$6 billion. It will be situated at the Karashor valley and according to the government will prevent the 4,060 square km large lowlands from being flooded, stop desalinisation of the land and return the area to crop growing. Environmentalists claim it will undermine the agricultural sector and contribute to water loss.

Mining
There are large deposits of iodine-bromine, sodium sulphate, magnesium, sulphur, potassium and other salts in Turkmenistan. Prime deposits of ore and rock are located in Tourakyr, Bolshoy Balkhan, Kopet Dag, Badkhyz, Govurdak, Kugitang, Cheleken, Turkmenbashi peninsula, central and south-east Garagum and northern Turkmenistan. Of these, the Zulfagar alunite deposit in Badkhyz in the south contains several million tonnes of ore with a 50 per cent alunite content. Turkmenistan has the third largest deposits of sulphur in the world, located in the Kara Kum desert. Deposits of industrial minerals, notably kaolin and building granite, are also exploited. Non-ferrous and rare metals are mined and used for the production of chemicals. Gold and platinum are also present.
Despite Turkmenistan's vast resources, mineral deposits are under-exploited and not used significantly in domestic industry. Turkmenistan has not traditionally extracted or processed any significant amounts of metal ores, although the government has shown interest in attracting foreign investment to build its own metal-producing facilities.

Hydrocarbons
Turkmenistan's oil reserves stood at 500 million barrels in 2004. It remains difficult to estimate Turkmenistan's potential oil reserves as much will depend on negotiations to define ownership and prospecting rights in the Caspian Sea. Oil production increased to 260,000 barrels per day (bpd) in 2004. The government plans to increase oil production to two million bpd by 2010, despite difficulties in meeting goals because of shortage of foreign investment.. Turkmenistan exported around 170,000 bpd in 2004. Turkmenistan has two oil refineries – Turkmenbashi and Chardzhou – with a combined capacity of 237,000bpd.
State-owned Turkmenneft accounts for 90.5 per cent of oil extraction and state-owned gas producer Turkmengaz produces another 3 per cent. The rest is produced by foreign companies in production-sharing arrangements.
Turkmenistan had proven natural gas reserves of 2.90 trillion cubic metres in 2004, making it one of the world's largest deposits, although the government claims the actual figure may be closer to 20 trillion cubic metres. Gas production was 55.6 billion cubic metres in 2004. State-owned Turkmengaz accounts for 85 per cent of production.
In 1998, a natural gas pipeline to Iran was opened. A number of alternatives for further gas pipelines have been put forward, including a trans-Caspian pipeline (TCP), which would run across the Caspian to Azerbaijan through Georgia to Turkey, and an alternative pipeline south, through Afghanistan to Pakistan. Turkmenistan does not produce or import coal.

Energy
Turkmenistan has an electricity generating capacity of 3.9GW and generates 60 per cent more electricity than it consumes. All power stations run on natural gas. Turkmenistan is connected to Iranian power lines for export of electricity. Iran and Turkmenistan may exchange electricity during periods of peak energy consumption, usually summer in Turkmenistan and winter in Iran. Electricity is also exported to Kazakhstan.
Turkmenistan plans to sell electricity through Iran to other countries of the Economic Co-operation Organisation (ECO), which includes six former Soviet republics. The government aims to increase electricity production to 25.5 billion by 2012, but reaching this target will require significant investment in energy infrastructure.

Financial markets
Commodity exchange
The State Commodity and Raw Materials (SC&RM) exchange trades commodities only.

Banking and insurance
The economic crisis of 1997–98 led to all banks in Turkmenistan becoming 'government commercial banks'. Prior to this move, Turkmenistan had 67 banks, two of which were state-owned banks (Vneshekonombank and Sberbank). Vneshekonombank has become one of the largest banks in Central Asia since its

Turkmenistan

creation in 1991. The bank dominates import/export operations and is a key institution for the operation of foreign investment in Turkmenistan. Sberbank holds 95 per cent of all household deposits. The banking sector is widely viewed as corrupt and inefficient, failing to channel funds effectively, and is constrained by the government's tight control of the credit and foreign exchange markets.

Central bank
Central Bank of Turkmenistan
Main financial centre
Ashgabat

Time
GMT plus five hours

Geography
Turkmenistan is the second largest Central Asian republic and shares lengthy borders with Iran to its south and Uzbekistan to its north and east. The country also borders Kazakhstan to the north-west and Afghanistan to the south-east. The Caspian Sea, where the major port of Turkmenbashi is located, is to the west. The Kara Kum desert comprises over 80 per cent of Turkmenistan's total area. The Kopet Dag mountains extend along Turkmenistan's southern border with Iran and Afghanistan.

Climate
Temperatures in Ashgabat range between 0 and 40 degrees Celsius (C). Turkmenistan can be very hot in the summer, with temperatures of 35 degrees C common and a maximum of up to 50 degrees C in some provinces. Winters in the Ashgabat area tend to be mild and temperatures do not usually fall below freezing. However, in mountainous southern areas it is not uncommon for temperatures as low as minus 33 degrees C to be recorded. Ashgabat is the southernmost capital city of the former Soviet republics, on the same latitude as San Francisco and Cordoba.

Dress codes
Smart clothes are required for business visitors.

Entry requirements
Passports
Required by all. Passports must be valid six months after date of departure.
Visa
Required by all. Business visitors require a full itinerary and an invitation, certified by the Ministry of Foreign Affairs in Ashgabat, from a local, private individual or company to support their application. The Turkmen Chamber of Commerce can provide new business visitors with such a letter. For tourists, these can be obtained from authorised travel agents in Ashgabat. All visitors must provide evidence of sufficient funds for the visit and return/onwards passage.
For further information visit www.turkmenistanembassy.org.
All visa applications made overseas are referred to Ashgabat for a decision. This can take several weeks. There is an accelerated 24 hours service, but a supplementary fee charged at approximately US$150 is levied.
On arrival visitors must complete a migration card and pay a US$10 migration fee. The authorities retain one copy and the other must be handed back, by the visitor, on departure.
Visitors must register within three days of their arrival, excluding weekends and holidays, with the Turkmenistan State Registration Service. This is carried out by the inviting organisation or individual, and a registration fee is paid. Tourists should register with the State Committee of Turkmenistan for Tourism and Sports. Registration is for the period of the visa; three days before departure, visitors must de-register with the same authorities. Visitors not staying in Ashgabat should register at the local velayat office of their place of residence (there is no need to register both in Ashgabat and regionally).
Visitors transiting the country can be registered at entry and exit points if their stay is not longer than five days and they hold a valid transit visa. Transit visitors cannot change their visas in-country, and need to notify the authorities if they intend to vary their route through the country.

Currency advice/regulations
Import and export of the national currency is not allowed. A refund is possible against exchange receipts. Import of foreign currencies is subject to restrictions and persons should check with the central bank for up-to-date regulations.
Ensure you bring enough US dollars to cover all potential needs, although services can only be paid for with the manat, the local currency. Turkmenistan is a cash-only economy. Traveller's cheques and credit cards are not commonly accepted.

Customs
On arrival declare all foreign currency and valuable items such as jewellery, cameras, computers etc.

Prohibited imports
Prohibited imports include generally restricted items (arms, unlicensed drugs etc), carpets and wool rugs.

Health (for visitors)
A reciprocal health agreement for urgent medical treatment exists with the United Kingdom. Proof of UK residence will be required.

Mandatory precautions
Vaccination certificate required for yellow fever if travelling from an infected area.

Advisable precautions
Water precautions recommended: water purification tablets may be useful or drink bottled water.
It is advisable to be 'in date' for the following immunisations: polio (within 10 years), tetanus (within 10 years), typhoid, hepatitis 'A' (moderate risk only), tick-borne encephalitis, tuberculosis. Also hepatitis 'B' if you are spending more than 6–8 working weeks in a year in the region.
There has been a significant increase in the number of cases of diphtheria. Anti-malarial precautions are advisable. Inoculation against rabies is advisable if travelling to rural areas. It could be wise to have precautionary antibiotics if going outside major urban centres. A travel kit including a disposable syringe is a reasonable precaution.

Hotels
Hotels often in short supply and expensive. Advisable to book in advance through Intourist or other specialist travel agents. A number of major hotel renovations and new building projects are being undertaken in the centre of Ashgabat.

Credit cards
Credit cards are accepted.

Public holidays
Fixed dates
1 Jan (New Year's Day), 12 Jan (Remembrance Day), 18 Feb (President's Birthday), 19 Feb (National Flag Day), 8 Mar (Women's Day), 20 Mar (Novruz Bairam/Persian New Year), 9 May (Victory Day), 18 May (Constitution Day), 21 Jun (Day of Election of First President), 6 Oct (1948 Earthquake Commemoration), 27–28 Oct (Independence Day, two days), 12 Dec (Day of Neutrality).
Variable dates
Eid al Adha, Eid al Fitr (three days).
The Islamic year contains 354 or 355 days, with the result that Muslim feasts advance by 10–12 days against the Gregorian calendar. Dates of feasts vary according to the sighting of the new moon, so cannot be forecast exactly. Islamic year 1426: 10 February 2005 to 30 January 2006.

Working hours
Banking
Mon–Fri: 0930–1730.
Business
Mon–Fri: 0900–1800.
Shops
Mon–Sat: 0900–1800.

Telecommunications
Telecommunications have improved with the completion of the Turkmen section of the Trans-Asia-Europe fibre-optic communications line. However, businesses continue to complain of high costs and inefficiency, particularly with regards to Internet and email facilities.

Electricity supply
220V AC 50Hz. Round two-pin continental plugs are standard.

Social customs/useful tips
Local customs are in a period of change. In general, the direction of change is toward liberalisation and Westernisation of attitudes and customs, although courtesy and respect for traditions are still important. Turkmens can be wary of new commitments and decision-making can be very slow. Gratuities are becoming more customary, particularly in international hotels. Visitors are advised to carry some form of identity at all times.

Security
It is unwise to venture out on the streets alone at night. Incidents of mugging, theft and pickpocketing are increasing in all cities. Visitors should be vigilant and are advised to dress down. Keep expensive jewellery, watches and cameras out of sight.

Getting there
Air
National airline: Turkmenistan Airlines
International airport/s: Ashgabat Airport (Code: ASB), 4km from city centre. National carrier, Khova Yollary Airways, allocated about US$100m for the 1998 civil aviation development plan. Seven new international air routes are to open and three routes to Russia are to be relaunched. A new guidance system and runway (completed April 1998) at Ashgabat Airport will allow more traffic to be handled. An airport complex is to be built at the southern town of Mary, the landing strip at Neitdag near the shores of the Caspian Sea is to be reconstructed, and an arrival terminal at eastern Charzhou airport is to be built.
Other airport/s: Mary airport in southern Turkmenistan meets international flight standards from January 2002.
Airport tax: There is no airport departure tax.
Surface
Road: Primary roads are few; secondary roads, particularly in desert areas, are of poor quality.
There are border crossings with Iran, Afghanistan, Kazakhstan and Uzbekistan. A road links Chardhzhou and Mazar-e-Sharif in Afghanistan.
Rail: A railway service operates between Iran and Turkmenistan. It runs nearly 300km from the Iranian Silk Road city of Mashhad, crosses the Turkmen border at Sarakhs and joins the Soviet-era Turksib railway at Tedzhen. It gives Turkmenistan access to the Iranian Gulf port of Bandar Abbas.
Main port/s: Turkmenbashi (formerly Krasnovodsk) has ferry links to Baku, Azerbaijan.

Getting about
National transport
Air: Akhal Air Company (division of Turkmenistan Airlines) operates domestic services. Daily flights between Ashgabad and Mary.
Road: Roads are poorly maintained and sometimes dangerous. However, new highways are under construction.
Buses: Buses serve Turkmenbashi (formerly Krasnovodsk) and Mary.
City transport
Taxis: Volga taxis have a sign on top. Agree a price beforehand. It is safer to use officially marked taxis which you should not share with strangers.
Car hire
A national licence with authorised translation, or an international driving permit, is required.

BUSINESS DIRECTORY
The addresses listed below are a selection only. While World of Information makes every endeavour to check these addresses, we cannot guarantee that changes have not been made, especially to telephone numbers and area codes. We would welcome any corrections.

Telephone area codes
The international direct dialling (IDD) code for Turkmenistan is +993, followed by area code and subscriber's number:
Ashgabat   12
Mary   522
Turkmenabad (Chardhzhou)   378
Turkmenbashi (Krasnovodsk)   243

Useful telephone numbers
Fire: 01
Police: 02
Ambulance: 03
Gas leak: 04

Chambers of Commerce
Turkmenistan Chamber of Commerce and Industry, 17 Karreyeva Street, Ashgabat 744000 (tel: 355-594; fax: 355-381; e-mail: asccitm@online.tm).

Banking
Daykhanbank, 60 Atabayeva St, Ashgabat (tel: 419-873, 419-875; fax: 419-868).

Garashsyzlyk, 30 A Shevchenko St, Ashgabat (tel: 354-875, 397-393; fax: 397-892).

International Joint-Stock Bank Garaguma, 3 K Kuliyeva St, Ashgabat (tel: 354-062, 475-269; fax: 353-854).

National Bank of Pakistan, Sheraton Turkmen Hotel, 7 Gorogly St, 744000 Ashgabat (tel: 350-465, 512-050; fax: 350-465).

Obabank, 51 Ostrovskogo, Ashgabat (tel: 346-968, 346-558; fax: 246-968).

Prezidentbank, (temporarily at:) 22 Bitarap Turkmenistan Str, Ashgabat (tel: 357-943; fax: 510-812).

The Savings Bank of Turkmenistan, 86 Prospect Mahtumkuly, 744000 Ashgabat (tel: 394-298, 395-4671; fax: 396-553).

Senagat, 42 Turkmenbashy Shayoly Prospect, Ashgabat (tel: 510-305, 350-694; fax: 510-571).

The State Bank for Foreign Economic Affairs of Turkmenistan (Turkmenvnesheconombank), 22 Asudalyk St, 744000 Ashgabat (tel: 235-0252; fax: 239-7982).

Central bank
State Central Bank of Turkmenistan, Gogol Street 22, 744000 Ashgabat (tel: 356-131; fax: 510-812).

Travel information
Akhal Air Company, Ashgabat Airport, 744088 Ashgabat (tel: 225-6084/1052; fax: 229-0724, 225-4402).

Intourist, Hotel Ashgabat, Prospekt Makhtumkuli 74, 744023 Ashgabat (tel: 290-026).

Lufthansa Airport Office, Ashgabat Airport (tel: 510-697; fax: 510-728).

Turkmenintour, Ul Makhtumkhuli 74, Ashgabat (tel: 256-932, 255-191; fax: 293-169).

Turkmenistan Airlines, Ashgabat Airport (foreign economic relations) (tel: 290-766; fax: 254-402).

Ministry of tourism
Ministry of Culture and Tourism, Ulitsa Pushkin 14, Ashgabat 744000 (tel: 253-560; fax: 551-991).

National tourist organisation offices
The State Tourism Corporation of Turkmenistan (Turkmensiyakhat), 17, Pushkin Street, Ashgabat 744000 (tel: 354-777; fax: 396-740, 397-537; e-mail: travel@emtm.net; internet site: http://www.turkmens.com/asgabat.html).

Ministries
Ministry of Agriculture, Ulitsa Azadi 63, Ashgabat 744000 (tel: 256-691; fax: 253-557).

Ministry of Automobile Transport, Ulitsa Baba Annanova 2, Ashgabat 744025 (tel: 474-992; fax: 470-391).

Turkmenistan

Ministry of Communications, Ulitsa Zhitnikova 36, Ashgabat 744000 (tel: 256-665).

Ministry of Construction, Ulitsa Alishera Navoi 56, Ashgabat 744000 (tel: 256-060).

Ministry of Construction Materials Industry, Ulitsa Steklozavodskaya 1, Ashgabat 744000 (tel: 251-560; fax: 251-913).

Ministry of Consumer Goods, Ulitsa Annadurdieva 52, Ashgabat 744000 (tel: 255-442; fax: 254-833).

Ministry of Economy and Finance, Borodinskaya Street no 2, Ashgabat 744000 (tel: 251-653; fax: 256-511).

Ministry of Energy and Industry, Ulitsa N Pomma 6, Ashgabat 744000 (tel: 254-921; fax: 291-670).

Ministry of Foreign Affairs, Prospect Lenina no 11, Ashgabat 744000 (tel: 251-463).

Ministry of Foreign Economic Relations, Ulitsa Kemine 92, Ashgabat 744000 (tel: 297-511; fax: 297-524).

Ministry of Health, Prospect Magtymguly 95, Ashgabat 744000 (tel: 251-063; fax: 255-032).

Ministry of Information, Ulitsa Chekhova 8, Ashgabat (tel: 297-572).

Ministry of Interior Affairs (tel: 251-328).

Ministry of Melioration and Water Resources, Ulitsa Seidi 1, Ashgabat 744000 (tel: 253-032; fax: 298-589).

Ministry of Oil and Gas Industry and Mineral Resources, 28 Gogolia Street, Ashgabat 744000 (tel: 293-827; fax: 510-443).

Ministry of Trade, Pervomayskovo Street no 1, Ashgabat 744000 (tel: 251-047; fax: 295-108).

Office of the President (tel: 254-534).

Other useful addresses

American Business Liaison, Gogol Street no 17, Ashgabat 74000 (tel: 253-386).

British Embassy, 301-308 Office Building, Ak Altin Plaza Hotel, Ashgabat (tel: 251-0861; fax: 632-510).

Central Asia Research Forum, School of Oriental and African Studies, Thornhaugh Street, London WC1H 0XG, UK (tel: (0)20-7323-6300; fax: (0)20-7436-3844).

Department of Investments, Cabinet of Ministers, Ashgabat (tel: 254-954; fax: 255-112).

EU-TACIS, 92 Kemine Street, Ashgabat (tel: 512-117, 251-020; fax: 511-721).

Kuvyat (state energy corporation), 6 Nurberdi Pomma Street, Ashgabat; Foreign Economic Relations (tel/fax: 254-921).

State Agency for Foreign Investment of Turkmenistan, 53 Azadi Street, Ashgabat 74400 (tel: 350-231; fax: 350-415).

State Committee on Statistics, 72 Magtymgyly Avenue, Ashgabat 744000 (tel: 294-265, 253-596; fax: 254-379).

State Commodity and Raw Materials Exchange, Magtumguly Street 3111, Ashgabat (tel: 254-321; fax: 510-304).

State Customs Office, 7 Stepan Razin, 7440225 Ashgabat (tel: 470-455; fax: 470-221).

State Railway of Turkmenistan, 7 Saparmirat Turkmenbashi Street, 744007 Ashgabat; Engineering Department (tel: 473-936; fax: 473-958); International Services (tel: 473-958; fax: 510-632).

State TV and radio, Prospekt Svobody 89, Ashgabat (tel: 251-515).

Turkmenistan Embassy (USA), 2207 Massachusetts Svenue, NW, Washington DC 20008 (tel: 202-588-1500; fax: 202-588-0697; e-mail: turkmen@earthlink.net).

Turkmenintorg Foreign Trade Organisation, Hivinskaya Str 1, 744000 Ashgabat (tel: 298-774/684/975, 297-521; fax: 298-774/955, 295-987).

Internet sites

Turkmenistan Embassy, Washington, US: http://www.turkmenistanembassy.org

Turkmenistan Information Centre: http://www.turkmenistan.com

Turks and Caicos Islands

KEY FACTS

Official name: Turks and Caicos Islands

Head of State: Queen Elizabeth II, represented by Governor Richard Tauwhare (sworn in 11 Jul 2005)

Head of government: Chief Minister Michael Eugene Misick (sworn in 15 Aug 2003)

Ruling party: Progressive National Party (PNP)

Area: 430 square km

Population: 19,956 (2004)

Capital: Cockburn Town (on Grand Turk)

Official language: English

Currency: US dollar (US$) = 100 cents

GDP per capita: US$9,600 (2003)

GDP real growth: 4.90% (2003)

Labour force: 4,850 (2003)

Unemployment: 10.00% (2003)

Inflation: 4.00% (2003)

Balance of trade: -US$6.40 million (2003)

Visitor numbers: 155,600 (2003)

COUNTRY PROFILE

Historical profile
The first residents of the islands were Amerindians. There are claims that Christopher Colombus actually made his first landing (1492) in the Americas on Grand Turk, and not in the neighbouring Bahamas.
1512 Spanish explorer, Juan Ponce de León, arrived.
1678 British settlers came from Bermuda and set up a salt-panning industry.
1766 Having overridden French and Spanish claims to the islands, Britain appointed a colonial resident.
1799 The islands were annexed to the Bahamas.
1874–1959 The islands were administered by the British from Jamaica, after which time they were ruled directly from London by a governor.
1972 The islands received their own governor.
1973 The islands became a Crown colony.
1976 The first elections under a new constitution were won by the pro-independence People's Democratic Movement (PDM).
1980 The PDM lost the general election (if they had won, the UK would have granted the islands independence) to the Progressive National Party (PNP) which was committed to maintaining the status quo.
1985 Chief Minister Norman Saunders, the minister for development and commerce, and a PNP member of the Legislative Council, were arrested and subsequently convicted in the US on drug trafficking charges.
1986 After allegations of corruption in the local government, a commission of inquiry found the chief minister, Nathaniel Francis, and two of his ministers, unfit to govern. The governor dissolved the government and the Executive Council, and ruled through a special Advisory Council, of which he was chairman, until elections in 1988.
1988 The PDM won 11 of the 13 seats.
1991 The PNP returned to power after winning eight seats in the general election.
1995 The PDM won the election. Hugh Derek Taylor was sworn in as chief minister.
1999 In the general election, the PDM increased its representation from eight to nine seats.
2002 Jim Poston became governor.
2003 The ruling PDM won the parliamentary election; the opposition PNP won two seats in by-elections, giving it a majority in parliament. Chief Minister Taylor resigned on 15 August and Michael Eugene Misick was sworn in on the same day.
2004 In January, the government agreed to implement the EU's Savings Tax Directive.
2005 Richard Tauwhare was sworn in as governor on 11 July.

Political structure
Constitution
The 1976 constitution was suspended in 1986, restored and revised in 1988 and amended in 1993. It provides for the exercise of a ministerial type of government, through a governor appointed by the British monarch, an Executive Council (ExCo) which has general control of government, and a Legislative Council (LegCo).
Voting: universal suffrage 18 years and over.
Form of state
Caribbean dependency status: overseas territory of the UK.
The executive
The head of state, Queen Elizabeth II, is represented by an appointed governor who is responsible for external affairs, defence, internal security, the police service and civil service. The governor appoints the chief minister. The Executive Council (ExCo) consists of five ministers appointed by the governor from among the members of the LegCo and three ex-officio members.
National legislature
The 19-seat unicameral Legislative Council (LegCo) comprises 13 popularly elected members (four-year term in single-seat constituencies), three ex-officio members and three appointed members.
Legal system
The legal system is based on laws of England and Wales, with a small number of laws adopted from Jamaica and The Bahamas.
Last elections
24 April 2003 (parliamentary)
Results: Parliamentary: the PDM won seven seats out of 13 and the PNP six seats. On 7 August 2003, the opposition PNP won two seats in by-elections, giving it a majority in parliament with eight seats out of 13, against five seats for the PDM.
Next elections
May 2007 (parliamentary)

Turks and Caicos Islands

Political parties
Ruling party
Progressive National Party (PNP)
Main opposition party
People's Democratic Movement (PDM)
Political situation
The idea that the Turks and Caicos islands and Canada could become federated seems, at first, somewhat far-fetched but this idea has been discussed several times since 1917 when the prime minister of the day, Robert Borden first proposed it. Canada already has a financial stake in the tourist industry with 30 per cent of all hotels and resorts Canadian-owned and many retirees enjoying the sunnier climes. Not everyone in Turks and Caicos is in agreement with the proposals. It is feared that if there is some accommodation, income or sales taxes would be introduced. Canada is also mindful that such a federation might smack of neo-colonialism.

Population
19,300 (2004)
Ethnic make-up
Afro-Caribbean (95 per cent)
Religions
Baptist (41 per cent), Methodist (19 per cent), Anglican (18 per cent), Seventh-Day Adventist (2 per cent).

Education
The school system is constrained by insufficient infrastructure and is poorly equipped to deal with children of immigrants for whom English is not a first language.
The UK government has a number of projects, which it is working on through the Department for International Development (DFID). By improving teaching methods, the government hopes that around 80 per cent of children will achieve levels in reading and mathematics acceptable to their age.
The primary and secondary curriculum is also under review with plans that it will be standardised.
Compulsory years: Four to 16
Enrolment rate: 94 per cent primary enrollment of relevant age group, 80.2 per cent secondary enrollment.

Health
The UK government has designed an on-going programme of reforms to improve the health care system. Priorities include human resource development, greater access to financial resources and the prevention and control of HIV/Aids.
The hospital on the island of Grand Turk serves as a referral centre for all of the islands. There are nine community health care clinics throughout the islands.
HIV prevalence: Less than 1 per cent in 2004
Life expectancy: 77.7 years

Fertility rate/Maternal mortality rate:
4.61 births per woman

Welfare
There is a reciprocal health and welfare agreement with the UK, which entitles nationals of the Turks and Caicos islands to benefits such as income support, housing allowances and child benefits.

Main cities
Cockburn Town (capital, estimated population 5,000 in 2003) situated on Grand Turk island.

Main islands
Grand Turk (business centre), Providenciales (most tourism facilities), South Caicos (fishing and sailing), Salt Cay, Middle Caicos, North Caicos (natural bird sanctuary), Pine Cay and Parrot Cay.
Eight out of 30 islands are inhabited.

Languages spoken
Official language/s
English

Media
Press
There are no dailies. *Turks and Caicos Islands Free Press* is a bi-weekly newspaper featuring sports, entertainment, real estate, students and business. *Times of the Island* is an international quarterly magazine of the Turks and Caicos Islands.
Broadcasting
Radio: Local radio stations.
Television: Multi-channel satellite television is received from the US and Canada. There is a private television station. Cable TV is available from WIV Cable TV.

Economy
The economy is based on tourism and the financial services industry. The tourism sector is estimated to be worth over US$200 million each year. Worries regarding geographically unbalanced growth are abating as tourism development spreads outside the island of Providenciales. A US$35 million cruise ship terminal is being constructed. Strong economic growth in 2004 was based to a large extent on expanding tourism and construction activity. Financial services continued to be adversely affected during 2004 by international regulatory and supervisory obligations and the need to develop new products, but investor confidence remained high in 2004. The opening of investment and promotion offices in London and New York in 2004 will benefit both the financial and the tourism sectors.
In August 2004, the European Commission allocated US$10.1 million to Turks and Caicos to improve the islands' infrastructure.

External trade
The trade deficit is partly offset by earnings from tourism and offshore finance.
Imports
Principal imports are food and beverages, tobacco, clothing, manufactures and construction materials.
Main sources: UK, US
Exports
Principal reported exports are lobster, fish, dried and fresh conch, and conch shells.
Main destinations: UK, US

Agriculture
Farming
The agricultural sector is limited to small-scale production for domestic consumption and accounts for around 2 per cent of GDP. The growing tourism sector has encouraged production of fruit and vegetables for hotels and restaurants. Farming is confined to the rearing of livestock and the growing of maize, beans and some fresh fruit. A hydroponics facility has been developed at Providenciales.
Fishing
The fishing industry grew as the salt industry declined. Over-fishing, low prices and better paid jobs in the growing tourism industry in the 1990s led to a decline in fishing. However, as export prices started to improve, particularly for conch, and the government started to improve conservation techniques and encourage value-added processing, so the industry has rebounded.
Fishing for lobster and conch production accounts for just under 2 per cent of

KEY INDICATORS — Turks and Caicos Islands

	Unit	2000	2001	2002	2003	2004
Population	m	0.02	0.02	0.02	0.02	0.02
Gross domestic product (GDP)	US$bn	0.23	0.13	0.23	0.23	–
GDP per capita	US$	10,709	11,030	10,806	9,600	–
GDP real growth	%	4.7	0.1	2.0	4.9	–
Exports (fob) (goods)	US$m	8.8	7.3	6.9	169.2	–
Imports (fob) (goods)	US$m	148.7	156.9	153.2	175.6	–
Balance of trade	US$m	-139.9	-149.6	-146.3	-6.4	–

GDP. There is a commercial conch farm on Providenciales.
The typical total annual fish catch is over 1,300mt; shellfish, molluscs and cephalopods account for another 1,000mt per annum.

Industry and manufacturing
The manufacturing sector accounts for less than 1 per cent of GDP. Activity is confined to fish processing (mainly lobsters and conch) and construction work. A rice-milling and packaging plant, supplied with rice from Guyana, is the only significant industrial enterprise.
Construction activity has increased with new tourist and residential developments. The Turks and Caicos Investment Agency is promoting the islands as a location for manufacturing electronic goods.

Tourism
Tourism is the mainstay of the Turks and Caicos economy and continues to expand rapidly, despite the effects of recession in the US and the 2001 terrorist attacks in the US. Cruise ship arrivals showed a remarkable rise in 2003, to 24,867 from 2,411 in 2002. Increase in total passenger arrivals in 2003 was around 20 per cent. The main factor influencing growth in the tourism sector has been promotion efforts and improved airline access from North America to Providenciales. 77 per cent of total arrivals come from the US. Wishing to diversify away from dependence on this market, promotions are being targeted at Europe and Asia. Resort and other facilities continue to be developed, together with a strategic tourism plan for 2004–07. In December 2004, the ground-breaking ceremony for the construction of a cruise terminal and pier project in Grand Turk, scheduled to open in 2006, was held.

Hydrocarbons
The Turks and Caicos Islands do not produce any hydrocarbons. They rely entirely on imports of refined oil products. The Islands do not import either natural gas or coal.

Banking and insurance
Legislation enacted to combat money laundering in response to international regulatory and supervisory obligations led to a slowdown in the growth of financial services. The uncertainty occasioned by the scrutiny the sector is subject to, together with a lack of new products, have caused financial services to stagnate in recent years. A review was undertaken in 2004 to identify ways of modernising the sector and developing new products. Investment offices to market the financial services and also tourism were opened in London and New York in 2004.

Under an EU tax directive introduced in July 2005 in a number of associate and dependent EU countries, the Turks and Caicos began imposing a withholding tax to be passed to the relevant EU depositor's country but retaining the anonymity of the saver. Withholding taxes begin at 15 per cent, rising to 35 per cent by 2011. Turks and Caicos has also agreed to supply information on tax fraud, for criminal or civil trials, and notify EU member states about additional malpractices.

Central bank
There is no central bank.

Main financial centre
Cockburn Town, Grand Turk.

Offshore facilities
The Financial Services Commission is an independent statutory body responsible for licensing and supervising all finance-related entities and registering companies.

Time
GMT plus five hours (GMT plus four hours from April–October)

Geography
The Turks and Caicos Islands consist of more than 30 low-lying islands forming the south-eastern end of the Bahamas chain of islands, lying about 145km north of Haiti.

Climate
Tropical, tempered by trade winds. Winter nights sometimes cool, summers are hot. Mean temperature range from 25–29 degrees Celsius.

Entry requirements
Passports
Required by all except visitors from North America, who may enter without passport if they have a birth certificate and one piece of ID bearing a photograph. A return ticket is also required for visitors. Visitors may stay for 30 days.

Visa
No visas are required for citizens of North America, EU or most Commonwealth countries. Proof of return/onward passage is required upon entry. Contact the nearest British High Commission or embassy for further details.

Currency advice/regulations
There are no restrictions on the import/export of local or foreign currency.

Health (for visitors)
Mandatory precautions
Yellow fever vaccination certificate required if arriving from an infected area.

Advisable precautions
Typhoid and polio vaccinations. Water precautions.

Hotels
Accommodation available on Grand Turk, Salt Cay, South Caicos, Pine Cay, North Caicos and Providenciales. Eight per cent room tax and 10–15 per cent service charge added to bill. Guest-houses on Middle Caicos.

Public holidays
Fixed dates
1 Jan (New Year's Day), 12 Jun (Queen's Birthday), 1 Aug (Emancipation Day), 25 Dec (Christmas Day), 26 Dec (Boxing Day).

Variable dates
Good Friday, Easter Monday, Commonwealth Day (second Mon in Mar), National Heroes' Day (last Mon in May), National Youth Day (last Fri in Sep), Columbus Day (second Mon in Oct).

Working hours
Banking
Mon–Thu: 0830–1430; Fri: 0830–1230, 1430–1630.

Business
Mon–Fri: 0830–1600.

Government
Winter: Mon–Thu: 1300–1730, 1900–2130; Fri: 1300–1730, 1900–2100.
Summer: Mon–Thu: 1200–1630, 1800–2030; Fri: 1200–1630, 1800–2000.

Telecommunications
Telephone/fax
IDD is available on all islands in the Turks & Caicos Islands. Phone cards are required in phone booths. Toll-free 1-800, cellular and internet services available.

Electricity supply
120/240 V, 60 cycles

Weights and measures

Getting there
Air
National airline: Turks and Caicos Airways.
International airport/s: Grand Turk (GDT); South Caicos International (XSC); Providenciales (PDS), duty-free shop, car-hire.
Airport tax: Adult international departures US$23.
Surface
Main port/s: Cockburn Harbour (South Caicos), Grand Turk, Providenciales.

Getting about
National transport
Air: Turks and Caicos Airways serves Middle Caicos, North Caicos, Pine Cay, Providenciales, Salt Cay, South Caicos and Grand Turk.
Charter companies also operate between the islands at competitive rates.
Road: Main roads on Grand Turk, South Caicos and Providenciales are surfaced.

Turks and Caicos Islands

Car hire
Available on Grand Turk, Providenciales and South Caicos. International driving licence required. Driving is on the left.

BUSINESS DIRECTORY

The addresses listed below are a selection only. While World of Information makes every endeavour to check these addresses, we cannot guarantee that changes have not been made, especially to telephone numbers and area codes. We would welcome any corrections.

Telephone area codes
The international direct dialling code (IDD) for Turks and Caicos Islandsis +1 649 followed by subscriber's number.

Chambers of Commerce
Grand Turk Chamber of Commerce, PO Box 148, Grand Turk (tel: 946-2324; fax: 946-2504).

Banking
Barclays Bank plc, PO Box 61, Grand Turk (tel: 946-2831; fax: 946-2695); PO Box 236, Butterfield Square, Providenciales (tel: 946-4254, 946-4246; fax: 946-4573).

Bordier International Bank and Trust Ltd, PO Box 5, Caribbean Place, Providenciales (tel: 946-4535; fax: 946-4540).

First National Bank Ltd, PO Box 58, The Arch Plaza, Leeward Highway, Providenciales (tel: 946-4060; fax: 946-4061).

Turks and Caicos Banking Co Ltd (private international banking services), PO Box 123, Harbour House, Front Street, Grand Turk (tel: 946-2368; fax: 946-2365).

Travel information
Turks and Caicos Airways, (tel: 946-4255; fax: 941-5781).

Turks & Caicos Islands Tourist Board, PO Box 128, Front Street, Grand Turk (tel: 946-2321/2322; fax: 946-2833/2723; e-mail: tci.tourism@tciway.tc; internet site: http://www.turksandcaicostourism.com).

National tourist organisation offices
Turks and Caicos Tourist Board, Front Street, PO Box 128, Grand Turk (tel: 946-2321/2; fax: 946-2733; e-;mail: tci.tourism@tciway.tc; internet site: http://www.turksandcaicostourism.com).

Turks & Caicos Islands Tourist Board, Stubbs Diamond Plaza, Providenciales (tel: 946-4970/4971, 941-5494).

Ministries
Governor's Office, Government House, Waterloo, Grand Turk (tel: 946-2309; fax: 946-2903; e-mail: govhouse@tciway.tc).

Main Government Offices, Cockburn Town, Grand Turk (tel: 946-2801).

Ministry of Education, Youth, Sports and Women's Affairs (tel: 946-2801, ext 142; fax: 946-1337; e-mail tci.sports@tciway.tc).

Ministry of Finance, Commerce and Development (tel: 946-2935, 946-2937; fax: 946-2557; e-mail: fsc@tciway.tc).

Ministry of Health and Education (tel: 946-2801; fax: 946-2722).

Other useful addresses
Development Board, PO Box 105, Hibiscus Square, Pond Street, Grand Turk (tel: 946-2058).

Financial Services Commission, Harry Francis Building, Pond Street, Grand Turk (tel: 946-2802; fax: 946-2821).

General Trading Company (Turks & Caicos) Ltd, PMBI, Cockburn Town, Grand Turk (tel: 946-2464).

Government Information Service (GIS), Government Square, Grand Turk (tel: 946-2301 ext 40505/40506; fax: 946-1120).

Immigration Department, South Base, Grand Turk (tel: 946-2939; fax:964-2924; e-mail: iam@tciway.tc).

TCInvest, Hibiscus Square, Box 105, Grand Turk (tel: 946-2058; fax: 946-1464; e-mail: tcinvest@tciway.tc; internet site: http://www.tcinvest.tc).

Turks & Caicos Hotel Association, Third Turtle Inn, Providenciales (tel: 946-4230).

Turks Islands Importers Ltd (TIMCO), Front Street, PO Box 72, Grand Turk (tel: 946-2480).

Internet sites
Gateway Sites:
http://www.turksandcaicos.tc

Local Information: http://www.tc/info.htm

Tuvalu

KEY FACTS

Official name: Tuvalu

Head of State: Queen Elizabeth II, represented by Governor General Filoimea Telito (sworn in 15 Apr 2005)

Head of government: Prime Minister Maatia Toafa (elected and sworn in 11 Oct 2004)

Area: 26 square km (nine coral atolls)

Population: 11,600 (2004)

Capital: Vaiaku in Funafuti administrative division

Official language: Tuvaluan, English

Currency: Australian dollar (A$) = 100 cents

Exchange rate: A$1.31 per US$ (Oct 2005)

GDP per capita: US$2,020 (PPP, 2004)

GDP real growth: -4.00% (2004)

Labour force: 7,000 (2003)

Inflation: 2.80% (2004)

Balance of trade: -US$6.92 million (2003)

Visitor numbers: 1,377 (2003)

COUNTRY PROFILE

Historical profile
Tuvalu was formerly known as the Ellice (or Lagoon) Islands.
1892 A British protectorate was declared over the Ellice Islands and the group was linked administratively with the Gilbert Islands to the north.
1916 The UK annexed the protectorate, which was renamed the Gilbert and Ellice Islands colony.
1975 The Ellice Islands, under the old native name of Tuvalu (eight standing together), became a separate British dependency.
1978 Tuvalu became independent.
1989 A UN report on the greenhouse effect listed Tuvalu as one of the island groups which would completely disappear beneath the sea in the twenty-first century unless drastic action was taken.
1996 The 12-member parliament was forced out and Bikenibeu Paeniu became prime minister.
1998 Tomasi Puapua was appointed governor general.
1999 A no-confidence vote forced out Paeniu. Ionatana Ionatana was elected prime minister.
2000 Ionatana Ionatana died suddenly. Tuvalu was formally admitted to the UN.
2001 A by-election was held. Faimalaga Luka was elected prime minister by parliament. Koloa Talake was elected prime minister after Faimalaga Luka's government lost a no-confidence vote.
2002 Nine out of 15 MPs were re-elected and Prime Minister Koloa Talake and three of his ministers lost their seats. Saufatu Sopoanga was elected prime minister by parliament.
2003 Two by-elections in May resulted in the Sopoanga government losing its majority. In July, Prime Minister Sopoanga said he would delay the reconvening of parliament until he had regained majority support. Faimalaga Luka was sworn in on 9 September as governor general. In the October by-election, the new member for Nukufetau declared his allegiance to the government, giving it a one-seat majority.
2004 During the first six months of the year, there were several very high tides – 'king tides' – associated with the new moon. At only four metres above sea level, at their highest points, the islands experienced seawater swamping of homes and agricultural land. On 25 August, Prime Minister Saufatu Sopoanga's government was toppled in a no-confidence vote; Deputy Prime Minister Maatia Toafa became acting prime minister. He was elected prime minister on 11 October.
2005 On 15 April, Filoimea Telito was sworn in as governor general.

Political structure
Constitution
The constitution dates from 1978. The British sovereign is head of state, represented by a governor general with limited powers. The governor general's power to veto government measures was abolished under a constitutional amendment in 1986. Each island is ruled by a traditional council of chiefs which runs services and determines development priorities.
Form of state
Constitutional monarchy
The executive
Executive power is exercised by the prime minister and a cabinet appointed by the governor general upon the advice of the prime minister.
National legislature
Legislative authority is vested in a 13-member unicameral Palamene o Tuvalu (parliament) (12 members elected by universal suffrage for a four-year term in four double- and four single-seat constituencies and one *ex-officio* member). Parliament elects the prime minister and appoints a cabinet of up to four members.
Last elections
October 2003 (by-election); 25 July 2002 (parliamentary).
Results: By-election: the new member for Nukufetau declared his allegiance to the government, giving it a one-seat majority. Parliamentary: only non-partisans were elected (no political parties exist); Saufatu Sopoanga was elected prime minister by parliament, defeating Amasone Kilei by eight votes to seven.
Next elections
2006 (parliamentary)

Political parties
There are no political parties, although there is an opposition group within parliament.

Political situation
The politics of Tuvalu are dominated by the very real possibility that this low-lying atoll will disappear as global warming raises the sea level. While still prime minister, Saufatu Sopoaga had spoken at UN conferences pleading with all countries to take measures to cut greenhouse gases; a global environmental problem for everyone has been refined into a local

catastrophe for just 11,600 people on Tuvalu, so now their domestic political response has an international direction. Niue, despite its own problems of depopulation, has offered to take as many Tuvaluan families as may wish to emigrate; and New Zealand has agreed to take 75 Tuvaluans per year (although the high entry requirement has meant that by June 2004 – after two years – only 32 Tuvaluans had been accepted).

In May 2004 the government announced that it would consider removing the Queen as head of state and for Tuvalu to become a republic, following a referendum.

Population
11,600 (2004)

Ethnic make-up
Tuvalu's population is Polynesian in origin.

Religions
Christianity, under which the Church of Tuvalu (Congregationalists) accounts for 97 per cent of the population.

Education
Compulsory years: Seven to 14.

Health
Life expectancy: 63.5 years (WHO).
Fertility rate/Maternal mortality rate: 2.9 births per woman (WHO).
Head of population per physician/bed: 0.3 physicians per 1,000 people.

Main cities
Vaiaku in Funafuti administrative division (capital, estimated population 5,300 in 2003).

Languages spoken
Official language/s
Tuvaluan, English

Media
Press
The Tuvalu Broadcasting and Information Office provides a fortnightly publication in Tuvaluan *Sikuleo o Tuvalu* and *Tuvalu Echoes* in English. It has 10 pages covering local news, public notices and tide tables.

Broadcasting
Media freedom is respected in Tuvalu but the market is very small. The government operates Radio Tuvalu but there is no TV station. Tuvalu Broadcasting Services transmits daily radio programmes in Tuvaluan with English news broadcasts. Many islanders have satellite dishes for receiving foreign TV.

Radio: Radio Tuvalu is a government-owned station.

Advertising
Radio and press advertisements are accepted by the Broadcasting and Information Officer in Funafuti.

Economy
Tuvalu is a mere 26 square kilometres in size and has an economy to match. The small subsistence economy accounts for approximately 30 per cent of GDP. It is supplemented by copra exports and official transfers and investment income from overseas assets. Its smallness means that even a slight change in economic activity will affect GDP. In 2003 two construction projects (a hospital renovation and extention and a government office block) were almost equal to the total value of GDP for the previous year. As a result of these projects labour income rose by over 10 per cent in 2003, internal revenue collection was up (but fell by 12 per cent in 2004) and import duties declined by around 20 per cent in 2004, reflecting the decline in imports of construction materials.

Tuvalu has had to take its revenue where it can and when it was allocated .tv as its country-level domain (CLD) indicator it went into business with a California corporation to take advantage of it. The government sold its share in DotTV Corporation in 2001 for A$20 million (US$10 million) and continues to receive a small royalty.

Other sources of revenue are fishing licences for the exclusive economic zone and remittances from seafarers (some 20 per cent of GDP). The Tuvalu Maritime Training Institute is being upgraded over the period 2005–07. This is an important project as it not only boosts economic activity but also ensures the Institute retains its accreditation from the International Maritime Organisation. The government also anticipates a grant from Japan to rebuild the electricity generation and distribution system on Funafuti over 2005–06. The Tuvalu Trust Fund (TTF) invests in equities and is normally an important source of income. The government invests its budget surpluses in the TTF as a financial stockpile for years when it runs a deficit. A second fund, for the outer islands – the Falekaupule Trust Fund – has been provided with funds by a loan from the Asian Development Bank (ADB).

The ADB forecasts that the economy will pick up in 2005. A proposal to introduce a value added tax (VAT) is being considered. This will become important if the Pacific Island Countries Trade Agreement is ratified since Tuvalu will loose revenue on imports from the region.

External trade
Tuvalu is a signatory of the Pacific Island Countries Free Trade Agreement (PICTA), under which all tariffs between member states have to be removed by 2016. The Pacific Agreement on Closer Economic Relations (PACER), signed by the Pacific Forum countries (including Tuvalu), will see the reduction on tariffs on products from Australia and New Zealand in stages, until 2011.

Imports
Principal imports are food, animals, mineral fuels, machinery and manufactured goods.

Main sources: Fiji (43.1 per cent total, 2004), Japan (20.0 per cent), Australia (10.6 per cent), Poland (9.9 per cent)

Exports
Copra is the major export, followed by fish. Tuvalu postage stamps are traded worldwide. Coconut oil is exported to New Zealand. Exports totalled US$276,000 in 2003.

Main destinations: Germany (34.6 per cent total, 2004), Poland (25.9 per cent), Philippines (12.5 per cent), Fiji (8.4 per cent), Italy (6.7 per cent), UK (4.7 per cent)

Agriculture
Farming
About 80 per cent of the population survive through subsistence agriculture. Much of the soil is infertile, rainfall is variable and crops are liable to cyclone damage. Copra is the only export crop. Family smallholdings produce subsistence crops of pulaka, taro and other vegetables, bananas and coconuts. Agriculture is under threat from salinisation of the soil caused by rising ocean waters.

Crop production in 2004 included: 1,600 tonnes (t) coconuts, 700t cereal in total, 140t roots & tubers, 270t bananas, 208t oilcrops, 735t fruit in total, 530t vegetables in total, 50t citrus fruit. Livestock production included: 138t meat in total, 93t pig meat, 45t poultry, 22t eggs, 3t honey.

Fishing
Fishing and exploitation of the sea are important to the economy, serving mainly local consumption. There is potential to increase income by negotiating fisheries

KEY INDICATORS — Tuvalu

	Unit	2000	2001	2002	2003	2004
Population	m	0.01	0.01	0.01	0.01	0.01
GDP real growth	%	13.4	5.9	1.2	3.0	-4.0
Inflation	%	5.3	1.8	3.3	2.5	2.8
Exchange rate	per US$	1.80	1.82	1.86	1.55	1.36

agreements with other countries. The typical annual marine fish catch is 500t.

Industry and manufacturing
A small industry sector (baking, construction, boat building, coconut oil mill, soap making etc) serves local needs, some handicrafts are exported.

Tourism
There is no developed tourist industry owing to Tuvalu's remote location, infrequent flights and lack of amenities, although a Tourism Action Plan has been developed. Air access from Fiji has improved, but the number of visitors, mainly on official or other business and relatives, is small. There were 1,377 visitors in 2003, of whom only 184 were classified as holiday-makers.
Facilities, including the airport, the sole hotel and some guest houses, are concentrated on Funafuti. The other islands are relatively unspoilt, but are not easily accessible.

Environment
The government has publicly acknowledged the problem of the rising sea levels, but feels the situation has been exaggerated by the world media. Claims that the islands will be washed away by 2050 are debateable.

Mining
Tuvalu has no known mineral resources.

Hydrocarbons
There are no known hydrocarbons reserves. The UN Law of the Sea gave Tuvalu an exclusive economic zone of 12,949 square km for exploration.

Banking and insurance
The state-owned National Bank of Tuvalu (NBT) dominates the country's banking sector. Its monopoly position ensures that it remains in profit.
Tuvalu's currency is the Australian dollar and interest rates are determined by the Reserve Bank of Australia (RBA), so the government has little control over monetary policy. The royalty revenues generated by the '.tv' domain name (after the sale of the DotTV Corporation) have been lower than expected and are paid irregularly.
Central bank
National Bank of Tuvalu

Time
GMT plus twelve hours

Geography
Tuvalu is a scattered group of nine small atolls, extending about 560km (350 miles) from north to south in the western Pacific Ocean. Fiji lies to the south, Kiribati to the north and the Solomon Islands to the west. At their highest point, these islands are only four metres above sea level, and vulnerable to the rise in sea levels caused through global warming.

Climate
Hot and humid, temperatures 26–32 degrees Celsius. Rainfall varies considerably, up to 3,000mm in a year, falling most heavily from November–February. Hurricanes possible.

Entry requirements
Passports
Required by all.
Visa
None required, however visitors must have return/onward tickets and sufficient funds for their stay.
Currency advice/regulations
No restrictions on import and export of local and foreign currency.
Customs
Personal effects allowed duty-free. There are quarantine regulations for plants and animals, and it is inadvisable to carry fruit or plant material. Certain goods may be subject to regulation or import licensing, such as arms, fireworks, drugs, motorcycles, jewellery.

Health (for visitors)
Health facilities are basic.
Mandatory precautions
Vaccination certificate for yellow fever required if travelling from an infected zone.
Advisable precautions
There is rabies risk. Vaccinations for diphtheria, tuberculosis, hepatitis 'A' and 'B', polio, tetanus and typhoid are recommended.

Hotels
There is only one hotel, the government owned Vaiaku Lagi Hotel. Reservations should be made well in advance. Visitors may be asked to share rooms when there are accommodation shortages. Private guest houses are also available.
Tipping is optional and not expected.

Public holidays
Fixed dates
1 Jan (New Year's Day), 12 Jun (Queen's Official Birthday), 5 Aug (National Children's Day), 1–2 Oct (Tuvalu Days, Anniversary of Independence), 11 Nov (Prince of Wales' Birthday), 25–26 Dec (Christmas Holiday).
Variable dates
Commonwealth Day (second Mon in Mar), Good Friday, Easter Monday.

Working hours
Banking
Mon–Thu: 0930–1300; Fri: 0830–1200.
Business
Mon–Fri: 0800–1600.
Government
Mon–Thu: 0730–1615; Fri: 0730–1245.
Shops
Mon–Sat: 0630–1730.

Electricity supply
240V AC (on island of Funafuti only)

Weights and measures
Imperial system (metric units allowed in some instances).

Social customs/useful tips
Tipping is not customary. In business an informal attitude prevails. It is customary to shake hands on meeting and taking leave. Sometimes business cards are exchanged after introduction. Business is conducted in English. Visitors should be perceptive to unfamiliar local customs. Alcohol is generally available, but there are some limitations on consumption outside licensed premises. The minimum drinking age is 20 years.

Getting there
Air
Air Fiji offers return flights to Funafuti from Fiji. Air Marshall Islands also operates return flights from the Marshall Islands.
National airline: Tuvalu has no national airline.
International airport/s: Funafuti International (FUN), east of Funafuti.
Airport tax: International departures A$14; not applicable to direct transit passengers by same flight.
Surface

Getting about
National transport
Road: The only tar roads are on Funafuti. Elsewhere there are tracks. There is a limited number of vehicles, including some minibuses.
Water: An inter-island service is available which also calls at Suva (Fiji) at times.
City transport
Taxis: There are a few taxis from the airport to the city centre. Hotels offer an airport pick-up service.

BUSINESS DIRECTORY
The addresses listed below are a selection only. While World of Information makes every endeavour to check these addresses, we cannot guarantee that changes have not been made, especially to telephone numbers and area codes. We would welcome any corrections.

Telephone area codes
The international direct dialling (IDD) code for Tuvalu is +688 followed by subscriber's number.

Useful telephone numbers
Police and fire: 20-726
Ambulance: 20-749

Chambers of Commerce
Tuvalu Chamber of Commerce, PO Box 27, Funafuti (tel: 208-46; fax:208-29).

Tuvalu

Banking
Development Bank of Tuvalu, PO Box 9, Vaiaku, Funafuti (tel: 201-99; fax: 208-50).

Central bank
National Bank of Tuvalu; PO Box 13, Vaiaku, Funafuti (tel: 208-03; fax: 208-02; e-mail: gmbt@tuvalu.tu).

Travel information
Air Marshall Islands, PO Box 1319, Majuro MH 96960, Republic of the Marshall Islands (tel: (692)625-3731; fax: (692)625-33730).

Flight information (tel: 20-847, 20-737).

Funafuti International Airport, Department of Civil Aviation, Ministry of Works and Communication, Private Mail Bag, Funafuti (tel: 20-737, 20-725, 20-721; fax: 20-722).

Travel Office, Ministry of Works and Communication, Vaiaku, Funafuti (tel: 20-737).

Ministry of tourism
Ministry of Commerce and Natural Resources (tourist information), Vaiaku, Funafuti.

Ministries
Ministry of Commerce and Natural Resources, Vaiaku, Funafuti.

Ministry of Finance, Viaiku, Funafuti (tel: 20-840).

Statistics Division, c/o Finance Ministry, Viaiku, Funafuti (tel: 20-839).

Other useful addresses
Asian Development Bank (ADB), South Pacific Regional Mission, La Casa di Andrea, Fr. Dr. W. H. Lini Highway; PO Box 127, Port Vila (tel: +678 2 23-300; fax: +678 2 23-183; email: adbsprm@adb.org; internet: http://www.adb.org/SPRM).

Broadcasting and Information Office, Vaiaku Funafuti.

Business Development Advisory Board, PO Box 9, Funafuti (tel: 20-850).

Department of Civil Aviation, Ministry of Works and Communications, Private Mail Bag, Funafuti (tel: 20-737, 20-725, 20-721; fax: 20-722).

Department of Commerce, PO Box 33, Funafuti (tel: 20-839).

Internet sites
South Pacific Tourism Organisation: http://www.tcsp.com/tuvalu/index.html

Uganda

KEY FACTS

Official name: Republic of Uganda

Head of State: President Yoweri Kaguta Museveni (Movement) (since 1986 Revolution; last re-elected 2001)

Head of government: President Yoweri Kaguta Museveni; Prime Minister Apolo Nsimbabi heads the cabinet (re-appointed by the President Jul 2001)

Ruling party: Non-party 'Movement' government

Area: 236,036 square km

Population: 25.52 million (2004)

Capital: Kampala

Official language: English

Currency: Ugandan shilling (Ush) = 100 cents

Exchange rate: Ush1,865.50 per US$ (Oct 2005)

GDP per capita: US$265 (2004)

GDP real growth: 5.90% (2004)

Labour force: 12.52 million (2004)

Inflation: 5.90% (2004)

Balance of trade: -US$755.00 million 2004

Foreign debt: US$3.90 billion (2003)

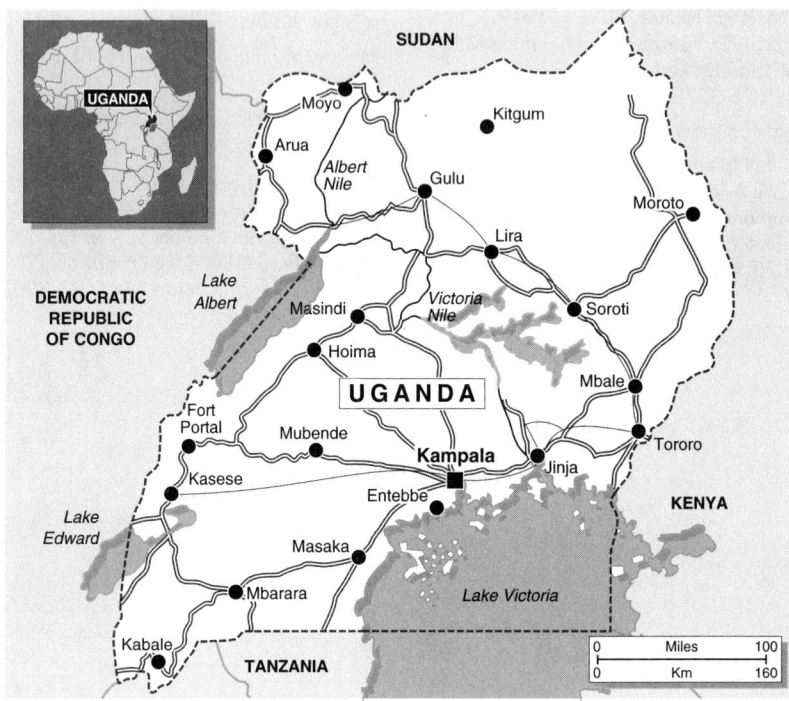

The foundation for the economic turnaround of Uganda was laid when the National Resistance Movement, under the leadership of President Yoweri Museveni, assumed control of the government in 1986. Uganda's annual average growth rate over the past decade of nearly 6.0 per cent was exceptional, given that Uganda is a landlocked country and has been buffeted by deteriorating terms of trade since the mid-1990s.

Donors and creditors have also been very active in Uganda. United Kingdom, the Netherlands, Ireland, Sweden, Norway, and Germany have provided budget support, while the European Commission and the African Development Bank budget support programmes are also closely harmonised with those of the IMF.

The key challenge for Uganda is to revive and sustain growth so as to reduce poverty. It should focus on promoting productivity growth, reducing vulnerability to external shocks, diversifying the economy to high value added activities, and expanding private sector participation.

Economy

A stable macroeconomic environment is necessary for sustaining high growth rates and Uganda's must alleviate constraints in absorbing donor inflows while ensuring macroeconomic stability. What is needed is a careful sequencing of structural reforms to ease supply constraints and deepen domestic financial markets to enhance financial intermediation and the economy's capacity to absorb the donor money.

More attention will need to be paid to developing indirect monetary instruments. Government spending financed by aid might threaten fiscal sustainability, undermine international competitiveness and export diversification efforts, and raise the cost of finance for the private sector.

Uganda and its partners should take steps to enhance the effectiveness of aid. The authorities should strive to strengthen public expenditure management to ensure that resources reach their intended purposes and reassure donors that their funds are well spent. A rising domestic revenue-to-GDP ratio would allow higher spending on poverty programmes. A stronger revenue effort would relieve pressures to withdraw liquidity stemming from government operations, thereby mitigating the crowding out of private sector operations.

Transparency and accountability is essential for improving the business environment and promoting private sector growth. The authorities should curb corruption by imposing criminal sanctions for corrupt practices. There is an immediate need to implement civil service reform. Reducing the costs of starting and closing a business and registering land titles is also important.

More spending must be directed toward agriculture, in particular, rural infrastructure and the services provided to farmers. The focus has been on raising spending on poverty-reducing programmes, yet the lack of adequate and functioning infrastructure, including at the regional level, is a serious obstacle to Uganda's medium-term growth prospects.

In 2000, Uganda qualified for enhanced Highly Indebted Poor Countries (HIPC) debt relief worth US$1.3 billion and Paris Club debt relief worth US$145 million. These amounts combined with the original HIPC debt relief added up to about US$2 billion. Foreign borrowing will now need to be tightly controlled to ensure debt sustainability. This is because the ratio of debt to exports is projected to remain high in the medium term. As a result, the bulk of foreign inflows will have to come in the form of grants and their macroeconomic consequences assessed on a continuous basis. The authorities should also focus on further developing the capacity to effectively manage foreign debt.

Uganda has no prolonged need for IMF financing. Over the years, Fund financing to support Uganda's reform efforts has declined sharply, and the amount of resources the Fund provides is not needed to support the country's balance of payments. In contrast, donor funds cover over one-half of public spending. There is a case for continued Fund engagement, possibly in a non-borrowing arrangement, which would provide for policy advice and a basis for continued donor support and to mobilise foreign private investment.

Politics

Since the late 1980s Uganda has rebounded from civil war and economic catastrophe to become relatively peaceful, stable and prosperous. In the 1970s and early 1980s Uganda was notorious for its human rights abuses, first during the military dictatorship of Idi Amin from 1971–79 and then after the return to power of Milton Obote, who had been ousted by Amin. During this time up to half a million people were killed in state-sponsored violence. Since becoming president in 1986 Yoweri Museveni has introduced democratic reforms and has been credited with substantially improving human rights, notably by reducing abuses by the army and the police. Western-backed economic reforms have produced solid annual growth.

Uganda, along with five other countries, intervened in the Democratic Republic of Congo's 1998–2003 civil war. The DR Congo accuses Uganda of maintaining its influence in the mineral-rich east of that country. Uganda says DR Congo has failed to disarm Ugandan rebels on its soil. At home, military action and tentative peace talks have not halted the massacres and mutilations perpetrated by the Lord's Resistance Army – a cult-like group that for 20 years has been fighting to run the country along the lines of the biblical Ten Commandments. This violence has displaced more than 1.6 million people and tens of thousands have been killed.

Yoweri Museveni took power on the back of his National Resistance Army in 1986. He won the country's first direct presidential election 10 years later and was re-elected in 2001. Parliament voted to abolish a constitutional limit on presidential terms, to pave the way for him to seek re-election in 2006. The March 2006 poll will be the first to be contested by opposition parties in almost two decades. Severe restrictions on multi-party politics were imposed by Museveni when he took power in 1986; only the president's 'Movement' system was allowed to take part in elections. When the president maintained that the country's factional rifts had been healed, Ugandans voted to lift the curbs.

Risk assessment

Economic	Fair
Political	Good
Regional stability	Poor
Stock market	Poor

COUNTRY PROFILE

Historical profile

Uganda has produced more than its fair share of surprises since it gained independence. It was unique at the time of independence from Britain in 1962, in that the rights of its four constituent kingdoms were embedded in a rather complicated constitution which, with the benefit of hindsight, was never going to hold sway against the pressures of African nationalism. In Humpty Dumpty fashion, the Kings fell. After four years of independence, the Kabaka (King) of Buganda was forcefully removed. Three years later the three other kings were deposed, following the introduction of a republican constitution. Unaware of what lay in store, Uganda settled uneasily into the by then common pattern of a one party state. Then came the military and, in 1971, the infamous rule of Idi Amin, a jumped up former sergeant in the King's African Rifles. For decades, Uganda reeled from the economic and political shocks of Amin's rule.

By the eighteenth century, the territory was occupied by Nilotic peoples in the north –

KEY INDICATORS — Uganda

	Unit	2000	2001	2002	2003	2004
Population	m	22.21	22.80	23.46	24.49	25.52
Gross domestic product (GDP)	US$bn	5.70	5.80	5.90	6.30	*6.83
GDP per capita	US$	257	255	250	234	265
GDP real growth	%	4.4	5.4	6.6	5.2	5.9
Inflation	%	6.3	2.0	-2.0	6.1	5.9
Exports (fob) (goods)	US$m	439.0	442.0	403.0	498.0	705.3
Imports (fob) (goods)	US$m	1,513.0	1,501.0	1,600.0	1,151.0	1,460.3
Balance of trade	US$m	-1,070.0	-1,059.0	-1,190.0	-653.0	-755.0
Current account	US$m	-861.0	-819.0	-633.0	-852.0	-130.0
Foreign debt	US$bn	3.7	3.1	3.8	3.9	0.0
Total reserves minus gold	US$m	808.0	983.4	934.0	1,080.3	1,308.1
Foreign exchange	US$m	804.5	981.5	931.1	1,075.5	1,307.4
Exchange rate	per US$	1,644.50	1,755.70	1,800.75	1,898.50	1,810.30

the Acholi and Langi – and by Bantus and Bagandas, from whom the country gets its name, in the south.
1886–1890 The UK colonised Uganda.
1900 Bugunda in western Uganda became an autonomous region with its own constitutional monarchy.
1958 The UK allowed Uganda self-government.
1962 Uganda became an independent state within the Commonwealth.
1963 Uganda became a republic. Sir Edward Mutesa II, the King of Bugunda, became Uganda's first president.
1966 Milton Obote, the defence minister, seized power with the help of Colonel Idi Amin, second-in-command of the army. Obote repressed the Baganda and re-integrated Bugunda.
1967 The constitutional role of kings was abolished, along with federal system of government.
1971 Obote was ousted by Idi Amin, who expelled the large Asian (mainly Indian) community and carried out purges in which thousands died. Asians had owned 90 per cent of Uganda's businesses and the economy collapsed.
1979 Tanzania invaded Uganda, causing Amin to flee to Saudi Arabia. Yusufu Lule was briefly appointed president before being replaced by Godfrey Binaisa.
1980 Obote won the presidential election and started to pursue liberal economic policies to obtain aid from western donors, and the economy began to improve.
1985 Ethnic feuding resulted in a coup removing Obote from power.
1986 Yoweri Museveni came to power at the head of the National Resistance Movement (NRM), which had waged a guerrilla war since 1981. He banned multi-party politics, saying they led to ethnic fighting.
1996 President Museveni was elected president for a five-year term.
1998 Uganda intervened in the Democratic Republic of Congo (DRC) on behalf of the rebels, against the Kabila government.
2001 President Museveni was re-elected. In legislative elections, the supporters of the 'No Party' Movement – formerly the NRM – secured a majority but over 50 MPs, including 10 ministers, lost their seats. President Museveni's cabinet was headed by incumbent Prime Minister Apolo Nsimbabi. A peace agreement was signed by Rwanda and Uganda in London.
2002 A peace deal was signed with the Uganda National Rescue Front (UNRF) rebels after more than five years of negotiations.
2003 The Lord's Resistance Army (LRA) announced a cease-fire, but attacks continued and the government ordered an all-out offensive against the rebels. In May, Uganda withdrew the last of its troops from eastern DRC. Tens of thousands of DRC civilians sought asylum in Uganda.
2004 In February, the LRA rebels killed some 200 people at a camp for displaced persons in the north; President Museveni blamed poor military co-ordination. President Museveni was promoted to general in May, and then retired from the army. In August, the military offensive against the LRA rebels by the UPDF halted the planned peace talks between the government and the rebels.
2005 In July, The Ugandan parliament voted for a constitutional amendment to allow President Yoweri Museveni to stay longer in office; he should stand down in 2006. Opposition presidential candidate, Kizza Besgiye, went on trial in December for treason and rape, pleading not guilty. Dr Besgiye also faces charges of terrorism and unlawful possession of firearms and was due to appear before a military court on 20 December; however, the High Court put the trial on hold until the Constitutional Court 'resolves certain matters'. He was returned to prison but released on the orders of the High Court on 1 January 2006.
2006 On a radio talk show on 4 January Museveni said he would be ready to 'give out the keys officially when elections are well conducted and I lose.'

Political structure
In a referendum held on 29 June 2000, over 90 per cent of voters chose to continue the 'No Party' Movement system, in operation following the election of the National Resistance Movement (NRM) in 1986. Less than 10 per cent of the electorate voted. The Movement system allows parties to exist in name but not to function. All candidates in parliamentary elections run as individuals.

Constitution
An elected constituent assembly drafted a constitution which was promulgated on 8 October 1995. It retains the system of non-party government.
In July 2005, the Ugandan parliament voted for a constitutional amendment to allow President Yoweri Museveni to stay longer in office; he should stand down in 2006.

Form of state
Unitary republic

The executive
The president is elected for a five-year term. The president appoints a prime minister and a cabinet composed of representatives of a number of political parties.

National legislature
The Ugandan parliament has 292 members including 214 elected constituency representatives, 53 district women representatives, 10 Uganda People's Defence Forces (UPDF) representatives, five youth representatives, five representatives of disabled people and five workers' representatives.
The Movement system allows parties to exist in name but not to function. All candidates in parliamentary elections run as individuals.

Legal system
The legal system is based on English common law and the 1995 constitution.

Last elections
26 June 2001 (parliamentary); 6/14 March 2001 (presidential).
Results: Presidential: President Museveni was re-elected.
Parliamentary: the supporters of the Non Party 'Movement' – formerly the NRM – secured a majority but over 50 MPs, including 10 ministers, lost their seats.

Next elections
2006 (presidential and parliamentary)

Political parties
Political parties can exist, although public political activities like fund-raising and campaigning are banned.

Ruling party
Non-party 'Movement' government

Population
25.52 million (2004)

Ethnic make-up
There are over 20 ethnic groups of which the Baganda, Banyankole and Basoga are the largest. Approximately 99 per cent of the population is of African descent and 1 per cent European or Asian.

Religions
Christianity (71 per cent), traditional beliefs (13 per cent), Islam (5 per cent), others (11 per cent).

Education
Unesco reported that a government's education programme launched in 1997, had successfully increased primary school enrolment from 2.5 million in 1997 to 6.5 million in 2001. The programme provided free primary education to four children including orphaned and disabled children from each household.
Primary school lasts for seven years and, having successfully undertaken exams, students then follow either an acedemic or vocational secondary schooling.
Literacy rate: 70 per cent, adult rate (2003).
Compulsory years: None.
Enrolment rate: 74 per cent gross primary; 12 per cent gross secondary; of relevant age groups, (including repeaters) (World Bank).
Pupils per teacher: 35 in primary schools.

Uganda

Health
Annual expenditure in the health sector was US$6 per person and is targetted to increase to US$11, which is still less than the recommended US$12 minimum. The lack of resources and an extreme dependence on foreign aid has resulted in a high infant and maternal mortality rate and low immunisation coverage.
Annual government spending is around 58 per cent, and foreign spending approximately 25 per cent, of the total expenditure on health, which is about 6 per cent of GDP.
Improved water sources are available to 42 per cent of the population.

HIV/Aids
In 2005 there were an estimated 800,000 people living with HIV/Aids, with 100,000 new infections each year. Even though the prevalence has been falling – down to 6 per cent in 2005 from the high of 30 per cent in the early 1990s – those who are developing Aids is increasing and putting social and economic pressure on the country's resources. The number of people living longer with HIV has been rising due to anti-retroviral (ARV) drugs; there are over 65,000 patients currently receiving ARV medication. Since the beginning of the pandemic in Uganda, an estimated one million people have died of Aids and the government expects another to be treating over 50,000 Aids suffers each year.

Uganda was the first country in sub-Saharan Africa to show a decrease in the number of HIV positive sufferers, due to an extensive, long-term government initiative to combat the spread of the disease (one of the best instituted in Africa). UNAIDS granted US$250 million (2001–06) for government sponsored projects from the Global Fund to fight HIV/Aids, Tuberculosis and Malaria.

Rural areas have been badly hit with productivity and output in the agricultural sector significantly fallen as Aids has taken its toll of workers and those that curtail their time in the fields to care for the sick. In April 2005 US researchers upheld findings of a 1997 Ugandan study that claimed the Aids drug Nevirapine was safe and effective. The use of the drug, to limit HIV mother-to-child infection, was embroiled in a politicised row in 2004 when it was claimed poor record keeping had invalidated the trial of the drug and that is was unsafe and causing thousands of severe side effects, including deaths.

HIV prevalence: 4.1 per cent aged 15–49 in 2003 (World Bank)
Life expectancy: 43.2 years (World Bank)
Fertility rate/Maternal mortality rate: 6.0 births per woman (2003); maternal mortality rate 510 per 100,000 live births (World Bank).
Birth rate/Death rate: 46.6 births and 17 deaths per 1,000 people (2003).
Infant mortality rate: 81 per 1,000 live births (2003); 38 per cent of children aged under five are malnourished (World Bank).
Head of population per physician/bed: 0.9 hospital beds per 1,000 of the population.

Welfare
The distribution of income in Uganda is less unequal than most countries in Africa, with the richest 20 per cent of the country owning 44.9 per cent of the national wealth while the bottom 20 per cent earning 7.1 per cent of the country's income. Around 10 per cent of the rural population lives under the national poverty line, while around 40 per cent of the urban population is classified as poor. The informal sector employs over 80 per cent of the urban population, implying a high degree of job insecurity and casual labour.

Main cities
Kampala (capital, estimated population 1.3 million in 2004), Gulu (116,500).

Languages spoken
KiSwahili, Luganda and Luo are widely spoken.
Official language/s
English

Media
Press
Uganda has over 14 regularly published newspapers and periodicals, some of which are in local languages.
Dailies: *The Monitor* is the only daily independent newspaper. The other major daily is *The New Vision*, a government-owned newspaper. *Ngabo* is a national daily and Sunday newspaper.
Weeklies: Bi-weekly newspaper (Tue and Fri) *The Monitor*.
Periodicals: *Musizi* is a monthly publication containing religious and political information.

Broadcasting
Radio and television services are controlled by the government under the Ministry of Information and Broadcasting.
Radio: Radio Uganda is the only radio station in the country. It broadcasts on two channels: the Blue Channel and the Red Channel, in English, KiSwahili and 20 local languages.
Television: Uganda Television Service (UTS) is a state-owned commercial service, which broadcasts programmes mainly in English, KiSwahili and Luganda. Cable Sat Television (CTV) is a privately owned television network which is only received in areas within 50km from the Kololo television mast in Kampala.

Economy
The country's main problem concerns its reliance on coffee exports, which account for 70 per cent of export revenues and which have declined in unit value due to the depressed world coffee market. Good macroeconomic indicators hide the fact that many Ugandans are not enjoying the fruits of growth, with a strong divide between the south-east and the troubled north and south-west. With monetary tools having a limited effect on macroeconomic indicators due to the effects of climate change and declining external markets on the economy, fiscal policy plays an important role in achieving economic goals. Despite the government's attempts at fiscal sustainability, it faces problems with revenue collection and overspending which are largely linked to factors outside its control, such as droughts and depressed export prices.

The budget in 2004 estimated that government spending would rise by 7.8 per cent, largely due to increased spending on the military. Revenues are hoped to be raised by a greater efficiency in tax collection and reduced corruption, along with increased taxes on alcohol and cigarettes.

External trade
The East African Community (EAC) pledges to work towards common action on the movement of labour and goods between Uganda, Kenya and Tanzania and the integration of transport, tourism and telecommunications. It has considerable economic potential as a regional bloc with a combined population of 80 million, a land area of 1.8 million square kilometres, common languages such as English and KiSwahili and large amounts of natural resources, including minerals, water, energy, forestry and wildlife. However, the issue of tariffs is an obstacle for the Tanzanian government in particular, which is concerned that complete free trade would heighten economic disparities within the EAC and undermine the country's struggling industrial sector.

On 31 December 2002, the US approved Uganda as being eligible for tariff preferences under the African Growth and Opportunities Act (AGOA). The legislation requires that countries are only eligible for greater access to US markets provided they have made continued progress toward a market-based economy, the rule of law, free trade, poverty reduction and the protection of workers' rights. This process is reviewed annually.

Imports
Principal imports are capital equipment, vehicles, petroleum, medical supplies and cereals.
Main sources: Kenya (27.9 per cent total, 2004), India (8 per cent), UAE (7.4 per

cent), South Africa (6.9 per cent), UK (5.9 per cent), China (5.6 per cent), Japan (5.1 per cent), US (4.6 per cent)

Exports
Principal exports are agricultural products – coffee (typically 70 per cent of total), tea, cotton, fish and fish products, horticultural products – flowers, gold.
Main destinations: Kenya (13.6 per cent total, 2004), Switzerland (11.2 per cent), The Netherlands (9.8 per cent), Belgium (8.6 per cent), France (4.2 per cent)

Re-exports
Gold, diamonds, coltan and niobium, mostly from neighbouring DRC.

Agriculture
Farming
Agriculture accounted for 32.2 per cent of GDP in 2004. Around 80 per cent of the population derive their livelihood from agriculture. The area under cultivation has only increased by one-third over the last 30 years. The situation has been worsened by irregular rainfall and climate change. This has eroded the farmers' confidence in applying improved technology to increase productivity, resulting in crop and livestock yields which have been ranked among the lowest in the world. Agricultural development is hampered by shortages of vital inputs, damage caused by civil war, low producer prices and corrupt purchasing bodies.

Uganda's varied climate allows the production of a wide range of produce. Around 75 per cent of Uganda's agricultural output is made up of food crop production, two-thirds of which is used for subsistence. Maize is one of the main food crops and is grown around Lake Victoria as a cash crop. The fertility of Ugandan land could make it a bread basket for East Africa, particularly if the effects of periodic droughts are ameliorated by adequate irrigation techniques.

Coffee is the main cash crop, providing around 70 per cent of agricultural export earnings. Most production is carried out on a small-scale basis. Rehabilitation of coffee holdings has been the main stimulus to economic growth in recent years. The government has encouraged planting of clone coffee which yields in a shorter period of around two years, is more disease resistant and gives higher yields.

The private sector controls over 90 per cent of the coffee trade in Uganda. Liberalisation of the coffee market has meant that producers can sell coffee on the open market to the highest bidder, although the dismantling of state marketing boards has meant that they are more vulnerable to price fluctuations and have to deal with often unscrupulous middlemen. The formation of co-operatives has become a basis for reducing the adverse effects of liberalisation.

Cotton was once an important cash crop, but due to its labour intensiveness, relatively high cost of production and a poor marketing system, farmers looked towards growing non-traditional cash crops which have a readily available market. Cotton growing is being revived in some eastern areas, and production has been boosted by reforms in agricultural pricing and marketing regimes introduced in the 1990s. Sugar is grown on several vast estates and production is creeping up after collapsing completely in the early 1980s. Tobacco and tea are also important cash crops.

The estimated crop production for 2004 included: 2,309,000 tonnes (t) cereals in total, 1,350,000t maize, 15,000t wheat, 5,500,000t cassava, 573,000t potatoes, 2,650,000t sweet potatoes, 420,000t sorghum, 140,000t rice, 615,000t bananas, 9,900,000t plantains, 711,300t pulses, 8,723,000t roots and tubers, 139.270t oilcrops, 33,000t tobacco, 4,000t cocoa beans, 186,000t green coffee, 70t vanilla, 2,100t pepper spice, 3,920t other spices, 1,600,000t sugar cane, 36,000t tea, 22,200t cotton lint, 158,000t soya beans, 700,000mt millet, 10,567,650t fruit in total, 556,000t vegetables in total. Estimated livestock production included: 258,620t meat in total, 106,000t beef, 60,000t pig-meat, 36,920t lamb and goat meat, 37,700t poultry, 20,000t eggs, 700,000t milk, 300t honey, 14,847t cattle hides, 1,392mt sheepskins.

Fishing
Uganda's fishing industry is important, both for domestic consumption and export. The annual catch is typically around 220,000 tonnes, 40 per cent of which is exported. In 2004, the industry is estimated to have added US$100 million or six per cent to the nation's economy.

The fisheries industry is mostly based on inland capture fisheries from lakes Victoria, Albert, Edward, George and Kyoga. Lake Victoria is Uganda's most important fishery, supplying some 50 per cent of the national catch. Nile perch obtained from Lake Victoria alone amount to 110,000 tonnes and remains the largest fish export item to the markets of Europe, Australia and South-East Asia. Estimates of Lake Kyoga put supplies at 30,000 tonnes, with the nature of the fishery shifting from a prolific Nile perch and tilapia fishery to increased supplies of mukene.

Forestry
Uganda is moderately forested with around 30 per cent forest cover and an additional 48 per cent of other wooded land. Deforestation accounted for an annual average loss of 1.9 per cent, the equivalent of 86,000ha of forest cover, between 1990–2000. There is a wide network of protected areas, including 50 parks and nature reserves. A large proportion of household energy needs are met by fuelwood. The sector produces sawnwood from local hardwood species and much of industrial roundwood is used for agricultural purposes. Paper is imported in large quantities.

The import of forest materials in 2004 amounted to US$29.4 million, exports amounted to US$1,115,000. Production in 2004 included: 39.4 million cubic metres (mcum) roundwood, 1.1mcum sawlogs and veneers, 264,000 cubic metres (cum) sawnwood, *4,600cum wood-based panels, 36.2mcum woodfuel, 792,417t charcoal.
* estimate

Industry and manufacturing
Industry accounts for around 21 per cent of GDP. The industrial sector is has seen relatively high levels of growth, particularly in food processing, tobacco, beverages, timber/paper and chemicals/soap. Underutilisation of factory capacity and lack of foreign exchange tend to inhibit progress.

Other industries are textiles, cement, plastics, steel, metal products and brewing. Most of these are operating well below capacity mainly due to shortages of imported materials, spares and fuel, inadequate infrastructure and a lack of skilled manpower.

The building industry is hampered by a lack of finance and skilled manpower and most local building equipment factories still produce at only 50 per cent of their installed capacities. Consequently, many finished products, such as cement, sanitary ware, plumbing pipes and glass are imported.

The textile sector has failed to take advantage of the US's African Growth and Opportunity Act (AGOA), which gives the textile industries from qualifying countries like Uganda access to US markets. Manufacturers have been unable to raise capacity, so they cannot fulfill the demands of US customers. The sector's decline is due to a fall in cotton producton, which has been adversely affected by political instability in the cotton-growing northern regions.

Tourism
The government is investing heavily in tourism to build it up as major currency earner. Insecurity in parts of the country continues to be a handicap, but visitor numbers in 2004 increased by 68 per cent over the previous year, registering around 512,000 arrivals. The sector is expected to contribute 4.6 per cent to GDP in 2005.

Uganda

Mining
Uganda has deposits of copper, cobalt and iron ore, as well as less viable fields of tungsten, beryl, columbo-tantalite, gold, bismuth, tin, limestone and phosphates. Uganda's mineral potential remains untested due to very little exploration to date.

Hydrocarbons
Uganda has no proven oil or gas reserves, but there have been indications of the presence of hydrocarbons. Exploration is being undertaken by three companies and oil deposits have been found in the Semliki valley near Lake Albert. Natural gas was also present. Canada's Heritage Oil and Energy Africa Uganda each has a 50 per cent interest in the area under exploration. If the oil reserves are found to support commercially viable levels of production, Uganda stands to benefit significantly, and notwithstanding proceeds from oil output, analysts estimate that investment could amount to US$60 million over 15 years. Heritage Oil and Gas started drilling the third oil well on the Turaco prospect in the Semliki Basin in October 2004.

The downstream industry is dependent on the importation of refined petroleum products and is the largest item of foreign exchange outflow. The majority of refined oil it consumes is imported from the Kenyan Mombassa Refinery. The development of the East African Community involving Uganda, Kenya and Tanzania will improve the pipeline infrastructure. A US$110 million pipeline from Kenya to Uganda is scheduled to begin construction in October 2006 and be completed in late 2007.

Neither natural gas nor coal is produced or imported.

Energy
Uganda relies on imported oil for around 50 per cent of its energy needs, the balance being provided by hydroelectricity. Nalubaale (Owen Falls) power station, operating since the mid-1950s, and its Kiira extension supply almost all of the electricity system's capacity of 380MW. Less than five per cent of the population has access to electricity, which due to growing demand has to be rationed. A 250MW hydro-plant is planned for construction at Bujagali, but has been dogged by controversy. In 2003, Eskom Uganda, a subsidiary of South Africa's Eskom Enterprises Africa, took over electricity distribution. Uganda exports some electricity to Kenya, Tanzania and Rwanda.

Financial markets
Stock exchange
The Kampala Stock Exchange (KSE) began trading in 1998.

Banking and insurance
Great efforts are being made to improve efficiency in the banking sector, including the placement of local banks under statutory management. However, Uganda's banking sector remains weak. In recent years, the Bank of Uganda's (BoU) (central bank) regulatory powers have been insufficient, with reports that troubled banks have failed to meet their reserve requirements.

In an effort to reverse the situation, the BoU increased the capital requirements of all banks and was granted power to close banks that failed to comply with a number of regulations. As a result, the ratio of non-performing loans to total assets has fallen and banking system profitability has improved. However, the BoU was forced to seize control of the Uganda Commercial Bank (UCB) after its privatisation due to fraudulent behaviour by the buyer. In 2002, an 80 per cent stake in UCB was sold to South Africa's Standard Bank Group.

The government is planning to increase the availability of credit to poor rural areas through micro-finance and a lighter regulatory framework.

Central bank
Bank of Uganda

Main financial centre
Kampala

Time
GMT plus three hours

Geography
Uganda is a landlocked country in East Africa, bordered by Sudan to the north, the Democratic Republic of Congo to the west, Kenya to the east and Rwanda, Tanzania and Lake Victoria to the south.

Climate
Equatorial, tempered by high altitude. Temperatures are fairly constant throughout the year, hottest months December–February, June–August, with daytime range (in Kampala) of 27–29 degrees Celsius (C) compared with an annual average of 26 degrees C (night-time average 16 degrees C). Heaviest rainfall occurs March–May, October–November; April is wettest month (average fall for month 175 mm).

Dress codes
Lightweight clothing is advisable all year round. Senior officials tend to wear suits, local businessmen and government officials wear suits or safari suits. Light cotton dresses, skirts and blouses or lightweight suits are advised for women. A lightweight raincoat may be needed at any time of the year.

Entry requirements
Passports
Required by all. Passports must be valid for six months.

Visa
Required by all, except citizens of countries found at www.ugandaembassy.com/visa.htm (countries with reciprocal visa-free entry). Visas may be obtained in advance or directly at the points of entry. A return/onward ticket is required.

Currency advice/regulations
No restrictions on import of foreign currency. It is best to carry US dollars, euros or British pounds sterling.

When changing traveller's cheques, a valid passport is required. Some agencies may ask for your sales advice slip. Small denomination bills of US$1, 5, 10 and 20 are changed at substantially reduced rates, as are torn and soiled notes.

Customs
Baggage and property accompanying the passenger may be imported into the country duty-free, providing the goods are re-exported at the end of the visit. Duty-free allowances are: one litre of spirits, wines and liqueurs; 500ml of perfume and toilet water; 250 grammes of cigarettes, cigars and tobacco.

Prohibited imports
Game trophies

Health (for visitors)
Mandatory precautions
A valid international certificate of vaccination against cholera is required for entry into and exit from Uganda. Vaccination must have taken place not less than seven days and no more than six months prior to entering the country. A valid international certificate of vaccination against yellow fever is also required for visitors arriving from infected areas. The certificate becomes valid 12 days after vaccination and lasts for 10 years.

Advisable precautions
There is a risk of malaria, typhoid is a risk outside main towns. Normal precautions for the tropics with regard to hygiene and drinking water should be taken. Bilharzia risk is present in the lakes and rivers and visitors are advised to swim only in well-maintained swimming pools. A mild form of dysentery is common. Rabies is a risk.

The Aids virus has reached epidemic proportions and precautions should be taken, including a travel kit with disposable syringe and needles. Any medicines required should be brought with the visitor and accompanied by their original packaging.

Medical facilities are limited and visitors should have sufficient insurance to ensure medical evacuation.

Hotels
Private and government-owned, variable standard, but available in all main centres. Should be booked in advance.

Credit cards
Most car hire firms and travel agencies refuse credit cards.

Public holidays
Fixed dates
1 Jan (New Year's Day), 26 Jan (Liberation Day), 8 Mar (Women's Day), 1 May (Labour Day), 3 Jun (Martyrs' Day), 9 Jun (National Heroes' Day), 9 Oct (Independence Day), 25 Dec (Christmas Day), 26 Dec (Boxing Day).
Variable dates
Good Friday, Easter Monday, Ascension Day, Eid al Adha, Eid al Fitr.

Working hours
Banking
Mon–Fri: 0900–1400. Some bureaux de change open Sat and Sun.
Business
Mon–Fri: 0830–1245, 1400–1700.
Government
Mon–Fri: 0830–1245, 1400–1700.
Shops
Mon–Fri: 0830–1700; Sat: 0900–1600.

Telecommunications
Telephone/fax
Service is good for calls abroad but can be unreliable within Uganda. Hotels charge very high prices for phone calls. Uganda's telecommunications industry has been liberalised, breaking the former monopoly of the Uganda Posts and Telecommunications Corporation.
Postal services
Not very reliable.
Courier services
Air courier services available.

Electricity supply
240V AC, 50 cycles.

Social customs/useful tips
Appointments are essential for business meetings. Ugandans have a less urgent sense of time than Europeans, and appointments often run late, particularly if it is raining.
The customary form of greeting is to shake hands. Exchanging business cards is an established ritual.
Visitors should remember that an increasing number of Hindus and Muslims are engaged in commerce and local advice should be obtained if any entertainment is planned. There are many local traditions, but few will affect business visitors and tourists.

Security
There are still areas of the country that are not under secure government control. Rebel activity occasionally targets tourists, and visitors are advised to check with local embassies if they intend to travel away from the main urban centres or main road and rail routes. The government has stepped up its campaign against lawlessness.
Due to rebel raids, including activity spilling over from neighbouring countries, visitors are warned against travelling to certain destinations, particularly the northern and south-western regions, where the Mountains of the Moon and several game parks are located.

Getting there
Air
International airport/s: Entebbe (Code: EBB), at Entebbe, 35km from Kampala; information desk, duty-free shop, restaurant, bank, post office, hotel reservations, car hire.
Airport tax: There is no airport departure tax.
Surface
Road: There is good road access from Kenya, although links with Rwanda may be disrupted by military activity.
Rail: It is possible to travel by train from Nairobi (Kenya) to Kampala via a connection at Tororo; this can be slow and uncomfortable.
Water: Water access is possible via Lake Victoria, from Mwanza (Tanzania) and Kisumu (Kenya).

Getting about
National transport
Road: Uganda has a road network of 27,540km. Main towns are connected by 2,096km of tarmac roads. Rehabilitation has started and many major roads are in good condition.
Buses: Regular services scheduled include Entebbe-Kampala (journey time: 30–45 minutes). There are services between most main centres but they tend to be crowded. An interstate bus service between Kampala and Kigali (Rwanda) is frequently suspended due to military activity. Akamba Bus regularly travels between Kampala and Nairobi (Kenya).
Rail: Approximately 1,200km of line exists, but only Kampala-Kasese and Kampala-Jinja-Mbale are functioning.
Water: Some freight and passenger transport is available on Lake Victoria.
City transport
Taxis: Available at airport and in Kampala at hotels, the railway station, main park and near major office blocks. The drive from Entebbe airport to Kampala city centre takes 45 minutes.
Matatus (public taxis) are available within Kampala, its suburbs and in all major towns.
Car hire
Car hire is expensive. Services are available, mainly with driver, from a number of rental firms, and through independent taxi drivers. Driving is on the left. A valid international driving licence is required.

BUSINESS DIRECTORY

The addresses listed below are a selection only. While World of Information makes every endeavour to check these addresses, we cannot guarantee that changes have not been made, especially to telephone numbers and area codes. We would welcome any corrections.

Telephone area codes
The international direct dialling (IDD) code for Uganda is +256, followed by area code:

Entebbe	42	Lugazi	44
Fort Portal	483	Masaka	481
Jinja	43	Mbale	45
Kampala	41	Mbarara	485
Kasese	483	Tororo	45

Useful telephone numbers
Ambulance, fire, police: 999
Directory enquiries: 901
International hospital: 340-531, 345-768

Chambers of Commerce
Uganda National Chamber of Commerce and Industry, PO Box 3809, Kampala (tel: 258-791; fax: 258-793; e-mail: uncci@uol.co.ug).

Banking
Allied Bank International Uganda Ltd PO Box 2750, Plot 24 Jinja Road, Kampala (tel: 236-535/6; fax: 230-439).

Bank of Baroda (Uganda) Ltd PO Box 7197, 18 Kampala Road, Kampala (tel: 233-680/3; fax: 258-263).

Barclays Bank of Uganda Ltd, PO Box 2971, 16 Kampala Road, Kampala (tel: 230-972/6, 232-594/7; fax: 259-467).

Centenary Rural Development Bank Ltd, PO Box 1872, 7 Entebbe Road, Kampala (tel: 251-276; fax: 251-273).

CitiBank (Uganda) Ltd, PO Box 7505, Centre Court, Ternan Avenue, Nakasero Plot 4, Kampala (tel: 340-625; fax: 340-624).

Development Finance Company of Uganda Ltd, PO Box 2767, Rwenzori Hse, Plot 1 Lumumba Ave, Kampala (tel: 256-125, 232-212; fax: 259-435).

East African Development Bank, PO Box 7128, East African Development Bank Building, 4 Nile Avenue, Kampala (tel: 230-021/5; fax: 259-763).

Uganda

HSBC Equator Bank plc, PO Box 23232, Cargen Hse, 13/14 Parliament Ave, Kampala (tel: 347-699; fax: 347-701).

Stanbic Bank Uganda Ltd, PO Box 72647, 45 Kampala Road, Kampala (tel: 231-151, 230-811; fax: 231-116).

Standard Chartered Bank Uganda Ltd, PO Box 7111, 5 Speke Road, Kampala (tel: 258-211/7; fax: 231-473).

Uganda Commercial Bank Ltd, PO Box 973, 12 Kampala Rd, Kampala (tel: 234-710, 258-012; fax: 259-012, 242-694).

Uganda Development Bank, PO Box 7210, 22 Hannington Rd, UDB Towers, Kampala (tel: 230-740/5; fax: 258-571).

Central bank
Bank of Uganda, PO Box 7120, 37–43 Kampala Rd, Kampala (tel: 258-441; fax: 230-878).

Travel information
East African Airlines (EAA) (regional airline commenced operating flights October 2002 to Lusaka, Harare, Johannesburg, Kigali, Bujumbura, Dubai and Kinshasa), Airways House, 6 Colville Street Kampala.

Uganda National Parks, Kanjokya Street, PO Box 3530, Kampala (tel: 530-158; fax: 530-159).

Uganda Tourist Board, PO Box 7211, Plot 13/15 Kimathi Avenue, Impala House, Kampala (tel: 342-196/7; fax: 342-188; e-mail: utb@starcom.co.ug; internet site: http://www.visituganda.co.ug).

Ministry of tourism
Ministry of Tourism, Trade and Industry, Farmers House, Plot 6/8 Parliament Avenue, PO Box 7103, Kampala (tel: 343-947; fax: 256-395; e-mail: uwa@uwa.or.ug).

National tourist organisation offices
Uganda Tourist Board, IPS Building, 9/11 Parliament Avenue, PO Box 7211, Kampala (tel: 242-196/7; fax: 242-188; e-mail: utb@starcom.com.ug).

Ministries
Ministry of Agriculture, Animal Industry and Fisheries, PO Box 102, Entebbe (tel: 20-981/9).

Ministry of Education and Sports, 17/19 Hannington Rd, PO Box 7063, Kampala (tel: 234-440/9).

Ministry of Energy, Minerals and Environment Protection, Amber House, 33 Kampala Rd, PO Box 7270, Kampala (tel: 230-070/415).

Ministry of Finance and Economic Planning (Finance), Apollo Kaggwa Rd, PO Box 8147, Kampala (tel: 234-700, 257-095).

Ministry of Finance and Economic Planning (Planning), Uganda House, 10 Kampala Rd, PO Box 7086, Kampala (tel: 235-051/4).

Ministry of Finance and Economic Planning (Statistics Department), PO Box 13, Entebbe.

Ministry of Foreign and Regional Affairs, Parliament Bldg, PO Box 7084, Kampala (tel: 257-525, 258-252; fax: 232-874, 256-722).

Ministry of Information and Broadcasting, Kampala.

Ministry of Land Housing and Urban Development, Jinja Rd, PO Box 7122, Kampala (tel: 242-931/4).

Ministry of Labour and Social Welfare, 1 Portal Ave, PO Box 7009, Kampala (tel: 254-964).

Ministry of Local Government, 10 Kampala Rd, PO Box 7037, Kamapal (tel: 241-279).

Ministry of Women in Development, Youth and Culture, 4 Jinja Rd, PO BOx 7136, Kampala (tel: 254-881/8).

Ministry of Works, Transport and Communications, PO Box 10, Entebbe (tel: 20-101).

Prime Minister's Office, Nile Ave, PO Box 341, Kampala (tel: 232-222).

Other useful addresses
British High Commission, Commercial Section, 120/12 Parliament Avenue, PO Box 7070, Kampala (tel: 257-301/4, 257-054/9; fax: 257-304).

Central Tender Board (responsible for administering most government and aid-funded tenders), PO Box 3925, Kampala.

Civil Aviation Authority, PO Box 5536, Kampala (tel: 256-874/5, 256-896; fax: 256-807).

Coffee Marketing Board Ltd, Plot 15 Kibira Rd, PO Box 7154, Kampala.

Commonwealth Development Corporation, Kampala (tel: 235-784).

Development Finance Company of Uganda, Kampala (tel: 256-125).

Export Policy Analysis and Development Unit (EPADU), Impala House, PO Box 10951, Kampala (tel: 231-390/363; fax: 231-329).

Immigration Department, PO Box 7165, Kampala.

Lint Marketing Board, PO Box 7018, Kampala.

National Housing and Construction Corporation, PO Box 659, Kampala.

Nile International Conference Centre, PO Box 3496, Kampala (tel: 258-619; fax: 259-130).

Privatisation Unit, Ministry of Finance and Economic Planning, IPS Building, 6th Floor, 14 Parliament Avenue, PO Box 10944, Kampala (tel: 256-467, 256-392; fax: 259-997, 242-403; e-mail: pmu@imul.com).

Public Enterprise Reform and Divestiture, IPS Building, 6-7 Floors, PO Box 10944, Kampala (tel: 256-467, 243-995, 259-997; fax: 259-997).

Radio Uganda, Nile Avenue, PO Box 2038, Kampala.

Statistics Department, PO Box 13, Entebbe (fax: 20-147).

Uganda Advisory Board of Trade, PO Box 6877, Kampala (tel: 233-311).

Uganda Development Corporation, UDC Building, Parliament Ave, PO Box 7042, Kampala (tel: 234-383, 241-588; fax: 241-588).

Uganda Export Promotion Council, Plot 17/19 Jinja Road, PO Box 5045, Kampala (tel: 259-779).

Uganda Industrial Development Corporation Ltd, PO Box 442, Kampala (tel: 234-281).

Uganda Investment Authority, Plot 28 Kampala Road, PO Box 7418, Kampala (tel: 251-562, 234-105; fax: 242-903; e-mail: info@ugandainvest.com; internet site: http://www.ugandainvest.com).

Uganda Manufacturers' Association, Kampala (tel: 220-285, 245-560).

Uganda News Agency (UNA), c/o Ministry of Information and Broadcasting, PO Box 7142, Kampala (tel: 254-461).

Uganda Railway Corporation, PO box 7150, Kampala (tel: 258-051; fax: 244-405).

Uganda Tea Corporation Ltd, Kasaku Estate, Jinja-Kampala Rd, PO Box 8955, Lugazi (tel: 48-230/45; fax: (041) 230-698).

Uganda Television Service, PO Box 4260, Kampala.

Ugandan Embassy (US), 5911 16th Street, NW, Washington DC 20011 (tel: 202-726-7100; fax: 202-726-1727; e-mail: ugembassy@aol.com).

Internet sites
Africa Business Network: http://www.ifc.org/abn

African Development Bank: http://www.afdb.org

Africa Online: http://www.africaonline.com

AllAfrica.com: http://allafrica.com

Mbendi AfroPaedia (information on companies, countries, industries and stock exchanges in Africa): http://mbendi.co.za

Ukraine

KEY FACTS

Official name: Ukraina (Ukraine)

Head of State: President Viktor Yushchenko (sworn in 23 Jan 2005)

Head of government: Prime Minister Yuri Yekhanurov (approved by parliament 22 Sep 2005)

Ruling party: Za Yedinu Ukrainu (ZYU) (For United Ukraine)

Area: 603,700 square km

Population: 47.25 million (2004)

Capital: Kiev (Kyiv)

Official language: Ukrainian

Currency: Hryvna (H) = 100 kopiyka (plural hryvni) (introduced Sep 1996)

Exchange rate: H5.05 per US$ (Oct 2005)

GDP per capita: US$1,366 (2004)

GDP real growth: 12.10% (2004)

Labour force: 25.18 million (2004)

Unemployment: 4.60% (2004); 9.50% (International Labour Organisation, 2004)*

Inflation: 9.00% (2004)

Balance of trade: US$3.74 billion 2004

Foreign debt: US$14.20 billion (2003)

Annual FDI: US$1,000.00 million (2003)*

* estimated figure

Ukraine has one of the simplest flags in the world – a strip of blue above a strip of yellow, representing corn fields under a bright sky. The flag is a reference to the country's agricultural history, so important that it used to be known as the bread basket of the Soviet Union.

Bread in no small part fuelled the country to be one of the most powerful states in Europe in the 10th and 11th centuries – it belonged to the first Slavic state, Kievan Rus. The Ukraine was incorporated into the Soviet Union until 1917, when it won its independence – albeit for a brief spell of three years. In 1920 it was conquered again and ruled by a fierce Soviet regime. Eight million people died when Stalin orchestrated two famines to break the spirit of the Ukrainian people in 1921–22 and 1932–33. The country endured further untold hardship during the second world war, with another eight million people dying. Ukraine was also the unfortunate victim of the 1986 Chernobyl disaster. The nuclear power station exploded and burst into flames after safety regulations were repeatedly flouted. It was the worst nuclear accident in history and eight per cent of Ukrainian land was contaminated. Five years later, the Soviet Union broke up and the Ukraine re-achieved its independence.

Independence and revolution

This was not the end of the Ukraine's troubles. Its early economic record was disastrous, as a result of inveterate corruption and sky-high inflation. Ukraine was still very much tied to Russia. Now, however, the economy has been reformed and the last decade has seen an upward trend. Political hopes – for reform, democracy and human rights – were pinned on the 'Orange Revolution' of 2004–05, although to a certain extent these hopes were dashed throughout the course of the year. The promised crackdown on corruption has not materialised although there has been progress on civil liberties and the country is no longer blacklisted by human rights groups.

When Viktor Yanukovych 'won' the November 2004 presidential elections, his incensed rival Viktor Yushchenko rallied his troops. It had been a hugely fraudulent poll and hundreds of thousands of pro-democracy activists marched peacefully in the streets for 10 days, demanding that a replacement ballot be held. This was the

Orange Revolution – 20 per cent of the population participated. In the capital, Kiev, 48 per cent of the population turned out to protest. Another election, this time not rigged, was held in December 2005, and sure enough the reformist Yushchenko won. He praised the country for setting 'an example for the millions of people who still cherish freedom and democracy'. This historic chain of events rattled President Vladimir Putin of neighbouring Russia who seeks to avoid mass public unrest at any cost. Since the late 1990s most states of the former Soviet Union have evolved towards authoritarian regimes and 'managed democracies'. Ukraine would have continued down such a path if Yanukovych had been confirmed as president in 2004. Progress is being hindered by the current composition of parliament. Only if Yushchenko and Tymoshenko form a coalition will there be a pro-reform ruling majority.

Electoral reform will be implemented in 2006. In March, Ukrainians will vote under a parliamentary-presidential system, to replace the previous presidential system which can lead to authoritarian regimes and executive abuse of office.

Greater freedoms

International media watchdog Reporters without Borders has recorded considerable improvement in press freedom. Since the Orange Revolution newspapers have become forums of debate and criticism rather than merely showcases of propaganda. Transparency International has said policies introduced last year to battle corruption are producing results. Ukraine is ranked 107 out of 158 countries in the corruption perception index.

There is now greater religious tolerance and freedom to practice. The Ukrainian (Uniate) Catholic Church has moved its headquarters to Kiev; which signals a move towards the unification of the Orthodox Churches in Ukraine.

Minimum pensions have been increased to the levels of minimum wages. Wages for those employed by the state have increased by 57 per cent. Social welfare spending, including child support to encourage population growth, grew in 2005 by 73 per cent. National integration has improved. Yushchenko is committed to nation-building and affirmative action for the Ukrainian language.

The security forces have been overhauled. Interior minister Yuriy Lutsenko has pushed through 5,000 voluntary resignations, 2,000 members failed re-certification and 400 members have been charged. Similar clean ups are being undertaken in the Customs and Tax services. The notoriously corrupt traffic police was disbanded, after one officer demanded a bribe from the driver of the car in which Yushchenko was travelling.

Foreign affairs

Foreign policy has totally changed direction. It is now driven by the need to 'return to Europe'. In October 2005, the president of the European Commission, José Manuel Barroso, declared to Ukraine: 'Our door remains open, the future of Ukraine is in Europe – the best way is not to talk all the time about membership but to achieve concrete results, show commitment to European standards and values'. By this, Barroso means laying down the roots of true democracy, and a market economy. The certification of free market status by the EU and US, subsequent membership of the WTO and an invitation from NATO inviting Ukraine into a Membership Action Plan, are all expected over 2006. Yushchenko visited the Washington in April 2005, and had a dialogue and photo opportunity with President George W Bush. The Ukrainian premier stated that his country's dreams were those of Western civilization. Bush then thanked Yushchenko 'for being an active partner in the war on terrorism', and the two discussed membership of NATO and the WTO.

Gas crisis

On 10 January 2006 the Ukrainian parliament sacked Prime Minister Yuri Yekhanurov's government over a controversial gas deal with Russia. Backed into a corner by Russia cutting Ukraine's supply of natural gas, Yekhanurov had agreed to a deal with Russia's state owned gas supplier Gazprom to pay US$95 per 1,000 cu m for future supplies of gas – this compares to the previous figure of US$50. Yekhanurov was to remain as acting prime minister until President Viktor Yushchenko named a successor. Russia's action not only affected Ukraine but many former Soviet republics, as well as a number of European Union countries, supplied by Gazprom via the Ukrainian pipeline.

Politics

Former Ukrainian prime minister (Ms) Yulia Tymoshenko was sacked by Yushchenko in September 2005 after the partnership that swept them to power in Ukraine's Orange Revolution turned sour and has since seized every opportunity to criticise the man who replaced her. Vowing to fight the five-year gas deal, she was the driving force behind the no confidence vote that ousted Yekhanurov. Tymoshenko has now joined forces with

KEY INDICATORS — Ukraine

	Unit	2000	2001	2002	2003	2004
Population	m	48.78	48.39	48.01	47.62	47.25
Gross domestic product (GDP)	US$bn	31.80	37.60	41.40	49.50	*65.15
GDP per capita	US$	630	770	890	1,250	1,366
GDP real growth	%	5.9	9.1	4.6	8.5	12.1
Inflation	%	28.2	12.0	0.8	6.0	9.0
Unemployment	%	5.3	3.9	3.8	3.7	3.5
Natural gas output	bn cum	16.8	17.1	17.2	17.7	18.3
Coal output	mtoe	42.1	43.6	43.0	41.6	41.9
Exports (fob) (goods)	US$m	15,722.0	17,091.0	19,140.0	21,225.0	33,432.0
Imports (fob) (goods)	US$m	14,943.0	16,893.0	18,590.0	20,029.0	29,691.0
Balance of trade	US$m	779.0	198.0	550.0	1,196.0	3,741.0
Current account	US$m	1,481.0	1,402.0	3,174.0	3,059.0	7,160.0
Foreign debt	US$bn	10.5	12.5	13.6	14.2	–
Total reserves minus gold	US$m	1,352.7	2,955.4	4,241.0	6,730.7	9,302.4
Foreign exchange	US$m	1,103.6	2,704.3	4,213.0	6,709.5	9,301.3
Foreign direct investment (FDI)	US$bn	0.0	0.8	0.7	1.0	1.9
Exchange rate	per US$	5.44	5.37	5.35	5.33	5.32

* estimated figure

pro-Moscow opposition parties and will fight Yuschenko in the March 26 poll. Yekhanurov was to have headed the People's Union-Our Ukraine bloc in the 2006 elections to give voters the chance to decide for themselves about the achievements of the government. Now the odds are on a Yushchenko-Tymoshenko coalition, considered internationally and domestically the best chance for a reformist, Western-oriented government.

Yushchenko is committed to democratisation, economic reform and Euro-Atlantic integration. Tymoshenko is respected for her political skills. Muddled policy in the first nine months of the Orange Revolution was not solely the fault of the Tymoshenko government. Other factors were the creation of a parallel government in the National Security and Defence Council, Yushchenko's lack of leadership and inability to take decisive decisions except in crises. His extensive travels abroad also distracted him from domestic policies.

If they unite during, or after the 2006 elections, they could balance one another to promote all-embracing reform.

Economy

After Russia, Ukraine was the most important economic component of the former Soviet Union. It generated more than one quarter of Soviet agricultural output. Its diversified heavy industry supplied the equipment and raw materials to industrial and mining sites in other regions of the USSR. Shortly after independence in December 1991, Ukraine liberalised most prices and erected a legal framework for privatisation, but widespread resistance to reform within the government and the legislature stalled the effort. Output by 1999 had fallen to less than 40 per cent of the 1991 level.

Dependence on Russia for energy and the lack of structural reform have made the economy vulnerable to external shocks. Outside institutions – particularly the International Monetary Fund (IMF) have encouraged Ukraine to quicken the pace and scope of reforms.

Quarrels among senior leaders, expensive social policies and unclear plans for privatisation, have led to an incoherent policy and government malaise. Growth slumped from 12 per cent in 2004 to 4.4 per cent in 2005. Increased gas prices will seriously impact on growth over 2006.

Foreign debt rose by 20.2 per cent to US$36.861 billion over the first nine months of 2005, up from US$30.65 billion on January 1. The National Bank of Ukraine has expressed alarm at the higher figure. The state and private sector had started to borrow heavily from abroad. Corporate foreign debt now exceeds the European average and the bank planned to tighten control over corporate liabilities to avoid surprise surges in demand on the currency market.

Outlook

Ukraine will need to focus on economic reform and growth next year if it is to realise its ambitions to be an eventual member of certain key international organisations. Growth in 2005 was disappointing and 2006 is expected to bring a similar figure of 5.4 per cent. However, the country is definitely moving in the right direction.

Risk assessment

Economic	Moderate
Political	Moderate
Regional stability	Good

COUNTRY PROFILE

Historical profile

Ukraine first came under Russian suzerainty in the 1650s, as an alternative to invasion by the Poles.

Although some parts of Ukraine were initially annexed by the Poles, by the end of the eighteenth century the whole of Ukraine had been taken over by Russia.
1917 The Bolsheviks consolidated control over Ukraine, until the incorporation of the republic into the Soviet Union. The Russians retained direct control of eastern Ukraine from 1918 until the country's independence from Russia in 1991. The city of Lviv (formerly Lvov) near the western border was seized from the collapsing Austro-Hungarian Empire.
1920s Russia lost control of parts of western Ukraine to Poland, Czechoslovakia and Romania during the civil war between the Bolsheviks and counter-revolutionary forces supported by Western European armies. Soviet dictator, Josef Stalin, initiated a system of collective agriculture which forced Ukrainian farmers to render fixed quantities of produce to the authorities. These quotas were unrealistic, creating entirely artificial famine conditions during which over five million Ukrainians were estimated to have died.
1945 Following the end of the Second World War, the Soviet Union regained control of the lost areas of western Ukraine.
1954 Responsibility for the government of Crimea, an autonomous republic within Ukraine, was transferred from Russia to Ukraine as part of reforms initiated by Nikita Kruschev after Stalin's death.
1986 The Chernobyl nuclear reactor based in Ukraine exploded, causing widespread damage in both Ukraine and neighbouring Belarus.
1991 Under pressure from the opposition parties, in particular Narodniy Rukh Ukrayiny (Rukh) (People's Movement of Ukraine), the government gradually moved towards independence. Political power was transferred from the government of the former Soviet Union to Ukrainian national authorities in Kiev.
A majority voted for independence in a referendum, leading to a declaration of independence and the recognition of Ukraine as an independent state by the international community. Leonid Kravchuk won the presidential elections.
1992 Disagreements over economic policy saw the resignation of Ukraine's first prime minister, Vladimir Fokin, who was replaced by Leonid Kuchma.
1993 Arguments over economic policy and labour strikes led to the resignation of Kuchma and Yukhlym Zvyahilsky assumed the post.
1994 Kuchma returned as the main challenger to Kravchuk in the presidential elections, finally defeating Kravchuk in the run-off. Kuchma's attempts to swing the balance of power from parliament in favour of the presidency, in order to reduce the opposition to his economic programme, achieved mixed success.
1996 A new constitution gave the president the power to appoint a government formed by parliamentary deputies.
1997 Valeriy Pustovoitenko became prime minister.
1998 After elections, the Komunistychna Partiya Ukrainy (KPU) (Communist Party of Ukraine) emerged as the largest single party.
1999 Kuchma was re-elected president. He appointed reformist independent deputy Viktor Yuschenko as prime minister.
2000 Over 80 per cent of voters in a referendum supported President Kuchma's proposals for constitutional reform, designed to increase the powers of the presidency.
2001 Yushchenko's pro-reform government was toppled by the KPU-dominated parliament. Anatoly Kinakh became prime minister.
2002 In September, Russia, Ukraine, Kazakhstan and Belarus signed an economic union treaty. Two mass demonstrations called for the president to resign due to corruption and misconduct.
2003 There were demonstrations in Kiev in March, demanding the resignation of Kuchma. Ukraine and Russia signed an agreement on the joint use of the Kerch Strait and the status of the Azov Sea. The constitutional court ruled that Kuchma could run for a third term as president.

2004 Kuchma failed to stand in the October 2004 presidential election, which was won by the Russian-backed Viktor Yanukovych. Opposition supporters gathered in Kiev to protest against election fraud (the Orange Revolution) and the Supreme Court negated the result. Viktor Yushchenko won the re-run election on 26 December.

2005 Yushchenko was sworn in as president on 23 January. Yuliya Tymoshenko was approved as prime minister on 4 February. Yushchenko dismissed Tymoshenko and her cabinet on 8 September. Yuri Yekhanurov was appointed prime minister on 22 September. Russia cut off gas supplies in December after Ukraine refused to agree to a four-fold increase in the price of gas.

2006 A final agreement was reached on 4 January for a five-year gas supply deal. The price per 1,000 cubic metres (cum) of gas from Russia was set at US$230 (up from US$50), but in a complex deal the Russian gas will be sold to Gazprom-owned Roskurenergo, which will mix this gas with cheaper gas from Turkmenistan, Uzbekistan and Kazakhstan and then sell it to Ukraine at US$95 per 1,000 cum. Ukraine is able to buy a mix of gas from Kazakhstan and Turkmenistan at US$95 per cum. This agreement was not signed by Ukraine and on 10 January Prime Minister Yekhanurov was sacked, for agreeing the deal, but agreed to stay on until a replacement was named.

Political structure
Constitution
The 1996 constitution defines Ukraine as a sovereign, unitary state answerable to individual citizens, with the protection of citizens' rights as its foremost responsibility. The constitution forbids multiple nationality for Ukrainian citizens. The development and protection of the Ukrainian language is a constitutional obligation, but the constitution also guarantees free use of Russian and other minority languages, and requires the state to promote the study of languages of 'international communication'.

The constitution recognises and guarantees the right to local self-government. Local government is based on 24 *oblasts* (regional divisions) and one autonomous republic (Crimea). The *oblasts* are further divided into *rayons* (districts).

The Autonomous Republic of Crimea is bound by the Ukrainian constitution and by acts of the Verkhovna Rada (Supreme Council). However, it has the power to legislate separately on matters such as transport, planning, land use and healthcare.

Form of state
Presidential democratic republic

The executive
The highest executive authority rests with the president, who is directly elected for a five-year term and nominates the prime minister and regional governors, whose appointment are subject to the approval of parliament. The president has the power to appoint the cabinet, although parliament must approve it. Members of the cabinet do not necessarily need to be drawn from parliament. The president may rule by decree and did so in 1998, during deadlock in the legislature. Under normal circumstances, the prime minister shares some executive powers with the president and both can propose and approve legislation. This creates the potential for conflict between the two executive branches.

National legislature
The Verkhovna Rada (Supreme Council) (commonly called the Rada) is the legislature and its 450 members are elected for a five-year term: 225 by proportional representation and 224 in single-seat constituencies (in addition to the speaker). Only parties that obtain over 4 per cent of the vote are allocated PR seats. The Rada elects a speaker and plays an active role in proposing and enacting legislation.

Legal system
The legal system is based on a civil law code and, since the collapse of communism, has been engaged in an ongoing process of reform. The Constitutional Court is the highest interpreter of the constitution and is permitted to carry out judicial review of legislation. There are 18 Supreme Court judges, six each appointed for a nine-year non-renewable term by the president, parliament and a congress of Ukrainian judges.

The Supreme Court is the court of final appeal for civil and criminal cases originally heard in the lower courts. The Supreme Court's judges are appointed by a plenary session of existing judges. The lower courts are organised according to both geography and legal specialisation. The constitution encourages trial by jury and forbids the creation of emergency courts. Judges are granted legal immunity and can only be dismissed by a verdict of the Supreme or Constitutional Courts, or by an order of parliament.

Last elections
26 December 2004 (re-run presidential); 31 October/21 November 2004 (presidential); 31 March 2002 (parliamentary).
Results: Presidential (re-run): Viktor Yushchenko won 52 per cent of the vote and Viktor Yanukovych 44.2 per cent. Presidential (first round): Prime Minister Viktor Yanukovych won 40.1 per cent of the vote against 39.2 per cent for former prime minister Viktor Yushchenko, 5.8 per cent for Oleksandr Moroz and 5 per cent for Petro Symonenko.
Presidential (second round): Viktor Yanukovych, backed by Russia, won with 49.5 per cent of the vote, against pro-West Viktor Yushchenko with 46.6 per cent. Parliament passed a resolution declaring the presidential elections invalid. Parliamentary: although the reformist bloc of Viktor Yushchenko, Nasha Ukraina, won 23 per cent of the vote and the Komunistychna Partiya Ukrainy 20 per cent, the Za Yedinu Ukrainu (ZYU) (For United Ukraine), which received just 12 per cent of the vote and 102 seats, was able to muster enough support from other pro-Kuchma parties and deputies to emerge as the largest party.

Next elections
2007 (parliamentary); 2009 (presidential).

Political parties
Ruling party
Za Yedinu Ukrainu (ZYU) (For United Ukraine)
Main opposition party
The opposition is composed of the Povstan, Ukrayino! (Arise, Ukraine!) movement, comprising the Komunistychna Partiya Ukrainy (KPU) (Communist Party of Ukraine) and Sotsialistychna Partiya Ukrainy (SPU) (Socialist Party of Ukraine). The movement is backed by the largest party in the Rada, the Nasha Ukraina (NU) (Our Ukraine).

Population
47.25 million (2004)
Ethnic make-up
Ukrainian (72 per cent), Russian (22 per cent), Belarussian, Moldovan, Polish, Romanian and Tatar (in Crimea). Over 10 million ethnic Russians live in eastern Ukraine; Crimea is about 63 per cent Russian.

Religions
The principal religion is Christianity, of various denominations including Ukrainian Orthodox, Autocephalous Orthodox, and Ukrainian Greek Catholic (Uniate) Church. There is a small Jewish minority, and a Muslim minority mostly located in Crimea.

Education
The reversal of the Russian dominated education system is the primary aim of the government.

Literacy is almost universal in Ukraine, reflecting the high level of educational participation and high quality of teaching. Increased emphasis has also been placed on Ukrainian history, culture and literature.

Elementary schooling must begin by aged seven (parents may choose to enrol their children in school at aged six), and lasts until aged 10. This is followed by secondary basic education, which lasts until aged 15 when examinations determine academic upper secondary education until aged 18, or vocational education which lasts until aged 20. Ukraine has large scientific and educational centres in Kiev, Odessa, Lviv, Kharkiv and Donetzk, with more than 200 higher educational institutes. There are 10 universities.

Literacy rate: 99.7 per cent, adult rate (2003)

Compulsory years: 6/7 to 16.

Enrolment rate: 78 per cent gross primary enrolment; 105 per cent gross secondary enrolment, of relvant age groups (including repeaters), (Unicef 2004)

Pupils per teacher: 21 in primary schools.

Health

The precipitous economic decline since 1991 has significantly lowered living standards in Ukraine and adversely affected health. Although high soil fertility enables most Ukrainians to enjoy a sufficient diet, nutrition levels remain lower than optimum and high alcohol and tobacco consumption does little to improve matters. Moreover, lacking adequate funds, many health facilities have closed or reduced their level of service since independence. Although the number of doctors is well above the Organisation for Economic Co-operation and Development (OECD) average, they lack the training, facilities and medicines to provide adequate preventative or primary healthcare. One result of this has been outbreaks of tuberculosis, which reached epidemic levels in the late 1990s.

HIV prevalence: 0.1 per cent aged 15–49 in 2003 (World Bank)

Life expectancy: 68.3 years (World Bank)

Fertility rate/Maternal mortality rate: 1.2 births per woman (World Bank)

Birth rate/Death rate: 10 births and 16.4 deaths per 1,000 population (2003)

Infant mortality rate: 15 per 1,000 live births (World Bank)

Welfare

As part of its plan to reduce the fiscal deficit and meet IMF spending restrictions, the government has been forced to alter its social security structure.

More targeting of assistance to vulnerable groups is being planned, with reforms to family benefits, sickness benefits and the employment fund. A social insurance system provides benefits for old age pensions, sickness, maternity, work injury, and employee family allowances.

The pension system is being reformed, with preferential pensions being scaled down. The retirement age is 60 and 55 for men and women, with 25 or 20 years contributions, respectively. Reforms being enacted in 2004 intend to raise this and introduce additional voluntary and mandatory savings schemes. There are also plans to increase the pension age gradually.

The insurance scheme is funded by employee earnings of 1 per cent on wages up to H150 and 2 per cent on wages of H150 or more (capped at wage of H1,600 per month); employers pay 37 per cent of payroll and central and local governments provide subsidies as needed. There are an estimated 2.2 million Ukrainians who are eligible for extra social security payments as victims of the 1986 Chernobyl disaster.

Main cities

Kiev (Kyiv) (capital, estimated population 2.6 million in 2004), Kharkiv (Kharkov) (1.4 million), Odessa (1.0 million), Dnepropetrovsk (1.0 million), Donetsk (984,900), Zaporizhzhya (783,000), Lviv (Lvov) (700,100); Sevastapol (330,900); Simferopol (338,600) and Yalta are the major centres of Crimea.

Languages spoken

Ukrainian, Polish and German are widely spoken in western Ukraine, while Russian is widely spoken in the east. Romanian, Bulgarian, Hungarian and Belarusian are also spoken.

Official language/s

Ukrainian

Media

Press

The press in Ukraine is routinely censored, assisted by the large state-owned printing press, Presa Ukrayiny. The president's office also regularly takes legal action for defamation against any newspapers which criticise government policy, expose corruption among ministers or the country's powerful business oligarchs.

Dailies: National publications in English include *IntelNews* (www.brama.com/news) and *Ukrainian Independent Agency* (www.proua.com). Daily newspapers include *Golos Ukraina, Uriadoviy Kurier, Kievski Vedomosti, Komsomolskaya Pravda* and *Izv*. Other dailies in Ukrainian language include *The Day, Postup, Vechirniy Kyiv* and those in Russian are *Segodnya, Slobidskyi Kray* and *Facty i Kommentarii*.

Local dailies include *Kiev Post* in English, *Aviso* is an Ukrainian free-ads newspaper, with Kiev and regional issues. Others are *New Day* and *Vechernij Kharkov*.

Weeklies: The important weeklies include *Slovo, ATV Digest* (Ukrainian, Russian) *Gorod Weekly* (Russian), *InformBulletin* (Ukrainian), *Selski Visti, Kyiv Post* (English), *Slovo Weekly* (Russian), *Stolichnye Novosti (Capital News)* (Russian), *UNIAR* (Russian) and *Zerkalo Nedeli (Mirror Weekly)* (Russian). *Zagranitsa* is a weekly newspaper with features on immigration, travel and business. *Ukrainian Weekly* carries news about Ukraine and Ukrainians around the world. *Kharkovsky Courier* is published twice in the week, covering entertainment and news.

Business: The principal business newspaper is *Eastern Economist Daily*, published in Ukrainian and English. *Finansovaya Ukraina* covers financial news.

Broadcasting

Russian TV and radio stations are restricted from broadcasting in Ukraine. The border areas are the only regions that can receive uncensored programmes from Russia. In February 2004, the Ukrainian language broadcasts of US-funded Radio Liberty were shut down, as were radio stations endeavouring to re-broadcast the transmissions. In one case the director of the radio station died in a car accident. In an unprecedented development in March 2004, Presdient Kuchma agreed to stop media 'checks' (normally taking the form of tax inspections and supervisory examinations, during the period leading up to the October 2004 presidential elections. Such 'checks' normally resulted in stations being taken off the air for some time, or services being resumed conditionally.

Radio: There are 14 radio stations, 10 of which are commercial. The state-run Radios 1, 2 and Promin Radio (Channel 3) dominate the radio sector.

Television: There are 20 TV stations, 17 of which are commercial. A Polish channel can be received in the Lviv area and the Russian channel Ostankino can be received in most areas. There are at least 33 television stations (plus 21 repeater stations that relay broadcasts from Russia) (1997).

Advertising

The advertising industry is concentrated in Kiev. International advertisers dominate.

Economy

Despite its great potential for strong economic growth, Ukraine disappointed observers with poor economic development in the years following independence. The transition years of the 1990s were marred by a lack of political consensus on how to best provide the country with the conditions for a market economy.

The re-election of President Leonid Kuchma in 1999 led to the acceleration of structural economic reforms, and to Ukraine's first annual GDP growth in 2000.

Sales of steel to China are fuelling Ukraine's economy. Improvements in the economy and better investor confidence brought about significant increases in foreign direct investment (FDI) to US$1.9

Ukraine

billion in 2004, up from US$700 million in 2002 and US$1 billion in 2003. New tax laws and a law introducing international mortgage lending have added improvements to the business environment.

External trade
Imports
Principal imports include energy, machinery and equipment, and chemicals.
Main sources: Russia (31.9 per cent total, 2004), Germany (11.9 per cent), Turkmenistan (5.8 per cent), Italy (4.5 per cent)

Exports
Principal exports are ferrous and non-ferrous metals, fuel and petroleum products, chemicals, machinery and transport equipment, and food products.
Main destinations: Russia (17.4 per cent total, 2004), Turkey (7.1 per cent), Italy (5.7 per cent)

Agriculture
Farming
Historically known as the 'bread basket' of the former Soviet Union, Ukraine used to produce 25 per cent of the total Soviet agricultural output. The agricultural sector, despite Ukraine's rich land resources (with one-third of the world's total acreage of black soil), went into decline for several years as a result of general inefficiency, late payments and a lack of finance for fuel, fertilisers and machinery.
In 2004, agriculture accounted for around 12 per cent of GDP, compared to 25 per cent at independence in 1991, but is gradually returning to positive growth. Progress of agricultural sector reforms since 1992, including price and trade reforms, and agriculture-specific institutional reforms will have a significant impact on the future of agricultural production. Economy-wide reforms will allow the sector to absorb technological advances more rapidly.
The main agricultural products are wheat, barley, potatoes, sugar beet and flax. Ukraine is the world's largest producer of sugar beet.
The grain harvest in 2003 was at a record low due to extreme weather conditions and locust infestation, but the 2004 harvest was much improved.
Crop production in 2004 included: 41.0 million tonnes (t) cereals in total, 17.5 million t wheat, 8.8 million t maize, 20.7 million t potatoes, 11.0 million t barley, 1.6 t rye, 739,200t pulses, 500,000t grapes, 1.2 million t tomatoes, 1.4 million t oilcrops, 16.5 million t sugar beet, 850,000t apples, 1.0 million t oats, 130,000t chillies, 2.1 million t fruit in total, 6.9 million t vegetables in total. Livestock production included: 1.5 million t meat in total, 658,000t beef, 570,000t pig-meat, 15,500t lamb and goat meat, 295,000t poultry, 681,000t eggs, 13.7 million t milk.

Fishing
The fishery sector is an elaborate organisational complex of oceanic fisheries, pond fish farms, co-operatives, scientific research and education as well as enterprises dealing with processing and the sale of fish products, stock protection and restoration. The sector typically employs more than 60,000 people. The Black Sea fishing industry is concentrated around the ports of Odessa, Mariupol, Sevastopol, Berdyansk and Izmail.
Ukraine has a potential capacity to harvest and rear between 700,000 and 800,000 tonnes of fish, with an annual output of food fish products from vessels and coastal enterprises amounting to more than 600,000 tonnes. The country exports over a third of its fish catch and the industry makes a substantial contribution to the country's trade balance.

Forestry
Ukraine has mainly mixed and steppe forests, which account for one-sixth of the land area, with forest cover estimated at 9.5 million hectares (ha). Nearly two-thirds of the forest is available for wood supply, although consumption of forest products per capita is significantly below the European average. The state owns all the forest area.
The Zavarpattska and Polisia regions are the main centres for the forestry and paper industries. Apart from the smaller wood processing enterprises, most of the forest industry is privatised and caters to domestic demand. The industry is being modernised by improving the sawmills and other manufacturing operations. Small quantities of roundwood and half-finished products are exported to the Middle East and European countries. Wood pulp and paper, mainly from the Russian Federation are imported.
Exports of forest material in 2004 amounted to US$644 million, while imports amounted to US$576 million. Production in 2004 included 14,861,800 cubic metres (cum) roundwood, 6,465,700cum industrial roundwood, 2,019,100cum sawnwood, 4,570,500cum sawlogs and veneers, 1,308,000cum wood-based panels, 8,396,000cum woodfuel.

Industry and manufacturing
The industrial sector, hich contributed around 37 per cent to GDP in 2004, is essentially divided into two. Most of the sector is concentrated on heavy industry, principally in metallurgy, mining and mechanical engineering. The iron and steel industry is the main earner of hard currency revenues. It is dominated by large companies, such as JSC Zaporozhstal, and the government has been reluctant to introduce privatisation and other reforms. Ukraine has benefited from China's increasing demand for steel.
The high-technology industry, having been located in Ukraine in Soviet times, is modern and internationally competitive.

Tourism
The tourism sector is at an early stage of development, having to construct infrastructure practically from scratch after years of Soviet-era neglect. Ukraine's rich cultural and environmental resources offer considerable potential. Tourism is treated as an essential instrument in the modernisation of the economy, but its contribution is as yet modest. Around six million arrivals were recorded in 2004 and the sector is expected to contribute 3.2 per cent of GDP in 2005.

Environment
Extensive pollution is one of the more persistent legacies of the Soviet regime when massive industrialisation was pursued at any cost. The most obvious example is the Chernobyl nuclear power explosion which increased rates of thyroid cancer, leukaemia and birth defects in the surrounding areas. All Ukraine's cities suffer from pollution, both in the air as well as rivers and agricultural land. The Lviv region has the most polluted water in the country. Only about 55 per cent of the Ukranian population has access to safe water.

Mining
The mining sector traditionally accounts for 10 per cent of GDP and employs 3 per cent of the workforce.
Ukraine possesses an estimated 5 per cent of the world's mineral reserves. It has the world's largest supply of titanium, the third-largest deposit of iron ore (more than 200 billion tonnes) and 30 per cent of the world's manganese ore. It also has deposits of mercury, uranium and nickel, and a small amount of gold.
The largest iron ore deposits are in the Krivoy Roj area, with estimated reserves of 18 billion tonnes, Kremenchuk with 4.5 billion tonnes and Kerch and Belozerskie in the Donetsk region. The manganese deposits around Nikopol are thought to be the largest in the world. Gold deposits containing an average of between five and six grammes of gold per tonne of ore exist in the Trans-Carpathian region. The area also contains deposits of zinc and lead.
Other natural resources present in Ukraine include salt, lime, limestone, china clay, sulphur (around Lviv) and granite. Phosphorus deposits of about 20 billion tonnes are also present.

Ukraine typically produces 50 million tonnes per year (tpy) of iron, 1,000 tpy of nickel and 500 tpy of uranium.

Hydrocarbons
Ukraine's proven oil and gas reserves were not exploited during the Soviet era, when other regions (Siberia and Central Asia) could be developed more cheaply. The country has large hydrocarbon reserves and an extensive network of pipelines carrying Russian oil and gas to Western Europe.

Ukraine has oil reserves of 395 million barrels, the majority of which are located in the Dnieper-Donetsk basin in the eastern part of Ukraine. 80 per cent of Ukraine's oil consumption is met by imports, mostly from Russia. Efforts to reduce dependence on Russian oil have included the construction of an international oil terminal at Odessa port.

Ukraine has natural gas reserves of 1.4 trillion cubic metres. Annual production was 17.2 billion cubic metres supplies little more than 20 per cent of total domestic consumption, with the remainder being imported from Russia and Turkmenistan. A disagreement over prices led to Russia turning off its supply of gas to Ukraine in December 2005. An agreement was reached in January 2006, after pressure was put on both countries by the EU and others. The price per 1,000 cubic metres (cum) of gas from Russia was set at US$230 (up from US$50), but in a complex deal the Russian gas will be sold to Gazprom-owned Roskurenergo, which will mix this gas with cheaper gas from Turkmenistan, Uzbekistan and Kazakhstan and then sell it to Ukraine at US$95 per 1,000 cum.

Ukraine has 34.2 billion tonnes of coal reserves, but these are under-exploited. Ukraine is a net importer of coal. Reserves are set to last for the next 300 years.

Energy
Ukraine has 54.8GW of installed electricity capacity. There are four major thermal power stations and four nuclear power plants. The last working nuclear reactor at the Chernobyl plant was closed in December 2000. Thermal power, much of which is gas-fired, accounts for nearly 50 per cent of the electricity produced in Ukraine, while nuclear energy provides 40 per cent and hydroelectric plants supply the remainder.

A state-owned company, Enerhoatom, oversees the nuclear power plants. Lack of funding has meant that safety standards continue to be lax and strike action and power breakdowns are frequent.

A second reactor at the Khmelnitsky nuclear power plant was switched on in August 2004, the first new nuclear reactor since Chernobyl.

Financial markets
Stock exchange
The Ukrainian Stock Exchange (USE) was founded in 1991. The Interbank Currency Exchange conducts secondary trading in government securities daily and has benefited from restructuring of government debt.

The Russian financial crisis of 1998 devastated the USE, with market capitalisation falling to under 5 per cent as a proportion of GDP. Recovery in dollar terms since has been muted due to the devaluation of the hryvna.

There are only 11 listed companies on the exchange, and trading volume is negligible. Total market capitalisation in 2003 was US$88.5 million.

Banking and insurance
There are seven domestic banks operating in the banking sector, two of which are state-owned and originate from the Soviet era. Foreign investors are permitted to participate in the banking sector, but are only granted a licence after at least a year of running an office in the country.

In February 2004, Ukraine was removed from the OECD Financial Action Task Force (FATF) list of non-co-operative countries on money-laundering after reforms had been implemented.

Central bank
National Bank of Ukraine

Time
GMT plus two hours (GMT plus three hours from late March to late September); Crimea GMT plus three hours.

Geography
Ukraine is situated in Eastern Europe. The largest country entirely within Europe, Ukraine covers 603,700 square kilometres, stretching 2,000km from east to west and 1,000km from north to south. The Crimean peninsula in the south juts into the Black Sea, and has the Sea of Azov to the east.

In eastern Ukraine, the country is bordered by Russia to the east and north. In the western part of the country the northern border is with Belarus, and there are western borders with Poland and Slovakia. There are also short borders with Hungary, Romania and Moldova to the south-west, and a small salient of land south of Moldova which borders Bulgaria and has access to the Danube River delta. The average height above sea level in Ukraine is only 175 metres, and most of the land area is composed of rolling steppes and wooded plains. About two-thirds of the country is covered by a thick layer of humus-rich soil, making it one of the most fertile regions in the world.

The only mountains are in the south on the Crimean peninsula (maximum height 1,545 metres) and the Carpathians in the west (maximum height 2,061 metres). The main rivers are the Dnepr which drains the central regions of the country and flows into the Black Sea near Kherson and the Dnestr which flows through western Ukraine and Moldova before entering the Black Sea near Odessa.

Climate
The moderate continental climate varies little across the country. The Black Sea resorts around Odessa and Yalta are usually warmer and drier than the rest of Ukraine. The average rainfall per year is 1,440mm, with the Crimea receiving only 400mm. Average temperatures in Kiev range from 20 degrees Celsius (C) in July to minus 7 degrees C in January. Average temperatures in Lviv in western Ukraine range from 16 degrees C in July, to minus 5 degrees C in January.

Dress codes
Business clothes are appropriate for meetings, including a suit or jacket with a tie for men and formal clothing for women.

Entry requirements
Passports
Required by all.
Visa
Required by all, except citizens of Romania, Mongolia, Serbia and Montenegro, and the CIS (except Turkmenistan). Business visas require an original invitation from a legal entity duly registered in Ukraine, containing the official address and telephone number typed on its letterhead, and signed by an authorised officer of the entity, other than the applicant. The invitation must bear the entity's seal and be accompanied, when applicable, by a clear copy of its valid Certificate of Registration in Ukraine. The invitation should detail the purpose and if necessary, the number of visits, detailed itinerary, and provide basic passport data of the visitor. Letters of invitation are not required, for either business or tourist visits, by citizens of the EU, US, Canada, Japan, Switzerland, Slovakia, or Turkey. For all other tourists a letter of invitation from a Ukrainian or local tourist agency or a confirmation from a Ukrainian hotel is necessary. An application can be downloaded from www.ukremb.com/consular/docs/visa.pdf.
Currency advice/regulations
Hard currency can be changed in hotels or at the numerous street kiosks.

The most easily exchanged currency is the US dollar, and travellers' cheques are accepted only at selected bureaux in the major cities. All imported hard currency must be declared on arrival, and visitors are not usually permitted to re-export

Ukraine

more than the originally declared amount. The import or export of local currency is prohibited.

It is possible to withdraw money from automated teller machines (ATMs) in Kiev, using cards belonging to the leading Western networks.

Customs
Small amount of personal goods are allowed duty free. On arrival, declare all valuable items such as jewellery, cameras, computers and musical instruments.

There are strict regulations governing the export of antiques and items of historical interest. If in doubt seek prior permission from customs authorities.

Prohibited imports
Weapons, narcotics and certain pharmaceutical and communications products are subject to import restrictions and licences are issued by the relevant government ministries.

Health (for visitors)
Mandatory precautions
Vaccination certificates if travelling from a cholera or yellow fever infected area. An HIV/Aids test is required for long-stay visitors only. A UK-issued certificate is usually accepted. All visitors entering Ukraine are required to purchase health insurance at the airport of entry and prior to passing through immigration control. British passport holders are exempt due to a reciprocal agreement between the Ukrainian and British governments.

Advisable precautions
It is advisable to be 'in date' for the following immunisations: polio (within 10 years), tetanus (within 10 years), typhoid fever and hepatitis 'A' (moderate risk only). There is a rabies risk. Any medicines required by the traveller should be imported and it is advisable to have precautionary antibiotics if travelling outside the major urban centres. However, there are restrictions on the import of some pharmaceuticals and visitors are advised to check with their local Ukrainian embassy prior to travel. A travel kit including a disposable syringe is a reasonable precaution. Water precautions are recommended (water purification tablets may be useful).

Hotels
Kiev has a shortage of hotels. It is worth booking rooms several weeks in advance through the Intourist travel agency.

Credit cards
Credit cards are not widely accepted.

Public holidays
Fixed dates
1 Jan (New Year's Day), 7 Jan (Orthodox Christmas Day), 14 Jan (Orthodox New Year), 8 Mar (Women's Day), 1–2 May (Labour Days), 9 May (Victory Day), 28 Jun (Constitution Day), 24 Aug (Independence Day).

Variable dates
Orthodox Good Friday, Orthodox Easter Monday, Orthodox Whit Monday.

Working hours
Banking
Mon–Fri: 0930–1730.
Open 24 hours at Kiev Borispol airport, but only until noon at Odessa.
Business
Mon–Fri: 0900–1800.
Government
Mon–Thu: 09700–1700; Fri: 0900–1200.
Shops
Mon–Sat: 0900–1900.

Social customs/useful tips
Tips are not expected at most cafes, although at more expensive restaurants a tip of between 5 and 10 per cent is appropriate.

Small gifts for your host are appreciated in the event of personal hospitality. Handshaking is customary on meeting and on leaving. The formal mode of address, *Pan* (Mr) or *Pani* (Mrs) is usual even after several meetings. The use of business cards is widespread. It is important to be on time for meetings and appointments.

Referring to Ukraine as part of the Soviet Union or, even worse, as part of Russia, is a serious insult. The post-independence reaction to decades of 'Russification' led to strong nationalistic feelings, particularly in western Ukraine.

Security
Normal precautions should be taken when visiting Ukraine – avoid displaying large amounts of cash or expensive personal belongings. Avoid travelling alone at night in Kiev, particularly on the metro or in the city's parks.

Getting there
Air
National airline: Air Ukraine International.
International airport/s: Kiev-Borispol International Airport (KBP), 27km from city centre, duty-free and tax-free shops.
Other airport/s: Zhulhany Airport (domestic flights), 11km from Kiev; Lviv Airport, 7km from city centre.
Airport tax: There is no airport departure tax.

Surface
Road: The main roads into Ukraine enter from Slovakia and Uzhgorod, Belarus near Kovel and Chernigov and Russia at Kharkov and Stakhanov.
Rail: There are links connecting Kiev with all Commonwealth of Independent States (CIS) member states. Direct rail connections are available to Warsaw in Poland, Budapest in Hungary and Bucharest in Romania. Trains may be slow and uncomfortable.
Water: There are ferry services from Russia to the Crimean ports. Odessa and Yalta on the Black Sea have regular arrivals from Haifa, Istanbul, Limassol, Piraeus and Port Said. Riverboats from Odessa go to a number of Central European cities via the Danube.
Main port/s: The main Crimean ports are Yalta and Sevastopol, with Kerch the main port for the Sea of Azov. Izmail is the main Danube River port, and Odessa is the largest Black Sea port.

Getting about
National transport
Air: The main airports at Kiev, Odessa, Lviv and Ivano-Frankivsk all handle domestic traffic, as do 19 other regional airports. Smaller airports are subject to temporary closures due to power failures and fuel shortages.
Road: There is an extensive road network comprising approximately 172,315km of road, with around 29,227km of these being main or national roads. Many roads are poorly surfaced and in need of modernisation.
Buses: Ukraine has an extensive bus network, with routes to every city and most smaller towns. Most buses are overcrowded, but well heated.
Taxis: Using taxis for long-distance journeys is an option as they are reasonably cheap. Payment is usually requested in hard currency. Agree a price before setting off.
Rail: The Ukrainian rail network links the major cities, most of which are at least one night's travel apart. There are three types of sleeper carriage: the *spalny vahon* is the first class compartment for two people; the *kupe* or *kupeyny* is the second class compartment for four people; and the *platskart* is the third class open carriage with groups of six bunks in each alcove, with more beds along the aisles – avoid the *platskart* unless absolutely necessary.

Remember to take your own food and drink, although the carriage attendants usually provide cups of tea at the start and finish of the journey.

It is advisable to pre-book tickets before arriving in Ukraine. Foreigners can usually buy rail tickets from separate offices with English-speaking clerks, although the price will be slightly higher.

Although journey times are slower than air, rail travel is more reliable during the winter months.
Water: Passenger transport is available on Ukraine's rivers, the Dnepr and Dnestr, which traverse large areas of the country, but price increases, lack of spare parts

and cheaper land-based transport have caused a sharp decline in these services.

City transport
Taxis: In most cities there are official taxis with set fares, unofficial 'gypsy cabs' with negotiated fares and fixed-route, fixed price shared taxis which operate as minibus services. The taxi journey from Borispol airport to Kiev city centre takes about 40 minutes.

Car hire
International agencies are represented in the capital city. Private garages are available, although a shortage of spare parts still exists. Availability of suitable petrol remains problematic, as unleaded petrol is unavailable. In addition, insurance cover can be difficult to arrange.

Speed limits are 60kph (37mph) in built-up areas, 90kph (55mph) in open areas and 110kph (69mph) on motorways. Traffic drives on the right and an international driving permit is required. The use of right-hand-drive cars is prohibited. It is illegal to drive having consumed any amount of alcohol.

BUSINESS DIRECTORY

The addresses listed below are a selection only. While World of Information makes every endeavour to check these addresses, we cannot guarantee that changes have not been made, especially to telephone numbers and area codes. We would welcome any corrections.

Telephone area codes
The international direct dialling code (IDD) for Ukraine is + 380, followed by area code and subscriber's number:

Dnepropetrovsk	562	Odessa	482
Donetsk	622	Sevastopol	692
Kharkov	572	Simferopol	652
Kiev	44	Yalta	654
Lviv	322		

Useful telephone numbers
Address enquiries: 061
Directory enquiries: 09
Fire brigade: 01
Hospital enquiries: 003
Lost property office: 229-7844
Militia (Police): 02
Paid enquiries service: 009
Railway timetable: 09
River port: 416-1268
Taxi: 058
Taxi enquiries: 225-0396
Time: 060

Chambers of Commerce
American Chamber of Commerce in Ukraine, 42 Shovkovychna Street, 01601 Kiev (tel: 490-5800; fax: 490-5801; e-mail: acc@amcham.ua).

British-Ukrainian Chamber of Commerce, 34a Grushevskogo Street, 01021 Kiev (tel: 410-5720; fax: 230-2151; e-mail: administrator@bucc.com.ua).

Crimea Chamber of Commerce and Industry, 45 Sevastopolskaya Street, 95013 Simferopol (tel: 499-731; fax: 445-813; e-mail: cci@cci.crimea.ua).

Dnipropetrovsk Chamber of Commerce and Industry, 3 Vakulenchuka Street, 49061 Dnipropetrovsk (tel: 362-258; fax: 362-259; e-mail: miv@dcci.dp.ua).

Donetsk Chamber of Commerce and Industry, 12 Dzerzinskogo Avenue, 83000 Donetsk (tel: 928-060; fax: 928-048; e-mail: dcci@dtpp.donetsk.ua).

Kharkov Chamber of Commerce and Industry, 3a Kartsarskaya Street, 61012 Kharkov (tel: 149-690; fax: 149-682; e-mail: info@kcci.kharkov.ua).

Kiev Chamber of Commerce and Industry, 55 Bogdana Khmelnitskogo Street, 01054 Kiev (tel: 246-8301; fax: 246-9966; e-mail: info@kiev-chamber.org.ua).

Lviv Chamber of Commerce and Industry, 14 Stryisky Park, 79011 Lviv (tel: 764-611; fax: 767-972; e-mail: lcci@cscd.lviv.ua).

Odessa Chamber of Commerce and Industry, 47 Bazarna Street, 65011 Odessa (tel: 286-610; fax: 224-822; e-mail: orccii@orccii.odessa.ua).

Sevastopol Chamber of Commerce and Industry, 34 Velyka Morska, 99011 Sevastopol (tel: 543-536; fax: 540-644; e-mail: stpp@optima.com.ua).

Ukrainian Chamber of Commerce and Industry, 33 Velyka Zhytomyrska Street, 01601 Kiev (tel: 212-291; fax: 212-3353; e-mail: ucci@ucci.org.ua).

Banking
Aggio Joint Stock Bank, 9 Leskova Street, 252011 Kiev (tel: 295-0305; fax 295-3164).

Commercial Bank (Ekspobank), 2-4 Volodarskogo Street, 254025 Kiev (tel: 216-1676; fax: 216-6073).

First Ukrainian International Bank (under full management of Bank Mees and Hpe Pierson NV, ABN/AMRO), 8 Prorizna Street, 252034 Kiev (tel: 224-2187; fax: 224-2055).

Gradobank, 1 Dimitrova Street, 252650 Kiev (tel: 261-9191; fax: 268-1530).

Inki Bank, 10/2 Mechnikova Street, 252023 Kiev (tel: 294-9219; fax: 290-6292).

Legbank Commercial Bank for Light Industry, 8/10 Esplanadna (Kuybysheva) Street, 252601 Kiev (tel: 220-6125; fax: 220-8684).

Ukreximbank, 8 Kreshchatyk Street, Kiev (tel: 226-3363; fax: 229-8082).

Ukrainian Bank for Foreign Economic Affairs, 8 Kreshchatyk Street, 252001 Kiev (tel: 293-1698).

Ukrainian Financial Group Joint Stock Commercial Bank, 7 Vokzalnaya Street, 252032 Kiev (tel: 245-4560; fax: 245-4587).

Central bank
National Bank of Ukraine, 9 Institutska Street, Kiev 01601 (tel: 253-0180; fax: 230-2033; e-mail: info@bank.gov.ua).

Travel information
Borispol Airport, Kiev (tel: 296-7454, 225-2252, 212-2592).

International Touristic Corporation, Golden Shore, 4 Nahimov Avenue, 335000 Sevastopol, Crimea (tel: 524-114, 523-001; fax: 523-213).

Ukrainian International Airlines, Kiev (tel: 216-7040, 296-7293, 221-8380, 296-7455; internet site: http://www.ukraine-international.com/eng/).

National tourist organisation offices
Ukrintour (Ukrainian Foreign Tourism Association), 26 Bohdana Khmelnitskoho Street, 252030 Kiev (tel: 212-5570; fax: 212-4524).

Ministries
Ministry of Agriculture and Foodstuffs, 24 Kreshchatyk Street, 252001 Kiev (tel: 226-2772; fax: 229-8756).

Ministry of the Coal Industry, 4 Bohdana Khmelnitskoho Street, 252001 Kiev (tel: 226-2273, 228-0372; fax: 228-2131).

Ministry of Communications, 22 Kreshchatyk Street, Kiev (tel: 226-2140; fax: 228-6141).

Ministry of Culture, 19 Ivana Franka Street, 252030 Kiev (tel: 224-4911, 226-2645, 226-2902; fax: 225-3257).

Ministry of Defence, 6 Povitroflotsky Avenue, 252168 Kiev (tel: 224-7152; fax: 226-2015).

Ministry of Education, 10 Peremogy Avenue, 252135 Kiev (tel: 216-7210, 216-7763, 216-1575; fax: 274-1049).

Ministry of Engineering, the Defence Industry and Conversion, 6 Pushkinska Street, 252034 Kiev (tel: 229-0390; fax: 228-7653).

Ministry of Environment Protection, 5 Kreshchatyk Street, 252001 Kiev (tel: 226-2428, 228-0644; fax: 229-8383).

Ministry of Finance, 12/2 Hrushevskoho Street, 252008 Kiev (tel: 226-2044; fax: 293-2178).

Ministry of Foreign Affairs, 1 Mihaylivska Square, 252018 Kiev (tel: 226-3379, 293-1581; fax: 226-3169, 293-3302).

Ministry of Foreign Economic Relations, 8 Lvivska Square, 254655 Kiev (tel: 212-3005; fax: 212-5259).

Ukraine

Ministry of Forestry, 5 Kreshchatyk Street, 252001 Kiev (tel: 226-3253, 226-2735, 228-5666; fax: 228-7794).

Ministry of Health, 7 Hrushevskoho Street, 252021 Kiev (tel: 293-6194; fax: 293-6975).

Ministry of Industry, 34 Kreshchatyk Street, 252001 Kiev (tel: 226-2623; fax: 227-4104).

Ministry of Information, 2 Prorizna Street, 252601 Kiev (tel: 226-2871).

Ministry of Internal Affairs, 10 Bogomoltsa Street, 252021 Kiev (tel: 291-3333, 226-3317; fax: 291-3182).

Ministry of Justice, 13 Karl Marx Street, 252001 Kiev (tel: 226-2416; fax: 226-2416).

Ministry of Labour, 28 Pushkinska Street, 252004 Kiev (tel: 226-2445, 226-2639, 226-3215; fax: 224-5905).

Ministry for Nationalities, Migration and Cults Issues, 21/8 Instytutska Street, 252021 Kiev (tel: 293-5335; fax: 293-3531).

Ministry of Power Engineering and Electrification, 30 Kreshchatyk Street, 252001 Kiev (tel: 224-9388; fax: 224-4021).

Ministry for Protection of the Population against the Consequences of Chernobyl, 8 Lvivska Square, 254655 Kiev (tel: 212-5049; fax: 212-5069).

Ministry of Social Welfare, 26-28 Kudriavka Street, 252053 Kiev (tel: 222-5555, 226-2401; fax: 212-2535).

Ministry of Statistics, 3 Shota Rustaveli Street, 252023 Kiev (tel: 226-2021, 227-7057; fax: 227-0783, 227-4266).

Ministry of Transport, 51 Horkoho Street, 252005 Kiev (tel: 226-2266, 227-1029, 227-7087; fax: 227-7351).

Ministry of Youth and Sports Issues, 42 Esplanadna Street, 252023 Kiev (tel: 220-0200, 220-1461; fax: 220-1294).

Ukrainian Ministry for Economics and Issues of European Integration, 12/2 Hrushevskoho Street, 252008 Kiev (tel: 293-4005, 293-9329; fax: 293-6371).

Other useful addresses

British Embassy, 9 Desyatinna, 01025 Kiev (tel: 462-0011/15; fax: 462-0013; internet: wwwbritemb-ukraine.net).

Cabinet of Ministers, 12/2 Hrushevskoho Street, 252001 Kiev (tel: 226-3263; fax: 293-2093).

Committee for Standardisation, Methodology and Certification, 10 Kypska Street, 252021 Kiev (tel: 226-2971).

EBRD Kiev Office, c/o National Hotel, 5 Lipska Street, 252021 Kiev 21 (tel: 291-8847, 291-8977; fax: 291-6246).

EU Co-ordination Unit – TACIS Programme, Agency for International Co-operation and Investment, 1 Mihailivska Ploscha, 252018 Kiev (tel: 212-8312; fax: 230-2513).

European Centre for Macroeconomic Analysis of Ukraine, Kiev (tel & fax: 228-3283; e-mail: ecman@gv.kiev.va).

Foreign Trade Organisation (UKRIMPEX), 22 Vorovsky Street, 252054 Kiev (tel: 216-2174; fax: 216-1926, 216-2996).

International Finance Corporation Field Office, Suite 7, 28-A Lyuteranska Street, 252024 Kiev (tel: 293-4857, 293-8341; fax: 293-0539).

Kiev City Administration, 36 Khreshchatyk Street, Kiev (tel: 220-8065; fax: 228-4718).

Kiev Universal Commodity Exchange (KUCE), 1 Kudryashova Street, 252035 Kiev (tel: 276-7129, 244-0143, fax: 276-7129).

Soros International Economic Advisory Group, Kiev (tel: 296-9877; fax: 269-5263).

State Ukrainian Property Fund, 18/9 Kutuzova Street, 252133 Kiev (tel: 296-6963; fax: 296-6984).

Ukrainian Association of Industrialists and Entrepreneurs, 34 Kreshchatik Street, 252001 Kiev (tel: 224-3122, 228-3069; fax: 226-3152).

Ukrainian Embassy (USA), Suite 711, 3350 M Street, NW, Washington DC 20007 (tel: 202-333-0606; fax: 202-333-0606; e-mail: vmar@aol.com).

Ukrainian Exchange (commodities and stock exchange), 15 Proreznaya Street, 252601 Kiev (tel: 228-6481; fax: 229-6376).

Ukrainian League of Enterprises with Foreign Capital, 19A Lyuteranska Street, 252073 Kiev (tel: 229-3544; fax: 229-8739).

Ukrainian National News Agency (UKRINFORM), 8-16b Khemlnitski Street, 252601 Kiev (tel: 226-2469, 229-0143; fax: 229-2439/8007, 228-1659).

Ukrainian Universal Commodity Exchange, 1 Academika Glushkova Avenue, 252085 Kiev (tel: 261-6333, 261-6375; fax: 261-6362).

UKRINTERENERGO (State Foreign Trade Company), 27 Komintern Street, 252032 Kiev (tel: 291-7296; fax: 220-1885).

World Bank Field Office, Suite 2/3, 26 Shovkovychna Street, 252024 Kiev (tel: 293-1110, 293-4045; fax: 293-4236).

Internet sites

Ukraine gateway site:
http://www.brama.com

Ukraine Embassy, London:
http://www.ukrainet.org

Ukraine Embassy, Washington:
http://www.ukremb.com

General information:
http://www.bizukraine.com

Tourism and travel:
http://www.ukraine.com

Ukraine International Airlines:
http://www.ukraine international.com

History and culture:
http://www:uazone.net

News on Ukraine:
http://www.infoukes.com

Travel and tourism:
http://www.travel.kyiv.org

United Arab Emirates

KEY FACTS

Official name: Al Imarat al Arabiyya al Muttahida (United Arab Emirates) (UAE)

Head of State: President Sheikh Khalifa bin Zaid al Nahayan (ruler of Abu Dhabi) (elected 3 Nov 2004)

Head of government: Prime Minister Sheikh Maktoum bin Rashed al Maktoum (ruler of Dubai). Sheikh Maktoum died on 4 Jan 2006 and is expected to be succeeded by his brother Sheikh Mohammed bin Rashed al Maktoum.

Area: 83,600 square km

Population: 3.34 million (2004)

Capital: Abu Dhabi (federal capital); Dubai (commercial capital)

Official language: Arabic

Currency: Dirham (Dh) = 100 fils

Exchange rate: Dh3.67 per US$ (fixed)

GDP per capita: US$22,017 (2004)

GDP real growth: 5.70% (2004)

Labour force: 2.11 million (2004)

Inflation: 3.80% (2004)

Oil production: 2.67 million bpd (2004)

Balance of trade: US$23.82 billion 2004

Foreign debt: US$18.50 billion (2003)

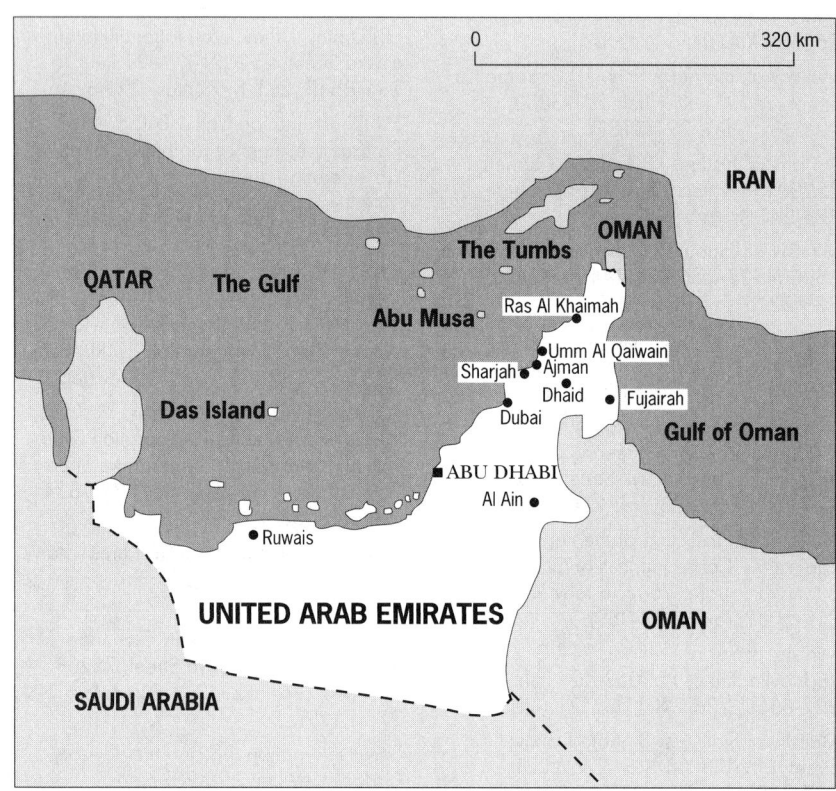

It was a transitional year in many respects for the United Arab Emirates (UAE) in 2005. It was President Sheikh Khalifa bin Zaid al Nahayan's first year in office. The country's founding president, Sheikh Zaid bin Sultan al Nahayan, had died in November 2004. Moreover, more change was to come, with the death in office of vice president and prime minister Sheikh Maktoum bin Rashid al Maktoum on 4 January 2006.

A diversifying economy

The UAE economy grew by around 6.5 per cent in 2005, much of it fuelled by the booming emirate of Dubai. In September, Dubai launched an ambitious plan to become the financial services centre of the Middle East, in competition with Bahrain, when it officially opened the Dubai International Financial Exchange (DFIX). The DFIX forms part of the Dubai International Financial Centre (DIFC), established in 2002. Both of these projects were the brainchild of the then de facto Emir of Dubai, Sheikh Mohammed bin Rashid al Maktoum. Sheikh Mohammed succeeded his brother Sheikh Maktoum as Emir of Dubai and prime minister and vice president of the UAE in January 2006.

The UAE sits on about 10 per cent of the world's proven oil reserves and also has t

he fifth largest gas reserves in the world. About 30 per cent of its GDP is based on oil exports, although recent developments in Dubai and elsewhere in the country have seen large strides taken in the financial and petrochemical sectors.

Dynastic musical chairs

With the death of founding president Sheikh Zaid in November 2004, a new member of the al Nahayan clan stepped forward to inherit not only the family emirate of Abu Dhabi but also the virtually hereditary presidency of the UAE itself. A

United Arab Emirates

similar change took place in January 2006, when Sheikh Mohammed inherited the emirate of Dubai and the UAE's vice-presidency and prime ministerial office.

Democratic reform, sort of, some time

In December 2005, President Sheikh Khalifa announced plans to institute a partially-elected advisory council. Khalifa also stated that suffrage would be limited to a small number of electors who would in turn be chosen by the country's seven emirs. No date was given for the election and political parties will remain banned.

Also in December, the Emirate of Abu Dhabi held its first ever elections for its Chamber of Commerce and Industry. Women were also allowed to vote and two seats were reserved for women candidates.

Camel reform

In July and September 2005, the UAE government announced new laws regulating camel racing in the country. Camel racing is one of the most popular sports in the Gulf region but the UAE and others states such as Qatar have been criticised in recent years by anti-slavery groups and Western governments. These accuse the UAE of turning a blind eye to the trafficking of children into the country, where the victims live in virtual slavery as camel jockeys. The reforms raised the minimum age of camel jockeys from 16 to 18 and instituted an ID card system to enforce this regulation.

Outlook

The UAE has remained violence-free in a region hyper-charged in the wake of the US-led invasion of Iraq. There have been no reports of Islamist terrorism or politically inspired attacks on the UAE's large expatriate population. There is also little to suggest so far that the country's citizens are agitating for democratic reform. The combination of public quiescence and restricted political freedom look set to continue as long as economic prosperity continues.

Risk assessment

Politics	Stable
Economy	Booming
Regional stability	Fragile

COUNTRY PROFILE

Historical profile
The people of the UAE are descended from tribespeople who were settled for much of the year and engaged in agriculture, fishing or pearl diving, and from nomadic Bedouins. To have created the richest state in the Middle East out of a disparate group of sheikhdoms in the space of 30 years is no mean achievement. Not more than a few decades ago, Dubai was still sending raiding parties out to neighbouring Sharjah and minor wars continued to be fought between Dubai and Abu Dhabi. More often than not the opposing armies were led by the same personalities who subsequently became the federation's greatest supporters. The UAE was established under the sponsorship of the British in 1971. In the framework of its withdrawal from 'east of Suez' the British Foreign Office had recognised the vulnerability of the individual sheikhdoms. The tiny emirate of Fujairah, for example, had already been targetted as a mafia base.

In three decades, the transformation from the Trucial States as they were known prior to federation, to a modern nation state has been dramatic. Sheikh Zayed bin Sultan al Nahayan, ruler of the richest emirate Abu Dhabi and president of the UAE from its inception until his death in November 2004, trod a delicate path between the interests of the new nation and the authority of the other six ruling sheikhs. The federation has grown alongside the development of a federal structure and is today a fine balance, allowing each ruler to determine the style and economic future of his emirate, while Abu Dhabi provides the infrastructure and (with the exception of Dubai, which in commercial terms follows its own path) a platform for greater prosperity. Not that the UAE has not had its moments: in 1976 Sheikh Zayed threatened to resign in frustration over slow progress, which caused the other rulers to realise that without Abu Dhabi and its massive oil revenues, the union could lose its one financial backer. Gradually, common cause enabled the individual emirates to put their rivalries aside, or at least to express them in commercial, rather than in military terms.

1498 The Portuguese occupied the region.
1633 The Dutch turned the Portuguese out of their trading posts, to be ousted in their turn, by the British.
1820 Britain and a number of rulers in the Gulf signed a treaty to combat piracy. This began a series of agreements which led to the area becoming known as the Trucial Coast, comprising the Trucial states (Abu Dhabi, Dubai, Sharjah, Ras al Khaimah, Umm al Qaiwain, Fujairah and Ajman).
1892 Exclusive Agreements between the Trucial States and Britain were signed, which effectively gave the British control over foreign affairs, while each emirate retained control over internal affairs.
1952 The seven emirates formed a Trucial council to promote increased co-operation.
1958 Oil was discovered off Abu Dhabi.
1962 Oil was exported for the first time from Abu Dhabi.
1966 Oil was discovered off Dubai.
1968 Britain announced its intention to withdraw from the Gulf by 1971. A British plan to form a single state consisting of Bahrain, Qatar and the Trucial States did not take place.
1971 The independence of Bahrain and Qatar was negotiated. Iran occupied the islands of Greater and Lesser Tumb and Abu Musa. Abu Dhabi, Dubai, Sharjah,

KEY INDICATORS — United Arab Emirates

	Unit	2000	2001	2002	2003	2004
Population	m	2.88	3.00	3.00	3.17	3.34
Gross domestic product (GDP)	US$bn	67.40	67.80	71.40	80.40	70.96
GDP per capita	US$	27,189	20,659	19,173	19,048	22,017
GDP real growth	%	5.0	2.9	-0.9	4.6	5.7
Inflation	%	1.4	2.0	2.8	3.2	3.8
Oil output	'000 bpd	2,491.0	2,429.0	2,270.0	2,520.0	2,667.0
Natural gas output	bn cum	39.8	41.3	46.0	44.4	45.8
Exports (fob) (goods)	US$m	39,900.0	46,100.0	45,970.0	60,800.0	69,480.0
Imports (fob) (goods)	US$m	34,300.0	32,876.0	37,320.0	51,955.0	45,660.0
Balance of trade	US$m	5,600.0	13,224.0	8,640.0	8,845.0	23,820.0
Current account	US$m	12,625.0	12,700.0	6,170.0	6,751.0	16,140.0
Total reserves minus gold	US$m	13,522.7	14,146.4	*15,219.4	15,087.8	18,529.9
Foreign exchange	US$m	13,303.9	13,918.2	*14,897.2	14,731.5	18,209.0
Exchange rate	per US$	3.67	3.67	3.67	3.67	3.67

* estimated figure

Fujairah, Umm al Qaiwain and Ajman formed the United Arab Emirates (UAE), a loose federation; Sheikh Zayed bin Sultan al Nahayan (ruler of Abu Dhabi) was elected president of the federation. Ras al Khaimah's ruler did not join at this point since he optimistically hoped that successful oil exploration would enable him to stick out for a better deal.
1972 Ras al Khaimah joined the federation; the Federal National Council (FNC) was created as a 40-member consultative body, appointed by the seven rulers of the UAE.
1980s The UAE supported Iraq during the Iran-Iraq war.
1981 The UAE became a founding member of the Gulf Co-operation Council (GCC). The GCC's inaugural meeting was held in Abu Dhabi.
1991 The UAE joined the US-led alliance against Iraq. The Bank of Credit and Commerce International (BCCI), in which the Abu Dhabi royal family owned a 77.4 per cent stake, collapsed.
1992 Iran insisted that visitors to the islands of Abu Musa and Greater and Lesser Tumb must have Iranian visas.
1993 Abu Dhabi sued BCCI's executives for damages.
1994 A court in Abu Dhabi convicted 11 of the 12 former BCCI executives accused of fraud. They were given prison sentences and ordered to pay compensation.
1996 Iran's dispute with the UAE over the islands of Abu Musa and the Tumbs was further fuelled by Iran when it built an airport on Abu Musa and a power station on Greater Tumb. Two BCCI executives were cleared of fraud charges on appeal.
1998 Diplomatic relations with Iraq were restored – the UAE had severed them at the outbreak of the Gulf War.
1999 The GCC reiterated its support for the UAE over the three disputed islands of Greater and Lesser Tumb and Abu Musa.
2001 Six thousand prisoners were pardoned by the President on humanitarian grounds. The government ordered financial institutions to freeze the assets of 62 organisations and individuals suspected of funding terrorist movements.
2002 The UAE and Oman signed a final agreement delineating their entire 1,000km border.
2003 The minister of higher education said that the employment of women graduates was an important factor for the UAE.
2004 President Sheikh Zayed bin Sultan al Nahayan died on 2 November. Sheikh Khalifa bin Zaid al Nahayan succeeded his father as ruler of Abu Dhabi, and on 3 November, the Federal National Council elected him as president of the UAE.
2005 A new terminal for Abu Dhabi International Airport was opened in August. In December Sheikh Zayed announced plans to elect half of the 40 members of the FNC; no date for the elections was announced.
2006 Sheikh Maktoum bin Rashed al Maktoum, ruler of Dubai and vice president and prime minister of the UAE, died on 4 January. He was succeeded by Sheikh Mohammed bin Rashid al Maktoum.

Political structure
Constitution
Highest government authority is vested in the Supreme Council of Rulers, which consists of the rulers of the seven emirates – Abu Dhabi, Dubai, Sharjah, Ras al Khaimah, Umm al Qaiwain, Fujairah and Ajman – which comprise the UAE. It is responsible for most internal and external affairs. Abu Dhabi and Dubai hold the power of veto on the Supreme Council. The Supreme Council meets four times a year, and elects the president and vice president (each for terms of five years). The president appoints the prime minister and the Council of Ministers.
The 40 members of the Federal National Council (FNC), drawn proportionately from each emirate, are appointed by the rulers.
The individual emirates have retained a great degree of autonomy and all local powers which are not specifically reserved for the federal government belong to them. Since 1971, the president has been the ruler of Abu Dhabi and the prime minister and vice president the ruler of Dubai, suggesting that elections are a matter of form and that in fact the two emirates with the largest economic and political muscle tend to dominate the federation.
A constitutional amendment in 1996 removed the word 'interim' from the constitution and designated Abu Dhabi the capital of the UAE.
Form of state
Federal monarchy
The executive
The Council of Ministers is formally the executive body. However, real power resides with senior members of the ruling families, especially those of Dubai and Abu Dhabi, as expressed by the decisions of the Supreme Council of Rulers.
National legislature
The 40-member Federal National Council (FNC) has consultative functions and is the closest approximation the UAE has to a law-making national assembly. Every two years, the emirates of Abu Dhabi and Dubai appoint eight members each, Sharjah and Ras al Khaimah appoint six members each and Ajman, Fujairah and Umm al Qaiwain appoint four members each.

In December 2005 Sheikh Kalifa bin Zayed announced that half the FNC would be elected, although he did not give a date for the elections.
Legal system
The federal courts, which consist of the Union Supreme Court and primary tribunals, were established by law in 1979. The former primary tribunals in Abu Dhabi, Sharjah, Ajman and Fujairah became federal primary tribunals and the former primary tribunals of other towns became circuits of the federal primary tribunals. The law applied is *Sharia* (Islamic Law).
Last elections
Nov 2004 (president and vice president; open only to members of the Supreme Council of Rulers).
Results: Presidential: Sheikh Zayed Bin Sultan al Nahyan (ruler of Abu Dhabi) was re-elected.
Next elections
2006 (president and vice president; open only to members of the Supreme Council of Rulers).

Political parties
Party political activity is not officially permitted in the UAE.

Population
3.34 million (2004)
Ethnic make-up
UAE nationals make up a fifth of the population. Around 80 per cent of the population are expatriates, with those from the Indian subcontinent accounting for about 40 per cent of the population. The second largest group is Iranians, who make up about 17 per cent. Non-UAE Arabs make up about 13 per cent and Westerners about 5 per cent.
Abu Dhabi is dominated by the Bani Yas tribe of which the al Bu Falasah is the most important section (to which the al Maktoums of Dubai belong).
Religions
The majority are Sunni Muslims; about 20 per cent are Shi'a Muslims. Many expatriates from the Indian subcontinent are Christian. The constitution guarantees full religious rights to all. The Apostolic Vicariate of Arabia is in Abu Dhabi.

Education
Primary education is compulsory and is followed by three years' preparatory education which qualifies students for general or technical secondary education. The language of instruction is English.
General secondary education lasts for three years. It consists of a common first year followed by specialisation in science or the humanities. At aged eighteen, students take an examination for progression to higher education.

United Arab Emirates

Technical secondary education lasts for six years following primary school and comprises three main streams: technical, agricultural and commercial in both preparatory and secondary cycles. At aged eighteen, a Technical Secondary Diploma is awarded.

Secondary education is also offered in religious institutions.

Higher education is offered in public and private universities and Higher Colleges of Technology. These include the United Arab Emirates (UAE) University, and the Dubai University College, (a private college).

Emirate and federal politics can at times threaten academic standards. Education is allocated some 20 per cent of the federal budget.

Literacy rate: 77.3 per cent, male; 80.7 per cent, female; adult rate in 2002 (World Bank).

Compulsory years: 6 to 12.

Enrolment rate: 89 per cent gross primary enrolment; 80 per cent gross secondary enrolment, of relevant age groups (including repeaters) (World Bank).

Pupils per teacher: 16 in primary schools.

Health

Life expectancy: 75.4 years (World Bank)

Fertility rate/Maternal mortality rate: 3.0 births per woman; maternal mortality 3 per 100,000 live births (World Bank).

Infant mortality rate: 7.0 per 1,000 live births; 7 per cent of children aged under five are malnourished (World Bank).

Head of population per physician/bed: 1.8 physicians and 2.6 hospital beds available per 1,000 people.

Welfare

There is an extensive and generous welfare system in the UAE, in many ways a model of a successful welfare state. However, this reflects the unique characteristics of the UAE – no social security contributions are levied on employers or employees, and there is no personal taxation. Many services remain free, and there are numerous grants, loans, and subsidies.

Main cities

Abu Dhabi (federal capital estimated population 539,800 in 2003), Dubai (commercial capital, 906,100), Sharjah (433,400), Ajman (154,900), Ras al Khaimah (105,000), Fujairah (44,900), Umm al Qaiwain (33,900).

Languages spoken

Languages of the Indian sub-continent are widely spoken among the expatriate community. Persian (Farsi), Urdu and English are also spoken.

Official language/s
Arabic

Media

Press
The press is largely independent, although criticism of rulers is not allowed.

Dailies: Main daily Arabic newspapers include *Al-Jareeda*, Sharjah's *Al-Khaleej*, Abu Dhabi's *Al-Ittihad* and *Al-Wahda* and Dubai's *Al-Bayan*. *Al-Khaleej* and *Al-Ittihad* tend to be the market leaders. English language dailies include *Dubai News*, *UAE Today*, *Gulf News*, *Gulf News Tabloid*, *Gulf News Classified*, *Khaleej Times* and *Khaleej Times Features*. Major news agencies providing daily news include Emirates Media Inc. (www.emi.co.ae/) and Emirates News Agency (www.wam.org.ae).

Weeklies: Weeklies are *Al-reyadha wa Al-shabab*, *Al-Sada Magazine* and *Emirates Today*.

Business: Business publications include the monthly publication *Gulf Business Magazine*.

Periodicals: There are over 30 magazines in Arabic and English. *What's On* magazine lists cultural events.

Broadcasting
Radio: Abu Dhabi Radio, which has stations in Abu Dhabi, Dubai, Ras Al-Khaimah and Umm Al-Qaiwain, broadcasts in Arabic, English, French, Bengali and Urdu. The government-owned Capital Radio broadcasts in English from Abu Dhabi.

A shortwave world service broadcasts to North America, the Far East and Europe.

Television: Dubai Radio and Colour Television broadcasts domestic Arabic and European programmes. UAE Radio and Television also broadcasts from Dubai in Arabic and English to the USA, India and Pakistan, the Far East, Australia and New Zealand, Europe and North and East Africa.

In addition, Ras Al-Khaimah Broadcasting Station has two stations broadcasting in Arabic; Sharjah Broadcasting Station puts out programmes in Arabic and French and Umm Al-Qaiwain Broadcasting Station broadcasts in Arabic. Abu Dhabi television programmes incorporate information, entertainment, religion, culture, news and politics.

Advertising
The UAE is the region's marketing gateway. Dual English and Arabic usage is common on signs and in many publications. Newspaper share of total advertising is typically just over half, usually representing advertising worth over US$100 million per annum.

Economy

The UAE has a buoyant economy, underpinned by its vast oil and gas resources. GDP, boosted by rising oil prices and investor confidence, grew by 6.4 per cent in 2004. Abu Dhabi and Dubai account for approximately 60 per cent and 25 per cent respectively of overall GDP. Abu Dhabi, which possesses over 90 per cent of the country's oil wealth, is financially dominant, providing almost 75 per cent of federal revenues and grants to smaller emirates.

Oil accounts for 30 per cent of GDP, but successful efforts are being made to diversify the economy. Dubai, for example, has developed a range of manufacturing industries, financial services and tourism, and is emerging, because of its favourable tax regime, as an important international diamond centre.

The leading non-oil sectors are manufacturing (including Dubai's state-owned aluminium smelter, Dubal), commerce and government services (each contributing around 15 per cent to GDP), real estate (14 per cent), construction (12 per cent) and transport and communications (9 per cent). The UAE has made good progress in privatising small agricultural enterprises and has broadened the programme to include larger-scale industrial projects and public utilities.

External trade

The UAE is essentially an export-based economy with exports almost entirely based on crude oil and related products. Dubai is the main trade centre and accounts for over 70 per cent of UAE's imports and re-exports and half of its non-oil exports. The Dubai Ports Authority is the thirteenth-largest container handling body in the world.

Imports
Main imports are machinery and transport equipment, chemicals and food. US goods to be imported during 2006 will be US$10.2 billion.

Main sources: China (10.4 per cent total, 2004), India (8.3 per cent), Japan (7.2 per cent), Germany (6.6 per cent), France (6.4 per cent), UK (6.2 per cent), US (6.0 per cent), Italy (4.1 per cent)

Exports
Main exports are crude oil (45 per cent total), natural gas, re-exports, dried fish and dates.

Main destinations: Japan (28.5 per cent total, 2004), South Korea (9.5 per cent), Thailand (5.9 per cent)

Re-exports
Aluminium, from Dubai.

Agriculture

Farming
Agriculture contributes around 4 per cent to GDP and employs 8 per cent of the workforce. A harsh climate and sandy soil make self-sufficiency in food production an unlikely prospect. The northern Emirates of Ras al Khaimah, Fujairah (on the western Gulf of Onan coast) and

Ajman supply 25 per cent of local demand. Ajman is the most productive and has been a focal region for agricultural development. Ras al Khaimah and Fujairah produce a more diverse selection of agricultural produce as a result of the higher rainfall they receive. Very few nationals still work on farms, where labour is mostly from Bangladesh and Baluchistan in south-west Pakistan.

Government farm subsidies are generous. Many farms are supported through funding available on easy credit terms, seed allocations and technical advice on fertilisation, irrigation, mechanisation and marketing of crops. Earth-moving and wells are free, and seeds, fertilisers and insecticides are half the market price. Abu Dhabi gives land to its citizens without charge, as well as underwriting other Emirates' grants of land to other UAE citizens via its financing of the federal budget. The main state-funded agricultural research centres and extension services are at al Dhafra, Liwa and Madina Zayed. The Arid Lands Research Centre operates experimental vegetable greenhouses on Saadiyat Island near Abu Dhabi town. The UAE is self-sufficient in various winter vegetables and excess crops of vegetables are sometimes dumped in the desert, due to a lack of processing facilities. The government already buys crops at 'favourable' prices, before selling them at discounted rates in the market.

Water shortages and soil salinity are constant problems. Agriculture is dependent on fast depleting underground aquifers. When these run dry, irrigation will depend almost entirely on desalinated water. The country's largest dairy farm at Digdagga has a herd of Friesians producing meat and milk for local consumption. Estimated crop production in 2004 included: 7,094 tonnes (t) potatoes, 760,000t dates, 15,000t cabbages, 16,184t citrus fruit, 240,000t tomatoes, 10,000t cauliflowers, 4,255t mangoes, 15,000t cucumbers, 786,010t fruit in total, 506,492t vegetables in total. Estimated livestock production included: 74,380t meat in total, 9,750t beef, 15,386t camel meat, 9,000t lamb and goat meat, 30,000t poultry, 17,000t eggs, 97,890t milk, 1,500t sheepskins.

Fishing
Catches cover over 80 per cent of domestic consumption. The UAE ranks fourth in the Arab world in the volume of its annual catch. Around 20 fishing ports and 25 repair workshops have been established along the coastline in Dubai, Sharjah and Ras al Khaimah. Over 15,000 tonnes of fish are imported to supplement domestic sources.

Forestry
The UAE has around 3.8 per cent forest cover, almost all of which is plantation. The government has initiated a long-term programme of afforestation. Abu Dhabi's western region now has about 5,000 hectares of mature tree plantations, including 120 million tamarind, tamarisk, acacia, neem and cork trees, as well as some 30 million date palms. Between 1990–2000, forest cover grew by an average of 8,000 hectares or 2.84 per cent per annum. The rate of growth has slowed since 2000.

Industry and manufacturing
The industrial sector typically accounts for under 20 per cent of GDP and employs 45 per cent of the workforce. Non-oil industry, particularly manufacturing and re-exports, is concentrated in free trade zones.

The government is placing increased emphasis on the expansion of non-oil manufacturing, such as cement, building materials, aluminium, fertilisers, foodstuffs, garments, furniture, plastics, fibreglass and processed metals.

Most non-oil export production is located on Dubai. Dubai has intensified efforts to promote foreign investment and attract regional and global capital. In April 2002, the Dubai Authority for Investment and Development (DAID) was set up to grant concessions, franchises and incentives and to issue licences to large investors. The DAID is authorised to set up, own and develop investment companies on its own or with other organisations.

Dubai's largest manufacturing enterprise, the state-owned Dubai Aluminium Company (Dubal), is expanding production from 536,000 tonnes in 2001 to 710,000 tonnes by 2007. Dubal is based in the thriving free trade area, the Jebel Ali Free Zone. Dubai is also keen to develop information technology (IT); the Dubai Internet City was set up in 2001. IT spending in the UAE was estimated at US$550 million to US$600 million during the first six months of 2004, putting spending for the full year on course to surpass the 2003 total of US$1.1 billion. Abu Dhabi is planning to develop an industrial base, including petrochemicals, steel and aluminium. A seven-year, US$100 billion investment programme was initiated in 2005. It will be mainly government funded, but it is hoped to attract private private sector and foreign direct investment.

Tourism
Dubai is the largest tourism market in the Emirates, attracting both business travellers and an increasing number of leisure tourists. Tourism is a key element in Dubai's development strategy. With the aim of making Dubai a major tourist destination, investment has been poured into infrastructure, including hotels, a new conference centre, a cruise terminal and, with a view to becoming an aviation hub, airport and airline fleet expansion. The annual growth rate in visitors to Dubai is typically between 10–15 per cent. Tourism is expected to contribute 1.2 per cent to GDP in 2005.

Shortage of prime building land has not deterred planners. The Palm (previously known as the Palm Islands) is a US$3 billion scheme, involving the construction of two man-made islands off the Dubai coast, each in the shape of a palm tree.

Mining
The development of non-hydrocarbon minerals plays a role in the government's policy of diversification away from dependence on the oil sector. Limestone, gypsum and dolerite are exploited. Celestite is known to exist but has not yet been extracted.

Copper is known to exist in Fujairah and Ras al Khaimah. There is also thought to be talc in Fujairah, chromium in Sharjah, Ajman, Fujairah and Ras al Khaimah, and manganese throughout the northern Emirates. Mineral studies are being undertaken in the Madah region of Fujairah, in Al-Siji in Sharjah and in the Masfouyt and Manama areas of Ajman. Ras al Khaimah already has two quarries, four cement companies and further downstream factories, with annual cement production of 2.3 million tonnes.

Hydrocarbons
The UAE is one of the world's largest producers of crude oil and natural gas, which account for around 30 per cent of GDP. Oil reserves total 97.8 billion barrels, with production at around 2.7 million barrels per day (bpd). Approximately 94 per cent is held by Abu Dhabi; Dubai holds just under 4 per cent, with 4 billion barrels, while Sharjah and Ras al Khaimah hold 1.5 billion and 100 million barrels respectively. Under the constitution, each emirate is responsible for its own production and resource development. Refinery capacity in the UAE is 645,000 bpd, an increase of around two-thirds over the past decade. A 300,000 bpd refinery is projected for construction at Fujairah. Gas reserves total 6.06 trillion cubic metres, the world's fifth-largest, with production of around 46 billion cubic metres. Abu Dhabi holds 92.5 per cent of the total reserves, with 5.0 per cent in Sharjah, 1.9 per cent in Dubai and 0.5 per cent in Ras al Khaimah. Reserves are expected to last for another 150–170 years.

Coal is neither produced or imported in the UAE.

United Arab Emirates

Energy
Electricity generation capacity is estimated at 5.8GW. The government is seeking to open up the sector with limited privatisation in order to inject new capital and increase capacity to meet soaring demand. Abu Dhabi is leading the way, with the creation of new independent power and water projects and joint ventures with minority interests held by foreign firms. The Abu Dhabi government has rejected full privatisation of the water and power sector.

The UAE is participating in a US$1 billion project to build a regional power grid linking the GCC countries. The UAE will join the regional grid, along with Oman, as part of the second phase of the project after it has connected all the power stations in the Emirates. The first phase, linking Saudi Arabia, Bahrain, Kuwait and Qatar, is scheduled for completion in 2009.

Financial markets
Stock exchange
There are two stock markets in the UAE: the Abu Dhabi Stock Market (ADSM) and the Dubai Financial Market (DFM). The stock exchanges are likely to experience strong growth in the future, particularly in corporate bonds. This will be strengthened by Dubai's intention to tap the markets for funds to help with infrastructure development. The DIFC bourse does not impose currency restrictions or limit the involvement of international portfolio investors.

Banking and insurance
Financial services constitute a key sector throughout the Emirates, with Dubai at the leading edge and hoping to overtake Bahrain as the Gulf's leading financial centre. The UAE's banking sector has attracted more foreign interest than other Gulf states due to its liberal banking regime and low level of taxation.

Development of the sector is focussed on the Dubai International Financial Sector (DIFC), which was launched in February 2001 as a link between the financial markets of Africa, Asia, the Middle East and the West. The DIFC has concentrated on the development of asset management, administration, reinsurance and Islamic finance in an attempt to develop a niche market.

Continuing large-scale infrastructure projects, growing prospects in the tourism industry and the creation of an automated stock exchange all represent considerable opportunities for banks. WTO membership, effective from 2003, obliges the UAE authorities to admit new foreign banks and help to increase competition in the sector. On the downside, the UAE's banking sector lacks transparency, although the OECD's Financial Action Task Force (FATF) declared the UAE's performance in 2002 as 'satisfactory'.

Sometimes the UAE's banking sector has attracted the wrong sort of attention, with money laundering being a particular blight on the banking sector. The 11 September 2001 terrorist attacks in the US focussed attention on the UAE, particularly its informal money transfer system known as *hawala*, in which funds are transferred from one country to another via a broker. The lack of paperwork and the fact that no money physically crosses borders has made *hawala* a channel for terrorist financing. In November 2002, the central bank tightened regulations on *hawala* brokers by introducing a certification system, which required brokers to provide details of their overseas clients and to notify the authorities if there are any suspicious transactions.

Central bank
Central Bank of the United Arab Emirates

Time
GMT plus four hours

Geography
The UAE is bordered by Oman to the east, Saudi Arabia to the west and south, Qatar to the north, and by a coastline of approximately 650km on the southern shore of the Gulf. Much of the land is sand desert or salt flats. Six of the Emirates lie on the Arabian Gulf coast. Fujairah, the seventh, lies on the Gulf of Oman. The region is one of shallow seas and offshore islands and coral reefs. The UAE's two coasts are divided by the Hajjar Mountains stretching through the Musandam Peninsula to the Straits of Hormuz.

Climate
Summer temperatures are hot, reaching 49 degrees Celsius (C) in the shade, while January, the coldest winter month, sees temperatures ranging from three to 28 degrees C. Humidity, particularly on the coast, can be extreme. Average annual rainfall is very low, ranging between 100mm and 200mm.

Dress codes
A lightweight suit or lightweight jacket and trousers are advised. A tie is de rigueur at business meetings but a jacket need not be worn. Long-sleeved shirts should be worn at business and official meetings. In public places, women should dress discretely and men should wear shirts and long trousers. Bikinis are allowed on certain beaches.

Entry requirements
Passports
Required by all.

Visa
Required by all, except citizens of EU, North America, Australasia, Japan and a few other Asian countries, for visits up to one month. For a full list of exceptions visit http://www.uae-embassy.org/consular.htm where a visa application form can also be found.

All visitors that require visas must include a letter of invitation from a sponsor in the UAE, giving details of the sponsor's residency permit, and a copy of their passport.

Prohibited entry
Holders of Israeli passports.

Currency advice/regulations
Import of Israeli currency is prohibited.

Customs
Personal effects are duty-free. Trade with Israel is prohibited, as are goods originating from that country. Imports of pork products, alcoholic beverages, firearms and ammunition require a special permit. Most goods may be imported freely, but importers must hold a general import licence permitting trade only in the categories of goods specified in the licence.

Prohibited imports
Irradiated foods. The importation and possession of poppy seeds in any and all forms is strictly prohibited. Persons found to possess even very small quantities of controlled substances listed by the UAE are subject to prosecution by the authorities and may be given lengthy prison terms of up to 15 years.

Legislation enacted in January 1996 imposes the death sentence for convicted drug traffickers.

Health (for visitors)
Mandatory precautions
None.

Advisable precautions
Hepatitis 'A', polio, tetanus and typhoid vaccinations and anti-malaria precautions are recommended.

NB Some drugs normally taken under a doctor's supervision are classified as narcotics in the UAE. A doctor's prescription should be carried along with any medication that is brought into the country. If suspected of being under the influence of drugs or alcohol, individuals may be required to submit to blood and/or urine tests and may be subject to prosecution.

Hotels
Excellent standards in Abu Dhabi and Dubai, and rooms are generally in adequate supply however advance booking is always advisable.

A 20 per cent tax is included in all bills.

Credit cards
Major credit cards are accepted.

Public holidays
Fixed dates
1 Jan (New Year's Day), 6 Aug (Sheikh Zayed's Accession), 2 Dec (National Day).
Variable dates
Eid al Adha (three days), Eid al Fitr (two days), Islamic New Year, Birth of the Prophet, Ascension of the Prophet.
The Islamic year has 354 or 355 days, with the result that Muslim feasts advance by 10–12 days against the Gregorian calendar each year. Dates of the Muslim feasts vary according to sightings of the new moon, so cannot be forecast exactly. Islamic year 1426: 10 February 2005 to 30 January 2006.

Working hours
Working hours vary between Emirates, and change from summer to winter. The weekend starts on Thursday afternoon and extends to Saturday.
During Ramadan, the Muslim holy month of fasting during daylight hours, most officials work 0900–1300, but many useful contacts can be made and renewed during and after the evening *Iftar* meal.
Banking
Sat–Wed: 0800–1200; Thu in Abu Dhabi: 0800–1200/1600–1730; Thu, in northern Emirates: 0800–1100 . Some banks only open Mon–Wed: 1630–1830.
Business
Sat–Wed: 0700/0800–1300/1400–1600–1900/1930; Thu: 0730–1100/1200.
Government
Sat–Wed: 0700/0800–1300/1400; Thu: 0730–1100/1200 .

Telecommunications
Telephone/fax
The telephone system is fully automated. Telephone calls within each emirate are free.
Postal services
The postal service is modern.
Mobile phones
GSM cell phones can be rented from Avis or Budget; SIM cards are also available.
Internet/e-mail
Internet access is available in internet cafes. ISDN is available.

Electricity supply
240/415V AC (Abu Dhabi) and 220/380V AC (Northern Emirates), with three-pin round or flat type plug fittings.

Weights and measures
Metric system (imperial system and local units also used).

Social customs/useful tips
Pork should not be eaten in the presence of Muslims. It is discourteous to eat, drink or smoke in front of Muslims in daylight hours during Ramadan (when it is illegal to do so in public).
Avoid using the term 'Mohammedan'. Avoid asking personal questions, especially about wives.
Always shake hands on meeting and leaving. You may find the handshake lasts longer than in the West, but this is a sign of friendship. If you have made a good impression, the handshake on departure will be longer than that on arrival.
If coffee is served it is courteous to accept it. Cups will generally be refilled automatically unless the cup is shaken from side to side as it is returned to the server. To take only one cup of coffee is an insult, and to take three or more is considered greedy in some quarters – if in doubt follow the example of your host.
Most restaurants and hotels have bars and licensed restaurants, although a licence, which lays down a monthly quota, is required for purchase for consumption at home. Licences are not issued to Muslims.

Security
The level of street crime has been traditionally far lower than in the West because of the severity of the penalties imposed. The influx of expatriate workers since the early 1970s has encouraged incidents of theft. Murder and violent crimes such as mugging and rape remain rare. Generally speaking the UAE has a very low incidence of crime.

Getting there
Air
National airline: Air Arabia; Emirates Airlines; Etihad Airways (launched November 2003)
International airport/s: Abu Dhabi International Airport (ADIA); 35km from city. The ADIA's expansion is taking place in two phases: in the first phase, a new terminal is being built and will be ready by August 2005; in the second phase, a totally new airport will be built, to become operational in 2009.
Dubai International (DXB), 4km from city, with duty-free shop, bar, buffet, bank, hotel reservations, post office, shops, car hire.
Sharjah International (SHJ), 10km from city, with duty-free shop, bar, buffet, restaurant, bank (restricted hours), hotel reservations.
Ras al Khaimah International (RKT).
Other airport/s: Fujairah has an airport.
Airport tax: None
Surface
Road: Road links are through Oman and Saudi Arabia. Buses run between Dubai and Muscat.
Water: Passenger services run between Sharjah and Bandar-é Abbas in Iran.

Getting about
National transport
Air: Scheduled services are infrequent. Small light aircraft and helicopters may be chartered.
Road: Good, surfaced roads along the coast link all Emirates. It takes about two hours to travel by road from Dubai to Abu Dhabi. There are numerous oases, the best known are Al-Ain and Liwa in Abu Dhabi and Dhaid in Sharjah.
Rail: There is no railway in the UAE.
City transport
Taxis: Taxis are plentiful and cheap and English is widely understood if not spoken. Metered taxis are available in Abu Dhabi and the rounding-up of the charge is typical for a tip. It is advisable to negotiate fares in advance in other Emirates as taxis are not usually metered.
City traffic in Dubai has become very congested and it is advisable to allow plenty of time to reach a destination. Taxis on stands outside hotels charge more than those flagged in the street. Fixed fares are available for pre-paid journeys from Dubai airport to the city.
Some hotels offer a courtesy pick-up service; others offer the service but charge. A limousine can be booked through the hotel.
Helicopter: Helicopter services are available between Dubai's airport and some premier hotels.
Car hire
General and chauffeur-driven car hire is available. International licences are acceptable only for short-term visitors and requirements should be checked on arrival. Driving is on the right, with speed limits of 60kph in towns and 80–100kph elsewhere.

BUSINESS DIRECTORY
The addresses listed below are a selection only. While World of Information makes every endeavour to check these addresses, we cannot guarantee that changes have not been made, especially to telephone numbers and area codes. We would welcome any corrections.

Telephone area codes
The international direct dialling (IDD) code for The United Arab Emirates is +971 followed by the area code:

Abu Dhabi	2	Fujairah	70
Ajman	6	Ras al Khaimah	77
Al-Ain	3	Sharjah	6
Dubai	4	Umm al Quwain	6

Useful telephone numbers
Directory enquiries: 180
Operator: 100
Call enquiries: 160
Call bookings: 150

United Arab Emirates

Police (Abu Dhabi): 461-461

Chambers of Commerce

Abu Dhabi Chamber of Commerce and Industry, PO Box 662, Abu Dhabi (tel: 621-4000; fax: 621-5867; e-mail: service@adcci-gov.ae).

American Business Council (Dubai and Northern Emirates), PO Box 9281, Dubai (tel: 331-4735; fax: 331-4227; e-mail: amchamdx@emirates.net.ae).

American Business Group (Abu Dhabi), PO Box 43710, Abu Dhabi (tel: 626-2086; fax: 626-2087; e-mail: abgroup@emirates.net.ae).

Ajman Chamber of Commerce and Industry, PO Box 662, Ajman (tel: 742-2177; fax: 742-7591; e-mail: ajmchmbr@emirates.net.ae).

British Business Group (Abu Dhabi), PO Box 43635, Abu Dhabi (tel: 457-234; fax: 450-605; e-mail: bbgauh@emirates.net.ae).

British Business Group (Dubai and Northern Emirates), PO Box 9333, Dubai (tel: 397-0303; fax: 397-0939; e-mail: britbiz@emirates.net.ae).

Dubai Chamber of Commerce and Industry, PO Box 1457, Dubai (tel: 228-1181; fax: 221-1646; e-mail: dcciinfo@dcci.org).

Federation of UAE Chambers of Commerce and Industry, PO Box 3014, Abu Dhabi (tel: 621-4144; fax: 633-9210; e-mail: fcciauh@emirates.net.ae).

Federation of UAE Chambers of Commerce and Industry, PO Box 8886, Dubai (tel: 221-2977; fax: 223-5498; e-mail: fccidxb@emirates.net.ae).

French Business Council (Dubai), PO Box 25775, Dubai (tel: 352-362; fax: 352-120; e-mail: fbc@emirates.net.ae).

French Business Group (Abu Dhabi), PO Box 73390, Abu Dhabi (tel: 674-1137; fax: 678-6650; e-mail: fbgad@emirates.net.ae).

Fujairah Chamber of Commerce and Industry, PO Box 738, Fujairah (tel: 222-2400; fax: 222-1464; e-mail: fujccia@emirates.net.ae).

Ras Al-Khaimah Chamber of Commerce and Industry, PO Box 87, Ras Al-Khaimah (tel: 233-3511; fax: 233-0233; e-mail: rkchmbr@emirates.net.ae).

Sharjah Chamber of Commerce and Industry, PO Box 580, Sharjah (tel: 554-1444; fax: 554-1119; e-mail:scci@sharjah.gov.ae).

Umm Al-Quwain Chamber of Commerce and Industry, PO Box 436, Umm Al-Quwain (tel: 765-1111; fax: 765-7056; e-mail: uaqcci@emirates.net.ae).

Banking

Abu Dhabi Commercial Bank, Al-Salam Street, PO Box 939, Abu Dhabi (tel: 720-000; fax: 776-499).

Arab Bank for Investment & Foreign Trade, PO Box 46733, Abu Dhabi (tel: 721-900; fax: 770-550).

Commercial Bank of Dubai Ltd, PO Box 2668, Dubai (tel: 523-355; fax: 520-444).

Emirates Bank International, PO Box 2923, Dubai (tel: 256-256; fax: 221-005).

Mashreq Bank, P.O. Box 1250, Omar Ibn Al Khatab Rd, Next to Al Ghurair Retail City, Deira, Dubai (tel: 222-9131).

National Bank of Abu Dhabi, PO Box 4, Abu Dhabi (tel: 666-800; fax: 655-329).

National Bank of Dubai, PO Box 777, Dubai (tel: 267-000; fax: 268-939).

National Bank of Fujairah, PO Box 786, Abu Dhabi (tel: 333-300; fax: 24-516).

National Bank of Sharjah, PO Box 4, Sharjah (tel: 547-745; fax: 543-483).

National Bank of Umm Al-Qawain, PO Box 17888, Al-Ain (tel: 513-000; fax: 665-440).

RakBank (National Bank of Ras Al-Khaimah), PO Box 5300, Oman Street, Al-Nakheel, Ras Al-Khaimah (tel: 228-1127; fax: 228-3238; email: nbrakho@emirates.net.ae).

Union National Bank, PO Box 865, Abu Dhabi (tel: 741-600; fax: 786-080).

Central bank

Central Bank of the United Arab Emirates, PO Box 854, Abu Dhabi (tel: 665-2220; fax: 666-7494; e-mail: uaecb@cbuae.gov.ae).

Travel information

Abu Dhabi International Airport (tel: 757-500).

Abu Dhabi National Hotels Company, PO Box 6806, Abu Dhabi (tel: 447-228; fax: 448-495).

Dubai Airport (tel: 245-333).

Emirates Air, PO Box 686, Airline Centre, Flame Roundabout, Dubai (tel: 228-151; fax: 214-560).

Gulf Air, Hamdan St/Airport Road, Abu Dhabi (tel: 332-600).

Oman Air, PO Box 1058, Central Post Office Seeb International Airport, Muscat, Oman (tel: 519-237; fax: 510-805).

Qatar Airways, Almana Tower, Airport Road, PO Box 22550, Doha, Qatar (tel: 430-707; fax: 352-433).

Ras Al-Khaimah National Travel Agency, Ras Al-Khaimah (tel: 331-100).

Ministry of tourism

Department of Tourism and Commerce Marketing, PO Box 594, Dubai (tel: 223-0000; fax: 223-0022; e-mail: info@dubaitourism.co.ae; internet site: http://www.dubaitourism.co.ae).

Ministries

Ministry of Agriculture & Fisheries, PO Box 213, Abu Dhabi (tel: 662-781; fax: 654-787).

Ministry of Communication, PO Box 900, Abu Dhabi (tel: 651-900; fax: 661-575).

Ministry of Defence, PO Box 2838, Dubai (tel: 532-330; fax: 531-974).

Ministry of Economy & Commerce, PO Box 901, Abu Dhabi (tel: 215-455; fax: 260-000).

Ministry of Education and Youth, PO Box 295, Abu Dhabi (tel: 213-800; fax: 351-164).

Ministry of Electricity & Water, PO Box 629, Abu Dhabi (tel: 335-099; fax: 213-738).

Ministry of Finance & Industry, PO Box 433, Abu Dhabi (tel: 726-000; fax: 773-301).

Ministry of Foreign Affairs, PO Box 1, Abu Dhabi (tel: 652-200; fax: 653-849).

Ministry of Health, PO Box 848, Abu Dhabi (tel: 330-000; fax: 313-525).

Ministry of Higher Education & Scientific Research, PO Box 45253, Abu Dhabi (tel: 669-422; fax: 645-277).

Ministry of Information & Culture, PO Box 17, Abu Dhabi (tel: 453-000; fax: 451-155).

Ministry for the Interior, PO Box 398, Abu Dhabi (tel: 414-666; fax: 415-780).

Ministry for Justice and Islamic Affairs & Awqaf, PO Box 2272, Abu Dhabi (tel: 212-300; fax: 316-003).

Ministry for Labour & Social Affairs, PO Box 809, Abu Dhabi (tel: 651-890; fax: 665-889).

Ministry of Petroleum & Mineral Resources, PO Box 59, Abu Dhabi (tel: 651-810; fax: 663-414).

Ministry of Planning, PO Box 904, Abu Dhabi (tel: 211-699; fax: 311-375).

Ministry of Public Works & Housing, PO Box 878, Abu Dhabi (tel: 651-778; fax: 665-598).

Ministry of State for Cabinet Affairs, PO Box 899, Abu Dhabi (tel: 651-113; fax: 652-184).

Minister of State for Supreme Council Affairs, PO Box 545, Abu Dhabi (tel: 343-921; fax: 344-137).

Ministry of Youth & Sports, PO Box 539, Abu Dhabi (tel: 393-919; fax: 293-919).

Other useful addresses

Abu Dhabi Company for Onshore Oil Operations (ADCO), PO Box 270, Abu Dhabi (tel: 366-100).

Abu Dhabi Gas Liquifaction Co Ltd, PO Box 3500, Abu Dhabi (tel: 333-888).

Abu Dhabi National Oil Co (ADNOC), PO Box 898, Abu Dhabi (tel: 366-000).

Abu Dhabi Water and Electricity Authority, ADWEA Building, Al Falah Street, PO Box 6120, Abu Dhabi (tel: 694-3333).

Ajman Independent Studios, PO Box 442, Ajman (tel: 424-000; fax: 428-087).

Arab Monetary Fund (headquarters), PO Box 2818, Abu Dhabi (tel: 328-500).

British Embassy, Khalid Bin-Walid Street, Abu Dhabi (tel: 326-600; fax: 341-744).

British Embassy, Al-Seef, Dubai (tel: 521-893; fax: 527-095).

Department of Information, Dubai Municipality, PO Box 67, Dubai (tel: 221-141).

Dubai International Trade Centre, PO Box 9292, Dubai (tel: 372-200; fax: 373-493).

Dubai TV, PO Box 1695, Dubai (tel: 370-255; fax: 374-111).

Jebel Ali Free Zone Authority, PO Box 3258, Dubai (tel: 815-000; fax: 815-001).

Gulf Arab Marketing & Exhibition Co (GAME), PO Box 610, Abu Dhabi (tel: 376-900; fax: 378-894).

Ports Authority of Dubai, PO Box 3258, Dubai (tel: 56-578).

Ports Authority of Sharjah, PO Box 510, Sharjah (tel: 541-666).

UAE Embassy (USA), 1010 Wisconsin Avenue, NW, Washington DC 20007 (tel: 202-672-1050; fax: 202-672-1082).

UAE Radio & TV Dubai, PO Box 2765, Dubai (tel: 370-599; fax: 379-275).

UAE Television & Broadcasting Corporation, PO Box 17, Abu Dhabi (tel: 311-417; fax: 452-059).

UAE TV Sharjah, PO Box 111, Sharjah (tel: 361-111; fax: 541-755).

Internet sites

Arab Net: http://www.arab.net/welcome.html

Arabia OnLine: http://www.arabia.com

Dubai Tourism: http://dubaitourism.co.ae

Gulf business explorer: http://www.igulf.com/main.htm

UAE Government: http://www.fedfin.gov.ae

UAE interact: http://www.uaeinteract.com/

Yellow Pages: http://www.uae-ypages.com

United Kingdom

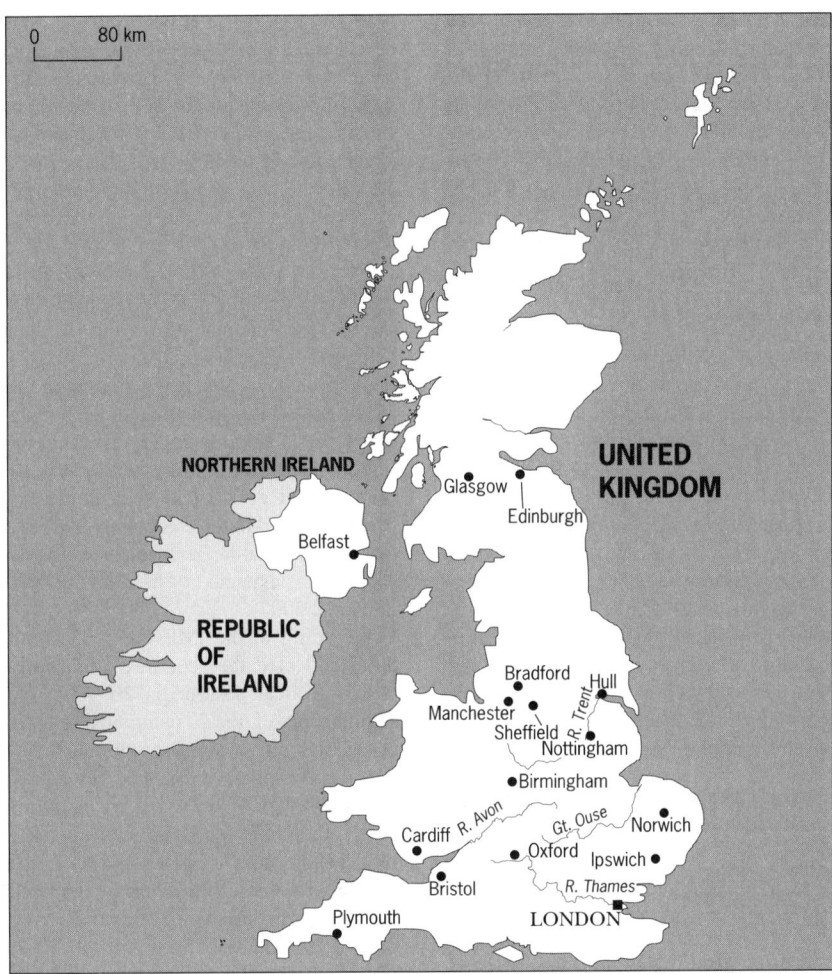

KEY FACTS

Official name: The United Kingdom of Great Britain and Northern Ireland (UK)

Head of State: Queen Elizabeth II (crowned 2 Jun 1953)

Head of government: Prime Minister Tony Blair (since 1997; re-elected 2001 and 5 May 2005)

Ruling party: Labour Party (since 1997; re-elected 2001 and 5 May 2005)

Area: 244,103 square km

Population: 59.60 million (2004)

Capital: London

Official language: English; English and Welsh in Wales. Scottish Gaelic is spoken in Scotland.

Currency: Pound sterling (£) = 100 pence

Exchange rate: £0.57 per US$ (Oct 2005)

GDP per capita: US$35,460 (2004)

GDP real growth: 3.10% (2004)

Labour force: 29.47 million (2003)

Unemployment: 4.60% (OECD, 2004)

Inflation: 1.30% (2004)

Oil production: 2.03 million bpd (2004)

Balance of trade: -US$106.07 billion (2004)

Foreign debt: US$6,785.92 billion (2004)

Annual FDI: US$534.30 billion (cumulative, 1995–2004, OECD); US$78.50 billion (OECD, 2004)*

* estimated figure

Many of the UK's voters saw the 2005 election as an almost single issue referendum on Prime Minister Tony Blair. On his general integrity and more specifically on his handling of the Iraq war, which claimed the life of its hundredth British soldier in February 2006. That so many of the electorate saw the election this way suggested that there were not that many issues on which they did consider the prime minister to be in need of replacement. The economy barely featured as an election issue, nor were the traditional labour weaknesses of health, education and taxation perceived to be major liabilities. Conservative election tactics to focus on Mr Blair's honesty – or lack of it – were at best half hearted. The Conservatives – under their former leader, the hapless Ian Duncan Smith US$692 million had supported the Labour government's policy on the Iraq war. To make a U-turn under his replacement, Michael Howard, would have been branded as opportunistic, something they had already been accused of over their immigration policy. More than ever, the Conservatives came up against the reality that Mr Blair had very astutely stolen the political middle ground from them.

Mr Howard's election campaign was not an easy ride. He had to accept that Labour's successful management of the economy had moved the political argument on to less straightforward issues. The general prosperity that had benefited most Britons for a period of eight years or more meant that tax cuts had ceased to be an election winner. Yet to promise greater expenditure than Labour on health and education without at the same time raising taxes looked an equally doubtful option. Mr Howard had also shot himself in the foot by his party's 'opportunistic' opposition to increased tuition fees for university students.

Mr Blair was, nevertheless, seen by many of the electorate – and by a number of his party membership – as a busted flush following his announcement that he would, at some point during Labour's third term in government, be stepping down as prime minister. The general assumption was that he would be replaced by his Chancellor of the Exchequer (finance minister) Gordon Brown. Despite the electorate's misgivings over the reportedly tense relationship between Mr Blair and Mr Brown, which was also reported to have divided the labour Party into two warring camps, the fact that Mr Brown had managed the economy so successfully for a period of eight years was a good enough reason for many for voting Labour.

In the event, the labour Party lost 57 seats in the election, ending up with 355, still a majority in the 646-member house. Most commentators attributed this to his support for the Iraq war and close alliance with US President George W Bush. Despite the manifest weakness of Mr Blair's personal position, the Conservatives only managed to gain 32 seats, giving them a total of 198. After the election their leader Mr Howard announced that he was to stand down as leader. The lesser opposition party, the Liberal Democrats under their leader Charles Kennedy (who was also to resign in late 2005 admitting that he had an alcohol problem) gained 10 seats, giving them 62. In Scotland the Scottish Nationalist Party gained one seat to six, and in Northern Ireland the Democratic Unionists increased their parliamentary presence by four, to a total of nine, mostly at the expense of the United Unionist Party, lead by Nobel Prize winner John Trimble.

IMF praise

In March 2005 the IMF had congratulated the UK government on its 'state of the art' policy frameworks. Up until mid-2005 the IMF and a number of respected economic authorities, including the OECD and the EU had been forced to eat humble-pie over their unduly pessimistic projections for the UK economy. In some cases forecasts of dramatic tax increases had proved wrong, in others projected growth estimates had been dismissed as wishful thinking.

In the second half of 2005, however, things changed. The downturn in the UK economy, although less dramatic than elsewhere in Europe, nevertheless stifled growth to well below the levels projected in Mr Brown's forecasts, to the extent that official forecasts had to be revised downwards. In 2004–05 the UK's deficit rose to US$66 billion – 2.9 per cent of GDP. In the period 2000–04 public expenditure rose by 4.4 per cent a year, double the rate of economic growth. However, in Labour's second term, from 2001–05, tax revenues had dropped by 1.2 per cent. Like all good things, Mr Brown's expansionary phase eventually had to end. In the financial year 2006–07 total government expenditure is due to grow at a more manageable rate, in tandem with the economy. Tax revenues are also due to increase by 2 per cent in the two years up to 2007–08.

In its December 2005 report on the British economy, the IMF concluded that macro-economic stability in the UK had held up remarkably well. According to the IMF report, over the previous decade the UK's real GDP growth had been both strong and stable; unemployment and inflation had both been low, while the current account deficit had been moderate. The IMF noted that the economy had hit a 'soft patch' in 2005, but also observed that growth was expected to pick up again in 2006 and 2007.

According to the IMF the 2005 slowdown reflected the economy's relatively strong cyclical position in 2003–04, the stabilisation of the housing market, the earlier tightening of monetary policy and the significant increase in the energy prices that the UK had experienced in line with other developed economies. The IMF's short term forecast was very much in line with that of the Bank of England, showing growth rising to around 2.25 per cent in 2006, and 2.75 per cent in 2007. The UK treasury had, by the end of 2005, already revised downwards its 2005–06 forecast.

Consumption and investment were expected to accelerate as the adverse factors that have affected the economy in 2005 declined. Export demand was expected to grow in line with a general recovery in the euro-zone and other EU member countries. Inflation was expected to fall below 2 per cent in 2006, rising moderately, but within forecast targets, in 2007.

The IMF drew attention to possible risks in the UK's economic equation. Home prices were still considered to be over-valued, although 2005 had been a year of more modest growth, assuaging fears of an abrupt house price adjustment. Immigration, particularly from the EU's new eastern Europe member states, is changing

KEY INDICATORS — United Kingdom

	Unit	2000	2001	2002	2003	2004
Population	m	58.66	58.79	59.23	59.42	*59.60
Gross domestic product (GDP)	US$bn	1,424.92	1,422.30	1,552.40	1,743.44	*2,140.90
GDP per capita	US$	23,900	23,700	26,300	29,493	35,460
GDP real growth	%	3.9	2.3	1.8	2.2	3.1
Inflation	%	2.9	1.8	2.2	1.3	1.3
Unemployment	%	3.8	5.0	5.2	5.0	4.8
lOil output	'000 bpd	2,667.0	2,503.0	2,463.0	2,245.0	2,029.0
Natural gas output	bn cum	108.1	105.8	103.1	102.7	95.9
Coal output	mtoe	19.5	19.6	18.3	17.2	15.3
Exports (fob) (goods)	US$m	283,950.0	275,950.0	276,000.0	305,000.0	349,310.0
Imports (fob) (goods)	US$m	329,910.0	324,200.0	339,810.0	376,282.0	455,380.0
Balance of trade	US$m	-45,960.0	-48,250.0	-51,800.0	-71,282.0	-106,070.0
Current account	US$m	-27,840.0	-29,370.0	-13,010.0	-24,000.0	-47,040.0
Total reserves minus gold	US$m	43,890.0	37,280.0	39,360.0	41,850.0	45,340.0
Foreign exchange	US$m	39,280.0	31,940.0	32,790.0	35,150.0	39,480.0
Exchange rate	per US$	0.64	0.68	0.66	0.59	0.55

* estimated figure

the structure of the labour market, creating the potential for a larger workforce and more stable wage growth.

The UK's monetary policy appears to have been successful in addressing the combined effects of both a cyclical slowdown and rising energy prices. Interest rate increases in 2003 and 2004 had helped cool demand and appeared to have contained the effects of energy price increases. A modest cut in interest rates in August 2005 – by 0.25 per cent – was in response to a faster than anticipated drop in demand. The IMF drew attention to the UK's recent deficits, which followed a series of surpluses. The deficits were caused by significant increases in government expenditure.

The IMF noted that the UK has a relatively low level of public debt, but as the overall deficit had been averaging around 3 per cent of GDP, it risks giving cause for concern. If the UK's net debt figure is to be held below a ceiling of 40 per cent, then the deficit will certainly have to be reined in. The IMF also noted that the UK's 2005/06 budget appeared to be on track to reduce the overall deficit in relation to GDP; in part this reflected the rise in government revenues as a result of higher energy prices, as well as strong personal income and corporate tax revenues. The IMF noted that if the UK succeeded in containing the growth in public spending by the year 2008/09, there would be a reduction in the overall deficit to some 2 per cent of GDP by the year 2009/10. This, in turn, would stabilise net debt at about 40 per cent of GDP. The IMF also considered that the UK's forecast of an overall deficit of 1.5 per cent of GDP was optimistic and would require tougher measures than those spelt out in the UK Treasury's *Pre-Budget Report*.

Foreign relations

Early 2005 was dominated by persistent talk of the proposed EU constitution, but this issue was effectively sidelined as an election topic by the government's decision to call a referendum on the matter. The debate was really put to bed however, when in the space of three days at the end of May and beginning of June the French and Dutch voted 'no' to the proposed document. Elsewhere on the EU front Blair found himself on the rack once again, as several of Britain's Europhobic tabloids criticised the prime minister for caving in to Continental governments on the UK's EU rebate. In truth Blair left himself exposed to such attacks, having stated that he would not negotiate the UK's prized rebate at all, 'period'. He then went on to modify his stance slightly, claiming that the rebate could be put on the table for negotiation if the Common Agricultural Policy (CAP) was likewise altered. Though the CAP was not officially part of the eventual negotiation settlement Blair claimed that the final settlement of a £4 billion (US$2.3 billion) reduction in the rebate was necessary in order to pay for enlargement and all the long-term benefits that EU expansion is likely to bring to the UK.

During 2005 the UK held both the EU and G8 presidency. The major summit for the latter was disrupted when multiple bombs were detonated on the London transport network on 7 July, leading to 52 deaths and hundreds of casualties, in addition to mass disruption. The attacks were carried out by suicide bombers and were reported to be the work of the al Qaeda terrorist network. Hours after the attacks, speaking against a backdrop of world leaders, Blair talked of his and others' 'determination to defend our values and our way of life' adding that this resolve was 'greater than their determination to cause death and destruction to innocent people in a desire to impose extremism on the world'. The 7/7 bombings, as they have subsequently become known, re-opened the debate on Britain's policy toward the countries of the Muslim world and in particular the occupations of Iraq and Afghanistan. Blair was able to ride out any immediate political difficulty created by the attacks however, and in fact received praise from right across the political spectrum for the way in which he responded to the atrocities.

The 7/7 bombings did seriously divert the news agenda away from the G8 summit in Gleneagles in July. The summit had been focused on achieving a new aid and debt reduction deal for the world's poor and indeed a US$50 billion agreement was reached. The new deal was reached after mass protests in addition to a world wide series of rock concerts was organised by aid campaigner Bob Geldof. The Blair government's marshalling of the EU during its presidency came under fire throughout 2005 from opposition parties. The Conservative Party were particularly critical of the government's approach to the presidency, claiming that it lacked direction and purpose. In response the Labour leadership often pointed to the commencement of Turkey's EU membership negotiations under the UK presidency.

Legislative liabilities

Just six months after he led his party to an historic third term in government, Blair received his first ever legislative defeat in the House of Commons as prime minister. On 9 November 2005 49 Labour MPs voted with the opposition to defeat the anti-terrorism legislation by 322 votes to 291. The major sticking point for both the opposition and the Labour rebels was the prime minister's insistence that a clause allowing for terrorist suspects to be held for up to 90 days without trial be included in the bill. Blair was criticised for playing hard and fast with democracy, and allegations of authoritarianism were repeatedly made by members of his own party. Having rejected the bill, MPs voted to extend the detention period without trial to 28 days.

In the aftermath of his substantial legislative defeat, Blair's authority began to look increasingly shaky. Opposition leader Michael Howard's call for the prime minister to 'consider his position' was hardly a new trick, but it has been generally acknowledged that Blair's date of departure was hastened by the Commons defeat on such a fundamental plank of the government's domestic and national security policy. Whispers as to Blair's eventual departure from a political stage that he has dominated for so long only intensified after the government received two more defeats in the Commons in early 2006, one of which was caused by the prime minister himself failing to turn up to vote! Further legislative troubles remain on the horizon for Blair as his proposed education reforms have come in for severe criticism from the left wing of his party.

Opposition shake-up

The consequences for the Conservative Party of Blair's third victory at the polls were almost immediately evident. At around lunchtime on 6 May, Conservative leader Howard announced his intention to stand down as party leader, though not with immediate effect. His decision to linger on as a lame duck leader was immediately criticised by both the Tory and non-Tory press as being an open invitation for infighting, recriminations and general bloodletting within Conservative ranks. Other notable Tory figures however, welcomed the pause, claiming that a period of six months or so (proposed by Howard) was just what the party needed in order to debate its future direction.

The immediate frontrunner in the race was David Davis, the hard line shadow

Nations of the World: A Political, Economic and Business Handbook

home secretary. But as the autumn conference season approached the young, dynamic figure of David Cameron emerged. Cameron wowed the party faithful in Blackpool with his twenty-minute speech delivered entirely from memory, as Davis bombed. His drab delivery contrasted unfavourably with the vigour and promise of the young turk Cameron and the press battered the veteran Davis for days afterwards. Back in Westminster, the self-proclaimed 'Big Beast' and former Chancellor Ken Clarke was knocked out in the first round ballot of MPs. As his supporters climbed on board the 'Cameroon' (as his supporters are known) bandwagon the 39-year old old-Etonian surged ahead of Davis and the other right wing candidate Liam Fox. When Davis' and Cameron's names went to the country in a run off contest soon after, it was the latter than ran away with the race, winning by a comfortable margin of two to one.

As Cameron and his fellow modernisers set about revamping the Conservatives with talk of new liberal objectives, it wasn't just the Tories that felt the winds of change. Cameron's victory also put the squeeze on the centre-left Liberal Democrat party and in particular its leader Charles Kennedy. Rumours of Kennedy's expansive social life and regular drinking had filled the corridors of Westminster for years. These rumours combined with the arrival of the fresh-faced Cameron turned up the heat on Kennedy who had had a poor election campaign. Kennedy had led the Liberals to a record number of seats but his failure to capitalise on perfect political weather coupled with his seemingly laid back style meant that his party were in danger of ceding some of their hard won centre-ground to the moderate Cameron.

In early January, prompted by imminent press reports Kennedy admitted to alcoholism, or a 'problem with drink' as he put it. He was forced to resign just days later in the midst of the furore, as Liberal Democrat MPs opened fire on their leader. An election campaign was immediately set in motion and the final ballot of party members is due to take place in March 2006. The Liberals must now decide which way they will turn having straddled both wings of the political spectrum successfully for so long under Kennedy. The current frontrunner is veteran foreign affairs spokesman Sir Menzies Campbell, though left-wing candidate Simon Hughes and the telegenic former journalist and MEP Chris Hume are close behind.

Outlook

The economic outlook for the UK is not quite as rosy as it was just a couple of years ago. Some analysts claim that Chancellor Gordon Brown's economic miracle is unravelling and that the UK is slowly heading toward a major recession, though it is probably more accurate to say that the economy is entering a slowdown, from which it will likely recover. There are serious economic worries for Brown however, including very poor productivity growth and severe criticisms of what many believe to be an economic management approach grounded in over-burdensome regulation. The IMF predicts growth of 1.9 per cent for 2005 and 2.2 per cent for 2006. This figure is lower than that achieved in recent years but with the 2012 Olympics having been awarded to London, the prospects of the Games and all that comes with it may provide a welcome fillip to the economy in years to come.

Indeed, Brown has made no secret of his desire to get out of the treasury and into No 10 Downing Street. He has often remarked, half in jest, that there are two types of Chancellor: those that fail and those that get out in time. With the economy taking a downturn and Blair struggling with his own party, Brown's urgency to move next door will only intensify. Blair has a big date in his legislative diary in early 2006 – a parliamentary vote on education at which he will presumably turn up to vote! Rebels on the left of his own party are out to get Blair and would relish the opportunity to hammer the final nail into his political coffin. But Brown and the Labour Party, having seen the way in which the opposition Conservative Party imploded following the political assassination of Margaret Thatcher, want nothing of the same. For this reason alone, Blair is likely to survive 2006, provided he makes enough concessions to his parliamentary enemies, before stepping aside for Brown some time in 2006-07.

Risk assessment

Politics	Stable
Economy	Fair
Regional stability	Excellent

COUNTRY PROFILE

Historical profile

After a thousand year period of Roman, Saxon and Viking occupation, feudal England was invaded by the Normans in 1066. The Norman-ruled Kingdom eventually emerged as an organised English state, headed by a monarch. Wales was united with England in 1536, while the 1707 Act of Union united England and Scotland as part of the United Kingdom (UK) of Great Britain. Ireland was united with Great Britain in 1801. By the eighteenth century, Great Britain had emerged as a major industrial, colonial and military power.

1837–1901 The long reign of Queen Victoria saw the British Empire at the height of its power.

1914–1918 The British Empire was involved in the First World War against Germany and its allies.

1922 The Irish Free State (Eire) was created in southern Ireland. The remaining six north-eastern counties of Ireland remained part of Great Britain.

1939–45 The British Empire was joined by the US and the Soviet Union in the Second World War against the Axis powers of Germany, Italy and Japan. Facing near economic collapse as a result of the war, the UK began to relinquish control of its colonies after 1945 and its role in the world as a major power declined.

1945–51 The Labour Party was elected into government. Led by Prime Minister Clement Attlee, the government implemented reforms to education, healthcare, housing and the social security system.

1953 Queen Elizabeth II was crowned on 2 June.

1969 The start of 'The Troubles' in Northern Ireland as violence between the Catholic civil rights movement and the Unionists, who perceived it as republicanism, intensified.

1973 The UK joined the European Economic Community.

1979 Following a decade marred by economic stagnation and endemic inflation, the Conservative Party gained a parliamentary majority in the general election, and Margaret Thatcher, leader of the party, became the UK's first woman prime minister.

1979–1990 Thatcher's radical domestic policies, including privatisation and local government reforms, did not prevent her securing two further election victories, in addition to gaining a victory in the 1982 Falklands conflict.

1990 Introduction of the community charge and a loss of party confidence stemming from her vociferous opposition to the European Community finally led to Thatcher being replaced by John Major as leader of the Conservative Party and prime minister.

1992 The Treaty on European Union (also known as the Maastricht Treaty) was signed. The Treaty harmonised legislation in key areas of European Union (EU) social policy, immigration and finance, although the UK successfully opted out of the Social Chapter. The UK was forced out of the European Exchange Rate Mechanism (ERM) after the pound dropped below the permitted parity with the deutschmark. The Conservatives won the general election.

1997 The Labour Party, under the leadership of Tony Blair, won an overwhelming victory in the general election.

1998 The UK and Irish governments attempted to bring to an end the problems in Northern Ireland through the signing of the Good Friday Peace Agreement. The political settlement established a precedent for Ireland's direct involvement in Northern Ireland's affairs, with cross-border co-operation and the decommissioning of paramilitary arms.

1999 Scotland's first legislature for 300 years and Wales' first for 600 years were opened in June. Power and conditional authority were also devolved in Northern Ireland in December.

2000 The first case of BST – foot and mouth – was identified on 20 February. By 30 September when the last case was confirmed, four million animals had been culled and compensation totalling £1.1 billion (US1.5 billion) had been allocated to farmers.

2001 The Labour Party was returned to power in a second landslide victory.

2003 British forces joined a US-led invasion of Iraq in March. The Northern Ireland legislature was suspended after Sinn Féin was accused of bugging offices in Stormont.

2004 The Butler Inquiry into the quality of intelligence used to justify UK participation in the Iraq war found no evidence of 'deliberate distortion or culpable negligence' by the government.

2005 The Labour Party won the 5 May parliamentary elections with a significantly reduced majority. On 7 July, there were four bomb explosions (on three underground trains and a bus) during the morning rush hour in London, killing 52 people and injuring over 700. Another series of suicide bombers two weeks later did not succeed when the detonators failed.

Political structure
Constitution
There is no formal written constitution, instead constitutional law is based on legal precedent and legislation both within the UK and from EU supranational institutions. Power within the UK is partially devolved to Scotland, Wales and Northern Ireland. Local councils operate at the level of metropolitan boroughs, counties, districts and parishes, delivering a number of public services such as education and policing, although their powers, particularly regarding taxation and spending, are circumscribed by central government.

Form of state
Parliamentary democratic monarchy

The executive
The monarch is head of state. The monarchy is governed by convention and may not participate in politics or government affairs. It has, however, by unspoken agreement three rights: to be consulted, to encourage and to warn.

The monarch, in regard to democratic principles, accedes to the results of the popular vote and appoints the winner of any general election, and only in extreme circumstances may a monarch dismiss the government.

While government ministers act nominally in the name of the Crown, almost all power rests with the prime minister as head of government and his cabinet of ministers (part of the executive but drawn from the legislature).

The prime minister chooses and chairs the cabinet, who are members of the political party which typically has most seats in the House of Commons. The cabinet consists of around 20 ministers, although its exact composition is not fixed and there are some ministers without portfolio. Secretaries of state are ministers who head specific government departments. Major figures of importance in the cabinet include the chancellor of the exchequer (responsible for economic management), the foreign secretary (foreign policy) and the home secretary (responsible for law and order). Other ministers deal on a functional basis with trade and industry, health, energy, transport and so on. Cabinet ministers head departments of civil servants and have junior ministers (who do not, as a rule, have a seat in the cabinet) to assist them. These ministries are effectively the executive arm of central government, implementing decisions of the cabinet and parliament.

National legislature
The parliament is based on two chambers, the House of Commons (lower house – with 646 members of parliament (MPs)) and the House of Lords (upper house – with 713 members: 595 life peers, 92 hereditary peers and 26 Church of England archbishops and bishops). There are no fixed dates for general elections, although they must be held at least every five years. MPs are elected in a simple majority system (first-past-the-post) in single member constituencies.

The government is in the process of reforming the House of Lords (upper house). All but 10 per cent of the hereditary peers were removed from the Lords in 1999. Life peers are appointed by the Crown at the behest of the prime minister and new appointments generally include retired politicians, businessmen and academics. The government is planning further reform of the Lords, including the introduction of directly-elected members. No date has been set for the next round of reforms. Parliament meets to consider government policies, pass laws and raise taxation for the purposes of government. Laws, known as bills before their successful passage through parliament, must be passed by the House of Commons. The House of Lords can suggest amendments to, or refuse to pass, most (but not budget) bills. The House of Commons is ultimately under no obligation to accept the Lords' amendments. It can overrule a House of Lords' refusal to pass a bill as a last resort.

Devolution of power to Scotland and Wales took place in 1999 and was Scotland's first legislature for 300 years and Wales' first for 600 years. Elections to the 129-member Scottish Parliament and the 60-member Welsh Assembly are conducted under a system of proportional representation. The Scottish Parliament may raise taxes, however the Welsh Assembly must seek funds from Westminster.

Legal system
The judiciary is independent of both the legislature and executive. The legal system in Scotland and Northern Ireland differs from that in England and Wales.

In England and Wales around 300 county courts deal with minor civil cases. Magistrates courts deal with minor criminal cases. Civil and criminal appeals from these courts are heard by crown courts, which sit in about 90 venues. Scotland and Northern Ireland have slightly different judicial systems. The main purpose of a crown court is to try the more important criminal cases. The High Court of Justice is the main civil court, divided into three sections: Chancery Division, Queens Bench Division and the Family Division. The ultimate court of appeal and the supreme judicial authority for the UK (excluding Scottish criminal cases appeal) is the House of Lords. When sitting as a court of appeal, it consists of the Lord Chancellor, together with the Law Lords (formally called the Lords of Appeal in Ordinary) and deals only with appeals based on points of law.

Since the signing of the Single European Act in 1988, the European Court of Justice (ECJ) has supreme jurisdiction over some aspects of UK law, although this is not often exercised.

Last elections
5 May 2005 (parliamentary); 10 June 2004 (European Parliament); 26 November 2003 (Norther Ireland parliamentary); 1 May 2003 (Scotland and Wales parliamentary).

Results: United Kingdom parliamentary: Prime Minister Tony Blair's Labour Party won 356 seats out of 646 (35.2 per cent of the vote), the Conservative Party 198 (32.3 per cent), the Liberal Democrats 62 (22.1 per cent), the Democratic Unionist Party (DUP) nine, the Scottish National Party (SNP) six, Sinn Féin five, the Social Democratic and Labour Party three, Plaid Cymru three, the Ulster Unionist Party (UUP) one, Health Concern one, RESPECT one and independents one. Turnout was about 61 per cent.

European Parliament: the Conservatives won 27.4 per cent of the vote (27 seats out of 78), Labour 22.3 per cent (19), UK Independence Party (UKIP) 16.8 per cent (12), Liberal Democrats 15.1 per cent (12), Green Party 6.2 per cent (two), SNP 3 per cent (two), Plaid Cymru 1.1 per cent (one), UUP 1 per cent (one), DUP 1 per cent (one) and Sinn Féin 1 per cent (one); turnout 38.9 per cent.

Northern Ireland parliamentary: the Democratic Unionist Party (DUP) won 30 ^ seats out of 108 (25.7 per cent of first-preference votes), the Ulster Unionist Party (UUP) 27 ^ seats (22.7 per cent), Sinn Féin 24 seats (23.5 per cent), the Social Democratic and Labour Party (SDLP) 18 seats (17 per cent), the Alliance Party six seats (3.7 per cent) and independents three seats (7.5 per cent); turnout was 63.1 per cent. *^ Three of the members elected to the Assembly for the UUP subsequently defected to the DUP, so when the Assembly convened the DUP had 33 seats and the UUP 24.*

Scotland parliamentary: Labour won 50 seats out of 129, Scottish National Party (SNP) 27, Conservatives 18, Liberal Democrats 17, Green Party seven, Scottish Socialist Party six, Scottish Senior Citizens Unity Party one and independents three; turnout was 49.4 per cent.

Wales parliamentary: Labour won 30 seats out of 60, Plaid Cymru 12, Conservatives 11, Liberal Democrats six and independents one; turnout was 38.2 per cent.

Next elections
By 3 June 2010 (parliamentary). A referendum on the EU constitution was due to be held in March 2006. However, after the French and Dutch 'No's' in June 2005, it was postponed indefinitely.

Political parties
Ruling party
Labour Party (since 1997; re-elected 2001 and 5 May 2005)
Main opposition party
Conservative Party

Population
59.60 million (2004)
Ethnic make-up
The English, Scots, Welsh and Irish peoples combined make up over 90 per cent of the population of the UK; the largest ethnic minorities are those of Caribbean or African descent (875,000 people). The next largest ethnic groups are Indians (840,255 people) and Pakistani and Bangladeshis (639,390 people). Ethnic minority groups represent just under 6 per cent of the population.
Religions
Church of England (25 million (baptised)), Roman Catholic (4.12 million), Muslim (1.5 million), Presbyterian (1.1 million), Methodist (800,000), Sikh (500,000), Hindu (320,000), Jewish (285,000).

Education
The UK has a devolved education system. Alongside the state system are independent schools, often denominational, which are financed by fees, endowments and the state. Pre-school education is not state-funded; it is available for ages two to five, through playgroups and nursery schools. There is a national curriculum and assessment targets for all primary schools and a minimum attainment is set for all children.

The usual age for transfer to secondary schools is 11 in England, Wales and Northern Ireland and 12 in Scotland. About 90 per cent of state secondary school pupils in England, Wales and Scotland attend comprehensive schools, which provide a wide range of secondary education for most children of all abilities. In other areas, the grammar school system has been retained alongside the comprehensive system, with admission through some form of testing at the age of 10 or 11.

All children are tested at the ages of 7, 11 and 14 years, and take General Certificate of Secondary Education (GCSE) or Scottish Certificate of Education (SCE) examinations at 15–16 years. Students can then opt to study at further education institutions for a range of academic and vocational qualifications, such as Advanced level (A-level) or the National Vocational Qualification (NVQ).

Tertiary education typically starts at aged 18, when students go on to university or colleges of higher education. UK higher education has expanded so that first degrees and further post-graduate qualifications are taken at over 162 universities and other colleges of higher education.

Compulsory years: 5 to 16 in England, Wales and Scotland; 4 to 16 in Northern Ireland.
Enrolment rate: 101 per cent gross primary enrolment of relevant age group (including repeaters); 158 per cent gross secondary enrolment; 59 per cent tertiary enrolment (World Bank).
Pupils per teacher: 19 in primary schools

Health
The National Health Service (NHS) benefits from major government spending, with UK citizens provided with free treatment. Most people are required to pay an initial fee for some aspects of treatment such as eye tests, dental care and prescriptions. The NHS accounts for 85 per cent of total healthcare provision in the UK.

The service provided by the NHS is generally of high quality, but delays for many non-urgent operations have encouraged people to take out private health insurance policies. Private health cover is becoming increasingly common as a company benefit.

In May 2004 a World Health Organisation report on obesity stated 22 per cent of UK adults were obese.

Latest figures show 83 per cent of children were immunised against measles before aged one year. Many parents have withdrawn their infants from the programme and questioned the efficacy of the triple MMR (measles, mumps and rubella) vaccine, following a hotly contested report that claimed the onset of autism and the MMR vaccination were linked.

The government announced that it would take measures to prohibit visitors or 'health tourists' from accessing NHS services, limiting treatment to accidents and emergency cases only.

In 2003/04 the government introduced treatment centres to undertake routine medical and surgical services – such as cataract removal operations – aimed at reducing waiting lists. Overseas providers were hired to provide all the necessary treatment, outside the administration of local health authorities. This has provided competition for the NHS, to match the provision of treatment at a reduced cost with speedier flow-through.

HIV prevalence: 0.2 per cent aged 15–49 in 2003 (World Bank)
Life expectancy: 77.6 years (World Bank)
Fertility rate/Maternal mortality rate: 1.6 births per woman (World Bank)
Birth rate/Death rate: 12 births and 11 deaths per 1,000 people (World Bank)
Infant mortality rate: 5.3 per 1,000 live births (World Bank)

Welfare
The UK has long-established social security and welfare systems. Jobseekers Allowance is provided to most of those registered as unemployed. Additional benefits are paid to families on low incomes or with special needs, for example through the Family Credit Scheme. There is also a wide range of allowances for disabled people. The Housing Benefit Scheme is administered by local authorities and provides assistance with rent and other payments.

Pensions
The UK has an ageing population, with the number of over 65 year-olds projected

United Kingdom

to outnumber the numbers below 16 years by 2008. The number of those past retirement age is expected to peak at around 15 million in the 2030s. Bills for healthcare and pensions are set to rise significantly, while revenue from income tax falls. Government policy is to actively encourage private pension schemes for all employees, and most people now entering the labour market do not expect to receive a sufficient state pension on retirement. Private pension schemes allow retirement at any time between age 50 and 75.

The State Retirement Pension is paid to men at age 65 and women at age 60, although for women this age is starting to increase with the state retirement age to be equalised at age 65 by April 2020.

A report published in October 2004 found that state pensions were underfunded, and that 9–12 million people (or 40 per cent of the workforce) were not saving enough for their retirement. In March 2005 the unfunded public workers' pensions liability was estimated at £690 billion (US$1.2 trillion) or 1.5 times the net public sector debt. The government has begun taking action to alleviate the problem but much more will be required and may include some combination of higher taxes, compulsory savings and/or an increase in the retirement age over 65.

In April 2005 the Pension Protection Fund (PPF) began operation. The fund is aimed at workers who lose their pension when their employer declares bankruptcy. The scheme is an insurance plan, to which all final salary pension schemes must belong. Pension schemes pay fees for each member into a fund and when a business collapses the employees should receive at least 90 per cent of the sum they were due when they retire and retired members should receive 100 per cent of the sum. Critics claim this measure will discourage businesses from running final salary pensions, if they are to shoulder yet another financial burden, and that one large enterprise that collapsed could overwhelm the fund.

Main cities

London (capital, estimated population 7.5 million in 2004), Glasgow (Scotland) (1.1 million), Birmingham (971,800), Liverpool (461,900), Edinburgh (Scotland) (460,000), Sheffield (417,900), Leeds (417,000), Bristol (406,500), Manchester (390,700), Leicester (316,900), Cardiff (Wales) (280,800), Belfast (Northern Ireland) (246,200).

Languages spoken

Other communities such as Indian, Pakistani, Jewish and Chinese maintain their languages.

The Gaelic Language (Scotland) Bill 2004 was introduced on 27 September 2004. It established Bòrd na Gàidhlig (the Bòrd) as a statutory body which will work to secure the status of Gaelic as an official language of Scotland.

Official language/s

English; English and Welsh in Wales. Scottish Gaelic is spoken in Scotland.

Media

Press

There are over 2,000 newspapers in the UK. All major newspapers are in English. The national and regional press is dominated by nine dailies which have a combined circulation of over 12 million.

Dailies: The most influential newspapers include *The Daily Telegraph*, *The Times*, *The Guardian*, *Financial Times* and *The Independent*. The four newspapers with the largest circulation are all tabloids – *The Sun*, *Daily Mail*, *The Mirror* and *Daily Express*. The London evening newspaper is the *Evening Standard*. Other regional dailies include *Western Mail* (Wales), *Daily Record*, *The Herald* (Scotland), *Belfast Telegraph*, *The Irish News* and *Irish Times* (Northern Ireland).

Weeklies: There are several Sunday newspapers. The most influential include *The Independent on Sunday*, *The Sunday Times*, *The Observer* and *The Sunday Telegraph*. Other popular Sunday newspapers are *News of the World*, *Mail on Sunday*, *Sunday Mirror*, *Sunday People* and *Sunday Express*, *Sunday Life* (Belfast), *Sunday World* (Northern Ireland edition).

Business: There are a large number of publications covering all aspects of business, with international circulation, including *Business Standard*, *Business Week*, *Euro Business*, *Independent Business Today*, *UK Weekly Financial News Summary*, *Business & Finanace UK*, *Financial News*, *Financial Times* (daily), *The Economist* (weekly, worldwide) and *Investors Chronicle* (weekly). Other regional publications include *Business Brief Channel Islands*, *London Business Matters* and *Business and Finance in Scotland*.

Periodicals: Periodicals of general interest with national and international circulation include *Private Eye*, *Prospect*, *Spectator* and *New Statesman*.

Broadcasting

Public television and radio broadcasting is controlled by the British Broadcasting Corporation (BBC), which is financed by a licence fee and does not carry advertising. There are a number of commercial television and radio stations, at national and local levels, which are financed by sale of advertising time.

Nationwide digital television services are due to be fully implemented by 2012, when all analogue services will be suspended.

Radio: There are 216 radio stations, of which 172 are commercial.

The BBC operates nine radio stations and 32 local radio stations. There are an increasing number of privately-operated commercial radio stations. BBC Radio One and Radio Two regularly command the highest listening audiences for both age-related programming and general audience ratings.

Television: There are five national terrestrial television networks in operation – BBC1 and BBC2 controlled by BBC; and ITV, Channels 4 and 5. Channel 4 also provides a Welsh language television network for Wales called S4C.

Cable, digital and satellite systems are growing, particularly the Sky network which includes news and sports channels.

Advertising

There is a highly developed industry covering all forms of media. Television advertising is particularly important, with ITV, Channel 4 and Channel 5 accepting advertisements (limited to a daily average of six minutes per hour). Radio advertising is also effective (limited to nine minutes per hour). The majority of newspapers and magazines carry advertising and relatively high circulation figures make this a particularly useful form of promotion. Newspapers account for around 30 per cent of the media market compared to 40 per cent for television. Cinemas carry short advertisements and posters. Billboards and public transport are also widely used.

Economy

The UK economy is a large and open mixed economy, characterised by an export-oriented manufacturing sector. It has a major financial centre and is one of the world's largest exporters of financial services.

The UK it is the third richest country in Europe and a member of the G8, a bloc of the wealthiest countries worldwide. This status is in no small measure based on its financial and service industries including insurance, banking and financial transaction services; the London Stock exchange is Europe's oldest and largest trading forum and globally second only to Wall Street.

The economy was restructured in the 1980s when heavy industries stagnated and investment swung in favour of new technology and service industries, which account for two-thirds of GDP. This rise of service industries and the decline of the traditional industrial base has led to higher GDP per capita, employment and disposable income levels. The economy has steadily improved since the 1990s, in spite of occasional upsets, and the Labour government, which has been in power since 1997, has adopted a policy of maintaining macroeconomic stability. In 1997, the Bank of England was given operational independence and charged with keeping inflation low by setting interest rates.

The OECD has commended the resilience of the UK's economic growth, in the face of the last global downturn, and the reduction in structural unemployment, which has fallen to low levels. It has highlighted the productivity gap with other leading OECD economies, which remains large. The OECD, in its 2005 publication *Economic Policy Reforms*, recommended:
reform disability benefit schemes
improve access by young people to vocational training
improve public infrastructure, especially in transport.

External trade
The traditional deficit on non-oil visible trade is offset by invisible earnings, which account for 30 per cent of total export earnings.

Imports
Main imports are manufactured goods, machinery, fuels and foodstuffs.
Main sources: Germany (13 per cent total, 2004), US (9.2 per cent), France (7.5 per cent), Netherlands (6.6 per cent), Belgium (5.0 per cent), Italy (4.3 per cent), China (4.2 per cent)

Exports
The UK typically ranks among the top five trading nations in the world, behind the US, Germany, Japan and France. Main exports are manufactured goods, fuels, chemicals; food, beverages and tobacco.
Main destinations: US (15 per cent total, 2004), Germany (10.7 per cent), France (9.2 per cent), Ireland (6.8 per cent), Netherlands (6.1 per cent), Belgium (5.2 per cent), Spain (4.5 per cent), Italy (4.2 per cent)

Agriculture
Farming
Agriculture contributes one per cent to GDP, employs 2 per cent of the workforce and meets over two-thirds of domestic food consumption needs. The sector is highly efficient and is a significant exporter of agricultural produce, fertilisers and foodstuffs. The farming industry remains stuck in long-term recession. The National Farmers' Union (NFU), which represents a third of UK farmers, estimated that by February 2005 British farmers owed the banks £12 billion (US$22.6 billion), the highest debt level in 20 years, and the average wage for full time farmers was estimated at £15,000 (US$28,282) per annum. Setbacks have included Bovine Spongiform Encephalopathy (BSE) in the mid 1990s, resulting in the death of nearly 200,000 diseased cattle and the destruction 4.5 million asymtomatic cattle; extensive flooding in 2000; and the foot-and-mouth outbreak of 2001 which resulted in the culling of over 4 million animals. Government policy is to keep the agricultural industry competitive by reducing subsidies and allowing market forces to determine a farm's viability.

UK membership of the EU has created policy disputes between the farmers' organisations, the UK government and the EU. Most of UK agriculture is now governed by the EU's Common Agricultural Policy (CAP), leaving only a few issues to the UK government. The CAP is based on three broad principles:
- the EU is treated as a single market for agricultural produce
- EU farmers are given preference over outside suppliers
- EU member governments meet the cost of the CAP.

Fundamental reform to the CAP was introduced on 1 January 2005 in the UK. The subsidies paid on farm output, which tended to benefit large farms and encourage overproduction, were replaced by single farm payments not conditional on production. This is expected to reward farms that provide and maintain a healthy environment, food safety and animal welfare standards. The changes are also intended to encourage market conscious production and cut the cost of CAP to the EU taxpayer.

Crop production in 2004 included: 22.3 million tonnes (t) cereals in total, 15.7 million t wheat, 5.9 million t barley, 6.0 million t potatoes, 652,000t oats, 28,000t flax fibre, 968,000t pulses, 1,200t grapes, 80,000t tomatoes, 623,060t oilcrops, 7.6 million t sugar beet, 125,000t apples, 247,610t fruit in total, 2.7 million t vegetables in total. Livestock production included: 3.2 million t meat in total, 700,000t beef, 675,000t pig-meat, 310,000t lamb, 1.5 million t poultry, 718,000t eggs, 14.6 million t milk, 7,000t honey, 63,000t cattle hides, 62,000t sheepskins, 3,080t horsemeat, 60,000t greasy wool.

Fishing
Once an important contribution to the economy, the UK's fishing industry is in decline. The total annual marine catch is typically 750,000 tonnes. Cod stocks in the North Sea, Skagerrak, Irish Sea and waters west of Scotland have been in decline for a number of years.

Forestry
Forests cover 24,000 square kilometres, accounting for nearly 10 per cent of total land use. Careful management and replanting programmes mean that forests in the UK are growing by almost 130 square kilometres per annum. Much of the forest plantations have been in the form of non-indigenous coniferous trees, such as the Norwegian Spruce, but in 2005 the government announced a change in policy in favour deciduous woodlands.

The UK typically produces around 7.5 million cubic metres of timber per annum. The UK is far from being self-sufficient in timber or wood products, importing up to 90 per cent of its requirements.

The UK is one of the largest markets for forest products in Europe, with consumption per capita remaining around the European average. Most of the internal demand for pulp and sawnwood is met by imports, although the paper industry depends on the large domestic supply of recovered paper.

Exports of forest products in 2004 amounted to US$2.6 billion, while imports amounted to US$11.2 billion. Production in 2004 included 8,100,389 cubic metres (cum) roundwood, 7,871,389cum industrial roundwood, 2,762,788cum sawnwood, 4,928,389cum sawlogs and veneers, 2,600,000cum pulpwood, 3,533,000cum wood-based panels, 229,000cum woodfuel; 7,642,000 tonnes (t) recovered paper, 1,117,000t newsprint, 1,515,000t printing and writing paper, 3,871,000t other paper and paperboard.

Industry and manufacturing
The manufacturing industry is centred in northern England and the Midlands. Heavy industry and mining have steadily declined since the nineteenth century industrial revolution, but more rapidly in recent decades. Regions where heavy industry and manufacturing were once important typically have lower GDP per capita and higher unemployment than in the south-east. Northern England, the Midlands and Wales were dealt several blows between the late 1990s and 2002 as foreign-owned plants, notably in the vehicle manufacturing sector, closed, causing tens of thousands of redundancies. The sector's contribution to GDP has fallen in the last twenty years from over 40 per to around 25 per cent.

The government's involvement in industry has decreased since the 1980s. Policy has focused on small- and medium-sized enterprises (SMEs) and on the development of high-tech industry. The government has reformed its subsidies system to the larger industries, including the phased abolition of subsidies to ship-building operations. The long-awaited turnaround in manufacturing investment has been delayed by rising oil and commodity prices pushing up costs and putting pressure on profit margins.

United Kingdom

Tourism
Tourism is firmly established as one of the UK's top industries. The sector, which employs around one million people, is expected to contribute four per cent to GDP in 2005.. The UK ranks fifth in the international tourism earnings league behind the US, Spain, France and Italy.
Around 26 million arrivals were recorded in 2004, a number that matched the previous high of 25.7 million in 1998. Scotland accounted for the largest growth at 20 per cent against 12 per cent for the rest of the UK.

Mining
The UK is a significant producer of zinc, lead and limestone. There are also deposits of silver, copper, gold, iron ore and potash. Lead and tin production typically reach 2,000 tonnes per annum. Potash production is around 890,000 tonnes, placing UK in the top 10 producers in the world. An estimated 14.6 million tonnes of sandstone, 104.6 million tonnes of sand/gravel and 95.7 million tonnes of limestone are also produced.

Hydrocarbons
The UK has proven oil reserves of 4.5 billion barrels of oil and produces 730 million barrels per annum. Since production peaked in 1999 there has been a steady fall, underscoring the rapid rundown in the UK's domestic oil supplies. Around 2.3 million barrels per day (bpd) were produced in 2005, but it could be half that amount by 2010.
UK has proven gas reserves of 20.8 trillion cubic metres (cum) and produces 95.9 billion cum. Gas production peaked in 2000, but consumption has continued to grow, due mainly to its use in electricity generation. In 2005, the UK became a net importer of gas for the first time in decades.
The UK has estimaated coal reserves of 1.5 billion tonnes and produces around 28.2 million tonnes (less than 10 per cent of that mined in 1900). Imports amounted to 31.9 million tonnes.
The Office of Gas and Electricity Markets (Ofgem), the official regulator of the oil and gas industries, is charged with securing gas and electricity supplies and regulating markets to allow for competition and restrict business monopolies.

Energy
The UK has almost 80GW of installed electricity capacity, 77 per cent of which is thermal, 15 per cent nuclear, five per cent hydroelectric and two per cent renewable. The net power generation is over 377 billion kilowatt hours (bkwh), while electricity consumption is over 400 bkwh. The bulk of UK imported electricity comes from France.
The largest producer of power is British Energy (BE), which operates eight nuclear power stations and generates about 20 per cent of the total electricity supply for the UK. There are 33 reactors; construction of the last new reactor, the 1188MW Sizewell B in East Anglia, was completed in 1994.
The government approved the development of three large offshore windfarms, at an estimated US$10 billion, in 2003. It is expected that when they become operational in 2010 they will generate as much electrical capacity as six nuclear power stations and five per cent of total power needs. The UK is reported to have Europe's best wind resources.
Wave power became the latest provider of electricity to the national grid, when the Pelamis project off the coast of Orkney delivered its first supply in 2004.

Financial markets
Stock exchange
The London Stock Exchange (LSE) is Europe's oldest and largest trading forum with a £2.8 trillion traded (US$5.2 trillion) in 2004. Almost 1,000 new companies were admitted to the lists since 2003. Two leading European exchanges the Deutsche Borse, in December 2004, and Euronext, in February 2005, made bids of takeover but both were rejected.

Banking and insurance
The UK's high street banks have been very profitable since the mid-1990s, despite being the focus of criticism. The UK banking sector is generally regarded as highly concentrated, but the rise of internet and telephone banking has put renewed pressure on high street banks. One consequence has been the decision by several leading banks to reduce the number of small branches in areas of low population density.
It is not yet clear whether a radical switch to internet banking will appeal to customers, or whether the combined (so-called 'clicks and mortar') approach will prove more successful). There is evidence that cost-cutting among British banks has given them a better chance of breaking into European markets. Likewise, to compete in a tighter market, banks are being forced into mergers and take-overs. In 2004 the Banco Santander Central Hispano successful bid for the Abbey National Bank in a £8.5bn (US$15.6 billion) deal that created the world's eighth largest and Europe's fourth largest banking group.
Independent financial centres within the UK, Jersey, Guernsey, and the Isle of Man, are adhering to a new EU tax agreement, which was introduced in July 2005. They are imposing a withholding tax, up to 35 per cent, to be passed to the tax department of an EU citizen's country, while retaining the anonymity of the saver, instead of informing the relevant EU country about the amount of money in savings accounts and allowing tax to be levied from the home country.
They also supply information on tax fraud, for criminal or civil trials, and notify EU member states about additional malpractices.

Central bank
Bank of England. Monetary policy and the Exchange Equalisation Account is managed by the Bank of England. In 1997, the government authorised the Bank of England to set interest rates independently.

Main financial centre
The City of London is a major international financial centre.

Time
GMT. British Summer Time is GMT plus one hour (April–October, variable dates).

Geography
The UK consists of a major island (divided into England, Wales and Scotland) together with the northern part of the island of Ireland and a number of other smaller islands, including the Channel Islands, the Isle of Man (both dependencies of the Crown) and other islands which are part of the main countries constituting the UK. There are extensive, though not particularly high, mountain and hill ranges in Wales, Scotland and parts of England. The rest of the country includes flatlands (as in East Anglia) and more gently rolling agricultural land.

Climate
The climate is temperate, with a reasonable amount of rainfall. Very hot summers or very cold winters, such as are found on continental Europe, are rare. The temperature rarely goes above 25 degrees Celsius (C), or much below zero, except in mountainous regions such as the Scottish highlands. Rainfall is around 75mm per month on average, although it is higher in Scotland at up to an average of 280mm per month. The wettest month is usually November.

Dress codes
In general, British dress codes follow the conventional North American or European pattern. A suit and tie for men and smart attire for women are advisable at most business occasions.

Entry requirements
Passports
Passports should be valid until at least six months after the intended departure date. Required by all visitors, as the UK is not a signatory of the Schengen Accords allowing EU citizens to enter without a passport.

Nations of the World: A Political, Economic and Business Handbook

Visa
Visas are required by all, except nationals of North America, Australasia, Japan and other EU members. For further exceptions and advice visit www.ukvisas.gov.uk/ (includes application forms). All visas must be applied for before travelling.
In 2003, the UK introduced a requirement for visas for Jamaicans entering the UK.

Currency advice/regulations
There are no restrictions on the transfer of UK or foreign currencies. Currencies and travellers' cheques can be exchanged in banks, hotels and numerous bureaux de change.

Customs
Personal effects duty-free (other than alcoholic drink, tobacco products, perfume), plus small duty-free allowance. EU regulations apply.

Prohibited imports
Imports of firearms require special permission, which may be refused unless proof is provided that the weapon is to be used for sporting purposes and will be re-exported upon departure.

Health (for visitors)
Mandatory precautions
There are no mandatory vaccination certificates required, although evidence of good health may be requested if travelling from areas infected with, for instance, yellowfever.

Advisable precautions
There are no major health hazards for foreign visitors. It is recommended that visitors have up-to-date tetanus immunisation.

Hotels
Classified from one- to five-star by AA and RAC (automobile associations), with five being the best. Rating system in Northern Ireland – A star, A, B star, B, C and D. Prices usually includes a 10–15 per cent service charge, but tipping is also expected.

Credit cards
Major credit cards are widely accepted.

Public holidays
Fixed dates
1 Jan (New Year's Day), 25 Dec (Christmas Day), 26 Dec (Boxing Day).
If New Year's Day, Christmas Day or Boxing Day falls at the weekend, an extra day is taken the following Monday/Tuesday.
There are two additional fixed dates in Northern Ireland, St Patrick's Day on 17 Mar and Battle of the Boyne (Orangemen's Day) on 12 Jul.

Variable dates
Good Friday, Easter Monday, May Day Bank Holiday (first Mon in May), Spring Bank Holiday (last Mon in May) and Summer Bank Holiday (last Mon in Aug). Scotland has an additional Bank Holiday (first Mon in Aug).

Working hours
Banking
Mon–Fri: 0930–1530 or 1630. Some banks open Saturday morning and there are variations in hours in Scotland and Northern Ireland.

Business
Mon–Fri: usually 0900–1700.

Government
0900–1700 (Mon–Fri). As flexible working hours are often adopted in government departments, it is advisable to make an appointment before a visit.

Shops
Mon–Sat: generally 0900–1730. An increasing number of shops are also taking advantage of Sunday shopping hours (a maximum of 6 hours) and are open 1000–1600 or 1100–1700.

Telecommunications
Telephone/fax
British Telecom, although no longer having a statutory monopoly to provide telecommunication services, continues to operate the majority of services. Mercury Communications is the second-largest telecom provider.
Direct dialling is available on all local and overseas calls.
For international telephone enquiries dial 153; for international operator assistance 155.
Public telephones can be found at railway stations, hotels and restaurants and in the street. A growing number are operated by telephone cards, which can be purchased at post offices and many shops.

Postal services
On 1 January 2006 the Royal Mail will lose its monopoly on the collection and delivery of letters in the UK. All licenced operators will be able to delivery business and residential mail from that date. The market has an estimated £4.5 billion (US$8.4 billion) turnover and only 30 per cent of letters delivered and specialised bulk mailing is open to competition. The new market will include separate collection boxes and mail tracking services.
A new regulatory body – Postcomm – will monitor future services.
The Royal Mail provides guaranteed overnight delivery services and parcel post. There are also a number of other privately owned courier companies. UK mail has two rates for standard letters up to 60 grammes, first class mail is expected to be delivered within one working day, and second class mail is slower. Stamps can be purchased at supermarkets, tobacconists and newsagents as well as post offices.

Electricity supply
230V AC. The electricity supply voltage throughout the EU is standard.

Social customs/useful tips
A reasonable degree of punctuality is required by those in business. Business cards are usually exchanged at meetings. Gifts are not usually offered to business acquaintances, although when visiting a private home it may be appropriate to take chocolates or wine.
There are few unusual or particularly strict laws. Alcoholic drinks are not allowed into some sporting fixtures, notably football matches. Smoking is now actively discouraged in many public place and only a minority of transport services provide for passengers who smoke; expect a ban to be in place.

Security
Street crime is still much less prevalent in the UK than, for instance, the USA. The police, with a few exceptions, remain unarmed. The number of firearms used in criminal activity is relatively low, although it has increased in recent years.

Getting there
Air
National airline: There are no state-owned airlines, but British Airways offers the most extensive choice of destinations.
International airport/s: London Heathrow (LHR), 24km west of London is the principal UK airport. Other satellite airports serve regional cities that provide short-haul international flights. London City (LCY) 10KM east of city; London Gatwick (LGW), 46km south of London; London Stansted (STN), 55km north-east of London.
Channel Islands: Guernsey (GCI), 6km south-west of St Peter Port; Jersey (JER), 8km west of St Helier.
Northern Ireland: Belfast International (BFS), 29km north-west of city.
Scotland: Aberdeen (ABZ), 11km north-west of city; Edinburgh (EDI), 11km west of city; Glasgow (Int) (GLA), 14km west of city.
Wales: Cardiff (Int) (CWL), 19km south-west of city.
The Heathrow Express connects Heathrow Airport to west London's Paddington station. Services run, every 15 minutes, between 05.00 and 23.45. The slower London underground connects, initially via the Piccadilly Line, to all mainline stations and city centre.
An extensive airbus service operates from Heathrow airport to the city, including Victoria coach station, Russell Square and Liverpool Street Station.
Rapid train services are available from other London airports to the city centre.

United Kingdom

Other airport/s: London Luton (LTN), 51.2km north-west of London; Birmingham International (Int) (BHX), 13km east of city; Bournemouth Int (BOH), Bristol Int (BRS), East Midlands Int (EMA), Humberside Int (HUY), Leeds Bradford Int (LBA), Liverpool John Lennon (LPL), 11km south of Liverpool; Manchester Int (MAN); Newcastle Int (NCL), 8km north-west of Newcastle; Norwich (NWI), Plymouth City (PLH), Southampton Int (SOU), Teeside Int (MME).

Airport tax: There are three taxes levied which vary according to UK departure airport and domestic or international destination airport. All three are paid when purchasing an airline ticket.

Surface

Road: There are major road links to all parts of the UK and from the Republic of Ireland to Northern Ireland.

Rail: Eurostar connects to Paris and Brussels via the channel tunnel which carries passenger and freight vehicles and foot passengers.

Water: Regular ferry and hovercraft connections with the continent and Ireland.

Main port/s: The main ports are London, Liverpool, Grimsby, Southampton, Milford Haven, Tees and Hartlepool, Dover, Felixstowe, Larne and Holyhead.

Getting about

National transport

Air: Most major cities are linked by regular flights to 21 main commercial airports. A number of small, 'no-frills' airlines have introduced cheap domestic flights, including connections to Ireland and Scotland and other regional cities, which has led to air travel competing with rail travel for the first time.

Approximate flight times from London to: Aberdeen (1 hour 25 mins), Belfast (1 hour 10 mins), Edinburgh (1 hour 10 mins), Jersey (50 mins), Manchester (50 mins) and Newcastle (1 hour).

Road: There is an extensive network of about 370,000km (free to all users), including 2,800km of motorway, linking all major cities and towns. The M25 circles London as a hub linking other motorways in a network. Traffic can be heavy on these routes, especially as road haulage (wholly in the private sector) use them extensively. Major towns and cities are connected by trunk roads ('A' roads). Note that roads in rural areas ('B' roads) can be slow and winding.

Information on planning motorway journeys can be obtained through: www.highways.gov.uk/travel/index.htm

Buses: Express buses between towns and cities are fully in the private sector. Urban and local buses are often still run by local authorities, although private companies operate some routes. For details of services contact www.traveline.org.uk/.

Rail: There is a network of about 18,400km, with relatively expensive first- and second-class services. All principal towns in the UK are connected by regular inter-city services.

Regional companies operate network services. It is advisable to book tickets in advance. These can be obtained on-line (www.thetrainline.com/). For more information on UK train services and fare prices, contact: National Rail Enquiries on 08457 484950.

Water: There are public and private ferry and car ferry links between Hampshire and the Isle of Wight. Services also provide links with the isles of Scotland, subject to weather conditions, and Northern Ireland. Inshore and inland waterways, are under the control of the British Waterways Board.

City transport

Taxis: Available in all major cities and towns. Taxis can be hailed in the street, at taxi ranks or contacted by telephone. Taxis may charge extra – over and above the metered charge – depending on the number of passengers, the size of luggage items, for journeys at night and at weekends and for journeys exceeding 8km. Tipping is usually in the region of 10 per cent.

Buses, trams & metro: Extensive network linking all parts of the capital. Central London buses are the only ones still formally protected from private competition. Good bus services are also available in all other major towns. London is served by an extensive metro system. Reliable metro services also operate in Glasgow, Liverpool, Manchester (metrolink train system) and Newcastle.

Ferry: There are passenger and car ferry services across the Thames in London and the Mersey in Liverpool.

Car hire

Widely available at airports and in main towns. All major international hire firms are represented. International driving licence or full national licence required. Driving is on the left. Speed limits: motorways/dual carriageways maximum 70mph (113kph), normal roads 40-70mph (64-97kph) (signposted) and built-up areas 30 or 40mph (48 or 64kph) (signposted). Speed cameras are in operation on motorways and other roads and imposed fines are usually forwarded as per car rental agreements.

BUSINESS DIRECTORY

The addresses listed below are a selection only. While World of Information makes every endeavour to check these addresses, we cannot guarantee that changes have not been made, especially to telephone numbers and area codes. We would welcome any corrections.

Telephone area codes

The international direct dialling (IDD) code for United Kingdom is +44, followed by area code and subscriber's number.

Aberdeen	1224	London (central)	207
Belfast	2890 2	Manchester	161
Birmingham	121	Newcastle	191
Cambridge	1223	Nottingham	115
Cardiff	2920	Oxford	1865
Coventry	2476	Perth	1738
Dundee	1382	Plymouth	1752
Edinburgh	131	Portsmouth	2392
Exeter	1392	Sheffield	114
Glasgow	141		
Liverpool	151		
London (outer)	208		

Useful telephone numbers

Emergency services	999
Directory enquiries (BT, fee service)	118-500
International directory enquiries (BT, fee service)	118-505

Chambers of Commerce

Birmingham Chamber of Industry and Commerce, 75 Harbourne Road, Birmingham B15 3DH (tel: 454-6171; fax: 455-8670; e-mail: info@birminghamchamber.org.uk).

British Chambers of Commerce, 50 Broadway, St James Park, London SW1H 0RG (tel: 7152-4046; fax: (0)20-7565-2049).

Cardiff Chamber of Commerce, Trade and Industry, St David's House East, Wood Street, Cardiff CF10 1ES (tel: 2034-8280; fax: 2037-7653; e-mail: enquiries@cardiffchamber.co.uk).

Edinburgh Chamber of Commerce, 27 Melville Street, Edinburgh EH3 7JF (tel: 477-7000; fax: 477-7002; e-mail: information@ecce.org).

Leeds Chamber of Commerce, 102 Wellington Street, Leeds LS1 4LT (tel: 0113-247-0000; fax: 0113-247-111; e-mail: info@leedschamber.co.uk).

London Chamber of Commerce and Industry, 33 Queen Street, london EC4R 1AP (tel: 7248-4444; fax: 7489-0391; e-mail: lc@londonchamber.co.uk).

Manchester Chamber of Commerce and Industry, Churchgate House, 56 Oxford Street, Manchester M60 7HJ (tel: 237-4102; fax: 237-3277; e-mail: info@mcci.org.uk).

Sheffield Chamber of Commerce and Industry, Albion House, Savile Street, Sheffield S4 7UD (tel: (0)114-201-8888; fax: (0)114-272-0950; e-mail: info@scci.org.uk).

Nations of the World: A Political, Economic and Business Handbook

Banking
Abbey National, 2 Triton Square, Regent's Place, London NW1 3AN (tel: 7612-4000; fax: 7612-4230; e-mail: investor@abbeynational.com).

Bank of Scotland, The Mound, Edinburgh EH1 1YZ (tel: 470-7777; fax: 243-5640).

Barclays Bank, 54 Lombard Street, London EC3P 3AH (tel: 7699-5000; fax: 7699-2680).

British Bankers' Association, Pinners Hall, 105-108 Old Broad Street London EC2N 1EX (tel: 7216-8800; fax: 7216-8811).

Chartered Institute of Bankers in Scotland, Drumsheugh House, 38b Drumsheugh Gardens, Edinburgh EH3 7SW (tel: 473-7777; fax:473-7788; e-mail: info@ciobs.org.uk).

Clydesdale Bank, 30 St Vincent Place, Glasgow G1 2HL (tel: 248-7070; fax: 223-2559).

Halifax Plc, Trinity Road, Halifax HX1 2RG (tel: 01422-333-333; fax: 01422-391-777).

HSBC, 10 Lower Thames Street, London EC3R 6AE (tel: 7260-0500; fax: 7260-0501).

Lloyds TSB, 71 Lombard Street, London EC3P 3BS (tel: 7626-1500; fax: 7356-1731).

National Westminster Bank, 135 Bishopsgate, London EC2M 3UR (tel: 7375-5000; fax: 7375-5050).

Royal Bank of Scotland, 36 St Andrew Square, Edinburgh EH2 2YB (tel: 556-8555; fax: 557-6565).

Central bank
Bank of England, Threadneedle Street, London EC2R 8AH (tel: 7601-4444; fax: 7601-5460; e-mail: enquiries@bankof england,co.uk).

Travel information
Aberdeen Airport, Dyce, Aberdeen AB21 7DU (tel: 1224-722-331; fax: 1224-775-845; e-mail: glal@baa.com).

Belfast International Airport, Aldergrove, Belfast BT 29 4AB (tel: 448-4848; fax: 448-4849; e-mail: info.desk@bial.co.uk).

Birmingham International Airport, Birmingham B26 3QJ (tel: 767-5511; fax: 782-8802; e-mail: custsrvs@bhx.co.uk).

British Airways, Waterside, PO Box 365, Harmondsworth, Middlesex (tel: 8738-5100; fax: 8738-9838).

Cardiff International Airport, Rhoose CF62 3BD (tel: 1446-711-111; fax: 1446-711-675; e-mail: info@cial.co.uk).

Edinburgh Airport, Edinburgh EH12 9DN (tel: 333-1000; fax: 344 3470; e-mail: glal@baa.com).

VisitBritain, Thames Tower, Blacks Road, Hammersmith, London W6 9EL (tel: 8563-3000; fax: 8563-3234; e-mail: comments@englishtourism.org.uk).

Gatwick Airport, West Sussex RH6 0NP (tel: 0870-000-2468; fax: 1293-503-794; e-mail: gatwick_feedback@baa.com).

Glasgow Airport, Paisley, Renfrewshire PA3 2SW (tel: 887-1111; fax: 848-4769; e-mail: glal@baa.com).

Heathrow Airport, 234 Bath Road, Harlington, Middlesex UB3 5AP (tel: 0870-0000-123; fax: 8745-4290; e-mail: lhr1feedback@baa.com).

Manchester Airport, Manchester M90 1QX (tel: 489-3000; fax: 489-3813; e-mail: info@manchesterairport.co.uk).

Northern Ireland Tourist Board, 59 North Street, Belfast BT1 1NB (tel: 231-221; fax: 240-960; e-mail: info@nitb.com).

Passport Office, Globe House, 89 Ecclestone Square, London SW1V 1PN (tel: 0870-521-0410; fax: 7271-8403; e-mail: london@ukpa.gov.uk).

Glasgow Prestwick International Airport, Aviation, Prestwick, Ayrshire KA9m 2PL (tel: 1292-511-000; fax: 1292-511-010; e-mail: info@gpia.co.uk).

Stansted Airport, Essex CM24 1QW (tel: 0870-0000-303; fax: 1279-662-066; e-mail: stansted_feedback@baa.com).

VisitScotland, 23 Ravelston Terrace, Edinburgh EH4 3TP (tel: 332-2433; fax: 343-1513; e-mail: info@visitscotland.com).

Wales Tourist Board, Brunel House, 2 Fitzalan Road, Cardiff CF24 0UY (tel: 499-909; fax: 485-031; e-mail: info@visitwales.com).

Ministry of tourism
Department of Culture, Media and Sport, 2-4 Cockspur Street, London SW1Y 5DH (tel: 7211 6200; email: enquiries@culture.gov.uk)

National tourist organisation offices
VisitBritain, Thames Tower, Blacks Road, Hammersmith, London W6 9EL (tel: 8846-9000; fax: 8563-0302).

Ministries
Cabinet Office, 70 Whitehall, London SW1A 2AS (tel: 7270-1234).

Department of Culture, Media and Sport, 2-4 Cockspur Street, London SW1Y 5DH (tel: 7211-6000; e-mail: enquiries@culture.gov.uk)

Department of Education and Skills, Sanctuary Building, Great Smith Street, London SW1P 3BT (tel: 0870-000-2288; fax: 01928-79-4248; e-mail: info@dfes.gov.uk).

Department of Environment, Food and Rural Affairs, Nobel House, 17 Smith Square, London SW1P 3JR (tel: 7238-6000; fax: 7238-6591).

Department of Health, Richmond House, 79 Whitehall, London SW1A 2NS (tel: 7210-4850; e-mail: dhmail@doh.gsi.gov.uk).

Department of International Development, 94 Victoria Street, London SW1E 5JL (tel: 7917-7000; fax: 7917-0019; e-mail: enquiry@dfid.gov.uk).

Department of Trade and Industry, 1 Victoria Street, London SW1H 0ET (tel: 7215-5000; e-mail: dti.enquiries@dti.gsi.gov.uk).

Department of Transport, Local Government and Regions, Eland House, Bressenden Place, London SW1E 5DU (tel: 7944-3000).

Department of Work and Pensions, Richmond House, 79 Whitehall, London SW1A 2NS (tel: 7238-0800; fax: 238-0763; peo@dwp.gsi.gov.uk).

Foreign and Commonwealth Office, King Charles Street, London SW1A 2AH (tel: 7270-1500).

Home Office, 50 Queen Annes Gate, London SW1H 9AT (tel: 7273-4000; fax: 7273-2065; e-mail: public.enquiries@homeoffice.gti.gov.uk).

Lord Chancellor's Department, Selborne House, 54-60 Victoria Street, London SW1E 6QW (tel: 7210-8500; e-mail: general.enquiries.@lcdhq.gsi.gov.uk).

Ministry of Defence, Main Building, Horse Guards Avenue, London SW1A 2HB (tel: 0870-607-4455).

Northern Ireland Office, 11 Millbank, London SW1P 4PN (tel: 7210-3000; fax: 7210-0249; e-mail: press.nio@nics.gov.uk).

Prime Ministers Office, 10 Downing Street, London SW1A 2AA (tel: 7270-3000).

Scotland Office, Dover House, London SW1A 2AU (tel: 7270-6754; fax: 7270-6812; e-mail: scottish.secretary@scotland.gov.uk).

Treasury, Parliament Street, London SW1P 3AG (tel: 7270-4558; fax: 7270-5244; e-mail: public.enquiries@hm-treasury.gov.uk).

Wales Office, Gwydyr House, London SW1A 2ER (e-mail: wales.office@wales.gsi.gov.uk).

Other useful addresses
Aberdeen Exhibition and Conference Centre, Bridge of Don, Aberdeen (tel: 1224-824-824; fax:1224-825-276; e-mail: aecc@aecc.co.uk).

United Kingdom

Advertising Standards Authority, 2 Torrington Place, London WC1E 7HW (tel: 7580-5555; fax: 7631-3051; e-mail: inquiries@asa.org.uk).

BBC Television, Television Centre, Wood Lane, London W12 7RJ (tel: 8743-8000; fax: 8749-7520; e-mail: info@bbc.co.uk).

British Council, 10 Spring Gardens, London SW1A 2BN (tel: 7930-8466; fax: 7389-6347; e-mail: general.enquiries@britishcouncil.org).

British Embassy (USA), 3100 Massachusetts Avenue, NW, Washington DC 20008 (tel: 202-588-7800; fax: 202-588-7870).

British Sky Broadcasting Group (BSkyB), 6 Centaurs Business Park, Grant Way, Isleworth TW7 5QD (tel: 7705-3000; fax: 7705-3060).

British Waterways Board, Willow Grange, Church Road, Watford WD17 4QA (tel: 01923-201-120; e-mail: enquiries.hq@britishwaterways.co.uk).

Chartered Institute of Marketing, Moor Hall, Cookham, Maidenhead, Berkshire SL6 9QH (tel: 1628-427-500; fax: 1628-427-499; e-mail: info@cim.co.uk).

Confederation of British Industry (CBI), Centre Point, 103 New Oxford Street, London WC1A 1DU (tel: 7395-8247; fax: 7240-1578; e-mail: enquiry.desk@cbi.org.uk).

Crown Estate, 16 Carlton House Terrace, London SW1Y 5AH (tel: 7210-4377; fax: 7210-4236; e-mail: pr@crownestate.co.uk).

Customs and Excise, New King's Beam House, 22 Upper Ground, London SE1 9PJ (tel: 7620-1313; fax: 7865-4975; e-mail: enquiries.lon@hmce.gsi.gov.uk).

Design Council, 34 Bow Street, London WC2E 7DL (tel: 7420-5200; fax:7420-5300; e-mail: info@designcouncil.org.uk).

Guild of Registered Tourist Guides, The Guild House, 52d Borough High Street, London SE1 1XN (tel: 7403-1115; fax: 7378-1705; e-mail: guild@blue-badge.org.uk).

Independent Television News (ITN), 200 Gray's Inn Road, London WC1X 8HF (tel: 7833-3000; fax: 7430-4868; e-mail: info@itn.co.uk).

Institute of Export, Export House, Minerva Business Park, Lynch Wood, Peterborough PE2 6FT (tel: 1733-404-400; fax: 1733-404-444; e-mail: Institute@export.org.uk).

Institute of Linguists, Saxon House, 48 Southwark Street, London SE1 1UN (tel: 7940-3100; fax: 7940-3101; e-mail: info@iol.org.uk).

ITV Network Centre, 200 Gray's Inn Road, London WC1X 8HF (tel: 7843-8000; fax: 7843-8158; e-mail: info@itv.co.uk).

Kings Hall Exhibition and Conference Centre, Balmoral, Belfast (tel: 028-9066-5225; fax: 028-9066-1264; e-mail: info@kingshall.co.uk).

London Stock Exchange, Old Broad Street, London EC2N 1HP (tel: 7797-1000; e-mail: enquiries@londonstockexchange.com).

National Exhibition Centre, Birmingham B40 1NT (tel: 780-4141; fax: 780-2517; e-mail: centre-exhibitions@necgroup.co.uk).

Office for National Statistics, 1 Drummond Gate, London SW1V 2QQ (tel: 7233-9233; fax: 7533-6262; e-mail: info@statistics.gov.uk).

Press Complaints Commission, 1 Salisbury Square, London EC4Y 8JB (tel: 7353-1248; fax: 7353-8355; e-mail: pcc@pcc.org.uk).

Scottish Exhibition and Conference Centre, Exhibition Way, Fenniston Street, Glasgow G3 8YW (tel: 248-3000; fax: 226-3423; e-mail: info@secc.co.uk).

Trades Union Congress (TUC), Congress House, 23-28 Great Russell Street, London WC1B 3LS (tel: 7636-4030; fax: 7636-0632; e-mail: info@tuc.org.uk).

Internet sites

Bank of England: http://www.bankofengland.co.uk

British Airways: http://www.british-airways.com

British Chambers of Commerce: http://www.britishchambers.org.uk/internet_home_page.htm

Confederation of British Industry: http://www.cbi.org.uk

Department of Trade and Industry: http://www.dti.gov.uk

Eurostar: http://www.eurostar.com

Kelly's Directory - the search engine for UK industry: http://www.kellys.reedinfo.co.uk

UK export (database of British exporters): http://www.export.co.uk

UK Online - gateway to all UK government websites: http://www.ukonline.gov.uk

UK trade information: http://www.ukinfo.com

UK yellow pages: http://www.yell.co.uk

United States of America

KEY FACTS

Official name: United States of America

Head of State: President George W Bush (Republican Party) (sworn in 20 Jan 2001; re-elected 2 Nov 2004 and sworn in for a second term on 20 Jan 2005)

Head of government: President George W Bush

Ruling party: Republican Party

Area: 9,300,000 square km

Population: 296.47 million (US Census Bureau, 27 Jun 2005)

Capital: Washington DC

Official language: A bill to recognise English as the official language was introduced in the House of Representatives in February 2003. Spanish is regarded as the unofficial second national language.

Currency: US dollar (US$) = 100 cents

GDP per capita: US$39,934 (2004)

GDP real growth: 4.40% (2004); 4.1% (3rd quarter 2005)

Labour force: 147.40 million (2004)

Unemployment: 5.50% (OECD, 2004)

Inflation: 2.70% (2004)

Oil production: 7.24 million bpd (2004)

Balance of trade: -US$662.04 billion (2004)

Foreign debt: US$8,360.17 billion (2004)

Annual FDI: US$1,461.40 billion (cumulative, 1995–2004, OECD); US$106.80 billion (OECD, 2004)*

* estimated figure

The United States of America remains the world's foremost economic and military power. The country's unique status as a melting pot for so many of the globe's cultures has set it apart from many other capitalist democracies. The US's nascent rise to emerge as the world's only superpower by the turn of the twenty-first century is attributable to an exceptional entrepreneurial talent among its people and a desire to build things better, bigger and faster than any other society on earth.

But in recent years the US's status as the sole global superpower has begun to be challenged by the irresistible rise of China. Furthermore, the inherent belief among much of the nation that its country is an impenetrable fortress where disaster cannot strike has been destroyed. The horrifying spectacle of the terrorist attacks of 11 September 2001 put paid to that. But it was another equally horrifying, yet natural disaster that really brought home this fact in 2005.

Katrina et al

In August hundreds of people were killed and many thousands more were left homeless when Hurricane Katrina, the most destructive tropical storm to hit the United States in decades, wreaked havoc throughout the southern states. Louisiana was very hard hit and in particular the famous 'Big Easy' city of New Orleans was left flooded and abandoned for days afterwards. Katrina was just one of 15 hurricanes during the 2005 Atlantic hurricane season that officially ran from June 1 to November 30, but it was the most severe, along with fellow category 5 hurricanes Rita and Wilma.

Katrina formed on 23 August and made landfall twice. First in Florida where lives were lost and damage caused and then on the southern coast of Louisiana on 29 August, where a storm surge breached the levee system that protected New Orleans from Lake Pontchartrain and the Mississippi River. The breach resulted in mass flooding throughout the city, destroying homes, businesses and lives. The Mississippi and Alabama coasts were also heavily hit and deaths from Katrina, directly and indirectly caused by the hurricane were over the 1,400 mark. However, by mid-January 2006 some 3,200 remained officially unaccounted for, so a substantial rise in the total death toll is almost assured.

Prior to Katrina's landfall approximately 1.2 million people were under order to evacuate. Many however, did not have the means to flee while others remained in their houses in the expectation that they could ride out the storm. As the scale of the disaster was revealed, under much criticism for their response, the authorities began to evacuate people by bus to nearby states. Over 1.5 million people were displaced by the hurricane, making Katrina the biggest humanitarian disaster in the United States since the Great Depression in the 1930s. The Federal Disaster Zone for Katrina covered 90,000 square miles, an area almost equivalent to the total landmass of the United Kingdom; some three million people were also left without electricty. With a total cost of US$75 billion dollars, according to the National Hurricane Centre (NHC), Katrina is the most expensive natural disaster in the history of the United States.

Some of the most shocking elements of the aftermath of the catastrophe were captured on television and in the national print media. Images and stories of New Orleans residents, including members of the city's police force, undertaking violent looting shocked the world. Though much of the looting involved the necessary collection of basic goods for survival such as water and foodstuffs, non-essential high quality goods were also hoarded. The French Quarter, famous, among other things for its jewelry shops, was probably the most looted area of the city. Gunmen and snipers, reportedly armed with M16s, began to take de facto control of parts of the city. Some police were also reported to have turned in their badges as the level of violence escalated out of control. Troops were eventually put on the streets of New Orleans to restore some semblance of order to the city and the surrounding area.

New Orleans Mayor Ray Nagin designated the Louisiana Superdome, along with the New Orleans Convention Centre, as a 'refuge of last resort' for those who

United States of America

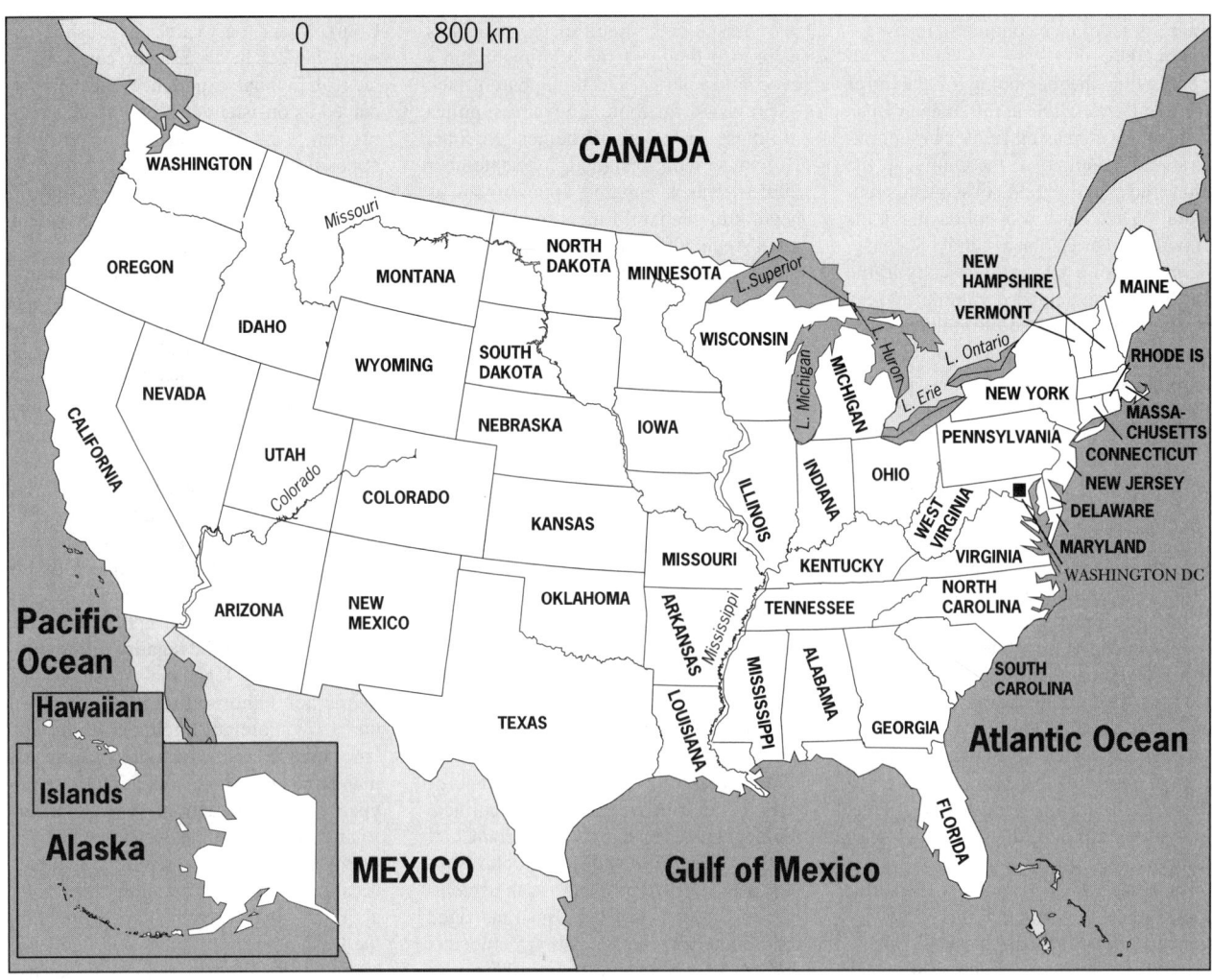

were unable to leave the city. Some 60,000 people were thought to have sought refuge inside the dome. As Katrina passed overhead two huge holes were ripped open in the ceiling and heating, air-conditioning and water supplies all failed or expired. Reports of the enclosure degenerating into a state of mayhem – a 'Terrordome' in the words of one British tabloid newspaper – may well have been inflated, but order was undoubtedly lost for a period inside the dome. Many put the blame for the state of chaos in the city at the door of the authorities and a national debate as to the appropriateness of the preparation for and subsequent management of the Katrina disaster was sparked.

Bush's annus horribilis

Following his re-election as president in November 2004, George W Bush claimed that he 'had earned political capital and I intend to spend it'. With a new mandate that included a Republican majority in both the Senate and Congress, he looked set to do so. But throughout 2005 Bush spent much of the year picking up loose change from the floor rather than cashing substantial politically-partisan cheques, as the first year of his second term turned into something of a political public relations nightmare.

Following criticism of his inauguration for being too extravagant at a time of war, Bush took his plans for social security reform on a road show across America. The reform package included a fractional privatisation of the system whereby employees could pay some payroll taxes into their own designated private account. During the tour the White House's plans came under heavy attack from the opposition Democrats, who claimed the Republicans were over-emphasising the current system's problems in order to push through a partisan reform. Bush even suffered the embarrassment of being jeered by some Democrats as he delivered the traditionally non-partisan State of the Union address. As the year wore on the reforms were further scrutinised before other more pressing national issues allowed them to stall and run into the sand.

Bush met the ire of the Democratic Party once more when he nominated self-professed neo-conservative and leading hawk John Bolton as US Ambassador to the United Nations (UN). After Bolton's appointment was held up for months following a Democrat orchestrated filibuster, Bush was forced to resort to a recess appointment – which will last until January 2007 when a new legislature convenes – in order to put his man in the post. Problems were compounded for the White House when two of the administration's most high profile advisors, Karl Rove and Lewis 'Scooter' Libby Jr were heavily criticised in July 2005 for their respective roles in 'outing' undercover CIA agent Valerie Plame in what became known as the *Plame affair*. On October 28, vice-presidential advisor Libby was indicted on five counts of felony and perjury, while Rove, known as 'Bush's brain', is set to face continuing investigation in 2006.

Following the beginning of the furor over the *Plame affair* in the summer Bush came under increasing fire for his administration's handling of the run-up to the 2003 Iraq invasion and subsequent occupation. While Bush was holidaying at his Crawford, Texas ranch Cindy Sheehan, the mother of a US army casualty in the conflict, led an extended vigil outside the 'Western White House'. Simultaneously, the president's already shaky approval rating went into free fall, as did the approval ratings of his administration's performance in the post-war rebuilding effort.

The Bush administration then came under severe attack for the way in which it prepared for and reacted to hurricane Katrina. Even as Katrina wreaked havoc throughout Louisiana, Alabama and Mississippi Bush remained at his ranch and, in a mis-timed public relations move, he even attended a Republican Party fund-raising event in California. Many opponents of the administration piled on the agony by claiming that the advent of the Iraq war had depleted the US army's capability to deal with disasters at home. Criticism of the White House was fierce, though perhaps not all of it was totally deserved.

The Bush administration was undoubtedly slow off the mark in terms of the federal response to the disaster and Bush's personal performance in not visiting the disaster zone for some time afterward was misguided. Legitimate criticisms were also made of the administration's evacuation policy and the apparent lack of provision for food and water supplies to those affected. Whether Michael Brown – who resigned in September 2005 – was a suitable appointment as head of the Federal Emergency Management Agency (FEMA) has also been disputed owing to his dearth of disaster management experience prior to taking on the role. But there were also question marks beneath the federal government level. Doubts as to whether local and state government agencies successfully executed the evacuation plan, whether the evacuation plan was properly circulated prior to landfall and whether the correct provisions were made by local authorities to distribute necessary supplies of water and staple foodstuffs have all been expressed. And, most shockingly for Americans (and those watching their TV screens around the World) was the uncomfortable feeling that had New Orleans been a predominantly white, northern city, help would have been faster and better managed.

Following the fall out from the events of the summer, Bush regained some political momentum when his nominee for Chief Justice of the Supreme Court, John Roberts, was accepted by Congress in September. In October however, Bush managed to infuriate both the opposition Democrats and his Republican colleagues by nominating Harriet Miers to the Supreme Court. Miers' past career as Bush's personal lawyer in Texas, her comparative lack of judicial experience and her perceived inconsistency on important constitutional issues ensured powerful opposition from within Bush's conservative base, which in turn led to Miers' offering her withdrawal to the president. Bush eventually withdrew his nomination of Miers following a humiliating climb-down amid accusations of cronyism. He went on to nominate the 'safe' figure of Samuel Alito for the vacant position on the bench on 31 October 2005. Alito was promptly confirmed as a Supreme Court member by the Senate on 31 January 2006.

Bush ended 2005 as badly as he started the year when it emerged, to great public criticism, that he had signed an executive order facilitating the surveillance of US citizens by the National Security Agency without a warrant in 2002. A national debate ensued as to the legality of the measure with many legal analysts suggesting it was not authorised under the terms of the 1978 Foreign Intelligence Surveillance Act (FIST). The White House has maintained that there is existing legal provision for such action, with President Bush claiming that the decision taken was 'crucial to our national security' and inextricably linked to the ongoing 'threat from al Qaeda'. In a worrying development for the Bush administration, a poll published by an online research and polling agency in January 2006 claimed that 52 per cent of Americans believed it appropriate for Congress to impeach the president if the claims that he broke the law are substantiated.

Economy: goodbye Greenspan

The world's most famous central banker left the world's most famous central bank in the world's most important economy at the end of January 2006. After eighteen and a half years in the top job at the United States Federal Reserve, or 'the Fed' as it is popularly known, Alan Greenspan took a bow. The 79-year old economic guru is succeeded by Ben Bernanke as Chairman of the Board of Governors, arguably the most important economic decision making position in the Western World.

Greenspan will be sorely missed and his successor has a challenging job on his hands. Greenspan's record as Fed Chairman is impressive, having successfully steered the US economy through stormy weather. His handling of the Black Monday stock market crash in 1987 shortly after he assumed the position and more

KEY INDICATORS — United States of America

	Unit	2000	2001	2002	2003	2004
Population	m	281.42	284.40	285.42	288.40	296.47
Gross domestic product (GDP)	US$bn	9,872.90	10,082.10	10,360.00	10,819.81*	11,667.51
GDP per capita	US$	35,120	35,500	36,300	37,312	39,934
GDP real growth	%	3.7	0.8	1.9	3.0	4.4
Inflation	%	3.4	2.8	1.6	2.3	2.7
Unemployment	%	4.0	4.7	5.8	6.1	–
Oil output	'000 bpd	7,733.0	7,717.0	7,698.0	7,454.0	7,241.0
Natural gas output	bn cum	555.6	555.4	547.7	549.5	542.9
Coal output	mtoe	570.7	590.7	571.7	551.3	567.2
Exports (fob) (goods)	US$m	774,860	723,830	693,520	724,006	811,080
Imports (fob) (goods)	US$m	1,224,830	1,147,500	1,202,500	1,305,648	1,473,120
Balance of trade	US$m	-449,570	-423,670	-500,000	-581,642	-662,040
Current account	US$m	-413,450	-385,700	-473,940	-530,670	-665,940
Total reserves minus gold	US$m	56,600.0	57,630.0	67,960.0	74,890.0	75,890.0
Foreign exchange	US$m	31,240.0	28,980.0	33,820.0	39,720.0	42,720.0

* estimated figure

recently his steady management of the world's biggest economy in the aftermath of the 9/11 terrorist attacks won him high praise. Though in recent years his closeness to the current Bush administration has perturbed many, Greenspan is still considered the best brain around when it comes to monetary and economic policy.

Bernanke, a distinguished Princeton economist with much less practical experience than his predecessor, will need to overcome some tough challenges in order to win the confidence of the financial markets. Not least among them is the need to keep inflation low. Mr Bernanke has reiterated his belief in a system of institutionalisation of inflation targets. He has stated on many occasions since rising to prominence as Chairman of the Council of Economic Advisors in June, that so-called 'inflation targetting' is the way forward for the US economy. In this respect, Bernanke's advocacy of a strict inflationary goal puts him at odds with his forerunner who liked to keep the markets guessing. Bernanke's method is similar to that of both the European Central Bank and the Bank of England, both of whom are practitioners of 'inflation targetting'.

The IMF predicts growth of 3.5 per cent for the US economy in 2005 and 3.3 per cent for 2006. Since 2001, when real GDP growth of below 1 per cent was recorded following the slowdown created by the 11 September 2001 attacks, the US economy has recovered to its 2000 GDP growth rate of 3–4 per cent per annum. The rate of inflation remains under 3 per cent and is set to fall to near 2 per cent by 2006, according to the IMF. The unemployment rate, though higher than the early part of the decade, is now beginning to fall.

While net exports in 2004–05 showed a deficit of under 1 per cent, exports of goods and services increased as a percentage in volume. The US economy is dominated by its service industries which generate over half its GDP; financial institutions are the largest single industry contributor. IT, arts and entertainment products, incorporating intellectual property, are an important component of exports. Manufacturing accounts for less than 25 per cent of GDP, with exports consisting of machinery, such as transport, aerospace and defence equipment and electrical goods as well as chemicals and food. An apparent trend, for over two decades, is the rise in health spending as a share of GDP, growing from 10 per cent in 1985 to around 15 per cent in 2003.

The Bush administration has pursued expansionary monetary and fiscal policies, with low interest rates and a series of fiscal stimulus packages, so that expansion has continued steadily. Private domestic demand has not been depressed by energy prices or interest rate increases. Sustained wealth gains and favourable financial conditions have supported household and business spending. Nevertheless net exports have contracted, the external account has deteriorated and inflation is rising due to an increase in production costs. Although some monetary stimuli have been removed it is expected that further tightening is needed to curtail emerging inflationary pressures; long-term interest rates have remained unusually low. The government's higher spending has been offset by faster revenue growth. However, projected deficits remain high and underscore the need to adjust tax and spending levels and contain debt accumulation.

The problem of Iran

Whichever way you turned in 2005, there was a story about Iran's plans, ambitions or intent regarding nuclear technology. At stake was Iran's claim, reiterated by President Ahmadinejad before the UN General Assembly in September, that it had the right to nuclear power. Iran first began its nuclear programme in 1974, froze it in 1979 and resumed operations in 1992. The stated intent has been since 1974 that Iran wants to build nuclear power stations, not nuclear weapons. The US, EU and the International Atomic Energy Agency (IAEA) point out that, as a signatory of the Nuclear non-Proliferation Treaty (NPT), Iran is bound to open its facilities to international inspection. This inspection regime was instituted with the intent of preventing the development of nuclear arsenals by states other than the 'official' nuclear states – The US, Britain, France, China and Russia.

In November 2004, Iran agreed to suspend its uranium enrichment programme and enter into negotiations with the EU over a permanent solution to Iran's nuclear ambitions. This followed months of pressure from the US, both directly and via the IAEA, to refer Iran to the UN Security Council. The US alleged that Iran was trying to manufacture a nuclear bomb, with uranium enrichment being a key stage in the process, and argued that only the Security Council could wave a big enough stick to deter Iran. The EU deal meant that the US had to cool its heels until diplomacy ran its course. The scene was therefore set for both Iran and the EU to deliver a deal in 2005, with the US having suffered a diplomatic setback.

Negotiations were rocky from the start, with an IAEA inspection team claiming that it had only been given partial access to an Iranian nuclear facility at Parchin. In February, Iran rejected an EU offer to give Iran a light-water nuclear reactor in exchange for closing down Iran's efforts to develop a heavy-water reactor. The latter type of reactor is capable of producing plutonium for use in a nuclear bomb. In March, the US, EU and IAEA presented a united front in demanding full 'transparency' from Iran regarding its nuclear programme. Iran-EU talks broke down again in March and definitively in June. In August, the IAEA accused Iran of having conducted illegal experiments with plutonium in 1995 and 1998, when Iran revealed that it had effectively lied in earlier assurances given to the UN body.

Matters came to a head in September, when the IAEA officially paved the way for Iran's nuclear activities to be referred to the UN Security Council. A caveat was that there was no date set for the referral to take place. The key reason for this was that the IAEA felt room should be allowed for a Russian proposal to deal with Iran. The Russians proposed that they enrich uranium of Iran's behalf and keep any nuclear waste generated in the process. Thus Iran would not be in possession of an enrichment process or the materials needed to produce a nuclear bomb. In November, the IAEA publicly agreed to delay any referral to the Security Council until Iran considered Russia's proposal.

Outlook

Politically, 2005 was a very bad year for President Bush. In almost every respect 2006 can only get better. However, Bush remains in considerable difficulty going in to the new year, with allegations of constitutional violations, an abysmal approval rating and the festering sore of the *Plame affair*. A poor performance in the 2006 mid-term elections for the Republican Party would effectively make President Bush into a very lame duck, with a full two years of his second term left to run. On the other hand, a resurgence in Republican Party fortunes may embolden the president and re-energise his conservative base.

On the economic front, 2005 saw solid growth of 3.5 per cent (according to IMF estimates) as well as the exit of Greenspan from his all-powerful policy making role. His replacement at the Fed, Benanke, faces key challenges ahead, one of which is keeping inflation under control. Bernanke is a prominent advocate of inflation targetting and has stated his desire to keep inflation in check by setting an inflationary ceiling for the economy. Whether he will be able to successfully operate such a system as international oil prices continue to rise is another question. The US economy's reliance on highly priced imported oil from geopolitical hotspots throughout the world may continue to have a knock effect for consumers who could see prices on the high street rise owing to an inflation 'domino effect' throughout the economy.

Risk assessment

Politics	Stable
Economy	Stable
Regional stability	Excellent

COUNTRY PROFILE

Historical profile
The first inhabitants of North America included the Pueblo people in New Mexico, the Apache in Texas, the Navajo in Arizona, Colorado and Utah, and the Hopi in Arizona, the Crow in Montana, the Cherokee in North Carolina and Mohawks and Iroquois in New York State.
1565–07 The Spanish, French and British founded settlements across North America.
1619 The first African slaves were brought into North America by the British.
1700s As the eighteenth century progressed, an increasing number of European settlers arrived. British attempts to assert authority over its 13 North American colonies led to conflicts with the French and the indigenous population. In order to recoup losses after winning the conflict the British imposed higher taxes, which led to civil unrest and the first stirrings of an independence movement.
1776 Independence from Britain was declared by the colonies.
1781 Rebel states set up a loose confederation, codified in Articles of Confederation, after defeating the British at the Battle of Yorktown.
1783 The British accepted the loss of their colonies under the Treaty of Paris.
1787 The 'founding fathers' drew up the constitution, which created a federal structure for the United States of America.
1788 The constitution came into effect.
1789 George Washington was elected the first US president.
1800s During the nineteenth century, populations expanded across the plains to the west coast. By 1850, a combination of land purchases, war and diplomacy had created much of the modern-day US.
After 1850, immigrants began arriving from all over the world, mainly attracted by the industrial jobs in the north.

The south remained committed to agriculture and the use of slaves.
1860 When the abolitionist Abraham Lincoln became president, the south seceded from the north and civil war was declared in 1861.
1865 The north won the civil war, but after Lincoln's assassination blacks in the south remained disenfranchised and segregated.
1898 The US's emergence as a world power was demonstrated when Spain lost control of its colonies in Cuba, Guam, the Philippines and Puerto Rico, after being defeated in Cuba by the US.
1914 The US declared its neutrality at the start of the First World War.
1917 The US declared war on Germany after a torpedo attack on the passenger vessel *Lusitania* a year earlier. Over one million US troops had served on the Allied side by the time the war ended in 1918.
1929 The Wall Street crash resulted in a lengthy economic recession referred to as the 'Great Depression'.
1941 After remaining neutral at the outbreak of the Second World War in 1939, the US declared war on the Axis powers following the Japanese air attack on Pearl Harbour.
1944 The US led the Allied liberation of Nazi-occupied Western Europe.
1945 Following the victory in Europe, the US dropped two atomic bombs on the Japanese cities of Hiroshima and Nagasaki, ending the Pacific War.
1947–50s The US's Marshall Plan was instrumental in the rebuilding of post-war Western Europe and Japan, providing financial aid. The Cold War emerged between the capitalist US and Western Europe and the communist Soviet Union and its Eastern European bloc.
1950–53 The US led a UN military force against communist North Korea after it had invaded South Korea. When the Chinese intervened on the side of the North Koreans the war became attritional. A cease-fire was signed in 1953.
1962 Tensions between the Soviet Union and the US reached a climax during the Cuban missile crisis.
1963 John F Kennedy, the youngest-ever US president, was assassinated in Dallas, Texas in November.
1964–73 The US was embroiled in the Vietnam War. The US government provided South Vietnam with military assistance against communist North Vietnam, but was forced to withdraw in 1973 when the war was lost and there was mounting domestic opposition to the high number of casualties.
1974 President Richard Nixon, who was elected in 1969, was forced to resign over the Watergate scandal involving a break-in at Democrat headquarters; tape recordings made in the White House showed he had sanctioned the burglary and subsequent cover-up.
1970s and 1980s was a period of great technological advancement and declining industrialisation when US corporations became worldwide leaders and US brands in computers, fast-food and entertainment became global brands. The collapse of the Soviet Union by 1991 left the US as the world's sole superpower.
1979 Iranian students attacked the US embassy in Tehran and held 63 hostages for 444 days. A failed military rescue mission in 1980 damaged the chances of incumbent Jimmy Carter winning the 1980 presidential election.
1980 Ronald Reagan became president. As a conservative popularist his policies were based on reducing federal services and tax cuts, particularly for high income earners, later dubbed Reagonomics.
1989 US troops invaded Panama to oust General Manuel Noriega from power.
1991 In the first Gulf War, a US-led coalition forced Iraq to withdraw from Kuwait.
1992 The Democratic candidate Bill Clinton defeated the Republican incumbent, George Bush, in the presidential election.
1995 A bomb in Oklahoma killed over 160 people; it was the worst case involving domestic terrorists in US history.
1996 Clinton was re-elected as president.
1999 The US led a NATO military campaign against Yugoslavia in response to Serbian violence towards ethnic Albanians in the Kosovo region.
2000 George W Bush was elected president but only after controversial vote counting was declared valid by Florida's Supreme Court.
2001 On 11 September, two passenger jets were flown into the twin towers of the World Trade Centre in New York, demolishing both towers. A third jet was crashed into the Pentagon in Washington. In all, 3,025 people died in the attacks. President Bush declared a 'war on terrorism'. In October, the US launched military action in Afghanistan against the Taliban and Osama Bin Laden's al Qaeda group, blamed for being behind the terrorist attacks of 11 September.
The giant energy provider Enron declared bankruptcy when massive accountancy frauds were discovered.
2002 Bush declared that if Saddam Hussein could not prove to the UN weapons inspectors that he had disposed of his weapons of mass destruction as stipulated by UN resolutions, the US would conduct a war against Iraq. Troop deployment in Kuwait began at the end of the year. UN weapons inspectors were allowed into Iraq for the first time in four years, evidence they were shown was not sufficient to

United States of America

convince the US that all materials had been destroyed.
WorldCom declared itself bankrupt when it revealed accountancy fraud, it was the biggest US business failure, eclipsing the Enron failure
2003 US-led coalition invaded Iraq in March. On 2 May, President Bush declared that 'major combat operations in Iraq have ended'.
2004 On 29 June, the US and Libya restored diplomatic relations after a break of 24 years. In Iraq, by September, there had been 647 US deaths since the president had declared an end to combat missions in 2003; the total number of dead since the beginning of the war was 1,002. A Senate report declared the US-led war on Iraq was based on 'flawed' information. Institutional failings in intelligence agencies and the government were held to be responsible for the failure to prevent the 11 September 2001 attack. Bush was re-elected president.
2005 On 20 January, George W Bush was sworn in as President for a second term. In November allegations were made against the Bush regime alleging the CIA was running prisons in Eastern Europe where terrorist suspects were being held. There were also allegations of the rendition of suspects to regimes where they could be tortured. The Patriot Act, which President Bush describes as a vital tool in the fight against terrorism, was extended for one month in December. The deal is seen as a compromise as Bush had wanted a permanent extension of the bill. Democrats and some Republican senators have said the law does not provide enough civil liberty safeguards. In December a federal judge ruled that it would be 'unconstitutional to teach Intelligent Design (ID) as an alternative to evolution in a public school science classroom'.

Political structure
Constitution
The constitution of 17 September 1787 came into effect on 4 March 1789. The constitution strictly separates powers between the executive (presidential administration), legislature (Congress – Senate and House of Representatives) and judiciary (Supreme Court).
Form of state
Federal presidential democratic republic
The executive
The president, elected for a maximum of two terms of four years by an electoral college of representatives elected from each state, wields executive power. The president is both the chief of state and head of government.
National legislature
Legislative power is vested in a bicameral Congress consisting of a 435-member House of Representatives, elected for a two-year term, and a 100-member Senate, one-third of whose members are elected every two years.
Legal system
The legal system is based on English common law. There are judicial reviews of legislative acts. The US accepts compulsory International Court of Jurisdiction (ICJ) authority, although only with reservations. The nine justices of the Supreme Court are appointed for life by the president, with confirmation by the Senate.
Last elections
2 November 2004 (presidential and legislative)
Results: House of Representatives: Republican Party 49.9 per cent of the vote (232 seats); Democratic Party 47.4 per cent (202 seats); Libertarian Party 0.9 per cent (no seats); independents (one seat).
Senate: Republican Party 46.7 per cent of the vote (55 seats); Democratic Party 51.0 per cent (44 seats); Libertarian Party 0.9 per cent (no seats); independents (one seat).
Presidential: incumbent George W Bush (Republican Party) won 51 per cent of the vote (carrying 31 states with 286 electoral votes), John Kerry (Democratic Party) 48 per cent (19 states and the District of Columbia, totalling 252 electoral votes), Ralph Nader (independent) 0.3 per cent.
Next elections
2006 (legislative); 2008 (presidential).

Political parties
Ruling party
Republican Party
Main opposition party
Democratic Party

Population
296.47 million (US Census Bureau, 27 Jun 2005)
Ethnic make-up
The US has the fourth-largest population in the world and contains a varied social and ethnic mix.
The US is not following the trend of an ageing population as seen in many OECD countries. All categories of ages show an increase, except the 5–13 years old, which declined by 380,000 in 2003–04. This growth in population indicates a high rate of immigration rather than a fertility rate no greater than 2.0 per cent. Approximately 22 per cent of the population is under 14 years of age. Some 20 per cent of the total population claim British ancestry, 20 per cent German and 18 per cent Irish ancestry.
In January 2003, the Census Bureau announced that Hispanics (Latinos) (13 per cent of the population) had overtaken blacks (12 per cent) as the largest minority group. In July it also reported that the legal Latino population grew by 4.6 million people between 2000–03, accounting for half the nation's total population growth during the period. The Asian population is also growing (around 4 per cent). Native Americans and native Alaskans combined are less than 1 per cent of the population.
Religions
There are some 90 religious organisations in the US with over 50,000 members each. There are approximately 86 million Protestants, 58 million Catholics, six million Jews and over six million members of other faiths. The total number of members of religious groups is estimated to be about 156 million. In the southern United States, the 'bible belt' stretches from California to Florida where the Baptist Church and Evangelism is strong. Numerous protestant sects can be found, each with their own unique outlook.

Education
Under a federal system, each state sets its own educational cycles; each year is a grade, from 1–12. Whichever cycle is adopted it incorporates 12 years. Education is mainly funded at local and state levels with policy set by the local school boards and state education authorities. Some federal funding is available to meet special needs. Schooling is generally compulsory from the age of six (states vary) to 16 years. Pupils at elementary and high schools (up to age 18) generally pay no tuition fees; further education establishments in general charge tuition fees. There is no state assistance for either tuition or living expenses for most university and undergratuate students, although loans are available. Some grant assistance is provided for students from low income and disadvantaged categories and scholarships are available on a competitive and special category basis.
High school graduates who decide to continue their education may enter a technical or vocational institution, a two-year college, or a four-year college or university.
The latest census reports that there are over 32 million elementary school children and over 15 million in high school; combined the projected number is expected to exceed 53 million, a figure not reached since the baby boomers swelled numbers in the early 1960s. The majority of high school students go on to college. Altogether, the system caters for over 72 million individuals in education.
Educational expenditure is typically around 7 per cent of the annual GDP. Elementary and secondary schools spent about 60 per cent of this total, and colleges and universities accounted for the remaining 40 per cent.
Compulsory years: 6 to 16

Enrolment rate: 101 per cent gross primary enrolment; 95.5 per cent gross secondary enrolment, of relevant age groups (including repeaters). (Unicef 2004).
Pupils per teacher: 16 in primary schools.

Health

Total expenditure on health is around 13–14 per cent of GDP, of which government spending is 44–45 per cent. Prepaid plans account for 64 per cent of private spending on health.

Healthcare is largely a private-sector concern. Exceptions include the extensive Medicare programme for the elderly and the lesser Medicaid programme for those on welfare. Some emergency hospital treatment is free of charge for the poor. Health expenditure of 13 per cent of GDP is greater than the Organisation of Economic Co-operation and Development (OECD) average of 8 per cent.

Most people have private health insurance, either as a job benefit or paid for by themselves and is becoming a major financial burden, both for individuals and for the companies who pay for employee health schemes. The premiums for family coverage is over US$9,000 per annum; and for those in worker's health schemes, an employee's share averaged US$2,084, for family cover. The number of Americans without health insurance in 2004 rose for the fourth year in succession, to 45.8 million, some 15.7 per cent of the population, according to the Census Bureau.

The rise in health insurance costs (double digits for three consecutive years from 2000) has left employers with a growing insurance premium, which in turn has led many to pass on these costs directly to employees, or closing down their schemes entirely. This loss has prompted an alliance, which may have political ramifications, as companies and workers align themselves to challenge the power of the 'medical industrial complex' of private insurance companies, the pharmaceutical industry and the large private hospitals.

In May 2004 a report on obesity ranked US citizens the most obese in the developed world, with 31 per cent of adults grossly fat and of the rest, two out of three are merely overweight. Obesity rates have doubled in number since 1980.

HIV prevalence: 0.6 per cent aged 15–49 in 2003 (World Bank)
Life expectancy: 77.4 years (World Bank)
Fertility rate/Maternal mortality rate: 2.0 births per woman (World Bank)
Infant mortality rate: 7.0 per 1,000 live births; 1 per cent of children aged under five are malnourished (World Bank).

Welfare

Income security programmes are in general a mixture of federal and state funding and vary from state to state. The major programmes are unemployment compensation, housing subsidies for low income families and individuals, food stamps, child nutrition, payments to the disabled and family support payments. While states provide some limited form of income security, federal government policy concentrates on encouraging recipients back to work. In addition, the federal government makes social security payments to one in six Americans, either aged or disabled.

Pensions

Medicare trustees, in 2004, reported that the finance for the programme, set up to pay retirees, was deeply underfunded. Retirement payments were made from current revenue and the US$72 billion obligation (inluding the social security pension), to expected numbers of retirees, will outstrip assets and budgets by 2014, leaving the government to either make up the shortfall with tax increases or cut the pension benefits.

A trend by private companies to convert defined benefit and final salary schemes into defined contribution schemes (with uncertain benefits) has increased, with 75 per cent conversion in two decades, and US underfunding of defined benefit schemes estimated at US$278.6 billion. One of the largest providers of a defined benefit pension – United Airlines – has proposed transferring assets to the Pensions Benefit Guaranty Corporation (PBGC), a federal insurer, and divesting itself of a costly legacy. Worry has been expressed that if this and other businesses do likewise it could bankrupt the PBGC and require a government bail out costing tens of billions of dollars.

Main cities

Washington (capital, estimated population 563,384 in 2004), New York (8.1 million), Los Angeles (3.8 million), Chicago (2.9 million), Houston (2.0 million), Philadelphia (1.5 million), Phoenix (1.4 million), San Diego (1.3 million), San Antonio (1.2 million), Dallas (1.2 million), Detroit (911,402), San José (898,349), Indianapolis (783,438), Jacksonville (773,781), San Francisco (751,682), Columbus (728,432), Louisville (699,017), Austin (672,011), Memphis (645,978), Baltimore (628,670), Milwaukee (586,941), Fort Worth (585,122), Charlotte (584,658), El Paso (584,113), Boston (581,616), Seattle (569,101), Denver (557,478), Nashville (544,765), Portland (538,544), Oklahoma City (523,303), Las Vegas (517,017), Tucson (507,658).

Languages spoken

English is the national language, spoken by approximately 85 per cent of the population. Spanish is common in areas of Hispanic concentration (parts of Florida, Texas, California, New Mexico, Arizona and New York City).

Official language/s

A bill to recognise English as the official language was introduced in the House of Representatives in February 2003. Spanish is regarded as the unofficial second national language.

Media

The US Constitution guarantees both the press and broadcasters freedom of speech, subject to the laws of libel and slander; even in the latter cases, there are well established public interest defences to these charges. Broadcasters are compelled to be fair in their coverage of political events such as election campaigns and (at least in theory) their licence could be at risk in event of excessive bias in their reporting.

Press

There is no official news agency. The US Information Service, a government controlled agency, is responsible for dissemination of information about the US, especially through its Voice of America radio network, which broadcasts in over 40 languages to all parts of the world.

Dailies: In total, there are some 1,600 daily newspapers, approximately 1,000 evening papers and 600 morning papers, mostly serving a city, state or region. Most newspapers and magazines are published in English. There are also newspapers serving ethnic communities published in other languages. The main national dailies include *USA Today*, *New York Times*, *Washington Post*, *Los Angeles Times*, *Christian Science Monitor*, *Nando Times*, *Washington Times*, distributed nationally in main centres. Other major publications include, the *Philadelphia Enquirer*, *Boston Globe*, *Chicago Sun-Times*, *San Francisco Chronicle*, *Detroit Free Press* and *Chicago Tribune*.

Weeklies: There are over 7,600 weekly papers and 550 semi-weekly papers. National and widely read weeklies include *Time* and *Newsweek*.

Business: The *Wall Street Journal*, a financial and business daily, is published in four regional editions. The major business magazines are *Business Week*, *Forbes* and *Fortune*. Others business news is carried by *Financial Times*, *Investor's Business Daily* and *Washington Business Journal*.

Broadcasting

Radio: CBS, NBC and ABC all have radio networks. Other major radio networks include Keystone Broadcasting, Mutual

United States of America

Broadcasting, Sheridan Broadcasting and National Public Radio (public service network).There are more than 5,000 private radio stations. Virtually all US households have a radio.

Television: There are four major commercial TV broadcasting networks, which compete fiercely with each other for viewers and advertising revenue: Columbia Broadcasting System (CBS), National Broadcasting Corporation (NBC), Capital Cities/ABC (ABC) and Fox. There is also a national public broadcasting network (PBS) which is supported by donations from the government and 'pledges' from viewers.

One phenomenon which has caused a steep erosion in viewer numbers for the traditional broadcast stations is the growth of cable-based pay-TV services such as Turner Broadcasting (CNN, TNT and others). In the large cities, a cable viewer might have 50 or more channels to choose from, allowing advertisers to target their audience.

In addition to the national networks and their affiliates, there are many small networks and independent TV and radio stations, often serving one locality. Most broadcasting is in English, but there are also TV and radio stations serving local ethnic communities in their own languages. The Spanish-speaking community is relatively well served in Florida, California and New York City.

Virtually all US households have a television set and 60 per cent have cable TV. There are well over 1,000 TV stations in the overwhelmingly commercial broadcasting system.

Economy

The IMF predicts growth of 3.5 per cent for the US economy in 2005 and 3.3 per cent for 2006. Since 2001, when real GDP growth of below 1 per cent was recorded following the slowdown created by the 11 September 2001 attacks, the US economy has recovered to its 2000 GDP growth rate of ~4 per cent GDP per annum. The rate of inflation remains under 3 per cent and is set to fall to near 2 per cent by 2006, according to the IMF. The unemployment rate, though higher than the early part of the decade, is now beginning to fall.

While net exports in 2004–05 showed a deficit of under 1 per cent, exports of goods and services increased as a percentage in volume. The US economy is dominated by its service industries which generate over half its GDP; financial institutions are the largest single industry contributor. IT, arts and entertainment products, incorporating intellectual property, are an important component of exports. Manufacturing accounts for less than 25 per cent of GDP, with exports consisting of machinery, such as transport, aerospace and defence equipment and electrical goods as well as chemicals and food. An apparent trend, for over two decades, is the rise in health spending as a share of GDP, growing from 10 per cent in 1985 to around 15 per cent in 2003. The Bush administration has pursued expansionary monetary and fiscal policies, with low interest rates and a series of fiscal stimulus packages, so that expansion has continued steadily. Private domestic demand has not been depressed by energy prices or interest rate increases. Sustained wealth gains and favourable financial conditions have supported household and business spending. Nevertheless net exports have contracted, the external account has deteriorated and inflation is rising due to an increase in production costs.

Although some monetary stimuli have been removed it is expected that further tightening is needed to curtail emerging inflationary pressures; long-term interest rates have remained unusually low.

The government's higher spending has been offset by faster revenue growth. However, projected deficits remain high and underscore the need to adjust tax and spending levels and contain debt accumulation.

Labour productivity and employment rates have remained high since the mid-1990s. The OECD 2005 *Economic Policy Reforms* makes a number of employment related recommendations including: restraining health costs and reforming 'Medicare' to focus on reducing the unit cost per member and curtailing over-consumption, improving educational achievement in primary and secondary levels by monitoring current schemes and preparing to fund more if necessary, reducing agricultural support and rolling back the extra support given to farmers in the last few yearsand reversing the recent move away from market based outcomes.

External trade

Having been the world's greatest creditor during the early 1980s, the United States has now accumulated a large current account deficit.

Since the early 1990s, the US has offset much of its merchandise trade deficit with an increase in its surplus on services – financial, tourism, transport. That means that while the merchandise trade deficit is large (and growing), the overall balance of payments deficit is much lower. A large external deficit and increases of 20 per cent a year in foreign direct investment led Congress to adopt the 1988 Trade Act, which allowed retaliatory action against barriers to US imports and the blocking of foreign takeovers where these endangered national security.

President Bush wishes to create a Middle East Free Trade Area by 2013. To this end, the US has free trade agreements with Israel and Jordan and in 2004, concluded an agreement with Morocco.

Imports

Principal imports are industrial supplies (32.9 per cent of total), agricultural products, capital goods, computers, telecommunications equipment, vehicles and parts, office machines, electric power machinery, consumer goods.

Main sources: Canada (17.1 per cent total, 2004), China (13.7 per cent), Mexico (10.4 per cent), Japan (8.8 per cent), Germany (5.2 per cent)

Exports

The US is the top trading nation worldwide, nevertheless as a member of the North American Free Trade Association (Nafta), it exports the majority of its goods and services to Canada and Mexico. Main exports are telecommunications and computers equipment (49 per cent of total), agricultural products, industrial supplies, capital goods – transistors, aircraft, vehicles and parts, consumer goods, and medicines.

Main destinations: Canada (23 per cent total, 2004), Mexico (13.6 per cent), Japan (6.7 per cent), UK (4.4 per cent), China (4.3 per cent)

Agriculture

Farming

Agriculture now accounts for just 2 per cent of total GDP and employs approximately 3 per cent of the country's workforce. However, despite its relatively small contribution to total US GDP, the agricultural sector continues to account for half of the world's corn production and over 20 per cent of world grain output. The US is the world's largest agricultural exporter and exports account for about 25 per cent of farmers' receipts. Capital-intensive farming techniques produce dairy produce, potatoes, fruit, vegetables and poultry for urban markets in the north-eastern states; wheat, barley, maize, oats, soya beans, fodder crops, pigs and cattle in the mid-west and central plains; cotton, tobacco, peanuts, citrus fruits, rice and sugar cane in the south; cattle and sheep in the central and western states; apples, berries and nuts in the Pacific north-west; and vines, apples, citrus fruits, peaches, tomatoes, olives, cotton and rice in California.

The US and Canada have long (since 2003) been at odds over the import of live cattle. One case of bovine spongiform encephalopathy (BSE) was detected in a Canadian cattle herd and a US ban was imposed. Just as the ban was about to be lifted in 2005 another two cases were reported and the ban was reinstated. There had been plans for two million head of cattle to be imported from Canada and the ban has hit US meat processors in particular. Meanwhile in 2005 a US Senate decided not to designate Canada as an area of 'minimal risk' from BSE, and R-Calf, a Montana cattle association, was successful in having a temporary injunction blocking any US government move to reopen the border to live cattle imports. The dispute is part of a larger problem, with US beef exports banned from important markets in Asia, US local interests believe maintaining the ban will keep domestic wholesale prices high.

The estimated crop production for 2004 included: 389,067,930 tonnes (t) cereals in total, 58,737,800t wheat, 299,917,120t maize, 20,680,770t potatoes, 10,469,730t rice, 26,320,150t sugar cane, 27,175,630t sugar beets, 85,483,904t soya beans, 1,567,750t pulses, 11,554,970t sorghum, 21,413,960t roots and tubers, 14,907,660t citrus fruit, 4,571,440t apples, 5,418,160t grapes, 12,766,000t tomatoes, 17,927,919t oilcrops, 398,810t tobacco, 12,539,350t seed cotton, 5,062,240t cotton lint, 1,326,410t treenuts, 29,912,640t fruit in total, 39,185,160t vegetables in total. Livestock production included: 38,890,500t meat in total, 11,261,000t beef, 9,312,000t pig meat, 90,00t sheep and goat meat, 18,007,500t poultry, 5,288,000t eggs, 77,470,000t milk, 82,000t honey, 1,045,557t cattle hides, 8,718t sheepskins, 18,000t greasy wool.

Fishing
The fishing industry is well established in the United States and the sector is highly developed on both the Pacific and Atlantic coasts.
Total seafood exports typically amount to over US$3 billion, mainly comprising ground fish (38 per cent), salmon (18 per cent), herring, lobster, shrimps, squid and crab. The top US export markets include Japan (37 per cent), Canada (21 per cent) and the EU (18 per cent). Shrimps account for approximately 36 per cent of total fish and seafood imports.

Forestry
One third of the total land area- 225.9 million hectares (ha)- of the Unites States is covered in forested land. Forests and other wooded areas are mainly concentrated in the east and west of the central plain.
The major part of the forest is classed as semi-natural, with less than a tenth remaining undisturbed, located mainly in Alaska and the west. About nine-tenths of the forest is available for wood supply.

The government owns nearly two fifths of forest and other wooded land, while the remainder is shared among private individuals and institutions, forest industries and some by indigenous peoples.
Forestry is widespread and about half domestic timber needs are met by Oregon and Washington states, with the south-east producing increasing quantities of softwood for pulp. About 30 per cent of global industrial roundwood comes from the US. The US produces and consumes large quantities of sawn timber, wood-based panels and paper. It is also the largest importer and the second-largest exporter, of forest products.
Exports of forest material in 2004 amounted to US$15.7 billion, while imports amounted US$31.3 billion. Production in 2004 included: 458,310,187 cubic metres (cum) roundwood, 414,702,008cum industrial roundwood, 87,436,000cum sawnwood, 234,673,008cum sawlogs and veneers, 171,024,000cum pulpwood, 44,262,134cum wood-based panels, 43,608,179cum wood fuel, 930,300t charcoal.

Industry and manufacturing
The industrial sector remains a relatively significant contributor to the US economy. The sector employs over 20 per cent of the total workforce and contributes approximately 22 per cent to total GDP. The manufacturing sector has declined in significance over recent years as the services sectors have expanded.
There has been a shift in the manufacturing sector away from 'smokestack' industries, such as cars, primary metals and heavy machinery, towards high-technology industries, such as aerospace, communications equipment, electronic components and computers. Food, printing and publishing and textiles and clothing are also important.

Tourism
The tourism industry expanded over 2005 and now accounts for over 10 per cent of total US GDP. Approximately 11.9 per cent of the country's total employment is accounted for by the sector, an increase on the 2004 percentage.
Florida, California and New York are the top three destinations for international travellers to the US and their spending exceeds US$30 billion in these states alone. Of all visitors flying to the US, about 40 per cent arrive through either Miami International, Los Angeles or New York JFK. The Trade Industry Association of America (TIA) has lobbied the US government to minimise the disruption stricter security measures (put in place as a result of the 9/11attacks) have on international tourists to America.

Despite growth in the tourism industry overall, visitor numbers have declined, from 50,945,000 in 2000 to 414,838,000 in 2004. The top international destination for US citizens in 2004 was Italy, with Alaska being the top domestic destination.

Environment
The US is not a signatory to the Kyoto Protocol.

Mining
The mining sector contributes approximately 4 per cent to total US GDP. The sector also employs approximately 4 per cent of the total US workforce.
While there are economically exploitable reserves of virtually every mineral within the US, these are insufficient to meet the needs of the economy in almost all circumstances. The country is 100 per cent dependent on imports for its consumption of bauxite, graphite and manganese among others. Mineral resources include ores of iron, copper (about 13 per cent of worldwide production), lead (17 per cent of worldwide production), gold (15 per cent), silver (12 per cent) and nickel.
The US accounts for approximately 17 per cent of worldwide aluminium production, totalling 3.8 million tonnes.

Hydrocarbons
Total proven oil reserves currently stand at 21.4 billion barrels. This figure equates to the eleventh largest proven reserves in the world with 80 per cent of proven reserves located in just four states: Texas, Louisiana, Alaska and California. Despite large proven reserves, total reserves have actually fallen by approximately 17 per cent since 1990.
Oil production amounts to 7.6 million barrels per day (bpd), the vast majority of which was crude oil (5.4 million bpd). US oil production has fallen sharply since the mid-1980s due to a decline in oil prices. In the period 2000–02, oil production was at a 50-year low. However, production has increased as more deepwater oil wells in the Gulf of Mexico and onshore oil fields in Alaska have come on-stream. Oil production suffered considerably following Hurricane Katrina and other severe storms in the Gulf of Mexico during the summer and autumn months of 2005. Several refineries as well as oil platforms were damaged.
The US has estimated proven natural gas reserves of 5.29 trillion cubic metres. Gas production is estimated at 542.9 billion cubic metres while consumption is 646.7 billion cubic metres. Net imports amount to approximately 99 billion cubic metres. The vast majority of natural gas imports come from Canada, approximately 94 per cent of total gas imports.

United States of America

US coal reserves account for around a quarter of the world's total reserves; estimated at 246 billion tonnes. The US produces 567.2 million tonnes of oil equivalent, (as at end 2004). The states with the largest coal production include Wyoming, West Virginia and Kentucky. More than 90 per cent of US coal output is consumed by the electricity sector. In a typical year for the US, the country imports somewhere in the region of 36 million tonnes of coal. There is a trend towards consumption of coal with lower sulphur content in order to meet environmental targets for sulphur dioxide emissions.

Energy
Total electricity generation was 3,953 billion KW (as at end 2004).
Coal-fired power stations account for approximately 50 per cent of generation, nuclear 21 per cent, gas 16 per cent, hydroelectricity 7 per cent, oil 2 per cent and other sources 1 per cent.
US power demand is increasing rapidly, with the government forecasting 1.8 per cent average annual growth in electricity sales between 2000–20. This increase will require a significant addition in generating capacity and the government forecasts that 1,300 new power plants will be needed between 2002 and 2020.
Privately owned local monopolies regulated by state public utility commissions account for 80 per cent of electricity sales. Coal inputs for electricity generation have risen and are expected to continue to grow, as are those of natural gas.

Financial markets
Stock exchange
The New York Stock Exchange (NYSE), the largest equities marketplace in the world, is home to some 2,800 companies valued at about US$15 trillion in market capitalisation. The Chicago Board of Trade is the largest of 11 commodity and financial futures exchanges. The National Association of Securities Dealers Automated Quotation System (Nasdaq) is a computer-based over-the-counter market in securities.

Banking and insurance
The banking and financial services industry in the US is noted for its complicated regulations, which are overseen by numerous federal and state authorities with overlapping jurisdictions.
Regulatory agencies include the Federal Reserve, the Federal Deposit Insurance Corp (FDIC), the Securities and Exchange Commission, the Comptroller of the Currency, the Department of Justice and state bank departments. Depositors in banks or savings and loan associations which are members of the FDIC or Federal Savings and Loan Insurance Corporation have their deposits guaranteed to a limit of US$100,000 by the government's system of deposit insurance.
Central bank
Federal Reserve System

Time
Eastern Standard Time = GMT minus five hours
Central Standard Time = GMT minus six hours
Mountain Standard Time = GMT minus seven hours
Pacific Standard Time = GMT minus eight hours (minus seven hours April to October)

Geography
The US is about half the size of Russia and covers a total area of about nine million square km. It stretches from the North Atlantic Ocean to the North Pacific Ocean. The US has borders with Canada (8,893km) (including 2,477km Alaska/Canada), Cuba 29km (US Naval Base at Guantanamo Bay) and Mexico (3,326km).
The western part of the country is dominated by the two major mountain ranges, the Rockies and Sierras. In the eastern US, the lower Appalachian and Allegheny mountains provide the western boundary to the coastal plain. The lowest point is Death Valley, -86 metres; the highest point is Mount McKinley, 6,194 metres. The central part of the country, the mid-west, is a vast plain, much of it flat and featureless. This is the breadbasket of the US.
Alaska has mountains and broad river valleys. Hawaii is rugged and volcanic.

Climate
The size of the land area and the natural mountain barriers give a wide range of climates. It is tropical in Hawaii and Florida, arctic in Alaska, semi-arid in the great plains west of the Mississippi River and arid in the Great Basin of the south-west. California (especially the south) has a Mediterranean-style climate with mild winters and hot summers. The south and Gulf of Mexico areas have a semi-tropical climate. The east coast and the mid-west are invariably very cold in winter and very hot in summer. Snow can be heavy at times, but most cities are equipped for swift snow removal from major streets and the transportation system can cope fairly well in poor weather. Most buildings, cars and public transport are well heated or air-conditioned, according to the season.

Dress codes
There are no overriding dress codes. In the Wall Street financial district of New York and other financial centres, business suits are *de rigueur*, while on the west coast, senior executives might wear anything from suits or sports jackets and trousers to jeans and T-shirts. The more normal business attire would be a business suit, shirt and tie. Despite the reputation US businessmen have for flashy dressing, formal colours are more acceptable, with dark suits, dark socks and sombre ties being the most acceptable form.

Entry requirements
Passports
Required by all. Canadians need only proof of citizenship. Following the 11 September terrorist attacks, security at US airports has been stepped up and passengers should expect delays during flight check-in.
The US has a rolling programme of introducing biometric scanning technology to enhance security measures screening visitors into and out of the US. From October 2005, only machine readable passports (MRP), will be acceptable from citizens of visa-free nations.
Visa
A reciprocal visa-waiver programme allows citizens of the EU, Australasia, Japan (with biometric, machine readable passports (MRP)) entry without a visa if they have a return/onward ticket. The 'Visa Waiver Program' (VWP), allows business and tourist visits up to 90 days. Further information can be found at http://travel.state.gov and follow link to 'visas for foreign citizens'.
From October 2005 all citizens of visa-free countries who do not have a MRP must apply for a visa. All other visitors must apply for a visa.
For information of specific business visas and extended stays visit: www.usvisas.gov/business_temp.html.
Currency advice/regulations
Amounts of US$10,000 or more in currency or other negotiable form should be declared.

Health (for visitors)
Mandatory precautions
No vaccination certificates are required, unless visitor has been in infected areas within the previous six months.
Advisable precautions
There are no major health hazards for visitors, and no inoculations or vaccinations are necessary. However, visitors from countries where cholera or yellow fever are rife will require vaccination certificates.
As health costs can be extremely high in the US, it is strongly suggested that travellers take out an adequate travel insurance policy before they leave home.

Hotels
Major hotels have toll-free telephone numbers (with an 800 area code) for

Nations of the World: A Political, Economic and Business Handbook

reservations. Unless a deposit has been paid, a hotel room will often not be held after 1700/1800, even when the hotel is notified of late arrival. Check-out times vary from 1000–1300 and short extensions can be arranged. Visitors may be charged for overstaying check-out time without making arrangements. Most good hotels have restaurant facilities, bars, free parking and swimming pools. Many hotels provide courtesy transport or an airport bus service.

Credit cards
Considerable use is made of credit cards, and it is advisable to carry an internationally recognised card such as American Express, Mastercard or Visa. A credit card is essential for car hire.

Public holidays
Fixed dates
1 Jan (New Year's Day), 14 Jun (Flag Day), 4 Jul (Independence Day), 11 Nov (Veterans' Day), 25 Dec (Christmas Day). Any holiday falling on a Sunday is taken on the next day; any holiday on a Saturday is taken on the day before.
Variable dates
Martin Luther King's Birthday (third Mon in Jan), Washington's Birthday (third Mon in Feb), Memorial Day (last Mon in May), Labour Day (first Mon in Sep), Columbus Day (second Mon in Oct), Thanksgiving Day (fourth Thu in Nov).
Statutory and public holidays are fixed by state legislation and vary considerably between states.

Working hours
Most offices remain closed on the Friday following Thanksgiving. Working hours vary considerably depending on the industry.
Banking
0900–1500 (Mon-Fri).
Business
0900–1700 (Mon-Fri).
Government
0830–1730 (Mon-Fri).
Shops
0930–1800 (Mon-Fri); 1200–1700 (Sun).

Telecommunications
Telephone/fax
Ringing tone lasts two seconds, followed by a four-second silence; number unobtainable is indicated by a recorded message; number engaged is indicated by rapid pips.
Postal services
The US has a reliable and extensive postal service, although surface mail is often slower than in Europe.
Courier services
The US is home to some of the world's leading express courier services with excellent global distribution networks.

Electricity supply
110–120V AC, 60 cycles single phase, with flat two-point plug fittings and screw-type light sockets. It is advisable to purchase any adapters which may be required before travelling to the US.

Weights and measures
Units of measurement used in the US are in general the same as the imperial system, but the old winchester bushel and wine gallon are still in use. Wine gallon = 0.83268 Imperial gallon; bushel = 0.969 Imperial bushel; 1 pint = 16 fl oz. A short hundredweight contains 100lb and a short ton contains 2,000lb. Conversion to metric system is taking place very slowly and on a voluntary basis, with the US Metric Board co-ordinating the process.

Social customs/useful tips
One seemingly universal taboo, especially in professional circles, is smoking. Many corporations forbid their employees to smoke at work, except perhaps in designated smoking areas. If you must smoke, be careful to ask permission from your hosts first and do not be offended if they refuse your request.
People are likely to use first names in discussions with you. They are also likely to refer to someone else by their surname only. Neither of these usages is considered impolite.
The main cultural role model in the US is that of the pioneer, the isolated man or woman battling against the odds, the story of someone rising from a deprived background to become rich and/or famous. This has led to an admiration for hard work, free enterprise and determination. Gun ownership by civilians is considered, by many, to be a part of American heritage.

Security
The US has a reputation for crime and violence. New York, Baltimore, Chicago, Detroit, Washington and Los Angeles have a high rate of robbery. Washington, Detroit, Baltimore, Dallas, Houston, Philadelphia, Atlanta and Los Angeles have high murder rates.
However, much of the trouble is concentrated in parts of each city and avoiding these neighbourhoods will considerably reduce any risk. Elementary precautions should prevent visitors having too much trouble. Avoid walking in deserted streets, and try to walk on the street-side rather than next to buildings. Always be aware of the kind of neighbourhood it is. At night, except in lively and well-lit areas, call a cab to collect you rather than walking to look for a cab.
Although the risk of being mugged is often exaggerated (and crime figures have been falling since the mid-1990s), it is recommended not to resist a robbery attempt. As a precaution, have two wallets, one with your credit cards, identification and some cash, the other with say US$20 cash in it to hand over if you are challenged. Keep your valuables (especially expensive jewellery) out of sight.

Getting there
Air
International airport/s: The US is accessible by air from all continents and a vast number of countries. Some of the most important international airports are in New York (John F. Kennedy International Airport, Newark), Boston (Logan Airport), Chicago (O'Hare), Dallas (Fort William International), Houston, Los Angeles, San Francisco, Atlanta (Hartfield Internationa), Denver (Stapleton International), Detroit (Metro Wayne) Washington DC, Baltimore and St Louis.
Airport tax: Departure taxes are included in the price of a ticket, though the local airport departure tax may not have been included if your ticket was purchased outside the US.
There is a passenger facility charge of US$3 in Baltimore Washington International, Wayne County in Detroit, International in Miami, Sky Harbor International in Phoenix, Portland International in Pittsburgh and Lambert-St Louis International in St Louis.
Surface
Road: The US has land borders with Mexico in the south and Canada in the north and there are plenty of efficient overland border crossings between the US and those countries. Border crossings are strictly controlled, especially from the south.
Rail: There are rail services between the US, Canada and Mexico.
Water: The US has numerous sea and inland water ports and is well served by the international shipping lines.

Getting about
National transport
National transport is variable depending upon city. However, the US is generally perceived to have one of the most advanced transportation structures in the world, including metro systems in most major cities and sufficient bus networks. Transportation by ferries and helicopters is also widely available.
Air: A highly developed network of airline services connects most towns of importance. Fare systems have been deregulated, leading to sharp competition (and some insolvencies). Major savings can be made by shopping with care.
Road: In most parts of the US the car is the best way of getting around. The country is well-served by many interstate freeways that connect the entire country.

United States of America

During the winter even the interstates can be closed or slowed by snow. There is an extensive secondary road system.

Buses: There is a wide network of air-conditioned long-distance buses linking all major cities, but smaller cities and rural areas are generally not well served by public transport. Greyhound is the main bus system in the US and plays an important transportation role in most parts of the country.

Rail: Around 245,000km of grade one railroad links approximately 500 stations. Most long-distance trains are air-conditioned and equipped with dining cars, bar cars and sleeping accommodation. Amtrak is generally comfortable and runs a popular shuttle service between New York and Washington; the New York to Boston route is also well travelled. Much of the national network is in need of new equipment, however, and in terms of time and cost, rail travel compares poorly to air travel on most inter-city routes.

City transport

Public transport is usually good, especially in New York where the subway is cheap and quick. Buses are an adequate but much slower alternative in most cities. At night, taxis are the safer option for travel. Fares vary in different cities. Public transport is woefully inadequate in Los Angeles and the cable cars of San Francisco are a special treat. Commuter rail services throughout the US are usually safe and reliable.

Most cities have severe parking problems in downtown areas and it is more convenient to travel by public transport or taxi.

Taxis: It is wise to confirm the approximate cost when entering a cab.

In Los Angeles, taxis do not cruise streets looking for passengers, but there are taxi stands at airports, major hotels, and train and bus terminals.

Taxi fares in Washington DC are based on the unmetered zone system with a basic fare and each zone charged extra; drivers may stop and pick up several passengers following the same general route. Enquire in advance how many zones you will ride.

Buses, trams & metro: There are bus services in all main cities. Many hotels have courtesy bus services to and from airports. In New York City, buses are slower than the subway, and especially crowded during rush hours, but the routes are more varied and the stops more frequent, usually every two blocks.

The subway in New York City is the fastest way to get around. Trains are identified by number or letter which are displayed on the front and sides of the cars. Some are local and some express so be sure the train you board stops where you need to get off. If travelling after 2200, wait for the train in the areas marked for off-peak hours.

A subway connects downtown Chicago and O'Hare International Airport with fast, cheap and frequent services. Pick up the subway at Terminal 2. From the city, catch the Dearborn Street subway to the airport. Union Station is the transportation hub in Washington DC. Connections between Metrorail and Metrobus are available at all Metrorail stations.

Car hire

Car hire is widely available in major cities. A valid overseas or international driving licence and an international credit card are required. Other methods of payment may not be accepted. Driving is on the right-hand side of the road. States are free to set their own speed limits: Montana has no day-time limit but at nigth the limit is 55mph; 75mph in Kansas, Nevada and Wyoming; 70mph in California, Missouri, Oklahoma, South Dakota and Texas. For further information on state highways see www.us-highways.com with links to other relevant sites.

BUSINESS DIRECTORY

The addresses listed below are a selection only. While World of Information makes every endeavour to check these addresses, we cannot guarantee that changes have not been made, especially to telephone numbers and area codes. We would welcome any corrections.

Telephone area codes

The international direct dialling code (IDD) for the United States of America is +1, followed by area code and subscriber's number:

Alaska	907	New Orleans	504
Albuquerque	505	New York	718
Atlanta	404	NY - Manhattan	212
Austin	512	Newark	201
Boston	617	Montana	406
Chicago	312	Oklahoma City	405
Denver	303	Philadelphia	215
Des Moines	515	Phoenix	602
Detroit	313	Pittsburgh	412
Hawaii	808	Portland	503
Houston	713	Sacramento	916
Kansas City	816	St Louis	314
Indianapolis	317	St Paul	612
Las Vegas	702	Salt Lake City	801
Los Angeles	213	San Francisco	415
Louisville	502	Seattle	206
Memphis	901	Washington DC	202
Miami	305	Wichita	316

Useful telephone numbers

Emergency services: 911

Chambers of Commerce

British-American Business Council, 52 Vanderbilt Avenue, 20th Floor, New York NY 10017 (tel: 661-5660; fax: 661-1886; e-mail: info@babc.org).

United States Chamber of Commerce, 1615 H Street, NW, Washington DC 20062 (tel: 659-6000; e-mail: intl@uschambers.com).

Banking

Bank of America, 555 California Street, San Francisco, California, 94104 (tel: 415-622-3456; fax: 510-675-8170).

Bankers Trust, 280 Park Avenue, New York, New York, 10017 (tel: 212-250-2500; fax: 212-250-4029).

Chase Manhattan, 1 Chase Manhattan Plaza, New York, New York, 10081 (tel: 212-552-2222).

Chemical Bank, 270 Park Avenue, New York, New York, 10017 (tel: 212-270-6000; fax: 212-682-3761).

Citibank, 399 Park Avenue, New York, New York, 10043 (tel: 212-559-1000; fax: 212-223-2681).

First National Bank of Chicago, 1 First National Plaza, Chicago, Illinois, 60670 (tel: 312-732-4000; fax: 312-732-5965).

Inter-American Development Bank, 1300 New York Avenue NW, Washington DC 20577 (tel: 202-623-3900; fax: 202-623-2360).

Morgan Guaranty Trust, 60 Wall Street, New York, New York, 10260 (tel: 212-483-2323; fax: 212-233-2623).

Nations Bank, 100 North Tryon Street, Charlotte, North Carolina, 28255 (tel: 704-386-5000; 704-386-0645).

Central bank

Federal Reserve System, 20th Street and Constitution Avenue, NW, Washington DC 20551 (tel: 452-3000; fax: 452-3819).

Travel information

United States Travel and Tourism Administration, United States Department of Commerce, Washington DC 20230 (tel: 377-2000).

Ministries

Bureau of Competition, Federal Trade Commission, 6th State and Pennsylvania Avenue, NW, Washington DC 20530.

Department of Agriculture, 14th street and Independence Avenue, SW, Washington DC 20250 (tel: 720-8732).

Department of Commerce, 14th Street and Constitution Avenue, NW, Washington DC 20230 (tel: 377-2000; fax: 377-5270).

Nations of the World: A Political, Economic and Business Handbook

Department of Defence, The Pentagon, Washington DC 20301 (tel: 545-6700).

Department of Energy, 1000 Independence Avenue, SW, Washington DC 20585 (tel: 586-5000).

Department of Homeland Security, 3801 Nebraska Avenue, NW, Washington DC 20528 (fax: 282-8404).

Department of Transportation, 400 7th Street, SW, Washington DC 20570 (tel: 366-4000).

Environmental Protection Agency, 401 M Street, SW, Washington DC 20460 (tel: 382-4700; fax: 382-7886).

Federal Trade Commission, 6th Street and Pennsylvania Avenue, NW, Washington DC 20530 (tel: 326-2100).

United States and Foreign Commercial Service Office, Department of Commerce, 14th Street and Constitution Avenue, NW, Washington DC 20230.

United States Information Agency, 301 Fourth Street, SW, Washington DC 20547 (tel: 485-8752).

Other useful addresses

British Embassy, 3100 Massachusetts Avenue, NW, Washington DC 20008 (tel: 462-1340; fax: 898-4255, 898-4225, 898-4654).

Consumer Product Safety Commission, 5401 Westbard Avenue, Bethseda, Maryland 20207.

Council of Economic Advisers, Old Executive Office Bldg, 17th St and Pennsylvania Ave, NW, Washington, DC 20500-0001 (tel: 395-5042).

New York Stock Exchange, 11 Wall Street, New York, NY 10005 (tel: 656-3000; fax: 656-2294).

Office of Science and Technology Policy, Old Executive Office Building, Washington DC 20506 (tel: 456-7116).

Office of the United States Trade Representative, 600 17th Street, Washington DC 20506 (tel: 395-3204; fax: 395-3911).

Securities and Exchange Commission, 450 5th Street, NW, Washington DC 20549 (tel: 272-2650; fax: 272-7050).

Internet sites

Alamo Rent A Car: http://www.freeways.com

American Airlines: http://www.amrcorp.com/aa_home/aa_home.ht

American Chamber of Commerce: http://www.amcham.com

American Stock Exchange: http://www.amex.com

Big Book (information on 16m businesses):http://www.bigbook.com

Big yellow pages (business and residential information):http://www.bigyellow.com

Continental Airlines: http://www.flycontinental.com.

Delta Airlines: http://www.com-stock.com/dave/delta.htm

Export and Trade Information: http://www.stat.usa.gov

Federal Agencies: http:www.fedworld.gov

Lookup USA (locate addresses and telephone numbers of US businesses): http://abii.com

Northwest Airlines: http://www.winternet.com/~tela/nwa-info.html

Southwest Airlines: http://www.iflyswa.com

Trade US: http://www.tradeUS.com

United Airlines: http://www.ual.com

US Bureau of Census: www.census.gov

US Department of Commerce: http://www.commerce.gov/

US Government gateway site: http://firstgov.gov/

US Office of Insular affairs: http://www.doi.gov/oia

US International Trade Administration: www.ita.doc.gov/ita_home

US Virgin Islands

COUNTRY PROFILE

Historical profile
1493 The islands were first sighted by Columbus.
1494–1670 The indigenous Carib and Arawak Indian population endured various waves of European invasions and settlement, including African slaves who were used on sugar cane plantations.
1670 The islands of St John and St Thomas were colonised by Denmark.
1733 Denmark purchased St Croix from France.
1917 Denmark sold he islands to the US for US$25 million.
1927 US citizenship was granted to the islands' population.
1936 Universal suffrage was provided for by the Organic Act of the Virgin Islands.
1954 An elected 15-member Senate was created.
1970 A governor was elected for the first time, following the 1968 Elective Governor Act.
1973 The US Virgin Islands elected a non-voting delegate to the US House of Representatives for the first time.
1989 Hurricane Hugo caused a total disruption of the power system
1995 Damage to the power system was incurred when Hurricane Marilyn hit the islands.
1998 Governor Charles W Turnbull was elected. There was less damage from Hurricane George, due to the reconstruction of buildings after the previous hurricanes, to withstand a Category 2 storm.
2002 Charles Turnbull was re-elected governor and the Democrats won a majority in the parliamentary election.

Political structure
Constitution
The islands are under full US jurisdiction. One non-voting member is elected to the US House of Representatives.
Form of state
Overseas territory of the United States of America
The executive
Executive authority is exercised by the governor (elected for a four-year term by popular vote) who makes other executive appointments with the concurrence of the legislature.
National legislature
The unicameral legislature, the Senate, has 15 members elected by popular vote for a two-year term in two multi-seat constituencies; its measures are subject to the governor's approval.

Legal system
The legal system is based on US laws.
Last elections
4 November 2002 (governor); 4 November 2004 (parliamentary)
Results: Governor: Charles W Turnbull was re-elected with 50.5 per cent of the vote. Parliamentary: The Democratic Party of the Virgin Islands (Dem) won 10 of the 15 seats in the Senate and the Independent Citizens Movement (ICM) won 4, the remaining seat going to an independent candidate.
Next elections
November 2006 (governor and parliamentary)

Political parties
Ruling party
Democratic Party of the Virgin Islands, affiliated to the US Democratic Party
Political situation
Social tensions came to a head in October 2005 with citizens of St Croix and St Thomas converged on St John to protest at the hate crimes perpetrated in the US Virgin Islands. The protest was sparked by the perceived delay in the investigation into an attack on a black woman by four white men. Friction has increased in the community as a whole as white people have taken up residence in certain areas and changed the demographics to a fifty/fity mix with West Indian residents. Measures to defuse the tension include inter-communal discussion panels to deal with issues of race, property tax, housing, education, crime and health.

Population
122,600 (2004)
Ethnic make-up
Descendants of former African slaves form the majority (80 per cent) of the population. Whites make up a further 15 per cent. Almost three-quarters (74 per cent) of inhabitants are West Indians (45 per cent Virgin Islands-born, 29 per cent from elsewhere in the Caribbean). Puerto Ricans make up 5 per cent of the population.
Religions
Various Christian denominations predominate, (Baptist, Roman Catholic and Episcopalian).

Health
Life expectancy: 78.3 years (World Bank)
Fertility rate/Maternal mortality rate: 2.2 births per woman (World Bank)
Infant mortality rate: 8.3 per 1,000 live births (World Bank).

KEY FACTS

Official name: Virgin Islands of the United States

Head of State: George W Bush

Head of government: Governor Charles W Turnbull (since 1998; re-elected 5 Nov 2002)

Ruling party: Democratic Party of the Virgin Islands, affiliated to the US Democratic Party

Area: 355 square km

Population: 122,600 (2004)

Capital: Charlotte Amalie (on St Thomas)

Official language: English

Currency: US dollar (US$) = 100 cents

GDP per capita: US$19,000 (2003)

GDP real growth: 2.00% (2003)

Labour force: 49,000 (2003)

Unemployment: 4.90% (2003)

Inflation: 2.00% (2003)

Main cities
Charlotte Amalie on the island of St Thomas (capital, estimated population 12,100 in 2003), Christiansted and Frederiksted on St Croix. The third major island and the least populous is St John (Cruz Bay).

Languages spoken
Spanish and Creole are also spoken.
Official language/s
English

Media
Press
Dailies: The two major dailies are *Virgin Islands Daily News* and *St Croix Avis*. Other publications include an independent community newspaper *St John Times*. The island is served by on-line news services (www.onepaper.com). The *St Croix Source* provides an alternative news and information source for and about the St Croix community. It is the sister publication of *St Thomas Source* and *St John Source*.
Weeklies: *Tradewinds St. John Newspaper* (www.stjohntradewindsnews.com) is published and distributed weekly on St John, as well as to international subscribers. Since 1972, Tradewinds Newspaper has been the island authority. A general tourist publication, *St Thomas This Week Magazine*, is available on-line (www.st-thomas.com/week).
Business: Publications include *Virgin Islands Business Journal*.
Broadcasting
There are cable and television stations and several commercial radio stations operating on the islands.

Economy
Tourism is the main economic activity, accounting for some 80 per cent of GDP. Financial services are increasing in importance. Agriculture makes little contribution to the economy. St John, the smallest island, with a population of about 5,000, has the strongest economy in the group.

External trade
There is a heavy reliance on imports and aid from the US, with which there are direct links by air and freighter, and an indirect link via Puerto Rico. The US Virgin Islands are not part of the Federal Customs Area, an arrangement which confers certain advantages.

Imports
Main imports are crude oil, foodstuffs, consumer goods and building materials.
Main sources: US, Puerto Rico
Exports
Petroleum products, chemicals, clocks and watches, meat and ethanol.
Main destinations: US and Puerto Rico.

Agriculture
Farming
The agricultural sector contributes around 1 per cent to GDP. The US Virgin Islands are mainly hilly with little flat land. The poor quality of the soil and lack of rain precludes large-scale cultivation. Small quantities of sorghum, fruit and vegetables are produced on St Croix and St Thomas. Cattle are the main agricultural product; a special breed of Senepol cattle hardened to the hot temperatures was developed on St Croix for meat export. Livestock production in 2004 included 730 tonnes (t) meat in total, 520t beef, 105t pig meat, 33t lamb and goat meat, 72t poultry, 160t eggs, 1,960t milk.
Fishing
There is some commercial fishing, mainly of lobsters, but fishing is mostly for game, not commercial purposes. The typical total fish catch is over 300t, plus over 36t of other seafood, per annum.

Industry and manufacturing
The industrial sector contributes around 17 per cent to GDP. Manufacturing is better developed here than in much of the Caribbean; it is small-scale and export-based (mainly to the US). Manufacturers have the right to stamp 'Made in America' on their products. The main activities are rum distilling (3–4 million gallons per year), watch/clock assembly, ethanol refining, woollen textiles and garments.
The largest single employer is the Hovensa oil refinery on St Croix, which has a capacity of around 500,000 barrels per day (bpd). Hovensa, one of the world's largest refineries, won the Gold Award at the 2004 annual convention of the National Petrochemical and Refiners' Association for its achievements in safe operations in 2003.

Tourism
The tourism sector forms the mainstay of the economy, accounting for 80 per cent of GDP and employment. Visitor numbers, which passed the two million mark in 1997, peaked at 2,562,600 in 2001, but have since declined due to the 11 September 2001 terrorist attacks in the US and the global economic downturn. The cruise ship business was particularly affected, especially following the withdrawal of calls to St Croix in 2002. The sector recovered in 2003 and 2004 saw a record 2,623,327 visitors, with cruise ship passengers accounting for nearly two million of these, over 10 per cent up on 2003.

Hydrocarbons
The US Virgin Islands do not produce any hydrocarbons. They rely entirely on crude imports from Trinidad and Tobago. The largest refinery in the western hemisphere and one of the world's biggest, with a capacity of around 500,000 barrels per day (bpd), is located on St Croix. Less than a quarter of oil imports is consumed locally, the rest being re-exported as refined oil products, mainly to the US.
The US Virgin Islands do not import natural gas; around 283,000 short tonnes of coal per annum are imported.

Banking and insurance
Central bank
Federal Reserve System

Time
GMT minus four hours

Geography
The US Virgin Islands consist of three main inhabited islands (St Croix, St Thomas and St John) and about 50 smaller, mostly uninhabited, islands. They are situated at the eastern end of the Greater Antilles, about 64km (40 miles) east of Puerto Rico in the Caribbean Sea.

Climate
Sub-tropical with a mean annual temperature of 26 degrees Celsius. Low levels of humidity. Rainy season runs May–November.

Entry requirements
Passports
Not required by US citizens with an identity card. Citizens of other countries should follow the regulations required by the US for their countries.
Visa
US entry requirements apply. Visas required by all, except US and Canadian citizens with proof of identity, and foreign nationals from countries with visa free entry to the US and are in possession of machine-readable passports under the 'Visa Waiver Program' (VWP) due to be introduced in October 2005. All passport holders must apply for a visa. Visits, (for both tourism and business) and visas are valid for up to 90 days. A return/onward ticket is also required.

KEY INDICATORS — US Virgin Islands

	Unit	2000	2001	2002	2003	2004
Population	m	0.12	0.12	0.12	0.12	0.12
Gross domestic product (GDP)	US$bn	1.80	1.80	1.81	2.40	–
GDP per capita	US$	15,000	15,000	15,000	19,000	–

US Virgin Islands

Further information can be found at http://travel.state.gov/ including information on temporary business visas. See http://uscis.gov/graphics/services/visa_info.htm for more detailed information.

Currency advice/regulations
The US dollar circulates. Import/export over US$5,000 must be declared.

Customs
There are no sales or luxury taxes and no customs duties on tourist-related items.

Health (for visitors)
Mandatory precautions
Yellow fever vaccination certificate if arriving from infected area.

Advisable precautions
Health insurance is strongly advised. Adopt precautions when drinking water in rural areas. There is a bilharzia (schistosomiasis) risk when swimming – chlorinated pools are safe. Visitors should consider immunisation against hepatitis 'A'.

Hotels
Advisable to book in advance, especially in winter months. There is an 8 per cent hotel tax. A 15 per cent tip is usual.

Public holidays
Fixed dates
1 Jan (New Year's Day), 6 Jan (Three Kings' Day), 19 Jan (Martin Luther King Day), 3 Jul (Emancipation Day), 4 Jul (US Independence Day), 25 Jul (Hurricane Supplication Day), 17 Oct (Virgin Islands Thanksgiving Day), 1 Nov (D Hamilton Jackson Day), 11 Nov (Veterans' Day), 25 Dec (Christmas Day).

Variable dates
President's Day (second Mon in Feb), Maundy Thursday, Good Friday, Easter Monday, Memorial Day (fourth Mon in May), Labour Day (first Mon in Sep), Columbus Day (second Mon in Oct), US Thanksgiving Day (fourth Thu in Nov).

Working hours
Banking
Mon–Fri: 0900–1430; Fri: 1530–1700.
Government
Mon–Fri: 0800–1700.
Shops
Mon–Sat: 0900–1700. Some Sunday opening when cruise ships are in port.

Telecommunications
Telephone/fax
Modern, 100 per cent automatic service is in operation.
Fax international services available.
Postal services
Airmail to US and Europe takes under one week. Post offices are open Mon–Fri 0900–1700, and Sat 0900–1200.

Electricity supply
110/120V AC, 60 Hz

Getting there
Air
International airport/s: St Croix-Alexander Hamilton (STX), 14km south-west of Christiansted, car rental; St Thomas-Cyril E. King (STT), 3km west of Charlotte Amalie, duty-free shop, bar, restaurant, bank, shops, car hire.
Airport tax: None
Surface
Water: Regular ferry service with the British Virgin Islands.
Main port/s: Charlotte Amalie (St Thomas), Christiansted, Frederiksted, South Shore cargo port (St Croix).

Getting about
National transport
Air: There are frequent services between St Thomas and St Croix (by Sunaire Express).
Road: Over 800km. Surfaces are good.
Buses: Public service on all main routes and group tours available.
Water: Regular ferry service between St Thomas and St John and the British Virgin Islands.
City transport
Taxis: Widely available; fixed-rate system applies but is not always strictly adhered to.
Higher charges are made for extra passengers, luggage and at night. Taxi vans usually carry multiple passengers; private taxis can be arranged for extra cost.
Car hire
A wide selection of cars is available. National licences are accepted and required. Traffic drives on the left. Speed limit is 35kph in towns and 55kph elsewhere.

BUSINESS DIRECTORY
The addresses listed below are a selection only. While World of Information makes every endeavour to check these addresses, we cannot guarantee that changes have not been made, especially to telephone numbers and area codes. We would welcome any corrections.

Telephone area codes
The international direct dialling code (IDD) for the US Virgin Islands is +1 340 followed by the subscriber's number.

Chambers of Commerce
St Croix Chamber of Commerce, PO Box 4369, Kingshill, St Croix 00851 (tel: 773-1435; fax: 773-8172; e-mail: stcroixchamber@vipowernet.net).

St Thomas-St John Chamber of Commerce, 6 Main Street, PO Box 324, Charlotte Amalie, St Thomas 00804 (tel: 776-0100; fax: 776-0588; e-mail: chamber@islands.vi).

Banking
Banco Popular de Puerto Rico, Church St, Christiansted, St Croix, VI 00820 (tel: 773-0077).

First Virgin Islands Federal Savings Bank, 50 Kronprindesens Gade, Charlotte Amalie, St Thomas, VII 00803 (tel: 776-9494).

Central bank
Federal Reserve Bank of Atlanta, 1000 Peachtree Street NE, Atlanta, Georgia 30309-4470, USA (tel: +1-404 498-8500; fax: +1-404-498-8073).

Travel information
National tourist organisation offices
USVI Department of Tourism, PO Box 6400, St Thomas, VI 00804 (tel: 800-372; internet site: http://www.usvitourism.vi).

Other useful addresses
Department of Economic Development and Agriculture (responsible for promotion and development of tourism), PO Box 6400, St Thomas 00804 (tel: 774-8784).

Industrial Development Commission, PO Box 3499, St Croix (tel: 773-6499); PO Box 6400, St Thomas (tel: 774-8784).

Office of the Governor, Government House, 21–22 Kongens Gade, Charlotte Amalie, St Thomas, VI 00801 (tel: 774-0001).

St Croix Hotel and Tourism Association, PO Box 24238, Gallows Bay, St Croix, USVI 00824 (tel: 773-7117; fax: 773-5883, e-mail: hax@noc.usvi.net).

St Thomas and St John Hotel Association, 4-D Contant, St Thomas, USVI 00803 (tel: 774-6835).

Virgin Islands Port Authority, Cyril E King Airport, St Thomas, VI 00801 (tel: 774-1629).

Internet sites
Tourist information: http://www.here.vi

US Office of Insular Affairs: http://www.doi.gov/oia

US Virgin Islands Guide: http://www.usvi.net/

Uruguay

KEY FACTS

Official name: República Oriental del Uruguay (Oriental Republic of Uruguay)

Head of State: President Tabaré Vázquez (Frente Amplio) (sworn in 1 Mar 2005)

Head of government: President Tabaré Vázquez

Ruling party: Frente Amplio (Broad Front) coalition party (elected Oct 2004)

Area: 176,215 square km

Population: 3.43 million (2004)

Capital: Montevideo

Official language: Spanish

Currency: Peso Uruguayo (Ur$) = 100 centavos

Exchange rate: Ur$24.08 per US$ (Oct 2005)

GDP per capita: US$3,543 (2004)

GDP real growth: 12.00% (2004)

Labour force: 1.55 million (2004)

Unemployment: 13.10% (2004)

Inflation: 9.20% (2004)

Balance of trade: US$20.00 million (2003)

Foreign debt: US$11.80 billion (2003)

On 31 October 2004 Uruguay's voters elected the country's first left-wing government in its 174-year history.

The inauguration of President Tabaré Ramón Vázquez Rosas (Frente Amplio) (Broad Front), a former physician and football club chief, was billed as something of a fête for Latin America's left-wing leaders. Hugo Chávez, Venezuela's radical nationalist president, Bolivia coca growers' leader Evo Morales (soon himself to be president) and the Cuban foreign minister all attended the ceremony in Montevideo. Reports even suggested that Fidel Castro was due to attend but was forced to cancel due to an injured knee.

A moderate leftward shift

It is another group of the region's leaders, however, that the Vázquez government now most closely resembles. US fears of another left-wing nationalist in a South American presidential palace were allayed throughout 2005 as the new government appeared to be similar to the coalition of President Luiz Inácio 'Lula' da Silva in Brazil and other such centre-left governing alliances throughout the continent.

The make-up of the ruling coalition (Frente Amplio, Encuentro Progresista and Nueva Mayoria), with its selection of communists, hard line trade union leaders and former guerrilla fighters, at first sight

Uruguay

appeared to constitute a shift to the hard left of the Uruguayan political spectrum. Vázquez's vow to form a 'government of change' in his inaugural address only increased expectations of a radical transformation. As 2005 wore on however, the new government's approach, particularly to economic policy, remained consistent with mainstream left-of-centre thinking.

Economic policy: Astori's approach

Following the Argentine economic crisis of 1999–2002 and the knock on effect on Uruguay, the country embarked on an economic recovery. There were devastating contractions of 1.3, 3.1 and 10.8 per cent respectively recorded in 2000–02, before a turnaround was achieved in 2003. Growth of 12 per cent was recorded in 2004 as the economy rebounded and a rate of 6 per cent has been projected for 2005. The IMF forecasts growth of 4 per cent for 2006. Some 30 per cent of the 3.43 million population still live in poverty however, and the country's public debt was close to 100 per cent of GDP at the beginning of 2005. The large debt is particularly debilitating for the government, as it consumes approximately 5.1 per cent of total GDP in interest payments annually.

Integral to the new government's economic policy has been finance minister Danilo Astori. More radical figures on the far left of the governing coalition have suggested Uruguay was foolish to have negotiated a cordial agreement with the IMF in 2003. They claim that the country should have gone the way of Argentina in driving a hard bargain with the fund. Astori has rejected such approaches, underlining a policy of respectful co-operation with international institutions: 'Uruguay adopted the best strategy for its interests… this is a small, fragile country but we have one intangible asset, which is our seriousness… we share much of the same vision with IMF staff'.

The finance minister's assumptions appear to be correct thus far, as his country has been rewarded for its actions with a new IMF deal. The new pact will run for three years and facilitate the rolling over of 60 per cent of IMF loans (US$2.7 billion) for the duration of the programme. On its part, Uruguay agreed to a primary fiscal surplus equivalent to 3.5 per cent of total GDP, which will rise to 4 per cent by 2007. Inflation will fall by 1 percentage point a year to 3.5 per cent by 2008 and growth is expected to average 4 per cent under the programme. Government officials have also stated their intention to reduce the country's total debt to 60 per cent of GDP by the end of its five year term.

Astori has also advocated the implementation of a structural reform programme that will allow the central bank increased independence, reform the tax code and improve the business environment. The latter objective is aimed at increasing the amount of private capital in the economy. In an interview with the *Financial Times* (*FT*) of London vice president Rodolfo Nin Novoa said that there was 'a huge place for the private sector – much more than the public sector – to develop the country'. The government's desire to attract a higher level of private investment was further evidenced by an attempt to push through parliament an agreement with the US to protect outside investments. Uruguay's improving relationship with international investors was confirmed when the government issued some US$300 million in sovereign bonds, which covered the country's financing requirements for the whole of 2005.

Rapprochement with Cuba

One of the first executive decisions taken by President Vázquez was the re-establishment of diplomatic relations with Cuba. Uruguay and Cuba had previously fallen out in April of 2002, when former president Jorge Batlle enraged Castro by suggesting the United Nations send an official observer to scrutinise human rights on the island. The decision to recognise Cuba was taken almost immediately after the presidential election result was known and initially alarmed Washington. In subsequent months however, the United States has reduced its concerns of developments in Uruguay, as Vázquez has steered a moderate path. A traditional tenet of the country's foreign and trade policy has been its forthright advocacy of Mercosur, which has been reconfirmed by the new president on numerous occasions throughout 2005.

Outlook

The political and economic outlook for Uruguay looks relatively promising. The Vázquez government has secured a new deal with the IMF and has improved its image and reputation with external investors. The continued maintenance of the broad governing coalition may prove to be a challenge throughout 2006 however, as far-left members of the governing coalition may well begin to voice their disquiet at the hitherto austere policy measures of the leadership. In a revealing statement given during an interview with the *FT* Astori talked of dividing 'our five year term into two halves, and in the first half there is absolutely no room for flexibility'. The finance minister's reference to a lack of room for flexibility may well signal that the second half of the Vázquez term will see a loosening of fiscal policy. In 2006 however, a prudent macroeconomic course looks set to continue.

Risk assessment

Economy	Stable
Politics	Stable
Regional stability	Stable
Stock market	Stable

KEY INDICATORS — Uruguay

	Unit	2000	2001	2002	2003	2004
Population	m	3.33	3.36	3.38	3.40	*3.43
Gross domestic product (GDP)	US$bn	20.10	18.20	13.50	10.93	*13.14
GDP per capita	US$	6,004	5,424	4,004	3,210	3,543
GDP real growth	%	-1.3	-3.1	-10.8	2.5	12.0
Inflation	%	4.8	-4.4	14.0	19.5	9.2
Unemployment	%	13.5	14.9	16.7	18.4	–
Exports (fob) (goods)	US$m	2,400.0	2,144.0	2,040.0	2,127.0	–
Imports (fob) (goods)	US$m	3,460.0	2,911.0	2,260.0	2,107.0	–
Balance of trade	US$m	-1,060.0	-767.0	-221.0	-7.0	–
Current account	US$m	-592.8	-475.0	-365.0	288.0	-40.0
Total reserves minus gold	US$m	2,479.0	3,097.0	769.0	2,083.0	2.5
Foreign exchange	US$m	2,432.0	3,050.0	763.0	2,079.0	2,507.0
Exchange rate	per US$	12.10	13.32	20.65	28.35	28.70

* estimated figure

Nations of the World: A Political, Economic and Business Handbook

COUNTRY PROFILE

Historical profile
1516 Spanish explorer Juan Díaz de Solis was killed by indigenous people while he was navigating the Rio de la Plata. His death discouraged European exploration for more than a century afterwards.
In the seventeenth century, the Portuguese began colonising Uruguay.
1726 The Spanish founded Montevideo and took over Uruguay.
1776 Uruguay became part of the vice royalty of La Plata, which was run from Buenos Aires in Argentina.
1808 The defeat of the Spanish monarchy by Napoleon weakened La Plata, leading to a rebellion in Uruguay which overthrew the vice royalty. The Uruguayans resisted Argentine and Brazilian invaders.
1825 Uruguay achieved formal independence from Spain.
1830 A constitution was approved.
1838–65 Uruguay became embroiled in civil war between the conservative Colorados (reds) and the liberal Blancos (whites).
1865–70 Uruguay joined Argentina and Brazil and fought a war against Paraguay, which was eventually defeated.
1904 The Colorados and Blancos fought their last civil war. The Blancos became the Partido Nacional (PN) (National Party) and the Colorados the Partido Colorado (PC).
1903–07 and 1911–16 President José Batlle y Ordonez (Colorado party), introduced the welfare state, extended the right to vote to women, disestablished the Roman Catholic Church and abolished the death penalty.
1933 A military coup led to the abolition of opposition parties.
1951 A new constitution replaced the post of president with a nine-member council.
1962–73 The Tupamaros guerrillas engaged in a campaign of insurgency.
1973–85 A military dictatorship took power, unleashing a campaign of harsh repression.
1984 Violent protests erupted against military rule. The military dictatorship agreed to step down and return the country to constitutional government.
1985 Julio María Sanguinetti, a Colorado, was installed as president after democratic elections
1989 Luis Alberto Lacalle won the presidential election. An amnesty for human rights abusers endorsed by referendum.
1994 Sanguinetti won the presidential election.
1999 Jorge Batlle Ibañez (PC) was elected president.
2000 A commission was set up to investigate 'disappearances' under the military regime.
2002 The financial crisis that began in Asia and weakened many economies in Latin America, particularly Argentina, prompted Batlle to introduce fiscal measures including tax increases to prevent the crisis spilling into Uruguay. Banks were closed to stop the mass withdrawal of savings and a general strike was called.
2003 The government managed to restructure almost half of its US$11 billion foreign debt, pushing the repayment dates back five years. A referendum rejected proposals for the sale of state oil assets to foreign investment.
2004 The management of the Uruguay Energy Efficiency Project, funded by a US$6.80 million grant from the Global Environment Facility (in May 2003) was approved by the World Bank. Left-wing Tabaré Vázquez (Frente Amplio) won presidential elections in November, marking a dramatic political shift. The Frente Amplio coalition party won the parliamentary elections.
2005 Tabaré Vázquez was sworn in as president on 1 March. Within hours of taking office the new president restored diplomatic relations with Cuba and signed an energy deal with Venezuela. In December, forensic experts found remains of individuals thought to have been killed during Uruguay's period of military rule.

Political structure
Constitution
The constitution dates from 1967, with a period of suspension during military rule between 1973 and 1985. Voting is by secret ballot and is obligatory for all citizens aged 18 and over. The electorate has to vote in support of a single party list for president, mayors and legislators. A reform to permit cross-party voting for the different positions was defeated at a referendum in 1994.
Form of state
Presidential democratic republic
The executive
Executive power is vested in the president, who is directly elected every five years, usually in October or November. The president is assisted by a vice president and an appointed council of ministers. The president has the power to veto parliamentary resolutions, but the veto can be overturned by a three-fifths majority of Congress.
National legislature
Legislative power is vested in a bicameral Congress, comprising a 31-member Senate and a 99-member Chamber of Deputies, with at least two representatives for each department of the country. Both houses are elected on a proportional representation basis every five years, usually at the same time as presidential elections.

Legal system
The legal system is based on Spanish civil law. Written law is passed by parliament and promulgated by the president. The ultimate source of the law is the constitution.
Judicial power is exercised by the Supreme Court of Justice which has five members elected by Congress. The Court nominates all other judges and officials.
Last elections
31 October 2004 (presidential and parliamentary)
Results: Presidential: Tabaré Vázquez (Frente Amplio) won 50.7 per cent of the vote, Jorge Larrañaga (PN) 34.1 per cent and Guillermo Stirling (PC) 10.3 per cent. Turnout was 89.6 per cent.
Parliamentary: the Frente Amplio (Broad Front) won 53 seats out of 99 in the Chamber of Deputies (17 seats out of 31 in the Senate), the Partido Nacional-Blancos (PN) (National-White Party) 34 (10), the ruling Partido Colorado (PC) (Colorado Party, *Colorados*) 10 (three) and the Partido Independiente (PI) (Independent Party) two (no seats in the Senate).
Next elections
2009 (presidential and parliamentary)

Political parties
Ruling party
Frente Amplio (Broad Front) coalition party (elected Oct 2004)
Main opposition party
Partido Nacional-Blancos (PN) (National-White Party)

Population
3.43 million (2004)
Ethnic make-up
Around 90 per cent are of European descent, with approximately one-quarter of the population of Italian origin. Minorities are black and *mestizo* (mixed race), but there are no pure Indian groups.
Religions
The majority of Uruguayans are Roman Catholic (66 per cent) with a small minority of Protestants (2 per cent) and Jews (1 per cent). Secular traditions are strong and a third of the population have no professed religious faith.

Education
All education, including university tuition, is provided free of charge. The curriculum is the same in both public and private schools. Secondary education is available from aged 12 and divided into two three-year courses. Technical studies are offered in technical schools and last between two and seven years. There are five universities and enrolment in tertiary education is typically 30 per cent.

Uruguay

Literacy rate: 97.7 per cent, total; 98.1 per cent, female; adult rates in 2002 (Word Bank).
Compulsory years: Six to 14
Enrolment rate: 109.5 per cent gross primary enrolment; 98.5 per cent gross seconday enrolment, of relevant age groups (including repeaters) (Unicef 2004).
Pupils per teacher: 20 in primary schools

Health
Total expenditure on health is around 10–11 per cent of GDP, of which government spending is about 46 per cent; almost 70 per cent of private expenditure is spent on pre-paid plans. This funding is relatively high, in regional terms, offering comparatively good medical provision.
HIV prevalence: 0.3 per cent aged 15–49 in 2003 (World Bank)
Life expectancy: 75.4 years (World Bank)
Fertility rate/Maternal mortality rate: 2.2 births per woman (2003); maternal mortality 26 per 100,000 live births (World Bank).
Infant mortality rate: 12 per 1,000 live births (World Bank)
Head of population per physician/bed: 3.7 doctors and 4.4 hospital beds per 1,000 people

Welfare
Uruguay maintains one of the most comprehensive systems of social security in Latin America, including free education, state medical care, pensions and unemployment benefits. Social security spending accounts for around 15 per cent of GDP.
The largest welfare expenditure is the payment of old age pensions. The long tradition of healthcare provision and a relatively low mortality rate have produced an ageing population. The pension age is low (with sometimes less than 30 years' service required). There are some 800,000 old-age pensioners out of a total population of three million and compared to a workforce of only one million, producing one of the highest ratios of pensioners to workers in the world.
There is widespread and vociferous opposition to any modification of the social security system. Many of the welfare benefits, including a workers' charter stipulating maximum hours, minimum wages and paid holidays, date from the beginning of the twentieth century.
Social security is covered by the state budget with about 50 per cent of contributions coming from tax revenues. Despite attempts by the government to raise the percentage derived from taxes, the remaining 50 per cent is still split roughly equally between contributions from workers and employers. Almost 90 per cent of the population is covered for all benefits.

Housewives, who are ineligible for retirement benefit, only receive separate pensions after their husbands have died. Benefits include: a retirement pension at 60 for men, 55 for women or after 30 years of recognised service; an invalidity pension after 10 years of recognised service; an early retirement pension for citizens fulfilling political duties; free maternity care for working women and workers' wives; and sick pay of up to three months for all workers. Unemployment pay of up to six months is provided for all workers who have paid contributions for a year or more. This can reach up to 75 per cent of nominal salary. All medical costs are met by the state during the six-month period.

Main cities
Montevideo (capital, estimated population 1.4 million in 2004), Salto (102,400), Paysandú (78,200), Las Piedras (71,600), Rivera (67,200).

Languages spoken
Business languages: English and Portuguese. French and Italian are also widely spoken.
Official language/s
Spanish

Media
Press
Dailies: The most important dailies are published in Montevideo and are in Spanish. These include *El País*, *Cambio*, *El Telégrafo*, *El Observador*, *La Mañana*, *La Hora*, *Gaceta Comercial* and *La República* (morning), *El Diario* and *Ultimas Noticias* (evening).
Weeklies: There are 12 weeklies available in Montevideo, covering a variety of subjects. *Brecha*, available on-line (http://www.brecha.com.uy/), is an important Spanish-language weekly. *Semanario Manos* is a weekly of general interest.
Business: The leading weekly business publications are *Crónicas Económicas* and *Búsqueda*.
Periodicals: Several regional newspapers are available in main centres outside Montevideo. The main Buenos Aires papers can also be found. There are numerous periodicals and a few trade publications. *El Correo de la Costa* features issues of general interest.
Broadcasting
Radio: There are more than 100 radio stations, a third of which are in Montevideo.
Television: Four TV stations (one run by the state and three private), transmit from Montevideo and 16 others serve towns outside the capital.
About 71 per cent of households own television sets.

Advertising
Television advertising claims nearly half of all media advertising expenditure. The next largest share, about one-quarter, goes to newspapers. Less than 20 per cent goes to radio advertising. Several major advertising companies have offices in Montevideo. Advertising placement fees, in particular on radio and television, are high by regional standards.

Economy
Following three successive contractions, in 2000, 2001 and 2002, Uruguay's economy has grown in every year since 2003. Growth of 2.5 per cent was recorded in 2003, a figure that jumped to 12 per cent in 2004. The IMF has forecast growth of 6 per cent for 2005 and the country's economy is expected to expand by 4 per cent in 2006. The annual rate of inflation now stands at around 7 per cent having reached almost 20 per cent in 2003. Uruguay has a highly centralised economy. Approximately 17 per cent of the labour force is employed by the state. The economy is among the most developed in Latin America with one of the highest per capita incomes in the region, at over US$6,000 in 2000 (although it dropped dramatically in 2003 to US$3210). The economy is largely driven by services (a major feature of which is the well-run offshore financial sector), industry and commodity exports. Tourism also plays a small but increasingly important role.
Uruguay has always been cause for concern, placed between Latin America's two largest economies, Brazil and Argentina. The country is highly exposed to economic fluctuations in its neighbours' economies and consequently, the Argentine crisis dominated Uruguay's economic performance. The country depends on the Argentine and Brazilian markets for its agricultural exports. In 2001 and 2002, the Argentinian and Brazilian markets dried up and Uruguay found itself in its third year of recession.
Uruguay has traditionally been seen by many as a haven within South America, attracting large amounts of flight capital from neighbouring countries. For years, Argentinians have been storing money in Uruguay's banks, mostly due to a lack of confidence in Argentina's financial system. After the banking freeze, many Argentinians turned to their deposits in Uruguayan banks. This had a ruinous effect on the country's financial system, which was forced to consolidate in 2003. A left-wing president was elected in March 2005, the first in Uruguay's 174 year history. Despite the fears of many external observers, the government of Tabaré Ramón Vázquez Rosas has toned down its leftist electoral rhetoric since coming to

power. In June 2005 Uruguay signed a new deal with the IMF worth US$1.1 billion that will run for three years. Under the terms of the new programme, an inflation target of 3.5 is to be reached by 2008 and annual average growth is expected to be in the region of 4 per cent.

The new government has also stated that it sees a viable role for private capital in the economy over the next few years. A recent statement to this effect by vice president Rodolfo Nin Navoa was somewhat surprising given that the new administration comprises, among others, communists and former revolutionary guerillas. However, the government has explicitly stated that state run monopolies in sectors such as water, telecommunications and energy will not be sold off. Privatisation of these state owned enterprises would be virtually politically impossible, as the vast majority of Uruguay's 3.4 million population is fervently opposed to privatisation.

External trade
Uruguay is a full member of the Mercosur trade group, established in 1995. Other members include Argentina, Brazil and Paraguay.

The South American Community of Nations, of which Uruguay is a member, intends to fully integrate Mercosur with the Andean Pact by 2007.

Imports
Main imports are machinery, chemicals, vehicles and crude oil.
Main sources: Argentina (21.3 per cent total, 2004), Brazil (17.1 per cent), US (12.3 per cent), China (6.9 per cent), Russia (5.1 per cent)

Exports
Main exports are meat, rice, leather products, wool, fish and dairy products.
Main destinations: Brazil (19.4 per cent total, 2004), US 18 per cent), Germany (6.6 per cent), Argentina (6.4 per cent)

Agriculture
Farming
Though agricultural production accounts for approximately 6 per cent of total GDP, agricultural-related products make up more than half of the country's exports. The sector also employs around 11 per cent of Uruguay's workforce.

Traditional exports have been hit by protectionism and tough competition from the EU. An outbreak of foot-and-mouth disease throughout the region also affected Uruguayan meat exports, although by 2003 the situation was under control and trade had resumed.

The sector is also an important supplier of raw materials (sugar, oilseeds, etc) to industry. It is expanding more rapidly than industry.

Livestock rearing forms the basis of the sector with cattle and sheep being produced for domestic consumption and for export (as meat, wool, hides and skins). Poultry and pigs are largely produced for the home market but exports of dairy products are increasing in importance. Exports of butter and cheese to Mercosur countries are substantial.

There is virtual self-sufficiency in food, although imports of wheat are required at times of low harvests.

Principal crops are wheat (mainly grown on mixed farms), rice (the main export crop, grown almost entirely in the north-east), sugar cane and beet, maize, barley, sorghum, linseed, sunflower seed, vegetables (mainly grown by smallholders) and citrus fruits (mainly oranges and tangerines).

The estimated crop production for 2004 included: 3,670,543 tonnes (t), 1,262,600t rice, 532,600t wheat, 223,000t maize, 377,000t soya beans, 136,345t potatoes, 30,000t sweet potatoes, 69,682t sorghum, 406,500t barley, 26,300t oats, 242,177t citrus fruit, 147,057t grapes, 60,000t tomatoes, 72,478t apples, 142,619t oilcrops, 3,000t tobacco, 181,500t sugar cane, 508,495t fruit in total, 205,429t vegetables in total. Livestock production included: 602,451t meat in total, 496,498t beef, 16,000t pig meat, 41,527t lamb, 54,219t poultry, 36,248t eggs, 1,500,000t milk, 13,200t honey, 66,419t cattle hides, 26,504t sheep and goat meat.

Fishing
The fishing industry typically generates US$80 million in exports per annum. Uruguay suffers from water pollution from its meat and leather industries, which has hit the fishing sector in previous years. If this problem can be permanently erradicated the prospects for the fishing industry will improve markedly.

Forestry
Uruguay has approximately 1.2 million hectares of forested land, which constitutes 5 per cent of the country's total landmass.

Assisted by fiscal incentives, forestry has become a dynamic sector, attracting both foreign and domestic investment. Local forest resources produce modest quantities of sawn timber and pulp with most of paper products imported.

It is estimated that 1.7 million tonnes of timber per year could be exported, but improvements and remodelling of existing facilities and infrastructure would be needed in order to transport the timber. Export of forest materials in 2004 amounted to US$131 million, while imports total US$63 million.

Production in 2004 included: 5,399,152 cubic metres (cum) roundwood, 2,132,000cum industrial roundwood, 1,637,000cum pulpwood, 230,000cum sawnwood, 485,000cum sawlogs and veneers, 4,267,152cum wood fuel, 117,655 tonnes charcoal.

Industry and manufacturing
Uruguay's industrial sector has been in recession in recent years and has suffered significant reductions in investment. The industry still accounts for a sizeable percentage of the workforce, though this is now falling.

Government industrial policy has promoted export operations, based mainly on agricultural processing and related labour-intensive industries. Although traditional key sectors are still meat processing and packing and while the wool industry and fisheries still have priority, attention has turned to other sectors such as textiles and leather. The penetration of new markets has been a key feature of plans to stimulate manufacturing industry and exports.

Despite a number of new trade agreements with Mercosur, the US and Mexico, industry still suffers deep-seated structural problems. These have included high levels of debt, obsolete machinery and poor investment.

Tourism
Tourism is of considerable importance to Uruguay's economy, accounting for just under 10 per cent of total GDP and employing 10.7 per cent of the country labour force.

The travel and tourism industry suffered a major decline in previous years following the economic crisis in Argentina, which, along with Brazil, is its most important market. However, the sector is now recovering and visitor numbers are rising, which has, in turn, resulted in an increase in capital investment in the sector.

Mining
Mining and quarrying combined make up less than 1 per cent of Uruguay's total GDP. The country has few known mineral reserves and is wholly dependent on imports for raw materials ranging from oil to aluminium.

There are known deposits of iron ore, gold, manganese, copper, zinc and lead. Regulations in 1990 opened up the sector to foreign investment but very few foreign companies are active. Argentina has been the main purchaser of sand from Uruguay while Spain, South Africa and the US have purchased semi-precious stones and granite. Japan and Argentina are also important markets for granite exports. However, most mine production is consumed domestically.

Hydrocarbons
With no proven oil reserves of its own and a significant demand for oil, Uruguay

Uruguay

relies heavily on imports. The country has only one oil refinery, situated near Montevideo, which outputs 50,000 barrels per day (bpd).

Uruguay has looked increasingly to Venezuela to supply it with oil. In a deal struck in August 2005 the Venezuelan government agreed to supply Uruguay with 43,600 bpd of crude oil.

The National Administration of Fuel, Alcohol and Portland Cement (ANCAP), a state enterprise, has a monopoly on oil importing and refining. Intermittent oil exploration is carried out but results have been disappointing so far.

The importance of natural gas in the country's energy sector will increase with the construction of new pipelines and distribution systems. The government is hoping to increase gas usage to be 30 per cent of primary energy consumption, however the country's economic problems have hindered this target. Currently only small quantities are being imported.

There are known deposits of low-grade coal although no coal is produced and Uruguay relies on imports of approximately two million tonnes per annum.

Energy

Uruguay has approximately 2,100 megawatts (MW) of instilled electricity generating capacity. About half of the country's energy needs are produced domestically and the shortfall is covered by imports, predominantly from Argentina and Brazil. The 1,890MW hydropower plant at Salto Grande (built with Argentina), the 300MW Palmar plant, and two plants on the Rio Negro are sufficient to meet local demand and provide surplus for export.

Financial markets
Stock exchange

The Uruguayan stock market is the Bolsa de Montevideo, which runs an electronic listing system, the Bolsa Electrónica de Valores del Uruguay SA (Bevsa). Owing to the low levels of privatisation in Uruguay, there are few companies listed and many do not trade actively. Liquidity has traditionally been thin, with a high proportion of family businesses concentrating shares among a small number of people and eliminating speculators. However, the government's reforms to the state sector through a series of capital injections have helped improve liquidity levels.

Banking and insurance

Uruguay's banking and financial services sector continues to be dominated by three public banks. The Banco Central del Uruguay (BCU), which does not offer private credit, the Banco de la República Oriental de Uruguay (BROU) and the Banco Hipotecario de Uruguay (BHU) are the kingpins of the financial system.

The BROU is multi-purpose and is the largest credit provider, offering 40 per cent of overall private credit in Uruguay and receiving 33 per cent of deposits. The Banco Hipotecario specialises in mortgage lending.

The largest private bank was the Banco Comercial. In the early 1990s Banco Comercial was successfully re-privatised as part of a programme to return all these institutions to the private sector after their accounts have been put in order. Banco Comercial, the country's oldest bank, was sold to a consortium comprising Crédit Suisse, Chemical Bank, Dresdner Bank and Banco General de Negocios.

At the end of the 1990s, the banking sector's non-performing loan rate was about 6 per cent, which was very low by regional standards. However, the level of non-performing loans has risen sharply due to the deepening economic recession since then, which has seen many businesses close. The situation was made worse by a drain of US dollar liquidity caused by worsening regional conditions and political instability in Uruguay.

Uruguay's banking reputation has been undermined in recent years by money laundering scandals and, in 2002, a suspension in trading due to massive withdrawals from hard currency deposit accounts during the debt repayment crisis in neighbouring Argentina. Non-residents' deposits account for around 40 per cent, a large proportion of which are from Argentinians and are in high-interest, hard currency accounts. The Argentine banking crisis of 2002 affected Uruguay's banking system as Argentinians withdrew large amounts of money from Uruguayan deposit accounts. This prompted panic withdrawals by Uruguayans. During this time nearly US$6 billion, or 40 per cent of total deposits, was withdrawn from the banking system. This led to government action, including an investigation into illegal capital flight by Banco Comercial and the freezing of long-term foreign currency savings under an emergency law. Savers in Uruguayan banks were denied access to around US$2.2 billion in high interest, three-year deposit accounts. In July 2002, the government ordered the temporary closure of the banking system to head off a dangerous run on bank accounts, which had drained the country's foreign reserves from US$3.1 billion at the end of 2001 to US$655 million by mid-2002.

In 2003, the Banco Comercial, the Banco de Montevideo and the Banco la Caja Obrera merged into a new institution, the Nuevo Banco Comercial, which opened in March, while the Banco de Crédito was liquidated.

Central bank
Banco Central del Uruguay

Main financial centre
Montevideo

Time
GMT minus three hours (GMT minus two hours from December to February)

Geography

Uruguay has an area of 176,215 square km and is bordered by Argentina to the west, by Brazil in the north and by the Atlantic and the wide River Plate estuary to the south-east. The largest river, the Uruguay, runs along the border with Argentina.

About 95 per cent of the country is rolling grassland, with few hills above 300 metres. The highest point is the Cerro Catedral at 514 metres. Only about 6 per cent of the land is naturally forested.

The River Negro (Río Negro), the main tributary of the River Uruguay, cuts across the centre of the country, separating the two main ranges of hills, the Cuchilla de Haedo and the Cuchilla Grande. Artificial lakes on the Rio Negro cover 1,199 square km.

Climate

The climate is temperate and rainfall is abundant, with an average of about 100 days of rain a year. In January, the hottest summer month, average temperatures range between 21.4 degrees Celsius (C) on the coast and 26.2 degrees C inland. In July the average temperatures are between 10.8 degrees C on the coast and 13.3 degrees C in the interior, with temperatures occasionally falling to freezing point at night.

Dress codes

Clothing is mostly informal, but jackets and ties or suits for men and skirts for women are usual for business. Uruguayans generally wear more conservative colours than their neighbours in Brazil and Argentina.

Entry requirements
Passports

Required by all except nationals of Argentina, Bolivia, Brazil, Chile, Colombia, Costa Rica, Dominican Republic, Ecuador, Guatemala, Honduras, Paraguay, Peru and the US. Nationals from these countries need a national identity card.

Visa

Required by all except nationals of EU, US, Canada, Japan, Norway, Switzerland, most Latin American countries and certain others for visits up to three months. A Tourist Card will be issued when travellers enter the country (usually given to airline passengers before landing), and must be kept until departure.

Nations of the World: A Political, Economic and Business Handbook

Business travellers from the countries mentioned do not require visas either. All other business visitors must have a letter of authorisation from their company or organisation.
The visitor is advised to check with the nearest consulate to determine the validity of their status before travelling.

Currency advice/regulations
No restrictions on import/export of local or foreign currency. Most currencies and travellers' cheques can be changed at banks or the *casas de cambio*, with the latter sometimes offering lower rates.

Customs
Personal effects are allowed in duty-free, precious jewels and gold (worth more than US$500) must be declared.

Prohibited imports
Import and export of precious jewels, gold, firearms, pornography, subversive literature, inflammable articles, acids, prohibited drugs (medications), plants, seeds, and foodstuffs as well as some antiquities and business equipment must be declared.

Health (for visitors)
Mandatory precautions
None
Advisable precautions
A typhoid vaccination may be necessary. Water precautions should be taken outside Montevideo.
Excellent health care is available but foreign visitors must pay the full cost.

Hotels
Graded into four classes by the National Tourism Bureau – de luxe, 1, 2A and 2B. There is a 20 per cent value added tax on hotel bills. Service charge is normally included – if not, usually 10 per cent tip.

Credit cards
Accepted in many places.

Public holidays
Fixed dates
1 Jan (New Year's Day), 6 Jan (Epiphany), 19 Apr (Landing of the 33 Patriots), 1 May (Labour Day), 18 May (Battle of Las Piedras), 19 Jun (Birth of General Artigas), 18 Jul (Constitution Day), 25 Aug (Independence Day), 12 Oct (Discovery of America), 2 Nov (All Souls' Day), 25 Dec (Christmas Day).
Variable dates
Carnival (Feb), Maundy Thursday, Good Friday.

Working hours
Banking
Mon–Fri: 1300–1700 in Montevideo; summer variations may apply in other areas.

Business
Mon–Fri: 0830–1200, 1430–1830/1900. (Some business offices open Sat mornings.)
Government
From mid-Mar to mid-Dec: Mon–Fri: 1200–1900. From mid-Dec to mid-Mar: Mon–Fri: 0730–1330.

Electricity supply
220V AC, 50 cycles

Social customs/useful tips
Punctuality is expected and business cards are essential. Uruguay's population is mostly of Italian or Spanish descent, and maintains many European customs, ranging from diet to dress. There is a long tradition of liberal legislation in contrast to many South American countries. Divorce and gambling, for example, are both legal. There is provision in the law for duels in matters of honour, something which much of the population considers an anachronism but which is nevertheless invoked from time to time.

Security
Residents consider the capital relatively safe to walk around at night compared with other South American cities.

Getting there
Air
Many flights to Montevideo include a stopover at Buenos Aires in Argentina.
National airline: Pluna (Primeras Líneas Uruguayas de Navegación Aérea).
International airport/s: Montevideo-Carrasco International (MVD), 19km from city; duty-free shop, bar, restaurant, bank, post office.
Airport tax: International departures US$6 to Buenos Aires and US$12 to all other destinations; departure taxes are not applicable for international transit passengers.
Surface
Road: A US$176 million programme to improve primary highways is under way. There are a number of border crossings from Brazil, the crossing from Argentina is preferable by boat.
Water: There is a night-ferry service from Buenos Aires to Montevideo (10 hours). High-speed ferries also operate between Montevideo and Buenos Aires (2 hours 30 minutes) (internet: www.buquebus.com). There are also services from Colonia (160km west of Montevideo) to Buenos Aires by ferry and a hydrofoil service (three times daily).
A port departure tax may be levied.
Main port/s: Montevideo River Plate (Rio Plate) harbour includes all the country's main port facilities, served by cargo lines from the USA and Europe.

Getting about
National transport
Air: The only internal destinations currently offered are domestic legs of international flights.
Road: Ninety per cent of roads are paved and while urban roads are good, rural roads are only fair. The highway network radiates from Montevideo towards the borders of Brazil and Argentina.
Buses: ONDA, CITA and COT run fast and frequent lines, connecting most towns over all the country (routes include: Montevideo-Punta del Este, two hours; Montevideo-Paysandú, six hours).
Rail: The rail system connects only a few villages and this slow service is under threat of closure.
Water: Some Buenos Aires-Montevideo ferries call at Colonia; there are various other services on the rivers Plate, Uruguay and Negro to suit local needs.
City transport
Taxis: Taxis are widely available in towns and from airports. They can be hailed. Fares are metered, with higher charges for extra passengers and at night; can be hired on a time basis, in which case fare should be negotiated in advance. A 10 per cent tip is usual.
Buses, trams & metro: An extensive bus service links all the capital's suburbs. There is an airport bus to the city centre, travelling time 35 minutes.
Car hire
International driving licence must be accompanied by two photographs; traffic conditions within Montevideo can be difficult and chauffeur-driven cars often recommended. A driving permit for 90 days can be obtained from Montevideo town hall.

BUSINESS DIRECTORY
The addresses listed below are a selection only. While World of Information makes every endeavour to check these addresses, we cannot guarantee that changes have not been made, especially to telephone numbers and area codes. We would welcome any corrections.

Telephone area codes
The international dialling code (IDD) for Uruguay is +598 followed by area code and subscriber's number:

Canelones	33	Minas	44
Florida	352	Montevideo	2
Las Piedras	2	Paysandú	72
Maldonado	42	Punta del Este	42
Mercedes	53	San José De Carrasco	2

Useful telephone numbers
Emergency 911
Emergency, outside Montevideo 02911
Roadside assistance 1707

Uruguay

Chambers of Commerce
American-Uruguayan Chamber of Commerce, Plaza Independencia 831, Edificio Plaza Mayor, 11100 Montevideo (tel: 908-9186; fax: 908-9187; e-mail: info@ccuruguayusa.com).

British-Uruguayan Cámara de Comercio, Avenida Libertador Brigadier General Lavalleja 1641, Montevideo (tel: 908-0349; fax: 908-0936; e-mail: camurbri@netgate.com.uy).

Uruguay Cámara Nacional de Comercio y Servicios, Rincón 454, 11000 Montevideo (tel: 916-1277; fax: 916-1243; e-mail: info@cncs.com.ny).

Banking
Banco de la República Oriental del Uruguay, Cerrito No. 351 Casa Central, Montevideo (tel: 950-205, 950-157; fax: 962-855).

Banco Exterior, Sarandi No. 402, 11000 Montevideo (tel: 960-042; fax: 961-089).

Banco Holandés Unido, Sucursal Montevideo, 25 de Mayo No. 501, 11000 Montevideo (tel: 960-702; fax: 960-121).

Banco Pan de Azucar, Rincón No. 518/528, 11000 Montevideo (tel: 960-925, 960-469; fax: 961-493).

Banco Santander, Cerrito No. 449, 11000 Montevideo (tel: 960-715, 960-802; fax: 963-685).

Banco Sudameris, Rincón No. 500, Montevideo (tel: 961-050, 961-309; fax: 964-292).

Banco Surinvest, Rincón No. 530, Montevideo (tel: 960-177; fax: 960-241).

Banesto-Banco Uruguay, 25 de Mayo No. 401, 11000 Montevideo (tel: 961-444/48; 960-838).

Citibank, Cerrito No. 455, Montevideo (tel: 950-374, 962-838; fax: 963-665).

Discount Bank (Latin America), Rincón No. 390, Montevideo (tel: 959-525; fax: 960-890).

The First National Bank of Boston, Zabala No. 1463, 11000 Montevideo (tel: 960-127; fax: 962-209).

ING Bank S.A., Misiones No. 352/60, Montevideo (tel: 960-961, 959-0692; fax: 958-955).

Lloyds Bank (BOLSA), Zabala No. 1500, Montevideo (tel: 961-370/74; fax: 961-262).

Nuevo Banco Comercial (NBC), Cerrito No. 400, 11100 Montevideo (tel: 960-394/97; fax: 963-569).

Central bank
Banco Central del Uruguay, Diagonal Fabini 777, 11100 Montevideo. (tel/fax: 1967; e-mail: info@bcu.gub.uy).

Travel information
Pluna Airlines, Colonia 1021, Montevideo (tel: 980-606, 983-516; fax: 921-478).

Ministry of tourism
Ministerio de Turismo, Av. Libertador, Brig. Gral Lavalleja 1409 Montevideo (tel: 914-340, 913-243; fax: 921-624).

Ministries
Ministerio de Defensa Nacional (National Defence), Edificio 'Gral.Artigas', Avda. 8 de Octubre 2628, Montevideo (tel: 809-707/9, 472-828; fax: 809-397).

Ministerio de Economía y Finanzas (Economy and Finance), Colonia 1089 - P.3, Montevideo (tel: 921-017; fax: 921-277).

Ministerio de Educación y Cultura (Education and Culture), Reconquista 535, Montevideo (tel: 950-103; fax: 962-632).

Ministerio de Ganadería, Agricultura y Pesca (Livestock, Agriculture and Fisheries), Constituyente 1476 (tel: 404-155/59, 413-622; fax: 499-623).

Ministerio de Industria, Energía y Minería (Industry, Energy and Mines), Rincón 747, Montevideo (tel: 900-231, 900-233, 912-924, 908-120; fax: 921-245).

Ministerio del Interior (Home Office), Mercedes 993, Montevideo (tel: 989-310; fax: 920-716).

Ministerio de Relaciónes Exteriores (Foreign Affairs), Av. 18 de Julio 1205, Montevideo (tel: 921-007/08/10; fax: 921-327).

Ministerio de Salud Pública (Public Health), Av. 18 De Julio 1892, Montevideo (tel: 400-101/04; fax: 488-676).

Ministerio de Trabajo y Seguridad Social (Labour and Social Security), Juncal 1511, Montevideo (tel: 962-681, 962-790, 962-806, 961-668; fax: 963-767).

Ministerio de Transporte y Obras Públicas (Transport and Public Works), Rincón 561, Montevideo (tel: 957-386, 957-544, 957-940, 958-245; fax: 962-883).

Ministerio de Vivienda, Ordenamiento Territorial y Medio Ambiente (Housing, Territorial Regulation and Environment), Zabala 1427, Montevideo (tel: 950-211, 950-421, 950-560, 950-324; fax: 962-914).

Oficina de Planeamiento y Presupuesto (OPP) (Planning and Budget Office), Dr. Luis A. de Herrera 3350, Montevideo (tel: 472-110, 819-525; fax: 299-730).

Other useful addresses
Aero Consultora Uruguaya, Florida 1280-202, Montevideo (tel: 987-312).

Asociación de Importadores y Mayoristas de Almacén, Ed de la Bolsa de Comercio, Rincón 454, Montevideo.

British Embassy, Calle Marco Bruto 1073, Montevideo (tel: 623-657; fax: 627-815).

Comisión Para el Desarrollo de la Inversión (Committee for Investment Development), Plaza Independencia 776, P.1 - 11100 Montevideo (tel: 980-318; fax: 908-298).

Cenci (Centro de Estadísticas Naciónales y Comercio Internacional del Uruguay) Misiones 136, 1 Montevideo (tel: 954-578).

Comisión Sectorial para el Mercosur, Paysandú esq, Florida, Montevideo (tel: 915-556; fax: 923-655).

Compañía Uruguaya de Exportaciónes S.A. (Comurex), Misiones 1372 - Ofic 303, Montevideo (tel: 960-086; fax: 962-514).

Dirección General de Comercio Exterior (Bureau of Foreign Affairs), Cuareim 1384, P.2 - 11100 Montevideo (tel: 920-319; fax: 921-726).

Dirección General de Estadísticas y Censos (DGEC), Cuareim 2052, Montevideo (tel: 947-056/58).

Dirección Nacional de Aduanas, Rbla. 25 de Agosto esq. Yacaré, Montevideo (tel: 961-335; fax: 964-691).

Export Trade Uruguay S.A., Caramurú 6092, Montevideo (tel: 605-217; fax: 605-217).

Laboratorio Tecnológico del Uruguay, Av Italia 6201, Montevideo (tel: 613-730; fax: 604-753).

Latin American Integration Association, Cebollati 1461, Casilla de Correo 577, Montevideo (tel: 401-121/28).

Unidad Asesora de Promoción Industrial, Rincón 723, P.2, Montevideo (tel: 986-402; fax: 914-434).

Unión de Exportadores, Rincón 454, P.2, Montevideo (tel: 961-117).

Uruguayan Embassy (USA), 1913 'I' Street, NW, Washington DC 20006 (tel: 202-331-1313; fax: 202-331-8142; e-mail: uruwashi@uruwashi.org).

Internet sites
El Observador Económico (Spanish): http://www.observador.com.uy

El Pais digital edition (Spanish): http://www.diarioelpais.com.edicion

Crónicas Económicas: http://www.cronicas.com.uy

Montevideo Free Zone (Zona France de Montevideo): http://www.zfm.com

Uzbekistan

KEY FACTS

Official name: Ozbekiston Respublikasy (Republic of Uzbekistan)

Head of State: President Islam Abduganievich Karimov (since 1991; re-elected Jan 2000)

Head of government: Prime Minister Shavkat Mirziyayev (appointed 11 Dec 2003)

Ruling party: Coalition government: Chalk Demokratik Partijasi (CDP) (People's Democratic Party) and independents

Area: 447,400 square km

Population: 27.95 million (2004)

Capital: Tashkent

Official language: Uzbek

Currency: Sum (Sum)

Exchange rate: Sum1,140.86 per US$ (Oct 2005); (central bank realigned official rate 1 Nov 2001)

GDP per capita: US$375 (2004)

GDP real growth: 7.10% (2004)

Labour force: 11.95 million (2004)

Unemployment: 0.60% (official, 2004); 20.00% (underemployment, 2004)*

Inflation: 8.80% (2004)

Oil production: 152,000 bpd (2004)

Balance of trade: US$880.00 million 2004

Foreign debt: US$4.60 billion (2003)

* estimated figure

Russia conquered Uzbekistan in the late 19th century. Stiff resistance to the Red Army after the First World War was eventually suppressed and a socialist republic set up in 1924. During the Soviet era, intensive production of cotton and grain led to overuse of agrochemicals and the depletion of water supplies, which have left the land poisoned and the Aral Sea and several rivers half dry. Independent since 1991, the country seeks to gradually lessen its dependence on agriculture while developing its mineral and petroleum reserves. Current concerns include terrorism by Islamic militants, economic stagnation, and the curtailment of human rights and democratisation. Uzbekistan has the largest population of any of the former Soviet republics, most recently counted at nearly 28 million.

Foreign affairs

While both the US and the European Union (EU) had during the 1990s courted Uzbekistan, its strategic importance emerged more forcefully after the 9/11 terror attacks on New York and the Pentagon. US intelligence and military forces used former Soviet military bases in Uzbekistan to mount their campaign to oust the Taliban government in Afghanistan, and have maintained a presence in the predominantly Muslim country, but were asked to leave in July after the regime became deeply suspicious of their on-going activities.

Despite Western pressure, President Islam Karimov has outlawed opposition parties, harassed and imprisoned dissidents, and, despite his own promises, failed to take meaningful steps to stop the routine use of torture against perceived opponents. Scores of dissidents have been executed after sham trials. He appears to be increasingly reliant on his National Security Service chief, Rustam Inoyatov.

Karimov's most recent display of resistance to opening meaningful political space for the opposition – or for civil-society groups – came late in 2004 when his government blocked the holding of a conference on the death penalty, saying the New York based sponsors had not registered in Uzbekistan. International human rights groups noted Karimov's long history of refusing to register independent human rights or other issue-oriented groups, often treating their activities as illegal.

Karimov's intransigence is embarrassing not only to the Bush administration, which continues to want Uzbekistan as a strategic ally in Washington's war on terror, but also to Western Europe. The European Bank for Reconstruction and

Uzbekistan

Development has given Karimov warning that it will cut funding to Uzbekistan unless he meets certain benchmarks toward human-rights and political reform.

The US is clearly in a quandary. Karimov hosted US Agriculture Secretary Ann Veneman late in 2004. Veneman praised the country's leadership, repeatedly describing Uzbekistan as a 'strategic ally of the US'. She offered both food aid and assistance in developing Uzbekistan's agricultural sector. She did not speak publicly about the human rights situation in the country.

In a speech before the National Endowment of Democracy, in which he criticised what he said were decades of Western tolerance for repression practiced by Western-allied Muslim governments, President Bush omitted any reference to Uzbekistan.

The overall thrust of geopolitics in Central Asia in 2005 was illustrated by the evolution of the Shanghai Co-operation Organization (SCO), which includes Uzbekistan. The SCO was increasingly active in 2005, leading some analysts to see the emergence of a potentially powerful regional grouping serving the interests of its heavyweight members, China and Russia. A summit of SCO leaders in July called for the US-led anti-terrorism coalition to provide a timeframe for withdrawal from military facilities on SCO territory, a thinly veiled reference to the US bases in Uzbekistan. In July, Karimov gave the US six months to vacate the Karshi-Khanabad air base it had used to support operations in Afghanistan.

Karimov was angry at US criticism of the killing of prisoners who broke out of an Andijan jail. They attempted an armed uprising, which Karimov says was an Islamic coup attempt supported by the West. Political analysts said his belief was that the US had gone from a useful strategic partner to a meddlesome plotter that threatened his hold on power. The state-run newspaper *Narodnoe slovo* said: 'Certain countries of the West, which would like to see the Central Asian countries fall into line with their expansionist policy, are using any and all means to export to this region forms and principles of democracy acceptable to them. The West is using the drama in Andijan in its great, dirty game to 'advance democracy,' which is in fact (aimed at) surrounding the potential rivals of Russia and China, which the West ceaselessly portrays as 'bad guys'.' Russia went further and its foreign ministry called Andijan 'a purely American operation. The US and the British transported militants from Afghanistan to Andijan to conduct the operation'.

Economy

Uzbekistan is a dry, landlocked country of which 11 per cent of the land area consists of intensely cultivated, irrigated river valleys. More than 60 per cent of the population lives in densely populated rural communities. Uzbekistan is now the world's second-largest cotton exporter and fifth largest producer; it relies heavily on cotton production as the major source of export earnings. Other exports include gold, oil and steel.

Following independence at the collapse of the USSR, the government sought to prop up its Soviet-style command economy with subsidies and tight controls on production and prices. Uzbekistan responded to the negative external conditions generated by the Asian and Russian financial crises by emphasising import substitute industrialisation and tightening export and currency controls within its already largely closed economy.

The government, while aware of the need to improve the investment climate, sponsors measures that often increase, not decrease, its control over business decisions. A sharp increase in the inequality of income distribution has hurt the lower ranks of society.

Potential investment by Russia and China in Uzbekistan's gas and oil industry would increase economic growth prospects.

Uzbekistan raised crude steel output 2.8 per cent year-on-year January to November 2004–05 to 565,812 tonnes. The state-owned Uzmetkombinat plant produces 99 per cent of Uzbekistan's crude steel and all of the country's roll and milling balls. It smelts scrap metal and has the capacity to produce 750,000 tonnes of crude steel per year.

The state continues to maintain a dominant ownership position in the economy. Serious restrictions in foreign as well as domestic trade remain. Nevertheless, led by strong growth in trade and agriculture, real growth in 2004 was an estimated 7.1 per cent. While fiscal policy was tight, rapid growth of monetary aggregates in the second half of the year led to higher inflation – while the official estimate of CPI inflation was only 3.7 per cent, the IMF estimated up to 15.5 per cent.

The current account registered a surplus of 10.1 per cent of GDP as export growth of 31.6 per cent outpaced import growth of 27.3 per cent. Foreign direct investment was US$187 million, up substantially from 2003, but at 1.5 per cent of GDP modest compared to the size of the economy.

After a mid-2005 meeting, the IMF said that in view of Uzbekistan's lagging transformation to a market economy, significant reforms were needed to enable Uzbekistan to reach its economic potential, attract foreign direct investment, and improve living standards and reduce poverty. In particular, decisive efforts were called for to further liberalise domestic and foreign trade and improve the business climate and governance.

Risk assessment

Economic	Poor
Political	Poor
Regional stability	Poor

KEY INDICATORS — Uzbekistan

	Unit	2000	2001	2002	2003	2004
Population	m	24.64	25.40	25.76	26.85	27.95
Gross domestic product (GDP)	US$bn	7.34	9.10	9.00	9.90	*11.96
GDP per capita	US$	298	358	348	386	375
GDP real growth	%	4.0	4.5	2.8	3.2	7.1
Inflation	%	25.0	27.2	27.0	10.0	8.8
Unemployment	%	0.6	0.4	0.4	0.5	–
Oil output	'000 bpd	177.0	172.0	171.0	166.0	152.0
Natural gas output	bn cum	52.2	53.5	53.8	53.6	55.8
Exports (fob) (goods)	US$m	2,771.0	2,740.0	2,510.0	3,065.0	3,700.0
Imports (fob) (goods)	US$m	2,380.0	2,814.0	2,430.0	2,554.0	2,820.0
Balance of trade	US$m	392.0	-74.0	83.0	511.0	880.0
Current account	US$m	72.0	-113.0	220.0	659.0	80.0
Foreign debt	US$bn	4.4	4.6	4.4	4.6	–
Exchange rate	per US$	409.00	504.59	819.42	975.00	1,020.00

* estimated figure

Nations of the World: A Political, Economic and Business Handbook

COUNTRY PROFILE

Historical profile
In the first century BC, Central Asia, including present-day Uzbekistan, formed an important part of the overland trade route known as the Great Silk Road, linking China with the Middle East and Imperial Rome. The Uzbeks are the second-largest community of Turkic people in the world. Lying between the Ferghana Basin and the Amu Darya River, the lands of modern Uzbekistan were the cradle of Central Asian civilisation until overcome by Mongol Tatar horsemen in the first century AD. Arabs conquered Uzbekistan in the seventh to eighth centuries and introduced Islam. In the fourteenth century, Uzbekistan became part of the empire of the Mongol leader, Timur, also known as Tamerlane, with Samarkand as its capital. The decline of Timur's empire saw the rise of the nomadic Uzbeks, who by the mid-nineteenth century had established the emirate of Bukhara, and khanates of Samarkand, Khiva and Kokand.

The Islamic Movement of Uzbekistan (IMU), based in Afghanistan and Tajikistan, poses a genuine armed threat to Uzbekistan. The activities of the IMU, which aims to overthrow Uzbekistan and establish a separate Islamic polity in the Ferghana valley, has made the Tajikistan-Uzbekistan border a zone of continual near-war. The government severely represses those it suspects of Islamic extremism.

1865–1876 The Russians took Tashkent and made it the capital of Turkestan, incorporating vast areas of Central Asia. They annexed the emirate of Bukhara and the khanates of Samarkand, Khiva and Kokand

1917 Following the October Revolution in Russia, the Tashkent Soviet was established.

1920 The Tashkent Soviet ousted the emir of Bukhara and the other khans.

1921 Uzbekistan became part of the Turkestan Autonomous Soviet Socialist Republic (ASSR).

1924 The Uzbek Soviet Socialist Republic (SSR) was formed from the Turkestan ASSR, the Bukharan People's Soviet Republic and the Khorezmian People's Soviet Republic; it was given Union Republic status in the Union of Soviet Socialist Republics (USSR).

1930s The Uzbek capital was transferred from Samarkand to Tashkent.

1944 The Soviet leader, Stalin, deported 160,000 Meskhetian Turks from Georgia to Uzbekistan.

1950s–80s Cotton production was boosted as the government undertook major irrigation projects on Uzbekistan's rivers and lakes. The country's water levels were drastically reduced.

1984 Thousands of Uzbek officials were arrested on corruption charges over the 'cotton affair' when millions of roubles went missing as a result of invented crop yields.

1989 Islam Karimov became the leader of the Communist Party of Uzbekistan. Ethnic violence broke out against the Meskhetian Turks and other minorities in the Ferghana Valley. Birlik (Unity), a nationalist movement, was founded.

1990 The Communist Party of Uzbekistan declared economic and political sovereignty and Islam Karimov became president.

1991 Independence from the USSR was declared. Uzbekistan joined the Commonwealth of Independent States (CIS). The first presidential elections were won by Islam Karimov; only a few opposition groups were allowed to field candidates.

1992 President Karimov banned the political parties Birlik and Erk (Freedom) Democratic Party and members of the opposition were arrested.

1994 Uzbekistan signed an economic integration treaty with Russia and an economic, military and social co-operation treaty with Kazakhstan and Kyrgyzstan.

1995 The ruling Chalk Demokratik Partijasi (CDP) (People's Democratic Party), formerly the Communist Party of Uzbekistan, won the elections. A referendum extended President Karimov's term of office until the year 2000.

1996 Uzbekistan, Kazakhstan and Kyrgyzstan agreed to create a single economic market.

1999 The president blamed bomb blasts in Tashkent on the IMU. A declaration of *jihad* was broadcast by the IMU from a radio station in Iran, demanding the resignation of the Uzbek leadership. The IMU, operating from mountain hideouts, attacked government forces (the first of many future cross-border incursions).

2000 President Karimov was re-elected. Western observers deemed the elections neither free nor fair.

2001 Tajikistan, China, Russia, Kazakhstan, Kyrgyzstan and Uzbekistan formed the Shanghai Co-operation Organisation (SCO) and agreed to fight ethnic and religious militancy, while promoting investment and trade. Uzbekistan allowed US troops to be based on its soil and the use of its airspace for the US-led military operation in Afghanistan.

2002 Uzbekistan's citizens voted in favour of a two-year extension of President Karimov's term in office from five to seven years and to convert the parliament to two chambers.

2003 Although the Birlik movement and the Erk opposition party were able to hold official meetings for the first time since they were banned in 1992, political parties were denied registration under restrictive registration procedures. On 11 December, President Karimov dismissed Prime Minister Otkir Sultanov and appointed Shavkat Mirziyayev in his place.

2004 There were shootings and bombings in March, April and July; the authorities blamed Islamic exteMists. In April, the European Bank for Reconstruction and Development reduced aid because of Uzbekistan's poor record on economic reform and human rights. An agreement with Turkmenistan on water resources was signed in November. Opposition parties were barred from taking part in the December parliamentary elections.

2005 After the second round of parliamentary elections on 9 January, the government was formed by the former ruling party, CDP, and independents. On 13 May, thousands of people protested in Andijan, a city near the Kyrgyz border, demanding the release of 23 men detained on charges of belonging to an Islamic group that advocates the overthrow of the secular government; protesters were killed and wounded in violent clashes with police.

Political structure
Uzbekistan has one of the most stable polity of all the countries of the former Soviet Union. The government of President Karimov keeps a firm hold of all branches of government and civil society. Consequently, the political environment is heavily centralised around the personality of the President and the dangers of political as well as economic stagnation are high.

Constitution
The constitution was adopted in December 1992. It guarantees respect for all citizens, regardless of language, custom or tradition, and forbids any group or individual to exercise power on behalf of the people of Uzbekistan except for the elected president and legislature. The creation of a state ideology and censorship of the media are also contrary to the constitution; however, media censorship is still practised.

The autonomous region of Karakalpakstan has its own constitution, but is subject to the laws of Uzbekistan. Karakalpakstan has the right to withdraw from Uzbekistan depending on support via a referendum.

On 8 December 1992, Uzbekistan became the second Central Asian state to adopt a post-independence constitution. The already considerable powers of the president were increased, giving him the

Uzbekistan

right to appoint regional governors who report directly to him. The constitution also included guarantees of freedom, of conscience and of travel, and a statement that the country should be a secular democracy. President Karimov has pointed to the Turkish state as his country's model. On 27 January 2002, a nationwide referendum agreed with the extension of the president's constitutional term in office from five to seven years and authorised the election of a bicameral parliament.

Form of state
Secular, (theoretically) democratic and presidential republic.

The executive
The president is head of state, holds supreme executive power and is directly elected for no more than two consecutive terms. A January 2002 referendum approved a two-year extension of the president's constitutional term of office from five to seven years (it was originally due to expire in 2005 and has been extended to 2007).

The president appoints the prime minister and ministers, subject to confirmation by the legislature, appoints the judges of the lower courts and the governors of the regions.

The Cabinet of Ministers is the government of the country; it is subordinate to the president.

National legislature
A January 2002 referendum approved increasing the country's parliament from a one-chamber legislature to two.

From December 2004, parliament comprises a lower house (Legislative Assembly with 120 seats, elected for a term of five years), responsible for formulating legislation and considering ministerial nominations, and an upper house (Senate), which will be responsible for approving legislation. President Islam Karimov selects 16 of the Senate's 100 representatives, with the remaining 84 elected from the ranks of regional, district and city legislative councils for each of the country's 12 regions, the city of Tashkent and the autonomous Republic of Karakalpakstan.

Legal system
Judicial power is nominally independent of government, but as the judges of the higher courts are selected from among lower court judges, who are themselves appointed by the president, there is in practice significant political control over the system.

The three highest courts are the Constitutional Court, the Supreme Court and the High Commercial Court. The first rules on the validity of legislation and on disputes between the government of Uzbekistan and the Karakalpakstan autonomous region. The second is the highest court of appeal for criminal and civil cases initiated in the lower courts. The third is the highest court of arbitration for civil cases initiated in the lower courts.

Last elections
9 January 2005 (second round parliamentary); 26 December 2004 (first round parliamentary); 2002 (referendum); 9 January 2000 (presidential).

Results: Parliamentary second round: after the second round of parliamentary elections, the Liberal-Democratic Party held a total of 41 seats out of 120, followed by the People's Democratic Party with 33.

Parliamentary first round: 62 out of 120 constituencies were decided. The Liberal-Democratic Party won 21 seats, the Chalk Demokratik Partijasi (CDP) (Democratic People's Party) 18, the Fidokorlar National-Democratic Party nine, the National Renaissance Democratic Party six, the Adolat Social-Democratic Party two and initiative-group candidates six.

Referendum: Ninety-one per cent of Uzbekistan's citizens voted in favour of a possible two-year extension of Karimov's term in office and to increase the country's parliament from a one-chamber legislature to two.

Presidential: President Islam Karimov was re-elected with 91.9 per cent of the vote against 4.1 per cent for his opponent, Abdulhasiz Dzhalalov.

Next elections
December 2007 (presidential); 2009 (parliamentary).

Political parties
In 1997, legislation came into force prohibiting parties based on ethnic or religious lines, or those advocating war or subversion of the constitutional order. As a result of amendments to the Law on Elections in August 2003, only registered political parties and voters' initiative groups have the right to field candidates for election.

Ruling party
Coalition government: Chalk Demokratik Partijasi (CDP) (People's Democratic Party) and independents

Main opposition party
All parties in the Supreme Assembly are loyal to the president. The banned O'zbekiston Erk Demokratik Partiyasi (OEDP) (Erk Democratic Party) is considered to be the main opposition party to the Karimov regime.

Population
27.95 million (2004)

Ethnic make-up
Uzbek (72 per cent), Russian (8 per cent), Tajik (7 per cent), Kazakh (4 per cent), others (9 per cent). There is a Korean minority estimated at 7 per cent. The Uzbeks are the second most numerous Turkic people in the world after the Turks themselves.

Religions
Muslim (88 per cent, mostly Sunni); Christian Eastern Orthodox (9 per cent).

Education
Although Uzbekistan's overall literacy rate is high, the government is implementing a long-term programme of transition from Cyrillic to Latin script, and in the short-term there is likely to be some changes in the literacy rate.

Primary education begins at aged six and last until aged 10. General secondary education lasts until aged 15, when students may choose between a technical, vocational or academic course for two years. From aged 17, specialised secondary schools offer advanced vocational or academic two-year courses.

There are 16 universities and 42 research institutes in the country, including the state-run Tashkent Islamic University. The government initiated a National Programme for Personnel Training, giving high priority to introducing new educational technologies and attracting international donors. The reform programme replaced existing schools and it is estimated that seven million pupils will enrol in these new schools, and in sharp contrast with the past, 90 per cent (an unprecedented amount in the New Independent States) of these pupils are expected to enrol in vocational education and training.

In February 2005 a report by the International Crisis Group alleged that thousands of children are forced out of school to work in cotton fields. Uzbekistan is the world's fifth largest cotton producer and during the harvest season children of all ages are used to pick the cotton. Pay for this work may be denied and refusal to work may lead to expulsion from school.

Literacy rate: 99.3 per cent total; 98.9 per cent female; adult rates (World Bank 2004).

Compulsory years: Six to 15

Enrolment rate: 100 per cent gross primary school enrolment rate in 2000, 94 per cent at secondary level and 36 per cent at tertiary level.

Pupils per teacher: 21 in primary schools.

Health
Healthcare standards were fairly uniform across the former Soviet Union, but the breakdown in trade and economic crises have brought about a severe shortage of medicines and equipment.

According to a presidential decree in 1999, private healthcare institutions, were exempted from tax in order to facilitate investment in medical equipment; it also included a programme for the development

of medical treatment centres in villages over 2001–05. The government also plans to make premises and funds available for private healthcare institutions.
HIV prevalence: 0.1 per cent aged 15–49 in 2003 (World Bank)
Life expectancy: 66.7 years (World Bank)
Fertility rate/Maternal mortality rate: 2.3 births per woman; maternal mortality 21 per 100,000 live births (World Bank).
Birth rate/Death rate: 23 births and 6 death per 1,000 people (World Bank)
Infant mortality rate: 57 per 1,000 live births; 7.9 per cent of children aged under five are malnourished (World Bank).
Head of population per physician/bed: 3.3 physicians and 8.3 hospital beds per 1,000 people.

Welfare
Social spending is relatively high compared to most other transitional countries. Social assistance is channelled through traditional local structures using the national Malhalla foundation, which is responsible for meeting the needs of the poor. The Malhalla collects information on the claimants' needs independently of the state. Wages in the agricultural sector have tended to fall behind the national average as a result of high taxes, contributing to increased risks of civil unrest. Expenditure on the social safety net continues to account for 3.5 per cent of GDP and benefits are usually increased in line with wages rather than with official inflation.
There is a comprehensive system of benefits for sickness, disability, maternity and unemployment, as well as a combined state and private pension scheme. However, many of these payments are linked to the declining minimum wage, with the result that those depending on benefits are likely to drop below the poverty line. There are special payments to veterans of the Soviet war in Afghanistan. The government also provides benefits through budget subsidies for housing maintenance and public utilities.

Main cities
Tashkent (capital, estimated population 2.3 million in 2004), Namangan (432,000), Samarkand (374,900), Andizhan (354,500), Bukhara (272,400), Nukus (262,100), Karshi (226,400).

Languages spoken
Uzbek is of Turkic origin and is the most commonly used language, although Russian remains the language of inter-ethnic communication and business. Turkish and Arabic are also spoken. English and other Western languages are increasingly common, particularly in Tashkent and other urban areas.

Official language/s
Uzbek

Media
Although the Uzbek Constitution and the Law on Mass Media forbids censorship, Uzbekistan still practises it. The government controls much of the printing and distribution infrastructure.

Press
Pre-publication censorship of the press by the state was abolished in 2002, but self-censorship is widespread.
Dailies: State-run dailies include: *Khalq Sozi*, the Russian-language newspapers *Narodnoe Slovo* (People's World) and *Pravda Vostoka* (Truth of the East).
Weeklies: Weeklies include the *Mohiyat*.
Business: Business news is carried by *Business Partner Uzbekistana*, *Business-vestnik Vostoka* (Business News of the East); English language publications include *Business Partner* and *Business Review*.

Broadcasting
Private TV and radio stations operate alongside the state-run broadcasters. Foreign channels are available via cable TV.

Economy
Following independence in 1991, Uzbekistan faced a loss of subsidies from Russia and contracting regional markets. Uzbekistan resisted the shock economic reforms of other ex-Soviet countries, following instead a more cautious restructuring approach. This resulted in a much smaller contraction in the economy than was experienced in other states in the region.
Uzbekistan's economic growth remains largely dependent on cotton. The agricultural sector accounts for over 30 per cent of GDP and cotton exports for 28 per cent of foreign exchange earnings.
The government has introduced a gradual economic liberalisation programme (termed 'evolutionary reform' by President Karimov), which is being monitored by the IMF. It has pledged to privatise 'non-strategic' state-owned industries, rationalise the financial sector and attempt to attract much-needed foreign investment in an effort to increase know-how and economic efficiency. The government's ability to find buyers for medium- and large-scale enterprises, such as the oil and gas company Uzbekneftegaz and the telecommunications company Uzbektelecom, will ultimately depend on the pace of economic reform and asking prices. Many analysts suspect the government has traditionally inflated the latter in order to delay the privatisation programme, a process which will expose the inefficiencies of Uzbekistan's company-base and lead to a period of politically sensitive labour-shedding.

In recent years, international financial organisations have become wary of lending to Uzbekistan, although the Asian Development Bank has provided financial aid as part of a development programme. In 2004, the European Bank for Reconstruction and Development withdrew aid because of Uzbekistan's poor record on economic reform and human rights and its failure to meet key economic targets. The government's medium-term objective is to liberalise trade, attract foreign investment and realise the benefits of currency convertibility.

External trade
Uzbekistan still relies heavily on trade with former Soviet Union states, particularly Russia. It has signed a number of trade agreements with regional countries. It has an agreement with Kazakhstan and Kyrgyzstan permitting free movement of capital, goods and labour between the three countries and the co-ordination of monetary and fiscal policy.

Imports
Principal imports are machinery and equipment, foodstuffs, chemicals and metals.
Main sources: Russia (26.4 per cent total, 2004), South Korea (10.8 per cent), Germany (9.4 per cent), China (8.3 per cent), Kazakhstan (6.0 per cent), Turkey (6.0 per cent)

Exports
Principal exports are cotton, gold, energy products, mineral fertilisers, ferrous metals, textiles, food products and vehicles. Export tariffs and bans are being phased out.
Main destinations: Russia (21.2 per cent total, 2004), China (14 per cent), Ukraine (7.0 per cent), (Turkey 6.3 per cent), Tajikistan (5.8 per cent), Bangladesh (4.2 per cent)

Agriculture
Farming
The agricultural sector contributed around 31 per cent to GDP in 2004 and employs around a third of the working population. Only 9 per cent of the land is suitable for cultivation.
Over 1,500 farms operate on a co-operative basis. Family farms dominate 99 per cent of the cotton sector and 93 per cent of the corn sector.
Cotton is the main crop, around a million tonnes a year being produced, three-quarters of it for export. In a report published in early 2005 – *The Curse of Cotton: Central Asia's destructive monoculture* – the International Crisis Group (ICG) said that while the former Soviet cotton producing countries of Uzbekistan, Tajikistan and Turkmenistan continued to exploit their cotton growers there was little hope of improving economic development

Uzbekistan

and tackling poverty. The cotton industry is vital to the economy of Uzbekistan, yet while the industry continues to rely on cheap labour (including children), land ownership is uncertain, state intervention discourages competition and the rule of law is limited, there is little incentive for the powerful vested interests to reform the system.

In addition to the economic and social costs to the rural populations, the environmental costs of the monoculture have been devastating. The degradation of the Aral Sea in particular has lead to international concern.

Crop production in 2004 included: 5.37 million tonnes (mt) wheat, 181,230 tonnes (t) rice, 156,400t maize, 589,110t grapes, 1,000t pistachios, 11,100t pulses, 895,730t potatoes, 1.24mt tomatoes, 1.36mt fruit in total, 3,48mt vegetables in total. Livestock production included: 592,300t meat in total, 490,500t beef, 12,600t pig-meat, 70,500t lamb, 16,700t poultry, 104,390t eggs, 4.27mt milk, 2,250t honey, 16,799t cocoons (silk).

Fishing
Crop production in 2004 included: 5.37 million tonnes (mt) wheat, 181,230 tonnes (t) rice, 156,400t maize, 589,110t grapes, 1,000t pistachios, 11,100t pulses, 895,730t potatoes, 1.24mt tomatoes, 1.36mt fruit in total, 3,48mt vegetables in total. Livestock production included: 592,300t meat in total, 490,500t beef, 12,600t pig-meat, 70,500t lamb, 16,700t poultry, 104,390t eggs, 4.27mt milk, 2,250t honey, 16,799t cocoons (silk).

Forestry
Only 8 per cent of Uzbekistan is forested and commercial exploitation is for domestic purposes only as fuel. There is low production of industrial roundwood, because the government has placed restrictions on harvesting due to the poor condition of forests.

Production in 2004 included 24,980 cubic metres (cum) roundwood, 6,000cum pulpwood, 18,980cum woodfuel.

Industry and manufacturing
Industry contributed around 25 per cent to GDP in 2004 and employs 18 per cent of the working population.

Main industries include chemical and gas production, heavy engineering, specialising in machinery for the cotton-growing and textile industries, aircraft construction, metal works, textiles and cotton derivatives, canned foods and nitrogenised fertilisers.

Tourism
Uzbekistan, situated on the route of the ancient Silk Road, is a country rich in historical and cultural heritage, giving it considerable tourist potential. Infrastructure is improving and attractions, including skiing, are being developed.

Environment
The Aral Sea is drying up due to the overuse of water from the two main rivers which feed into it and has lost 40 per cent of its water, dropping by up to 19 metres. This has resulted in desertification of the surrounding land. A UN study published in 2004 reported that there was no possibility of restoring the water and the need must be on preserving what is left.

The government has endorsed a 2004 joint strategy to resolve the demands of its water requirements with its neighbours. Uzbekistan has numerous environmental problems, apart from the management of water resources and the Aral Sea Basin. More than half of irrigated land is heavily salinated and eroded. Surface and underground water sources used for human consumption in parts of the country have also been polluted by industrial and communal discharges.

Mining
Uzbekistan is rich in unexplored mineral deposits – its potential mineral wealth amounts to a value of US$3,000 billion. There are around 100 deposits of various metals, including gold, silver, uranium, zinc, copper and tungsten, which need developing. Uzbekistan is the fourth-largest uranium producer in the world. Uzbekistan is the ninth-largest gold producer in the world. Its commercial reserves are associated with open-cast mines of the Muruntau field in the Kyzylkum desert in central Uzbekistan, which have been developed by the main state gold producer Kyzylkumredmetzoloto (Navoi Integrated Mining and Metallurgical Plant) since 1967. Its annual output amounts to 55–60 tonnes, producing 70 per cent of Uzbekistan's total gold production.

The Zarafshan-Newmont joint-venture between Uzbekistan and the US mining company Newmont, set up in 1995, processes about 200 million tonnes of low-grade ore, previously regarded as waste, from the Muruntau open gold pit. The project is due to end in 2012.

Dzhetymtau, located in the Kyzylkum desert is estimated to hold reserves of 400 tonnes of gold and 350,000 tonnes of tungsten ores.

There are silver deposits in the central Kyzylkum region, which also contain gold, platinum group metals, cobalt and nickel, which can be recovered as by-products. Uzbekistan is the only producer of enriched uranium in the former Soviet Union. All output is exported, since Uzbekistan has no nuclear reactors.

Uzbekistan's proven uranium reserves are around 80,000 tonnes, while estimated reserves are around 178,000 tonnes. Sugraly is one of Central Asia's biggest uranium fields and holds an estimated 38,000 tonnes of uranium. Kyzylkumredmetzoloto (Kyzylkum Precious Metals and Gold) is Uzbekistan's only uranium producer and exporter. Uzbekistan possesses considerable reserves of lead and zinc.

Copper production in Uzbekistan averages 80,000 tonnes per year, principally from the Kalmakir open mine, with the remainder mined at the Sari Checku open pit. The ore is processed at the Almalyk concentrator.

Uzbekistan produces over 100,000 tonnes per year of feldspar, about one-third of the output of the former Soviet Union. The non-ferrous metal industry includes the mining of bismuth, tungsten and molybdenum. Other natural resources include rock salt, potassium salts, anthracite, graphite, ozokerite, sulphur, quartz, limestone, gypsum, bentonites and semi-precious stones.

Hydrocarbons
Uzbekistan had proved oil reserves of 600 million barrels in 2004 and produced 152,000 barrels per day (bpd). Production meets domestic demand of 131,000 bpd. Thereare three refineries –at Fergana, Alty-Arik and Bukhara with total capacity of 222,000 bpd.

Uzbekistan had proved reserves of natural gas of 1.86 trillion cubic metres in 2004 and is the tenth-largest natural gas producer in the world. Gas production was 55.8 billion cubic metres in 2004. Principal oil and gas fields include Kuanish, Shakhpakthy and Chembar. Other fields have been discovered in the Mamangan and Ferghana regions. Whereas neighbouring Kazakhstan, Azerbaijan and increasingly Turkmenistan have signed numerous multi-million and even multi-billion dollar oil and gas production agreements with foreign energy companies, external involvement in the Uzbekistani sector only began in 2004, when agreements were signed with Russian and Chinese companies. The industry is almost entirely state-controlled, with 14 companies grouped around Uzbekneftegaz (Uzbek Oil and Gas), which is responsible for all aspects of exploration, production, distribution and processing in the hydrocarbons sector.

Uzbekistan has abundant reserves of coal, about one-third of which is highly valued anthracite, but production has rapidly declined and the industry is in need of modernisation. Production meets nearly all domestic needs of around one million tonnes per annum.

Energy

The energy sector is almost entirely state-controlled. Natural gas provides most of the necessary energy for local power generation facilities. Uzbekistan is the largest electricity producer among the Central Asian republics and a net exporter of electricity, supplying regional countries, such as Tajikistan.

Uzbekistan is part of the Central Asian power distribution system along with Kyrgyzstan, southern Kazakhstan, Tajikistan and Turkmenistan. In May 2002, the Uzbekistan government signed an agreement with the interim Afghan government to supply 30MW of electricity to northern Afghanistan.

Uzbekistan has 37 electric power plants with an overall capacity of over 11.2GW. There are hydroelectric power plants on the Syr Darya, Narin and Chirchik rivers, and thermal power stations at Syr Darya, Tashkent, Novo-Angren, Tachiatasch and Ferghana. Hydroelectric plants produce 15 per cent of Uzbekistan's electricity and thermal–powered plants 85 per cent. Work began on the construction of five hydro-electric power plants in 2002. The largest is the Topalang hydroelectric power station in southern Uzbekistan, which will produce 175MW of electricity annually when fully constructed.

Financial markets
Stock exchange

The Republican Stock Exchange (RSE) 'Tashkent' opened in 1994. It houses a securities exchange, real estate traders, the national investment fund and the national securities depositary. It does not trade all joint-stock companies each month and therefore market capitalisation varies widely.

Banking and insurance

Three state-owned banks dominate the banking sector: Bank Asaka, National Bank of Uzbekistan (NBU) and Narodny Bank.

Central bank
National Bank of Uzbekistan (NBU)

Main financial centre
Tashkent

Time

GMT plus five hours

Geography

Uzbekistan is located in the heart of Central Asia. The fourth-largest republic in the former Soviet Union, Uzbekistan measures approximately 925km from north to south and 1,400km from west to east at its widest points. The republic has a short border with Afghanistan to the south, Kazakhstan lies to the north, Kyrgyzstan and Tajikistan to the east and south-east and Turkmenistan to the south-west.

The western region, including the Karakalpakstan oblast, marks the eastern fringe of the Turkmen desert. The Kyzylkum desert covers most of the area between Tashkent and the Aral Sea. The western reaches of the Tien Shan mountain range protrude from Kyrgyzstan and Tajikistan into south-eastern Uzbekistan. The fertile Ferghana Valley runs from the north-eastern finger of Uzbekistan, east of Tashkent, across the border into Kyrgyzstan. Half of the Aral Sea lies within Uzbekistan, the other half in Kazakhstan. There are two main rivers. The Amu Darya, which enters from Afghanistan at Termez and runs along the border with Turkmenistan before turning north at Khiva and flowing into the southern end of the Aral Sea. The Syr Darya flows from the Tien Shan mountains northwards, east of Tashkent and into Kazakhstan, eventually reaching the northern end of the Aral Sea.

Climate

Uzbekistan comprises mostly desert and semi-desert, with extreme continental temperatures: the average stands at -8 degrees Celsius (C) in January and 26 degrees C in June. Temperatures in Tashkent vary from -1 degree C in January to 29–40 degrees C or more in summer. Rainfall averages between 80 and 90mm per annum on the plains and 890 to 1,000mm per annum in the mountains.

Dress codes

Smart clothes are required for business visitors. Otherwise dress is not overly formal but modest, particularly outside Tashkent.

Entry requirements
Passports

Passports are required by all and must be valid for at least six months after the intended date of departure.

Visa

Required by all. Business travellers must obtain an invitation from a local company or organisation. The Uzbek contact should submit a visa support letter to the Ministry of Foreign Affairs in Tashkent before the visitor applies for a visa. When an approval to visit has been agreed a confirmation is sent by the ministry to the embassy and the visitor should contact the consular section to ensure that a visa issuance confirmation of the Ministry of Foreign Affairs is in place before submitting their application.

To download a visa application visit www.uzbekistanembassy.uk.net/main/visas/VisaApplicationForm.pdf.

However citizens of UK, US, Austria, Belgium, Germany, Italy, France, Japan, Spain and Switzerland, travelling on business, are not required to obtain an invitation and may travel on a visitor's visa. Multiple entry visas, for up to one year, are obtainable by these citizens, except those of the US who may obtain them for up to four years.

Travellers on visitor's visas whose stay in Uzbekistan exceeds three days are required to register with the Local Department of the Ministry of Internal Affairs within three working days of arrival. Hotel administration should take care of such registration automatically.

Transit visas issued in other CIS countries are no longer recognised.

Currency advice/regulations

Imported foreign currency must be declared on arrival, as re-export is only allowed within the limits of the declaration given. The import of amounts over US$20 million requires permission from the Ministry of Foreign Economic Relations. The import and export of domestic currency is forbidden. Travellers cheques can rarely be exchanged outside the commercial areas of Tashkent.

Customs

Goods to the value of US$5,000 can be imported for personal use. On arrival, valuable items such as jewellery, cameras, computers should be declared.

Health (for visitors)
Mandatory precautions

Vaccination certificates are required for yellow fever if travelling from an infected area.

Advisable precautions

Water precautions recommended: water purification tablets may be useful or drink bottled water. It is advisable to be 'in date' for the following immunisations: polio (within 10 years), tetanus (within 10 years), typhoid fever, hepatitis 'A' (moderate risk only), tick-borne encephalitis, tuberculosis. Anti-malarial precautions advisable. There is a risk of rabies. Any medicines required by the traveller should be brought into the country and it would be wise to have precautionary antibiotics if going outside major urban centres. A travel kit including a disposable syringe is a reasonable precaution. A reciprocal health agreement exists with the UK for urgent medical treatment. Proof of UK residence will be required.

Hotels

Advisable to book in advance through Uzbektourism or other specialist travel agents.

Credit cards

Credit cards are not widely accepted outside Tashkent's top hotels and restaurants.

Public holidays
Fixed dates

1 Jan (New Year's Day), 8 Mar (Women's Day), 20–22 Mar (Nawruz/Persian New

Uzbekistan

Year), 1 May (Labour Day), 9 May (Day of Memory and Respect), 1 Sep (Independence Day), 18 Nov (Flag Day), 8 Dec (Constitution Day).

Variable dates
Eid al Adha, Eid al Fitr, Birth of the Prophet.
The Islamic year contains 354 or 355 days, with the result that Muslim feasts advance by 10–12 days against the Gregorian calendar. Dates of feasts vary according to the sighting of the new moon, so cannot be forecast exactly. Islamic year 1426: 10 February 2005 to 30 January 2006.

Working hours
Banking
Mon–Fri: 0800–1300, 1400–1700. Banks are generally open Saturday mornings but it is advisable to make appointments weekdays only. Banks at Tashkent airport are open only at arrival of international flights.

Business
Mon–Fri: 0800–1300, 1400–1700. Business hours generally include Saturday mornings but appointments should be made.

Government
Mon–Fri: 0800–1300, 1400–1700. Some government offices are open Saturday mornings.

Shops
Mon–Fri: 0800–2000/2100. Shops are closed for lunch for one hour at any time between 1100 and 1500.

Telecommunications
In 2003, Uzbekistan is implementing the first stage of the modernisation plan for its telecommunications infrastructure, through the Agency of Posts and Telecommunications.
The National Programme for the reconstruction and development of telecommunications in Uzbekistan up to 2010 provides for the modernisation of international and local networks in Uzbekistan and the replacement of outdated analogue telecommunications systems with new digital networks to meet with international standards.
The modernisation is being partially funded through credit from OECF Japan Fund.

Mobile phones
Coverage in areas outside Tashkent is extremely limited.

Internet/e-mail
By January 2005, there were around 675,000 Internet users (government statistics).

Electricity supply
220V AC

Social customs/useful tips
Business is conducted formally. Appointments are essential when business cards are exchanged.
Personal relationships are the key to doing business in Uzbekistan, with the hierarchy confined to a small group of influential families. Establishing contact within that group can be vital.
Gratuities are illegal.
The giving of small gifts is widely practised, not as bribes but as social niceties. Uzbek hospitality is renowned. It may be regarded as insulting to decline an invitation to a private function. Offering basic food is considered insulting. It is polite to see a visitor off at a train station. If travelling on public transport, make sure to give up your seat to the old, parents with children and the disabled. Superstitions are taken somewhat seriously: for example, do not give an even number of flowers, as this is funereal; do not greet people in a doorway – this is considered unlucky. Local customs of note are ram butting and wrestling, and wedding ceremonies in September which take place in the street. Alcohol is available and smoking is widespread.

Security
Terrorist bombings in Tashkent have prompted many Western government to advice their citizens not to visit Uzbekistan unless absolutely necessary. Visitors should alert their presence to their own embassies on arrival and take all precautions and advice given regarding safety measures.
It is unwise to venture out on the streets alone at night. Dress inconspicuously, as wealthy-looking foreigners can be a target for muggers. Identification should be carried at all times, and visitors should avoid photographing official buildings. If taking photographs in the vicinity of police or soldiers, it is best to ask their permission first.
Since 1999, there has been an increasing terrorist and kidnapping threat in the north-east of the country, especially in the Ferghana Valley and mountainous regions on the Kyrgyz and Tajik borders. Visitors should register with the Uzbek authorities before entering these areas. Outbreaks of violence can lead to strong reactions from the Uzbekistani army, including widespread road blocks and the closure of some destinations. If stopped by police, visitors should remain calm and polite.

Getting there
Air
National airline: Ozbekiston Havo Yollari (Uzbekistan Airlines)
International airport/s: Tashkent International airport (TAS), 11km from city centre. Facilities include duty free, bureau de change, left luggage, restaurants and bar. Tashkent airport is Central Asia's main international airport. The airport is served by a handful of airlines from Western and Eastern Europe, the Middle East and the Far East. A new passenger air terminal was constructed in early 2002.
Airport tax: No tax is levied.

Surface
There are border crossings with Afghanistan, Kazakhstan, Kyrgyzstan, Tajikistan and Turkmenistan, however since December 2002 some border crossings may be closed due to import disputes.
Road: Primary roads along trade routes are being upgraded to increase access for freight. Secondary roads are in poor condition especially in desert areas such as the borders with Turkmenistan and the western borders with Kazakhstan.
Rail: Tashkent is the hub of rail services in Central Asia. Lines run west to Ashgabat (Turkmenistan), south to Samarkand and on to Dushanbe (Tajikistan), east to Bishkek (Kyrgyzstan) and Almaty (Kazakhstan) and north to Moscow (Russia). The distances involved do not make this the most convenient means of travel, services are few and slow, and tickets must be purchased with hard currency, preferably US dollars.

Getting about
National transport
Air: There are many cheap internal flights between cities, and these tend to be the most convenient way to travel over long distances. Tashkent, Bukhara, Samarkand and Urgench are all served by internal flights.
Road: The road network is deteriorating and many published statistics on paved and unpaved roads are often a decade out-of-date. Driving can be hazardous for the visitor and it is recommended that arrangements should be made to use a local driver and a four-wheel drive vehicle, particularly if travelling to the Tien Shan mountain ranges. Tashkent roads are relatively well maintained with street lighting. Outside the city however the risks of driving, especially at night, include livestock and farm vehicles (often animal-drawn). There are security checkpoints at the city limits of Tashkent and other towns throughout the country. A permit is necessary if travelling to Termez and other areas of the Surkhandarya region. The permit can be applied for in Tashkent and usually takes five days to process. Uzbekistan has a large highway police force, and drivers are frequently stopped for minor infractions or document checks. Foreign drivers may also face the solicitation of bribes, from the highway police; minor corruption of this kind is commonplace.

Buses: Routes between the main cities are served by modern air-conditioned coach services which are reliable but infrequent. Other regional services are irregular and often used for transporting goods and livestock.

Rail: Tashkent, Samarkand and Bukhara are all connected by a modern, electrified railway. Some other routes are in varying states of disrepair, and long-distance travel by train should be avoided.

City transport

Taxis: In each city there are official taxis (with sign on top) and unofficial taxis. Agree rates in advance when using the official taxis. A few dollars are sufficient for a local journey in an unofficial taxi. In Tashkent it is safer to use official taxis or hire cars. Journey time from the airport to the city centre is 15–20 minutes.

Buses, trams & metro: A trolleybus service operates in Tashkent. Buses from the airport take 30–60 minutes to the city and are not recommended.

Trains: Journey time from the airport to the city centre is 10–20 minutes.

Car hire

A national licence with authorised translation or international driving permit is required.

BUSINESS DIRECTORY

The addresses listed below are a selection only. While World of Information makes every endeavour to check these addresses, we cannot guarantee that changes have not been made, especially to telephone numbers and area codes. We would welcome any corrections.

Telephone area codes

International direct dialling code (IDD) for Uzbekistan is +998, followed by area code and subscriber's number:
Bukara 65 Samarkand 66
Ferghana 73 Tashkent 71

Useful telephone numbers

Police: 02
Fire: 01
Ambulance: 03

Chambers of Commerce

American Chamber of Commerce in Uzbekistan, 41 Buyok Turon Street, Tashkent 700000 (tel: 120-6077; fax: 120-7077; e-mail: office@amcham-uzbekistan.org).

Uzbekistan Chamber of Commodity Producers and Entrepreneurs, 6 Bukhoro Street, Tashkent 700047 (tel: 133-0699; fax: 133-3799; e-mail: root@ptp.co.uz).

Banking

Bank Asaka (specialised state joint stock commercial), 67 Nukus Str, 700015 Tashkent (tel: 120-8111; fax: 540-659).

Narodny Bank (People's Bank), Tashkent.

National Bank for Foreign Economic Activity of the Republic of Uzbekistan, 101 Amir Temur St, 700084 Tashkent (tel: 137-6077; fax: 133-3200).

National Bank of Uzbekistan, Tashkent.

Pakhta Bank, 43 Mukimi Street, 700096 Tashkent (tel: 781-296; fax: 120-8818).

Uzbekistan-Turkish Bank, No.15/B Drujba Naradov Street, Tashkent (tel: 173-8323, 173-8324; fax: 120-6362).

Uzpromstroybank, Tashkent.

Central bank

Central Bank of Uzbekistan (CBU), Prospekt Uzbekistana 6, 700003 Tashkent (tel: 133-6829; fax: 133-3509).

Travel information

Aeroflot, Tashkent (tel: 336-456).

Intourist, 45 Hamza St, Tashkent (tel: 335-970, 332-773).

Uzbekistan Airways, 41 Movaraunnakhr Street, Tashkent 700060 (tel: 332-860; fax: 557-470).

National tourist organisation offices

Uzbektourism, 47 Khorezm St, 700047 Tashkent (tel: 335-414; fax: 327-948; internet: www.uzbektourism.uz).

Ministries

Ministry of Agriculture, 4 Navoi St, 700004 Tashkent (tel: 411-353, 410-020; fax: 410-053).

Ministry of Communication, 1 Alexei Tolstoi St, 700000 Tashkent (tel: 338-503; fax: 331-695).

Ministry for Cultural Affairs, 30 Navoi St, 700129 Tashkent (tel: 394-957).

Ministry of Defence, 100 Academician Abdullaev St, 700000 Tashkent (tel: 336-667).

Ministry of Energy and Electrification, 6 Horezm St, 700000 Tashkent (tel: 336-128; fax: 362-700).

Ministry of Finance, 5 Mustaqillik Sq, 700078 Tashkent (tel: 391-943; fax: 445-643).

Ministry of Foreign Affairs, 9 Uzbekistan Ave, 700029 Tashkent (tel: 336-475; fax: 394-348; internet: http://jahon.mfa.uz/englishnew.htm).

Ministry of Foreign Economic Relations, Elyor Madjidovich Ganiev, 75 Buyuk Ipak Yuli St, 700077 Tashkent (tel: 670-734, 689-256, 344-480; fax: 687-231, 687-477).

Ministry of Health, 12 Navoi St, 700012 Tashkent (tel: 411-680; fax: 411-641).

Ministry of Higher and Special Secondary Education, 6 Mustaqillik Sq, 700078 Tashkent (tel: 394-808; fax: 394-329).

Ministry of Internal Affairs, 1 Herman Lopatin St, 700029 Tashkent (tel: 583-614; fax: 338-934).

Ministry of Justice, 5 Hamza St, 700047 Tashkent (tel: 335-039; fax: 335-176).

Ministry of Labour, 4 Abai St, 700195 Tashkent (tel: 417-628; fax: 397-821).

Ministry of Land Improvement and Water Economy, 5-a Abdulla Qodiri St, 700128 Tashkent (tel: 411-353; fax: 414-924).

Ministry of Public Education, 5 Mustaqillik Sq, 700078 Tashkent (tel: 394-214; fax: 391-173).

Ministry of Social Security, 20-a Abdulla Avioni St, 700100 Tashkent (tel: 535-371).

Other useful addresses

Business-Vestnik Vostoka (BVV) (weekly information in English on the region), Tashkent (e-mail: bvv@bvv.bcc.com.uz).

Cabinet of Ministers, 5 Mustakillik Maidoni, Tashkent (tel: 398-188; fax: 398-121).

Central Asia Research Forum, School of Oriental and African Studies, Thornhaugh St, London WC1H 0XG, UK (tel: (0)171-323-6300; fax: (0)171-436-3844).

EU Co-ordinating Unit, Tarasa Chevchenka St Dom 4, 700029 Tashkent (tel: 384-018, 563-479, 560-417; fax: 320-652).

Foreign Investment Agency, 4th Floor, 16A Navoi Street, Tashkent (tel: 415-541, 415-752; fax: 891-201).

Government House, 700008 Tashkent (tel: 398-295/260; fax: 398-601/463).

National Agency for Telecommunications and Postal Services, 1 Tolstoy Street, Tashkent (tel: 336-503, 336-645; fax: 398-732).

National Association of Gold Mining and Diamond Processing Companies, 26 Turaqorghan Thoroughfare, 700019 Tashkent (tel: 480-720; fax: 442-603).

National Joint Stock Corporation for Construction in the City of Tashkent, 16-a Uzbekistan Ave, 700027 Tashkent (tel: 339-033; fax: 364-788).

SME Development Agency, 89 Gargarin St. Samarkand, PO Box 703029 (tel: 242-966; fax: 310-107; e-mail: ravshan@samarkand.silk.glas.apc.org).

State Company for Television and Radio Broadcasting, 69 Navoi St, 700011 Tashkent (tel: 338-106; fax: 440-021).

State Committee on Agriculture and Construction of the Republic of Uzbekistan, 6 Abai St, 700011 Tashkent (tel: 440-084/700/485).

State Committee on Forecasting and Statistics of the Cabinet of Ministers, 45a Uzbekistanskii Ave, 700008 Tashkent (tel:

Uzbekistan

398-216, 398-669; fax: 672-509, 677-816).

State Committee on Forests, 49-a Uzbekistan Ave, 700017 Tashkent (tel: 459-180).

State Committee on Geology and Mineral Resources, 11 Taras Shevchenko St, 700060 Tashkent (tel: 337-206; fax: 560-283).

State Committee on Precious Metals, 26 Turk-Kurganskiy Proezd, 700019 Tashkent (tel: 480-720, 480-663; fax: 442-603, 480-481).

State Committee for Privatisation (GKI), Mustaqillik Maydoni 6, Tashkent (tel: 398-768; fax: 398-548).

State Committee on the Protection of Nature, 5-a Abdulla Qodyri St, 700000 Tashkent (tel: 410-442; fax: 413-990).

State Committee on Science and Technology, 29 Hadicha Syleimonova St, 700017 Tashkent (tel: 391-843; fax: 391-243).

State Committee for Television and Radio, Ulitsa Khoremzskaya 49, Tashkent (tel: 443-287).

State Corporation on Industrial and Civil Engineering Construction, 17 Proletar St, 700060 Tashkent (tel: 337-725; fax: 331-041).

State Corporation of Local Industries, 5 Mustaqillik Sq, 700078 Tashkent (tel: 391-058; fax: 394-853).

State Joint-Stock Association on Trade, 6 Mustaqillik Sq, 700078 Tashkent (tel: 394-971; fax: 391-282).

State Property Committee of the Republic of Uzbekistan, Prospekt Uzbekistanskij 55, 700003 Tashkent (fax: 139-4617; 139-2236).

Uzbek Embassy (USA), 1746 Massachusetts Avenue, NW, Washington DC 20036 (tel: 202-887-5300; fax: 202-293-6804; e-mail: emb@uzbekistan.org).

Uzbek Information Agency (state news agency), Ulitsa Khamza 2, Tashkent (tel: 394-982, 331-622).

Uzbekinvest, 5 Mustaqillik Sq, 700078 Tashkent (tel: 391-989/069; fax: 891-538, 445-186).

Uzbekneftgas (national corporation of the oil and gas industry), 21 Akhunbabaev St, 700047 Tashkent (tel: 335-757; fax: 321-062).

Uzbek Post Office, 1 Tolstoy Street, Tashkent (tel: 133-5747; fax: 136-0921).

Internet sites

The Times of Central Asia:
http://www.times.kg

News and commercial information:
http://www.uzreport.com

General and government information:
http://www.uzland.uz

Regional news and links:
http://www.eurasianet.org

Vanuatu

KEY FACTS

Official name: Ripablik blong Vanuatu (Republic of Vanuatu)

Head of State: President Kalkot Mataskelekele (elected 16 Aug 2004)

Head of government: Prime Minister Ham Lini (elected 11 Dec 2004)

Ruling party: National unity government (formed 18 Aug 2004)

Area: 11,880 square km (82 islands)

Population: 212,576 (2004)

Capital: Port Vila (on Efate)

Official language: Bislama (Ni-Vanuatu Pidgin), English, French

Currency: Vatu (V) = 100 centimes

Exchange rate: V112.15 per US$ (Oct 2005)

GDP per capita: US$1,484 (2004)

GDP real growth: 3.00% (2004)

Inflation: 2.80% (2004)

Balance of trade: -US$71.00 million (2003)

Foreign debt: US$68.60 million (2003)

COUNTRY PROFILE

Historical profile

1606 European contact with the islands dates back to 1606, when Ferdinand de Quiros arrived at Big Bay.
1792 Captain Cook explored the islands in 1792, calling the group the New Hebrides.
1980 The country gained independence, having been formerly run as a condominium.
1995 The general election led to a coalition government of the Union of Moderate Parties (UMP) (Francophone) and the National United Party (NUP) (Anglophone). Parliament elected Serge Vohor as prime minister.
1998 A general election was held and Donald Kalpokas formed a coalition government comprising his Vanua'atu Party (VP) (Party of Our Land) and the NUP.
1999 John Bernard Bani was elected president by a consensual vote of all parties, with the exception of the NUP. Parliament elected Barak Sopé prime minister by four votes, effectively ousting Donald Kalpokas, who resigned.
2001 Sopé and his government were ousted following a no-confidence vote, reaffirmed by the Supreme Court. A new government was formed with a coalition of the UMP and the VP, with Edward Natapei appointed as prime minister.
2002 An earthquake struck Vanuatu, causing US$700,000 of damage. The UMP won the parliamentary elections.
2003 A new police commissioner, Robert Diniro Obed, was appointed in February. In November, UMP was ousted from the governing coalition.
2004 In February, Cyclone Ivy caused flooding in many areas and some 1,000 people were evacuated to temporary shelters in Port Vila. Prime Minister Edward Natapei's party, VP, delivered him an ultimatum – resign or face a vote of no confidence. The Prime Minister dissolved parliament; a caretaker government took over. The snap elections on 6 July resulted in no clear majority. VP, NUP, Vanuatu Republican Party (VRP), National Community Association (NCA) and People's Progressive Party (PPP) agreed to form a coalition government.
On 24 March, Roger Abiut, speaker of parliament, became acting president following the expiration of John Bani's term. In the first, second and third round of presidential elections, no candidate won a two-thirds majority. On 12 April, in the fourth round, the electoral college elected Alfred Masing Nalo, who was sworn in the same day. On 11 May, President Masing was removed from office by the Supreme Court and the speaker of parliament, Roger Abiut, again became acting president. On 29 July, parliament elected Josias Moli as speaker, and also acting president. Serge Vohor (leader of the UMP) was elected prime minister. A coalition government was formed. On 16 August, the Electoral College failed to elect a president, but the chief justice ordered the electors to continue sitting until a president was chosen, and they finally elected Kalkot Mataskelekele.
On 18 August, Prime Minister Vohor formed a national unity government. On 13 September, the government said it had lost confidence in the country's police commissioner, Robert Di Niro, and suspended him after he had issued orders for the arrest of the prime minister for contempt of court, following comments he made on the floor of parliament concerning a recent ruling of the country's chief justice. After negotiations by the prime minister's lawyers, the arrest order was replaced by a summons requiring him to appear in court. In December, Prime Minister Serge Vohor was ousted in a no-confidence motion and Ham Lini was elected to the post.

Political structure

Constitution
Republic
There are six provincial governments (Shefa, Sanma, Penama, Tafea, Malampa and Torba).
A Malvatumauri (National Council of Chiefs) advises the government on matters of custom, land tenure and the preservation of Vanuatu's traditions. Members of the council are hereditary peers and may not sit in parliament unless given leave to and elected by their peers.

Form of state
Independent democratic republic

The executive
The executive consists of a Council of Ministers headed by the prime minister who is elected by parliament from among its members. The prime minister and the 12 co-members of the Council of Ministers oversee the administration of the 13 government ministries.
The president, who is head of state, is elected for a five-year term by an electoral college made up of the members of parliament and the presidents of the six

provincial governments. A two-thirds majority is required.

National legislature
The 52-member parliament is elected by universal adult suffrage for a four-year term in multi-seat constituencies.

Legal system
Based on English law.

Last elections
13 and 16 August 2004 (presidential); 6 July 2004 (snap parliamentary).
Results: Presidential: The Electoral College failed to elect a president on 13 August 2004, the leading contenders being Willie David Saul with 27 votes and Donald Kalpokas with 26. On 16 August, the College reconvened and several votes were again inconclusive, but the chief justice ordered the electors to continue sitting until a president was chosen, and they finally elected Kalkot Mataskelekele with 49 votes against seven for Willie David Saul. Parliamentary: the mainly English-speaking VP and the NUP, together with their coalition partner, the Greens, 20 seats, and the French-speaking parties 14 seats; there was an increase in the number of independent members of parliament, from six to nine.

Next elections
2008 (parliamentary); 2009 (presidential).

Political parties
Union of Moderate Parties (UMP) (Francophone); Vanua'atu Party (VP) (Party of Our Land); Greens Confederation; National United Party (NUP) (Anglophone); Vanuatu Republican Party (VRP); National Community Association (NCA); People's Progressive Party (PPP)

Ruling party
National unity government (formed 18 Aug 2004)

Political situation
Political strife ensued when former prime minister, Serge Vohor, officially recognised Taiwan in November 2004, without agreement from his cabinet and colleagues. Parliament was outraged and within six weeks a motion of no confidence had removed him from office. The new prime minister, Ham Lini, revoked all agreements and reaffirmed Vanuatu's 'one China' policy, ensuring good relations with its distant neighbour and resulting in a US$3 million grant from China. About US$1 million will be used to underpin the 2005 budget and the rest allocated to government development projects.

Population
212,576 (2004)

Ethnic make-up
The great majority of the population is Melanesian in origin, with around 5 per cent of European descent.

Religions
About 80 per cent of the population is Christian, although animism is still in evidence, and the cargo cult remains on Tanna Island. There have been localised secessionist movements in Santo, Malekula, Ambrym, Aoba, Pentecost and Maewo.

Education
In November 2003, the EU awarded a grant of eur8 million to 14 pacific countries to be used to enhance basic education, and in the case of Vanuatu, to extend compulsory schooling to eight years.
Literacy rate: 53 per cent adult rate in 2004
Compulsory years: Six to 12.
Enrolment rate: 117 per cent gross primary enrolment; 28.5 per cent gross secondary enrolment, of relevant age groups (including repeaters) (Unicef 2004).

Health
HIV/Aids
In August 2004, Vanuatu had two confirmed HIV/Aids cases.
Life expectancy: 68.7 years (World Bank)
Fertility rate/Maternal mortality rate: 4.3 births per woman (World Bank)
Infant mortality rate: 31 per 1,000 live births (World Bank)

Main cities
Port Vila, on Efate (capital, estimated population 35,300 in 2003).

Languages spoken
English is spoken by 60 per cent of the population and French by 40 per cent. There are 115 indigenous languages.

Official language/s
Bislama (Ni-Vanuatu Pidgin), English, French

Media
Press
There are a number of English language weekly publications including *Trading Post*, *Vanuatu Post* (Sunday newspaper), *Viewpoint* (available free), and the government-run newspaper *Vanuatu Weekly/Hebdomadaire* published on Saturdays in English, French and Bislama.

Broadcasting
Radio: Radio Vanuatu programmes are broadcast 16 hrs/day in Bislama, English and French.

Economy
The majority of Vanuatu's population is engaged in subsistence agriculture. Vanuatu's main export, copra, is a commodity subject to wide fluctuations in price on the world market. However, steps have been taken to reduce dependence on it by developing exports of cocoa, timber, beef and fish. Earnings from tourism and the tax-free financial centre help offset trade deficits and provide employment. The financial sector opened in 1971 and is an important foreign exchange earner. Since the mid-1990s, macroeconomic performance has deteriorated rapidly due to structural problems, external factors and political instability. GDP growth stagnated in much of the late 1990s, recovering to 2.7 per cent in 2000, then falling again in 2001 and 2002, until it picked up in 2003 to 2.4 per cent and 3.0 per cent in 2004. Inflation has generally been stable at between 2–4 per cent.
The problems afflicting the Vanuatu economy arise from its narrow export base,

KEY INDICATORS — Vanuatu

	Unit	2000	2001	2002	2003	2004
Population	m	0.19	0.20	0.21	0.21	0.21
Gross domestic product (GDP)	US$bn	0.23	0.22	0.23	0.28	*0.32
GDP per capita	US$	1,202	1,113	1,095	1,150	1,484
GDP real growth	%	2.7	-2.1	-2.8	2.4	3.0
Inflation	%	2.3	3.7	2.2	3.0	2.8
Consumer prices	1995=100	–	–	–	–	*2.8
Exports (fob) (goods)	US$m	31.7	21.0	22.5	22.0	*34.2
Imports (fob) (goods)	US$m	82.7	87.9	90.5	93.0	*92.0
Balance of trade	US$m	-51.0	-66.9	-68.0	-71.0	–
Current account	US$m	-14.0	-15.0	-31.0	-4.1	-10.0
Total reserves minus gold	US$m	38.9	37.7	36.5	43.8	61.8
Foreign exchange	US$m	34.8	33.5	32.0	38.8	56.5
Exchange rate	per US$	135.66	145.31	139.20	122.56	111.79

* estimated figure

which made it vulnerable in the Asian crisis, and currency devaluations in competing economies such as Fiji, the Solomon Islands and Papua New Guinea. The volatility of coalition governments in the recent past has deterred foreign investors who were already put off by the country's poor infrastructure and a lack of skills and education.

The tourism sector is recognised by the government as a key sector in its economic development to provide employment opportunities for its young and rapidly growing population. Although bureaucracy is one of the issues facing new investment, there have been some successful investment proposals approved by the Vanuatu Foreign Investment Board, which have centred on the tourism, international finance and agricultural sectors. Vanuatu's beef industry has been a success, mainly due to access to export markets, since domestic demand for beef is not sufficient to keep the enterprise going. Overall economic growth is low, in contrast to population growth, which is estimated to be growing by 2.6 per cent per year.

In April 2004, a new US$1.4 million five-year plan for Australian aid was agreed between the two countries.

External trade
Imports
Principal imports are machinery and equipment, foodstuffs and fuels.
Main sources: Taiwan (34.6 per cent total, 2004), Australia (15.5 per cent), Japan (10.7 per cent), Singapore (8.0 per cent), New Zealand (6.0 per cent), Fiji (4.6 per cent)
Exports
Main exports are copra, beef, cocoa, timber, kava and coffee.
Main destinations: Thailand (46.3 per cent total, 2004), Malaysia (18.1 per cent), Japan (7.4 per cent), Belgium (5.3 per cent), Indonesia (5.3 per cent)

Agriculture
Farming
The agricultural sector accounts for around 20 per cent of GDP, employs 70 per cent of the workforce and provides up to 80 per cent of the country's exports. Agricultural production and livestock rearing is mainly carried out by smallholding farmers. More than 90 per cent of all the fruit and vegetables consumed in Vanuatu are imported.

Around 41 per cent of the land area is cultivatable, although only half is utilised. The soil is generally fertile and rainfall adequate, although crops can be subject to cyclone damage. The sector is hampered by a general lack of capital and investment, technical skills as well as the isolation of farmers.

Copra is Vanuatu's main export crop, accounting for approximately one-third of total export earnings and 6 per cent of GDP. Copra prices had been falling up to 2004 when world prices rose at a time when the Vanuatu Commodities Marketing Board (VCMB) opened up the market to competitive buyers in 2003. Output of copra reached 36,000 tonnes in 2004, and the sector has made a move towards coconut oil processing with exports generating US$9.3 million. In 2003 a new mechanised coconut-desiccating factory opened, in the northern region, capable of processing 24,000 coconuts per day. It is projected that this plant will produce 44 tonnes of coconut oil and 118 tonnes of coconut meat per day expanding export markets

Kava, used for manufacturing tranquilliser drugs, has become an important export commodity, although production was scaled back due to plant disease and medical concerns over the substance's effects on the liver. Australia and New Zealand lifted a ban on kava after finding that these claims could not be substantiated.

Cattle rearing and forestry are becoming increasingly important foreign exchange earners.

Crop production in 2004 included: 240,000 tonnes (t) coconuts, 2,400t cassava, 700t maize, 500t yams, 13,500t bananas, 2,000t cocoa beans, 110t spices, 40,000t roots & tubers, 2,500t groundnuts, 20,900t fruit in total, 31,950t oilcrops, 10,300t vegetables, 50t coffee, green. Livestock production included: 6,640t meat in total, 3,300t beef, 2,805t pig meat, 26t goat meat, 500t poultry, 320t eggs, 2,900t milk.

Fishing
An experimental project to seed reefs with trochus raised in hatcheries is under way (the shells are collected and sold as buttons). Investment project permits have been issued for fish farming.

The typical annual fish catch is over 27,000t, with 850t other seafood and 100,000 units pearls and shells.

Forestry
Access only by sea to exploitable forests has limited timber production. The government is working to achieve certification by the International Tropical Timber Organisation (ITTO) to prove that the country's forests are being sustainably managed. This would increase the added value of timber products.

In 2003 forest exports amounted to US$3.0 million, and imports amounted to US$1.8 million.

Timber production in 2003 included: 119,000 cubic metres (cum) roundwood, 28,000cum industrial roundwood, 91,000cum wood fuel.

Industry and manufacturing
The industrial sector accounts for approximately 12 per cent of GDP and employs 5 per cent of the workforce. Manufacturing contributes about 5 per cent of GDP. Main industries include copra processing, meat canning, fish processing, soft drinks bottling, furniture making, timber production, metalwork and handicrafts for the growing tourist market.

Japan has played an important part in helping to improve regional commercial centres for transporting and distributing agricultural products and other goods, providing investment for wharves on Tanna and Malekula Islands.

Industrial production increased by 1 per cent in 2003.

Tourism
Tourism is the main source of foreign exchange. The sector passed through a difficult period after its best year in 2000, when 57,591 visitors were recorded and the sector accounted for 40 per cent of GDP. Affected in 2001 by the general downturn in tourist activity, arrivals fell to 53,300. The decline continued in 2002, due to a high exchange rate, competition from other Pacific destinations and cyclones. Aided by improving air connections and increased cruise ship tours, the sector began to recover slowly in 2003, but took off again in 2004 with a record 60,611 visitors. Australia continues to be the main market.

Mining
Production of manganese from the large-scale mine on Efate has ceased. While Vanuatu has mineral resources, including precious metals, these have yet to be exploited.

Hydrocarbons
Vanuatu does not have any hydrocarbon reserves. Refined oil is imported to meet domestic requirements. The government is encouraging renewable energy companies to invest in Vanuatu.

Energy
Vanuatu has around 32MW of installed generating capacity, entirely based on refined oil imports.

In 2000, Vanuatu became the first country in the Asia-Pacific region to attempt to base its entire economy on renewable energy. It plans to reach that goal by 2020, with electricity generated by geothermal heat, wind and solar power and locally manufactured hydrogen-based fuels, which could also be exported.

Banking and insurance
The introduction in 1983 of the International Companies Act helped Vanuatu to develop as an offshore banking centre, attracting some 100 banks. Following the

Vanuatu

11 September 2001 terrorist attacks in the US, the US cut off all direct financial dealing with Vanuatu. The aim was to block all financial transactions that could be linked to terrorists, although Vanuatu was not considered to be a haven for terrorist assets. Vanuatu complied with the requirements of the OECD and was removed from the list of nations with 'tax havens' in 2003.

Central bank
Reserve Bank of Vanuatu
Main financial centre
Port Vila

Time
GMT +11hrs. Summer time +12 hours

Geography
Vanuatu comprises an irregular archipelago of about 80 islands in the south-west Pacific Ocean, spread over a distance of about 900km (560 miles) from north to south. The islands lie about 1,000km (600 miles) west of Fiji and 400km (250 miles) north-east of New Caledonia.

Climate
Temperatures can range from 16–33 degrees Celsius and rainfall varies from 1,000–2,000mm per annum. Cyclones may occur from December to April.

Entry requirements
Passports
Required by all. Must be valid four months from date of arrival.
Visa
Required by all except citizens of the Commonwealth, EU, Fiji, Japan, Norway, Philippines, South Korea, South Africa, Switzerland and the US for stays of up to 30 days. All travellers must hold onward/return tickets and sufficient funds for their stay.
Visas are only obtainable from the Principal Immigration Officer, The Immigration Department, Port Vila, Vanuatu. PMB 014 and must be approved before entry.
Prohibited entry
Anyone whose demeanour is not considered acceptable is prohibited entry.
Currency advice/regulations
No restrictions on import and export of local and foreign currency.

Health (for visitors)
Mandatory precautions
Vaccination certificate for yellow fever if travelling from an infected area.
Advisable precautions
Vaccination for diphtheria, tuberculosis, hepatitis 'A' and 'B', polio, tetanus, typhoid. Anti-malarial precautions should be taken.

Hotels
A 10 per cent tax is added to hotel bills. There are three luxury hotels now operating.

Public holidays
Fixed dates
1 Jan (New Year's Day), 21 Feb (Father Lini Day), 5 Mar (Custom Chief's Day), 1 May (Labour Day), 24 Jul (Children's Day), 30 Jul (Independence Day), 15 Aug (Assumption Day), 5 Oct (Constitution Day), 29 Nov (Unity Day), 25 Dec (Christmas Day), 26 Dec (Family Day).
Variable dates
Good Friday, Easter Monday, Ascension Day.

Working hours
Banking
Mon–Fri: 0830–1500.
Business
Mon–Fri: 0730–1700.
Government
Mon–Fri: 0730–1700.
Shops
Mon–Fri: 0800–1200; 1400–1800. Sat: 0800–1200.

Telecommunications
Telephone/fax
Domestic and international telecommunications are operated by Telecom Vanuatu. Formed in 1989, this is jointly owned by the government of Vanuatu and British and French telecommunications companies. A domestic firm, Communication Services (Vanuatu) Ltd, was granted a telecommunications licence in 1999.

Electricity supply
220/280V AC, 50 cycles

Weights and measures
Metric system

Social customs/useful tips
Tipping is considered contrary to Melanesian customs of hospitality. Bartering is also frowned upon. It is customary to shake hands on meeting and taking leave. An informal attitude prevails in business. Sometimes business cards are exchanged after introduction. Business is often conducted in Pidgin or in English or French.

Getting there
Air
National airline: Air Vanuatu
International airport/s: Port Vila-Bauerfield (VLI), 6km from Port Vila (on Efate); duty-free shop, buffet, currency exchange, hotel reservations, post office, shops, car hire.
Airport tax: A departure tax of V2,500, to be paid in local currency.
Surface
Main port/s: Port Vila and Luganville (Santo)

Getting about
National transport
Tours by minibus, airplane, car and boat are available.
Air: Van Air operates inter-island services to 16 destinations from Port Vila-Bauerfield airport. Charter services are available.
Road: There are some 150km of surfaced road on Efate, and 100km on Espiritu Santo, which are passable in dry weather.
Water: Sea links between the islands are generally good. Inter-island boats taking deck passengers are irregular.
City transport
Taxis: Taxi service is available in Port Vila and Luganville. All taxis are metered. Journey time from the airport to the city centre is about 10 minutes.
Buses, trams & metro: Buses serve the whole of Port Vila. Journey time from airport to city centre is 10 minutes.
Car hire
Car hire is available in Port Vila and Luganville. International, French and UK licences are acceptable.

BUSINESS DIRECTORY
The addresses listed below are a selection only. While World of Information makes every endeavour to check these addresses, we cannot guarantee that changes have not been made, especially to telephone numbers and area codes. We would welcome any corrections.

Telephone area codes
The international direct dialling code (IDD) for Vanuatu is +678 followed by subscriber's number.

Useful telephone numbers
Police: 22222
Fire: 22333
Ambulance: 22100

Chambers of Commerce
Vanuatu Chamber of Commerce and Industry, PO Box 189, Port Vila (tel: 27-543; fax: 27-542; e-mail: vancci@vanuatu.com.vu).

Banking
ANZ Bank (Vanuatu) Ltd, Private Mail Bag 003, Port Vila (tel: 22-536; fax: 22-814).

Banque d'Hawaii (Vanuatu) Ltd, PO Box 29, Lini Highway, Port Vila (tel: 22-412; fax: 23-579).

European Bank Ltd, PO Box 65, International Bldg, Kumul Highway, Port Vila (tel: 27-700; fax: 22-884).

National Bank of Vanuatu, PO Box 249, Air Vanuatu House, Rue de Paris, Port Vila (tel: 22-201; fax: 22-761).

Central bank
Reserve Bank of Vanuatu, PMB 62, Port Vila, Vanuatu (tel: 23-333; fax: 24-231).

Travel information
Air Vanuatu (international) (tel: 23-848). Bauerfield Port Vila International Airport, Civil Aviation Department, PMB068, Port Vila (tel: 22-993, 22-819; fax: 23-783).

The Principal Immigration Officer, Private Mail Bag PMB014, Vila.

Tour Vanuatu, PO Box 409, Port Vila (tel: 22-733; fax: 23-442).

VanAir (domestic) (tel: 22-643, 22-753).

National tourist organisation offices

National Tourism Office of Vanuatu, PO Box 209, Port Vila (tel: 22-515, 22-685; fax: 23-889; internet site: http://www.vanuatutourism.com).

Ministries

Ministry of Finance and Housing, PO Box 31, Port Vila (tel: 22-951).

Ministry of Postal Services, Telecommunications and Meteorology, Private mail Bag 011, Port Vila (tel: 25-059; fax: 23-142).

Ministry of Trade, Co-operatives, Energy and Industry, Port Vila (tel: 23-979).

Prime Minister's Office, Private Mail Bag 053, Port Vila (tel: 22-413).

Other useful addresses

Asian Development Bank (ADB), South Pacific Regional Mission, La Casa di Andrea, Fr. Dr. W. H. Lini Highway; PO Box 127, Port Vila (tel: 23-300; fax: 23-183; email: adbsprm@adb.org; internet: http://www.adb.org/SPRM).

Department for Foreign Affairs, Port Vila (tel: 22-913, 22-347; fax: 23-142).

The Immigration Department, Port Vila, PMB 014, (tel: 22-354; fax: 25-492).

Internet sites

Investment promotion authority: http://www.investinvanuatu.com

Telephone directory (English): http://www.teldir.com/tdred/eng/128334

Vanuatu government: http://www.vanuatu.gov.vu/

Vanuatu Online: http://www.vol.com.vu/

Vanuatu Broadcasting and Television Corporation: http://www.vbtc.com.vu/

Vatican City (The Holy See)

COUNTRY PROFILE

Historical profile
1917 The Code of Canon Law was devised. The Law provides codified information and rules on the operations of the Catholic Church.
1922 Achilles Ratti became Pope Pius XI.
1929 The Pope was instrumental in defining the Vatican's position within Italy, which was confirmed by the signing of the Lateran Treaty, when the Vatican City State was formed as a separate state.
1939 When Pius XI died, Eugenio Pacelli became Pope Pius XII, the 261st Pope.
1958 After Pius XII died, Pope John XXIII was elected.
1963 Second Vatican Council assembled (the first council sat in 325 AD), to debate the role of the Church in the modern world, particularly regarding church administration, doctrine and discipline. Foremost in the 16 decrees issued were the reforms in the format of the mass and the liturgy, adoption of local languages instead of Latin for services, and the promotion of ecumenicalism within Christian churches.
1964 Paul VI, appointed Pope in 1963, made the first ever papal visit to Israel.
1965 Paul VI made the first papal trip to the Western hemisphere, with a visit to the UN headquarters in New York. The Vatican published a document that proclaimed the the Jews were not to blame for the death of Jesus Christ.
1967 The Apostolic Constitution was ratified.
1974 The Vatican intervened in Italian politics by urging voters to reject, in a referendum, a recently passed law that made divorce legal.
1978 John Paul I was elected Pope, but died one month later, which made his the shortest reign as Pope. A Polish national, Karol Jozef Wojtyla, succeeded him as John Paul II.
1981 An assassination attempt was made on Pope John Paul II's life. The Vatican intervened in Italian politics by urging voters to reject in a referendum a recently passed law that made abortion legal.
1983 A new and revised Code of Canon Law was introduced.
1990 Cardinal Angelo Sodano became the secretary of state of The Holy See.
1993 The Vatican officially recognised Israel as an independent state.
1998 In May, the commandant of the Pope's Swiss Guard and his wife were murdered by a fellow Guardsman. Commandant Alois Estermann protected John Paul II from an assassination attempt in 1981. It was the first murder case in the Holy See within living memory.
1999: The Istituto per le Opere di Religione (IOR) (the Institute for Religious Works, otherwise known as the Bank of the Holy See or the Vatican Bank) was sued in the US for helping to conceal in 1945 Nazi-era assets looted from Holocaust survivors and Nazi sympathisers from Croatia.
2000 In March, on a visit to Israel, John Paul II apologised for anti-Semitism by Christians throughout the ages and called for the formation of an independent Palestinian state.
2001 Pope John Paul II appointed 44 new cardinals. The Pope issued a worldwide apology to victims of sexual abuse by Roman Catholic priests and other officers of the Church.
2002 The IOR was sued in the US over a charity scandal. The Pope sent an envoy, Cardinal Roger Etchegaray, to the Middle East to help with the Israeli-Palestinian peace process. The Capuchin friar, Padre Pio, was canonised. After the Vatican ordered that management of Padre Pio's sanctuary in the south-eastern town of San Giovanni Rotondo should be taken from the local Capuchins and given to the regional archdiocese, the town's residents barricaded the entrance to the shrine. An internal Vatican report showed that the Holy See had one of the highest crime rates in the world, it suggested that the high number of tourists and attendant pick-pockets as the reason.
2003 The Vatican hosted a closed-door seminar of top officials and international medical experts on the problem of paedophilia, within the Church
2004 The Vatican library, which houses nearly two million books and manuscripts, adopted radio frequency identification (RFID) tags. The library used to close for one month each year in order to check its contents, but with RFID, it will take half a day. In October, the Vatican weighed into a dispute between Italy and the EU parliament over the suitability of an Italian candidate for the European Commission. The Vatican criticised opponents of the Italian government's choice for commissioner, accusing them of conducting a 'lay inquisition'.
2005 Pope John Paul II, aged 84, who had been suffering from Parkinson's disease and severe arthritis, died on 2 April; the chamberlain, Eduardo Cardinal

KEY FACTS

Official name: Stato della Città del Vaticano (Vatican City State). Santa Sede (The Holy See) — the head organisation of the Roman Catholic Church — operates from the territory of the Vatican City State.

Head of State: Pope Benedict XVI (inaugurated 24 Apr 2005)

Head of government: There is no head of government, but Secretary of State of The Holy See Cardinal Angelo Sodano (appointed 1991 and confirmed again 21 Apr 2005) handles diplomatic and political activity.

Area: 0.44 square km

Population: 880 (2004)

Capital: Vatican City

Official language: Latin; Italian is most commonly spoken.

Currency: Vatican City Lira and Euro (VCL and eur)

Exchange rate: VCL and eur0.83 per US$ (Oct 2005); (the Vatican City State has its own currency which, by agreement with the Italian state, is also legal tender in Italy; its value is pegged to that of the euro).

Martínez Somalo, became acting head of state. The conclave to elect a new pope began on 18 April, and on 19 April, Joseph Cardinal Ratzinger was elected and chose the name Benedictus XVI. On 21 April, he confirmed Cardinal Angelo Sodano as secretary of state and Giovanni Lajolo as foreign minister. Pope Benedictus XVI was inaugurated on 24 April. In June, the Pope intervened in Italian politics by successfully urging a boycott of a referendum on Italy's fertility laws. A diplomatic row between the Vatican and Israel broke out in July when Israel demanded to know why the Pope did not mention Israeli victims during a speech deploring terrorism. In November, the Vatican published a new policy document on homosexualtiy and the clergy, sparking controversy among liberal and conservative Catholics alike.

2006 A Vatican official announce that the Vatican wants to join the Schengen borderless zone. This would allow for an exchange of information and joint operations and preventative measures to ensure the security of all people.

Political structure

The Vatican City and the Holy See are two different entities: the Vatican is the physical state, while the Holy See is a non-geographical sovereign entity. The Holy See participates in a number of international organisations, such as the UN, as an observer. Italy is in charge of defending the city state, although the Pope's personal guards, the Swiss Guards, belong to the Vatican City.

The Vatican City State employs 1,534 people. It is a sovereign country recognised as a separate subject under international law. The Pope is its absolute monarch and chief of state, but its general administration is overseen by an executive called the Pontifical Commission, appointed by the Pope and headed by a president. The Pope plays little part in the Commission's administration. The Commission runs a police force and post office, has a railway station and issues car licence plates. The term 'Vatican' is commonly used to describe the residence of the Pope – the Apostolic Palace.

The Holy See is exclusively made up of ecclesiastical dignitaries, being the head organisation of the Roman Catholic Church and consisting of the Pope and the Roman Curia. It operates from the territory of the Vatican City State and constitutes a sovereign institution with the status of a subject of international law. The Curia is headed by the Secretariat of State which is presided over by a Cardinal who assumes the title of Secretary of State. The Cardinal Secretary of State is the person primarily responsible for the diplomatic and political activity of The Holy See, in some circumstances representing the person of the Supreme Pontiff himself.

Central offices of The Holy See are: Secretariat of State (two sections), nine congregations, three tribunals, 11 pontifical councils, the Apostolic Chamber, the Administration of the Patrimony of the Apostolic See (APSA) (sometimes referred to as the Vatican Bank), Prefecture of the Economic Affairs of The Holy See, Prefecture of the Papal Household, Office of the Liturgical Celebrations of the Supreme Pontiff, The Holy See Press Office, Vatican Information Service, Central Office of Church Statistics, five pontifical commissions and committees, nine institutions linked to The Holy See, the Synod of Bishops and six pontifical academies. In addition to these central offices, there are 118 pontifical representations to nations and to international organisations. There are 2,674 people working in the Roman Curia: 755 ecclesiastics, 344 religious and 1,575 lay people. There are about 1,000 retired persons.

The Pope is elected for life by a Conclave composed of members of the College of Cardinals. Pope John Paul II changed the rules to make a simple majority sufficient to elect a Pope if no-one has the traditional two-thirds majority after 30 rounds of voting. The College of Cardinals consists of 183 cardinals, of which 117 are electors. Suffrage is limited to cardinals less than 80 years old.

After the Pope's death, the chamberlain becomes acting head of state. An official nine-day mourning period, known as the *novemdiales*, follows the death of the Pope. The Pope's body lies in state in St Peter's Basilica in the Clementine Chapel until the funeral, which takes place between four and six days following the Pope's death. A Conclave, consisting of all the Cardinals under 80 years, meets to elect the next pope no less than 15 days, and no more than 20 days, after the death of the Pope.

Constitution

In 2001, a new basic law, incorporating constitutional amendments adopted since the creation of the Vatican City State under the 1929 Lateran Treaty with Italy, entered into force. It replaced the 1967 document *Regimini Ecclesiae Universae* as the Vatican's constitutional text. It distinguishes between the legislative, executive and judicial branches, continuing to vest absolute authority over all three branches in the Pope as supreme pontiff and sovereign.

Form of state

Theocratic state governed by the head of the Roman Catholic church.

The executive
All executive power is vest in the Pope. He appoints his own advisors.
When a Pope is unable to perform his duties important decisions on the confirmation of bishops, doctrinal issues and the promulgation of laws within the Catholic Church are left in abeyance.

Population
880 (2004)
Ethnic make-up
Italians and Swiss.
Religions
Roman Catholic.

Main cities
Vatican City (capital)

Languages spoken
Mainly Italian and Latin.
Official language/s
Latin; Italian is most commonly spoken.

Media
Press
The only daily newspaper is *L'Osservatore Romano* which covers religious matters plus some general news items. Also weekly editions published in several languages. The official bulletin of the Holy See is *Acta Apostolicae Sedis*, published monthly. All of the Holy See's media actvities incur substantial annual trading losses.

Broadcasting
Radio: Vatican Radio broadcasts in 40 languages, providing a link between the Holy See and Catholics throughout the world. The broadcasting centre at Santa Maria di Galeria, about 20km from the Holy See, has diplomatic privileges similar to foreign embassies. In 2001, Vatican Radio agreed to end some broadcasts because the Italian authorities claimed the antennae were emitting dangerous levels of radiation.

Television: Centro Televisivo Vaticano (CTV) (Vatican Television Centre) was established in 1983 and provides live broadcasts on religious and papal matters. It also provides footage for foreign news broadcasters and acts as a press centre for broadcast journalists.

Economy
The main sources of income are The Holy See's book of real estate and from an internationally diversified portfolio of stocks and bonds.

Other income includes *Obolo di San Pietro* (Peter's Pence) (voluntary annual contributions from dioceses), the sale of postage stamps, tourist mementos and publications, and fees for admission to museums. The Istituto per le Opere di Religione (IOR) (Bank of The Holy See) collects money from residents.

Vatican City (The Holy See)

No special agreements exist between the EU and The Holy See.

The 2004 Peter's Pence collection totalled US$51.7 million. The money was used for charitable purposes – to help the populations of countries struck by calamities and to aid Roman Catholic works in countries suffering strife. Following a series of sex scandals in the US involving clergymen, analysts predict that the Peter's Pence collection for 2005 will be significantly less than 2004's.

In 2004, the Holy See posted a budget surplus of US$3.7 million, the first surplus since 2000.

Tourism
Tourism and tourist numbers for the Holy See are difficult to ascertain as there is no practical border between the Holy See and Italy; however it is estimated that there are some 18 million visitors each year. Up to 100,000 people attend the Pope's annual Easter Message. Around 15,000 people visit the Musei Vaticani (Vatican Museums) per day (2005 estimate).

Banking and insurance
The Vatican's banking sector has been embroiled in a number of transnational controversies over the past three decades. The IOR acknowledged 'moral involvement' in the collapse of the Italian private bank, the Banco Ambrosiano, in 1982 and paid US$241million to creditors. Roberto Calvi, who headed the Banco Ambrosiano, fled Italy pending a trial for corruption and was found dead in London in June 1982. Five people, all alleged to have mafia ties, were charged in Rome with Calvi's murder in April 2005.

In November 1999, survivors of Nazi-run concentration camps filed a law suit claiming that the IOR helped conceal assets looted from camp victims by the then pro-Nazi Croatian government.

Central bank
Istituto per le Opere di Religione (IOR) (Bank of The Holy See); European Central Bank (ECB).

Time
GMT plus one hour (GMT plus two hours late Mar to late Sep).

Geography
The State of the Vatican City (The Holy See) is situated entirely within the city of Rome, Italy.

Climate
Mediterranean, with hot summers and mild winters. Temperatures range from 4–30 Celsius (C).

Dress codes
Dress should be modest – no shorts or sundresses. Lightweight clothing for summer; medium-weight and light topcoat for winter.

Entry requirements
No formal regulations exist, however visitors must adhere to Italian entry requirements before entry to the city.
Italy: no visa requirements for citizens of most of Europe, the Americas, Australasia and some Asian countries, visiting for up to 90 days. For a full list, and further information for those citizens not included on the list of visa-free travel, visit www.italyemb.org/Visti.htm. A Schengen visa application (offered in several languages) can be downloaded on www.eurovisa.info/ApplicationForm.htm.

Currency advice/regulations
The Vatican City State has its own currency, the Vatican City Lira (VCL), which, by agreement with the Italian state, is also legal tender in Italy. Its value is pegged to that of the euro. The Vatican City State mints its own metal coinage each year at the Italian mint. The cut, weight and measure are precisely equal to those of the euro coinage, which is also accepted.

Health (for visitors)
As for Italy.

Public holidays
Fixed dates
1 Jan (New Year's Day), 6 Jan (Epiphany), 25 April (Liberation Day), 1 May (Labour Day), 2 Jun (Anniversary of the Republic), 15 Aug (Assumption Day), 1 Nov (All Saints' Day), 8 Dec (Immaculate Conception), 25 Dec (Christmas Day), 26 Dec (St Stephen's Day).

Variable dates
Easter Monday

Getting there
Air
A heliport is used by Vatican City officials and visiting dignitaries.
International airport/s: Rome, served by Leonardo da Vinci (Fiumicino) (FCO), 35km from the Vatican City.
Surface
By road or rail through Rome. There is a speed limit of 30kph in the Vatican City.

Getting about
National transport
Rail: The Vatican City has its own small railway which runs into Italy. It covers 862 metres before leaving the City.

BUSINESS DIRECTORY
The addresses listed below are a selection only. While World of Information makes every endeavour to check these addresses, we cannot guarantee that changes have not been made, especially to telephone numbers and area codes. We would welcome any corrections.

Telephone area codes
The international direct dialling (IDD) code for Vatican City is +39 followed by the area code 066982; this is complete in itself, giving access to a central switchboard/operator.

Banking
Central bank
Istituto per le Opere di Religione (IOR), 00120 Città del Vaticano, Rome (tel: 83-354; fax: 85-195); European Central Bank (ECB), Kaiserstrasse 29, D-60311 Frankfurt am Main, Germany (tel: +49(69)13-440; fax: +49(69)1344-6000).

Other useful addresses
Agenzia Internazionale Fides (AIF) (International Fides Agency), Palazzo di Propaganda Fide, Via di Propaganda 1c, 00187 Rome (tel: 679-2414).

American Embassy, Via Delle Terme Deciane 26, 00153 Rome (tel: 646-741; fax: 5730-0682; e-mail: Usinb.holysee@agora.it).

Annuario Pontificio, Palazzo Apostolico, 00120 Città del Vaticano (tel: 698-3064); Press Room, Via della Conciciazione, 54, 00193 Roma (tel: 698-3466).

Apostolic Nunciature (UK), 54 Parkside, Wimbledon, London SW19 5NE, UK (tel: (020) 8946-1410; fax: (020) 8947-2494; e-mail: gb nuntius@eaglenet.co.uk).

British Embassy, Via dei Condotti 91, 00187 Rome (tel: 6992-3561; fax: 6994-0684).

Centro Televisivo Vaticano, Palazzo Belvedere, 00120 The Holy See (tel: 698-5467).

Prefecture of the Economic Affairs of the Holy See, Palazzo delle Congregazioni, Largo del Colonnato 3, 00193 Rome (tel: 84-263; fax: 85-011).

Radio Vaticana, Palazzo Pio, Piazza Pia 3, 00120 Roma (tel: 6988-3551; fax: 6988-3237).

Secretariat of State, Palazzo Apostolico, 00120 The Holy See (tel: 6982).

Internet sites
Vatican City: http://www.vatican.va

Vatican Facts: http://www.vaticanfacts.com

Agenzia Internazionale Fides: http://www.fides.org

KEY FACTS

Official name: República Bolivariana de Venezuela (Bolivarian Republic of Venezuela)

Head of State: President Hugo Chávez Frías (MVR) (re-elected 4 Dec 2005)

Head of government: President Hugo Chávez Frías

Ruling party: Movimiento V República (MVR) (Movement for the Fifth Republic) (re-elected Dec 2005)

Area: 916,490 square km

Population: 25.51 million (2004)

Capital: Caracas

Official language: Spanish

Currency: Bolívar (B) = 100 céntimos

Exchange rate: B2,602.56 per US$ (Oct 2005); (the bolívar was devalued in Jan 2005)

GDP per capita: US$4,148 (2004)

GDP real growth: 17.30% (2004); *7.8% (2005)

Labour force: 11.11 million (2004)

Unemployment: 17.10% (2004)

Inflation: 21.70% (2004)

Oil production: 2.98 million bpd (2004)

Balance of trade: US$21.43 billion 2004

Foreign debt: US$38.20 billion (2003)

Annual FDI: US$1.14 billion (2004)

* estimated figure

Venezuela

The self-destruction of the political opposition, a controversial foreign policy and the Chávez government's continued implementation of its 'revolutionary' agenda were all features of the Venezuelan political arena in 2005. The government's economic policy is closely intertwined with its agenda for social change. Though the economy has grown strongly as oil revenues have increased, it has not yet returned to the level of performance achieved prior to the social unrest and political disruption of 2002–03.

Easy win for Chávez

President Hugo Rafael Chávez Frías was handed an easy victory in Venezuela's parliamentary elections in December 2005 when all five main opposition parties staged a boycott. The opposition parties had accused the Consejo Nacional Electoral (CNE) (National Election Council) of bias and claimed the CNE was unable to ensure that voting was secret, even though international bodies had previously approved the voting machines to be used. Chávez' own party won a total of 114 seats, with pro-Chávez parties wining the remainder of the 167 total seats. However, just 25 per cent of registered voters turned out to vote. While the European Union (EU) praised the CNE for the way it handled the vote, the Organisation of American States (OAS) criticised the CNE's decision to extend voting hours in certain districts, amid concerns that some public workers had been pressurised to vote.

The Chávistas were heading for an approximate two-thirds majority prior to the opposition boycott and it has been suggested that the opposition made a calculated move by choosing not to participate in the poll. Outside observers have noted that Acción Democrática (AD) (Democratic Action) and Primero Justicia (Justice First) may have calculated a political 'cost-benefit analysis'. The parties may have reasoned it would be more beneficial to their cause to boycott the elections and discredit the returned Chávez government rather than stand and face almost certain defeat, as polls predicted. After all, the eventual turn-out was very low and the government received a two-thirds majority, which was predicted regardless of whether the election was contested.

As with the 2004 recall election however, in which Chávez was successful, the opposition seem to have misjudged the public mood once more. Venezuelan voters may be dissatisfied with the democratic process, but the major opposition parties will now no longer be represented in the National Assembly, which will run for the next five years. With a two-thirds majority behind him Chávez will most likely be able to amend the country's constitution, thereby eradicating the present two term presidential limit. Furthermore, two of the most likely challengers to oppose Chávez in the December 2006 presidential elections, Julio Borges and Manuel Rosales, will not be able to count on a national institutional infrastructure – ie a power base within the National Assembly – with which to launch their presidential campaigns. Consequently, their respective prospects of beating Chavez at the polls will be severely diminished. Many external observers hope that in the absence of the traditional opposition parties, opposition to Chávez will arise from within his own ranks so as to provide some sort of democratic challenge.

The Bolivarian Revolution continues

Chávez continued to implement his Bolivarian Revolution throughout 2005. One of the main tenets of the reform programme has been land reform. The president ordered his minister of the interior to carry out a nationwide revision of land titles, to redistribute idle or unproductive areas to the poor. The most high profile victim of the state land grab was English meat magnate Lord Vestey, who's 32,000 acre cattle ranch was seized by the authorities.

Vestey's *El Charcote* ranch was redistributed among what the Venezuelan authorities called 'landless' peasants, but there are doubts as to the long-term advantages the poorest sector of the country will derive from the government's *latifundo* drive. Firstly the state, not the individual landowner, will retain subsoil ownership rights, ensuring that it will remain difficult for farmers to gain access to crucial loans. Without credit the small landowners will be unable to purchase new technology, the like of which is imperative to high levels of production. Second, Venezuela, in common with the rest of Latin America, is much more urbanised today than it was 30 or 40 years previously. With 90 per cent of the population living in urban areas the country's demographic structure would be better served by larger estates with a network supply able to deliver food to cities, rather than relying upon smaller farmers each with just a parcel of land. Regardless of the potential long-term detriments, Chávez' land reform programme looks set to continue for the foreseeable future.

The Chávez government's reform package also included the seisure of some US$5 billion of the central bank's international reserves. Venezuela's US$29 billion reserves are the largest in Latin America, if measured by equivalent weeks' worth of wages. Chávez has stated on several occasions that the central bank should 'belong to the people' and that the reserves are not properly maximised if left unused. The government also initiated a new oversight programme for foreign private banks in 2005. Under the new regulations up to two government officials will be allocated governing board seats. The new rules are most likely to affect Banco Santander and BBVA, two Spanish banks with large stakes in the country.

The Bolivarian Revolution has also been evident in the government's dealings with oil companies and agribusiness during 2005. President Chávez' father, Hugo de los Reyes Chávez, the governor of Barinas province, issued an expropriation order against a flour mill owned and operated by the conglomerate Polar. The energy minister, Rafael Ramirez, issued several ultimatums to foreign oil interests throughout 2005. On 16 December Ramirez announced that oil giants Anglo Dutch/Royal Dutch Shell, BP, Total, Exxon-Mobil and Chevron had all agreed to hand over majority ownership of their new concessions to Petróleos de Venezuela SA (PdVSA), the Venezuelan state oil company. Ramirez also confirmed that all of the major companies had agreed to sign new contracts complete with higher tax rates.

Economic performance

Given its status as the fifth-largest oil exporter in the world, it is unsurprising that the Venezuelan economy is hugely dependent on its natural resource wealth to generate growth. Thus, when the employees of the state oil company PdVSA struck in December 2002–February 2003 the country's economy had suffered greatly. The after effect of the industrial action organised by the country's political opposition was a contraction of 13 per cent in 2003 and the fall out from the events of three years ago is still being felt.

Growth rebounded in 2004 with a 17.3 per cent expansion, though this figure must be considered in the context of a low GDP base following the industrial action of 2002–03. The latest IMF estimate for Venezuela indicates strong growth of 7.8 per cent for 2005 and a reduced rate of 4.5

KEY INDICATORS — Venezuela

	Unit	2000	2001	2002	2003	2004
Population	m	24.39	24.66	25.16	25.33	*25.51
Gross domestic product (GDP)	US$bn	120.50	125.00	95.40	85.50	*109.32
GDP per capita	US$	4,939	5,070	3,800	3,350	4,148
GDP real growth	%	3.2	2.7	-8.9	-13.0	17.3
Inflation	%	16.2	12.5	22.4	34.1	21.7
Unemployment	%	13.9	12.1	18.1	21.2	–
Oil output	'000 bpd	3,321.0	3,418.0	2,942.0	2,987.0	2,980.0
Natural gas output	bn cum	27.2	28.9	27.3	29.4	28.1
Coal output	mtoe	–	–	–	–	6.6
Exports (fob) (goods)	US$m	33,035.0	27,056.0	26,470.0	19,708.0	38,748.0
Imports (fob) (goods)	US$m	15,491.0	17,282.0	16,640.0	7,578.0	17,318.0
Balance of trade	US$m	17,544.0	9,774.0	9,800.0	12,130.0	21,430.0
Current account	US$m	13,111.0	4,364.0	2,200.0	6,494.0	14,510.0
Total reserves minus gold	US$m	13,088.0	9,239.0	8,487.0	16,035.0	18,375.0
Foreign exchange	US$m	12,633.0	8,825.0	8,038.0	–	17,867.0
Exchange rate	per US$	679.96	723.67	1,074.51	2,124.25	1,887.78

* estimated figure

per cent in 2006. Inflation, which rose significantly in 2002 and 2003 is now heading downward, but remains at a high level of 21.7 per cent (2004). Historically, an overvalued currency has been problematic in terms of the competitiveness of other Venezuelan exports aside from oil, thus retarding the country's diversification efforts and continued development. Significantly, the government chose to guard against this element of the 'Dutch disease' phenomenon by devaluing the bolívar on 1 January 2005, from 1,920 to 2,150 per US dollar.

The Chávez government has continued its expansionary fiscal policy, as public spending rose considerably throughout 2004 and 2005. Despite high oil revenues and increased growth the economy has not yet fully recovered from the disturbances of late 2002 and early 2003. The value of GDP and per capita income remain lower than in 2001. Unemployment has also increased in every year since 2001.

Problems with Colombia

Never a shrinking violet, Chávez went head to head with Colombia in January and February 2005 over the capture of a guerrilla fighter on Venezuelan soil. Urged to take a tough line on the matter by his supporters the Venezuelan president criticised Bogotá for what he considered the illegal 'kidnapping' of the rebel after Colombian authorities seized the individual. Chávez also blamed the United States for the episode by claiming that Washington had engineered an 'imperialist plot' in an attempt to play the two neighbours off against one another. Venezuela suspended commercial ties with Colombia and withdrew its ambassador as tensions escalated. Aware of their economic interdependence – bilateral trade is worth US$5.2 billion per annum – Colombian President Alvaro Uribe scheduled a summit with Chávez, before cancelling at the final hour, citing a mysterious attack of food poisoning. Despite this apparent snub, the presidents did eventually meet in Caracas in February and full diplomatic relations were restored.

Venezuela entered Mercado Común del Sur (Mercosur) (Southern Common Market), on 9 December 2005. Other members of Mercusor include Argentina, Brazil, Paraguay and Uruguay. On the day of his country's full accession Chávez underlined his intention to re-design the trading bloc: 'we have to politicise Mercosur', he emphatically stated. Underlining his popular appeal, he added '… we cannot allow this to be purely an economic project, one for the elites and for the transnational companies'. Undoubtedly, Chávez' views Mercusur as a medium through which to spread his leftist political platform throughout South America and weaken US influence on the continent. Observers in Washington are likely to have been alarmed by such overt references to the politicisation of what was originally intended simply to be a trading bloc.

El Commandante Petrolero

A unique feature of Chávez's approach to foreign policy has been his use of natural resources to build alliances, increase Venezuela's influence in Latin America and generally antagonise the United States. Throughout 2005 the Venezuelan president continued to play 'petrol politics' on the international stage. Traditionally an OPEC hawk – a state keen to raise oil prices – Venezuela enlisted fellow cartel-member Iran in a bid to steer oil away from the US domestic market. In January 2005, the ministry of energy arranged for a group of PdVSA traders to undergo training by Iranian officials in London in how to strategically place oil in Asian energy markets. The move was undoubtedly part of a larger strategy to strengthen ties with China, who's vice president had been fêted by Chávez when he visited Caracas in 2004. The episode is likely to further aggravate Washington, which will not have liked the fact its South American menace was colluding with an Axis of Evil member.

Venezuela has striven to secure regional alliances by offering its natural resources as a huge carrot. The *Petrocaribe* initiative was created in order to sell oil to 13, mostly Caribbean countries on credit terms as low as 1 per cent for up to 25 years. Other high profile deals included an agreement struck with Ecuador and an economic and energy pact signed with Argentina. In August 2005 Chávez, in a classic example of his trademark lighting diplomacy, visited Uruguay, Argentina and Brazil in under two days to discuss energy security. Then, in December 2005, in a cheeky move designed to further iritate Washington, Venezuela struck an oil deal with the Bronx borough of New York. Chávez' decision to complete the 40 per cent discount deal, somewhat contradictory given his stated desire to divert oil from the US, was designed to win him sympathy in Latin America. Significantly, almost 50 per cent of the Bronx borough population is of hispanic origin.

The nuclear question

A further worry to Washington, and indeed to the international community at large in 2005, was Venezuela's apparent willingness to re-stock its weapons arsenal including, ominously, the acquisition of nuclear technology. In March, Iranian President Mohammad Khatami visited Caracas and the two countries were rumoured to have been making plans for a nuclear partnership. Chávez secured a weapons deal with Brazil in March, involving the importation of 100,000 AK-47s and 50 Mig-29 warplanes. In October, Washington began something of a charm offensive designed to isolate Chávez in the region. However, the Venezuelan president's oil diplomacy throughout 2005 has won him several allies, particularly the larger states in Latin America. During a visit to Brazil in May for example, US Secretary of State Donald Rumsfeld was rebuked by President Luiz Inácio 'Lula' da Silva. In reply to Rumsfeld's disparaging remarks concerning the Venezuelan leader Lula said that he '… didn't accept defamation and insinuations against a friend'!

Outlook

Venezuela's domestic political scene will continue to remain as quirky as ever in 2006. A presidential election, one of seven in Latin America in 2006, will no doubt be colourful and exciting. But the traditional opposition has made life difficult for itself by choosing to boycott the 2006 parliamentary poll and will struggle to build a national political profile for their respective candidates when they take on Chávez. The president has stated his desire to amend the constitution so he can run again in 2006 and this looks likely given his new two-thirds majority in the national assembly.

The country's economic performance remains volatile, with a consistent level of growth having not yet been found. The economy will continue to grow however, as long as international oil prices continue to rise. Chávez recently transferred a sizeable portion of the country's reserves out of US treasuries apparently for political reasons, and relations with the US continue to remain poor. The simulation of a mock US invasion by Venezuelan armed forces, the curtailment of anti-narcotics co-operation with the US and Chávez' repeated denouncements of the Bush administration are symptomatic of the ill feeling between Caracas and Washington. This kind of sabre-rattling will undoubtedly continue throughout 2006.

Venezuela

Risk assessment

Politics	Stable
Economy	Poor
Regional stability	Stable
Stock market	Poor

COUNTRY PROFILE

Historical profile
1498 Christopher Columbus landed at the mouth of the Orinoco River on 2 August.
1499 Alonso de Ojeda first saw Lake Maracaibo and called the area 'little Venice', or Venezuela, after the houses the local inhabitants built on stilts.
1520s Spanish colonisation began. The most exploitable resource was cocoa.
1567 Caracas was founded.
1620 By this time cocoa had become the principal export. Production attracted many Spanish immigrants.
1749 First rebellion against Spanish rule.
1810–21 Simón Bolívar defeated the Spanish army in a long war and created Greater Colombia out of Venezuela, Colombia, Ecuador, Bolivia and Peru.
1823 The last battles for independence gained Venezuela its freedom from Spanish control.
1830 Bolívar died, José Antonio Paez assumed the presidency.
1859–63 A civil war erupted in a power struggle between conservative centralists and federalists forces. The liberal federalists won the war.
1870–88 General Antonio Guzmán ruled the country, increasing its international prestige, and developed the country's colonial bureaucracy into a modern state and commercial outpost of the industrialising countries around the North Atlantic.
1908–1935 General Juan Vicente Gómez ruled the country, instituting a harsh policy of repression while developing Venezuela into an oil-based, technocratic economy. The influence of foreign petroleum interests on domestic policies increased with the increase in direct foreign investment.
1935–41 General Eleazar Lopez Contreras became president and began a policy of liberal capitalist democracy.
1945 After decades of rule by dictators, political violence erupted in Caracas. A coup led by a group of young military men and Rómulo Ernesto Betancourt Bello (Acción Democrática (AD) (Democratic Action)), set up a new government committed to democracy and social and land reforms. Foreign powers were suspicious of the government's left-wing credentials until Betancourt announced prompt elections would be held, acceptable reforms implemented and no radical action would be taken against foreign oil interests.
1947 A new constitution that provided for a popular vote, by secret ballot, to elect a president was promulgated. Romulo Gallegos Freire (AD) became the first Venezuelan president to be elected by democratic vote.
1948 The government was overthrown in a military *coup d'état* backed by conservative elements opposed to the reforms. A succession of *juntas* formed governments.
1952 Marcos Evangelista Pérez Jiménez seized power and became the next dictator president.
1953 The United States of Venezuela was renamed the Bolivian Republic of Venezuela.
1958 Pérez Jiménez was deposed by the military and a governing council allowed free elections, in which Betancourt (AD) was elected president. A pact between the main parties, including the AD and the Partido Demócrata Cristiano de Venezuela (Copei) (Christian Democrat Party of Venezuela), agreed to share power and maintain a pluralistic democracy. Moderate economic reforms, with regard for US interests, were slowly introduced.
1969 Rafael Caldera Rodríguez became Venezuela's first Copei president and managed to achieve a degree of political and economic stability.
1973 Venezuela joined the Andean Community, which also included Ecuador, Colombia, Peru and Bolivia.
1974–79 Carlos Andrés Pérez Rodríguez (AD) held presidential office and used massive oil revenues to nationalise industries and diversify the economy.
1979–84 The election of President Herrera (Copei) coincided with a downturn in global oil prices which led to a series of problems, including rising corruption, capital flight, economic stagnation and high levels of external debt.
1988 Presidential and legislative elections were held in December. Pérez became the first former president to be re-elected.
1989 Public protests against the government's austerity programme, which involved drastic government spending cut-backs in order to stabilise the economy, broke out around the country. The first-ever direct elections of state governors were held.
1992 Lieutenant Colonel Hugo Rafael Chávez Frías led an unsuccessful coup attempt against President Pérez.
1998 The presidential election was won by Hugo Chávez of the Movimiento V República (MVR) (Movement for the Fifth Republic), with more than 56 per cent of the vote.
1999 President Chávez's government began his 'Bolívarian Revolution' that included a unicameral National Assembly, a new constitution, a reduced civilian control of the military and an increased control by government of the economy. A referendum approved all the amendments. Torrential rains caused severe flooding in December, killing approximately 30,000 people.
2000 In the first elections under the new constitution Chávez was re-elected president. His coalition won 99 out of 165 assembly seats but not enough to rule unfettered. The assembly granted him the right to legislate by decree.
2001 There were calls for the president's resignation after he passed 49 laws under his special powers of decree, regarding land redistribution and the oil sector.
2002 Civil unrest interrupted oil exports. President Chávez was briefly ousted from power on 12 April. Other Latin American countries refused to recognise Pedro Carmona Estanga as interim president and Chávez's supporters counter-demonstrated until he was reinstated. Chávez formally resumed his presidency on 15 April. On 2 December, an opposition-led general strike began.
2003 In January, the government imported petrol from Brazil and attempted to regain control of the strike-bound oil facilities. The strike ended in February. The opposition failed to force a referendum on whether Chávez should serve out his remaining presidential term in office.
2004 In June the electoral authority ruled that opponents of Chávez had collected enough signatures for a referendum. President Chávez won 58 per cent of the vote in the 15 August recall referendum.
2005 A decree for land distribution was signed by the president. During a state visit to Cuba in May, President Chávez and Fidel Castro signed several trade and co-operation agreements. In November Venezuela agreed to supply heating oil to poor residents of Boston and New York at 40 per cent below the market rate. In December, elections took place, with Chávez loyalists making big gains. Opposition parties staged a boycott of the poll.

Political structure
Constitution
A referendum in December 1999 voted for a new constitution which set out to strengthen democracy and the judiciary, but consolidated presidential powers and the role of the state in the economy.
The federal republic comprises 72 federal dependencies, 23 states, two federal territories and one federal district. The La Guaira-based Vargas District became Venezuela's 23rd state in 1999.
Voting is compulsory for all Venezuelan nationals over 18 years old.
Form of state
Federal presidential republic

Nations of the World: A Political, Economic and Business Handbook

The executive
Executive power rests with the president who is elected by direct, compulsory, universal suffrage for a renewable six-year term.

National legislature
A 165-member unicameral National Assembly headed by the president replaced the bicameral Congress which was abolished by the 1999 constitution.

Legal system
The Supreme Court appoints judges in consultation with civil society groups.

Last elections
December 2005 (parliamentary); 15 August 2004 (recall referendum); July 2000 (presidential).
Results: Recall referendum: President Chávez won 58 per cent of the vote; turnout 60 per cent.
Presidential: Hugo Rafael Chávez Fríaz (MVR) 59.5 per cent of the vote, Francisco Arias Cárdnas 37.5 per cent.
Parliamentary: MVR 114 seats; various pro-Chávez parties 53 seats. The turnout was 25 per cent, but due to a boycott by AD the results have been subject to claims of under-representation and questions of legitimacy.

Next elections
2006 (presidential); 2009 (parliamentary).

Political parties
Ruling party
Movimiento V República (MVR) (Movement for the Fifth Republic) (re-elected Dec 2005)

Main opposition party
Acción Democrática (AD) (Democratic Action) boycotted the 2005 election and has no parliamentary seats.

Population
25.51 million (2004)

Ethnic make-up
Mestizo (67 per cent), White (21 per cent), Black (10 per cent), Indian (2 per cent).

Religions
Roman Catholic (96 per cent), Protestant (2 per cent).

Education
Pre-primary (one year) and basic education lasts until aged 15. Exams then determine whether students progress onto an academic course for two years or a vocational course for three years. Many institutes of higher education have a selection procedure and often run preparatory courses as part of the admission process. Professional courses last for three years, catering for the industrial, farming, commercial and health sectors.
Universities, institutes, two ecclesiastic university institutes and three military institutes, provide higher education. Institutes and University Colleges generally provide for short courses of study lasting between two and three years. Long courses lasting for five to six years are also available. The universities are both public and private. National public universities are both autonomous and experimental institutions.
Literacy rate: 93.1 per cent, total; 92.7 per cent, female; adult rates in 2002 (World Bank).
Compulsory years: Five to 17
Enrolment rate: 91 per cent gross primary enrolment; 40 per cent gross seconday enrolment of relevant age groups (including repeaters).
Pupils per teacher: 21 in primary schools

Health
Venezuela has achieved significant long-term advances with regard to health in hospital care but preventive and primary health care remains on a very small scale. Venezuela is vulnerable to natural disasters, the most frequent of which are floods with concurrent landslides, and there is also a risk of earthquakes. The Ministry of Family has assisted non-governmental organisations (NGOs) and community-based groups to participate in social programmes at a household level. The armed forces, which are already active in a social welfare programme known as Bolivar 2000, were used in the fight against a dengue epidemic in 2001.
HIV prevalence: 0.7 per cent aged 15–49 in 2003 (World Bank)
Life expectancy: 73.9 years (World Bank)
Fertility rate/Maternal mortality rate: 2.7 births per woman (2003); maternal mortality 60 per 100,000 live births (World Bank).
Birth rate/Death rate: 4 deaths per 24 births per 1,000 people; infant mortality 19 per 1,000 live births (World Bank).
Infant mortality rate: 18 per 1,000 live birth; 4 per cent of children under aged five are malnourished (World Bank).
Head of population per physician/bed: Typically 2.4 physicians and 1.5 hospital beds per 1,000 people.

Welfare
Venezuela operates a social insurance system covering employees in private and public employment, unemployed and family members.
The welfare system of benefits covers sickness, maternity, work injury, unemployment and family allowances. Pensioners are also covered for medical benefits. Sickness benefits are covered for up to 52 weeks. Maternity benefit is payable up to six months before and after confinement. Workers' medical benefits include free general and specialist care and hospitalisation. Unemployment benefit covers 60 per cent of the average weekly salary of the last 50 weeks and is paid for up to 13 weeks after waiting for one month following loss of employment. Unemployed persons are entitled to transportation subsidy, training and guidance services.

Pensions
A new system of private pensions was introduced in 1998. In 1999, Venezuela moved away from a pay-as-you-go pension system to one based on 'individual capitalisation funds', along the lines of the Chilean model. Under the mandatory pay-as-you-go system all participants receive pensions in proportion to their contributions, amounting to 12–13 per cent of base salary, and on the basis of the accumulation of the individual fund. The government pays for any deficiency between the accumulated value of the individual capitalised fund and the minimum amount of pension.
Full pensions are paid at aged 60, provided 240 months of contributions have been paid. At the age of 60, the employee has the option of either buying a life annuity from an insurance company, or withdrawing fixed monthly amounts from their individual capitalisation account.
A disability pension is available with 250 weeks of contribution, plus 30 per cent of workers' average earnings, payable after six months of disability.

Main cities
Caracas (capital, estimated population 1.7 million in 2004), Maracaibo (1.9 million), Valencia (1.6 million), Barquisimeto (948,900), Ciudad Guayana (818,600), Petare (518,800), Maracay (491,200), Ciudad Bolívar (372,400).

Languages spoken
Spanish is spoken by the majority of the population. Indian dialects are spoken by about 200,000 Amerindians in the remote interior.

Official language/s
Spanish

Media
Press
There are approximately 50 newspapers, all with limited circulation in proportion to the population. There are an estimated 15 daily newspapers published in Caracas. The major Caracas papers include *El Nacional*, *El Universal*, *El Diario*, *Meridiano*, *El Mundo*, *Ultimas Noticias*, *Economía Hoy* and *The Daily Journal* (English). A number of regional dailies are published in main centres. There are also numerous periodicals including *El Carabobeño* and the monthly *Cabala* of consumer interest.

Broadcasting
Radio: There is a total of 280 radio stations. *Radio Nacional* operates the state

broadcasting service of eight radio stations. There are also two cultural and a large number of commercial stations. All broadcasts are in Spanish.

Television: Four national TV stations, one of which is government-owned, as well as 12 regional and six local channels. All are commercial. The private TV stations broadcast in Spanish nationwide. About 96 per cent of the population have a TV set.

Advertising

Television accounts for around 60 per cent of advertising expenditure.

Economy

The economy of Venezuela performed inconsistently throughout the 2000s. The economy suffered from stagflation, (a decline in real GDP coupled with inflation), in 2002 and 2003, but has since improved on the back of an increase in the oil price. Real GDP growth of 17.3 per cent was achieved in 2004 and the IMF forecasts growth of 7.8 per cent for 2005 and 4.5 per cent in 2006. High inflation however, remains a serious problem. Venezuela's economic performance is largely dependent on oil, which in a typical year accounts for over 40 per cent of government revenues and up to 30 per cent of total GDP.

While oil has generated growth, it has also distorted the Venezuelan economy and prevented diversification. Furthermore, volatile international oil prices have had damaging political repercussions. The nationwide strike in 2002 included employees from state owned oil company Petróleos de Venezuela SA (PdVSA). This brought oil production almost to a standstill and severely worsened the Venezuelan recession. Against expectations of the World Bank and IMF, several months after the strike oil production levels returned to those before the strike, starting an impetus for growth.

The restructuring programme has not generated enough foreign investment to diversify the economy. Domestic investment has been curtailed by high interest rates and a general feeling of insecurity created by the President's unpredictability and the opposition's attempts to undermine the political order through economic sabotage. A move in 2003 to stem capital flight through currency controls has helped prevent further deterioration of the bolívar and stabilised the economy, however this has led to a shortage of imported products due to the slow release of dollars by Caldivi, the agency set up in 2003 to manage currency control.

President Chávez's hawkish approach to oil prices suggests that, like his predecessors, he believes that oil revenues will enable Venezuela to avoid the type of structural changes that have taken place in the rest of the region.

In December 2005, for the first time since President Chávez came to power, a multilateral institution has given the go-ahead for a substantial loan for the country. The Inter-American Development Bank (IADB) agreed to lend US$768 million to Venezuela, a large portion of which is earmarked for development of the country's hydroelectric infrastructure.

External trade

Venezuela became an associate member of Mercosur midway through 1994 and a full member of the trade group in December 2005.

Venezuela is a member of the South American Community of Nations, which aims to integrate the Mercosur and Andean Community trade agreements by 2007 in order to eliminate tariffs for non-sensitive products by 2014 and sensitive products by 2019.

Imports

Principal imports are raw materials, machinery and equipment, transport equipment and construction materials.

Main sources: US (33.2 per cent total, 2004), Colombia (5.7 per cent), Brazil (5.0 per cent), Germany (4.0 per cent)

Exports

Principal exports are petroleum, bauxite and aluminium, steel, chemicals, agricultural products and basic manufactures.

Main destinations: US (58.7 per cent total, 2004), The Netherlands Antilles (4.1 per cent), Canada (2.5 per cent)

Agriculture

Farming

Land use is divided between arable land (3 per cent), permanent crops cultivation (1 per cent), meadows and pastures (20 per cent), forest and woodland (50 per cent) and other use (26 per cent). The country is subject to periodic droughts. Venezuela's main arable centres are Acarigua, El Tigre, Maracay, Valencia and Barquisimeto.

The agricultural sector is not hugely important to the economy of Venezuela, constituting just 5 per cent of total GDP. There has been little investment in modern farm technology. Inefficient marketing, poor farm management and scant irrigation are all features of the Venezuelan agricultural industry.

The major crops are rice, maize, sorghum, sugar cane, coffee (the main export crop), cocoa and cotton. Tropical fruits, cassava, beans, groundnuts and other vegetables are staple crops for small farmers. Poultry and pig-farming are of growing importance with small quantities of meat exported. Beef production has, however, slumped due to the smuggling of cattle to Colombia (where prices are higher), and cheap imports.

Throughout the 1990s, the government liberalised agricultural imports through lowering tariffs and removing quantitative restrictions in the form of import licences. The overall aim was to boost agricultural efficiency and to refocus production on areas where the country has a comparative advantage.

An agricultural programme is under way, involving the improvement and irrigation of 350,000 hectares of existing agricultural land and the use of about one million new hectares for cultivation. The programme aims to increase output of cereals, sugar and oilseeds (to reduce dependence on imports), and promote crop diversification.

Since the election of Hugo Chávez as president in 1999, the government has introduced land reform measures designed to bring disused agricultural land into production and redistribute land to the rural poor. The measures have been resisted by the land-owning oligarchy in the countryside, particularly cattle ranchers. The national government accelerated its land reform programme and continued to expropriate local agribusinesses throughout 2005.

Crop production in 2004 included: 3,670,543 tonnes (t) cereals in total, 2,068,465t maize, 9,832,005t sugar cane, 336,894t potatoes, 989,478t rice, 612,450t sorghum, 428,450t plantains, 549,628t bananas, 594,567t citrus fruit, 183,707t tomatoes, 15,931t cocoa beans, 65,559t green coffee, 1,012,939t roots and tubers, 97,342t oilcrops, 45,205t pulses, 2,364,222t fruit in total, 1,405,975t vegetables in total. Livestock production included: 1,242,764t meat in total, 433,010t beef, 117,579t pig meat, 7,495t lamb and goat meat, 684,680t poultry, 149,291t eggs, 1,237,107t milk.

Fishing

Since coming to power President Chávez has passed legislation that regulates the activities of large trawlers in order to protect small fishing communities.

Generally, the fishing industry has seen good growth, owing to an increase in the tuna catch. The overall typical fish catch is in the region of 435,000mt, including 318,000mt marine fish and 79,000mt shellfish.

Forestry

Approximately half of Venezuela's total landmass is covered with forests and woodland, the majority of which are in the south and east of the country. The forestry sector remains undeveloped and around half the country's wood-derived products are imported.

Exports of forest materials in 2004 amounted to US$ 98.2 million, while imports constituted US$190.1 million. Timber production in 2004 included 5,033,503 cubic metres (cum) roundwood, 1,289,000cum industrial roundwood, 501,000cum sawnwood, 231,000cum pulpwood, 1,058,000cum sawlogs & veneer logs, 302,000cum wood-based panels, 3,744,503cum wood fuel, 379,199t charcoal.

Industry and manufacturing

Over time heavy industries have arisen with the intention of using local materials as inputs including the refining of aluminium (an increasingly significant export), petrochemicals (ammonia, sulphuric acid, fertilisers, plastics etc) and cement and steel production.

Import-dependent industries include motor vehicle assembly, tyres, rubber, pharmaceuticals, electrical goods and machinery. The traditional home market industries are beverages, textiles, food processing, ceramics and paper/pulp. Major state enterprises include Sidor (steel), Venalum and Alcasa (aluminium) and Pequiven (petrochemicals). Venezuela's aluminium industry is inefficient and heavily indebted.

Manufacturing production remains highly concentrated, with around 10 per cent of all firms accounting for 75 per cent of output. Joint ventures involving state, domestic and foreign private capital were developed in the 1990s to expand the petrochemical and aluminium industries. Manufacturing increased in 2004, on the wave of a general economic upswing in the economy during the year. In the first seven months of the 2004 calender year the manufacturing sector expanded by 38 per cent more than the same seven month period in 2003.

Tourism

The travel and tourism industry of Venezuela has been hampered by the political and economic stability in the country. Though capital investment in the sector has risen to represent almost 12 per cent of total capital investment in the economy, employment in the sector is down, as is the industry's percentage contribution to total GDP.

Mining

Venezuela is endowed with a significant range of mineral resources. However, these deposits remain largely undeveloped. The sectors of the industry retaining the most importance include iron ore, bauxite, gold, diamond and nickel laterites. Other sources include zinc, copper, lead, silver, manganese, titanium, nickel, marble, sulphur, phosphates, mercury and uranium.

At present, the mining industry contributes just 1 per cent of the country's total GDP. The government reformed its mining law in 1999, converting mining contracts signed with Corporacion Venezolana de Guayana (CVG) into mining concessions. The government eliminated exploration and surface taxes in the first three years of a concession.

Several foreign investment and joint ventures have propped up the sector. Venezuelan, Canadian and US companies have combined to exploit the extensive kimberlite sills in the region of Guaniamo and aid in the marketing of diamonds. Nickel is mined at Loma de Niquel. The main mineral exploited is iron ore; reserves are estimated at 2,800 million tonnes, 80 per cent high-grade. The largest deposits are located at Cerro Bolívar and San Isidro. Estimated reserves of bauxite at Los Pijiguaos typically amount to some four billion tonnes of high-grade ore.

In September President Chávez suggested that the Las Cristinas gold mining region would be re-nationalised at some point in the future. Crystallex, a Canadian mining company operating in the region and currently planning to build the what would be the largest gold mine in Venezuela, saw a sharp decline in its share price on the back of the news.

Hydrocarbons

Venezuela continues to be one of the world's most important oil exporters. The country is endowed with the most extensive proven oil reserves in the Western Hemisphere and the petroleum industry is the mainstay of the economy.

Total proven conventional oil reserves are estimated at 77.2 billion barrels, which should last at least 65 years at present production levels. This figure does not include significant extra-heavy and bitumen deposits, which are thought to be as high as 270 billion barrels.

Production is restricted by Venezuela's OPEC quota, which was officially set at 2.3 million barrels per day (bpd) in 2002. An opposition-led general strike in 2002 shut down the country's oil industry, causing oil output to fall to under 400,000bpd. By 2003, the strike in the oil sector had ended and oil production was rising to near normal levels. About 58 per cent of oil exports are destined for the US, which has become increasingly reliant on Venezuelan oil in recent years; Venezuela accounts for around 12 per cent of the US's oil supply.

By 2004, there were large proven natural gas reserves estimated at 4.2 trillion cubic metres, the eighth-largest in the world. Production of natural gas was 28.1 billion cubic metres in 2004. An estimated 60 per cent of gas production is consumed by the oil industry, 10 per cent is used for power generation, 6 per cent for petrochemical production and the rest is consumed by industrial and commercial customers in urban areas. The gas infrastructure consists of over 3,000 miles of pipeline and private companies are planning to extend the network, possibly to neighbouring countries such as Colombia and Brazil.

Exploitation of gas reserves is a priority, although output has slowly fallen year-by-year since the mid-1990s. Venezuela is the second largest producer of coal in Latin America, after Colombia, and has 479 million tonnes of coal reserves (2004). PdVSA operates, through joint ventures between its subsidiary Carbozulia and foreign companies, four mines with production at 6.6 million tonnes of oil equivalent (2004). Domestic consumption is only around 15,000 tonnes per annum and most of Venezuela's mainly bituminous coal is exported to markets in North and South America and Europe. The government intends to increase production to around 18 million tonnes per annum by 2008.

Energy

Venezuela has an electricity generation capacity of 21.3 gigawatts (GW). Approximately 62 per cent of total electricity generated is hydroelectric, with traditional thermal sources constituting the remainder.

Almost half of Venezuela's electricity generating capacity is provided by the 10GW Raul Leoni hydroelectric dam on the Caroní River.

Venezuela's grid is connected to that of Colombia, enabling the country to export surplus electricity. However, there have been serious electricity shortages in recent years due to low rainfall and electricity theft, which is estimated to account for a quarter of Venezuelan energy consumption.

The electricity sector is dominated by the state-owned Electrificación de Caroni (EDELCA). Cadafe, which includes Cadela, Elecentro, Eleoriente, Eleoccidente, Desurca, and Semda, is the second-largest state-owned electricity company.

The Caruachia dam project began operations in early 2003 and will increase Venezuela's electricity generating capacity by 11 per cent, providing 2.2GW of power when it is completed in 2010. Another dam, the 2.2GW Tocoma hydroelectric dam, is scheduled for completion by 2010. In December 2005 the Inter-American Development Bank (IADB) approved a US$768 million loan for Venezuela, US$750 million of which is to be devoted

Venezuela

to the construction and operation of the Tocoma dam.

Financial markets
Stock exchange
The Bolsa de Valores de Caracas (BCV) (Caracas Stock Exchange) is the largest stock exchange in the country. The Comisión Nacional de Valores (CNV) (National Securities Commission) authorises bond issues and the public share offerings of domestic and foreign companies, but foreign shares can be traded on the exchange only if the government has given prior authorisation. Shares are not widely traded as the major domestic companies are privately held. Latin American fund managers invest on average 2 per cent of their total portfolios in Venezuela, compared to an average of 30 per cent in Mexico and 15 per cent in Argentina.

Banking and insurance
With the bankruptcy of the second biggest bank in the country, Banco Latino, in 1994, the Venezuelan banking and financial services system went into meltdown. About a third of Venezuela's banks subsequently went into insolvency as depositors panicked, closing accounts and forcing under-capitalised banks to close. Since then, the financial sector in Venezuela has undergone a vigorous restructuring, ensuring that the banks of today are well capitalised with relatively clean balance sheets.

The government has been able to recuperate its losses through the privatisation of several leading banks, and Venezuela's financial system is largely controlled by foreign interests. Foreign participation in Venezuela's banking system had risen to around 70 per cent of total banking assets by 2002 compared to less than 5 per cent in 1994. As elsewhere in Latin America, it is the Spanish banks which have had the most influence in Venezuela's banking system, with Banco Santander Central Hispano (BSCH) engaged in aggressive take-overs of indigenous banks. In September Venezuela's banking superintendent privately told several of the country's large banks that President Chávez intends to place official government representatives on their governing boards. Banco Santander and BBVA, two Spanish banks currently in ownership of Banco de Venezuela and Banco Provincial respectively, would be directly affected by the new arrangements.

Central bank
Banco Central de Venezuela

Main financial centre
Caracas

Time
GMT minus four hours

Geography
Venezuela is on the north coast of South America, bordered by Colombia to the west, Guyana to the east and Brazil to the south.

Climate
Tropical, hot and humid, with more moderate temperatures in highlands. Dry season from December–April, with mean temperature in Caracas 19 degrees Celsius (C), rising to 28 degrees C during the day; nights are cool. Rainy season from May–November, with mean daytime temperature in Caracas 23 degrees C.

Entry requirements
Passports
Required by all and valid for six months.
Visa
Required by some, many may visit on tourist visas for up to 90 days. The only requirement is filling out the tourist card provided by the transport carrier or airline. For further information visit www.embavenez-us.org/ and view the information on visas for a full list of exemptions.
Business travellers must contact the nearest consulate for further information concerning their visas. Information expected to be requested include a company letter, stating names and addresses of companies to be visited in Venezuela and purpose of trip.
Currency advice/regulations
There are no restrictions on the import or export of foreign or local currency.

Health (for visitors)
Mandatory precautions
None (yellow fever vaccination certificates may be required by visitor leaving for other countries).
Advisable precautions
Yellow fever, cholera, typhoid, polio vaccinations. Malaria prophylaxis recommended for visits to some rural areas. Rabies is present and dengue fever is becoming more common. There are occasional outbreaks of viral encephalitis.
In north-central regions, to avoid the risk of Bilharzia use only chlorinated swimming pools for bathing.
Bottled water is advisable for new visitors. Unwashed raw foods and undercooked meats are not safe to eat.
Healthcare facilities are good in main cities, but the cost is high, therefore, medical insurance is recommended.

Hotels
The selection of first-rate hotels is rather limited. Good standard in Caracas and main centres. Graded into classes by Tourism Department on a one- to five-star basis. Booking in advance is essential. There are some seasonal variations of rates. There is a 10 per cent tourist tax.

Public holidays
Fixed dates
1 Jan (New Year's Day), 19 Apr (Declaration of Independence), 1 May (Labour Day), 24 Jun (Battle of Carabobo), 5 Jul (Independence Day), 24 Jul (Simon Bolívar's Birthday), 15 Aug (Assumption Day), 12 Oct (Columbus Day), 1 Nov (All Saints' Day), 8 Dec (Immaculate Conception), 25 Dec (Christmas Day), 31 Dec (New Year's Eve).
Variable dates
Epiphany (first Mon in Jan), Carnival (Feb), Maundy Thursday, Good Friday.

Working hours
Banking
Mon–Fri: 0830–1130, 1400–1630.
Business
Mon–Fri: 0800–1800 (with long lunch break from noon to 1430).
Government
Mon–Fri: range from 0730–1530 to 0930–1730; long lunch break from noon to 1430.
Shops
Mon–Sat: 0900–1300, 1500–1900.

Telecommunications
Mobile phones
A GSM 900 network is limited to coverage in Caracas and main towns.

Electricity supply
110V AC, 60 cycles

Social customs/useful tips
The normal form of greeting is a handshake or an *abrazo*, a cross between a handshake and a hug. Luncheons are frequently heavy. Wine in restaurants tends to be expensive.
Public services are inefficient and it is advisable to hire professional help to carry out official transactions.
Punctuality is not a strong point and the traffic is often blamed for delays. Business meetings may be cancelled or rescheduled at the last moment.
There is no numbering system for streets in Caracas, and many street names are not marked. Directions are given by building or residence name and the neighbourhood or *urbanización*.

Security
Carry identification at all times because police make spot checks and a person without identification may be detained. Beware of pickpockets as they are everywhere. If unlucky enough to be robbed, do not argue as criminals can quickly become violent. Many Caracas residents carry handguns for personal defence and are prepared to use them.

Getting there
Air
National airline: Aeropostal (Alas de Venezuela) (VH), and Avensa and

Servivensa (which does not fly to Europe) (VC).

International airport/s: Caracas-Simón Bolívar (Maiquetía) (CCS), 22km north of city, duty-free, bank/bureau de change (0800–1800), restaurant, tourist information and car hire. Journey time to city by bus 45 minutes running every hour. Taxis are located at a rank.

Other airport/s: Maracaibo-La Chinita (MAR), 17km from city, restaurant, car hire.

Airport tax: International departures approximately US$17 and domestic departures B600.

Surface

Road: It is possible to cross from Colombia by the Caribbean Coastal Highway, or by the Pan-American Highway via San Cristobal. The only road from Brazil (via Santa Elena de Uairen) is very rough and is difficult in the rainy season. There is no direct access from Guyana.

Main port/s: Guanta, La Guaira, Maracaibo, Puerto Cabello.

Getting about
National transport

Air: This is the best means of internal travel with several carriers offering many destinations.

Overbooking is common and it is advisable to arrive at the airport well before minimum check-in time. Cancellations and schedule changes are also likely to occur. Unlimited travel tickets are available.

Road: Those between main cities are of a high standard, with 17,050km paved motorways, 13,500km macadam highways and 5850km other roads. The Pan-American Highway runs from Caracas, via Valencia and Barquisimeto, to the Colombian border. Other main highways include: Valencia-Puerto Cabello; Coro-La Ceiba; Caracas-Ciudad Bolívar.

Buses: Services are not luxurious but relatively efficient with frequent journeys between major cities (eg Caracas-Maracaibo: journey time approximately 10hrs.) It is advisable to book in advance.

Rail: A very limited service available, (Barquisimeto-Puerto Cabello; around four trains per day).

City transport

Taxis: Within Caracas taxis are not metered and passengers should negotiate a fare before travelling.

Tips are customary. Higher fares are charged for late night journeys. Shared taxis (*por puestos*) widely used.

Outside Caracas fares are by negotiation and tend to be expensive for long trips.

Buses, trams & metro: The metro reaches main points all along the Valley of Caracas. It is fast, cheap, clean, comfortable and safe, although pickpockets abound. It links with the metrobus services although services have deteriorated in recent years.

Shared taxis are main form of public transport in main towns.

Car hire

Most international rental car companies are available in main towns and at airports. National or international licence accepted. A credit card is required. Insurance cover is recommended.

BUSINESS DIRECTORY

The addresses listed below are a selection only. While World of Information makes every endeavour to check these addresses, we cannot guarantee that changes have not been made, especially to telephone numbers and area codes. We would welcome any corrections.

Telephone area codes
The international direct dialling (IDD) code for Venezuela is +58, followed by area code and subscriber's number:

Barquisimeto	251	Maturin	291
Caracas	212	Merida	274
Ciudad Bolivar	285	Pt Cabello	242
Cumana	293	San Cristobal	276
Maracaibo	261	Valencia	241
Maracay	243		

Chambers of Commerce
American-Venezuelan Cámara de Comercio, Torre Credival, 2da Avenida de Campo Alegre, Caracas (tel: 263-0833; fax: 263-1829; e-mail: vanamcham@venamcham.org).

British-Venezuelan Chamber of Commerce, Avenida Francisco de Miranda, Multicentro Empresarial del Este, Caracas (tel: 267-3112; fax: 263-0362; e-mail: britcham@ven.net).

Caracas Cámara de Comercio, Calle Andrés Eloy Blanco 215, Los Caobos, Caracas (tel: 571-3222; fax: 571-0050; e-mail: comercioccs@cantv.net).

Valencia Cámara de Comercio, Avenida Bolivar Norte, Edificio Cámara de Comercio, Valencia (tel: 857-5109; fax: 857-5147; e-mail: camaracomercio@cantv.net).

Venezualan Federación de Cámaras y Asociaciones de Comercio y Producción, Avenida El Empalme, Urbanizacion El Bosque, PO Box 2568, Caracas (tel: 731-1711, 731-0246; e-mail: direje@fedecamaras.org.ve).

Banking
Banco Industrial de Venezuela, Av Universidad Esquina de Traposos, Zona postal 1010, Apartado postal 2054, Caracas (tel: 545-9222/541-8622; fax: 545-8315).

Banco Mercantil, Av Andrés Bello No 1, Edif Mercantil, Aportado postal 789, Caracas 1010-A (tel: 541-4320, 541-6666; fax: 507-1239, 574-3216; e-mail: mercan24@bancomercantil.com; internet site: http://www.bancomercantil.com).

Banco Provincial, Av Este 'O', San Bernardo, Zona postal 1010-A, Apartado postal 1269, Caracas (tel: 574-5611, 574-6611; fax: 574-9408, 574-2065).

Central bank

Banco Central de Venezuela, Avenida Urdaneta esq Las Carmelitas, Apartado 2017, Caracas 1010 (tel: 801-5111; fax: 861-1649; e-mail: info@bcv.org.ve).

Travel information
Caracas International airport (internet site: http://www.aeropuerto-maiquelia.com.ve).

National tourist organisation offices

Venezuelan Tourist Corporation (Corpoturismo), Torre Oeste, Piso 37, Parque Central, Caracas 1010 (tel: 574-1968, 2124; fax: 574-2220).

Ministries
Conicit (Ministry of State for Higher Education, Science and Technology), Edif Maploca, Final Avda Principal Los Cortijos de Lourdes, Caracas (tel: 239-0433; fax: 239-8677).

Dirección General Sectorial de Minas y Geología (Division of the Ministry of Energy and Mines responsible for minerals policy), Torre Oeste, 4 Piso, Parque Central, Caracas.

Instituto de Comercio Exterior (ICE – Export Authority attached to the Ministry of Foreign Affairs), Centro Comercial Los Cedros, Apdo 51852, Caracas 1050 (tel: 729-960; fax: 716-061).

Ministry of Agriculture and Livestock, Torre Este, Piso 14, Caracas (tel: 509-0445; fax: 574-2432).

Ministry of Defence, Fuerta Tiuna, Conejo Blanco, Caracas 1090(tel: 622-2745, 693-0626; fax: 662-4078).

Ministry of Education, Esquina de Salas, Edificio Sede Del Ministerio de Educación, Caracas (tel: 564-0672; fax: 564-0379).

Ministry of Energy, Torre Oeste, Parque Central, Piso 16, Caracas (tel: 507-6604; fax: 571-3953).

Ministry of the Environment, Torre Sur, Centro Simon Bolivar, Piso 25, Caracas (tel: 481-6275/1049/2209; fax: 483-1148).

Ministry of Family Affairs, Torre Oeste, Parque Central, Piso 51, Caracas (tel: 575-3690/8901; fax: 573-7481).

Ministry of Finance, Edif Banco la Guaira, Piso 12, Av Mexico, Caracas (tel: 509-8281; fax: 509-7831).

Venezuela

Ministry of Foreign Affairs, Conde a Carmelitas, Torre M.R.E., Piso 2, Caracas 1010 (tel: 862-4484/4668; fax: 861-0894).

Ministry of Foreign Trade, Centro Comercial los Cedros, Mezzanina 3, Avda Libertador, Caracas (tel: 762-2777, 531-0009; fax: 762-3883).

Ministry of Health and Social Security, Edif, Sur, Centro Simón Bolívar, Caracas (tel: 483-1566).

Ministry of Home Affairs, Esquina de Carmelitas, Caracas 1010 (tel: 83-4334; fax: 861-1967).

Ministry of Housing (tel: 509-8676, 574-9813; fax: 509-8437).

Ministry of Industrial Development, Edif Sur, Piso 9, Centro Simón Bolívar, Caracas (tel: 419-296, 419-341/396; fax: 483-2607).

Ministry of Justice, Torre Norte, Centro Simón Bolívar, Piso 25 (tel: 483-1170; fax: 483-7515).

Ministry of Labour, Torre Sur, Piso 5, Centro Simón Bolívar, Caracas (tel: 483-1881; fax: 483-5940).

Ministry of Planning (Cordiplan), Parque Central, Torre Oeste, Piso 26, Caracas (tel: 507-7902; fax: 573-2834).

Ministry of Public Works and Commercial Affairs, Centro Simón Bolívar, Torre Sur, Piso 6, Caracas (tel: 483-2124-2371/4518/4318; fax: 412-553, 481-4916, 483-8552).

Ministry of Trade and Industry, Av Libertador Centro Comercial Los Cedros, Piso 2, Caracas (tel: 531-0026; fax: 762-9869).

Ministry of Transport and Communications, Torre Este, Parque Central, Piso 50, Caracas (tel: 509-1076/1071; fax: 509-1769).

Ministry of Urban Development, Torre Oeste, Parque Central, Piso 51, Caracas (tel: 574-5349/8649; fax: 571-1767).

President's Office, Palacio de Miraflores, Avenida Urdeneta, Caracas 1010 (tel: 81-0811; fax: 861-1101).

Other useful addresses

Asociación Nacional de Comerciantes e Industriales, Plaza Panteón Norte 1, Apdo 33, Caracas.

CVG Bauxita de Venezuela S.A. (Raw Material for Aluminun), Av. La Estancia, Edif, Diamen, Piso 2, Chuao, Caracas (tel: 922-311, 916-187, 916-487; fax: 918-176).

British Embassy, Edificio Torre Las Mercedes, 3 Piso, Avenida La Estancia, Chuao, Caracas 1060 (tel: 911-255, 993-4111, 926-542, 914-253; fax: 993-9989).

Caracas Stock Exchange (fax: 952-2640; internet site: http://www.caracasstock.com).

Central Information Office (OCI), Parque Central, Torre Oeste, Piso 18, Caracas (tel: 572-7110; fax: 572-2675).

The Commission for State Reform, Torre Oeste, Piso 38, Parque Central, Caracas (tel: 507-8934/8931; fax: 572-3178).

Conapri (National Council for Investment Promotion), Centro Banavén, PB, Local 4, Chuao, Caracas (tel: 923-801; fax: 926-498).

Consejo Venezolana de la Industria, Edif Cámara de Industriales, Esq de Puente Anauco, Caracas.

Corporación Venezolana de Guayana (CVG) (Main Company), Edif. de Administración, Via Caracas, Puerto Ordaz, Ciudad Guayana, C.P. 80915, Edo. Bolivar (tel: 303-333; fax: 226-300, 225-311).

CVG Ferrominera del Orinoco A.A. (Iron), Av La Estancia, Chuao, Edif, Torre Las Mercedes, Piso 9, Caracas 1070-A (tel: 911-166; fax: 911-639).

Fondo de Inversiones de Venezuela (Privatisation Programme Information), Torre Financiera del Banco Central de Venezuela, Piso 20, Esq de Santa Capilla, Avda Urdaneta, Caracas (tel: 806-5974; fax: 819-169).

PdVSA (Petróleos de Venezuela), Avda Liberator, La Campina, Apdo 169, Caracas 1010-A (tel: 708-1111; fax: 708-4661).

CVG Siderúrgica del Orinoco C.A. SIDOR. (Aluminium, Iron and Steel), Av La Estancia, Chuao, Edif. General de Seguros, Caracas, 1070-A (tel: 912-333, 911-462).

Superintendencia de Inversiones Extranjeras (SIEX – Superintendency of Foreign Investment), Apdo 213, Edif La Perla, Piso 3, Bolsa a Mercaderes, Caracas (tel: 483-6666; fax: 484-4368, 481-7919).

Unión Patronal Venezolana de Comercio, Edif General Urdaneta, Piso 2, Marrón a Pelota, Apdo 6578, Caracas.

US Embassy, Avda Principal de la Floresta, Esq Francisco de Miranda, La Floresta, Caracas (tel: 285-3111; fax: 285-0336).

Venezuelan Embassy (USA), 1099 30th Street, NW, Washington DC 20007 (tel: 202-342-2214; fax: 202-342-6820; e-mail: despacho@embavenez-us.org).

Internet sites

Venezuela Export Directory: http://www.ddex.com/

Venezuela trade: http://www.trade-venezuela.com

Vietnam

KEY FACTS

Official name: Cong Hoa Xa Hoi Chu Nghia Viet Nam (The Socialist Republic of Vietnam) (SRV)

Head of State: President Tran Duc Luong (DCSV) (since 1997; re-appointed 24 Jul 2002)

Head of government: Prime Minister Phan Van Khai (DCSV) (since 1997; re-appointed 25 July 2002)

Ruling party: Dang Cong San Viet Nam (DCSV) (Communist Party of Vietnam)

Area: 329,556 square km

Population: 83.03 million (2004)

Capital: Hanoi

Official language: Vietnamese

Currency: Dong (D) = 100 xu

Exchange rate: D15,892.50 per US$ (Oct 2005)

GDP per capita: US$535 (2004)

GDP real growth: 7.70% (2004)

Labour force: 43.98 million (2004)

Unemployment: 1.90% (2004)

Inflation: 7.70% (2004)

Oil production: 427,000 bpd (2004)

Balance of trade: -US$2.59 billion 2004

Foreign debt: US$14.10 billion (2003)

In 2005, Vietnam struggled to contain a worsening outbreak of the avian flu H5N1. Vietnam also marked important anniversaries, namely the 60th anniversary of its declaration of independence from French rule, and the 30th anniversary of the fall of the South Vietnamese government, which heralded the unification of the country under communist rule.

In 2005, Vietnam's GDP continued to grow at more than 7 per cent. The IMF praised the government for its macroeconomic management but also urged it to speed up privatisation reforms. Vietnam's hopes of WTO membership were raised during the year, after constructive talks with the US government and bilateral trade agreements with the EU and Singapore.

In July, the ruling Dang Cong San Viet Nam (DCSV) (Communist Party of Vietnam) initiated unprecedented steps to allow members to run private companies and for entrepreneurs to join the party.

In March, state oil companies from Vietnam, China and the Philippines signed an agreement to exploit jointly oil fields in the vicinity of the disputed Spratly Islands. All three countries claim all or some of the islands, most of which are no more than atolls. Taiwan, Malaysia and Brunei also contest ownership of the Spratlys.

Bird flu

Since 2003, more than 50 people have died in Vietnam after contracting the H5N1 virus. In 2005, 12 died in January alone. Vietnam appealed to the UN for help and, in November, became the first affected country to manufacture under licence the only known effective treatment for H5N1, Tamiflu.

Anniversaries

In September 2005, Vietnam marked the 60th anniversary of its declaration of independence from French colonial rule. The Vietnamese, led by future president Ho Chi Min, had to fight until 1954 before the French were to relinquish their claims.

In April 2005, Vietnam marked the 30th anniversary of the defeat of South Vietnam by DCSV-led North Vietnam. The victory in 1975 brought to an end 18 years of fighting between the US-backed South Vietnam and the Soviet and Chinese-backed North. The fighting, which saw US combat troops enter the war in 1965 and remain until 1973, cost the lives of an estimated 3–4 million Vietnamese, as well as the lives of more than 58,000 American military personnel.

Thaw

In June, the first official visit by a Vietnamese leader to the US since the end of the Vietnam War took place. Prime Minister Phan Van Khai visited the White House and held talks with US president George W Bush. Trade links between the two countries had been growing since the 1990s but relations remain strained over a number of points including the fate of 1,800 US servicemen classified as Missing in Action (MIA) since the Vietnam War, and US criticism of Vietnam's human rights record. In December 2004, the first commercial flight linking Vietnam and the US was made.

Human rights

In 2005, the US-based Human Rights Watch (HRW) commended Vietnam for improving its human rights record. Twelve prominent political and religious dissidents were freed during the year. The government also continued to ease pressure on the country's 5–7 million strong Catholic community, even hosting a senior Vatican official in November. Vietnam does not have diplomatic relations with the Vatican, and has traditionally seen the Holy See as an unwelcome competitor for the allegiance of its people. However, it wasn't all good news for those expressing dissent in Vietnam in 2005. The government kept up the pressure on its minority Montagnard communities, jailing six in November for 'threatening national security'. The government had launched a crackdown in 2004 when Montagnards began protesting against state-sanctioned confiscations of their tribal lands. Montagnards have also long been distrusted by the DCSV, as many Montagnards had sided with US forces during the Vietnam War. The

Vietnam

government also stepped up efforts in 2005 to control or shut down newspapers and online news sites that took a line not in accordance with government views.

The sex trade

The arrest by Vietnamese police, in November, of former rock star Gary Glitter (real name Paul Gadd), on charges of obscene acts against minors, highlighted a growing and worrying problem in Vietnam. Every year hundreds of Vietnamese women and girls are trafficked by people smugglers into brothels, both in Vietnam and, increasingly, China. UN officials warned in 2005 that Vietnam risks becoming the new people trafficking centre of south-east Asia.

Outlook

It is quite possible that Vietnam will successfully conclude its negotiations to join the WTO in 2006. Further trade reforms can be expected in order to achieve this result. As a net oil exporter, Vietnam can probably look forward to further oil revenue windfalls, due to continuing high oil prices. The Vietnamese economy is forecast to continue growing at around 7 per cent.

Avian flu will probably continue to affect Vietnam, although experts expect steps taken in 2005 to deal with the outbreak to bear results in 2006.

Although there has been little public dispute about the fate of the Spratly Islands in the past twelve months, there is always the possibility that this will change, as Vietnam is one of the more aggressive claimants to the island chain.

Risk assessment

Politics	Stable
Economy	Booming
Regional stability	Stable

COUNTRY PROFILE

Historical profile

The Red River (Song Hong) Delta in the north is considered the 'Cradle of the Nation'. It was from here in the tenth century that the Nam Tien Movement was begun by General Le Han. The southward expansion occurred because of the need to seek new ricelands.

The Vietnamese expanded south, during the fourteenth to eighteenth centuries, conquering the Cham people and Mekong Delta.

1428 After a long period of rule by successive Chinese rulers, Vietnam gained independence from the Ming dynasty's control. The Le dynasty ruled until 1527.

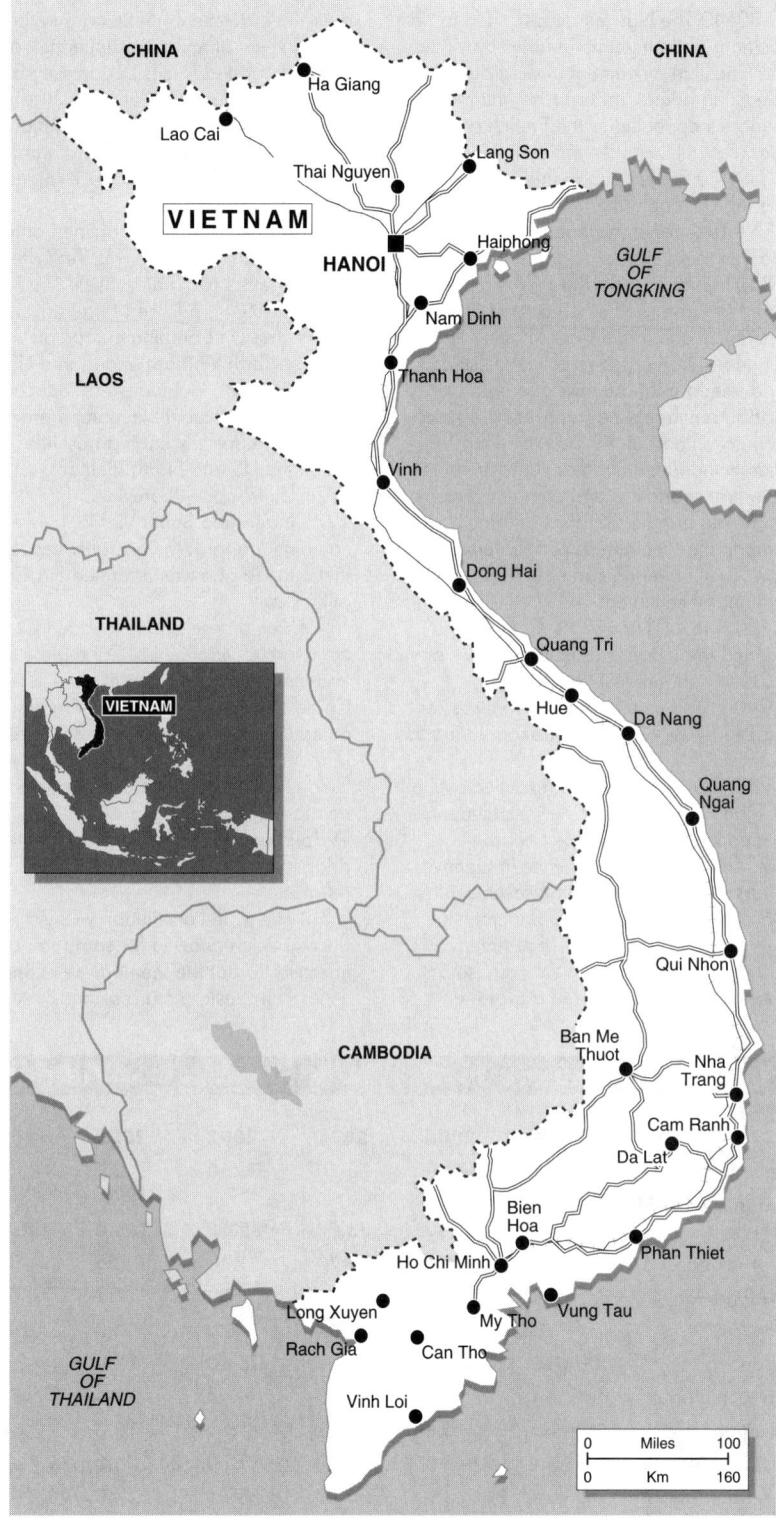

1680 The Portuguese, Dutch, English and French established trading posts in Vietnam.

1771–1802 The Tai Son Rebellion years. The Tai Son brothers wrested control from the ruling Nguyen family. They aimed to seize the wealth of the rich and aid the poor. Most of the members of the Nguyen family were killed except for Nguyen Anh, the nephew of a Nguyen lord.

1802 Vietnam was unified under the leadership of Nguyen Anh who recaptured much of Vietnam from the Tai Son brothers.

1830–40 The Nguyen dynasty tried to rid Vietnam of French missionaries by forcing the Christian movement underground and executing priests. In response, the missionaries appealed to the French government for military intervention in Vietnam.
1859 The French began their attack on the region, capturing the city of Danang.
1861 The French captured Saigon (now Ho Chi Minh city).
1862 Vietnam agreed to the Treaty of Saigon that gave the French control of three provinces and the island of Poulo Condore, free passage of French ships and freedom for the missionaries.
1883 French rule began over the whole country as part of the Indochina territory that included Cambodia. Under colonial rule, transportation and communications improved but the standard of living among the Vietnamese people remained low. Their suffering contributed to rising nationalist sentiment.
1930 A revolutionary, Ho Chi Minh, formed the Indochinese Communist Party (ICP) to fight against French rule.
1940 The French administration was replaced by Japanese occupation during the war.
1945 The Japanese were expelled by the ICP and French forces. A war of independence against France began.
1954 At a peace conference in Geneva, Vietnam was divided at the seventeenth parallel into communist Democratic Republic of Vietnam (north) and American-backed Republic of Vietnam (south). North Vietnam sponsored a growing guerrilla movement (Viet Cong) in the south, which aimed to re-unite Vietnam.
1964 US armed forces began their official intervention in support of South Vietnam after the US Gulf of Tonkin resolution. The US was committed to South Vietnam.
1967 The US military presence totalled nearly 500,000 troops.
1968 The Communists launched an attack on South Vietnam. This 'Tet Offensive' targetted five major cities. The Communists were forced to retreat within weeks. The US bombing campaign against North Vietnam ended and US troops in South Vietnam were reduced.
1973 The Paris peace accords were signed, temporarily ending hostilities between the US and North Vietnam.
1975 US troops withdrew.
1976 North and South Vietnam were combined to form the Socialist Republic of Vietnam. Saigon was renamed Ho Chi Minh City.
1979 Vietnamese troops invaded Cambodia overthrowing the Pol Pot regime and instituting their own puppet government; Chinese troops invaded Vietnam but were defeated. During this time Vietnam established close relationships with the Soviet Union, which was necessary for its economic development.
1986 Economic reform began with the adoption of the *doi moi* (renovation) reforms.
1992 The state constitution was introduced, which allowed for some liberalisation of the Vietnamese economy.
1993 Full Western aid resumed.
1995 A Vietnamese and American rapprochement began. Vietnam joined the Association of Southeast Asian Nations (Asean).
1997 Tran Duc Luong was elected president by the National Assembly, and Phan Van Khai was appointed prime minister.
2000 Vietnam and the US signed an agreement enabling normal trading relations between the two countries.
2001 Nong Duc Manh was appointed secretary general of the Dang Cong San Viet Nam (DCSV) (Communist Party of Vietnam). The bilateral trade agreement between Vietnam and the US came into effect.
2002 Russia closed its naval base in Cam Ranh. Vietnam signed an accord with Russia to construct a US$100 million hydroelectric power station in Vietnam's central highlands. DCSV members won most seats in the National Assembly elections. President Tran Duc Luong was reappointed for a second term by the National Assembly.
2003 In April, the World Health Organisation (WHO) officially certified Vietnam as the first country to be removed from the danger list of Severe Acute Respiratory Syndrome (Sars) countries.
2004 In January, Vietnam confirmed the first human deaths from bird 'flu.
2005 Prime Minister Phan Van Khai visited the US, the first visit by a Vietnamese leader since the end of the Vietnam War.

Political structure
Constitution
Vietnam has adopted, in broad terms, a Marxist-Leninist political ideology. A number of its political systems are derived from those of China and the former USSR. The political structure is dominated throughout by the Dang Cong San Viet Nam (DCSV) (Communist Party of Vietnam).
Under the 1992 state constitution, the DCSV continues to be ultimately responsible for policy, but the government assumed greater administrative and executive responsibility.
Twenty-four amendments to the 1992 constitution were passed in December 2001. The most important gave equality to the private sector of the economy. Local government is vested in elected provincial, municipal and district councils.
Form of state
Socialist republic
The executive
Executive power is officially exercised by a Western-style council of ministers under a prime minister. However, in practice, there is a two-way balance with the presidency and party. The president is elected by the National Assembly for a five-year term. Between sessions of the National

KEY INDICATORS — Vietnam

	Unit	2000	2001	2002	2003	2004
Population	m	77.69	78.70	80.50	81.77	*83.03
Gross domestic product (GDP)	US$bn	31.30	33.00	35.10	39.20	*45.21
GDP per capita	US$	396	420	420	455	535
GDP real growth	%	5.5	6.8	7.0	7.2	7.7
Inflation	%	-1.8	-0.4	4.0	4.0	7.7
Oil output	'000 bpd	328.0	350.0	354.0	372.0	427.0
Natural gas output	bn cum	1.6	2.0	2.4	2.4	4.2
Coal output	mtoe	6.4	7.2	8.6	10.7	14.8
Exports (fob) (goods)	US$m	14,448.0	15,100.0	16,710.0	20,176.0	23,720.0
Imports (fob) (goods)	US$m	14,073.0	16,000.0	19,730.0	25,227.0	26,310.0
Balance of trade	US$m	375.0	-900.0	-3,000.0	-5,051.0	-2,590.0
Current account	US$m	960.0	593.0	-522.0	-1,853.0	-2,020.0
Foreign debt	US$bn	15.6	12.6	14.1	14.1	–
Total reserves minus gold	US$m	3,416.5	3,674.6	4,121.1	6,224.2	–
Foreign exchange	US$m	3,416.2	3,660.0	4,121.0	6,222.0	–
Exchange rate	per US$	14,168.00	14,725.00	15,253.50	15,524.00	15.75

* estimated figure

Vietnam

Assembly, affairs of state are dealt with by the president and the National Assembly's standing committee, the council of state. In any case, membership of the Council of Ministers generally coincides with that of the Politburo and Secretariat of the DCSV, and executive decisions may, *de facto*, be taken by the DCSV even without the co-operation of the government.

The DCSV's 166-member Central Committee meets once or twice a year and is responsible for selecting the Politburo, which has 17 members. The Politburo oversees the DCSV's daily functions and has the power and authority to issue directives to the government. It is the highest policy-making body.

National legislature
The Council of Ministers is responsible to and appointed by the legislative Quoc Hoi (National Assembly), itself elected to a five-year term by universal adult suffrage (voting is mandatory).

The Quoc Hoi is the highest representative and legislative body of the people of Vietnam and the only institution with the authority to enact the constitution, codes and laws and elect the president and vice president, prime minister, president of the supreme people's court and procurator general, among other high officials.

The National Assembly, which is dominated by the ruling DCSV, meets twice a year in plenary session for about two to three weeks at a time. The Assembly's principal purpose is the (generally automatic) approval of Politburo decisions and DCSV-inspired legislation.

Legal system
Vietnam applied French law in the colonial period, but assumed a legal system based on the Soviet mould after the communist takeover. The country has a civil law system, but much of the law is underdeveloped and in the process of being innovated, for example in the case of foreign investment. Civil cases involving such matters as family law are distinguished from 'economic' cases, which include disputes arising from trade, investment and payments involving foreign entities. 'Economic' cases are dealt with by a separate arbitration system, in which the Vietnam International Arbitration Centre (VIAC) is a prominent body. The People's Supreme Court is Vietnam's highest court. Under it are People's Courts for each province, municipality and district.

The legal system is in the process of being reformed.

Last elections
2002 (presidential and parliamentary)
Results: Presidential: President Tran Duc Luong was re-appointed by the National Assembly for a second term.
Parliamentary: Dang Cong San Viet Nam (DCSV) (Communist Party of Vietnam) members won 447 of 498 seats; turnout was 99.7 per cent.

Next elections
2007 (presidential and parliamentary)

Political parties
Ruling party
Dang Cong San Viet Nam (DCSV) (Communist Party of Vietnam)
Main opposition party
Vietnam has no opposition parties.

Population
83.03 million (2004)
Ethnic make-up
Vietnamese (84 per cent) and Chinese (2 per cent). The remainder are Khmers, Chams and members of some 51 ethnic groups.
Religions
Although the country is officially atheist, many Vietnamese profess to being Buddhists. Christians are a significant minority (five million, mostly Catholics), followed by Caodaists, Hoa Hao Buddhists, Muslims and Hindus. There is a religious revival in Vietnam.

Education
Primary school lasts until age 11. Secondary school education is divided into lower secondary and upper secondary school lasting for four and three years, respectively. There is also provision for technical and vocational secondary education. Universities, specialised colleges, community and junior colleges provide higher education. There are currently over 100 higher education institutions. Distance education is offered in two open universities and other provincial centres.

The Ministry of Labour, Invalids and Social Affairs is expected to build a vocational training school in each province and a job training centre in each district by 2005. Since 1998, the state has invested US$12 million to upgrade infrastructure in job training centres and set up 39 new vocational schools. Trainees at vocational schools have annually increased by 20 per cent. Vietnam will provide vocational training to 1.3 million people annually, including 200,000 technicians, until 2010. As a result, the number of untrained workers will be reduced by 1.6 per cent by that year.

Public expenditure on education typically amounts to 3 per cent of annual gross national income.
Literacy rate: 94 per cent, adult rate (2003).
Compulsory years: Six to 14.
Enrolment rate: 105.6 per cent gross primary enrolment; 67.1 per cent gross secondary enrolment, of relevant age groups (including repeaters) (World Bank 2004).
Pupils per teacher: 28, in primary schools.

Health
The government has sought to improve the country's deteriorating healthcare system, which suffers from chronic underfunding and resultant shortages of medicine and equipment, recruitment problems and low staff morale. In 2001, an agreement was signed by the International Finance Corporation to invest US$8 million to establish a foreign-owned, Western-style hospital in Ho Chi Minh City. The new hospital will have modern equipment and advanced medical facilities. It is the first hospital project to be partly funded by private investors and reflects the government's promotion of investment in Vietnam's healthcare system. The parlous state of Vietnam's healthcare system today dates back to the end of the war in 1975. Although on paper the results are impressive, including the establishment of 9,000 communal clinics and the training of an additional 23,000 doctors to give a ratio of approximately 40 doctors per 10,000 population, the reality is that many clinics are not equipped or stocked and are given inadequate budgets. Many doctors prefer to concentrate their efforts on the more remunerative private treatment of better-off patients. Annual total expenditure on health is about 5 per cent, of which government spending is 28–29 per cent; private expenditure is 71–72 per cent, of which spending on pre-paid plans is 4.2 per cent. This difference between private and public expenses partly reflects the system of health fees introduced in the 1990s to supplement the health budget. The new charges (from which civil servants and war veterans are exempt) backfired, resulting in lower bed-occupancy rates – in some cases drops of 40 per cent were registered.

In 2004, avian flu broke out twice killing 20 people and prompting the slaughter of more than 100 million poultry.
HIV/Aids
The US has named Vietnam as the first country, outside Africa or the Caribbean, to benefit from the US$15 billion fund set aside to aid 15 countries in a five-year programme starting in 2004. While estimates of 200,000 people living with HIV is relatively low at 0.5 per cent of the population, the disease is reported to be spreading fast.
HIV prevalence: 0.4 per cent aged 15–49 in 2003 (World Bank)
Life expectancy: 69.9 years (2003)
Fertility rate/Maternal mortality rate: 1.9 births per woman (2003)
Birth rate/Death rate: 12.7 births and six deaths per 1,000 people (2003).

Infant mortality rate: 19 per 1,000 live births (2003); 37 per cent of children aged under five are malnourished (World Bank).

Welfare
Vietnam's transition to a market economy has increased problems of unemployment and the availability of social security benefits. The country has about 46.6 million people of working age, accounting for 59 per cent of the total population. Vietnam aims to create 1.4 million jobs annually in the period between 2001–05. The country also plans to reduce unemployment to 5 per cent and increase working time in rural areas.

Although there are social security systems for the victims of war, the collapse of the co-operative system has affected benefits in rural areas. With the introduction of a new Labour Code in 1994, and the Law on Co-operatives in 1996, the Vietnamese government declared its willingness to provide social insurance to workers in all economic sectors. The Vietnam Social Security Organisation, founded in 1995, has a social insurance scheme covering both state and private employees for benefits including retirement, survivorship, sickness, maternity and compensation for work related injuries. The pension scheme is supported by 10 per cent and 5 per cent contributions from the employer and the employee, respectively.

The Ministry of Public Security has undertaken education programmes aimed at halting the increase in the traffic, to China each year, estimated at thousands of women, and young girls aged under 18 – who account for one in six cases.

Main cities
Hanoi (capital, estimated population 1.4 million in 2004), Ho Chi Minh City (formerly Saigon) (3.5 million), Hai Phong City (581,600), Da Nang City (452,700), Bien Hoa (374,800), Hue (271,900), Na Trang (270,100),

Languages spoken
The Vietnamese alphabet is an adaptation from the Roman, using tonal marks. French is spoken in official circles and some English is spoken in business circles, especially in the south. Business is usually conducted in Vietnamese or English, although many executives speak French and Russian, and a few speak Chinese.
English and French are officially taught in secondary schools.

Official language/s
Vietnamese

Media
Press
The press is largely state-owned. The liberalisation of the media has not yet significantly reduced party and government control of the press. There are around 177 newspapers and 313 magazines available in Vietnam.

Dailies: *Saigon Times Daily* and *Viet Nam News* are national English language dailies. The most popular publications published in Vietnamese include *Nhan Dan* (People) – the official publication of the CPV – *Quan Doi Nhan Dan* (People's Army), *Nguoi Viet Daily News* (daily outside Vietnam) and *Viet Luan Newspaper*.

Weeklies: *Doanh Nghiep* (weekly) is published by the Union of Co-operatives.

Business: Weekly business publications include *Market Weekly* (Institute for the Study of Market and Prices of the State Price Commission) and *Vietnam Business* (Trade Information Centre of the Ministry of Commerce and Tourism). *Vietnam Investment Review (VIR)* is the first weekly international business newspaper, written, produced and circulated in Vietnam, and distributed throughout Asia, Europe and the US.

Business monthlies are *Vietnam Economic Times* (analysis and business tips), *Nghien Cuu Kinh Te* (Economic Institute in Hanoi) and *Vietnam Foreign Trade* (Chamber of Commerce and Industry).

Periodicals: Several periodicals that have recently begun publishing in Vietnamese to an international standard include *Nha Dep* (Beautiful Home), *Dinh Cao* (Sports and Fitness), *M* (Fashion) and *Phu Nu The Gioi* (Woman's World). Other popular publications include *Tuoi Tre* (youth), *Saigon Giai Phong* (Saigon Liberation) and *Lao Dong* (Labour). English language periodicals are *Vietnam Courier* (monthly) and *Vietnamese Studies* (quarterly).

Broadcasting
Radio: The national radio service, Voice of Vietnam (VOV) broadcasts in Vietnamese on short-wave, AM and FM, with external services in numerous languages. News bulletins are in Vietnamese, English, French and Russian. There are three major stations besides VOV. Recent improvements in programming have brought English lessons and international music to the airwaves.

Television: There are five major television stations and one national broadcaster (VTV). There are over 50 provincial stations. VTV-4 broadcasts overseas and has foreign-language content. Satellite TV is widely available.

Advertising
Advertising has only been permitted since 1990. The content of advertising remains heavily regulated, but regulations are somewhat arbitrarily policed. In theory, only companies licensed in Vietnam may advertise in Vietnam, while advertisements for liquor and beer, as well as cigarettes, are prohibited. Certain products such as pharmaceuticals, agro-chemicals, cosmetics and toiletries require the permission of the relevant ministry before they can be advertised.

About 20 international advertising agencies are present in Vietnam, mainly to support a small number of global accounts. Television is the favoured medium of foreign advertisers, despite high airtime costs of between US$600–US$1,200 for 30-second slots. Less popular broadcasters such as VTV-4 sell advertising at much lower rates.

Economy
Vietnam is a medium-sized country with a population of 83 million, split between a more Western-oriented, relatively infrastructure-rich south and the more highly populated but relatively impoverished north. Although the numbers of people living below the poverty line dropped below 40 per cent during the 1990s, Vietnam remains one of the world's poorest countries, with a GDP per capita of only US$535 (up from US$455 in 2003). The initial reform policies, collectively known as *doi moi* (change to the new), aimed to move from a centrally planned to a multi-sectoral economy based on market principles, with the objective of doubling Vietnam's GDP between 1991 and 2000. Deeper reform has been very slow, as some of the more conservative members of the Communist Party have wanted to maintain the state-controlled economy. Full privatisation on the Western model is not envisaged.

GDP real growth increased to 7.7 per cent in 2004, up from 7.2 per cent in 2002 – the fastest growth since 1997. Although Vietnam's growth is the fastest in south-east Asia, it trails China, South Korea, Taiwan and Thailand when they were at similar stages of development. Vietnam's economic expansion was led by exports of clothing to the US. The industrial and construction sectors accounted for 40 per cent of the economy in 2004; the services sector, which is growing by around six per cent per annum, accounted for around 38 per cent. Agriculture, forestry and fisheries accounted for the remaining 22 per cent of GDP, expanding at around three per cent.

Vietnam aims to become an industrialised country by the year 2020.

External trade
Trade is through state and private agencies. Japan, Singapore, Hong Kong, Thailand, France and Australia all have significant trading links with Vietnam. Due to shortage of hard currency, many Vietnamese companies still prefer trading on a barter basis.

A US-Vietnam bilateral trade agreement came into effect in December 2001, which opened the US market for

Vietnam

Vietnamese exports. The US has agreed to cut tariffs on a number of Vietnamese imports. In return, Vietnam will ease investment procedures for US firms. Following this agreement, Vietnam's exports to the US are expected to rise by 60 per cent from 2000 levels to reach an estimated US$1.3 billion by 2006.

Imports

Principal imports include machinery and equipment, petroleum products, fertiliser, steel products, raw cotton, grain, cement and motorcycles.

Main sources: China (13.6 per cent total, 2004), Japan (11.5 per cent), Singapore (11.5 per cent), Taiwan (10.2 per cent), South Korea (9.8 per cent), Thailand (6.7 per cent), Hong Kong (4.4 per cent), US (4.1 per cent), Malaysia (4.1 per cent)

Exports

Principal exports include crude oil, marine products, rice, coffee, rubber, tea, garments and shoes.

Main destinations: US (19.8 per cent total, 2004), Japan (13.7 per cent), China (8.4 per cent), Australia (7.0 per cent), Germany (5.7 per cent), Singapore (4.8 per cent), UK (4.6 per cent)

Agriculture

Farming

Agriculture accounts for around 22 per cent of GDP and employs 67 per cent of the workforce. Agricultural goods, including forestry and fishery products, account for more than 50 per cent of total export revenues.

About 15–18 per cent of the total land area is cultivated arable. In the south especially, climate and soils are ideal for rice production. Considerable losses can be sustained from typhoons, flooding and drought.

In the south, 60 per cent of the land is privately farmed; in the north, 95 per cent of farms have been turned into substantial collectives. A contract system on the land spurred a marked improvement in agricultural production.

Record exports of almost 90,000 tonnes of pepper, in 2004, showed a 32 per cent increase on 2003 figures and confirmed Vietnam as the world's largest exporter. The value of the 2004 exports amount to US$133.7 million even though the average world price declined by US$54.4 per tonne.

Ambitious plans include increased use of fertilisers, development of irrigation systems and resettlement of small farmers. Farmers have boosted rice production by planting high-yield varieties and using more modern farming techniques; government credit of about US$100 million was used mainly in the Mekong Delta. Half of Vietnam's rice is grown along the Mekong Delta.

Other main food crops include sugar cane, coconut, soya beans, silk, rubber, coffee, tea, tobacco, jute. Livestock raised includes pigs, buffaloes, cattle, sheep, goats, horses and poultry.

The Vietnam National Rubber Corporation development plans for the rubber industry will increase the area under cultivation from 250,000 hectares (ha) to 700,000ha. VNRC estimates 1.7 million ha of total natural land is available for rubber cultivation. The private sector is expected to take a 30–50 per cent share in the development of the industry.

The Vietnam National Coffee Corporation (Vinacaphe) has increased the total area of coffee cultivation to around 200,000ha, principally in the central highlands. Much cultivation in the coffee-growing highlands is under-reported due to a special tax regime. Annual production is thought to be as high as 40,000 tonnes and the government plans to increase production to 100,000 tonnes per year (tpy) by 2010.

Avian flu broke out twice in 2004 and prompted the slaughter of millions of birds.

Crop production in 2004 included: 39.3 million tonnes (mt) cereals in total, 35.9mt rice, 3.4mt maize, 5.5mt cassava, 1.5mt sweet potatoes, 365,000 tonnes (t) potatoes, 1.35mt bananas, 252,800t pulses, 7.5mt roots and tubers, 930,600t coconuts, 560,200t citrus fruit, 21,000t sesame seed, 422,200 pineapples, 314,230t oilcrops, 27,500t tobacco, 833,796t treenuts, 834,600t green coffee, 14,200t jute, 400,100t natural rubber, 95,700t pepper spice, 91,800t various herbs and spices, 15.8mt sugar cane, 108,422t tea, 11,722t cotton lint, 314,200t mangoes, 242,100 soya beans, 5.5mt fruit in total, 7.8mt vegetables in total. Livestock production included: 2.7mt meat in total, 220,839 beef, 101,050t buffalo meat, 2.0mt pig-meat, 7,800t goat meat, 405,609t poultry, 197,000t eggs, 182,314t milk, 10,701 honey, 1,980t horsemeat, 3,000t cocoons, silk.

Fishing

Fishing has traditionally been an important source of export earnings. The sector is facing severe depletion of inshore stocks. Coastal waters were typically overfished by the poorly equipped Vietnamese fleet, whose boats could only stay at sea for short periods of time. Poor infrastructure and processing technology is compounded by a lack of skills required for deep-water fishing on the part of fishermen.

Main fish products are shrimp, freshwater fish, catfish, dried squid and tuna.

Forestry

About 50 per cent of the total land area is forested. Forestry is developing, with 12–15 per cent of the removed volume of timber classified as industrial wood. Legal exploitation from around one million hectares (ha) of plantations produces a domestic supply of approximately three million cubic metres of wood annually, but insufficient for the processing industry. The industry is estimated to have the potential to approach a turnover of US$1 billion annually, especially following the relaxation of import licences and quotas for domestic processors importing wood. The domestic industry is likely to remain dependent on felled and imported wood of dubious legal status at least over the medium-term. In the longer term, a government replanting programme designed to add five million ha of forest cover by 2010 should change this.

Annual exports of forest materials amount to an estimated US$64 million, while imports amount to around US$167 million.

Industry and manufacturing

Industry contributed 40 per cent to GDP in 2004 and employs 10 per cent of the workforce.

The heavy industrial base is mostly located in the north, and in the past was adversely affected by conflicts with China. The economy's leading industries were incorporated into the state sector following the Communist takeover and despite limited 'equitisation' (distribution of shares to the public and employees), most remain in state hands. They include oil and gas, food and foodstuff processing, synthetic yarns and fabrics, textiles, engineering, cement, fertilisers, glass, rubber products, tobacco, chemicals, paper and steel. Of some 6,000 state-owned enterprises, only 400 have been equitised, while 2,000 have been organised into 17 'general corporations' (akin to conglomerates) and 77 'special corporations', tending to reinforce monopoly conditions.

Since the *doi moi* reforms of the 1980s, the government has been prioritising lighter, export-oriented and labour-intensive industries. Most of the government's special industrial zones have not yet been fully occupied, and much industry outside the 'legacy' sectors of command-economy industrialisation has been affected by ambivalent sentiment among foreign direct investors.

Tourism

Vietnam is developing as a tourist destination. More facilities are becoming available, although quality and infrastructure, such as roads and power, are inadequate, especially compared to competitors in the region. Visitor numbers have improved year-on-year, despite the presence of

Sars. There were 3.43 million arrivals in 2005, an increase of 15.4 per cent on 2004. The main markets are China, the US, Taiwan, Japan, Hong Kong, Thailand, France, UK and Canada. Tourism is expected to contribute 2.2 per cent to GDP in 2005.

Mining
Vietnam is believed to possess a wide range of minerals. The sector is relatively undeveloped, owing to lack of investment and a discouraging legislative environment.

Mining is largely concentrated in the north. Commercially significant quantities of iron ore, apatite, chromite, rubies and gold exist. There are reserves of manganese, titanium ore, bauxite, tin, copper, zinc, lead, nickel, graphite and mica. Other minerals include phosphates, salt, tin, chromium, wolfram, silver, antimony, pirit, kaolin and limestone.

Vietnam imports a number of metals, including steel.

Hydrocarbons
Vietnam had proven oil reserves of around 3 billion barrels in 2004 and produced 427,000 barrels per day (bpd). The largest oil fields are Back Ho, Rang Dong, Hang Ngoc and Dai Hung. Vietnam has no refinery capacity and has to import petroleum products. A refinery is being built at Dung Quat and a second is planned for Nghi Son. Vietnam is a net exporter of oil, exporting around 193,000 bpd in 2004.

Upstream activities in the oil sector are largely controlled by the government-owned Vietnam Oil and Gas Corporation (PetroVietnam). This is the only firm licensed to conduct petroleum activities. Operations conducted by foreign investors must be conducted in co-operation with PetroVietnam.

Vietnam had proven natural gas reserves of 240 billion cubic metres (cum) in 2004 and produced 20.3 billion cum. Production and consumption are set to increase as new fields come into production. Current production is absorbed by the domestic market. Domestic gas consumption is expected to increase to an annual 10 billion cubic metres by 2010.

Vietnam had coal reserves of 150 million tonnes in 2004, mostly anthracite, located in the north of Vietnam, where the province of Quang Ninh holds a significant proportion. Coal is the principal source of commercial energy, meeting about half of Vietnam's annual primary energy needs. Production totalled 14.8 million tonnes oil equivalent in 2004, up 38.6 per cent on 2003 output. Vietnam exports around five million tonnes of coal, mainly to China and Japan.

Energy
Vietnam has installed electricity generating capacity of around 8.5GW, supplied mainly by hydro-power and coal-fired thermal plants. Domestic demand is increasing faster than supply. Vietnam imports electricity from China and is seeking other sources, including Laos. The government plans to add over 1,000MW annually over 2002–10. A mixture of additional gas, coal-fired and hydroelectric plants are planned, together with a nuclear station.

Work has begun on creating a national electricity grid, which is due for completion in 2020.

Financial markets
Stock exchange
Vietnam's Securities Trading Centre (STC), located in Ho Chi Minh City, began operations in July 2000.

Banking and insurance
VietcomBank regulates matters relating to exchange control and is responsible for all transactions involving foreign exchange, including bills of exchange, foreign remittances, traveller's cheques and foreign currencies.

In 2005 the government decided that VietcomBank will be the first state bank to be offered for partial privatisation and ostensibly to operate on purely commercial principles. The decision is based on the government's need to sustain economic growth.

There are four large state banks, which account for around 70 per cent of total lending, of which 60 per cent of loans are awarded to state entities and some are of dubious financial viability. Official figures for bad debt levels do not exist but officials in the state bank estimate it could be as high as 20 per cent. In preparation for public ownership VietcomBank reduced its portfolio of state enterprised down to 50 per cent and reported a first-half year gross profit of US$82 million in 2005, up by 41 per cent on the previous year.

Central bank
State Bank of Vietnam
Main financial centre
Hanoi

Time
GMT plus seven hours

Geography
Vietnam is bordered to the north by the People's Republic of China, to the west and south-west by Laos and Cambodia and to the east by the South China Sea. The country has 3,200km of coastline, 1,150km of land border with China and 1,650km of land border with Laos.

The country is broad in the north and south and narrow in its central region. There are two main cultivated areas, the Red River Delta (15,000 square km) in the north and the Mekong Delta (60,000 square km) in the south. Three-quarters of the country consists of mountains and hills, the highest point being Phan Si Pan mountain in the Hoang Lien Son range in the far north-west of Vietnam.

Climate
Located in the tropical monsoon zone, Vietnam's climate is hot and humid. There is abundant seasonal rainfall.

In the north, climatic changes occur in four seasons: spring (January–April) brings light rain and constant humidity; summer (May to July) is very hot, humid and rainy; autumn (August–October) brings drier weather but sometimes includes storms; winter (October–early January) is cooler. In the centre and the south it is hot year round and there are only two seasons: a rainy season (May–October) and a dry season (October–April).

Average annual temperatures in Hanoi are 29.2 degrees Celsius (C) in the hot season and 17.2 degrees C in the cold season; Hue in central Vietnam: 29.3 degrees C and 20.5 degrees C; Ho Chi Minh City: 29.7 degrees C and 24 degrees C.

The average annual rainfall in Hanoi is 1,680mm; Hue: 2,890mm; Ho Chi Minh City: 1979mm.

The best times to visit are November–January in Ho Chi Minh City and September–December in Hanoi.

Dress codes
In Hanoi in the summer (officially from 15 April to 15 October), no jackets are required even for the most formal occasions. In winter, a jacket is more usual but a bush jacket is acceptable even when the weather is warm.

In the south, informal tropical-weight clothing is all that is needed at any time of the year. A jacket and tie is not necessary. In the highlands, where it is cooler, a bush jacket is acceptable any time.

Entry requirements
Passports
Required by all. Business visitors should ensure that the validity of their passports will extend beyond the duration of their visit before making visa applications.
Visa
Required by all. Tourist visas are only issued for visits up to one month long. Business visas are issued only after authorities in Vietnam have approved sponsorship by a local company or organisation. If the business visitor does not have a local sponsor, assistance can be obtained from the embassy. UK visitors can gain further information at www.vietnamembassy.org.uk, and US visitors at, www.vietnamembassy-usa.org/.

Vietnam

All visitors must retain the yellow portion of the immigration arrival-departure card, to be surrendered to authorities when leaving.

Currency advice/regulations
Visitors can bring in an unlimited amount of foreign currency, but amounts over US$3,000 should be declared to customs authorities on arrival, as only the balance or an amount of foreign currency less than that declared on arrival can be expatriated. Vietnamese dong may not be brought in or taken out of Vietnam.
US dollars can be used freely. Currency can be exchanged at all licensed banks, including foreign banks, and at hotels and airports. The official rate is usually the same or close to the parallel market rate. Do not enter into exchange transactions with individuals.

Customs
Items of high value need a declaration at the time of entry; sometimes tax is charged on arrival and refunded on departure.
Visitors may take into Vietnam, free of duty, personal effects for use during their stay, 200 cigarettes or 50 cigars and alcoholic drinks up to two litres; jewellery must be declared at customs on arrival. The import of cameras and video tapes is restricted; small-size tourist cameras present no problem.
On departure customs officials are likely to check baggage. Antiques cannot be exported. Caution is advised when purchasing souvenirs made of ivory, silver, gold and stone, as you may require a permit from customs to take them out of Vietnam.

Prohibited imports
Prohibited imports include 'dangerous and unhealthy' cultural products, firecrackers, second-hand consumer goods, children's toys with the potential for harmful influence and cigarettes over quota. Used equipment may be brought in if greatly superior to newer equivalents and complies with labour, hygiene, safety and other codes. Other products may be temporarily banned.
Drug smuggling carries the death penalty.

Health (for visitors)
Mandatory precautions
Vaccination certificate required for yellow fever if travelling from an infected area.
Advisable precautions
Medical facilities are poor. Accidents or illness will leave the visitor relying on arrangements for medical treatment being made by their sponsor. The Swedish clinic (tel: 845-2464) in Hanoi can provide aid. Evacuation may be the only option for most patients in the rest of the country and travel insurance should always provide such cover.

It is advisable to be 'in date' for the following immunisations: tetanus (within 10 years), typhoid fever (within three years), rabies if travelling in rural areas (within three years), hepatitis 'A' and 'B', diphtheria, tuberculosis, Japanese B encephalitis. Anti-malarial precautions should be taken. Malaria, dengue fever and Japanese encephalitis are common in many parts of Vietnam. Typhoid is a problem in the Mekong Delta. There is no vaccine available against dengue fever. Care should accordingly be taken to avoid mosquito bites. Visitors should use safe skin repellent against day-biting mosquitoes and consider a mosquito net.
A small first aid kit is advisable, or at least a few sterilised syringes and needle, as a precaution against becoming infected with HIV, as Aids is becoming more of a problem. Ask to see syringes unwrapped in front of you.
Strict food and water hygiene is advisable: boil or purify all drinking water; use of an iodine resin water purifier is advised. Drinking from carafes supplied in major hotel bedrooms is generally safe. Bottled water is widely available.
The climate in the north can aggravate respiratory problems and rheumatism.

Hotels
There is a shortage of hotel accommodation in both Ho Chi Minh City and Hanoi. The standard of hotel accommodation is reasonable. Most leading hotels accept traveller's cheques.
Tipping is discretionary. It is not a Vietnamese tradition. Waiters and waitresses at restaurants and doormen at hotels may expect to be tipped.

Credit cards
Can only be used in the larger hotels, restaurants and clubs.

Public holidays
Fixed dates
1 Jan (New Year's Day), 30 Apr (Liberation of Ho Chi Minh City/Saigon), 1 May (May Day), 2 Sep (National Day).
Variable dates
Tet Nguyen Dan (Vietnamese New Year) (Jan/Feb)

Working hours
Banking
Mon–Fri: 0800–1630; Sat: 0800–1200.
Business
Mon–Sat: 0730–1130, 1230–1630 in summer (15 Apr to 15 Oct); 0800–1200, 1230–1630 in winter (16 Oct to 14 Apr).
Government
Mon–Sat: 0730–1130, 1230–1630 in summer; 0800–1200, 1230–1630 in winter.

Shops
Many small privately owned shops stay open seven days a week, often until late at night.

Telecommunications
Mobile phones
Vietnam Mobile Service, an affiliate of VNPT, operates the Vinaphone service in competition with the Mobiphone network, directly owned by VNPT.
Both use the GSM standard. Coverage is mostly in the Hanoi and Ho Chi Minh City areas, with pockets of coverage available along the coast.
Internet/e-mail

Electricity supply
Electric current is 220V, 50 cycles. Round two-pin plugs are used. There are electricity shortages and frequent surges in current. Sensitive electronic equipment should be shielded with a surge suppressor.

Social customs/useful tips
Business is conducted slowly with many familiarisation meetings. Be patient with language difficulties and red tape. The combination of Confucian interaction norms and communist bureaucracy may create large amounts of the latter.
It is rude to show the soles of the feet/shoes. Do not touch anyone's head, not even that of a child. When handing over or receiving anything, the right hand should generally be used. On formal occasions it is considered polite to use both hands. Etiquette for male visitors is to shake hands with a man but not with a woman, unless she offers her hand.
Shoes must be removed before entering any religious building. It is also customary to remove shoes before entering a Vietnamese home, but in modern residences the requirement is no longer observed.
Most Vietnamese names consist of a family name, a middle name and a given name, in that order. The given name is used in address but to do so without a title is considered as expressing either great intimacy between friends or arrogance of the sort a superior would use with his or her inferior. The titles, *Bac* or *Ong* (Mr) (in increasing seniority), *Ba* (Mrs), *Co* or *Chi* (Miss) precedes a Vietnamese given name (sometimes full name). Wives may retain their own names and children take their father's family name. The middle name may be common to all the male members of a given family.

Security
Most visits to Vietnam are trouble-free and serious or violent crimes against foreigners are rare. There have been some reports of aggravated theft and assault in areas frequented by tourists in Ho Chi Minh City, prompting the city police chief,

Nguyen Chi Dung, to say that tourists who were robbed would receive an apology from the police.

Outside Hanoi and Ho Chi Minh City, the provision of prompt consular assistance is difficult because of poorly developed infrastructure throughout Vietnam, meaning travel and health insurance are well advised. Travel is restricted near military installations and in some border areas. Unexploded mines, bombs and shells are a hazard in former battlefield areas.

Getting there
Air
National airline: Vietnam Airlines (formerly Hang Khong Vietnam and the General Civil Aviation Administration of Vietnam).

International airport/s: Tan Son Nhat (SGN), 7km from Ho Chi Minh City; benefits from a modern air traffic control system; capacity has been increased to five million from three million passengers a year; two runways have been upgraded to accommodate all kinds of aircraft; a US$240 million project is planned to build a new terminal capable of receiving seven million passengers a year, completion 2006.

Noi Bai (HAN), 38km from Hanoi; modern passenger terminal, able to receive four million passengers annually.

Danang International Airport, five-minute drive to Danang City; two runways; a feasibility study has been submitted to the government for a modern terminal capable of receiving four million passengers a year.

Airport tax: International departures US$12, excluding transit passengers and infants under two years; domestic departures D20,000.

Surface
Road: There is overland access to Vietnam via China (Quang Ninh and Lang Son border gates in the north), Cambodia (Moc Bai border gate) and Laos (Lao Bao border gate). This should not be attempted without proper preparation and visas which specifically permit entry at one of the three border crossings. Status of overland routes should be checked, as passage has not always been practicable.

Rail: Hanoi and Nanning, in China's Guangxi province, are linked by rail. China and Vietnam have also started a second cross-border rail service. The 761km route links Hanoi with Kunming, the capital of China's south-western province of Yunnan, and runs through the northern Vietnamese border town of Lao Cai.

The rail connection linking Hanoi with Pingxiang in China's Guangxi province via the Dong Dang border point in Lang Son province, 200km north of Hanoi, was re-opened in 1996. A further link, through the Lao Cai province border point 300km northwest of Hanoi, has been re-opened.

Main port/s: Ho Chi Minh City is the biggest port in Vietnam. Haiphong is also important. Danang has a modern sea port.

Getting about
National transport
Air: Vietnam Airlines, the state-controlled air service, provides regular services between Hanoi, Hue, Danang and Ho Chi Minh City. Flights should be booked well in advance.

Road: There is a 88,000km road network in relatively poor condition. Roads are better in the south. The coastal Route 1 between Hanoi and Ho Chi Minh City can become impassable in heavy rain. A four-wheel drive vehicle is advisable outside the major centres.

In 1998, the Asian Development Bank (ADB) approved loans amounting to US$40 million and US$100 million to Cambodia and Vietnam, respectively, from the ADB's Special Fund resources for rehabilitation of parts of the Phnom Penh-Ho Chi Minh City (HCMC) Highway Project over the 10-year period from 2002 to 2012.

Rail: There is a 3,200km rail network. Railways need extensive work. Vietnam Railways operate regular services in the national network from northern provinces near the Sino-Vietnamese border to Ho Chi Minh City.

There are two-class rail services between main centres, including Hanoi-Ho Chi Minh City, Hanoi-Haiphong, Hanoi-Lao Cai, Loc Ninh-Ho Chi Minh City-My Tho and Hanoi-Lang Son. The 'express' train journey from Hanoi to Ho Chi Minh City can take over 24 hours. Long-distance trains are more reliable and comfortable, as well as offering a faster service. Fares for foreigners are comparable to internal air fares.

Water: Cruise facilities may be available. A local network of services runs between ports.

City transport
Taxis: In Hanoi, cycle-rickshaws (the famous *cyclo*) are available, but slow and best for sightseeing. Taxi cars and motorbikes are a faster form of hired transport. When travelling by taxi it is advisable to note down the registration number of the driver (displayed on the rear side of the vehicle), for security reasons.

Taxis serving the hour-long route between downtown Hanoi and the city's airport will typically be ancient and non-air-conditioned vehicles. In Ho Chi Minh City, taxis are modern. Tipping is discretionary; taxi drivers do not expect to be tipped.

Car hire
Car transport is normally arranged by Vietnam Tourism. Car hire bills must be settled in US dollars. An international driving licence and a test taken in Vietnam are required, as a Vietnamese driving licence must be obtained from the Vietnamese Road Administration in Hanoi (fax: 857-1440) before driving any vehicle. Right hand drive vehicles are not permitted. Self-drive car and motorcycle hire are not recommended. Always check with the hire company about accident liability. Chauffeur-driven cars may be hired. Road signs are poor and city traffic erratic and fast-moving. Driving is on the right. A four-wheel-drive vehicle is required outside major cities.

BUSINESS DIRECTORY
The addresses listed below are a selection only. While World of Information makes every endeavour to check these addresses, we cannot guarantee that changes have not been made, especially to telephone numbers and area codes. We would welcome any corrections.

Telephone area codes
The international direct dialling code (IDD) for Vietnam is +84, followed by area code and subscriber's number:

Da Nang	51	Ho Chi Minh City	8
Haiphong	31	Lang Son	25
Hanoi	4	Lao Cai	20

Useful telephone numbers
English-language directory enquiries: 108
Police: 113
Fire: 114
Ambulance: 115

Chambers of Commerce
American Chamber of Commerce in Vietnam - Hanoi, Press Club, 59A Ly Thai To Street, Hanoi (tel: 934-2790; fax 934-2787; e-mail: info@amchamhanoi.com).

American Chamber of Commerce in Vietnam - Ho Chi Minh City, New World Hotel, 76 Le Lai Street, Ho Chi Minh City (tel: 824-3562; fax: 824-3572; e-mail: amcham@hcm.vnn.vn).

British Business Group Vietnam - Hanoi, Metropole Hotel, 56 Ly Thai To Street, Hanoi (tel: 936-2420; fax: 936-2419; e-mail: eurochamhanoi@hn.vnn.vn).

British Business Group Vietnam - Ho Chi Minh City, 25 Le Duan Boulevard, Ho Chi Minh City (tel: 829-8430; fax: 822-5172; e-mail: bbgv.hcmc@hcm.fpt.vn).

Vietnam Chamber of Commerce and Industry, 9 Dao Duy Anh Street, Hanoi (tel: 574-3084; fax: 574-2020; e-mail: vcci@hn.vnn.vn).

Vietnam

Banking

ANZ International Merchant Banking Division, 14 Le Thai To Street, Hanoi (tel: 825-8190; fax: 825-8188/9).

Bank of America, 27 Ly Thuong Kiet St, Hanoi (tel: 824-9316; fax: 824-9322).

Crédit Lyonnais, Han Man Officetel, 65 Nguyen du St., Quan 1, Ho Chi Minh City (tel: 299-226; fax: 296-465).

Indovina Bank Ltd (first joint-venture bank), 36 Ton That Dam, D1, Ho Chi Minh City (tel: 822-4995, 823-0130; fax: 823-0131).

Thai Military Bank, Unit 113, 1 Floor, Saigon Trade Center, No. 37 Ton Due Thang Street, Ben Nghe Ward, District 1, Ho Chi Minh City (tel: 910-0606, 910-1388/90; fax: 910-0505).

Industrial and Commercial Bank of Vietnam, 108 Tran Hung Dao, Hanoi (tel: 942-1066, 942-1186; fax: 942-1143).

Central bank

State Bank of Vietnam, 49 Ly Thai To Street, Hanoi (tel: 825-8388; fax: 825-8385).

Travel information

Ben Thanh Tourist Service, 165 Pham Ngui Lao Street, 1st District, Ho Chi Minh City (tel: 886-0635; fax: 836-1953).

Cathay Pacific Airways, 58 Dong Khoi Road, District 1, Ho Chi Minh City (tel: 822-3203; fax: 822-2679); also at 27 Ly Thuong Kiet Street, Hanoi (tel: 824-9427; fax: 822-2679).

Quang Nam-Da Nang Tourist Company (Da Nang Tourism), 68 Bach Dang Street, Da Nang (tel: 822-112, 821-423, 822-213).

Thua Thien-Hue Tourist Company, No. 9 Ngo Quyen Street, Hue City (tel: 83-288, 82-369).

Vietnamtourism, 30A Ly Thuong Kiet Street, Hanoi (tel: 825-5552, 826-4148; fax: 855-7583).

Vietnam Airlines (formerly Hang Khong Vietnam and the General Civil Aviation Administration of Vietnam), Gailem Airport, Hanoi (tel: 827-2643; fax: 827-2291).

National tourist organisation offices

Vinatour, 54 Nguyen Du Street, Hanoi (tel: 825-2986, 825-7245; 825-2707).

Ministries

Ministry of Agriculture and Rural Development, 6 Ngoc Ha Street, Hanoi; International Relations Department (tel: 845-9670/71/72; fax: 845-4319).

Ministry of Construction, 37 Le Dai Hanh Street, Hanoi; International Relations Department (tel: 825-5497; fax: 825-2153).

Ministry of Culture and Information, 51-53 Ngo Quyen, Hanoi.

Ministry of Education & Training, 49 Dai Co Viet Street, Hanoi; International Relations Department (tel: 869-4961; fax: 826-3243).

Ministry of Energy, 18 Tran Nguyen Han, Hanoi.

Ministry of Finance, 8 Phgan Huy Chu Street, Hanoi; International Relations Section (tel: 826-2061, 824-0437; fax: 826-2266).

Ministry of Fisheries, 57 Ngoc Khanh, Hanoi.

Ministry of Foreign Affairs, 1 Ton That Dam Street, Hanoi; International Organisation Department (tel: 845-6525, 845-5900; fax: 845-9205).

Ministry of Forestry, 123 Lo Duc, Hanoi.

Ministry of Health, 138 Duong Giang Vo, Hanoi.

Ministry of Industry, 7 Trang Thi Street, Hanoi (fax: 826-9033); International Relations Department (tel: 826-7988, 825-9887).

Ministry of Justice, 25a Cat Linh Street, Hanoi; Internatinal Relations Department (tel: 843-0931; fax: 825-4835).

Ministry of Labour, War Invalids and Social Affairs, 2 Dinh Le Street, Hanoi; International Relations Department (tel: 826-9534; fax: 824-8036).

Ministry of Marine Products, 57 Ngoc Khanh Street, Hanoi; International Relations Department (tel: 832-5607; fax: 832-6702).

Ministry of National Defence, 28A Dien Bien Phy Street, Hanoi (tel: 826-8101; fax: 845-7195); International Relations Department, 33 A Pham Ngu Lao Street, Hanoi (tel: 825-3646).

Ministry of Planning and Investment (background information on aid-financed projects), 2 Hoanag Van Thu, Hanoi; External Economic Relations Department (tel: 845-8241 (ext 3505); fax: 823-0161).

Ministry of Public Health, 138 A Giango Vo, Hanoi; International Relations Department (tel: 844-2463, 846-4050; fax: 846-4051).

Ministry of Sciences, Technology and Environment, 39 Tran Hung Dao Street, Hanoi; International Relations Department (tel: 826-3388; fax: 825-2733).

Ministry of Trade, 31 Trang Tien Street, Hanoi; (tel: 826-2522; fax: 826-4696).

Ministry of Transport, 80 Tran Hung Dao Street, Hanoi; International Relations Department (tel: 825-3301; fax: 825-5851).

Office of the National Assembly, 35 Ngo Quyen, Hanoi (tel: 252-861).

Other useful addresses

ASEAN Investment Promotion Agency, Ministry of Planning and Investment, c/o ASEAN Vietnam, 7 Chu Van An Street, Hanoi (fax: 435-758).

ASEAN Secretariat, 70 A Jl Sisingamangaraja, Jakarta 12110, Indonesia (tel: 62(21)726-2991, 724-3372; fax: 724-3504, 739-8234; E-mail: asean.or.id).

Asian Development Bank, Vietnam Resident Mission, c/o State Bank of Vietnam, Room 401, 16 Tong Dan Street, Hanoi (tel: 824-5908; fax: 824-6171).

British Consulate General, 25 Le Duan, District 1, Ho Chi Minh City (tel: 829-2433; fax: 822-5740).

British Embassy, 31 Hai Ba Trung, Hanoi (tel: 825-2510; fax: 826-5762).

British Embassy Commercial Office, 100 Tue Tinh Street, Hanoi (tel: 822-6875, 822-9455, 822-9457; fax: 822-9457).

Commerical and Tourist Services Centre, 1 Ba Trieu Street, Hanoi (tel: 268-499; fax: 265-388).

Department General for Post and Telecomunication, 18 Nguyen Du Street, Hanoi; International Relations Department (tel: 822-6622; fax: 822-6590).

Electricity of Vietnam (EVN), 18 Tran Nguyen Han Street, Hanoi (tel: 826-3725; fax: 824-9462).

Foreign Trade & Investment Development Centre, 92-96 Nguyen Hue Ave, District 1, Ho Chi Minh City (tel: 822-2982; fax: 822-2983).

Investip (will provide business contacts), 1 bis Yet Kieu Street, Hanoi (tel: 826-4707; fax: 826-6185).

The National Oil Service Company of Vietnam, 2 Le Loi Street, Vung Tau Srv, Ho Chi Minh City (tel: 897-562; fax: 897-664).

Petrovietnam, 22 Ngo Quyen Street, Hanoi; International Relations Department (tel: 825-2526; fax: 826-5942).

Saigon Shipping Company (Saigonship), 9 Nguyen Cong Tru Street, District 1, Ho Chi Minh City (tel: 896-316, 896-302; fax: 825-067).

State Committee for Co-operation and Investment Consultancy Service Centre (will provide business contacts), 56 Quoc Tu Giam Street, Hanoi (tel: 825-4970; fax: 825-9271).

Tea Estate Agencies Ltd, 31 Nguyen Gia Thieu Street, Hanoi (tel: 822-8556; fax: 822-7923).

Trade Service Company (will provide business contacts), Vietnam Chamber of Commerce, 33 Ba Trieu Street, Hanoi (tel: 826-6780; fax: 825-6446).

Tea Estate Agencies Ltd, 31 Nguyen Gia Thieu Street, Hanoi (tel: 822-8556; fax: 822-7923).

Trade Service Company (will provide business contacts), Vietnam Chamber of Commerce, 33 Ba Trieu Street, Hanoi (tel: 826-6780; fax: 825-6446).

US Embassy, 7 Lang Ha, Dong Da District, Hanoi (tel: 843-1500).

Vietnam Civil Aviation, Gia Lam Airport, Hanoi; International Relations Department (tel: 827-2241).

Vietnam Fund Management Co Ltd (investment into Vietnamese companies and projects), 3 Trieu Viet Vuong Street, Hanoi (tel: 822-8632, 826-6315; fax: 822-8648); 4 Dong Khoi, District 1, Ho Chi Minh City (tel: 829-1074, 829-7206; fax: 823-0685).

Vietnam National Foreign Trade Corporation (TRANSAF), 46 Ngo Quyen, Hanoi.

Vietnamese Embassy (US), Suite 400, 1233 20th Street, NW, Washington DC 20036 (tel: 202-861-0737; fax: 202-861-0917; e-mail: info@vietnamembassy-usa.org).

Internet sites

Asian Development Bank: http://www.adb.org/vrm

General Statistics Office (GSO): http://www.gso.gov.vn

Vietnam Access (trade fairs and business opportunities): http://vietnamaccess.com

Vietnam Business Journal: http://www.viam.com

Wallis and Futuna

COUNTRY PROFILE

Historical profile
Futuna and Alofi were originally settled by Samoans, and around 1450AD Uvea was settled by Tongans.
1616 Futuna and Alofi were sighted by two Dutch navigators, Willem Cornelius van Schouten and Jacob le Maire, who re-named them the Hoorn Islands.
1767 Samuel Wallis, the English navigator, sighted the island of Uvea, which was re-christened Wallis.
1820 The Takumasiva royal dynasty was restored in the kingdom of Uvea (Wallis).
1842 The authorities in Wallis requested French protection, which was granted.
1886–87 Queen Amelia of Uvea signed a protectorate treaty, which was ratified by the French in April 1887. In September 1887, the Kings of Alo and Sigave (the kingdoms of Futuna) also requested French protection and this was granted.
1924 The islands assumed the official status of a French colony.
1942 US and French forces arrived during the Second World War and the islands were used as a strategic air base.
1958 The French constitution was adopted.
1959 Tomasi Kulimoetoke II became the *Lavelua* (King of Uvea), ending a period of instability within the royal family.
1961 Wallis and Futuna became a French Territoire d'Outre-Mer (TOM) (Overseas Territory).
1999 Sagato Alofi became the the *Tuiagaifo* (King of Alo); Pasilio Keletaona became the *Keletaona* (King of Sigave).
2000 Atalo Tao Fifanua, the *kivalu* (prime minister) of the kingdom of Uvea, resigned.
2001 Tisimasi Heofala was endorsed as the *kivalu* of Uvea.
2002 The ruling right-wing Rassemblement pour la République (RPR) (Rally for the Republic) and its affiliates retained a majority in the Territorial Assembly elections. Christian Job was appointed *administrateur supérieur*, replacing Alain Waquet. Wallis and Futuna's only newspaper, the weekly *Te Fenua Fo'ou*, closed down in April after being subjected to threats and raids from the local (traditional) authorities.
2004 On 15 December, Xavier de Furst was appointed administrateur supérieur.
2005 The grandson of the *Lavelua*, Tomasi Tuhagala, was found guilty of unintentional homicide after a road accident in 2004, in which a man was killed. The *Lavelua* refused to allow him to be jailed, saying the matter had already been settled in the traditional manner, but Tuhagala was put in jail after the three royal families in Wallis and Futuna intervened. The French government, which pays the King's salary, also influenced the outcome.

Political structure
Constitution
28 September 1958 (French Fifth Republic)
In 1961, Wallis and Futuna became a Térritoire d'Outre-Mer (TOM) (Overseas Territory) of France.
Wallis and Futuna is administered by an administrator (administrateur supérieur) appointed by France and is represented in the French parliament by a deputy and a senator.
The islands are divided into three administrative districts based on the ancient kingdoms: *Uvea* (Wallis), *Alo* (Futuna) and *Sigave* (Futuna).
Wallis and Futuna is the only French territory where a native system of monarchy has been allowed to survive. There are three traditional kings: the Lavelua (King of Uvea), the Tuiagaifo (King of Alo) and the Keletaona (the title of King of Sigave depends on family heritage, and therefore, he has the title of Tui Sigave, Tamolevai or Keletaona).
In *Uvea*, there is a kivalu, the equivalent of a prime minister, who is appointed by the King.
Form of state
Térritoire d'Outre-Mer (TOM) (Overseas Territory) of France
The executive
The President of France is the head of state, represented by an appointed administrator.
National legislature
Local affairs are conducted by an elected Territorial Assembly with legislative powers (20 members elected by proportional representation for five years – 13 members are elected from Wallis and seven from Futuna) and traditional councils of rulers and leaders. The administrator has veto power over many of the Assembly's decisions.
Legal system
French law is applied while the traditional kings deal with customary law.
Last elections
March 2002 (Territorial Assembly)
Results: Parliamentary: the ruling right-wing RPR and its affiliates retained a majority in the Territorial Assembly

KEY FACTS

Official name: Wallis and Futuna

Head of State: President of France; Administrateur Supérieur M le *Préfét* Xavier de Furst (took office 18 Jan 2005)

Ruling party: Rassemblement pour la République (RPR) (Rally for the Republic)

Area: 144 square km – Wallis (or Uvea): 77.6km; Futuna: 64.4km

Population: 15,300 (2004)

Capital: Mata Utu (on Wallis)

Official language: Wallisian, Futunian, French

Currency: Comptoirs Français du Pacifique franc (CFPf) = 100 centimes

Exchange rate: CFPf98.91 per US$ (Oct 2005); (pegged CFPf119.25 per euro)

GDP per capita: US$2,000 (2003)

Balance of trade: -US$50,000 (2003)

elections, winning 13 seats. The remaining seven seats were won by the Socialist party and its affiliates (they gained one seat). Turnout was just under 83 per cent.
Next elections
2007 (Territorial Assembly)

Political parties
Ruling party
Rassemblement pour la République (RPR) (Rally for the Republic)
Main opposition party
Union Populaire pour Wallis et Futuna (UPWF) (People's Union for Wallis and Futuna) (allied to France's Parti Socialiste (PS) (Socialist Party)

Population
15,300 (2004)
Ethnic make-up
Polynesian
Religions
Roman Catholic

Health
Life expectancy: 73 years for men and 74 for women.
Infant mortality rate: 21 per 1,000 live births.

Main cities
Mata Utu, on Wallis (capital, estimated population 1,300 in 2003)

Languages spoken
Official language/s
Wallisian, Futunian, French

Media
Press
Weeklies: The only newspaper dedicated to Wallis and Futuna – *Te Fenua Fo'ou (TFF)*, written in French and Wallisian, closed down in April 2002; a new weekly publication took over in September 2002 – *Fenua Magazine* – but ceased publication in September 2003.

Economy
The economy is based on subsistence agriculture and fishing. Licensing of fishing rights, import taxes, remittances from migrant workers and grants from France are the other sources of income.

External trade
Imports
Principal imports are chemicals, machinery, ferries and consumer goods.
Main sources: France (97 per cent total, 2004), Australia (2 per cent), New Zealand (1 per cent)
Exports
Exports are copra, chemicals and construction materials.
Main destinations: Italy (40 per cent total, 2004), Croatia (15 per cent), US (14 per cent), Denmark (13 per cent)

Agriculture
Farming
Approximately 80 per cent of the labour force depend on agriculture for their livelihood. The soil of the main islands is volcanic and rainfall is adequate.
Crop production in 2004 included: 2,300 tonnes (t) coconuts, 2,400t cassava, 1,600t taro, 4,100t bananas, 18t tobacco, 8,667t fruit in total, 615t vegetables in total, 50t citrus fruit, 500t yams, 299t oilcrop. Livestock production included: 379t meat in total, 3t beef, 315t pig meat, 15t goat meat, 46t poultry, 33t eggs, 30t milk, 11t honey.
Fishing
Tuna is fished for local consumption. Licensing of fishing rights to Japan and South Korea provide an important source of revenue.
The typical annual fish catch, for local consumption, is 300t with 4t other seafood.
Forestry
Timber is logged for local consumption and some pine reafforestation has been undertaken.

Industry and manufacturing
Industrial activity is limited to handicrafts.

Banking and insurance
The only bank is Banque de Wallis et Futuna (a subsidiary of BNP, the French multinational bank).
Central bank
The Paris-based Institut d'Emission d'Outre-Mer (IEOM) provides all central banking services except foreign exchange reserves.

Time
GMT plus twelve hours

Geography
Wallis and Futuna comprises two groups of islands – Wallis Islands, including Wallis Island (also known as Uvea) and 22 islets on the surrounding reef, and, to the south-east, Futuna (or Hooru), comprising the two small islands of Futuna and Alofi. They are north-east of Fiji and west of Samoa.

Climate
Hot and humid, although May–October can be dry and cooler. Rainy season from November to April. Average temperature 27 degrees Celsius.

Entry requirements
Passports
Required by all except certain French nationals.
Visa
Required by all, except citizens of EU, North America, Australasia and Japan, for stays up to one month; this includes business trips by representatives of foreign entities with an invitation from a local company or organisation. Proof of adequate funds for stay, an itinerary, a guarantee of repatriation if necessary and return/onward ticket are also required. For further exceptions, full details and a copy of the application form visit www.diplomatie.gouv.fr/thema/dossier.gb.asp and follow the path (entering France) to the database.
Currency advice/regulations
As there are only two banks in the country (none at the airport), it is advisable to enter the country with cash, the most practical currency being Comptoirs Français du Pacifique franc (CFPf). Travellers cheques can be exchanged at the banks, but each transaction is accompanied by a large commission; the banks will give advances of up to US$235 a week on Visa or MasterCard.

Health (for visitors)
Mandatory precautions
Vaccination certificates required for yellow fever if travelling from an infected area.
Advisable precautions
Vaccinations for diphtheria, tuberculosis, hepatitis 'A' and 'B', polio, tetanus and typhoid are recommended. Rabies risk.

Hotels
There are less than 50 hotel rooms available.

Working hours
Banking
The bank in Mata Utu opens every weekday.

Telecommunications
On 18 July 2002, the French Development Agency loaned the territory CFPf360 million over 15 years to modernise the telephone network of the two islands, with the aim of increasing the number of subscribers from 1,700 to 2,400 in 2005.
Telephone/fax
Communications are by satellite, although a limited radio link is maintained.

Weights and measures
Metric system

Getting there
Air
The most regular connections to Wallis and Futuna are flights from New Caledonia and Tahiti.
National airline: Wallis and Futuna is planning to set up its own airline.
International airport/s: Wallis Hihifo Airport (WLS), 6km from Mata Utu; bureau de change, bars, VIP lounge, duty-free shop, newsagent/tobacconist, chemist shop, tourist help desk.
Surface
Water: There are no regular passengership services to the islands.
Main port/s: Mata Utu; Leava

Wallis and Futuna

Getting about
National transport
There is no public transport.
Air: New Caledonia-based Aircalin operates an inter-island service between Wallis and Futuna islands (five flights weekly).
Road: There are surfaced roads in Mata Utu and a road network links the main towns on Wallis.
Buses: Minibus services operate on Wallis.
Car hire
Car hire is available on Wallis.

BUSINESS DIRECTORY

The addresses listed below are a selection only. While World of Information makes every endeavour to check these addresses, we cannot guarantee that changes have not been made, especially to telephone numbers and area codes. We would welcome any corrections.

Telephone area codes
The international direct dialling (IDD) code for Wallis and Futuna is +681 followed by the subscriber's number.

Banking
Banque de Wallis et Futuna, PO Box 59, Mata Utu (tel: 722-124; fax: 722-156).

Central bank

Institut d'Emission d'Outre-Mer (IEOM), 5 rue Roland Barthes, 75598 Paris Cedex 12, France (tel : +33 1 5344-4141; fax : +33 1 4347-5134; e-mail: contact@ieom.fr).

Travel information
Aircalin, 8 Rue Frédéric Surleau, BP 3736, Noumea 98846 CEDEX, New Caledonia (tel: (687)283-333; fax: (687)272-772).

Wallis Hihifo Airport, BP 1, Mata Utu 98600 (tel: 722-660; fax: 720-183).

Other useful addresses
Service des Postes et Télécommunications, BP 00 98600, Mata Utu (tel: 720-700; fax: 722-500; e-mail: spt.get@wallis.co.nc).

Internet sites
Wallis and Futuna (in French): www.wallis.co.nc

Yemen

KEY FACTS

Official name: Jamhuriya al Yamaniya (Republic of Yemen)

Head of State: President Ali Abdullah Saleh (GPC) (elected Sep 1999)

Head of government: Prime Minister Abdul Qader Bagammal (GPC) (since Mar 2001)

Ruling party: General People's Congress (GPC) (re-elected 27 Apr 2003)

Area: 527,968 square km

Population: 19.42 million (2004)

Capital: Sana'a

Official language: Arabic

Currency: Rial (YR) = 100 fils

Exchange rate: YR193.46 per US$ (Oct 2005)

GDP per capita: US$518 (2004)

GDP real growth: 2.70% (2004)

Labour force: 5.95 million (2004)

Unemployment: 30.00% (2003)

Inflation: 12.50% (2004)

Oil production: 429,000 bpd (2004)

Balance of trade: US$734.00 million 2004

Foreign debt: US$6.20 billion (2003)

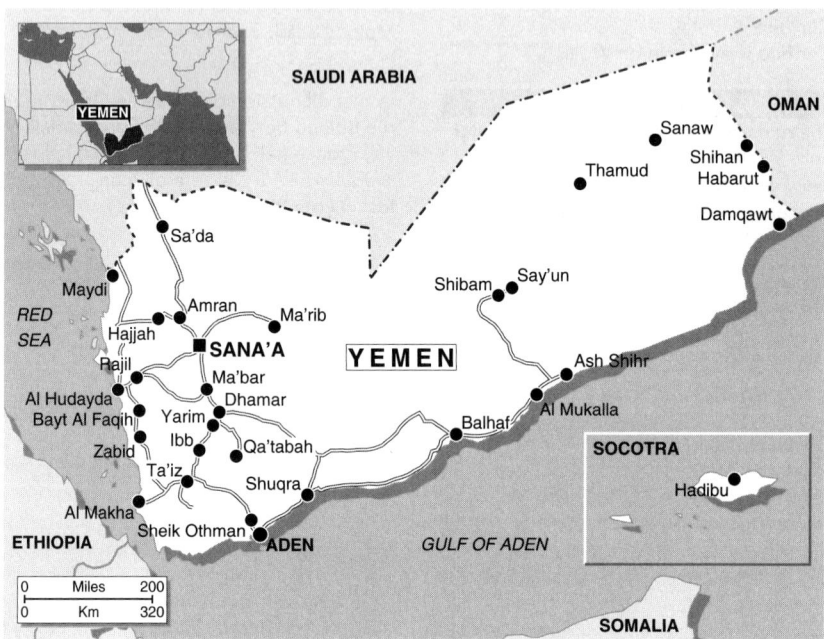

In 2005, Yemen endured a second year of violent clashes between security forces and a mixture of Islamist rebels and disgruntled tribal levies. The government faced broader unrest due to the implementation of unpopular economic reforms. Yemen's struggling economy was given a boost in 2005 through an increase in oil production and the sharp global rise in the price of oil.

A struggling economy

Yemen's GDP is forecast by the IMF to grow 3.7 per cent in 2005 – a significant advance on 2004's growth of 2.7 per cent. However, much of this growth was due to a surge in world oil prices and a timely boost in Yemeni oil production. Inflation is still over 12 per cent, public sector reform has stalled, and continued fighting between the government and Islamist and tribal dissidents has deterred many investors. This fighting has also helped to stymie a budding tourist sector.

As of November 2005, the government is in dispute with the US-based Hunt Oil company over the extension of an oil field lease.

The rebellion reignites

After a major outbreak of fighting between June and September 2004, the government must have hoped that 2005 would be a quieter year. Hussein al Houthi, a cleric of the Zaidi Shi'a sect, had led an uprising against government authority in the northern Saada province. By September 2004, Houthi had been killed along with up to 800 of his followers and members of the security services. The government struck a deal with Houthi's remaining followers, allowing for a cease-fire and an amnesty.

However, fighting broke out again in March and April of 2005, killing up to 200 Zaidis, soldiers and police. The government blamed Houthi's father, Badr al Din al Houthi, who in turn accused the government of continuing to arrest followers the late cleric. By May, serious fighting had subsided although minor clashes continued.

Kidnappings

The government was also forced to deploy troops in the restive Marib province, near the country's capital Sana'a. Tribes in the province took issue with a government decree ordering all Yemenis to stop carrying arms in public. When the government moved to enforce the ban in February 2005, tribesmen in Marib resisted. Mass arrests followed. Between November and December, Marib tribesmen began kidnapping foreign tourists in order, they say, to highlight the government's campaign against them. Sensitive to foreign criticism and anxious not to further jeopardise the country's growing tourism sector, the government has been keen to negotiate with the kidnappers.

Riots

In March and July 2005, widespread demonstrations and riots hit Yemen. The government had implemented long-stalled attempts to reform various sectors of the economy. Of these reforms, the introduction of a sales tax and a reduction in fuel subsidies were the most unpopular. In July, up to 36 people were killed during demonstrations against the government, mainly due to the police opening fire on demonstrators.

Outlook

Yemen will go to the polls in 2006 (date yet to be announced) to elect a president. Incumbent, Ali Abdullah Saleh has indicated that he will not be running, although analysts predict a last minute change of heart could take place. President Saleh ruled the Yemen Arab Republic (North Yemen) from 1978–1990 and has since ruled as president of the united Republic of Yemen. The fact that Saleh may not run therefore represents the possibility of a major change in Yemeni politics. There is speculation that Saleh's son, Colonel Ahmad Ali Abdullah Saleh, may run for office. The younger Saleh is currently commander of the elite Republican Guard and, since 1997, an MP. If Saleh's son does succeed him, this will be the second Arab republic in recent years (after Syria in 2000), to take on a dynastic flavour.

Yemen can expect further kidnappings until the government finds a way to engage constructively with tribal elements of the population. Zaidi militants are also likely to mount further challenges to government rule in Saada province, although the extent of the insurgency will depend upon how the government administers its amnesty programme for ex-combatants.

In February 2006, a jailbreak in Sana'a led to the escape of 13 convicted Islamist militants, some of whom are linked to the al Qaeda attack on the USS *Cole* in 2000. An international manhunt is under way.

Risk assessment

Politics	
Stable	
Economy	Fragile
Regional stability	Stable

COUNTRY PROFILE

Historical profile

Yemen is the reputed home of the Queen of Sheba. Holding a key position on the ancient spice routes, it has been at the crossroads of Africa, the Middle East and Asia for thousands of years. The north/south division of Yemen took shape in the nineteenth century when the British occupied Aden and established control over its hinterland, restricting Ottoman influence to the north. For much of the twentieth century, north and south developed in very different ways: the north under the rule of hereditary Imams, the south under British colonial rule.

After years of border wars, the traditionalist north and Marxist south merged in 1990 and the modern Republic of Yemen was established. In 1994, a brief civil war ended in defeat for separatist southerners and the survival of the unified Yemen. Since unification, the country has been modernising and opening up to the outside world, but still maintains much of its tribal character and old ways. Many Afghan Arabs made their home in Yemen after the end of the Soviet occupation of Afghanistan and as a result, the government has come under close international scrutiny in the US-led war on terrorism.

1500s–1600s The Ottomans controlled most of Yemen.
1839 Aden came under British rule, serving as a major refuelling port after the opening of the Suez Canal in 1869.
1918–62 The Ottoman empire broke up and north Yemen gained independence under Imam Yahya. His son, Imam Ahmad succeeded him in 1948 and ruled until his death in 1962. A *coup d'état* overthrew his son and the Yemen Arab Republic (YAR), was established by the military. A civil war between royalists, supported by Saudi Arabia, and republicans, backed by Egypt ensued.
1967 British withdrew from Aden as local resistance to their presence grew steadily more violent. A communist state in the south was established, comprising Aden and the former protectorate of South Arabia. It was officially known as the People's Democratic Republic of Yemen (PDRY). A nationalisation programme began.
1970s–80s The YAR and the PDRY were in conflict. Ali Abdullah Saleh became president of the YAR in 1978. President Ali Nasser Mohammed of the PDRY fled the country in 1986, after thousands died in political conflict.
1990 The YAR and the PDRY were unified and became the Republic of Yemen, with Ali Abdullah Saleh as president.
1991 A constitution was adopted. Yemen's support for Iraq in the Gulf War, led to around a million migrant workers from other gulf states being evicted and returning home.
1993 Democratic elections (the first in the Arabian Peninsula) led to a three-party coalition comprising the former ruling party of the YAR, General People's Congress (GPC), led by Ali Abdullah Saleh, the former ruling party of the PDRY, Yemeni Socialist Party (YSP), led by al

KEY INDICATORS — Yemen

	Unit	2000	2001	2002	2003	2004
Population	m	18.02	18.65	19.32	19.37	*19.42
Gross domestic product (GDP)	US$bn	8.60	8.40	10.30	11.10	*12.83
GDP per capita	US$	469	444	535	558	518
GDP real growth	%	5.1	1.8	4.1	3.1	2.7
Inflation	%	8.5	11.9	12.3	10.7	12.5
Oil output	'000 bpd	438.0	458.0	473.0	454.0	429.0
Exports (fob) (goods)	US$m	4,094.0	3,317.0	3,050.0	3,400.0	4,468.0
Imports (fob) (goods)	US$m	2,484.0	2,771.0	2,830.0	2,900.0	3,734.0
Balance of trade	US$m	1,610.0	546.0	220.0	500.0	734.0
Current account	US$m	1,260.0	510.0	540.0	130.0	130.0
Total reserves minus gold	US$m	2,900.3	3,658.1	4,410.5	4,986.9	5,664.8
Foreign exchange	US$m	2,815.6	3,639.6	4,365.6	4,982.0	5,613.5
Exchange rate	per US$	161.72	168.67	175.48	177.95	184.78

* estimated figure

Beedh, and a mainly northern Islamic tribal grouping, the Congregation for Reform (Islah). Disputes within the coalition resulted in an escalating political crisis.
1994 The constitution was amended. In spite of the signing of a conciliation agreement, a series of military confrontations broke out, leading to a full-scale civil war between northern and southern forces. Unity was restored and President Saleh was re-elected by parliament. A coalition government was formed, comprising the GPC and Islah, with the YSP and other smaller parties in opposition.
1995 Yemen and Eritrea clashed over the Hanish islands in the Red Sea.
1997 The ruling GPC won the first election since the 1994 civil war.
1998 Eritrea and Yemen accepted the ruling of the Permanent Court of Arbitration in the Hague that Yemen should have the island of Greater Hanish.
2000 Yemen and Saudi Arabia signed a treaty resolving a 65-year dispute over land and sea boundaries. The US naval vessel, *USS Cole*, was damaged in a suicide attack in Aden; a bomb exploded at the British Embassy.
2001 A referendum approved the extension of the president's term of office by two years to seven years and the parliamentary term by two years to six years. In response to the attack on New York, President Saleh told US President Bush that Yemen would join the fight against terrorism.
2002 Jarallah Omar, secretary general of the opposition party, YSP, was assassinated by an Islamic militant. Yemen expelled more than 100 foreign Islamic scholars, suspected of being al Qaeda members. The supertanker *Limburg* was badly damaged in an explosion off the coast of Yemen.
2003 The ruling GPC was re-elected. The 10 chief suspects in the bombing of the *USS Cole* escaped from custody in Aden.
2004 In March, the last two 2003 escapee terrorists, suspected of masterminding the bombing of the *USS Cole* were re-arrested. Fifteen men were sentenced in August on terror charges some for bombing the supertanker *Limburg* and in September two more for bombing the *USS Cole*. Government troops killed rebel cleric, Hussein al Houthi, the leader of an insurrection in the north.
2005 There was more fighting during March–April between government forces and al Houthi supporters causing hundreds of deaths. In May the UN WHO confirmed 83 cases of polio; Yemen had been free of the disease, it is thought pilgrims from the *Haj* may have been exposed to the disease.

Political structure
Constitution
The constitution was adopted in 1991 and was amended in 1994 and 2001. Voting eligibility: 18 years.
A 2001 referendum approved the extension of the president's and parliament's terms of office from five to seven years, and from four to six years, respectively.
Form of state
Republic
The executive
Power is vested in the post of president, who is the Head of State.
The president is elected by popular vote from at least two candidates, endorsed by parliament. He sets a national agenda and is empowered to rule by decree in the case of parliament's absence, call for parliamentary elections, appoint a prime minister to form a government, call for general referenda and form the National Defence Council.
The president can serve a maximum of two, seven-year terms.
The prime minister, in consultation with the president, selects the cabinet to assist in the duties of the executive branch.
National legislature
The bicameral parliament is composed of an upper house, the Consultative Council, and a lower house, the House of Representatives.
The House of Representatives, with 301 elected members who serve six-year terms, has legislative powers.
The Shura, Consultative Council, is composed of 111 members, appointed by the president, and serves only as advisory body.
There are 17 administrative provinces (11 in the north and six in the south).
Legal system
An independent judiciary was established under the constitution. It is based on *Sharia* (Islamic law), Turkish law, English common law and local tribal customary law. The Supreme Court is based in the capital.
Last elections
27 April 2003 (parliamentary)
Results: Parliamentary: the ruling GPC won 238 seats out of 301, followed by Islah with 46 seats.
Next elections
2006 (presidential), 2009 (parliamentary)
Political parties
Ruling party
General People's Congress (GPC) (re-elected 27 Apr 2003)
Main opposition party
Islah (Yemeni Congregation for Reform) (Islamist party)

Population
19.42 million (2004)

Ethnic make-up
Arabs form 96 per cent of the population. There are ethnic tensions between Arabs and Afro-Arab and South Asian minorities. European communities are concentrated in the major metropolitan areas.
Religions
Muslim (more than 99 per cent), including Shi'ite, Sunni and Zaydi (members of a Shi'ite subsect). Small number of Jews.

Education
Primary education begins at the age of six and lasts for nine years.
Secondary education is provided for academic and vocational courses both lasting three years. The first year comprises a common curriculum, with the option to choose either the scientific or literary subjects for the remaining two years. There are some technical secondary schools, three vocational training centres, a Veterinary Training School and several agricultural secondary schools. There are also religious institutions, which concentrate on Islamic education. Higher education is provided by the University of Sana'a (1970), the University of Aden (1973) and the University of Science and Technology, Sana'a.
Literacy rate: 49 per cent, total; 28.5 per cent, female; adult rates in 2002 (World Bank).
Compulsory years: Six to 15.
Enrolment rate: 70 per cent gross primary enrolment; 34 per cent gross secondary enrolment, of relevant age groups (including repeaters) (World Bank).
Pupils per teacher: 30 in primary schools.

Health
In April 2005 an outbreak of polio infected 22 children in the port city of al Hudaydah. The UN had been working to eradicate the disease worldwide by the end of 2005, this outbreak may spread and jepodise this plan.
HIV prevalence: 0.1 per cent aged 15–49 in 2003 (World Bank)
Life expectancy: 57.7 years (World Bank)
Fertility rate/Maternal mortality rate: 6.0 births per woman; maternal mortality 350 per 100,000 live births (World Bank).
Infant mortality rate: 82 per 1,000 live births; 46 per cent of children under aged five are malnourished (World Bank).
Head of population per physician/bed: 0.2 physicians and 0.6 hospital beds per 1,000 people.

Main cities
Sana'a (capital, estimated population 1.5 million in 2004), Aden (568,700), Ta'iz (453,400), Hodeida (426,100), Mukalla (174,700).

Yemen

Languages spoken
English is the second language and is often understood in business circles.
Official language/s
Arabic

Media
Press
Dailies: The official daily newspaper is *Al Thawra*. Other dailies are *Al Ayyam*, *Al Yumhuriyya* and *Al Ttariq*. *Yemen Online* (www.yemenonline.tsx.org/) provides daily news. *Yemen Observer* (www.yobserver.com/) is an independent English online newspaper covering current events.
Weeklies: Weeklies in Arabic are *26 September*, *Al Ray News*, *Al Soura* and the English language weekly *Yemen Times*.
Broadcasting
Radio: Four radio stations broadcast in English; BBC World Service available on short wave.
Television: TV stations in Aden and Sana'a, including commercial advertising. English-language news at 1930.

Economy
With GDP per capita falling to US$518 in 2004, from US$558 in 2003, Yemen's population remains among the poorest in the world with 40 per cent of the population living below the national poverty line. One of the challenges facing Yemen has been to reduce its dependence on its rapidly depleting oil reserves by turning to non-oil sectors and to attract private investment.

The economy slowed in 2004 as oil production declined by 5.9 per cent – even though higher oil prices provided a stable current account of US$130 million. Non-oil production grew at 4.1 per cent, fuelled by domestic demand and supported by a boost in construction, transport and the trade sector; although these, in turn, pushed up inflation to 12.5 in 2004, from 10.7 in 2003.

Privatisation, liberalisation and opening the economy to the world market system have resulted in an enhanced international position for Yemen. International investors, including Gulf Co-operation Council (GCC) sources, in co-operation with the EU, Japan, the US and the World Bank/IMF, have combined to develop an improving economic position.

Industry, in 2004, was 37.5 per cent of GDP, of which 4.9 per cent was manufacturing, while agricultural production contributed 13.8 per cent.

Reform measures have been incorporated into the 2005 budget and macroeconomic indicators were used for the first time, nevertheless the IMF in its appraisal of the economy considers Yemen 'at a crossroads'. The government has the challenge of rapidly declining oil revenue against the need to promote growth and diversity. Progress and structural reforms have begun and while the short-term outlook is manageable, without a long-term strategy, including prioritising and sequencing, the fiscal momentum is unlikely to be sustained.

External trade
The government's policy of opening up the economy and liberalising import controls, as well as a stable political climate, has encouraged international investors to take a new approach to the possibilities of this emerging market.
Imports
Main imports are food and live animals, machinery and equipment, and chemicals.
Main sources: UAE (12.8 per cent total, 2004), Saudi Arabia (10.2 per cent), China (9.0 per cent), France (7.9 per cent), Kuwait (4.4 per cent), US (4.4 per cent), India (4.3 per cent), Turkey (4.1 per cent)
Exports
Apart from crude oil, which has dominated exports since the late 1980s, coffee, dried and salted fish.
Main destinations: China (33.5 per cent total, 2004), Thailand (31.4 per cent), Singapore (7.2 per cent), South Korea (6.1 per cent)

Agriculture
Farming
With its fertile soil and relatively high levels of rainfall, Yemen possesses the best climatic conditions for agriculture on the Arabian peninsula. Due to its mountainous terrain, terrace agriculture is common practice. In the east and north, herding is the chief activity. In southern Yemen, fertile areas are severely limited and confined to the wadis, comprising only 1 per cent of the total land area.

Agriculture employs nearly 70 per cent of the total workforce and generated 13.8 per cent of GDP in 2004. The main crops are sorghum, wheat, barley, maize, millet, sesame, cotton, coffee, vegetables, dates, fruit, tobacco and qat (a legal narcotic). The cultivation of qat, a widely used mild narcotic shrub dominates production. It is estimated that up to 25 per cent of irrigated land is given over to qat, which generates a value added equivalent of 25 per cent of GDP.

Cereals, fruit and vegetables account for 75 per cent of output, but annual imports of grain are still required. Cereal yields are low and the climate is more suitable for fruit production. Private sector trading companies have invested in agriculture in Tihama and Marib, concentrating on bananas and citrus fruits.

Drought in some places and floods in others, plus general manpower shortages remain serious problems. The Marib Dam provides irrigation and for a region adjacent to the desert (Empty Quarter).

The estimated crop production for 2004 included: 487,944 tonnes (t) cereals in total, 105,273t wheat, 31,066t maize, 213,197t potatoes, 263,428t sorghum, 99,000t bananas, 60,800t pulses, 201,620t citrus fruit, 169,000t grapes, 200,438t tomatoes, 11,242t oilcrops, 11,900t tobacco, 33,300t dates, 11,600t green coffee, 9,800t cotton lint, 73,800t papayas, 646,220t fruit in total, 736,643t vegetables in total. Estimated livestock production included: 202,720t meat in total, 59,800t beef, 3,120t camel meat, 30,300t lamb, 26,000t goat meat, 83,500t poultry, 31,980t eggs, 263,393t milk, 681t honey, 11,169t cattle hides, 6,000t sheepskins.
Fishing
Fisheries are one of Yemen's greatest potential sources of wealth after oil. There are some fish exports to Europe and the Middle East.

Industry and manufacturing
The industrial sector contributed 37.5 per cent of GDP, of which manufacturing was 4.9 per cent in 2004. The sector employs around 10 per cent of the working population. Excluding the petroleum sector, industry accounts for only 4 per cent of GDP.

Heavy industry is mostly government-owned while the private sector is encouraged to participate in joint ventures and light industries including food processing, clothing, textiles, leather goods, jewellery, cosmetics, mineral water, fertilisers and cigarettes.

Fish processing is a growth area.

Industrial production increased by 5.0 per cent, and manufacturing by 5.3 per cent, in 2004.

Tourism
The government has been seeking to develop tourism as a potential source of revenue. The country has a moderate climate all-year-round and an ancient civilisation which would prove of great interest to visitors. However, with the rise of terrioist activities tourism has been hampered.

Travel and tourism, in 2005, is expected to contribute around US$253 million or 1.9 per cent of GDP and 13 per cent of total exports, and employ 8.6 per cent of all workers. Around US$283 million or 12.8 per cent of total capital investment is expected to be invested in the sector in 2005.

Environment
Yemen has water shortages, especially in the increasingly urbanised areas around Sana'a and other cities.

Mining
Salt is mined at Salif, where deposits total 25 million tonnes. Gypsum and marble are extracted. There are also deposits of zinc, lead, iron, sulphur, gold, silver, copper and nickel.

Hydrocarbons
In 2004, oil reserves stood at 4 billion barrels. Oil production was 420,000 barrels per day (bpd). Over 80 per cent of total oil production is exported. Exploration is ongoing, and in August 2003 a new field of four wells was announced, although the quality of oil has yet to be determined.

Downstream, Yemen has a refining capacity of 130,000bpd with two refineries at Aden (120,000bpd) and Marib (10,000bpd).

Reserves of natural gas were estimated at 478 billion cubic metres in 2004. Yemen does not exploit this resource yet, it could be used for power generation and industry in the future, although two-thirds of its reserves is earmarked for export. A US$5 billion liquefied natural gas (LNG) project was scheduled to come on line by 2006, but ExxonMobil left the consortium in 2002. The project found Chinese and Indian backers and is expected to be completed by 2009 and will involve construction of gas-gathering facilities, a pipeline to the Gulf of Aden and an LNG plant. An estimated 6.2 million tonnes of LNG will be exported per annum. A second pipeline will carry gas for local consumption to Sana'a.

Yemen neither produces nor imports coal. In February 2004, Syria and Yemen signed a co-operation agreement in the field of oil, gas and mineral resources.

Energy
Installed electricity generating capacity is estimated at 810MW, all of it produced by oil-fired power stations. Yemen has power problems and expansion of electricity is a major priority. Plans include thermal power stations and grid extension.

Banking and insurance
Domestic banks are burdened by red tape and private sector credit is crowded out by the state, although the government has announced a reform programme to develop the financial sector.

Central bank
Central Bank of Yemen

Main financial centre
Sana'a

Time
GMT plus three hours

Geography
Yemen is situated in the south of the Arabian peninsula, bordered to the north by Saudi Arabia, to the east by Oman, to the south by the Gulf of Aden, and to the west by the Red Sea. The islands of Perim and Kamaran at the southern end of the Red Sea, the island of Socotra at the entrance to the Gulf of Aden, and the Kuria Muria islands near the coast of Oman, are also part of the Republic.

Climate
The semi-desert coastal plain known as the Tihama is hot, humid and dusty. The highlands, which are agreeable in summer but cold in winter, enjoy most of the unreliable rainfall (March–April and July–September).

Entry requirements
Passports
Required by all.

Visa
Required by all, except for a few Arab nationals (visit the consular section of www.yemenembassy.org.uk for further information and confirmation).
Tourist visas valid for visits up to two months require a confirmation letter from a tour company and proof of return/onward passage.
Business visas require: a letter from the applicant's company explaining the purpose of the visit and the nature of business; proof of return/onward passage. If several journeys are proposed beyond the standard six months visa validity, a letter of invitation from a Yemeni company is also required.
Travellers with Pakistani or Iranian visas, or Israeli stamps in their passports are likely to be subject to long delays on arrival.

Prohibited entry
Israeli nationals or holders of passports with Israeli visas are forbidden entry.

Customs
Personal effects are free of duty.

Prohibited imports
No alcohol is allowed. All goods from Israel are prohibited, and permitted imports require import licences.

Health (for visitors)
Mandatory precautions
Certificate of vaccination against yellow fever if travelling from infected area.

Advisable precautions
Vaccinations against typhoid and polio are recommended, also anti-malaria precautions (malaria has been endemic in Tihama).
Water precautions are essential; water and milk should be boiled. Local dairy products should be avoided as milk is unpasteurised; vegetables, meat and fish should be well cooked and eaten hot. Use only well maintained, chlorinated, swimming pools as bilharzia can be contracted from streams and rivers. Gastric upsets common.

Hotels
Sana'a has several first-class hotels. It is advisable to book in advance. The major hotels have good restaurants.

Credit cards
Major credit cards are acceptable.

Public holidays
Fixed dates
1 Jan (New Year's Day), 1 May (Labour Day), 22 May (Unity Day), 26 Sep (Revolution Day), 14 Oct (National Day), 30 Nov (Independence Day).

Variable dates
Eid al Adha (four days), Eid al Fitr (four days), Islamic New Year, Birth of the Prophet.
The Islamic year contains 354 or 355 days, with the result that Muslim feasts advance by 10–12 days against the Gregorian calendar. Dates of feasts vary according to the sighting of the new moon, so cannot be forecast exactly.

Working hours
Banking
Sat–Wed: 0800–1200, Thu: 0800–1130 (closed Fri); in summer: Sat–Wed: 0730–1130, Thu: 0730–1100 (closed Fri).

Business
Sat–Wed: 0800–1230, 1600–1900; Thu: 0800–1200 (closed Fri).

Government
Sat–Thu: 0900–1300.

Telecommunications
Telephone/fax
The telephone directory is in Arabic. For help, ask the telephone operator at your hotel or ring 18 (English spoken).

Electricity supply
Generally 220V AC, with two-pin plug fittings.

Weights and measures
Metric system

Social customs/useful tips
Islamic culture and customs are strictly observed, but visitors are allowed to drink alcohol in hotels or private homes.

Getting there
Air
National airline: Yemenia Airline
International airport/s: Sana'a International (Code: SAH), 13km north of Sana'a, with duty-free shop (no alcohol), restaurant, bank; Khormaksar (ADE), 11km north-east of Aden; al Ganad (TAI) 22km from Ta'iz; al Mukalla in Riyan; Say'un and Hodeida.
Airport tax: Departure tax US$20.

Surface
There are very few road connections between Yemen and neighbouring countries (Saudi Arabia and Oman).
Main port/s: Aden, Hodeidah and Mukalla

Yemen

Getting about
National transport
Internal travel may be affected by local night-time curfews and military check points.
Air: Regular scheduled services linking Sana'a, Aden, Hodeida, Ta'iz and Marib.
Road: There are metalled roads between all major cities.
Buses: There are scheduled services between Sana'a and all major centres.

City transport
Most hosts will send a car to the airport to meet guests.
Taxis: Taxis have yellow licence plates and black stripes, and wait on ranks outside the major hotels and terminals. Fare is by negotiation and there is a minimum charge system in cities. Always fix fare before setting off – ask at the hotel what the price should be and bargain from there. Also ask the hotel for directions before setting off, as most taxi drivers, even those from the hotels, are likely to get lost in the city.
A fixed fare is charged between Sana'a airport and the city centre.
Dahabs (shared taxis) are minibuses which ply set routes in the city. Prices are fixed between destinations and are reasonably cheap.
Buses, trams & metro: Buses wait outside the airport.

Car hire
Available in Sana'a.

BUSINESS DIRECTORY
The addresses listed below are a selection only. While World of Information makes every endeavour to check these addresses, we cannot guarantee that changes have not been made, especially to telephone numbers and area codes. We would welcome any corrections.

Telephone area codes
The international direct dialling (IDD) code for Yemen is +967, followed by the area code and subscriber's number:

Aden	2	Sana'a	1
Almahra	5	Taiz	4
Amran	7	Yarim	4
Hodeidah	3	Zabid	3

Chambers of Commerce
Aden Chamber of Commerce, Queen Arwa Road, PO Box 473, Crater, Aden (tel: 221-176; fax: 255-660; e-mail: cciaden@y.net.ye).

Federation of Yemen Chambers of Commerce and Industry, Al-Qiyadah Road, PO Box 16992, Sana'a (tel: 265-038; fax: 261-269; e-mail: fucci@y.net.ye).

Hadhramout Chamber of Commerce and Industry, Mukalla Main Street, PO Box 8302, Mukalla (tel: 353-258; fax: 303-437; e-mail: hdramoutchamber@y.net.ye).

Hodeidah Chamber of Commerce and Industry, Liberty Squaret, PO Box 3370, Hodeidah (tel: 217-401; fax: 211-528; e-mail: hodcii@y.net.ye).

National Chamber of Commerce and Industry, PO Box 5029, Crater, Aden (tel: 51203; fax: 232-412).

Sana'a Chamber of Commerce and Industry, Airport Road, PO Box 195, Sana'a (tel: 232-361; fax: 232-412; e-mail: sanaacomyemen@y.net.ye).

Ta'iz Chamber of Commerce and Industry, Chamber Street, PO Box 5029, Taiz (tel: 210-581; fax: 212-335; e-mail: taizchamber@y.net.ye).

Banking
Arab Bank Plc, PO Box 5130, Madram Street, Maala, Aden (tel: 242-099, 240-043; fax: 242-098).

Credit Agricole Indosuez, PO Box 651, Al Ma'ala Main St, Aden (tel: 247-4024; fax: 247-282).

International Bank of Yemen YSC, PO Box 819, al Maidan - Crater, Off Queen Arwa Rd, Crater, Aden (tel: 255-795; fax: 252-016).

National Bank of Yemen, PO Box 5, Crater, Aden (tel: 252-875, 253-327; fax: 252-875).

Watani Bank for Trade and Investment, PO Box 4424, Queen Arwa St, Agaba, Aden (tel: 2506-1017; fax: 250-618).

Yemen Bank for Reconstruction and Development, PO Box 239, Aden (tel: 252-104, 254-046; fax: 252-141).

Yemen Commercial Bank, PO Box 4230, Aden (tel: 255-813, 253-384; fax: 255-428).

Central bank
Central Bank of Yemen, PO Box 59, Ali Abdulmoghni Street, Sana'a (tel: 274-310 fax: 274-057; e-mail: info@centralbank.gov.ye).

Travel information
Sana'a Airport information (tel: 200-818).
Yemenia, PO Box 1183, Al Hasaba Airport Road, Sana'a (tel: 232-380/87, 232-401; fax: 252-991, 231-470).

Ministries
Ministry of Agriculture and Water Resources, PO Box 2805 (tel: 200-999; fax: 209-509).

Ministry of Civil Service and Administration Reform, PO Box 1992, Sana'a (tel: 200-404; fax: 274-456).

Ministry of Communications, PO Box 17045, Sana's (tel: 271-100; fax: 251-150).

Ministry of Construction, PO Box 1180, Sana'a (tel: 202-288; fax: 274-145).

Ministry of Culture and Tourism (tel: 200-002; fax: 252-316).

Ministry of Defence (tel: 250-330; fax: 251-559).

Ministry of Economy, Supply & Trade, PO Box 1704, Sana'a (tel: 202-471).

Ministry of Education (tel: 274-548; fax: 274-558).

Ministry of Electricity and Water, PO Box 11422, Sana'a (tel: 250-143; fax: 251-554).

Ministry of Finance, PO Box 190, Sana'a (tel: 260-375; fax: 263-040).

Ministry of Fishery Wealth, PO Box 19179, Sana'a (tel: 262-866; fax: 263-165).

Ministry of Foreign Affairs, PO Box 1994, Sana'a (tel: 202-555; fax: 209-540).

Ministry of Higher Education and Scientific Research, PO Box 11327, Sana'a (tel: 200-463; fax: 262-001).

Ministry of Housing and Urban Planning, PO Box 1445, Sana'a (tel: 262-614; fax: 215-613).

Ministry of Immigrants Affairs, PO Box 1299, Sana'a (tel: 215-666; fax: 263-027).

Ministry of Industry, PO Box 607, Sana'a (tel: 252-339; fax: 252-366).

Ministry of Information (tel: 200-050; fax: 282-050).

Ministry of the Interior and Security (tel: 252-701; fax: 251-529).

Ministry of Justice (tel: 252-158; fax: 252-138).

Ministry of Labour and Vocational Training, PO Box 60, Sana'a (tel: 274-922; fax: 274-107).

Ministry of Legal Affairs, PO Box 1292, Sana'a (tel: 262-047; fax: 262-047).

Ministry of Local Government, PO Box 2198, Sana'a (tel: 250-626; fax: 251-513).

Ministry of Oil and Mineral Resources, PO Box 81, Sana'a (tel: 202-312; fax: 202-314).

Ministry of Planning and Development, PO Box 175, Sana'a (tel: 250-118; fax: 251-503).

Ministry of Provision and Trade, PO Box 804, Sana'a (tel: 252-337; fax: 251-366).

Ministry of Public Health, PO Box 274160, Sana'a (tel: 252-222; fax: 244-143).

Ministry of Securities and Social Affairs (tel: 262-809; fax: 209-547).

Ministry of State for Cabinet Affairs (tel: 200-677; fax: 209-518).

Ministry of State for Foreign Affairs, PO Box L994, Sana'a (tel: 202-544; fax: 209-540).

Ministry of State for House of Deputies Affairs (tel: 200-671; fax: 209-518).

Ministry of Transport, PO Box 2781 (tel: 260-904; fax: 263-169).

Ministry of Tourism, PO Box 129, Sana'a (tel: 252-319; fax: 260-186).

Ministry of WAQF and Guidance (tel: 274-438; fax: 274-17).

Ministry of Youth and Sport, PO Box 2701, Sana'a (tel: 215-653; fax: 263-181).

Other useful addresses

British Consulate-General, PO Box 6304, Khormaksar, Aden (tel: 232-712; fax: 231-256).

British Embassy, PO Box 1287, Sana'a (tel: 264-081; fax: 263-059).

Central Planning Organisation, PO Box 175, Sana'a (tel: 250-1018).

Foreign Trade Corporation, PO Box 77, Sana'a (tel: 72-058).

General Post Office, Liberation (Tahreer) Square, (tel: 71-401/2).

Ports and Marine Affairs Corporation, PO Box 3183, Hodeidah.

Republic of Yemen Embassy (USA), Suite 705, 2600 Virginia Avenue, NW, Washington DC 20037 (tel: 965-4760; fax: 337-2017; e-mail: information@yemenembassy.org).

United Nations Development Programme, PO Box 551 Sana'a (tel: 70-593/70-596).

Internet sites

ArabNet: http://www.arab.net/welcome.html

Arabia.On.Line: http://www.arabia.com

Embassy of the Republic Yemen, Washington DC:
http://www.yemenembassy.org

Yemen gateway site:
http://www.al-bab.com/yemen/Default.htm

Yemen Times On-line:
http://www.yementimes.com

Zambia

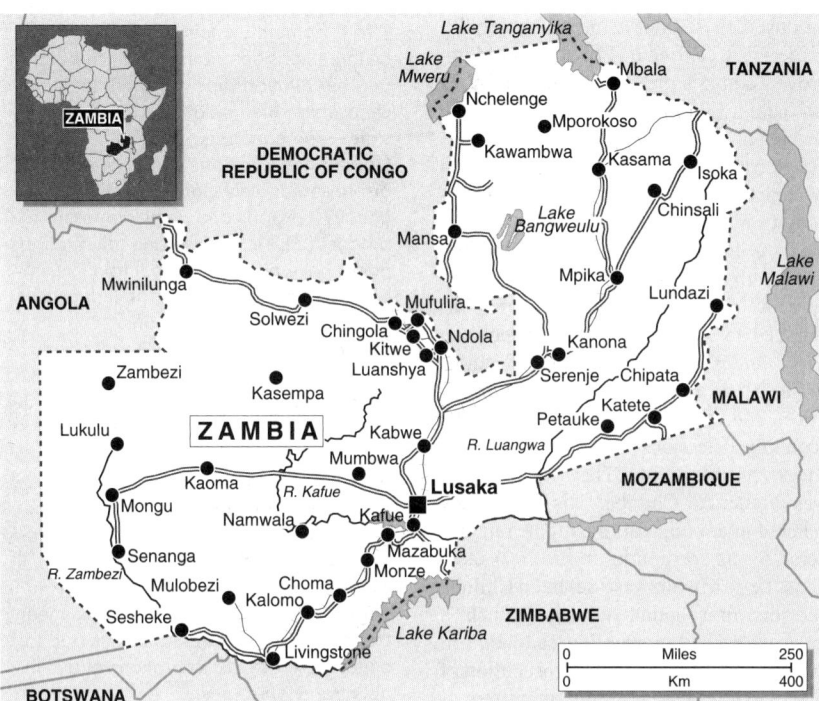

KEY FACTS

Official name: Republic of Zambia

Head of State: President Levy Mwanawasa (MMD) (elected 27 Dec 2001; inaugurated 2 Jan 2002)

Head of government: President Levy Mwanawasa

Ruling party: Movement for Multi-party Democracy (MMD) (re-elected 27 Dec 2001)

Area: 752,614 square km

Population: 11.00 million (2004)

Capital: Lusaka

Official language: English

Currency: Kwacha (K) = 100 ngwee

Exchange rate: K4,475.00 per US$ (Oct 2005)

GDP per capita: US$478 (2004)

GDP real growth: 5.00% (2004)

Labour force: 4.47 million (2004)

Unemployment: 50.00% (2003)

Inflation: 18.00% (2004)

Balance of trade: -US$29.00 million 2004

Foreign debt: US$6.50 billion (2003)

In December 2005, the International Monetary Fund (IMF) approved relief for Zambia on all outstanding debt to the IMF incurred before January 1, 2005. This amounted to approximately US$577 million.

The medium-term development strategy for Zambia is to reduce poverty through strong economic growth and economic diversification driven by the private sector. The strategy targets real growth of at least five per cent a year, single-digit inflation by 2007, and a strengthened international reserve position.

Reforms are needed to create an environment more conducive to private sector development. Implementation of the reform agenda is now key. Spending will escalate during 2006 to cover the cost of elections. Financing gaps in 2006 and 2007 will need to be filled through a combination of additional grants and offsetting measures.

The IMF is collaborating with the World Bank in many areas of Zambia's development. In some areas the Fund leads and its analysis serve as inputs into World Bank policy formulation and advice; these include macroeconomic stability, fiscal, monetary, and exchange rate policies. The Fund and the Bank share responsibility in the areas of trade, the financial sector, public expenditure management, including debt management, and economic governance. The Bank takes the lead in the social sectors, including health, education, social protection, water and sanitation, agriculture and rural development, private sector development including regulatory issues and the environment.

Economic policies highlight diversification away from reliance on copper revenues – even though the fortunes of the Copperbelt are clearly in a bull phase. The drivers are investments in private sector operations. However, investment remains at less than six per cent of gross domestic product in the face of annual population growth of three per cent.

A key challenge is to attract new investment that will ensure diversified sources of growth. Long term, copper is not the mainstay of the Zambian economy. It will continue to be extremely important, but by the nature of that industry, growth in the main accrues to those who finance it. It can create only so much employment, it is the kind of growth that, while good for the economy, is not as broad based as Zambia needs. It is not the type of growth that improves people's lives.

The main areas for which the World Bank and government agencies are seeking investments are agriculture and tourism, both offer broad based growth that is sustainable in the long haul. All that is required is the infrastructure to open the country up.

Copper

The copper crisis years are over. Copper prices are in an upswing. A new Copperbelt has started. Many believe the Anglo American pull out in 2002 was a wake up call for new and better planning, but the core problem remains, Zambia is not in control of the final destiny of its copper mining industry. Prices are set on the London Metal Exchange and in 1999 were at their lowest for 15 years.

Zambia is still a major producer, but mines in the landlocked country have to contend with high transport costs, ageing infrastructure and growing competition from Australia and Chile and even closer to home. Canadian companies are fast-tracking developments in the Democratic Congo, Australians are looking in Botswana.

Influenced by the bull phase of the industry, the mining companies disagree. There are good years left, technology is good, the challenge is to keep costs down, but Zambia is in for the long term is their view. They do not go along with World Bank forecasts that the copper price will decline to 81 cents/lb by 2007 from 2005's estimate of 99 cents. Industrial sources say prices will hold 'for at least four years' and 'more optimistic forecasts are over exuberant'.

The historical production high is 700,000 tonnes/year, 450,000 tonnes were produced over 2004. A 'new Copperbelt', to the West, centred on Solwezi, could improve Zambia's present production by 25 per cent within two years, 60 per cent within six.

The territory of Northern Rhodesia was administered by the South Africa Company from 1891 until it was taken over by the UK in 1923. During the 1920s and 1930s, advances in mining spurred development and immigration. The name was changed to Zambia on independence in 1964, under President Kenneth Kaunda. In the 1980s and 1990s, declining copper prices and a prolonged drought hurt the economy. Elections in 1991 brought an end to one-party rule. The new president was Frederick Chiluba. His presidency ushered in era that will mostly be remembered for its corruption. In the 2001 elections, Levy Mwanawasa defeated Chiluba and his first action was to launch a far-reaching anti-corruption campaign in 2002, which resulted in the prosecution of CHILUBA and many of his supporters.

Mwanawasa narrowly won the presidential elections, which opposition parties claimed was subject to fraud and ballot-rigging. Yet, Mwanawasa's supporters and detractors alike agree that he displays a high level of integrity in his public life.

Risk assessment

Economic	Poor
Political	Improving
Regional stability	Poor

COUNTRY PROFILE

Historical profile

Following independence from Britain in 1964, Zambia's affairs were dominated by three considerations: the price of copper, her relationships with what for years were white-ruled neighbouring African states, and communications.

Copper has traditionally accounted for a disproportionately high proportion of the country's exports and gross domestic product (GDP). The rise and fall of copper prices have played a critical role in Zambia's economic fortunes. The independence struggles in neighbouring Zimbabwe, Mozambique, Angola and South Africa placed Zambia squarely in the front line of Black African states facing a white controlled south. Zambia's relations with her neighbours have always been coloured by the landlocked country's dependence on communications. To export copper, Zambia needs constant access to major ports along railways or roads capable of handling large bulk tonnages of her copper. For years this meant that political considerations have had to be tempered by considerations of available transport routes.

Shona people arrived in the area in the twelfth century, establishing the empire of Mwene Mutapa, which included southern Zambia.

In the sixteenth century, people from the Luba and Lunda around the Congo River set up small kingdoms in Zambia. Portuguese explorers visited the region in the late eighteenth century. Migration and slave-trading by the Portuguese and Arabs led to instability in the region.

1851 British missionary David Livingstone visited central Africa.

1880s British settlers followed Livingstone and the British South Africa Company, headed by British imperialist and financier, Cecil John Rhodes, opened its first copper mine at Broken Hill (later Kabwe) in 1908.

1924 The colony was put under direct British rule.

1953–63 Northern Rhodesia (later Zambia) was part of the British-sponsored Federation of Rhodesia and Nyasaland.

1960 The United National Independence Party (UNIP) was formed by Kenneth Kaunda to campaign for independence and the dissolution of white minority rule.

1964 Zambia gained independence under the presidency of Kenneth Kaunda.

KEY INDICATORS — Zambia

	Unit	2000	2001	2002	2003	2004
Population	m	10.42	10.57	10.70	10.85	*11.00
Gross domestic product (GDP)	US$bn	3.90	3.70	4.10	4.80	*5.39
GDP per capita	US$	375	355	381	447	448
GDP real growth	%	3.6	4.0	3.0	3.1	5.0
Inflation	%	26.1	21.4	22.2	21.5	18.0
Exports (fob) (goods)	US$m	789.0	871.0	945.0	1,117.0	1,548.0
Imports (fob) (goods)	US$m	1,008.0	1,253.0	1,200.0	1,633.0	1,519.0
Balance of trade	US$m	-219.0	-382.0	-250.0	-516.0	29.0
Current account	US$m	-571.0	-743.0	-470.0	-628.0	-620.0
Foreign debt	US$bn	5.6	5.9	5.4	6.5	–
Total reserves minus gold	US$m	244.8	183.4	535.1	247.7	337.1
Foreign exchange	US$m	222.5	116.5	464.8	247.2	312.2
Exchange rate	per US$	3,110.84	3,610.94	4,425.00	4,502.50	4,757.11

* estimated figure

Zambia

The government supported Marxist rebels in Mozambique, independence movements in Rhodesia (later Zimbabwe) and the African National Congress (ANC) in South Africa. This led to internal security problems and financial difficulties as Zambia's colonial neighbours attempted to destabilise the country.

1964–1970s Key enterprises and land were nationalised.

1972 Zambia became a one-party state with UNIP as the only legal party.

1975 The Tanzania-Zambia Railway Authority (Tazara) opened, linking the Zambian Copperbelt to the Tanzanian port of Dar es Salaam, reducing the country's dependence on Rhodesia and South Africa for port access.

1976 Zambia gave support to Rhodesia's bid for independence and its eventual transformation from white minority rule into Zimbabwe.

1989 Zambia began a programme of austerity measures to stabilise the economy, following a long-term fall in the price of Zambia's chief export, copper.

1990 Food riots heightened calls for an end to one-party rule.

1991 Multi-party elections were held in which Kaunda was defeated by Frederick Chiluba and the Movement for Multi-party Democracy (MMD).

1996 The MMD and President Chiluba were re-elected in a landslide victory.

1999 There was a spate of Angolan terrorist attacks in Lusaka. The Indeni Oil Refinery in Ndola was sabotaged.

2000 Kaunda resigned as leader of UNIP.

2001 Even though the MMD voted to change the constitution and allow the president to run for a third term in office, Chiluba announced he would not stand. The MMD was re-elected although the opposition said the elections were flawed.

2002 Levy Mwanawasa (MMD) was inaugurated as president; the opposition filed a petition to have the result of the presidential election nullified, alleging vote-rigging by the ruling party. The government said it would not accept genetically modified (GM) maize to help alleviate severe food shortages.

2003 Former president Frederick Chiluba's immunity from prosecution was removed and he was arrested in January and charged on 59 counts, including abuse of office.

2004 The court case against Chiluba was dropped in September. In October he was charged, with two others, of 'siphoning off' from state funds US$488,000.

2005 The Japanese cancelled Zambia's outstanding debt – about US$692 million – in December.

2006 President Mwanawasa has said that election laws will be amended in time for the elections later in 2006. The opposition, however, expressed doubts that this would happen.

Political structure
Constitution
In November 1991, Zambia's one-party state was replaced by a multi-party democratic system based on a new constitution. In 1995 the ruling Movement for Multi-party Democracy (MMD) revised the constitution. The Zambia Law Association criticised the new constitution on the grounds that it allows parliament to make retrospective laws and that a president could be elected on receiving the highest number of votes cast even if these amounted to less than 50 per cent. It also condemned amendments to the Bill of Rights of the 1991 Constitution without a referendum. A controversial Bill passed by President Chiluba on 28 May 1996 made further amendments to the constitution: future presidential candidates must be second-generation Zambians.

Form of state
Republic

The executive
Executive power is held by the president elected by universal suffrage for a five-year term. The constitution provides for a cabinet appointed from within parliament and gives it extra powers. The president does not have the right to declare martial law. The president must obtain parliamentary approval to impose a state of emergency longer than seven days.

National legislature
Legislative power is held by a unicameral National Assembly. The National Assembly has 159 members, including 150 members elected in single seat constituencies for a five-year term, eight members appointed by the president and a speaker.

Legal system
The president appoints judges and nominates the chief justice. Courts include the Supreme Court of Zambia and the High Court.

Last elections
27 December 2001 (presidential and legislative)
Results: Presidential: Levy Mwanawasa (MMD) won 29.1 per cent of the vote; Anderson Mazoka 27.2 per cent.
Parliamentary: Movement for Multi-party Democracy (MMD) won 27.5 per cent of the vote (69 seats out of 159); United Party for National Development (UPND) 23.3 per cent (49 seats); Forum for Democracy and Development (FDD) 15.3 per cent (12 seats); United National Independence Party (UNIP) 10.4 per cent (13 seats); Heritage Party 7.4 per cent (4 seats); Patriotic Front 2.8 per cent (1 seat); Zambia Republican Party 5.5 per cent (1 seat); non-partisan 1; appointed members 8; Speaker 1.

Next elections
2006 (presidential and legislative)

Political parties
Ruling party
Movement for Multi-party Democracy (MMD) (re-elected 27 Dec 2001)
Main opposition party
United Party for National Development (UPND)

Population
11.00 million (2004)
Ethnic make-up
There are 73 ethnic groups in Zambia. The largest single group, comprising 34 per cent of the population, is the Bemba (north-east and Copperbelt areas). Other important groups include the Tonga of the southern province with 16 per cent of the population; the Nyanja of the eastern provinces (14 per cent) who are well represented in the capital, Lusaka; and the Lozi (9 per cent) of the west.
The European population live and work mostly in the urban areas, or on the farmlands along the railway lines. A high proportion of the Asian community is to be found on the Copperbelt and other urban centres.
Religions
Christian, Muslim and indigenous beliefs. Approximately 70 per cent of the population is Christian (mainly Roman Catholic and Protestant).

Education
The HIV/Aids crisis in sub-Saharan Africa has not only undermined public investment in education but has also contributed to the shortage of trained teachers, in 2001 815 primary school teachers, or 45 per cent of teachers trained that year, died of Aids. This has resulted in declining literacy rates and low levels of school enrolment. Enrolment rates for the richest households are more than one-third higher than for the poorest households. A first cycle primary education begins at age seven, lasting until age 11, then three years in a second cycle primary school prepares children for exams to determine progression to a junior secondary school for two years until aged 16 when successfully completed exams allow progression into senior secondary school for the last two years. There are two universities that provide higher education and several specialist institutions providing professional and vocational training.
The government has developed a strong education sector reform through the Basic Education Sub-sector Investment Programme (Bessip), which has set a target of universal primary school enrolment for just under half a million children by

2005. Annual government expenditure during the first phase of the reform amounted to US$56 million, excluding contributions from international donors for the projects. The scheme aims to construct 2,000 additional classrooms and improve training in rural schools. Zambia spends typically less than 3 per cent of GDP on education.

Literacy rate: 79.9 per cent, total; 73.8 per cent, female; adult rates (World Bank); an improvement on the estimated 78 per cent total rate over the period 1994–2000.

Compulsory years: Seven to 13.

Enrolment rate: 89 per cent gross primary enrolment; 27 per cent gross secondary enrolment, of relevant age groups (including repeaters) (World Bank).

Pupils per teacher: 39 in primary schools.

Health

Government spending was 53.1 per cent, and foreign spending was 48.7 per cent of the total expenditure on health in 2001, which was 5.7 per cent of GDP. Healthcare is provided free in state-funded hospitals and commercially in private sector clinics. Rural health care is rudimentary and frequently provided only by missionary hospitals and clinics. State funding cut-backs have led to severe shortages of medical equipment and staff. Many medical posts are unfilled for lack of funds. The government is keen to encourage private investment in hospitals and believes foreign investment provides the key to the redevelopment of the health sector.

Improved water sources are available to 64 per cent of the population.

HIV/Aids

Zambia has one of the highest rates of HIV in Africa. It is estimated that 42 per cent of hospital beds are occupied by HIV/Aids sufferers. The World Bank reported that the Aids epidemic would radically reduce the rate of population growth; it fell from 2.8 per cent annually in 1990–97 to 1.5 per cent in 2003. The impact on households is severe, with children often kept from attending school in order to help with harvesting of subsistence crops. Studies show that around 55 per cent of households affected by HIV/Aids are unable to pay school fees. Households affected by HIV/Aids have on average 30–35 per cent less income than those who are not affected. Around 60 per cent of families of Aids sufferers endure food shortages and malnutrition as a direct result of the disease.

Nationally HIV/Aids also poses a significant economic threat, with a projected annual loss in GDP growth per capita of 1.15 per cent forecast for the period 2000–10. Government spending on intervention plans was budgeted at US$560 million between 2002–05, of which US$88 million was allocated to antiretroviral treatment and US$126 million to hospital treatment. Zambia, as one of the poorest countries in the world, has been identified as in need of international aid to fight the disease.

A disturbing aspect of the disease that has been identified since 2001 is the gender disparity that has developed. Whereas the highest risk group was previously sexually active males, now women in general and young women in particular lead the male rates – by over 10 per cent in urban areas and over 5 per cent in rural areas. A UN taskforce studying this shift in the demographics has identified socio-economic forces that have left females vulnerable to the disease.

HIV prevalence: 15.6 per cent aged 15–49 in 2003 (World Bank)

Life expectancy: 36.5 years (World Bank)

Fertility rate/Maternal mortality rate: 5.0 births per woman; maternal mortality 6.5 per l,000 (World Bank).

Infant mortality rate: 102 per 1,000 live births; 28.1 per cent of children aged under 5 arre malnourished (World Bank).

Welfare

Zambia is one of the poorest countries in the world, with an estimated 80 per cent of its 11 million people living in desperate poverty. In December 2003 the statistics office stated that 'the food basket... was K528,529 for a family of six. The same family on average was expected to live on K758,961 for all their basic needs'.

The government provides some basic welfare for pensioners, children and people affected by disasters.

The Pension Scheme Regulation Act of 1996 provides a regulatory framework for private pension schemes. The Zambia National Provident Fund (ZNPF) was successfully transformed into the National Pension Scheme Authority (Napsa) in early 2000. The weaknesses of ZNPF, which included poor benefits, delays in payment and ineffective record keeping were critically examined to overcome similar problems for the Napsa. The economic difficulties in Zambia and the low retirement age of 55 made it necessary for Napsa to begin with modest benefits. The scheme offers three principal benefits namely retirement, invalidity and survivors' benefits. Additionally, it provides a funeral grant.

The scheme is based on the principle of social insurance and requires compulsory financial contributions from both employees and their employers at a rate of 5 per cent each. Retirement benefit is paid on the basis of a minimum contributory period of 15 years. The scheme is basic to allow the development of private occupational pension schemes.

Main cities

Lusaka (capital, estimated population 1.3 million in 2004), Ndola (349,300), Kitwe (306,200), Kabwe (219,600), Chingola (151,100), Mufulira (131,500), Luanshya (125,300), Livingstone (111,200).

Languages spoken

English is the usual medium for business. There are 73 identified African languages, all Bantu, of which seven are recognised as official vernaculars – Tonga, Lozi, Bemba, Kaonde, Luvale, Lunda and Nyanja. Zambian traders usually have a working knowledge of English.

Official language/s

English

Media

Press

Dailies: There are two principal national daily newspapers, *Times of Zambia* and *Zambia Daily Mail*.

Weeklies: Major weeklies including Sunday papers are *Zambezi Times Weekly*, *Sunday Mail*, *Sunday Times*, *Sun*, *Zambian Citizen*, *The Monitor* and *The Weekly Express*. *The Post* is Zambia's leading independent newspaper, published twice weekly.

Business: Publications include *The Financial Review* and *Financial Mail*.

Periodicals: Include the bi-monthly publication *National Mirror* and the monthly *New Age*. The Community Voice media, an organisation of young writers in Lusaka, launched the first community newspaper in March 1999 called *Community Voice*.

Broadcasting

Radio: A domestic service, in English and seven local languages, is provided by Zambia National Broadcasting Corporation (three channels).

Television: There are services broadcast in English and seven vernacular languages by Zambia National Broadcasting Corporation in Lusaka, Livingstone and Copperbelt towns and all provincial towns, namely Kasama, Chipata, Mongu, Solwezi, Mansa, Kabwe.

Economy

Zambia's main economic zone follows the rail-line southwards from the Copperbelt, around Ndola and Kitwe, through Lusaka, the capital, to Victoria Falls. This area has been subject to urbanisation, although the rest of the country is relatively sparsely inhabited. Approximately 52 per cent of GDP output is from the services sector, 27 per cent from industry and 21 per cent from agriculture.

Zambia

The main economic activity is mining, with copper making up 58 per cent of exports and cobalt around 19 per cent. The decline in the economy has mirrored the fall in both copper production and world copper prices. Economic restructuring since 1991 has focussed on the development of non-copper sectors, which have subsequently recorded growth. However, this has not stopped falling incomes, increased poverty, rising unemployment, increased debt and a growing informal sector. By 2002, the formal sector employed only 11 per cent of the labour force, while the informal sector employed 60 per cent. Two-thirds of Zambians, mainly in rural areas, face expenditure limits well below the cost of their basic needs and over a third spend at least 85 per cent of their income on food, making them vulnerable to price fluctuations caused by food shortages. Government statistics show that in December 2003 a family of six annually paid K528,529 for its food, whereas the average earnings for the family was K758,961. The country also faces high inflation and a widening current account deficit which are worsened by the continuing depreciation of the kwacha.

Full donor support and free market reform has had little impact on poverty and the economy still depends on the volatile price of copper while agricultural output is severely restricted by climatic change. In 2002, fears of an economic downturn were heightened when the mining conglomerate, Anglo American, withdrew from the Konkola Copper Mines (KCM) venture. Analysts estimated that if the Konkola mines close, 3 per cent of the workforce would be made redundant, with adverse consequences for the entire economy. Despite this, the economy managed growth in 2003 of 3.1 per cent. Unemployment was a significant problem with half the population unemployed and inflation was high at 21 per cent.

External trade

There are no restrictions on the importation of equipment.

Export formalities have been streamlined and exporters are free to trade in any currency at the current market rate.

On 31 December 2002, the US approved Zambia as being eligible for tariff preferences under the Africa Growth and Opportunities Act (AGOA). The legislation requires that countries are only eligible for greater access to US markets provided they have made continued progress toward a market-based economy, the rule of law, free trade, poverty reduction and the protection of workers' rights. This process is reviewed annually.

Regional trade is expected to improve with the opening in May 2004 of a road bridge across the River Zambezi between Namibia and Zambia.

Imports

Principal imports are machinery, transportation equipment, petroleum products, electricity, fertiliser; foodstuffs and clothing.

Main sources: South Africa (50.3 per cent total, 2004), Zimbabwe (13.2 per cent), UAE (5.3 per cent)

Exports

Principal exports are copper/cobalt (64 per cent), cobalt, electricity, tobacco, flowers and cotton.

Main destinations: Tanzania (14.1 per cent total, 2004), South Africa (13.2 per cent), China (9.1 per cent), Japan (7.9 per cent), Thailand (7.9 per cent), Switzerland (7.3 per cent), Belgium (6.7 per cent), Malaysia (4.0 per cent)

Agriculture

Farming

About 10 per cent of Zambia's 600 million hectares is arable land but only around 30 million hectares are under cultivation. There are more than 300,000 smallholders, mostly subsistence farmers, earning cash from growing mainly cotton and tobacco. About 500 highly mechanised commercial farms and estates account for 40 per cent of marketed crops and animal produce. The country has abundant perennial and underground water resources. Power generated by hydroelectric installations has been extended to some farming areas. In the wetter northern part of the country, tea and coffee thrive at the higher altitudes, with maize and millet at lower levels. The climate of the central province suits maize, soya beans, cotton and tobacco. The south and west are drier and suit sorghum, tobacco, cotton and groundnuts.

Agriculture accounts for approximately 21 per cent of GDP. Most state-run farms have been privatised. One problem that the industry faces is that much of the land is under tribal authority and difficult to access. In order to tackle this problem, the government has set up areas of virgin land, such as the Tazara Corridor Services (Tazcor), which are open for investment. Government policy has long been to achieve self-sufficiency in food production, increase exports and improve the supply of inputs to peasant farmers. Measures have included a wide range of production incentives, comprising preferential tax and loan rates, the encouragement of foreign investment and improvements in producer prices. The 2004 budget included a proposal to give away land to local and foreign investors.

Official policy has also encouraged new crops for export which include coffee, flowers and exotic vegetables for European markets. In contrast to these successful new crops, cashew nut production has failed to penetrate European markets. Regional integration means that farmers are finding foreign competition difficult as high production costs, high taxation levels and cheap imports continue to undermine their competitiveness. The country is marginally self-sufficient in food with maize surpluses in times of good weather.

The estimated crop production for 2004 included: 1,161,000 tonnes (t) maize, 1,800,000t sugar cane, 950,000t cassava, 135,000t wheat, 11,000t potatoes, 53,000t sweet potatoes, 19,000t sorghum, 2,200t barley, 12,000t rice, 17,000t pulses, 1,014,000t roots and tubers, 3,500t citrus fruit, 25,000t tomatoes, 25,640t oilcrops, 4,800t tobacco, 4,100t green coffee, 4,160t various spices, 750t tea, 22,000t cotton lint, 101,200t fruit in total, 267,400t vegetables in total. Estimated livestock production included: 127,074t meat in total, 40,800t beef, 11,000t pig-meat, 546t lamb, 4,728t goat meat, 36,500t poultry, 46,400t eggs, 64,200t milk, 200t honey, 5,355t cattle hides, 33,500t game meat.

Fishing

Annual commercial fish production is estimated at 70,000 tonnes. The sector suffers due to infrastructural difficulties, including lack of input supply, such as nets and boats, poor transport and storage facilities. The private sector has stepped up investment in fish marketing and distribution, fish farming and manufacturing of nets and boats.

The Department of Fisheries in Zambia and the Department of National Parks and Wildlife Management in Zimbabwe, with the co-operation of Norway and Denmark, have undertaken a project to facilitate the sustainable utilisation of the shared fisheries resources on Lake Kariba.

Forestry

Forest and other wooded land accounts for 42 per cent and 37 per cent of the total land area respectively. In 1990–2000, deforestation accounted for an annual average loss of 2.38 per cent of forest cover. Although nearly half of Zambia's land area is covered by forest, there are only a few commercially exploitable tree species. It is estimated that forests cover some 31.2 million hectares (ha), with most being open savannah woodlands and *miombo* woodland comprising around 80 per cent of the country's vegetation. There are large networks of protected areas constituting 32 per cent of the forests with around 20 national parks and more than 30 game management areas.

Charcoal is a significant cooking and heating fuel in rural areas but, in some regions, woodland has been ravaged and a severe shortage of charcoal is expected unless there is government sponsored replanting. There is some export of sawn timber, while most of the demand for paper products is met by imports.

Exports of forest materials in 2004 amounted to US$935,000 and imports amounted to US$3.8 million. Production in 2004 included 8,053,000 cubic metres (cum) roundwood, 515,000cum industrial roundwood, 157,000cum sawnwood, 319,000cum sawlogs and veneers, 17,900cum wood-based panels, 7,219,000cum wood fuel, 1,041,000t charcoal.

Industry and manufacturing

Industry contributes around 27 per cent to GDP in 2004. The sector employs 8 per cent of the labour force.

Macroeconomic stabilisation and divestiture of state assets has led to a severe contraction in these sectors of the economy. The government is no longer willing to subsidise the industrial and manufacturing sector. This change contrasts vividly with policy in the 1960s and 1970s whereby vast copper profits were used to establish one of the largest parastatal economies in Africa.

Targetted sectors for development include agriculture-derived processed products and non-traditional exports such as textiles, chemicals and engineering products. Industrial production increased by 5.1 per cent in 2003.

Tourism

Tourism is a growing sector, forecast to account for some 4.5 per cent of GDP in 2005 and generate over 55,000 jobs. Infrastructure remains underdeveloped, including air connections. The cost of air fuel is a serious problem. Nevertheless, visitor numbers continue to grow, rising from 577,526 in 2003 to 610,109 in 2004. The collapse of neighbouring Zimbabwe's tourist industry has benefitted the Zambian tourism, as visitors discover that the Victoria Falls can be viewed from the Zambian side. The government recognises the sector's importance and is aiming to attract a million visitors annually by 2010.

Mining

Zambia has enormous mineral wealth, with major deposits of copper, cobalt, lead, zinc, emeralds, aquamarine, amethyst and tourmaline. It also has small reserves of selenium, manganese, tin, nickel, iron, gold, silver and diamonds. The mining sector contributes around a fifth of GDP and employs around 10 per cent of the workforce. Copper and its by-products, mostly cobalt, account for around 90 per cent of mining production and mining exports. Zambia is also the second largest producer of cobalt (9,000 tons in 2004) after the Democratic Republic of Congo (DRC) (11,000 tons in 2004) and has one of the world's largest reserves. Substantial amounts of cobalt can be recovered from the copper slag heaps, for which Canada's Colossus Resources obtained a 25-year contract with the Zambia Consolidated Copper Mines (ZCCM) signed in 2000. The Nkana and Mufulira cobalt mines and refineries produce 1,800 tonnes per year (tpy) of cobalt. The Nkana and Nchanga mines produce more than half of Zambia's copper and 70 per cent of its cobalt.

In August 2002, Anglo American decided to formally quit its mining operations at the Konkola Copper Mines (KCM), which sought a new strategic equity partner. Anglo American's withdrawal followed nine years of negotiations over the privatisation of the mines and two years of operation. The decision was prompted by the drop in KCM's assets and high running costs (including US$350 million expenditure on upgrading facilities), while world metal prices were at the time low. The government pledged to keep the mines open and finally in August 2004 a formal agreement with Vedanta Resources Plc was announced whereby Vedanta Resources acquired a 51 per cent controlling stake in KCM for US$48.2 million in cash. Vedanta plans to expand production from the current (2005) 2 million tonnes per year (tpy) to 6 million tpy.

There is very little mining activity outside the Copperbelt although base metal exploration has continued in other regions. Zambia is prospecting for chromium, nickel, tin, tantalite and iron ore. The government allows private sector purchase and export of gemstones. Mining companies can retain 50 per cent of foreign exchange earnings.

Zambia contains approximately a quarter of the world's gem emeralds and accounts for an estimated 20 per cent of output of rough emeralds. Other gemstones mined on a smaller scale include amethysts in the Southern Province near Lake Kariba and Kalomo. Deposits of aquamarine and tourmaline are mined for the jewellery trade. Production of gemstones is estimated to be worth US$200 million annually.

Hydrocarbons

Zambia has no known oil or gas reserves and the country is dependent on imported fuel supplies. The 1,710km Tazama pipeline from Dar es Salaam, Tanzania, supplies oil to the Indeni refinery at Ndola. Oil imports are significant, accounting for about one-fifth of the total import bill, although imports have been cut back steadily since the mid-1980s in order to save foreign exchange. With Zambia's deal to buy crude oil directly from Iran oil prices in Zambia are likely to drop. Zambia does not import natural gas. Most coal is locally produced at the Maamba Collieries, which has reserves of over 50 million tonnes. Due to a variety of problems production has never exceeded 800,000 tonnes per year (tpy), compared with a rated capacity of 1.2 million tpy. The Maamba Collieries were privatised, with an 80 per cent share sold to Benicon Limited, in 1998. Zambia uses coal in the mining transformation process. All coal produced is consumed domestically and fulfils all domestic demand.

Energy

Almost 70 per cent of total domestic energy needs are met by hydroelectricity, mostly from plants at Kafue Gorge, Kariba North and Livingstone, which, together with several smaller hydroelectric and diesel plants, have a capacity of 1,700MW. The national demand for power is about 1,000MW, of which 70 per cent is accounted for by the mining industry. However, only 10 per cent of the population has access to electricity.

The Zambian Electricity Supply Company (Zesco) is the national electricity authority responsible for transmission and distribution. It is up for privatisation, although divestment has been delayed due to ongoing political disputes and its lengthy reorganisation in preparation for privatisation.

Zambia also owns the Central African Power Corporation (CAPC) with Zimbabwe. CAPC operates the two Kariba power stations. The country is able to export power to Zimbabwe, Botswana, Namibia and Tanzania and is connected to the Democratic Republic of Congo (DRC) (from which Zambia has imported electricity) and South Africa.

In September 2004, Zesco signed a memorandum of understanding with Farab International of Iran for construction of the US$100 million Itezhi-tezhi hydropower plant on the Kafue River, in Zambia's southern province, which will have a capacity of 120 megawatts.

Financial markets

Stock exchange

The Lusaka Stock Exchange (LuSE) was launched in 1994. There has been a slow response from foreign investors, despite Zambia's complete relaxation of controls on foreign exchange.

The Exchange performed relatively wel in 2004. The All Share Index ended the year 447.46 compared to 371.99 in 2003. The upward trend was as a result of significant gains recorded in Chilanga Cement,

Zambia

Farmers House and National Breweries Plc. This was as a result of increasing investor awareness, the favourable results these companies have been reporting, and the reduction in interest rates, which have made the capital market an attractive investment forum.

The Exchange recorded share volumes of 327,429,911 (against 820,43,079 in 2003) and a turnover of K47, 560,824,870 (K14, 064,081,461in 2003).

Banking and insurance

Zambia's banking sector has undergone a period of crisis and change. The liberalisation of the economy during the 1990s gave rise to the launch of a number of banks. Poor management and over-banking led to the closure of a number of these banks, prompting a wave of concern among investors and depositors who lost money.

In March 2003 the government first directed the Zambia Privatisation Agency (ZPA) to privatise the main state owned commercial bank, Zambia National Commercial Bank. 49 per cent of its shares were to be sold to a qualified investor with management rights, 25.8 per cent were to be offered to the Zambian public through the Zambia Privatisation Trust Fund (ZPTF), 25 per cent were to be retained by the government and the existing minority shareholders, who held 0.2 per cent, were to retain their shares. The ZPA called for tenders to be received by September 2005.

The largest commercial banks, Barclays Bank of Zambia and Standard Chartered Bank Zambia, are foreign-owned. However, since January 1972 all foreign-owned banks have been required to incorporate locally.

There are several state-owned development banks and other private financial institutions. The Development Bank of Zambia offers medium- and long-term loans and business consultancy services.The Agricultural Finance Company and Zambia Agricultural Development Bank were merged and renamed the Lima Bank. The government-owned Zambia State Insurance Corporation (ZSIC) is the major insurance company in Zambia. Other development banks include the state-owned Zambia National Building Society.

Central bank
Bank of Zambia

Main financial centre
Lusaka

Time
GMT plus two hours

Geography

Zambia is landlocked, bordered to the south by Zimbabwe and the Caprivi Strip (an extension of Namibia); to the south-east by Mozambique; to the east by Malawi; to the north-east by Tanzania; to the north and north-west by the Democratic Republic of Congo (DRC); and to the west by Angola.

About nine-tenths of the country is a high rolling plateau (900–1,200 metres above sea level) covered by savannah bush and woodland. The only relief from the monotony of the plateau is the Zambezi and Luangwa rift system. The Luapula River, part of the Congo River system, cuts into the northern part of the plateau.

Zambia takes its name from the Zambezi River. At 2,655km long, this is the third longest river in Africa.

Climate

Altitude governs Zambia's climate and it is generally cooler than its neighbours. There are three distinct seasons: cool and dry from May to August; hot and dry from September to October; and rainy from November to April. Rainfall varies widely across the country. The average temperature is 16 degrees Celsius (C) in the winter and 24 degrees C in summer.

The Zambezi and Luangwa river valleys can remain hot and humid all year, typical of tropical lowlands. They are particularly uncomfortable in the rainy season.

Dress codes

The contrast between morning, midday and evening temperatures means that a sweater is often required in the early morning and after sunset between April and September. A light raincoat or umbrella is useful during the wet season from November to April.

Dress is generally informal. Lightweight suits can be worn for most of the year; during the hot season tropical suits are preferable. Tailored safari suits are popular. A hat and sunglasses are useful for protection against the sun.

Most women wear cotton or other lightweight dresses during the day and evening. Warm dresses and lightweight coats are needed during the coldest season, June to August.

Entry requirements

Passports
Required by all.

Visa
Required by all, exceptions include those listed on the *Visa Application Instructions* (items 4 and 5) for tourist visits only, at http://www.zambiaembassy.org. Tourist visas can be obtained at all border crossings, fees will be levied in cash, usually sterling or dollars (exact amounts as change may not be available).

All business visits require a visa, obtained in advance. Applications should include a letter from a local company or organisation giving brief details of the nature of business and a full itinerary.

Currency advice/regulations
Foreign currency can be imported without limitation.

Health (for visitors)

Mandatory precautions
A yellow fever vaccination certificate is required if travelling from an infected area. Passengers travelling to Zambia by air should have a yellow fever vaccination certificate in case the aircraft is unavoidably detained in central Africa. A certificate of inoculation against cholera is required by travellers who have visited an infected area.

Advisable precautions
Malaria is present (especially the malignant falciparum strain which is resistant to chloroquine) from November to May throughout the country and all year in the Zambezi valley (both weekly nivaquine and daily paludrine should be taken). Rabies and bilharzia are also present, and visitors should avoid swimming or paddling in standing water. There is a worsening HIV/Aids epidemic in Zambia. Typhoid and typhus are rare. All water for drinking, brushing teeth or making ice should be sterilised. Milk is pasteurised and therefore safe. Vegetables should be cooked and fruit peeled.

Hotels

Several good quality hotels are available. Hotels are graded from one to five stars by the Hotels Board. A service charge of 10 per cent, plus 10 per cent sales tax are added to all bills. Room charges must be settled in foreign currency. Some hotels require a deposit to cover the room rate and an element for food and drink to be converted to Kwacha on arrival. Tipping not customary in Zambia but is acceptable.

Credit cards

Not widely accepted, except by hotels and duty-free shops.

Public holidays

Fixed dates
1 Jan (New Year's Day), 12 Mar (Youth Day), 1 May (Labour Day), 25 May (African Day), 24 Oct (Independence Day), 25 Dec (Christmas Day).

Variable dates
Good Friday, Easter Monday, Heroes' Day (first Mon of Jul), Unity Day (first Tue of Jul), Farmers' Day (first Mon of Aug).

Working hours

Banking
Mon–Fri: 0815–1430.

Business
Mon–Fri: 0800–1230, 1400–1630.
Government
Mon–Fri: 0800–1300, 1400–1700.
Shops
Privately owned: Mon–Fri: 0800–1700, Sat: 0800–1300; state-owned: Mon–Sat: 0800–1800, Sun: 0800–1200.
Note: There are wide variations outside city centres.

Telecommunications
Telephone/fax
Domestic service is limited and expensive.

Electricity supply
230V AC

Social customs/useful tips
Visitors normally entertain business guests in hotels or restaurants, while residents prefer to entertain informally at home or at their clubs. Temporary membership of clubs can normally be obtained on an introduction from friends.

Security
The stealing of cheques has become a problem in Zambia. Visitors are advised to carry travellers' cheques in small denominations and to cash only sufficient for current needs. There has also been a rise in violent crime due to the economic decline and care must be taken when travelling after dark. It is not regarded as advisable to travel by car between Lusaka and the Copperbelt after dark.

Getting there
Air
National airline: There is no national airline.
International airport/s: Lusaka International (Code: LUN), 26km from city; duty-free shop, bar, restaurant, bank, shops, car hire; Livingstone International Airport (LVI).
Airport tax: Adult international departures US$20, excluding transit passengers. Domestic departures, K12,000.
Surface
Road: There are tarred roads from Zimbabwe, Botswana, Namibia (Caprivi Strip), Democratic Republic of Congo (DRC), Tanzania and Malawi; motorists should check border post hours, and regulations concerning their vehicles. A customs bond may be required for the import of cars.
During the rainy season many rural roads are impassable. It is not advisable to travel by car between Lusaka and the Copperbelt after dark.
A road bridge across the River Zambezi, between Namibia and Zambia, opened in May 2004.
Rail: The Tanzania Zambia Railway Authority (Tazara) railway links Zambia to Tanzania – the connection is at Kapiri Mposhi.
Zambia Railways Limited (ZRL) connects with Zimbabwe, Mozambique, South Africa, Botswana and DRC.
Water: Services include ferries from Botswana (Kazungula) and steamers from Kigoma, Tanzania across Lake Tanganyika to Mpulungu.

Getting about
National transport
Air: There are regular flights from Lusaka to Livingstone and to the Copperbelt in the north. There are several flights a week from Lusaka to other centres including Mfuwe in the Luangwa valley. There is also a scheduled service to Johannesburg. Charter companies also operate but are in heavy demand. There is a total of around 150 airfields and airstrips.
Road: The total network is almost 40,000km, of which about 6,500km are main roads. Surfaced roads link main centres. During the rainy season many rural roads are impassable.
Buses: Eagle Travel runs regular coach services to numerous locations including tourist sites. Non-tourist services can be irregular and crowded.
Rail: A passenger service called the Kafubu Express, run by Zambia Railways Limited (ZRL), links Lusaka with Ndola, Livingstone and Kitwe. The total network is over 2,000km.
City transport
Taxis: These are available between airports and hotels and within town centres. They are generally unmetered.
Buses, trams & metro: A number of privately-owned companies run domestic services over a number of routes. Buses are irregular and crowded, especially during the rush hour.
Car hire
The Zambia Tourist Board has authorised over 16 car-hire firms serving mainly Lusaka, Livingstone and the Copperbelt which are the major urban and tourist centres. Car hire is usually on a chauffeur-driven basis. This is available from BIG-5 in foyer of Holiday Inn, Church Road, PO Box 30666, Lusaka (tel: 229-222). On special request, firms may offer self-drive car-hire services.

BUSINESS DIRECTORY
The addresses listed below are a selection only. While World of Information makes every endeavour to check these addresses, we cannot guarantee that changes have not been made, especially to telephone numbers and area codes. We would welcome any corrections.

Telephone area codes
The international direct dialling (IDD) code for Zambia is +260, followed by the area code and subscriber's number:

Chingola	2	Livingstone	3
Chipata	6	Luanshya	2
Choma	3	Lusaka	1
Kabwe	2	Mongu	7
Kasama	4	Ndola	2
Kitwe	2	Solwezi	8

Chambers of Commerce
Livingstone Chamber of Commerce and Industry, 29 Airport Road, PO Box 60648, Livingstone (tel/fax: 323-656; e-mail: denmar@zamtel.zm).

Lusaka Chamber of Commerce and Industry, Farmers House, Cairo Rod, PO Box 37997, Lusaka (tel: 221-266; fax: 224-114; e-mail: luschamb@zamnet.zm).

Zambia Association of Chambers of Commerceand Industry, Showgrounds, Great East Road, PO Box 30844, Lusaka (tel: 255-046; fax: 253-007; e-mail: zacci@zamnet.zm).

Banking
Barclays Bank of Zambia, Cairo Rd, PO Box 31936, Lusaka (tel: 228-858/66; fax: 222-519, 226-185).

Cavmont Merchant Bank Ltd, Fourth Floor, Tazara House, Independence Avenue, PO Box 38474, Lusaka (tel: 224 280; fax: 221 643; e-mail: info@cavmont.com.zm).

Citibank, Citibank House, PO Box 30037, Lusaka (tel: 229-025/6/7/8; fax: 226-264).

Indo Zambia Bank, 686 Cairo Rd, PO Box 35411, Lusaka (tel: 225-080, 222-622; fax: 225-090).

Investrust Bank Plc, Investrust House, Plot 4527/8, Freedom Way, PO Box 32344, Lusaka (tel: 238-733; fax: 237 060; e-mail: inquiries@investrustbank.co.zm).

Stanbic Bank, Cairo Rd, Woodgate House, PO Box 31955, Lusaka (tel: 229-071/3, 229-285/6; fax: 221-152, 225-380).

Standard Chartered Bank, PO Box 32238, Lusaka (tel: 229-242; fax: 222-092).

Union Bank, Zimco House, PO Box 34940, Lusaka (tel: 229-397/8; fax: 221-866).

Zambia National Commercial Bank, Cairo Rd, PO Box 33611, Lusaka (tel: 228-979, 221-355; fax: 224-006).

Central bank
Bank of Zambia, Bank Square, Cairo Road, PO Box 30080, Lusaka 10101 (tel: 228-888 fax: 221-764; e-mail: pr@boz.zm).

Zambia

Travel information
Tourism Council of Zambia, PO Box 36561, Lusaka (tel: 251-666; fax: 251-501; e-mail: tcz@zamnet.zm; internet: http://www.zambiatourism.com).

Zambian Express, Lusaka (tel: 222-060, 238-162/65; fax: 238-166; e-mail: zamex@zamnet.zm).

Ministry of tourism
Ministry of Tourism, PO Box 30575, Lusaka (tel: 227-645; fax: 225-174).

National tourist organisation offices
Zambia National Tourist Board (ZNTB), Tourist Centre, Mosi-oa-Tunya Road, PO Box 60342, Livingstone (tel: 321-404/5; fax: 321-487; e-mail: zntblive@zamnet.zm); Century House, Cairo Road, Lusaka Square, PO Box 30017, Lusaka (tel: 229-087/90; fax: 225-174; e-mail: zntb@zamnet.zm).

Zambian Airways, 5309 Dedan Kimathi Street, Mukuba Pension House, Lusaka (tel: 225-151; fax: 223-227; email: roanair@zamnet.zm).

Ministries
Ministry of Agriculture, Food and Fisheries, Mulungushi House, Box RW 50291, Lusaka (tel: 251-537/233; fax: 252-029).

Ministry of Commerce, Trade and Industry, Kwacha House Annex, PO Box 31968/34373, Lusaka (tel: 228-301, 221-184; fax: 226-673).

Ministry of Communication and Transport, PO Box 50065, Lusaka (tel: 251-444/938/740/759; fax: 002-601, 253-260).

Ministry of Community Development and Social Services, Fidelity House, PO Box 31958, Lusaka (tel: 227-840, 228-321; fax: 225-327).

Ministry of Defence, PO Box RW 17X, Lusaka (tel: 251-211, 254-667; fax: 254-670, 221-339, 253-875).

Ministry of Education, PO Box 50093, Lusaka (tel: 227-636; fax: 222-396).

Ministry of Energy and Water Development, Ministerial Headquarters, Lusaka (tel: 263-870; fax: 252-339).

Ministry of Environment and Natural Resources, Mulungushi House, PO Box 30055, Lusaka (tel: 252-711, 250-186; fax: 252-952).

Ministry of Finance, PO Box RW 50062, Lusaka (tel: 250-544, 227-668; fax: 250-501).

Ministry of Foreign Affairs, PO Box 50069, Lusaka (tel: 262-666; fax: 250-634/240, 252-867).

Ministry of Health, PO Box 30205, Lusaka (tel: 227-745, 223-435; fax: 223-435).

Ministry of Home Affairs, PO Box 50997, Lusaka (tel: 254-261/362; fax: 224-656, 254-669).

Ministry of Information and Broadcasting Services, PO Box 50200, Lusaka (tel: 251-766, 253-965; fax: 254-013, 252-391, 250-524).

Ministry of Labour and Social Security, PO Box 32186, Lusaka (tel: 227-640).

Ministry of Lands, Mulungushi House, PO Box 30069, Lusaka (tel: 252-288; fax: 250-130).

Ministry of Legal Affairs, PO Box 50106, Lusaka (tel: 251-588; fax: 253-695).

Ministry of Local Government and Housing, PO Box 34204, Lusaka (tel: 253-077; fax: 252-680).

Ministry of Mines and Minerals Development, PO Box 31969, Lusaka (tel: 252-990; fax: 251-224).

Ministry of Science, Technical Education and Vocational Training, PO Box 50464, Lusaka (tel: 229-673; fax: 252-951).

Ministry of Sports, Youth and Child Development, 4th Floor, Memaco House, Sapele Rd, Lusaka (tel: 227-168; fax: 223-996).

Ministry of Works and Supply, PO Box 50236, Lusaka (tel: 253-266; fax: 222-360).

Other useful addresses
Central Statistics Office, PO Box 31908, Lusaka.

Chilanga Cement plc, Kafue Road, PO Box 32639, Lusaka (tel: 225-2853, 701-297; fax: 252-853, 252-655).

Export Board of Zambia, PO Box 30064, Third Floor, State Lottery Building, Cairo Road, North End, Lusaka (tel: 228-106/7; fax: 222-509).

Lusaka Stock Exchange Ltd, Lusaka (tel: 228-594, 228-391; fax: 228-608, 225-969; e-mail: luse@zamnet.zm).

Metal Marketing Corp of Zambia, PO Box 35570, 10101 Lusaka (tel: 228-131/140).

National Air Charters, PO Box 33650, 10101 Lusaka (tel: 229-154, 228-274).

National Commission for Development Planning, PO Box 50268, Lusaka.

National Import & Export Corporation, PO Box 30282, 10101 Lusaka (tel: 228-018).

Nitrogen Chemicals, PO Box 360226, Kafue (tel: 311-531/5; fax: 311-313).

Zambia Consolidated Copper Mines Ltd (ZCCM), 5309 Dedan Kimathi Road, PO Box 30048, Lusaka (tel: 229-115; fax: 221-057).

Zambia Electricity Supply Corporation Ltd (Zesco), PO Box 33304, Stand 6949 Great East Road, Lusaka 10101 (tel: 223-970, 239-343, 225-074; fax: 223-971, 237-601, 239-343, 222-753).

Zambian Embassy (USA), 2419 Massachusetts Avenue, NW, Washington DC 20008 (tel: 202-265-9717; fax: 202-332-0826; e-mail: info@zambiainfo.org).

Zambia Industrial & Commercial Copper Industry Service Bureau, PO Box 22100, Kitwe.

Zambia Investment Centre, 5th Floor, Ndeke House, Haile Selassie Avenue, PO Box 34580, Lusaka (tel: 252-130, 252-152; fax: 252-150; e-mail: invest@zamnet.zm).

Zambia National Broadcasting Corporation, PO Box 50015, 10101 Lusaka (tel: 229-648).

Zambia National Oil Company Limited (ZNOC), Lusaka (tel: 222-135; fax: 220-144, 221-265).

Zambia Privatisation Agency (ZPA), Privatisation House, Nasser Road, PO Box 30819, Lusaka (tel: 227-851, 223-859, 227-791; fax: 225-270; e-mail: zpa@zamnet.zm).

Zambia Railways Ltd (ZRL), PO Box 80935, Kabwe (tel: 223-822, 222-201/209; fax: 228-023/025).

Zambia Telecommunications Co Ltd, Lusaka (tel: 611-111, 612-399; fax: 613-055, 615-855).

Internet sites
Zambian Express: http://www.africa-insites.com

Zambian gateway website: http://www.zamnet.zm

Zambian Statistical Office: http://www.zamstats.gov.zm

Africa Business Network: http://www.ifc.org/abn

AllAfrica.com: http://allafrica.com

African Development Bank: http://www.afdb.org

Africa Online: http://www.africaonline.com

Harambee Afrika (UK business club for traders with east, central and southern Africa; includes annotated web resource list): http://www.harambee.co.uk

Mbendi AfroPaedia (information on companies, countries, industries and stock exchanges in Africa): http://mbendi.co.za

Zimbabwe

KEY FACTS

Official name: Republic of Zimbabwe

Head of State: President Robert Gabriel Mugabe (Zanu-PF) (since 1980)

Head of government: President Robert Gabriel Mugabe

Ruling party: Zimbabwe African National Union-Patriotic Front (Zanu-PF) (re-elected 31 Mar 2005)

Area: 391,109 square km

Population: 14.71 million (2004)

Capital: Harare

Official language: English, Shona and Ndebele

Currency: Zimbabwe dollar (Z$) = 100 cents (a Z$50,000 bearer note went into circulation Jan 2005, pending introduction of a new currency)

Exchange rate: Z$26,003.40 per US$ (Oct 2005); (weighted average auction rate from 31 Jan 2004; the Z$ was devalued by 4.3 per cent on 27 Jul 2004 – the third devaluation in eight months.)

GDP per capita: US$496 (2004)

GDP real growth: -4.80% (2004)

Labour force: 5.94 million (2004)

Unemployment: 70.00% (2003)

Inflation: 282.40% (2004)

Balance of trade: -US$190.00 million 2004

Foreign debt: US$3.90 billion (2003)

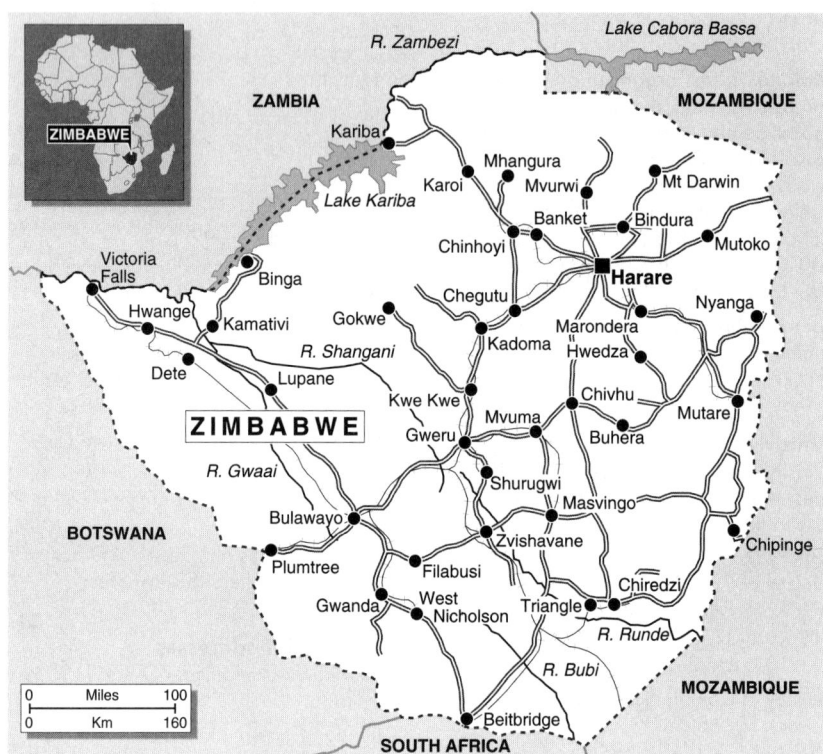

Zimbabwe's living standards and social indicators have deteriorated rapidly over the last few years. The estimated proportion of the population living below the official poverty line has more than doubled to 80 per cent since the mid-1990s due to decreasing real incomes and rising unemployment. The ability of the government to increase spending on social programmes is limited by the continuous economic decline and the resulting rise in the demand for social assistance.

Politics

The political situation remains difficult. Relations with the international community have become increasingly strained and external financial support is confined to humanitarian assistance. The ruling Zimbabwe African National Union Patriotic Front (ZANU-PF) party won a two-thirds majority in the parliamentary elections held on 31 March 2005. Although less violence was reported than in previous elections, the opposition party and Western governments criticised the elections as being neither free nor fair. Nevertheless, governments in the region, as well as the Southern African Development Community (SADC) and the African Union accepted the results.

Difficult living conditions

The plight of the poor in Zimbabwe has been further worsened by food insecurity. There has been an overall contraction in agricultural production. About 40 per cent of the population is expected to continue to be food insecure through 2006. There has been a sharp deterioration of the medical infrastructure and shortages of essential drugs and equipment, particularly in public hospitals. Remuneration for health sector staff is inadequate and protective working materials are lacking. The public sector has a deficit of 843 medical doctors from an established complement of 1,530, and a deficit of 4,700 nurses from an established complement of 11,640.

Zimbabwe

Students increasingly drop out from school. Primary school enrolment rates over the last five years have dropped substantially. Many households are too poor to afford the US$4 a term school fees. As with health care, the standard of education has fallen significantly due to staff attrition. Increasingly unattractive working conditions, low salaries, heavy workloads and inadequate basic teaching materials have lowered the morale of teachers.

Zimbabwe has experienced a substantial brain drain, with an estimated 30 per cent of the population now living outside the country. To stop the outflow of labour from the public sector, the government substantially increased wages in the 2005 budget. As a result, the public sector wage bill share of gross domestic product (GDP) doubled to 18 per cent, creating substantial fiscal pressures.

Land reform

A land reform programme adversely affected various social dimensions. More than 80 per cent of commercial farmland was redistributed to indigenous experienced and would-be farmers. Few of the owners were compensated. Rural social infrastructure which had been provided by the mainly white farmers collapsed. Food insecurity increased. About 300,000 farm workers and their families lost their homes and their incomes. There were significant losses in agricultural capital stock and production, uneven distribution of land and infrastructure and a lack of security of tenure. Large scale commercial farming has been effectively destroyed. The number of large-scale farming units declined from 3,217 at the beginning of 2000 to about 250 partially-operational as of 2005. The output of the commercial agricultural sector is down to between five to 20 per cent of 2000 levels. Much of the on-farm infrastructure was removed, stolen, or vandalised in the process of taking over farms.

The recent Operation Restore Order that entailed the demolition of illegal dwellings and structures has created a humanitarian crisis. The United Nations has estimated that 700,000 people across the country have lost either their homes, or their source of livelihood, or both. A further 2.4 million have been indirectly affected in varying degrees.

Economy in free fall

Inflation rose to an annual rate of 320 per cent in 2005, while the exchange rate fell from Z$24 per US dollar in 2000 to nearly Z$100,000 per US cent in early 2006. Zimbabwe is now issuing 50,000 dollar banknotes, the 20,000 dollar bill is only enough to buy half a loaf of bread.

Net donor aid flows have fallen from around US$375 million in 1996 to an estimated US$240 million. In absolute terms less aid has been provided while the need for it has drastically risen. Badly needed support from the International Monetary Fund (IMF) remains suspended because of the country's failure to meet budgetary goals and repay US$136 million owed to the IMF.

Members of the IMF visited Zimbabwe in February 2006 to conduct a review of the current economic situation. The delegation emphasised that without comprehensive economic and political reforms, Zimbabwe's prospects would be bleak. The fund stood ready to assist the authorities in designing an appropriate package to help achieve macroeconomic stability and growth. A further meeting to review Zimbabwe's overdue financial obligations to the IMF was tentatively scheduled for early March.

The World Bank lending programme in Zimbabwe is inactive due to arrears. The Bank's role is now limited to technical assistance and analytical work focusing on macroeconomic policy, food security issues, social sector expenditures, social service delivery mechanisms and HIV/Aids.

Outlook

Robert Mugabe played a key role in ending white rule in Rhodesia and he and his Zanu-PF party have dominated Zimbabwe's politics since independence in 1980. He is an African leader of the 1960s – strong and ruthless, anti-Western, suspicious of capitalism and deeply intolerant of dissent and opposition.

For years Zimbabwe was a major tobacco producer and a potential bread basket for surrounding countries. Now, its economy is in tatters, poverty and unemployment are endemic and political strife and repression commonplace.

The main challenge to Mugabe comes from the opposition Movement for Democratic Change (MDC). The MDC says its members have been killed, tortured and harassed by Zanu-PF supporters. The president says the party is a tool of the West. In late 2005/early 2006 the MDC split. Morgan Tsvangerai was accused of being weak and ineffective. Gibson Sibanda, who had been instrumental in launching the MDC with Tsvangerai heads the splinter group.

In 2005 Zanu-PF won more than two-thirds of the votes in parliamentary elections, again said by the MDC to be fraudulent. This enabled Mugabe to change the constitution, paving the way for the creation of an upper house of parliament, the Senate.

The future for Zimbabwe rests with Mr Mugabe and how much longer he can hang on. In early 2006 there were rumours of defections from the ruling ZANU party, some even joining the United People's Movement (UPM) under former information minister Jonathan Moyo. However, until a safe exit route for Mr Mugabe and his cronies (and wife) can be agreed, it seems unlikely that Zimbabwe's situation will change for the better.

KEY INDICATORS — Zimbabwe

	Unit	2000	2001	2002	2003	2004
Population	m	12.63	12.30	12.31	13.51	14.71
Gross domestic product (GDP)	US$bn	5.40	4.70	4.80	4.60	–
GDP per capita	US$	428	365	373	359	496
GDP real growth	%	-4.2	-7.3	-5.6	-13.1	-4.8
Inflation	%	55.9	76.7	140.0	431.7	282.4
Coal output	mtoe	2.6	3.2	2.7	1.9	2.1
Exports (fob) (goods)	US$m	1,801.0	1,715.0	1,730.0	1,225.0	1,409.0
Imports (fob) (goods)	US$m	1,500.0	1,455.0	1,410.0	1,914.0	1,599.0
Balance of trade	US$m	301.0	260.0	317.0	-689.0	-190.0
Current account	US$m	-10.0	-460.0	-5,700.0	410.0	-310.0
Foreign debt	US$bn	3.9	3.8	4.0	3.9	4.7
Total reserves minus gold	US$m	193.1	64.7	83.4	–	–
Foreign exchange	US$m	192.5	64.3	82.9	–	–
Exchange rate	per US$	46.66	55.28	55.45	438.72	4,303.28

Nations of the World: A Political, Economic and Business Handbook

Risk assessment

Economic	Disastrous
Political	Uneasy
Regional Stability	Good

COUNTRY PROFILE

Historical profile
In the eleventh century, the Shona people of Great Zimbabwe began trading with the Swahili traders on the Mozambique coast. Great Zimbabwe became southern Africa's richest and most powerful nation. In the 1500s, as Great Zimbabwe began to decline, the various Shona tribes broke up into autonomous states. Alliances between Shona states led to the formation of the Rozwi state.
1830–1890 European venturers and missionaries explored much of the south. Cecil John Rhodes was one who gained great wealth from the diamonds found in the area.
1834 The Ndebele people, push out of present day South Africa, invaded and established the Ndebele state.
1889 Rhodes founder of the British South Africa Company (BSA) and was granted the territories that today comprise Zimbabwe, under a British mandate as Southern Rhodesia.
1890 White migration began as settlers arrived.
1893 The BSA crushed a Ndebele uprising.
1922 The white minority voted to become a self-governing British dominion.
1930s Opposition to colonial rule began to grow.
1953 The Central African Federation (CAF) was created, merging Southern Rhodesia (Zimbabwe), Northern Rhodesia (Zambia) and Nyasaland (Malawi).
1960s The Zimbabwe African People's Union (Zapu, mainly Ndebele) and the Zimbabwe African National Union (Zanu mainly Shona) were formed.
1963 The CAF collapsed after Zambia and Malawi elected to become separate independent states.
1964 Ian Smith of the Rhodesian Front (RF) became prime minister. He gained independence from Britain with an electoral system that would preserve white minority rule.
1965 The RF made a unilateral declaration of independence (UDI). Despite international sanctions, Smith managed to keep his regime intact until 1980, with the support of apartheid South Africa and Portugal's colonialist regime in Mozambique. Zapu and Zanu began a campaign of guerrilla warfare.
1976 Although Zanu and Zapu formed the Patriotic Front (PF) alliance, co-operation between the two remained limited.
The civil war continued and intensified towards the end of the 1970s.
1979 A new constitution, favourable to the PF, was drawn up at Lancaster House in the UK.
1980 Robert Mugabe's Zanu party won the general election and Zimbabwe gained independence from Britain. Mugabe became prime minister. Opposition leader Joshua Nkomo was appointed to the cabinet.
1982 Nkomo was sacked after Mugabe accused him of plotting to overthrow the government. Zapu was largely destroyed by the North Korean-trained Fifth Brigade which Mugabe sent into Matabeleland. According to the Catholic church a systematic campaign of terror was carried out against the rural population.
1987 Zanu and Zapu put their differences behind them and merged to form the Zimbabwe African National Union-Patriotic Front (Zanu-PF). Mugabe changed the constitution and became executive president.
1997 The economy crashed due to concerns about compensation payments to former guerrillas and the consequences of seizing 1,480 of mostly white-owned farms. Mass, violent demonstrations ensued.
1998 A national general strike due to soaring food prices, gained 80 per cent commitment. Mugabe decided, without consulting parliament, to intervene in the war in Democratic Republic of Congo (DRC) by sending troops.
2000 So-called 'squatters' seized hundreds of white-owned farms in a campaign of intimidation. Mugabe lost a referendum vote for constitutional amendments. Zanu-PF won the parliamentary election by a narrow majority, against the Movement for Democratic Change's (MDC). Protests in Harare, against rises in food prices and demanding Mugabe's resignation, turned into riots.
2001 The finance minister declared that foreign reserves had run out. The World Bank and IMF cut aid due to ongoing land seizure programme. A list of 2,030 white-owned farms required to be handed over under the new land-acquisition law, was published.
2002 New legislation outlawed criticism of the president and gave sweeping powers to the police to maintain public order. The EU imposed sanctions on 20 members of the Zimbabwean government, including the president, after its team of election observers was expelled. Robert Mugabe was re-elected in controversial circumstances. His opponent, Morgan Tsvangirai, was arrested on trumped up charges of treason. Zimbabwe was suspended from the Commonwealth. The opposition failed in its legal challenge to the election results. Media freedom was curtailed.
2003 The currency was devalued by 93 per cent. The US imposed economic sanctions on President Mugabe and 76 other high-ranking government officials, freezing their assets and barring Americans from conducting business with them. Zimbabwe withdrew from The Commonwealth after it refused to end Zimbabwe's suspension, citing Mugabe's election-rigging and persecution of dissidents.
2004 After their plane was impounded in Harare, 70 mercenaries planning a coup in Equatorial Guinea, were detained and charged.
2005 The ruling Zanu-PF was re-elected in the 31 March parliamentary elections with an increased majority; the opposition MDC claimed the elections were rigged. In May/June, thousands of shanty homes and businesses were demolished by the government, and around 200,000 people made homeless. As a result of the increased majority, in August the government passed a number of constitution amendments, including the re-introduction of a 66-seat upper house (Senate). Also in August charges of treason against Morgan Tsvangirai, leader of the opposition, were dropped. Elections to the upper house were held on 26 November. The Consumer Council reported at the end of the year that the cost of buying groceries increased almost 10-fold during the year. Bread rose by some 1,157 per cent.

Political structure
Constitution
The constitution was first instigated in 1979, based on articles agreed in the Lancaster House accord. An amendment in 1987 resulted in the appointment of an executive president as Head of State.
The election laws were amended in January 2002 to ban independent election monitors and deny voting rights to Zimbabweans living abroad.
Further amendments to the constitution, in 2005, included the re-introduction of an upper house – the Senate. The Senate has 66 members – 50 members elected for five-year terms (five from each of the 10 provinces), 10 traditional chiefs and six members appointed by the president.

Form of state
Republic

The executive
Executive power is vested in the president (elected by universal suffrage every six years), vice presidents and cabinet. Both the vice presidents and cabinet are appointed by the president.

National legislature
Legislative power is vested in the parliament, comprising a 150-member House of Assembly (lower house) and

Zimbabwe

66-member Senate (upper house). The lower house is made up of 120 directly elected members; twenty are nominated by the president and the remaining 10 are traditional chiefs' representatives and provincial governors. The Assembly is also elected every five years. It comprises five members directly elected from each of the 10 provinces, 10 traditional chiefs and six appointed by the president.

Legal system
Based on the constitution and English common law.

Last elections
31 March 2005 (parliamentary); 9–11 March 2002 (presidential).
Results: Parliamentary: the ruling Zanu-PF was re-elected with 58.8 per cent of the vote (78 seats out of 150); the MDC won 37.5 per cent (41 seats); one independent won a seat; there are 20 presidential appointees and 10 *ex-officio* members (traditional chiefs).
Presidential: controversially Robert Mugabe (Zanu-PF) was re-elected with 55 per cent of the vote, against 42 per cent for Morgan Tsvangirai (MDC).

Next elections
14 January 2006 (local authority); 2008 (presidential); 2010 (parliamentary).

Political parties
Ruling party
Zimbabwe African National Union-Patriotic Front (Zanu-PF) (re-elected 31 Mar 2005)
Main opposition party
Movement for Democratic Change (MDC)

Population
14.71 million (2004)
Ethnic make-up
Shona (75 per cent) (including the Zezuru clan (18 per cent) and the Karanga clan (22 per cent)); Ndebele (18 per cent); white (1 per cent). There are several minor ethnic groups, and a small number of inhabitants of Asian or mixed racial descent.
Religions
Dual Christian/indigenous beliefs (50 per cent), Christian (25 per cent), indigenous beliefs (24 per cent).

Education
The educational system was one of the best in the region with universal primary school enrolment and secondary education reaching about 50 per cent of those eligible.
The worsening public finances has put the country's education facilities at risk as the government rationalises non-military expenditure. With increases in education levies of between 400 per cent and 2,000 per cent in 2003–04, impoverished families are increasingly unable to find the money to send their children to school.
Primary enrolment has declined from 93 per cent in 2000 to 65 per cent in 2003. When schools reassembled for the winter term 2004, they were forced to turn away 800,000 orphans because President Mugabe's government has run out of money to pay their fees.
Literacy rate: 90 per cent, total; 86.3 per cent, female; adult rates (World Bank).
Compulsory years: Five to 12.
Enrolment rate: 95.0 per cent gross primary enrolment; 44.5 per cent gross secondary enrolment, of relevant age groups (including repeaters) (World Bank).
Pupils per teacher: 37 in primary schools.

Health
The state of Zimbabwe's healthcare was mixed in the 1990s. Spending on private healthcare (such as private household expenditure and insurance) averaged 3.7 per cent of GDP.
Estimates in 2002 showed that 24 per cent of health workers' posts were vacant and 73 per cent of health facilities had no drugs.
In 2005 the UK gave over US$17.9 million to UN and non-governmental agencies (NGO) to provide food for five million people affected by food shortages. Around US$1 million will be allocated to help those who have returned to their rural homes after being evicted under the government's Operation Murambatsvina.

HIV/Aids
The UN stated, in April 2005, that one million children have been made orphans and another 160,000 would lose a parent in 2005. Unicef called on donor countries to look beyond the political administration of Zimbabwe and focus on the victims of the disease. Only US$14 is contributed for each Zimbabwean compared to US$68 for citizens of neighbouring Namibia or US$111 in Mozambique. With one of the highest infection rates in the region, with an estimated 1.8 million people HIV positive in 2003 Zimbabwe's sick can ill-afford international neglect. Poor governance, profligacy and the politicisation of relief by President Mugabe has left donors averse to giving more. The HIV prevalence rate for females aged 15–24 years is 33 per cent and the incidence of mother-to-child transmission of HIV/Aids is 12 per cent, and these pose another serious impediment to Zimbabwe's embattled population.
HIV prevalence: 24.65 per cent aged 15–49 in 2003 (World Bank)
Life expectancy: 33 years in 2003 (Unicef)
Fertility rate/Maternal mortality rate: 3.9 births per woman; maternal mortality 400 per 100,000 live births (World Bank).
Infant mortality rate: 78 per 1,000 live births; 13 per cent of children under aged five are malnourished (World Bank).
Head of population per physician/bed: 6 physicians and 50 hospital beds available per 100,000 people

Welfare
Many companies operated some form of social security plan for their employees, which usually included medical aid but the deteriorating economy has curtailed welfare measures. Workers may individually contribute to private insurance and medical aid funds.

Main cities
Harare (capital, estimated population 2.0 million in 2004), Bulawayo (1.0 million), Mutare (189,000), Gweru (154,900).

Languages spoken
Local languages, Shona and Ndebele spoken by the majority of the population, are written languages and are taught in schools.
Official language/s
English, Shona and Ndebele

Media
The government operates a highly repressive policy towards the media and members of Zanu-PF have occasionally bombed the offices of some newspapers. In 2002, criticism of President Mugabe was outlawed by the Public Order and Security Act (POSA). The *Access to Information* law makes it an offence to report from Zimbabwe unless state-registered; only Zimbabwean citizens or residents of the country are eligible for registration. Foreign journalists are only allowed into the country to cover specific events and a registration levy of US$12,000 is imposed; through these measures the government is able to limit independent investigation and press freedom.

Press
Dailies: Major English-language dailies include *The Herald*, published in Harare, *The Chronicle* and *Zimbabwe Independent*.
The Daily News, the only privately owned daily paper, published by Associated Newspapers of Zimbabwe, was closed down in September 2003.
Weeklies: Weekly newspapers include *Zimbabwe Standard* and *The Gweru Times* (bi-lingual weekly in English and Shona). *Kwayedza* and *The Manica Post* cover current and political affairs. National Sunday newspapers are *The Sunday Mail* and *The Sunday News*.
Business: *The Financial Gazette* is the country's only wholly independent newspaper, published in Harare. *The Farmer* published weekly covers agricultural matters. Business news is also covered by *The Chronicle*, published in Bulawayo, *Manica*

Post, published in Mutare, and some regional publications.
Periodicals: *Journal of Social Development in Africa* is published twice annually featuring development issues. *Skyhost* covers travel and *Moto* current affairs.
Broadcasting
Radio: There are radio services in English, Shona and Ndebele.
Television: Two television channels, broadcasting for about 45 hours per week, are transmitted by the Zimbabwe Broadcasting Corporation (ZBC). Satellite systems are available.

Economy
Since 1999, when Zimbabwe began a programme of land-resettlement – mainly white farmers dispossessed and their land given to black Zimbabweans, who were largely inexperienced farmers. Zimbabwe has been characterised by food shortages, lack of foreign exchange and hyperinflation. Agriculturally, Zimbabwe was largely self-sufficient in the 1990s, but by 2005, over 33,000 tonnes of maize had to be imported each week to feed the population and over 40 per cent of the population relied on international food aid. The UN Food Agency warned that following poor harvests in 2004 there were no seed stocks for the 2005 planting and food insecurity was growing. Hyperinflation in 2004 reached 282.4 per cent and resulted in foodstuffs becoming absent from markets.

For over five years GDP growth has been negative. In 2004, GDP contracted by 4.8 per cent, showing a slight improvement on the -13.1 per cent of 2003. Nevertheless, GDP is projected to decline by around 7 per cent in 2005.

Agricultural exports have halved since 2000 from US$855 million to US$400 million in 2004. The principal export used to be tobacco leaves but in 2004 only 64,000 tonnes were exported compared to 230,000 tonnes in 2000.

Minerals now constitute the main export commodities and are the mainstay of the economy. Zimbabwe has the second-largest reserves of platinum, which is easy to extract and has lower production costs than the first ranking, South Africa. Two mining companies, currently active, wish to expand their operations but are leery of government plans for land tenure and 'economic empowerment provisions' – where companies would be required to sell a 20 per cent stake to local Zimbabweans and 30 per cent within 10 years. The mineral reserves have attracted the attention of the Chinese, who are assiduously investing in Africa, and may have backed the government diplomatically and financially and allowed it to repay IMF US$120 million loan in August 2005.

The economy at the domestic level is all but stagnated and at the international level is constrained by hyperinflation and the black market.

The Zimbabwe dollar has been devalued dramatically and was the worst performing currency in 2004, falling 85.6 per cent against the US dollar. Official rates at the beginning of 2005 pegged it at Z$5,711, by May it was Z$9,000 and in July it was anywhere between Z$10,800–17,500 (representing, within three months, a cumulative devaluation of 182 per cent). In October 2005, with the Zimbabwe dollar trading officially at Z$26,000 per US$, and unofficially at Z$90,000, and inflation running at 360 per cent the Central bank allowed the currency to trade freely in order to allow exporters to trade 70 per cent of their foreign currency earnings at the market rate, as long as they 'surrendered' the other 30 per cent to the central bank. This measure is intended to encourage business to increase exports. Observers consider this a positive move but one that will take time to benefit the economy.

The IMF has warned that the continued difficulties will cause GDP growth to decline by as much as 7 per cent in 2005 and a widening fiscal deficit will push up inflation to over 400 per cent.

External trade
Zimbabwe's competitiveness on international markets was severely hampered by the country's currency, which was set at an overvalued peg against the US dollar until 2005 when it was allowed to float. Exports by Zimbabwe's key commercial farming sector have plumeted since 2003. Coupled with declining foreign investment and a lack of hard currency, this led to continued problems for Zimbabwe's external trade balance in 2004/05. In an effort to ease the situation, in January 2006 the RBZ announced a number of incentives for exporters.

Imports
Main imports are machinery and transport equipment, other manufactures, chemicals and fuels.
Main sources: South Africa (47.2 per cent total, 2004), Democratic Republic of the Congo (6.2 per cent), China (4.4 per cent)

Exports
Main exports are gold, cotton, tobacco, ferroalloys, textiles and clothing.
Main destinations: South Africa (11.9 per cent total, 2004), Zambia (6.3 per cent), China (3.4 per cent)

Agriculture
Farming
Agriculture used to be the dominant sector of the economy. Since 1999 government policy has skewed typical patterns. Whereas Zimbabwe was almost self-sufficient in food with annual exports of around US$70 million, in 2004, imports of food were estimated at US$280 million, in addition to the immense aid provided through the World Food Programme. Since 2000, the government has appropriated white-owned farm property with little or no compensation. Over 200,000 black agricultural workers lost their jobs when corporate and white-owned farms were confiscated and the land given to 124,000 black families. The government has not sought to combine land transfers with the necessary capital and expertise to run the farms and this has resulted in the virtual destruction of the commercial farming sector. The agricultural sector is now firmly small scale, poorly invested, subsistence farming. It is estimated that 85 per cent of Zimbabwe households rely on farm wages for food and other needs.

In June 2004, President Mugabe's government said that, in future, all land would be owned by the state and then leased back to farmers.

Concerted measures employed to ensure increased agricultural production are hampered by a lack of farm machinery and foreign exchange to purchase the necessary equipment.

It is estimated that the country has to import 250,000 tonnes of maize to meet expected shortfalls.

Primary crop production for 2004 was 1,227,280 metric tonnes (t) cereals in total (2,538,429t in 2000), *1,000,000t maize (2,108,110t in 2000), 80,000t wheat (250,000t in 2000), 25,000t barley (32,000t in 2000), 84,000t soya beans (143,592t in 2000), *4,100,000t sugar cane (4,227,500t in 2000) *80,000 tobacco leaves (227,277t in 2000)
* estimate

Fishing
Despite the existence of five major flood plains, the country has little fishery potential. There are no natural lakes of any significant size and large man-made reservoirs are primarily used for hydro-electric and farming purposes.

Lake Kariba accounts for approximately 80 per cent of the country's total fish production. The industrial fishery thrives on fresh water sardines (kapenta) which were introduced to the lake from Lake Tanganyika. Lake Kariba also supports an artisanal gillnet fishery, which is based on 40 indigenous species near the lake's shores. This type of activity is important for the local economy, as most of the land available along the shore is unsuitable for crop cultivation.

The catch from reservoirs other than Lake Kariba is typically estimated at 2,000 tonnes per year. The bulk of the catch from these small reservoirs is not usually marketed but kept for domestic consumption. The catch from small dams typically constitutes another 2,000 tonnes, while rivers and fish farms are estimated to yield 1,000 tonnes of fish.

Forestry
Around half of Zimbabwe's land area is forested; between 1990–2000, it lost over 320,000 hectares (ha), an average 1.54 per cent of forest cover each year, which was twice the African average. Forests are primarily used for fuelwood, which at an annual average of eight million cubic metres of roundwood, provides three-quarters of domestic energy supplies. The country's main exported forest product is sandalwood.

Industry and manufacturing
Zimbabwe's industrial sector was one of the most advanced and diversified in sub-Saharan Africa. Since 2000, the sector has been undermined by capital flight, a lack of foreign exchange, an overvalued exchange rate, severe fuel shortages and the constant threat of forced nationalisation. The largely liberalised textile sector is also struggling against competition from countries such as South Africa where subsidies and tariffs operate as barriers to free trade.

Other problems include a lack of capacity which can only be improved with increased foreign investment. As supporters of the Zanu-PF begin to attack foreign companies operating in Zimbabwe, prospects for industrial expansion are bleak. Successful and successive general stikes were called through 2004–05 to register the growing plight of low wages. Zimbabwe's heavy industries are also facing hard times, despite being targetted by the government as essential to developing import substitutes, which would reduce the loss in foreign exchange. In recent years, Zimbabwe has experienced an expansion in the chemicals and cement sectors. Growth in industrial production in 2004 was a negative -3.5 per cent in 2004.

Tourism
Tourism has stagnated as Zimbabwe is becoming increasingly viewed as a pariah state. Repressive regimes do not attract much tourism and Zimbabwe is losing much foreign exchange from this potentially lucrative industry. The continuing perception in important markets, such as the US, UK and Australia is that Zimbabwe is unsafe, compounded by government travel warnings. Hotels have become dependent on NGOs for business, but this is threatened by proposed government legislation to curb NGO activity.

Government statistics are unreliable. The World Travel and Tourism Council regards the country as one of the lowest ranked for contributions to national GDP – 1.4 per cent in 2005. The sector may grow, but not from Western foreign tourists. The expectation is that tourism will decline by around 3.3 per cent between 2006–15. The tourist sector is estimated to have attracted 8.4 per cent of total capital investment but this is a 2.6 per cent fall on previous years.

A symptom of the sector's malaise is the collapse of Victoria Falls as a centre, since tourists find that they can view the falls from Zambia, where tourism has benefited considerably from its neighbour's troubles. Zimbabwe is courting the fledgling Asian market, especially China, which has granted Approved Destination Status to the country.

Mining
The mining sector accounts for around 8 per cent of GDP and employs 5 per cent of the workforce. Many minerals, including chromite, copper and nickel ores, iron ore, tin ore, gold ore, phosphate rock, limestone and iron pyrites are converted to downstream products. The main exceptions are coal, phosphate rock, pyrites and limestone, which, along with a substantial proportion of iron, steel, copper and asbestos production are sold on the domestic market. Import substitution is encouraged. However, high fuel prices have increased costs markedly.

The government's policy on land and assets tenure has left foreign companies concerned that their assets could be seized without cause or warning. The 'economic empowerment provisions' require companies to sell a 20 per cent stake to local black investors and 30 per cent by 2015.

Illegal trade in gold has risen due to the low prices paid to small gold producers.

Hydrocarbons
There are no proven oil deposits in Zimbabwe. Zimbabwe has no refining capacity and traditionally imports its oil from South Africa. The National Oil Company of Zimbabwe (Nocizm) is responsible for supplying the country with oil, but supplies are unreliable due to a high fuel prices and its inability to pay its bills.

Coal is for domestic use only. Around 60 per cent of coal production is used for electricity generation. The Wankie Coal Company (WCC) is the country's only coal producer and is 40 per cent owned by the government. Annual production is typically around four million tonnes. There are no proven natural gas deposits in Zimbabwe.

Energy
Coal provides 60 per cent of local electricity generating capacity with wood, oil and hydroelectric power providing the rest. Zimbabwe continues to face problems relating to the rising cost of oil and electricity imports. This has resulted in severe debts within the electricity sector and continual threats to the power supply. Emphasis is on developing local energy resources, particularly coal and hydropower. Projects under way involve expansion of the huge Hwange coal field, including two new thermal power stations, and the building of hydroelectric stations on the Zambezi River.

The Zimbabwe Electricity Supply Authority (Zesa), which oversees generation, transmission and distribution of electricity, has plans for a number of projects aimed at rehabilitating existing power generators, as well as creating new ones. Zimbabwe is keen to co-operate with neighbouring states and will be largely helped by the growing ties within the Southern African Development Community (SADC). The government also has ambitious, and probably unrealistic, plans to provide hundreds of rural districts with electricity through solar power to provide lighting as well as helping rural industries.

Financial markets
Stock exchange
Zimbabwe's first stock exchange was formed in 1896, but lasted just six years. The current Zimbabwe Stock Exchange (ZSE) was founded in 1946 and was located in Bulawayo. In 1974, the Zimbabwe Stock Exchange Act was promulgated and the ZSE was relocated to Harare.

Banking and insurance
Before the economic crisis that began in 2000, Zimbabwe had a sophisticated banking system. Performance has been adversely affected by the macroeconomic environment, including the government's foreign exchange regime, negative interest rates and the high level of domestic borrowing.

The banking sector comprises the Reserve Bank of Zimbabwe (RBZ) (central bank), five commercial banks, four merchant banks, five finance houses (mainly engaged in hire purchase), two discount houses serving the money market, three building societies and the Post Office Savings Bank. In addition, state-owned corporations invest and lend for specific development purposes.

Central bank
Reserve Bank of Zimbabwe
Main financial centre
Harare

Nations of the World: A Political, Economic and Business Handbook

Time
GMT plus two hours

Geography
Zimbabwe is a landlocked country in southern central Africa. It is bounded by the Limpopo river and South Africa to the south, by the Zambezi river and Zambia to the north, by Mozambique to the east and by Botswana to the west.

The country falls into three geographical areas: the Highveld, the Lowveld and the Eastern Highlands. The Highveld comprises the major part of the country extending across its central area and rising gradually from the south-west to the north-east, with an average altitude of 1,200 metres. The two main cities, Harare (altitude 1,472 metres) and Bulawayo (altitude 1,343 metres) lie in this area. The Lowveld comprises the Sabi-Limpopo valleys in the south (altitude 600 metres to 800 metres) and the Zambezi valley in the north (altitude 400 metres to 600 metres). The Eastern Highlands borders Mozambique and contains two ranges, the Chimanimani Mountains, with peaks reaching 2,436 metres, and the Inyanga Mountains, with peaks up to 2,595 metres.

A spectacular natural feature is the Victoria Falls on the Zambezi river, the border with Zambia, in the north-western corner of the country. Further east, the Zambezi is dammed for electricity generation at Kariba, forming a lake 250km long.

Climate
Most of the country is semi-tropical with day temperatures of 30 degrees Celsius (C), or slightly above on hot days in the rainy season, but falling as low as 0 degrees C at night in the dry winter season. Rainfall is largely confined to the months November to March and is subject to wide annual variations with considerable influence on agricultural production. Heavier rain falls in the Eastern Highlands.

Dress codes
Business dress is generally formal, suits or jacket with a tie and trousers for men. Many hotels and restaurants require smart casual attire, particularly in the evening, with some insisting on jacket and tie, thus excluding denim jeans. Women normally dress conservatively in European style.

Entry requirements
Passports
Required by all.
Visa
Are required by all, except citizens of countries with reciprocal visa-free entry. Foreign nationals are being advised by their representatives to apply for visas before arrival to avoid fees, increasing with inflation, that may be imposed locally with little notice.

Contact the consular section of the nearest embassy for further advice and requirements for a visa, and confirmation the visitor requires a visa. All visitors must have an onward/return ticket and 'sufficient' money for their stay.

Currency advice/regulations
No limit on foreign currency brought into country, but the amount must be declared and must not be exceeded by amount taken out at departure.

The low value of the Z$ means that carrying any amount of cash, even in high denomination notes, is so bulky as to be inconvenient. A Z$50,000 bearer note went into circulation in January 2006, pending the introduction of a new currency later in the year. ATMs are designed to issue a maximum of 40 notes, which has led to long queues while clients make several withdrawals.

Health (for visitors)
Mandatory precautions
Yellow fever vaccination certificate if travelling from an infected area.
Advisable precautions
Cholera, hepatitis 'A' and 'E' and typhoid immunisations are strongly advised. Anti-malarial prophylaxis is necessary for visitors to Zambezi valley and other low-lying areas from Nov–Jun, elsewhere precautions are necessary throughout the year. Bilharzia is endemic, to avoid the risk, only use well maintained, chlorinated swimming pools. Water precautions are necessary, use only boiled or bottled water. Hot cooked meals and peeled fruit are advisable.

There is an AIDS risk: 10 per cent of the population is infected with HIV.

Medical services are good in main towns, hospitals and the services of private doctors, may be charged in full before treatment, health insurance is essential.

Hotels
Several hotels of various standards are available in the main cities, rated from one to five stars by the Tourist Board. Most of the larger ones are air-conditioned. The government imposes a bed tax per person per night, and it is usual to tip 10 per cent.

Public holidays
Fixed dates
1 Jan (New Year's Day), 18 Apr (Independence Day), 1 May (Labour Day), 25 May (Africa Day), 11 Aug (Heroes' Day), 12 Aug (Defence Forces' Day), 22 Dec (Unity Day), 25 Dec (Christmas Day), 26 Dec (Boxing Day).
Variable dates
Good Friday, Easter Monday.

Working hours
Banking
Mon–Fri: 0830–1500, (Wed) 0830–1300; Sat: 0830–1130.
Business
Mon–Fri: 0745/0830–1600/1700.
Government
Mon–Fri: 0745/0830–1600/1700.

Electricity supply
230V AC

Social customs/useful tips
Zimbabweans generally rise early and go to bed early, particularly on weekdays. Punctuality is generally appreciated in business circles, though not uniformly reciprocated, particularly by members of the government. Hospitality, particularly for meals, is widely offered and may be freely reciprocated. The formal address (Mr, Mrs or Miss with surname) is usual and Christian-name terms are only adopted on closer acquaintance. The giving or receiving of gifts, other than between personal friends, is not customary. No particular proscriptions apply to eating, drinking or smoking and there are no particular religious observances or taboos. Tipping (for example, 10 per cent of a restaurant bill) is common.

It is unwise to photograph major government buildings, military personnel or equipment without prior official permission. Photographers should bring their own film as it is not generally available locally.

Security
Physical attacks, car-jacking and credit card fraud are increasing problems. Foreign nationals who are perceived to be wealthy could be targetted by criminals operating in the vicinity of hotels, restaurants and shopping malls in Harare and other major tourist areas. Caution should be exercised at all times.

Visitors should make two photocopies of the biographic page of their passport; one copy should be retained at home and the other carried at all times for identification purposes.

Getting there
Air
National airline: Air Zimbabwe
International airport/s: Harare International Airport (HRE), 12km from city; post office, restaurant, duty-free shop and bank/bureau de change.
Bulawayo Airport (BUQ), 24km from city.
Other airport/s: Victoria Falls Airport (VFA); Kariba Airport (KAB).
Airport tax: Departure tax US$30, transit passenger are exempt.
Surface
Road: Direct route from Lusaka (Zambia) to Harare, via Victoria Falls, Kariba and Chirundu. Entry from South Africa at

Beitbridge and from Botswana at Plumtree. Most of the border posts are closed from 1800 to 0600 hours every day although specific hours vary.

Rail: Regular services from Zambia, via Victoria Falls, from Beira, from South Africa and from Maputo, Mozambique.

Getting about
National transport
Air: Regular inexpensive daily flights to all major destinations.

Road: Network of over 85,000km, of which about one-quarter are classed as main or secondary roads and half are surfaced with gravel. Good roads connect major towns.

Buses: Good inter-city network operated by Express Motorways Africa Ltd, Zimbabwe Omnibus Company, plus numerous local operators. Express coach services from Harare to Bulawayo, Mutare, Kariba, Chipinge, Masvingo. Advisable to book in advance.

Rail: National Railways of Zimbabwe operate services between Harare and Gweru, Bulawayo, Victoria Falls, Mutare, Masvingo, Chinhoyi and intermediate towns (there are also certain places served by branch lines). Two classes – some trains carry restaurant cars and couchette sleeping accommodation. (NB Bedding is charged). Advisable to book tickets (and bedding) in advance.

City transport
Taxis: These are not usually hailed in the street, they are available at ranks near main hotels. A 10 per cent tip is usual.

Buses, trams & metro: Urban services in some centres can be sporadic.

Car hire
Self-drive cars are available in main cities and at Harare airport, although their condition may not be well maintained. However, they are a useful method of transport as most main intercity roads tend to be of good quality. Traffic drives on the left and a foreign or international driving licence is acceptable during short visits.

BUSINESS DIRECTORY

The addresses listed below are a selection only. While World of Information makes every endeavour to check these addresses, we cannot guarantee that changes have not been made, especially to telephone numbers and area codes. We would welcome any corrections.

Telephone area codes
The international direct dialling code (IDD) for Zimbabwe is + 263, followed by area code and subscriber's number:

| Bulawayo | 9 | Harare | 4 |
| Chiredze | 31 | Mutare | 20 |

Chambers of Commerce
Zimbabwe National Chamber of Commerce, 115 Nelson Mandela Avenue, PO Box 1934, Harare (tel: 799-692; fax: 799-695; e-mail: info@zncc.co.zw).

Banking
Barclays Bank of Zimbabwe Ltd, PO Box 1279, Barclay House, Jason Moyo Avenue/First Street, Harare (tel: 758-280/1/2/3; fax: 752-913).

First Merchant Bank of Zimbabwe, PO Box 2786, FMB House, 67 Samora Machel Avenue, Harare (tel: 703-071, 727-294; fax: 250-682).

Merchant Bank of Central Africa, PO Box 3200, 14th Floor, Old Mutual Centre, Third Street, Jason Moyo Avenue, Harare (tel: 738-081; fax: 708-005).

NMB Bank, PO Box 2564, 1st Floor, Unity Court, Corner 1st Street/Union Avenue, Harare (tel: 759-651/9, 759-601/6; fax: 759-648).

Stanbic Bank Zimbabwe Ltd, PO Box 300, Stanbic Bank Centre, 59 Samora Machel Avenue, Harare (tel: 759-480/3, 759-471/9, 759-479; fax: 749-030).

Standard Chartered Bank Zimbabwe Ltd, PO Box 373, John Boyne House, 38 Speke Ave, Harare (tel: 752-864; fax: 758-076).

Zimbabwe Banking Corporation Ltd, PO Box 3198, Zimbank House, 46 Speke Avenue, Harare (tel: 757-471/94; fax: 757-497, 751-741).

Central bank
Reserve Bank of Zimbabwe, PO Box 1283, 80 Samora Machel Avenue, Harare (tel: 703-000; fax: 707-800; e-mail: rbzmail@rbz.co.zw).

Travel information
Air Zimbabwe, PO Box AP1, Harare Airport, Harare (tel: 575-111; fax: 575-068).

National tourist organisation offices
Zimbabwe Tourism Authority, 9th Floor, Kopje Plaza, 1 Jason Moyo Avenue, Cnr Jason Moyo/Rotten Row, PO Box CY286, Causeway, Harare (tel: 758-730/34, 752-570, 758-712/14; fax: 758-726/28; e-mail: mktg@ztazim.org; zta@africaonline.co.zw; internet site: http://www.tourismzimbabwe.co.zw).

Ministries
Ministry of Agriculture, Ngungunyana Building 1, Borrowdale Road, P.Bag 7701, Causeway, Harare (tel: 706-081, 700-596; fax: 734-646).

Ministry of Defence, Munhumutapa Building, Samora Machel Avenue, P.Bag 7713, Causeway, Harare (tel: 700-155, 728-271).

Ministry of Education, Ambassador House, Union Avenue, PO Box CY121, Causeway, Harare (tel: 734-051, 734-067; fax: 734-075).

Ministry of Environment and Tourism, 14th Floor Karigamombe Centre, 53 Samora Machel Avenue, P.Bag, 7753, Causeway, Harare (tel: 794-455, 704-701; fax: 794-450).

Ministry of Finance, Munhumutapa Building, Samora Machel Avenue, P.Bag, 7705, Causeway, Harare (tel: 794-571, 796-191; fax: 792-750).

Ministry of Foreign Affairs, Munhumutapa Building, Samora Machel Avenue, P.Box 4240, Harare (tel: 727-005, 794-681; fax: 706-293).

Ministry of Health and Child Welfare, Kaguvi Building, 4th Street, P.O. Box CY198, Causeway, Harare (tel: 730-011, 794-411; fax: 793-634).

Ministry of Higher Education: Old Mutual Centre, 1st Floor, 3rd Street/J.Moyo Avenue, PO Box UA 275, Union Avenue, Harare (tel: 702-361, 796-441; fax: 790-923, 728-730).

Ministry of Home Affairs, 11th Floor, Mukwati Building, P.Bag 505D, Harare (tel: 723-653, 703-642; fax: 728-768).

Ministry of Industry and Commerce, 13th Floor, Mukwati Building, 4th Street/Livingston Avenue, P.Bag 7708, Causeway, Harare (tel: 702-731, 729-801).

Ministry of Information, Posts and Telecommunications, 8th-11th Floor, Linquenda House, Baker Avenue, PO Box CY1276 & CY825, Causeway, Harare (tel: 703-891, 706-891; fax: 735-640).

Ministry of Justice, Legal and Parliamentary Affairs, Corner House, Leopold Takawira Street, P.Bag 7704, Causeway, Harare (tel: 790-902, 790-905; fax: 790-901).

Ministry of Lands and Water Development, Ngungunyana Building, 1 Borrowdale Road, P.Bag 7701, Causeway, Harare (tel: 706-081, 700-596).

Ministry of Local Government, Rural and Urgan Development, 16th-20th Floors, Mukwati Building, P.Bag 7706, Causeway, Harare (tel: 790-601, 728-601).

Ministry of Mines, Zimre Centre, L.Takawira Street/Union Avenue, P.Bag 7709, Causeway, Harare (tel: 732-881, 732-885; fax: 790-704).

Ministry of National Affairs, Employment Creation and Co-operatives, Zanu PF Building, Rotten Row/S.Machel Avenue, PO Box 4530, Harare (tel: 734-691, 730-893; fax: 735-338).

Ministry of National Security, Chaminuka Building, 5th Street, Causeway, Harare (tel: 795-965).

Ministry of Public Construction and National Housing, Corner L.Takawira Street & H. Chitepo Avenue, PO Box CY441, Causeway, Harare (tel: 704-561, 704-021; fax: 702-271).

Ministry of Public Service, Labour and Social Welfare, 12th Floor Compensation House, Central Avenue/4th Street, P.Bag 7707, Causeway, Harare (tel: 790-871, 796-451).

Ministry of Sports Recreation and Culture, Pax House, 89 Union Avenue, Harare (tel: 707-411, 794-450; fax: 707-580).

Ministry of Transport and Energy, 4th Floor Atlas House, 62 Robert Mugabe Road, Private Bag 7742, Causeway, Harare (tel: 706-446, 706-161; fax: 708-225, 752-923).

Office of the President and Cabinet, Munhumutapa Building, Samora Machel Avenue/3rd Street, Private Bag 7700, Causeway, Harare (tel: 707-091, 707-098; fax: 734-644, 792-044).

Parliament of Zimbabwe, Baker Avenue Box 8055, Causeway, Harare (tel: 729-722, 795-548).

Other useful addresses

Agricultural Marketing Authority (AMA), Royal Mutual House, 45 Baker Avenue, PO Box 8094, Harare (tel: 730-944).

Attorney-General's Office, Corner House, Leopold Takawira Street, P.Bag 7704, Causeway, Harare (tel: 790-902, 790-905).

Chamber of Mines of Zimbabwe, 4 Central Avenue, PO Box 712, Harare (tel: 702-843; fax: 707-983).

Cold Storage Commission (CSC), Josiah Chinamano Road, Bulawayo (tel: 68-961; fax: 67-522).

Commercial Farmers' Union, Agriculture House, PO Box 1241, Leopold Takawira Street, Harare (tel: 791-881).

Confederation of Zimbabwe Industries, Industry House, 109 Rotten Row, PO Box 3794, Harare (tel: 739-833; fax: 702-873).

Cotton Marketing Board (CMB), Kurima House, 89 Baker Avenua, Harare (tel: 739-061; fax: 66-429).

Dairy Marketing Board (DMB), Dolphin House, Leopold Takawira Street, Harare (tel: 705-700).

Grain Marketing Board (GMB), Kurima House, 89 Baker Avenue, Harare (tel: 732-011; fax: 732-019).

Minerals Marketing Corporation of Zimbabwe, Globe House, 51 Jason Moyo Avenue, PO Box 2628, Harare (tel: 703-402, 705-862; fax: 722-441).

Parliament of Zimbabwe, Baker Avenue Box 8055, Causeway, Harare (tel: 729-722, 795-548).

Zimbabwe Broadcasting Corporation (ZBC), Broadcasting Centre, Pockets Hill, PO Box HG444, Highlands, Harare (tel: 486-670, 481-252/9; fax: 498-613).

Zimbabwean Embassy (USA), 1608 New Hampshire Avenue, NW, Washington DC 20009 (tel: 202-332-7100; fax: 202-483-9326; e-mail: zimemb@erols.com).

Zimbabwe International Trade Fair, Zift, PO Famona, Bulawayo (tel: 64-911).

Zimbabwe Investment Centre, 109 Rotten Row, PO Box 5950, Harare (tel: 757-931/5; fax: 757-937).

Zimbabwe State Trading Corporation, Globe House, 51 Jason Moyo Avenue, Harare (tel: 729-353).

Zimbabwe Stock Exchange, PO Box UA234, 8th Floor, Southampton House, Union Avenue, Harare (tel: 736-861; fax: 791-045).

Zimbabwe Tourist Development Corporation, PO Box 8052, Causeway, Harare (tel: 793-666).

Internet sites

Africa Business Network: http://www.ifc.org/abn

AllAfrica.com: http://www.allafrica.com

African Development Bank: http://www.afdb.org

Africa Online: http://www.africaonline.com

Harambee Afrika (UK business club for traders with east, central and southern Africa; includes annotated web resource list): http://www.harambee.co.uk

Mbendi AfroPaedia (information on companies, countries, industries and stock exchanges in Africa): http://mbendi.co.za

The world in 2005

This piece last year noted that a chain reaction had begun on 9/11 in New York City when the twin towers came down, and hoped that the 'Sarajevo Syndrome', which in 1914 drew in so many countries, wouldn't engulf the world again. Well, as the man who jumped from the twentieth floor said as he passed the tenth floor, 'so far, so good'. In the war on terrorism, only a bit of the West (the US and its allies) are fighting only a few of the terrorists (in Iraq mostly). But while in the First and Second World Wars, the 'enemy' was plain to see, in this war the enemy can be right there, unrecognised – as was shown in London on 7 July 2005 (7/7 or saba saba day) when 52 people died in three bomb explosions on the London transport system.

The 'big' powers are in a dilemma. The war in Iraq, it is generally acknowledged, has proved to be a disaster. The Americans and their allies, principally the British and Australians, but also around 20 other nationalities, say they can't leave until... what? Democracy is installed? But there were three elections in Iraq in 2005, so why not go now? Well, there is the Iranian issue, and Israel, the other two 'I's' of 2005 (see page 1720).

But 2005 will perhaps be remembered not for man-made wars, but for natural disasters. First was the *tsunami*, that giant wave created by an earthquake, on 26 December 2004, off the coast of Indonesia that swept six thousand miles, destroying lives and communities and finally expiring on the beaches of East Africa. The statistics alone are horrifying – 13 countries around the Indian Ocean; over 230,000 killed, and more than a million persons made homeless; 350 million cubic feet of waste generated on Banda Aceh (most of which was swept out to sea, destroying the fishing areas) and 95 million cubic feet in Sri Lanka (mostly dumped in lagoons and other environmentally sensitive areas) – compared to just 42 million cubic feet after the 9/11 attacks in New York; US$5 billion in aid donated by private individuals and US$7 billion by governments – the highest figures raised for any disaster.

One year later, some communities had been completely rebuilt, tourists were returning to the beaches of Thailand, fishermen had new boats. But in some countries, especially Sri Lanka, the money hadn't been spent, boxes of aid still stood on quay sides and the initial solidarity and comradship between all the people – governments, NGOs, rebels (in Sri Lanka and Indonesia) and international aid agencies – had faded.

The third natural disaster was the earthquake in Kashmir in October 2005. Again, the world was slow to grasp the size of the destruction. But so was the government of Pakistan, not particularly through any fault of its own, but because the area was so inaccessible. The death toll rose to almost 75,000 – 73,000 of whom were in Pakistani administered Kashmir – as the remote areas were finally reached and a full assessment was made. Donors pledged some US$5.4 billion, the largest donations coming from Saudi Arabia, Kuwait, the United Arab Emirates and Turkey. Again, it was difficult to spend the funds. Winter was approaching and winter tents were needed, medical facilities were in short supply, or in the wrong places, childen needed shoes. Of the money donated US$3.5 billion has been allocated to rebuilding local infrastructure and homes, the rest to surviving the harsh winter.

The second natural disaster to hit the headlines had been Hurricane Katrina and the havoc it wrecked on New Orleans in the southern United States at the end of August. Here, unlike the Asian *tsunami* and the Kashmir earthquake yet to come, it was the aftermath as much as the hurricane that took the world by surprise. This was not some third world country without an adequate infrastructure or communications. This was the world's Number One superpower, with, it was expected, all the money and equipment to sort itself out. And Hurricane Katrina had been tracked for days; New Orleans knew it was coming. Yet it was not until almost a week after Katrina struck that what was described as the US's largest airlift operation got underway and those still there, around 10,000 people, many stranded in the Superdome stadium, were evacuated.

Americans were shocked as much by what didn't happen in New Orleans, as what did happen. They, and the world, expected their relief agencies to swing into action. Why this didn't happen, and what part race may have played in the reasons why not, has fundamentally changed the way some Americans see their government. The cost of reconstruction could run as high as US$200 billion. Congress has already pledged US$62 billion.

Natural disasters in 2005 have cost as much as any war. More people have died and more homes and livelihoods destroyed than ever before. And more individuals have given more money to help others than in any other year.

> This was not some third world country... this was the world's Number One superpower, with... all the money and equipment to sort itself out.

Africa map

What's on the menu for Africa?

> Not so much doom and gloom, says Barry Baxter. After 45 years working as a journalist in southern Africa, he feels Africa is finally turning that corner and is finding its own way to prosperity. Here he gives a personal view.

Conflict in Africa will continue for some years yet and make the headlines, but less reported is an unrelenting war that is being fought to 'put Africa right'. This time the war is a bloodless conflict to earn for the continent its rightful place in world affairs; it is being waged by a well-educated and increasingly world-wise younger generation of politicians and businesspeople who do not expect to be offered Africa-on-a-plate. They are well-prepared to work for what they want.

They are showing their muscle, not through the barrel of Kalishnikov, but at negotiating tables in capitals in Africa and around the world. Africa still has a lot to offer the world, but only in return for respect and fair dealing.

In many cases their inspiration is a new generation of African leaders; trained economists, skilled politicians who know how to fight wars of words. Many others are now the elder statesmen of Africa, with no need to seek more stature than they have and willing to share freely their wisdom.

The despôts are still there, but many people even in their own governments are beginning to question them. There are still leaders who seek to hang on to power at all costs. It is usually their own people who pay the price in continuing conflict while neighbouring countries begin to win their battles against poverty.

Yes, many Africans do still live on less than one dollar a day, aid is abused by their leaders and the people around them; but daily they become more of a minority as more of their people see there is a way out of their misery and demand the men and women who want to rule them take that road.

The discussions about cultural changes, the domination of the ideas of the West over the traditions of Africa, persist. The past must not determine what Africana will become, but it must always be a part of them. It is inevitable that from Cape Town to Cairo people will want the best the West has to offer. Many have it already. Millionaires in Africa are not rare.

It's hard to argue against these material ambitions and the new Africans don't. Why should they? An African elite has grown up alongside the shanties and that was an inevitable part of development; it is not all the result of corruption or double dealing as the critics are wont to describe it.

Business is business and the prosperity of Africa depends on more and more of it. From huge internationally funded projects to the growing informal sectors of Africa's towns and cities business is being done daily and more millionaires are in the making.

It is said that the rich stay rich because they hold on to their money tightly. There is no doubt this is true, but as much as the new governments encourage free enterprise, they try to ensure that the trickle down effect of the new wealth will mean that the children of those people who today cannot afford to buy from a hawker on a sandy 'sidewalk', tomorrow will be shopping at the supermarket around the corner.

In many cases, accelerated development schemes have sucessfully put people there already. The obstinate governments will come around. If they do not, they will be left in situations that cannot persist and the prices their leaders will have to pay will result in change anyway.

Pie in the sky? I do not think so. There is a gap between rhetoric and reality, it is growing smaller. There will inevitably be some compromises along the way but enough African countries have identified the road they have to travel to eventually take the rest with them.

Worldwide, politicians can be economical with the truth, but in reviewing the 53 countries of Africa featured in this volume, I saw clearly that economics and development is the story of Africa – and that the rest of the world is finally taking notice. I cannot visualise an Africa where politics is as public as in the West, but the sometimes difficult to understand politics of those 53 countries is clearly taking a back seat to the developing business of Africa.

Globalisation or as it is now often called, the external situation, is a regular topic. You can hate it or not, but particularly at this stage of weak domestic markets, the money has to come from somewhere. Unashamedly a globalised thinker, I believe those African leaders that take down the barriers to business first and open up their economies – and indeed their countries – will be first past the post, particularly in the poverty eradication stakes, which is what achieving peace and development in Africa is all about. It will at times be a difficult political balancing act for both Africa, the East and the West, but they all must make an equal effort.

Africa has a lot to offer the world, and the world has a lot Africa wants and needs. Africa is open for business and the long-term beneficiaries can be not only its people, but also those in the lands it does business with.

China in Africa

China is back in Africa, in a big way. Africa has much of what China needs in the way of natural resources, especially oil, copper and other minerals. And it is making sure that it gets what it wants by offering loans and finance without attaching the strings that the West now insists upon – such as transparency, good governence and fiscal probity – rather than the lop-sided trade and unsuitable purchases of earlier deals.

In Angola, which in 2005 was already exporting around a quarter of its oil to China, a US$2 billion soft loan to help build schools, hospitals, railways, roads and other infrastructure probably ensured that China was the winner of oil exploration rights to a large bloc offered in 2005. In the Sudan, where the West pulled out of developing their oil industry because of the civil war in the south and the US's concern for Sudan's apparent support for the al Qaeda network, China, together with Malaysia, have enabled Sudan to become a net oil exporter. In Zambia China has invested some US$170 million in mining; in Uganda a Chinese pharmaceutical firm is making a new anti-malerial drug; in Sierra Leone a luxury hotel complex is being developed by China (Sierra Leone has good beaches and tourism used to be a considerable foreign exchange earner before the civil was); in the Democratic Republic of Congo, a country shunned by the West for being too unstable, the Chinese are investing in copper mines and are building the roads on which to transport their exports.

All this is a far cry from the Friendship Halls of the 1980s when China made friends who would not be friends with Taiwan. Now it is the raw materials to fuel China's rapidly expanding industry that are attractive, and if that means going where the West fears to tread, or attaches conditions to aid, then so much the better. Zimbabwe, especially, is a case in point – China has supported Robert Mugabe since the pre-independence days of rivalry between Mugabe and Joshua Nkoma. China chose the right side then and has supported Mugabe ever since, despite Zimbabwe's current disastrous situation. Zimbabwe has the minerals that China needs, and China has invested accordingly.

Africa may eventually find that China's apparent largesse is not quite so open handed afterall. While China is generous with its offers of aid, it is also firm when it comes to defending its rights under the World Trade Organisation. Cheap Chinese exports, expecially textiles, are undercutting African production, not only within Africa but also as Africa tries to export itself. In Lesotho, 10 clothing factories had to close, throwing some 10,000 workers out of work, as China's cheaper textiles reached America's markets.

Currencies (units per US$) – Africa

	Unit	Jan 2001	Jan 2002	Jan 2003	Jan 2004	Jan 2005
Algeria	Algerian dinar	72.03	76.35	78.93	72.54	72.10
Angola	Readjusted kwanza	17.68	32.12	58.86	78.83	85.72
Benin	CFA franc	691.39	733.16	629.73	520.05	482.58
Botswana	Pula	5.46	7.02	5.40	4.43	4.27
Burkina Faso	CFA franc	691.39	733.16	629.73	520.05	482.58
Burundi	Burundi franc	790.09	863.96	1,070.00	1,060.00	1,060.00
Cameroon	CFA franc	691.39	733.16	629.73	520.05	482.58
Cape Verde	Cape Verde escudo	116.01	119.80	108.95	108.95	81.15
Central African Republic	CFA franc	691.39	733.16	629.73	520.05	482.58
Chad	CFA franc	691.39	733.16	629.73	520.05	482.58
Comoros	Comoros franc	515.35	548.06	470.36	454.33	361.94
Congo	CFA franc	691.39	733.16	629.73	520.05	482.58
Democratic Republic of Congo	Congolese franc	4.50	313.00	360.00	378.00	440.50
Côte d'Ivoire	CFA franc	691.39	733.16	629.73	520.05	482.58
Djibouti	Djibouti franc	175.40	170.00	175.00	175.00	175.85
Egypt	Egyptian pound	3.86	4.58	4.64 (a)	6.17	6.07
Equatorial Guinea	CFA franc	691.39	733.16	629.73	520.05	482.58
Eritrea	Nakfa	8.24	8.47	8.30	8.55	13.50
Ethiopia	Ethiopian birr	8.24	8.47	8.30	8.55	8.60
Gabon	CFA franc	691.39	733.16	629.73	520.05	482.58
Gambia	Dalasi	15.58	17.48	22.38	29.50	29.50
Ghana	Cedi	7,175.00	7,402.50	8,400.00	8,850.00	9,000.00
Guinea	Guinean franc	1,855.00	1,965.00	1,985.00	2,005.00	2,805.00
Guinea-Bissau	CFA franc	691.39	733.16	629.73	520.05	482.58
Kenya	Kenya shilling	78.60	78.82	77.58	76.00	78.65
Lesotho	Maloti	7.84	12.09	8.44	6.68	5.63
Liberia	Liberian dollar	1.00	1.00	1.00	1.00	47.00
Libya	Libyan dinar	0.54	0.64	1.23	1.31	1.25
Madagascar	Franc Malgache	6,491.00	6,364.00	6,380.00	5,700.00	9,275.00
Malawi	Kwacha	80.25	67.00	86.66	107.00	108.00
Mali	CFA franc	691.39	733.16	629.73	520.05	482.58
Mauritania	Ouguiya	247.15	264.01	268.23	264.61	261.64
Mauritius	Mauritius rupee	27.83	30.25	29.10	26.20	28.18
Morocco	Moroccan dirham	10.55	11.46	10.22	8.78	8.24
Mozambique	Metical	17,191.50	22,885.00	23,343.00	23,352.50	18,603.50
Namibia	Namibian dollar	7.84	12.09	8.44	6.68	5.63
Niger	CFA franc	691.39	733.16	629.73	520.05	482.58
Nigeria	Naira	110.70 (m)	115.75	130.40	139.55	133.15
Réunion	French franc/Euro	6.91	1.12 (*)	0.96	0.79	0.74
Rwanda	Rwanda franc	359.03	454.00	500.00	556.55	554.05
São Tomé and Príncipe	Dobra	2,390.00	8,937.20	9,019.70	8,700.00	9,040.00
Senegal	CFA franc	691.39	733.16	629.73	520.05	482.58
Seychelles	Seychelles rupee	6.35	5.62	5.62	5.50	5.52
Sierra Leone	Leone	2,036.08	2,241.00	2,010.00	2,450.00	2,455.00
Somalia	Somali shilling	2,620.00	2,620.00	2,620.00	2,620.00	3,068.00
South Africa	Rand	7.84	12.09	8.44	6.68	5.63
Sudan	Sudanese dinar	258.70	258.70	258.70	259.80	250.63
Swaziland	Lilangeni	7.84	12.09	8.44	6.68	5.63
Tanzania	Tanzania shilling	803.00	918.00	978.00	1,057.54	1,040.00
Togo	CFA franc	691.39	733.16	629.73	520.05	482.58
Tunisia	Tunisian dinar	1.36	1.46	1.34	1.21	1.20
Uganda	Ugandan shilling	1,855.00	1,730.00	1,860.00	1,937.00	1,737.50
Zambia	Kwacha	4,650.00	3,820.00	4,455.00	4,550.00	4,700.00
Zimbabwe	Zimbabwe dollar	55.13	55.45	55.45	824.00	5,729.27

(a) Egyptian pound floated 29 Jan 2003; (*) euro single currency from 1 Jan 2002; (m) market rate; (o) official rate.

Nations of the World: A Political, Economic and Business Handbook

Key indicators 2004/05 – Africa

	Population (m)	Area ('000 sq km)	GDP per capita (US$)	Inflation (%)	GDP real growth (%)	Balance of trade (US$m)
Algeria	32.16	2,381.70	2,521	3.6	5.3	16,910
Angola	15.94	1,246.70	1,305	43.6	11.2	7,864
Benin	6.94	112.60	565	2.6	3.0	-213
Botswana	1.80	582.00	5,740	6.3	5.2	685
Burkina Faso	12.44	274.00	412	-0.4	4.8	-448
Burundi	7.80	27.80	91	7.9	5.5	-106
Cameroon	16.79	475.40	831	0.3	4.3	466
Cape Verde	0.46	4.00	2,097	-1.9	4.0	-326
Central African Republic	4.09	623.00	331	-2.2	0.9	32
Chad	8.21	1,284.00	523	-4.8	30.5	-690
Comoros	0.77	2.20	582	4.3	1.9	-24
Congo	3.47	342.00	1,427	2.0	4.0	1,474
Democratic Republic of Congo	58.78	2,345.40	112	3.9	6.8	-223
Côte d'Ivoire	18.95	322.50	852	1.5	-0.9	1,764
Djibouti	0.77	23.20	793	3.0	3.0	–
Egypt	70.83	1,001.50	1,111	8.1	4.1	-8,210
Equatorial Guinea	0.49	28.10	4,120	8.0	34.2	1,604
Eritrea	4.27	125.00	138	21.4	1.8	-557
Ethiopia	72.04	1,251.30	116	9.0	11.6	-1,541
Gabon	1.38	267.70	5,469	1.0	1.9	2,485
Gambia	1.42	11.30	276	14.6	7.7	-67
Ghana	20.35	239.50	434	12.6	5.5	-1,513
Guinea	8.47	245.90	403	17.5	1.2	37
Guinea-Bissau	1.38	36.10	208	3.0	4.3	–
Kenya	33.52	582.70	482	11.5	3.1	-1,601
Lesotho	2.59	30.40	652	5.5	2.3	-246
Liberia	3.85	111.40	127	7.8	21.8	-87
Libya	5.81	1,775.50	5,121	-1.0	0.9	11,426
Madagascar	17.66	592.00	251	13.8	5.3	-279
Malawi	11.65	118.50	151	11.6	4.3	-18
Mali	11.79	1,241.20	404	-3.1	2.2	–
Mauritania	2.83	1,030.70	462	10.4	5.2	–
Mauritius	1.27	1.90	4,829	4.4	4.4	-233
Morocco	29.90	711.00	1,629	2.0	3.5	-6,494
Mozambique	18.58	799.40	292	12.6	7.8	-284
Namibia	1.97	824.30	2,261	5.5	4.4	-117
Niger	12.67	1,267.00	258	0.4	0.9	–
Nigeria	141.60	923.80	500	15.0	3.5	16,850
Réunion	0.78	2.50	–	–	2.5	–
Rwanda	8.59	26.30	215	12.0	4.0	-190
São Tomé and Príncipe	0.16	0.90	402	12.8	6.0	-34
Senegal	10.63	196.20	733	0.5	6.0	-754
Seychelles	0.08	0.50	8,499	4.0	-2.0	-137
Sierra Leone	4.85	72.30	201	13.7	7.4	–
Somalia	11.56	738.00	–	–	2.8	–
South Africa	47.56	1,127.20	4,500	1.4	3.7	115
Sudan	38.00	2,505.80	617	8.4	7.3	-192
Swaziland	1.10	17.40	2,172	3.5	2.1	-240
Tanzania	36.58	945.10	295	4.6	6.3	-724
Terres Australes	(a)	439.80	–	–	–	–
Togo	5.25	56.00	375	1.2	2.9	-162
Tunisia	9.90	164.20	2,855	3.6	5.8	-2,434
Uganda	25.52	236.00	264	5.9	5.9	-755
Zambia	11.00	752.60	478	18.0	5.0	-29
Zimbabwe	14.71	391.10	496	282.4	-4.8	-190

(a) 90 people

South America map

Nations of the World: A Political, Economic and Business Handbook

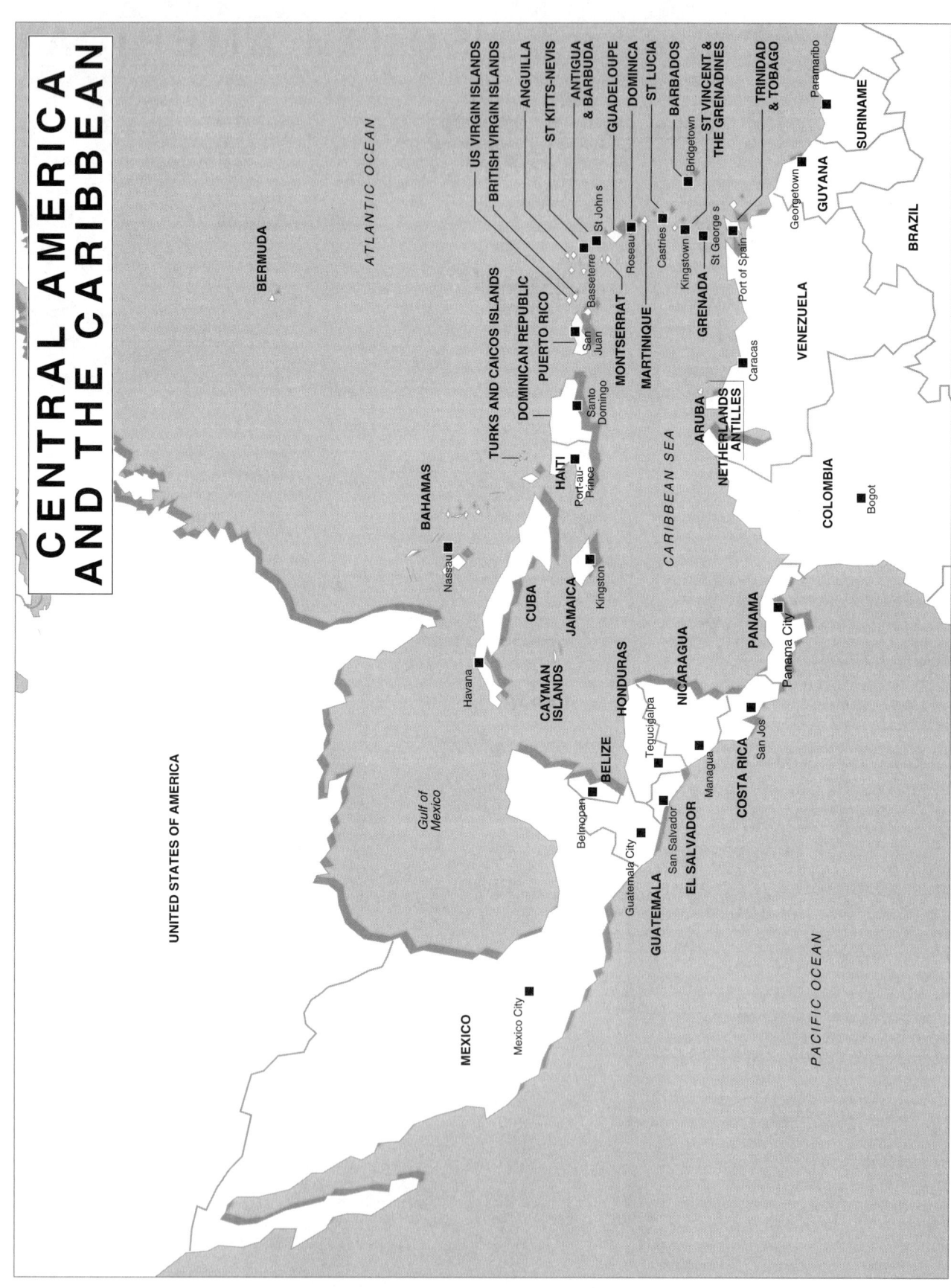

Maps

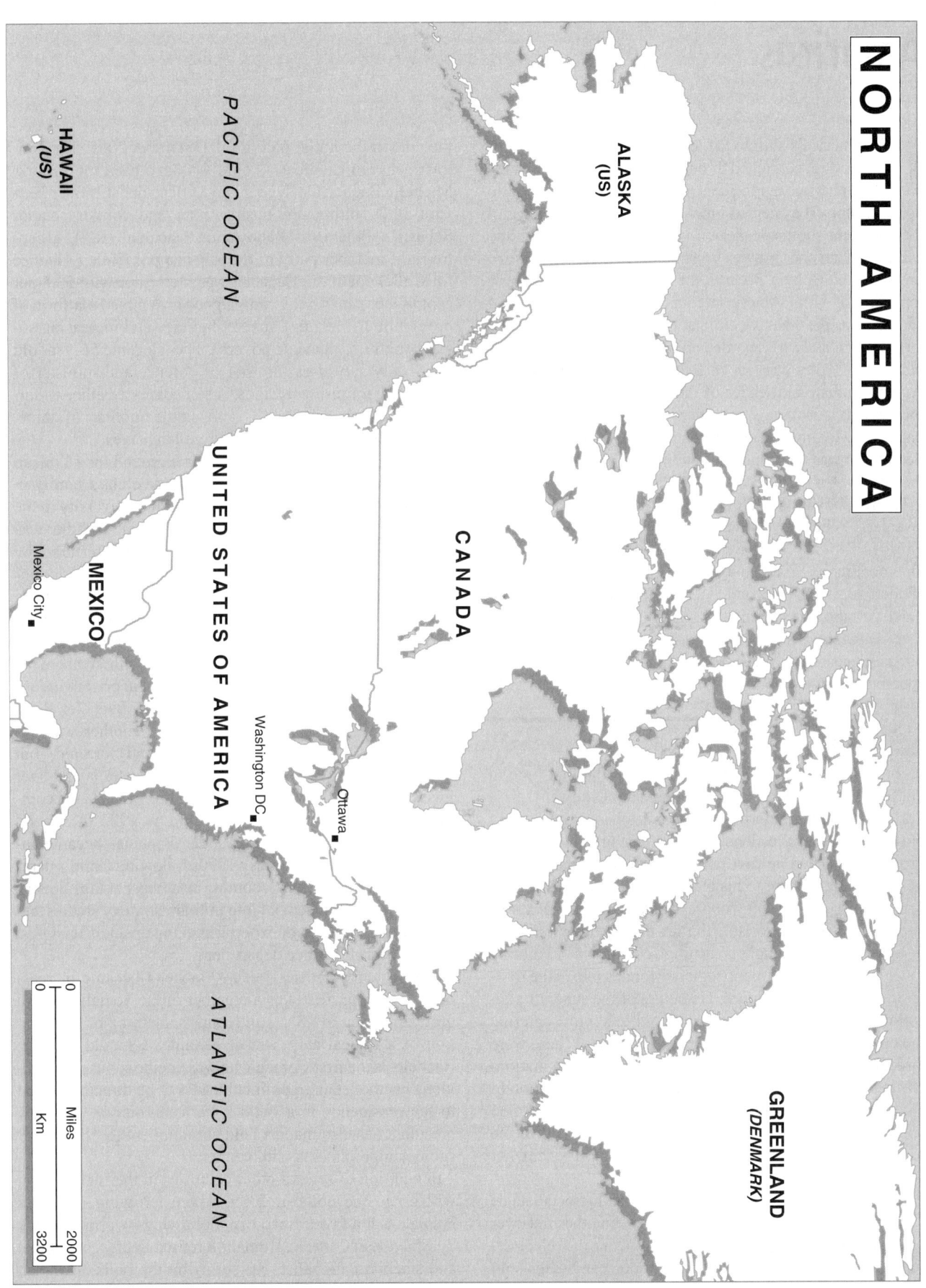

Americas

Latin America's shift to the left of the international political spectrum continued throughout 2005. Throughout the year Venezuelan President Hugo Chávez continued to confirm himself as heir to Fidel Castro's throne as King of the continent's leftist leaders. Toward the end of 2005 however, Bolivian coca grower's champion Evo Morales rose to prominence. Bolivia became the latest in an increasingly long line of Latin American countries to elect a left-wing candidate as president when Juan Evo Morales Aima (popularly known as Evo) recorded an absolute majority with 54 per cent of votes cast on 18 December 2005. Morales, an Aymara Indian and leader of the *cocalero* (coca growers) movement, is Bolivia's first ever indigenous president. His party, the Movimiento al Socialismo (MAS) (Movement for Socialism) was confirmed as having won 72 of 130 seats in the chamber of deputies and 12 of 27 in the senate.

The flamboyant Morales, noted for his trademark striped sweater, beat Jorge Quiroga of Poder Democratico Nacional (Podemos) into second place in the presidential race. However, MAS was not as successful in the respective regional gubernatorial races and this could well restrict Morales' power. The regional governor posts were contested electorally for the first time in 2005 and are expected to wield considerable power.

Charismatic and unorthodox, Morales has an interesting past. The *cocalero* leader shot to national and international prominence when he first ran for president, finishing runner-up, in 2002. Prior to his bid for the presidency Morales was dismissed from his congressional seat on charges of connections with terrorist activities during riots in Sacaba in January 2002. Brought up in tough conditions in a mining town in Bolivia's Altiplano region, Morales joined the military at the age of seventeen. He boasts of the superior education he received at the 'university of life', before entering the cut-throat world of Bolivian union politics. There were three major tenets to Morales electoral programme: nationalisation of Bolivia's natural gas reserves, the formation of a constituent assembly in order to rewrite the constitution with a commitment to indigenous rights, and, third, the 'depenalisation' (Morales' own phrase) of the coca leaf, but not the drug itself.

Verónica Michelle Bachelet Jeria of Partido Socialista de Chile (SP) (Socialist Party of Chile) became the first-ever Chilean female president when she won the electoral run-off on 15 January 2006, after various candidates split the vote in the initial poll on 11 December 2005. The contrast between candidates could not have been more stark: Michelle Bachelet, a dyed in the wool socialist, verses Harvard PhD, billionaire businessman and former senator Sebastián Piñera, of Renovación Nacional (RN), a centre-right member party of the Alianza por Chile (Alliance for Chile) coalition. Bachelet was victorious with 53.5 per cent of the vote, having campaigned on a mixed platform of promoting Chile's free-market heritage and increasing social benefits to alleviate poverty. The telegenic 55-year old previously served as minister of defence and minister of health under President Lagos. A self confessed atheist – unusual in Catholic Chile – and single mother of three, Bachelet is competent in 5 different languages.

Bachelet has an unconventional background for a Chilean presidential candidate. Born into a middle class family in Santiago she went to medical school at the university in the city. Bachelet's father was detained and tortured by the Chilean authorities under instruction from Pinochet in 1973, having disobeyed orders and been charged with treason; he later died in prison. In January 1975 Bachelet along with her mother was detained and tortured, but both were later allowed to seek exile in Australia and later East Germany. Bachelet returned to Chile in 1979 and completed her medical degree, graduating in 1983. A shrewd networker and relationship builder Bachelet became involved in politics in the early 1990s following Chile's democratic transition. After becoming an advisor at the ministry of health she branched out into military strategy studies and transformed her area of expertise, taking up an official post in the Chilean defence department.

During her time as a student Bachelet became increasingly left-wing, firstly as a member of the Socialist Youth group and then SP. She still retains something of a reputation of a radical and is most certainly a mould breaker. Bachelet is the first woman who was not the spouse of a previous head of state or political leader to be directly elected to the presidency in a Latin American country. The new president has also made a bold commitment to fill half her cabinet appointments with women.

In addition to several other countries in the region, Peru will go to the polls in 2006, where left-winger Ollanta Humala is hot favourite to win. Following a warm embrace by Chávez, in Caracas, Humala, a retired lieutenant colonel and staunch nationalist, has surged in the polls. The man

> Morales, an Aymara Indian and leader of the *cocalero* (coca growers) movement, is Bolivia's first ever indigenous president.

who led a failed coup in 2000 has drawn obvious comparisons with his leftist Venezuelan sponsor and the recent victory of fellow firebrand Evo Morales in Bolivia has only added to his campaign's momentum. Furthermore, Peru's electoral history has traditionally thrown up victories for outsider 'insurgent' candidates, Alberto Fujimori's victory in 1990 and Toledo's in 2001 being cases in point. Humala's recent rise in the polls and his unique brand of leftist rhetoric has alarmed many within the governing Perú Posible (PP) (Peru Possible) party. He has claimed, in a similar manner to Morales in Bolivia, that the coca trade would be legalised under his watch, and has categorically stated his desire to nationalise several industries. Ominously for foreign business interests in the country, he has talked of the 'colonisation' of natural resources by international companies: 'nationalism is about defending national markets and national interests' is a mantra he has repeated on several occasions.

Inter-Continental relations

Throughout 2005 Chávez continued his rhetorical war with the government of the United States, constantly referring to George W Bush as 'Mr Danger'! Behind the flamboyant rhetoric however, lies a strategic plan on Chávez' part to dilute Washington's influence in the Latin American and Caribbean region. The cornerstone of this policy is the Petrocaribe initiative. Petrocaribe is the name given to a programme allowing 13 different countries in the Caribbean region to purchase Venezuelan oil at reduced prices. Venezuela, the world's fifth largest oil exporter produces approximately 3.1 million barrels a day and the Petrocaribe initiative is just the latest in a line of energy security deals that the Venezuelan president has signed with countries in the region.

The terms of Petrocaribe allow each of the 13 Caribbean signatories – who have little oil of their own – to purchase Venezuelan oil at a 40 per cent discount as long as the international oil price remains above US$50 dollars per barrel. The deal also includes a clause allowing for a further discount should the oil price break the US$100 per barrel mark. Petrocaribe is a fine example of Chávez' not-so-subtle oil diplomacy and though the Venezuelan president claims not to be interested in gaining political leverage in the region, it does not take a geopolitical genius to realise an encroachment into Washington's strategic territory is just what is on his mind.

An extremely important development for the region occurred in August 2005 when the WTO ruled that the EU's decision to impose import tariffs on bananas was illegal. The EU tariff, which was due to come into effect in January 2006 would have meant that banana imports from Latin America would have faced a steep tariff of eur230 (US$280.30),although quotas would have been abolished, but bananas from the African Caribbean and Pacific (ACP) countries would remain tariff-free. The ACP countries are mostly former EU colonies, and in the case of the Caribbean islands, have traditionally exported bananas to the EU which have been grown by smallholders. The effect of this ruling will mean a loss of exports from these small growers in favour of bananas grown on large plantations owned by US fruit growers such as Del Monte and Chiquita. Coupled with a similar loss of sugar exports to the EU, these countries face an up-hill battle to replace these traditional exports.

Outlook

Taking the Latin American and Caribbean region in its entirety, there is evidence of healthy economic growth. The real GDP of the region expanded by 4.3 per cent in 2005 and the region's economy looks set to grow throughout 2006. However, this growth is not uniform and particular areas have suffered from stagnation while other sub-regions have boomed. Overall though, the region's economic condition is relatively stable.

Politically, the region is shifting ever leftward. With the old stalwart of the left, Castro, now a pale imitation of his former charismatic self, Chávez is now leading the charge against US designs for the region. Increasingly, he is being joined by more leftist populist figures, such as Evo Morales in Bolivia. Morales' victory in late 2005 in such an important natural resource state, has further increased the pressure on Washington. Should Humala, another leftist with a populist streak, win in Peru in 2006 as polls currently suggest, then Latin America will have moved to by far its most left wing position in the international political spectrum for many years.

> With the old stalwart of the left, Castro, now a pale imitation of his former charismatic self, Chávez is now leading the charge against US designs for the region.

Nations of the World: A Political, Economic and Business Handbook

Currencies (units per US$) – Americas

	Unit	Jan 2001	Jan 2002	Jan 2003	Jan 2004	Jan 2005
Argentina	Peso	1.00	1.00	3.35	2.93	2.97
Belize	Belize dollar	2.00	1.97	1.97	1.97	1.98
Bolivia	Peso Boliviano	6.40	6.85	7.51	7.80	8.04
Brazil	Real	1.95	2.31	3.46	2.89	2.66
Chile	Chilean peso	573.25	651.70	713.35	592.55	555.75
Colombia	Colombian peso	2,253.25	2,297.90	2,843.80	2,779.70	2,352.50
Costa Rica	Colón	318.45	341.69	378.66	418.67	458.60
Ecuador	Sucre/US dollar	**1.00	1.00	1.00	1.00	1.00
El Salvador	Colón	8.74	8.75	8.75	8.75	8.75
French Guiana	French franc/Euro	6.91	1.12 (e)	0.96	0.79	0.74
Guatemala	Quetzal	7.82	7.94	7.81	8.02	7.75
Guyana	Guyana dollar	180.50	180.50	179.00	179.00	179.00
Honduras	Lempira	15.13	15.92	16.92	17.74	18.63
Mexico	Mexican peso	9.86	9.14	10.38	11.24	11.15
Nicaragua	Gold Córdoba	12.90	13.77	14.57	15.43	16.20
Panama	Balboa	1.00	1.00	1.00	1.00	1.00
Paraguay	Guarani	3,557.00	4,760.00	7,290.00	6,100.00	6,115.00
Peru	New sol	3.52	3.44	3.50	3.46	3.28
Suriname	Suriname guilder	981.00	2,178.50	2,178.50	2,515.00	2.74
Uruguay	Peso Uruguayo	12.55	14.75	27.38	29.32	26.41
Venezuela	BolGreek Centuryívar	698.95	760.25	1,396.76	2,851.74	2,578.29
NORTH AMERICA						
Canada	Canadian dollar	1.50	1.60	1.57	1.29	1.20
United States of America	US dollar	1.00	1.00	1.00	1.00	–
CARIBBEAN						
Anguilla	EC dollar	2.70	2.70	2.70	2.67	2.70
Antigua	EC dollar	2.70	2.70	2.70	2.67	2.70
Aruba	Aruba guilder	1.79	1.79	1.79	1.79	1.79
Bahamas	Bahamian dollar	1.00	1.00	1.00	1.00	1.00
Barbados	Barbados dollar	1.99	1.99	1.99	1.99	2.00
Bermuda	Bermuda dollar	1.00	1.00	1.00	1.00	1.00
British Virgin Islands	US dollar	1.00	1.00	1.00	1.00	1.00
Cayman Islands	Cayman Islands dollar	0.82	0.82	0.82	0.82	0.82
Cuba	Cuban peso	21.00	21.00	21.00	21.00	1.00
Dominica	EC dollar	2.70	2.70	2.70	2.67	2.70
Dominican Republic	Dominican Republic peso	16.11	16.50	20.00	33.70	28.50
Grenada	EC dollar	2.70	2.70	2.70	2.67	2.70
Guadeloupe	French franc/Euro	6.91	1.12 (e)	0.96	0.79	0.74
Haiti	Gourde	23.00	26.00	36.00	40.00	36.00
Jamaica	Jamaican dollar	45.15	47.05	49.85	59.80	61.00
Martinique	French franc/Euro	6.91	1.12 (e)	0.96	0.79	0.74
Montserrat	EC dollar	2.70	2.70	2.70	2.67	2.70
The Netherlands Antilles	NA guilder	1.78	1.78	1.78	1.78	1.79
Puerto Rico	US dollar	1.00	1.00	1.00	1.00	1.00
St Kitts Nevis	EC dollar	2.70	2.70	2.70	2.67	2.70
St Lucia	EC dollar	2.70	2.70	2.70	2.67	2.70
St Vincent	EC dollar	2.70	2.70	2.70	2.67	2.70
Trinidad and Tobago	Trinidad and Tobago dollar	6.24	6.14	6.16	6.15	6.23
Turks and Caicos Islands	US dollar	1.00	1.00	1.00	1.00	1.00
US Virgin Islands	US dollar	1.00	1.00	1.00	1.00	1.00

(o) official rate; (e) euro single currency from 1 January 2002; ** Ecuador adopted US dollar, 2000

Key indicators 2004/05 – Americas

	Population (m)	Area ('000 sq km)	GDP per capita (US$)	Inflation (%)	GDP real growth (%)	Balance of trade (US$m)
Argentina	38.47	2,766.90	3,912	4.4	9.0	13,267
Belize	0.27	23.00	3,977	2.7	3.0	-178
Bolivia	8.88	1,098.60	1,125	4.4	3.8	391
Brazil	181.20	8,512.00	3,417	6.6	5.2	33,693
Chile	15.48	756.60	5,856	1.1	6.0	9,019
Colombia	45.30	1,138.90	2,099	5.9	4.0	1,134
Costa Rica	4.27	51.10	4,361	12.3	4.2	-1,658
Ecuador	13.18	270.70	2,145	2.7	6.6	-90
El Salvador	6.70	21.40	2,335	4.5	1.5	-2,619
French Guiana	0.20	91.00	6,000	1.5	–	-470
Guatemala	12.39	108.90	1,953	7.0	2.6	-3,760
Guyana	0.87	215.00	1,024	4.7	1.6	-80
Honduras	6.94	112.10	1,035	8.1	4.2	-1,267
Mexico	102.80	1,958.20	6,506	4.7	4.4	-8,811
Nicaragua	5.98	148.00	788	8.2	4.0	-1,270
Panama	3.04	77.10	4,524	0.5	6.0	-1,585
Paraguay	5.85	407.00	1,155	5.2	2.1	-394
Peru	27.55	1,285.20	2,349	3.7	5.1	2,728
Suriname	0.46	164.00	2,401	9.0	4.6	–
Uruguay	3.43	176.20	3,543	9.2	12.0	–
Venezuela	25.51	916.50	4,148	21.7	17.3	21,430
NORTH AMERICA						
Canada	31.75	9,976.10	31,209	1.8	2.8	51,734
United States of America	296.50	9,300.00	39,934	2.7	4.4	-665,940
CARIBBEAN						
Anguilla	0.01	0.01	–	–	–	–
Antigua	0.07	0.02	11,270	-1.3	4.1	–
Aruba	0.09	0.02	–	2.5	3.5	–
Bahamas	0.33	13.90	17,486	1.5	3.3	-1,206
Barbados	0.27	0.40	10,334	1.5	3.0	-946
Bermuda	0.07	0.01	36,000	–	–	–
British Virgin Islands	0.02	0.15	16,000	1.0	1.0	–
Cayman Islands	0.05	0.30	33,300	*4.4	2.0	–
Cuba	11.91	110.90	2,900	3.0	3.0	-3,192
Dominica	0.07	0.80	3,643	2.3	1.0	–
Dominican Republic	8.79	48.40	2,190	51.5	2.0	-2,647
Grenada	0.09	0.34	4,386	2.3	-3.2	-202
Guadeloupe	0.44	1.80	–	–	–	–
Haiti	8.67	27.80	419	27.1	-3.5	-746
Jamaica	2.68	11.00	3,237	11.5	2.5	-1,940
Martinique	0.42	1.10	–	–	–	–
Montserrat	(+)	0.01	–	–	–	-21
Netherlands Antilles	0.22	0.80	–	2.5	1.0	–
Puerto Rico	3.90	8.90	12,659	6.5	2.7	–
St Kitts Nevis	0.05	0.30	10,351	2.4	5.1	-123
St Lucia	0.16	0.60	4,021	1.0	2.0	-304
St Vincent	0.12	0.40	3,512	2.0	2.8	–
Trinidad and Tobago	1.30	5.10	9,084	3.9	6.2	2,021
Turks and Caicos Islands	0.02	0.43	–	–	–	–
US Virgin Islands	0.12	0.40	–	–	–	–

* Estimated figure, (+) 9,341 people

Nations of the World: A Political, Economic and Business Handbook

Asia and Pacific maps

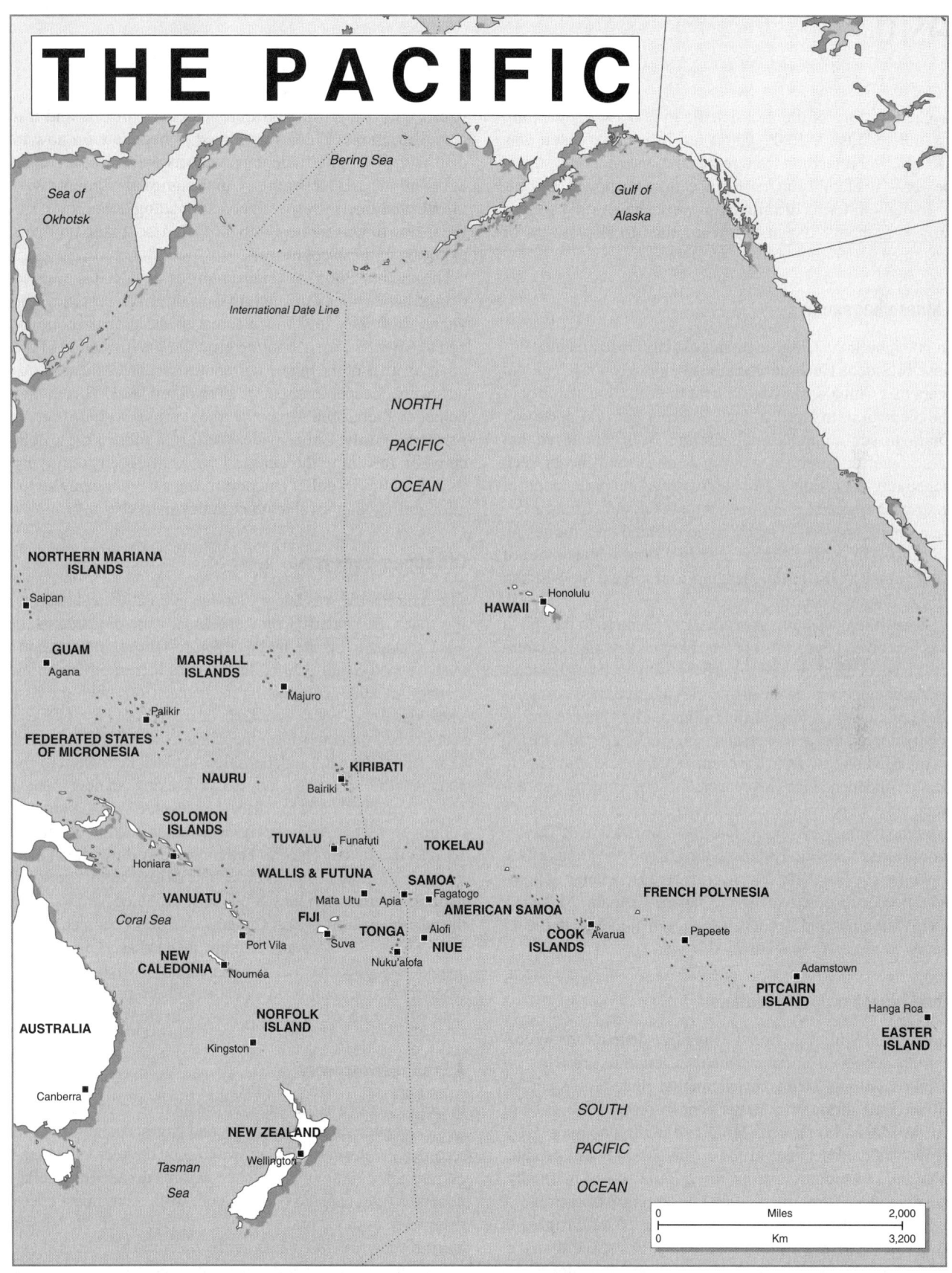

Asia

The big story of the Asia-Pacific in 2005 was, by a long mile, China. In 2005, China left little doubt that it was amidst a transition from regional to international superpower – irrefutably in terms of economic power and increasingly in terms of military power. The world's second largest economy, Japan, also continued to show signs of sustained economic recovery in 2005.

Chinese hegemony?

In 2005, both the Chinese premier Wen Jiabao and the Chinese president Hu Jintao sought to allay growing regional fears that China's rise was a threat to peace and stability in the the region. In April, at the 26-nation Asia Co-operation Dialogue summit in Pakistan, Premier Wen announced that 'a stronger and more developed China... will never seek hegemony'. President Hu, addressing the parliament of long-time regional rival Vietnam, stated that 'China's development poses an obstacle to no one and undermines no one'. Also in April, China signed an accord with another of its regional rivals, India, pledging to resolve a Sino-Indian border dispute peaceably.

Clearly there was some sensitivity in China as to the way it was perceived beyond its borders. However, while the country's leaders did their best to push a positive message, events in March underscored the difficulties and at times contradictory realities of the task ahead of them. The Chinese parliament adopted an 'anti-secession' law, officially authorising an invasion of Taiwan in the event of a Taiwanese attempt to declare independence. Moreover, the government also announced a 12 per cent increase in defence spending. China's growing military power, the fact that any invasion of Taiwan would almost inevitably draw in the US and its various allies, as well as the fact that China was involved in a range of maritime border disputes, involving Japan, Vietnam, Malaysia, The Philippines and Brunei all suggest that unease in the region was not entirely unjustified.

The Chinese economy matters

Concurrent with this growth was huge demand for hydrocarbon-generated energy. China's economic growth contributed, along with environmental disasters such as Hurricane Katrina, to a 30 per cent increase in the price of oil in 2005. Moreover, combined with booming GDP growth-related demand in India, the gap between production and consumption of oil in 2005 narrowed markedly, raising fears of sustained, global inflationary pressure.

China's trade surplus with the rest of the world tripled in 2005, to US$102 billion. This imbalance caused many in the US and the EU to call for restrictions on Chinese exports, particularly manufactured goods such as textiles. Faced with American and European tariff threats and import restrictions, China was forced to negotiate on how to deal with widening trade gaps with its major trading partners. In June and November, China signed agreements with the EU and the US respectively, stipulating temporary artificial slowdowns in the number of Chinese textile products exported to these countries.

Throughout 2005, several countries and NGOs warned China that its policy of keeping the value of its currency, the yuan, artificially low was a threat to the global economy and to China's own economic growth. The low value of the yuan against other major currencies meant Chinese products were cheaper to import than rival products. This in turn helped to fuel China's massive trade surplus with its trading partners. In July, China made an effort to address these concerns by revaluing the yuan 2.1 per cent higher, removing its peg to the US dollar and permitting a 0.3 per cent fluctuation in the yuan's value on currency markets.

Old superpower versus new?

The Asia-Pacific was hungry for energy in 2005 and its leading states, particularly China and India were prepared to do what it takes to secure hydrocarbon resources. India assiduously wooed Saudi Arabia, the world's largest oil-exporting country, in 2005, culminating in January 2006 with the first state visit by a Saudi monarch in 51 years. Two Chinese state-owned oil companies, the China National Offshore Oil Company (CNOOC) and the China National Petroleum Company (CNPC) were especially active, seeking out new sources of oil, from the Pacific to Africa. However, CNOOC attracted controversy when, in June, it placed a multi-billion dollar bid for US oil company Unocal. The controversy drew attention to a growing feeling in the US that China's rise was not necessarily in its interests. Senior US politicians lobbied hard to block the take-over, arguing that China was in direct competition to the US and therefore any attempt to purchase Unocal was against US interests. CNOOC eventually withdrew its bid when it became clear that Unocal would accept a less contentious offer from American company Chevron.

A Japanese recovery

In 2005, there was further confirmation of a cautious economic recovery in the world's second largest economy. Japan recorded 2.7 per cent GDP growth during the year – the highest rate since 2000. In November, Japan's decade-long deflationary cycle appeared at an end, with consumer prices recording sustained price increases. In December, the Nikkei index reached 16,400 points for the first time in 5 years. Consumer and business confidence and foreign investment also reached new highs in Japan in 2005.

Currencies (units per US$) – Asia

	Unit	Jan 2001	Jan 2002	Jan 2003	Jan 2004	Jan 2005
Afghanistan	Afghani	4,750.00	4,750.00	43.00 (a)	43.00	43.00
Australia	Australian dollar	1.80	1.93	1.77	1.33	1.28
Bangladesh	Taka	54.10	56.95	57.90	58.88	59.69
Bhutan	Ngultrum	46.56	48.25	47.98	45.63	43.47
Brunei	Brunei dollar	1.73	1.85	1.74	1.70	1.63
Cambodia	Riel	3,886.00	3,835.00	3,835.00	3,990.00	3,846.00
China	Renminbi yuan	8.28	8.28	8.28	8.28	8.28
Fiji	Fijian dollar	2.16	2.28	2.08	1.72	1.65
Hong Kong	Hong Kong dollar	7.80	7.80	7.80	7.76	7.77
India	Rupee	46.56	48.25	47.98	45.63	43.47
Indonesia	Rupiah	9,600.50	10,415.00	8,927.50	8,422.50	9,282.50
Japan	Yen	117.98	131.09	119.78	107.17	102.47
Kazakhstan	Tenge	145.39	151.47	155.85	143.25	129.96
North Korea	Won	2.20	2.20	2.20	2.20	900.00
South Korea	Won	1,278.20	1,308.70	1,196.95	1,191.50	1,035.20
Kyrgyzstan	Som	49.22	47.72	46.10	43.88	40.91
Laos	New kip	7,600.00	7,600.00	7,600.00	7,882.00	7,842.00
Macao	Pataca	7.99	8.03	7.99	7.97	8.01
Malaysia	Ringgit	3.80	3.80	3.80	3.80	3.80
Maldives	Rufiyaa	11.72	11.77	12.75	12.80	12.80
Marshall Islands	US dollar	1.00	1.00	1.00	1.00	1.00
Federated States of Micronesia	US dollar	1.00	1.00	1.00	1.00	1.00
Mongolia	Tugrik	1,075.00	1,102.00	1,125.00	1,126.00	1,209.00
Myanmar	Kyat	6.53	6.75	6.28	6.42	6.42
Nepal	Rupee	74.38	76.64	76.50	73.00	69.55
New Zealand	New Zealand dollar	2.24	2.34	1.91	1.52	1.38
Pakistan	Rupee	58.90	60.10	58.25	57.39	59.43
Papua New Guinea	Kina	3.36	3.74	3.95	3.27	3.10
Philippines	Peso	51.60	51.65	53.51	55.52	56.13
Samoa	Tala	3.32	3.53	3.22	2.78	2.68
Singapore	Singapore dollar	1.73	1.85	1.74	1.70	1.63
Sri Lanka	Rupee	84.95	93.15	96.76	96.95	104.48
Taiwan	Taiwanese dollar	32.70	34.99	34.81	33.95	31.69
Tajikistan	Tajik rouble	2.35 (c)	2.40	2.79	2.79	2.79
Thailand	Baht	43.33	43.93	43.03	39.62	38.85
Timor-Leste	US dollar	1.00	1.00	1.00	1.00	1.00
Turkmenistan	Manat	5,200.00 (o)	5,200.00 (o)	5,200.00 (o)	5,200.00 (o)	^5148.00
Uzbekistan	Sum	325.00 (o)	688.00 (1)	970.00	980.00	1,058.00
Vietnam	New dong	14,529.50	15,088.00	15,406.00	15,642.00	15,773.00

^ Jan 2006
(1) central bank realigned official rate 1 Nov 2001; (a) new re-denominated afghani from 31 January 2003; (b) June 2000; (c) somoni introduced 30 October 2000; (o) official

Nations of the World: A Political, Economic and Business Handbook

Key indicators 2004/05 – Asia

	Population (m)	Area ('000 sq km)	GDP per capita (US$)	Inflation (%)	GDP real growth (%)	Balance of trade (US$m)
Afghanistan	25.79	647.50	194	13.0	7.5	-3,313
Australia	20.23	7,682.30	30,445	2.3	3.2	-18,215
Bangladesh	146.39	144.00	376	6.1	5.4	-2,552
Bhutan	2.22	47.00	817	4.5	7.0	–
Brunei	0.37	5.80	15,612	0.9	1.1	–
Cambodia	13.81	181.00	314	2.0	4.3	-818
China	1,335.84	9,597.10	1,269	3.9	9.5	30,700
Fiji	0.84	18.30	2,143	2.4	3.8	-1,030
Hong Kong	7.84	1.10	23,667	-0.4	8.1	-9,312
India	1,088.06	3,287.60	608	3.8	7.3	-20,150
Indonesia	221.78	1,919.40	1,165	6.1	5.1	24,790
Japan	127.94	377.70	36,575	-0.7	2.6	132,130
Kazakhstan	13.89	2,717.30	2,715	6.9	9.4	6,786
North Korea	22.70	122.40	–	–	1.0	–
South Korea	47.72	99.10	14,098	3.6	4.6	38,161
Kyrgyzstan	5.32	198.50	425	4.1	6.0	-128
Laos	5.69	236.80	416	11.2	6.0	-214
Macau	0.45	(a)	18,096	1.1	28.0	–
Malaysia	24.65	330.40	4,625	1.4	7.1	24,200
Maldives	0.29	0.30	2,318	6.4	8.8	-285
Marshall Islands	0.06	0.20	1,800	2.4	-1.5	–
Federated States of Micronesia	0.12	0.70	*2,090	1.5	-3.3	–
Mongolia	2.61	1,565.00	512	5.0	6.0	-147
Myanmar	52.81	676.60	167	9.0	5.0	383
Nepal	26.41	147.20	239	4.0	3.5	–
New Zealand	4.04	268.70	23,899	2.3	5.0	-1,433
Pakistan	157.06	804.00	550	6.7	6.5	-3,382
Papua New Guinea	5.50	462.80	686	7.4	2.5	1,084
Philippines	83.41	300.40	1,014	5.5	6.1	-6,381
Samoa	0.17	2.80	1,750	2.4	3.2	–
Singapore	4.22	0.60	24,740	1.7	8.4	18,800
Sri Lanka	20.48	65.60	989	7.6	5.2	-1,959
Taiwan	23.07	36.00	13,260	1.6	5.7	5,100
Tajikistan	6.54	143.10	329	7.1	10.6	-136
Thailand	64.34	514.00	2,522	2.7	6.1	11,124
Timor-Leste	0.98	19.00	357	4.1	1.0	-159
Turkmenistan	5.74	488.10	2,469	5.9	7.5	1,150
Uzbekistan	27.95	447.40	375	8.8	7.1	880
Vietnam	83.03	329.60	535	7.7	7.7	-2,590

* Estimated figure, (a) area 25.8 square km

Europe

The year 2005 was not the best of years for the European Union (EU). In mid-May, French voters flatly rejected the new European Constitution lovingly drawn up by former French president Valéry Giscard d'Estaing. One week later, an even larger percentage of Dutch voters rejected the proposed constitution. For the first time in the EU's short history, the rift between the politicians and the bureaucrats on the one hand, and Europe's citizens on the other was not only apparent, it had made its mark on the way in which the EU was to develop. The automatic assumption, long cherished by an older generation of European politicians, that the EU was a 'good thing', no longer held up.

If this awareness was a shock to many in Brussels, Europe's leaders showed few signs of actually responding to the challenge. The late June summit of the EU's leaders, presided over by Luxembourg, was principally characterised by an acrimonious row between the EU's would-be economic reformers – the 'herring-eaters' of the North – lead by Tony Blair as the UK assumed the EU's presidency in mid-year, and the so called 'pasta-eaters' of the 'old' Europe. The latter, lead by Jaques Chirac, supported by those countries for whom the EU's social model was paramount, and those that shared with France an attachment to the EU's absurd agricultural policy under which a staggering 40 per cent of all EU expenditure goes on agriculture.

Displaying a characteristic ability not to bite the bullet, the end year EU leaders' summit opted for 'dither' rather than ' decision' and settled for a less than far-reaching review of EU budgetary reforms – in 2008.

Lisbon reforms

In 2000, at a meeting in Lisbon, Portugal's capital, the EU had adopted what became known as the Lisbon strategy for reform, aimed at making Europe 'the most competitive and dynamic knowledge-based economy in the world' by 2010. But since 2000 not too much in the way of structural reform had happened in those countries that most needed it. In part, this was due to the reluctance of Europe's politicians to rock the electoral boat. In France, Italy and Germany, shorter working hours, longer holidays and greater state provision for ill-health and old-age were seen by voters as natural developments. For governments, the easy option was to do nothing in the hope that something would simply 'turn up'. Possibly improved global trading conditions, possibly cheaper energy prices.

What did turn up, however, was not always what had been hoped for. In France, where a nervous government was still coming to terms with the referendum loss, November saw the country plunged into widespread race riots in which thousands of cars were burnt. Interior minister (and presidential hopeful) Nicholas Sarkozy described the rioters as 'scum', which did little to lessen racial tensions. Sarkozy's rival in the presidential race, the unelected 'énarque' Prime Minister Dominic de Villepin, was rushed into introducing a series of ill-thought out job creation and urban re-generation schemes. French unemployment remained stuck at 100 per cent by the end of 2005.

If things looked bad in France, however, in Italy they looked even worse. Bogged down by recession and confronted with steadily worsening public finances, Italy's political leadership remained more concerned with self-preservation than with economic reform as the April 2006 elections approached. Italy's national debt reached 107 per cent of GDP, which itself was on a downward, recessionary trend. The relative strength of the euro did little to help. The Frankfurt based European Central Bank has kept interest rates around 2.00 per cent for over two years. Unable to resort to the traditional tool of devaluation, Italy saw exports slump as exporters found it increasingly difficult to compete with competition from Asia – notably China. For Italy, there were no easy answers. One answer that was proposed by Italian welfare minister Roberto Maroni was the re-adoption of the lira (and the rejection of the euro). In the post referendum shock, similar views were also expressed in France and Germany (where a poll showed a substantial majority in favour of re-adopting the Deutschmark). One central banker observed that the euro agreement had been drafted as a 'marriage with no divorce clause', and the very thought of again having to change slot machines and re-printing bank notes was enough to give rise to second thoughts.

The high hopes pinned on Germany's newly elected Chancellor, Angela Merkel of the CDU, soon dissipated as the reality of Mrs Merkel's position became clear. Such was the narrowness of her victory over former Chancellor Schroeder of the CSU, that she was obliged to form a Grand Coalition cabinet. A number of key ministerial positions went to opposition members, making it difficult for Mrs Merkel to implement her original manifesto. But, in contrast to France and Italy, by late 2005 it appeared that the German economy was responding to increased consumer confidence and greater business optimism. The Schroeder government's 'Hartz' reforms had cut unemployment benefits – especially for the longer-term unemployed. Additionally, a number of large German companies such as Siemens, DaimlerChrysler and Volkswagen had introduced local working agreements.

Slow growth throughout the euro-zone, combined with an increasingly painful realisation of the relentless strength of economies such as China and India have, possibly for the first time, caused an awareness in European public and political opinion that something will have to change. In those countries where economic reform has been at best patchy, 2005 may turn out to have been the year in which the tide turned.

Nations of the World: A Political, Economic and Business Handbook

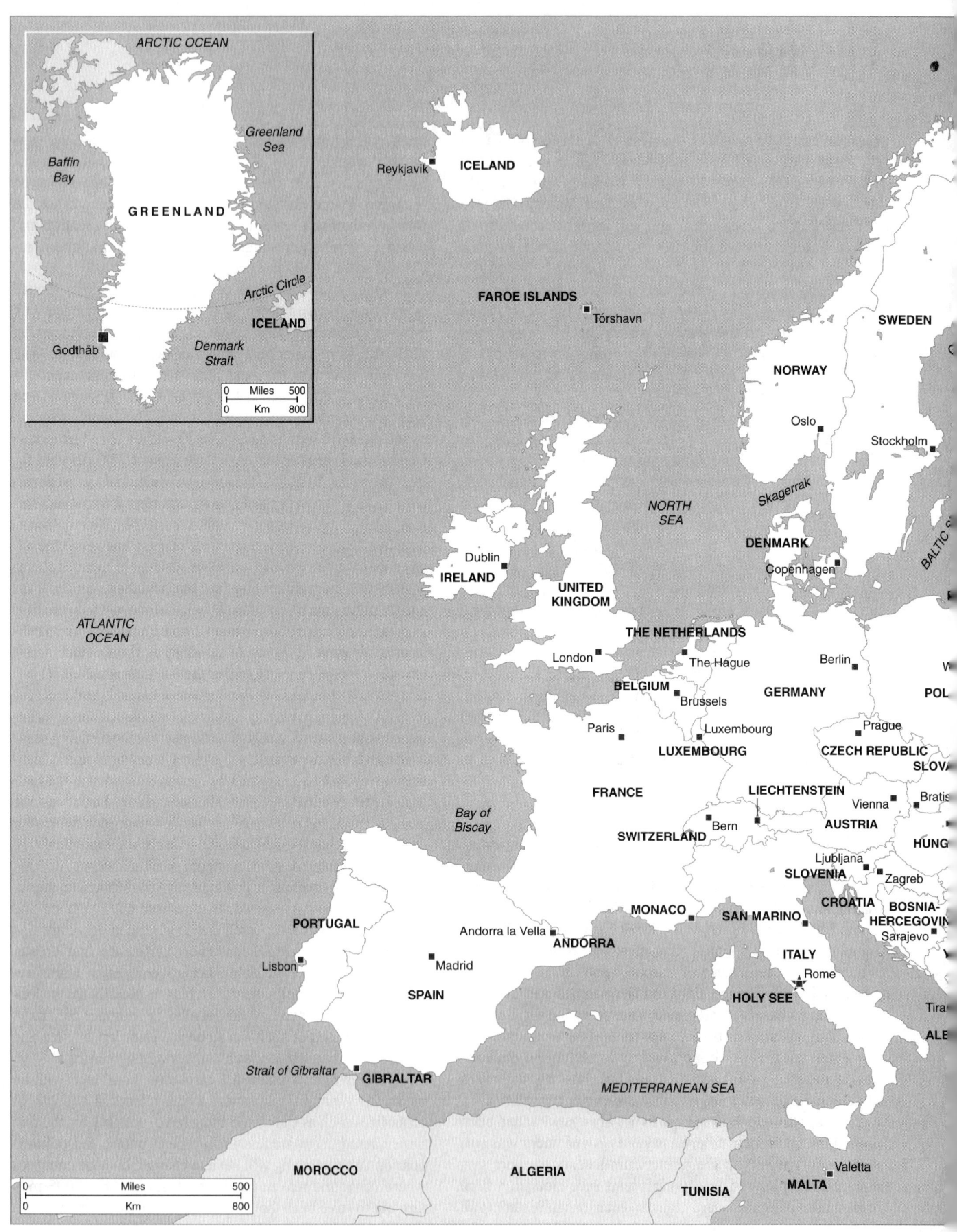

Europe map

Nations of the World: A Political, Economic and Business Handbook

Currencies (units per US$) – Europe

	Unit	Jan 2001	Jan 2002	Jan 2003	Jan 2004	Jan 2005
Albania	Lek	141.00	137.15	133.94	106.40	92.35
Andorra	French franc/Euro	6.91	1.12 (*)	0.96	0.79	0.74
Armenia	Dram	553.97	561.81	558.14	558.14	484.00
Austria	Schilling/Euro	14.50	1.12 (*)	0.96	0.79	0.74
Azerbaijan	Manat	4,558.00	4,780.00	4,901.00	4,923.00	4,915.50
Belarus	Belarus rouble	1,244.00	1,618.00	1,930.00	2,162.50	2,176.00
Belgium	Belgian franc/Euro	42.52	1.12 (*)	0.96	0.79	0.74
Bosnia-Herzegovina	Bosnian dinar/marka	2.06	2.19	1.87	1.56	1.44
Bulgaria	Lev	2.06	2.18	1.88	1.55	1.44
Croatia	Kuna	8.02	8.30	7.22	6.06	5.63
Cyprus	Cyprus pound	0.61	0.64	0.55	0.47	0.43
Czech Republic	Czech koruna	37.20	35.69	30.11	25.68	22.33
Denmark	Danish krone	7.87	8.32	7.13	5.90	5.47
Estonia	Kroon	16.49	17.48	15.02	12.41	11.51
Faroe Islands	Faroese krone	7.87	8.32	7.13	5.90	5.47
Finland	Markka/Euro	6.27	1.12 (*)	0.96	0.79	0.74
France	French franc/Euro	6.91	1.12 (*)	0.96	0.79	0.74
Georgia	Lari	1.97	2.17	2.18	2.11	1.82
Germany	Deutsche mark/Euro	2.06	1.12 (*)	0.96	0.79	0.74
Gibraltar	Gibraltar pound	0.68	0.69	0.62	0.56	0.52
Greece	Drachma/Euro	359.16	1.12 (*)	0.96	0.79	0.74
Greenland	Danish krone	7.87	8.32	7.13	5.90	5.47
The Holy See	Italian lira/Euro	2,040.86	1.12 (*)	0.96	0.79	0.74
Hungary	Forint	279.33	272.25	226.41	207.42	180.73
Iceland	Icelandic krona	84.51	101.17	81.07	70.90	61.48
Ireland	Punt/Euro	0.83	1.12 (*)	0.96	0.79	0.74
Italy	Italian lira/Euro	2,040.86	1.12 (*)	0.96	0.79	0.74
Latvia	Lat	0.62	0.63	0.59	0.53	0.51
Liechtenstein	Swiss franc	1.62	1.65	1.40	1.24	1.14
Lithuania	Lit	4.00	4.00	3.32 (a)	2.74	2.54
Luxembourg	Luxembourg franc/Euro	42.52	1.12 (*)	0.96	0.79	0.74
Macedonia	Macedonian denar	64.05	68.08	58.77	49.05	46.45
Malta	Maltese lira	0.43	0.45	0.40	0.34	0.32
Moldova	Moldovan leu	12.80	13.11	13.90	13.10	12.38
Monaco	French franc/Euro	6.91	1.12 (*)	0.96	0.79	0.74
The Netherlands	Guilder/Euro	2.32	1.12 (*)	0.96	0.79	0.74
Norway	Norwegian krone	8.66	8.93	6.96	6.65	6.06
Poland	Zloty	4.12	3.94	3.83	3.74	2.99
Portugal	Escudo/Euro	211.31	1.12 (*)	0.96	0.79	0.74
Romania	Romanian leu	26,185.00	32,160.00	33,500.00	32,596.00	28,979.20
Russia	Rouble	28.32 (m)	30.54	31.88	29.24	27.72
San Marino	San Marino lira/Euro	2,040.86	1.12 (*)	0.96	0.79	0.74
Serbia	Dinar	13.65	66.48	59.50	54.29	58.30
and Montenegro	Deutsche mark/Euro	2.06	1.12 (*)	0.96	0.79	0.74
Slovakia	Slovak koruna	45.98	47.86	39.63	32.64	28.50
Slovenia	Slovene tolar	226.28	243.27	221.07	187.79	176.28
Spain	Peseta/Euro	175.37	1.12 (*)	0.96	0.79	0.74
Sweden	Swedish krone	9.34	10.33	8.72	7.20	6.65
Switzerland	Swiss franc	1.62	1.65	1.40	1.24	1.14
Turkey	Turkish lira	667,675.00	1,414,000.00	1,647,450.00	1,405,000.00	1,348,500.00
Ukraine	Hryvna	5.43	5.31	5.33	5.33	5.31
United Kingdom	UK pound	0.68	0.69	0.62	0.56	0.52
Euro	(introduced 1 Jan 1999)	1.05	1.12	0.96	0.79	0.74

(a) litas pegged to the US dollar until February 2002, when it was re-pegged to the euro at a rate of Lt3.4528; (m) market rate; (*) euro single currency from 1 January 2002.

Key indicators 2004/05 – Europe

	Population (m)	Area ('000 sq km)	GDP per capita (US$)	Inflation (%)	GDP real growth (%)	Balance of trade (US$m)
Albania	3.16	28.80	2,131	2.9	5.9	-1,522
Andorra	0.07	0.73	–	–	–	–
Armenia	3.00	29.80	1,093	7.0	10.1	-465
Austria	8.07	83.90	35,809	2.0	2.0	4,205
Azerbaijan	8.32	86.60	1,024	8.1	10.1	161
Belarus	9.88	208.00	2,641	18.1	11.0	-2,100
Belgium	10.41	30.50	34,244	1.9	2.7	8,993
Bosnia and Hercegovina	4.36	0.46	2,129	0.8	5.2	-4,570
Bulgaria	7.91	111.00	3,074	6.1	5.7	-3,353
Croatia	4.38	56.50	7,378	2.1	3.8	-8,346
Cyprus	0.96	9.30	19,202	2.3	3.7	-4,043
Czech Republic	10.29	78.90	10,480	2.8	4.0	-1,680
Denmark	5.41	43.10	44,929	1.2	2.3	9,610
Estonia	1.24	45.10	8,287	3.0	6.2	-1,966
Faroe Islands	0.05	1.40	–	–	–	–
Finland	5.22	338.10	35,670	0.1	3.7	12,821
France	60.30	544.00	32,663	2.3	2.3	-7,940
Georgia	5.32	69.70	866	5.7	8.5	-916
Germany	82.63	357.00	32,695	1.8	1.7	191,780
Gibraltar	0.03	(+)	–	–	–	–
Greece	11.07	132.00	18,722	3.1	4.2	-38,780
Greenland	0.06	2,166.10	20,000	1.6	1.8	-39
Hungary	10.12	93.00	10,129	6.8	4.0	-2,922
Iceland	0.30	103.10	43,576	3.1	5.7	-519
Ireland	4.02	70.30	44,888	2.3	5.1	39,562
Italy	57.30	301.30	29,219	2.3	1.2	7,100
Latvia	2.26	64.60	5,822	6.3	8.0	-1,680
Liechtenstein	0.04	0.20	–	–	–	–
Lithuania	3.49	65.20	6,404	1.2	6.6	-2,317
Luxembourg	0.46	2.60	69,929	2.2	4.4	-3,157
Macedonia	2.13	25.70	2,295	-0.3	2.3	-1,048
Malta	0.40	0.40	13,734	2.7	1.5	-871
Moldova	4.21	34.00	716	12.3	7.0	-800
Monaco	0.03	(++)	–	–	–	–
Netherlands	16.37	41.50	35,416	1.4	1.3	40,400
Norway	4.60	324.00	54,521	0.4	2.9	33,576
Poland	38.20	312.70	6,227	3.5	5.3	-5,584
Portugal	10.50	92.10	16,375	2.5	1.0	-17,888
Romania	21.48	237.50	3,207	11.9	8.3	-4,390
Russia	146.74	17,075.00	4,093	10.9	7.1	87,145
San Marino	0.03	0.01	–	–	–	–
Serbia and Montenegro	11.03	102.20	2,893	9.5	7.2	-6,284
Slovakia	5.43	49.00	7,603	7.5	5.5	-430
Slovenia	2.00	20.30	16,447	3.6	4.4	-1,044
Spain	41.90	504.80	24,144	3.1	2.7	-64,524
Sweden	9.00	449.00	38,449	1.1	3.5	23,730
Switzerland	7.43	41.30	49,305	0.8	1.7	15,547
Turkey	72.80	779.50	4,251	10.6	8.0	-23,830
Ukraine	47.25	603.70	1,366	9.0	12.1	3,741
United Kingdom	56.60	244.10	35,460	1.3	3.1	-106,070

(+) area 5.8 square km; (++) area 1.8 square km

Middle East

In 2005, the Middle East was dominated by events in, and stemming from, the three 'I's': Iran, Iraq and Israel. Iraq, with its volatile cocktail of insurgent violence and elections, continued to transfix policy makers both inside the region and out, not the least in Iran, Syria, Turkey, the US and the EU.

Iraq

After a half-century of democratic hiatus, Iraqis went to the polls three times in 2005. As a result, for the first time in the history of the modern Iraqi state, members of the country's Shi'a and Kurdish communities won key positions of power. The US and its allies had banked on elections in Iraq constituting a turning point in the post-Saddam Hussein era. However, as much as this was a watershed, there were complications, at least from the US perspective. Parliamentary elections in January and December, and a referendum in October, split largely along sectarian and ethnic lines. While US relations with the Iraqi Kurds have long been strong, relations with Iraq's Shi'a majority were complex and at times violent – witness the US occupation force's clashes with the Mehdi Army in 2004. Neighbouring states were even more alarmed at the reality of a Shi'a-dominated government in Iraq, particularly Saudi Arabia. Gulf Arab states had backed Saddam Hussein in the 1980s Iran-Iraq Gulf War, largely because of their fear of Iranian regional power and the fact that it was a predominantly Shi'a country. Many Gulf states have restive Shi'a populations of their own. On the other hand, Turkey continued to express dissatisfaction over the direction of the new Iraqi constitution as it concerned Iraqi Kurds. The constitution, adopted in October, formally recognised the autonomy of the *de facto* Kurdish statelet in the country's north. Turkey has made it clear it will not tolerate any move towards Kurdish independence from Iraq, fearful of the consequences for its own Kurdish minority. Syria and Iran also expressed such reservations, as they too have Kurdish minorities.

Iran

A drawn out collapse of the 2005 negotiations between Iran and the international community over Iran's nuclear ambitions ensured that Iran was increasingly centre stage in US and EU diplomacy in the region. Iran and the EU failed to reach an agreement on an alternative approach to acquiring nuclear energy – namely an approach that did not entail the enrichment of uranium. The US and the EU fear that such enrichment could lead to the development of a nuclear bomb. Iran repeatedly denied that it sought such a weapon. The fall out of the collapse of negotiations included a majority vote, in September, on the International Atomic Energy Agency (IAEA) to refer Iran to the UN Security Council. This development paved the way for the imposition of a sanctions regime and, theoretically, discussion of a military action. Although the UK stated that military action was 'inconceivable', US president George W Bush has not ruled out such a course. A temporary stay in the IAEA's referral was granted in order to allow Russia to negotiate a compromise deal with Iran.

Matters were not helped by the surprise election, in June 2005, of Mahmoud Ahmadinejad to the Iranian presidency. The newly elected president confirmed his reputation as a hard line hawk in foreign policy, by threatening, in October, to wipe Israel 'off the map'. Iran's increasing isolation also led it to seek solace in the company of Syria – itself considered a pariah state by the US.

> After a half-century of democratic hiatus, Iraqis went to the polls three times in 2005.

Israel

Politics in Israel and the Palestinian Occupied Territories, comprising jointly some 10 million people in the region of many hundreds of millions, again managed to command international attention in 2005. Palestinians voted for a president in January, for the first time in nine years. Mahmoud Abbas emerged as the victor, officially becoming the Palestinian's first new leader in 37 years. Yasser Arafat, who had died in November 2004, had led the Palestinians since 1968. In Israel, Ariel Sharon, long serving prime minister and renowned 'superhawk' in his dealings with the Palestinians and the Arab world in general, confounded his foes and allies alike. Between August and September, he oversaw the first withdrawal of Israeli settlers and soldiers from occupied territory since peace was reached with Egypt, in 1982. Moreover, in November, after having struggled to rein in rebels in his own party, Sharon abandoned the Likud, a party he had co-founded in 1973, to form his own, centrist political party – Kadima. Sharon and Kadima immediately captured the public imagination and polls suggested that the party would easily win most seats in an election due in March 2006. Central to Sharon's platform was a pledge to reach a final agreement with the Palestinians, thus ending more than half a century of conflict. Analysts promptly stated that this was the best chance for peace since the collapse of the US-brokered Camp David talks in 2000. But then after suffering a minor stroke on 18 December, Sharon was felled by a second, more serious stroke on 4 January 2006. By early February, Sharon was still in a critical condition in a coma, but was, nominally, still head of government. His deputy, Ehud Olmert, was still deputy prime minister (and Sharon's chair at cabinet meetings empty). Kadima, however, moved to elect Olmert their leader in Sharon's place, and continued to dominate the polls.

A democratic awakening?

Democratic development exercised the minds of many Middle Eastern rulers in 2005. Compared to Western standards, the democratic reform on display was at times microscopic, but relative to the region, some of the changes were unprecedented. The region's regimes, dynastic and republican, have been under pressure to reform from the US government since President Bush outlined his vision of a democratic 'Greater Middle East' in November 2003. Parliamentary and plebiscitary elections in Iraq captured most headlines in 2005 but there were significant developments elsewhere in the region. The issue of full political rights for women and an almost universal ban on the formation of political parties were constant refrains. Reforms were also tempered by the continuation of tight controls over the media and the frequent jailing of dissidents deemed to have taken their liberties 'too far'.

Between February and April, the region's biggest monarchy Saudi Arabia held countrywide municipal elections. Voters were asked to elect local councils, which will have advisory powers only. Women, who make up more than 50 per cent of the population, were not allowed to participate. The government announced that women would be able to vote and stand for office when the country next elects its local councils, in 2009.

In May, Kuwait's parliament passed legislation allowing for full political rights for women. In December, the United Arab Emirates (UAE) government announced plans to allow partial elections to the Federal National Council. However, suffrage will be limited to a relatively small number of locally-appointed men. Long ahead of the regional pack in matters of democratic reform (women have had full political rights since 1999), Qatar adopted its first written constitution in June. The constitution guarantees freedom of expression, assembly and religion. Women are already allowed to vote and stand for office in the emirate.

Islamist militancy

The issue of Islamist militancy continued to trouble many governments in the Middle East, not to mention scores of innocent bystanders. Since the US-led invasion of Iraq in March 2003, anti-government and anti-Western violence in the Middle East has escalated dramatically. Again, while the bloody struggle between US forces and their allies in Iraq dominated headlines, clashes took place elsewhere. In 2005, Islamist militants, espousing causes ranging from the violent overthrow of government to the removal of all Western influence, were involved in a string of shoot-outs and bombings across the region. Many of these militants claimed affinity with or membership of al Qaeda.

As in 2004, Saudi Arabia was at the heart of this maelstrom. On several occasions, Saudi security services clashed with militants in the capital Riyadh, as well as in the west of the country, around Jeddah. Dozens have been killed. King Abdullah, who succeeded his half-brother to the throne in August, vowed to crush the al Qaeda network in Saudi Arabia. A 'most-wanted' list of 36 issued by the government in June was largely emptied by December, through the killing, arrest or surrender of wanted militants, but there appeared to be no let up in the violence.

Attacks against government security services and expatriate communities also took place in Kuwait, in January, and Qatar, in March. In August, militants aligned with the Jordanian-born leader of al Qaeda in Iraq, Abu Musab al Zarqawi launched attacks against a US navy ship near Aqaba. In November, the same grouping launched suicide bomb attacks in the Jordanian capital Amman, killing 57 people.

The Middle East's own 'colour' revolution

The assassination of Lebanon's former prime minister Rafik Hariri in February 2005 precipitated what has been called by many the 'cedar revolution', with reference to recent people-power driven revolutions in Kyrgyzstan, Ukraine and Georgia. The assassination was blamed by many Lebanese on Syria and its proxies within Lebanon's government. Hundreds of thousands took to the streets of the capital Beirut, calling for the withdrawal of Syrian troops and intelligence services, present in Lebanon since 1976. The US, the EU, Russia, as well as most of Syria's traditional allies, including Egypt and Saudi Arabia, joined the calls for a withdrawal. This represented a major realignment of the region's main political players, usually tolerant of Syria's activities in Lebanon.

In March, Syria bowed to pressure and initiated what it called a 'redeployment', in effect the full-scale evacuation of Lebanon by its forces. This cleared the way for elections in May and June, the first to be held in Lebanon free of overt Syrian influence in 29 years. Anti-Syrian political parties, led by Hariri's son Saad secured a landslide majority in parliament.

Oil surge

With oil reaching an unprecedented US$66 per barrel in 2005, the Middle East's oil producing countries reaped massive export returns. Even Yemen, long the poorest country in the region, posted a budget surplus on the back of the oil export surge. Prices were boosted by the impact of Hurricane Katrina on US refinery capacity and rapid growth in demand from China and India. With the recent escalation of tensions between Iran and the IAEA, oil prices may well again advance towards 2005's record levels, precipitating further large-scale windfalls of cash in the Middle East. Efforts in Qatar, the UAE, Bahrain, Saudi Arabia and Oman to develop offshore gas fields in 2005 also heralded a renewal of the Middle East's domination of the hydrocarbon sector.

Nations of the World: A Political, Economic and Business Handbook

THE MIDDLE EAST AND NORTH AFRICA

ISRAEL: Jerusalem official capital (disputed by Arab states); Tel Aviv commercial centre

KAZAKHSTAN: Akmola official capital; Almaty commercial and administrative centre

PAKISTAN: Islamabad official capital; Karachi commercial centre

SOMALIA: Mogadishu capital of Somalia; Hargeisa capital of Somaliland (not recognised)

TURKEY: Ankara official capital; Istanbul commercial centre

WESTERN SAHARA: Laayoune unrecognised capital

Middle East map

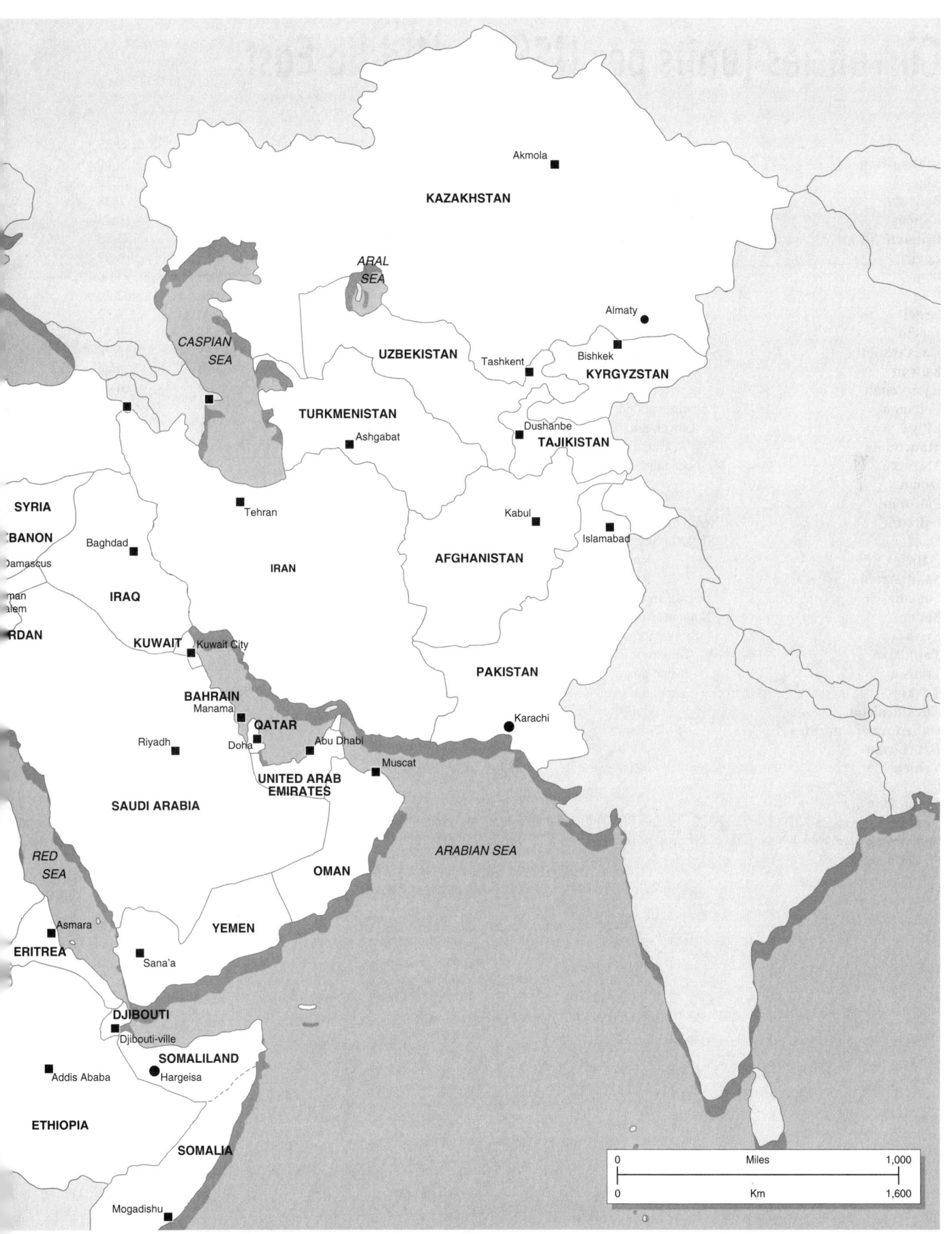

Nations of the World: A Political, Economic and Business Handbook

Currencies (units per US$) – Middle East

	Unit	Jan 2001	Jan 2002	Jan 2003	Jan 2004	Jan 2005
Afghanistan	Afghani	4,750.00	4,750.00	43.00 (b)	43.00	43.00
Algeria	Algerian dinar	72.03	76.35	78.93	72.53	72.10
Bahrain	Bahraini dinar	0.38	0.38	0.38	0.38	0.38
Cyprus	Cyprus pound	0.61	0.64	0.55	0.47	0.43
Djibouti	Djibouti franc	175.40	170.00	175.00	175.00	175.85
Egypt	Egyptian pound	3.86	4.58	4.64 (d)	6.17	6.07
Iran	Rial	1,747.50 (o)	1,750.00 (o)	7,971.00 (e)	8,303.00	8,793.00
Iraq	Dinar	0.31	0.31	0.31	0.31	1,462.50
Israel	Shekel	4.11	4.48	4.79	4.40	4.32
Jordan	Jordanian dinar	0.71	0.71	0.71	0.71	0.71
Kazakhstan	Tenge	145.39	151.47	155.85	143.25	129.96
Kuwait	Kuwaiti dinar	0.31	0.31	0.30	0.29	0.29
Kyrgyzstan	Som	49.22	47.72	46.10	43.88	40.91
Lebanon	Lebanese pound	1,509.00	1,513.75	1,501.00	1,514.00	1,513.50
Libya	Libyan dinar	0.54	0.64	1.23	1.31	1.25
Mauritania	Ouguiya	247.15	264.01	268.23	264.61	261.64
Morocco	Moroccan dirham	10.55	11.46	10.22	8.78	8.24
Oman	Rial	0.39	0.39	0.39	0.39	0.39
Pakistan	Rupee	58.90	60.10	58.25	57.39	59.43
Palestine	Dinar (Jordanian)	0.71	0.71	0.71	0.71	0.71
	Shekel (Israeli)	4.11	4.48	4.79	4.40	4.32
Qatar	Riyal	3.64	3.64	3.64	3.64	3.64
Saudi Arabia	Riyal	3.75	3.75	3.75	3.75	3.75
Somalia	Somali shilling	2,620.00	2,620.00	2,620.00	2,620.00	3,068.00
Sudan	Sudanese dinar	258.70	258.70	258.70	259.80	250.63
Syria	Syrian pound	52.50	45.90	51.58	48.83	52.21
Tajikistan	Tajik rouble	2.35 (*)	2.40	2.79	2.79	2.79
Tunisia	Tunisian dinar	1.36	1.46	1.34	1.21	1.20
Turkey	Turkish lira	667,675.00	1,414,000.00	1,647,450.00	1,405,000.00	1,348,500.00
Turkmenistan	Manat	5,200.00 (o)	5,200.00 (o)	5,200.00 (o)	5,200.00 (o)	^5148.00
United Arab Emirates	Dirham	3.67	3.67	3.67	3.67	3.67
Uzbekistan	Sum	325.00 (o)	688.00 (c)	970.00	980.00	1,058.00
Yemen	Rial	164.39	170.70	177.89	178.01	185.71

^ Jan 2006
(*) somoni introduced 30 October 2000; (a) Jun 2000; (b) new re-valued Afghani currency from 31 January 2003; (c) central bank re-aligned official rate 1 Nov 2001; (d) Egyptian pound floated 29 January 2003; (e) managed float rate from 21 March 2002; (o) official rate

Key indicators 2004/05 – Middle East

	Population (m)	Area ('000 sq km)	GDP per capita (US$)	Inflation (%)	GDP real growth (%)	Balance of trade (US$m)
Afghanistan	25.79	647.50	194	13.0	7.5	-3,313
Algeria	32.16	2,381.70	2,521	3.6	5.3	16,910
Bahrain	0.70	0.70	13,848	4.9	5.5	1,485
Cyprus	0.96	9.30	19,202	2.3	3.7	-4,043
Djibouti	0.77	23.20	793	3.0	3.0	–
Egypt	70.83	1,001.50	1,111	8.1	4.1	-8,210
Iran	67.42	1,648.20	2,473	15.6	6.6	7,490
Iraq	25.39	434.90	1,303	7.0	37.3	200
Israel	6.70	20.80	17,695	-0.4	4.3	-2,397
Jordan	5.80	91.90	1,947	3.4	6.7	-4,400
Kazakhstan	13.89	2,717.30	2,715	6.9	9.4	6,786
Kuwait	2.39	17.80	19,559	1.8	7.2	19,301
Kyrgyzstan	5.32	198.50	425	4.1	6.0	-124
Lebanon	4.43	10.50	5,225	3.0	5.0	-6,379
Libya	5.81	1,775.50	5,121	-1.0	0.9	11,426
Mauritania	2.83	1,030.70	462	10.4	5.2	–
Morocco	29.89	711.00	1,629	2.0	3.5	-6,494
Oman	3.23	320.00	10,339	1.6	2.5	6,767
Pakistan	157.06	803.90	550	6.7	6.5	-3,382
Palestine	3.53	6.30	–	–	–	–
Qatar	0.65	11.40	37,610	7.5	9.9	8,850
Saudi Arabia	23.34	2,149.70	9,972	0.2	5.3	85,222
Somalia	11.60	738.00	–	–	2.8	–
Sudan	38.00	2,505.80	617	8.4	7.3	-192
Syria	19.23	185.20	1,308	3.5	3.4	-115
Tajikistan	6.54	143.10	329	7.1	10.6	-136
Tunisia	9.92	164.20	2,855	3.6	5.8	-2,434
Turkey	72.80	779.50	4,251	10.6	8.0	-23,830
Turkmenistan	5.74	488.10	2,469	5.9	7.5	1,150
United Arab Emirates	3.34	83.60	22,017	3.8	5.7	23,820
Uzbekistan	27.95	447.40	375	8.8	7.1	880
Yemen	19.42	528.00	518	12.5	2.7	734

US Embassies

Albania
2100 S Street NW
Washington, DC 20008
Phone: (202) 223-4942
Fax: (202) 628-7342
www.albaniaembassy.org

Afghanistan
2341 Wyoming Ave. NW
Washington, DC 20008
Phone: (202) 234-3770
Fax: (202) 328-3516

Algeria
2118 Kalorama Rd.
Washington, DC 20008
Phone: (202) 265-2800
Fax: (202) 667-2174
E-mail: embalgus@cais.com
www.algeria-us.org

Andorra
2 United Nations Plaza
25th Floor
New York, NY 10017

Angola
1615 M Street NW
Suite 900
Washington, DC 20036
Phone: (202) 785-1156
Fax: (202) 785-1258
E-mail: angola@angola.org
www.angola.org

Antigua
3216 New Mexico Ave. NW
Washington, DC 20016
Phone: (202) 362-5122
Fax: (202) 362-5225

Argentina
1600 New Hampshire Ave. NW
Washington, DC 20009
Phone: (202) 238-6400
Fax: (202) 332-3171
E-mail: info@embajadaargentinaeeuu.org
www.embajadaargentinaeeuu.org

Armenia
2225 R Street
Washington, DC 20008
Phone: (202) 219-1976
Fax: (202) 319-2982
E-mail: amembusadm@msn.com
www.armeniaemb.org

Australia
1601 Massachusetts Ave. NW
Washington, DC 20036
Phone: (202) 797-3000
Fax: (202) 797-3168

Austria
3524 International Court NW
Washington, DC 20008-3035
Phone: (202) 895-6700
Fax: (202) 895-6750

Azerbaijan
927 15th Street NW
Suite 700
Washington, DC 20035
Phone: (202) 337-3500
Fax: (202) 337-5911
E-mail: azerbaijan@azembassy.com
www.azembassy.org

Bahamas
2220 Massachusetts Ave. NW
Washington, DC 20008
Phone: (202) 319-2660
Fax: (202) 319-2668

Bahrain
3502 International Drive NW
Washington, DC 20008
Phone: (202) 342-0741
Fax: (202) 362-2192
E-mail: info@bahrainembassy.org
www.bahrainembassy.org

Bangladesh
3510 International Drive NW
Washington, DC 20007
Phone: (202) 244-2745
Fax: (202) 244-5366
E-mail: bdenq@bangladoot.org
www.bangladoot.org

Barbados
2144 Wyoming Ave. NW
Washington, DC 20008
Phone: (202) 939-9200
Fax: (202) 332-7467

Botswana
1531-3 New Hampshire Avenue NW
Washington, DC 20009
Phone: (202) 244-4990
Fax: (202) 244-4164
www.botswanaembassy.org

Belarus
1619 New Hampshire Avenue
Washington, DC 20009
Phone: (202) 986-1606
Fax: (202) 986-1805
E-mail: embassy@capu.net
www.belarusembassy.org

Belgium
3330 Garfield Street NW
Washington, DC 20008
Phone: (202) 333-6900
Fax: (202) 333-3079
E-mail: Washington@diplobel.org
www.diplobel.us

Belize
2535 Massachusetts Avenue
Washington, DC 20008
Phone: (202) 332-9636
Fax: (202) 332-6888
E-mail: belize@oas.org
www.embassyofbelize.org

Benin
2124 Kalorama Road NW
Washington, DC 20008
Phone: (202) 232-6656
Fax: (202) 265-1996

Bhutan
2 UN Plaza
27th Floor
New York, NY 10017
Phone: (212) 826-1919
Fax: (212) 826-2998

Bolivia
3014 Massachusetts Avenue NW
Washington, DC 20008
Phone: (202) 483-4410
Fax: (202) 328-3712
www.bolivia-usa.org

Bosnia
2109 E Street NW
Washington, DC 20037
Phone: (202) 337-1500
Fax: (202) 337-1502
E-mail: info@bosniaembassy.org
www.bosniaembassy.org

Brazil
3006 Massachusetts Avenue NW
Washington, DC 2000
Phone: (202) 238-2700
Fax: (202) 238-2827
E-mail: webmaster@brasilemb.org
www.brasilemg.org

Brunei Darussalam
1621 22nd Street NW
Washington, DC 20008
Phone: (202) 237-1838
Fax: (202) 885-0560
E-mail: info@bruneiembassy.org
www.bruneiembassy.org

Bulgaria
1621 22nd Street NW
Washington, DC 20008
Phone: (202) 237-1838
Fax: (202) 885-7973
E-mail: office@bulgaria-embassy.org
www.bulgaria-embassy.org

Burkina Faso
2340 Massachusetts Avenue NW
Washington, DC 20008
Phone: (202) 332-5577
Fax: (202) 667-1882
E-mail: bf@burkinaembassy-usa.org
www.burkinaembassy-usa.org

Burundi
2233 Wisconsin Avenue NW
Suite 212
Washington, DC 20007
Phone: (202) 342-2574
Fax: (202) 342-2578

Cambodia
4500 16th Street NW
Washington, DC 20011
Phone: (202) 726-7741
Fax: (202) 726-8381
E-mail: cambodia@embassy.org
www.embassy.org/cambodia

Cameroon
2349 Massachusetts Avenue
Washington, DC 20008
Phone: (202) 265-8790
Fax: (202) 387-3826

Canada
501 Pennsylvania Avenue NW
Washington, DC 20001
Phone: (202) 682-1740
Fax: (202) 682-7726
E-mail: webmaster@canadianembassy.org
www.candandianembassy.org

Cape Verde
3415 Massachusetts Avenue NW
Washington, DC 20007
Phone: (202) 965-6820
Fax: (202) 965-1207
E-mail: ambacvus@sysnet.net
www.capeverdeusa.org

Central African Republic
1618 22nd Street NW
Washington, DC 20008
Phone: (202) 483-7800
Fax: (202) 332-9893

Chad
2002 R Street NW
Washington, DC 20009
Phone: (202) 462-4009
Fax: (202) 265-1937
E-mail: info@chadembassy.org
www.chadembassy.org

Chile
1732 Massachusetts Avenue
Washington, DC 20036
Phone: (202) 785-1746
Fax: (202) 887-5579
www.chile-usa.org

China
2300 Connecticut Avenue NW
Washington, DC 20008
Phone: (202) 328-2500
Fax: (202) 588-0032
E-mail: chinaembassy_us@fmprc.gov.cn
www.china-embassy.org

Colombia
2118 Leroy Place NW
Washington, DC 20008
Phone: (202) 387-8338
Fax: (202) 232-8643
E-mail: emwas@columbiaemb.org
www.colombiaemb.org

Comoros
420 E 50th Street
New York, NY 10022
Phone: (212) 750-1637
Fax: (212) 983-4712

Congo, Republic of
4891 Colorado Avenue NW
Washington, DC 20011
Phone: (202) 726-5500
Fax: (202) 726-1860
E-mail: info@embassyofcongo.org
www.embassyofcongo.org

Congo, Democratic Republic of
1800 New Hampshire Avenue NW
Washington, DC 20009
Phone: (202) 234-7690
Fax: (202) 234-2609

Costa Rica
2114 S Street NW
ashington, DC 20008
Phone: (202) 234-2945
Fax: (202) 265-4795
E-mail: embassy@costarica-embassy.org
www.costarica-embassy.org

Cote d'Ivoire
424 Massachusetts Avenue NW
Washington, DC 20008
Phone: (202) 797-0300

Croatia
2343 Massachusetts Avenue NW
Washington, DC 20008
Phone: (202) 588-5899
Fax: (202) 588-8936
E-mail: webmaster@croatiaemb.org
www.croatiaemb.org

Cuba
2630 and 2639 16th Street
Washington, DC 20009
Phone: (202) 797-8518
Fax: (202) 986-7283
E-mail: cubaseccion@igc.apc.org

Cyprus
2211 R Street NW
Washington, DC 20008
Phone: (202) 462-5772
Fax: (202) 483-6710
E-mail: cypembwash@earthlink.net
www.cyprusembassy.net

Denmark
3200 Whitehaven Street NW
Washington, DC 20008
Phone: (202) 234-4300
Fax: (202) 328-1470
E-mail: wasamb@wasamb.um.dk
www.denmarkemb.org

Djibouti
1156 15th Street NW
Suite 515
Washington, DC 20005
Phone: (202) 331-0270
Fax: (202) 331-0302

Dominica
3216 New Mexico Avenue
Washington, DC 20016
Phone: (202) 364-6781
Fax: (202) 364-6791
E-mail: embdomdc@aol.com

Dominican Republic
1715 22nd Street NW
Washington, DC 20008
Phone: (202) 332-6280
Fax: (202) 265-8059
E-mail: embdomrepusa@msn.com
www.domrep.org

Ecuador
2535 15th Street NW
Washington, DC 20009
Phone: (202) 234-7200
Fax: (202) 667-3482
E-mail: mecuawaa@erols.com
www.ecuador.org

Egypt
3521 International Court NW
Washington, DC 20008
Phone: (202) 895-5400
Fax: (202) 244-4319
E-mail: embassy@egyptembdc.org
www.egyptembassy.us

El Salvador
2308 California Street NW
Washington, DC 20008
Phone: (202) 265-9671
E-mail: cbartoli@elsalvador.org

Equatorial Guinea
2020 16th Street NW
Washington, DC 20009
Phone: (202) 518-5700
Fax: (202) 518-5252

Eritrea
1707 New Hampshire Avenue NW
Washington, DC 20009
Phone: (202) 319-1991
E-mail: veronica@embassyeritrea.org

Czech Republic
3900 Spring of Freedom Street NW
Washington, DC 20008
Phone: (202) 274-9100
Fax: (202) 966-8540
E-mail: Washington@embassy.mzv.cz
www.mzv.cz/washington/

Estonia
1730 M Street NW
Suite 503
Washington, DC 20008
Phone: (202) 588-0101
Fax: (202) 588-0108
E-mail: info@estemb.org
www.estemb.org

Ethiopia
3506 International Drive NW
Washington, DC 20008
Phone: (202) 364-1200
Fax: (202) 686-9551

Fiji
2233 Wisconsin Avenue NW
Suite 240
Washington, DC 20007
Phone: (202) 337-8320
Fax: (202) 337-1996
E-mail: fijiemb@earthlink.net

Finland
3301 Massachusetts Avenue NW
Washington, DC 20008
Phone: (202) 298-5800
Fax: (202) 298-6030
E-mail: info@finland.org
www.finland.org

France
4101 Reservoir Road NW
Washington, DC 20007
Phone: (202) 944-6000
Fax: (202) 944-6072
E-mail: info@amb-wash.fr
www.info-france-usa.org

Gabon
2034 20th Street NW
Suite 200
Washington, DC 20009
Phone: (202) 797-1000
Fax: 202-332-0668

Gambia
1155 15th Street NW
Suite 1000
Washington, DC 20005
Phone: (202) 785-1399
Fax: (202) 785-1430
E-mail: gamembdc@gambia.com
www.gambia.com/index.html

Georgia
1615 New Hampshire Avenue NW
Suite 300
Washington, DC 20009
Phone: (202) 387-2390
Fax: (202) 393-4537
www.georgiaemb.org

Germany
4645 Reservoir Road NW
Washington, DC 20007-1998
Phone: (202) 298-4000
Fax: (202) 298-4249
www.germany-info.org

Ghana
3512 International Drive NW
Washington, DC 20008
Phone: (202) 686-4529
Fax: (202) 686-4527
E-mail: ghtrade@cais.com
www.ghana-embassy.org

Greece
2221 Massachusetts Avenue NW
Washington, DC 20008
Phone: (202) 939-1300
Fax: (202) 939-1324
www.greekembassy.org

Grenada
1701 New Hampshire Avenue NW
Washington, DC 20009
Phone: (202) 265-2561
Fax: (202) 265-2468
www.grenadaembassyusa.org

Guatemala
2220 R Street NW
Washington, DC 20008
Phone: (202) 745-4952
Fax: (202) 745-1908
E-mail: info@guatemala-embassy.org
www.guatemala-embassy.org

Guinea
2112 Leroy Place NW
Washington, DC 20008
Phone: (202) 986-4300

Guniea-Bissau
15929 Yukon Lake
Rockville, MD 20855
Phone: (301) 947-3958

Guyana
2490 Tracy Place NW
Washington, DC 20008
Phone: (202) 265-6900
Fax: (202) 232-1297
E-mail: guyanaembassy@hotmail.com
www.guyana.org/govt/embassy.html

Haiti
2311 Massachusetts Avenue NW
Washington, DC 20008
Phone: (202) 332-4090
Fax: (202) 745-7215
E-mail: embassy@haiti.org
www.haiti.org

Holy See, The (Vatican City)
3339 Massachusetts Avenue NW
Washington, DC 20008
Phone: (202) 333-7121

Honduras
3007 Tilden Street NW
Suite 4M
Washington, DC 20008
Phone: (202) 966-7702
Fax: (202) 966-9751
E-mail: embhondu@aol.com
www.hondurasemb.org

Hungary
3910 Shoemaker Street NW
Washington, DC 20008
Phone: (202) 362-6730
Fax: (202) 966-8135
E-mail: office@huembwas.org
www.huembwas.org

Iceland
1156 15th Street NW
Suite 1200
Washington, DC 20005-1704
Phone: (202) 265-6653
Fax: (202) 265-6656
E-mail: icemb.wash@utn.stjr.is
www.iceland.org

India
2107 Massachusetts Avenue NW
Washington, DC 20008
Phone: (202) 939-7000
Fax: (202) 265-4351
www.indainembassy.org

Indonesia
2020 Massachusetts Avenue NW
Washington, DC 20036
Phone: (202) 775-5200
Fax: (202) 775-5365

Iran
2209 Wisconsin Avenue NW
Washington, DC 20007
Phone: (202) 965-4990
Fax: (202) 965-1073
www.daftar.org/default_eng.htm

Iraq
1801 P Street NW
Washington, DC 20036
Phone: (202) 483-7500
Fax: (202) 462-5066
www.iraqembassy.org

Ireland
2234 Massachusetts Avenue NW
Washington, DC 20008
Phone: (202) 462-3939
Fax: (202) 232-5993
E-mail: ireland@irelandemb.org
www.irelandemb.org

Israel
3514 International Drive NW
Washington, DC 20008
Phone: (202) 364-5500
Fax: (202) 364-5423
E-mail: ask@israelemb.org
www.israelemb.org

Italy
3000 Whitehaven Street NW
Washington, DC 20008
Phone: (202) 612-4400
Fax: (202) 518-2154
www.italyemb.org

Jamaica
1520 New Hampshire Avenue NW
Washington, DC 20036
Phone: (202) 452-0660
Fax: (202) 452-0081
E-mail: info@emjamusa.org
www.emjamusa.org

Japan
2520 Massachusetts Avenue NW
Washington, DC 20008
Phone: (202) 238-6700
Fax: (202) 328-2187
www.embjapan.org

Jordan
3504 International Drive NW
Washington, DC 20008
Phone: (202) 966-2664
Fax: (202) 966-3110
E-mail: HKJEmbassyDC@aol.com
www.jordanembassyus.org

Kazakhstan
1401 16th Street NW
Washington, DC 20036
Phone: (202) 232-5488
E-mail: kazak@intr.net
www.kazakhembus.com

Kenya
2249 R Street NW
Washington, DC 20008
Phone: (202) 387-6101
Fax: (202) 462-3829
E-mail: info@kenyaembassy.com
www.kenyaembassy.com

Korea
2450 Massachusetts Avenue NW
Washington, DC 20008
Phone: (202) 939-5600
Fax: (202) 797-0595
www.koreaembassyusa.org

Kuwait
2940 Tilden Street NW
Washington, DC 20008
Phone: (202) 966-0702
Fax: (202) 364-2868

Kyrgyzstan
1732 Wisconsin Avenue NW
Washington, DC 20007
Phone: (202) 338-5141
Fax: (202) 338-5139
E-mail: embassy@kyrgyzstan.org
www.kyrgyzstan.org

Laos
2222 S Street NW
Washington, DC 20008
Phone: (202) 332-6416
Fax: (202) 332-4923
www.laoembassy.com

Latvia
4325 17th Street NW
Washington, DC 20011
Phone: (202) 726-8213
Fax: (202) 726-6785
E-mail: embassy@latvia-USA.org
www.latvia-usa.org

Lebanon
2560 28th Street NW
Washington, DC 20008
Phone: (202) 939-6300
Fax: (202) 939-6324
E-mail: info@lebanonembassyus.org
www.lebanonembassyus.org

Lesotho
2511 Massachusetts Avenue NW
Washington, DC 20008
Phone: (202) 797-5333
Fax: (202) 234-6815

Liberia
5201 16th Street NW
Washington, DC 20011
Phone: (202) 723-0437
Fax: (202) 723-0436
E-mail: liberianembassy@urbanafrica.com
www.liberian-connection.com/embassy.htm

Lithuania
2622 16th Street NW
Washington, DC 20009-4202
Phone: (202) 234-5860
Fax: (202) 328-0466
E-mail: admin@ltembassyus.org
www.ltembassyus.org

Luxembourg
2200 Massachusetts Avenue NW
Washington, DC 20008
Phone: (202) 265-4171
Fax: (202) 328-8270
E-mail: infos@luxembourg-usa.org
www.luxembourg-usa.org

Macedonia
1101 30th Street NW
Suite 302
Washington, DC 20007
Phone: (202) 337-3063
Fax: (202) 337-3093
E-mail: usoffice@macedoniaembassy.org
www.macedonianembassy.org

Madagascar
2374 Massachusetts Avenue NW
Washington, DC 20008
Phone: (202) 265-5525
E-mail: malagasy@embassy.org
www.embassy.org/madagascar/

Malawi
2408 Massachusetts Avenue NW
Washington, DC 20008
Phone: (202) 797-1007

Malaysia
3516 International Court NW
Washington, DC 20008
Phone: (202) 572-9700
Fax: (202) 483-7661

Mali
2130 R Street NW
Washington, DC 20008
Phone: (202) 332-2249
Fax: (202) 332-6603
E-mail: info@maliembassy-usa.org
www.maliembassy-usa.org

Malta
2017 Connecticut Avenue NW
Washington, DC 20008
Phone: (202) 462-3611
Fax: (202) 387-5470
E-mail: Malta_Embassy@compuserve.com

Marshall Islands
2433 Massachusetts Avenue NW
Washington, DC 20008
Phone: (202) 234-5414
Fax: (202) 232-3236
E-mail: info@rmiembassyus.org
www.rmiembessay-usa.org

Mauritania
2129 Leroy Place NW
Washington, DC 20008
Phone: (202) 232-5700
Fax: (202) 319-2623
E-mail: info@mauritaniembassy-usa.org
www.maurianiembassy-usa.org

Mauritius
4301 Connecticut Avenue NW
Suite 441
Washington, DC 20008
Phone: (202) 244-1491
Fax: (202) 966-0983
E-mail:MAURITUS.EMBASSY@prodigy.net
www.idsonline.com/usa/embasydc.html

Mexico
1911 Pennsylvania Avenue NW
Washington, DC 20006
Phone: (202) 728-1600
Fax: (202) 728-1698
E-mail: mexembusa@sre.gob.mx
www.embassyofmexico.org

Micronesia
1725 N Street NW
Washington, DC 20036
Phone: (202) 223-4383
Fax: (202) 223-4391
E-mail: fsm@fsmembassy.org
www.fsmembassy.org

Moldova
2101 S Street NW
Washington, DC 20008
Phone: (202) 667-1130
Fax: (202) 667-1204
E-mail: moldova@dgs.dgsys.com

Mongolia
2833 M Street NW
Washington, DC 20007
Phone: (202) 333-7117
Fax: (202) 298-9227
E-mail: esyam@mongolianembassy.us
www.mongolianembassy.us

Morocco
1601 21st Street NW
Washington, DC 20009
Phone: (202) 462-7979
Fax: (202) 265-0161

Mozambique
1990 M Street NW
Suite 570
Washington, DC 20036
Phone: (202) 293-7146
Fax: (202) 835-0245
E-mail: embamoc@aol.com
www.embamoc-usa.org

Myanmar
2300 S Street NW
Washington, DC 20008
Phone: (202) 332-9044
Fax: (202) 332-0946
E-mail: info@mewashingtondc.com
www.mewashingtondc.com

Namibia
1605 New Hampshire Avenue NW
Washington, DC 20009
Phone: (202) 986-0540
Fax: (202) 986-0443
www.namibianembassyusa.org

Nepal
2131 Leroy Place NW
Washington, DC 20008
Phone: (202) 667-4550
Fax: (202) 667-5534
E-mail: nepali@erols.com

Netherlands
4200 Linnean Avenue NW
Washington, DC 20008
Phone: (202) 244-5300
Fax: (202) 362-3430
www.netherlands-embassy.org

New Zealand
37 Observatory Circle
Washington, DC 20008
Phone: (202) 328-4800
Fax: (202) 667-5227
E-mail: nz@nzemb.org
www.nzemb.org

Nicaragua
1627 New Hampshire Avenue NW
Washington, DC 20009
Phone: (202) 939-6570
Fax: (202) 939-6542

Niger
2204 R Street NW
Washington, DC 20008
Phone: (202) 483-4224
Fax: (202) 483-3169
E-mail: embassyofniger@ioip.com
www.nigerembassyusa.org

Nigeria
1333 16th Street NW
Washington, DC 20036
Phone: (202) 986-8499
Fax: (202) 462-7124
www.nigeriaembassyusa.org

Norway
2720 34th Street NW
Washington, DC 20008
Phone: (202) 333-6000
Fax: (202) 337-0870
www.norway.org

Oman
2535 Belmont Road NW
Washington, DC 20008
Phone: (202) 387-1980
Fax: (202) 745-4933

Pakistan
3517 International Court
Washington, DC 20008
Phone: (202) 243-6500
Fax: (202) 686-1534
E-mail: info@embassyofpakistan.org
www.embassyofpakistan.org

Palau
1800 K Street NW
Suite 714
Washington, DC 20006
Phone: (202) 452-6814
Fax: (202) 452-6281
E-mail: info@palauembassy.com

Panama
2862 McGill Terrance NW
Washington, DC 20008
Phone: (202) 483-1407

Papua New Guinea
1779 Massachusetts Avenue NW
Suite 805
Washington, DC 20036
Phone: (202) 745-3680
Fax: (202) 745-3679
E-mail: Kunduwash@aol.com
www.pngembassy.org

Paraguay
2400 Massachusetts Avenue NW
Washington, DC 20008
Phone: (202) 483-6960
Fax: (202) 234-4508

Peru
1700 Massachusetts Avenue NW
Washington, DC 20036
Phone: (202) 833-9860
Fax: (202) 659-8124
E-mail: webmaster@embassyofperu.us
www.Peruvianembassy.us

Philippines
1600 Massachusetts Avenue NW
Washington, DC 20036
Phone: (202) 467-9300
Fax: (202) 467-9417
www.philippineembassy-usa.org

Poland
2640 16th Street NW
Washington, DC 20009
Phone: (202) 234-3800
Fax: (202) 328-6271
E-mail: information@ioip.com
www.polandembassy.org

Portugal
2125 Kalorama Road NW
Washington, DC 20008
Phone: (202) 328-8610
Fax: (202) 462-3726
E-mail: portugal@portugalemb.org
www.protugalemb.org

Qatar
4200 Wisconsin Avenue NW
Suite 200
Washington, DC 20016
Phone: (202) 274-1600
Fax: (202) 237-0061
E-mail: info@qatarembassy.org
www.qatarembassy.net

Romania
1607 23rd Street NW
Washington, DC 20008
Phone: (202) 332-4848
Fax: (202) 232-4748
E-mail: romania1@roembus.org
www.roembus.org

Russia
2650 Wisconsin Avenue NW
Washington, DC 20007
Phone: (202) 298-5700
Fax: (202) 298-5735
www.russianembassy.org

Rwanda
1714 New Hampshire Avenue NW
Washington, DC 20009
Phone: (202) 232-2882
Fax: (202) 232-4544
E-mail: rwandemb@rwandemb.org
www.rwandaemb.org

Saint Kitts/Nevis
3216 New Mexico Avenue NW
Washington, DC 20016
Phone: (202) 686-2636
Fax: (202) 686-5740
E-mail: info@stkittsnevis.org
www.stkittsnevis.org

Saint Lucia
3216 New Mexico Avenue NW
Washington, DC 20016
Phone: (202) 364-6792
Fax: (202) 364-6723

Saint Vincent
3216 New Mexico Avenue NW
Washington, DC 20016
Phone: (202) 364-6730
Fax: (202) 364-6736

Saudi Arabia
601 New Hampshire Avenue NW
Washington, DC 20037
Phone: (202) 337-4076
E-mail: info@saudiembassy.net
www.saudiembassy.net

Senegal
2112 Wyoming Avenue NW
Washington, DC 20008
Phone: (202) 234-0540
E-mail: erahay@senegalembassy-us.org
www.senegalembassy-us.org

Seychelles
800 2nd Avenue
Suite 400
New York, NY 10017
Phone: (212) 687-9766
Fax: (212) 972-1786

Sierra Leone
1701 19th Street NW
Washington, DC 20009
Phone: (202) 939-9261
Fax: (202) 483-1793

Singapore
3501 International Place
Washington, DC 20008
Phone: (202) 537-3100
Fax: (202) 537-0876
E-mail: singemb@bellatlantic.net
www.gov.sg/mfa/washington/

Slovak Republic
3523 International Court NW
Washington, DC 20008
Phone: (202) 237-1054
Fax: (202) 237-6438
E-mail: info@slovakembassy-us.org
www.slovakembaassy-us.org

Slovenia
1525 New Hampshire Avenue NW
Washington, DC 20036
Phone: (202) 667-5363
Fax: (202) 667-4563
E-mail: slovenia@embassy.org
www.gov.si/mzz/dkp/vwa

South Africa
3051 Massachusetts Avenue NW
Washington, DC 20008
Phone: (202) 232-4400
Fax: (202) 265-1607
E-mail: info@saembassy.org
www.saembassy.org

Spain
2375 Pennsylvania Avenue NW
Washington, DC 20037
Phone: (202) 452-0100
Fax: (202) 833-5670
E-mail: spain@spainemb.org
www.spainemb.org

Sri Lanka
2148 Wyoming Avenue NW
Washington, DC 20008
Phone: (202) 483-4025
Fax: (202) 232-7181
E-mail: slembassy@starpower.net
www.slembassyusa.org

Sudan
2210 Massachusetts Avenue NW
Washington, DC 20008
Phone: (202) 338-8565
Fax: (202) 667-2406
E-mail: info@sudanembassyus.org
www.sudanembassy.org

Suriname
4301 Connecticut Avenue NW
Suite 460
Washington, DC 20008
Phone: (202) 244-7488
Fax: (202) 244-5878

Swaziland
3400 International Drive NW
Washington, DC 20008

Sweden
1501 M Street NW
Washington, DC 20005
Phone: (202) 467-2600
Fax: (202) 467-2656
E-mail: embassaden.washington@foreign.ministry.se
www.swedish-embassy.org

Switzerland
2900 Cathedral Avenue NW
Washington, DC 20008
Phone: (202) 745-7900
Fax: (202) 387-2564
E-mail: vertretung@was.rep.admin.ch
www.swissemb.org

Syria
2215 Wyoming Avenue NW
Washington, DC 20008
Phone: (202) 232-6313
Fax: (202) 234-9548

Taiwan
4201 Wisconsin Avenue NW
Washington, DC 20016
Phone: (202) 895-1800
Fax: (202) 966-0825

Tanzania
2139 R Street NW
Washington, DC 20008
Phone: (202) 939-6125
Fax: (202) 797-7408
E-mail: balozi@tanzaniaembassy-us.org
www.tanzaniaembassy-us.org

Thailand
1024 Wisconsin Avenue NW
Suite 401
Washington, DC 20007
Phone: (202) 944-3600
Fax: (202) 944-3611
E-mail: thai.wsn@thaiembdc.org
www.thaiembdc.org

Togo
2208 Massachusetts Avenue NW
Washington, DC 20008
Phone: (202) 234-4212
Fax: (202) 232-3190

Tonga
800 2nd Avenue, Suite 400B
New York, NY 10017

Trinidad and Tobago
1708 Massachusetts Avenue NW
Washington, DC 20036
Phone: (202) 467-6490
Fax: (202) 785-3130
E-mail: embttgo@erols.com
http://ttembassy.cjb.net

Tunisia
1515 Massachusetts Avenue NW
Washington, DC 20005
Phone: (202) 862-1850
Fax: (202) 862-1858

Turkey
2525 Massachusetts Avenue NW
Washington, DC 20008
Phone: (202) 612-6700
Fax: (202) 612-6744
E-mail: info@turkey.org
www.turkey.org

Turkmenistan
2207 Massachusetts Avenue
Washington, DC 20008
Phone: (202) 588-1500
Fax: (202) 588-0697
E-mail: turkmen@earthlink.net
www.turkmenistanembassy.org

Uganda
5911 16th Street NW
Washington, DC 20011
Phone: (202) 726-7100
Fax: (202) 726-1727
E-mail: ugemassy@.aol.com
www.ugandaembassy.com

Ukraine
3350 M Street NW
Washington, DC 20007
Phone: (202) 333-0606
Fax: (202) 338-0817
E-mail: infolook@aol.com
www.ukremb.com

United Arab Emirates
3522 International Court NW
Suite 400
Washington, DC 20008
Phone: (202) 243-2400
Fax: (202) 243-2432

United Kingdom
3100 Massachusetts Avenue NW
Washington, DC 20008
Phone: (202) 588-6500
Fax: (202) 588-7870
www.britainusa.com

Uruguay
1913 I Street NW
Washington, DC 20006
Phone: (202) 331-1313
Fax: (202) 331-8142
E-mail: uruwashi@uruwashi.org
www.uruwashi.org

Uzbekistan
1746 Massachusetts Avenue NW
Washington, DC 20036
Phone: (202) 887-5300
Fax: (202) 293-6804
E-mail: emb@uzbekistan.org
www.uzbekistan.org

Venezuela
1746 Massachusetts Avenue NW
Washington, DC 20007
Phone: (202) 342-2214
Fax: (202) 342-6820
E-mail: prensa@embavenez-us.org
www.embavenez-us.org

Vietnam
1233 20th Street NW
Suite 400
Washington, DC 20007
Phone: (202) 861-0737
Fax: (202) 861-0917
E-mail: info@vietnamembassy-usa.org
www.vietnamembassy-usa.org

Western Samoa
800 2nd Avenue
Suite 400
Washington, DC 20037
Phone: (212) 599-6196
Fax: (212) 599-0797

Yemen
2600 Virginia Avenue NW
Suite 705
Washington, DC 20037
Phone: (202) 965-4760
Fax: (202) 337-2017
E-mail: info@yemenembassy.org
www.yemenembassy.org

Yugoslavia
2134 Kalorama Road NW
Washington, DC 20008
Phone: (202) 332-0333
Fax: (202) 332-3933
www.yuembusa.org

Zambia
2419 Massachusetts Avenue NW
Washington, DC 20008
Phone: (202) 265-9717
Fax: (202) 332-0826

Zimbabwe
1608 New Hampshire Avenue NW
Washington, DC 20009
Phone: (202) 332-7100
Fax: (202) 483-9326
E-mail: zimemb@erols.com
www.zimebassy-usa.org

Mackenzie & Harris
General Reference Titles

The Value of a Dollar 1600-1859, The Colonial Era to The Civil War

Following the format of the widely acclaimed, T*he Value of a Dollar, 1860-2004*, *The Value of a Dollar 1600-1859, The Colonial Era to The Civil War* records the actual prices of thousands of items that consumers purchased from the Colonial Era to the Civil War. Our editorial department had been flooded with requests from users of our Value of a Dollar for the same type of information, just from an earlier time period. This new volume is just the answer – with pricing data from 1600 to 1859. Arranged into five-year chapters, each 5-year chapter includes a Historical Snapshot, Consumer Expenditures, Investments, Selected Income, Income/Standard Jobs, Food Basket, Standard Prices and Miscellany. There is also a section on Trends. This informative section charts the change in price over time and provides added detail on the reasons prices changed within the time period, including industry developments, changes in consumer attitudes and important historical facts. This fascinating survey will serve a wide range of research needs and will be useful in all high school, public and academic library reference collections.

600 pages; Hardcover ISBN 1-59237-094-2, $135.00

The Value of a Dollar 1860-2004, Third Edition

A guide to practical economy, *The Value of a Dollar* records the actual prices of thousands of items that consumers purchased from the Civil War to the present, along with facts about investment options and income opportunities. This brand new Third Edition boasts a brand new addition to each five-year chapter, a section on Trends. This informative section charts the change in price over time and provides added detail on the reasons prices changed within the time period, including industry developments, changes in consumer attitudes and important historical facts. Plus, a brand new chapter for 2000-2004 has been added. Each 5-year chapter includes a Historical Snapshot, Consumer Expenditures, Investments, Selected Income, Income/Standard Jobs, Food Basket, Standard Prices and Miscellany. This interesting and useful publication will be widely used in any reference collection.

"Recommended for high school, college and public libraries." –ARBA

600 pages; Hardcover ISBN 1-59237-074-8, $135.00

Working Americans 1880-1999
Volume I: The Working Class, Volume II: The Middle Class, Volume III: The Upper Class

Each of the volumes in the *Working Americans 1880-1999* series focuses on a particular class of Americans, The Working Class, The Middle Class and The Upper Class over the last 120 years. Chapters in each volume focus on one decade and profile three to five families. Family Profiles include real data on Income & Job Descriptions, Selected Prices of the Times, Annual Income, Annual Budgets, Family Finances, Life at Work, Life at Home, Life in the Community, Working Conditions, Cost of Living, Amusements and much more. Each chapter also contains an Economic Profile with Average Wages of other Professions, a selection of Typical Pricing, Key Events & Inventions, News Profiles, Articles from Local Media and Illustrations. The *Working Americans* series captures the lifestyles of each of the classes from the last twelve decades, covers a vast array of occupations and ethnic backgrounds and travels the entire nation. These interesting and useful compilations of portraits of the American Working, Middle and Upper Classes during the last 120 years will be an important addition to any high school, public or academic library reference collection.

"These interesting, unique compilations of economic and social facts, figures and graphs will support multiple research needs. They will engage and enlighten patrons in high school, public and academic library collections." –Booklist

Volume I: The Working Class ♦ 558 pages; Hardcover ISBN 1-891482-81-5, $145.00
Volume II: The Middle Class ♦ 591 pages; Hardcover ISBN 1-891482-72-6; $145.00
Volume III: The Upper Class ♦ 567 pages; Hardcover ISBN 1-930956-38-X, $145.00

Working Americans 1880-1999 Volume IV: Their Children

This Fourth Volume in the highly successful *Working Americans 1880-1999* series focuses on American children, decade by decade from 1880 to 1999. This interesting and useful volume introduces the reader to three children in each decade, one from each of the Working, Middle and Upper classes. Like the first three volumes in the series, the individual profiles are created from interviews, diaries, statistical studies, biographies and news reports. Profiles cover a broad range of ethnic backgrounds, geographic area and lifestyles – everything from an orphan in Memphis in 1882, following the Yellow Fever epidemic of 1878 to an eleven-year-old nephew of a beer baron and owner of the New York Yankees in New York City in 1921. Chapters also contain important supplementary materials including News Features as well as information on everything from Schools to Parks, Infectious Diseases to Childhood Fears along with Entertainment, Family Life and much more to provide an informative overview of the lifestyles of children from each decade. This interesting account of what life was like for Children in the Working, Middle and Upper Classes will be a welcome addition to the reference collection of any high school, public or academic library.

600 pages; Hardcover ISBN 1-930956-35-5, $145.00

To preview any of our Directories Risk-Free for 30 days, call (800) 562-2139 or fax to (518) 789-0556

Working Americans 1880-2003 Volume V: Americans At War
Working Americans 1880-2003 Volume V: Americans At War is divided into 11 chapters, each covering a decade from 1880-2003 and examines the lives of Americans during the time of war, including declared conflicts, one-time military actions, protests, and preparations for war. Each decade includes several personal profiles, whether on the battlefield or on the homefront, that tell the stories of civilians, soldiers, and officers during the decade. The profiles examine: Life at Home; Life at Work; and Life in the Community. Each decade also includes an Economic Profile with statistical comparisons, a Historical Snapshot, News Profiles, local News Articles, and Illustrations that provide a solid historical background to the decade being examined. Profiles range widely not only geographically, but also emotionally, from that of a girl whose leg was torn off in a blast during WWI, to the boredom of being stationed in the Dakotas as the Indian Wars were drawing to a close. As in previous volumes of the *Working Americans* series, information is presented in narrative form, but hard facts and real-life situations back up each story. The basis of the profiles come from diaries, private print books, personal interviews, family histories, estate documents and magazine articles. For easy reference, *Working Americans 1880-2003 Volume V: Americans At War* includes an in-depth Subject Index. The *Working Americans* series has become an important reference for public libraries, academic libraries and high school libraries. This fifth volume will be a welcome addition to all of these types of reference collections.

600 pages; Hardcover ISBN 1-59237-024-1; $145.00
Five Volume Set (Volumes I-V), Hardcover ISBN 1-59237-034-9, $675.00

Working Americans 1880-2005 Volume VI: Women at Work
Unlike any other volume in the *Working Americans* series, this Sixth Volume, is the first to focus on a particular gender of Americans. *Volume VI: Women at Work*, traces what life was like for working women from the 1860's to the present time. Beginning with the life of a maid in 1890 and a store clerk in 1900 and ending with the life and times of the modern working women, this text captures the struggle, strengths and changing perception of the American woman at work. Each chapter focuses on one decade and profiles three to five women with real data on Income & Job Descriptions, Selected Prices of the Times, Annual Income, Annual Budgets, Family Finances, Life at Work, Life at Home, Life in the Community, Working Conditions, Cost of Living, Amusements and much more. For even broader access to the events, economics and attitude towards women throughout the past 130 years, each chapter is supplemented with News Profiles, Articles from Local Media, Illustrations, Economic Profiles, Typical Pricing, Key Events, Inventions and more. This important volume illustrates what life was like for working women over time and allows the reader to develop an understanding of the changing role of women at work. These interesting and useful compilations of portraits of women at work will be an important addition to any high school, public or academic library reference collection.

600 pages; Hardcover ISBN 1-59237-063-2; $145.00

Working Americans 1880-2005 Volume VII: Social Movements
The newest addition to the widely-successful *Working Americans* series, *Volume VII: Social Movements* explores how Americans sought and fought for change from the 1880s to the present time. Following the format of previous volumes in the Working Americans series, the text examines the lives of 34 individuals who have worked -- often behind the scenes -- to bring about change. Issues include topics as diverse as the Anti-smoking movement of 1901 to efforts by Native Americans to reassert their long lost rights. Along the way, the book will profile individuals brave enough to demand suffrage for Kansas women in 1912 or demand an end to lynching during a March on Washington in 1923. Each profile is enriched with real data on Income & Job Descriptions, Selected Prices of the Times, Annual Incomes & Budgets, Life at Work, Life at Home, Life in the Community, along with News Features, Key Events, and Illustrations. The depth of information contained in each profile allow the user to explore the private, financial and public lives of these subjects, deepening our understanding of how calls for change took place in our society. A must-purchase for the reference collections of high school libraries, public libraries and academic libraries.

600 pages; Hardcover ISBN 1-59237-101-9; $145.00
Seven Volume Set (Volumes I-VII), Hardcover ISBN 1-59237-133-7, $945.00

The Encyclopedia of Warrior Peoples & Fighting Groups
Many military groups throughout the world have excelled in their craft either by fortuitous circumstances, outstanding leadership, or intense training. This new second edition of The Encyclopedia of Warrior Peoples and Fighting Groups explores the origins and leadership of these outstanding combat forces, chronicles their conquests and accomplishments, examines the circumstances surrounding their decline or disbanding, and assesses their influence on the groups and methods of warfare that followed. This edition has been completely updated with information through 2005 and contains over 20 new entries. Readers will encounter ferocious tribes, charismatic leaders, and daring militias, from ancient times to the present, including Amazons, Buffalo Soldiers, Green Berets, Iron Brigade, Kamikazes, Peoples of the Sea, Polish Winged Hussars, Sacred Band of Thebes, Teutonic Knights, and Texas Rangers. With over 100 alphabetical entries, numerous cross-references and illustrations, a comprehensive bibliography, and index, the Encyclopedia of Warrior Peoples and Fighting Groups is a valuable resource for readers seeking insight into the bold history of distinguished fighting forces.

"This work is especially useful for high school students, undergraduates, and general readers with an interest in military history." –Library Journal

Pub. Date: May 2006; Hardcover ISBN 1-59237-116-7; $95.00

To preview any of our Directories Risk-Free for 30 days, call (800) 562-2139 or fax to (518) 789-0556

The Encyclopedia of Invasions & Conquests, From the Ancient Times to the Present

Throughout history, invasions and conquests have played a remarkable role in shaping our world and defining our boundaries, both physically and culturally. This second edition of the popular Encyclopedia of Invasions & Conquests, a comprehensive guide to over 150 invasions, conquests, battles and occupations from ancient times to the present, takes readers on a journey that includes the Roman conquest of Britain, the Portuguese colonization of Brazil, and the Iraqi invasion of Kuwait, to name a few. New articles will explore the late 20th and 21st centuries, with a specific focus on recent conflicts in Afghanistan, Kuwait, Iraq, Yugoslavia, Grenada and Chechnya. Categories of entries include countries, invasions and conquests, and individuals. In addition to covering the military aspects of invasions and conquests, entries cover some of the political, economic, and cultural aspects, for example, the effects of a conquest on the invade country's political and monetary system and in its language and religion. The entries on leaders – among them Sargon, Alexander the Great, William the Conqueror, and Adolf Hitler – deal with the people who sought to gain control, expand power, or exert religious or political influence over others through military means. Revised and updated for this second edition, entries are arranged alphabetically within historical periods. Each chapter provides a map to help readers locate key areas and geographical features, and bibliographical references appear at the end of each entry. Other useful features include cross-references, a cumulative bibliography and a comprehensive subject index. This authoritative, well-organized, lucidly written volume will prove invaluable for a variety of readers, including high school students, military historians, members of the armed forces, history buffs and hobbyists.

"Engaging writing, sensible organization, nice illustrations, interesting and obscure facts, and useful maps make this book a pleasure to read." –ARBA

Pub. Date: March 2006; Hardcover ISBN 1-59237-114-0; $95.00

Encyclopedia of Prisoners of War & Internment

This authoritative second edition provides a valuable overview of the history of prisoners of war and interned civilians, from earliest times to the present. Written by an international team of experts in the field of POW studies, this fascinating and thought-provoking volume includes entries on a wide range of subjects including the Crusades, Plains Indian Warfare, concentration camps, the two world wars, and famous POWs throughout history, as well as atrocities, escapes, and much more. Written in a clear and easily understandable style, this informative reference details over 350 entries, 30% larger than the first edition, that survey the history of prisoners of war and interned civilians from the earliest times to the present, with emphasis on the 19th and 20th centuries. Medical conditions, international law, exchanges of prisoners, organizations working on behalf of POWs, and trials associated with the treatment of captives are just some of the themes explored. Entries range from the Ardeatine Caves Massacre to Kurt Vonnegut. Entries are arranged alphabetically, plus illustrations and maps are provided for easy reference. The text also includes an introduction, bibliography, appendix of selected documents, and end-of-entry reading suggestions. This one-of-a-kind reference will be a helpful addition to the reference collections of all public libraries, high schools, and university libraries and will prove invaluable to historians and military enthusiasts.

"Thorough and detailed yet accessible to the lay reader. Of special interest to subject specialists and historians; recommended for public and academic libraries." - Library Journal

Pub. Date: March 2006; Hardcover ISBN 1-59237-120-5; $95.00

The Religious Right, A Reference Handbook

Timely and unbiased, this third edition updates and expands its examination of the religious right and its influence on our government, citizens, society, and politics. From the fight to outlaw the teaching of Darwin's theory of evolution to the struggle to outlaw abortion, the religious right is continually exerting an influence on public policy. This text explores the influence of religion on legislation and society, while examining the alignment of the religious right with the political right. A historical survey of the movement highlights the shift to "hands-on" approach to politics and the struggle to present a unified front. The coverage offers a critical historical survey of the religious right movement, focusing on its increased involvement in the political arena, attempts to forge coalitions, and notable successes and failures. The text offers complete coverage of biographies of the men and women who have advanced the cause and an up to date chronology illuminate the movement's goals, including their accomplishments and failures. This edition offers an extensive update to all sections along with several brand new entries. Two new sections complement this third edition, a chapter on legal issues and court decisions and a chapter on demographic statistics and electoral patterns. To aid in further research, The Religious Right, offers an entire section of annotated listings of print and non-print resources, as well as of organizations affiliated with the religious right, and those opposing it. Comprehensive in its scope, this work offers easy-to-read, pertinent information for those seeking to understand the religious right and its evolving role in American society. A must for libraries of all sizes, university religion departments, activists, high schools and for those interested in the evolving role of the religious right.

" Recommended for all public and academic libraries." - Library Journal

Pub. Date: November 2006; Hardcover ISBN 1-59237-113-2; $95.00

To preview any of our Directories Risk-Free for 30 days, call (800) 562-2139 or fax to (518) 789-0556

From Suffrage to the Senate, An Encyclopedia of American Women in Politics

From Suffrage to the Senate is a comprehensive and valuable compendium of biographies of leading women in U.S. politics, past and present, and an examination of the wide range of women's movements. Up to date through 2006, this dynamically illustrated reference work explores American women's path to political power and social equality from the struggle for the right to vote and the abolition of slavery to the first African American woman in the U.S. Senate and beyond. This new edition includes over 150 new entries and a brand new section on trends and demographics of women in politics. The in-depth coverage also traces the political heritage of the abolition, labor, suffrage, temperance, and reproductive rights movements. The alphabetically arranged entries include biographies of every woman from across the political spectrum who has served in the U.S. House and Senate, along with women in the Judiciary and the U.S. Cabinet and, new to this edition, biographies of activists and political consultants. Bibliographical references follow each entry. For easy reference, a handy chronology is provided detailing 150 years of women's history. This up-to-date reference will be a must-purchase for women's studies departments, high schools and public libraries and will be a handy resource for those researching the key players in women's politics, past and present.

"An engaging tool that would be useful in high school, public, and academic libraries looking for an overview of the political history of women in the US." –Booklist

Pub. Date: March 2006; Two Volume Set; Hardcover ISBN 1-59237-117-5; $195.00

An African Biographical Dictionary

This landmark second edition is the only biographical dictionary to bring together, in one volume, cultural, social and political leaders – both historical and contemporary – of the sub-Saharan region. Over 800 biographical sketches of prominent Africans, as well as foreigners who have affected the continent's history, are featured, 150 more than the previous edition. The wide spectrum of leaders includes religious figures, writers, politicians, scientists, entertainers, sports personalities and more. Access to these fascinating individuals is provided in a user-friendly format. The biographies are arranged alphabetically, cross-referenced and indexed. Entries include the country or countries in which the person was significant and the commonly accepted dates of birth and death. Each biographical sketch is chronologically written; entries for cultural personalities add an evaluation of their work. This information is followed by a selection of references often found in university and public libraries, including autobiographies and principal biographical works. Appendixes list each individual by country and by field of accomplishment – rulers, musicians, explorers, missionaries, businessmen, physicists – nearly thirty categories in all. Another convenient appendix lists heads of state since independence by country. Up-to-date and representative of African societies as a whole, An African Biographical Dictionary provides a wealth of vital information for students of African culture and is an indispensable reference guide for anyone interested in African affairs.

"An unquestionable convenience to have these concise, informative biographies gathered into one source, indexed, and analyzed by appendixes listing entrants by nation and occupational field." –Wilson Library Bulletin

Pub. Date: July 2006; Hardcover ISBN 1-59237-112-4; $125.00

American Environmental Leaders, From Colonial Times to the Present

A comprehensive and diverse award winning collection of biographies of the most important figures in American environmentalism. Few subjects arouse the passions the way the environment does. How will we feed an ever-increasing population and how can that food be made safe for consumption? Who decides how land is developed? How can environmental policies be made fair for everyone, including multiethnic groups, women, children, and the poor? American Environmental Leaders presents more than 350 biographies of men and women who have devoted their lives to studying, debating, and organizing these and other controversial issues over the last 200 years. In addition to the scientists who have analyzed how human actions affect nature, we are introduced to poets, landscape architects, presidents, painters, activists, even sanitation engineers, and others who have forever altered how we think about the environment. The easy to use A–Z format provides instant access to these fascinating individuals, and frequent cross references indicate others with whom individuals worked (and sometimes clashed). End of entry references provide users with a starting point for further research.

"Highly recommended for high school, academic, and public libraries needing environmental biographical information." –Library Journal/Starred Review

Two Volume Set; Hardcover ISBN 1-57607-385-8 $175.00

World Cultural Leaders of the Twentieth Century

An expansive two volume set that covers 450 worldwide cultural icons, World Cultural Leaders of the Twentieth Century includes each person's works, achievements, and professional careers in a thorough essay. Who was the originator of the term "documentary"? Which poet married the daughter of the famed novelist Thomas Mann in order to help her escape Nazi Germany? Which British writer served as an agent in Russia against the Bolsheviks before the 1917 revolution? These and many more questions are answered in this illuminating text. A handy two volume set that makes it easy to look up 450 worldwide cultural icons: novelists, poets, playwrights, painters, sculptors, architects, dancers, choreographers, actors, directors, filmmakers, singers, composers, and musicians. World Cultural Leaders of the Twentieth Century provides entries (many of them illustrated) covering the person's works, achievements, and professional career in a thorough essay and offers interesting facts and statistics. Entries are fully cross-referenced so that readers can learn how various individuals influenced others. A thorough general index completes the coverage.

"Fills a need for handy, concise information on a wide array of international cultural figures."–ARBA

Two Volume Set; Hardcover ISBN 1-57607-038-7 $175.00

To preview any of our Directories Risk-Free for 30 days, call (800) 562-2139 or fax to (518) 789-0556

Grey House Publishing
Business Directories

The Directory of Business Information Resources, 2006

With 100% verification, over 1,000 new listings and more than 12,000 updates, this 2006 edition of *The Directory of Business Information Resources* is the most up-to-date source for contacts in over 98 business areas – from advertising and agriculture to utilities and wholesalers. This carefully researched volume details: the Associations representing each industry; the Newsletters that keep members current; the Magazines and Journals - with their "Special Issues" - that are important to the trade, the Conventions that are "must attends," Databases, Directories and Industry Web Sites that provide access to must-have marketing resources. Includes contact names, phone & fax numbers, web sites and e-mail addresses. This one-volume resource is a gold mine of information and would be a welcome addition to any reference collection.

"This is a most useful and easy-to-use addition to any researcher's library." –The Information Professionals Institute

2,500 pages; Softcover ISBN 1-59237-078-0, $195.00 ◆ Online Database $495.00

Sports Market Place Directory, 2005

For over 20 years, this comprehensive, up-to-date directory has offered direct access to the Who, What, When & Where of the Sports Industry. With over 20,000 updates and enhancements, the *Sports Market Place Directory* is the most detailed, comprehensive and current sports business reference source available. In 1,800 information-packed pages, *Sports Market Place Directory* profiles contact information and key executives for: Single Sport Organizations, Professional Leagues, Multi-Sport Organizations, Disabled Sports, High School & Youth Sports, Military Sports, Olympic Organizations, Media, Sponsors, Sponsorship & Marketing Event Agencies, Event & Meeting Calendars, Professional Services, College Sports, Manufacturers & Retailers, Facilities and much more. *The Sports Market Place Directory* provides organization's contact information with detailed descriptions including: Key Contacts, physical, mailing, email and web addresses plus phone and fax numbers. Plus, nine important indexes make sure that you can find the information you're looking for quickly and easily: Entry Index, Single Sport Index, Media Index, Sponsor Index, Agency Index, Manufacturers Index, Brand Name Index, Facilities Index and Executive/Geographic Index. For over twenty years, *The Sports Market Place Directory* has assisted thousands of individuals in their pursuit of a career in the sports industry. Why not use "THE SOURCE" that top recruiters, headhunters and career placement centers use to find information on or about sports organizations and key hiring contacts.

1,800 pages; Softcover ISBN 1-59237-077-2, $225.00 ◆ CD-ROM $479.00

The Directory of Mail Order Catalogs, 2006

Published since 1981, this updated edition features 100% verification of data and is the premier source of information on the mail order catalog industry. Details over 12,000 consumer catalog companies with 44 different product chapters from Animals to Toys & Games. Contains detailed contact information including e-mail addresses and web sites along with important business details such as employee size, years in business, sales volume, catalog size, number of catalogs mailed and more. Four indexes provide quick access to information: Catalog & Company Name Index, Geographic Index, Product Index and Web Sites Index.

"This is a godsend for those looking for information." –Reference Book Review

1,700 pages; Softcover ISBN 1-59237-103-5 $250.00 ◆ Online Database (includes a free copy of the directory) $495.00

The Directory of Business to Business Catalogs, 2006

The completely updated *Directory of Business to Business Catalogs*, provides details on over 6,000 suppliers of everything from computers to laboratory supplies... office products to office design... marketing resources to safety equipment... landscaping to maintenance suppliers... building construction and much more. Detailed entries offer mailing address, phone & fax numbers, e-mail addresses, web sites, key contacts, sales volume, employee size, catalog printing information and more. Jut about every kind of product a business needs in its day-to-day operations is covered in this carefully-researched volume. Three indexes are provided for at-a-glance access to information: Catalog & Company Name Index, Geographic Index and Web Sites Index.

"An excellent choice for libraries... wishing to supplement their business supplier resources." –Booklist

800 pages; Softcover ISBN 1-59237-105-1, $165.00 ◆ Online Database (includes a free copy of the directory) $325.00

To preview any of our Directories Risk-Free for 30 days, call (800) 562-2139 or fax to (518) 789-0556

Thomas Food and Beverage Market Place, 2006

Thomas Food and Beverage Market Place is bigger and better than ever with thousands of new companies, thousands of updates to existing companies and two revised and enhanced product category indexes. This comprehensive directory profiles over 18,000 Food & Beverage Manufacturers, 12,000 Equipment & Supply Companies, 2,200 Transportation & Warehouse Companies, 2,000 Brokers & Wholesalers, 8,000 Importers & Exporters, 900 Industry Resources and hundreds of Mail Order Catalogs. Listings include detailed Contact Information, Sales Volumes, Key Contacts, Brand & Product Information, Packaging Details and much more. *Thomas Food and Beverage Market Place* is available as a three-volume printed set, a subscription-based Online Database via the Internet, on CD-ROM, as well as mailing lists and a licensable database.

> "*An essential purchase for those in the food industry but will also be useful in public libraries where needed. Much of the information will be difficult and time consuming to locate without this handy three-volume ready-reference source.*" –ARBA

8,500 pages, 3 Volume Set; Softcover ISBN 1-59237-096-9, $495.00 ♦ CD-ROM $695.00 ♦ CD-ROM & 3 Volume Set Combo $895.00 ♦ Online Database $695.00 ♦ Online Database & 3 Volume Set Combo, $895.00

The Grey House Biometric Information Directory, 2006

With 100% updated information, this latest edition offers a complete, current look, in both print and online form, of biometric companies and products – one of the fastest growing industries in today's economy. Detailed profiles of manufacturers of the latest biometric technology, including Finger, Voice, Face, Hand, Signature, Iris, Vein and Palm Identification systems. Data on the companies include key executives, company size and a detailed, indexed description of their product line. Plus, the Directory also includes valuable business resources, and current editorial make this edition the easiest way for the business community and consumers alike to access the largest, most current compilation of biometric industry information available on the market today. The new edition boasts increased numbers of companies, contact names and company data, with over 700 manufacturers and service providers. Information in the directory includes: Editorial on Advancements in Biometrics; Profiles of 700+ companies listed with contact information; Organizations, Trade & Educational Associations, Publications, Conferences, Trade Shows and Expositions Worldwide; Web Site Index; Biometric & Vendors Services Index by Types of Biometrics; and a Glossary of Biometric Terms. This resource will be an important source for anyone who is considering the use of a biometric product, investing in the development of biometric technology, support existing marketing and sales efforts and will be an important acquisition for the business reference collection for large public and business libraries.

800 pages; Softcover ISBN 1-59237-121-3, $225

The Grey House Homeland Security Directory, 2006

This updated edition features the latest contact information for government and private organizations involved with Homeland Security along with the latest product information and provides detailed profiles of nearly 1,000 Federal & State Organizations & Agencies and over 3,000 Officials and Key Executives involved with Homeland Security. These listings are incredibly detailed and include Mailing Address, Phone & Fax Numbers, Email Addresses & Web Sites, a complete Description of the Agency and a complete list of the Officials and Key Executives associated with the Agency. Next, *The Grey House Homeland Security Directory* provides the go-to source for Homeland Security Products & Services. This section features over 2,000 Companies that provide Consulting, Products or Services. With this Buyer's Guide at their fingertips, users can locate suppliers of everything from Training Materials to Access Controls, from Perimeter Security to BioTerrorism Countermeasures and everything in between – complete with contact information and product descriptions. A handy Product Locator Index is provided to quickly and easily locate suppliers of a particular product. Lastly, an Information Resources Section provides immediate access to contact information for hundreds of Associations, Newsletters, Magazines, Trade Shows, Databases and Directories that focus on Homeland Security. This comprehensive, information-packed resource will be a welcome tool for any company or agency that is in need of Homeland Security information and will be a necessary acquisition for the reference collection of all public libraries and large school districts.

> "*Compiles this information in one place and is discerning in content. A useful purchase for public and academic libraries.*" –Booklist

800 pages; Softcover ISBN 1-59237-084-5, $195.00 ♦ Online Database (includes a free copy of the directory) $385.00

The Grey House Transportation Security Directory & Handbook, 2005

This brand new title is the only reference of its kind that brings together current data on Transportation Security. With information on everything from Regulatory Authorities to Security Equipment, this top-flight database brings together the relevant information necessary for creating and maintaining a security plan for a wide range of transportation facilities. With this current, comprehensive directory at the ready you'll have immediate access to: Regulatory Authorities & Legislation; Information Resources; Sample Security Plans & Checklists; Contact Data for Major Airports, Seaports, Railroads, Trucking Companies and Oil Pipelines; Security Service Providers; Recommended Equipment & Product Information and more. Using the *Grey House Transportation Security Directory & Handbook*, managers will be able to quickly and easily assess their current security plans; develop contacts to create and maintain new security procedures; and source the products and services necessary to adequately maintain a secure environment. This valuable resource is a must for all Security Managers at Airports, Seaports, Railroads, Trucking Companies and Oil Pipelines.

800 pages; Softcover ISBN 1-59237-075-6, $195

To preview any of our Directories Risk-Free for 30 days, call (800) 562-2139 or fax to (518) 789-0556

The Grey House Safety & Security Directory, 2006
The Grey House Safety & Security Directory is the most comprehensive reference tool and buyer's guide for the safety and security industry. Arranged by safety topic, each chapter begins with OSHA regulations for the topic, followed by Training Articles written by top professionals in the field and Self-Inspection Checklists. Next, each topic contains Buyer's Guide sections that feature related products and services. Topics include Administration, Insurance, Loss Control & Consulting, Protective Equipment & Apparel, Noise & Vibration, Facilities Monitoring & Maintenance, Employee Health Maintenance & Ergonomics, Retail Food Services, Machine Guards, Process Guidelines & Tool Handling, Ordinary Materials Handling, Hazardous Materials Handling, Workplace Preparation & Maintenance, Electrical Lighting & Safety, Fire & Rescue and Security. The Buyer's Guide sections are carefully indexed within each topic area to ensure that you can find the supplies needed to meet OSHA's regulations. This comprehensive, up-to-date reference will provide every tool necessary to make sure a business is in compliance with OSHA regulations and locate the products and services needed to meet those regulations.

"Presents industrial safety information for engineers, plant managers, risk managers, and construction site supervisors…" –Choice

1,500 pages, 2 Volume Set; Softcover ISBN 1-59237-104-3, $225.00

The Grey House Performing Arts Directory, 2005
The Grey House Performing Arts Directory is the most comprehensive resource covering the Performing Arts. This important directory provides current information on over 8,500 Dance Companies, Instrumental Music Programs, Opera Companies, Choral Groups, Theater Companies, Performing Arts Series and Performing Arts Facilities. Plus, this edition now contains a brand new section on Artist Management Groups. In addition to mailing address, phone & fax numbers, e-mail addresses and web sites, dozens of other fields of available information include mission statement, key contacts, facilities, seating capacity, season, attendance and more. This directory also provides an important Information Resources section that covers hundreds of Performing Arts Associations, Magazines, Newsletters, Trade Shows, Directories, Databases and Industry Web Sites. Five indexes provide immediate access to this wealth of information: Entry Name, Executive Name, Performance Facilities, Geographic and Information Resources. *The Grey House Performing Arts Directory* pulls together thousands of Performing Arts Organizations, Facilities and Information Resources into an easy-to-use source – this kind of comprehensiveness and extensive detail is not available in any resource on the market place today.

"Immensely useful and user-friendly … recommended for public, academic and certain special library reference collections." –Booklist

1,500 pages; Softcover ISBN 1-59237-023-3, $185.00 ◆ Online Database $335.00

The Directory of Venture Capital & Private Equity Firms, 2006
This edition has been extensively updated and broadly expanded to offer direct access to over 2,800 Domestic and International Venture Capital Firms, including address, phone & fax numbers, e-mail addresses and web sites for both primary and branch locations. Entries include details on the firm's Mission Statement, Industry Group Preferences, Geographic Preferences, Average and Minimum Investments and Investment Criteria. You'll also find details that are available nowhere else, including the Firm's Portfolio Companies and extensive information on each of the firm's Managing Partners, such as Education, Professional Background and Directorships held, along with the Partner's E-mail Address. *The Directory of Venture Capital & Private Equity Firms* offers five important indexes: Geographic Index, Executive Name Index, Portfolio Company Index, Industry Preference Index and College & University Index. With its comprehensive coverage and detailed, extensive information on each company, *The Directory of Venture Capital & Private Equity Firms* is an important addition to any finance collection.

"The sheer number of listings, the descriptive information provided and the outstanding indexing make this directory a better value than its principal competitor, Pratt's Guide to Venture Capital Sources. Recommended for business collections in large public, academic and business libraries." –Choice

1,300 pages; Softcover ISBN 1-59237-102-7, $450.00 ◆ Online Database (includes a free copy of the directory) $889.00

New York State Directory, 2005/06
The New York State Directory, published annually since 1983, is a comprehensive and easy-to-use guide to accessing public officials and private sector organizations and individuals who influence public policy in the state of New York. *The New York State Directory* includes important information on all New York state legislators and congressional representatives, including biographies and key committee assignments. It also includes staff rosters for all branches of New York state government and for federal agencies and departments that impact the state policy process. Following the state government section are 25 chapters covering policy areas from agriculture through veterans' affairs. Each chapter identifies the state, local and federal agencies and officials that formulate or implement policy. In addition, each chapter contains a roster of private sector experts and advocates who influence the policy process. The directory also offers appendices that include statewide party officials; chambers of commerce; lobbying organizations; public and private universities and colleges; television, radio and print media; and local government agencies and officials.

New York State Directory - 800 pages; Softcover ISBN 1-59237-093-4; $129.00
New York State Directory with Profiles of New York – 2 volumes; 1,600 pages; Softcover ISBN 1-59237-095-0; $195

To preview any of our Directories Risk-Free for 30 days, call (800) 562-2139 or fax to (518) 789-0556

Profiles of New York, 2005/06 ♦ Profiles of Florida, 2005/06 ♦ Profiles of Texas, 2005/06

Packed with over 50 pieces of data that make up a complete, user-friendly profile of each state, these directories go even further by then pulling selected data and providing it in ranking list form for even easier comparisons between the 100 largest towns and cities! The careful layout gives the user an easy-to-read snapshot of every single place and county in the state, from the biggest metropolis to the smallest unincorporated hamlet. The richness of each place or county profile is astounding in its depth, from history to weather, all packed in an easy-to-navigate, compact format. No need for piles of multiple sources with this volume on your desk. Here is a look at just a few of the data sets you'll find in each profile: History, Geography, Climate, Population, Vital Statistics, Economy, Income, Taxes, Education, Housing, Health & Environment, Public Safety, Newspapers, Transportation, Presidential Election Results, Information Contacts and Chambers of Commerce. As an added bonus, there is a section on Selected Statistics, where data from the 100 largest towns and cities is arranged into easy-to-use charts. Each of 22 different data points has its own two-page spread with the cities listed in alpha order so researchers can easily compare and rank cities. A remarkable compilation that offers overviews and insights into each corner of the state, *Profiles of New York*, *Profiles of Florida* and *Profiles of Texas* go beyond Census statistics, beyond metro area coverage, beyond the 100 best places to live. Drawn from official census information, other government statistics and original research, you will have at your fingertips data that's available nowhere else in one single source. Data will be published on additional states in 2006 and 2007.

Profiles of New York, 2005/06: 800 pages; Softcover ISBN 1-59237-108-6; $129.00
Profiles of Florida, 2005/06: 800 pages; Softcover ISBN 1-59237-110-8; $129.00
Profies of Texas, 2005/06: 800 pages; Softcover ISBN 1-59237-111-6; $129.00

International Business and Trade Directories

Completely updated, the Third Edition of *International Business and Trade Directories* now contains more than 10,000 entries, over 2,000 more than the last edition, making this directory the most comprehensive resource of the worlds business and trade directories. Entries include content descriptions, price, publisher's name and address, web site and e-mail addresses, phone and fax numbers and editorial staff. Organized by industry group, and then by region, this resource puts over 10,000 industry-specific business and trade directories at the reader's fingertips. Three indexes are included for quick access to information: Geographic Index, Publisher Index and Title Index. Public, college and corporate libraries, as well as individuals and corporations seeking critical market information will want to add this directory to their marketing collection.

"Reasonably priced for a work of this type, this directory should appeal to larger academic, public and corporate libraries with an international focus." –Library Journal

1,800 pages; Softcover ISBN 1-930956-63-0, $225.00 ♦ Online Database (includes a free copy of the directory) $450.00

The Rauch Guide to the US Adhesives & Sealants, Cosmetics & Toiletries, Ink, Paint, Plastics, Pulp & Paper and Rubber Industries

The Rauch Guides are known worldwide for their comprehensive marketing information. Acquired by Grey House Publishing in 2005, new updated and revised editions will be published throughout 2005 and 2006. Each Guide provides market facts and figures in a highly organized format, ideal for today's busy personnel, serving as ready-references for top executives as well as the industry newcomer. *The Rauch Guides* save time and money by organizing widely scattered information and providing estimates for important business decisions, some of which are available nowhere else. Each Guide is organized into several information-packed chapters. After a brief introduction, the ECONOMICS section provides data on industry shipments; long-term growth and forecasts; prices; company performance; employment, expenditures, and productivity; transportation and geographical patterns; packaging; foreign trade; and government regulations. Next, TECHNOLOGY & RAW MATERIALS provide market, technical, and raw material information for chemicals, equipment and related materials, including market size and leading suppliers, prices, end uses, and trends. PRODUCTS & MARKETS provide information for each major industry product, including market size and historical trends, leading suppliers, five-year forecasts, industry structure, and major end uses. For easy access, each *Guide* contains a chapter on INDUSTRY ACTIVITIES, ORGANIZATIONS & SOURCES OF INFORMATION with detailed information on meetings, exhibits, and trade shows, sources of statistical information, trade associations, technical and professional societies, and trade and technical periodicals. Next, the COMPANY DIRECTORY profiles major industry companies, both public and private. Generally several hundred companies are analyzed. Information includes complete contact information, web address, estimated total and domestic sales, product description, and recent mergers and acquisitions. Each Guide also contains several APPENDICES that provide a cross-reference of suppliers, subsidiaries and divisions. The Rauch Guides will prove to be an invaluable source of market information, company data, trends and forecasts that anyone in these fast-paced industries.

The Rauch Guide to the U.S. Paint Industry Softcover ISBN 1-59237-127-2 $595 ♦ The Rauch Guide to the U.S. Plastics Industry Softcover ISBN 1-59237-128-0 $595 ♦ The Rauch Guide to the U.S. Adhesives and Sealants Industry Softcover ISBN 1-59237-129-9 $595 ♦ The Rauch Guide to the U.S. Ink Industry Softcover ISBN 1-59237-126-4 $595 ♦ The Rauch Guide to the U.S. Rubber Industry Softcover ISBN 1-59237-130-2 $595 ♦ The Rauch Guide to the U.S. Pulp and Paper Industry Softcover ISBN 1-59237-131-0 $595 ♦ The Rauch Guide to the U.S. Cosmetic and Toiletries Industry Softcover ISBN 1-59237-132-9 $895

To preview any of our Directories Risk-Free for 30 days, call (800) 562-2139 or fax to (518) 789-0556

Universal Reference Publications
Statistical & Demographic Reference Books

America's Top-Rated Cities, 2006
America's Top-Rated Cities provides current, comprehensive statistical information and other essential data in one easy-to-use source on the 100 "top" cities that have been cited as the best for business and living in the U.S. This handbook allows readers to see, at a glance, a concise social, business, economic, demographic and environmental profile of each city, including brief evaluative comments. In addition to detailed data on Cost of Living, Finances, Real Estate, Education, Major Employers, Media, Crime and Climate, city reports now include Housing Vacancies, Tax Audits, Bankruptcy, Presidential Election Results and more. This outstanding source of information will be widely used in any reference collection.

"The only source of its kind that brings together all of this information into one easy-to-use source. It will be beneficial to many business and public libraries." –ARBA

2,500 pages, 4 Volume Set; Softcover ISBN 1-59237-076-4, $195.00

America's Top-Rated Smaller Cities, 2004/05
A perfect companion to *America's Top-Rated Cities*, *America's Top-Rated Smaller Cities* provides current, comprehensive business and living profiles of smaller cities (population 25,000-99,999) that have been cited as the best for business and living in the United States. Sixty cities make up this 2004 edition of *America's Top-Rated Smaller Cities*, all are top-ranked by Population Growth, Median Income, Unemployment Rate and Crime Rate. City reports reflect the most current data available on a wide-range of statistics, including Employment & Earnings, Household Income, Unemployment Rate, Population Characteristics, Taxes, Cost of Living, Education, Health Care, Public Safety, Recreation, Media, Air & Water Quality and much more. Plus, each city report contains a Background of the City, and an Overview of the State Finances. *America's Top-Rated Smaller Cities* offers a reliable, one-stop source for statistical data that, before now, could only be found scattered in hundreds of sources. This volume is designed for a wide range of readers: individuals considering relocating a residence or business; professionals considering expanding their business or changing careers; general and market researchers; real estate consultants; human resource personnel; urban planners and investors.

"Provides current, comprehensive statistical information in one easy-to-use source... Recommended for public and academic libraries and specialized collections." –Library Journal

1,100 pages; Softcover ISBN 1-59237-043-8, $160.00

Profiles of America: Facts, Figures & Statistics for Every Populated Place in the United States
Profiles of America is the only source that pulls together, in one place, statistical, historical and descriptive information about every place in the United States in an easy-to-use format. This award winning reference set, now in its second edition, compiles statistics and data from over 20 different sources – the latest census information has been included along with more than nine brand new statistical topics. This Four-Volume Set details over 40,000 places, from the biggest metropolis to the smallest unincorporated hamlet, and provides statistical details and information on over 50 different topics including Geography, Climate, Population, Vital Statistics, Economy, Income, Taxes, Education, Housing, Health & Environment, Public Safety, Newspapers, Transportation, Presidential Election Results and Information Contacts or Chambers of Commerce. Profiles are arranged, for ease-of-use, by state and then by county. Each county begins with a County-Wide Overview and is followed by information for each Community in that particular county. The Community Profiles within the county are arranged alphabetically. *Profiles of America* is a virtual snapshot of America at your fingertips and a unique compilation of information that will be widely used in any reference collection.

A Library Journal Best Reference Book "An outstanding compilation." –Library Journal

10,000 pages; Four Volume Set; Softcover ISBN 1-891482-80-7, $595.00

The Comparative Guide to American Suburbs, 2005
The Comparative Guide to American Suburbs is a one-stop source for Statistics on the 2,000+ suburban communities surrounding the 50 largest metropolitan areas – their population characteristics, income levels, economy, school system and important data on how they compare to one another. Organized into 50 Metropolitan Area chapters, each chapter contains an overview of the Metropolitan Area, a detailed Map followed by a comprehensive Statistical Profile of each Suburban Community, including Contact Information, Physical Characteristics, Population Characteristics, Income, Economy, Unemployment Rate, Cost of Living, Education, Chambers of Commerce and more. Next, statistical data is sorted into Ranking Tables that rank the suburbs by twenty different criteria, including Population, Per Capita Income, Unemployment Rate, Crime Rate, Cost of Living and more. *The Comparative Guide to American Suburbs* is the best source for locating data on suburbs. Those looking to relocate, as well as those doing preliminary market research, will find this an invaluable timesaving resource.

"Public and academic libraries will find this compilation useful...The work draws together figures from many sources and will be especially helpful for job relocation decisions." – Booklist

1,700 pages; Softcover ISBN 1-59237-004-7, $130.00

To preview any of our Directories Risk-Free for 30 days, call (800) 562-2139 or fax to (518) 789-0556

The Asian Databook: Statistics for all US Counties & Cities with Over 10,000 Population

This is the first-ever resource that compiles statistics and rankings on the US Asian population. *The Asian Databook* presents over 20 statistical data points for each city and county, arranged alphabetically by state, then alphabetically by place name. Data reported for each place includes Population, Languages Spoken at Home, Foreign-Born, Educational Attainment, Income Figures, Poverty Status, Homeownership, Home Values & Rent, and more. Next, in the Rankings Section, the top 75 places are listed for each data element. These easy-to-access ranking tables allow the user to quickly determine trends and population characteristics. This kind of comparative data can not be found elsewhere, in print or on the web, in a format that's as easy-to-use or more concise. A useful resource for those searching for demographics data, career search and relocation information and also for market research. With data ranging from Ancestry to Education, *The Asian Databook* presents a useful compilation of information that will be a much-needed resource in the reference collection of any public or academic library along with the marketing collection of any company whose primary focus in on the Asian population.

1,000 pages; Softcover ISBN 1-59237-044-6 $150.00

The Hispanic Databook: Statistics for all US Counties & Cities with Over 10,000 Population

Previously published by Toucan Valley Publications, this second edition has been completely updated with figures from the latest census and has been broadly expanded to include dozens of new data elements and a brand new Rankings section. The Hispanic population in the United States has increased over 42% in the last 10 years and accounts for 12.5% of the total US population. For ease-of-use, *The Hispanic Databook* presents over 20 statistical data points for each city and county, arranged alphabetically by state, then alphabetically by place name. Data reported for each place includes Population, Languages Spoken at Home, Foreign-Born, Educational Attainment, Income Figures, Poverty Status, Homeownership, Home Values & Rent, and more. Next, in the Rankings Section, the top 75 places are listed for each data element. These easy-to-access ranking tables allow the user to quickly determine trends and population characteristics. This kind of comparative data can not be found elsewhere, in print or on the web, in a format that's as easy-to-use or more concise. A useful resource for those searching for demographics data, career search and relocation information and also for market research. With data ranging from Ancestry to Education, *The Hispanic Databook* presents a useful compilation of information that will be a much-needed resource in the reference collection of any public or academic library along with the marketing collection of any company whose primary focus in on the Hispanic population.

> *"This accurate, clearly presented volume of selected Hispanic demographics is recommended for large public libraries and research collections."* –Library Journal

1,000 pages; Softcover ISBN 1-59237-008-X, $150.00

Ancestry in America: A Comparative Guide to Over 200 Ethnic Backgrounds

This brand new reference work pulls together thousands of comparative statistics on the Ethnic Backgrounds of all populated places in the United States with populations over 10,000. Never before has this kind of information been reported in a single volume. Section One, Statistics by Place, is made up of a list of over 200 ancestry and race categories arranged alphabetically by each of the 5,000 different places with populations over 10,000. The population number of the ancestry group in that city or town is provided along with the percent that group represents of the total population. This informative city-by-city section allows the user to quickly and easily explore the ethnic makeup of all major population bases in the United States. Section Two, Comparative Rankings, contains three tables for each ethnicity and race. In the first table, the top 150 populated places are ranked by population number for that particular ancestry group, regardless of population. In the second table, the top 150 populated places are ranked by the percent of the total population for that ancestry group. In the third table, those top 150 populated places with 10,000 population are ranked by population number for each ancestry group. These easy-to-navigate tables allow users to see ancestry population patterns and make city-by-city comparisons as well. Plus, as an added bonus with the purchase of *Ancestry in America*, a free companion CD-ROM is available that lists statistics and rankings for all of the 35,000 populated places in the United States. This brand new, information-packed resource will serve a wide-range or research requests for demographics, population characteristics, relocation information and much more. *Ancestry in America: A Comparative Guide to Over 200 Ethnic Backgrounds* will be an important acquisition to all reference collections.

> *"This compilation will serve a wide range of research requests for population characteristics … it offers much more detail than other sources."* –Booklist

1,500 pages; Softcover ISBN 1-59237-029-2, $225.00

Crime in America's Top-Rated Cities, 2000

This volume includes over 20 years of crime statistics in all major crime categories: violent crimes, property crimes and total crime. *Crime in America's Top-Rated Cities* is conveniently arranged by city and covers 76 top-rated cities. *Crime in America's Top-Rated Cities* offers details that compare the number of crimes and crime rates for the city, suburbs and metro area along with national crime trends for violent, property and total crimes. Also, this handbook contains important information and statistics on Anti-Crime Programs, Crime Risk, Hate Crimes, Illegal Drugs, Law Enforcement, Correctional Facilities, Death Penalty Laws and much more. A much-needed resource for people who are relocating, business professionals, general researchers, the press, law enforcement officials and students of criminal justice.

> *"Data is easy to access and will save hours of searching."* –Global Enforcement Review

832 pages; Softcover ISBN 1-891482-84-X, $155.00

To preview any of our Directories Risk-Free for 30 days, call (800) 562-2139 or fax to (518) 789-0556

The American Tally: Statistics & Comparative Rankings for U.S. Cities with Populations over 10,000

This important statistical handbook compiles, all in one place, comparative statistics on all U.S. cities and towns with a 10,000+ population. *The American Tally* provides statistical details on over 4,000 cities and towns and profiles how they compare with one another in Population Characteristics, Education, Language & Immigration, Income & Employment and Housing. Each section begins with an alphabetical listing of cities by state, allowing for quick access to both the statistics and relative rankings of any city. Next, the highest and lowest cities are listed in each statistic. These important, informative lists provide quick reference to which cities are at both extremes of the spectrum for each statistic. Unlike any other reference, *The American Tally* provides quick, easy access to comparative statistics – a must-have for any reference collection.

"A solid library reference." -Bookwatch

500 pages; Softcover ISBN 1-930956-29-0, $125.00

The Grey House Handbook on Alternative Energy, 2006

This is the first ever resource to pull together information, resources and statistics for all types of Alternative Energy, including Hydro, Wind, Solar, Coal, Natural Gas and Atomic Energy sources. The Handbook begins with an informative Introduction to Alternative Energy Resources, including editorial on the history of energy, the necessity of using alternative energy, conservation and the economics of using alternative energy sources. Plus, handy charts are also included that cover uses of energy sources today; forecasts of energy sources and the availability of energy sources in the future. Next, readers will find chapters on each Type of Energy Source. Chapters begin with an Introduction to the specific energy source, History, Strengths & Drawbacks, Industrial & Residential Use and Trends. Several articles are also included for each energy source, followed by Resources, including Associations, Magazines, Trade Shows and Vendors. The Grey House Handbook on Alternative Energy also contains a informative, useful section on Statistics. These charts allow for easy location of very specific data. A handy Glossary and section on Public Energy Companies is also included for easy reference. Three indexes, Product Index, Subject Index and Entry Name Index allow the user to locate specific resources quickly and easily. As the need for alternative energy sources continues to grow, having access to these resources will become more and more important. This first edition will prove useful to the reference collections public and academic libraries.

800 pages; Softcover ISBN 1-59237-134-5; $165.00

The Environmental Resource Handbook, 2005/06

The Environmental Resource Handbook is the most up-to-date and comprehensive source for Environmental Resources and Statistics. Section I: Resources provides detailed contact information for thousands of information sources, including Associations & Organizations, Awards & Honors, Conferences, Foundations & Grants, Environmental Health, Government Agencies, National Parks & Wildlife Refuges, Publications, Research Centers, Educational Programs, Green Product Catalogs, Consultants and much more. Section II: Statistics, provides statistics and rankings on hundreds of important topics, including Children's Environmental Index, Municipal Finances, Toxic Chemicals, Recycling, Climate, Air & Water Quality and more. This kind of up-to-date environmental data, all in one place, is not available anywhere else on the market place today. This vast compilation of resources and statistics is a must-have for all public and academic libraries as well as any organization with a primary focus on the environment.

"…the intrinsic value of the information make it worth consideration by libraries with environmental collections and environmentally concerned users." –Booklist

1,000 pages; Softcover ISBN 1-59237-090-X, $155.00 ◆ Online Database $300.00

Weather America, A Thirty-Year Summary of Statistical Weather Data and Rankings

This valuable resource provides extensive climatological data for over 4,000 National and Cooperative Weather Stations throughout the United States. *Weather America* begins with a new Major Storms section that details major storm events of the nation and a National Rankings section that details rankings for several data elements, such as Maximum Temperature and Precipitation. The main body of *Weather America* is organized into 50 state sections. Each section provides a Data Table on each Weather Station, organized alphabetically, that provides statistics on Maximum and Minimum Temperatures, Precipitation, Snowfall, Extreme Temperatures, Foggy Days, Humidity and more. State sections contain two brand new features in this edition – a City Index and a narrative Description of the climatic conditions of the state. Each section also includes a revised Map of the State that includes not only weather stations, but cities and towns.

"Best Reference Book of the Year." –Library Journal

2,013 pages; Softcover ISBN 1-891482-29-7, $175.00

To preview any of our Directories Risk-Free for 30 days, call (800) 562-2139 or fax to (518) 789-0556

Sedgwick Press
Health Directories

The Complete Directory for People with Disabilities, 2006

A wealth of information, now in one comprehensive sourcebook. Completely updated, this edition contains more information than ever before, including thousands of new entries and enhancements to existing entries and thousands of additional web sites and e-mail addresses. This up-to-date directory is the most comprehensive resource available for people with disabilities, detailing Independent Living Centers, Rehabilitation Facilities, State & Federal Agencies, Associations, Support Groups, Periodicals & Books, Assistive Devices, Employment & Education Programs, Camps and Travel Groups. Each year, more libraries, schools, colleges, hospitals, rehabilitation centers and individuals add *The Complete Directory for People with Disabilities* to their collections, making sure that this information is readily available to the families, individuals and professionals who can benefit most from the amazing wealth of resources cataloged here.

"No other reference tool exists to meet the special needs of the disabled in one convenient resource for information." –Library Journal

1,200 pages; Softcover ISBN 1-59237-083-7, $165.00 ♦ Online Database $215.00 ♦ Online Database & Directory Combo $300.00

The Complete Directory for People with Chronic Illness, 2005/06

Thousands of hours of research have gone into this completely updated 2005/06 edition – several new chapters have been added along with thousands of new entries and enhancements to existing entries. Plus, each chronic illness chapter has been reviewed by an medical expert in the field. This widely-hailed directory is structured around the 90 most prevalent chronic illnesses – from Asthma to Cancer to Wilson's Disease – and provides a comprehensive overview of the support services and information resources available for people diagnosed with a chronic illness. Each chronic illness has its own chapter and contains a brief description in layman's language, followed by important resources for National & Local Organizations, State Agencies, Newsletters, Books & Periodicals, Libraries & Research Centers, Support Groups & Hotlines, Web Sites and much more. This directory is an important resource for health care professionals, the collections of hospital and health care libraries, as well as an invaluable tool for people with a chronic illness and their support network.

"A must purchase for all hospital and health care libraries and is strongly recommended for all public library reference departments." –ARBA

1,200 pages; Softcover ISBN 1-59237-081-0, $165.00 ♦ Online Database $215.00 ♦ Online Database & Directory Combo $300.00

The Complete Learning Disabilities Directory, 2005

The Complete Learning Disabilities Directory is the most comprehensive database of Programs, Services, Curriculum Materials, Professional Meetings & Resources, Camps, Newsletters and Support Groups for teachers, students and families concerned with learning disabilities. This information-packed directory includes information about Associations & Organizations, Schools, Colleges & Testing Materials, Government Agencies, Legal Resources and much more. For quick, easy access to information, this directory contains four indexes: Entry Name Index, Subject Index and Geographic Index. With every passing year, the field of learning disabilities attracts more attention and the network of caring, committed and knowledgeable professionals grows every day. This directory is an invaluable research tool for these parents, students and professionals.

"Due to its wealth and depth of coverage, parents, teachers and others... should find this an invaluable resource." -Booklist

900 pages; Softcover ISBN 1-59237-092-6, $145.00 ♦ Online Database $195.00 ♦ Online Database & Directory Combo $280.00

The Complete Mental Health Directory, 2006

This is the most comprehensive resource covering the field of behavioral health, with critical information for both the layman and the mental health professional. For the layman, this directory offers understandable descriptions of 25 Mental Health Disorders as well as detailed information on Associations, Media, Support Groups and Mental Health Facilities. For the professional, *The Complete Mental Health Directory* offers critical and comprehensive information on Managed Care Organizations, Information Systems, Government Agencies and Provider Organizations. This comprehensive volume of needed information will be widely used in any reference collection.

"... the strength of this directory is that it consolidates widely dispersed information into a single volume." –Booklist

800 pages; Softcover ISBN 1-59237-124-8, $165.00 ♦ Online Database $215.00 ♦ Online & Directory Combo $300.00

To preview any of our Directories Risk-Free for 30 days, call (800) 562-2139 or fax to (518) 789-0556

Older Americans Information Directory, 2004/05

Completely updated for 2004/05, this Fifth Edition has been completely revised and now contains 1,000 new listings, over 8,000 updates to existing listings and over 3,000 brand new e-mail addresses and web sites. You'll find important resources for Older Americans including National, Regional, State & Local Organizations, Government Agencies, Research Centers, Libraries & Information Centers, Legal Resources, Discount Travel Information, Continuing Education Programs, Disability Aids & Assistive Devices, Health, Print Media and Electronic Media. Three indexes: Entry Index, Subject Index and Geographic Index make it easy to find just the right source of information. This comprehensive guide to resources for Older Americans will be a welcome addition to any reference collection.

"Highly recommended for academic, public, health science and consumer libraries..." –Choice

1,200 pages; Softcover ISBN 1-59237-037-3, $165.00 ◆ Online Database $215.00 ◆ Online Database & Directory Combo $300.00

The Complete Directory for Pediatric Disorders, 2004/05

This important directory provides parents and caregivers with information about Pediatric Conditions, Disorders, Diseases and Disabilities, including Blood Disorders, Bone & Spinal Disorders, Brain Defects & Abnormalities, Chromosomal Disorders, Congenital Heart Defects, Movement Disorders, Neuromuscular Disorders and Pediatric Tumors & Cancers. This carefully written directory offers: understandable Descriptions of 15 major bodily systems; Descriptions of more than 200 Disorders and a Resources Section, detailing National Agencies & Associations, State Associations, Online Services, Libraries & Resource Centers, Research Centers, Support Groups & Hotlines, Camps, Books and Periodicals. This resource will provide immediate access to information crucial to families and caregivers when coping with children's illnesses.

"Recommended for public and consumer health libraries." –Library Journal

1,200 pages; Softcover ISBN 1-59237-045-4, $165.00 ◆ Online Database $215.00 ◆ Online Database & Directory Combo $300.00

The Complete Directory for People with Rare Disorders

This outstanding reference is produced in conjunction with the National Organization for Rare Disorders to provide comprehensive and needed access to important information on over 1,000 rare disorders, including Cancers and Muscular, Genetic and Blood Disorders. An informative Disorder Description is provided for each of the 1,100 disorders (rare Cancers and Muscular, Genetic and Blood Disorders) followed by information on National and State Organizations dealing with a particular disorder, Umbrella Organizations that cover a wide range of disorders, the Publications that can be useful when researching a disorder and the Government Agencies to contact. Detailed and up-to-date listings contain mailing address, phone and fax numbers, web sites and e-mail addresses along with a description. For quick, easy access to information, this directory contains two indexes: Entry Name Index and Acronym/Keyword Index along with an informative Guide for Rare Disorder Advocates. The Complete Directory for People with Rare Disorders will be an invaluable tool for the thousands of families that have been struck with a rare or "orphan" disease, who feel that they have no place to turn and will be a much-used addition to the reference collection of any public or academic library.

"Quick access to information... public libraries and hospital patient libraries will find this a useful resource in directing users to support groups or agencies dealing with a rare disorder." –Booklist

726 pages; Softcover ISBN 1-891482-18-1, $165.00

The Directory of Drug & Alcohol Residential Rehabilitation Facilities

This brand new directory is the first-ever resource to bring together, all in one place, data on the thousands of drug and alcohol residential rehabilitation facilities in the United States. *The Directory of Drug & Alcohol Residential Rehabilitation Facilities* covers over 1,000 facilities, with detailed contact information for each one, including mailing address, phone and fax numbers, email addresses and web sites, mission statement, type of treatment programs, cost, average length of stay, numbers of residents and counselors, accreditation, insurance plans accepted, type of environment, religious affiliation, education components and much more. It also contains a helpful chapter on General Resources that provides contact information for Associations, Print & Electronic Media, Support Groups and Conferences. Multiple indexes allow the user to pinpoint the facilities that meet very specific criteria. This time-saving tool is what so many counselors, parents and medical professionals have been asking for. *The Directory of Drug & Alcohol Residential Rehabilitation Facilities* will be a helpful tool in locating the right source for treatment for a wide range of individuals. This comprehensive directory will be an important acquisition for all reference collections: public and academic libraries, case managers, social workers, state agencies and many more.

"This is an excellent, much needed directory that fills an important gap..." –Booklist

300 pages; Softcover ISBN 1-59237-031-4, $135.00

To preview any of our Directories Risk-Free for 30 days, call (800) 562-2139 or fax to (518) 789-0556

Sedgwick Press
Education Directories

Educators Resource Directory, 2005/06

Educators Resource Directory is a comprehensive resource that provides the educational professional with thousands of resources and statistical data for professional development. This directory saves hours of research time by providing immediate access to Associations & Organizations, Conferences & Trade Shows, Educational Research Centers, Employment Opportunities & Teaching Abroad, School Library Services, Scholarships, Financial Resources, Professional Consultants, Computer Software & Testing Resources and much more. Plus, this comprehensive directory also includes a section on Statistics and Rankings with over 100 tables, including statistics on Average Teacher Salaries, SAT/ACT scores, Revenues & Expenditures and more. These important statistics will allow the user to see how their school rates among others, make relocation decisions and so much more. For quick access to information, this directory contains four indexes: Entry & Publisher Index, Geographic Index, a Subject & Grade Index and Web Sites Index. *Educators Resource Directory* will be a well-used addition to the reference collection of any school district, education department or public library.

"Recommended for all collections that serve elementary and secondary school professionals." –Choice

1,000 pages; Softcover ISBN 1-59237-080-2, $145.00 ◆ Online Database $195.00 ◆ Online Database & Directory Combo $280.00

The Comparative Guide to American Elementary & Secondary Schools, 2004/05

The only guide of its kind, this award winning compilation offers a snapshot profile of every public school district in the United States serving 1,500 or more students – more than 5,900 districts are covered. Organized alphabetically by district within state, each chapter begins with a Statistical Overview of the state. Each district listing includes contact information (name, address, phone number and web site) plus Grades Served, the Numbers of Students and Teachers and the Number of Regular, Special Education, Alternative and Vocational Schools in the district along with statistics on Student/Classroom Teacher Ratios, Drop Out Rates, Ethnicity, the Numbers of Librarians and Guidance Counselors and District Expenditures per student. As an added bonus, *The Comparative Guide to American Elementary and Secondary Schools* provides important ranking tables, both by state and nationally, for each data element. For easy navigation through this wealth of information, this handbook contains a useful City Index that lists all districts that operate schools within a city. These important comparative statistics are necessary for anyone considering relocation or doing comparative research on their own district and would be a perfect acquisition for any public library or school district library.

"This straightforward guide is an easy way to find general information. Valuable for academic and large public library collections." –ARBA

2,400 pages; Softcover ISBN 1-59237-047-0, $125.00

Sedgwick Press
Hospital & Health Plan Directories

The Comparative Guide to American Hospitals

This brand new title is the first ever resource to compare all of the nation's hospitals by 17 measures of quality in the treatment of heart attack, heart failure and pneumonia. This data is based on the recently announced Hospital Compare, produced by Medicare, and is available in print and in a unique and user-friendly format from Grey House Publishing, along with extra contact information from Grey House's *Directory of Hospital Personnel*. *The Comparative Guide to American Hospitals* provides a snapshot profile of each of the nations 6,000 hospitals. These informative profiles illustrate how the hospital rates in 17 important areas: Heart Attack Care (% who receive Aspirin at Arrival, Aspirin at Discharge, ACE Inhibitor for LVSD, Beta Blocker at Arrival, Beta Blocker at Discharge, Thrombolytic Agent Received, PTCA Received and Adult Smoking Cessation Advice); Heart Failure (% who receive LVF Assessment, ACE Inhibitor for LVSD, Discharge Instructions, Adult Smoking Cessation Advice); and Pneumonia (% who receive Initial Antibiotic Timing, Pneumococcal Vaccination, Oxygenation Assessment, Blood Culture Performed and Adult Smoking Cessation Advice). Each profile includes the raw percentage for that hospital, the state average, the US average and data on the top hospital. For easy access to contact information, each profile includes the hospitals address, phone and fax numbers, email and web addresses, type and accreditation along with 5 top key administrations. These profiles will allow the user to quickly identify the quality of the hospital and have the necessary information at their fingertips to make contact with that hospital. Most importantly, *The Comparative Guide to American Hospitals* provides an easy-to-use Ranking Table for each of the data elements to allow the user to quickly locate the hospitals with the best level of service. This brand new title will be a must for the reference collection at all public, medical and academic libraries.

2,500 pages; Softcover ISBN 1-59237-109-4 $175.00

To preview any of our Directories Risk-Free for 30 days, call (800) 562-2139 or fax to (518) 789-0556

The Directory of Hospital Personnel, 2006

The Directory of Hospital Personnel is the best resource you can have at your fingertips when researching or marketing a product or service to the hospital market. A "Who's Who" of the hospital universe, this directory puts you in touch with over 150,000 key decision-makers. With 100% verification of data you can rest assured that you will reach the right person with just one call. Every hospital in the U.S. is profiled, listed alphabetically by city within state. Plus, three easy-to-use, cross-referenced indexes put the facts at your fingertips faster and more easily than any other directory: Hospital Name Index, Bed Size Index and Personnel Index. *The Directory of Hospital Personnel* is the only complete source for key hospital decision-makers by name. Whether you want to define or restructure sales territories… locate hospitals with the purchasing power to accept your proposals… keep track of important contacts or colleagues… or find information on which insurance plans are accepted, *The Directory of Hospital Personnel* gives you the information you need – easily, efficiently, effectively and accurately.

"Recommended for college, university and medical libraries." –ARBA

2,500 pages; Softcover ISBN 1-59237-107-8 $275.00 ♦ Online Database $545.00 ♦ Online Database & Directory Combo, $650.00

The Directory of Health Care Group Purchasing Organizations, 2006

This comprehensive directory provides the important data you need to get in touch with over 800 Group Purchasing Organizations. By providing in-depth information on this growing market and its members, *The Directory of Health Care Group Purchasing Organizations* fills a major need for the most accurate and comprehensive information on over 800 GPOs – Mailing Address, Phone & Fax Numbers, E-mail Addresses, Key Contacts, Purchasing Agents, Group Descriptions, Membership Categorization, Standard Vendor Proposal Requirements, Membership Fees & Terms, Expanded Services, Total Member Beds & Outpatient Visits represented and more. Five Indexes provide a number of ways to locate the right GPO: Alphabetical Index, Expanded Services Index, Organization Type Index, Geographic Index and Member Institution Index. With its comprehensive and detailed information on each purchasing organization, *The Directory of Health Care Group Purchasing Organizations* is the go-to source for anyone looking to target this market.

"The information is clearly arranged and easy to access…recommended for those needing this very specialized information." –ARBA

1,000 pages; Softcover ISBN 1-59237-0091-8, $325.00 ♦ Online Database, $650.00 ♦ Online Database & Directory Combo, $750.00

The HMO/PPO Directory, 2006

The HMO/PPO Directory is a comprehensive source that provides detailed information about Health Maintenance Organizations and Preferred Provider Organizations nationwide. This comprehensive directory details more information about more managed health care organizations than ever before. Over 1,100 HMOs, PPOs and affiliated companies are listed, arranged alphabetically by state. Detailed listings include Key Contact Information, Prescription Drug Benefits, Enrollment, Geographical Areas served, Affiliated Physicians & Hospitals, Federal Qualifications, Status, Year Founded, Managed Care Partners, Employer References, Fees & Payment Information and more. Plus, five years of historical information is included related to Revenues, Net Income, Medical Loss Ratios, Membership Enrollment and Number of Patient Complaints. Five easy-to-use, cross-referenced indexes will put this vast array of information at your fingertips immediately: HMO Index, PPO Index, Other Providers Index, Personnel Index and Enrollment Index. *The HMO/PPO Directory* provides the most comprehensive information on the most companies available on the market place today.

"Helpful to individuals requesting certain HMO/PPO issues such as co-payment costs, subscription costs and patient complaints. Individuals concerned (or those with questions) about their insurance may find this text to be of use to them." –ARBA

600 pages; Softcover ISBN 1-59237-100-0, $275.00 ♦ Online Database, $495.00 ♦ Online Database & Directory Combo, $600.00

The Directory of Independent Ambulatory Care Centers

This first edition of *The Directory of Independent Ambulatory Care Centers* provides access to detailed information that, before now, could only be found scattered in hundreds of different sources. This comprehensive and up-to-date directory pulls together a vast array of contact information for over 7,200 Ambulatory Surgery Centers, Ambulatory General and Urgent Care Clinics, and Diagnostic Imaging Centers that are not affiliated with a hospital or major medical center. Detailed listings include Mailing Address, Phone & Fax Numbers, E-mail and Web Site addresses, Contact Name and Phone Numbers of the Medical Director and other Key Executives and Purchasing Agents, Specialties & Services Offered, Year Founded, Numbers of Employees and Surgeons, Number of Operating Rooms, Number of Cases seen per year, Overnight Options, Contracted Services and much more. Listings are arranged by State, by Center Category and then alphabetically by Organization Name. Two indexes provide quick and easy access to this wealth of information: Entry Name Index and Specialty/Service Index. *The Directory of Independent Ambulatory Care Centers* is a must-have resource for anyone marketing a product or service to this important industry and will be an invaluable tool for those searching for a local care center that will meet their specific needs.

"Among the numerous hospital directories, no other provides information on independent ambulatory centers. A handy, well-organized resource that would be useful in medical center libraries and public libraries." –Choice

986 pages; Softcover ISBN 1-930956-90-8, $185.00 ♦ Online Database, $365.00 ♦ Online Database & Directory Combo, $450.00

To preview any of our Directories Risk-Free for 30 days, call (800) 562-2139 or fax to (518) 789-0556

FREE CD-ROM

Grey House Publishing
PO Box 860 ◆ 185 Millerton Road ◆ Millerton, NY 12546
(800) 562-2139 ◆ (518) 789-8700 ◆ FAX (518) 789-0556
www.greyhouse.com ◆ e-mail: books@greyhouse.com

FREE CD-ROM WITH YOUR PURCHASE

Nations of the World, 2006 – CD-Rom

With your FREE CD-Rom, you can quickly and easily view and print out Country Reports as ready-to-use resources – right from PDF files - great for all types of users. Just attach this coupon to your payment and we'll ship your CD-Rom at no cost.

FREE CD-ROM COUPON

☐ I have enclosed my payment for *Nations of the World, 2006*. Send my FREE CD-Rom to the address below.

Name: _____ Invoice#: _____

Company Name: _____

Address: _____

City: _____ State: _____ Zip Code: _____

Telephone Number: _____ Fax Number: _____

Authorization Signature: _____ Date: _____

FREE CD-ROM

Grey House Publishing
PO Box 860 ◆ 185 Millerton Road ◆ Millerton, NY 12546
(800) 562-2139 ◆ (518) 789-8700 ◆ FAX (518) 789-0556
www.greyhouse.com ◆ e-mail: books@greyhouse.com

FREE CD-ROM WITH YOUR PURCHASE

Nations of the World, 2006 – CD-Rom

With your FREE CD-Rom, you can quickly and easily view and print out Country Reports as ready-to-use resources – right from PDF files - great for all types of users. Just attach this coupon to your payment and we'll ship your CD-Rom at no cost.

FREE CD-ROM COUPON

☐ I have enclosed my payment for *Nations of the World, 2006*. Send my FREE CD-Rom to the address below.

Name: _____ Invoice#: _____

Company Name: _____

Address: _____

City: _____ State: _____ Zip Code: _____

Telephone Number: _____ Fax Number: _____

Authorization Signature: _____ Date: _____